RELIGIOUS BOOKS
1876-1982

This edition of RELIGIOUS BOOKS 1876-1982 was prepared
by the R.R. Bowker Company's Department of
Bibliography in collaboration with the
Publications Systems Department

Senior staff of the Department of Bibliography includes:
Peter Simon, Database Manager.
Dean Hollister, Senior Product Manager.
Andrew Grabois, Editorial Coordinator.

Michael B. Howell, Manager, Systems Development.

Andrew H. Uszak, Senior Vice President, Data Services/Systems.
Gertrude Jennings, Manager, Product Research and Development,
Data Services.
Debra K. Brown, Manager, Technical Development, Data Services.

RELIGIOUS BOOKS
1876-1982

SUBJECT INDEX

AUTHOR INDEX

TITLE INDEX

R.R. BOWKER COMPANY

New York & London

Published by the R.R. Bowker Company (a Xerox Publishing Company)
1180 Avenue of the Americas, New York, N.Y. 10036

International Standard Book Number (Set) 0-8352-1602-0
International Standard Book Number (Vol. 1) 0-8352-1739-6
International Standard Book Number (Vol. 2) 0-8352-1741-8
International Standard Book Number (Vol. 3) 0-8352-1742-6
International Standard Book Number (Vol. 4) 0-8352-1743-4

Printed and bound in the United States of America

Library of Congress Cataloging in Publication Data
Main entry under title:

Religious books, 1876-1982.

"Prepared by the R.R. Bowker Company's Department of Bibliography in collaboration with the Publications Systems Department"—T.p. verso.
Includes indexes.
1. Religion—Bibliography. 2. Theology—Bibliography. 3. Religions—Bibliography. I. R.R. Bowker Company. Dept. of Bibliography. II. R.R. Bowker Company. Publications Systems Dept.
Z7751.R385 1983 [BL48] 016.2 83-6028
ISBN 0-8352-1602-0 (set)

Contents

FOREWORD VII
PREFACE IX

VOLUME 1
Subject Index
Aaen, Bernhard, 1918- to Clergy—Washington, D.C.—Biography 1-1302

VOLUME 2
Subject Index
Clergymen's families to More, Sir Thomas, Saint, 1478-1535—
Juvenile Literature 1303-2596

VOLUME 3
Subject Index
Morea, Andre to Zyburn, John S. 2597-3900

VOLUME 4
Author Index 3901-4069
Title Index 4071-4389

Foreword

Stephen Lee Peterson
Librarian, Yale Divinity School Library
New Haven, Connecticut

Religious Books 1876-1982 is a bibliographic instrument which will prove to be exceptionally useful in libraries, and to bibliographers and students of the humanities. This usefulness is due to the scope of the work, its format, its structure and its timely publication. More than being a useful bibliographic tool, however, *Religious Books 1876-1982* is a major contribution to the bibliography of religion and to the bibliography of the humanities generally.

Students of religion know, or soon learn, the substantial complexities presented by the literature of this field. Even to speak of religion as one field represents a simplification which most specialists would question. Religion has spawned an extensive and diverse literature. It is international in range and much of it ancient in origin. The diversity of this literature, of course, reflects the presence of religious practice in almost every society, ancient or modern. The literate religions have their own sacred writings and canonical interpretations or commentaries which sacred texts evoke. Each of these literary traditions is extensive, each has its own peculiarities of codification and access, and most often includes unusual languages.

Primal religions have their own texts and practices which are generally known through a body of technical literature produced in the main by social scientists. The fact that much of this literature is relatively recent does not reduce the complexity facing the bibliographer. Indeed, the diverse ways in which scholars have studied religion adds to the bibliographic complexity of the field. While the philosophy of religion and the psychology of religion have been well established disciplines for centuries,[1] the comparative study of religion and the phenomenological study of religion as well as the history of religion are somewhat newer approaches. Together, they have contributed a substantial body of literature to the traditional corpus of religious writing.

Beyond the traditional and the technical, i.e., scholarly, literature of religion, there is an even more voluminous body of writing given to the propagation of religion and the encouragement of religious practice. These popular or semi-popular publications now account for a large portion of the output of the American religious press.

Thus, the librarian, the bibliographer, the scholar, the student welcome the publication of *Religious Books 1876-1982*. The scope of this bibliographic work embraces the diversity and complexity of the field of religion. It does so without prejudice. It reflects the actual publication of religious writing to the extent this material has been reported in the book trade.

Not only does *Religious Books 1876-1982* bring a substantial measure of order to the bibliographic complexities of the field of religion, it also helps redress the rather uneven development of libraries in this field. In North America, there are few truly comprehensive library collections in religion. Some general educational institutions have collections covering most religions, but these libraries are not likely to have highly detailed literature pertaining to specific religions. The specifically religious institutions such as theological schools tend to have collections focused on the particular religious or intellectual traditions of the school. Thus, *Religious Books 1876-1982* brings together the description of a greater range of books important to the study of religion than the catalogues of all but the very largest and most comprehensive libraries in North America. Yet, *Religious Books 1876-1982* stands essentially as a bibliography rather than a library catalogue. In that even the Library of Congress does not keep for its collections all of the books it receives or catalogues, it is doubtful if any library holds all or most of the works cited in this tool.

Religious Books 1876-1982 is based on the large and old book publishing records of the Bowker Company. These files have been augmented by entries from the Library of Congress *National Union Catalog* and other sources. There is considerable coverage of British books. Cataloging-in-source records have been completed and the file has been read against MARC records. The result is simply the most comprehensive bibliography of books on religion for North American usage.

It is, of course, truly advantageous to have *Religious Books 1876-1982* organized primarily as a subject bibliography. Subject bibliography in religion is not well developed. The most comprehensive subject index to periodical literature began only in 1949.[2] Most of the other large continuing subject bibliographies are based in Europe and, while they include many English language materials, they necessarily concentrate on publications originating in Europe. The *Library of Congress Subject Catalog* began publication only in 1950. While bibliographers may use this work with benefit, students generally have not found it a convenient tool to use. The *Subject Index of Modern Books,* of the British Museum Library, begun in 1881, is an improvement in this regard, but its infrequent cumulations and its English and European orientation render it less helpful to North Amer-

[1]The modern discipline of the psychology of religion, however, may be said to have begun with the research of William Starbuck reported in his *The Psychology of Religion,* New York: Charles Scribner's Sons, 1901.

ican students. *Religious Books 1876-1982* then, occupies a place of singular importance in the constellation of subject bibliography in religion, particularly for North American scholars and institutions.

The author and title indexes, while not containing full bibliographic description, do not have diminished importance. Certainly there is no comparable bibliography listed by title in the field. In this regard as with the subject index, *Religious Books 1876-1982* makes a fresh and needed contribution to the bibliography of religion. Only the full *National Union Catalog* surpasses *Religious Books 1876-1982* as a comprehensive author file. Of course, cost alone makes the *NUC* inaccessible to many libraries. Furthermore, persons primarily interested in religion will find *Religious Books 1876-1982* the far easier and more efficient resource to consult.

In essence, this tool now makes it possible for the specialist and the non-specialist alike to make maximum use of the Library of Congress subject heading system as a source both of subject bibliography and of comprehensive bibliography.

A sound grasp of the structure of this bibliography will extend considerably its usefulness. The approximately 130,000 titles are organized under the first subject heading assigned by the Library of Congress. The result is that some 27,000 subject descriptors are used. These, of course, represent the historic practice of the Library of Congress so that some headings appear here which are not currently assigned. New headings appear as they have been introduced.

Bowker's decision to enter titles only under the first subject heading but to list all of the tracings for each entry must, in most cases, be considered prudential. It is a decision representing sound bibliographic theory. In a straightforward way, the user of this tool can extend his search to related or alternative topics simply by referring to the subject tracings. Indeed, the inexperienced bibliographer can construct a quite complex subject search in this manner. The tracings also will call the user's attention to uniform titles. Uniform titles are used frequently to describe religious works, particularly works containing sacred texts. These uniform titles, indirectly, constitute an important aspect of subject searches. The more sophisticated bibliographer will use *Religious Books 1876-1982* in tandem with *Library of Congress Subject Headings*. The "see" and "see also" references in this aid will provide important clues for other useful headings in *Religious Books 1876-1982*. As a result, subject access to the literature of religion is greatly enhanced by this publication.

Who will use *Religious Books 1876-1982*? Certainly it may be anticipated that this tool will become the principal source of retrospective bibliography in religion in most libraries. Indeed, in many libraries it may supplant the card file for subjects as the source for first consultation in subject searches.

Synagogue and church libraries will find this work indispensable. Individual scholars will acquire and use this tool, and if not individuals, surely teaching groups and academic departments will want it in their offices. Libraries cooperating together will find that this work readily aids the work of resource sharing as well as providing a way of sharing bibliographic data effectively. At a time when many libraries are actively working on collection preservation, *Religious Books 1876-1982* will provide the foundation for this effort.

The R.R. Bowker Company is to be congratulated on bringing its considerable experience, its rich data base, modern technology, and its record of excellence in library service together to produce its series of large subject bibliographies. Specialists in religion should be grateful that their field is one of the early beneficiaries of this initiative. Subject access to information and literature must not be hindered by the conventions of local ownership of resources. *Religious Books 1876-1982* provides the broadest possible coverage to the field of religion and all persons interested in this field will find their interest and inquiry greatly assisted by this bibliography.

Stephen Lee Peterson, Ph.D
Librarian of the Yale University Divinity School

Dr. Peterson holds the following degrees: B.A. Bethel College, St. Paul, Minnesota; B.D. Colgate Rochester Divinity School, Rochester, New York; A.M.L.S. College and University Librarianship and A.M. New Eastern Languages and Literatures, University of Michigan, Ann Arbor, Michigan; Ph.D Religion, Vanderbilt University, Nashville, Tennessee. He has served in the library profession since 1968 at Vanderbilt University as Divinity Librarian and as Assistant Director for Bibliographic Services. Since 1972, Dr. Peterson has been Librarian of the Divinity School at Yale, serving also during 1978–1980 as Acting Librarian of the Beinecke Rare Book and Manuscript Library. These are a selection of Dr. Peterson's publications, lectures and projects: "The Theological Tasks of the Seminary Library," Lecture given at the Garrett-Evangelical Theological Seminary, Evanston, Illinois, March 1983. "Collection Development in Religion in the Library of Congress," *Proceedings of the American Theological Library Association 35:26-33 (1981).* "Collection Development in Theological Libraries: A New Model—A New Hope," *in Essays on Theological Librarianship Presented to Calvin Henry Schmidt,* American Theological Library Association: Philadelphia, 1980. "The Subject Approach to Theology: An Alternative System for Libraries," *Proceedings of the American Theological Library Association 31:135-147 (1977).* Director, Project 2000, sponsored by the Association of Theological Schools and the American Theological Library Association, 1981. This is a research project to develop planning strategies for theological libraries to the end of this century. It is funded by the Lilly Endowment.

[2]*Index to Religious Periodical Literature*, now *Religion Index One*, published by the American Theological Library Association.

Preface

As publishers of *Religious Books And Serials In Print*, the R.R. Bowker Company is especially pleased to be able to publish *Religious Books 1876-1982*. While *Religious Books And Serials In Print* provides current ordering and price information on in-print titles, *Religious Books 1876-1982* provides over one-hundred years of Library of Congress cataloging on religious titles published or distributed in the United States. This comprehensive bibliography of some 130,000 entries covers all aspects of the world's religions, including the religious implications of such topics as abortion, homosexuality, and business ethics. In addition, this collection provides broad coverage of areas related to religion such as philosophy, magic, astrology and occult sciences. Because of their extensive and complete coverage, these volumes offer a historical perspective of literature in religious and related fields and can serve as a basic resource for reference and research, collection assessment and development, and acquisitions and cataloging.

SURVEY OF PROFESSIONAL LIBRARIANS AND INFORMATION SPECIALISTS

It is an established routine at Bowker in designing new reference works to consult professional librarians and others involved in developing information before publishing. The surveys we made seek to establish a definite need for the reference work as well as to obtain practical direction from potential users as to content and format. This interaction has been most satisfying since it has resulted in direct hands on influence on the final design of *Religious Books 1876-1982* as well as enthusiastic acceptance of the concept by a great majority of those surveyed.

We mailed questionnaires to the users of *Religious Books And Serials In Print* and to others who use information in these subjects. Over 75 percent responded affirmatively to questions asking whether they would purchase *Religious Books 1876-1982*, and with comments such as these, confirmed the validity of our concept:

"...Religion is a major emphasis in our university and is one of the subjects for which we would need comprehensive retrospective coverage..."

"...This book would be a real asset to our collection because of its subject index and title index. Also having the author index in one alphabetical arrangement will save time in verfication...The price seems low for such a massive project."

DATA ACQUISITION

Entries were selected from the over 1.8 million titles in the *American Book Publishing Record* database, which represents all United States monographs in the National Union catalog, MARC tapes and titles cataloged at Bowker for the period covered. Titles were initially selected by Dewey Decimal and Library of Congress classification numbers for both core religious areas in these classification systems as well as all identifiable peripheral areas, ranging from astrology to philosophy. Each entry was then individually reviewed to determine its appropriateness for publication in *Religious Books 1876-1982*. The final book was produced from records stored on magnetic tape, edited by computer programs, and set in type by computer-controlled photocomposition.

ARRANGEMENT AND CONTENT OF ENTRIES

The user can access the information in *Religious Books 1876-1982* by subject, author and title. Complete entries appear in the subject index under Library of Congress subject headings and are arranged by main entry within the subject. Over 27,000 Library of Congress subject headings, including names when used as subjects, are listed. Each full entry represents cataloging prepared by the Library of Congress. Entry information includes: main entry, title (in italics), subtitle, author statement, publication place, publisher, publication date, collation, series statement, general note or contents note, LC classification number (in brackets), Dewey Decimal number, LC card number and tracings.

General Editorial Policies

In order to insure that the integrity of original Library of Congress cataloging is maintained in the subject index, and that entries are uniform and easy to find, the following editorial policies have been maintained:

Subject headings were made uniform whereas the entries listed within may contain variant forms of the tracing.

Dual listings are provided when an entry contains both subject and name tracings.

Entries without subject or name tracings in the original cataloging were assigned by editorial staff to appropriate subject headings. In this publication, over 20,000 titles without tracings were assigned subjects.

Subject Index

Entries are arranged alphabetically by main entry within subject.

Headings were derived from the primary subject and uniform name tracings in the original cataloging entries. Some of these headings were made uniform due to variances in the styling of tracings in these entries.

Subject headings are arranged alphabetically.

Abailard, Pierre, 1079-1142
Baptism
Convenants (Theology)

Many of the main headings are broken down still further:

Church
Church—Administration
Church—Authority
Church—Biblical Teachings

Headings, as used in Library of Congress cataloging practice, are explicit rather than general—thus books on God (Hinduism) are under God (Hinduism), not God.

Author and Title Indexes

The author and title indexes are alphabetically arranged by their authors and titles respectively. Page references are provided to the main entries in the subject index.

ACKNOWLEDGEMENTS

We extend special gratitude to Dr. Stephen L. Peterson, Librarian, Yale Divinity School Library for his support and encouragement and for preparation of the Foreword. Gertrude Jennings, Manager, Product Research and Development, Data Services Division, developed the concept of *Religious Books 1876-1982*. She, Peter Simon, Database Manager, and Dean Hollister, Senior Product Manager, were responsible for the design, planning, and production of this product. The book indexes were produced with the help of Andrew Grabois, Editorial Coordinator, Subject Guide Department, whom we thank for his conscientious and dedicated efforts. Data Processing support was received from Francis J. McWade, Data Processing Manager, John Murphy, Computer Operations Supervisor, and Joyce Edwards, Data Conversion Control Supervisor. Our thanks to all members of the Data Services/Systems Division who worked on this publication.

Peter Simon,
Database Manager

Gertrude Jennings,
Manager, Product Research
and Development,
Data Services Division

Dean Hollister,
Senior Product Manager,
Department of Bibliography

RELIGIOUS BOOKS
1876-1982

VOLUME 3

Subject Index

Morea, Andre
to
Zyburn, John S.

Morea, Andre.

MOREA, Andre. 274.98
The book they couldn't ban : the miraculous experiences of a Bible courier in Romania / [by] Andre Morea. London : Lakeland, 1976. 157 p. ; 18 cm. [BV2369.5.E852M66] 77-353521 ISBN 0-551-00589-0 : £0.75
1. Morea, Andre. 2. Bible—Publication and distribution—Europe, Eastern. I. Title.

MOREA, Andre. 266'.023'0924 B
Surrounded by angels : the miraculous story of a Bible courier behind the Iron Curtain / Andre Morea. 1st U.S. ed. Minneapolis : Bethany Fellowship, 1976. 157 p. ; 18 cm. (Dimension books) [BV2369.5.E852M67 1976] 76-22930 ISBN 0-87123-503-X pbk. : 1.95
1. Morea, Andre. 2. Bible—Publication and distribution—Europe, Eastern. I. Title.

Moreau, Basile Antoine Marie, 1799-1873.

BARROSSE, Thomas. 271'.79 B
Moreau; portrait of a founder. Notre Dame, Ind., Fides Publishers [1969] viii 392 p. 23 cm. Includes bibliographical references. [BX4705.M72B37] 75-92021
1. Moreau, Basile Antoine Marie, 1799-1873. 2. Congregation of Holy Cross.

CATTA, Etienne. 922.244
Basil Anthony Mary Moreau, by Etienne Catta and Tony Catta. English translation by Edward L. Heston. Milwaukee, Bruce Pub. Co. [c1955] 2v. illus. 24cm. [BX4705.M72C33] 55-11616
1. Moreau, Basile Antolne Marie, 1799-1878. 2. Congregation of Holy Cross. I. Catta, Tony, joint author. II. Title.

CATTA, Etienne. 922.244
Mother Mary of the Seven Dolors and the early origins of the Marinites of Holy Cross (1818-1900) [by] Etienne Catta and Tony Catta. English translation by Edward L. Heston. Milwaukee, Catholic Life Publications [1959] 495p. illus. 24cm. Includes bibliography. [BX4705.M3815C3] 59-43143
1. Moreau, Basile Antoine Marie, 1799-1873. 2. Marie des Sept. Doubleurs, 1818-1900. 3. Sisters Marianites of Holy Cross. I. Catta, Tony, joint author. II. Title.

FITZGERALD, Gerald 922.244
Michael Joseph Cushing, father, 1894-
Juxta crucem, the life of Basil Anthony Moreau, 1799-1873, founder of the Congregation of holy cross and of the Marianite sisters of holy cross by Gerald, M. C. Fitzgerald... New York, P. J. Kenedy & sons [c1937] xix, 300 p. front., plates. ports. 24 1/2 cm. "Works consulted": p. [viii] [Secular name: Gerald Cushing Fitzgerald] [BX4705.M72F5] 38-3711
1. Moreau, Bastle Antoine Marie, 1799-1873. 2. Congregation of the holy cross. 3. Sisters Marianites of holy cross. I. Title.

MACEOIN, Gary, 1909- 922.244
Father Moreau, founder of Holy Cross. Milwaukee, Bruce [c.1962] 194p. front. port. 23cm. 62-16633 3.50
1. Moreau, Basile Antoine Marie, 1799-1873. 2. Congregation of Holy Cross. I. Title.

MARY Immaculate, Sister, 922.244
1908-
The cross against the sky; a book for children based on the life of Father Basil Anthony Moreau, the founder and first Superior General of the Congregation of the Holy Cross. With drawings by Sister M. Rose Ellen and Dorothy Van V. Young. South Bend [Ind.] Fides Publishers [1950] 133 p. col. illus. 23 cm. Secular name: Helen Creek. [BX4705.M72M3] 50-14978
1. Moreau, Basile Antoine Marie, I. Title.

MARY, Immaculate 1908 922.244
Sister, 1908-
The cross against the sky; a book for children based on the life of Father Basil Anthony Moreau, the founder and first Superior General of the Congregation of the Holy Cross. With drawings by Sister M. Rose Ellen and Dorothy Van V. Young. South Bend [Ind.] Fides Publishers [1949] 133 p. col. illus. 23 cm. Secular name: Helen Creek. [BX4705.M72M3] 50-14978
1. Moreau, Basile Antoine Marie, 1799-1873. I. Title.

Morecraft, James Edward.

FORKER, Cora, 1918- 284'.1'0924 B
Daystar : the story of the Rev. James Edward Morecraft, the God to whom he belonged, and the people he loved and served / by Cora Forker and Lois Wiley. Harrisburg, Pa. : Stackpole Books, [1975] p. cm. [BX8080.M567F67] 75-23241
1. Morecraft, James Edward. I. Wiley, Lois, 1931- joint author. II. Title.

Morehead, John Alfred, 1867-1936.

TREXLER, Samuel Geiss, 922.473
1877-
John A. Morehead who created world Lutheranism, by Samuel Trexler ... with portrait. New York, London, G. P. Putnam's sons, 1938. xiv p., 1 l., 17-167, [1] p. front. (port.) 21 cm. On cover: John A. Morehead, a biography. [BX8080.M57T7] 38-14038
1. Morehead, John Alfred, 1867-1936. I. Title.

Morehouse, Henry Lyman, 1834-1917.

CRANDALL, Lathan Augustus, 920.
1850-
Henry Lyman Morehouse; a biography, by Lathan A. Crandall, D.D. Philadelphia, Boston [etc.] The American Baptist publication society [c1919] 6 p. l., 240 p. front., plates, ports. 20 cm. [BX6495.M6C7] 20-770
1. Morehouse, Henry Lyman, 1834-1917. I. Title.

Moreno, Maria.

STEARN, Jess. 133.9'1'0924 B
A matter of immortality : dramatic evidence of survival / Jess Stearn. 1st ed. New York : Atheneum Publishers, 1976. 300 p. ; 22 cm. [BF1283.M587S73 1976] 76-11543 ISBN 0-689-10721-8 : 9.95
1. Moreno, Maria. 2. Spiritualism. I. Title.

STEARN, Jess. 133.9'1'0924
A matter of immortality : dramatic evidence of survival / Jess Stearn. 1st ed. New York : New American Library, 1977,c1976. 245p. ; 18 cm. [BF1283.M587S73 1976] ISBN 0-451-07652-4 pbk. : 1.95
1. Moreno, Maria. 2. Spritualism. I. (A Signet Book) II. Title.
L.C. card no. for 1976 Atheneum ed:76-11543.

Morgan, Arthur Ernest, 1878—

MORGAN, Lucy (Griscom) Mrs. 218
Finding his world; the story of Arthur E. Morgan, by Lucy Griscom Morgan. Yellow Springs [O.] Kahoe & Spieth, 1927. 4 p. l., 108 p. 24 cm. [BD431.M88] 27-20593
1. Morgan, Arthur Ernest, 1878- I. Title.

Morgan, Edward, 1751?-1844.

MORGAN, Clarita 287'.632'0924 B
Hutchison, 1908-
Reverend Edward Morgan, 1751?-1844; pioneer local preacher of the Methodist Episcopal Church in southwest Virginia. Ordained by Bishop Francis Asbury, 1801. [Radford? Va.] 1973. iv, 121, 14 p. illus. 29 cm. "One hundred copies ... printed." Includes bibliographical references. [BX8495.M617M67] 74-158969
1. Morgan, Edward, 1751?-1844. 2. Morgan family.

Morgan, George Campbell, 1863-1945.

MORGAN, George Campbell, 1863-
...The teaching of the lesson; a commentary on the International Sunday school lessons for the year 1910, by G. Campbell Morgan, D.D. [1st year New York and London, Hodder and Stoughton [c1909- v. 14 x 6 1/2 cm. $0.25 9-29571
I. Title.

MORGAN, Jill. 285'.8'0924
A man of the word; life of G. Campbell Morgan. New York, F. H. Revell [1951] 404p. plates. 22cm. [BX7260.M] A53
1. Morgan, George Campbell, 1863-1945. I. Title.

MORGAN, Jill. 285'.8'0924
A man of the word; life of G. Campbell Morgan. New York, F. H. Revell [1951] 404p. plates. 22cm. [BX7260.M] A53
1. Morgan, George Campbell, 1863-1945. I. Title.

WAGNER, Don M 251
The expository method of G. Campbell Morgan. [Westwood, N.J.] Revell [1957] 128 p. 20 cm. Includes bibliography. [BS501.M6W3] 57-5409
1. Morgan, George Campbell, 1863-1945. 2. Bible — Hermeneutics. I. Title.

WAGNER, Don M 251
The expository method of G. Campbell Morgan. [Westwood, N.J.] Revell [1957] 128 p. 20 cm. Includes bibliography. [BS501.M6W3] 57-5409
1. Morgan, George Campbell, 1863-1945. 2. Bible — Hermeneutics. I. Title.

Morgan, Geraldine, 1927-

MORGAN, Geraldine, 1927- 248'.2 B
Shadows in the sunshine. Philadelphia, Dorrance [1973] 92 p. 22 cm. [BX7020.Z8M58] 73-77629 ISBN 0-8059-1858-2 4.00
1. Morgan, Geraldine, 1927- 2. Church of God—Sermons. 3. Sermons, American. I. Title.

Morgan, Justin.

BANDEL, Betty, 783'.02'60924 B
1912-
Sing the Lord's song in a strange land : the life of Justin Morgan / Betty Bandel ; with a musical appendix compiled and edited by James G. Chapman. Rutherford, N.J. : Fairleigh Dickinson University Press, c1981. 263 p. : ill., music ; 22 cm. Includes the complete musical works of Justin Morgan. Includes index. Bibliography: p. 235-243. [ML410.M779B3] [M2092.4] 78-73309 ISBN 0-8386-2411-1 : 17.50
1. Morgan, Justin. 2. Composers—United States—Vermont—Biography. 3. Choruses, Sacred (Mixed voices, 4 parts), Unaccompanied. 4. Anthems. 5. Morgan horse. I. Chapman, James G. II. Morgan, Justin. Works. 1981. III. Title.

Morgan memorial, Boston.

HELMS, Edgar James, 1863-
Pioneering in modern city missions, by Edgar James Helms; with an introduction by Bishop Frederick B. Fisher ... Boston, Mass., Morgan memorial printing department, 1927. 1 p. l., 7-136 p. front., plates, ports. 23 1/2 cm. Illustrations on covers. A 35
1. Morgan memorial, Boston. 2. Boston—Social conditions. I. Title.

Morgan, William, 1774-ca. 1826.

BERNARD, David, 1798-1876.
Light on masonry, a collection of all the most important documents on the subject of speculative free masonry: embracing the reports of the Western committees in relation to the abduction of William Morgan ... with all the degrees of the order conferred in a master's lodge as written by Captain William Morgan ... By Elder David Bernard ... Utics, W. Williams, printer, 1829. x. [2], [13]-506, 54, [1] p. front. (port.) pl. 18 cm. The author was a minister of the Genesee (N. Y.) Baptist association, who had takes fifteen degrees of masonry and was intimate secretary of the Lodge of perfection. He was among the first in that section of the country to recede from the order. cf. J. Q. Adams, Letters on the masonic institution, 1847, p. 228 et seq. C. T. McClenachan, History of freemasonry in New York, 1888-1894, while going very fully into the Morgan affair, v. 2, p. 458-506, does not mention Bernard's book. In 1883, Robert Morris published his "William Morgan: or, Political antimasonry, its rise, growth, and decadence," by which," says McClenachan. "It was endeavored to show the innocence of our brotherhood, with a seal almost as great as the fanatics of 1829 exercised to condemn the institution for the acts of a few over-sealous, unworthy members." [H8527.B5] 2-10527
1. Morgan, William, 1774-ca. 1826. 2. Freemasons—Rituals. 3. Anti-masonic party I. Title.

MOCK, Stanley Upton. 366.1
The Morgan episode in American free masonry, by Stanley Upton Mock. East Aurora, N.Y., The Roycrofters, 1930. 2 p. l., 9-152 p., 1 l. front. (port.) plates. 23 cm. [HS525.M6] 32-17276
1. Morgan, William, 1774-ca. 1826. 2. Freemasons. 3. Freemasons, Batavia, N.Y. 4. Antimasonic party. I. Title.

A Narrative of the facts and circumstances relating to the kidnaping [!] and murder of William Morgan and of the attempt to carry off David C.p Miller, and to burn or destroy the printing-office of the latter for the purpose of preventing the printing and publishing of a book, entitled "Illustrations of masonry." Prepard under the direction of the several committees appointed at meetings of the citizens of the counties of Genesee, Livingston, Ontario, Monroe and Niagara, in the state of New York: containing most of the depositions and other documents to substantiate the statements made, and disclosing many particulars of the transactions. Batavia, Printed by D. C. Miller, under the direction of the committees, 1827. Also,the supplementary report of the committee, containing the report of the coroner's inquest on the body of Wm. Morgan, etc. "Cynosure ed." Chicago, Ill., E. A. Cook & co., 1873. iv p., 1 l., [8]-95 p. 17 cm. Cover-title: History of the abduction and murder of Capt. William Morgan. [HS527.N3] ca 18
1. Morgan, William, 1774-ca. 1826. 2. Antimasonic party.

A 'narrative of the facts and circumstances relating to the kidnapping and presumed murder of William Morgan. And of the attempt to carry off David C. Miller, and to burn or destroy the printing office of the latter, for the purpose of preventing the printing and publishing of a book entitled "Illustrations of masonry." Prepared under the direction of the several committees appointed at the meetings of the citizens of the counties of Genesee, Livingston, Ontario, Monroe, and Niagara, in the state of New York. With an appendix containing most of the deposition and other documents, to substantiate the statements made, and disclosing many particulars of the transactions, not in the narrative. To which is added, the late trials at Canadaigua. Brookfield, E. and G. Merriam, printers, 1827. 84 p. 19 cm. [HS527.N3 1827] 18-22952
1. Morgan, William 1774-ca. 1826. 2. Antimasonic party.

A narrative of the facts and circumstances relating to the kidnapping and presumed murder of William Morgan: and of the attempt to carry off David C. Miller, and to burn or destroy the printing-office of the latter, for the purpose of preventing the printing and publishing of a book entitled "Illustrations of masonry". Prepared under the direction of the several committees appointed at the meetings of the citizens of the counties of Genesee, Livingston, Ontario, Monroe, and Niagara in the state of Newesee, Livingston, Ontario, Monroe, and Niagara in the state of New-York: with an appendix, containing most of the depositions and other documents to substantiate the statements made, and disclosing many particulars of the transaction, not in the narrative. [3d ed.] Rochester, N. Y., Printed by E. Scrantom, 1828. 72 p. 20 cm. Title-page blurred. [HS527.N3 1828] 22-15942
1. Morgan, William, 1774-ca. 1826. 2. Antimasonic party.

O'RIELLY, Henry, 1806-1886.
American political-antimasonry, with its

"Good-enough Morgan." "One of the most singular features in American social, religious and political history, as well as in the annals of the masonic institution throughout the world" ... Brief notices of some events in the history of the political-antimasonic excitement ... By Henry O'Rielly ... Including also notices of indictments and civil suits for alleged libels concerning the "Good-enough Morgan" and its "inventor" [i. e. Thurlow Weed] New York, The American news company [c1880] xvi, 9-55 p. 24 cm. Ms. letter from author inserted before p. [i] [Name originally: Henry O'Reilly] [HS527.O69] 9-26891
1. Morgan, William, 1774-ca. 1826. 2. Weed, Thurlow, 1797-1882. 3. Antimasonic party. I. Title.

WANDELL, Samuel Henry, 1860- 366.1
The myth of William Morgan; anti-masonic period, 1826-1832, by Samuel H. Wandell ... Introduction by Walter F. McCaleb, PH.D. [New York, 1943] 3 p. l., vii, 166 p. incl. facsim. 24 cm. [HS511.M83W3] 43-2327
1. Morgan, William, 1774-ca. 1826. 2. Freemasons. U.S—Hist. I. Title.

Morganton, N.C. Grace church.

STONEY, William Shannon, 1896- 283.756
Historical sketch of Grace church, Morganton, North Carolina, [by] Rev. William S. Stoney. [n.p.] 1935. 50 p. illus. (incl. ports.) 22 1/2 cm. [BX5980.M6G78] 35-14137
1. Morganton, N.C. Grace church. I. Title.

Moriarty, Frederick L.

THE Word in the world; 201'.1
essays in honor of Frederick L. Moriarty, S.J. Edited by Richard J. Clifford & George W. MacRae. [Cambridge, Mass.] Weston College Press, 1973. x, 282 p. port. 23 cm. [BR50.W63] 72-97356 3.50 (pbk.)
1. Moriarty, Frederick L. 2. Moriarty, Frederick L.—Bibliography. 3. Theology—Addresses, essays, lectures. I. Moriarty, Frederick L. II. Clifford, Richard J., ed. III. MacRae, George W., ed. Publisher's Address: 3 Phillips Place Cambridge, Mass. 02138.

Morin, Jean Baptiste, 1583-1656.

SCHWICKERT, Friedrich "Sindbad." 133.5
Cornerstones of astrology; volume I, synthesis, by Friedrich "Sindbad" Schwickert and Adolf Weiss. Dallas, Sangreal Foundation [1972] ix, 342 p. illus. 24 cm. (Morin de Villefranche) [BF1679.S38] 73-151846 ISBN 0-87913-000-8
1. Morin, Jean Baptiste, 1583-1656. 2. Astrology—History. I. Weiss, Adolf, joint author. II. Title.

Moriscos.

CHEJNE, Anwar G. 306'.089927046
Islam and the West : the Moriscos, a cultural and economic history / by Anwar G. Chejne. Albany : State University of New York Press, c1982. p. cm. Includes index. Bibliography: p. [DP104.C45] 19 82-703 ISBN 0-87395-606-0 : 44.50 ISBN 0-87395-603-6 pbk. : 16.95
1. Moriscos. I. Title.

LEA, Henry Charles, 1825-1909.
The Moriscos of Spain; their conversion and expulsion, By Henry Charles Lea, LL. D. Philadelphia, Lea brothers & co., 1901. xii, 463 p. 21 cm. [DP104.L43] 1-30496
1. Moriscos. 2. Inquisition. Spain. I. Title.

Mormon, Book of.

see also Book of Mormon

THE book of Mormon: 289.3
an account written by the hand of Mormon, upon plates taken from the plates of Nephi ... Translated by Joseph Smith, jun. Division into chapters and verses, with references, by Orson Pratt, sen. Salt Lake City, Utah, Juvenile instructor office, 1888. xii, 623 p. 25 1/2 cm. [BX8623 1888] 36-25137
I. Smith, Joseph, 1805-1844, tr. II. Pratt, Orson, 1811-1881. III. Book of Mormon.

THE Book of Mormon; 289.3
an account written by the hand of Mormon upon plates taken from the plates of Nephi ... Translated by Joseph Smith, jun. Monongahela, Pa., The Church of Jesus Christ, 1934. 7 p. l., 519 p. 1 illus. 19 1/2 cm. "Errats" slip mounted on lining-paper. [BX8623 1934] 37-977
I. Smith, Joseph, 1805-1844. II. Book of Mormon.

THE book of Mormon;
an account written by the hand of Mormon, upon plates taken from the plates of Nephi ... Translated by Joseph Smith, jun. Division into chapters and verses, with references, by Orson Pratt, sen. Chicago, Northern states mission, 1908. 4 p. l., [vii]-xii, 623 p. 17 cm. Fourth Chicago edition. [BX8623 1908] 9-31980
I. Smith, Joseph, 1805-1844, tr. II. Pratt, Orson, 1811-1881. III. Book of Mormon.

THE book of Mormon,
an account written by the hand of Mormon upon plates taken from the plates of Nephi ... Tr. by Joseph Smith, jun. Salt Lake City, Utah, The Church of Jesus Christ of latter-day saints, 1920. 4 p. l., 568 p. 20 cm. "First edition published in 1830." "First issued, as divided into chapters and verses with references by Orson Pratt, in 1879." "First issued, in double-column pages, with chapter headings, chronological data, revised foot-note references, pronouncing vocabulary and index, in 1920." [BX8623 1920] 21-5409
I. Smith, Joseph, 1805-1844. II. Book of Mormon.

THE book of Mormon;
an account written by the hand of Mormon upon plates taken from the plates of Nephi ... Tr. by Joseph Smith, jun. Salt Lake City, Utah, The Church of Jesus Christ of latter-day saints, 1921. 4 p. l., 508 p. 20 cm. "First edition published in 1830." "First issued, as divided into chapters and verses with references by Orson Pratt, in 1879." "First issued in double-column pages, with chapter headings, chronological data, revised foot-note references, pronouncing vocabulary and index, in 1920." [BX8623 1921] 22-1355
I. Smith, Joseph, 1805-1844. II. Book of Mormon.

BOOK of Mormon. 289.3
The Book of Mormon; an account written by the hand of Mormon, upon plates taken from the plates of Nephi. By Joseph Smith, Junior. Palmyra [N. Y.] Printed by E. B. Grandin for the author, 1830. [Salt Lake City; W. C. Wood, 1958] [33] p., facsim. (588 p.), [27] p. illus., ports., map. facsims. 24cm. (Joseph Smith begins his work; [edited by] Wilford C. Wood, v. 1) Reproduced from uncut sheets of the 1st ed. in the possession of Wilford C. Wood. [BX8621.W6 vol. 1] 58-2405
I. Smith, Joseph, 1805- 1844. II. Title. III. Series: Wood, Wilford C., ed. Joseph Smith begins his work, v. 1

BOOK of Mormon.
The Book of Mormon. Translated by Joseph Smith, Jr. Compared with the original manuscript and the Kirtland edition of 1837, which was carefully re-examined and compared with the original manuscript by Joseph Smith and Oliver Cowdery. Authorized ed. Independence, Mo., Board of Publication of the Reorganized Church of Jesus Christ of Latter Day Saints [1962, 1953] 838 p. 68-25045
I. Smith, Joseph, 1805-1844. II. Cowdery, Oliver. III. Reorganized Church of Jesus Christ of Latter-Day Saints. Board of Publication. IV. Title.

BOOK of Mormon.
The book of Mormon. Translated by Joseph Smith, Jr. Reprinted from the 3d. American edition, carefully revised by the translator. New York, Jas. O. Wright [n. d.] xix, 380 p. 20 cm. NUC67
I. Smith, Joseph, 1805-1844. II. Church of Jesus Christ of Latter-Day Saints. III. Title.

BOOK of Mormon.
The Book of Mormon; an account written by the hand of Mormon upon plates taken from the plates of Nephi ... Translated by Joseph Smith, jun. Salt Lake City, Church of Jesus Christ of Latterday Saints, 1961. 568 p. 20 cm. 65-28197
I. Title.

BOOK of Mormon.
The Book of Mormon; an account written by the hand of Mormon upon plates taken from the plates of Nephi. Translated by Joseph Smith, jun. Salt Lake City, The Church of Jesus Christ of Latter-day Saints, 1963 [c1961] 588 p. col. illus. 18 cm. 67-76087
I. Church of Jesus Christ of Latter-Day Saints. II. Smith Joseph, 1805-1844, tr. III. Title.

BOOK of Mormon. 289.3'22
The Book of Mormon; an account written by the hand of Mormon upon plates taken from the plates of Nephi. Translated by Joseph Smith, Jr. Salt Lake City, Church of Jesus Christ of Latter-Day Saints, 1964 [c1963] 558 p. 18 cm. [BX8623 1964] 72-8846
I. Smith, Joseph, 1805-1844. II. Church of Jesus Christ of Latter-Day Saints.

BOOK of Mormon. 289.3
The Book of Mormon, translated by Joseph Smith, jr. Compared with the original manuscript and the Kirtland edition of 1837, which was carefully re-examined and compared with the original manuscript by Joseph Smith and Oliver Cowdery. Authorized ed. Independence, Mo., The Board of publication of the Reorganized church of Jesus Christ of latter day saints, 1943. viii p., 1 l., 818 p. 26 cm. I. Smith, Joseph, 1805-1844. II. Reorganized church of Jesus Christ of latter-day saints. Board of publication. [BX8623 1943] 43-11787
I. Title.

BOOK of Mormon.
The book of Mormon: an account written by the hand of Mormon, upon plates taken from the plates of Nephi ... Translated by Joseph Smith, jun. Division into chapters and verses with references, by Orson Pratt, sen. [5th Chicago ed.] Salt Lake City Utah, The Church of Jesus Christ of Latter-Day Saints [n. d.] 623 p. 17 cm. 67-4106
I. Smith, Joseph, 1805-1844, tr. II. Pratt, Orson, 1811-1881. III. Title.

BOOK of Mormon. 289.3
Book of Mormon commentary, by Eldin Ricks. [1st ed. Salt Lake City] Deseret News Press, 1951- v. 19cm. Contents.v.1. The first book of Nephl. Includes bibliographies. [BX8623 1951] 55-42346
I. Ricks, Eldin, ed. II. Title.

THE Book of Mormon message and evidences. 2d ed. [Salt Lake City, Church of Jesus Christ of Latter-day Saints, c1961] 217p. front. 20cm. Includes bibliography.
I. Harris, Franklin Stewart, 1912-

FARNSWORTH, Dewey.
Book of Mormon evidences in ancient America. Compiled by Dewey Farnsworth [and] Edith Wood Farnsworth. Salt Lake City, Utah, Deseret Book Co., 1964, c1953. 176 p. illus., maps, facsims. 31 cm. Bibliography, p. 175-176. 67-86556
1. Mormon, Book of. I. Farnsworth, Edith Wood, joint author. II. Title.

HUNTER, Milton Reed, 1902-.
Ancient America and the Book of Mormon, by Milton R. Hunter [and] Thomas Stuart Ferguson. Oakland, Calif., Kolob Book Co. 1964 [c1950] xv, 450 p. illus., port., maps. "Essentially a comparison of the Book of Mormon with an ancient Mexican history, known as the Works of Ixtlilxochittl." Bibliographical footnotes. 67-89851
I. Title.

NIBLEY, Hugh, 1910-
An approach to the Book of Mormon... 2d ed. Salt Lake City, Utah, Deseret Book Company, 1964. xxii, 416 p. 24 cm. Bibliographical references included in "Footnotes" (p. [377]-416) 67-51397
I. Title.

REYNOLDS, George.
A dictionary of the Book of Mormon, comprising its biographical, geographical and other proper names, by Elder George Rynolds ... Salt Lake City, Utah, J. H. Parry, 1891. 2 p. l., 364 p. 19 cm. 13-9988
I. Title.

SMITH, Joseph, 1805-1844. 289.322
The Book of Mormon. Translated by Joseph Smith, Jr. Compared with the original manuscript and the Kirkland Edition of 1837, which was carefully re-examined and compared with the original manuscript by Joseph Smith and Oliver Cowdery. Foreword by Marcus Bach. New York, Family Library [1973, c.1966] xxvii, 414 p. 18 cm. (Family Library, FY3034) [BX8623 1966] ISBN 0-515-03034-1 1.75 (pbk)
I. Cowdery, Oliver. II. Reorganized Church of Jesus Christ of Latter-Day Saints. III. Book of Mormon. IV. Title. L.C. card no. for the hardbound edition: 66-15423.

A voice from the dust; 289.3
a sacred history of ancient Americans. The Book of Mormon; this edition edited and arranged by Genet Bingham Dee. [Salt Lake City, The Deseret news press, c1939] xv, [1] p., 3 l., [3]-860 p. incl. front., illus. (part col., 1 mounted) pl. 24 cm. Map on lining-paper. [BX8623 1939] 39-24677
I. Dee, Mrs. Genet (Bingham) ed. II. Smith, Joseph, 1805-1844, tr. III. Book of Mormon.

WIGHT, Levi Lamoni, 1836-1918. 289.3'0924 B
The reminiscences and Civil War letters of Levi Lamoni Wight; life in a Mormon splinter colony on the Texas frontier. Davis Bitton, editor. Salt Lake City, University of Utah Press [1970] 191 p. facsim., geneal. table, map, ports. 24 cm. (University of Utah publications in the American West, v. 4) Includes bibliographical references. [BX8678.W5A3 1970] 74-120412 ISBN 0-87480-060-9
I. Title. II. Series: Utah. University. Publications in the American West, v. 4

Mormon Church—Anecdotes, facetiae, satire, etc.

CARD, Orson Scott. 289.3'3
Saintspeak, the Mormon dictionary / Orson Scott Card ; cartoons by Calvin Grondahl. Salt Lake City, Utah : Orion Books, 1981. [63] p. : ill. ; 22 cm. [BX8637.C37 1981] 19 81-52879 ISBN 0-941214-00-1 pbk. : 3.95
1. Mormon Church—Anecdotes, facetiae, satire, etc. I. Title.
Publisher's address: Nine Exchange Place, Suite 716, Salt Lake City, UT 84111

Mormon Church—Catechisms and creeds—Juvenile literature.

LAEMMLEN, Ann, 1959- 238'.933
Articles of faith : learning book / Ann Laemmlen and Jackie Owen. Salt Lake City, Utah : Deseret Book Co., c1982- v. <1 > : ill. ; 28 cm. A workbook of activities relating to the first four Articles of Faith of the Church of Jesus Christ of Latter-day Saints. [BX8649.L33 1982] 19 82-5018 ISBN 0-87747-878-3 (v. 1) : 3.95
1. Mormon Church—Catechisms and creeds—Juvenile literature. 2. [Mormon Church—Catechisms and creeds.] I. Owen, Jackie, 1958- II. Title.

Mormon Church—Doctrinal and controversial works.

ANDERSON, Einar, 1909- 230'.933
History and beliefs of Mormonism / by Einar Anderson. Grand Rapids, MI : Kregel Publications, [1981] p. cm. Revision of: Inside story of Mormonism. Grand Rapids : Kregel Publications, 1973. [BX8645.A67 1981] 19 81-13671 ISBN 0-8254-2122-5 (pbk.) : 4.95
1. Mormon Church—Doctrinal and controversial works. I. Title.

GEER, Thelma. 289.3
Mormonism, mama, and me! / Thelma Geer. 2nd ed. Tucson, Ariz. (P.O. Box 13532, Tucson 85732) : Calvary Missionary Press, c1980. xi, 207 p. : ill. ; 22 cm. Includes bibliographical references

and index. [BX8645.G43 1980] 19 81-146846 3.95 (pbk.)
1. Mormon Church—Doctrinal and controversial works. 2. Geer, Thelma. I. Title.

LUDLOW, Victor L. 221.6'1
Unlocking the Old Testament / Victor L. Ludlow. Salt Lake City, Utah : Deseret Book Co., 1981. ix, 239 p. : ill. ; 24 cm. Includes index. Bibliography: p. 234. [BS1171.2.L84] 19 81-68266 ISBN 0-87747-873-2 pbk. : 6.95
1. Mormon Church—Doctrinal and controversial works. 2. Bible. O.T.—Criticism, interpretation, etc. I. Title.

MCCONKIE, Bruce R. 236'.3
The millennial Messiah : the second coming of the Son of Man / Bruce R. McConkie. Salt Lake City, Utah : Deseret Book Co., c1982. xxiii, 726 p. ; 24 cm. Includes index. [BT886.M42 1982] 19 81-19599 ISBN 0-87747-896-1 : 15.95
1. Mormon Church—Doctrinal and controversial works. 2. Second Advent. I. Title.

MILLER, Ken, 1938- 238'.933
What the Mormons believe : an introduction to the teachings of The Church of Jesus Christ of the Latter-day Saints / Ken Miller. Bountiful, Utah : Horizon, c1981. 259 p. : ill. ; 24 cm. Includes index. [BX8635.2.M54] 19 81-80958 ISBN 0-88290-177-X : 9.95
1. Mormon Church—Doctrinal and controversial works. I. Title.

PEARSON, Glenn Laurentz. 221.6
The Old Testament : a Mormon perspective / Glenn L. Pearson. Salt Lake City, Utah : Bookcraft, c1980. 232 p. ; 24 cm. Includes index. Bibliography: p. [223]-225. [BS1171.2.P36] 19 80-68069 ISBN 0-88494-406-9 : 6.95
1. Mormon Church—Doctrinal and controversial works. 2. Bible. O.T.—Criticism, interpretation, etc. I. Title.

PETERSEN, Mark E. 248.4'8933
Family power! / Mark E. Petersen. Salt Lake City, Utah : Bookcraft, c1981. vii, 119 p. ; 23 cm. [BX8643.F3P47] 19 80-68473 ISBN 0-88494-417-4 : 5.50
1. Mormon Church—Doctrinal and controversial works. 2. Family—Religious life. I. Title.

PETERSEN, Mark E. 224'.106
Isaiah for today / Mark E. Petersen. Salt Lake City, Utah : Deseret Book Co., 1981. p. cm. Includes index. [BS1515.2.P47] 19 81-12476 ISBN 0-87747-882-1 : 6.95
1. Mormon Church—Doctrinal and controversial works. 2. Bible. O.T. Isaiah—Criticism, interpretation, etc. I. Title.

Mormon Church—Doctrinal and controversial works, Popular.

WARD, Maurine. 261.8'3442
From Adam's rib to women's lib / Maurine Ward. Salt Lake City, Utah : Bookcraft, c1981. 173 p. ; 23 cm. Includes bibliographical references and index. [HQ1233.W29] 19 81-71069 ISBN 0-88494-425-5 : 6.50
1. Mormon Church—Doctrinal and controversial works, Popular. 2. Feminism—Religious aspects. 3. Feminism—Religious aspects—Mormon Church. 4. Women (Mormon theology) I. Title.

Mormon Church—doctrine.

OSBORN, A. C.
The Mormon doctrine of God and heaven. An address delivered before the Baptist ministers' conference of South Carolina, November, 1898. By Rev. A. C. Osborn ... Nashville, Tenn., Sunday school board, Southern Baptist convention [1899] 63 p. 17 cm. Apr
I. Title.

PARRISH, Mary Pratt.
This is the truth; a discussion of the first principles of the Gospel. Salt Lake City, Deseret Book Co., 1963. 95 p. 23 cm. The lesson book used for 1962-63 in-service lessons of the Primary Association. 68-76378
1. Mormon Church—doctrine. 2. Church of Jesus Christ of Latter-day Saints. Primary Association—Manuals. I. Title.

RIGGS, Timberline Wales, 1890-
A skeptic discovers Mormonism. Salt Lake City, Utah, Deseret Book, 1961 [c1946] 201 p. 21 cm. 68-19765
1. Mormon Church—Doctrine. I. Title.

SMITH, Joseph, 1805-1844.
The doctrine and covenants of the Church of Jesus Christ of Latter-day Saints; containing revelations given to Joseph Smith, the prophet, with some additions by his successors in the presidency of the church. Salt Lake City, The Church of Jesus Christ of Latter-day Saints, c1957. ix, 312 p.
I. Title.

SMITH, Joseph, 1805-1844. 230.
The doctrine and covenants of the Church of Jesus Christ of latter-day saints; containing revelations given to Joseph Smith, the prophet, with some additions by his successors in the presidency of the church. Salt Lake City, Utah, The Church of Jesus Christ of latter-day saints, 1921. ix, 312 p. 19 cm. With this is bound: The pearl of great price; a selection from the revelations, translations, and narrations of Joseph Smith ... Salt Lake City, 1921. "Certain parts were issued at Zion, Jackson county, Missouri, in 1833, under the title, Book of commandments for the government of the Church of Christ. An enlarged compilation was issued at Kirtland, Ohio, in 1835, under the title Doctrine and covenants of the Church of the latter-day saints. First issued as divided into chapters and verses, by Orson Pratt in 1876. First issued with foot-notes in 1879. First published in double-column pages, with present chapter headings, revised foot-note references, and index, in 1921." [BX8628.A3 1921] 22-5313
I. Church of Jesus Christ of latter-day saints. II. Title.

SMITH, Joseph, 1805-1844. 230.
The doctrine and covenants, of the Church of Jesus Christ of latter-day saints containing the revelations given to Joseph Smith, jun., the prophet, for the building up of the kingdom of God in the last days. Divided into verses, with references, by Orson Pratt, sen. Salt Lake City, Utah, Deseret news company, 1880. 2 p. l., 508 p. 17 cm. [BX8628.A3 1880] 15-16189
I. Pratt, Orson, 1811-1881. II. Church of Jesus Christ of latter-day saints. III. Title.

SMITH, Joseph, 1805-1844.
Doctrine and covenants of the Church of the Latter day saints: carefully selected from the revelations of God, and compiled by Joseph Smith, junior, Oliver Cowdery, Sidney Rigdon, Frederick G. Williams, (presiding elders of said church) Proprietors. Kirtland, O., Printed by F. G. Williams & co. for the proprietors, 1835. iv, [5]-257, xxv p. 15 1/2 cm. 2-15094
I. Title.

Mormon Church—Doctrine—Lamanites.

LARSEN, Dean L
You and the destiny of the Indian, by Dean L. Larsen. Salt Lake City, Bookcraft [c1966] 105 p. 23 cm. 68-107575
1. Mormon Church—Doctrine—Lamanites. I. Title.

Mormon Church—Doctrine—Restoration of the Gospel.

CLUNY, Russell F
Positive evidence of the restored church. 6th ed. [Salt Lake City, Nibley Park Press] 1958 [1953] 56 p. 18 cm. 68-81394
1. Mormon Church—Doctrine—Restoration of the Gospel. 2. Mormon Church—Doctrine—Salvation. I. Title.

Mormon Church—Doctrine—Zion.

DOXEY, Roy Watkins, 1908-
Zion in the last days, by Roy W. Doxey. [1st ed.] Salt Lake City, Olympus Pub. Co. [1965] xi, 104 p. 18 cm. Bibliography: p. [83]-84. 68-33251
1. Mormon Church—Doctrine—Zion. I. Title.

Mormon Church-Education.

GARDINER, Erma Y
Three steps to good teaching by Erma Y. Gardiner. Illustrations by LaFawn G. Holt. Salt Lake City, Church of Jesus Christ of Latter-day Saints, General Board of Primary Association, 1960. 107 p. illus. 23 cm. 66-40952
1. Mormon Church-Education. I. Title.

Mormon Church — Education, Elementary.

CHURCH of Jesus Christ of Latter-day Saints. Primary Association. General Board.
Blazing the trail, lessons for nine, ten, and eleven-year-old trail builders. Salt Lake City, 1961. 331 p. illus. 22 cm. 67-34406
1. Mormon Church — Education, Elementary. I. Title.

CHURCH of Jesus Christ of Latter-Day Saints. Primary Association. General Board.
Guiding ... along the trail. Salt Lake City, 1959. 251 p. illus. 23 cm. 66-47212
1. Mormon Church — Education, Elementary. I. Title.

CHURCH of Jesus Christ of Latter-Day Saints. Primary Association. General Board.
Handbook for guide patrol leaders. Salt Lake City, 1961. 187 p. illus. 30 cm. 67-87493
1. Mormon Church — Education, Elementary. 2. Boy Scouts of America. I. Title.

CHURCH of Jesus Christ of Latter-Day Saints. Primary Association. General Board.
Lesson book for top pilots, children eight years old. Salt Lake City, 1962. 274 p. illus. 23 cm. 66-47211
1. Mormon Church — Education, Elementary. I. Title. II. Title: Top pilot lessons.

CHURCH of Jesus Christ of Latter-Day Saints. Primary Association. General Board.
Mission primary lessons for compass pilots, children 7 and 8 years of age. Salt Lake City, 1956. 245 p. illus. 23 cm. 67-36725
1. Mormon Church — Education, Elementary. I. Title. II. Title: Compass pilot lessons.

CHURCH of Jesus Christ of Latter-Day Saints. Primary Association. General Board.
Mission primary lessons for radar pilots. Salt Lake City, 1957. 237 p. illus. 23 cm. 66-47210
1. Mormon Church — Education, Elementary. I. Title. II. Title: Radar pilot lessons.

CHURCH of Jesus Christ of Latter-Day Saints. Primary Association. General Board.
Trekking along the trail, lessons for nine, ten, and eleven-year-old trail builders. Salt Lake City, 1963. 320 p. illus. 23 cm. 67-33915
1. Mormon Church — Education, Elementary. I. Title.

Mormon Church—Education, Religious.

SMITH, Virgil B
How to spark gospel learning, a handbook for parents, teachers, missionaries, servicemen, speakers, advisers, firesides and students of the Church of Jesus Christ of Latter-day Saints. [Salt Lake City, Inland West Distributors, c1961] 134 p. illus. 68-58523
1. Mormon Church—Education, Religious. I. Title.

Mormon Church — History — 1891—

ALLEN, James B
Mormonism in the twentieth century, by James B. Allen and Richard O. Cowan. Provo, Utah, Extension Publications, Brigham Young University Press, c1964. 162 p. 28 cm. NUC66
1. Mormon Church — History — 1891- I. Cowan, Richard Olsen, joint author. II. Title.

KING, Hannah Tapfield.
An epic poem. A synopsis of the rise of the church of Jesus Christ of Latter-day saints, from the birth of the prophet Joseph Smith to the arrival on the spot which the prophet Brigham Young pronounced to be the site of the future Salt Lake City. By Hannah Tapfield King. Salt Lake City, Pub. at the Juvenile instructor office, 1884. 62 p. 18 1/2 cm. 10-31336
I. Title.

Mormon Church—Missions—Anecdotes, facetiae, satire, etc.

NIELSON, Larry. 818'.5407
How would you like to see the slides of my mission? / Larry Nielson. Bountiful, Utah : Horizon, 1981, c1980. 157 p. : ill. ; 22 cm. [PN6231.M675N5] 19 80-82708 ISBN 0-88290-153-2 pbk. : 4.95
1. Mormon Church—Missions—Anecdotes, facetiae, satire, etc. I. Title.

Mormon church-Missions-Finnish.

SUOMI calls,
compiled and edited by Alvin S. Anderson, Udell E. Poulsen, and Phileon B. Robinson. [Salt Lake City, Finnish Mission Society, c1957] 239p. illus., ports.
1. Mormon church-Missions-Finnish. 2. Mormons-Biography. I. Anderson, Alvin S

Mormon Church—Missions—Hawaii.

PACK, Alice C
Building missionaries in Hawaii, 1960-1963. [Laie, Hawaii, Church College of Hawaii, 1963?] [168] p. (chiefly illus.) 29 cm. On cover: The Church building missionaries.
1. Mormon Church—Missions—Hawaii. I. Church College of Hawaii. II. Title.

Mormon Church — Music

CHURCH of Jesus Christ of Latter-Day Saints. Primary General Board Music Committee.
Teaching the gospel through music. [Salt Lake City? n.d.] 99 p. illus. 23 cm. Cover-title. "Music manual for primary choristers and organists." 66-49021
1. Mormon Church — Music I. Title.

Mormon Church—Negroes.

RICHARDSON, Arthur M
That ye may not be deceived; a discussion of the racial problem; segregation or integration? [Salt Lake City?, n. d.] 15 p. 19 cm. Includes bibliography. 68-30364
1. Mormon Church—Negroes. I. Title. II. Title: Segregation or integration?

Mormon Church—Sacred books.

BENNION, Lowell L. 1908- 289.3'2
(Lowell Lindsay),
Understanding the Scriptures / Lowell L. Bennion. Salt Lake City, Utah : Deseret Book Company, c1981. vii, 88 p. ; 24 cm. Includes index. [BS511.2.B46] 19 81-66422 ISBN 0-87747-863-5 : 5.95
1. Mormon Church—Sacred books 2. Bible—Criticism, interpretation, etc. I. Title.

BIBLE. English. 1944. 220.52
Smith.
... *The Holy Scriptures,* containing the Old and New Testaments; an inspired revision of the Authorized version, by Joseph Smith, junior. A new corr. ed., the Reorganized church of Jesus Christ of latter day saints. Independence, Mo., Herald publishing house [c1944] 1418, 159 p. 20 1/2 cm. At head of title: Inspired version. "Concordance, especially prepared for use with the inspired version of the Holy Scriptures": 159 p. at end. [BX8630.A2 1944] 45-1690
I. Bible. English. 1944. Authorized. II. Smith, Joseph, 1805-1844 III. Reorganized church of Jesus Christ of latter-day-saints. IV. Title.

BIBLE. English. 1944. 220.52
Smith.
... *The Holy Scriptures,* containing the Old and New Testaments; an inspired revision of the Authorized version, by Joseph Smith, junior. A new corr. ed.; the Reorganized church of Jesus Christ of latter day saints. Independence, Mo., Herald publishing house [c1944] 1418, 159 p. 20 1/2 cm. At head of title: Inspired version. "Concordance, especially prepared for use with the inspired version of the Holy Scriptures": 159 p. at end. [BX8630.A2 1944] 45-1690
I. Bible. English. 1944. Authorized. II. Smith, Joseph, 1805-1844 III. Reorganized church of Jesus Christ of latter-day-saints. IV. Title.

BIBLE. English. Smith. 220.5'2
1974.
The Holy Scriptures. Inspired version: containing the Old and New Testaments, an inspired revision of the Authorized version, by Joseph Smith, Jr. Independence, Mo., Herald Pub. House [1974] 1201, 88 p. 21 cm. A publication of the Reorganized Church of Jesus Christ of Latter Day Saints. "Concordance, especially prepared for use with the Inspired version of the Holy Scriptures": p. 1-80 (2d group) [BX8630.A2 1974] 73-87524 9.00; 25.00 (deluxe ed.)
I. Smith, Joseph, 1805-1844. II. Reorganized Church of Jesus Christ of Latter-Day Saints. III. Bible. English. Authorized. 1974.

BIBLE. English. Smith. 220.5'2
1974.
The Holy Scriptures. Inspired version: containing the Old and New Testaments, an inspired revision of the Authorized version, by Joseph Smith, Jr. Independence, Mo., Herald Pub. House [1974] 1201, 88 p. 21 cm. A publication of the Reorganized Church of Jesus Christ of Latter Day Saints. "Concordance, especially prepared for use with the Inspired version of the Holy Scriptures": p. 1-80 (2d group) [BX8630.A2 1974] 73-87524 9.00; 25.00 (deluxe ed.)
I. Smith, Joseph, 1805-1844. II. Reorganized Church of Jesus Christ of Latter-Day Saints. III. Bible. English. Authorized. 1974.

BOOK of Mormon. 289.3
The New Testament of ancient America; adapted from the third book of Nephi of the Book of Mormon. Independence, Mo., Herald House [c1955] 216p. 12cm. [BX8623 1955] 56-7615
I. Title.

BOOK of Mormon.
[The Book of Mormon; an account written by the hand of Mormon upon plates taken from the plates of Nephi ... Tr. by Joseph Smith, jun.] New York, Pub. for the Deseret university, by Russell bros., 1869. 3 p. l., [v]-xi, 443 p. 23 cm. Title and text printed in the Deseret alphabet. cf. Bancroft, Hist., of Utah, 1889, p. 712-714. [BX8624 1869]
I. Smith, Joseph, 1805-1844, tr. II. Title.

Mormon Church—Sacred books—Study and teaching.

BIBLE. English. 1959. Smith.
The Holy Scriptures, containing the Old and New Testaments; an inspired revision of the Authorized version, by Joseph Smith, junior. A new, corr. ed. The Reorganized church of Jesus Christ of latter day saints. Independence, Mo., Herald Publishing House [1959] 1418, 159 p. 20 cm. Concordance in last 159 p. NUC66
I. Bible. English. 1959. Authorized. II. Smith, Joseph, 1805-1844. III. Reorganized Church of Jesus Christ of Latter-Day Saints. IV. Title.

PACKARD, Dennis J. 220'.07
Feasting upon the word / Dennis & Sandra Packard ; foreword and afterword by Arthur Henry King. Salt Lake City, Utah : Deseret Book Co., 1981. xv, 242 p. ; 24 cm. Includes index. [BS600.2.P28] 19 81-12446 ISBN 0-87747-879-1 : 6.95
1. Mormon Church—Sacred books—Study and teaching. 2. Bible—Study. I. Packard, Sandra, 1950- II. Title.

WIDTSOE, John Andreas, 1872-
Rational theology; as taught by the Church of Jesus Christ of Latter-day saints, by John A. Widtsoe. Pub. for the use of the Melchizedek priesthood, by the General priesthood committee. [Salt Lake City, Printed by the Deseret news] 1915. viii, 190 p. 20 cm. "References": p. [179]-184. 15-3403
I. Title.

Mormon Church—Sermons.

SILL, Sterling W. 252'.0933
The upward reach / by Sterling W. Sill. Bountiful, Utah : Horizon Publishers, c1980. 407 p. : port. ; 24 cm. Reprint. Originally published: Salt Lake City : Bookcraft, 1962. Includes index. [BX8639.S5U6 1980] 19 80-83863 ISBN 0-88290-167-2 : 9.95
1. Mormon Church—Sermons. 2. Sermons, American. I. Title.

Mormon Church — Temples — Oakland, Calif.

IMPROVEMENT Era.
Oakland Temple issue. [Salt Lake City, c1964] 80 p. illus. Issued as a special number of the Improvement Era. 67-52685
1. Mormon Church — Temples — Oakland, Calif. I. Title.

Mormons and Mormonism.

ALLEN, Edward Jones, 289.3'3
1898-
The second United Order among the Mormons, by Edward J. Allen. New York, AMS Press, 1967 [c1936] 148 p. 23 cm. (Studies in history, economics and public law, no. 419) Originally presented as the author's thesis, Columbia University. Bibliography: p. 144-145. [BX8611.A47 1967] 71-29858
1. Mormons and Mormonism. I. Title. II. Series: Columbia studies in the social sciences, 419.

ALLEN, Edward Jones, 1898- 289.3
The second United order among the Mormons, by Edward J. Allen, PM.D. New York, Columbia university press; London P.S. King & son, ltd., 1936. 148 p. 23 cm. (Half-title: Studies in history, economics and public law, ed. by the Faculty of political science of Columbia university, no. 419) Issued also as thesis (PH.D.) Columbia university. [H31.C7 no. 419] [BX8611.A47 1936 a]]308.2: 36-34560
1. Mormons and Mormonism. I. Title. II. Title: United order among the Mormons, The second.

ALWARD, Benjamin B comp
A look at Mormonism; pictorial highlights of the Church and its people. Salt Lake City, Utah, Deseret Book Co., 1962. [c1956] 184 p. (chiefly illus.) 28 cm. NUC65
1. Mormons and Mormonism. I. Title.

ANDERSON, Edward Henry, 289.8
1858-
A brief history of the Church of Jesus Christ of latter-day saints, from the birth of the prophet Joseph Smith to the present time, by Edward H. Anderson ... Independence, Mo., Press of Zion's printing and publishing company, 1928. 245 p. illus. (incl. ports.) 14 cm. Includes preface to 4th edition, 1925. [BX8611.A48 1923] 37-11140
1. Mormons and Mormonism. I. Title.

ANDERSON, Nephi. 280.
A young folks' history of the Christ of Latter-day saints, by Nephi Anderson ... Salt Lake City, Utah, Deseret Sunday school union, 1917. 1 p. l., viii, [9]-184 p. front. illus. (incl. maps) ports. 20 cm. [BX8611.A5 1917] 17-14115
1. Mormons and Mormonism. I. Title.

ANDRUS, Hyrum Leslie, 1924-
Anticipation of the Civil War in Mormon thought, and Joseph Smith and the West. Provo, Extension Publications, Division of Continuing Education, Brigham Young University, 1966. 54 p. 28 cm. Includes bibliographies. 68-55581
1. Mormons and mormonism. 2. U. S.—Hist.—Civil War—Miscellanea. I. Title.

ARBAUGH, George 289.8
Bartholomew, 1905-
Gods, sex, and saints; the Mormon story. Rock Island, Ill., Augustana Press [1957] 61p. 20cm. [BX8645.A7] 57-857
1. Mormons and Mormonism I. Title.

ARBAUGH, George 280.3
Bartholomew, 1905-
Revelation in Mormonism, its character and changing forms, by George Bartholomew Arbaugh. Chicago, Ill., The University of Chicago press [1932] x p., 1 l., 252 p. illus. (incl. facsim.) diagr. 23 1/2 cm. Thesis (PH.D.)--University of Iowa, 1931. Without thesis note. Bibliography: p. 235-241. [BX8643.R4A7 1931] 33-3811
1. Smith, Joseph, 1805-1844. 2. Mormons and Mormonism. 3. Book of Mormon. I. Title.

AUSTIN, Emily M. 917.3'03'50924 B
Mormonism; or, Life among the Mormons: being an autobiographical sketch; including an experience of fourteen years of Mormon life [by] Emily M. Austin. Madison, Wis., M. J. Cantwell, Book and Job Printer, 1882. [New York, AMS Press, 1971] 253 p. 22 cm. [BX8695.A95A3] 74-134388 ISBN 0-404-08480-X 10.00
I. Title. II. Title: Life among the Mormons.

BAILEY, Paul Dayton 289.3
Grandpa was a polygamist; a candid remembrance. Los Angeles, Westernlore Press, c.1960. 181p. illus. 21cm. 60-13175 5.50
1. Mormons and Mormonism. I. Title.

BAILEY, Paul Dayton, 1906- 289.3
Grandpa as a polygamist; a candid remembrance. Los Angeles, Westernlore Press, 1960. 181p. illus. 21cm. [BX8638.B3] 60-13175
1. Mormons and Mormonlsm. I. Title.

BAILEY, Paul Dayton, 922.8373
1906-
Jacob Hamblin, buckskin apostle. [Limited ed.] Los Angeles, Westernlore Press, 1948. 408 p. illus., port., map (on lining-papers) 23 cm. Bibliography: p. 401-402. [F826.H2B3] 48-5696
1. Hamblin, Jacob, 2. Mormons and Mormonism. I. Title.

BAILEY, Paul Dayton, 1906-
Jacob Hamblin, buckskin apostle. Los Angeles, Westernlore Press, 1961 [c1948] 408 p. illus., port., map (on lining-papers) 23 cm. Bibliography: p. 401-402. NUC64
1. Hamblin, Jacob, 1819-1886. 2. Mormons and Mormonism. I. Title.

BAILEY, Paul Dayton, 289.3'3 B
1906-
Polygamy was better than monotony. With some home-town primitives by Don Louis Perceval. Los Angeles, Westernlore Press, 1972. 200 p. illus. 22 cm. [BX8638.B32] 72-83538 7.95
1. Mormons and Mormonism. I. Title.

BEADLE, John Hanson, 1840- 289.
1897.
Life in Utah; or, The mysteries and crimes of Mormonism. Being an expose of the secret rites and ceremonies of the Latter-day saints, with a full and authentic history of polygamy and the Mormon sect from its origin to the present time. By J. H. Beadle ... Philadelphia, Pa., Chicago, Ill. [etc.] National publishing company [1870] 608 p. front., illus., plates, ports., fold. map, facsim. 22 cm. [BX8645.B4 1870] 30-5377
1. Mormons and Mormonism. I. Title.

BEADLE, John Hanson, 1840- 289.
1897.
Polygamy; or, The mysteries and crimes of Mormonism, being a full and authentic history of this strange sect from its origin to the present time ... by J. W. Beadle ... assisted by Hon. O. J. Hollister ... with an introduction by Hon. Murat Halstead ... Philadelphia, Pa., National publishing co. [1904] 1 p. l., xvi, 604 p. illus., plates. 24 cm. [BX8645.B4 1904] 4-28228
1. Mormons and Mormonism. I. Hollister, Ovande James, 1834-1892, joint author. II. Title.

BEAN, Willard, W. 280.
A.B.C. History of Palmyra and the beginning of "Mormonism," by Willard Bean... Palmyra, N.Y. Palmyra courier co., inc., 1938. 94 p. illus. 22 1/2 cm. "This book is made up of a series of articles appearing in the Palmyra courier-journal." [BX8611.B3] A 41
1. Mormons and Mormonism. 2. Palmyra, N.Y.—Hist. I. Title.

BEARDSLEY, Harry Markle, 922.8373
1893-
Joseph Smith and his Mormon empier, by Harry M. Beardsley ... Boston and New York, Houghton Mifflin company, 1931. xii p., 2 l., 3-421 p. front., plates, ports. 22 1/2 cm. Bibliography: p. [405]-412. [BX8695.S6B4] 31-33418
1. Smith, Joseph, 1805-1844. 2. Mormons and Mormonism. I. Title.

BENNETT, Frances 289.3'0922
Grant.
Glimpses of a Mormon family. Salt Lake City, Deseret Book Co., 1968. xi, 308 p. illus. 24 cm. [CT275.B56223A3] 68-25349
I. Title.

BENNETT, John C. 289.
The history of the saints; or, An expose of Joe Smith and Mormonism. By John C. Bennett. 3d ed. Boston, Leland & Whiting; New York, Bradbury, Soden, & co.; [etc., etc.] 1842. 1 p. l., ii, [3]-344 p. incl. plates, plan. 2 port. (incl. front.) 18 cm. Cover-title: Mormonism exposed. [BX8645.B45 1842b] 35-32577
1. Smith, Joseph, 1805-1844. 2. Mormons and Mormonism. 3. Mormons and Mormnism in Illinois, I. Title. II. Title: Mormonism exposed.

BENNETT, Wallace Foster. 289.3
Why I am a Mormon. New York, T. Nelson [1958] 256p. 21cm. [BX8635.B39] 58-8020
1. Mormons and Mormonism. I. Title.

BENNETT, Wallace Foster.
Why I am a Mormon [3d ed.] Salt Lake City, Deseret Book, 1964 [c1958] 276 p. 22 cm. NUC68
1. Mormons and Mormonism. I. Title.

BENNETT, Wallace Foster.
Why I am a Mormon. Boston, Beacon Press [1965, c1958] 256 p. 21 cm. NUC68
1. Mormons and Mormonism. I. Title.

BENNION, Adam S. 289.
What it means to be a Mormon, written for the Deseret Sunday school union, by Adam S. Bennion. Salt Lake City, Utah, The Deseret Sunday school union, 1917. vi, [7]-176 p. 19 cm. [BX8635.B4] 17-14535 0.75
1. Mormons and Mormonism. I. Deseret Sunday school union, Salt Lake City. II. Title.

BENNION, Lowell Lindsay, 289.3
1908-
The religion of the Latter-day saints. (Rev. and enl. ed.) [By] Lowell L. Bennion ... Salt Lake City, Utah, L. D. S. Department of education [c1940] 309 p. diagrs. 20 cm. Contents.--pt. 1. Mormon doctrine and philosophy.--pt. ii. The restored church of Christ.--pt. iii. Joseph Smith and the restoration. Includes bibliographies. [BX8635.B42 1940] 40-29600
1. Mormons and Mormonism. I. Title.

BERRETT, William Edwin. 289.3
The restored church; a brief history of the growth and doctrines of the Church of Jesus Christ of Latter-Day Saints. 10th ed. [Salt Lake City] Deseret Book Co., 1961. 490p. illus. 27cm. Includes bibliography. [BX8611.B35 1961] 61-65165
1. Mormons and Mormonism. I. Title.

BERRETT, William Edwin.
The restored church; a brief history of the growth and doctrines of the Church of Jesus Christ of Latter-Day Saints. 13th ed. [Salt Lake City] Deseret Book Co., 1965. 490 p. illus. 27 cm. Includes bibliography. 67-39700
1. Mormons and Mormonism. I. Title.

BERRETT, William Edwin. 289.3
The restored church; a brief history of the origin, growth and doctrines of the Church of Jesus Christ of latter-day saints, by William Edwin Berrett. [Salt Lake City] Department of education of the Church of Jesus Christ of latter-day saints, 1936. xxx

p., 1 l., 560 p. incl. front. (port.) illus. fold. map. 23 cm. Written "for use as a text in the senior seminaries of the L. D. S. church." of. Pref. "Selected bibliography": p. [559]-560. [BX8611.B35] 37-2367
1. Mormons and Mormonism. I. Church of Jesus Christ of latter-day saints. Dept. of education. II. Title.

BIBLE. English. 1959. Authorized. 289.3
Holy Scriptures of the Church of Jesus Christ of Latter-Day Saints: Holy Bible. Book of Mormon. Doctrine and covenants. Pearl of great price. Including indexes, concordances, and the combination reference to the four standard works, masterpieces of religious art, a pictorial history of the church, family genealogical records, Bible maps, and other inspirational and informative features. [1st ed.] Salt Lake City, Published by Deseret Book Co., for Wheelwright Publications [1960] 1v. (various pagings) col. illus., col. maps, col. ports. 30cm. Each work has special t. p. [BX8621.D4 1960] 60-2641
1. Mormons and Mormonism. I. Book of Mormon. II. Smith, Joseph, 1805-1844. The doctrine and covenants of the Church of Jesus Christ of Latter—Day Saints. III. Smith, Joseph, 1805-1844. Pearl of great price. IV. Church of Jesus Christ of Latter-Day Saints. V. Title.

BIRNEY, Hoffman, 1891- 289.3
Zealots of Zion, by Hoffman Birney, drawings by Charles Hargens. Philadelphia, The Penn publishing company [c1931] 317 p. front., illlus. (incl. double map) plates, ports. 21 cm. Illustrated lining-papers. [Full name: Herman Hoffman Birney] Bibliography: p. [315]-317. [BX8611.B45] 31-32319
1. Mormons and Mormonism. 2. Frontier and pioneer life—Utah. 3. Mountain Meadows massacre, 1857. I. Title.

BOOK of Mormon. 289.3
Gospel teachings in the Book of Mormon, compiled by Ezra L. Marler. Salt Lake City, Deseret Book Co., 1956. 155p. 16cm. [BX8623 1956a] 56-45154
I. Marler, Ezra L., comp. II. Title.

BOOK of Mormon. 289.3
Gospel teachings the Book of Mormon, compiled by Ezra L. Marler. Salt Lake City, De5eret Book Co., 1956. 155p. 16cm. [BX8623 1956a] 56-45154
I. Marler, Ezra L. comp. II. Title.

BRAMWELL, Enoch Ernest, 1869- 289.
Why do I believe? by E. Ernest Bramwell ... Salt Lake City, Utah, The Desert news press, 1926. 238, [2] p. illus. 20 cm. [BX8621.B7] 27-1512
1. Mormons and Mormonism. I. Title.

BROWN, Hugh B. 289.3
Mormonism . . . address . . . delivered on Monday, Feb. 26, 1962, to the students at the Pittsburgh Theological Seminary, Pittsburgh, Pa. Salt Lake City, Utah, Deseret [c.1962] 62p. illus. 20cm. 62-3768 .50 pap.,
1. Mormons and Mormonism. I. Title.

BROWN, Hugh B 289.3
Mormonism . . . address . . . delivered on Monday, Feb. 26, 1962, to the students at the Pittsburgh Theological Seminary, Pittsburgh, Pa. Salt Lake City, Deseret Book Co. [1962] 62p. illus. 20cm. [BX8637.B7] 62-3768
1. Mormons and Mormonism. I. Title.

BROWN, James Stephens, b.1828.
Giant of the Lord; life of a pioneer. Salt Lake City, Bookcraft [1960] 524 p. illus. 24 cm. 66-13354
1. Mormons and Mormonism. I. Title.

BROWN, John, 1820-1896. 922.8373
Autobiography of pioneer John Brown, 1820-1896, arranged and published by his son, John Zimmerman Brown... Salt Lake City, Utah, [Press of Stevens & Wallis, inc.] 1941. 6 p. l., 15-491 p. front., illus. (incl. ports.) facsims. 28 1/2 cm. Pages 469-472 blank. "Errata" slip inserted. "Pioneer John Brown's genealogy, prepared for publication by his daughter, Rose B. Hayes": p. [431]-468. [F826.B88] 41-15379
1. Mormons and Mormonism. I. Brown, John Zimmerman, 1873- II. Hayes, Mrs. Harriet Rose Ann (Brown) 1860- III. Title.

BROWN, John Elward. 289.
"In the cult kindgom" Mormonism, Eddyism, Russellism, by John Elward Brown ... Chicago, Siloam Springs, Ark. [etc.] International federation publishing company [1918] 124 p. 19 cm. [BX8645.B8] 18-3542
1. Russell, Charles Taze, 1852-1916. 2. Mormons and Mormonism. 3. Christian Science. I. Title.

[CAMAN, William Cooper]
Rattling, roaring rhymes on Mormon Utah and her institutions. Life among the Rocky Mountain saints, the land of many wives and much silver; or, The follies and crimes of Bigamy Young and his po-lig. divines. By "Will Cooper" [pseud.] Chicago, Union publishing company, 1874. iv, 7-140 p. 20 cm. [F827.C28] 12-9294
1. Mormons and Mornonism. 2. Utah. I. Title.

CANNON, Elaine. 808.066'92
Putting life in your life story / Elaine Cannon. Salt Lake City : Desert Book Co., 1977. 94 p. ; 23 cm. Includes index. [BX8638.C36] 77-15451 ISBN 0-87747-679-9 pbk. : 2.95
1. Mormons and Mormonism. 2. Diaries—Authorship. 3. Biography (as a literary form) I. Title.

CANNON, Frank Jenne, 1859- 922
Brigham Young and his Mormon empire, by Frank J. Cannon and George L. Knapp ... New York, Chicago [etc.] Fleming H. Revell company [1913]. 398 p. front., plates, ports. 21 cm. [F826.Y7] 13-24816 1.50.
1. Young, Brigham, 1801-1877. 2. Mormons and Mormonism. 3. Utah==Hist. I. Knapp, George Leonard, 1872- joint author. II. Title.

CANNON, Frank Jenne, 1859- 922
Under the prophet in Utah; the national menace of a political priestcraft, by Frank J. Cannon ... and Harvey J. O'Higgins ... Boston, Mass., The C. M. Clark publishing co., 1911. 402 p. front. (port.) 19 1/2 cm. First published in Everybody's magazine. [F826.C22] 12-1307
1. Mormons and Mormonism. 2. Utah—Pol. & govt. I. O'Higgins, Harvey Jerrold, 1876-1929. II. Title.

CANNON, George Quayle, 1827-1901. 266.
My first mission. By George Q. Cannon ... Salt Lake City, Utah, Juvenile instructor office, 1879. 3 p. l, 66 p. 18 cm. (Faith promoting series). [BX8661.C3] 16-3269
1. Mormons and Mormonism. 2. Missions—Hawaiian Islands. I. Title.

CANNON, George Quayle, 1827-1901. 289.3'08
Writings from the Western standard. New York, Paladin Press [1969] xv, 512 p. 22 cm. Reprint of the 1864 ed. [BX8609.C3 1969] 69-19547 25.00
1. Mormons and Mormonism. I. Title.

CARMER, Carl Lamson, 1893- 289.3
The farm boy and the angel [by] Carl Carmer. [1st ed.] Garden City, N.Y., Doubleday, 1970. 237 p. 22 cm. Bibliography: p. 220-229. [BX8635.2.C36] 76-105616 5.95
1. Mormons and Mormonism. I. Title.

CHURCH of Jesus Christ of latter-day saints. Church radio, publicity and missionary literature committee. 266.93
The missionary's hand book. Independence, Mo., Zion's printing and publishing company, 1937. 160 p. 19 1/2 cm. Preface signed: Church radio, publicity and missionary literature committee. "Literature": p. [61]-65. [BX8061.C45] 38-1803
1. Mormons and Mormonism. I. Title.

CHURCH of Jesus Christ of latter-day saints. Church radio, publicity and missionary literature committee. 280.3
A short history of the Church of Jesus Christ of latter-day saints. [Salt Lake City] The Church of Jesus Christ of latter-day saints [c1938] 4 p. l., 232 p. front., illus. (incl. ports.) 19 1/2 cm. Preface signed: Church radio, publicity and missionary literature committee. "Prepared ... chiefly by John Henry Evans."--Pref. Edited by G. B. Hinckley. [BX8611.A32] 38-17923
1. Mormons and Mormonism. I. Evans, John Henry, 1872- II. Hinckley, Gordon Bitner, ed. III. Title.

CHURCH of Jesus Christ of latter-day saints. Council of the twelve apostles. 289.2
Priesthood and church welfare; a study course for the quorums of the Melchizedek priesthood for the year 1939, prepared under the direction of the Council of the twelve, by Dr. George Stewart, Dr. Dilworth Walker [and] E. Cecil McGavin. [Salt Lake City] Deseret book company, c1938. 2 p. l., [3]-304 p. front. 19 1/2 cm. "References" at end of some of the chapters. [BX8643.W4A5 1938] 49-5689
1. Mormons and Mormonism. 2. Sociology, Christian—Mormon authors. 3. Natural resources. I. Stewart, George, 1888- II. Walker, Dilworth, 1806- III. McGavin, Elmer Cecil. IV. Title. V. Title: The Melchizedek priesthood, A study course for the quorums of.

CLAYTON, William, 1814-1879. 922
William Clayton's journal; a daily record of the journey of the original company of "Mormon" pioneers from Nauvoo, Illinois, to the valley of the Great Salt Lake, pub. by the Clayton family association. Salt Lake City, Utak. The Deseret news, 1921. x, 376 p. front. (port.) 19 1/2 cm. [F826.C6] 21-12983
1. Mormons and Mormonism. I. Title.

CONSTITUTIONAL and governmental rights to the Mormon, as defined by Congress and the Supreme court of the United States, containing the full text of the Declaration of independence, the Constitution of the United States, Washington's farewell address, the organic act of Utah territory, the Anti-polygamy law of 1862, the Poland law of 1874, the Edmunds law of 1882, the Edmunds-Tucker law of 1887, the United States statute of limitations, the poor convict release act, and the Idaho test oath law. To which is appended a digest of the decisions of the Supreme court of the United States applicable to "Mormon" cases. Carefully arranged and compiled from authentic sources. Salt Lake City, J. H. Parry, 1890. 116 p. 20 1/2 cm. 33-25487
1. Mormons and Mormonism. I. Parry, Joseph Hyrum, pub. II. U.S. Laws, statutes, etc. III. U.S. Supreme court.

CORBETT, Pearson Harris, 1900- 922.8373
Jacob Hamblin, the peacemaker. Salt Lake City, Deseret Book Co. [1952] 538p. illus. 24cm. Includes bibliography. [F826.H2C6] 53-26139
1. Hamblin, Jacob, 1819-1886. 2. Mormons and Mormonism. 3. Indians of North America—Missions. I. Title.

[COYNER, John McCutchen] comp. 289.
Hand-book on Mormonism ... Salt Lake City, Hand-book publishing co., 1882. cover-title, 95, [1] p. illus. (incl. plans) 22 cm. [BX8645.C7] 1-2085
1. Mormons and Mormonism. I. Title.

CROWE, W L. 289.
The Mormon Waterloo, being a condensed and classified array of testimony and arguments against the false prophet, Joseph Smith, his works, and his church system and doctrines, based upon standard history, science, the Bible, and Smith against himself, by Elder W. L. Crowe ... [St. Paul, Neb., 1902?] 160 p. 20 cm. [BX8645.C85] 22-10331
1. Smith, Joseph, 1805-1844. 2. Mormons and Mormonism. I. Title.

CURTIS, T W.
The Mormon problem the nation's dilemma. New data, new method, involving leading questions of the day. By T. W. Curtis. New Haven, Hoggson & Robinson, printers, 1885. vii, 62 p. 24 cm. 4-34601
I. Title.

DARTER, Francis M. 220
"The time of the end." Daniel identifies Latter day temples and Jesus as the Christ. The voice of God. The mysteries of Daniel unveiled. God sets a date for the restoration of the gospel of Jesus Christ, including His holy Latter day sanctuary--the temple. The approaching end. By Francis M. Darter. Los Angeles, Calif. [Printed by Wetzel publishing company[1928. 295 p. fold. pl. 21 cm. Folded plate mounted on inside of front cover. [BX8631.D3] 28-22711
1. Mormons and Mormonism. 2. Bible. O. T. Daniel—Criticism. interpretation, etc. 3. Bible—Prophecies. I. Title.

DARTER, Francis M. 289.3
Zion's redemption; the return of John the Revelator, the Elias, the Restorer, the gatherer of all Israel and forerunner of Christ's second coming; Latter-day saints and the Jews to be gathered by men "Like as Moses," the "marred" servant, "a root of Jesse", the "one mighty and strong," "the branch", by Francis M. Darter ... Salt Lake City, Utha, Deseret news publishing co., 1933. 224 p. incl. front. (port.) fold. pl. 20 cm. Folded plate mounted on p. [3] of cover. [BX8638.D3] 36-17786
1. Mormons and Mormonism. 2. Bible—Prophecies. I. Title.

DAVIS, Inez (Smith) 1889- 289.3
The story of the church; a history of the Church of Jesus Christ of Latter Day Saints, and of its legal successor, the Reorganized Church of Jesus Christ of Latter Day Saints. 4th ed., rev. Independence, Mo., Herald Pub. House, 1948. 645 p. ports. 23 cm. Full name: Vida Ines (Smith) Davis. Bibliographical footnotes. [BX8611.D3 1948] 48-2868
1. Mormons and Mormonism. 2. Reorganized Church of Jesus Christ of Latter-Day Saints—Hist. I. Title.

DAVIS, Inez (Smith) Mrs. 1889- 289.3
The story of the church, by Inez Smith Davis; a history of the Church of Jesus Christ of latter day saints, and of its legal successor, the Reorganized church of Jesus Christ of latter day saints. Independence, Mo., Herald publishing house, 1938. 480 p. 23 cm. [Full name: Mrs. Ida Inez (Smith) Davis] [BX8611.D3] 39-33142
1. Mormons and Mormonism. I. Title.

DAVIS, Inez (Smith) 1889- 289.3
The story of the church, by Inez Smith Davis; a history of the Church of Jesus Christ of latter day saints, and of its legal successor, the Reorganized church of Jesus Christ of latter day saints. 3d ed. Independence, Mo., Herald publishing house, 1943. 575 p. illus. (facsims.) ports. 22 1/2 cm. [Full name: Vida Inez (Smith) Davis] Bibliographical foot-notes. [BX8611.D3 1943] 43-16986
1. Mormons and Mormonism. I. Title.

DE JONG, Gerrit, 1892- 289.3
The Gospel today [by] Gerrit de Jong, Jr. Salt Lake City, Deseret Book Co., 1966. viii, 387 p. col. illus. 24 cm. "Recommended readings": p. [379]-383. Bibliographical footnotes. [BX8635.2.D4] 66-29995
1. Mormons and Mormonism. I. Title.

DYER, Alvin Rulon. 071'.92'25
The Lord speaketh, the true significance of the Sacred Grove interview with the Prophet, Joseph Smith. Salt Lake City, Deseret Book Co., 1964. xxiii, 337 p. 24 cm. Bibliographical footnotes. [BX8635.2.D92] 64-3444
1. Mormons and Mormonism. I. Title.

EDMUNDS, John K. 289.3'3
Through temple doors / John K. Edmunds. Salt Lake City : Bookcraft, c1978. viii, 147 p. ; 24 cm. Includes bibliographical references and index. [BX8643.T4E35] 78-61502 ISBN 0-88494-348-8 : 4.95
1. Mormons and Mormonism. 2. Temples. I. Title.

EDWARDS, Francis Henry, 1897-
Studies in the life and ministry of Jesus, [Rev. ed.] Independence, Mo., Herald, 1959. 64-33375
1. Mormons and Mormonism. I. Title.

EDWARDS, Francis Henry, 1897-
Studies in the life and ministry of Jesus, [Rev. ed.] Independence, Mo., Herald, 1959. 390 p. 21 cm. 64-33375
1. Jesus Christ. 2. Mormons and Mormonism. I. Title.

ERICKSEN, Ephraim Edward. 301.6'35
The psychological and ethical aspects of Mormon group life / by Ephraim Edward

Ericksen ; introductory essay, The religious thought of E. E. Ericksen, by Sterling M. McMurrin. Salt Lake City : University of Utah Press, [1975] xxii, 101 p. : port. ; 24 cm. "A Bonneville Books reprint edition." Reprint of the 1922 ed. published by the University of Chicago Press, Chicago; with a new introd. Includes bibliographical references and index. [BX8611.E7 1975] 75-310523 ISBN 0-87480-090-0 : 6.50
1. Mormons and Mormonism. I. Title.

ERICKSEN, Ephraim Edward. 280.
The psychological and ethical aspects of Mormon group life... by Ephraim Edward Ericksen. Chicago, Ill., University of Chicago press [1922] 2 p. l., vii-x, 101 p. 24 cm. Thesis (PH.D.)--University of Chicago, 1918. Published also without thesis note. [BX8611.E7] 22-24136
1. Mormons and Mormonism. I. Title.

ETERNAL quest,
selected, arranged, and ed. by Charles Manley Brown. Salt Lake City, Bookcraft, 1956. 448p. port.
1. Mormons and Mormonism. I. Brown, Hugh B II. Brown, Charles Manley, ed.

EVANS, John Henry, 1872- 922.8373
Charles Coulson Rich; pioneer builder of the West, by John Henry Evans. New York, The Macmillan company, 1936. xv p., 2 l., 400 p. front., illus. (map) plates, ports. 22 1/2 cm. "First printing." Bibliography: p. 391-392. [BX8695.R46E8] 36-13440
1. Rich, Charles Coulson, 1809-1883. 2. Mormons and Mormonism. I. Title.

EVANS, John Henry, 1872- 289.3
The heart of Mormonism, by John Henry Evans ... Written for the senior seminaries of the Church of Jesus Christ of latter-day saints ... Salt Lake City, Utah, Pub. for the Department of education by the Deseret book company, 1930. xii, 529 p. illus. (incl. ports.) 22 1/2 cm. [BX8635.E85] 30-28324
1. Mormons and Mormonism. I. Title.

EVANS, John Henry, 1872- 922.8373
Joseph Smith, an American prophet, by John Henry Evans. New York, The Macmillan company, 1933. xi p., 2 l., 3-447 p. front., plates, ports., facsim. 24 cm. Bibliography: p. 435-437. [BX8695.S6E85] 33-8271
1. Smith, Joseph, 1805-1844. 2. Mormons and Mormonism. I. Title.

EVANS, John Henry, 1872- 280.
Our church and people, written for the Deseret Sunday school union, by John Henry Evans ... Salt Lake City, Utah, The Deseret book company, 1924. 298 p. incl. plates, ports. front. 20 cm. [BX8611.E87] 25-4302
1. Mormons and Mormonism. I. Deseret Sunday school union, Salt Lake City. II. Title.

EVANS, John Henry, 1872- 289.3
Step a little higher, by John Henry Evans. Salt Lake City, Deseret book company [c1937] 196 p. 20 1/2 cm. [BX8638.E8] 38-7430
1. Mormons and Mormonism. I. Title.

FALLOWS, Samuel, bp., 1835- 289.
1922.
The Mormon menace, by Rt. Rev. Samuel Fallows ... and Helen M. Fallows, A. M. Chicago, Woman's temperance publishing association, 1903. 122 p., 1 l. 20 cm. [BX8645.F3] 3-10059
1. Mormons and Mormonism. I. Williams, Helen May (Fallows) Mrs. joint author. II. Title.

FERRIS, Benjamin G. Mrs. 922
The Mormons at home; with some incidents of travel from Missouri to California, 1852-3. In a series of letters. By Mrs. B. G. Ferris... New York, Dix & Edwards: [etc., etc.] 1856. viii, 299 p. 19 cm. [F826.F39] 17-28705
1. Mormons and Mormonism. 2. The West—Descr. & trav. I. Title.

FERRIS, Benjamin G. 289.3'792
Utah and the Mormons. The history, government, doctrines, customs, and prospects of the Latter-day Saints. From personal observation during a six months' residence at Great Salt Lake City. New York, AMS Press [1971] 377 p. illus. 22 cm. Reprint of the 1854 ed. [BX8635.F47 1971] 77-134394 ISBN 0-404-08436-2 15.00
1. Mormons and Mormonism. I. Title.

FERRIS, Benjamin G. 922
Utah and the Mormons. The history, government, doctrines, customs, and prospects of the Latter-day saints. From personal observation during a six months' residence at Great Lake City. By Benjamin G. Ferris... New York, Harper & brothers, 1854. xii, [12]-347 p. incl. front. (port.) illus., plates. 20 cm. [F826.F4] 17-28706
1. Mormons and Mormonism. I. Title.

FISH, Joseph, 1840- 289.3'0924 B
1926.
The life and times of Joseph Fish, Mormon pioneer. Edited by John H. Krenkel. Danville, Ill., Interstate Printers & Publishers [1970] 543 p. 3 maps (2 on lining papers), port. 24 cm. Includes bibliographical references. [BX8695.F57A3 1970] 70-110886
1. Mormons and Mormonism. I. Title.

[FITCH, T Mrs.]
A brief history of the Church of Jesus Christ of Latterday saints, from the birth of the prophet Joseph Smith to the present time. By the author of the "Life of Brigham Young" ... Salt Lake City, G. Q. Cannon & sons co. 1893. viii, [9]-173 p. 19 cm. A11
1. Smith, Joseph, 1805-1844. 2. Mormons and Mormonism. I. Title.

FOLK, Edgar Estes, 1856- 289.
1917.
The Mormon monster; or, The story of Mormonism...with a full discussion of the subject of polygamy, by Edgar E. Folk...with an introduction by George A. Lofton. Chicago, New York [etc.] Fleming H. Revell company, 1900. 6 p. l., 5-372 p. front., plates, ports. 21 1/2 cm. [BX8645.F6] 1-7157
1. Mormons and Mormonism. I. Title.

FREECE, Hans P. 289.
The letters of an apostate Mormon to his son, by Hans P. Freece; illustrated by Verona P. Turini. [New York, The Wolfer press, c1908] 73 p. incl. front. (port.) illus. 21 cm. [BX8645.F75] 9-13972
1. Mormons and Mormonism. I. Title.

FROISETH, Jennie Anderson. Mrs.
The women of Mormonism; or, The story of polygamy as told by the victims themselves. Edited by Jennie Anderson Froiseth ... with an introduction by Miss Frances E. Willard, and supplementary papers by Rev. Leonard Bacon ... Hon. P. T. Van Zile, and others ... Detroit, Mich., C. G. G. Paine, 1882. xviii, 19-416 p. front., illus., plates, p orts. 20 cm. [BX8641.F8] 33-39236
1. Mormons and Mormonism. 2. Polygamy. I. Title.

FROISETH, Jennie Anderson. Mrs.
The women of Mormonism; or, The story of polygamy as told by the victims themselves. Edited by Jennie Anderson Froiseth ... With an introduction by Miss Frances E. Willard, and supplementary papers by Rev. Leonard Bacon ... Hon P. T. Van Zile, and others ... Detroit, Mich., C. G. G. Paine, 1887. xviii, 19-416 p. front., illus., plates, ports. 20 cm. [BX8641.F8 1887] 41-28175
1. Mormons and Mormonism. 2. Polygamy. I. Title.

GATES, Susa (Young) 289.3'0924 B
1856-1933.
The life story of Brigham Young: Mormon leader, founder of Salt Lake City, and builder of an empire in the uncharted wastes of Western America, by Susa Young Gates, in collaboration with Leah D. Widtsoe. Freeport, N.Y., Books for Libraries Press [1971] 287 p. illus., map, ports. 24 cm. Reprint of the 1930 ed. [BX8695.Y7G3 1971] 74-164602 ISBN 0-8369-5886-1
1. Young, Brigham, 1801-1877. 2. Mormons and Mormonism. I. Widtsoe, Leah Eudora (Dunford) 1874- joint author. II. Title.

GATES, Susa (Young) Mrs., 922.83
1856-1933.
The life story of Brigham Young, by Susa Young Gates (one of his daughters) in collaboration with Leah D. Widtsoe, with a foreword by Reed Smoot. New York, The Macmillan company, 1930. xviii p., 1 l., 388 p. front., plates. ports. 24 1/2 cm. [BX8695.Y7G3] 30-25731
1. Young, Brigham, 1801-1877. 2. Mormons and Mormonism. I. Widtsoe, Mrs. Leah Eudora (Dunford) 1871- joint author. II. Title.

GIBBS, Josiah Francis, 1845- 289.
Lights and shadows of Mormonism [by] J. F. Gibbs. [Salt Lake City, Salt Lake tribune publishing company? c1909] 535 p. incl. front., illus., ports. 21 cm. [BX8645.G5] 10-839
1. Mormons and Mormonism. I. Title.

GOLDER, Frank Alfred, 1877-
1929, ed.
The march of the Mormon battalion from Council Bluffs to California; taken from the journal of Henry Standage, by Frank Alfred Golder in collaboration with Thomas A. Bailey and J. Lyman Smith. New York, London, The Century co. [c1928] xiii, 295 p. illus. (map) plates, ports. (incl. front.) 21 cm. Maps on lining-papers. Bibliography: p. 276-280. [E409.5.I 72G6] 28-23976
1. Mormons and Mormonism. 2. U. S.—Hist.—War with Mexico, 1845-1848—Regimental histories—Ia. inf.—Mormon battalion. 3. Iowa infantry. Mormon battalion, 1846-1847. I. Standage, Henry, 1818-1899. II. Bailey, Thomas Andrew, 1902- joint ed. III. Smith, John Lyman. IV. Title.

GRAY, Albert Frederick, 289.
1886-
The menace of Mormonism, by A. F. Gray. Anderson, Ind., Gospe trumpet company, [c1926] 128 p. front. (port.) illus. (map, facsim.) plates, diagr. 19 cm. [BX8645.G65] 26-8210
1. Mormons and Mormonism. I. Title.

GREEN, Doyle L.
Meet the Mormons; a pictorial introduction to the Church of Jesus Christ of Latter-day Saints and its people [by] Doyle L. Green [and] Randall L. Green. Salt Lake City, Desert Book Co., 1965. 115 p. illus. (part col.) 29 cm. 67-92336
1. Mormons and Mormonism. I. Green, Randall L., joint author. II. Title.

GREEN, Nelson Winch. 922.
Fifteen years among the Mormons: being the narrative of Mrs. Mary Ettie V. Smith, late of Great Salt Lake City: a sister of one of the Mormon high priests ... By Nelson Winch Green. New York, H. Dayton; Indianapolis, Ind., Asher & company, 1859. xvi, 17-408 p. 19 cm. [BX8695.S7G7] 22-19204
1. Smith, Mrs. Mary Ettie V. (Coray) 2. Mormons and Mormonism. I. Title.

GREEN, Nelson Winch. 922.
Fifteen years amont the Mormons; being the narrative of Mrs. Mary Ettie V. Smith, late of Great Salt Lake City: a sister of one of the Mormon high priests, she having been personally acquainted with most of the Mormon leaders, and long in the confidence of the "Prophet", Brigham Young. By Nelson Winch Green. New York, C. Scribner, 1858. xvi, 17-388 p. front. (port.) 19 cm. Mrs. Smith's narrative is in the first person, but the authorship is claimed by Green in the Introduction. [BX8695.S7G] A 24
1. Smith, Mrs. Mary Ettie V. (Coray) b. 1829. 2. Mormons and Mormonism. I. Title.

GREEN, Nelson 289.3'3'0924 B
Winch.
Mormonism: its rise, progress, and present condition. Embracing the narrative of Mrs. Mary Ettie V. Smith, of her residence and experience of fifteen years with the Mormons; containing a full and authentic account of their social condition—their religious doctrines, and political government ... By N. W. Green. Hartford, Belknap & Bliss, 1870. [New York, AMS Press, 1972] 472 p. illus. 22 cm. [BX8695.S7G74 1972] 79-134401 ISBN 0-404-08445-1 19.50
1. Smith, Mary Ettie V. (Coray) 2. Mormons and Mormonism. I. Title.

GUNNISON, John Williams, 289.3
1812-1853.
The Mormons, or, Latter-day saints, in the valley of the Great salt lake: a history of their rise and progress, peculiar doctrines, present condition, and prospects, derived from personal observation, during a residence among them. By Lieut. J. W. Gunnison ... Philadelphia, Lippincott, Grambo & co., 1852. vi, [1], vii-ix, 13-163 p. incl. front., illus. 14 cm. [BX8611.G8 1852] 35-35226
1. Mormons and Mormonism. I. Title.

GUNNISON, John Williams, 289.3'3
1812-1853.
The Mormons, or, Latter-day Saints, in the valley of the Great Salt Lake: a history of their rise and progress, peculiar doctrines, present condition, and prospects, derived from personal observation, during a residence among them. Freeport, N.Y., Books for Libraries Press [1972] ix, 13-168 p. front. 23 cm. Reprint of the 1852 ed. [BX8611.G8 1972] 70-38355 ISBN 0-8369-6772-0
1. Mormons and Mormonism. I. Title.

GUNNISON, John Williams, 289.3
1812-1853.
The Mormons, or Latter-day saints, in the valley of the Great Salt Lake: a history of their rise and progress, peculiar doctrines, present condition, and prospects, derived from personal observation, during a residence among them. By Lieut. J. W. Gunnison ... Philadelphia, Lippincott, Grambo & co., 1853. ix, 13-168 p. front., illus. 20 cm. [BX8611.G8 1853] 35-35202
1. Mormons and Mormonism. I. Title.

GUNNISON, John Williams, 289.3
1812-1853.
The Mormons, or, Latter-day saints, in the valley of the Great salt lake: a history of their rise and progress, peculiar doctrines, present condition, and prospects, derived from personal observation, during a residence among them. By Lieut. J. W. Gunnison ... New York, J. W. Lovell company [1884] 1 p. l., [1], vi-xvii, 13-168 p. illus. 19 cm. (On cover: Lovell's library. v. 8, no. 440) [BX8611.G8 1884] 35-35225
1. Mormons and Mormonism. I. Title.

HADEN, Lila Carpenter. 241
Bits of truth; essays of love and faith according to the teachings of the Church of Latter-Day Saints, by Aunt Lila [pseud. 1st ed.] New York, Greenwich Book Publishers [1961] 114p. 21cm. [BX8638.H25] 61-10886
1. Mormons and Mormonism. I. Title.

HAMBLIN, Jacob 922.8373
Jacob Hamblin, buckskin apostle. Los Angeles, Westernlore Pr. [1961, c.1948] 408p. illus. Bibl. 7.50
1. Hamblin, Jacob, 1819-1886. 2. Mormons and Mormonism. I. Title.

HANSEN, Klaus J. 289.3'73
Mormonism and the American experience / Klaus J. Hansen. Chicago : University of Chicago Press, c1981. xviii, 257 p. ; 21 cm. (Chicago history of American religion) Includes index. Bibliography: p. 245-249. [BX8635.2.H36] 19 80-19312 ISBN 0-226-31552-5 : 17.50
1. Mormons and Mormonism. 2. Mormons and Mormonism in the United States. I. Title.

HANSON, Paul M 1878- 289.3
Jesus Christ among the ancient Americans. [Completely rev. ed.] Independence, Mo., Herald Pub. House, 1959. 204p. illus. 21cm. Includes bibliography. [BX8638.H3 1959] 59-8363
1. Mormons and Mormonism. I. Title.

HANSON, Paul M., 1878- 289.3
Jesus Christ among the ancient Americans, by Paul M. Hanson ... Independence, Mo., Herald publishing house, 1945. 256 p. xxv pl. (incl. front., map, facsims.) on 13 l. 22 1/2 cm. Bibliography: p. 221-230. [BX8638.H3] 45-5010
1. Mormons and Mormonism. I. Title.

HARRIS, Franklin Stewart, 289
1884-
The fruits of Mormonism, by Franklin Stewart Harris ... and Newbern Isaac Butt ... New York, The Macmillan company, 1925. ix p., 2 l., 146 p. diagrs. 20 cm. [F826.H28] 25-20252
1. Mormons and mormonism. 2. Utah—Soc. condit. I. Butt, Newbern Isaac, joint author. II. Title.

HARRIS, William.
Mormonism portrayed; its errors and absurdities exposed, and the spirit and designs of its authors made manifest: by William Harris, with emendations by a citinen [!] To which is added an appendix, containing the testiomony of the most prominent witnesses as taken at the trial of Joe Smith, jr., and others for high treason against the state of Missouri, before Judge King of the Fifth judical district. Warsaw, Ill., Sharp & Gamble, 1841. 64 p. 22 cm. A 24
1. Mormons and Mormonism. 2. Smith, Joseph, 1805-1844. I. Title.

HEMENWAY, Charles W. 1860- 920
Memoirs of my day. In and out of Mormondom. By Charles W. Hemenway ... Written in prison ... Salt Lake City, Utah [Printed by the Deseret news company] 1887. ix, 265 p. front. (port.) 18 1/2 cm. [CT275.H55A3] CA 17
1. Mormons and Mormonism. I. Title.

HINCKLEY, Gordon Bitner, 289.3
1910-
What of the Mormons? A brief study of the Church of Jesus Christ of Latter-Day Saints. [Salt Lake City] Church of Jesus Christ of Latter-Day Saints, 1947. 222 p. illus., ports. 22 cm. [BX8635.H5] 48-819
1. Mormons and Mormonism. I. Title.

HOWE, Eber D., b.1798.
Mormonism unveiled: or, A faithful account of that singular imposition and delusion, from its rise to the present time. With sketches of the characters of its propagators. By E. D. Howe. Painesville [O.] Printed and pub. by the author, 1834. ix, [11]-290 p. front. 18 1/2 cm. A 24
1. Mormons and Mormonism. I. Title.

HUNTER, Milton Reed. 289.373
Brigham Young, the colonizer, by Milton R. Hunter, PH.D. Salt Lake City, Utah, The Deseret news press, 1940. xvi p., 1 l., 383 p. front., illus. (maps) plates, ports. 22 1/2 cm. Bibliography: p. [368]-378. [BX8695.Y7H8] 41-4197
1. Young, Brigham, 1801-1877. 2. Mormons and Mormonism. I. Title.

HUNTER, Milton Reed. 289.373
The Mormons and the American frontier, by Milton R. Hunter ... Salt Lake City, Utah, L.D.S. Dept. of education, 1940. 280 p. 20 cm. "Supplementary readings" at end of each chapter. Bibliography: p. [267]-273. [BX8611.H8] 41-3525
1. Mormons and Mormonism. I. Title.

HUNTER, Milton 289.3'092'4 B
Reed, 1902-
Brigham Young the colonizer, by Milton R. Hunter. [4th ed., rev.] Santa Barbara, Calif., Peregrine Smith, 1973. xviii, 399 p. illus. 23 cm. A revision of the author's thesis, University of California, Berkeley, 1935. Bibliography: p. [384]-389. [BX8695.Y7H8 1973] 73-85421 ISBN 0-87905-017-9 8.95
1. Young, Brigham, 1801-1877. 2. Mormons and Mormonism. I. Title.

HUNTER, Rodello. 289.3
A daughter of Zion. Drawings by Allan P. Nielson. [1st ed.] New York, Knopf, 1972. xiv, 285 p. illus. 22 cm. [BX8695.H83A3] 74-171116 ISBN 0-394-47032-X 6.95
1. Mormons and Mormonism. I. Title.

HYDE, John, 1833-1875. 289.8
Mormonism; its leaders and designs. By John Hyde, Jun. ... New York, W. P. Fetridge & company, 1857. xii, [13]-335 p. front., illus, plates, ports. 19 cm. [BX8645.H94 1857] 40-18688
1. Mormons and Mormanisms. I. Title.

HYDE, John, 1833-1875. 289.
Mormonism: its loaders and designs. By John Hyde jun. ... 2d ed. New York, W. P. Fetridge & company, 1857. xii, [13]-335 p. front., illus., plates, ports. 20 cm. [BX8645.H94] A 21
1. Mormons and Mormonism. I. Title.

IVINS, Anthony Woodward, 366.1
1852-1934.
The relationship of "Mormonism" and freemasonry [by] Anthony W. Ivins. Salt Lake City, Utah, The Deseret news press [c1934] 254 p. front., illus., plates, ports. 22 cm. "Masonic authorities reviewed by the author": p. [5] [HS495.I 7] 35-25776
1. Mormons and Mormonism. 2. Freemasons. I. Title.

JACOBSON, Marsha T. 264'.083
Through the eyes of little saints / written by Marsha T. Jacobson ; ill. by Bill Kuhre. Salt Lake City, Utah : Bookcraft, c1978. [23] p. : col. ill. ; 26 cm. Labeled pictures and brief text explain activities at the Church of Jesus Christ of Latter-Day Saints' meetinghouses. [BX8638.J3] 78-72277 ISBN 0-88494-355-0 pbk. : 2.95
1. Church of Jesus Christ of Latter-Day Saints—Juvenile literature. 2. [Church of Jesus Christ of Latter-Day Saints.] 3. [Mormons and Mormonism.] I. Kuhre, William. II. Title.

JENSON, Andrew, 1850- 922.
Latter-day Saint biographical encyclopedia. A compilation of biographical sketches of prominent men and women in the Church of Jesus Christ of Latter-day Saints: by Andrew Jenson ... Salt Lake City, A. Jenson history company, 1901- v. front. (port.) 25 cm. Index to v. 1-2 in v. 2. [BX8693.J4] 26-1583
1. Mormons and Mormonism. I. Title.

JOHNSON, Thomas Cary, 1859- 290
Some modern isms, by Thos. Cary Johnson ... Richmond, Va., Presbyterian committee of publication [c1919] 192 p. illus. (port. group) 20 cm. "The lectures in this volume, on Mormonism, on Christian science, and on Russellism, were delivered to the senior class in Union theological seminary in Virginia, in January, 1918."--Pref. "Literature on Mormonism": p. [9]; "Literature on Christian science": p. 45; "Literature on Russellism": p. 97; "Literature on Nietzscheism": p. 158. Contents.--Mormonism.--Eddyism, or Christian science.--Wayward children of Mother Eddy: or The new thought people's ism; and the ism of the Unity school of Christianity.--Russellism.--Nietzscheism. [BL98.J6] 19-8309
1. Russell, Charles Taze, 1852-1916. 2. Nietzsche Friedrich Wilhelm, 1844-1900. 3. Mormons and Mormonism. 4. Christian science. 5. New thought. I. Title.

JOSEPHSON, Marba C. 289.3
A thumbnail sketch of Mormonism, by Marba C. Josephson. Salt Lake City, Utah, Bookcraft [1946] 95 p. incl. illus., port. 16 cm. "First edition." "Extracts from Joseph Smith's own story": p. 76-95. [BX8637.J6] 47-17735
1. Mormons and Mormonism. I. Smith, Joseph, 1805-1844. II. Title.

KANE, Thomas Leiper, 1822- 264
1883.
The Mormons. A discourse delivered before the Historical society of Pennsylvania: March 26, 1950. By Thomas L. Kane ... Philadelphia, King & Baird, printers, 1850. 84 p. 22 cm. [Miscellaneous pamphlets, v. 2, no. 10] A sympathetic account of the Mormon removal from Illinois to Utah. [AC901.M5 vol. 20-12565]
1. Mormons and Mormonism. I. Title.

KANE, Thomas Leiper, 289.373
1822-1883.
The private papers and diary of Thomas Leiper Kane, a friend of the Mormons; with an introduction and edited by Oscar Osburn Winther. San Francisco, Gelber-Lilienthal, inc., 1937. ix, [1] p., 1 l., 78, [2] p. front., (port.) pl., facsim. 20 cm. "Five hundred copies printed at the Grabhora press, October; 1937." [BX861.K25A4] 38-17812
1. Mormons and Mormonism. I. Winther, Scsar Osburn, ed. II. Title. III. Title: A friend of the Mormons.

KENNEDY, James Henry, 1849- 280.
1934.
Early days of Mormonism, Palmyra, Kirtland, and Nauvoo, by J. H. Kennedy ... New York, C. Scribner's sons, 1888. vii, 275 p. front. (2 port.) illus. (plan) pl., facsims. 20 cm. [BX8611.K4] 38-20558
1. Mormons and Mormonism. I. Title.

KIDDER, Daniel Parish, 280.2
1815-1891.
Mormonism and the Mormons: a historical view of the rise and progress of the sect self-styled Latter-day saints. By Daniel P. Kidder ... New-York, G. Lane & P. P. Sandford, for the Methodist Episcopal church, 1842. 342 p. 1 illus. 14 cm. [BX8611.K45 1842] 35-36268
1. Mormons and Mormonism. I. Title.

KIDDER, Daniel Parish, 1815- 280.
1891.
Mormonism and the Mormons: a historical view of the rise and progress of the sect self-styled Latter-day saints. By Daniel P. Kidder ... New-York, Carlton & Phillips, 1856. 342 p. 15 cm. [BX8611.K45 1856] 23-10323
1. Mormons and Mormonism. I. Title.

KIDDER, Daniel Parish, 1815-
1891.
Mormonism and the Mormons: a historical view of the rise and progress of the sect self-styled Latter-day saints. By Daniel P. Kidder ... New York, G. Lane & C. B. Tippett, for the Methodist Episcopal church, 1844. 343 p. 15 1/2 cm. [BX8811.K45] A 22
1. Mormons and Mormonism. I. Title.

KINNEY, Bruce, 1865-1936.
Mormonism; the Islam of America, by Bruce Kinney ... New York, Chicago [etc.] Fleming H. Revell company [c1912] 3 p. l., 5-189 p. front., plates. 20 cm. (On verso of half-title: Interdenominational home mission study course. 9) At head of title: Issued under the direction of the Council of women for home missions. [Full name: Edwin Bruce Kinney] Bibliography: p. 183-185. [BN8635.K5] 12-18075
1. Mormons and Mormonism. I. Title.

LA RUE, William Earl. 280.
The foundations of Mormonism; a study of the fundamental facts in the history and doctrines of the Mormons from original sources, by William Earl La Rue, B. D., with introduction by Alfred Williams Anthony, D. D. New York, Chicago [etc.] Fleming H. Revell company [c1919] 243 p. front. (port.) 20 cm. On verso of t.-p.: Published for the Home mission's council, and the Council of women for home missions. Bibliography: p. 240-243. [BX8611.L3] 19-18540
1. Mormons and Mormonism. I. Title.

[LATHAM, Henry Jepson] 922
Among the Mormons. How an American and an Englishman went to Salt Lake City, and married seven wives apiece. Their lively experience. A peep into the mysteries of Mormonism. By Ring Jepson [pseud.] San Francisco, The San Francisco news company, 1879. 115 p. 17 cm. p. 7-8 blank. [F826.L35] 16-3748
1. Mormons and Mormonism. 2. Utah—Descr. & trav. I. Title.

LAYTON, Christopher, 1821- 922
1898.
Autobiography of Christopher Layton, with an account of his funeral, a personal sketch, etc., and genealogical appendix; ed. by John Q. Cannon. Salt Lake City, Utah, The Deseret news, 1911. v p., 1 l., 317 p. front. (port) 18 cm. [F826.L42] 12-1308
1. Mormons and Mormonism. I. Cannon, John Q., ed. II. Title.

LAYTON, 289.373'0924 (B)
Christopher, 1821-1898.
Christopher Layton. Edited by Myron W. McIntyre and Noel R. Barton. [2d ed. Kaysville, Utah] Christopher Layton Family Organization [c1966] vii, 438 p. illus., ports. 24 cm. First ed. published in 1911 under title: Autobiography of Christopher Layton. "Genealogical appendix": p. [253]-408. Bibliographical references included in "Notes" (p. 221-252) [F826.L43 1966] 67-7931
1. Layton family. 2. Mormons and Mormonism. I. McIntyre, Myron W., 1923- ed. II. Barton, Noel R., 1942- ed. III. Title.

LEE, John Doyle, 1812- 922.8373
1877.
A Mormon chronicle: the diaries of John D. Lee, 1848-1876. Edited and annotated by Robert Glass Cleland and Juanita Brooks. San Marino, Calif., Huntington Library, 1955. 2v. illus. (part col.) port., map (on lining papers) 24cm. (Huntington Library publications) [BX8695.L4A32] 55-11914
1. Mormons and Mormonism. I. Cleland, Robert Glass, 1885- ed. II. Brooks, Juanita, 1898- ed. III. Title. IV. Series: Henry E. Huntington Library and Art Gallery, San Marino, Calif. Huntington Library publications

LEE, John Doyle, 1812-1877. 922
The Mormon menace; being the confession of John Doyle Lee, Danite, an official assassin of the Mormon church under the late Brigham Young; introduction by Alfred Henry Lewis ... New York, Home protection publishing co. [1905] 1 p. l., xxii, [23]-368 p. front., 3 pl., port. 19 1/2 cm. An abridged reprint of an earlier edition (St. Louis, 1881) published under title: Mormonism unveiled; including the remarkable life and confessions of John D. Lee ... [F826.L475] 5-2764
1. Mormons and Mormonism. 2. Mountain Meadows massacre, 1857. I. Lewis, Alfred Henry, 1857-1914. II. Title.

LEE, John Doyle, 1812-1877. 922
Mormonism unveiled; or, The life and confessions of the late Mormon bishop, John D. Lee; (written by himself) embracing a history of Mormonism from its inception down to the present time, with an exposition of the secret history, signs, symbols and crimes of the Mormon church. Also the true history of the horrible butchery known as the Mountain meadows massacre ... St. Louis, Mo., Bryan, Brand & co., 1877. 1 p. l., v-xiv, [15]-390 p. front., plates, ports. 22 cm. Edited by W. W. Bishop. [F826.L473] 19-10552
1. Mormons and Mormonism. 2. Mountain meadows massacre, 1857. 3. Young, Brigham, 1801-1877. I. Bishop, William W., ed. II. Title.

LEE, John Doyle, 1812-1877. 922
Mormonism unveiled; including the remarkable life and confessions of the late Mormon bishop, John D. Lee; (written by himself.) And complete life of Brigham Young, embracing a history of Mormonism from its inception down to the present time ... also the true history of the horrible butchery known as the Mountain Meadows massacre ... St. Louis, Moffat publishing company; Cleveland, O., C. C. Wick & co., 1881. xiv, [15]-413 p. incl. front. plates, ports. 22 cm. Edited by William W. Bishop. [F826.L474] 4-27969
1. Mormons and Mormonism. 2. Mountain Meadows massacre, 1857. 3. Young, Brigham, 1801-1877. I. Bishop, William W. II. Title.

LEE, John Doyle, 1812-1877. 922
Mormonism unveiled; including the remarkable life and confessions of the late Mormon bishop, John D. Lee; (written by himself) and complete life of Brigham Young, embracing a history of Mormonism from its inception down to the present time, with an exposition of the secret history, signs, symbols, and crimes of the Mormon church. Also the true history of the horrible butchery known as the Mountain Meadows massacre. Illustrated with wood engravings and colored plates. St. Louis, Mo., J. H. Mason, 1891. xiii, [1], [15]-413 p. incl. col. front. plates (part col.) ports. 21 1/2 cm. Edited by William W. Bishop. [F826.L4745] 16-8171
1. Mormons and Mormonism. 2. Mountain meadows massacre, 1857. 3. Young, Brigham, 1801-1877. I. Bishop, William W., ed. II. Title.

LEONE, Mark P. 301.5'8
Roots of modern Mormonism / Mark P. Leone. Cambridge, Mass. : Harvard University Press, 1979. ix, 250 p., [1] leaf of plates : ill. ; 24 cm. Includes index. Bibliography: p. [242]-244. [BX8611.L46] 78-25965 ISBN 0-674-77970-3 : 15.00
1. Mormons and Mormonism. I. Title.

LINN, William Alexander, 289.3
1846-1917
The story of the Mormons: from the date of their origin to the year 1901. New York, Russell, 1963. 637p. illus. 23cm. 63-12565 10.00
1. Mormons and Mormonism. 2. Utah—Hist. I. Title.

LINN, William Alexander, 289.
1846-1917.
The story of the Mormons, from the date of their origin to the year 1901, by William Alexander Linn. New York, The Macmillan company; London, Macmillan & co., ltd., 1902. xxv, 637 p. facsims., diagrs. 24 cm. [BX8611.L5] 2-4701

1. Mormons and mormonism. 2. Utah—Hist. I. Title.

LINN, William Alexander, 1846-1917. 289.3
The story of the Mormons; from the date of their origin to the year 1901. from the date of their origin to the year 1901. New York, Russell & Russell, 1963. 637 p. illus. 23 cm. [BX8611.L5 1963] 63-12565
1. Mormons and Mormonism. 2. Utah — Hist. I. Title.

LITTLE, James A. 280.
From Kirtland to Salt Lake City, by James A. Little ... Salt Lake City, Utah, J. A. Little, 1890. viii, [9]-260 p. illus. 23 cm. "This book may be considered an epitome of the motives and experiences of the saints who rejoiced and suffered in the prosecution and exoduses attending the early growth of the Latter-day work."--Pref. [BX8611.L55] 13-20443
1. Mormons and Mormonism. 2. Utah—Hist. I. Title.

LUKER, R G ed.
First ward historical review. (Church of Jesus Christ of Latter-Day Saints. First quorum of elders service project, 7) Limited ed. 66-32118
1. Mormons and Mormonism. 2. Salt Lake City — Genealogy. I. Title. II. Series.

LUKER, R G ed.
First ward historical review. [Salt Lake City, Utah, Moench, 1965] 143 p. illus. 29 cm. (Church of Jesus Christ of Latter-Day Saints. First quorum of elders service project, 7) Limited ed. 66-32118
1. Mormons and Mormonism. 2. Salt Lake City — Genealogy. I. Title. II. Series.

LUNDWALL, Nels Benjamin, 1884- comp. 289.3
Temples of the Most High ... N. B. Lundwall, compiler and publisher. Salt Lake City, Utah, 1941. x, 358 p. incl. col. front., illus. (1 col.; incl. ports. plans) 23 cm. [BX8643.T4L8] 44-26685
1. Mormons and Mormonism. 2. Temples. I. Title.

MCGAVIN, Elmer Cecil. 366.1
Mormonism and masonry. [Enl. ed.] Salt Lake City, Stevens & Wallis, 1947. 7,200 p. illus. 24 cm. Bibliographical footnotes. [HS495.M3 1947] 49-17747
1. Mormons and Mormonism. 2. Freemasons. I. Title.

MCGAVIN, Elmer Cecil. 366.1
"Mormonism" and masonry, by E. Cecil McGavin. Salt Lake City, Utah, The Desert news press [c1935] 87 p. 1 illus., pl. 19 1/2 cm. [HS495.M3] 36-16906
1. Mormons and Mormonism. 2. Freemasons. I. Title. II. Title: Masonry.

MACGREGOR, Daniel. 289.
A marvelous work and a wonder; the Gospel restored. 4th ed. Thirty-third thousand. By Daniel Macgregor. Independence, Mo., The Reorganized church of Jesus Christ of latter day saints, 1923. 250 p. incl. front. (port.) illus., diagrs. 20 cm. "Authors referred to": p. 246-250. [BX8635.M3 1923] 23-6609
I. Title.

MCNIFF, William John 289.3
Heaven on earth; a planned Mormon society, by William J. McNiff. Philadelphia, Porcupine Press, [1973 c.1972] 262, 134-174 p. 22 cm. (The American utopian adventure) Reprint of the 1940 ed. published by the Mississippi Valley Press, Oxford, Ohio, which was issued as v. 1 of Annals of America; together with H. Gardner's Communism among the Mormons, reprinted from the Quarterly journal of economics, v. 37 (1922) Bibliography: p. [239]-247. [BX8635.M332] 72-187474 ISBN 0-87991-001-1 12.50
1. Mormons and Mormonism. I. Gardner, Hamilton, 1859- Communism among the Mormons. 1972. II. Title.

MCNIFF, William John. 289.3
Heaven on earth; a planned Mormon society, by William J. McNiff... Oxford, O., The Mississippi valley press, 1940. viii p., 1 l., [11]-262 p. front. (facsim.) 23 cm. (Half-title: Annals of America; editors, Philip D. Jordan, Charles M. Thomas. vol. i) Bibliography: p. [237]-247. [BX8635.M33] 40-10036
1. Mormons and Mormonism. I. Title.

MCNIFF, William John. 289.3
Heaven on earth; a planned Mormon society, by William J. McNiff. Oxford, Ohio, Mississippi Valley Press, 1940. [New York, AMS Press, 1974] 261 p. 23 cm. (Communal societies in America) Bibliography: p. [239]-247. [BX8635.M332 1974] 72-8632 ISBN 0-404-11007-X 14.00
1. Mormons and Mormonism. I. Title.

MAJOR, Gertrude Keene. Mrs. 289.
The revelation in the mountain, by Gertrude Keene Major, with an introduction by Judge C. C. Goodwin. New York, Cochrane publishing co., 1909. 160 p. front. (port.) illus. (incl. plans) plates. 19 1/2 cm. [BX8645.M37] 25-12316
1. Mormons and Mormonism. I. Title.

MARRIAGE, monogamy and polygamy on the basis of divine law ... An open letter to the Massachusetts members of Congress by one of their constituents, with observations on the opinion of the Supreme court in Reynolds vs. United States, 98 U. S. Supreme court reports. By a citizen of Massachusetts ... Boston, J. Campbell, 1882. 76 p. 24 cm. Cover-title: The Mormon problem. [BX8641.M35] 9-10722
1. Mormons and Mormonism. 2. Reynolds, George. I. A citizen of Massachusetts.

A marvelous work and a wonder.
Salt Lake City, Deseret Book Co., 1950 [c1958] XVIII, 452 p. 23cm. An expansion of the author's mimeographed outline, The message of Mormonism.
I. Richards, Le Grand, Bp., 1886-

[MAYHEW, Henry] 1812-1887. 280.
History of the Mormons; or, Latter-day saints. With memoirs of the life and death of Joseph Smith, the "American Mahomet." Auburn [N.Y.] Derby and Miller, 1852. vii p., 1 l., [17]-399 p. incl. plates. front. 20 cm. First published in London in 1851, under title: The Mormons: or Latter-day saints. Edited by Charles Mackay. [BX8611.M3 1852] 39-17850
1. Smith, Joseph, 1805-1844. 2. Mormons and Mormonism. I. Mackay, Charles, 1814-1889, ed. II. Title.

[MAYHEW, Henry] 1812-1887. 280.
...History of the Mormons: or Latter-day saints. With memoirs of the life and death of Joseph Smith, the "American Mahomet". Auburn [N.Y.] Derby and Miller, 1853. vii p., 1 l., [17]-399 p. incl. plates. front. 20 cm. At head of title: Second thousand. First published in London in 1851, under title: The Mormons: or Latter-day saints. Edited by Charles Mackay. [BX8611.M3 1853] 5-28796
1. Smith, Joseph, 1805-1844. 2. Mormons and Mormonism. I. Mackay, Charles, 1814-1889, ed. II. Title.

[MAYHEW, Henry] 1812-1887. 280.
...History of the Mormons: or, Latter-day saints. With memoirs of the life and death of Joseph Smith, the "American Mahomet." Auburn and Buffalo, Miller, Orton & Mulligan, 1854. vii, [1], [17]-399 p. incl. plates. front. 19 1/2 cm. At head of title: Third thousand. First published in London in 1851, under title: The Mormons: or Latter-day saints. Edited by Charles Mackay. [BX8611.M3 1854] 35-34755
1. Smith, Joseph, 1805-1844. 2. Mormons and Mormonism. I. Mackay, Charles, 1814-1889, ed. II. Title.

MAYHEW, Henry, 1812-1887. 289.3'09
The Mormons; or Latter-day Saints: a contemporary history. New York, AMS Press [1971] 326 p. illus. 22 cm. Reprint of the 1852 ed. [BX8611.M3 1971] 71-134398 ISBN 0-404-08440-0 12.50
1. Smith, Joseph, 1805-1844. 2. Mormons and Mormonism. I. Title.

[MAYHEW, Henry] 1812-1887. 280.
The religious, social, and polictical history of the Mormons, or Latter-day saints, from their origin to the present time; containing full statements of their doctrines, government and condition, and memoirs of their founder, Joseph Smith. Edited, with important additions, by Samuel M. Smucker ... New York, Hurst & company [c1881) viii, [7]-466 p. incl. front., plates. 20 cm. First published in London in 1851, under title: The Mormons: or Latter-day saints. [BX8611.M3 1881] 28-25245
1. Smith, Joseph, 1805-1844. 2. Mormons and Mormonism. I. Schmucker, Samuel Moshelm, 1823-1863, ed. II. Title.

[MAYHEW, Henry] 1812-1887. 280.
The religious, social, and political history of the Mormons, or Latter-day saints, from their origin to the present time; containing full statements of their doctrines, government and condition, and memoirs of their founder, Joseph Smith, Edited, with important additions, by Samuel M. Smucker... New York and Auburn, Miller, Orton & Mulligan, 1856. viii, [17]-460 p. incl. plates. 18 cm. First published in London in 1851, under title: The Mormons: or Latter-day saints. [BX8611.M3 1856] 28-25244
1. Smith, Joseph 1805-1844. 2. Mormons and Mormonism. I. Schmucker, Samuel Moshelm, 1823-1863, ed. II. Title.

[MAYHEW, Henry] 1812-1887. 280.
The religious, social, and political history of the Mormons, or Latter-day saints, from their origin to the present time; containing full statements of their doctrines, government and condition, and memoirs of their founder, Joseph Smith. Edited, with important additions, by Samuel M. Smucker... New York, C. M. Saxton, 1858. viii, [17]-460 p. incl. plates. col. front. 20 cm. First published in London in 1851, under title The Mormons: or Latter-day saints. [BX8611.M3 1858] 36-3416
1. Smith, Joseph, 1805-1844. 2. Mormons and Mormonism. I. Schmucker, Samuel Moshelm, 1823-1863, ed. II. Title.

MEAKIN, John Phillips, 1851- 289.
Leaves of truth; Utah and the Mormons, by John Phillips Meakin. Papers, poems and letters. An appeal for a nobler manhood. Salt Lake City, Utah, 1909. 2 p. l., [iii]-viii, 274, [2] p. front., pl., port. 20 cm. [BX8635.M4] 9-9241
1. Mormons and Mormonism. I. Title.

MERKLEY, Christopher, 1808- 289.3'3 B
Biography of Christopher Merkley. Written by himself. Freeport, N.Y., Books for Libraries Press [1972] 46 p. 23 cm. Reprint of the 1887 ed. [BX8695.M35A3 1972] 70-38363 ISBN 0-8369-6780-1
1. Mormons and Mormonism.

METCALF, Anthony, b.1827. 922.8373
Ten years before the mast. Shipwrecks and adventures at sea! Religious customs of the people of India and Burmah's empires. How I became a Mormon and why I became an infidel! By A. Metcalf. [Malad City, Id., 1888] 1 p. l., 81 p. illus. 18 cm. [BX8695.M4A3] 36-30783
1. Mormons and Mormonism. I. Title.

MEYER, Eduard, 1855-1930.
The origin and history of the Mormons, with reflections on the beginnings of Islam and Christianity. Tr. by Heinz F. Rahde and Eugene Seaich. [Salt Lake City? Utah, 1961] 216 p. 29 cm. 65-46678
1. Mormons and Mormonism. I. Title.

MORMONIAD. 811.3
Boston, A. Williams & co., 1858. 100 p. 18 1/2 cm. In verse. [BX8645.M6] 36-34773
1. Mormons and Mormonism.

MORMONISM and masonry.
Salt Lake City, 1956 [c1947] 7, 200p. illus. 'Fourth enlarged edition, 1956.'
1. Mormons and Mormonism. 2. Freemasons. I. McGavin, Elmer Cecil.

MORRIS, Nephi Lowell. 922.
Prophecies of Joseph Smith and their fulfillment, by Nephi Lowell Morris. Salt Lake City, Deseret book company, 1920. vi, [2], 198 p. illus. (incl. facsims.) 19 cm. [BX8695.S6M6] 20-22060
1. Smith, Joseph, 1805-1844. 2. Mormons and Mormonism. I. Title.

MORRIS, Nephi Lowell. 922.
Prophecies of Joseph Smith and their fulfillment, by Nephi Lowell Morris. Salt Lake City, Deseret book company, 1926. xiii, [1], 329 p. illus. (incl. facsims.) port. 19 1/2 cm. [BX8695.S6M6 1926] 26-21779
1. Smith, Joseph, 1805-1844. 2. Mormons and Mormonism. I. Title.

MORTON, William Albert, 1866-
Mother stories from the Book of Mormon, by William A. Morton ... Salt Lake City, Utah, W. A. Morton [c1911] 2 p. l., 139 p. 19 1/2 x 16 cm. $0.50. 11-14109
I. Title.

THE Most holy principle. [Murray, Utah] GEMS [1970-71] 3v. 24 cm. Contents.Contents.—v. 1. The law and the testimony, 5 Dec. 1805-3 Mar. 1887.—v. 2. The horn made war with the saints and prevailed, 3 Mar. 1887-2 Sep. 1898.—v. 3. A history problem, 23 Dec. 1805-Jun. 1970. [BX8641.M65] 72-16602 261.8'3
1. Mormons and Mormonism. 2. Polygamy.

MULLEN, Robert Rodolf, 1908- 289.309
The Latter-Day Saints; the Mormons yesterday and today [by] Robert Mullen. [1st ed.] Garden City, N.Y., Doubleday, 1966. xvi, 316 p. illus., map (on lining papers) ports. 24 cm. "Bibliography and notes": p. [289]-303. [BX8635.2.M8] 66-20920
1. Mormons and Mormonism. I. Title.

NELSON, Nels Lars, 1862- 289.
Scientific aspects of Mormonism; or, Religion in terms of life, by Nels L. Nelson ... New York and London, G. P. Putnam's sons, 1904. xi, 347 p. 21 cm. [BX8635.N4] 4-19645
1. Mormons and Mormonism. I. Title.

NIBLEY, Hugh, 1910- 289.3
The world and the prophets. Salt Lake City, Deseret Book Co. [1954] 250p. 24cm. [BX8635.N5] 55-20567
1. Mormons and Mormonism. I. Title.

NIBLEY, Hugh Winder, 1910- 289.3
The world and the prophets. Enl. ed. Salt Lake City, Deseret, 1962[c.1954] 281p. 14cm. 62-52146 3.95
1. Mormons and Mormonism. I. Title.

NIBLEY, Preston. 922.8373
Brigham Young, the man and his work, by Preston Nebley... Salt Lake City, Utah, Deseret news press, 1936. 2 p. l., 551 p. front., ports. 23 1/2 cm. "This book is the out-growth of a series of articles which appeared in the church section of the Desert news during the years 1934 and 1935." [BX3695.Y7N5] 37-789
1. Young, Brigham, 1801-1877. 2. Mormons and Mormonism. I. Title.

NIBLEY, Preston, comp. 242
Inspirational talks for youth, compiled under the direction of the presiding bishopric, by Preston Nibley. Salt Lake City, Utah, The Deseret news press, 1941. 15, 320 p. 20 cm. [BX8608.N5] 41-25782
1. Mormons and Mormonism. 2. Conduct of life. 3. Youth—Religious life. I. Title.

NIBLEY, Preston, comp. 289.3
Three Mormon classics: Leaves from my journal[by] Wilford Woodruff; My first mission [by] George Q. Cannon; Jacob Hamblin [by] James A. Little. Compiled by Preston Nibley. Salt Lake City, Utah, Stevens & Wallis, inc., 1944. 2 p. l., vii-ix, [1] p., 1 l., 340, [1] p. ports. 23 1/2 cm. "First edition, April 1944." [BX8608.N53] 44-4257
1. Mormons and Mormonism. I. Woodruff, Wilford, 1807-1898. Leaves from my journal, II. Cannon, George Quayle, 1827-1902. My first mission. III. Hamblin, Jacob, 1819-1886. Jacob Hamblin. IV. Title.

O'DEA, Thomas F. 289.3
The Mormons. Chicago, Univ. of Chic. Pr. [1964, c.1957] 288p. 21cm. (Phoenix bk., P 162) 1.95 pap.,
1. Mormons and Mormonism. I. Title.

OSWALT, Martin Luther. 289.
Pen pictures of Mormonism, by Rev. M. L. Oswalt ... Philadelphia, American Baptist publication society, 1899. 95 p. 20 cm. [BX8645.O8] 18-8669
1. Mormons and Mormonism. I. Title.

PARRY, Edwin Francis, 1860- comp. 922.8373
Stories about Joseph Smith, the prophet; a collection of incidents related by friends who knew him ... Compiled by Edwin F. Parry. Salt Lake City, Utah, The Deseret news press, 1934. 192 p. illus. 16 cm. "A companion volume to 'Joseph Smith's teachings'." [BX8695.S6P3] 35-2674
1. Smith, Joseph, 1805-1844. 2. Mormons and Mormonism. I. Title.

PENROSE, Charles William, 1832- 289.
Blood atonement, as taught by leading elders of the Church of Jesus Christ of latter-day saints. An address, delivered in the Twelfth ward assembly hall, Salt Lake, City, October 12, 1884, by Elder Charles W. Penrose. Reported by John Irvine. Salt Lake City, Utah, Printed at Juvenile instructor office, 1884. 54 p. 18 cm. [BX8643.B6P4] 22-814
1. Mormons and Mormonism. I. Title.

PRATT, Parley Parker, 1807-1857. 289.8
A voice of warning and instruction to all people, containing a declaration of the faith and doctrine of the Church of the latter day saints, commonly called Mormons. By P. P. Pratt ... New-York, Printed by W. Sandford, 1837. x, [11]-216 p. 16 cm. [BX8635.P88 1837] 33-25832
1. Mormons and Mormonism. I. Title.

PRATT, Parley Parker, 1807-1857. 289.
A voice of warning, and instruction to all people, or An introduction to the faith and doctrine of the Church of Jesus Christ, of latter day saints. By P. P. Pratt ... 2d ed., rev. New-York, J. W. Harrison, printer, 1839. viii, [9]-216 p. 16 cm. [BX8635.P88 1839] 22-13522
1. Mormons and Mormonism. I. Title.

PRATT, Parley Parker, 1807-1857. 289.3
A voice of warning, and instruction to all people, or, An introduction to the faith and doctrine of the Church of Jesus Christ, of later day saints. By Parley P. Pratt ... 3d American ed. Nauvoo [Ill.] Printed by J. Taylor, 1844. x, [11]-284 p. 13 cm. [BX8635.P88 1844] 33-25817
1. Mormons and Mormonism. I. Title.

THE religion of the Latter-Day Saints. Salt Lake City, Utah, L. D. S. Department of Education [1959, c1940] 299p. 20cm.
1. Mormons and Mormonism. I. Bennion, Lowell Lindsay, 1908-

REMY, Jules, 1826-1893. 289.3'792
A journey to Great-Salt-Lake City by Jules Remy and Julius Brenchley; with a sketch of the history, religion, and customs of the Mormons, and an introduction on the religious movement in the United States. By Jules Remy. With 10 steel engravings and a map. London, W. Jeffs, 1861. [New York, AMS Press, 1972] 2 v. illus. 22 cm. Translation of Voyage au pays des Mormons. Bibliography: v. 2, p. 561-569. [F826.R3913 1972] 75-134399 ISBN 0-404-08441-9 (set) 42.00
1. Mormons and Mormonism. 2. Utah—Description and travel. 3. California—Description and travel—1848-1869. 4. Nevada—Description and travel. 5. Overland journeys to the Pacific. I. Title.

REORGANIZED church of Jesus Christ of latter-day saints, complainant. 267.
... The Reorganized church of Jesus Christ of latter day saints, complainant, vs. the Church of Christ at Independence, Missouri; Richard Hill, trustee; Richard Hill, Mrs. E. Hill, C. A. Hall [and others] ... as members of and doing business under the name of the Church of Christ, at Independence, Missouri, respondents. In equity. Complainant's abstract of pleading and evidence ... Lamoni, Ia., Herald publishing house, 1893. In the Circuit court of the United States, Western district of Missouri, Western division, at Kansas City. Binder's title: Abstract of evidence, Temple lot suit. [BX8671.A6 1893] 5-3209
1. Mormons and Mormonism. I. Independence, Mo. Church of Christ, respondent. II. U.S. Circuit court (8th circuit) III. Temple lot suit. IV. Title.

THE restored church; a brief history of the growth and doctrines of the Church of Jesus Christ of Latter-day Saints. 8th ed., 1956. Salt Lake City, Department of Education of the Church of Jesus Christ of Latter-day Saints: distributed by the Deseret Book Co., 1949 [i.e. 1956] xxx, 710p. illus., ports., maps (one fold.) 24cm. Includes bibliography.
1. Mormons and Mormonism. I. Berrett, William Edwin.

REYNOLDS, George. 289.
The story of the Book of Mormon. By Elder George Reynolds ... With original illustrations by G. M. Ottinger, Wm. T. Armitage, John Held, W. C. Morris and others. Salt Lake City, J. H. Parry, 1888. xv, [17]-494 p. incl. illus., plates. fornt. 23 cm. [BX8627.R4] 6-4156
1. Mormons and Mormonism. I. Title.

REYNOLDS, George, 1842-1909. 289.3
The story of the Book of Mormon. Salt Lake City, Distributed by Deseret Book Co., 1957. 364p. illus. 24cm. [BX8627.R4 1957] 57-59114
1. Mormons and Mormonism. I. Book of Mormon. II. Title.

RICHARD, Claude. 249
Home evening handbook for use of parents and older children, by Claude Richards. Adopted as official guide by the Highland stake of the Church of Jesus Christ of latter-day saints ... 1st ed., 1936. Salt Lake City, Deseret book company [c1936] 2 p. l., 84 p. incl. forms. plates, ports. 19 1/2 cm. [BX8643.F3R5] 36-33118
1. Mormons and Mormonism. 2. Family—Religious life. I. Title.

RICKS, Eldin. 289.3
Combination reference, a simple and orderly arrangement of selected references to the standard works of the Church of Jesus Christ of latter-day saints, prepared by Eldin Ricks. [Salt Lake City] Deseret book company, 1943. 58 p. 20 cm. [BX8621.R5] 44-27346
1. Mormons and Mormonism. I. Title.

RIEGEL, Oscar Wetherhold, 1902- 922.8373
Crown of glory, the life of James J. Strang, Moses of the Mormons, by O. W. Riegel. New Haven, Yale university press, 1935. 4 p. l., 281 p. front. (port.) 24 cm. "Published on the foundation established in memory of Amasa Stone Mather of the class of 1907, Yale college."--1st prelim. leaf. "Sources of information": p. [274]-276. [BX8695.S8R5] 35-23615
1. Strang, James Jesse, 1813-1856. 2. Mormons and Mormonism. 3. Beaver island, Mich.—Hist. I. Title.

RIGGS, Timberline Wales, 1890- 289.3
A skeptic discovers Mormonism, by Timberline W. Riggs. Los Angeles, Calif., Wetzel publishing co., inc. [1943] 200 p. 21 cm. [BX8635.R5] 43-14358
1. Mormons and Mormonism. I. Title.

RIGGS, Timberline Wales, 1890- 289.3
A skeptic discovers Mormonism, by Timberline W. Riggs. Overton, Nev., T. W. Riggs [c1944] 200 p. 21 cm. "Third edition." [BX8635.R5 1944] 45-12484
1. Mormons and Mormonism. I. Title.

RIGGS, Timberline Wales, 1890- 222.16
The Ten commandments and other subjects, by Timberline Riggs. [Overton, Nev., 1946] 130 p. 16 cm. [BV4655.R5] 47-16899
1. Mormons and Mormonism. 2. Commandments, Ten. I. Title.

RILEY, Isaac Woodbridge, 1869-1933. 922.
The founder of Mormonism: a psychological study of Joseph Smith, jr., by I. Woodbridge Riley ... with an introductory preface by Prof. George Trumbull Ladd. New York, Dodd, Mead & company, 1902. xix, 446 p. facsim. 20 cm. Bibliography: p. 427-446. [BX8695.S6R5] 2-16103
1. Smith, Joseph, 1805-1844. 2. Mormons and Mormonism. I. Title.

ROBERTS, Brigham Henry, 1857- 289.3
A comprehensive history of the Church of Jesus Christ of latter-day saints, century i ... by B. H. Roberts ... Published by the church. Salt Lake, City, Utah, Deseret news press, 1930. 6 v. fronts., plates, ports., maps (part fold.) facsims. (1 fold.) 26 cm. Most of the plates accompanied by guard sheets with descriptive letterpress. Published in the "American" from June 1909 to July 1915 under title, "History of the Mormon church": now revised. cf. Pref. An exact reproduction of "The Latter-day saints' eemigrants' guide ... By W. Clayton, St. Louis, Mo. Republican steam power press--Chambers & Knapp, 1848" (vol. iii, p. [547]-572) has special t.-p. [BX8611.R65] 30-24609
1. Mormons and Mormonism. I. Church of Jesus Christ of latterday saints. II. Title.

ROBERTS, Brigham Henry, 1857- 289.
New witnesses for God ... Salt Lake City, The Deseret news, 1895-19 v. 20 cm. Vol. 1 has title: A new witness for God. By Elder B. H. Roberts ... Salt Lake City, Utah, G. Q. Cannon & sons company, 1895. [BX8635.R62 1895] 9-12413
1. Mormons and Mormonism. I. Title.

RUMBLE, Leslie, 1892-
The Mormons or Latter-Day Saints. Completely revised and enl. ed. With a preface by Paul G. Dyer. [St. Paul, Minn., Radio Replies Press Society, 1957] 52 p. 17 cm. 66-17438
1. Mormons and Mormonism. I. Title.

SCOTT, Reva Lucile (Holdaway) 1900- 922.8373
A biography of Parley P. Pratt, the Archer of Paradise [by] Reva Stanley [pseud.] Illustrated with rare photographs. Caldwell, Id., The Caxton printers, ltd., 1937. 349 p. front., plates, ports., facsims. 23 1/2 cm. Cover-title: The Archer of Paradise. "First printing." Bibliographical references included in "Notes" (p. [334]-337) Bibliography: p. [338]-340. [BX8695.P7S35] 37-34656
1. Pratt, Parley Parker, 1807-1857. 2. Mormons and Mormonism. I. Title.

SCRAPS of biography. 922.8373
Tenth book of the Faith-promoting series. Designed for the instruction and encouragement of young Latter-day saints. Salt Lake City, Juvenile instructor office, 1883. viii, [9]-104 p. 19 cm. [BX8698.S3] 36-31806
1. Mormons and Mormonism.

SEIBEL, George, 1872- 289.
The Mormon problem; the story of the Latter-day saints, with an expose of their beliefs and practices, by George Seibel. Pittsburgh, Pa., Pittsburgh printing company, 1899. 88 p. 19 cm. [BX8645.S4] 3-85997
1. Mormons and Mormonism. I. Title.

SEIBEL, George, 1872- 289.
The Mormon saints; the story of Joseph Smith, his golden bible, and the church he founded, by George Seibel. Pittsburgh, The Lessing company, 1919. 103 p. 17 cm. [BX8635.S4] 19-15408
1. Smith, Joseph, 1805-1844. 2. Mormons and Mormonism. I. Title.

SHELDON, Henry Clay, 1845-1928. 289.
A fourfold test of Mormonism, by Henry C. Sheldon ... New York, Cincinnati, The Abingdon press [c1914] New York, Cincinnati, The Abingdon press [c1916] 151 p. 17 1/2 cm. 1 p. l., 153-192 p. 17 cm. --[Appendix] Failure of pro-Mormon apology to impair the test, by Henry C. Sheldon ... "A brief reply to the attempt of Robert C. Webb to refute my treatise in his book entitled, The case against Mormonism." [BX8645.S5] [BX8645.S5 App.] 289. 14-16787
1. Webb, Robert C. The case against Mormonism. 2. Mormons and Mormonism. I. Title.

SHOOK, Charles Augustus, 1876-
The true origin of Mormon polygamy, by Charles A. Shook ... Mendota, Ill., The W[estern] a[dvent] C[hristian] p[publication] ass'n [c1910] 223 p. 19 cm. $0.50. [HQ994.S5] 11-646
1. Mormons and Mormonism. I. Title.

SHOOK, Charles Augustus, 1876-
The true origin of Mormon polygamy, by Charles A. Shook ... [2d ed.] Cincinnati, The Standard publishing company, 1914. viii, 213 p. front., plates, ports. 20 cm. "The first edition ... was published in the year 1910."--Foreword. [BX8641.S5 1914] 14-2919
1. Mormons and Mormonism. I. Title.

SLATER, Nelson. 922
Fruits of Mormonism, or A fair and candid statement of facts illustrative of Mormon principles, Mormon policy, and Mormon character by more than forty eye-witnesses, comp.by N. Slater, A. M. Coloma, Cal., Harmon & Springer, 1851. 1 p. 6, 96, [1] p. 17 cm. An attack on the Mormons for their alleged ill-treatment of emigrants to California. [F826.S625] 18-2279
1. Mormons and Mormonism. 2. Utah—Hist. 3. Overland journeys to the Pacific. I. Title.

SLOAN, Robert W. 922
The great contest. The chief advocates of anti-Mormon measures reviewed by their speeches in the House of representatives, January 12, 1887, on the bill reported by J. Randolph Tucker as a substitute for Senator Edmund's bill against the Mormon church. By R. W. Sloan. Salt Lake City, Utah [Printed by the Deseret news co.] 1887. vii, 98 p. 18 cm. [F826.S629] 17-30836
1. Mormons and Mormonism. I. Title.

SMITH, George Albert, 1817-1875. 280.
The rise, progress, and travels of the Church of Jesus Christ of latter-day saints, being a series of answers to questions, including the revelation on celestial marriage, and a brief account of the settlement of Salt Lake Valley, with interesting statistics, by President George A. Smith ... Salt Lake City, Printed at the Deseret news office, 1869. 49 p. 22 1/2 cm. [BX8611.S6 1869] 27-11397
1. Mormons and Mormonism. 2. Church of Jesus Christ of latter-day saints. I. Title.

SMITH, Jesse Nathaniel, 1834-1906. 922.8373
Journal of Jesse N. Smith, compiled and edited by Nephi Jensen. [Salt Lake City, Stevens & Wallis, inc., c1940] 136 p. incl. front., ports. (1 double) 19 1/2 cm. [BX8695.S55A35] 40-33662
1. Smith family. 2. Mormons and Mormonism. I. Jensen, Nephi, 1876- ed. II. Title.

SMITH, Joseph, 1805-1844.
Teachings of the prophet Joseph Smith, Taken from his sermons and writings as they are found in the Documentary history and other publications of the Church and written or published in the days of the Prophet's ministry. Selected and arranged by the historian, Joseph Fielding Smith and his assistants in the Historian's Office of the Church of Jesus Christ of Latter Day Saints. [Salt Lake City Deseret Book Co.] 1956 [c1938] 410 p. 24 cm.
1. Mormons and Mormonism. I. Smith, Joseph Fielding, 1876- comp. II. Title.

SMITH, Joseph, 1805-1844. 289.3
Teachings of the prophet Joseph Smith, taken from his sermons and writings as they are found in the Documentary history and other publications of the church and written or published in the days of the Prophet's ministry. Selected and arranged by the historian, Joseph Fielding Smith, and his assistants in the historian's office of the Church of Jesus Christ of latter-day saints. [Salt Lake City] Deseret news press, 1938. 408 p. 23 1/2 cm. [BX8621.S55] 38-8207
1. Mormons and Mormonism. I. Smith, Joseph Fielding, 1876- comp. II. Title.

SMITH, Joseph, 1832-1914.
Joseph Smith III and the Restoration. Edited by his daughter Mary Audentia Smith Anderson, and condensed by his granddaughter Bertha Audentia Anderson Hulmes. Independence, Mo., Herald House, 1965. 639 p. illus. 23 cm. 68-7181
1. Mormons and mormonism. I. Anderson, Mary Audentia (Smith) ed. II. Hulmes, Bertha Audentia (Anderson) 1892- III. Title.

SMITH, Joseph Fielding, 1838-1918. 289.
Gospel doctrine; selections from the sermons and writings of Joseph F. Smith ... Salt Lake City, Utah, The Deseret news, 1919. xv, 696 p. port. 20 cm. Compiled by Dr. John A. Widstoe and others. cf. Introd. [BX8635.S6] 19-9854
1. Mormons and Mormonism. I. Widstoe, John Andreas, 1872- comp. II. Title.

SMITH, Joseph Fielding, 1876- comp. 922.8373
Life of Joseph F. Smith, sixth president of the Church of Jesus Christ of latter-day saints ... compiled by Joseph Fielding Smith ... [Salt Lake City] The Deseret news press, 1938. 490 p. front., ports., facsim. 23 1/2 cm. [BX8695.S6S57] 39-3104
1. Smith, Joseph Fielding, 1838-1918. 2. Smith, Hyrum, 1800-1844. 3. Mormons and Mormonism. I. Title.

SNOWDEN, James Henry, 1852-1936. 289.
The truth about Mormonism, by James H. Snowden. New York, George H. Doran company [1926] xix p., 1 l., 25-369 p. front., plates, ports. 21 cm. "The literature of Mormonism and list of books consulted": p. ix-xiv. [BX8611.S7] 26-15360
1. Mormons and Mormonism. I. Title.

SPENCER, Clarissa (Young) 1860- 922.8373
Brigham Young at home, by Clarissa Young Spencer with Mabel Harmer. Salt Lake City, Deseret Book Co., 1961 [c1940] 301 p. illus. 24 cm. [BX8695.Y7S58 1961] 61-3053
1. Young, Brigham, 1801-1877. 2. Mormons and Mormonism. I. Title.

SPENCER, Clarissa (Young) Mrs., 1860- 922.
One who was valiant, by Clarissa Young Spencer, with Mabel Harmer; illustrated with photographs. Caldwell, Id., The Caxton printers, ltd., 1940. 279 p., 1 l. front., plates, ports. 23 1/2 cm. [BX8695.Y7S6] 922 ISBN 40-3943
1. Young, Brigham, 1801-1877. 2. Mormons and Mormonism. I. Harmer, Mabel, 1894- II. Title.

STANLEY, Reva. 922.8373
A biography of Parley P. Pratt, the archer of paradise [by] Reva Stanley; illustrated with rare photographs. Caldwell, Id., The Caxton printers, ltd., 1937. 349 p. front., plates, ports., facsims., geneal. tables. 23 1/2 cm. "Notes": p. [334]-337. Bibliography: p. [338]-340. [BX8695.P7S7] 37-34656
1. Pratt, Parley Parker, 1807-1857. 2. Mormons and Mormonism. I. Title.

STANLEY, Reva. 922.8373
A biography of Parley P. Pratt, the archer of paradise [by] Reva Stanley; illustrated with rare photographs. Caldwell, Id., The Caxton printers, ltd., 1937. 349 p. front., plates, ports., facsims., geneal. tables. 23 1/2 cm. "Notes": p. [334]-337. Bibliography: p. [338]-340. [BX8695.P7S7] 37-34656
1. Pratt, Parley Parker, 1807-1857. 2. Mormons and Mormonism. I. Title.

STENHOUSE, Fanny, "Mrs. T. B. H. Stenhouse," 1829-
Expose of polygamy in Utah. A lady's life among the Mormons. A record of personal experience as one of the wives of a Mormon elder during a period of more than twenty years. By Mrs. T. B. H. Stenhouse ... Illustrated by H. L. Stephens. American news company, New-York, American news company, 1872. 221 p. front., plates. 20 cm. [BX8641.S75] 9-8208
1. Mormons and Mormonism. I. Title.

STENHOUSE, Fanny, "Mrs. T. B. H. Stenhouse," 1829-
A lady's life among the Mormons. A record of personal experience as one of the wives of a Mormon elder, during a period of more than twenty years. By Mrs. T. B. H. Stenhouse ... Illustrated by H. L. Stephens. 2d ed. New York, Russell brothers, 1872. 221 p. front., plates. 21 cm. First published in 1872 under title: Expose of polygamy in Utah. [BX8641.S75 1872 a] 36-3417
1. Mormons and Mormonism. I. Title.

STEWART, John J
The glory of Mormonism. Salt Lake City, Mercury Pub. Co. [1963] 256 p. illus., ports. 24 cm. Bibliographical footnotes. 68-7211
1. Mormons and Mormonism. I. Title.

STEWART, John J
Joseph Smith, the Mormon prophet, by John J. Stewart. Salt Lake City, Mercury Pub. Co. [c1966] 257 p. illus. 68-6683
1. Smith, Joseph, 1805-1844. 2. Mormons and mormonism. I. Title.

STEWART, John J
Mormonism vs. Communism. With a foreword by Ezra Taft Benson. Salt Lake City Utah, Mercury Pub. Co. [1961] 93 p. (A Mercuryette book) Bibliographical footnotes. 65-103737
1. Mormons and Mormonism. 2. Communism and religion. I. Title.

STOWELL, Earl. 289.3
The magic of Mormonism. Salt Lake City, Bookcraft [c1965] 264 p. 24 cm. Bibliography: p. 245-246. [BX8635.2.S75] 66-6717
1. Mormons and Mormonism. I. Title.

SUNDERLAND, La Roy, 1802-1885. 133
Mormonism exposed and refuted. By La Roy Sunderland. New York, Piercy & Reed, printers, 1838. iv, [5]-54 p. 15 cm. [BF1999.S85] 34-15708
1. Mormons and Mormonism. I. Title.

TALMAGE, James Edward, 1862- 289.
The great apostasy, considered in the light of scriptural and secular history, by James E. Talmage ... Salt Lake City, Utah, The Deseret news, 1909. vii, 176 p. 20 cm. [BX8635.T34] 9-28747
1. Mormons and Mormonism. I. Title.

TALMAGE, James Edward, 1862- 289.3
The story of "Mormonism", by James E. Talmage ... 7th ed. in English, including forty-sixth to fiftieth thousand. Salt Lake City, Utah, The Deseret news, 1920. 146 p. 18 cm. "The philosophical basis of 'Mormonism'": p. [97]-145. [BX8611.T3 1920] 33-35631
1. Mormons and Mormonism. I. Title. II. Title: The philosophical basis of "Mormonism".

TALMAGE, James Edward, 1862- 289.3
The story of "Mormonism", by James E. Talmage ... 10th ed. in English, including the sixtieth thousand, rev. by the author. Salt Lake City, Utah, The Deseret book company, 1930. 165 p. 18 cm. "The philosophical basis of 'Mormonism'": p. 109-165. [BX8611.T3 1930] 30-22341
1. Mormons and Mormonism. I. Title. II. Title: The philosophical basis of "Mormonism".

TALMAGE, James Edward, 1862-
The story of "Mormonism" and the Philosophy of "Mormonism," by James E. Talmage ... Salt Lake City, The Deseret news, 1914. 136 p. 18 cm. First published in The Improvement era. cf. Pref. 14-9869
I. Title.

TALMAGE, James Edward, 1862-
The story of "Mormonism," by James E. Talmage ... 2d ed. Salt Lake City, Bureau of information, 1910. 87 p. 15 1/2 cm. "A revised and reconstructed form of lectures delivered ... at the University of Michigan ... and elsewhere. The 'Story' first appeared in print as a lecture report, in the Improvement era, vol. iv; and was afterward issued as a booklet from the office of the 'Millennial star,' Liverpool."--Pref. 10-9632
I. Title.

TALMAGE, James Edward, 1862- 289.
The vitality of Mormonism; brief essays on distinctive doctrines of the Church of Jesus Christ of Latter-day saints, by James E. Talmage ... Boston, R. G. Badger [c1919] 1 p. l., 7-361 p. 20 1/2 cm. [BX8635.T4] 19-8230
1. Mormons and Mormonism. I. Title.

TALMAGE, James Edward, 1862-1933.
The great apostasy, considered in the light of scriptural and secular history. Salt Lake City, Utah, Deseret Book Co., 1964. vii, 176 p. 20 cm. 68-14565
1. Mormons and Mormonism. I. Title.

TALMAGE, James Edward, 1862-1933. 289.33
The house of the Lord; a study of holy sanctuaries, ancient and modern. Salt Lake City, Bookcraft Publishers [1962] 333 p. illus. 23 cm. [BX8643.T4T3 1962] 62-6078
1. Mormons and Mormonism. 2. Temples. I. Title.

TALMAGE, James Edward, 1862-1933.
The vitality of Mormonism; brief essays on distinctive doctrines of the Church of Jesus Christ of Latter-Day-Saints. Salt Lake City, Deseret book Co., 1957 [1919] 346 p.
1. Mormons and Mormonism. I. Title.

TANNER, Jerald.
Changes in Joseph Smith's History, by Jerald & Sandra Tanner. Salt Lake City, Modern Microfilm Co. [1965] 88 p. illus. 29 cm. Loose-leaf. 66-63301
1. Smith, Joseph, 1805-1844. 2. Mormons and Mormonism. I. Tanner, Sandra, joint author. II. Title.

TAYLOR, John, 1808-1887. 289.3
The gospel kingdom; selections from the writings and discourses of John Taylor ... selected, arranged, and annotated, with an introduction, by G. Homer Durham. [Salt Lake City] The Bookcraft company [c1943] xxx p., 2 l., 401 p. 2 front. (ports.) 23 cm. "First edition." "Notes on sources and abbreviations": p. [vii]-viii. [BX8609.T3] 44-19080
1. Mormons and Mormonism. I. Durham, G. Homer, comp. II. Title.

TOWNSEND, George Alfred, 1841-1914. 922
The Mormon trials at Salt Lake city. By Geo. Alfred Townsend. New York, American news company, 1871. 49 p. 20 1/2 x 16 1/2 cm. "Letters from Utah to the Cincinnati commercial, October, 1871." [BX8641.T7] [F826.T74] 8-18582
1. Mormons and Mormonism. I. Title.

TRAUM, Samuel Wegner, 1868-
Mormonism against itself, by Samuel W. Traum ... Cincinnati, The Standard publishing company, 1910. xx, [21]-321 p. front., ports., facsims. 20 cm. $1.00 10-14681
I. Title.

TUCKER, Pomeroy, 1802-1870. 289.3
Origin and progress of Mormonism. Biography of its founders and history of its church. Personal remembrances and historical collections hitherto unwritten. By Pomeroy Tucker ... New York, D. Appleton and company, 1867. 302 p. front., ports. 20 cm. [BX8611.T8] 35-35201
1. Mormons and Mormonism. I. Title.

TULLIDGE, Edward Wheelock. 922.8373
Life of Joseph the prophet. By Edward W. Tullidge. Plano, Ill., Published by the Board of publication of the Reorganized church of Jesus Christ of latter day saints, 1880. xii, 827 p. 4 port (incl. front.) 22 cm. [BX8695.S6T8] 36-31811
1. Smith, Joseph, 1805-1844. 2. Mormons and Mormonism. I. Reorganized church of Jesus Christ of latter-day saints. Board of publication. II. Title.

TULLIDGE, Edward Wheelock.
The women of Mormondom. New York, 1877. [Salt Lake City, 1957] 552 p. illus. 23 cm. Limited ed. 68-101202
1. Mormons and Mormonism. I. Title.

TURNER, Wallace, 1921- 289.373
The Mormon establishment. Boston, Houghton, 1966. 343p. illus. 22cm. [BX8635.2.T8] 66-19476 6.00
1. Mormons and Mormonism. I. Title.

URSENBACH, Octave F.
Why I am a "Mormon," by O. F. Ursenbach ... Salt Lake City, Utah, 1910. iv p., 1 l., 212 p. 17 1/2 cm. $1.00 10-14962
I. Title.

URSENBACH, Octave F.
Why I am a "Mormon," by O. F. Ursenbach ... Salt Lake City, Utah, 1910. iv p., 1 l., 212 p. 17 1/2 cm. $1.00 10-14962
I. Title.

UTAH Academy of Sciences, Arts and Letters. 289.3
Symposium on Mormon culture; papers presented at the fall meetings of the Jtah Academy of Sciences, Arts, and Letters, held at Utah State Agricultural College, Logan, Utah, November 14, 1952. [Logan 1952] 1v. (various pagings) 28cm. [BX8638.U8 1952a] 54-24165
1. Mormons and Mormonism. I. Title.

WAITE, Catharine (Van Valkenburg) Mrs. 1829-1913. 922.8373
The Mormon prophet and his harem; or, An authentic history of Brigham Young, his numerous wives and children. By Mrs. C. V. Waite ... Cambridge [Mass.] Printed at the Riverside press, and for sale by Hurd & Houghton, New York; [etc., etc] 1866. x, 280 p. front., plates, ports., plan. 19 cm. [BX8695.Y7W3] 36-31808
1. Young, Brigham, 1801-1877. 2. Mormons and Mormonism. I. Title.

WAITE, Catharine (Van Valkenburg) Mrs., 1829-1913. 922.83
The Mormon prophet and his harem; or, An authentic history of Brigham Young, his numerous wives and children. By Mrs. C. V. Waite ... 3d ed. Cambridge [Mass.] Printed at the Riverside press, and for sale by Hurd & Houghton, New York; [etc., etc.] 1867. x, 280 p. pl., 4 port. (incl. front.) 19 1/2 cm. [F826.Y73] 19-19021
1. Young, Brigham, 1801-1877. 2. Mormons and Mormonism. I. Title.

WALLACE, Irving 922.8373
The twenty-seventh wife. New York, New Amer. Lib. [1962, c.1961] 400p. 18cm. (Signet Bk. T2133) Bibl. .75 pap.,
1. Young, Ann Eliza (Webb) b.1844. 2. Mormons and Mormonism. 3. Polygamy. I. Title.

WALLACE, Irving, 1916- 992.8373
The twenty-seventh wife. New York, Simon and Schuster, 1961. 443 p. illus. 24 cm. Includes bibliography. [BX8641.Y7W3] 61-9599
1. Young, Ann Eliza (Webb) b. 1844. 2. Mormons and Mormonism. 3. Polygamy. I. Title.

WEBB, Robert C. 289.
The case against Mormonism; a plain discussion and analysis of the stock allegations and arguments against the Church of Jesus Christ of latter-day saints and its founder, Joseph Smith, with the intention of determining their evidential value, also their actual significance to the claims made for the system of teaching and practice, popularly known as "Mormonism". By Robert C. Webb, non-"Mormon" ... New York, L. L. Walton, 1915. 1 p. l., 157 p. illus. 19 1/2 cm. [BX8635.W4] 15-27775
1. Mormons and Mormonism. I. Title.

WEBB, Robert C. 289.3'3
The real Mormonism : a candid analysis of an interesting but much misunderstood subject in history, life, and thought / by Robert C. Webb. New York : AMS Press, 1975. xii, 463 p. ; 23 cm. (Communal societies in America) Reprint of the 1916 ed. published by Sturgis & Walton Co., New York. Includes index. [BX8635.W44 1975] 72-2971 ISBN 0-404-10736-2 : 29.00
1. Mormons and Mormonism. I. Title.

WEBB, Robert C. 289.
The real Mormonism; a candid analysis of an interesting but much misunderstood subject in history, life and thought, by Robert C. Webb ... New York, Sturgis & Walton company, 1916. 2 p. l., iii-xii, 463 p. 21 1/2 cm. [BX8635.W44] 16-8831
1. Mormons and Mormonism. I. Title.

WERNER, Morris Robert, 1897- 289.3'092'4 B
Brigham Young / by M. R. Werner. Westport, Conn. : Hyperion Press, 1975, c1925. p. cm. Reprint of the ed. published by Harcourt, Brace, New York. Includes index. Bibliography: p. [BX8695.Y7W4 1975] 75-351 ISBN 0-88355-254-X : 26.50
1. Young, Brigham, 1801-1877. 2. Mormons and Mormonism.

WERNER, Morris Robert, 1897- 922.
Brigham Young, by M. R. Werner... New York, Harcourt, Brace and company [1925] xvi, 478 p. front., illus., plates, ports. 22 1/2 cm. "First edition." Bibliography: p. 463-469. [BX8695.Y7W4] 25-11448
1. Young, Brigham, 1801-1877. 2. Mormons and Mormonism. I. Title.

WESTON, Joseph Harry, 1911-
These amazing Mormans! 12th ed. Salt Lake City, Weston [1961] 87 p. illus. 28 cm. 67-23037
1. Mormons and Mormonism. I. Title.

WESTON, Joseph Harry, 1911- 289.3
These amazing Mormons! Salt Lake City, Deseret News Press distributed by Advertiser's Service, 1948. 87 p. port. 29 cm. [BX8637.W4] 48-3388
1. Mormons and Mormonism. I. Title.

WHALEN, William Joseph. 289.3
The Latter-Day Saints in the modern day world; an account of contemporary Mormonism. New York, John Day Co. [1964] 319 p. illus., ports. 21 cm. Bibliography: p. 309-314. [BX8635.2.W5] 64-10944
1. Mormons and Mormonism. I. Title.

[WHITMER, David] 1805-1888. 230.
An address to all believers in Christ. By a witness to the divine authenticity of the Book of Mormon. Richmond, Mo., D. Whitmer, 1887. 75 p. 22 1/2 cm. [BX8637.W5 1887] 38-31398
1. Mormons and Mormonism. 2. Book of Mormon. I. Title.

WHITMER, David, 1805-1888. 230.
An address to all believers in Christ, by a witness to the divine authenticity of the Book of Mormon. Richmond, Mo., D. Whitmer, 1887 [c1926] 95 p. 22 cm. This book is a reprint of a book by David Whitmer, dictated to John J. Snyder and published in 1887. cf. Pref. [BX8637.W5 1926] 26-10715
1. Mormons and Mormonism. 2. Book of Mormon. I. Snyder, John Jacob, 1853- II. Title.

WHITMER, David, 1805-1888. 289.3
An address to all believers in Christ, by a witness to the divine authenticity of the Book of Mormon... Richmond, Mo., D. Whitmer, 1887. Reprint 1938. 97 p. 22 cm. "Fourteen revelations reprinted from the Book of commandments": p. 74-97. [BX8637.W5 1938] 38-29583
1. Mormons and Mormonism. 2. Book of Mormon. I. Church of Jesus Christ of latter-day saints. A book of commandments. II. Title.

WHITNEY, Helen Mar (Kimball) Mrs. 1828-
Why we practice plural marriage. By a "Mormon" wife and mother--Helen Mar Whitney. Salt Lake City, Utah, The Juvenile instructor office, 1884. 72 p. 17 1/2 cm. [HQ994.W5] 17-7865
1. Mormons and Mormonism. I. Title.

WHITNEY, Orson Ferguson, 1855- 289.
Saturday night thoughts; a series of dissertations on spiritual, historical and philosophic themes, by Orson F. Whitney... Salt Lake City, Utah, The Deseret news, 1921. 323 p. 20 cm. [BX8609.W4] 21-18190
1. Mormons and Mormonism. I. Title.

WILLIAMS, Marion Moffet, Mrs.
My life in a Mormon harem, by Mrs. Marion Moffet Williams. Minneapolis, Minn., 1920. 198 p. 2 port. (incl. front.) 20 cm. [BX8641.W55] 21-19952
1. Mormons and Mormonism. I. Title.

WILLIAMS, Nancy Clement. 922.8373
After 100 years. [Salt Lake City? 1951] 234 p. illus. 21 cm. [BX8695.W546W5] 51-39054
1. Williams, Rebecca (Swain) 1798-1861. 2. Williams, Frederick Granger, 1787-1842. 3. Mormons and Mormonism. I. Title.

WILSON, Lycurgus A[rnold] 1856-
Outlines of Mormon philosophy; or, The answers given by the gospel, as revealed through the prophet Joseph Smith, to the questions of life. By Lycurgus A. Wilson ... Salt Lake City, Utah, The Deseret news 1905. 3 p. l., [iii]-xiii p., 1 l., [17]-123 p. 1 illus. 20 cm. 5-33902
I. Title.

WISHARD, Samuel Ellis, 1825-
The Mormons, by Samuel E. Wishard ... New York, Literature department, Presbyterian home missions, 1904. ix p., 1 l., 121 p. front., 2 pl., 3 port. 16 1/2 cm. (Lettered on cover: Home missions of the Presbyterian church, U.S.A.) [BV2627.W5] 4-24538
1. Mormons and Mormonisn. I. Title.

WOOD, Wilford C ed. 289.322
Joseph Smith begins his work. Salt Lake City? 1958- v. illus., ports., map, facsims. 24 cm. Contents.-- v. 1. Book of Mormon. [BX8621.W6] 58-2314
1. Smith, Joseph, 1805-1844. 2. Mormons and Mormonism. I. Title.

[WYL, W.] 289.
... Joseph Smith, the prophet, his family and his friends. A study based on facts and documents. With fourteen illustrations. Salt Lake City, Tribune printing and publishing company, 1886. 4 p. l., [5]-320 p. illus. 17 cm. (Added t.-p.: Mormon portraits, or The truth about the Mormon leaders from 1830 to 1886 ... by Dr. W. Wyl. [v. 1]) [BX8645.W9] 5-28265
1. Smith, Joseph, 1805-1844. 2. Mormons and Mormonism. I. Title.

[WYMETAL, Wilhelm von Ritter 1838-1896. 289.
Joseph Smith the prophet, his family and his friends, A study based on facts and documents. Salt Lake City, Tribune Print. and Pub. Co., 1886. 320 p. illus. 17 cm. (His Mormon portraits; or, The truth about the Mormon leaders from 1830 to 1886. [v. 1]) [BX8645.W9] 5-28265
1. Smith, Joseph, 1805-1844. 2. Mormons and Mormonism. I. Title.

YOUNG, Ann Eliza (Webb) b.1844. 289.3'3
Wife no. 19. New York, Arno Press, 1972 [c1875] 605 p. illus. 23 cm. (American women: images and realities) [BX8641.Y7 1972] 72-2634 ISBN 0-405-04488-7 27.00
1. Mormons and Mormonism. 2. Polygamy. I. Title. II. Series.

YOUNG, Brigham, 1801-1877. 289.
Discourses of Brigham Young ... selected and arranged by John A. Widtsoe Salt Lake City, Utah, Desert book company [c1925] xv, 760 p. front., plates, ports. 19 1/2 cm. [BX8609.Y57] 26-12674
1. Mormons and Mormonism. I. Widtsoe, John Andreas, 1872- ed. II. Title.

YOUNG, John R., 1837- 922.
Memoirs of John R. Young, Utah pioneer, 1847, written by himself. Salt Lake City, Utah, The Deseret news, 1920. viii, [9]-341 p. front. (port.) 19 1/2 cm. [BX8695.Y8A4] 20-20023
1. Mormons and Mormonism. I. Title.

ZION'S printing and publishing company, Independence, Mo. 230.98
Handbook of the restoration; a selection of gospel themes discussed by various authors; also other items of interest to gospel students, compiled and published by Zion's printing and publishing co. [Independence, c1944] xv, [1], 704 p. illus. (incl. ports.) 22 cm. "First edition." [BX8635.Z5] 45-973
1. Mormons and Mormonism. I. Title.

ZOBELL, Albert L., comp. 289.3
Minute sermons, compiled by Albert L. Zobell, jr. Salt Lake City, Utah, Bookcraft [1946] 103 p. 16 cm. "First edition." [BX8608.Z6] 46-16247
1. Mormons and Mormonism. I. Title.

ZOBELL, Albert L., comp. 289.3
Moments with the prophets. Salt Lake City, Utah, Deseret Book Co. [c.1960] 218p. 16cm. 61-596 1.00
1. Mormons and Mormonism. 2. Aphorisms and apothegms. I. Title.

ZOBELL, Albert L comp.
Moments with the prophets. Salt Lake City, Deseret Book Co. [1960] 218 p. 16 cm.
1. Mormons and Mormonism. 2. Aphorisms and apothegms. I. Title.

ZOBELL, Albert L comp. 289.33
Words of life; continuing moments with the prophets. [Salt Lake City] Deseret Book Co., 1961. 112 p. 16 cm. [BX8608.Z65] 62-1135
1. Mormons and Mormonism. 2. Aphorisms and apothegms. I. Title.

Mormons and Mormonism—Addresses, essays, lectures.

ANDERSON, James Henry, 1857- 252.098
The present time and prophecy, being a selection of addresses made by Elder James H. Anderson, uniting this subject with the divine testimony of the prophet Joseph Smith ... Salt Lake City, Utah, The Deseret news press, 1933. 648 p. incl. illus., ports., map, plans. 23 cm. [BX8639.A6] 34-1447
1. Mormons and Mormonism—Addresses, essays, lectures. I. Title.

ASHTON, Wendell J
Bigger than yourself; short discussions on more abundant living, by Wendell J. Ashton. Salt Lake City, Bookcraft [c1965] 244 p. 24 cm. 68-26245
1. Mormons and Mormonism—Addresses, essays, lectures. I. Title.

BENNION, Adam Samuel, 1886- 252.093
The candle of the Lord. Salt Lake City, Deseret Book Co., 1958. 339p. 24cm. [BX8609.B4] 58-27485
1. Mormons and Mormonism—Addresses, essays, lectures. I. Title.

BENSON, Ezra Taft. 289.3081
... so shall ye reap; [selected addresses. Compiled by Reed A. Benson. Salt Lake City. Deseret Book Co., 1960 351p. illus. 24cm. [BX8609.B43] 60-51164
1. Mormons and Mormonism—Addresses, essays, lectures. I. Title.

BENSON, Ezra Taft. 289.3
This nation shall endure / Ezra Taft Benson. Salt Lake City : Deseret Book Co., 1977. 152 p. ; 24 cm. Includes index. [BX8639.B42T47] 77-21466 ISBN 0-87747-658-6 : 5.95
1. Mormons and Mormonism—Addresses, essays, lectures. 2. United States—Civilization—Addresses, essays, lectures. I. Title.

BOWEN, Albert E. 280.3
Constancy amid change, by Albert E. Bowen ... Radio addresses delivered over station KSL from the Tabernacle in Salt Lake City, Utah. [Salt Lake City, The Deseret news press, c1944] 211, [1] p. front. (port.) col. illus. 24 cm. [BX8639.B6C6] 46-774
1. Mormons and Mormonism—Addresses, essays, lectures. I. Title.

BRIGHAM Young University, Provo, Utah. Adult Education and Extension Services. 289.304
Our leaders speak; eternal truths spoken at Brigham Young University. Compiled by the Brigham Young University, Adult Education and Extension Services, Extension Publications. Selected and arranged by Soren F. Cox. Salt Lake City, Deseret Book Co., 1957. 206p. illus. 24cm. [BX8639.A1B7] 58-27399
1. Mormons and Mormonism—Addresses, essays, lectures. I. Cox, Soren F., ed. II. Title.

BROWN, Hugh B 289.3
Continuing the quest. Salt Lake City, Deseret Book Co., 1961. 542p. illus. 24cm. Selections from the author's radio and conference addresses, etc. [BX8609.B68] 62-738
1. Mormons and Mormonism—Addresses, essays, lectures. I. Title.

BROWN, Hugh B 289.3
Eternal quest. Selected, arr. and edited by Charles Manley Brown. Salt Lake City, Bookcraft [c1956] 448p. 24cm. [BX8609.B7] 58-48849
1. Mormons and Mormonism— Addresses, essays, lectures. I. Title.

BROWN, Hugh B. 289.3
Vision and valor [by] Hugh B. Brown. Salt Lake City, Bookcraft, 1971. x, 262 p. port. 24 cm. [BX8609.B73] 70-154210
1. Mormons and Mormonism—Addresses, essays, lectures. I. Title.

CALLIS, Charles A. 289.304
Fundamentals of religion, a series of radio addresses by Charles A. Callis ... Independence, Mo., Zion's printing and publishing company [1945] 2 p. l., 236, [3] p. 18 1/2 cm. [BX8639.C3F8] 45-7678
1. Mormons and Mormonism—Addresses, essays, lectures. I. Title.

CHURCH of Jesus Christ of Latter-Day Saints. 289.3082
Life's directions; a series of fireside addresses, by the general authorities of the Church of Jesus Christ of Latter-Day Saints. Salt Lake City, Deseret Book Co., 1962. 191p. illus. 24cm. [BX8639.A1A3] 62-38083
1. Mormons and Mormonism—Addresses, essays, lectures. I. Title.

CHURCH of Jesus Christ of Latter-Day Saints. 289.304
Messages of inspiration; selected addresses of the general authorities of the Church of Jesus Christ of Latter-Day Saints. Salt Lake City, Deseret Book Co., 1957. 356p. illus. 24cm. [BX8608.A4] 57-2587
1. Mormons and Mormonism—Addresses, essays, lectures. I. Title.

COWLEY, Matthew, 1897-1953. 252.093
Matthew Cowley speaks; discourses of Elder Matthew Cowley of the Quorum of the Twelve of the Church of Jesus Christ of Latter-Day Saints. Salt Lake City, Deseret Book Co., 1954. 456p. illus. 24cm. [BX8639.C6M3] 54-2010
1. Mormons and Mormonism—Addresses, essays, lectures. I. Title.

A Decade of the best; 289.3
the Elbert A. Smith award winning articles of 1961-1970. [Independence, Mo., Herald Pub. House, 1972] 239 p. front. 21 cm. Collection of articles published in the Saints' herald. [BX8637.D4] 72-182435 ISBN 0-8309-0058-6
1. Mormons and Mormonism—Addresses, essays, lectures. 2. Theology—Addresses, essays, lectures. I. Saints' herald.

EVANS, Richard Louis, 1906- 252.093
... and "the spoken word," by Richard L. Evans. New York and London, Harper & brothers [1945] xviii p., 1 l., 155 p. 19 1/2 cm. A third volume of selections from the author's "spoken word" which accompanies the Sunday morning program of sacred music by the Tabernacle choir from Salt Lake City. cf. Foreword. "First edition." [BX8639.E8A5] 45-6083
1. Mormons and Mormonism—Addresses, essays, lectures. I. Title.

EVANS, Richard Louis, 1906- 252.093
The everlasting things, [1st ed.] New York, Harper [1957] 255p. 22cm. Seventh vol. of selections from the author's 'spoken word' which accompanies the CBS Sunday morning broadcast of sacred music by the Tabernacle choir in Salt Lake City. [BX8639.E8E9] 57-10532
1. Mormons and Mormonism—Addresses, essays, lectures. I. Title.

EVANS, Richard Louis, 1906- 248.4893
Faith in the future. New York, Harper [c.1963 524p. 22cm. Tenth vol. of selections from the author's 'spoken word' which accompanies the CBS Sunday broadcast of sacred music by the Tabernacle Choir in Salt Lake City. 63-21589 3.00
1. Mormons and Mormonism—Addresses, essays, lectures. I. Title.

EVANS, Richard Louis, 1906- 248.4893
Faith in the future. [1st ed.] New York, Harper & Row [1963] 224 p. 22 cm. Tenth vol. of selections from the author's "spoken word" which accompanies the CBS Sunday broadcast of sacred music by the Tabernacle Choir in Salt Lake City. [BX8639.E8F3] 63-21589
1. Mormons and Mormonism — Addresses, essays, lectures. I. Title.

EVANS, Richard Louis, 1906- 242
Faith, peace, and purpose [by] Richard L.

Evans. Cleveland, World Pub. Co. [1966] xiv, 242 p. 21 cm. Twelfth vol. of selections from the author's "spoken word" which accompanies the CBS Sunday broadcast of sacred music by the Tabernacle Choir in Salt Lake City. [BX8639.E8F32] 66-25880
1. Mormons and Mormonism—Addresses, essays, lectures. I. Title.

EVANS, Richard Louis, 1906- 252.093
From the crossroads . . . [1st ed.] New York, Harper [1955] 256p. 22cm. A 6th vol. of selections from the author's talks which accompany the CBS Sunday morning broadcast of sacred music by the Tabernacle choir and organ in Salt Lake City. [BX8639.E8F7] 55-9688
1. Mormons and Mormonism—Addresses, essays, lectures. I. Title.

EVANS, Richard Louis, 1906- 252.093
This day ... and always, by Richard L. Eavns. New York and London, Harper & brothers [1942] xv, 200 p., 1 l. 21 1/2 x 13 cm. A second volume of selections from the author's "spoken word" which accompanies the Sunday morning program of sacred music by the Taberncale choir from Salt Lake City. The first volume has title: Unto the hills. cf. Foreword. "First edition." [BX8639.E8T45] 42-50833
1. Mormons and Mormonism—Addresses, essays, lectures. I. Title.

EVANS, Richard Louis, 1906-
Thoughts ... for one hundred days as heard on radio; selected from Thought for the day and the Spoken word as heard on radio. [1st ed.] Salt Lake City, Publishers Press [1966] [228] p. 21 cm. 68-31018
1. Mormons and Mormonism—Addresses, essays, and lectures. I. Title.

EVANS, Richard Louis, 1906- 252.003
Unto the hills, by Richard L. Evans. New York and London, Harper & brothers [c1940] xiv, 151 p. 22 cm. Selections arranged by topic from the "announcer's 'spoken word'" which during the past ten years has accompanied the Sunday morning broadcast of the Mormon tabernacle choir and organ from Temple square in Salt Lake City. cf. Foreword. "First edition." [BX8639.E8U5] 40-8173
1. Mormons and Mormonism—Addresses, essays, lectures. 2. Homiletical illustrations. I. Title.

HACKWORTH, Dorothy South, comp. 252.093
The Master's touch. Salt Lake City, Bookcraft [1962, c1961] 290p. 24cm. [BX8676.H3 1962] 62-53005
1. Mormons and Mormonism—Addresses, essays, lectures. 2. Witness bearing (Christianity) I. Title.

JOURNAL of discourses digest / compiled by Joseph Fielding McConkie. 230'.9'3 Salt Lake City : Bookcraft, c1975- v. ; 24 cm. Includes index. [BX8639.A1J682] 75-29769 ISBN 0-88494-290-2 (v. 1) : 6.95 (v. 1)
1. Mormons and Mormonism—Addresses, essays, lectures. I. McConkie, Joseph F.

KIRKHAM, Oscar A 1880- 289.3
Say the good word. Salt Lake City, Deseret Book Co.. 1958. 273p. illus. 24cm. [BX8609.K5] 58-35735
1. Mormons and Mormonism—Addresses, essays, lectures. I. Title.

LEA, Leonard J. 248.4893
Views from the mountain. Independence, Mo., Herald House [c.]1961. 220p. 61-9682 2.75
1. Mormons and Mormonism—Addresses, essays, lectures. I. Title.

LUNDWALL, Nels Benjamin, 1884- comp. 231.3
Discourses on the Holy Ghost; also, lectures on faith, as delivered at School of the Prophets at Kirtland, Ohio. Salt Lake City, Bookcraft [1959] 154p. 24cm. [BX8608.L8] 59-37369
1. Mormons and Mormonism—Addresses, essays, lectures. 2. Mormons and Mormonism—Doctrinal and controversial works. 3. Holy Spirit. I. Title.

MCKAY, David Oman, 1873- 289.304
Cherished experiences, from the writings of David O. McKay. Compiled by Clare Middlemiss. Salt Lake City, Deseret co. [1955] 209p. illus. 24cm. [BX8609.M25] 55-30116
1. Mormons and Mormonism—Addresses, essays, lectures. I. Title.

MCKAY, David Oman, 1873-1970. 289.3'3 B
Cherished experiences, from the writings of President David O. McKay / compiled by Clare Middlemiss. Rev. and enl. Salt Lake City : Deseret Book Co., 1976. xii, 204 p. : ill. ; 24 cm. Includes index. [BX8609.M25 1976] 76-5178 ISBN 0-87747-030-8 5.95
1. McKay, David Oman, 1873-1970. 2. Mormons and Mormonism—Addresses, essays, lectures. I. Title.

MCKAY, David Oman, 1873-1970. 289.3
Stepping stones to an abundant life. Compiled by Llewelyn R. McKay. Salt Lake City, Utah, Deseret Book Co., 1971. x, 445 p. port. 24 cm. [BX8609.M27] 77-158727 ISBN 0-87747-442-7 5.95
1. Mormons and Mormonism—Addresses, essays, lectures. I. Title.

THE Mormon people, their character and traditions / Thomas G. 289.3'3 Alexander, editor. Provo, Utah : Brigham Young University Press, [1980] p. cm. (Charles Redd monographs in Western history ; no. 10) [BX8637.M66] 80-18051 ISBN 0-8425-1834-7 pbk. : 6.95
1. Mormons and Mormonism—Addresses, essays, lectures. I. Alexander, Thomas G. II. Series.

NIBLEY, Hugh, 1910- 289.3'3
Nibley on the timely and the timeless : Classic essays of Hugh W. Nibley / with an autobiographical introd. by Hugh W. Nibley ; foreword by Truman G. Madsen. [Provo, Utah] : Religious Studies Center, Brigham Young University, c1978. xxviii, 323 p. ; 24 cm. (Religious studies monograph series ; v. 1) Bibliography: p. 307-323. [BX8639.N5N5] 78-4382 ISBN 0-88494-338-0 : 7.50
1. Mormons and Mormonism—Addresses, essays, lectures. I. Title. II. Series.

PETERSEN, Mark E 289.3
Patterns for living. Salt Lake City, Bookcraft [1962] 325p. 24cm. [BX8609.P44] 62-5331
1. Mormons and Mormonism— Addresses, essays, lectures. I. Title.

PETERSEN, Mark E 289.3
Toward a better. life. Salt Lake City, Deseret Book Co., 1960. 345p. 24cm. [BX8609.P45] 60-34861
1. Mormons and Mormonism—Addresses, essays, lectures. I. Title.

RICHARDS, Stephen L., 1879- 289.3
The church in war and peace, by Stephen L. Richards ... [Salt Lake City] Zion's printing & publishing co., 1943. viii, 221 p. 20 cm. [BX8639.R5C47] 44-19372
1. Mormons and Mormonism—Addresses, essays, lectures. I. Title.

RICHARDS, Stephen L 1879- 289.304
Where is wisdom? Addresses. Salt Lake City, Deseret Book Co. [1955] 432p. illus. 24cm. [BX8609.R53] 56-17872
1. Mormons and Mormonism—Addresses, essays, lectures. I. Title.

ROBERTS, Brigham Henry, 1857-1933. 289.3
Discourses of B. H. Roberts of the First Council of the Seventy. Salt Lake City, Deseret Book Co., 1948. 128 p. port. 24 cm. "Other works of Elder B. H. Roberts": p. [127]-128. [BX8609.R6] 49-27884
1. Mormons and Mormonism—Addresses, essays, lectures. I. Title.

ROBINSON, Christine Hinckley. 230.893
Living truths from the Doctrine and covenants. Salt Lake City, Deseret Book Co., 1961. 151p. 20cm. [BX8639.R6L5] 61-2976
1. Mormons and Mormonism— Addresses, essays, lectures. 2. Smith, Joseph, 1806-1844. Doctrine and covenants. I. Title.

ROMNEY, Marion G., 1897- 248.4'8'933
Look to God and live; discourses of Marion G. Romney. Compiled by George J. Romney. Salt Lake City, Utah, Deseret Book Co., 1971. xv, 291 p. port. 24 cm. [BX8639.R64L66] 70-176091 ISBN 0-87747-451-6 4.95
1. Mormons and mormonism—Addresses, essays, lectures. I. Title.

SILL, Sterling W 252.097
The glory of the sun. Salt Lake City, Bookcraft [1961] 387 p. 24 cm. Fifty-two messages from the radio program: "Sunday evening from Temple Square." [BX8639.S5G5] 61-7643
1. Mormons and Mormonism — Addresses, essays, lectures. I. Title.

SILL, Sterling W 289.33
The upward reach. Salt Lake City, Bookcraft [1962] 407 p. illus. 24 cm. [BX8639.S5U6] 62-53317
1. Mormons and Mormonism—Addresses, essays, lectures. I. Title.

SMITH, Joseph Fielding, 1876- 289.3
The restoration of all things; a series of radio talks by Elder Joseph Fielding Smith on fundamental principles of the gospel, given over KSL commencing June 4, 1944 and concluding December, 1944. [Salt Lake City] The Deseret news press [1945] 334 p. 20 cm. [BX8639.S57R4] 46-15778
1. Mormons and Mormonism—Addresses, essays, lectures. I. Title.

SPERRY, Sidney Branton, 1895- 252.093
Knowledge is power. Salt Lake City, Bookcraft [1958] 269 p. 24 cm. [BX8609.S67] 58-43141
1. Mormons and Mormonism — Addresses, essays, lectures. I. Title.

TO the glory of God; 230'.93'3 Mormon essays on great issues—environment—commitment—love—peace—youth—man. Contributors: Hugh W. Nibley [and others] Salt Lake City, Deseret Book Co., 1972. xi, 234 p. 24 cm. Includes bibliographical references. [BX8639.A1T6] 72-78244 ISBN 0-87747-475-3 4.95
1. Mormons and Mormonism—Addresses, essays, lectures. I. Nibley, Hugh, 1910-

WIDTSOE, John Andreas, 1872- 289.304
Man and the dragon, and other essays by John A. Widtsoe. [Salt Lake City] The Bookcraft company, 1945. 263 p. 20 1/2 cm. "First edition." "The eighty-four essays ... appeared, with one exception, as editorials in the Latter-day saints' Millennial star ... January 1928 to October 1933, inclusive."--Prefatory note. [BX8609.W5] 45-11402
1. Mormons and mormonism—Addresses, essays, lectures. I. Title.

YARN, David H 252.093
Faith in a day of unbelief. Salt Lake City, Deseret Book Co. [1960] 189 p. 20 cm. "Prepared originally as radio addresses which were delivered weekly on the Sunday evening hour of the Church of Jesus Christ of Latter-Day Saints on radio station KSL in Salt Lake City from February 10, 1952 through June 29, 1952." [BX8639.Y3F3] 60-3651
1. Mormons and Mormonism — Addresses, essays, lectures. I. Title.

Mormons and Mormonism—Apologetic works.

NIBLEY, Hugh, 1910- 289.3
The myth makers. Salt Lake City, Bookcraft [1961] 293p. 24cm. Includes bibliography. [BX8635.5.N5] 61-59773
1. Smith, Joseph, 1805-1844. 2. Mormons and Mormonism—Apologetic works. I. Title.

Mormons and Mormonism—Bibliography

EBERSTADT (Edward) and Sons, New York.
A collection of rare books, manuscripts, paintings, etc., relating to Utah and the Mormons offered for sale . . . New York [195?] 119 p. illus., port. 33 cm. 65-32963
1. Mormons and Mormonism—Bibl. I. Title. II. Title: Rare books, manuscripts, paintings, etc., relating to Utah and the Mormons.

FLAKE, Chad J. 016.2893
A Mormon bibliography, 1830-1930 : books, pamphlets, periodicals, and broadsides relating to the first century of Mormonism / edited by Chad J. Flake ; introd. by Dale L. Morgan. Salt Lake City : University of Utah Press, 1978. xxxi, 825 p., [24] leaves of plates : facsims. ; 29 cm. Includes bibliographical references and index. [Z7845.M8F55] [BX8635.2] 74-22639 ISBN 0-87480-016-1 : 75.00
1. Mormons and Mormonism—Bibliography. I. Title.

MORGAN, Dale Lowell, 1914- 016.2893
A bibliography of the churches of the dispersion. [n. p., 1953] 107-181p. facsims, 26cm. 'The introduction is reprinted from the Western humanities review. vol. VII, no. 3 [p. 255-266] Summer 1953. This is the third in a series of bibliographies on the leaser Mormon churches.' [Z7845.M8M6] 54-26202
1. Mormons and Mormonism—Bibl. I. Title. II. Title: Churches of the dispersion.

NEW York. Public library. 016.
... List of works in the library relating to the Mormons. New York, 1909. Cover-title, 57 p. 26 cm. "Reprinted from the Bulletin, March, 1909." "A large majority of the books ... was collected by the late William Berrian, from whose estate they were bought in December, 1899, by Miss Helen Miller Gould and presented to the library." [Z7845.M8N5] CA 9
1. Mormons and Mormonism—Bibl. I. Berrian, William, book collector. II. Title.

UTAH. University. Library. 016.2893
Holdings of the University of Utah on Utah and the Church of Jesus Christ of Latter-Day Saints [by] L. H. Kirkpatrick. Salt Lake City, 1954. 285p. 28cm. [Z7845.M8U8] 55-62434
1. Mormons and Mormonism—Bibl. 2. Utah—Bibl. I. Kirkpatrick, Leonard Henry, 1907- II. Title.

VERSTEEG, Harvey.
The Mormon archives. [Detroit, 1965?] 12 [2] 1. Caption title. Bibliographical footnotes. NUC68
1. Mormons and Mormonism—Bibl. 2. Genealogical Society of the Church of Jesus Christ of Latter-Day Saints. Library 3. Michigan—Authors. I. Genealogical Society of the Church of Jesus Christ of Latter-Day Saints. II. Title.

Mormons and Mormonism—Bibliography—Exhibitions.

CRAWLEY, Peter, 1936- 016.2893
Notable Mormon books, 1830-1857 : an exhibition in conjunction with the sixth annual Mormon Festival of Arts / selected and described by Peter Crawley and Chad J. Flake. Provo : Friends of the Brigham Young University Library, 1974. 19 p. ; 23 cm. [Z7845.M8C7] [BX8635.2] 75-332918
1. Mormons and Mormonism—Bibliography—Exhibitions. I. Flake, Chad J., joint author. II. Mormon Festival of Arts, 6th, Brigham Young University, 1974. III. Title.

Mormons and Mormonism-Bibliography Title.

NASH, William Verlin, 1928-
Library resources for the study of Mormons and Mormonism. Urbana, Ill., 1960. 131, [150] 1. illus., maps. 30 cm. Bibliography: leaves 121-127 (1st group) 64-49509
1. Mormons and Mormonism-Bibl. Title. I. Title.

Mormons and Mormonism—Bio-bibliography.

BITTON, Davis, 1930- 016.2893'3 B
Guide to Mormon diaries & autobiographies / Davis Bitton. Provo,

Utah : Brigham Young University Press, c1977. xi, 417 p. ; 29 cm. Includes index. [Z7845.M8B58] [BX8693] 77-1138 ISBN 0-8425-1478-3 : 29.95
1. Mormons and Mormonism—Bio-bibliography. 2. Diaries—Bibliography. 3. Autobiographies—Bibliography. I. Title.

Mormons and Mormonism—Biography

ARRINGTON, Leonard J. 288.3'3 B
From Quaker to Latter-Day Saint : Bishop Edwin D. Woolley / Leonard J. Arrington. Salt Lake City : Deseret Book Co., 1976. xiii, 592 p. ; 24 cm. Includes index. Bibliography: p. 497-500. [BX8695.W57A77] 76-43171 ISBN 0-87747-591-1 : 6.95
1. Woolley, Edwin Dilworth, 1897-1881. 2. Mormons and Mormonism—Biography. I. Title.

ASHTON, Wendell J. 289.3'0922 B
Theirs is the kingdom [by] Wendell J. Ashton. Pen sketches by Nelson White. [2d ed.] Salt Lake City, Bookcraft, 1970. x, 300 p. ports. 24 cm. Bibliography: p. [291]-295. [BX8693.A8 1970] 74-126081
1. Mormons and Mormonism—Biography. I. Title.

ASHTON, Wendell J. 922.83
Theirs is the kingdom, by Wendell J. Ashton. Salt Lake City, Utah, Bookcraft company, 1945. xiv, 371 p. incl. ports. 20 1/12 cm. Bibliography: p. 361-366. [BX8696.A8] 45-11400
1. Mormons and Moronism—Biog. I. Title.

BROWN, James Stephens, 289.3'3 B b.1828.
Life of a pioneer : being the autobiography of James S. Brown. New York : AMS Press, 1977. p. cm. (Communal societies in America) Reprint of the 1900 ed. published by G. Q. Cannon, Salt Lake City. [BX8695.B7A3 1977] 77-17574 ISBN 0-404-08432-X : 21.00
1. Brown, James Stephens, b. 1828. 2. Mormons and Mormonism—Biography. I. Title.

BURGESS-OLSON, Vicky, 289.3'3 B 1945-
Sister saints / by Vicky Burgess-Olson. Provo, Utah : Brigham Young University Press, c1978. xiv, 494 p. : ports. ; 23 cm. (Studies in Mormon history ; v. 5) Includes bibliographical references. [BX8693.B87] 78-5080 ISBN 0-8425-1235-7 : 5.95
1. Mormons and Mormonism—Biography. 2. Women—United States—Biography. I. Title. II. Series.

CHEVILLE, Roy 289.3'092'2 B Arthur, 1897-
Joseph and Emma Smith, companions for seventeen and a half years, 1827-1844 / by Roy A. Cheville. Independence, Mo. : Herald Pub. House, c1977. 206 p. ; 21 cm. [BX8695.S6C53] 76-44549 ISBN 0-8309-0174-4 : 8.00
1. Smith, Joseph, 1805-1844. 2. Smith, Emma Hale. 3. Mormons and Mormonism—Biography. I. Title.

DURRANT, George D. 248'.83
Someone special : starring youth / George D. Durrant. Salt Lake City : Bookcraft, 1976. viii, 119 p. : ill. ; 24 cm. [BX8695.D8A35] 76-45722 ISBN 0-88494-311-9 pbk. : 3.50
1. Durrant, George D. 2. Mormons and Mormonism—Biography. 3. Youth—Conduct of life. 4. Youth—Religious life. I. Title.

GREEN, Doyle L. ed. 922.8373
Our leaders. Salt Lake City, Deseret Book Co. [1951] 112 p. illus. 19 cm. [BX8693.G7] 52-16007
1. Mormons and Mormonism—Blog. I. Title.

HART, Edward LeRoy, 289.3'092'4 B 1916-
Mormon in motion : the life and journals of James H. Hart, 1825-1906, in England, France, and America / by Edward L. Hart. [s.l.] : Windsor Books, 1978. xix, 313 p. : ill. ; 24 cm. Includes bibliographical references and index. [BX8695.H34H34] 78-60386 ISBN 0-932100-00-7 : 15.00
1. Hart, James H., 1825-1906. 2. Mormons and Mormonism—Biography. I. Hart, James H., 1825-1906. II. Title.
Publisher's address: PO Box 280, Brightwaters, NY 11718

HETTRICK, Ric. 289.3'3 B
From among men : biographies of 26 Latter-Day apostles / Ric and Marcia Hettrick. Independence, Mo. : Herald Pub. House, c1976. 220 p. : ports. ; 21 cm. [BX8693.H44] 76-27242 ISBN 0-8309-0170-1
1. Mormons and Mormonism—Biography. I. Hettrick, Marcia, joint author. II. Title.

HILL, Donna. 289.3'092'4 B
Joseph Smith, the first Mormon / by Donna Hill. 1st ed. Garden City, N.Y. : Doubleday, 1977. xviii, 527 p., [8] leaves of plates : ill. ; 25 cm. Includes index. Bibliography: p. [495]-513. [BX8695.S6H54] 73-15345 ISBN 0-385-00804-X : 12.50
1. Smith, Joseph, 1805-1844. 2. Mormons and Mormonism—Biography. I. Title.

HILTON, Eugene, 289.3'0924 B 1889-
My second estate; the life of a Mormon. [Oakland, Calif., Hilton Family, 1968] 245 p. illus., facsims., ports. 28 cm. Cover title. "Volume of family lore and pictures ... prepared especially for the families descended from Eugene Hilton and Ruth Naomi Savage." Bibliographical footnotes. [BX8695.H5A3] 70-11040
I. Title.

HINCKLEY, Bryant S 1867- 922.8373
The faith of our pioneer fathers. Salt Lake City, Deseret Book Co., 1956. 268p. illus. 24cm. [BX8693.H5] 56-2877
1. Mormons and Mormonism—Biog. I. Title.

IMPROVEMENT Era.
Presidents of the Church. [Salt Lake City, 1958] 1 v. (unpaged) ports. 67-50069
1. Mormons and Mormonism — Biography. 2. Mormon Church — General Authorities — First Presidency. I. Title.

THE Instructor (Salt Lake 230.93 City)
Our prophets and principles; writings on our Articles of faith and prophets who made them live. Salt Lake City [1956] 172p. illus. 24cm. [BX8693.I5] 56-2876
1. Mormons and Mormonism—Biog. 2. Smith, Joseph, 1805-1844. The pearl of great price. 3. Apostles. I. Title.

KIMBALL, Edward L., 289.3'3 B 1930-
Spencer W. Kimball, twelfth president of the Church of Jesus Christ of Latter-day Saints / Edward L. Kimball, Andrew E. Kimball, Jr. Salt Lake City : Bookcraft, 1977. x, 438 p. : ill. ; 24 cm. Includes index. [BX8695.K53K55] 77-14714 ISBN 0-88494-330-5 : 8.50
1. Kimball, Spencer W., 1895- 2. Mormons and Mormonism—Biography. I. Kimball, Andrew E., joint author. II. Title.

NIBLEY, Preston.
The presidents of the Church, by Preston Nibley ... Salt Lake City, Utah, Deseret book company [1965, c1941] 477 p. ports. 24 cm. "Tenth printing." 68-10415
1. Mormons and Mormonism—Biog. I. Title.

NIBLEY, Preston. 922.83
The presidents of the Church, by Preston Nibley... Salt Lake City, Utah, The Deseret book company, 1941. 321 p. ports. 23 1/2 cm. [BX8693.N5] 41-25074
1. Mormons and Mormonism—Biog. I. Title.

NIBLEY, Preston. 922.8373
Stalwarts of Mormonism. Salt Lake City, Deseret Book Co., 1954. 215p. illus. 24cm. [BX8693.N53] 54-4997
1. Mormons and Mormonism—Biog. I. Title.

PEARSON, Carol Lynn. 289.3'3 B
The flight and the nest / Carol Lynn Pearson. Salt Lake City : Bookcraft, 1975. xiii, 121 p. : ill. ; 24 cm. Includes bibliographical references and index. [BX8693.P4] 75-31079 ISBN 0-88494-288-0 : 3.50
1. Mormons and Mormonism—Biography. 2. Women—Biography. 3. Women. I. Title.

REECE, Colleen L. 288.3'092'2 B
The unknown witnesses, by Colleen L. Reece. [Independence, Mo., Herald Pub. House, 1974] 159 p. 18 cm. [BX8693.R43] 73-87642 ISBN 0-8309-0107-8 5.00
1. Bible—Biography. 2. Mormons and Mormonism—Biography. I. Title.

SESSIONS, Gene Allred. 289.3'3 B
Latter-day patriots : nine Mormon families and their Revolutionary War heritage / Gene Allred Sessions. Salt Lake City : Deseret Book Co., 1975. xiv, 219 p., [1] leaf of plates : ill. ; 24 cm. Includes bibliographical references and index. [BX8693.S47] 75-37276 ISBN 0-87747-600-4
1. Mormons and Mormonism—Biography. 2. United States—History—Revolution, 1775-1783. I. Title.

YORGASON, Blaine M., 289.3'3 B 1942-
Tall timber : the struggles of James Yorgason, a Mormon polygamist / by Blaine M. Yorgason. [Rexburg, Idaho] : Ricks College Press, 1976. xx, 315 p. : ill. ; 29 cm. Includes index. Bibliography: p. 224-228. [BX8695.Y67Y67] 76-28588 25.00
1. Yorgason, James, 1847-1917. 2. Mormons and Mormonism—Biography. I. Title.

YOUNG, Brigham, 289.3'092'4 B 1801-1877.
Letters of Brigham Young to his sons / edited and introduced by Dean C. Jessee ; with a foreword by J. H. Adamson. Salt Lake City : Deseret Book Co., 1974. xliv, 375 p. : ports. ; 25 cm. (The Mormon heritage series ; v. 1) Includes bibliographical references and index. [BX8695.Y7A4 1974] 74-80041 ISBN 0-87747-522-9 : 9.95
1. Young, Brigham, 1801-1877. 2. Mormons and Mormonism—Biography. I. Jessee, Dean C., ed. II. Title.

Mormons and Mormonism—Biography—Indexes.

MERRILL Library. Special 289.3'3 Collections Dept.
Name index to the Library of Congress collection of Mormon diaries. Logan, Utah State University Press, 1971. 391 p. 28 cm. (Western Text Society series, v. 1, no. 2) [BX8693.M47 1971] 75-636249
1. Mormons and Mormonism—Biography—Indexes. I. Title. II. Title: Library of Congress collection of Mormon diaries. III. Series: Western Text Society. Western Text Society series, v. 1, no. 2.

Mormons and Mormonism—Charities.

CHURCH of Jesus Christ of 258 latter-day saints. General board of the Relief society.
A centenary of Relief society, 1842-1942. Relief society women's auxiliary of the Church of Jesus Christ of latter-day saints. Salt Lake City, Utah, General board of Relief society, 1942. 96 p. illus. (incl. ports., facsim.) diagrs. 30 1/2 x 28 cm. [BX8603.R4A4] 43-132
1. Mormons and Mormonism—Charities. I. Title.

Mormons and Mormonism—Collected works.

BURTON, Alma P., 1913- 289.3'3 comp.
Doctrines from the prophets; choice selections from the Latter-Day leaders, compiled and arranged by Alma P. Burton. Salt Lake City, Bookcraft, 1970. x, 476 p. 24 cm. [BX8608.B85] 76-115487
1. Mormons and Mormonism—Collections. I. Title.

CANNON, George Quayle, 230.93 1827-1901.
Gospel truth; discourses and writings. Selected, arr. and edited by Jerreld L. Newquist. [Salt Lake City] Zion's Book Store, 1957- v. illus. 24cm. [BX8609.C29] 57-35445
1. Mormons and Mormonism—Collected works. I. Title.

CANNON, George Quayle, 230'.9'3 1827-1901.
Gospel truth; discourses and writings of president George Q. Cannon. Selected, arr., and edited by Jerreld L. Newquist. [2d ed.] [Salt Lake City] Deseret Book Co., 1974- c1957- v. 24 cm. [BX8609.C292] 74-165262 ISBN 0-87747-519-9 4.95 (v. 1)
1. Mormons and Mormonism—Collected works. I. Newquist, Jerreld L., ed. II. Title.

CHURCH of Jesus Christ of Latter-Day Saints.
Messages of the First Presidency of the Church of Jesus Christ of Latter-Day Saints, 1833-1964. Introd., notes, and index, by James R. Clark. Salt Lake City, Bookcraft 1965- v. 24 cm. [BX8607.A1C48] 66-1214
1. Mormons and Mormonism — Collections. I. Clark, James Ratcliffe, 1910- ed. II. Title.

GRANT, Heber Jeddy, 1856- 230.98
Gospel standards; selections from the sermons and writings of Heber J. Grant ... compiled by Dr. G. Homer Durham under the direction of John A. Widtsoe and Richard L. Evans ... [Salt Lake City, The Improvement era] 1941. xix, p., 2 l., [3]-384 p. col. front. (port.) 24 cm. "Key to abbreviations and note on sources": leaf proceeding p. [2] [BX8609.G7] 42-3561
1. Mormons and Mormonism—Collected works. I. Durham, G. Homer, comp. II. Widtsoe, John Andreas, 1872- III. Evans, Richard Louis, 1906- IV. Improvement era. V. Title.

LEE, Harold B., 1899- 230'.9'3
Stand ye in holy places; selected sermons and writings of president Harold B. Lee. Salt Lake City, Deseret Book Co., 1974. 398 p. port. 24 cm. [BX8609.L43] 74-77591 ISBN 0-87747-526-1 5.95
1. Mormons and Mormonism—Collected works. I. Title.

LEE, Harold B., 1899- 289.3'3 1973.
Ye are the light of the world : selected sermons and writings of president Harold B. Lee. Salt Lake City : Deseret Book Co., 1974. x, 364 p. ; 24 cm. Companion volume to the author's Stand ye in holy places. Includes bibliographical references and index. [BX8609.L44 1974] 74-28800 ISBN 0-87747-542-3 : 5.95
1. Mormons and Mormonism—Collected works. I. Title.

NEWQUIST, Jerreld L., comp. 261
Prophets, principles and national survival Salt Lake City, Publishers Pr., 1881 WN Temple [1964] 575p. 24cm. Bibl. [BX8608.N4] 64-57193 4.95
1. Mormons and Mormonism—Collections. 2. Sociology, Christian (Mormon)—Collections. I. Title.

PRATT, Orson, 1811-1881 289.3081
Masterful discourses and writings [N. B. Lundwall, comp.] Salt Lake City, Bookcraft [1963, c.1962] 656p. ports. 24cm. 63-5908 price unreported
1. Mormons and Mormonism—Collected works. I. Title.

PRATT, Orson, 1811-1881. 289.3081
Masterful discourses and writings of Orson Pratt ... Salt Lake City, Utah, N. B. Lundwall [1946] 620 (i.e. 622) p. 2 ports. on 1 l. 23 1/2 cm. Includes extra numbered pages 424A-424B. [BX8609.P68] 47-18890
1. Mormons and Mormonism—Collected works. I. Title.

PRATT, Orson, 1811-1881. 289.3081
Orson Pratt's works on the doctrines of the gospel, by Orson Pratt ... Salt Lake City, Utah, The Deseret news press [1945- v. front. (port.) 22 cm. Preface signed: Parker Pratt Robison. [BX8609.P74] 45-10793
1. Mormons and Mormonism—Collected works. I. Robison, Parker Pratt, ed. II. Title.
Contents omitted.

PRATT, Parley Parker, 1807- 289.3 1857.
Writings of Parley Parker Pratt, one of the first missionaries and a member of the First Quorum of the Twelve Apostles of the Church of Jesus Christ of Latter-Day

Saints, edited and published by his grandson Parker Pratt Robinson. 1st ed. Salt Lake City, 1952. 385p. illus. 24cm. [BX8609.P75] 53-15574
1. Mormons and Mormonism—Collected works. 2. Theology— Collected works—19th cent. I. Title.

RICHARDS, Le Grand, Bp., 1886- 289.3'3
Le Grand Richards speaks. Compiled by G. LaMont Richards. Salt Lake City, Deseret Book Co., 1972. xvi, 292 p. ports. 24 cm. [BX8609.R52] 72-76068 ISBN 0-87747-469-9 4.95
1. Mormons and Mormonism—Collected works. I. Title.

SMITH, Joseph Fielding, 1876- 230.93
Doctrines of salvation: sermons and writings. Compiled by Bruce R. McConkie. Salt Lake City, Bookcraft [c1954-56] 3v. port. 24cm. Bibliographical footnotes. [BX8609.S63] 56-34495
1. Mormons and Mormonism—Collected works. I. Title.

TANNER, Nathan Eldon, 1898- 289.3'3
Seek ye first the Kingdom of God, by N. Eldon Tanner. Compiled by LaRue Sneff. Salt Lake City, Deseret Book Co., 1973. ix, 303 p. port. 24 cm. [BX8609.T28] 73-91712 ISBN 0-87747-510-5 4.95
1. Mormons and Mormonism—Collected works. I. Title.

Mormons and Mormonism—Congresses.

MORMONISM : 230'.9'33
a faith for all cultures / F. LaMond Tullis, editor ; Arthur Henry King, Spencer J. Palmer, Douglas F. Tobler, assistant editor[s]. Provo, Utah : Brigham Young University Press, c1978. p. cm. "Edited versions of remarks made at the regional sessions of the Expanding Church Symposium." Includes index. [BX8605.M67] 78-7665 ISBN 0-8425-1282-9 : 8.95
1. Mormons and Mormonism—Congresses. I. Tullis, F. LaMond, 1935-

REFLECTIONS on Mormonism 289.3
: Judaeo-Christian parallels : papers delivered at the Religious Studies Center symposium, Brigham Young University, March 10-11, 1978 / edited, with an introductory essay, by Truman G. Madsen. Provo, Utah : The Center ; Salt Lake City : produced and distributed by Bookcraft, 1978. xviii, 245 p. : ill. ; 24 cm. (The Religious studies monograph series ; v. 4) Includes indexes. Bibliography: p. 223-226. [BX8635.2.R43] 78-69990 ISBN 0-88494-358-5 : 6.95
1. Bible—Criticism, interpretation, etc.—Addresses, essays, lectures. 2. Mormons and Mormonism—Congresses. 3. Mormons and Mormonism—Sacred books—Addresses, essays, lectures. I. Madsen, Truman G. II. Brigham Young University, Provo, Utah. Religious Studies Center. III. Series.

Mormons and Mormonism—Dictionaries.

BROOKS, Melvin R 289.303
L. D. S. reference encyclopedia. Salt Lake City, Bookcraft, 1960. 540p. 24cm. [BX8605.5.B7] 60-44463
1. Mormons and Mormonism—Dictionaries. I. Title.

BROOKS, Melvin R 289.303
L.D.S. Reference encyclopedia. Salt Lake City, Bookcraft, 1960-65. 2 v. 24 cm. [BX8605.5.B7] 60-44463
1. Mormons and Mormonism — Dictionaries. I. Title.

JENSON, Andrew, 1850- 289.309
Encyclopedic history of the Church of Jesus Chirst of latter-day saints, by Andrew Jenson ... Salt Lake City, Utah, Printed by Deseret news publishing company, 1941. iv p., 1 l., 976 p. 24 cm. [BX8605.5.J4] 41-8948
1. Mormons and Mormonism—Dictionaries. I. Title.

MCCONKIE, Bruce R 230.93
Mormon doctrine. Salt Lake City, Bookcraft, 1958. 776p. 24cm. [BX8605.5.M3] 58-10837
1. Mormons and Mormonism—Dictionaries. I. Title.

MCCONKIE, Bruce R. 230.9'3
Mormon doctrine, by Bruce R. McConkie. 2d ed. Salt Lake City, Bookcraft, 1966. 856 p. 24 cm. [BX8605.5.M3 1966] 67-2237
1. Mormons and Mormonism—Dictionaries. I. Title.

Mormons and Mormonism—Doctrinal and controversial works.

ALLRED, Byron Harvey. 230.93
A leaf in review of the words and acts of God and men relative to the fullness of the Gospel [by] B. Harvey Allred. Caldwell, Id., The Caxton printers, ltd., 1933. 2 p. l., [7]-222 p., 1 l. 21 1/2 cm. [BX8635.A6] 33-13889
1. Mormons and Mormonism—Doctrinal and controversal works. I. Title.

ALWARD, Benjamin B comp. 289.3
Handy Scripture guide. 1st ed. Salt Lake City, Deseret Book Co., 1957. 225p. 18cm. [BX8631.A7] 57-47818
1. Mormons and Mormonism—Doctrinal and controversial works. 2. Bible—Indexes, Topical. I. Title.

ALWARD, Benjamin B comp. 289.3
Know the Latter-Day Scriptures. Salt Lake City, Deseret Book Co., 1958. 571p. 23cm. 'Thirty-eight basic subjects of the Gospel supported by more than one thousand scriptural passages taken from the Book of Mormon, Doctrine and covenants, and Pearl of great price.' [BX8631.A72] 58-30624
1. Mormons and Mormonism—Doctrinal and controversial works. I. Book of Mormon. II. Smith. Joseph. 1805-1844. The pearl of great price. III. Smith, Joseph, 1805-1844. Doctrine and covenants. IV. Title.

ANDERSON, Einar. 289.3
I was a Mormon. Grand Rapids, Zondervan Pub. House [1964] 186 p. illus., ports. 23 cm. Bibliography: p. 183-186. [BX8645.A65] 64-15556
1. Mormons and Mormonism — Doctrinal and controvesial works. I. Title.

ANDERSON, Einar, 1909- 230'.9'3
Inside story of Mormonism. Grand Rapids, Kregel Publications [1973] 162 p. illus. 22 cm. [BX8645.A67] 72-93354 ISBN 0-8254-2111-X 2.95
1. Mormons and Mormonism—Doctrinal and controversial works. I. Title.

ANDRUS, Hyrum Leslie, 1924- 230.9'3'0924
Foundations of the millennial kingdom of Christ [by] Hyrum L. Andrus. Salt Lake City, Bookcraft, 1968- v. 24 cm. Contents.Contents.—v. 1. God, man, and the universe.—v. 2. Principles of perfection.—v. 3. Doctrines of the kingdom. Bibliographical footnotes. [BX8635.2.A5] 68-56891 5.95 (v. 1)
1. Smith, Joseph, 1805-1844. 2. Mormons and Mormonism—Doctrinal and controversial works. I. Title.

BANKHEAD, Reid E. 289.3'22
The word and the witness; the unique mission of the Book of Mormon [by] Reid E. Bankhead [and] Glenn L. Pearson. Salt Lake City, Bookcraft, 1970. ix, 246 p. 24 cm. [BX8627.B3] 74-127953
1. Book of Mormon. 2. Mormons and Mormonism—Doctrinal and controversial works. I. Pearson, Glenn Laurentz, joint author. II. Title.

BARKER, James Louis, 1880-1958. 230.93
Apostasy from the divine church. [Salt Lake City?] K. M. Barker [1960] 805p. 24cm. Includes bibliography. [BX8635.2.B3] 60-32793
1. Mormons and Mormonism—Doctrinal and controversial works. 2. Church history. I. Title.

BENNION, Lowell Lindsay, 1908- 289.3
An introduction to the Gospel. Course no. 28 for the Sunday schools of the Church of Jesus Christ of Latter-Day Saints. Salt Lake City, Deseret Sunday School Union Board [1955] 319p. illus. 24cm. [BX8G10.B4] 56-16954
1. Mormons and Mormonism—Doctrinal and controversial works. 2. Church of Jesus Christ of Latter-Day Saints. Deseret Sunday School Union. I. Title.

BENNION, Lowell Lindsay, 1908- 289.3
Religion and the pursuit of truth. Salt Lake City, Deseret Book Co., 1959. 180p. 24cm. [BX8635.2.B4] 59-33737
1. Mormons and Mormonism—Doctrinal and controversial works. 2. Religion and science—1900- I. Title.

BLOSSOM, Rose B. 289.3
The four standard works of the Church of Jesus Christ of latter-day saints, by Rose B. Blossom. Los Angeles, Calif., Triple S publishers, [c1939] 8 p. l., [19]-124 p. 1 l. fold. mounted plates. 18 1/2 cm. "Second edition of part one, first edition of all except part one." [BX8621.B5 1939] 39-18801
1. Mormons and Mormonism—Doctrinal and controversial works. I. Title.

BOUCHER, Theophiel. 289.3
Mormonism -- faith or fallacy. [1st ed.] New York, Pageant Press [1960, c1959] 432p. 21cm. [BX8645.B64] 59-14473
1. Mormons and Mormonism—Doctrinal and controversial works. I. Title.

BRAMWELL, Enoch Ernest, 1869- 280.93
The exalted life [by] Ernest Bramwell ... [Salt Lake City, The Desert news press, c1941] 208 p. 21 cm. Bibliography: p. [6] [BX8638.B7] 42-900
1. Mormons and Mormonism—Doctrinal and controversial works. I. Title.

BROWN, Hugh B 248
The abundant life, by Hugh B. Brown. Salt Lake City, Bookcraft [1965] 371 p. 24 cm. [BX8635.2.B7] 65-29175
1. Mormons and Mormonism — Doctrinal and controversial works. I. Title.

BURTON, Alma P. 1913- 230.93
Understanding the things of God [by] Alma P. Burton. 1st ed. Salt Lake City, Deseret, 1966. x, 206p. 24cm. [BX8635.2.B8] 66-20704 2.95
1. Mormons and Mormonism—Doctrinal and controversial works. I. Title.

CHEVILLE, Roy Arthur, 1897- 230.293'3
When teen-agers talk theology; a guide in exploring together, by Roy A. Cheville [Independence, Mo., Herald Pub. House, 1968] 445 p. 21 cm. At head of title: For youth ... and all who live with youth. [BX8643.Y6C5] 68-57672
1. Mormons and mormonism—Doctrinal and controversial works. 2. Youth—Religious life. I. Title.

CLARK, James Ratcliffe, 1910-
The story of the pearl of great price. 5th ed. Salt Lake City, Bookcraft, Inc., [1960] 253 p. illus. 24 cm. Smith, Joseph, 1805-1844. Pearl of great price. 66-31846
1. Mormons and Mormonism — Doctrinal and controversial works. I. Title.

CLARK, Joshua Reuben, 1871- 230.93
On the way to immortality and eternal life; a series of radio talks. With appendix. Salt Lake City, Deseret Book Co., 1949. xii, 469 p. 24 cm. [BX8635.C5] 49-3131
1. Mormons and Mormonism—Doctrinal and controversial works. I. Title.

CLARK, Joshua Reuben, 1871-1961. 289.3
Behold the Lamb of God; selections from the sermons and writings published and unpublished by J. Reuben Clark, Jr., on the life of the Savior. Salt Lake City, Deseret Book Co., 1962. 382 p. illus. 24 cm. [BX8639.C5B4] 63-1083
1. Mormons and Mormonism — Doctrinal and controversial works. I. Title.

COOK, Alonzo Laker. 289.3
A study of the gospel of Our Savior. [Independence, Mo., Zion's Print. and Pub. Co., 1946-50. 2v. port. 19cm. Vol. 2 has imprint: Tremonton, Utah. [BX8635.C6] 47-17025
1. Mormons and Mormonism—Doctrinal and controversial works. I. Title.

COWAN, Richard O., 1934- 289.3
Doctrine and covenants : our modern scripture / by Richard O. Cowan. Rev. ed. Provo, Utah : Brigham Young University, [1978] p. cm. Includes index. Bibliography: p. [BX8628.C69 1978] 78-19190 ISBN 0-8425-1316-7 pbk. : 5.95
1. Smith, Joseph, 1805-1844. Doctrine and covenants. 2. Mormons and Mormonism—Doctrinal and controversial works. I. Title.

COWAN, Richard O., 1934- 289.3
The Doctrine and covenants, our modern scripture [by] Richard O. Cowan. 2d ed. rev. Provo, Utah, Brigham Young University Press [1969] xix, 151 p. illus. 28 cm. Bibliography: p. 145-146. [BS8628.C69 1969] 76-243194
1. Smith, Joseph, 1805-1844. Doctrine and covenants. 2. Mormons and Mormonism—Doctrinal and controversial works. I. Title.

COWLEY, Matthias Foss. 230.93
Talks on doctrine. Chicago, Missions of

the Church of Jesus Christ of Latter-day Saints [19-] 287 p. 14 cm. [BX8637.C65] 48-44263
1. Mormons and moronism—Doctrinal and controversial works. I. Title.

CROSSFIELD, R. C. 289.3'2
Book of Onias, by R. C. Crossfield. New York, Philosophical Library [1969] vii, 62 p. 23 cm. [BX8638.C7] 70-86503 3.50
1. Mormons and Mormonism—Doctrinal and controversial works. I. Title.

CROWTHER, Duane S. 236'.2
Life everlasting [by] Duane S. Crowther. Salt Lake City, Bookcraft [1967] xix, 399 p. port. 24 cm. Bibliography: p. 371-373. [BX8635.2.C73] 67-25433
1. Mormons and Mormonism—Doctrinal and controversial works. 2. Future life. I. Title.

CURTIS, Bardella Shipp. 289.3
Mrs.
Sacred scriptures and religious philosophy, a comparative study by Bardella Shipp Curtis. Caldwell, Id., The Caxton printers, ltd., 1942. 320 p. 24 cm. Bibliography: p. [317]-320. [BX8635.C8] 42-14145
1. Mormons and Mormonism—Doctrinal and controversial works. I. Title.

DARTER, Francis M 1881- 289.3
Celestial marriage; the sermons that cost Francis M. Darter ... his membership, by Francis M. Darter ... [Salt Lake City, c1937] 78 p. 19 cm. [BX8643.C5D3] 37-23657
1. Mormons and Mormonism—Doctdrinal and controversial works. 2. Marriage. I. Title.

DE JONG, Gerrit, 1892- 230.93
Greater dividends from religion; a discussion of the practicality of some religious teachings of a peculiar people. Foreword by Milton Bennion. Salt Lake City, Deseret Book Co. [1950] 137 p. 23 cm. [BX8635.D4] 51-696
1. Mormons and Mormonism—Doctrinal and controversial works. I. Title.

DICKINSON, Ellen E. Mrs. 289.
New light on Mormonism, by Mrs. Ellen E. Dickinson, with introduction by Thurlow Weed. New York, Funk & Wagnalls, 1885. 4 p., 2 l., [11]-272 p. 20 cm. Includes a discussion of the relationship of the "Book of Mormon" to Spaulding's Manuscript found". [BX8645.D5] 11-21984
1. Spaulding, Solomon, 1761-1816. 2. Mormons and Mormonism—Doctrinal and controversial works. 3. Book of Mormon. I. Title.

DOXEY, Roy Watkins, 230'.9'33
1908- ed.
Latter-day prophets and the Doctrine and covenants / compiled by Roy W. Doxey. Salt Lake City : Deseret Book Co., 1978. 4 v. ; 21 cm. Includes indexes. Bibliography: v. 4, p. 505-508. [BX8628.D69 1978] 78-17475 15.95
1. Smith, Joseph, 1805-1844. Doctrine and covenants. 2. Mormons and Mormonism—Doctrinal and controversial works. I. Smith, Joseph, 1805-1844. Doctrine and covenants. II. Title.

DOXEY, Roy Watkins, 1908- 289.3'2
Prophecies and prophetic promises, from the Doctrine and covenants [by] Roy W. Doxey. Salt Lake City, Utah, Deseret Book Co., 1969. xiii, 349 p. 24 cm. Bibliography: p. [330]-333. [BX8628.D694] 74-101993 4.95
1. Mormons and Mormonism—Doctrinal and controversial works. I. Smith, Joseph, 1805-1844. Doctrine and covenants. 1969. II. Title.

DYER, Alvin Rulon. 071'.92'25
The fallacy, Salt Lake City, Deseret Book Co., 1964. xi, 153 p. col. illus., col, ports. 24 cm. Bibliographical footnotes. [BX8635.2.D9] 64-3037
1. Mormons and Mormonism—Doctrinal and controversial works. 2. Reorganized Church of Jesus Christ of Latter-Day Saints—Doctrinal and controversial works. I. Title.

DYER, Alvin Rulon. 230.9'3
The meaning of truth, by Alvin R. Dyer. [Rev. ed.] Salt Lake City, Deseret Book Co., 1961 [i.e. 1970] 199 p. illus., maps (part col.), ports. 24 cm. 1961-62 ed. published under title: The day of the gentile. Contains three articles: The day of the gentile, The meaning of truth, and The kingdom of evil. Includes bibliographical references. [BX8635.2.D923 1970] 72-130324 4.95
1. Mormons and Mormonism—Doctrinal and controversial works. 2. Demonology. I. Title.

DYER, Alvin Rulon 230.93
Who am I? A sequel volume to This age of confusion. Revealed answers to whence am I? Who am I? And whither am I going? Salt Lake City, Deseret 1966. xxix, 589p. port. 24cm. Bibl. [BX8635.2.D93] 66-21408 5.95
1. Mormons and Mormonism—Doctrinal and controversial works. 2. Man (Theology) I. Title.

ETZENHOUSER, Rudolph, 289.3'22
1856-
From Palmyra, New York, 1830, to Independence, Missouri, 1894. Independence, Mo., Ensign Pub. House, 1894. [New York, AMS Press, 1971] 444 p. 22 cm. The Book unsealed, rev. and enl., which was first published in 1892, forms part one of this work. [BX8627.E78 1971] 73-134393 ISBN 0-404-08435-4 17.50
1. Smith, Joseph, 1805-1844. 2. Book of Mormon. 3. Mormons and Mormonism—Doctrinal and controversial works. I. Title.

FLINDERS, Neil J. 301.1
Leadership and human relations; a handbook for parents, teachers, and executives, by Neil J. Flinders. Salt Lake City, Utah, Deseret Book Co., 1969. xxi, 254 p. illus. 24 cm. Bibliography: p. 239-247. [BX8635.2.F57] 79-82864 4.95
1. Mormons and Mormonism—Doctrinal and controversial works. 2. Christian leadership. I. Title.

FRASER, Gordon Holmes. 230'.9'3
Is Mormonism Christian? / By Gordon H. Fraser. Chicago : Moody Press, c1977. p. cm. A consolidation and revision of the author's 1965 ed. of Is Mormonism Christian? and 1964 ed. of What does the Book of Mormon teach? Bibliography: p. [BX8645.F73] 77-6227 ISBN 0-8024-4169-6 pbk. : 1.75
1. Mormons and Mormonism—Controversial literature. I. Fraser, Gordon Holmes. What does the Book of Mormon teach? II. Title.

GREEN, Forace, comp. 289.3
Cowley & Whitney on doctrine. Salt Lake City, Bkcraft [c.1963] 517p. illus. 24cm. Orig. pub. as Cowley's Talks on doctrine and [Whitney's] Saturday night thoughts. 63-4149 4.00
1. Mormons and Mormonism—Doctrinal and controversial works. I. Cowley, Matthias Foss, 1858-Talks on doctrine. II. Whitney, Orson Ferguson, 1855-1931. Saturday night thoughts. III. Title.

GREEN, Forace, comp. 230.93
Testimonies of our leaders, compiled and rev. by Forace Green. Salt Lake City, Bookcraft, 1958. 336p. illus. 23cm. [BX8637.G83] 59-24140
1. Momons and Mormonism— Doctrinal and controversial works. I. Title.

HANCOCK, Golman Bluford, 289.
1839-
Mormonism exposed. Joseph Smith an imposter and the book of Mormon a fraud. By Elder G. B. Hancock. Marionville, Mo., A Doggett, printer, 1902. 151 p. front. (port.) plates, 20 1/2 cm. [BX8645.H28] 2-24730
1. Mormons and Mormonism—Doctrinal and controversial works. I. Title.

HANKS, Marion D., comp. 248.8'3
How glorious is youth. Compiled and edited by Marion D. Hanks, Doyle L. Green [and] Elaine Cannon. Salt Lake City, Deseret Book Co., 1968. xi, 233 p. 24 cm. Articles previously published in the Improvement era. [BX8643.Y6H3] 68-58286 3.50
1. Mormons and Mormonism—Doctrinal and controversial works. 2. Youth—Religious life. I. Green, Doyle L., joint comp. II. Cannon, Elaine, joint comp. III. Improvement era. IV. Title.

HOWE, Eber D., b.1798. 289.3'3
Mormonism unvailed : or, A faithful account of that singular imposition and delusion, from its rise to the present time : with sketches of the characters of its propagators, and a full detail of the manner in which the famous Golden Bible was brought before the world ... / by E. D. Howe. New York : AMS Press, [1976] p. cm. (Communal societies in America) Reprint of the 1834 ed. printed and published by the author, Painesville, Ohio. [BX8635.H64 1976] 72-2967 ISBN 0-404-10730-3 : 15.00
1. Mormons and Mormonism—Doctrinal and controversial works. I. Title.

HUNTER, Milton Reed. 230.93
The gospel through the ages, by Milton R. Hunter ... Salt Lake City, Utah, Stevens and Wallis, inc., 1945. xv, 320 p. diagrs. 23 1/2 cm. "Written and published under the direction of the General priesthood committee of the Council of the twelve of the Church of Jesus Christ of latter-day saints." "Supplementary readings" at end of most of the chapters. [BX8635.H8] 45-21956
1. Mormons and Mormonism—Doctrinal and controversial works. I. Church of Jesus Christ of latter-day saints. Council of the twelve apostles. II. Title.

HUNTER, Milton Reed, 1902- 289.3
ed.
Pearl of great price commentary; a selection from the revelations, translations and narrations of Joseph Smith. 1st ed. Salt Lake City, Stevens & Wallis, 1948. xii, 264 p. illus. 24 cm. [BX8629.P52 1948] 49-222
1. Smith, Joseph, 1805-1844. Pearl of great price. 2. Mormons and Mormonism—Doctrinal and controversial works. I. Title.

JENSEN, Nephi, 1876- 230.93
The world's greatest need: salvation from the evils of the world through the restored saving power of Jesus Christ. Salt Lake City, Deseret News Press, 1950. xi, 216 p. 20 cm. [BX8635.J4] 51-18539
1. Mormons and Mormonism—Doctrinal and controversial works. I. Title.

JONAS, Larry W. 230.93
Mormon claims examined. Grand Rapids, Mich., Baker Book House, 1961. 85p. 61-4439 1.00 pap.,
1. Mormons and Mormonism—Doctrinal and controversial works. I. Title.

JONES, Milton Jenkins. 230.93
The Gospel plan; an encyclopedia of the steps in the Gospel plan. [Salt Lake City] Deseret News Press, 1947. 88 p. diagr. 20 cm. [BX8637.J55] 47-26895
1. Mormons and Mormonism—Doctrinal and controversial works. I. Title.

KIRBAN, Salem. 291'.08 s
Mormonism. Huntingdon Valley, Pa., S. Kirban Inc. [1971] 61 p. illus. (part col.), ports. 22 cm. (His Doctrines of devils, no. 2) [BL85.K56 no. 2] [BX8645] 289'.3'3 72-196423 1.50
1. Mormons and Mormonism—Doctrinal and controversial works. I. Title.

LAMB, Martin Thomas. 289.
The Mormons and their Bible, by Rev. M. T. Lamb. Philadelphia, The Griffith & Rowand pres, 1901. 152 p. illus., 4 port. (incl. front.) 20 cm. Revision of his "Golden Bible", published 1887. [BX8627.L35] 2-3295
1. Mormons and Mormonism—Doctrinal and controversial works. 2. Book of Mormon. I. Title.

LARSEN, John. 289.
Mormonism refuted in the light of Scripture and history; a testimony to the historical church, written by John Larsen ... San Francisco, Protestant publishing house, 1899. 2 p. l., [7]-75 p., 1 l. 21 cm. [BX8645.L3] 0-6542
1. Mormons and Mormonism—Doctrinal and controversial works. I. Title.

LEFGREN, John C., 1945- 232.9'21
April sixth / John C. Lefgren ; foreword by Truman G. Madsen. Salt Lake City, Utah : Deseret Book Co., 1980. xv, 71 p. : ill. ; 24 cm. Includes index. [BX8643.J4L43] 80-11199 ISBN 0-87747-810-4 : 5.95
1. Jesus Christ—Nativity—Miscellanea. 2. Mormons and Mormonism—Doctrinal and controversial works. I. Title.

LUNDSTROM, Harold, comp. 230.93
Motherhood, a partnership with God. Salt Lake City, Bookcraft [1956] 348p. 24cm. [BX8641.L8] 56-57282
1. Mormons and Mormonism—Doctrinal and controversial works. 2. Mothers—Religious life. I. Title.

LUNDWALL, Nels Benjamin, 289.3
1884- comp.
Assorted gems of priceless value ... N. B. Lundwall, compiler and publisher. Salt Lake City, Utah [1944] viii, 376 p. 23 1/2 cm. "First edition." Includes bibliographies. [BX8621.L8] 47-15259
1. Mormons and Mormonism—Doctrinal and controversial works. I. Title.

LUNDWALL, Nels Benjamin, 230.93
1884- comp.
Inspiredp rophetic warnings to all inhabitants of the earth. 5th ed., enl. Being a compilation of ancient and modern prophecies. Salt Lake City, 1943. 160 p. 19 cm. [BX8637.L812 1943] 48-41841
1. Mormons and mormonism—Doctrinal and controversial works. I. Title.

LUNDWALL, Nels Benjamin, 230.93
1884- comp.
Masterpieces of Latter-Day Saint leaders; a compilation of discourses and writings of prominent leaders of the Church of Jesus Christ of Latter-Day Saints. Salt Lake City, Deseret Book Co. [1954, c1953] 151p. 24cm. [BX8635.L8] 54-20749
1. Mormons and Mormonism— Doctrinal and controversial works. I. Title.

LUNDWALL, Nels Benjamin, 289.3
1884- comp.
The vision; or, The degrees of glory (Doc. and cov. section 76) being a compilation of rare and invaluable writings by authorities of the Church of Jesus Christ of Latter-Day Saints, as well as quotations from eminent historians, philosophers, Catholic fathers and Protestant leaders on the doctrine of salvation for the living and the dead. Salt Lake City [1939?] 148 p. 24 cm. [BX8628.L8 1939] 47-39686
1. Smith, Joseph, 1805-1844. Doctrine and covenants. 2. Mormons and Mormonism—Doctrinal and controversial works. I. Title.

MCKAY, David Oman, 1873- 252.093
Gospel ideals; selections from the discourses of David O. McKay. [Salt Lake City] 1953. 598 p. illus. 24 cm. "An Improvement era publication." [BX8635.M325] 54-17880
1. Mormons and Mormonism—Doctrinal and controversial works. I. Title.

MCKINLAY, Lynn A 289.3
For behold ye are free; a series of lectures. Salt Lake City, Deseret Book Co., 1956. 158p. illus. 24cm. [BX8635.M326] 57-17934
1. Mormons and Mormonism—Doctrinal and controversial works. 2. Free will and determinism. I. Title.

MCKINLAY, Lynn A 252.093
Life eternal; a series of lectures, delivered to the Young People's Temple Group of the South Davis Stake. Life eternal [n.p., c1950] 189p. illus. 24cm. [BX8635.M327] 54-31232
1. Mormons and Mormonism—Doctrinal and controversial works. I. Title.

MCKINLAY, Lynn A 289.3
The spirit giveth life; a series of five lectures. Salt Lake City, Deseret Book Co., 1955. 144p. illus. 24cm. [BX8635.M328] 55-35833
1. Mormons and Mormonism—Doctrinal and controversial works. I. Title.

MCMILLAN, Duncan Bhann
The Bible search light thrown onto mormonism, by D. B. McMillan ... [n. p., 1901] 75 pp. port. 18 cm. 2-5209
1. Mormons and mormonism—Doctr. & controv. works. I. Title.

MCMURRIN, Sterling M. 230.93
The Theological foundations of the Mormon religion. Salt Lake City, Univ. of Utah Pr. [c.1965] 151p. 21cm. Bibl. [BX8635.2.M3] 65-26131 3.00; 2.00 pap.,
1. Mormons and Mormonism—Doctrinal and controversial works. I. Title.

MARLER, Ezra L. 289.3
Highway helps, by Ezra L. Marler. Short discussions on the meaning and purpose of life, with emphasis on the fact of its continuity after death, and the elements contributing to its fullest enjoyment. [Independence, Mo., Zion's printing and publishing co., c1945] 2 p. l., vii-xv, 384 p. fronts. (ports.) 21 1/2 cm. [BX8635.M36] 46-13095
1. Mormons and Mormonism—Doctrinal and controversial works. I. Title.

MARTIN, Walter Ralston, 1928- 289.3
The maze of Mormonism. Grand Rapids, Zondervan Pub. House [1962] 186p. 21cm. (The Modern cult library) Includes bibliography. [BX8645.M39] 62-7372
1. Mormons and Mormonism—Dictrinal and controversial works. I. Title.

MARTIN, Walter Ralston, 1928- 289.3
The maze of Mormonism / Walter Martin. Rev. and enl. Santa Ana, Calif. : Vision House Publishers, 1978. 377 p. : ill. ; 21 cm. Bibliography: p. [361]-377. [BX8645.M39 1978] 78-66067 ISBN 0-88449-017-3 pbk. : 5.95
1. Mormons and Mormonism—Doctrinal and controversial works. I. Title.

MAXWELL, Neal A. 230'.9'33
Things as they really are / Neal A. Maxwell. Salt Lake City : Deseret Book Co., 1978. xiv, 127 p. ; 24 cm. Includes index. Bibliography: p. 121. [BX8635.2.M38] 78-26077 ISBN 0-87747-730-2 : 5.95
1. Mormons and Mormonism—Doctrinal and controversial works. I. Title.

MORGAN, Stephen G., 1940- 230.9'3
Are you Mormons ignoramuses? By Stephen G. Morgan. [Salt Lake City] N. G. Morgan, Sr. [1966] xviii, 256 p. illus., map, port. 24 cm. [BX8635.2.M6] 67-2016
1. Mormons and Mormonism—Doctrinal and controversial works. I. Title.

MUSSER, Joseph W
Michael, our Father and our God; the Mormon conception of deity, as taught by Joseph Smith, Brigham Young, John Taylor and their associates in the priesthood. 4th ed. Salt Lake City, Utah, Truth Pub. Co., 1963. 139 p. 24 cm. 66-20967
1. Mormons and Mormonism — Doctrinal and controversial works. 2. God. I. Smith, Joseph, 1805-1844. II. Title.

PEARSON, Glenn Laurentz. 289.3
The Book of Mormon, key to conversion. Salt Lake City, Bookcrraft [1963] 64 p. 21 cm. [BX8635.5.P4] 63-23862
1. Mormons and Mormonism—Controversial works. 2. Book of Mormon. I. Title.

PEARSON, Glenn Laurentz. 230.93
Know your religion. Salt Lake City, Bookcraft [1961] 248p. 24cm. [BX8635.2.P4] 61-30602
1. Mormons and Mormonism—Doctrinal and controversial works. I. Title.

PETERSEN, Mark E. 230'.9'33
The forerunners / Mark E. Petersen. Salt Lake City, Utah : Bookcraft, c1979. 145 p. ; 24 cm. Includes index. [BX8635.2.P448] 79-53831 ISBN 0-88494-376-3 : 5.50
1. John the Baptist. 2. Smith, Joseph, 1805-1844. 3. Mormons and Mormonism—Doctrinal and controversial works. I. Title.

PETERSEN, Mark E 289.3
One Lord, one faith! Salt Lake City, Deseret Book Co., 228p. 24cm. [BX8639.P4O4] 62-52926
1. Mormons and Mormonism—Doctrinal and controversial works. I. Title.

POND, Douglas V., 1908- 230'.9'3
Pillars of Mormonism : a kindly review of Mormonism in a careful comparison with the Bible / by Douglas V. Pond. Washington : Review and Herald Pub. Association, c1978. 271 p. ; 21 cm. Bibliography: p. 269-271. [BX8645.P66] 78-1380 7.95 pbk. : 4.95
1. Mormons and Mormonism—Doctrinal and controversial works. I. Title.

PRATT, Parley Parker, 1807-1857 289.3
Key to the science of theology, designed as an introduction to the first principles of spiritual philosophy, religion, law and government, as delivered by the ancients, and as restored in this age, for the final development of universal peace. truth, and knowledge. 9th ed. Salt Lake City, Deseret, 1965. 170p. 20cm. [BX8635.P85] 65-25454 price unreported
1. Mormons and Mormonism—Doctrinal and controversial works. I. Title.

PRATT, Parley Parker, 1807-1857. 289.
Key to the science of theology; designed as an introduction to the first principles of spiritual philosophy; religion; law and government; as delivered by the ancients, and as restored in this age, for the final development of universal peace, truth and knowledge. By Parley P. Pratt ... 3d ed. Salt Lake City, Deseret news steam printing establishment, 1874. xv, 178 p. 18 cm. [BX8635.P85 1874] 24-1482
1. Mormons and Mormonism—Doctrinal and controversial works. I. Title.

PRATT, Parley Parker, 1807-1857. 230'.93
Key to the science of theology : A voice of warning / by Parley P. Pratt. Salt Lake City : Deseret Book Co., 1978. 127 p. ; 24 cm. (Classics in Mormon literature) Includes indexes. [BX8635.P85 1978.] 77-21220 ISBN 0-87747-674-8 lib. bdg. : 4.95
1. Mormons and Mormonism—Doctrinal and controversial works. I. Pratt, Parley Parker, 1807-1857. A voice of warning. 1978. II. Title.

A rational theology,
as taught by the Church of Jesus Christ of Latter-day Saints. 7th ed. Salt Lake City, Deseret Book Co., 1965 [c1937] viii, 203 p. 20 cm. Bibliography: p. [191]-196. [Widtsoe, John Andreas,] 1872 67-72122
1. Mormons and Mormonism — Doctrinal and controversial works. 2. Theology.

RICH, Wendell O 289.3
Distinctive teachings of the restoration. 1st ed. [Salt Lake City] Printed by Deseret News Press [1962] 216 p. 24 cm. "Originally presented to ... Utah State University ... as a doctoral thesis." Includes bibliography. [BX8635.2.R5] 63-4804
1. Mormons and mormonism — Doctrinal and controversial works. 2. Mormons and Mormoniam — Education. I. Title.

RICHARDS, Claude. 230.93
The temple letters; a rewarding path to happiness on earth and everlasting treasures in heaven. Salt Lake City, Deseret Book Co., 1956. 198p. illus. 24cm. [BX8638.R5] 56-30631
1. Mormons and Mormonism—Doctrinal and controversial works. I. Title.

RICHARDS, Henry W
A reply to "The Church of the Firstborn of the Fulness of Times." Salt Lake City, Deseret Book Co., 1965. 159 p. illus. 24 cm. 67-4211
1. Mormons and Mormonism — Doctrinal and controversial works. 2. Mormons and Mormonism — Government. 3. Church of the Firstborn of the Fulness of Times. I. Title.

RICHARDS, Le Grand, Bp., 1886- 230'.9'33
A marvelous work and a wonder / LeGrand Richards. Rev. and enl. ed. Salt Lake City : Deseret Book Co., 1976. xiv, 424 p. ; 18 cm. Includes bibliographical references and index. [BX8635.2.R52 1976] 76-2237 ISBN 0-87747-161-4 pbk. : 1.50
1. Mormons and Mormonism—Doctrinal and controversial works. I. Title.

RICHARDS, Le Grand, Bp., 1886- 289.3
A marvelous work and a wonder. Salt Lake City, Deseret Book Co., 1950. xvi, 376 p. 23 cm. An expansion of the author's mimeographed outline, The message of Mormonism. [BX8635.R45] 51-18844
1. Mormons and Mormonism—Doctrinal and controversial works. I. Title.

RICHARDS, Le Grand, Bp., 1886-
A marvelous work and a wonder. [Rev. ed.] Salt Lake City, Deseret Book Co., 1967 [c1958] xviii, 452 p. 22 cm. An expansion of the author's mimeographed outline, The message of Mormonism. 68-78829
1. Mormons and Mormonism—Doctrinal and controversial works. I. Title.

RICKS, Eldin, comp. 289.3
New Bible ready reference; a compilation of useful Bible passages for Latter-Day Saint missionaries, teachers, and students. A companion volume to the Combination reference. [1st ed. Salt Lake City] Deseret Book Co., 1961. 262p. 15cm. [BX8631.R5] 61-45730
1. Mormons and Mormonism—Doctrinal and controversial works. 2. Bible—Indexes, Topical. I. Title.

ROBERTS, Brigham Henry, 1857-
The gospel: an exposition of its first principles; and man's relationship to Deity, by Elder B. H. Roberts ... 3d ed. (rev. by the author) Salt Lake City, Utah, The Deseret news, 1901. vii, [2], 10-294 p. 20 cm. 1-24607
1. Mormons and Mormonism—Doctrinal and controversial works. 2. Theology, Doctrinal. 3. Salvation. I. Title.

ROBERTS, Brigham Henry, 1857- 289.
The Mormon doctrine of deity; the Roberts-Van der Donckt discussion, to which is added a discourse, Jesus Christ: the revelation of God, by B. H. Roberts. Also a collection of authoritative Mormon utterances on the being and nature of God ... Salt Lake City, Utah, The Deseret news, 1903. xii, [9]-296 p. 20 cm. [BX8635.R58] 4-59
1. God. 2. Mormons and Mormonism—Doctrinal and controversial works. I. Van der Donckt, Cyril, 1856- II. Title.

ROBERTS, Brigham Henry, 1857- 230.93
Rasha--the Jew; a message to all Jews, by Elder B. H. Roberts ... Salt Lake City, Utah, Deseret news press, 1932. xxiv, 156 p. incl. front. port. 23 cm. Frontispiece accompanied by leaf and portrait accompanied by guard sheet, each with descriptive letterpress. [BX8638.R6] 33-14657
1. Mormons and Mormonism—Doctrinal and controversial works. 2. Jews—Religion. 3. Bible. O. T.—Prophecies. 4. Bible—Prophecies—O. T. 5. Book of Mormon. I. Title.

ROBERTS, Brigham Henry, 1857-1933 289.3
The Gospel; an exposition of its first principles, and man's relationship to deity, 10th ed. Salt Lake City, Deseret, 1965 ix, 292p. 24cm. Cover title: The Gospel and man's relationship to deity. [BX8631.R6] 65-25455 price unreported
1. Mormons and Mormonism—Doctrinal and controversial works. I. Title. II. Title: The Gospel and man's relationship to deity.

ROBERTS, Brigham Henry, 1857-1933. 231
The Mormon doctrine of deity : the Roberts-Van der Donckt discussion, to which is added a discourse, Jesus Christ, the revelation of God : also a collection of authoritative Mormon utterances on the being and nature of God / by B. H. Roberts. Bountiful, Utah : Horizon Publishers, [1976?], c1903. xii, 296 p. ; 23 cm. Reprint of the ed. published by the Deseret news, Salt Lake City. [BX8635.R58 1976] 76-359769 ISBN 0-88290-058-7 : 5.95
1. Mormons and Mormonism—Doctrinal and controversial works. 2. God. I. Van der Donckt, Cyril, 1865- II. Title.

ROBERTS, Brigham Henry, 1857-1933. 289.
The seventy's course in theology. First-[fifth] year... Compiled and edited by Elder B. H. Roberts ... Salt Lake City, The Deseret news, 1907-12. 5 v. 23 cm. Vol. 2 has imprint: Salt Lake City, Skelton publishing co., v. 3: Salt Lake City, The Caxton press. No more published? Includes "References." [BX8635.R63] 8-11510
1. Mormons and mormonism—Doctrinal and controversial works. I. Title.

ROPP, Harry L. 289.3'2
The Mormon papers : are the Mormon scriptures reliable? / Harry L. Ropp. Downers Grove, Ill. : InterVarsity Press, c1977. 118 p. : ill. ; 21 cm. Based on the author's thesis (M.A.) Lincoln Christian Seminary, 1974. Bibliography: p. [117]-118. [BX8645.R66] 77-2681 ISBN 0-87784-789-4 pbk. : 2.95.
1. Mormons and Mormonism—Doctrinal and controversial works. 2. Mormons and Mormonism—Sacred books. I. Title.

SKOUSEN, Willard Cleon, 1913- 289.3
The challenge of our times. [1st ed.] Salt Lake City, Bookcraft Publishers [1953] 167p. 23cm. [BX8635.S55] 53-37091
1. Mormons and Mormonism—Doctrinal and controversial works. I. Title.

SMITH, Heman Conoman.
The truth defended, or, A reply to Elder D. H. Bays' Doctrines and dogmas of Mormonism. By Elder Heman C. Smith... Lamoni, Ia., Board of publication of the Reorganized church of Jesus Christ of Latter day saints, 1901. 241 p. pl. facsim. 19 cm. 1-25580
1. Bays, David H. Doctrines and dogmas of Mormonism. 2. Mormons and Mormonism—Doctr. & controv. works. I. Title.

SMITH, Heman Conoman, 1850- 267.
True succession in church presidency of the Church of Jesus Christ of latter day saints. Being a reply to Elder B. H. Roberts on "Succession in the presidency of the church." By Elder Heman C. Smith... 2d ed. Lamoni, Ia., Board of publication to the Reorganized church of Jesus Christ of latter day saints, 1900. 1 p. l., 234 p. 17 1/2 cm. [BX8671.S6 1900] 38-20547
1. Roberts, Brigham Henry, 1857-1933. Succession in the presidency of the church. 2. Mormons and Mormonism—Doctrinal and controversial works. I. Title.

SMITH, Joseph, 1805-1844. 289.3'3
A book of commandments for the government of the Church of Christ, organized according to law on the 6th of April 1830. Zion [Mo.] W. W. Phelps, 1833. [Independence, Mo., Herald House, 1972] [8], 160 p. facsim. 12 cm. Half title: Herald heritage reprint of the Book of commandments. Facsim. reproduction, with a pref., of a part of a 1st ed. of the Book of doctrine and covenants, printed at Independence, Mo., but never published. Cf. Pref. [BX8628.A3 1833a] 72-181703 ISBN 0-8309-0066-7 3.50
1. Mormons and Mormonism—Doctrinal and controversial works. I. Church of Jesus Christ of Latter-Day Saints. II. Reorganized Church of Jesus Christ of Latter Day Saints. III. Title.

SMITH, Joseph, 1805-1844. 230.93
Discourses. Compiled and arr. by Alma P. Burton. 1st ed. Salt Lake City, Descret Book Co., 1956. 237 p. illus. 24 cm. [BX8621.S5] 57-17601
1. Mormons and Mormonism — Doctrinal and controversial works. I. Title.

SMITH, Joseph, 1805-1844. 230.93
Discourses. Compiled and arr. by Alma P. Burton. 3d ed., Rev and enl. Salt Lake City, Deseret Bolk Co., 1965. viii, 280 p. col. port. 27 cm. [BX8621.S5 1965] 65-29687
1. Mormons and Mormonism — Doctrinal and controversial works. I. Burton, Alma P., 1913- comp. II. Title.

SMITH, Joseph, 1805-1844. 289.3'2
The doctrine and covenants, of the Church of Jesus Christ of Latter-Day Saints, containing the revelations given to Joseph Smith, Jun., the prophet, for the building up of the Kingdom of God in the last days. Divided into verses, with references, by Orson Pratt, Sen. Westport, Conn., Greenwood Press [1971] 503 p. 23 cm. Reprint of the 1880 ed. [BX8628.A3 1971b] 69-14082 ISBN 0-8371-4101-X
1. Mormons and Mormonism—Doctrinal and controversial works. I. Pratt, Orson, 1811-1881. II. Church of Jesus Christ of Latter-Day Saints.

SMITH, Joseph, 1805-1844. 230.9'3
Doctrine and covenants of the Church of the Latter Day Saints: carefully selected

from the revelations of God, and compiled by Joseph Smith, Jr. [and others] Kirtland, Ohio, Printed by F. G. Williams, 1835. [Independence, Mo., Herald House, 1971] 257, xxv p. 16 cm. [BX8628.A3 1971] 77-26627 ISBN 0-8309-0041-1
1. Mormons and Mormonism—Doctrinal and controversial works. I. Church of Jesus Christ of Latter-Day Saints. II. Title.

SMITH, Joseph, 1805-1844. 230.93
Lectures on faith, delivered in Kirtland Temple in 1834 and 1835; with the revelation on the Rebellion as an appendix. Independence, Mo., Herald House, 1952 [i.e. 1953] 56p. illus. 20cm. 'These lectures were published as part one of the first edition (1835) of the Book of doctrine and covenants.' [BX8628.A4 1953] 53-32190
1. Mormons and Mormonism—Doctrinal and controversial works. 2. Faith. I. Title.

SMITH, Joseph, 1805-1844.
The pearl of great price; a selection from the revelations, translations, and narrations of Joseph Smith, first prophet, seer and revelator to the Church of Jesus Christ of latter-day saints. Salt Lake City, Utah, The Church of Jesus Christ of latter-day saints, c1957. iv, 65 p.illus. (facsims.)
1. Mormons and Mormonism — Doctrinal and controversial works. I. Title.

SMITH, Joseph, 1805-1844. 230.
The pearl of great price; a selection from the revelations, translations, and narrations of Joseph Smith, first prophet, seer and revelator to the Church of Jesus Christ of latter-day saints. Salt Lake City, Utah, The Church of Jesus Christ of latter-day saints, 1921. iv, 63 p. illus. (facsims.) 19 cm. [With his The doctrine and covenants of the Church of Jesus Christ of latter-day saints ... Salt Lake City, 1921] "First issued, as divided into chapters and verses with references, by James E. Talmage, in 1902. First published in double-column pages, with index, in 1921." [BX8628.A2 1921] 22-5314
1. Mormons and Mormonism—Doctrinal and controversial works. I. Title.

SMITH, Joseph, 1805-1844. 289.
The pearl of great price: being a choice selection from the revelations, translations, and narrations of Joseph Smith, first prophet, seer, and revelator to the Church of Jesus Christ of Latter-day saints. Salt Lake City, Utah, Printed at the Latter-day saints' printing and publishing establishment, 1878. 2 p. l., 71 p. illus., fold. pl. 23 cm. [BX8629.P52 1878] 4-20691
1. Mormons and Mormonism—Doctrinal and controversial works. I. Title.

SMITH, Joseph Fielding, 1838-1918. 289.3
Gospel doctrine; selections from the sermons and writings of Joseph F. Smith ... 7th ed. Salt Lake City, Utah, Deseret book company, 1946. 3 p. l., [v]-xiv, 553 p. front. (port.) 23 1/2 cm. Compiled by Dr. John A. Widtsoe and others. cf. Introd. [BX8635.S6 1946] 47-4692
1. Mormons and Mormonism—Doctrinal and controversial works. I. Wildtsoe, John Andreas, 1872- comp. II. Title.

SMITH, Joseph Fielding, 1876- 230.93
Answers to gospel questions. Salt Lake City, Deseret Book Co. [1957- v. 23 cm. [BX8638.S48] 57-29432
1. Mormons and Mormonism — Doctrinal and controversial works. 2. Questions and answers — Theology. I. Title.

SMITH, Joseph Fielding, 1876- 230.93
Elijah the prophet and his mission. Salt Lake City, Deseret Book Co., 1957. 123 p. 20 cm. [BX8638.S484] 57-31389
1. Elijah, the prophet. 2. Mormons and Mormonism — Doctrinal and controversial works. I. Title.

SMITH, Joseph Fielding, 1876- 289.3
Man, his origin and destiny. Salt Lake City, Deseret Book Co., 1954. 563p. 24cm. [BX8635.S65] 54-1762
1. Mormons and Mormonism—Doctrinal and controversial works. 2. Man (Theology) 3. Religion and science—1900- I. Title.

SMITH, Joseph Fielding, 1876-
The way to perfection; short discourses on Gospel themes dedicated to all who are interested in the redemption of the living and the dead. 11th ed. [Salt Lake City] Genealogical Society of the Church of Jesus Christ of Latter-Day Saints, 1956. 365p. 20cm.
1. Mormons and Mormonism—Doctrinal and controversial works. I. Title.

SMITH, Joseph Fielding, 1876-
The way to perfection; short discourses on Gospel themes dedicated to all who are interested in the redemption of the living and the dead. 11th ed. [Salt Lake City] Genealogical Society of the Church of Jesus Christ of Latter-Day Saints, 1956. 365 p. 20 cm.
1. Mormons and Mormonism — Doctrinal and controversial works. I. Title.

SMITH, Joseph Fielding, 1876-
Way to perfection. 12th ed. [Salt Lake City] Published for the Genealogical Society by Deseret Book Co., 1963. 365 p. 20 cm. 65-35681
1. Mormons and Mormonism — Doctrinal and controversial works. I. Title.

SMITH, Joseph Fielding, 1913- 230.93
Religious truths defined; a comparison of religious faiths with the restored gospel. Salt Lake City, Bookcraft [1959] 411 p. 24 cm. [BX8635.2.S55] 59-48894
1. Mormons and Mormonism — Doctrinal and controversial works. I. Title.

SMITH, Willard J., 1858- 231
What the restoration movement teaches concerning God, by Willard J. Smith ... Port Huron, Mich. [c1935] iv, [5]-111 p. front. (port.) 19 cm. "My ... endeavor to answer the follies and foibles as set forth in Brother Wood's booklet ... "The infinite God'."--Foreword. [BT101.S627] 35-15605
1. Wood, Samuel, 1874- The infinite God. 2. Mormons and Mormonism—Doctrinal and controversial works. I. Title.

[SMITH JOSEPH] 1805-1844. 230.
A book of commandments for the government of the Church of Christ, organized according to law on the 6th of April 1830. Zion [Mo.] W. W. Phelps, 1833. 160 p. 12 cm. L. C. copy imperfect: part of t. p. and parts of p. 17-18 lacking. Part of a 1st ed. of the Book of doctrine and covenants, printed at Independence, Mo., but never published, as the sheets were burned by a mob. Cf. Berrian. Cat. of books ... on Mormonism; Woodward. Bibl. scallawagiana; Sabin. --Microfilm copy h (negative) Mirofilm BX-14 [BX8628.A3 1833] 8-25600
1. Mormons and Mormonism—Doctrinal and controversial works. I. Church of Jesus Christ of Latter-Day Saints. II. Title.

STENHOUSE, Fanny, 1829- 289.3'792'25
Tell it all; the tyranny of Mormonism; or, An Englishwoman in Utah, by Mrs. T. B. H. Stenhouse. New York, Praeger [1971] xii, 404 p. illus. 23 cm. (Travellers' classics) 1888 ed. published under title: The tyranny of Mormonism. [BX8645.S67 1971] 73-148137 29.50
1. Mormons and Mormonism—Doctrinal and controversial works. I. Title.

STEWART, Ora (Pate) 1910- 230.93
A letter to my son. [3d ed.] Salt Lake City, Bookcraft [1951] 109p. 17cm. [BX8643.Y6S7 1951] 54-31772
1. Mormons and Mormonism—Doctrinal and controversial works. 2. Young men—Religious life. 3. Sexual ethics. I. Title.

STILSON, Max. 230.93
How to deal with Mormons. Grand Rapids, Zondervan Pub. House [1965] 61 p. 21 cm. Bibliography: p. 61-62. [BX8645.S7] 64-15557
1. Mormons and Mormonism — Doctrinal and controversial works. I. Title.

STOKES, Jeremiah, 1877- ed. 289.3
Modern miracles, by Jeremiah Stokes. Salt Lake City, Utah, Bookcraft [1945] 5 p. l., 196 p. 20 cm. "Second edition." [BX8638.S85 1945] 46-3248
1. Mormons and Mormonism—Doctrinal and controversial works. 2. Faith-cure. I. Title.

STRONG, Leon Marshal, 1893- 230.93
Three timely treasures: Dispensations of the gospel, The ten lost tribes [and] From the Kingdom of Judah to John the Baptist. [Independence, Mo., 1949] 103 p. illus. 21 cm. Bibliographical footnotes. [BX8638.S88] 49-5599
1. Mormons and Mormonism—Doctrinal and controversial works. 2. Covenants (Theology) 3. Lost Tribes of Israel. I. Title.

TALMAGE, James Edward, 1802-
The articles of faith; a series of lectures on the principal doctrines of the church of Jesus Christ of Latter-day saints, by Dr. James E. Talmage. Written by appointment; and published by the church. Salt Lake City, Utah, The Deseret news, 1901. ix, [1], 485 p. 20 cm. 2-1449
1. Mormons and Mormonism—Doctrinal and controversial works. I. Title.

TALMAGE, James Edward, 1862- 289.
The articles of faith. A series of lectures on the principal doctrines of the Church of Jesus Christ of Latter-day saints, by Dr. James E. Talmage. Written by appointment; and published by the church. Salt Lake City, Utah, The Deseret news, 1899. viii, 490 p. 20 cm. [BX8635.T3 1899] 99-2349
1. Mormons and Mormonism-Doctrinal and controversial works. I. Title.

TALMAGE, James Edward, 1862- 230.93
The articles of faith; a series of lectures on the principal doctrines of the Church of Jesus Christ of Latter-day saints. By James E. Talmage ... Prepared by appointment and published by the church. 20th thousand. Salt Lake City, Utah, The Deseret news, 1901. ix, [1], 485 p. 20 cm. Second edition. [BX8635.T3 1901a] 33-7482
1. Mormons and Mormonism—Doctrinal and controversial works. I. Title.

TALMAGE, James Edward, 1862- 289.
A study of the articles of faith, being a consideration of the principal doctrines of Church of Jesus Christ of latter-day saints, by James E. Talmage ... Rev. and in parts rewritten. 12th ed. in English, including the 57th thousand. Salt Lake City, Utah, The Church of Jesus Christ of latter-day saints, 1924. ix, [1], 537 p. 20 cm. [BX8635.T3 1924] 24-10616
1. Mormons and Mormonism—Doctrinal and controversial works. I. Title.

TALMAGE, James Edward, 1862-1933.
Jesus the Christ; a study of the Messiah and his mission according to Holy Scriptures, both ancient and modern. Salt Lake City, Utah, Deseret Book Comp., 1962. xi, 804 p. 68-66733
1. Mormons and Mormonism—Doctrinal and controversial works. I. Title.

TALMAGE, James Edward, 1862-1933.
Jesus the Christ; a study of the Messiah and His mission according to Holy Scriptures both ancient and modern. Pub. by the Church. 30th ed. including the 127th thousand. Salt Lake City, Utah, Deseret Book Co., 1960. 804 p. 20 cm. Bibliographical references included in "Notes" (after each chapter) 67-69101
1. Jesus Christ-Biog. 2. Mormons and Mormonism-Doctrinal and controversial works. I. Title.

TALMAGE, James Edward, 1862-1933.
Jesus the Christ; a study of the Messiah and His mission according to Holy Scriptures both ancient and modern. Published by the church. 35th ed. Salt Lake City, Deseret Book Co., 1963. 804 p. 20 cm. 66-65258
1. Jesus Christ-Biog. 2. Mormons and Mormonism-Doctrinal and controversial works. I. Title.

TALMAGE, James Edward, 1862-1933. 289.
Jesus the Christ; a study of the Messiah and his mission according to Holy Scriptures both ancient and modern. Published by the church. 6th ed. Salt Lake City, Deseret Book Co., 1922. 804 p. 20 cm. [BX8643.J4T3 1922] 52-56531
1. Jesus Christ—Biog. 2. Mormons and Mormonism—Doctrinal and controversial works. I. Title.

TALMAGE, James Edward, 1862-1933.
A study of the articles of faith, being a consideration of the principal doctrines of the Church of Jesus Christ of latter-day saints, by James E. Talmage... 47th ed. in English including the two hundred sixty-eight thousand. Salt Lake City, Utah, The Church of Jesus Christ of latter-day saints, 1966. ix, [1], 536 p. 20 cm. 68-69376
1. Mormons and Mormonism—Doctrinal and controversial works. I. Title.

TALMAGE, James Edward, 1862-1933.
A study of the articles of faith; being a consideration of the principal of doctrines of the church of Jesus Christ of Latter-day Saints. 42d ed. in English, including the 243d thousand. Salt Lake City, Church of Jesus Christ of Latter-Day Saints, 1961. ix, 536 p. 20 cm. 63-73788
1. Mormons and Mormonism-Doctrinal and controversial works. I. Title. II. Title: Articles of faith.

TALMAGE, James Edward, 1862-1933.
A study of the Articles of faith; being a consideration of the principal doctrines of the Church of Jesus Christ of Latter-day Saints, by James E. Talmage. 44th ed. in English, incl. the 253d thousand. Salt Lake City, Church of Jesus Christ of Latter-day Saints, 1962. ix, 536 p. 19 cm. Cover title: Articles of faith. 67-69177
1. Mormons and Mormonism-Doctrinal and controversial works. I. Title. II. Title: Articles of faith.

TALMAGE, James Edward, 1862-1933
A study of the articles of faith; being a consideration of the principal doctrines of the Church of Jesus Christ of Latter-day Saints, by James E. Talmage 46th ed. in English ... Salt Lake City, Church of Jesus Christ of Latter-Day Saints, 1965. ix, 536 p. 20 cm. 67-65663
1. Mormons and Mormonism—Doctrinal and controversial works. I. Title.

TALMAGE, James Edward, 1862-1933.
A study of the articles of faith, being a consideration of the principal doctrines of the Church of Jesus Christ of Latter-day Saints. 36th ed. Salt Lake City, Church of Jesus Christ of Latter-day Saints [c1957] 536 p.
1. Mormons and Mormonism — Doctrinal and controversial works. I. Title.

TANNER, Jerald.
The case against Mormonism. [Salt Lake City, 1967- v. (loose-leaf) illus., facsims. 30 cm. 68-14075
1. Mormons and Mormonism—Controversial works. I. Tanner, Sandra, joint author. II. Title.

TAYLOR, John, 1808-1887. 232.3
An examination into and an elucidation of the great principle of the mediation and atonement of Our Lord and Savior Jesus Christ. [1st ed. with concordance. Salt Lake City 1950] 206 p. 24 cm. Cover title: The mediation and atonement. "A concordance of The mediation and atonement, by Peter C. Cariston": . 190-206. [BX8643.B6T3 1950] 50-1763
1. Mormons and Mormonism — Doctrinal and controversial works. 2. Atonement. I. Title. II. Title: The mediation and atonement.

TAYLOR, John, 1808-1887. 232.3
An examination into and an elucidation of the great principle of the mediation and atonement of Our Lord and Saviour Jesus Christ. By President John Taylor ... Salt Lake City, Utah, Deseret news company, 1882. 205 p. 22 1/2 cm. On cover: The mediation and atonement. [BX8643.B6T3 1882a] 38-11157
1. Mormons and Mormonism—Doctrinal and controversial works. 2. Atonement. I. Title.

TVEDTNES, John A. 262
The church of the Old Testament / John A. Tvedtnes. Rev. ed. Salt Lake City, Utah : Deseret Book Co., 1980. p. cm. Includes index. Bibliography: p. [BX8635.2.T86 1980] 80-18595 5.95

1. Bible. O.T.—Criticism, interpretation. 2. Dead Sea scrolls. 3. Mormons and Mormonism—Doctrinal and controversial works. 4. Church. I. Title.

URSENBACH, Octave Frederick, 1870- 215
Deity and law, by Octave F. Ursenbach. Los Angeles, Calif., The Aetna press [c1933] 122 p. 20 cm. [BX8638.U7] [230.93] 33-24709
1. Mormons and Mormonism—Doctrinal and controversial works. 2. Religion and science—1900- 3. Religion—Philosophy. I. Title.

WESTENSKOW, Melvin, 1909- 289.3
Treasures to share. Dedicated to all who are seeking religious truth. Salt Lake City, Deseret News Press [1948] viii, 170 p. 23 cm. [BX8635.W47] 49-340
1. Mormons and Mormonism—Doctrinal and controversial works. I. Title.

WIDTSOE, John Andreas, 1872- 230.93
A rational theology as taught by the Church of Jesus Christ of latter-day saints, by Elder John A. Widtsoe ... 4th ed. (rev.) Salt Lake City, Deseret book co., 1937. viii, 202 p. 20 cm. "References": p. [191]-196. [BX8635.W6 1937] 38-3713
1. Mormons and Mormonism—Doctrinal and controversial works. I. Title.

WIDTSOE, John Andreas, 1872-1952. 230.93
Evidences and reconciliations. Arr. by G. Homer Durham. Salt Lake City, Bookcraft [1960] 412 p. 24 cm. [BX8635.W582] 60-29867
1. Mormons and Mormonism — Doctrinal and controversial works. I. Title.

WILSON, Lycurgus Arnold, 1856- 289.
Outlines of Mormon philosophy; or, The answers given by the gospel, as revealed through the prophet Joseph Smith, to the questions of life. By Lycurgus A. Wilson ... Salt Lake City, Utah, The Deseret news, 1905. 3 p. l., [iii]-xiii p., 1 l., [17]-128 p. illus. (port.) 20 cm. [BX8635.W67] 5-33902
1. Mormons and Mormonism—Doctrinal and controversial works. I. Title.

WOODRUFF, Wilford, 1807-1898. 289.3
The discourses of Wilford Woodruff, fourth president of the Church of Jesus Christ of latter-day saints. Selected, arranged and edited by G. Homer Durham, with a foreword by John A. Widtsoe ... [Salt Lake City] Bookcraft, 1946. xxii p., 1 l., 357 p. front. (port.) 23 1/2 cm. "First edition." [BX8635.W7] 47-18728
1. Mormons and Mormonism—Doctrinal and controversial works. I. Durham, George Homer, 1911- ed. II. Title.

YARN, David H. 230.93
The Gospel: God, man, and truth [by] David H. Yarn. Salt Lake City, Deseret, 1965. viii, 211p. 24cm. [BX8635.2.Y3] 65-18575 price unreported
1. Mormons and Mormonism—Doctrinal and controversial works. I. Title.

YOUNG, Seymour Dilworth, 1897- 248.4893
More precious than rubies; a Mormon boy and his priesthood. Salt Lake City, Bookcraft [c1959] 110 p. illus. 24 cm. [BX8643.Y6Y6] 60-29866
1. Mormons and Mormonism — Doctrinal and controversial works. 2. Youth — Religious life. I. Title.

YOUNG, Thomas W. 289.
Mormonism: its origin, doctrines and dangers. Ann Arbor, Mich., G. Wahr [1900] 71 p. 19 1/2 cm. Bibliography: p. [5]-6. [BX8645.Y7] 0-3155
1. Mormons and Mormonism—Doctrinal and controversial works. I. Title.

ZIEGLER, Wesley Moody, 1911- 289.3
An analysis of the Articles of faith. [Pasadena, Calif., 1949] 236, vii p. 24 cm. [BX8629.P6Z5] 49-6859
1. Smith, Joseph. 1805-1844. The pearl of great price. 2. Mormons and Mormonism—Doctrinal and controversial works. I. Title.

Mormons and Mormonism—Doctrinal and controversial works—Church of Christ authors.

SCOTT, Latayne Colvett, 1952- 230'.9'33
The Mormon mirage : a former Mormon tells why she left the church / Latayne Colvett Scott. Grand Rapids : Zondervan Pub. House, c1979. xi, 276 p. ; 24 cm. Includes indexes. Bibliography: p. 257-261. [BX8645.S35] 79-17717 ISBN 0-310-38910-0 10.95
1. Scott, Latayne Colvett, 1952- 2. Mormons and Mormonism—Doctrinal and controversial works—Church of Christ authors. I. Title.

Mormons and Mormonism—Doctrinal and controversial works—Congresses.

PEARL of Great Price Symposium, Brigham Young University, 1975. 230'.9'33
Pearl of Great Price Symposium : a centennial presentation, November 22, 1975 / sponsored by the Department of Ancient Scripture. 1st ed. Provo, Utah : Brigham Young University, 1976. iii leaves, 103 p. ; 28 cm. Includes bibliographical references. [BX8629.P5P4 1975] 76-370968 pbk. : 2.00
1. Smith, Joseph, 1805-1844. The pearl of great price—Congresses. 2. Mormons and Mormonism—Doctrinal and controversial works—Congresses. I. Brigham Young University, Provo, Utah. Dept. of Ancient Scripture.

Mormons and Mormonism—Doctrinal and controversial works—History and criticism

NIBLEY, Hugh, 1910- 289.3
Sounding brass; informal studies of the lucrative art of telling stories about Brigham Young and the Mormons. Salt Lake City, Bookcraft [1964] 286[8]p. illus. 24cm. Bibl. 64-5722 price unreported
1. Mormons and Mormonism—Doctrinal and controversial works—Hist. & crit. I. Title.

Mormons and Mormonism—Doctrinal and controversial works—Lutheran authors.

HULLINGER, Robert N. 289.3'22
Mormon answer to skepticism : Why Joseph Smith wrote the book of Mormon / by Robert N. Hullinger. St. Louis, Mo. : Clayton Pub. House, c1980. xiv, 201 p. : ill. ; 23 cm. Includes index. Bibliography: p. [181]-188. [BX8627.H78] 19 79-54055 ISBN 0-915644-18-5 (pbk.) : 14.95
1. Smith, Joseph, 1805-1844. 2. Book of Mormon. 3. Mormons and Mormonism—Doctrinal and controversial works—Lutheran authors. I. Title.

Mormons and Mormonism—Doctrinal and controversial works—Mormon authors.

PETERSEN, Mark E. 222'.110924 B
Joseph of Egypt / Mark E. Petersen. Salt Lake City, Utah : Deseret Book Co., 1981. 156 p. ; 24 cm. Includes index. [BX8643.J67P47] 19 81-531 ISBN 0-87747-861-9 : 6.95
1. Joseph (Biblical patriarch) 2. Mormons and Mormonism—Doctrinal and controversial works—Mormon authors. I. Title.

Mormons and Mormonism—Doctrinal and controversial works—Protestant authors.

TANNER, Jerald, 1938- 230'.9'33
The changing world of Mormonism / by Jerald and Sandra Tanner. Chicago : Moody Press, c1979. p. cm. Bibliography: p. [BX8645.T26] 79-18311 ISBN 0-8024-1234-3 : 9.95
1. Mormons and Mormonism—Doctrinal and controversial works—Protestant authors. I. Tanner, Sandra, 1941- joint author. II. Title.

Mormons and mormonism—Doctrine.

RICHARDS, Stephen L 1879-1959.
About Mormonism. [Salt Lake City] Church of Jesus Christ of Latter-day Saints [1961] 1 v. Cover--title. 68-10494
1. Mormons and mormonism—Doctrine. I. Title.

STEWART, John J
Mormonism and the Negro; an explanation and defense of the doctrine of the Church of Jesus Christ of Latter-day Saints in regard to Negroes and others of Negroid blood. [1st ed. Logan, Utah, c1960] 54 p. 19 cm.
I. Title.

Mormons and Mormonism—Education.

BENNION, Milton Lynn, 1902- 377.898
Mormonism and education [by] Milton Lynn Bennion ... [Salt Lake City] The Department of education of the Church of Jesus Christ of latter-day saints [c1939] xi, 297 p. illus. (incl. maps) diagrs. 16 cm. Bibliography: p. [283]-292. [LC586.M6B4] 40-12796
1. Mormons and Mormonism—Education. I. Church of Jesus Christ of latter-day saints. Dept. of education. II. Title.

BURTON, Alma P 1913- 922.8373
Karl G. Maeser, Mormon educator. Salt Lake City, Deseret Book Co., 1953. 79p. illus. 23cm. 'Condensation of a thesis . . . for the degree of master of science . . . Brigham Young University.' [BX8695.M3B8] 53-35200
1. Maeser, Karl Gottfried, 1828-1901. 2. Mormons and Mormonism—Education. I. Title.

CHEVILLE, Roy Arthur, 1897-. 377.893
... The Latter day saints and their changing relationship to the social order, a sociological approach to religious education; the digest of a research study, "The role of religious education in the accommodation of a sect." By Roy A. Cheville. Independence, Mo., Herald publishing house, Reorganized church of Jesus Christ of latter-day saints, 1942. 77 p. 19 1/2 cm. (Church school leadership series) Bibliography: p. 77. [BX8671.C45] 42-22633
1. Mormons and Mormonism—Education. 2. Sociology, Christian—Mormon authors. I. Reorganized church of Jesus Christ of latter-day saints. II. Title.

CHEVILLE, Roy Arthur, 1897-. 377.893
... The role of religious education in the accommodation of a sect ... by Roy A. Cheville. Independence, Mo., Herald publishing house, 1942. 77 p. 20 cm. Part of thesis (PH. D.)--University of Chicago, 1942. Published also without thesis note under title: The Latter day saints and their changing relationship to the social order. Bibliography: p. 77. [BX8671.C45 1942a] A42
1. Mormons and Mormonism—Education. 2. Sociology, Christian—Mormon authors. I. Title.

CHURCH of Jesus Christ of latter-day saints. Deseret Sunday school union. 268
Jubilee history of Latter-day saints Sunday schools. 1849-1899 ... Salt Lake City, Utah, Deseret Sunday school union, 1900. viii, [9]-546, [16] p. front., plates, ports. 23 cm. Prepared by a committee of the Deseret Sunday school union board. Sixteen pages at end blank for "Sunday school and personal history memoranda." [BX8610.A53] 22-23420
1. Mormons and Mormonism—Education. I. Title.

DESERET Sunday school union, Salt Lake City.
Jubilee history of Latter-day saints Sunday schools. 1849-1899 ... Salt Lake City, Utah, Deseret Sunday school union, 1900. viii, [9]-546 p. front., plates. ports. 23 cm. Prepared by a committee of the Deseret Sunday school union board. Sixteen blank pages at end for "Sunday school and personal history memoranda." [BX8610.D45] 22-23420
1. Mormons and Mormonism—Education. I. Church of Jesus Christ of latter-day saints. II. Title.

HOOLE, Daryl (Van Dam) 207
The art of teaching children, by Daryl V. Hoole. Illus. [by] Dick and Mary Scopes. Salt Lake City, Deseret Book Co., 1964. xix, 230 p. illus. 24 cm. "Oh! hang up the baby's stocking, author of words unknown, music arranged [for voice and piano] by Ellen F. Bentley": (p. 64) [BX8610.H6] 64-4289
1. Mormons and Mormonism — Education. 2. Religious education of children. I. Bentley, Ellen F., arr. Hang up the baby's stocking. II. Title.

THE Instructor (Salt Lake City) 268.893
A reader for the teacher; an anthology of ideas and teaching helps taken from the Instructor, the teacher's magazine of the church. Compiled by A. Hamer Reiser. Salt Lake City, Deseret Book Co., 1960. 362p. 24cm. Includes bibliography. [BX8610.15] 60-29868
1. Mormons and Mormonism—Education. 2. Religious education. I. Reiser, A. Hamer, comp. II. Title.

Mormons and Mormonism — Fiction.

EVENTFUL narratives ... 289.3
Designed for the instruction and encouragement of young Latter-day saints. Salt Lake City, Utah, Juvenile instructor office, 1887. vii, [9]-98 p. 19 cm. (Faith-promoting series. 13th book) [BX8637.E8] 38-12922
1. Mormons and Mormonism—Fiction. I. Aveson, Robert. II. Huntington, O. B.
Contents omitted.

MOFFETT, Grant.
Jewels of the valleys. New York, Carlton press [1964] 168 p. 21 cm. (A reflection book) 66-95470
1. Mormons and Mormonism — Fiction. I. Title.

[RICHARDS, Robert]
The Californian Crusoe; or, The lost treasure found. A tale of Mormonism. London, J. H. Parker; New York, Stanford and Swords, 1854. iv, 162 p. front. 17 cm. This work purports to be by an Englishman named Richards. A 22
1. Mormons and Mormonism—Fiction. I. Title.

TOURGEE, Albion Winegar, 1838-1905.
Button's inn. By Albion W. Tourgee... Boston, Roberts brothers, 1887. x, 418 p. 18 cm. A story of Mormonism in the early part of the century. [PZ3087.B8 1887] 8-29835
1. Mormons and Mormonism—Fiction. I. Title.

[WARD, Maria, Mrs.]
The Mormon wife; a life story of the sacrifices, sorrows and sufferings of woman. A narrative of many years' personal experience. by the wife of a Mormon elder... Hartford, Conn., Hartford publishing company, 1873. xvii, [9]-449 p. front., plates, ports. 21 cm. [BX8641.W35 1873] S-34314
1. Mormons and Mormonism—Fiction. I. Title.

Mormons and Mormonism—Finance.

REORGANIZED church of Jesus Christ of latter-day saints. 254
Handbook of the financial law, by the Presiding bishopric for the Reorganized church of Jesus Christ of latter day saints. [Independence, Mo., Herald publishing house, c1941] 58 p. 19 1/2 cm. Revised edition. [BX8671.A53] 42-5720
1. Mormons and Mormonism—Finance. I. Title.

Mormons and Mormonism—Genealogy

JACOBSON, Gladys (Slaugh) comp.
Legacy; the story of George Alfred Slaugh and Rachel Maria Goodrich, their children and their children's children. Salt Lake City, 1964. 287 p. illus., geneal. tables. 29 cm. 68-49888

1. Slaugh family (George Alfred Slaugh, 1868-1945) 2. Mormons and Mormonism—Geneal. I. Title.

Mormons and Mormonism—Genealogy—Miscellanea.

THE Celestial connection 248.2
: faith-promoting stories on family research / compiled by Connie Rector & Diane Deputy. Salt Lake City, Utah : Bookcraft, c1980. viii, 207 p. ; 23 cm. "A companion volume to Links of forever, by the same compilers."—jacket. [CS49.C44] 19 80-67379 ISBN 0-88494-407-7 : 5.95
1. Mormons and Mormonism—Genealogy—Miscellanea. 2. United States—Genealogy—Miscellanea. I. Rector, Connie. II. Deputy, Diane.

Mormons and Mormonism — Government.

CLARK, Harold Glen, 1902- 262.4
Millions of meetings. Salt Lake City, Deseret Book Co. [1955] 118p. illus. 24cm. [BX8657.C55] 55-30108
1. Mormons and Mormonism—Government. I. Title.

DURHAM, Reed C. 289.3'3
Succession in the church [by] Reed C. Durham, Jr. [and] Steven H. Heath. Salt Lake City, Bookcraft, 1970. viii, 207 p. 24 cm. [BX8657.D8] 72-119915
1. Mormons and Mormonism—Government. I. Heath, Steven H., joint author. II. Title.

KEELER, Joseph Brigham, 1855- 289.
First steps in church government; what church government is and what it does. A book for young members of the lesser priesthood. By Joseph B. Keeler. Salt Lake City, The Deseret news, 1906. viii, 152 p. 16 cm. [BX8635.K4] 7-3088
1. Mormons and Mormonism—Government. I. Title.

WIDTSOE, John Andreas, 1872- 289.3
Priesthood and church government; a handbook and study course for the quorums of the Melchizedek priesthood of the Church of Jesus Christ of latter-day saints, compiled under the direction of the Council of the twelve, by John A. Widtsoe ... [Salt Lake City] Deseret book company, 1939. 2 p. l., [iii]-xiv, 410 p. front., diagrs. 20 1/2 cm. [BX8657.W5] 40-11394
1. Mormons and Mormonism—Government. I. Title.

WIDTSOE, John Andreas, 1872-1952.
Priesthood and church government in the Church of Jesus Christ of Latter-day Saints, compiled under the direction of the Council of the Twelve, by John A. Widtsoe. [Salt Lake City] Deseret Book Co., 1963 [c1939] xvi, 397 p. front. 20 cm. 67-71586
1. Mormons and Mormonism — Government. I. Church of Jesus Christ of Latter-Day Saints. Council of the Twelve Apostles. II. Title.

YOUNG, Fred L. 262.9
Ministry of reconciliation and church court procedure. Independence, Mo., Herald House [c.1961, c.]1960. 200p. (Pastor's reference library) 60-53060 2.50
1. Mormons and Mormonism—Government. I. Reorganized Church of Jesus Christ of Latter-Day Saints. II. Title.

YOUNG, Fred L 262.9
Ministry of reconciliation and church court procedure. Independence, Mo., Herald House, 1960. 200 p. 18 cm. (Pastors' reference library) At head of title: Reorganized Church of Jesus Christ of Latter Day Saints. "The offical court procedures and decisions of the quorums and councils -- have been included." [BX8657.Y57] 60-53060
1. Mormons and Mormonism — Government. I. Reorganized Church of Jesus Christ of Latter-Day Saints. II. Title.

Mormons and Mormonism — History

ANDERSON, Nels, 1889- 289.3
Desert saints: the Mormon frontier in Utah. Chicago, University of Chicago Press [1966] xxxvi, 459 p. illus., ports. 21 cm. First published 1942. Bibliography: p. 447-452. [BX8611.A49 1966] 66-19134
1. Mormons and Mormonism—History. I. Title.

ANDERSON, Nels, 1889- 280.3
Desert saints; the Mormon frontier in Utah, by Nels Anderson. Chicago, Ill., The University of Chicago press [1942] xx, 459 p. incl. illus. (incl. ports., facsims.) tables, diagr. maps (2 fold.) 24 cm. Bibliographical references included in "Notes" at end of each chapter, Bibliography: p. 447-452. [BX8611.A49] 42-9220
1. Mormons and Mormonism—Hist. I. Title.

ARRINGTON, Leonard J. 289.3'73
Building of the city of God : community & cooperation among the Mormons / Leonard J. Arrington, Feramorz Y. Fox, Dean L. May. Salt Lake City : Deseret Book Co., 1976. xiii, 497 p. : ill. ; 24 cm. Includes bibliographical references and index. [BX8611.A77] 76-27141 ISBN 0-87747-590-3 : 7.95
1. Mormons and Mormonism—History. 2. Collective settlements—History. I. Fox, Feramorz Y., 1881-1957, joint author. II. May, Dean L., joint author. III. Title.

BACH, Marcus, 1906- 289.3
The Mormon. [Salt Lake City] Deseret Book Co., by special arrangement with the Bobbs-Merrill Co. [1951] 63 p. 20 cm. "From [the author's] Faith and my friends." [BX8611.B3] 51-8642
1. Mormons and Mormonism—Hist. I. Title.

BACKMAN, Milton Vaughn. 270
American religions and the rise of Mormonism, by Milton V. Backman, Jr. Salt Lake City, Deseret Book Book Co., 1965. xiii, 466 p. illus., maps (on lining papers) ports. 24 cm. Bibliography: p. 431-442. [BX8611.B314] 65-27488
1. Mormons and Mormonism—Hist. 2. Church history. 3. U.S.—Church history. I. Title.

BARKER, James Louis, 1880-1958. 289.3
Restoration of the divine church. Salt Lake City, K. M. Barker [c1960] 140p. 24cm. Includes bibliography. [BX8611.B32] 61-37758
1. Mormons and Mormonism—Hist. I. Title.

BERRETT, William Edwin, ed. 289.309
Readings in L. D. S. Church history from original manuscripts, by William E. Berrett and Alma P. Burton. 1st ed. Salt Lake City, Deseret Book Co., 1953-58. 3v. facsims. 24cm. Includes bibliographies. [BX8611.B346] 53-23418
1. Mormons and Mormonism—Hist. I. Burton, Alma P., 1913- joint ed. II. Title.

BURTON, Alma P 1913- 289.309
Mormon trail from Vermont to Utah; a guide to historic places of the Church of Jesus Christ of Latter-Day Saints. [Rev. ed.] Salt Lake City, Deseret Book Co., 1960. 103p. illus. 23cm. Includes bibliography. [BX8611.B78 1960] 60-50906
1. Mormons and Mormonism—Hist. I. Title.

BURTON, Alma P 1913- 289.309
Mormon trail from Vermont to Utah; a guide to historic places of the Church of Jesus Christ of Latter-Day Saints. [2d ed. Salt Lake City, Deseret Book Co., 1953] 84p. illus. 23cm. [BX8611.B78] 53-36467
1. Mormons and Mormonism— Hist. I. Title.

BURTON, Alma P 1913- comp. 289.3
Stories from Mormon history, by Alma P. Burton and Clea M. Burton. 1st ed. Salt Lake City, Deseret Book Co. [1960] 310p. 24cm. [BX8611.B79] 60-33251
1. Mormons and Mormonism—Hist. I. Burton, Clea M., joint comp. II. Title.

CHURCH of Jesus Christ of latter-day saints. Deseret Sunday school union. 268.
Bible and church history stories for the Primary department of the Sunday School. Salt Lake City, Utah, The Deseret Sunday School union, 1922. 190, 164, 113 p. illus. (incl. ports., facsims.) 19 1/2 cm. [BX8610.A45] 22-20148
1. Mormons and Mormonism—Hist. 2. Bible—Study—Text-books. I. Title.

DAY, Robert B. 289.3'09
They made Mormon history [by] Robert B. Day. Salt Lake City, Deseret Book Co., 1968. viii, 364 p. illus., ports. 24 cm. Bibliography: p. [345]-354. [BX8611.D34] 68-58285 4.95
1. Mormons and Mormonism—History. I. Title.

EVANS, John Henry, 1872-
One hundred years of Mormonism, a history of the Church of Jesus Christ of latter-day saints from 1805 to 1905, by John Henry Evans ... Salt Lake City, The Deseret news, 1905. xxxviii, 528 p. 20 1/2 cm. 5-39855
I. Title.

FIFE, Austin E 289.309
Saints of sage & saddle; folklore among the Mormons, by Austin and Alta Fife. Bloomington, Indiana University Press, 1956. 367 p. illus. 22 cm. [BX8611.F5] 56-11997
1. Mormons and Mormonism — Hist. 2. Folk-lore — U.S. I. Fife, Alta (Stephens) II. Title.

FIFE, Austin E 289.309
Saints of sage & saddle; folklore among the Mormons, by Austin and Alta Fife. Gloucester, Mass., P. Smith, 1966 [c1956] xiv, 367 p. illus., map (on lining papers) 21 cm. Includes unacc. melodies. Bibliography: p. 339-342. [BX8611.F5 1966] 66-31847
1. Mormons and Mormonism — Hist. 2. Folk-lore — U.S. I. Fife, Alta (Stephens) joint author. II. Title.

FIFE, Austin E. 289.309
Saints of sage & saddle; folklore among the Mormons, by Austin and Alta Fife. Bloomington, Indiana University Press, 1956. 367 p. illus. 22 cm. [BX8611.F5] 56-11997
1. Mormons and Mormonism—History. 2. Folk-lore—U.S. I. Fife, Alta (Stephens). II. Title.

GRANT, Carter Eldredge. 289.309
The kingdom of God restored. Salt Lake City, Deseret Book Co., 1955. 602p. illus. 24cm. [BX8611.G7] 55-12598
1. Mormons and Mormonism—Hist. I. Title.

[HARMER, Earl W.] comp. 289.3
Our destiny a brief historical outline of Gods covenant race from patriarchal times to the present 1st ed., 1940; 2d ed., 1942. Salt Lake City, Utah, E. W. Harmer, 1942. 159 p. illus., fold. geneal. tab. 19 cm. "The first sections of this pamphlet are a brief outline from our fathers Abraham, Isaac and Jacob to the birth of the U.S.A....written by... W. J. Cameron for the magazine 'Destiny'...The concluding pages and pedigree chart are selections from 'God's convenant race' by James H. Anderson."--Pref. [BX8611.H3 1942] 43-17469
1. Mormons and Mormonism—Hist. I. Cameron, William John, 1879- II. Anderson, James Henry, 1857- God's covenant race. III. Title.

HILL, Marvin S., comp. 289.3'3
Mormonism and American culture. Edited by Marvin S. Hill and James B. Allen. New York, Harper & Row [1972] vii, 189 p. 21 cm. (Interpretations of American history) Bibliography: p. 185-189. [BX8611.H55] 72-82900 ISBN 0-06-042819-8 Pap. $2.95
1. Mormons and Mormonism—History. I. Allen, James B., joint comp. II. Title.

HUNTRESS, Keith Gibson, 1913- ed. 289.373
Murder of an American prophet: events and prejudices surrounding the killing of Joseph and Hyrum Smith, Carthage, Illinois, June 27, 1844; materials for analysis. San Francisco, Chandler [1963, c.1960] 232p. illus. 23cm. 63-9886 2.25 pap.,
1. Mormons and Mormonism—Hist. I. Title.

KJELGAARD, James Arthur, 1910- 289.3
The coming of the Mormons; illustrated by Stephen J. Voorhies. New York, Random House [1953] 183 p. illus. 22 cm. (Landmark books, 37) [BX8611.K55] 53-6257
1. Mormons and Mormonism—History. I. Title.

KJELGAARD, James Arthur, 1910-1959. 289.3
The coming of the Mormons; illustrated by Stephen J. Voorhies. New York, Random House [1953] 183 p. illus. 22 cm. (Landmark books, 37) A brief history of the Mormons in America: their journey westward, their founding of Salt Lake City, and their influence on and development of the West. [BX8611.K55] AC 68
1. Mormons and Mormonism—History. I. Voorhies, Stephen J., illus. II. Title.

LARSON, Gustive Olof, 1897- 289.3'73
Prelude to the kingdom : Mormon desert conquest, a chapter in American cooperative experience / by Gustive O. Larson. Westport, Conn. : Greenwood Press, c1978. ix, 287 p. : ill. ; 24 cm. Includes bibliographical references and index. [BX8611.L29 1978] 78-5694 ISBN 0-313-20452-7 lib.bdg. : 21.00
1. Mormons and Mormonism—History. 2. Utah—History. I. Title.

LITTLEFIELD, Lyman Omer. 280.
Reminiscences of Latter-day Saints, giving an account of much individual suffering endured for religious conscience. Logan, Utah, Utah Journal Co.,printers, 1888. 206 p. port. 22 cm. Errata slip inserted. [BX8611.L62]
1. Mormons and Mormonism—Hist. 2. Persecution. I. Title.

MCGAVIN, Elmer Cecil. 978
The Mormon pioneers. Salt Lake City, Stevens & Wallis 1947. vii. 234 p. 24 cm. [BX8611.M2] 49-2009
1. Mormons and Mormonism—Hist. I. Title.

MELVILLE, J. Keith, 1921- 320.9'792
Highlights in Mormon political history, by J. Keith Melville. [Provo, Utah] Brigham Young University [1967] viii, 99 p. illus., facsims., 4 maps, ports. 23 cm. (Charles E. Merrill monograph series in the humanities and social sciences, no. 2) Bibliographical footnotes. [BX8611.M34] 70-18511
1. Mormons and Mormonism—History. 2. Utah—History. I. Title. II. Series.

THE Mormon role in the settlement of the West 289.3'0978
/ Richard H. Jackson, editor. Provo, UT : Brigham Young University Press, c1978. xiii, 169 p. : ill. ; 23 cm. (Charles Redd monographs in Western history ; no. 9) Includes bibliographical references and index. [BX8611.M67] 78-24728 ISBN 0-8425-1321-3 : 6.95
1. Mormons and Mormonism—History. 2. The West—History—To 1848. I. Jackson, Richard H., 1941- II. Title. III. Series.

NIBLEY, Preston, comp. 289.3082
Pioneer stories, compiled under the direction of the presiding bishopric for the youth of the church, by Preston Nibley. Salt Lake City, Utah, The Deseret new press, 1940. 328 p. 20 1/2 cm. [BX8611.N5] 41-6971
1. Mormons and Mormonism—Hist. I. Church of Jesus Christ of latter-day saints. II. Title.

PETERSEN, Emma Marr. 289.309
The story of our church for young Latter-Day Saints; illustrated by Milton E. Swensen. [1st ed.] Salt Lake City, Bookcraft Pub. Co. [1952] 311p. illus. 24cm. [BX8611.P4] 53-28738
1. Mormons and Mormonism—Hist. I. Title.

PETERSEN, Emma Marr. 289.309
The story of our church for young Latter-Day Saints; illustrated by Milton E. Swensen. [4th ed.] Salt Lake City,

Bookcraft Pub. Co. [1958] 311p. illus. 24cm. [BX8611.P4 1958] 58-48853
1. Mormons and Mormonism—Hist. I. Title.

ROBERTS, Brigham Henry, 1857-
... *Mormonism.* The relation of the church to Christian sects. Origin and history of Mormonism. Doctrines of the church. Church organization. Present status. By B. H. Roberts. Published by the church. Salt Lake City, Deseret news print [1903] 1 p. l., 68 p. 19 cm. 3-11588
I. Title.

SLETTEN, Nettie. 289.309
God and mankind versus Satan; tracts on divine judgment and salvation. [1st ed.] New York, Exposition Press [1957] 192 p. 21 cm. [BX8611.S56] 57-9225
1. Mormons and Mormonism — Hist. I. Title.

SMITH, Joseph Fielding, 289.309 1876-
Church history and modern revelation, covering the first period: Joseph Smith, the prophet. Alphabetical index and digest of the above study course, by Andrew K. Smith. [Salt Lake City] Council of the Twelve Apostles of the Church of Jesus Christ of Latter-Day Saints [1953] 2v. 24cm. [BX8611.S66] 54-22110
1. Smith, Joseph, 1805-1844. 2. Mormons and Mormonism— Hist. I. Title.

SMITH, Joseph Fielding, 1876-
Essentials in church history; a history of the church from the birth of Joseph Smith to the present time, with introductory chapters on the antiquity of the gospel and the "falling away." 17th ed. [Salt Lake City] Published by the Deseret Book Company for the Church of Jesus Christ of Latter-Day Saints, 1961 [1950] vii, 748 p. illus., ports., maps, facsims. 20 cm. 65-35743
1. Mormons and Mormonism — Hist. I. Title.

SMITH, Joseph Fielding, 1876-
Essentials in church history; a history of the church from the birth of Joseph Smith to the present time, with introductory chapters on the antiquity of the gospel and the "Falling away." 18th ed. [Salt Lake City, Utah] Deseret Book Co., 1963. 748 p. illus. Imperfect: p. [529]-530 mutilated. 65-35680
1. Mormons and Mormonism — Hist. I. Title.

STENHOUSE, Thomas B H.
The Rocky Mountain saints; a full and complete history of the Mormons, from the first vision of Joseph Smith to the last courtship of Brigham Young ... and the development of the great mineral wealth of the territory of Utah. By T. B. H. Stenhouse ... Illustrated with twenty-four full-pageengravings, a steel plate frontispiece, an autographic letter of Brigham Young, and numerous woodcuts. New York, D. Appleton and company, 1873. xxiv, 761 p. incl. illus., plates, port., maps, facsims. front., pl., double facsim. 24 cm. "Writers on Mormonism": p. 741-746. 16-24014
I. Title.

STENHOUSE, Thomas B H.
The Rocky Mountain saints: a full and complete history of the Mormons ... and the development of the great mineral wealth of the territory of Utah ... New York, D. Appleton & co., 1873 [c1900] xxiv, 761 p. incl. illus., pl. front. (port.) 8 degrees. 0-4787
I. Title.

TANNER, Jerald.
Mormonism; a study of Mormon history and doctrine. Salt Lake City, Jerald Tanner [1961?] 262 p. 65-61753
I. Title.

TAYLOR, Philip A. M. 289.373
Expectations westward; the Mormons and the emigration of their British converts in the nineteenth century [by] P. A. M. Taylor. Ithaca, N. Y., Cornell University Press, 1966. xvi, 277 p. illus., maps (part fold.) 23 cm. Bibliography: p. [250]-266. [BX8611.T36 1966] 66-13812
1. Mormons and Mormonism—History. 2. U.S.—Emigration and immigration. I. Title.

TAYLOR, Samuel Woolley, 289.3'3 B 1907-
The Kingdom or nothing : the life of John Taylor, militant Mormon / by Samuel W. Taylor. New York : Macmillan, c1976. x, 406 p. ; 24 cm. Includes index. Bibliography: p. 386-396. [BX8695.T3T39] 75-38962 ISBN 0-02-616600-3 : 8.95
1. Taylor, John, 1808-1887. 2. Mormons and Mormonism—History. I. Title.

WEST, Ray Benedict, 1908- 289.309
Kingdom of the saints; the story of Brigham Young and the Mormons. New York, Viking Press, 1957. 389 p. illus. 22 cm. [BX8611.W4] 57-6437
1. Young, Brigham, 1801-1877. 2. Mormons and Mormonism—History. I. Title.

WHITE, Sheryl. 289.3'3
Mormon, 150 years / text by Sheryl White. Beaverton, Or. : Beautiful America Pub. Co., c1980. p. cm. [BX8611.W525] 19 80-24117 ISBN 0-89802-177-4 : 12.95 ISBN 0-89802-201-0 (pbk.) : 6.95
1. Mormons and Mormonism—History. I. Title.

WHITMER, John, 1802- 289.3'73 1878.
An early Latter Day Saint history : the book of John Whitmer kept by commandment / edited by F. Mark. McKiernan and Roger D. Launius. Independence, Mo. : Herald Pub. House, c1980. 213 p. ; 23 cm. Includes index. Bibliography: p. 179-202. [BX8611.W53 1980] 79-25512 ISBN 0-8309-0269-4 pbk. : 8.50
1. Church of Jesus Christ of Latter-Day Saints—History. 2. Mormons and Mormonism—History. I. McKiernan, F. Mark. II. Launius, Roger D. III. Title.

YOUNG, T. W.
Mormonism: its origin, doctrines and dangers. Ann Arbor, Mich., G. Whar [1900] 71 p. 12°. Jul
I. Title.

Mormons and Mormonism—History—Addresses, essays, lectures.

MULDER, William. 289.3'73
The Mormons in American history / by William Mulder. Salt Lake City, Utah : University of Utah Press, 1980, c1957. p. cm. Reprint of the ed. published by Extension Division, University of Utah, Salt Lake City, which was issued as the Frederick William Reynolds lecture, 1957, and v. 48, no. 11 of the Bulletin of the University of Utah. [BX8611.M8 1980] 19 80-27308 ISBN 0-87480-184-2 : pbk. : 5.00
1. Mormons and Mormonism—History—Addresses, essays, lectures. I. Title. II. Series: Frederick William Reynolds memorial lecture ; 1957.

Mormons and mormonism—History, Military.

BAILEY, Paul Dayton, 1906- 289.3
The armies of God [by] Paul Bailey. Garden City, N.Y., Doubleday, 1968. ix, 300 p. illus. 22 cm. Bibliography: p. [285]-291. [BX8611.B317] 68-29282 5.95
1. Mormons and mormonism—History, Military. I. Title.

Mormons and Mormonism—History—Sources.

MULDER, William, ed. 289.373
Among the Mormons; historic accounts by contemporary observers, edited by William Mulder and A. Russell Mortensen. [1st ed.] New York, Knopf, 1958. 482p. illus. 25cm. [BX8611.M79] 58-5825
1. Mormons and Mormonism—Hist.—Sources. I. Mortensen, Arlington Russell, 1911- joint ed. II. Title.

MULDER, William. 289.33
Among the Mormons; historic accounts by contemporary observers. Edited by William Mulder & A. Russell Mortensen. Lincoln, Univ. of Nebraska Pr. [1973, c.1958] xiv, 482, xiv p. 20 cm. (Bison Book, BB568) [BX8611.M79] ISBN 0-8032-5778-3 pap., 2.45
1. Mormons and Mormonism—History—Sources. 2. Reorganized Church of Jesus Christ of Latter Day Saints—History—Sources. I. Mortensen, Arlington Russell, 1911- joint ed. II. Title.

TERRY, Keith. 289.3
From the dust of decades; a saga of the papyri and mummies [by] Keith Terry and Walter Whipple. Salt Lake City, Bookcraft, 1968. 118 p. illus., facsims. 24 cm. Includes bibliographical references. [BX8622.T44] 68-29490
1. Smith, Joseph, 1805-1844. 2. Mormons and Mormonism—History—Sources. I. Whipple, Walter, joint author. II. Title.

Mormons and Mormonism—History—Sources—Bibliography.

BERRETT, LaMar 016.2893'092'4 S C.
An annotated catalog of documentary-type materials in the Wilford C. Wood Collection, by LaMar C. Berrett. [1st ed. Bountiful, Utah] Wilford C. Wood Foundation, 1972. ix, 236 p. port. 29 cm. (His The Wilford C. Wood Collection, v. 1) [Z6616.W58B4 vol. 1] 016.2893'092'4 73-160582
1. Wood, Wilford C.—Archives. 2. Smith, Joseph, 1805-1844—Archives. 3. Mormons and Mormonism—History—Sources—Bibliography. I. Title. II. Series.

BERRETT, LaMar C. 016.2893'092'4
The Wilford C. Wood Collection, by LaMar C. Berrett. [1st ed. Bountiful, Utah] Wilford C. Wood Foundation, 1972- v. port. 29 cm. Catalog of the collection. [Z6616.W58B4] 73-160583
1. Wood, Wilford C.—Archives. 2. Smith, Joseph, 1805-1844—Archives. 3. Mormons and Mormonism—History—Sources—Bibliography. I. Wilford C. Wood Foundation. II. Title.

CHURCH of Jesus Christ of 929.3 Latter-Day Saints.
Register of L.D.S. Church records. Classified by the Library of the Genealogical Society of The Church of Jesus Christ of Latter-Day Saints. Compiled by Laureen Richardson Jaussi [and] Gloria Duncan Chaston. Salt Lake City, Deseret Book Co., 1968. xiv, 400 p. 24 cm. Bibliographical footnotes. [Z7845.M8C48] 68-25348
1. Mormons and Mormonism—History—Sources—Bibliography. I. Jaussi, Laureen Richardson. II. Chaston, Gloria Duncan. III. Genealogical Society of the Church of Jesus Christ of Latter-Day Saints. Library. IV. Title.

Mormons and Mormonism—Hymns.

CHURCH of Jesus Chirst of 245. latter-day saints.
Sacred hymns and spirtual songs for the Church of Jesus Christ of latter-day saints. 25th ed. Salt Lake City Utah, The Deseret news company, 1912. 486 p. 12 1/2 cm. On spine: L.D.S. hymns. Without music. [BV420.A3 1912] 45-40054
1. Mormons and Mormonism—Hymns. I. Title.

CHURCH of Jesus Christ of 245. latter-day saints.
Sacred hymns and spiritual songs. For the Church of Jesus Christ of latter-day saints. 14th ed. Salt Lake city, G. Q. Cannon, 1871. 432 p. 12 1/2 cm. On spine: L.D.S. hymns. Without music. [BV420.A3 1871] 45-40053
1. Mormons and Mormonism—Hymns. I. Title.

Mormons and Mormonism—Hymns—History and criticism

CHEVILLE, Roy Arthur, 245.2093 1897-
They sang of the Restoration; stories of Latter Day Saint hymns. [Independence, Mo., Herald Pub. House, 1955] 267p. 21cm. [BV420.A1C4] 55-5413
1. Mormons and Mormonism—Hymns—Hist. & crit. I. Title.

Mormons and Mormonism in Arizona.

MCCLINTOCK, James H., 1864- 979
Mormon settlement in Arizona; a record of peaceful conquest of the desert, by James H. McClintock ... Phoenix, Ariz., 1921. xi, 307 p. front., plates, ports., maps (1 fold.) 21 1/2 cm. Plates printed on both sides. One plate laid in. "Printing and binding by the Manufacturing stationers inc., Phoenix; illustrations by Phoenix engraving company, Phoenix; maps by Jas. M. Barney, Phoenix; art work by David Swing, Phoenix. Bibliography: p. 279-280. [F811.M124] [BX8615.A6M2] 21-10693
1. Mormons and Mormonism in Arizona. 2. Arizona—Hist. I. Title.

MCCLINTOCK, James H., 289.3'791 1864-1934.
Mormon settlement in Arizona; a record of peaceful conquest of the desert. Phoenix, Ariz., 1921. [New York, AMS Press, 1971] xi, 307 p. illus. 22 cm. Bibliography: p. 279-[280] [F811.M124 1971] 78-134397 ISBN 0-404-08439-7 14.00
1. Mormons and Mormonism in Arizona. 2. Arizona—History—To 1950. I. Title.

PETERSON, Charles S. 289.3'791'33
Take up your mission : Mormon colonizing along the Little Colorado Rriver, 1870-1900. [by] Charles S. Peterson. Tucson, University of Arizona Press [1973] xii, 309 p. illus. 24 cm. Bibliography: p. 273-295. [F817.L5P47] 72-89621 ISBN 0-8165-0397-4 9.50
1. Mormons and Mormonism in Arizona. 2. Little Colorado Valley, Ariz.—History. I. Title.

Mormons and Mormonism in Cache Co., Utah.

SIMMONDS, A. J. 277.92'12
The gentile comes to Cache Valley : a study of the Logan apostacies of 1874 and the establishment of non-Mormon churches in Cache Valley, 1873-1913 / A. J. Simmonds. Logan : Utah State University Press, 1976. p. cm. Bibliography: p. [BX8611.S5] 76-28513 ISBN 0-87421-088-7 : 5.00
1. Mormons and Mormonism in Cache Co., Utah. 2. Cache, Co., Utah—Church history. 3. Cache, Co., Utah—History. I. Title.

Mormons and Mormonism in Germany.

SCHARFFS, Gilbert W. 289.3'43
Mormonism in Germany; a history of the Church of Jesus Christ of Latter-Day Saints in Germany between 1840 and 1970, by Gilbert W. Scharffs. Salt Lake City, Deseret Book Co., 1970. xiv, 256 p. illus., maps. 24 cm. Based on the author's thesis, Brigham Young University. Bibliography: p. [227]-231. [BX8617.G4S3 1970] 70-136240 ISBN 0-87747-368-4 5.50
1. Mormons and Mormonism in Germany. I. Title.

Mormons and Mormonism in Great Britain.

EVANS, Richard Louis, 289.342 1906-
A century of "Mormonism" in Great Britain; a brief summary of the activities of the Church of Jesus Christ of latterday saints in the United Kingdom. with emphasis on its introduction one hundred years ago, by Richard L. Evans ... [Salt Lake City, The Deseret news press, 1937. viii, [9]-256 p. front., plates. ports. 21 cm. Bibliography: p. iv. [BX8617.G7E85] 38-30638
1. Mormons and Mormonism in Great Britain. I. Title.

KIMBALL, Heber Chase, 922.8373 1801-1868.
Journal of Heber C. Kimball, an elder of the Church of Jesus Christ of latter day saints. Giving an account of his mission to Great Britain, and the commencement of the work of the Lord in that land. Also the success which has attended the labors of the elders of the present time. By R. R. Thompson... Nauvoo, Ill: Printed by Robinson and Smith, 1840. viii, [9]-60 p. 20 cm. [BX8695.K5A3] 36-30784

1. Mormons and Mormonism in Great Britain. I. Thompson, Robert Biatsell, 1811?-1841, ed. II. Title.

Mormons and Mormonism in Idaho—History.

WELLS, Merle W. 289.3'796
Anti-Mormonism in Idaho, 1872-92 / Merle W. Wells. Provo, Utah : Brigham Young University Press, c1978. p. cm. (Studies in Mormon history ; v. 4) Includes index. Bibliography: p. [BX8615.I2W44] 77-89975 ISBN 0-8425-0904-6 pbk. : 5.95
1. Mormons and Mormonism in Idaho—History. 2. Idaho—Politics and government. 3. Polygamy—Idaho. I. Title. II. Series.

Mormons and Mormonism in Illinois.

ROBERTS, Brigham Henry, 1857-1933. 289.
The rise and fall of Nauvoo, by Elder B. Roberts ... Salt Lake City, Utah, The Deseret news, 1900. vi, [9]-457 p. 20 cm. [BX8615.I 3R6] A 37
1. Mormons and Mormonism in Illinois. 2. Nauvoo, Ill.—History. I. Title.

Mormons and Mormonism in Illinois—History—Bibliography.

KIMBALL, Stanley Buchholz. 016.286
Sources of Mormon history in Illinois, 1839-48, an annotated catalog of the microfilm collection at Southern Illinois University, compiled by Stanley B. Kimball. Carbondale, Library, Southern Illinois University, 1964. xii, 76 p. 28 cm. ([Illinois] Southern Illinois University, Carbondale. Library. Bibliographic contributions, no. 1) [Z7845.M8K5] A 65
1. Mormons and Mormonism in Illinois — Hist. — Bibl. 2. Microfilms — Catalogs. I. Title. II. Series. III. Series: Illinois. Southern Illnois University, Cabrondale. University Libraries. Bibliographic contributions, no. 1

KIMBALL, Stanley Buchholz. 016.262'001
Sources of Mormon history in Illinois, 1839-48; an annotated catalog of the microfilm collection at Southern Illinois University, compiled by Stanley B. Kimball. 2nd ed., rev. and enl. Carbondale, Central Publications, Southern Illinois University, 1966. xii, 104 p. 28 cm. (Southern Illinois University, Carbondale. Library. Bibliographic contributions, no. 1) [Z7845.M8K5 1966] A 67
1. Mormons and Mormonism in Illinois—History—Bibliography. 2. Microfilms—Catalogs. I. Title. II. Series: Illinois. Southern Illinois University, Carbondale. University Libraries. Bibliographic contributions, no. 1

Mormons and Mormonism in Italy.

RICHARDS, Daniel Brigham. 289.345
... The Scriptural allegory, in three parts ... by Dr. Daniel B. Richards ... Salt Lake City, Utah, Magazine printing company, 1931. iv, [4], 320 (i.e. 324) p. front., ports. 23 1/2 cm. Versos of leaves 1-4 numbered 1A-4A. Contents.History of the Church of Jesus Christ of latter-day saints in Italy.--History of the Waldensian church.--Ten consecutive years of the author's missionary labors. [BX8609.R5] 34-9060
1. Mormons and Mormonism in Italy. 2. Waldenses. 3. Mormons and Mormonism—Missions. I. Title.

Mormons and Mormonism in Kirtland, Ohio—History.

HILL, Marvin S. 289.3'3
The Kirtland economy revisited : a market critique of sectarian economics / Marvin S. Hill, C. Keith Rooker, Larry T. Wimmer. Provo, Utah : Brigham Young University Press, [1978] c1977. viii, 85 p., [4] leaves of plates : ill. ; 23 cm. (Studies in Mormon history ; v. 3) Includes index. Bibliography: p. 83-85. [BX8615.O3H54 1978] 78-3848 ISBN 0-8425-1230-6 pbk. : 3.95
1. Kirtland Safety Society Bank. 2. Smith, Joseph, 1805-1844. 3. Mormons and Mormonism in Kirtland, Ohio—History. 4. Mormons and Mormonism—Finance. 5. Kirtland, Ohio—Economic conditions. 6. Kirtland, Ohio—Church history. I. Rooker, C. Keith, 1937- joint author. II. Wimmer, Larry T., 1935- joint author. III. Title. IV. Series.

Mormons and Mormonism in Manchester, Eng.

CLAYTON, William, 1814-1879. 289.3'427'2
Manchester Mormons; the journal of William Clayton, 1840 to 1842. Edited by James B. Allen and Thomas G. Alexander. Santa Barbara [Calif.] Peregrine Smith, 1974. 248 p. illus. 23 cm. (Classic Mormon diary series, v. 1) Includes bibliographical references. [BX8617.G7C55 1974] 73-89749 ISBN 0-87905-024-1 8.95
1. Clayton, William, 1814-1879. 2. Mormons and Mormonism in Manchester, Eng. 3. Manchester, Eng.—Religion. I. Title.

Mormons and Mormonism in Mexico.

ROMNEY, Thomas Cottam. 289.3721
The Mormon colonies in Mexico, by Thomas Cottam Romney ... Salt Lake City, Utah, The Deseret book company, 1938. 338 p. front., plates., ports., fold. map. 24 cm. [BX8617.M4R6] 39-12954
1. Mormons and Mormonism in Mexico. I. Title.

YOUNG, Karl E., 1903- 289.3'72'1
The long hot summer of 1912 episodes in the flight of the Mormon colonists from Mexico by Karl E. Young [Provo, Utah, Brigham Young University, 1967] vii, 67 p. 23 cm. (Charles E. Merrill monograph series in the humanities and social sciences, [v. 1] no. 1) Bibliography: p. 67. [F1392.M6Y59] 72-188006 1.00
1. Mormons and Mormonism in Mexico. I. Title. II. Series.

Mormons and Mormonism in Missouri.

DYER, Alvin Rulon. 289.3778
The refiner's fire; historical highlights of Missouri. Salt Lake City, Deseret Book Co., c1960] 141 p. illus. 24 cm. Includes bibliography. [BX8615.M8D9] 61-22324
1. Mormons and Mormonism in Missouri. I. Title.

DYER, Alvin Rulon. 289.3'778
The refiner's fire; the significance of events transpiring in Missouri, by Alvin R. Dyer. [2d ed. rev. and enl.] Salt Lake City, Deseret Book Co., 1968. 334, [3] p. illus. (part col.), facsims., maps, plans. 24 cm. Includes music. Bibliography: p. [335]-[337] [BX8615.M8D9 1968] 68-29075
1. Mormons and Mormonism in Missouri. I. Title.

GEDDES, Joseph A. 289.
The United order among the Mormons (Missouri phase) an unfinished experiment in economic organization, by Joseph A. Geddes ... Salt Lake City Utah, The Deseret news press., 1924. 172 p. 24 cm. "Bibliography--collections": p. [165]-167. [BX8615.M8G4] 24-10827
1. Mormons and Mormonism in Missouri. I. Title.

GEDDES, Joseph Arch, 1884- 289.3'778
The United Order among the Mormons (Missouri phase) : an unfinished experiment in economic organization / by Joseph A. Geddes. New York : AMS Press, 1975, c1924. 172 p. ; 23 cm. (Communal societies in America) Reprint of the ed. published by the Desert News Press, Salt Lake City. Originally presented as the author's thesis, Columbia University, 1924. Includes bibliographical references and index. [BX8615.M8G4 1975] 72-8247 ISBN 0-404-11001-0 : 10.00
1. Mormons and Mormonism in Missouri. I. Title.

WILCOX, Pearl. 289.3'778
The Latter Day Saints on the Missouri frontier. [Independence? Mo., 1972] 367 p. illus. 21 cm. Bibliography: p. 351-355. [BX8615.M8W5] 72-83317
1. Reorganized Church of Jesus Christ of Latter-Day Saints—History. 2. Mormons and Mormonism in Missouri. I. Title.

Mormons and Mormonism in Nauvoo, Ill.

HAWTHORNE, Paul. 289.3'773'43
Nauvoo / by Paul Hawthorne. Decatur : House of Illinois, [1974] 54 p. : ill. ; 21 cm. [BX8615.I3H38] 74-18145
1. Mormons and Mormonism in Nauvoo, Ill. I. Title.

TAYLOR, Samuel Woolley, 1907- 289.3'773'43
Nightfall at Nauvoo [by] Samuel W. Taylor. New York, Macmillan [1971] x, 403 p. 21 cm. Bibliography: p. [375]-391. [BX8615.I3T39] 72-139965 7.95
1. Mormons and Mormonism in Nauvoo, Ill. I. Title.

Mormons and Mormonism in Orderville, Utah.

PARR, Lucy. 289.3'792'51
Not of the world : a living account of the United Order / Lucy Parr. Bountiful, Utah : Horizon Publishers, [1975] 231 p. : ill. ; 24 cm. Pages 128-141 printed in incorrect order. Includes index. Bibliography: p. 225-228. [BX8611.P34] 75-5320 ISBN 0-88290-047-1 : 5.95
1. Mormons and Mormonism in Orderville, Utah. 2. Orderville, Utah—History. I. Title.

Mormons and Mormonism in Scandinavia.

JENSEN, Andrew, 1850-1941. 289.
History of the Scandinavian mission, by Andrew Jensen ... Salt Lake City, Utah, Deseret news press, 1927. xvi, 570 p. front., illus. (incl. ports.) 24 cm. [BX8617.S3J4] 44-52321
1. Mormons and Mormonism in Scandinavia. I. Title.
Contents omitted.

JENSON, Andrew, 1850-1941. 266'.93'48
History of the Scandinavian mission / Andrew Jenson. New York : Arno Press, 1979. xvi, 570 p. : ill. ; 24 cm. (Scandinavians in America) Reprint of the 1927 ed. published by the Deseret News Press, Salt Lake City, Utah. Includes index. [BX8617.S3J4 1979] 78-15190 ISBN 0-405-11643-8 : 40.00
1. Mormons and Mormonism in Scandinavia. 2. Missions—Scandinavia. 3. Scandinavia—Church history. I. Title. II. Series.

ZOBELL, Albert L [266.93] 289.348
Under the midnight sun; centennial history of Scandinavian missions. Salt Lake City, Deseret Book Co., 1950. viii, 197 p. illus., port. 23 cm. [BX8617.S3Z6] 50-29209
1. Mormons and Mormonism in Scandinavia. 2. Mormons and Mormonism — Missions. I. Title.

Mormons and Mormonism in the United States—Biography.

CONKLING, J. Christopher, 1949- 289.3'092'4 B
A Joseph Smith chronology / J. Christopher Conking ; prepared for BEI Productions, inc. Salt Lake City : Deseret Book Company, 1979. ix, 276 p. : map ; 25 cm. Includes index. Bibliography: p. 253-266. [BX8695.S6C64] 79-896 ISBN 0-87747-734-5 : 7.95
1. Smith, Joseph, 1805-1844—Chronology. 2. Mormons and Mormonism in the United States—Biography. I. BEI Productions. II. Title.

DURRANT, George D. 929'.1'072073
Fun & names : or, How to dig your family history without really prying / disclosed by George D. Durrant ; undercover work by Noel R. Barton. Salt Lake City, Utah : Bookcraft, c1980. viii, 102 p. : ill. ; 24 cm. [BX8695.D8A34] 19 80-65244 ISBN 0-88494-392-5 pbk. : 4.95
1. Durrant, George D. 2. Durrant family. 3. Mormons and Mormonism in the United States—Biography. 4. Genealogy—Handbooks, manuals, etc. I. Barton, Noel R., 1942- II. Title.

GIBBONS, Francis M., 1921- 289.3'092'4 B
Heber J. Grant, man of steel, prophet of God / Francis M. Gibbons. Salt Lake City, Utah : Deseret Book Co., 1979. ix, 240 p. ; 24 cm. Includes index. [BX8695.G7G52] 79-11649 ISBN 0-87747-755-8 : 6.95
1. Grant, Heber Jeddy, 1856-1945. 2. Mormons and Mormonism in the United States—Biography. I. Title.

GIBBONS, Francis M., 1921- 289.3'092'4 B
Joseph Smith, martyr, prophet of God / Francis M. Gibbons. Salt Lake City : Deseret Book Co., 1977. ix, 377 p. ; 23 cm. Includes index. Bibliography: p. 366-368. [BX8695.S6G52] 77-2019 ISBN 0-87747-637-3 : 6.95
1. Smith, Joseph, 1805-1844. 2. Mormons and Mormonism in the United States—Biography. 3. Mormons and Mormonism—History. I. Title.

GRIFFITHS, Iris. 289.3'3 B
The vindicator / Iris Griffiths. Independence, Mo. : Herald Pub. House, c1977. 214 p. : port. ; 20 cm. A biography of the Welsh immigrant to Utah whose disillusionment leads him to California where he finds the Reorganized Church and serves as its missionary to Wales. [BX8678.G74G74] 92 77-1808 ISBN 0-8309-0172-8 : 6.50
1. Griffiths, John, 1826-1891. 2. [Griffiths, John, 1826-1891.] 3. Mormons and Mormonism in the United States—Biography. 4. Missionaries—Wales—Biography. 5. Missionaries—United States—Biography. 6. [Mormons and Mormonism in the United States—Biography.] 7. [Missionaries.] I. Title.

JACKSON, Ronald Vern. 289.3'092'4 B
The seer, Joseph Smith, his education from the Most High / by Ronald Vern Jackson. 3d ed., expanded and bound. Salt Lake City : Hawkes Pub. Inc., c1977. 248 p. : ill. ; 23 cm. Includes bibliographical references. [BX8695.S6J25 1977] 77-77303 ISBN 0-89036-088-X : 3.95
1. Smith, Joseph, 1805-1844. 2. Mormons and Mormonism in the United States—Biography. I. Title.
Publisher's address 3775 S. 500W. Box 15711, Salt Lake City, UT 84115

KIMBALL, Stanley Buchholz. 289.3'3 B
Heber C. Kimball : Mormon patriarch and pioneer / Stanley B. Kimball. Urbana : University of Illinois Press, c1981. xv, 343 p., [11] leaves of plates : ill. ; 24 cm. Includes bibliographical references and index. [BX8695.K5K55] 19 80-21923 ISBN 0-252-00854-5 : 17.95
1. Kimball, Heber Chase, 1801-1868. 2. Mormons and Mormonism in the United States—Biography.

MADSEN, Truman G. 289.3'3 B
Defender of the faith : the B. H. Roberts story / Truman G. Madsen. Salt Lake City, Utah : Bookcraft, c1980. xiv, 455 p., [3] leaves of plates : ill. ; 23 cm. Includes index. Bibliography: p. [441]-443. [BX8695.R58M29] 19 79-54895 ISBN 0-88494-395-X : 9.50
1. Roberts, Brigham Henry, 1857-1933. 2. Mormons and Mormonism in the United States—Biography. I. Title.

PEARSON, Carol Lynn. 289.3'3 B
Will I ever forget this day? : Excerpts / from the diaries of Carol Lynn Pearson ; edited by Elouise M. Bell. Salt Lake City, Utah : Bookcraft, c1980. 130 p. : ill. ; 24 cm. [BX8695.P42A38] 79-54897 ISBN 0-88494-390-9 pbk. : 5.50
1. Pearson, Carol Lynn. 2. Mormons and Mormonism in the United States—Biography. I. Bell, Elouise M. II. Title.

SILL, Sterling W. 289.3'3 B
The nine lives of Sterling W. Sill : an autobiography. Bountiful, Utah : Horizon Publishers, c1979. 286 p. ; 24 cm. Includes index. [BX8695.S38A36] 80-111657 ISBN 0-88290-118-4 : 6.50
1. Sill, Sterling W. 2. Mormons and Mormonism in the United States—

Mormons and Mormonism—United States—Biography.

STURLAUGSON, Mary Frances. 289.3'3 B
A soul so rebellious / Mary Frances Sturlaugson. Salt Lake City, Utah : Deseret Book Co., 1980. 88 p. ; 24 cm. [BX8695.S85A37] 19 80-69271 ISBN 0-87747-841-4 : 5.95
1. Sturlaugson, Mary Frances. 2. Mormons and Mormonism—United States—Biography. I. Title.

WILCOX, Brad. 248'.48'933
The super baruba success book for under-achievers, over-expecters, and other ordinary people / Brad Wilcox. Salt Lake City : Bookcraft, c1979. xi, 116 p. ; 24 cm. [BX8695.W544A37] 79-53050 ISBN 0-88494-372-0 pbk. : 4.50
1. Wilcox, Brad. 2. Mormons and Mormonism—United States—Biography. I. Title.

Mormons and Mormonism in the United States — Historic buildings, monuments, etc.

BURTON, Alma P 1913- 289.309
Mormon trail: Vermont to Utah; a guide to historic places of the Church of Jesus Christ of Latter-Day Saints, by Alma P. Burton. Rev. and enl. Salt Lake City, Deseret Book Co., 1966. 103 p. (p. 100-103, blank for "Notes") illus., maps (part fold.) port. 23 cm. Cover title: Mormon trail from Vermont to Utah. Earlier editions published with title: Mormon trail from Vermont to Utah. Bibliography: p. 99. [BX8611.B78] 66-8721
1. Mormons and Mormonism in the U.S. — Historic buildings, monuments, etc. I. Title.

WALKER, Charles L., 1832-1904. 289.3'3 B
The diary of Charles L. Walker / edited by A. Karl Larson and Katharine Miles Larson. Logan, Utah : Utah State University Press, 1980. p. cm. Includes bibliographical references and index. [BX8695.W3A32] 19 80-21200 ISBN 0-87421-106-9 (set) : 30.00
1. Walker, Charles L., 1832-1904. 2. Mormons and Mormonism in the United States—Biography. I. Larson, Andrew Karl. II. Larson, Katharine Miles. III. Title.

Mormons and Mormonism in the United States — Historic houses, etc.

OSCARSON, R Don. 289.373
The travelers' guide to historic Mormon America, by R. Don Oscarson, with Stanley B. Kimball, research and text and Leslie F. Medley, art and layout. Salt Lake City, Bookcraft, 1965. 84 p. illus., facsims., col. maps, plans, ports. 16 x 24 cm. Bibliography: p. 84. [BX8611.O8] 66-6608
1. Mormons and Mormonism in the U.S. — Historic houses, etc. I. Kimball, Stanley Buchholz. II. Medley, Leslie F., illus. III. Title.

Mormons and Mormonism in the West—Biography—Juvenile literature.

PARR, Lucy. 920'.078
True stories of Mormon pioneer courage / Lucy Parr. Bountiful, Utah : Horizon Publishers, c1977. 192 p. ; 24 cm. Bibliography: p. 188-192. Presents twenty-two stories of lesser-known pioneers who have made contributions to the Mormon Church. [F593.P3] 920 76-29310 ISBN 0-88290-073-0 : 4.95
1. [Church of Jesus Christ of Latter-Day Saints.] 2. Mormons and Mormonism in the West—Biography—Juvenile literature. 3. Pioneers—The West—Biography—Juvenile literature. 4. The West—History—1848-1950—Juvenile literature. 5. Frontier and pioneer life—The West—Juvenile literature. 6. [Mormons and Mormonism in the West.] 7. [Frontier and pioneer life—The West.] I. Title.

Mormons and Mormonism in Utah.

DALTON, Luella Adams comp.
History of the Iron County mission and Parowan, the mother town. [n. p., 196-] x, 474 p. ports. 23 cm. Bibliographical footnotes. 67-5893
1. Mormons and Mormonism in Utah. 2. Mormons and Mormonism — Biog. 3. Iron Co., Utah — Hist. 4. Parowan, Utah — Hist. I. Title.

RELIEF society memories.
A history of Relief Society in St. George Stake, 1867-1956. Compiled by Verna L. Dewsnup [and] Katharine M. Larson. [Springville, Utah, Art City Publishing Co., 1956] xvi, 238p. illus., ports. 24cm.
1. Mormons and Mormonism in Utah. I. Church of Jesus Christ of Latter-Day Saints. St. George Stake. Relief Society. II. Dewsnup, Verna L., ed. III. Larson, Katharine M., ed.

Mormons and Mormonism in Utah—Biography.

KAPP, Ardeth Greene, 1931- 289.3'3 B
Miracles in pinafores & bluejeans / Ardeth Greene Kapp. Salt Lake City : Deseret Book Co., 1977. 81 p. ; 24 cm. A woman shares the experiences of herself and others which exemplify the principles of living a spiritually enriched life. [BX8695.K35A35] 92 77-4268 ISBN 0-87747-644-6 : 3.95
1. Kapp, Ardeth Greene, 1931- 2. [Kapp, Ardeth Greene, 1931-] 3. Mormons and Mormonism in Utah—Biography. 4. [Mormons and Mormonism—Biography.] 5. [Christian life.] I. Title.

REEVE, Becky. 289.3'3 B
The spirit knows no handicap / Becky Reeve. [Salt Lake City? Utah] : Bookcraft, c1980. 94 p., [4] leaves of plates : ports. ; 24 cm. [BX8695.R42A34] 19 80-65245 ISBN 0-88494-397-6 : 4.95
1. Reeve, Becky. 2. Mormons and Mormonism in Utah—Biography. 3. Quadriplegics—Utah—Biography. 4. Utah—Biography. I. Title.

SEALY, Shirley. 289.3'3 B
Forever after / Shirley Sealy. Salt Lake City : Deseret Book Co., 1979. 137 p., [1] leaf of plates : port. ; 24 cm. [BX8695.S32S42] 79-17933 ISBN 0-87747-779-5 : 5.95
1. Sealy, Gayle Burch. 2. Sealy, Devro. 3. Sealy, Shirley. 4. Mormons and Mormonism in Utah—Biography. 5. Toxemia of pregnancy—Biography. I. Title.

Mormons and Mormonism in Utah—History.

TAYLOR, Samuel Woolley, 1907- 289.3'3
Rocky Mountain Empire : the Latter-day Saints today / Samuel W. Taylor. New York : Macmillan, 1978. p. cm. Includes index. Bibliography: p. [BX8611.T37] 78-9655 ISBN 0-02-616610-0 : 12.95
1. Church of Jesus Christ of Latter-day Saints—History. 2. Mormons and Mormonism in Utah—History. 3. Utah—Church history. I. Title.

Mormons and Mormonism is Missouri.

BILLETER, Julius Caesar, 1903- 289.3778
The temple of promise, Jackson county, Missouri, by Julius C. Billeter. Independence, Mo., Press of Zion's printing and publishing company [1946] viii, ,55 p. illus. (incl. maps, plan.) 20 cm. [BX8615.M8B5] 46-8546
1. Mormons and Mormonism is Missouri. 2. Reorganized church of Jesus Christ of latter-day saints. I. Title.

Mormons and Mormonism—Juvenile literature.

ELGIN, Kathleen, 1923- 289.3'09
The Mormons: the Church of Jesus Christ of Latter-Day Saints, written and illustrated by Kathleen Elgin. With a foreword by Ray Knell. New York, D. McKay Co. [1969] 96 p. illus., maps. 26 cm. (The Freedom to worship series) Bibliography: p. 94. An introduction to the history, organization, theology, and present-day position of the Mormon Church. Includes a biography of one early Mormon pioneer and lawmaker, Charles Coulson Rich. [BX8635.2.E4] 74-81898 3.95
1. Mormons and Mormonism—Juvenile literature. 2. [Mormons and Mormonism.] I. Title.

LINFORD, Marilynne Todd. 289.3
ABC's for young LDS. Illustrated by Joyce Bigelow Mann. Salt Lake City, Bookcraft, 1971. 60 p. col. illus. 29 cm. Brief alphabetically arranged entries, from Adam to Zion, define basic concepts of Mormon theology. [BX8635.2.L55] 70-175138
1. Mormons and Mormonism—Juvenile literature. 2. [Mormons and Mormonism.] 3. [Alphabet books.] I. Mann, Joyce Bigelow, illus. II. Title.

Mormons and Mormonism—Missions.

ALLRED, G. Hugh. 266'.9'33
How to make a good mission great / G. Hugh Allred, Steve H. Allred. Salt Lake City : Deseret Book Co., 1978. 61 p. ; 24 cm. Bibliography: p. 59. [BX8661.A44] 78-7974 ISBN 0-87747-703-5 : 3.95
1. Mormons and Mormonism—Missions. 2. Evangelistic work. I. Allred, Steve H., 1952- joint author. II. Title.

ASTON, Willard A 266.93
Teaching the gospel with prayer and testimony. [San Francisco? 1956] 255p. illus. 24cm. [BX8661.A8] 56-41460
1. Mormons and Mormonism—Missions. I. Title.

BASSETT, Henry Lawrence, 1864- 279.61
Adventures in Samoa, by Henry L. Bassett. Los Angeles, Calif., Wetzel publishing co., inc. [c1940] 224 p. plates, ports. 21 cm. [BX8061.B3] 266.93 40-35633
1. Mormons and Mormonism—Missions. 2. Missions—Samoan islands. I. Title.

BUTLER, Florence G. 266.93
The art of being a member missionary, by Florence G. Butler. Salt Lake City, Deseret Book Co., 1968. xii, 108 p. 20 cm. Includes bibliographies. [BX8661.B8] 68-25347
1. Mormons and Mormonism—Missions. I. Title.

DAYNES, Robert W. 266.9'3
Missionary helps, by Robert W. Daynes. Salt.Lake City, Bookcraft [1967] 59p. 21cm. [BX8661.D3] 67-17927 price unreported
1. Mormons and Mormonism—Missions. 2. Evangelistic work. I. Title.

DYER, Alvin R. 266.93
The challenge. [Salt Lake City] Deseret [1963, c.1962] 216p. 24cm. 63-880 2.75
1. Mormons and Mormonism—Missions. I. Title.

HATCH, William Whitridge. 266.9'3'75
There is no law; a history of Mormon civil relations in the Southern States, 1865-1905. [1st ed.] New York, Vantage Press [1968] 133 p. illus., ports. 21 cm. Bibliography: p. 129-133. [BX8661.H3] 78-3018 4.50
1. Mormons and mormonism—Missions. 2. Missions—Southern States—History. 3. Polygamy. I. Title.

JACOBS, Barbara Tietjen. 266.93
So you're going on a mission! Provo, Utah, Press Pub. Co. [1968] 392 p. illus. 24 cm. [BX8661.J25] 68-3225
1. Mormons and Mormonism—Missions. I. Title.

NIBLEY, Preston, comp. 266'.9'30922 B
Missionary experiences / compiled under the direction of the Presiding Bishopric for the youth of the church by Preston Nibley. Salt Lake City : Bookcraft, c1975. 320 p. ; 24 cm. [BX8661.N5 1975] 75-327696 4.95
1. Mormons and Mormonism—Missions. I. Title.

NIBLEY, Preston, comp. 266.93
Missionary experiences, compiled under the direction of the Presiding bishopric for the youth of the church, by Preston Nibley. Salt Lake City, Utah, The Deseret news press, 1943. 320 p. 20 cm. "Second printing." [BX8661.N5] 44-33374
1. Mormons and Mormonism—Missions. I. Title.

Mormons and Mormonism, Negro.

LUND, John Lewis.
The Church and the Negro; a discussion of Mormons, Negroes and the priesthood. [Salt Lake City? Paramount Publishers] 1967. 129 p. 23 cm. Bibliography: p. 127-129. 68-95504
1. Mormons and Mormonism, Negro. I. Title.

STEWART, John J. 261.8'34'5196073
Mormonism and the Negro; an explanation and defense of the doctrine of the Church of Jesus Christ of Latter-Day Saints in regard to Negroes and others of negroid blood, by John J. Stewart. With a historical supplement, The church and the negroid people, by William E. Berrett. [3d ed. Orem, Utah, Bookmark, 1967, c1960] 55, 23 p. 19 cm. Includes bibliographical references. [BX8643.N4S8 1967] 73-172525
1. Mormons and Mormonism, Negro. I. Berrett, William Edwin. The church and the negroid people. 1967. II. Title.

Mormons and Mormonism—Periodicals

LIGHT on Mormonism. 289.3
The little cyclopedia of Mormonism; being the ... volumes of Light on Mormonism ... v. [1]-1922/27- Cleveland, O., The Utah gospel mission, 1907 [i. e. 1927]- v. illus. 27 cm. Vols. [1]- edited by J. D. Nutting. Vol. [1] covers v. 1-5 (Apr. 1922-Mar. 1927) of Light on Mormonism; v. 2 covers v. 6-10 (Apr. 1927-Mar. 1932) [BX8601.L5] 34-28830
1. Mormons and Mormonism—Period. I. Nutting, John Danforth, 1854- ed.

Mormons and Mormonism—Periods.—Indexes.

EASTWOOD, Laurie T
Index guide to periodicals of the Church of Jesus Christ of Latter-day Saints: Improvement era, Children's friend, Instructor, Church news, Relief Society magazine. Compiled by Laurie T. Eastwood and M. Lovelle Mortenson. Salt Lake City, Deseret Book Co. [1964] 123 p. 23 cm.
1. Mormons and Mormonism—Periods.—Indexes. I. Mortenson, M. Lovelle, joint author. II. Title.

Mormons and Mormonism—Pictorial works.

EVANS, John Henry, 1872-
Birth of Mormonism in picture; scenes and incidents in early church history from photographs by George E. Anderson ... narrative and notes by Prof. John Henry Evans. Salt Lake City, Utah. Deseret Sunday school union [c1909] 62, [2] p. illus. 19 x 23 1/2 cm. 10-4251
I. Title.

WARNER, James A. 289.3'3
The Mormon way / photos./text by James A. Warner and Styne M. Slade. Englewood Cliffs, N.J. : Prentice-Hall, c1976. 173 p. : ill. ; 24 cm. [BX8638.W37] 76-7624 ISBN 0-13-601088-1 : 25.00
1. Mormons and Mormonism—Pictorial works. I. Slade, Styne M., joint author. II. Title.

Mormons and Mormonism—Pictures, illustrations, etc.

ALWARD, Benjamin B comp. 289.3
A look at Mormonism: pictorial highlights of the church and its people. 1st ed. Salt Lake City, Deseret Book Co., 1956. 202p. illus. 28cm. [BX8638.A6] 57-32594

1. Mormons and Mormonism—Pictures, illustrations, etc. I. Title.

HOWELLS, Rulon Stanley, 1902- 289.3
The Mormon story; a pictorial account of Mormonism. 11th ed. Salt Lake City, Bookcraft, 1963. 179p. illus. 32cm. 63-3998 3.95
1. Mormons and Mormonism—Pictures, illustrations, etc. I. Title.

HOWELLS, Rulon Stanley, 1902- 289.3
The Mormon story; a pictorial account of Mormonism. 21st ed. Salt Lake City, Bookcraft, 1964. 100p. illus. (pt. col.) maps (pt. col.) ports. (pt. col.) 32cm. 64-6467 price unreported
1. Mormons and Mormonism—Pictures illustrations, etc. I. Title.

HOWELLS, Rulon Stanley, 1902- 289.3
The Mormon story; a pictorial account of Mormonism. [1st ed.] Salt Lake City, Bookcraft [1957] 179p. illus. 28cm. [BX8638.H64] 57-14509
1. Mormons and Mormonism—Pictures, illustrations, etc. I. Title.

HOWELLS, Rulon Stanley, 1902-
The Mormon story; a pictorial account of Mormonism. 9th ed. Salt Lake City, Bookcraft, c1957, 1962. 179 p. illus. 28 cm. 64-18264
1. Mormons and Mormonism—Pictures, illustrations, etc. I. Title.

HOWELLS, Rulon Stanley, 1902-
The Mormon story; a pictorial account of Mormonism. 10th ed. Salt Lake City, Utah Bookcraft, 1962, c1957. 179 p. illus. (part col.) 27 cm. 64-18361
1. Mormons and Mormonism—Pictures, illustrations, etc. I. Title.

Mormons and Mormonism — Poetry.

SMITH, Eliza Roxey (Snow) 1804-1887.
Eliza R. Snow; an immortal; selected writings. [Salt Lake City, Utah] Pub. by Nicholas G. Morgan, Sr. Foundation, 1957. iv, 370 p. 23 cm.
1. Mormons and Mormonism — Poetry. I. Title.

[SMITH, Eliza Roxey (Snow)] Mrs., 1804-1887. 245
Poems, religious, historical, and political. Also two articles in prose. By Eliza R. Snow ... Comp. by the author. Vol. II. Salt Lake City, Printed at the Latter-day saints' printing and publishing establishment, 1877. iv, 284 p. front. (port.) 18 cm. Vol. 1 published in Liverpool in 1856. [PS2859.S76P6 vol. 2] 30-9286
1. Mormons and Mormonism—Poetry. I. Title.

Mormons and Mormonism—Political activity.

MELVILLE, J. Keith, 1921- 320.9'79
Conflict and compromise : the Mormons in mid nineteenth-century American politics / J. Keith Melville. 1st ed. Provo, Utah : Printed for the Political Science Dept. by the Brigham Young University Printing Service, 1974. viii, 121 p. : ill. ; 23 cm. Includes bibliographical references. [BX8643.P6M44] 74-195954
1. Mormons and Mormonism—Political activity. 2. United States—Politics and government—1845-1861. I. Title.

Mormons and Mormonism—Quotations, maxims, etc.

SENTENCE sermons / 230'.9'3
compiled by Dean R. Zimmerman. Salt Lake City : Deseret Book Co., 1978. xvii, 282 p. ; 23 cm. [BX8608.5.S46] 78-2568 ISBN 0-87747-672-1 : 4.95
1. Mormons and Mormonism—Quotations, maxims, etc. I. Zimmerman, Dean R.

ZOBELL, Albert L comp.
At the fountain, comp. by Albert L. Zobell. Salt Lake City, Deseret Book Co., 1963. 96 p. 16 cm. 68-23080
1. Mormons and Mormonism—Quotations, maxims, etc. I. Title.

ZOBELL, Albert L., Jr., comp. 289.3
The glorious purpose; more moments with the prophets. [Salt Lake City, Utah] Deseret [1963, c.]1962. 104p. 16cm. 63-1321 1.00
1. Mormons and Mormonism—Quotations, maxims, etc. I. Title. II. Title: Moments with the prophets.

ZOBELL, Albert L comp. 230'.9'33
The joy that endures. Salt Lake City, Deseret Book Co., 1963. 96 p. 16 cm. [BX8608.5.Z62] 63-4967
1. Mormons and Mormonism — Quotations, maxims, etc. I. Title.

ZOBELL, Albert L comp.
Quills of truth, compiled by Albert L. Zobell. Salt Lake City, Bookcraft [1963] 114 p. 16 cm. 68-78332
1. Mormons and Mormonism—Quotations, maxims, etc. I. Title.

Mormons and Mormonism—Relations—Judaism.

GLANZ, Rudolf 289.3
Jew and Mormon: historic group relations and religious outlook. New York, 620 W. 711 St., Author, 1963. 379p. 24cm. Bibl. 63-16229 6.00
1. Mormons and Mormonism—Relations—Judaism. 2. Judaism—Relations—Mormonism. I. Title.

Mormons and Mormonism—Sacred books—Concordances.

A Topical guide to the scriptures of the Church of Jesus Christ of Latter-Day Saints. 289.3'2'03
Salt Lake City, Utah : Deseret Book Co., 1977. 500 p. ; 24 cm. Includes index. [BX8622.T64] 77-87963 ISBN 0-87747-677-2 : 7.95 ISBN 0-87747-678-0 pbk. : 5.95
1. Mormons and Mormonism—Sacred books—Concordances. I. Church of Jesus Christ of Latter-day Saints.

Mormons and Mormonism—Sacred books—Inspiration.

FREE, Jack 289.3
Mormonism and inspiration; a study. Concord, Calif. Pacific Pub. Co. [1963, c.1962] 381p. 21cm. 63-2729 4.50
1. Mormons and Mormonism—Sacred books—Inspiration. I. Title.

Mormons and mormonism—Sermons.

BENNION, Samuel O 1874- 252.093
Radio addresses, by Elder Samuel O, Bennion ... Addresses delivered over radio station KSL, April 10 to June 5, 1938, as a part of the regular Sunday evening radio program of the Church of Jesus Christ of latter-day saints. Independence, Mo., Zion's printing and publishing company [c1938] 70 p., 1 l. 20 cm. "These sermons were published in the Church section of the Deseret news and in pamphlet form ... [and] now ... in booklet form."--Pref. Bibliography: 1 leaf at end. [BX8639.B4R3] 39-274
1. Mormons and Mormonism—Sermons. 2. Sermons, American. I. Title.

CRITCHLOW, William J., 1892-1968. 252.09'3
Gospel insights, from the sermons and stories of William J. Critchlow, Jr. Compiled by Eleanor Knowles. Salt Lake City, Deseret Book Co., 1969. viii, 149 p. 24 cm. [BX8639.C7G6] 78-82120 3.95
1. Mormons and Mormonism—Sermons. 2. Sermons, American. I. Knowles, Eleanor, ed. II. Title.

RICHARDS, Claude. 922.8373
J. Golden Kimball; the story of a unique personality, by Claude Richards ... Salt Lake City, Utah, Deseret news press, 1934. 2 p. l., vii-xi, 398 p. front., pl., ports. 22 cm. "Tabernacle talks, abridged by Claude Richards and approved by J. Golden Kimball": p. [139]-387. [BX8695.K52R5] 34-34754
1. Kimball, Jonathan Golden, 1853- 2. Mormons and Mormonism—Sermons. I. Title.

SILL, Sterling W. 252.09'3
The power of believing [by] Sterling W. Sill. Salt Lake City, Bookcraft, 1968. x, 330 p. illus. 24 cm. [BX8639.S5P6] 68-59023 3.75
1. Mormons and Mormonism—Sermons. 2. Sermons, American. I. Title.

SMITH, George Albert, 1879- 252.093
Sharing the gospel with others; excerpts from the sermons of President Smith, selected and comp. by Preston Nibley. [Salt Lake City, Deseret Book Co., 1948] 219 p. port. 24 cm. [BX8639.S53S5] 49-4203
1. Mormons and Mormonism—Sermons. 2. Sermons, American. I. Title.

SMITH, Joseph Fielding, 1876- 201
Seek ye earnestly ... Salt Lake City, Utah, Deseret Book Co., 1970. viii, 459 p. col. port. 24 cm. [BX8639.S57S4] 77-136242 ISBN 0-87747-367-6 5.95
1. Mormons and Mormonism—Sermons. 2. Sermons, American. 3. Mormons and Mormonism—Addresses, essays, lectures. I. Title.

SMITH, Joseph Fielding, 1876- 252.0893
Take heed to yourselves, by Joseph Fielding Smith. Salt Lake City, Deseret, 1966. viii, 453p. port. 24cm. [BX8639.S57T3] 66-25511 4.95
1. Mormons and Mormonism—Sermons. 2. Sermons, American. I. Title.

SPERRY, Sidney Branton, 1895- 252.093
Themes of the restored gospel; a series of gospel discourses as contained in the sermons and articles of Sidney B. Sperry. Salt Lake City, Bookcraft Pub. Co., 1950. 165 p. 20 cm. [BX8639.S8T45] 52-64564
1. Mormons and Mormonism — Sermons. 2. Sermons, American. I. Title.

WIRTHLIN, Joseph Leopold, 1893- 252.0893
A heritage of faith, by Joseph L. Wirthlin. Richard Bitner Wirthlin, compiler. Salt Lake City, Utah, Deseret Book Co., 1964. x, 262 p. port. 24 cm. [BX8639.W5H4] 64-66456
1. Mormons and Mormonism — Sermons. 2. Sermons, American. I. Wirthlin, Richard Bitner, comp. II. Title.

YOUNG, Brigham, 1801-1877.
Discourses of Brigham Young; selected and arranged by John A. Widtsoe. Salt Lake City, Deseret Book, 1961 [c1954] 498 p. illus., front. 24 cm. 68-25127
1. Mormons and mormonism—Sermons. I. Widtsoe, John Andreas, 1872-1952. II. Title.

Mormons—Doctrine.

A marvelous work and a wonder.
Salt Lake City, Desert Book Co., 1950 [i.e. 1957] xviii, 456p. An expansion of the author's mimeographed outline, The message of Mormonism.
1. Mormons—Doctrine. I. Richards, Le Grand, Bp., 1886-

Mormons — Mormonism — History

SMITH, Joseph Fielding, 1876-
Essentials in church history; a history of theChurch from the birth of Joseph Smith to the present time, with introductory chapters on the antiquity of the Gospel and the "Falling Away" 19th.ed. [Salt Lake City? Published by the Deseret Book Co., for the Church of Jesus Christ of Latter-Day Saints, 1964. 748 p. illus., ports., maps, facsims. 66-43867
1. Mormons — Mormonism — Hist. I. Title.

Mormons—United States.

FIFE, Austin E. 289.3'09
Saints of sage and saddle : folklore among the Mormons / by Austin and Alta Fife. Reprint ed. Salt Lake City : University of Utah Press, 1980. xviii, 367 p. : map ; 22 cm. Reprint. Originally published: Bloomington : Indiana University, 1956. Includes index. Bibliography: p. [339]-342. [BX8611.F5 1980] 19 81-137868 ISBN 0-87480-180-X pbk. : 20.00
1. Mormons—United States. 2. Folklore—United States. I. Fife, Alta Stephens. II. Title.

Mormons—United States—Biography.

ARRINGTON, Leonard J. 289.3'3 B
Saints without halos : the human side of Mormon history / Leonard J. Arrington and Davis Bitton. Salt Lake City : Signature Books, c1981. viii, 158 p. ; 24 cm. Bibliography: p. 156-158. [BX8693.A77] 19 82-119402 ISBN 0-941214-01-X : 11.95
1. Mormons—United States—Biography. I. Bitton, Davis, 1930- II. Title.

BACKMAN, Milton Vaughn. 289.3'092'4 B
Joseph Smith's first vision : confirming evidences and contemporary accounts / Milton V. Backman, Jr. 2nd ed., rev. and enl. Salt Lake City, Utah : Bookcraft, c1980. xiv, 227 p. : ill., ports., maps ; 24 cm. Includes index. Bibliography: p. [211]-222. [BX8695.S6B3 1980] 19 80-65981 ISBN 0-88494-399-2 : 6.95
1. Smith, Joseph, 1805-1844. 2. Mormons—United States—Biography. 3. Visions. 4. New York (State)—Church history. I. Title.

DALTON, Lee. 289.3'3 B
Tag / Lee Dalton. Bountiful, Utah : Horizon Publishers, c1982. 177 p. ; 24 cm. [BX8695.D34A37 1982] 19 81-82053 ISBN 0-88290-193-1 : 6.95
1. Dalton, Lee. 2. Mormons—United States—Biography. I. Title.

EYER, Mary Sturlaugson. 289.3'3 B
He restoreth my soul / Mary Sturlaugson Eyer. Salt Lake City, Utah : Deseret Book Co., c1982. 98 p. ; 24 cm. [BX8695.S85A33] 19 82-1363 ISBN 0-87747-908-9 : 6.95
1. Eyer, Mary Sturlaugson. 2. Mormons—United States—Biography. I. Title.

GIBBONS, Francis M., 1921- 289.3'3 B
Brigham Young, modern Moses, prophet of God / Francis M. Gibbons. Salt Lake City, Utah : Deseret Book Co., 1981. 286 p. ; 24 cm. Includes index. Bibliography: p. 277-278. [BX8695.Y7G53] 19 81-7766 ISBN 0-87747-858-9 : 8.95
1. Young, Brigham, 1801-1877. 2. Mormons—United States—Biography. I. Title.

HUNT, Larry E. 289.3'3 B
F.M. Smith : Saint as reformer, 1874-1946 / by Larry E. Hunt. Independence, Mo. : Herald Pub. House, c1982. 2 v. (488 p.) ; 20 cm. Originally presented as the author's thesis (doctoral—Missouri-Columbia, 1978) Bibliography: p. 476-488 (v. 2) [BX8695.S73H86 1982] 19 81-7213 ISBN 0-8309-0320-8 : 11.00
1. Smith, Frederick Madison, 1874-1946. 2. Mormons—United States—Biography. I. Title.

JOHNSON, Sonia. 289.3'3 B
From housewife to heretic / Sonia Johnson. 1st ed. Garden City, N.Y. : Doubleday, 1981. p. cm. Includes index.

[BX8695.J65A34] 19 80-2964 ISBN 0-385-17493-4 : 12.95
1. Johnson, Sonia. 2. Mormons—United States—Biography. 3. Feminists—United States—Biography. I. Title.

LINDER, Ted. 289.3'3 B
Ben Nelson, defender of the faithful / by Ted Linder. Independence, Mo. : Herald Pub. House, c1981. p. cm. [BX8695.N37L56] 19 81-7190 ISBN 0-8309-0321-6 : Write for information.
1. Nelson, Ben. 2. Mormons—United States—Biography. I. Title.

MINER, Caroline Eyring. 289.3'3 B
Camilla, a biography of Camilla Eyring Kimball / Caroline Eyring Miner, Edward L. Kimball. Salt Lake City, Utah : Deseret Book Co., 1980. viii, 216 p. : ill. ; 24 cm. Includes index. [BX8695.K49.M56] 19 80-69723 ISBN 0-87747-845-7 : 7.95
1. Kimball, Camilla E. 2. Mormons—United States—Biography. I. Kimball, Edward L. II. Title.

SESSIONS, Gene Alfred. 289.3'3 B
Mormon thunder : a documentary history of Jedediah Morgan Grant / Gene A. Sessions. Urbana : University of Illinois Press, c1982. xvii, 413 p. : ill. ; 24 cm. Includes bibliographical references and index. [BX8695.G72S47 1982] 19 81-16075 ISBN 0-252-00944-4 : 16.95
1. Grant, Jedediah M. 2. Mormons—United States—Biography. I. Title.

VAN WAGONER, Richard S. 289.3'092'2 B
A book of Mormons / Richard S. Van Wagoner and Steven C. Walker. Salt Lake City, Utah : Signature Books, c1982. x, 454 p. : ill., ports. ; 24 cm. Includes index. Bibliography: p. [419]-440. [BX8693.V36 1982] 19 82-173783 ISBN 0-941214-06-0 : 14.95
1. Mormons—United States—Biography. I. Walker, Steven C. II. Title.
Publisher's address : 9 Exchange Place, Suite 716, Salt Lake City, UT 84111.

THE Words of Joseph Smith : the contemporary accounts of the Nauvoo discourses of the Prophet Joseph / compiled and edited by Andrew F. Ehat and Lyndon W. Cook ; with a foreword by Truman G. Madsen. Provo, Utah : Religious Studies Center, Brigham Young University ; Salt Lake City, Utah : Distributed by Bookcraft, c1980. xxv, 447 p. ; 24 cm. (Religious studies monograph series ; v. 6) Includes indexes. [BX8695.S6W67] 19 80-70806 ISBN 0-88494-419-0 : 10.95 289.3'092'4
1. Smith, Joseph, 1805-1844. 2. Mormon Church—Doctrinal and controversial works. 3. Mormons—United States—Biography. I. Ehat, Andrew F. II. Cook, Lyndon W. III. Series.

Mormons—Utah—History—Fiction.

YORGASON, Blaine M., 1942- FIC
The courage covenant / Blaine M. Yorgaston. Salt Lake City, Utah : Bookcraft, 1982, c1979. viii, 183 p. ; 23 cm. Reprint. Originally published: Massacre at Salt Creek. Garden City, N.Y. : Doubleday, 1979. [PS3575.O57M37 1982] 813'.54 19 82-165010 ISBN 0-88494-455-7 : 6.95
1. Mormons—Utah—History—Fiction. 2. Ute Indians—Fiction. 3. Indians of North America—Utah—Fiction. I. [Massacre at Salt Creek] II. Title.

Morning Star (Ship)

BINGHAM, Hiram, 1831-1908.
Story of the Morning Star, the children's missionary vessel. Boston, American Board [of Commissioners for Foreign Missions] 1866. 71 p. illus., map. 17 cm. [BV3677.B5] 50-42070
1. Morning Star (Ship) 2. Missions—Micronesia. I. Title.

Moro Sheeba.

KING, Beztrice (Tannehill) 922
Moro Sheeba. Chicago, Moody Press [1957] 128p. 22cm. [BV3625.C63M6] 57-20942
1. Moro Sheeba. I. Title.

Morris, George Sylvester, 1840-1869.

JONES, Marc Edmund, 1888- 921.1
George Sylvester Morris; his philosophical career and theistic idealism. Philadelphia, D. McKay Co., 1948. xvi, 430 p. 21 cm. Issued also as thesis, Columbia Univ. "Friedrich Adolf Trandelenburg article by Morris in the New Englander, volume 32, April, 1874)" 335-384. "Revised draft of unused introduction. (For Morris translation of Hegel's Philosophy of the state and of history)": p. 385-412. Bibliography: p. 413-416. [B945.M54J6 1948a] 49-7314
1. Morris, George Sylvester, 1840-1869. I. Title.

Morris, Myron Newton, 1810-1885.

MEMORIAL of Rev. Myron Newton Morris. Published by the Congregational church, West Hartford, Conn. Hartford, Conn., Press of the Case, Lockwood & Brainard company, 1886. 122 p. front. (mounted port.) 20 cm. [BX7260.M565M4] 35-37819 922.
1. Morris, Myron Newton, 1810-1885. I. West Hartford, Conn Congregational church.
Contents omitted.

Morris, Robert, 1818-1888.

DENSLOW, Ray Vaughn, 1885- 366.1
The masonic conservators, written for the Masonic service association of Missouri, by Ray V. Denslow. [St. Louis] Grand lodge, Ancient free and accepted masons of the state of Missouri, 1931. 132 p. 24 cm. [HS517.D37] 33-12636
1. Morris, Robert, 1818-1888. 2. Freemasons. 3. Masonic service association of Missouri. I. Title. II. Title: Conservators, The masonic.

MORRIS, Robert Hugh. 243
The fifth horseman, and other sermons, by Robert Hugh Morris ... foreword by Edgar P. Hill ... New York, Chicago [etc.] Fleming H. Revell company [c1922] 160 p. 19 1/2 cm. [BX9178.M6F5] 23-4813
I. Title.

Morris, Samuel, 1873-1893.

BALDWIN, Lindley J. 248.2'4
The ebony saint: Samuel Morris's miraculous journey of faith, by Lindley J. Baldwin. Evesham, (Worcs), James, 1967. 125 p. front (port), illus. 18 1/2 cm. 9/6 SBN 85305-001-5 (B67-26224) [BV4935.M63B3 1967] 68-116300
1. Morros, Samuel, 1873-1893. I. Title.

BALDWIN, Lindley J. 922
The march of faith; the challenge of Samuel Morris to undying life and leadership, by Lindley J. Baldwin ... Victory center ed. New York, N.Y., Distributed by Christian business men's committee, inc., of N.Y. [1944] 2 p. l., [7]-94 p. illus., port. 19 cm. [E185.97.M85] 44-6554
1. Morris, Samuel, 1873-1893. I. Title.

MASA, Jorge O. 920
The angel in ebony; or, The life and message of Sammy Morris, by Jorge O. Mass; published by class of 1928 of Taylor university. Upland, Ind., Taylor university press [c1928] 131 p. front., plates, ports. 17 1/2 cm. [E185.97.M86] 29-3768
1. Morris, Samuel, 1873-1893. I. Title.

Morris, Thomas Asbury, bp., 1794-1874.

MARLAY, John F. 922.
The life of Rev. Thomas A. Morris, D. D., late senior bishop of the Methodist Episcopal church. By Rev. John F. Marlay, A. M. With an introduction by Bishop E. S. Janes. Cincinnati, Hitchcock and Walden; New York, Nelson and Phillips, 1875. 7, [1], iv, 9-407 p. front. (port.) 20 cm. [BX8495.M63M3] 12-36753
1. Morris, Thomas Asbury, bp., 1794-1874. I. Title.

Morrisite War, 1862.

ANDERSON, C. LeRoy. 289.3'3
For Christ will come tomorrow : the saga of the Morrisites / C. LeRoy Anderson. Logan, Utah : Utah State University Press, [1981] p. cm. Includes index. Bibliography: p. [BX8680.M64A83] 19 81-16226 ISBN 0-87421-109-3 : 12.50
1. Church of the First Born (Morrisites)—History. 2. Morris, Joseph, 1824-1862. 3. Church of the First Born (Morrisites)—Biography. 4. Morrisite War, 1862. I. Title.

Morrison, Henry Clay, 1857-1942.

MORRISON, Henry Clay, 1857- 258
Remarkable conversions, interesting incidents and striking illustrations, by Rev. H. C. Morrison ... Louisville, Ky., Pentecostal publishing company [c1925] 125 p. 19 1/2 cm. [BV4014.M6] 25-9315
I. Title.

MORRISON, Henry Clay, 1857-1942. 922.773
Some chapters of my life story [by] Rev. H. C. Morrison. Louisville, Ky., Pentecostal publishing company [c1941] 269 p. front., ports. 21 cm. [BX8495.M68A3] 42-16427
I. Title.

WESCHE, Percival A 287.10924
Henry Clay Morrison; crusador saint. [Berne, Ind., Herald Press, c1963] 208 p. 21 cm. Imprint on mounted label. Bibliographical references included in "Footnotes" (p. 206-208) [BX8495.M68W4] 64-1036
1. Morrison, Henry Clay, 1857-1942. I. Title.

WIMBERLY, Charles Franklin, 1866- 922.
A biographical sketch of Henry Clay Morrison, p.p., editor of "The Pentecostal herald"; the man and his ministry, by C. F. Wimberly ... New York, Chicago [etc.] Fleming H. Revell company [1922] 214 p. front. (port.) pl. 19 1/2 cm. [BX8495.M68W5] 23-5929
1. Morrison, Henry Clay, 1857- I. Title.

Morrison, Joseph Grant.

CORBETT, C T 922.89
Soldier of the cross; the life story of J. G. Morrison, 1871-1939. Kansas City, Mo., Beacon Hill Press [1956] 128p. 19cm. [BX8699.N32M63] 56-33591
1. Morrison, Joseph Grant. I. Title.

Morristown, N.J. St. Peter's Church.

LINDSLEY, James Elliott. 233.749
A history of Saint Peter's Church, Morristown, New Jersey. Morristown? 1952 102 p. illus. 21 cm. [BX5980.M67S3] 52-31358
1. Morristown, N.J. St. Peter's Church. I. Title.

Morse, Eugene.

MORSE, Eugene. 266'.0092'4 B
Exodus to a hidden valley. [1st ed.] New York, Reader's Digest Press; distributed by E. P. Dutton, 1974. 215 p. map. 22 cm. [BV3270.M67] 73-21673 ISBN 0-88349-021-8 7.95
1. Morse, Eugene. 2. Missions—Burma. I. Title.

Morse, Henry, 1595-1645.

CARAMAN, Philip, 1911- 922.242
Henry Morse, priest of the plague. New York, Farrar, Straus and Cudahy [1957] 201p. illus. 22cm. Includes bibliography. [BX4705.M7254C3] 57-1742
1. Morse, Henry, 1595-1645. I. Title.

Morse, Henry, 1595-1645—Juvenile literature.

NASH, Roy, 1929- 92
Death is my parish, Illus. by Carolyn Lee Jagodits. Notre Dame. Ind. 46556, Dujarie Pr. [1965] 94p. illus. 24cm. [BX4700.M65N3] 65-27761 2.25
1. Morse, Henry, 1595-1645—Juvenile literature. I. Title.

Morse, Horace Bassett, 1804-1825.

BURROUGHS, Charles, 1787-1868. 922
Memoirs and select papers of Horace B. Morse, A.B. of Haverhill, N.H. who was drowned near Portsmouth harbour, June 22, 1825. By Charles Burroughs ... Portsmouth, N.H. Printed by Miller and Brewster, 1829. vi, [7]-203 p. 17 1/2 cm. "A discourse, delivered in St. John's church, Portsmouth, N.H. June 26, 1825 ... by Charles Burroughs, rector": p. [131]-203. [BR1725.M55B8] 38-7492
1. Morse, Horace Bassett, 1804-1825. 2. Protestant Episcopal church in the U.S.A.—Sermons. I. Title.

Morse, Jedidiah, 1761-1826.

MORSE, James King, 1906- 922.573
Jedidiah Morse, a champion of New England orthodoxy [by] James King Morse. New York, Columbia university press, 1939. ix, 179, [1] p. 23 1/2cm. (Columbia studies in American culture, no. 2). Issued also as thesis (PH.D.) Columbia university. Bibliography: p. 163-[172] [BX7260.M57M37 1939] 39-11247
1. Morse, Jedidiah, 1761-1826. 2. New England—Church history. 3. New England—Religion. I. Title.

Morse, Samuel, 1792-1859.

WEBSTER, John Calvin, 1810-1884. 922.573
Worship and work: or, The life of Dea. Samuel Morse, of Hopkinton, Mass. By J. C. Webster. Introduction, by Rev. E. Dowse. Written for the Massachusetts Sabbath school society, and approved by the Committee of publication. Boston, Massachusetts Sabbath school society [c1860] xiv, [15]-214 p. front. (port.) 16 cm. [BX7260.M58W4] 36-3222
1. Morse, Samuel, 1792-1859. I. Massachusetts Sabbath school society. Committee of publication. II. Title.

Mortality.

CROTHERS, Samuel McChord, 1857-1927. 237.
... The endless life, by Samuel McChord Crothers. Boston and New York, Houghton, Mifflin and company, 1905. 3 p. l., 55, [1] p. 19 cm. (The Ingersoil lecture, 1905) [BT921.C785] 5-36511
1. Mmortality. I. Title.

Mortgages (Canon law)

STENGER, Joseph Bernard, 1908- 254
... The mortgaging of church property; a historical synopsis and commentary, by Rev. Joseph Bernard Stenger ... Washington, D.C., The Catholic university of America press, 1942. 186 p. 23 cm. (The Catholic university of America, 1942. "Biographical note": p. 173. Bibliography: p. 162-170. [BX1939.M68S75] A 43
1. Mortgages (Canon law) 2. Catholic church. Codex juris canonici. C. 1530-1533. I. Title.

Mortimer, Elizabeth (Ritchie)

BULMER, Agnes (Collinson) Mrs 1775-1836. 920.7
Memoirs of Mrs. Elizabeth Mortimer: with selections from her correspondence. By Agnes Bulmer ... New-York, Pub. by T. Mason and G. Lane, for the Methodist Episcopal church, 1836. 287 p. front. (port.) 14 cm. [BR1725.M57B8] 7-27747
1. Mortimer, Elizabeth (Ritchie) Mrs I. Title.

Morton, David, 1833-1898.

HOSS, Elijah Embree, bp., 1849-1919. 922.
David Morton, a biography, by Bishop Elijah Embree Hoss ... Nashville, Tenn., Publishing house of the Methodist

Episcopal church, South, Smith & Lamar, agents, 1916. x, 214 p. front., plates, ports., fold. map, fold. geneal. tab., facsim. 21 cm. $1.50 [BX8495.M7H6] 16-11218
1. Morton, David, 1833-1898. I. Title.

Mosaics—Istanbul.

KAHLER, Heinz. 726'.5'094961
Hagia Sophia. With a chapter on the mosaics by Cyril Mango. Translated by Ellyn Childs. New York, Praeger [1967] 74 p. 103 illus. (part col.), fold. plans. 31 cm. Bibliography:p. 70-[72] [NA5870.A9K33] 67-29605
1. Istanbul. Ayasofya Muzesi. 2. Mosaics—Istanbul. I. Title.

Moses.

AUERBACH, Elias, 1882- 222'.1'0924
Moses. Translated and edited by Robert A. Barclay and Israel O. Lehman, with annotations by Israel O. Lehman. Detroit, Wayne State University Press, 1975. 253 p. ; 24 cm. Includes bibliographical references. [BS580.M6A813] 72-6589 ISBN 0-8143-1491-0
1. Moses. 2. Bible. O.T. Pentateuch—Criticism, interpretation, etc.

BAUGHEN, Michael A. 253
The Moses principle : leadership and the venture of faith / Micheal Baughen. Wheaton, Ill : H. Shaw, c1978. 118 p. ; 21 cm. [BS580.M6B29 1978] 78-27498 ISBN 0-87788-558-3 pbk. : 2.95
1. Moses. 2. Bible. O.T.—Biography. 3. Christian life—1960- I. Title.

BEDELL, Gregory Townsend, 1793-1834. 221.92
The life of Moses. By G.T. Bedell ... Written for the American S. union, and revised by the Committee of publication. Philadelphia, American Sunday-school union, 1832. iv, 5-213 p. front., illus. 15 cm. [BS580.M6B4] 36-31435
1. Moses. I. American Sunday-school union. II. Title.

BEEGLE, Dewey M. 222'.1'0924 B
Moses, the servant of Yahweh [by] Dewey M. Beegle. Grand Rapids, Mich., Eerdmans [1972] 368 p. illus. (on lining paper) 23 cm. Includes bibliographical references. [BS580.M6B44] 73-162029 ISBN 0-8028-3406-X 7.95
1. Moses. I. Title.

BISHOP, Charles Cloophus, 1854- 232.9
The two most wonderful babies who became the two greatest men in the world [by] Charles C. Bishop. [Nashville, Tenn., Consolidated development co., c1934] 48 p. plates. 23 cm. [BT302.B45] 34-8968
1. Jesus Christ—Biog.—Juvenile literature. 2. Moses. I. Title.

BORK, Paul F., 1924- 222'.12'095
The world of Moses / Paul F. Bork. Nashville : Southern Pub. Association, c1978. 128 p. : ill. ; 20 cm. Bibliography: p. 125-128. [BS1245.5.B67] 78-5022 ISBN 0-8127-0166-6 pbk. : 4.95
1. Moses. 2. Bible. O.T. Exodus—History of contemporary events. I. Title.

BUBER, Martin, 1878-1965. 221.92
Moses; the revelation and the covenant. New York, Harper [1958] 226 p. 21 cm. (Harper torchbooks, TB27) "First published in 1946 under the title: Moses." Includes bibliography. [BS580.M6B8 1958] 58-5216
1. Moses.

CAMERON, Edwin Ray, 1897- 221.92
My servant Moses, by E. Ray Cameron... New York [etc.] Fleming H. Revell company [c1937] 187 p. 19 1/2 cm. [BS580.M6C23] 37-13553
1. Moses. I. Title.

CAMPBELL, Samuel Miner, 1823-1892. 221.92
Across the desert. A life of Moses. By the Rev. S. M. Campbell... Philadelphia, Presbyterian board of publication [1873] 342 p. incl. front., illus., plates, maps, plans. 19 1/2 cm. [BS580.M6C25] 36-31437
1. Moses. I. Presbyterian church in the U.S.A. Borad of publication. II. Title.

DAICHES, David, 1912- 222'.1'0924 B
Moses, the man and his vision / David Daiches. New York : Praeger, 1975. 264 p. : ill. ; 26 cm. Includes index. Bibliography: p. 257-258. [BS580.M6D3] 74-11918 ISBN 0-275-33740-5 : 19.95
1. Moses. I. Title.

DUNGAN, David Roberts, 1837- 221.
Moses, the man of God, by D. R. Dungan. St. Louis, Christian publishing company, 1899. 303 p. front., illus. 20 cm. [BS580.M6D8] 0-4375
1. Moses. I. Title.

ENTWISTLE, Mary. 221.92
Baby Moses, by Mary Entwistle; illustrated by Roberta F. C. Waudby. New York, T. Nelson and sons, 1935. [50] p. col. illus. 14 x 11 cm. (Bible books for small people... no. 8) [BS551.B396 no. 8] 37-16286
1. Moses. I. Waudby, Roberta F. C., illus. II. Title.

FLEG, Edmond, 1874- 221.
The life of Moses, by Edmond Fleg; translated from the French by Stephen Haden Guest. New York, E. P. Dutton & co., inc. [c1928] xii, 276 p. 21 cm. [BS580.M6F62 1928a] 28-29464
1. Moses. I. Guest, Stephen Haden, tr. II. Title.

FLUEGEL, Maurice, 1831?-1911. 222.
Exodus, Moses and the Decalogue legislation. The central doctrine and regulative organum of Mosaism... By Maurice Fluegel... Baltimore, Md., M. Fluegel co., c1910. 3 p. l., [5]-308 p. 1 l. 23 1/2 cm. [BS1245.F4] 10-8630
1. Moses. 2. Jews—Hist.—To entrance into Canaan. 3. Commandments, Ten. I. Title.

FREUD, Sigmund, 1856- 221.92
Moses and monotheism [by] Sigmund Freud. New York, A. A. Knopf, 1939. 5 p. l., 3-218, v, [1] p., 1 l. 23 cm. "Translated from the German by Katherine Jones." "Parts I and II of this book were published in German in 'Imago' in 1937: part III has not previously appeared in print."--Translator's note. "First American edition." [BS580.M6F7 1939a] 39-27591
1. Moses. 2. Monotheism. 3. Jews—Religion—Relations—Egyptian. 4. Psychology, Religious. I. Jones, Katherine, tr. II. Title.

FREUD, Sigmund, 1856-1939. 221.92
Moses and monotheism. Translated from the German by Katherine Jones. New York, Vintage Books, 1955 [c1939] viii, 178, iv p. 19cm. (A Vintage book, K-14) Translation of Der Mann Moses und die monotheistische Religion. Bibliographical footnotes. [BS580] 55-152
1. Moses. 2. Monotheism. 3. Judaism—Relations—Egyptian. 4. Psychology, Religious. I. Title.

GAEBELEIN, Arno Clemens, 1861- 221.92
Moses, his first and second coming; the exodus in the light of prophecy, by earno Clemens Gaebelein ... New York, N. Y., Publication office "Our hope" (A. C. Gaebelein, inc.); London, Pickering & Inglis; [etc., etc., c1940] 183 p. 21 cm. [BS580.M6G25] 40-35379
1. Moses. 2. Typology (Theology) I. Title.

GAGE, Joy P. 222'.10924
Lord, can we talk this over? / By Joy P. Gage. Chicago : Moody Press, c1980. 93 p. ; 22 cm. [BS580.M6G257] 80-16014 ISBN 0-8024-4011-8 pbk. : 2.50
1. Moses. 2. Bible. O.T. Exodus—Study. 3. Bible. N.T. Hebrews XI, 23-29—Study. 4. Faith—Biblical teaching. I. Title.

GILPIN, Richard O. 222'.1'0924 B
Moses—born to be a slave, but God ... / Richard O. Gilpin. 1st ed. Hicksville, N.Y. : Exposition Press, c1977. 119 p. ; 22 cm. [BS580.M6G48] 77-366950 ISBN 0-682-48843-7 : 5.50
1. Bible. O.T.—Biography. 2. Moses. I. Title.

GLASSON, Thomas Francis. 226.506
Moses in the fourth Gospel. Naperville, Ill., A. R. Allenson [1963] 115 p. 22 cm. (Studies in Biblical theology, no. 40) Includes bibliography. [BS2615.2.G6] 63-5666
1. Moses. 2. Bible. N.T. John — Theology 3. Wilderness (Theology) 4. Typology (Theology) I. Title.

GOLDING, Louis, 1895- 221.92
In the steps of Moses, by Louis Golding. Philadelphia, The Jewish publication society of America, 5703-1943. 4 p. l., 3-556 p. plates. 22 cm. Maps on lining-papers. First published in two volumes under the titles: In the steps of Moses the lawgiver and In the steps of Moses the conquerer. Bibliography: p. 553-556. [BS580.M6G55] 43-10138
1. Moses. 2. Egypt—Descr. & trav. 3. Sinaitic peninsula—Descr. & trav. 4. Levant—Descr. & trav. 5. Jews—Hist.—To entrance into Canaan. I. Jewish publication society of America. II. Title.

GOLDING, Louis, 1895- 221.92
In the steps of Moses the lawgiver, by Louis Golding. New York, The Macmillan company, 1938. xiii, 355 p. front., plates. 19 cm. "Printed in Great Britain." [BS580.M6G6 1938] 38-30992
1. Moses. 2. Egypt—Descr. & trav. 3. Sinal—Descr. I. Title.

GRANT Watson, Elliot Lovegood, 1885- 221.
A prophet and his God; the story of Moses, by E. L. Grant Watson. New York, H. Liveright, 1930. 7 p. l., 11-304, [1] p. 22 cm. London edition (T. Butterworth, limited, 1929) has title: Moses, the lord of the prophets. [BS580.M6G7 1930] 30-3990
1. Moses. I. Title.

GREENE, Carla, 1906- 221.92
Moses; the great lawgiver. Illustrated by Anne Lewis. Irvington-on-Hudson, N.Y., Harvey House [1968] 45 p. illus. 27 cm. A brief biography of the Biblical prophet who led his people out of Egypt to the Promised Land and gave them the Ten Commandments. [BS580.M6G72] AC 68
1. Moses. I. Lewis, Anne, illus. II. Title.

GREGORIUS, Saint, Bp. of Nyssa, fl.379-394. 222'.1'0924
The life of Moses / Gregory of Nyssa ; translation, introd. and notes by Abraham J. Malherbe and Everett Ferguson ; pref. by John Meyendorff. New York : Paulist Press, c1978. xvi, 208 p. ; 23 cm. (The Classics of Western spirituality) Translation of De vita Moysis. Includes indexes. Bibliography: p. 139-140. [BS580.M6G7313] 78-56352 ISBN 0-8091-2112-3 pbk. : 6.95
1. Moses. 2. Bible. O.T.—Biography. 3. Mysticism—Early church, ca.30-600. I. Title. II. Series.

HALLAM, Robert Alexander, 1807-1877. 221.92
Moses; a course of lectures delivered in the chapel of St. James' church, New London. By Robert A. Hallam. New York, Boston, E. P. Dutton and company, 1869. x, 295 p. 19 cm. [BS580.M6H25] 37-7034
1. Moses. I. Title.

HALLOCK, Mary Angeline (Ray) Lathrop, Mrs. b.1810. 221.92
Story of Moses; or, Desert wanderings from Egypt to Canaan. By Mrs. M. A. Hallock ... Illustrated ed. Philadelphia, New York, The American Sunday-school union, c1888. 246 p. incl. front., illus., plates. 19 1/2 cm. [BS580.M6H3] 37-7035
1. Moses. I. American Sunday-school union. II. Title. III. Title: Desert wanderings from Egypt to Canaan.

HAUGHTON, Rosemary. 221.92
The young Moses. Illustrated by the author. New York, Roy Publishers [1966] 136 p. illus. 21 cm. The boyhood of Moses of the Bullrushes, who grew up to lead the Jews out of Egypt back to their intended country. [BS580.M6H368] AC 67
1. Moses. 2. Egypt—Social life and customs—To 640 A.D. I. Title.

HUBBARD, Elbert, 1856-1915. 920.
Little journeys to the homes of great teachers ... written by Elbert Hubbard ... East Aurora, N.Y., The Roycrofters, 1908. 2 v. ports. 20 1/2 cm. (His Little journeys, vol. xxii-xxiii) Originally issued in monthly parts. Contents.[book 1] Moses. Confucius. Pythagoras. Plato. King Alfred. Friedrich Froebel.--[vook 2] Booker T. Washington. Thomas Arnold. Erasmus. Hypatia. St. Bendeict. Mary Baker Eddy. [CT101.H8 vol. 22, 23] 8-34965
1. Moses. 2. Confucious. 3. Pythagoras. 4. Plato. 5. Alfred the Great, king of England, 849-901. 6. Froebel, Fredrich Wilhelm August, 1782-1852. 7. Washington, Booker Taliaferro, 1859?-1915. 8. Arnold, Thomas, 1795-1842. 9. Erasmus, Desiderius, d. 1536. 0. Hypatia, d. 415. 1. Benedictus, Saint, abbot of Monte Cassino. 2. Eddy, Mrs. Mary (Baker) 1821-1910. I. Title.

KENNEDY, James Hardee 248.4
The commission of Moses and the Christian calling. Grand Rapids, Mich., Eerdmans [c.1964] 74p. 21cm. Five lectures delivered to the Annual Pastors Conference at the New Orleans Baptist Theological Seminary in June of 1962. Bibl. 64-16585 2.00 bds.,
1. Moses. I. Title.

KENNEDY, James Hardee. 248.4
The commission of Moses and the Christian calling. Grand Rapids, Eerdmans [1964] 74 p. 21 cm. "Five lectures delivered to the Annual Pastors Conference at the New Orleans Baptist Theological Seminary in June of 1962." Bibliographical footnotes. [BS580.M6K4] 64-16585
1. Moses. I. Title.

KINNS, Samuel.
Moses and geology; or, The harmony of the Bible with science. Thoroughly rev. and the astronomical facts brought up to date. With a special preface. By Rev. Samuel Kinns ... 9th thousand. London, Paris, New York & Melbourne, Cassell & co., limited, 1886. xxviii, 514 p. col. front., illus., pl. 20 1/2 cm. 4-30763
I. Title.

KLAGSBRUN, Francine. 221.92'4
The story of Moses. New York, Watts [1968] xvii., 171p. map. 22cm. Immortals of phil. & religion) [BS580.M6K55] 68-27403 3.95; 2.96 lib. ed.,
1. Moses. I. Title.

KLAGSBRUN, Francine. 222'.1'0924 B
The story of Moses. London, New York, Franklin Watts Ltd. [1971] xvii, 171 p. map. 23 cm. (Immortals of philosophy and religion) Bibliography: p. v-vii. [BS580.M6K55 1971] 72-180143 ISBN 0-85166-290-0 £1.25
1. Moses. I. Title.

THE life of Moses. 221.92
Written by a friend of little children, particularly for their use. Embellished with eight engravings. New York, W. Burgess, 1830. iv, [5]-108 p. front., plates. 15 cm. [BS580.M6L5] 36-37407
1. Moses.

LONG, Laura. 221.92
The chosen boy; a story of Moses, who led his people from slavery to the Promised Land. Drawings by Clotilde Embree Funk. [1st ed.] Indianapolis, Bobbs-Merrill [1952] 192 p. illus. 20 cm. [BS580.M6L58] 52-10704
1. Moses. I. Title.

LOWRIE, John Marshall, 1817-1867. 221.92
The Hebrew lawgiver. By John M. Lowrie ... Philadelphia, Presbyterian board of publication [1865] 2 v. 18 cm. [BS580.M6L6] 36-37401
1. Moses. I. Presbyterian church in the U. S. A. (Old school) Board of publication. II. Title.

LUZZATTO, Moses Hayyim, 1707-1747.
Moses Haym Luzzatto's Lah-y' shaw-riem tehilaw "Praise for righteousness") tr. from the Hebrew by Rabbi Herbert S. Goldstein and Rebecca Fischel, March 7, 1915. New York, Block publishing company, 1915. 55 p. 17 cm. $0.35. 16-1702
I. Goldstein, Herbert S., tr. II. Fischel, Rebecca, joint tr. III. Title. IV. Title: Lah-y' shaw-riem tehilaw. V. Title: Praise for righteousness.

MEYER, Frederick Brotherton, 1847-1929. 221.92
Moses. the servant of God. Grand Rapids,

Zondervan Pub. House [1954] 189p. 20cm. [BS580.M6M4 1954] 53-13076
1. Moses. I. Title.

MILLER, Basil William, 1897- 221.92
Moses, builder of altars, by Basil Miller. Grand Rapids, Mich., Zondervan publishing house [1943] 2 p. l. [7]-154 p. 20 cm. [BS580.M6M5] 44-24729
1. Moses. I. Title.

MOSES, Edward P.
Moses' primer. Richmond, Va., B. F. Johnson pub. co., 1901. 79 p. illus. 12°. 1-20337
I. Title.

MOSES, God's servant.
Westchester, Ill., Good News Publishers, 1961. 64p. (A 'one evening' condensed book)
1. Moses. I. Meyer, Frederick Brotherton, 1847-1929. II. Series.

NEHER, Andre. 221.92
Moses and the vocation of the Jewish people. Translated by Irene Marinoff. New York, Harper Torchbooks, c1959. 191p. illus. 18cm. (Men of wisdom, MW7) Includes bibliography. [BS580.M6N43] 59-6652
1. Moses. 2. Judaism—Hist.—Ancient period. I. Title.

PEARLMAN, Moshe, 1911- 222'.12'09
Moses; where it all began. Photography by David Harris. [1st American ed.] New York, Abelard-Schuman [1974, c1973] 224 p. illus. 28 cm. "An adaptation of the title The first days of Israel by Moshe Pearlman." [BS580.M6P39 1973] 73-21320 ISBN 0-200-00138-8 8.95
1. Moses. 2. Jews—History—To 953 B.C. 3. Levant—Description and travel—Views. I. Pearlman, Moshe, 1911- The first days of Israel in the footsteps of Moses. II. Title.

PETERSEN, Mark E. 222'.1'0924 B
Moses : man of miracles / Mark E. Petersen. Salt Lake City : Deseret Book Co., 1977. 198 p. ; 24 cm. Includes index. [BS580.M6P445] 77-21553 ISBN 0-87747-651-9 : 4.95
1. Bible. O.T.—Biography. 2. Moses. 3. Mormons and Mormonism—Doctrinal and controversial works.

PETERSHAM, Maud (Fuller) 1890- 221.92
Moses, from the story told in the Old Testament [by] Maud and Miska Petersham. New York, Macmillan, 1958 [c1938] [32] p. illus. 24 cm. Retells the Bible story of Moses, who was hidden from the Egyptians as a baby, and who led his people across the Red Sea and into the wilderness in search of the Promised Land. [BS580.M6P45 1958] AC 68
1. Moses. 2. Bible stories—Old Testament. I. Petersham, Miska, 1888- joint author. II. Title.

PINKERTON, Frank C. 221.92
... The man Moses. New York, The Paebar company, 1945. 3 p. l., ix-xvii p., 2 l., 132 p. 21 cm. "First edition." [BS580.M6P5] 45-5370
1. Moses. 2. Christianity—20th cent. I. Title.

RAD, Gerhard von, 1901- 221.92
Moses. New York, Association Press [1960?] 80p. 19cm. (World Christian books, no. 32. Second series) [BS580.M6R23] 60-8945
1. Moses. I. Title.

RAWLINSON, George, 1812-1902. 221.
... Moses, his life and times, by George Rawlinson ... New York, Chicago [etc.] F. H. Revell company [pref. 1887] viii, 205 p. 20 cm. (Men of the Bible ... ed. by J. S. Exell) [BS580.M R] A 13
1. Moses. I. Title.

ROSHWALD, Mordecai, 1921- 222'.1'0924
Moses: leader, prophet, man; the story of Moses and his image through the ages [by] Mordecai and Miriam Roshwald. New York, T. Yoseloff [1969] 233 p. illus. 22 cm. Bibliography: p. 215-228. [BS580.M6R62] 69-15773 6.00
1. Moses. I. Roshwald, Miriam, joint author. II. Title.

ROYCE, G. Monroe.
The son of Amram ... New York, T. Whittaker [1901] 324 p. 12 degrees. "An attempt, in the form of fiction, at a true and complete account of Moses and the beginnings of Israel."--Pref. May
I. Title.

SCHULTZ, Samuel J. 225.9'5
The gospel of Moses [by] Samuel J. Schultz. [1st ed.] New York, Harper & Row [1974] x, 165 p. 21 cm. Bibliography: p. 66-67. [BS635.2.S32 1974] 74-4619 ISBN 0-06-067132-7 ISBN 0-06-067132-7 5.95
1. Moses. 2. Bible—History of Biblical events. I. Title.
Pbk. 2.95, ISBN 0-06-067133-5.

SCHULTZ, Samuel J. 221.6
The gospel of moses / Samuel J. Schultz. Chicago : Moody Press, 1979, c1974. x, 165 p. ; 22 cm. Original ed. published by Harper & Row, New York. Bibliography: p. 66-67. [BS635.2.S32 1979] 78-11662 ISBN 0-8024-3197-6 : 5.95
1. Moses. 2. Bible—History of Biblical events. I. Title.

SCHURE, Edouard, 1841-1929. 291.6
The mysteries of ancient Egypt: Hermes/Moses. Introd. by Paul M. Allen. Blauvelt, N.Y., Rudolf Steiner Publications [1971] 11-134 p. 18 cm. (Steinerbooks) Published also in 1961 as the 3d and 4th chapters of the author's The great initiates which was G. Rasberry's translation of Les grands inities. Includes bibliographical references. [BL2441.S3513] 72-150260 1.45
1. Moses. 2. Egypt—Religion. I. Schure, Edouard, 1841-1929. Les grands inities. Moses. English. 1971. II. Title. III. Title: Hermes/Moses.

SILVER, Daniel Jeremy. 222'.10924
Images of Moses / Daniel Jeremy Silver. New York : Basic Books, c1982. p. cm. Includes index. [BS580.M6S483 1982] 19 82-72386 ISBN 0-465-03201-X : 15.95
1. Moses (Biblical leader) 2. Bible. O.T. Pentateuch—Criticism, interpretation, etc.—History. I. Title.

SMITH, Daniel, 1806-1852. 221.92
The life of Moses. By the Rev. Daniel Smith... New York, Pub. by T. Mason and G. Lane, for the Sunday school union of the Methodist Episcopal church, 1839. 224 p. incl. plates. front. 14 cm. (On cover: S[unday] s[chool] & y[ouths] library. 189) [BS580.M6S5] 36-37405
1. Moses. I. Sunday school union of the Methodist Episcopal church. II. Title.

SOUTHON, Arthur Eustace, 1887- 221.92
On eagles' wings. New York, McGraw-Hill [1954, c1939] 296 p. 21 cm. The story of Moses. [BS580.M6S55 1954] 53-12057
1. Moses. I. Title.

STEFFENS, Joseph Lincoln, 1866- 221.
Moses in red; the revolt of Israel as a typical revolution, by Lincoln Steffens. Philadelphia, Dorrance and company [c1926] 144 p. 20 cm. [BS580.M6S7] 26-17842
1. Moses. 2. Jews—Hist.—To B. C. 953. 3. Revolutions. I. Title.

STOCK, Augustine. 234
The way in the wilderness; Exodus, wilderness, and Moses themes in Old Testament and New. Collegeville, Minn., Liturgical Press [1969] xii, 156 p. 23 cm. Bibliographical footnotes. [BS680.E9S86] 72-13548 4.75
1. Moses. 2. Exodus, The—Biblical teaching. I. Title.

SZEKELY, Edmond Bordeaux. 222'.11
The Essene book of creation; our spiritual heritage for the space age. [San Diego, Calif.] First Christians' (Essene) Church, 1968. 71 p. illus., port. 31 cm. Contents.Contents.—Genesis; an Essene interpretation.—Moses; a modern revaluation. [BS580.M6S9] 74-14717
1. Moses. 2. Bible. O.T. Genesis I-III—Criticism, interpretation, etc. I. Title.

TAYLOR, William Mackergo, 1829-1895. 221.92
Moses, the law-giver, by the Rev. William M. Taylor ... New York and London, Harper & brothers, 1905. iv p., 1 l., [7]-482 p. front. 19 cm. [BS580.M6T3 1905] 13-23937
1. Moses. I. Title.

TAYLOR, William Mackergo, 1829-1895. 221.
Moses the law-giver, by the Rev. William M. Taylor ... New York and London, Harper & brothers, 1907. iv p., 1 l., [7]-482 p. front. 19 1/2 cm. [BS580.M6T3 1907] 7-9584
1. Moses. I. Title.

THURBER, Robert Bruce, 1882- 221.
...The story of Moses, by Robert Bruce Thurber. Nashville, Tenn., Atlanta, Ga. [etc.] Southern publishing association [c1924] 64 p. incl. col. front., col. illus. 19 1/2 cm. (Bible stories series, no. 2) [BS580.M6T4] 25-5743
1. Moses. I. Title.

TIEDE, David Lenz. 291.2'11
The charismatic figure as miracle worker. [Missoula? Mont.] Published by Society of Biblical Literature for the Seminar on the Gospels, 1972. vi, 324 p. 22 cm. (Society of Biblical Literature. Dissertation series, no. 1) Originally presented as the author's thesis, Harvard. Bibliography: p. 293-312. [BJ1521.T48 1972] 72-87359
1. Moses. 2. Jesus Christ—Person and offices. 3. Virtue. 4. Miracles. I. Title. II. Series.

TODD, John, 1800-1873. 221.92
Questions on the life of Moses. Embracing the books of Exodus, Leviticus, Numbers, and Deuteronomy. By John Todd... Northampton, Mass., Hopkins, Bridgman & co.; Boston, Massachusetts Sabbath school society; [etc., etc.] 1858. 144 p. 14 1/2 cm. [BS580.M6T6] 36-37406
1. Moses. I. Title.

WADIA, Ardaser Sorabjee N. 1882- 221.92
The message of Moses, by Ardaser Sorabjee N. Wadia ... with frontispiece by E. J. Sullivan ... London and Toronto, J. M. Dent & sons, ltd.; New York, E. P. Dutton & co., inc. [1929] xiv, 100 p. incl. map. front. 18 cm. (Half-title: Message series, no. 4) "First published 1929." [BS580.M6W3] 34-8089
1. Moses. 2. Jews—Religion. I. Title.

WEE, Mons Olson, 1871- 221.
Moses, faith in decision, by M. O. Wee... Minneapolis, Minn., Augsburg publishing house [c1929] 122, [4] p. illus. 20 cm. "In part, a translation from a previously printed Norwegian text,--somewhat revised."--Pref. Bibliography: p. [125] [BS580.M6W4] 29-23809
1. Moses. I. Title.

WEISFELD, Israel Harold, 1906- 221.92
This man Moses, by Israel H. Weisfeld. New York, Bloch Pub. Co. [1966] xxii, 234 p. illus. 25 cm. Bibliography: p. [229]-230. [BS580.M6W43] 66-24260
1. Moses. I. Title.

WILLIAMSON, Adolph Ancrum, 1883- 221.92
Moses, who first saw our pyramid of life; a grand philosophy of evolution. New York, Philosophical Library [1950] viii, 231 p. 23 cm. Bibliography: p.229-231. [BS580.M6W5] 50-1115
1. Moses. I. Title.

Moses—Art.

MELLINKOFF, Ruth. 246'.55
The horned Moses in medieval art and thought. Berkeley, University of California Press, 1970. xix, 210 p. 130 illus. 27 cm. (California studies in the history of art, 14) Bibliography: p. 185-201. [BL604.H6M44] 77-85450 ISBN 0-520-01705-6 16.50
1. Moses—Art. 2. Horns (in religion, folk-lore, etc.) I. Title. II. Series.

NEWMAN, Louis Israel, 1893-
From the Nile to Mount Pisgah. An oratorio on the life of Moses. New York, Congregation Rodeph Sholom, 1965. 26 p. 19 cm. 67-51256
I. New York. Congregation Rodeph Sholom. II. Title.

Moses ben Maimon, 1135-1204.

ABRAVANEL, Isaac, 1437-1508. 200
Maimonides and Abrabanel on prophecy, by Alvin Jay Reines. Cincinnati, Hebrew Union College Press, 1970. lxxxi, 239 p. 24 cm. Translation of selections from Perush 'al Sefer Moreh nevukhim (romanized form) Includes bibliographical references. [BS1198.A2713] 73-119106
1. Moses ben Maimon, 1135-1204. Dalalat al-ha'irin. 2. Prophets. I. Reines, Alvin Jay, 1926- ed. II. Title.

BOKSER, Ben Zion, 1907- 181.3
The legacy of Maimonides. [Rev. ed.] New York, Hebrew Pub. Co. [1962] 146p. illus. 24cm. 62-37013 2.50
1. Moses ben Maimon, 1135-1204. I. Title.

BRATTON, Fred Gladstone, 1896- 296.1'72
Maimonides, medieval modernist. Boston, Beacon Press [1967] ix, 159 p. 21 cm. Bibliography: p. 152-154. [BM755.M6B7] 67-24893
1. Moses ben Maimon, 1135-1204. I. Title.

BURSTEIN, Abraham, 1893- 921.9
The boy of Cordova; an incident in the youth of Moses Maimonides, by Abraham Burstein; illustrated by Reuben Leaf. New York, Bloch publishing co., 1935. xx, 124 p. front., plates. 19 cm. "First printing." [BM755.M6B8] 35-6212
1. Moses ben Malmon, 1135-1204 I. Leaf, Reuben, illus. II. Title.

EFROS, Israel Isaac, 1890- 181'.3'03
Philosophical terms in the Moreh nebukim, by Israel Efros. New York, AMS Press, 1966 [c1924] xi, 157 p. 23 cm.Original ed. issued as v. 22 of Columbia University oriental studies. "Notes by Prof. Louis Ginzberg": p. [127]-144. [BM545.D35E33 1966] 72-185386
1. Moses ben Maimon, 1135-1204. Dalalat al-ha'irin. 2. Philosophy—Dictionaries—Hebrew. I. Ginzberg, Louis, 1873-1953. II. Title. III. Series: Columbia University oriental studies, v. 22.

ELEFANT, William L. 296.6'1 B
The educational ideas and related philosophical concepts in the writings of Maimonides, by William L. Elefant. 1972. vi, 166, 3 l. 28 cm. Thesis—University of Denver. Photocopy of typescript. Bibliography: leaves 165-166. [BM755.M6E4 1972] 73-154594
1. Moses ben Maimon, 1135-1204. I. Title.

ESSAYS on Maimonides; 189
an octocentennial volume. Edited by Salo Wittmayer Baron. New York, AMS Press, 1966 [c1941] 316 p. 24 cm. Includes bibliographical references. [B759.M34E8 1966] 296'.01 79-160004
1. Moses ben Maimon, 1135-1204. I. Moses ben Maimon, 1135-1204. II. Baron, Salo Wittmayer, 1895- ed.

FELSHIN, Max, 1895- 921.9
Moses Maimonides, Rambam. New York, Book Guild, 1956. 205p. 21cm. [BM755.M6F4] 57-59236
1. Moses ben Maimon, 1135-1204. I. Title.

[GINZBERG, Asher] 1856-1927.
... The supremacy of reason, by Achad Ha-Am [pseud.] Translated from the Hebrew by Leon Simon ... New York city, Maimonides octocentennial committee, 1935. 52 p. 23 cm. (Maimonides octocentennial series, no. i) A38

1. Moses ben Maimon, 1135-1204. 2. Reason. I. Simon, Leon, 1881- tr. II. Title.

GOLDMAN, Solomon, 1893- 181.3
The Jew and the universe, by Solomon Goldman. New York and London, Harper & brothers, 1936. xi p., 1 l., 184 p., 1 l., 185-257 p. 21 cm. [B755.G6] 36-21330
1. Moses ben Maimon, 1135-1204. 2. Philosophy, Jewish. I. Title.

GOLDMAN, Solomon, 1893- 181'.3
1953.
The Jew and the universe. New York, Arno Press, 1973 [c1936] xi, 257 p. 23 cm. (The Jewish people: history, religion, literature) Reprint of the ed. published by Harper, New York. Includes bibliographical references. [B755.G6 1973] 73-2200 ISBN 0-405-05265-0 15.00
1. Moses ben Maimon, 1135-1204. 2. Philosophy, Jewish. I. Title. II. Series.

HARTMAN, David. 181'.3
Maimonides : Torah and philosophic quest / David Hartman ; foreword by Shlomo Pines. 1st ed. Philadelphia : Jewish Publication Society of America, 1976. xv, 296 p. ; 22 cm. Includes index. Bibliography: p. 269-288. [B759.M34H36] 76-6305 ISBN 0-8276-0083-6 : 7.95
1. Moses ben Maimon, 1135-1204. 2. Philosophy, Jewish. 3. Philosophy, Medieval. 4. Jewish law—Philosophy. I. Title.

JEWISH Theological 016.2961'72
Seminary of America. Library.
Maimonides' Mishneh Torah : a collection of manuscripts from the Library of the Jewish Theological Seminary : an index to the microfilm collection, reels 1-9. Ann Arbor, Mich. : University Microfilms International, 1980. vii, 20 p. ; 28 cm. Added t. p.: Mishneh Torah leha-Rambam. [Z6374.L4J48 1980] [BM520.84.A2] 19 80-23113 ISBN 0-8357-0530-7 : 21.00
1. Moses ben Maimon, 1135-1204. Mishneh Torah—Manuscripts—Catalogs. 2. Jewish Theological Seminary of America. Library—Catalogs. 3. Jewish law—Bibliography—Catalogs. 4. Manuscripts, Hebrew—New York (City)—Catalogs. I. Title. II. Title: Mishneh Torah leha-Rambam.

KLEIN, Carol. 181.3
The credo of Maimonides, a synthesis. New York, Philosophical Library [1958] 143p. 23cm. Includes bibliography. [B759.M34K55] 58-2115
1. Moses ben Malmon, 1135-1204. I. Title.

KLEIN, Carol. 181.3
The credo of Maimonides, a synthesis. New York, Philosophical Library [1958] 143p. 23cm. Includes bibliography. [B759.M34K55] 58-2115
1. Moses ben Malmon, 1135-1204. I. Title.

KOHUT, Alexander, 1842- 24-17624
1894.
Notes on a hitherto unknown exegetical, theological and philosophical commentary to the Pentateuch composed by Aboo Manzur al Dhameri with appendices containing Hebrew and Arabic extracts. A contribution to the critical study of Maimuni's writings, by Alexander Kohut ... [New York city, A Ginsberg, printer, 1892] 56, xxxviii p. diagr. 22 cm. "Appendix the first. Hebrew selections from Aboo Manzur al Dhamari's Hebrew-Arablc commentary: p. 1-xxi. Appendix the second. Arabic selections from the Sirag al-akul ... of Aboo Manzur al-Dhamari": p. [xxxviii. [BS1225.K65]
1. Moses ben Maimon, 1135-1204 2. Bible. O. T. Pentateuch—Commentaries. 3. Bible—Commentaries—O. T. Pentateuch. I. Abu Manzur al-Dhamari. II. Title.

MAIMONIDES 296.6'1'0924 B
octocentennial series, numbers I-IV. New York, Arno Press, 1973. 52, 27, 32, 31 p. 23 cm. (The Jewish people: history, religion, literature) Reprint of The supremacy of reason, by Achad ha-am; Moses Maimonides, by Alexander Marx; Maimonides as codifier, by Chaim Tchernowitz; and of The philosophy of Maimonides, by Isaac Husik; all published by Maimonides Octocentennial Committee, New York, 1935. [BM755.M6M276] 73-2214 ISBN 0-405-05278-2 9.00
1. Moses ben Maimon, 1135-1204. I. Ginzberg, Asher, 1856-1927. Al parashat derakhim. Shilton ha-sekhel. English. 1973. II. Marx, Alexander, 1878-1953. Moses Maimonides. 1973. III. Tchernowitz, Chaim, 1870-1949. Maimonides as codifier. 1973. IV. Husik, Isaac, 1876-1939. The philosophy of Maimonides. 1973. V. Title. VI. Series.

MELBER, Jehuda. 181.3
The universality of Maimonides. [Brighton? Mass., c1960] 158, 3 l. 28cm. Copyright date stamped on t. p. Bibliography: 3 l. at end. [B759.M34M4] 60-45998
1. Moses ben Malmon, 1135-1204. I. Title.

MELBER, Jehuda. 181.3
The universality of Maimonides. [Brighton? Mass., c1960] 158, 3 l. 28cm. Copyright date stamped on t. p. Bibliography: 3 l. at end. [B759.M34M4] 60-45998
1. Moses ben Malmon, 1135-1204. I. Title.

MELBER, Jehuda. 181'.3
The universality of Maimonides. New York, Jonathan David [1968] 174 p. 22 cm. Includes bibliographical references. [B759.M34M4 1968] 68-19959
1. Moses ben Maimon, 1135-1204. I. Title.

MINKIN, Jacob Samuel, 1885- 181.3
The world of Moses Maimonides, with selections from his writings. New York, T. Yoseloff [1957] 448p. 24cm. 'Chronology of the life and works of Moses Maimonides': p. 428-431. Bibliography: p. 432-434. Bibliographical references included in 'Notes' (p. 435-440) [BM755.M6M5] 57-7874
1. Moses ben Maimon, 1135-1204. I. Moses ben Maimon, 1135-1204. Selections. II. Title.

MOSES ben Maimon, 1135- 181'.3
1204.
Rambam : readings in the philosophy of Moses Maimonides / selected and translated, with introduction and commentary, by Lenn Evan Goodman. New York : Viking Press, [1975] p. cm. (The Jewish heritage classics) Includes index. Bibliography: p. [B759.M32E5 1975] 75-14476 ISBN 0-670-58964-0 : 12.50
1. Moses ben Maimon, 1135-1204. 2. Philosophy, Jewish. 3. Philosophy, Medieval. 4. Ethics, Jewish. I. Goodman, Lenn Evan, 1944- II. Title. III. Series.

MOSES ben Maimon, 1135- 181'.3
1204.
Rambam : readings in the philosophy of Moses Maimonides / selected and translated with introd. and commentary by Lenn Evan Goodman. New York : Schocken Books, 1977, c1976. xiv, 444 p. ; 21 cm. Selections from the author's Dalalat al-ha'irin and Thamaniyat fusul. Includes index. Bibliography: p. [B759.M33D3132 1977] 76-48856 ISBN 0-8052-0569-1 pbk. : 5.95
1. Moses ben Maimon, 1135-1204. 2. Philosophy, Jewish. 3. Philosophy, Medieval. 4. Ethics, Jewish. I. Goodman, Lenn Evan, 1944- II. Moses ben Maimon, 1135-1204. Thamaniyat fusul. English. Selections. 1977. III. Title. IV. Title: Readings in the philosophy of Moses Maimonides.

MUNZ, Isak, 1857- 921.9
Maimonides (The Rambam) the story of his life and genius, by Dr. J. Munz; translated from the German, with an introduction, by Henry T. Schnittkind, PH. D. Octocentennial ed.: 1935. Boston, Winchell-Thomas company [c1935] 3 p. l., xiii-xxx, 238 p. 21 cm. (Half-title: The Jewish bookshelf) [BM755.M6M82] 35-3983
1. Moses ben Maimon, 1135-1204. I. Schnittkind, Henry Thomas 1888 tr Translation of Moses ben Maimon maimonides) II. Title.

SARACHEK, Joseph, 1892- 181'.3
Faith and reason; the conflict over the rationalism of Maimonides, by Joseph Sarachek. New York, Hermon Press [1970] 285 p. 24 cm. Reprint of the 1935 ed. Bibliography: p. 275-278. [B759.M34S27 1970] 77-136766 ISBN 0-87203-024-5 9.75
1. Moses ben Maimon, 1135-1204. 2. Judaism—History—Medieval and early modern period, 425-1789. 3. Philosophy, Jewish. 4. Philosophy, Medieval. 5. Faith and reason.

SARACHEK, Joseph, 1892- 181.3
... *Faith and reason:* the conflict over the rationalism of Maimonides, by Joseph Sarachek ... Williamsport, Pa., The Bayard press, 1935- v. 21 cm. (Oriental series) Vol. 1 issued also as thesis (PH. D.) Columbia university. Bibliography: vol. I, p. 275-278. [BM755.M6S3] 36-9650
1. Moses ben Maimon, 1135-1204. 2. Jews—Religion. 3. Philosophy, Jewish. 4. Philosophy, Medieval. 5. Philosophy and religion. 6. Religion and science—1900- I. Title. II. Title: The rationalism of Maimonides.

SILVER, Daniel Jeremy 296.172
Maimonidean criticism and the Maimonidean controversy, 1180-1240. Leiden, E. J. Brill [dist. Cleveland, Temple Lib., Univ. Circle at Silver Park [c.]1965.
1. Moses ben Maimon, 1135-1204. I. Title.

TWERSKY, Isadore. 296.1'72
Introduction to the Code of Maimonides (Mishneh Torah) / by Isadore Twersky. New Haven : Yale University Press, 1980. p. cm. (Yale Judaica series ; v. 22) Includes index. Bibliography: p. [BM520.84.T83 1980] 79-10347 ISBN 0-300-02319-7 : 40.00
1. Moses ben Maimon, 1135-1204. Mishneh Torah. 2. Jewish law. 3. Philosophy, Jewish. I. Title. II. Series.

YELLIN, David, 1864- 922.
Maimonides; by David Yellin and Israel Abrahams. Philadelphia, Jewish publication society of America, 1903. xii, 239 p. front. (port.) 3 pl., 2 facsim. 19 cm. Based on Yellin's Warsaw, 1898. ("Tushiah" series) [BM755.M6Y4] 3-15368
1. Moses ben Maimon, 1135-1204. I. Abrahams, Israel, 1858-1925 joint author II. Jewish publication society of America. III. Title.

YELLIN, David, 296.6'1'0924 B
1864-1941.
Maimonides: his life and works, by David Yellin and Israel Abrahams. 3d rev. ed., with introd., bibliography and supplementary notes, by Jacob I. Dienstag. New York, Hermon Press [1972 i.e. 1973] xxxiv, 193 p. illus. 20 cm. Reprint of the 1903 ed. published by Jewish Publication Society of America, Philadelphia; with new material. Bibliography: p. xvii-xxix. [BM755.M6Y4 1972] 72-83937 ISBN 0-87203-031-8 7.95
1. Moses ben Maimon, 1135-1204. I. Abrahams, Israel, 1858-1925, joint author.

ZEITLIN, Solomon, 1892- 921.9
Maimonides, a biography. 2d ed. New York, Bloch Pub. Co., 1955. 234p. illus. 21cm. [B759.M34Z4 1955] 55-8133
1. Moses ben Maimon, 1135-1204. I. Title.

ZEITLIN, Solomon, 1892- 921.9
Maimonides; a biography, by Solomon Zeitlin, PH.D. New York, Bloch publishing co., 1935. xi, 234 p. front. (port.) facsim. 21 cm. Bibliographical references in "Notes" (p. 216-223) [B759.M34Z4] 35-6282
1. Moses ben Maimon, 1135-1204. I. Title.

Moses ben Maimon, 1135-1204—Addresses, essays, lectures.

MOSES ben Maimon, 296.6'1'0924 B
1135-1204.
Letters of Maimonides / translated and edited with introductions and notes by Leon D. Stitskin. New York : Yeshiva University Press, 1977. 199 p. ; 24 cm. Includes bibliographical references. [BM545.A45S8 1977] 77-78152 ISBN 0-89362-006-8 : 10.00
1. Moses ben Maimon, 1135-1204—Addresses, essays, lectures. 2. Judaism—Addresses, essays, lectures. 3. Rabbis—Egypt—Biography—Addresses, essays, lectures. I. Stitskin, Leon D.

Moses ben Maimon, 1135-1204. Dalalat al-ha'irin.

EFROS, Israel Isaac, 1890- 181.
... *Philosophical terms in the Moreh nebukim,* by Israel Efros, PH. D. New York, Columbia university press, 1924. xi p., 1 l., 157 p. 24 cm. (Columbia university oriental studies, vol. xxii) "Notes by Prof. Louis Ginzberg": p. 129-144. "Works consulted": p. [ix]-x. [B759.M34E4] [PJ25.C6] 203 25-1408
1. Moses ben Malmon, 1135-1204. Dainlatal-ba'Irin. 2. Philosophy—Terminology. 3. Hebrew language, Post-Biblical—Terms and phrases. I. Ginsberg, Louis, 1873- II. Title.

EFROS, Israel Isaac, 1890- 181.
... *Philosophical terms in the Moreh nebukim,* by Israel Efros, PH. D. New York, Columbia university press, 1924. xi p., 1 l., 157 p. 24 cm. (Columbia university oriental studies, vol. xxii) "Notes by Prof. Louis Ginzberg": p. 129-144. "Works consulted": p. [ix]-x. [B759.M34E4] [PJ25.C6] 203 25-1408
1. Moses ben Malmon, 1135-1204. Dainlatal-ba'lrin. 2. Philosophy—Terminology. 3. Hebrew language, Post-Biblical—Terms and phrases. I. Ginsberg, Louis, 1873- II. Title.

ROTH, Leon, 1896- 181.3
The guide for the perplexed [by] Moses Maimonides. London, New York, Hutchinson's University Library [1948] 141 p. 19 cm. (Hutchinson's university library: Jewish religion, 11) Bibliography: p. 135. [BM545.D35R6] 50-13601
1. Moses ben Maimon, 1135-1204. Dalalat al-ha'irin. 2. Philosophy, Jewish. 3. Philosophy, Medieval. 4. Jews—Religion. I. Title.

Moses ben Maimon, 1135-1204—Juvenile literature.

MARCUS, Rebecca B. 296.6'1'0924 B
Moses Maimonides: rabbi, philosopher, and physician, by Rebecca B. Marcus. New York, F. Watts [1969] ix, 114 p. illus., facsims., ports. 22 cm. (Immortals of philosophy and religion) Bibliography: p. 108-109. A biography of the Spanish-born Jewish philosopher, rabbi, and physician of the Middle Ages who spent a good deal of his life in Egypt and whose works influenced the thinking of Jews, Christians, and Moslems. [BM755.M6M28] 92 69-12594 3.95
1. Moses ben Maimon, 1135-1204—Juvenile literature. 2. [Moses ben Maimon, 1135-1204.] I. Title.

Moses ben Nahman, ca. 1195-ca. 1270.

CHAVEL, Charles Ber, 296.0924
1906-
Ramban, his life and teachings. New York, P. Feldheim [c1960] 128 p. 23 cm. Includes bibliography. [BM755.M62C4] 63-1543
1. Moses ben Nahman, ca. 1195-ca. 1270. I. Title.

Moses—Fiction.

HASKIN, Dorothy (Clark) 221.92
1905-
The royal brickyard. Grand Rapids, Baker Book House, 1959. 69p. 21cm. (Valor series, 4) [BS580.M6H36] 59-15529
1. Moses—Fiction. I. Title.

Moses, ha-Kohen, of Tordesillas.

SHAMIR, Yehuda, 1936- 296.3
Rabbi Moses ha-Kohen of Tordesillas and his book 'Ezer ha-emunah—a chapter in the history of the Judeo-Christian controversy. Coconut Grove, Fla., Field Research Projects, 1972. 2 v. map. 28 cm. Vol. 2 "includes the [Hebrew] text of Sefer 'Ezer ha-emunah and an appendix presenting Sefer 'Ezer ha-dat." Bibliography: v. 1, p. 223-236. [BM648.M673S52] 72-172722
1. Moses, ha-Kohen, of Tordesillas. 2. Abner of Burgos. 3. Judaism—Apologetic works. I. Moses, ha-Kohen, of Tordesillas. 'Ezer ha-emunah. 1972. II. Title: 'Ezer ha-emunah. III. Ti

Moses, Helen Elizabeth (Turney) 1853-1906.

MOSES, Jasper Turney, 1880- ed. 922
Helen E. Moses, of the Christian woman's board of missions; bio- graphical sketch, memorial tributes, missionary addresses by Mrs. Moses, sonnets and other verses; ed. by Jasper T. Moses ... New York, Chicago [etc.] F. H. Revell company [1909] 192 p. front., ports. 20 cm. [BV3705.M77M6] 9-27019
1. Moses, Helen Elizabeth (Turney) 1853-1906. I. Title.

Moses — Juvenile literature.

DOLAN, William M 211.9
Moses and the liberation from Egypt. Garden City, N.Y. [Coubleday, 1962] 64 p.illus. 21 cm. (The Catholic know-your-Bible-program) [BS580.M6D59] 63-3128
1. Moses — Juvenile literature. 2. Bible stories, English — O.T. — Exodus. I. Title.

GREENE, Carla, 1906- 92 (j)
Moses; the great lawgiver. Illustrated by Anne Lewis. Irvington-on-Hudson, N.Y., Harvey House [1968] 45 p. illus. 27 cm. [BS580.M6G72] 68-22985 2.95
1. Moses—Juvenile literature. I. Title.

KLAGSBRUN, Francine. 222'.1'0924 B
The story of Moses. New York, F. Watts [1968] vxii, 171 p. map. 22 cm. (Immortals of philosophy and religion) Presents the life and teachings of the prophet and lawgiver who, after a revelation from God, devoted his life to leading his people out of slavery to the promised land. [BS580.M6K55] 68-27403 3.95
1. Moses—Juvenile literature. 2. [Moses.] 3. [Prophets.] I. Title.

LIBBEY, Scott 222.1095
Rebels and God. Illus. by Shirley Hirsch. [Philadelphia] United Church [1964] 89p. illus. (pt. col.) 22cm. Pt. of the United Church curriculum, prepared, pub by the Div. of Christian Educ. and the Div. of Pubn. of the United Church Bd. for Homeland Ministries. 64-14494 1.50
1. Paul, Saint, apostle—Juvenile literature. 2. Moses—Juvenile literature. I. United Church for Homeland Ministries. Division of Christian Education. II. United Church of Christ. III. United Church Board Division of Publication. IV. Title.

MACMASTER, Eve, 1942- 222'.109505
Moses, the servant of God : stories of God and His people : Exodus, Leviticus, Numbers, and Deuteronomy / retold by Eve B. MacMaster ; illustrated by James Converse. Scottdale, Pa. : Herald Press, 1982. p. cm. (Story Bible series ; bk. 2) [BS580.M6M28] 19 82-2849 ISBN 0-8361-1994-0 (pbk.) : 5.95
1. Moses (Biblical leader)—Juvenile literature. 2. Bible stories, English—O.T. Pentateuch. I. Title. II. Series.

MUNOWITZ, Ken. 222'.1'0924 B
Moses, Moses / pictures by Ken Munowitz ; text by Charles L. Mee, Jr.. 1st ed. New York : Harper & Row, c1977. [32] p. : ill. ; 26 cm. Retells the early events in the life of Moses. [BS580.M6M8 1977] 76-41516 ISBN 0-06-024178-0 : 4.95. lib.bdg. : 4.79
1. Bible. O.T.—Biography—Juvenile literature. 2. Moses—Juvenile literature. 3. [Moses.] 4. [Bible stories—O.T.] I. Mee, Charles L. II. Title.

SAPORTA, Raphael, 1913- 222
A basket in the reeds. Illus. by H. Hechtkopf. Minneapolis, Lerner [1965, c.1964] 1v. (unpaged) col. illus. 31cm. [BS580.M6S32] 64-25640 3.79
1. Moses—Juvenile literature. I. Hechtkopf, H., illus. II. Title.

YOUNG, William Edgar, 1928- 222'.1'0924 B
Moses : God's helper / William E. Young ; illustrated by J. William Myers. Nashville : Broadman Press, c1976. 48 p. : col. ill. ; 24 cm. (Biblearn series) Discusses the life of Moses who led the Hebrews out of Eygpt and received the Ten Commandments from God. [BS580.M6Y68] 76-382766 ISBN 0-8054-4225-1 : 3.95
1. Moses—Juvenile literature. 2. [Moses.] 3. Bible. O.T.—Biography—Juvenile literature. 4. [Bible stories—O.T.] I. Myers, James William. II. Title.

Moses—Legends.

WIESEL, Elie, 1928- 221.9'22 B
Messengers of God : Biblical portraits and legends / Elie Wiesel ; translated from the French by Marion Wiesel. 1st American ed. New York : Random House, c1976. xiv, 237 p. ; 22 cm. Translation of Celebration biblique. Bibliography: p. 237. [BM516.W513 1976] 75-43425 ISBN 0-394-49740-6 : 8.95
1. Moses—Legends. 2. Job, the patriarch. 3. Midrash—Legends. 4. Bible. O.T. Genesis—Legends. 5. Aggada. 6. Tales, Hasidic. I. Title.

Mosques—Addresses, essays, lectures.

NIYAZI, Kausar. 297'.65
Role of the mosque / Kausar Niazi. 1st ed. Lahore : Sh. Muhammad Ashraf, 1976. 40 p. ; 22 cm. Includes quotations from the Koran and Hadith. Paper read at the conference organized by the Rabitat al-'Alam al-Islami at Mecca, 1974. Bibliography: p. 39-40. [BP187.6.A1N59] 76-938560 Rs4.00
1. Mosques—Addresses, essays, lectures. I. Title.

Motazilites.

FRANK, Richard M. 181'.07
Beings and their attributes : the teaching of the Basrian school of the Mu'tazila in the classical period / Richard MacDonough Frank. Albany : State University of New York Press, 1978. 216 p. ; 24 cm. (Studies in Islamic philosophy and science) Includes bibliographical references and indexes. [BP195.M6F73] 78-6957 ISBN 0-87395-378-9 : 25.00
1. Motazilites. 2. Islamic theology—History. 3. Ontology. I. Title. II. Series.

Mother-goddesses.

JAMES, Edwin Oliver, 1886- 291.211
The cult of the mother-goddess; an archaeological and documentary study. New York, Barnes & Noble [1961, c.1959] 300p. Bibl. 61-3056 6.50
1. Mother-goddesses. I. Title.

JAMES, Edwin Oliver, 1886- 291.211
The cult of the mother goddess; an archaeological and documentary study. New York, Praeger [1959] 300 p. 23 cm. (Books that matter) Includes bibliography. [BL325.M6J3 1959] 59-8623
1. Mother-goddesses. I. Title.

NEUMANN, Erich. 291.214
The great mother; an analysis of the archetype. Translated from th e German by Ralph Manheim. [New York] Pantheon Books [1955] xiiii, 380p. illus. 27cm. (Bollingen series, 47) Bibliography: p. 339-352. [BL85.N4] 55-10026
1. Mother-goddesses. 2. Religions. I. Title. II. Series.

NEUMANN, Erich.
The great mother; an analysis of the archetype. Translated from the German by Ralph Manheim. [2d ed. New York] Pantheon Books [1963] xliii, 381 p. illus. (Bollingen series, 47) Includes bibliography. 65-55993
1. Mother-goddesses. 2. Religions. I. Title.

PATAI, Raphael, 1910- 296.3'11
The Hebrew goddess. [New York] Ktav Pub. House [1968, c1967] 349 p. illus. 24 cm. Bibliography: p. 329-336. [BM530.P28] 67-22753
1. Mother-goddesses. 2. Mythology, Jewish. I. Title.

Mother goddesses, Greek.

PRICE, Theodora Hadzisteliou. 292'.2'11
Kourotrophos : cults and representations of the Greek nursing deities / by Theodora Hadzisteliou Price. Leiden : Brill, 1978. xiv, 241 p., 31 p. of plates : ill. ; 25 cm. (Studies of the Dutch Archaeological and Historical Society ; v. 8) Based on the author's thesis, Oxford, 1966. Includes indexes. Bibliography: p. [xi]-xiv. [BL820.M65P74] 78-372726 ISBN 90-040-5251-8 : 50.00
1. Mother goddesses, Greek. I. Title. II. Series: Dutch Archaeological and Historical Society. Studies ; v. 8.
Distributed by Humanities Press, Atlantic Highlands, NJ

Mothers.

BAKER, Joseph Baer, 1877-
Sermons on our mothers and those other heroic, selfsacrificing souls who, from time immemorial, have taken the places and performed the duties of mother, by Rev. Joseph B. Baker ... introduction by Rev. Francis E. Clark ... Philadelphia, Pa., H. M. Shelley [c1926] 5 p. l., 7-125 p. 19 cm. [BV4281.B3] 26-6276
1. Mothers. I. Title.

BYRUM, Isabel Coston, 1870-
The value of a praying mother, by Isabel C. Byrum. Anderson, Ind., Gospel trumpet company [c1911] 173 p. 19 cm. 11-32222 0.50
I. Title.

COOLIDGE, Herbert, 1874- 242
Mother's might and how to use it, by Herbert Coolidge; how mothers may build the body, mind and spirit of the child through prayer. The same principle and method may be applied by anyone of either sex who wishes to minister to the well being of another regardless of age or sex or distance. Holyoke, Mass., The Elizabeth Towne co., inc.; [etc., etc.] 1919. 3 p. l., 5-113 p. front., plates. 19 cm. [BV4529.C6] 20-630
1. Mothers. 2. Prayer. I. Title.

THE faithful mother's reward:
a narrative of the conversion and happy death of J. B. who died in the tenth year of his age. With an introduction, by Rev. Charles Hodge, D. D. Philadelphia, Presbyterian board of publication, 1853. xvi, 323 p. 16 cm. 8-6847

*HUGHES, Elmer R. 220.92
Famous mothers from the Bible and history: the stories of great men and the women behind them. New York, Exposition [c.1963] 156p. 21cm. 3.00
I. Title.

HUGHES, Elmer Ray. 920.7
Famous mothers from the Bible and history; the stories of great men and the women behind them. [1st ed.] New York, Exposition Press [c1963] 156 p. 22 cm. [CT3203.H8] 64-3101
1. Mothers. I. Title.

HUGHES, Elmer Ray 920.02
More famous mothers from the Bible and history, by Elmer R. Hughes. [1st ed] New York, Exposition [1966] 96p. 21cm. Companion vol. to the author's Famous mothers from the Bible and history. [CT3203.H82] 66-31668 3.50
1. Mothers. I. Title.

MACADAM, George. 232.
Mary the mother, and all mothers, in holy lands and all lands, on holy days and all days, by George MacAdam. New York, Cincinnati, The Abingdon press [c1924] 218 p. illus. 19 1/2 cm. [BT601.M15] 25-4632
1. Mary, Virgin. 2. Mothers. I. Title.

MINDSZENTY, Jozsef, Cardinal, 1892- 248
The face of the Heavenly Mother. New York, Philosophical Library [1951] 150 p. 22 cm. Translation, by Charles Donahue, of Mutter in Gottes Augen, originally published in Hungarian as v. 2 of Az edesanya. Name originally: Jozsef Pehm. [BX2353.M553] 51-14179
1. Mothers. I. Title.

MINDSZENTY, Jozsef, Cardinal, 1892- 248
The mother; tr. from the German by Benedict P. Lenz. [American ed.] St. Paul, Radio Replies Press [1949] xix, 160 p. ports. 22 cm. Name originally: Jozsef Pehm. [BX2353.M552] 49-10223
1. Mothers. I. Title.

THORNE, R. A. ed. 173
Beauties of home and the life beyond... Ed. by R. A. Thorne, with an introduction by Rev. Robert Collyer... Chicago, People's publishing company, 1889. xviii p., 1 l., [21]-507 p. incl. col. front. illus. col. plates. 25 cm. [HQ734.T5] 9-6926
1. Mothers. 2. Home. 3. Heaven. I. Title.

THORNE, Rosella A. comp. 173
Treasury of thought. Mother, Home, and Heaven. Selections from the best English and American authors. Comp. by Rosella A. Thorne. With an introduction by Rev. Robert Collyer... New York, Bryan, Taylor & co., 1884. 1 p. l., [iii]-xv, [1], 448 p. front., plates. 25 cm. Pub. in 1889 under title: Beauties of home and the life beyond. [HQ734.T47] 15-12794
1. Mothers. 2. Home. 3. Heaven. I. Title.

VANDER DONCKT, Cyril, 1865-
Christian motherhood and education, adapted mainly from French authorities, by Rev. C. Van der Donckt. New York and Cincinnati, Frederick Protet co. (inc.) 1926. 1 p. l., v-xv, 269 p. 19 1/2 cm. [BX2353.V3] 27-879
1. Mothers. 2. Catholic church—Education. I. Title.

Mother's Day sermons.

BAKER, Joseph Baer, 1877- 252.6
Sermons on our mothers. Grand Rapids, Mich., Baker Bk., 1963. 125p. 20cm. First pub. in 1926 under title: Sermons on our mothers and those other heroic, self-sacrificing souls. 63-12753 1.95 bds.,
1. Mother's Day sermons. 2. Lutheran Church—Sermons. 3. Sermons, English. I. Title.

Mothers—Prayer-books and devotions.

BRENNEMAN, Helen Good. 242'.6
Meditations for the expectant mother; a book of inspiration for the lady-in-waiting. Drawings by Esther Rose Graber. Scottdale, Pa., Herald Press [1968] 80 p. illus. 27 cm. "Acknowledgments" (bibliographical): p. 77-78. [BV4847.B69] 68-12025
1. Mothers—Prayer-books and devotions. I. Title.

FRANZISKUS, Pius. 248
Mother love. A manual for Christian mothers, with instructions for the Archconfraternity of Christian mothers, by Rev. Pius Franziskus ... rev. by a Capuchin father of St. Augustine's province. New York and Cincinnati, F. Pustet co., inc. [c1926] 1 p. l., viii, 684 p. front., illus. 15 cm. [BX2353.F7] 26-8343
I. Title.

FROST, Marie. 242'.6'43
Mother's meditations. Wheaton, Ill., Tyndale House Publishers [1969, c1968] 59 p. illus. 20 cm. (Heritage edition) [BV283.M7F76] 68-56397
1. Mothers—Prayer-books and devotions. I. Title.

Mothers—Prayer-books and devotions—English.

BLAIR, Caroline Grant. 242'.6'43
Prayers for mothers / Caroline Grant Blair ; illustrated by Pat Traub. Valley Forge : Judson Press, c1980. [47] : ill. ; 22 cm. [BV4847.B5] 79-19958 ISBN 0-8170-0864-0 pbk. : 1.95
1. Mothers—Prayer-books and devotions—English. I. Title.

BRENNEMAN, Helen Good. 242
Meditations for the new mother, a devotional book for the new mother during the first month following the birth of her baby. Drawings by Esther Rose Graber. Scottdale, Pa., Herald Press, 1953. 78p. illus. 28cm. [BV4847.B7] 53-7585
1. Mothers—Prayer-books and devotions—English. I. Title.

BURROW, Barbara. 242'.6'33
We planted miracles today, Lord; a mother's meditations and prayers. Illustrated by Lilian Weytjens. [Kansas City, Mo., Hallmark Cards, 1973] 1 v. (unpaged) col. illus. 16 cm. (Hallmark editions) [BV283.M7B87] 72-75046 ISBN 0-87529-289-5 2.00
1. Mothers—Prayer-books and devotions—English. I. Title.

COURTNEY, Star L. 242'.8
Now is too soon [by] Star L. Courtney. Old Tappan, N.J., F. H. Revell [1974] 64 p. illus. 19 cm. [BV283.M7C68] 73-22358 ISBN 0-8007-0652-8 2.95
1. Mothers—Prayer-books and devotions—English. 2. Parent and child. I. Title.

ESPECIALLY for mother 242'.6'43
/ [compiled by] Mildred Tengbom. Old Tappan, N.J. : Revell, c1977. 125 p. ; 21 cm. [BV4847.E86] 77-16027 ISBN 0-8007-0911-X : 5.95. ISBN 0-8007-0915-2 gift ed. : 7.95
1. Mothers—Prayer-books and devotions—English. I. Tengbom, Mildred.

GILLESPIE, Julia Berford 248
(Wall) Mrs. 1850-
A mother's morning prayers, by Julia B. Gillespie. New York [etc.] Fleming H. Revell company [c1937] 370 p. 16 cm. [BV283.M7G5] 27-15881
1. Mothers—Prayer-books and devotions—English—English. 2. Calendars. I. Title.

GLAZIER, Donna L. 242'.6'43
Heaven help me; devotions for young mothers, by Donna L. Glazier. Minneapolis, Augsburg Pub. House [1970] vii, 139 p. 23 cm. [BV283.M7G55] 75-101109 3.95
1. Mothers—Prayer-books and devotions—English. I. Title.

HARRELL, Irene Burk. 242'.6'43
Ordinary days with an extraordinary God; prayerables II, by Irene Harrell. Waco, Tex., Word Books [1973, c.1971] 125 p. 18 cm. (A Word pbk., 90036) [BV283.M7H37] 72-144360 0.95 (pbk.)
1. Mothers—Peayerbooks and devotions—English. I. Title. II. Title: Prayerables II.

HOLMES, Deborah Aydt, 242'.6'43
1949-
Survival prayers for young mothers / by Deborah Aydt Holmes. Atlanta : John Knox Press, c1977. 111 p. ; 21 cm. [BV4847.H55] 76-12390 ISBN 0-8042-2195-2 : 4.95
1. Mothers—Prayer-books and devotions—English. I. Title.

HOLMES, Marjorie, 1910- 242'.6'43
As tall as my heart; a mother's measure of love. McLean, Va., EFM Publications; distributed by Hawthorn Books [New York] 1974. 120 p. illus. 23 cm. (A Love and laughter book) [BV283.M7H64] 74-75733 ISBN 0-914440-03-9 4.95
1. Mothers—Prayer-books and devotions—English. I. Title.

HOLMES, Marjorie, 1910- 242.643
As tall as my heart; a mother's measure of love. New York, Bantam Books, [1975] 117 p. 18 cm. [BV283.M7H46] 1.25 (pbk.)
1. Mothers—Prayer-books and devotions—English. I. Title.
L.C. card no. for original edition: 74-75733

IKERMAN, Ruth C. 242'.6'32
Prayers of a homemaker [by] Ruth C. Ikerman. Nashville, Abingdon Press [1966] 72 p. 12 cm. [BV283.M7I4] 66-28024
1. Mothers—Prayer-books and devotions—English. I. Title.

MALL, E. Jane, 1920- 241'.6'43
A mother's gifts : a book of praise and inspiration / E. Jane Mall, drawings by Billie Jean Osborne. Nashville : Abingdon Press, c1976. 62 p. : ill. ; 20 cm. [BV283.M7M33] 75-33082 ISBN 0-687-27249-1 : 3.50
1. Mothers—Prayer-books and devotions—English. I. Title.

MATTISON, Judith N. 242'.8'43
Prayers from a mother's heart / Judith Mattison ; ill. by Audrey Teeple. Minneapolis : Augsburg Pub. House, [1975] 95 p. : ill. ; 20 cm. [BV283.M7M37] 74-14177 ISBN 0-8066-1460-9 pbk. : 2.95
1. Mothers—Prayer-books and devotions—English. I. Teeple, Audrey. II. Title.

MURPHY, Mary Maloney. 242'.6'33
Creating; reflections during pregnancy. New York, Paulist Press [1974] 53 p. illus. 18 cm. [BV283.M7M87] 73-90086 ISBN 0-8091-1815-7 1.50 (pbk.)
1. Mothers—Prayer-books and devotions—English. I. Title.

PIUS Franziskus Father. 248.37
Mother love; a manual for Christian mothers with instructions for the Archconfraternity of Christian Mothers. English revision of 1960 by Bertin Roll. New York, F. Pustet Co. [1960] 691p. illus. 15cm. [BX2353.P513 1960] 60-794
1. Mothers—Prayer-books and devotions—English. 2. Catholic Church—Prayer-books and devotions—English. I. Cathokic Church. Liturgy and ritual. English. II. Archconfraternity of Christian Mothers. III. Title.

PIUS Franziskus father 264.02
Mother love; a manual for Christian mothers, with instructions for the Archconfraternity of Christian Mothers, by Rev. Pius Franciscus. English revision of 1951 by Bertin Roll. New York, F. Pustet Co. [1951] 691 p. illus. 15 cm. [BX2353.P513 1951] 52-400709
1. Mothers — Prayer-books and devotions — English. 2. Catholic Church — Prayer-books and devotions — English. I. Catholic Church. Liturgy and ritual. English. II. Archconfraternity of Christian Mothers. III. Title.

PIUS Franziskus, Father.
Mother love; a manual for Christian mothers, with instructions for the Archconfraternity of Christian mothers, by Rev. Pius Franziskus ... Rev. by a Capuchun father of St. Augustine's province. New York and Cincinnati, F. Pustet co., inc. [1926] 1 p. l., viii, 684 p. front., illsu. 14 1/2 cm. [BX2353.P513 1926] 26-8343
1. Mothers—Prayer-books and devotions—English. 2. Catholic church—Prayer-books and devotions—English. I. Catholic church. Liturgy and ritual. English. II. Archconfraternity of Christian mothers. III. Title.

REID, Frances P 264.1
None so small: reflections and prayers of a mother. Nashville, Broadman Press [1958] 66p. 19cm. [BV4847.R4] 58-5414
1. Mothers—Prayer-books and devotions—English. I. Title.

STARCK, Johann Friedrich, 243
1680-1756.
Starck's motherhood prayers for all occasions, from the German edition of Dr. F. Pieper; translated and edited by W. H. T. Dau. St. Louis, Mo., Concordia publishing house, 1921. 1 p. l., [535]-612 p. 22 1/2 cm. Taken from Starck's prayer-book (C. P. H. edition) with original pagination and index. cf. Publisher's note. [BV283.M7S8] 36-32739
1. Mothers—Prayer-books and devotions—English. 2. Lutheran church—Prayer-books and devotions—English. I. Pieper, Frans August Otto, 1852-1931. II. Dau, William Herman Theodore, 1864- tr. III. Title. IV. Title: Motherhood prayers.

WHEATCROFT, Anita. 242
Preface for parents; counsels for the expectant mother and father. Foreword by Dora P. Chaplin. Illustrated by Berit Homstead. Greenwich, Conn., Seabury Press, 1955. 95p. illus. 20cm. [BV4847.W46] 55-8741
1. Mothers—Prayer-books and devotions—English. I. Title.

Mothers—Religious life.

ALDRICH, Doris Coffin. 242
Musings of a mother. Chicago, Moody Press [1949] 124 p. 17 cm. (Colportage library, 197) [BV4529.A4] 50-1039
1. Mothers—Religious life. I. Title.

BOIGELOT, Rene 612.6
Maternity; a baby is born; the wonderful adventure of the human cell from conception to birth, by Pierre Dufoyer [pseud.] Tr. [from French] adapted by David M. Murphy. Staten Island, N.Y., Alba [1965, c.1964] vii, 143p. illus. 22cm. (Cana ser., 3) [BX2353.B613] 64-21802 3.95
1. Mothers—Religious life. I. Title.

BOWMAN,Mary D. 242.643
Hey, Mom! Illus. by Don Sampson. Westwood, N.J., Revel [c.1965] 31p. col. illus. 19cm. [BV4847.B6] 65-23622 2.00
1. Mothers—Religious life. I. Title.

BOWMAN, Mary D. 248.8
Mom, you gotta be kiddin' [by] Mary D. Bowman. With illus. by Don Sampson. Old Tappan, N.J., F. H. Revell [1968] 62 p. col. illus. 16 x 21 cm. [BV4847.B62] 68-28435 2.95
1. Mothers—Religious life. I. Title.

DAVIS, Elisabeth Logan. 920.7
Mothers of America: the lasting influence of the Christian home. [Westwood, N. J.] F. H. evell Co. [1954] 191p. sWomen in the U. S.--Biog. [CT3260.D39] 54-7999
I. Title.

HERTZ, Jacky. 248'.843
The Christian mother : a Mary-Martha balance / Jacky Hertz. New York : Hawthorn Books, c1976. xii, 162 p. ; 22 cm. [BV4529.H47 1976] 76-15427 ISBN 0-8015-1280-8 : 6.95
1. Mothers—Religious life. I. Title.

JOHNSTON, Dorothy Grunbock 248.4
Hey, Mom! Wheaton, Ill., Scripture Pr. 1825 College Ave. [c.1965] 96p. illus. 23cm. [BV4829.J6] 65-22376 1.25 pap.,
1. Mothers—Religious life. 2. Children—Management. I. Title.

JOHNSTON, Dorothy Grunbock. 248.4
Hey, Mom! Wheaton, Ill., Scripture Press Publications [1965] 96 p. illus. 23 cm. [BV4829.J6] 65-22376
1. Mothers — Religious life. 2. Children — Management. I. Title.

KOOIMAN, Helen W 242.643
Joyfully expectant; meditations before baby comes [by] Helen W. Kooiman. Westwood, N.J., F. H. Revell Co. [1966] 121 p. 21 cm. [BV4529.K6] 66-21898
1. Mothers — Religious life. I. Title.

MATTISON, Judith N. 242'.6431
Mom has a second job : prayer thoughts for working mothers / Judith Mattison. Minneapolis : Augsburg Pub. House, c1980. 96 p. : ill. ; 20 cm. [BV4529.M37] 19 80-65548 ISBN 0-8066-1793-4 pbk. : 3.95
1. Mothers—Religious life. I. Title.

PERKINS, Mary, 1912- 242
Mind the Baby! A mother's various attempts in the course of the days' routine, to appreciate by observation, reason and faith the wonders of God's making and remaking of one small Christian ... New York, Sheed & Ward, 1949. 122 p. 20 cm. Full name: Mary Elizabeth (Perkins) Ryan. [BX2353.P47] 49-11046
1. Mothers—Religious life. 2. Children—Management. I. Title.

Motilon Indians—Missions.

KUNG, Andres, 1945- 266'.0092'4
Bruce Olson : missionary or American colonizer? / Andres Kung ; [translated by Frederic Love]. Chappaqua, N.Y. : Christian Herald Books, c1981. p. cm. Translation of: Bruce. [F2319.2.M6O43513] 19 80-69309 ISBN 0-915684-83-7 : 6.95
1. Olson, Bruce. 2. Kung, Andres, 1945- 3. Motilon Indians—Missions. 4. Indians of South America—Colombia—Missions. I. [Bruce.] English II. Title.
Publisher's address : 40 Overlook Dr., Chappaqua, NY 10514.

OLSON, Bruce. 266'.023'0987
Bruchko by Bruce Olson. Carol Stream, Ill. : Creation House, 1978. 208p. ; 18 cm. First ed. published in 1973 under title: For this cross I'll Kill you [F2319.2M6044 1978] 78-107540 ISBN 0-88419-133-8 pbk. : 1.95
1. Olson, Bruce. 2. Motilon Indians — Missions. 3. Yuko Indians — Missions. 4. Indians of South America — Venezuela — Missions. 5. Missionaries — Venezuela — Biography. 6. Missionaries — United States — Biography. I. Title.

OLSON, Bruce. 266'.023'0987
For this cross I'll kill you. [1st ed.] Carol Stream, Ill., Creation House [1973] 221 p. illus. 24 cm. [F2319.2.M6O44] 73-81494 ISBN 0-88419-038-2 4.95
1. Olson, Bruce. 2. Motilon Indians—Missions. 3. Yuko Indians—Missions. I. Title.

Motion.

BUCKLEY, Michael J. 211
Motion and motion's God; thematic variations in Aristotle, Cicero, Newton, and Hegel, by Michael J. Buckley. [Princeton, N.J.] Princeton University Press, 1971. 287 p. 22 cm. Includes bibliographical references. [BD620.B8] 73-132234 ISBN 0-691-07124-1 10.00
1. Motion. 2. God—Proof. 3. Dialectic. I. Title.

Motivation (Psychology)

AUSTGEN, Robert J. 227.06
Natural motivation in the Pauline Epistles [by] Robert J. Austgen. Notre Dame, Ind., University of Notre Dame Press, 1966. viii, 156 p. 23 cm. Thesis—University of Fribourg. Bibliography: p. 137-146. [BS2652.A88] 66-31813
1. Bible. N.T. Epistles of Paul—Theology. 2. Bible. N.T. Epistles of Paul—Psychology. 3. Motivation (Psychology) I. Title.

Motor bus driving-Moral and religious aspects.

*GENTRY, Gardiner. 253.'7'3
Bus them in / by Gardiner Gentry. Grand Rapids : Baker Book House, 1976c1973. [ix], 151p. : ill. ports. ; 22 cm. [BV1523.A7] ISBN 0-8010-3705-0 pbk. : 2.95
1. Motor bus driving-Moral and religious aspects. 2. Evangelistic work-United States. I. Title.

*GOODMAN, Carlton T. 253.'7'3
How to be a successful bus pastor or bus captain / Carlton T. Goodman. Grand Rapids : Baker Book House, 1976c1974. 183p. ; 22 cm. First published 1974 by Church Growth Publications. [BV1523.A7] ISBN 0-8010-3661-5 pbk. : 2.95
1. Motor bus driving-Moral and religious aspects. 2. Evangelistic work-United States. I. Title.

Mott, John Raleigh 1865-1955.

FISHER, Galen Merriam, 1873-- 922
John R. Mott, Architect of co-operation and unity. New York, Association Press [c1952] 214p. illus. 21cm. [BV1085.M75F5] 53-6601
1. Mott, John Raleigh, 1865- I. Title.

HOPKINS, Charles 267'.392'4 B
Howard, 1905-
John R. Mott, 1865-1955 : a biography / by C. Howard Hopkins. Grand Rapids : Eerdmans, c1979. xvii, 816 p., [12] leaves of plates : ill. ; 23 cm. Includes index. Bibliography: p. 779-780.

[BV1085.M75H66] 19 79-15069 ISBN 0-8028-3525-2 : 19.95
1. Mott, John Raleigh, 1865-1955. 2. Young Men's Christian Associations—Biography.

MACKIE, Robert C. 267.0924
Layman extraordinary: John R. Mott, 1865-1955, by Robert C. Mackie, others, Foreword by W. A. Visser't Hooft [New York] Association [1965] 127p. 18cm. [BV1085.M75M26] 65-27832 1.25 pap.,
1. Mott, John Raleigh 1865-1955. I. Title.

MATHEWS, Basil Joseph, 1879- 922
John R. Mott, world citizen, by Basil Mathews... New York and London, Harper & brothers, 1934. xiii, 469 p. front., plates. ports., facsims. 22 cm. Maps on lining-papers. "First edition." "Published works of John R. Mott": p. 455-461. [BV1085.M75M3] 34-2163
1. Mott, John Raleigh, 1865- I. Title.

Mounier, Emmanuel, 1905-1950.

HELLMAN, John, 1940- 194
Emmanuel Mounier and the new Catholic left, 1930-1950 / John Hellman. Toronto ; Buffalo : University of Toronto Press, c1981. viii, 357 p. ; 24 cm. Includes index. Bibliography: p. [333]-336. [B2430.M694H44] 19 81-182626 ISBN 0-8020-2399-1 : 35.00
1. Mounier, Emmanuel, 1905-1950. 2. Esprit; revue internationale. 3. Catholics—France—History—20th century. 4. Personalism—History—20th century. I. Title.

RAUCH, Rufus William. 261.7'0944
Politics and belief in contemporary France: Emmanuel Mounier and Christian democracy, 1932-1950, by R. William Rauch, Jr. The Hague, Nijhoff, 1972. 363 p. 24 cm. Includes bibliographical references. [B2430.M694R38] 73-160173 ISBN 9-02-471281-5
1. Mounier, Emmanuel, 1905-1950. 2. Mouvement republicain populaire. 3. Esprit; revue internationale. 4. Center parties—France. I. Title.
Distributed by Humanities; 15.00.

Mt. Calvary Holy Church of America (Boston, Mass.)

PARIS, Arthur E., 1945- 289.9
Black Pentecostalism : Southern religion in an urban world / Arthur E. Paris. Amherst : University of Massachusetts Press, 1982. vii, 183 p. ; 23 cm. Includes index. Bibliography: p. [175]-180. [BX8770.A4P37 1982] 19 81-16169 17.50
1. Mt. Calvary Holy Church of America (Boston, Mass.) 2. Afro-Americans—Massachusetts—Boston—Religion. 3. Boston (Mass.)—Church history. I. Title.

Mount Hermon Association.

GUDNASON, Kay. 269'.2'0979465
Rings in the redwoods; the story of Mount Hermon. Mount Hermon, Calif., Mount Hermon Association, 1972. 439 p. illus. 31 cm. [BV3799.M6G82] 73-160698
1. Mount Hermon Association. I. Title.

SMITH, Harry R 1900- 269
Apart with Him; fifty years of the Mount Hermon conference. Oakland, Calif., Western Book & Tract Co. [1956] 137 p. illus. 21 cm. [BV3799.M6S56] 56-36225
1. Mount Hermon Association. I. Title.

Mount Holyoke college.

THOMAS, Louise Porter, Mrs. 266
Seminary militant; an account of the missionary movement at Mount Holyoke seminary and college, by Louise Porter Thomas. South Hadley, Mass., Department of English, Mount Holyoke college, 1937. ix, 117 p., 1 l. 22 cm. (Half-title: Mount Holyoke college centennial publications) "Of this book ... eleven hundred copies have been printed." [BV2416.M6T5] 37-11646
1. Mount Holyoke college. 2. Missions. 3. Missionaries. I. Mount Holyoke college. Dept. of English. II. Title. III. Title: Missionary movement at Mount Holyoke seminary and college.

Mount Mercy academy, Buffalo.

FITZGERALD, Mary Innocentia, sister. 271.92
A historical sketch of the Sisters of mercy in the diocese of Buffalo, 1857-1942, by Sister Mary Innocentia Fitzgerald ... with a foreword by His Excellency, the Most Reverend John A. Duffy ... Buffalo, N.Y., Mount Mercy academy, 1942. xviii, [2], 132 p. front. (port.) plates, map, diagrs. 20 cm. "Principal sources": p. 121-122. [BX4484.B9F5] 43-4803
1. Sisters of mercy. Buffalo. 2. Mount Mercy academy, Buffalo. I. Title.

Mount Moriah African Methodist Episcopal Church, Annapolis, Md.

GREENE, Carroll, comp. 287'.8752'56
The Mount Moriah A.M.E. Church; a documentary report—background and potential. Compiled by Carroll Greene, Jr. Baltimore, Commission on Negro History and Culture [1972] 1 v. (various pagings) 28 cm. Includes bibliographical references. [BX8481.A56M683] 73-622655
1. Mount Moriah African Methodist Episcopal Church, Annapolis, Md. I. Title.

Mt. Pisgah church (Presbyterian) Woodford co., Ky.

SHEWMAKER, William Orpheus, 1869- 285.1769
Pisgah and her people, 1784-1934; a memorial to the past; a testimonial to the present; a reminder to the future ... By William Orpheus Shewmaker ... [Lexington, Ky., Printed by the Commercial printing company, c1935] 7 p. l., 269 p. illus., plates. 21 1/2 cm. "Sources": 269. [BX9211.M8S45] 35-13398
1. Mt. Pisgah church (Presbyterian) Woodford co., Ky. 2. Presbyterian church in Kentucky. 3. Presbyterians in Kentucky. 4. Pisgah, Ky. I. Title.

Mount Pleasant, Ohio—History.

BURKE, James Lee, 1935- 289.6'771'69
Mount Pleasant and the early Quakers of Ohio / James L. Burke, Donald E. Bensch. [Columbus] : Ohio Historical Society, [1975] vi, 45 p. : ill. ; 25 cm. "Text previously appeared in Ohio history, volume 83, number 4, autumn 1974, in a somewhat different format." Bibliography: p. 43-44. [BX7649.M68B87] 75-315472
1. Friends, Society of—Mount Pleasant, Ohio. 2. Friends, Society of. Ohio Yearly Meeting. 3. Mount Pleasant, Ohio—History. I. Bensch, Donald E., joint author. II. Title.

Mount Scholastica Convent, Atchison, Kan.

SCHUSTER, Mary Faith 271.9790978136
The meaning of the mountain; a history of the first century at Mount St. Scholastica. Helicon [dist. New York Taplinger c.1963] 329p. illus., ports., 23cm. (Benedictine studies, 6) Bibl. 63-19401 6.00
1. Mount Scholastica Convent, Atchison, Kan. 2. Mount St. Scholastica College, Atchison, Kan. I. Title. II. Series.

Mount Vernon, Ind. Trinity Evangelical and Reformed Church.

LANG, Elfrieda Wilhelmina Henrietta, 1904- 285.7772
The history of Trinity Evangelical and Reformed Church, 1853-1953, Mount Vernon, Indiana. St. Louis, Eden Pub. House, 1953. 206p. illus. 24cm. [BX7481.M6L3] 53-39549
1. Mount Vernon, Ind. Trinity Evangelical and Reformed Church. I. Title.

Mount Vernon, N. Y. First Methodist Episcopal church.

ANDERSON, William S ed. 287.
Threescore and ten, seventieth anniversary of the First Methodist Episcopal church, Mount Vernon, New York, edited by William S. Anderson. [Mt. Vernon, N. Y., Printing house of W. E. Rudge] 1922. 3 p. l., 3-162, [2] p. front., illus., ports. 24 cm. "Fifteen hundred copies." Errata on end lining-paper. [BX8481.M77A5] 24-10829
1. Mount Vernon, N. Y. First Methodist Episcopal church. I. Title.

Mount Vernon Place United Methodist Church.

HISTORY, Mount Vernon Place United Methodist Church, 1850-1976 / Royce L. Thompson, editor. 287'.6753 Washington : The Church, 1977. 136 p. : ill. ; 23 cm. Bibliography: p. 127-136. [BX8481.W325H57] 77-74710
1. Mount Vernon Place United Methodist Church. I. Thompson, Royce L.

Mountain, Jacob, Bp., 1749-1825.

MILLMAN, Thomas Reagh. 922.371
Jacob Mountain, first lord bishop of Quebec, a study in church and state, 1793 1825. Toronto, Univ of Toronto Press, 1947. viii, 320 p. plates, ports., fold. maps. 23 cm. (University of Toronto studies. History and economics series, v. 10) Toronto. University. University of Toronto studies. History and economic series, v. 10. Bibliography: p. [303]-310. [H31.T6 vol. 10] [BX5620.M62M5] 47-27138
1. Mountain, Jacob, Bp., 1749-1825. 2. Church of England in Canada—Hist. 3. Church and state in Canada. I. Title. II. Series.

Mountain Valley United Methodist Church.

ARRINGTON, Mary Marie Koontz. 287'.6755'922
A white church on a high hill; a historical sketch of Mountain Valley Evangelical United Brethren Church, 1833-1970. [Harrisonburg, Va., Printed at Park View Press, 1970] xxi, 307 p. illus., ports. 23 cm. [BX8481.M78A9] 73-21638
1. Mountain Valley United Methodist Church. I. Title.

Mountain whites (Southern states)

HURST, Samuel Need, 1867- 277.
The mountains redeemed; the romance of the mountains, a true story of life and love in Southwest Virginia, interwoven with an exposition of her mountain life and the weird religion of the mountains, embracing scores of humorous, ridiculous, laughable, and tragic stories, episodes, and incidents and the religious, moral, educational, industrial and political redemption of the mountains, by Sam N. Hurst ... illustrated by S. N. Hurst, jr. ... Appalachia, Va., Hurst and company, 1929. xvii, 384 p. front., illus., plates, ports. 20 cm. Based on the life of the author. [F227.H96] 29-9416
1. Mountain whites (Southern states) I. Title.

WILSON, Samuel Tyndale, 1858- 277.
The southern mountaineers, by Samuel Tyndale Wilson ... New York city, Literature department, Presbyterian home missions, 1906. xii, 164 p. front., 9 pl. 16 1/2 cm. (On cover: Home missions of the Presbyterian church, U.S.A.) [BV2793.W7] 6-17852
1. Mountain whites (Southern states) 2. Presbyterian church in the U.S.A.—Missions. I. Title.

Mountains (in religion, folk-lore, etc.)

CLIFFORD, Richard J. 398'.36
The cosmic mountain in Canaan and the Old Testament [by] Richard J. Clifford. Cambridge, Mass., Harvard University Press, 1972. 221 p. illus. 22 cm. (Harvard Semitic monographs, v. 4) A revision of the author's thesis, Harvard, 1970. Bibliography: p. 203-211. [BL447.C57 1972] 71-188968 ISBN 0-674-17425-9
1. Mountains (in religion, folk-lore, etc.) 2. Mountains in the Bible. I. Title. II. Series.

COSSUM, William Henry, 1863-
Mountain peaks of prophecy and sacred history, by W. H. Cossum, m. a. Chicago, The Evangel publishing house [c1911] 2 p. l., 7-195 p. maps. 20 cm. 11-5345 0.65
I. Title.

HEADLEY, Joel Tyler, 1813-1897 220.81
The sacred mountains. By J. T. Headley ... New York, Baker and Scribner, 1847. x p., 1 l., [18]-175 p. front., illus., plates. 15 1/2 cm. Added t.-p. engraved. [BS690.H4] 33-37786
1. Mountains (in religion, folk-lore, etc.). I. Title.

HEADLEY, Joel Tyler, 1813-1897. 220.91
The sacred mountains. By J. T. Headley ... New York, Baker and Scribner, 1851. x p., 1 l., [18]-175 p. front., illus., plates. 19 1/2cm. [BS630.H4 1851] 33-36470
1. Mountains (in religion, folk-lore, etc.). I. Title.

HEADLEY, Joel Tyler, 1813-1897. 220.91
The sacred mountains. By J. T. Headley ... New York, J. S. Taylor, 1851. 8 p. l., [v]-xii, [18]-204 p. plates. 18cm. Added t.-p. engraved. [BS630.H4 1851a] 35-25953
1. Mountains (in religion, folk-lore, etc.) I. Title.

HEADLEY, Joel Tyler, 1813-1897. 220.
Sacred mountains, characters, and scenes in the Holy Land. By Rev. J.T. Headley ... New York, Scribner, Armstrong & co., 1875. xv p., 1 l., [19]-441 p. incl. front., plates. 19 1/2cm. Added t.-p., engraved. Contains all the material included in the author's The sacred mountains, first published in 1847, and sixteen additional chapters. [BS630.H4 1875] 36-4363
1. Mountains (in religion, folk-lore, etc.) 2. Bible—History of Biblical events. I. Title.

Mountains in the Bible.

LEE, G. Avery. 248'.4'61
I want that mountain! [By] G. Avery Lee. Nashville, T. Nelson [1974] p. cm. Includes bibliographical references. [BX6333.L395I22] 74-13017 3.50 (pbk.).
1. Mountains in the Bible. 2. Baptists—Sermons. 3. Sermons, American. I. Title.

POLHAMUS, William Robert. 252.
Mountain scenes from the Bible; or, "Soul heights in Scriptural geography", by William Robert Polhamus ... New York, Chicago [etc.] Fleming H. Revell company [c1922] 350 p. 21 cm. [BX8333.P6M6] 23-618
I. Title.

ROBINSON, Reuben.
Mountain peaks of the Bible, by Bud Robinson. Louisville, Ky., Pentecostal publishing company, c1913. 164 p. front. (port.) 18 1/2 cm. $0.50 13-5400
I. Title.

SUMMERBELL, Joseph James.
Mountains of the Bible, by J. J. Summerbell ... Boston, Sherman, French & company, 1912. 4 p. l., 85, [1] p. 19 1/2 cm. $1.00. 12-24499
I. Title.

Mountains—Palestine.

MACARTNEY, Clarence Edward Noble, 1879- 252.051
Mountains and mountain men of the Bible. New York, Abingdon-Cokesbury Press [1950] 188 p. 20 cm. [BX9178.M174M6] 50-7310
1. Mountains—Palestine. 2. Bible—Biog. 3. Presbyterian Church—Sermons. 4. Sermons, American. I. Title.

Mourning customs, Jewish.

KLEIN, Isaac. 296.4'45
A time to be born, a time to die = ('Et la-ledet ve-'et la-mut) Ecclesiastes 3:2 / by Isaac Klein. New York : Dept. of Youth Activities, United Synagogue of America, c1976. vi, 106 p. ; 21 cm. In English. Bibliography: p. 104-105. [BM712.K565] 77-356147
1. Mourning customs, Jewish. 2. Death

(Judaism)—Meditations. I. Title. II. Title: 'Et la-ledet ve-'et la-mut.

LAMM, Maurice. 393'.09174'924
The Jewish way in death and mourning. New York, J. David [1969] xvii, 265 p. 23 cm. Bibliography: p. 249-250. [BM712.L3] 69-11684 5.95
1. Mourning customs, Jewish. I. Title.

RABINOWICZ, Harry M., 1919- 296.4'45
A guide to life; Jewish laws and customs of mourning [by] H. Rabinowicz. New York, Ktav Pub. House [1967, c1964] 186 p. 19 cm. Includes the English and Hebrew texts of mourning prayers. Bibliography: p. 181. [BM712.R3 1967] 67-19371
1. Mourning customs, Jewish. I. Title.

TALMUD Minor tractates Semahot. English. 1966. 296.445
The tractate 'Mourning' (Semahot) (Regulations relating to death. burial. and mourning) Tr. from Hebrew. introd. notes, by Dov Zlotnick. New Haven, Conn., Yale [c.]1966. x, 233p. 22cm. (Yale Judaica ser., v. 17) With an appendix: The Hebrew text of the tractate. ed. from mss. by Dov Zlotnick. Vocalized by Eduard Y. Kutscher. Bibl. [BM506.4.S4E5] 66-12517 7.50
1. Mourning customs, Jewish. I. Title. II. Series.

TALMUD. Minor tractates. Semahot. English. 1966. 296.445
The tractate "Mourning" (Semahot) (Regulations relating to death, burial, and mourning). Translated from the Hebrew, with introd. and notes, by Dov Zlotnick. New Haven, Yale University Press, 1966. x, 233 p. 22 cm. Yale Judaica series, v. 17) "With an appendix The Hebrew text of the tractate, edited from manuscripts by Dov Zlotnick. Vocalized by Eduard Y. Kutscher." Bibliographical references included in "Notes" (p. [97]-169) [BM506.4.S4E5] 66-12517
1. Mourning customs, Jewish. I. Zlotnick, Dov, ed. and tr. II. Talmud, Minor tractates. Semahot. III. Title.

Mourning (Jewish law)

FELDER, Aaron. 296.4'45
[Sefer Yesode semabot (romanized form)] Yesodei smochos : a compilation of Jewish laws and traditions dealing with death and mourning, with the addition of detailed studies of related problems arising from modern life situations / by Aaron Felder. New York : Felder, 1974. xii, 156 p. ; 22 cm. Text in English, notes in Hebrew. Includes index. Bibliography: p. 142-143. [BM712.F44] 75-309123
1. Mourning (Jewish law) 2. Mourning customs, Jewish. I. [Yesode semahot] II. Title: Yesode semahot. III. Title: Yesodei smochos.

GOLDSTEIN, Israel, 1896- comp. 296
Mourner's devotions arranged and compiled by Israel Goldstein ... adapted to orthodox, conservative and reform requirements. New York, Bloch publishing company, 1941-5702. 4 p. l., 103 p. 20 cm. "Yahrzeit calendar for ten years [1941-1950]": p. [89]-108. Bibliographical references included in Foreword (4th prelim. leaf) [BM667.M7G6] 42-7722
I. Jews. Liturgy and ritual. II. Title.

Movimento de Educacao de Base.

DE KADT, Emanuel Jehuda. 322'.44'0981
Catholic radicals in Brazil, by Emanuel de Kadt. London, New York, Oxford U.P., 1970. xii, 304 p. 23 cm. Issued under the auspices of the Royal Institute of International Affairs. Based on author's thesis, University of London. Bibliography: p. 291-296. [F2538.2.D45] 72-20402 ISBN 0-19-214984-9 60/-
1. Movimento de Educacao de Base. 2. Brazil—Politics and government—1954- 3. Catholics in Brazil. I. Royal Institute of International Affairs. II. Title.

Moving pictures—Catalogs.

WORLD Council of Christian Education and Sunday School Association. North American Administrative Committee. 268.63530838
Slide and film strip evaluations for use in Christian churches around the world. Published cooperatively by the North American Administrative Committee, World Council of Chirstian Education and Sunday School Association, and Committee on Radio, Audio Visual Education and Mass Communication, Division of Foreign Missions, National Council of Churches of Christ in the U. S. A. New York [1953- v. illus. 22cm. Introd. to pt. 1 signed: Erich F. Voehringer. [BV1643.W62] 53-34243
1. Moving pictures—Catalogs. I. National Council of the Churches of Christ in the United States of America Division of Foreign Missions. Committee on Radio Audio Visual Education and Mass Communication. II. Voehringer. Erich Frederick, 1905- III. Title.

Moving-pictures in church work.

JONES, George William, 1931- 791.43'015
Sunday night at the movies, by G. William Jones. Richmond, John Knox Press [1967] 127 p. illus. 21 cm. Includes bibliographical references. [BV1643.J6] 67-23338
1. Moving-pictures in church work. 2. Moving-picture criticism. I. Title.

SUMMERS, Stanford. 260
Secular films and the church's ministry. New York, Seabury Press [1969] 64 p. illus. 28 cm. Includes bibliographical references. [BV1643.S9] 73-19430 1.95
1. Moving-pictures in church work. I. Title.

Moving-pictures—Moral and religious aspects.

RICE, John R 1895-
What is wrong with the movies? By John R. Rice. Murfreesboro, Tenn., Sword of the Lord Publishers [1964, c1938] 112 p. 22 cm. 68-78415
1. Moving-pictures—Moral and religious aspects. I. Title.

SMITH, Roy Lemon, 1887- 268.
Moving pictures in the church, by Roy L. Smith ... New York, Cincinnati, The Abingdon press [c1921] 74 p. front., plates. 19 cm. [BV1643.S6] 22-1223
1. Moving-pictures—Moral and religious aspects. I. Title.

Mowers, Charles.

HORTON, Roy F 1902- 268
Inspiration Point and its personalities. St. Louis, Bethany Press [1961] 96p. illus. 23cm. [BX7330.I6H6] 61-12217
1. Mowers, Charles. 2. Scoville, Charles Beign, 1869-1938. 3. Inspiration Point, Ark. 4. Disciples of Christ. I. Title.

Mowes, Heinrich, 1798-1834.

THE bruised reed: 922.448
a memoir of the Rev. Henry Mowes, late pastor of Altenhausen and Ivenrode, Prussia ... Revised by the Committee of publication of the American Sunday-school union. Philadelphia, American Sunday-school union [1843] 129 p. 15 1/2 cm. [BX8080.M55B7] 36-33019
1. Mowes, Heinrich, 1798-1834. I. American Sunday-school union.

Mowry, Salome Lincoln, 1807-1841.

DAVIS, Almond H. 253'.2'0924 B
The female preacher; or, Memoir of Salome Lincoln, by Almond H. Davis. New York, Arno Press, 1972 [c1843] viii, 162 p. 20 cm. (American women: images and realities) [BR1725.M68D38 1972] 72-2599 ISBN 0-405-04489-5 7.00
1. Mowry, Salome Lincoln, 1807-1841. I. Title. II. Series.

Moye, Jean Martin, 1730-1793.

CALLAHAN, Mary Generosa, 1901- 922.2
The life of Blessed John Martin Moye. Milwaukee, Bruce Press [1964] ix, 262 p. maps, port. 24 cm. (Catholic life publications) [BX4700.M68C3] 65-364
1. Moye, Jean Martin, 1730-1793. I. Title.

FOUCAULT, Alphonse Gabriel, bp., 1843-1929. 922.2
The Venerable Jean-Martin Moye, apostolic missionary: founder of the Sisters of providence in Lorraine: and the Christian virgins in China; translated from the French of the Most Reverend A. G. Foucault ... by the Sisters of divine providence of Kentucky; foreword to the English translation by Reverend Peter Gilday ... Melbourne, Ky., Sisters of divine providence of Kentucky [c1932] xii, 108 p., 1 l. incl. front. (mounted port.) plates. 19 cm. [BX4705.M74F6] 33-6354
1. Moye, Jean Martin, 1730-1793. 2. Sisters of divine providence. 3. Christian virgins. I. Sisters of divine providence. Kentucky, tr. II. Title.

PLUS, Raoul, 1882- 922.2
Shepherd of untended sheep; John Martin Moye, priest of the Society of the Foreign Missions of Paris, founder of the Sisters of Divine Providence. Translated from the French by Sister James Aloysius [and] Sister Mary Generose. Westminster, Md., Newman Press, 1950. xv, 180 p. illus., ports. 21 cm. Translation of J. M. Moye. [BX4705.M74P52] 51-9450
1. Moye, Jean Martin, 1730-1793. 2. Sisters of Divine Providence. I. Title.

Moyer, Kenneth Allan, 1913-

MOYER, Kenneth Allan, 1913- 287'.92'0924 B
Preacher on the roof / by Kenneth A. Moyer ; illustrated by Joanne Jackson. [s.l. : s.n.], c1976. 74 p. : ill. ; 28 cm. Cover title. [BX9883.M65A35] 77-366089
1. Moyer, Kenneth Allan, 1913- 2. United Church of Canada—Clergy—Biography. 3. Clergy—Canada—Biography. I. Title.

Mpongwe language—Texts.

BIBLE. N. T. Gospels. Mpongwe. 1879.
The four Gospels; translated from the original Greek, into the Mpongwe language, by American missionaries at the Gaboon, West Africa. 3d ed. New York, American Bible society, 1879. 153 p. 20 cm. [BS325.M77 Gospels 1879] 26-9063
1. Mpongwe language—Texts. I. Title.

BIBLE. O. T. Mpongwe. Selections. 1879. 221.5988
The books of Ecclesiastes, Song of Solomon, Daniel and the Minor prophets, translated into the Mpongwe languge at the Gaboon and Corisco mission, Gaboon, West Africa. New York, American Bible society, 1879. 119 p. 20 cm. "Translated by A. Bushnell."--British and foreign Bible see Hist. est. Contains also Issiah, chapt. 1-29. Lettered on cover: Mpongwe Sctipture. [BS225.M71 1879] ca25
1. Mpongwe language—Texts. I. Bushnell, Albert, 1819-1879 tr. II. American Bible society. III. Title.

BIBLE. O. T. Selections. Mpongwe. 1859.
The books of Genesis, part of Exodus, Proverbs, and Acts, translated into the Mpongwe language, at the mission of the A. B. C. F. M., Gaboon, West Africa. New York, American Bible society, 1859. 434 p., 1 l., 18 cm. [BS325.M71 1859] 26-10904
1. Mpongwe language—Texts. I. Title.

Mrage—Catholic Church.

HEILLY, Alphonse 265'.5
Love and sacrament. Tr. by Sister Mary Augusta. Notre Dame, Ind., Fides [1966] cix, 118p. 20cm. Bibl. [BX2250.H4513] 65-24106 3' 2.25 pap.,
1. Mrage—Catholic Church. I. Title.

Mtusu, Daniel, d. 1917.

FRASER, Donald, 1870-1933. 286'.6'0924 B
The autobiography of an African; retold in biographical form & in the wild African setting of the life of Daniel Mtusu. Westport, Conn., Negro Universities Press [1970] 209 p. illus., port. 23 cm. Reprint of the 1925 ed. [BV3625.N82F7 1970] 78-138006 ISBN 0-8371-5653-X
1. Mtusu, Daniel, d. 1917. 2. Missions to Angoni. I. Title.

Mublenberg, William Augustus, 1796-1877.

NEWTON, William Wilberforce, 1843-1914. 922.
...Dr. Mublenberg, by William Wilberforce Newton, D.D. Boston and New York, Houghton Mifflin and company, 1890. x p. 1 l., 272 p. 18 1/2 cm. (American religious leaders) [BX5995.M8N5] 12-37231
1. Mublenberg, William Augustus, 1796-1877. I. Title.

Mudge, James, 1844-1918. Growth in holiness toward perfection.

DUNN, Lewis Romaine, 1822-1898.
A manual of holiness and review of Dr. James B. Mudge. By Rev. Lewis R. Dunn ... Cincinnati, Cranston & Curts; New York, Hunt & Eaton, 1895. 152 p. 20 cm. [BT67.M9D8] 41-35230
1. Mudge, James, 1844-1918. Growth in holiness toward perfection. 2. Perfection. I. Title.

STEEL, Daniel, 1824-1914. 234.
A defense of Christian perfection; or, A criticism of Dr. James Mudge's "Growth in holiness toward pefection," by Daniel Steele ... New York, Hunt & Eaton; Cincinnati, Cranston & Curtis, 1896. 136 p. 19 cm. [BT767.M9S8] 41-25231
1. Mudge, James, 1844-1918. Growth in holiness toward perfection. 2. Perfection. I. Title.

Muelder, Walter George, 1907-— Bibliography.

TOWARD a discipline of social ethics: essays in honor of Walter George Muelder. 177
Paul Deats, Jr., editor. Boston, Boston University Press, 1972. viii, 328 p. port. 25 cm. Contents.Contents.—Walter G. Muelder: an appreciation of his life, thought, and ministry, by C. E. Lincoln and P. Deats, Jr.—The tasks and methods of social ethics: The quest for a social ethic, by P. Deats, Jr. The relevance of historical understanding, by J. M. Gustafson. The struggle for political consciousness, by A. F. Geyer. The logic of moral argument, by R. B. Potter, Jr.—Ethics, power, and strategy: Toward a Christian understanding of power, by T. S. Sample. The disciplines of power: the necessity and limits of coercion, by J. D. Stamey. The dilemma of Christian social strategy, by J. P. Wogaman. The demand for economic justice: southern Africa and the Portuguese colonies, by F. Houtart.—The church and social responsibility: Political participation—a Christian view, by G. McGovern. The social gospel and race relations: a case study of a social movement, by P. N. Williams. Institutions, unity, and mission, by J. K. Matthews. Public and private dimensions of ethical responsibility, by L. H. DeWolf.—Communitarian Christian ethics: a personal statement and a response, by W. G. Muelder.—A bibliography of the writings of Walter G. Muelder (p. 321-328) [BT738.T68] 70-189020 10.00
1. Muelder, Walter George, 1907-— Bibliography. 2. Sociology, Christian—Addresses, essays, lectures. 3. Social ethics—Addresses, essays, lectures. I. Deats, Paul, ed. II. Muelder, Walter George, 1907-

Muench, Aloisius Joseph, Abp., 1889-1962.

BARRY, Colman James, 1921- 262'.135'0924 B
American nuncio: Cardinal Aloisius Muench [by] Colman J. Barry. Collegeville,

Minn., Saint John's University Press, 1969. xii, 379 p. illus. 25 cm. Bibliography: p. 289-293. [BX4705.M755B37] 71-83090
1. Muench, Aloisius Joseph, Abp., 1889-1962. I. Title.

Muenster, Tex. Sacred heart church.

FUHRMANN, Joseph Paul, 1894- 282.764
A golden jubilee history of the Sacred heart parish, 1889-1939, Muenster, Texas, by Joseph P. Fuhrmann ... San Antonio, Tex., Standard printing company, 1939. 170 p. illus. (incl. ports., facsim.) 24 cm. Bibliography: p. [7]--[8] [BX4603.M87S3] 40-30836
1. Muenster, Tex. Sacred heart church. I. Title.

Muggeridge, Malcolm, 1903-

MUGGERIDGE, Malcolm, 1903- 248'.4
A twentieth century testimony / by Malcolm Muggeridge. Nashville : T. Nelson, [1978] p. cm. Includes index. [BV4501.2.M74] 78-15925 ISBN 0-8407-5143-5 : 10.95
1. Muggeridge, Malcolm, 1903- 2. Christian life—1960- I. Title.

Muhammad 'Abduh, 1849 (cs)-1905.

ADAMS, Charles Clarence. 297'.61'0924
Islam and modernism in Egypt; a study of the modern reform movement inaugurated by Muhammad @Abduh. New York, Russell & Russell [1968] viii, 283 p. 23 cm. (American University at Cairo. Oriental studies) Reprint of the 1933 ed. First part of the author's thesis, University of Chicago, 1928. Bibliography: p. [269]-274. [BP80.M8A63 1968] 68-25061
1. Muhammad @Abduh, 1849-1905. 2. Islam—20th century. 3. Egypt—Politics and government—1882-1952. I. Title. II. Series.

ADAMS, Charles Clarence. 922.97
Islam and modernism in Egypt; a study of the modern reform movement inaugurated by Muhammad 'Abduh, by Charles C. Adams ... London, Oxford university press, H. Milford, 1933. viii p. 1 l. 280 (1) 22 1/2 cm. (The American university at Cairo, Oriental studies) The first part of a dissertation submitted in 1928 to the Graduate faculty of the University of Chicago Department of Old Testament, for degree of doctor of philosophy. It forms an introductory study for a translation into English, not yet published, of a work on the Islamic callphate by 'Ali 'Ahd al-Rasik. cf. Pref. Bibliography: p. [269]-274 [BP80.M8A5] 33-20433
1. Muhammad 'Abduh, 1849 (cs)-1905. 2. Jamal al-Din, al-Husaini, al-Afghani, bey, 1839-1897 3. Muhammad Rashid Rija 4. Ali Abd al Razik, 1888- 5. Panislamism 6. Egypt—Pol. & govt. 1882- I. Title.

AMIN, 'Uthman, 1905- 922.97
Muhammad 'Abduh [by] Osman Amin; translated from the Arabic by Charles Wendell. Washington, American Council of Learned Societies. 1953. vi. 103 p. 23 cm. (American Council of learned Societies. Near Eastern Translation Program. [Publication] no. 4) Bibliographical references included in "Notes" (p. 100-103) [BP80.M8A713] 54-781
1. Muhammad 'Abduh, 1849-1905. I. Title. II. Series: American Council of Learned Societies Devoted to Humanistic Studies. Near Eastern Translation Program. [Publication] no. 4

Muhammad, the prophet.

ANDRA, Tor, Bp., 1885-1947. 922.97
Mohammed, the man and his faith. Translated by Theophil Menzel. New York, Harper [1960] 194 p. 21 cm. (Harper torchbooks, TB62. The Cloister library) [BP75.A57 1960] 60-5489
1. Muhammad, the prophet.

ANDRAE, Tor, 1885- 922.97
...Mohammed, the man nad his faith, translated by Theophil Menzel... New York, C. Scribner's sons, 1936. 274 p. front. (facsim.) 20 cm. [Full noms: Ter Julius Efraim Andrae] [BP75.A57] 36-16210
1. Muhammad, the prophet. I. Menzel, Theophil William, 1902- II. Title.

ANDRAE Tor, Bp. 1885-1947. 297
Mohammed, the man and his faith. Tranlsated by Theophil Menzel. New York, Barnes and Noble [1957] 196p. illus. 22cm. Bibliographical footnotes. [BP75.A] A 58
1. Muhammad, the prophet. I. Title.

ANDRa, Tor, Bp., 1885-1947. 297'.63 B
Mohammed; the man and his faith. Translated by Theophil Menzel. Freeport, N.Y., Books for Libraries Press [1971] 274 p. facsim. 23 cm. Reprint of the 1936 ed. Includes bibliographical references. [BP75.A57 1971] 79-160954 ISBN 0-8369-5821-7
1. Muhammad, the prophet.

ARCHER, John Clark 1881- 297
...Mystical elements in Mohammed, by John Clark Archer. New Haven, Yale University press; [etc., etc.] (1924) 86 p. 1 l. 26 cm. (Yale oriental series. Researches, vol. xi. pt. 1) The author's doctoral dissertation, Yale university, 1932, but not published as a thesis. [BP75.A7] 24-
1. Muhammad, the prophet. 2. Mysticism—Mohammodanism. I. Title.

*AZZAM, Abdel Rahman, 1893- 297
The eternal message of Muhammad. Tr. from Arabic by Caesar E. Farah. Introd. by Vincent Sheean. New York, New Amer. Lib. [1965, c.1964] 254p. 18cm. (Mentor bk., MT634) .75 pap.,
I. Title.

BENGALEE, Mutiur Rahman. 922.97
The life of Muhammad, by Sufi Mutiur Rahman Bengalee, M. A. Chicago, Ill., The Moslem sunrise press, 1941. ix, 286 p. front., plates, map. 20 cm. Bibliography: p. 281-282. [BP75.B4] 42-5460
1. Muhammad, the prophet. I. Title.

BODLEY, Ronald Victor Courtenay, 1892- 297'.63 B
The messenger; the life of Mohammed, by R. V. C. Bodley. New York, Greenwood Press [1969, c1946] xiv, 368 p. 23 cm. Bibliography: p. 360. [BP75.B56 1969] 70-92296
1. Muhummad, the prophet. I. Title.

BODLEY, Ronald Victor Courtenay, 1892- 922.97
The messenger; the life of Mohammed, by R. V. C. Bodley ... Garden City, New York, Doubleday & company, inc., 1946. xiv p., 1 l., 368 p. 22 cm. "First edition." Bibliography: p. 360. [BP75.B56] 46-2458
1. Muhammad, the prophet. I. Title.

BUSH, George, 1796-1859. 297
The life of Mahommed; founder of the religion of Islam, and of the empire of the Saracens. By the Rev. George Bush, A.M. 1st Canada ed. Niagara, H. Chapman, 1831. 112 p. 20 cm. [BP75.B8 1831] 2-5539
1. Muhammad, the prophet. I. Title.

BUSH, George, 1796-1859. 297
...The life of Mohammed; founder of the religion of Islam, and of the empire of the Saracens. By the Rev. George Bush, A.M. New York, Printed by J. & J. Harper, 1831. 261 p. front. (fold. plan) 16 cm. (On cover: Harper's family library, no x) At head of title: Harper's stereotype edition. Cover dated 1830. [BP75.B8 1831a] 39-22836
1. Muhammad, the prophet. I. Title.

BUSH, George, 1796-1859. 922.
... The life of Mohammed; founder of the religion of Islam, and of the empire of the Saracens. By the Rev. George Bush, A.M. New York, Harper & brothers, 1837. 261 p. front. (fold. plan) 16 cm. (On cover: The Family library. No. 10) At head of title: Harper's stereotype edition. [BP75.B8 1837] 44-27298
1. Muhammad, the prophet. I. Title.

BUSH, Gorge, 1796-1859. 297
...The life of Mohammed; founder of the religion of Islam, and of the empire of the Saracens. By the Rev. George Bush... New York, Printed by J. & J. Harper, 1830. 261 p. front. (fold. plan) 16 cm. On cover: Harper's family library, no. x) At head of title: Harper's stereotype edition. [BP75.B8 1830] 22-22541
1. Muhammad, the prophet. I. Title.

DERMENGHEM, Emile, 1872- 297'.63 B
Muhammad and the Islamic tradition. Translated from the French by Jean M. Watt. Westport, Conn., Greenwood Press [1974, c1958] 191 p. illus. 22 cm. (Men of wisdom, MW6) Reprint of the ed. published by Harper, New York, which was issued as no. MW6 of Men of wisdom. Bibliography: p. 188-191. [BP75.D393 1974] 73-15204 ISBN 0-8371-7163-6 12.25
1. Muhammad, the prophet. 2. Islam. I. Title. II. Series.

DIBBLE, Roy Floyd, 1887- 297
Mohammed, by R. F. Dibble. New York, The Viking press, 1926. 257 p. 23 cm. [BP75.D45] 26-17132
1. Muhammed, the prophet. I. Title.

DRAYCOTT, Gladys M. 297
Mahomet, founder of Islam, by G. M. Draycott. New York, Dodd, Mead & company, 1916. 2 p. l., 7-351 p. 22 1/2 cm. Printed in Great Britain. [BP75.D7] 17-248
1. Muhammad, the prophet. I. Title.

ESSAD, Bey. 922.97
Mohammed; a biography, by Essad bey. Translated by Helmut L. Ripperberger. New York, Toronto, Longmans, Green and co., 1936. vi, 376 p. 21 cm. "First edition." [BP75.E8] 37-27173
1. Muhammad, the prophet. I. Ripperger, Helmut Lother, 1897- tr. II. Title.

FINGER, Charles J. 297
... Mahomet [by] Charles J, Finger. Girard, Kan., Haldeman-Julius company [c1923] 64 p. 13 cm. (Ten cent pocket series, no. 412, ed. by E. Haldeman-Julius) Advertising matter: p. 57-64. Bibliography: p. 56. [BP75.F5] CA 24
1. Muhammad, the prophet. I. Title.

GIBBON, Edward. 1737-1794.
Life of Mahomet. By Edward Gibbon. With notes by Dean Milman and Dr. William Smith. Boston, Houghton, Mifflin and company, 1881. xii, [9]-236 p. 16 cm. (On cover: Biographical series) "Editor's preface", March 1859, signed O. W. Wight. A 33
1. Muhammad, the prophet. I. Wight, Orlando William, 1824-1888, ed. II. Milman, Henry Hart, 1791-1868. III. Smith, William, Sir. 1813-1893. IV. Title.

GLUBB, John Bagot, Sir, 1897- 297.63 B
The life and times of Muhammad, by John Bagot Glubb (Glubb Pasha). New York, Stein and Day [1970] 416 p. geneal. tables, maps. 25 cm. Bibliography: p. [403]-405. [BP75.G58] 74-87954 10.00
1. Muhammad, the prophet. I. Title.

HOLLAND, Edith.
Mohammed, by Edith Holland; with frontispiece in color and eight black and white illustrations. New York, Frederick A. Stokes company [c1914] 191, [1] p. col. front., illus. (map) plates. 19 1/2 cm. (On verso of half title: Heroes of all time) $0.75 Published in Great Britain under title: The story of Mohammed. 14-17657
1. Muhammad, the prophet. I. Title.

HOSAIN, Safdar. 297'.63'0924
Who was Mohammed. [Hyderabad, India, 1967] 122 p. 22 cm. Rs 3 [BP75.H67] S A
1. Muhammad, the prophet. I. Title.

HUSAIN, Athar, 1920- 297.63
Prophet Muhammad and his mission. Bombay, New York, Asia Pub. [1967] xi. 214p. 23cm. Bibl. [BP75.H8] SA 67 5.25
1. Muhammad, the prophet. I. Title. Distributed by Taplinger.

IRVING, Washington, 1783-1859. 922.97
Life of Mahomet [by] Washington Irving. London, J. M. Dent & sons, ltd.; New York, E. P. Dutton & co., inc. [1935] xx, 265, [1] p. 17 1/2 cm. (Half-title: Everyman's library, ed. by Ernest Rhys. Biography. [no. 513]) "First published in this edition, 1911; reprinted ... 1935." "Introduction by Prof. E. Vernon Arnold." [AC1.E8 no. 513] 36-37423
1. Muhammad, the prophet. 2. Mohammedanism. I. Title.

IRVING, Washington, 1783-1859.
Life of Mahomet, by Washington Irving. London, J. M. Dent & sons, ltd.; New York, E. P. Dutton & co. [1911] xx, 265 p. 17 1/2 cm. (Half-title: Everyman's library, ed. by Ernest Rhys. Biography. [no. 513]) Introduction by Prof E. Vernon Arnold. Bibliography: p. XV. A 12
1. Muhammad, the prophet. 2. Mohammedanism. I. Title.

IRVING, Washington, 1783-1859. 297'.63 B
Mahomet and his successors. New York, Putnam. [New York, AMS Press, 1973] 2 v. illus. 19 cm. (The works of Washington Irving, v. 15-16) At head of title: Hudson edition. Reprint of the 1889 ed. [DS38.3.I76 1973] 73-8685 20.00 ea.
1. Muhammad, the prophet. 2. Islamic Empire—History. I. Title.

IRVING, Washington, 1783-1859. 297'.63 B
Mahomet and his successors. Edited by Henry A. Pochmann and E. N. Feltskog. Madison, University of Wisconsin Press, 1970. xiv, 651 p. facsims., map. 24 cm. (The Complete works of Washington Irving) Includes bibliographical references. [DS38.3.I76 1970] 77-15207
1. Muhammad, the prophet. 2. Islamic Empire—History. I. Pochmann, Henry August, 1901- ed. II. Feltskog, E. N., ed. III. Title.

IRVING, Washington, 1783-1859. 297
Mahomet and his successors. By Washington Irving. [Knickerbocker ed.] ... New York, G. P. Putnam and son, 1868-69. 2 v. fronts., pl. 19 1/2 cm. Added title-pages, engraved. [BP75.I 73] 7-19341
1. Muhammad, the prophet. 2. Mohammedanism. 3. Mohammedan empire. I. Title.

IRVING, Washington, 1783-1859. 922.97
... Mahomet and his successors, by Washington Irving ... New York and London, G. P. Putnam's sons [1897] 3 v. fronts. 18 cm. At head of title: Knickerbocker edition. Contents.--v. 1-2. Mahomet and his successors.--v. 3, Mahomet and his successors. The legend of Don Roderick. The legend of Pelayo. Abderahman. [DS238.A1 I 7 1897] 4-21974
1. Muhammad, the prophet. 2. Mohammedanism. 3. Mohammedan empire. 4. Caliphs. I. Title.

IRVING, Washington, 1783-1859. 922.97
... Mahomet and his successors, by Washington Irving ... New York, G. P. Putnam's sons [1902] 2 v. fronts. 21 cm. At head of title: Hudson edition. Added t.-p., engraved. Publishers' lettering: Irving's works. [v. 15-16] [PS2050.F02 vol. 15-16] (817.24) 4-17612
1. Muhammad, the prophet. 2. Mohammedanism. 3. Mohammendan empire. 4. Caliphs. I. Title.

IRVING, Washington, 1783-1859.
Mahomet and his successors, By Washington Irving. [New York, Belford company, 188-?] 499 p. 19 cm. (With, as issued, his Life of Oliver Goldsmith. New York [188-?]) [PS2052.B4] 44-44744
1. Muhammad, the prophet. 2. Mohammedanism. I. Title.

JEFFERY, Arthur, ed. 297.082
Islam; Muhammad and his religion. Edited, with an introd. by Arthur Jeffery. New York, Liberal Arts Press [1958] 252p. 21cm. (The Library of religion, no. 6) [BP161.J4] 58-9958
1. Muhammad, the prophet. 2. Mohammedanism. I. Title.

JEFFERY, Arthur, ed.
Islam: Muhammad and his religion. Edited, with an introd. by Arthur Jeffery. Indianapolis, New York. Bobbs-Merrill [c1958] 252 p. 21 cm. (The Library of liberal arts) 66-15465
1. Muhammad, the prophet. 2. Islam. I. Title.

JOHNSTONE, Peirce De Lacy 922.97
Henry, 1850-
... Muhammad and his power, by P. De Lacy Johnstone ... New York, C. Scribner's sons, 1901. xviii, 238 p. 19 cm. (Half-title: The world's epoch-makers, ed. by O. Smeaton. [vii]) Series title also at head of t.-p. "Some leading dates in the history": p. xiii-xiv. [BP75.J6] 2-9884
1. Muhammad, the prophet. I. Title.

KHAN, Muhammad 297'.63 B
Zafrulla, Sir, 1893-
Muhammad, seal of the prophets / Muhammad Zafrulla Khan. London ; Boston : Routledge & Kegan Paul, 1980. viii, 289 p. ; 21 cm. Includes index. Bibliography: p. 284. [BP75.K4973] 19 80-40570 ISBN 0-7100-0610-1 (pbk.) : 12.50
1. Muhammad—Biography. 2. Muslims—Saudi Arabia—Biography. I. Title.

KHEIRALLAH, George Ibrahim, 297
1879-
Islam, and the Arabian prophet, by Dr. G. I. Kheirallah ... From Arabian and Islamic sources. New York city, Islamic publishing company [c1938] 6 p. l., 176 p. illus., facsim. 28 1/2 cm. Title also in Arabic. [BP75.K5] 39-25417
1. Muhammad, the prophet. 2. Mohammedanism. I. Title.

THE life of Mahomet; 922.97
or, The history of that imposture which was begun, carried on, and finally established by him in Arabia; and which was subjugated a larger portion of the globe, than the religion of Jesus has yet set at liberty. 2d American ed. New-York: Published by Evert Duyckinck, no. 102 Pearl-street. J. C. Totten, printer, 1813. vi, [7]-118 p. 14 cm. [BP75.L5 1813] 32-11970
1. Muhammad, the prophet.

MARGOLIOUTH, David Samuel, 297
1858-
Mohammed and the rise of Islam, by D. S. Margoliouth. 3d ed. New York and London, G. P. Putnam's sons [19-] 2 p. l., iii-xxvi p., 1 l., 481 p. front., plates, facsims., fold. maps. 20 cm. (Half-title: Heroes of the nations) First edition, 1905. Bibliography: p. xxiii-xxvi. [BP75.M3] 21-19550
1. Muhammad, the prophet. 2. Mohammedanism—Hist. I. Title.

MARGOLIOUTH, David 297'.63 B
Samuel, 1858-1940.
Mohammed and the rise of Islam. Freeport, N.Y., Books for Libraries Press [1972] xxvi, 481 p. illus. 23 cm. Reprint of the 1905 ed., issued in series: Heroes of the nations. Bibliography: p. xxiii-xxvi. [BP75.M3 1972] 73-38361 ISBN 0-8369-6778-X
1. Muhammad, the prophet. I. Title. II. Series: Heroes of the nations.

MARGOLIOUTH, David Samuel, 297
1858-1940.
Mohammed and the rise of Islam, by D. S. Margoliouth. New York [etc.] G. P. Putnam's sons, 1905. 2 p. l., iii-xxvi p., 1 l., 481 p. front., plates, 2 fold. maps. 20 cm. (Half-title: Heroes of the nations) Bibliography: p. xxiii-xxvi. [BP75.M2] 5-32424
1. Muhammad, the prophet. 2. Mohammedanism—Hist. I. Title.

RODINSON, Maxime. 297'.63 B
Mohammed. Translated by Anne Carter. New York, Vintage Books [1974, c1971] xix, 360 p. maps. 19 cm. Bibliography: p. 343-[346] [BP75.13.R613 1974] 73-14953 ISBN 0-394-71011-8 2.45 (pbk.)
1. Muhammad, the prophet.

RODINSON, Maxime. 297'.63 B
Mohammed. Translated by Anne Carter. [1st American ed.] New York, Pantheon Books [1971] xix, 360 p. illus. 22 cm. Bibliography: p. 315-324. [BP75.R5713 1971] 69-20189 ISBN 0-394-47110-5 8.95
1. Muhammad, the prophet.

STOBART, James William 297
Hampson.
... Islam & its founder. By J. W. H. Stobart ... Published under the direction of the Committee of general literature and education appointed by the Society for promoting Christian knowledge. London, Society for promoting Christian knowledge; New York, Pott, Young, & co. [1877] 1 p. l., 254 p. incl. geneal tab. fold. front. (map) 17 1/2 cm. (Non-Christian religious systems) [BP75.S67] 42-4109
1. Muhammad, the prophet. 2. Mohammedanism. I. Society for promoting Christian knowledge. London. General literature committee. II. Title.

SUGANA, Gabriele Mandel. 297'.63
The life and times of Mohammed; translator [from the Italian] Francis Koval. London, New York, Hamlyn, 1968. [1], 77 p. (chiefly illus. (chiefly col.) col. maps) 30 cm. (Portraits of greatness) German translation has title: Mohammed und seine zeit. Col. illus. on lining papers. [BP75.S9 1968] 70-433824 ISBN 0-600-03149-7 17/6
1. Muhammed, the prophet. I. Title.

WARREN, Ruth. 922.97
Muhammad, prophet of Islam. New York, F. Watts [1965] 133 p. 22 cm. (Immortals of philosophy and religion) [BP75.W296] 65-13070
1. Muhammad, the prophet.

WARREN, Ruth 922.97
Muhammad, prophet of Islam. New York, Watts [c.1965] 133p. 22cm. (Immortals of philo. and rel.) [BP75.W296] 65-13070 2.95
1. Muhammad, the prophet. I. Title.

WATT, William Montgomery 922.97
Muhammad: prophet and statesman [New York] Oxford [1964, c.1961] 250p. map. 19cm. (78) Abridgement of the author's Muhammad at Mecca and Muhammad at Medina. Bibl. 1.85 pap.,
1. Muhammad, the prophet. I. Title.

WATT, William Montgomery. 922.97
Muhammad: prophet and statesman. [London] Oxford University Press, 1961. 250 p. illus. 19 cm. "Essentially an abridgement of the [author's] . . . Muhammad at Mecca and Muhammad at Medina." Includes bibliography. [BP75.W33] 61-2473
1. Muhammad, the prophet. I. Title.

WATT, William Montgomery, 922.97
Muhammad at Mecca. Oxford, Clarendon Press, 1953. xvi. 192p. 23cm. Sequel: Muhammad at Medina. Bibliography: p. [viii]-ix. [BP75.W3] 53-13179
1. Muhammad. the prophet. I. Title.

WATT, William Montgomery, 922.97
Muhammad at Mecca. Oxford, Clarendon Press, 1953. xvi. 192p. 23cm. Sequel: Muhammad at Medina. Bibliography: p. [viii]-ix. [BP75.W3] 53-13179
1. Muhammad. the prophet. I. Title.

WATT. William Montgomery. 922.97
Muhammad at Medina. Oxford. Clarendon Press, 1956. xiv. 418p. map. 23cm. 'Sequel to Muhammad at Mecca.' Bibliographical footnotes. [BP75.W32] 56-4035
1. Muhammad. the prophet. I. Title.

WATT, William Montgomery 922.97
Muhammad: prophet and statesman. [New York] Oxford Univ. Press [c.]1961. 250p. illus. Bibl. 61-2473 4.00
1. Muhammad, the prophet. I. Title.

WATT, William 297'.63 B
Montgomery.
Muhammad: prophet and statesman [by] W. Montgomery Watt. London, New York, Oxford University Press [1974, c1961] 250 p. 21 cm. (A Galaxy book, 409) "Essentially an abridgement of the ... [author's] Muhammad at Mecca and Muhammad at Medina." Includes bibliographical references. [BP75.W33 1974] 74-163338 ISBN 0-19-881078-4 2.95 (pbk.)
1. Muhammad, the prophet.

Muhammad, the prophet—Addresses, essays, lectures.

NIYAZI, Kausar. 297'.38
To the Prophet / Kausar Niazi ; [translated by Saeed-ul-Hassan and edited by Karam Hydri]. 1st ed. Lahore : Sh. Muhammad Ashraf, 1976. xi, 150 p. ; 22 cm. Translation of Zikr-i Rasul. Includes quotations in Arabic with Urdu translation. [BP75.N59] 76-938515 Rs16.00
1. Muhammad, the prophet—Addresses, essays, lectures. 2. Mawlid al-Nabi—Addresses, essays, lectures. I. Title.

Muhammad, the prophet—Biography.

RODINSON, Maxime. 297'.63 B
Mohammed / Maxime Rodinson ; translated from the French by Anne Carter ; with a new introd. on contemporary Islam by the author. New York : Pantheon Books, 1979. p. cm. Translation of Mahomet. Reprint of the 1971 ed. published by Pantheon Books, New York. Includes index. Bibliography: p. [BP75.13.R613 1979] 79-17158 ISBN 0-394-50908-0 : 15.00 ISBN 0-394-73822-5 pbk. : 4.95
1. Muhammad, the prophet—Biography. 2. Muslims—Saudi Arabia—Biography. I. Title.

Muhammad the prophet—Campaigns.

AL-WAQIDI, Muhammad ibn 297.63
'Umar 747-or8-823.
The kitab al-maghazi of al-Waqidi, ed. by Marsden Jones. London, Oxford Univ. Pr., 1966. 3v. (46, xiii, 1321p.) 8 plates. 25cm. Includes bibls., and a pref. and bibl. in English. Text in Arabic [BP75.W3] NE67 20.20 set.,
1. Muhammad the prophet—Campaigns. I. Jones, Marsden, ed. II. Title.

Muhammad, the Prophet—Juvenile literature.

KELEN, Betty. 297'.63 B
Muhammad : the messenger of God / by Betty Kelen. 1st ed. Nashville: T. Nelson, [1975] 278 p. ; 21 cm. Includes index. Bibliography: p. 261. [BP75.K43] 75-5792 ISBN 0-8407-6440-5 : 6.95
1. Muhammad, the prophet—Juvenile literature.

PIKE, Edgar Royston, 1896- 297
Mohammed, founder of the religion of Islam. New York, Roy [1964, c.1962] 127p. illus. 19cm. (Roy's pathfinder biographies) 64-10672 3.50 bds.,
1. Muhammad, the Prophet—Juvenile literature. I. Title. II. Title: Founder of the religion of Islam.

PIKE, Edgar Royston, 297'.63 B
1896-
Mohammed; prophet of the religion of Islam [by] E. Royston Pike. New York, F. A. Praeger [1969, c1965] viii, 117 p. illus. 23 cm. (Praeger pathfinder biographies) 1962 and 1964 editions published under title: Mohammed, founder of the religion of Islam. Bibliography: p. 113-114. A biography of the founder of Islam who is revered by his followers as the first prophet of Allah. Includes chapters of the Koran, what a Muslim believes, and how he practices his faith. [BP75.P5 1969] 92 68-55017
1. Muhammad, the prophet—Juvenile literature. 2. [Muhammad, the prophet.] I. Title.

Muhammad, the prophet—Political career.

IQBAL, Afzal. 327'.2'0924 B
The Prophet's diplomacy : the art of negotiation as conceived and developed by the Prophet of Islam / by Iqbal Afzal ; foreword by S. A. Rahman ; pref. by Muhammad Daud Rahbar. Cape Cod, Mass. : C. Stark, [1975] xxxiii, 142 p. ; 23 cm. Earlier ed. published under title: Diplomacy in Islam. Includes index. Bibliography: p. [138]-139. [BP77.69.I65 1975] 74-20174 ISBN 0-89007-006-7 : 8.00
1. Muhammad, the prophet—Political career. 2. Diplomacy. I. Title.

Muhammad, the prophet—Spiritual life.

ARCHER, John Clark, 1881- 297'.63
1957.
Mystical elements in Mohammed / by John Clark Archer. New York : AMS Press, [1980] c1924. 86 p. ; 24 cm. Reprint of the ed. published by Yale Univeristy Press, New Haven, which was issued as v. 11, pt. 1 of Yale oriental series, Researches. Includes bibliographical references. [BP75.A7 1980] 19 80-26396 ISBN 0-404-60281-9 : 22.50
1. Muhammad, the prophet—Spiritual life. I. Title. II. Series: Yale oriental series : Researches ; v. 11, pt. 1.

Muhammadijah.

PEACOCK, James L. 301.29'59
Muslim puritans : reformist psychology in Southeast Asian Islam / James L. Peacock. Berkeley : University of California Press, c1978. xi, 276 p. ; 22 cm. Includes index. Bibliography: p. 251-269. [BP63.I5P4] 76-55571 ISBN 0-520-03403-1 : 18.75
1. Muhammadijah. 2. Islam—Indonesia. 3. Islam—Singapore. 4. Islam—Malaysia. 5. Islam—Psychology. I. Title.

PEACOCK, James L. 297'.8
Purifying the faith : the Muhammadijah movement in Indonesian Islam / James L. Peacock. Menlo Park, Calif. : Benjamin/Cummings Pub Co., c1978. x, 118 p. : ill. ; 24 cm. (The Kiste and Ogan social change series in anthropology) Includes index. Bibliography: p. [112]-[114] [BP10.M83P4] 78-61992 ISBN 0-8053-7824-3 : 11.95
1. Muhammadijah. I. Title. II. Series: Kiste and Ogan social change series in anthropology.

Muhlenberg Co., Ky. Unity Baptist church.

ROTHERT, Otto Arthur, 1871-
A history of Unity Baptist church, Muhlenberg County, Kentucky, by Otto A. Rothert. Louisville, Ky., Press of J. P. Morton & company, incorporated, 1914. 2 p. l., 59 p. illus. (incl. facsim.) 21 cm. 14-13566 0.30
1. Muhlenberg Co., Ky. Unity Baptist church. I. Title.

Muhlenberg, Henry Melchior, 1711-1787.

FRICK, William Keller, 1850- 922.
Henry Melchior Muhlenberg, "patriarch of the Lutheran church in America." By Rev. William K. Frick ... Philadelphia, Lutheran publication society [1902] iv, 5-200 p. front. (port.) 16 cm. (On cover: Lutheran handbook series) [BX8080.M9F8] 2-22723
1. Muhlenberg, Henry Melchior, 1711-1787. I. Title.

MANN, William Julius, 922.473
1819-1892.
Life and times of Henry Melchior Muhlenberg. By William J. Mann ... Philadelphia, G. W. Frederick, 1887. xvi, 547 p. front. (port.) 23 cm. [BX8080.M9M3] 12-36528
1. Muhlenberg, Henry Meichlor, 1711-1787. I. Title.

MUHLENBERG, Henry 922.473
Melchiar
The notebook of a colonial clergyman, condensed from the Journals of Henry Melchior Muhlenberg. Translated [from the German]and edited by Theodore G. Tappert and John W. Doberstein, Philadelphia, Muhlenberg Press. [c.]1959. vi, 250p. 21 cm. 59-10536 3.50
I. Title.

MUHLENBERG, Henry Melchior, 1711-1787. 922.473
The journals of Henry Melchior Muhlenberg. Translated by Theodore G. Tappert and John W. Doberstein. Philadelphia, Evangelical Lutheran Ministerium of Pennsylvania and Adjacent States, 1942-58. 3v. port. 27cm. [BX8080.M9A4] 42-18316
I. Title.

MUHLENBERG, Henry Melchior, 1711-1787. 922.473
The journals of Henry Melchior Muhlenberg ... translated by Theodore G. Tappert and John W. Doberstein ... Philadelphia, The Evangelical Lutheran ministerium of Pennsylvania and adjacent states and the Muhlenberg press, 1942- v. front. (port.) 27 cm. [BX8080.M9A4] 42-18316
I. Tappert, Theodore Gerhardt, 1904- tr. II. Doberstein, John W., joint tr. III. Evangelical Lutheran ministerium of Pennsylvania and adjacent states. IV. Title.

MUHLENBERG, Henry Melchior, 1711-1787. 284'.1'0924 B
The notebook of a colonial clergyman : condensed from The journals of Henry Melchior Muhlenberg / translated and edited by Theodore G. Tappert and John W. Doberstein. Philadelphia : Fortress Press, 1975, c1959. vi, 249 p. ; 20 cm. Includes index. [BX8080.M9A43 1975] 75-24119 ISBN 0-8006-1804-1 pbk. : 3.50
1. Muhlenberg, Henry Melchoir, 1711-1787. I. Title.

RIFORGIATO, Leonard R., 1939- 284.1'092'4 B
Missionary of moderation : Henry Melchior Muhlenberg and the Lutheran Church in English America / Leonard R. Rigorgiato. Lewisburg [Pa.] : Bucknell University Press ; London : Associated University Presses, c1980. p. cm. Includes index. Bibliography: p. [BX8080.M9R53] 78-75203 ISBN 0-8387-2379-9 : 14.50
1. Muhlenberg, Henry Melchior, 1711-1787. 2. Lutheran Church—Clergy—Biography. 3. Lutheran Church in the United States—History. 4. Clergy—United States—Biography. I. Title.

SEEBACH, Margaret Rebecca (Himes) Mrs., 1875- 922.
An eagle of the wilderness; the story of Henry Melchior Muhlenberg, by Margaret R. Seebach... Philadelphia, Pa., The United Lutheran publication house [c1924] 139 p. front., plates. 19 cm. [BX8080.M9S4] 24-24076
1. Muhlenberg, Henry Melchior, 1711-1787. I. Title.

STOEVER, Martin Luther, 1820-1870. 922.473
Memoir of the life and times of Henry Melchior Muhlenberg ... By M. L. Stoever ... For the Lutheran board of publication. Philadelphia, Lindsay & Blakiston, 1856. xii, 13-120 p. incl. front. (port.) 17 1/2 cm. Advertising matter: p. [l] [BX8080.M9S8] 36-33020
1. Muhlenberg, Henry Melchior, 1711-1787. I. Lutheran board of publication. II. Title.

SUSQUEHANNA synod of the Evangelical Lutheran church in the United States. 922.473
In memoriam. Henry Melchior Muhlenberg, 1711. 1742. 1787. Commemorative exercises held by the Susquehanna synod of the Evangelical Lutheran church, at Selinsgrove, Penna., October 18 and 19, 1887. Published for the synod's committee. Philadelphia, Lutheran publication society, 1888. 62 p. front. (port.) 22 cm. [BX8080.M9S85] 23-3539
1. Muhlenberg, Henry Melchior, 1711-1787. 2. Muhlenberg family. I. Title.
Contents omitted.

Muhlenberg, William Augustus, 1796-1877.

AYERS, Anne, 1816-1896. 922.373
The life and work of William Augustus Muhlenberg, by Anne Ayres ... New York, A. D. F. Randolph & company [1884] 2 p. l., [iii] xiv, 524 p. incl. pl., facsim., port. front. 20 cm. [BX5995.M8A9 1884] 34-24955
1. Muhlenberg, William Augustus, 1796-1877. I. Title.

AYRES, Anne, 1816-1896. 922.973
The life and work of William Augustus Muhlenberg, by Anne Ayres ... New York, Harper & brothers, 1880. 4, [v]-xiv, 524 p. incl. pl., facsim. 2 port. (incl. front.) 24 cm. [BX5995.M8A9 1890] 34-24954
1. Muhlenberg, William Augustus, 1796-1877. I. Title.

AYRES, Anne, 1816-1896. 922.373
The life and work of William Augustus Muhlenberg ...by Anne Ayres ... 4th ed. New York, T. Whittaker, 1889. 2 p. l., [iii] -xiv, 384, 387-524 p. incl. pl. 2 port. (incl. front.) 2. facsim. on 4 pl. 23 cm. [BX5995.M8A9 1889] 12-30474
1. Muhlenberg, William Augustus, 1796-1877. I. Title.

SKARDON, Alvin Wilson, 1912- 283'.0924 B
Church leader in the cities: William Augustus Muhlenberg [by] Alvin W. Skardon. Philadelphia, University of Pennsylvania Press [1971] 343 p. illus., geneal. tables, ports. 24 cm. Originally presented as the author's thesis, University of Chicago, 1960, under the title: William Augustus Muhlenberg: pioneer urban church leader. Bibliography: p. 312-334. [BX5995.M8S54 1971] 70-92853 ISBN 0-8122-7596-9 15.00
1. Muhlenberg, William Augustus, 1796-1877. I. Title.

Muhtasib (Mohammedan official)

MUHAMMAD ibn'Abd Allan, called Ibn al-Ukhuwah, d.1329. 892.78
The Ma'alim al-qurba fi ahkam al-hisba of Diya' al-Din Muhammad ibn Muhammad al-Qurashi al-Shafi'i, known as Ibn al-Ukhuwwa; edited, with abstract of contents, glossary and indices by Reuben Levy ... [Cambridge, Eng.] Printed by the Cambridge university press for the Trustees of the "E. J. W. Gibb memorial": London, Luzac & co., 1938. xvii, [1], 113, 247 p. 26 cm. (Half-title: "E. J. W. Gibb memorial" series. New series, xii) Arabic text paged with Arabic numeral characters. [PJ709.G62 vol. 12] 892.708 41-18311
1. Muhtasib (Mohammedan official) 2. Mohammedanism. 3. Mohammedans—Soc. life & cust. I. Levy, Reuben, ed. II. Title.

Muilenburg, James.

ANDERSON, Bernhard W., ed. 221.6
Israel's prophetic heritage; essays in honor of James Muilenburg. Ed. by Bernhard W. Anderson, Walter Harrelson. New York, Harper [c.1962] xiv, 242p. port. 22cm. 62-11122 5.00
1. Muilenburg, James. 2. Bible. O. T.—Addresses, essays, lectures. 3. Bible. O. T. Prophets—Criticism, interpretation, etc. I. Harrelson, Walter J., joint ed. II. Title.

RHETORICAL criticism 809'.935'22
: essays in honor of James Muilenburg / edited by Jared J. Jackson and Martin Kessler. Pittsburgh : Pickwick Press, [1974] xviii, 287 p. : port. ; 22 cm. (Pittsburgh theological monograph series ; no. 1) Contents.Contents.—Introduction: Anderson, B. W. The new frontier of rhetorical criticism; a tribute to James Muilenburg.—Pentateuch: Kessler, M. Rhetorical criticism of Genesis 7. Kikawada, I. M. The shape of Genesis 11:1-9. Hamlin, E. J. The liberator's ordeal; a study of Exodus 4:1-9.—Former prophets: Rose, A. S. The "principles" of divine election; wisdom in 1 Samuel, 16. Ritterspach, A. D. Rhetorical criticism and the Song of Hannah. Ridout, G. The rape of Tamar.—Latter prophets: Jackson, J. J. Style in Isaiah 28 and a drinking bout of the gods (RS 24.258). Sacon, K. K. Isaiah 40:1-11; a rhetorical-critical study. Fisher, R. W. The herald of good news in Second Isaiah. Holmgren, F. Yahweh the avenger; Isaiah 63:1-6. Brueggemann, W. Israel's sense of place in Jeremiah. Raitt, T. M. Jeremiah's deliverance message to Judah.—Writings: Kuntz, J. K. The canonical wisdom psalms of ancient Israel: their rhetorical, thematic and formal dimensions.—Miscellanea biblica: Gottwald, N. K. Were the early Israelites pastoral nomads? March, W. E. Laken: its functions and meanings. Ball, I. J. Additions to a bibliography of James Muilenburg's writings (p. [285]-287) Includes bibliographical references. [BS1192.R48] 74-22493 ISBN 0-915138-00-X : 7.95
1. Muilenburg, James. 2. Muilenburg, James—Bibliography. 3. Bible. O.T.—Addresses, essays, lectures. I. Muilenburg, James. II. Jackson, Jared Judd, 1930- ed. III. Kessler, Martin, 1927- ed. IV. Title. V. Series.

Muktananda Paramhamsa, Swami.

MUKTANANDA Paramhamsa, Swami. 294.5'6 B
Guru: Chitshaktivilas; the play of consciousness. [1st ed.] New York, Harper & Row [1971] xxx, 175 p. illus. 22 cm. [BL1175.M77A313 1971] 77-148442 ISBN 0-06-066045-7 5.95
1. Muktananda Paramhamsa, Swami. 2. Spiritual life (Hinduism) I. Title.

MUKTANANDA Paramhamsa, Swami. 294.5'43
Play of consciousness = Chitshakti vilas / Swami Muktananda. [2d ed.]. San Francisco : Harper & Row, 1978. xl, 322 p., [3] leaves of plates : ill. ; 22 cm. Translation of Citsakti vilasa. Includes index. [BL1228.M813 1978] 78-62769 ISBN 0-914602-37-3 pbk. : 5.95
1. Muktananda Paramhamsa, Swami. 2. Spiritual life (Hinduism) I. Title. II. Title: Chitshakti vilas.

PEARCE, Joseph Chilton. 291.4'3
The bond of power / Joseph Chilton Pearce. 1st ed. New York : Dutton, c1981. 179 p. ; 22 cm. Includes bibliographical references. [BL627.P4 1981] 19 80-22860 ISBN 0-525-06950-X : 10.95
1. Muktananda Paramhamsa, Swami. 2. Meditation. 3. Gurus. 4. Consciousness. 5. Creative ability. 6. Reality. I. Title.

Mulla Sadra, Muhammad ibn Ibrahim, d. 1641.

RAHMAN, Fazlur, 1919- 181'.07
The philosophy of Mulla Sadra (Sadr al-Din al-Shirazi) / Fazlur Rahman. 1st ed. Albany : State University of New York Press, 1975. vii, 277 p. ; 24 cm. (Studies in Islamic philosophy and science) Includes bibliographical references and indexes. [B753.M84R3] 75-31693 ISBN 0-87395-300-2 : 20.00
1. Mulla Sadra, Muhammad ibn Ibrahim, d. 1641. I. Title. II. Series.

Mullany, Patrick Francis, 1847-1898.

SMITH, John Talbot, 1855-1923. 922.273
Brother Azarias; the life story of an American monk, by Rev. John Talbot Smith ... New York, W. H. Young & company, 1897. 2 p. l., [iii]-vii, 280 p. 5 pl., 3 port. (incl. front.) 20 1/2 cm. [BX4705.M8S6] 4-16972
1. Mullany, Patrick Francis, 1847-1898. I. Title.

Mulleaburg, James.

ANDERSON, Bernhard W ed. 221.6
Israel's prophetic heritage: essays in honor of James Muilenburg. Edited by Bernhard W. Anderson and Walter Harrelson. 1st ed. New York, Harper [1962] xiv, 242p. port. 22cm. [BS1192.A4] 62-11122
1. Mulleaburg, James. 2. Bible. O. T.—Addresses, essays, lectures. 3. Bible. O. T. Prophets—Criticism. interpretation, etc. I. Harreison, Walter., joint ed. II. Title.
Contents omitted.

Muller, Friedrich Max, 1823-1900.

†BROWN, Robert, 1844- 292'.1'3
Semitic influence in Hellenic mythology / Robert Brown. New York : Arno Press, 1977. xv, 228 p. ; 23 cm. (International folklore) Reprint of the 1898 ed. published by Williams and Norgate, London. Includes index. [BL785.B7 1977] 77-70583 ISBN 0-405-10084-1 : 14.00
1. Muller, Friedrich Max, 1823-1900. Contributions to the science of mythology. 2. Lang, Andrew, 1844-1912. Modern mythology. 3. Mythology, Greek. 4. Mythology, Semitic. 5. Mythology. I. Title. II. Series.

Mullings, Gwedolyn Lydia, 1928-

MULLINGS, Gwendolyn Lydia, 1928- 209'.2'4 B
My pilgrim journey : the making of an evangelist / by Gwendolyn Lydia Mullings. New York : William-Frederick Press, 1976. 91 p. ; 22 cm. [BX8809.M84A35] 76-47764 ISBN 0-87164-035-X : 3.50
1. Mullings, Gwedolyn Lydia, 1928- 2. Plymouth Brethren in New York (City)—Biography. 3. New York (City)—Biography. I. Title.

Mullins, Edgar Young, 1860-1928.

MULLINS, Isla May (Hawley) Mrs. 1859-1936. 922.673
Edgar Young Mullins, an intimate biography, by Isla May Mullins. Nashville, Tenn., Sunday school board of the Southern Baptist convention [c1929] 216 p. plates, ports. 20 cm. [BX6495.M8M8] 42-483
1. Mullins, Edgar Young, 1860-1928. I. Southern Baptist convention. Sunday school board. II. Title.

Mulry, Thomas Maurice, 1855-1916.

MEEHAN, Thomas F. 922.
Thomas Maurice Mulry, by Thomas F. Meehan. New York, The Encyclopedia press, inc. [c1917] 3 p. l., 247 p. front. (port.) 21 cm. "Papers and addresses": p. 120-240. [BX4705.M9M4] 17-18042 1.50
1. Mulry, Thomas Maurice, 1855-1916. I. Title.

MEEHAN, Thomas Francis, 1854-1942. 922.
Thomas Maurice Mulry. New York, Encyclopedia Press [1917] 247 p. port. 21 cm. "Papers and addresses": p. 120-240. [BX4705.M9M4] 17-18042
1. Mulry, Thomas Maurice, 1855-1916. I. Title.

Muncie, Ind. First Presbyterian church.

THOMAS, Belle. 285.177265
... The first one hundred years; a history of the First Presbyterian church, Muncie, Indiana, by Belle Thomas. Publication sponsored by the Women's auxiliary and the Flower mission, 1938. [Muncie, ind., Scott printing company, c1938] vii, [1], 9-137 p. plates 22 cm. At head of title: 1838-1938. [BX9211.M85F5] 39-24403
1. Muncie, Ind. First Presbyterian church. I. Title.

Mundahoi.

ROTH, Don A., 1927- 248'.246'0924 B
Mundahoi, Borneo witch doctor / by Don A. Roth. Nashville : Southern Pub. Association, c1975. 126 p. : ports. ; 21 cm. (A Crown book) [BV3342.M86R67] 75-11398 ISBN 0-8127-0098-8 pbk. : 2.95
1. Mundahoi. 2. Seventh-Day Adventists—Missions. 3. Missions—Sabah.

Mundelein, George William, 1872-1939.

KANTOWICZ, Edward R. 282'.092'4 B
Corporation sole : Cardinal Mundelein and Chicago Catholicism / Edward R. Kantowicz. Notre Dame, Ind. : University of Notre Dame Press, c1982. p. cm. (Notre Dame studies in American Catholicism) [BX4705.M95K36 1982] 19 82-13420 ISBN 0-268-00738-1 : 19.95 ISBN 0-268-00739-X (pbk.) : 9.95
1. Mundelein, George William, 1872-1939. 2. Catholic Church—Bishops—Biography. 3. Catholic Church. Archdiocese of Chicago—History—20th century. 4. Bishops—United States—Biography. I. Title. II. Series.

MARTIN, Paul Revere, 1884- comp. 922.273
The first cardinal of the West; the story of the church in the archdiocese of Chicago, under the administration of His Eminence George cardinal Mundelein, third archbishop of Chicago and first cardinal of the West, compiled from the New world files and other authentic sources by Paul R. Martin; illustrated by Walter Krawiec. [Chicago, The New world publishing co., c1934] xvi, 17-215 p. illus., pl., ports. 24 cm. "Edited and arranged by the Rev. Timothy Rowan."--p. v. [Full name: Paul Revere Francis Martin] [BX4705.M95M3] 34-33075
1. Mundelein, George William, cardinal, 1872- 2. Catholic church in Chicago. I. Rowan, Timothy, ed. II. Title.

MUNDELEIN, George William, cardinal, 1872- 204
Letters of a bishop to his flock, by His Eminence George cardinal Mundelein ... New York, Cincinnati [etc.] Benziger brothers, 1927. 317 p. front. (port.) fold. pl. 19 cm. [BX890.M8] 27-25824
I. Title.

Mundurucu Indians—Missions.

BURKS, Arthur J., 1898- 922.281
Bells above the Amazon. New York, McKay [1951] 241 p. illus. 21 cm. "A Story Press book." [BV2853.B6B8] 51-14366
1. Mense, Hugo, 1879- 2. Mundurucu Indians—Missions. I. Title.

Mundurucu Indians—Religion and mythology.

MURPHY, Robert Francis, 1924- 299.8
Mundurucu religion. Berkeley, University of California Press, 1958. iv, 146p. illus., maps. 26cm. (University of California publications in American archaeology and ethnology, v. 49, no. 1) Bibliography: p. 145-146. [E51.C15 vol. 49, no. 1] A58
1. Mundurucu Indians—Religion and mythology. 2. Mundurucu Indians—Rites and ceremonies. I. Title. II. Series: California. University. University of California publications in American archaeology and ethnology, v. 49, no. 1

Munger, Theodore Thornton, 1830-1910.

BACON, Benjamin Wisner, 1860-1932. 920.
Theodore Thornton Munger, New England minister, by Benjamin Wisner Bacon. New Haven, Yale university press; London, H. Milford, Oxford university press, 1913. xxiii, 409 p. incl. front. (port.) plates. 23 cm. "Selected writings": p. [xvii]-xxiii. [BX7260.M8B3] 14-39
1. Munger, Theodore Thornton, 1830-1910. I. Title.

Munhall, Pa. Anne Ashley memorial Methodist Episcopal church.

SMELTZER, Wallace Guy, 1900- 287.674885
Homestead Methodism (1830-1933) the history of Methodism in Mifflin township, Allegheny county, Pa., being the story of the first Methodist Episcopal church in that township, variously named Whitaker church, the Franklin church, "The Neck" church, and the Anne Ashley memorial church, located at Twenty-second street, Munhall, Pa., in its background, origin, and work through the century, along with: the expansion of Methodism in the community from this original parent society; the coming of other religious communions to the vicinity; and an account of the settlement, and the industrial and social development of the Homestead district. By Wallace Guy Smeltzer...Published in connection with the centennial anniversary of the erection of the original church building, May 14th through 21st, 1933. [Pittsburg, Printed by the D. K. Murdoch company, c1933. 167 p. front., plates, ports., map. 20 cm. 32 p. incl. plan. 19 cm. Homestead Methodism supplement, being historical and informational material concerning the Anne Ashley memorial Methodist Episcopal church, Munhall, Pa., not included in the centennial volume, Homestead Methodism. Issued on May 27, 1934, on the ocassion of the 104th anniversary of the founding of the Anne Ashley memorial church [by] Wallace Guy Smeltzer...[Munhall? Pa.] The author [1943?] Autographed from typewritten copy. "A bibliography of the more important records consulted": p. 167. [BX8481.M8S5] 33-14156
1. Whitaker family. 2. Munhall, Pa. Anne Ashley memorial Methodist Episcopal church. 3. Methodist Episcopal church in Pennsylvania. I. Title.

Munich. Bayerische staatsbibliothek. Mss. lat. 6224

BIBLE. N. T. Gospels. Latin. 1888. Old Latin.
... The four Gospels from the Munich ms. (q) now numbered lat. 6224 in the Royal library at Munich; with a fragment from St. John in the Hof-bibliothek at Vienna (cod. lat. 502); edited, with the aid of Tischendorf's transcript (under the direction of the Bishop of Salisbury) by Henry J. White ... With a facsimile. Oxford, The Clarendon press, 1888. iv, [1], 166 p. front. (fold. facsim.) 23 x 20 cm. (Old-Latin Biblical texts: no. iii) Facsimile: Codex monaceusis (q) fol. 202 recto [St. Mark xvi, 16-20] "Additions and corrections to Old-Latin Biblical texts, nos. i and ii": p. [165]-166. [BS1989.A106 no. iii] 24-32107
1. Munich. Bayerische staatsbibliothek. Mss. lat. 6224 2. Vienna. National bibliothek. Mss. lat. 502. 3. Bible. N. T. Gospels. Latin—Versions—Old Latin. 4. Bible. Latin—Versions—Old Latin—N. T. Gospels. I. Bible. Latin. N. T. Gospels. 1888. Old Latin. II. Bible. N. T. John. Latin. 1888. Old Latin. III. Bible. Latin. N. T. John. 1888. Old Latin. IV. Bible. Manuscripts. Latin. N. T. Gospels. V. White, Henry Julian, 1859-1934, ed. VI. Wordsworth, John. bp. of Salisbury, 1843-1911. VII. Title.

Munroe, Elizabeth, 1793-1873.

JAMES, Mary Dagworthy (Yard) Mrs. 1810-1883. 922.773
"Mother Munroe." The shining path: as illustrated in the life and experienceof Elizabeth Munroe. By Mrs. Mary D. James ... Boston, J. H. Earle, 1880. 192 p. front. (port.) 17 cm. [BR1725.M8J3] 38-3077
1. Munroe, Elizabeth, 1793-1873. I. Title.

Munzer, Thomas, 1490 (ca.)-1525.

GRITSCH, Eric W. 284'.3 B
Reformer without a church; the life and thought of Thomas Muentzer, 1488?-1525, by Eric W. Gritsch. Philadelphia, Fortress Press [1967] xiv, 214 p. map, port. 24 cm. Bibliography: p. 199-208. [BX4946.M8G7] 67-20144
1. Munzer, Thomas, 1490 (ca.)-1525. I. Title.

Munzer, Thomas, 1490 (ca.)-1525—Addresses, essays, lectures.

THE Anabaptists and Thomas Muntzer / translated and edited by James M. Stayer, Werner O. Packull. Dubuque, Iowa : Kendall/Hunt Pub. Co., c1980. vii, 167 p. ; 24 cm. Bibliography: p. 165-167. [BX4931.2.A5] 19 80-81977 ISBN 0-8403-2235-6 pbk. : 9.95 284'.3
1. Munzer, Thomas, 1490 (ca.)-1525—Addresses, essays, lectures. 2. Anabaptists—Europe—History—16th century—Addresses, essays, lectures. I. Stayer, James M. II. Packull, Werner O., 1941-

Munzer, Thomas, 1490 (ca.)-1525—Bibliography.

HILLERBRAND, Hans Joachim. 016.284'3
Thomas Muntzer : a bibliography / Hans J. Hillerbrand. St. Louis : Center for Reformation Research, 1976. 34 p. ; 22 cm. (Sixteenth century bibliography ; 4) Includes index. [Z8604.5.H54] [BX4946.M8] 76-359502 2.00
1. Munzer, Thomas, 1490 (ca.)-1525—Bibliography. I. Title. II. Series.

Mural painting and decoration.

VINCENT IRENÉ (VONGEH)
The sacred oasis; caves of the thousand Buddhas, Tun Huang. With a pref. by Pearl Buck. Chicago, University of Chicago Press [1953] xix, 114p. illus. (1 col.) fold. map. 25cm. Bibliography: p. 111-112. A53
1. Tun-huang, Kansu. 2. Mural painting and decoration. 3. Decoration and ornament—China—Kansu. 4. Art, Buddhist. I. Title.

Mural painting and decoration, Thai.

WRAY, Elizabeth. 294.3'82
Ten lives of the Buddha; Siamese temple paintings and Jataka tales, by Elizabeth Wray, Clare Rosenfield, and Dorothy Bailey, with photos. by Joe D. Wray. [1st ed.] New York, Weatherhill [1972] 154 p. illus. (part col.) 27 cm. Bibliography: p. 151-154. The ten most popular Jataka tales, stories of Buddha's previous incarnations, accompanied by photographs of Siamese temple paintings depicting them. Includes background essays on the Jatakas and Siamese temple painting. [BL1411.J32W7] 73-179982 ISBN 0-8348-0067-5 12.95
1. Jatakas—Illustrations—Juvenile literature. 2. [Jatakas.] 3. Mural painting and decoration, Thai. 4. [Art, Thai.] I. Rosenfield, Clare, joint author. II. Bailey, Dorothy, joint author. III. Wray, Joe D., illus. IV. Jatakas. English. Selections. Wray. V. Title.

Murch, James DeForest, 1892-

MURCH, James DeForest, 1892- 269'.2'0924 B
Adventuring for Christ in changing times; an autobiography of James DeForest Murch. [Louisville, Ky.] Restoration Press, 1973. 348 p. port. 25 cm. [BX7343.M8A33] 73-84633
1. Murch, James DeForest, 1892- I. Title.

Murchison, Anne Ferrell.

MURCHISON, Anne Ferrell. 230
Milk for babes : using the Bible to find the answers to life's questions / Anne Ferrell Murchison. Waco, Tex. : Word Books, c1979. 255 p. ; 22 cm. [BV4501.2.M776] 78-63745 ISBN 0-8499-2868-0 : 6.95
1. Murchison, Anne Ferrell. 2. Christian life—1960- 3. Theology, Doctrinal—Popular works. I. Title.

Murder.

WRIGHT, Henry Clarke, 1797-1870. 179.
Man-killing, by individuals and nations, wrong--dangerous in all cases. By Henry C. Wright. Boston, M. A. Dow, 1841. 61 p. 15 cm. [BV4627.M8W7] 44-36763
1. Murder. 2. Capital punishment. 3. War. 4. Evil, Non-resistance to. I. Title.

Murder—Louisiana—New Orleans.

GAMBINO, Richard. 264.1'523'0976335
Vendetta : a true story of the worst lynching in America, the mass murder of Italian-Americans in New Orleans in 1891, the vicious motivitations behind it, and the tragic repercussions that linger to this day / Richard Gambino. 1st ed. Garden City, N.Y. : Doubleday, 1977. xi, 198 p., [12] leaves of plates : ill. ; 22 cm. Bibliography: p. 194-198. [HV6534.N45G35] 76-18345 ISBN 0-385-12273-X : 7.95
1. Murder—Louisiana—New Orleans. 2. Italian Americans. 3. Lynching—New Orleans. I. Title.

Murdock, Stephen.

MURDOCK, Alma. 248'.2'0924
Crowned. San Antonio, Tex., Naylor Co. [1962] 51p. illus. 23cm. [BV4935.M8M8] 62-13062
1. Murdock, Stephen. I. Title.

Murphey, Cecil B.

MURPHEY, Cecil B. 266'.5'20924 B
But God has promised / Cecil B. Murphey. Carol Stream, Ill. : Creation House, c1976. 169 p. ; 22 cm. [BV3625.K42M87 1976] 76-16283 ISBN 0-88419-001-3 pbk. : 2.95
1. Murphey, Cecil B. 2. Missionaries—Kenya—Biography. 3. Missionaries—United States—Biography. I. Title.

MURPHEY, Cecil B. 248'.4
Somebody knows I'm alive / by Cecil B. Murphey. Atlanta : John Knox Press, c1977. vi, 168 p. ; 21 cm. [BX9225.M8A37] 76-44967 ISBN 0-8042-2206-1 : 4.95
1. Murphey, Cecil B. 2. Presbyterian Church—Clergy—Biography. 3. Clergy—Georgia—Biography. I. Title.

Murphy, Bob.

MURPHY, Bob. 248'.246 B
Christianity rubs holes in my religion / by Bob Murphy. Houston : Hunter Ministries Pub. Co., c1976. 113 p. ; 20 cm. [BV4935.M84A33] 76-150938 1.95
1. Murphy, Bob. 2. Converts—United States—Biography. 3. Christian life—1960- I. Title.

Murphy, Carol R.

MURPHY, Carol R. 248'.3
O inward traveller / Carol R. Murphy. Wallingford, Pa. : Pendle Hill Publications, 1977. 31 p. ; 20 cm. (Pendle Hill pamphlet ; 216 ISSN 0031-4250s) Bibliography: p. 30-31. [BL627.M88] 77-91637 ISBN 0-87574-216-5 : 0.95
1. Murphy, Carol R. 2. Meditation. I. Title.

Murphy, Daniel Richard, 1802-1875.

MUSTAIN, Claud J 266.60924
Wilderness prophet; a biography of Daniel Richard Murphy, pioneer preacher, missionary, colporteur, 1802-1875 [by] Claud J. Mustain. Springfield, Mo., Cain-Service Print. Co. [1966] ii, 54 p. illus. 22 cm. [BX6495.M85M8] 66-6533
1. Murphy, Daniel Richard, 1802-1875. I. Title.

Murphy, Edgar Gardner, 1869-1913.

BAILEY, Hugh C. 283'.0924 B
Edgar Gardner Murphy, gentle progressive, by Hugh C. Bailey. Coral Gables, Fla., University of Miami Press [1968] xii, 274 p. illus., ports. 21 cm. Bibliography: p. [247]-258. [BX5995.M85B3] 68-29705 8.50
1. Murphy, Edgar Gardner, 1869-1913. 2. Southern States—History—1865- I. Title.

Murphy, Francis, 1836-1907.

VANDERSLOOT, Jacob Samuel, 1834-1882. 178.
The true path; or, Gospel temperance; being the life, work and speeches of Francis Murphy, Dr. Henry A. Reynolds, and their co-laborers. Embracing also a history of the Women's Christian temperance union. By Rev. J. Sam'l Vandersloot... New York, H. S. Goodspeed & co.; Boston, Crocker & co.; [etc., etc.] c1878] xi p., 1 l., 13-642 p. incl. plates,

ports., front., port. 19 1/2 cm. [HV5292.V3] 10-7143
1. Murphy, Francis, 1836-1907. 2. Reynolds, Henry Augustus, 1839- 3. Temperance. 4. Woman's Christian temperance union. I. Title.

VANDERSLOOT, Jacob Samuel, 1834-1882. 178.
The true path; or, The Murphy movement and gospel temperance. A complete history of the...great reformatory wave now deluging our land; together with the biography, addresses, incidents and anecdotes of Francis Murphy... By Rev. J. Saml. Vandersloot... Philadelphia, W. Flint; Minneapolis, Minn., Haber brothers; [etc., etc.] 1877. 2 p. l., [3]-408 p. front., (port.) 19 cm. [HV5292.V28] 10-7144
1. Murphy, Francis, 1836-1907. 2. Temperance. I. Title.

Murphy, Willie, 1933-

†MURPHY, Willie, 1933- 269'.2'0924 B
Black and trying / by Willie Murphy. Harrison, Ark. : New Leaf Press, c1976. 165 p. : port. ; 23 cm. Written by W. Murphy with C. Dudley. [BV4935.M86A33] 76-22272 ISBN 0-89221-023-0 : 5.95
1. Murphy, Willie, 1933- 2. Converts—United States—Biography. 3. Evangelists—United States—Biography. I. Dudley, Cliff, joint author. II. Title.

Murray, Florence J., 1894-

MURRAY, Florence J., 1894- 266'.025'0924 B
At the foot of Dragon Hill / Florence J. Murray. 1st ed. New York : E. P. Dutton, 1975. xiii, 240 p. ; 22 cm. [R722.M8 1975] 75-14424 6.95
1. Murray, Florence J., 1894- 2. Missionaries, Medical—Korea—Correspondence, reminiscences, etc. 3. Women physicians—Correspondence, reminiscences, etc. I. Title.

Murray, Hannah, Lindley, 1777-1836.

SPRING, Gardiner, 1785-1873. 920.7
A pastor's tribute to one of his flock. The memoirs of the late Hannah L. Murray. By Gardiner Spring ... New York, R. Carter & brothers, 1849. vi, [7]-312 p. front. (port.) 23 1/2 cm. [BR1725.685S6] 38-3189
1. Murray, Hannah, Lindley, 1777-1836. I. Title.

Murray, John, 1741-1815.

BISBEE, Frederick Adelbert, 1855-1923. 289.
1770-1920, from Good Luck to Gloucester, the book of the pilgrimage; being the record of the celebration by means of a great pageant of the one hundred and fiftieth anniversary of the landing of John Murray, his reception by Thomas Potter, and the preaching of the first Universalist sermon at Good Luck, New Jersey, and the establishing of the first Universalist Church at Gloucester, Massachusetts, by the Rev. Frederick A. Bisbee ... Boston, The Murray press, 1920. 4 p. l., 373 p. front., plates, ports. 21 1/2 cm. [BX9933.B5] 21-945
1. Murray, John, 1741-1815. 2. Universalist church—U.S. I. Title. II. Title: From Good Luck to Gloucester.

HEWITT, S C. 133.91
Messages from the superior state; communicated by John Murray, through John M. Spear, in the summer of 1852 ... Carefully prepared for publication, with a sketch of the author's earthly life, and a brief description of the spiritual experience of the medium. By S. C. Hewitt ... Boston, B. Marsh, 1852. viii, [9]-167 p. 18 cm. [BF1291.S72] 10-33816
1. Murray, John, 1741-1815. I. Spear, John Murray, b. 1804. II. Title.

SKINNER, Clarence Russell, 1881- 922.8173
Hell's ramparts fell, the life of John Murray [by] Clarence R. Skinner and Alfred S. Cole. Boston, Mass., The Universalist publishing house, 1941. 5 p. l., 177, [6] p. front., ports. 20 1/2 cm. "References": [6] p. at end. [BX9969.M8S55] 41-26030
1. Murray, John, 1741-1815. I. Cole, Alfred Storer, joint author. II. Title.

Murray, John Courtney.

LOVE, Thomas T. 261.7
John Courtney Murray: contemporary church-state theory. Garden City, N.Y., Doubleday, 1965[c.1964, 1965] 239p. 22cm. Bibl. [BX4705.M977L6] 65-12357 4.95
1. Murray, John Courtney. 2. Church and state—Catholic Church. I. Title.

*MURRAY, John Courtney 231.09
The problem of God, yesterday and today New Haven, Conn., Yale [1965, c.1964] vii, 121p. 21cm. (St. Thomas More lects., 1; Y-138) [BT98.M8] 1.45 pap.,
I. Title.

PELOTTE, Donald E. 261.7'092'4
John Courtney Murray : theologian in conflict / by Donald E. Pelotte. New York : Paulist Press, c1976. xi, 210 p. ; 24 cm. Includes index. Bibliography: p. 191-206. [BX4705.M977P44] 76-18046 ISBN 0-8091-0212-9 : 9.95
1. Murray, John Courtney. 2. Catholic Church—Biography. 3. Theologians—United States—Biography.

Murray, Nicholas, 1802-1861.

PRIME, Samuel Irenaeus, 1812-1885. 922.573
Memoirs of the Rev. Nicholas Murray, D. D. (Kirwan.) By Samuel Irenaeus Prime ... New York, Harper & brothers, 1862. xii, [13]-438 p. incl. front. (port.) 20 cm. [BX9225.N83P7] 36-22130
1. Murray, Nicholas, 1802-1861. I. Title.

Murray, Robert Lindley, 1825-1874

[MURRAY, Ruth Shearman (Taber)] 922.
Under His wings; a sketch of the life of Robert Lindley Murray. New York, A.D.F. Randolph, 1876. 164 p. illus. 19 cm. [BX7795.M8M8] 52-50303
1. Murray, Robert Lindley, 1825-1874 I. Title.

Murrinsville, Pa. St. Alphonsus church.

[CANOVA, John L] 282.
History of St. Alphonsus church, Murrinsville, Pennsylvania. written on the occasion of the diamond jubilee of the church, 1842-1917. [Murrinsville 1917 87 p. pl. 3 port. 23 1/2 c, Preface signed: J.L. Canova. [BX4603. M9S3] 18-184
1. Murrinsville, Pa. St. Alphonsus church. I. Title.

Murugan (Hindu deity)

CLOTHEY, Fred W. 294.5'2'11
The many faces of Murukan : the history and meaning of a South Indian god / Fred W. Clothey with the poem Prayers to Lord Murukan / by A. K. Ramanujan. The Hague ; New York : Mouton, c1978. xvi, 252 p. ; 24 cm. (Religion and society ; 6) Includes index. Bibliography: p. [239]-248. [BL1225.M8C58] 78-319059 ISBN 9-02-797632-5 : 37.10
1. Murugan (Hindu deity) I. Ramanujan, A. K., 1929- Prayers to Lord Murukan. 1978. II. Title. III. Series: Religion and society (The Hague) ; 6.

Musar movement.

GOLDBERG, Hillel. 296.8'3
Musar anthology. [Hillel Goldberg, editor. 1st ed. Hyde Park, Mass., Harwich Lithograph, 1972] 64 p. illus. 28 cm. Cover title. Includes bibliographical references. [BJ1285.5.M8G65] 72-91473
1. Musar movement. I. Title.

URY, Zalman F. 296.8'3
The Musar movement : a quest for excellence in character education / by Zalman F. Ury. New York : Yeshiva University Press, Dept. of Special Publications : selling agents, Bloch Pub. Co., 1970, c1969. 84 p. ; 23 cm. (Studies in Torah Judaism ; 12) Bibliography: p. 79-81. [BJ1285.5.M8U79 1970] 74-191759
1. Lipkin, Israel, 1810-1883. 2. Musar movement. I. Title. II. Series.

Musar movement—History.

ECKMAN, Lester Samuel. 296.8'3
The history of the Musar movement, 1840-1945 / by Lester Samuel Eckman New York : Shengold Publishers, [1975] 174 p. ; 25 cm. Includes index. Bibliography p. 169-172. [BJ1285.5.M8E25] 75-24183 ISBN 0-88400-041-9 : 8.95
1. Musar movement—History. I. Title.

Musculus, Wolfgang, 1497-1563.

SCHWAB, Paul Josiah. 922.443
... The attitude of Wolfgang Musculus toward religious tolerance, by Paul Josiah Schwab ... Scottdale, Pa., Printed by the Mennonite press, 1933. 62, [1] p. illus. (port.) 26 cm. (Yale studies in religion. no. 6) "An essay based upon a dissertation submitted to the faculty of the Graduate school of Yale university ... for the degree of doctor of philosophy [1923]" Bibliography: p. 57-[69] [BR350.M8S42 1928] 34-8173
1. Musculus, Wolfgang, 1497-1563. 2. Toleration. I. Title.

Muse, Dan Thomas, Bp., 1882-

ODEN, Margaret (Muse) 1916- 922.89
Steps to the sun. Franklin Springs, Ga., Publishing House of the Pentecostal Holiness Church [1955] 129p. illus. 21cm. [BX8795.P25O3] 55-36602
1. Muse, Dan Thomas, Bp., 1882- I. Title.

Mushrooms (in religion, folk-lore, etc.)

ALLEGRO, John Marco, 1923- 200
The sacred mushroom and the cross; a study of the nature and origins of Christianity within the fertility cults of the ancient Near East, by John M. Allegro. [1st ed. in U.S.] Garden City, N.Y., Doubleday [1970] xxii, 349 p. illus. (part col.), maps. 24 cm. Includes bibliographical references. [BL444.A44 1970b] 73-111140 7.95
1. Mushrooms (in religion, folk-lore, etc.) 2. Fertility cults—Near East. 3. Christianity—Origin. I. Title.

Music.

BENHAM, Asahel. 783.
Federal harmony; containing, in a familiar manner, the rudiments of psalmody; together with a collection of church music. (Most of which are entirely new.) By Asahel Benham. The 6th ed. Middletown [Conn.] Printed by M. H. Woodward [1795?] 58 (i. e. 64) p. 12 x 19 cm. Nos. 9-10, 15-16 repeated in paging. [M2116.B46F26] 5-7976
I. Title.

DANE, Susan Martha, 1849-1896.
Sunshine gleams from a sick room, or, Songs of faith and hope, by Susan Martha Dane. With brief memorial sketches by Rev. B. P. Snow, Rev. George Lewis, D. D. [Portland, Me., W. M. Marks, printer] 1898. 136 p. 21 cm. 2-9980
I. Title.

EDWARDS, John Harrington, 1834-1918? 783.
God and music, by John Harrington Edwards ... New York, The Baker & Taylor co. [1903] 319 p. 20 cm. [ML3920.E26] 3-6996
1. Music. I. Title.

EDWARDS, John Harrington, 1834-1918? 783.
God and music, by John Harrington Edwards ... [New ed.] New York, The Baker & Taylor co., 1907. 319 p. 20 cm. [ML3920.E262] 9-8638
1. Music. I. Title.

LITTLE, William.
... The easy instructor; or, A new method of teaching sacred harmony. Containing, i. The rudiments of music on an improved plan ... ii. A choice collection of psalm tunes and anthems ... By William Little and William Smith ... Easy instructor or A new method of teaching sacred harmony Albany, Printed for Websters & Skinners and D. Steele & son. Packard & Benthuysen, printers [pref. 1798] 127, [1] p. 13 x 23 cm. At head of title: Revised and enlarged edition. A 18
I. Smith, William, joint author. II. Title.

Music—Addresses, essays, lectures.

STEBBINS, George Coles, 1846- comp. 783.
The male quartet, compiled and arranged by Geo. C. Stebbins and I. Allan Sankey: for use in Young men's Christian associations, glee clubs, college Sunday night class meetings and all religious gatherings; with a selection of secular and patriotic songs for special occasions. Chicago, New York, The Biglow & Main co. [1902] 160 p. 19 cm. [M2198.S8M2] 3-557
I. Sankey, Ira Allan, 1874- joint comp. II. Title.

STEBBINS, George Coles, 1846- 783.
The male quartet, compiled and arranged by Geo. C. Stebbins and I. Allan Sankey: for use in Young men's Christian associations, glee clubs, college Sunday night class gatherings; with a selection of secular and patriotic songs for special occasions. Chicago, New York, The Biglow & Main co. [c1902] 128 p. 19 cm. [M2198.S8M21] 30-5301
I. Sankey, Ira Allan, 1874- joint comp. II. Title.

Music—Almanacs, yearbooks, etc.

THE Catholic choirmaster's diary. 783.2059 Boston, McLaughlin & Reilly Co. v. 28 cm. annual. [ML19.C37] 51-15219
1. Music—Almanacs, yearbooks, etc. 2. Church music—Catholic Church.

Music—Bibliography—Catalogs.

OAKLAND, Cal. Free public library. 781.9731
Sacred and secular music list, including the Vesper, Hughes and Dow gifts. Oakland public library ... [Oakland] 1937. 2 p. l., 62 p. 21 cm. [ML136.O16S2] 41-7398
1. Music—Bibl.—Catalogs. I. Title.

Music, Byzantine.

TILLYARD, Henry Julius Wetenhall, 1881- 783.9
Byzantine music and hymnography / by H. J. W. Tillyard. New York : AMS Press, 1976. p. cm. Reprint of the 1923 ed. published by Faith Press, London. Includes index. Bibliography: p. [ML188.T5 1976] 74-24242 ISBN 0-404-13116-6 : 11.50
1. Music, Byzantine. 2. Hymns, Greek—History and criticism. 3. Church music—Orthodox Eastern Church. 4. Musical notation. I. Title.

Music, Byzantine—Addresses, essays, lectures.

STRUNK, William Oliver, 1901- 783 .026'19
Essays on music in the Byzantine world / Oliver Strunk ; foreword by Kenneth Levy. New York : W. W. Norton, [1975] p. cm. Includes bibliography and index.

[ML188.S87] 74-23928 ISBN 0-393-02183-1 : 12.50
1. Music, Byzantine—Addresses, essays, lectures. 2. Church music—Orthodox Eastern Church. 3. Paleography, Musical. I. Title.

Music Byzantine—History and criticism

WELLESZ, Egon, 1885- 783.2
Eastern elements in Western chant. Studies in the early history of ecclesiastical music. 2nd printing. Copenhagen, Munksgaard, 1967. 16, 212p. 11 plates. 26cm. Bibl. footnotes. [ML3082.W44] 68-88712 7.00
1. Music Byzantine—Hist. & crit. 2. Chants (Plain, Gregorian, etc.)—Hist. & crit. 3. Church music—Hist. & crit. I. Title.

Music—Collected works.

BEALL, B. B. 783
Bright beautiful bells. A collection of songs for Sunday schools, gospel meetings ... and all other religious and musical endeavor. By B. B. Beall ... Birmingham, Ala., Buchanan, Ga., B. B. Beall & co. [c1900] [120] p. 20 cm. Edition with round notes. [M2193.B36B6 Copyright] Aug
I. Title.

BEALL, B. B.
Bright beautiful bells. A collection of songs for Sunday school, gospel meetings, revivals, young people's meetings, and all other religious and musical endeavor. Birmingham, Ala., Buchanan, Ga., B. B. Beall & co. [c1900] 60 pp. 8° 1-42
I. Title.

BLISS, Philip Paul.
Sunshine for Sunday schools: a new collection of original and selected music. Cincinnati, J. Church & co; Chicago, G. F. Root & sons, 1910. 160 p. 24 degrees. Aug
I. Title.

CLEMENT, Jecques. 16th cent. [Works] 783.2054
Opera omnia, edidit K. Ph. Bernet Kempers. Rome, American Institute of Musicology in Rome, 1951- v. 35 cm. (Corpus mensurabilis musices, 4) Contents.1. Missa misericorde. [M3.C6] 52-64546
1. Music—Collected works. 2. Masses—To 1800—Vocal scores. I. Bernet Kempers, Karel Philippus, 1897- ed. II. Title. III. Series.

LARCOM, Lucy, 1824-1893.
At the beautiful gate, and other songs of faith, by Lucy Larcom. Boston and New York, Houghton, Mifflin and company, 1892. xi, 117 p. 17 cm. [PS2222.A7 1892] 12-34960
I. Title.

Music—History and criticism—Medieval.

HUGHES, Anselm, 1889- ed. 296
Early medieval music. up to 1300. London, New York, Oxford University Press, 1954. 1955] xviii, 434p. map. facsims., music. 26cm. (New Oxford history of music, v. 2) Bibliography: p. [405]-417. [ML160.N44 vol.2] 54-14955
1. Music—Hist. & crit.—Medieval. I. Title. II. Title: —Another issue. III. Series.

Music in Christian education.

LUNDE, Alfred E. 264'.2
Christian education thru music / by Alfred E. Lunde. 1st ed. Wheaton, Ill. : Evangelical Teacher Training Association, 1978. 80 p. : ill. ; 21 cm. (Evangelical leadership preparation series) Bibliography: p. 56. [ML3000.L86] 78-51509 ISBN 0-910566-83-6 pbk. : 2.90
1. Music in Christian education. I. Title. II. Series.

Music in churches.

ADAMS, Zabdiel, 1739-1801. 783.
The nature, pleasure and advantages of church-musick. A sermon preached at a lecture in the First parish of Lancaster, on Thursday April 4th, 1771. By Zabdiel Adams ... Published at the request of the choir... Boston: Printed by Richard Draper. 1771. 2 p. l., 3-86 p. 18 a/2 cm. [ML3001.A31] 27-1419
1. Music in churches. I. Title.

ARE, Thomas L., 1932- 264'.2
Faithsong : a new look at the ministry of music / Thomas L. Are. 1st ed. Philadelphia : Westminster Press, c1981. p. cm. [ML3001.A73] 19 81-4789 ISBN 0-664-24375-4 pbk. : 6.95
1. Music in churches. 2. Church music—United States. 3. Church music—Protestant Churches. I. Title.

BALES, James D., 1915- 264'.2
Instrumental music and New Testament worship, by James D. Bales. Searcy? Ark. [1973] 299 p. 22 cm. Bibliography: p. 281-294. [ML3001.B2] 73-169351
1. Music in churches. I. Title.

BOOK, Morris Butler, 1907- 264.2
Book-Miller debate on instrumental music in worship, held in Orlando, Florida, March 15-17, 1955 [by] Morris B. Book [and] James P. Miller. [Gainesville, Fla., Phillips Publications, 1955] 140p. group ports. 23cm. [BV290.B63] 55-57985
1. Music in churches. 2. Disciples of Christ—Doctrinal and controversial works. 3. Churches of Christ—Doctrinal and controversial works. I. Miller, James Parker. II. Title.

BOSWELL, Ira Matthews, 1866- 783.
Boswell-Hardeman discussion on instrumental music in the worship, conducted in the Ryman auditorium, Nashville, Tenn., May 31, to June 5, 1923. Nashville, Tenn., Gospel advocate company, 1924. 239 p. ports. 23 1/2 cm. [ML3001.B6] 24-15687
1. Music in churches. I. Hardeman, N. B. II. Title.

BOYD, James Shields, 1830-
Homilies, hymns and harmonies; or, Food to strengthen and songs to cheer, by Rev. J. S. Boyd ... Kirksville, Mo., The Journal printing co., c1912. 255 p. 20 cm. 12-20213 1.25
I. Title.

BROWN, Hugh, 1811?-1888. 783.
Discourses on Scripture psalmody in praising God; and against instrumental music in public worship: by the Rev. Hugh Brown... North White Creek, N.Y., R.K. Crocker, Washington co. post print, 1859. 64 p. 29 cm. [ML3001.B86]
1. Music in churches. 2. Psalmody. I. Title. II. Title: Scripture psalmody in praising God.

BUNTING, Robert H 264.2
Both sides of the music question discussed; a written discussion between Robert H. Bunting of the Church of Christ and J. D. Marion of the Christian Church. Athens, Ala., C. E. I. Store c1957. 61p. 21cm. (Freedom booklets) [ML3001.B9] 59-45627
1. Music in churches. I. Marion, Johnie D. II. Title.

CLUBB, Merrel Dare, 1865- 783.
Discussion; Is instrumental music in Christian worship scriptural? Between M. D. Clubb (affirmant)...and H. Leo Boles (negant)... Nashville, Tenn., Gospel advocate company, 1927. 155 p. 23 1/2 cm. [ML3001.C6] 27-7288
1. Music in churches. I. Boles, Henry Leo, 1874- joint author. II. Title. III. Title: Is instrumental music in Christian worship scriptural?

DARNTON, Charles 1836- 783.
The Sea of Galilee, scenes and lessons from the life of Christ. A sacred cantata, designed for church use. The words written or selected by P. W. Darnton, B. A., music by Charles Darnton ... London [etc.] Bayley & Ferguson; Boston, Oliver Ditson company, c1902. iv, 75 p. 27 cm. (Sacred cantatas) Vocal score with planoforte accompeniment. [M2023.D223S3] 2-27994
I. Title.

GABRIEL, Charles H.
King of Israel; a scriptural oratorio cantata for church choirs and choruses, by Chas. H. Gabriel ... Cincinnati, New York, Fillmore bros., 1901. 60 pp. 25 cm. Vocal score. 2-1188
I. Title.

GARSIDE, Charles. 264'.2'0924
The origins of Calvin's theology of music, 1536-1543 / Charles Garside. Philadelphia : American Philosophical Society, 1979. 36 p. ; 29 cm. (Transactions of the American Philosophical Society ; v. 69, pt. 4 ISSN 0065-9746s) Includes index.IBibliography: p. 33-35.I[ML3001.G27] 78-73171 ISBN 0-87169-694-0 pbk. : 10.00
1. Calvin, Jean, 1509-1564—Music. 2. Music in churches. I. Title. II. Series: American Philosophical Society, Philadelphia. Transactions ; v. 69, pt. 4.

GIRARDEAU, John Lafauette, 1825-1898. 264.2
Instrumental music in the public worship of the church. By John L. Girardeau ... Richmond, Va., Whittet & Sheperson, printers, 1888. 208 p. 20 cm. [ML3001.G51] 6-11582
1. Music in churches. I. Title. II. Title: Instrumental music in the ... church.

HAMMETT, John, 1678or9-1773. 783.
Promiscuous singing no divine institution; having neither president nor precept to support it, either from the musical institution of David, or from the gospel dispensation. Therefore it ought to be exploded, as being a humane invention, tending rather to gratify the carnal ears of men, than to be acceptable and pleasing worship to God. By John Hammett ... [n. p.] Printed in the year 1739. 1 p. l., iii, 29 p. 17 cm. "Newport? Printed by the Widow Franklin?"--Evans, American bibliography, v. 2, p. 140. [ML3001.H22] 6-3692
1. Music in churches. I. Title.

HUNT, J[oseph] M[arion]
Music in the church; a series of practical talks upon all the departments of music in public services. Kansas City, Mo., The J. M. Hunt music co. [1900] 64 p. 16 cm. Sep
I. Title.

HUNTER, William C. 783'.02'6
Music in your church / by William C. Hunter. Valley Forge, PA : Judson Press, [1981] p. cm. [ML3001.H88] 19 81-4933 ISBN 0-8170-0917-5 : 4.50
1. Music in churches. 2. Church music. I. Title.

LUTKIN, Peter Christian, 1858-1931. 783'.026
Music in the church. New York, AMS Press [1970] xii, 274 p. 23 cm. Reprint of the 1910 ed. Bibliography: p. 257-263. [ML3001.L95 1970] 72-135722
1. Music in churches. I. Title.

MARSHALL, William, of Philadelphia. 783.
The propriety of singing the Psalms of David in New Testament worship. A sermon preached at Middle-Octoraro, April 13th, 1774. At the opening of the Associate Presbytery of Pensylvania. By William Marshall ... Perth: Printed for A. Sharp [etc.] 1776. 68 p. 17 cm. [ML3001.M28] 9-2113
1. Music in churches. I. Title.

THE music of Holy Week;
a choir book in accord with the newly restored Holy Week liturgy, including chants, mass ordinaries, selected part-music, hymns and the Easter Sunday proper. Compiled and edited by the staff of the Gregorian institute. Toledo, Ohio, Gregorian institute of America [1957] xv, 207p.

PAYNE, O E. 783.
Instrumental music is scriptural ... by O. E. Payne. Cincinnati, The Standard publishing company [c1920] 2 p. l., 3-352 p. 20 cm. [ML3001.P19] 20-11683
1. Music in churches. I. Title.

STEWART, H J.
The Nativity: a church oratorio. The words comp., and the music composed by H. J. Stewart ... Cincinnati, New York [etc.] The John Church company, c1901. 2 p. l., vi, 3-104 p. 29 cm. Vocal score. [M2003.S] 1-553
I. Title.

TROBIAN, Helen Reed 264.2
The instrumental ensemble in the church. Nashville, Abingdon [c.1961-1963] 96p. 19cm. (Basic music bk.) Bibl. 62-16125 1.50 pap.,
1. Music in churches. 2. Instrumental music—Hist. & crit. I. Title.

TROBIAN, Helen Reed. 264.2
The instrumental ensemble in the church. New York, Abindgon Press [1963] 96 p. 19 cm. (A Basic music book) Includes bibliographies. [ML3001.T86] 62-16125
1. Music in churches. 2. Instrumental music — Hist. & crit. I. Title.

WALLACE, Gervias Knox, 1903- 264.2
Wallace-Hunt debate, held at Ottumwa, Iowa, April 24-27, 1951, between G. K. Wallace and Julian O. Hunt. Tape recorded. Longview, Wash., Telegram Book Co., 1953. 276p. 21cm. [BV290.W28] 54-20984
1. Music in churches. I. Hunt, Julian O. II. Title.

Music in religious education.

WRIGHT, Kathryn S. 268'.432
Let the children sing; music in religious education [by] Kathryn S. Wright. New York, Seabury Press [1974] p. cm. "A Crossroad book." [BV1534.8.W74] 73-17915 ISBN 0-8164-0256-6 5.95
1. Music in religious education. I. Title.

Music, Influence of.

REYNOLDS, Isham E. 1879- 783.
Ministry of music in religion [by] L. E. Reynolds ... Nashville, Tenn., Sunday school board of the Southern Baptist convention [c1929] 195 p. 19 cm. [ML3920.R39] A 30
1. Music, Influence of. I. Title.

Music—Italy—Venice.

MOORE, James Harold. 783.2'4
Vespers at St. Mark's : music of Alessandro Grandi, Giovanni Roretta, and Francesco Cavalli / by James H. Moore. Ann Arbor, Mich. : UMI Research Press, c1980. p. cm. (Studies in musicology ; no. 30) Includes index. Bibliography: p. [ML290.8.V26M66] 19 80-39497 ISBN 0-8357-1143-9 : 84.95
1. Grandi, Alessandro, d. 1630. Works. 2. Roretta, Giovanni, ca. 1596-1668. Works. 3. Cavalli, Pier Francesco, 1602-1676. Works. 4. Music—Italy—Venice. 5. Church music—History and criticism. 6. Vespers (Music)—History and criticism. I. Title. II. Series.

Music, Jewish — Bibliography

NATIONAL Jewish Music Council. 222'.1'07
Bridging Israel and America through music and honoring four American Jewish composers. [Program guides prepared for the Jewish Music Festival theme, 1963-64. New York, 1963-64] 2 v. ports. 28 cm. Contents.-- v.1. Music of Israel today. -- v.2. The music of Gershon Ephros, Solomon Rowosky, Heinrich Schalit, Jacob Weinburg; edited by Lewis Appleton. [ML3776.N31B7] 65-5865
1. Music, Jewish — Bibl. 2. Composers, Jewish. I. Title. II. Title: Honoring four American Jewish composers.

Music, Jewish—History and criticism.

CONTRIBUTIONS to a 781.7'2'924
systematic study of Jewish music / edited by Eric Werner. [New York] : Ktav Pub. House, 1975. p. cm. Includes bibliographical references. [ML3195.C66] 75-14024 25.00
1. Music, Jewish—History and criticism. I. Werner, Eric.

IDELSOHN, Abraham Zebi, 1882-1938. 783'.02'96
Jewish music in its historical development / by A. Z. Idelsohn. Westport, Conn. : Greenwood Press, 1980, c1929. p. cm. Reprint of the 1948 ed. published by Tudor Pub. Co., New York. Includes index. [ML3776.I3 1980] 19 80-24235 ISBN 0-313-22749-7 lib. bdg. : 35.00
1. Jews. Liturgy and ritual. 2. Music,

Jewish—History and criticism. 3. Folk-songs, Jewish. 4. Musicians, Jewish. I. Title.

WERNER, Eric. 783'.029'6
From generation to generation; studies on Jewish musical tradition. New York, American Conference of Cantors [1967?] 168 p. illus. 24 cm. "This limited edition has been published in honor of Dr. Eric Werner's forthcoming retirement from the faculty of the School of Sacred Music, Hebrew Union College-Jewish Institute of Religion." Contents.Contents.—Music in the Bible.—Musical instruments in the Bible.—The music of post-Biblical Judaism.—Role of tradition in the music of the Synagogue.—What function has Synagogue music today?—Ideas and practices of liturgical music.—Practical applications of (Jewish) musical research.—Rise and fall of American Synagogue music.—Solomon Sulzer, statesman and pioneer.—Abraham Zvi Idelsohn, in memoriam. Includes bibliographical references. [ML3195.W38] 74-182184
1. Werner, Eric. 2. Jews. Liturgy and ritual. 3. Music, Jewish—History and criticism. 4. Synagogue music—History and criticism. I. Title.

Music—Jews.

A Collection of Sabbath school hymns. Comp. by a Sabbath school teacher, for the benefit oif the children in the Confederate States ... Raleigh [N. C.] Raleigh register steam-power press, 1863. 62, ii p. 14 cm. 17-8249

STAINER, John, Sir 1840-1901. 220.
The music of the Bible, with some account of the development of modern musical instruments from ancient types, by John Stainer ... New ed.: with additional illustrations and supplementary notes, by the Rev. F. W. Galpin ... London, Novello and company, limited; New York, The H. W. Gray co. [1914] xii, 230 p. front., illus., plates. 22 cm. [ML166.S783] 14-17691
1. Music—Jews. 2. Bible—Music. 3. Musical instruments. I. Galpin, Francis William, 1858- ed. II. Title.

WEISSER, Albert. 780.95694
The modern renaissance of Jewish music, events and figures, Eastern Europe America. New York, Bloch Pub. Co., 1954. 175p. ports., map. music. 24cm. Includes biographies, and lists of works, of Joel Engel, Joseph Achron, Moses Milner, Lazare Saminsky, Alexander Krein, and Michael Gnlessen. 'Complete list of publications of the Society for Jewish folk music in St. Petersburg': p. [66]-[68] Bibliography: p. 165-169. [ML300.W35] 781.72 54-5789
1. Music—Jews. 2. Folk-songs, Jewish—Hist. & crit. 3. Obahchestvo evreiskol narodnoi muzykl. 4. Music—Russia— Hist. & crit. 5. Music—U.S.—Hist. & crit. I. Title.

WERNER, Eric. 783'.029'6
A voice still heard : the sacred songs of the Ashkenazic Jews / Eric Werner. University Park : Pennsylvania State University Press, c1976. p. cm. Includes bibliographical references and index. [ML3195.W43] 75-26522 ISBN 0-271-01167-X : 18.75
1. Music—Jews. 2. Synagogue music—History and criticism. I. Title.

Music—Jews—Bibliography.

WEISSER, Albert, comp. 016.7817'2'924
Bibliography of publications and other resources on Jewish music. New York, National Jewish Music Council, 1969. 117 p. 29 cm. "Revised and enlarged edition based in part upon 'The Bibliography of books and articles on Jewish music' prepared by Joseph Yasser and published in 1955." [ML128.J4W4] 70-3537 3.00
1. Music—Jews—Bibliography. I. National Jewish Music Council.

Music—Jews—History and criticism

IDELSON, Abraham Zebi, 1882-1938. 781.7'2'924
Jewish music in its historical development, by A. Z. Idelsohn. New York, Schocken Books [1967, c1956] xi, 535 p. facsims., music. 21 cm. Contents.Contents.—pt. 1. The song of the synagogue.—pt. 2. Folk-song. Contains bibliographies; also bibliographical footnotes. [ML3776.13 1967] 67-25236
1. Jews. Liturgy and ritual. 2. Music—Jews—History and criticism. 3. Folk-songs, Jewish. 4. Musicians, Jewish. I. Title.

SAMINSKY, Lazare, 1882- 781.72
Music of the ghetto and the Bible, by Lazare Saminsky... New York, Bloch publishing company, 1934. vii, 261 p. illus. (music) 22 cm. [ML3776.S3M8] (781.733) 35-2375
1. Music—Jews—Hist. & crit. 2. Bible—Music. 3. Jews, Liturgy and ritual. 4. Folk-sons, Jewish. 5. Musicians, Jewish. I. Title.

Music—Jews, Yemenite—Bibliography.

MARKS, Paul F. 016.7817'53'32
Bibliography of literature concerning Yemenite-Jewish music, by Paul F. Marks. Detroit, Information Coordinators, 1973. 50 p. 23 cm. (Detroit studies in music bibliography, 27) Includes selected discography (p. 49-50). [ML128.J4M37] 72-90431 ISBN 0-911772-57-X 5.00
1. Music—Jews, Yemenite—Bibliography. I. Title. II. Series.

Music—Juvenile literature.

MACKAY, Ruth (Clarage) 783.9
They sang a new song; stories of great hymns. Illustrated by Gordon Laite. New York, Abingdon Press [1959] 128p. illus. 25cm. [ML3930.A2M34] 59-11188
1. Music—Juvenile literature. 2. Hymns—Hist. & crit. I. Title.

MOORE, John Travers 783
The story of Silent night. Illus. by Bob Hyskell, Leonard Gray. St. Louis, Concordia [c.1965] 1v. (unpaged) col. illus. 27cm. Includes 2-voice musical setting of Silent night! Holy night! [ML3930.G84M66] 65-19252 1.25 bds.,
1. Gruber, Franz Xaver, 1787-1863. Stille Nacht. 2. Music—Juvenile literature. I. Title.

WATSON, Nancy Dingman. 783.6'5'54
Carol to a child, and a Christmas pageant. Music by Clyde Watson. Illus. by Aldren A. Watson. New York, World Pub. Co. [1969] [31] p. col. illus. 22 cm. Includes musical setting in close score. A poem celebrating the birth of Jesus and music to which it can be sung are accompanied by suggestions for using both in a Christmas pageant. [ML3925.A2W37] 73-82770 3.95
1. Music—Juvenile literature. 2. [Christmas poetry.] 3. [Christmas music.] I. Watson, Aldren Auld, 1917- illus. II. Title.

Music—Manuals, text-books, etc.

BENNETT, Clifford Alvin, 1904- ed. 783.282
Catholic choirmasters correspondence course. A course of 110 college accredited lessons in sacred music and liturgy, edited by Clifford A. Bennett ... Pittsburgh, Pa., Gregorian institute [c1942-45] 6 v. illus. (incl. music) 28 1/2 x 21 1/2 cm. Vols. 2, 4 and 6 have title "Catholic choir-masters course" and imprint: Toledo, O., Gregorian institute of America. Contents.[v. 1] 1st quarter (27 lessons)--[v. 2] 2d quarter. Lessons 28-44: Children's and boy's choirs, by Dom Ermin Vitry. Lessons 45-54: Male choir training, by R. M. Silby.--[v. 3] Polyphony (lessons 55-59)--[v. 4] 3d quarter. Lessons 60-65: Elementary theory of Greogorian chant. Lessons 66-85; Rhythm and chironomy.--[v. 5] Gregorian chant modality (lessons 86-95)--[v. 6] 4th quarter. Lessons 96-107: Psalmody, by J. T. Kush. Lessons 108-110: The divine office, by Dom Godfrey Dickmann. [MT88.B46] 42-19677
1. Music—Manuals, text-books, etc. 2. Choral singing—Instruction and study. 3. Chants (Plain, Gregorian, etc.)—Instruction and study. 4. Church music—Catholic church. 5. Catholic church, Liturgy and ritual. I. Gregorian institute of America. II. Title.

GREENISH, Arthur James, 1860- 783'.026'203
The student's dictionary of muscial terms. [New ed.] London, J. Williams New York, Mills Music [c1953] xi,131p. 19 cm. (The Joseph Williams series of handbooks on music) [ML108.G85 1953] 56-33410
I. Title. II. Series.
Contents omitted

PITTS, Lilla Belle. 783.8
Guide and teaching suggestions, by Lilla Belle Pitts, Mabelle Glenn [and] Lorrain E. Watters. Boston, Ginn [1952] 2 v. 24 cm. (Our singing world) For use with Our singing world. Contents.[1] Kindergarten and grades one, two, and three, -- [2] Grades four, five, and six. [MT935.P589] 52-11021
1. Music — Manuals, text-books, etc. 2. Choral singing, Juvenile — Instruction and study. I. Title. II. Series.

Music—Manuscripts.

WOLFENBUTTEL, Herzog-August-bibliothek, Mss. (677(Helmst. 628] 781.969
... An old St. Andrews music book (Cod. Helmst, 628) published in facsimile, with an introduction by J. H. Baxter ... London, Pub. for St. Andrews university by H. Milford, Oxford university press; [etc., etc.] 1931. xix, [1] p. facsim: [394] p. 19 cm. 41 p. 18 cm. (St. Andrews university publications, no. xxx) Index to the facsimile edition of ms. Wolfenbuettel 677, prepared by Dom Anselm Hughes ... Edinburgh & London, W. Blackwood & sons ltd., 1939 [M2.W86 Index] 33-14392
1. Music—Manuscripts. 2. Manuscripts—Facsimiles. 3. Church music—Catholic church. 4. Songs, Medievel—Dictionaries, indexes, etc. I. Baxter, James Houston, 1894- ed. II. Hughes, Anselm, father, 1889- III. Title. IV. Title: St. Andrews music book.

Music—Manuscripts—Facsimiles.

WOLFENBUTTEL. Herzog-August-Bibliothek. MSS. (Cod. Helmst. 628) 783'.026'2
An old St. Andrews music book (Cod. Helmst. 628) published in facsimile, with an introduction by J. H. Baxter, London, Published for St. Andrews University by H. Milford, Oxford University Press, 1931. [New York, AMS Press, 1973] xix, [1], 394 p. 19 cm. Original ed. issued as no. 30 of St. Andrews University publications. Bibliography: p. [xx] [M2.W86 1973] 70-178515 ISBN 0-404-56525-5
1. Music—Manuscripts—Facsimiles. 2. Church music—Catholic Church. 3. Part-songs, Sacred—To 1800. 4. Organum. I. Baxter, James Houston, 1894- ed. II. Title. III. Title: St. Andrews music book. IV. Series: St. Andrews University, Scot. Publications, no. 30.

Music—Pennsylvania—Bethlehem.

WALTERS, Raymond, 1885- 783.8'09748'22
The Bethlehem Bach Choir; an historical and interpretative sketch. New York, AMS Press [1971] x, 289 p. illus., ports. 22 cm. Reprint of the 1918 ed. [ML200.8.B562B34 1971] 77-135726 ISBN 0-404-07200-3
1. Bach Choir, Bethlehem, Pa. 2. Music—Pennsylvania—Bethlehem. I. Title.

Music—Periodicals

ACCENT, 783.05
church music library. [Minneapolis, etc.] v. illus. ports. 27cm. 10 no. a year. Subtitle varies slightly. Editor: J. W. Brewer. Includes choral music. [ML1.A113] 58-27772
1. Music—Period. 2. Church music—Period. I. Brewer, James W., ed.

Music—Russia—History and criticism.

BAKST, James. 780.947
A history of Russian-Soviet music. New York, Dodd, Mead [1966] x, 406 p. 24 cm. Includes 16 p. of illus. between p. 118-119. "Notes": p. 379-390; bibliography: p. 391-393. [ML300.B28] 66-18349
1. Music—Russia—History and criticism. 2. Music—Russia—1917- —History and criticism. I. Title.

Musical accompaniment.

BUCK, Dudley, 1839-1909. 783.
Illustrations in choir accompaniment., with hints in registration. A hand-book (provided with marginal notes for reference) for the use of organ students, organists, and those interested in church music. By Dudley Buck. New York, G. Schirmer, 1877. 3 p. l., 177 p. 31 cm. [MT190.B92] 5-42078
1. Musical accompaniment. 2. Organ—Instruction and study. I. Title.

BUCK, Dudley, 1839-1909. 783.
Illustrations in choir accompaniment, with hints in registration. A hand-book (provided with marginal notes for reference) for the use of organ students, organists, and those interested in church music. By Dudley Buck. New York, G. Schirmer, 1905. 3 p. l., 177 p. 30 cm. First published 1877. [MT190.B922] 5-42077
1. Musical accompaniment. 2. Organ—Instruction and study. I. Title.

RICHARDS, Henry W., 1865- 783.
The organ accompaniment of the church services; a practical guide for the student, by H. W. Richards ... Boston, Mass., The Boston music co. G. Schirmer (inc.); New York, G. Schirmer; [etc., etc., c1911] viii, 187 p. 19 1/2 cm. $1.50 [MT190.R29] 11-17491
1. Musical accompaniment. 2. Organ—Instruction and study. 3. Church music—Church of England. I. Title.

RICHARDS, Henry W., 1865- 783.
... The organ accompaniment of the church services; a practical guide for the student, by H. W. Richards ... London, J. Williams, limited; Boston, Mass., The Boston music company (G. Schirmer, inc.) c1911. viii, 142 p. 22 cm. (The Joseph Williams series of handbooks on music under the editorship of Stewart Macpherson) [MT190.R291] 12-2247
1. Musical accompaniment. 2. Organ—Instruction and study. 3. Church music—Church of England. I. Title.

Musical instruments, Jewish.

FINESINGER, Sol Baruch, 1900- 220.
Musical instruments in the Old Testament, by Sol Baruch Finesinger ... Baltimore, 1926. 64 p., 1 l. illus. 22 1/2 cm. Thesis (PH.D.)--Johns Hopkins university, 1925. Vita. "Reprinted from the Hebrew union college annual, vol. III, 1926." Bibliography: p. 61-63. [ML166.F47] 27-3948
1. Musical instruments, Jewish. 2. Bible—Music. I. Title.

Musical instruments—Pictorial works.

BONNER, Stephen. 726'.5'094223
Early Norman secular musicians on the church of Barfreston in Kent; drawings by Roy Bishop. Cambridge, Bois de Boulogne, 1969. [14] p. 5 illus. (1 col.). 22 cm. "This first edition is limited to sixty copies only, of which this is no. 28." Bibliography: p. [14] [ML85.B635] 72-463152 20/-
1. Barfreston, Church. 2. Musical instruments—Pictorial works. 3. Music in art. I. Title.

Musical notation.

THOMASON, Jean Healan. 090
Shaker manuscript hymnals from South Union, Kentucky. With comment on the musical notation by Fann R. Herndon. Introd. by Julia Neal. Bowling Green, Kentucky Folklore Society, c1967. v, 56 p. facsims., music. 22 cm. (Kentucky folklore series no. 3) Discussion of 15 manuscript

hymnals in the library of Western Kentucky University. [ML3178.S5T5] 78-3026 1.00
1. Shakers—Hymns—History and criticism. 2. Musical notation. I. Kentucky Library. II. Herndon, Fann R. III. Title. IV. Series.

Musicians, American.

METCALF, Frank Johnson, 1865- 783
American writers and compilers of sacred music, by Frank J. Metcalf ... New York, Cincinnati, The Abingdon press [c1925] 373 p. front., ports., facsims. (incl. music) 21 cm. [ML106.U3M3] 25-18159
1. Musicians, American. 2. Church music—U. S. 3. Hymns, English—Hist. & crit. I. Title.

Musicians, American—Biography.

METCALF, Frank Johnson, 1865-1945. 783'.0922
American writers and compilers of sacred music, by Frank J. Metcalf. New York, Russell & Russell [1967, c1925] 373 p. facsims. (incl. music), ports. 21 cm. "Reissued." [ML106.U3M3 1967] 66-24731
1. Musicians, American—Biography. 2. Church music—United States. 3. Hymns, English—History and criticism. I. Title.

Muslim pilgrims and pilgrimages—Jerusalem.

IBN al-Firkah, Ibrahim ibn 'Abd al-Rahman, 1262-1329. 297'.095694
Palestine, Mohammedan Holy Land / [compiled] by Charles D. Matthews ; with a foreword by Julian Obermann. New York : AMS Press, [1980], c1949. xxx, 176 p. ; 24 cm. Translation of Ibn al-Firkah's Ba'ith al-nufus ila ziyarat al-Quds al-mahrus and al-Tadmuri's Muthir al-gharam fi fadl ziyarat al-Khalil 'am. Reprint of the ed. published by Yale University Press, New Haven, which was issued as v. 24 of Yale oriental series : Researches. Includes index. Bibliography: p. 157-158. [BP187.5.P19I2313 1980] 19 78-63568 ISBN 0-404-60324-6 : 34.50
1. Muslim pilgrims and pilgrimages—Jerusalem. 2. Muslim pilgrims and pilgrimages—Jordan—Hebron. 3. Palestine in Islam. I. Matthews, Charles D., 1901- II. Tadmuri, Ishaq ibn Ibrahim, d. 1430? Muthir al-gharam fi fadl ziyarat al-Khalil 'am. English. 1980. III. Title. IV. Series: Yale oriental series : Researches ; v. 24.

Muslim pilgrims and pilgrimages—Saudi Arabia—Mecca.

LONG, David E. 297'.38
The Hajj today : a survey of the contemporary Makkah pilgrimage / David Edwin Long. Albany : State University of New York Press, c1979. 180 p. : ill. ; 23 cm. Includes index. Bibliography: p. [147]-156. [BP187.3.L66] 78-7473 ISBN 0-87395-382-7 : 30.00
1. Muslim pilgrims and pilgrimages—Saudi Arabia—Mecca. I. Title.

Muslim pilgrims and pilgrimages—Saudi Arabia—Mecca—Addresses, essays, lectures.

HAJJ studies / 297'.55
edited by Ziauddin Sardar and M. A. Zaki Badawi. London : Croom Helm for Hajj Research Centre, King Abdul Aziz University, Jeddah, [1978]- v. : ill. ; 23 cm. (Hajj Research Centre studies ; 2) Includes bibliographies and index. [BP187.3.H247] 78-308933 ISBN 0-85664-681-4 (v. 1) : 19.50
1. Muslim pilgrims and pilgrimages—Saudi Arabia—Mecca—Addresses, essays, lectures. I. Sardar, Ziaddin. II. Badawi, M. A. Zaki. III. Series: Jami'at al-Malik 'Abd al-Aziz al-Ahliyah. Hajj Research Centre. Hajj Research Centre studies ; 2.
Dist. by Biblio Distribution Ctr. Totowa, N J

Muslim pilgrims and pilgrimages—Saudi Arabia—Mecca—Pictorial works.

GUELLOUZ, Azzedine. 297'.38
Mecca, the Muslim pilgrimage / photos. by Abdelaziz Frikha ; text by Ezzedine Guellouz. New York : Paddington Press : distributed by Grosset & Dunlap, c1979. 124 p. : col. ill. ; 30 cm. Translation of Pelerinage a la Mecque. [BP187.3.G8313] 79-1125 ISBN 0-448-22301-5 : 14.95
1. Muslim pilgrims and pilgrimages—Saudi Arabia—Mecca—Pictorial works. I. Frikha, Abdelaziz. II. Title.

Muslim saints—Morocco—Boujad.

EICKELMAN, Dale F., 1942- 297'.0964
Moroccan Islam : tradition and society in a pilgrimage center / by Dale F. Eickelman. Austin : University of Texas Press, c1976. xx, 303 p. : ill. ; 24 cm. (Modern Middle East series ; no. 1) Includes index. Bibliography: p. 287-296. [BP64.M62B653] 75-45136 ISBN 0-292-75025-0 15.95
1. Muslim saints—Morocco—Boujad. 2. Islam—Morocco. 3. Boujad, Morocco—Social life and customs. 4. Morocco—Social life and customs. I. Title. II. Series: Modern Middle East series (Austin, Tex.) ; no. 1.

Muslims.

BROOMHALL, Marshall, 1866- 297'.0951
Islam in China; a neglected problem. Preface by John R. Mott, Harlan P. Beach [and] Samuel M. Zwemer. New York, Paragon Book Reprint Corp., 1966. xx, 332 p. illus., maps (part fold.) 25 cm. "Unaltered and unabridged reprint of the work first published in ... 1910." "Chinese Mohammedan literature": p. 301-302. Bibliography: p. 307-310. [BP63.C5B7 1966] 66-30337
1. Muslims. I. Title.

Muslims in Egypt—Biography.

MUHAMMAD Zaki Badawi. 301.24'2'0962
The reformers of Egypt / M. A. Zaki Badawi. London : Croom Helm, c1978. 160 p. ; 23 cm. Includes bibliographical references and index. [BP64.E3M84 1978] 78-312985 ISBN 0-85664-651-2 : 19.00
1. al-Afghani, Jamal al-Din, 1838-1897. 2. Muhammad 'Abduh, 1849-1905. 3. Muhammad Rashid Rida. 4. Muslims in Egypt—Biography. 5. Islam—Egypt—History. I. Title.
Distributed by Biblio Distribution Centre, Totowa, NJ

Muslims in India.

RAM GOPAL, 1912- 325.3420954
Indian Muslims; a political history, 1858-1947. Bombay, New York, Asia Pub. House [1964] x, 351 p. 23 cm. Rs 18. Bibliographical footnotes. [DS463.R32] 67-158
1. Muslims in India. 2. India—Pol. & govt.—1765-1947. I. Title.

Muslims in Saudi Arabia—Biography.

MARGOLIOUTH, David Samuel, 1858-1940. 297'.63 B
Mohammed and the rise of Islam / by D. S. Margoliouth. New York : AMS Press, 1978. xxvi, 481 p., [27] leaves of plates (1 fold.) : ill. ; 19 cm. Reprint of the 1905 ed. published by Putnam, New York, in series: Heroes of the nations. Includes index. Bibliography: p. xxiii-xxvi. [BP75.M3 1978] 73-14455 ISBN 0-404-58273-7 : 30.00
1. Muhammad, the prophet. 2. Muslims in Saudi Arabia—Biography. I. Title. II. Series: Heroes of the nations.

Muslims in West Africa.

LEVTZION, Nehemia. 297'.0966
Muslims and chiefs in West Africa: a study of Islam in the Middle Volta Basin in the pre-colonial period. Oxford, Clarendon Pr., 1968. xxvi, 228p. 2 maps. 23cm. (Oxford studies in African affairs) Bibl. [BP64.A4W36] 68-106555 8.00
1. Muslims in West Africa. I. Title. II. Series.
Available from Oxford Univ. Pr., New York.

Muslims—Saudi Arabia—Biography.

KHAN, Muhammad Zafrulla, Sir, 1893- 297'.63 B
Muhammad, seal of the prophets / Muhammad Zafrulla Khan. London ; Boston : Routledge & Kegan Paul, 1980. viii, 289 p. ; 21 cm. Includes index. Bibliography: p. 284. [BP75.K4973] 19 80-40570 ISBN 0-7100-0610-1 (pbk.) : 12.50
1. Muhammad—Biography. 2. Muslims—Saudi Arabia—Biography. I. Title.

RODINSON, Maxime. 297'.63 B
Mohammed / Maxime Rodinson ; translated from the French by Anne Carter ; with a new introd. on contemporary Islam by the author. New York : Pantheon Books, 1979. p. cm. Translation of Mahomet. Reprint of the 1971 ed. published by Pantheon Books, New York. Includes index. Bibliography: p. [BP75.13.R613 1979] 79-17158 ISBN 0-394-50908-0 : 15.00 ISBN 0-394-73822-5 pbk. : 4.95
1. Muhammad, the prophet—Biography. 2. Muslims—Saudi Arabia—Biography. I. Title.

Musser, Daniel. The Reformed Mennonite church.

FUNK, John F. 1835-1930. 289
The Mennonite church and her accusers. A vindication of the character of the Mennonite church of America from her first organization in this country to the present time. By John F. Funk. Elkhart, Ind., Mennonite publishing company, 1878. iv, [5]-210 p. 19 cm. [BX8121.F8] 46-28144
1. Musser, Daniel. The Reformed Mennonite church. 2. Mennonites—Doctrinal and controversial works. I. Title.

Mussolini, Benito, 1883-

HEARLEY, John. 261.
Pope or Mussolini, by John Hearley. New York, The Maccaulay company [c1929] xiii p., 1 l., 17-256 p. 21 cm. [BX1545.H35] 29-14114
1. Mussolini, Benito, 1888- 2. Church and state in Italy. 3. Roman question. 4. Popes—Temporal power. 5. Concordat of 1929. 6. Fascism—Italy. I. Catholic church. Treatise, etc., 1922- (Pius XI) II. Title. III. Title: Italy. Treatise, etc., 1900- (Victor Emmanuel III).

PIROLO, Nicholas. 220.1
Babylon, political and ecclesiastical, showing characteristics of anti-Christ and false prophet, considering Mussolini and the Pope with their respective, "Vv il Duce" and "Vicarius Filii Dei", 666, by Evangelist Nicholas Pirolo... Milwaukee, Wis., [Word and witness publishing company, c1937] 2 p. l., 7-109 p. 22 cm. On cover: The Pope, Mussolini, Babylon, 666. [BS647.P55] 37-23526
1. Mussolini, Benito, 1883- 2. Papacy. 3. Catholic church—Doctrinal and controversial works—Protestant authors. 4. Bible—Prophecies. I. Title. II. Title: The Pope, Mussolini, Babylon, 666.

Mustard seed (Parable)

MARY Reparata, sister, 1892-1927. 242
A grain of mustard seed: memoirs and utterances of Sister Mary Reparata, O.P.: edited by a member of her community, Monastery of the Holy Name, Cincinnati, Ohio. New York, Cincinnati [etc.] Benziger brothers, 1932. 114 p. front. (port.) 15 1/2 cm. [Secular name: Marie Gautier] [BX2182.M37] 32-20107
I. Mary St. Peter, sister, 1859- ed. II. Title.

WALLEY, Barbara Ann. 226'.8
Mustard seed faith; an exposition of the Biblical mustard seed. Menomonie, Wis., Mustard Seed Press [1968] 3 p. illus. 15 cm. "One hundred and sixty copies were printed ... number 5." [BT378.M8W3] 68-7795
1. Mustard seed (Parable) 2. Faith—Biblical teaching. I. Title.

Muze'on 'al shem Sir Aizik ve-Leidi Volfson be-Hekhal Shelomoh.

JEWISH life in art and tradition : 296.4
based on the collection of the Sir Isaac and Lady Edith Wolfson Museum, Hechal Shlomo, Jerusalem / Yehuda L. Bialer, Estelle Fink ; photos. by David Harris. 1st American ed. New York : Putnam, 1976. 189 p. : ill. (some col.) ; 26 cm. [BM657.A1J48 1976] 75-33424 ISBN 0-399-11695-8 : 16.95
1. Muze'on 'al shem Sir Aizik ve-Leidi Volfson be-Hekhal Shelomoh. 2. Liturgical objects—Judaism—Pictorial works. 3. Jews—Rites and ceremonies. I. Bialer, Judah Loeb. II. Fink, Estelle. III. Muze'on 'al shem Sir Aizik ve-Leidi Volfson be-Hekhal Shelomoh.

Mvthology. Hindu.

NARAYAN, R. K., 1906- 294.521
God, demons, and others. Decorations by R. K. Laxman. New York, Viking [c.1964] 241p. illus. 24cm. 64-12225 6.50
1. Mvthology. Hindu. I. Title.

Mycenae—Religion.

EVANS, Arthur John, Sir 1851- 292
The Mycenaean tree and pillar cult and its Mediterranean relations; with illustrations from recent Cretan finds, by Arthur J. Evans ... with a coloured plate and seventy figures in the text. London, Macmillan and co., limited; New York, The Macmillan company, 1901. xii p., 1 l., 106 p. illus., col. pl. 28 cm. "Reproduced, by permission, from the Journal of Hellenic studies." [BL793.M8E8] 2-9354
1. Mycenae—Religion. 2. Tree-worship. 3. Cultus, Greek. 4. Crete—Antiq. I. Title. II. Title: Pillar cult. The Mycenian.

Myers, Frederic William Henry, 1843-1901.

DALLAS, Helen A. 133.
Death, the gate of life? (Mors janua vitae?) A discussion of certain communications purporting to come from Frederic W. H. Myers, by H. A. Dallas; with an introduction by Professor W. F. Barrett ... New York, E. P. Dutton & company [1919] xix, 147, [1] p. illus. 19 cm. Previously published (London, 1910) under title: Mors janua vitae? [BF1301.M9] 19-13017
1. Myers, Frederic William Henry, 1843-1901. 2. Psychical research. I. Title.

Myers, Jacob Martin, 1904-

A Light unto my path; 221.6
Old Testament studies in honor of Jacob M. Myers. Edited by Howard N. Bream, Ralph D. Heim [and] Carey A. Moore. Philadelphia, Temple University Press [1974] xxv, 529 p. 24 cm. (Gettysburg theological studies, 4) Includes bibliographical references. [BS1192.L53] 73-85042 ISBN 0-87722-026-3 15.00
1. Myers, Jacob Martin, 1904- 2. Myers, Jacob Martin, 1904- —Bibliography. 3. Bible. O.T.—Addresses, essays, lectures. I. Myers, Jacob Martin, 1904- II. Bream, H. N., ed. III. Heim, Ralph Daniel, 1895- ed. IV. Moore, Carey A., 1930- ed. V. Title. VI. Series.

Myers, Rawley.

MYERS, Rawley. 282'.092'4 B
Journal of a parish priest / by Rawley Myers. Huntington, Ind. : Our Sunday Visitor, c1982. 118 p. ; 21 cm. [BX4705.M988A34 1982] 19 81-82022 ISBN 0-87973-675-5 (pbk.) : 3.75
1. Myers, Rawley. 2. Catholic Church—Clergy—Biography. 3. Clergy—United States—Biography. I. Title.

Mysteries and miracle-plays—Bibliography

STODDARD, Francis Hovey, 1847- 016.
... *References for students* of miracle plays and mysteries. By Francis H. Stoddard ... Berkeley [University of California] 1887. 67, [1] p. fold. tab. 22 1/2 cm. (University of California. Library bulletin no. 8) Supplement to the Report of the secretary of the Board of regents. Contents.I. Histories, essays and works for reference.--II. Editions of plays not English.--III. Mysteries and miracle plays in England.--IV. Table of extant English mysteries. [Z5784.M6S8] 1-10236
1. Mysteries and miracle-plays—Bibl. I. Title.

Mysteries and miracle-plays, Cornish.

THE Creacion of the world : a critical edition and translation / edited and translated by Paula Neuss. New York : Garland Pub., 1983. p. cm. (Garland medieval texts ; no. 3) Cornish and English. According to colophon of original manuscript, written by William Jordan; he is believed to have been the scribe and not the author—cf. Introd. Translation of: Gwreans an bys. Bibliography: p. [PB2591.G8E5 1983] 19 81-23528 ISBN 0-8240-9447-6 : 50.00 891.6'72
1. Mysteries and miracle-plays, Cornish. 2. Cornish drama. I. Neuss, Paula. II. Jordan, William, fl. 1611. III. [Gwreans an bys.] English & Cornish IV. Title. V. Series.

Mysteries and miracle plays, English—Concordances.

PFLEIDERER, Jean D. 822'.0516
A complete concordance to The Chester mystery plays / Jean D. Pfleiderer, Michael J. Preston. New York : Garland, 1981. xxii, 513 p. ; 29 cm. (Garland reference library of the humanities ; v. 249) "Based upon the R.M. Lumiansky and David Mills edition, The Chester mystery cycle, vol. I., London: Oxford University Press, 1974"—Pref. [PR644.C4P47 1981] 19 80-8519 ISBN 0-8240-9465-4 : 100.00
1. Chester plays—Concordances. 2. Mysteries and miracle plays, English—Concordances. 3. English drama—To 1500—Concordances. 4. English language—Middle English, 1100-1500—Glossaries, vocabularies, etc. I. Preston, Michael J. II. Chester plays. Chester mystery cycle. V. 1. III. Title. IV. Series.

Mysteries and miracle-plays—History and criticism

CARGILL, Oscar, 1898- 792.1
Drama and liturgy, by Oscar Cargill. New York, Columbia university press, 1930. ix, 151 p., 1 l. 21 cm. (Half-title: Columbia university studies in English and comparative literature) Published also as thesis (PH. D.) Columbia university. Bibliography: p. 145-148. [PR641.C35 1930 a] 30-29284
1. Mysteries and miracle-plays—Hist. & crit. 2. Drama, Medieval—His. & crit. 3. Liturgies. I. Title.

Mysteries of the Rosary.

ROSS, Kenneth Needham, 1908- 248.36
The Christian mysteries. Derby [Eng.] P. Smith [dist. New York, Morehouse, 1965] 164p. 17cm. [BT303.R67] 64-1804 2.75 bds.,
1. Mysteries of the Rosary. I. Title.

Mysteries of the Rosary—Sermons.

WALLS, Ronald. 242'.742
The glory of Israel; scriptural background on the mysteries of the Rosary. Huntington, Ind., Our Sunday Visitor [1972] 94 p. illus. 21 cm. [BT303.W26] 72-75088 ISBN 0-87973-813-8 1.95
1. Catholic Church—Sermons. 2. Mysteries of the Rosary—Sermons. 3. Sermons, English—Scotland. I. Title.

Mysteries, Religious.

ANGUS, Samuel, 1881- 291.
The mystery religions and Christianity; a study in the religious background of early Christianity, by S. Angus ... New York, C. Scribner's sons [1928] xvi, 359 p. 23 cm. "First edition February 1925 ... cheaper edition April 1928." Printed in Great Britain. Bibliography: p. 315-352. [BL610.A6 1928] 29-25342
1. Mysteries, Religous. 2. Christianity and other religions. I. Title.

ANGUS, Samuel, 1881-1943. 200'.9'015
The mystery-religions : a study in the religious background of early Christianity / by S. Angus. New York : Dover Publications, 1975. xvi, 359 p. ; 22 cm. Reprint of the 2d ed. published in 1928 by Scribner, New York under title: The mystery-religions and Christianity. Includes indexes. Bibliography: p. 315-352. [BL610.A6 1975] 74-12657 ISBN 0-486-23124-0 pbk. : 3.95
1. Mysteries, Religious. 2. Christianity and other religions. I. Title.

ANGUS, Samuel, 1881-1943 299
The mystery-religions and Christianity; a study in the religious background of early Christianity. Introd. by Theodore H. Gaster. New Hyde Park, N. Y., University Bks. [1967c.1966] xxiv, 359p. 24cm. (Univ. lib. of comp. relig.) Bibl. [BL610.A6 1966] 66-27423 10.00
1. Mysteries, Religious. 2. Christianity and other religions. I. Title.

BONOMELLI, Geremia, bp., 1831-
Christian mysteries; or, Discourses for all the great feasts of the year, except those of the Blessed Virgin, by the Right Rev. Jeremias Bonomelli, D.D., bishop of Cremona; tr. by the Right Rev. Thomas Sebastian Byrne, D.D., bishop of Nashville. New York, Cincinnati [etc.] Benziger brothers, 1910. 4 v. 20 1/2 cm. 11-411 5.00.
I. Byrne, Thomas Sebastian, bp., 1842- tr. II. Title.

GODWIN, Joscelyn. 291'.044
Mystery religions in the ancient world / Joscelyn Godwin. 1st U.S. ed. San Francisco : Harper & Row, c1981. p. cm. Includes index. Bibliography: p. [BL610.G63 1981] 19 81-47423 ISBN 0-06-063140-6 pbk. : 9.95
1. Mysteries, Religious. 2. Religions. I. Title.

HEINDEL, Max, d.1919. 212
Ancient and modern initiation, by Max Heindel. 1st ed. Oceanside, Calif., The Rosicrucian fellowship; London, L. & [i.e. N.] Fowler & co. [c1931] 148 p. front., plates. 20 cm. Contents.pt. i. The tabernacle in the wilderness.--pt.ii. The Christian mystic initiation. [BF1623.R7H25] 32-7584
1. Mysteries. Religious. 2. Jews—Rites and ceremonies. 3. Christianity. 4. Rosicrucians. I. Title.

KNOCHE, Grace Frances. 291.3
... *The mystery-schools,* by Grace Frances Knoche. Covina, Calif., Theosophical university press, 1943. 3 p. l., 124, [3] p. 15 cm. (Theosophical manual no. XIV) "Second printing, 1943." "Books for further study": p. [125] [BL610.K6] 44-46070
1. Mysteries, Religious. 2. Theosophy. I. Title.

LARKEY, Mabel A. 133.3
Greatest mystery of the ages revealed. New York, Vantage [c.1962] 102p. 21cm. 2.50 bds.,
I. Title.

LIEVEGOED, B. C. J. 1905- (Bernardus Cornelis Johannes), 299'.935
Mystery streams in Europe and the new mysteries / by B.C.J. Lievegoed. Spring Valley, N.Y. : Anthroposophic Press, c1982. xv, 87 p. : ill. ; 21 cm. Translation of: Mysteriestromen in Europa en die nieuwe mysterien. Bibliography: p. 87. [BL610.L5313 1982] 19 82-150360 ISBN 0-88010-002-8 pbk. : 8.95
1. Mysteries, Religious. 2. Anthroposophy. I. [Mysteriestromen in Europa en die nieuwe mysterien.] English II. Title.

MACCHIORO, Vittorio D., 1880- 292
From Orpheus to Paul; a history of Orphism, by Vittorio D. Macchioro. New York, H. Holt and company [c1930] 6 p. l., 3-262 p. front., plates (1 fold.) 22 1/2 cm. (Half-title: Studies in religion and culture) "Schermerhorn lectures, I." "Notes": p. 227-258. [BL795.07M3] 30-13999
1. Orpheus. 2. Paul, Saint, apostle. 3. Mysteries, Religious. 4. Christianity and other religions. I. Title. II. Title: Orphism.

*MCNEILLY, Elizabeth H. 230
The three greatest mysteries. New York, Carlton [c.1964] 70p. 21cm. 2.50
I. Title.

SCHURE, Edouard, 1841-1929. 182'.2
The ancient mysteries of Delphi: Pythagoras. Introd. by Paul M. Allen. Blauvelt, N.Y., Rudolf Steiner Publications, 1971. 130 p. 18 cm. (Steinerbooks) Originally published as chapter 6 of the author's Les grands inities. [BL610.S3713] 70-150529 1.45
1. Mysteries, Religious. 2. Pythagoras and Pythagorean school. I. Title.

SCHURE, Edouard, 1841-1929. 291.6
The mysteries of ancient Greece: Orpheus/Plato. Blauvelt, N.Y., Rudolf Steiner Publications, 1971. 11-134 p. illus. 18 cm. (Steinerbooks) Published also in 1961 as the 5th and 7th chapters of the author's The great initiates which was G. Rasberry's translation of Les grands inities. Includes bibliographical references. [BL795.O7S3813] 76-150261 1.45
1. Orpheus. 2. Plato. 3. Mysteries, Religious. I. Schure, Edouard, 1841-1929. Les grands inities. Plato. English. 1971. II. Title. III. Title: Orpheus/Plato.

SHELDON, Henry Clay, 1845-1928.
The mystery religions and the New Testament, by Henry C. Sheldon ... New York, Cincinnati, The Abingdon press [c1918] 1 p. l., 5-155 p. 17 1/2 cm. [BS2380.S5] 18-19135
1. Mysteries, Religious. 2. Christianity and other religions. I. Title.

SPENCE, Lewis, 1874-1955. 299'.2762
The mysteries of Egypt; or, The secret rites and traditions of the Nile. Edited, with an introd., by Paul M. Allen. Blauvelt, N.Y., Rudolf Steiner Publications [1972] 260 p. 18 cm. (Steinerbooks, 1727) Includes bibliographical references. [BL2441.S68 1972] 79-183056 1.95
1. Mysteries, Religious. 2. Egypt—Religion. 3. Mythology, Egyptian. I. Title.

WHITNEY, Wilson, 1845-
The Christian mysteries, and other sermons and papers, by Rev. Wilson Whitney... [Detroit, Mich., Times printing company, c1914] 4 p. l., 190 p. port. 20 cm. $1.00 14-2799
I. Title.

WILLOUGHBY, Harold Rideout 292.3
Pagan regeneration; a study of mystery initiations in the Graeco-Roman world, by Harold R. Willoughby. Chicago, University of Chicago Press [1960, c.1929] xi, 307p. 22cm. (Chicago reprint series) (Bibls.) 4.50
1. Mysteries, Religious. 2. Greece—Religion. 3. Rome—Religion. I. Title. II. Title: Regeneration, Pagan.
Contents omitted.

WILLOUGHBY, Harold Rideout, 1890- 292
Pagan regeneration; a study of mystery initiations in the Graeco-Roman world. [Chicago] University of Chicago Press [1960, c1929] 307 p. 22 cm. (Chicago reprint series) Includes bibliography. [BL727.W5 1960] 60-51202
1. Mysteries, Religious. 2. Initiations (in religion, folk-lore, etc.) 3. Greece — Religion. 4. Rome — Religion. I. Title.

WILLOUGHBY, Harold Rideout, 1890- 292.
Pagan regeneration; a study of mystery initiations in the Graeco-Roman world, by Harold R. Willoughby ... Chicago, Ill., The University of Chicago press [c1929] xi, 307 p. 21 cm. Bibliography at end of each chapter. [BL727.W5] 29-22404
1. Mysteries, Religious. 2. Greece—Religion. 3. Rome—Religion. I. Title. II. Title: Regeneration Pagan.
Contents omitted.

Mystery.

SCOTT, John Martin, 1913- 248
Phenomena of our universe : mysteries that influence our lives / John M. Scott. Huntington, Ind. : Our Sunday Visitor, c1976. 136 p. : ill. ; 18 cm. [BT127.5.S35] 75-28977 ISBN 0-87973-797-2 pbk. : 1.75
1. Mystery. 2. Supernatural. I. Title.

Mystery—Biblical teaching.

BISAGNO, John R. 220.6
Great mysteries of the Bible / John R. Bisagno. Nashville, Tenn. : Broadman Press, 1982, c1981. 142 p. ; 22 cm. [BS2545.M87B57] 19 81-67997 ISBN 0-8054-1952-7 : 6.95
1. Bible. N.T.—Criticism, interpretation, etc. 2. Mystery—Biblical teaching. I. Title.

WILSON, Thomas Ernest, 1902- 231'.74
Mystery doctrines of the New Testament : God's sacred secrets / T. Ernest Wilson. 1st ed. Neptune, N.J. : Loizeaux Bros., 1975. 123 p. ; 20 cm. Bibliography: p. 119-123. [BS2545.M87W54] 74-78881 ISBN 0-87213-962-X pbk. : 1.95
1. Bible. N.T.—Criticism, interpretation, etc. 2. Mystery—Biblical teaching. I. Title.

Mystical union.

ANABEL du Coeur de Jesus, Mother. 149.3
The doctrine of the divine indwelling; a commentary on the prayer of Sister Elizabeth of the Trinity. Translated into English by a Discalced Carmelite. Westminster, Md., Newman Press, 1950. 150 p. 20 cm. Bibliography: p. 15-16. [BV5082.E6A6] 50-12392
1. Elizabeth de la Trinite, Sister, 1880-1906. 2. Mystical union. 3. Mysticism—Catholic Church. I. Title.

BALDWIN, Harmon Allen, 1869-
The indwelling Christ, by Harmon A. Baldwin; with an introduction by Bishop Burton R. Jones ... Vandergrift Heights, Pa., The author [c1912] 282 p. 20 cm. [BT205B16] 12-18069
1. Mystical union. I. Title.

BRENT, Charles Henry, bp., 1862-1929. 220
Presence, by Charles H. Brent... New York, London [etc.] Longmans, Green and co., 1914. viii, 53 p. 18 1/2 cm. [BR125.B7217] 14-9926
1. Mystical union. I. Title.

CABASILAS, Nicolaus, 14thcent. 234'.16
The life in Christ / Nicholas Cabasilas ; translated from the Greek by Carmino J. deCatanzaro ; with an introduction by Boris Bobrinskoy. Crestwood, N.Y. : St. Vladimir's Seminary Press, 1982, c1974. p. cm. Translation of: Peri tes en Christoi Zoes. Includes bibliographical references. [BT767.7.C313 1982] 19 82-16870 ISBN 0-913836-12-5 : 7.95
1. Orthodox Eastern Church—Doctrinal and controversial works. 2. Mystical union. 3. Sacraments—Orthodox Eastern Church. I. [Peri tes en Christoi Zoes.] English II. Title.
Publisher's address : 575 Scarsdale Rd., Crestwood, NY 10707.

CAMPBELL, James Mann, 1840-1926. 232
The indwelling Christ, by James M. Campbell. Chicago, New York [etc.] Fleming H. Revell company [1895] 3 p. l., 5-178 p. 19 cm. Introduction by Prof. A. B. Bruce, D.D. [BT205.C2] 37-31962
1. Mystical union. I. Title.

CUNNINGHAM, Francis L B 231
The indwelling of the Trinity; a historico-doctrinal study of the theory of St. Thomas Aquinas. Dubuque, Priory Press, 1955. 414p. 24cm. (The Aquinas library) Includes bibliography. [BT769.C77] 55-2521
1. Thomas Aquinas, Saint, 1225?-1274. 2. Mystical union. I. Title.

CUTHBERT, father, 1866- 234
In Christ; a brief exposition of the Christian life, by Father Cuthbert, O. S. F. C. New York, Cincinnati [etc.] Benziger brothers [1933] 5 p. l., 213 p. 19 cm. "Printed in Great Britian." [Secular name: Lawrence Cuthbert Hess] [BT769.C8] 34-13737
1. Mystical union. 2. Catholic church—Doctrinal and controversial works—Catholic authors. I. Title.

GORDON, Adoniram Judson, 248
1836-1895.
In Christ or, The believer's union with his Lord. Grand Rapids, Baker Book House, 1964. 209 p. 20 cm. "Reprinted from the edition issued in 1872." Bibliographical references included in "Notes" (p. [208]-209) [BT769.G6 1964] 64-14563
1. Mystical union. I. Title.

GORDON, Adoniram Judson, 234.
1836-1895.
In Christ; or, The believer's union with his Lord. By A. J. Gordon ... 6th ed. Boston, H. Gannett, 1883. iv p., 2 l., [9]-209 p. 19 cm. [BT769.G6 1883] 45-50703
1. Mystical union. I. Title.

JAEGHER, Paul de. 234
One with Jesus; or, The life of identification with Christ. Translated from the French. [New enl. ed.] Westminster, Md., Newman Press, 1956. 59p. 21cm. Translation of La vie d'identification au Christ Jesus. [BT769.J313] 57-59535
1. Mystical union. I. Title.

JOHNSON, Elbert Neil. 232
The Master is here; Jesus' presence in fact and experience. [1st ed.] New York, American Press [1955] 141p. 22cm. [BT205.J6] 55-7998
1. Mystical union. I. Title.

JUAN De La Cruz Saint, 1542- 245.6
1591.
Spiritual canticle. 3d rev. ed. Translated, edited, and with an introd. by E. Allison Peers from the critical ed. of P. Silverio de Santa Teresa. Garden City, N. Y., Image Books [1961] 520p. 18cm. (A Doubleday image book, D110) [BV5080.J773 1961] 61-1028
1. Mystical union. I. Title.

LAUBACH, Frank Charles, 1884- 242
Christ liveth in me, and Game with minutes. [Westwood, N.J.] Revell [c.1961] 64p. 61-9241 1.00 bds.,
1. Mystical union. 2. Christian life. I. Title.

MURA, Ernest, 1900- 231
In Him is life. Translated by Angeline Bouchard. St. Louis, B. Herder Book Co. [1956] 226p. 21cm. (Cross and crown series of spirituality, no. 8) Translation of L'humanite vivifiante du Christ. [BX2350.M915] 56-10797
1. Mystical union. 2. Spiritual life—Catholic authors. I. Title.

PIERSON, Arthur Tappan, 234.8
1837-1911.
Vital union with Christ. Grand Rapids, Mich., Zondervan [1961] 120p. 'Formerly published as: Shall we continue to sin?' 61-19957 1.95; 1.00 bds., pap.,
1. Mystical union. I. Title.

PLUS, Raoul, 1882-
In Christ Jesus, by Raoul Plus, S.J. Rev. and corr. ed. Tr. by Peter Addison. Westminster, Md., Newman Bookshop, 1948. xiii, 207 p. 19 cm. A 48
1. Mystical union. 2. Spiritual life. 3. Sanctification. I. Addison, Peter, tr. II. Title.

PLUS, Raoul, 1882- 248
Progress in divine union, by the Reverend Raoul Plus, S. J., translated from the French by Sister Mary Bertille and Sister Mary St. Thomas ... New York, Cincinanti, Frederick Pustet co. (inc.) 1941. viii, 9-142 p. 19 cm. [BX2350.P54] 41-26057
1. Mystical union. 2. Spiritual life—Catholic authors. 3. Prayer. I. Mary Bertille, sister, 1905- tr. II. Mary St. Thomas sister, 1905- joint tr. III. Title.

STARR, Irina. 200
The sound of light; experiencing the transcendental. New York, Philosophical Library [1969] xiii, 131 p. 22 cm. [BT769.S7] 69-20335 4.95
1. Mystical union. 2. Experience (Religion) I. Title.

STRONG, Augustus Hopkins, 260
1836-1921.
Union with Christ; a chapter of Systematic theology, by Augustus Hopkins Strong ... Philadelphia, Boston [etc.] American Baptist publication society [c1913] 84 p. 20 cm. "Reprint in compendious form [of] the chapter of my 'Systematic theology' on Union with Christ."--Pref. [BT75.S87] 13-21320
1. Mystical union. I. Title.

THOMPSON, Colin P. 861'.3
The poet and the mystic : a study of the Cantico espiritual of San Juan de la Cruz / by Colin P. Thompson. Oxford [Eng.] ; New York : Oxford University Press, 1977. p. cm. (Oxford modern languages and literature monographs) Includes index. Bibliography: p. [BV5080.J7755T48] 77-9326 ISBN 0-19-815531-X 22.00
1. Juan de la Cruz, Saint, 1542-1591. Cantico espiritual. 2. Mystical union. I. Title.

UPHAM, Thomas Cogswell, 1799- 231
1872.
A treatise on divine union, designed to point out some of the intimate relations between God and man in the higher forms of religious experience. By Thomas C. Upham... Boston, C. H. Peirce and company, 1851. 8, 435 p. 19 cm. [BT165.U6] 40-24466
1. Mystical union. I. Title. II. Title: Divine union, A treatise on.

Mystical union—Early works to 1800.

HOOKER, Thomas, 1586-1647. 234
The soules exaltation / by T.H. New York : AMS Press, 1981. p. cm. (A Library of American Puritan writings ; v. 18) [BT767.7.H66 1981] 19 78-298 ISBN 0-404-60818-3 : 57.50
1. Mystical union—Early works to 1800. I. Title. II. Title: Soul's exaltation. III. Series. Contents omitted.

Mysticism.

ADDISON, Charles Morris, 248
1856-
The theory and practice of mysticism, by Charles Morris Addison... New York, E.P. Dutton & company [c1918] viii p., 2 l., 3-216 p. 19 1/2 cm. "The lectures which form the substance of this volume were written at the request of the Faculty of the Episcopal theological school in Cambridge and were delivered there in May, 1915."--Pref. [BV5082.A4] 18-7412
1. Mysticism. I. Title.

ADDISON, Charles Morris, 248
1856-
What is mysticism? A study of man's search for God, by the Rev. Charles Morris Addison, D.D. New York, The Macmillan company, 1923. 3 p. l. 54 p. 18 cm. [BV5082.A45] 23-8084
1. Mysticism. I. Title.

ARKUS, Karen A. 248'.22
A trip into the mystic mind / by Karen A. Arkus. Anaheim, Ca. : Arkus House Publications, 1977. 163 p. ; 21 cm. Includes bibliographical references. [BL625.A74] 76-27490 ISBN 0-917596-01-3 pbk. : 3.95
1. Mysticism. I. Title.

BAUMGARDT, David, 1890- 149.3
Great Western mystics: their lasting significance. New York, Columbia Univ. Press, 1961. xii, 99p. (Matchette Foundation lectures, no. 4) Bibl. 60-10165 3.00
1. Mysticism. I. Title. II. Series.

BENNETT, Charles Andrew 141
Armstrong, 1885-1930.
A philosophical study of mysticism, an essay, by Charles A. Bennett ... New Haven, Yale university press; [etc., etc.] 1923. 7 p. l., [3]-194 p. 24 cm. "The present volume is the third work published by the Yale university press on the Amasa Stone Mather memorial publication fund." Contents.--pt. 1. The mystical ambition.--pt. ii. Revelation.--pt. iii. Religion and morality. [B828.B4] 23-16500
1. Mysticism. I. Yale university. Amasa Stone Mather memorial publication fund. II. Title.

BERBERICH, Wilhelm August, 242
1861-1929.
Seeing God; a manual of spiritual readings from which may be learned the art of the holy contemplation or spiritual vision of God; from the German original of William A. Berberich by Rev. Laurence P. Emery ... New York, Cincinnati [etc.] Benziger brothers, 1934. vii, 454 p. incl. front., ports. 17 cm. [BV5091.C7B42] 34-40313
1. Mysticism. I. Emery, Laurence Peter Ernest, tr. II. Title. III. Title: Contemplation, A manual of Translation of Die hellige beschauung.

BJERREGAARD, Carl Henrick
Andreas 1845-
Mysticism; or, Teachings of the ages on the inner or spiritual life, by C. H. A. Bjerregaard ... and Robert Arnot ... New York, Knight & Brown, 1902. 55 p. front., pl. 25 cm. Specimen pages. 2-1164
1. Mysticism. I. Title.

BJERREGAARD, Carl Henrik
Andreas.
Lectures on mysticism and nature worship 2d ser. Chicago, M. R. Kent, 1897. 132 p. 8 cm. 1-1582
I. Title.

*BLOFELD, John 149.3
Beyond the gods Taoist and Buddhist mysticism. New York, E. P. Dutton, 1974 164 p. 19 cm. [BV5082] ISBN 0-525-47383-1 2.45 (pbk.)
1. Mysticism. I. Title.

BOEHME, Jakob, 1575-1624. 149.3
The signature of all things, with other writings, by Jacob Boehme. London & Toronto, J. M. Dent & sons ltd.; New York, E. P. Dutton & co. [1926] xiv, 295 p. 17 1/2 cm. (Half-title: Everyman's library, ed. by Ernest Rhys. Philosophy & theology) Introduction signed: Clifford Bax. Contents.Signatura rerum.--Of the supernatural life.--The way from darkness to true illumination. Bibliography: p. [xii] [BV5080.B64E3] 33-36661
1. Mysticism. I. Bax, Clifford, 1886- ed. II. Title.

BOEHME, Jakob, 1575-1624. 149.3
The signature of all things, with other writings by Jacob Boehme. London & Toronto, J. M. Dent & sons, ltd.; New York, E. P. Dutton & co. [1934] xiv, 295 p. 17 1/2 cm. (Half-title: Everyman' library, ed. by Ernest Rhys. Philosophy & Theology. [no. 563]) "First published in this edition, 1912; reprinted...1934." Introduction by Clifford Bax. Contents.Signatura rerum.--Of the supernatural life.--The way from darkness to true illumination. Bibliogrpahy: p. [xii] [AC1.E8 no.569] 36-37588
1. Mysticism. I. Title.

BOHME, Jakob, 1575-1624. 149.3
Jacob Boehme's The way to Christ, in a new translation by John Joseph Stoudt, with a foreword by Rufus M. Jones. New York and London, Harper & brothers [1947] xxxix p., 2 l., 3-254 p., 1 l. incl. front. (port.) 2 illus. (incl. facsim.) 22 cm. "First edition." "Selected bibliography": p. 251-254. [BV5080.B7W414] 47-4175
1. Mysticism. I. Stoudt, John Joseph, tr. II. Title. III. Title: The way to Christ.

BOHME, Jakob, 1575-1624. 248'.22
Jacob Boehme's The way to Christ : in a new translation / by John Joseph Stoudt ; with a foreword by Rufus M. Jones. Westport, Conn. : Greenwood Press, 1979, c1947. xxxix, 254 p. : port. ; 23 cm. Translation of Der Weg zu Christo. Reprint of the 1st ed. published by Harper, New York. Bibliography: p. 251-254. [BV5080.B7W413 1979] 78-13976 ISBN 0-313-21075-6 lib. bdg. : 19.75
1. Mysticism. I. Title. II. Title: The way to Christ.

BOHME, Jakob, 1575-1624. 204
Six theosophic points and other writings, by Jacob Bohme; newly translated into English by John Rolleston Earle, M.A. New York, A. A. Knopf, 1920. 220 p. 21 1/2 cm. Contents.Six theosophic points.--Six mystical points.--On the earthly and heavenly mystery.--On the divine intuition. [BV5072.B7 1920] 20-4124
1. Mysticism. I. Earle, John Rolleston, 1864-1933, tr. II. Title.

BRINTON, Howard Haines, 1884- 922
The mystic will, based on a study of the philosophy of Jacob Boehme, by Howard H. Brinton ... with an introduction by Rufus M. Jones ... New York, The Macmillan company, 1930. xiii p., 2 l., 3-269 p. diagr. 20 1/2 cm. Bibliography: p. 259-262. [BV5095.B7B7] 30-15635
1. Boehme, Jakob, 1575-1624. 2. Mysticism. I. Title.

BROWNING, Louise 149.
Starkweather, Mrs.
Missing links and mystic kinks, by Louise Starkweather Browning. Boston, The Christopher publishing house [c1924] 103 p. 20 1/2 cm. [BV5085.B7] 24-23078
I. Title.

BUCKHAM, John Wright, 1864- 230.
Mysticism and modern life, by John Wright Buckham ... New York, Cincinnati, The Abingdon press [c1915] 256 p. 20 cm. [BV5081.B8] 15-26890
1. Mysticism. I. Title.

BURROWS, Ruth. 248'.22
Guidelines for mystical prayer / [by] Ruth Burrows. London : Sheed and Ward, 1976. x, 149 p. ; 20 cm. [BV5082.2.B87] 77-354225 ISBN 0-7220-7663-0 : £2.50
1. Mysticism. I. Title.

BUTLER, Charles, 1750-1832.
Reminiscences of Charles Butler ... With 1. An essay on the mystical devotions of Catholics and Protestants: 2. A correspondence between the late Dr. Parr and Mr. Butler: 3. And,--Considerations on the present proceedings for the reform on the English courts of equity:--on a charge brought against conveyancers, solicitors, and attornies:--and on Mr. Humphreys' "Observations on the actual state of real property in England" ... Boston, Wells and Lilly, 1827. iv, [12]-294 p. 20 cm. Second volume of the Reminiscences. An American edition of the 1st volume was published, New York, 1824. 29-753
1. Mysticism. 2. Equity pleading and procedure—Gt. Brit. 3. Law reform—Gt. Brit. 4. Lawyers—Gt. Brit. 5. Conveyancing—Gt. Brit. 6. Real property—Gt. Brit. I. Humphreys, James d. 1830. Observations on the actual state of the English laws of real property. II. Parr, Samuel, 1747-1825. III. Title.

BUTLER, Edward Cuthbert, 248'.22
1858-1934.
Western mysticism : the teaching of SS. Augustine, Gregory, and Bernard on contemplation and the contemplative life / Cuthbert Butler. New York : Gordon Press, [1975] p. cm. Reprint of the 1922 ed. published by Constable, London. [BV5075.B8 1975] 75-20378 ISBN 0-87968-244-2 lib.bdg. : 34.95
1. Augustinus, Aurelius, Saint, Bp. of Hippo. 2. Bernard de Clairvaux, Saint, 1091?-1153. 3. Gregorius, the Great, Saint, Pope, 540 (ca.)-604. 4. Mysticism. 5. Contemplation. I. Title.

BUTLER, Edward Cuthbert, 248.2'2
1858-1934.
Western mysticism; the teaching of Augustine, Gregory, and Bernard on contemplation and the contemplative life. 3d ed. with Afterthoughts, and a new foreword by David Knowles. New York, Barnes & Noble [1968, c1967] lxxii, 242 p. 22 cm. Bibliographical footnotes. [BV5075.B8 1968] 68-6959
1. Augustinus, Aurelius, Saint, Bp. of Hippo. 2. Bernard de Clairvaux, Saint, 1091?-1153. 3. Gregorius I, the Great, Saint, Pope, 540 (ca.)-604. 4. Mysticism. 5. Contemplation. I. Title.

CHANDLER, Arthur, bp. of 230.
Bloemfontein, 1860-
First-hand religion: suggestions towards the practice of Christian mysticism, by Arthur Chandler ... London, A. R. Mowbray & co. ltd.; Milwaukee, The Morehouse publishing co. [1922] xi, 81, [1] p. 19 cm. "Originally delivered in the form of lectures ... in the diocese of Winchester."--Pref. "A list of a few books": p. 81. [BV5081.C55] 23-4187
1. Mysticism. I. Title.

CHANEY, Robert Galen, 1913- 248'.22
Mysticism—the journey within / Robert Chaney. Upland, Calif. : Astara, c1979. v, 192 p. ; 23 cm. (Astara's library of mystical classics) [BL625.C47] 79-52959 pbk. : 12.50
1. Mysticism. I. Title.
Publisher's Address, 1916 Race St., Philadelphia, PA 19103

CLYMER, Reuben Swinburne 1878- 133
Ancient mystic oriental masonry, its teachings, rules, laws and present usages which govern the order at the present day... By Dr. R. Swinburne Clymer... Allentown, Pa., The Philosophical publishing co. [c1907] 196 p. 18 1/2 cm. [BF1611.C56] 7-18301
I. Title.

COBB, Stanwood, 1881- 248
The essential mysticism, by Stanwood Cobb. Boston, The Four seas company, 1918. 144 p. 19 cm. [BV5082.C6] 18-22881
1. Mysticism. I. Title.

CONFESSIONS. 248
Compiled and edited by W. Scott Palmer [pseud.] With an introd. by Evelyn Underhill. New York, Harper [1954] 188p. 14cm. [BV5080.B65E5 1954] [BV5080.B65E5 1954] 149.3 53-10976 53-10976
1. Mysticism. I. Bohme, Jakob, 1575-1624.

CRONK, Walter. 248
The golden light. Los Angeles, DeVorse [1964] 196 p. illus. 24 cm. [BV5095.C7A3] 64-15645
1. Mysticism. I. Title.

CURTISS, Harriette Augusta. Mrs. 133
The temple of silence, transcribed by Harriette Augusta Curtiss in collaboration with F. Homer Curtiss ... San Francisco, Cal., The Curtiss philosophic book co. [c1920] 3 p. l., 9-60 p. 13 cm. (Gems of mysticism series) [BF1999.C86] 22-21419
1. Mysticism. I. Curtiss, Frank Homer, 1875- joint author. II. Title.

DASGUPTA, Surendra Nath, 1887- 294
Hindu mysticism; six lectures, by S. N. Dasgupta ... (Norman Wait Harris foundation lectures, 1926) Northwestern, Evaston, Ill. Chicago, London, The Open court publishing co., 1927. xx, 168 p. front. (port.) 20 cm. [BL2015.M8D3] 27-15507
1. Mysticism. I. Harris, N. W., Lectures, Northwestern university, Evanston, Ill. II. Title.

DAWKINS, Muriel (Bacheler) Mrs.
Mysticism an epistemological problem ... by Muriel Bachelor Dawkins ... [New Haven, The Tuttle, Morehouse & Taylor company, 1916] 100 p. 24 cm. Thesis (PH. D.)--Yale university, 1915. Bibliography: p. [96]-100. 16-14469
I. Title.

DE QUINCEY, Thomas, 1785-1859.
The ecstasies of Thomas De Quincey, chosen by Thomas Burke. New York, Doubleday, Doran & co. [1929] 319, [1] p. 19 cm. Printed in Great Britain. [PR4532.B8] 29-3738
I. Burke, Thomas, 1887- comp. II. Title.
Contents omitted.

DHAMMAPADA. English. 294.3
The wayfarer, an interpretation of the Dhammapada [by] Wesley La Violette. Los Angeles, De Vorss, 1956. 125p. 24cm. [BL1411.D5E6] 56-59217
I. La Violette, Wesley, 1894- II. Title.

DUNLAP, Knight, 1875- 131.
Mysticism, Freudianism and scientific psychology, by Knight Dunlap ... St. Louis, C. V Mosby company, 1920. 173 p. 20 cm. [BF636.D8] 21-4094
1. Mysticism. 2. Psychoanalysis. 3. Psychology. I. Title. II. Title: Freudlanism.

EUSTACE, Cecil John, 1903- 248.2
An infinity of questions; a study of the religion of art, and of the art of religion in the lives of five women [by] Cecil Johnson Eustace. With an introd. by Michael de la Bedoyere. Freeport, N.Y., Books for Libraries Press [1969] 170 p. ports. 23 cm. (Essay index reprint series) Reprint of the 1946 ed. Contents.Contents.—The bent world.—The poetic instinct: Helen Foley.—The genius: Katherine Mansfield.—The artist in agony: France Pastorelli.—The mystic: Elizabeth Leseur.—The lover: St. Therese of Lisieux.—Epilogue. Bibliography: p. 169-170. [BV5095.A1E8 1969] 70-84356
1. Foley, Helen, 1896-1937. 2. Mansfield, Katherine, 1888-1923. 3. Pastorelli, France, Mme. 4. Leseur, Elisabeth (Arrighi) 1866-1914. 5. Therese, Saint, 1873-1897. 6. Mysticism. I. Title.

EUSTACE, Cecil John, 1903- 920.7
An infinity of questions a study of the religion of art, and of the art of religion in the lives of five women. With an introd. by Michael de la Bedoyere. New York, Toronto, Longmans, Green, 1946. 170 p. ports. 19 cm. [[BV5095.A1E]] A 48
1. Foley, Helen, 1896-1937. 2. Mansfield, Katherine, 1888-1923. 3. Pastorelli, Mme, France. 4. Leseur, Elizabeth (Arrigha) 1866-1914. 5. Therese, Saint, 1873-1897. 6. Mysticism. I. Title.

EVANS, Helen (Fiske) 149.3
The garden of the Little Flower, and other mystical experiences, by Helen Fiske Evans. With foreword by the Bishop of Maryland and preface by the Bishop of Northern Indiana. [Baltimore, The Sutherland press, 1947] xii, 138 p. front. 20 1/2 cm. [BV5095.E9A3] 17-21746
1. Mysticism. 2. Therese, Saint, 1873-1897. I. Title.

FORT, Adele Brooks. 149.3
Splendor in the night, recording a glimpse of reality, by Adele Brooks Fort; with foreword by Rufus M. Jones ... Portland, Me., The Mosher press, 1934. xxi, [1], 64, [1] p., 1 l. 17 cm. "First edition, May, 1963 ... Third edition, December, 1884." "Five hundred copies ... printed. [BV5005.F6A4 1934 a] 41-20703
1. Mysticism. I. Title.

FURSE, Margaret Lewis. 291.4'2
Mysticism, window on a world view / Margaret Lewis Furse. Nashville : Abingdon Press, c1977. 220 p. ; 22 cm. Includes bibliographical references and indexes. [BL625.F87] 76-56816 ISBN 0-687-27674-8 pbk. : 5.95
1. Mysticism. I. Title.

GHOSE, Sisirkumar. 291.4'2
Mystics and society; a point of view. Foreword by Aldous Huxley. New York, Asia Pub. [c.1968] xv, 116p. 23cm. Bibl. refs. included in Notes [BL625.G47 1968] 68-7335 3.75
1. Mysticism. I. Title.
Available from Taplinger.

GILBREATH, Joseph Earl. 201
The vision of God and the social order, by J. Earl Gilbreath; foreword by Rufus M. Jones. New York [etc.] Fleming H. Revell company [c1936] 191 p. 20 cm. [BV5083.G5] 36-33924
1. Mysticism. 2. Sociology, Chritstian. I. Title.

GREGG, Richard Bartlett, 1885- 149.3
The self beyond yourself. Philadelphia, Lippincott [1956] 287p. 21cm. Includes bibliography. [BL625.G68] 56-10811
1. Mysticism. I. Title.

GRIERSON, Francis, 1848- 141
Modern mysticism, and other essays, by Francis Grierson. [4th ed.] London, John Lane; New York, John Lane company; [etc., etc.] 1914. 180 p. 20 cm. Preface signed: L. W. T. Contents.--Preface.--Modern mysticism.--Beauty and morals in nature.--The tragedy of Macbeth.--Modern melancholy.--Tolstoy.--Imitation and originality.--Physical courage and moral cowardice.--Parsifalitis--Authority individualism.--The new criticism.--Amiel.--Culture.--The artistic faculty in literature. [B828.G8 1914] 15-13726
I. Title.

GROSS, Josiah.
Ondell and Dolee; a story of mysticism, by Josiah Gross. New York, London [etc.] The Abbey press [1902] 260 p., 1 l. 21 cm. 2-19996
I. Title.

GROUP for the Advancement of Psychiatry. Committee on Psychiatry and Religion. 291.4'3
Mysticism : spiritual quest or psychic disorder? / Formulated by the Committee on Psychiatry and Religion. New York : Group for the Advancement of Psychiatry, 1976. p. 705-825 ; 23 cm. (Publication - Group for the Advancement of Psychiatry ; v. 9, no. 97) Includes bibliographical references. [RC321.G7 no. 97] [BL625] 76-45931 ISBN 0-87318-134-4 : 4.00
1. Mysticism. I. Title. II. Series: Group for the Advancement of Psychiatry. Report ; no. 97.

HALL, Manly Palmer. 133
What the ancient wisdom expects of its disciples; a study concerning the mystery schools, by Manly P. Hall. 2d rev. ed. Los Angeles, Cal., Hall publishing co. [c1929] 64 p. 17 cm. Advertising matter: p. 59-64. [BF1999.H337 1929] ca 30
1. Mysticism. I. Title.

HALL, Manly Palmer, 1901- 149.3
The mystical Christ; religion as a personal spiritual experience. 1st ed. Los Angeles, Philosophical Research Society [1951] 248 p. illus. 24 cm. [BV5082.H34] 52-18341
1. Mysticism. I. Title.

HANSON, Virginia, comp. 149'.3
The silent encounter : reflections on mysticism / edited by Virginia Hanson. Wheaton, Ill. : Theosophical Pub. House, [1974] 240 p. ; 21 cm. (A Quest book) Includes bibliographical references. [BL625.H24] 74-4168 ISBN 0-8356-0448-9 pbk. : 2.75
1. Mysticism. I. Title.

HAPPOLD, Frederick Crossfield, 1893- 248.22
Mysticism; a study and an anthology. Baltimore, Penguin [c.1963] 364p. 19cm. (Pelican bks., A568) 63-3395 1.45 pap.,
1. Mysticism. I. Title.

HAPPOLD, Frederick Crossfield, 1893- 291.4'2
Mysticism: a study and an anthology, [by] F. C. Happold. Revised ed. Harmondsworth, Penguin, 1970. 407 p. 18 cm. (Pelican books) [BL625.H25 1970] 73-159216 ISBN 0-14-020568-3 £0.45
1. Mysticism. I. Title.

HARKNESS, Georgia Elma, 1891- 248'.22
Mysticism: its meaning and message [by] Georgia Harkness. Nashville, Abingdon Press [1973] 192 p. 23 cm. Includes bibliographical references. [BV5082.2.H37] 72-10070 ISBN 0-687-27667-5 5.50
1. Mysticism. I. Title.

HATCHER, William Eldridge, 1834-1912. 920.
Along the trail of the friendly years, by William E. Hatcher... New York, Chicago [etc.] Fleming H. Revell company [c1910] 359 p. front. (port.) 21 1/2 cm. [BX6495.H285.A3] 10-13160
I. Title.

HERMAN, Emily, 1876-1923. 248.2'2
The meaning and value of mysticism. 3d ed. Freeport, N.Y., Books for Libraries Press [1971] xvi, 397 p. 23 cm. Reprint of the 1923 ed. Bibliography: p. 379-389. [BV5082.H395 1971] 72-164607 ISBN 0-8369-5891-8
1. Mysticism. I. Title.

HERMES Trismegistus. 231
The divine pymander, and other writings of Hermes Trismegistus. Translated from the original Greek by John D. Chambers. New York, S. Weiser, 1972. xxiv, 170 p. 21 cm. Reprint of the 1882 ed. published by T. & T. Clark, Edinburgh, under title: The theological and philosophical works of Hermes Trismegistus. Contents.Contents.—Poemandres.—Excerpts from Hermes by Stobaeus.—Notices of Hermes in the Fathers. Includes bibliographical references. [BF1598.H5E5 1972] 70-184564 ISBN 0-87728-193-9 3.50
I. Chambers, John David, 1805-1893, tr. II. Title.

HERMES Trismegistus. 231
The divine pymander, and other writings of Hermes Trismegistus. Translated from the original Greek by John D. Chambers. New York, S. Weiser, 1972. xxiv, 170 p. 21 cm. Reprint of the 1882 ed. published by T. & T. Clark, Edinburgh, under title: The theological and philosophical works of Hermes Trismegistus. Contents.Contents.—Poemandres.—Excerpts from Hermes by Stobaeus.—Notices of Hermes in the Fathers. Includes bibliographical references. [BF1598.H5E5 1972] 70-184564 ISBN 0-87728-193-9 3.50
I. Chambers, John David, 1805-1893, tr. II. Title.

HERMES Trismegistus. 299'.31
The divine pymander of Hermes Mercurius Trismegistus. Translated from the Arabic by Dr. Everard. With introd. & preliminary essay by Hargrave Jennings. Madras, India, P. Kailasam Bros., 1884. Minneapolis, Wizards Bookshelf, 1973. xiv, 112 p. 22 cm. (Secret doctrine reference series) Translation of Poemander. [BF1598.H5E5 1973] 73-84044 ISBN 0-913510-07-6 6.00
I. Everard, John, 1575?-1650? tr. II. Title.

HERMES Trismegistus. 299'.31
The divine pymander of Hermes Mercurius Trismegistus. Translated from the Arabic by Dr. Everard. With introd. & preliminary essay by Hargrave Jennings. Madras, India, P. Kailasam Bros., 1884. Minneapolis, Wizards Bookshelf, 1973. xiv, 112 p. 22 cm. (Secret doctrine reference series) Translation of Poemander. [BF1598.H5E5 1973] 73-84044 ISBN 0-913510-07-6 6.00
I. Everard, John, 1575?-1650? tr. II. Title.

HODGSON, Geraldine Emma, 1865- 281.
English mystics, by Geraldine E. Hodgson ... London [etc.] A. R. Mowbray & co., ltd. Milwaukee, U.S.A., The Morehouse publishing co. [1922] xi, 387, [1] p. 19cm. "Principal books mentioned in the text": p. 380-382. [BV5077.G7H6] 23-6047
1. Mysticism. I. Title.

HOLMES, Walter Herbert Greame.
The presence of God; a study in divine immanence and transcendence, by W. H. G. Holmes ... With a preface by Charles Gore ... London, Society for promoting Christian knowledge; New York and Toronto, The Macmillan co., 1923. xiv, 114 p. 20cm. A23
1. Mysticism. I. Title.

HOPKINS, Emma Curtis. 149.3
High mysticism; a series of twelve studies in the wisdom of the sages of the ages. By Emma Curtis Hopkins. Cornwall Bridge, Conn., Emma Curtis Hopkins fund, 1928-35. 13 v. 16 cm. Contents.I. The silent edict, 9th ed., 1935.--II. Remission, 6th ed., 1930.--III. For-giveness, 6th ed., 1930.--IV. Faith, 6th ed., 1928.--V. Works, 5th ed., 1932.--VI. Understanding, 5th ed.--VII-VIII. Ministry, 4th ed.--IX. Ministry, 5th ed.--X-XI. Ministry, 4th ed.--XII. Ministry, 5th ed.--[XIII] Resume, practice book for the twelve chapters in high mysticism--first sent forth in 1892. 10th ed., 1928. [BV5082.H57] 40-18258
1. Mysticism. 2. Christian science. I. Title.
Contents omitted.

HOPKINSON, Arthur Wells, 1874- 149'.3
Mysticism: old and new, by Arthur W. Hopkinson. Port Washington, N.Y., Kennikat Press [1971] 153 p. 22 cm. Reprint of the 1946 ed. Includes bibliographical references. [BV5083.H57 1971] 77-118528
1. Mysticism.

HUNTER, Joseph Boone. 286'.6'0924 B
Along the way. Fort Worth, Tex., Branch-Smith, 1972. xiii, 171 p. port. 22 cm. Autobiographical. [BX7343.H83A3] 71-188574 ISBN 0-87706-020-7
I. Title.

INGE, William Ralph 248.2
The awakening of the soul; an introduction to Christian mysticism. Edited by A. F. Judd. [New York, Morehouse-Barlow] [1959] 61p. 19cm. 59-4793 1.00 pap.,
1. Mysticism. I. Title.

INGE, William Ralph, 1860- 149.3
Mysticism in religion. London, New York , Hutchinson's Univ. Library [1947] 168 p. 24 cm. (The senior series) [BL625.I5 1947] 48-16150
1. Mysticism. I. Title. II. Series.

INGE, William Ralph, 1860-
Christian mysticism considered in eight lectures delivered before the University of Oxford, by William Ralph Inge ... New York, C. Scribner's sons; [etc., etc.] 1899. xv, 379, [1] p. 23 cm. (Half-title: The Bampton lectures, 1899) [BS28.I45] [BR45.B] A14
1. Mysticism. I. Title.

INGE, William Ralph, 1860- 149.3
Mysticism in religion. Chicago, Univ. of Chicago Press [1948] 168 p. 24 cm. "Bibliography of modern books": p. 166. [BL625.I5 1948] 48-8494
1. Mysticism. I. Title.

INGE, William Ralph, 1860- 149.3
1954.
Christian mysticism. [7th ed.] New York, Meridian Books, 1956. xx, 332 p. 19 cm. (Living age books, 3) [BV5082.I6 1956] 56-9239
1. Mysticism. I. Title.

INGE, William Ralph, 248'.22
1860-1954.
Mysticism in religion / by W. R. Inge. Westport, Conn. : Greenwood Press, 1976, c1948. 168 p. ; 24 cm. Reprint of the ed. published by University of Chicago Press, Chicago. Includes index. Bibliography: p. 166. [BL625.I5 1976] 76-15407 ISBN 0-8371-8953-5 lib. bdg. : 12.25
1. Mysticism. I. Title.

JACOBY, John E 149.3
Across the night; adventures in the supranormal. New York, Philosophical Library [1958] 110p. 22cm. Includes bibliography. [BL625.J2] 59-60
1. Mystricism. I. Title.

JAEGHER, Paul de. ed. 149.3
An anthology of mysticism; edited with an introd. and biographical notes by Paul de Jaegher, S. J., and translated by Donald Attwater and others. Westminster, Md., Newman Press, 1950. viii, 281 p. 19 cm. [BV5072.J] A51
1. Mysticism. I. Title.

JAMES, Joseph, of Harrow 149.3
Weald. ed.
The way of mysticism, an anthology. New York, Harper [1951] 274 p. 20 cm. [BV5072.J35] 51-14123
1. Mysticism. I. Title.

JEFFERYS, William Hamilton, 149.3
1871-
The key to the door of divine reality, by W. H. Jefferys ... Philadelphia, The American press, 1934. 70, [1] p. incl. front. 19 cm. [BV5085.J4] 34-31086
1. Mysticism. I. Title.

JOHNSON, Raynor Carey 248.2
Watcher on the hills. London, Hodder &Stoughton [1959] 188p. 23cm. Bibl. [BL625.J6] 59-65444 4.50
I. Title.
A testimony to the validity of mystical experience. Now available from Verry, Mystic, Conn.

JOHNSON, Raynor Carey 248.22
Watcher on the hills; a study of some mystical experiences of ordinary people. New York, Harper [1960, c.1959] 188p. illus. 22cm. 60-11779 3.50 half cloth
1. Mysticism. I. Title.

JOHNSTON, William, 1924- 291.4'2
The inner eye of love : mysticism and religion / William Johnston. San Francisco : Harper & Row, [1978] p. cm. Includes index. Bibliography: p. [BL625.J62] 78-4428 ISBN 0-06-064195-9 : 7.95
1. Mysticism. I. Title.

JONES, Rufus Matthew, 1863- 248
New studies in mystical religion; the Ely lectures delivered at Union theological seminary, New York, 1927, by Rufus M. Jones ... New York, The Macmillan company, 1927. 205 p. 20 cm. [BV5082.J6] 27-22176
1. Mysticism. I. Title.

JONES, Rufus Matthew, 1863- 149.
... Some exponents of mystical religion, by Rufus M. Jones ... New York, Cincinnati [etc.] The Abingdon press [c1930] 237 p. 20 cm. (The New era lectureship, University of Southern California--5th ser.) [BV5075.J55] 30-2332
1. Mysticism. I. Title. II. Title: Mystical religion, Some exponents of.

JONES, Rufus Matthew, 291.4'2
1863-1948.
New studies in mystical religion; the Ely lectures delivered at Union Theological Seminary, New York. New York, Krishna Press, 1974. 205 p. 24 cm. Reprint of the 1927 ed. published by Macmillan, New York, and issued in series: Elias P. Ely lectures on the evidence of Christianity, 1927. Includes bibliographical references. [BV5082.J6 1974] 73-15412 ISBN 0-87968-102-0 35.00 (lib. bdg.).
1. Mysticism. I. Title. II. Series: Elias P. Ely lectures on the evidence of Christianity, 1927.

JONES, Rufus Matthew, 1863- 248.2
1948.
Spiritual reformers in the 16th and 17 centuries. Boston, Beacon Press [1959, c1914] 362p. 21cm. (Beacon paperback no. 81) Includes bibliography. [BV5075.J6 1959] 59-6392
1. Mysticism. 2. Reformers. I. Title.

JUAN de la Cruz, Saint, 248'.22
1542-1591.
Counsels of light and love / St. John of the Cross ; introd. by Thomas Merton. New York : Paulist Press, 1978, c1977. 78 p. ; 18 cm. (The Spiritual masters) Adapted from the Complete works of St. John of the Cross edited by E. A. Peers. [BV5085.J8213 1978] 78-64359 ISBN 0-8091-2069-0 pbk. : 1.95
1. Mysticism. I. Peers, Edgar Allison. II. Title.

KNAPP, Ida C. 248
Myself the challenger. New York, Island Press Cooperative [1952] 80 p. 22 cm. [BV5082.K6] 149.3 52-7187
1. Mysticism. I. Title.

LAREDO, Bernardino de, 1482- 248
1545?
The ascent of Mount Sion, being the third book of the treatise of that name translated with an introduction and notes by E. Allison Peers. New York, Harper [1952] 275 p. 21 cm. (Classics of the contemplative life) [BV5080.L263 1952a] 52-4612
1. Mysticism. I. Title.

LAUBACH, Frank Charles, 1884-
Letters by a modern mystic. [Westwood, N. J.] Revell [1958] 62p. 17cm. (Revell's inspirational classics) [BV5085.L3] 58-11016
1. Mysticism. I. Title.

LAW, William, 1686-1761. 149.3
Liberal and mystical writings of William Law: with an introduction, by William Scott Palmer [pseud.] and a preface, by W. P. Du Bose ... London, New York [etc.] Longmans, Green, and co., 1908. xviii, 166 p. 20 cm. [BV5080.L28] 10-399
1. Mysticism. I. Dowson, Mary Emily, Mrs. 1848- ed. II. Dubose, William Porcher, 1836-1918. III. Title.
Contents omitted.

LAW, William, 1686-1761. 149.3
Selected mystical writings, ed. with notes and twenty-four studies in the mystical theology of William Law and Jacob Boehme and an enquiry into the influence of Jacob Boehme on Isaac Newton by Stephen Hobhouse. Foreword by Aldous Huxley. [2d ed. rev.] New York, Harper, 1948. xxiii, 425 p. facsim. 22 cm. "Short bibliography": p. 391-392. [BV5080.L3 1948] 48-7408
1. Bohme, Jakob, 1575-1624. 2. Newton, Sir Isaac, 1642-1727. 3. Mysticism. I. Hobhouse, Stephen Henry, 1881- ed. II. Title.

LUDLOW, James Meeker, 1841- 285.
Along the friendly way; reminiscences and impressions, by James M. Ludlow. New York, Chicago [etc. Fleming H. Revell company [c1919] 363 p. front. (port.) 21 cm. [BX9225.L8A5] 19-16116
I. Title.

MCCANN, Leonard A 149.3
The doctrine of the void ; as propounded by S. John of the Cross in his major prose works and as viewed with the light of Thomistic principles. Toronto, Rochester [N. Y.] Basilian Press [c1955] 146p. 23cm. Bibliography: p. 142-146. [BX4700.J7M3] 56-58978
1. Juan de la Cruz, Saint, 1542-1591. 2. Mysticism. I. Title.

MCNAMARA, William. 248.2'2
Christian mysticism : a psychotheology / William McNamara. Chicago, Ill. : Franciscan Herald Press, c1981. xix, 154 p. ; 21 cm. Includes bibliographical references. [BV5082.2.M25] 80-13193 ISBN 0-8199-0793-6 : 9.95
1. Mysticism. 2. Mysticism—Psychology. I. Title.

MALONEY, George A., 1924- 248'.22
The breath of the mystic / by George A. Maloney. Denville, N.J. : Dimension Books, c1974. 204 p. ; 21 cm. Includes bibliographical references. [BV5082.2.M34] 75-316128 6.95
1. Mysticism. 2. Prayer. I. Title.

MARIE de la Trinite, sister 248
1901-1942.
The spiritual legacy of Sister Mary of the Holy Trinity, Poor Clare of Jerusalem (1901-1942) Edited by Silvere van den Broek; translated from the French. Westminster, Md., Newman Press, 1950. 364 p. illus., port. 19 cm. Secular name: Louisa Jacques. [BV5082.M342] 50-4895
1. Mysticism. I. Broek, Silvere van den, 1880-1949, ed. II. Title.

MARTINEZ, Luis Maria, Abp., 248
1881-
Secrets of the interior life; translated by H. J. Beutler. St. Louis, B. Herder Book Co., 1949. viii, 207 p. 21 cm. Translation of Simientes divinas. [BV5082.M355] 50-4335
1. Mysticism. I. Title.

MENZEL, Addalena. 220
Mystical vision and revelation, by Addalena Menzel. New York city, T. Gaus' sons, inc. [c1929] 268 p. 20 cm. [BR125.M488] 29-19205
I. Title.

MERTON, Thomas, 1915- 291.4'2
1968.
Mystics and Zen masters. New York, Farrar, Strauss and Giroux [1967] x, 303 p. 22 cm. Bibliographical references included in "Notes" (p. 289-303) [BL625.M38] 66-20167
1. Mysticism. 2. Zen Buddhism. I. Title.

MUKERJEE, Radhakamal, 291.14
1889-
The theory and art of mysticism. Foreword by William Ernest Hocking. [dist. New York, Taplinger, 1961, c.1960] 352p. Bibl. 5.25
I. Title.

THE new life in Christ 230.
Jesus. Essays on subjects relating to spiritual life, to which is added, Listening to Jesus and The law of love, edited by Julian Field with an introduction by the Very Reverend F. W. Farrar, D. D., dean of Canterbury ... New York, Printed privately, 1896. xxx p., 1 l., 240 p. 17 cm. "First published in parts anonymously in Germany in 1738 to 1740." [BV5080.N4] 27-3779
1. Mysticism. I. Field, Julian. II. Farrar, Frederic William, 1831-1903.

NICOL, William Robertson, 248
Sir, 1851-1923.
The garden of nuts; mystical expositions with an essay on Christian mysticism, by the Rev. W. Robertson Nicoll ... New York, A. C. Armstrong and son; London, Hodder and Stoughton, 1905. x, 232 p. 19 cm. "The song of the obscure night, by St. John of The Cross. With translations by Jane T. Stoddart and David Lewis" (with "Books of reference"): p. 1-13. [BV5082.N5] 46-36649
1. Mysticism. I. Juan de in Cruz, Saint, 1542-1591. II. Title.

OSENDE, Victorino, 1879- 248
Pathways of love; translated by a Dominican sister of the Perpetual Rosary, Milwaukee, Wisconsin. St. Louis, B. Herder Book Co. [1958] 268p. 21cm. (Cross and crown series of spirituality, no. 12) Translation of Las grandes etapas de la vida espiritual. [BV5082.O753] 58-13828
1. Mysticism. I. Title.

OTTO, Rudolf, 1869-1937. 149.3
Mysticism east and west; a comparative analysis of the nature of mysticism, by Rudolf Otto ... translated by Bertha L. Bracey [and] Richenda C. Payne. New York, The Macmillan company, 1932. xvii, 262 p. 23 cm. An enlarged form of the Haskell lectures delivered at Oberlin college, Oberlin, Ohio, in the winter of 1923-1924. cf. Foreword. Translation of Westostliche mystik. [Full name: Karl Ludwig Rudolf Otto] [BL625.O73] 32-3276
1. Mysticism. 2. Philosophy and religion. I. Bracey, Bertha L., tr. II. Payne, Richenda C., joint tr. III. Title.

THE papers of John Pererin, 220
by a modern mystic. Boston, Mass., The Murray press [c1923] 272 p. 18 1/2 cm. First published 1922 in the Universalist leader. [BR125.P173] 23-12556
I. A modern mystic.

PATTON, Kenneth Leo, 1911- 190
Man's hidden search, an inquiry into naturalistic mysticism. Boston, Meeting House Press [1954] 123p. 21cm. [B828.P3] [B828.P3] 149.3 54-9546 54-9546
1. Musticism. I. Title.

PEDRICK, Katharine Francis. 230.
How to make perfection appear, by Katharine Francis Pedrick. Boston, Lothrop, Lee & Shepard co. [c1919] 235 p. 20 cm. Previous edition has title: The practical mystic; or, How to make perfectionappear. [BV5081.P4 1919] 19-16909
1. Mysticism. 2. Idealism. I. Title.

PENINGTON, Isaac, 1616- 230.96
1679.
The name is living: the life and teachings of Isaac Penington, edited by M. Whitcomb Hess, with foreword by Rufus M. Jones. Chicago, New York, Willett, Clark & company, 1936. 4 p. l., 151 p. 20 cm. Bibliography: p. 149-151. [BV5080.P4] 38-9575
1. Mysticism. 2. Friends, Society of—Doctrinal and controversial works. I. Hess, Mary (Whitcomb) Mrs. 1893- ed. II. Title.

PIERRE, Joseph H. 291.4'2
The road to Damascus / Joseph H. Pierre, Jr. New York, N.Y. : Irvington Publishers, 1981. p. cm. Includes index. Bibliography: p. [BL625.P5] 19 80-28816 ISBN 0-8290-0449-1 pbk. : 8.95
1. Mysticism. 2. Reality. I. Title.

THE plain path to Christian 230.
perfection, showing that we are to seek for reconsiliation and union with God, solely by renouncing ourselves, denying the world, and following Our Blessed Saviour in the regeneration. Translated from the French. Philadelphia, Printed by J. Crukshank, 1780. xi, 91 p. 10 cm. Translated by Anthony Beneset. "The treatise of which the following is an extract was written in the German language about two hundred and fifty years ago, and since translated into the French." Bound with Webb, Elizabeth. A letter to Anthony William Boehm. Philadelphia, 1783. [BV5080.P55 1780] 50-1762
1. Mysticism. I. Benezet, Anthony, 1713-1784, tr.

THE plain path to Christian 230.
perfection, shewing that we are to seek for reconciliation and union with God, solely by renouncing ourselves, denying the world, and following our Blessed Savior, in the regeneration. Translated from the French ... Philadelphia, Printed by Joseph Crukshank, in Third-street, opposite the Work-house, MDCCLXXII. xi, 124 p. 16 1/2 cm. Translated by Anthony Benezet. "The treatise of which the following is an extract, was written in the German language about two hundred and fifty years ago, and since translated into the French.""-Pref. [BV5080.P55] 46-28947
1. Mysticism. I. Benezet, Anthony 1713-1784, tr.

PRESCOTT, Latimer Howard.
History of Criterion lodge, no. 68 Knights of Pythias (of Cleveland, Ohio). Cleveland, O., The Imperial press, 1899. 167 p. pl., tab. 8 degrees. No. 549 of a limited ed. of 550 copies. May
I. Title.

PRESCOTT, Latimer Howard.
History of Criterion lodge, no. 68 Knights of Pythias (of Cleveland, Ohio). Cleveland, O., The Imperial press, 1899. 167 p. pl., tab. 8 degrees. No. 549 of a limited ed. of 550 copies. May
I. Title.

RAYON, M[esha]
The mystic self; uncommon sense versus common sense. Chicago, 1900. 4 p. l., 70 p., 1 l. front., pl. 16 degree. Nov
I. Title.

RECEJAC, E. 201
Essay on the bases of the mystic knowledge ... by E. Recejac ... tr. by Sara Carr Upton. New York, C. Scribner's sons, 1899. 3 p. l., [v]-xi, 287 p. 21 cm. [B828.R3] 99-738
1. Mysticism. I. Upton, Sara Carr, 1843- tr. II. Title.

REINHOLD, Hans Ansgar, 1897- ed. 149.3
The soul afire; revelations of the mystics, edited by H. A. Reinhold. New York, Meridian Bks. [1960, c.1944] xxiii, 413p. (MG28) 1.95 pap.,
1. Mysticism. I. Title.

*REINHOLD, Hans Ansgar, 1897- ed. 149'.3
The soul afire; revelations of the mystics; ed. by H. A. Reinhold. Garden City, N.Y., Image Books, 1973. 480 p. 18 cm. (Image bk., D320) First published in 1960. [BL695] pap., 1.95
1. Mysticism. I. Title.

REINHOLD, Hans Ansgar, 1897- ed. 149.3
The soul afire; revelations of the mystics, edited by H. A. Reinhold. [New York] Pantheon books [1944] xxiii, 413 p. 23 1/2 cm. "First edition." [BV5072.R4] 45-4210
1. Mysticism. I. Title.

*RICCARDO, Martin. 248.22
Mystical consciousness : exploring an extraordinary state of awareness / by Martin Riccardo. Burbank, Ill. : MVR Books, c1977. 144p. ; 22 cm. Includes bibliographical references. [BL625] pbk. : 3.50
1. Mysticism. I. Title.
Publisher's address: 7809 So. LaPorte Ave., Burbank Illinois 60459.

RIENCOURT, Amaury de. 291.1'75
The eye of Shiva : Eastern mysticism and science / Amaury de Riencourt. 1st U.S. ed. New York : Morrow, 1981. 221 p. ; 22 cm. Includes index. Bibliography: p. [209]-212. [BL625.R5 1981] 19 80-22032 ISBN 0-688-00036-3 : 8.95 ISBN 0-688-00038-X pbk. : 4.95
1. Mysticism. 2. Religion and science—1946- I. Title.

RIHBANY, Abraham Mitrie, 1869- 149.3
Seven days with God, by Abraham Mitrie Rihbany ... Boston and New York, Houghton Mifflin company, 1926. 4 p. l., 253, [1] p. 21 cm. [BV5082.R48] 26-5405
1. Mysticism. I. Title.

RILEY, Isaac Woodbridge, 1869-1933. 291.4'2
The meaning of mysticism / by Woodbridge Riley. Folcroft, Pa. : Folcroft Library Editions, 1975, c1930. p. cm. Reprint of the ed. published by R. R. Smith, New York. [BV5082.R5 1975] 75-26512 ISBN 0-8414-7227-0 lib. bdg. : 15.00
1. Mysticism. I. Title.

RILEY, Isaac Woodbridge, 1869-1933. 149.3
The meaning of mysticism, by Woodbridge Riley, PH. D. New York, R. R. Smith, inc., 1930. 5 p. l., 3-102 p. 20 cm. [BV5082.R5] 30-11394
1. Mysticism. I. Title.

ROSTOVTSEV, Mikhail Ivanovich, 1870- 292
... *Mystic Italy,* by Michael I. Rostovtzeff. New York, H. Holt and company, [c1927] xxi, 176 p. incl. front., illus. 23 cm. (Brown university. The Colver lectures, 1927) "Notes": p. 159-176. [BL815.M8R6] 28-8827
1. Mysticism. 2. Mystries, Religious. 3. Rome—Religion. I. Title.

SAVAGE, David S., 1910- 149'.3
Mysticism and Aldous Huxley : an examination of Heard-Huxley theories / by D. S. Savage. Folcroft, Pa. : Folcroft Library Editions, 1977 [c1947] 21 p. ; 26 cm. Reprint of the ed. published by O. Baradinsky at the Alicat Book Shop, Yonkers, N.Y., which was issued as no. 10 of the Outcast series of chapbooks. [B828.S28 1977] 77-23247 ISBN 0-8414-7805-8 : 6.00
1. Huxley, Aldous Leonrad, 1894-1963. 2. Heard, Gerald, 1889-1971. 3. Mysticism. I. Title. II. Series: The Outcast chapbooks ; no. 10.

*SCHARFSTEIN, Ben-Ami. 149.3
Mystical experience. Indianapolis, Bobbs-Merrill Co. [1973] 195 p. 23 cm. Bibliography: p. [176]-190. [BV5082.2] 72-14014 6.95.
1. Mysticism. I. Title.

SCHWEITZER, Albert, 1875- 227
The mysticism of Paul the apostle, by Albert Schweitzer ... translated into English by William Montgomery ... with a prefatory note by F. C. Burkitt ... New York, H. Holt and company [c1931] xv, 411 p. 22 cm. [BS2655.M9S43 1931 a] 32-1464
1. Paul, Saint, apostle. 2. Mysticism. 3. Bible. N. T. Epistles of Paul—Theology. 4. Bible—Theology—N. T. Epistles of Paul. I. Montgomery, William, 1871-1930- tr. II. Title.

SCHWEITZER, Albert, 1875-1965. 227
The mysticism of Paul the apostle. Translated into English by William Montgomery. With a prefatory note by F. C. Burkitt. New York, Macmillan, 1955 [c1931] xv, 411 p. 22 cm. [BS2655.M9S43 1955] 56-967
1. Paul, Saint, apostle. 2. Bible. N. T. Epistles of Paul—Theology. 3. Mysticism. I. Title.

SHARPE, Alfred B.
Mysticism, its true nature and value; with a translation of the "Mystical theology" of Dionysius, and of the letters to Caius and Dorotheus (1, 2 and 5) by A. B. Sharpe ... London [etc.] Sands & company; St. Louis, Mo., B. Herder [1910] 2 p. l., vii-xi, 233 p., 1 l. 19 1/2 cm. Contents.I. Two ideas of mysticism.--II. Supernatural mysticism.--III. The nature of mystical experience.--IV. The object of mystical knowledge.--V. The psychology of mysticism.--VI. Evil.--VII. Immanence and transcendence.--VIII. Plotitus.--IX. Heretical mystics.--X. Mysticism, philosophy and religion.--XI. Dionysius.--XII. The "Mystical theology" of Dionysius the Aeropagite, Letter: I. To Caius the monk--The ignorance by means of which God is known is above sense-knowledge, not below it. II. To the same--In what sense God is above the principle of divinity. V. To Dorotheus the deacon--The divine darkness further explained. A 11
1. Mysticism. I. Dionysius Aeropagita. II. Title.

SHEARER, John Bunyan, 1832-1919. 261.
... *Modern mysticism;* or, The covenants of the spirit, their scope and limitations. By Rev. J. B. Shearer ... Richmond, Va., Presbyterian committee of publication [c1905] 116 p. 20 cm. (Davidson college divinity lectures, Otts foundation. 3d series. mdccccv) [BT121.85] 5-36514
I. Title.

SHEINER, Ben, 1925- 291.4'2
Intellectual mysticism / Ben Sheiner. New York : Philosophical Library, c1978. 120 p. : ill. ; 22 cm. [BL625.S46] 78-50531 ISBN 0-8022-2228-5 : 7.50
1. Mysticism. I. Title.

SINGH, Sundar, 1889- 922
The cross is heaven; the life and writings of Sadhu Sundar Singh. Edited by A. J. Appasamy. New York, Association Press [1957] 96p. 20cm. (World Christian books) [BV5082.S52 1957] 57-6879
1. Mysticism. I. Title.

SINGH, Sundar, 1889- 922
The cross is heaven; the life and writings of Sadhu Sundar Singh. Edited by A. J. Appasamy. New York, Association Press [1957] 93 p. 20 cm. (World Christian books) [BV5082.S52 1957] 57-6879
1. Mysticism. I. Title.

SINGH, Sundar, 1889- 248
Reality and religion; meditations on God, man and nature. With an introd. by Canon Streeter. New York, Macmillan, 1924. xvi, 30 p. 18 cm. [BV5082.S54 1924a] 24-9366
1. Mysticism. I. Title.

SIX theosophic points, 190
and other writings. With an introductory essay, Unground and freedom, by Nicholas Berdyaev. [Translated by John Rolleston Earle. Ann Arbor] University of Michigan Press [1958] xii, 208p. 21cm. (Ann Arbor paperbacks, AA17) [BV5080.B64E4 1958] [BV5080.b64E4 1958] 149.3 58-969 58-969
1. Mysticism. I. Bohme, Jakob, 1575-1624.

SMITH, Margaret. 149.3
Studies in early mysticism in the Near and Middle east; being an account of the rise and development of early Christian mysticism in the Near and Middle east up to the seventh century, and of the subsequent development of mysticism in Islam known as Sufism, together with some account of the relationship between early Christian mysticism and the earliest form of Islamic mysticism, by Margaret Smith... London, The Sheldon press; New York and Toronto, The Macmillan co., 1931. x, 276 p. 22 1/2 cm. "Bibliography of authors consulted": p. 258-263. [BV5075.S6] 32-878
1. Mysticism. 2. Sufism. 3. Christianity and other religions—Mohammedanism. I. Title.

SNEATH, Elias Hershey, 1857- ed. 291.326
At one with the invisible; studies in mysticism, edited by E. Hershey Sneath ... New York, The Macmillan company, 1921. 5 p. l., 293 p. 20 cm. [BL625.S6] 21-2941
1. Mysticism. 2. Psychology, Religious. I. Title.

SONTAG, Frederick. 248'.22
Love beyond pain : mysticism within Christianity / by Frederick Sontag. New York : Paulist Press, c1977. v, 137 p. ; 21 cm. Includes bibliographical references. [BV5082.2.S64] 76-44928 ISBN 0-8091-1998-6 pbk. : 4.50
1. Mysticism. 2. Spiritual life. I. Title.

SPLENDOR in the night; 149.3
recording a glimpse of reality by a pilgrim, with foreword by Rufus M. Jones. Portland, Me., The Mosher press, 1933. xxi, [1], 64 p., 2 l. 17 cm. "Five hundred copies of this book have been printed ... on Blue Hill text in the month of May MCMXXXIII." [BV5082.S65] 33-17365
1. Mysticism. I. Jones, Rufus Matthew, 1863-

STACE, Walter Terence, 1886- ed. 291.14
The teachings of the mystics being selections from the great mystics and mystical writings of the world. New York New American Library [1972] 240 p. 18 cm. (A Mentor book, MJ1181) [BL625.S75] 60-15528 Pap. 1.95
1. Mysticism. I. Title.

STACE, Walter Terence, 1886- 149.3
Mysticism and philosophy. Philadelphia, Lippincott [c.1960] 349p. Bibl. notes 22cm. 60-13581 6.00
1. Mysticism. 2. Philosophy. 3. Philosophy and religion. I. Title.

STARCKE, Walter. 248.2'2
This double thread. [1st ed.] New York, Harper & Row [1967] xiv, 146 p. 22 cm. [BV5082.2.S7] 67-14937
1. Mysticism. I. Title.

STEINER, Rudolf, 1861-1925. 149.
Mystics of the renaissance and their relation to modern thought, including Meister Eckhart, Tauler, Paracelsus, Jacob Boehme, Giordano Bruno, and others, by Rudolf Steiner ... authorized translation from the German by Bertram Keightley ... New York and London, G. P. Putnam's sons, 1911. xii p., 1 l. 278 p. 19 cm. [BV5075.S83] 11-29053
1. Mysticism. I. Keightley, Bertram, tr. II. Title.

STIERNOTTE, Alfred P ed. 149.3082
Mysticism and the modern mind. New York, Liberal Arts Press [1959] 206 p. 24 cm. Includes bibliography. [B828.S83] 59-11686
1. Mysticism. I. Title.

SUMMERS, Montague, 1880- 149.3
The physical phenomena of mysticism, with especial reference to the stigmata, divine and diabolic. London, New York, Rider [1950] 262 p. illus., ports. 24 cm. Full name: Alphonsus Joseph-Mary Augustus Montague Summers. Includes bibliographical references. [BV5090.S8 1950] 50-4368
1. Mysticism. 2. Stigmatization. I. Title.

SUMMERS, Montague, 1880- 149.3
The physical phenomena of mysticism, with especial reference to the stigmata, divine and diabolic. New York, Barnes & Noble [c1950] 262 p. illus., ports. 24 cm. Full name: Alphonsus Joseph-Mary Augustus Montague Summers. Includes bibliographical references. [BV5090.S8 1950a] 51-2283
1. Mysticism. 2. Stigmatization. I. Title.

SUZUKI, Daisetz Teitaro, 1870- 149.3
Mysticism: Christian and Buddhist. New York, Collier [1962, c.1957] 160p. (AS159V) Bibl. .95 pap.,
1. Mysticism. I. Title.

SUZUKI, Daisetz Teitaro, 1870- 149.3
Mysticism: Christian and Buddhist. [1st ed.] New York, Harper [c1957] 214 p. 20 cm. (World prespectives, v.12) [BL625.S85] 56-11086
1. Mysticism. I. Title.

SUZUKI, Daisetz Teitaro, 1870- 149.3
Mysticism: Christian and Buddhist. [1st ed.] New York, Harper [c1957] 214p. 20cm. (World prespectives, v. 12) [BL625.S85] 56-11086
1. Mysticism. I. Title.

SUZUKI, Daisetz Teitaro, 1870-1966. 291.4'2
Mysticism, Christian and Buddhist / by Daisetz Teitaro Suzuki. Westport, Conn. : Greenwood Press, 1975, c1957. xix, 214 p. ; 23 cm. Reprint of the ed. published by Harper, New York, which was issued as v. 12 of World perspectives. Includes bibliographical references. [BL625.S85 1975] 75-31442 ISBN 0-8371-8516-5 lib. bdg. : 13.50
1. Mysticism. I. Title.

SUZUKI, Daisetz Teitaro, 1870-1966. 291.4'2
Mysticism: Christian and Buddhist; the Eastern and Western way. [New York] Macmillan [1969, c1957] 160 p. 18 cm. Bibliographical footnotes. [BL625.S85 1969] 77-82562 1.45
1. Mysticism. I. Title.

THORNTON, Edward, 1907- 291.4'2
The diary of a mystic; foreword by C. A. Meier. London, Allen & Unwin, 1967 3-180p. 23cm. [BL625.T47] 67-114174 4.00 bds.,
1. Mysticism. I. Title.
Distributed by Hillary House, New York

THURSTON, Herbert, 1856-1939. *248 149.3
The physical phenomena of mysticism; edited by J. H. Crehan. Chicago, H. Regnery Co., 1952. 419 p. 23 cm. Full name: Herbert Henry Charles Thurston. [BV5090.T45] 52-4542
1. Mysticism. I. Title.

TILLYARD, Aelfrida Catharine Wetenhall. 248
The making of a mystic [by] Aelfrida Tillyard. Cambridge, W. Heffer & sons ltd., 1917. vii, 109 p. 19 1/2 cm. [BV5082.T5] 18-15646
1. Mysticism. I. Title.

TILLYARD, Aelfrida Catharine Wetenhall. 201
Spiritual exercises and their results; an essay in psychology and comparative religion, by Aelfrida Tillyard. London, Society for promoting Christian knowledge. New York and Toronto, The Macmillan

co. [c1927] viii, 216 p. 19 1/2 cm. [BL53.T6] 28-12840
1. Mysticism. 2. Devotional exercises. 3. Psychology, Religious. 4. Religions. I. Title.
Contents omitted.

UNDERHILL, Evelyn 248.22
Practical mysticism. New York, Dutton 1960 (Dutton Everyman paperback) 1.25 pap.,
1. Mysticism. I. Title.

UNDERHILL, Evelyn, 1875- 248
The essentials of mysticism and other essays, by Evelyn Underhill. London & Toronto, J. M. Dent & sons ltd.; New York, E. P. Dutton & co., 1920. vii, 245 p. 20 cm. [BV5082.U5] 21-1752
1. Myticism. I. Title.

UNDERHILL, Evelyn, 1875- 149.3
Mysticism: a study in the nature and development of man's spiritual consciousness, by Evelyn Underhill ... Rev. ed. New York, E. P. Dutton and company, inc. [1930] xviii p., 1 l., 515, [1] p. 22 1/2 cm. "Printed in Great Britain." Bibliography: p. 475-504. [BV5081.U55 1930] 31-26805
1. Mysticism. I. Title.

UNDERHILL, Evelyn, 1875- 149.
The mystics of the church, by Evelyn Underhill ... New York, George H. Doran company [1926] 259, [1] p. 20 cm. "Illustrative works" at end of each chapter. [BV5075.U6 1926] 26-5586
1. Mysticism. I. Title.

UNDERHILL, Evelyn, 1875- 230.
Practical mysticism; a little book for normal people, by Evelyn Underhill ... London, J. M. Dent & sons ltd. New York, E. P. Dutton & co., 1914. xv. 163. [1] p. 18 1/2 cm. [BV5081.U6 1914] 14-22566
1. Mysticism. I. Title.

UNDERHILL, Evelyn, 1875- 230.
Practical mysticism; a little book for normal people, by Evelyn Underhill ... New York, E. P. Dutton & company [c1915] xiii p., 1 l., 169 p. 20 cm. [BV5081.U6 1915] 15-4658
1. Mysticism. I. Title.

UNDERHILL, Evelyn, 1875-1941. 204
Collected papers of Evelyn Underhill, edited by Lucy Menzies, with an introduction by Lumsden Barkway ... New York, London [etc.] Longmans, Green and co., inc., 1946. 240 p. 19 1/2 cm. "First American edition." "List of Evelyn Underhill's writings": p. 37-38. [BV5072.U5 1946] 46-3613
1. Mysticism. I. Menzies, Lucy, ed. II. Title.

UNDERHILL, Evelyn, 1875-1941. 248
Light of Christ; addresses given at the House of retreat, Pleshey, in May, 1932, by Evelyn Underhill ... with a memoir by Lucy Menzies. London, New York [etc.] Longmans, Green and co. [1945] 107 p. incl. front. 17 1/2 cm. "First American edition." [BV5081.U48] 45-4942
1. Mysticism. 2. Spiritual life. 3. Retreats. I. Title.

UNDERHILL, Evelyn, 1875- 248.22
1941.
The Mount of Purification, with Meditations and prayers, 1949, and Collected papers, 1946. [New York] Longmans [c.1960] 333p. (Inner life series) 61-101 3.00 bds.,
1. Mysticism. I. Title.

UNDERHILL, Evelyn, 1875- 248'.22
1941.
The mystic way : a psychological study in Christian origins / by Evelyn Underhill. Folcroft, Pa. : Folcroft Library Editions, 1975. p. cm. Reprint of the 1913 ed. published by J. M. Dent, London ; Dutton, New York. Includes index. Bibliography: p. [BV5081.U5 1975] 75-34166 ISBN 0-8414-8854-1 lib. bdg. : 35.00
1. Mysticism. I. Title.

UNDERHILL, Evelyn, 1875- 248.22
1941.
Mysticism; a study in the nature and development of man's spiritual consciousness. New York, Dutton, 1961. 519p. (Everyman paperback D73) 1.95 pap.,
1. Mysticism. I. Title.

UNDERHILL, Evelyn, 1875-1941. 190
Mysticism; a study in the nature and development of man's spiritual consciousness. New York, Noonday Press, 1955. 519 p. 21 cm. (Meridian books, MG1) [BV5081.U55 1955] 55-5159
1. Mysticism.

UNDERHILL, Evelyn, 1875-1941. 081
Practical mysticism. New York, Dutton, 1960 [c1943] 169 p. 19 cm. (A Dutton everyman paperback, D49) [BV5081.U6] 62-1687
1. Mysticism. I. Title.

VANN, Vicki. 248'.22
The growth of the soul : from impiety to ecstasy / by Vicki Vann. Marina del Rey, Calif. : DeVorss, c1977. 100 p. ; 22 cm. [BL625.V36] 77-78828 ISBN 0-87516-235-5 pbk. : 3.25
1. Mysticism. 2. Ecstasy. 3. Identification (Religion) I. Title.

LA Vie spirituelle. 248
Mystery and mysticism [by] A. Ple [and others] New York, Philosophical Library [1956] v. 137p. 22cm. First published in French as a special issue of La Vie spirituelle. Bibliographical footnotes. [BV5072.V5 1956a] [BV5072.V5 1956a] 149.3 56-4331 56-4331
1. Mysticism. I. Pie, Albert. II. Title.
Contents omitted.

WAITE, Arthur Edward. 149.
Lamps of western mysticism; essays on the life of the soul in God, by Arthur Edward Waite. London, K. Paul, Trench, Trubner & co., ltd.; New York, A. A. Knopf, 1923. viii, 334 p. 24 1/2 cm. [BV5075.W3] 24-8669
1. Mysticism. I. Title.

WAITE, Arthur Edward, 149'.3
1851-1942.
Lamps of Western mysticism. Introd. by Paul M. Allen. New York, Rudolf Steiner Publications, 1973. viii, 334 p. illus. 18 cm. [BV5075.W3 1973] 70-159505 2.45 (pbk.)
1. Mysticism. I. Title.

WATKIN, Edward Ingram, 1888- 248
The philosophy of mysticism, by Edward Ingram Watkin ... New York, Harcourt, Brace & Howe, 1920. 4 p. l., 11-412 p. 22 cm. Printed in Great Britain. [BV5082.W] a21
1. Mysticism. I. Title.

WATSON, Evelyn Mabel Palmer, 248
1886-
Inner radiance; paragraphs on Christian mysticism, by Evelyn Mabel Watson, introduction by Theodore S. Henderson... New York, Cincinnati, The Abingdon press [c1926] 137 p. 17 1/2 cm. [BV5082.W36] 26-11573
1. Mysticism. I. Title.

WATTS, Alan Wilson, 1915- 291
Behold the spirit; a study in the necessity of mystical religion [by] Alan Watts. [New ed.] New York, Pantheon Books [1971] xxviii, 257 p. 22 cm. Bibliography: p. 253-257. [BV5082.W37 1971] 79-162581 ISBN 0-394-47341-8 5.95
1. Mysticism. I. Title.

WATTS, Alan Wilson, 1915- 149.3
Behold the spirit, a study in the necessity of mystical religion. [New York] Pantheon [1947] 254 p. 21 cm. Bibliography: p. 249-254. [BV5082.W37] 47-11186
1. Mysticism. I. Title.

WATTS, Alan Wilson, 1915- 294.329
This is it, and other essays on Zen and spiritual experience. [New York] Pantheon Books [1960, c.1958, 1960] 158p. 22cm. Bibl.: p.155-158. 60-11758 3.50
1. Mysticism. 2. Zen (Sect) I. Title.

WATTS, Alan Wilson, 1915- 294.3'4
This is it, and other essays on Zen and spiritual experience [by] Alan Watts. New York, Vintage Books [1973] 158 p. 19 cm. Reprint of the 1960 ed. [BL625.W35 1973] 72-8394 ISBN 0-394-71904-2 1.65 (pbk)
1. Mysticism. 2. Zen Buddhism. I. Title.

WILLIAMSON, Benedict, 1868- 248
Supernatural mysticism, by Benedict Williamson; with an introduction by His Eminence Cardinal Bourne ... and a foreword on the call to contemplation, by the Lord Bishop of Plymouth. London, K. Paul, Trench, Trubner & co., ltd; St. Louis, B. Herder book company, 1921. xvi, 268 p., 1 l. 23 cm. [BV5082.W5] 32-5638
1. Mysticism. I. Title.

WOODS, Richard. 291.4'2
Mysterion : an approach to mystical spirituality / by Richard Woods. Chicago, Ill. : Thomas More Press, c1981. 371 p. ; 23 cm. "A revised and slightly expanded version of a study program published by the Thomas More Association in 1979-80"—Pref. Includes bibliographies. [BL625.W66] 19 81-132597 ISBN 0-88347-127-2 : 14.95
1. Mysticism. I. Title.

YOUNGHUSBAND, Francis 149'.3
Edward Sir 1863-1942.
Modern mystics. Freeport, N. Y., Books for Libraries Press [1967] viii, 315 p. 22 cm. (Essay index reprint series) Reprint of the 1935 ed. [BL625.Y6] 67-28774
1. Mysticism. I. Title.

YOUNGHUSBAND, Francis 149'.3
Edward, Sir, 1863-1942.
Modern mystics. New Hyde Park, N.Y., University Books [1970] xv, 315 p. 23 cm. Reprint of the 1935 ed., with a new foreword by Leslie Shepard. [BL625.Y6 1970] 72-118603 7.95
1. Mysticism. I. Title.

YUNGBLUT, John R. 248'.22
Discovering God within / John R. Yungblut. 1st ed. Philadelphia : Westminster Press, c1979. 197 p. ; 21 cm. Includes bibliographical references. [BV5082.2.Y86] 78-21713 ISBN 0-664-24231-6 pbk. : 6.95
1. Mysticism. I. Title.

ZAEHNER, Robert Charles. 149.3
Mysticism, sacred and profane; an inquiry into some varieties of praeter-natural experience. Oxford, Clarendon Press, 1957. xviii, 256p. 25cm. Bibliographical footnotes. [BL625.Z18] 57-2468
1. Mysticism. I. Title.

Mysticism—1450-1800.

BOHME, Jakob, 1575-1624. 248'.22
The way to Christ / Jocob Boehme ; translation and introd. by Peter Erb ; pref. by Winfried Zeller. New York : Paulist Press, c1978. xviii, 307 p. ; 23 cm. (The Classics of Western spirituality) Translation of Der weg zu Christo. Includes bibliographical references and indexes. [BV5080.B7W413 1978] 77-95117 ISBN 0-8091-2102-6 pbk. : 6.95
1. Mysticism—1450-1800. I. Erb, Peter, 1943- II. Title. III. Series.

Mysticism—20th century

CURTISS, Harriette Augusta. 133
Mrs.
The divine mother [by] Harriette Augusta Curtiss and F. Homer Curtiss ... San Francisco, The Curtiss philosophic book co., 1921. ix, 11-79 p. 14 cm. (Gems of mysticism series) [BF1999.C78] ca 22
I. Curtiss, Frank Homer, 1875- joint author. II. Title.

CURTISS, Harriette Augusta. 133
Mrs.
The divine mother [by] Harriette Augusta Curtiss and F. Homer Curtiss ... San Francisco, The Curtiss philosophic book co., 1921. ix, 11-79 p. 14 cm. (Gems of mysticism series) [BF1999.C78] ca 22
I. Curtiss, Frank Homer, 1875- joint author. II. Title.

HODGES, Herman. 248.2'2
How I reached the celestial heaven. [1st ed.] Taylors, S. C., Faith Print. Co. [1967] 160p. illus., port. 21cm. [BV5095.H57A3] 66-22428 2.95 pap.,
1. Mysticism—20th cent. I. Title.
Available from the author at 1115 N. Main St., Danville, Va. 24541.

Mysticism—Addresses, essays, lectures.

DUPRE, Louis K., 1925- 248.2'2
The deeper Life : an introduction to Christian mysticism / Louis Dupre. New York : Crossroad, 1981. p. cm. [BV5082.2.D86] 19 81-3275 ISBN 0-8245-0007-5 (pbk.) : 4.95
1. Mysticism—Addresses, essays, lectures. I. Title.

GHOSE, Sisirkumar. 149'.3
Mystics and society; a point of view. With a foreword by Aldous Huxley. Bombay, New York, Asia Pub. House [1968] xv, 116 p. 23 cm. Bibliographical references included in "notes": p. 105-113. [BL625.G47 1968c] SA 68 14.00
1. Mysticism—Addresses, essays, lectures. I. Title.

JOHNSTON, William, 1925- 248.4
The mirror mind : spirituality and transformation / William Johnston. 1st ed. San Francisco, CA : Harper & Row, 1981, c1980. p. cm. Includes index. [BL625.J625 1981] 19 80-8350 ISBN 0-06-064197-5 : 10.95
1. Mysticism—Addresses, essays, lectures. 2. Spiritual life—Addresses, essays, lectures. 3. Christianity and other religions—Buddhism—Addresses, essays, lectures. 4. Buddhism—Relations—Christianity—Addresses, essays, lectures. I. Title.

MYSTICISM and 291.4'2
philosophical analysis / edited by Steven T. Katz. New York : Oxford University Press, 1978. 264 p. ; 23 cm. Includes bibliographical references and index. [BL625.M89 1978] 78-5958 ISBN 0-19-520027-6 pbk. : 3.50
1. Mysticism—Addresses, essays, lectures. I. Katz, Steven T., 1944-

SAMPSON, Holden Edward, 1859-
The true mystic; three lectures on mysticism, by the Rev. Holden E. Sampson... 1st ed. London, W. Rider & son, limited; New York, Macoy publishing and masonic supply company, 1914. 2 p. l., 7-219 p. 19 1/2 cm. $1.00. 14-12219
I. Title.

SILENT fire : 248'.22'0922 B
an invitation to Western mysticism / by Walter Holden Capps and Wendy M. Wright [editors]. 1st ed. San Francisco : Harper & Row, c1978. p. cm. (A Harper forum book) Includes index. Bibliography: p. [BV5072.S54 1978] 78-3366 ISBN 0-06-061314-9 pbk. : 5.95
1. Mysticism—Addresses, essays, lectures. 2. Mystics—Biography—Addresses, essays, lectures. I. Capps, Walter H. II. Wright, Wendy M.

UNDERHILL, Evelyn, 1875- 248'.22
1941.
The essentials of mysticism, and other essays / by Evelyn Underhill. New York : AMS Press, [1976] p. cm. Reprint of the 1920 ed. published by J. M. Dent, London and Dutton, New York. [BV5082.U5 1976] 75-41277 ISBN 0-404-14620-1 : 15.00
1. Mysticism—Addresses, essays, lectures. I. Title.

WHITE, John Warren, 1939- 149'.3
comp.
The highest state of consciousness. Edited by John White. [1st ed.] Garden City, N.Y., Anchor Books, 1972. xxi, 484 p. 19 cm. Bibliography: p. [472]-480. [BL625.W48] 70-171340 2.95
1. Mysticism—Addresses, essays, lectures. 2. Ecstasy—Addresses, essays, lectures. 3. Experience (Religion)—Addresses, essays, lectures. I. Title.

Mysticism—Asia—Collected works.

CHUANG-TZU. 181'.09'514
Musings of a Chinese mystic : selections from the philosophy of Chuang Tzu / with an introd. by Lionel Giles. San Francisco : Chinese Materials Center, [1977] i.e. 1978. 112 p. ; 20 cm. (Reprint series - Chinese Materials Center ; no. 73) Translation of selections from Nan-hua ching. "The extracts in this volume are drawn, with one or two very slight modifications, from the translation by Professor H. A. Giles (Quaritch, 1889)"—Note, p. 7. Reprint of

the ed. published by J. Murray, London, in the Wisdom of the East series. [BL1900.C5E5 1977] 78-309484 5.20
1. Giles, Herbert Allen, 1845-1935. II. Title. III. Series: Chinese Materials Center. Reprint series — Chinese Materials Center ; no. 73. IV. Series: The Wisdom of the East series.
Publisher's address: 809 Taraval St., San Francisco, CA 94116

EASTERN mysticism / 291.4'2'095
edited with an introd. and commentary by Raymond Van Over. New York : New American Library, 1977- v. ; 18 cm. (A Mentor book) Contents.Contents.—v. 1. The Near East and India. Includes bibliographical references. [BL625.E28] 77-73988 pbk. : 2.50
1. Mysticism—Asia—Collected works. 2. Mysticism—Near East—Collected works. I. Van Over, Raymond.

Mysticism—Bahaism.

SHOOK, Glenn Alfred, 1882-1954. 297'.89'42
Mysticism, science, and revelation. [1st American ed.] Wilmette, Ill., Baha'i Pub. Trust [1967] x, 145 p. 20 cm. Bibliographical footnotes. [BP370] 67-9571
1. Mysticism—Bahaism. I. Title.

Mysticism—Biblical teaching.

SCHWEITZER, Albert, 1875-1965. 227'.08'24822
The mysticism of Paul the apostle. With a prefatory note by F. C. Burkitt. [Translated from the German by William Montgomery] New York, Seabury Press [1968, c1931] xv, 411 p. 21 cm. (A Seabury paperback, SP51) Translation of Die Mystik des Apostels Paulus. Bibliographical footnotes. [BS2655.M9S43 1968] 68-28707 2.95
1. Paul, Saint, apostle. 2. Bible. N.T. Epistles of Paul—Theology. 3. Mysticism—Biblical teaching. I. Title.

Mysticism—Bibliography.

BOWMAN, Mary Ann. 016.2914'2
Western mysticism : a guide to the basic works / compiled by Mary Ann Bowman. Chicago, Ill. : American Library Association, c1978. vi, 113 p. ; 23 cm. Includes indexes. [Z7819.B68] [BL625] 78-18311 ISBN 0-8389-0266-9 pbk. : 8.00
1. Mysticism—Bibliography. I. Title.

Mysticism—Catholic Church.

ARINTERO, Juan Gonzalez, 1860-1928. 230.2
The mystical evolution in the development and vitality of the Church; tr. by Jordon Aumann. St. Louis, B.Herder Book Co., 1949- v. port 24 cm. Transiation of La evolucion mistics. Bibliographical footnotes. [BV5081.A73] 49-4505
1. Mysticism—Catholic Church. I. Title.

BLOIS, Louis de, 1506-1566. 248
A book of spiritual instruction (Institutio spiritualis) Translated from the Latin by Bertrand A. Wilberforce; edited by a Benedictine of Stanbrook Abbey. [Rev. ed.] Westminster, Md., Newman Press [1955] xxvi, 143p. 20cm. (The Orchard books) [BV5080.B484 1955] 55-8651
1. Mysticism—Catholic Church. I. Title. II. Title: Spiritual Instruction. III. Series.

[BONA, Giovanni] cardinal, 1609-1674. 230.
A treatise of spiritual life; translated from the Latin of Mgr. Charles Joseph Morozzo ... by Rev. D. A. Donovan ... 2d rev. ed. New York & Cincinnati, F Pustet & co. [c1901] x, 11-513 p. 19 cm. Commonly attributed to Carlo Giuseppe Morozzo since its first publication in 1674. The authorship of Giovanni Bona is affirmed by Marco Vattasso in his edition of Bona's Hortus cuelestium deliciarum (Roma, 1918) p. xxxix. [BV5080.B83C82 1901] 2-16089
1. Mysticism—Catholic church. I. Morozzo, Carlo Giuseppe, bp., 1645-1729, supposed author. II. Donovan, Daniel A., tr. III. Title.

BONAVENTURA, Saint, Cardinal, 1221-1274. 248'.22
The mind's journey to God = Itinerarium mentis ad Deum / Saint Bonaventure ; newly translated from the Latin with an introd. by Lawrence S. Cunningham. Chicago : Franciscan Herald Press, [1979] p. cm. (Tau series) Bibliography: p. [BT100.B56 1979] 79-1449 ISBN 0-8199-0765-0 : 6.95
1. Mysticism—Catholic Church. I. Cunningham, Lawrence. II. Title.

BRICE, father, 1905- 149.3
Journey in the night; a practical introduction to St. John of the Cross, and, in particular, a companion to the first book of the "Ascent of mt. Carmel," by the Rev. Father Brice, C.P. New York and Cincinnati, Frederick Pustet co., inc., 1945. 4 pl l., 158 p., 1 l. 22 1/2 cm. [Secular name: Frank Bernard Zurmuehlen] Bibliographical foot-notes. [BV5080.J776B7] 45-20016
1. Juan de la Cruz, Saint, 1542-1591. Subida del monte Carmelo. 2. Mysticism—Catholic church. I. Title.

BRICE, father, 1905- 149.3
Spirit in darkness; a companion to book two of the "Ascent of mt. Carmel" by the Rev. Fr. Brice ... New York and Cincinnati, Frederick Pustet co., inc., 1946. 4 p. l., 356 p. diagrs. 22 1/2 cm. [Secular name: Frank Bernard Zurmuchlen] Bibliographical foot-notes. [BV5080.J776B72] 46-16804
1. Juan de la cruz, Saint, 1542-1591. Subida del monte Carmelo. 2. Mysticism—Catholic church. I. Title.

BRUNO de Jesus-Marie Father, ed. 922.246
Three mystics: El Greco, St. John of the Cross, St. Teresa of Avila. New York, Sheed & Ward, 1949. 187 p. illus. 28 cm. [BV5095.A1B7] 49-6955
1. Theotocopuli, Dominico, called El Greco, d. 1614. 2. Juan de la Cruz, Saint, 1542-1591. 3. Teresa, Saint, 1515-1582. 4. Mysticism—Catholic Church. I. Title.

CASEL, Odo [Secular name: Johannes Casel] 1886-1948. 208.1
The mystery of Christian worship, and other writings. Ed. by Burkhard Neunheuser; Pref. by Charles Davis. Westminster, Md., Newman [c.1962] 212p. 22cm. Tr. of the 4th German ed. of Das christliche Kultmysterium and of the other writings which appeared with it in 1960. 62-5084 5.75
1. Mysticism—Catholic Church. I. Title.

CAUSSADE, Jean Pierre de, d.1751. 248
Abandonment; or, Absolute surrender to divine providence, posthumous work of J. P. de Caussade. Rev. and corr. by H. Ramiere. Translated from the 8th French ed. by Ella McMahon. New York, Benziger Bros. [1952] 192 p. 16 cm. [BV5080.C3 1952] 52-4982
1. Mysticism—Catholic Church. 2. Spiritual life—Catholic authors. I. Title. II. Title: Absolute surrender to divine providence.

CAUSSADE, Jean Pierre de, d.1751. 248
Abandonment; or, Absolute surrender to Divine providence. Posthumous work of Rev. J. P. de Caussade, S. J. Revised and corrected by Rev. H. Ramiere, S. J. Translated from the eighth French edition by Miss Ella McMahon. New York, Cincinnati and St. Louis, Benziger brothers; London, R. Washbourne; [etc., etc.] 1887. 192 p. 14 cm. [BV5080.C3] 37-36744
1. Mysticism—Catholic church. 2. Spiritual life—Catholic authors. I. Ramiere, Henri, 1821-1884, ed. II. McMahon, Ella, tr. III. Title.

CAUSSADE, Jean Pierre de, d.1751. 248
Abandonment; or, Absolute surrender to divine providence, posthumous work of Rev. J. P. De Caussade, S.J. Revised and corrected by Rev. H. Ramiere, S. J. Translated from the eighth French edition by Ella McMahon. New York, Boston [etc.] Benziger brothers, inc. [c1945] 192 p. 13 cm. [BV5080.C3 1945] 46-21157
1. Mysticism—Catholic church. 2. Spiritual life—Catholic authors. I. Ramiere, Henri, 1821-1884, ed. II. MacMahon, Ella J., tr. III. Title.

CAUSSADE, Jean Pierre de, d.1751. 248'.22
Abandonment to divine providence / by Jean-Pierre de Caussade ; newly translated, with an introd. by John Beevers. 1st ed. Garden City, N.Y. : Image Books, 1975. 119 p. ; 18 cm. (An Image book original) Translation of L'abandon a la providence divine. [BV5080.C3 1975] 74-2827 ISBN 0-385-02544-0 pbk.: 1.45
1. Mysticism—Catholic Church. 2. Spiritual life—Catholic authors. I. Title.

DICKEN, E W Trueman. 922.246
The crucible of love; a study of the mysticism of St. Teresa of Jesus and St. John of the Cross. New York, Sheed and Ward [1963] xv, 548 p. illus., ports., facisms. 22 cm. Bibliography: p. 524-525. [BX4700.T4D5] 63-18069
1. Teresa, Saint, 1515-1582. 2. Juan de la Cruz, Saint, 1542-1591. 3. Mysticism — Catholic Church. I. Title.

ELIZABETH DE LA TRINITE, Sister, 1880-1906 248.22
Spiritual writings: letters, retreats, and unpublished notes. Edited by M. M. Philipon. New York, P. J. Kenedy [c1962] 180 p. illus. 22 cm. Secular name: Elisabeth Catez. 62-21053
1. Mysticism — Catholic Church. I. Title.

GRAEF, Hilda C. 922.2
Mystics of our times. Garden City, N.Y., Hanover House, [c]1962. 240p. Bibl. 62-7636 4.50
1. Mysticism—Catholic Church I. Title.

GRAEF, Hilda C 922.2
Mystics of our times. Glen Rock, N.J., Paulist Press [1963, c1962] 240 p. 18 cm. (Deus books) Bibliography: p. [239]-240. [BV5095.A1G68 1963] 63-20220
1. Mysticism — Catholic Church. 2. Catholic Church — Biog. I. Title.

GRAEF, Hilda C 149.3
The way of the mystics. Westminister, Md., Newman Bookshop [1948] 160 p. 22 cm. Bibliography: p. 159-160. [BV5095.A1G7] 49-2860
1. Mysticism—Catholic Church. I. Title.

HARROW, Katharine.
Allegorical visions of the pathways of life; of the heights and depths; of the hearts of men; of the soul of the infinite. [By] Katharine Harrow. New York, The New-way publishing company [c1913] 85 p. 2 pl. 20 cm. 13-22108 1.25
I. Title.

HEAVENLY converse ... 242
by a Poor Clare Colettine. New York, Sheed & Ward, 1940. vii, 136 p. 19 cm. "Printed in Great Britain." "A sequel to Songs in the night."--Pref. [BV5082.H38] 40-30135
1. Mysticism—Catholic church. 2. Love (Theology). 3. Spiritual life—Catholic authors. I. A Poor Clare Colettine

*JUAN de la Cruz, Saint, 1542-1591. 149.3
Ascent of Mount Carmel, by Saint John of the Cross. Trans. & edited with a general introd., by E. Allison Peers, from the critical edition of P. Silverio de Santa Teresa. 3d rev. ed. Garden City, N.Y., Doubleday [1972] 478 p. 18 cm. (Image Books) Bibliographical footnotes. [BV5080.J77493 1958] ISBN 0-385-01111-3 pap., 1.95
1. Mysticism—Catholic Church. I. Peers, Edgar Allison, ed. II. Title.

JUAN De La Cruz Saint, 1542-1591. 149.3
The dark night of the soul, translated, abridged, and edited by ,kurt F. Reinhardt. New York, F. Ungar Pub. Co. [1957] xxxiii. 222p. illus. 21cm. (Milestones of thought in the history of ideas) Bibliography:p. [xxvi] [BV5080.J77572] 56-12399
1. Mysticism—Catholic Church. I. Juan de la Cruz, Saint, 1542-1591. The ascent of Mount Carmel. II. Reinhardt, Kurt Frank, 1896- ed. and tr. III. Title.
Contents omitted.

JUAN De La Cruz, Saint 1542-1591 149.3
Living flame of love. Tr., ed., introd. by E. Allison Peers, from the critical ed. of P. Silverio de Santa Teresa. Garden City, N. Y., Doubleday [1962] 272p. 18cm. (Image bk., D129) Bibl. 62-4311 .85 pap.,
1. Mysticism—Catholic Church. I. Peers, Edgar Allison, ed. and tr. II. Title.

JUAN de la Cruz, Saint, 1542-1591. 149.3
The mystical doctrine of St. John of the Cross; an abridgement made by C. H., with an introduction by R. H. J. Steuart, S. J. New York, Sheed and Ward, inc., 1934. xxiii, 213 p. 17 cm. "Printed in Great Britain." "From the authorized translation made by David Lewis and revised by Dom Benedict Zimmerman, O. C. D." "The arrangement of this book--the selection of passages and sub-headings--is taken from the French work, Abrege de toute la doctrine mystique de S. Jean de la Crois."--Publisher's note. [BV5080.J75 1934] 35-2887
1. Mysticism—Catholic church. I. H., C., comp. II. C. H., comp. III. Lewis, David, 1814-1895, tr. IV. Zimmerman, Benedict, father, 1859 ed. V. Title.

JUAN De La Cruz Saint, 1542-1591. 149.3
Ascent of Mount Carmel. Translated and edited, with a general introd., by E.-Allison Peers from the critical edition of P. Silverio de Santa Teresa. 3d rev. ed. Garden City, N. Y., Image Books [1958] lxxxiv. 386p. 19cm. (A Doubleday image book, D63) [BV5080.J77593 1958] 57-59521
1. Mysticism—Catholic Church. I. Peers, Edgar Allison, ed. and tr. II. Title.

JUAN de la Cruz, Saint, 1542-1591. 149.3
Dark night of the soul. Translated and edited, with an introd., by E. Allison Peers from the critical edition of P. Silverio de Santa Teresa. 3d rev. ed. Garden City, N.Y., Image Books [1959] 193 p. 18 cm. (A Doubleday image book, D78) [BV5080.J77572 1959] 59-6380
1. Mysticism—Catholic Church. I. Peers, Edgar Allison, ed. and tr. II. Title.

JUAN De Los Angeles Father, d. 1609. 149.3
Conquest of the kingdom of God. Translated by Cornelius J. Crowley. St. Louis, Herder [1957] 216p. 21cm. (Cross and crown series of spirituality, no. 10) Translation of Dialogos de la conquista del espiritual y secreto reyno de Dios. [BV5080.J77683] 57-13267
1. Mysticism—Catholic Church. I. Title.

KERNS, H. J. 220.6
Secrets of wisdom; the mystery of His sacred name revealed. New York, Exposition [c.1963] 105p. 21cm. 3.00
I. Title.

KNOWLES, David, 1896- 248.22
The nature of mysticism, by M. D. Knowles. [1st ed.] New York, Hawthorn Books [1966] 140 p. 21 cm. (Twentieth century encyclopedia of Catholicism, v. 38. Section IV: The Means of redemption) Bibliography: p. 136-140. [BV5082.2.K6] 66-15244
1. Mysticism—Catholic Church. I. Title.

KOLBE, Frederick Charles, 1854- 282
The four mysteries of the faith, by Monsignor Kolbe ... with a foreword by. His Eminence Cardinal Gasquet. London, New York [etc.] Longmans, Green and co., 1926. xvi, 204 p. illus. (plan.) 20 cm. [BX1751.K7] 26-15629
I. Title.

MCCABE, Francis Xavier, 1872- 230.
The Catholic church, the mystic body of Christ, animated by the spirit of God, the teacher of the world, by Francis Xavier McCabe ... St. Louis, Mo., The Vincentian press [1925] 5 p. l., 56 p., 1 l. 15 1/2 cm. Cover-title: His mystic body. [BX1753.M2] 25-8800
I. Title.

MALFITANO, Gilbert Jacques. 248'.22
The seven steps on how to become a

mystic and enjoy the most exhilarating pleasure available to man on this earth / Gilbert Jacques Malfitano. Albuquerque, N.M. : Gloucester Art Press, [1979] 30 leaves : ill. ; 28 cm. Cover title. [BV5082.2.M33] 79-22985 ISBN 0-930582-37-3 : 27.50
1. Mysticism—Catholic Church. I. Title.

MENENDEZ, Josefa, Sister, 1890-1923. 241
Christ's appeal for love to His humble servant Josefa Menendez, translated by L. Keppel. Newman Press 1951 176p. illus. 19cm. 'A revised, abridged edition of [the author's] The way of divine love.' Translation of Un liamamiento al amor. [BV5082.M42 1951] 53-26456
1. Mystiusm—Catholic Church. 2. Love (Theology) I. Title.

MENENDEZ, Josefa, 1890-1923. 241
The way of divine love; or, The message of the Sacred Heart to the world, and a short biography of His messenger, Sister Josefa Menendez, coadjutrix sister of the Society of the Sacred Heart of Jesus, 1890-1923. Westminster, Md., Newman Press [1956] 504p. illus. 22cm. 'Translation of Un Hamamiento al amor. [BV5082.M415 1956] 57-1484
1. Mysticism—Catholic Church. 2. Love (Theology) I. Title.

MILITZ, Annie (Rix) Mrs. 248
All the way; a handbook for those who have entered the path and have determined to walk all the way with Christ to the heights of the ascension, by Annie Rix Militz. Los Angeles, Calif., The Master mind publishing co. [c1922] 3 p. l., [11]-60 p. 18 cm. [BV4510.M45] 22-24892
I. Title.

MOROZZO, Carlo Giuseppe, bp., 1645-1729. 149.
A treatise of spiritual life; translated from the Latin of Mgr. Charles Joseph Morozzo ... by Rev. D. A. Donovan ... 2d rev. ed. New York & Cincinnati, F. Pustet & co. [c1901] x, 11-513 p. 19 cm. [BV5080.M62 1901] 2-16089
1. Mysticism—Catholic church. I. Donovan, Daniel A., tr. II. Title.

OSUNA, Francisco de, d.ca.1540. 149.3
The third spiritual alphabet, by Fray Francisco de Osuna; translated from the Spanish by a Benedictine of Stanbrook, with an introduction by Father Cuthbert, O. S. F. C., and notes showing the influence of the book on St. Teresa. New York, Cincinnati [etc.] Benziger brothers [1931] 2 p. l., vii-xxxvi, 490 p. 1 l. 23 cm. [BV5080.O83] 32-22676
1. Teresa, Saint, 1515-1582. 2. Mysticism—Catholic church. 3. Meditation. I. A Benedictine of Stanbrook, tr. II. Title.

OSUNA, Francisco de, d.ca.1840. 149.
The third spiritual alphabet, tr. from the Spanish by a Benedictine of Stanbrook, with an introd. by Father Cuthbert, o. s. f. c., and notes showing the influence of the book of St. Teresa. Westminster, Md., Newman Bookshop, 1948. xxxvi, 490 p. 22 cm. Translation of Tercera parte d'l libro liamado Abecedario espual. [BV5080.O] A 48
1. Teresa, Saint, 1515-1582. 2. Mysticism—Catholic Church. 3. Meditation. I. A Benedictine of Stanbrook, tr. II. Title.

PARENTE, Paschale P. 149.3
The mystical life, by Pascal P. Parente ... St. Louis, Mo., and London, B. Herder book co., 1946. ix, 272 p. 22 cm. Bibliography: p. 258-266. [BV5081.P3] 46-2356
1. Mysticism—Catholic church. I. Title.

PEPLER, Conrad, 1908- 149.3
The three degrees; a study of Christian mysticism. St. Louis, Herder [1957 or 8] 256p. 19cm. [BV5082.P4] 58-2002
1. Mysticism—Catholic Church. I. Title.

SONGS in the night ... 242
by a Poor Clare Colettine. New York, Sheed & Ward, inc., 1936. vi p., 2 l., 217 p. front. 19 cm. "Printed in Great Britain." [BV5082.S63] 39-5112
1. Mysticism—Catholic church. 2. Love (Theology) 3. Spiritual life—Catholic authors. I. A Poor Clare Colettine.

STOLZ, Anselm, father, 1900- 149.3
The doctrine of spiritual perfection, by Rev. Anselm Stolz ... translated by Rev. Aidan Williams ... St. Louis, Mo., and London, B. Herder book co., 1938. v, 250 p. 21 cm. [Secular name: Julius Stolz] [BV5082.S68] 38-25906
1. Mysticism—Catholic church. 2. Translation of Theologie der mystik. I. Williams, Aidan, father, 1904- tr. II. Title. III. Title: Spiritual perfection, The doctrine of.

TEILHARD de Chardin, Pierre 210.81
Hymn of the universe [Tr. by Simon Bartholomew] New York, Harper [c.1961, 1965] 157p. 22cm. [B2430.T373H93] 65-10375 3.00
1. Mysticism—Catholic Church. 2. Cosmology. 3. Creation. I. Title.

TEILHARD de Chardin, Pierre. 248.2'2
Hymn of the universe. [Translated by Gerald Vann] New York, Harper & Row [1969, c1965] 157 p. 21 cm. (Harper colophon books, CN 173) [B2430.T373] 78-8361 1.95
1. Mysticism—Catholic Church. 2. Cosmology. 3. Creation.

THURSTON, Herbert, 1856-1939. 149.3
Surprising mystics. Edited by J. H. Crehan. Chicago, H. Regnery Co., 1955. 238p. 23cm. [BV5095] 56-2164
1. Mysticism—Catholic Church. I. Title.

VANN, Gerald, 1906- 248
The paradise tree; on living the symbols of the church. New York, Sheed and Ward [1959] 820 p. 22 cm. Includes bibliography. [BV5083.V3] 59-8236
1. Mysticism — Catholic Church. 2. Sacraments — Catholic Church. 3. Symbolism. I. Title.

WATKIN, Edward Ingram, 1888- 248.2'2
Poets and mystics, by E. I. Watkin. Freeport, N. Y., Books for Libraries Press [1968] ix, 318 p. 23 cm. (Essay index reprint series) Reprint of the 1953 ed. Includes bibliographical references. [BV5077.G7W35 1968] 68-55862
1. Mysticism—Catholic Church. I. Title.

WILLIAMSON, Benedict, 1868- 248
The triumph of love, by Benedict Williamson, with a foreword by the Lord Bishop of Plymouth. London, K. Paul, Trench, Trubner & co.; St Louis, B. Herder book company, 1923. xxiii, 230 p. 22 1/2 cm. [BV5082.W52] 23-8630
1. Mysticism—Catholic church. 2. Love (Theology) I. Title.

Mysticism—Catholic Church—Early works to 1800.

OSUNA, Francisco de, d.ca.1540. 248.2'2
The third spiritual alphabet / Francisco de Osuna ; translation and introduction by Mary E. Giles ; preface by Kieran Kavanaugh. New York : Paulist Press, c1981. xvi, 624 p. ; 23 cm. (The Classics of Western spirituality) Translation of: Tercer abecedario espiritual. Includes indexes. Bibliography: p. 610. [BV5080.O813 1981] 19 81-84067 ISBN 0-8091-2145-X (pbk.) : 11.95
1. Catholic Church—Doctrinal and controversial works—Catholic authors. 2. Mysticism—Catholic Church—Early works to 1800. I. [Tercer abecedario espiritual.] English II. Title. III. Series.

Mysticism—China—Collections.

VAN OVER, Raymond, comp. 291.4'2
Chinese mystics. Edited and with an introd. by Raymond Van Over. [1st ed.] New York, Harper & Row [1973] xxx, 183 p. 21 cm. [BL1802.V3 1973] 72-78072 pap 2.45
1. Mysticism—China—Collections. 2. Religious literature, Chinese. I. Title.

Mysticism—Collected works.

BOHME, Jakob, 1575-1624. 230
The works of Jacob Behmen, the Teutonic theosopher : to which is prefixed the life of the author ; with figures illustrating his principles, left by the Reverend William Law, M.A. New York : Gordon Press, 1976. p. cm. Reprint of the 1764-1781 ed. printed for M. Richardson, London and other publishers. Contents.Contents.—v. 1. The aurora. The three principles.—[2] The threefold life of man. The answers to forty questions concerning the soul. The treatise of the Incarnation. The clavis.—v. 3. The mysterium magnum; or, An explanation of the first Book of Moses, called Genesis. Four tables of divine revelation.—v. 4. Signatura rerum. Of the election of grace; or, Of God's will towards man, commonly called predestination. The way to Christ. A discourse between a soul hungry and thirsty after the fountain of life, the sweet love of Jesus Christ; and a soul enlightened. Of the four complexions. Of Christ's testaments, baptism, and the supper. [BV5072.B58 1976] 76-21647 ISBN 0-87968-465-8 lib.bdg. : 600.00(4 vols.)
1. Mysticism—Collected works. 2. Theology—Collected works—16th century.

FREMANTLE, Anne (Jackson) 1909- ed. 248.22082
The Protestant mystics. Introd. by W. H. Auden [New York] New Amer. Lib. [1965, c.1964] 317p. 18cm. (Mentor bk. MQ628) Bibl. [BV5072.F7] .95 pap.,
1. Mysticism—Collections. 2. Protestantism—Collections. I. Title.

FREMANTLE, Anne (Jackson) 1909- 248.22082
The Protestant mystics. Introd. by W. H. Auden. Boston, Little [c.1964] xi, 396p. 22cm. Bibl. 64-10472 6.75
1. Mysticism—Collections. 2. Protestantism—Collections. I. Title.

HALL, Manly Palmer. 244
The ways of the lonely ones; a collection of mystical allegories, by Manly Hall; illustrated by J. Augustus Knapp. 4th rev. ed. Los Angeles, Calif., The Phoenix press, 1934. 2 p. l., 3-89 p. plates. 24 cm. [BV4515.H3 1934] 36-7782
I. Title.

HAYWOOD, Harry LeRoy, 1886-1956. 248.2'1
Christian mysticism and other essays / by Harry LeRoy Haywood. New York : Gordon Press, 1980. p. cm. Reprint of the 1917 ed. published by Murray Press, Boston. [BV5085.H39 1980] 80-10187 ISBN 0-87968-862-9 lib. bdg. : 49.95
1. Mysticism—Collected works.

JUAN De La Cruz Saint, 1542-1591. 208.1
Collected works. Translated by Kieran Kavanaugh and Otilio Rodriguez. With introduction by Kieran Kavanaugh. [1st ed.] Garden City, N.Y., Doubleday, 1964. 740 p. illus., facsim. 25 cm. [BX890.J6233] 64-11725
1. Mysticism — Collected works. 2. Theology — Collected works — 16th cent. 3. Catholic Church — Collected works — 16th cent. 4. Catholic Church — Collected works. I. Title.

Mysticism — Comparative studies.

BENNETT, John Godolphin, 1897- 149.3
Christian mysticism and Subud. New York, Dharma Book Co. [1961] 69p. 18cm. [BL625.B44] 61-19679
1. Mysticism—Comparative studies. I. Title.

*CHENEY, Sheldon. 291.42.
Men who have walked with God; being the story of mysticism through the ages told in the biographies of representative seers and saints with experts from their writings and saying. [New York, Dell, 1974, c1945]. xiv, 395 p. illus. 21 cm. (A Delta book) [BL625] 3.45 (pbk.)
1. Mysticism—Comparative studies. 2. Mysticism (comparative religion). I. Title.

DE MARQUETTE, Jacques. 149.3
Introduction to comparative mysticism. New York, Philosophical Library [1949] 229 p. 22 cm. "Lectures ... given at the Lowell Institute of Boston in December of 1944 and repeated at the Forum of the School of Philosophy, University of Southern California, in March and April of 1945." Bibliography: p. 209-211. [BL625.D4] 49-10035
1. Mysticism—Comparative studies. I. Title.

ELLWOOD, Robert S., 1933- 291.4'2
Mysticism and religion / Robert S. Ellwood, Jr. Englewood Cliffs, N.J. : Prentice-Hall, c1980. xiii, 194 p. ; 24 cm. Includes bibliographical references and index. [BL625.E44] 79-15395 ISBN 0-13-608810-4 : 10.95 ISBN 0-13-608802-3 (pbk.) : 5.95
1. Mysticism—Comparative studies. I. Title.

JOHNSTON, William, 1925- 294.3'4'42
The still point : reflections on Zen and Christian mysticism. New York, Fordham University Press, 1970. xiii, 193 p. 21 cm. Includes bibliographical references. [BL625.J63] 75-95713 ISBN 0-8232-0860-5 7.50
1. Mysticism—Comparative studies. 2. Zen Buddhism—Relations—Christianity. 3. Christianity and other religions—Zen Buddhism. I. Title.

JOHNSTON, William, 1925- 294.3'4'42
The stillpoint : reflections on Zen and Christian mysticism / by William Johnston. New York : Fordham University Press, 1977,c1970. viii, 202p. ; 20 cm. Includes index. [BL625.J63] ISBN 0-8232-0861-3 pbk. : 6.00
1. Mysticism — Comparative studies. 2. Zen Buddhism — Relations — Christianity. 3. Christianity and other religions — Zen Buddhism. I. Title.
L.C. card no. for 1970 Fordham University Press ed.: 75-95713.

OTTO, Rudolf [Karl Ludwig Rudolf Otto] 1869-1937 149.3
Mysticism East and West; a comparative analysis of the nature of mysticism. Tr. [from German] by Bertha L. Bracey, Richenda C. Payne. New York, Collier [1962, c.1932, 1960] 282p. 18cm. (BS30) 62-5884 1.50 pap.,
1. Mysticism—Comparative studies. 2. Philosophy and religion. I. Title.

PARRINDER, Edward Geoffrey. 291.4'2
Mysticism in the world's religions / [by] Geoffrey Parrinder. London : Sheldon Press, 1976. viii, 210 p. ; 21 cm. Includes index. Bibliography: p. 199-203. [BL625.P37 1976] 76-369829 ISBN 0-85969-085-7 : £4.95. ISBN 0-85969-086-5 pbk.
1. Mysticism—Comparative studies. I. Title.

SPENCER, Sidney, 1888- 149.3
Mysticism in world religion [Cranbury, N.J.] A. S. Barnes [1966, c.1963] 363p. 22cm. Bibl. [BL625.S65] 66-15189 6.00
1. Mysticism — Comparative studies. I. Title.

SPENCER, Sidney, 1888- 291.14
Mysticism in world religion. Baltimore,

Penguin [c.1963] 363p. 19cm. (Pelican bks. A594) Bibl. 63-3923 1.65 pap.,
1. Mysticism—Comparative studies. I. Title.

SPENCER, Sidney, 1888- 291.4'2
Mysticism in world religion. Gloucester, Mass., P. Smith, 1971 [c1963] 363 p. 21 cm. (Pelican books, A594) Bibliography: p. [341]-354. [BL625.S65 1971] 70-22894
1. Mysticism—Comparative studies. I. Title.

STEVENS, Edward, 1928- 181
Oriental mysticism. New York, Paulist Press [1973] 186 p. illus. 18 cm. (Deus books) Cover title: An introduction to oriental mysticism. Includes bibliographical references. [BL625.S76] 73-87030 ISBN 0-8091-1798-3 1.95 (pbk.)
1. Mysticism—Comparative studies. 2. Meditation. I. Title. II. Title: An introduction to oriental mysticism.

WAINWRIGHT, William J. 291.4'2
Mysticism : a study of its nature, cognitive value, and moral implications / William J. Wainwright. Madison, Wis. : University of Wisconsin Press, c1981. xv, 245 p. ; 22 cm. Includes index. Bibliography: p. 234-242. [BL625.W27] 19 81-12922 ISBN 0-299-08910-X : 40.00
1. Mysticism—Comparative studies. I. Title.

WALKER, Kenneth Macfarlane, 291.4
1882-
The mystic mind. New York, Emerson [c.1962, 1965] 176p. 22cm. First ed. pub. in London in 1962 under title: The conscious mind, a commentary on the mystics. Bibl. [BL625.W28] 65-16758 3.95
1. Mysticism—Comparative studies. I. Title.

WHITSON, Robley Edward 291.42
Mysticism and ecumenism. New York, Sheed [1966] xv, 209p. 22cm. Bibl. [BL625.W53] 66-12260 4.95
1. Mysticism—Comparative studies. I. Title.

WINSKI, Norman. 291.4
Mysticism for the millions; a primer on mysticism. With an introd. by Gerald Heard. [1st ed.] Los Angeles, Sherbourne Press [1965] xiv, 98 p. 22 cm. Bibliography: p. [97]-98. [BL625.W54] 65-15791
1. Mysticism — Comparative studies. I. Title.

Mysticism—Comparative studies—Addresses, essays, lectures.

UNDERSTANDING mysticism 291.4'2
/ edited by Richard Woods. 1st. ed. Garden City, N.Y. : Image Books, 1980. xi, 586 p. ; 21 cm. Includes index. Bibliography: p. [564]-575. [BL625.U52] 78-22743 ISBN 0-385-15117-9 pbk. : 7.95
1. Mysticism—Comparative studies—Addresses, essays, lectures. 2. Mysticism—Psychology—Addresses, essays, lectures. I. Woods, Richard.

ZAEHNER, Robert Charles. 291
Concordant discord: the interdependence of faiths: being the Gifford lectures on natural religion delivered at St. Andrews in 1967-1969, by R. C. Zaehner. Oxford, Clarendon P., 1970. ix, 464 p. 24 cm. (Gifford lectures, 1967/69) Includes bibliographical references. [BL625.Z17] 76-540412 ISBN 0-19-826624-3 80/-
1. Mysticism—Comparative studies—Addresses, essays, lectures. I. Title. II. Series.

Mysticism—Comparative studies—Dictionaries.

FERGUSON, John, 291.4'2'0321
1921-
Encyclopedia of mysticism and mystery religions / John Ferguson. New York : Crossroad, 1982, c1976. 228 p. : ill. ; 23 cm. Bibliography: p. 217-227. [BL625.F43 1982] 19 82-123902 ISBN 0-8245-0429-1 (pbk.) : 9.95
1. Mysticism—Comparative studies—Dictionaries. 2. Mysteries, Religious—Dictionaries. I. Title.

Mysticism—Dictionaries.

FERGUSON, John, 1921- 291.4'2
An illustrated encyclopaedia of mysticism and the mystery religions / [by] John Ferguson. London : Thames and Hudson, 1976. 228 p. : ill., ports. ; 25 cm. American ed. published under title: An illustrated encyclopedia of mysticism and the mystery religions. Bibliography: p. 217-227. [BL625.F44 1976] 77-352543 ISBN 0-500-01140-0 : £6.50
1. Mysticism—Dictionaries. 2. Religions—Dictionaries. I. Title.

Mysticism—Early church.

*BUTLER, Dom Cuthbert 248.22
Western mysticism the teaching of Augustine, Gregory and Bernard on contemplation and the contemplative life. 2d ed., with afterthoughts New York, Harper, 1966 xii, 242p. 21cm. (Torchbk., TB 312 K. Cathedral Lib.) 1.75 pap.,
I. Title.

CAYRE, Fulbert. 281.1
Spiritual writers of the early church. Translated from the French by W. Webster Wilson. [1st ed.] New York, Hawthorn Books [1959] 126, [1]p. 21cm.. (The Twentieth century encyclopedia of Catholicism, v. 39. Section 4: The means of redemption) Translation of Spirituels et mystiques des premiers temps. Bibliography: p. [127] [BV5075.C313] 59-6725
1. Mysticism—Early church. I. Title. II. Series: The Twentieth century encyclopedia of Catholicism, v. 39

GREGORIUS, Saint, Bp. of 248.22
Nyssa, fl. 379-394.
From glory to glory; texts from Gregory of Nyssa's mystical writings, selected and with an introd. by Jean Danielou. Translated and edited by Herbert Musurillo, New York, Scribner [1961] xiv, 298p. illus. 22cm. Includes bibliographical references. [BV5080.G73] 61-13370
1. Mysticism—Early church. I. Danielou, Jean, ed. II. Musurillo, Herbert Anthony, ed. and tr. III. Title.

SAINT GREGORIUS, Bp. of 248.22
Nyssa, fl.379-394
From glory to glory; texts from Gregory of Nyssa's mystical writings, selected, introd. by Jean Danielou. Tr., ed. by Herbert Musurillo. New York. Scribners [c.1961] xiv, 298p. illus. Bibl. 61-13370 4.95
1. Mysticism—Early church. I. Danielou, Jean, ed. II. Musurillo, Herbert Anthony, ed. and tr. III. Title.

Mysticism—Early church, ca.30-600.

GREGORIUS, Saint, Bp. of 248'.22
Nyssa, fl.379-394.
From glory to glory : texts from Gregory of Nyssa's mystical writings / selected and with an introd. by Jean Danielou ; translated and edited by Herbert Musurillo. Crestwood, N.Y. : St. Vladimir's Seminary Press, 1979. p. cm. Reprint of the 1961 ed. published by Scribner, New York. [BR65.G74E53 1979] 79-38 ISBN 0-913836-54-0 pbk. : 8.95
1. Mysticism—Early church, ca. 30-600. I. Title.

GREGORIUS, Saint, Bp. 222'.1'0924
of Nyssa, fl.379-394.
The life of Moses / Gregory of Nyssa ; translation, introd. and notes by Abraham J. Malherbe and Everett Ferguson ; pref. by John Meyendorff. New York : Paulist Press, c1978. xvi, 208 p. ; 23 cm. (The Classics of Western spirituality) Translation of De vita Moysis. Includes indexes. Bibliography: p. 139-140. [BS580.M6G7313] 78-56352 ISBN 0-8091-2112-3 pbk. : 6.95
1. Moses. 2. Bible. O.T.—Biography. 3. Mysticism—Early church, ca.30-600. I. Title. II. Series.

LOUTH, Andrew. 248.2'2'09015
The origins of the Christian mystical tradition from Plato to Denys / Andrew Louth. Oxford : Clarendon Press ; New York : Oxford University Press, 1981. xvii, 215 p. ; 22 cm. Includes index. Bibliography: p. [205]-210. [BV5075.L68] 19 80-41057 ISBN 0-387-10503-4 : 29.95
1. Mysticism—Early church, ca. 30-600. I. Title.

Mysticism—Early works to 1800.

CLOUD of unknowing. 248.2'2
The cloud of unknowing / edited, with an introduction, by James Walsh ; preface by Simon Tugwell. New York : Paulist Press, c1981. xxvi, 293 p. ; 23 cm. (The Classics of western spirituality) Includes indexes. Bibliography: p. 267-272. [BV5080.C5 1981] 19 81-82201 ISBN 0-8091-2332-0 (pbk.) : 7.95 ISBN 0-8091-0314-1 : 11.95
1. Mysticism—Early works to 1800. I. Walsh, James, 1920- II. Title. III. Series.

LULL, Ramon, d.1315. 248.2'2
The art of contemplation / translated from the Catalan of Ramon Lull with an introductory essay by E. Allison Peers. New York : Gordon Press, 1980. p. cm. Translation of Art de contemplacio, a part of his Blanquerna. Reprint of the 1925 ed. published by Society for Promoting Christian Knowledge, London ; Macmillian, New York. [BV5080.L7713 1980] 80-10263 ISBN 0-8490-1451-4 lib. bdg. : 55.00
1. Mysticism—Early works to 1800. I. Peers, Edgar Allison. II. Title.

Mysticism—Early works to 1800—Addresses, essays, lectures.

ECKHART, Meister, 252'.02
d.1327.
Meister Eckhart / [compiled] by Franz Pfeiffer ; translation with some omissions and additions by C. de B. Evans. New York : Gordon Press, 1981. p. cm. (Studies in Religious Mysticism.) Reprint. Originally published: London : J.M. Watkins, 1956 (v.1). 1952 (v.2). Vol. 2 has title: The works of Meister Eckhart. Includes bibliographies. [BV5080.E3213 1981] 19 81-7242 ISBN 0-8490-2222-3(2 vol set.) : 250.00
1. Catholic Church—Sermons. 2. Mysticism—Early works to 1800—Addresses, essays, lectures. 3. Sermons, English—Translations from Latin. 4. Sermons, Latin—Translations into English. I. Pfeiffer, Franz, 1815-1868. II. Evans, C. de. B. III. [Selections.] English. 1981 IV. Title. V. Series.

ECKHART, Meister, 248.2'2
d.1327.
Meister Eckhart, the essential sermons, commentaries, treatises, and defense / translation and introduction by Edmund Colledge, and Bernard McGinn ; preface by Huston Smith. New York : Paulist Press, c1981. xviii, 366 p. ; 24 cm. (The Classics of Western spirituality) Includes indexes. Contents.Contents. Latin works / translated by Bernard McGinn. Documents relating to Eckhart's condemnation: Selections from Eckhart's Defense. The bull, "In agro dominco" (March 27, 1329). Selections from the Commentary on John — German works / translated by Edmund Colledge. Selected sermons. Treatises: The book of "Benedictus": The book of divine consolation. The book of "Benedictus": Of the nobleman Counsels on discernment. On detachment. Bibliography: p. 349-353. [BV5080.E3213 1981a] 19 81-82206 ISBN 0-8091-0322-2 : 12.95 ISBN 0-8091-2370-3 pbk. : 8.95
1. Catholic Church—Sermons. 2. Mysticism—Early works to 1800—Addresses, essays, lectures. 3. Sermons, Latin—Translations into English. 4. Sermons, English—Translations from Latin. I. Colledge, Edmund, 1910- II. McGinn, Bernard, 1937- III. [Selections.] English. 1981. Paulist Press IV. Title. V. Series.
Contents omitted.

Mysticism—England—History.

THE cell of self-knowledge:
seven early English mystical treatises printed by Henry Pepwell in 1521; ed. with an introduction and notes by Edmund G. Gardner, m. a. London, Chatto & Windus; New York, Duffield & co., 1910. xxvii, 134, [2] p. front. 17 cm. (Half-title: The new medieval library) Added t.-p. within ornamental border. [PN665.N4 vol. 9] 10-9627
1. Pepwell, Henry, d. 1540, comp. II. Gardner, Edmund Garratt, 1809- ed.
Contents omitted.

*KNOWLES, David 248.220942
The English mystical tradition. New York, Harper [1965, c.1961] viii, 197p. 21cm. (Harper torchbks., TB302) 1.35 pap.,
I. Title.

TUMA, George Wood. 248'.22'0942
The fourteenth century English mystics : a comparative analysis / George Wood Tuma. Salzburg : Inst. f. Engl. Sprache u. Literatur, Univ. Salzburg, 1977- v. ; 21 cm. (Elizabethan & Renaissance studies ; 61) Au77-17/18-192 (v. 1) Originally presented as the author's thesis, Michigan State University. Includes bibliographical references. [BV5077.G7T85 1977] 77-377075 pbk. (v.1 & v.2) : 17.50 each vol.
1. Mysticism—England—History. 2. Mystics—England. 3. Mysticism—Middle Ages, 600-1500. I. Title. II. Series. III. Salzburg studies in English literature
Distributed by Humanities Press

Mysticism—England—History—Bibliography.

LAGORIO, Valerie 016.2482'2'0942
Marie, 1925-
The 14th-century English mystics : a comprehensive annotated bibliography / Valerie Marie Lagorio, Ritamary Bardley. New York : Garland Pub., 1981. p. cm. (Garland reference library of the humanities ; v. 190) Includes index. [Z7819.L33] [BV5077.G] 19 79-7922 ISBN 0-8240-9535-9 : 30.00
1. Mysticism—England—History—Bibliography. 2. Mysticism—History—Middle Ages, 600-1500—Bibliography. 3. Mystics—England—Bibliography. I. Bradley, Ritamary, 1916- joint author. II. Title.

Mysticism—England—Quotations, maxims, etc.

THE Wisdom of the 248'.22'0941
English mystics / compiled by Robert Way. New York : New Directions, c1978. p. cm. (Wisdom series) [BV5085.W59 1978] 78-6435 ISBN 0-8112-0700-5 : 3.75
1. Mysticism—England—Quotations, maxims, etc. I. Way, Robert. II. Series: Wisdom series (New York)

Mysticism—Friends, Society of.

BRINTON, Howard Haines, 248.2'2
1884-
Ethical mysticism in the Society of Friends [by] Howard H. Brinton. [Wallingford, Pa., Pendle Hill Publications, 1967] 36 p. 19 cm. (Pendle Hill pamphlet 156) [BX7748.M9B7] 67-31429
1. Mysticism—Friends, Society of. I. Title.

PECK, George Terhune, 248'.22
1916-
The triple way : purgation, illumination, union / George Peck. Wallingford, Pa. : Pendle Hill Publications, 1977. 32 p. ; 20 cm. (Pendle Hill pamphlet ; 213 ISSN 0031-4250s) Bibliography: p. 30-32. [BX7748.M9P42] 77-79824 ISBN 0-87574-213-0 : 0.95
1. Mysticism—Friends, Society of. I. Title.

Mysticism—Germany.

CLARK, James Midgley, 149'.3
1888-1961.
The great German mystics: Eckhart, Tauler, and Suso. Folcroft, Pa., Folcroft Press [1969] vii, 121 p. 25 cm. Reprint of the 1949 ed., which was issued as no. 5 of Modern language studies. Bibliography: p. 110-117. [BV5077.G3C58 1969] 72-193479
1. Eckhart, Meister, d. 1327. 2. Tauler, Johannes, 1300 (ca.)-1361. 3. Suso, Heinrich, 1300?-1366. 4. Mysticism—Germany. I. Title.

CLARK, James Midgley, 248.2'2
1888-1961.
The great German mystics, Eckhart, Tauler and Suso. New York, Russell & Russell [1970] 121 p. 22 cm. Reprint of the 1949

ed. Bibliography: p. 110-117. [BV5077.G3C58 1970] 73-81493
1. Eckhart, Meister, d. 1327. 2. Tauler, Johannes, 1300 (ca.)-1361. 3. Suso, Heinrich, 1300?-1366. 4. Mysticism—Germany. I. Title.

Mysticism—Great Britain

COLEMAN, Thomas William, 1884- 248.2'2'0922
English mystics of the fourteenth century, by T. W. Coleman. Westport, Conn., Greenwood Press [1971] 176 p. 23 cm. Reprint of the 1938 ed. Contents.Contents.—Christian mysticism.—The times of the English mystics.—The Ancren riwle.—Richard Rolle.—The Cloud of unknowing.—Walter Hilton.—The Lady Julian.—Margery Kemp. Includes bibliographical references. [BV5077.G7C6 1971] 74-109723 ISBN 0-8371-4213-X
1. Mysticism—Gt. Brit. I. Title.

COLLEDGE, Eric, ed. 248.22
The mediaeval mystics of England. [Elmer O'Brien general ed.] New York, Scribners [c.1961] 309p. Bibl. 61-6030 4.95 bds.,
1. Mysticism—Gt. Brit. 2. Mysticism—Middle Ages. I. Title.

HODGSON, Geraldine Emma, 1865-1937. 248'.22'0942
English mystics. [Folcroft, Pa.] Folcroft Library Editions, 1973. xi, 387 p. 24 cm. Reprint of the 1922 ed. published by A. R. Mowbray, London; Morehouse Pub. Co., Milwaukee, Wis. Bibliography: p. 380-382. [BV5077.G7H6 1973] 73-13663 ISBN 0-8414-4756-X (lib. bdg.)
1. Mysticism—Great Britain. I. Title.

INGE, William Ralph, 1860-1954. 248.2'2'0922
Studies of English mystics. Freeport, N.Y., Books for Libraries Press [1969] vi, 239 p. 23 cm. (Essay index reprint series.) (St. Margaret's lectures, 1905) Reprint of the 1906 ed. Contents.Contents.—On the psychology of mysticism.—The Ancren riwle and Julian of Norwich.—Walter Hylton.—William Law.—The mysticism of Wordsworth.—The mysticism of Robert Browning. [BV5077.G7I6 1969] 69-17578
1. Mysticism—Gt. Brit. 2. Mysticism in literature. I. Title. II. Series.

KNOWLES, David, 1896- 248.220942
The English mystical tradition. [1st ed.] New York, Harper [1961] 197p. 22cm. Includes bibliography. [BV5077.G7K58] 61-7343
1. Mysticism—Gt. Brit. I. Title.

KNOWLES, David [Michael Clive Knowles] 1896- 248.220942
The English mystical tradition. New York, Harper [c.1961] 197p. Bibl. 61-7343 3.75 bds.,
1. Mysticism—Gt. Brit. I. Title.

PEPLER, Conrad, 1908- 248
The English religious heritage. St. Louis, Herder [1958] 444p. 23cm. Originally published in The life of the spirit. [BV5077.G7P4] 58-3295
1. Mysticism—Gt. Brit. I. Title.

WALSH, James, 1920- ed. 248.220942
Pre-Reformation English spirituality New York, Fordham [1966] xiii, 287p. 23cm. Bibl. [BV5077.G7W3] 65-12885 5.75
1. Mysticism—Gt. Brit. 2. Religious literature, English—Hist. &crit. I. Title.

Mysticism—Hinduism.

MENEN, Aubrey. 294.5'42
The mystics. Photos. by Graham Hall. New York, Dial Press, 1974. 239 p. illus. 26 cm. Bibliography: p. 233. [BL1215.M9M46] 74-5258 ISBN 0-8037-6204-6
1. Mysticism—Hinduism. I. Title.

Mysticism—History.

BAILEY, Raymond. 248'.22'0924
Thomas Merton on mysticism / Raymond Bailey. Garden City, N.Y. : Doubleday, 1975. 239 p. ; 22 cm. Originally presented as the author's thesis, Southern Baptist Theological Seminary, Louisville. Includes bibliographical references. [BX4705.M542B28 1975] 75-22742 ISBN 0-385-07173-6 : 7.95
1. Merton, Thomas, 1915-1968. 2. Mysticism—History. I. Title.

BASTIDE, Roger. 149.3
The mystical life, by Roger Bastide; translated from the French by H. F. Kynaston-Snell and David Waring. New York, C. Scribner's sons, 1935. 2 p. l., 7-256 p. 19 cm. [BV5083.B32] 37-12806
1. Mysticism—Hist. 2. Mysticism—Psychology. 3. Psychology, Pathological. I. Kynaston-Snell, Harold F. tr. II. Waring, David, joint tr. III. Title. IV. Title: Translation of Los problemes de la vie mystique.

CHENEY, Sheldon, 1886-. 149.3
Men who have walked with God, being the story of mysticism through the ages told in the biographies of representative seers and saints, with excerpts from their writings and sayings, by Sheldon Cheney. New York, A. A. Knopf, 1945. xiv p., 1 l., 395, viii p., 1 l. plates. 22 cm. "First edition." [BL625.C5] 45-8427
1. Mysticism—Hist. I. Title.
Contents omitted.

FAIRWEATHER, William. 248.2'2'09
Among the mystics. Freeport, N.Y., Books for Libraries Press [1968] xvi, 145 p. 22 cm. (Essay index reprint series) Reprint of the 1936 ed. Bibliographical footnotes. [BV5075.F3 1968] 68-20298
1. Mysticism—History. I. Title.

GAUDREAU, Marie M. 248'.22'0924
Mysticism and image in St. John of the Cross / Marie M. Gaudreau. Bern : Herbert Lang, 1976. 256 p. ; 23 cm. (European university papers : Series 23, Theology ; v. 66) Bibliography: p. 231-256. [BV5075.G36] 77-467124 ISBN 3-261-01932-8 : 35.00F
1. Juan de la Cruz, Saint, 1542-1591. 2. Mysticism—History. 3. Image of God—History of doctrines. I. Title. II. Series: Europaische Hochschulschriften : Reihe 23, Theologie ; Bd. 66.

GODWIN, George Stanley, 1889- 149'.3
The great mystics, by George Godwin. [Folcroft, Pa.] Folcroft Library Editions, 1974. v, 106 p. 24 cm. Reprint of the 1945 ed. published by Watts, London, which was issued as no. 106 of The Thinker's library. Bibliography: p. 105. [BV5075.G6 1974] 74-2430 ISBN 0-8414-4499-4 (lib. bdg.)
1. Mysticism—History. I. Title.

GRAEF, Hilda C. 248.2209
The story of mysticism [by] Hilda Graef. [1st ed.] Garden City, N. Y., Doubleday, 1965. 286 p. 22 cm. Bibliography: p. [283]-286. [BV5075.G7] 65-19934
1. Mysticism—History. I. Title.

JONES, Rufus Matthew, 1863-1948. 248.2'2
Studies in mystical religion. New York, Russell & Russell [1970] xxxviii, 518 p. 23 cm. Reprint of the 1909 ed. [BV5075.J62 1970] 79-102509
1. Mysticism—History. I. Title.

KATSAROS, Thomas. 291.4'2
The Western mystical tradition; an intellectual history of Western civilization, by Thomas Katsaros and Nathaniel Kaplan. New Haven, College & University Press [1969- v. 21 cm. Includes bibliographical references. [BV5075.K33] 71-92544 7.50
1. Mysticism—History. I. Kaplan, Nathaniel, joint author. II. Title.

O'BRIEN, Elmer 291.14
Varieties of mystic experience, an anthology and interpretation. New York, New Amer. Lib. [1965, c.1964] 252p. 18cm. (Mentor-Omega bk. MT631) [BV5082.2025] .75 pap.,
1. Mysticism—Hist. 2. Mysticism—Collections. I. Title.

O'BRIEN, Elmer. 291.14
Varieties of mystic experience, an anthology and interpretation. [1st ed.] New York, Holt, Rinehart and Winston [1964] x, 321 p. 24 cm. [BV5082.2.O25] 64-21918
1. Mysticism—History. 2. Mysticism—Collections. I. Title.

SMITH, Margaret. 149.3
An introduction to the history of mysticism, by Margaret Smith... London, Society for promoting Christian knowledge; New York and Toronto, The Macmillan co. [1930] vi, 121, [1] p. 19 cm. Bibliography: p. 117-118. [BL625.S55] 30-30123
1. Mysticism—Hist. I. Title.

SMITH, Margaret, 1884- 297'.4
The way of the mystics : the early Christian mystics and the rise of the Sufis / Margaret Smith. London : Sheldon Press, 1976. xii, 276 p. ; 22 cm. Reprint of the 1931 ed. published under title: Studies in early mysticism in the Near and Middle East. Includes index. Bibliography: p. 258-263. [BV5075.S6 1976] 76-381586 ISBN 0-85969-072-5 : £2.95
1. Mysticism—History. 2. Sufism. 3. Christianity and other religions—Islam. 4. Islam—Relations—Christianity. I. Title.

STEINER, Rudolf, 1861-1925. 189.5
Mysticism at the dawn of the modern age. Tr. from German by Karl E. Zimmer. Introd., Paul M. Allen. Englewood, N. J., 25 Pershing Rd. Rudolf Steiner Publications, [c.1960] 253p. (His Major writings, v. 3) 60-15703 5.00
1. Mysticism—Hist. I. Title.

STEINER, Rudolf, 1861-1925. 189.5
Mysticism at the dawn of the modern age. Translated from the German by Karl E. Zimmer. Introductory comment by Paul M. Allen. [1st. ed.] Englewood, N.J., Rudolf Steiner Publications [1960] 253 p. 22 cm. (His Major writings, v. 3) Translation of Die Mystik im Aufgange des neu;eitilchen Geisteslebens und thr Verhilltnis zur modernen Weltanschauung. [BV5075.S813] 60-15703
1. Mysticism — Hist. I. Title.

UNDERHILL, Evelyn 248.2209
The mystics of the church. New York, Schocken [1964] 259p. 21cm. Bibl. 64-22607 5.00; 1.95 pap.,
1. Mysticism—Hist. I. Title.

WALSH, James, 1920, ed. 248
Spirituality through the centuries; ascetics and mystics of the Western Church. New York, Kenedy [1964] ix, 342p. 23cm. Bibl. [BV5075.W34] 64-21181 5.50
1. Mysticism—Hist. I. Title.

Mysticism—History—20th century.

NEWELL, William Lloyd. 291.4'2
Struggle and submission : R.C. Zaehner on mysticisms / by William Lloyd Newell ; foreword by Gregory Baum. Washington, D.C. : University Press of America, c1981. xvii, 383 p. ; 22 cm. Includes index. Bibliography: p. 321-343. [BL625.N4] 19 80-6295 ISBN 0-8191-1696-3 : 21.75 ISBN 0-8191-1697-1 (pbk.) : 12.75
1. Zaehner, R. C. (Robert Charles), 1913-1974. 2. Mysticism—History—20th century. I. Title.

Mysticism—History of doctrines.

THOMAS, Father, ed. 922.246
St. Teresa of Avila studies in her life, doctrine, and times. Ed. by Father Thomas, Father Gabriel, Westminster, Md., Newman [1964] 249p. plates, ports. 23cm. Bibl. 64-969 4.75
1. Teresa, Saint. 1515-1582. 2. Mysticism—History of doctrines. I. Gabriele di Santa Maria Maddalena, Father Gabriel, joint ed. II. Title.

THOMAS, Father, ed. 922.246
St. Teresa of Avila; studies in her life, doctrine, and times. Edited by Father Thomas and Father Gabriel. Westminster, Md., Newman Press [1963] 249 p. plates, ports. 23 cm. Includes bibliographical references. [BX4700.T4T5] 64-969
1. Teresa, Saint, 1515-1582. 2. Mysticism — History of doctrines. I. Gabriele di Santa Maria Maddelena, Father, joint ed. II. Title.

Mysticism in literature.

JONES, Rufus Matthew, 1863-1948. 821'.8
Mysticism in Robert Browning. New York, Macmillan, 1924. New York, Haskell House, 1971. 28 p. 23 cm. "Originally written for the Boston Browning Society and ... printed in the Biblical review for April 1923." [PR4242.R4J6 1971] 70-117596 ISBN 0-8383-1029-X
1. Browning, Robert, 1812-1889—Religion and ethics. 2. Mysticism in literature. I. Title.

MERRELL-WOLFF, Franklin. 133
Pathways through to space; a personal record of transformation in consciousness, by Franklin Merrell-Wolff. New York, R. R. Smith, 1944. xii p., 1 l., 288 p. 24 1/2 cm. [BF1999.M48] 44-36221
I. Title.

MEYER, Frederick Brotherton, 1847- 252.
The call and challenge of the unseen, by F. B. Meyer ... New York, Chicago [etc.] Fleming H. Revell company [c1928] 184 p. 20 cm. "Many ... of these addresses were delivered in various parts of the United States, during my recent tour."--Pref. [BX6333.M4C2] 28-31128
I. Title.

Mysticism — India.

DASGUPTA, Surendra Nath 149.30954
Hindu mysticism. [Six lectures] New York, F. Ungar Pub. Co. [1959] xx, 168p. Includes bibliography. 21cm. (Atlantic paperbacks 501) 58-11626 1.25 pap.,
1. Mysticism—India. I. Title.

MUKERJEE, Radhakamal, 1889- 149.3
The theory and art of mysticism. With a foreword by William Ernest Hocking. [1st Indian ed.] Bombay, New York, Asia Pub. House [1960] xix, 352 p. 23 cm. [BL2015.M9M8 1960] SA 65
1. Mysticism — India. 2. Mysticism — Comparative studies. I. Title.

MUKERJEE, Radhakamal, 1889- 149.3
Theory and art of mysticism, by Radhakamal Mukerjee ... with a foreword by William Ernest Hocking ... London, New York [etc.] Longmans, Green and co., [1937] xvi, 308 p. 26 cm. "First published 1937." [BL2015.M9M8] 38-9015
1. Mysticism—India. 2. Mysticism. I. Title.

ZAEHNER, Robert Charles 291.14
Hindu and Muslim mysticism. [dist. New York, Oxford Univ. Press, c.]1960[ ] 234p. (Jordan lectures in comparative religion, 5) Bibl. 61-1206 4.80
1. Mysticism—India. 2. Mysticism—Mohammedanism. I. Title.

ZAEHNER, Robert Charles. 294.5'42
Hindu and Muslim mysticism [by] R. C. Zaehner. New York, Schocken Books [1969, c1960] viii, 234 p. 21 cm. "Consists of eight lectures delivered (in a slightly abridged form) in May 1959 at the School of Oriental and African Studies in the University of London." Bibliographical footnotes. [BL2015.M9Z3 1969] 74-83675 2.45
1. Mysticism—India. 2. Mysticism—Islam. I. Title.

Mysticism—India—Collected works.

DE LAURENCE, Lauron William, 1868-
The mystic test book of " The Hindu occult chambers"; The magic and occultism of India; Hindu and Egyptian crystal gazing; The Hindu magic mirror. By Dr. L. W. de Laurence ... Chicago, Ill., De Laurence, Scott & company [1909] 3 p. l., 177 p. front. (ports.) illus., 2 pl. (1 col.) 20 cm. 9-16947
I. Title.

DIXON, James Qallan, 1851-
... Mystic spirit voice of the Hindoo "Senam," mysterious, facinating, by James Qallan Dixon, author and compiler. Buffalo, N. Y., Sovereign publishing co., c1916. cover-title, 57 p. 22 cm. Prose and verse. [PS1543.D36M8 1916] 16-6164 0.25
I. Title.

MASSON, Jeffrey Moussaleff, 1941- 294.5'01'9
The oceanic feeling : the origins of religious sentiment in ancient India / by J. Moussaieff Masson. Dordrecht, Holland ; Boston : D. Reidel Pub. Co. ; Hingham, MA : distributed in the U.S.A. and Canada by Kluwer Boston, inc., c1980. xv, 213 p. ; 23 cm. (SC1 ; 3) Includes index. Bibliography: p. 143-207. [BL2015.M9M36] 80-11682 34.00
1. Mysticism—India—Collected works. 2. Mysticism—Hinduism—Collected works. 3. Psychoanalysis and religion—Collected works. 4. Psychology, Religious—Collected works. 5. Mysticism—Psychology—Collected works. I. Title. II. Series: Studies of classical India ; v. 3.

Mysticism—Judaism.

ABELSON, Joshua, 1873-1940. 296.7'1
Jewish Mysticism; an introduction to the Kabbalah. New York, Hermon Press [1969] ix, 182 p. 20 cm. Reprint of the 1913 ed. Bibliography: p. [176]-178. [BM723.A4 1969] 68-9535 4.95
1. Mysticism—Judaism. 2. Cabala. I. Title.

ALTMANN, Alexander, 1906- 910'.03'924 s
Leo Baeck and the Jewish mystical tradition. [New York, Leo Baeck Institute, 1973] 28 p. 23 cm. (Leo Baeck memorial lecture 17) Includes bibliographical references. [DS135.G3A263 no. 17] [BM755] 296.6'1 B 73-93000
1. Baeck, Leo, 1873-1956. 2. Mysticism—Judaism. I. Title. II. Series.

BEN Zion, Raphael, tr. 296
The way of the faithful; an anthology of Jewish mysticism, translated from the Hebrew by Raphael Ben Zion. Los Angeles, Calif. [Printed by Haynes corporation] 5605-1945. xiii, 233 p. 20 1/2 cm. [BM723.B4] 45-20014
1. Mysticism—Judaism. I. Title.
Contents omitted.

BUBER, Martin 181.3
I and Thou. With a postscript by the author added. Translated [from the German] by Ronald Gregor Smith. 2d ed. New York, Scribner [c.1958] xii, 137p. (bibl. footnotes) 21cm. (Scribner lib. SL15) 1.25 pap.,
1. Mysticism—Judaism. 2. Ontology. 3. God (Theory of Knowledge) I. Title.

BUBER, Martin, 1878-1965. 181.3
I and Thou. With a postscript by the author added. Translated by Ronald Gregor Smith. 2d ed. New York, Scribner [1958] 137 p. 20 cm. [BM723.B753 1958] 58-12686
1. Mysticism—Judaism. 2. Ontology. 3. God knowableness. I. Title.

NEHER, André. 224'.06
The prophetic existence. Translated from the French by William Wolf. South Brunswick [N.J.] A. S. Barnes [1969] 355 p. 22 cm. Translation of L'essence du prophetisme. Includes bibliographical references. [BS1198.N413] 68-27259 10.00
1. Bible. O.T. Prophets—Theology. 2. Mysticism—Judaism. I. Title.

POSY, Arnold, 1893- 296.8'33
Mystic trends in Judaism. New York, J. David [1966] 213 p. 23 cm. [BM723.P65] 66-21592
1. Mysticism—Judaism. 2. Jewish sects. I. Title.

SCHOLEM, Gershom Gerhard, 1897- 296.833
Major trends in Jewish mysticism [3d rev. ed.] New York, Schocken Books [1961, c.1946, 1954] 460p. illus. (Schocken paperbacks, SB5) Bibl. 61-8991 2.25 pap.,
1. Mysticism—Judaism. I. Title.

SCHOLEM, Gershom Gerhard, 1897- 296
Major trends in Jewish mysticism. Based on the Hilda Stroock lectures delivered at the Jewish Institute of Religion, New York, 3d rev. ed. New York, Schocken Books [1954] 456p. 24cm. [BM723.S35 1954] 55-1150
1. Mysticism—Judaism. I. Title.

SCHOLEM, Gershom Gerhard, 1897- 296.833
Major trends in Jewish mysticism. New York, Schocken Books [1961, c1954] 460 p. illus. 21 cm. (Schocken paperbacks, SB5) "Reprinted from the third revised edition." Includes bibliography. [BM723.S35 1961] 61-8991
1. Mysticism—Judaism. I. Title.

SCHOLEM, Gershom Gerhard, 1897-
Major trends in Jewish mysticism. [Rev. ed.] New York, Schocken Books [c1946] xiv, 454 p. 24 cm. (The Hilda Strook [?] lectures, 1938, delivered at the Jewish Institute of Religion, New York) An enl. version of nine lectures, tr. in part by George Lichthelm, seven of which were delivered at the Jewish Institute of Religion, two on other occasions. Bibliography: p. [425]-438. A 49
1. Mysticism—Judaism. I. Lichthelm, George, tr. II. Title. III. Series: Jewish Institute of Religion, New York. The Hilda Stich Stroock lectures, 1938

WEINER, Herbert, 1919- 135.4
9 1/2 mystics; the Kabbala today. [1st ed. New York, Holt, Rinehart and Winston [1969] ix, 310 p. 22 cm. [BM723.W37 1969] 67-12906 6.95
1. Mysticism—Judaism. 2. Judaism—20th century. I. Title.

Mysticism—Judaism—Addresses, essays, lectures.

MYSTICS and medics : 296.7'1
a comparison of mystical and psychotherapeutic encounters / edited by Reuven P. Bulka. New York, NY : Human Sciences Press, c1979. 120 p. ; 23 cm. "This book is a revised and expanded version of Mystics and medics, a special issue of the Journal of psychology and Judaism. In altered form, it gathers essays which appeared originally in that and other issues of the Journal." Includes bibliographies. [BM723.M97] 79-87593 ISBN 0-87705-377-4 : 4.95
1. Mysticism—Judaism—Addresses, essays, lectures. 2. Psychotherapy—Addresses, essays, lectures. I. Bulka, Reuven P. II. Journal of psychology and Judaism.

Mysticism—Judaism—Historiography.

BIALE, David, 1949- 296.7'1 B
Gershom Scholem : Kabbalah and counter-history / David Biale. 2nd ed. Cambridge, Mass. : Harvard University Press, 1982. p. cm. Includes index. Bibliography: p. [BM755.S295B5 1982] 19 82-9295 ISBN 0-674-36332-9 pbk. : 7.95
1. Scholem, Gershom Gerhard, 1897- 2. Mysticism—Judaism—Historiography. 3. Scholars, Jewish—Germany—Biography. 4. Scholars, Jewish—Israel—Biography. I. Title.

Mysticism—Judaism—History—Sources.

BOKSER, Ben Zion, 1907- 296.7'1
The Jewish mystical tradition / Ben Zion Bokser. New York : Pilgrim Press, c1981. 277 p. ; 24 cm. Bibliography: p. 275-277. [BM723.J485] 19 80-27627 ISBN 0-8298-0435-8 : 14.95 ISBN 0-8298-0451-X ISBN pbk. : 9.95
1. Mysticism—Judaism—History—Sources. 2. Cabala—History—Sources. 3. Hasidism—History—Sources. I. Title.

JEWISH mystical testimonies 296.7'1
/ [edited by] Louis Jacobs. New York : Schocken Books, 1977, c1976. ix, 270 p. ; 21 cm. Bibliography: 261-264. [BM723.J48 1977] 76-46644 ISBN 0-8052-3641-4 : 14.95
1. Mysticism—Judaism—History—Sources. I. Jacobs, Louis.
Contents omitted

Mysticism—Juvenile literature.

NORDBERG, Robert B. 291.4'2
The teenager and the new mysticism [by] Robert B. Nordberg. [1st ed.] New York, R. Rosen Press [1973] xii, 126 p. port. 22 cm. Includes bibliographies. Discusses the many different methods, old and new, currently being used by those in search of mystical experience. [BL625.N67] 72-92837 ISBN 0-8239-0278-1 3.99
1. Mysticism—Juvenile literature. 2. [Mysticism.] I. Title.

Mysticism - Middle Ages, 600-1500.

ANGELA, of Foligno, 1248?-1309. 242'.1
The book of divine consolation of the Blessed Angela of Foligno. Translated from the Italian by Mary G. Steegmann. Introd. by Algar Thorold. New York, Cooper Square Publishers, 1966. xliv, 265 p. illus., facsims. 17 cm. (The Medieval library) Translation of Liber de vera fidelium experientia. [BV5080.A52 1966] 66-30731
1. Mysticism—Middle Ages. I. Steegmann, Mary G., tr. II. Thorold, Algar Labouchere, 1866-1936. III. Title.

CATERINA da Siena, Saint, 1347-1380. 248.2'2
The dialogue / Catherine of Siena ; translation and introd. by Suzanne Noffke ; pref. by Giuliana Cavallini. New York : Paulist Press, c1980. xvi, 398 p. ; 23 cm. (The Classics of Western spirituality) Translation of Libro della divina dottrina. [BV5080.C2613 1980] 79-56755 ISBN 0-8091-2233-2 (pbk.) : 7.95
1. Mysticism—Middle Ages, 600-1500. I. Noffke, Suzanne. II. Series: Classics of Western spirituality.

CATERINA Da Siena, Saint 1347-1380. 242
The orcherd of Syon; edited from the early manuscripts of Phyllis Hodgson and Gabriel M. Liegey. London, New York [etc.] Published for the Early English Text Society by the Oxford U. P., 1966- v. front. (facsims.) 22 1/2 cm. (Early English Text Society. [Publications. Original series] no. 258) v. 1:84/ (v. 1:B 66-19173) "The orcherd is an early fifteenth-century translation of the work perhaps now best known as The dialogue of St. Catherine of Siena." Contents.CONTENTS. -- v. 1. Text. [PR1119.A2 no. 258] 67-74981
1. Mysticism — Middle Ages. I. Hodgson, Phyllis, ed. II. Liegey, Gabriel Michael, 1904- ed. III. Title.

CLOUD of unknowing. 149.3
The cloud of unknowing; a new translation of a classic guide to spiritual experience revealing the dynamics of the inner life from a particular historical and religious point of view. Introductory commentary and translation by Ira Progoff. New York, Julian Press, 1957. 243p. 22cm. [BV5080.C53 1957] 58-1038
1. Mysticism— Middle ages. I. Progoff, Ira. ed. and tr. II. Title.

CLOUD of unknowing 149.3
The cloud of unknowing. Tr. into modern English with an introd. by Clifton Wolters. Baltimore, Penguin [1967] 143p. 18cm. (Penguin classic L108) [BV5080.C53 1961] 61-3501 1.25 pap.,
1. Mysticism—Middle Ages. I. Wolters, Clifton. ed. and tr. II. Title.

CLOUD of unknowing. 149.3
The cloud of unknowing; a new translation of a classical guide to spiritual experience revealing the dynamics of the inner life from a particular historical and religious point of view. Introductory commentary and translation by Ira Progoff [New York] [Dell] [1973, c.1957] 143 p. 20 cm. (Delta book) [BV5080.C53 1957] pap., 2.45
1. Mysticism—Middle Ages. I. Progoff, Ira, ed. and tr. II. Title.

CLOUD of unknowing. 149.3
The cloud of unknowing; a version in modern English of a fourteenth century classic. [1st ed.] New York, Pub. in assn. with Pendle Hill by Harper [1948] xxvii. 146 p. 14 cm. [BV5080.C52] 48-5987
1. Mysticism—Middle ages. I. Title.

CLOUD of unknowing. 149.3
The cloud of unknowing and the Book of privy counselling, edited from the manuscripts with introduction, notes and glossary by Phyllis Hodgson ... London, Pub. for the Early English text society by H. Milford, Oxford university press, 1944. lxxxvi p., 1 l., 227, [1] p. front. (facsim.) 22 1/2 cm. (Half-title: Early English text society. Original series no. 218. 1944 (for 1943)) "A shortened form of two dissertations [by Phyllis Hodgson] originally presented to the University of Oxford in supplication for the degrees of bachelor of letters and doctor of philosophy."--Pref. Bibliography: p. [lxxxvii] [PR1119.A2 no. 218] (820.82) 45-8154
1. Mysticism—Middle ages. I. Hodgson, Phyllis, ed. II. Title. III. Title: Book of privy counselling.

THE cloud of unknowing, and other treatises, 248
by an English mystic of the fourteenth century; with a commentary on the Cloud by Father Augustine Baker;edited by Justin McCann. [6th and rev. ed.] Westminster, Md., Newman Press [1952] xxix, 220p. 20cm. (The Orchard books) [BV5080.C5 1952] [BV5080.C5 1952] 149.3 52-14308 52-14308
1. Mysticism—Middle Ages. I. Cloud of unknowing. II. Baker, Augustine, Father, 1575-1641. III. McCann, Justin, 1882- ed. IV. Dionysius Areopagita. De mystica theologia. V. Title: A book of contemplation. VI. Series.
Contents omitted.

CLOUD of unknowing, (The) 149.3
Tr. into modern English with an introd. by Clifton Wolters. Penguin [dist. New York, Atheneum, c.1961] 143p. (Penguin classics, L108) Bibl. 61-3501 .95 pap.,
1. Mysticism—Middle Ages. I. Wolters, Clifton, ed. and tr.

CLOUD of unknowing. 248'.22
The Cloud of unknowing, and other works / translated [from Middle English] into modern English with an introduction by Clifton Wolters. Harmondsworth ; New York : Penguin, 1978. 232 p. ; 18 cm. (Penguin classics) Contents.Contents.—The cloud of unknowing.—The epistle of privy counsel.—Dionysius' mystical teaching.—The epistle of prayer. Bibliography: p. 30-[34] [BV5080.C5 1978] 79-305465 ISBN 0-14-044385-1 pbk. : 2.95
1. Mysticism—Middle Ages, 600-1500. I. Wolters, Clifton. II. Dionysius Areopagita, Pseudo-. De mystica theologia. English. 1978.

CLOUD of unknowing. 149'.3
The cloud of unknowing and The book of privy counseling. Newly edited, with an introd., by William Johnston. [1st ed.] Garden City, N.Y., Image Books [1973] 195 p. 18 cm. (An Image book original) Text based on the 1944 ed., edited by P. Hodgson. [BV5080.C53 1973] 73-79737 ISBN 0-385-03097-5 1.45
1. Mysticism—Middle Ages, 600-1500. I. Johnston, William, 1925- ed. II. The book of privy counseling. 1973.

DOBBINS, Dunstan John. 282.
... *Franciscan mysticism,* a critical examination of the mystical theology of the seraphic doctor, with special reference to the sources of his doctrines (Essay crowned by Oxford university) by Dunstan Dobbins ... New York. J. F. Wagner [1927] 207 p. front. (port.) 23 cm. (Franciscan studies no. 6. September, 1927) Bibliography: p. [203]-207. [BX3601.F7 no. 6] 29-4160
1. Mysticism—Middle ages. 2. Bonaventura, Saint, cardinal, 1221-1274. I. Title.

ECKHART, Meister, d.1327. 189'.5
Meister Eckhart; a modern translation, by Raymond Bernard Blakney. New York, Harper & Row [1969? c1941] xxviii, 338 p. 21 cm. (Harper torchbooks. The Cloister library, TB-8) Bibliography: p. 306-307. [BV5080] 78-8467 2.95
1. Mysticism—Middle Ages, 600-1500. I. Blakney, Raymond Bernard, ed.

ECKHART, meister, d.1327. 149.3
Meister Eckhart, a modern translation, by Raymond Bernard Blakney. New York and London, Harper & brothers, [c1941] xxviii, 333 p. 21 cm. "First edition." [BV5080.E45E4] 41-25506
1. Mysticism—Middle ages. I. Blakney, Raymond Bernard, ed. and tr. II. Title.

ECKHART, Meister, d. 1327. 248
Meister Eckehart speaks; a collection of the teachings of the famous German mystic, with an introd. by Otto Karrer.

Translated from the German by Elizabeth Strakosch. New York, Philosophical Library [1957] 72p. 19cm. [BV5080.E45E57] 57-14137
1. Mysticism—Middle Ages. I. Title.

ECKHART, Meister, d. 1327 189.5
Treatises and sermons. Selected, tr. from Latin & German with introd., notes by James M. Clark, John V. Skinner. London, Faber & Faber [Mystic, Conn., Verry, 1966, c.1958] 267p. 21cm. (Classics of the contemplative life) First pub. in 1957 under title: Meister Eckhart, an introduction to the study of his works, with an anthology of his sermons. ,bb anthology of his sermons. Bibl. [BV5080.E45E43]
1. Eckhart, Meister, d. 1327. 2. Mysticism — Middle Ages. I. Clark, James Midgley, 1888- ed. and tr. II. Skinner, John Vass, ed. and tr. III. Title.

GERTRUDE, Saint, surnamed the Great, 1256-1302? 149.3
Exercises. Introd., commentary, and translation by a Benedictine nun of Regina Laudis. Westminster, Md., Newman Press, 1956. 191p. 23cm. [BV5080.G433] 56-8469
1. Mysticism—Middle Ages. I. Title.

GILSON, Etienne Henry, 1884- 922.244
The mystical theology of Saint Bernard, by Etienne Gilson ... translated by A. H. C. Downes. New York, Sheed & Ward, 1940. ix, [1], 226 p. front. 22 cm. "Printed in Great Britian." Lectures delivered in 1933 at University college of Wales, Aberystwith. cf. Pref. "Around St. Bernard, men and movements" (p. [153]-214): Curiositas. Abelard. Berenger the scholastic. St. Bernard and courtly love. Notes on William of Saint-Thierry. Bibliography: p. 252-258. [BX4700.B5G53] 40-10261
1. Bernard de Clairvaux, Saint, 1091?-1153. 2. Mysticism—Middle ages. 3. Courtly love. 4. Aballard, Pierre, 1079-1142. 5. Berenger, Pierre, 12th cent. 6. Guilaume de Saint-Thierry, 1085 (ca.)-1148. I. Downes, Alfred Howard Campbell, 1882- tr. II. Title.

JAN VAN RUYSBROECK, 1293-1381. 248
The spiritual espousals. Translated from the Dutch with an introd. by Eric Colledge. New York, Harper [1953] 195p. 21cm. (Classics of the contemplative life) [BV5080.J5273 1953] 149.3 53-1009
1. Mysticism—Middle Ages. I. Title.

JOHNSTON, William, 1925- 248.2'2
The mysticism of the Cloud of unknowing; a modern interpretation. With a foreword by Thomas Merton. New York, Desclee Co. [1967] xvi, 285 p. 22 cm. Bibliography: p. [257]-280. [BV5080.C6J6] 67-17678 5.50
1. Cloud of unknowing. 2. Mysticism—Middle Ages, 600-1500. I. Title.

MECHTHILD, of Magdeburg(ca 1212-ca. 1282. 248.2'2
The revelations of Mechthild of Magdeburg (1210-1297); or, The flowing light of the Godhead. Translated from the manuscript in the library of the Monastery of Einsiedeln by Lucy Menzies. London, New York, Longmans, Green [1953] xxxvii, 263p. 22cm. Bibliography: p. xxxv-xxxvii. [BV5080.M] A54
1. Mysticism—Middle Ages. I. Title. II. Title: The flowing light of the Godhead.

MEDIAEVAL mystical tradition and Saint John of the Cross, by a Benedictine of Stanbrook Abbey. Westminster, Md., Newman Press, 1954. 161p. 22cm. [BV5075.M4 1954a] 54-12580 248-22
1. Juan de la Crus, Saint, 1542-1591. 2. Mysticism—Middle Ages. I. A Benedictine of Stanbrook Abbey.

MERSWIN, Rulman, 1307-1382. 248.2
Mystical writings. Edited and interpreted by Thomas S. Kepler. Philadelphia, Westminster Press [1960] 143p. 21cm. Contains a translation of the author's Vier anfangende Jahre (The four beginning years) and Das Buch von den neun Felsen (The book of the nine rocks) Bibliography: p.35-36. [BV5080.M46] 60-5053
1. Mysticism—Middle Ages. I. Merswin, Rulman, 1307-1382. Vier anfangende Jahre. II. Merswin, Rulman, 1307-1382. Das Buch von den neun Felsen. III. Kepler, Thomas Samuel, 1897- ed. and tr. IV. Title.

MOMMAERS, Paul, 1935- 248'.22'0924
The land within : the process of possessing and being possessed by God according to the mystic Jan van Ruysbroeck / by Paul Mommaers ; translated by David N. Smith. Chicago : Franciscan Herald Press, c1975. vii, 143 p. ; 21 cm. p. cm. Translation of Waar naartoe is nu de gloed van de liefde? Includes bibliographical references. [BV5095.J3M6513] 75-19472 ISBN 0-8199-0583-6 : 6.95
1. Jan van Ruysbroeck, 1293-1381. 2. Mysticism—Middle Ages, 600-1500. I. Title.

NICHOLAUS Cusanus, cardinal, 1401-1464. 149.
... The vision of God; translated by Emma Gurney Salter, with an introduction by Evelyn Underhill. London [etc.] J. M. Dent & sons, ltd.; New York, E. P. Dutton & co. [1928] xxx, 130 p. 18 1/2 cm. At head of title: Nicholas of Cusa. [Name originally: Nicolaus Krebs (Khrypffs, Chrypffs) of Cues or Cusa] [BV5080.N5] 29-4654
1. Mysticism—Middle ages. I. Gurney-Salter, Emma, 1875- tr. II. Title.

NICOLAS, Cusanus [Name originally: Nicolas Krebs (Khrypffs, Chrypffs) of Cues of Cusa.] Cardinal [Name originally: Nicolaus Krebs (Khrypffs, Chrypffs) of Cues or Cusa.] 248.22
The vision of God; with an introd. by Evelyn Underhill. [Translated from the Latin by Emma Gurney Salter] New York, Unger Pub. Co. [1960] xxx, 130p. 18cm. (Atlantic Paperbacks 503) 60-9104 1.25 pap.,
1. Mysticism—Middle Ages. I. Title.

PETRY, Ray C., 1903- ed. 248
Late medieval mysticism. Philadelphia, Westminister Press [1957] 424 p. 24 cm. (The Library of Christian classics, v. 13) [BV5072.P4] 149.3 57-5092
1. Mysticism—Middle ages. I. Title.

PROGOFF, Ira, ed. and tr. 149.3
The cloud of unknowing; a new translation of a classic guide to spiritual experience revealing the dynamics of the inner life from a particular historical and religious point of view. Introductory commentary and translation by Ira Progoff. New York, Julian Press, 1957. 243 p. 22 cm. [BV5080.C53 1957] 58-1038
1. Mysticism—Middle Ages. I. Cloud of unknowing.

ROLLE, Richard, of Hampole, 1290?-1349. 248.2
The Contra amatores mundi of Richard Rolle of Hampole. Edited, with introd. and translation, by Paul F. Theiner. Berkeley, University of California Press, 1968. viii, 196 p. 24 cm. (University of California publications. English studies, 33) "This edition follows the text as given in MS. 18932 of the John Rylands Library in Manchester (M)."—p. 61. Based on the editor's thesis, Harvard University, 1962. "Textual notes": p. 113-144. Bibliography: p. 63-64. [BV5039.L3R57 1968] 68-64641
1. Mysticism—Middle Ages, 600-1500. 2. Asceticism—Middle Ages, 600-1500. I. Theiner, Paul F., ed. II. Title. III. Series: California. University. University of California publications. English studies, 33

SUSO, Heinrich, 1300?-1336. 248.2'2
The exemplar; life and writings of Blessed Henry Suso, O.P. Complete ed. based on mss., with a critical introd. and explanatory notes by Nicholas Heller. Translated from the German by Ann Edward. Dubuque, Iowa, Priory Press [1962] 2 v. illus. 22 cm. Issued in a case. Translation of Des Mystikers Heinrich Seuse, O.P.R., deutsche Schriften. Bibliographical footnotes. [BV5080.S913 1962] 62-14456
1. Mysticism—Middle Ages. I. Heller, Nikolaus, ed. II. Title.

SUSO, Heinrich, 1300-1366. 180
Little book of eternal wisdom and Little book of truth. Translated with an introd. and notes by James M. Clark. New York, Harper [1953] 212p. 21cm. (Classics of the contemplative life) [BV5080.S818 1953] 149.3 53-11224
1. Mysticism—Middle Ages. I. Suso, Heinrich, 1300-1366. Little book of truth. II. Title. III. Title: Little book of truth.

TAULER, Johannes, 1300(ca.)-1361.Spuriousanddoubtfulworks. 149.3
The book of the poor in spirit, by a Friend of God (fourteenth century) A guide to Rhineland mysticism; edited, translated, and with an introd. by C. F. Kelley. New York, Harper [1954] xv, 288p. 22cm. First published in 1621 under title: Nachfolgung des armen Lebens Christi. Bibliographical references included in 'Notes' (p. 271-287) and 'Addenda' (p. 287-288) [BV5080.T42] 55-108
1. Mysticism—Middle Ages. I. Kelley, Carl Franklin, 1914- ed. and tr. II. Title.

TAULER, Johannes, ca., 1300-1361. 149.
The sermons and conferences of John Tauler, of the Order of preachers, surnamed "the illuminated doctor"; being his spiritual doctrine. First complete English translation, with introduction and index, by Very Rev. Walter Elliott ... Brookland Station, Washington, D.C. Apostolic mission house, 1910. 13 p. l., [3] -780, [6] p. 23 1/2 cm. [BV5080.T25 1910] 11-1071
1. Mysticism—Middle ages. I. Elliott, Walter, 1843-1936, tr. II. Title.

Mysticism—Middle Ages, 600-1500—Collected works.

ECKHART, Meister, d.1327. 230'.2
Breakthrough, Meister Eckhart's creation spirituality, in new translation / introd. and commentaries by Matthew Fox. Garden City, N.Y. : Image Books, 1980. p. cm. Includes bibliographical references and indexes. [BV5080.E3213 1980b] 80-18900 ISBN 0-385-17034-3 (pbk.) : 14.95
1. Mysticism—Middle Ages, 600-1500—Collected works. 2. Mysticism—Germany—Collected works. I. Fox, Matthew, 1940- II. Title.

ECKHART, Meister, d.1327. 230'.2
Breakthrough, Meister Eckhart's creation spirituality, in new translation / introd. and commentaries by Matthew Fox. Garden City, N.Y. : Doubleday, 1980. p. cm. Includes bibliographical references and indexes. [BV5080.E3213 1980] 19 80-909 ISBN 0-385-17045-9 : 14.95
1. Mysticism—Middle Ages, 600-1500—Collected works. 2. Mysticism—Germany—Collected works. I. Fox, Matthew, 1940- II. Title.

Mysticism - Mohammedanism

ARCHER, John Clark 1881- 297
...Mystical elements in Mohammed, by John Clark Archer. New Haven, Yale University press; [etc., etc.] (1924) 86 p. 1 l. 26 cm. (Yale oriental series. Researches, vol. xi. pt. 1) The author's doctoral dissertation, Yale university, 1932, but not published as a thesis. [BP75.A7] 24-
1. Muhammad, the prophet. 2. Mysticism—Mohammodanism. I. Title.

*NICHOLSON, Reynold A. 297.4
The mystics of Islam. London, Routledge & Kegan Paul [Chester Springs, Pa., Dufour, 1965] vi, 178p. 20cm. Bibl. 3.50 bds.,
I. Title.

Mysticism—Orthodox Eastern Church.

GREGERSON, Jon 248.2
The transfigured cosmos; four essays in Eastern Orthodox Christianity. New York. Ungar [c.1960] 111p. 21cm. (bibl. notes: p. 99-107, footnotes) illus. 59-9153 3.50
1. Mysticism—Orthodox Eastern Church. 2. Hesychasm. I. Title.

†LOSSKY, Vladimir, 1903-1958. 230'.1'9
The mystical theology of the Eastern Church / by Vladimir Lossky ; [translated from the French by members of the Fellowship of St. Alban and St. Sergius]. Crestwood, N.Y. : St. Vladimir's Seminary Press, 1976, c1957. p. cm. Translation of Essai sur la theologie mystique de l'Eglise d'Orient. Reprint of the ed. published by J. Clarke, London. Includes bibliographical references. [BV5082.2.L6713 1976] 76-25448 ISBN 0-913836-31-1 pbk. : 5.95
1. Mysticism—Orthodox Eastern Church. I. Title.

Mysticism—Psychological aspects.

DEIKMAN, Arthur. 150
The observing self : mysticism and psychotherapy / Arthur J. Deikman. Boston, Mass. : Beacon Press, c1982. xiii, 194 p. ; 21 cm. Includes bibliographical references. [BL625.D39 1982] 19 81-70486 ISBN 0-8070-2950-5 : 12.50
1. Mysticism—Psychological aspects. 2. Psychotherapy. I. Title.

Mysticism—Psychology.

BASTIDE, Roger, 1898- 149.3
The mystical life, by Roger Bastide; translated from the French by H. F. Kynaston-Snell and David Waring. New York C. Scribner's sons, 1935. 2p. 1, 7-256 p. 19 cm. Translation of Les problemes de la vie mystique. [BV5083.B32] 37-12806
1. Mysticism—Psychology. 2. Psychology, Pathological. I. Kynaston-Snell, Harold F., tr II. Waring, David, joint tr. III. Title.

LEUBA, James Henry, 1868- 201
The psychology of religious mysticism, by James H. Leuba ... London, K. Paul, Trench, Trubner & co., ltd. New York, Harcourt, Brace & company, inc., 1925. xii, 336 p. 22 1/2 cm. (Half-title: International library of psychology, philosophy and scientific method) [BV5083.L4] 25-5217
1. Mysticism—Psychology. 2. Psychology, Religious. I. Title.

LEUBA, James Henry, 1868-1946. 248'.22'019
The psychology of religious mysticism. Revised ed. London, Boston, Routledge and K. Paul, 1972. xii, 336 p. 22 cm. (International library of psychology, philosophy and scientific method) Reprint of revised ed., London, K. Paul, 1929. Includes bibliographical references. [BV5083.L4 1972] 73-159944 ISBN 0-7100-7317-8 4.00
1. Mysticism—Psychology. 2. Psychology, Religious. I. Title. II. Series.

MALLORY, Marilyn May. 248'.22
Christian mysticism : transcending techniques : a theological reflection on the empirical testing of the teaching of St. John of the Cross / Marilyn May Mallory. Assen : Van Gorcum, 1978. xix, 300 p. ; 23 cm. Includes index. Bibliography: p. 284-291. [BV5083.M275] 78-311564 ISBN 9-02-321535-4 pbk.: 28.00
1. Juan de la Cruz, Saint, 1542-1591. 2. Mysticism—Psychology. 3. Asceticism. 4. Contemplation. 5. Experience (Religion) 6. Body, Human (in religion, folk-lore, etc.) I. Title.
Distributed by Humanities Press, Atlantic Highlands, NJ

MARECHAL, Joseph, 1878-1944 291.4
Studies in the psychology of the mystics. Tr. [from French] introductory foreword, by Algar Thorold. Albany, Magi Bks., 33 Buckingham Dr. [1965] v, 344p. 21cm. First pub. in Eng. by Burns, Oates and Washbourne, 1927. Bibl. [BL625.M3] 65-1694 3.75 pap.,
1. Mysticism—Psychology. 2. Psychology, Religious. I. Title.

Mysticism—Quaker authors.

KING, Rachel Hadley, 1904- 922.86
George Fox and the light within, 1650-1660, by Rachel Hadley King... Philadelphia, Friends book store, 1940. 177 p. 21 cm. "Presented in partial fulfillment of the requirements for the PH.D. degree at Yale university [1937]"--Pref. "Published by grant of Philadelphia monthly meeting from the Rebecca White fund." Bibliography: p. 173-177. [BX7795.F7K47 1937] 40-34633
1. Fox, George, 1624-1691. 2. Mysticism—Quaker authors. I. Title.

Mysticism—Russia.

FEDOTOV, Georgii 248.2'2'0947
Petrovich, 1886-1951, ed.
A treasury of Russian spirituality. Compiled and edited by G. P. Fedotov. Gloucester, Mass., P. Smith, 1969. xviii, 12-501 p. illus., ports. 21 cm. Reprint of the 1950 ed. Bibliography: p. 500-501. [BV5077.R8F4 1969] 76-11004 6.50
1. Mysticism—Russia. 2. Mysticism—Orthodox Eastern Church. I. Title.

FEDOTOV, Georgil 281.947
Petrovich, 1886- ed.
A treasury of Russian spirituality. New York, Sheed & Ward, 1948. xvi, 501 p. illus., ports. 23 cm. "A short bibliography of Russian spirituality": p. 500-501. [BV5077.R8F4] 48-4585
1. Mysticism—Russia. 2. Mysticism—Orthodox Eastern Church. I. Title.

Mysticism—Russia—History.

BOLSHAKOFF, Serge. 248'.22'0922 B
Russian mystics / by Sergius Bolshakoff ; introd. by Thomas Merton. Kalamazoo, Mich. : Cistercian Publications, 1977, c1976. xxx, 303 p. ; 23 cm. (Cistercian studies series ; no. 26) Italian translation has title: I mistici russi. Bibliography: p. 285-303. [BV5077.R8B6413] 76-15485 ISBN 0-87907-826-X : 13.95 ISBN 0-87907-926-6 pbk. : 5.50
1. Mysticism—Russia—History. 2. Mysticism—Orthodox Eastern Church, Russian—History. 3. Monasticism and religious orders—Russia—History. I. Title. II. Series.

Mysticism—Spain.

CUGNO, Alain, 1942- 248.2'2'0924
Saint John of the Cross : reflections on mystical experience / Alain Cugno ; translated by Barbara Wall. New York : Seabury Press, 1982. 153 p. ; 22 cm. Translation of: Saint Jean de la Croix. 1979. Includes bibliographical references and index. [BX4700.J7C8313 1982] 19 81-14430 ISBN 0-8164-2359-8 : 13.95
1. John of the Cross, Saint, 1542-1591. 2. Mysticism—Spain. 3. Mysticism—1450-1800. I. [Saint Jean de la Croix.] English II. Title.

[HUBBARD, Alice Philena] 922.246
Seven Spanish mystics, original studies by Sister Felicia. Cambridge, Mass., Society of Saint John the Evangelist, 1947. x, 70 p. 10 plates. 24 cm. Name in religion: Felicia, Sister. [BV5077.S7H8] 47-5819
1. Mysticism—Spain. 2. Catholic Church—Biog. I. Title.
Contents omitted.

LULL, Ramon, d.1315. 149.
The book of the lover and the beloved; translated from the Catalan of Ramon Lull with an introductory essay, by E. Allison Peers. London, Society for promoting Christian knowledge; New York and Toronto, The Macmillan company, 1923. 2 p. l., vii-viii, 105, [1] p. 17 cm. Translated from his Blanquerna, of which it forms a part. [BV5080.L8 1923a] 24-4197
1. Mysticism—Spain. I. Peers, Edgar Allison, tr. II. Title.

LULL, Ramon, d.1315. 149.
The book of the lover and the beloved; tr. from the Catalan of Ramon Lull, with an introductory essay by E. Allison Peers. New York, The Macmillan company, 1923. 4 p. l., 115 p. 17 1/2 cm. Translated from his Blanquerna, of which it forms a part. [BV5080.L8] 23-14690
1. Mysticism—Spain. I. Peers, Edgar Allison, tr. II. Title.

LULL, Ramon, d.1315. 242'.2
The book of the Lover and the Beloved / edited by Kenneth Leech from the E. Allison Peers translation of Ramon Lull. New York : Paulist Press, 1978. vii, 116 p. ; 19 cm. (The Spiritual masters) Translation of Libre de Amich e Amat, a part of the author's Blanquerna. "May have been written before Blanquerna, and was subsequently incorporated into it as chapter 99." Includes bibliographical references. [BV5080.L8 1978] 78-61666 ISBN 0-8091-2135-2 pbk. : 2.25
1. Mysticism—Spain. I. Leech, Kenneth. II. Peers, Edgar Allison. III. Lull, Ramon, d. 1315. Blanquerna. Chapter 99. IV. Title.

PEERS, Edgar Allison. 149.3
Studies of the Spanish mystics. 2d ed., rev. London, S. P. C. K.? New York, Macmillan, 1951- v. 22cm. Includes bibliography. [BV5077.S7P52] 57-22935
1. Mysticism—Spain. 2. Spanish literature—Hist. & crit. I. Title. II. Title: Spanish mystics.

PEERS, Edgar Allison. 281.
Studies of the Spanish mystics, by E. Allison Peers ... London, The Sheldon press; New York and Toronto, The Macmillan co., 1927- v. 23 cm. Bibliography: v. 1, p. 407-462. [BV5077.S7P5] 27-18044
1. Mysticism—Spain. 2. Spanish literature—Hist. & crit. I. Title. II. Title: Spanish mystics.

POND, Kathleen, 1898- 149.3082
ed. and tr.
The spirit of the Spanish mystics; an anthology of Spanish religious prose from the fifteenth to the seventeenth century. New York, P. J. Kenedy [1958] 170p. 23cm. [BV5072.P6] 58-5668
1. Mysticism—Spain. I. Title.

RIVET, Mary Majella, mother, 289
1897-
... The influence of the Spanish mystics on the works of Saint Francis de Sales ... by Mother Mary Majella Rivet ... Washington, D. C., The Catholic university of America press, 1941. xii, 113 p. 23 cm. Thesis (PH. D.)--Catholic university of America, 1941. "Editions of Spanish authors which were available during the lifetime of Saint Francis de Sales and which he probably used": p. 105-107. [Secular name: Marcelle Marie River] "Select bibliography": p. 111-113. [BX4700.F5R5 1941] 41-11843
1. Francois de Sales, Saint, bp. of Geneva, 1587-1622. 2. Mysticism—Spain. I. Title.

RUBIO, David, 1884- 149.3
The mystic soul of Spain, by David Rubio ... New York, Cosmopolitan science & art service, inc., 1946. 3 p. l., 94 p. 19 1/2 cm. [BV5077.S7R8] 47-2606
1. Mysticism—Spain. I. Title.

VELA, Maria. 922.246
The third mystic of Avila; the self revelation of Maria Vela, a sixteenth century Spanish nun. Foreword and translation by Frances Parkinson Keyes. New York, Farrar, Straus and Cudahy [1960] 300 p. illus. 22 cm. Autograph by translator inside front cover. [BX4705.V427A3] 60-9735
I. Keyes, Frances Parkinson (Wheeler) 1885- II. Title.

Mysticism—Spain—Collected works.

THE Wisdom of the 248'.22'0946
Spanish mystics / selected by Stephen Clissold. New York : New Directions Pub. Co., c1977. 88 p. ; 21 cm. Bibliography: p. 86-88. [BV5072.W5] 77-7650 ISBN 0-8112-0663-7 : 7.50 ISBN 0-8112-0664-5 pbk. : 2.95
1. Mysticism—Spain—Collected works. 2. Mysticism—Catholic Church—Collected works. I. Clissold, Stephen.

Mysticism—Study and teaching.

STAAL, Frits. 291.4'2
Exploring mysticism : a methodological essay / Frits Staal. Berkeley : University of California Press, [1975] xix, 230 p., [9] leaves of plates : ill. ; 25 cm. Includes index. Bibliography: p. 215-224. [BL625.S73] 74-76391 ISBN 0-520-02726-4 : 15.00 pbk. : 4.95
1. Mysticism—Study and teaching. I. Title.

STAAL, Frits. 291.4'2
Exploring mysticism / Frits Staal. Harmondsworth : Penguin, 1975. [1], 224 p. : 1 ill. ; 18 cm. (A Pelican book) Includes index. Bibliography: p. 209-218. [BL625.S73 1975] 75-328922 ISBN 0-14-021847-5 : £0.70
1. Mysticism—Study and teaching. I. Title.

Mysticism—Taoism—Collected works.

THE Wisdom of the 299'.51442
Taoists / compiled by D. Howard Smith. New York : New Directions, 1980. p. cm. (Wisdom series) [BL1923.W57] 80-15629 ISBN 0-8112-0786-2 pbk. : 4.95
1. Mysticism—Taoism—Collected works. I. Smith, David Howard. II. Title. III. Series. IV. Series: Wisdom series (New York)

Mysticism—Terminology.

L'HEUREUX, Aloysius 248.2'2
Gonzaga, Mother.
The mystical vocabulary of Venerable Mere Maria de l'Incarnation. New York, AMS Press [1969, c1956] xi, 193 p. 22 cm. (Catholic University of America. Studies in Romance languages and literatures, v. 53) First published under title: The mystical vocabulary of Venerable Mere Marie de l'Incarnation and its problems. Originally presented as the author's thesis, Catholic University of America. Bibliography: p. 184-190. [BV5080.M29L4 1969] 72-94190
1. Marie de l'Incarnation, Mother, 1599-1672. La relation de 1654. 2. Mysticism—Terminology. I. Title. II. Series.

Mysticism—United States—History.

BRIDGES, Leonard Hal, 149'.3
1918-
American mysticism : from William James to Zen / Hal Bridges. Lakemont, Ga. : CSA Press, [1977?] c1970. ix, 206 p. ; 21 cm. Includes index. Bibliography: p. 175-188. [BL625.B7 1977] 76-55054 ISBN 0-87707-191-8 pbk. : 3.95
1. Mysticism—United States—History. I. Title.

Mystics—England—Biography.

BULLETT, Gerald William, 149'.3
1894-1958.
The English mystics / Gerald Bullett. Folcroft, Pa. : Folcroft Library Editions, 1979. p. cm. Reprint of the 1950 ed. published by M. Joseph, London. Includes index. Bibliography: p. [BV5095.A1B84 1979] 79-547 ISBN 0-8414-9831-8 lib. bdg. : 17.50
1. Mystics—England—Biography. 2. Mysticism—England. I. Title.

Myth.

BARNARD, Mary. 291'.13
The mythmakers. Athens, Ohio University Press [1967, c1966] 213 p. 22 cm. Bibliography: p. [195]-203. [BL304.B3] 66-20061
1. Myth. I. Title.

BOLLE, Kees W. 291'.13
The freedom of man in myth [by] Kees W. Bolle. [Nashville] Vanderbilt University Press, 1968. xiv, 199 p. 20 cm. Bibliographical footnotes. [BL304.B6] 68-8564 ISBN 0-8265-1125-2 5.00
1. Myth. 2. Mysticism. I. Title.

BUCHLER, Ira R. 398
A formal study of myth, by Ira R. Buchler and Henry A. Selby. Austin, University of Texas, 1968. iv, 166 l. illus. 28 cm. (University of Texas. Center for Intercultural Studies in Folklore and Oral History. Monograph series, no. 1) Cover title. Bibliography: p. 159-166. [BL304.B8] 68-66061
1. Myth. I. Selby, Henry A., joint author. II. Title. III. Series: Texas. University. Center for Intercultural Studies in Folklore and Oral History. Monograph series, no. 1

COOK, Albert Spaulding. 401'.9
Myth and language / Albert Cook. Bloomington : Indiana University Press, c1980. ix, 332 p. ; 24 cm. Includes index. Bibliography: p. 311-324. [BL304.C66] 79-84259 ISBN 0-253-14027-7 : 22.50
1. Levi-Strauss, Claude. 2. Myth. 3. Language and languages. 4. Greek literature—History and criticism. 5. Folk literature—History and criticism. I. Title.

DE SANTILLANA, Giorgio, 200.4
1902-
Hamlet's mill; an essay on myth and the frame of time [by] Giorgio de Santillana and Hertha von Dechend. Boston, Gambit, 1969. xxv, 505 p. illus. 24 cm. Bibliography: p. [453]-484. [BL304.D43] 69-13267 10.00
1. Myth. 2. Knowledge, Theory of. I. Dechend, Hertha von, 1915- joint author. II. Title.

DUGGAN, William J. 204.5
Myth and Christian belief [by] William J. Duggan. Notre Dame, Ind., Fides [1971] viii, 141 p. illus. 20 cm. Bibliography: p. 141. [BL304.D84] 76-140145 ISBN 0-8190-0431-6 2.95
1. Myth. 2. Religion and language. I. Title.

ELIADE, Mircea, 1907- 291.13
Myth and reality. Tr. from French by Willard R. Trask. [1st Amer. ed.] New York. Harper [1968,c.1963] v. 212p. 20cm. (World perspectives, v. 31 Harper torchbks., TB 1369) Bibl. [BL304.E413] 63-16508 1.75 pap.,
1. Myth. 2. Mythology—Addresses, essays, lectures. I. Title. II. Series.

ELIADE, Mircea, 1907- 291.13
Myth and reality. Translated from the French by Willard R. Trask. [1st American ed.] New York, Harper & Row [1963] xiv, 204 p. 20 cm. (World perspectives, v. 31) "Basic bibliography": p. 203-204. Bibliographical footnotes. [BL304.E413] 63-16508
1. Myth. 2. Mythology—Addresses, essays, lectures. I. Title.

ELIADE, Mircea, 1907- 291.1'3
Myths, rites, symbols : a Mircea Eliade reader / edited by Wendell C. Beane and William G. Doty. New York : Harper & Row, 1976, c1975. 2 v. (xxviii, 465 p.) ; 21 cm. (Harper colophon books ; CN 510) Includes bibliographical references. [BL304.E43 1976] 75-7931 ISBN 0-06-090510-7(V.1) pbk. : 3.95
1. Myth. 2. Rites and ceremonies. 3. Symbolism. I. Title.

FONTENROSE, Joseph Eddy, 291.13
1903-
The ritual theory of myth [by] Joseph Fontenrose. Berkeley. Univ. of Calif. Pr. 1966. 77p. 27cm. (Univ. of Calif. pubns., Folklore studies. 18) Bibl. [BL304.F6] 66-8139 2.50 pap.,
1. Myth. I. Title. II. Series: California. University of California publications. Folklore studies, 18

*JAMES, E. O. 200.4
Christian myth and ritual; a historical study. Gloucester, Mass., Peter Smith, 1973. 341 p. 21 cm. First published in London by John Murray, 1933. Bibliography: p. 328-340. [BL304] ISBN 0-8446-2307-5 6.00
1. Myth. 2. Folk-lore. 3. Religion, Primitive. I. Title.

KELSEY, Morton T. 291.1'3
Myth, history, and faith : the remythologizing of Christianity / by Morton T. Kelsey. New York : Paulist Press, [1974] v, 185 p. ; 21 cm. Includes bibliographical references. [BL304.K38] 73-94216 ISBN 0-8091-1827-0 pbk. : 4.50
1. Myth. 2. Theology. I. Title.

KNOX, John, 1900- 201
Myth and truth; an essay on the language of faith. Charlottesville, Univ. Pr. of Va. [1964] vii, 87p. 21cm. (Richard lects., Univ. of Va., 1963-64] Bibl. 64-25858 2.50
1. Myth. I. Title. II. Series.

LARSEN, Stephen. 291.1'3
The shaman's doorway : opening the mythic imagination to contemporary consciousness / Stephen Larsen. 1st ed. New York : Harper & Row, c1976. xii, 244 p. : ill. ; 22 cm. Includes bibliographical references. [BL304.L37 1976] 75-9337 ISBN 0-06-064929-1 : 10.00
1. Myth. 2. Mythology. 3. Consciousness. I. Title.

LARSEN, Stephen. 291.1'3
The shaman's doorway : opening the mythic imagination to contemporary consciousness / Stephen Larsen. New York : Harper & Row, 1977c1976. xii, 244p. : ill ; 21 cm. (Harper Colophon Books) Includes bibliographical references.

[BL304.L37] ISBN 0-06-090547-6 pbk. : 3.95
1. Myth. 2. Consciousness. 3. Mythology. I. Title.
L.C. card no. for original ed.:75-9337.

MALINOWSKI, Bronislaw, 1884-1942. 398'.042
Myth in primitive psychology. Westport, Conn., Negro Universities Press [1971, c1926] 94 p. 19 cm. On spine: Primitive psychology. Original ed. issued in series: The New science series. Includes bibliographical references. [BL304.M3 1971] 79-152394 ISBN 0-8371-5954-7
1. Myth. 2. Ethnopsychology. I. Title.

MULLER, Karl Otfried, 1797-1840. 291.1'3
Introduction to a scientific system of mythology / Karl Otfried Muller. New York : Arno Press, 1978. p. cm. (Mythology) Reprint of the 1884 ed. published by Longman, Brown, Green and Longmans, London. Translation of Prolegomena zu einer wissenschaftlichen Mythologie. [BL310.M7513 1978] 77-79144 ISBN 0-405-10553-3 lib. bdg. : 22.00
1. Myth. 2. Mythology, Greek. I. Title. II. Series.

NORMAN, Dorothy, 1905- 200.4
The hero: myth, image, symbol. New York, World Pub. Co. [1969] xvii, 238 p. illus. 26 cm. "An NAL book." Bibliographical footnotes. [BL304.N6] 68-57956 10.00
1. Myth. 2. Symbolism. 3. Art and mythology. I. Title.

O'BRIEN, William James. 209
Stories to the dark : explorations in religious imagination / by William James O'Brien. New York : Paulist Press, c1977. vii, 163 p. ; 23 cm. "A Newman book." Includes bibliographical references. [BL311.O27] 77-74577 ISBN 0-8091-0222-6 : 10.00 ISBN 0-8091-2032-1 pbk. : 5.95
1. Myth. 2. Religion and literature. 3. Story-telling (Christian theology) 4. Spiritual life—Catholic authors. I. Title.

PATAI, Raphael, 1910- 301.2'1
Myth and modern man. Englewood Cliffs, N.J., Prentice-Hall [1972] viii, 359 p. 24 cm. Includes bibliographical references. [BL304.P38] 70-163399 ISBN 0-13-609123-7 9.95
1. Myth. 2. Mythology. I. Title.

RAINE, Kathleen Jessie, 1908- 016.2911'3
On the mythological / by Kathleen Raine. Selected bibliography of myth in literature / James A. S. McPeek. Fullerton, Calif. : College English Association, 1969. 39 p. ; 23 cm. (CEA chap book) "Distributed as a supplement to the CEA critic, vol. xxxii, no. 1." [BL304.R33] 75-308075
1. Myth. 2. Mythology. 3. Mythology—Bibliography. I. McPeek, James Andrew Scarborough. Selected bibliography of myth in literature. 1969. II. CEA critic. III. Title. IV. Series: American English Association. A CEA chap book.

VIGNOLI, Tito, 1828-1914. 291.1'3
Myth and science / Tito Vignoli. New York : Arno Press, 1978. 330 p. ; 21 cm. (Mythology) Translation of Mito e scienza. Reprint of the 1882 ed. published by D. Appleton, New York, which was issued as v. 40 in the International scientific series. Includes bibliographical references and index. [BL304.V513 1978] 77-79156 ISBN 0-405-10565-7 : 19.00
1. Myth. 2. Psychology, Religious. 3. Religion—Philosophy. I. Title. II. Series. III. Series: The International scientific series (New York) ; v. 40.

WILLIAMS, Jay G., 1932- 232
Yeshua Buddha : an essay in Christian mythology / Jay G. Williams. Wheaton, Ill. : Theosophical Pub. House, c1978. p. cm. (Quest books) Includes bibliographical references and index. [BT304.97.W54] 78-8789 ISBN 0-8356-0515-9 pbk. : 3.95
1. Jesus Christ—Theosophical interpretations. 2. Myth. I. Title.

Myth—Addresses, essays, lectures.

AMERICAN Catholic Philosophical Association. 108 s
Myth and philosophy. Edited by George F. McLean. Washington, Office of the National Secretary of the Association, Catholic University of America [1971] 202 p. 23 cm. (Its Proceedings, v. 45) Includes bibliographical references. [B11.A4 no. 45] [BL304] 398'.042 72-184483
1. Myth—Addresses, essays, lectures. I. McLean, George F., ed. II. Title. III. Series.

CAMPBELL, Joseph, 1904- 291'.13
The flight of the wild gander; explorations in the mythological dimension. New York, Viking Press [1969] viii, 248 p. illus. 22 cm. Bibliographical references included in "Notes" (p. 227-240) [BL304.C35 1969] 69-18803 7.50
1. Myth—Addresses, essays, lectures. I. Title.

CAMPBELL, Joseph, 1904- 291.1'3
The flight of the wild gander; explorations in the mythological dimension. Chicago, Regnery [1972, c1969] viii, 248 p. illus. 21 cm. "A Gateway edition." Includes bibliographical references. [BL304.C35 1972] 70-183820 2.65
1. Myth—Addresses, essays, lectures. I. Title.

MYTH and the crisis of historical consciousness / edited by Lee W. Gibbs and W. Taylor Stevenson. Missoula, Mont. : Published by Scholars Press for the American Academy of Religion, c1975. ix, 107 p. ; 24 cm. Essays from the seminar held during the annual meetings of the American Academy of Religion, 1972-1974. Includes bibliographical references. [BL304.M86] 75-33049 ISBN 0-89130-053-8 : 4.20 901
1. Myth—Addresses, essays, lectures. 2. History—Philosophy—Addresses, essays, lectures. I. Gibbs, Lee W. II. Stevenson, W. Taylor. III. American Academy of Religion.

MYTH, symbol, and reality / edited by Alan M. Olson. Notre Dame, Ind. : University of Notre Dame Press, c1980. xiv, 189 p. ; 23 cm. (Boston University studies in philosophy and religion ; v. 1) Includes bibliographical references and index. [BL304.M87] 80-11617 ISBN 0-268-01346-2 : 14.95 291.1'3
1. Myth—Addresses, essays, lectures. 2. Symbolism—Addresses, essays, lectures. 3. Hermeneutics—Addresses, essays, lectures. 4. Reality—Addresses, essays, lectures. I. Olson, Alan M. II. Series: Boston University. Boston University studies in philosophy and religion ; v. 1.

MYTHS, dreams, and religion. Edited by Joseph Campbell. New York, E. P. Dutton, 1970. 255 p. 21 cm. Series of lectures sponsored by the Society for the Arts, Religion and Contemporary Culture. Includes bibliographical references. [BL304.M93 1970] 70-87201 7.95 398.2
1. Myth—Addresses, essays, lectures. 2. Dreams—Addresses, essays, lectures. I. Campbell, Joseph, 1904- ed.

OHMANN, Richard Malin, ed. 291.13
The making of myth. New York, Putnam [1963, c.] 1962. 179p. 21cm. (Controlled essay materials, v.1) Bibl. 62-12846 2.00 pap.,
1. Myth—Addresses, essays, lectures. I. Title.

Myth—Collected works.

PANIKKAR, Raymond, 1918- 291
Myth, faith, and hermeneutics : cross-cultural studies / R. Panikkar. New York : Paulist Press, c1979. xxiii, 500 p. ; 24 cm. Includes indexes. Bibliography: p. 462-478. [BL304.P32] 77-99306 ISBN 0-8091-0232-3 : 19.95
1. Myth—Collected works. 2. Faith—Comparative studies—Collected works. 3. Religion—Philosophy—Collected works. 4. Hermenenties—Collected works. 5. East and West—Collected works. 6. Theology—Collected works. I. Title.

Myth in literature.

RIGHTER, William. 809'.933'1
Myth and literature / William Righter. London ; Boston : Routledge & Paul, 1975. 132 p. ; 20 cm. (Concepts of literature) Bibliography: p. [129]-132. [PN56.M94R5] 75-319878 ISBN 0-7100-8137-5 : 10.95
1. Myth in literature. I. Title.

RUTHVEN, K. K. 291.1'301
Myth / [by] K. K. Ruthven. London : Methuen, 1976. [8], 104 p. ; 20 cm. (The Critical idiom ; 31) Distributed in the USA by Harper & Row, Barnes & Noble Import Division. Includes index. Bibliography: p. [84]-100. [PN56.M94R8 1976] 77-354267 5.75
1. Myth in literature. 2. Mythology in literature. I. Title.

SEIDEN, Morton Irving, 1921- 821'.8
William Butler Yeats: the poet as a mythmaker, 1865-1939. New York, Cooper Square Publishers, 1975 [c1962] xiv, 397 p. front. 24 cm. Reprint of the ed. published by Michigan State University Press, East Lansing. Bibliography: p. 339-354. [PR5908.M8S4 1975] 74-79395 ISBN 0-8154-0491-3 12.50
1. Yeats, William Butler, 1865-1939—Criticism and interpretation. 2. Myth in literature.

STILLMAN, Peter R. 809'.933'7
Introduction to myth / Peter R. Stillman. Rochelle Park, N.J. : Hayden Book Co., c1977. 214 p. ; 23 cm. (Hayden series in literature) Bibliography: p. 213-214. [PN56.M94S8] 77-2904 ISBN 0-8104-5890-X pbk. : 5.31
1. Myth in literature. 2. Literature—Collections. I. Title.

VICKERY, John B., ed. 809.933
Myth and literature; contemporary theory and practice, edited by John B. Vickery. Lincoln, University of Nebraska Press [1966] xii, 391 p. 25 cm. Bibliography: p. 377-381. [PN56.M94V5] 65-11563
1. Myth in literature. I. Title.

Myth in literature—Addresses, essays, lectures.

LUKE, Helen M., 1904- 809'.15
The inner story : myth and symbol in the Bible and literature / Helen M. Luke. New York : Crossroad, 1982. viii, 118 p. ; 22 cm. [PN56.M94L84 1982] 19 81-17473 ISBN 0-8245-0443-7 : 8.95
1. Myth in literature—Addresses, essays, lectures. 2. Symbolism in literature—Addresses, essays, lectures. 3. Myth in the Bible—Addresses, essays, lectures. 4. Symbolism in the Bible—Addresses, essays, lectures. I. Title.

Myth in the Old Testament.

DAHER, Paul. 922.2569
A cedar of Lebanon. Dublin, Browne and Nolan [1956] 169p. illus. 23cm. 'Translated. With additions. and index, from the French of Vie, survie et prodiges de l'ermite Charbel Makhlouf, by Rev. L. E. Whatmore.' [BX4705.M2635D312] 57-23160
I. Makhiuf, Sharbal, Father, 1828-1898. II. Title.

ROGERSON, John William. 221'.08 s
Myth in Old Testament interpretation / J. W. Rogerson. Berlin ; New York : De Gruyter, 1974. vi, 206 p. ; 24 cm. (Beiheft zur Zeitschrift fur die alttestamentliche Wissenschaft ; 134) Includes indexes. Bibliography: p. [190]-201. [BS410.Z5 vol. 134] [BS1183] 221.6'8 73-78234 ISBN 3-11-004220-7 : 33.80
1. Myth in the Old Testament. I. Title. II. Series: Zeitschrift fur die alttestamentliche Wissenschaft. Beihefte ; 134.

TANNEHILL, James B.
Naamah and Nimrod, a defense of the faith of our fathers, by J. B. Tannehill ... Columbus, O., The New Franklin printing co. [c1916] x, 358 p. illus. (incl. maps, charts, tables) plates. 29 cm. $1.50 Bibliography: p. [iv] 16-17386
I. Title.

The myth of God Incarnate—Congresses.

INCARNATION and myth : the debate continued / edited by Michael Goulder. Grand Rapids : Eerdmans, c1979. p. cm. Papers from a meeting held at the University of Birmingham, July 10-12, 1978, sponsored by the Cadbury Trust and the Dept. of Extramural Studies, University of Birmingham. Includes indexes. [BT220.I52] 79-16509 ISBN 0-8028-1199-X pbk. : 5.95 232'.1
1. The myth of God Incarnate—Congresses. 2. Incarnation—Congresses. I. Goulder, M. D. II. Cadbury Trust. III. Birmingham, Eng. University. Dept. of Extra-Mural Studies.

Mythology.

AGARD, Walter Raymond, 1894- 731.87
Classical myths in sculpture. [Madison] University of Wisconsin Press [1951] xvi, 203 p. illus. 26 cm. "Bibliography and catalog": p. [177]-183. [NB1920.A35] 51-62409
1. Mythology. 2. Sculpture. I. Title.

ANDERSON, Mary Gooch.
... Stories of the golden age, by Mary Gooch Anderson. New York, The Macmillan company, 1914. viii, 231 p. illus. 18 cm. (Everychild's series) [FZ8.1.A548S] 14-18125 0.40
1. Mythology. I. Title.

BAKER, Rannie Belle, 1889- comp. 291
In the light of myth; selections from the world's myths, complied and interpreted by Rannie B. Baker ... art selection by Ruth C. Stebbins, illustrations by Alexander Key. Chicago, New York, Row, Peterson & company [c192554 xiv, 334 p. incl. front., illus. 19 cm. [BL310.B3] 25-8796
1. Mythology. I. Title.

BANIER, Antoine, 1673-1741. 292'.1'3
The mythology and fables of the ancients explain'd from history : London, 1739-40 / Antoine Danier. New York : Garland Pub., 1976. 4 v. ; 23 cm. (The Renaissance and the gods ; 40) Translation of La mythologie et les fables expliquees par l'histoire. Reprint of the 1739-1740 ed. printed for A. Millar, London. Includes bibliographical references and index. [BL305.B3 1976] 77-140 ISBN 0-8240-2089-8 : 40.00 per vol.
1. Mythology. 2. Folk-lore. I. Title. II. Series.

BELL, Louie M.
... Mythology in marble, by Louie M. Bell. Boston, New York [etc.] Educational publishing company [1901] 167 p. incl. front., pl. 25 cm. Bibliography: p. 166. [NB1920.B4] 2-14890
1. Mythology. 2. Sculpture. I. Title.

BLACKWELL, Thomas, 1701-1759. 291.1'3
Letters concerning mythology, London, 1748 / Thomas Blackwell. New York : Garland Pub., 1976. p. cm. (The Renaissance and the gods ; 42) Reprint of the 1748 ed. printed in London. [BL305.B55 1976] 75-27887 ISBN 0-8240-2091-X lib.bdg. : 40.00
1. Mythology. I. Title. II. Series.

[BLANCHARD, Edward Litt Laman] 1820-1889. 291
Freaks and follies of fabledom. A little Lempriere. London, J. Ollivier, 1852. 2 p. l., 119, [1] p. 22 1/2 cm. Caption title: Mythology made easy. A burlesque, in dictionary form. [BL730.B6] 31-31294
I. Title. II. Title: Mythology made easy.

BRATTON, Fred Gladstone, 1896- 398.2'093
Myths and legends of the ancient Near East. New York, Crowell [1970] xv, 188 p. illus., geneal. tables, map. 24 cm. Bibliography: p. 179-184. [BL311.B7 1970] 79-101938 7.95
1. Mythology. I. Title.

BRYANT, Jacob, 1715-1804. 291
A new system : or, An analysis of ancient mythology / Jacob Bryant ; introd. by

Burton Feldman. New York : Garland Pub., 1979- v. : ill. ; 26 cm. (Myth and romanticism ; 5) Reprint of the 2d ed. (1775-1776) published by T. Payne, London. Includes bibliographical references. [BL305.B7 1979] 78-60881 ISBN 0-8240-3554-2: 180.00
1. Mythology. 2. History, Ancient. I. Title. II. Series.

BULFINCH, Thomas, 1796-1867 291.13
The age of fable. Afterword, bibl. by Martin Bucco. New York, Harper [c.1966] 377p. 19cm. (Harper perennial classic) Bibl. [BL310.B82] 66-2059 1.75; .75 pap.,
1. Mythology. I. Title.

*BULFINCH, Thomas, 1796-1867 291.13
The age of fable [Introd. by Earle Toppings] New York, Airmont [c.1965] 292p. illus. 18cm. (Classics ser., CL80) .60 pap.,
I. Title.

BULFINCH, Thomas, 1796-1867 290
The age of fable. Garden City, N.Y., Doubleday [1961] 389p. (Dolphin bk. C132 .95 pap.,
I. Title.

BULFINCH, Thomas, 1796-1867 290
The age of fable, Introd. by Daniel B. Dodson. Greenwich, Conn., Fawcett [c.1961] 336p. (Premier bk., d144) .50 pap.,
1. Mythology. I. Title.

BULFINCH, Thomas, 1796-1867. 290
The age of fable; or, Stories of gods and heroes. Introductory essay by Dudley Fitts. Illustrated by Joe Mugnaini. New York, Heritage Press [1959, c1958] xix, 230p. illus. 29cm. [BL310.B82 1959] 59-16165
1. Mythology. I. Mugnaini, Joe, illus. II. Title.

BULFINCH, Thomas, 1796-1867. 291.13
The age of fable. Afterword and bibliography by Martin Bucco. New York, Harper & Row [1966] 377 p. 19 cm. (A Harper perennial classic) Bibliography:p. 365. [BL310.B82] 66-2059
1. Mythology. I. Title.

BULFINCH, Thomas, 1796-1867. 290
The age of fable; or, Beauties of mythology, by Thomas Bulfinch. A new enl. and illustrated ed., edited by E. E. Hale ... Boston, S. W. Tilton & co. [etc.]; New York, C. T. Dillingham, 1882. 2 p. l., vii-xxi, 472 p. illus. 22 cm. [BL310.B8 1882] 8-16307
1. Mythology. 2. Chivalry. 3. Folk-lore. 4. Charlemagne (Romances, etc.) I. Hale, Edward Everett, 1822-1900, ed. II. Title.

BULFINCH, Thomas, 1796-1867. 291
The age of fable; or, Beauties of mythology. By Thomas Bulfinch ... Boston, S. W. Tilton & co. [189-?] 2 p. l., 3-488 p. 20 cm. Published also under title: Stories of gods and heroes. [BL310.B815] 39-7339
1. Mythology. 2. Folk-lore. I. Title.

BULFINCH, Thomas, 1796-1867. 291
The age of fable; or, Beauties of mythology, by Thomas Bulfinch. A new, rev. and enl. ed.; edited by Rev. L. Loughran Scott ... With a classical index and dictionary, and nearly two hundred illustrations. Philadelphia, D. McKay [1898] xxiii, 501 p. front., illus., 15 pl. fold. tab. 22 cm. [BL310.B8 1898] 4-10420
1. Mythology. I. Scott, John Loughran, 1846-1919, ed. II. Title.

BULFINCH, Thomas, 1796-1867. 290
The age of fable, by Thomas Bulfinch. London, J. M. Dent & sons, ltd.; New York, E. P. Dutton & co. [1910] x, 371, [1] p. 18 cm. (Half-title: Everyman's library, ed. by Ernest Rhys. For young people. [no. 472]) Bibliography: p. viii. [BL310.B82 1910] A 11
1. Mythology. 2. Folk-lore. I. Title.

BULFINCH, Thomas, 1796-1867- 291
The age of fable; or, Beauties of mythology, by Thomas Bulfinch. New ed., rev. and enl. ... New York, Review of reviews company, 1913. 2 v. fronts., plates, ports., map. 18 cm. Paged continuously. Contents.--i--ii, Stories of gods and heroes.--iii. King Arthur and his knights. The Mabinogeon. Hero myths of the British race.--iv. Legends of Charlemagne. [BL310.B8 1913] 13-26578
1. Mythology. 2. Chivalry. 3. Folk-lore. 4. Charlemagne (Romances, etc.) I. Title.

BULFINCH, Thomas, 1796-1867. 290
The age of fable [by] Thomas Bulfinch. London, J. M. Dent & sons, ltd.; New York, E. P. Dutton & co., inc. [1931] x, 371, [1] p. 18 cm. (Half-title: Everyman's library, ed. by Ernest Rhys. For young people. [no. 472]) "First published in this edition 1920; reprinted ... 1981." "The works of Thomas Bulfinch": p. viii. [AC1.E8 no. 472] 36-37586
1. Mythology. I. Title.

BULFINCH, Thomas, 1796-1867. 291
The age of fable; or, Beauties of mythology, by Thomas Bulfinch. With notes, revisions and additions by William H. Klapp ... With nearly two hundred illustrations and a complete index. New York, Tudor publishing company [1935] xv, 456 p. illus., 16 pl. (incl. front.) geneal. tab. 22 cm. [BL310.B8 1935] [BL310.B] 291 A 38
1. Mythology. I. Klapp, William Henry, 1849-1924, ed. II. Title.

BULFINCH, Thomas, 1796-1867. 291
... *The age of fable;* or, Stories of the gods of Greece and Rome, the deities of Egypt, and the eastern and Hindu mythology, by Thomas Bulfinch ... New York, G. H. McKibbin [1900] 2 p. l., 9-256 p. col. front., illus. (part col.) 17 cm. (The Manhattan young people's library) [BL310.B8 1900] 0-4672
I. Title.

BULFINCH, Thomas, 1796-1867.
The age of fable; or, Stories of gods and heroes. Boston, Sanborn, Carter & Bazin, 1855. 1 p. l., 485 p. pl. 12 degrees. 1-120
I. Title.

BULFINCH, Thomas, 1796-1867. 290
A book of myths; selections from Bulfinch's Age of fable, with illustrations by Helen Sewell. New York, Macmillan [1966, c1942] 126, [2] p. illus. (part col.) 26 cm. "Eleventh printing". [BL310.B85 1966]
1. Mythology. I. Sewell, Helen, 1896- illus. II. Title.

BULFINCH, Thomas, 1796-1867. 290
A book of myths; selections from Bulfinch's Age of fable, with illustrations by Helen Sewell. New York, The Macmillan company, 1942. 126 [2] p. illus. (part col.) 25 1/2 cm. [BL310.B85] 42-25450
1. Mythology. I. Sewell, Helen, 1896- illus. II. Title.

BULFINCH, Thomas, 1796-1867 291
Bulfinch's mythology: The age of chivalry and Legends of Charlemagne, or romance of the Middle Ages. Foreword by Palmer Bovie [New York] New Amer. Lib. [c.1962] 608p. 18cm. (Mentor classic, MT450) .75 pap.,
1. Mythology. 2. Chivalry. 3. Folk-lore—Europe. 4. Charlemagne (Romances, etc.) I. Title. II. Title: The age of fable. III. Title: The age of chivalry. IV. Title: Legends of Charlemagne.

BULFINCH, Thomas, 1796-1867. 290
Bulfinch's mythology; The age of fable; The age of chivalry; Legends of Charlemagne, by Thomas Bulfinch; complete in one volume, revised and enlarged with illustrations. New York, Thomas Y. Crowell company [c1913] xv, [2] p., 1 l., 912 p. front., plates, double map. 21 cm. [BL310.B76] A 15
1. Mythology. 2. Chivalry. 3. Folk-lore. 4. Charlemagne (Romances, etc.) I. Title. II. Title: The age of fable. III. Title: The age of chivalry. IV. Title: Legends of Charlemagne.

BULFINCH, Thomas, 1796-1867. 290
Bulfinch's mythology; The age of fable; the age of chivalry; Legends of Charlemagne. New York, The Modern library [1934] xi, 778 p. xvi pl. 21 cm. (Half-title: The modern library of the world's best books) "First Modern librawry edition. 1934." [BL310.B76 1934] 34-27086
1. Mythology. 2. Chivalry. 3. Folk-lore. 4. Charlemagne (Romances, etc.) I. Title. II. Title: The age of fable. III. Title: The age of chivalry. IV. Title: Legends of Charlemagne.

BULFINCH, Thomas, 1796-1867. 398.2
Bulfinch's Mythology. New York : Avenel Books : distributed by Crown Publishers, [1978] p. cm. The three works, popularly known as Bulfinch's mythology, were originally written and published separately. Includes index. Contents.Contents.—The age of fable.—The age of chivalry.—Legends of Charlemagne. [BL310.B82 1978] 78-13042 ISBN 0-517-26277-0 pbk. : 5.98
1. Charlemagne, 742-814—Romances. 2. Mythology. 3. Chivalry. 4. Folk-lore—Europe. I. Title. II. Title: Mythology.

BULFINCH, Thomas, 1796-1867. 291
Bulfinch's mythology: The age of fable, The age of chivalry, Legends of Charlemagne; with dictionary index. illus. by Elinore Blaisdell. New York, T. Y. Crowell Co. [1947] xv, 957 p. col. plates. map. 22 cm. [BL310.B82 1947] 47-4613
1. Mythology. 2. Chivalry. 3. Folk-lore—Europe. 4. Charlemagne (Romances, etc.) I. Blaisdell, Elinore, 1904- illus. II. Title. III. Title: The age of fable. IV. Title: The age of chivalry. V. Title: Legends of Charlemagne.

BULFINCH, Thomas, 1796-1867 290
Collier Mythology of Greece and Rome; v.1. New York, [1962] 380p. 18cm. (HS24) .65 pap.,
1. Mythology. I. Title.

BULFINCH, Thomas, 1796-1867. 290
The golden age of myth & legend, being a revised & enlarged edition of "The age of fable", by Thomas Bulfinch ... edited by George H. Godfred. New York, Frederick A. Stokes company [1915] xviii, [2], 495, [1] p. col. front., plates, (part col.) maps (1 double) 23 cm. Printed in Great Britain. [BL310.B8 1915] 18-20041
1. Mythology. 2. Folk-lore. I. Godfrey, George H., ed. II. Title.

BULFINCH, Thomas, 1796-1867 290
Mythology: The age of fable, or beauties of mythology. Foreword by Palmer Bovie [New York] New Amer. Lib. [c.1962] 408p. 18cm. (Mentor classics, MP449) .60 pap.,
1. Mythology. I. Title.

BULFINCH, Thomas, 1796-1867. 290
Mythology, a modern abridgement, by Edmund Fuller. [New York, Dell Pub. Co., 1959] 448p. 17cm. (Laurel edition, LXIII) [BL310.B82 1959a] 59-4132
1. Mythology. 2. Chivalry. 3. Folk-lore—Europe. 4. Charlmagne (Romances, etc I. Fuller, Edmund, 1914- II. Title.

BULFINCH, Thomas, 1796-1867. 291'.13
Mythology: the age of fable. With a foreword by Robert Graves. Illustrated by Joseph Papin. Garden City, N.Y., International Collectors Library [1968] xvi, 383 p. illus. 22 cm. [BL310.B82 1968] 68-3624
1. Mythology. I. Graves, Robert, 1895-

BULFINCH, Thomas, 1796-1867. 398.2
Mythology: The age of fable, The age of chivalry, Legends of Charlemagne. New York, Crowell [1970] 980 p. illus., maps. 21 cm. The three works, popularly known as Bulfinch's mythology, were originally written and published separately. [BL310.B82 1970] 69-11314 6.95
1. Charlemagne, 742-814—Romances. 2. Mythology. 3. Chivalry. 4. Folk-lore—Europe.

BULFINCH, Thomas, 1796-1867. 290
Stories of gods and heroes, by Thomas Bulfinch. New York, T. Y. Crowell company [192-] xiii p., 1 l., 399 p. col. front., col. plates, double map, geneal. tab. 21 cm. Published originally under title: The age of the fable. [BL310.B8] 36-32753
1. Mythology. 2. Folk-lore. I. Title.

BURDICK, Lewis Dayton. 290
Oriental studies, by Lewis Dayton Burdick... Oxford, N.Y., The Irving company, 1905. 5 p. l., [3]-150 p. 21 cm. [BL313.B65] 6-1486
1. Mythology. 2. Mythology, Oriental. I. Title.

BURLAND, Cottie Arthur, 1905- 291.2'11
Gods and heroes of war / C. A. Burland ; with ill. by Honi Werner. New York : Putnam, [1974] 127 p. : ill. ; 22 cm. Includes index. [BL311.B87 1974] 73-88518 ISBN 0-399-20383-4. ISBN 0-399-60873-7 lib. bdg. : 4.49
1. Mythology. I. Title.

BURLAND, Cottie Arthur, 1905- 291.1'3
Myths of life & death / C. A. Burland. New York : Crown Publishers, 1974. 256 p. : ill. ; 24 cm. Includes index. Bibliography: p. [252] [BL311.B88 1974] 74-79865 12.50
1. Mythology. I. Title.

CAMPBELL, Joseph, 1904- 291
The hero with a thousand faces. New York, Meridian Books, 1956 [c1949] 416 p. illus. 19 cm. (Meridian books, M22) [BL313] 56-6574
1. Mythology. 2. Psychoanalysis. I. Title.

CAMPBELL, Joseph, 1904- 291'.13
The hero with a thousand faces. [2d ed. Princeton, N.J.] Princeton University Press [1968, c1949] xxiii, 416 p. illus. 24 cm. (Bollingen series, 17) Bibliographical footnotes. [BL313.C28 1968] 68-7394 6.00
1. Mythology. 2. Psychoanalysis. I. Title. II. Series.

CAMPBELL, Joseph, 1904- 291
The hero with a thousand faces. [New York]Pantheon Books [1949] xxiii. 416 p. illus. 24 cm. (The Bollingen series, 17) Bibliographical footnotes. [BL313.C28] 49-8590
1. Mythology. 2. Psychoanalysis. I. Title. II. Series.

CAMPBELL, Joseph, 1904- 292
The masks of God: Occidental mythology. New York, Viking, 1964. x, 564p. illus. 22cm. 64-2011 7.95
1. Mythology. I. Title.

CAMPBELL, Joseph, 1904- 291'.13
The masks of God. New York, Viking, 1959-[68] 4v. illus. 22cm. Contents.[4] Creative mythology. Bibl. [GN470.C32] 59-8354 10.00
1. Mythology. I. Title.

CAMPBELL, Joseph, 1904- 291'.13
The masks of God. New York, Viking Press [1969, c1959- v. illus. 22 cm. Contents.Contents.—[1] Primitive mythology. Includes bibliographical references. [BL311.C272] 71-9761 7.95 (v. 1)
1. Mythology. I. Title.

CAMPBELL, Joseph, 1904- 291'.13
Occidental mythology / Joseph Campbell. New York : Penguin Books, [1976] p. cm. (His The masks of God ; v. 3) Includes bibliographical references and index. [BL311.C276] 76-23179 8.95 ISBN 0-670-003-00-X pbk. : 3.95
1. Mythology. I. Title. II. Series.

CARPENTER, Edward, 1844-1929. 290
Pagan & Christian creeds: their origin and meaning, by Edward Carpenter. New York, Harcourt, Brace and Howe, 1920. 319 p. 21 cm. [BL313.C3] 20-5669
1. Mythology. 2. Religion, Primitive. 3. Christianity and other religions. I. Title.

CARTWRIGHT, Thomas.
... *The old, old myths of Greece & Rome;* by Thos. Cartwright. New York, E. P. Dutton and company [1908] 4 p. l., 124, [1] p. 8 col. pl. (incl. front.) illus. 17 cm. (Every child's library) Series note at head of title and of caption title. Title within ornamental border. W 8
1. Mythology. I. Title.

CHADWICK, Mara Louise Pratt. Mrs.
World history in myth and legend, by Mara L. Pratt Chadwick ... Boston, New York [etc.] Educational publishing company [c1906] 154 p. incl. illus., pl. 18 cm. [JZ8.1.C346W] 6-9293
1. Mythology. I. Title.

CHASE, Richard Volney, 1914- 291
Quest for myth. Baton Rouge, Louisiana State Univ. Press [1949] xi, 150 p. 24 cm. Thesis--Columbia Univ. Pub. also without thesis statement. Vita. "Notes"

(bibliographical): p. 133-148. [BL313.C47 1949a] A 49
1. Mythology. I. Title.

CHASE, Richard Volney, 1914-1962. 398
Quest for myth. New York, Greenwood Press [1969, c1949] xi, 150 p. 23 cm. Includes bibliographical references. [BL313.C47 1969] 77-90483
1. Mythology. I. Title.

CLARKE, Helen Archibald, d.1926. 290
A child's guide to mythology, by Helen A. Clarke ... New York, The Baker & Taylor company, 1908. 399 p. front., 11 pl. 20 1/2 cm. Published later under title: A guide to mythology for young readers. [BL310.C45] 8-33422
1. Mythology. 2. Folk-lore. I. Title.

CLARKE, Helen Archibald, d.1926. 291
A guide to mythology for young readers, by Helen A. Clarke ... New York, The Baker & Taylor company, 1910. 399 p. front., plates. 19 cm. (On cover: The Guide series). [BL310.C5] 11-6951
1. Mythology. I. Title.

CLODD, Edward, 1840-1930. 398'.042
Myths and dreams. 2d ed., rev. London, Chatto & Windus, 1891. Ann Arbor, Mich., Gryphon Books, 1971. x, 251 p. 22 cm. Includes bibliographical references. [BL313.C5 1971] 70-159918
1. Mythology. 2. Dreams. 3. Folk-lore. I. Title.

COLUM, Padraic, 1899- 1881- 291
... Orpheus: myths of the world. Twenty engravings by Boris. Artzybasheff. New York, The Macmillan company, 1930. 4 p. l., vii-xxxi, 327 p. illus., plates. 28 cm. "This edition ... is limited to three hundred fifty copies, each of which has been signed by the author and the artist. This is number 345." [BL310.C55] 30-25512
1. Mythology. 2. Legends. I. Title.

COLUM, Padraic, 1881-1972. 291
Myths of the world. 20 engravings by Boris Artzybasheff. New York, Grosset & Dunlap [1959? c1930] 327 p. illus. 21 cm. (The Universal library, UL-50) First published in 1930 under title: Orpheus: myths of the world. [BL310.C55 1959] 59-1389
1. Mythology. 2. Legends. I. Title.

COOLIDGE, Olivia E. 293
Legends of the North; illustrated by Edouard Sandoz. Boston, Houghton Mifflin, 1951. x, 260 p. illus. 24 cm. [BL860.C65] 51-9247
1. Mythology. I. Title.

COX, George William, 1827-1902. 291'.13
An introduction to the science of comparative mythology and folklore. 2d ed. London, K. Paul, Trench, 1883. Detroit, Singing Tree Press, 1968. xvi, 380 p. 22 cm. Bibliographical footnotes. [BL310.C6 1968] 68-20124
1. Mythology. 2. Folklore. I. Title. II. Title: Comparative mythology and folklore.

COX, George William, 1827-1902. 291
An introduction to the science of comparative mythology and folklore, by the Rev. Sir George W. Cox ... New York, H. Holt and company, 1881. xvi, 380 p. 21 cm. [BL310.C6] 12-31632
1. Mythology. 2. Folk-lore. I. Title.

CREIGHTON, David. 291
Deeds of gods and heroes [by] David Creighton. New York, St. Martin's Press [1967] 216 p. illus., map (on lining paper) 22 cm. Includes bibliographical references. Examines the mythologies of Greece, Rome, Egypt, Babylon, Troy, North America and Scandinavia. [PZ8.1.C873De] AC 67
1. Mythology. I. Title.

DARLINGTON, William. 234
A catechism of mythology; containing a compendious history of the heathen gods and heroes, indispensable to a correct knowledge of the ancient poets and the classics: with seventy-five engravings. To which is added, The mythology of northern Europe, translated from the French ... By William Darlington ... Baltimore, W. R. Lucas, 1832. x, [1], [13]-305 p. front. (port.) xvi pl. 20 cm. Each plate has guard sheet with descriptive letterpress. [BL310.D6] 32-35371
1. Mythology. I. Title. II. Title: The mythology of northern Europe.

DOANE, Thomas William, 1852-1885. 291'.13
Bible myths and their parallels in other religions, being a comparison of the Old and New Testament myths and miracles with those of heathen nations of antiquity, considering also their origin and meaning. New foreword by Leslie Shepard. 4th ed. New Hyde Park, N.Y., University Books [1971] xxxiii, 589 p. illus. 25 cm. Reprint of the 1908 ed. Bibliography: p. xxi-xxxiii. [BL2775.D5 1971] 70-120900 10.00
1. Bible—Criticism, interpretation, etc. 2. Mythology. I. Title.

DRAKE, Samuel Adams, 1833-1905.
The myths and fables of today; illustrations by F.T. Merrill. Boston, Lee & Shepard, 1900. v. 266 pl front., illus. 12 cm. 0-4178
I. Title.

EDWARDS, S. A. 291
A handbook of mythology. For the use of schools and academies. By S. A. Edwards ... Philadelphia, Eldredge & brother, 1883. viii, 9-253 p. illus. 17 cm. [BL310.E3 1883] 32-35370
I. Title.

EDWARDS, S. A. 291
A hand-book of mythology; for the use of schools and academies. By S. A. Edwards ... Rev. ed. Philadelphia, Eldredge & brother, 1898. viii, 9-290 p. illus. 17 cm. [BL310.E3 1898] 98-1119
1. Mythology. I. Title.

ELIADE, Mircea, 1907- 291.13
Myths, dreams, and mysteries; the encounter between contemporary faiths and archaic realities. Translated by Philip Mairet. New York, Harper [1961, c1960] 256 p. 22 cm. (The Library of religion and culture) Includes bibliography. [BL311.E413 1961] 60-15616
1. Mythology. 2. Dreams. 3. Mysteries, Religious. I. Title.

FARMER, Florence Virginia.
Nature myths of many lands, by Florence V. Farmer. New York, Cincinnati etc. American book company 1910 224 p. illus. 19 cm. (On cover: Eclectic readings) 10-13486
I. Title.

FISKE, John, 1842-1901. 291
Myths and myth makers; old tales and superstitions interpreted by comparative mythology. By John Fiske ... Boston, J. R. Osgood and company, 1873. vi p., 1 l., 251 p. 1 illus. 20 cm. "Modern works [on] ... the legend of William Tell": p. [241] [BL313.F5] 31-47
1. Mythology. 2. Folk-lore. I. Title.

FISKE, John, 1842-1901. 291
Myths and myth-makers; old tales and superstitions interpreted by comparative mythology, by John Fiske ... Boston and New York, Houghton, Mifflin and company, 1900. vi p., 1 l., 251 p. 1 illus. 20 cm. Modern works on the legend of William Tell: p. [241] [BL313.F5 1900] 0-2978
1. Mythology. 2. Folk-lore. I. Title.

FRAZER, James George Sir 291
The golden bough a study in magic and religion. 1 volume. Abriged ed. New York, Macmillan, [1960, c.1922, 1950] xvi, 864p. 22cm. (Macmillan paperbacks, 5) 2.50 pap.,
1. Mythology. 2. Religion, Primitive. 3. Magic. 4. Superstition. I. Title.

FRAZER, James George Sir, 1854- 291
The golden bough; a study in comparative religion, by J. G. Frazer ... New York and London, Macmillan and co., 1894. 2 v. front. 22 cm. [BL310.F63] 38-4128
1. Mythology. 2. Religion, Primitive. 3. Magic. 4. Superstition. I. Title.

FRAZER, James George, Sir, 1854- 291
The golden bough: a study in magic and religion, by J. G. Frazer ... 2d ed., rev. and enl. ... London, Macmillan and co., limited; New York, The Macmillan company, 1900. 3 v. front. 23 cm. Contents.-v. 1. The king of the wood. The perils of the soul.-v. 2. Killing the god.-v. 3. Killing the god (cont'd) The golden bough. [BL310.F65] 1-25066
1. Mythology. 2. Religion, Primitive. 3. Magic. 4. Superstition. I. Title.

[FRAZER, James George Sir] 1854- 291
The golden bough: a study in magic and religion. 3d ed. ... [New York, The Macmillan company, 1935] 12 v. front. 23 cm. Contents.-[vol. i-ii] pt. 1. The magic art and the evolution of kings.-[vol. iii.] pt. ii. Taboo and the perils of the soul.-[vol. iv] pt. iii. The dying god.-[vol. v-vi] pt. iv. Adonis, Attis, Osiris.--[vol. vii-viii] pt. v. Spirits of the corn and of the wild.--[vol. ix] pt. vi. The scapegoat.--[vol. x-xv] pt. vii. Balder the Beautiful.--vol. xii. Bibliography and general index. 3d ed., rev. and enl. [BL310.F 1935] 35-35398
1. Mythology. 2. Religion, Primitive. 3. Magic. 4. Superstition. I. Title.

FRAZER, James George, Sir, 1854-1941. 291.1'3
Aftermath : a supplement to The golden bough / by Sir James George Frazer. New York : AMS Press, [1976] p. cm. Reprint of the 1937 ed. published by Macmillan, New York. Includes index. [BL310.F715 1976] 75-41104 ISBN 0-404-14543-4 : 28.50
1. Mythology. 2. Religion, Primitive. 3. Magic. 4. Superstition. I. Frazer, James George, Sir, 1854-1941. The golden bough. II. Title.

FRAZER, James George, Sir 1854-1941. 291
Aftermath; a supplement to The golden bough, by Sir James George Frazer ... New York, The Macmillan company, 1937. xx p., 1 l., 494 p. 23 cm. [BL310.F715 1937] 37-27240
1. Mythology. 2. Religion, Primitive. 3. Magic. 4. Superstition. I. Frazer, James George, Sir, 1854-1941. The golden bough. II. Title.

FRAZER, James George, Sir, 1854-1941. 291'.13
The golden bough; a study in magic and religion. With an introd. by Stanley Edgar Hyman and illus. by James Lewicki. New York, Limited Editions Club, 1970. 2 v. (xxiii, 884 p.) illus. (part col.) 30 cm. Issued in case. [BL310.F72 1970] 75-13057
1. Mythology. 2. Religion, Primitive. 3. Magic. 4. Superstition. I. Title.

FRAZER, James George, Sir, 1854-1941. 291
The golden bough; a study in magic and religion. Abridged ed. New York, Macmillan, 1951 [c1950] xvi, 864 p. 22 cm. [BL310.F72 1951] A 52
1. Mythology. 2. Religion, Primitive. 3. Magic. 4. Superstition. I. Title.

FRAZER, James George, Sir, 1854-1941. 291
The golden bough; a study in magic and religion, by Sir James George Frazer ... Abridged ed. New York, The Macmillan company, 1940. xiv, 752 p. 22 cm. [BL310.F] A41
1. Mythology. 2. Religion, Primitive. 3. Magic. 4. Superstition. I. Title.

FRAZER, James George, Sir, 1854-1941. 291
The golden bough : the roots of religion and folklore / by James G. Frazer ; with a new foreword. 1981 ed. New York : Avenel Books, c1981. ca 480 p., [47] p., of plates : ill. ; 24 cm. Reprint. Originally published: London : Macmillan, 1890. Includes index. [BL310.F7 1981] 19 81-925 ISBN 0-517-33633-2 : 7.98
1. Mythology. 2. Religion, Primitive. 3. Magic. 4. Superstition. I. Title.

FRAZER, James George, Sir, 1854-1941. 291
The illustrated golden bough / Sir James George Frazer ; general editor, Mary Douglas ; abridged and illustrated by Sabine MacCormack. 1st ed. in the U.S. Garden City, N.Y. : Doubleday, 1978. 253 p., [8] leaves of plates : ill. (some col.) ; 26 cm. Includes index. [BL310.F72 1978] 78-3229 ISBN 0-385-14515-2 : 14.95
1. Mythology. 2. Religion, Primitive. 3. Magic. 4. Superstition. I. Douglas, Mary Tew. II. MacCormack, Sabine. III. Title.

FRAZER, James George, Sir 1854-1941 291
The new Golden bough; a new abridgment of the classic work. Ed., notes, foreword. by Theodor H. Gaster. Garden City, N.Y., Doubleday 1961 [c.1959] xx, 426p. (Doubleday anchor magnum A270) Bibl. 1.95 pap.,
1. Mythology. 2. Religion, Primitive. 3. Magic. 4. Superstition. I. Title.

FRAZER, James George, Sir 1854-1941 291
The new Golden bough; a new abridgment of the classic work. Ed., notes, foreword. by Theodor H. Gaster [New York] New Amer. Lib. [1964, c.1959] 832p. 18cm. (Mentor bk., MY594) Bibl. 1.25 pap.,
1. Mythology. 2. Religion, Primitive. 3. Magic. 4. Superstition. I. Title.

FRAZER, James George, Sir, 1854-1941. 291
The new Golden bough: a new abridgment of the classic work. Edited, and with notes and foreword, by Theodor H. Gaster. New York, Criterion Books [1959] xxx, 738 p. 24 cm. Bibliographical references included in "Notes" and in "Additional notes." [BL310.F72 1959] 59-6125
1. Mythology. 2. Religion, Primitive. 3. Magic. 4. Superstition. I. Title.

FRAZER, James George, Sir, 1854-1941. 291.13
The new golden bough; a new abridgement of the classic work. Edited, and with notes and foreword, by Theodor H. Gaster. [New York] New American Library [1964, c1959] 832 p. 19 cm. (A Mentor book) Includes bibliographical references. [BL310] 66-1736
1. Mythology. 2. Religion, Primitive. 3. Magic. 4. Superstitution. I. Gaster, Theodor Herzl, 1906- ed. II. Title.

THE Golden treasury of myths and legends; adapted from the world's great classics, by Anne Terry White. Illustrated by Alice and Martin Provensen. De luxe ed. New York, Golden Press [1959] 164 p. col. illus. 29 cm. (A Giant golden book) [BL310.G6] 59-1560 292
1. Mythology. 2. Legends. I. White, Anne Terry.

GOODRICH, Norma Lorre 291.13
The ancient myths. [New York] New American Library [c.1960] 256p. illus. maps (A Mentor book, MD313) Bibl. 60-16972 .50 pap.,
1. Mythology. I. Title.

GRAY, Louis Herbert, 1875-1955,ed. 291
The mythology of all races. Louis Herbert Gray, editor. George Foot Moore, consulting editor. New York, Cooper Square Publishers, 1964 [c1916-32] 13 v. illus., maps (part fold.) plates (part col.) 24 cm. Vols. 2, 4-5, 7-8, 13 are edited by J. A. Macculloch and G. F. Moore. Includes bibliographies. [BL25.M8] 65-3246
1. Mythology. I. Macculloch, John Arnott, 1868-1950 ed. II. Title.

GRIMAL, Pierre, ed. 291
Larousse world mythology [Tr. from French by Patricia Beardsworth] New York, Putnam [c.1965] 560p. illus., col. plates. 30cm. Bibl. [BL311.G683] 65-19763 25.00; until Jan. 1, 19.95
1. Mythology. I. Title.

GRIMAL, Pierre, 1912- ed. 291
Larousse world mythology. [Translated by Patricia Beardsworth] New York, Putnam [1965] 560 p. illus., col. plates. 30 cm. Translation "from Mythologies de la Mediterranee au Gange and Mythologies des steppes, des iles et des forets." Bibliography: p. 546-547. [BL311.G683 1965] 65-19763
1. Mythology. I. Title.

GUERBER, Helene Adeline, d.1929. 292
Myths of Greece and Rome, narrated with special reference to literature and art, by H. A. Guerber ... New York, Chicago [etc.] American book company [1893] 428

p. incl. front., illus., maps, geneal. tab. 19 cm. [BL725] 4-4210
1. Mythology. I. Title.

HAIGH, Madelon. 200.4
Myths are somebody's religion. Los Angeles, Tinnon-Brown [1968] v, 64 p. 23 cm. [BL311.H34] 68-57775
1. Mythology. I. Title.

*HAMILTON, Edith 292
Mythology [Reissue] Illus. by Steele Savage [New York] New Amer. Lib. [1964, c.1940, 1942] 335p. illus. 18cm. (Mentor bk. MP520) .60 pap.,
I. Title.

*HAMILTON, Edith. 292
Mythology. Illus. by Steele Savage. Large type ed. New York, Watts [1966,c1942] xiv, 497p. illus. 29 cm. (Keith Jennison bk.) 8.95
1. Mythology. I. Title.

HAMILTON, Edith. 290
Mythology, by Edith Hamilton, illustrated by Steele Savage. Boston, Little, Brown and company, 1942. xiv, 497 p. incl. front, illus. plates, geneal, tables, 22 1/2 cm. "First edition." [BL310.H3] 42-12948
1. Mythology. I. Savage, Steele, illus. II. Title.

HAMILTON, Edith, 1867- 292
Mythology. Illus. by Steele Savage. [New York] Grosset [1961, c.1940, 1942] 497p. (Little, Brown & Co. ed.; Universal Library, UL933) 1.95 pap.,
1. Mythology. I. Title.

HAMILTON, Edith, 1867- 292
Mythology. Illustrated by Steele Savage. [New York] New American Library [1953, c1942] 335p. illus. 18cm. (A Mentor book, Ma 86) [BL310] 53-2244
1. Mythology. I. Title.

HAMILTON, Edith, 1867-1963. 292
Mythology. Illustrated by Steele Savage. [New York] Grosset & Dunlap [1963, c1942] xiv. 497 p. illus., geneal. tables. 21 cm. (The Universal library. UL93) "A Little, Brown & Company edition." [BL310.H3] 64-5048
1. Mythology. I. Title.

HARTLAND, Edwin Sidney, 398'.042
1848-1927.
Mythology and folktales; their relation and interpretation. New York, AMS Press [1972] 53 p. 19 cm. Reprint of the 1900 ed., which was issued as no. 7 of the Popular studies in mythology, romance and folklore. Bibliography: p. 41-53. [BL310.H34 1972] 76-139170 5.50
1. Mythology. 2. Folk-lore. I. Title. II. Series: Popular studies in mythology, romance and folklore, no. 7.

HERZBERG, Max John, 1886- 290
Myths and their meaning. Boston, Allyn and Bacon, 1962. v, 359 p. illus. 21 cm. (The Academy classics) [BL310.H45 1962] 78-9413
1. Mythology. I. Title.

HERZBERG, Max John, 1886- 291
... Myths and their meaning, by Max J. Herzberg ... Boston, New York [etc.] Allyn and Bacon [c1928] xiii, 502 p. front., illus., plates, double map, diagrs. 18 cm. (Academy classics for junior high schools) "Reading list" at end of each chapter. [BL310.H45] 28-13009
1. Mythology. I. Title.

HERZBERG, Max John, 1886- 290
... Myths and their meaning, by Max J. Herzberg ... Boston, New York [etc.] Allyn and Bacon [c1931] xiv, 504 p. front., illus., plates, double map, diagrs. 18 cm. (Academy classics for junior high schools) "Reading list" at end of each chapter. [BL310.H45 1931] 31-30736
1. Mythology. I. Title.

INGERSOLL, Robert Green, 1833-
1899.
Myth and miracle. A lecture by Robert G. Ingersoll. The only correct and authorized ed., rev. and enl. New York, C. P. Farrell, 1895. 63 p. 21 cm. 12-34563
I. Title.

IONS, Veronica. 291.1'3
The world's mythology in colour / Veronica Ions ; introduction by Jacquetta Hawkes. London ; New York : Hamlyn, 1974. 350 p. : chiefly ill. (chiefly col.) ; 29 cm. Includes index. Bibliography: p. 340-341. [BL311.I54] 76-350372 ISBN 0-600-31301-8 : £4.95
1. Mythology. I. Title.

JOBES, Gertrude. 291.212
Outer space: myths, name meanings, calendars from the emergence of history to the present day, by Gertrude and James Jobes. New York, Scarecrow Press, 1964. 479 p. charts. 22 cm. Bibliography: p. 411-417. [BL438.J6] 64-11783
1. Mythology. 2. Astronomy. 3. Stars (in religion, folk-lore, etc.) I. Jobes, James, joint author. II. Title.

JUNG, Carl Gustav, 1875- 291.214
Essays on a science of mythology; the myths of the divine child and the divine maiden, by C. G. Jung, C. Kerenyi. Tr. [from German] by R. F. C. Hull. Rev. ed. New York, Harper [1963,c.1949, 1959] 200p. 21cm. (Harper torchbks.; Bollingen lib., TB2014) Bibl. 1.85 pap.,
1. Mythology. 2. Psychonalaysis. I. Kerenyi, Karoly, 1897. II. Title.

JUNG, Carl Gustav, 1875- 291.214
Essays on a science of mythology; the myth of the Divine Child and the mysteries of Eleusis, by C. G. Jung and C. Kerenyi. Translated by R. F. C. Hull. [New York] Pantheon Books [c1949] 289 p. illus. 24 cm. (The Bollingen series, 22) Transation of Einfuhrung in das Wesen der Mythologie. Bibliographical footnotes. [BL313.J83] 50-6248
1. Mythology. 2. Psychoanalysis. I. Kerfenyl, Karoly, 1897- II. Title. III. Series.

JUNG, Carl Gustav, 1875- 291.1'3
1961.
Essays on a science of mythology; the myth of the divine child and the mysteries of Eleusis, by C. G. Jung and C. Kerenyi. Translated by R. F. C. Hull. [Rev. ed. Princeton, N.J.] Princeton University Press [1969, c1963] viii, 200 p. 21 cm. (Bollingen series, 22) Translation of Einfuhrung in das Wesen der Mythologie. Bibliography: p. 184-196. [BL313.J83 1969] 76-88547 ISBN 0-691-09851-4 ISBN 0-691-01756-5 (pbk.)
1. Mythology. 2. Psychoanalysis. I. Kerenyi, Karoly, 1897-1973. II. Title. III. Series.

JUNG, Carl Gustav, 1875- 291.13
1961.
Essays on a science of mythology; the myths of the divine child and the divine maiden, by C. G. Jung and C. Kerenyi. Translated by R. F. C. Hull. Rev. ed. New York, Harper & Row [1963] viii, 200 p. 21 cm. (The Bollingen library, v. 22) Harper torchbooks, TB2014. Translation of Einfuhrung in das Wesen der Mythologie. Bibliography: p 184-196. [BL313.J83 1963] 63-3824
1. Mythology. 2. Psychoanalysis. I. Kerenyi, Karoly, 1897- joint author. II. Title. III. Series: Bollingen series, 22

KINGSLEY, Charles, 1819-1875.
Phaethon; or, Loose thoughts for loose thinkers. By the Rev. Charles Kingsley ... From the 2d London ed. Philadelphia, H. Hooker, 1854. 91 p. 18 1/2 cm. [PR4842.P4 1854] 15-10778
I. Title. II. Title: Loose thoughts for loose thinkers.

KNIGHT, Richard Payne, 1750- 291
1824.
The symbolical language of ancient art and mythology. An inquiry. By Richard Payne Knight ... A new ed. With introduction, additions, notes, translated into English, and a new and complete index. By Alexander Wilder, M. D. New York, J. W. Bouton, 1876. xxvii, 240 p. 25 cm. Bibliographical foot-notes. [BL313.K6 1876] A 19
1. Mythology. 2. Symbolism. 3. Art, Ancient. I. Wilder, Alexander, 1823-1908, ed. II. Title.

KNIGHT, Richard Payne, 1750- 291
1824.
The symbolical language of ancient art and mythology; an inquiry, by Richard Payne Knight ... New ed., with introduction, additions, notes translated into English and a new and complete index, by Alexander Wilder, M. D. With 348 illustrations by A. L. Rawson. New York, J. W. Bouton, 1892. xxvii, [1], 452 p. front., illus., plates. 25 cm. (Half-title: Bouton's archaic, library. vol. ii) [BL313.K6 1892] 31-48
1. Mythology. 2. Symbolism. 3. Art, Ancient. I. Wilder, Alexander, 1823-1908, ed. II. Title.

KOMROFF, Manuel, 1890- 292
Gods and demons. New York, Lion Books [1954] 189p. 18cm. (Lion library edition, LL 8) [BL310.K63] 55-21995
1. Mythology. I. Title.

KRAMER, Samuel Noah, 1897- 291
ed.
Mythologies of the ancient world. Chicago, Quadrangle Books [c.1961] 480p. illus. Bibl. 7.50
1. Mythology. I. Title.

KRAMER, Samuel Noah, 1897- 291
ed.
Mythologies of the ancient world. With contributions by Rudolf Anthes [and others. 1st ed.] Garden City, N.Y., Doubleday, 1961. 480 p. illus. 18 cm. (Anchor books, A229) Includes bibliography. [BL311.K7] 60-13538
1. Mythology. I. Title.

LANG, Andrew, 1844-1912. 291.1'3
Custom and myth / by Andrew Lang. 2nd ed., revised. Wakefield : EP Publishing, 1974 [i.e.1976] [7], 312 p. : ill. ; 19 cm. Reprint of the 2d, rev. ed. published in 1885 by Longmans, London. Includes index. [BL310.L3 1974] 74-189327 12.95
1. Mythology. I. Title.
Distributed by British Book Center, New York.

LANG, Andrew, 1844-1912. 291'.13
Magic and religion. New York, Greenwood Press [1969] x, 316 p. 23 cm. Reprint of the 1901 ed. Contents.Contents.—Science and superstition.—The theory of loan-gods, or borrowed religion.—Magic and religion.—The origin of the Christian faith.—The approaches to Mr. Frazer's theory.—Attemps to prove the Sacaean criminal divine.—Zakmuk, Sacaea, and Purim.—Mordecai, Esther, Vashti, and Haman.—Why was the mock-king of the Sacaea whipped and hanged?—Calvary.—The ghastly priest.—South African religion.—"Cup and ring:" An old problem solved.—First-fruits and taboos.—Walking through fire.—Appendices. Mr. Tylor's theory of borrowing. The martyrdom of Dasius. The ride of the beardless one. Bibliographical footnotes. [BL310.L34 1969] 69-13964
1. Mythology. 2. Religion, Primitive. I. Title.

LANG, Andrew, 1844-1912. 291.13
Magic and religion, by Andrew Lang ... London, New York and Bombay, Longmans, Green, and co., 1901. x, 316 p. 24 cm. [BL310.L34] 2-5201
1. Mythology. 2. Religion, Primitive. I. Title.
Contents omitted.

LANG, Andrew, 1844-1912. 291'.13
Modern mythology. London, Longmans, Green, 1897. New York, AMS Press [1968] xxiv, 212 p. 22 cm. Contents.Contents.—Introduction.—Recent mythology.—The story of Daphne.—The question of allies.—Mannhardt.—Philology and Demeter Erinnys.—Totemism.—The validity of anthropological evidence.—The philological method in anthropology.—Criticism of fetishism.—The riddle theory.—Artemis.—The fire-walk.—The origin of death.—Conclusion. Bibliographical footnotes. [BL310.L35 1968] 68-54279
1. Mythology. I. Title.

LANG, Andrew, 1844-1912. 291
Modern mythology, by Andrew Lang ... London, New York and Bombay, Longmans, Green, and co., 1897. xxiv p., 1 l., 212 p. 23 cm. "Most of chapter xii, appeared in the 'Contemporary review', and most of chapter xiii, in the 'Princeton review'."--p. xxiv. [BL310.L35] 12-34979
1. Mythology. I. Title.
Contents omitted.

LANG, Andrew, 1844-1912. 291'.13
Myth, ritual, and religion. New York, AMS Press [1968] 2 v. in 1. 23 cm. Reprint of the 1906 ed. Bibliographical footnotes. [BL310.L4 1968] 68-54280
1. Mythology. 2. Myth. 3. Religion, Primitive. 4. Rites and ceremonies. I. Title.

LANG, Andrew, 1844-1912. 291
Myth, ritual and religion, by Andrew Lang ... New ed. London, New York [etc.] Longmans, Green, and co., 1899. 2 v. 20 cm. (The Silver library) "First printed, August, 1887." [BL310.L4] 12-34980
1. Mythology. 2. Religion, Primitive. 3. Rites and ceremonies. I. Title.

LANG, Andrew, 1844-1912. 291.
Myth, ritual and religion, by Andrew Lang ... New impression. London, New York [etc.] Longmans, Green, and co., 1906. 2 v. 19 1/2 cm. (On cover: The Silver library) "First printed, August, 1887; reset ... February, 1899; reprinted ... September, 1906." Bibliographical foot-notes. [BL310.L4 1906] 44-29216
1. Mythology. 2. Religion, Primitive. 3. Rites and ceremonies. I. Title.

LAROUSSE encyclopedia of 290
mythology. With an introd. by Robert Graves. [Translated by Richard Aldington and Delano Ames, and rev. by a panel of editorial advisers from the Larousse mythologie generale, edited by Felix Guirland] New York, Prometheus Press, 1959. viii, 500p. illus., col. plantes, maps. 30cm. Bibliography: p. [493]-494. [BL310.G853] 59-11019
1. ythologie generalle. 2. Mythology. 3. Folk-lore. I. Fuirand, Fellx ed.

LARUE, Gerald A. 301.2'1
Ancient myth and modern man [by] Gerald A. Larue. Englewood Cliffs, N.J., Prentice-Hall [1975] ix, 230 p. 23 cm. Bibliography: p. 218-225. [BL311.L32] 74-9527 ISBN 0-13-035493-7 ISBN 0-13-035493-7 9.95
1. Mythology. I. Title.
Pbk. 4.95; ISBN 0-13-035485-6.

LEVI-STRAUSS, Claude 291'.13
The raw and the cooked. Translated from the French by John and Doreen Weightman. [1st U.S. ed.] New York, Harper & Row [1969] xiii, 387 p. illus., chart, maps, 25 cm. (His Introduction to a science of mythology, 1) Translation of Le cru et le cuit. Bibliography: p. 361-370. [BL304.L4813 1969] 67-22501 10.00
1. Mythology. I. Title.

MABIE, Hamilton Wright, 1846-
1916, ed.
... Myths, edited by Hamilton Wright Mabie. Garden City, N.Y., Nelson Doubleday, inc., 1927. xvi p., 1 l., 3-351 p. col. front. 19 1/2 cm. (The children's library) Title within ornamental border in colors. Illustrated lining-papers. Running title: Myths every child should know. A 27
1. Mythology I. Title. II. Title: Myths every child should know.

MALINOWSKI, Bronislaw, 291.13
1884-
Myth in primitive psychology, by Bronislaw Malinowski ... New York, W. W. Norton & company, inc. [c1926] ix, 11-94 p. 17 cm. [The new science series, ed. by C. K. Ogden. vol. I] [BL313.M33] 27-8132
1. Mythology. 2. Ethnopsychology. I. Title.

MASSEY, Gerald, 1828-1907. 291
A book of the beginnings, containing an attempt to recover and reconstitute the lost origines of the myths and mysteries, types and symbols, religion and language, with Egypt for the mouthpiece and Africa as the birthplace / by Gerald Massey ; introd. by Leslie Shepard. Secaucus, N.J. : University Books, [1974] 2 v. ; 24 cm. Reprint of the 1881 ed. published by Williams and Norgate, London. Contents.Contents.—v. 1. Egyptian origines in the British Isles.—v. 2. Egyptain origines in the Hebrew, Akkado-Assyrian and Maori. Includes bibliographical references. [BL313.M37 1974] 74-75172 ISBN 0-8216-0211-X : 30.00
1. Mythology. 2. Religion, Primitive. 3. Folk-lore. 4. Language and languages—Etymology. 5. Egyptian language—Etymology—Names. I. Title: A book of the beginnings ...

MASSEY, Gerald, 1828-1907. 291.1'3
The natural genesis : or, Second part of A book of the beginnings, containing an attempt to recover and reconstitute the lost origins of the myths and mysteries, types and symbols, religion and language, with Egypt from the mouthpiece and Africa as the birthplace / by Gerald Massey. New York : S. Weiser, 1974. 2 v. : ill. ; 27 cm. "Comparative vocabulary of Sanskrit and Egyptian": v. 2, p. [507]-519. Reprint of the 1883 ed. published by Williams and Norgate, London. Includes bibliographical references and index. [BL313.M38 1974] 73-92166 ISBN 0-87728-248-X : 50.00
1. Mythology. 2. Mythology, Egyptian. 3. Folk-lore. 4. Christianity and other religions. I. Title.

MAYO, Robert, 1784-1864. 291.13
A new system of mythology, in two volumes; giving a full account of the idoltry of the pagan world, illustrated by analytical tables, and 50 elegant copperplate engravings, representing more than 200 subjects, in a third volume, particularly adapted to the capacity of junior students, compiled, digested, and arranged, by Robert Mayo... Philadelphia, Printed for the author, by T. S. Manning, N.w. corner of Sixth and Chesnut streets, 1815-19. 4 v. plates, fold., tab. 22 cm. Imprint varies slightly. Volume numbers appear only on half-titles. Vols. II-III: A new system of mythology, in three volumes...illustrated by analytical tables...in a fourth volume. Vol. IV has engraved t.-p.: A mythology of the pagan world illustrated by 52 plates, engraved by Tanner, Vallance, Kearny & co.: Philadelphia, Published by Geo: Mayo & co.: 1819. Printed by Cammeyer & Acock. [BL310.M3] 32-35163
1. Mythology. 2. Idols and images—Worship. 3. Religion, Primitive. 4. Art, Ancient. I. Title.

MEES, Gualtherus Hendrik, 1903- 290
The revelation in the wilderness dealing with the revelation of the meaning of the symbolism contained in the traditions of old in the wilderness of the mind and of the modern world); an exposition of traditional psychology. Deventer, N. Kluwer, 1951-54. 3v. illus. 25cm. Contents.v. 1. The book of signs [with Supplement]--v. 2. The book of battles [with Supplement]--v. 3. The book of stars [with Supplement] [BL313.M4] 53-33702
1. Mythology. 2. Symbolism. 3. Religion, Primitive. I. Title. II. Title: The book of signs.

METCALFE, James S[tetson]
Mythology for moderns ... New York, Life pub. co. 1899. 117 p. illus. 8 degree. 0-1474
I. Title.

MILLS, Charles De Berard, 1821-1900. 291.13
The tree of mythology, its growth and fruitage; genesis of the nursery tale, saws of folk-lore, etc.; a study by Charles De B. Mills ... Syracuse, N.Y., C. W. Bardeen, 1889. vii, [9]-288 p. 23 cm. [BL310.M5] 12-36785
1. Mythology. 2. Folk-lore. 3. Symbolism. I. Title.

MONTAGU, Ashley, 1905- 398'.04
The ignorance of certainty [by] Ashley Montagu and Edward Darling. [1st ed.] New York, Harper & Row [1970] xvi, 240 p. 22 cm. Includes bibliographical references. [BL311.M64 1970] 78-123955 6.95
1. Mythology. 2. Folk-lore. I. Darling, Edward, joint author. II. Title.

MULLER, Friedrich Max, 1823-1900. 291.1'3
Comparative mythology / Friedrich Max Muller. New York : Arno Press, 1977. p. cm. (International folklore) Reprint of the 1909 ed. published by G. Routledge, London. Includes index. [BL311.M8 1977] 77-70612 ISBN 0-405-10111-2 : 14.00
1. Mythology. I. Title. II. Series.

MULLER, Friedrich Max, 1823-1900. 291.13
Contributions to the science of mythology, by the Right Hon. Professor F. Max Muller ... London, New York and Bombay, Longmans, Green, and co., 1897. 2 v. 23 cm. Paged continuously. [BL310.M78] 12-36948
1. Mythology. I. Title.

MUNZ, Peter, 1921- 291.1'3
When the golden bough breaks; structuralism or typology? London, Boston, Routledge & K. Paul [1973] xii, 143 p. 23 cm. Bibliography: p. 131-138. [BL311.M83] 73-87315 ISBN 0-7100-7650-9 7.50
1. Mythology. 2. Myth. 3. Symbolism. I. Title.

MURRAY, Alexander Stuart, 1841-1904. 291
Manual of mythology, for the use of schools, art students and general readers. Founded on the works of Petiscus, Preller, and Welcker. By Alexander S. Murray ... with thirty-five plates and toned papers, representing seventy-six mythological subjects. New York, Scribner, Welford and Armstrong, 1873. viii, 399 p. plates. 18 cm. [BL310.M85 1873] 32-35160
1. Mythology. I. Title.

MURRAY, Alexander Stuart, 1841-1904. 291
Manual of mythology. Greek and Roman, Norse, and old German, Hindoo and Egyptian mythology. By Alexander S. Murray ... Reprinted from the second revised London edition. With 45 plates on tinted paper ... New York, C. Scribner's sons [1888?] xi, 368 p. front., xlv pl. 21 cm. [BL310.M85] 41-30622
1. Mythology. I. Title.

MURRAY, Alexander Stuart, 1841-1904. 291
Manual of mythology. Greek and Roman, Norse and Old German, Hindoo and Egyptian mythology, by Alexander S. Murray ... revised and corrected on the basis of the 20th ed. of Petiscus, with ten full-page plates and one hundred illustrations in text. Philadelphia, D. McKay [c1895] 2 p. l., 7-408 p. front., illus., plates. 20 cm. [BL310.M85 1895] 12-36985
1. Mythology. I. Title.

MURRAY, Alexander Stuart, 1841-1904. 291
Manual of mythology. Greek and Roman, Norse and Old German, Hindoo and Egyptian mythology, by Alexander S. Murray ... With notes, revisions and additions by William H. Klapp ... Philadelphia, H. Altermus, 1898. xv, 427 p. illus., 16 pl. (incl. front.) geneal, tab. 20 cm. [BL310.M85 1898] 4-4205
1. Mythology. I. Klapp, William Henry, 1849-1924, ed. II. Title.

MURRAY, Alexander Stuart, 1841-1904. 291
Manual of mythology; Greek and Roman, Norse and Old German, Hindoo and Egyptian mythology, by Alexander S. Murray ... With notes revisions and additions by William H. Klapp ... With two hundred illustrations and a complete index. New York, Tudor publishing company [1935] xv, [1], 427 p. front., illus., plates. 22 cm. [BL310.M85 1935] 36-6098
1. Mythology. I. Klapp, William Henry, 1849-1924, ed. II. Title.

MURRAY, Alexander Stuart, 1841-1904. 398
Manual of mythology: Greek and Roman, Norse and Old German, Hindoo and Egyptian mythology. Detroit, Gale Research Co., 1970. xi, 368 p. plates. 23 cm. "A facsimile reprint of the 1885 edition." [BL310.M85 1885a] 75-130452
1. Mythology. I. Title.

**MYTHOLOGY* 291
[notes] by Julia Wolfe Loomis Edit. bd. of consultants: Stanley Cooperman, Charles Leavitt. Unicio J. Violi. New York, Monarch Pr. [c.1965] 155p. 22cm. (Monarch notes and study guides 523-1) Cover title. Bibl. 1.00 pap.,

MYTHOLOGY : 291.1'3
an illustrated encyclopedia / edited by Richard Cavendish ; consultant editor, Trevor O. Ling. New York : Rizzoli, c1980. 303 p. : ill. (some col.) ; 30 cm. Includes index. Bibliography: p. 293-295. [BL311.M95] 19 79-92600 ISBN 0-8478-0286-8 : 35.00
1. Mythology. 2. Religions. I. Cavendish, Richard. II. Ling, Trevor Oswald.

THE Mythology of all races 294.
... Louis Herbert Gray ... editor George Foot Moore ... consulting editor. Boston, Marshall Jones company, 1916-32. 13 v. fronts. (part col.) illus., plates (part col.) maps (part fold.) 25 cm. Vols. 2, 4-5, 7-8, 13 are edited by J. A. Macculloch and G. F. Moore, and have imprint: Boston, Archaeological institute of America, Marshall Jones company. Contents.--i. Greek and Roman, By W. S. Fox. 1916--ii. Eddic, by J. A. Macculloch. 1930.--iii. Celtic, by J. A. Macculloch; Slavic by Jan Machal. 1918.--iv. Finno-Ugric. Siberian, by Uno Holmberg. 1917--v. Semitic, by S. H. Langdon. 1931.--vi. Indian, by A. B. Keith; Iranian, by A. J. Carnoy, 1917.--vii. Armenian, by M. H. Annikian; African, by Alice Werner. 1925.--viii. Chinese, by J. C. Ferguson; Japanese, by Masaharu Anesaki. 1928--ix. Ceanic, by R. B. Dixon. 1916--x. North American, by H. B. Alexander. 1916.--xi. Latin-American, by H. B. Alexander. 1920.--xii. Egyptian, by W. M. Muller; Indo-Chinese, by J. G. Scott. 1918.--xiii. Complete index to volumes 1-xii. 1932. Bibliography at end of each volume. [BL25.M8] 17-26477
1. Mythology 2. Mythology I. Gray, Louis Herbert, 1875- ed. II. Moore, George Foot, 1851-1931, joint ed. III. Macculloch, John Arnott, 1868- joint ed.

... Myths and legends; 291
ed. by Thomas J. Shahan ... Boston, Hall and Locke company [c1902] xix, 391, [1] p., 1 l. incl. col. front., illus. col. plates. 22 cm. (Young folks' library. [3d ed.] v) Issued in 1901 under title: A book of famous myths and legends. "Suggestions for supplementary reading": 1 leaf at end of book. [AC5.Y69 vol. 5] 3-8905
1. Mythology. 2. Legends. I. Shahan, Thomas Joseph, bp., 1857-1932, ed.

MYTHS and symbols; 200.4
studies in honor of Mircea Eliade. Edited by Joseph M. Kitagawa and Charles H. Long. With the collaboration of Gerald C. Brauer and Marshall G. S. Hodgson. Chicago, University of Chicago Press [1969] 438 p. port. 23 cm. [BL25.M85] 69-12132
1. Mythology. 2. Symbolism. I. Eliade, Mircea, 1907- II. Kitagawa, Joseph Mitsuo, 1915- ed. III. Long, Charles H., ed.

NEW Larousse 200.4'03
encyclopedia of mythology. Introd. by Robert Graves. [Translated by Richard Aldington and Delano Ames, and rev. by a panel of editorial advisers from the Larousse mythologie generale edited by Felix Guirand. New ed. New York] Putnam [1968, c1959] xi, 500 p. illus., col. plates. 30 cm. Bibliography: p. [486]-487. [BL311.N43 1968] 68-57758 17.95
1. Mythology. 2. Folk-lore. I. Guirand, Felix, ed. Mythologie generale. II. Title: Larousse encyclopedia of mythology.

NEW Larousse encyclopedia 291'.13
of mythology. Introduction by Robert Graves [translated from the French by Richard Aldington & Delano Ames, & revised by a panel of editorial advisors from the Larousse mythologie generale edited by Felix Guirand] New ed. London, New York, Hamlyn, 1968. xi, 500 p. 32 plates, illus. (some col.) 30 cm. First ed. published in 1959 under title: Larousse encyclopedia of mythology. Bibliography: p. [486]-487. [BL311.L33 1968] 78-436741 84/-
1. Mythology. 2. Folk-lore. I. Guirand, Felix, ed. Mythologie generale.

PARKER, Derek. 291.2'11
The immortals / Derek & Julia Parker. New York : McGraw-Hill, c1976. 207 p. : ill. (some col.) ; 30 cm. "A Webb & Bower book." Includes index. Bibliography: p. 204-205. [BL311.P37] 76-6940 ISBN 0-07-048493-7 : 19.95
1. Mythology. 2. Folk-lore. I. Parker, Julia. II. Title.

PARKER, Derek. 291.1'3
The immortals / [by] Derek & Julia Parker. London : Barrie and Jenkins, 1976. 208 p. : ill. (some col.), facsim., port. ; 30 cm. "A Webb & Bower book" Ill. on lining papers. Includes index. Bibliography: p. 204-205. [BL311.P37 1976b] 77-357776 ISBN 0-214-20283-6 : £7.95
1. Mythology. 2. Folk-lore. I. Parker, Julia, joint author. II. Title.

POOR, Laura Elizabeth. 291.2
Sanskrit and its kindred literatures; studies in comparative mythology. Boston, Milford House [1973, c1880] p. Reprint of the ed. published by Roberts Bros., Boston. Bibliography: p. [BL313.P6 1973] 73-13748 ISBN 0-87821-179-9 30.00 (lib. bdg.)
1. Mythology. 2. Literature, Ancient. 3. Literature, Medieval. I. Title.

POOR, Laura Elizabeth. 291
Sanskrit and its kindred literatures, Studies in comparative mythology. By Laura Elizabeth Poor. Boston, Roberts brothers, 1880. 2 p. l., [iii]-iv p., 1 l., 468 p. 126 cm. "Partial list of books consulted": p. [453]-455. [BL313.P6] 31-1130
1. Mythology. 2. Literature, Ancient. 3. Literature, Medeval. I. Title.

RANK, Otto, 1884-1939. 290
The myth of the birth of the hero; a psychological interpretation of mythology, translated by F. Robbins and Smith Ely Jelliffe. New York, R. Brunner, 1952. 100 p. 23 cm. Bibliographical footnotes. [BL313.R3 1952] 52-9509
1. Mythology. 2. Psychology, Pathological. 3. Heroes. I. Title.

RANK, Otto, 1884-1939. 290
The myth of the birth of the hero, and other writings. Edited by Philip Freund. New York, Vintage Books, 1959. xiv, 315, xv p. 19 cm. (A Vintage book, K-70) Bibliographical footnotes. [BL313.R263] 59-593
1. Mythology. 2. Psychology, Pathological. 3. Heroes. 4. Psychoanalysis—Addresses, essays, lectures. I. Title.

ROBINSON, Herbert Spencer. 291.1'3
Myths and legends of all nations / by Herbert Spencer Robinson and Knox Wilson. Totowa, N.J. : Littlefield, Adams, 1976. xii, 244 p. ; 21 cm. (A Littlefield, Adams quality paperback ; no. 319) Includes indexes. [BL310.R6 1976] 75-35613 ISBN 0-8226-0319-5 : 2.95
1. Mythology. 2. Legends. 3. Folk-lore. I. Wilson, Knox, 1901- joint author. II. Title.

ROBINSON, Herbert Spencer. 290
Myths and legends of all nations, by Herbert Spencer Robinson and Knox Wilson. [1st ed.] Garden City, N.Y. Garden City Pub. Co. [1950] xii, 244 p. 22 cm. [BL310.R6] 50-6035
1. Mythology. 2. Legends. 3. Folk-Lore. I. Wilson, Knox, 1901- II. Title.

RYNO, Wakeman, 1849-1918. 299.31
Amen, the god of the Amonians: or, A key to the mansions in heaven, by Wakeman Ryno, M.D. New York, Baltimore [etc.] Broadway publishing co., 1910. 3 p. l., 5-138 p. front., plates. 20 cm. [BL313.R8] 11-651
1. Mythology. 2. Astrology. 3. Symbolism. I. Title.

SPENCE, Lewis. 291
The outlines of mythology. Introd. by Daniel B. Dodson [Gloucester, Mass., Peter Smith, 1963, c.1944, 1961] 144p. 19cm. (Premier bk. rebound) Bibl. 2.50
1. Mythology. I. Title.

SPENCE, Lewis, 1874- 291
An introduction to mythology, by Lewis Spence ... New York, Farrar & Rinehart [1931] 334, [1] p. front. 22 cm. (Lettered on cover: The myths series) Printed in Great Britain. [Full name: James Lewis Thomas Chalmers Spence] [BL310.S7 1931] 31-28238
1. Mythology. I. Title.

SPENCE, Lewis, 1874- 291.13
The outlines of mythology. Introd. by Daniel B. Dodson. Greenwich, Conn., Fawcett [c.1944, 1961] 144p. (Premier bk., d143) Bibl. .50 pap.,
1. Mythology. I. Title.

SPENCE, Lewis, 1874-1955. 291.1'3
The outlines of mythology / by Lewis Spence. Folcroft, Pa. : Folcroft Library Editions, 1977. p. cm. Reprint of the 1944 ed. published by Watts, London, which was issued as no. 99 of Thinker's library.

Includes index. Bibliography: p. [BL311.S68 1977] 77-3223 ISBN 0-8414-7803-1 lib. bdg. : 15.00
1. Mythology. I. Title. II. Series: The Thinker's library ; no. 99.

TICHENOR, Henry Mulford, 1858- 291.
Mythologies, a materialistic interpretation, analyzing the class character of religion, by Henry M. Tichenor ... St. Louis, Mo., The Melting pot publishing co. [c1919] 198 p. 19 cm. [BL310.T5] 19-14538
I. Title.

VIGNOLI, Tito, 1828-1914. 290
... Myth and science. An essay. By Tito Vignoli. New York, D. Appleton and company, 1882. 2 p. 330 p. 19 1/2 cm. (The international scientific series [40]) [BL313.V5] 12-39768
1. Mythology. 2. Psychology. Religious. 3. Religious—Philosophy. I. Title.

WATTS, Alan Wilson, 1915- 230
Myth and ritual in Christianity. New York, Vanguard Press [1953] ix. 262p. illus. 23cm. (Myth and man) A Thames and Hudson book. [BR135.W3] 54-6992
1. Mythology. 2. Christian art and symbolism. I. Title. II. Series.

*WEIGEL, James. 291.13
Mythology; including Egyptian, Babylonian, Indian, Greek, Roman, and Norse mythologies, Arthurian legends, introduction to mythology, narratives and commentaries; biographical essay, recommended reading, genealogical tables ... by James Weigel, Jr. Lincoln, Neb., Cliff's Notes [1973] 210 p. 21 cm. Bibiography: p. 194-195. [BL310] ISBN 0-8220-1485-8 1.95 (pbk.)
1. Mythology. I. Title.

WHITE, Catherine Ann, 1825-1878. 291.
The student's mythology: a compendium of Greek, Roman, Egyptian, Assyrian, Persian, Hindoo, Clune[!], Thibetian, Scandinavian, Celtic, Aztec, and Peruvian mythologies, in accordance with standard authorities. Arranged for the use of schools and academies. By C. A. White. New ed., rev. and cor. New York, A. C. Armstrong & son, 1882. 1 p. l., 315 p. 19 cm. [BL310.W5 1882] 19-7139
1. Mythology. I. Title.

WHITE, Catherine Ann, 1825-1878. 291.
The student's mythology; a compendium of Greek, Roman, Egyptian, Assyrian, Persian, Hindoo, Chinese, Thibetian, Scandinavian, Celtic, Aztec, and Peruvian mythologies ... arranged for the use of schools and academies, by C. A. White. New ed., rev. and cor. New York, A. C. Armstrong & son, 1891. 1 p. l., 315 p. 19 cm. [BL310.W5 1891] 3-26450
1. Mythology. I. Title.

WHITE, Catherine Ann, 1825-1878. 291.
Student's mythology: a compendium of Greek, Roman, Egyptian, Assyrian, Persian, Hindoo, Chinese, Hibetian, Scandinavian, Celtic, Aztec, and Peruvian mythologies ... arranged for the use of schools and academies, by C. A. White. New ed., rev. and cor. New York, A. C. Armstrong & son, 1894. 1 p. l., 315 p. 19 cm. [BL310.W5 1894] 3-26448
1. Mythology. I. Title.

WITTGENSTEIN, Ludwig, 1889-1951. 291
Remarks on Frazer's Golden bough / by Ludwig Wittgenstein ; edited by Rush Rhees ; translated by A. C. Miles and Rush Rhees. Atlantic Highlands, N.J. : Humanities Press, 1979. p. cm. Translation of Bemerkungen uber Frazers Golden bough. [BL310.F73W5713] 79-4038 ISBN 0-391-00984-2 : 6.00
1. Frazer, James George, Sir, 1854-1941. The golden bough. 2. Mythology. 3. Religion, Primitive. 4. Magic. 5. Superstition. I. Rhees, Rush. II. Title.

WOOLSEY, John Martin, 1833-
The original Garden of Eden discovered and the final solution of the mystery of the woman the tree and the serpent, being the lunar theory of mythology by J. M. Woolsey ... [Mt. Vernon? N.Y., c1910] 5 p. l., [5]-512 p. 21 cm. $1.50. [1910; A271489; J. M. Woolsey, Mt.] 10-20290
I. Title.

WOOLSEY, John Martin, 1833-
Symbolic mythology and translation of a lost and forgotten language, by J. M. Woolsey ... [New York, Printed by T. Taylor, c1917] 2 p. l., [7]-224 p. 21 cm. [BL603.W8] 17-28084
1. Mythology. 2. Symbolism. I. Title.

Mythology— Addresses, essays, lectures.

CAMPBELL, Joseph, 1904- 398'.042
Myths to live by. Foreword by Johnson E. Fairchild. New York, Viking Press [1972] x, 276 p. 22 cm. Based on thirteen lectures delivered at the Cooper Union Forum between 1958 and 1971. [BL315.C27] 78-181974 ISBN 0-670-50359-2 6.95
1. Mythology—Addresses, essays, lectures. I. Title.

MIDDLETON, John, 1921- comp. 291.1'3
Myth and cosmos : readings in mythology and symbolism / edited by John Middleton. Austin : University of Texas Press, [1976] c1967. p. cm. (Texas Press sourcebooks in anthropology ; 5) Reprint of the ed. published for the American Museum of Natural History by the Natural History Press, Garden City, N.Y., issued in series: American sourcebooks in anthropology. Includes index. Bibliography: p. [BL313.M48 1976] 75-43817 ISBN 0-292-75030-7 pbk. : 5.95
1. Mythology—Addresses, essays, lectures. 2. Symbolism—Addresses, essays, lectures. I. Title. II. Series. III. Series: American Museum sourcebooks in anthropology.
Contents omitted.

MIDDLETON, John, 1921- comp. 291'.13
Myth and cosmos; readings in mythology and symbolism. Garden City, N.Y., Published for the American Museum of Natural History [by] the Natural History Press, 1967. xi, 368 p. illus. 21 cm. (American Museum sourcebooks in anthropology) Bibliography: p. [349]-356. [BL313.M48] 67-12883
1. Mythology—Addresses, essays, lectures. 2. Symbolism—Addresses, essays, lectures. I. American Museum of Natural History, New York. II. Title. III. Series.

MURRAY, Henry Alexander, 1893- ed. 291.13
Myth and mythmaking. New York, G. Braziller, 1960. 381 p. 22 cm. [BL311.M85] 59-12232
1. Mythology—Addresses, essays, lectures. I. Title.

MYTHS / 291.1'3
Alexander Eliot ... [et al.] New York : McGraw-Hill, c1976. 320 p. : ill. ; 33 cm. Includes index. Bibliography: p. 302-304. [BL315.M95] 76-20186 ISBN 0-07-019193-X : 39.95
1. Mythology—Addresses, essays, lectures. 2. Myth—Addresses, essays, lectures. I. Eliot, Alexander.

SEBEOK, Thomas Albert, 1920- ed. 291.13
Myth: a symposium. Bloomington, Ind. Univ. Pr. [c.1958, 1965] 180p. illus. 21cm. (Midland bk. MB83) Bibl. [BL310.S37] 65-29803 2.45 pap.,
1. Mythology—Addresses, essays, lectures. I. Title.

SEBEOK, Thomas Albert, 1920- ed. 291.04
Myth: a symposium. Philadelphia, American Folklore Society, 1955. 110p. diagrs. 26cm. (Bibliographical and special series of the American Folklore Society, v. 5) [BL310.S37] 56-1838
1. Mythology— Addresses, essays, lectures. I. Title. II. Series: American Folklore Society. Bibliographical and special series, v. 5

SEBEOK, Thomas Albert, 1920- ed. 291.13
Myth: a symposium. Edited by Thomas A. Sebeok. Bloomington, Indiana University Press [1965] 180 p. illus. 21 cm. (A Midland book, MB83) Contents.—Myth, symbolism, and truth, by D. Bidney.—The eclipse of solar mythology, by R. M. Dorson.—Myth, metaphor, and simile, by R. Th. Christiansen.—The structural study of myth, by C. Levi-Strauss.—The personal use of myth in dreams, by D. Eggan.—Myth and ritual, by Lord Ragian.—The ritual view of myth and the mythic, by S. E. Hyman.—The semantic approach to myth, by P. Wheelwright.—Myth and folktales, by S. Thompson. Includes bibliographies. [BL310.S37 1965] 65-29803
1. Mythology—Addresses, essays, lectures. I. Title.

Mythology, Armenian.

ANANIKIAN, Mardiros Harootioon, 1875-1924. 294.
... Armeniun [mythology] by Mardiros H. Ananikian ... African [mythology] by Alice Werner ... Boston, Archaelogical institute of America, Marshall Jones company, 1925. viii, 448 p. illus., xxxiv pl. (part col., incl. fronr.) map. 25 cm (The mythology of all races ... Canon J. A. MacCulloch ... editor ...vol.viii) Each plate accompanied by guard sheet with descriptive letterpress. Bibliography: p. [443]-448. [BL25.M3 vol. 7] [BL1760.A6] 25-19195
1. Mythology, Armenian. 2. Mythology, African. 3. Tales, Arnenian. 4. Tales, African. 5. Folk-lore—Armenia. 6. Folk-lore—Africa, East. 7. Animals, Legends and stories of. I. Werner, Allice, 1859-1935. II. Title.

Mythology, Aryan.

COX, George William, 1827-1902. 291'.13
The mythology of the Aryan nations. Port Washington, N.Y., Kennikat Press [1969] 2 v. 23 cm. Half-title: Aryan mythology. Reprint of the 1870 ed. Bibliographical footnotes. [BL660.C6 1969] 68-8202
1. Mythology, Aryan. 2. Aryans. I. Title. II. Title: Aryan mythology.

GUBERNATIS, Angelo de, conte, 1840-1913. 291.2'12
Zoological mythology; or, The legends of animals. London, Trubner, 1872. Detroit, Singing Tree Press, 1968. 2 v. 22 cm. Bibliographical footnotes. [BL325.A6G8 1968] 68-58904
1. Mythology, Aryan. 2. Animal lore. 3. Animals, Legends and stories of. 4. Folk-lore. I. Title. II. Title: Legends of animals.

Mythology, Aryan—Addresses, essays, lectures.

MYTH and law among the Indo-Europeans; 291'.13 studies in Indo-European comparative mythology. Edited by Jaan Puhvel. Berkeley, University of California Press, 1970. x, 276 p. 24 cm. (Publications of the UCLA Center for the Study of Comparative Folklore and Mythology, 1) "Most of the works ... were originally presented at a symposium held under the joint auspices of the Center [for the Study of Comparative Folklore and Mythology] and of the Section of Indo-European Studies [of the University of California, Los Angeles] on March 17-18, 1967." Bibliography: p. [247]-268. [BL660.M9] 75-627781 ISBN 0-520-01587-8 10.00
1. Mythology, Aryan—Addresses, essays, lectures. I. Puhvel, Jaan, ed. II. California. University. University at Los Angeles. Center for the Study of Comparative Folklore and Mythology. III. Series: California. University. University at Los Angeles. Center for the Study of Comparative Folklore and Mythology. Publications, 1

MYTH in Indo-European antiquity. 291.1'3 Edited by Gerald James Larson. Co-edited by C. Scott Littleton and Jaan Puhvel. Berkeley, University of California Press, 1974. vi, 197 p. 24 cm. (Publications of the UCSB Institute of Religious Studies) Essays resulting from a conference held in Mar. 1971 at the University of California, Santa Barbara. Bibliography: p. [191]-192. [BL660.M93] 72-93522 ISBN 0-520-02378-1 10.00
1. Dumezil, Georges, 1898- —Addresses, essays, lectures. 2. Mythology, Aryan—Addresses, essays, lectures. I. Larson, Gerald James, ed. II. Littleton, C. Scott, ed. III. Puhvel, Jaan, ed. IV. Series: California. University, Santa Barbara. Institute of Religious Studies. Publications.

Mythology, Assyro-Babylonian.

GASTER, Theodor Herzl, 1906- ed. and tr. 299.2
The oldest stories in the world, originally translated and retold, with comments, by Theodor H. Gaster. New York, Viking Press, 1952. 238 p. illus. 25 cm. [BL1600.G3] 52-13711
1. Mythology, Assyro-Babylonian. 2. Mythology, Hittite. 3. Mythology, Canaanite. I. Title.

KING, Leonard William, 1869-1919. 299'.2'1
Babylonian religion and mythology / by L. W. King. New York : AMS Press, [1976] p. cm. Reprint of the 1899 ed. published by K. Paul, Trench, Trubner, London, which was issued as v. 4 in series: Books on Egypt and Chaldaea. [BL1620.K5 1976] 73-18854 ISBN 0-404-11352-4 : 12.00
1. Mythology, Assyro-Babylonian. 2. Assyro-Babylonian religion. I. Title. II. Series: Books on Egypt and Chaldaea ; v. 4.

SMITH, George, 1840-1876.
The Chaldean account of Genesis, containing the description of the creation, the fall of man, the deluge, the tower of Babel, the times of the patriarchs, and Nimrod: Babylonian fables, and legends of the gods; from the cuneiform inscriptions. By George Smith ... New York, Scribner, Armstrong & co., 1876. xvi, 319 p. incl. front. (mounted phot.) illus. 4 pl. 24 1/2 cm. [BS1236.S6 1876a] 8-17084
1. Mythology, Assyro-Babylonian. 2. Bible. O.T. Genesis—Criticism, interpretation, etc. 3. Cosmogony, Babylonian. 4. Bible—Criticism, interpretation, etc. O.T. Genesis. I. Title.

Mythology, Australian.

ROBINSON, Roland E. 398.4'0994
Aboriginal myths and legends [by] Roland Robinson. Melbourne, Sun Books [1966] xvi, 218 p. illus. 19 cm. [BL2610.R6] 67-88063 1.25 Aust.
1. Mythology, Australian. I. Title.

Mythology, Australian (Aboriginal)

MOUNTFORD, Charles Pearcy, 1890- 398.2
The dreamtime; Australian aboriginal myths in paintings by Ainslie Roberts, with text by Charles P. Mountford. Adelaide, Rigby; San Francisco, TriOcean [1966, c.1965] 79p. illus. (pt. col.) 24cm. [BL2610.M6] 65-23900 4.50 bds.,
1. Mythology, Australian (Aboriginal) I. Roberts, Ainslie, illus. II. Title.

ROBERTS, Ainslie. 759.994
The dawn of time; Australian aboriginal myths in paintings by Ainslie Roberts, with text by Charles P. Mountford. Line illus. by Ainslie Roberts. New York, Taplinger Pub. Co. [1972, c1969] 79 p. illus. (part col.) 25 cm. [BL2610.R58 1972] 77-175042 ISBN 0-8008-2121-1 6.95
1. Mythology, Australian (Aboriginal) 2. Art and mythology. I. Mountford, Charles Pearcy, 1890- II. Title.

ROBERTS, Ainslie. 759.994
The first sunrise; Australian aboriginal myths in paintings by Ainslie Roberts, with text by Charles P. Mountford. Line illus. by Ainslie Roberts. New York, Taplinger Pub. Co. [1972, c1971] 79 p. illus. (part col.) 25 cm. [BL2610.R593 1972] 70-175043 ISBN 0-8008-2745-7 6.95
1. Mythology, Australian (Aboriginal) 2. Art and mythology. I. Mountford, Charles Pearcy, 1890- II. Title.

ROBINSON, Roland E. 398.2'0994
Aboriginal myths and legends [by] Roland Robinson. Melbourne, Sun Books [1968] xvi, 218 p. illus. 18 cm. [BL2610.R6 1968] 73-541174 0.95
1. Mythology, Australian (Aboriginal) I. Title.

Mythology, Australian (Aboriginal)—Juvenile literature.

ROBINSON, Roland E., 398.2'0994
comp.
Wandjina, children of the Dreamtime; aboriginal myths & legends selected by Roland Robinson. With illus. by Roderick Shaw. [Brisbane] Jacaranda [1968] 112 p. col. illus. 28 cm. [BL2610.R62] 73-384644 2.50
1. Mythology, Australian (Aboriginal)—Juvenile literature. I. Shaw, Roderick, illus. II. Title.

Mythology, Celtic.

ARBOIS de Jubainville, 299'.1'6
Henry d', 1827-1910.
The Irish mythological cycle and Celtic mythology. Translated from the French, with additional notes, by Richard Irvine Best. New York, Lemma Pub. Corp., 1970. xv, 240 p. 23 cm. Reprint of the 1903 ed. Translation of Le cycle mythologique irlandais et la mythologie celtique. Includes bibliographical references. [BL980.I7A7 1970] 70-112679 ISBN 0-87696-006-9
1. Mythology, Celtic. 2. Epic literature, Irish. 3. Tuatha de Danaan. I. Title.

MACBAIN, Alexander, 299'.1'6
1855-1907.
Celtic mythology and religion : with chapters upon Druid circles and Celtic burial / by Alexander Macbain ; with introductory chapter & notes by W. J. Watson. Folcroft, Pa. : Folcroft Library Editions, 1976. xviii, 252 p., 8 leaves of plates : ill. ; 24 cm. Reprint of the 1917 ed. published by E. Mackay, Stirling, Scot. Includes bibliographical references. [BL900.M3 1976] 76-1877 ISBN 0-8414-6043-4 lib. bdg. : 17.50
1. Mythology, Celtic. 2. Druids and Druidism. 3. Cultus, Celtic. I. Title.

MACBAIN, Alexander, 299'.1'6
1855-1907.
Celtic mythology and religion, with chapters upon Druid circles and Celtic burial / by Alexander Macbain ; with introductory chapter & notes by W. J. Watson. Norwood, Pa. : Norwood Editions, 1975. 252 p., [8] leaves of plates : ill. ; 23 cm. Reprint of the 1917 ed. published by E. Mackay, Sterling, Scot. [BL900.M3 1975] 75-33767 ISBN 0-88305-911-8 lib. bdg. : 25.00
1. Mythology, Celtic. 2. Druids and druidism. 3. Cultus, Celtic. I. Title.

MACCULLOCH, John Arnott, 290
1868-
... Celtic [mythology] by John Arnott Macculloch ... Slavic [mythology] by Jan Machal ... with a chapter on Baltic mythology by the editor ... Boston, Marshall Jones company, 1918. x, 398 p. xxxvii (i.e. 40) pl. (incl. col. front.) 25 cm. (The mythology of all races ... L. H. Gray ... editor, vol. iii) Each plate accompanied by guard sheet with descriptive letterpress. "Slavic [mythology]" largely based on the author's Bajeslovl slovanske, has been translated by F. Krupicka. cf. Editor's pref. Bibliography: p. [363]-398. [BL25.M8 vol. 3] [BL900.M4] (290.8) 18-14207
1. Mythology, Celtic. 2. Mythology, Slavic. 3. Legends, Celtic. 4. Folk-lore, Slavic. I. Machal, Jan. II. Gray, Louis Herbert, 1875- III. Krupicka, F., tr. IV. Title.

SQUIRE, Charles. 299'.16
Celtic myth and legend / Charles Squire. Hollywood, Calif. : Newcastle Pub. Co., [1975] p. cm. (A Newcastle mythology book) First ed. published in 1905 under title: The mythology of the British Islands. Reprint of the 191-? ed. published by Gresham Pub. Co., London, in series: Myth and legend in literature and art. Bibliography: p. [BL900.S6 1975] 74-26576 ISBN 0-87877-030-5 : 4.95
1. Mythology, Celtic. 2. Folk-lore, Celtic. 3. Legends, Celtic. I. Title. II. Series: Myth and legend in literature and art.

SQUIRE, Charles. 299'.16
Celtic myth & legend, poetry & romance. With illus. in colour & monochrome after paintings by J. H. F. Bacon & other artists. Boston, Milford House [1974] p. First ed. published in 1905 under title: The mythology of the British Islands. Reprint of the 1910 ed. published by Gresham Pub. Co., London, in series: Myth and legend in literature and art. Bibliography: p. [BL900.S6 1974] 73-16082 ISBN 0-87821-194-2 40.00 (lib. bdg.).
1. Mythology, Celtic. 2. Folk-lore, Celtic. 3. Legends, Celtic. I. Title. II. Series: Myth and legend in literature and art.

SQUIRE, Charles. 299'.1'6
Celtic myth & legend, poetry & romance / by Charles Squire ; with ill. by J. H. F. Bacon & other artists and with a foreword by Cary Wilkins. New York : Bell Pub. Co., 1979. x, 450 p., [10] leaves of plates : ill. ; 24 cm. First published in 1905 under title: The mythology of the British Islands. Reprint of the 191-? ed. published by Gresham Pub. Co., London, in series: Myth and legend in literature and art. Includes bibliographical references and index. [BL900.S6 1979] 79-19633 ISBN 0-517-30490-2 : 5.98
1. Mythology, Celtic. 2. Folk-lore, Celtic. 3. Legends, Celtic. I. Title. II. Series: Myth and legend in literature and art.

SQUIRE, Charles. 299'.16
Celtic myth & legend, poetry & romance / by Charles Squire. San Bernardino, Calif. : Borgo Press, 1980. p. cm. First ed. published in 1905 under title: The mythology of the British Islands. Reprint of the 191-? ed. published by Gresham Pub. Co., London, in series: Myth and legend in literature and art. Includes index. Bibliography: p. [BL900.S6 1980] 19 80-53343 lib. bdg. : 12.95
1. Mythology, Celtic. 2. Folklore, Celtic. 3. Legends, Celtic. I. Title. II. Series: Myth and legend in literature and art.

SQUIRE, Charles. 299'.1'6
The mythology of ancient Britain and Ireland. [Folcroft, Pa.] Folcroft Library Editions, 1973. p. Reprint of the 1909 ed. published by Constable, London. Bibliography: p. [BL980.G7S6 1973] 73-13769 10.00 (lib. bdg.).
1. Mythology, Celtic. 2. Legends, Celtic. I. Title.

Mythology, Chinese.

FERGUSON, John Calvin, 299.51
1866-
...Chinese [mythology] by John C. Ferguson, Japanese [mythology] by Masaharu Aneski... Boston, Archaeological institute of America, Marshall Jones company, 1928. xii, 416 p. illus., xliv pl. (part col., incl. front.) on 321., map. 24 1/2 cm. (The mythology of all races ... Canon J. A. MacCulloch ... editor ... vol. viii) Each plate accompanied by guard sheet with descriptive letterpress. Bibliography: p. [389]-400. [BL25.M8 vol. viii] [BL1801.F4] (290.82) 28-14539
1. Mythology, Chinese. 2. Mythology, Japanese. 3. China—Religion. 4. Japan—Religion. 5. Tales, Chinese. 6. Tales, Japanese. 7. Art, Chinese. 8. Art, Japanese. I. Anesaki, Masaharu, 1873- II. Title.

FERGUSON, John Calvin, 299.51
1866-1945.
Chinese mythology, Japanese mythology by Masaharu Anesaki. New York, Cooper Square Publishers, 1964 [c1928] xii, 416 p. illus., map, 44 plates (part col.) 24 cm. (The Mythology of all races, v. 8) Bibliography: p. [389]-400. [BL25.M8 1964 vol. 8] 63-19093
1. Mythology, Chinese. 2. Mythology, Japanese. I. Anesaki, Masaharu, 1873-1949. II. Title. III. Series.

MACKENZIE, Donald 291.1'3'0951
Alexander, 1873-1936.
Myths of China and Japan / by Donald A. Mackenzie. Boston : Longwood Press, 1977. xvi, 404 p., [34] leaves of plates : ill. ; 22 cm. Reprint of the 1923 ed. published by Gresham Pub. Co., London, in series: Myth and legend in literature and art. Includes bibliographical references and index. [BL1802.M33 1977] 77-6878 ISBN 0-89341-149-3 lib.bdg. : 45.00
1. Mythology, Chinese. 2. Mythology, Japanese. 3. Folk-lore—China. 4. Folk-lore—Japan. 5. China—Civilization. 6. Japan—Civilization. I. Title. II. Series: Myth and legend in literature and art.

SANDERS, Tao Tao Liu. 299'.51
Dragons, gods & spirits from Chinese mythology / text by Tao Tao Liu Sanders ; illustrations by Johnny Pau. New York : Schocken Books, 1982, c1980. p. cm. (World mythologies series) [BL1802.S26 1982] 19 82-790 ISBN 0-8052-3799-2 : 14.95
1. Mythology, Chinese. I. Title. II. Title: Dragons, gods, and spirits from Chinese mythology. III. Series.

WERNER, Edward Theodore 299.51
Chalmers, 1864-
Myths & legends of China, by E. T. C. Werner ... With thirty-two illustrations in colors by Chinese artists. New York, Farrar & Rinehart [1933] 2 p. l., 7-453, [1] p. col. front., col. plates, 21 1/2 cm. (Lettered on cover: The myths series) Printed in Great Britain. [GR335.W35 1933] 33-38011
1. Mythology, Chinese. 2. Legends—China. I. Title. II. Series.

WERNER, Edward Theodore 299'.51
Chalmers, 1864-1954.
Myths & legends of China. [New York] B. Blom [1971] 453 p. illus. 21 cm. Reprint of the 1922 ed. [BL1825.W46 1971] 71-172541
1. Mythology, Chinese. 2. Legends—China. I. Title.

Mythology, Chinese—Dictionaries.

WERNER, Edward Theodore 398.3
Chalmers, 1864-1954.
A dictionary of Chinese mythology. Introd. by Hyman Kublin. New York, Julian Press, 1961. xxiii, 627 p. 24 cm. Bibliography: p. 625-627. [BL1801.W35 1961] 61-17239
1. Mythology, Chinese — Dictionaries. I. Title.

WERNER, Edward Theodore 299'.51
Chalmers, 1864-1954.
A dictionary of Chinese mythology. Boston, Milford House [1974] p. cm. Reprint of the 1932 ed. published by Kelly and Walsh, Shanghai. Bibliography: p. [BL1801.W35 1974] 70-186794 ISBN 0-87821-046-6 6.00 (lib. bdg.).
1. Mythology, Chinese—Dictionaries. I. Title.

WERNER, Edward Theodore 299'.51
Chalmers, 1864-1954.
A dictionary of Chinese mythology / by E. T. C. Werner. Portland, Me. : Longwood Press, 1977. p. cm. Reprint of the 1932 ed. published by Kelly and Walsh, Shanghai. Includes index. Bibliography: p. [BL1801.W35 1977] 76-27521 ISBN 0-89341-034-9 : 60.00
1. Mythology, Chinese—Dictionaries. I. Title.

Mythology, Classical.

BATMAN, Stephen, 292'.1'3
d.1584.
The golden booke of the leaden gods : London 1577 / Stephen Batman. The third part of ... Yvychurch : London 1592 / Abraham Fraunce. The fountaine of ancient fiction : London 1599 / [translated by] Richard Lynche. New York : Garland Pub., 1976. p. cm. (The Renaissance and the gods ; 13) The third work, by V. Cartari, is a translation of Le imagini de i dei gli antichi. [BL720.B37] 75-27856 ISBN 0-8240-2062-6 lib.bdg. : 40.00
1. Mythology, Classical. 2. Heresies and heretics. I. Fraunce, Abraham, fl. 1582-1633. The third part of the Countesse of Pembrokes Yuychurch. 1976. II. Cartari, Vincenzo, b. ca. 1500. Le imagini de i dei gli antichi. English. 1976. III. Title. IV. Series.

BEMENT, R B. 292
The pantheon, a key to the hidden meaning of the Greek and Roman pagan poets ... By R. B. Bement ... Clyde, O., Independent printing co., 1874. 72 p. 21 cm. [BL730.B4] 31-29559
1. Mythology, Classical. I. Title.

BERENS, E M. 292
A hand-book of mythology; myths and legends of ancient Greece and Rome, illustrated from antique sculptures. By E. M. Berens. New York, Maynard, Merrill & co. [c1894] 1 p. l., xiii., [7]-334 p. front., illus., plates. 17 cm. London edition, 1879, has title: The myths and legends of ancient Greece and Rome. [BL725.B4] 31-25468
1. Mythology. Classical. I. Title.

BERENS, E. M. 292'.2'11
The myths and legends of ancient Greece and Rome / by E. M. Berens. Boston : Longwood Press, 1978. p. cm. Reprint of the 1880 ed. published by Blackie, London. Includes index. [BL720.B47 1978] 79-91528 ISBN 0-89341-029-2 lib.bdg. : 30.00
1. Mythology, Classical. I. Title.

BULFINCH, Thomas, 1796- 292'.1'3
1867.
Bulfinch's mythology : the Greek and Roman fables illustrated, from The age of fable by Thomas Bulfinch : with 200 works of art by artists from Praxiteles to Picasso / compiled by Bryan Holme ; with an introd. by Joseph Campbell. New York : Viking Press, [1979] p. cm. (A Studio book) [BL721.B84 1979] 79-14830 ISBN 0-670-19464-6 : 15.95
1. Mythology, Classical. 2. Mythology, Classical, in art. I. Holme, Bryan, 1913- II. Title.

BULFINCH, Thomas, 1796- 292'.13
1867.
Myths of Greece and Rome / compiled by Bryan Holme ; with an introduction by Joseph Campbell. New York, N.Y. : Penguin, 1981. p. cm. An edition of The age of fable, the first book of the author's Mythology. Includes index. [BL721.B84 1981] 19 81-2264 ISBN 0-14-005643-2 pbk. : 10.95
1. Mythology, Classical. 2. Mythology, Classical, in art. I. Holme, Bryan, 1913- II. [Age of fable] III. Title.

CARTARI, Vincenzo, 292'.1'3
b.ca.1500.
Le imagini ... degli dei / Vincenzo Cartari. New York : Garland Pub., 1976. p. cm. (The Renaissance and the gods ; 12) Reprint of the 1571 ed. published by V. Valgrisi, Venice, under title: Le imagini de i dei de gli antichi. [BL720.C2 1976] 75-27855 ISBN 0-8240-2061-8 : 40.00
1. Mythology, Classical. I. Title. II. Series.

CASTANIS, Christophoros 292
Plato, b.1814.
Interpretations of the attributes of the principal fabulous deities, with an essay on the history of mythology. Originally given in lectures by Christophoros Plato Castanis ... Portland [Me.] W. Hyde, 1844. 3 p. l., [iii]-v, [7]-102, [2] p. 23 cm. [BL721.C35] 31-25475
1. Mythology, Classical. I. Title.

CONTI, Natale, 1520?- 291'.1'3
1580?
Mythologiae : Venice, 1567 / Natalis Comes. New York : Garland Pub., 1976. p. cm. (The Renaissance and the gods ; no. 11) Reprint of the 1567 ed. published by Comin da Trino, Venice. [BL720.C6 1976] 75-27853 ISBN 0-8240-2060-X : 40.00
1. Mythology, Classical. I. Title. II. Series.

CONTI, Natale, 1520?- 292'.1'3
1580?
Mythologiae / Natale Conti Mythologia, Padua, 1616 / M. Antonio ; introductory notes by Stephen Orgel. New York : Garland Pub., 1979. 2 v. in 1 : ill. ; 24 cm. (The Philosophy of images ; 13) Reprint of two works first published in Padua in 1616. Includes index. [BL720.C6 1979] 78-68194 ISBN 0-8240-3687-5 lib. bdg. : 60.00
1. Mythology, Classical. I. Tritonio, Marco Antonio, 16th cent. Mythologia. 1979. II. Title. III. Series.

DWIGHT, Mary Ann 1806-1858. 292
Grecian and Roman mythology. By M. A. Dwight. With a series of illustrations. 2d abridged ed. New York, A. S. Barnes & co., 1857. 312 p. incl. front., illus. 19 cm. [BL721.D6 1857] 16-4823
1. Mythology, Classical. I. Title.

DWIGHT, Mary Ann, 1806-1858. 292
Grecian and Roman mythology. By M. A. Dwight. With an introductory notice by Tayler Lewis... Also a series of illustrations in outline. 3d ed. New York and Chicago, A. S. Barnes & company, 1876. 451 p. incl. front., illus. 22 cm. [BL721.D8 1876] 31-25474
1. Mythology, Classical. I. Lewis, Tayler, 1802-1877. II. Title.

DWIGHT, Mary Ann, 1806-1858. 292
Grecian and Roman mythology. By M. A. Dwight. With an introductory notice by Tayler Lewis... Also a series of illustrations in outline. New York and Chicago, A. S. Barnes & company [c1882] 451 p. incl. front., illus. 21 1/2 cm. First edition, 1849. [BL721.D8 1882] 12-32038
1. Mythology, Classical. I. Lewis, Tayler, 1802-1877. II. Title.

ELY, Talfourd. 292
Olympos: tales of the gods of Greece and Rome. By Talfourd Ely ... Based on the German of Dr. Hans Dutschke. With an index, six photographic plates, and forty-seven illustrations in the text. New York, G. P. Putnam's sons; London, H. Grevel & co., 1891. xviii, 298 p. illus., vi pl. (incl. front.) 20 1/2cm. [BL721.E520] A31
1. Mythology, Classical. I. Dutschke, Hans, 1848- Der Olymp. II. Title.

FAIRBANKS, Arthur, 1864- 292
... The mythology of Greece and Rome, presented with special reference to its influence on literature, by Arthur Fairbanks. New York, D. Appleton and company, 1908. xvii, 408, [1] p. illus., 2 fold. maps (incl. front.) iv geneal. tab. (1 fold) 20 cm. (Half-title: Twentieth century text-books, Classical section) Series title in part also at head of t.-p. [BL721.F3 1908] 14-6765
1. Mythology, Classical. I. Title.

FAIRBANKS, Arthur, 1864- 292
... The mythology of Greece and Rome, presented with special reference to its influence on literature, by Arthur Fairbanks. New York, D. Appleton and company, 1907. xvii, 408, [1] p. illus., 2 fold. maps. (incl. front.) Iv General tab. (1 fold.) 20 cm. (Half-title: Twentieth century text-books. Classical section ...) Series title in part also at head of t.-p. [BL721.F3 1907] 7-6167
1. Mythology, Classical. I. Title.

FOX, William Sherwood, 1878- 292
Greek and Roman [mythology] New York, Cooper Square Publishers, 1964 [c1916] lxii, 354 p. illus., 63 plates (part col.) 24 cm. (The Mythology of all races, v. 1) Bibliography: p. [333]-354. [BL25.M8 1964 vol. 1] 63-19086
1. Mythology, Classical. I. Title. II. Series.

FOX, William Sherwood, 1878. 292
... Greek and Roman [mythology] by William Sherwood fox ... Boston, Marshall Jones company, 1916. ixii, 354 p. illus., lxiii pl. (incl. front.; part col.) 20 cm. (The mythology of alPraces ... L. H. Gray ... editor ... vol. i) Each plate accompanied by guard sheet with descriptive letterpress. Bibliography: p. [335]-354. [BL25.M8 vol. 1] [BL721.F7] 294.
1. Mythology, Classical. I. Title.

FOX, William Sherwood, 1878- 292
Greek and Roman mythology, by William Sherwood Fox ... Boston, Mass., Marshall Jones company [c1928] 3 p. l., [ix]-ixii, 402 p. illus., lxiii pl. (incl. front.: col.) 23 cm. Bibliography: p. [333]-354. [BL721.F7 1928] 28-25253
1. Mythology, Classical. I. Title.

FRANCILLON, Robert Edward, 1841-1919.
Gods and heroes; or, The kingdom of Jupiter, by Robert Edward Francillon; illustrated by Sears Gallagher. Boston, New York [etc.] Ginn and company [1915] xii, 361 p. incl. front., illus., map. 18 cm. [PZ28.1.F846G] 15-19999
1. Mythology, Classical. I. Title.

GAUTRUCHE, Pierre, 1602-1681. 291.1'3
The poetical histories, London 1671 / Pierre Gautruche ; translated by Marius D'Assigny. Appendix de Diis et heroibus poeticis, Roven 1705 /Joseph de Jouvency. New York : Garland Pub., 1976. 540 p. in various pagings ; 23 cm. (The Renaissance and the gods) Reprint of The poetical histories, a translation of L'histoire poetique pour l'intelligence des poetes and De diis & heroibus poeticis, an appendix to the ed. of Ovid's Metamorphoseon published by R. Lallemant. Includes index. [BL720.G35 1976] 76-23078 ISBN 0-8240-2081-2 lib.bdg. : 40.00
1. Mythology, Classical. 2. Hieroglyphics. I. D'Assigny, Marius, 1643-1717. II. Jouvency, Joseph de, 1643-1719. Appendix de Diis et heroibus poeticis. 1976. III. Title. IV. Series.

GAYLEY, Charles Mills, 1858-1932, ed. 292
The classic myths in English literature; based chiefly on Bulfinch's "Age of fable." (1855) Accompanied by an interpretative and illustrative commentary, edited by Charles Mills Gayley ... Boston, U.S.A., Ginn & company, 1893. xxxviii, 539 p. illus., 6 maps (4 double) geneal. tab. 19 cm. Short bibliography in Preface. [BL721.G3 1893] 4-4204
1. Mythology, Classical. 2. Mythology, Norse. 3. English poetry (Selections: Extracts, etc.) I. Bulfinch, Thomas, 1796-1867. Age of fable. II. Title.

GAYLEY, Charles Mills, 1858-1932. 292.211
The classic myths in English literature and in art. Accompanied by an interpretative and illustrative commentary. New ed. rev. and enl. New York, Blaisdell Pub. Co. [1963, c1911] xii, 597 p. illus. (part col.) geneal. tab., maps (part fold. col.) 20 cm. "Based originally on Bulfinch's Age of fable (1855)" Bibliographical references included in "Preface" (p. v-xi) (Selections: Extracts, etc.) [BL721.G3 1963] 65-6686
1. Mythology, Classical. 2. Mythology, Norse 3. English poetry (Selections: Extracts, etc.) I. Bulfinch, Thomas, 1796-1867. Age of fable. II. Title.

GAYLEY, Charles Mills, 1858-1932, ed. 292'.2'11
The classic myths in English literature and in art, based originally on Bulfinch's "Age of fable" (1855), accompanied by an interpretative and illustrative commentary. New ed., rev. and enl. Boston, Milford House [1973] p. Reprint of the 1911 ed. published by Ginn, Boston. [BL721.G3 1973] 73-13946 ISBN 0-87821-186-1 50.00 (lib. bdg.)
1. Mythology, Classical. 2. Mythology, Norse. 3. English poetry (Selections: Extracts, etc.) 4. Mythology, Classical, in art. I. Bulfinch, Thomas, 1796-1867. Age of fable. II. Title.

GAYLEY, Charles Mills, 1858-1932, ed. 292
The classic myths in English literature and in art based originally on Bulfinch's "Age of fable" (1855) accompanied by an interpretative and illustrative commentary by Charles Mills Gayley ... New ed., rev. and enl. Boston, New York [etc.] Ginn and company [c1911] xii, 597 p. front., illus., plates, 3 maps (2 fold.) fold. geneal. tab. 20 cm. Short bibliography in Preface. [BL721.G3 1911] 11-1253
1. Mythology, Classical. 2. Mythology, Norse. 3. English poetry (Selections: Extracts, etc.) I. Bulfinch, Thomas, 1796-1867. Age of fable. II. Title.

GAYLEY, Charles Mills, 1858-1932, ed. 292
The classic myths in English literature and in art, based originally on Bulfinch's "Age of fable" (1855); accompanied by an interpretative and illustrative commentary, by Charles Mills Gayley ... New ed., rev. and enl. Boston, New York [etc.] Ginn and company [c1939] xii, 597 p. front., illus., plates, 3 maps (2 fold.) fold. geneal tab. 20 cm. Bibliography in preface. [BL721.G3 1939] 41-8950
1. Mythology, Classical. 2. Mythology, Norse. 3. English poetry (Selections: Extracts, etc.) I. Bulfinch, Thomas, 1796-1867. Age of fable. II. Title.

GENEST, Emile 398.2
Myths of ancient Greece and Rome. Ed., tr., from French by Barbara Whelpton. Illus. by Rene Peron. Cleveland, World [1965, c.1947, 1963] 196p. illus. (pt. col.) map. 19cm. Myths and legends; Holly bk.) [BL721.G453] 65-17998 2.50
1. Mythology, Classical. I. Peron, Rene, illus. II. Title.

GRANT, Michael, 1914- 292
Myths of the Greeks and Romans [New York] New Amer. Lib. [1964, c.1962] 432p. illus. 18cm. (Mentor bk., MQ562) Bibl. .95 pap.,
1. Mythology, Classical. I. Title.

GRANT, Michael, 1914- 292
Myths of the Greeks and Romans. [1st ed.] Cleveland, World Pub. Co. [1962] 487 p. illus. 23 cm. [BL722.G7] 62-15713
1. Mythology, Classical. I. Title.

HARRISON, Jane Ellen, 1850-1928. 292'.1'3
Myths of Greece and Rome / by Jane Harrison. Folcroft, Pa. : Folcroft Library Editions, 1976. 79 p. ; 23 cm. Reprint of the 1927 ed. published by E. Benn, London, in series: Benn's sixpenny library. Bibliography: p. 79. [BL721.H35 1976] 76-46570 ISBN 0-8414-4907-4 lib. bdg. : 10.00
1. Mythology, Classical. I. Title.

HARRISON, Jane Ellen, 1850-1928. 292
... Myths of Greece and Rome, by Jane Harrison ... Garden City, N. Y., Doubleday, Doran & company, inc., 1928. 3 p. l., 71 p. 17 cm. (The little books of modern knowledge) Bibliography: p. 71. [BL725.H25] 34-17137
1. Mythology, Classical. I. Title.

HART, John Seely, 1810-1877. 292
Epitome of Greek and Roman mythology. With explanatory notes and a vocabulary, by John S. Hart ... Philadelphia, Lippincott, Grambo & co., 1853. xi, 13-162 p. 20 cm. In Latin. "Latin text of the following volume...was prepared by some of the same band of eminent scholars to whom we are indebted for the 'Historia sacra', 'Historia graeca'...It was intended originally to follow those works, and hence was called...'Appendix dediis et heroibus poeticis!"--Pref. [BL725.H3] 31-29549
1. Mythology, Classical. I. Title.

HAWTHORNE, Nathaniel, 1804-1864.
... A wonder-book, and Grandfather's chair. By Nathaniel Hawthorne ... Boston, James R. Osgood and company, 1876. 2 v. in l. front., pl. 19 1/2 cm. At head of title: Hawthorne's works. Illustrated library edition. A34
1. Mythology, Classical. I. Title. II. Title: Grandfather's chair.

HENDRICKS, Rhoda A., comp. 292'.08
Classical gods and heroes; myths as told by the ancient authors. Translated and introduced by Rhoda A. Hendricks. New York, Morrow, 1974 [c1972] xi, 322 p. 22 cm. "Morrow paperback editions." Bibliography: p. 294. [BL722.H45 1974] 74-2014 ISBN 0-688-05279-7 3.95 (pbk.).
1. Mythology, Classical. I. Title.

HERZBERG, Max John, 1886- 292
Classical myths, by Max J. Herzberg ... Boston, New York [etc.] Allyn and Bacon [c1935] xiv p., 1 l., 517, 27 p. col. front., illus., 2 col. pl., double maps. 20 cm. Illustrated lining-papers. "Northern and Celtic stories have been included although the chief emphasis has been placed ... on our classical heritage."--Pref. "Reading lisr" at end of each chapter. [BL725.H4] 35-19700
1. Mythology. Classical. 2. Mythology. Germanic. 3. Mythology, Norse. 4. Mythology, Celtic. I. Title.

HORT, William Jillard. 292
The new pantheon: or, An introduction to the mythology of the ancients, in question and answer. Compiled principally for the use of young persons. By W. Jillard Hort. With plates. Boston: Printed by Manning and Loring, for John Norman. Sold by him; also by William Polham, no. 59, and Manning & Loring, no. 2, Cornhill ... 1809. viii, 161, [9] p. plates. 14 1/2 cm. Imperfect: t.-p. mutilated. [BL310.H6 1809] 32-35362
1. Mythology, Classical. I. Title.

HUTCHINSON, Winifred Margaret Lambart, 1868-
Orpheus with his lute: stories of the world's spring-time, by W. M. L. Hutchinson ... With illustrations. New York, Longmans, Green & co.; London, E. Arnold, 1909. xi, 292 p. 8 pl. (incl. front.) 20 cm. W 10
1. Mythology, Classical. I. Title.

IRVING, Christopher, d.1856. 292
Irving's Catechism of mythology: being a compendious history of the heathen gods, goddesses and heroes; designed chiefly as an introduction to the study of the ancient classics ... 2d American ed. rev. and improved, by M. J. Kerney ... Adapted to the use of schools in the United States. Baltimore, J. Murphy & co.; Philad'a, Kay & Troutman; [etc., etc.] 1850. 2 p. l., [7]-96 p. front., pl. 14 cm. Printed in London, 1821. cf. British museum catalogue. [BL725.I 6 1850] 1-1248
1. Mythology, Classical. I. Kerney, Martin Joseph, 1819-1861, ed. II. Title. III. Title: Catechism of mythology.

KING, William, 1663-1712 292.21
An historical account of the heathen gods and heroes, necessary for the understanding of the ancient poets. Introd. by Hugh Ross Williamson. Carbondale, Southern Ill. Univ. Pr. [c.1965] 256p. 6 plates. 23cm. (Centaur classics) [BL720.K5] 64-18550 12.00
1. Mythology. Classical. I. Title. II. Title: The heathen gods and heroes.

LEMMI, Charles William, 1882- 292'.13
The classic deities in Bacon; a study in mythological symbolism, by Charles W. Lemmi. New York, Octagon Books, 1971 [c1933] ix, 224 p. 24 cm. Bibliography: p. 215-221. [B1199.M8L4 1971] 70-120639
1. Bacon, Francis, Viscount, St. Albans, 1561-1626. 2. Bacon, Francis, Viscount St. Albans, 1561-1626. De sapientia veterum. 3. Mythology, Classical. 4. Mythology in literature. 5. Symbolism in literature. 6. Literature, Comparative—Classical and English. 7. Literature, Comparative—English and classical. I. Title.

LEMMI, Charles William, 1882- 292'.1'3
The classic deities in Bacon; a study in mythological symbolism, by Charles W. Lemmi. Folcroft, Pa., Folcroft Press [1969, c1933] ix, 224 p. 26 cm. Originally presented as the author's thesis, Johns Hopkins, 1935. Bibliography: p. 215-221. [B1199.M8L4 1969] 72-193482
1. Bacon, Francis, Viscount St. Albans, 1561-1626. 2. Bacon, Francis, Viscount St. Albans, 1561-1626. De sapientia veterum. 3. Mythology, Classical. 4. Mythology in literature. 5. Symbolism in literature. 6. Literature, Comparative—Classical and English. 7. Literature, Comparative—English and classical. I. Title.

LEMMI, Charles William, 1882- 292'.13
The classic deities in Bacon : a study in mythological symbolism / by Charles W. Lemmi. Folcroft, Pa. : Folcroft Library Editions, 1978 [c1933] ix, 224 p. ; 25 cm. Reprint of the ed. published by Johns Hopkins Press, Baltimore. Originally presented as the author's thesis, Johns Hopkins University. Includes index. Bibliography: p. 215-221. [B1199.M8L4 1978] 76-28258 ISBN 0-8414-5805-7 lib. bdg. : 25.00
1. Bacon, Francis, Viscount, St. Albans, 1561-1626. 2. Bacon, Francis, Viscount, St. Albans, 1561-1626. De sapienta veterum. 3. Mythology, Classical. 4. Mythology in literature. 5. Symbolism in literature. I. Title.

LOVERDO, Costa de, 1921- 292'.13
Gods with bronze swords. Translated by Nancy Amphoux. [1st ed.] Garden City, N.Y., Doubleday, 1970. x, 273 p. illus., maps. 22 cm. Translation of Les dieux aux epees de bronze. Bibliography: p. [258]-260. [BL722.L613] 70-114752 6.95
1. Mythology, Classical. I. Title.

MCGRADY, Samuel Hugh, 1885- ed. 292
Legends and myths of Greece and Rome, edited by S. H. McGrady, M.A.; illustrated by T. H. Robinson. London, New York [etc.] Longmans, Green and co. [1936] 2 p. l., 7-191, [1] p. col. front., illus., pl. 19 1/2 cm. "School edition first published January 1936; library edition first published September 1906." [BL725.M3 1936a] 37-3711
1. Mythology, Classical. I. Title.

MILEY, Cora E. 292
Myths and legends of Greece and Rome, by Cora E. Miley. Oklahoma City, Harlow publishing company, 1925. v p. l., 146 p. illus. 20 cm. [BL725.M5] 25-20035
1. Mythology, Classical. I. Title.

MONCRIEFF, Ascott Robert 292
Hope, 1846-1927.
Classic myth and legend, by A. R. Hope Moncrieff; with illustrations in colour & monochrome from famous paintings & statuary. New York, W. H. Wise & company, 1934. xvi, 443 p. col. front., plates (part col.) 23 cm. (On cover: Myths and legends of mankind) [BL721.M6] 34-31963
1. Mythology, Classical. I. Title.

MONCRIEFF, Ascott Robert 292'.1'3
Hope, 1846-1927.
Classic myth and legend / by A. R. Hope Moncrieff. Boston : Longwood Press, 1977. p. cm. Reprint of the 1912 ed. published by Gresham Pub. Co., London. Includes index. [BL721.M6 1977] 77-85616 ISBN 0-89341-317-8 lib.bdg. : 45.00
1. Mythology, Classical. I. Title.

MONSIGNY, Mary. Mme. 292
Mythology: or, A history of the fabulous deities of the ancients: designed to facilitate the study of history, poetry, painting, &c. By Madame Monsigny. 1st American ed. Randolph [Vt.]: Printed by Sereno Wright, for Thomas and Merrifield, booksellers and stationers, Windsor, Vt. 1809. 298 p. 18 cm. Published in London, 1780? cf. Brit. mus. Catalogue. [BL720.M6] 31-24949
1. Mythology, Classical. I. Title.

MORFORD, M. P. O. 292
Classical mythology / Mark P. O. Morford, Robert J. Lenardon. 2d ed. New York : McKay, 1977. xvi, 524 p. : ill. ; 24 cm. Includes indexes. Bibliography: p. 493-494. [BL722.M67 1977] 77-2230 ISBN 0-679-30336-7 : 14.95. ISBN 0-679-30344-8 pbk. : 7.95
1. Mythology, Classical. I. Lenardon, Robert J., 1928- joint author. II. Title.

MORFORD, M. P. O. 292
Classical mythology, by Mark P. O. Morford and Robert J. Lenardon. New York, McKay [1971] x, 498 p. illus., maps. 22 cm. Bibliography: p. 461-462. [BL722.M67] 78-124550 4.95
1. Mythology, Classical. I. Lenardon, Robert J., 1928- joint author.

NORTON, Daniel Silas, 1908- 292
1951.
Classical myths in English literature [by] Dan S. Norton and Peters Rushton, with an introd. by Charles Grosvenor Osgood. New York, Rinehart [1952] 444 p. illus. 21 cm. [BL313.N6] 52-5597
1. Mythology, Classical. 2. Mythology in literature. I. Title.

NORTON, Daniel Silas, 1908- 292
1951.
Classical myths in English literature [by] Dan S. Norton and Peters Rushton. With an introd. by Charles Grosvenor Osgood. New York, Greenwood Press [1969, c1952] xvi, 444 p. 22 cm. [BL727.N67 1969] 70-92305 ISBN 0-8371-2440-9
1. Mythology, Classical. 2. Mythology in literature. I. Rushton, Peters, 1915-1949. II. Title.

OSGOOD, Charles Grosvenor, 821.4
1871-1964
The classical mythology of Milton's English poems. Brooklyn, N.Y., Gordian Pr., 84 Bway, [c.]1964. 1xxxv. 111p. 23cm. (Yale studies in Eng., 8) [PR3592.M807] 64-8180 4.50
1. Milton, John, 1608-1674—Criticism and interpretation. 2. Mythology, Classical. I. Title. II. Series.

PETISCUS, August Heinrich, 292
b.1780.
The gods of Olympos; or, Mythology of the Greeks and Romans; translated and edited from the twentieth edition of A. H. Petiscus, by Katherine A. Raleigh, with a preface by Jane E. Harrison ... New York, Cassell publishing company [1893] xv, 271 p. illus., viii pl. (incl. front.) 21 cm. Bibliographies interspersed. [BL721.P4 1893] 31-25460
1. Mythology, Classical. I. Raleigh, Katherine A., ed. and tr. II. Title.

POMEY, Francois 292'.1'3
Antoine, 1618-1673.
The Pantheon : London, 1694 / Antoine Pomey ; translated by J. A. B. New York : Garland Pub., 1976. p. cm. (The Renaissance and the gods ; 34) Translation of Pantheum mythicum. Reprint of the 1694 ed. printed by B. Motte for R. Clavel and C. Harper, London. [BL720.P65 1976b] 75-27879 ISBN 0-8240-2083-9 lib.bdg. : 40.00
1. Mythology, Classical. I. Title. II. Series.

[POMEY, Francois Antoine] 292
1618-1673.
Tooke's Pantheon of the heathen gods, and illustrious heroes. Revised for a classical course of education, and adapted for the use of students of every age and of either sex ... Baltimore, E. J. Coale, 1825. 2 p. l., [iii]-iv p., 1 l., [13]-305, [11] p. plates. 18 cm. Half-title engraved. A revision of Tooke's translation of Pomey's Pantheum mythicum. "From the thirtythird London edition, revised and corrected so as to adapt it to persons of every age & of every sex, by a gentleman of Baltimore." [BL720.P65 1825] 34-41719
1. Mythology, Classical. I. Tooke, Andrew, 1673-1732, tr. II. Title.

[ROBBINS, Eliza] 1786-1853. 292
Elements of mythology: or, Classical fables of the Greeks and Romans: to which are added some notices of Syrian, Hindu, and Scandinavian superstitions, together with those of the American nations: the whole comparingpolytheism with true religion. For the use of schools. By the author of "American popular lessons" ... Philadelphia, Towar, J. & D. M. Hogan; Pittsburgh, Hogan & co., 1830. xii, 348 p. illus. 15 cm. [BL725.R57] 31-25462
1. Mythology, Classical. I. Title.

ROSE, Herbert Jennings, 292.018
1883-
Modern methods in classical mythology; three lectures delivered at University college, London, in February, 1930, by H. J. Rose ... St. Andrews, W. C. Henderson & son, ltd., University press, 1930. 50 p. 21 cm. Cover-title. [BL727.R6] 32-32008
1. Mythology, Classical. I. Title.

ROSS, Alexander, 1590- 292'.1'3
1654.
Mystagogus poeticus : or, The muses interpreter / Alexander Ross. New York : Garland Pub., 1976. p. cm. (The Renaissance and the gods ; 30) Reprint of the 1648 ed. printed by T. W. for T. Whitaker, London. [BL720.R7 1976] 75-27875 ISBN 0-8240-2079-0 lib.bdg. : 40.00
1. Mythology, Classical. I. Title. II. Series.

SABIN, Frances Ellis, 1870- 292
Classical myths that live today. Ralph V. D. Magoffin, classical editor. Chicago, S. Burdett Co. [1958] 347, lxii p. illus. 20 cm. Includes bibliography. [BL725.S15 1958] 58-4572
1. Mythology, Classical. 2. English poetry (Selections: Extracts, etc.) I. Magoffin, Ralph Van Deman, 1874-1942, ed.

SABIN, Frances Ellis, 1870- 292
Classical myths that live today, by Frances E. Sabin ... Ralph Van Deman Magoflin ... classical editor. New York, Newark [etc.] Silver, Burdett and company [c1927] xxv p., 1 l., 348 p., 1 l., xivi p. incl. front., illus. double map. 19 1/2 cm. "Additional reading" and "Poems for reference" at end of most of the chapters. [BL725.S15] 27-8217
1. Mythology, Classical. 2. English poetry (Selections: Extracts, etc.) I. Magoflin, Ralph Van Deman, 1874- ed. II. Title.

*SCHWAB, Gustav 292
Gods and heroes; myths and epics of ancient Greece. Greenwich. Conn., Fawcett [1965, c.1946] xiii, 736p. illus. 18cm. (Premier bk., p289) 1.25 pap.,
1. Mythology, Classical. 2. Mythology—Greece. I. Title.

SEEMAN, Otto, 1825-1901. 292
The mythology of Greece and Rome. With special reference to its use in art. From the German of O. Seeman. Ed. by G. H. Bianchi...With sixty-four illustrations. New York, Harper & brothers, 1887. 2 p. l., [7]-311 p. front., illus. 17 cm. [BL721.S] A 14
1. Mythology, Classical. 2. Art, Roman. 3. Art, Greek. I. Bianchi, George Henry, ed. II. Title.

SEZNEC, Jean.
The survival of the pagan gods; the mythological tradition and its place in Renaissance humanism and art. Translated by Barbara F. Sessions. New York, Harper [1961] xiv, 376 p. illus. (Harper torchbooks. The Bollingen library, TB 2004) Bollingen series, 38. Translation of La survivance des dieux antiques.
I. Title. II. Series.

SHELDON, William. 292
History of the heathen gods, and heroes of antiquity. To which is added an original translation of the Battle of the gods and giants. The whole newly arranged, corrected and enlarged with the addition of several original and valuable articles. By William Sheldon, F.A.S. 1st ed., ornamented with a number of elegant cuts. Published at Worcester. By Isaiah Thomas, Jun. Sold at his bookstore in Boston and Worcester, Isaac Sturtevant, printer [1809] xxiv, [25]-216 p. front., plates. 14 1/2 cm. "Battle of the gods and titans. From the Theogony of Heslod": p. 179-183. Appendix: Explanation of the constellations, planets, times and seasons. Represented on the Farnese globe. [BL725.S5] 6-22427
1. Mythology, Classical. I. Hesiodus. II. Title.

SMITH, Lloyd E. 292.
...A dictionary of classical mythology [by] Lloyd E. Smith. Girard, Kan., Haldeman-Julius company [c1924] 64 p. 12 1/2 cm. (Little blue book, no. 499, ed. by E. Haldeman-Julius) [BL715.S5] CA 24
1. Mythology, Classical. I. Title.

SMITH, Lloyd E. 292
...Legends of Greek and Roman heroes [by] Lloyd E. Smith. Girard, Karn., Halderman-Julius company [c1924] 64 p. 12 1/2 cm. (Little blue book, no. 497, ed. by E. Haldeman-Julius) "This...is...a sequel to 'Greek and Roman mythology'." [BL730.S6] CA 24
1. Mythology, Classical. I. Title.

STEUDING, Hermann, 1850-1917. 292
... Greek and Roman mythology, based on Steuding's Griechische and romische mythologie, by Karl Pomeroy Harrington ... and Herbert Cushing Tolman ... Boston, New York [etc.] Leach, Shewell, and Sanborn, 1897. ix, 179 p. 18 cm. (The students' series of Latin classics) "Brief bibliography": p. v-vi. [BL725.S6 1897] 31-29551
1. Mythology, Classical. I. Harrington, Karl Pomeroy, 1861- II. Tolman, Herbert Cushing, 1865-1923. III. Title.

TATLOCK, Jessie May, 1878- 292
Greek and Roman mythology, by Jessie M. Tatlock ... New York, The Century co., 1917. xxviii, 372 p. incl. illus., plates. 21 cm. "A brief list of poems and dramas based on the myths": p. 356-361. [BL721.T3] 17-3155
1. Mythology, Classical. I. Title.

TOOKE, Andrew, 1673- 292'.1'3
1732.
The Pantheon : London, 1713 / [written by Fra. Pomey] ; [translated and adapted by] Andrew Tooke. New York : Garland Pub., 1976. p. cm. (The Renaissance and the gods ; 35) Adaptation of F. A. Pomey's Pantheum mythicum. Reprint of the 1713 ed. printed for C. Harper, London. Includes index. [BL720.T8 1976] 75-27880 ISBN 0-8240-2084-7 : 40.00
1. Mythology, Classical. I. Title. II. Series.

Mythology, Classical—Bibliography

D'OOGE, Benjamin Leonard, 016.62
1860-
Helps to the study of classical mythology, for the lower grade and secondary schools, by Benjamin L. D'Ooge ... Ann Arbor, G. Wahr, 1899. x, 180 p. 18 cm. [Z7836.D65] 99-3018
1. Mythology, Classical—Bibl. I. Title.

Mythology, Classical—Dictionaries.

BELL, Robert E. 292'.13'0321
Dictionary of symbols, attributes, and associations in classical mythology / Robert E. Bell. Santa Barbara, CA : ABC-Clio, 1981. p. cm. Includes index. [BL715.B44] 19 81-19141 ISBN 0-87436-305-5 : 47.50
1. Mythology, Classical—Dictionaries. I. Title.

SCHMIDT, Joel. 292'.13'0321
Larousse Greek and Roman mythology / by Joel Schmidt ; edited by Seth Benardete. New York : McGraw-Hill, c1980. p. cm. Translation of Dictionnaire de la mythologie grecque et romaine. Includes index. [BL715.S313] 80-15046 6.95
1. Mythology, Classical—Dictionaries. I. Benardete, Seth. II. Title.

STAPLETON, Michael. 292'.003
A dictionary of Greek and Roman mythology / Michael Stapleton ; introd. by Stewart Perowne. New York : Bell Pub. Co., c1978. 224 p. : ill. ; 23 cm. Includes bibliographical references and index. [BL715.S7 1978b] 78-14466 ISBN 0-517-26281-9 pbk. : 3.98
1. Mythology, Classical—Dictionaries. I. Title.

Mythology, Classical, in art.

ALBRICUS, philosophus. 704.94'7
Allegoriae poeticae : Paris, 1520 / Albricus. Theologia mythologica : Antwerp, 1532 / Georgius Pictorius. Apotheoseos ... : Basel, 1558 / Georgius Pictorius. New York : Garland Pub., 1976. p. cm. (The Renaissance and the gods ; no. 4) Reprint of the 1520 ed. of Allegoriae poeticae, of the 1532 ed. of Theologia mythologica, and of the 1558 ed. of Apotheoseos. [N7760.A44 1976] 75-27845 ISBN 0-8240-2053-7 : 40.00
1. Mythology, Classical, in art. 2. Mythology, Classical. I. Pictorius, Georg, 1500 (ca.)-1569. Theologia mythologica, 1976. II. Pictorius, Georg, 1500 (ca.)-1569. Apotheoseos ... 1976. III. Title. IV. Series.

MAROLLES, Michel de, 704.94'7
1600-1681.
Tableaux du temple des muses : Paris, 1655 / Michel de Marolles. Iconologia : or, Moral emblems : London, 1709 / Cesare Ripa. New York : Garland Pub., 1976. p. cm. (The Renaissance and the gods ; no. 31) Reprint of the 1655 ed. of the Tableaux du temple des muses, published by N. L'Anglois, Paris, and of the 1709 ed. of the Iconologia, published by P. Tempest, London. [NE1680.M32 1976] 75-27876 ISBN 0-8240-2080-4 : 40.00
1. Mythology, Classical, in art. 2. Engravings. I. Ripa, Cesare, fl. 1600. Iconologia. English. 1976. II. Title. III. Series.

MAYERSON, Philip. 700
Classical mythology in literature, art, and music. Waltham, Mass., Xerox College Pub. [1971] xv, 509 p. illus., geneal. tables, map. 26 cm. Bibliography: p. 483-487. [NX650.M9M38] 77-138393
1. Mythology, Classical, in art. I. Title.

MAYERSON, Philip. 700
Classical mythology in literature, art, and music / Philip Mayerson. Glenview, Ill. : Scott, Foresman, [1982] c1971. p. cm. Reprint. Originally published: New York : Wiley, c1971. Includes index. Bibliography: p. [NX650.M9M38 1982] 19 82-772 ISBN 0-673-15690-7 : 26.95
1. Mythology, Classical, in art. 2. Arts. I. Title.

Mythology, Classical—Juvenile literature.

ELGIN, Kathleen, 1923- 292
The first book of mythology, Greek-Roman written and illustrated by Kathleen Elgin. New York, F. Watts, c1955. 61p. illus. 23cm. (The First books, 67) [BL725.E4] 55-9600
1. Mythology, Classical- juvenile literature. I. Title.

[GOODRICH, Samuel Griswold] 292
1793-1860.
A book of mythology, for youth, containing descriptions of the deities, temples, sacrifices and superstitions of the ancient Greeks and Romams. Adapted to the use of schools. Boston, Richardson, Lord and Holbrook, 1832. ix, [11]-121 p. incl. front., illus. 16 x 13 cm. Illustrated t.-p. [BL725.G6] 31-25465

1. Mythology, Classical—Juvenile literature. I. Title.

HAWTHORNE, Nathaniel, 1804-1864. JUV
Tanglewood tales, by Nathaniel Hawthorne; illustrated by Fern Bisel Peat. Akron, O., New York, The Saalfield publishing company [c1930] 4 p. l., 13-252 p. front., illus. 19 cm. (Half-title: Every child's library) [PZ8.1.H318Ta45] 292 30-13385
1. Mythology, Classical—Juvenile literature. I. Peat, Mrs. Fern Bisel, illus. II. Title.
Contents omitted.

HAWTHORNE, Nathaniel, 1804-1864.
Tanglewood tales for girls and boys; being a second Wonder-book by Nathaniel Hawthorne; with an introduction by Katherine Lee Bates. New York, T. Y. Crowell & company [1902] xv, 180 p. pl. 21 cm. (His Works... [Popular ed.] New York [1902, v. 14]) With "A wonder book for boys and girls," the two forming a double volume of the Works, which complete comprise 14 vols. in 7 (unnumbered) [PS1850.F02 vol. 13-14] 2-20807
1. Mythology, Classical—Juvenile literature. I. Title.
Contents omitted.

HAWTHORNE, Nathaniel, 1804-1864.
...A wonder book: the Gorgon's head, The golden touch, The three golden apples, by Nathaniel Hawthorne; with biographical sketch and notes. New York, Maynard, Merrill & co. [c1895] 96 p. illus. 17 cm. (On cover: Maynard's English classics, no. 168) Series title also at head of t.-p. [H318.W14] 7-3765
1. Mythology, Classical—Juvenile literature. I. Title.

HAWTHORNE, Nathaniel, 1804-1864. 292
A wonder book, and Tanglewood tales. [Fredson Bowers, textual editor. Columbus] Ohio State University Press [1972] xi, 463 p. illus. 25 cm. (The centenary edition of the works of Nathaniel Hawthorne, v. 7. Writings for children, 2) A collection of Greek myths retold as fairy tales. [PS1850.F63 vol. 7] [PZ8.1] 77-150221 ISBN 0-8142-0158-X
1. Mythology, Classical—Juvenile literature. 2. [Mythology, Classical.] I. Bowers, Fredson Thayer, ed. II. Hawthorne, Nathaniel, 1804-1864. III. Title. IV. Title: Tanglewood tales.

HAWTHORNE, Nathaniel, 1804-1864. JUV
Wonder book for girls and boys, by Nathaniel Hawthorne; with 60 designs by Walter Crane. Boston, Houghton, Mifflin and company, 1902. x, 210 p. col. front., col. illus., 18 col. pl. 28 1/2 cm. Title in colors within ornamental border. [PZ8.1.H318W5] 292 4-17572
1. Mythology, Classical—Juvenile literature. I. Crane, Walter, 1845-1915, illus. II. Title.
Contents omitted.

HAWTHORNE, Nathaniel, 1804-1864. JUV
A wonder-book for girls and boys, by Nathaniel Hawthorne, illustrated by Fern Bisel Peat. Akron, O., New York,,The Saalfield publishing company [1930] 4 p. l., 13-234 p. col. front., illus., plates. 23 cm. (On cover: Companion series) [PZ8.1.H318W68] 292 30-18301
1. Mythology, Classical—Juvenile literature. I. Peat, Mrs. Fern Bisel, illus. II. Title.

HAWTHORNE, Nathaniel, 1804-1864.
A wonder-book for girls and boys, by Nathiel Hawthorne; with an introduction by Katherine Lee Bates... New York, T. Y. Crowell & company [1902] 1 p. l., xviii, 159 p. front., pl. 21 cm. (Added t.-p.: The works of Nathaniel Hawthorne... [Popular ed. v. 13]) Forms with "Tanglewood tales", a double volume of the Works, which complete comprise 14 vols. in 7 (unnumbered) [PS1850.F02 vol. 13-14] 2-20806
1. Mythology, Classical—Juvenile literature. I. Title.
Contents omitted.

KEIGHTLEY, Thomas, 1789-1872. 282
The mythology of ancient Greece and Italy: for the use of schools. By Thomas Keightley ... 1st American ed., enl. and improved. New York, D. Appleton & co., 1837. xii, [13]-232 p. illus. 16 cm. Designed as an introduction to the author's larger work, bearing the same title. cf. Introd. [BL721.K42 1837] 33-39249
1. Mythology, Classical—Juvenile literature. I. Title.

KEIGHTLEY, Thomas, 1789-1872. 292
The mythology of ancient Greece and Italy for the use of schools by Thomas Keightley ... 12th American ed., enl. and improved. New York, D. Appleton and company, 1878. xii, [13]-232 p. illus. 16 cm. Designed as an introduction to the author's larger work, bearing the same title. cf. Pref. [BL725.K4 1878] 31-29555
1. Mythology, Classical—Juvenile literature. I. Title.

MOORE, Patrick. 398'.362'0938
Legends of the planets / [by] Patrick Moore. London : Luscombe, 1976. [5], 115 p. : ill. (some col.) ; 27 cm. [BL722.M66 1976] 77-375287 ISBN 0-86002-122-X : £4.50
1. Mythology, Classical—Juvenile literature. 2. Planets (in religion, folklore, etc.)—Juvenile literature. I. Title.

MOORE, Patrick. 292'.1'3
Legends of the planets / Patrick Moore. Sandton [South Africa] : Valiant Publishers, 1976. 115 p. : ill. (some col.) ; 27 cm. [BL722.M66 1976b] 77-373989 ISBN 0-86884-017-3 : R7.50
1. Mythology, Classical—Juvenile literature. 2. Planets (in religion, folklore, etc.)—Juvenile literature. I. Title.

SCHWAB, Gustav Benjamin, 1792-1850. 292
...Gods & heroes; myths & epics of ancient Greece. [New York] Pantheon [1946] 764 p.illus. 23 1/2 cm. At head of title: Gustav Schwab. "Translated from the German text and its Greek sources by Olga Marx and Ernst Morwitz. Introduction by Werner Jaeger."--p. [5]. [BL725.S32] 47-873
1. Marx, Olga, 1894- tr. 2. Morwitz, Ernst, 1887- joint tr. 3. Mythology, Classical—Juvenile literature. I. Title. II. Title: Translation of Die schonsten sagen des klassischen altertums.

Mythology, Classical—Outlines, syllabi, etc.

WOLVERTON, Robert E. 292.0202
An outline of classical mythology [by] Robert E. Wolverton. Totowa, N.J., Littlefield, Adams, 1966. xviii, 127p. geneal. tables. 21cm. (Littlefield, Adams quality paperback, no. 97) [BL722.W6] 66-18149 1.50 pap.,
1. Mythology, Classical—Outlines, syllabi, etc. I. Title. II. Title: Classical mythology.

Mythology—Collected works.

LEEMING, David Adams, 1937- 291.1'3
Mythology, the voyage of the hero / David Adams Leeming. 2d ed. New York : Harper & Row, c1981. p. cm. Includes index. Bibliography: p. [BL311.L326 1981] 80-12703 ISBN 0-06-043942-4 pbk. : 5.50
1. Mythology—Collected works. I. Title.

LEEMING, David Adams, 1937- 200'.4
Mythology; the voyage of the hero. Philadelphia, Lippincott [1973] vii, 338 p. 23 cm. Bibliography: p. 322-326. [BL311.L326] 73-913 ISBN 0-397-47276-5 4.95
1. Mythology—Collections. I. Title.

MCKENZIE, Cary Blair.
Classic myth-lore in rhyme, founded on Bullfinch's Age of fable, by Cary Blair McKenzie; illustrated by J. Gardner Scott. Los Angeles, Cal., E. K. McKenzie [c1905] 104 p. illus. 22 1/2 cm. 5-39031
I. Title.

MARANDA, Pierre, comp. 398'.08
Mythology; selected readings. [Harmondsworth, Eng., Baltimore] Penguin Books [1972] 320 p. 18 cm. (Penguin modern sociology readings) (Penguin education) Bibliography: p. 299-309. [BL315.M37] 72-197307 ISBN 0-14-080158-8 Pap. $3.95
1. Mythology—Collections. I. Title.

Mythology, Cretan.

MACKENZIE, Donald Alexander, 1873-1936. 913.391'8'03
Myths of Crete & pre-Hellenic Europe. With illus. in colour by John Duncan and from photos. Boston, Milford House [1973] p. Reprint of the 1917 ed. published by Gresham Pub. Co., London, in series: Myth and legend in literature and art. [BL793.C7M32 1973] 73-14711 ISBN 0-87821-192-6
1. Mythology, Cretan. 2. Art, Cretan. 3. Crete—Civilization. I. Title.

MACKENZIE, Donald Alexander, 1873-1936. 939.1'8
Myths of Crete and pre-Hellenic Europe / by Donald A. Mackenzie ; with ill. in colour by John Duncan. Boston : Longwood Press, 1977. liv, 361 p., [32] leaves of plates : ill. ; 22 cm. Reprint of the 1918 ed. published by the Gresham Pub. Co., in series: Myth and legend in literature and art. Includes bibliographical references and index. [BL793.C7M3 1977] 76-27522 ISBN 0-89341-035-7 : 40.00
1. Mythology, Cretan. 2. Art, Cretan. 3. Crete—Civilization. I. Title. II. Series: Myth and legend in literature and art.

Mythology, Dagari.

GOODY, John Rankine, comp. 299'.6
The myth of the Bagre [by] Jack Goody. Oxford, Clarendon Press, 1972. x, 381 p. illus. 22 cm. (Oxford library of African literature) Includes the White Bagre and the Black Bagre in Dagari and English. Bibliography: p. [117] [BL2480.D3G66] 73-155639 ISBN 0-19-815134-9 £9.00
1. Mythology, Dagari. I. White Bagre. English and Dagari. 1972. II. Black Bagre. English and Dagari. 1972. III. Title.

Mythology—Dictionaries.

AKEN, Andreas Rudolphus Antonius van. 292.03
The encyclopedia of classical mythology [by A. R. A. van Aken. Translated from the Dutch by D. R. Welsh] Englewood Cliffs, N.J., Prentice-Hall [1965] 155 p. illus., maps. 22 cm. (A Spectrum book) "Originally entitled: Elseviers mythologische encyclopedie." [BL715.A413] 64-23566
1. Mythology—Dictionaries. I. Title.

BELL, John, 1745-1831. 291.2'1
Bell's New pantheon / John Bell ;introd. by Robert D. Richardson, Jr. New York : Garland Pub., 1979. 2 v. : ill. ; 24 cm. (Myth & romanticism ; 4) Reprint of the 1790 ed. printed by and for J. Bell, London. [BL303.B4 1979] 78-60919 ISBN 0-8240-3553-4 : 120.00
1. Mythology—Dictionaries. I. Title. II. Title: New pantheon. III. Series: Myth and romanticism.

*BRAY, Frank Chapin, 1866- 291.03
Bray's university dictionary of mythology. New York, Apollo [1964, c.1935] 323p. 20cm. (A-81) 1.95 pap.,
1. Mythology—Dictionaries. I. Title.

COTTERELL, Arthur. 291.1'3
A dictionary of world mythology / Arthur Cotterell. 1st American ed. New York : Putnam, 1980, c1979. 256 p. : ill. ; 24 cm. Includes index. Bibliography: p. [246]-249. [BL303.C66 1980] 79-65889 ISBN 0-399-12464-0 : 12.95
1. Mythology—Dictionaries. I. Title.

DAIGLE, Richard J. 200'.4
The Mentor dictionary of mythology and the Bible, by Richard J. Daigle and Frederick R. Lapides. New York, New American Library [1973] vi, 202 p. 18 cm. (A Mentor book) [BL715.D24] 73-76392 1.95 (pbk.)
1. Bible—Dictionaries. 2. Mythology—Dictionaries. I. Lapides, Frederick R., joint author. II. Title.

EVANS, Bergen, 1904- 398
Dictionary of mythology, mainly classical. Lincoln [Neb.] Centennial Press [1970] xviii, 293 p. illus. 22 cm. Bibliography: p. 269-270. [BL303.E9] 70-120115 6.95
1. Mythology—Dictionaries. I. Title.

GRANT, Michael, 1914- 292'.003
Gods and mortals in classical mythology [by] Michael Grant and John Hazel. Springfield, Mass., G. & C. Merriam Co. [1973] 447 p. illus. (part col.) 26 cm. "A Merriam-Webster." Bibliography: p. 444-446. [BL715.G67 1973] 73-5650 ISBN 0-87779-087-6 15.00
1. Mythology—Dictionaries. I. Hazel, John, joint author. II. Title.

HENDRICKS, Rhoda A 290
Mythology pocket crammer. New York, Ken Pub. Col,; distributed to the book trade by Doubleday, Garden City, N. Y. [1963] 160 p. 14 cm. (The Pocket crammer series) [BL303.H46] 63-5155
1. Mythology — Dictionaries. I. Title.

HENDRICKS, Rhoda A. 290
Mythology pocket grammer. Garden City, N.Y. Ken Pub. Co.; dist. Doubleday, [c.1963] 160p. 14cm. (Pocket grammer ser.) 63-5155 1.00 pap., plastic bds.
1. Mythology—Dictionaries. I. Title.

HOWE, George, 1876-1936. 398.2
A handbook of classical mythology, by George Howe and G. A. Harrer. Detroit, Gale Research Co., 1970. vii, 301 p. 22 cm. Facsim. of the 1947 ed. Includes bibliographical references. [BL715.H6 1947a] 77-121209
1. Mythology—Dictionaries. I. Harrer, Gustave Adolphus, 1886-1943 joint author. II. Title.

KASTER, Joseph. 290.3
Putnam's concise mythological dictionary. Based upon Gods, by Bessie Redfield. New York, Putnam [1963] [9], 180 p. 20 cm. Bibliography: 7th-8th prelim. pages. [BL31.K3] 63-9663
1. Mythology—Dictionaries. 2. Religion—Dictionaries. I. Redfield, Bessie Gordon, 1868- comp. Gods. II. Title. III. Title: Mythological dictionary.

KIRKWOOD, Gordon MacDonald, 1916- 292.03
A short guide to classical mythology. New York [Holt] Rinehart [and Winston, 1960, c.1959] 109p. (Rinehart English pamphlets) Includes bibl. 60-1973 1.00 pap.,
1. Mythology—Dictionaries. I. Title.

KRAVITZ, David, 1939- 292'.003
Who's who in Greek and Roman mythology / David Kravitz ; illustrations by Lynne S. Mayo. 1st American ed. New York : C. N. Potter : distributed by Crown Publishers, [1976] c1975. 246 p. : ill. ; 24 cm. Published in 1975 by New English Library, London, under title: The dictionary of Greek & Roman mythology. [BL715.K7 1976] 76-29730 ISBN 0-517-52746-4 : 10.00 ISBN 0-517-52747-2 pbk. : 3.95
1. Mythology—Dictionaries. I. Title.

MCGOVERN, Thomas.
The pronouncing dictionary of mythology and antiquities ... New York, The Chiswick pub. co. [1899] 163 p. 24° Apr
I. Title.

MYTHOLOGIES of the world : a concise encyclopedia / Max S. Shapiro, executive editor ; compiled by Rhoda A. Hendricks, research editor. 1st ed. Garden City, N.Y. : Doubleday, 1979. xviii, 218 p. : ill. ; 22 cm. Bibliography: p. [219]. [BL303.M95] 78-1221 ISBN 0-385-13667-6 : 8.95 291.1'3
1. Mythology—Dictionaries. I. Shapiro, Max S. II. Hendricks, Rhoda A.

MYTHOLOGIES of the world : a concise encyclopedia / by Rhoda A. Hendricks ; Max S. Shapiro, executive editor. 1st McGraw-Hill pbk. ed. New York : McGraw-Hill, 1981. p. cm. Originally published: Garden City, N.Y. : Doubleday, 1979. [BL303.M95 1981] 19 81-532 ISBN 0-07-056421-3 (pbk.) : 4.95 291.1'3
1. Mythology—Dictionaries. I. Hendricks, Rhoda A. II. Shapiro, Max S.

SYKES, Egerton. 290.3
Everyman's dictionary of non-classical mythology. London, Dent; New York, Dutton [1952] xviii, 262 p. plates. 20 cm. (Everyman's reference library) Bibliography: p. xvi-xviii. [BL303.S9] 52-3946
1. Mythology — Dictionaries. I. Title.

TRIPP, Edward 398
The meridian handbook of classical mythology. N.Y., New American Library, [1974, c1970] ix, 631 p. geneal. table, maps. 21 cm. (A Meridian book) Originally published under title: Crowell's handbook of classical mythology [BL303.T75 1974] 74-127614 5.95 (pbk.)
1. Mythology—Dictionaries. I. Title.

WOODCOCK, Percival George. 290.3
Short dictionary of mythology. New York, Philosophical Library [1953] 156 p. 24 cm. [BL303.W6] 53-7910
1. Mythology—Dictionaries. I. Title.

ZIMMERMAN, John Edward, 1901- 292.03
Dictionary of classical mythology. [1st ed.] New York, Harper & Row [1964] xx, 300 p. 21 cm. Bibliography: p. 295-300. [BL715.Z5] 63-20319
1. Mythology—Dictionaries. I. Title.

Mythology—Dictionaries, indexes, etc.

BECHTEL, John Hendricks, 1841- 292.
A dictionary of mythology; containing short and interesting sketches of characters found in Grecian and Roman mythology, with all proper names carefully pronounced, by John H. Bechtel ... Philadelphia, The Penn publishing company, 1899. 221 p. 15 cm. [BL715.B4] 99-2706
1. Mythology—Dictionaries, indexes, etc. 2. Mythology, Classical. I. Title.

BECHTEL, John Hendricks, 1841- 290.
A dictionary of mythology, by John H. Bechtel ... containing short and interesting sketches of characters found in Grecian and Roman mythology, with all proper names correctly pronounced. Philadelphia, The Penn publishing company, 1927. 221 p. 15 1/2 cm. [BL303.B35 1927] 27-11376
1. Mythology—Dictionaries, indexes, etc. I. Title.

BLACK, Jane. 292
Mythology for young people, by Jane Black. New York, Chicago [etc.] C. Scribner's sons [c1925] viii p., 1 l., 141 p. 16 1/2 cm. In form of a dictionary. [BL725.B45] 25-16682
1. Mythology—Dictionaries, Indexes, etc. 2. Mythology, Classical—Juvenile literature. I. Title.

BRAY, Frank Chapin, 1866- 290.3
The world of myths; a dictionary of mythology, by Frank Chapin Bray. New York, Thomas Y. Crowell company [c1935] x, 328 p. 20 cm. [BL306.B67] 35-24306
1. Mythology—Dictionaries, indexes, etc. I. Title.

ELLIS, Edward Ellis, 1840-1916. 290.3
1000 mythological characters briefly described, adapted to private schools, high schools, and academies, edited by Edward S. *ellis New York, Nobel and Noble [c1927] 162 p. front., plates. 17 cm. First published, 1895, with title: The youth's dictionary of mythology. [BL303.E4 1927] 27-17088
1. Mythology—Dictionaries, indexes, etc. I. Title.

ELLIS, Edward Sylvester, 1840-1916. 290.3
1000 mythological characters briefly described; adapted to private schools, high schools and academies; edited by Edward S. Ellis New York city, Hinds & Noble [1899] 146 p. front., plates. 17 cm. First published, 1895, with title: The youth's dictionary of mythology. [BL303.E4] 0-1011
1. Mythology—Dictionaries, indexes, etc. I. Title.

ELLIS, Edward Sylvester, 1840-1916. 290.3
The youth's dictionary of mythology for boys and girls, containing brief and accurate accounts of the gods and goddesses of the ancients; edited with introduction by Edward S. Ellis ... New York, The Woolfall company, 1895. 146 p. 16 cm. (Lettered on cover: Woolfall's Home and school library) Published later with title: 1000 mythological characters briefly described. [BL303.E45] 30-33825
1. Mythology—Dictionaries, indexes, etc. I. Title.

HOWE, George, 1876-1936. 292.03
A handbook of classical mythology, by George Howe and G. A. Harrer ... New York, F. S. Crofts & co., 1929. vii, 301 p. 19 1/2 cm. Contains "Literature". [BL715.H6] 29-14609
1. Mythology—Dictionaries, indexes, etc. 2. Mythology, Classical. I. Harrer, Gustave Adolphus, 1886- joint author. II. Title.

Mythology, Egyptian.

BUDGE, Ernest Alfred Thompson Wallis, Sir, 1857-1934. 299'.3'1
The gods of the Egyptians; or, Studies in Egyptian mythology. New York, Dover Publications [1969] 2 v. illus. (part fold., col.) 24 cm. Reprint of the 1904 ed. Includes bibliographical references. [BL2441.B83 1969] 72-91925 4.50 per vol.
1. Mythology, Egyptian. I. Title.

CLARK, Robert Thomas Rundle. 299.31
Myth and symbol in ancient Egypt. New York, Grove Press [1960, c1959] 292 p. illus. 23 cm. (Myth and man) [BL2441.2.C55 1960a] 60-9260
1. Mythology, Egyptian. I. Title.

CLARK, Robert Thomas Rundle. 299.3
Myth and symbol in ancient Egypt / R.T. rundle Clark. London ; New York : Thames and Hudson, [1978]c1959. 292p., [8] leaves of plates : ill. ; 22 cm. Includes bibliographical references and index. [BL2441.2.C55] 77-92262 ISBN 0-500-27112-7 pbk. : 7.95
1. Mythology, Egyptian. I. Title.

EGYPTIAN mythology. 299.31
New York, Tudor Pub. Co. [1965] 152 p. illus. (part col.) map. 29 cm. "Based on the text translated by Delano Ames from Mythologie generale Larousse." [BL2441.2.E4] 65-9171
1. Mythology, Egyptian. I. Guirand, Felix, ed. Mythologie generale. II. Larousse encyclopedia of mythology.

JAMES, Thomas Garnet Henry. 299'.3'1
Myths and legends of ancient Egypt, by T. G. H. James. Illustrated by Brian Melling. New York, Grosset & Dunlap [1971] 159 p. col. illus. 22 cm. (A Grosset all-color guide, 27) Bibliography: p. [157] [BL2441.2.J3 1971] 73-136363 ISBN 0-448-00866-1 3.95
1. Mythology, Egyptian. I. Melling, Brian, illus. II. Title.

JAMES, Thomas Garnet Henry. 299'.3'1
Myths and legends of Ancient Egypt, by T. G. H. James; illustrated by Brian Melling. Feltham, Hamlyn, 1969. 160 p. col. illus., col. map. 19 cm. (Hamlyn all-colour paperbacks) [BL2441.2.J3 1969] 78-530247 6/-
1. Mythology, Egyptian. I. Title.

MACKENZIE, Donald Alexander, 1873-1936. 299'.3'2
Egypt myth and legend : with historical narrative notes on race problems, comparative beliefs, etc. / by Donald A. Mackenzie. Portland, Me. : Longwood Press, 1976. xlix, 404 p., [38] leaves of plates : ill. ; 22 cm. Reprint of the 1907 ed. published by Gresham Pub. Co., London, issued in series: Myth and legend in literature and art. Includes index. [BL2441.M3 1976] 76-27520 ISBN 0-89341-033-0 lib.bdg. : 45.00
1. Mythology, Egyptian. 2. Legends, Egyptian. 3. Egypt—History. I. Title. II. Series: Myth and legend in literature and art.

MACKENZIE, Donald Alexander, 1873-1936. 299'.3'1
Egyptian myth and legend. With historical narrative notes on race problems, comparative beliefs, etc. Boston, Milford House [1973] p. Reprint of the 1913 ed. published by Gresham Pub. Co., London, in series: Myth and legend in literature and art. [BL2441.M3 1973] 73-13910 ISBN 0-87821-184-5 40.00 (lib. bdg.)
1. Mythology, Egyptian. 2. Legends, Egyptian. 3. Egypt—History. I. Title. II. Series: Myth and legend in literature and art.

MACKENZIE, Donald Alexander, 1873-1936. 299'.3'1
Egyptian myth and legend : with historical narrative notes on race problems, comparative beliefs, etc. / by Donald A. Mackenzie. New York : Bell Pub. Co., 1978. p. cm. This ed. first published in 1907 by Gresham Pub. Co., London, in series: Myth and legend in literature and art; with plates in color. [BL2441.M3 1978] 78-17839 ISBN 0-517-25912-5 pbk. : 4.98
1. Mythology, Egyptian. 2. Legends, Egyptian. 3. Egypt—History. I. Title. II. Series: Myth and legend in literature and art.

MULLER, Wilhelm Max, 1862-1919. 299.31
Egyptian [mythology] by W. Max Muller. New York, Cooper Square Publishers, 1964 [c1918] xiv, 450 p. illus., 21 plates (part col.) 24 cm. (The Mythology of all races, v. 12) Bibliography: p. [431]-450. [BL25.M8] 63-19097
1. Mythology, Egyptian. 2. Mythology, Indochinese. I. Scott, Sir James George, 1851-1935. II. Title. III. Title: Indo-Chinese [mythology] IV. Series.

MULLER, Wilhelm Max, 1862-1919. 299.
... Egyptian [mythology] by W. Max Muller ... Indo-Chinese [mythology] by Sir James George Scott ... Boston, Marshall Jones company, 1918 xiv p., 21., 3-450 p. illus. xxi pl. (incl. front., part col.) 25 cm. (The mythology of all races ... L. H. Grary ... editor ... vol. xii) Each plate accompained by guard sheet with descriptive letterpress. Bibliography: p. [431]-450. [BL25.M8 vol. 12] [BL2441.M8] 294. 18-8775
1. Mythology, Egyptian. 2. Mythology, Indo-Chinese. I. Scott, James George, Sir 1851-1935. II. Title.

MYTHOLOGICAL papyri. 299.31
Translated with introd. by Alexandre Piankoff; edited, with a chapter on the symbolism of the papyri, by N. Rambova. [New York] Pantheon Books [1957] 2 v. col. front, illus., 30 fold. plates. 32cm. (Bollingen series, 40:3 Egyptian religious texts and representations, v. 3) Contents.1. Texts.--2. Plates. [PJ1551.E3 vol. 3] 58-697
1. Mythology, Egyptian. 2. Egyptian language—Papyri. I. Plankoff, Alexander, tr. II. Series: Bollingen series, 40: III. Egypian religious texts and representations, v. 3

Mythology, Egyptian—Addresses, essays, lectures.

STEINER, Rudolf, 1861-1925. 299'.3'1
Egyptian myths and mysteries; twelve lectures, Leipzig, September 2-14, 1908. [Translated by Norman Macbeth] New York, Anthroposophic Press [1971] vi, 151 p. 22 cm. "Translated from shorthand reports unrevised by the lecturer, from the German edition published with the title, Aegyptische Mythen und Mysterien (vol. 106 in the Bibliographical survey, 1961)" Includes bibliographical references. [BL2441.S7513] 70-144034
1. Mythology, Egyptian—Addresses, essays, lectures. 2. Anthroposophy—Addresses, essays, lectures. I. Title.

Mythology, Egyptian—Dictionaries.

MERCATANTE, Anthony S. 299'.3'1
Who's who in Egyptian mythology / Anthony S. Mercatante ; foreword by Robert S. Bianchi ; illustrated by the author. 1st ed. New York : C. N. Potter : distributed by Crown Publishers, c1978. xxi, 231 p. : ill. ; 24 cm. Bibliography: p. 219-231. [BL2428.M47 1978] 78-14477 ISBN 0-517-53445-2 : 14.95 ISBN 0-517-53446-0 pbk. : 5.95
1. Mythology, Egyptian—Dictionaries. I. Title.

Mythology, English.

BRANSTON, Brian, 1914- 293
The lost gods of England. [2d ed.] London, Thames and Hudson [1974] 216 p. illus. (part col.) 25 cm. [BL980.G7B7 1974] 74-179873 ISBN 0-500-11013-1
1. Mythology, English. 2. Mythology, Anglo-Saxon. I. Title.
Distributed by Oxford University Press, New York, 10.00.

BRANSTON, Brian, 1914- 293
The lost gods of England / Brian Branston. New York : Oxford University Press, 1974. 216 p. : ill. (some col.) ; 25 cm. Includes index. [BL980.G7B7 1974b] 74-78753 ISBN 0-19-519796-8 : 10.00
1. Mythology, English. 2. Mythology, Anglo-Saxon. I. Title.

Mythology, Finno-Urgrian.

HARVA, Uno, 1882-1949. 299.45
Finno-Ugric, Siberian [mythology] by Uno Holmberg. New York, Cooper Square Publishers, 1964. xxv, 587 p. illus., map, 63 plates (part col.) 24 cm. (The Mythology of all races, v. 4) Bibliography: p. [561]-587. [BL25.M8] 63-19089
1. Mythology, Finno-Urgrian. 2. Mythology, Siberian. I. Title. II. Series.

Mythology, Germanic.

CHANTEPIE de la Saussaye, Pierre Daniel, 1848-1920. 293
The religion of the Teutons. Translated from the Dutch by Bert J. Vos. [Boston] Milford House [1973] p. Translation of Geschiedenis van den Godsdienst der Germanen. Reprint of the 1902 ed. published by Ginn, Boston, which was issued as v. 3 of Handbooks on the history of religions. Bibliography: p. [BL860.C45 1973] 73-186792 ISBN 0-87821-097-0 50.00 (lib. bdg.)
1. Mythology, Germanic. 2. Mythology, Norse. 3. Germanic tribes—Religion. I. Title. II. Series: Handbooks on the history of religions, v. 3.

CHANTEPIE de la Saussaye, Pierre Daniel, 1848-1920. 293
The religion of the Teutons / by P. D. Chantepie de la Saussaye ; translated from the Dutch by Bert J. Vos. Portland, Me. : Longwood Press, 1977. vii, 504 p., [2] leaves of plates : maps ; 22 cm. Translation of Geschiedenis van den godsdienst ger Germanen. Reprint of the 1902 ed. published by Ginn, Boston, which was issued as v. 3 of Handbooks on the history of religions. Includes bibliographical references and index. [BL860.C413 1977] 76-27519 ISBN 0-89341-030-6 : 50.00
1. Mythology, Germanic. 2. Mythology, Norse. 3. Germanic tribes—Religion. I. Title. II. Series: Handbooks on the history of religions ; v. 3.

CHANTEPIE de la Saussaye, Pierre Daniel, 1848-1920. 293
... The religion of the Teutons, by P. D. Chantepie de la Saussaye ... translated from the Dutch by Bert J. Vos ... Boston and London, Ginn & company, 1902. vii, [1] 504 p. 1 illus., maps. 22 cm. (Half-title: Handbooks on the history of religion v. 3) Series title in part also at head of t.-p. Bibliography: p. 417-463. [BL860.C45] 2-16440
1. Mythology, Germanic. 2. Mythology, Norse. 3. Germanic tribes—Religion. I. Vos, Bert John, 1867- tr. II. Title.

DAVIDSON, Hilda Roderick (Ellis) 293.211
Gods and myths of northern Europe. Baltimore, Penguin [c.1964] 251p. 19cm. (Pelican bk. A670) Bibl. 64-56969 1.25 pap.,
1. Mythology, Germanic. 2. Mythology, Norse. 3. Europe, Northern—Religion—Hist. I. Title.

GRIMM, Jakob Ludwig Karl, 1785-1863. 293
Teutonic mythology. Translated from the fourth ed. with notes and appendix by James Steven Stallybrass. New York, Dover Publications [1966] 4 v. (viii, 1887 p.) 22 cm. "Unabridged and unaltered republication of the work first published ... in 1883 ... [to] 1888." [BL860.G753] 66-15933
1. Mythology, Germanic. 2. Mythology, Norse. 3. Germanic tribes—Religion. 4. Magic, Germanic. 5. Superstition. 6. Names, Germanic. I. Stallybrass, James Steven, 1826-1888, ed. and tr. II. Title.

GRIMM, Jakoh Ludwig Karl 1785-1863 293
Teutonic mythology. Tr. from the 4th ed. with notes. appendix by James Steven Stalllybrass [Magnolia, Mass., P. Smith. 1967] 4v. (viii, 1887p.) 22cm. (Dover bks. rebound) Unabridged, unaltered repubn. of the work first pub. 1883-1888 by George Bell [BL860.G753] 4.75 ea.,
1. Mythology, Germanic. 2. Mythology, Norse. 3. Germanic tribes—Religion. 4. Magic, Germanic. 5. Superstition. 6. Names. Germanic. I. Stallybrass, JamesSteven, 1826-1888, ed. and tr. II. Title.

MACKENZIE, Donald Alexander, 1873- 293
Teutonic myth and legend, by Donald A. Mackenzie; an introduction to the Eddas & sagas, Beowulf, the Nibelungenlied, etc. New York, W. H. Wise & company, 1934. xivii, 469 p. incl. col. front. plates (1 double, part col.) 22 1/2 cm. (On cover: Myths and legends of mankind) [BL860.M3 1934] 34-31769
1. Mythology, Germanic. 2. Legends, Germanic. I. Title.

MACKENZIE, Donald Alexander, 1873-1936. 293
Teutonic myth and legend / by Donald A. Mackenzie. Boston : Longwood Press, 1978. xlvii, 469 p., [31] leaves of plates : ill. ; 22 cm. Reprint of the ed. published by Gresham Pub. Co. in series: Myth and legend in literature and art. Includes index. [BL860.M3 1978] 77-91530 ISBN 0-89341-313-5 lib.bdg. : 45.00
1. Mythology, Germanic. 2. Legends, Germanic. I. Title. II. Series: Myth and legend in literature and Art.

SCHWARTZ, Stephen P., 1938- 830
Poetry and law in Germanic myth, by Stephen P. Schwartz. Berkeley, University of California Press, 1973. 61 p. 26 cm. (University of California publications. Folklore studies, 27) Bibliography: p. 59-61. [BL865.S37] 72-83099 ISBN 0-520-09461-1 2.25 (pbk.)
1. Mythology, Germanic. I. Title. II. Series: California. University. University of California publications. Folklore studies, 27.

Mythology, Germanic—Addresses, essays, lectures.

BAUSCHATZ, Paul C., 1935- 293'.24
The well and the tree : world and time in early Germanic culture / Paul C. Bauschatz. Amherst : University of Massachusetts Press, 1982. xx, 256 p. : ill. ; 24 cm. Includes index. Bibliography: p. [229]-243. [BL863.B38 1982] 19 81-14766 ISBN 0-87023-352-1 : 25.00
1. Mythology, Germanic—Addresses, essays, lectures. 2. Germanic tribes—Religion—Addresses, essays, lectures. 3. Language and culture—Addresses, essays, lectures. 4. Time—Addresses, essays, lectures. I. Title.

Mythology, Germanic—Juvenile literature.

HOSFORD, Dorothy G. 293
Thunder of the gods; illustrated by Claire & George Louden. [1st ed.] New York, Holt [1952] 115 p. illus. 21 cm. [BL865.H64] 52-9038
1. Mythology, Germanic—Juvenile literature. I. Title.

Mythology, Greek.

APOLLODORUS. 292'.2'11
Gods and heroes of the Greeks : The library of Appolodorus / translated with introd. and notes by Michael Simpson ; drawings by Leonard Baskin. Amherst : University of Massachusetts Press, 1976. vi, 311 p. : ill. ; 24 cm. Translation of Viviotheke, often formerly believed to be the work of Apollodorus, the Athenian grammarian, but now generally ascribed to a later Apollodorus. Includes index. Bibliography: p. [305]-306. [PA3870.A55A28] 75-32489 ISBN 0-87023-205-3 : 12.00. ISBN 0-87023-206-1 pbk. : 5.95
1. Mythology, Greek. I. Apollodorus, of Athens. Vivliotheke. II. Simpson, Michael, 1934- III. Baskin, Leonard, 1922- IV. Title.

BACON, Francis, Viscount St. Albans, 1561-1626. 292'.2'11
De sapientia veterum : London, 1609, and The wisedome of the ancients : translated by Arthur Gorges : London, 1619 / Francis Bacon. New York : Garland, 1976. p. cm. (The Renaissance and the gods ; no. 20) Reprints of the 1609 ed. of De sapientia veterum published by R. Barker, London, and the 1619 ed. of The wisedome of the ancients published by J. Bill, London. [B1180.D6 1976] 75-27863 ISBN 0-8240-2068-5 : 40.00
1. Mythology, Greek. I. Gorges, Arthur, Sir, 1557 (ca.)-1625. II. Title. III. Title: The wisedome of the ancients. IV. Series.

BACON, Francis, Viscount St. Albans, 1561-1626. 292'.2'11
The wisedome of the ancients. New York, Da Capo Press, 1968. 175 p. 16 cm. (The English experience, no. 1) Translation of De sapientia veterum. [B1180.D62E5 1968] 68-54614
1. Mythology, Greek. I. Title.

BARNES, Hazel Estella. 292'.2'11
The meddling gods; four essays on classical themes [by] Hazel E. Barnes. Lincoln, University of Nebraska Press [1974] 141 p. 21 cm. Contents.Contents.—The look of the Gorgon.—Death and cocktails: The Alcestis theme in Euripides and T. S. Eliot.—Homer and the meddling gods.—The case of Sosia versus Sosia. Includes bibliographical references. [BL785.B3] 73-92003 ISBN 0-8032-0838-3 25.00 (lib. bdg.)
1. Mythology, Greek. I. Title.
Contents omitted.

BARTHELL, Edward E. 292'.2'11
Gods and goddesses of ancient Greece, by Edward E. Barthell, Jr. Coral Gables, Fla., University of Miami Press [1971] xi, 416 p. 28 cm. Bibliography: p. [397]-398. [BL782.B36] 72-129664 ISBN 0-87024-165-6 25.00
1. Mythology, Greek. I. Title.

†BROWN, Robert, 1844- 292'.1'3
Semitic influence in Hellenic mythology / Robert Brown. New York : Arno Press, 1977. xv, 228 p. ; 23 cm. (International folklore) Reprint of the 1898 ed. published by Williams and Norgate, London. Includes index. [BL785.B7 1977] 77-70583 ISBN 0-405-10084-1 : 14.00
1. Muller, Friedrich Max, 1823-1900. Contributions to the science of mythology. 2. Lang, Andrew, 1844-1912. Modern mythology. 3. Mythology, Greek. 4. Mythology, Semitic. 5. Mythology. I. Title. II. Series.

BROWN, Robert, 1844- 292'.13
Semitic influence in Hellenic mythology, with special reference to the recent mythological works of the Rt. Hon. Prof. F. Max Muller and Mr. Andrew Lang. Clifton, N.J., Reference Book Publishers, 1966. xv, 228 p. 23 cm. (Library of religious and philosophical thought) On cover: Library of religious and philosophic thought. Reprint of the 1898 ed. [BL785.B7] 65-27053
1. Mythology, Greek. 2. Mythology, Semitic. 3. Muller, Friedrich Max, 1823-1900. Contributions to the science of mythology. 4. Lang, Andrew, 1844-1912. Modern mythology. I. Title.

BROWN, Robert F., 1941- 292'.2'11
Schelling's treatise on "The deities of Samothrace" : a translation and an interpretation / by Robert F. Brown. Missoula, Mont. : Published by Scholars Press for American Academy of Religion, c1977. viii, 65 p. ; 24 cm. (Studies in religion ; no. 12) Bibliography: p. 64-65. [BL793.S3S332 1977] 76-42239 ISBN 0-89130-087-2 : 4.20
1. Schelling, Friedrich Wilhelm Joseph von, 1775-1854. Ueber die Gottheiten von Samothrace. 2. Mythology, Greek. 3. Samothrace—Religion. I. Schelling, Friedrich Wilhelm Joseph von, 1775-1854. Ueber die Gottheiten von Samothrace. English. 1976. II. Title. III. Series: American Academy of Religion. AAR studies in religion ; no. 12.

BULFINCH, Thomas, 1796-1867. 290
The Trojan War, with introductory notes on the Grecian divinities. Adapted from The age of fable. [New York] Priv. print. by K. H. Volk, 1957. 54p. (on double leaves) mounted illus. 26cm. [BL310.B82 1957] 58-49556
1. Mythology, Greek. I. Title.

BURKERT, Walter, 1931- 292'.13
Structure and history in Greek mythology and ritual / Walter Burkert. Berkeley : University of California Press, c1979. xix, 226 p. : ill. ; 24 cm. (Sather classical lectures ; v. 47) Includes index. Bibliography: p. 211-218. [BL785.B83] 78-62856 ISBN 0-520-03771-5 : 15.00
1. Mythology, Greek. 2. Rites and ceremonies—Greece. I. Title. II. Series.

COX, George William, 1827-1902. 292
Tales of ancient Greece. By the Rev. G. W. Cox ... 4th ed. Chicago, J. McClurg and co., 1879. xiiii, 372 p. 18 cm. "The tales collected in this volume have, with one exception, appeared in the 'Tales from Greek mythology', 'The gods and heroes', and 'Tales of Thebes and Argos'."--Pref. [BL781.C6 1879] 15-16191
1. Mythology, Greek. 2. Legends, Greek. I. Title.

COX, George William, 1827-1902. 292
Tales of ancient Greece, by Sir George W. Cox, bart. London & Toronto, J. M. Dent & sons, ltd.; New York, E. P. Dutton & co. [1915] x, 325 p. 17 cm. (Half-title: Everyman's library, ed. by Ernest Rhys. For young people. [no. 721]) Bibliography: p. viii. [BL781.C] A 16
1. Mythology, Greek. 2. Legends, Greek. I. Title.
Contents omitted.

COX, George William, 1827-1902. 292
Tales of ancient Greece [by] Sir George W. Cox. London, J. M. Dent & sons, ltd.; New York, E. P. Dutton & co., inc. [1927] viii, 325 p. 18 cm. (Half-title: Everyman's library, ed. by Ernest Rhys. For young people. [no. 721]) "First published in this edition 1915. Reprinted ... 1927." "Editor's note" signed: J. C. "List of the works of Sir George Cox": p. viii. [AC1.E8 no. 721] 37-5624
1. Mythology, Greek. 2. Legends, Greek. I. Title.

DALL, Caroline Wells (Healey) 1822-1912. 398.2'0938
Margaret and her friends; or, Ten conversations with Margaret Fuller upon the mythology of the Greeks and its expression in art. New York, Arno Press, 1972 [c1895] 162 p. 22 cm. (The Romantic tradition in American literature) [BL785.D3 1972] 72-4961 ISBN 0-405-04633-2 8.00
1. Mythology, Greek. 2. Mythology, Classical, in art. I. Ossoli, Sarah Margaret (Fuller) marchesa d', 1810-1850. II. Title. III. Title: Ten conversations with Margaret Fuller. IV. Series.

DALL, Caroline Wells (Healey) Mrs. 1822-1912. 292
Margaret and her friends; or, Ten conversations with Margaret Fuller upon the mythology of the Greeks and its expression in art held at the house of the Rev. George Ripley ... Boston, beginning March 1, 1841. Reported by Caroline W. Healey. Boston, Roberts brothers, 1895. 3 p. l., [5]-162 p. 21 cm. [BL785.D3] 31-31272
1. Mythology, Greek. 2. Art and mythology. I. Ossoll, Sarah Margaret (Fuller) marchesa d', 1810-1850. II. Title.

DIEL, Paul, 1893- 292'.3'7
Symbolism in Greek mythology : human desire and its transformations / Paul Diel ; pref. by Gaston Bachelard ; translated from the French by Vincent Stuart, Micheline Stuart, and Rebecaa Folkman. Boulder : Shambhala ; [New York] : distributed in the U.S. by Random House, 1980. xx, 218 p. ; 22 cm. Translation of Le symbolisme dans la mythologie grecque. [BL785.D513] 79-67686 ISBN 0-87773-178-0 ISBN 0-394-51083-6 (Random House) : 12.50
1. Mythology, Greek. 2. Symbolism. I. Title.

DOWRICK, Stephanie. 292'.08
Land of Zeus : the Greek myths retold by geographical place of origin / Stephanie Dowrick. 1st ed. in the U.S.A. Garden City, N.Y. : Doubleday, 1976, c1974. xiv, 223 p. : maps ; 22 cm. "A consolidation of ... Greek Island mythology and Land of Zeus: myths of the Greek gods and heroes." Includes index. Bibliography: p. [213] [BL782.D7 1976] 74-25102 ISBN 0-385-05629-X : 7.95
1. Mythology, Greek. I. Title.

DUTHIE, Alexander 292
The Greek mythology, a reader's handbook. Philadelphia, Dufour, 1961[ ] 168p. illus. 61-14085 2.95 bds.,
1. Mythology, Greek. I. Title.

DUTHIE, Alexander. 292'.1'3
The Greek mythology : a reader's handbook / by Alexander Duthie. Westport, Conn. : Greenwood Press, 1979. 168 p. : ill. ; 23 cm. Reprint of the 1949 2d ed. published by Oliver and Boyd, Edinburgh. Includes index. [BL781.D8 1979] 78-13988 ISBN 0-313-21077-2 lib. bdg. : 15.00
1. Mythology, Greek. I. Title.

ELIOT, Alexander. 292'.2'1
Creatures of Arcadia, and creatures of a day. Illustrated by Eugene Berman. Indianapolis, Bobbs-Merrill [1967] xl, 157 p. illus. 22 cm. Based chiefly on Greek myths. Contents.Contents.—The sense of myth.—The white heifer.—The children of Nemesis.—The gorgon.—The bull blood.—The beggar by the fire.—The fox and the grapes.—The full glory.—The wisdom of Cheiron.—The eagle and the tortoise.—The incredible crayfish.—The asp and the file.—The fond companions.—The trials of Psyche. [BL782.E55] 67-25174
1. Mythology, Greek. I. Title.

ESPELAND, Pamela, 1951- 291.1'3'0938 E
The story of Arachne / Pamela Espeland ; pictures by Susan Kennedy. Minneapolis : Carolrhoda Books, c1980. [32] p. : col. ill. ; 24 cm. Because she boasts that she weaves better than anyone, Arachne is turned into a spider. [PZ8.1.E83Ss 1980] 80-15621 ISBN 0-87614-130-0 (lib. bdg.) : 5.95
1. Arachne—Juvenile literature. 2. [Arachne.] 3. [Mythology, Greek.] I. Kennedy, Susan. II. Title.

ESPELAND, Pamela, 1951- 292'.13
The story of Baucis and Philemon / Pamela Espeland ; pictures by George Overlie. Minneapolis : Carolrhoda Books, c1981. [32] p. : ill. ; 24 cm. (A Myth for modern children) An old, impoverished couple are the only ones in Phrygia to take pity on two tired, hungry travelers who turn out to be Jupiter and Mercury in disguise. [BL820.B28E84] 19 80-27674 ISBN 0-87614-140-8 : 5.95
1. Baucis and Philemon (Greek mythology)—Juvenile literature. 2. [Baucis and Philemon (Greek mythology)] 3. [Mythology, Greek.] I. Overlie, George. II. Title.

EVSLIN, Bernard. 883'.01
Greeks bearing gifts : the epics of Achilles and Ulysses / by Bernard Evslin ; illustrated by Lucy Martin Bitzer. New York : Four Winds Press, [1976] c1971. p. cm. [BL782.E89 1976] 76-16039 ISBN 0-590-17431-2 : 9.95
1. Mythology, Greek. I. Homerus. Ilias. II. Homerus. Odyssea. III. Title.

EVSLIN, Bernard. 292
Heroes, gods and monsters of the Greek myths. Illustrated by William Hofmann. New York, Four Winds Press [1967] 223 p. illus. 22 cm. Bibliography: p. 223. Retellings of the ancient Greek myths,

arranged in four sections: the Gods, Nature Myths, Demigods, and Fables. Includes a brief section on words from the Greek myths which are part of the English language. [BL782.E9] AC 68
1. Mythology, Greek. I. Hofmann, William, illus. II. Title.

EVSLIN. BERNARD. 292'.2'11
Heroes, gods and monsters of the Greek myths. Illustrated by William Hofmann. New York, Four Winds Press [1967] 223 p. illus. 22 cm. Bibliography: p. 223. [BL782.E9] 67-23541
1. Mythology, Greek. I. Title.

FARRAR, Francis Albert.
Old Greek nature stories, by F. A. Farrar ... With eight plates after originals in the principal galleries ... New York, L. Macveagh, The Dial press [1926] 256 p. front., plates. 19 cm. (Half-title: Told through the ages) Printed in Great Britain. A 2
1. Mythology, Greek. 2. Mythology—Juvenile literature. I. Title.

FISCHER, Carl John, 1936- 292'.2'11
The myth and legend of Greece [by] Carl Fischer. Dayton, Ohio, G. A. Pflaum [1968] v, 202 p. 19 cm. [BL782.F57] 68-54898 0.95
1. Mythology, Greek. I. Title.

GATES, Doris, 1901- JUV
A fair wind for Troy / Doris Gates ; drawing by Charles Mikolaycak. New York : Viking Press, [1976] p. cm. Retells the events leading up to the Trojan War including Helen's capture by Paris and the sacrifice of Iphigenia at Aulis. [PZ8.1.G1684Fai] 292'.1'3 398.2 76-27738 ISBN 0-670-30505-7 lib. bdg. : 6.95
1. [Mythology, Greek.] I. Mikolaycak, Charles. II. Title.

GIBSON, Michael. 292'.13
Gods, men & monsters from the Greek myths / illustrations by Giovanni Caselli ; texts by Michael Gibson. American ed. New York : Schocken Books, 1982, c1977. p. cm. Includes index. A collection of myths relating the exploits and adventures of the gods and heroes of ancient Greece. [BL782.G53 1982] 19 81-14542 ISBN 0-8052-0691-4 : 14.95
1. Mythology, Greek. 2. [Mythology, Greek.] I. Caselli, Giovanni, fl. 1976- ill. II. Title. III. Title: Gods, men, and monsters from the Greek myths.

GRAVES, Robert, 1895- 292
The Greek myths [2.v.] Baltimore, Penguin [dist. New York, Atheneum, 1961, c.1955] 370; 412p maps (1 fold-out) (Pelican bk., A508; A509) 1.45 pap., ea.,
1. Mythology, Greek. I. Title.

GRAVES, Robert, 1895- 292
The Greek myths. Baltimore, Penguin Books [1955] 2 v. 2 maps (1 fold. col.) 19 cm. (Penguin books, 1026-1027) Bibliographical footnotes. [BL781.G65 1955a] 55-8278
1. Mythology, Greek. I. Title.

GREEN, Roger Lancelyn. 292.21
Heroes of Greece and Troy, retold from the ancient authors. With drawings by Heather Copley and Christopher Chamberlain. New York, H. Z. Walck, 1961. 337 p. illus. 24 cm. "First published in 1958 ... in two volumes entitled Tales of the Greek heroes and The tale of Troy." [BL782.G7 1961] 61-14925
1. Mythology, Greek. 2. Troy—Romances, legends, etc. I. Title.

GREEN, Roger Lancelyn. 292.21
Tales of the Greek heroes, retold from the ancient authors. Illustrated by Betty Middleton-Sandford. [Harmonds-worth, Middlesex] Penguin Books [1958] 205p. illus. 18cm. (Puffin books, PS119) [BL781.G66] 59-17233
1. Mythology, Greek. I. Title.

HAMILTON, Mary Agnes (Adamson) Mrs. 1883-
Greek legends, told by Mary Agnes Hamilton. Oxford, The Clarendon press, 1912. 192 p. incl. front., illus. 19 cm. W 13
1. Mythology, Greek. I. Title.

HARRISON, Jane Ellen, 1850- 292
Mythology, by Jane Ellen Harrison ... Boston, Mass., Marshall Jones company [c1924] xx, 155 p. illus. 19 cm. (Half-title: Our debt to Greece and Rome [26]; editors, G. D. Hadzsits ... D. M. Robinson) Bibliography: p. 154-155. [BL781.H28] 25-821
1. Mythology, Greek. I. Title.

HARRISON, Jane Ellen, 1850- 1928. 292
Mythology. [Illustrated ed.] New York, Harcourt, Brace & World [1963, c1924] 111 p. illus. 21 cm. (A Harbinger book, Ho24) [BL781.H28] 63-3642
1. Mythology, Greek. I. Title.

HARRISON, Jane Ellen, 1850- 1928. 292
Mythology. New York, Cooper Square Publishers, 1963. xviii, 155 p. illus. 19 cm. (Our debt to Greece and Rome) Bibliographical references included in "Notes" (p. 151-153) Bibliography: p. 154-155. [BL781.H28 1963a] 63-10305
1. Mythology, Greek. I. Title. II. Series.

HERMES, Trismegistus.
Hermetica, the ancient Greek and Latin writings which contain religious or philosophic teachings ascribed to Hermes Trismegistus, edited with English translation and notes, by Walter Scott ... Oxford, The Clarendon press, 1924-36. 4 v. front. 23 cm. Contents.--i. Introduction, texts and translation.--ii. Notes on the Corpus Hermeticum.--iii. Notes on the Latin Asclepius and the Hermetic excerpts ofStobaeus.--iv. Testimonia, with introduction, addenda and indices by A. S. Ferguson. [PA3998.H5 1924] 25-15541
I. Scott, Walter, 1855-1925, ed. II. Ferguson, Alexander Stewart, 1883- ed. III. Title.

HUTCHINSON, Winifred Margaret Lambart, 1868- 292
The muses' pageant; myths & legends of ancient Greece, retold by W. M. L. Hutchinson ... London & Toronto, J. M. Dent & sons, ltd.; New York, E. P. Dutton & co. [1914?-29] 3 v. 18 cm. (Half-title: Everyman's library, ed. by E. rhys. Classical. [581, 606, 671]) Vols. 1-2 first publishing in this edition, 1912; v. 1 reprinted 1927; v. 2, 1929; v. 3 undated (1914?) Title within ornamental border. Contents.--v. 1. Myths of the gods.--v. 2. Myths of the heroes.--v. &. The lengths of Thebes. [AC1.E8 no. 581,606,671] 36-37600
1. Mythology, Greek. I. Title.

HUTCHINSON, Winifred Margaret Lambart, 1868-
The muses' pageant: myths and legends of ancient Greece, retold by W. M. L. Hutchinson ... London, J. M. Dent & sons, ltd.; New York, E. P. Dutton & co. [1912] 3 v. 18 cm. (Half-title: Everyman's library, ed. by Ernest Rhys. Classical. no. 581) Title within ornamental border. Contents.--v. 1. Myths of the god.--v. 2. Myths of the horses.--v. 3 Legends of Thebes. A 12
1. Mythology, Greek. I. Title.

KERENYI, Karoly 292
The heroes of the Greeks. Translated by H. J. Rose. New York, Grove Press [1960, c1959] xxiv, 439p. illus. 23cm. (Myth and man) (Bibl. notes: p.381-412) 60-8387 6.50
1. Mythology, Greek. 2. Heroes. I. Title.

KERENYI, Karoly, 1897- 292
The gods of the Greeks. [German text has been rendered into English by Norman Cameron] London, New York, Thames, and Hudson [1951] xvi, 304 p. illus. 23 cm. (Myth and man) [BL781.K363] 51-14117
1. Mythology, Greek. I. Title. II. Series.

KERENYI, Karoly, 1897- 1973. 292'.13
Goddesses of Sun and Moon : Circe, Aphrodite, Medea, Niobe / Karl Kerenyi ; translated from German by Murray Stein. Irving, Tex. : Spring Publications, 1979. 84 p. ; 21 cm. (Dunquin series ; 11) Translation of selections from Tochter der Sonne and Niobe. Includes bibliographical references. [BL785.K4213 1979] 79-127206 ISBN 0-88214-211-9 pbk. : 7.00
1. Mythology, Greek. 2. Sun (in religion, folk-lore, etc.)—Greece. I. Kerenyi, Karoly, 1897-1973. Niobe. Niobe. English. 1979. II. Title.
Publishers Address: Box 1, Univ. of Dallas, Irving TX 75061

KERENYI, Karoly, 1897- 1973. 292'.2'13
The heroes of the Greeks / C. Kerenyi ; [translated by] H. J. Rose. [London; New York] : Thames & Hudson, 1978, c1959. 439p. : ill. ; 22 cm. Includes bibliographical references and index. [BL782.K413] pbk. : 7.95
1. Mythology, Greek. 2. Heroes. I. Title.
Book carries L.C. card no.: 77-99200.

KIRK, Geoffrey Stephan. 292'.1'3
The nature of Greek myths / G. S. Kirk. Woodstock, N.Y. : Overlook Press, 1975, c1974. 332 p. ; 24 cm. Includes index. Bibliography: p. [305]-[306] [BL782.K57 1975] 74-21683 15.00
1. Mythology, Greek. I. Title.

KIRK, Geoffrey Stephen. 292'.1'3
The nature of Greek myths / [by] G. S. Kirk. Harmondsworth : Penguin, 1974. 332 p. ; 19 cm. (A Pelican book) Includes index. Bibliography: p. [305]-306. [BL782.K57] 74-196296 ISBN 0-14-042175-0 pbk. : 3.75
1. Mythology, Greek. I. Title.
Distributed by Penguin, Baltimore, Md.

LECOMTE, Edward Semple, 1916-
Endymion in England; the literary history of a Greek myth; by Edward S. LeComte. New York, King's crown press, 1944. xii, [2], 189 p. 23 cm. Issued also as thesis (PH.D.) Columbia university. Bibliographical foot-notes. A 44
1. Mythology, Greek. 2. Literature, Comparative—English and classical. 3. Literature, Comparative—Classical and English. 4. Literature, Comparative—Themes, motives. I. Title.

MANN, Charles Eben, 1844- 292
Greek myths and their art; the Greek myths as an inspiration in art and in literature; a supplementary reader prepared for use in the fourth, fifth and sixth grades of school, by Charles E. Mann... New York, Chicago, The Prang educational company [c1907] xxii, 155 p. front., illus., 28 pl., double map. 20 1/2 cm. [BL781.M3] 8-2746
1. Mythology, Greek. 2. Art and mythology. I. Title.

MOFFITT, Frederick James, 1896- 292
Diary of a warrior king; adventures from the Odyssey, by Frederick J. Moffitt. Consultant: M. A. Jagendorf [and] Carolyn W. Field. Illustrated by Bill Shields. Morristown, N.J., Silver Burdett Co. [1967] 90 p. col. illus., col. map. 25 cm. (Folk literature around the world) A diary of Odysseus which begins seven days after leaving Troy and records the many misfortunes that stripped him of crew and ship on the long journey home. [PZ8.1.M698Di] AC 68
1. Mythology, Greek. I. Shields, Bill, illus. II. Homerus. Odyssea. III. Title.

NEIBUHR, Barthold Georg, 1776- 1831.
The Greek heroes; stories translated from Neibuhr, with additions, with four coloured plates and numerous other illustrations by Arthur Rackham ... London, New York [etc.] Cassell and company, limited, 1910. 96 p. col. front., illus., col. plates. 19 cm. A 10
1. Mythology, Greek. I. Rackham, Arthur. II. Title.

NILSSON, Martin Persson, 1874- 292
The Mycenaean origin of Greek mythology. New York, Norton [1963, c1932] 258 p. 20 cm. (The Norton library, N234) Bibliographical footnotes. [BL793.M8N53] 63-23840
1. Mythology, Greek. 2. Civilization, Mycenaean. I. Title.

NILSSON, Martin Persson, 1874- 292
The Mycenaean origin of Greek mythology, by Martin P. Nilsson ... Berkeley, Calif., University of California press, 1932. 3 p. l., 258 p. 23 cm. (Half-title: Sather classical lectures, v. 8, 1932) [Full name: Nils Martin Persson Nilsson] [BL793.M8N53] 32-4396
1. Mythology, Greek. 2. Civilization, Mycenaean. I. Title.

NILSSON, Martin Persson, 1874-1967. 292'.08
The Mycenaean origin of Greek mythology. A new introd. and bibliography by Emily Vermeule. Berkeley, University of California Press [1972, c1932] xv, 258 p. 22 cm. Original ed. issued as v. 8 of Sather classical lectures. Bibliography: p. xiv-xv. [BL793.M8N53 1972] 70-181440 ISBN 0-520-01951-2 3.65
1. Mythology, Greek. 2. Civilization, Mycenaen. I. Vermeule, Emily. II. Title. III. Series: Sather classical lectures, v. 8.

PATRICK, Richard. 292'.211
All colour book of Greek mythology, by Richard Patrick; introduction by Barbara Leonie Picard. London, New York, Octopus Books Ltd, 1972. 103 p., chiefly col. illus. 30 cm. [BL782.P3 1972] 73-152184 ISBN 0-7064-0071-2 £0.99
1. Mythology, Greek. I. Title.

PFISTER, Friedrich, 1883- 292
Greek gods and heroes. Tr. from German by Mervyn Savil. London, Macgibbon & Kee [dist. Chester Spring, Pa., Dufour, 1962, c.1961] 272p. illus. 22cm. 61-65881 8.50 bds.,
1. Mythology, Greek. I. Title.

PINSENT, John, 1922- 292'.08
Greek mythology. London, New York, Hamlyn, 1969. 5-141 p. illus. (some col.) 29 cm. Illus. on lining papers. Bibliography: p. 136. [BL782.P53] 78-449216 25/-
1. Mythology, Greek. I. Title.

PINSENT, John, 1922- 398.2'0938
Myths and legends of ancient Greece. Illustrated by Jan Parker. New York, Grosset & Dunlap [1970] 159 p. col. illus., col. map. 22 cm. (A Grosset all-color guide, 22) Bibliography: p. 156. Retellings of the ancient Greek myths and legends introduced by notes on their origins, variations, and significance. Illustrated by ancient and modern works of art. [BL782.P54 1970] 70-120443 3.95
1. Mythology, Greek. 2. [Mythology, Greek.] I. Parker, Jan, illus. II. Title.

PLATO.
The myths of Plato; tr., with introductory and other observations, by J. A. Stewart ... London, New York, Macmillan and co., limited, 1905. xii, 532 p. 23 cm. [B355 1905] 5-33030
I. Stewart, John Alexander, 1846- tr. II. Title.
Contents omitted.

PRICE, Margaret (Evans) 1888- 292
Myths and enchantment tales, adapted from the original text. Illustrated by Evelyn Urbanowich. New York, Rand McNally [1960] 192 p. illus. 23 cm. Twenty-six myths which encompass most of the rich folk heritage left by the ancient Greeks. [PZ8.1.P933My4] AC 68
1. Mythology, Greek. I. Urbanowich, Evelyn, illus. II. Title.

ROSE, Herbert Jennings, 1883- 292
Gods and heroes of the Greeks; an introduction to Greek mythology [Gloucester, Mass., Peter Smith, 1963, c.1958] 202p. 19cm. (Meridian bks., M59 rebound) Bibl. 3.50
1. Mythology, Greek. I. Title.

ROSE, Herbert Jennings, 1883- 1961. 292
Gods and heroes of the Greeks; an introduction to Greek mythology. New York, Meridian Books [1958] 202 p. 19 cm. (Meridian books, M59) [BL785.R7 1958] 58-11926
1. Mythology, Greek. I. Title.

ROSENBERG, Donna. 292'.13
Mythology and you : classical mythology and its relevance to today's world / Donna Rosenberg, Sorelle Baker. Skokie, IL : National Textbook Co., c1981. 295 p. : ill. ; 23 cm. (NTC language arts books) [BL782.R67] 19 80-80563 price unreported
1. Mythology, Greek. I. Baker, Sorelle, joint author. II. Title. III. Series: National Textbook Company. NTC language arts books.

ROUSE, William Henry Denham, 1863-1950. 292
Gods, heroes and men of ancient Greece. [New York New American Library [1957] 189p. 18cm. (A Signet key book, KD357) [BL781] 57-3981
1. Mythology, Greek. I. Title.

RUSKIN, John, 1819-1900. 292
The Queen of the air; being a study of the Greek myths of cloud and storm, by John Ruskin, LL. D. New York, The Mershon company [18-] 2 p. l., 247 p. 15 cm. [PR5259.A1] 42-286
1. Mythology, Greek. 2. Athena. 3. Art, Greek. I. Title.
Contents omitted.

RUSKIN, John, 1819-1900. 292
The Queen of the air: being a study of the Greek myths of cloud and storm. By John Ruskin, LL. D. New York, J. Wiley & son, 1871. vii, 178 p. 21 cm. [PR5259.A1 1871] 40-38209
1. Mythology, Greek. 2. Athena. 3. Art, Greek. I. Title.
Contents omitted.

RUSKIN, John, 1819-1900. 292
The Queen of the air: being a study of the Greek myths of cloud and storm. By John Ruskin, LL. D. New York, J. Wiley & sons, 1878. vii, 178 p. 21 cm. [PR5259.A1 1878] 15-10437
1. Mythology, Greek. 2. Athena. 3. Art, Greek. I. Title.
Contents omitted.

RUSKIN, John, 1819-1900. 292
The queen of the air; being a study of the Greek myths of cloud and storm, by John Ruskin ... With an introduction by Charles Eliot Norton. Brantwood ed. New York, Maynard, Merrill, & co., 1893. xx p., 2 l., 233 p. 20 cm. [PR5259.A1 1893] 4-14171
1. Mythology, Greek. I. Title.
Contents omitted.

RUSKIN, John, 1819-1900. 292
The queen of the air; being a study of the Greek myths of cloud and storm, by John Ruskin, LL. D. Chicago, W. B. Conkey company [1900] 190 p. front. (port.) plates. 16 cm. [PR5259.A1 1900] 0-4783
1. Mythology, Greek. I. Title.

RUSKIN, John, 1819-1900.
The Queen of the air, being a study of the Greek myths of cloud and storm, by John Ruskin, LL. D. New York, John W. Lovell company [1885] 130 p. 19 cm. (On cover: Lovell's library. v. 10, no. 516) [PR5250.E85 vol. 4] 28-17847
1. Mythology, Greek. 2. Athena. 3. Art, Greek. I. Title.
Contents omitted.

RUSKIN, John, 1819-1900.
The queen of the air: being a study of the Greek myths of cloud and storm, by John Ruskin ... With an introduction by Charles Eliot Norton. Brantwood ed. New York, C. E. Merrill & co. [1891] xx p., 2 l., 233 p. 20 cm. 13-33964
I. Title.
Contents omitted.

RUSKIN, John, 1819-1900. 292'.211
The queen of the air : being a study of Greek myths of cloud and storm / by John Ruskin. Boston : Longwood Press, 1978. p. cm Reprint of the 1869 ed. published by W. L. Allison Co., New York. [PR5259.A1 1978] 78-58190 ISBN 0-89341-322-4 lib.bdg. : 25.00
I. Title.

SAINT VICTOR, Paul Jacques Raymond Binsse comte de, 1827-1881.
Men and gods, by Paul de Saint-Victor; translated by John Myers O'Hara. Portland, Me., Smith and Sale [1925] 5 p. l., 3-63, [1] p., 1 l. 18 1/2 cm. Contents.The Venus of Melos.-- Diana.-- Ceres and Proserpine--Helen.--Melaeger.-- Hellenic death. [BL790.S32] 26-1958
1. Mythology, Greek. I. O'Hara, John Myers, 1870-tr. II. Title.

*SCHWAB, Gustav. 292'.08
Gods and heroes : myths and epics of ancient Greece / Gustav Schwab ; introd. by Werner Jaeger. New York : Pantheon Books [1977]. 764p. : ill. ; 24 cm. Translated from the German text and it's Greek sources by Olga Marx and Ernst Morwitz. [BL780.S37] 47-873 12.95 ISBN 0-394-73402-5 pbk. : 5.95
1. Mythology, Greek. 2. Mythology, Classical. I. Marx, Olga, tr. II. Morwitz, Ernst, tr. III. Title.

SCULL, Sarah Amelia. 292
Greek mythology systematized. By S. A. Scull. Philadelphia, Porter & Coates [1880] 397 p. illus., geneal. tables. 20 cm. "Sources of materials": p. 27. [BL781.S4] 31-31279
1. Mythology, Greek. 2. Emblems. I. Title.

SELTMAN, Charles Theodore 292.211
The twelve Olympians. New York, Crowell [c.1960] 208p. illus., map, 22cm. (Bibl.: p.[11] and bibl. footnotes) 60-9164 4.50
1. Mythology, Greek. I. Title.

SELTMAN, Charles Theodore, 1886- 292.211
The twelve Olympians. New York. [Apollo Eds., 1962, c.1960] 208p. illus., map (A33) 1.95 pap.,
1. Mythology, Greek. I. Title.

SERRES, Michel. 844'.914
Hermes—literature, science, philosophy / by Michel Serres ; edited by Josue V. Harari & David F. Bell. Baltimore : Johns Hopkins University Press, c1982. xl, 168 p. ; 24 cm. Contents.Contents. The apparition of Hermes, Don Juan — Knowledge in the classical age — Michelet, the soup — Language and space, from Oedipus to Zola — Turner translates Carnot — Platonic dialogue — The origin of language — Mathematics and philosophy — Lucretius, science and religion — The origin of geometry — Dynamics from Leibniz to Lucretius / by Ilya Prirogine and Isabelle Stengers. Includes bibliographical references and indexes. [PQ2679.E679A2 1982] 19 81-47601 ISBN 0-8018-2454-0 : 14.00
I. Harari, Josue V. II. Bell, David F. III. Title.

SMITH, Lloyd E. 292
...Greek and Roman mythology [by] Lloyd E. Smith. Girard, Kan., Haldeman-Julius company [c1924] 64 p. 12 1/2 cm. (Little blue book, no. 498, ed. by E. Halderman-Julius) Advertising matter: p. 62-64. [BL725.S54] CA 24
1. Mythology, Greek. 2. Mythology, Roman. I. Title.

WARNER, Rex, 1905- 292
Men and gods. Illustrated by Elizabeth Corsellis. New York, Farrar, Straus and Young, 1951. 223 p. illus. 21 cm. [BL781.W3] 51-10289
1. Mythology, Greek. I. Title.

WARNER, Rex, 1905- 292
Men and gods. Illustrated by Edward Gorey. New York, Looking Glass Library; distributed by Random House [1959] 287 p. illus. 19 cm. (Looking glass library, 4) [BL782.W35] 59-13336
1. Mythology, Greek. I. Title.

WARNER, Rex, 1905- 292'.08
The stories of the Greeks. New York, Farrar, Straus & Giroux [1967] x, 405 p. illus. 24 cm. Contents.Contents.— Introduction.—Men and gods.—Greeks and Trojans.—The vengeance of the gods. [BL782.W36] 67-18535
1. Mythology, Greek. I. Title.

WARNER, Rex, 1905- 292
The vengeance of the gods. Illustrated by Susan Einzing. [East Lansing] Michigan State College Press, 1955. 192p. illus. 20cm. [BL781] 55-7698
1. Mythology, Greek. I. Title.

WHITE, Anne Terry. JUV
Odysseus comes home from the sea, told by Anne Terry White. Illustrated by Arthur Shilstone. New York, Crowell [1968] x, 192 p. illus., map. 21 cm. (Crowell hero tales) An adaptation of Homer's Odyssey. Retells the story of Odysseus' adventurous journey home from the Trojan War past Calypso, Cyclops, Circe, and other dangers. [PZ8.1.W58Od] 292 AC 68
1. Mythology, Greek. I. Homerus. Odyssea. II. Shilstone, Arthur, illus. III. Title.

YOUNG, Arthur Milton, 1900- 292
Legend builders of the West. [Pittsburgh] University of Pittsburgh Press [1958] 255 p. illus. 25 cm. [BL785.Y6] 58-9160
1. Mythology, Greek. 2. Art and mythology. 3. Literature, Comparative — Themes, motives. I. Title.

Mythology, Greek—Addresses, essays, lectures.

MYTH, religion, and society : structuralist essays / by M. Detienne ... [et al.] ; edited by R. L. Gordon. Cambridge [Eng.] ; New York : Cambridge University Press, 1982. p. cm. English translations of essays previously published in French. Includes index. Bibliography: p. [BL790.M95] 19 80-40783 ISBN 0-521-22780-1 : 39.50 ISBN 0-521-29640-4 pbk. : 12.50 292'.13
1. Mythology, Greek—Addresses, essays, lectures. I. Gordon, Raymond L. II. Detienne, Marcel.

Mythology, Greek—Bibliography.

†LAW, Helen Hull. 016.821'009'37
Bibliography of Greek myth in English poetry / by Helen H. Law. Folcroft, Pa. : Folcroft Library Editions, 1977. 39 p. ; 34 cm. Reprint of the 1955 ed. published by the American Classical League, Service Bureau, Oxford, Ohio, which was issued as its Bulletin 27. [Z7836.L4 1977] [BL782] 77-9519 ISBN 0-8414-5827-8 lib. bdg. : 7.50
1. Mythology, Greek—Bibliography. 2. English poetry—Bibliography. I. Title. II. Series: American Classical League. Service Bureau. Bulletin ; 27.

Mythology, Greek—Dictionaries.

THE New Century handbook of Greek mythology and legend. Edited by Catherine B. Avery. New York, Appleton-Century-Crofts [1972] viii, 565 p. 21 cm. "Selected from the New Century classical handbook." [BL782.N45] 75-183796 ISBN 0-390-66946-6 7.95 292'.08'03
1. Mythology, Greek—Dictionaries. I. Avery, Catherine B., ed. II. The New Century classical handbook.

Mythology, Greek—Handbooks, manuals, etc.

BOSWELL, Fred. 292'.13
What men or gods are these? : A genealogical approach to classical mythology / by Fred and Jeanetta Boswell. Metuchen, N.J. : Scarecrow Press, 1980. vii, 315 p. ; 19 x 25 cm. Includes indexes. Bibliography: p. 245-250. [BL782.B6] 80-13780 ISBN 0-8108-1314-9 : 19.50
1. Mythology, Greek—Handbooks, manuals, etc. I. Boswell, Jeanetta, 1922- joint author. II. Title.

Mythology, Greek—Juvenile literature.

AULAIRE, Ingri (Mortenson) d', 1904-- 292
Ingri and Edgar Parin d'Aulaire's Book of Greek myths. Garden City, N.Y., Doubleday [c.1962] 192p. illus. (pt. col.) 32cm. 62-15877 4.95
1. Mythology, Greek—Juvenile literature. I. Aulaire, Edgar Parin d', 1898- joint author. II. Title. III. Title: Book of Greek myths.

AULAIRE, Ingri (Mortenson) d', 1904- JUV
Ingri and Edgar Parin d'Aulaire's Book of Greek myths. [1st ed.] Garden City, N. Y., Doubleday [1962] 192p. illus. 32cm. [PZ8.1.A86 In] 292 62-15877
1. Mythology, Greek—Juvenile literature. I. Aulaire, Edgar Parin d', 1898- joint author. II. Title. III. Title: Book of Greek myths.

FORBUSH, William Byron, 1868-1927, comp. JUV
Myths and legends of Greece and Rome, compiled by William Byron Forbush ... illustrated by Frederick Richardson. Philadelphia, Chicago [etc.] The John C. Winston company [c1928] xii, 337 p. col. front., illus., col. plates. 21 cm. (On cover: The Winston clear-type popular classics) "Literary references" at end of each story except one. [PZ8.1.F745My] 292 28-18423
1. Mythology, Greek—Juvenile literature. 2. Mythology, Roman—Juvenile literature. I. Title.

FOUR old Greeks; JUV
Achilles, Hernkles, Donysos, Alkestis, by Jennie Hall ... Chicago, New York, Rand, McNally & co. [c1901] 224 p. incl. front., illus. 18 cm. Title within ornamental border. "A bibliography": p. 222-224. [PZ8.1.H143F] 292 9-17527
1. Mythology, Greek—Juvenile literature. I. Title: Four old Greeks;

GRAVES, Robert, 1895- JUV
Greek gods and heroes. Illustrated by Dimitris Davis. [1st ed.] Garden City, N.Y., Doubleday, 1960. 160 p. illus. 25 cm. [PZ8.1.G75Gr] 292'.'3 60-12438
1. Mythology, Greek—Juvenile literature. I. Title.

GREEN, Roger Lancelyn. JUV
The tale of Thebes / [selected and retold by] Roger Lancelyn Green ; illustrated by Jael Jordan. Cambridge, [Eng.] ; New York : Cambridge University Press, 1977. xiii, 102 p., [3] leaves of plates : ill. ; 23 cm. The stories of Cadmus, Dionysus, Oedipus, Antigone, and others collectively present the mythology associated with Thebes, some of the most famous of the Greek classical myths. [PZ8.1.G77Taj] 292'.1'3 398.2 76-22979 ISBN 0-521-21410-6 : 6.50 ISBN 0-521-21434-3 pbk. : 2.95
1. Mythology, Greek—Juvenile literature. 2. [Mythology, Greek.] I. Jordan, Jael. II. Title.

GREEN, Roger Lancelyn. 398.2
Tales the Muses told; ancient Greek myths. Illustrated by Don Bolognese. New York, H. Z. Walck, 1965. 137 p. illus. 22 cm. [BL782.G73] 65-22661
1. Mythology, Greek—Juvenile literature. I. Title.

HARSHAW, Ruth (Hetzel) Mrs. JUV
The council of the gods, by Ruth Harshaw; illustrations by Nicolas Kaissaroff. Chicago, Thomas S. Rockwell company, 1931. xxii, 23-198 p. incl. front., illus., plates. 24 cm. [PZ8.1.H251Co] 292 31-20660
1. Mythology, Greek—Juvenile literature. I. Title.

KINGSLEY, Charles, 1819-1875 292
The heroes. Illus. with 4 colour plates & line drawings by Joan Kiddell-Monroe. New York, Dutton [1963] 210p. illus. (pt. col.) 22cm. (Children's illus. classics, 58) 63-4140 3.25
1. Mythology, Greek—Juvenile literature. I. Title.

KINGSLEY, Charles, 1819-1875. 292
The heroes. Illustrated by Ron King. Santa Rosa, Calif., Classic Press [1968] 215 p. illus., map. 29 cm. (Educator classic library, 10) Stories based on the Greek myths about Perseus, Jason and the Argonauts, Theseus, and the twelve labors of Heracles. [PZ8.1.K614H42] 74-2316
1. Mythology, Greek—Juvenile literature. 2. [Mythology, Greek.] I. King, Ron, illus. II. Title.

KINGSLEY, Charles, 1819-1875. JUV
The heroes, or, Greek fairy tales for my children. By Charles Kingsley. With illustrations by the author. New York, The Macmillan company, 1902. 320 p. incl. front. plates. 19 cm. [PZ8.1.K614H5] 292 4-15351
1. Mythology, Greek—Juvenile literature. I. Title.
Contents omitted.

KINGSLEY, Charles, 1819-1875. JUV
The heroes; or, Greek fairy tales for my children [by] Charles Kingsley; drawings by Helen H. Kihn. New York, R. M. McBride & company, 1930. xx, 238 p. incl. front., illus., plates. 20 1/2 cm. [PZ8.1.K614H 27] 292 31-26061
1. Mythology, Greek—Juvenile literature. I. Title.
Contents omitted.

KINGSLEY, Charles, 1819-1875.
The heroes, by Charles Kingsley. London, J. M. Dent & co.; New York, E. P. Dutton & co. [1908] lxvii, 229, [1] p. incl. plates. 17 1/2 cm. (Half-title: Everyman's library, ed. by Ernest Rhys. Children's books. [no.

113]) Title within ornamental border: illustrated lining-papers. Bibliography: p. [vii] A11
1. Mythology, Greek—Juvenile literature. I. Rhys, Grace. II. Title.
Contents omitted.

KINGSLEY, Charles, 1819-1875. 292'.1'3
The heroes / by Charles Kingsley. New York : Mayflower Books, [1980] p. cm. (Facsimile classics series) Photoreprint of the 1962 ed. published by Macmillan, London. Stories based on the Greek myths concerning Perseus, the Argonauts, and Theseus. Illustrated by H. M. Brock. Presents the adventures of Perseus, Jason and the Argonauts, and Theseus. [PZ8.1.K614H 1980] 79-21470 8.95
1. Mythology, Greek—Juvenile literature. 2. [Mythology, Greek.] I. Brock, Henry Matthew, 1875- II. Title. III. Series.

LANG, Andrew, 1844-1912 292
Tales of Troy and Greece. Illus. by Edward Bawden. New York, Roy [1963] 299p. illus. 21cm. 63-10578 3.95
1. Mythology, Greek—Juvenile literature. I. Title.

LARNED, Augusta, 1835- 292
Old tales retold from Grecian mythology in talks around the fire. By Augusta Larned ... Fifteen illustrations. New York, Nelson & Phillips; Cincinnati, Hitchcock & Walden [1876] 498 p. incl. front. 10 pl. 20 cm. [BL781.L3] 31-31283
1. Mythology, Greek—Juvenile literature. I. Title.

MCLEAN, Mollie. JUV
Adventures of the Greek heroes [by] Mollie McLean Anne Wiseman. Illustrated by Witold T. Mars. Boston, Houghton Mifflin, 1961. 174p. illus. 22cm. [PZ8.1.M2Ad] 292 61-10628
1. Mythology, Greek—Juvenile literature. I. Wiseman, Anne, joint author. II. Title.

SISSONS, Nicola Ann, comp. JUV
Myth and legends of the Greeks. Illustrated by Rafaello Busoni. New York, Hart Pub.Co. [1962, c1960] 189 p. illus. 23 cm. Published in 1960 under title: World-famous myths and legends of the Greeks. [PZ8.1.S58My 2] j 292 62-12233
1. Mythology, Greek — Juvenile literature. I. Title.

SISSONS, Nicola Ann, comp. 292
Myths and legends of the Greeks. Illus. by Rafaello Busoni. New York, Hart [1962, c.1960] 189p. illus. Pub. in 1960 under the title: World-famous myths and legends of the Greeks. 62-12233 2.95
1. Mythology, Greek—Juvenile literature. I. Title.

SISSONS, Nicola Ann, comp. JUV
Myths and legends of the Greeks. Illustrated by Rafaello Busoni. New York, Hart Pub. Co. [1962, c1960] 189 p. illus. 23 cm. (Sunrise library) Published in 1960 under title: World-famous myths and legends of the Greeks. [PZ8.1.S58My 2] j 292 62-12233
1. Mythology, Greek — Juvenile literature. I. Title.

WITTING, Alisoun 292
A treasury of Greek mythology. Illus. by James Barry. Irvington-on-Hudson, N.Y., Harvey House [1966, c.1965] 125p. col. illus. 27cm. [BL782.W57] 65-24973 3.50; 3.36 lib. ed.,
1. Mythology, Greek—Juvenile literature. I. Barry James E., illus. II. Title.

Mythology, Hawaiian.

BECKWITH, Martha Warren, 1871- 290.92
Hawaiian mythology, by Martha Beckwith, Published for the Folklore foundation of Vassar college. New Haven, Yale university press; London, H. Milford, Oxford University press, 1940. x p., 1 l., 575 p. 24 1/2 cm. Illustrations on t.-p. "The publication of this book was made possible by the Lucy Maynard Salmon fund established at Vassar college, June, 1926." "References": p. [545]-555. [BL2620.H3B4] 40-8309
1. Mythology, Hawaiian. 2. Folk-lore—Hawaiian islands. 3. Legends—Hawaiian islands. I. Vassar college, Lucy Maynard Salmon fund for research. II. Title.

BECKWITH, Martha Warren, 1871-1959. 398.2'09969
Hawaiian mythology. With a new introd. by Katharine Luomala. Honolulu, University of Hawaii Press, 1970. xxxiii, 575 p. 24 cm. Originally published in 1940. Bibliography: p. [545]-555. [BL2620.H3B4 1970] 70-97998 12.00
1. Mythology, Hawaiian. 2. Folk-lore—Hawaii. 3. Legends—Hawaii.

KEPELINO, ca.1830-ca.1878. 398.309969
Kepelino's Traditions of Hawaii, edited by Martha Warren Beckwith ... Honolulu, Hawaii, The Museum, 1932. 2 p. l., [3]-206 p. 1 illus. 23 1/2 cm. (Bernice P. Bishop museum. Bulletin 95) Translated, with notes and supplementary material, by Martha Warren Beckwith from a typed copy of a Hawaiian manuscript (in the Bernice P. Bishop museum) written in the hand of Bishop Malgret, who seems either to have copied it from an original by the accredited composer, Kepelino, or to have taken it down from dictation. cf. Introd. Hawaiian and English on opposite pages. "List of references": p. 201-203. [GN670.B4 no. 95] [BL2620.H3K4] (572.996) 33-16446
1. Mythology, Hawaiian. 2. Folk-lore—Hawaiian islands. 3. Hawaiian language—Texts. I. Beckwith, Martha Warren, 1871- ed. and tr. II. Title.

MELVILLE, Leinani. 299'.9
Children of the rainbow; a book concerning the religion, legends, and gods of the natives of pre-Christian Hawaii. Wheaton, Ill., Theosophical Pub. House [1969] xvii, 183 p. illus. 21 cm. (AQuest book) [GR385.H3M4] 69-17715 1.95 (pbk)
1. Mythology, Hawaiian. 2. Hawaii—Religion. I. Title.

Mythology, Hindu.

BARBORKA, Geoffrey A. 891.21
Gods and heroes of the Bhagavad-gita; a brief description of the mythology of ancient India as contained in the Bhagavad-gita, including technical terms and explanations in the light of theosophy [by] Geoffrey A. Barborka. Point Loma, Calif., Thesophical university press, 1939. xii, 134, 10 p. 15 1/2 cm. [BL1130.B3] [[294.51]] 39-18647
1. Mythology, Hindu. 2. Mahabharate. Bhagavadgita. I. Title.

BHATIVEDANTA, A.C. Swami 1896- JUV
Prahlad : a story for children from the ancient Vedas of India / A. C. Bhaktivedanta Swami Prabhupada ; publisher and editor, Mohanananda das Adhikari ; [ill. by Goursundar das and Govinda devi dasi]. Dallas, Tex. : Iskcon Children's Press, c1973. [32] p. : col. ill. ; 28 cm. Relates the tale of the child Prahlad whose devotion for and love of Krishna helped him endure severe tortures and win for his father liberation from a curse. [PZ8.1.B48Pr] 294'.1 75-319632
1. Prahlada—Juvenile literature. 2. [Prahlada.] 3. [Mythology, Hindu.] I. Das, Goursundar. II. Govinda Devi. III. Title.

ELWIN, Verrier, 1902- 294.5
Myths of middle India. [Bombay, New York] Indian Branch, Oxford University Press [1949] xvi, 532 p. 23 cm. (His Specimens of the oral literature of middle India, 4) Full name: Harry Verrier Holman Elwin. Includes bibliographies. [BL2003.E55] 50-1528
1. Mythology, Hindu. I. Title.

GOPINATHA Rao, T. A., 1872- 294.5'21'8
Elements of Hindu iconography, by T. A. Gopinatha Rao. 2d ed. New York, Paragon Book Reprint Corp., 1968. 2 v. in 4. illus., plates. 25 cm. "An unaltered and unabridged reprint of the Madras 1914 edition." "Published under the patronage of the government of His Highness the Maharaja of Travancore." Selections from relevant texts in Sanskrit and Tamil: v. 1, pt. 2, p. 33-[160] (at end); v. 2, pt. 2, p. [1] -279 (at end) "List of the important works consulted": v. 1, pt. 1, p. xxix-[xxx]; v. 2, pt. 1, p. xxvii. [BL1201.G7 1968] 68-29408
1. Mythology, Hindu. 2. Art, Hindu. 3. Idols and images. I. Title. II. Title: Hindu iconography.

GOPINATHA RAO, T. A., 1872-1919. 732'.44
Elements of Hindu iconography / T. A. Gopinatha Rao. New York : Garland Pub., 1980. p. cm. Includes selections from relevant texts in Sanskrit and Tamil. Reprint of the 1914-1916 ed. published by the Law Printing House, Madras. Includes index. Bibliography: p. [BL1205.G65 1980] 78-74265 ISBN 0-8240-3902-5 (set) : 160.00
1. Mythology, Hindu. 2. Art, Hindu. 3. Idols and images—India. I. Title.

GREENE, Joshua. JUV
Krishna, master of all mystics / retold by Joshua Greene (Yogesvara Dasa) ; ill. by Dominique Amendola (Dirgha Dasi). New York, N.Y. : Bala Books, [1980] p. cm. Krishna uses his mystic powers to replace the calves and cowherders stolen by Lord Brahma. [BL1220.G692] [E] 19 80-23415 ISBN 0-89647-010-5 pbk. : 2.95
1. Krishna—Juvenile literature. 2. [Mythology, Hindu.] I. Amendola, Dominique. II. Title.

HINDU myths : 294.5'1'308
a sourcebook / translated from the Sanskrit with an introduction by Wendy Doniger O'Flaherty. Harmondsworth ; Baltimore : Penguin, 1975. 358 p. ; 19 cm. (The Penguin classics) Includes index. Bibliography: p. 302-309. [BL2001.2.H56] 75-323936 ISBN 0-14-044306-1 : £0.80 ($3.50 U.S.)
1. Mythology, Hindu. I. O'Flaherty, Wendy Doniger.

HOPKINS, Edward Washburn, 1857-1932. 294.5'922
Epic mythology. New York, Biblo and Tannen, 1969. 277 p. 26 cm. The mythology of the two epics of India, the Mahabharata and the Ramayana. Reprint of the 1915 ed. [BL1130.H6 1969] 76-75358
1. Mahabharata. 2. Valmiki. Ramayana. 3. Mythology, Hindu. I. Title.

KEITH, Arthur Berriedale, 1879- 294.
... *Indian [mythology]* by A. Berriedale Keith ... Iranian, by Albert J. Carnoy ... Boston, Marshall Jones company, 1917. ix, 404 p. illus., xliv pl. (part col., incl. front.) 25 cm. (The mythology of all races ... L. H. Gray ... editor ... v. vi) Each plate accompanied by guard sheet with descriptive letterpress. Bibliography: p. [389]-404. [BL25.M8] 17-6787
1. Mythology, Hindu. 2. Mythology, Aryan. I. Carney, Albert Joseph, 1878- II. Title.

KIRK, James A., comp. 294.5
Stories of the Hindus; an introduction through texts and interpretation, by James A. Kirk. New York, Macmillan [1972] xviii, 269 p. 22 cm. Bibliography: p. 256-259. [BL1145.5.K57] 72-77651
1. Mythology, Hindu. 2. Hindu literature. I. Title.

MACDONELL, Arthur Anthony, 1854-1930. 294'.1
Vedic mythology. New York, Gordon Press, 1974. 174 p. 24 cm. (Series: Buhler, Georg, 1837-1898, ed. Grundriss der indo-arischen Philologie und Altertumskunde, Bd. 3, Hft. 1 A.) Reprint of the 1897 ed. published by K. J. Trubner, Strassburg, which was issued as Bd. 3, Hft. 1 A, of Grundriss der indo-arischen Philologie und Altertumskunde, hrsg. von G. Buhler. [BL2001.M23 1974] 74-8799 ISBN 0-87968-153-5 29.95 (lib. bdg.)
1. Mythology, Hindu. I. Title. II. Series.

MACKENZIE, Donald Alexander, 1873-1936. 294
Indian myth and legend / Donald A. Mackenzie. Boston : Longwood Press, 1978 xlviii, 463 p., [32] leaves of plates : ill. ; 22 cm. Reprint of the 1913 ed. published by Gresham Pub. Co., London. Includes index. [BL1201.M3 1978] 77-85615 ISBN 0-893-41-316-X pbk. : 50.00
1. Mythology, Hindu. 2. Legends—India. I. Title.

†MOOR, Edward, 1771-1848. 294.3'4'211
The Hindu pantheon / by Edward Moor ; introductory preface by Manly P. Hall. Los Angeles : Philosophical Research Society, 1976. xiv, 467 p., 105 leaves of plates : ill. ; 32 cm. On spine: Moor's Hindu pantheon. At head of title: Sri Sarvva Deva Sabha. Reprint of the 1810 ed. printed for J. Johnson by T. Bensley, London. [BL1201.M63 1976] 76-26759 ISBN 0-89314-409-6 : 40.00
1. Mythology, Hindu. 2. Gods, Hindu. 3. Art, Hindu. I. Title.

NARAYAN, R. K., 1906- 294.521
God, demons, and others. Decorations by R. K. Laxman. New York, Viking [c.1964] 241p. illus. 24cm. 64-12225 6.50
1. Mvthology. Hindu. I. Title.

NARAYAN, R K 1906- 294.521
Gods, demons, and others. Decorations by R. K. Laxman. New York, Viking [1967, c.1964] 241p. illus. 20cm. (Compass bks., C202) 1.45 pap.,
1. Mythology, Hindu. I. Title.

NOBLE, Margaret Elizabeth, 1867-1911 294.5'1'13
Myths of the Hindus & Buddhists, by Anda K. Coomaraswamy, and the Sister Nivedita (Margaret E. Noble) With 32 illus. by Indian artists under the supervision of Abanindro Nath Tagore i[Magnolia, Mass., P. Smith 1967] xii, 399p. illus. 22cm. (Dover bk. rebound) Authors' names in reverse order in other eds. Unabridged repubn. of the work orig. pub. in 1913 [BL2001.N6 1967] 5.00
1. Mythology, Hindu. 2. Buddha and Buddhism. I. Coomaraswamy, Ananda Kentish, 1877-1947, joint author. II. Title.

NOBLE, Margaret Elizabeth, 1867-1911. 294.5'1'3
Myths of the Hindus & Buddhists, by Ananda K. Coomaraswamy and Sister Nivedita (Margaret E. Noble) With 32 illus. by Indian artists under the supervision of Abanindro Nath Tagore. New York, Dover Publicatons [1967] xii, 399 p. illus. 22 cm. Author's names in reverse order in other editions. "An unabridged republication of the work originally published ... in 1913." [BL2001.N6 1967] 67-14131
1. Mythology, Hindu. 2. Buddha and Buddhism. I. Coomaraswamy, Ananda Kentish, 1877-1947, joint author. II. Title.

NOBLE, Margaret Elizabeth, 1867-1911. 294
Myths of the Hindus & Buddhists, by the Sister Nivedita (Margaret E. Noble) of Ramakrishna-Vivekananda and Ananda K. Coomaraswamy; with thirty-two illustrations in colour by Indian artists under the supervision of Abanindro Nath Tagore, c. i. e. New York, Farrar & Rinehart [1934] 1 p. l., v-xii, 425, [1] p. col. front., 31 col. pl. 22 cm. (On cover: The myths series) Printed in Great Britain. [BL2001.N6 1934] 35-1183
1. Mythology, Hindu. 2. Buddha and Buddhism. I. Coomaraswamy, Ananda Kentish, 1877- joint author. II. Title.

NOBLE, Margaret Elizabeth, 1867-1911.
Myths of the Hindus & Buddhists, by the Sister Nivedita (Margaret E. Noble) ... and Ananda K. Coomaraswamy; with thirty-two illustrations in colour by Indian artists under the supervision of Abanindro Nath Tagore, c. i. e. New York, H. Holt & company, 1914. xii, 399, [1] p. col. front., col. plates. 24 cm. A 14
1. Mythology, Hindu. 2. Buddha and Buddhism. I. Coomaraswamy, Ananda Kentish, 1877- joint author. II. Title.

O'FLAHERTY, Wendy Doniger. 294.5'2'1
Women, androgynes, and other mythical beasts / Wendy Doniger O'Flaherty. Chicago : University of Chicago Press, c1980. xviii, 382 p., [4] leaves of plates : ill. ; 24 cm. Includes index. Bibliography: p. 345-362. [BL2001.2.O36] 19 79-16128 ISBN 0-226-61849-8 lib. bdg. : 27.00
1. Mythology, Hindu. 2. Sex. 3. Animals, Mythical. 4. Androgyny (Psychology) I. Title.

PURANAS. English. Selections. 294.5'925
Classical Hindu mythology : a reader in the Sanskrit Puranas / [edited by] Conelia Dimmitt and J. A. B. van Buitenen. Philadelphia : Temple University Press, c1978. p. cm. Includes index. Bibliography: p. [BL1135.P6213] 77-92643 ISBN 0-87722-117-0 : 17.50. ISBN 0-87722-122-7 pbk. : 9.95
1. Dimmitt, Cornelia, 1938- II. Buitenen, Johannes Adrianus Bernardus van. III. Title.

ZIMMER, Heinrich Robert, 1890-1943 294.5
Myths and symbols in Indian art and civilization. Ed. by Joseph Campbell. New York, Harper [1962, c.1946] 248p. illus. (Bollingen lib.; Harper torckbk., TB2005) 2.25 pap.,
1. Mythology, Hindu. 2. Symbolism. 3. Art, Hindu. 4. India—Civilization. I. Campbell, Joseph, 1904- ed. II. Title.

ZIMMER, Heinrich Robert, 1890-1943. 294.5'1'3
Myths and symbols in Indian art and civilization. Edited by Joseph Campbell. [Princeton, N.J.] Princeton University Press [1972, c1946] xiii, 248 p. plates. 22 cm. (Bolingen series, 6) Reprint of the ed. published by Pantheon Books, New York. [BL2003.Z5 1972] 74-163422 ISBN 0-691-09800-X ISBN 0-691-01778-6 (pbk.)
1. Mythology, Hindu. 2. Symbolism. 3. Art, Hindu. 4. India—Civilization. I. Campbell, Joseph, 1904- ed. II. Title. III. Series.

ZIMMER, Heinrich Robert, 1890-1943. 294.5'1'3
Myths and symbols in Indian art and civilization. Edited by Joseph Campbell. New York, Harper [1962, c1946] xiii, 248 p. plates. 21 cm. (Harper torchbooks, TB 2005. The Bollingen library, 6) Reprint of the ed. published by Pantheon Books, New York. [BL2003.Z5 1962] 74-163423
1. Mythology, Hindu. 2. Symbolism. 3. Art, Hindu. 4. India—Civilization. I. Campbell, Joseph, 1904- ed. II. Title.

ZIMMER, Heinrich Robert, 1890-1943. 294.5
... Myths and symbols in Indian art and civilization. Edited by Joseph Campbell ... [New York] Pantheon books [1946] xiii, 248 p., 1 l. plates. 23 1/2 cm. (Half-title: The Bollingen series, VI) At head of title: Heinrich Zimmer. "Lecture course delivered at Columbia university the winter term of 1942." [BL2003.Z5] 46-7144
1. Mythology, Hindu. 2. Symbolism. 3. Art, Hindu. 4. India—Civilization. I. Campbell, Joseph, 1904- ed. II. Title.

Mythology, Hindu—Dictionaries.

DOWSON, John, 1820-1881. 294.5'03
A classical dictionary of Hindu mythology and religion, geography, history, and literature. Boston, Milford House [1973] p. Reprint of the 1879 ed. published by Trubner, London, which was issued as no. 6 of Trubner's oriental series. [BL1105.D6 1973] 73-13680 ISBN 0-87821-185-3 35.00
1. Mythology, Hindu—Dictionaries. 2. Sanskrit literature—Dictionaries. I. Title.

Mythology—History.

FELDMAN, Burton, comp. 398'.042
The rise of modern mythology, 1680-1860 [compiled by] Burton Feldman and Robert D. Richardson. Bloomington, Indiana University Press [1972] xxvii, 564 p. front. 24 cm. Bibliography: p. 528-554. [BL311.F43] 71-135005 ISBN 0-253-35012-3 19.95
1. Mythology—History. I. Richardson, Robert D., 1934- joint comp. II. Title.

MOORS, Kent F. 184
Platonic myth : an introductory study / Kent F. Moors. Washington, D.C. : University Press of America, c1982. x, 137 p. ; 23 cm. Based on the author's thesis (Ph.D.)—Northern Illinois University. Includes bibliographical references. [B398.M8M66 1982] 19 81-43816 ISBN 0-8191-2314-5 : 18.25 ISBN 0-8191-2315-3 (pbk.) : 7.75
1. Plato. 2. Mythology—History. I. Title.

Mythology in literature.

MOORMAN, Charles. 820.993
Arthurian triptych; mythic materials in Charles Williams, C. S. Lewis, and T. S. Eliot. Berkeley, University of California Press, 1960. ix, 163p. 23cm. (Perspectives in criticism, 5) Bibliographical references included in 'Notes'(p. 157-163) [PR6045.I5Z85] 59-14476
1. Williams, Charles, 1886-1945. 2. Lewis, Clive Staples, 1898- 3. Eliot, Thomas Stearnis, 1888- 4. Arthur, King. 5. Mythology in literature. I. Title. II. Series.

SLOCHOWER, Harry, 1900- 809.9'33
Mythopoesis: mythic patterns in the literary classics. Detroit, Wayne State University Press, 1970. 362 p. illus. 24 cm. Includes bibliographies. [PN56.M95S5 1970] 69-11337
1. Mythology in literature. I. Title.

Mythology, Indic.

BHATTACHARJI, Sukumari. 291'.13'0934
The Indian theogony; a comparative study of Indian mythology from the Vedas to the Puranas. [London] Cambridge University Press, 1970. xiii, 396 p. 24 cm. Bibliography: p. 364-374. [BL2001.2.B48] 79-96080 7/-/- ($22.00)
1. Mythology, Indic. I. Title.

DUMEZIL, Georges, 1898- 294.5'1'3
The destiny of a king. Translated by Alf Hiltebeitel. Chicago, University of Chicago Press [1973] 155 p. 24 cm. Translation of part three of Mythe et epopee, vol. 2: Types epiques indo-europeens: un heros, un sorcier, un roi. Includes bibliographical references. [BL2003.D8513 1973] 73-75311 ISBN 0-226-16975-8 10.00
1. Mythology, Indic. I. Title.

ELWIN, Verrier, 1902-1964, ed. and tr. 294
Tribal myths of Orissa / Verrier Elwin. New York : Arno Press, 1980. lv, 700 p. ; 23 cm. (Folklore of the world.) Reprint of the 1954 ed. published by Oxford University Press, Bombay, New York, which was issued as no. 5 in the author's series: Specimens of the oral literature of middle India. Includes indexes. Bibliography: p. [647]-648. [BL2003.E56 1980] 19 80-746 ISBN 0-405-13312-X : 65.00
1. Mythology, Indic. I. Title. II. Series: Folklore of the world (New York)

KEITH, Arthur Berriedale, 1879-1944. 294
Indian [mythology] by A. Berriedale Keith. Iranian [mythology] by Albert J. Carnoy. New York, Cooper Square Publishers, 1964 [c1917] ix, 404 p. illus., 44 plates (part col.) 24 cm. (The Mythology of all races, v. 6) Bibliography: p. [369]-404. [BL25.M8 1964 vol. 6] [BL1031.K4036] 63-19091
1. Mythology, Indic. 2. Mythology, Aryan. I. Carnoy, Albert Joseph, 1878- II. Title. III. Series.

Mythology, Indo-European.

TILCOMB, Sarah E. 299
Aryan sun-myths : the origin of religions / by Sarah E. Tilcomb ; with an introd. by Charles Morris. Boston : Longwood Press, 1979. p. cm. Reprint of the 1889 ed. published by Nims and Knight, Troy, N.Y. Includes index. Bibliography: p. [BL660.T47 1979] 78-31508 ISBN 0-89341-323-2 : 20.00
1. Mythology, Indo-European. 2. Religion, Primitive. I. Title.

Mythology, Indonesian.

HAINUWELE / 291.1'3'09598
[hrsg. von] Adolf E. Jensen. New York : Arno Press, 1978. xi, 455 p., [9] leaves of plates (1 fold.) : ill. ; 24 cm. (Mythology) Reprint of the 1939 ed. published by V. Klostermann, Frankfurt am Main, which was issued as v. 1 of Ergebnisse der Frobenius-Expedition, 1937-38 in die Molukken und nach Hollandisch Neu-Guinea. Includes bibliographical references. [BL2120.C47H34 1978] 77-79133 ISBN 0-405-10543-6 : 28.00
1. Mythology, Indonesian. 2. Ceram—Religion. 3. Sacrifice. I. Jensen, Adolf Ellegard, 1899-1965. II. Frobenius-Expedition, 1937-1938. Ergebnisse der Frobenius-Expedition, 1937-38 in die Molukken und nach Hollandisch Neu-Guinea. v. 1.

Mythology, Iranian.

HINNELLS, John R. 295'.1'3
Persian mythology / [by] John R. Hinnells. London ; New York : Hamlyn, 1973. 2-143 p. : ill., (some col.), map, ports. ; 29 cm. Includes index. Bibliography: p. 138-139. [BL2270.H56] 74-193695 ISBN 0-600-03090-3 : £1.95
1. Mythology, Iranian. 2. Zoroastrianism. I. Title.

Mythology, Irish—Dictionaries.

KAVANAGH, Peter. 293
Irish mythology, a dictionary. New York, P. Kavanagh Hand-Press [1958-59] 3v. 23cm. 'Limited to 100 numbered copies of which this is number 50.' Slip inserted in v. 1: There are also 17 extra series copies numbered 101-116. The 17th is unnumbered. [BL980.I7K3] 58-48141
1. Mythology, Irish—Dictionaries. I. Title.

Mythology, Japanese.

PIGGOTT, Juliet. 299'.5611'3
Japanese mythology. Feltham, New York, Hamlyn, 1969. 5-141 p. illus. (some col.), map. 29 cm. Illus. on lining papers. Bibliography: p. 138. [BL2202.P5 1969] 74-458795 ISBN 0-600-02113-0 25/-
1. Mythology, Japanese. I. Title.

Mythology, Javanese.

ANDERSON, Benedict R O'G 299.5
Mythology and the tolerance of the Javanese [by] Benedict R. O'G Anderson. Ithaca, N.Y., Modern Indonesia Project, Southeast Asia Program, Dept. of Asian Studies, Cornell University, 1965. x, 77 p. illus. 28 cm. (Cornell University. Modern Indonesia Project. Monograph series) [BL2120.J3A7] 67-2748
1. Mythology, Javanese. 2. National characteristics, Javanese 3. Toleration. I. Title. II. Series.

Mythology, Jewish.

GOLDZIHER, Ignac, 1850-1921. 296.1
Mythology among the Hebrews and its historical development. Translated from the German, with additions by the author, by Russell Martineau. New York, Cooper Square Publishers, 1967. xxxv, 457 p. 24 cm. "A Marandell book." Translation of Der Mythos bei den Hebraern und seine geschichtliche Entwickelung. Includes two essays by H. Steinthal. [BM530.G6 1967] 66-23969
1. Mythology, Jewish. 2. Judaism—History—To 70 A.D. I. Steinthal, Heymann, 1823-1889. II. Title.

GRAVES, Robert, 1895- 296
Hebrew myths; the book of Genesis, by Robert Graves and Raphael Patai. [1st ed.] Garden City, N.Y., Doubleday, 1964. 311 p. maps. 25 cm. "Abbrevations, sources, and annotated bibliography": p. 281-294. [BS1236.G7] 63-19845
1. Bible. O.T. Genesis—Criticism, interpretation, etc. 2. Mythology, Jewish. 3. Mythology, Semitic. I. Patai, Raphael, 1910- joint author. II. Title.

PATAI, Raphael, 1910- 296
Man and temple in ancient Jewish myth and ritual. 2d enl. ed., with a new introd. & postscript. New York, Ktay [1967] xiv, 247p. 24cm. Bibl. [BM530.P3 1967] 67-22754 5.95 bds.,
1. Mythology, Jewish. 2. Cultus, Jewish. 3. Jerusalem. Temple. I. Title.

Mythology—Juvenile literature.

BARBER, Richard W. 291.2'11
A companion to world mythology / Richard Barber ; illustrated by Pauline Baynes. New York : Delacorte Press, [1980] c1979. viii, 312 p. : ill. (some col.) ; 24 cm. Includes indexes. Alphabetically lists the gods of such diverse cultures as Polynesia, Japan, and ancient Greece, with substantial accounts of their exploits. [BL311.B35 1980] 292 19 79-16843 ISBN 0-440-00750-X : 14.95
1. Mythology—Juvenile literature. 2. [Mythology.] I. Baynes, Pauline. II. Title.

COX, George William, 1827-1902. 291
A manual of mythology in the form of question and answer. By the Rev. George W. Cox ... 1st American, from the 2d London edition. New York, Leypoldt & Holt, 1868. 300 p. incl. illus., geneal. tables. 18 cm. "Mythical genealogies": p. [283]-290. [BL310.C63 1868] [BL725.C87M] A 31
1. Mythology—Juvenile literature. I. Title.

FAHS, Sophia Blanche (Lyon) Mrs. 291.212
Beginnings of earth and sky; stories old and new, by Sophia L. Fahs; drawings by Marjorie Cole. Boston, The Beacon press, inc., 1937. vii, 155 p. illus. 25 cm. [Beacon books in religious education. Children's series on beginnings. v. 1] [BV1561.B33 vol. 1] 268.61 38-4279
1. Mythology—Juvenile literature. 2. Earth. 3. Astronomy—Juvenile literature. I. Title.

GREEN, Roger Lancelyn. JUV
A book of myths, selected and retold by Roger Lancelyn Green. Illustrated by Joan Kiddell-Monroe. London, J. M. Dent. New York, Dutton [1965] viii, 184 p. illus. (part col.) 22 cm. (The C.I.C. series, no. 66) [PZ8.1.G77Bo] 291 65-3519
1. Mythology—Juvenile literature. I. Title.

SCHREIBER, Morris 292
Stories of gods and heroes; famous myths and legends of the world, adapted by Morris Schreiber. Illus. by Art Seiden. New York, Grosset [1964]c. 1960 101p. col. illus. 33cm. 60-52135 3.95; 4.05 bds., lib. ed.,
1. Mythology—Juvenile literature. 2. Legends—Juvenile literature. I. Title.

SMITH, Evelyn. 291
Myths and legends of many lands, retold by Evelyn Smith. With eight coloured plates and chapter headings by A. E. Bestall. London, New York [etc.] T. Nelson and sons, ltd. [1930] x, 11-221 p., 1 l. col. front., illus., col. plates. 23 cm. (Half-title: Highroads of modern knowledge) "Sources of the myths told in this book": p. vii-viii. [BL310.S6] 31-15207
1. Mythology—Juvenile literature. 2. Legends. I. Title.

Mythology, Maori.

SMITH, Stephenson Percy, 1840-1922, ed. and tr. 398.2'09931
The lore of the Whare-wananga: or, Teachings of the Maori College on religion, cosmogony, and history / written down by H. T. Whatahoro from the teachings of Te Matorohanga and Nepia Pohuhu, priests of the Whare-wananga of the East coast, New Zealand ; translated by S. Percy Smith. New York : AMS Press, [1978] p. cm. Vol. 1 has also special t.p. in Maori. Vol. 2 has alternative title: Teachings of the Maori College on their history and migrations, etc. English and Maori. Reprint of the 1913-1915 ed. printed for the Polynesian Society in New Plymouth, N.Z. and issued as v. 3-4 of its Memoirs. Includes indexes. Contents.Contents.—pt. 1. Te Kauwae-runga; or, Things celestial.—pt. 2. Te Kauwae-raro; or, Things terrestrial. [BL2615.S6 1978] 75-35272 ISBN 0-404-14370-9 : 41.50
1. Mythology, Maori. 2. Maori language—Texts. I. Whatahoro, H. T. II. Matorohanga, Te, d. 1884. III. Pohuhu, Nepia, d. 1882. IV. Title. V. Series: Polynesian Society, Wellington. Memoirs ; v. 3-4.

Mythology—Methodology.

LITTLETON, C. Scott. 291.1'3
The new comparative mythology: an anthropological assessment of the theories of Georges Dumezil [by] C. Scott Littleton. Rev. ed. Berkeley, University of California Press, 1973. xv, 271 p. 23 cm. Bibliography: p. 239-259. [BL43.D8L5 1973] 72-89243 ISBN 0-520-02404-4 11.95
1. Dumezil, Georges, 1898- 2. Mythology—Methodology. I. Title.
Pbk., 3.65, ISBN 0-520-02403-6.

LITTLETON, C. Scott. 291.13
The new comparative mythology; an anthropological assessment of the theories of Georges Dumezil. Berkeley, University of California Press, 1966. xiii, 242 p. 25 cm. Bibliography: p. 215-233. [BL43.D8L5] 66-23181
1. Dumezil, Georges, 1898- 2. Mythology—Methodology. 3. Mythology, Aryan. I. Title.

Mythology, Minoan.

HERBERGER, Charles F. 292'.08
The thread of Ariadne; the labyrinth of the calendar of Minos [by] Charles F. Herberger. New York, Philosophical Library [1972] xi, 158 p. illus. 22 cm. Bibliography: p. 156-158. [BL793.C7H47] 72-78167 ISBN 0-8022-2089-4 12.00
1. Mythology, Minoan. 2. Calendar, Minoan. 3. Cnossus, Crete. Palace of Minos. Toreador Fresco. I. Title.

Mythology—Miscellanea.

MACKEY, Sampson Arnold. 398'.362
The mythological astronomy of the ancients demonstrated by restoring to their fables & symbols their original meanings. Norwich, Printed by R. Walker. Minneapolis, Wizards Bookshelf, 1973. 200 p. illus. 15 cm. (Secret doctrine reference series) Reprint of the 1822-23 ed. Bibliography: p. 199. [BL313.M3 1973] 73-84043 ISBN 0-913510-06-8
1. Mythology—Miscellanea. I. Title.

Mythology, Norse.

ANDERSON, Rasmus 293'.2'11
Bjorn, 1846-1936.
Norse mythology; or, The religion of our forefathers, containing all the myths of the Eddas, systematized and interpreted. With an introd., vocabulary and index. 5th ed. [Boston] Milford House [1974] p. cm. Reprint of the 1891 ed. published by S. C. Griggs, Chicago. Bibliography: p. [BL860.A6 1974] 76-186790 ISBN 0-87821-086-5 45.00
1. Mythology, Norse. 2. Icelandic and Old Norse literature. 3. Northmen—Religion. I. Title.

ANDERSON, Rasmus 293'.2'11
Bjorn, 1846-1936.
Norse mythology : or, The religion of our forefathers, containing all the myths of the Eddas / systematized and interpretated, with an introd., vocabulary and index, by R. B. Anderson. Boston : Longwood Press, 1977. p. cm. Reprint of the 2d ed. published in 1891 by S. C. Griggs, Chicago. Bibliography: p. [BL860.A6 1977] 77-6879 ISBN 0-89341-147-7 lib.bdg. : 25.00
1. Mythology, Norse. 2. Icelandic and Old Norse literature. 3. Northmen—Religion. I. Title. II. Title: The religion of our forefathers.

ANDERSON, Rasmus Bjorn, 1846- 293
1936.
Norse mythology; or, The religion of our forefathers, containing all the myths of the Eddas, systematized and interpreted. With an introduction vocabulary and index. By R. B. Anderson ... Chicago, S. C. Griggs and company; London, Trubner & co., 1875. 473 p. front. 21 cm. "List of works consulted": p. 13-14. [BL860.A6 1875] 32-1033
1. Mythology, Norse. 2. Icelandic and Old Norse literature. 3. Northmen—Religion. I. Title.

ANDERSON, Rasmus Bjorn, 1846- 293
1936.
Norse mythology; or, The religion of our forefathers, containing all the myths of the Eddas, systematized and interpreted. With an introduction vocabulary and index. By R. B. Anderson ... 4th ed. Chicago, S. C. Griggs and company; London, Trubner & co., 1884. 473 p. front. 20 cm. "List of works consulted": p. 13-16. [BL860.A6 1884] 40-25667
1. Mythology, Norse. 2. Icelandic and Old Norse literature. 3. Northmen—Religion. I. Title.

ANDERSON, Rasmus Bjorn, 1846- 293
1936.
Norse mythology; or, The religion of our forefathers, containing all the myths of the Eddas, systematized and interpreted. With an introduction, vocabulary and index. By Rasmus B. Anderson ... 7th ed. Chicago, Scott, Foresman and company, 1901. 473 p. front. 21 cm. "List of works consulted": p. 13-14. [BL860.A6 1901] 3-27917
1. Mythology, Norse. 2. Icelandic and Old Norse literature. 3. Northmen—Religion. I. Title.

AULAIRE, Ingri (Mortenson) 293
d', 1904-
Norse gods and giants [by] Ingri and Edgar Parin d'Aulaire. [1st ed.] Garden City, N.Y., Doubleday [1967] 154 p. illus. (part col.) 32 cm. A collection of the myths of the Norsemen, containing stories of the gods Odin, Thor, Loki, Njord, Frey, and the others of the Aesir. [PZ8.1.A86No] AC 67
1. Mythology, Norse. I. Aulaire, Edgar Parin d', 1898- joint author. II. Title.

BOULT, Katherine F. Mrs. 293
Asgard & the Norse heroes retold by Katherine F. Boult. London & Toronto, J. M. Dent & sons, ltd.; New York, E. P. Dutton & co. [1926]. x p. 1 l, 268 p. 17 1/2 cm. [Half-title: Everyman's library, ed. by Ernest Rhys. For young people 4dno. 689 5d]. "First issue of this edition 1914. Reprinted ... 1926". "List of Authorities consulted": p. vii. [AC1.E8 no. 689] 37-5606
1. Mythology, Norse. I. Title.

BOULT, Katherine F. Mrs.
Asgard & the Norse heroes, retold by Katherine F. Boult. London, J. M. Dent & sons, ltd.: New York E. P. Dutton & co., [1914]. x p., 1 l. 268 p. 17 cm. [Half-title: Everyman's library, ed. by Ernes Rhys. For Young People. (no. 689)). List of authorities consulted: p. vii. A14
1. Mythology, Norse. 2. Icelandic and Old Norse literature. I. Title.

BRANSTON, Brian, 1914- 293'.13
Gods & heroes from Viking mythology / text by Brian Branston ; illustrations by Giovanni Caselli. American ed. New York : Schocken Books, 1982, c1978. p. cm. Includes index. A collection of myths about Thor, Balder, King Gylfi and other Nordic gods and heroes. [BL860.B66 1982] 19 81-14540 ISBN 0-8052-3794-1 : 14.95
1. Mythology, Norse. 2. [Mythology, Norse.] I. Caselli, Giovanni, fl. 1976- ill. II. Title. III. Title: Gods and heroes from Viking mythology.

BRANSTON, Brian, 1914- 293
Gods of the North. New York, Vanguard Press [1955] 318 p. illus. 23 cm. (Myth and man) A Thames and Hudson book. [BL860.B67] 55-7888
1. Mythology, Norse. I. Title.

BRANSTON, Brian, 1914- 293'.13
Gods of the North / Brian Branston. 1st paperback ed. published with revisions in the USA. New York : Thames and Hudson, 1980. x, 318 p. : ill. ; 22 cm. Includes index. Bibliography: p. 309-310. [BL860.B67 1980] 19 79-66130 ISBN 0-500-27177-1 pbk. : 7.95
1. Mythology, Norse. I. Title.
Distributed by W. W. Norton, NYC

BROWN, Abbie Farwell, FIC
d.1927.
In the days of giants; a book of Norse tales, by Abbie Farwell Brown; with illustrations by E. Boyd Smith. Boston and New York, Houghton, Mifflin and co. 1902. 6 p.,l., 159, [1] p.front., plates. 19 cm. Retold from Edda Snorra Sturlusonar. Six of these tales are reprinted from "The Churchman." [PZ8.1.B812I] 293 2-12213
1. Mythology, Norse. I. Edda Snorra Sturlusonar. II. Title.

BUGGE, Sophus, 1833- 839'.6'1
1907.
The home of the Eddic poems; with especial reference to the Helgi-lays. Translated from the Norwegian by William Henry Schofield. Rev. ed., with a new introd. concerning the Old Norse mythology. London, D. Nutt, 1899. [New York, AMS Press, 1972] lxxix, 408 p. 19 cm. Original ed. issued as no. 11 of Grimm library. Translation of Helge-digtene i den Aldre Edda. Includes bibliographical references. [PT7235.B713 1972] 74-144524 ISBN 0-404-53554-2 21.00
1. Edda Samundar. Helgakvida Hjorvardssonar. 2. Edda Samundar. Helgakvida Hundingsbana. 3. Mythology, Norse. I. Title.

CARTWRIGHT, Thomas.
One for Wod and one for Lok; or, Asgard, Midgard and Utgard, by Thomas Cartwright ... New York, E. P. Dutton and company [1908] 4 p. l., 120 p. 8 col. pl. (incl. front.) illus. 17 cm. (Every child's library) Series note in title and at head of caption title. W 8
1. Mythology, Norse. I. Wilson, Patten, illus. II. Title.

CRAIGIE, William Alexander, 293
Sir, 1867-1957.
The religion of ancient Scandinavia. Freeport, N.Y., Books for Libraries Press [1969] xi, 71, [1] p. 23 cm. (Select bibliographies reprint series) Reprint of the 1906 ed. Bibliography: p. 71-[72] [BL860.C7 1969] 74-99657
1. Mythology, Norse. I. Title.

CROSSLEY-HOLLAND, Kevin. 293'.13
The Norse myths / introduced and retold by Kevin Crossley-Holland. 1st American ed. New York : Pantheon Books, 1980. xli, 276 p. : ill. ; 24 cm. ([The Pantheon fairy tale and folktale library]) Includes index. Bibliography: p. 254-261. [BL860.C76 1980] 80-7718 ISBN 0-394-50048-2 : 14.95
1. Mythology, Norse. I. Title. II. Series: Pantheon fairy tale and folklore library.

DAVIDSON, Hilda Roderick 293'.13
(Ellis)
Scandinavian mythology [by] H. R. Ellis Davidson. London, New York, Hamlyn, 1969. 2-143 p. illus. (some col.), map. 29 cm. Bibliography: p. 138. [BL860.D384] 76-497286 25/-
1. Mythology, Norse. I. Title.

DUMEZIL, Georges, 293'.2'11
1898-
Gods of the ancient Northmen. Edited by Einar Haugen; introd. by C. Scott Littleton and Udo Strutynski. Berkeley, University of California Press, 1973. xlvi, 157 p. 24 cm. (UCLA Center for the Study of Comparative Folklore and Mythology. Publications, 3) Translation of Les dieux des Germains and 4 articles written between 1952 and 1959. Includes bibliographical references. [BL860.D7813] 74-157819 ISBN 0-520-02044-8 9.00
1. Mythology, Norse. 2. Germanic tribes—Religion. I. Title. II. Series: California. University. University at Los Angeles. Center for the Study of Comparative Folklore and Mythology. Publications, 3.

EDDA, Snaorra Sturlusonar
The Younger Edda: also called Snorre's Edda, or the Prose Edda. An English version of the foreword; The fooling of Gylfe, the afterword; Brage's talk, the afterword to Brege's talk, and the important passages in the Poetical diction (Skaldskaparhal), with an introduction, notes, vocabulary, and index. By Rasmus B. Anderson. Chicago, S. C. Griggs and company; [etc., etc.] 1880. 302 p. 20 cm. [PT7313.E5A5] 12-30336
1. Mythology, Norse. 2. Scalds and scaldic poetry. I. Snorri Sturluson, 1178-1241. II. Anderson, Rasmus Bjorn, 1846- tr. III. Title.

EDDA Snorra. Sturlusonar 839.6
Selections
The prose Edda of Snorri Sturluson; tales from Norse mythology, Introduced by Sigurdur Nordal; selected and translated by Jean I. Young. Berkely, University of California Press, 1964. 131 p. 22 cm. [PT7313.E5Y6 1964] 64-25941
1. Mythology, Norse. 2. Scalds and scaldic poetry. I. Snorri Sturluson, 1178-1241. II. Young, Jean Isobel, tr III. Title.

EDDA, Snorra Sturlusonar
The Prose Edda, by Snorri Sturluson, tr. from the Icelandic, with an introduction, by Arthur Gilchrist Brodeur ... New York, The American-Scandinavian foundation; [etc., etc.] 1916. xxii, 266 p. 19 1/2 cm. (Half-title: Scandinavian classics. vol. v) Translations of the prose Edda: p. xix-xxi. [PT7313.E5B7] 16-22078
1. Mythology, Norse. 2. Scalds and scaldic poetry. I. Snorri Sturluson, 1178-1241. II. Brodeur, Arthur Glichrist, 1888- tr. III. Title.

EDDA Snorra Sturlusonar. 839.6
Selections.
The prose Edda of Snorri Sturluson; tales from Norse mythology. Introduced by Sigurdur Nordal; selected and translated by Jean I. Young. [Cambridge, Eng.] Bowes & Bowes [1954] 131p. 19cm. [PT7313.E5Y6] 55-3196
1. Mythology, Norse. 2. Scalds and scaldic poetry. I. Snorri Sturluson, 1178-1241. II. Young, Jean Isobel, tr. III. Title.

FARADAY, Lucy 398.2'0948
Winifred, 1872-
The Edda, by Winifred Faraday. New York, AMS Press [1972] 51, 60 p. 19 cm. Reprint of the 1902 ed., which was issued in two parts as no. 12-13 of Popular studies in mythology, romance, and folklore. "Appendix: Thrymskvida": p. [42]-45 (1st group) Contents.Contents.—The divine mythology of the North.—The heroic mythology of the North. Includes bibliographical references. [BL860.F34 1972] 74-139175 ISBN 0-404-53512-7 11.00
1. Edda Samundar. 2. Mythology, Norse. I. Edda Samundar. rymskviEa. 1972. II. Title. III. Series: Popular studies in mythology, romance, and folklore, no. 12-13.

GELLING, Peter. 293'.13
The chariot of the sun, and other rites and symbols of the northern bronze age, by Peter Gelling and Hilda Ellis Davidson. Foreword by Christopher Hawkes. New York, Praeger [1969] ix, 200 p. illus. (part col.), map. 26 cm. Bibliography: p. 185-189. [BL863.G4 1969] 68-54466 7.50
1. Mythology, Norse. 2. Sun (in religion, folk-lore, etc.) I. Davidson, Hilda Roderick (Ellis) joint author. II. Title.

GREEN, Roger Lancelyn 293
Myths of the Norsemen; retold from the old Norse poems and tales by Roger Lancelyn Green. Drawings by Brian Wildsmith [Chester Springs, Pa.] Dufour [1964, c.1960] 190p. illus. 22cm. Pub. in Harmondsworth, Eng., in 1960 under title: The saga of Asgard. 64-12718 3.50 bds.,
1. Mythology, Norse. I. Title.

GREEN, Roger Lancelyn. 293'.2'11
Myths of the Norsemen, retold from the old Norse poems and tales. Illustrated by Brian Wildsmith. [Harmondsworth, Eng.] Penguin Books [1970, c1960] 208 p. illus. 18 cm. (Puffin books, 464) First puboished in 1960 under title: The saga of Asgard. [BL860.G68 1970] 72-24349 0.95 (U.S.)
1. Mythology, Norse. I. Title.

GUERBER, Helene Adeline, 293'.8
d.1929.
Myths of northern lands; narrated with special reference to literature and art. Detroit, Singing Tree Press, 1970. 319 p. illus., ports. 23 cm. Reprint of the 1895 ed. [BL860.G8 1970] 70-124583
1. Mythology, Norse. 2. Mythology, Germanic. 3. Legends, Germanic. I. Title.

GUERBER, Helene Adeline, 203
d.1929.
Myths of northern lands, narrated with special reference to literature and art, by H. A. Guerber ... New York, Chicago [etc.] American book company, 1895. 319 p. 24 pl. (incl. front.) 19 cm. [BL860.G8] 4-4207
1. Mythology, Norse. 2. Mythology, Germanic. 3. Legends, Germanic. I. Title.

HODGES, Margaret. JUV
Baldur and the mistletoe; a myth of the Vikings, retold by Margaret Hodges. Illustrated by Gerry Hoover. [1st ed.] Boston, Little, Brown [1973, c1974] 30 p.

col. illus. 24 cm. (Her Myths of the world) Based on the Norse myths contained in The younger Edda. Baldur, a young Norse god, is protected from all things except mistletoe. [PZ8.1.H69Bal] 293'.2'11 73-608 ISBN 0-316-36787-7 5.95
1. [Mythology, Norse.] I. Hoover, Gerry, illus. II. Edda Snorra Sturlusonar. III. Title. IV. Title: A myth of the vikings.

KAUFFMANN, Friedrich, 1863-1941. 293'.1'3
Northern mythology / by Friedrich Kauffmann ; [translated by M. Steele Smith] Folcroft, Pa. : Folcroft Library Editions, 1976. xii, 106 p. ; 23 cm. Translation of Deutsche Mythologie. Reprint of the 1903 ed. published by Dent, London, in series: The Temple primers. Includes index. Bibliography: p. 99-100. [BL860.K33 1976] 76-5464 ISBN 0-8414-5524-4 lib. bdg. : 12.50
1. Mythology, Norse. 2. Mythology, Germanic. I. Title.

KAUFFMANN, Friedrich, 1863-1941. 293'.1'3
Northern mythology / by Friedrich Kauffmann ; [translated by M. Steele Smith] Folcroft, Pa. : Folcroft Library Editions, 1976. xii, 106 p. ; 23 cm. Translation of Deutsche Mythologie. Reprint of the 1903 ed. published by Dent, London, in series: The Temple primers. Includes index. Bibliography: p. 99-100. [BL860.K33 1976] 76-5464 ISBN 0-8414-5524-4 lib. bdg. : 12.50
1. Mythology, Norse. 2. Mythology, Germanic. I. Title.

KEYSER, Rudolph, 1803-1864. 293
The religion of the Northmen; by Rudolph Keyser ... Translated by Barclay Pennock. New York, C. B. Norton, 1854. 346 p., 1 l. 20 cm. "The Eddas and sagas of Iceland": p. 42-76 (chapter ii of translator's introduction) Translation of Nordmendenes religionsforfatning hedendommen. [Full bname:Jacob Rudolph Keyser] [BL860.K43] 32-1034
1. Mythology, Norse. 2. Northmen—Religion. 3. Icelandic and Old Norse literature. I. Pennock, Barclay, 1821-1859, tr. II. Title.

LARNED, Augusta, 1835-
Tales from the Norse grandmother, (the Elder Edda.) By Augusta Larned ... New York, Phillips & Hunt; Cincinnati, Walden & Stowe, 1881. 432 p. front. 19 cm. [PT7235.L3] 20-16545
1. Mythology, Norse. I. Edda Saemundar. II. Title.

MACCULLOCH, John Arnott, 1868- 293
... *Eddic [mythology]* by John Arnott MacCulloch ... Boston, Archaeological institute of America, Marshall Jones company, 1930. x p., 2 l., [3]-400 p. xlvii pl. (1 col.; incl. col. front.) 24 1/2 cm. (The mythology of all races ... Canon J. A. MacCulloch ... editor ... vol. ii) Each plate accompanied by guard sheet with descriptive letterpress. Bibliography: p. [387]-400. [BL25.M8 vol. 2] [BL860.M25] (291) 30-9990
1. Mythology, Norse. I. Title.

MADELEY, Dora Ford.
The heroic life and exploits of Siegfried, the dragonslayer; an old story of the north, retold by Dora Ford Madeley, with twelve illustrations by Stephen Reid. New York, T. Y. Crowell & company [1910] vii, 166 p., 1 l. col. front., col. pl. 20 cm. A 10
1. Siegfried. 2. Mythology, Norse. I. Title.

MORTENSEN, Karl Andreas, 1867- 293
A handbook of Norse mythology, by Karl Mortensen ... translated from the Danish by A. Clinton Crowell ... New York, Thomas Y. Crowell company [1913] viii, 206 p. illus. 17cm. [BL860.M6] 13-5411
1. Mythology, Norse. I. Crowell, Asa Clinton, tr. II. Title.

MUNCH, Peter Andreas, 1810-1863. 293
Norse mythology; legends of gods and heroes. In the revision of Magnus Olsen. Translated from the Norwegian by Sigurd Bernhard Hustvedt. New York, American-Scandinavian Foundation, 1926 [c1927] Detroit, Singing Tree Press 1968. xvii, 392 p. 20 cm. Translation of Norrone gude- og heltesagn. Bibliography: p. 279-280. [BL860.M86 1968] 68-31092
1. Mythology, Norse. 2. Legends, Norse. I. Olsen, Magnus Bernhard, 1878-1963.

MUNCH, Peter Andreas, 1810-1863. 298
Norse mythology, legends of gods and heroes, by Peter Andreas Munch, in the revision of Magnus Olsen; translated from the Norwegian by Sigurd Bernhard Hustvedt. New York, The American-Scandinavian foundation; London, H. Milford, Oxford university press, 1926. xvii p., 1 l., 397 p. 19 cm. (Half-title: Scandinavian classics, vol. xxvii) Bibliography: p. 279-280. [BL860.M86] 27-26452
1. Mythology, Norse. 2. Legends, Norse. I. Olsen, Magnus Bernhard, 1878- II. Hustvedt, Sigurd Bernhard, 1882- tr. III. Title.

MUNCH, Peter Andreas, 1810-1863. 293'.11
Norse mythology; legends of gods and heroes, by Peter Andreas Munch, in the revision of Magnus Olsen. Translated from the Norwegian by Sigurd Bernhard Hustvedt. New York, AMS Press [1970] xvii, 392 p. 23 cm. Translation of Norrone gude- og heltesagn. Reprint of the 1926 ed., which was issued as no. 27 of Scandinavian classics. Bibliography: p. 279-280. [BL860.M86 1970] 74-112002 ISBN 0-404-04538-3
1. Mythology, Norse. 2. Legends, Norse. I. Olsen, Magnus Bernhard, 1878-1963. II. Title. III. Series: Scandinavian classics, no. 27.

PIGOTT, Grenville, 1796-1865. 291.1'3'0948
A manual of Scandinavian mythology / Grenville Pigott. New York : Arno Press, 1978. xliv, 370 p. ; 21 cm. (Mythology) "Illustrated by translations from A. G. Oehlenschlager's Danish poem The gods of the North." Reprint of the 1839 ed. published by W. Pickering, London. Includes index. [BL860.P5 1978] 77-79152 ISBN 0-405-10561-4 : 25.00
1. Eddas. 2. Mythology, Norse. I. Oehlenschlager, Adam Gottlob, 1779-1850. Nordens guder. II. Edda Snorra Sturlusonar. III. Title. IV. Series.

RYDBERG, Viktor, 1828-1895. 293
Teutonic mythology; gods and goddesses of the Northland ...by Viktor Rydberg...Authorised translation from the Swedish by Rasmus B. Anderson...Hon. Rasmus B. Anderson...editor in chief; J. W. Buel, PH.D., managing editor. London, New York [etc.] Norroena society, 1906. 3 v. col. front., plates. 23 1/2 cm. (Half-title: Norroena, the history and romance of northern Europe; a library of supreme classics printed in complete form. Viking ed.) Paged continuously. "Of the Viking edition there are but six hundred and fifty sets made for the world." This set not numbered. [Full name: Abraham Viktor Rydberg] [BL860.R83 1906] 6-16491
1. Mythology, Norse. 2. Mythology, Germanic. 3. Legends, Norse. I. Anderson, Rasmus Bjorn, 1846-1936, ed. and tr. II. Buel, James William, 1849-1920, joint ed. III. Title.

STERN, Herman Isidore, 1854- 293
The gods of our fathers, a study of Saxon mythology. By Herman I. Stern. New York and London, Harper & brothers, 1898. xxviii, [1], 268, [1] p. 19 cm. [BL860.S7] 12-38935
1. Mythology, Norse. I. Title.

STERN, Herman Isidore, 1854- 293'.1'3
The gods of our fathers : a study of Saxon mythology / by Herman I. Stern. Road Town, Tortola, British V.I. ; Boston : Longwood Press, 1979. p. cm. Reprint of the 1898 ed. published by Harper, New York. [BL860.S7 1979] 77-85623 ISBN 0-89341-303-8 : 30.00
1. Mythology, Norse. 2. Legends, Norse. I. Title.

THOMAS, Edward, 1878-1917.
Norse tales, by Edward Thomas ... Oxford, The Clarendon press, 1912. 159, [1] p. 19 cm. W 13
1. Mythology, Norse. I. Title.

TOFFTEEN, Olof A.
Myths and Bible; some hints to the value of Scandinavian mythology upon Biblical research, by Olof A. Toffteen... Minneapolis, Minn., 1899. 57 p. 20 cm. 3-19948
I. Title.

TURVILLEPETRE, Edward Oswald Gabriel 293'.0948
Myth and religion of the North : the religion of ancient Scandinavia / E. O. G. Turville-Petre. Westport, Conn. : Greenwood Press, 1975, c1964. ix, 340 p., [12] leaves of plates : ill. ; 23 cm. Reprint of the ed. published by Holt, Rinehart and Winston, New York. Includes index. Bibliography: p. 321-329. [BL860.T8 1975] 75-5003 ISBN 0-8371-7420-1 lib.bdg. : 19.75
1. Mythology, Norse. 2. Scandinavia—Religion. I. Title.

WALSH, John Herbert. 293
Norse legends and myths. Illustrated by Tom Taylor. London, New York, Longmans, Green [1957] 182 p. 17 cm. (The Heritage of literature series. Section A, no. 68) [BL860.W33] 58-1468
1. Mythology, Norse. I. Title.

WHITE, Isabella, ed.
...Gods and heroes of the North; selections from early Scandinavian literature, ed. with explanatory notes, by Isabella White. New York, Maynard, Merrill & co., 1893. 60 p. 17 cm. [English classic series. no. 143] [PT7228.W5] 14-6762
1. Mythology, Norse. I. Title.

ZIMMERN, Alice, 1855-
... Gods and heroes of the north; by Alice Zimmern ... London, New York [etc.] Longmans, Green, and co., 1907. x, 142 p. front., illus. 19 cm. (Longmans' class-books of English literature) W 8
1. Mythology, Norse. I. Title.

Mythology, Norse—Juvenile literature.

PYLE, Katharine. JUV
Tales from Norse mythology; retold and illustrated by Katharine Pyle; 8 illustrations in color. Philadelphia & London, J. B. Lippincott company [c1930] 256 p. col. front., col. plates. 24 cm. Illustrated lining-papers. [PZ8.1.P995Tan] 293 30-30017
1. Mythology, Norse—Juvenile literature. I. Title.

Mythology, Oceanic.

DIXON, Roland Burrage, 1875-1934. 299.9
Oceanic [mythology] New York, Cooper Square Publishers, 1964 [c1916] xv, 364 p. illus., fold. map, 24 plates. 24 cm. (The Mythology of all races, v. 9) Bibliography: p. [345]-364. 63-19094
1. Mythology, Oceanic. I. Title. II. Series.

DIXON, Roland Burrage, 1875-1934. 294.
... *Oceanic [mythology]* by Roland B. Dixon ... Boston, Marshall Jones company, 1916. xv, 364 p. illus., xxiv (i. e. 25) pl. (incl. front.; part col.) fold. map. 25 cm. (The mythology of all races ...v. 9) Each plate accompanied by guard sheet with descriptive letterpress. Bibliography: p. [345]-364. [BL25.M8 vol. 9] [BL2600.D5] 16-22069
1. Mythology, Oceanic. I. Title.

Mythology, Oriental.

ASIATIC mythology; 291.13
a detailed description and explanation of the mythologies of all the great nations of Asia, by J. Hackin [others] Introd. by Paul-Louis Couchoud. Tr. by F. M. Atkinson. New York, Crowell [1963] 459p. illus., col. plates. 30cm. 63-20021 12.50
1. Mythology, Oriental. 2. Art, Oriental. 3. Asia—Religion. I. Hackin, Joseph, 1886-1941.

Mythology—Outlines, syllabi, etc.

LOOMIS, Julia Wolfe 291.13
Mythology. New York, Monarch Pr. [1966, c.1965] 155p. illus. 22cm. (Monarch notes and study guides, 523-1) Bibl. [BL311] 66-1768 2.50
1. Mythology—Outlines, syllabi, etc. I. Title.

Mythology, Polynesian.

ANDERSEN, Johannes Carl, 1873- 299.9
Myths & legends of the Polynesians, by Johannes C. Andersen ... with sixteen plates in colour by Richard wallwork ... thirty-two plates in half- tone and other illustrations. New York, Farrar & Rinehart [1931] 511, [1] p. col. front., illus., plates (part col.) fold. map. 24 cm. (Lettered on cover: The myths series) Printed in Great Britain. "Authorities": p. 469-470. [BL2300.A5 1931] 31-28225
1. Mythology, Polynesian. 2. Legends—Polynesia. 3. Folk-lore—Polynesia I. Title.

GILL, William Wyatt, 1828-1896. 299'.9
Myths and songs from the South Pacific / William Wyatt Gill. New York : Arno Press, 1977. p. cm. (International folklore) Reprint of the 1876 ed. published by H. S. King, London. [BL2620.P6G54] 77-70596 ISBN 0-405-10095-7 : 19.00
1. Mythology, Polynesian. 2. Mangaia—Religion. I. Title. II. Series.

GREY, George, Sir 1812-1898 299.94
Polynesian mythology, and ancient traditional history of the Maori as told by their priests and chiefs. Ed. by W. W. Bird. Illus. by Russell Clark [Illus. New Zealand ed. Christchurch] Whitcombe Tombs [dist. South Pasadena. Calif., Hutchins, 1964] 250p. illus. 23cm. 57-41672 6.00
1. Mythology. Polynesian. 2. Legends—New Zealand. I. Title.

GREY, George, Sir, 1812-1898. 299'.9
Polynesian mythology and ancient traditional history of the Maori as told by their priests and chiefs. Edited by W. W. Bird. Illustrated by Russell Clark. New York, Taplinger Pub. Co. [1970, c1956] 249 p. illus. 23 cm. First published in London in 1854 under title, "Mythology and traditions of the New Zealanders. Ko nga mahinga a nga tupuna Maori he mea kohikohi mai," with Maori text only. An English translation was published under title: Polynesian mythology and ancient traditional history of the New Zealand race, as furnished by their priests and chiefs. A 2d ed., with the same title as the English translation, included a reprint of the original Maori text. The 3d ed., with Maori text only, was published under title: Nga mahi a nga tupuna. [BL2615.G7 1970] 78-82687 4.95
1. Mythology, Polynesian. 2. Legends—New Zealand. I. Title.

GREY, George, Sir 1812-1898.
Polynesian mythology & ancient traditional history of the New Zealanders as furnished by their priests and chiefs, by Sir George Grey ... London, G. Routledge & sons, limited; New York, E. P. Dutton & co. [1906] 2 p. l., vii-xv, 247, [1] p. illus. (music) 16 cm. (Half-title: The new universal library) [BL2615.G] A 33
1. Mythology, Polynesian. I. Title.

LUOMALA, Katharine. 299.9
Voices on the wind; Polynesian myths and chants. Illustrated by Joseph Feher. [Honolulu] Bishop Museum Press [c1955] 191p. illus. 26cm. [BL2620.P6L82] 56-21816
1. Mythology, Polynesian. I. Title.

STIMSON, John Francis, 1883- comp. and tr. 299.9
The legends of Maui and Tahaki, translated by J. F. Stimson ... Honolulu, Hawaii, The Museum, 1934. 100 p. illus. (music) 25 1/2 cm. (Bernice P. Bishop museum. Bulletin 127) "The present material comes from the island of Fagatau in the Tusmotu archipelago and derives from Farius-a-Makitua, a former chief of Fatagau."--Introd. Legends in Tuamatuan and English in parallel columns. "Music of the Tahaki chants, by E. G. Burrows": p. 78-88. "Bibliography: annotated lists of references to versions of the Tahaki legend from parts of Polynesia other than Fagatau,

compiled by K. P. Emory": p. 89-90. [GN670.B4 no. 127] (572.996) 35-18675
1. Mythology, Polynesian. 2. Legends—Polynesia. 3. Maui (Polynesian deity) 4. Tawhaki (Polynesian deity) 5. Tusinotuan language—Texts. 6. Music—Tuamotu islands. I. Burrows, Edwin G. II. Emory, Kenneth Pike, 1897- III. Title.

STIMSON, John Francis, 1883- comp. and tr. 299.9
Tuamotuan legends (island of Anaa) ... translated by J. F. Stimson ... Honolulu, Hawaii, The Museum, 1937- v. 25 1/2 cm. (Bernice P. Bishop museum. Bulletin 148) Includes texts of chants, without music. [GN670.B4 no. 148] (572.996) 38-36750
1. Mythology, Polynesian. 2. Legends—Polynesia. 3. Tuamotuan language—Texts. I. Title.

Mythology, Roman.

DUMEZIL, Georges, 1898- 292'.07
Camillus : a study of Indo-European religion as Roman history / by Georges Dumezil ; edited, with an introd., by Udo Strutynski ; translations by Annette Aronowicz and Josette Bryson. Berkeley : University of California Press, c1980. p. cm. Translation of portions of Mythe et epopee (v. 3) and Fetes romaines d'ete et d'automne suivi de Dix questions romaines. Includes bibliographical references and index. [BL805.D77] 80-36771 ISBN 0-520-02841-4 : 16.95
1. Camillus, Marcus Furius, d. B.C. 365. 2. Mythology, Roman. 3. Mythology, Indo-European. 4. Rome—History—To 510 B.C. I. Strutynski, Udo. II. Title.

GRANT, Michael, 1914- 292'.07
Roman myths. New York, Scribners [1973, c.1971] xvi, 293 p. illus. 20 cm. (Lyceum editions) [BL802.G7 1972] 75-162749 ISBN 0-684-13237-0 pap., 3.50
1. Mythology, Roman. I. Title.

PEROWNE, Stewart, 1901- 292'.1'3
Roman mythology. London, New York, Hamlyn, 1969. 141 p. illus. (some col.), maps, ports. 29 cm. Illus. on lining papers. Bibliography: p. 138. [BL802.P46] 79-499664 ISBN 0-600-03347-3 25/-
1. Mythology, Roman. I. Title.

WINTER, John Garrett, 1881- 292
The myth of Hercules at Rome, by John Garrett Winter ... New York, The Macmillan company; London, Macmillan & co., ltd., 1910. 2 p. l., p. [171]-273 diagr. 22 1/2 cm. (Half-title: University of Michigan studies. Humanistic series, vol. IV, pt. II) [BL820.H5W5] 12-6532
1. Hercules. 2. Mythology, Roman. I. Title.

Mythology, Samoan.

STUEBEL, C. 299'.9
Myths and legends of Samoa = Tala o le Vavau / Samoan text by C. Stuebel ; English translation by Brother Herman ; illustrated by Iosua Toafa. Wellington [N.Z.] : A. H. & A. W. Reed, 1976. 157 p. : ill. ; 24 cm. [BL2620.S35S85] 76-380070 ISBN 0-589-00968-0
1. Mythology, Samoan. 2. Samoan Islands—Social life and customs. I. Title. II. Title: Tala o le Vavau.

Mythology, Semitic.

DAVIS, John D., 1854-1926. 222'.1106
Genesis and Semitic tradition / John D. Davis ; introd. by Ronald Youngblood. Grand Rapids, Mich. : Baker Book House, 1980. xi, 150 p. : ill. ; 22 cm. (Twin brooks series) Reprint of the 1894 ed. published by Scribner, New York. Includes bibliographical references. [BS1235.D37 1980] 80-112354 4.95
1. Bible. O.T. Genesis I-XI—Criticism, interpretation, etc. 2. Mythology, Semitic. 3. Assyro-Babylonian literature—Relation to the Old Testament. I. Title.

HOOKE, Samuel Henry, 1874- 291.13
Middle Eastern mythology. Baltimore, Penguin [c.1963] 198p. illus. 18cm. (Pelican bks., A546) 63-2044 .95 pap.,
1. Mythology, Semitic. 2. Mythology, Egyptian. I. Title.

LANGDON, Stephen Herbert, 1876- 299.2
... Semitic [mythology] by Stephen Herbert Langdon ... Boston, Archaeological institute of America, Marshall Jones company, 1931. xx p., 1 l., 454 p. illus., plates. 25 cm. (The mythology of all races ... Canon J. A. MacCulloch ... editor ... vol. v) Bibliography: p. 423-431. [BL25.M8 vol. 5] [BL1600.L3] 290.8 31-25060
1. Mythology, Semitic. I. Title.

LANGDON, Stephen Herbert, 1876-1937. 299.2
Semitic [mythology] New pyork, Cooper Square Publishers, 1964[1931] xx, 454 p. 102 illus. 24 cm. (The Mythology of all races, v. 5) Bibliography: p. [419] 431. [BL25.M8 1964 vol. 5] 63-19090
1. Mythology, Semitic. I. Title. II. Series.

Mythology, Semitic—Addresses, essays, lectures.

WENSINCK, Arnet Jan, 1882-1939. 291.1'3
Studies of A. J. Wensinck. New York : Arno Press, 1978. 220 p. in various pagings : ill. ; 24 cm. (Mythology) Reprint of articles published in Verhandelingen der Koninklijke Akademie van Wetenschappen, 1917-1921. Contents.Contents.—The ideas of the western Semites concerning the navel of the earth.—The ocean in the literature of the western Semites.—Tree and bird as cosmological symbols in western Asia. Includes bibliographies. [BL1600.W42 1978] 77-82275 15.00
1. Mythology, Semitic—Addresses, essays, lectures. 2. Navel (in religion, folk-lore, etc.)—Addresses, essays, lectures. 3. Sea in literature—Addresses, essays, lectures. 4. Folk-lore of trees—Addresses, essays, lectures. 5. Folk-lore of birds—Addresses, essays, lectures. I. Title. II. Series.

Mythology—Study and teaching.

FAHS, Sophia Blanche (Lyon) Mrs. 291.212
Beginnings of earth and sky; a guide book for teachers and parents, by Sophia L. Fahs and Mildred T. Tenny. Boston, the Beacon press, inc., 1938. vii, 67 p. 25 cm. [Beacon books in religious education. Children's series on beginnings] On cover: Beginnings of earth and sky. Leader's guide. Guide to Mrs. Faha' Beginning of earth and sky; stories old and new. Includes bibliographies. [BV1561.B33 vol. 1] 268.61 38-12100
1. Mythology—Study and teaching. 2. Earth. 3. Astronomy—Study and teaching. 4. Religious education. I. Tenny, Mildred T., joint author. II. Title.

Mythology, Sumerian.

KINNIER Wilson, J. V. 299'.21
The rebel lands : an investigation into the origins of early Mesopotamian mythology / J. V. Kinnier Wilson and Herman Vanstiphout. Cambridge : Cambridge University Press, 1977. p. cm. (University of Cambridge Oriental publications ; 29) Includes indexes. Bibliography: p. [BL1615.K56] 77-1272 ISBN 0-521-21469-6 : 19.95
1. Mythology, Sumerian. 2. Mythology, Assyro-Babylonian. I. Vanstiphout, Herman, joint author. II. Title. III. Series: Cambridge. University. Oriental publications ; 29.

KRAMER, Samuel Nathan. 299.2
Sumerian mythology, a study of spiritual and literary achievement in the third millennium, B.C. [by] S. N. Kramer ... Philadelphia, The American philosophical society, 1944. xiv, 125 p. front., illus. (incl. map) XX pl. 24 cm. (Half-title: Memoirs of the American philosophical society ... vol. XXI, 1944) Frontispiece accompanied by leaf with descriptive letterpress. "References and notes": p. 104-119. [PJ4047.K7] 45-2810
1. Mythology, Sumerian. I. Title.

KRAMER, Samuel Noah, 1897- 299.2
Sumerian mythology; a study of spiritual and literary achievement in the third millennium B. C. Rev. ed. [Gloucester, Mass., Peter Smith, 1962, c.1961] 130p. illus. 21cm. (Harper torchbks., Acad. lib., TB1055 rebound) Bibl. 3.50
1. Mythology, Sumerian. I. Title.

KRAMER, Samuel Noah, 1897- 299.2
Sumerian mythology; a study of spiritual and literary achievement in the third millennium B.C. Rev. ed. New York, Harper [c.1961] 130p. illus. (Harper torchbks., Academy lib. TB1055) Bibl. 1.45 pap.,
1. Mythology, Sumerian. I. Title.

KRAMER, Samuel Noah, 1897- 299.2
Sumerian mythology, a study of spiritual and literary achievement in the third millennium, B.C. [by] S. N. Kramer... Philadelphia, The American philosophical society, 1944. xiv, 125 p. front., illus. (incl. map) xx pl. 24 cm. (Half-title: Memoirs of the American philosphical society... vol. xxi, 1944) Frontispiece accompanied by leaf with descriptive letterpress. "References and notes": p. 104-119. [PJ4047.K7] 45-2810
1. Mythology, Sumerian. I. Title.

Mythology, Syrian.

SELDEN, John, 1584-1654. 299.23
The fabulous gods denounced in the Bible. Translated from Selden's "Syrian deities" by W. A. Hauser. Philadelphia, J. B. Lippincott & co., 1880. 178 p. 19 cm. [BL1640.S4] 33-400
1. Mythology, Syrian. I. Hauser, W. A., tr. II. Title.

Mythology, Thracian.

THRACIAN legends / 292'.1'3
Alexander Fol ... [et al.] ; tranl. [from the Bulgarian by] Y. Pencheva. Sofia : Sofia-Press, 1976. 144 p., 30 leaves of plates : ill. ; 22 cm. Bibliography: p. 139-143. [BL975.T5T48] 77-550819
1. Mythology, Thracian. 2. Thracians—Religion. I. Fol, Aleksandur.

Mythology, Yoruba.

GLEASON, Judith Illsley. 299'.6
Orisha: the gods of Yorubaland, by Judith Gleason. Art by Aduni Olorisa. [1st ed.] New York, Atheneum, 1971. 122 p. illus. 25 cm. [BL2480.Y6G57 1971] 70-134809 5.25
1. Mythology, Yoruba. I. Title.

Naaman, the Syrian.

ROGERS, Ebenezer Platt, 1817-1881. 221.92
The Syrian leper; or, The Sinner's malady and the sinner's cure. By Rev. E. P. Rogers... New York, American tract society [1867] 100 p. 15 1/2 cm. [BS580.N2R6] 36-37404
1. Naaman, the Syrian. I. Title. II. Title: The sinner's malady. III. Title: American tract society.

Naaman, the Syrian—Drama.

BOXER, James.
Sacred dramas. By Rev. James Boxer. i. Naaman the Syrian. ii. The finding of Moses. iii. Jephthah's daughter. Boston, Lee and Shepard; New York, Lee, Shepard, and Dillingham, 1875. 174 p. 20 cm. [PS1114.B5S3] 20-17341
1. Naaman, the Syrian—Drama. 2. Moses—Drama. I. Title. II. Title: Naaman the Syrian. III. Title: The finding of Moses. IV. Title: Jephthah's daughter.

Naaman, the Syrian—Juvenile literature.

GREENE, Carol. 222'.54'09505
Seven baths for Naaman : the healing of Naaman for beginning readers : 2 Kings 5:1-15 for children / by Carol Greene ; illustrated by Aline Cunningham. St. Louis : Concordia Pub. House, c1977. [46] p. : col. ill. ; 23 cm. (I can read a Bible story.) Retells the Bible story in which Naaman, a wealthy Syrian travels to Israel in hopes that Elisha will cure him of his illness. [BS580.N2G73] 77-6801 ISBN 0-570-07321-9 : 3.95. ISBN 0-570-07315-4 pbk. : 1.95
1. Naaman, the Syrian—Juvenile literature. 2. [Naaman, the Syrian.] 3. Bible. O.T.—Biography—Juvenile literature. 4. [Bible stories—O.T.] I. Cunningham, Aline. II. Title.

Nabataeans.

LAWLOR, John Irving. 220.9'3
The Nabataeans in historical perspective. Grand Rapids, Baker Book House [1974] 159 p. illus. 22 cm. (Baker studies in Biblical archaeology) Bibliography: p. 144-150. [DS154.2.L38] 74-156928 ISBN 0-8010-5536-9 3.95 (pbk.).
1. Nabataeans. I. Title.

NacNally, David Rice, 1810-1895.

HILLIARD, Frances McAnally Blackburn. 287'.631'0924 B
Stepping stones to glory : from circuit rider to editor and the years in between : life of David Rice McAnally, 1810-1895 / by Frances McAnally Blackburn Hilliard. Baltimore : Gateway Press, 1975. 139 p. : ill. ; 23 cm. [BX8495.M14H54] 75-18536 10.00
1. McAnally, David Rice, 1810-1895. I. Title.

Nadapada.

GUENTHER, Herbert V. 294.32
The life and teaching of Naropa. Tr. from Tibetan with a philosophical commentary based on the Oral transmission. [New York] Oxford [c.]1963. xvi, 292p. 23cm. (UNESCO collection of representative works; Titbetan ser.) This first English tr. of the life and teachings of Naropa is based on an old Tibetan ed. of the work by lHa'i btsun-pa Rin-chen rnamrgyal of Brad-dkar. Appendix contains the complete text of the twelve instructions of Nadapada in Tibetan (transliterated) Bibl. 63-23887 10.00
1. Nadapada. I. lHa'l btsun-pa Rin-chen rNamrgyal,12th cent. II. Nadapada. III. Title. IV. Series.

GUENTHER, Herbert V 294.32
The life and teaching of Naropa. Translated from the original Tibetan with a philosophical commentary based on the oral transmission. Oxford, Clarendon Press, 1963. xvi, 292 p. 23 cm. (UNESCO collection of representative works; Tibetan series) "This first English translation of the life and teachings of Naropa is based on an old Tibetan edition" of the work by lHa'i btsun-pa Rin-chen rnamrgyal of Brad-dkar. Appendix contains the complete text of the twelve instructions of Nadapada in Tibetan (transliterated) Bibliography: p. [281]-285. [BL1473.N3G83] 63-23887
1. Nadapada. I. 1Ha'l btsun-pa Rin-chen rNamrgyal, 12th cent. Nadapada. II. Title. III. Series.

Nagarjuna, Siddha.

NAGARJUNA, Siddha. 294.3'4
The precious garland and The song of the four mindfulnesses / Nagarjuna and Kaysang Gyatso, Seventh Dalai Lama ; translated and edited by Jeffrey Hopkins and Lati Rimpoche, with Anne Klein ; foreword by Tenzin Gyatso, Fourteenth Dalai Lama. 1st U.S. ed. New York : Harper & Row, [1975] 119 p. ; 21 cm. (The Wisdom of Tibet series ; 2) Translation of Rajaparikatharatnamala by Nagarjuna and a poem by the Seventh Dalai Lama. [BQ2872.E5 1975] 74-25688 ISBN 0-06-063541-X : 5.95
I. Bskal-bzan-rgya-mtsho, Dalai Lama VII, 1708-1757. The song of the four mindfulnesses causing the rain of achievements to fall. English. 1975. II. Title.

STRENG, Frederick J. 294.3'01
Emptiness; a study in religious meaning [by] Frederick J. Streng. Nashville, Abingdon Press [1967] 252 p. 24 cm. Bibliography: p. 229-247. [BL1416.N33S7] 67-11010
1. Nagarjuna, Siddha. 2. Sunyata. I. Title.

Nagle, Nano, 1718-1784.

LEAHY, Maurice, 1900- 922.2415
The Flower of Her Kindred, a biographical study of Nano Nagle of Ireland, foundress, pioneer of popular education and noted leader in sociology in the eighteenth century, by Maurice Leahy, with a preface by His Grace the Most Reverend John J. Glennon... New York, N.Y., M. Leahy [1944] xv, 294 p. 21 cm. [BX4705.N2L4] 44-9000
1. Nagle, Nano, 1728-1784. II. Title.

LEAHY, Maurice, 1900- 922.2415
The Flower of Her Kindred, a biographical study of Nano Nagle of Ireland, foundress, pioneer of popular education and noted leader in sociology in the eighteenth century, by Maurice Leahy, with a preface by His Grace the Most Reverend John J. Glennon... New York, N.Y., M. Leahy [1944] xv, 294 p. 21 cm. [BX4705.N2L4] 44-9000
I. Nagle, Nano, 1728-1784. II. Title.

MARY Thomas, Sister, P.B.V.M. 255'.977'0924 B
Not words but deeds; the story of Nano Nagle. Illustrated by Carolyn Lee Jagodits. Notre Dame, [Ind.] Dujarie Press [1968] 92 p. illus. 22 cm. A biography of the Irish woman who, despite the strictness of the English Penal Laws, opened schools for poor Catholic children, and founded the order of the Sisters of the Presentation. [PZ7.M3688No] 92 AC 68
1. Nagle, Nano, 1718-1784. I. Jagodits, Carolyn Lee, illus. II. Title.

O'CALLAGHAN, Rosaria. 271'.977'0924
Flame of love; a biography of Nano Nagle, foundress of the Presentation Order, 1718-1784. Milwaukee, Bruce Press [1960] 192p. illus. 23cm. (Catholic life publications) Includes bibliography. [BX4511.Z8N3] 61-1445
1. Nagie, Nano, 1718-1784. 2. Sisters of the Presentation of the Blessed Virgin Mary—Hist. I. Title.

O'CALLAGHAN, Rosaria. 271'.977'0924
Flame of love; a biography of Nano Nagle, foundress of the Presentation Order, 1718-1784. Milwaukee, Bruce Press [1960] 192p. illus. 23cm. (Catholic life publications) Includes bibliography. [BX4511.Z8N3] 61-1445
1. Nagie, Nano, 1718-1784. 2. Sisters of the Presentation of the Blessed Virgin Mary—Hist. I. Title.

Nahman ben Simhah, of Bratzlav, 1770?-1810?

FLEER, Gedaliah. 296.6'1 B
Rabbi Nachman's fire : an introduction to Breslover Chassidus / by Gedaliah Fleer. 2d, rev. ed. New York : Hermon Press, 1975, c1972. 110 p. ; 21 cm. [BM198.F56 1975] 75-20993 ISBN 0-87203-057-1 pbk. : 3.95
1. Nahman ben Somhah, of Bratzlav, 1770?-1810? 2. Bratslav Hasidim. I. Title.

GREEN, Arthur, 1941- 296.6'1'0924 B
Tormented master : a life of Rabbi Nahman of Bratslav. University : University of Alabama Press, 1979. p. cm. (Judaic studies series ; 9) Bibliography: p. [BM755.N25G73] 78-16674 ISBN 0-8173-6907-4 : 19.50
1. Nahman ben Simhah, of Bratzlav, 1770?-1810? 2. Rabbis—Poland—Biography. 3. Hasidim—Poland—Biography. I. Title. II. Series: Judaic studies ; 9.

GREEN, Arthur, 1941- 296.6'1'0924 B
Tormented master : a life of Rabbi Nahman of Bratslav / Arthur Green. New York : Schocken Books, 1981, c1979. viii, 395 p. : ill. ; 23 cm. Reprint of the 1979 ed. published by University of Alabama Press, University, which was issued as no. 9 of Judaic studies series. Includes indexes. Bibliography: p. 381-388. [BM755.N25G73 1981] 80-14668 ISBN 0-8052-0663-9 pbk. : 11.95
1. Nahman ben Simhah, of Bratzlav, 1770?-1810? 2. Rabbis—Poland—Biography. 3. Hasidim—Poland—Biography. I. Title. II. Series: Judaic studies ; 9.

NAHMAN ben Simhah, of Bratzlav, 1770?-1810? 296.8'33
Rabbi Nachman's wisdom: Shevachay haRan, Sichos haRan, by Nathan of Nemirov. Translated and annotated by Aryeh Kaplan. Edited by Zvi Aryeh Rosenfeld. [1st ed. Brooklyn, 1973] 458 p. illus. 24 cm. Translation of Shivhe ha-Ran. Includes bibliographical references. [BM198.N3313] 74-168205
1. Nahman ben Simhah, of Bratzlav, 1770?-1810? 2. Hasidism. 3. Tales, Hasidic. I. Nathan ben Naphtali Herz, of Nemirov, comp. II. Title.

Nahuas-Religion and mythology.

BURNING water;
thought and religion in ancient Mexico. With 82 drawings. New York, Grove Press [1960] 192p. illus. 21cm. First Evergreen edition.
1. Nahuas-Religion and mythology. 2. Quetzalcoatl. I. Sejourne, Laurette.

SEJOURNE, Laurette 299.7
Burning water; thought and religion in ancient Mexico. With 82 drawings [by Abel Mendoza] and 22 photographs. New York, Grove Press [1960] xiii, 192p. illus. 21cm. (Myth and man series: Evergreen ed. E-241) Bibl. notes, 1.95 pap.,
1. Nahuas—Religion and mythology. 2. Quetzalcoatl. I. Title.

Naipaul, V. States (Vidiadhar Surajprasad), 1932-

NAIPAUL, V. S. 1932- (Vidiadhar Surajprasad), 297'.095
Among the believers : an Islamic journey / V.S. Naipaul. 1st ed. New York : Knopf, 1981. p. cm. [BP63.A1N35] 19 81-47503 ISBN 0-394-50969-2 : 15.00
1. Naipaul, V. S. (Vidiadhar Surajprasad), 1932- 2. Islam—Asia. 3. Islamic countries—Description and travel. I. Title.

NAIPAUL, V. S. 1932- (Vidiadhar Surajprasad), 297'.095
Among the believers : an Islamic journey / V.S. Naipaul. 1st Vintage Books ed. New York : Vintage Books, 1982, c1981. viii, 430 p. ; 21 cm. Reprint. Originally published: New York : Knopf, 1981. [BP63.A1N35 1982] 19 82-40048 ISBN 0-394-71195-5 : 5.95
1. Naipaul, V. S. (Vidiadhar Surajprasad), 1932- 2. Islam—Asia. 3. Islamic countries—Description and travel. I. Title.

Names, Geographical—Palestine.

LIGHTFOOT, John, 1602-1675. 226'.06
A commentary on the New Testament from the Talmud and Hebraica, Matthew — I Corinthians / John Lightfoot ; [introd. by R. Laird Harris]. Grand Rapids, Mich. : Baker Book House, c1979- v. ; 23 cm. Reprint of the 1859 ed. published by Oxford University Press, Oxford, England, under title: Horae hebraicae et talmudicae. Originally written in Latin and published at intervals between 1658 and 1674. It is not known by whom the translation was made. Contents.Contents.—v. 1. Place names in the Gospels. [BS2335.L5313 1979] 79-126350 ISBN 0-8010-5590-3 : 45.00
1. Bible. N.T.—Commentaries. 2. Bible. N.T. Gospels—Names. 3. Talmud. 4. Names, Geographical—Palestine. I. Title.

Names, Personal.

GRUSSI, Alphonse Maria, 1859-
Chats on Christian names, by Rev. A. M. Grussi. Boston, Mass, The Stratford company, 1925. 3 p. l., 449 p. 20 cm. Reprinted from the Beechive, Perkin, iii. The volume is intended chiefly as a book for daily spiritual reading for Catholics. cf. Foreword. [C52367.G7] 25-5981
1. Names, Personal. I. Title.

SMYTH-VAUDRY, Telesphor, 1847-
A daily miracle in a name; or, The Catholic name, by T. Smyth-Vaudry ... (A new and enl. ed.) ... Techny. Ill., Printed by the Society of the Divine word [c1907] 3 p. l., [9]-269 p. 20 cm. 11-26262
I. Title.

SMYTH-VAUDRY, Telesphor, 1847-
... A daily miracle in a name; or, The Catholic name, by T. Smyth- Vaudry ... (A new and enl. ed.) ... San Antonio, Tex., Guessaz & Ferlet co., 1907. 3 p. l., [5]-220 p. 20 cm. At head of title: Notes on the divine plan of the church. 8-16405
I. Title.

Names, Personal—Jewish—Bibliography.

SINGERMAN, Robert. 016.9294
Jewish and Hebrew onomastics : a bibliography / Robert Singerman. New York : Garland Pub., 1977. p. cm. (Garland reference library of the humanities ; v. 92) Includes indexes. [Z6824.S5] [CS3010] 76-52684 ISBN 0-8240-9881-1 lib.bdg. : 17.50
1. Bible—Names—Bibliography. 2. Names, Personal—Jewish—Bibliography. I. Title.

Nanak, 1st guru of the Sikhs, 1469-1538.

MCLEOD, W. H. 294.5'53'0924 B
Guru Nanak and the Sikh religion [by] W. H. McLeod. Oxford, Clarendon P., 1968. xii, 259 p. 24 cm. Bibliography: p. 233-240. [BL2017.9.N3M27] 74-373992 50/-
1. Nanak, 1st guru of the Sikhs, 1469-1538. 2. Sikhism. I. Title.

Nanking. University.

WHEELER, William Reginald, 1889- 922.551
John E. Williams of Nanking, by W. Reginald Wheeler ... New York [etc.] Fleming H. Revell company [c1937] 222 p. front., plates, ports. 21 cm. [BV3427.W5W5] 37-5195
1. Williams, John Elias, 1871-1927. 2. Nanking. University. I. Title.

Nansa Valley, Spain—Religious life and customs.

CHRISTIAN, William A., 1944- 209'.46'1
Person and God in a Spanish valley [by] William A. Christian, Jr. New York, Seminar Press, 1972. xiii, 215 p. illus. 24 cm. (Studies in social discontinuity) Bibliography: p. 195-198. [BR1027.N36C56 1972] 72-7697 ISBN 0-12-816150-7 8.95
1. Nansa Valley, Spain—Religious life and customs. I. Title. II. Series.

Napoleon i, emperor of the French, 1769-1821.

ROBB, Stewart. 133.5
Nostradamus on Napoleon. Translated and interpreted by Stewart Robb. [1st American ed.] New York, Oracle Press [1961] 140p. illus. 21cm. [BF1815.N8R57 1961] 61-2913
1. Napoleon I, Emperor of the French, 1769-1821. I. Notredame, Michel de, 1503-1566. II. Title.

ROBB, Stewart. 133.3
Nostradamus on Napoleon, Hitler and the present crisis, by Stewart Robb ... New York, C. Scribner's sons, 1942. xii, 228 p. illus., plates, ports. 21 cm. "Bibliographical note": p. 217-218. [BF1815.N8R57 1942] 43-3310
1. Napoleon I, emperor of the French, 1769-1821. 2. Hitler, Adolf, 1889- I. Notredame, Michel de, 1503-1566. Les propheties. II. Title.

ROBB, Stewart. 133.3
Nostradamus on Napoleon, Hitler and the present crisis, by Stewart Robb ... New York C. Scribner's sons, 1941. xiv, 218 p. illus. (incl. map, facsims.) plates, ports., diagrs. 21 cm. "Bibliographical note": p. 217-218. [BF1815.N8R57] 159.9613 41-24922
1. Napoleon i, emperor of the French, 1769-1821. 2. Hitler, Adolf, 1889- I. Notredame, Michel de, 1503-1566. Les propheties. II. Title.

Narayanaswami Aiyar, K.

UPANISHADS. English. Selections. 294'.5'9218
Thirty minor Upanishads, including the Yoga Upanishads / [translated by] K. Narayansvami Aiyar. [El Reno, OK] : Santarasa Publications, 1980. p. cm. Reprint of the 1914 ed. published by K. Narayanasvami Aiyar, Madras. [BL1120.N37 1980] 79-27326 ISBN 0-935548-00-9 : 16.95
1. Narayanaswami Aiyar, K. I. Title.
Publishers Address: Mason Hall Apartments, 1420 W. Abingdon Dr., Apt. 237, Alexandria, VA 22314

Narcotic addicts—New York (State)—Brooklyn—Biography.

TORRES, Victor. 248'.2 B
Son of evil street / Victor Torres with Don Wilkerson. 2d ed. Minneapolis : Bethany Fellowship, 1977. 166 p. ; 18 cm. (Dimension books) [BV4935.T65A37 1977] 77-150672 ISBN 0-87123-516-1 pbk. : 1.95
1. Torres, Victor. 2. Narcotic addicts—New York (State)—Brooklyn—Biography. 3. Converts—New York (State)—Brooklyn—Biography. 4. Brooklyn—Biography. I. Wilkerson, Don, joint author. II. Title.

Narcotic addicts—Personal narratives.

TORRES, Victor. 248'.2 B
Son of evil street, by Victor Torres, with Don Wilkerson. Minneapolis, Bethany Followship [1973] 160 p. 21 cm. [BV4935.T65A37] 73-10828 ISBN 0-87123-516-1 1.95
1. Torres, Victor. 2. Narcotic addicts—Personal narratives. 3. Conversion. I. Title.

Narcotic habit.

BUNTING, Charles A. 178
Hope for the victims of alcohol, opium, morphine, cocaine, and other vices. A narrative of successful efforts during ten years of personal labor, devoted as Christ's instrument to redeem the slave of such habits, in the New York Christian home for intemperate men... By Charles A. Bunting... New York, Christian home building, 1888. 120, [4] p. 2 pl., 3 port. (incl. front.) 18 cm. [RC364.B94] 7-32791
1. Narcotic habit. 2. Alcoholism. I. New York Christian home for intemperate men, Mount Vernon, N.Y. II. Title.

Nardi, Michele, 1850-1914.

SIMPSON, Albert B., 1844- comp.
Michele Nardi, the Italian evangelist; his life and work, comp. by Rev. A. B. Simpson. New York, Blanche P. Nardi [c1916] 143 p. front., plates, ports. 18 1/2 cm. $0.75 16-13193
1. Nardi, Michele, 1850-1914. I. Title.

Naropa Institute.

LOKA : 294
a journal from Naropa Institute / edited by Rick Fields. 1st ed. Garden City, N.Y. : Anchor Press, 1975. 142 p. : ill. ; 28 cm. [BP605.N3L64] 74-31515 ISBN 0-385-02312-X : 4.00
1. Naropa Institute. I. Fields, Rick. II. Naropa Institute.

Narration in the Bible.

CULLEY, Robert C. 221.6'7
Studies in the structure of Hebrew narrative / by Robert C. Culley. Philadelphia : Fortress Press, c1976. vi, 122 p. ; 22 cm. (Semeia supplements) Bibliography: p. 119-122. [BS1205.2.C84] 75-37159 ISBN 0-8006-1504-2 pbk. : 3.95
1. Bible. O.T. Historical books—Criticism, Form. 2. Narration in the Bible. I. Title. II. Series.

RUNDQUIST, Alfred.
The dawn of truth; an exposition of Biblical narratives, by a layman ... Written and published by Alfred Rundquist. Chicago, Ill., 1915. 200 p. 20 cm. 15-24851 2.00

I. Title.

Nascapee Indians—Religion and mythology.

SPECK, Frank Gouldsmith, 1881-1950. 299'.7
Naskapi : the savage hunters of the Labrador peninsula / Frank G. Speck ; foreword by J. E. Michael Kew. New ed. Norman : University of Oklahoma Press, c1977. xii, 257 p. : ill. ; 24 cm. (The Civilization of the American Indian series ; v. 10) Includes bibliographical references and index. [E99.N18S7 1977] 77-365978 ISBN 0-8061-1412-6 : 8.95
1. Nascapee Indians—Religion and mythology. 2. Indians of North America—Newfoundland—Labrador—Religion and mythology. 3. Nascapee Indians—Hunting. 4. Indians of North America—Newfoundland—Labrador—Hunting. I. Title. II. Series.

Nash, Elsie.

THOMSON, Mary. 133.9'1'0924 B
To Elsie with love : an adventure into the unknown / by Mary Thomson. London ; New York : Regency Press, 1975. 160 p., plate : port. ; 23 cm. [BF1283.N3T47] 75-325201 ISBN 0-7212-0395-7 : 12.95
1. Nash, Elsie. 2. Spiritualism. I. Title.

Nash, John B., 1809-

TRIALS and travels of brother John Israel ... ex--John B. Nash, former "Gingseng king" ... [Los Angeles, Printed by Giles publishing co.] c1922. cover-title, 3-74 p. 17 cm. [BR1719.N3T7] 37-25843 922
1. Nash, John B., 1809-

Nashua, N.H. First Congregational church.

CHURCHILL, John Wesley, 1839-1900. 277.
History of the First church in Dunstable-Nashua, N.H., and of later churches there, as sketched by Prof. John Wesley Churchill in an address to the Nashua historical society, December 16, 1885, with an introduction and editorial notes and a biographic sketch of Prof. Churchill, by Charles Carroll Morgan. Boston, Mass., The Fort Hill press [c1918] xv, 99 p. plates, ports. 20 1/2 cm. [BR560.N25C5] 18-18801
1. Nashua, N.H. First Congregational church. 2. Nashua, N.H.—Churches. I. Morgan, Charles Carroll, 1832- ed. II. Title.

Nashville—Church history—Addresses, essays, lectures.

HOOPER, Robert E., 1932- 286'.63 B
A call to remember : chapters in Nashville restoration history / by Robert E. Hooper. [Nashville : Gospel Advocate Company], 1978, c1977 x, 111 p. ; 22 cm. Bibliography: p. 107-111. [BX7075.Z6N24] 78-101025 ISBN 0-89225-183-2 pbk. : 3.75
1. Churches of Christ—Tennessee—Nashville—History—Addresses, essays, lectures. 2. Lipscomb, David, 1831-1918—Addresses, essays, lectures. 3. David Lipscomb College, Nashville—History—Addresses, essays, lectures. 4. Nashville—Church history—Addresses, essays, lectures. I. Title.
Publisher's address : P.O. Box 150, Nashville, TN 37202

Nashville. First Baptist church.

BURROUGHS, Prince Emanuel, 1871- 286.1768
The spiritual conquest of the second frontier; the biography of an achieving church, 1820-1942, by P. E. Burroughs ... Nashville, Tenn., Broadman press [1942] x, 222 p. front., plates, ports., map. 23 cm. [BX6480.N3F5] 43-628
1. Nashville. First Baptist church. I. Title.

MAY, Lynn E. 286'.1'76855
The First Baptist Church of Nashville, Tennessee, 1820-1970 [by Lynn E. May, Jr. [Nashville, First Baptist Church, 1970] 331 p. illus., ports. 24 cm. Includes bibliographical references. [BX6480.N3F55] 72-136021
1. Nashville. First Baptist Church. I. Title.

Nason, Tara.

NASON, Donna. 248'.2 B
Tara, child of hopes & dreams / by Donna Nason. Wheaton, Ill. : Tyndale House Publishers, c1978. 223 p. : ill. ; 21 [RJ496.B7N37] 78-54087 ISBN 0-8423-6920-1 (pbk.) : 4.95
1. Nason, Tara. 2. Brain-damaged children—California—Orange Co.—Biography. 3. Christian biography—California—Orange Co. I. Title.

Nassau, Mrs. Mary Brunette (Foster) 1849-1884.

[NASSAU, Robert Hamill] 1835-1921. 922.
The path she trod, a memorial of Mary Brunette (Foster) Nassau, by her husband. Philadelphia, Press of Allen, Lane & Scott, 1909. 204 p., 1 l. ports. 24 cm. [BV3542.N28N3] 11-13347
1. Nassau, Mrs. Mary Brunette (Foster) 1849-1884. I. Title.

Nassau, Mrs. Mary Cloyd (Latta) 1831-1870.

[NASSAU, Robert Hamill] 1835-1921. 922.
Crowned in palm-land. A story of African mission life ... Philadelphia, J. B. Lippincott & co., 1874. 390 p. front. (port.) plates, map. 19 cm. A memoir of Mrs. Mary Cloyd Nassau. Genealogy of Latta family: p. 13-14. [BV3542.N3N3] 33-18572
1. Nassau, Mrs. Mary Cloyd (Latta) 1831-1870. 2. Latta family. 3. Missions—Africa. I. Title.

Nast, William, 1807-1899.

WITTKE, Carl Frederick, 1892- 922.743
William Nast, Patriarch of German Methodism, Detroit, Wayne State University Press, 1959 [c1960] 248 p. illus. 21 cm. Includes bibliography. [BX8495.N323W5] 60=5382
1. Nast, William, 1807-1899. I. Title.

Natchez-Jackson (Diocese)

PILLAR, James L. 282.762
The Catholic Church in Mississippi, 1837-65. New Orleans, Hauser [c.1964] xviii, 380p. illus., ports., maps. 24cm. Bibl. 63-23197 8.00
1. Natchez-Jackson (Diocese) 2. Catholic Church in Mississippi. I. Title.

PILLAR, James L. 282.762
The Catholic Church in Mississippi, 1837-65 New Orleans. Hauser Press, [1964] xviii, 380 p. illus. ports., maps. 24 cm. Bibliography: p. [349]-359. [BX1415.M7P5] 63-23197
1. Natchez-Jackson (Diocese) 2. Catholic Church in Mississippi. I. Title.

TENTH Diocesan Synod, Diocese of Natchez-Jackson, held in St. Peter's Co-cathedral, Jackson, May 23, 1957. [Presided over by Most Reverend R. O. Gerow] [Natchez, Miss., 1957] ix, 113p. 23cm.
I. Natchez-Jackson, Miss. (Diocese) Synod. 10th, 1957. II. Gerow, Richard Oliver, Bp., 1885-

Natchez, Miss. Cathedral of Our Lady of sorrows.

GEROW, Richard Oliver, bp., 1885- 282.762
Cradle days of St. Mary's at Natchez, by Most Rev. R. O. Gerow ... Natchez, Miss. 1941. xiii, 302 p. incl. front. plates, ports. 24 cm. Bibliography: p. 281-184. [BX4603.N34A3] 41-32557
1. Natchez, Miss. Cathedral of Our Lady of sorrows. I. Title.

Natchez, Miss. Trinity church.

STIETENROTH, Charles. 283.762
One hundred years with "Old Trinity" church, Natchez, Miss., by Chas. Stietenroth. Natchez, Miss., Natchez printing & stationery co., 1922. 77 p. front., plates, ports., facsim. 26 1/2 cm. [BX5980.N27T7] 263.762 35-22769 35-22760
1. Natchez, Miss. Trinity church. I. Title.

Nathdwara, India—Religious life and customs.

JINDEL, Rajendra. 301.5'8
Culture of a sacred town : a sociological study of Nathdwara / Rajendra Jindel. Bombay : Popular Prakashan, 1976. ix, 233 p., [2] leaves of plates : ill. ; 23 cm. A revision of the authoress' thesis, University of Rajasthan, 1970. Includes index. Bibliography: p. 221-228. [BL1227.N36A16 1976] 76-905789 Rs45.00
1. Nathdwara, India—Religious life and customs. 2. Hindu shrines—India—Nathdwara. I. Title.

National association for the promotion of holiness. Missionary society.

CARY, William Walter, 1887- 275.1
... *Story of the National holiness missionary society*, by W. W. Cary ... Chicago, Ill., National holiness missionary society, 1940. xii, 353 p. double front, plates, ports., maps. 20 cm. Bibliography: p. 351-353. [BV2360.N35C3] 266.99 42-28772
1. National association for the promotion of holiness. Missionary society. 2. Missions—China. I. Title.

National Association of Evangelicals.

SHELLEY, Bruce Leon, 1927- 269
Evangelicalism in America, by Bruce L. Shelley. Grand Rapids, Eerdmans [1967] 134 p. 21 cm. Bibliographical references included in "Notes" (p. 133-134) [BR513.S5] 67-21466
1. National Association of Evangelicals. 2. Evangelicalism—United States. I. Title.

National Association of Temple Educators. Survey Committee.

RELIGIOUS school organization and administration. New York, National Association of Temple Educators, U. A. H. C., 1961. xvii, 120p. charts. 28cm. (Educational Research Survey, no. 3) Cover title. Nate survey committee.
1. National Association of Temple Educators. Survey Committee. I. Bennett, Alan D II. Series.

National Baptist Convention of the United States of America—Collected works.

MORRIS, E. C., 1855- 286'.133
Sermons, addresses, and reminiscences, and important correspondence / E. C. Morris. New York : Arno Press, 1980. 322 p. : ill. ; 23 cm. (The Baptist tradition) Reprint of the 1901 ed. published by the National Baptist Pub. Board, Nashville. [BX6447.M67 1980] 79-52598 ISBN 0-405-12465-1 : 24.00
1. National Baptist Convention of the United States of America—Collected works. 2. Morris, E. C., 1855- 3. National Baptist Convention of the United States of America—Clergy—Directories. 4. Afro-American Baptists—Portraits. I. Title. II. Series: Baptist tradition.

National Baptist Convention of the United States of America. Foreign Mission Board—History.

FREEMAN, Edward Anderson, 1914- 266'.6'133
The epoch of Negro Baptists and the Foreign Mission Board / Edward A. Freeman. New York : Arno Press, 1980, [c1953] xv, 301 p. ; 24 cm. (The Baptist tradition) Reprint of the ed. published by Central Seminary Press, Kansas City. Bibligraphy: p. 219-224. [BV2521.F73 1980] 79-52593 ISBN 0-405-12460-0 : 23.00
1. National Baptist Convention of the United States of America. Foreign Mission Board—History. 2. Afro-American Missionaries. 3. Afro-American Baptists—Missions. I. Title. II. Series: Baptist tradition.

National Baptist Convention of the United States of America—History.

JACKSON, Joseph Harrison, 1900- 286'.133
A story of Christian activism : the history of the National Baptist Convention, U.S.A., inc. / by J. H. Jackson. Nashville, Tenn. : Townsend Press, 1980. p. cm. Includes index. Bibliography: p. [BX6443.J28] 80-17408 ISBN 0-935990-01-1 : 19.50
1. National Baptist Convention of the United States of America—History. I. Title.

PELT, Owen D 286.173
The story of the National Baptists, by Owen D. Pelt and Ralph Lee Smith. [1st ed.] New York, Vantage Press [1960] 272p. illus. 22cm. Includes bibliography. [BX6443.P4] 60-15470
1. National Baptist Convention of the United States of America—Hist. I. Smith, Ralph Lee, joint author. II. Title.

National Baptist Memorial Church, Washington, D.C.

WANN, John L. 286'.1753
A compilation and history of National Baptist Memorial Church (formerly Immanuel Baptist Church), Washington, D.C., 1906 to about 1976 / by John L. Wann. [Washington : s.n.], c1976. ix, 459 p. : ill. ; 24 cm. [BX6480.W3N378] 76-150944
1. National Baptist Memorial Church, Washington, D.C. I. Title: A compilation and history of National Baptist Memorial Church (formerly Immanuel Baptist Church) ...

National Benevolent Association.

BURKE, Jessie May, ed.
Benevolence. Edited by Jessie M. Burke. [St. Louis, National Benevolent Association of the Christian pchurches (Disciples of Christ) 1960] 62 p. Cover title. "Published . . . at the request of Decade of decision committee through the Council of agencies." 64-60176
1. National Benevolent Association. 2. Decade of Decision. I. Disciples of Christ. Council of Agencies. II. Title.

National Benevolent Association of the Christian church.

THE concern for benevolence among Disciples of Christ, a study course for older young people and adults. St. Louis, National Benevolent Association of the Christian Churches (Disciples of Christ) and the Christian Board of Publication [1957] 60p. 22cm.
1. National Benevelont Association of the Christian Church. 2. Disciples of Christ—Charities. I. Moseley, Joseph Edward, 1910-

THE concern for benevolence among Disciples of Christ, a study course for older young people and adults. St. Louis, National Benevolent Association of the Christian Churches (Disciples of Christ) and the Christian Board of Publication [1957] 60p. 22cm.
1. National Benevelont Association of the Christian Church. 2. Disciples of Christ — Charities. I. Moseley, Joseph Edward, 1910-

National Bible Society of Scotland.

THE lively oracles ...
Illus. by Robert Hodgson. London, New York, Thomas Nelson [1959] 186p. illus. 23cm.

1. National Bible Society of Scotland. I. McFarlan, Donald Maitland.

National Catholic Welfare Conference. Catholic Relief Services.

EGAN, Eileen Mary, 1922-
The works of peace, by Eileen Egan. Introd. by Patrick A. O'Boyle. Afterword by Barbara Ward. New York, Sheed and Ward [1965] xi, 212 p. 22 cm.
1. National Catholic Welfare Conference. Catholic Relief Services. I. Title.

SIXTEEN encyclicals of 282.081
His Holiness Pope Pius xi, 1926-1937. [Washington, D. C., National Catholic welfare conference, 1938] [553] p. 19 cm. Without general t.-p.: title taken from cover. Each item has special t.-p. and separate paging. [BX860.A45] 40-34102
I. National Catholic welfare conference. II. Catholic church. Pope, 1922-1939 (Pius xi)
Contents omitted.

National Catholic women's union.

LUTZ, Bernard E. 267.442
The National Catholic women's union, a quarter-century of effort and achievement, by Bernard E. Lutz ... St. Louis, Mo., 1941. 2 p. l., 7-108, 1 p. illus. (incl. ports.) 24 cm. [BX810.N3L8] 42-17404
1. National Catholic women's union. I. Title.

National committee on Congregational young people.

STOCK, Harry Thomas. 285.
A year's program for young people [by] Harry Thomas Stock ... with the collaboration of the National committee on Congregational young people. Boston, Chicago, The Pilgrim press [c1926] xii, 82 p. 19 1/2 cm. [BX7105.N3S7] 26-22092
1. National committee on Congregational young people. I. Title.

National Conference on Church and State. 15th, Denver, 196-?

PROTESTANTS and Other Americans United for Separation of Church and State.
The current challenge to church-state separation. Selected addresses from the 15th National Conference on Church and State, Denver, Colorado. [Washington D. C.] Protestants and other Americans United for Separation of Church and State [196-] 61 p. 68-41372
1. National Conference on Church and State. 15th, Denver, 196-? I. Title.

National convention of Methodist men, Indianapolis, 1913.

DOWNEY, David George, 287.606373
1838-1935, ed.
Militant Methodism; the story of the first National convention of Methodist men, held at Indianapolis, Indiana, October twenty-eight to thirty-one, nineteen hundred and thirteen ... Edited by David G. Downey, E. W. Halford [and] Ralph Welles Keeler. Cincinnati, New York, The Methodist book concern [1913] 379 p. 21 cm. [BX8207.N4 1913] 31-35777
1. National convention of Methodist men, Indianapolis, 1913. 2. Methodist Episcopal church. I. Halford, Elijah Walker, 1843- joint ed. II. Keeler, Ralph Welles, 1877- joint ed. III. Title.

National Council of Juvenile Court Judges.

LIPPITT, Gordon L
Judges look at themselves; a new approach to judicial education. The first year's evaluation study of the National Council of Juvenile Court Judges training University, 1963. 171 p. forms. 28 cm. 66-87944
1. National Council of Juvenile Court Judges. 2. Judges. 3. Juvenile courts. I. McCune, Shirley, joint author. II. George Washington University, Washington, D.C. Center for the Behavioral Sciences. III. Title.

National Council of the Churches of Christ in the U.S.A Department of

NATIONAL Study Conference on the Church and Ecobomic Life. 3d, Pittsburgh,1956.
American abundance; Ossibilities and problems from the perspective of the Christian conscience. Message and reports. New York, Dept. of the Church and Economic Life, National Council of the Churches of Christ in the U.S.A [1956?] 63 p. 65-57889
1. National Council of the Churches of Christ in the U.S.A Dept. of I. Title.

National Council of the Churches of Christ in the United States of America.

CHURCH League of America. 261.8
The record of the National Council of Churches. Wheaton, Ill. [1969] 161 p. 28 cm. [BX6.N2C49] 73-289636 3.00
1. National Council of the Churches of Christ in the United States of America. I. Title.

THE emerging perspective;
response and prospect. With an introd. by Glenn W. Moore. Proceedings of the conference on the churches and social welfare. [New York] National Council of the Churches of Christ in the U.S.A., [1956] xvi, 303p. (Churches and social welfare, vol.3)
1. National Council of the Churches of Christ in the United States of America. I. Bachmann, Emest Theodore, ed.

THE emerging perspective;
response and prospect. With an introd. by Glenn W. Moore. Proceedings of the conference on the churches and social welfare. [New York] National Council of the Churches of Christ in the U. S. A., [1956] xvi, 303p. (Churches and social welfare, vol. 3)
1. National Council of the Churches of Christ in the United States of America. I. Bachmann, Emest Theodore, ed.

ERVIN, Spencer, 1886- ed. 283.73
The Episcopal Church in the United States and the National Council of Churches. Bala-Cynwyd, Pa., 1954. 69p. 24cm. [BX6.N2E7] 55-3566
1. National Council of the Churches of Christ in the United States of America. 2. Protestant Episcopal Church in the U. S .A. 3. Protestantism. I. Title.

KNOCK and it shall be opened
unto you; refugee resettlement program 1953-1957. July/August 1957. New York [c1957] 61p. illus. 22cm.
I. National Council of the Churches of Christ in the United States of America. Central Dept. of Church World Service.

MCINTIRE, Carl, 1906- ed.
Eugene Carson Blake, the chief church spokesman for leftist causes. How the leading American churchman has aided communist causes especially through the National Council of Churches. [Collingswood, N.J., 20th Century Reformation Hour, n.d.] 71 p. illus. 31 cm. (20th Century Reformation Hour. Scrapbook no. 6) Cover title. 68-54524
1. National Council of the Churches of Christ in the United States of America. I. Title.

METHODIST Church (United 262'.001
States). Committee Appointed to Study the National Council of the Churches of Christ in the U.S.A.
Report to the South Carolina Annual Conference, Southeastern Jurisdiction of the Methodist Church. [Columbia? S.C.] 1965. 95 p. 23 cm. Bibliography: p. 61-69. [BX6.N2M45] 75-19322
1. National Council of the Churches of Christ in the United States of America. I. Methodist Church (United States). Conferences. South Carolina. II. Title.

METROPOLITAN 286'.673
Nicolai—agent in Soviet Secret Police; how the Communists are using the National Council of the Churches of Christ in the United States of America. [Compiled by Carl McIntire. Collingswood, N.J., 20th Century Reformation Hour, 1959] 70 p. illus. 31 cm. [BX6.N2M46] 73-172526
1. National Council of the Churches of Christ in the United States of America. 2. Nikolai, Metropolitan of Krututsy and Kolomna, 1892-1961. 3. Communism and Christianity. I. McIntire, Carl, 1906- comp.

MURCH, James DeForest, 280'.4'09B
1892-
The Protestant revolt; road to freedom for American churches. Foreword by Edmund A. Opitz. Arlington, Va., Crestwood Books, 1967. 326 p. ports. 21 cm. [BR516.M82] 67-21695
1. National Council of the Churches of Christ in the United States of America. 2. Protestant churches—United States. I. Title.

NATIONAL Convocation on the Church in Town and Country, St. Louis, 1956.
New horizons for town and country churches. [New York, Department of Town and Country Church, Division of Home Missions, National Council of the Churches of Christ in the U.S.A., 1956] iv, 116 p. 20 cm. Rural churches -- Congresses. 63-34681
I. National Council of the Churches of Christ in the United States of America. Dept. of Town and Country Church. II. Title.

NATIONAL Council of the 266.06273
Churches of Christ in the United States of America. Division of Foreign Missions.
Report. 2d- 1952- New York. v. illus. 23-28cm. annual. The Minutes of the division's first meeting are included in v. 57 (1950) of the Report of the Foreign Missions Conference on North America. Includes Report of the 58th- meetings of the Foreign Missions Conference of North America. [BV2390.N273] 55-43961
I. Title.

NATIONAL Council of the 280.6273
Churches of Christ in the United States of America. General Board. National Lay Committee.
The chairman's final report to the members of the National Lay Committee. June 16, 1950-June 30, 1955. [J. Howard Pew, chairman. Philadelphia? 1955?] xi, 316p. 24cm. [BX6.N2A457] 60-19256
I. Pew, John Howard. 1882- II. Title.

PRATT, Henry J., 1934- 286'.6'73
The liberalization of American Protestantism; a case study in complex organizations [by] Henry J. Pratt. Detroit, Wayne State University Press, 1972. 303 p. 24 cm. Bibliography: p. [293]-299. [BX6.N2P7] 74-38837 ISBN 0-8143-1475-9 15.95
1. National Council of the Churches of Christ in the United States of America. 2. Christianity and politics. I. Title.

SEARCH: a national consultation
on personnel needs in church planning and research. Sponsored by the Division of Home Missions and the Bureau of Research and Survey of the National Council of the Churches of Christ, and made possible by a grant from the Lilly Endowment, inc. [New York, Published for the Division of Home Missions, National Council of the Churches of Christ in the U. S. A., by the Office of Publication and Distribution, 1960] x, 133p. diagr. 22cm. 'A report of the National Consultation on Personnel Needs in Church Planning and Research.'
I. Norton, Perry L ed.

SINGER, Charles Gregg, 262'.001
1910-
The unholy alliance : a study of the National Council of Churches / C. Gregg Singer. New Rochelle, N.Y. : Arlington House, [1975] p. cm. Includes index. Bibliography: p. [BX6.N2S56] 75-11598 ISBN 0-87000-327-5 : 11.95
1. National Council of the Churches of Christ in the United States of America. 2. Federal Council of the Churches of Christ in America. I. Title.

THIRD National Study Conference
on the Church and Economic Life. Pittsburgh, Pennsylvania, April 12-15, 1956. Theme: The Christian conscience and an economy of abundance. Conference message and group reports. New York, Published for Dept. of the Church and Economic Life, Division of Christian Life and Work, National Council of the Churches of Christ in the U. S. A. by the Office of Publication and Distribution [1956?] 63p. 22cm. Cover title: American abundance, possibilities and problems from the perspective of the Christian conscience.
I. National Council of the Churches of Christ in the United States of America. Dept. of the Church and Economic Life.

TULGA, Chester Earl, 280.6273
1896-
The case against the National Council of Churches. Chicago, Conservative Baptist Fellowship [1951] 60 p. 18 cm. (His Little books on big subjects) [BX6.N218T8] 51-7432
1. National Council of the Churches of Christ in the United States of America. I. Title.

National Council of the Churches of Christ in the United States of America. General Board.

ESPY, R H Edwin.
Church-state policies and the National Council of Churches. Statement to the General Board New York City, June 2, 1966. [New York, 1966] 1 v. 68-42934
1. National Council of the Churches of Christ in the United States of America. General Board. I. Title.

National council of the Congregational churches of the United States—History

HOOD, Edmund Lyman, 1858-1931.
The National council of Congregational churches of the United States, by Rev. E. Lyman Hood... Boston, Chicago, The Pilgrim press [1901] 253 p. front. (port.) 19 1/2 cm. [BX7107.A54] 3-3894
1. National council of the Congregational churches of the United States—Hist. I. Title.

NATIONAL council of
Congregational churches, Boston, 1865.
Debates and proceedings of the National council of Congregational churches, held at Boston, Mass., June 14-24, 1865. From the phonographic report by J. M. W. Yerrinton and Henry M. Parkhurst. Boston, American Congregational association, 1866. xlv p., 1 l., 530 p. 24 cm. [BX7107.A4 1865] 10-27514
I. Yerrinton, James M. W., d. 1893, reporter. II. Parkhurst, Henry Martyn, 1825- joint reporter. III. Title.

NATIONAL council of the 285.873
Congregational churches of the U. S.
The National council digest; a compilation of all the important acts of the National council of Congregational churches in the United States, with page references to statements and reports, from the date of its organization at Oberlin, Ohio, on November 17, 1871, and incorporating a revision of the issue of 1905 by Asher Anderson, D. D., by Charles Emerson Burton ... Published under direction of the Executive committee of the National council.New York, N. Y. [Boston, Chicago, The Pilgrim press] 1930. 347 p. 24 cm. [BX7107.A45 1930] 33-15324
I. Anderson, Asher, 1846-1925, ed. II. Burton, Charles Emerson, 1869-1940, ed. III. Title.

National Federation of Priests' Councils.

STEWART, James H, 1927- 282'.73
American Catholic leadership : a decade of turmoil 1966-1976 : a sociological analysis of the National Federation of Priests' Councils / James H. Stewart. 2514 GC 's-Gravenhage, [Noordeinde 41] : Mouton, 1978. xx, 200 p. ; 23 cm. (Religion and society ; 11) Bibliography: p. [193]-199. [BX1407.C6S74] 78-326261 ISBN 9-02-797884-0 pbk. : 14.70
1. National Federation of Priests' Councils. I. Title. II. Series: Religion and society (The Hague) ; 11.
Available from Mouton, New York.

National Federation of Priests' Councils—History.

BROWN, Francis F., 1916- 262'.14
Priests in council : a history of the National Federation of Priests' Councils / Francis F. Brown. Kansas City, Kan. : Andrews and McMeel, c1979. xxvi, 184 p. ; 24 cm. Includes bibliographical references and index. [BX1407.C6B76] 79-18906 ISBN 0-8362-3301-8 : 20.00
1. National Federation of Priests' Councils—History. I. Title.

National Fellowship of Brethren Churches — History

KENT, Homer A 289.92
250 years conquering frontiers; a history of the Brethren Church. Winona Lake, Ind., Brethren Missionary Herald Co. [1958] 233p. illus. 23cm. [BX7829.N33K4] 286.5 58-38245
1. National Fellowship of Brethren Churches—Hist. I. Title.

KENT, Homer Austin, 1898- 286'.5
Conquering frontiers; a history of the Brethren Church (the National Fellowship of Brethren Churches) by Homer A. Kent, Sr. [Rev. ed.] Winona Lake, Ind., BMH Books [1972] 245 p. illus. 24 cm. 1958 ed. published under title: 250 years conquering frontiers. Bibliography: p. 228-230. [BX7829.N33K4 1972] 72-187886
1. National Fellowship of Brethren Churches—History. I. Title.

National Holiness Association.

ROSE, Delbert R. 287.673
A theology of Christian experience; interpreting the historic Wesleyan message. Minneapolis, Bethany [c.1965] 314p. ports. 22cm. Bibl. [BX6.N42R6] 65-20789 4.95
1. Smith, Joseph H. 2. National Holiness Association. I. Title.

ROSE, Delbert R 287.673
A theology of Christian experience; interpreting the historic Wesleyan message, by Delbert R. Rose. [2d ed.] Minneapolis, Bethany Fellowship [1965] 314 p. ports. 22 cm. Revision of thesis, State University of Iowa. Bibliography: p. 307-314. [BX6.N42R6] 65-20789
1. Smith, Joseph H. 2. National Holiness Association. I. Title.

National Jewish Welfare Board. Jewish Center Division.

PERETZ, Isaac Loeb, 892.4081
1851-1915.
Isaac Loeb Peretz; a source book for programming, compiled and edited by Philip Goodman. New York, Jewish Center Division, National Jewish Welfare Board, c1951. 64 p. illus. 29 cm. "Issued on the occasion of the one hundredth anniversary of the birth of Peretz." [PJ5129.P4A6 1951] 52-9114
1. National Jewish Welfare Board. Jewish Center Division. I. Title.

National Lutheran Council.

WENTZ, Frederick K. 284'.173
Lutherans in concert; the story of the National Lutheran Council, 1918-1966 [by] Frederick K. Wentz. Minneapolis, Augsburg Pub. House [1968] ix, 221 p. illus., ports. 22 cm. Bibliography: p. 199-200. [BX8041.A44] 68-13727
1. National Lutheran Council. 2. Lutheran Church in the U.S. I. Title.

National Lutheran Educational Conference.

WICKEY, Gould, 1891- 377.8'41
Lutheran cooperation through Lutheran higher education; a documentary history of the National Lutheran Educational Conference, 1910-1967. Washington, Lutheran Educational Conference of North America, 1967. xii, 185 p. illus., ports. 24 cm. [LC573.N3W5] 67-21390
1. National Lutheran Educational Conference. I. Title.

National seminar of Catholics, Jews and Protestants. 1st, Washington, D. C., 1932.

LASKER, Bruno, 1880- 206.373
Religious liberty and mutual understanding; an interpretation of the National seminar of Catholics, Jews and Protestants, Washington, D. C., March 7-9, 1932, by Bruno Lasker. New York city, The National conference of Jews and Christians [1932] 76 p. 23 cm. [BL21.N3 1932 d] 32-26996
1. National seminar of Catholics, Jews and Protestants. 1st, Washington, D. C., 1932. 2. Religions—Congresses. 3. Religious liberty. 4. Toleration. I. National conference of Jews and Christians. II. Title.

National socialism.

WIENER, Peter F.
... Martin Luther Hitler's spiritual ancestor, by Peter F. Wiener ... London, New York [etc.] Hutchinson & co., ltd. [1945] 34 p. 18 1/2 cm. (Win the peace pamphlet, no. 3) A45
1. Luther, Martin, 1483-1546. 2. National socialism. I. Title.

National songs, American—History and criticism.

WELCH, Helena. 783.9'5'2
Songs to sing forever. Nashville, Southern Pub. Association [1968] 79 p. 22 cm. Includes each song in 4-pt. harmony. [ML3551.W45] 68-30795
1. National songs, American—History and criticism. 2. Hymns, English—History and criticism. I. Title.

National Study Conference on the Church and Economic Life, 4th, Pittsburgh, 1962.

NATIONAL Study Conference on the Church and Economic Life. 4th, Pittsburgh,1962.
The church in a world that won't hold still;-general and group reports. [New York, Published for Dept. of the Church and Economic Life, National Council of the Churches of Christ in the U.S.a., by the Office of Publication and Distribution, 1962] 64 p. Cover title. 65-57890
I. Title.

OBENHAUS, Victor.
The churches and change; the significance of technology and rapid economic development for Christian faith and life today; report and interpretation of The Fourth National Study Conference on The Church and Economic Life. [n.p., 1962?] 1514-1536 p. Supplement to the Christian Century, Dec. 12, 1962. 65-22764
1. National Study Conference on the Church and Economic Life, 4th, Pittsburgh, 1962. I. Title.

Nationalism and religion.

BARON, Salo Wittmayer, 1895- 291
Modern nationalism and religion. New York, Meridian Books [1960, c1947] 363p. 21cm. (Jewish Publications Society series, JP18) [BL65.N3B3 1960] 60-14922
1. Nationalism and religion. I. Title.

BARON, Salo Wittmayer, 261.7
1895-
Modern nationalism and religion. Freeport, N.Y., Books for Libraries Press [1971, c1947] x, 363 p. 24 cm. (Essay index reprint series) Includes bibliographical references. [BL65.N3B3 1971] 79-134050 ISBN 0-8369-2142-9
1. Nationalism and religion. I. Title.

BARON, Salo Wittmayer, 1895- 291
Modern nationalism and religion. [1st ed.] New York, Harper [1947] x, 363 p. 25 cm. (Rauschenbusch lectures, Colgate-Rochester Divinity School, Rochester, N.Y.) Bibliographical references included in "Notes" (p. [273]-349) [BL65.N3B3] 47-11474
1. Nationalism and religion. I. Title.

KOENKER, Ernest Benjamin 261.7
Secular salvations; the rites and smybols of political religions. Philadelphia, Fortress [c.1965] xii, 220p. 22cm. Bibl. [BL65.N3K6] 65-22554 3.75
1. Nationalism and religion. 2. Rites and ceremonies—Germany. 3. Rites and ceremonies—Communist countries. I. Title.

WOOD, James Edward. 322'.1
The problem of nationalism in church-state relationships, by James E. Wood, Jr. Scottdale, Pa., Herald Press [1969] 31 p. 20 cm. (Focal pamphlet no. 18) Reprinted from a Journal of church and state, Spring 1968. Bibliography: p. 29. [BL65.N3W65] 74-12014
1. Nationalism and religion. 2. Church and state. I. Title.

Nationalism and religion—Asia, Southeastern.

VON DER MEHDEN, Fred R 261.7
Religion and nationalism in Southeast Asia: Burma, Indonesia, the Philippines. Madison, University of Wisconsin Press, 1963. 253 p. illus. 23 cm. [BL65.N3V6] 63-13743
1. Nationalism and religion—Asia, Southeastern. 2. Asia, Southeastern—Religion. I. Title.

VON DER MEHDEN, Fred R. 261.7
Religion and nationalism in Southeast Asia: Burma, Indonesia, the Philippines. Madison, University of Wisconsin Press, 1963. 253 p. illus. 23 cm. [BL65.N3V6] 63-13743
1. Nationalism and religion—Asia, Southeastern. 2. Asia, Southeastern—Religion. I. Title.

Nationalism and religion—Philippine Islands.

DEATS, Richard L. 279.14
Nationalism and Christianity in the Philippines [by] Richard L. Deats. Dallas, Southern Methodist University Press [1968, c1967] ix, 207 p. 24 cm. Bibliography: p. [181]-200. [BR1260.D4] 67-28035
1. Nationalism and religion—Philippine Islands. 2. Missions—Philippine Islands. 3. Indigenous church administration. 4. Philippine Islands—Church history. I. Title.

Nationalism and religion—Rome.

GRANT, Robert McQueen, 270.1
1917-
The sword and the cross. New York, Macmillan, 1955. 144 p. 22 cm. [BL805.G7] 55-806
1. Nationalism and religion—Rome. 2. Rome—Religion. 3. Church history—Primitive and early church. I. Title.

GUTERMAN, Simeon 322'.1'0937
Leonard, 1907-
Religious toleration and persecution in ancient Rome, by Simeon L. Guterman. Westport, Conn., Greenwood Press [1971] 160 p. 23 cm. Reprint of the 1951 ed. Includes bibliographical references. [BL805.G8 1971] 70-104269 ISBN 0-8371-3936-8
1. Nationalism and religion—Rome. 2. Judaism—Relations—Roman. 3. Rome—Religion. 4. Persecution—Early church, ca. 30-600. I. Title.

Nationalism and religion—U.S.

HUDSON, Winthrop Still, 260.7
1911- comp.
Nationalism and religion in America: concepts of American identity and mission, edited by Winthrop S. Hudson. [1st ed.] New York, Harper & Row [1970] xxxiii, 211 p. 21 cm. (Harper forum books, RD 10) Includes bibliographical references. [BL65.N3H8 1970] 76-109063 3.50
1. Nationalism and religion—U.S. 2. Messianism, American. 3. Religion and state—U.S. I. Title.

PETERSEN, Arnold, 1885- 261.73
Theocracy for democracy? By Arnold Petersen. New York, N.Y., New York labor news company, 1944. 191 p. illus. (incl. ports., facsims.) 24 cm. The major portion of this volume appeared in Socialist labor party. Fifty years of American Marxism. cf. book-jacket. [BR516.P4] A 44
1. Nationalism and religion—U.S. 2. Theocracy. 3. Democracy. I. Title.
Contents omitted.

Nationalism—Biblical teaching.

CHRISTENSEN, Duane L. 224'.06'6
Transformations of the war oracle in Old Testament prophecy : studies in the oracles against the nations / by Duane L. Christensen. Missoula, Mont. : Published by Scholars Press for Harvard theological review, 1976c1975 xii, 305 p. : maps ; 22 cm. (Harvard dissertations in religion ; no. 3) Originally presented as the author's thesis, Harvard, 1971. Bibliography: p. 285-305. [BS1199.N3C4 1975] 75-34264 ISBN 0-89130-064-3 pbk. : 6.00
1. Bible. O.T. Prophets—Criticism, interpretation, etc. 2. Bible. O.T. Prophets—History of contemporary events, etc. 3. Nationalism—Biblical teaching. 4. War—Biblical teaching. I. Title. II. Series.

Nationalism—India.

MOOKERJI, Radha Kumud, 294.51
1884-
Nationalism in Hindu culture. 2d ed. Delhi, S. Chand [1957] ii, 104p. 19cm. [DS423.M55 1957] SA66 2.50 bds.,
1. Nationalism—India. 2. Civilization, Hindu. I. Title.
Available from Verry in Mystic, Conn.

PANDEY, Dhanpati. 320.9'54'035
The Arya Samaj and Indian nationalism, 1875-1920. Foreword by Dukhan Ram. [1st ed.] New Delhi, S. Chand [1972] xi, 203 p. 23 cm. Bibliography: p. 195-203. [BL1253.P36] 72-906205
1. Arya-samaj. 2. Nationalism—India. I. Title.
Dist. by Verry, 7.50.

Nationalism—Jews.

FARMER, William Reuben. 933
Maccabees, Zealots, and Josephus; an inquiry into Jewish nationalism in the Greco-Roman period. Westport, Conn., Greenwood Press [1973, c1956] xiv, 239 p. 22 cm. Reprint of the ed. published by Columbia University Press, New York. Bibliography: p. [211]-220. [DS109.912.F37 1973] 73-15052 ISBN 0-8371-7152-0 11.25
1. Jews—History—168 B.C.-135 A.D. 2. Josephus, Flavius. 3. Bible. N.T.—History of contemporary events, etc. 4. Nationalism—Jews. I. Title.

Native American Church of North America.

MARRIOTT, Alice Lee, 1910- 299'.7
Peyote [by] Alice Marriott and Carol K. Rachlin. New York, Crowell [1971] x, 111 p. illus. 22 cm. Bibliography: p. 99-102. [E98.R3M3 1971] 75-146284 ISBN 0-690-61697-X 6.95
1. Native American Church of North America. 2. Peyotism. I. Rachlin, Carol K., joint author. II. Title.

SLOTKIN, James Sydney, 299'.7
1913-1958.
The peyote religion : a study in Indian-white relations / J. S. Slotkin. New York : Octagon Books, 1975, c1956. vii, 195 p. : ill. ; 24 cm. Reprint of the ed. published by the Free Press, Glencoe, Ill. Bibliography: p. 143-187. [E98.R3S5 1975] 74-23409 ISBN 0-374-97480-2 : 10.50

1. Native American Church of North America. 2. Peyotism. 3. Indians of North America—Government relations. I. Title.

Nativistic movements.

LANTERNARI, Vittorio. 290
The religions of the oppressed; a study of modern messianic cults. Translated from the Italian by Lisa Sergio. [1st American ed.] New York, Knopf, 1963. 343 p. 22 cm. Translation of Movimenti religiosi di liberta e di salvezza dei popoli oppressi. Includes bibliography. [BL85.L363 1963] 62-15568
1. Nativistic movements. I. Title.

Nativistic movements—India.

FUCHS, Stephen 275.4
Rebellious prophets; a study of messianic movements in Indian religions. New York, Asia Pub. [dist., Taplinger, 1966, c.1965] vix, 304p. 23cm. (Pubns. of the Indian branch of the Anthropos Inst., no. 1) Title. (Series: Anthropos Institute. Indian Branch. Publications, no. 1) Bibl. [BL2015.N3F8] 66-3997 10.75
1. Nativistic movements—India. 2. India—Religion. I. Title. II. Series.

Natural law.

DOW, Lorenzo, 1777-1834. 267.
A journey from Babylon to Jerusalem, or The road to peace and true happiness: prefaced with An essay on the rights of man. By Lorenzo Dow. It being the essence of twenty years experience, observations and reflections ... Lynchburg, Va., Printed by Haas & Lamb, 1812. 96, 143, [2] p. front. (port.) 18 cm. Imperfect: p. 109-120 wanting. [BX8332.D615] 4-32105
1. Natural law. 2. Methodism—Doctrinal and controversial works. I. Title.

DRUMMOND, Henry, 1851-1897.
Natural law in the spiritual world. New York, Mershon Company [n.d.]C391 p. 68-21063
I. Title.

DRUMMOND, Henry, 1851-1897. 215
Natural law in the spiritual world. By Henry Drummond. New York, Hurst & co., [1888] 285 p. 19 cm. [BL240.D6 1886] 12-31926
I. Title.

HUNT, Mary A.
Scientific Bible. Reason--revelation--rapture. Twentieth century testimony. Nature and "me"--one. Knowable, human, natural, personal God. Self-eternal substance. Natural law. [Poem by] Mary A. Hunt. Chicago, F. E. Ormsby & co. [c1901] 76 p. 23 1/2 cm. 2-16105
I. Title.

STRAUSS, Leo. 227.91
Natural right and history. Chicago, University of Chicago Press [1957] 327 p. 22 cm. (Charles R. Walgreen Foundation lectures) [BS2785.S85] 56-45703
1. Natural law. I. Title.

Natural resources.

EARTHKEEPING, Christian 261.8'5
stewardship of natural resources / by the fellows of the Calvin Center for Christian Scholarship, Calvin College, Peter De Vos ... [et al.] ; [edited by Loren Wilkinson] Grand Rapids, Mich. : Eerdmans, c1980. viii, 317 p. ; 23 cm. Bibliography: p. 310-314. [HC55.E27] 19 80-15900 ISBN 0-8028-1834-X pbk. : 7.95
1. Natural resources. 2. Environmental protection. 3. Stewardship, Christian. I. De Vos, Peter. II. Wilkinson, Loren. III. Calvin Center for Christian Scholarship.

Natural theology.

ANDERSON, James Francis, 210
1910-
Natural theology; the metaphysics of God. Milwaukee, Bruce Pub. Co. [1962] 179p. 24cm. (Christian culture and philosophy series) Includes bibliography. [BL182.A5] 62-10339
1. Natural theology. 2. Thomas Aquinas, Saint—Theology. I. Title.

BABBAGE, Charles, 1792-1871 210
The ninth Bridgewater treatise: a fragment. 2nd ed., reprinted. London, Cass, 1967. viii, xxi, 23-273p. tables, diagrs. 23cm. (Cass Lib. of sci. classics, no. 6) New impression, with index, of the Second (London) ed. [BL175.B89 1838a] 67-110707 14.50
1. Natural theology. I. Title. II. Series. Distributed by Barnes & Noble, New York.

BANKS, Natalie N.
The golden thread; the continuity of esoteric teaching. London, Lucis Press; New York, Lucis Pub. Co. [1963] 95, [1] p. 18 cm. Bibliography: p. 95-[96] NUC67
1. Natural theology. I. Title.

BASCOM, John, 1827-1911. 210
Natural theology. by John Bascom ... New York. G. P. Putnam's sons. 1880. xiii, 306 p. 19 cm. [BL181.B3] 12-30559
1. Natural theology. 2. God. I. Title.

BENEDETTO, Arnold J. 210
Fundamentals in the philosophy of God. New York, Macmillan [c.1963] 330p. illus. 22cm. Bibl. 63-7394 5.00
1. Natural theology. I. Title. II. Title: Philosophy of God.

BOEDDER, Bernard, 1841- 290
... *Natural theology,* by Bernard Boedder, S. J. 2d ed. (New impression) London, New York [etc.] Longmans, Green and co., 1921. 2 p. l., [vii]-xii, 480 p. 19 cm. (Stonyhurst philosophical series) [BL181.B6 1921] 26-9199
1. Natural theology. 2. God. I. Title.

BOLIGHAM and Vaux, Henry 210
Peter Brougham baron, 1778-1868.
A discourse of natural theology, showing the nature of the evidence and the advantages of the study. By Henry lord Brougham ... Philadelphia, Carey, Lea & Blanchard, 1835. viii, [9]-190 p. 19 1/2 cm. [BL181.B77 1835d] 33-20496
1. Natural theology. I. Title.

[BRANAGAN, Thomas] b.1774. 210
The pleasures of contemplation, being a desultory investigation of the harmonies, beauties, and benefits of nature: including a justification of the ways of God to man, and a glimpse of his sovereign beauty ... By the author of "The pleasures of death". To which is added, Some causes of popular poverty ... By Dr. Blatchly ... Philadelphia. Published by Eastwick & Stacy, 1817. 240 p. illus. (port.) 19 cm. Imperfect: frontispiece wanting. "Some causes of popular poverty ... by C. C. Blatchey", has special t.-p. [BL181.B7 1817] 26-7305
1. Natural theology. 2. Poverty. I. Blatchly, Cornelius C. II. Title.

BRUNNER, Heinrich Emil, 1889-
Natural theology, comprising "Nature and grace" by Emil Brunner and the reply "No" by Karl Barth. Translated from the German by Peter Fraenkel. With an introd. by John Baillie. Longdon, G. Bles: The Centenary Press, 1946. [Ann Arbor, Mich., 1962] 128 p. (on double leaves) Photocopy (positive) made by University Microfilms. 64-8068
1. Barth, Karl, 1886- 2. Natural theology. 3. Grace (Theology) I. Barth, Karl, 1886- No! II. Title.

CAROTHERS, J. Edward. 210
The pusher and puller; a concept of God [by] J. Edward Carothers. Nashville, Abingdon Press [1968] 223 p. 23 cm. Bibliography: p. 213-216. [BL182.C26] 68-17435
1. Natural theology. I. Title.

CASSERLEY, Julian Victor 210
Langmead, 1909-
Graceful reason; the contribution of reason to theology. Foreword by John Heuss. Greenwich, Conn., Seabury Press, 1954. 163p. 22cm. [BL181.C28] 54-9008
1. Natural theology. I. Title.

CASSERLEY, Julian Victor 210
Langmead, 1909-
Graceful reason; the contribution of reason to theology. Foreword by John Heuss. London, New York, Longmans, Green [1955] 163p. 23cm. [BL181.C28 1955] 55-2014
1. Natural theology. I. Title.

CHADBOURNE, Paul Ansel, 1823- 210
1883.
Lectures on natural theology; or, Nature and the Bible from the same author. Delivered before the Lowell institute, Boston. By P. A. Chadbourne ... New York, G. P. Putnam & son, 1867. xvi, [17]-320 p. 20 cm. [BL181.C5] 30-24915
1. Natural theology. 2. Science. I. Lowell institute lectures. II. Title.

CHALMERS, Thomas, 1780-1847. 215
On the power, wisdom, and goodness of God, as manifested in the adaptation of external nature, to the moral and intellectual constitution of man. By the Rev. Thomas Chalmers ... Philadelphia, Carey, Lea & Blanchard, 1833. xiv, [15]-308 p. 19 cm. (Half-title: The Bridgewater treatises on the power, wisdom, and goodness of God, as manifested in the creation. Treatise i) [BL175.B81 1833a] 30-24896
1. Natural theology. 2. Man. I. Title. II. Title: Adaptation of nature to man.

CHALMERS, Thomas, 1780-1847. 215
On the power, wisdom, and goodness of God, as manifested in the adaptation of external nature to the moral and intellectual constitution of man. By the Rev. Thomas Chalmers ... New ed. Philadelphia, Carey, Lea & Blanchard, 1836. xii, [13]-276 p. 22 cm. (Half-title: The Bridgewater treatises on the power, wisdom, and goodness of God, as manifested in the creation. Treatise i) With this bound: Treatise viii, Chemistry meteorology, and the function of digestion ... By William Prout ... Philadelphia, 1836. [BL175.B81 1836] 8-6824
1. Natural theology. 2. Man. I. Title. II. Title: Adaptation of nature to man.

[CHEEVER, George Barrell] 210
1807-1890.
Voices of nature to her foster-child, the soul of man: a series of analogies between the natural and the spiritual world, By the author of "A reel in a bottle." Edited by Rev. Henry T. Cheever. New York, C. Scribner, 1852. ix p., 2 l., [15]-430 p. 20 cm. [BL181.C6] 31-31277
1. Natural theology. 2. Analogy (Religion) I. Cheever, Henry Theodore, 1814-1897, ed. II. Title.

COBB, John B. 210
A Christian natural theology, based on the thought of Alfred North Whitehead, by John B. Cobb, Jr. Philadelphia, Westminster Press [1965] 288 p. 21 cm. Bibliographical footnotes. [B1674.W354C6] 65-11612
1. Whitehead, Alfred North, 1861-1947. 2. Natural theology. I. Title.

DIALOGUES concerning natural religion; edited with introduction by Henry D. Aiken. New York, Hafner Pub. Company, 1957. xviii, 95p. 21cm. (The Hafner Library of classics, 5) 'Selected bibliography': p. xviii.
1. Natural theology. I. Hume, David, 1711-1776. II. Aiken, Henry David, 1912- ed.

DONCEEL, Joseph F., 1906- 210
Natural theology. New York, Sheed [1962] 178p. 21cm. 62-9106 3.00
1. Natural theology. I. Title.

DUNCAN, Henry, 1774-1846. 215
Sacred philosophy of the seasons, illustrated the perfections of God in the phenomena of the year. By the Rev. Henry Duncan ... With important additions and some modifications to adapt it to American readers, by F. W. P. Greenwood ... Boston, Marsh, Capen, Lyon, and Webb, 1839. 4 v. 20 cm. First published in England in 1836. [BL240.D85] 31-11679
1. Natural theology. 2. Religion and science—1800-1859 I. Greenwood, Francis William Pitt, 1797-1843, ed. II. Title.

DUNCAN, Henry, 1774-1846. 215
Sacred philosophy of the seasons; illustrating the perfections of God in the phenomena of the year. By the Rev. Henry Duncan ... With important additions and some modifications to adapt it to American readers. By Rev. F. W. P. Greenwood ... New York, Harper & brothers, 1847. 4 v. 20 cm. [BL240.D85 1847] 38-20546
1. Natural theology. 2. Religion and science—1800-1859. I. Greenwood, Francis William Pitt, 1797-1843, ed. II. Title.

DUNS, Joannes, Scotus, 1265?- 211
1308?
A treatise on God as first principle; a revised Latin text of the De primo principio translated into English along with two related questions from an early commentary on the Sentences, by Allan B. Wolter. [Chicago?] Forum Books [1966] xxiii, 189 p. 21 cm. (A Quincy College publication) English and Latin on opposite pages. Includes bibliographical references. [B765.D73D43 1966] 65-28880
1. Natural theology. 2. God—Proof, Ontological. I. Wolter, Allan Bernard, 1913- ed. II. Title. III. Series: Quincy, Ill. College. Publications

FISHER, George Park, 1827- 210
1909.
Manual of natural theology, by George Park Fisher... New York, C. Scribner's sons, 1893. x, 94 p. illus. 17 1/2 cm. [BL181.F5] 30-24917
1. Natural theology. 2. Theism. I. Title.

FISKE, John, 1842-1901. 210
Through nature to God, by John Fiske ... Boston and New York, Houghton, Mifflin and company, 1899. xv, 194, [2] p. 18 cm. [BL181.F74] 99-1680
1. Natural theology. 2. Theism. I. Title. Contents omitted.

FLEW, Antony Garrard Newton, 210
1923-
God & philosophy [by] Antony Flew. [1st American ed.] New York, Harcourt, Brace & World [1966] 208 p. 21 cm. Bibliography: p. [195]-204. [BL182.F55 1966] 66-23807
1. Natural theology. I. Title.

FREMANTLE, William Henry, 1831-
Natural Christianity, by the Hon. W. H. Fremantle ... London and New York, Harper & brothers, 1911. 14, 194, [1] p. 18 cm. (Half-title: Harper's library of living thought) Added t.-p., illus. W 11
I. Title.

GALLAUDET, Thomas Hopkins, 215
1787-1851.
The youth's book on natural theology, illustrated in familiar dialogues, with numerous engravings. By Rev. T. H. Gallaudet ... Hartford, Cooke & co., 1832. viii, [9]-248 p. incl. illus., plates. 18 cm. [BL185.G2 1882] 30-30808
1. Natural theology. I. Title.

GALLAUDET, Thomas Hopkins, 210
1787-1851.
The youth's book on natural theology; illustrated in familiar dialogues, with numerous engravings. By Rev. T. H. Gallaudet ... New-York, The American tract society [1832] 231 p. illus. 16 cm. [BL185.G2] 21-7934
1. Natural theology. I. American tract society. II. Title.

GALLAUDET, Thomas Hopkins, 210
1787-1851.
The youth's book on natural theology; illustrated in familiar dialogues, with numerous engraving. By Rev. T. H. Gallaudet ... New York, American tract society [184-?] 269 p. illus. 16 cm. [BL185.G2 1840] 32-1013
1. Natural theology. I. American tract society. II. Title.

GILLETT, Ezra Hall, 1823- 210
1875.
God in human thought: or, Natural theology traced in literature, ancient and modern, to the time of Bishop Butler. With a closing chapter on the moral system, and an English bibliography, from Spenser to Butler. By E. H. Gillett ... New York, Scribner, Armstrong & co., 1874. 2 v. 24 cm. Paged continuously. "The attempt to prepare a historical and critical introduction to Bishop Butler's 'Analogy', to be delivered in the form of lectures ... has resulted in ... this work."--Pref. Bibliography: v. 2, p. [793]-825. [BL181.G5] 30-28767
1. Butler, Joseph, bp. of Durham, 1692-1752. The analogy of religion. 2. Natural

theology. 3. Literature and morals. 4. Natural theology—Bibl. 5. Philosophy—Hist. I. Title.

HARTSHORNE, Charles, 1897- 210
A natural theology for our time. La Salle, Ill., Open Court [1967] xi, 145 p. 22 cm. (The Open Court library of philosophy.) (Morse lectures, 1964) "Somewhat extended and revised versions of ... [the] lectures." [BL182.H34] 66-14722
1. Natural theology. I. Title. II. Series.

HEARD, Gerald, 1889- 210
Is God evident? An essay toward a natural theology. New York, Harper [1948] xx, 254 p. 22 cm. [BL181.H4] 48-2695
1. Natural theology. I. Title.

HEYDON, Joseph Kentigern.
The God of reason, by J. K. Heydon. New York, Sheed & Ward, 1940. v, 151 p. 19 cm. "Printed in Great Britain." A 41
1. Natural theology. I. Title.

HICKS, Lewis Ezra, 1839-1922. 210
A critique of design-arguments; a historical review and free examination of the methods of reasoning in natural theology, by L. E. Hicks ... New York, C. Scribner's sons, 1883. xi, 417 p. 21 cm. [BL181.H5] 30-24918
1. Natural theology. 2. Religion—Philosophy. 3. Teleology. I. Title. II. Title: Design-arguments, A critique of.

HILL, Thomas, 1818-1891. 215
Geometry and faith; a supplement to the Ninth Bridgewater treatise, by Thomas Hill ... 3d ed. greatly enlarged. Boston, Lee and Shepard; New York, C. T. Dillingham, 1882. 6 p. l., 109 p. 19 1/2 cm. [BL175.B893 1883] 12-34098
1. Natural theology. 2. Geometry. I. Title.

HOBART, Richard. 289
Hobart's Analysis of Bishop Butler's Analogy of religion, natural and revealed, to the constitution and course of nature. With notes. Also Craufurd's questions for examination. Revised and adapted to the use of schools. By Charles E. West ... New York, Harper & brothers, 1848. xii, [13]-298 p. 16 cm. [BT1100.B97H64] 43-40399
1. Butler, Joseph, bp. of Durham, 1692-1752. The analogy of religion. 2. Natural theology. 3. Apologetics—18th cent. I. Craufurd, Sir George William, bart., 1797-1881. II. West, Charles Edwin, 1809-1900, ed. III. Title. IV. Title: Analysis of Bishop Butler's Analogy of religion.

HOLLOWAY, Maurice R 210
An introduction to natural theology. New York, Appleton-Century-Crofts [1959] 492p. 22cm. [BL181.H63] 59-6522
1. Natural theology. I. Title.

HUME, David, 1711-1776 210
Dialogues concerning natural religion, 2d. ed. Ed., introd. by Norman Kemp Smith. Indianapolis, Bobbs [1963, c.1947] 249p. 21cm. (Lib. of liberal arts 174) 1.45 pap.,
1. Natural theology. I. Title.

HUME, David, 1711-1776. 210
Dialogues concerning natural religion; ed. with an introd. by Norman Kemp Smith. 2d ed., with suppl. London, New York, T. Nelson [1947] xii, 249 p. 23 cm. "Editions, reprints, and translations of the Dialogues": p. x. [BL180.H8 1947] 47-5315
1. Natural theology. I. Smith, Norman Kemp, 1872- ed. II. Title.

HUME, David, 1711-1776. 210
Dialogues concerning natural religion; ed. with introd. by Henry D. Aiken. New York, Hafner Pub. Co., 1948. xviii, 95 p. 21 cm. (The Haftner library of classics, no. 5) "Selected bibliography": p. xviii. [BL180.H8 1948] 48-8099
1. Natural theology. I. Aiken, Henry David, ed. II. Title.

HUME, David, 1711-1776. 210
Dialogues concerning natural religion; edited with an introd. by Norman Kemp Smith. 2d ed., with suppl. New York, Social Sciences Publishers [1948] xii, 249 p. 23 cm. "Editions, reprints, and translations of the Dialogues": p. x. [BL180.H8 1948a] 50-11527
1. Natural theology. I. Title.

HUME, David, 1711-1776. 210
Hume's Dialogues concerning natural religion; edited with an introduction by Norman Kemp Smith ... Oxford, The Clarendon press, 1935. xii, 283, [1] p. 19 1/2 cm. "Editions, reprints, and translations of the Dialogues": p. xii. [BL180.H8] 36-7787
1. Natural theology. I. Smith, Norman Kemp, 1872- ed. II. Title.

JOYCE, George Hayward, 1864- 210
... Principles of natural theology, by George Hayward Joyce ... London, New York [etc.] Longmans, Green & co., 1923. xxviii, 612 p. 19 cm. (Stonyhurst philosophical series) Contents.--The existence of God.--Nature and attributes of God.--God in his relation to the world. [BL181.J6] 24-5913
1. Natural theology. 2. God. I. Title.

JOYCE, George Hayward, 1864- 210
1943.
Principles of natural theology. London, Longmans, Green, 1923. [New York, AMS Press, 1972] xxviii, 612 p. 19 cm. Original ed. issued in series: Stonyhurst philosophical series. [BL181.J6 1972] 79-170829 ISBN 0-404-03609-0
1. Natural theology. 2. God. I. Title. II. Series: Stonyhurst philosophical series.

KIDD, John, 1775-1851. 215
On the adaptation of external nature to the physical condition of man, principally with reference to the supply of his wants, and the exercise of his intellectual faculties. By John Kidd ... New ed. Philadelphia, Carey, Lea & Blanchard, 1836. viii, [vii]-viii, [xi]-xii, [13]-196 p. 22 1/2 cm. (Half-title: The Bridgewater treatises on the power, wisdom, and goodness of God, as manifested in the creation. Treatise ii) Bound with this: Whewell, William. Astronomy and general physics. Philadelphia, 1836. Treatise iii. and Bell, Sir Charles. The hand. Philadelphia, 1836. Treatise iv. [BL175.B82 1836] 8-6820
1. Natural theology. 2. Man. 3. Nature. I. Title. II. Title: Adaptation of nature to man.

KIRBY, William, 1759-1850. 215
On the power, wisdom and goodness of God, as manifested in the creation of animals, and in their history, habits and instincts. By the Rev. William Kirby ... Philadelphia, Carey, Lea & Blanchard, 1836. ixxii, 519 p. xvi (i. e. 20) pl. (incl. front.) 22 1/2 cm. (Half-title: The Bridgewater treatises on the power, wisdom and goodness of God, as manifested in the creation. Treatise vii) [BL175.B87 1836] 8-4269
1. Natural theology. 2. Animals, Habits and behavior of. I. Title.

KREYCHE, Robert J 1920- 211
God and reality; an introduction to the philosophy of God [by] Robert J. Kreyche. New York, Holt, Rinehart and Winston [1965] xiv, 124 p. 21 cm. Bibliography: p. 119-120. [BL182.K7] 65-21065
1. Natural theology. I. Title.

LEE, Luther, 1800-1889. 210
Natural theology, or The existence, attributes, and government of God. Including the obligations and duties of men, demonstrated by arguments drawn from the phenomena of nature. By Luther Lee ... Syracuse, Wesleyan Methodist publishing house, 1866. 183 p. 18 1/2 cm. [BL181.L4] 28-12126
1. Natural theology. I. Title.

LONG, John Elbert, 1832- 213
Natural theology and Genesis. By Rev. J. E. Long. Ithaca, Mich., Gratiot county herald, 1905. 83 p. 23 cm. [BL181.L7] 5-14460
1. Natural theology. 2. Creation. I. Title.

MARCH, Daniel, 1816-1909. 210
Our Father's house, or, The unwritten word. By Rev. Daniel March ... Philadelphia, Pa. [etc.] Zeigler, McCurdy & co., 1870. 7 p. l., 9-500 p. front., plates, 23 cm. [BL181.M4] 30-24932
1. Natural theology. I. Title.

MASCALL, Eric Lionel, 1905- 210
The openness of being; natural theology today [by] E. L. Mascall. Philadelphia, Westminster Press [1972, c1971] xiii, 278 p. 23 cm. (The Gifford lectures, 1970-71) Bibliography: p. [267]-274. [BL182.M35 1972] 72-75839 ISBN 0-664-20944-0 9.75
1. Natural theology. 2. Theism. I. Title. II. Series.

MATHER, Cotton, 1663-1728. 210
The Christian philosopher, a collection of the best discoveries in nature, with religious improvements. By Cotton Mather ... The style made easy and familiar. Charlestown [Mass.]: Published at the Middlesex bookstore. J. M'Kown, printer, 1815. 324 p. 18 cm. Dedication signed: The Bradbury. [BL180.M4 1815] 45-45054
1. Natural theology. I. Title.

MULLER, Friedrich Max, 1823- 290
1900.
Natural religion; the Gifford lectures delivered before the University of Glasgow in 1888, by F. Max Muller ... London and New York, Longmans, Green, and co., 1889. xix, 608 p. 20 cm. [BL181.M8] 210 12-36946
1. Natural theology. 2. Religion Primitive. 3. Language and languages. I. Title.

MURPHY, Joseph John, 1827- 210
1894.
Natural selection and spiritual freedom by Joseph John Murphy ... London and New York, Macmillan and co., 1893. xxvii, 241 p. 17 cm. [BL181.M83] 38-19171
1. Natural theology. 2. Evolution. I. Drummond, Henry, 1851-1897. Natural law in the spiritual world. II. Title.

NELSON, Thomas Hiram, 1863- 210
Nature's revelation of God and the Bible supplement, by Evangelist Thomas H. Nelson ... New York, American tract society [c1940] 208 p. 21 cm. [BL181.N4] 40-12145
1. Jesus Christ—Person and offices. 2. Natural theology. I. American tract society. II. Title.

[NICHOLS, Ichabod] 1784- 210
1859.
A catechism of natural theology ... Portland [Me.] Shirley and Hyde, 1829. 184 p., 1 l. illus. 18 1/2 cm. [BL181.N6] 30-24928
1. Natural theology. 2. Anatomy. I. Title.

PALEY, William, 1743-1805. 210
Natural theology: or, Evidences of the existence and attributes of the Deity, collected from the appearances of nature. By William Paley... Hallowell [Me.] Glazier & co., 1826. iv, [6]-288 p. 17 cm. [BL181.P3 1826] 27-4887
1. Natural theology. I. Title.

PALEY, William, 1743-1805. 210
... Natural theology; or evidence of the existence and attributes of the Deity, collected from the appearances of nature. By William Paley...Illustrated by the plates, and by a selection from the notes of James Paxton...with additional notes, original and selected, for this edition. And a vocabulary of scientific terms. Boston, Lincoln & Edmands, 1829. vi, [2], [5]-308, [2] p. 38 l. front., XXXIX pl. (incl. diagr.) 19 cm. At head of title: Paley's theology, with illustrations. Preface signed: J. W. [i.e. John Ware] [BL181.P3 1829] 30-24926
1. Natural theology. 2. Natural history. I. Paxton, James, 1788-1860. II. Ware, John, 1795-1864, ed. III. Title.

PALEY, William, 1743-1805. 210
...Natural theology: or, Evidences of the existence and attributes of the Deity, collected from the appearances of nature. By William Paly... Illustrated by the plates, and by a selection from the notes of James Paxton...with additional notes, original and selected, for this edition. And a vocabulary of scientific terms. Stereotype ed. Boston, Gould, Kendall and Lincoln, 1848. iv, 344 p. front., XXXIX pl. (incl. diagr.) 19 cm. At head of title: Paley's theology, with illustrations. Preface signed: J. W. [i.e. John Ware] [BL181.P3 1848] 33-25266
1. Natural theology. 2. Natural history. I. Paxton, James, 1786-1860. II. Ware, John, 1795-1864, ed. III. Title.

PALEY, William, 1743-1805. 210
...Natural theology: or, evidences of the existence and attributes of the Deity, collected from the appearances of nature, by William Paley, D.D. Illustrated by the plates, and by a selection from the notes of James Paxton. With additional notes, original and selected, for this edition, and a vocabulary of scientific terms. By John Ware, M.D. Boston, Gould, Kendall, and Lincoln, 1850. iv, 344 p. front., XXXIX pl. (incl. diagr.) 20 cm. At head of title: Paley's theology, with illustrations. [BL181.P3 1850] 31-35776
1. Natural theology. 2. Natural history. I. Paxton, James, 1786-1860. II. Ware, John, 1795-1864, ed. III. Title.

PALEY, William, 1743-1805. 210
...Natural theology: or, Evidences of the existence and attributes of the Deity, collected from the appearances of nature, by William Paley, D.D. Illustrated by the plates, and by a selection from the notes of James Paxton. With additional notes, original and selected, for this edition, and a vocabulary of scientific terms. By John Ware, M.D. Boston, Gould and Lincoln, 1854. iv, 420 p. XXXIX pl. (incl. diagr.) 20 cm. At head of title: Paley's theology, with illustrations. [BL181.P3 1854] 30-24921
1. Natural theology. 2. Natural history. I. Paxton, James, 1786-1860. II. Ware, John, 1795-1864, ed. III. Title.

PALEY, William, 1743-1805. 210
Natural theology and tracts. By William Paley... New-York, S. King, 1824. 2 p. l., [iii]-v, [2], [9]-368 p. pl. 13 1/2 cm. Added t.-p., engraved. On cover: Paley's works. 3. [BL181.P3 1824] 39-32786
1. Natural theology. 2. Natural history. I. Title.

PALEY, William, 1743-1805. 210
Paley's Natural theology, with selections from the illustrative notes, and the supplementary dissertations, of Sir Charles Bell, and Lord Brougham; the whole newly arranged, and edited by Elisha Bartlett, M.D. With...wood cuts, and a life and portrait of the author... Boston, Marsh, Capen, Lyon, and Webb, 1839. 2 v. front. (port.) illus. 19 1/2 cm. [BL181.P3 1839] 30-24920
1. Natural theology. 2. Natural history. I. Brougham and Vaux, Henry Peter Brougham, 1st baron, 1778-1868. II. Bell, Sir Charles, 1774-1842. III. Bartlett, Elisha, 1804-1855, ed. IV. Title.

PALEY, William, 1743-1805. 210
Paley's Natural theology, with illustrative notes, &c. By Henry lord Brougham...and Sir Charles Bell...with numerous woodcuts. To which are added, preliminary observations and notes. By A. Potter... New-York, Harper and brothers, 1840. 2 v. illus. 16 cm. (On cover: Harper's family library. no. XCVI-XCVII. Stereotype edition) [BL181.P] A 31
1. Natural theology. 2. Natural history. I. Brougham and Vaux, Henry Peter Brougham, baron, 1778-1868. II. Bell, Sir Charles, 1774-1842. III. Potter, Alonzo, bp., 1800-1865. IV. Title.

PALFREY, John Gorham, 1796- 210
1881.
The theory and uses of natural religion; being the Dudleian lecture, read before the University of Cambridge, May 8th, 1839. By John Gorham Palfrey... Boston, F. Andrews, 1839. 76 p. 22 1/2 cm. [BL185.P3] 35-35195
1. Natural theology. I. Title.

PEABODY, Andrew Preston, 290
1811-1893.
Christianity the religion of nature. Lectures delivered before the Lowell institute. By A. P. Peabody ... Boston, Gould and Lincoln; New York, Sheldon and company; [etc., etc.] 1864. xii, [13]-256 p. 20 1/2 cm. [BL181.P4] 42-40829
1. Natural theology. 2. Revelation. I. Lowell institute lectures, 1862-63. II. Title.

PEARL, Leon 110
Four philosophical problems: God, freedom, mind, and perception. New York, Harper [c.1963] 244p. 22cm. Bibl. 63-7290 4.75
1. Natural theology. 2. Free will and determinism. 3. Mind and body. 4. Perception. I. Title.

PEARL, Leon. 110
Four philosophical problems: God, freedom, mind, and perception. New York, Harper & Row [1963] 244 p. 22 cm. Includes bibliography. [BD21.P32] 63-7290
1. Natural theology. 2. Free will and determinism. 3. Mind and body. 4. Perception. I. Title.

READ, Hollis, 1802-1887. 210
The palace of the Great King; or, The power, wisdom and goodness of God, illustrated in the multiplicity and variety of His works. By Rev. Hollis Read ... New York, C. Scribner, 1859. 408 p. 19 cm. [BL181.R3] 30-24924
1. Natural theology. I. Title.

ROYCE, Josiah 111
The world and the individual. [2 v.] With an introd. by John E. Smith. New York, Dover Publications [c.1959] xxii, 588p.; xx, 480p. 21cm. 2.25 pap., ea.
1. Natural theology. 2. Ontology. 3. Reality I. Title.
Contents omitted.

ROYCE, Josiah, 1855-1916. 111
The world and the individual [2v.] Introd. by John E. Smith [Gloucester, Mass., Peter Smith, 1961, c.1899, 1959] 2v. 588p.; 480p. (Dover bks. rebound in cloth) 4.25 ea.,
1. Natural theology. 2. Ontology. 3. Reality. I. Title.
Contents omitted.

ROYCE, Josiah, 1855-1916. 111
The world and the individual. With an introd. by John E. Smith. New York, Dover Publications [1959] 2 v. 21 cm. Contents.Contents.—1st ser. The four historical conceptions of being.—2d ser. Nature, man, and the moral order. [B945.R63W7 1959] 59-14226
1. Natural theology. 2. Ontology. 3. Reality. I. Title.

ROYCE, Josiah, 1855-1916. 123
The world and the individual; Gifford lectires delivered before the University of Aberdeen. 1st series: The four historical conceptions of being, by Josiah Royce ... New York, The Macmillan company; London, Macmillan & co., ltd., 1900. xvi, 588 p. 21 cm. [B945.R63W7 1st ser.] 0-402
1. Natural theology. 2. Ontology. 3. Reality. I. Title.

ROYCE, Josiah, 1855-1916. 123
The world and the individual; Gifford lectures delivered before the University of Aberdeen. 1st series: The four historical conceptions of being, by Josiah Royce ... New York, The Macmillan company; London, Macmillan & co., ltd., 1920. xvi, 588 p. 21 cm. [B945.R63W7 1st ser. 1920] 38-38926
1. Natural theology. 2. Ontology. 3. Reality. I. Title.

[SEELY, John Robert, Sir] 210
1834-1895.
Natural religion. by The author of "Ecce homo"... Boston, Roberts brothers, 1882. vi p., 1 l., 251 p. 17 1/2 cm. [BL181.S4 1882] 14-8136
I. Title.

SENTIMENTS upon the religion 210
of reason and nature, carefully translated from the original French manuscript, communicated by the author. 3d ed. [Philadelphia? 1795?] vii, 9-160 p. 16 1/2 cm. With this is bound: Some doubts respecting the death, resurrection, and ascension of Jesus Christ. New York, 1797. Preface signed: T. C. [BL180.S42] 30-28772
1. Natural theology. I. C., T., tr. II. T. C., Tr.

SMART, Ninian, 1927- 291'.1
The yogi and the devotee: the inter play between the Upanishads and Catholic theology. London, Allen & Unwin, 1968. 174p. 23cm. Bibl. [BR128.H5S6] 68-105847 5.00
1. Natural theology. 2. Christianity and other religions—Hinduism. 3. Hinduism—Relations—Christianity. I. Title.
Distributed by Humanities, New York.

SMYTH, Newman, 1843-1925. 290
Constructive natural theology, by Newman Smyth. New York, C. Scribner's sons, 1913. viii p., 1 l., 123 p. 20 cm. [Full name: Samuel Phillips Newman Smyth] [BL181.S6] 13-19088
1. Natural theology. I. Title.

TEMPLE, William, Abp of
Canterbury, 1881-1944.
Nature, man and God; being the Gifford lectures delivered in the University of Glasgow in the academical years 1932-1933 and 1933-1934. London, Macmillan; New York, St. Martin's Press, 1960. 530 p. (Gifford lectures, Glasgow University, 1932-33, 1933-34)
1. Natural theology. 2. Religion — Philosophy. 3. Transcendentalism. 4. Knowledge, Theory of (Religion) I. Title.

TEMPLE, William, Abp. of 210
Canterbury, 1881-1944.
Nature, man, and God / by William Temple. [1st AMS ed.]. New York : AMS Press, [1979] xxxii, 530 p. ; 22 cm. Reprint of the 1934 ed. published by Macmillan, London, which was issued as the Gifford lectures, 1932-1934. Includes bibliographical references and index. [BL181.T4 1979] 77-27190 ISBN 0-404-60493-5 : 40.00
1. Natural theology. 2. Religion—Philosophy. 3. Immanence of God. 4. Transcendentalism. 5. Knowledge, Theory of (Religion) I. Title. II. Series: Gifford lectures ; 1932-1934.

VALENTINE, Milton, 1825-1906. 210
Natural theology; or, Rational theism. By M. Valentine ... Chicago, S. C. Griggs and company, 1885. viii, 274 p. 19 1/2 cm. "This volume presents the substance of lectures on the subject, given to students ... of Pennsylvania college."--Pref. [BL181.V3] 30-30815
1. Natural theology. I. Title. II. Title: Rational theism.

WALKER, James Barr, 1805- 210
1887.
...God revealed in the process of creation, and by the manifestation of Jesus Christ; including an examination of the development theory contained in the "Vestiges of the natural history of creation." By James B. Walker... Boston, Gould and Lincoln; New York, Sheldon, Lamport & Blakeman, 1855. x, [2], [13]-273 p. front. 20 cm. At head of title: Sacred philosophy. [BL181.W2] 22-15340
1. Natural theology. 2. Chambers, Robert, 1802-1871. Vestiges of the natural history of creation. I. Title.

WALLACE, William, 1844-1897.
Lectures and essays on natural theology and ethics, by William Wallace...edited with biographical introduction, by Edward Caird...with a portrait. Oxford, The Clarendon press, 1898. xi, 566 p., 1 l. front. (port.) 23 cm. [BL131.W3] 8-22428
1. Natural theology. 2. Ethics. I. Caird, Edward, 1835-1908, ed. II. Title.

WEBB, Clement Charles Julian, 210
1865-
Studies in the history of natural theology, by Clement C. J. Webb ... Oxford, The Clarendon press, 1915. vi p., 1 l., 363, [1] p. 23 cm. The substance of three courses of lectures delivered by the author as Wilde lecturer on natural and comparative religion ... Oxford ... 1911-12 and 1912-13."--Pref. [BL181.W4] 16-6131
I. Title.

WEST, Robert Frederick. 230.66
Alexander Campbell and natural religion. New Haven, Yale Univ. Press, 1948. ix, 250 p. 24 cm. (Yale studies in religious education, 21) Bibliography: p. [231]-240. [BX7343.C2W4] 48-9950
1. Campbell, Alexander, 1788-1866. 2. Natural theology. 3. Religion. I. Title. II. Series: Yale studies in the history and theory of religious education, 21

WHEELER, Herschel 210
My Father's world. by Herschel & Ruth Wheeler. Mountain View, Calif., Pacific Pr. Pub [1966. c.1965] 119p. illus. 26cm. Bibl. [BL182.W5] 65-23811 4.50 bds.,
1. Natural theology. I. Wheeler, Ruth Lellah (Carr) 1899- joint author. II. Title.

WHEWELL, William, 1794-1866. 215
Astronomy and general physics considered with reference to natural theology. By the Rev. William Whewell ... Philadelphia, Carey, Lea & Blanchard, 1833. 2 p. l., [7]-284 p. 19 cm. (Half-title: The Bridgewater treatises on the power, wisdom, and goodness of God as manifested in the creation. Vol. 3) [BL175.B83 1833] 5-6404
1. Natural theology. 2. Cosmical physics. 3. Astronomy. I. Title.

WHEWELL, William, 1794-1866. 215
Indications of the Creator. by William Whewell ... Philadelphia, Carey and Hart, 1845. xiii, [13]-86 p.19 cm. Extracts, bearing upon theology, from the author's "History of the inductive sciences," and "Philosophy of the inductive sciences". cf. Preface. [BL181.W5 1845] 30-28781
1. Natural theology. I. Title. II. Title: History of the inductive sciences. III. Title: Philosophy of the inductive sciences.
Contents omitted.

WILSON, Daniel, bp., 1778- 210
1858.
Analogy of religion, natural and revealed, to the constitution and course of nature: consisting of a criticism of Butler's treatise on the subject, together with a view of the connexion of the arguments of the analogy with the other main branches of the evidence of Christianity not noticed in Bulter's work. By Daniel Wilson ... Boston, J. Loring, 1834. 235 p. 15 1/2 cm. [BT1100.B9W5] 33-39492
1. Butler, Joseph, bp. of Durham, 1692-1763. The analogy of religion. 2. Natural theology. I. Title.

WOOD, Barry, 1940- 230
The magnificent frolic. Philadelphia, Westminster Press [1970] 223 p. 20 cm. Bibliography: p. [215]-223. [BL182.W65] 78-101698 ISBN 0-664-20886-X 4.95
1. Natural theology. I. Title.

Natural theology—Addresses, essays, lectures.

MORRISS, Frank. 210
The forgotten revelation; essays on God and nature. Chicago, Franciscan Herald Press [1964] 91 p. 22 cm. [BL182.M6] 64-24286
1. Natural theology — Addresses, essays, lectures. I. Title.

WILLIAMS, William George, 231
1822-1902, ed.
The Ingham lectures. A course of lectures on the evidences of natural and revealed religion. Delivered before the Ohio Wesleyan university, Delaware, Ohio. Cleveland, Ingham, Clarke and company; New York, Nelson & Phillips; [etc., etc.] 1872. viii, 365 p. 20 cm. Preface signed: W. G. Williams. Through the liberality of William A. Ingham, this course of lectures was delivered during the years 1869, 1870 and 1871. cf. Pref. [BT1101.W6] 17-31606
I. Ingham, William A. II. Foster, Randolph Sirks, bp. 1820-1903. III. Hahan, Asa. 1800-1889. IV. Thomson, Edward, bp. 1810-1879. V. Clark, Davis Wasgatt, bp. 1812-1871. VI. Warren, William Fairfield, 1833-1929. VII. Newhall, Fales Henry, 1827-1883. VIII. Curry, Daniel, 1809-1887. IX. Godman, William Davis, 1829-1908. X. Title.

Natural theology—Collections.

ALSTON, William P., ed. 201
Religious belief and philosophical thought; readings in the philosophy of religion. New York, Harcourt [1963] 626p. 24cm. 63-13110 7.50
1. Natural theology—Collections. 2. Religion—Philosophy—Collections. I. Title.

BAISNEE, Jules Albert, 210.82
1879- ed.
Readings in natural theology. Westminster, Md., Newman Press, 1962. 321 p. 22 cm. (The College readings series, no. 7) [BL175.B3] 62-16556
1. Natural theology—Collections. I. Title.

Natural theology—Early works to 1900.

†DERHAM, William, 1657-1735. 210
Physico-theology : or, A demonstration of the being and attributes of God from His works of creation / William Derham. New York : Arno Press, 1977. 444 p., [1] leaf of plates : ill. ; 21 cm. (History of ecology) Reprint of the 4th ed., corr., 1716, printed for W. Innys, London. [BL180.D4 1977] 77-74212 ISBN 0-405-10383-2 : 28.00
1. Natural theology—Early works to 1900. 2. Natural history—Pre-Linnean works. 3. God—Attributes. I. Title. II. Series.

HUME, David, 1711-1776. 210
Dialogues concerning natural religion. Edited and with commentary by Nelson Pike. Indianapolis, Bobbs-Merrill [1970] xxiii, 238 p. 21 cm. (The Bobbs-Merrill text and commentary series, TC6) Bibliography: p. xxi-xxii. [BL180.H8 1970] 77-132933 2.95
1. Natural theology—Early works to 1900. I. Pike, Nelson, ed. II. Title.

HUME, David, 1711-1776. 210
Dialogues concerning natural religion and the posthumous essays, Of the immortality of the soul and Of suicide / David Hume ; edited, with an introd., by Richard H. Popkin. Indianapolis : Hackett Pub. Co., c1980. xxiii, 105 p. ; 23 cm. Bibliography: p. xxi-xxiii. [BL180.H78 1980] 79-25349 ISBN 0-915144-46-8 : 10.00 ISBN 0-915144-45-X (pbk.) : 1.95
1. Natural theology—Early works to 1900. 2. Immortality—Early works to 1800—Addresses, essays, lectures. 3. Suicide—Early works to 1800—Addresses, essays, lectures. I. Popkin, Richard Henry, 1923- II. Title.

MATHER, Cotton, 1663-1728. 210
The Christian philosopher: a collection of the best discoveries in nature, with religious improvements. Gainesville, Fla., Scholars' Facsimiles & Reprints, 1968. xiii, vii, 304 p. 23 cm. Reprint of the 1721 ed., with an introd. by Josephine K. Piercy. [BL180.M4 1968] 68-29082
1. Natural theology—Early works to 1900. I. Title.

MULLER, Friedrich Max, 1823- 210
1900.
Natural religion : the Gifford lectures delivered before the University of Glasgow in 1888 / by F. Max Muller. New York : AMS Press, [1975] xix, 608 p. ; 19 cm. Reprint of the 1889 ed. published by Longmans, Green, London, in series: Gifford lectures, 1888. Includes bibliographical references and index. [BL181.M8 1975] 73-18810 ISBN 0-404-11450-4 : 31.00
1. Natural theology—Early works to 1900. 2. Religion. 3. Mythology. I. Title. II. Series: Gifford lectures, 1888.

PALEY, William, 1743-1805. 210
Natural theology; selections. Edited with an introd., by Frederick Ferre. Indianapolis, Bobbs-Merrill [c1963] xxxv, 88 p. 21 cm. (The Library of liberal arts) "184." Bibliography: p. xxiii-xxxiv. [BL180.P3] 63-12201
1. Natural theology — Early works to 1900. 2. Natural history. I. Title.

RAY, John, 1627-1705. 210
The wisdom of God manifested in the works of the creation / John Ray. Nachdr. d. Ausg. London 1691. Hildesheim ; New York : Olms, 1974. 249 p. ; 17 cm. (Anglistica & Americana ; 122) Reprint of the 1691 ed. printed for S. Smith, at the Princes Arms in S. Pauls Church Yard, London. [BL180.R3 1974] 75-329441 ISBN 3-487-05403-5 : DM39.80
1. Natural theology—Early works to 1900. 2. Science—Early works to 1800. I. Title. II. Series.

†RAY, John, 1627-1705. 210
The wisdom of God manifested in the works of creation / John Ray. New York : Arno Press, 1977. 405 p. : port. ; 21 cm. (History of ecology) Reprint of the 1717 ed. printed by R. Harbin for W. Innys, London. [BL180.R3 1977] 77-74250 ISBN 0-405-10419-7 : 30.00
1. Natural theology—Early works to 1900. 2. Science—Early works to 1800. I. Title. II. Series.

RAY, John, 1627-1705. 210
The wisdom of God manifested in the works of thhe creation : 1691 / John Ray. New York : Garland Pub., 1979. 249 p. ; 19 cm. (British philosophers and theologians of the 17th & 18th centuries) Reprint of the ed. printed for S. Smith, London. [BL180.R3 1979] 75-11250 ISBN 0-8240-1801-X : 29.50
1. Natural theology—Early works to 1900. 2. Science—Early works to 1800. I. Title. II. Series.

STOKES, George Gabriel, Sir, 210
bart., 1819-1903.
Natural theology / by Sir G. G. Stokes,

bart. 1st AMS ed. New York : AMS Press, 1979. viii, 272 p. ; 18 cm. Reprint of the 1891 ed. published by A. and C. Black, London, which was issued as Gifford lectures, 1891. [BL181.S67 1979] 77-27232 ISBN 0-404-60452-8 : 22.50
1. Natural theology—Early works to 1900. I. Title. II. Series: Gifford lectures ; 1891.

WALLACE, Robert, 1697-1771. 210
Various prospects of mankind, nature and providence. 1761. To which is added Ignorance and superstition, a source of violence and cruelty, a sermon preached in the High Church of Edinburgh, January 6, 1746. New York, A. M. Kelley, 1969. viii, 406, 39 p. 22 cm. (Reprints of economic classics) Reprint of the 1761 ed. and 1746 ed., respectively. [BL180.W3 1969] 69-19550 ISBN 0-678-00491-9
1. Natural theology—Early works to 1900. I. Wallace, Robert, 1697-1771. Ignorance and superstition. II. Title.

WILKINS, John, Bp. of Chester, 1614-1672. 210
Of the principles and duties of natural religion. With a new introd. by Henry G. Van Leeuwen. New York, Johnson Reprint Corp., 1969. xxxvii, 410 p. 19 cm. (Texts in early modern philosophy) Reprint of the 1693 ed. Bibliography: p. xxxvi-xxxvii. [BL180.W5 1969] 68-58291
1. Natural theology—Early works to 1900. I. Title.

WOLLASTON, William, 1660-1724. 170
The religion of nature delineated / William Wollaston. New York : Garland, 1978. 218 p. ; 24 cm. (British philosophers and theologians of the 17th & 18th centuries) Reprint of the 1724 ed. printed by S. Palmer, London, and sold by B. Lintott, J. Osborn, and W. and J. Innys. [BL180.W6 1978] 75-11267 ISBN 0-8240-1816-8 : 29.50
1. Natural theology—Early works to 1900. I. Title. II. Series.

Natural theology—Early works to 1900—Addresses, essays, lectures.

REID, Thomas, 1710-1796. 210
Thomas Reid's Lectures on natural theology (1780) / transcribed from student notes, edited, and with an introd. by Elmer H. Duncan ; with a new essay "Reid, first principles and reason in the Lectures on natural theology" by William R. Eakin. Lanham, MD : University Press of America, 1981. p. cm. Includes bibliographical references. [BL180.R36 1981] 19 80-26200 ISBN 0-8191-1354-9 : 19.00 ISBN 0-8191-1355-7 (pbk.) : 9.00
1. Natural theology—Early works to 1900—Addresses, essays, lectures. I. Duncan, Elmer H. II. Title.

Natural theology—Early works to 1900—Collected works.

JOHNSON, Samuel, 1822-1882. 230
Selected writings of Samuel Johnson / edited and with an introd. by Roger C. Mueller. Delmar, N.Y. : Scholars' Facsims. & Reprints, 1977. xix, 164 p. : port. ; 23 cm. A collection of articles which previously appeared in various journals. Bibliography: p. xviii-xix. [BL181.J57 1977] 77-25885 ISBN 0-8201-1305-0 : 22.00
1. Natural theology—Early works to 1900—Collected works. 2. Rationalism—Collected works. 3. Transcendentalism—Collected works. I. Mueller, Roger C. II. Title.

Natural theology—History of doctrines.

LEMAHIEU, D. L., 1945- 230'.3'0924
The mind of William Paley : a philosopher and his age / D. L. LeMahieu. Lincoln : University of Nebraska Press, c1976. xi, 215 p. ; 23 cm. Based on the author's thesis, Harvard University. Includes bibliographical references and index. [BL182.L45] 75-22547 ISBN 0-8032-0865-0 : 12.95
1. Paley, William, 1743-1805. Natural theology. 2. Paley, William, 1743-1805. 3. Natural theology—History of doctrines. I. Title.

SHEPHERD, William C. 230.2'0924
Man's condition; God and the world process [by] William C. Shepherd. [New York] Herder and Herder [1969] 266 p. 22 cm. Bibliographical footnotes. [BT761.2.S5] 68-55091
1. Rohner, Karl, 1904- 2. Natural theology—History of doctrines. 3. Grace (Theology)—History of doctrines. I. Title.

Natural theology—History of doctrines—Addresses, essays, lectures.

CURREY, Cecil B. 210
Reason and revelation : John Duns Scotus on natural theology / Cecil B. Currey. Chicago : Franciscan Herald Press, [1977] p. cm. (Synthesis series) Includes bibliographical references. [BL182.C87] 77-9614 ISBN 0-8199-0717-0 pbk. : 0.65
1. Duns, Joannes Scotus, 1265?-1308?—Addresses, essays, lectures. 2. Natural theology—History of doctrines—Addresses, essays, lectures. I. Title.

Natural truths association.

KUHN, Julius. 210
Fundament of all teaching [by Julius] Kuhn ... [Serial no. 1]-6. [Conshohocken, Pa., The Natural truths association, c1903] 6 v. 16 x 14 cm. [BL185.K8] 30-30810
1. Natural truths association. I. Title.

Naturalism.

KRIKORIAN, Yervant Hovhannes, 1892- ed.
... Naturalism and the human spirit. New York, Columbia university press, 1944. x, 397 p. 23 1/2 cm. (Half-title: Columbia studies in philosophy, ed. under the Dept. of philosophy, Columbia university. No. 8) At head of title: Edited by Yervant H. Krikorian. A 44
1. Naturalism. I. Title.
Contents omitted.

LEWIS, Tayler, 1802-1877. 239.
Nature, progress, ideas. A discourse on naturalism, in its various phases, as opposed to the true Scriptural doctrine of the divine imperium. Delivered at Union college, Schenectady, July 24, 1849. Before the New-York alpha of the Phi beta kappa society. By Tayler Lewis... Schenectady, G. Y. Van Debogert, 1850. 56 p. 21 cm. [BT1210.L45] 43-38731
1. Naturalism. 2. Providence and government of God. 3. Apologetics—19th cent. I. Title.

OTTO, Rudolf, 1869- 215
Naturalism and religion, by Dr. Ruddolf Otto .. tr. by J. Arthur Thomson ... and Margaret R. Thomson; ed. with an introduction by Rev. W. D. Morrison, LL. D. London, Williams & Norgate; New York, G. P. Putnam's sons, 1907. xi, 374 p. 19 cm. (Half-title: Crown theological library, vol. xvii) [Full name: Karl Ludwig Rudolf Otto] [BL240.O8 1907] 7-18190
I. Thomson, John Arthur, Sir 1861- tr. II. Thomson, Margaret R., joint tr. III. Morrison, William Douglas, 1853- ed. IV. Title.

PRATT, James Bissett, 1875- 201
Naturalism, by James Pratt ... New Haven, Yale university press; London, H. Milford, Oxford university press, 1939. x, 180 p. 21 cm. (Half-title: Powell lectures on philosophy at Indiana university, Daniel S. Robinson, editor. 3d ser.) "Published for Indiana university." [B828.2.P7] 39-12947
1. Naturalism. I. Title.

RIEPE, Dale Maurice, 1918- 181'.4
The naturalistic tradition in Indian thought / by Dale Riepe. Westport, Conn. : Greenwood Press, 1982, c1981. xi, 308 p. : ill. ; 22 cm. Reprint. Originally published: Seattle : University of Washington Press, 1961. Includes index. Bibliography: p. 255-285. [B132.N3R5 1982] 19 82-9185 ISBN 0-313-23622-4 lib. bdg. : 35.00
1. Naturalism. 2. Philosophy, Indic. I. Title.

Naturalists.

OSBORN, Henry Fairfield, 1857-1935.
Impressions of great naturalists: Darwin, Wallace, Huxley, Leidy, Cope, Balfour, Roosevelt, and others, by Henry Fairfield Osborn ... 2d ed. completely rev. with additions and new illustrations. New York, London, C. Scribner's sons, 1928. x p., 3 l., 3-294 p. front., pl., ports., facsims. 20 cm. "volume ii of Biological series." "Biographies by the author": p. [277]-285. [QH26.O7 1928] 28-25538
1. Naturalists. I. Title.
Contents omitted.

Nature.

COSPER, Wilbert Le Roy.
Nature's way, by Bishop Wilbert Le Roy Cosper ... San Francisco, Cal., C. P. I. publishing co. [c1917] 4 p. l., 15-126 p. front. (port.) 19 cm. [BX6799.C7C8] 17-25999 1.50
I. Title.

HAY, Marian Margaret, 1908- 215
God's out-of-doors, by Marian M. Hay. Takoma Park, Washington, D.C., Peekskill, N.Y. [etc.] Review and herald publishing assn. [1933] 95 p. 19 1/2 cm. [BL262.H3] 33-33469
1. Nature. 2. God. I. Title.

HUTTON, [w. Rev.]
Hutton's book of nature laid open; revised and improved, by Rev. J. L. Blake ... New York, Harper & brothers, 1846. vi, 7-252 p. 16 cm. (Harper & brothers. School district library, no. 289) Added t.-p., engr. 5-25589
I. Blake, John Lauris, 1788-1857. II. Title.

KENEN, Peter B. 1932-
Nature, capital, and trade. [New York, 1965] cover-title, 438-460 p. 24 cm. (Columbia University. School of International Affairs. [Publications, no. 1]) Reprinted from the Journal of political economy, v. 73, no. 5, Oct. 1965. Bibliographical footnotes. 66-81715
I. Title.

LACEY, Thomas Alexander, 1853-
Nature, miracle and sin: a study of St. Augustine's conception of the natural order. By T. A. Lacey ... London, New York [etc.] Longmans, Green, and co., 1916. xiii, 165 p. 23 cm. (The Pringle Stuart lectures for 1914) 16-22751
I. Title.

MILL, John Stuart, 1806-1873. 215
Nature, and Utility of religion. [Essays] Edited with an introd. by George Nakhnikian. New York, Liberal Arts Press [1958] xxx, 80p. 21cm. (The Library of liberal arts, no. 81) Bibliography: p. xxix. [BL51.M58] 58-59889
1. Nature. 2. Religion. I. Title. II. Title: Utility of religion.

RICE, Merton Stacher, 1872-1943. 215
My Father's world [by] Merton S. Rice ... New York, Nashville, Abingdon-Cokesbury press [1943] 103 p. incl. front., illus. 25 1/2 cm. [BL262.R5] 43-16168
1. God. 2. Nature. I. Title.

SIMPSON, James Young, 1873-1934.
Nature: cosmic, human and divine, by James Young Simpson ... New Haven, Yale university press; London, H. Milford, Oxford university press, 1929. ix, 157, [1] p. 19 1/2 cm. (Half-title: The Terry lectures) Printed in Great Britain. [BD581.S5] 30-6635
1. Nature. 2. Philosophy of nature. I. Title.

URBAN, Abram Linwood. 210
A temple of the spirit: a mystical approach to meanings in the world of nature, and the world of man. [By] Abram Linwood Urban ... Boston, R. G. Badger [c1930] 91 p. 20 cm. [BR125.U65] 31-3087
I. Title.

Nature conservation—Moral and religious aspects.

GRABER, Linda H. 170
Wilderness as sacred space / Linda H. Graber. Washington : Association of American Geographers, c1976. xiv, 124 p. : ill. ; 22 cm. (Monograph series - Association of American Geographers ; 8) Bibliography: p. 117-124. [QH75.G66] 76-19927 ISBN 0-89291-111-5 pbk. : 4.95
1. Nature conservation—Moral and religious aspects. 2. Wilderness areas—United States. 3. Environmental psychology. 4. Geographical perception. I. Title. II. Series: Association of American Geographers. Monograph series ; 8.

Nature in literature.

BRENTANO, Mary Bernarda. 210
Nature in the works of Fray Juis [i.e. Luis] de Granada. New York, AMS Press [1969, c1936] xix, 160 p. 22 cm. (The Catholic University of America. Studies in Romance languages and literatures, v. 15) Originally presented as the author's thesis, Catholic University of America, 1936. Bibliography: p. 154-156. [PQ6412.L8Z57 1969] 75-94164
1. Luis de Granada, 1504-1588. 2. Nature in literature. I. Title. II. Series.

BRENTANO, Mary Bernarda sister. 208.1
Nature in the works of Fray Luis De Granda... by Sister Mary Bernarda Brentano... Washington, D.C., The Catholic university of America, 1936. xix, 160 p. 22 1/2 cm. (The Catholic university of America. Studies in Romance language and literature. vol. XV) Thesis (Ph. D.)--Catholic university of America, 1936. "Select bibliography": p. 154-156. [PQ6412.L8Z57 1936] 36-22938
1. Luis de Granada, 1504-1588. 2. Nature in literature. I. Title.

Nature in the Bible.

ARCHIBALD, Andrew Webster, 1851-1926. 220.
Biblical nature studies, by Rev. Andrew W. Archibald... Boston, New York [etc.] The Pilgrim press [c1915] xi, 230 p. 19 1/2 cm. [BS660.A7] 15-17792
1. Nature is the Bible. I. Title.

*LINDEMANN, Henry 242
God's silent preachers reflections on nature. New York, Exposition [c.194] 125p. 22cm. 3.50
I. Title.

MARVIN, Francis Merton, 1884- 220.85
Nature appreciation. Saylorsburg, Pa., Country Press, 1948. 70 p. illus., port. 22 cm. "Issue limited." [BS660.M3] 49-2270
1. Nature in the Bible. I. Title.

SADLER, Alfred John, 1875- 242
Out of doors with God [by] Alfred J. Sadler, with introduction by Norman Vincent Peale ... New York, Nashville, Abingdon-Cokesbury press [c1940] 173 p. 17 1/2 cm. [BS660.S23] 40-34438
1. Nature in the Bible. 2. Meditations. I. Title.

STEARNS, John M[ilton] 1810-1898.
The Bible in harmony with nature. Atheism abnormal and monstrous. Spirit life and material entities. By John M. Stearns ... Brooklyn, D. S. Holmes [1881] [iii]-vi, [7]-87 p. 19 cm. Cover-title: Tom Paine on trial, and the infidels in court. 4-2024
I. Title.

Nature—Religious aspects—Juvenile literature.

DEVINE, Bob. 231.7'65
God in creation / by Bob Devine. Chicago : Moody Press, c1982. p. cm. Describes several complex phenomena in nature, including the hatching of an egg, the homing instincts of salmon, and the life cycle of the cicada, which give evidence of the handiwork of the Creator. [BL205.D48 1982] 19 82-8147 ISBN 0-8024-3027-9 pbk. : 3.25
1. Nature—Religious aspects—Juvenile literature. 2. [Nature—Religious aspects.] 3. [God.] 4. [Creation.] 5. [Christian life.] I. Title.

Nature— Religious interpretations.

[MCDANIELS, Johnson Beauregard] 1862- 211
Voice of nature, the true word; a scrap book of truth, based upon the fidelity of historical, religious, and scientific research. By the author, Guy Thotmus (nom de guerre.) ... [Parsons, Kan., c1929] 1 p. l., [5]-215 p. 20 1/2 cm. Label mounted on verso of t.-p.: "Copyright ... by J. B. McDaniels." [BL2775.M23] 29-14779
I. Title.

A New ethic for a new earth. 261.8'3
Edited by Glenn C. Stone. [New York] Published by Friendship Press for the Faith-Man-Nature Group and the Section on Stewardship and Benevolence of the National Council of Churches [1971] 176 p. 19 cm. (F/M/N papers, no. 2) Includes papers presented at the Faith-Man-Nature Group's 4th national conference, Airlie House, Nov. 28-30, 1969. Pages 173-176 blank for "Notes." Bibliography: p. 163-172. [BL435.N48] 77-152084 1.95
1. Nature—Religious interpretations. 2. Human ecology—Moral and religious aspects. I. Stone, Glenn C., ed. II. Faith-Man-Nature Group. III. Series: Faith-Man-Nature Group. F/M/N papers, no. 2

SCHOOLLAND, Marian M 1902- 242
When I consider -- With 40 illus. by Reynold H. Weidenaar Grand Rapids, Eerdmans, 1956. 124p. illus. 23cm. [BV4832.S38] 56-12135
1. Nature— Religious interpretations. I. Title.

SHEARER, John, 1862- 261
Christianity with nature, by John Shearer. New York, W. Neale, 1929. 55 p. 20 1/2 cm. [BR123.S35] 29-16510
I. Title.

Nature—Religious interpretations—Addresses, essays, lectures.

DANNEN, Kent, 1946- 242
Listen to the sparrow's song / by Kent Dannen ; photos. by Kent and Donna Dannen. St. Louis : Bethany Press, c1979. 94 p. : ill. ; 16 cm. [BV4832.2.D344] 79-10169 ISBN 0-8272-2116-9 pbk. : 3.00
1. Nature—Religious interpretations—Addresses, essays, lectures. I. Title.

Nature—Religious interpretations—Juvenile literature.

DEVINE, Bob. 210
The soil factory / by Bob Devine. Chicago : Moody Press, c1978. p. cm. Contents.Contents.—The soil factory.—Who goes there?.—The underground seismograph.—Earth's white cocoon.—God's fireworks. [BL185.D43] 78-18310 ISBN 0-8024-8109-4 pbk. : 1.50
1. Nature—Religious interpretations—Juvenile literature. 2. [Nature—Religious interpretations.] I. Title.

REID, John Calvin, 1901- 248.8'2
Secrets from field & forest / John Calvin Reid ; [illustrated by Rick Tuma]. Wheaton, Ill. : Tyndale House Publishers, 1980, c1979. 106 p. : ill. ; 19 cm. A collection of 10 stories about wildlife characters whose behavior demonstrate many of God's teachings. Also includes prayers, poems, and Bible references. [BT695.5.R44] 19 79-63458 ISBN 0-8423-5858-7 (pbk.) : 2.95
1. Nature—Religious interpretations—Juvenile literature. 2. Animals, Legends and stories of—Juvenile literature. 3. [Nature—Fiction.] 4. [Animals—Fiction.] 5. [Christian life—Fiction.] 6. [Short stories.] I. Tuma, Rick. II. Title.

Nature study.

LANTRY, Eileen E. 207
A family guide to Sabbath nature activities / Eileen E. Lantry ; [illustrated by Tim Mitoma]. Mountain View, Calif. : Pacific Press Pub. Association, c1980. 127 p. : ill. ; 27 cm. Includes index. Bibliography: p. 120-124. [QH53.L29] 19 79-84350 7.95
1. Nature study. 2. Sabbath. 3. Family—Religious life. 4. Games in Christian education. I. Title.

SAINT-PIERRE, Jacques Henri Bernardin de, 1737-1814
St.-Pierre's Studies of nature. Tr. by Henry Hunter, D.D. Philadelphia, J. & J. L. Gihon [184-] 398 p. front. 23 cm. Added t.-p., engraved, has imprint: Philadelphia, W. A. Leary & co. [PQ2065.E6E5 1840] 16-12443
I. Hunter, Henry, 1741-1802, tr. II. Title. III. Title: Studies of nature.

Nature (Theology)

BARNETTE, Henlee H. 261.8'3
The church and the ecological crisis, by Henlee H. Barnette. Grand Rapids, Eerdmans [1972] 114 p. 22 cm. Bibliography: p. 112-114. [BT695.5.B37] 72-77175 ISBN 0-8028-1457-3 (pbk) 2.25 (pbk)
1. Nature (Theology) 2. Human ecology—Moral and religious aspects. I. Title.

HENDRY, George Stuart, 1904- 231.7
Theology of nature / George S. Hendry. 1st ed. Philadelphia : Westminster Press, c1980. 258 p. ; 21 cm. (The Warfield lectures ; 1978) Includes bibliographical references and index. [BT695.5.H46] 79-27375 ISBN 0-664-24305-3 : 12.95
1. Nature (Theology) 2. Religion and sciences—1946- 3. Creation. 4. Holy Spirit. I. Title. II. Series: Annie Kinkead Warfield lectures ; 1978.

HUME, David, 1711-1776.
Dialogues concerning natural religion. Edited, with an introduction, by Norman Kemp Smith. Indianapolis, Bobbs-Merrill [1964? c1947] xii, 249 p. (The Library of liberal arts, 174) Bibliography: p. x. Bibliographical footnotes. 65-52715
I. Title.

PROTESTANT Episcopal church in the U. S. A. National council. Dept. of religious education. 268.
... Christian nature series, course ... prepared for the General board of religious education ... Milwaukee, The Young churchman co., 19 v. 19 cm. At head of title: Teacher's manual. Contains bibliographies. [BX5874.A4] 17-28085
I. Title.

RUST, Eric Charles. 230
Nature—garden or desert? An essay in environmental theology, by Eric C. Rust. Waco, Tex., Word Books [1971] 150 p. 23 cm. Includes bibliographical references. [BT695.5.R88] 76-157751 4.95
1. Nature (Theology) I. Title.

SANTMIRE, H. Paul. 500.9'01
Brother Earth; nature, God, and ecology in time of crisis [by] H. Paul Santmire. New York, T. Nelson [1970] 236 p. 20 cm. Includes bibliographical references. [BT695.5.S25] 71-127072
1. Nature (Theology) 2. Human ecology—Moral and religious aspects. I. Title.

Nature (Theology)—History of doctrines.

CHERRY, C. Conrad. 230
Nature and religious imagination : from Edwards to Bushnell / Conrad Cherry. Philadelphia : Fortress Press, c1980. x, 242 p. ; 23 cm. Includes bibliographical references and index. [BT695.5.C47] 79-7374 ISBN 0-8006-0550-0 : 12.95
1. Nature (Theology)—History of doctrines. 2. Theology, Doctrinal—New England—History. 3. United States—Religion—To 1800. 4. United States—Religion—19th century. I. Title.

Nature (Theology)—Juvenile literature.

DEVINE, Bob. 213'.5
The oyster thief / by Bob Devine ; pictures by Carolyn Bowser. Chicago : Moody Press, c1979. 32 p. : ill. (some col.) ; 21 cm. (God in creation series) Examines phenomena in nature that reflect Christian beliefs. [BT695.5.D486] 78-20904 ISBN 0-8024-6267-7 pbk. : 1.50
1. Nature (Theology)—Juvenile literature. 2. [Nature (Theology)] 3. [Christian life.] I. Bowser, Carolyn Ewing. II. Title. III. Series.

DEVINE, Bob. 213'.5
The trap-door spider / by Bob Devine. Chicago : Moddy Press, c1979. 32 p. : ill. (some col.) ; 21 cm. (God in creation series) Examines phenomena in nature that reflect Christian beliefs. [BT695.5.D487] 78-20905 ISBN 0-8024-8847-1 pbk. : 1.50
1. Nature (Theology)—Juvenile literature. 2. [Nature (Theology)] 3. [Christian life.] I. Bowser, Carolyn Ewing. II. Title. III. Series.

NIXON, Joan Lowery. 231'.7
When God speaks / by Joan Lowery Nixon ; illustrated by James McIlrath. Huntington, Ind. : Our Sunday Visitor, c1978. [30] p. : col. ill. ; 29 cm. "An OSV read-along book." A young boy learns that God uses many ways to speak of His love through the natural world. [BT695.5.N58] 78-56879 ISBN 0-87973-358-6 pbk. : 4.95
1. Nature (Theology)—Juvenile literature. 2. [God.] 3. [Nature.] I. McIlrath, James. II. Title.

Nature (Theology)—Meditations.

ROBERTSON, Josephine. 242'.4
Garden meditations / Josephine Robertson ; ill. by Billie Jean Osborne. Nashville : Abingdon, c1977. 111 p. : ill. ; 21 cm. [BT695.5.R62] 77-23316 ISBN 0-687-14000-5 : 5.95
1. Nature (Theology)—Meditations. 2. Gardening—Meditations. I. Title.

SMITH, Don Ian, 1918- 242'.1
Sagebrush seed / Don Ian Smith. Nashville : Abingdon, c1977. 111 p. : ill. ; 20 cm. [BT695.5.S64] 77-4347 ISBN 0-687-36746-8 : 5.95
1. Nature (Theology)—Mediations. I. Title.

WALKER, Raymond B., 1888-1974. 210
Beside still waters / by Raymond B. Walker. 1st ed. Portland, Or. : Binford & Mort, [1976] c1975. 165 p. : ill. ; 28 cm. Includes bibliographical references. [BT695.5.W34] 75-32601 ISBN 0-8323-0264-3 : 12.50
1. Nature (Theology)—Meditations. I. Title.

Nature (Theology)—Sermons.

HEZMALL, Everett F. 210
God speaks through nature / by Everett F. Hezmall. Lincoln, Neb. : Venture Pub., 1975. 102 p. ; 18 cm. [BT695.5.H49] 75-29556 1.25
1. Presbyterian Church—Sermons. 2. Nature (Theology)—Sermons. 3. Sermons, American. I. Title.

Nature-worship.

FRAZER, James George, Sir 1854-
The worship of nature, by Sir James George Frazer ... New York, The Macmillan company, 1926- v. 23 cm. Vol. 1, The Gifford lectures, University of Edinburgh, 1924-1925. [BL435.F7 1926 a] 26-7353
1. Nature-worship. I. Title.

FRAZER, James George, Sir, 1854-1941. 291.2'12
The workship of nature / by James George Frazer. Volume I. New York : AMS Press, [1974, i.e.1975] p. cm. No more published. Reprint of the 1926 ed. published by Macmillan, New York, which was issued as the Gifford lectures, 1924-1925. [BL435.F7 1974] 73-21271 ISBN 0-404-11427-X : 35.00
1. Nature worship. 2. Religion, Primitive. I. Title. II. Series: Gifford lectures ; 1924-1925.

SENDER, Ramon. 291.2'12
Being of the sun, written by Ramon Sender & Alicia Bay Laurel. Drawn & lettered by Alicia with musical notation by Ramon. Songs: music by Ramon & words by Alicia except where otherwise noted. [1st ed.] New York, Harper & Row [1973] 202 p. illus. 28 cm. [BL435.S46] 73-4060 ISBN 0-06-012523-3 4.95
1. Nature-worship. I. Laurel, Alicia Bay, joint author. II. Title.

Naude, Beyers.

BRYAN, G. McLeod. 285'.732'0924 B
Naude, prophet to South Africa / G. McLeod Bryan. Atlanta : John Knox Press, c1978. vii, 151 p. : group port. ; 21 cm. [BX9595.S63N383] 77-15746 ISBN 0-8042-0942-1 pbk. : 5.95
1. Naude, Beyers. 2. Reformed Church—Clergy—Biography. 3. Clergy—South Africa—Biography. I. Title.

Nauer, Barbara.

NAUER, Barbara. 248'.2'0924 B
Rise up and remember / Barbara Nauer. 1st ed. Garden City, N.Y. : Doubleday, 1977. viii, 110 p. ; 21 cm. [BX4705.N284A37] 76-54011 ISBN 0-385-12955-6 pbk. : 2.95
1. Nauer, Barbara. 2. Catholics in the United States—Biography. 3. Pentecostalism—Catholic Church. I. Title.

Nauvoo, Ill.—History

FLANDERS, Robert Bruce. 289.377343
Nauvoo; kingdom on the Mississippi. Urbana, University of Illinois Press, 1965. vii, 304 p. illus., map (on lining papers) ports. 24 cm. Bibliography: p. 342-350. [F549.N37F55] 65-19110
1. Nauvoo, Ill. — Hist. 2. Church of Jesus Christ of Latter-Day Saints. 3. Mormons and Mormonism in Illinois. I. Title.

FLANDERS, Robert Bruce. 289.377343
Nauvoo; Kingdom on the Missippi. Urbana, University of Illinois Press [1975] c1965 vii., 364 p. illus., 23 cm. Bibliography: p. 342-350. [F549.N37F55] 65-19110 ISBN 0-252-00561-9 3.95 (pbk.)
1. Nauvoo, Ill.—History. 2. Church of Jesus Christ of Latter-Day Saints. 3. Mormons and Mormonism in Illinois. I. Title.

Nauvoo, Ill. Temple.

HARRINGTON, Virginia S. 917.73'43
Rediscovery of the Nauvoo Temple; report on the archaeological excavations, by Virginia S. Harrington & J. C. Harrington. Salt Lake City, Nauvoo Restoration, 1971. 54 p. illus., col. plate. 29 cm. Bibliography: p. 51-52. [NA5235.N3H3] 76-31744
1. Nauvoo, Ill. Temple. I. Harrington, Jean Carl, 1901- joint author. II. Title.

MCGAVIN, Elmer Cecil 289.3773
The Nauvoo Temple. Salt Lake City, Deseret [1963, c.1962] 185p. illus. 24cm. 63-1780 2.50
1. Nauvoo, Ill. Temple. I. Title.

Navaho Indians.

HAILE, Berard, 1874-
Head and face masks in Navaho ceremonialism. St. Michaels, Ariz., St. Michaels Press, 1947. xiv, 122 p. illus., plates (part col.) 24 cm. A50
1. Navaho Indians. 2. Masks. 3. Navaho Indians—Rites and ceremonies. I. Title.

Navaho Indians—Legends.

KING, Jeff. 970.62
Where the two came to their father, a Navaho war ceremonial, given by Jeff King; text and paintings recorded by Maud Oakes, commentary by Joseph Campbell ... New York, Pantheon books inc. [1943] 5 p. l., 3-84 p., 2 l. 30 1/2 x 23 cm. and portfolio of 18 col. pl. 62 x 37 1/2 cm. (The Bollingen series. I) [E99.N3K45] [299.7] 44-5981
1. Navaho Indians—Legends. 2. Navaho Indians—Religion and mythology. 3. Navaho Indians—Art. I. Oakes, Maud. II. Campbell, Joseph, 1904- III. Title.

Navaho Indians—Masks.

HAILE, Berard, 1874-1961. 299'.7
Head and face masks in Navaho ceremonialism / Berard Haile. 1st AMS ed. New York : AMS Press, 1978. xiv, 122 p., [14] leaves of plates (2 fold.) : ill. ; 22

cm. Reprint of the 1947 ed. published by St. Michaels Press, St. Michaels, Ariz. [E99.N3H23 1978] 76-43722 ISBN 0-404-15565-0 : 17.50
1. Navaho Indians—Masks. 2. Indians of North America—Southwest, New—Masks. 3. Navaho Indians—Rites and ceremonies. 4. Indians of North America—Southwest, New—Rites and ceremonies. I. Title.

Navaho Indians—Missions.

DOLAGHAN, Thomas, 1927- 280'.4'097913
The Navajos are coming to Jesus / by Thomas Dolaghan, David Scates. South Pasadena, Calif. : William Carey Library, c1978. xiii, 176 p. : ill. ; 22 cm. Bibliography: p. [167]-176. [E99.N3S32] 78-3609 ISBN 0-87808-162-3 pbk. : 5.95
1. Navaho Indians—Missions. 2. Indians of North America—Southwest, New—Missions. 3. Navaho Indians—Religion and mythology. 4. Indians of North America—Southwest, New—Religion and mythology. 5. Christianity—Southwest, New. I. Scates, David 1932- joint author. II. Title.

STIRLING, Betty 266.6779
Mission to the Navajo. Mountain View, Calif., Pacific Pr. Pub. Assn. [c.1961] 147p. illus. 61-10880 3.50
1. NavajoIndians—Missions. 2. Seventh-Day Adventists—Missions. 3. Missions—Arizona. 4. Missions—New Mexico. I. Title.

WALLIS, Ethel Emily. 266'.022'0924 B
God speaks Navajo. [1st ed.] New York, Harper & Row [1968] x, 146 p. illus., map, ports. 22 cm. [E98.M6W27] 68-29560 4.95
1. Edgerton, Faye, 1889-1968. 2. Navaho Indians—Missions. I. Title.

Navaho Indians — Religion and mythology.

ABERLE, David Friend, 1918- 299.7
The peyote religion among the Navaho, by David F. Aberle. With field assistance by Harvey C. Moore and with an appendix on Navaho population and education by Denis F. Johnston. Chicago, Aldine Pub. Co. [1966] xxvi, 454 p. illus., maps. 27 cm. (Viking Fund publications in anthropology, no. 42) Bibliography: p. 423-436. [E99.N3A2] 65-26751
1. Navaho Indians — Religion and mythology. 2. Peyotism. I. Title. II. Series.

ABERLE, David Friend, 1918-
The peyote religion among the Navaho, by David F. Aberle. With field assistance by Harvey C. Moore and with an appendix on Navaho population and education by Denis F. Johnston. Subscriber's ed. [New York] Distributed through Current anthropology for the Wenner-Gren Foundation for Anthropological Research, 1966. xxvi, 454 p. illus., maps. 27 cm. (Viking Fund publications in anthropology, no. 42) Bibliography: p. 423-436. NUC67
1. Navaho Indians — Religion and mythology. 2. Peyotism. I. Title.

FRANCISCANS, St. Michaels, Ariz.
A Navaho-English catechism of Christian doctrine for the use of Navaho children. St. Michaels, Ariz., The Franciscan fathers, 1910. 1 p. l., [5]-125, [1] p., 1 l. 16 x 12 cm 10-21332
I. Title.

GILL, Sam D., 1943- 299'.78
Sacred words : a study of Navajo religion and prayer / Sam D. Gill. Westport, Conn. : Greenwood Press, 1981. xxvi, 257 p. ; 22 cm. (Contributions in intercultural and comparative studies ; no. 4 ISSN 0147-1031s) Includes index.IBibliography: p. [237]-243.V[E99.N3G49] 80-659 ISBN 0-313-22165-0 lib. bdg. : 29.95
1. Navaho Indians—Religion and mythology. 2. Indians of North America—Southwest, New—Religion and mythology. I. Title.

HAILE, Berard, 1874-1961. 299'.7
Starlore among the Navaho / by Berard Haile. Santa Fe, N.M. : W. Gannon, 1977, c1947. 44 p., [7] leaves of plates (2 fold.) : ill. ; 23 cm. Reprint of the ed. published by the Museum of Navajo Ceremonial Art, Santa Fe, N.M. Bibliography: p. 44. [E99.N3H27 1977] 76-53085 ISBN 0-88307-532-6 : 15.00
1. Navaho Indians—Religion and mythology. 2. Stars (in religion, folk-lore, etc.) 3. Indians of North America—Southwest, New—Religion and mythology. I. Title.

HALL, Manly Plamer. 133
From a philosopher's scrap-book, the sand magic of the Navahos, the mystery of the thunderbird, ju=jutsu, a secret of the samurai, the whirling dervishes, Java's dancing shadows, the Temple of heaven, the seven days of creation, by Manly P. Hall. 1st ed. Los Angeles, Calif., Hall publishing company, 1929. 64 p. illus. 17 cm. Advertising matter: p. 61-64. [BF1999.H3245] ca 30
I. Title.

KLAH, Hasteen. 970.62
Navajo creation myth; the story of the emergence, by Hasteen Klah, recorded by Mary C. Wheelwright ... Santa Fe, N. M., Museumo cermecenial art, 1942. 237 (i.e. 239), [1] p. front. (port.) col. illus. 25 cm. (Navajo religion series, vol. 1) [E99.N3K5] 299.7 42-13214
1. Navaho Indians—Religion and mythology. 2. Creation. I. Wheelwright, Mary C. II. Title.

KLAH, Hasteen. 299'.72
Navajo creation myth / [by Hasteen Klah ; recorded by Mary C. Wheelwright]. New York : AMS Press, [1980] 237 p. : ill. ; 22 cm. Reprint of the 1942 ed. published by the Museum of Navajo Ceremonial Art, Santa Fe, N.M., which was issued as v. 1 of Navajo religion series. [E99.N3K5] 76-43762 ISBN 0-404-15615-0 : 24.50
1. Navaho Indians—Religion and mythology. 2. Creation. 3. Indians of North America—Southwest, New—Religion and mythology. I. Wheelwright, Mary C. II. Title. III. Series: Navajo religion series ; v. 1.

[KLAH, Hasteen] 970.62
The story of the Navajo Hail chant, by Gladys A. Reichard. New York, N.Y., Gladys A. Reichard, 1944. 2 p. l., [vii]-xii, 155 p. illus. 27 1/2 cm. Reproduced from type-written copy. Recorded by dictation from the chanter, Hasteen Klah, and interpreted by his niece, Lucy Tabaha. cf. Introd. Navaho and English on opposite pages. [E99.N3K52] (299.7) 44-51372
1. Navaho Indians—Religion and mythology. 2. Navaho language—Texts. I. Tabaha, Lucy. II. Reichard, Gladys Amanda, 1893- tr. III. Title. IV. Title: Hail chant.

MCNELEY, James Kale. 299'.78
Holy wind in Navajo philosophy / James Kale McNeley. Tucson, Ariz. : University of Arizona Press, c1981. xvii, 115 p. ; 24 cm. Includes index. Bibliography: p. 105-109. [E99.N3M317] 19 80-27435 ISBN 0-8165-0710-4 : 14.95 ISBN 0-8165-0724-4 (pbk.) : 6.95
1. Navaho Indians—Religion and mythology. 2. Navaho Indians—Philosophy. 3. Indians of North America—Southwest, New—Religion and mythology. 4. Indians of North America—Southwest, New—Philosophy. I. Title.

†*NAVAJO Mountain and Rainbow Bridge religion* / [compiled by] Karl W. Luckert ; with English translations by Irvy W. Goossen and Harry Bilagody, Jr. ; with field assistance by Harry Bilagody, Jr., Zhunie Yellowhair, and Wilson R. Yazzie ; and with an additional text recorded by Hoffman Birney. Flagstaff : Museum of Northern Arizona, 1977. viii, 157 p. : ill. ; 23 cm. (American tribal religions : v. 1) Bibliography: p. 155-157. [E99.N3N353] 77-153661 pbk. : 6.95 299'.7
1. Navaho Indians—Religion and mythology. 2. Indians of North America—Southwest, New—Religion and mythology. I. Luckert, Karl W., 1934- II. Series.

... Navajo religion series, v. 1- Santa Fe, N. M., Museum of Navajo ceremonial art, 1942- v. 25 cm. 42-13213
I. Santa Fe, N. M. Museum of Navajo ceremonial art.

REICHARD, Gladys Amanda, 1893- 299.7 970.62
Navaho religion, a study of symbolism. [New York] Pantheon Books [1950] 2 v. (xxxvi, 800 p.) illus. 24 cm. (Bollingen series, 18) Bibliography: v. 2, p. 747-759. [E99.N3R38] 50-6769
1. Navaho Indians — Religion and mythology. 2. Symbolism. I. Title. II. Series.

REICHARD, Gladys Amanda, 1893-
Prayers: the compulsive word. Seattle, University of Washington Press [1966, c1944] x, 97 p. illus. 24 cm. (American Ethnological Society, New York. Monographs, 7) 67-62749
1. Navaho Indians — Religion and mythology. 2. Prayers. 3. Navaho language — Texts. I. Title. II. Series.

REICHARD, Gladys Amanda, 1893-1955. 299'.7
Navaho religion : a study of symbolism / Gladys A. Reichard. 2d ed. Princeton : Princeton University Press, 1974, c1950. xlvii, 804 p. : ill. ; 22 cm. (Princeton/Bollingen paperbacks ; 318) (Bollingen series ; 18) "First Princeton/Bollingen paperback edition." Includes index. Bibliography: p. [747]-761. [E99.N3R38 1974] 75-306306 ISBN 0-691-09801-8 : 16.50 ISBN 0-691-01798-0 pbk. : 6.95
1. Navaho Indians—Religion and mythology. 2. Symbolism. I. Title. II. Series.

SCHEVILL, Margaret Erwin. 970.62
Beautiful on the earth, by Margaret Erwin Schevill, with five illustrations reproduced from the author's drawings in serigraph by Louie Ewing. Santa Fe, N.M., Hazel Dreis editions [1947] xv, 155, [1] p. col. front., col. plates. 26 1/2 cm. Each plate accompanied by guard sheet with descriptive letterpress. "Five hundred copies ... have been printed ... at the Merrymount press, Boston." [E99.N3S37] 299.7 47-19962
1. Navaho Indians—Religion and mythology. 2. Navaho Indians—Rites and ceremonies. I. Title.

SPENCER, Katherine. 299.7
Mythology and values; an analysis of Navaho chantway myths. Philadelphia, American Folklore Society, 1957. viii, 240p. 23cm. (Memoirs of the American Folklore Society. v.48) Errata leaf inserted. Bibilography: p. 235--240. [GR1.A5 vol. 48] [GR1.A5 vol. 48] 970.62 57-13891 57-13891
1. Navaho Indians—Religion and mythology. I. Title. II. Series: American Folklore Society. Memoirs, v. 481

THE Upward moving and emergence way : the Gishin Biye' version / [recorded by] Berard Haile ; Karl W. Luckert, editor ; Navajo orthography by Irvy W. Goossen. Lincoln : University of Nebraska Press, [1982], c1981. xv, 238 p. : ill. ; 23 cm. (American tribal religions ; v. 7) "A Bison book."—Cover. [E99.N3U76 1982] 19 81-7441 ISBN 0-8032-2320-X : 17.95 299'.78
1. Navaho Indians—Religion and mythology. 2. Navaho Indians—Rites and ceremonies. 3. Indians of North America—Southwest, New—Religion and mythology. 4. Indians of North America—Southwest, New—Rites and ceremonies. I. Begay, Gishin. II. Haile, Berard, 1874-1961. III. Luckert, Karl W., 1934- IV. Goossen, Irvy W. V. Title. VI. Series.

WOMEN versus men : 299'.72
a conflict of Navajo emergence / the Curly To Aheedliinii version ; [recorded by] Berard Haile ; Navajo orthography by Irvy M. Goossen ; Karl W. Luckert, editor. Lincoln : University of Nebraska Press, 1982. viii, 118 p. ; 23 cm. (American tribal religions ; v. 6) English and Navaho. [E99.N3W74] 19 81-7433 ISBN 0-8032-2319-6 : 14.95 ISBN 0-8032-7211-1 pbk. : 9.95
1. Navaho Indians—Religion ad mythology. 2. Indians of North America—Southwest, New—Religion and mythology. 3. Navaho Indians—Legends. 4. Indians of North America—Southwest, New—Legends. I. Curly, To Aheedliinii. II. Haile, Berard, 1874-1961. III. Goossen, Irvy W. IV. Luckert, Karl W., 1934- V. Series.

Navaho Indians —Rites and ceremonies.

BEAUTYWAY: 299.7
a Navaho ceremonial. Myth recorded and translated by Father Berard Haile; with a variant myth recorded by Maud Oakes;and sandpaintings recorded by Laura A. Armer, Franc J. Newcomb, and Maud Oakes. [New York] Pantheon Books [1957] xii, 218p. illus., 16 col. plates. 26cm. (Bollingen series, 53) 'Supplement to Beautyway: a Navaho ceremonial. The myth, told by Singer man. recorded in the Navaho language by Father Berard Halle. Edited by Leland C. Wyman' (83p.) in pocket. Bibliography: p.199-201. [E99.N3W93] 970.62 57-7170
1. Navaho Indians —Rites and ceremonies. 2. Navaho Indians—Religion and mythology. 3. Navaho language—Texts. 4. Sandpaintings. I. Wyman, Leland Clifton, 1897- ed. II. Haile, Berard, 1874- III. Series.

LOVE-MAGIC and Butterfly People : the Slim Curly version of the ajilee and Mothway myths / [compiled by] Berard Haile ; Irvy W. Goossen, linguist in Navajo ; Karl W. Luckert, editor. Flagstaff : Museum of Northern Arizona Press, c1978. xi, 172 p. : port. ; 23 cm. (American tribal religions ; v. 2) English and Navaho. [E99.N3L79] 78-59705 ISBN 0-89734-026-4 : 13.95 299'.7
1. Navaho Indians—Rites and ceremonies. 2. Navaho Indians—Religion and mythology. 3. Indians of North America—Southwest, New—Rites and ceremonies. 4. Indians of North America—Southwest, New—Religion and mythology. 5. Navaho language—Texts. I. Slim Curly. II. Haile, Berard, 1874-1961. III. Goossen, Irvy W. IV. Luckert, Karl W., 1934- V. Title. VI. Series.

LUCKERT, Karl W., 1934- 299'.7
A Navajo bringing-home ceremony : the Claus Chee Sonny version of Deerway AjiLee / Karl Luckert ; Johnny C. Cooke, Navajo interpreter ; Irvy W. Goossen, linguist in Navajo. Flagstaff : Museum of Northern Arizona Press, c1978. xiv, 208 p. : ill. ; 23 cm. (American tribal religions ; v. 3) Bibliography: p. 205-208. [E99.N3L817] 78-59701 ISBN 0-89734-027-2 : 14.95
1. Navaho Indians—Rites and ceremonies. 2. Ajilee (Navaho rite) 3. Indians of North America—Arizona—Rites and ceremonies. I. Title. II. Series.

NAVAHO figurines called dolls. Original drawings by Harry Walters. Santa Fe, N.M., Museum of Navaho Ceremonial Art [1973? c.1972] 75 p. illus. 28 cm. Bibliography (p. 73-75) [E99.N3N27] 72-97250 299'.7
1. Navaho Indians—Rites and ceremonies. 2. Dolls (in religion, folk-lore, etc.) I. Kelly, Roger E. Navaho ritual human figurines: form and function, 1972. II. Lang, R. W. The remaking rites of the Navaho: causal factors of illness and its nature. 1972.
Contents omitted. Publisher's address: 704 Camino Lejo Santa Fe, N.M.

WATERWAY : 299'.7
a Navajo ceremonial myth / told by Black Mustache Circle ; [recorded by] Berard Haile ; orthography by Irvy W. Goossen ; appendix by Karl W. Luckert. [Flagstaff] : Museum of Northern Arizona Press, c1979. vi, 152 p. : 14 ill. ; 23 cm. (American tribal religions ; v. 5) English and Navaho. Bibliography: p. 152. [E99.N3W29] 79-66605 ISBN 0-89734-030-2 : 12.95
1. Navaho Indians—Rites and ceremonies. 2. Navaho Indians—Religion and mythology. 3. Indians of North America—Southwest, New—Rites and ceremonies. 4. Indians of North America—Southwest, New—Religion and mythology. I. Black Mustache Circle. II. Haile, Berard, 1874-1961. III. Goossen, Irvy W. IV. Series.

WYMAN, Leland Clifton, 1897- ed. [299.7] 970.62
Beautyway: a Navaho ceremonial. Myth recorded and translated by Father Berard Haile; with a variant myth recorded by Maud Oakes; and sandpaintings recorded by Laura A. Armer, Franc J. Newcomb, and Maud Oakes. [New York] Pantheon Books [1957] xii, 218 p. illus., 16 col. plates. 26 cm. (Bollingen series, 53)

"Supplement to Beautyway: a Navaho ceremonial. The myth, told by Singer man, recorded in the Navaho language by Father Berard Haile. Edited by Leland C. Wyman" (83 p.) in pocket. Bibliography: p. 199-201. [E99.N3W93] 57-7170
1. Navaho Indians — Rites and ceremonies. 2. Navaho Indians — Religion and mythology. 3. Navaho language — Texts. 4. Sandpaintings. I. Haile, Berard, 1874- II. Title. III. Series.

WYMAN, Leland Clifton, 1897- 299'.7
Blessingway [by] Leland C. Wyman. With three versions of the myth recorded and translated from the Navajo by Berard Haile. Tucson, University of Arizona Press [1970] xxviii, 660 p. illus., facsims., ports. 24 cm. Bibliography: p. 635-637. [E99.N3W9323] 66-28786 19.50
1. Navaho Indians—Rites and ceremonies. I. Haile, Berard, 1874-1961. II. Title.

WYMAN, Leland Clifton, 1897- 299.7
The red antway of the Navaho [by] Leland C. Wyman. Santa Fe, N.M., Museum of Navajo Ceremonial Art, 1965. 276 p. illus. (part col.) 22 cm. (Navajo religion series, v. 5) Bibliography: p. 235-237. [E99.N3W9] 65-18506
1. Navaho Indians — Rites and ceremonies. 2. Navaho Indians — Religion and mythology. 3. Sand paintings. 4. Ants (in religion, folk-lore, etc.) I. Title. II. Series.

Nayler, James, 1617?-1660.

BRAILSFORD, Mabel Richmond. 922.
A Quaker from Cromwell's army: James Nayler, by Mabel Richmond Brailsford. New York, The Macmillan company, 1927. 200 p. front. (port.) 2 pl. 21 cm. Printed in Great Britain. Bibliography: p. [7]-9. [BX7795.N3B7] 28-2662
1. Nayler, James, 1617?-1660. 2. Friends, Society of. England. I. Title.

Ndembu (African tribe)—Rites and ceremonies.

TURNER, Victor Witter. 299'.6
Revelation and divination in Ndembu ritual / Victor Turner. Ithaca, N.Y. : Cornell University Press, 1975. 354 p. : ill. ; 22 cm. (Symbol, myth, and ritual) Includes index. Bibliography: p. 343-344. [DT963.42.T83] 75-1623 ISBN 0-8014-0863-6 : 17.50 ISBN 0-8014-9151-7 pbk. : 4.95
1. Ndembu (African tribe)—Rites and ceremonies. 2. Ndembu (African tribe)—Religion. 3. Symbolism. I. Title.

Neale, John Mason, 1818-1866.

TOWLE, Eleanor A. (Taylor) Mrs. 922.
John Mason Neale, D.D., a memoir, by Eleanor A. Towle... London, New York [etc.] Longmans, Green, and co., 1906. xiii, [1], 338 p. front. (port.) plates, double facsim. 23 cm. "Chronological list of the works of the late Rev. J. M. Neale, from the Catalogue in the British museum": p. 322-327. [BX5199.N5T7] 7-29047
1. Neale, John Mason, 1818-1866. I. Title.

Neale, Mrs. Mary (Peisley) 1717-1757.

NEALE, Mary (Peisley) Mrs. 1717-1757.
Some account of the life and religious exercises of Mary Neale, formerly Mary Peisley. Principally compiled from her own writings. Dublin--Printed: Philadelphia: Reprinted for, and sold by, Joseph Crukshank, no. 87, High-street, 1796. v, [7]-118 p. 18 cm. Preface signed: Samuel Neale. A 31
1. Neale, Mrs. Mary (Peisley) 1717-1757. I. Neale, Samuel, 1729-1792, ed. II. Title.

Neale, Rollin Heber, 1803-1879.

HAGUE, William, 1808-1887. 922-673
Christian greatness in the minister. A discourse on the life and character of Rollin Heber Neale, D. D., forty years pastor of the First Baptist church of Boston; delivered before the church October 17, 1880, the forty-second anniversary of his settlement, by William Hague, D. D. Published by request of the church. Boston, H. Gannett, 1880. 76 p. 18 1/2 x 15 cm. [BX6495.N4H3] 36-24363
1. Neale, Rollin Heber, 1803-1879. I. Boston. First Baptist church. II. Title.

Near East—Antiquities.

ARCHAEOLOGY and the Bible 220.9'3
: an introductory study / D. J. Wiseman and Edwin Yamauchi. Grand Rapids : Zondervan, c1979. 122 p. ; 21 cm. (Contemporary evangelical perspectives) "The two chapters of this book have been selected from the introductory articles that make up volume 1 of The Expositor's Bible commentary." Includes indexes. Contents.Contents.—Wiseman, D. J. Archaeology and the Old Testament.—Yamauchi, E. Archaeology and the New Testament. Bibliography: p. 108-109. [BS620.A7] 79-10859 ISBN 0-310-38341-2 pbk. : 3.95
1. Bible—Antiquities. 2. Near East—Antiquities. I. Wiseman, Donald John. Archaeology and the Old Testament. 1979. II. Yamauchi, Edwin M. Archaeology and the New Testament. 1979.

PRITCHARD, James Bennett, 1909- 221.95
The ancient Near East; supplementary texts and pictures relating to the Old Testament, edited by James B. Pritchard. Princeton, N.J., Princeton University Press, 1969. viii, 274 p. illus., plans. 29 cm. Contains supplementary materials for the author's The ancient Near East in pictures and Ancient Near Eastern texts. Bibliographical footnotes. [BS1180.P826] 78-76500 15.00
1. Bible. O.T.—Antiquities. 2. Bible. O.T.—History of contemporary events. 3. Near East—Antiquities. 4. Oriental literature—Translations into English. 5. English literature—Translations from Oriental literature. I. Title.

Near East—Church history—Sources.

RABBATH, Antoine, 1867-1913, comp. 281'.5
Documents inedits pour servir a l'histoire du christianisme en Orient. New York, AMS Press [1973] 2 v. 23 cm. Texts in French and/or Italian, Latin, Arabic, Portuguese; some summaries in French. Reprint of the 1905?-1911? ed. published by A. Picard, Paris. [BR1070.R3 1973] 72-174293 ISBN 0-404-05202-9
1. Near East—Church history—Sources. I. Title.

Near East—Civilization.

PEOPLES of Old Testament times, 221.9'1
edited by D. J. Wiseman for the Society for Old Testament Study. Oxford, Clarendon Press, 1973. xxi, 402 p. illus. 22 cm. Includes bibliographies. [DS57.P44] 73-179589 ISBN 0-19-826316-3 17.75
1. Near East—Civilization. 2. Near East—History—To 622. I. Wiseman, Donald John, ed. II. Society for Old Testament Study.
Distributed by Oxford University Press, New York; Library edition 14.02

Near East—Description and travel.

BALY, Denis. 220.91
Atlas of the Biblical world [by] Denis Baly and A. D. Tushingham. Consultants: R. P. Roland de Vaux [and others] New York, World Pub. Co. [1971] xiii, 208 p. illus. (part col.), maps (part col.), plans. 29 cm. Bibliography: p. 177-185. [BS630.B337 1971] 71-107641 12.95
1. Bible—Geography. 2. Bible—History of contemporary events, etc. 3. Near East—Description and travel. I. Tushingham, A. Douglas, 1914- joint author. II. Title.

Near East—Description and travel—Guide-books.

BERRETT, LaMar C. 220.9'1
Discovering the world of the Bible [by] LaMar C. Berrett. Provo, Utah, Young House [1973] xxi, 701 p. illus. 23 cm. Bibliography: p. 662-665. [DS43.B43] 72-80275 ISBN 0-8425-0598-9 14.95
1. Near East—Description and travel—Guide-books. I. Title.
Pbk; 10.95, ISBN 0-8425-0599-7.

DUFFIELD, Guy P., 1909- 220.91
Handbook of Bible lands, by Guy P. Duffield. Glendale, Calif., G/L Regal Books [1969] 186 p. illus., maps. 18 cm. Bibliography: p. 181-182. [BS630.D8] 77-80446 1.65
1. Bible—Geography. 2. Near East—Description and travel—Guide-books. I. Title. II. Title: Bible lands.

MEINARDUS, Otto Friedrich August. 914.5
St. Paul's last journey / Otto F. A. Meinardus. New Rochelle, N.Y. : Caratzas Bros., 1979. xiv, 159 p., [1] leaf of plates : ill. ; 21 cm. (In the footsteps of the saints) Includes index. Bibliography: p. 149-151. [BS2506.M42] 78-51247 ISBN 0-89241-073-6 : 7.50 ISBN 0-89241-046-9 (pbk.) : 4.95
1. Paul, Saint, apostle—Journeys. 2. Near East—Description and travel—Guide-books. 3. Italy—Description and travel—1945- —Guide-books. 4. Spain—Description and travel—1951- —Guide-books. 5. Malta—Description and travel—Guide-books. I. Title. II. Series.

Near East—History—Addresses, essays, lectures.

WRIGHT, George Ernest, 1909- ed. 221.6
The Bible and the ancient Near East; essays in honor of William Foxwell Albright. [1st ed.] Garden City, N.Y., Doubleday, 1961. 409 p. illus., port. 25 cm. "Bibliography of W. F. Albright": p. [363]-389. Includes bibliographical references. [BS1188.W7] 61-8699
1. Albright, William Foxwell, 1891- 2. Bible. O.T.—Criticism, interpretation, etc. 3. Near East—History—Addresses, essays, lectures. 4. Religions—History—Addresses, essays, lectures. I. Title.

Near East—History—To 622.

HARRISON, Roland Kenneth. 220.95
Old Testament times, by R. K. Harrison. Grand Rapids, Mich., Eerdmans [1970] xvi, 357 p. illus., maps. 24 cm. Bibliography: p. 341-342. [BS1197.H27] 69-12314 6.95
1. Bible. O.T.—History of Biblical events. 2. Near East—History—To 622. I. Title.

Near East—Periodicals—Bibliography.

MCGILL University, Montreal. Institute of Islamic Studies. Library. 016.91'003'1767105
Periodica Islamica; a check-list of serials available at McGill Islamics Library, compiled by Muzaffar Ali. Montreal, McGill University, Institute of Islamic Studies, 1973. 28 p. 28 cm. [Z883.M342 1973] 74-158834
1. McGill University, Montreal. Institute of Islamic Studies. Library. 2. Near East—Periodicals—Bibliography. 3. Islamic countries—Periodicals—Bibliography. 4. Islam—Periodicals—Bibliography. I. Muzaffar Ali. II. Title.
Publisher's address: 136 S. Broadway, Irvington, N.Y. 10533

Near East—Periodicals—Bibliography—Union lists.

GOLDSTEIN, Marianne. 016.05
Selected serials in Judaic, Biblical, and Near Eastern studies in the FAUL Consortium and SUNY University Centers libraries : a union list / compiled by Marianne Goldstein. Buffalo : Lockwood Memorial Library, State University of New York at Buffalo, 1975. ix, 52 leaves ; 28 cm. Bibliography: leaf 52. [Z6367.G65] [DS101] 76-352602
1. Jews—Periodicals—Bibliography—Union lists. 2. Five Associated University Libraries. 3. New York (State). State University at Stony Brook. Library. 4. New York (State). State University, Albany. Library. 5. Bible—Periodicals—Bibliography—Union lists. 6. Near East—Periodicals—Bibliography—Union lists. I. Title: Selected serials in Judaic, Biblical, and Near Eastern studies ...

Near East—Politics and government—Miscellanea.

WALVOORD, John F. 236'.3
Armageddon : oil and the Middle East crisis ; what the Bible says about the future of the Middle East and the end of Western civilization / John F. Walvoord with John E. Walvoord. Grand Rapids : Zondervan Pub. House, 1974. 207 p. : ill. ; 18 cm. [BS647.2.W27] 74-4946 pbk. : 1.75
1. Bible—Prophecies. 2. Near East—Politics and government—Miscellanea. I. Walvoord, John E., joint author. II. Title.

Near East—Religion.

ARBERRY, Arthur John, 1905- 200'.956
Religion in the Middle East: three religions in concord and conflict; general editor A. J. Arberry. London, Cambridge U.P., 1969. 2 v. 32 plates, 41 illus., facsim., 25 maps. 24 cm. Contents.Contents.—v. 1. Juduism and Christianity.—v. 2. Islam. Bibliography: v. 2, p. 659-690. [BL1600.A7] 68-21187 7/-/- ($22.50)
1. Near East—Religion. I. Title.

GASTER, Theodor Herzl, 1906- 291.093
Thespis; ritual, myth.,and drama in the ancient Near East.Foreword by Gilbert Murray. New York, Harper [1966, c.1950] 512p. 21cm. (Torchbk.; Acad. Lib., TB1281) Bibl. [BL96.G3 1961] 2.95 pap.,
1. Near East—Religion. 2. Rites and ceremonies—Near East. 3. Mythology. 4. Religious drama—Hist. & crit. 5. Seasons. I. Title.

GASTER, Theodor Herzl, 1906- 291.1'3
Thespis : ritual, myth, and drama in the ancient Near East / Theodor H. Gaster ; foreword by Gilbert Murray. New and rev. ed. New York : Gordian Press, 1975. p. cm. Reprint of the 1961 ed. published by Anchor Books, Garden City, N.Y. Includes indexes. Bibliography: p. [BL96.G3 1975] 75-15735 ISBN 0-87752-188-3 : 15.00
1. Near East—Religion. 2. Rites and ceremonies—Near East. 3. Mythology. 4. Religious drama—History and criticism. 5. Seasons. I. Title.

GASTER, Theodor Herzl, 1906- 291.1'3
Thespis : ritual, myth, and drama in the ancient Near East / Theodor H. Gaster ; foreword by Gilbert Murray. New York : Norton, [1977] c1961. p. cm. (The Norton library) Originally published in 1966 by Harper & Row, New York. Includes index. Bibliography: p. [BL96.G3 1977] 77-14475 ISBN 0-393-00863-0 pbk. : 5.95
1. Near East—Religion. 2. Rites and ceremonies—Near East. 3. Mythology. 4. Religious drama—History and criticism. 5. Seasons. I. Title.

GASTER, Theodor Herzl, 1906- 291.1'3
Thespis : ritual, myth, and drama in the ancient Near East / Theodor H. Gaster ; foreword by Gilbert Murray. New York : Norton, [1977] c1961. p. cm. (The Norton library) Originally published in 1966 by Harper & Row, New York. Includes index. Bibliography: p. [BL96.G3 1977] 77-14475 ISBN 0-393-00863-0 pbk. : 5.95
1. Near East—Religion. 2. Rites and ceremonies—Near East. 3. Mythology. 4. Religious drama—History and criticism. 5. Seasons. I. Title.

GASTER, Theodor Herzl, 1906- 291.1'3
Thespis; ritual, myth, and drama in the ancient Near East. Foreword by Gilbert Murray. New and rev. ed. Garden City, N.Y., Doubleday, 1961. 515 p. 19 cm.

(Anchor books, A230) Includes bibliography. [BL96.G3 1961] 61-7650
1. Near East—Religion. 2. Rites and ceremonies—Near East. 3. Mythology. 4. Religious drama—History and criticism. 5. Seasons. I. Title.

JURJI, Edward Jabra, 1907- 290.956
The Middle East, its religion and culture. Philadelphia, Westminster Press [1956] 159p. 22cm. [BL1060.J8] 56-9553
1. Near East—Religion. 2. Near East—Civilization. I. Title.

JURJI, Edward Jabra, 1907- 200'.956
The Middle East; its religion and culture, by Edward J. Jurji. Westport, Conn., Greenwood Press [1973, c1956] 159 p. 22 cm. Bibliography: p. 156-159. [BL1060.J8 1973] 72-9809 ISBN 0-8371-6597-0 8.50
1. Near East—Religion. 2. Near East—Civilization.

TEIXIDOR, Javier. 200'.956
The pagan god : popular religion in the Greco-Roman Near East / by Javier Teixidor. Princeton, N.J. : Princeton University Press, c1977. xii, 192 p. ; 23 cm. Includes index. Bibliography: p. 165-174. [BL1060.T44] 76-24300 ISBN 0-691-07220-5 : 10.00
1. Near East—Religion. I. Title.

Near East—Religion—Addressess, essays, lectures.

SCRIPTURE in context : 221.6
essays on the comparative method / edited by Carl D. Evans, William W. Hallo, John B. White. Pittsburg : Pickwick Press, 1980. xiv, 328 p. ; 22 cm. (Pittsburgh theological monograph series ; no. 34) Originally presented at a seminar held at Yale University, summer of 1978. Includes bibliographical references and indexes. [BS1171.2.S35] 80-10211 ISBN 0-915138-43-3 pbk. : 13.50
1. Bible. O.T.—Criticism, interpretation, etc.—Addresses, essays, lectures. 2. Bible. O.T.—Comparative studies—Addresses, essays, lectures. 3. Near East—Religion—Addressess, essays, lectures. I. Evans, Carl D. II. Hallo, William W. III. White, John Bradley, 1947-
Contents omitted Contents omitted

Near East—Religion—Collected works.

KAPELRUD, Arvid Schou, 1912- 221.6
God and his friends in the Old Testament / Arvid S. Kapelrud. [Oslo] : Universitetsforlaget, c1979. 202 p. ; 22 cm. Includes bibliographical references. [BS511.2.K36] 79-322297 ISBN 8-200-01890-3 : 23.00
1. Bible. O.T.—Criticism, interpretation, etc.—Collected works. 2. Dead Sea scrolls—Collected works. 3. Near East—Religion—Collected works. I. Title.
Distributed by Columbia University Press, NYC

Near East—Religion—History—Sources.

ment. Engl
RELIGIONSGESCHICHTLICHES Textbuch zum Alten Testament. English *Near Eastern religious texts relating to the Old Testament* / edited by Walter Beyerlin, in collaboration with Hellmut Brunner ... [et al. ; translated by John Bowden from the German]. Philadelphia : Westminster Press, c1978. xxviii, 288 p., 4 leaves of plates : ill. ; 23 cm. (The Old Testament library) Translation of Religionsgeschichtliches Textbuch zum Alten Testament, which is a translation of ancient Egyptian, Mesopotamian, Hittite, Ugaritic, and North Semitic texts, with commentary. Includes bibliographical references and indexes. [BL1060.R4413] 77-28284 ISBN 0-664-21363-4 : 22.50
1. Bible. O.T.—History of contemporary events, etc.—Sources. 2. Near East—Religion—History—Sources. I. Beyerlin, Walter. II. Title. III. Series.

Near East—Social life and customs.

EWING, Joseph Franklin, 1905- 225.9
The ancient way: life and landmarks of the Holy Land [by] J. Franklin Ewing. New York, Scribner [1964] 224 p. illus., map, plan. 22 cm. [BS621.E9] 64-23524
1. Bible—History of contemporary events, etc. 2. Near East—Social life and customs. I. Title.

Nebraska. University—Religion.

WERNER, Oscar Helmuth, 1888- 371.8
... A religious welfare survey at the University of Nebraska, 1941- 43. Reported by Oscar H. Werner for the faculty representatives on the Religious welfare council. [Lincoln, The University of Nebraska, 1943] viii, 9-77 p. incl. tables. 23 cm. (University of Nebraska publication ... no. 144, May 1943) Bibliographical footnotes. [BV1610.W4] A 44
1. Nebraska. University—Religion. I. Nebraska. University. Council of religious welfare. II. Title.

Necedah, Wis. Queen of the Holy Rosary Mediatrix of Peace Shrine.

VAN HOOF, Mary Ann, 1909- 232.91
Revelations and messages as given through Mary Ann Van Hoof at Necedah, Wisconsin, 1950-1970. [Necedah, Wis., For My God and My Country, inc., 1971] lxx, 634 p. illus., ports. 19 cm. "The contents of the first edition of the Revelations and message book was compiled and edited by Myrtle Sommers ... The additional work since Myrtle's death has been carried on by other dedicated workers." [BT660.N4V35 1971] 77-25776
1. Necedah, Wis. Queen of the Holy Rosary Mediatrix of Peace Shrine. I. Sommers, Myrtle, ed. II. Title.

Needleman, Jacob.

NEEDLEMAN, Jacob. 230
Lost Christianity / Jacob Needleman. 1st ed. Garden City, N.Y. : Doubleday, 1980. ix, 228 p. ; 22 cm. Includes index. [BR121.2.N38] 79-6663 ISBN 0-385-00011-1 : 9.95
1. Needleman, Jacob. 2. Christianity—Essence, genius, nature. 3. Christianity—20th century. 4. Christianity and other religions. 5. Spirituality. I. Title.

Needlework.

ANTROBUS, Mary (Symonds), Mrs.
Needlework in religion; an introductory study of its inner meaning, history, and development; also a practical guide to the construction and decoration of altar clothing and of the vestments required in church services. By M. Symonds (Mrs. G. Antrobus) and L. Preece ... London, New York [etc.], Sir I. Pitman & sons, ltd., [1924.] xxiii, 229, [1] p., 4 l. illus. (part col.) xxxv pl. (incl. col. front.) 23 1/2 cm. Blank leaves for "Notes" (4 at end). "Books for reference": p. 223. [NK9310.A5] 34-23722
1. Needlework. 2. Embroidery. 3. Christian art and symbolism. 4. Church vestments. I. Preece, Louisa, joint author. II. Title.

DEAN, Beryl 746.44
Church needlework. [dist. Newton, Mass., Branford, 1962, c.1961] 136p. illus. 23cm. 4.95 bds.,
1. Needlework. 2. Embroidery. 3. Church vestments. I. Title.

Needlework, Church.

DEAN, Beryl.
Church needlework. Newton, Mass., Branford [1962] 136 p. 79 illus. 23 cm. 63-8130
1. Needlework, Church. 2. Embroidery, Church. 3. Costume, Ecclesiastical. I. Title.

Neem Karoli Baba.

RAM Dass. 294.5'6'10924
Miracle of love : stories about Neem Karoli Baba / by Ram Dass. 1st ed. New York : Dutton, c1979. xvi, 414 p. : ill. ; 24 cm. [BL1175.N43R35 1979] 79-10745 ISBN 0-525-47611-3 : 9.95
1. Neem Karoli Baba. 2. Hindus in India—Biography. I. Title.

Neerskov, Hans Kristian.

NEERSKOV, Hans Kristian. 266'.0092'4 B
Mission possible / Hans Kristian, with Dave Hunt. Old Tappan, N.J. : Revell, [1975] 191 p. ; 21 cm. [BV3777.E93N43] 74-26808 ISBN 0-8007-0717-6 pbk. : 2.95
1. Neerskov, Hans Kristian. 2. Evangelistic work—Europe, Eastern. I. Hunt, Dave, joint author. II. Title.

Neesima, Joseph Hardy, 1843-1890.

DAVIS, Jerome Dean, 1838-1910. 275.
A maker of new Japan Rev. Joseph Hardy Neesima, LL. D., president of Doshisha university, Kyoto, by Rev. J. D. Davis ... [3d ed.] New York, Chicago [etc.] Fleming H. Revell company [1905] 9 p., 1 l., [2], 13-156 p. front., illus. (coat of arms) plates, ports. 20 cm. First published in 1890 under title: A sketch of the life of Rev. Joseph Hardy Neesima. [BV3457.N4D3] 12-31770
1. Neesima, Joseph Hardy, 1843-1890. I. Title.

DAVIS, Jerome Dean, 1838-1910. 275.
A sketch of the life of Rev. Joseph Hardy Neesima, LL.D., president of Doshisha university, Kyoto, by Rev. J. D. Davis ... [2d ed.] New York, Chicago [etc.] Fleming H. Revell company [c1894] 156 p. front., illus. (coat of arms) plates, ports. 19 1/2 cm. [BV3457.N4D35] 12-13251
1. Neesima, Joseph Hardy, 1843-1890. I. Title.

HARDY, Arthur Sherburne, 1847-1930. 922.
Life and letters of Joseph Hardy Neesima. By Arthur Sherburne Hardy. Boston and New York, Houghton, Mifflin and company, 1891. vi, 350 p. 2 port. (incl. front.) facsim. 20 1/2 cm. [BV3457.N4H3 1891] 8-11261
1. Neesima, Joseph Hardy, 1848-1890. I. Title.

HARDY, Arthur Sherburne, 1847-1930. 922.
Life and letters of Joseph Hardy Neesima, by Arthur Sherburne Hardy. Boston and New York, Houghton, Mifflin and company, 1892. vi, 350 p. 2 port. (incl. front.) facsim. 20 cm. "Sixth edition." [BV3457.N4H3 1892] 8-16221
1. Neesima, Joseph Hardy, 1843-1890. I. Title.

Neff, Felix, 1798-1829.

GILLY, William Stephen, 1789-1855. 922.444
A memoir of Felix Neff, pastor of the High Alps. And of his labours among the French Protestants of Dauphine, a remnant of the primitive Christians of Gaul. By William Stephen Gilly ... Philadelphia, Carey & Lea, 1832. 5 p. l., [13]-320 p. 16 cm. [BR1722.N4G5 1832 a] 38-3071
1. Neff, Felix, 1798-1829. I. Title.

GILLY, William Stephen 1789-1855. 922.444
A memoir of Felix Neff. pastor of the High Alps. By William Stephen Gilly ... Abridged for the Massachusetts Sabbath school society, and revised by the Committee of publication. Boston, Massachusetts Sabbath school society, 1833. 2 p. l., [9]-128 p. front. 15 cm. [BR1725.N4G5 1833] 38-3067
1. Neff, Felix, 1798-1829. I. Massachusetts Sabbath school society, Committee of publication. II. Title.

Neff, LaVonne.

NEFF, LaVonne. 248'.246 B
A heart of flesh. Mountain View, Calif., Pacific Press Pub. Association [1973] 94 p. 22 cm. (A Destiny book D-139) [BX6193.N43A3] 73-78988
1. Neff, LaVonne. I. Title.

Negro churches.

FRAZIER, Edward Franklin, 1894-1962. 277.3
The Negro church in America. New York, Schocken Books [1964, c1963] xii, 92 p. 23 cm. (Studies in sociology) Bibliographical footnotes. [BR563.N4F7] 62-19390
1. Negro churches. I. Title.

MAYS, Benjamin Elijah, 1895- 277.3
The Negro's church, by Benjamin Elijah Mays and Joseph William Nicholson. New York, Russell & Russell [1969] xiii, 321 p. maps. 20 cm. Reprint of the 1933 ed. Bibliographical footnotes. [BR563.N4M3 1969] 68-15142
1. Negro churches. I. Nicholson, Joseph William, joint author. II. Title.

MAYS, Benjamin Elijah, 1895- 277'.3
The Negro's church [by] Benjamin Elijah Mays & Joseph William Nicholson. New York, Arno Press, 1969. xiii, 321 p. map, plans. 22 cm. (Religion in America) Reprint of the 1933 ed. Includes bibliographical references. [BR563.N4M3 1969c] 70-83430
1. Negro churches. I. Nicholson, Joseph William, joint author. II. Title.

Negro churches—Addresses, essays, lectures.

NELSEN, Hart M., comp. 301.5'8'0973
The Black church in America, edited by Hart M. Nelsen, Raytha L. Yokley [and] Anne K. Nelsen. New York, Basic Books [1971] vii, 375 p. 25 cm. Includes bibliographies. [BR563.N4N44] 79-147014 ISBN 0-465-00691-4 10.00
1. Negro churches—Addresses, essays, lectures. 2. Negro clergy—United States—Addresses, essays, lectures. I. Yokley, Raytha L., joint comp. II. Nelsen, Anne K., joint comp. III. Title.

Negro churches—Bibliography.

LEFFALL, Dolores C., 1931- 016.26
The Black church; an annotated bibliography. Compiled by Dolores C. Leffall. Washington, Minority Research Center [1973] 92 p. 29 cm. (Minority group series) Cover title: Focus on the Black church. [Z1361.N39L383] 73-176035 7.50
1. Negro churches—Bibliography. 2. Negroes—Religion—Bibliography. I. Title. II. Title: Focus on the Black church. III. Series.

Negro churches—United States.

FRAZIER, Edward Franklin, 1894-1962. 301.5'8
The Negro church in America [by] E. Franklin Frazier. The Black church since Frazier [by] C. Eric Lincoln. New York, Schocken Books [1974] vi, 216 p. 21 cm. (Sourcebooks in Negro history) "The Black church since Frazier originated as the James Gray lectures given at Duke University in 1970." Bibliography: p. [207]-208. [BR563.N4F7 1974] 72-96201 ISBN 0-8052-3508-6 10.00
1. Negro churches—United States. 2. Negroes—Religion. I. Lincoln, Charles Eric. The Black church since Frazier. 1974. II. Title. III. Title: The Black church since Frazier. IV. Series.

GEORGE, Carol V. R. 287'.83 B
Segregated Sabbaths; Richard Allen and the emergence of independent Black churches 1760-1840 [by] Carol V. R. George. New York, Oxford University Press, 1973. x, 205 p. front. 21 cm. Bibliography: p. 184-198. [BX8449.A6G46] 73-76908 7.95

1. Allen, Richard, Bp., 1760-1831. 2. African Methodist Episcopal Church. 3. Negro churches—United States. I. Title.

Negro churches—United States—Congresses.

NATIONAL United Methodist 287'.6 Convocation on the Black Church, Atlanta, 1973.
Experiences, struggles, and hopes of the Black church / edited by James S. Gadsden. Nashville : Tidings, c1975. x, 149 p. ; 18 cm. Includes bibliographical references. [BR563.N4N37 1973] 75-3633
1. Negro churches—United States—Congresses. I. Gadsden, James S. II. United Methodist Church (United States) III. Title.

Negro clergy—United States.

HAMILTON, Charles V. 253
The Black preacher in America [by] Charles V. Hamilton. New York, Morrow, 1972. 246 p. 21 cm. Includes bibliographical references. [BR563.N4H34] 78-170231 ISBN 0-688-00006-1 ISBN 0-688-05006-9 (pbk)
1. Negro clergy—United States. I. Title.

Negro clergy—United States—Biography.

BODDIE, Charles 253'.2'0922 B Emerson.
God's "bad boys." Valley Forge [Pa.] Judson Press [1972] 125 p. ports. 23 cm. [BR563.N4B64] 72-75360 ISBN 0-8170-0534-X 4.95
1. Negro clergy—United States—Biography. I. Title.

Negro clergy—United States—Biography—Dictionaries.

WILLIAMS, Ethel L. 280'.092'2 B
Biographical directory of Negro ministers / by Ethel L. Williams. 3d ed. Boston : G. K. Hall, 1975. p. cm. Includes index. Bibliography: p. [BR563.N4W5 1975] 74-34109 ISBN 0-8161-1183-9 lib.bdg. : 28.00
1. Negro clergy—United States—Biography—Dictionaries. I. Title.

WILLIAMS, Ethel L. 262.140922 B
Biographical directory of Negro ministers, by Ethel L. Williams. New York, Scarecrow Press, 1965. xi, 421 p. 22 cm. Bibliography: p. 407-412. [BR563.N4W5] 65-13562
1. Negro clergy—United States—Biography—Dictionaries. I. Title.

WILLIAMS, Ethel L. 262'.14'0922 B
Biographical directory of Negro ministers, by Ethel L. Williams. 2d ed. Metuchen, N.J., Scarecrow Press, 1970. 605 p. 22 cm. Bibliography: p. 575-580. [BR563.N4W5 1970] 78-18496 ISBN 8-10-803283-
1. Negro clergy—U.S.—Biography—Dictionaries. I. Title.

Negro literature—History and criticism

MAYS, Benjamin Elijah, 810.9 1895-
The Negro's God as reflected in his literature [by] Benjamin E. Mays...lithographs by James L. Wells. Boston, Chapman & Grimes, inc. [c1938] viii p., 1 l., 269 p. 20 cm. Bibliography: p. 257-268. [PS158.N5M3] 231 38-37550
1. God. 2. Negro literature—Hist. & crit. 3. Negroes—Religion. 4. Religion in literature. I. Title.

Negro Muslims.

DIARA, Agadem L. 297'.197'83451
Islam and Pan-Africanism [by] Agadem L. Diara. [Detroit, Agascha Productions, 1973] xx, 95 p. port. 22 cm. Bibliography: p. 81-83. [BP62.N4D5] 72-91318 ISBN 0-913358-04-5 1.50 (pbk.)
1. Negro Muslims. 2. Pan-Africanism. 3. Islam—Africa. I. Title.

Negro race.

NOTT, Josiah Clark, 1804-1873.
Two lectures on the connection between the Biblical and physical history of man. Delivered by invitation from the Chair of political economy, etc., of theLouisiana university, in December 1848. By Josiah C. Nott ... New York, Bartlett and Welford, 1849. 146 p. front. (fold. map) 23 cm. Contents.--Physical history of man.--Man intellectually viewed.--Geography of the Bible.--Ethnography of the Bible.--Chronology.--New Testament.--Universal terms.--Appendix: a Original language of the Bible. B. Pentateuch. C. History of text and canon of the Old Testament. [GN356.N91] 4-28665
1. Negro race. 2. Monogenism and polygenism. I. Title.

Negro race—Addresses, essays, lectures.

BLYDEN, Edward Wilmot, 291'.17'83 1832-1912
Christianity, Islam and the Negro race [by] Edward W. Blyden; Introd. by Christopher Fyfe. Edinburgh, University Pr., 1967. xviii, ix, 407p. 23cm. (African heritage bks., I) Bibl. [DT4.B54 1967] 67-105041 6.50
1. Negro race—Addresses, essays, lectures. 2. Christianity—Africa—Addresses, essays, lectures. 3. Islam—Africa—Addresses, essays, lectures. I. Title. II. Series.
American distributor: Aldine, Chicago.

Negro race in the Bible.

DUNSTON, Alfred 221.8'30145'196 G., 1915-
The Black man in the Old Testament and its world / by Alfred G. Dunston, Jr. Philadelphia : Dorrance, [1974] 161 p. ; 22 cm. Bibliography: p. 159-161. [BS1199.N4D86] 74-78665 ISBN 0-8059-2016-1 : 6.95
1. Negro race in the Bible. I. Title.

Negro race—Religion.

LANDERS, Ruth, 1908- 299.6
The city of women. New York, Macmillan, 1947. vi, 248 p. 22 cm. "The material for this book about Brazil was gathered during an anthropological field trip in Bahia and Rio de Janeiro in 1938 and 1939 ... It ... describes the life of Brazilians of the Negro race." [BL2490.L3] 47-3896
1. Negro race—Religion. 2. Negroes in Brazil. 3. Folk-lore, Negro. I. Title.

Negro songs.

BARTON, William Eleazar, 784.7'56 1861-1930.
Old plantation hymns. New York, AMS Press [1972] 45 p. illus. 24 cm. Original t.p. reads: Old plantation hymns; a collection of hitherto unpublished melodies of the slave and the freeman, with historical and descriptive notes. Reprint of the 1899 ed. [ML3556.B29 1972] 72-38499 ISBN 0-404-09918-1 5.00
1. Negro songs. I. Title.

DETT, Robert Nathaniel, 784.7'56 1882-1943, ed.
Religious folk-songs of the Negro as sung at Hampton Institute. Hampton, Va., Hampton Institute Press, 1927. [New York, AMS Press, 1972] xxvii, 236, ii, xiii p. 24 cm. [M1670.H3 1972] 72-1595 ISBN 0-404-09920-3 12.50
1. Negro songs. I. Hampton Institute, Hampton, Va. II. Title.

GRISSOM, Mary Allen. 784.756
The Negro sings a new heaven, by Mary Allen Grissom. Chapel Hill, The University of North Carolina press, 1930. 4 p. l., 101 p. 24 cm. [The University of North Carolina. Social study series] Songs with music. "Most of the songs included in this volume have been taken directly from the Negroes in their present-day worship and have been selected from those sung in the neighborhood of Louisville, Kentucky, and certain rural sections in Adair county."--Foreword. [M1670.G8N3] 39-28863
1. Negro-songs. 2. Negroes—Kentucky. I. Title.

JOHNSON, James Weldon, 784.756 1871-1938, ed.
The book of American Negro spirituals, edited with an introduction by James Weldon Johnson; musical arrangements by J. Rosamond Johnson, additional numbers by Lawrence Brown. New York, The Viking press, 1925. 187 p. 26 cm. [M1670.J67] 25-230720
1. Negro songs. I. Johnson, John Rosamond, 1873- II. Brown, Lawrence. III. Title. IV. Title: Spirituals.

JOHNSON, John Rosamond, 784.756 1873- ed.
Rolling along in song; a chronological survey of American Negro music, with eighty-seven arrangements of Negro songs, including ring shouts, spirituals, work songs, plantation ballads, chain-gang, jail-house, and minstrel songs, street cries, and blues, edited and arranged by J. Rosamond Johnson. New York, The Viking press, 1937. 224 p. 26 cm. [M1670.J65R6] 37-27426
1. Negro songs. I. Title.

MCILHENNY, Edward Avery, 784.756 1872- comp.
Befo' de war spirituals; words and melodies, collected by E. A. McIlhenny ... Boston, The Christopher publishing house [c1933] 255 p. plates, ports. 21 1/2 cm. "The numbers ... represent the real singing of real Louisiana spirituals by real Louisiana Negroes."--Introd. to music, signed: Henri Wehrmann. [M1670.M15B4] 34-383
1. Negro songs. 2. Negroes—Louisiana. I. Wehrmann, Henry, 1870- II. Title. III. Title: Spirituals.

STILL, William Grant, 784.756 1895-
Twelvy Negro spirituals [arranged] by William Grant Still. Illustrated by Albert Barbelle ... [New York] Handy brothers, music co., inc. [c1937- v. illus. (incl. ports.) 30 1/2 x 23 cm. Title from cover. Vol. 1 has special t.-p. With stories of Negro life by Ruby Berkley Goodwin. Edited by Wellington Adams. Contents.v. 1. "Gwinter sing all along de way." "All God's chillum got shoes." "Lis'n to de lam's." "Keep me from sinkin' down." "Lawd, ah wants to be a Christian." "Great camp meeting." [M1670.S86N4] 37-22232
1. Negro songs. I. Goodwin, Ruby Berkley. II. Adams, Wellington Alexander, 1879- ed. III. Title. IV. Title: Spirituals, Twelve Negro.

WORK, John Wesley, 1901- 784.756 ed.
American Negro songs and spirituals; a comprehensive collection of 230 folk songs, religious and secular, with a foreword by John W. Work. New York, Crown publishers [c1940] 1 p. l., [v]-vii p., 1 l., 259 p. 26 cm. With music. Bibliography: p. 252-256. [M1670.W93A] A 42
1. Negro songs. I. Title.

Negro spirituals.

CRITE, Allan Rohan, 704.948'4 1910- illus.
Were you there when they crucified my Lord; a Negro spiritual in illustrations. College Park, Md., McGrath Pub. Co. [1969, c1944] [93] p. illus. 29 cm. Music for the spiritual: p. [13] [N8053.C7 1969] 70-84107
1. Jesus Christ—Art. 2. Jesus Christ—Crucifixion. 3. Negro spirituals. I. Title.

HANDY, William 784.756 Christopher, 1873- arr.
W. C. Handy's collection of Negro spirituals for mixed voices, male voices, also vocal solos with piano accompaniment ... New York, N.Y., Handy brothers music co. inc. [1938] cover-title, 116 p. 26 cm. [M1670.H33O6] 43-20557
1. Negro spirituals. I. Title.

[HAWKINS, John Dewey] 784.756 comp.
Daily food in Negro spirituals. Henderson, N.C., Dr. J. D. Hawkins, c1943. [101] p. illus.(ports.) 19 cm. Without music. [M1670.H38D3] 44-5799
1. Negro spirituals. I. Title.

JOHNSON, James Weldon, 1871-1938.
The books of American Negro spirituals, including The book of American Negro spirituals, and The second book of Negro spirituals [by] James Weldon Johnson and J. Rosamond Johnson. New York, Viking Press [1964] 2 v. in 1. First published as 2 v. in 1, 1940. 67-42157
1. Negro spirituals. I. Johnson, John Rosamond, 1873- II. Title. III. Title: The book of American Negro spirituals. IV. Title: The second book of Negro spirituals.

Negro spirituals—History and criticism.

CONE, James H. 784.7'56
The spirituals and the blues: an interpretation [by] James H. Cone. New York, Seabury Press [1972] viii, 152 p. 21 cm. (A Seabury paperback, SP 74) Includes bibliographical references. [ML3556.C66] 73-186165 ISBN 0-8164-0236-1 ISBN 0-8164-2073-4 (pbk) 2.95 (pbk)
1. Negro spirituals—History and criticism. 2. Blues (Songs, etc.)—History and criticism. I. Title.

HEILBUT, Tony. 783.7
The gospel sound; good news and bad times. New York, Simon and Schuster [1971] 350 p. ports. 22 cm. [ML3556.H37] 76-156151 ISBN 0-671-20983-3 7.95
1. Negro spirituals—History and criticism. 2. Negro musicians. I. Title.

THURMAN, Howard, 1899- 784.756
Deep river; reflections on the religious insight of certain of the Negro spirituals. Illustrated by Elizabeth Orton Jones. [Rev. and enl.] New York. Harper 1955. 93 p. illus. 22 cm. [ML3556.T55 1955] 55-11483
1. Negro spirituals—Hist. & crit. I. Title.

THURMAN, Howard, 784.7'56'09 1899-
Deep river; reflections on the religious insight of certain of the Negro spirituals. Illustrated by Elizabeth Orton Jones. Port Washington, N.Y., Kennikat Press [1969, c1955] 93 p. illus. 21 cm. [ML3556.T55 1969] 71-79302
1. Negro spirituals—History and criticism. I. Title.

THURMAN, Howard, 1899- 783.6'7
Deep river and The Negro spiritual speaks of life and death / by Howard Thruman. Richmond, Ind. : Friends United Press, c1975. 136 p. : ill. ; 22 cm. "Originally separate books, but now in a single volume, Deep river was copyrighted in 1945 and 1955, and The Negro spiritual speaks of life and death in 1947." [ML3556.T55 1975] 75-27041 ISBN 0-913408-20-4 pbk. : 2.95
1. Negro spirituals—History and criticism. I. Thurman, Howard, 1899- The Negro spiritual speaks of life and death. 1975. II. Title: Deep river. III. Title: The Negro spiritual speaks of life and death.

THURMAN, Howard, 1899- 784.7'56
The Negro spiritual speaks of life and death. New York, Harper & Row [1969, c1947] 55 p. 22 cm. (J. & J. Harper editions.) (The Ingersoll lecture, Harvard University, 1947) [ML3556.T56 1969] 76-80802
1. Negro spirituals—History and criticism. I. Title. II. Series.

THURMAN, Howard, 1899- 784.756
The Negro spiritual speaks of life and death. New York, Harper [1947] 55 p. 18 cm. (The Ingersoll lecture, Harvard University, 1947) Series. [ML3556.T56] 47-12396
1. Negro spirituals—Hist.& crit. I. Title. II. Series.

Negro spirituals—Meditations.

OWENS, James Garfield. 264'.2
All God's chillun; meditations on Negro spirituals [by] J. Garfield Owens. Nashville, Abingdon Press [1971] 144 p. 20 cm. [BV4832.2.O9] 79-134251 ISBN 0-687-01020-9 3.75
1. Negro spirituals—Meditations. I. Title.

Negro theological seminaries.

DANIEL, William Andrew, 1895- 207'.11
The education of Negro ministers, by W. A. Daniel. Based upon a survey of theological schools for Negroes in the United States made by Robert L. Kelly and W. A. Daniel. New York, Negro Universities Press [1969] 187 p. 23 cm. Reprint of the 1925 ed. "The Institute of Social and Religious Research ... is responsible for this publication." [BV4080.D3 1969] 71-78581 ISBN 0-8371-1410-1
1. Negro theological seminaries. 2. Theology—Study and teaching. 3. Negroes—Education. I. Institute of Social and Religious Research. II. Title.

Negroes.

GILLARD, John Thomas, 1900- 261
Christ, color & communism [by] Rev. John T. Gillard ... [Baltimore, The Josephite press, 1937] v, 138 p. 19 cm. [BX1407.N4G52] 37-20301
1. Negroes. 2. Communism—U. S. 3. Socialism and Catholic church. 4. Sociology, Christian—Catholic authors. I. Title.
Contents omitted.

OLIVER, French Earl, 1879- comp. 252
Famous Negro sermons, by French E. Oliver, D. D. Hollywood, Calif., He Oliver press [c1927] 173 p. 11 cm. [BV4241.5.O5] 28-32
I. Title. II. Title: Negro sermons.

Negroes—Addresses, essays, lectures.

AHMANN, Matthew, II ed. 261.8'3
The Church and the urban racial crisis, edited by Mathew Ahmann and Margaret Roach. Techny, Ill., Divine Word Publications [1967] viii, 262 p. 22 cm. "The major addresses and background papers prepared for the August, 1967, convention of the National Catholic Conference for Interracial Justice held at Rockhurst College in Kansas City, Missouri." [E185.615.C58] 67-29364
1. Negroes—Addresses, essays, lectures. 2. Church and race problems—U. S.—Addresses, essays, lectures. I. Roach, Margaret, ed. II. National Catholic Conference for Interracial Justice. III. Rockhurst College, Kansas City, Mo. IV. Title.

CHURCH and the urban racial crisis (The). ed. by Mathew Ahmann, Margaret Roach. Techny, Ill., Divine World [1967] viii, 262p. 22cm. The major addresses and background papers prepd. for the Aug. 1967, convention of the Natl. Catholic Conf. for Interracial Justice held at Rockhurst Coll. in Kansas City, Mo. [E185.615.C58] 67-29364 2.95 261.8'3
1. Negroes—Addresses, essays, lectures. 2. Church and race problems—U. S.—Address essays, lectures. I. Ahmann. Mathew H. ed. II. Roach, Margaret. ed. III. National Catholic Conference for Interracial Justice. IV. Rockhurst College, Kansas City, Mo.

Negroes—Atlanta.

ENGLISH, James W. 286'.133'0924
Handyman of the Lord: the life and ministry of the Rev. William Holmes Borders, by James W. English. [1st ed.] New York, Meredith Press [1967] ix, 177 p. 21 cm. Published in 1973 under title: The prophet of Wheat Street. [BX6455.B63E5] 67-12637
1. Borders, William Holmes, 1905- 2. Negroes—Atlanta. I. Title.

ENGLISH, James W. 286'.133'0924 B
The prophet of Wheat Street; the story of William Holmes Borders, a man who refused to fail, by James W. English. Elgin, Ill., D. C. Cook Pub. Co. [1973] 205 p. 18 cm. First ed. published in 1967 under title: Handyman of the Lord. [BX6455.B63E5 1973] 73-78715 ISBN 0-912692-19-7 1.25
1. Borders, William Holmes, 1905- 2. Negroes—Atlanta. I. Title.

[Negroes—Biography.]

HASKINS, James, 1941- 301.45'19'6073024 B
The picture life of Malcolm X, by James S. Haskins. New York, F. Watts, 1975. 43 p. illus. 22 cm. (Picture lives) Brief text and photographs present the life of the controversial black Muslim leader who was assassinated in 1965. [BP223.Z8L574] 92 74-7441 ISBN 0-531-02771-6 3.90 (lib. bdg.)
1. Little, Malcolm, 1925-1965—Juvenile literature. 2. [Little, Malcolm, 1925-1965.] 3. [Negroes—Biography.] I. Title.

WHITE, Florence Meiman, 1910- 301.45'19'6073024 B
Malcolm X: Black and proud, by Florence M. White. Illustrated by Victor Mays. Champaign, Ill., Garrard Pub. Co. [1975] 95 p. illus. (part col.) 24 cm. (Americans all) A biography of the black man who, as leader of the Black Muslims and later of the Organization of Afro-American Unity, sought a better life for his people. [BP223.Z8L578] 92 74-16264 ISBN 0-8116-4582-7 3.28 (lib. bdg.)
1. Little, Malcolm, 1925-1965—Juvenile literature. 2. [Little, Malcolm, 1925-1965.] 3. [Negroes—Biography.] I. Mays, Victor, 1927- illus. II. Title.

Negroes—Civil rights.

GOLDWIN, Robert A. 1922- ed. 232.41
100 years of emancipation; four essays by Roy Wilkins others. Chicago] Public Affairs Conf. Center, Univ. of Chic., c.1963. 30cm. 63-2611 apply
1. Negroes—Civil rights. 2. U. S.—Legal status, laws, etc. 3. Emancipation proclamation. I. Wilkins, Roy, 1901- II. Title.

ROOT, Robert. 261.83
Struggle of decency; religion and race in modern America [by] Robert Root and Shirley W. Hall. New York, Friendship Press [1965] 174 p. 19 cm. [E185.61.R77] 65-11440
1. Negroes — Civil rights. 2. Church and race problems — U.S. I. Hall, Shirley W., joint author. II. Title.

SHEARES, Reuben A., 1933- 323.4'0973
Next steps toward racial justice; a primer on shalom and racial justice, by Reuben A. Sheares [and] S. Garry Oniki. Published for Joint Educational Development. Philadelphia, United Church Press [1974] 127 p. 22 cm. (A Shalom resource) Bibliography: p. 117-124. [E185.615.S47] 74-4035 ISBN 0-8298-0278-9 2.95 (pbk)
1. Negroes—Civil rights. 2. United States—Race question. 3. Church and race problems—United States. I. Oniki, S. Garry, 1920- joint author. II. Joint Educational Development. III. Title.

THOMAS, Howard E 323.4'071'52
Organizing for human rights; a handbook for teachers and students, by Howard E. Thomas and Sister Mary Peter. Dayton, Ohio, G. A. Pflaum [c1966] 64 p. illus. 24 cm. "Resource section": p. 39-58. [E185.615.T5] 67-1874
1. Negroes — Civil rights. 2. Civil rights — Study and teaching. 3. Church and race problems — Catholic Church. I. Mary Peter, Sister, joint author. II. Title.

Negroes—Education.

BRAWLEY, James P. 377'.87'673
Two centuries of Methodist concern : bondage, freedom, and education of Black people. [by] James P. Brawley. [1st ed.] New York, Vantage Press [1974] 606 p. illus. 24 cm. Bibliography: p. 588-593. [LC2801.B76] 74-162882 ISBN 0-533-00649-X 12.00
1. Methodist Church (United States)—Education. 2. Negroes—Education. I. Title.

JONES, Charles Colcock, 1804-1863. 268'.0973
The religious instruction of the Negroes in the United States. Freeport, N.Y., Books for Libraries Press, 1971. xiii, 277 p. 23 cm. (The Black heritage library collection) Reprint of the 1842 ed. [LC2751.J7 1971] 70-149869 ISBN 0-8369-8718-7
1. Negroes—Education. 2. Christian education. I. Title. II. Series.

JONES, Charles Colcock, 1804-1863. 268'.0973
The religious instruction of the Negroes in the United States. New York, Negro Universities Press [1969] xiii, 277 p. 23 cm. Reprint of the 1842 ed. [LC2751.J7 1969] 73-82466 ISBN 0-8371-1645-7
1. Negroes—Education. 2. Christian education. I. Title.

MCKINNEY, Richard Ishmael, 1906- 377
Religion in higher education among Negroes, by Richard I. McKinney. New York, Arno Press, 1972 [c1945] xvi, 165 p. 24 cm. (Religion in America, series II) Original ed. issued as vol. 18 of Yale studies in religious education. Bibliography: p. [149]-161. [BV1610.M33 1972] 75-38785 ISBN 0-405-04075-X
1. Negroes—Education. 2. Negroes—Religion. 3. Universities and colleges—Religion. I. Title. II. Series: Yale studies in religious education, v. 18

MCKINNEY, Richard Ishmael, 1906- 248
Religion in higher education among Negroes, by Richard I. McKinney ... New Haven, Yale university press; London, H. Milford, Oxford university press, 1945. xvi, 165, [1] p. incl. tables. 23 1/2 cm. (Half-title: Yale studies in religious education, XVIII) "The complete results of this study were presented as a dissertation ... for the degree of doctor of philosophy in Yale university [1942]"--p. xii. Bibliography: p. [149]-161. [BV1610.M33] A 45
1. Negroes—Education. 2. Negroes—Religion. 3. Universities and colleges—Religion. I. Title.

Negroes—Housing.

CLARK, Henry, 1930- 261.83
The church and residential desegregation; a case study of an open housing covenant campaign. New Haven, College & University Press [1965] 254 p. 21 cm. Bibliographical references included in "Notes" (P. 234-254) [E185.89.H6C55] 64-20663
1. Negroes — Housing. 2. Discrimination in housing — U.S. 3. Church and race problems — U.S. I. Title.

Negroes in America—Religion.

BASTIDE, Roger, 1898- 200'.97
African civilisations in the New World. Translated from the French by Peter Green, with a foreword by Geoffrey Parrinder. New York, Harper & Row [1971] vi, 232 p. 23 cm. (A Torchbook library edition) Translation of Les Ameriques noires, les civilisations africaines dans le Nouveau monde. Includes bibliographies. [E29.N3B4213 1971] 75-158981 ISBN 0-06-136057-0 12.50
1. Negroes in America—Religion. 2. Negroes in America. 3. Africa—Religion. I. Title.

Negroes in Cuba—Religion.

CABRERA, Lydia. 133.4'7'097291
El monte : igbo, finda, ewe orisha, vititi nfinda : notas sobre las religiones, la magia, las supersticiones y el folklore de los negros criollos y el pueblo de Cuba / Lydia Cabrera. 4. ed. Miami, Fla. : Ediciones Universal, 1975. 564 p., [13] leaves of plates : ill. ; 22 cm. (Coleccion del chichereku en el exilio) Includes index. [BL2530.C9C32 1975] 75-26416
1. Negroes in Cuba—Religion. 2. Cuba—Religion. 3. Magic—Cuba. 4. Folk-lore—Cuba. 5. Folk-lore, Negro. I. Title.

Negroes—Kentucky.

MARRS, Elijah P. 1840- 920
Life and history of the Rev. Elijah P. Marrs ... Louisville, Ky., The Bradley & Gilbert company, 1885. 146 p. 1 l. front. (port.) 20 cm. [E185.97M36M3] 12-27743
1. Negroes—Kentucky. 2. U. S. artillery. 12th colored regt., 1863-1865. 3. U. S.—Hist.—Civil war—Personal narratives. I. Title.

Negroes—Memphis.

FULLER, Thomas Oscar, 1867- 277.68
The story of the church life among Negroes in Memphis, Tennessee, for students and workers, 1900-1938, by T. O. Fuller ... Memphis. Tenn. [c1938] 3 p. l., 52 p. front. (port.) illus. 22 cm. [BR563.N4F8] 38-39348
1. Negroes—Memphis. 2. Memphis—Churches. I. Title. II. Title: Church life among Negroes in Memphis.

Negroes—Philadelphia.

DOUGLASS, William. 283.74811
Annals of the first African church, in the United States of America, now styled the African Episcopal church of St. Thomas, Philadelphia, in its connection with the early struggles of the colored people to improve their condition, with the co-operation of the Friends, and other philanthropists; partly derived from the minutes of a beneficial society, established by Absalom Jones, Richard Allen and others, in 1787, and partly from the minutes of the aforesaid church. By the Rev. Wm. Douglass, rector. Philadelphia, King & Baird, printers, 1862. 172 p. 19 cm. Philadelphia. St. Thomas' church. [N5980.P5A35] 35-34414
1. Negroes—Philadelphia. I. Title.

Negroes—Race identity.

CLEAGE, Albert B. 200
The black Messiah [by] Albert B. Cleage, Jr. New York, Sheed and Ward [1968] 278 p. 22 cm. [E185.7.C59] 68-9370 6.50
1. Jesus Christ—Negro interpretations. 2. Negroes—Race identity. I. Title.

Negroes-Religion.

BANKS, William L. 209'.73
The Black church in the U.S.; its origin, growth, contributions, and outlook, by William L. Banks. Chicago, Moody Press [1972] 160 p. 22 cm. Bibliography: p. 154-156. [E185.7.B3] 76-175492 ISBN 0-8024-0870-2 2.25
1. Negroes—Religion. I. Title.

BARRETT, Leonard E. 299'.6
Soul-force: African heritage in Afro-American religion, by Leonard E. Barrett. [1st ed.] Garden City, N.Y., Anchor Press, 1974. viii, 251 p. 22 cm. (C. Eric Lincoln series on Black religion) Bibliography: p. [237]-240. [E185.7.B33 1974] 73-83612 ISBN 0-385-07410-7 7.95
1. Negroes—Religion. I. Title. II. Series.

BEN-JOCHANNAN, Yosef. 299'.6
The Black man's religion, and Extracts and comments from the Holy Black Bible. [New York, Alkebu-lan Books Associates, 1974] 1 v. (various pagings) illus. 22 cm. (African-American heritage series) Cover title. Includes v. 2-3 of the author's The Black man's religion; v. 1 published in 1970 under title: African origins of the major "Western religions". Includes bibliographical references. [BR563.N4B462] 74-162930
1. Bible—Criticism, interpretation, etc. 2. Negroes—Religion. I. Ben-Jochannan, Yosef. Extracts and comments from the Holy Black Bible. 1974. II. Title. III. Series.

CARTER, Harold A. 264'.1
The prayer tradition of Black people / Harold A. Carter. Valley Forge, PA : Judson Press, c1976. 142 p. ; 23 cm. Includes index. Bibliography: p. 133-139. [BR563.N4C37] 75-35881 ISBN 0-8170-0698-2 : 6.95
1. Negroes—Religion. 2. Prayer—History. I. Title.

FAUSET, Arthur Huff, 1899- 200'.973
Black gods of the metropolis :, Negro religious cults of the urban North. New York, Octagon Books, 1970 [c1944] ix, 126 p. illus., ports. 24 cm. (Publications of the Philadelphia Anthropological Society,

v. 3) (Brinton memorial series, [no. 2]) "A study of five Negro religious cults in the Philadelphia of today." Issued also as the author's thesis, University of Pennsylvania. [BR563.N4F3 1970] 73-120251
1. Negroes—Religion. 2. Negroes—Philadelphia. 3. Sects—U.S. I. Title. II. Series. III. Series: Philadelphia Anthropological Society. Publications, v. 3.

FAUSET, Arthur Huff, 1899- 200'.973
Black gods of the metropolis; Negro religious cults of the urban North. [Philadelphia] University of Pennsylvania Press [1971] xi, 128 p. illus., group ports. 21 cm. "Originally published in 1944 as volume 111 of the Brinton memorial series, Publications of the Philadelphia Anthropological Society." Bibliography: p. 123-126. [BR563.N4F3 1971] 75-133446 ISBN 0-8122-1001-8
1. Negroes—Religion. 2. Negroes—Philadelphia. 3. Sects—U.S. I. Title.

FAUST, Arthur Huff, 1899- 289.9
... Black gods of the metropolis, Negro religious cults of the urban North, by Arthur Hoff Fauset. Philadelphia, University of Pennsylvania press; London, H. Milford, Oxford university press, 1944. x, 126 p. plates, ports. 23 1/2 cm. (Publications of the Philadelphia anthropological society. Vol. III) Half-title: ... Brinton memorial series. [No. 2] Issued also as thesis (PH.D.) University of Pennsylvania. "A study of five Negro religious cults in the Philadelphia of today."--Pref. [BR563.N4F3 1944 a] 44-3761
1. Negroes—Religion. 2. Negroes—Philadelphia. 3. Sects—U.S. I. Title.

FELTON, Ralph Almon, 1882- 277.5
These my brethren; a study of 570 Negro churches and 1542 Negro homes in the rural South. Madison, N. J., Dept. of the Rural Church, Drew Theological Seminary [1950] 102 p. 23 cm. Cover title. [BR563.N4F4] 50-2257
1. Negroes—Religion. 2. Negroes—Moral and social conditions. 3. Rural churches—Southern States. I. Title.

FISK University, Nashville. Social Science Institute. 248.2'46
God struck me dead; religious conversion experiences and autobiographies of ex-slaves. Clifton H. Johnson, editor. Foreword by Paul Radin. Philadelphia, Pilgrim Press [1969] xix, 171 p. 22 cm. [BV4930.F5 1969] 78-77839 3.45
1. Negroes—Religion. 2. Conversion. I. Johnson, Clifton H., ed. II. Title.

FORDHAM, Monroe, 1939- 209'.73
Major themes in Northern Black religious thought, 1800-1860 / Monroe Fordham. 1st ed. Hicksville, N.Y. : Exposition Press, [1975] xii, 172 p. ; 22 cm. (An Exposition-university book) Includes index. Bibliography: p. 159-167. [BR563.N4F65] 75-10618 ISBN 0-682-48256-0 : 8.50
1. Negroes—Religion. 2. Negro churches—United States. 3. Religious thought—19th century. I. Title.

FRAZIER, Edward Franklin, 1894-1962 277.3
The Negro church in America. New York, Schocken [1966, c.1963] xii, 92p. 21cm. (SB135) Bibl. 1.45 pap.,
1. Negroes—Religion. I. Title.

FRAZIER, Edward Franklin, 1894-1962.
The Negro church in America. New York, Schoken Books, 1962. xii, 92 p. 23 cm. 68-44234
1. Negroes-Religion. I. Title.

HAYNES, Leonard L 1923- 261.8
The Negro community within American Protestantism, 1619-1844. Boston, Christopher Pub. House [1953] 264p. 21cm. [BR563.N4H38] 53-4230
1. Negroes—Religion. 2. Protestant churches—U. S. I. Title.

JOHNSON, Joseph Andrew, 1914- 253
The soul of the Black preacher, by Joseph A. Johnson, Jr. Philadelphia, Pilgrim Press [1971] 173 p. 22 cm. Contents.Contents.—The soul of the Black preacher.—Conflict, challenge, defeat, victory.—The triumphant adequacy of Jesus.—Wholeness through Jesus Christ.—Man's helplessness and the power of Christ.—The principle of identical harvest.—Jesus, the leader.—Jesus, the disturber.—Jesus, the emancipator.—Jesus, the liberator.—Jesus, the word of life.—The Christian's call, commitment, and commission.—"All is of grace and grace is for all."—"Even we have believed in Jesus Christ."—The imperative of beyondness.—The Christian faith and the Black experience. Includes bibliographical references. [BR563.N4J58] 70-162411 ISBN 0-8298-0193-6 4.95
1. Negroes—Religion. 2. Negro clergy. I. Title.

JOHNSTON, Ruby Funchess. 277.3
The development of Negro religion. New York, Philosophical Library [1954] 202p. illus. 23cm. [BR563.N4J6] 54-7966
1. Negroes—Religion. I. Title.

JOHNSTON, Ruby Funchess. 277.3
The religion of Negro Protestants; changing religious attitudes and practices. New York, Philosophical Library [1956] xxvi, 224p. tables. 24cm. Bibliography:p. 214-217. [BR563.N4J62] 56-13828
1. Negroes—Religion. 2. Protestant churches-U.S. I. Title.

JONES, Howard O. 261.8'34'5196073
White questions to a Black Christian / by Howard O. Jones. Grand Rapids, Mich. : Zondervan Pub. House, [1975] 215 p. ; 18 cm. Bibliography: p. 211-215. [BR563.N4J63] 74-11859 pbk. : 1.75
1. Negroes—Religion. I. Title.

JONES, Major J., 1919- 241'.6'99
Black awareness: a theology of hope [by] Major J. Jones. Nashville, Abingdon Press [1971] 143 p. 19 cm. Includes bibliographical references. [BR563.N4J64] 77-148067 ISBN 0-687-03585-6
1. Negroes—Religion. 2. Negroes—Race identity. I. Title.

LINCOLN, Charles Eric, comp. 200
The Black experience in religion, edited by C. Eric Lincoln. Garden City, N.Y., Anchor Press, 1974. xii, 369 p. 21 cm. (C. Eric Lincoln series on Black religion) Includes bibliographical references. [BR563.N4L56] 73-16508 ISBN 0-385-01884-3 3.95 (pbk.).
1. Negroes—Religion. I. Title. II. Series.

LYON, Ernest, 1860-
The negro's view of organic union, by Ernest Lyon ... introduction by George A. Owens. New York, Cincinnati, The Methodist book concern [c1915] 64 p. 17 1/2 cm. $0.25. "The question of organic union of the Methodist Episcopal church and the Methodist Episcopal church, South."--Introd. 16-7676
I. Title.

MAYS, Benjamin Elijah, 1895- 325.260973
The Negro's church, by Benjamin Elijah Mays and Joseph William Nicholson. New York, Institute of social and religious research [c1933] xiii, 321 p. illus. (maps) 19 1/2 cm. "The Institue of social and reilgious research...is responsible for this publication."--p. [ii] [BR563.M4M3] 261 33-6349
1. Negroes—Religion. 2. Churches—U.S. I. Nicholson, Joseph William, joint author. II. Institue of social and religious research III. Title.

MILLER, Harriet Parks. 286'.133'0975
Pioneer colored Christians. Freeport, N.Y., Books for Libraries Press, 1971. 103 p. illus. 23 cm. (The Black heritage library collection) Reprint of the 1911 ed. [E185.7.M5 1971] 73-37313 ISBN 0-8369-8950-3
1. Carr family. 2. Negroes—Religion. 3. Negroes—Southern States. I. Title. II. Series.

MITCHELL, Henry H. 299'.6
Black belief : folk beliefs of Blacks in America and West Africa / Henry H. Mitchell. 1st ed. New York : Harper & Row, [1975] xiii, 171 p. ; 21 cm. Includes index. Bibliography: p. [164]-168. [BR563.N4M57 1975] 74-4632 ISBN 0-06-065762-6 : 6.95
1. Negroes—Religion. I. Title.

[NEWCOMB, Harvey, 1803-1863] 261.83'4'493
The "Negro pew": being an inquiry concerning the propriety of distinctions in the house of God, on account of color. Freeport, N.Y., Books for Libraries Press, 1971. 108 p. 23 cm. (The Black heritage library collection) Reprint of the 1837 ed. [E185.7.N48 1971] 76-149873 ISBN 0-8369-8753-5
1. Negroes—Religion. 2. Negroes—Segregation. I. Title. II. Series.

PARKER, Robert Allerton. 922
The incredible messiah; the deification of Father Divine, by Robert Allerton Parker. Boston, Little, Brown and company, 1937. xiii, 323 p. front. (port.) 22 cm. "First edition." Bibliography: p. 321-323. [BX7350.P3] 37-9706
1. Baker, George, self-named Father Divine. 2. Negroes—Religion. I. Title. II. Title: Messiah, The incredible.

PARKER, Robert Allerton. 922
The incredible messiah; the deification of Father Divine, by Robert Allerton Parker. Boston, Little, Brown and company, 1937. xiii, 323 p. front. (port.) 22 cm. "First edition." Bibliography: p. 321-323. [BX7350.P3] 37-9706
1. Baker, George, self-named Father Divine. 2. Negroes—Religion. I. Title. II. Title: Messiah, The incredible.

PERKINS, Benjamin Paul, 1934- 262'.001
Black Christians' tragedies; an analysis of Black youth and their church [by] Benjamin Paul Perkins, Sr. [1st ed.] New York, Exposition Press [1972] 64 p. 22 cm. [E185.7.P4] 72-185996 ISBN 0-682-47510-6 3.00
1. Negroes—Religion. 2. Negro youth. I. Title.

PIPES, William Harrison, 1912- 251
Say amen, brother! Old-time Negro preaching: a study in American frustration. New York, William-Frederick Press, 1951. 1, 210 p. 24 cm. Bibliography: p. 201-205. [BR563.N4P53] 51-11631
1. Negroes — Religion. 2. Preaching — Hist. — U.S. I. Title. II. Title: Old-time Negro preaching.

PIPES, William Harrison, 1912- 251'.00973
Say amen, brother! Old-time Negro preaching: a study in American frustration, by William H. Pipes. Westport, Conn., Negro Universities Press [1970, c1951] i, 210 p. 24 cm. Bibliography: p. 201-205. [BR563.N4P53 1970] 73-111585 ISBN 0-8371-4611-9
1. Negroes—Religion. 2. Preaching—History—U.S. I. Title.

REED, William J.
Rome and the negro; lives of the noted African bishops, saints, martyrs, holy women and fathers of deserts. Taken from the lives of the saints, Roman and African calenders. Author: William J. Reed ... [Louisville, Ky.] Press of the Louisville anzeiger, 1907. 144 p. 19 cm. 7-7184
I. Title.

RICHARDSON, Harry Van Buren. 277.5
Dark glory, a picture of the church among Negroes in the rural South. New York, Pub. for Home Missions Council of North America and Phelps Stokes Fund by Friendship Press [1947] xiv, 209 p. 19 cm. "A selected reading list": p. 194-197. [BR563.N4R5] 47-24753
1. Negroes—Religion. I. Title.

RILEY, Willard D 241
Widsom in Ethiopia 1st ed. New York, Vantage Press [1959] 66p. 22cm. [BR563.N4R54] 59-3659
1. Negroes— Religion. I. Title.

SERNETT, Milton C., 1942- 280'.4'0975
Black religion and American evangelicalism : white Protestants, plantation missions, and the flowering of Negro Christianity, 1787-1865 / by Milton C. Sernett ; with a foreword by Martin E. Marty. Metuchen, N.J. : Scarecrow Press, 1975. 320 p. : ill. ; 23 cm. (ATLA monograph series ; no. 7) A revision of the author's thesis, University of Delaware. Includes index. Bibliography: p. 239-288. [BR563.N4S47 1975] 75-4754 ISBN 0-8108-0803-X : 16.50
1. Negroes—Religion. 2. Evangelicalism—Southern States. I. Title. II. Series: American Theological Library Association. ATLA monograph series ; no. 7.

TUCKER, Joseph Louis, 1842-1906. 277.
The relations of the church to the colored race. Speech of the Rev. J. L. Tucker ... before the Church congress, held in Richmond, Va., on the 24-27 Oct., 1882 ... Jackson, Miss., C. Winkley, steam book and job print, 1882. cover-title, 91 p. 22 cm. "Somewhat enlarged, but adheres to the line of argument adopted at the congress." [BR563.N4T8] 46-37685
1. Negroes—Religion. I. Title.

WASHINGTON, Joseph R. 277.3
Black religion; the Negro and Christianity in the United States [by] Joseph R. Washington, Jr. Boston, Beacon Press [1964] ix, 308 p. 22 cm. Bibliographical references included in "Notes" (p. 298-303) [BR563.N4W3] 64-13529
1. Negroes—Religion. I. Title. II. Title: The Negro and Christianity in the United States.

WASHINGTON, Joseph R. 280
Black sects and cults, by Joseph R. Washington, Jr. [1st ed.] Garden City, N.Y., Doubleday, 1972. xii, 176 p. 22 cm. (The C. Eric Lincoln series on Black religion) Bibliography: p. [167]-170. [BR563.N4W32] 72-86649 ISBN 0-385-00209-2 5.95
1. Negroes—Religion. I. Title. II. Series.

WASHINGTON, Joseph R. 280
Black sects and cults, by Joseph R. Washington, Jr. Garden City, N.Y., Anchor Press/Doubleday, 1973 [c.1972] xii, 176 p. 21 cm. (Anchor Book, A0-102) (C. Eric Lincoln series on Black religion) [BR563.N4W32] -72 ISBN 0-385-00252-1 2.95 (pbk.)
1. Negroes—Religion. I. Title. II. Series.

WASHINGTON, Joseph R. 260
The politics of God, by Joseph R. Washington, Jr. Boston, Beacon Press [1967] ix, 234 p. 21 cm. Bibliographical footnotes. [BR563.N4W33] 67-14108
1. Negroes—Religion. 2. Church and race problems—United States. I. Title.

WILLIAMS, Melvin D., 1933- 301.5'8
Community in a Black Pentecostal church; an anthropological study [by] Melvin D. Williams. [Pittsburgh] University of Pittsburgh Press [1974] xii, 202 p. 24 cm. Bibliography: p. 189-198. [BR563.N4W523] 74-5108 ISBN 0-8229-3290-3 9.95
1. Negroes—Religion. 2. Pentecostal churches—Pennsylvania—Pittsburgh. 3. Negroes—Pittsburgh. I. Title.

WILMORE, Gayraud S. 200
Black religion and Black radicalism. Garden City, N.Y., Anchor Pr./Doubleday, 1973 [c.1972] xiii, 344 p. 21 cm. (Anchor Books, AO-91) (C. Eric Lincoln series on Black religion) Bibliography: p. [307]-329. [BR563.N4W53] 75-180116 ISBN 0-385-09125-7 3.50 (pbk.)
1. Negroes—Religion. I. Title. II. Series.

WOODSON, Carter Godwin, 1875- 277.
The history of the Negro church, by Carter G. Woodson ... Washington, D.C., The Associated publishers [c1921] x, 330 p. front., plates, ports. 20 1/2 cm. [BR563.N4W6] 22-935
1. Negroes—Religion. I. Title. II. Title: Negro church, The history of the.

WOODSON, Carter Goodwin, 1875- 277.3
The history of the Negro church, by Carter G. Woodson ... 2d ed. Washington, D.C., The Associated publishers [1945] xi, 322 p. illus. (incl. ports.) 20 1/2 cm. [BR563.N4W6 1945] 46-279
1. Negroes—Religion. I. Title.

Negroes—Religion—Addresses, essays, lectures.

MCCALL, Emmanuel L., comp. 277*.3
The Black Christian experience. Emmanuel L. McCall, compiler. Nashville, Broadman Press [1972] 126 p. 21 cm. [BR563.N4M23] 72-79173 ISBN 0-8054-6514-6 3.95
1. Negroes—Religion—Addresses, essays, lectures. I. Title.

QUEST for a Black 201'.1
theology. Edited by James J. Gardiner, and J. Deotis Roberts. Philadelphia [Pilgrim Press, 1971] xiii, 111 p. 22 cm. Five of six essays originally presented at an interdenominational conference held in Washington, D.C., May 2-3, 1969, and jointly sponsored by the Graymoor Ecumenical Institute and the Georgetown University Dept. of Theology. Includes bibliographical references. [BR563.N4Q4] 76-151250 ISBN 0-8298-0196-0 5.95
1. Negroes—Religion—Addresses, essays, lectures. 2. Negroes—Race identity. I. Gardiner, James J., ed. II. Roberts, James Deotis, ed. III. Graymoor Ecumenical Institute. IV. Georgetown University, Washington, D.C. Dept. of Theology.

Negroes—Religion—Bibliography.

DAVIS, Lenwood G. 016.3092'08 s
A history of Black religion in Northern areas : a preliminary survey / Lenwood G. Davis. Monticello, Ill. : Council of Planning Librarians, 1975. 12 p. ; 28 cm. (Exchange bibliography ; 734) Cover title. [Z5942.C68 no. 734] [Z1361.N39] [BR563.N4] 016.2 75-331469 pbk. : 1.50
1. Negroes—Religion—Bibliography. 2. Negroes—Bibliography. 3. Negroes—Periodicals—Bibliography. I. Title. II. Series: Council of Planning Librarians. Exchange bibliography ; 734.

DAVIS, Lenwood G. 016.3092'08 s
A history of Black religion in southern areas : a preliminary survey / Lenwood G. Davis. Monticello, Ill. : Council of Planning Librarians, 1975. 13 p. ; 28 cm. (Exchange bibliography ; 733) Cover title. [Z5942.C68 no. 733] [Z1361.N39] [BR563.N4] 209'.75 75-306461 1.50
1. Negroes—Religion—Bibliography. I. Title. II. Series: Council of Planning Librarians. Exchange bibliography ; 733.

DISCIPLES of Christ 016.286'6
Historical Society.
Preliminary guide to Black materials in the Disciples of Christ Historical Society. Nashville, Tenn., 1971. v, 32 l. 28 cm. [Z1361.N39D56] 72-194135
1. Negroes—Religion—Bibliography. 2. Negroes—Bibliography. I. Title.

Negroes—Religion—Bibliography—Catalogs.

JACKSON, Giovanna R. 016.261
Afro-American religion and church and race relations, compiled by Giovanna R. Jackson. [Bloomington] Indiana University Libraries, 1969. 18 p. 28 cm. (Focus: Black America bibliography series) [Z1361.N39J29] 73-620739
1. Indiana. University. Libraries. 2. Negroes—Religion—Bibliography—Catalogs. 3. Church and race problems—Bibliography—Catalogs. I. Indiana. University. Libraries. II. Title. III. Series.

Negroes—Religion—Bibliography—Union lists.

WILLIAMS, Ethel 016.301451'96073
L.
Afro-American religious studies: a comprehensive bibliography with locations in American libraries. Compiled by Ethel L. Williams and Clifton L. [i.e. F.] Brown. Metuchen, N.J., Scarecrow Press, 1972. 454 p. 22 cm. [Z1361.N39W55] 78-166072 ISBN 0-8108-0439-5
1. Negroes—Religion—Bibliography—Union lists. 2. Missions—Africa—Bibliography—Union lists. 3. Catalogs, Union—United States. I. Brown, Clifton F., 1943- joint author. II. Title.

Negroes—Segregation.

REIMERS, David M. 261.83
White Protestantism and the Negro [by] David M. Reimers. New York, Oxford University Press, 1965. ix, 236 p. 21 cm. Bibliographical references included in "Notes" (p. 190-222) Bibliography: p. 223-227. [E185.61.R36] 65-22800
1. Negroes—Segregation. 2. Church and race problems—United States. 3. Protestant churches—United States. I. Title.

Negroes—Virginia.

RANDOLPH, Edwin Archer, 920.
1854-
The life of Rev. John Jasper, pastor of Sixth Mt. Zion Baptist church, Richmond, A.; from his birth to the present time, wit his theory on the rotation of the sun. By E. A. Randolph, ll. b. Richmond, Va., R. T. Hill & co., 1884. xii, 167 p. front. (port.) 20 cm. [E185.97.J39] 12-10713
1. Jasper, John, 1812-1901. 2. Negroes—Virginia. I. Title.

Nehemiah.

ALDEN, Joseph, 1807-1885. 221.92
The Jewish Washington; or, Lessons of patriotism and piety suggested by the history of Nehemiah. By Rev. Joseph Alden, D.D. Written for the Massachusetts Sabbath school society, and revised by the Committee of publication. Boston, Massachusetts Sabbath school society, 1846. 90 p. incl. front. 19 cm. Tall-pieces. [BS580.N45A6] 37-7012
1. Nehemiah. 2. Patriotism. I. Massachusetts Sabbath school society. Committee of publication. II. Title. III. Title: Lessons of patriotism and piety.

BARBER, Cyril J. 222'.8'06
Nehemiah and the dynamics of effective leadership / by Cyril J. Barber. Neptune, N.J. : Loizeaux Bros., [1976] p. cm. Bibliography: p. [BS1365.2.B37] 76-22567 pbk. : 2.75
1. Nehemiah. 2. Bible. O.T. Nehemiah—Criticism, interpretation, etc. 3. Leadership—Biblical teaching. I. Title.

GETZ, Gene A. 222'.806
Nehemiah : a man of prayer and persistence / Gene A. Getz. Ventura, Calif. : Regal Books, c1981. 175 p. ; 21 cm. Includes bibliographical references. [BS580.N45G47] 19 80-53102 ISBN 0-8307-0778-6 pbk. : 4.95
1. Nehemiah. 2. Bible O.T. Nehemiah—Criticism, interpretation, etc. I. Title.

SEUME, Richard H. 221.9'24 B
Nehemiah : God's builder / by Richard H. Seume. Chicago : Moody Press, c1978. 121 p. ; 22 cm. Bibliography: p. 120-121. [BS580.N45S48] 77-29141 ISBN 0-8024-5868-8 : 2.95
1. Nehemiah. 2. Bible. O.T. Nehemiah—Criticism, interpretation, etc. 3. Bible. O.T.—Biography.

SWINDOLL, Charles R. 301.15'53
Hand me another brick / by Charles R. Swindoll. Nashville : T. Nelson, c1978. 207 p. ; 21 cm. Includes bibliographical references. [BV652.1.S94] 78-4170 ISBN 0-8407-5650-X pbk. : 3.95
1. Nehemiah. 2. Christian leadership. 3. Leadership. I. Title.

Neher, Minneva Josephine, 1896-1937.

MOW, Anetta Cordula, 1899- 275.1
comp.
In memoriam; Minneva J. Neher, Alva C. Harsh, Mary Hykes Harsh- Elgin, Ill., Brethren Pub. House [1947] 160 p. illus., ports., map. 20 cm. [BV3427.A1M7] 266 48-13840
1. Neher, Minneva Josephine, 1896-1937. 2. Harsh, Alva Carlton, 1910-1937. 3. Harsh, Mary (Hykes) 1903-1937. I. Title.

Nelson, Ben.

LINDER, Ted. 289.3'3 B
Ben Nelson, defender of the faithful / by Ted Linder. Independence, Mo. : Herald Pub. House, c1981. p. cm. [BX8695.N37L56] 19 81-7190 ISBN 0-8309-0321-6 : Write for information.
1. Nelson, Ben. 2. Mormons—United States—Biography. I. Title.

Nelson, Bert N., 1888-1932.

NELSON, Daniel, 1902- 922.451
The apostle to the Chinese communists, by Daniel Nelson. Minneapolis, The Board of foreign missions of the Norweigian Lutheran church of America [c1935] xi, 139 p. incl. front. (port.) facsims. 21 cm. Facsimiles (1 folded) in collephane pocket mounted on p. [vi] "Second edition." [BV3427.N4N4 1935] 36-20230
1. Nelson, Bert N., 1888-1932. 2. Missions—China. I. Norwegian Lutheran church of America. Board of foregn missions. II. Title.

Nelson, Erik Alfred, 1862-1939.

BRATCHER, Lewis Malen, 922.673
1888-
The apostle of the Amazon. Nashville, Broadman Press ['1951] 138 p. illus. 20 cm. [BV2853.B6B719] 52-6512
1. Nelson, Erik Alfred, 1862-1939. 2. Missions—Brazil. I. Title.

Nelson, Frank Howard, 1869-1939.

HERRICK, Warren Crocker, 922.373
1898-
Frank H. Nelson of Cincinnati, by Warren C. Herrick, a sometimes assistant; with a foreword by Charles P. Taft. Louisville, The Cloister press, 1945. x, 110 p. front., (port.) 19 1/2 cm. [BX5995.N36H4] 46-12025
1. Nelson, Frank Howard, 1869-1939. I. Title.

Nelson, Rebecca Jewel (Francis)

NELSON, Joseph Raleigh.
Lady unafraid. Decorations by Richard A. Huff. Calumet, Mich., R. W. Drier, 1965 c1951] 278 p. illus., maps. (on lining papers) 24 cm. 67-94438
1. Nelson, Rebecca Jewel (Francis) 2. Indians, N.A. — Tribes — Chippewa — Missions. I. Title.

Nelson, Reuben Emmanuel, 1905-1960.

TORBET, Robert George, 922.673
1912-
Reuben E. Nelson: free churchman [by] Robert G. Torbet, Henry R. Bowler. Chicago, Judson Pr. [c.1961] 64p. illus. 61-12687 1.50
1. Nelson, Reuben Emmanuel, 1905-1960. I. Bowler, Henry R., joint author. II. Title.

TORBET, Robert George, 922.673
1912-
Reuben E. Nelson: free churchman [by] Robert G. Torbet and Henry R. Bowler. [1st ed.] Chicago, Judson Press [1961] 64 p. illus. 20 cm. [BX6207.A38N46] 61-12687
1. Nelson, Reuben Emmanuel, 1905-1960. I. Bowler, Henry R., joint author. II. Title.

Nelson, Ruth Youngdahl.

NELSON, Ruth 284.1'332'0924 B
Youngdahl.
God's joy in my heart / Ruth Youngdahl Nelson, written with Karen Matison Hess. Minneapolis, Minn. : Augsburg Pub. House, c1980. 254 p. : ill. ; 24 cm. [BX8080.N43A33] 19 80-65544 ISBN 0-8066-1789-6 pbk. : 7.95
1. Nelson, Ruth Youngdahl. 2. Lutherans—United States—Biography. I. Hess, Karen M., 1939- joint author. II. Title.

Neo-Confucianism.

CHANG, Chia-sen, 1886- 181.1
The development of Neo-Confucian thought, by Carsun Chang. New York, Bookman Associates [c1957-62] 2 v. 23 cm. Includes bibliographies. [BL1851.C5] 58-177
1. Neo-Confucianism. I. Title.

TAYLOR, Rodney Leon, 299'.512
1944-
The cultivation of sagehood as a religious goal in Neo-Confucianism : a study of selected writings of Kao P'an-lung (1562-1626) / by Rodney Leon Taylor. Missoula, Mont. : Scholars Press, 1978, c1974. p. cm. (Dissertation series - American Academy of Religion ; 22 ISSN 0145-272Xs) Originally presented as the author's thesis, Columbia, 1974. "Chinese texts": p. Bibliography: p. [B127.N4T38 1978] 78-18685 ISBN 0-89130-239-5 pbk. : 7.50
1. Kao, P'an-lung, 1562-1626. 2. Neo-Confucianism. 3. Self-culture. I. Title. II. Series: American Academy of Religion. Dissertation series — American Academy of Religion ; 22.

Neo-orthodoxy.

BRADSHAW, Marion John, 1886- 230
Baleful legacy, a faith without foundations; an examination of neo-orthodoxy. Oklahoma City, Modern Publishers, 1955. 113p. 24cm. Includes bibliography. [BT78.B7] 56-17870
1. Neo-orthodoxy. I. Title.

HORDERN, William. 230
The case for a new reformation theology. Philadelphia, Westminster Press [1959] 176p. 22cm. Includes bibliography. [BT78.H58] 59-5410
1. Neo-orthodoxy. I. Title. II. Title: New reformation theology.

RELIGIOUS liberals reply, 230
by Henry N. Wieman [and others] Boston, Beacon Press, 1947. viii, 177 p. 21 cm. [BT78.R45] 47-12451
1. Neo-orthodoxy. 2. Liberalism (Religion) I. Wieman, Henry Nelson, 1884-
Contents omitted.

RYRIE, Charles Caldwell, 230
1925-
Neo-orthodoxy [Rev. ed.] Chicago, Moody [1966, c.1956] 64p. 18cm. (Christian forum bk.) [BT78.R9] 58-44331 .95 pap.,
1. Neo-orthodoxy. I. Title.

RYRIE, Charles Caldwell, 230
1925-
Neo-orthodoxy: what it is and what it does. Chicago, Moody Press [1956] 62p. 22cm. [BT78.R9] 58-44331
1. Neo-orthodoxy. I. Title.

TULGA, Chester Earl, 1896- 230
The case against neo-orthodoxy. Chicago, Conservative Baptist Fellowship [1951] 64 p. 18 cm. (His Little books on big subjects) [BT78.T815] 51-23627
1. Neo-orthodoxy. I. Title.

Neoplatonism.

BIGG, Charles, 1840-1908.
... Neoplatonism, by C. Bigg ... Pub. under the direction of the general literature committee. London [etc.] Society for promoting Christian knowledge; New York, E. & J. B. Young & co., 1895. 2 p. l., [vii]-viii, [9]-355, [1] p. 17 cm. (Chief ancient philosophies) [B517.B6] 4-18044
1. Neoplatonism. I. Title.

DODDS, Eric Robertson, 1893-
ed. and tr.
Select passages illustrating Neoplatonism. translated with an introduction by E. R. Dodds ... London, Society for promoting Christian knowledge: New York and Toronto. The Macmillan co., 1923. v. [1], [7]-127 p. 19 cm. (On cover: Translations of early documents) Selections largely from the Enmeads of Plotinus. Bibliography: p. 126-127. [B517.A2D6] 25-6246
1. Neoplationism. I. Title. II. Title: Plotinus.

DODDS, Eric Robertson, 1893-
comp. and ed.
... Select passages illustrative of Neoplatonism, arranged and edited by E. R. Dodds ... London, Society for promoting Christian knowledge: New York and Toronto, The Macmillan co., 1924. 1 p. l., iv, 91, 15, [1] p., 1 l. 19 cm. (Texts for students. no. 36) A 25
1. Neoplatonism. I. Title.

ELSEE, Charles.
Neoplatonism in relation to Christianity; an essay, by Charles Elsee ... Cambridge, The University press, 1908. xii, 144 p. 19 1/2cm. "The expansion of an essay which was awarded the Hulsean prize in 1901."--Pref. "List of modern works consulted": p. [xi]-xii. [B517.E4] 9-9818
1. Neoplatonism. 2. Church history—Primitive and early church. I. Title.

PLOTINUS. 281
Select works of Plotinus, tr. from the Greek, with an introduction containing the substance of Porphyry's life of Plotinus, by Thomas Taylor. New ed., with preface and bibliography by G. R. S. Mead ... London and New York, G. Bell & sons, 1909. lxxiv, 343 p. 18 1/2cm. (Bohn's philosophical library). Bibliography: p. xxxv-xxxviii. [PA3606.B6] A10
I. Taylor, Thomas, 1758-1835, tr. II. Mead, George Robert Stow, 1863-1933, ed. III. Title.

WHITTAKER, Thomas, 1856-
The Neo-Platonists: a study in the history of Hellenism. By Thomas Whittaker... Cambridge, The University press, 1901. xiii, [1], 231 p. 23 cm. [HV6117.W73] E16
1. Neoplatonism I. Title.

WHITTAKER, Thomas, 1856-
The Neo-Platonists; a study in the history of Hellenism, by Thomas Whittaker. 2d ed., with a supplement on the Commentaries of Proclus. Cambridge [Eng.] The University press, 1928. xv, [1], 318 p., 1 l. 23 cm. "First edition 1901; second edition (enlarged) 1918, reprinted 1928." [B517.W5 1928] 29-948
1. Proclus Lycius, surnamed Diadochus. Commentarii. 2. Neoplatonism. I. Title.

Neoplatonism—Addresses, essays, lectures.

NEOPLATONISM and early 186'.4
Christian thought : essays in honour of A.H. Armstrong / edited by H.J. Blumenthal and R.A. Markus. London : Variorum Publications, 1981. x, 256 p. ; 24 cm. Includes bibliographical references and index. [B517.N45 1981] 81-195828 ISBN 0-86078-085-6 : 60.00
1. Armstrong, A. H. (Arthur Hilary) 2. Neoplatonism—Addresses, essays, lectures. 3. Christianity—Philosophy—History—Addresses, essays, lectures. I. Armstrong, A. H. (Arthur Hilary) II. Blumenthal, H. J. III. Markus, R. A. 1924- (Robert Austin), Contents omitted.

Nepal—Description and travel

FLETCHER, Grace (Nies) 266
The fabulous Flemings of Kathmandu; the story of two doctors in Nepal. New York, Dutton [c.]1964. 219p. illus., map, ports. 21cm. 64-11095 4.95
1. Fleming, Robert Leland, 1905- 2. Fleming, Bethel. 3. Nepal—Descr. & trav. I. Title.

Nepal—Religion.

SNELLGROVE, David L. 299.54
Himalayan pilgrimage; a study of Tibetan religion, by a traveller through western Nepal. Oxford B. Cassirer. [Mystic, Conn., Verry, 1966] xvi, 304p. illus. (col.front.) maps. 23 cm. First pub. in England in 1961. Bibl. [BL2030.N3S5] 61-42472 bds., 7.50
1. Nepal—Religion. 2. Nepal—Descr. & trav. I. Title.

Nephites.

LEE, Hector. 289.3
The three Nephites; the substance and significance of the legend in folklore. Albuquerque, University of New Mexico Press, 1949. 162 p. map. 23 cm. (University of New Mexico publications in language and literature, no. 2) (New Mexico. University. University of New Mexico publications in language and literature no. 2) Bibliography: p. 127-134. [BX8627.L44] 49-47373
1. Nephites. I. Title. II. Title: Nephites. III. Series.

LEE, Hector Haight, 1908- 289.3
The three Nephites; the substance and significance of the legend in folklore. Albuquerque, University of New Mexico Press, 1949. 162 p. map. 23 cm. (University of New Mexico publications in language and literature, no. 2) Bibliography: p. 127-134. [BX8627.L44] 49-47373
1. Nephites. I. Title. II. Series: New Mexico. University. University of New Mexico publications in language and literature, no. 2

LEE, Hector Haight, 398'.352
1908-
The three Nephites / Hector [Haight] Lee. New York : Arno Press, 1977. p. cm. (International folklore) Reprint of the 1949 ed. published by University of New Mexico Press, Albuquerque, which was issued as no. 2 of University of New Mexico publications in language and literature. Originally presented as the author's thesis, University of New Mexico. Bibliography: p. [BX8627.L44 1977] 77-70608 ISBN 0-405-10105-8 : 10.00
1. Nephites. I. Title. II. Series. III. Series: New Mexico. University. University of New Mexico publications in language and literature ; no. 2.

Nerinckx, Charles, 1761-1824.

CATHOLIC Church. 255'.97
Congregatio de Propaganda Fide.
Documents: Nerinckx—Kentucky—Loretto, 1804-1851, in archives Propaganda Fide, Rome. Co-editors: Augustin C. Wand and M. Lilliana Owens. St. Louis, Mo., Mary Loretto Press, 1972. 305 p. 23 cm. Bibliography: p. 292-305. [BX4705.N4C37 1972] 76-189662
1. Nerinckx, Charles, 1761-1824. 2. Sisters of Loretto at the Foot of the Cross. I. Wand, Augustin C., ed. II. Owens, Lilliana, 1898- ed. III. Title.

MAES, Camillus Paul, 922.273
bp., 1846-1915.
The life of Rev. Charles Nerinckx: with a chapter on the early Catholic missions of Kentucky; copious notes on the progress of Catholicity in the United States of America from 1800 to 1825; an account of the establishment of the Society of Jesus in Missouri; and an historical sketch of the Sisterhood of Loretto in Kentucky, Missouri, New Mexico, etc. By Rev. Camillus P. Maes... Cincinnati, R. Clarke & co., 1880. xvii, 635 p. front. (port.) 23 cm. [BX4705.N4M3] 37-16268
1. Nerinckx, Charles, 1761-1824. 2. Sisters of Loretto at the foot of the cross. 3. Catholic church in Kentucky. 4. Jesuits in Missouri. I. Title.

MAGARET, Helene, 1906- 922.273
Giant in the wilderness, a biography of Father Charles Nerinekx. Milwaukee, Bruce Pub. Co. [1952] 200 p. illus. 22 cm. [BX4705.N4M33] 52-1753
1. Nerinckx, Charles, I. Title.

Nessima, Joseph Hardy, 1843-1890.

MCKEEN, Phebe Fuller, 1831- 922.
1880.
A sketch of the early life of Joseph Hardy Nessima; with an introd. by Philena McKeen. Boston, D. Lothrop Co. [1890] 52 p. plates, ports. 17 cm. [BV3457.N4M3] 48-33825
1. Nessima, Joseph Hardy, 1843-1890. 2. Nessinia, Joseph Hardy, 1843-1890. I. Title.

Nestorian church—History

MALECH, George David, 1837- 281.8
1909.
History of the Syrian nation and the old evangelical-apostolic church of the East, from remote antiquity to the present time, by Prof. George David Malech ... after his death edited, with numerous pictures and illustrations, by his son, the Reverend Nestorius George Malech, archdeacon. Minneapolis, Minn, [c1910] xxii, 449 p. incl. front. (port.) illus., maps. 28 cm. [BX153.M3] 11-4786
1. Nestorian church—Hist. I. Malech, Nestorius George, d. 1927, ed. II. Title.

STEWART, John, 1861- 281'.8
Nestorian missionary enterprises. New York : AMS Press, [1980] xxxiv, 352 p., [2] leaves of plates : map ; 23 cm. Reprint of the 1928 ed. published by T. & T. Clark, Edinburgh. Includes index. bibliography: p. [340]-343. [BX153.S7 1980] 78-63172 ISBN 0-404-16187-1 : 32.50
1. Nestorian Church—History. 2. Nestorian Church—Missions. I. Title.

VINE, Aubrey Russell, 281'.8
1900-
The Nestorian churches. New York : AMS Press, [1980] p. cm. Reprint of the 1937 ed. published by Independent Press, London. Includes index. Bibliography: p. [BT1440.V5 1980] 78-63173 ISBN 0-404-16188-X : 21.50
1. Nestorian Church—History. I. Title.

Nestorian church. Liturgy and ritual.

NARSAI, 413(ca.)-503. 230
The liturgical homilies of Narsai, translated into English with an introduction by Dom R. H. Connolly ... with an appendix by Edmund Bishop. Cambridge [Eng.] The University press, 1909. lxxvi, 176 p. 23 cm. (Added t.-p.: Texts and studies: contributions to Biblical and patristic literature, ed. by J. A. Robinson. vol. viii, no. 1) [BR45.T43 vol. 8, no. 1] 25-12306
1. Nestorian church. Liturgy and ritual. I. Connolly, Richard Hugh, 1873- tr. II. Bishop, Edmund, 1846-1917. III. Title. Contents omitted.

NESTORIAN Church. 264.01'8
Liturgy and ritual.
The Liturgy of the Holy Apostles Adai and Mari, together with 2 additional liturgies to be said on certain feasts and other days, and the Order of Baptism. Complete and entire; collated from many MSS. from various places. New York, AMS Press [1970] ix, 89 p. 29 cm. Translated from the Syriac ed. published by the Archbishop of Canterbury's Mission to the Assyrian Christians at Urmi. Reprint of the 1893 ed. [BX157.A3 1970] 79-131032 ISBN 0-404-03997-9
I. [Liturgy of the Holy Apostles Adai and Mari. English] II. Title.

Nestorian church—Pastoral letters and charges.

ISHO'YABH III, patriarch 281'.8
of the Nestorians, d.657or8.
The book of consolations : or, The pastoral epistles of Mar Isho -yahbh of Kuphlana in Adiabene : the Syriac text / edited with an English translation by Philip Scott-Moncrieff. Part. I. The Syriac text. 1st AMS ed. New York : AMS Press, 1978. lvi, 101 p. ; 22 cm. Reprint of the 1904 ed. published by Luzac, London, in series: Luzac's Semitic text and translation series. No more published. [BX151.I78 1978] 77-87669 ISBN 0-404-11350-8 : 21.50
1. Nestorian church—Pastoral letters and charges. I. Scott-Moncrieff, Philip David, 1882-1911. II. Title. III. Series: Luzac's Semitic text and translation series.

Nestorian tablet of Sian-fu.

HOLM, Frits, 1881-
My Nestorian adventure in China; a popular account of the Holm- Nestorian expedition to Sian-fu and its results, by Frits Holm...with an introduction by the Rev. Prof. Abraham Yohannan...illustrated with a map and thirty-three photographs by the author and a frontispiece. New York, Chicago [etc.] Fleming H.Revell company, 1923. 335 p. plates, 2 port. (incl. front.) 23 1/2 cm. Maps on lining-papers. [BX154.C4H6] 23-11339
1. Nestorian tablet of Sian-fu. 2. China—Descr. & trav. I. Title.

NESTORIAN tablet of 266.00951
Sian-fu
The Nestorian monument of Hsi-an Fu in Shen-hsi,China, relation to the diffusion of Christianity in China in the seventh and eighth centuries; with the Chinese text of the inscription, a translation, and notes, and a lecture on the monument with a sketch of subsequent Christian missions in China and their present state, by James Legge. London, Trubner, 1888. New York, Reprinted by Paragon, 1966. iv, 65p. illus. 23cm. [BX154.C4N414 1966] 66-18959 5.00
1. Nestorian tablet of Sian-fu. 2. Missions—China. I. Legge, James, 1815-1897. II. Title.

NESTORIAN tablet of 266.00951
Sian-fu.
The Nestorian monument of Hsi-an Fu in Shen-hsi, China, relating to the diffusion of Christianity in China in the seventh and eighth centuries; with the Chinese text of the inscription, a translation, and notes, and a lecture on the monument with a sketch of subsequent Christian missions in China and their present state, by James Legge. London, Trubner, 1888. New York, Reprinted by Paragon Book Reprint Corp., 1966. iv, 65 p. illus. 23 cm. [BX154.C4N414 1966] 66-18959
1. Nestorian tablet of Sian-fu. 2. Missions — China. I. Legge, James, 1815-1897. II. Title.

Nestorians.

EMHARDT, William 281'.8'09
Chauncey, 1874-
The oldest Christian people; a brief account of the history and traditions of the Assyrian people and the fateful history of the Nestorian church, by William Chauncey Emhardt and George M. Lamsa. Introd. by John Gardiner Murray. New York, AMS Press [1970] 141 p. map. 23 cm. Reprint of the 1926 ed. Bibliography: p. 137-138. [BX153.E6 1970] 71-126651 ISBN 4-04-023398-
1. Nestorians. I. Lamsa, George Mamishisho, 1893- joint author. II. Title.

EMHARDT, William Chauncey, 281.
1874-
The oldest Christian people; a brief account of the history and traditions of the Assyrian people and the fateful history of the Nestorian church, by William Chauncey Emhardt...and George M. Lamsa...introduction by Rt. Reverend John Gardiner Murray... New York, The Macmillan company, 1926. 141 p. map. 19 1/2 cm. Bibliography: p. 137-138. [BX153.E6] 26-18120
1. Nestorians. I. Lamsa, George Mamishisho, 1898- joint author II. Title.

Nestorians—History

JOSEPH, John. 281.8
The Nestorians and their Muslim neighbors, a study of western influence on their relations. Princeton, Princeton University Press, 1961. xv, 281p. maps. 23cm. (Princeton Oriental studies, 20) Bibliography: p. 239-269. [DS39.J6] 61-7417
1. Nestorians— Hist. I. Title. II. Series.

Nestorius, patriarch of Constantinople, fl. 428.

BETHUNE-BAKER, James 281.8
Franklin, 1861-
Nestorius and his teaching: a fresh examination of the evidence, by J. F. Bethune-Baker, B.D. With special reference to the newly recoverd Apology of Nestorius (The bazaar of Heraclides) Cambridge [Eng.] The University press, 1908. xviii, 232 p. 19 1/2 cm. "Errata" slip inserted after p. xviii. [BT1440.B45] A 12
1. Nestorius, patriarch of Constantinople. fl. 428. I. Title.

LOOFS, Friedrich, 230'.1'40924 B
1858-1928.
Nestorius and his place in the history of Christian doctrine / by Friedrich Loofs. New York : B. Franklin, [1975] p. cm. Reprint of the 1914 ed. published by the University Press, Cambridge, Eng. [BR65.N384L66 1975] 75-1225 ISBN 0-8337-4903-X
1. Nestorius, Patriarch of Constantinople, fl. 428. I. Title.

LOOFS, Friedrich, 1858-1928.
Nestorius and his place in the history of Christian doctrine, by Friedrich Loofs ... Cambridge, University press, 1914. vii, [1], 132 p. 19 cm. A 14

1. Nestorius, patriarch of Constantinople, fl. 428. I. Title.

MACARTHUR, John Stewart. 232.
Chalcedon, by J. S. MacArthur ... London, Society for promoting Christian knowledge; New York and Toronto, The Macmillan co. [1931] v, [7]-191 p. 20 cm. [BT220.M2] A 35
1. Nestorius, patriarch of Constantinople, fl. 428. 2. Eutyches, 378-ca. 454. 3. Incarnation. 4. Chalcedon, Council of, 451. I. Title.

Netherlands—Church history—20th century

BOAS, J. H. 274.92
Resistance of the churches in the Netherlands, by J. H. Boas. With a foreword by H. P. Van Dusen. New York city, Netherlands information bureau, 1944. 99, [1] p. 23 1/2 cm. (On cover: Booklets of the Netherlands information bureau ... No. 13) [BR906.B6] 45-7675
1. Netherlands—Church history—20th cent. 2. World war, 1939—-Religious aspects. 3. Netherlands—Hist.—German occupation, 1940-1945. I. Title.

Netherlands—History

TORCHIANA, Henry Albert Willem van Coenen, 1867-
Holland, the birthplace of American political, civil and religious liberty; an historical essay, by H. A. Van Coenen Torchiana... San Francisco, P. Elder & company [c1915] 3 p. l., lx-xviii, 89, [1] p. mounted front., mounted plates, mounted ports. 24 1/2 cm. Cover-title and half-title: Holland; an historical essay... [DJ114.T7] 15-14506
1. Netherlands—Hist. 2. Dutch in the U.S. I. Title.

Nettleton, Asahel, 1783-1844.

SMITH, R. S. 269
Recollections of Nettleton, and the great revival of 1820, By Rev. R. Smith. Albany, E. H. Pease & co., 1848. 150 p. 15 cm. [BV3785.N36S5] 37-37664
1. Nettleton, Asabel, 1783-1844. 2. Revivals—U.S. I. Title.

TYLER, Bennet, 1783-1858. 922.
Memoir of the life and character of Rev. Asahel Nettleton, D.D. By Bennet Tyler ... Hartford, Robins & Smith, 1844. xi, [13]-372 p. front. (port.) 19 cm. [BX7260.N4T8] 14-11452
1. Nettleton, Asahel, 1783-1844. I. Title.

TYLER, Bennet, 1783-1858. 922.
Memoir of the life and character of Rev. Asahel Nettleton, D.D. /By Bennet Tyler ... 2d ed. Hartford, Robins and Smith, 1845. x, [11]-367 p. front. (port.) 20 cm. [BX7260.N4T8] 14-11453
1. Nettleton, Asahel, 1783-1844. I. Title.

Neuharth, Steven, 1952-1975.

UTT, Richard H. 286'.73 B
Once you start climbing-don't look down : the story of Steve Neuharth / by Richard H. Utt, with Ruben and Nancy Neuharth. Mountain View, Calif. : Pacific Press Pub. Association, c1978. 122 p. : ill. ; 18 cm. (A Redwood paperback ; 110) [BX6193.N48U77] 78-50438 pbk. : 2.50
1. Neuharth, Steven, 1952-1975. 2. Seventh-Day Adventists—United States—Biography. I. Neuharth, Ruben, joint author. II. Neuharth, Nancy, joint author. III. Title. IV. Title: Don't look down.

Neuman, Therese, 1898-

SCHIMBERG, Albert Paul, 1885- 922.243
The story of Therese Neumann. Bruce paperback pub. in collaboration with All Saints. New York. [1962,c.1947] 211p. 17cm. (AS-233) .50 pap.,
1. Neuman, Therese, 1898- 2. Stigmatization. I. Title.

Neumann, Abraham Aaron,

DROPSIE College for Hebrew and Cognate Learning, Philadelphia. 492.082
Studies and essays in honor of Abraham A. Newman, president, Dropsie College for Hebrew and Cognate Learning, Philadelphia. Ed. by Meir BenHorin, Bernard D. Weinryb, Solomon Zeitlin. Philadelphia, Dropsie College, Broad bel. York St. [c.] 1962. xiii, 649p. port. 25cm. Added t.p. in Hebrew. Some articles in Hebrew. Bibl. 62-52536 7.50
1. Neumann, Abraham Aaron, 2. Judaism—Addresses, essays, lectures. 3. Jews-Hist.—Addresses, essays, lectures. 4. Hebrew philology—Addresses, essays, lectures. I. Ben-Horin, Meir, 1918- ed. II. Title.

Neumann, John Nepomucene, Bp., 1811-1860.

BERGER, Johann, 1845- 922.273
Life of Right Rev. John N. Neumann, D. D., of the Congregation of the Most Holy Redeemer. Fourth bishop of Philadelphia. From the German of Rev. John A. Berger, C. S. S. R., by Rev. Eugene Grimm, C. S. S. R. New York, Cincinnati [etc.] Benziger brothers, 1884. 457 p. incl. front. (port.) pl. 20 cm. [Full name: Johann Nepomuk Berger] [BX4705.N52B42] 37-15209
1. Neumann, John Nepomucene, bp., 1811-1800. I. Grimm, Eugene, 1835-1891, tr. II. Title.

FLAVIUS, Brother, 1927- 92
The house on Logan Square; a story of Blessed John Neumann. Illus. by Carolyn Lee Jagodits. Notre Dame, Ind., Dujarie Press [1964] 94 p. illus., port. 24 cm. [BX4700.N4F5] 65-934
1. Neumann, John Nepomucene, Bp., 1811-1860. I. Title.

GALVIN, James J., 1911- 922.273
Blessed John Neumann, Bishop of Philadelphia. Foreword by John J. Krol. Helicon [dist. New York, Taplinger, c.1964] ix, 261p. 21cm. 64-14665 4.95
1. Neumann, John Nepomucene, Bp., 1811-1860. I. Title.

GALVIN, James J 1911- 922.273
Blessed John Neumann, Bishop of Philadelphia. Forword by John J. Krol. Baltimore, Helicon [1964] ix, 261 p. 21 cm. [BX4700.N4G28] 64-14665
1. Neumann, John Nepomucene, Bp., 1811-1860. I. Title.

LANGAN, Tom. 282'.092'4 B
John Neumann : harvester of souls / Tom Langan. Huntington, IN : Our Sunday Visitor, c1976. 155 p. ; 21 cm. [BX4700.N4L35] 76-21416 ISBN 0-87973-758-1 pbk. : 2.95
1. Neumann, John Nepomucene, Bp., 1811-1860. 2. Catholic Church—Bishops—Biography. 3. Bishops—Pennsylvania—Philadelphia—Biography. 4. Philadelphia—Biography.

NEUMANN, John Nepomucene, Saint, 1811-1860. 271'.64'024 B
Autobiografia de San Juan Neumann, C.S.S.R., cuarto obispo de Filadelfia / introd., commentario y epilogo por Alfred C. Rush ; pref. por John Cardinal Krol ; traduccion al espanol, Amarilda Rivera Munoz. Boston : Daughters of St. Paul, 1980. p. cm. Translation of Autobiography of Saint John Neumann. Includes bibliographical references and index. [BX4700.N4A3318] 80-13768 ISBN 0-8198-0704-4 pbk. : 2.50
1. Neumann, John Nepomucene, Saint, 1811-1860. 2. Christian saints—Pennsylvania—Philadelphia—Biography. 3. Philadelphia—Biography. I. Rush, Alfred Clement, 1910- II. Title.

PHILADELPHIA. St. Peter's church (Catholic) 922
The venerable servant of God, John Nepomucene Neumann, of the Congregation of the Most Holy Redeemer, and fourth bishop of Philadelphia. Philadelphia, Redemptorist fathers, St. Peter's church, 1898. 56 p. front. (port.) pl. 13 cm. [BX4705.N52P45] 41-33869
1. Neumann, John Nepomucene, bp., 1811-1860. I. Title.

WILSON, Robert H. 282'.092'4 B
St. John Neumann, 1811-1860, fourth Bishop of Philadelphia / Robert H. Wilson. Philadelphia : Institutional Services, Archdiocese of Philadelphia, c1977. 39 p. : ill. (some col.) ; 24 cm. [BX4705.N45W54] 77-70313
1. Neumann, John Nepomucene, Bp., 1811-1860. 2. Catholic Church—Bishops—Biography. 3. Bishops—Pennsylvania—Philadelphia—Biography. 4. Philadelphia—Biography. I. Title.

Neumann, John Nepomucene, Saint, 1811-1860.

NEUMANN, John Nepomucene, Saint, 1811-1860. 271'.64'024 B
Autobiografia de San Juan Neumann, C.S.S.R., cuarto obispo de Filadelfia / introd., commentario y epilogo por Alfred C. Rush ; pref. por John Cardinal Krol ; traduccion al espanol, Amarilda Rivera Munoz. Boston : Daughters of St. Paul, 1980. p. cm. Translation of Autobiography of Saint John Neumann. Includes bibliographical references and index. [BX4700.N4A3318] 80-13768 ISBN 0-8198-0704-4 pbk. : 2.50
1. Neumann, John Nepomucene, Saint, 1811-1860. 2. Christian saints—Pennsylvania—Philadelphia—Biography. 3. Philadelphia—Biography. I. Rush, Alfred Clement, 1910- II. Title.

Neumann, John Nepomucene, Saint, 1811-1860—Juvenile literature.

HINDMAN, Jane F. 282'.092'4 B
An ordinary saint : the life of John Neumann / by Jane F. Hindman. New York : Arena Lettres, c1977. ix, 146 p. ; 18 cm. A biography of the bishop renowned for his good deeds who was proclaimed a saint in 1977. [BX4700.N4H56] 92 77-75429 ISBN 0-88479-004-5 : 1.95
1. Neumann, John Nepomucene, Saint, 1811-1860—Juvenile literature. 2. [Neumann, John Nepomucene, Saint, 1811-1860.] 3. Christian saints—United States—Biography—Juvenile literature. 4. [Saints.] I. Title.

READY, Dolores. 271'.64'024 B
Traveler for God : a story about John Neumann / written by Dolores Ready ; illustrated by Constance Crawford. Minneapolis : Winston Press, c1977. [32] p. : ill. (some col.) ; 21 cm. (Stories about Christian heroes) A brief biography of the Roman Catholic saint responsible for organizing the first Catholic school system in America. [BX4700.N4R43] 92 77-77679 ISBN 0-03-022111-0 pbk. : 1.50
1. Neumann, John Nepomucene, Saint, 1811-1860—Juvenile literature. 2. [Neumann, John Nepomucene, Saint, 1811-1860.] 3. Christian saints—United States—Biography—Juvenile literature. 4. [Saints.] I. Crawford, Constance. II. Title. III. Series.

SHEEHAN, Elizabeth Odell, 1919- 92
John Neumann, the children's bishop. Illus. by Harry Barton. New York, Farrar [1965] xiv, 178p. illus. 22cm. (Vision bks.) [BX4700.N4S5] 65-11814 2.25
1. Neumann, John Nepomucene, Bp., 1811-1860—Juvenile literature. I. Title.

Neumann, Kaspar, 1648-1715.

HABERMANN, Johann, 1516-1590.
The Christian's companion; containing morning & evening prayers, for every day in the week; together with other devotions. By Dr. John Haberman. To which is added, Dr. Neuman's Prayer of prayers; and a collection of morning and evening hymns. Tr. from the German. Harrisburg, Pa., G. S. Peters, 1829. iv, [5]-144 p. front. 13 1/2 x 7 1/2 cm. 5-17673
1. Neumann, Kaspar, 1648-1715. I. Title.

Neumann, Therese, 1898-1962.

GRAEF, Hilda C. 922.243
The case of Therese Neumann. Westminster, Md., New man Press, 1951. xix, 162 p. 23 cm. Bibliographical footnotes. [BX4705.N47G7] 51-10857
1. Neumann, Therese, 1898- 2. Stigmatization. I. Title.

HOVRE, Eugene de. 922.243
The riddle of Konnersreuth, by Eugene canon De Hovre translated by Reverend P. M. Van Dorpe, S.T.B. Chicago, Ill., Benedictine press [c1933] 396, [3] p. incl. illus., ports. 19 cm. Translation of Therese Neumann, het levend raadael van Konnersreuth. [BX4705.N47H6] 33-33273
1. Neumann, Therese, 1898- 2. Stigmatisation. I. Van Dorpe, Paul Mary, 1899- tr. II. Title.

LAMA, Fredrich, ritter von, 1876- 922.243
Further chronicles of Therese Neumann, by Fredrich ritter von Lama; translated by Albert Paul Schimberg. Milwaukee, New York [etc.] The Bruce publishing company [c1932] vii, [5], 259 p. front., pl. 20 cm. [BX4705.N47L33] 32-9245
1. Neumann, Therese, 1898- 2. Stigmatization. I. Schimberg, Albert Paul, tr. II. Title.

LAMA, Friedrich, ritter, von, 1876- 922.
Therese Neumann; a stigmatist of our days, by Friedrich ritter von Lama, translated by Albert Paul Schimberg. Milwaukee, Wis., New York [etc.] The Bruce publishing company c[1929] 5 p. l., 249 p. pl. 2 port. (incl. front.) 21 cm. "References": p. [243]-249. [BX4705.N47L32] 30-3995
1. Neumann, Therese, 1898- 2. Stigmatization. I. Schimberg, Albert Paul, tr. II. Title.

LAMA, Friedrich, ritter von, 1876- 922.243
Therese of Konnersreuth; a new chronicle, by Friedrich ritter von Lama; translated by Albert Paul Schimberg. Milwaukee, The Bruce publishing company [c1935] xiii p., 1 l., 267 p. front., plates, ports. 20 cm. [BX4705.N47L35] 35-10466
1. Neumann, Therese, 1898- 2. Stigmatization. I. Schimberg, Albert Paul, tr. II. Title.

MESSMER, Josef. 922.
A visit to the stigmatized seer, Therese Neumann, by Msgr. Joseph Messmer [and] Rt. Rev. Bishop Sigismund Waltz, D. D.; translated from the German by a member of the Dominican order. Chicago, Ill., John P. Daleiden co. [c1929] 117 p. front. (port.) 20 cm. "The message of Konnersreuth, by the Right Reverend Bishop Sigismund Waltz": p. 79-110. Translated of Die stigmatislerte seherin, Theresia Neumann. [BX4705.N47M4] 29-15060
1. Neumann, Therese, 1898- 2. Stigmatization. 3. Miracles. I. Waitz, Siegmund, bp., 1864- II. A member of the Dominican order, tr. III. Title.

[MOEWS, Guy Albert] 1904- 922.243
Soldiers saw Resl. Cincinnati, O., St. Francis book shop [1947] 71 p. front., plates, ports. 17 cm. On cover: Story of Theres Neumann. [BX4705.N47M6] 47-3879
1. Neumann, Therese, 1808- 2. Stigmatization. I. Title.

ROY, Charles Eugene. 922.243
Theresa Neumann of Konnersreuth, by Rev. C. E. Roy ... and Rev. W. A. Joyce ... St. Louis, Mo., B. Herder book company [1936] vii, 198 p. front. (facsim.) 19 cm. "Printed in Great Britain." Based on a series of addresses given by the author in St. Mary's church, London, in August 1935. cf. Pref. [BX4705.N47R6] 38-11609
1. Neumann, Theresa, 1898- 2. Stigmatization. 3. Joyce, William Alphonsus, 1886- joint author. I. Title.

SCHIMBERG, Albert Paul, 1885- 922.243
The story of Therese Neumann. Milwaukee, Bruce Pub. Co. [1947] ix, 232 p. illus., ports. 21 cm. [BX4705.N47S34] 47-12337
1. Neumann, Therese, 1898- 2. Stigmatization. I. Title.

SIWEK, Paul. 922.243
The riddle of Konnersreuth, a psychological and religious study; translated by Ignatius McCormick.

Milwaukee, Bruce Pub. Co. [1953] xvi, 228p. 23cm. Translation and revision of Une stigmatisee de nos jours. Bibliographical footnotes. [BX4705.N47S52] 53-13490
1. Neumann, Therese, 1898- 2. Stigmatization. I. Title.

STEINER, Johannes, 1902- 282'.0924
Therese Neumann; a portrait based on authentic accounts, journals, and documents. Staten Island, N.Y., Alba House [1967] 278 p. illus., facsims., map, ports. 22 cm. Translation of Theres Neumann von Konnersreuth. Includes bibliographical references. [BX4705.N47S73] 66-27536
1. Neumann, Therese, 1898-1962.

STEINER, Johannes, 1902- 248'.2 B
The visions of Therese Neumann / by Johannes Steiner. New York : Alba House, c1976. xii, 244 p. : ill. ; 22 cm. Translation of Visionen der Therese Neumann. [BX4705.N47S7513] 75-34182 ISBN 0-8189-0318-X : 5.95
1. Neumann, Therese, 1898-1962. 2. Visions. I. Title.

TEODOROWICZ, Jozef, abp., 1864- 922.243
Mystical phenomena in the life of Theresa Neumann, by Most Reverend Josef Teodorowicz ... translated by Rev. Rudolph Kraus ... St. Louis, Mo., and London, B. Herder book co., 1940. xi, 519 p. 22 1/2cm. [BX4705.N47T42] 40-4930
1. Neumann, Therese, 1898 2. Stigmatization. I. Kruas, Rudolph, 1895- tr. Translation of Konnersreuth im lichte der mystik and psychologie. II. Title.

THOMAS, F., c.m.f. 922.243
The mystery of Konnersreuth, facts, personal experiences, critical remarks [by] Rev. F. Thomas, C.M.F. ... Los Angeles, Calif., F. Thomas [1941] 8 p. l., 5-136 p. front., plates, ports., facsim. 19 cm. "Fifth edition." [BX4705.N4TT46] 41-22306
1. Neumann, Therese, 1898 I. Title.

THE two stigmatists,
Padre Pio and Teresa Neumann; containing the autobiography of Teresa Neumann, a critical account of the phenomena in her life and a comparison with Padre Pio. A reply to the apostles of hysteria. 2d ed. St. Paul, Radio Replies Press Society, [1956?] xxxii, 212p. illus. 22cm.
1. Neumann, Therese, 1898- 2. Pio da Pietralcina, Father, 1887- 3. Stigmatization. I. Carty, Charles Mortimer. II. Neumann, Therese, 1898-

Neuropsychology—Philosophy.

SPERRY, Roger Wolcott, 1913- 174'.95
Science and moral priority : the merging of mind, brain, and values / Roger W. Sperry. New York : Columbia University Press, 1982. p. cm. (Convergence) Includes index. Bibliography: p. [QP360.S63] 19 81-24206 ISBN 0-231-05406-8 : 16.95
1. Neuropsychology—Philosophy. 2. Ethics. 3. Intellect. 4. Science—Philosophy. I. Title.

Nevada—Church history.

LOOFBOUROW, Leonidas Latimer, 1877- 277.93
Steeples among the sage; a centennial story of Nevada's churches, by Leon L. Loofbourow. [Oakland, Calif., Lake Park Press, 1964] 160 p. illus., ports. 22 cm. 'A Nevada centennial book." [BR555.N76L6] 64-56952
1. Nevada — Church history. I. Title.

Neve, Rosemary, 1923-

NEVE, Rosemary, 1923- 283'.092'4 B
At the name of Jesus / by Rosemary Neve. Evesham : James, 1976. 110 p. ; 19 cm. [BX5199.N53A34] 77-363320 ISBN 0-85305-189-5 : £2.25
1. Neve, Rosemary, 1923- 2. Anglicans—Biography. I. Title.

Neville family.

NICHOLS, John Gough, 1806-1873.
The armorial windows erected, in the reign of Henry VI. By John, viscount Beaumount, and Katharine, duchess of Norfolk, in Woodhouse chapel, by the park of' Beaumont, in Charnwood forest, Leicestershire, including an investigation of the differences of the coat of Neville. By John Gough Nichols, F. S. A. [Westminster, J. B. Nichols and sons] 1860. 2 p. l., 50 p., 1 l. illus. (incl. coats of arms) 2 geneal. tab. (incl. front.) 25 cm. "Read at the Annual meeting of the Leicestershire architectural and archaeological society of Loughborough, July 27th, 1859." Printed at the expense of William Perry Herrick. [CR1627.L4N5] 21-3222
1. Neville family. 2. Beaumont family. 3. Heraldry—England—Leicestershire. 4. Woodhouse chapel. Leicestershire. I. Herrick, William Perry, 1794-1876. II. Title.

Nevin, John Williamson, 1803-1886.

APPEL, Theodore, 1823-1907. 285'.7'0924 B
The life and work of John Williamson Nevin. New York, Arno Press, 1969. 776 p. facsim., port. 24 cm. (Religion in America) Reprint of the 1889 ed. [BX9593.N4A6 1969] 71-83409
1. Nevin, John Williamson, 1803-1886. I. Title.

APPEL, Theodore, 1823-1907. 922.
The life and work of John Williamson Nevin ... by Theodore Appel ... Philadelphia, Reformed church publication house, 1889. xxii, 1 l., 25-776 p. front. (port.) 24 1/2 cm. [BX9593.N4A6] 6-42760
1. Nevin, John Williamson, 1808-1886. I. Title.

APPEL, Theodore, 1823-1907. 922.
The life and work of John Williamson Nevin ... by Theodore Appel ... Philadelphia, Reformed church publication house, 1889. xxii, 1 l., 25-776 p. front. (port.) 24 1/2 cm. [BX9593.N4A6] 6-42760
1. Nevin, John Williamson, 1808-1886. I. Title.

WEISER, Reuben, 1807-1885. 269
... The mourner's bench. By R. Weiser ... [Bedford? Pa.] W. T. Chapman, jr., pr. [pref. 1844] cover-title, 32 p. 21 cm. At head of title: A tract for the people. Caption title: The mourner's bench; or, An humble attempt to vindicate new measures. A reply to John W. Nevin's The anxious bench. [BV3790.N38W4] 44-25660
1. Nevin, John Williamson, 1803-1886. The anxious bench. 2. Revivals. I. Title.

Nevin, Robert Peebles, 1820-1908.

THE sacredness of the 285.
Sabbath. A review of the case of Robert P. Nevin, in the presbytery of Allegheny. By a member of presbytery ... Allegheny, Pa., Ogden & Vance, printers, 1876. 49 p. 17 cm. [BX9193.N4S3] 37-37671
1. Nevin, Robert Peebles, 1820-1908. 2. Sunday. I. A member of presbytery. II. Presbyterian church in the U.S.A. Presbytery of Allegheny.

Nevius, John Livingston, 1829-1893.

NEVIUS, Helen Sanford (Coan) Mrs. 1833-1910. 922.
The life of John Livingston Nevius, for forty years a missionary in China, by his wife Helen S. Coan Nevius; introduction by W. A. P. Martin ... with illustrations from original photographs and a map of eastern Shantung. New York, Chicago [etc.] Fleming H. Revell company [c1895] 2 p. l., 3-476 p. front. (port.) plates, fold. map. 22 cm. [BV3427.N5N4] 12-37082
1. Nevius, John Livingston, 1829-1893. I. Title.

New Alexandria, Pa. Reformed Presbyterian church.

ELDER, John Calvin, 1862- comp. 285.
History of the Reformed Presbyterian church of New Alexandria, Pa. From its organization, September 16, 1816, to September 16, 1916. By J. Calvin Elder--1816 to 1868; J. Oliver Beatty--1868 to 1916; Rev. D. C. Matthews, pastor... [New Alexandria? 1917] 2 p. l., 60 p. plates, ports. 22 1/2 cm. Cover-title: Centennial of the New Alexandria Reformed Presbyterian church, Pittsburgh Presbytery, October 11, 1916... [BX9211.N4E5] 18-6661
1. New Alexandria, Pa. Reformed Presbyterian church. I. Beatty, John Oliver, 1863- joint comp. II. Title.

New Bedford, Mass.—Churches.

[KELLEY, Jesse Fillmore] 277.
History of the churches of New Bedford; to which are added notices of various other moral and religious organizations. Together with short memoirs of Rev. Messrs. Wheelock Craig, John Girdwood, Timothy Stowe, Daniel Webb, and Rev. Messrs. Henniss and Tallon, of St. Mary's church. New Bedford [Mass.] E. Anthony & sons, printers, 1869. 148 p., 1 l. 19 cm. Written by Jesse Fillmore Kelley and Adam Mackie cf. W. Cushing, Anonyms. [BR560.N3K4] 5-1570
1. New Bedford, Mass.—Churches. 2. New Bedford, Mass.—Biog. I. Mackie, Adam, 1818-1884, joint author. II. Title.

New Bedford, Mass. First Congregational soceity.

POTTER, William James, 1830-1893. 288.
The First Congregational society in New Bedford, Massachusetts; its history as illustrative of ecclesiastical evolution. By William James Potter ... New Bedford, Mass., Printed for the Society, 1889. 151 p. 24 cm. [BX9861.N4F5] 12-16806
1. New Bedford, Mass. First Congregational soceity. I. Title.

New Bern, N. C. Christ Church.

CARRAWAY, Gertrude S. 283.756
Crown of life; history of Christ church, New Bern, N. C., 1715-1940, by Gertrude S. Carraway ... New Bern, O. G. Dunn, 1940. 245 p. front., plates. ports. 26 cm. Bibliography: p. [223]-228. "Other sources": p. [229] [BX5980.N3C45] 41-13651
1. New Bern, N. C. Christ Church. I. Title.

New Bethel Methodist Church, Harrison Co., W. Va.

WASHBURN, Charles Henry, 1875-1956. 287.675457
History of the New Bethel Methodist Church, Good Hope, W. Va.; June 1, 1956. [Lost Creek, W. Va., New Bethel Methodist Church, 1960] 109 p. illus. 24 cm. [BX8481.N34W3] 60-10794
1. New Bethel Methodist Church, Harrison Co., W. Va. I. Title.

New Braunfels, Tex. First Protestant Evangelical and Reformed Church.

NEW Braunfels, Tex. First Protestant Evangelical and Reformed Church.
The first Protestant Church, New Braunfels, Texas: its history and its people. Supplement, 1955-1965. [New Braunfels, Tex., 1965] 60 p. ports. 23 cm. Supplements The First Protestant Church, by Oscar Haas, published in 1955. 67-94096
1. New Braunfels, Tex. First Protestant Evangelical and Reformed Church. I. Haas, Oscar, 1885- II. Title.

New Britain, Conn. Saint Mark's church.

SHEPARD, James, 1838- 283.
History of Saint Mark's church, New Britain, Conn., and of its predecessor Christ church, Wethersfield and Berlin, from the first Church of England service in America to nineteen hundred and seven, by James Shepard. New Britain, Conn. [The Tuttle, Morehouse & Taylor company] 1907. xi p., 1 l., [15]-707 p. front. (port.) illus., 36 pl. (incl. ports., facsims.) 24 cm. [BX5980.N33S4] 7-23976
1. New Britain, Conn. Saint Mark's church. I. Title.

New Brunswick, N. J. Church of St. John the Evangelist.

KIRK, Rudolf, 1898- 283.74942
The Church of St. John the Evangelist; a parish history, by Rudolf Kirk and Clara Marburg Kirk. New Brunswick, N. J., 1961. 97p. illus: 24cm. Includes bibliography. [BX5980.N35C53] 62-1938
1. New Brunswick, N. J. Church of St. John the Evangelist. I. Kirk, Clara (Marburg) 1903- joint author. II. Title.

New Brunswick, N.J. First Presbyterian Church.

JONES, Joseph Huntington, 1797-1868. 285.
Outline of a work of grace in the Presbyterian congregation at New Brunswick, N.J., during the year 1837. Philadelphia, H. Perkins, 1839. 148 p. 16 cm. Cover title:Revival in New Brunswick [BX9211.N435F55] 50-46174
1. New Brunswick, N.J. First Presbyterian Church. 2. Revivals—New Brunswick, N.J. I. Title. II. Title: Revival in New Brunswick.

New Brunswick, N. J. First Reformed Dutch church.

STEELE, Richard Holloway, 1824-1900. 261
Historical discourse delivered at the celebration of the one hundred and fiftieth anniversary of the First Reformed Dutch church. New-Brunswick, N. J., October 1, 1867. By Richard H. Steele ... New Brunswick, N. J., Pub. by the Consistory, 1867. v, [3], [9]-223 p. 24 cm. [F144.N5S8] 6-37984
1. New Brunswick, N. J. First Reformed Dutch church. I. Title.

New Brunswick, N. J. Theological seminary of the Reformed church in America—Biography

NEW Brunswick, N. J. Theological seminary of the Reformed church in America. 207.74942
Biographical record, Theological seminary, New Brunswick, New Jersey, 1784-1934, compiled by John Howard Raven, D. D., biographer of the Alumni association. Printed for the Seminary by the Rev. Archibald Laidlie, D. D., LL. D., memorial fund. [New Brunswick?] 1934. 276 p. 24 cm. [BV4070.N34 1934] 34-42814
1. New Brunswick, N. J. Theological seminary of the Reformed church in America—Biog. I. Raven, John Howard, 1870- comp. II. Title.

NEW Brunswick, N. J. Theological seminary of the Reformed church in America. 207.74942
The one hundred fiftieth anniversary of the founding of New Brunswick theological seminary, October second and third, nineteen hundred thirty-four. New Brunswick, N. J. [1934] 1 p. l., 108 p. 23 cm. [BV4070.N365 1934] 35-17930
I. Title.

New Canaan, Conn. Methodist Episcopal church.

NEW Canaan, Conn. Congregational church. 285.87469
... Canaan parish, 1733-1933, being the story of the Congregational church of New Canaan, Connecticut, as told by the observance of its two hundredth

anniversary, June 20 to December 20, 1933. Also the history and addresses of the Methodist Episcopal and St. Mark's churches given upon the occasion of their 100th and 150th anniversaries, respectively. [New Canaan, Conn., New Canaan advertiser, 1935. v. illus. (incl. ports., map, facsims.) Stamped on fly-leaf; First edition of which this copy is no. 134. Edited by Stephen Benjamin Hoyt. "History of the Methodist Episcopal church of New Canaan. Conn., by Clifford W. Hall": v. 1, p. 215-222; An historical address delivered in St. Mark's, New Canaan, Sunday, May 13th, 1934, on the occasion of the centennial of the consecration of the present church. By the Rt. Rev. Stephen E. Keeler": v. 1, p. 223-249. Blank pages for "Genealogy" (v. 1, p. 261-265) Bibliography: v. 1, p. 251-260. [BX7255.N34C6] 85-14129
1. New Canaan, Conn. Methodist Episcopal church. 2. New Canaan, Conn. St. Mark's church. I. Hall Clifford Watson, 1880- II. Keeler, Stephen Edward, 1887- III. Hoyt, Stephen Benjamin, ed. IV. Title.

New Castle, Pa. Central Presbyterian Church.

STERLING, Alice M 285.174893
Central Presbyterian Church; a history, 1851-1953. New Castle, Pa. [1953] unpaged. illus. 23cm. [BX9211.N45C4] 54-38487
1. New Castle, Pa. Central Presbyterian Church. I. Title.

New Covenant Baptist Association.

SEXTON, Mark S., 286'.1755'7 1952-
The chalice and the covenant : a history of the New Covenant Baptist Association, 1868-1975 / by Mark S. Sexton. Winston-Salem, N.C. : Hunter Pub. Co., 1976. xvi, 319 p. : ill. ; 24 cm. Includes indexes. [BX6444.N8S49] 76-150888 15.00
1. New Covenant Baptist Association. 2. Afro-American Baptists—North Carolina. 3. Afro-American Baptists—Virginia. I. Title.

New England—Bibliography

BOSTON. Public library. 016. Prince collection.
Catalogue of the library of Rev. Thomas Prince, former pastor of Old South church. Presented by him to the Old South church and society. Boston, Crocker and Brewster, 1846. 112 p. 24 cm. "Compiled by G. H. Whitman." Collection deposited in Boston public library, 1866. [Z997.P957] 4-4679
1. New England—Bibl. I. Prince, Thomas, 1687-1758. II. Whitman, G. H. III. Boston. Old South church. IV. Title.

New England Catholic historical society, Boston.

... Memorial volume of the one hundredth anniversary celebration of the dedication of the Church of the Holy Cross, Boston. [Boston] The New England Catholic historical society, 1904. 137 p., 1 l., [4] p. illus., (incl. ports.) 25 cm. At head of title: 1803--September--1903. Added t.-p., illus. 5-3186
1. New England Catholic historical society, Boston.

New England—Church history.

BACKUS, Isaac, 1724-1806. 284.
An abridgment of the Church history of New-England from 1602 to 1804, containing a view of their principles and practice, declensions and revivals, oppression and liberty. With a concise account of the Baptists in the southern parts of America and a chronological table of the whole. Pub. according to act of Congress. Boston, Printed for the author by E. Lincoln, 1804. 271 p. 22 cm. [BR530.B2 1804] 48-40425
1. New England—Church history. I. Title. II. Title: Church history of New England from 1620 to 1804.

BACKUS, Isaac, 1724-1806. 284.
Church history of New England from 1620 to 1804, containing a view of the principles and practice, declensions and revivals, oppression and liberty of the churches, and a chronological table. With a memoir of the author. Philadelphia, American Baptist Publ. and S. S. Society, 1844. 250 p. port. 20 cm. [BR530.B2 1844] 48-35693
1. New England—Church history. I. Title.

BACKUS, Isaac, 1724-1806. 284.
Church history of New England from 1620 to 1804, containing a view of the principles and practice, declensions and revivals, oppression and librty of the churches, and a chronological table. With a memoir of the author. Philadelphia, American Baptist Publ. Society, 1853. 250 p. port. 20 cm. [BR530.B2 1853] 48-35694
1. New England—Church history. I. Title.

BAINTON, Roland Herbert, 280.1 1894-
Christian unity and religion in New England. Boston, Beacon Press [1964] 294 p. illus., maps. 21 cm. (His Collected papers in church history, ser. 3) Bibliography: p. [283]-289. [BR530.B34] 64-13530
1. New England—Church history. 2. Christian union—New England. 3. Sects—New England. I. Title.

[BURGESS, George, bp.] 1809- 277. 1866.
Pages from the ecclesiastical history of New England, during the century between 1740 and 1840. Boston, J. B. Dow, 1847. 126 p. 19 cm. [BR530.B7] 43-19470
1. New England—Church history. 2. Unitarianism. I. Title.

FORD, David Barnes, 1820- 284. 1903.
New England's struggles for religious liberty, by Rev. David B. Ford... Philadelphia, American Baptist publication society, 1896. 275 p. 21 cm. [BR530.F7] 12-32250
1. New England—Church history. 2. Religious liberty—New England. I. Title.

MATHER, Cotton, 1663-1728 277.4
Magnalia Christi Americana; or, The ecclesiastical history of New-England from its first planting in the year 1620 unto the year of Our Lord 1698, in seven books. With an introd. and occasional notes, by Thomas Robbins and translations of the Hebrew, Greek and Latin quotations, by Lucius F. Robinson. To which is added a memoir of Cotton Mather, by Samuel G. Drake. Also, a comprehensive index by another hand. New York, Russell & Russell [1967] 2 v. ports. 25cm. Reissue of the text of the 1853-55 ed., each bk. having special t.p. Contents.v.1 Book 1. Antiquities. Book 2. Ecclesiarum clypei. Book 3. Polybius.--v. 2. Book 4. Sal gentium. Book 5. Acts and monuments Book 6. Thaumaturgus. Book 7. Ecclesiarum praelia. [BR520.M4 1967] 66-24730 35.00 set,
1. Mather, Cotton, 1663-1728. 2. New England—Church history. 3. New England—Biog. 4. New England—Hist.—Colonial period. I. Title.

MATHER, Cotton, 1663-1728. 277.4
Magnalia Christi Americana : or, The ecclesiastical history of New-England from its first planting in the year 1620 unto the year of our Lord 1698 / Cotton Mather. New York : Arno Press, 1972. 7 v. in 1 : ill. ; 27 cm. (Research library of colonial Americana) Reprint of the 1702 ed. printed for T. Parkhurst, London. [BR530.M34 1972] 74-141092 ISBN 0-405-03297-8
1. New England—Church history. 2. New England—History—Colonial period, ca. 1600-1775. 3. New England—Biography. I. Title. II. Series.

MATHER, Cotton, 1663-1728. 277.
Magnalis Christi americana; or, The ecclesiastical history of New England; from its first planting, in the year 1620, unto the year of Our Lord 1698. In seven books. By...Cotton Mather...With an introduction and occasional notes, by the Rev. Thomas Robbins, D.D., and translations of the Hebrew, Greek, and Latin quotations, by Lucius F. Robinson, LL.D. To which is added a memoir of Cotton Mather, by Samuel G. Drake, M.A. ... Also, a comprehensive index, by another hand... Hartford, S. Andrus and son, 1855, '53. 2 v. fronts., ports., geneal. tab. 23 1/2 cm. Each book has special t.-p. Contents.--I. book I. Antiquities, 1855, book II. Ecclesiarum ciypei 1853. book III. Polybius. 1853--II. book IV. Sal gentium. 1853. book V. Acts and monuments 1853. book VI. Thaumaturgus. 1853. book VII. Ecclesiarum praelia. 1853. [BR520.M4] 3-4343
1. Mather, Cotton, 1663-1728. 2. New England—Church history. 3. New England—Biog. 4. New England—Hist.—Colonial period. I. Robbins, Thomas, 1777-1856. II. Drake, Samuel Gardner, 1796-1875. III. Robinson, Lucius Franklin, 1826-1861, tr. IV. Title.

MATHER, Increase, 1639-1723. 285.
The order of the gospel, professed and practised by the churches of Christ in New England, justified, by the Scripture, and by the writings of many learned men, both ancient and modern divines; in answer to several questions, relating to church discipline. By Increase Mather, president of Harvard colledge in Cambridge, and teacher of a church at Boston in New England... Boston, Printed by B. Green, & J. Allen, for Benjamin Eliot, at his shop under the west end of the town house, 1700. 143 [1] p. 15 cm. [BX7230.M26] 22-2674
1. New England—Church history. I. Title.

MORSE, James King, 1906- 922.573
Jedidiah Morse, a champion of New England orthodoxy [by] James King Morse. New York, Columbia university press, 1939. ix, 179, [1] p. 23 1/2cm. (Columbia studies in American culture, no. 2). Issued also as thesis (PH.D.) Columbia university. Bibliography: p. 163-[172] [BX7260.M57M37 1939] 39-11247
1. Morse, Jedidiah, 1761-1826. 2. New England—Church history. 3. New England—Religion. I. Title.

THE Religious history of New England; 284. King's chapel lectures, by John Winthrop Platner, William W. Fenn ... [and others] Cambridge, Harvard university press; [etc., etc.] 1917. v. 856 p., 1 l. 24 1/2 cm. Contents.The Congregationalists, by J. W. Platner.--The revolt against the standing order, by W. W. Fenn.--The Baptists, by G. E. Horr.--The Quakers, by R. M. Jones.--The Episcopalians, by G. Hodges.--The Methodists, by W. E. Huntington.--The Universalists, by J. C. Adams.--The Swedenborgians, by W. L. Worcester. [BR530.R4] 17-15979
1. New England—Church history. I. Platner, John Winthrop, 1865-1921. II. Fenn, William Wallace, 1862-1932. III. Horr, George Edwin, 1856-1927. IV. Jones, Rufus Matthew, 1863- V. Hodges, George, 1856-1919. VI. Huntington, William Edwards, 1844-1930. VII. Adams, John Coleman, 1849-1922. VIII. Worcester, William Loring, 1859- IX. King's chapel lectures, 1914 15-1915 16.

RIEGLER, Gordon Arthur, 1901- 261
Socialization of the New England clergy, 1800 to 1860 [by] Gordon A. Riegler. Greenfield, O., The Greenfield printing and publishing company, 1945. 4 p. l., 187 p. 16 cm. Bibliographical references included in "Foot notes" (p. 139-167) Bibliography: p. 169-177. [BR530.R5] 45-6874
1. New England—Church history. 2. Clergy—New England. 3. Church and social problems—New England. I. Title.

RIEGLER, Gordon Arthur, 277.4 1901-
Socialization of the New England clergy, 1800 to 1860 / Gordon A. Riegler. Philadelphia : Porcupine Press, 1978 p. cm. (Perspectives in American history ; no. 37) Reprint of the 1945 ed. published by Greenfield Print. and Pub. Co., Greenfield, Ohio. Includes index. Bibliography: p. [BR530.R5 1979] 79-13027 ISBN 0-87991-361-4 lib.bdg. : 14.00
1. New England—Church history. 2. Clergy—New England. 3. Church and social problems—New England. I. Title. II. Series: Perspectives in American history (Philadelphia) ; no. 37.

SMITH, Chard Powers, 1894- 277.74
Yankees and God. [1st ed.] New York, Hermitage House [1954] 528 p. 22 cm. [BR530.S6] 54-11978
1. New England—Church history. 2. New England—Intellectual life. 3. Puritans. 4. Religious thought—U.S. 5. Philosophy, American. I. Title.

VAN NESS, Thomas, 1859- 220
The religion of New England, by Thomas Van Ness, Pub. for the Second Unitarian society of Brookline, Mass. Boston, The Beacon press, inc. [c1926] xi, 205 p. 18 cm. [BS530.V3] 26-120221
1. New England—Church history. I. Brookline, Mass. Second Unitarian society. II. Title.

WASHBURN, Owen Redington, 284.274 1866-
John Calvin in New England, 1620-1947 [i.e. 1943] North Montpelier, Vt., Driftwind Press, 1948. 111 p. 21 cm. "References": p. 110-111. [BR530.W33] 48-1777
1. New England—Church history. 2. Calvinism—Controversial literature. I. Title.

WINSLOW, Ola Elizabeth. 277.4
Meetinghouse Hill, 1630-1783. With a new pref. New York, Norton [1972] x, 344 p. illus. 20 cm. (The Norton library, N632) Reprint of the 1952 ed., with a new pref. [BR530.W5 1972] 79-39172 ISBN 0-393-00632-8 2.95
1. New England—Church history. I. Title.

WINSLOW, Ola Elizabeth. 277.4
Meetinghouse Hill, 1630-1783. New York, Macmillan, 1952. 344 p. illus. 22 cm. [BR530.W5] 52-11102
1. New England—Church history. I. Title.

New England—History

CHILD, Frank Samuel, 1854- 277.
The colonial parson of New England; a picture, by Frank Samuel Child ... New York, The Baker & Taylor co. [c1896] 3 p. l., 9-226 p. 19 cm. [BR520.C49] 2-24737
I. Title.

CRAWFORD, Mary Caroline, 920.073 1874-
The romance of old New England churches, by Mary Caroline Crawford ... Boston, L. C. Page & company, [1907] 5 p. l., vii-ix, [1], 11-377, [2] p. front., plates, ports. 20 cm. "Second impression, April, 1907." [F5.C91 1907] 31-30059
1. New England—Hist. 2. New England—Church history. I. Title.

New England—Intellectual life.

BROWN, Jerry Wayne. 220.6'3'0974
The rise of Biblical criticism in America, 1800-1870; the New England scholars. [1st ed.] Middletown, Conn., Wesleyan University Press [1969] vi, 212 p. 22 cm. Includes bibliographical references. [BS500.B7] 69-17793 10.00
1. Bible—Criticism, interpretation, etc.—History—19th century. 2. New England—Intellectual life. I. Title.

WARREN, Austin, 1899- 209'.74
New England saints / Austin Warren. Westport, Conn. : Greenwood Press, 1976. p. cm. Reprint of the 1956 ed. published by University of Michigan Press, Ann Arbor. Bibliography: p. [F4.W36 1976] 76-28302 ISBN 0-8371-9086-X lib.bdg. : 13.25
1. New England—Intellectual life. 2. Religious thought—New England. I. Title.

New England—Religion.

CHAUNCY, Charles, 1705-1787. 277.
Seasonable thoughts on the state of religion in New-England, a treatise in five parts ... With a preface giving an account of the antinomians, familists and libertines, who infected these churches, above an hundred years ago: very needful for these days; the like spirit and errors prevailing now as did then. The whole being intended,and calculated,to serve the interest of Christ's kingdom. By Charles Chauncy ... Boston, Printed by Rogers and Fowle, for Samuel Eliot in Cornhill 1743. xxx, 18, 424 p. 19 cm. [BR520.C45] 45-31137
1. New England—Religion. I. Title.

EDWARDS, Jonathan, 1703-1758. 277.
Some thoughts concerning the present revival of religion in New-England, and the way in which it ought to be acknowledged and promoted, humbly offered to the publick, in a treatise on that subject ... By Jonathan Edwards ... Boston: Printed and sold by S. Kneeland and T. Green in Queen-street, 1742. 1 p. l., iv-378 p. 15 1/2 cm. [BR520.E5 1742] 26-24348
1. New England—Religion. 2. Revivals. I. Title.

EDWARDS, Jonathan, 1703-1758. 277.
Some thoughts concerning the present revival of religion in New-England, and the way in which it ought to be acknowledged and promoted; humbly offer'd to the publick, in a treatise on that subject ... By Jonathan Edwards ... Boston, Printed: Edinburgh, Reprinted by T. Lumisden and J. Robertson, and sold at their printing-house in the Fish-market, 1743. iv, 221 p. 19 cm. [BR520.E5 1743] 26-24349
1. New England—Religion. 2. Revivals. I. Title.

New England—Social life and customs.

BLISS, William Root, 1825-1906. 285'.9'0974
Side glimpses from the colonial meeting-house. Detroit, Gale Research Co., 1970. 256 p. 22 cm. Reprint of the 1894 ed. [F7.B64 1970] 70-140410
1. New England—Social life and customs. 2. Puritans—New England. 3. Witchcraft—New England. I. Title.

New England spiritualist campmeeting association.

BUDINGTON, Henry Aaron, 1831-
History of the New England spiritualist campmeeting association at Lake Pleasant, Mass.; by H. A. Budington. Springfield, Mass., Star publishing company, c1907. cover-title, 88 p. plates, ports. 20 cm. [BF1228.N6] 10-32973
1. New England spiritualist campmeeting association. I. Title.

New England theology.

BANGS, Nathan, 1778-1862.
The reformer reformed: or, A second part of the Errors of Hopkinsianism detected and refuted: being an examination of Mr. Seth Williston's "Vindication of some of the most essential doctrines of the reformation." By Nathan Bangs ... New York, Printed by John C. Totten, no. 9 Bowery. 1816. viii, [9]-353, [2] p. 18 cm. [BX7251.B3 1816] 7-39364
1. Williston, Seth, 1770-1851. Vindication of some of the most essential doctrines of the reformation. 2. New England theology. I. Title.

BOARDMAN, George Nye, 1825-1915. 277
A history of New England theology, by George Nye Boardman ... New York, A. D. F. Randolph company, 1899. 1 p. l., 314 p. 20 cm. [BX7250.B6] 99-2387
1. New England theology. 2. New England—Church history. I. Title.

DE JONG, Peter Ymen. 231
The covenant idea in New England theology, 1620-1847, by Peter Y. De Jong. Grand Rapids, Mich., Wm. B. Eerdmans publishing company, 1945. 264 p. 20 cm. "Submitted in somewhat another form and at greater length to the faculty of the Hartford theological seminary, Hartford, Conn., as partial fulfilment of the requirements for the degree of doctor of philosophy."--Pref. Bibliography: p. 251-259. [BX7250.D4] 45-4086
1. New England theology. 2. Covenants (Theology) 3. Covenants (Church polity) I. Title.

DOW, Daniel, 1772-1849.
New Haven theology, alias Taylorism, alias neology; in its own language, with notes appended ... By Daniel Dow ... Thompson [Conn.] Printed by G. Roberts, 1834. iv, [5]-56 p. 21 cm. [BX7252.N5D6] 6-21175
1. New England theology. I. Title.

FOSTER, Frank Hugh, 1851-1935 285.874
A genetic history of the New England theology. New York, Russell, 1963. 568p. 22cm. Bibl. 63-12564 10.00
1. New England theology. I. Title.

FOSTER, Frank Hugh, 1851-1935. 285.
A genetic history of the New England theology of Chicago press, 1907. xv, 568 p. 23 cm. Biographical and bibliographical foot-notes. [BX7250.F7] 7-8502
1. New England theology. I. Title.

HAROUTUNIAN, Joseph, 1904- 285.874
Piety versus moralism; the passing of the New England theology. Hamden, Conn., Archon [dist. Shoe String] 1964[c.1932] xxv, 329p. 22cm. Bibl. 64-24715 8.00
1. New England theology. I. Title.

HAROUTUNIAN, Joseph, 1904- 285.874
Piety versus moralism; the passing of the New England theology, by Joseph Haroutunian. New York, H. Holt and company [c1932] xxv, 329 p. 22 cm. (Half-title: Studies in religion and culture. American religion series, iv) Issued also as thesis (P.H. D.) Columbia university. Bibliography: p. 307-322. [BX7250.H3 1932 a] 32-11666
1. New England theology. I. Title.

[TYLER, Bennet] 1783-1858.
Letters on the origin and progress of the New Haven theology. From a New England minister to one at the South. New York, R. Carter and E. Collier, 1837. iv, [5]-180 p. 16 cm. [BX7252.N5T9] 38-24326
1. New England theology. I. Title.

WALLACE, David Alexander, 1826-1883. 285.874
The theology of New England. An attempt to exhibit the doctrines now prevalent in the orthodox Congregational churches of New England. By David A. Wallace...With an introduction by Daniel Dana, D.D. Boston, Crocker & Brewster, 1856. 106 p. 19 1/2 cm. [BX7250.W3] 30-34025
1. New England theology. I. Title.

WILLISTON, Seth, 1770-1851.
A vindication of some of the most essential doctrines of the reformation: being a reply to objections raised against these doctrines in a late publication, entitled: "The errors of Hopkinsianism detected and refuted; in six letters, by Nathan Bangs ..." addressed to the author of the present work. To which is added a sermon, on the goodness of God, manifested in governing the hearts of His enemies. By Seth Williston ... Hudson, N.Y., Printed by Ashbel Stoddard, 1817. 264 p. 18 1/2 cm. [BX7251.B295W5] 42-32830
1. Bangs, Nathan, 1778-1862. The errors of Hopkinsianism detected and refuted. 2. New England theology. I. Title.

New France — Discovery and exploration

HABIG, Marion A. 922.273
The Franciscan Pere Marquette; a critical biography of Father Zenobe Membre, O. F. M., La Salle's chaplain and missionary companion, 1645 (ca.)-1689, with maps and original narratives; by Marion A. Habig... New York, J. F. Wagner, inc. [1934] xiii p., 1 l., 301 p. front., plates, maps. 23 cm. [Franciscan studies, no. 13] Appendix: Letter of Father Membre (translation) Letter of Henri de Tonti (original and translation) Letter of Father Christian Le Ciercq, containing an abridgment of Father Membre's letter (translation) Official report of La Salle's expedition of 1682: A. The author: Father Membre. B. Translation [of the Official report] Bibliography: p. [257]-285. [BX8601.B7 no. 13] [271.9032] 34-37974
1. Membre, Zenobe, 1645?-1687? 2. La Salle, Robert Cavelier, sieur de, 1643-1687. 3. New France—Disc. & explor. 4. Mississippi river—Disc. & explor. I. Tonti, Henri de, d. 1704. II. Le Clercq Chretiem, fl. 1641-1695. III. Title.

JESUITS. Letters from missions (North America) 922.271
The Jesuit relations and allied documents; travel and explorations of the Jesuit missionaries in New France, 1610-1791; the original French, Latin, and Italian texts, with English translations and notes. Edited by Reuben Gold Thwaites. Cleveland, Burrows Bros. Co., 1896-1901. 73 v. illus., plates, ports., maps (part fold.) facsims., plans. 23 cm. Vols. 72-73: Index. [F1030.7.C96] 3-6351
1. Jesuits — Missions. 2. New France — Disc. & explor. 3. Indians of North America — Missions. 4. Canada — Hist. — Sources. 5. New France — Bibl. 6. Indians of North American — Bibl. I. Thwaites, Reuben Gold, 1853-1913, ed. II. Title.

New Gilead United Church of Christ.

SHEPHERD, Banks D. 285'.8756'72
New Gilead Church; a history of the German Reformed people on Coldwater, by Banks D. Shepherd. [Concord? N.C., 1966] 63 p. illus., facsims., ports. 29 cm. Bibliography: p. 59. [BX9567.C6S5] 74-6086
1. New Gilead United Church of Christ. I. Title.

New Hampshire Bible society.

AIKEN, Edwin J.
The first hundred years of the New Hampshire Bible society. 1812-1912. Rev. Edwin J. Aiken, secretary, 1898-1912. Concord, N.H., The Rumford press, 1912. iv p. 1 l., 86 p. front., ports., facsim. 24 1/2 cm. A 13
1. New Hampshire Bible society. I. Title.

New Hampshire—Biography

CARTER, Nathan Franklin, 1830-1915. 261.
The native ministry of New Hampshire ... By Rev. N. F. Carter. Concord, N. H., Rumford printing co., 1906. iv, 1017 p. front. (port.) 24 cm. [BR555.N4C3] 6-7344
1. New Hampshire—Biog. I. Title.

New Haven. Christ Church.

LYON, Josephine A 1862-1939.
The chronicle of Christ Church. With an introd. by Chauncey Brewster Tinker. [New Haven? introd. 1941] 166 p. illus. 24 cm.
1. New Haven. Christ Church. I. Title.

LYON, Josephine A 1862-1939. 283.7468
The chronicle of Christ Church. With an introd. by Chauncey Brewster Tinker. [New Haven? introd. 1941] 166 p. illus. 24 cm. [BX5980.N37C5] 63-56481
1. New Haven. Christ Church. I. Title.

New Haven. First Baptist Church.

BRUSH, John W
A history of the First Baptist Church in New Haven, 1816-1966. [New Haven, 1966] 85 p. illus. 22 cm. 68-6688
1. New Haven. First Baptist Church. I. New Haven. First Baptist Church. II. Title.

New Haven. First church of Christ.

MAURER, Oscar Edward, 1878- 285.87468
A Puritan church and its relation to community, state, and nation; addresses delivered in preparation for the three hundredth anniversary of the settlement of New Haven, by Oscar Edward Maurer ... New Haven, Pub. for the First church of Christ in New Haven by Yale university press; London, H. Milford, Oxford university press, 1938. iv p., 1 l., 208 p. front. 21 cm. "The first four addresses summarize Dr. Leonard Bacon's Historical discourses, published ... in 1838, besides including ... new material ... The four following relate the history of the First church from 1825." --Foreword. [BX7255.N35F52] 38-16639
1. New Haven. First church of Christ. 2. Congregational churches in Connecticut. I. Bacon, Leonard, 1802-1881. Thirteen historical discourses. II. Title.

New Haven. St. Thomas' Episcopal church.

BEARDSLEY, William Agur, 1865- 283.7468
History of St. Thomas's Episcopal church, New Haven, Connecticut, 1848-1941. By Rev. William A. Beardsley ... [New Haven, The Tuttle, Morehouse & Taylor company, 1940?] 6 p. l., 125 p. front., plates, ports. 21 1/2 cm. [BX5980.N37S3] 42-1017
1. New Haven. St. Thomas' Episcopal church. I. Title.

New Haven. United church (Congregational)

MITCHELL, Mary (Hewitt) Mrs. 285.87468
History of the United church of New Haven, by Mary Hewitt Mitchell, PH.D., written in commemoration of the two hundredth anniversary, 1742-1942. New Haven, Conn. The United church, 1942. viii, 286 p. front., illus. (incl. ports.) 23 1/2 cm. [Full name: Mrs. Mary Cornwell (Hewitt) Mitchell] "Bibliographical note": p. 270-271. [BX7255.N35U5] 42-14259
1. New Haven. United church (Congregational) I. Title.

New Hope church, Chapel Hill township, Orange co., N. C.

CRAIG, David Irvin, 1849-19259 285.1756
A historical sketch of New Hope church, in Orange county, N. C. (Rev. ed.) By Rev. D. I. Craig ... Reidsville, N. C., 1891. 54 p. 22 cm. Includes "Family history" (p. 41-53) of the Strayhorn, Craig, Blackwood and Kirkland families. [BX9211.N47C7 1891] 37-16734
1. New Hope church, Chapel Hill township, Orange co., N. C. 2. Presbyterians in North Carolina. 3. North Carolina—Geneal. I. Title.

New Jersey—Church history.

FLEMINGTON, N.J. Baptist church. 286.
One hundredth anniversary exercises of the Baptist church, Flemington, N.J. June 17th, 18th and 19th, 1898. Flemington, N.J., The church, 1898. 175 p. front., illus., ports. 20 1/2 cm. [BX6480.F6A5] 3-12140
I. Title.

HACKENSACK, N.J. Third Reformed Church.
One hundredth anniversary . . . the Third Reformed Church, the church on the heights . . . [Hackensack ?] 1958. 1 v. (unpaged) port. 24 cm. Lettered on cover: 1858. 1958. 66-45796
I. Title.

JAMISON, Wallace N. 209.749
Religion in New Jersey: a brief history. Princeton, N.J., Van Nostrand [c.]1964. xiii, 183p. illus., fold maps. (on lining papers) 22cm. (N.J. hist. ser., v.13) Bibl. 64-23966 3.95 bds.,
1. New Jersey—Church history. I. Title. II. Series.

NEWARK, N.J. Trinity Cathedral. 283.749
Two hundred years of Old Trinity, 1746-1946. Newark, 1946. 72 p. illus., ports. 23 cm. [BX5980.N29T7] 47-26775
I. Title.

New Jersey—Church history—Sources.

AMERICAN tract society. 261.
Colporteur reports to the American Tract Society. 1841-1846. Prepared by the New Jersey Historical records survey projects, Division of professional and service projects, Work projects administration. Sponsored by New Jersey State planning board. Newark, N. J., The Historical records survey, 1940. 3 p. l., 123 numb. l., 1. l. incl. maps, tables. 27 cm. (Transcriptions of early church records of New Jersey) Reproduced from type-written

copy. "Other publications of the New Jersey Historical records survey project": leaf at end. [BR555.N5A5] 277 ISBN 40-28789 Revised
1. New Jersey—Church history—Sources. I. Historical records survey. New Jersey. II. Title.

New Jersey. Laws, statutes, etc.

A brief account of 285.
associated presbyteries; and a general view of their sentiments concerning religion and ecclesiastical order. By a convention of said prespyteries [!] Printed in Catskill, by M. Croswell-- 1796. 2 p. l., 102, [6] p. 17 1/2 x 11cm. An act, to incorporate sundry persons as trustees of the society, instituted in Morris-County, for the promotion of learning and religion. (6 p. at end) [BX8999.A9B7] 3-16694
1. New Jersey. Laws, statutes, etc.

New Jerusalem church.

BLOCK, Marguerite (Beck) 289.4'73
1889-
The New Church in the New World; a study of Swedenborgianism in America. With a new introd. by Robert H. Kirven. New York, Octagon Books, 1968 [c1932] xxiii, 464 p. port. 24 cm. (Studies in religion and culture. American religion series, 5) Bibliography: p. 437-449. [BX8716.B6 1968] 67-18752
1. New Jerusalem Church. I. Title. II. Series.

BLOCK, Marguerite (Beck) 289.4
Mrs., 1889-
The New church in the new world; a study of Swedenborgianism in America, by Marguerite Beck Block. New York, H. Holt and company [c1932] xi p., 2 l., 3-464 p. front. (port.) 22 cm. (Half-title: Studies in religion and culture. American religion series, v) Issued also as thesis (Ph.D.) Columbia university, 1962. [Full name: Mrs. Marguerite Hall (Beck) Block] Bibliography : p. 437-449. [BX8716.B6 1932a] 32-18712
1. New Jerusalem church. I. Title. II. Series.

DOLE, George Henry.
The New church; what, how, why [by] George Henry Dole. New York, The New church board of publication, 1901. 64 pp. 18 cm. 2-8104
1. New Jerusalem church. I. Title.

FERNALD, Woodbury M. 289.4
A new age for the New church; wherein is contained a condensed view of its past stages and future prospects; a review of the celestial sense of the divine word, through Rev. T. L. Harris; some notice of the authority of Swedenborg; and the coming judgment upon all the earth. By Woodbury M. Fernald... Boston, Mass., 1860. ix, [3]-85 p. 21 1/2 cm. No. [2] in a volume lettered: Spiritual miscellanies. [BF1235.S65] 34-13685
1. New Jerusalem church. 2. Harris, Thomas Laek, 1828-1906. Arcana of Christianity. 3. Swedenborg, Emanuel, 1688-1772. I. Title.

GENERAL church of the New
Jerusalem.
A liturgy for the General church of the New Jerusalem. Bryn Athyn, Pa., Academy book room, 1908. v, 814 p. 21 cm. 8-19231
I. Title.

GENERAL Church of the New
Jerusalem. Liturgy and ritual.
A liturgy for the General Church of the New Jerusalem. Bryn Athyn, Pa., Academy Book Room, 1908. v, 811 p. 20 1/2 cm. 8-19231
I. Title.

[HOBART, Nathaniel] 922.84
Life of Emanuel Swedenborg, with some account of his writings, together with a brief notice of the rise and progress of the New Church. Boston, Allen and Goddard, 1831. iv, [6]-188 p. 20 cm. [BX8748.H6 1831] 32-30343
1. Swendenshorg, Emanuel, 1894-1772. 2. New Jersulem church. I. Title.

HOBART, Nathaniel. 922.84
Life of Emanuel Swedenborg; with some account of his writings. By Nathaniel Hobart. 4th ed. Containing, in addition, a lecture on the mission of Swedenborg, by Sampson Reed, and an article on the New Jerusalem church, prepared for the new American cyclopedia. Boston, W. Carter & brother, 1862. iv, 246 p. front. (port.) 19 1/2 cm. [BX8748.H6 1862] 32-30344
1. Swedenborg, Emanuel, 1688-1772. 2. New Jerusalem church. I. Reed, Sampson, 1809-1880. II. Title.

HOLCOMBE, William Henry, 220
1825-1893.
Letters on spiritual subjects in answer to inquiring souls. By William H. Holcombe ... 2d ed. Philadelphia, Porter & Coates, 1889. 1 p. l., v-xiv, 15-405 p. 19 cm. [BR125.H67 1889] 20-7825
1. New Jerusalem church. I. Title.

INTRODUCTION to Swedenborg's religious thought. New York, Swedenborg pub. association, 1956. 235p. 21cm. 'Published some years ago under the title: 'The kingdom of heaven as seen by Swedenborg', the book hasnow been revised and condensed.'
1. Swedenborg, Emanuel, 1688—1772. 2. New Jerusalem church. I. Spalding, John Howard.

MERCER, Lewis Pyle, 1847- 289.
1906.
Emanuel Swedenborg and the New Christian church, by Rev. L. P. Mercer ... With a fraternal address to the church universal. Chicago, Western New-church union, 1893. 109 p. 13 cm. "Swedenborg's works": p. [95]-109. [BX8723.M38] 38-20528
1. Swedenborg, Emanuel, 1688-1772. 2. New Jerusalem church. I. Title.

NEW Jerusalem church. 783.
Liturgy and ritual.
Book of worship, containing services, prayers, sacraments and rites and a complete Psalter with chants, prepared for the use of the New-church, and printed by order of the General convention. [Tentative ed., being the joint report of the committees on "Liturgy revision" and "Prayers and rites" ...] New York city, New-church Board of publication, 1912. 2 p. l., iii-xxiv, 797 p. 19 cm. [M2131.S8B5] 12-15491
I. Title.

POWELL, David, 1805-1854?
Autobiography of the Rev. David Powell, a minister of the New church signified by the New Jerusalem in the Apocalypse: together with eight of his sermons. Ed. by the Rev. Wm. H. Benade. Philadelphia, Committee of the Darby society of the New church, 1856. 168 p. front. (port.) 23 cm. 5-130126
I. Benade, William Henry, 1816- ed. II. Title.

SWEDENBORG, Emanuel, 1688- 228
1772.
The divine Providence, by Emanuel Swedenborg. London, J. M. Dent & sons, ltd.; New York, E. P. Dutton & co. [1912] xvii, [1], 319, [1] p. 17 cm. (Half-title: Everyman's library, ed. by Ernest Rhys. Theology and philosophy) Title within ornamental border. Introduction by J. Howard Spalding. Bibliography: p. [xviii] [BX8712.D] A 14
1. New Jerusalem church. I. Spalding, J. Howard, ed. II. Title.

SWEDENBORG, Emanuel, 1688- 228
1772.
The four leading doctrines of the New church, signified by the New Jerusalem in the Revelation: being those concerning the Lord; the Sacred Scripture; faith; and life. By Emanuel Swedenborg ... New York, American Swedenborg printing and publishing society, 1857. 247 p. 23 1/2 cm. In 4 parts, each with special t.-p. [BX8712.D8 1857] 22-24325
1. New Jerusalem church. I. Title.

SWEDENBORG, Emanuel, 1688-1772.
Heaven and its wonders, and hell. From things heard & seen, by Emanuel Swedenborg. London, J. M. Dent & co.; New York, E. P. Dutton & co. [1909] xviii, 340 p. 17 1/2 cm. (Half-title: Everyman's library, ed. by Ernest Rhys. Theology and philosophy) Title within ornamental border: illustrated lining-papers. Introduction by J. Howard Spalding. Bibliography: p. xiv. A 11
1. New Jerusalem church. I. Title.

WOODS, Leonard, 1774-1854. 289.4
Lectures on Swedenborgianism. Delivered in the Theological seminary, Andover, February, 1846. By Leonard Woods ... Boston, Crocker and Brewster, 1846. 166 p. 18 1/2 cm. [BX8721.W7] 34-7189
1. New Jerusalem church. I. Title.

WUNSCH, William Frederic, 1882-
An outline of New-church teaching, with illustrative standard passages, by William F. Wunsch ... New York, The New-church press [c1926] xi, 260 p. 21 cm. "Standard passages from the theological works of Emanuel Swedenborg": p. 153-258. [BX8714.W8] 26-24281
1. New Jerusalem church. I. Swedenborg, Emanuel, 1688-1772. II. Title.

WUNSCH, William 230'.9'4
Frederic, 1882-
An outline of Swedenborg's teachings : with readings from his theological works / by William F. Wunsch. New York : Swedenborg Pub. Association, [1975] p. cm. Reprint of the 1926 ed. published by New-church Press, New York, under title: An outline of New-church teaching. Includes index. [BX8714.W8 1975] 74-23796 ISBN 0-87785-151-4 pbk. : 3.95
1. New Jerusalem Church. I. Title.

New Jerusalem church—Addresses, essays, lectures.

BUSH, George, 1796-1859. 208.
New church miscellanies; or, Essays ecclesiastical, doctrinal and ethical, by George Bush ... New York, W. McGeorge; Boston, O. Clapp; [etc., etc.] 1855. 372 p. 18 1/2 cm. Republished from the New church repository. [BX8713.B8] 38-35222
1. New Jerusalem church—Addresses, essays, lectures. I. Title.
Contents omitted.

PARSONS, Theophilus, 1797- 208.
1882.
Essays, by Theophilus Parsons. Boston, O. Clapp, 1845. 228 p. 20 cm. [BX8713.P3] 22-25636
1. New Jerusalem church—Addresses, essays, lectures. I. Title.
Contents omitted.

PARSONS, Theophilus, 1797- 208.
1882.
Essays. By Theophilus Parsons. (2d ser.) Boston, Crosby, Nichols, and company, 1856. 3 p. l., [3]-285 p. 19 cm. [BX8713.P32] 22-25635
1. New Jerusalem Church—Addresses, essays, lectures. I. Title.
Contents omitted.

PARSONS, Theophilus, 1797- 208.
1882.
Essays. By Theophilus Parsons. 3d ser. Boston, W. Carter and brother, 1862. 304 p. 19 cm. [BX8713.P33] 22-24328
1. New Jerusalem church—Addresses, essays, lectures. I. Title.
Contents omitted.

PENDLETON, Nathaniel 208.1
Dandridge, bp., 1865-1937.
Selected papers and addresses, by Nathaniel Dandridge Pendleton ... Bryn Athyn, Pa., The Academy of the New church, 1938. xxiii, 251 p. front. (port.) 23 cm. "A bibliography of principal papers, addresses and sermons (published and unpublished) by Nathaniel Dandridge Pendleton": p. 245-251. [BX8713.P42] 39-4458
1. New Jerusalem church—Addresses, essays, lectures. I. Title.

VROOMAN, Hiram. 252.094
Life after death [by] Hiram Vrooman ... 35 radio talks, WMAQ, Chicago daily news station ... [Chicago, Western New church union, c1931] cover-title, 191 p. 19 1/2 cm. [BX8724.V7 L5] 31-21209
1. New Jerusalem church—Addresses, essays, lectures. I. Title.

New Jerusalem church—Bibliography

NEW Jerusalem church.
Descriptive catalogue of New Church books and tracts, American and foreign, containing Swedenborg's works ... and works of other authors, including juvenile and Sunday school books, tracts. ... etc. [New York, New Church Board of publication] 1873. 71 p. 19 cm. A 10
1. Swedenborg, Emanuel, 1688-1772—Bibl. 2. New Jerusalem church—Bibl. I. Title.

[SWEDENBORG publishing 016.
association]
Is it worth while? Does it pay? [Philadelphia, The Nunc lieet press, 1905] cover-title, 23 p. 17 cm. Notices of recent publications, constitution, by-laws, etc., of the association. [Z7845.S9S9] 7-871
1. New Jerusalem church—Bibl. I. Title.

New Jerusalem church—Collected works.

SWEDENBORG, Emanuel, 1688- 289.4
1772.
Posthumous theological works of Emanuel Swedenborg ... Rev. John Whitehead ... editor and translator. New York, Swedenborg foundation incorporated, 1928. 2 v. 21 cm. Each work has also special t.-p. Contents.I. Autobiographical letters. The Coronis. The consummation of the age. Invitation to the New church. Additions to the true Christian religion. The canons of the New church. The doctrine of charity. Sketch of an ecclesiastical history of the New church. The word of the Lord from experience. The last judgment. Several minor works. Theological extracts from Swedenborg's correspondence. Gad and Asher.--II. Prophets and Psalms, translated by E. J. E. Schreck. Scripture confirmations. Precepts of the Decalogue. Marriage. Indexes on marriage.--Brief bibliography of Swedenborg's works. Index of publications. [BX8711.A25 1928] 38-24293
1. New Jerusalem church—Collected works. 2. Theology—Collected works—18th cent. 3. Whitehead, John, 1850- ed. and tr. I. Schreck, E. J. E., tr. II. Title.

SWEDENBORG, Emanuel, 1688- 230.
1772.
... *The Swedenborg library.* Edited by B. F. Barrett ... Philadelphia, Claxton, Remsen & Haffelfinger [1875-81] v. front. (v. 12, port.) 15 cm. Vols. 6-12 have imprint: Philadelphia, E. Claxton & co. [BX8711.A7B3] 45-28287
1. New Jerusalem church—Collected works. 2. Theology—Collected works—18th cent. I. Barrett, Benjamin Fiske, 1808-1892, ed. II. Title.
Contents omitted.

SWEDENBORG, Emanuel, 1688- 230.94
1772.
[Theological works] Boston and New York, Houghton, Miffin and company, 1907. 32 v. 19 cm. Rotch edition. Parts 1-4 of v. 22 and pt. 2 of v. 23 have each a special t.-p. Contents.[v. 1-19] The heavenly arcana disclosed ... which are in Genesis [v. 1-11] [and] in Exodus [v. 12-19]-[v. 20] Index to ... The heavenly arcana. [v. 21] Heaven and its wonders and hell.--[v. 22] Miscellaneous works: [pt. 1] Final judgment: [pt. 2] The white horse; [pt. 3] Earths in the universe; [pt. 4] Summary exposition.--[v. 22, pt. 1] The four doctrines of the New Jerusalem. [pt. 2] The New Jerusalem and its heavenly doctrine. [v. 24, pt. 1] Angelic wisdom concerning the divine love and concerning the divine wisdom. [pt. 2] The intercourse between the soul and the body. [v. 25] Angelic wisdom concerning the divine providence. [v. 26-28] The Apocalypse revealed. [v. 29] The delights of wisdom pertaining to marriage love. [v. 30-32] The true Christian religion. [BX8711.A2 1907] 13-11913
1. New Jerusalem church—Collected works. 2. Theology—Collected works—18th cent. I. Title.

New Jerusalem church — Doctrinal and controversial works.

BARNITZ, Harry W. 230.9'4
Existentialism and the new Christianity; a comparative study of existentialism and

Swedenborgianism: towards a new universal synthesis, by Harry W. Barnitz. New York, Philosophical Library [1969] xx, 509 p. 23 cm. Includes bibliographical references. [BX8721.2.B3] 69-14353 10.00
1. New Jerusalem Church—Doctrinal and controversial works. I. Title.

BARRETT, Benjamin Fiske, 1808-1892. 289.4
The golden city. By B. F. Barrett ... Philadelphia, Claxton, Remsen & Haffelfinger, 1874. xii, 13-253 p. 20 cm. [BX8721.B33] 38-11364
1. New Jerusalem church—Doctrinal and controversial works. I. Title.

BARRETT, Benjamin Fiske, 1808-1892. 222.
The question concerning the visible church, briefly considered. New-York [American Swedenborg Print. and Pub. Society] 1856. 108 p. 19 cm. An article (considerably enl.) originally published in the New Church repository, Nov., 1855 under title: Is the Church of the New Jerusalem a visible body? [BX8729.C5B3] 50-43958
1. New Jerusalem Church—Doctrinal and controversial works. 2. Church—Visibility. I. Title.

BARRETT, Benjamin Fiske, 1808-1892. 230.94
Swedenborg and Channing, Showing the many and remarkable agreements in the beliefs and teachings of these writers. By B. F. Barrett. Philadelphia, Claxton, Remsen & Haffelfinger, 1879. xx, 21-288 p. 20 cm. [BX8748.B28] 36-31813
1. Swedenborg, Emanuel, 1688-1772. 2. Channing, William Ellery, 1780-1842. 3. New Jerusalem church—Doctrinal and controversial works. 4. Unitarianism.—Doctrinal and controversial works. I. Title.

BIBLE. English. 1958. New Jerusalem Church.
The sacred scripture; or, the word of the Lord. Bryn Athyn, Pa., Academy Book Room, 1958. 1256 p. NUC66
I. Title. II. Title: The word of the Lord.

BUSH, George, 1796-1859. 230.94
Statement of reasons for embracing the doctrines and disclosures of Emanuel Swedenborg... By George Bush. New York, J. Allen; Boston, O. Clapp, 1846. 1 p. l., [67]-126, [129]-130 p. 23 cm. [With Swedenborg, Emanuel. The memorable..New York, 1846] [BX8711.A7B8] 1-17862
1. New Jerusalem church—Doctrinal and controversial works. 2. Swedenborg, Emanuel, 1688-1772. I. Title.

CARPENTER, Charles Thomas. 289.4
The new age of Christianity, by Charles Thomas Carpenter. Boston, Meador publishing company, 1935. 168 p. 21 cm. [BX8721.C3] 35-18659
1. New Jerusalem church—Doctrinal and controversial works. 2. Bible. N. T. Matthew xxiv—Commentaries. 3. Sociology, Christian—Swedenborgian authors. I. Title.

CARPENTER, Charles Thomas. 289.4
The spirituality and immortality of man. Placerville, Calif. [1947?] 200 p. 20 cm. [BX8721.C32] 48-15025
1. New Jerusalem Church—Doctrinal and controversial works. 2. Immortality. 3. Spirituality. I. Title.

[CLARKE, William Horatio], 1840-1913. 230.94
The face of Jesus; or, Thoughts for the mature concerning the nature of the word of God. By a believer in the internal evidence of divine revelation ... New York, R. Worthington; London, F. Pitman, 1883. iv, [5]-397 p. 22 1/2 cm. [BX8721.C47] 37-36514
1. New Jerusalem church—Doctrinal and controversial works. I. Title.

DOUGHTY, John. 222.11
The parable of creation, being a presentation of the spiritual sense of the Mosaic narrative as contained in the first chapter of Genesis, by Rev. John Doughty ... 5th ed. New Haven, Conn., Connecticut New church association, 1898. vii, 9-142 p. 15 1/2 cm. [BX8729.C7D6] 88-841
1. New Jerusalem church—Doctrinal and controversial works. 2. Creation. I. General convention of the New Jerusalem in the U. S. A. Connecticut association. II. Title.

ELLIS, John, 1815-1896. 230.
The new Christianity; an appeal to the clergy and to all men in behalf of its life of charity; pertaining to diseases, their origin and cure ... and the prevailing cruel treatment of girls and young men. New York, 1887. 511 p. illus. 19 cm. [BX8721.E56] 49-57584
1. New Jerusalem Church—Doctrinal and controversial works. 2. Temperance—Biblical arguments. I. Title.

[ELLIS, John] 1815-1896. 289.4
Skepticism; a divine revelation: and call to the New Jerusalem ... New York, The author & compiler, 1879. iv, 260 p. 18 1/2 cm. [BX8721.E6 1879] 36-33602
1. New Jerusalem church—Doctrinal and controversial works. I. Title.

EVANS, Warren Felt. 230.94
The new age and its messenger. By Rev. W. F. Evans ... Boston, T. H. Carter & company; London, C. P. Alvey, 1864. 110 p. 19 cm. [BX8721.E8] 32-22238
1. Swedenborg, Emanuel, 1688-1772. 2. New Jerusalem church—Doctrinal and controversial works. I. Title.

GILES, Chauncey, 1813-1893. 230.
Lectures on the nature of spirit, and of man as a spiritual being. By Chauncey Giles ... New York, General convention of the New Jerusalem in the United States of America, 1867. 206 p. 20 cm. Published in 1934 under title: The nature of spirit, and of man as a spiritual being. [BX8721.G5 1867] 11-22001
1. New Jerusalem church—Doctrinal and controversial works. 2. Soul. 3. Future life. I. General convention of the New Jerusalem in the U.S.A. II. Title.

GILES, Chauncey, 1813-1893. 230.
The nature of spirit, and of man as a spiritual being. By the Rev. Chauncey Giles ... 17th ed. Philadelphia, The American New-church tract and publication society, 1934. 232 p. 19 1/2 cm. Preface dated 1894. 1867 edition has title: Lectures on the nature of spirit, and of man as a spiritual being. [BX8721.G5 1934] 43-33728
1. New Jerusalem church—Doctrinal and controversial works. 2. Soul. 3. Future life. I. American New-church tract and publication society. II. Title.

GOULD, Edwin Miner Lawrence, 1886- 230.
Problems of the new Christianity, by E. M. Lawrence Gould ... with introduction by John Goddard. New York, The New-church press [1922] ix p., 1 l., 92 p. 19 cm. [BX8721.G7] 22-10552
1. New Jerusalem church—Doctrinal and controversial works. I. Title.

[HILLER, Margaret] 289.4
Religion and philosophy United; or, An attempt to show that philosophical principles form the foundation of the New Jerusalem church, as developed to the world in the mission of the Honourable Emanuel Swedenborg... Boston, Published for the subscribers, 1817. xii, [13]-55 p. 24 1/2 cm. [BX8721.H5] 5-21983
1. Swedenborg, Emanuel, 1688-1772. 2. New Jerusalem church—Doctrinal and controversial works. I. Title.

HINDMARSH, Robert, 1759-1835. 228
A compendium of the chief doctrines of the true Christian religion... by Robert Hindmarsh. Cincinnati, Reprinted from the Manchester edition by the Western New Jerusalem printing society and sold by Drake & Conclin, 1828-71. iv, [5]-197, [3] p. 13 cm. "--71", following the date of publication (1828) referes to the year 1757, considered the date of the founding of the New Jerusalem church as a spiritual system, as 1783 was the date of its founding as an external organization. cf. Encyclopaedia Britannica, 11th ed., vol. xix, p. 515. "List of the theological writings of Emanuel Swedenborg": p. [200] [BX8712.T89H5 1828] 39-18073
1. New Jerusalem church—Doctrinal and controversial works. 2. Theology, Doctrinal. I. Title.

HINDMARSH, Robert, 1759-1835. 232.8
A seal upon the lips of Unitarians, Trinitarians, and all others who refuse to acknowledge the sole, supreme, and exclusive divinity of Our Lord and Saviour Jesus Christ. Containing illustrations of one hundred and forty-four passages in the four Evangelists and the Apocalypse, in proof that Jesus Christ is the supreme and only God of heaven and earty ... By Robert Hindmarsh. Philadelphia: Printed for Johnson Taylor, by Lydia R. Bailey, no 10, North alley, 1815. 7 p. l., xii, 343 p. 21 1/2 cm. [BT215.H6] 37-24326
1. Jesus Christ—Divinity. 2. New Jerusalem church—Doctrinal and controversial works. I. Title.

KING, Thomas A.
Pearls from the Wonder-book [by] Rev. Thomas A. King... Germantown, Pa., Swedenborg pub. association, 1901. xvi, 217 p. 17 1/2 cm. 1-27081
1. New Jerusalem church—Doctr. & controv. works. 2. Bible. O.T.—Criticism, interpretation, etc. I. Title.

KINGSLAKE, Brian, 1907- 236'.2
The Aqueduct papers; twenty interviews with an angel concerning life after death. North Qunicy, Mass., Christopher Pub. House [1970] 197 p. port. 22 cm. [BX8729.F8K5] 70-116035 4.95
1. New Jerusalem Church—Doctrinal and controversial works. 2. Future life. I. Title.

KIP, Abraham Lincoln, 1865- 230.
Phases of the church universal, by A. L. Kip. New York, The Knickerbocker press [c1900] iii p., 1 l., 117 p. 21 cm. [BX8721.K5] 0-3033
1. New Jerusalem church—Doctrinal and controversial works. I. Title.

LATHBURY, Clarence. 230.
God winning us, by Rev. Clarence Lathbury. With a prefatory verse by Mary A. Lathbury ... Germantown, Pa., The Swedenborg publishing association, 1898. vii, 159 p. 16 cm. [BX8721.L3] 98-1576
1. New Jerusalem church—Doctrinal and controversial works. I. Title.

LATHBURY, Clarence, 1854- 230.
God winning us, by Clarence Lathbury ... 9th ed. New York, The New-church press [c1925] xii p., 1 l., 15-207 p. 18 cm. [BX8721.L3 1925] 25-12049
1. New Jerusalem church—Doctrinal and controversial works. I. Title.

MADELEY, Edward, 1801-1877. 230.
The science of correspondence elucidated. The key to the heavenly and true meaning of the Sacred Scriptures. By Rev. Edward Madeley, edited by his son; revised and greatly enlarged by B. F. Barrett... 6th American ed. Germantown, Pa., The Swedenborg publishing association; Philadelphia, M. S. Lantz [189-?] xii, 13-742 p. col. pl. 21 cm. Editor's preface signed: E. M. Contents.pt. 1. The science of correspondence elucidated.--pt. ii. Additional illustrations and confirmations of the doctrine of correspondence. By different authors [Rev. Thomas Goyder, Robert Hindmarsh, B. F. Barrett, and others] [BX8727.M3 1800] 24-16990
1. New Jerusalem church—Doctrinal and controversial works. 2. Bible—Criticsm, interpretation, etc. 3. Symbolism. I. Madeley, Edward. jr., ed. II. Barrett, Benjamin Fiske, 1808-1892. III. Goyder, Thomas, 1786-1849. IV. Hindmarsh, Robert, 1759-1835. V. Title.

MADELEY, Edward, 1801-1877. 230.94
The science of correspondences elucidated. The key to the heavenly and true meaning of the Sacred Scriptures. By Rev. Edward Madeley, edited by his son; revised and greatly enlarged by B. F. Barrett... 9th American ed. Germantown, Pa. The Swedenborg publishing association [189-?] xii, 13-742 p. col. pl. 21 cm. Editor's preface signed: E. M. [i.e. Edward Madeley, jr.] "Additional illustrations and confirmations of the doctrine of correspondence. By different authors [Rev. Thomas Goyder, Robert Hindmarsh, B. F. Barrett, and others]": p. 301-647. [BX8727.M3 1890c] 35-22750
1. New Jerusalem church—Doctrinal and controversial works. 2. Bible—Criticism, interpretation, etc. 3. Symbolism. I. Madeley, Edward, jr., ed. II. Barrett, Benjamin Fiske, 1808-1892. III. Goyder, Thomas, 1786-1849. IV. Hindmarsh, Robert, 1759-1835. V. Title.

MADELEY, Edward, 1801-1877. 230.94
The science of correspondences elucidated. The key to the heavenly and true meaning of the Sacred Scriptures. By Rev. Edward Madeley, edited by his son: revised and greatly enlarged by B. F. Barrett... 17th American ed. Germantown, Pa., The Swedenborg publishing association [19--] xii, 13-742 p. col. pl. 21 cm. Editor's preface signed: E. M. "Additional illustrations and confirmations of the doctrine of correspondence. By different authors [Rev. Thomas Goyder, Robert Hindmarsh, B. F. Barrett, and others]": p. 301-647. [BX8727.M3 1900] 35-30465
1. New Jerusalem church—Doctrinal and controversial works. 2. Bible—Criticism, interpretation, etc. 3. Symbolism. I. Madeley, Edward, jr., ed. II. Barrett, Benjamin Fiske, 1808-1892. III. Goyder, Thomas, 1786-1849. IV. Hindmarsh, Robert, 1759-1835. V. Title.

MAYER, Fred Sidney. 128
Why two worlds? By F. Sidney Mayer. [1st AMS ed.] New York, AMS Press [1972] 272 p. 22 cm. Reprint of the 1934 ed. [BX8721.M3 1972] 78-134425 ISBN 0-404-08465-6 12.00
1. New Jerusalem Church—Doctrinal and controversial works. 2. Mind and body. 3. Heaven. I. Title.

MERCER, Lewis Pyle, 1847-1906. 289.4
The New church; what it is, what it teaches. A manual of instruction compiled for the use of young people and inquirers, by Rev. L. P. Mercer. Chicago, Western New-church union, 1888. 69 p. 15 cm. [BX8723.M4] 38-19147
1. New Jerusalem church—Doctrinal and controversial works. I. Title.

NOBLE, Samuel, 1779-1853. 289.
An appeal in behalf of the views of the eternal world and state, and the doctrines of faith and life, held by the body of Christians who believe that a new church, is signified (in the Revelation, chapter xxi.) by the New Jerusalem, embracing answers to all principal objections, by the Rev. S. Noble ... 2d ed. Entirely re-modeled and much enlarged. New York, J. Allen, 1851. viii, [9]-537, [1] p. 20 cm. [BX8721.N6 1851] 23-3528
1. New Jerusalem church—Doctrinal and controversial works. I. Title.

NOBLE, Samuel, 1779-1853. 289.
An appeal in behalf of the views of the eternal world and state, and the doctrines of faith and life, held by the body of Christians who believe that a new church, is signified (in the Revelation, chapter xxi.) by the New Jerusalem, Embracing answers to all principal objections, by the Rev. S. Noble ... 2d ed. Entirely re-modeled and much enlarged. Boston, W. Carter & brother [1860?] viii, [9]-538 p. 20 cm. [BX8721.N6 1860] 23-3529
1. New Jerusalem church—Doctrinal and controversial works. I. Title.

ODHNER, C[arl] Th[eophilus] 1863-
Laws of order for the preservation of the conjugial. A review of a resolution and report adopted by the ministers of the General convention of the New Jerusalem church, on the subject of fornication and concubinage. By C. Th. Odhner. Philadelphia, Pa., The Academy of the New Church, 1904. 194 p. 20 cm. "The doctrine of the New Jerusalem respecting fornication and concubinage. (From The delights of wisdom respecting conjugial love ... By Emanuel Swedenborg ... nos. 423-476): p. [25]-88. 5-12183
I. Swedenborg, Emanuel, 1688-1772. II. Title.

ODHNER, C[arl] Th[eophilus] 1863-
Laws of order for the preservation of the conjugial. A review of a resolution and report adopted by the ministers of the General convention of the New Jerusalem church, on the subject of fornication and concubinage. By C. Th. Odhner. Philadelphia, Pa., The Academy of the

New church, 1904. 194 p. 20 cm. "The doctrine of the New Jerusalem respecting fornication and concubinage. (From The delights of wisdom repecting conjugial love ... By Emanuel Swedenborg ... nos. 423-476)": p. [25]-88. 5-12183
1. Swedenborg, Emanuel, 1688-1772. II. Title.

PARSONS, Theophilus, 1797- 1882. 230.94
Essays, by Theophilus Parsons. 2d ed. Boston, W. D. Ticknor and company, 1847. 181 p. 19 cm. [BX8713.P3 1847] 33-3425
1. New Jerusalem church—Doctrinal and controversial works. I. Title.
Contents omitted.

PARSONS, Theophilus, 1797- 1882. 289.
Outlines of the religion and philosophy of Swedenborg. By Theophilus Parsons. Boston, Roberts brothers, 1876. 318 p. 18 cm. [BX8721.P3 1876] 12-37430
1. Swedenborg, Emanuel, 1688-1772. 2. New Jerusalem church—Doctrinal and controversial works. I. Title.

PARSONS, Theophilus, 1797- 1882. 230.94
Outlines of the religion and philosophy of Swedenborg. By Theophilus Parsons. Rev. and enl. ed. New York city, The New church board of publication, 1903. 382 p. 18 cm. [BX8721.P3 1903] 12-37455
1. Swedenborg, Emanuel, 1688-1772. 2. New Jerusalem church—Doctrinal and controversial works. I. Title.

PITCAIRN, Theodore. 230
My Lord and my God; essays on modern religion, the Bible, and Emanuel Swedenborg. [1st ed.] New York, Exposition Press [1967] ix, 298 p. illus. (part col.), col. ports. 21 cm. [BX8721.2.P5] 67-9668
1. New Jerusalem Church—Doctrinal and controversial works. 2. Theology, Doctrinal—Popular works. I. Title.

SMITHSON, John Henry, 1803-1877. 230.94
Letters on the theology of the New church, signified by the New Jerusalem ... addressed, in a discussion, to the editor of the "Christian weekly news." By Rev. J. H. Smithson ... 21st American ed. Philadelphia, Swedenborg publishing association [19--] xxiii, 25-230 p. 15 cm. (New-church popular series. no. 2) Preface signed: B. F. B. [i. e. Benjamin Fiske Barrett] [BX8721.S6] 38-11167
1. New Jerusalem church—Doctrinal and controversial works. I. Barrett, Benjamin Fiske, 1808-1892, ed. II. Swedenborg publishing association. III. Title.

SMYTH, Julian Kennedy, 1856- 289.
Christian certainties of belief; the Christ, the Bible, salvation, immortality ... by Julian K. Smyth .. New York, The New-church press, incorporated [c1916] xi, 193 p. 19 cm. [BX8721.S65] 16-16696
1. New Jerusalem church—Doctrinal and controversial works. 2. Apologetics—20th cent. I. Title.

SWEDENBORG, Emanuel, 1688- 230.9'4
The four doctrines . . . English tr. by John Faulkner Potts. Newly ed. by Alice Spiers Sechrist. New York, Swedenborg Found., 1967. 329p. 18cm. [BX8712.D8 1967] 67-1465 1.00 pap.,
1. New Jerusalem Church—Doctrinal and controversial works. I. Sechrist, Alice Spiers, ed. II. Title.
Contents omitted.

SWEDENBORG, Emanuel, 1688- 1772 289.4
Arcana coelestia. The heavenly arcana, contained in the Holy Scripture or Word of the Lord unfolded, beginning with the book of Genesis. Together with wonderful things seen in the world of spirits and in the heaven of angels; v.1. Tr. from Latin. Thoroughly rev. ed. by John Faulkner Potts. Standard ed. New York, Swedenborg Found., 1963. 585p. 21cm. 63-1828 3.50; 2.50 text ed.,
1. New Jerusalem Church—Doctrinal and controversial works. 2. Bible. O. T. Genesis—Commentaries. 3. Bible. O. T. Exodus—Commentaries. I. Title.

SWEDENBORG, Emanuel, 1688- 1772. 228
Arcana coelestia. The heavenly arcana contained in the Holy Scriptures or word of the Lord unfolded beginning with the book of Genesis together with wonderful things seen in the world of spirits and in the heaven of angels. Translated from the Latin of Emanuel Swedenborg ... New York, American Swedenborg printing and publishing society, 1870-73. 10 v. 23 cm. Vols. 1-2, 4-5, 8 have imprint date 1873; v. 7: 1871; v. 3, 6, 9-10: 1870. On cover: Swedenborg. Works. [BX8712.A8 1870] 17-4661
1. New Jerusalem church—Doctrinal and controversial works. 2. Bible. O.T. Genesis—Commentaries. 3. Bible. O. T. Exodus—Commentaries. 4. Bible—Commentaries—O.T. Genesis. 5. Bible—Commentaries—O.T. Exodus. I. Bible. O. T. Genesis. English. 1870. II. Bible. O.T. Exodus. English. 1870. III. Bible. English. O. T. Genesis. 1870. IV. Bible. English. O. T. Exodus. 1870. V. Title.

SWEDENBORG, Emanuel, 1688- 1772. 228
Arcana coelestia; the heavenly arcana contained in the Holy Scriptures or word of the Lord unfolded beginning with the book of Genesis together with wonderful things seen in the world of spirits and in the heaven of angels, translated from the Latin of Emanuel Swedenborg ... New York, American Swedenborg printing and publishing society, 1882-92 [v. 1, '92] 10 v. 23 1/2 cm. Contents.I-VII'. Genesis.--VII"-x. Exodus. [BX8712.A8 1882] 17-4660
1. New Jerusalem church—Doctrinal and controversial works. 2. Bible. O. T. Genesis—Commentaries. 3. Bible. O. T. Exodus—Commentaries. 4. Bible—Commentaries—O.T. Genesis. 5. Bible—Commentaries—O.T.—Exodus. I. Bible. O.T. Genesis. English. 1882. II. Bible. O.T. Exodus. English. 1882. III. Bible. English. O.T. Genesis. 1882. IV. Bible. English. O.T. Exodus. 1882. V. Title.

SWEDENBORG, Emanuel, 1688- 1772. 228
Arcana coelestia: the heavenly arcana contained in the Holy Scripture, or Word of the Lord, unfolded, beginning with the book of Genesis together with wonderful things seen in the world of spirits and in the heaven of angels; translated from the Latin of Emanuel Swedenborg, thoroughly revised and edited by the Rev. John Faulkner Potts ... Library ed. New York, The American Swedenborg printing and publishing society, 1905-10. 12 v. 21 1/2 cm. [BX8712.A8 1905] 10-6156
1. New Jerusalem church—Doctrinal and controversial works. 2. Bible. O.T. Genesis—Commentaries. 3. Bible. O.T. Exodus—Commentaries. 4. Bible—Commentaries—O.T. Genesis. 5. Bible—Commentaries—O.T. Exodus. I. Potts, John Faulkner, ed. II. Bible. O.T. Genesis. English. 1905. III. Bible. O.T. Exodus. English. 1905. IV. Bible. English. O.T. Genesis. 1905. V. Bible. English O.T. Exodus. 1905. VI. Title.

SWEDENBORG, Emanuel, 1688- 1772. 228
A brief exposition of the doctrine of the New church, which is meant by the New Jerusalem in the Apocalypse. Translated from the Latin of Emanual Swedenborg, originally published at Amsterdam in the year 1769 ... Boston, O. Clapp, 1839. iv. 92 p. 18 cm. [BX8712.B8 1839] 43-46975
1. New Jerusalem church—Doctrinal and controversial works. I. Title.

SWEDENBORG, Emanuel, 1688- 1772. 230.
A compendium of the theological and spiritual writings of Emanual Swedenborg; being a systematic and orderly epitome of all his religious works; selected from more than 30 v. and embracing all his fundamental principles, with copious illus. and teachings. With an appropriate introd. prefaced by a full life of the author with a brief view of all his works on science, philosophy, and theology. Boston, Crosby and Nichols, 1853. 128, 574 (i. e. 446) p. port. 27 cm. [BX8711.A7F5] 52-56820
1. New Jerusalem Church—Doctorinal and controversial works. I. Title.

SWEDENBORG, Emanuel, 1688-1772. 230'.9'4
A compendium of the theological writings of Emanuel Swedenborg / [selected by] Samuel M. Warren. New York : Swedenborg Foundation, 1974. xl, 776 p. ; 23 cm. Reprint of the 1875 ed., with new introd. Includes bibliographical references and index. [BX8711.A7W3 1974] 73-94196 ISBN 0-87785-123-9 : 4.50
1. New Jerusalem Church—Doctrinal and controversial works. I. Warren, Samuel Mills, comp.

SWEDENBORG, Emanuel, 1688- 1772. 230.94
The divine love and wisdom, by Emanuel Swedenborg. London, J. M. Dent & sons, ltd.; New York, E. P. Dutton & co. [1912?] xxiii, 216 p. 17 cm. (Half-title: Everyman's library, ed. by Ernest Rhys. Theology and philosophy. [no. 635]) "The translation ... has been revised by Mr. F. Bayley, M.A., on the basis of the Fcap, 8vo. edition issued by the Swedenborg society." "Introduction by Sir Oliver Lodge." Bibliography: p. xvi. [AC1.E8 no. 635] A 13
1. New Jerusalem church—Doctrinal and controversial works. I. Bayley, Frank, 1871- tr. II. Title.

SWEDENBORG, Emanuel, 1688- 1772. 228
The doctrine of life for the New Jerusalem, from the commandments of the Decalogue, translated from the Latin of Emanuel Swedenborg, from the 6th London ed. New York, General convention of the New Jerusalem church in the United States, 1859. 54 p. 19 1/2 cm. "This edition ... printed for the Maryland association of the New Jerusalem."--Slip, inserted. [BX8712.D96 1859] 36-3441
1. New Jerusalem church—Doctrinal and controversial works. I. New Jerusalem church. Maryland association. II. Title.

SWEDENBORG, Emanuel, 1688- 1772. 230.94
The doctrine of life for the New Jerusalem, from the commandments of the Decalogue. From the Latin of Emanuel Swedenborg. Philadelphia, New Church tract and publication society [1907?] 102 p. 14 cm. Edited by Rev. C. Giles. [BX8712.D96] 40-17995
1. New Jerusalem church—Doctrinal and controversial works. I. Giles, Chauncey, 1813-1893, ed. II. Title.

SWEDENBORG, Emanuel, 1688- 1772. 230.94
The doctrine of the New Jerusalem concerning the Lord, by Emanuel Swedenborg. Originally published in Amsterdam in the year 1763; translated from the original Latin and edited by the Rev. John Faulkner Potts ... New York, The American Swedenborg printing and publishing society, 1906. xvii, 203, [1] p. 13 1/2 cm. Cover-title: Doctrine of the Lord. [BX8712.D92 1906] 36-29682
1. New Jerusalem church—Doctrinal and controversial works. I. Potts, John Faulkner, tr. II. Title. III. Title: Doctrine of the Lord.

[SWEDENBORG, Emanuel] 1688- 1772. 289.4
The doctrine of the New Jerusalem concerning the Sacred Scripture. Boston: Printed and sold by John W. Folsom, no. 30, Union-street, 1795. vi, [7]-186 p. 17 cm. Translated from the Latin by P. Provo. cf. J. Hyde. A bibliography of the works of E. Swedenborg. (no. 1797) [BX8721.S85] 32-15473
1. New Jerusalem church—Doctrinal and controversial works. I. Provo, Peter, fl. 1784, tr. II. Title.

SWEDENBORG, Emanuel, 1688-1772. 230.9'4
The four doctrines... English translation by John Faulkner Potts. Newly edited by Alice Spiers Sechrist. New York, Swedenborg Foundation, 1967. 329 p. 18 cm. Contents.Contents. -- The doctrine of the Lord for the New Jerusalem. -- The Doctrine of the Sacred Scripture for the New Jerusalem. -- The doctrine of life for the New Jerusalem. -- The doctrine of faith for the New Jerusalem. [BX8712.D8 1967] 67-1465
1. New Jerusalem Church — Doctrinal and controversial works. I. Sechrist, Alice Spiers, ed. II. Title.

SWEDENBORG, Emanuel, 1688-1772. 230'.9'4
The four doctrines : the Lord, Sacred Scripture, life, faith / by Emanuel Swedenborg ; English translation by John Faulkner Potts ; edited by Alice Spiers Sechrist. New York : Swedenborg Foundation, 1976. 328 p. ; 18 cm. Translation of Doctrina Novae Hierosolymae de Domino, Doctrina Novae Hierosolymae de Scriptura Sacra, Doctrina Novae Hierosolymae de fide, and Doctrina vitae pro Noya Hierosolyma ex praeceptis decalogi. [BX8711.A25 1976] 76-151239 ISBN 0-87785-064-X pbk. : 1.25
1. New Jerusalem Church—Doctrinal and controversial works. 2. Theology—Collected works—18th century. I. Title.

SWEDENBORG, Emanuel, 1688- 1772. 230.94
The four doctrines [by Emanuel] Swedenborg ... New York, The American Swedenborg printing and publishing society [1924] 4 v. in 1. 15 1/2 cm. Cover-title. Translated by the Rev. John Faulkner Potts. [BX8712.D8 1924] 36-29690
1. New Jerusalem church—Doctrinal and controversial works. I. Potts, John Faulkner, tr. II. Title.
Contents omitted.

SWEDENBORG, Emanuel, 1688- 1772. 228
The four doctrines with the Nine questions ... by Emanuel Swedenborg; translated from the original Latin works and edited by the Rev. John Faulkner Potts ... Library ed. New York, The American Swedenborg printing and publishing society, 1904. 6 pt. in 1 v. 21 1/2 cm. Five of the parts have special t.-p., and all have separate paging. [BX8712.D8 1904] 10-6150
1. New Jerusalem church—Doctrinal and controversial works. I. Potts, John Faulkner, ed. II. Hartley, Thomas, 1790?-1784. III. Hubbell, Chauncey Giles, ed. IV. Worcester, Samuel Howard, 1824-1891, comp. V. Mann, Charles Holbrook, 1839-1918, comp. VI. Title.
Contents omitted.

SWEDENBORG, Emanuel, 1688-1772. 230'.94
The four leading doctrines of the New Church, signified by the New Jerusalem in the revelation: being those concerning the Lord, the Sacred Scripture, faith, and life. New York, American Swedenborg Print. and Pub. Society, 1882. [New York, AMS Press, 1971] 247 p. 22 cm. Translations of Doctrina Novae Hierosolymae de Domino, Doctrina Novae Hierosolymae de Scriptura Sacra, Doctrina Novae Hierosolymae de fide, and Doctrina vitae pro Nova Hierosolyma ex praeceptis decalogi. [BX8711.A25 1971] 71-134426 ISBN 0-404-08466-4
1. New Jerusalem Church—Doctrinal and controversial works. 2. Theology—Collected works—18th century. I. Title.

SWEDENBORG, Emanuel, 1688-1772 222'.11'077
Heavenly secrets (Arcana caelestia), which are contained in the Holy Scripture or word of the Lord disclosed. From the Latin of Emanuel Swedenborg. New York, Swedenborg Found., 1967. v. 18cm. ontents.kv.1. Genesis, chapters 1-7, nos. 1-823. [BX8712.A8 1967] 67-9674 1.00 pap.,
1. New Jerusalem Church—Doctrinal and controversial works. 2. Bible. O.T. Genesis—Commentaries. 3. Bible. O.T. Exodus—Commentaries. I. Title.
Publisher's address: 139 E. 23rd St., New York, N.Y.

SWEDENBORG, Emanuel, 1688- 1772. 230.94
The memorabilia of Swedenborg: or, The spiritual world laid open ... Edited by George Bush. New York, J. Allen; Boston, O. Clapp, 1846. xvi, [17]-256, 16 p. 23 cm. Incomplete: p. 241-256 and 16 p. at end wanting. cf. Hyde, James, Bibliography of works of Swedenborg, p. 646. Cover-title: The Memorabilia of Swedenborg: or, Memorable relations of things seen and heard in heaven and hell. Imcomplete: p. [129]-144 and 16 p. at end wanting. [BX8711.A7B8] 1-22082
1. New Jerusalem church—Doctrinal and

controversial works. I. Bush, George, 1796-1859, ed. II. Title.

SWEDENBORG, Emanuel, 1688-1772.
Miscellaneous theological works of Emanuel Swedenborg. Standard edition. New York, Swedenborg Foundation, 1959. 634 p. 23 cm. Each work has special t. p. 67-71791
1. New Jerusalem church — Doctrinal and controversial works. 2. Theology — Collected works — 18th cent. I. Title.

SWEDENBORG, Emanuel, 230'.9'408
1688-1772.
Miscellaneous theological works of Emanuel Swedenborg / translation by John Whitehead. Standard ed. New York : Swedenborg Foundation, [1976] vii, 634 p. ; 22 cm. Contents.Contents.—The New Jerusalem and its heavenly doctrine.—A brief exposition of the doctrine of the new church.—The intercourse between the soul and the body.—The white horse mentioned in the Apocalypse, Chap.XIX.—Appendix to the treatise on The white horse.—The earths in the universe.—The last judgment.—Continuation concerning the last judgment. [BX8711.A25 1976b] 76-46143 ISBN 0-87785-071-2. ISBN 0-87785-070-4 (student)
1. New Jerusalem Church—Doctrinal and controversial works. 2. Theology—Collected works—18th century. I. Title.

SWEDENBORG, Emanuel, 1688- 230.94
1772.
Miscellaneous theological works of Emanuel Swedenborg ... New York, American Swedenborg printing and publishing society, 1909. 526 p. 23 cm. Each work has special t.-p. [BX8711.A25 1909] 13-25817
1. New Jerusalem church—Doctrinal and controversial works. 2. Theology—Collected works—18th cent. I. Title.
Contents omitted.

SWEDENBORG, Emanuel, 1688- 228
1772.
Of the New Jerusalem and its heavenly doctrine, as revealed from heaven, to which are prefixed some observations concerning the new heaven and the new earth. Tr. from the Latin of Emanuel Swedenborg. 4th American ed., from the 5th London ed. Boston, O. Clapp [1838] 72 p. 19 cm. "The extracts from the Arcana coelestia ... are omitted." [BX8712.H7 1838] 51-52193
1. New Jerusalem Church—Doctrinal and controversial works. I. Title.

SWEDENBORG, Emanuel, 1688- 230.94
1772
The true Christian religion, containing the universal theology of the New Church, foretold by the Lord in Daniel VII. 13, 14; and in Revelation XXI. 1, 2. 2v. Tr. from Latin ed. [by John C. Ager] Standard ed. New York, Swedenborg Found., 1963. 2.v. (588; 510p.) 21cm. 63-1799 ea., 3.50; text ed., ea., 2.50
1. New Jerusalem Church—Doctrinal and controversial works. 2. Theology, Doctrinal. I. Title.

SWEDENBORG, Emanuel, 1688- 230.94
1772.
The true Christian religion, containing the universal theology of the New church, foretold by the Lord in Daniel VII. 13, 14; and in Revelation XXI. 1, 2. By Emanuel Swedenborg ... A new translation from the original Latin edition, printed at Amsterdam, in the year 1771. Boston, J. Allen, 1833. xvi, 576 p. front. (port.) 25 1/2 cm. "Advertisement" (p. [iii]-iv) signed: T. G. W. "Translated by T. G. Worcester, and revised by the Rev. T. B. Hayward."--Hyde, J. A bibliography of the works of Emanuel Swedenborg (no. 2740) [BX8712.T8 1833] 36-30579
1. New Jerusalem church—Doctrinal and controversial works. 2. Theology, Doctrinal. I. Worcester, Taylor Gilman, 1799-1879, tr. II. Hayward, Tilly Brown, 1797-1878, ed. III. Title.

SWEDENBORG, Emanuel, 1688- 230.94
1772.
The true Christian religion; containing the universal theology of the New church, foretold by the Lord in Daniel, VII. 13, 14, and in the Apocalypse, XXI. 1, 2. Translated from the Latin of Emanuel Swedenborg ... New York, American Swedenborg printing and publishing society, 1853. xviii p., 1 l., 982 p. 23 1/2 cm. One of the reprints of the London edition of 1846, which was revised by H. Butter. cf. Hyde, J. A bibliography of the works of Emanuel Swedenborg, 1906, p. 553 (no. 2745) "The coronis, or Appendix, to the true Christian religion": p. 817-883. [BX8712.T8 1853] 36-6883
1. New Jerusalem church—Doctrinal and controversial works. 2. Theology, Doctrinal. I. Butter, Henry, 1794-1885, ed. II. Title.

SWEDENBORG, Emanuel, 38-37832
1688-1772.
The true Christian religion; containing the universal theology of the New church, foretold by the Lord in Daniel VII. 13, 14; and in Revelation XXI. 1, 2. By Emanuel Swedenborg ... A new translation from the original Latin edition, printed at Amsterdam, in the year 1771. New ed., with an index. New York, Published by the General convention of the New Jerusalem in the United States of America, 1866. xvi, 613 p. port. 23 1/2 cm. "Advertisement" (p. [iii]-iv) signed: T. G. W. [i. e. Taylor Gilman Worcester] Imperfect: portrait wanting. [BX8712.T8 1866]
1. New Jerusalem church—Doctrinal and controversial works. 2. Theology, Doctrinal. I. Worcester, Taylor Gilman, 1799-1879, tr. II. General convention of the New Jerusalem in the U.S.A. III. Title.

SWEDENBORG, Emanuel, 1688- 230.94
1772.
The true Christian religion: containing the universal theology of the New church, foretold by the Lord in Daniel VII. 13, 14: and in Revelation XXI. 1, 2. By Emanuel Swedenborg ... Rotch ed. New York, The New church board of publication; Boston, Massachusetts New church union; [etc., etc.] 1878. 2 v. 19 1/2 cm. Revised by Rev. S. H. Worcester. cf. J. Hyde. A bibliography of the works of Emanuel Swedenborg (nos. 2778 and 2779) [BX8712.T8 1878] 36-305576
1. New Jerusalem church—Doctrinal and controversial works. 2. Theology, Doctrinal. I. Worcester, Samuel Howard, 1824-1891, ed. II. Title.

SWEDENBORG, Emanuel, 1688- 230.94
1772.
The true Christian religion; containing the universal theology of the New church, foretold by the Lord in Daniel, VII, 13, 14 and in the Apocalypse, XXI, 1, 2. Translated from the Latin of Emanuel Swedenborg ... New York, American Swedenborg printing and publishing society, 1883. 3 p. l., [iii]-xviii, 982 p. 23 cm. "The coronis, or appendix to The true Christian religion": p. 817-[883] [BX8712.T8 1883] 34-36383
1. New Jerusalem church—Doctrinal and controversial works. 2. Theology, Doctrinal. I. Title.

SWEDENBORG, Emanuel, 1688- 230.94
1772.
The true Christian religion: containing the universal theology of the New church, foretold by the Lord in Daniel VII. 13, 14; and in Revelation XXI. 1, 2. By Emanuel Swedenborg ... Rotch ed. Philadelphia, J. B. Lippincott company, 1895. 2 p. l., [iii]-xvii, 1244 p. 19 1/2 cm. [BX8712.T8 1895] 36-30578
1. New Jerusalem church—Doctrinal and controversial works. 2. Theology, Doctrinal. I. Title.

SWEDENBORG, Emanuel, 1688- 228
1772.
The true Christian religion: containing the universal theology of the New church, foretold by the Lord in Daniel, VII. 13, 14, and in the Apocalypse, XXI. 1, 2. Translated from the Latin of Emanuel Swedenborg ... New York, American Swedenborg printing and publishing society, 1901. 2 p. l., [iii]-xviii, 982 p. 23 cm. [BX8712.T8 1901] 38-37825
1. New Jerusalem church—Doctrinal and controversial works. 2. Theology, Doctrinal. I. Title.

SWEDENBORG, Emanuel, 1688- 228
1772.
The true Christian religion, containing the universal theology of the New church foretold by the Lord in Daniel VII. 13, 14: and in Revelation XXI. 1, 2, by Emanuel Swedenborg ... translated from the original Latin ed., printed at Amsterdam, in the year 1771 ... Library ed. New York, The American Swedenborg printing and publishing society, 1906- 07. 2 v. 21 1/2 cm. Translated by J. C. Ager. [BX8712.T8 1906] 10-6152
1. New Jerusalem church—Doctrinal and controversial works. 2. Theology, Doctrinal. I. Ager, John Curtis, 1835-1913, tr. II. Title.

SWEDENBORG, Emanuel, 1688- 228
1772.
The true Christian religion: containing the universal theology of the New church, foretold by the Lord in Daniel, vii. 13, 14. and in the Apocalypse, xxi. 1, 2. Translated from the Latin of Emanuel Swedenborg ... New York, American Swedenborg printing and publishing society, 1912. 2 p. l., xviii, 982 p. 23 cm. [BX8712.T8 1912] 14-14959
1. New Jerusalem church—Doctrinal and controversial works. 2. Theology, Doctrinal. I. Title.

SWEDENBORG, Emanuel, 1688- 230.94
1772.
The true Christian religion, containing the universal theology of the New church; from the Latin of Emanuel Swedenborg ... London & Toronto, J. M. Dent & sons, ltd.; New York, E. P. Dutton & co., inc. [1933] xxxii, 928 p. 17 1/2 cm. (Half-title: Everyman's library, ed. by Ernest Rhys. Philosophy & theology. [no. 893]) "First published in this edition, 1933." Translated by F. Bayley. Introduction by Dr. Helen Keller. "Principal works of Emanuel Swedenborg": p. xiii-xiv. [AC1.S8 no. 893] A 33
1. New Jerusalem church—Doctrinal and controversial works. 2. Theology, Doctrinal. I. Bayley, Frank, 1871- tr. II. Title.

SWENDENBORG, Emanuel, 198'.5
1688-1772.
The essential Swedenborg: basic teachings of Emanuel Swedenborg, scientist, philosopher, and theologian. Selected and edited and with an introd. by Sig Synnestvedt. [New York] Swedenborg Foundation [1970] 202 p. 21 cm. "The theological writings of Emanuel Swedenborg": p. 181-190. [BX8711.A25 1970] 70-110362
1. New Jerusalem Church—Doctrinal and controversial works. 2. Theology—Collected works—18th century. I. Synnestvedt, Sigfried T., comp. II. Title.

VROOMAN, Hiram. 232.8
The divinity of Jesus Christ scientifically stated, by Hiram Vrooman. Chenoa, Ill., S. Vrooman, 1936. 120 p. 20 cm. [BT215.V7] 36-17866
1. Jesus Christ—Divinity. 2. New Jerusalem church—Doctrinal and controversial works. 3. Bible—Prophecies. I. Title.

VROOMAN, Hiram.
Science and theology; their co-ordination and differences ... 2d ed. Chicago, 1947. 187 p. 24 cm. A 48
1. New Jerusalem Church—Doctrinal and controversial works. 2. Religion and science—1900- I. Title.

VROOMAN, Hiram. 230.94
A skyline sketch of Emanuel Swedenborg's "True Christian religion," by Hiram Vrooman ... Chenoa, Ill., The author, 1943. 2 p. l., 75 p. 19 1/2 cm. [BX8712.T89V7] 44-1318
1. New Jerusalem church—Doctrinal and controversial works. I. Swedenborg, Emanuel, 1688-1772. Vera Christiana religio. II. Title.

New Jerusalem Church—Government.

ELLIS, John, 1815-1896.
The New Church; its ministry, laity, and ordinances. With an appendix on intoxicants and our New Church periodicals. New York, 1886. 124 p. 19 cm. [BX8737.E58] 49-57583
1. New Jerusalem Church—Government. 2. Temperance—Biblical arguments. I. Title.

New Jerusalem church—Hymns.

HIBBARD, John Randolph, 783.
b.1815.
The gloria. Psalms and hymns, with chants and tunes, for the New church. Compiled by Rev. J. R. Hibbard. Chicago, 1869. 1 p. l., 202 p. 17 1/2 cm. [M2131.S8H5] 45-44600
1. New Jerusalem church—Hymns. 2. Hymns, English. 3. Chants (Plain, Gregorian, etc.) I. Bible. English. Selections. 1869. II. Title.

HYMNS for the use of the New Jerusalem church. Philadelphia, T. S. Manning, 1833. 1 p. l., 224, viii p. 24 cm. 1-19630

New Jerusalem church in Chicago.

[WILLIAMS, Rudolph,] 1844-
The New church and Chicago; a history. [Chicago] W. B. Conkey company, 1906. 2 p. l., 9-408 p. incl. plates, ports. front. (port.) 20 cm. [BX8718.C4W5] 6-11296
1. New Jerusalem church in Chicago. I. Title.

New Jerusalem church in the United States

FIELD, George, 289.4'7
1809or10-1883.
Memoirs, incidents & reminiscences of the early history of the New Church in Michigan, Indiana, Illinois, and adjacent States; and Canada. New York, AMS Press [1971] vii, 368 p. 22 cm. Reprint of the 1879 ed. [BX8715.F5 1971] 70-134423 ISBN 0-404-08463-X
1. New Jerusalem Church in the United States. 2. New Jerusalem Church in Canada.

FIELD, George, 1809or10-1883.
Memoris, incidents & reminiscences of the early history of the New church in Michigan, Indiana, Illinois, and adjacent states; and Canada, by Rev. G. Field. Toronto, Can., R. Carswell & co.; New York, E. H. Swinney; [etc., etc.] 1879. vii, 368 p. 19 cm. [BX8715.F5] 44-31355
1. New Jerusalem church in the U.S. 2. New Jerusalem church in Canada. I. Title.

New Jerusalem church—Prayer-books and devotions—English.

SPERRY, Paul, 1870-
Words of life; practical mediations on sacred subjects, by Paul Sperry ... Philadelphia and London, J. B. Lippincott company [192-?] 278 p. 13 cm. [BX8735.S65] 43-46937
1. New Jerusalem church—Prayer-books and devotions—English. I. Title.

New Jerusalem church—Sermons.

DE CHARMS, Richard.
Sermons illustrating the doctrine of the Lord, and other fundamental doctrines of the New-Jerusalem church. Philadelphia, Brown, Bicking & Guilbert, 1840. viii, 376 p. 8 degree. 1-19605
I. Title.

EARTHLY problems in heavenly 252.
light. Bennett sermons, 1904. By James Reed [and] Henry Clinton Hay ... Boston, Massachusetts New-church union, 1905. 113 p. 18 cm. [BX8724.A1E3] 6-4707
1. New Jerusalem church—Sermons. 2. Sermons. American. I. Reed, James, 1834-1921. II. Hay, Henry Clinton, 1853-1935. III. Massachusetts New church union, Boston.
Contents omitted.

EDGERTON, Jedediah. 252.094
Spiritual truths, by Rev. Jedediah Edgerton ... foreword by Roger W. Babson. Good cheer broadcasts over station WBSO, Babson Park, Mass. Cambridge, Mass., The Powell publishing company, 1932. 215 p. 19 cm. "First edition." [BX8724.E4S6] 33-1604
1. New Jerusalem church—Sermons. 2. Sermons, American. I. Title. II. Title: Good cheer broadcasts.

PENDLETON, Nathaniel Dandridge, bp., 1865-1937. 252.094
The glorification; sermons and papers by Nathaniel Dandridge Pendleton ... Bryn Athyn, Pa., Academy book room, 1941. vi, 221 p. front. (port.) 23 cm. [BX8724.P4G55] 42-851
1. New Jerusalem church—Sermons. I. Title.

SMYTH, Julian Kennedy, 1856-1921. 252.094
Religion and life; a year book of short sermons on some phase of the Christian life for every week in the year, by the Rev. Julian K. Smyth ... New York, New-Church board of publication, 1911. 2 p. l., vii-x, 333 p. 19 cm. [BX8724.S6R4] 11-31750
1. New Jerusalem church—Sermons. 2. Sermons, American. I. Title.

SMYTH, Julian Kennedy, 1856-1921. 252.094
The stairway of life, by Julian Kennedy Smyth. New York, The New-church press [c1939] x, 227 p. front. (port.) 19 cm. [BX8724.S6S8] 40-6605
1. New Jerusalem church—Sermons. 2. Sermons, American. I. Title.

New Kensington, Pa. Saint Peter's church.

FUSCO, Nicola, 1888- 282.748
... *Mount Saint Peter;* story of Saint Peter's church in New Kensington, Pennsylvania. Pittsburgh, Pa., St. Joseph's protectory, 1944. xiv, 140 p. plates, ports. 20 1/2 cm. [BX4603.N44S3] 44-7793
1. New Kensington, Pa. Saint Peter's church. I. St. Joseph's protectory for homeless boys, Pittsburgh. II. Title.

A New library of the supernatural—Indexes.

INDEX to occult sciences. 133'.092'2 B
Garden City, N.Y. : Doubleday, 1977. 128 p. : ill. ; 27 cm. (A New library of the supernatural) Includes index to the 1st 19 volumes of the series. "Also published as guide to index." [BF1408.15] 76-40569 ISBN 0-385-11326-9 : 8.95
1. A New library of the supernatural—Indexes. 2. Occult sciences—Biography. 3. Psychical research—Biography.

New Madrid, Mo. Methodist church.

CLARK, Elmer Talmage, 1886- 287.
One hundred years of New Madrid Methodism, a history of the Methodist Episcopal church, South, in New Madrid, Missouri, by the Rev. Elmer T. Clark ... 1812-1912. [New Madrid, c1912] 3 p. l., 57, [8] p. plates, ports. 23 cm. [BX8481.N45M4] 12-16285
1. New Madrid, Mo. Methodist church. I. Title.

New Melleray, Iowa (Trappist abbey)

HOFFMAN, Mathias Martin, 1889- 271.125
Arms and the monk! The Trappist saga in Mid-America. Dubuque, Iowa, W. C. Brown Co. [1952] 233p. illus. 24cm. [BX2525.N4H6] 53-1677
1. New Melleray, Iowa (Trappist abbey) I. Title.

PERKINS, William Rufus, 1847-1895. 271.
... *History of the Trappist abbey of New Melleray, Dubuque county, Iowa.* By William Rufus Perkins ... Iowa City, The University, 1892. iv p., 1 l., 79 p. 25 cm. (State university of Iowa publications. Historical monograph no. 2) [BX2525.N4P4] [F616.I 78 no. 2] 9-1095
1. New Melleray, Ia. (Trappist abbey) 2. Trappist in the U. S. I. Title.

New Mexico—Description and travel

BENAVIDES Alonso de, 1630 266.2789
The memorial of Fray Alonso de Benavides, 1630. Tr. by Mrs. Edward E. Ayer. Annotated by Frederick Webb Hodge, Charles Fletcher Lummis. Albuquerque, N. M., Horn & Wallace [c.1965] xiii, 309p. illus., map (on lining papers) 24cm. Reprint of the 1916 ed. Includes facsim. of theoriginal Spanish ed. Bibl. [F799.B43] 65-9216 7.00
1. New Mexico—Descr. & trav. 2. Missions—New Mexico. 3. Indians of North America—New Mexico 4. Franciscans in New Mexico. I. Hodge, Frederick Webb, 1864-1956. II. Hodge, Frederick Webb, 1864-1956. III. Lummis, Charles Fletcher, 1859-1928. IV. Title.

BENAVIDES, Alonso de fl.1630. 266.2789
The memorial of Fray Alonso de Benavides, 1630. Translated by Mrs. Edward E. Ayer. Annotated by Frederick Webb Hodge and Charles Fletcher Lummis, Albuquerque, N.M., Horn and Wallace [1965] xiii, 309 p. illus. map (on lining papers) 24 cm. Reprint of the 1916 ed. Includes facism, of the original Spanish ed. with t.p. reading: Memorial ... hecho por el padre fray Alsonso de Benavides ... Madrid, Impr. Real., 1630. Bibliographical references included in "Notes" (p. 187-285) [F799.B43] 65-9216
1. New Mexico — Deser. & trav. 2. Missions — New Mexico. 3. Indians of North America — New Mexico. 4. franciscans in New Mexico. I. Hodge, Frederick Webb, 1864-1956. II. Lummis, Charles Fletcher, 1859-1928. III. Title.

New Mexico—Religion.

CHAVEZ, Angelico, 1910- 271'.7
My Penitente land : reflections on Spanish New Mexico / Angelico Chavez. 1st ed. Albuquerque : University of New Mexico Press, [1974] xiv, 272 p. ; 26 cm. [BR555.N6C48] 74-83380 ISBN 0-8263-0334-X : 12.00
1. Hermanos Penitentes. 2. New Mexico—Religion. I. Title.

New Munich, Minn. Immaculate Conception church.

ONE hundred years in Christ: Immaculate Conception parish, New Munich, 1857-1957. St. Cloud, Sentinal Publishing Co., 1957. 107p. front. (port.) illus. (ports.) 23cm. Preface signed P. M. B.
1. New Munich, Minn. Immaculate Conception church. I. Blecker, Paulin M 1931-

New Orleans. Baptist Theological Seminary.

MUELLER, William A. 207'.763'355
The school of providence and prayer; a history of the New Orleans Baptist Theological Seminary, by William A. Mueller. [New Orleans, Printed by the Print. Dept. of the New Orleans Baptist Theological Seminary, 1969] 143 p. illus., ports. 22 cm. Bibliographical references included in "Notes" (p. 140-143) [BV4070.N4356M8] 69-20321
1. New Orleans. Baptist Theological Seminary. I. Title.

New Orleans. Basilica of St. Louis King of France.

HUBER, Leonard Victor, 1903- 282.763355
The Basilica on Jackson Square and predecessors, dedicated to St. Louis King of France, 1727-1965, by Leonard V. Huber and Samuel Wilson, Jr. [1st ed. New Orleans? 1965] 80 p. illus., facsims., ports. 24 cm. Bibliography: p. 77-78. [BX4603.N46B33] 65-26657
1. New Orleans. Basilica of St. Louis King of France. I. Wilson, Samuel, 1911- joint author. II. Title.

New Orleans—History.

CLAPP, Theodore, 1792-1866. 285'.8'0924 B
Autobiographical sketches and recollections, during a thirty-five years' residence in New Orleans. Freeport, N.Y., Books for Libraries Press [1972] viii, 419 p. port. 23 cm. Reprint of the 1857 ed. [BX9225.C547A3 1972] 77-38346 ISBN 0-8369-6763-1
1. New Orleans—History. I. Title.

HACHARD, Marie Madeleine. 271'.974'024 B
The letters of Marie Madeleine Hachard, 1727-28 / translated by Myldred Masson Costa. 1st ed. New Orleans : [s.n.], 1974. 66 p. ; 19 cm. Translation of Relation du voyage des dames religieuses Ursulines de Rouen a la Nouvelle Orleans. On spine: Letters of an Ursuline, 1727-1728. [BX4705.H13A413 1974] 74-193362
1. Hachard, Marie Madeleine. 2. New Orleans—History. I. Title: Letters of an Ursuline, 1727-1728.

New Orleans—Sepulchral monuments—Bibliography.

GILBERT, Janice Dee. 016.726'8'0976335
"Cities of the dead"—New Orleans cemetery architecture / Janice Dee Gilbert. Monticello, Ill. : Vance Bibliographies, 1980. 6 p. ; 28 cm. (Architecture series : Bibliography ; A-252) ISSN 0194-1356) Cover title. [Z5943.S45G54] [NA6152.N48] 19 80-118345 pbk. : 2.00
1. New Orleans—Sepulchral monuments—Bibliography. I. Title. II. Series.

New Orleans. Temple Sinai.

HELLER, Maximilian, 1860- 296.
Jubilee souvenir of Temple Sinai, 1872-1922, comp. by Rabbi Max Heller New Orleans [American printing co., ltd.] 1922. 2 p. l., vi, 154 p. front., illus. (port.) 17 1/2 cm. [BM225.N4T4] 22-24883
1. New Orleans. Temple Sinai. I. Title.

New Orleans. Ursuline convent.

[SEMPLE, Henry Churchill] 1853-1925, ed. 271.
...*The Ursulines in New Orleans and Our Lady of Prompt Succor;* a record of two Centuries, 1727-1925. New York, P. J. Kenedy & sons, 1925. xiii, 319 p. front., plates, ports., facsims. 24 cm. At head of title: I. M. I. "First and only edition consisting of one thousand copies. This copy is no. 855." "Henry Churchill Semple, S.J., the editor." Publisher's note. [BX4544.N4S4] 25-24788
1. New Orleans. Ursuline convent. I. Title.

New Salem, Pa.—Church history.

KAUFMAN, Jean Troxell. 277.48'81
Salem X Roads' churches in the nineteenth century / by Jean Troxell Kaufman. Greensburg, Pa. : Research Committee, Westmoreland County Historical Society, 1977. 7 leaves ; 29 cm. (Westmoreland Co. church & cemetery history ; no. 2) Bibliography: leaf 7. [BR560.N38K38] 77-152585
1. New Salem, Pa.—Church history. I. Title. II. Series.

New Testament scholars—England—Biography.

DILLISTONE, Frederick William, 1903- 225.6'092'4 B
C. H. Dodd, interpreter of the New Testament / by F. W. Dillistone. Grand Rapids : Eerdmans, c1977. 255 p. ; 25 cm. Includes index. Bibliography: p. 249-251. [BS2351.D6D54 1977] 76-54324 ISBN 0-8028-3496-5 : 11.95
1. Dodd, Charles Harold, 1884-1973. 2. New Testament scholars—England—Biography. I. Title.

[HUGHES, Frederic Stephen] 225
Where is Christ? a question for Christians, by an Anglican priest in China; with a foreword by the Bishop of Edinburgh. Boston and New York, Houghton Mifflin company, 1919. 112 p. 19 1/2 cm. Printed in Great Britain. [BR121.H7] 20-21309
I. Title.

New Thought.

AIKEN, Alfred. 230.99
Lectures on reality. Series 1. New York, Hillier Press [1959] 251p. 21cm. [BF639.A12] 59-44075
1. New Thought. I. Title.

AIKEN, Alfred 230.99
Selected forums on absolute reality, Series I. New York 19, Box 378, Radio City Sta. Hillier Pr., [c.1964] 270p. 22cm. 64-3979 5.50 bds.,
1. New Thought. I. Title.

ALLEN, James, 1864-1912.
As a man thinketh. New York, Grosset & Dunlap [1959] 72 p. 16 cm. NUC64
1. New Thought. I. Title.

ALLEN, James, 1864-1912. 289.9
As a man thinketh. Edited for contemporary readers by William R. Webb. Illustrated by James Hamil. [Kansas City, Mo.] Hallmark Editions [1968] 61 p. illus. 20 cm. [BF639.A48 1968] 68-19597 2.50
1. New Thought. I. Title.

ALLEN, James, 1864-1912. 289.9
As a man thinketh; James Allen's greatest inspirational essays. Edited by William B. Franklin and William R. Webb. Illustrated by Bruce Baker. [Kansas City, Mo., Hallmark, 1971] 68 p. col. illus. 27 cm. (Hallmark crown editions) [BF639.A48 1971] 75-127755 ISBN 0-87529-155-4 5.00
1. New Thought. I. Morgan, James, 1944- ed. II. Webb, William R., ed. III. Title.

ANDERSON, Louis Catherine Vallet. 131.324
"Helps along the way" toward the attainment of spiritual consciousness, by Louise Catherine Vallet Anderson. [Sacramento, Calif., McArthur's, c1934] 103 p. incl. front. (port.) 17 cm. [BF645.A6] 159.91324 34-29345
1. New thought. I. Title.

ANDERSON, Uell Stanley, 1917-
The secret of secrets. Edinburgh, New York, Nelson [1958] 310 p. 22 cm. NUC64
1. New thought. 2. Meditations. I. Title.

ATKINSON, William Walker, 1862- 131.
Faith power; or, Your inspirational forces, by W. W. Atkinson and Edward E. Beals ... Detroit, Mich., Personal power company [etc., etc., c1922] 172 p., 1 l. 16 cm. (Lettered on cover: Personal power books. vol. iv) [BF638.P4 vol. iv] 22-24124
1. New thought. I. Beals, Edward E., joint author II. Title.

ATKINSON, William Walker, 1862- 131.
Spiritual power; or, The infinite fount, by W. W. Atkinson and Edward E. Beals ... Detroit, Mich., Personal power company; [etc., etc., c1922] 171 p., 1 l., 16 cm. (Lettered on cover: Personal power books. vol. vii) [BF638.P4 vol.vii] 22-24121
1. New thought. I. Beals, Edward e, joint author. II. Title.

ATZBAUGH, William, 1909- 131.324
Seek ye the Christ. San Gabriel, Calif., Willing Pub. Co. [1949] 127 p. 21 cm. [BF639.A89] 49-4420
1. New Thought. I. Title.

[AUSTIN, Dorothea] 230.99
Of God, by Dorothea. Boston, Christopher Pub. [c.1965] 83p. 21cm*2.50 [BF639.A94] 65-16478 2.50
1. New Thought. I. Title.

BISHOP, Tania Kroitor 289.9
Record of the spirit. San Gabriel, Calif., P. O. Box 51 Willing Pub. Co. [c.1959] 89p. 21cm. 60-1042 3.00
1. New Thought. 2. Lord's prayer. I. Title.

BOEHME, Kate Atkinson.
Realization made easy, for health, wealth, supply, self-direction, by Kate Atkinson Boehme. Holyoke, Mass., The Elizabeth Towne co., 1916. 125 p. illus. 19 cm. A revision of the author's "Thinking in the heart; or, Easy lesssons in realization," pub. 1902. [BF639B53 1916] 16-24091
1. New thought. I. Title.

[BROWN, Grace 3d Mann 4d] Mrs., 1859- 131.324
Studies in spiritual harmony, by Ione [pseud.] Denver, Col., The Reed publishing company, 1901. 5 p. l., [9]-134 p. front. (port.) 16 1/2 x 16 cm. [BF639.B7] [159.91324] 33-38482
1. New thought. I. Title.

CAMPBELL, James Mann, 1840-1926. 131
New thought Christianized, by James M. Campbell... New York, Thomas Y. Crowell company [c1917] v, 152 p. 19 1/2 cm. [BF640.C2] 17-13828
1. New thought. I. Title.

CARAKER, Andrew 289.9
The adventure into the reality of you. New York, Speller [1966, c.1965] x, 167p. 19cm. Bibl. [BF639.C24] 65-26568 3.95 bds.,
1. New Thought. I. Title.

CLARK, Chester A 230
Man and his Maker. [1st ed.] New York, Vantage Press [1956] 96p. 21cm. [BF639.C53] 56-7512
1. New Thought. I. Title.

CURTIS, Donald. 289.9
The golden bridge; science of mind in daily living. West Nyack, N.Y., Parker Pub. Co. [1969] xii, 211 p. 24 cm. [BF639.C884] 69-11732 6.95
1. New Thought. 2. Self-realization. 3. Success. I. Title. II. Title: Science of mind in daily living.

CURTIS, Donald. 248'.48'99
Live it up! / by Donald Curtis. Lekemont, Ga. : CSA Press, c1976. 112 p. : port. ; 22 cm. [BF639.C8844] 76-47419 ISBN 0-87707-187-X pbk. : 2.00
1. New Thought. I. Title.

CURTIS, Donald 248.4899
Your thoughts can change your life. Englewood Cliffs, N. J., Prentice-Hall [c.1961] 218p. illus. 61-13994 4.95 bds.,
1. New Thought. I. Title.

CUSTER, Dan 289.9
The miracle of mind power. Englewood Cliffs, N. J., Prentice-Hall [c.1960] xix, 263p. 24cm. 60-14196 4.95
1. New Thought. I. Title.

DEL MAR, Eugene.
Spiritual and material attraction; a conception of unity, by Eugene Del Mar. Denver, Col., The Smith-Brooks print. co., 1901. 79 p. 20 cm. 1-26893
1. New thought. I. Title.

DODDS, James E. 131.324
Six lessons on the silence. By James E. Dodds. (4th ed.) Portland, Or., Church of the truth [1939] 62 p. 19 cm. [BF645.D3 1939] 159.91824 42-32560
1. New thought. I. Portland, Or. Church of the truth. II. Title.

DRESSER, Horatio Willis, 1866- 131
Handbook of the new thought, by Horatio U. Dresser... New York and London, G. P. Putnam's sons, 1917. xiii p., 1 l., 263 p. 18 cm. $1.25 [BF639.D685] 17-13214
I. Title.

DRESSER, Horatio Willis, 1866- 131
Voices of hope, and other messages from the hills; a series of essays on the problem of life, optimism, and the Christ, by Horatio W. Dresser... Boston, G.H. Ellis, 1898. 213 p. 20 cm. Contents.The problem of life-The Basis of optimism.-Character building.-A sceptic's paradise.-The omnipresent spirit.-The problem of evil.-The escape from subjectivity.-Love.-The spiritual life.-The Christ.-The progressing God. [BF639.D725] 98-2063
1. New thought. I. Title.

DRESSER, Horatio Willis, 1866- 131
Voices of hope and other messages from the hills; a series of essays on the problems of life, optimism, and the Christ, by Horatio W. Dresser... New York & London, G.P. Putnam's sons, 1900. 213 p. 20 cm. [BF639.D725 1900] 32-16702
1. New thought. I. Title.

ERWOOD, William Joseph, 1874- 131.324
My Father God, by Will J. Erwood ... Minneapolis, Minn., The Life science publishing co. [1942] 100 p. port. 18 cm. Errata slip mounted on p. [5] [BF639.E72] 42-24912
1. God—Fatherhood. 2. New thought. I. Title.

FARGO, Gail B. 248
Talks to truth searchers with answers to puzzling "why" questions [by] Gail B. Fargo. New York, Philosophical Library [1974] 56 p. 23 cm. Bibliography: p. 55-56. [BF645.F28] 74-75082 ISBN 0-8022-2106-8 4.75
1. New Thought. I. Title.

FERRITER, Mary C.
Truth of life, love, liberty, by Mary C. Ferriter... Oakland, Calif., Key publishing company, 1923. 5 p. l., 160 p. 24 cm. [PFo.39.F37] 23-11101
1. New thought. I. Title.

FRANCIS, Geneieve Mae (Hilliard) Mrs. 1874- 131
On the path; lessons in the laws of life--self-unfoldment, psychology, metaphysics and occultism; seventy important questions on healing answered, with affirmations of tremendous power, by Genevieve Mae Francis ... San Francisco, Calif., Occult book publishers company, 1928. 154 p., 1 l. incl. front. (port.) 20 cm. [BF639.F68] 29-8287
1. New thought. I. Title.

FRANK, Henry, 1854- 242
The shrine of silence; a book of meditations, by Henry Frank. 3d ed. Washington, D. C., New way press [1905?] 2 p. l., iii-vi, [6], 9-273 p. 20 cm. [BV4832.F65 1905] 32-19339
1. New thought. I. Title.

FRANK, Henry, 1854-1933.
The shrine of silence; a book of meditations, by H. Frank, with some embellishments by H. B. Reissman. New York, London [etc.] The Abbey press [1901] 1 p. l., vi, [5]-273 p. port. 8 degrees. [n36b 1] 1-22861
1. New thought. I. Title.

FREDERIC, Del W 131.324
Passport to heaven. Boston, Christopher [1949] 161 p. 21 cm. [BF639.F695] 50-7943
1. New thought. I. Title.

FULTON, Lillian Britton. Mrs. 131
The Eden road, a series of eleven lessons on the life more abundant, by Rev. Lillian Britton Fulton; being a practical compendium of the principles and processes, step by step, that being the fulfilment of our desires through the Christ born within ... Jacksonville, Fla. [The Drew press] 1923. 84 p. 24 cm. [BF645.F8] 24-2577
1. New thought. I. Title.

GILLCHREST, Muriel Noyes 248.4899
The power of universal mind. Parker [dist. Englewood Cliffs, N.J., Prentice. 1966, c.1965] xiv, 242p. 24cm. Bibl. [BF639.G45] 65-28635 4.95 bds.,
1. New Thought. I. Title. II. Title: Universal mind.

GODDARD, Neville Lancelot, 1905- 230'.9'9
Immortal man : compilation of lectures / presented by Neville [i.e. N. L. Goddard] ; edited by Marge Broome. Lakemont, Ga. : CSA Press, c1977. 253 p. ; 22 cm. [BF638.G62] 77-81534 ISBN 0-87707-183-7 pbk. : 4.95
1. New Thought. I. Title.

GOD'S workshop, 131.324
by Rev. Robert A. Russell ... Denver, Col., R. A. Russell [c1935] 131 p. 15 cm. [HF639.R83] 159.91324 35-9998
1. New thought. 2. Mental healing.

GOLDEN, George Charles. 131
True stories by a metaphysician, by Rev. George C. Golden ... Holyoke, Mass., The Elizabeth Towne co., inc.; London, L. N. Fowler & co. [c1928] 2 p. l., 7-92 p. 18 cm. [BF639.G55] 29-5507
1. New thought. I. Title.

GOLDSMITH, Joel S. 242.6
The art of spiritual healing. New York, Harper [c.1959] 190p. 20cm. 59-14532 3.00 bds.,
1. New Thought I. Title.

GOLDSMITH, Joel S., 1892- 289.9
Beyond words and thoughts; from the metaphysical consciousness to the mystical [by] Joel S. Goldsmith. Edited by Lorraine Sinkler. New York, Julian Press, 1968. x, 180 p. 22 cm. [BF639.G5574] 68-19018
1. New Thought. I. Sinkler, Lorraine, ed. II. Title.

GOLDSMITH, Joel S 1892- 248.4899
Conscious union with God. New York, Julian Press, 1962. 253 p. 21 cm. [BF639.G5577 1962] 62-19298
1. New Thought. I. Title.

GOLDSMITH, Joel S., 1892- 230'.9'9
Conscious union with God / Joel S. Goldsmith. Secaucus, N.J. : University Books, c1962, 1974 printing. 253 p. ; 21 cm. Includes bibliographical references. [BF639.G5577 1974] 75-307045 ISBN 0-8216-0050-8 : 6.00
1. New Thought. I. Title.

GOLDSMITH, Joel S., 1892- 289.9
Consciousness unfolding. New York, Julian [c.]1962. 269p. 21cm. 62-19299 3.95
1. New Thought. I. Title.

GOLDSMITH, Joel S., 1892- 230'.9'9
Consciousness unfolding / Joel S. Goldsmith. Secaucus, N.J. : University Books, c1962, 1974 printing. 269 p. ; 21 cm. Includes bibliographical references. [BF639.G558 1974] 75-307046 ISBN 0-8216-0043-5 : 6.00
1. New Thought. I. Title.

GOLDSMITH, Joel S. 1892- 248
The contemplative life. New York, Julian [c.]1963. 209p. 22cm. 63-12486 4.50
1. New Thought. I. Title.

GOLDSMITH, Joel S 1892- 248
The contemplative life. New York, Julian Press, 1963. 209 p. 22 cm. [BF639.G5584] 63-12486
1. New Thought. I. Title.

GOLDSMITH, Joel S., 1892- 289.9
God, the substance of all form. New York, Julian [c.]1962. 174p. 21cm. 62-19301 3.50
1. New Thought. I. Title.

GOLDSMITH, Joel S 1892-
The infinite way. [8th ed.] San Gabriel, Calif., Willing Pub. Co.,[1958] 200 p. 16 cm. 63-12895
1. New Thought. I. Title.

GOLDSMITH, Joel S., 1892- 289.9
Leave your nets. Ed. by Lorraine Sinkler. New York, Julian [c.]1964. 150p. 22cm. [BF639.G563] 64-24789 3.50
1. New Thought. I. Title.

GOLDSMITH, Joel S 1892- 289.9
Leave your pets [by] Joel S. Goldsmith. Edited by Lorraine Sinkler. New York, Julian Press, 1964. 150 p. 22 cm. [BF639.G563] 64-24789
1. New Thought I. Title.

GOLDSMITH, Joel S 1892-
The letters, Honolulu, [1959, c1949] 307. p. 16 cm. 63-12896
1. New Thought. I. Title.

GOLDSMITH, Joel S. 1892- 289.9
Living now. Ed. by Lorraine Sinkler. New York, Julian [c.]1965. x, 212p. 22cm. First appeared in 1963 in the form of letters. [BF639.G5657] 65-26943 4.50
1. New Thought. I. Sinkler, Lorraine, ed. II. Title.

GOLDSMITH, Joel S 1892- 289.9
Living now [by] Joel S. Goldsmith. Edited by Lorraine Sinkler. New York, Julian Press, 1965. x. 212 p. 22 cm. "First appeared in 1963 in the form of letters." [BF639.G5657] 65-26943
1. New Thought. I. Sinkler, Lorraine, ed. II. Title.

GOLDSMITH, Joel S. 1892- 289.9
Living the infinite way. Rev. ed. New York, Harper [c.1961] 128p. 61-9646 2.50 bds.,
1. New Thought. I. Title.

GOLDSMITH, Joel S., 1892- 289.9
The Master speaks. New York, Julian [c.] 1962. 333p. 21cm. 62-19300 3.95
1. New thought. I. Title.

GOLDSMITH, Joel S., 1892- 231
The mystical I [by] Joel S. Goldsmith. Edited by Lorraine Sinkler. [1st ed.] New York, Harper & Row [1971] x, 145 p. 22 cm. [BF639.G5683] 73-149745 4.95
1. New Thought. I. Title.

GOLDSMITH, Joel S., 1892- 248.4
Our spiritual resources. New York, Harper & Row [c.1962] 190p. 20cm. 62-7965 3.50 bds.,
1. New Thought. I. Title.

GOLDSMITH, Joel S., 1892- 289.9
Realization of oneness; the practice of spiritual healing, by Joel S. Goldsmith, Ed. by Larraine Sinkler. New York, Julian, 1967. 209p. 22cm. [BF639.G5688] 67-17570 5.00
1. New thought. I. Title.

GOLDSMITH, Joel S., 1892- 289.9
Realization of oneness; the practice of spiritual healing, by Joel S. Goldsmith. Edited by Lorraine Sinkler. New York, Julian Press, 1967. 209 p. 22 cm. [BF639.G5688] 67-17570
1. New Thought. I. Title.

GOLDSMITH, Joel S., 1892- 289.9
The world is new. New York, Harper [c.1962] 209p. 62-7953 3.50 bds.,
1. New Thought. I. Title.

GOLDSMITH, Joel S., 1892-1964. 248.2'2
Awakening mystical consciousness / Joel S. Goldsmith ; edited by Lorraine Sinkler. 1st ed. San Francisco : Harper & Row, c1980. p. cm. Includes index. [BF639.G5573 1980] 79-3601 ISBN 0-06-063174-0 : 8.95
1. New Thought. 2. Mysticism. I. Sinkler, Lorraine. II. Title.

GOLDSMITH, Joel S., 1892-1964. 248.3'4
Horizons of consciousness : Joel S. Goldsmith's correspondence with Lorraine Sinkler / compiled and edited by Lorraine Sinkler. 1st ed. San Francisco : Harper & Row, c1981. p. cm. [BF639.G5595 1981] 19 81-47436 ISBN 0-06-063151-1 : 13.95 13.95
1. New Thought. I. Sinkler, Lorraine. II. Title.

GOLDSMITH, Joel S., 1892-1964. 230'.9'9
Man was not born to cry / Joel S. Goldsmith ; edited by Lorraine Sinkler. New Hyde Park, N.Y. : University Books, [1974] c1964. x, 210 p. ; 22 cm. [BF639.G567 1974] 75-307212 5.00
1. New Thought. I. Title.

GOLDSMITH, Joel S., 1892-1964. 248.4899
Man was not born to cry. Edited by Lorraine Sinkler. New York, Julian Press, 1964. x, 210 p. 22 cm. [BF639.G567] 64-15748
1. New Thought. I. Title.

GOLDSMITH, Joel S., 1892-1964. 289.9
Our spiritual resources / Joel S. Goldsmith ; edited by Lorraine Sinkler. San Francisco : Harper & Row, [1978] p. cm. Includes index. [BF639.G5686 1978] 78-16010 ISBN 0-06-063211-9 : 6.95
1. New Thought. I. Sinkler, Lorraine. II. Title.

GOLDSMITH, Joel S., 1892-1964. 289.9
A parenthesis in eternity. Edited by Lorraine Sinkler. [1st ed.] New York, Harper & Row [1964, c1963] viii, 366 p. 22 cm. [BF639.G5695] 64-10368
1. New thought. 2. Mysticism. I. Title.

GOLDSMITH, Joel S., 1892-1964. 289.9
The thunder of silence. [1st ed.] New York, Harper [1961] 192 p. 20 cm. [BF639.G58] 61-7340
1. New Thought. I. Title.

GOLDSMITH, Joel S., 1892-1964. 242
The world is new / Joel S. Goldsmith ; edited by Lorraine Sinkler. [2d ed.]. San Francisco : Harper & Row, c1978. x, 214 p. ; 20 cm. Includes index. [BF639.G59 1978] 78-105887 ISBN 0-06-063291-7 : 6.95
1. New Thought. I. Sinkler, Lorraine. II. Title.

GREY, Lisa Mae. Mrs. 131.324
Universal metaphysics, primary course, by Lisa Mae Grey and Georgie Fitzgerald: a textbook ... Los Angeles, DeVores & co. [c1934- v. front. (port.) 17 cm. [BF639.G685] 159.91324 34-38553
1. New thought. I. Fitzgerald, Georgie, joint author. II. Title. III. Title: Metaphysics, Unversal.

GRUMBINE, Jesse Charles Freemont. 131
The New thought religion, what it stands for in relation to the Christian theology and to divinity; the absolute, by J. C. F. Grumbine. Boston, Mass., The Order of the white rose [c1921] 1 p. l., 5-117 p. 16 cm. [BF639.G8] 21-13508 0.50
1. New Thought. I. Title.

HARDY, Ray Morton. 248
High adventure. San Gabriel, Calif., Willing Pub. Co. [1954] 112p. 21cm. [BF639.H435] 54-43975
1. New Thought. I. Title.

HERRING, Daniel Boone. 131
Arise and walk; or, Jesus the man, Christ the God, by Daniel Boone Herring. Holyoke, Mass., The Elizabeth Towne co., inc.; [etc., etc., c1930] 3 p. l., 9-265 p. 17 cm. [BR126.H385] 31-95
1. Jesus Christ. 2. New thought. I. Title.

HOLMES, Ernest Shurtleff. 131
The Bible in the light of religious science, by Ernest S. Holmes... New York, R. M. McBride & company, 1929. xiv, 206 p. 21 cm. [BF639.H615] 29-10525
1. New thought. 2. Bible—Criticism, interpretation, etc. I. Title.

HOLMES, Ernest Shurtleff. 131.324
The Ebell lectures on spiritual science, by Ernest S. Holmes... Los Angeles, De Vorss & co. [c1934] 124 p. 18 cm. [BF639.H634] 159.91324 34-33442
1. New thought. I. Title.

HOLMES, Ernest Shurtleff. 131.324
It's up to you! By Ernest Holmes in collaboration with Maude Lathem. Los Angeles, Institute of religious science, 1936. xvii, 172 p. 20 1/2 cm. "First edition." [BF639.H6343] 159.91324 37-1134
1. New thought. I. Lathem, Maude, joint author. II. Title.

HOLMES, Ernest Shurtleff. 230.99
A new design for living, by Ernest Holmes and Willis H. Kinnear. Englewood Cliffs, N. J., Prentice-Hall [1959] 236p. 22cm. Includes bibliography. [BF639.H6345] 59-8683
1. New Thought. 2. Peace of mind. I. Kinnear, Willis Hayes, 1907- joint author. II. Title.

HOLMES, Ernest Shurtleff. 131.324
Questions & answers on the science of mind, by Ernset Holmes and Alberta Smith. Los Angeles, Institute of religious science, 1935. 1 p. l., v-xiv p., 1 l., 132 p. 20 cm. [BF645.H57] 159.91324 40-34355
1. New thought. I. Smith, Mrs. Alberta, joint author. II. Title.

HOLMES, Ernest Shurtleff.
The science of mind. Completely rev. and enl. Editorial revision in collaboration with Maude Allison Lathem. New York, Dodd, Mead, 1964. 667 p. illus. 67-20749
1. New thought. I. Lathem, Maude Allison. II. Title.

HOLMES, Ernest Shurtleff.
This thing called life. New York, Dodd, Mead, 1964 [c1943] 153 p. 20 cm. Stamped on t.p.: Distributed by Scrivener and Co., Los Angeles. 67-103149
1. New thought. I. Title.

HOLMES, Ernest Shurtleff 237.2
You will live forever. New York, Dodd, Mead [c.]1960. 124p. 20cm. 60-15010 3.50
1. New Thought. I. Title.

HOLMES, Fenwicke Lindsay. 131
How to develop faith that heals, by Fenwicke Lindsay Holmes... Los Angeles, Calif., J. F. Rowny press, 1919. 100 p. front. (port.) 18 cm. [BF639.H645] 21-13290
1. New thought. I. Title.

HOLMES, Fenwicke Lindsay, 1883- 131
Religion and mental science, by Fenwicke L. Holmes. New York, R. M.McBride & company, 1929. viii p., 1 l., 228 p. 19 1/2 cm. [BF639.H665] 29-24211
1. New thought. I. Title.

HOLMES, Jerome Crane, 1885- 131.324
Self-measurement, by Jerome C. Polnes. Los Angeles,Calif., Institute of religious science [1942] 188 p. 19 1/2 cm. [BF639.H677] [[159.91324]] 42-16479
1. New thought. 2. Institute of religious science and school of philosophy,inc., Los Angeles I. Title.

HOOPER, Carrie Thomas, 1895- 131
Introduction copy of The power that lies in right thinking; educational psychology with Bible points; Carrie Thomas Hooper, author. [Nashville, Printed by the National Baptist publishing board, 1932] 111, [1] p. 2 port. (incl. front.) 20 cm. [BF645.H6] 32-18713
1. New thought. 2. Psychology, Applied. I. Title. II. Title: The power that lies in right thinking.

HOPKINS, Erasius Whitford. 131
Science of the new thought, by E. Whitford Hopkins... Bristol, Conn., The New thought book concern, 1904. 312 p. incl. illus., plates. 20 1/2 cm. 4-14205
I. Title.

HULL, Moses.
The spiritual Alps and how we ascend them, or A few thoughts on how to reach that altitude where spirit is supreme and all things are subject to it. By Moses Hull ... Chicago, M. Hull & co., 1893. 3 p. l., 11-106 p. front. (port.) 20 cm. [BF1262.H9] 11-3145
1. New thought. I. Title.

JACKSON, Loulia.
Heaven on earth; a work dealing with the new thought, by Loulia Jackson ... New York, Washington [etc.] Broadway publishing co. [c1911] 73 p. incl. front. (port.) 20 cm. 11-23715 1.00
I. Title.

JEWEL, Alice. 131
My healing gospel of eternal youth; twelve lessons on spiritual healing and the silence for the purpose of attaining eternal youth, by Alice Jewel ... Washington, D. C., Alice Jewel [c1926] xv, [1], 232 p. front. (port.) 19 cm. [Her Eternal youth series] [BF639.J45] 26-16606
1. New thought. 2. Mental healing. I. Title. II. Series.

KEELER, William Frederic, 1874-1943. 131.324
Christian victory instruction ... by W. Frederic Keeler; edited by Alma M. Morse. San Francisco, W. Kibbee & son 1945- v. port. 24 cm. [BF639.K38] 45-4083
1. New Thought. I. Morse, Alma M., ed. II. Title.

KENILWORTH, Walter Winston. 131
The life of the soul, by Walter Winston Kenilworth ... New York, R. F. Fenno & company [c1911] 261 p. 20 cm. [BF639.K45] 11-27662 1.00
1. New thought. I. Title.

KIPLINGER, Charles U. 131.324
How to live for health and spiritual attainment, by Dr. Charles U. Kiplinger ... St. Petersburg [Fla.] Printed by Dixie press, c1934. 1 p. l., 5-54 p. 18 1/2 cm. [BF645.K65] [159.91324] CA 34
1. New thought. I. Title.

LAMBERT, J Cameron. 289.9
Thoughts are things: attract what you want by thinking; a study in applied psychology. [New York? c1957] 144p. 23cm. [BF639.L12] 57-14864
1. New Thought. I. Title.

LANG, Celestia Root. Mrs.
Behold the Christ? An epic of the new theism, by Mrs. Celestia Root Lang ... Chicago, 1906. 128 p. 22 cm. On cover: Behold the Christ! In every one. A gospel of love. 7-6162
I. Title.

LANYON, Walter Clemow, 1887- 242
The eyes of the blind. [New York] Inspiration House [c1959] 220p. 21cm. [BF639.L205 1959] 60-32791
1. New Thought. I. Title.

LANYON, Walter Clemow, 1887- 131.324
The laughter of God, by Walter C. Lanyon. Los Angeles, Bookhaven press, Kellaway-Ide company [c1941] 4 p. l., 11-220 p. 22 cm. [BF639.L217] 159.91324 41-24914
1. New thought. I. Title.

LARSON, Christian Daa, 1874- 131
Healing yourself, by Christian D. Larson ... New York, Thomas Y. Crowell company [c1918] vi, 113 p. 20 cm. [BF639.L27] 18-18342 1.00
1. New thought. I. Title.

[LA TOUR, Victor] 131
The book of life, physical mental, spiritual. [Tacoma, Wash.] The True life publishing co., c1924. 116 p. 19 cm. On cover: Victor La Tour, PH. D. [BF645.L3] 24-28801
1. New thought. I. Title.

LORD, Christine. 131.324
Heaven's own doorstep, by Christine Lord. Los Angeles, Calif., DeVorss & co. [c1941] 2 p. l., 214 p. 20 cm. "First edition." [BF639.L87] [159.91324] 42-5995
1. New thought. I. Title.

LUNDE, Norman S. 289.9
You unlimited, through the secret power within you. New York, Dodd [c.1965] xiii, 173p. 21cm. [BF639.L883] 65-23608 3.50
1. New Thought. I. Title.

LUNDE, Norman S 289.9
You unlimited, through the secret power within you, by Norman S. Lunde. New York, Dodd, Mead [1965] xiii, 173 p. 21 cm. [BF639.L883] 65-23608
1. New Thought. I. Title.

MAGIC of faith.
[2d ed.] San Gabriel, California, Willing pub. co. [1956, c1954] 128p. 20cm.
1. New Thought. I. Murphy, Joseph, 1898-

MARY, pseud. 248
All that you are. Los Angeles, DeVorss [1959] 210p. 22cm. [BX639.M36] 60-616
1. New Thought. 2. Reincarnation. I. Title.

MISCELLANEOUS writings of Raymond Charles Barker. New York, First church of Religious science [Foreword, 1958] 75p. 17cm.
1. New Thought. I. Barker, Raymond Charles. II. New York. First Church of Religious Science.

MULLOWNEY, John James, 1878- 131.324
I believe, by Dr. John James Mullowney. [Tampa, Fla., The Florida grower press, 1944] 5 p. l., 96 p. incl. front. (port.) plates. 18 1/2 cm. "References": p. 96. [BF645.M85] 44-32027
1. Jesus Christ—Resurrection. 2. New thought. 3. Faith-cure. I. Title.

MURPHY, Joseph, 1898- 228
Pray your way through it. San Gabriel, Calif., Willing Pub. Co. [1958] 173p. 20cm. [BS2825.M79] 59-29210
1. New Thought. 2. Bible. N. T. Revelation—Miscellanea. I. Title.

MURPHY, Joseph, 1898- 248.32
Techniques in prayer therapy. San Gabriel, Calif., Willing Pub. Co. [1960] 213p. 20cm. [BF639.M838] 60-37398
1. New thought. 2. Faith-cure. I. Title.

MURPHY, Joseph, 1898- 289.9
You can change your whole life. San Gabriel, Calif:, Willing public co [1961] 185p. 21cm. [BF639.M843] 62-737
1. New Thought. I. Title.

MYRICK, Herbert, 1860-1927. 131
The promise of life; a preachment by Herbert Myrick to the New York churchman's association. New York, Orange Judd company, 1905. 2 p. l., 49 p. 18 cm. [BF639.M9] 5-33984
1. New thought. I. Title.

NIMICK, John A. 248.4
Be still and know, by John A. Nimick. New York, Philosophical Lib. [c.1966] 47p. 22cm. [BF641.N5] 67-11989 3.00
1. New Thought. I. Title.

NORTHRUP, Theodore G. 1839- 131.
Northrup's religion and business; the undreamed of possibilities which man may achieve through mastery of self. 4th ed. By Theodore G. Northrup. [New York, Smith & Smyth, c1921] 108 p. front. (port.) 16 cm. [BF640.N6 1921] 21-20560
1. New thought. I. Title. II. Title: Religion and business.

PALMER, Alma Kennedy. 289.9
The beautiful eternal now. Boston, Christopher [c.1963] 61p. 21cm. 63-11505 2.00
1. New Thought. I. Title.

PALMER, Alma Kennedy. 289.9
The beautiful eternal now. Boston, Christopher Pub. House [1963] 61 p. 21 cm. [BF639.P12] 63-11505
1. New Thought. I. Title.

PARKINSON, Merta Mary. 133.9
Love and laughter; a challenging adventure in daily living. Kansas City, Mo., F. Glenn Pub. Co. [1950] 220 p. 23 cm. [BF639.P14] 50-10908
1. New thought. I. Title.

RANDALL, John Herman, 1871- 131.
... *The rebirth of religion.* Spiritual consciousness. The rediscovery of Jesus. By J. Herman Randall. New York, Boston, H. M. Caldwell co. [1909] 3 p. l., 3-77 p. 18 cm. (The new philosophy of life series) [BF639.N4] 9-25429 0.60
1. New thought. I. Title.

RANDALL, John Herman, 1871- 131.
The supreme victory. The conquest of fear and worry. The psychology of prayer. By J. Herman Randall. New York, Boston, H. M. Caldwell co. [1909] 3 p. l., 3-83 p. 18 cm. (The ne wphilosophy of life series) [BF639.N4] 9-25428 0.60
1. New thought. I. Title.

RAWSON, Frederick Lawrence, 1859- 131.
True prayer in business; being one of the series of articles on right thinking (true prayer) appearing in "Active service" from March 31st to July 21st, and November 17th and 24th, 1917, revised and enlarged. By F. L. Rawson ... 2d ed. London and New York city, The Crystal press, limited [1920!] 1 p. l., 105 p. 18 cm. (On cover: Divine protection series, no. 6) [BF640.R33 1920] 23-15426
1. New thought. I. Title.

RAYMOND, Walter W. 131.
That unseen presence, by Walter W. Raymond ... Los Angeles, First church of divine science [c1927] 3 p. l., v-ix, 10-73 p. 20 cm. [BF639.R33] 28-14563
1. New thought. I. Title.

RAYMOND, Walter W. 289.9
Thoughts of a spiritual vagabond, by Walter W. Raymond. Dallas, Book Craft, 1969. 120 p. 22 cm. [BF639.R3315] 79-7541 4.95
1. New Thought. I. Title.

REGARDIE, Israel. 131.324
The romance of metaphysics, an introduction to the history, theory and psychology of modern metaphysics, by Israel Regardie. Chicago, The Aries press [1947] xi, 288 p. 23 1/2 cm. "Copyright 1946." [BF639.R3442] 47-18679
1. New thought. 2. Christian science. 3. Eddy, Mary (Baker) 1821-1910. 4. Unity school of Christianity, Kansas City, Mo. 5. Sects—U.S. I. Title.
Contents omitted.

RIX, Harriet Hale, 1863- 131.
Christian mind healing, by Harriet Hale Rix; a course of lessons in the fundamentals of new thought. Los Angeles, Cal., The Master mind publishing co., 1914. 1 p. l., 5-119 p. 23 cm. First published as a serial in the magazine the

Master mind. cf. Pref. [BF639.R75] 14-10255 1.00
1. New thought. I. Title.

ROBINSON, Grant. 131.324
...The orientation of the soul. by Grant Robinson. Philadelphia, Dorrance and company [c1938] 129 p. 20 cm. (Contemporary religious thought series, vol. XII) [BF639.R55] [159.91324] 38-2412
1. New thought. I. Title.

RUMMERFIELD, Walter Glen. 201
Psychology of religion applied to everyday living. San Gabriel, Calif., Willing Pub. Co. [1960] 178p. 20cm. [BF639.R78] 60-1043
1. New Thought. I. Title.

SCIENTIFIC Christian mental practice. [n.p.] High watch fellowship, 1958. 279p.
1. New thought. I. Hopkins, Emma Curtis.

SHAVER, John Edward.
The spirit and God's man. New York, Comet Press Books, 1960. 186 p. 21 cm. Vol. 2 of the author's tetralogy, the 1st of which is The spirit and the living seed, and the 3rd, The spirit of Christ within.
1. New Thought. I. Title.

SHAVER, John Edward 230.99
The spirit and the living seed. v. 2 New York, Comet Press Books [c.]1960. 183p. 21cm. (A Milestone book) Contents.v.2, The spirit and God's man. 60-676 3.00
1. New Thought. I. Title.

SHAVER, John Edward. 230.99
The spirit and the living seed. New York, Comet Press Books [1960] 183 p. 21 cm. (A Milestone book) [BF639.S518] 60-676
1. New Thought I. Title.

SHAVER, John Edward. 230.99
The spirit of Christ within. New York, Comet Press Books, 1960. 178 p. 21 cm. Vol. 3 of the author's projected tetralogy, the 1st of which is The spirit and the living seed, and the 2d, The spirit and God's man. [BF639.S519] 60-50386
1. New Thought. I. Title.

SHERMAN, Harold Morrow, 1898- 289.9
How to solve mysteries of your mind and soul; a way to find a philosophy of life that meets the needs of today and tomorrow [by] Harold Sherman. Los Angeles. DeVorss [1965] 212 p. 24 cm. [BF639.S549] 65-18958
1. New Thought. I. Title.

SINKLER, Lorraine. 289.9 B
The spiritual journey of Joel S. Goldsmith, modern mystic. [1st ed.] New York, Harper & Row [1973] xii, 194 p. 22 cm. Includes bibliographical references. [BF648.G64S57 1973] 72-13190 ISBN 0-06-067386-9 5.95
1. Goldsmith, Joel S., 1892-1964. 2. New Thought. I. Title.

SKARIN, Annalee. 248.4899
Secrets of eternity. Los Angeles, DeVorss [1960] 287 p. 23 cm. [BF639.S618] 60-3545
1. New Thought. I. Title.

SKARIN, Annalee. 289.9
The temple of God. Los Angeles, De Vorss [1958] 224 p. 22 cm. [BF639.S62] 59-24411
1. New thought I. Title.

SMITH, Alberta. Mrs. 131.324
I lift my lamp, by Alberta Smith, in collaboration with Maude Allison Lathem. Los Angeles, Calif., Institute of religious science, 1937. 198 p. 20 cm. "First edition." [BF639.S67] [159.91324] 37-5966
1. New thought. I. Lathem, Maude Allison, joint author. II. Institute of religious science and school of philosophy, inc., Los Angeles. III. Title.

TILBURNE, Edward Oliver. 131.
... Principles and practice of Christian psychology, by Edward Oliver Tilburne ... Los Angeles, Calif., The Universal prosperity partnership [c1921] 143, [1] p. front. (port.) 20 cm. (Christian psychology; the Universal prosperity partnership educational library) [BF639.T4] 22-4840
1. New thought. I. Title.

TNT, the power within you how to release the forces inside you and get what you want! by Claude M. Bristol and Harold Sherman. Englewood Cliffs, N. J., Prentice- Hall [1957] 238p. 24cm.
1. New Thought. I. Bristol, Claude Myron, 1891- II. Sherman, Harold Morrow, 1898- joint author.

TRINE, Ralph Waldo, 1866- 130
This mystical life of ours; a book of suggestive thoughts for each week through the year, from the complete works of Ralph Waldo Trine ... New York, T. Y. Crowell & co. [1907] ix, 190 p. 21 cm. [BF639.T667] 7-29412
1. New thought. I. Title.

TROWARD, Thomas, 1847-1916.
The hidden power, and other papers upon mental science, by T. Troward. New York, Dodd, Mead & Co., 1965 [c1921] 216 p. 19 cm. 68-103080
1. New thought. I. Title.

VALENTINE, John Marvin. 131.324
World temple science, "the key to success", by John Marvin Velentine. Trinidad, Col., The World temple science society, 1933. 3 p. l., 213 p. 19 1/2 cm. [BF640.V3] [159.91324] 33-12627
1. New thought. 2. Religious (Proposed, universal, etc.) I. Title.

WAKEFORD, Oneta. 289.9
Change your thoughts and alter your life. Minneapolis, Denison [1960] 166 p. 22 cm. [BF639.W15] 60-14933
1. New Thought. I. Title.

WALLACE, Helen Kelsey (Rhodes) Mrs. 135
Sleep as the great opportunity; or, Psychcoma, by Helen Rhodes-Wallace; with introduction by Elizabeth Towne. Holyoke, Mass., E. Towne, 1919. 155 p. front. (port.) 19 1/2 cm. [BF640.W3] 20-12976
1. New thought. I. Title. II. Title: Psychcoma.

WARBURTON, Amy. 131.824
Think by formula and insure your future, and Three basic laws of reincarnation, by Amy Warburton ... Oakland, Calif. [Berkeley, J. J. Rice, printer] 1941. 3 p. l., 9-78 p., 1 l. 20 1/2 cm. "First printing, January 1941." [BF640.W35] [159.91324] 41-2576
1. New thought. 2. Reincarnation. I. Title. II. Title: Three basic laws of reincarnation.

WERTZ, Clara Belle. 131.324
"Live power": a text-book on absolute sceince (the allness of God) by Clara Belle Wertz ... Los Angeles, Calif., DeVorss & co. [c1936] 2 p. l., 7-159 p. 18 1/2 cm. "First edition." [BF639.W45] 159.91324 36-12295
1. New thought. I. Title.

WHITING, Lilian 1859-1942.
The life radiant, by Lillian Whiting ... Boston, Little, Brown, and company, 1904. viii p., 2 l., [3]-375 p. 19 cm. [NBF639.W56] 3-28571
1. New thojght. 2. Spiritual life. I. Title.

WILSON, Floyd Baker, 1845- 131.
The man of to-morrow; human evolution-passing man in this age into God-consciousness, by Floyd B. Wilson ... New York, R. F. Fenno & company [c1914] 213 p. 19 1/2 cm. [BF639.W65] 14-6260
1. New thought. I. Title.

WOLFF, Mizanna. 131
The heart of healing; a journal of remarkable demonstrations of God's healing power, by Mizanna Wolff. Holyoke, Mass., The Elizabeth Towne co., inc.; London, L. N. Fowler & co. [c1927] 2 p. l., 7-85 p. 18 cm. [BF639.W75] 27-925
1. New thought. I. Title.

WOLHORN, Herman. 248'.4'0924
Emmet Fox's golden keys to successful living & reminiscences / Herman Wolhorn. 1st ed. New York : Harper & Row, c1977. viii, 229 p. ; 21 cm. [BF648.F6W64 1977] 76-62930 ISBN 0-06-069670-2 : 6.95
1. Fox, Emmet. 2. New Thought. 3. Clergy—United States—Biography. I. Title.

New thought—Bibliography

THE bibliography of progressive literature. Descriptive catalogue comprising a complete and classified list of works relating to science, philosophy ... telepathy, psychometry ... mind cure, massage, hydropathy and physical culture ... New York, New epoch publishing company [1899] 2 p. l., 95, [1] p. 26 cm. [Z6880.B58] 2-25575
1. New thought—Bibl. 2. Occult sciences—Bibl. I. New epoch publishing company.

New Thought—History

BRADEN, Charles Samuel, 1887- 289.9
Spirits in rebellion; the rise and development of new thought. Dallas, Southern Methodist University Press, 1963. 571 p. 23 cm. Includes bibliography. [BF639.B576] 63-13245
1. New Thought — Hist. 2. International New Thought Alliance. I. Title.

New thought I. Rellimeo.

WITHIN the holy of holies; 210 or, Attitudes of attainment, by Rellimeo. Rev. ed. Chicago, Ill., The Mastery publishing company, 1920. 95 p. 19 cm. Songs, with music: p. [25], [38], [88] [BF639.R3445W5 1920] 38-33127
1. New thought I. Rellimeo.

New Thought—United States—Directories.

BEEBE, Tom. 289.9 B
Who's who in New Thought : biographical dictionary of New Thought : personnel, centers, and authors' publications / by Tom Beebe. Lakemont, Ga. : CSA Press, c1977. 318 p. : maps ; 24 cm. Bibliography: p. 286-311. [BF648.A1B43] 77-152019 ISBN 0-87707-189-6 : 6.95
1. New Thought—United States—Directories. I. Title.

New Tribes Mission, Chicago.

JANK, Margaret, 1939- 266'.023'0987
Culture shock / by Margaret Jank. Chicago : Moody Press, c1977. p. cm. [F2520.1.Y3J36] 77-22658 ISBN 0-8024-1679-9 pbk. : 3.50
1. New Tribes Mission, Chicago. 2. Yanoama Indians—Missions. 3. Indians of South America—Venezuela—Missions. I. Title.

New Ulm, Tex. St. John Lutheran Church.

NEW Ulm, Tex. St. John Lutheran Church. 284'.1764'25
Hundredth anniversary 1867-1968 New Ulm, Tex. [1968] 1 v. (unpaged) illus., facsims., ports. 22 cm. [BX8076.N37S3V] 75-2682
1. New Ulm, Tex. St. John Lutheran Church. I. Title.

New West education commission.

HOOD, Edmund Lyman, 1858-1931.
The New West education commission 1880-1893 [by] Rev. E. Lyman Hood... Jacksonville, Fla., The H. & W. B. Drew company, 1905. 151 p. front. (port.) 20 1/2 cm. [LC564.N5H7] 5-42048
1. New West education commission. 2. Church schools—U.S. I. Title.
Contents omitted.

New Wilmington, Pa. Neshannock Presbyterian church.

JOHNSON, Hubert Rex, 1858- 285.
A history of the Neshannock Presbyterian church, New Wilmington, Pennsylvania, together with some account of the settlement of that part of northwestern Pennsylvania in which the church was organized, by Hubert Rex Johnson ... Washington, D. C., National capital press, inc., 1925. 463 p. incl. illus., tables, plans. front., plates, ports. 24 cm. [BX9211.N48N4] 25-24301
1. New Wilmington, Pa. Neshannock Presbyterian church. 2. Lawrence Co., Pa.—Hist. 3. Mercer Co., Pa.—Hist. I. Title.

New Windsor, Md. Presbyterian church.

A centennial history of the Presbyterian church of New Windsor, Maryland, 1839-1939. 285.175277 [Cincinnati, O., Priv. print. by the McDonald press, 1939] 4 p. l., 64 p., 1 l. incl. illus., ports., facsim. front. 23 cm. [BX9211.N485N4] 39-31827
1. New Windsor, Md. Presbyterian church.

New Year, Jewish-Sermons.

FRIEDMAN, Edwin H
Judaism and change; the opiates and illusions which answer for religion. High Holydays 1964-5725. [New York, 1964?] 1 v. (various pagings) 28 cm. 65-105969
1. New Year, Jewish-Sermons. 2. New Year — Sermons. 3. Atonement day — Sermons. I. Title.

New York. Allen street Presbyterian church.

YOUNG, Duncan McNeill, 1838-1891. 922.573
Gathering jewels; or, The secret of a beautiful life. In memoriam of Mr. & Mrs. James Knowles. Selected from their diaries... Edited by Rev. Duncan McNeill Young. New York, W. Knowles, 1887. xii p., 2 l., [15]-282 p. front., ports. 19 1/2 cm. "A brief historical sketch of the Allen street Presbyterian church": p. [70]-80. [BX9225.K7Y6] 36-24288
1. Knowles, James, 1811-1886. 2. Knowles, Mrs. Matilda (Darroch) 1811-1886. 3. New York. Allen street Presbyterian church. I. Title. II. Title: The secret of a beautiful life.

New York Bible society.

FANT, David Jones, 1897- 266.062747
The Bible in New York; the romance of Scripture distribution in a world metropolis from 1809 to 1948. New York, The Society [1948] 165 p. 24 cm. Cover title: Historical sketch of the New York Bible Society, 1809-1947. [BV2370.N53F3] 48-1122
1. New York Bible Society. 2. Bible—Publication and distribution. I. Title.

WATSON, Alexander, of New York. 206
History of the New York Bible society, from its origin in 1823 to the present time. By Alexander Watson ... New York, A. D. F. Randolph, 1858. 111 p. 22 1/2 cm. [BV2370.N53W3] 44-25653
1. New York Bible society. I. Title.

New York. Biblical Seminary.

EBERHARDT, Charles Richard. 922.573
The Bible in the making of ministers; the scriptural basis of theological education; the lifework of Wilbert Webster White. New York, Association Press, 1949. 254 p. port. 21 cm. Includes bibliographies. [BS501.W5E3] 49-5111
1. White, Wilbert Webster, 1863-1944. 2. New York. Biblical Seminary. 3. Bible—Study. I. Title.

New York. B'nai jeshurun congregation.

GOLDSTEIN, Israel, 1896- 296
A century of Judaism in New York: B'nai jeshurun, 1825-1925, New York's oldest ashkenazic congregation, by Israel Goldstein ... New York, Congregation B'nai jeshurun, 1930. xxix, 460 p. plates, ports. 24 cm. "Bibliography of works consulted": p. 445-449 [BM225.N5B6] 31-7159
1. New York. B'nai jeshurun congregation. 2. Jews in New York (City) I. Title.

New York Board of Rabbis.

GOODMAN, Philip, 1911- ed.
Jewish prayers and songs. New York, 1962. vii, 78 p. 23 cm. Philip Goodman, ed. 67-52107
1. New York Board of Rabbis. I. Title.

GOODMAN, Philip, 1911- ed.
A treasury of Jewish inspiration. New York, Board of Rabbis Inc., 1962. 150 p. 15 cm. 68-6488
1. New York Board of Rabbis. I. Title.

New York. Bowery mission and young mens home.

ST. John, Charles Jackson, 1895- 266
God on the Bowery, by Charles J. St. John ... New York [etc.] Fleming H. Revell company [c1940] 155 p. front. (port.) plates. 19 1/2 cm. [BV2656.N4S3] 40-34821
1. New York. Bowery mission and young mens home. 2. Evangelistic work. New York (City)—Soc. condit. I. Title.

New York. Broadway tabernacle church.

JUDD, Lewis Strong, 1858- 285.
The Broadway tabernacle church, 1901-1915; a historical sketch commemorative of the seventy-fifth anniversary of the church--October, 1915, by Lewis S. Judd. New York, Broadway tabernacle church, 1917. x, 130 p. front. 25 cm. [BX7255.N5B83] 19-16101
1. New York. Broadway tabernacle church. I. Title.

NEW York. Broadway tabernacle church.
Broadway tabernacle church; its history and work; with the documents relating to the resignation of its pastor, Rev. Joseph P. Thompson, D.D. New York, 1871. 51 pp. front. (port.) 8° 1-13635
I. Title.

WARD, Susan Hayes, 1838- 285.
The history of the Broadway tabernacle church, from its organization in 1840 to the close of 1900, including factors influencing its formation; by Susan Hayes Ward. New York [The Trow print] 1901. xxxi, 329 p. front., plates, ports. 24 cm. [BX7255.N5B85] 1-19635
1. New York. Broadway tabernacle church. I. Title.

New York. Calvary church.

REYNOLDS, Amelia (Stead) Mrs. 283.
New lives for old; what happens in Calvary Episcopal church in the city of New York as seen by a member of the staff, by Amelia S. Reynolds. New York, Chicago [etc.] Fleming H. Revell company [c1929] 96 p. 19 1/2 cm. [BX5980.N5C3] 29-14036
1. New York. Calvary church. I. Title.

New York. Calvary church (Protestant Episcopal)

CUYLER, John Potter, jr. 283.7471
Calvary church in action; being the record of the years 1932-3 in a down-town New York parish, by John Potter Cuyler, jr. ... foreword by the rector, Samuel M. Shoemaker. New York [etc.] Fleming H. Revell company [c1934] 79 p. front., plates, ports. 20 cm. [BX5980.N5C25] 34-42131
1. New York. Calvary church (Protestant Episcopal) 2. Oxford group. I. Title.

SHOEMAKER, Samuel Moor, 1893- 283.7471
Calvary church, yesterday and today; a centennial history, by Samuel M. Shoemaker ... New York [etc.] Fleming H. Revell company [c1936] xii, p., 1 l., 324 p. col. front., plates, ports., fold. plan 23 1/2 cm. [BX5980.N5C33] 36-8794
1. New York. Calvary church (Protestant Episcopal) I. Title.

New York. Cathedral of St. John the Divine.

HALL, Edward Hagaman, 1858- 283.
A guide to the Cathedral church of Saint John the Divine, in the city of New York, by Edward Hagaman Hall, L.H.D. New York, The Laymen's club of the Cathedral, 1920. 80 p. front., illus., plates, fold. plan. 17 1/2 cm. [BX5980.N5J65] 20-4898
1. New York. Cathedral church of Saint John the Divine. I. Title.

HALL, Edward Hagaman, 1858- 283.
A guide to the Cathedral church of Saint John the Divine in the city of New York, by Edward Hagaman Hall... 3d ed. New York, The Layman's club of the Cathedral, 1921. 88 p. incl. illus. , fold. plan. front., plates. 17 cm. [BX5980.N5J65 1921] 21-12251
1. New York. Cathedral church of Saint John the Divine. I. Title.

HALL, Edward Hagaman, 1858- 283.
A guide to the Cathedral church of Saint John the Divine in the city of New York, by Edward Hagaman Hall, L.H.D. 4th ed. New York, The Laymen's club of the cathedral, 1922. 115 p. incl. front., illus. 17 1/2 cm. [BX5980.N5J65 1922] 23-1658
1. New York. Cathedral church of Saint John the Divine. I. Title.

HALL, Edward Hagaman, 1858- 283.
A guide to the Cathedral church of Saint John the Divine in the city of New York, by Edward Hagaman Hall, L.H.D. 5th ed. New York, The Laymen's club of the Cathedral, 1924. 116 p. incl. front., illus. 17 cm. [BX5980.N5J65 1924] 24-17314
1. New York. Cathedral church of Saint John the Divine. I. Title.

HALL, Edward Hagaman, 1858- 283.
A guide to the Cathedral church of Saint John the Divine in the city of New York, by Edward Hagaman Hall, L.H.D. New York, The Laymen's club of the Cathedral, 1928. 182 p. incl. front., illus., plan, coats of arms. 17 1/2 cm. "Ninth edition." [BX5980.N5J65 1926] 26-30162
1. New York. Cathedral of St. John the Divine. I. Title.

HALL, Edward Hagaman, 1858- 726.6-97471
A guide to the Cathedral church of Saint John the Divine in the city of New York, by Edward Hagaman Hall, L.H.D. New York, The Laymen's club of the Cathedral, 1931. 142 p. incl. front., illus., plan, coats of arms. 17 1/2 cm. "Tenth edition." [BX5960.N5J65 1931] 31-3002
1. New York. Cathedral of St. John the Divine. I. Title.

HALL, Edward Hagaman, 1858-1936. 726.6097471
A guide to the Cathedral church of Saint John the Divine in the city of New York, by Edward Hagaman Hall, L.H.D. Rev. and enl. New York, The Laymen's club of the Cathedral, 1937. 195 p. incl. front., illus., double plan. 17 cm. "Eleventh edition." [BX5980.N5J65 1937] 39-4264
1. New York. Cathedral of St. John the Divine. I. Title.

HALL, Edward Hagaman, 1858-1936. 726.6067471
A guide to the Cathedral Church of Saint John the Divine in the City of New York, 16th ed. [New York] The Dean and Chapter of the Cathedral Church, 1955. 191 p. illus., port., plan. 18 cm. [BX5980.N5J65] 64-36624
1. New York. Cathedral of St. John the Divine. I. Title.

HALL, Edward Hagaman, 1858-1936. 726.6097471
A guide to the Cathedral Church of Saint John the Divine in the City of New York. 17th ed. New York, The Dean and Chapter of the Cathedral Church, 1965. 231 p. illus., ports. 23 cm [BX5980.N5J65] 66-813
1. New York. Cathedral of St. John the Divine. I. Title.

HALL, Edward Hagaman, 1858-1936. 726.
A guide to the Cathedral church of Saint John the Divine in the city of New York, by Edward Hagaman Hall, L.H.D. ... 7th ed. New York, The Laymen's club of the Cathedral, 1925. 126 p. incl. front., illus. 17 cm. [BX5980.N5J65 1925] 43-50476
1. New York. Cathedral of St. John the Divine. I. Title.

New York Catholic protectory.

NEW York Catholic protectory, West Chester, N.Y. 267
...N.Y. Catholic protectory. 1893. West Chester, N.Y., New York Catholic protectory print [1893?] 50 p. 3 l. fold. front. plates 22 cm. At head of title: 1863. [HV885.N5N5] E 15
1. New York Catholic protectory. 2. Children—Charities, protection, etc.—New York (City) I. Title.

New York. Church of Our Lady of esperanza.

ARMANET, Crescent. 282.
... Church of Our Lady of esperanza, descriptive book, by the Rev. Crescent Armanet, A.A. [New York, Wynkoop Hallenbeck Crawford co., printers] 1921. 4 p. l., 11-159 p. plates, ports. 23 1/2 cm. At head of title: A.R.T. [BX4603.N6O7] 21-11345
1. New York. Church of Our Lady of esperanza. I. Title.

NEW York, Church of Our Lady of Esperanza. 282.7471
Our Lady of Esperanza, New York: fiftieth anniversary. [New York, 624 W. 156 St., Author, 1963] unpaged. illus. 28cm. 63-17841 apply
I. Title.

New York. Church of Our Lady of Perpetual Help.

BYRNE, John F. 282.7471
Golden memories. Church of Our Lady of Perpetual Help, New York, 1887-1937. [By] John F. Byrne ... [New York? 1937?] xiii, [1], 98 p., 1 l. col. mounted front., illus. (incl. ports.) 28 cm. Includes advertising matter. [BX4603.N6O73] 39-425
1. New York. Church of Our Lady of Perpetual Help. I. Title.

New York, Church of St. Matthew and St. Timothy.

EHLE, John 283.7471
Shepherd of the streets; the story of the Reverend James A. Gusweller and his crusade on the New York West Side. Foreword by Harry Golden. New York, Sloane, [c.]1960. xi, 239p. illus. 22cm. 60-8997 4.00
1. Gusweller, James Alfred, 1923- 2. New York, Church of St. Matthew and St. Timothy. 3. Puerto Ricans in New York (City) 4. Building laws—New York (City) I. Title.

New York, Church of St. Michael.

BROWNE, Henry Joseph, 1919- 282.7471
The parish of St. Michael, 1857-1957; a century of grace on the West Side. New York, Church of St. Michael, 1957. 72p. 26cm. [BX4603.N6S4] 58-34895
1. New York, Church of St. Michael. I. Title.

New York, Church of the Ascension.

KENNEDY, James William, 1905- 283.7471
The unknown worshipper. New York, Morehouse-Barlow for the Church of the Ascension [1964] 202p. 46 illus. (incl. facsim., plan, ports.) 22cm. 64-20210 4.00
1. New York, Church of the Ascension. I. Title.

New York. Church of the Epiphany.

RUSSELL, Charles Howland, 1891- 283.747
The Church of the Epiphany, 1833-1958. New York, Published for the Church of the Epiphany by Morehouse-Gorham Co. [1956] 71p. illus. 24cm. [BX5980.N5E63] 56-14234
1. New York. Church of the Epiphany. I. Title.

New York. Church of the Good Shepherd.

[HOYT, Ralph] 1806-1878.
Echoes of memory and emotion. By the author of "Life and landscape". New York, A. D. F. Randloph: London, Hall, Virtue & co., 1861. 170 [1] p. front. (port.) illus., pl. 19 1/2 cm. On cover: Popular illustrated holiday edition. Hoyt's poems. New series. To aid in rebuilding the Good Shepherd free church. Press notices: p. [1-5] [PS2039.H6E3 1861] 27-11777
1. New York. Church of the Good Shepherd. I. Title.

New York, Church of the Holy Apostles.

EDELBLUTE, Lucius Aaron, 1876- 283.747
The history of the Church of the Holy Apostles (Protestant Episcopal) 1844-1944. New York, 1949. 280 p. illus., ports. 24 cm. On cover: A hundred years in Chelsea. Bibliography: p. 276-277. [BX5980.N5C38] 49-49559
1. New York, Church of the Holy Apostles. I. Title.

New York. Church of the sea and land.

BRUCKBAUER, Frederick, 1864- 285.
The kirk on Rutgers farm, by Frederick Bruckbauer; illustrated by Pauline Stone. New York, Fleming H. Revell company, 1919. 133 p. front., illus. (incl. ports.) 21 1/2 cm. Frontispiece on verso of half-title. Bibliography: p. 132-133. [BX9211.N3C5] 19-16120
1. New York. Church of the sea and land. 2. Rutgers, Henry, 1745-1830. 3. New York. Market street Dutch reformed church. I. Title.

New York. Church of the transfiguration.

MACADAM, George. 283.
The Little church around the corner, by George MacAdam ... New York & London, G. P. Putnam's sons, 1925. x, 347 p. front., plates, ports., facsims. (1 fold.) diagr. 22 1/2 cm. [F128.62.C56M12] [BX5980.N5T55 1925] 917. 25-5621
1. Houghton, George Hendric, 1820-1897. 2. Houghton, George Clarke, 1850-1923. 3. New York. Church of the transfiguration. I. Title.

ROSS, Ishbel. 283.7471
Through the lich-gate; a biography of the Little church around the corner, by Ishbel Ross; sixteen illustrations from dry points by Ralph L. Boyer. New York, W. F. Payson, 1931. 2 p. l., iii-v, 164 p. front., plates, ports. 28 cm. [F128.62.C56R8] 31-30853
1. New York. Church of the transfiguration. I. Boyer, Ralph L., 1879- illus. II. Title.

STUART, Suzette G. 283.7471
Guide book of the Little church around the corner, New York city, by Suzette O. Stuart. New York, Church of the transfiguration, 1930. 64 p., 1 l. 18 cm. [BX5980.N5T58] 32-4547
1. New York. Church of the transfiguration. I. Title.

STUART, Suzette Grundy. 283.7471
Guide book of the Little Church Around the Corner, New York City. New York, Church of the Transfiguration, 1930. 64 p. 18 cm. [BX5980.N5T58] 32-4547
1. New York. Church of the Transfiguration. I. Title.

New York. Church of Zion and St. Timothy.

[CLARKSON, David] 283.
History of the Church of Zion and St. Timothy of New York 1797-1894 ... Printed for private circulation. New York

& London, G. P. Putnam's sons [1894] xi, 353 p. front., plates. ports. 24 1/2 cm. Signed: David Clarkson. Plates accompanied by guard sheet with descriptive letterpress. [BX5980.N5Z7] 3-3713
1. New York. Church of Zion and St. Timothy. 2. Lutherans in New York (City). I. Title.

New York (City) Borough of the Bronx — Churches, Evangelical Lutheran — St. Matthews.

NEW York. Evangelical Lutheran Church of St. Matthew.
Our centennial year, 1862-1962 [by] William Jansen New York, 1962] 1 v. (unpaged) illus., ports. 28 cm. Limited ed. 67-56157
1. New York (City) Borough of the Bronx — Churches, Evangelical Lutheran — St. Matthews. I. Jansen, William. II. Title.

New York (City). Calvary Baptist Church.

DE PLATA, William R. 286'.1747'1
Tell it from Calvary; the record of a sustained Gospel witness from Calvary Baptist Church of New York City since 1847, by William R. De Plata. New York, Calvary Baptist Church [1973 c1972] xii, 189 p. illus. 24 cm. [BX6480.N5C33] 72-92842 4.95
1. New York (City). Calvary Baptist Church. 2. Baptists—Biography. 3. Baptists—Sermons. 4. Sermons, American. I. Title.
pap. 3.50.

New York (City). Chambers Memorial Baptist Church.

SCHOONOVER, Melvin E. 287'.87471
Making all things human; a church in East Harlem [by] Melvin E. Schoonover. Foreword by William Stringfellow. [1st ed.] New York, Holt, Rinehart and Winston, 1969] ix, 188 p. 22 cm. [BX6480.N577C45] 74-84680 4.95
1. New York (City). Chambers Memorial Baptist Church. I. Title.

New York (City) Chatham Square Cemetery.

POOL, David de Sola, 1885- 296
Portraits etched in stone; early Jewish settlers, 1682-1831. New York, Columbia University Press, 1952. xiv, 543 p. illus., ports. maps, geneal. tables. 26 cm. Bibliography: p. [513]-517. [F128.9.J5P6] 52-14151
1. New York (City) Chatham Square Cemetery. 2. Jews in New York (City) — Biog. 3. New York. Congregation Shearith Israel. I. Title.

New York (City)—Church history.

GREENLEAF, Jonathan, 1785-1865. 277.
A history of the churches, of all denominations, in the city of New York, from the first settlement to the year 1846. By Jonathan Greenleaf ... New York, E. French; Portland, Hyde, Lord & Duren, 1846. viii, 379, [1] p. 16 cm. [BR560.N4G8 1846] 22-13801
1. New York (City)—Church history. I. Title.

NEW York. Evangelical Lutheran Church of St. Matthew. 284.1747
Protocol of the Lutheran Church in New York City, 1702-1750. Translated by Simon Hart and Harry J. Kreider. New York, The Synod [i. e. United United Lutheran Synod of New York and New England] 1958. xxi, 523p. map, facsims. 28cm. Bibliography: p. xx. [BX8076.N4S27] 58-2867
1. New York (City)—Church history. 2. Lutheran Church in New York (City) I. Hart, Simon, tr. II. Kreider, Harry Julius, 1896- tr. III. United Lutheran Synod of New York and New England. IV. Title.

New York(City)—Churches.

BOMAR, Willie Melmoth, 1894- 252.00822
I went to church in New York, by W. Melmoth Bomar, PH.D. ... New York, The Graymont publishers, [c1937] ix, p., 1 l., 307 p. incl. plates. 23 1/2 cm. "Messages of representative religious leaders in New York,"--Foreword. [BR560.N4B6] 37-12277
1. New York (City)—Churches. 2. Sermons, American. I. Title.

CHURCH pictorial directory of New York City. New York. v. illus. 26 cm. annual. [BR560.N4C5] 49-35711 277.
1. New York (City)—Churches.

CHURCH year book and budget directory for Manhattan, Bronx, Queens [and] Staten island, 1933- New York, N.Y., Greater New York federation of churches, 1933- v. forms. 23 1/2 cm. Cover-title. In four parts; each part has special t.-p. [BR560.N4C5] 33-14005 277.471
1. New York (City)—Churches. 2. New York (City)—Direct. I. Greater New York federation of churches.

GREENLEAF, Jonathan, 1785-1865. 277.471
A history of the churches, of all denominations in the city of New York, from the first settlement to the year 1850. By Jonathan Greenleaf ... 2d ed. New York, E. French, 1850. viii, [9]-429, [1] p. 16 cm. [BR560.N4G8 1850] 33-28496
1. New York (City)—Churches. 2. New York (City)—Church history. I. Title.

*THE New York church and musical directory of New York and Brooklyn and other adjacent suburbs ...*with portraits of the leading artists and photographs of churches in New York and suburbs... Boston, Mass., W. G. James, c1908- v, illus. (incl. ports.) 20 cm. Editor: 1908- W. G. James. 8-19212
I. James, William Grant, ed.

NEW York. Fifth Avenue Presbyterian Church. 285.17471
A noble landmark of New York; the Fifth Avenue Presbyterian Church. 1808-1958. New York, 1960. 174p. illus. 23cm. [BX9211.N5FIS] 60-9133
I. Title.

NICKERSON'S illustrated church musical and school directory of New-York and Brooklyn ... New-York, Nickerson & Young [1895] 5-276 p. incl. front., illus., plates. 23 cm. Includes 18 pages of advertisements. [BR560.N4N5] [ML15.N3N5] 33-37798 277.471
1. New York (City)—Churches. 2. New York (City)—Schools. 3. Musicians—New York (City) 4. Church music—New York (City) 5. New York (City)—Direct. 6. Brooklyn—Direct.

PROTESTANT Council of the City of New York. Dept. of Church Planning and Research.
Morrisania, Melrose, Mott Haven, three Bronx communities. Prepared by the Dept. of church planning & research of the Protestant council of the city of New York. [New York] 1956. 83 p. illus., maps. 29 cm. 66-2133
1. New York(City)—Churches. 2. New York(City)—Soc. condit. I. Title.

New York (City) — Churches, Dutch Reformed — Marble church.

ACKERMAN, Ross D
Collegiate Reformed Protestant Dutch church of the city of New York. [Auburn? N. Y.] Men's league, Marble Collegiate church, 1965. 1 v. (various pagings) 28 cm. NUC66
1. New York (City) — Churches, Dutch Reformed — Marble church. I. New York. Collegiate Church. Marble Collegiate Church. II. Title.

New York (City)—Churches, Episcopal—St. James.

A history of Saint James' church in the city of New York, 1810-1860. [New York, Rector, wardens and vestrymen of St. James church, 1960] vi, 126p. illus., ports. 21cm.
1. New York (City)—Churches, Episcopal—St. James. I. Lindsley, J Elliott. II. New York, St. James Church, Manhattan (Protestant Episcopal)

New York (City). Interchurch Center.

HARMON, Francis Stuart, 1895- 262'.001
The Interchurch Center : reminiscences of an incorrigible promoter / by Francis Stuart Harmon. [New York] : Harmon, c1972. 385 p. : ill. ; 28 cm. Includes index. [BX6.N2H37] 70-185585
1. New York (City). Interchurch Center. 2. National Council of the Churches of Christ in the United States of America. I. Title.

New York (City). Metropolitan Museum of Art.

GRINNELL, Isabel Hoopes. 726'.1'208
Greek temples. New York, 1943. [New York] Arno Press, 1974. xxi, 59 p. illus. 32 cm. At head of title: The Metropolitan Museum of Art. Includes bibliographies. [NA275.G7 1974] 79-168420 ISBN 0-405-02258-1 20.00
1. New York (City). Metropolitan Museum of Art. 2. Temples, Greek. I. New York (City). Metropolitan Museum of Art.

New York City Mission Society.

MILLER, Kenneth Dexter, 1887- 266.022
The people are the city; 150 years of social and religious concern in New York City, by Kenneth D. Miller, Ethel Prince Miller. New York, Macmillan [c.]1962. 258p. illus. 62-7517 3.95
1. New York City Mission Society. I. Miller, Ethel (Prince) 1893- joint author. II. Title.

New York (City). Missionary Research Library.

NEW York (City). Missionary Research Library. 019'.1
Dictionary catalog of the Missionary Research Library, New York. Boston, G. K. Hall, 1968. 17 v. 37 cm. [Z7817.N54 1968] 74-169177
1. New York (City). Missionary Research Library. 2. Missions—Bibliography—Catalogs.

New York (City) St. Ignatius Loyola church.

[DOOLEY, Patrick Joseph] 282.
Fifty years in Yorkville, or, Annals of the parish of St. Ignatius Loyola and St. Lawrence O'Toole. New York [Frank Meany co., printers, inc.] 1917. vii, [2], 353, [1] p. front., illus., plates, ports. 21 2/2 cm. On cover: 1866-1916. Bibliographical references included in foreword. [BX4603.Y6S3] 47-43886
1. New York (City) St. Ignatius Loyola church. 2. Yorkville, N.Y. I. Title.

New York (City) St. Nicholas Cathedral.

ST. Nicholas Cathedral Study Group. 281.9'7471
St. Nicholas Cathedral of New York; history and legacy, edited by M. Pokrovsky. [1st ed.] New York, 1968. 103 p. illus., ports. 23 cm. [BX591.N57S2] 68-56203
1. New York (City) St. Nicholas Cathedral. I. Pokrovsky, M., ed. II. Title.

New York (City). St. Patrick's Cathedral.

COOK, Leland A. 282'.7471
St. Patrick's Cathedral / by Leland A. Cook ; foreword by Terence Cardinal Cooke ; introd. by Brendan Gill ; [cover photo. by David Frazier]. New York : Quick Fox, c1979. 160 p. : ill. ; 28 cm. Includes index. Bibliography: p. 157. [BX4603.N6S623] 79-88702 ISBN 0-8256-3169-6 : 24.95 ISBN 0-8256-3158-0 (pbk.) : 9.95
1. New York (City). St. Patrick's Cathedral. I. Title.

New York (City) St. Stephen's Methodist Church.

TIECK, William Arthur, 1908- 287.6747
God's house and the old Kingsbridge Road; the Story of St. Stephn's Methodist Church, Kingsbridge, New York City. Commemorating the golden jubilee of the present building, dedicated November 6-13, 1898. [New York? 1948] vii, 71 p. illus., ports., fold. map. 24 cm. [BX8481.N5S35] 48-11973
1. New York (City) St. Stephen's Methodist Church. I. Title.

New York (City). Trinity Church.

MESSITER, Arthur Henry, 1834- 783
A history of the choir and music of Trinity church, New York, from its organization, to the year 1897, by A. H. Messiter ... New York, E. S. Gorham, 1906. viii p., 2 l., 324 p. front., ports. 26 cm. [ML200.8.N5T7 Copyright] 7-20654
1. New York (City) Trinity church. I. Title.

MOREHOUSE, Clifford Phelps, 1904- 283'.747'1
Trinity: Mother of churches; an informal history of Trinity Parish in the city of New York [by] Clifford P. Morehouse. New York, Seabury Press [1973] xi, 338 p. illus. 22 cm. Bibliography: p. 325-327. [BX5980.N5T74] 72-94206 ISBN 0-8164-0246-9 8.95
1. New York (City). Trinity Church. I. Title.

New York (City). Union Theological Seminary. Library.

NEW York (City). Union Theological Seminary. Library. 016.2
Alphabetical arrangement of main entries from the shelf list / Union Theological Seminary Library, New York City. Boston : G. K. Hall, 1960. 10 v. ; 37 cm. [Z7755.N534 1960] [BR118] 75-313282
1. New York (City). Union Theological Seminary. Library. 2. Theology—Bibliography—Catalogs. I. Title.

New York. Collegiate church.

COE, Edward Benton, 1842-1914. 922.
A discourse commemorative of the Reverend Talbot Wilson Chambers, S.T.D., LL.D., by the Reverend Edward B. Coe ... New York [The Gilliss press] 1896. 76 p. front. (port.) 26 1/2 cm. The discourse was prepared at the request of, and printed by direction of, the Consistory of the Collegiate church. "Published writings": p. 72-76. [BX9543.C5C6] 9-14879
1. Chambers, Talbot Wilson, 1819-1896. 2. New York. Collegiate church. I. Title.

New York. Collegiate church—History

DEWITT, Thomas, 1791-1874. 252
A discourse delivered in the North Reformed Dutch church (Collegiate) in the city of New-York, on the last Sabbath in August, 1856. By Thomas DeWitt ... New-York, Board of publications of the Reformed Protestant Dutch church, 1857. 3 p. l., [5]-100 p. front., plates. 23 cm. Added t.-p., engraved, with vignette. [BX9531.N5C77] 24-6548
1. New York. Collegiate church—Hist. I. Title.

New York. Collegiate Church. Marble Collegiate Church.

NEW York. Collegiate Church. Marble Collegiate Church. Marble Club. 285.7747
The Marble Collegiate Church. [Blanche Tessaro Cleaver, editor] New York, 1954. unpaged. illus. 20cm. [BX9531.N5C715] 55-24617
1. New York. Collegiate Church. Marble

Collegiate Church. I. Cleaver, Blanche Tessaro, 1904- ed. II. Title.

New York, Congregation Shaaray teflia.

COHEN, Simon, 1894- 296
Shaaray tefila, a history of its hundred years, 1845-1945, by Simon Cohen, D. D. New York, Greenberg [1945] ix, 86 p. front., plates, ports. facsims. 20 cm. Bibliography: 85-86. [BM225.N5S4] 45-10485
1. New York, Congregation Shaaray teflia. I. Title.

New York. Congregation Shaare Zedek.

MONSKY, Jacob. 296.097471
Within the gates; a religious, social, and cultural history, 1837-1962. New York, Congregation Shaare Zedek [c1964] 180 p. illus., ports. 24 cm. Erratum slip inserted. [BM225.N5S43] 64-7517
1. New York. Congregation Shaare Zedek. 2. Jews in New York (City) I. Title.

New York. Congregation Shearith Israel.

GOLDSTEIN, Israel, 1896- 296
American Jewry comes of age; tercentenary addresses. New York, Bloch Pub. Co., 1955. 218p. illus. 21cm. [BM225.N5S457] 55-12321
1. New York. Congregation Shearith Israel. 2. Jews in the U. S. I. Title.

POOL, David de Sola, 1885- 296
An old faith in the New World; portrait of Shearith Israel, 1654-1954 [by] David and Tamar de Sola Pool. New York, Columbia University Press, 1955. xviii, 595p. illus., ports., maps, facsims., music 26cm. Bibliography: p. [555]-562. [BM225.N5S46] 55-6619
1. New York. Congregation Shearith Israel. 2. Judaism—U. S. I. Pool, Tamar (Hirschensohn) de Sola, 1893- joint author. II. Title.

New York. First Seventh Day Baptist Church.

RANDOLPH, Corliss Fitz, 286.3747
1863-
A century's progress; an historical sketch of the First Seventh Day Baptist Church of New York City, 1945-1945. Plainfield, N. J., Recorder Press, 1948. xix, 168 p. illus., ports. 21 m. Bibliographical references inclded in "Prefatory note". [BX6480.N5F57] 49-13646
1. New York. First Seventh Day Baptist Church. I. Title.

New York. French church the Saint Esprit.

MAYNARD, John Albert, 284-57471
1884-
The Huguenot church of New York; a history of the French church of Saint Esprit, by John A. F. Maynard... New York, 1938. 317 p. illus. (incl. ports.) 18 1/2 cm. [Full name: John Albert Fonsegrive Maynard] [BX9458.U5N4] 39-23633
1. New York. French church the Saint Esprit. I. Title.

New York. General Theological Seminary of the Protestant Episcopal Church in the United States—History.

DAWLEY, Powel Mills, 207'.7471
1907-
The story of the General Theological Seminary; a sesquicentennial history, 1817-1967. New York, Oxford University Press, 1969. xvii, 390 p. illus., ports. 24 cm. Bibliographical footnotes. [BV4070.G46D3] 69-17760 7.50
1. New York. General Theological Seminary of the Protestant Episcopal Church in the United States—History. I. Title.

New York. Grace church.

STEWART, William 726.
Rhinelander, 1852-
Grace church and old New York [by] William Rhinelander Stewart ... New York, E. P. Dutton & company [c1924] xix p., 1 l., 542 p. front., plates, ports. 24 cm. "This edition ... is limited to one thousand five hundred copies of which this is number 356." Bibliography: p. [511]-513. [BX5980.N5G7] 24-8510
1. New York. Grace church. I. Title.

New York. Heartsease home for women and babies.

KENNEDY, Annie Richardson. 176.
Mrs.
The Heartsease miracle; a record of God's answer to faith and prayer, by Annie Richardson Kennedy. New York, The Heartsease publishing co. [c1920] 113 p. plates. 19 cm. [HQ316.N6K4] 21-9691
1. New York. Heartsease home for women and babies. I. Title.

New York. John street Methodist church.

UPHAM, Francis Bourne, 287.67471
1862-
The story of old John street Methodist Episcopal church... New York city, 1766-1935 [by] Francis Bourne Upham... [New York? 1935] 84 p. illus. (incl. ports., plan, facsims,) 29 1/2 cm. [BX8481.N5J6] 35-12420
1. New York. John street Methodist church. I. Title.

New York. McAuley Water street mission.

HADLEY, Samuel Hopkins, 1842- 266
1906.
Down in Water street; a story of sixteen years life and work in Water street mission, a sequel to the life of Jerry McAuley, by Samuel H. Hadley... New York, London [etc.] Fleming H. Revell company [c1902] 3 p. l., 3-242 p., 1 l. front., plates, ports. 20 cm. [HV4046.N6H2] 2-20674
1. New York. McAuley Water street mission. I. Title.

WYBURN, Susie May (Patterson) 269
Mrs., 1880-
"But, until seventy times seven", Jeremiah, Samuel, John, by Mrs. S. May Wyburn. New York, Loizeaux brothers [c1936] 192 p. front., ports. 19 cm. The story of the McAuley Water street mission under Jerry McAuley, S. H. Hadley, J. H. Wyburn and Mrs. Wyburn. [HV4046.N6W9] 37-3299
1. McAuley, Jeremiah, 1839-1884. 2. Hadley, Samuel Hopkins, 1842-1906. 3. Wyburn, John Henry, 1858-1921. 4. New York. McAuley Water street mission. I. Title.

New York, N.y. Park Avenue Christian church—History

STARRATT, Rose M.
A sesquicentennial review of the Park Avenue Christian church, new York City [by] Rose M. Starratt. With an introd. by Hampton Adams. [St. Louis] Printed as a private edition by the Bethany Press, [1963] 159 p. Includes bibliography. 66-57054
1. New York, N.y. Park Avenue Christian church—Hist. I. L. Adams, Hampton, 1897- II. Title.

New York (N.Y.)—Synagogues—Pictorial works.

ISRAELOWITZ, 296.6'5'097471
Oscar.
Synagogues of New York City : a pictorial survey in 123 photographs / by Oscar Israelowitz. New York : Dover Publications, 1982. viii, 83, [2] p. : ill. (some col.) ; 28 cm. Bibliography: p. [85] [BM225.N49I85 1982] 19 81-69678 ISBN 0-486-24231-5 (pbk.) : 6.00
1. New York (N.Y.)—Synagogues—Pictorial works. 2. Synagogues—New York (N.Y.)—Pictorial works. I. Title.

New York. New School for Social Research. Research Division.

FIVE German Roman Catholic parishes. New York, Research Division of the New School for Social Research [1956?] 299p. 29cm. (Religion in Germany today, 4) Planographed copy.
1. New York. New School for Social Research. Research Division. I. Attansio, Salvator.

New York. Our Lady of Mercy (Church)

SCHUYLER, Joseph B. 254.22
Northern parish; a sociological and pastoral study. Chicago, Loyola University Press [c.]1960 xxi, 360p. Bibliography: p.333-341. illus., col. maps, diagrs. (part col.) tables. 24cm. (Jesuit studies; contributions to the arts and sciences by members of the Society of Jesus) 60-9600 8.00
1. New York. Our Lady of Mercy (Church) 2. Social survey — New York (City) 3. Church and social problems — New York (City) 4. Catholics in New York (City). I. Title.

New York. Riverside Church.

A brief history of the Riverside Church ... New York, The Riverside Church [c1957] 60p. 23cm. 'Corrections' inserted. Bibliography: p. 59-60.
1. New York. Riverside Church. I. Pendo, Mina.

New York. Rutgers Presbyterian Church.

BOGARDUS, Donald Fred, 285.1747
1915-
This house with glory; a history of Rutgers Presbyterian Church. New York, Rutgers Presbyterian Church [1948948] 62 p. illus., ports. 23 cm. [BX9211.N5R8] 48-4346
1. New York. Rutgers Presbyterian Church. I. Title.

New York. Sain Paul's chapel.

DIX, Morgan, 1827-1908. 283.
Historical recollections of St. Paul's chapel, New York, By the Rev. Morgan Dix ... To which is prefixed an account of the three days' services held in that chapel on occasion of the celebration of its centennial anniversary, Oct. 28th, 29th, and 30th, 1866. Printed by order of the Trinity church. New York, F. J. Huntington and company, 1867. 64 p. front., plan, facsim. 25 cm. [BX5980.N5P3] 1-13621
1. New York. Sain Paul's chapel. I. Title.

New York, St. Ann's Church (Catholle)

BROWNE, Henry Joseph, 282.747
1919-
St. Ann's on East Twelfth Street, New York City, 1852-1952. New York, Roman Catholic Church of St. Ann, 1952. 65 p. illus. 21 cm. [BX4603.N6S25] 52-64995
1. New York, St. Ann's Church (Catholle) I. Title.

New York, St. Bartholomew's parish.

CHORLEY, Edward Clowes, 283.7471
1865-
The centennial history of Saint Bartholomew's church in the city of New York, 1835-1935, by E. Clowes Chorley ... [New York, c1935] xix, 435 p. front., plates, ports. 24 cm. Bibliography: p. 415-418. [BX5980.N5B34] 35-3556
1. New York, St. Bartholomew's parish. 2. Episcopalians in New York (City) I. Title.

New York. St. George's Church.

ANSTICE, Henry, 1841-1922. 283.
History of St. George's church in the city of New York, 1752-1811- 1911, by the Rev. Henry Anstice ... New York, Harper & brothers, 1911. xiv, p., 1 l., 508 p. front., 1 illus., plates, ports., plan. 23 1/2 cm. [BX5980.N5G45] 11-20829
1. New York, St. George's church. I. Title.

HODGES, George, 1856-1919. 283.
The administration of an institutional church; a detailed account of the operation of St. George's parish in the city of New York, by George Hodges ... and John Reichert ... With introductions and comments by President Roosevelt, Bishop Potter and Dr. Rainsford. New York and London, Harper & brothers, 1906. xxii, [1] p., 1 l., 323, [1] p. front. (port.) illus. plates, plans, fold. facsims, tables (1 fold.) 23 cm. [BX5980.N5G47] 6-42355
1. New York. St. George's church. 2. Church work. I. Reichert, John, joint author. II. Title.

MOULTON, Elizabeth.
St. George's Church, New York. With a foreword by Reinhold Niebuhr. [New York, St. George's Church] 1964. xiii, 206 p. illus. 24 cm. 67-17907
1. New York. St. George's Church. I. New York. St. George's Church. II. Title.

New York. St. Luke's church.

TUTTLE, Penelope T. Sturgis 283.
(Cook) "Mrs. H. Croswell Tuttle," 1855-
History of Saint Luke's church in the city of New York 1820-1920, by Mrs. H. Croswell Tuttle. New York, Appeal printing company, 1926. 2 p. l., vi p., 1 l., 571 p. front., illus., plates, ports., map, facsim, 23 1/2 cm. [BX5980.N5L8] 27-8688
1. New York. St. Luke's church. 2. Protestant Episcopal church in the U.S.A.—Clergy. I. Title.

New York. Saint Mark's church.

ANTHON, Henry, 1795-1861. 283.
Parish annals. A sermon giving historical notices of St. Mark's church in the Bowery, N.Y., (from A.D. 1795 to A.D. 1845.) Delivered in said church, May 4, 1845. By Henry Anthon ... Published by the request of the vestry. New York, Stanford and Swords, 1845. 4 p. 1., [5]-58 p. 1 illus. 23 1/2 cm. [BX5980.M5M3] 1-13620
1. New York. Saint Mark's church. I. Title.

New York. St. Martin's Church.

JOHNSON, John Howard, 283.747
1897-
A place of adventure, and other articles and sermons. New York, 1954. 128p. 19cm. [BX5980.N5M34] 54-27861
1. New York. St. Martin's Church. 2. Protestant Episcopal Church in the U.S.A.—Sermons. 3. Sermons, American. I. Title.

JOHNSON, John Howard, 283.747
1897-
A place of adventure; essays and sermons. Foreword by Hughell E. W. Fosbroke. [Rev. ed.] Greenwich, Conn., Seabury Press, 1955. 130p. 19cm. [BX5980.N5M34 1955] 55-13760
1. New York. St. Martin's Church. 2. Protestant Episcopal Church in the U.S.A.—Sermons. 3. Sermons, American. I. Title.

New York. St. Monica's Church.

KELLY, George Anthony, 1916-
The story of St. Monica's parish, New York City, 1879-1954. New York, Monica Press, 1954. 154p. illus., ports. 24cm. A 55
1. New York. St. Monica's Church. I. Title.

New York. St. Patrick's cathedral.

BURTON, Katherine (Kurz) 282.7471
1890-
The dream lives forever : the story of St. Patrick's Cathedral. Foreword by Francis Cardinal Spellman. 1st ed. New York, Longmans, Green, 1960. 238p. illus. 21cm. [BX4603.N6A33] 60-10210
1. New York. St. Patrick's Cathedral. I. Title.

FARLEY, John Murphy, cardinal. 1842-1918. 282.
History of St. Patrick's cathedral, by Most Rev. John M. Farley ... New York city, Society for the propagation of the faith, archdiocese of New York [1908] xxii, 262 p. front., plates, ports., plan. 20 cm. [BX4603.N6A4] 9-15767
1. New York. St. Patrick's cathedral. I. Society for the propagation of the faith. New York (Archdiocese) II. Title.

MCNALLY, Augustin Francis, 1876- 726.6097471
... *Complete guide to St. Patrick's, New York* [by] Augustin McNally ... [New York? 1932] cover-title, 112 p. 6 pl. (incl. 4 port.) on 3 l. 23 1/2 cm. "The guide was put out in November 1931...3rd printing January, 1932." "15th centenary edition, 432-1932. St. Patrick's mission." [BX4603.N6A5 1932] 32-34775
1. New York. St. Patrick's cathedral. I. Title.

New York. St. Patrick's Church.

CARTHY, Mary Peter, Mother. 282.747
Old St. Patrick's, New York's first cathedral; ed. by Thomas J. McMahon. [New York] United States Catholic Historical Society, c1947. 109 p. illus. 23 cm. (United States Catholic Historical Society. Monograph series, 23) "In its original form, this study was a dissertation submitted to the faculty of the Graduate School of Arts and Sciences of the Catholic University of America in partial fulfillment of the requirements for the master of arts degree." Bibliography: p. 105-109. [BX4603.N6A35] 48-4344
1. New York. St. Patrick's Church. I. McMahon, Thomas J., 1909- ed. II. Title. III. Series.

New York. St. Peter's church.

ROCHE, Olin Scott, 1852- 922.3
Forty years of parish life and work, 1883-1923 an autobiography by the Reverend Olin Scott Roche... New York, The Friebele press, 1930. xix, p., 1 l., 388, iv p. front., plates, ports., facsims. 24 1/2 cm. "Selected sermons delivered at St. Peter's": p. 245-388. [BX5995.R57A3] 30-11529
1. New York. St. Peter's church. I. Title.

New York. St. Peter's church, Manhattan (Catholic)

RYAN, Leo Raymond. 282.7471
...Old St. Peter's, the mother church of Catholic New York (1785-1935) [by] Leo Raymond Ryan... New York, The United States Catholic historical society, 1935. xiii, 282 p. plates. 23 cm. (United States Catholic historical society. Monograph series. XV) Half-title: Historical records and studies. "Submitted in partial fulfillment of the requirements for the degree of doctor of philosophy in the Department of history at Fordham university."--Acknowledgments. Bibliography: p. 264-274. [BX4603.N6S63] 36-274
1. New York. St. Peter's church, Manhattan (Catholic) 2. Catholic church in New York (City) I. Title.

New York. St. Peter's church, Manhattan (Protestant Episcopal)

PATTERSON, Samuel White, 1883- 283.7471
Old Chelsea and Saint Peter's church; the centennial history of a New York parish, by Samuel White Patterson ... New York, The Friebele press, 1935. xii, 147 p. front., illus., plates, ports., map, plan, facsims. 24 cm. [BX5980.N5P4] 39-144
1. New York. St. Peter's church, Manhattan (Protestant Episcopal) I. Title. II. Title: Chelsea and Saint Peter's church.

New York. St. Stanislaus' Church.

MAKULEC, Louis L 1907- 282.747
Church of St. Stanislaus Bishop and Martyr. on East Seventh Street in New York City, 1874-1954. New York, Roman Catholic Church of St. Stanislaus, B. M., 1954. 240p. illus. 27cm. [BX4603.N6S72] 54-11904
1. New York. St. Stanislaus' Church. I. Title.

New York school of social work—Registers.

GRADUATE directory, 1898-1956. New York, New York school of social work, Columbia university [1956] 163p. 22cm.
1. New York school of social work—Registers. I. New York School of Social Work.

New York. Shearith Israel congregation. Crosby street synagogue.

POOL, David de Sola, 1885- 296
The Crosby street synagogue (1834-1860) of the Congregation Shearith Israel (founded in the city of New York--1655) By the Rev. D. de Sola Pool ... New York, 1934 52 p. illus. (incl. plan) 23 cm. [BM225.N5S48] 34-22383
1. New York. Shearith Israel congregation. Crosby street synagogue. I. Title.

New York. Shearith Israel congregation. Mill street synagogue.

POOL, David de Sola, 1885- 296
The Mill street synagogue (1730-1817) of the Congregation Shearith Israel (founded in the city of New York in 1655) By the Rev. D. de Sola Pool. New York, 1930. 72 p. illus. (incl. plans. facsims.) 23 cm. [BM225.N3S5] 33-37511
1. New York. Shearith Israel congregation. Mill street synagogue. I. Title.

New York, Sherburne.

SHERBURNE, N. Y. Christ Episcopal Church.
History of Christ Episcopal Church, Sherburne, New York. Copied from original records by Mrs. Edwin P. Smith. [Hamilton? N. Y.] 1955 [i. e. 1956?] 155 l. tables. 29cm. 'The one hundred and twenty-fifth anniversary of Christ Episcopal Church, Sherburne, N. Y., July 7th, 1828-1953': 46p. inserted.
1. New York. Sherburne. I. Smith, Gertrude Howard. I. Title.

SHERBURNE, N. Y. Christ Episcopal Church.
History of Christ Episcopal Church, Sherburne, New York. Copied from original records by Mrs. Edwin P. Smith. Hamilton? N. Y., 1955 [i.e. 1956?] 155 l. tables. 29 cm. "The one hundred and twenty-fifth anniversary of Christ Episcopal Church, Sherburne, N. Y., July 7th, 1828 -- 1953": 46 p. inserted.
1. New York, Sherburne. I. Smith Gertrude Howard. II. Title.

New York. Society of the free church of St. Mary the Virgin.

READ, Newbury Frost, ed. 283.7971
The story of St. Mary's; the Society of the free church of St. Mary the Virgin, New York city, 1868-1931, edited by Newbury Frost Read ... New York, Pub. for the Board of trustees, 1931. 4 p. l., 7-281 p. incl. front. plates, ports. 24 cm. [BX5980.N5M35] 31-9021
1. New York. Society of the free church of St. Mary the Virgin. I. Title.

New York (State)—Biography.

PETERS, Francis E. 271'.53'024
Ours, the making and unmaking of a Jesuit / F. E. Peters. New York : R. Marek Publishers, c1981. 215 p. ; 23 cm. [BX3706.2P47] 19 80-39536 ISBN 0-399-90113-2 : 11.95
1. Jesuits. 2. Peters, Francis E. 3. Jesuits—New York (State)—Biography. 4. New York (State)—Biography. I. Title.

New York (State)—Church history.

CROSS, Whitney R. 277.47
The burned-over district; the social and intellectual history of enthusiastic religion in western New York, 1800-1850 [Gloucester, Mass., P. Smith, 1966, c. 1950] xii, 383p. maps. 21cm. (Harper torchbk., Acad. lib., TB1242N rebound) Bibl. [BR555.N7C7] 4.50
1. New York (State)—Church history. 2. Enthusiasm. I. Title.

CROSS, Whitney R. 277.47
The Burned-over District; the social and intellectual history of enthusiastic religion in western New York, 1800-1850. New York, Harper [1965, c.1950] xiii, 383p. maps. 21cm. (Torchbk., TB1242 N. Acad. lib.) Bibl. [BR555.N7C7] 2.45 pap.,
1. New York (State)—Church history. 2. Enthusiasm. I. Title.

CROSS, Whitney R. 277.47
The Burned-over District : the social and intellectual history of enthusiastic religion in western New York, 1800-1850 / by Whitney R. Cross. New York : Octagon Books, 1981, c1950. xii, 383 p. : maps ; 21 cm. Reprint. Originally published: 1st Harper torchbook ed. New York : Harper & Row, 1965. (Harper tourchbooks. The Academy library) Includes bibliographical references and index. [BR555.N7C7 1981] 19 81-2636 ISBN 0-374-91932-1 : 27.50
1. New York (State)—Church history. 2. Enthusiasm—History. I. Title.

KEESEVILLE, N. Y. First Congregational church. 285.874753
One hundredth anniversary of the organization of the First Congregational church, Keeseville, N. Y. [Keeseville, 1906] 63 p. front., pl., ports. 26 cm. [BX7255.K45A3 1906] 33-22256
I. Title.

KREIDER, Harry Julius, 1896- 284'.1'747
Lutheranism in colonial New York. New York, Arno Press, 1972, [c1942] xviii, 158 p. 24 cm. (Religion in America, series II) Originally presented as the author's thesis, Columbia University, 1942. Bibliography: p. 149-158. [BX8042.N7K7 1972] 78-38452 ISBN 0-405-04072-5
1. Lutheran Church in New York (State) 2. Lutheran Church in New Jersey. 3. New York (State)—Church history. 4. New Jersey—Church history. I. Title.

SYRACUSE, N.Y. First Presbyterian church. 285.
One hundredth anniversary of the First Presbyterian society in the village of Syracuse, 1824-1924; commemorative exercises by the church and society, Friday, Saturday and Sunday, December 12, 13, and 14, 1924. Published by the society. Syracuse, N.Y., 1924. 1 p.l., 7-197 p. front., illus. (incl. ports.) fold. maps. 23 1/2 cm. [BX9211.S87F5] 26-7914
I. Title. II. Title: First Presbyterian society in the village of Syracuse.

TAPPAN, N.Y. Reformed Church. 285'.77'4728
Tappan Reformed Church, 1694-1969 : two and three quarter centuries of service. [Tappan? N.Y., 1969?] 1 v. (unpaged) illus., ports. 29 cm. On cover: Church at the crossroads for 275 years. [BX9531.T3A48] 70-14137
I. Title.

TAYLOR, Mary Christine. 282'.747
A history of the foundations of Catholicism in Northern New York / by Mary Christine Taylor. New York : United States Catholic Historical Society, 1976. xi, 440 p., [1] leaf of plates : ill. ; 23 cm. (Monograph series - United States Catholic Historical Society ; 32) Bibliography: p. 404-438. [BX1415.N7T39] 77-359034
1. Catholic Church in New York (State)—History. 2. New York (State)—Church history. I. Title. II. Series: United States Catholic Historical Society. Monograph series ; 32.

New York (State) — Dayton.

DAYTON, N. Y. St. Paul of the Cross Church.
100th anniversary, 1861-1961, St. Paul of the Cross Church, Dayton, New York. [Program and history. n.p., 1961] 1 v. (unpaged) illus., ports. 23 cm. Cover title. 63-8120
1. New York (State) — Dayton. I. Title.

New York (State) Ellicottville.

ELLICOTTVILLE, N.Y. Holy Name of Mary Church.
A book to commemorate the golden jubilee of Holy Name of Mary Church. Ellicottville, New York, 1909-1959, and the 109th anniversary of the founding of the parish, 1850-1859, July 26th, 27th and 28th. [n.p., 1959] 38 p. illus., ports. 24 cm. 63-20651
1. New York (State) Ellicottville. I. Title.

New York (State)—History—Colonial period, ca. 1600-1775.

ZWIERLEIN, Frederick James, 1881-1960. 277.47
Religion in New Netherland, 1623-1664. New York, Da Capo Press, 1971. vii, 351 p. map. 23 cm. (Civil liberties in American history) Thesis—University of Louvain. Reprint of the 1910 ed. Bibliography: p. 331-351. [F122.1.Z98 1971] 72-120851 ISBN 0-306-71960-6
1. New York (State)—History—Colonial period, ca. 1600-1775. 2. New York (State)—Church history. I. Title. II. Series.

New York (State)—Religion.

SMITH, George Leslie, 1940- 261
Religion and trade in New Netherland; Dutch origins and American development [by] George L. Smith. Ithaca, Cornell University Press [1973] xiii, 266 p. 23 cm. Bibliography: p. 249-259. [BR555.N7S62] 73-8403 ISBN 0-8014-0790-7 12.50
1. New York (State)—Religion. 2. New York (State)—Commerce. 3. Netherlands—Religion. 4. Netherlands—Commerce. 5. Christianity and economics—History. I. Title.

New York. Stephen Wise Free Synagogue.

GOLDSTEIN, Sidney Emanuel, 1879-1955. 296.38
The synagogue and social welfare, a unique experiment (1907-1953) New York, Published for Stephen Wise Free Synagogue and Hebrew Union College-Jewish Institute of Religion by Bloch, 1955. 376p. illus. 24cm. [BM225.N5S8] 55-7541
1. New York. Stephen Wise Free Synagogue. 2. Synagogues. 3. Sociology, Jewish. I. Title.

New York Sunday school commission, inc.

PALMER, Margaretta.
Teachers' notes on our book of worship, illustrated and explained, how to use the prayer book in services, part of the combined course of catechism, church year, and prayer book, or to be used separately as a distinct course, prepared for the Sunday school commission, inc. By Margaretta Palmer... [3d thousand] Milwaukee, Wis., Pub. for the New York Sunday school commission, inc. by the Young churchman co., 1914. xviii, 155 p. 18 1/2 cm. $0.25 "Suggested books and supplies for teachers": p. xii-xvii. 14-19025
1. New York Sunday school commission, inc. I. Title.

New York Sunday-school union, New York.

FERRIS, Isaac, 1798-1873.
Semi-centennial memorial discourse of the New-York Sunday-school union, delivered on the evening of the 25th February, 1866, in the Reformed Dutch church...New York. by Rev. Isaac Ferris...Published at the request of the Board of managers. New York, J. A. Gray & Green, printers, 1866. vi, [7]-120 p. 19 1/2 cm. [BV1503.N45F4] 7-30193
1. New York Sunday-school union, New York. 2. Religious education—New York (City) I. Title.

New York. Trinity church.

BERRIAN, William, 1787-1862. 283.747
Facts against fancy; or, A True and just view of Trinity church. By the Rev. William Berrian ... New York, Pudney & Russell, printers 1855. 74 p. 22 cm. [BX5980.N5T67 1855a] 35-36296
1. New York. Trinity church. I. Title.

CHORLEY, Edward Clowes, 1865- ed. 283.747
Quarter of a millennium; Trinity Church in the city of New York, 1697-1947; foreword by Frederic S. Fleming, rector. Philadelphia, Church Historical Society [1948,c1947] x, 162 p. illus., ports. 24 cm. (Church Historical Society publication 22) "A select bibliography": p. [139]-144. [BX5980.N5T685] 48-2422
1. New York. Trinity Church. 2. Series: Church Historical Society, Philadelphia. Publication 22. I. Title.

DIX, Morgan, 1827-1908, ed. 283.
A history of the parish of Trinity Church in the city of New York, compiled by order of the corporation, and edited by Morgan Dix... New York, Putnam, 1898-1950. 5 v. plates, ports., facsims. 26 cm. Pt. 5 compiled by John A. Dix, edited by Leicester C. Lewis and published for Trinity Church by Columbia University Press. Contents.--Pt. 1. To the close of the rectorship of Dr. Inglis, A. D. 1783--pt. 2. To the close of the rectorship of Dr. Moore, A. D. 1816.--pt. 3. The rectorship of Dr. Hobart from February, A.D. 1816 to August, A.D. 1830.--pt. 4. The close of the rectorship of Dr. Hobart and the rectorship of Dr. Berrian. --pt. 5. The rectorship of Dr. Morgan Dix. Includes bibliographies. [BX5980.N5T7] 98-1806
1. New York. Trinity Church I. Dix, John Adams 1880-1945, comp. II. Lewis, Leicester Crosby, 1887-1949, ed. III. Title.

DIX, Morgan, 1827-1908, ed. 283.
A history of the parish of Trinity church in the city of New York; compiled by order of the corporation, and edited by Morgan Dix ... New York, G. P. Putnam's sons, 1898-1906. 4 v. fronts., plates, ports., facsims. 26 cm. "Of this letter-press edition 750 copies have been prirnted for sale." Contents.--pt. i. To the close of the rectorship of Dr. Inglis, A. D. 1783.--pt. ii. To the close of the rectorship of Dr. Moore, A. D. 1816.--pt. iii. The rectorship of Dr. Hobart from February, A. D. 1816 to August, A. D. 1830--pt. iv. The close of the rectorship of Dr. Hobart and the rectorship of Dr. Berrian. Each volume contains bibliography. [BX5980.N5T7] 98-1806
1. New York. Trinity church. I. Title.

GRIDLEY, Willis Timothy.
Trinity! Break ye my commandments? By Willis Timothy Gridley, a disbarred New York attorney, illegally indicated March 2, 1928. Convicted and sentenced March 15, 1929, before Judge Arthur J. Tuttle, Detroit, Mich ... Grand Rapids, Mich., W. T. Gridley [c1930- v. front., illus., plates (1 fold.) ports., maps (part fold.) fold. plans, fold, facsims., forms (part fold.) 36 cm. Concerns the passing to the Trinity church corporation of the title to the lands on Manhattan island which had originally belonged to the children and heirs of Anneke Jans Bogardus. cf. Pref. "First edition of which 2500 volumes were printed." This copy not numbered. 31-3194
1. Bogardus family. 2. Bogardus, Annetje Jans, 1600?-1663. 3. New York. Trinity church. 4. Land grants—New York (City) I. Title.

JONES, Cave, 1769-1829. 922.373
A solemn appeal to the church: being a plain statement of facts in the matterspending between Dr. Hobart with others, and the author. By the Rev. Cave Jones, A. M., one of the assistant ministers of Trinity church, New-York. Together with an appendix, containing a statement of the case of the Rev. Mr. Feltus: under his own hand ... New-York, Printed for the author, 1811. 2 p. l., 104 p. 22 cm. "Appendix. A brief statement of the persecutions and mal-treatment experienced by the Rev. Henry J. Feltus": p. [89]-104. [BX5995.J7A3] 34-11503
1. Hobart, John Henry, bp., 1775-1830. 2. New York, Trinity church. I. Feltus, Henry James, 1775-1828. II. Title.

MESSITER, Arthur Henry, 1834-1916. 783.8'097471
A history of the choir and music of Trinity Church, New York, from its organization, to the year 1897. New York, AMS Press [1970] viii, 324 p. ports. 23 cm. Reprint of the 1906 ed. [ML200.8.N52T74 1970] 72-137317 ISBN 0-404-04313-5
1. New York. Trinity Church. I. Title.

MILLER, Rutger Blucker, 1805-1877.
Letter and authentic documentary evidence in relation to the Trinity church property, in the city of New York, submitted to the Commissioners of the land office, by Rutger B. Miller. June 21, 1855. Albany, H. H. Van Dyck, printer, 1855. 86 p., 1 l. front. (fold. map) 21 1/2 cm. 37-24937
1. New York. Trinity church. 2. Real property—New York (City) I. Title.

SICKELS, Daniel Edgar, 1825-1914. 200
Argument of the Hon. Daniel E. Sickles, in the Senate of the state of New York, April, 1857, on the Trinity church bill...Reported by Douglas A. Levien. Albany, J. Munsell, 1857. 85 p. 22 cm. [BX5980.N5T67 1857k] 39-18085
1. New York. Trinity church. I. Levien, Douglas. A. II. Title.

SICKLES, Daniel Edgar, 1819-1914. 726.
Argument of the Hon. Daniel E. Sickles, in the Senate of the state of New York, April, 1857, on the Trinity church bill ... Reported by Douglas A. Levien. Albany, J. Munsell, 1857. 85 p. 22 cm. [BX5980.N5T67 1857k] 39-18085
1. New York. Trinity church. I. Levien, Douglas A. II. Title.

THE Trinity Church Association and Trinity Mission House. New York, Trinity Parish, 1956. 87p.
I. Bridgeman, Charles Thorley.

TROUP, Robert, 1757-1832. 283.
Remarks on Trinity church bill, before the council of revision. By Robert Troup ... New York, Printed by T. and J. Swords, 1813; reprinted by J. A. Sparks, 1846. 69 p. 20 1/2 cm. [BX5980.N5T67 1846a] 39-13397
1. New York. Trinity church. I. Title.

New York. Union theological seminary.

COFFIN, Henry Sloane, 1877- 207.747
A half century of Union Theological Seminary, 1896-1945 an informal history. New York, Scribner, 1954. 261p. 21cm. [BV4070.U66C6] 54-6526
1. New York, Union Theological Seminary. I. Title.

NEW York. Trinity Church. 283.747
A guide book to Trinity Church and the Parish of Trinity Church in the city of New York, founded 1697. [rev. ed. New York, 1950] 59 p. illus. 22 cm. [BX5980.N5T675] 50-30969
I. Title.

NEW York. Union theological seminary. Founded 1836, by New school Presbyterians as New York theological seminary (open to students of all denominations and under no ecclesiastical control) Incorporated 1839 as Union theological seminary. At the union of the New school and Old school divisions of the Presbyterian church in the U.S.A. in 1870, the seminary conceded to the General assembly certain rights of control, but in 1892 this concession was formally withdrawn, and since that date it has been ecclesiastically independent. In 1905 the assent to the Westminster standards required of directors and professors was withdrawn, and it became completely undenominational. 20-21819

NEW York. Union theological seminary. 016.
Triennial catalogue. New York, J. A. Gray & Green, printers, 18 v. 23-23 1/2 cm. [BV4070.U64] CA 7
I. Title.

PRENTISS, George Lewis, 1816-1903.
The Union theological seminary in the city of New York: historical and biographical sketches of its first fifty years. By George Lewis Prentiss ... New York, A. D. F. Randolph and co., 1889. vi, 294 p. front., pl. 25 cm. E 12
1. New York. Union theological seminary. I. Title.

PRENTISS, George Lewis, 1816-1903. 016.
The Union theological seminary in the city of New York: its design and another decade of its history. With a sketch of the life and public services of Charles Butler, LL. D. By G. L. Prentiss. Asbury Park, N. J., M., W. & C. Pennypacker, 1899. viii p., 1 l., 576 p. incl. facsim. front (port.) 25 cm. [BV4070.U66P8] 99-5455
1. Butler, Charles, 1802-1897. 2. New York. Union theological seminary. I. Title.

New York. Union theological seminary-Alumni.

ALUMNI directory, 1836-1958. New York, Published by the Alumni office, 1958. xxx, 427p. 24cm.
1. New York. Union theological seminary-Alumni. I. New York. Union Theological Seminary.

New York. Washington Heights Baptist church.

[STOUT, Charles B.] 286.
A history of the Stanton street Baptist church, in the city of New York: with a sketch of its pastors, and a register of the entire membership. New York, Sheldon & company, 1860. viii, [9]-220 p. 17 cm. By Charles B. Stout and his associate in the clerkship of the church, Thomas J. Grout. cf. G. H. Hansell, Reminscences of Baptist churches ... in New York city. [BX6480.N5W3] 21-6488
1. New York. Washington Heights Baptist church. I. Title.

New York. Washington Heights congregation.

HERTZ, Emanuel, 1870-1940, ed. 296.097471
Washington Heights congregation; installation exercises of Rabbi Max Drob ... January 25, 1920 ... Edited and compiled by Emmanuel Hertz ... [New York, Madison square press, inc., 1920] 2 p. l., 9-69 p. illus. (ports.) 24 cm. [BM755.D7H4] 40-25671
1. Drob, Max, 1887- 2. New York. Washington Heights congregation. I. Title.

New Zealand—Economic conditions.

MARA Tautane (Society). 330.9'931
Trade, guns, and bibles / by Mara Tautane. [Auckland?] : Mara Tautane, 1976. 73 p. ; 20 cm. Includes index. Bibliography: p. [70]-71. [HC663.M37 1976] 77-372384
1. New Zealand—Economic conditions. 2. New Zealand—Colonization. 3. New Zealand—Foreign economic relations—Great Britain. 4. Great Britain—Foreign economic relations—New Zealand. I. Title.

Newark, N. J. First Presbyteran church.

STEARNS, Jonathan French, 1808-1889. 261
First church in Newark. Historical discourses, relating to the First Presbyterian church in Newark; originally delivered to the congregation of that church during the month of January, 1851. By Jonathan F. Stearns ... with notes ... Newark [N. J.] Printed at the Daily advertiser office, 1853. xiii, [1], 320 p. front., ports., fold. map. 24 cm. [F144.N6S7] 6-37983
1. Newark, N. J. First Presbyteran church. I. Title.

Newark, N. J. Grace church.

BASTAILLE, Edward Francis, 1904- 283.74932
Grace church in Newark; the first hundred years, 1837-1937 [by] Edward F. Bataille. [Newark, N. J., The Kenny press, inc., c1937] xi, 140 p. front., illus., plates, ports. 26 cm. [BX5980.N6G7] 37-8536
1. Newark, N. J. Grace church. I. Title.

Newark, N. J.—Nuns and nunneries.

THE nuns of Newark; brief sketches of the various religious communities of women in theArchdiocese of Newark. [Newark, N. J., 1956] 69p. illus.
1. Newark, N. J.—Nuns and nunneries. 2. Sisterhoods. I. Furlong, William F comp.

Newark, N.J. Second Presbyterian church.

MACE, John Wilson, 1885- 285.174932
Clee of the lighted tower, by John W. Mace and Irving T. Gumb. New York [etc.] Fleming H. Revell company [c1935] 159 p. front. (port.) illus. 19 1/2 cm. [BX9211.N55S37] 36-1894
1. Clee, Lester Harrison, 1888- 2. Newark, N.J. Second Presbyterian church. 3. Church work. I. Gumb, Irving Turple, 1892- joint author. II. Title.

Newbury, Mass. First church.

LITTLE, Eliza Adams, ed. 285.87445
The first parish, Newbury, Massachusetts 1635-1935; editors, Eliza Adams Little [and] Lucretia Little Ilsley. Contributors, Marion Stackpole Bailey, Harriot Withington Colman, Elizabeth Hale Little Ilsley [and others] ... Newburyport, News publishing co., inc., printers, 1935. 104 p. incl. front. plates, ports. 24 cm. Bibliography: p. 103-104. [BX7255.N33F5] 40-31210
1. Newbury, Mass. First church. I. Ilsley, Lucretia Little, 1906- joint ed. II. Title.

Newburyport, Mass. First Presbyterian church.

NEWBURYPORT, Mass. First Presbyterian church. 285.
Origin and annals of "The Old south," First Presbyterian church and parish, in Newburyport, Mass., 1746-1896. Edited by Horace C. Hovey ... Published for the society by a committee. Boston, Damrell & Upham, 1896. 4 p. l., 3-5 p., 1 l., 7-223 p. front., 1 illus., plates, ports. 23 cm. [BX9211.N6F46] 42-27032
I. Hovey, Horace Carter, 1833-1914, ed. II. Title.
Contents omitted.

WILLIAMS, Samuel Porter, 1779-1826. 285.
Historical account of the First Presbyterian church and society in Newburyport, Massachusetts, addressed to the congregation, worshipping in Federal street, July 9, 1826. By Samuel P. Williams ... Published at the request of the church. Saratoga Springs, G. M. Davison, 1826. 67, [1] p. 27 cm. [BX9211.N6F5] 1-9342
1. Newburyport, Mass. First Presbyterian church. I. Title.

Newby, Elizabeth Loza.

†NEWBY, Elizabeth Loza. 301.44'43'0924 B
A migrant with hope / Elizabeth Loza Newby. Nashville : Broadman Press, c1977. 138 p. ; 20 cm. [BX7795.N43A34] 76-53980 ISBN 0-8054-7218-5 : 4.95
1. Newby, Elizabeth Loza. 2. Friends, Society of—United States—Biography. 3. Mexican Americans—Biography. I. Title.

Newby, Grace V.

†NEWBY, Grace V. 133.9'3
A lamp unto our faith / by Grace V. Newby & Clarice Albritton. Marina del Rey, Calif. : DeVorss, c1976. iv, 144 p. ;

22 cm. [BF1283.N4A35] 76-24514 ISBN 0-87516-218-5 pbk. : 3.95
1. Newby, Grace V. 2. Albritton, Clarice. 3. Mediums—United States. I. Albritton, Clarice, joint author. II. Title.

Newell, Mrs. Harriet (Atwood) "Mrs. Samuel Newell," 1793-1812.

RAGLAND, Nathaniel M. 922
Leaves from mission fields; or, Memoirs of Mrs. Harriet Newell, Mrs. Ann Judson, Miss Hattie L. Judson, Mrs. Josephine Smith, Charles E. Garst, by N. M. Ragland ... St. Louis, Christian publishing company, 1900. x p., 1 l., 278 p. ports. 20 cm. [BV3700.R3] 0-5540
1. Newell, Mrs. Harriet (Atwood) "Mrs. Samuel Newell," 1793-1812. 2. Judson, Mrs. Ann (Hasseltine) 1789-1826. 3. Judson, Hattie L. 1861-1897. 4. Smith, Mrs. Josephine (Wood) 1850-1885. 5. Garst, Charles Elias, 1853-1808. 6. Missions, Foreign. I. Title.

Newhouse, Flower Arlene Sechler, 1909-

NEWHOUSE, Flower 248'.22'0924 B
Arlene Sechler, 1909-
Insights into reality : revelations through the extrasensory perception of Flower A. Newhouse / edited by Stephen and Phyllis Isaac. 1st ed. Escondido, Calif. : Christward Ministry, c1975. 191 p. ; 23 cm. [BP605.C5N424] 75-36869
1. Newhouse, Flower Arlene Sechler, 1909- 2. Christward Ministry. I. Isaac, Stephen, 1925- II. Isaac, Phyllis.

Newington, Conn. Congregational church.

BRACE, Joab, 1781-1861. 974
Half-century discourse. History of the church in Newington: its doctrine, its ministers, its experience: presented in the discourse delivered on Tuesday the 16th January, 1855, on his relinquishment of active service, at the close of half a century from his ordination in that place, by J. Brace, D. D. Pub. by the Ecclesiastical society. Hartford, Press of Case, Tiffany and company, 1855. 75 p. front. (port.) 23 cm. [BX7255.N64C55] [F104.N62B7] 285. 19-4226
1. Newington, Conn. Congregational church. I. Title.

Newlin, Mrs. Mary E. (York) ed.

NEWLIN, Alexander Willis, 922.773
1856-1895.
A successful life. Sketches of the life of Rev. Alex. W. Newlin, with some of his sermons and outlines. By Mary E. Newlin ... Alliance, O., The R. M. Scranton printing co. [1896] 191 p. port. 19 1/2 cm. [BX8495.N37A3] 36-37416
1. Newlin, Mrs. Mary E. (York) ed. 2. Methodism—Sermons. I. Title.

Newman, Albert Henry, 1852-1933.

EBY, Frederick, 1874- 922.673
Newman, the church historian; a study in Christian personality, by Frederick Eby ... Nashville, Tenn., Broadman press [1946] 10 p. l., 206 p. front., plates, ports. 23 cm. [BR139.N48E2] 46-8652
1. Newman, Albert Henry, 1852-1933. I. Title.

Newman clubs—History.

EVANS, John Whitney, 267'.62'2
1931-
The Newman movement : Roman Catholics in American higher education, 1883-1971 / John Whitney Evans. Notre Dame, Ind. : University of Notre Dame Press, c1980. xvi, 248 p. ; 24 cm. Includes bibliographical references and index. [BX810.E9] 79-18214 ISBN 0-268-01453-1 : 14.95
1. Newman clubs—History. 2. Church work with students—Catholic Church. 3. Church work with students—United States. 4. Church and college in the United States. 5. United States—Church history. I. Title.

Newman, John Henry, Cardinal, 1801-1890.

ABBOTT, Edwin Abbott, 1838- 922.
1926.
The Anglican career of Cardinal Newman, by Edwin A. Abbott.... London and New York, Macmillan and co., 1892. 2 v. 22 1/2 cm. [BX4705.N5A7] 1-22780
1. Newman, John Henry, cardinal, 1801-1890. I. Title.

ADAMS, Henry Austin, 1861- 204
Orations of Henry Austin Adams; introduction by His Eminence, Cardinal Gibbons. St. Paul, Minn., The Adams-Cannon company, 1902. xii, 214 p. front. (port.) 21 cm. Contents.Cardinal Newman.--Lee xxii.--D. Sir Thomas Mere--The destiny of Eria.--Dr. Wisdthurst. [BX890.A3] 2-30123
1. Newman, John Henry, cardinal, 1801-1890 2. Leo XIII, pope, 1810-1903 3. More, Sir Thomas, Saint, 1478-1535. 4. Windthorst, Ludwig Josef Ferdinand Custav, 1812-1891 5. Ireland. I. Title.

ATKINS, Gaius Glenn, 922.242
1868-
... Life of Cardinal Newman, by Gaius Glenn Atkins ... New York and London, Harper & brothers, 1931. xi p., 1 l., 338 p. front. (port.) 21 cm. (Creative lives) [BX4705.N5A8] 31-18017
1. Newman, John Henry, cardinal, 1801-1890. I. Title.

BARRY, William Francis, 922.242
1819-1930.
... Newman, by William Barry ... New York, C. Scribner's sons, 1904. x p., 1 l., 225 p. front., plates. ports. 20 cm. (Literary lives) [BX4705.N5B3] 4-6011
1. Newman, John Henry, cardinal, 1801-1899. I. Title.

BENARD, Edmond Darvil. 922.242
A preface to Newman's theology, by Rev. Edmond Darvil Benard ... St. Louis, Mo. and London, B. Herder book co., 1945. xv, 234 p. 21 cm. Bibliography: p. [208]-223. [BX4705.N5B4] 45-926
1. Newman, John Henry, cardinal, 1801-1890. 2. Theology, Doctrinal—Hist. 3. Dogma. I. Title.

BIEMER, Gunter. 231'.74'0924
Newman on tradition. Translated and edited by Kevin Smyth. [New York] Herder and Herder [1967] xx, 207 p. facsim. 22 cm. Revised version of the original German edition; Uberlieferung und Offenbarung published in 1961. Bibliography: p. 193-203. [BX4705.N5B513 1967b] 66-21076
1. Newman, John Henry, Cardinal, 1801-1890. 2. Tradition (Theology)—History of doctrines. I. Smyth, Kevin, ed. and tr. II. Title.

BOUYER, Louis 922.242
Newman; his life and spirituality [Tr. from the French by J. Lewis May] New York, Meridian Books [1960, c.1958] xii, 391p. (Bibl. footnotes) 19cm. (M87) 1.55 pap.,
1. Newman, John Henry, Cardinal, 1801-1890. I. Title.

BOUYER, Louis, 1913- 922.242
Newman; his life and spirituality. [Translated by J. Lewis May] New York, Meridian Books [1960, c1958] xiii, 391 p. 19 cm. (Meridian books) "M87." [BX4705.N5B653] 60-6782
1. Newman, John Henry, Cardinal, 1801-1890. I. Title.

CATHOLIC Renascence 922.242
Society.
A Newman symposium; report on the tenth annual meeting of the Catholic Renascence Society at the College of the Holy Cross, Worcester, Mass., April 1952. Edited by Victor R. Yanitelli. [New York] Fordham University [1952;] vi, 169p. 25cm. Bibliographical footnotes. [BX4705.N5C3] 53-1801
1. Newman, John Henry, Cardinal, 1801-1890. I. Yanitelli, Victor R., ed. II. Title.

CHETWOOD, Thomas B. 922.
Handbook of Newman, by Thomas B. Chetwood ... New York, Schwartz, Kirwin & Fause [c1927] v, 90 p. 18 cm. "A textbook for the beginning of Freshman English."--Foreword. [PR5109.C5] 27-16898
1. Newman, John Henry, cardinal, 1801-1890. I. Title.

CHETWOOOD, Thomas Bradbury, 922.
1881-.
Handbook of Newman, by Thomas B. Chetwood ... New York, Schwartz, Kirwin & Fauss [c1927] v. 90 p. 18 cm. "A textbook for the beginning of freshman English."--Foreword. [PR5109.C5] 27-16898
1. Newman, John Henry, cardinal, 1801-1890. I. Title.

COULSON, John, 1919- 262.7'0924
Newman and the common tradition: a study of the Church and society. Oxford, Clarendon, 1970. x, 279 p. 23 cm. Bibliography: p. [256]-265. [BV598.C67 1970] 70-17853 50/-
1. Newman, John Henry, Cardinal, 1801-1890. 2. Church—History of doctrines—19th century. 3. Religion and language. 4. Sociology, Christian. I. Title.

CULLER, Arthur Dwight. 922.242
The imperial intellect; a study of Newman's educational ideal. New Haven, Yale University Press, 1955. xii, 327p. illus., ports., facsims. 24cm. Bibliography: p.273-278. Bibliographical references included in 'Notes' (p. 279-316) [LB675.N45C8] 55-8700
1. Newman, John Henry, Cardinal, 1801-1890. I. Title.

D'ARCY, Martin Cyril, 121'.6
1888-
The nature of belief / by M. C. D'Arcy. Westport, Conn. : Greenwood Press, 1976, c1958. p. cm. Reprint of the ed. published by Herder, St. Louis. [BD215.D3 1976] 72-10693 ISBN 0-8371-6616-0 lib.bdg. : 15.50
1. Newman, John Henry, Cardinal, 1801-1890. An essay in aid of a grammar of assent. 2. Belief and doubt. 3. Knowledge, Theory of. 4. Faith. 5. Theism. I. Title.

DARK, Sidney, 262'.135'0924 B
1874-1947.
Newman. [Folcroft, Pa.] Folcroft Library Editions, 1973. p. Reprint of the 1934 ed. published by Duckworth, London, which was issued as no. 36 of Great lives. Bibliography: p. [BX4705.N5D3 1973] 73-7641 ISBN 0-8414-1870-5 (lib. bdg.)
1. Newman, John Henry, Cardinal, 1811-1890.

DESSAIN, Charles Stephen. 230'.2
The spirituality of John Henry Newman / C. S. Dessain ; [cover ill., Martha A. Nash]. Minneapolis, Minn. : Winston Press, [1980] c1977. 154 p. ; 22 cm. Edition of 1977 published under title: Newman's spiritual themes. Includes bibliographical references. [BX4705.N5D43 1980] 19 80-51108 ISBN 0-03-057843-4 (pbk.) : 4.95
1. Newman, John Henry, Cardinal, 1801-1890. I. Title.

DONAHUE, George Joseph. 922.
John Henry, cardinal Newman, by George J. Donahue ... Boston, Mass., The Stratford company, 1927. 4 p. l., [vii]-xviii, 21-224 p., 1 l. 2 t. (incl. front.) 19 cm. "Newman's choicest passages": p. [135]-224. Bibliography: 1 leaf at end. [BX4705.N5D6] 27-24790
1. Newman, John Henry, cardinal, 1801-1890. I. Title.

DONALD, Gertrude. 283'.43
Men who left the movement: John Henry Newman, Thomas W. Allies, Henry Edward Manning, Basil William Maturin. Freeport, N.Y., Books for Libraries Press [1967] viii, 422 p. 21 cm. (Essay index reprint series) Reprint of the 1933 ed. [BX5100.D6 1967] 67-23207
1. Newman, John Henry, Cardinal, 1801-1890. 2. Allies, Thomas William, 1813-1903. 3. Manning, Henry Edward, Cardinal, 1808-1892. 4. Maturin, Basil William, 1847-1915. 5. Oxford movement. I. Title.

ELBERT, John Aloysius, 234.2
1895-
Evolution of Newman's conception of faith [by] Rev. John A. Elbert ... Philadelphia, Pa., The Dolphin press [1933] 100 p. 23 cm. Issued also as thesis (PH.D) University of Cincinnati, under title; Newman's conception of faith prior to 1845; a genectic presentation and synthesis. Bibliography: p. 96-100. [BT771.N4E6 1933] 33-25964
1. Newman, John Henry, cardinal, 1801-1890. 2. Faith. I. Title.

ELWOOD, J. Murray. 201'.11
Kindly light : the spiritual vision of John Henry Newman / J. Murray Elwood ; [front cover line drawing after a portrait by George Richardson]. Notre Dame, Ind. : Ave Maria Press, c1979. 127 p. : ill. ; 23 cm. Includes bibliographical references. [BX4705.N5E48] 79-52444 ISBN 0-87793-185-2 (pbk.) : 2.95
1. Newman, John Henry, Cardinal, 1801-1890 2. Cardinals—England—Biography. I. Title.

FABER, Geoffrey 262'.135'0924 B
Cust, Sir, 1889-1961.
Oxford apostles : a character study of the Oxford movement / by Geoffrey Faber. New York : AMS Press, [1976] p. cm. Reprint of the 1936 ed. published by Faber and Faber, London. Includes index. Bibliography: p. [BX5100.F3 1976] 75-30022 ISBN 0-404-14027-0 : 32.50
1. Newman, John Henry, Cardinal, 1801-1890. 2. Church of England—Biography. 3. Oxford movement. I. Title.

FEMIANO, Samuel D. 262'.15
Infallibility of the laity; the legacy of Newman [by] Samuel D. Femiano. [New York] Herder and Herder [1967] xiii, 142 p. 22 cm. Includes bibliographical references. [BX4705.N5F4] 67-27737
1. Newman, John Henry, Cardinal, 1801-1890. 2. Laity—Catholic Church. I. Title.

FEY, William R., 234'.2'0924
1942-
Faith and doubt : the unfolding of Newman's thought on certainty / by William R. Fey ; with a pref. by Charles Stephen Dessain. Shepherdstown, W.Va. : Patmos Press, 1976. xix, 229 p. ; 23 cm. Includes index. Bibliography: p. 203-213. [BT50.F45] 75-38101 ISBN 0-915762-02-1 : 16.95
1. Newman, John Henry, Cardinal, 1801-1890. 2. Faith and reason. 3. Belief and doubt. I. Title.

FRIEDEL, Francis J. 922.
The Mariology of Cardinal Newman, by Rev. Francis J. Friedel ... New York, Cincinnati [etc.] Benziger brothers, 1928. xvi p., 1 l., 392 p. 19 cm. Bibliography: p. xv-xvi. [BX4705.N5F7] 29-781
1. Newman John Henry, cardinal, 1801-1890. 2. Mary, Virgin—Theology. I. Title.

GARNETT, Emmeline, 262.1350924
1924-
Tormented angel; a life of John Henry Newman. New York, Ariel Bks. [1966] 136p. 22cm. Bibl. [BX4705.N5G3] 66-18431 3.25
1. Newman, John Henry, Cardinal, 1801-1890. I. Title.
Ages 14-up. Available from Farrar.

GARNETT, Emmeline, 262.1350924 B
1924-
Tormented angel; a life of John Henry Newman. New York, Ariel Books [1966] 136 p. 22 cm. Bibliography: p. 133. [BX4705.N5G3] 66-18431
1. Newman, John Henry, Cardinal, 1801-1890. I. Title.

GRAEF. HILDA C. 248.2'0924
God and myself; the spirituality of John Henry Newman [by] Hilda Graef. [1st Amer. ed.] New York, Hawthorn [1968] 206p. 23cm. Bibl. [BX4705.N5G74 1968] 67-2465 5.95
1. Newman, John Henry, Cardinal, 1801-1890. I. Title.

GUITTON, Jean 262
The Church and the laity: from Newman to Vatican II. Tr. [from French] by Malachy Gerard Carroll. Staten Island, N.Y., Alba [c.1965] 176p. 22cm. [BX1920.G813] 65-15730 3.50
1. Newman, John Henry, Cardinal. 1801-1890. 2. Laity—Catholic Church. I. Title.

HARROLD, Charles 922.242
Frederick, 1897-
John Henery Newman; an expository and critical study of his mind, thought and art, By Charles Frederick Harrold. London, New York [etc.] Longmans, Green & co.,

inc., 1945. xv, 472 p. 21 1/2 cm. "First edition." Bibliographical references included in "Notes" (p. 378-439) "A select bibliography": p. 440-452. [BX4705.N5H33] 45-9046
1. Newman, John Henry, cardinal, 1801-1890. I. Title.

HARROLD, Charles Frederick, 1897-1948 262.1350924
John Henry Newman; an expository and critical study of his mind, thought and art. Hamden, Conn., Archon [dist. Shoe String] 1966[c.1945] xv, 472p. 21cm. Bibl. [BX4705.N5H33] 66-16086 11.00
1. Newman, John Henry, Cardinal, 1801-1890. I. Title.

HENRY, Caroline Vinton. 922.
Personal reminiscences of Cardinal Newman; a tribute by an American lady, Caroline Vinton Henry. Illustrated with numerous engravings. Introduction by Miss Eliza Allen Starr. Chicago, J. S. Hyland & company, 1899. 7 p. l., 9-181 p. incl. illus., plates, ports. 20 cm. [BX4705.N5H4] 0-497
1. Newman, John Henry, cardinal, 1801-1890. I. Title.

HOLLIS, Christopher, 1902- 262'.135'0924
Newman and the modern world. [1st ed. in the U.S.A.] Garden City, N. Y., Doubleday [1968, c1967] 230 p. 22 cm. Bibliography: p. 222-223. [BX4705.N5H63 1968] 67-11182
1. Newman, John Henry, Cardinal, 1801-1890. I. Title.

HOUGHTON, Walter Edwards, 1904- 230.2
The art of Newman's Apologia, by Walter E. Houghton. [Hamden, Conn.] Archon Books, 1970 [c1945] ix, 116 p. port. 21 cm. Includes bibliographical references. [BX4705.N5A38 1970] 78-120369
1. Newman, John Henry, Cardinal, 1801-1890. Apologia pro vita sua. I. Title.

HOUPPERT, Joseph W., comp. 262'.135'0924
John Henry Newman, edited by Joseph W. Houppert. Contributors: Northrop Frye [and others] St. Louis, Herder [1968] 108, [1] p. 18 cm. (The Christian critic series) Contents.Contents.—The problem of spiritual authority in the nineteenth century, by N. Frye.—Newman's essays on development in its intellectual milieu, by W. J. Ong.—Newman's idea of literature: a humanist's spectrum, by H. M. Petitpas.—Newman the poet, by J. Pick.—The thinker in the church: the spirit of Newman, by F. O'Malley.—Bibliography (p. [109]) [BX4705.N5H66] 68-25496
1. Newman, John Henry, 1801-1890. I. Frye, Northrop.

HUTTON, Richard Holt, 1826-1897. 262'.135'0924 B
Cardinal Newman / by Richard H. Hutton. 2d ed. New York : AMS Press, 1977. xi, 268 p. : port. ; 18 cm. Reprint of the 1891 ed. published by Methuen, London, in series: English leaders of religion. Includes bibliographical references. [BX4705.N5H8 1977] 75-30029 ISBN 0-404-14033-5 : 16.00
1. Newman, John Henry, Cardinal, 1801-1890. 2. Cardinals—England—Biography. I. Series: English leaders of religion.

HUTTON, Richard Holt, 1826-1897. 922.242
Cardinal Newman, by Richard H. Hutton. Boston and New York, Houghton, Mifflin and company, 1890. 3 p. l., 251 p. front. (port.) 20 cm. [BX4705.N5H3 1890] 37-6729
1. Newman, John Henry, cardinal, 1801-1890. I. Title.

HUTTON, Richard Holt, 1826-1897. 922.
Cardinal Newman, by Richard H. Hutton. 2d ed. Boston and New York, Houghton, Mifflin and company, 1891. 2 p. l., 251 p. front. (port.) 20 cm. [BX4705.N5H8 1891] 18-167
1. Newman, John Henry, cardinal, 1801-1890. I. Title.

JAEGER, A J. 783.
... The dream of Gerontius by Cardinal Newman, set to music for mezzo-soprano, tenor, and bass soli, chorus, and orchestra, by Edward Elgar. (Op. 38) Book of words, with analytical and descriptive notes by A. J. Jaeger ... London, Novello and company, limited; New York, Novello, Ewer and co. [1900!] 51 p. 25 x 19 cm. (Novello's series of the words of oratorios, cantatas, &c.) [MT115.E41] 6-2345
I. Elgar, Edward William, Sir, 1857- the dream of Gerontius. II. Title.

JUERGENS, Sylvester Peter, 1894- 248
Newman on the psychology of faith in the individual, by Sylvester P. Juergens ... New York, The Macmillan company, 1928. xvii p., 1 l., 288 p. 20 cm. Bibliography: p. 261-264. [BT771.N4J8] 28-21075
1. Newman, John Henry, cardinal, 1801-1890. 2. Faith. 3. Psychology, Religious. I. Title. II. Title: The psychology of faith in the individual.

KIENER, Mary Aloysi, sister, 1882. 922.242
John Henry Newman, the romantic, the friend, the leader, by Sister Mary Aloysi Kiener ... Foreword by Reverend John Cavanaugh ... introduction by G. K. Chesterton. Boston, Mass., Collegiate press corporation, 1933. 4 p. l., xxiii p., 2 l., 510 p. front., plates, ports. 24 1/2 cm. "First edition." [Secular name:Mary Agnes Kiener Bibliography: p. [457]-466. [BX4705.N5K5] 33-34985
1. Newman, John Henry, cardinal, 1801-1890. I. Title.

LAPATI, Americo D. 262'.135'0924
John Henry Newman, by Americo D. Lapati. New York, Twayne Publishers [1972] 161 p. 21 cm. (Twayne's English authors series, TEAS 140) Bibliography: p. 149-155. [BX4705.N5L28] 73-187619 5.500
1. Newman, John Henry, Cardinal, 1801-1890.

LASH, Nicholas. 230'.2
Newman on development : the search for an explanation in history / Nicholas Lash. Shepherdstown, W. Va. : Patmos Press, 1975. xiii, 264 p. ; 23 cm. Includes indexes. Bibliography: p. [209]-243. [BT21.L3] 75-16649 ISBN 0-915762-01-3 : 17.50
1. Newman, John Henry, Cardinal, 1801-1890. An essay on the development of Christian doctrine. 2. Catholic Church—Doctrinal and controversial works—Catholic authors. 3. Dogma, Development of. I. Title.

LESLIE, Shane, Sir, bart., 1885- 920.042
Studies in sublime failure. Freeport, N.Y., Books for Libraries Press [1970] 295, [1] p. ports. 23 cm. (Essay index reprint series) Reprint of the 1932 ed. Contents.Contents.—Cardinal Newman.—Charles Stewart Parnell.—Coventry Patmore.—Lord Curzon.—Moreton Frewen.—Bibliographical note (p. [296]) [CT782.L55 1970] 70-117817
1. Newman, John Henry, Cardinal, 1801-1890. 2. Parnell, Charles Stewart, 1846-1891. 3. Patmore, Coventry Kersey Dighton, 1823-1896. 4. Curzon, George Nathaniel Curzon, 1st marquis, 1859-1925. 5. Frewen, Moreton, 1853-1924. I. Title. II. Title: Sublime failure.

MCGRATH, Fergal, 1895-
Newman's university; idea and reality. London, New York, Longmans, Green [1951] xv. 537 p. 22 cm. "Works consulted": p. 512-522. A52
1. Newman, John Henry, Cardinal, 1801-1890. 2. Universities and colleges. 3. Education, Higher. 4. Catholic University of Ireland, Dublin. I. Title.

MAY, James Lewis, 1873- 922.242
Cardinal Newman. Westminster, Md., Newman Press, 1951. 309 p. port. 22 cm. "A list of Newman's works": p. 305-306. [BX4705.N5M43 1951] 51-8610
1. Newman, John Henry, Cardinal, I. Title.

MAY, James Lewis, 1873- 922.242
Cardinal Newman, by J. Lewis May. New York, L. MacVeagh, The Dial press; Toronto, Longmans, Green & co. [1930] xii p., 1 l., 15-309 p. front. (port.) 21 1/2 cm. "A list of Newman's works": p. 305-306. [BX4705.N5M43] 30-5073
1. Newman, John Henry, cardinal, 1801-1890. I. Title.

MAY, James Lewis, 1873- 922.242
Cardinal Newman; a study by J. Lewis May ... New York, Longmans, Green & co., 1937. x, 268 [1] p. 19 cm. "Printed in Great Britain." "A list of Newman's works": p. 259-260. [BX9705.N5M43 1937] 37-22377
1. Newman, John Henry, cardinal, 1801-1890. I. Title.

MIDDLETON, Robert Dudley. 262'.135'0924 B
Newman & Bloxam; an Oxford friendship, by R. D. Middleton. Westport, Conn., Greenwood Press [1971] x, 261 p. illus. 23 cm. Reprint of the 1947 ed. Includes bibliographical references. [BX4705.N5M5 1971] 74-104246 ISBN 0-8371-3986-4
1. Newman, John Henry, Cardinal, 1801-1890. 2. Bloxam, John Rouse, 1807-1891.

MIDDLETON, Robert Dudley. 922.242
Newman & Bloxam; an Oxford friendship. London, New York, Oxford Univ. Press, 1947. x, 261 p. illus., port., facsims. 22 cm. Bibliographical footnotes. [BX4705.N5M5] A 48
1. Newman, John Henry, Cardinal, 1801-1890. 2. Bloxman, John Rouse, 1807-1891. I. Title.

MIDDLETON, Robert Dudley. 922.242
Newman & Bloxam; an Oxford friendship. London, New York, Oxford Univ. Press, 1947. x, 261 p. illus., port., facsims. 22 cm. Bibliographical footnotes. [BX4705.N5M5] A 48
1. Newman, John Henry, Cardinal, 1801-1890. 2. Bloxman, John Rouse, 1807-1891. I. Title.

MIDDLETON, Robert Dudley. 922.242
Newman at Oxford; his religious development. London, New York, Oxford University Press, 1950. viii, 284 p. illus., ports. 23 cm. [BX4705.N5M52] 51-5457
1. Newman, John Henry, Cardinal, 1801-1890. I. Title.

MOODY, John, 1868- 922.242
John Henry Newman, by John Moody. New York, Sheed and Ward, 1945. ix p., 2 l., 353 p. 2 port. (incl. front.) 22 cm. Bibliography: p. 341-348. [BX4705.N5M6] 45-9074
1. Newman, John Henry, cardinal, 1801-1890. I. Title.

NEWCOMB, Covelle. 922.242
The red hat; a story of John Henry cardinal Newman, by Covelle Newcomb, illustrated by Addison Burbank. London, New York [etc.] Longmans, Green and co., 1941. vii, [1] p., 1 l., 278 p. illus. 22 cm. Illustrated lining-papers. "First edition." Bibliography: p. 277-278. [PR5108.N4] 41-24953
1. Newman, John Henry, cardinal, 1801-1890. I. Title.

NEWMAN, Bertram, 1886- 922.
Cardinal Newman; a biographical and literary study, by Bertram Newman. New York & London, The Century co. [c1925] ix, 223 p. 20 1/2 cm. "Short bibliography": p. 213-218. [BX4705.N5N4 1925 a] 25-17836
1. Newman, John Henry, cardinal, 1801-1890. I. Title.

NEWMAN, John Henry, cardinal, 1801-1890. 261
Discussions and arguments on various subjects, by John Henry cardinal Newman. New impression. London, New York [etc.] Longmans, Green, and co., 1899. 3 p. l., [v]-viii, 404 p. 19 cm. (On cover: The works of Cardinal Newman) [[BR85.N]] A 33
I. Title.
Contents omitted.

NEWMAN, John Henry, cardinal, 1801-1890. 261
Discussions and arguments on various subjects, by John Henry cardinal Newman. New impression. London, New York [etc.] Longmans, Green, and co., 1907. 3 p. l., [v]-viii, 404 p. 19 cm. [BR85.N43 1907] 10-24530
I. Title.
Contents omitted.

NEWMAN, John Henry, cardinal, 1801-1890. 261
Discussions and arguments on various subjects, by John Henry cardinal Newman. New impression. London, New York [etc.] Longmans, Green, and co., 1907. 3 p. l., [v]-viii, 404 p. 19 cm. [BR85.N43 1907] 10-24530
I. Title.
Contents omitted.

NEWMAN, John Henry, cardinal, 1801-1890.
The dream of Gerontius, by Cardinal Newman. 34th impression. London, New York and Bombay, Longmans, Green, and co., 1903. 59 p. 13 x 10 cm. [PR5107.D6 1903 a] 6-3635
I. Title.

NEWMAN, John Henry, cardinal, 1801-1890.
The dream of Gerontius, by Cardinal Newman; with introduction and notes by Maurice Francis Egan ... New York, London [etc.] Longmans, Green, and co., 1903. 3 p. l., 89 p. front. (port.) 18 1/2 cm. [PR5107.D6 1903] 3-25764
I. Egan, Maurice Francis, 1852-1924, ed. II. Title.

NEWMAN, John Henry, cardinal, 1801-1890.
... The dream of Gerontius, by Cardinal Newman; ed. for school use, with introduction questions and glossary, by John J. Clifford ... Chicago, Loyola university press [c1917] ix, 53 p. 18 1/2 cm. (Loyola English classics) $0.10 [PR5107.D6 1917] 17-10434
I. Clifford, John Joseph, ed. II. Title.

NEWMAN, John Henry, cardinal, 1801-1890.
The dream of Gerontius, by John Henry Newman (Cardinal) Arranged with concordance and chronicle by "Anglican". A contribution towards the centenary of the Oxford movement. London, New York [etc.] Longmans, Green and co. ltd., 1928. 103 p. 22 cm. $3.00 [PR5107.D6 1928] 28-8658
I. Dauglish, Alban Francis, 1865- ed. II. Title.

NEWMAN, John Henry, cardinal, 1801-1890.
... The dream of Gerontius, and other poems, By John Henry Newman. [Oxford ed.] London, New York [etc.] H. Milford, 1914. xi, 278 p. front. (port.) 19 cm. [PR5107.D6 1914] 15-26252
I. Title.
Contents omitted.

NEWMAN, John Henry, cardinal, 1801-1890.
Echoes from the Oratory. Selections from the poems of the Rev. John Henry Newman. New York, A. D. F. Randolph & company [c1884] 61 p. 18 cm. [PS5106.R3] 27-17996
I. Title.

NEWMAN, John Henry, cardinal, 1801-1890.
Essays, critical and historical, by John Henry cardinal Newman. New ed. ... London and New York, Longmans, Green, and co., 1895. 2 v. 19 cm. [PR5107.E8 1895] A 15
I. Title.

NEWMAN, John Henry, cardinal, 1801-1890.
Essays, critical and historical, by John Henry cardinal Newman. New impression. London, New York [etc.] Longmans, Green, and co., 1901. 2 v. 19 cm. (On cover: The works of Cardinal Newman) A 33
I. Title.

NEWMAN, John Henry, cardinal, 1801-1890. 208.1
The fine gold of Newman, collected from his writings by Joseph J. Reilly ... New York, The Macmillan company, 1931. 6 p. l., 11-245 p. 19 1/2 cm. "Works from

which selections have been taken": 5th prelim. leaf. [BX890.N42] (282) 31-17543
I. Reilly, Joseph John, comp. II. Title.

NEWMAN, John Henry, cardinal, 1801-1890. 208.1
The fine gold of Newman, collected from his writings by Joseph J. Reilly ... New York, The Macmillan company, 1931. 6 p. l., 11-245 p. 19 1/2 cm. "Works from which selections have been taken": 5th prelim. leaf. [BX890.N42] (282) 31-17543
I. Reilly, Joseph John, comp. II. Title.

NEWMAN, John Henry, cardinal, 1801-1890.
Hymns, by John Henry Newman. New York, E. P. Dutton & company, 1885. xx, 21-282 p. front. (port.) 14 1/2 cm. Preface signed: W. M. L. J. [PR5107.N8] 12-37243
I. Title.

NEWMAN, John Henry, cardinal, 1801-1890.
Introductory studies in Newman, with introduction, notes and inductive questions; a text-book for use in senior high school and college classes, study clubs and reading circles, by Sister Mary Antonia ... with foreword by the Rt. Rev. Thomas J. Shahan ... New York, Cincinnati [etc.] Benziger brothers, 1929. xv, 217 p. incl. front. (port.) 19 cm. [PR5106.D8] 29-19721
I. Durkin, Sister Mary Antonia, ed. II. Title.

NEWMAN, John Henry, cardinal, 1801-1890. 922.
Letters and correspondence of John Henry Newman during his life in the English church, with a brief autobiography; ed. at Cardinal Newman's request, by Anne Mozley ... London and New York, Longmans, Green, and co., 1890. 2 v. fronts. (ports.) 19 1/2 cm. [BX4705.N5A2] 12-37251
I. Mozley, Anne, 1809-1891, ed. II. Title.

NEWMAN, John Henry, cardinal, 1801-1890. 922.
Letters and correspondence of John Henry Newman during his life in the English church, with a brief autobiography; edited, at Cardinal Newman's request by Anne Mozley ... New edition. London, New York [etc.] Longmans, Green, and co., 1898. 2 v. fronts. (ports.) 19 cm. (On cover: The works of Cardinal Newman) [[BX4705.N5A]] A 33
I. Mozley, Anne, 1809-1891, ed. II. Title.

NEWMAN, John Henry, cardinal, 1801-1890.
... *Literary selections from Newman.* With introduction and notes by A sister of Notre Dame. London, New York [etc.] Longmans, Green and co., 1913. xv, 210 p. 19 cm. At head of title: Longmans' class-books of English literature. A 13
I. Title.
Contents omitted.

NEWMAN, John Henry, cardinal, 1801-1890. 242
Meditations and devotions of the late Cardinal Newman. New York and London, Longmans, Green, and co., 1893. xvi p., 2 l., [3]-438 p., 1 l. 19 1/2 cm. Prefatory notice signed: Wm. P. Neville. [BX2182.N5] 13-25806
I. Neville, William Paine, 1830?-1905, ed. II. Title.

NEWMAN, John Henry, cardinal, 1801-1890. 242
Meditations and devotions of the late Cardinal Newman. New York and London, Longmans, Green, and co., 1903. xvi p., 2 l., [3]-438 p., 1 l. 19 cm. (On cover: The works of Cardinal Newman) Prefatory notice signed: Wm. P. Neville. [[BX2182.N]] A33
I. Neville, William Paine, 1830?-1905, ed. II. Title.

NEWMAN, John Henry, Cardinal, 1801-1890 828.8
A Newman anthology: characteristics from his writings, being selections personal, historical, philosophical, and religious, from his various works, arr. by William Samuel Lilly with the author's approval. London, Dobson [dist. Chester Springs, Pa., Dufour, 1965] 355p. illus. 19cm. [BX4705] A63 3.95 bds.,
I. Lilly, William Samuel, 1840-1919, ed. II. Title.

NEWMAN, John Henry, Cardinal, 1801-1890. 230'.2'08
A Newman treasury : selections from the prose works of John Henry Cardinal Newman / selected and edited by Charles Frederick Harrold. New Rochelle, N.Y. : Arlington House, 1975, c1943. xii, 404 p. ; 24 cm. Reprint of the ed. published by Longmans, Green, London. Bibliography: p. 397-404. [PR5106.H3 1975] 74-31080 ISBN 0-87000-300-3 : 8.95
I. Harrold, Charles Frederick, 1897-1948, ed. II. Title.

NEWMAN, John Henry, Cardinal, 1801-1890.
Prose and poetry; selected by Geoffrey Tillotson. Cambridge, Harvard University Press, 1957. 842p. 21cm. (Reynard library) [PR5106.T] A57
I. Tillotson, Geoffrey, ed. II. Title.

NEWMAN, John Philip, 1826-1899.
Conversations with Christ. New York, Eaton & Mains [1900] 268 p. pl., port. 12 cm. 0-2127
I. Title.

O'FAOLAIN, Sean, 1900- 922.242
Newman's way. London, New York, Longmans, Green [1952] 286p. 22cm. [BX4705.N5O35 1952a] 54-2834
1. Newman, John Henry, Cardinal, 1801-1890. I. Title.

O'FAOLAIN, Sean, 1900- 922.242
Newman's way; the odyssey of John Henry Newman. New York, Devin-Adair Co., 1952. 335 p. illus. 23 cm. [BX4705.N5O35] 52-12280
1. Newman, John Henry, Cardinal, 1801-1890. I. Title.

PATTERSON, Webster T. 262'.15'0924
Newman: pioneer for the layman [by] Webster T. Patterson. Foreword by Robert W. Gleason. Washington, Corpus Books [1968] xxii, 193 p. 21 cm. Bibliography: p. 183-189. [BX4705.N5P3] 68-9475 7.50
1. Newman, John Henry, Cardinal, 1801-1890. 2. Laity. I. Title.

POWELL, Jouett Lynn. 262'.135'0924 B
Three uses of Christian discourse in John Henry Newman : an example of nonreductive reflection on the Christian faith / by Jouett Lynn Powell. Missoula, Mont. : Published by Scholars Press for the American Academy of Religion, 1976c1975 x, 232 p. ; 22 cm. (Dissertation series - American Academy of Religion ; no. 10) Originally presented as the author's thesis, Yale, 1972. Bibliography: p. 215-232. [BX4705.N5P65 1975] 75-29423 ISBN 0-89130-042-2 pbk. : 4.50
1. Newman, John Henry, Cardinal, 1801-1890. I. American Academy of Religion. II. Title. III. Series: American Academy of Religion. Dissertation series — American Academy of Religion ; no. 10.

REILLY, Joseph John, 1881- 922
Newman as a man of letters, by Joseph J. Reilly ... New York, The Macmillan company, 1925. ix p., 1 l., 329 p. 19 1/2 cm. [BX4705.N5R4] 25-11335
1. Newman, John Henry, cardinal, 1801-1890. I. Title.

REYNOLDS, Ernest Edwin, 1894- 922.242
Three cardinals: Newman, Wiseman, Manning. New York, Kenedy [1958] 278p. illus. 22cm. Includes bibliography. [BX4665.G7R4] 58-10991
1. Newman, John Henry, Cardinal, 1801-1890. 2. Wiseman, Nicholas Patrick Stephen, Cardinal, 1802-1895. 3. Manning, Henry Edward, Cardinal, 1808-1892. 4. Cardinals—Gt. Brit. I. Title.

RICKABY, Joseph John, 1845-1932. 261
Index to the works of John Henry cardinal Newman, by Joseph Rickaby... London, New York [etc.] Longmans, Green and co., 1914. viii, 156 p. 19 cm. [BR85.N5] 14-20393
1. Newman, John Henry, cardinal, 1801-1890. I. Title.

ROBBINS, William 262.1350924
The Newman brothers; an essay in comparative intellectual biography. Cambridge, Mass., Harvard [c.]1966. xii, 202p. ports. 23cm. Bibl. [BX4705.N5 R57] 66-4976 6.00
1. Newman, John Henry, Cardinal, 1801-1890. 2. Newman, Francis, 1805-1897. I. Title.

ROBBINS, William. 262.1350924
The Newman brothers; an essay in comparative intellectual biography. Cambridge, Harvard University Press, 1966. xii, 202 p. ports. 23 cm. Bibliographical footnotes. [BX4705.N5R57] 66-4976
1. Newman, John Henry, Cardinal, 1801-1890. 2. Newman, Francis, 1805-1897. I. Title.

ROBBINS, William. 262.1350924
The Newman brothers; an essay in comparative intellectual biography. London, Heinemann, 1966. xii, 202 p. front., 6 plates (ports.) 22 1/2 cm. 35/ -- [BX4705.N5R75] 66-71850
1. Newman, John Henry, Cardinal, 1801-1890. 2. Newman, Francis William, 1805-1897. I. Title.

ROSS, John Elliot, 1884- 922.242
... *John Henry Newman,* Anglican minister, Catholic priest, Roman cardinal. New York, W. W. Norton & company, inc. [c1933] xxi p., 1 l., 258 p. front. (port.) 22 cm. At head of title: By J. Elliot Ross. "First edition." "A short bibliography": p. 251-254. [BX4705.N5R6] 33-31106
1. Newman, John Henry, cardinal, 1801-1899. I. Title.

RUGGLES, Eleanor. 922.242
Journal into faith; the Anglican life of John Henry Newman [1st ed.] New York, W. W. Morton [1948] 336 p. port. 22 cm. [BX4705.N5R75] 48-6601
1. Newman, John Henry, Cardinal, 1801-1890. I. Title.

RYAN, Edwin. 922.2
A college handbook to Newman, by Edwin Ryan, D.D. Washington, D.C., The Catholic education press, 1930. v, 121 p. front. (port.) 20 cm. [PR5109.R8] 30-20275
1. Newman, John Henry, cardinal, 1801-1890. I. Title.

RYAN, John Kenneth, 1897- ed. 922.242
American essays for the Newman centennial, ed. by John K. Ryan and Edmond Darvil Benard. Washington, Catholic Univ. of America Press, 1947. xiii, 244 p. 24 cm. (p. [209]-227)--Biographical notes on contributors. [BX4705.N5R8] 47-30528
1. Newman, John Henry, Cardinal, 1801-1890. 2. Catholic Church—Addresses, essays, lectures. I. Benard, Edmond Darvil, 1914- joint ed. II. Title.
Contents omitted.

SELBY, Robin C. 230'.2'0924
The principle of reserve in the writings of John Henry Cardinal Newman / by Robin C. Selby. London ; New York : Oxford University Press, 1975. 108 p. ; 23 cm. (Oxford theological monographs) Includes indexes. Bibliography: p. [106]-108. [B1745.S44] 75-322798 ISBN 0-19-826711-8 : 16.00
1. Newman, John Henry, Cardinal, 1801-1890. 2. Reserve (Christian theology)—History of doctrines. I. Title. II. Series.

SHERIDAN, Thomas L., 1926- 234'.7'0924
Newman on justification; a theological biography, by Thomas L. Sheridan. Staten Island, N.Y., Alba [1967] 265p. 22cm. Bibl. [BX4705.N5S4] 67-21427 6.50
1. Newman, John Henry, Cardinal, 1801-1890. 2. Justification—History of doctrines. I. Title.

SNOW, Alpheus Henry, 1859-1920. 922
A study of the life and writings of John Henry Newman; an address delivered before the Indianapolis literary club, January 18, 1892 ... By Alpheus Henry Snow. Indianapolis [Press of the Sentinel printing company] 1892. 50 p. 17 cm. "Reprinted from 'Words and deeds' for May, 1892." [BX4705.N5S6] 39-13390
1. Newman, John Henry, cardinal, 1801-1890. I. Title.

STEPHEN, Leslie, Sir. 1832-1904. 211
An agnostic's apology, and other essays, by Leslie Stephen ... New York, G. P. Putnam's sons; London, Smith, Elder, & co., 1893. 3 p. l., 380 p. 21 cm. "Four ... chapters are republished (with alterations) from articles which originally appeared in the 'Fortnightly review', one from two articles in the 'Nineteenth century', and one from an article in the 'North American review'." [BL27.S7 1893 a] 38-19305
1. Newman, John Henry, cardinal, 1801-1890. 2. Agnosticism. I. Title.
Contents omitted.

TREVOR, Meriol. 922.242
Newman, the pillar of the cloud. Garden City, N.Y., Doubleday, 1962- v. illus. 22 cm. Includes bibliography. [BX4705.N5T662] 62-13341
1. Newman, John Henry, Cardinal, 1801-1890. Full name: Lucy Meriol Trevor. I. Title.

TREVOR, Meriol [Lucy Merial Trevor] 922.242
Newman, v.2. Garden City, N.Y., Doubleday, 1963[c.1962] 659p. illus. 22cm. Contents.v.2, Light in winter. Bibl. 62-13341 7.95
1. Newman, John Henry, Cardinal, 1801-1890. I. Title.

TREVOR, Meriol [Lucy Meriol Trevor] 922.242
Newman, the pillar of the cloud [v.1] Garden City, N.Y., Doubleday [c.]1962. 649p. illus. 22cm. Bibl. 62-13341 7.95
1. Newman, John Henry, Cardinal, 1801-1890. I. Title.

VARGISH, Thomas. 128'.2'0924
Newman: the contemplation of mind. Oxford, Clarendon P., 1970. xiv, 191 p. 23 cm. Based on author's thesis, Oxford. Includes bibliographical references. [B1649.N474V35] 78-532162 45/-
1. Newman, John Henry, Cardinal, 1801-1890. 2. Mind and body. I. Title.

WALGRAVE, J. H. 230.2
Newman the theologian; the nature of belief and doctrine as exemplified in his life and works. Translated [from the French] by A. V. Littledale. New York, Sheed & Ward [1960] 378p. Bibl.: p.373-378. 60-16895 8.50
1. Newman, John Henry, Cardinal, 1801-1890. 2. Dogma, Development of. I. Title.

WALGRAVE, Jan Henricus, 1911- 230.2
Newman the theologian; the nature of belief and doctrine as exemplified in his life and works, by J. H. Walgrave. Translated by A. V. Littledale. New York, Sheed & Ward [1960] xi, 378 p. 22 cm. "Translation of Newman, le developpement du dogme." Bibliography: p. 373-378. [BX4705.N5W233 1960] 60-16895
1. Newman, John Henry, Cardinal, 1801-1890. 2. Dogma, Development of. I. Title.

WALLER, Alfred Rayney, 1867-1922. 922.
John Henry, cardinal Newman, by A. R. Waller and G. H. S. Barrow. Boston, Small, Maynard & company, 1901. 5 p. l., ix-xviii p., 1 l., 150 p. front. (port.) 14 1/2 cm. (Added t.-p. illus.: The Westminster biographics) Bibliography: p. 148-150. [BX4705.N5W25] 2-1770
1. Newman, John Henry, cardinal, 1801-1890. I. Barrow, G. H. S., joint author. II. Title.

WALLER, Alfred Rayney, 1867-1922. 262'.135'0924 B
John Henry, Cardinal Newman / by A. R. Waller and G. H. S. Burrow [i.e. Barrow]. Norwood, Pa. : Norwood Editions, 1976. xviii, 150 p. ; 23 cm. Reprint of the 1901 ed. published by Kegan Paul, Trench, Trubner, London, in series: The Westminster biographies. Bibliography: p. [148]-150. [BX4705.N5W25 1976] 76-45369 ISBN 0-8482-2954-1 : 17.50
1. Newman, John Henry, Cardinal, 1801-1890. 2. Cardinals—England—Biography.

I. Barrow, G. H. S., joint author. II. Series: The Westminster biographies.

WARD, Maisie, 1889- 922.242
Young Mr. Newman. New York, Sheed & Ward, 1948. xvii, 477 p. illus., ports. 22 cm. Full name: Mary Josephine (Ward) Sheed. Bibliography: p. 468-471. [BX4705.N5W28 1948a] 48-8100
1. Newman, John Henry, Cardinal, 1801-1890. I. Title.

WARD, Wilfrid Philip, 1856- 922.
1916.
The life John Henry, cardinal Newman, based on his private journals and correspondence, cardinal Newman, based on his private journals and correspondence, by Wilfrid Ward...with portraits. New York [etc.] Longmans, Green, and co., 1912. 2 v. fronts., ports., facsims, 23 1/2 cm. [BX4705.N5W3 1912a] 12-3607
1. Newman, John Henry, cardinal, 1891-1890. I. Title.

WARD, Wilfrid Philip, 1856- 922.
1916.
The life of John Henry, cardinal Newman, based on his private journals and correspondence, by Wilfrid Ward ... with portraits. London, New York [etc.] Longmans, Green, and co., 1912. 2 v. fronts., ports., double geneal, tab., facsims. 23 1/2 cm. [BX4705.N5W3 1912] 12-2237
1. Newman, John Henry, cardinal, 1801-1890. I. Title.

WARD, Wilfrid Philip, 1856-1916.
The life of John Henry cardinal Newman based on his private journals and correspondence, by Wilfrid Ward...New Impression. London, New York [etc.] Longmans, Green and co. ltd., 1927. 2 v. in 1 front. (port.) 22 cm. [BX4705.N5W3 1927] 27-28094
1. Newman, John Henry, cardinal, 1801-1890. I. Title.

WARD, Wilfrid Philip, 1856- 261
1916.
Witnesses to the unseen and other essays, by Wilfrid Ward ... London and New York, Macmillan and co., 1893. xxix, 309 p. 23 cm. Reprinted with considerable additions from the Nineteenth century, the Contemporary review, and the National review. cf. Prefatory note. [BR85.W27] 1-5746
1. Newman, John Henry, cardinal, 1801-1890. 2. Catholic church—Addresses, essays, lectures. I. Title.
Contents omitted.

WEATHERBY, Harold 262'.135'0924 B
L., 1934-
Cardinal Newman in his age; his place in English theology and literature [by] Harold L. Weatherby. Nashville, Vanderbilt University Press, 1973. xv, 296 p. 23 cm. Includes bibliographical references. [BX4705.N5W4] 72-1347 ISBN 0-8265-1182-1 11.50
1. Newman, John Henry, Cardinal, 1801-1890. I. Title.

WHYTE, Alexander, 1837- 922.242
1921.
Newman; an appreciation, by Alexander Whyte, D.D.: with an appendix of letters not hitherto published. New York, Longmans, Green, and co., 1901. 68 p. 19 1/2 cm. [BX4705.N5W5] 1-27590
1. Newman, John Henry, Cardinal, 1801-1890. I. Title.

WHYTE, Alexander, 1837-1921. 922
Newman; an appreciation in two lectures: with the choicest passages of his writings selected and arranged by Alexander Whyte, D.D. The appendix contains six of His Eminence's letters not hitherto published. New York, Longmans, Green, and co., 1902. 252 p. facsim. 19 1/2 cm. [BX4705.N5W52] 2-3908
1. Newman, John Henry, cardinal, 1801-1890. I. Title.

YEARLEY, Lee H. 230'.2'0924
The ideas of Newman : Christianity and human religiosity / Lee H. Yearley. University Park : Pennsylvania State University Press, c1978. xii, 188 p. ; 24 cm. Includes index. Bibliography: p. [170]-175. [BX4705.N5Y4] 77-13894 ISBN 0-271-00526-2 : 12.50
1. Newman, John Henry, Cardinal, 1801-1890. I. Title.

Newman, John Henry, Cardinal, 1801-1890. Apologia pro vita sua.

HOUGHTON, Walter Edwards, 922.242
1904-
The art of Newman's Apologia, by Walter E. Houghton. New Haven, Pub. for Wellesley college by Yale university press; London, H. Milford, Oxford university press, 1945. ix, 116 p. front. (port.) 20 1/2 cm. Bibliographical foot-notes. [BX4705.N5A38] A 46
1. Newman, John Henry, cardinal, 1801-1890. Apologia pro vita sua. I. Wellesley college. II. Title.

[SYMPOSIUM on the 922.242
Apologia, Fordham University, 1963]
Newman's Apologia: a classic reconsidered. ed. by Vincent Ferrer Blehl, Francis X. Connolly. New York, Harcourt [1964] viii, 182p. 21cm. Papers of the symp. sponsored by the Fordham Univ. Ctr. of Newman Studies, Oct. 12, 1963, to commemorate the centenary of the pubn. of John Henry Newman's Apologia pro vita sua. Bibl. 64-18283 4.50
1. Newman, John Henry, Cardinal, 1801-1890. Apologia pro vita sua. I. Blehl, Vincent Ferrer, ed. II. Connolly, Francis Xavier, 1909- ed. III. Fordham University, New York. Center of Newman Studies. IV. Title.

Newman, John Henry, cardinal, 1801-1890. Grammar of assent.

D'ARCY, Martin Cyril, 1888- 121
The nature of belief, by M. C. D'Arcy ... New York, Sheed & Ward, 1945. xv, 17-250 p. 22 1/2 cm. "New edition." [[BD215.D]] A46
1. Newman, John Henry, cardinal, 1801-1890. Grammar of assent. 2. Belief and doubt. 3. Knowledge, Theory of. 4. Faith. I. Title.

TOOHEY,John Joseph, 1873- 201
An indexed synopsis of the "Grammar of assent", by John Joseph Toohey, S.J. New York,London [etc.] Longmans, Green, and co., 1906. vi, 220 p. 19 cm. [BR100.N45] 6-46340
1. Newman, John Henry, cardinal, 1801-1890. Grammar of assent. I. Title.

Newman, John Henry, Cardinal, 1801-1890—Juvenile literature.

SCHMID, Evan, 1920- 922.242
Cardinal from Oxford; a story of John Henry Cardinal Newman. Notre Dame, Ind., Dujarie Press [1959] 143p. illus. 22cm. [BX4705.N5S37] 59-3345
1. Newman, John Henry, Cardinal, 1801-1890—Juvenile literature. I. Title.

Newman, John Henry, Cardinal, 1801-1890—Knowledge, Theory of.

FERREIRA, M. Jamie. 201
Doubt and religious commitment : the role of the will in Newman's thought / M. Jamie Ferreira. Oxford [Eng.] : Clarendon Press ; New York : Oxford University Press, 1980. viii, 156 p. ; 23 cm. Includes index. Bibliography: p. [146]-151. [B1649.N474F47] 79-42785 ISBN 0-19-826654-5 : 28.50
1. Newman, John Henry, Cardinal, 1801-1890—Knowledge, Theory of. 2. Knowledge, Theory of. 3. Belief and doubt. 4. Certainty. 5. Faith and reason. I. Title.

Newman, John Henry, cardinal, 1801-1890. Lectures on the present position of Catholics in England.

SEMPER, Isidore Joseph, 230.2
1883-
...A study of four outstanding books of Christian apologetics, by I. J. Semper. Dubuque, Columbia college library, 1928. 3 p. l., [5]-27 p. 21 cm. (Books for the times, no. 1) [BX1755.S45] 34-19418
1. Newman, John Henry, cardinal, 1801-1890. Lectures on the present position of Catholics in England. 2. Chesterton, Gilbert Keith, 1874- Orthodoxy. 3. Belloc, Hilaire, 1870- Europe and the faith. 4. Stevenson, Robert Louis, 1850-1894. Father Damien. 5. Catholic church—Apologetic works. I. Title.
Contents omitted.

Newport News, Va. First Baptist church.

LITTLE, Lewis Peyton. 286.1755416
History of the First Baptist church of Newport News, Virginia, from 1883 to 1933, by Lewis Peyton Little. Newport News, Va., The Franklyn printing company, inc., 1936. xxi, [1], 218 p. incl. front., illus., ports., facsims. 24 cm. [BX6480.N575F5] 37-3274
1. Newport News, Va. First Baptist church. 2. Baptists—Newport News, Va. I. Title.

Newport, R. I. Touro Synagogue.

GUTSTEIN, Morris Aaron, 296.6
1905-
To bigotry no sanction; a Jewish shrine in America, 1658-1958. New York, Bloch Pub. Co., 1958. 191p. illus. 24cm. Includes bibliography. [BM225.N57T6] 58-14128
1. Newport, R. I. Touro Synagogue. I. Title.

Newport, R.I. Trinity church.

ISHAM, Norman 726.5097457
Morrison, 1864-
Trinity church in Newport, Rhode Island; a history of the fabric, by Norman Morrison Isham ... Boston, Printed for the subscribers [by D. B. Updike] 1936. xi, 111 p. front., illus. (incl. plans) plates, diagrs. 26 1/2 cm. [NA5235.N67T7] 36-23857
1. Newport, R.I. Trinity church. I. Title.

News—History—To 70 A. P.

PAYNE, John Barton, 1922- 220.95
An outline of Hebrew history. Grand Rapids, Baker Book House, 1954. 257p. 21cm. [DS117.P3] 54-11075
1. News—Hist.—To 70 A. P. 2. Bible—History of Biblical events. I. Title. II. Title: Hebrew history.

Newton, Adelaide Leaper, 1824-1854.

BAILLIE, John, d.1890. 922
A memoir of Adelaide Leaper Newton, by the Rev. John Baillie ... New York, R. Carter & brothers, 1862. xiii, [15]-364 p. front. (port.) 18 cm. [BR1725.N4B3] 24-6570
1. Newton, Adelaide Leaper, 1824-1854. I. Title.

Newton Center, Mass, Trinity church (Protestant Episcopal)

SULLIVAN, Edward Taylor, 283.744
1861-
A history of Trinity parish, Newton Centre, Massachusetts, by Edward T. Sullivan. [Newton Center] 1943. 2 p. l., iii-vi, 60 p. front., illus. 23 cm. [BX5980.N68S8] 44-23223
1. Newton Center, Mass, Trinity church (Protestant Episcopal) I. Title.

Newton, Isaac, 1642-1727.

HURLBUTT, Robert H. 211.3
Hume, Newton, and the design argument, by Robert H. Hurlbutt, III. Lincoln, University of Nebraska Press [1965] xiv, 221 p. 24 cm. Bibliographical footnotes. [BD541.H8] 65-10047
1. Newton, Isaac, 1642-1727. 2. Hume, David, 1711-1776. 3. Teleology — Hist. I. Title. II. Title: The design argument.

Newton, Isaac, Sir, 1642-1727—Religion and ethics.

MANUEL, Frank Edward. 283'.092'4
The religion of Isaac Newton / Frank E. Manuel. Oxford : Clarendon Press, 1974. vi, 141 p. ; 23 cm. (Fremantle lectures ; 1973) Includes bibliographical references and index. [QC16.N7M32] 75-302605 ISBN 0-19-826640-5 : 11.25
1. Newton, Isaac, Sir, 1642-1727—Religion and ethics. I. Title. II. Series.

Newton, John, 1725-1807.

[CECIL, Richard] 1748- 922.342
1810.
The life of John Newton ... Compiled for the American Sunday school union, and revised by the Committee of publication. Philadelphia, American Sunday school union, 1831. 160 p. front. (port.) 15 cm. "Taken from Newton's narrative of himself, and his memoirs by R. Cecil."--Advertisement, p. [3] [BX5199.N55C35] 30-33502
1. Newton, John, 1725-1807. I. American Sunday-school union. II. Title.

CECIL, Richard, 1748-1810. 922.
Memoirs of the Rev. John Newton, late rector of the united parishes of St. Mary Woolnoth, and St. Mary Woolchurch Haw, Lombard street, with general remarks on his life, connexions, and character. By Richard Cecil ... Philadelphia: Printed for B. & T. Kite, no. 20, North third street. J. Bouvier, printer, 1809. 257 p. 18 cm. [BX5199.N55C4 1809 a] 28-9937
1. Newton, John, 1725-1807. I. Title.

CECIL, Richard, 1748-1810. 922.
Memoirs of the Rev. John Newton ... with general remarks on his life, connexions, and character. By Richard Cecil ... New York, Published by Thomas A. Ronalds, book-seller and stationer, no. 188, Pearl street, 1809. 257, [1] p. 19 cm. [BX5199.N55C4] 30-31452
1. Newton, John, 1725-1807. I. Title.

DEAL, Williams 283'.092'4 B
John Newton, author of the song "Amazing grace," by William Deal. Westchester, Ill., Good News Publishers [1974] 80 p. 18 cm. (One evening book OE140) [BX5199.N55D35] 74-76011 0.95 (pbk.).
1. Newton, John, 1725-1807.

NEWTON, John, 1725-1807. 922.
An authentic narrative of some remarkable and interesting particulars in the life of John Newton. Communicated in a series of letters, to the Rev. Mr. Haweis... New-York, Printed by W. A. Davis, for C. Davis, no. 212, Water-street, 1796. 2 p. l., 248 p. front. (port.) 14 cm. [BX5199.N55A33 1796] 30-31456
I. Title.

NEWTON, John, 1725-1807. 922.
An authentic narrative of some remarkable and interesting particulars in the life of John Newton. Communicated in a series of letters to the Rev. Mr. Haweis... New-York, Published by Evert Duyckinck, no. 110 Pearl-street, 1806. 252 p. 14 cm. [BX5199.N55A33 1806] 36-31434
I. Haweis, Thomas, 1734-1820, ed. II. Title.

NEWTON, John, 1725-1807. 922.
An authentic narrative of some remarkable and interesting particulars in the life of the Rev. Mr. John Newton. Communicated, in a series of letters to the Rev. Mr. Haweis... 1st Hudson ed. Hudson: Printed by Ashbel Stoddard, and sold at his printing office, and book-store, corner of Warren and Third-streets, 1805. 1 p. l., [5]-112 p. 14 cm. [BX5199.N55A33 1805] 30-34009
I. Title.

NEWTON, John, 1725-1807. 922.342
Cardiphonia; or, The utterance of the heart in the course of a real correspondence. By the Reverend John Newton...With an introductory essay, by David Russell... Philadelphia, Presbyterian board of publication [185-?] 4, v-xxxvi, 37-494 p. front. (port.) 19 1/2 cm. [BX5199.N55A35 1850] 30-33501
I. Title. II. Title: The utterance of the heart.

NEWTON, John, 1725-1807. 922.
The life of John Newton, once a sailor, afterwards captain of a slave ship, and subsequently rector of St. Mary Woolnoth, London. "An authentic narrative", written by himself; to which some further particulars are added ... New York, Printed for the American tract society, by Pudney, Hooker & Russell, 1846. 116 p. 1 illus., plates. 18 cm. [BX5199.N55A33 1846] 30-31455
I. Title.

NEWTON, John, 1725-1807. 283'.3 B
Out of the depths : the autobiography of John Newton / introduction by Herbert Lockyer ; illustrations by Ron McCarty. Shepherd illustrated classic ed. New Canaan, Conn. : Keats, 1981. 135 p., [5] leaves of plates : ill. ; 21 cm. (A Shepherd illustrated classic) Original title: An authentic narrative of some remarkable and interesting particulars in the life of ******** "Written in the form of letters to the Rev. T. Haweis, D.D., and was first published in 1764"—Verso t.p. [BX5199.N55A33 1981] 19 80-85340 ISBN 0-87983-243-6 (pbk.) : 5.95
*1. Newton, John, 1725-1807. 2. Church of England—Clergy—Biography. 3. Clergy—England—Biography. I. Haweis, Thomas, 1734-1820. II. [Authentic narrative of some remarkable and interesting particulars in the life of ********] III. Title. IV. Series.*

NEWTON, John, 1725-1807. [248]922.342
Voice of the heart: Cardiphonia. With a biographical sketch of the author by William Culbertson. Chicago, Moody Press, 1950. 432 p. 23 cm. (The Wycliffe series of Christian classics) Previous editions published under title: Cardiphonia. Bibliography: p. 22. [BX5199.N55A35] 51-1389
I. Title. II. Series.

POLLOCK, John Charles. 283'.3 B
Amazing grace : the dramatic life story of John Newton / John Pollock. 1st ed. San Francisco : Harper & Row, c1981. p. cm. Bibliography: p. [BX5199.N55P64] 19 78-3142 ISBN 0-06-066653-6 : 9.95
1. Newton, John, 1725-1807. 2. Church of England—Clergy—Biography. 3. Clergy—England—Biography. I. Title.

Newton, John Brockenbrough, 1839-1897.

STANARD, Mary Mann Page (Newton) Mrs. 922.
John Brockenbrough Newton, a biographical sketch. By Mary Newton Stanard. [Richmond, Va., 1924] 60 [1] p. front., plates, ports. 21 1/2 cm. Reprint from the Virginia churchman, for private distribution, Richmond, Va., 1924. [BX5995.N38S8] 24-24508
1. Newton, John Brockenbrough, 1839-1897. I. Title.

Newton, Mass.—Directories

NEWTON church directory, 277.
1906, containing a list of churches, officers, members and attendants of the churches in Newton... Boston, F. H. Radford, 1906. 3-255 p. incl illus. 24 cm. Included advertising matter. No more published? [BR560.N45N4] 6-34376
1. Newton, Mass.—Direct. 2. Newton, Mass.—Churches.

Newton, Mass. Eliot Church.

FRAY, Harold R. 285'.8744'4
Conflict and change in the church, by Harold R. Fray, Jr. Boston, Pilgrim Press [1969] xiv, 113 p. 21 cm. [BV637.7.F7] 73-76085 2.95
1. Newton, Mass. Eliot Church. 2. Suburban churches—Case studies. I. Title.

Newton, N.C. First Baptist Church.

BRYSON, Jeter Lawrence, 1930- 286'.1756'785
The Lovely Lady of Catawba County; a history of the First Baptist Church, Newton, North Carolina, 1882-1967, by J. L. Bryson, Jr. [Newton, N.C., Printed by Epps Print. Co., 1967] 207 p. illus., ports. 22 cm. [BX6480.N58F5] 67-6601
1. Newton, N.C. First Baptist Church. I. Title.

Newton, Richard Heber, 1840-1914.

A service to honor the 922.373
memory of the Rev. R. Heber Newton, D.D., and to help perpetuate the ideals to which his life was dedicated, Church of the ascension, Fifth avenue and Tenth street, New York city, February the seventh, 1915. [New York, G. P. Putnam's sons] 1915. x, 79 p. 22 1/2 cm. Lettered on cover: In memoriam. Mounted portrait inserted. [BX5995.N4S4] 33-25259
1. Newton, Richard Heber, 1840-1914. I. New York. Church of the ascension.

Newton, Robert, 1780-1854.

JACKSON, Thomas, 1783-1873. 922.
The life of the Rev. Robert Newton, D. D. By Thomas Jackson ... New-York, Carlton & Phillips, 1855. 2 p. l., [iii]-xiv, 427 p. front. (port.) 20 cm. [BX8495.N4J3] 1-27489
1. Newton, Robert, 1780-1854. I. Title.

Newton, Samuel, d. 1810.

PHIPPS, Joseph, 1708-1787. 230.96
The original and present state of man, briefly considered: wherein is shewn, the nature of his fall, and the necessity, means and manner of his restoration, through the sacrifice of Christ, and the sensible operation of that divine principle of grace and truth, held forth to the world, by the people called Quakers. To which are added some remarks on the arguments of Samuel Newton, of Norwich. By Joseph Phipps ... London, Printed; New-York, Re-printed by William Ross, no. 33, Broad-street, m.dcc.lxxxviii. 2 p. l., 230 (i. e. 228) p. 22 cm. [BX7730.P6 1783] 2-642
1. Newton, Samuel, d. 1810. 2. Friends, Society of—Doctrinal and controversial works. I. Title.

Newton, Samuel, of Norwich. The leading sentiments of the people called Quakers examined.

PHIPPS, Joseph, 1708-1787. 230.96
The original and present state of man, briefly considered: wherein is shewn, the nature of his fall, and the necessity, means and manner of his restoration, through the sacrifice of Christ, and the sensible operation of that divine principle of grace and truth, held forth to the world, by the people called Quakers. To which are added, some remarks on the arguments of Samuel Newton, of Norwich. By Joseph Phipps ... Trenton [N. J.] Printed by Isaac Collins. m.dcc.xciii. 2 p. l., 228 p. 21 cm. [BX7790.P] A 33
1. Newton, Samuel, of Norwich. The leading sentiments of the people called Quakers examined. 2. Friends, Society of—Doctrinal and controversial works. I. Title.

Newton Theological institution, Newton Center, Mass.

HOVEY, Alvah, 1820-1903. 016.
Historical address delivered at the fiftieth anniversary of the Newton theological institution, June 8, 1975. By Alvah Hovey... Boston, Wright & Potter, 1875. 72 p. 23 cm. [BV4070.N76H7] 23-5043
1. Newton Theological institution, Newton Center, Mass. I. Title.

HOVEY, George Rice, 1860- 016.
Alvah Hovey, his life and letters, by George Rice Hovey. Philadelphia, Boston [etc.] The Judson press [c1928] 6 p. l., 267 p. front., plates, ports., facsim. 20 cm. "Writings of Alvah Hovey": p. 261-262. [BV4070.N759H6] 28-5686
1. Hovey, Alvah, 1820-1903. 2. Newton theological institution, Newton Center, Mass. I. Title.

NEWTON theological institution, Newton Centre, Mass. 252.
The Newton chapel; chapel talks by members of the faculty of the Newton theological institution. Philadelphia, Boston [etc.] The Judson press [1920] 5 p. l., 3-277 p. front. 20 cm. [BV4310.N4] 20-8357
I. Title.

Newton theological institutions, Newton Center, Mass.—Registers.

NEWTON theological institution, Newton Center, Mass. 016.
... *Historical catalogue.* 12th ed. Newton Centre, Mass., 1925. x, 278 p. 23 1/2 cm. [BV4070.N742 1925] 41-38417
1. Newton theological institutions, Newton Center, Mass.—Registers. I. Title.

Nez Perce Indians—Missions.

MORRILL, Allen Conrad. 266'.510922 B
Out of the blanket : the story of Sue and Kate McBeth, missionaries to the Nez Perces / by Allen Conrad Morrill, Eleanor Dunlap Morrill ; ill. & cover by Gregory Pole. Moscow : University Press of Idaho, c1978. 420 p. : ill. ; 21 cm. (A Gem book) Includes index. Bibliography: p. 412-416. [E99.N5M63] 78-54426 ISBN 0-89301-056-1 : 11.95
1. McBeth, Sue L., d. 1893. 2. McBeth, Kate C., 1832- 3. Nez Perce Indians—Missions. 4. Missionaries—Idaho—Biography. 5. Indians of North America—Idaho—Missions. I. Morrill, Eleanor Dunlap, joint author. II. Title.

Ngawang Lobsang Yishey Tenzing Gyatso, Dalai Lama, 1935-

THOMAS, Lowell Jackson, 1923- 922.943
The Dalai Lama. [1st ed.] New York, Duell, Sloan and Pearce [1961] 151 p. illus. 21 cm. [BL1489.N44T5] 61-7992
1. Ngawang Lobsang Yishey Tenzing Gyatso, Dalai Lama, 1935- I. Title.

Nicaea, Council of, 325.

BURN-MURDOCH, William Gordon, 1864-1927.
The Council of Nicaea; a memorial for its sixteenth centenary, by A. E. Burn ... London, Society for promoting Christian knowledge; New York and Toronto, The Macmillan co., 1925. xi, 146 p. front. (facsim.) 19 cm. [BR210.B87] 25-21661
1. Nicaea, Council of, 325. 2. Nicene creed. I. Title.

CHRYSTAL, James, 1832- tr.
Authoritative Christianity. The first ecumenical council ... which was held A.D. 325 at Nicaea in Bithynia. Vol. 1, which contains all its undisputed remains in Greek and English; the English translation by James Chrystal ... Jersey City, N.J., J. Chrystal, 1891. 4 p. l., xvi, 483 [4] p. 24 cm. No more published? [BR210.C5] 1-15076
1. Nicaes, Council of, 325. I. Title.

DUDLEY, Dean, 1823-1906.
History of the first Council of Nice: a world's Christian convention, A. D. 325: with a life of Constantine, 4th ed. By Dean Dudley ... Boston. D. Dudley & co. [c1886] 120 p. front. (port.) 19 cm. [BR210.D8 1886] 12-31891
1. Constantinus I, the Great. Emperor of Rome, d. 337 2. Nicaea, Council of, 325. I. Title.

Nicene creed.

BASSET, Bernard. 238'.142
And would you believe it! : Thoughts about the Creed / Bernard Basset. 1st ed. Garden City, N.Y. : Doubleday, 1976. 120 p. ; 22 cm. Includes bibliographical references. [BT999.B37] 76-3920 ISBN 0-385-12164-4 : 5.95
1. Nicene Creed. I. Title.

BASSET, Bernard. 238'.142
And would you believe it? : the story of the Nicene Creed / [by] Bernard Basset. London : Sheed and Ward, 1976. [5], 106 p. ; 21 cm. Includes bibliographical references. [BT999.B37 1976b] 76-378881 ISBN 0-7220-7601-0 : £2.95
1. Nicene Creed. I. Title.

BASSET, Bernard. 238'.142
And would you believe it! : Thoughts about the Creed / Bernard Basset. Garden City, N.Y. : Image Books, 1978, c1976. 156p. ; 18 cm. Includes bibliographical references. [BT999.B37] ISBN 0-385-13367-7 pbk. : 2.45
1. Nicene Creed. I. Title.
L.C. card no. for 1976 Doubleday ed.: 76-3920.

BINDLEY, Thomas Herbert, 1861-1931, ed. 238'.142
The oecumenical documents of the faith / edited with introd. and notes by T. Herbert Bindley. Westport, Conn. : Greenwood Press, 1980. viii, 246 p. ; 24 cm. Reprint of the 4th ed., rev. with introd. and notes by F. W. Green, published in 1950 by Methuen, London. Contents.Contents.—The Creed of Nicaea.—Three epistles of Cyril.—The tome of Leo.—The Chalcedonian definition. Includes bibliographical references and indexes. [BT999.B52 1980] 19 79-8708 ISBN 0-313-22197-9 lib. bdg. : 22.25
1. Chalcedon, Council of, 451. 2. Niceae Creed. 3. Constantinopolitan Creed. I. Green, Frederick Wastie, 1884- II. Title.

CLENDENIN, Frank Montrose, 1853-1930. 238.
The comfort of the catholic faith, by the Rev. Frank M. Clendenin ... New York, London [etc.] Longmans, Green and co., 1921. xiii, [1], 183 p. 19 cm. [BT999.C5] 21-21147
1. Nicene creed. I. Title.

FORELL, George Wolfgang. 238.142
Understanding the Nicene Creed, by George W. Forell. Philadelphia, Fortress Press [c1965] v. 122 p. 20 cm. [BT999.F6] 65-13407
1. Nicene Creed. I. Title.

FULTON, John, 1834-1907.
... *The Chalcedonian decree;* or, Historical Christianity, misrepresented by modern theology, confirned by modern science, and untouched by modern criticism, by John Fulton ... New York, T. Whittaker, 1892. vii p., 1 l., 213 p. 21 cm. (Charlotte Wood Slocum lectures) A 22
1. Nicene creed. 2. Trinity. 3. Apologetics. 4. [Chalcedon, Council of, 45] I. Title.

HARRISON, Charles George, 1855- 238.
The creed for the twentieth century, by C. G. Harrison ... London, New York [etc.] Longmans, Green and co., 1923. xx, 128 p. 19 cm. [BT999.H3] 23-7939
1. Nicene creed. I. Title.

ILEANA, Princess of Rumania, 1908- 238.1
Meditations on the Nicene creed. New York, Morehouse-Gorham Co. [1958] 144p. 18cm. [BT999.I4] 58-5310
1. Nicene creed. I. Title.

MACGREGOR, Geddes. 238'.142
The Nicene creed, illumined by modern thought / by Geddes MacGregor. Grand Rapids : Eerdmans, c1980. p. cm. [BT999.M32] 19 80-19348 ISBN 0-8028-1855-2 pbk. : 7.95
1. Nicene Creed. I. Title.

NEWLAND-SMITH, James Newland.
The creed of Christendom as expressed in the Nicene creed, short instructions for Bible classes, the senior classes in secondary schools, and others, by the Rev. J. N. Newland-Smith. London and Oxford, A. R. Mowbray & co.; Milwaukee, The Morehouse publishing co. [1920] 2 p. l., 224 p. 19 cm. A 20
1. Nicene creed. I. Title.

SCOTT, Hugh McDonald, 1848-1909. 238.1
Origin and development of the Nicene theology, with some reference to the Ritschlian view of theology and history of doctrine ... By Hugh M. Scott ... Chicago, Chicago theological seminary press, 1896. 2 p. l., ix, 5-390 p. 23 cm. Lectures delivered on the L. P. Stone foundation at Princeton theological seminary, in January, 1896. [BT999.S4] 38-31387
1. Ritschl, Albrecht Benjamin, 1822-1889. 2. Jesus Christ—History of doctrines. 3. Nicene creed. 4. Theology, Doctrinal—Hist. I. Title.

VINNEDGE, Hewitt Breneman, 1898- 238.1
I believe--so what? An inquiry concerning the faith of the Nicene Creed. West Park,

N.Y., Holy Cross Press, 1949. 59 p. 19 cm. [BT999.V5] 50-4488
1. Nicene Creed. I. Title.

WADDAMS, Herbert Montague. 238.14
Believing. New York, Morehouse-Gorham [1958] 98 p. 19 cm. [BT999.W3] 58-2241
1. Nicene Creed. 2. Creeds — Subscription. I. Title.

Nicene Creed—Congresses.

LUTHERANS and Catholics 234'.163 *in dialogue, I-III* / edited by Paul C. Empie and T. Austin Murphy. Minneapolis : Augsburg Pub. House, [1974?] 36, 87, 200 p. ; 20 cm. Papers and summary statements for meetings sponsored jointly by the Bishops' Committee for Ecumenical and Interreligious Affairs and the U.S.A. National Committee of the Lutheran World Federation, and held in various cities in 1965, 1966, and 1967. Reissue of the first three volumes of a series published under the same title by the U.S.A. National Committee of the Lutheran World Federation. Includes bibliographical references. [BX8063.7.C3L87] 74-187921 ISBN 0-8066-1451-X pbk. : 2.95
1. Catholic Church—Relations—Lutheran Church—Congresses. 2. Lutheran Church—Relations—Catholic Church—Congresses. 3. Nicene Creed—Congresses. 4. Baptism—Congresses. 5. Lord's Supper—Congresses. I. Empie, Paul C., ed. II. Murphy, Thomas Austin, 1911- ed. III. Catholic Church. National Conference of Catholic Bishops. Bishops' Committee for Ecumenical and Interreligious Affairs. IV. Lutheran World Federation. U.S.A. National Committee.
Contents omitted.

Nicene creed—Meditations.

THE school of charity; meditations on the Christian creed. The mystery of sacrifice; a meditation on the liturgy. London, New York, Longmans, Green [1956] vii, 111, [8] 77p. 18cm.
1. Nicene creed—Meditations. 2. Lord's Supper (Liturgy). 3. Lord's Supper—Rpayerbooks and devotions—English. I. Underhill, Evelyn, 1875-1941. II. Title: The mystery of sacrifice.

UNDERHILL, Evelyn, 1875- 238.1
The school of charity; meditations on the Christian creed, by Evelyn Underhill ... London, New York [etc.] Longmans, Green and co., 1934. xii p. 2 l., 111, [1] p. 19 1/2 cm. "Based upon the principal articles of the Nicene creed."--Pref. [BT999.U5] 34-12294
1. Nicene creed—Meditations. I. Title.

UNDERHILL, Evelyn, 1875-1941.
The school of charity; meditations on the Christian creed. The mystery of sacrifice; a meditation on the liturgy. London, New York, Longmans, Green [1956] vii, 111 [8] , 77 p. 18 cm.
1. Nicene creed — Meditations. 2. Lord's Supper (Liturgy). 3. Lord's Supper — Prayerbooks and devotions — English. I. Title. II. Title: The mystery of sacrifice.

Nicephorous, Saint, Patriarch of Constantinople.

ALEXANDER, Paul Julius, 1910- 246.3
The Patriarch Nicephorus of Constantinople; ecclesiastical policy and image worship in the Byzantine Empire. Oxford, Clarendon Press, 1958. xii, 287p. facsim. 22cm. Bibliography: p.[266]-280. [BR238.A4] 58-1693
1. Nicephorus, Saint, Patriarch of Constantinople. 2. Iconoclasm. I. Title.

ALEXANDER, Paul Julius, 1910- 270'.3'0924
The Patriarch Nicephorus of Constantinople : ecclesiastical policy and image worship in the Byzantine Empire / by Paul J. Alexander. New York : AMS Press, [1980] xii, 287 p. : facsim. ; 23 cm. Reprint of the 1958 ed. published by Clarendon Press, Oxford. Includes index. Bibliography: p. [266]-280. [BR238.A4 1980] 78-63177 ISBN 0-404-16195-2 : 25.00
1. Nicephorous, Saint, Patriarch of Constantinople. 2. Iconoclasm. I. Title.

Nichiren, 1222-1282.

ANESAKI, Masaharu, 1873- 922.94
Nichiren, the Buddhist prophet, by Masaharu Anesaki ... Cambridge, Harvard unviersity press; London, H. Milford, Oxford university press, 1916. xi, 160 p. front. (facsim.) 21 cm. [BL1473.N5A6] 16-17131
1. Nichiren, 1222-1282. 2. Buddha and Buddhism—Japan. I. Title.

ANESAKI, Masaharu, 1873-1949. 294.3'92'0924 B
Nichiren, the Buddhist prophet. Gloucester, Mass., P. Smith, 1966 [c1916] viii, 160 p. 21 cm. Bibliographical footnotes. [BL1442.N53A5 1966] 67-2824
1. Nichiren, 1222-1282. 2. Buddha and Buddhism—Japan. I. Title.

ELIOT, Charles Norton Edgecumbe Sir 294.32
Japanese Buddhism. With a memoir of the author by Harold Parlett. New York, Barnes &Noble, 1959 [i.e.1960] xxxiv, 449p. 23cm. (bibl. footnotes) 60-341 7.00
1. Nichiren, 1222-1282. 2. Buddha and Buddhism—Japan. I. Title.

RODD, Laurel Rasplica. 294.3'64 B
Nichiren, a biography / Laurel Rasplica Rodd. [Tempe] : Arizona State University, 1978. 86 p. ; 23 cm. (Occasional paper - Arizona State University ; no. 11) Contents.Contents.—Nichiren.—Letter from Sado.—Letter to the wife of Lord Shijo Kingo.—Letter from Mt. Minobu. Bibliography: p. 77-86. [BQ8349.N577R6] 78-624123 pbk. : 2.50
1. Nichiren, 1222-1282. 2. Priests, Nichiren—Japan—Biography. I. Title. II. Series: Arizona. State University, Tempe. Center for Asian Studies. Occasional paper ; no. 11.

Nichol, Charles Ready, 1876-

UNDERWOOD, Maude Jones. 922.89
C. R. Nichol, a preacher of righteousness. Clifton, Tex., Nichol Pub. Co., 1952. 320p. illus. 23cm. [BX7094.C95U57] 53-23289
1. Nichol, Charles Ready, 1876- I. Title.

Nichol, Francis David, 1897-1966.

WOOD, Miriam. 286'.73
His initials were F. D. N.; a life story of elder F. D. Nichol, for twenty-one years editor of the Review and herald, by Miriam and Kenneth Wood. [Washington] Review and Herald Publishing Association, 1967. 256 p. illus., ports. 22 cm. [BX6193.N5W6] 67-21872
1. Nichol, Francis David, 1897-1966. I. Wood, Kenneth H., joint author. II. Title.

Nicholas, Saint,

CHYZHEVS'KYI, Dmytro, 1894- 755.6
The icons of St. Nick [by] Dmitrij Tschizewskij. Translated by Hans Rosenwald. [n.p.] Catholic Art Book Guild; distributed by Taplinger Pub. Co. [New York, 1966, c1964] 80 p. 16 col. plates. 18 cm. (Pictorial library of Eastern Church art, v. 5) On cover: Icons: St. Nick. Translation of Der Hl. Nikolaus. [N8080.C543 1966] 66-9081
1. Nicholas, Saint, Pb. of Myra — Art. I. Title. II. Title: Icons: St. Nick.

INDEX to St. Nicholas; a complete, comprehensive index and dictionary catalogue to the first twenty-seven volumes of St. Nicholas ... comp. by Harriet Goss and Gertrude A. Baker ... Cleveland, O., Cumulative index co. [1901] 234 pp. 4 degree. Copyright by Cumulative index company, Cleveland, Ohio. Class A, XXc, no. 4137, Mar. 1, 1901; 2 copies rec'd June 17, 1901. 1-12744

Nicholas, Saint, bp. of Myra.

ANCELET-HUSTACHE, Jeanne 922.2392
Saint Nicholas. Tr. by Rosemary Sheed. New York, Macmillan, 1962[c.1959-1962] 96p. 18cm. (Your name--Your saint ser.) Bibl. 61-16725 2.50
1. Nicholas, Saint, Bp. of Myra. I. Title.

EBON, Martin. 282'.092'4 B
Saint Nicholas : life and legend / Martin Ebon. 1st ed. New York : Harper & Row, [1975] p. cm. Bibliography: p. [BX4700.N55E26 1975] 75-9329 ISBN 0-06-062113-3 : 8.95
1. Nicholas, Saint, Bp. of Myra. 2. Santa Claus.

GROOT, Adrianus Dingeman de 398.35
Saint Nicholas; a psychoanalytic study of his history and myth. The Hague, Mouton [dist. New York, Humanities, c.1965] 211p. 17 plates. 24cm. (Studies in the behavioral scis. 1) Bibl. [BX4700.N55G73] 65-6735 6.75
I. Nicholas, Saint, Bp. of Myra. II. Title.

GROOT, Adrianus Dingeman de. 398.35
Saint Nicholas; a psychoanalytic study of his history and myth [by] Adriaan D. de Groot. New York, Basic Books [c1965] 211 p. illus. 24 cm. (New Babylon; studies in the behavioral sciences, 1) Translation of Sint Nicolaas, patroon van liefde. Bibliography: p. [206]-207. [BX4700.N55G73 1965a] 66-26212
1. Nicholas, Saint, Bp. of Myra. I. Title.

JONES, Charles Williams, 1905- 264.02
The Saint Nicholas liturgy and its literary relationships (ninth to twelfth centuries) With an essay on the music by Gilbert Reaney. Berkeley, Univ. of Calif. Pr. [c.] 1963. x, 151p. music. 24cm. (Univ. of Calif. pubns. Engl. studies, 27) Liturgy ed. from British Museum ms. Cotton Nero E I, pt. II, leaves 153 verso-155 verso. Bibl. 64-63042 3.50 pap.,
1. Nicholas, Saint, Bp. of Myra. I. Catholic Church. Liturgy and ritual. Special Offices. Nicholas, Saint. Bp. of Myra. II. Title. III. Series: California. University. University of California publications in English, 27

JONES, Charles Williams, 1905- 264.02
The Saint Nicholas liturgy and its literary relationships (ninth to twelfth centuries) With an essay on the music by Gilbert Reaney. Berkeley, University of California Press, 1963. x, 151 p. music. 24 cm. (University of California publications. English studies, 27) Liturgy edited from British Museum manuscript Cotton Nero E. I, pt. II, leaves 153 verso-155 verso. "Bibliographic abbreviations": p. ix-x [BX4700.N55J6] 64-63042
1. Nicholas, Saint, Bp. of Myra. I. Catholic Church. Liturgy and ritual. Special Offices. Nicholas, Saint, Bp. of Myra. II. Title. III. Series. IV. Series: California. University. University of California publications. English studies, 27

JONES, Charles Williams, 1905- 282'.092'4 B
Saint Nicholas of Myra, Bari, and Manhattan : biography of a legend / Charles W. Jones. Chicago : University of Chicago Press, c1978. p. cm. Includes indexes. Bibliography: p. [BX4700.N55J63] 77-15487 ISBN 0-226-40699-7 lib. bdg. : 28.00
1. Nicholas, Saint, Bp. of Myra. 2. Christian saints—Turkey—Lysia—Biography. 3. Lysia—Biography. I. Title.

LORD, Daniel Aloysius, 1888-1955. 922.1
The man who was really Santa Claus. Illus. by Lee G. Hines. [St. Louis 1954] 71p. illus. 22cm. [BX4700.N55L6] 55-25501
1. Nicholas, Saint, Bp. of Myra. I. Title.

MCKNIGHT, George Harley, 1871-
St. Nicholas; his legend and his role in the Christmas celebration and other popular customs, by George H. McKnight ... New York and London, G. P. Putnam's sons, 1917. ix, 153 p. front., plates. 21 1/2 cm. [SV47.M3] 18-4719
1. Nicholas, Saint, bp. of Myra. 2. Christmas. I. Title.

PAULI, Hertha Ernestine, 1909- 922.1
St. Nicholas' travels, a miraculous biography as told by Hertha Pauli and pictured by Susanne Suba. Boston, Houghton Mifflin company, 1945. vi, 105 p. illus., col., plates. 21 cm. [BV47.P3] 45-10168
1. Nicholas, Saint, bp. of Myra. 2. Santa Claus. I. Suba, Susanne, 1913- illus. II. Title.

THOMPSON, Blanche Jennings, 1887- 922.1
Jolly old St. Nicholas; cover and illus. [by] Stanley S. Sessler [and] Frederick S. Beckman. Notre Dame, Ind., Ave Maria Press [1947] [72] p. illus. 25 cm. [BX4700.N55T5] 50-19913
1. Nicholas, Saint, Bp. of Myra. I. Title.

Nicholas, Saint, Bp. of Myra—Art.

CHYZHEVS'KYI, Dmytro, 1894- 755.6
The icons of St. Nick [by] Dmitrij Tschizewskij. Tr. by Hans Rosenwald. [n.p.] Catholic Art Bk. Guild, [New York, dist. Taplinger 1966, c.1964] 80p. 16 col. plates. 18cm. (Pictorial lib. of Eastean Church art, v.5) On cover: Icons: St. Nick. Tr. of Der Hl. Nikolaus. [N8080.C543 1966] 66-9081 2.50 bds.,
1. Nicholas, Saint, Bp. of Myra—Art. I. Title. II. Title: Icons: St. Nick.

Nicholas, Saint, bp of Myra—Drama.

ALBRECHT, Otto Edwin, 1899- ed. 879.2
Four Latin plays of St. Nicholas from the 12th century Fleury play-book; text and commentary, with a study of the music of the plays, and of the sources and iconography of the legends, by Otto E. Albrecht. Philadelphia, University of Pennsylvania press; London, H. Milford, Oxford university press, 1935. ix, 160 p. front., illus. (music) facsim. (music) 23 1/2 cm. "The ms. containing the four plays ... is preserved in the public library at Orleans (Ms. 201, olim 178, Miscellanea floriacensia saec. xiii) ...Originally in the possession of the monastery of Fleury, it passed at the revolution ... to the nearby library of Orleans."--p. 1. Issued also as thesis (PH. D.) University of Pennsylvania. Bibliography: p. 143-155. [PA8142.A4 1935] 35-34452
1. Nicholas, Saint, bp of Myra—Drama. 2. Mysteries and miracle-plays. Latin. 3. Latin drama, Medieval and modern. I. Orleans, France. Bibliotheque municipale. Mrs. (201) II. Title. III. Title: Fleury play-book.

Nicholas, Saint, Bp. of Myra—Juvenile literature.

BRYSON, Bernarda. 922.1
The twenty miracles of Saint Nicolas. With illus. by the author. [1st ed.] Boston, Little, Brown [1960] 88 p. illus. 28 cm. [BX4700.N55B7] 59-7338
1. Nicholas, Saint, Bp. of Myra—Juvenile literature. 2. [Nicholas, Saint, Bp. of Myra.] I. Title.

LUCKHARDT, Mildred Madeleine (Corell) 1898- 922.1
The story of Saint Nicholas. Illustrated by Gordon Laite. New York, Abingdon Press [1960] 112p. illus. 23cm. [BX4700.N55L8] 60-6815
1. Nicholas, Saint, Bp. of Myra—Juvenile literature. I. Title.

SMITH, Verena 92
The life of Saint Nicholas; pictures by Emile Probst. London, Burns &Oates; New York, Herder & Herder [1966, i.e., 1967] 26p. col. front., col. illus. 19x21cm. [BX4700.N55S6 1966] 67-82365 1.75 bds.,
1. Nicholas, Saint, Bp. of Myra— Juvenile literature. I. Probst, Emile, illus. II. Title.

Nicholas, Saint, of Tolentino, 13th century

COMPENDIUM of the life of 922. *Saint Nicholas of Tolentine, priest of the Order of Saint Augustine, patron of the holy souls in purgatory;* tr. from the Italian by Rev. V. C. Yannes, O. S. A. [New York, Printed by McClunn and company, c1918] 62 p. incl. pl. 17 cm. [BX4700.N6C6] 19-1725
1. Nicholas, Saint, of Tolentino, 13th cent. I. Yannes, Victor Camillus, 1885- tr.

Nicholites.

CARROLL, Kenneth Lane.
Joseph Nichols and the Nicholites; a look at the "New Quakers" of Maryland, Delaware, North and South Carolina. Easton, Md., Easton Pub. Co. [1962] 116 p. 24 cm. [BX7775.N5C3] 63-2540
1. Nichols, Joseph, 1730 (ca.)-1770. 2. Nicholites. I. Title.

Nicholls, Douglas Ralph, Sir, 1906-

CLARK, Mavis Thorpe 286.63
Pastor Doug: the story of an Aboriginal leader. Melbourne, Landsdowne; London, Newnes, 1966. [7] 245p. 12 plates (incl. ports.) 23cm. [BV3667.N5C55 1966] 66-72165 5.50 bds.,
1. Nicholls, Douglas Ralph, 1906- 2. Missions—Australia. I. Title.
Available from Ginn in Boston.

CLARK, Mavis Thorpe. 286'.63 B
Pastor Doug: the story of Sir Douglas Nicholls, Aboriginal leader [by] Mavis Thorpe Clark. Rev. ed. Melbourne, Lansdowne Press, 1972. 259 p., 6 plates. 23 cm. [BV3667.N5C55 1972] 73-176912 ISBN 0-7018-0017-8 6.95
1. Nicholls, Douglas Ralph, Sir, 1906- 2. Missions—Australia. I. Title.

Nichols, Harry Peirce, 1850-1940.

STEVENS, William Bertrand, bp., 1884- 922.373
Victorious mountaineer, a memoir of Harry Pierce Nichols, 1850-1940, by W. Bertrand Stevens; introduction [by] Frederick C. Grant; drawings [by] Carleton M. Winslow. Louisville [Ky.] The Cloister press, 1943. 3 p. l., [3]-78, [2] p. front. (port.) illus. 19 1/2 cm. [BX5995 N48S8] 44-751
1. Nichols, Harry Peirce, 1850-1940. I. Winslow, Carleton Monroe, 1876- illus. II. Title.

Nichols, James Albert—Addresses, essays, lectures.

ALPHA and omega : 231'.044
essays on the Trinity in honor of James A. Nichols, Jr. / edited by Caroleen Hillriegel, Lois Jones, Freeman Barton. Lenox, Mass. (200 Stockbridge Rd., Lenox, 01240) : Henceforth Publications, c1980. 140 p. ; 22 cm. Includes bibliographical references. [BT113.A46] 19 81-126219 4.50 (pbk.)
1. Nichols, James Albert—Addresses, essays, lectures. 2. Trinity—Addresses, essays, lectures. I. Nichols, James Albert. II. Hillriegel, Caroleen. III. Jones, Lois. IV. Barton, Freeman.

Nichols, Joseph, 1730 (ca.)-1770.

CARROLL, Kenneth Lane.
Joseph Nichols and the Nicholites; a look at the "New Quakers" of Maryland, Delaware, North and South Carolina. Easton, Md., Easton Pub. Co. [1962] 116 p. 24 cm. [BX7775.N5C3] 63-2540
1. Nichols, Joseph, 1730 (ca.)-1770. 2. Nicholites. I. Title.

Nicholson, Timothy, 1828-1924.

WOODWARD, Walter Carleton. 922.
Timothy Nicholson master Quaker; a biography by Walter C. Woodward ... Richmond, Ind., The Nicholson press, 1927. 2 p. l., vii-xiii, 252 p. front. (port.) 23 cm. [BX7795.N47W6] 27-21320
1. Nicholson, Timothy, 1828-1924. I. Title.

Nicodemus (Biblical character)

OTTS, John Martin Philip, 1838-1901. 225.92
Nicodemus with Jesus; or, Light and life for the dark and dead world. By Rev. J. M. P. Otts ... Philadelphia, J. S. Claxton, 1867. 1 p. l., [7]-230 p. 16 cm. [BS2500.N5O8] 39-10298
1. Nicodemus (Biblical character) I. Title.

Nicolaij, Paul Ernst Georg, friherre, 1860-1919.

LANGENSKJOLD, Margareta, 1889- 922
Baron Paul Nicolay, Christian statesman and student leader in northern and Slavic Europe, by Greta Langenskjold, translated from the Swedish by Ruth Evelyn Wilder ... New York, George H. Doran company [c1924] vi p., 3 l., 13-251 p. front., plates, ports., 20 cm. [BR1725.N5L3] 24-21165
1. Nicolaij, Paul Ernst Georg, friherre, 1860-1919. I. Wilder, Ruth Evelyn, tr. II. Title.

Nicolas, Armelle, 1606-1671.

[JEANNE, de la Nativite] fl. 1650. 922.
The holy life of Armelle Nicolas, a poor and ignorant servant-maid, commonly known as the "Good Armelle", born 1606, died 1671; translated and revised by Inanda [pseud.] Philadelphia, G. W. McCalla, 1899. 54 p. 20 cm. [BX4705.N57J4] 99-942
1. Nicolas, Armelle, 1606-1671. I. Lindley, Martha A., tr. II. Title.

Nicolaus Cusanus, Cardinal, 1401-1464.

BETT, Henry, 1876-1953. 230'.2'0924 B
Nicholas of Cusa / by Henry Bett. Merrick, N.Y. : Richwood Pub. Co., 1976. x, 210 p. ; 23 cm. Reprint of the 1932 ed. published by Methuen & Co., London, issued in series: Great medieval churchmen. Includes bibliographical references and index. [BX4705.N58B4 1976] 76-1131 ISBN 0-915172-05-4 lib.bdg. : 18.50
1. Nicolaus Cusanus, Cardinal, 1401-1464. I. Title. II. Series: Great medieval churchmen.

BURGEVIN, Frederick Haviland. 297'.122
Cribratio Alchorani; Nicholas Cusanus's criticism of the Koran in the light of his philosophy of religion. [1st ed.] New York, Vantage Press [1969] 128 p. 21 cm. Bibliography: p. 122-128. [BP169.B8] 76-6609 3.95
1. Nicolaus Cusanus, Cardinal, 1401-1464. Cribratio Alchorani. I. Title.

HEROLD, Norbert. 189.4
Menschliche Perspektive und Wahrheit : zur Deutung der Subjektivitat in den philosophischen Schriften des Nikolaus von Kues / Norbert Herold. Munster, Westf. : Aschendorff, 1975. x, 120 p. ; 24 cm. (Buchreihe der Cusanus-Gesellschaft ; Bd. 6) Abridgement of the author's thesis, Munster, 1973. Includes index. Bibliography: p. 113-118. [BX4705.N58C8 Bd. 6] [B765.N54] 189.4 75-511415 ISBN 3-402-03156-6
1. Nicolaus Cusanus, Cardinal, 1401-1464. 2. Subjectivity. I. Title. II. Series: Cusanus-Gesellschaft, Vereinigung zur Forderung der Cusanusforschung. Buchreihe ; Bd. 6.

SIGMUND, Paul E 262
Nicholas of Cusa and medieval political thought. Cambridge, Mass., Harvard University Press, 1963. viii, 335 p. port. 22 cm. (Harvard political studies) Bibliography: p. 317-330. [BX4705.N58S5] 63-20772
1. Nicolaus Cusanus, Cardinal, 1401-1464. 2. Conciliar theory. 3. Church and state—Catholic Church. I. Title. II. Series.

Nicolson, William, Abp. of Cashel, 1655-1727.

JAMES, Francis Godwin. 922.342
North Country bishop; a biography of William Nicolson. New Haven, Yale University Press, 1956. xiv, 330p. port., map, geneal. table. 25cm. (Yale historical publications. Miscellany, 65) Bibliographical essay': p. 281-295. [BX5595.N5J3] 56-11797
1. Nicolson, William, Abp. of Cashel, 1655-1727. I. Title. II. Series.

Niebuhr, Gustav, 1863-1913.

CHRYSTAL, William G., 1947- 285.7'3 B
A father's mantle : the legacy of Gustav Niebuhr / by William G. Chrystal. New York, N.Y. : Pilgrim Press, c1982. xx, 139 p. : ill. ; 21 cm. "A Gustav Niebuhr bibliography": P. 135-139. [BX7943.N53C48] 19 81-21108 ISBN 0-8298-0494-3 pbk. : 7.95
1. Niebuhr, Gustav, 1863-1913. 2. Evangelical Synod of North America—Clergy—Biography. 3. Clergy—United States—Biography. I. Title.

Niebuhr, Helmut Richard, 1894-1962.

FADNER, Donald Edward. 230'.092'4
The responsible God : a study of the Christian philosophy of H. Richard Niebuhr / by Donald Edward Fadner. Missoula, Mont. : Published by Scholars Press for the American Academy of Religion, c1975. xvi, 276 p. ; 21 cm. (Dissertation series - American Academy of Religion ; no. 13) Originally presented as the author's thesis, University of Chicago, 1974. Bibliography: p. 273-276. [BX4827.N47F3 1975] 75-29373 ISBN 0-89130-041-4 : 4.20
1. Niebuhr, Helmut Richard, 1894-1962. I. Title. II. Series: American Academy of Religion. Dissertation series — American Academy of Religion ; no. 13.

FOWLER, James W., 1940- 230'.092'4 B
To see the kingdom; the theological vision of H. Richard Niebuhr [by] James W. Fowler. Nashville, Abingdon Press [1974] xii, 292 p. illus. 24 cm. Bibliography: p. 277-286. [BX4827.N47F68] 74-688 ISBN 0-687-42300-7 10.95
1. Niebuhr, Helmut Richard, 1894-1962. I. Title.

GODSEY, John D. 230'.0924 B
The promise of H. Richard Niebuhr, by John D. Godsey. [1st ed.] Philadelphia, Lippincott [1970] 122 p. 22 cm. (The Promise of theology) Bibliography: p. 119-122. [BX4827.N47G6] 75-103600 3.95
1. Niebuhr, Helmut Richard, 1894-1962. I. Title.

HOEDEMAKER, Libertus Arend, 1935- 201'.1
The theology of H. Richard Niebuhr, by Libertus A. Hoedemaker. Philadelphia, Pilgrim Press [1970] xix, 204 p. 22 cm. A revision of the author's thesis entitled: Faith in total life, Utrecht, 1966. "Bibliography of the writings of H. Richard Niebuhr, compiled by Jane E. McFarland": p. 196-204. [BX4827.N47H6 1970] 78-139271 ISBN 0-8298-0186-3 10.00
1. Niebuhr, Helmut Richard, 1894-1962. I. Title.

KLIEVER, Lonnie D. 230'.092'4 B
H. Richard Niebuhr / by Lonnie D. Kliever. Waco, Tex. : Word Books, c1977. 205 p. ; 23 cm. (Makers of the modern theological mind) Bibliography: p. 203-205. [BX4827.N47K56] 77-92452 ISBN 0-8499-0078-6 : 7.95
1. Niebuhr, Helmut Richard, 1894-1962.

RAMSEY, Paul, ed. [Full name: Robert Paul Ramsey] 230.08
Faith and ethics; the theology of H. Richard Niebuhr [by] Waldo Beach [others] New York, Harper [1965, c.1957] 306p. port. 20cm. (Harper torchbk. TB129L) [BX4827.N47R3] 1.95 pap.,
1. Niebuhr, Helmut Richard, 1894- 2. Niebuhr, Helmut Richard, 1894- —Bibl. 3. Theology, Doctrinal—Addresses, essays, lectures. I. Title.

RAMSEY, Paul, ed. [Robert Paul Ramsey] 230.04
Faith and ethics: the theology of H. Richard Niebuhr [by] Waldo Beach [others.] [Magnolia, Mass., P. Smith, 1967,c.1957] xii, 314p. port. 21cm. [BX4827.N47R3] 4.00
1. Niebuhr, Helmut Richard. 1894- 2. Niebuhr, Helmut Richard, 1894-;Bibl. 3. Theology, Doctrinal — Addresses, essays, lectures. I. Title.
Contents omitted,

RAMSEY, Paul, ed. 230.04
Faith and ethics; the theology of H. Richard Niebuhr [by] Waldo Beach [and others. 1st ed.] New York, Harper [1957] xiv, 306p. port. 22cm. [BX4827.N47R3] 57-9882
1. Niebuhr, Helmut Richard, 1894- 2. Niebuhr, Helmut Richard, 1894- —Bibl. 3. Theology, Doctrinal—Addresses, essays, lectures. I. Title.
Onconnts omitted.

RAMSEY, Paul, ed.
Faith and ethics; the theology of H. Richard Niebuhr [by] Waldo Beach [and others] New York, Harper [1965, c1957] xii, 314, 10 p. port. (Harper Torchbooks) Bibliography of H. Richard Niebuhr's writings: p. 291-306. 66-43975
1. Niebuhr, Helmut Richard, 1894-1962. 2. Niebuhr, Helmut Richard, 1894-1962 — Bibl. 3. Theology, Doctrinal — Addresses, essays, lectures. I. Beach, Waldo. II. Title.

RAMSEY, Paul [Robert Paul Ramsey] 230.08
Faith and ethics; the theology of H. Richard Niebuhr [by] Waldo Beach [others] Ed. Paul Ramsey [Gloucester, Mass., P. Smith, 1965, c.1957] xii, 314p. port. 21cm. (Harper torchbk., Cloister lib., TB129L rebound) Bibl. [BX4827.N47R3] 4.00
1. Niebuhr, Helmut Richard, 1894- 2. Niebuhr, Helmut Richard, 1894- —Bibl. 3. Theology, Doctrinal—Addresses, essays, lectures. I. Title.

Niebuhr, Helmut Richard, 1894- —Bibliography

RAMSEY, Paul, ed. [Robert Paul Ramsey] 230.04
Faith and ethics: the theology of H. Richard Niebuhr [by] Waldo Beach [others.] [Magnolia, Mass., P. Smith, 1967,c.1957] xii, 314p. port. 21cm. [BX4827.N47R3] 4.00
1. Niebuhr, Helmut Richard. 1894- 2. Niebuhr, Helmut Richard, 1894-;Bibl. 3. Theology, Doctrinal — Addresses, essays, lectures. I. Title.
Contents omitted,

RAMSEY, Paul, ed. 230.04
Faith and ethics; the theology of H. Richard Niebuhr [by] Waldo Beach [and others. 1st ed.] New York, Harper [1957] xiv, 306p. port. 22cm. [BX4827.N47R3] 57-9882
1. Niebuhr, Helmut Richard, 1894- 2. Niebuhr, Helmut Richard, 1894- —Bibl. 3. Theology, Doctrinal—Addresses, essays, lectures. I. Title.
Onconnts omitted.

Niebuhr, Reinhold.

CARNELL, Edward John, 1919- 230.41
The theology of Reinhold Niebuhr. Grand Rapids, Eerdmans, 1951 ['1950] 250 p. 23 cm. Bibliographical footnotes. [BT78.N5C3] 51-9746
1. Niebuhr, Reinhold, 2. Dialectical theology. 3. Neo-orthodoxy. I. Title.

Niebuhr, Reinhold, 1892-1971.

BINGHAM, June, 1919- 230'.0924 B
Courage to change; an introduction to the life and thought of Reinhold Niebuhr. New York, Scribner [1972] xii, 414 p. illus. 24 cm. "Books by Reinhold Niebuhr": p. 405-406. Includes bibliographical references. [BX4827.N5B5 1972] 72-37467 ISBN 0-684-12789-X 10.00
1. Niebuhr, Reinhold, 1892-1971. I. Title.

BINGHAM, June, 1919- 922.473
Courage to change; an introduction to the life and thought of Reinhold Niebuhr. New York, Scribner [1961] 414 p. 24 cm. Includes bibliography. [BX4827.N5B5] 61-13362
1. Niebuhr, Reinhold, 1892-1971. I. Title.

CARNELL, Edward John, 1919- 230.41
The theology of Reinhold Niebuhr. [Rev. ed.] Grand Rapids, Eerdmans [1960] 250p. 22cm. Includes bibliography. [BX4827.N5C3 1960] 60-16193
1. Niebuhr, Reinhold, 1892- 2. Dialectical theology. 3. Neo-orthodoxy. I. Title.

CARNELL, Edward John, 1919- 230.41
The theology of Reinhold Niebuhr. Grand Rapids, Eerdmans, 1951 ['1950] 250 p. 23 cm. Bibliographical footnotes. [BT78.N5C3] 51-9746
1. Niebuhr, Reinhold, 2. Dialectical theology. 3. Neo-orthodoxy. I. Title.

DAVIES, David Richard, 1889- 922.473
Reinhold Niebuhr; prophet from America. New York, Macmillan Co., 1948. 102 p. 20 cm. [BX4827.N5D3 1948] 48-2696
1. Niebuhr, Reinhold, 1892- I. Title.

DAVIES, David Richard, 1889-1958. 230'.0924
Reinhold Niebuhr; prophet from America. Freeport, N.Y., Books for Libraries Press [1970, c1945] 94 p. 23 cm. "Books by Reinhold Niebuhr": p. [9] [BX4827.N5D3 1970] 71-117871
1. Niebuhr, Reinhold, 1892-

DIBBLE, Ernest F., 1929- 230'.092'4
Young prophet Niebuhr : Reinhold Niebuhr's early search for social justice / Ernest F. Dibble. Washington : University Press of America, 1978,c1977. viii, 320 p. ; 22 cm. Bibliography: p. 302-320. [BX4827.N5D5] 78-100405 ISBN 0-8191-0377-2 pbk. : 9.75
1. Niebuhr, Reinhold, 1892-1971. I. Title.

FACKRE, Gabriel J. 230'.0924
The promise of Reinhold Niebuhr, by Gabriel Fackre. [1st ed.] Philadelphia, Lippincott [1970] 101 p. 21 cm. (The Promise of theology) "A selected bibliography of works by Reinhold Niebuhr": p. 100-101. Includes bibliographical references. [BX4827.N5F3] 79-120329 3.50
1. Niebuhr, Reinhold, 1892- I. Title.

HARLAND, Gordon. 922.473
The thought of Reinhold Niebuhr. New York, Oxford University Press, 1960. xvii, 298 p. 22 cm. Bibliographical references included in "Notes" (p. [275]-294) [BX4827.N5H3] 60-7061
1. Niebuhr, Reinhold, 1892-1971. I. Title.

HOFMANN, Hans, 1923- 230.41
The theology of Reinhold Niebuhr. Translated by Louise Pettibone Smith. New York, Scribner, 1956. 269p. 22cm. [BX4827.N5H63] 56-5663
1. Niebuhr, Reinhold, 1892- 2. Sin—History of doctrines. I. Title.

HOFMANN, Hans F., 1923- 230.41
The theology of Reinhold Niebuhr Translated by Louise Pettibone Smith. New York Scribner 1956. 269 p. 22 cm. [BX4827.N5H63] 56-5663
1. Niebuhr, Reinhold, 1892- 2. Sin — History of doctrines. I. Title.

KEGLEY, Charles W. ed. 922.473
Reinhold Niebuhr: his religious, social, and political thought, edited by Charles W. Kegley and Robert W. Bretall. New York, Macmillan, 1956. xiv, 486 p. port. 22 cm. (The Library of living theology, v. 2) Contents.Contents.—Intellectual autobiography of Reinhold Niebuhr.—Essays of interpretation and criticism of the work of Reinhold Niebuhr.—Reply to interpretation and criticism, by R. Niebuhr.—Bibliography of the writings of Reinhold Niebuhr to 1956 (p. 455-478) [BX4827.N5K4] 56-13522
1. Niebuhr, Reinhold, 1892- I. Bretall, Robert Walter, 1913- joint ed.

KING, Rachel Hadley, 1904- 230.41
The omission of the Holy Spirit from Reinhold Niebuhr's theology. New York, Philosophical [c.1964] 209p. 22cm. Bibl. 64-13324 5.75
1. Niebuhr, Reinhold, 1892- I. Title.

LANDON, Harold R., ed. 230'.092'4 B
Reinhold Niebuhr: a prophetic voice in our time. Essays in tribute by Paul Tillich, John C. Bennett [and] Hans J. Morgenthau. Harold R. Landon, editor. Plainview, N.Y., Books for Libraries Press [1974, c1962] 126 p. 22 cm. (Essay index reprint series) Papers and discussions from the colloquium in honor of Reinhold Niebuhr on October 20, 1961, at the Cathedral Church of St. John the Divine, New York City. Reprint of the ed. published by the Seabury Press, Greenwich, Conn. Includes bibliographical references. [BX4827.N5L3 1974] 74-841 ISBN 0-518-10150-9 9.50
1. Niebuhr, Reinhold, 1892-1971.

LANDON, Harold R. ed. 922.473
Reinhold Niebuhr: a prophetic voice in our time; essays in tribute, by Paul Tillich, John C. Bennett [and] Hans J. Morgenthau. Greenwich, Conn., Seabury Press, 1962. 126 p. 21 cm. [BX4827.N5L3] 62-18023
1. Niebuhr, Reinhold, 1892- I. Tillich, Paul, 1886-

MCCANN, Dennis. 261.8
Christian realism and liberation theology : practical theologies in conflict / Dennis McCann. Maryknoll, N.Y. : Orbis Books, c1981. vi, 250 p. ; 24 cm. Includes index. Bibliography: p. 241-244. [BT738.M25] 19 80-23163 ISBN 0-88344-086-5 pbk. : 9.95
1. Niebuhr, Reinhold, 1892-1971. 2. Sociology, Christian—History—20th century. 3. Christian ethics—History—20th century. 4. Social ethics—History—20th century. 5. Liberation theology. I. Title.

MERKLEY, Paul. 200.92
Reinhold Niebuhr : a political account / Paul Merkley. Montreal : McGill-Queen's University Press, 1975. xii, 289 p. ; 24 cm. Includes index. Bibliography: p. [273]-277. [BX4827.N5M47] 76-351874 ISBN 0-7735-0216-5 : 13.50
1. Niebuhr, Reinhold, 1892-1971.
Distributed by McGill-Queen's University Press, Irvington, N.Y.

MEYER, Donald B. 261.7
The Protestant search for political realism, 1919-1941 [by] Donald B. Meyer. Westport, Conn., Greenwood Press [1973, c1960] x, 482 p. 23 cm. Bibliography: p. 463-474. [HN39.U6M45 1973] 72-12314 ISBN 0-8371-6698-5 19.25
1. Niebuhr, Reinhold, 1892-1971. 2. Church and social problems—United States. 3. Protestant churches—United States. 4. Christianity and politics. I. Title.

MOLIN, Lennart, 1944- 233
Hearts and structures : about man and society out of an American theological material / Lennart Molin. [Stockholm] : Gummesson, 1976. 212 p. ; 19 cm. Bibliography: p. 203-212. [BT701.2.M555] 77-366778 ISBN 9-17-070487-2 : kr40.00
1. Niebuhr, Reinhold, 1892-1971. 2. Niebuhr, Helmut Richard, 1894-1962. 3. Gustafson, James M. 4. Lehmann, Paul Louis, 1906- 5. Man (Theology)—History of doctrines—20th century. 6. Sociology, Christian—History. 7. Christian ethics—History. I. Title.

NIEBUHR, Reinhold, 1892-1971. 230'.092'4 B
Leaves from the notebook of a tamed cynic / by Reinhold Niebuhr. New York : Da Capo Press, 1976, c1929. p. cm. (Prelude to depression) Reprint of the ed. published by Willett, Clark & Colby, Chicago. [BX4827.N5A34 1976] 76-27833 ISBN 0-306-70852-3 : 15.00
1. Niebuhr, Reinhold, 1892-1971. 2. Clergy—Michigan—Detroit—Biography. 3. Detroit—Biography. I. Title.

NIEBUHR, Reinhold, 1892-1971. 280'.4'0924 B
Leaves from the notebook of a tamed cynic / Reinhold Niebuhr. San Francisco : Harper & Row, [1980] c1929. xii, 198 p. ; 21 cm. (Harper's ministers paperback library ; RD 311) [BX4827.N5A34 1980] 19 79-2992 ISBN 0-06-066231-X (pbk.) : 4.95
1. Niebuhr, Reinhold, 1892-1971. 2. Clergy—Michigan—Detroit—Biography. 3. Detroit—Biography. I. Title.

ODEGARD, Holtan Peter, 1923- 261.7
Sin and science; Reinhold Niebuhr as political theologian. Yellow Springs, Ohio. Antioh Press [1956] 245p. 22cm. Bibliography:p. [221]-234. [BX4827.N5O3] 56-8247
1. Niebuhr, Reinhold, 1892- 2. Sin. 3. Christianity and politics. I. Title.

ODEGARD, Holtan Peter, 1923- 261.7
Sin and science; Reinhold Niebuhr as political theologian, by Holtan P. Odegard. Westport, Conn., Greenwood Press [1972, c1956] 245 p. 22 cm. Bibliography: p. [221]-234. [BX4827.N5O3 1972] 72-6928 ISBN 0-8371-6505-9 11.25
1. Niebuhr, Reinhold, 1892-1971. 2. Sin. 3. Christianity and politics. I. Title.

ODEGARD, Holton P 261.7
Sin and science; Reinhold Niebuhr as political theologian. Yellow Springs, Ohio, Antioch Press [1956] 245p. 22cm. Bibliography: p. [221]-234. [BX4827.N5O3] 56-8247
1. Niebuhr, Reinhold, 1802- 2. Christianity and politics. 3. Sin I. Title.

PATTERSON, Bob E. 230'.092'4 B
Reinhold Niebuhr / by Bob E. Patterson. Waco, Tex. : Word Books, c1977. 163 p. ; 23 cm. (Makers of the modern theological mind) Bibliography: p. 161-163. [BX4827.N5P37] 76-46783 ISBN 0-87680-508-X : 6.95
1. Niebuhr, Reinhold, 1892-1971.

PLASKOW, Judith. 231
Sex, sin, and grace : women's experience and the theologies of Reinhold Niebuhr and Paul Tillich / by Judith Plaskow. Washington : University Press of America, [1980] p. cm. Based on the author's thesis, Yale, 1975. Includes index. Bibliography: p. [BT704.P56] 79-5434 ISBN 0-8191-0882-0 pbk. : 9.25
1. Niebuhr, Reinhold, 1892-1971. 2. Tillich, Paul, 1886-1965. 3. Women (Christian theology)—History of doctrines. 4. Sin—History of doctrines. 5. Grace (Theology)—History of doctrines. I. Title.

SCOTT, Nathan A. 230.41
Reinhold Niebuhr. Minneapolis, University of Minnesota Press; [distributed to high schools in the U.S. by McGraw-Hill, New York, 1963] 48 p. 21 cm. (University of Minnesota pamphlets of American writers, no. 31) Bibliography: p. 46-48. [BX4827.N5S3] 63-64003
1. Niebuhr, Reinhold, 1892-1971. I. Series: Minnesota. University. Pamphlets on American writers, no. 31

STONE, Ronald H. 261.7
Reinhold Niebuhr : prophet to politicians / Ronald H. Stone. Lanham, Md. : University Press of America, c1981. p. cm. Reprint. Originally published: Nashville : Abingdon Press, c1972. Includes bibliographical references and index. [BX4827.N5S74 1981] 19 81-3407 ISBN 0-8191-1540-1 : 19.25 ISBN 0-8191-1541-X (pbk.) : 10.50
1. Niebuhr, Reinhold, 1892-1971. 2. Christianity and politics—History—20th century. I. Title.

STONE, Ronald H. 230'.0924
Reinhold Niebuhr, prophet to politicians [by] Ronald H. Stone. Nashville, Abingdon Press [1971, c1972] 272 p. 24 cm. Includes bibliographical references. [BX4827.N5S74 1972] 71-172813 ISBN 0-687-36272-5 8.00
1. Niebuhr, Reinhold, 1892-1971. 2. Christianity and politics. I. Title.

Niebuhr, Reinhold, 1892-1971—Addresses, essays, lectures.

THE Legacy of Reinhold Niebuhr 230'.092'4
/ edited by Nathan A. Scott, Jr. Chicago : University of Chicago Press, 1975. xxiv, 124 p. : port. ; 24 cm. "This work also appeared as volume 54, number 4 (Oct. 1974), of the Journal of religion." Bibliography: p. 111-112. [BX4827.N5L4] 74-30714 ISBN 0-226-74297-0 : 6.95
1. Niebuhr, Reinhold, 1892-1971—Addresses, essays, lectures. I. Scott, Nathan A. II. The Journal of religion.

Niebuhr, Reinhold, 1892-1971—Bibliography.

ROBERTSON, D. B. 016.23
Reinhold Niebuhr's works : a bibliography / by D. B. Robertson. Syracuse, N.Y. : Wallon Book Bindery, 1976. 354 leaves ; 28 cm. [Z8628.R6 1976] [BX4827.N5] 76-374244
1. Niebuhr, Reinhold, 1892-1971—Bibliography.

ROBERTSON, D. B. 016.23
Reinhold Niebuhr's works : a bibliography / D. B. Robertson. Boston : G. K. Hall, c1979. xi, 238 p. ; 24 cm. Includes index. [Z8628.R6 1979] [BX4827.N5] 79-4037 ISBN 0-8161-8237-X lib. bdg. : 24.00
1. Niebuhr, Reinhold, 1892-1971—Bibliography.

Niebuhr, Richard R.

NIEBUHR, Richard R. 230.4
Schleiermacher on Christ and religion, a new introduction. New York, Scribners [c.1964] xv, 267p. 24cm. Bibl. [BX4827.S3N5] 64-22393 5.95
I. Schleiermacher, Friedrich Ernst Daniel, 1768-1834. II. Title.

PRIMEAUX, Patrick. 230'.583
Richard R. Niebuhr on Christ and religion : the four stage development of his theology / Patrick Primeaux. New York : E. Mellen Press, c1981. p. cm. (Toronto studies in theology ; v. 4) Includes index. Bibliography: p. [BX4827.N53P74] 19 81-38369 ISBN 0-88946-996-2 : 19.95
1. Niebuhr, Richard R. I. Title. II. Series.

Niemoller, Martin, 1892-

ALBUS, Harry James, 1920- 922.443
Concentration camp hero; the story of Martin Niemoeller for young people. by Harry Albus. Grand Rapids, Mich., Zondervan publishing house [1946] 2 p. l., 7-82 p. 20 cm. [BX8080.N48A6] 46-21563
1. Niemoller, Martin, 1892- I. Title.

DAVIDSON, Clarissa Start. 284'.1'0924 B
God's man : the story of Pastor Niemoeller / by Clarissa Start Davidson. Westport, Conn. : Greenwood Press, 1979, c1959. x, 242 p., [1] leaf of plates : port. ; 22 cm. Reprint of the ed. published by I. Washburn, New York. Bibliography: p. 241-242. [BX8080.N48D3 1979] 78-10131 ISBN 0-313-21065-9 lib. bdg. : 19.75
1. Niemoller, Martin, 1892- 2. Lutheran Church—Clergy—Biography. 3. Clergy—Germany, West—Biography. I. Title.

MILLER, Basil William, 1897- 922.443
Martin Niemoeller, hero of the concentration camp [by] Basil Miller. Grand Rapids, Mich., Zondervan publishing house [1942] 5 p. l. 9-160 p., 1 l. 20 cm. [BX8080.N48M5] 43-421
1. Niemoller, Martin, 1802. I. Title.

SCHMIDT, Dietmar. 922.443
Pastor Niemoller. Translated from the German by Lawrence Wilson. Garden City, N.Y., Doubleday, 1959. 224 p. illus. 22 cm. [BX8080.N48S343 1959a] 59-12275
1. Niemoller, Martin, 1892-

Nieto, David, 1654-1728.

PETUCHOWSKI, Jakob Josef, 1925- 296.3'0924
The theology of Haham David Nieto; an eighteenth-century defense of the Jewish tradition. New and rev. ed. by Jakob J. Petuchowski. [New York] Ktav Pub. House [1970] xix, 166 p. 24 cm. Bibliography: p. 161-166. [BM755.N5P4 1970] 79-105752
1. Nieto, David, 1654-1728. I. Title.

Nietzsche, Friedrich Wilhelm, 1844-1900.

ABRAHAM, Gerald Ernest Heal, 1904- 921.3
Nietzsche, by Gerald Abraham... New York, The Macmillan company, 1933. 144 p. 19 cm. (Great lives. (23] "Printed in Great Britain." Bibliography: p. 144. [B3316.A6] 34-120
1. Nietzsche, Friedrich Wilheim, 1844-1900. I. Title.

BRINTON, Clarence Crane, 1898- 921.3
Nietzsche, by Crane Brinton ... Cambridge, Mass., Harvard university press, 1941. xvii, 266 p. front., ports. 22 cm. (Half-title: Makers of modern Europe, ed. by Donald C. McKay in association with Dumas Malone) Bibliographical foot-notes. Bibliography: p. [245]-259. [B3316.B75] A 41

1. Nietzsche, Friedrich Wilhelm, 1844-1900. I. Title.

DOLSON, Grace Neal.
...Philosophy of Frederic Nietzsche, by Grace Neal Dolson... New York, The Macmillan company, 1901. v p., 1 l., 110 p. 25 cm. (Cornell studies in philosophy, no. 3) Bibliography: p. 104-110. 7-22423
I. Title.

DURANT, William James, 1885- 921.
... Nietzsche: who he was and what he stood for [by] Will Durant ... Girard, Kan., Haldeman-Julius company [c1924] 96 p. 13 cm. (Little blue book, no. 19, ed. by E. Haldeman-Julius) Advertising matter: p. 93-96. [B3316.D8] ca 25
1. Nietzsche, Friedrich Wilhelm, 1844-1900. I. Title.

FOSTER, George Burman, 921.3
1858-1918.
Friedrich Nietzsche, by George Burman Foster ... edited by Curtis W. Reese ... introduction by A. Eustace Haydon ... New York, The Macmillan company, 1931. xi p., 2 l., 250 p. 20 cm. [B3316.F78] 31-6808
1. Nietsche, Fredrich Wilhelm, 1844-1900. I. Reese, Curtis Williford, 1887- ed. II. Title.

KAUFMANN, Walter Arnold. 921.3
Nietzsche: Philosopher, psychologist, antichrist. New York, Meridian Books, 1956 [c1950] 412p. 19cm. (Meridian books, M25) [B3316] 56-6572
1. Nietzsche, Friedrich Wilhelm, 1844-1900. I. Title.

LUDOVICI, Anthony Mario, tr. 921.
The life of Nietzsche. tr. by Anthony M. Ludovici... New York, Sturgis and Walton company, 1912-15. 2 v. fronts., plates, ports., facsim. 25 cm. Printed in Great Britain. Vol. 2 translated by Paul V. Cohn. Contents.I. The young Nietzsche.--II. The lonely Nietzsche. [B3316.F65] 12-40067
1. Nietzsche, Friedrich Wilhelm, 1844-1900. I. Cohn, Paul Victor, tr. II. Ludovici, Anthony, Mario, tr. III. Cohn, Paul Victor, tr. IV. Ludovici, Anthony Mario, tr. V. Title.

MISTRY, Freny, 1944- 193
Nietzsche and Buddhism : prolegomenon to a comparative study / by Freny Mistry. Berlin ; New York : W. de Gruyter, 1981. p. cm. (Monographien und Texte zur Nietzsche-Forschung ; Bd. 6) Includes index. Bibliography: p. [B3318.B83M57] 19 81-3159 ISBN 3-11-008305-1 : 41.00
1. Nietzsche, Friedrich Wilhelm, 1844-1900. 2. Buddhism. 3. Eternal return. 4. Nirvana. 5. Nihilism (Philosophy) I. Title. II. Series.

MUGGE, Maximilian A 1878- 921.
Friedrich Nietzsche, by Maximilian A. Mugge. London, [etc.] T. C. & E. C. Jack; New York, Dodge publishing co. [1912] 94 p. incl. front. (port.) 17 cm. (On cover: The people's books. [68]) Bibliography: p. 91-92. [B3316.M87] A 14
1. Nietzsche, Friedrich Wilhelm, 1844-1900. I. Title.

NIETZSCHE, Friedrich Wilhelm,
1844-1900.
Nietzsche as critic, philosopher, poet and prophet; choice selections from his works, comp. by Thomas Common ... New York, E. P. Dutton & co.; London, G. Richards, 1901. ixv, 261 p. front. (port.) 21 cm. [B3312.E52C6] 3-17565
I. Common, Thomas, comp. II. Title.

NIETZSCHE, Friedrich Wilhelm,
1844-1900.
Thus spake Zarathustra. Translated by Thomas Common. New York, Carlton House [196-?] 368 p. 22 cm. 67-52315
I. Title.

NIETZSCHE, Friedrich Wilhelm,
1844-1900.
Thus spake Zarathustra. New York, Modern Library [1960?] 368 p. 65-81347
I. Title.

NIETZSCHE, Friedrich Wilhelm,
1844-1900.
Thus spake Zarathustra. Translated from the German by Thomas Common. With an introd. by Henry David Aiken and decorations by Arnold Bank. New York, Printed at the Thistle Press for the members of the Limited Editions Club, 1964. xv, 316 p. col. illus. 29 cm. In case. Title on two leaves. "Fifteen hundred copies ... have been printed. 65-85680
I. Title.

NIETZSCHE, Friedrich Wilhelm,
1844-1900.
... Thus spake Zarathustra, a book for all and none, translated by Thomas Common. New York, The Macmillan company, 1924. xxvi, 458 p. 20 cm. (Added t.-p.: The complete works of ... Nietzsche ... v. 11) At head of title: Friedrich Nietzsche. "Fifth edition, published May 1923, 2100 copies, of which this is no. 1829." Printed in Great Britain. Introduction by Mrs. Forster-Nietzsche. "Notes on "Thus spake Zarathustra.' By Anthony M. Ludovici": p. [405]-458. [B3312.E5L6 1923 vol. 11] 24-27428
I. Common, Thomas, tr. II. Ludovici, Anthony Mario. 1882- III. Forster-Nietzsche, Frau Elizabeth, 1846-1935. IV. Title.

NIETZSCHE, Friedrich Wilhelm,
1844-1900.
Thus spake Zarathustra, by Friedrich W. Nietzsche. London & Toronto, J. M. Dent & sons, ltd.; New York, E. P. Dutton & co., inc. [1933] xxiii, [1], 288 p. 18 cm. (Half-title: Everyman's library, ed. by Ernest Rhys. Theology & philosophy. [no. 892]) Title-page and page facing it (with quotation) with ornamental border: illustrated lining-papers. Translated by A. Tille and revised by M. M. Bosman; with an introduction by Ernest Rhys. "List of the chief works of Nietzsche": p. xvii-xviii. [B3312] A 33
I. Tille, Alexander, 1866-1913, tr. II. Bozman, Mildred Mary, 1893, tr. III. Title.

NIETZSCHE, Friedrich Wilhelm,
1844-1900.
Thus spoke Zarathustra; a book for all and no one. Translated by Marianne Cowan. Chicago, H. Regnery [c1965, c1957] vii, 340 p. 17 cm. (A Gateway edition, 6039)
I. Title.

NIETZSCHE, Friedrich Wilhelm,
1844-1900.
What Nietzsche taught, by Willard Huntington Wright ... New York, B. W. Huebsch, 1915. 333 p. front. (port.) 23 cm. Bibliography: p. 331-333. [B3312.E52W7] 15-4621
I. Wright, Willard Huntington, 1888- II. Title.

O'BRIEN, Edward Joseph 921.3
Harrington, 1890-
Son of the morning; a portrait of Friedrich Nietzsche [by] Edward J. O'Brien. New York, Brewer, Warren & Putnam [c1932] viii, 294 p. front., pl., ports., facsim. 22 1/2 cm. Bibliography: p. 289-294. [B3316.O2] 32-31171
1. Nietzsche, Friedrich Wilhelm, 1844-1900. I. Title.

ORAGE, Alfred Richard, 1873-
Nietzsche in outline & aphorism, by A. R. Orage ... Chicago, A. C. McClurg & co.; [etc., etc.] 1910. 2 p. l., vii-viii, 188. [1] p. 18 cm. 11-1499
I. Nietzsche, Friedrich Wilhelm, 1844-1900. II. Title.

PODACH, Erich Friedrich, 921.3
1894-
... The madness of Nietzsche, translated from the German by F. A. Voigt. London & New York, Putnam [1931] 236, [1] p. 20 cm. At head of title: E. F. Podach. "The German edition of this book was published last year [1930] under the title Nietzsche's zusammenbruch. It has been revised and greatly amplified by the author in collaboration with the translator,"--Pref. to the English ed. [B3316.P63] 32-10319
1. Nietzsche, Friederich Wilhelm 1844-1900. I. Voigt, Fritz August, 1802- tr. II. Title.

STEINER, Rudolfa 921.3
Friedrich Nietzsche, fighter for freedom. Translated from the German by Margaret Ingram deRis. Englewood, N.J., Rudolf Steiner Publications [25 Pershing Rd.] [c.1960] 222p. 22cm. (His Major writings, v.2) 60-11803 4.75
1. Nietzche, Friedrich Wilhelm, 1844-1900. I. Title.

ZUURDEEG, Willem 200'.1
Frederick.
Man before chaos. Prepared for publication by Esther Cornelius Swenson. Nashville, Abingdon Press [1968] 160 p. 20 cm. Bibliographical footnotes. [BD450.Z85] 68-11714
1. Nietzsche, Friedrich Wilhelm, 1844-1900. 2. Man. 3. Religion—Philosophy. 4. Civilization—Philosophy. I. Swenson, Esther Cornelius. II. Title.

Nietzsche, Friedrich Wilhelm, 1844-1900—Bibliography.

REICHERT, Herbert 016.193
William, 1917-
International Nietzsche bibliography, compiled and edited by Herbert W. Reichert [and] Karl Schlechta. Rev. and expanded. Chapel Hill, University of North Carolina Press, 1968. 162 p. 23 cm. (University of North Carolina studies in comparative literature, no. 45) [Z8628.85.R4 1968] 77-6896
1. Nietzsche, Friedrich Wilhelm, 1844-1900—Bibliography. I. Schlechta, Karl, 1904- joint author. II. Title. III. Series: North Carolina. University. Studies in comparative literature, no. 45

Nigeria—Social conditions

EAGLESFIELD, Carrol [266.61]
Frederick.
Listen to the drums; Nigeria and its people. Nashville, Broadman Press [1950] 82 p. illus. 19 cm. [DT515.E2] 276.69 50-14398
1. Nigeria—Soc. condit. 2. Missions—Nigeria. 3. Yorubas. I. Title.

Night.

HERVEY, James, 1714-1758. 242
Contemplations on the night. By James Hervey ... The thirty-third edition. New-York: Printed by James Rivington, near the Coffee-House: Of whom may be had Hervey's Meditations among the Tombs, 1774. 6, vii-viii, 75 p. 17 cm. Signatures: A, a, B-G, H. Numbered at foot of p. [3] "Vol. ii"; "The meditations" probably forming vol. i. [BV4831.H42 1774] 28-8861
1. Night. I. Title.

WIMBERLY, Charles Franklin, 270
1866-
The cry in the night; a book of the times, by Rev. C. F. Wimberly 2d ed. Louisville, Ky., Pentecostal publishing company [pref. 1913] 144 p. front. (port.) 19 1/2 cm. [BR125.W7] 17-24224
I. Title.

Nihilism.

THIELICKE, Helmut, 1908- 149.8
Nihilism, its origin and nature, with a Christian answer. Tr. [from German] by John W. Doberstein. New York, Harper [c.1961] 186p. (Religious perspectives, v. 4) Bibl. 61-7351 5.00
1. Nihilism. I. Title.

THIELICKE, Helmut, 1908- 149'.8
Nihilism; its origin and nature, with a Christian answer. Translated by John W. Doberstein. Introd. by Michael Novak. New York, Schocken Books [1969, c1961] ix, 190 p. 21 cm. Includes bibliographical references. [B828.3.T513 1969] 79-91549 6.50
1. Nihilism.

THIELICKE, Helmut, 1908- 149.8
Nihilism, its origin and nature, with a Christian answer. Translated by John W. Doberstein. [1st ed.] New York, Harper [1961] 186 p. 22 cm. (Religious perspectives, v. 4) Includes bibliography. [B828.3.T513] 61-7351
1. Nihilism. I. Title.

Nihilism—Addresses, essays, lectures.

THIELICKE, Helmut, 1908- 149'.8
Nihilism, its origin and nature, with a Christian answer / Helmut Thielicke ; translated by John W. Doberstein ; introduction by Michael Novak. Westport, Conn. : Greenwood Press, 1981, [c1969] p. cm. Translation of: Der Nihilismus. Reprint. Originally published: New York, Schocken Books. [1969, c1961] Includes bibliographical references and index. [B828.3.T513 1981] 19 81-7186 ISBN 0-313-23143-5 lib. bdg. : 19.75
1. Nihilism—Addresses, essays, lectures. 2. Apologetics—20th century—Addresses, essays, lectures. I. [Nihilismus.] English II. Title.

Nikephoros of Chios, Saint.

CAVARNOS, 281.9'092'4 B
Constantine.
St. Nikephoros of Chios, outstanding writer of liturgical poetry and lives of saints, educator, spiritual striver, and trainer of martyrs : an account of his life, character, and message, together with a comprehensive list of his publications, selections from them, and brief biographies of eleven neomartyrs and other Orthodox saints who are treated in his works / by Constantine Cåvarnos. Belmont, Mass. : Institute for Byzantine and Modern Greek Studies, c1976. 124 p. : port. ; 21 cm. (His Modern Orthodox saints ; 4) Includes index. Bibliography: p. 111-114. [BX395.N46C38] 76-3152 ISBN 0-914744-32-1 : 6.50. ISBN 0-914744-33-X pbk. : 3.95
1. Nikephoros of Chios, Saint. 2. Christian saints—Biography. I. Title: St. Nikephoros of Chios, outstanding writer of liturgical poetry ...

Nikko, Japan (Tochigi Prefecture)

NIKKO; 294.30035
the fine art and history, by Y. Okada [other. New York 1, 255 Seventh Ave., Perkins Oriental Bks., 1962] 256p. illus. (pt. col.) 22cm. Japanese text, with summary in English. Added t.p. J62 3.50 bds.,
1. Nikko, Japan (Tochigi Prefecture) I. Okada, Jo, 1911- II. Kuzunishi, Sosei.

Nikodemos Hagioreites, 1748 or 9-1809.

CAVARNOS, 281.9'092'4 B
Constantine.
St. Nicodemos the Hagiorite, great theologian and teacher of the Orthodox Church ... : an account of his life, character, and message ... / by Constantine Cavarnos. Belmont, Mass. : Institute for Byzantine and Modern Greek Studies, [1974] 167 p. : port. ; 21 cm. (His Modern Orthodox saints ; 3) Includes index. Bibliography: p. 157-158. [BX619.N5C38] 74-79388 ISBN 0-914744-17-8. ISBN 0-914744-18-6 pbk.
1. Nikodemos Hagioreites, 1748 or 9-1809. I. Title: St. Nicodemos the Hagiorite, great theologian and teacher ...

Nikolai, Metropolitan of Krutitsy and Kolomna, 1892-1961.

FLETCHER, William C. 281.9'0924 B
Nikolai; portrait of a dilemma, by William C. Fletcher. New York, Macmillan [1968] ix, 230 p. 22 cm. Includes bibliographical references. [BX597.N49F55 1968] 68-13209
1. Nikolai, Metropolitan of Krutitsy and Kolomna, 1892-1961.

Nikolaus von der Fliie, Saint, 1417-1487.

LAMB, George Robert. 922.2494
Brother Nicholas, a life of St. Nicholas of Flue. New York, Sheed and Ward [1955] 191p. 20cm. [BX4700.N66L3] 55-9450
1. Nikolaus von der Fliie, Saint, 1417-1487. I. Title.

Nikolaus von der Flue, Saint, 1417-1487.

LAMB, George Robert. 922.2494
Brother Nicholas, a life of St. Nicholas of Flue. New York, Sheed and Ward [1955] 191p. 20cm. [BX4700.N66L3] 55-9450
1. Nikolaus von der Fliie, Saint, 1417-1487. I. Title.

MCSWIGAN, Marie. 922.2494
Athelete of Christ: St. Nicholas of Flue, 1417-1487. Westminster, Md., Newman Press, 1959. 179p. illus. 23cm. Includes bibliography. [BX4700.N66M3] 59-14757
1. Nikolaus von der Flue, Saint, 1417-1487. I. Title.

MCSWIGAN, Marie 922.2494
Athlete of Christ: St. Nicholas of Flue, 1417-1487. Westminister, Md., Newman Press, [c.] 1959. [c.]1959. viii,179p. illus. (Bibl.) 59-14757 3.25
1. Nikolaus von der Flue, Saint, 1417-1487. I. Title.

Niles, John, 1775-1812.

PARKER, Sarah W 922.573
The Reverend John Niles, 1775-1812. Prepared for the one hundred and fiftieth anniversary of the Church of Christ in Bath, Presbyterian Congregation, January 3-5, 1958. Bath, N. Y., 1958. 80p. illus. 23cm. Includes bibliography. [BX9225.N47P3] 58-20659
1. Niles, John, 1775-1812. I. Title.

Nilotic tribes—Religion.

LINCOLN, Bruce. 299'.68
Priests, warriors, and cattle : a study in the ecology of religions / Bruce Lincoln. Berkeley : University of California Press, c1980. p. cm. (Hermeneutics, studies in the history of religions ; v. 10) [BL2480.N46L56] 78-68826 20.00
1. Nilotic tribes—Religion. 2. Indo-Iranians—Religion. 3. Cows (in religion, Folk-lore, etc.) 4. Nilotic tribes. 5. Indo-Iranians. I. Title. II. Series.

Nind, Mary (Clarke)

[NIND, John Newton] 1854-1921, ed. 923.
Mary Clarke Nind and her work: her childhood, girlhood, married life, religious experience and activity, together with the story of her labors on behalf of the Woman's foreign missionary society of the Methodist Episcopal church, by her children. Chicago, For the Woman's foreign missionary society, by J. N. Nind [c1906] 5 p. l., 221 p. front., plates, ports. 23 cm. [BV3705.N5N5] 7-3672
1. Nind, Mary (Clarke) Mrs. 2. Methodist Episcopal church. Women's foreign missionary society. 3. Missions, Foreign. I. Title.

Ninde, William Xavier, Bp., 1832-1901.

GAMEWELL, Mary Louise (Ninde) 1858-1947. 922.
William Xavier Ninde; a memorial by his daughter. New York, Eaton & Mains [c1902] 9, 290 p. plates, ports., facsims. 23 cm. [BX8495.N5G3] 2-21375
1. Ninde, William Xavier, Bp., 1832-1901. I. Title.

Nippon Seikokwai.

TUCKER, Henry St. George, bp., 1874- 275.2
... The history of the Episcopal church in Japan, by Henry St. George Tucker ... New York, C. Scribner's sons; London, C. Scribner's sons, ltd., 1938. 6 p. l., 228 p. 20 cm. (The Hale lectures) "Lectures, delivered in the autumn of 1937 at the Seabury-Western theological seminary, Evanston, Illnois."--Pref. Bibliography: p. 219-221. [BV3445.T8] 266.3 38-20742
1. Nippon Seikokwai. 2. Missions—Japan. 3. Japan—Hist. 4. Protestant Episcopal church in the U. S. A.—Missions. I. Title.

Nirvana.

ARUNDALE, George Sydney, 1878- 212
Nirvana, by George S. Arundale. Chicago, The Theosophical press [c1926] 7 p. l., 192 p. front., diagr. 19 1/2 cm. [BP573.N5A7] 27-436
I. Title.

JOHANSSON, Rune Edvin Andrews, 1918- 294.3'4'23
The psychology of nirvana; a comparative study of the natural goal of Buddhism and the aims of modern western psychology, by Rune E. A. Johansson. Garden City, Anchor Books [1970] 142 p. 19 cm. Bibliography: p. [137] [BL1456.66.J6 1970] 74-103789 1.45
1. Nirvana. 2. Buddha and Buddhism—Psychology. I. Title.

SHCHERBATSKOI, Fedor Ippolitovich, 1866-1942. 294.3'4'23
The conception of Buddhist nirvana (along with Sanskrta text of Madhayamaka-karika) by Th. Stcherbatsky. With comprehensive analysis & introd. [by Jaideva Singh] New York, Gordon Press, 1973. 1 v. (various pagings) 24 cm. Includes English translation and appended Sanskrit text of chapters 1 and 25 of Nagarjuna's Madhyamakakarika and of Candrakirti's commentary, Prasannapada. Includes bibliographical references. [BQ4263.S5 1973] 73-8277 ISBN 0-87968-058-X
1. Nirvana. 2. Madhyamika (Buddhism) I. Singh, Jaideva, ed. II. Nagarjuna, Siddha. Madhyamikasastra. 1973. III. Candrakirti. Prasannapada. 1973. IV. Title.

WELBON, Guy Richard. 294.3'4'23
The Buddhist nirvana and its Western interpreters. Chicago, University of Chicago Press [1968] xi, 320 p. 23 cm. Bibliography: p. 305-310. [BL1456.66.W42] 67-25535
1. Nirvana. I. Title.

Nishitani, Keiji, 1900-

WALDENFELS, Hans. 261.2'43
Absolute nothingness : foundations for a Buddhist-Christian dialogue / by Hans Waldenfels ; translated by J.W. Heisig. New York, N.Y. : Paulist Press, c1980. ix, 214 p. ; 23 cm. Translation of: Absolutes Nichts. Includes index. Bibliography: 190-203. [BR128.B8W3313] 19 80-81442 ISBN 0-8091-2316-9 (pbk.) : 7.95
1. Nishitani, Keiji, 1900- 2. Christianity and other religions—Buddhism. 3. Buddhism—Relations—Christianity. I. [Absolutes Nichts.] English II. Title.

Noah.

ALLEN, Don Cameron, 1904- 222.11
The legend of Noah; Renaissance rationalism in art, science, and letters. Urbana, Univ. of Ill. Pr., 1963, [c.1949] 221p. illus. 21cm. (Illini. bk. IB-12) Bibl. 1.45 pap.,
1. Noah. I. Title. II. Series: Illinois. University. Illinois studies in language and literature, v. 33, no. 3-4

COHEN, H. Hirsch. 222'.11
The drunkenness of Noah / by H. Hirsch Cohen. University : University of Alabama Press, [1974] xiii, 177 p. : map (on lining paper) ; 25 cm. (Judaic studies ; 4) Includes indexes. Bibliography: p. 160-164. [BS580.N6C63] 74-194696 ISBN 0-8173-6702-0 : 7.95
1. Noah. 2. Cain. 3. Bible. O.T. Genesis—Criticism, interpretation, etc. I. Title. II. Series.

LESSING, Erich. 221.95 (j)
The story of Noah. [Told in photographs by Erich Lessing. Text from the King James Bible. Pictures and text edited by Barbara Brakeley Miller. New York, Time-Life Books, 1968?] 1 v. (unpaged) illus. (part col.) 26 cm. [BS580.N6L4] 68-23127
1. Noah. 2. Bible. O.T. Genesis—Pictures, illustrations, etc. I. Miller, Barbara Brakeley, ed. II. Title.

Noah—Juvenile literature.

BERGEY, Alyce. 222
The first rainbow. Illus. by Ruth Brophy. Minneapolis, T. S. Denison [1965] 1 v. (unpaged) col. illus. 29 cm. [BS580.N6B4] 64-7705
1. Noah — Juvenile literature. I. Brophy, Ruth, illus. II. Title.

HUTTON, Warwick. 222'.11'09505
Noah and the great flood / Warwick Hutton. New York : Atheneum, 1977. p. cm. "A Margaret K. McElderry book." An interpretation of the familiar Bible story using a simple text based on the King James version. [BS658.H87] 77-3217 ISBN 0-689-50098-X : 7.95
1. Noah—Juvenile literature. 2. Bible. O.T.—Biography—Juvenile literature. 3. Deluge—Juvenile literature. 4. [Noah's ark.] 5. [Bible stories—O.T.] I. Title.

WYNANTS, Miche 222
Noah's ark. 1st Amer. ed. New York, Harcourt, c.1965. 1v. (unpaged)illus. (pt. col.) 28cm. [BS580.N6W9] 65-8155 3.25 bds.,
1. Noah—Juvenile literature. I. Title.

Noah's Ark.

*BALSIGER, Dave. 204.5
In search of Noah's ark / by Dave Balsiger & Charles E. Sellier Jr. Los Angeles : Sun Classic Books, 1976. 218, [32]p. : ill. ; 18 cm. (A Schick-Sun classic book) Includes bibliographical references. [BL325.D4] ISBN 0-917214-01-3 pbk. : 1.95
1. Noah's ark. I. Sellier, Charles E. joint author. II. Title.

BALSIGER, Dave. 222'.11
In search of Noah's ark / by Dave Balsiger & Charles E. Sellier, Jr. Los Angeles : Sun Classic Books, c1976. 218 p., [16] leaves of plates : ill. ; 18 cm. Bibliography: p. 216-217. [BS658.B34] 76-151887 ISBN 0-917214-01-3 : 1.95
1. Noah's ark. 2. Deluge. I. Sellier, Charles E., joint author. II. In search of Noah's ark. [Motion picture]

DUVOISIN, Roger Antoine, 1904-
A for the ark. New York, Lathrop, Lee & Shepard [1966, c1952] 1 v. (unpaged) illus. 28 cm. On udst cover: Library ed. 68-41881
1. Noah's Ark. 2. Alphabets. I. Title.

GERGELY, Tibor, 1900- JUV
The Noah's ark book. New York, Golden Press, c1966. [24] p. col. illus. 22 cm. (A Golden book for kindergarten) Illustrations show some of the animals that came two by two to Noah's ark. [PZ10.3.G34No] 221.95 AC 68
1. Noah's ark. I. Title.

[HEBERLING], Alma, 1856-
The Ark of Noah; or, The path of the just, by Alma of Iowa. Cedar Rapids, Ia., Republican printing co., 1902. 1 p. l., [5]-56. p. 17 cm. 272 p. incl. illus., charts. 23 1/2 x 31 cm. $4.00 2-16098
I. Title.

MCDOWELL, Josh. 220.1'3
Reasons skeptics should consider Christianity / Josh McDowell, Don Stewart. San Bernardino, Calif. : Here's Life Publishers, c1981. 249 p. ; 21 cm. "A Campus Crusade for Christ book"—T.p. verso. Bibliography: p. 222-249. [BS480.M385] 19 81-184386 ISBN 0-918956-98-6 (pbk.) : 4.95
1. Bible—Evidences, authority, etc. 2. Noah's ark. 3. Evolution. I. Stewart, Don Douglas. II. Title.
Publisher's address: P. O. Box 1576, 2700 Little Mountain Dr., Bldg. "b", San Bernardino, CA 92402.

NAVARRA, Fernand, 1915- 222'.11'093
Noah's ark: I touched it. Edited with Dave Balsiger. Plainfield, N.J., Logos International [1974] xv, 137 p. illus. 21 cm. [DS51.A66N35] 73-91761 ISBN 0-88270-064-2 2.95 (pbk.).
1. Noah's ark. 2. Ararat, Mt. I. Title.

NOORBERGEN, Rene. 933
The ark file / by Rene Noorbergen. Mountain View, Calif. : Pacific Press Pub. Association, c1974. 207 p., [8] leaves of plates : ill. ; 23 cm. [BS658.N66] 74-79956
1. Noah's ark. I. Title.

PAINE, Timothy Otis, 1824-1895.
Solomon's temple and capitol, ark of the flood and tabernacle: or, The holy houses of the Hebrew, Chaldee, Syriac, Samaritan, Septuagint, Coptic and Itala scriptures: Josephus, Talmud, and rabbis, by Timothy Otis Paine ... With forty-two full-page plates, and one hundred and twenty text-cuts, being photographic reproductions of the original drawings made by the author. Boston and New York, Houghton, Mifflin and company [etc.] 1885. x p., 1 l., 198 p. illus., plates. 38 cm. A 34
1. Noah's ark. 2. Jerusalem. Temple. 3. Tabernacle. I. Title.

TEEPLE, Howard Merle, 1911- 222'.11'09
The Noah's ark nonsense / Howard M. Teeple. Evanston, Ill. : Religion and Ethics Institute, 1978. 156 p. : ill. ; 23 cm. (Truth in religion ; 1) Bibliography: p. [150]-156. [BS658.T44] 78-53529 ISBN 0-914384-01-5 : 10.00
1. Noah's ark. 2. Deluge. I. Title. II. Series.

WIEMER, Rudolf Otto, 1905- JUV
Noah's Ark. [Text by Rudolph Otto Wiemer. Translation by Paul T. Martinsen. Minneapolis, Augsburg Pub. House, 1967] [24] p. col. illus. 27 cm. An interpretation of the story of Noah and the flood based on Genesis, chapters six through nine. [PZ7.W6355No] 221.95 AC 67
1. Noah's ark. I. Herrman, Reinhard, illus. II. Title.

WOOLSEY, John Martin, 1833-
The discovery of Noah's ark, final and decisive, by J. M. Woolsey ... New York, Cochrane publishing company, 1910. 62 p. 20 1/2 cm. $0.50. 10-30038
I. Title.

Noah's ark—Caricatures and cartoons—Juvenile literature.

WALSH, Bill. 222'.11'09505
Noah and the ark : a cartoon Bible story / by Bill Walsh ; with an afterword for parents and teachers by Charlie Sheed. Kansas City, [Kan.] : Sheed Andrews and McMeel, c1976. p. cm. (Cartoon Bible stories series) A cartoon version of how Noah builds the ark in preparation for the great flood. [BS658.W25] 76-57955 ISBN 0-8362-0697-5 pbk. : 1.95
1. Noah's ark—Caricatures and cartoons—Juvenile literature. 2. [Noah's ark—Caricatures and cartoons.] 3. [Bible stories—O.T.] 4. [Cartoons and comics.] I. Title.

Noah's ark—Juvenile literature.

BOLLIGER, Max. 221.9'505
Noah and the rainbow; an ancient story retold by Max Bolliger. Translated by Clyde Robert Bulla. With pictures by Helga Aichinger. New York, Crowell [1972] [25] p. col. illus. 31 cm. Translation of Der Regenbogen. Retells the Old Testament story of Noah who built an ark to hold his family and the animals during the great flood. [BS658.B6513] 72-76361 ISBN 0-690-58448-2 4.50
1. Noah's ark—Juvenile literature. 2. [Noah's ark.] I. Aichinger, Helga, illus. II. Title.

CHASE, Catherine. 222'.11'09505
Noah's ark / adapted from Genesis 6:5 to 9:17 by Catherine Chase ; illustrated by Elliot Ivenbaum. New York : Dandelion Press, 1979. [32] p. : col. ill. ; 18 x 23 cm. Retells the Old Testament story of Noah and the ark he built to withstand the flood which covered the earth. [BS658.C47] 78-64415 ISBN 0-89799-130-3 : 3.50 ISBN 0-89799-031-5 (pbk.) : 1.50
1. Noah's ark—Juvenile literature. 2. [Noah's ark.] 3. [Bible stories—O.T.] I. Ivenbaum, Elliot. II. Title.

HANCOCK, Sibyl. 222'.11'09505
An ark and a rainbow : Noah and the ark for beginning readers : Genesis 6-9 for children / by Sibyl Hancock ; illustrated by Aline Cunningham. St. Louis : Concordia Pub. House, c1976. [39] p. : col. ill. ; 23 cm. (I can read a Bible story) Easy-to-read retelling of the story of Noah and the ark he built to withstand a flood which covered the earth. [BS658.H25] 76-14924 ISBN 0-570-07309-X : 3.95
1. Noah's ark—Juvenile literature. 2. Deluge—Juvenile literature. 3. [Noah's ark.] 4. [Bible stories—O.T.] I. Cunningham, Aline. II. Title.

HANNON, Ruth. 222'.11
Noah's ark. Retold by Ruth Hannon. Pictures by Carolyn Bracken. New York,

Golden Press [1973] 33 p. illus. 28 cm. Retells the Old Testament story of Noah, who built an ark which held his family and a pair of every living creature on earth during the forty days of the flood. [BS658.H28] 73-77490 3.95
1. Noah's ark—Juvenile literature. 2. [Noah's ark.] I. Bracken, Carolyn, illus. II. Title.

JONES, Harold, 1904- 220.9
Noah and the ark, by Harold Jones, Kathleen Lines. New York, Watts [c.]1961. 1v. (chiefly col. illus.) 30x22cm. 61-12879 3.95
1. Noah's ark—Juvenile literature. I. Lines, Kathleen, joint author. II. Title.

*LATOURETTE, Jane 222.11
The story of the Noah's Ark: Genesis 6: 5-9: 17 for children. Illus. by Sally Mathews. St. Louis, Concordia, c.1965. 1v. (unpaged) col. illus. 21cm. (Arch bks., set 2, no. 59-1110) .35 pap.,
1. Noah58s Ark (Story)—Juvenile literature. I. Title.

LEMKE, Stefan. 222'.11'09505
Noah's ark / [art by Stefan Lemke and Marie-Luise Lemke-Pricken]. Philadelphia : Fortress Press, 1976. [20] p. : col. ill. ; 19 cm. "A Sunshine book." Retells the story of Noah and the huge ark that God asked him to build. [BS658.L45] 76-11269 ISBN 0-8006-1576-X pbk. : 1.75
1. Noah's ark—Juvenile literature. 2. [Noah's ark.] 3. [Bible stories—O.T.] I. Lemke-Pricken, Marie-Luise, joint author. II. Title.

MCKELLAR, Shona. 222'.1109505
The beginning of the rainbow / Shona McKellar ; Masahiro Kasuya, illustrator. Nashville : Abingdon, 1982, c1977. p. cm. A retelling of the Bible story of Noah and his ark. [BS658.M36 1981] 19 81-7954 ISBN 0-687-02770-5 : 7.95
1. Noah's ark—Juvenile literature. 2. [Noah's ark.] 3. [Bible stories—O.T.] I. Kasuya, Masahiro, ill. II. Title.

MARTIN, Charles E. 222'.11'09505
Noah's ark / illustrated Charles E. Martin ; retold by Lawrence T. Lorimer. New York : Random House, c1978. [32] p. : ill. ; 21 cm. (A Random House pictureback) A retelling of the Bible story of Noah and the huge ark God asked him to build. [BS658.M33] 77-92377 ISBN 0-394-83861-0 : 3.95. ISBN 0-394-93861-5 lib. bdg. : 4.99
1. Noah's ark—Juvenile literature. 2. [Noah's ark.] 3. [Bible stories—O.T.] I. Lorimer, Lawrence T. II. Title.

MUNOWITZ, Ken. 222'.1'09505
Noah / pictures by Ken Munowitz ; text by Charles L. Mee, Jr. 1st ed. New York : Harper & Row, c1978. p. cm. Retells the story of how Noah and his family built the ark and saved the animals from the Great Flood. [BS658.M78 1978] 77-11839 ISBN 0-06-024183-7 : 5.95. ISBN 0-06-024184-5 lib. bdg. : 5.79
1. Noah's ark—Juvenile literature. 2. [Noah's ark.] 3. [Bible stories—O.T.] I. Mee, Charles L. II. Title.

POMERANTZ, Charlotte. 222'.1109505
Noah's and Namah's ark / by Charlotte Pomerantz ; illustrated by Kelly K. M. Carson. New York : Holt, Rinehart, and Winston, c1981. [38] p. : ill. ; 24 cm. Retells in rhyme the story of how Noah and his family built the ark and saved the animals from the Great Flood. [BS1238.N6P65] 80-14595 ISBN 0-03-057629-6 : 9.95
1. Noah's ark—Juvenile literature. 2. [Noah's ark.] 3. [Bible stories—O.T.] I. Carson, Kelly K. M. II. Title.

STORR, Catherine. 222'.1109505
Noah and his ark / retold by Catherine Storr ; pictures by Jim Russell. Milwaukee : Raintree Childrens Books, c1982. p. cm. (People of the Bible) A retelling of the story of the Flood that lasted forty days, and the Ark on which Noah, his family, and a pair of each kind of animal took refuge. [BS658.S86 1982] 19 82-7712 ISBN 0-8172-1975-7 pbk. : 9.95
1. Noah's ark—Juvenile literature. 2. Bible stories, English—O.T. Genesis VI, 5-IX, 17. 3. [Noah's ark.] 4. [Bible stories—O.T. Genesis.] I. Russell, Jim, 1933- ill. II. Title. III. Series.

TESTER, Sylvia Root, 1939- 222'.11'09505
The great big boat / by Sylvia Root Tester ; illustrated by Robert Masheris. Elgin, Ill. : Child's World ; Cincinnati, Ohio : distributed by Standard Pub., c1979. 30 p. : col. ill. ; 25 cm. ([Bible story books]) Brief text retells the story of Noah and the flood. [BS658.T47] 79-12176 lib.bdg. : 4.95 4.95
1. Noah's ark—Juvenile literature. 2. Bible stories, English—O.T. Genesis VI, 5-IX, 17. 3. [Noah's ark.] 4. [Bible stories—O.T.] I. Masheris, Robert. II. Title. III. Series.

Noah's ark—Poetry.

KUSKIN, Karla. 221.95
The animals and the ark. New York, Harper [1958] [32] p. illus. 18 x 25 cm. A retelling in verse of the Biblical story of Noah and the ark in which he and the animals lived during the flood. [PZ8.3.K96An] AC 68
1. Noah's ark—Poetry. I. Title.

Noaillat, Marthe (Devuns) de, 1865-1926.

PONVERT, Simone (De Noaillat) 922.244
The King's advocate, translated from Simone de Nosillat-Ponvert's Marthe de Noaillat, 1865-1926, by Mary Golden Donnelly. Milwaukee, The Bruce publishing company [1942] xi, 260 p. 22 1/2 cm. (Half-title: Science and culture series: Joseph Husslein, general editor) [BX4705.N78P6] 43-3689
1. Noaillat, Marthe (Devuns) de, 1865-1926. 2. Jesus Christ the King, Feast of. I. Donnelly, Mary Golden, tr. II. Title.

Nobili, Roberto de', 1577-1656.

CRONIN, Vincent. 922.254
A pearl to India; the life of Roberto de Nobili. New York, Dutton, 1959. 297 p. illus. 21 cm. Includes bibliography. [BV3269.N6C7 1959] 59-5815
1. Nobili, Roberto de', 1577-1656. I. Title.

Noble, Margaret Elizabeth, 1867-1911.

ATMAPRANA, Pravrajika 921.9
Sister Nivedita of Ramakrishna-Vivekananda. [dist. Hollywood, Calif., Vendanta, 1962, c.1961] 297p. illus. 23cm. 62-3355 3.50 bds.,
1. Noble, Margaret Elizabeth, 1867-1911. I. Title.

REYMOND, Lizelle. 921.9
The dedicated, a biography of Nivedita. New York, J. Day Co. [1953] 374p. illus. 21cm. (An Asia book) Translation of Nivedita, fille de i'Inde. [B133.N64R43] 52-126814
1. Noble, Margaret Elizabeth, 1867-1911. I. Title.

Noble, William Alexander, 1895-

HANSEN, Lillian E. 266'.025'0924 B
The double yoke; the Story of William Alexander Noble, M.D., Fellow of the American College of Surgeons, Fellow of the International College of Surgeons, Doctor of Humanities, medical missionary extraordinary to India, his adopted land, by Lillian E. Hansen. Drawings by Ernest L. Reedstrom. New York, Citadel Press [1968] 268 p. illus., col. maps (on lining papers) 21 cm. [BX9743.N6H3 1968] 68-28451 5.95
1. Noble, William Alexander, 1895- 2. Missions, Medical—India. I. Title.

NOBLE, Margaret Elizabeth, 1867-1911.
Religion and Dharma, by Sister Nivedita (Margaret E. Noble) with a preface by S. K. Ratcliffe. London, New York [etc.] Longmans, Green and co., 1915. x, 156 p. 20 cm. A 16
I. Ratcliffe. Samuel Kerkham, 1868- II. Title.

Noblet, Marie Therese, 1889-1930.

ELLIOTT, Edmund E. R. 922.244
Child of Calvary, myrtyr [sic] of Satan; a biography of Mother Marie-Therese Noblet, miraculee of Lourdes, Little Mother of the Papuans. Prefatory letter by A. de Boismenu. [dist. Downers Grove, Ill., The Carmelite Third Order Press, Aylesford, Madden at Route 66, 1961] 171p. illus. map 61-3101 3.00
1. Noblet, Marie Therese, 1889-1930. I. Title.

Noel, Conrad, 1869-1942.

GROVES, Reginald, 1908- 283'.0924
Conrad Noel and the Thaxted Movement; an adventure in Christian socialism, by Reg Groves. New York, A. M. Kelley [1968] 334 p. port. 23 cm. Bibliographical references included in "Sources and acknowledgements" (p. 327-328) [BX5199.N65G7 1968] 68-3219
1. Noel, Conrad, 1869-1942. I. Title.

Non church-affiliated people.

GEIERMANN, Peter. 289
A mission to non-Catholics, by the Rev. Peter Geiermann ... St. Louis, Mo., and London, B. Herder book co., 1927. 2 p. l., iii-vii, 125 p. front. (port.) 20 cm. [BX1751.G44] 27-18485
I. Title.

HALE, James Russell. 306'.6
The unchurched : who they are and why they stay away / J. Russell Hale. 1st ed. San Francisco : Harper & Row, c1980. xiv, 206 p. ; 24 cm. Some of materials included are from the author's Who are the unchurched? published in 1977 by Glenmary Research Center, Washington, D.C. Includes index. Bibliography: p. [199]-202. [BL2747.H33 1980] 19 79-2993 ISBN 0-06-063560-6 : 9.95
1. Non church-affiliated people. 2. Irreligion and sociology. I. Title.

HALE, James Russell. 261.2
Who are the unchurched? : An exploratory study / J. Russell Hale. Washington : Glenmary Research Center, 1977. ix, 99 p. : map ; 28 cm. "GRC A-55/P-173." Includes bibliographical references. [BL2747.H34] 77-81922 ISBN 0-914422-06-5 : 2.00
1. Non church-affiliated people. 2. Irreligion and sociology. I. Title.

Non-institutional churches.

BOYD, Malcolm, 1923- 260
The underground church. Ed. by Malcolm Boyd. New York, Sheed [1968] x, 246p. 21 cm. Bibl. footnotes. [BV601.9.B6] 68-17361 4.95
1. Non-institutional churches. 2. Christianity—20th cent. I. Title.

BOYD, Malcolm, 1923- 260
The underground church, edited by Malcolm Boyd. [Rev. ed. Baltimore] Penguin Books [1969] xx, 271 p. 18 cm. (A Pelican book, A1109) [BV601.9.B6 1969] 76-5321 0.95
1. Non-institutional churches. 2. Christianity—20th century. I. Title.

PLOWMAN, Edward E. 248.8'3
The underground church; accounts of Christian revolutionaries in action, by Edward E. Plowman. Elgin, Ill., D. C. Cook Pub. Co. [1971] 128 p. 18 cm. [BV601.9.P57] 75-147214 0.95
1. Non-institutional churches. 2. Youth—Religious life. I. Title.

VINCENT, John J. 262'.001
Alternative church / by John J. Vincent. Belfast : Christian Journals Ltd, 1976. 149 p. ; 18 cm. Includes bibliographical references. [BV601.9.V56] 77-357079 ISBN 0-904302-22-9 : £0.90
1. Non-institutional churches. I. Title.

Nonjurors.

WAND, John William Charles, Bp. of London, 1885-
The High Church schism; four lectures on the Nonjurors. London, Faith Press; New York, Morehouse-Gorham Co. [1951] 88p. 19cm. Includes bibliography. A 53
1. Nonjurors. I. Title.

Nonviolence—Biblical teaching.

FERGUSON, John, 1921- 261.8
The politics of love : the New Testament and nonviolence / by John Ferguson. Nyack, N.Y. : Fellowship Publications, 1979. p. cm. Includes indexes. [BS2545.P4F47] 79-16508 pbk. : 3.00
1. Bible. N.T.—Criticism, interpretation, etc. 2. Nonviolence—Biblical teaching. I. Title.

TROCME, Andre, 1901-1971. 232.9'54
Jesus and the nonviolent revolution. Translated by Michael H. Shank and Marlin E. Miller. With introd. by Marlin E. Miller. Scottdale, Pa., Herald Press, 1973. 211 p. 22 cm. (The Christian peace shelf) Includes bibliographical references. [BS2417.P2T7613] 73-9934 ISBN 0-8361-1719-0 9.95
1. Jesus Christ—Person and offices. 2. Nonviolence—Biblical teaching. I. Title.

Nonviolence—Moral and religious aspects.

ARNETT, Ronald C., 1952- 261.8'3
Dwell in peace : applying nonviolence to everyday relationships / Ronald C. Arnett. Elgin, Ill. : Brethren Press, c1980. 156 p. ; 21 cm. Bibliography: p. [149]-156. [BT736.6.A76] 19 79-24639 ISBN 0-87178-199-9 pbk. : 5.95
1. Nonviolence—Moral and religious aspects. 2. Peace. 3. Interpersonal relations. I. Title.

DOUGLASS, James W. 301.6'32
Resistance and contemplation; the way of liberation. [New York, Dell, 1973, c.1972] 192 p. 21 cm. (Delta Book) Includes bibliographical references. [BT736.6.D68] 2.45 (pbk.)
1. Nonviolence—Moral and religious aspects. 2. Contemplation. I. Title.
L.C. card no. for the hardbound edition: 78-175368.

DOUGLASS, James W. 301.6'32
Resistance and contemplation; the way of liberation [by] James W. Douglass. [1st ed.] Garden City, N.Y., Doubleday, 1972. 192 p. 22 cm. Includes bibliographical references. [BT736.6.D68] 78-175368 5.95
1. Nonviolence—Moral and religious aspects. 2. Contemplation. I. Title.

DUIGNAN, Jim. 170
Prophetic resistance and hope : a primer on the history of non-violence / by Jim Duignan. Chicago : Sunburst Press, c1975. ix, 48 p. : ports. ; 22 cm. (Sunburst originals ; SB3) "Edition of 250 copies." [BT736.6.D84] 75-9290 ISBN pbk. : 1.25
1. Nonviolence—Moral and religious aspects. I. Title.

HARING, Bernhard, 1912- 261.8
A theology of protest [by] Bernhard Haring. New York, Farrar, Straus and Giroux [1970] xvii, 189 p. 22 cm. [BT736.6.H3 1970] 70-109556 5.95
1. Nonviolence—Moral and religious aspects. 2. Authority (Religion) I. Title.

SUGDEN, Christopher. 261.7
A different dream : non-violence as practical politics / by Christopher Sugden. Bramcote : Grove Books, 1976. 24 p. ; 22 cm. (Grove booklet on ethics ; no. 12 ISSN 0305-4241s) Includes bibliographical references. [BT736.6.S83] 77-374343 ISBN 0-901710-95-4 : £0.30
1. Nonviolence—Moral and religious aspects. I. Title.

Nonviolence—Moral and religious aspects—Addresses, essays, lectures.

GUINAN, Edward, comp. 261.8'73
Peace and nonviolence; basic writings. New York, Paulist Press [1973] ix, 174 p. 23 cm. On cover: Peace and nonviolence; basic writings by prophetic voices in the world religions. Includes bibliographies. [BT736.6.G84] 73-75741 ISBN 0-8091-1770-3 4.50

1. Nonviolence—Moral and religious aspects—Addresses, essays, lectures. 2. Peace (Theology)—Addresses, essays, lectures. I. Title.

Nonviolence—Moral and religious aspects—Collections.

ESTEY, George F., comp. 170
Nonviolence: a reader in the ethics of action [by] George F. Estey [and] Doris A. Hunter. Waltham, Mass., Xerox College Pub. [1971] xxi, 287 p. 21 cm. Includes bibliographies. [BT736.6.E83 1971] 72-135635
1. Nonviolence—Moral and religious aspects—Collections. I. Hunter, Doris A., 1920- joint comp. II. Title.

Nooksack Indians—Religion and mythology.

AMOSS, Pamela. 299'.7
Coast Salish spirit dancing : the survival of an ancestral religion / by Pamela Amoss ; with drawings by Ron Allen Hilbert. Seattle : University of Washington Press, c1978. xvii, 193 p. : ill. ; 22 cm. Includes index. Bibliography: p. 171-182. [E99.N84A47] 77-15184 ISBN 0-295-95586-4 : 15.00
1. Nooksack Indians—Religion and mythology. 2. Indians of North America—Religion and mythology. 3. Salishan Indians—Religion and mythology. 4. Trance. I. Title.

Norbert, Saint, abp. of Magdeburg. d. 1134.

KIRKFLEET, Cornelius James, 1881- 922.
History of Saint Norbert, Founder of the Norbertine (Premonstratensian) order, apostle of the blessed sacrament, archbishop of Magdeburg, by the Rev. Cornelius J. Kirkfleet ... (With twelve illustrations) St. Louis, Mo., and London, B. Herder, 1916. xvii p., 1 l., 364 p. front., plates, ports. 20 1/2 cm. "A list of biographies of St. Norbert": p. vi-ix. [BX4700.N8K5] 16-18298
1. Norbert, Saint, abp. of Magdeburg, d. 1134. 2. Premonstrants. I. Title.

KIRKFLEET, Cornelius James, 1881- 922.
History of Saint Norbert, founder of the Norbertine (Premonstratensian) order, apostle of the blessed sacrament, archbishop of Magdeburg, by the Rev. Cornelius J. Kirkfleet ... (With twelve illustrations) St. Louis, Mo., and London, B. Herder, 1916. xvii p., 1 l., 364 p. front., plates, ports. 21 cm. "A list of biographies of St. Norbert": p. vi-ix. [BX4700.N8K5] 16-18298
1. Norbert, Saint, abp. of Magdeburg. d. 1134. 2. Premonstrants. I. Title.

Nordtvedt, Matilda.

NORDTVEDT, Matilda. 248'.86
Defeating despair & depression / Matilda Nordtvedt. Chicago : Moody Press, [1975] 125 p. ; 22 cm. [BR1725.N54A33] 75-311320 ISBN 0-8024-2082-6 pbk. : 1.95
1. Nordtvedt, Matilda. 2. Depression, Mental—Personal narratives. 3. Christian life—1960- I. Title.

NORDTVEDT, Matilda. 248'.86
Living beyond depression / by Matilda Nordtvedt. Minneapolis, Minn. : Bethany Fellowship, c1978. 128 p. ; 18 cm. (Dimension books) Includes bibliographical references. [BR1725.N54A35] 78-58082 ISBN 0-87123-339-8 pbk. : 1.95
1. Nordtvedt, Matilda. 2. Christian biography—United States. 3. Christian life—1960- 4. Depression, Mental—Biography. I. Title.

Norfolk Co., Va.—Biography.

STEVENSON, Arthur Linwood, 1891- 287'.6755'51
Native Methodist preachers of Norfolk and Princess Anne Counties, Virginia / by Arthur L. Stevenson. Brevard, N.C. : Stevenson, 1975. 49 p. ; 22 cm. (His Native Methodist preacher series ; 6th) [BX8491.S69] 76-351183
1. Methodist Church in Norfolk Co., Va.—Clergy. 2. Methodist Church in Princess Anne Co., Va.—Clergy. 3. Norfolk Co., Va.—Biography. 4. Princess Anne Co., Va.—Biography. I. Title: Native Methodist preachers of Norfolk and Princess Anne Counties ...

Norfolk, Va.—History—Colonial period, ca. 1600-1775—Sources.

NORFOLK, Va. St. Paul's Church (Protestant Episcopal) 283'.755'52
Vestry book of Elizabeth River Parish, 1749-1761. Edited by Alice Granbery Walter. [New York?] 1967 [c1969] 43 p. facsims. 25 cm. [F234.N8N88] 71-254097
1. Norfolk, Va.—History—Colonial period, ca. 1600-1775—Sources. 2. Church records and registers—Norfolk, Va. I. Title.

Norfolk, Va. St. Paul's church (Protestant Episcopal)

NORFOLK, Va. St. Paul's church (Protestant Episcopal) Altar guild. 283.755521
St. Paul's church, 1832, originally the Borough church, 1739, Elizabeth river parish, Norfolk, Virginia. Norfolk, Va., The Altar guild of St. Paul's church, 1934. 1 p. l., 9-115, [5] p. incl. illus., pl., map, facsims. plates, ports. 28 cm. "Compiled under the auspices of the ladies of the Altar guild ... compiler, Mrs. Calvert R. Dey."--Pref. "Record of inscriptions on the tombstones in St. Paul's church yard": p. 63-115. [BX5980.N75S25] 35-11440
1. Norfolk, Va. St. Paul's church (Protestant Episcopal) 2. Epitaphs—Norfolk, Va. I. Dey, Margaret (Stuart) Mrs. 1877. II. Title.

Norman, Joyce.

NORMAN, Joyce. 248'.24 B
Personal assignment; a newspaperwoman's search for the good news. Old Tappan, N.J., F. H. Revell [1973] 127 p. 22 cm. [BV4935.N59A3] 73-16193 ISBN 0-8007-0639-0 3.95
1. Norman, Joyce. 2. Conversion. I. Title.

Norris, John Franklyn, 1877-1952.

THE Story of the Fort Worth Norris-Wallace debate; a documentary record of the facts concerning the Norris-Wallace debate, held in Fort Worth, Texas, November, 1934. Nashville, Tenn., F. E. Wallace, Jr. Publications [1969?] c1968. 346 p. facsims., ports. 24 cm. Compiled by F. E. Wallace. [BX6495.N59S7] 72-268696 230
1. Norris, John Franklyn, 1877-1952. 2. Wallace, Foy Esco, 1896- 3. Disputations, Religious. I. Wallace, Foy Esco, 1896- comp.

TATUM, E Ray. 286.100924(B)
Conquest or failure? Biography of J. Frank Norris by E. Ray Tatum. Dallas, Baptist Historical Foundation.[1966] 295 p. illus., ports. 21 cm. Bibliographical footnotes. [BX6495.N59T3] 66-8241
1. Norris, John Franklyn, 1877-1952. I. Title.

Norristown, Pa. Evangelical Lutheran church of the Trinity.

GANSER, Malcolm Hay, 1878- 384.174812
History of the Evangelical Lutheran church of the Trinity, Norristown, Pa., 1848-1938, written on the occasion of the celebration of the nintieth [?] anniversary, September 25, 1938, by Malcolm H. Ganser ... Norristown, Pa., Norristown herald, inc., 1938. 2 p. l., 107 p., 1 l., iix p. plates, ports. 23 1/2 cm. [BX8076.N6T72] 38-35770
1. Norristown, Pa. Evangelical Lutheran church of the Trinity. 2. Lutherans in Pennsylvania. I. Title.

Norristown, Pa. First Baptist church.

DELARME, Alonzo Alvin, 1862-1930. 286.
History of the First Baptist church of Norristown, Pa., from the organization, 1832, to the present time, 1897, by Alonzo Alvin DeLarne. [Philadelphia, Lehman & Bolton, 1897] 229, [2] p. incl. plates. ports. 21 cm. [BX6480.N8F5] 41-39795
1. Norristown, Pa. First Baptist church. I. Title.

North Africa Mission—History.

STEELE, Francis Rue, 1915- 266'.00961
Not in vain : the story of North Africa Mission / Francis R. Steele. Pasadena, Calif. : William Carey Library, c1981. xvi, 167 p., [8] p. of plates : ill. ;; 22 cm. Includes index. [BV3510.S74] 19 81-6122 ISBN 0-87808-182-8 pbk. : 4.95
1. North Africa Mission—History. I. Title.
Publisher's address 1705 N. Sierra Bonita Ave., P.O. Box 128-C, Pasadena, CA 91104.

North America—Church history.

HANDY, Robert T. 277
A history of the churches in the United States and Canada / Robert T. Handy. New York : Oxford University Press, 1977, c1976. ix, 471 p. : maps ; 24 cm. (Oxford history of the Christian Church) Includes index. Bibliography: p. 428-449. [BR510.H35 1977] 77-151281 ISBN 0-19-826910-2 : 19.95
1. North America—Church history. I. Title. II. Series.

HANDY, Robert T. 277
A history of the churches in the United States and Canada / Robert T. Handy. New York : Oxford University Press, 1978. p. cm. (Oxford history of the Christian Church) Includes index. Bibliography: p. [BR510.H35 1978] 77-15360 ISBN 0-19-826910-2 : 19.95
1. North America—Church history. I. Title. II. Series.

HOFFMAN, James W ed. 277
Concerns of a continent. With contributions by the editor and [others] New York, Friendship Press, 1958. 166p. illus. 20cm. [BR510.H6] 58-7035
1. North America—Church history. I. Title.

North Andover, Mass.—Biography.

MOFFORD, Juliet Haines. 288'.744'5
The history of North Parish Church of North Andover, 1645-1974 : and firm thine ancient vow / by Juliet Haines Mofford. North Andover, Mass. : Mafford, 1975. xxvi, 326 p. : ill. ; 25 cm. Includes index. Bibliography: p. [291]-301. [BX9861.N65N675] 75-39493
1. North Parish Church, North Andover, Mass. 2. North Andover, Mass.—Biography. I. Title. II. Title: And firm thine ancient vow.

North Carolina—Church history.

WEEKS, Stephen Beauregard, 1865-1918. 338.
...The religious development in the province of North Carolina. By Stephen Beauregard Weeks... Baltimore, The Johns Hopkins press, 1892. 68 p. 23 cm. (Johns Hopkins university studies in historical and political science. 10th ser., V-VI) "Sources of information on the religious development in North Carolina: p. [66]-68. [H31.J6] [F257.W39] 277 4-9367
1. North Carolina—Church history. I. Title.

WEEKS, Stephen Beauregard, 1865-1918. 973'.08 S
The religious development in the province of North Carolina. Baltimore, Johns Hopkins Press, 1892. [New York, Johnson Reprint Corp., 1973] 68 p. 22 cm. Pages also numbered 246-306. Original ed. issued as no. 5-6 of Church and state—Columbus and America, which forms the 10th series of Johns Hopkins University studies in historical and political science. Bibliography: p. [66]-68. [E18.C54 no. 5-6] [F257] 209'.756 72-14270 ISBN 0-384-66390-7 pap 4.00
1. North Carolina—Church history. I. Title. II. Series: Johns Hopkins University. Studies in historical and political science, 10th ser., 5-6. III. Series: Church and state—Columbus and America, no. 5-6.

North Carolina-Church history-Catholic.

MEMOIRS.
Durham [Christian Printing Co.] 1958. 108p. illus., port. 24cm.
1. North Carolina-Church history-Catholic. I. O'Brien, William Francis, 1872-

North Carolina — Church history — Methodist.

GRILL, Charles Franklin.
Methodism in the Upper Cape Fear Valley. Nashville, Tenn., Parthenon Press, 1966. 349 p. illus., ports. 24 cm. 67-94196
1. North Carolina — Church history — Methodist. I. Title.

North Carolina-Church history-Presbyterian.

LYTCH, William Elbert, 1928-
History of Bethesda Presbyterian Church, 1765-1965, Caswell County, N.C. [Yanceyville, 1965] 87 p. illjs., ports. 24 cm.
1. Bethesda Church, Caswell Co., N.C. 2. North Carolina-Church history-Presbyterian. I. Bethesda Presbyterian Church, Caswell Co., N.C. II. Title.

LYTCH, William Elbert, 1928-
History of Bethesda Presbyterian Church, 1765-1965, Caswell County, N.C. [Yanceyville, 1965] 87 p. illjs., ports. 24 cm. 66-37366
1. Bethesda Church, Caswell Co., N.C. 2. North Carolina-Church history-Presbyterian. I. Bethesda Presbyterian Church, Caswell Co., N.C. II. Title.

North Carolina—History—Revolution, 1775-1783—Religious aspects.

CALHOON, Robert McCluer. 261.7
Religion and the American Revolution in North Carolina / by Robert M. Calhoon. Raleigh : [North Carolina State University Graphics], 1976. x, 81 p. : ill. ; 23 cm. (North Carolina bicentennial pamphlet series ; 11) Bibliography: p. 79-80. [E263.N8C25] 76-383347
1. North Carolina—History—Revolution, 1775-1783—Religious aspects. I. Title. II. Series.

North Carolina—Religion.

BODE, Frederick A., 1940- 261.8'09756
Protestantism and the new South : Baptists and Methodists in political crisis, North Carolina, 1894-1903 / Frederick A. Bode. Charlottesville : University Press of Virginia, 1975. p. cm. Includes bibliographical references and index. [BR555.N78B62] 75-1289 ISBN 0-8139-0597-4 : 9.75
1. North Carolina—Religion. 2. Protestant churches—North Carolina. 3. North Carolina—Social conditions. I. Title.

North, Frank Mason, 1850-1935.

LACY, Creighton. 287'.632'0924
Frank Mason North: his social and ecumenical mission. Nashville, Abingdon Press [1967] 300 p. port. 24 cm. Bibliographical footnotes. [BX8495.N6L3] 67-14983
1. North, Frank Mason, 1850-1935. I. Title.

North Haven, Conn. St. John's Church.

STILES, H Nelson, comp. 283.7467
A chronicle of two hundred years of St. John's Church. North Haven, Conn., St. John's Episcopal Church, 1959. 103 p.

illus. 23 cm. Includes bibliography. [BX5980.N77S3] 59-35889
1. North Haven, Conn. St. John's Church. I. Title.

North, Mary E., 1843-1865.

CROUCH, Louisa J. 922
Early crowned: a memoir of Mary E. North. By Louisa J. Crouch ... With an introduction by Rev. R. S. Foster, D. D. New York, Carlton & Lanahan; Cincinnati, Hitchcock & Walden [1869] 263 p. front. (port.) 17 cm. Third edition. "Mary's brother. G. Adolphus North": p. [221]-268. [BR1725.N6C7 1869] 33-24580
1. North, Mary E., 1843-1865. 2. North, G. Adolphus, 1849-1866. I. Foster, Randolph Sinks, 1820-1908. II. Title.

CROUCH, Louisa J. 922
Early crowned: a memoir of Mary E. North. By Louisa J. Crouch ... With an introduction by Rev. R. S. Foster, D. D. New York, Carlton & Porter [1866] 256 p. front. (port.) 17 cm. "Mary's brother; G. Adolphus North": p. [223]-256. [BR1725.N6C7 1866] 38-3080
1. North, Mary E., 1843-1865. 2. North G. Adolphus, 1849-1866. I. Foster, Randolph Sinks, bp., 1820-1903. II. Title.

North Parish Church, North Andover, Mass.

MOFFORD, Juliet Haines. 288'.744'5
The history of North Parish Church of North Andover, 1645-1974 : and firm thine ancient vow / by Juliet Haines Mofford. North Andover, Mass. : Mafford, 1975. xxvi, 326 p. : ill. ; 25 cm. Includes index. Bibliography: p. [291]-301. [BX9861.N65N675] 75-39493
1. North Parish Church, North Andover, Mass. 2. North Andover, Mass.—Biography. I. Title. II. Title: And firm thine ancient vow.

North Stonington, Conn. First Baptist church.

PALMER, Albert Gallatin, 1813-1891. 286.17465
A discourse delivered at the one hundredth anniversary of the organization of the First Baptist church in North Stonington, September 20, 1843. With an appendix. By Albert G. Palmer... Boston, Gould, Kendall & Lincoln, 1844. 72 p. 16 cm. [BX6480.S85F5] 37-16704
1. North Stonington, Conn. First Baptist church. I. Title.

North Tarrytown, N.Y. First Reformed church.

NORTH Tarrytown, N.Y. First Reformed church. 285.
Two hundredth anniversary of the Old Dutch church of Sleepy Hollow, October 10 and October 11, 1897; 1697-1897. Tarrytown, N.Y., Printed by the De Vinne press for the Consistory of the First Reformed church, 1898. 4 p. l., 5-170 p. front., plates, ports., facsims. 24 1/2 cm. [BX9531.N6F5] 42-48558
I. Title.

STEWART, Abel T. 289
A historical discourse, delivered in the First reformed Protestant Dutch church of Tarrytown, N.Y., By Rev. Abel T. Stewart. May 13, 1866. New York, A. D. F. Randolph [1866] 19 p. front., pl. 23 cm. [BX9531.N6F55] 45-23090
1. North Tarrytown, N.Y. First Reformed church. I. Title.

North Yarmouth, Me.—Church history.

LETTERS to a friend,
on ecclesiastical councils, discipline and fellowship; comprising a history of the late dissentions in North-Yarmouth, (Maine.) Portland: Printed at the Mirror office, 1824. 80 p. 20 1/2 cm. [BX7149.N6L4] 27-9570
1. North Yarmouth, Me.—Church history.

Northampton, Eng. St. Matthew's Church

NICHOLAS, Michael. 942.5'5
Muse at St. Matthew's: a short history of the artistic traditions of St. Matthew's Church, Northampton; photographs by Ralph Meakins; cartoons by Stephen Meakins. Northampton, Michael Nicholas [117 Holly Rd. 1968] [27] p. 4 plates, illus. 25 cm. [BX5110.N6N5] 71-454057 5/6
1. Northampton, Eng. St. Matthew's Church I. Title.

Northampton, Mass.—Church history.

SPONSELLER, Edwin H. 285'.8'0924
Northampton and Jonathan Edwards [by] Edwin Sponseller. Shippensburg, Pa., Shippensburg State College, 1966. 32 p. 23 cm. (Shippensburg State College, Shippensburg, Pa. Faculty monograph series, v. 1, no. 1) "A note on the sources": p. 32. [BX7260.E3S66] 66-64511
1. Edwards, Jonathan, 1703-1758. 2. Northampton, Mass.—Church history. I. Title. II. Series: Pennsylvania. State College, Shippensburg. Faculty monograph series, v. 1, no. 1.

Northampton, Mass. St. Mary of the Assumption Church.

DWYER, Margaret Clifford. 282.744'23
Centennial history of St. Mary of the Assumption Church, Northampton, Massachusetts, 1866-1966. South Hackensack, N.J., Custombook, c1966. 1 v. (unpaged) illus. (part col.) ports. (part col.) 28 cm. Includes bibliography. [BX4603.N7S3] 66-30710
1. Northampton, Mass. St. Mary of the Assumption Church. I. Title.

Northern Baptist convention.

NATIONAL committee of northern Baptist laymen. Committee on survey. 286.
... Survey of the fields and work of the Northern Baptist convention by the special Committee on survey. [Report] to the Northern Baptist convention, Denver, Colorado, May, 1919. [New York, National committee of Northern Baptist laymen, 1919] 2 p. l., 151 p. illus. (incl. maps, charts) diagrs. 29 cm. At head of title: Report of the National committee of Northern Baptist laymen, section, ii. On cover: Final edition. [BX6207.A38] 19-19189
1. Northern Baptist convention. I. Title.

NORTHERN Baptist convention.
Annual of the Northern Baptist convention 1908- containing the proceedings of the 1st- meeting. St. Louis [etc., 1908- v. 23 cm. Prefixed to the Annual for 1908; Minutes of the meeting for the organization of the Northern Baptist contention held at Washington, D. C., May 16, 17, 1907 ... 10-28599
I. Title.

NORTHERN Baptist convention. 286.
A handbook of the Northern Baptist convention and its cooperating and affiliating organizations, 1919-1920. Pub. by order of the convention. Philadelphia, Boston American Baptist publication society [1919] 165 p. 24 cm. "Foreword" signed: W. C. Bitting. [BX6207.A35] 19-15960
I. Bitting, William Coleman, 1857-1931. II. Title.

NORTHERN Baptist convention. 286.
A manual of the Northern Baptist convention, prepared by request of the Executive committee, to commemorate the completion of ten years of service to the kingdom of God, 1908-1918. Philadelphia, For the Convention by the American Baptist publication society [1918?] viii, 135 p. 24 cm. "Foreword" signed: W. C. Bitting, editor. [BX6207.A349] 19-15961
I. Bitting, William Coleman, ed. II. Title.

NORTHERN Baptist convention. Committee on survey. 286.106373
Second survey of the fields and work of the Northern Baptist convention, presented by the Committee on survey to the Northern Baptist convention, Denver, Colorado, June 17, 1929. New York, The Northern Baptist convention board of missionary cooperation [1929] 2 p. l., 284 p. illus., maps, diagrs. 20 cm. [BX6207.A38 1929] 33-18555
I. Title.

Northern Baptist convention—Education.

NORTHERN Baptist convention. Board of education. 377.86
Baptist campus directory; a guide to Baptist-related schools, colleges, seminaries, student center. [Philadelphia] The Board of education of the Northern Baptist convention in co-operation with the schools [1945] 156 p. illus. (incl. ports.) 23 cm. [LC562.N58] 45-8083
1. Northern Baptist convention—Education. I. Title.

WHITE, Charles Lincoln, 1863- 266
Churches at work, by Charles L. White, edited by the Department of missionary education, Board of education of the Northern Baptist convention ... Philadelphia, Boston [etc.] The Judson press [1928] 8 p. l., 3-187 p. front., plates. 19 cm. [BV2765.W5 1928] 28-18408
I. Northern Baptist convention. Board of education. II. Title.

Northern Baptist convention. Ministers and missionaries benefit board.

NORTHERN Baptist convention. Ministers and missionaries benifit board. 254
Report of the Ministers and missionaries benefit board of the Northern Baptist convention ... [Rochester? N. Y., 19 v. 23 cm. [BX6345.5.N6] 35-24714
I. Title.

TOMLINSON, Everett Titsworth, 1859-1931. 254
The first twenty years of Ministers and missionaries benefit board of the Northern Baptist convention, by Everett T. Tomlinson... [Rahway, N.J., Quinn & Boden, inc., 1932] 2 p. l., 108 p. front., ports. 24 cm. "A tribute to the author, by P. C. Wright, D.D.": p. 1-5. [BX6347.T6] 32-29692
1. Northern Baptist convention. Ministers and missionaries benefit board. I. Wright, Peter Clark, 1870- II. Title.

Northern Baptist Convention — Missions.

LERRIGO, Peter Hugh James, 1875- ed. 266.61
All kindreds and tongues; an illustrated survey of the foreign mission enterprise of Northern Baptists, edited by P. H. J. Lerrigo, with the collaboration of Doris M. Amidon. Fourth issue, 1940. New York, American Baptist foreign mission society and Woman's American Baptist foreign mission society [1940] 3 p. l., 298 p. incl front., illus. maps (part double) 19 1/2 cm. "Missionary literature": p. 267-268. "Source material": p. [272] [BV2520.L37] 41-14823
1. Northern Baptist convention—Missions. 2. Baptists—Missions. I. Amidon, Doris M. II. American Baptist foreign mission society. III. Woman's American Baptist foreign mission society. IV. Title.

TULGA, Chester Earl, 1896- 266.6
The case against modernism in foregin missions. Chicago, Conservative Baptist Fellowship [1950] 64 p. 18 cm. (His Litte books on big subjects) [BV2520.T77] 50-4336
1. Northern Baptist Convention — Missions. 2. Missions, Foreign. 3. Modernist-fundamentalist controversy. I. Title.

TULGA, Chester Earl, 1896- 266.6
The foreign missions controversy in the Northern Baptist Convention, 1919-1949; 30 years of struggle. Chicago, Conservative Baptist Fellowship [1950] 201 p. 19 cm. [BV2520.T773] 50-4205
1. Northern Baptist Convention — Missions. 2. Missions, Foreign. 3. Modernist-fundamentalist controversy. I. Title.

Northwest, Canadian—Church history.

BROWN, Brian A., 1942- 971.9
The burning bush : a reformed ethic for the North / by Brian A. Brown. Dawson Creek, B.C. : Echo Pub., c1976. 165 p. : ill., map, ports. ; 20 cm. [BR575.N57B76] 77-367587 7.95
1. Campbell, Robert, 1808-1894. 2. Northwest, Canadian—Church history. 3. Northwest, Canadian—History. I. Campbell, Robert, 1808-1894. II. Title.

Northwest Regular Baptist Fellowship—Directories.

RUHLMAN, John J. 286'.179
A history of Northwest Regular Baptists : the General Association of Regular Baptist Churches in Washington, Oregon, and Idaho, 1939-1975 / by John J. Ruhlman, Jr. Schaumburg, Ill. : Regular Baptist Press, 1977,c1976 xiii, 334 p. : ill. ; 24 cm. Includes index. Bibliography: p. 319-325. [BX6389.34.W2R83] 76-12767 ISBN 0-87227-000-9 : 12.50
1. Northwest Regular Baptist Fellowship—Directories. I. Title.

Norton, Mrs. Sarah [Low] 1790-1856.

BALDWIN, Samuel Davies. 920.7
Life of Mrs. Sarah Norton; an illustration of practical piety. By Samuel D. Baldwin. Nashville, Tenn., J. B. M'Ferrin, agent, for the Methodist Episcopal church, South, 1858. iv p., 1 l., 7-187 p. front. (port.) 20 cm. [BR1725.N63B3] 34-40527
1. Norton, Mrs. Sarah [Low] 1790-1856. I. Title.

Norton, N.B. Christ Church.

HOYT, J. E.
History of the parish of Christ Church, Norton, N.B. [Norton, N.B.] 1961. 88 p. illus. 64-22137
1. Norton, N.B. Christ Church. I. Title.

Norton, Ralph C., 1868-1934.

NORTON, Edith (Fox) Mrs. 1881- 922
Ralph Norton and the Belgian gospel mission, by Edith F. Norton ... New York [etc.] Fleming H. Revell company [c1935] 2 p. l., 3-258 p. front., plates, ports. 20 cm. [Full name: Mrs. Edith Bland (Fox) Norton] [BV3785.N6N6] 35-34019
1. Norton, Ralph C., 1868-1934. 2. Missions—Belgium. 3. Evangelistic work. I. Title. II. Title: The Belgian gospel mission.

Norway—Church history.

HOYE, Bjarne, 1893- 284.7481
The fight of the Norwegian church against nazism, by Bjarne Hoye and Trygve M. Ager. New York, The Macmillan company, 1943. 4 p. l., 180 p. 19 1/2 cm. "First printing." [BR1006.H6] 43-4831
1. Norway—Church history. 2. Norske kirke—Hist. 3. Norway—Hist.—German occupation, 1940- I. Ager, Trygve Martinus, joint author. II. Title.

MOLLAND, Einar, 1908- 274.81
Church life in Norway, 1800-1950. Translated by Harris Kaasa. Minneapolis, Augsburg Pub. House [1957] 120 p. 21 cm. [BR1006.M6] 57-6474
1. Norway—Church history. I. Title.

MOLLAND, Einar, 1908- 274.81
Church life in Norway, 1800-1950 / by Einar Molland ; translated by Harris Kaasa. Westport, Conn. : Greenwood Press, 1978, c1957. p. cm. Reprint of the ed. published by Augsburg Pub. House, Minneapolis. Includes index. [BR1006.M6 1978] 78-2711 ISBN 0-313-20342-3 lib.bdg. : 13.00
1. Norway—Church history. I. Title.

Norwegian Americans—History.

STIANSEN, Peder, 1879- 286'.173
History of the Norwegian Baptists in America / P. Stiansen. New York : Arno Press, 1980 [c1939] 344 p. : ill. ; 23 cm. (The Baptist tradition) Reprint of the ed.

published by the Norwegian Baptist Conference of America. Includes index. Bibliography: p. 320-322. [BX6247.N6S8 1980] 79-52608 ISBN 0-405-12473-2 : 28.00
1. Norwegian Americans—History. 2. Baptists, Norwegian—History. I. Title. II. Series: Baptists tradition.

Norwegian Evangelical Lutheran Congregation at Coon Prairie.

HOLAND, Hjalmar 284'.1312'0977573
Rued, 1872-1963.
Coon Prairie : an historical report of the Norwegian Evangelical Lutheran Congregation at Coon Prairie, written on the occasion of its 75th anniversary in 1927 / by Hjalmar R. Holand ; translated by Oivind M. Hovde. Decorah, Iowa : [s.n.], 1977. 305 p. : ill. ; 24 cm. Includes index. [BX8076.N64H6413 1977] 77-361704
1. Norwegian Evangelical Lutheran Congregation at Coon Prairie. I. Title.

Norwegian Lutheran church of America.

BRUCE, Gustav Marius, 284.773
1879-
Ten studies on the Lutheran church, by Gustav M. Bruce ... Published under the auspices of the Board of elementary Christian education of the Norwegian Lutheran church of America. Minneapolis, Minn., Augsburg publishing house, 1932. 97 p. 1 illus. 20 1/2 cm. "First edition." "References for further study" at end of each chapter. [BX8065.B88] 32-20844
1. Norwegian Lutheran church of America. 2. Lutheran church. I. Norwegian Lutheran church of America. Board of elementary Christian education. II. Title.

UNITED Norwegian Lutheran 289
church of America. Liturgy and ritual.
The orders of service and ministerial acts of the Norwegian Luthern church. Minneapolis, Augsburg publishing house, 1902. 112, [2] p. 20 1/2 cm. "Translation of the Norwegian Lutheran 'Alterbog' ... made at the request of the Publishing committee of the United Norwegian Lutheran church."--Translator's note, signed: E. G. L. [i.e. Emil Gunerius Lund] [BX8067.A3 1902] 2-20334
I. Lund, Emil Gunerius, 1852- tr. II. Title.

Norwegian Lutheran church of America—History

DYBVIG, Philip S., 1899- 284.773
ed.
The forward march of faith; the story of a church which for a hundred years has struggled and grown ... edited by Philip S. Dybvig and Randolph E. Haugan, illustrated by John Ellingboe and Lee Mero, prepared by the Board of publication of the Norwegian Lutheran church of America. Minneapolis, Minn., Augsburg publishing house [c1943] 167 p. incl. illus. (part col.; incl. ports., maps) col. pl., diagrs. 36 cm. [BX8054.D9] 44-2161
1. Norwegian Lutheran church of America—Hist. I. Haugan, Randolph Edgar, 1902- joint ed. II. Norwegian Lutheran church of America. Board of publication. III. Title.

NORWEGIAN Lutheran church 284.773
of America. Centennial commission.
The centennial commemoration, a series of papers commemorating the one hundredth anniversary of the Norwegian Lutheran church of America ... v.1-. Minneapolis, Minn., The Centennial commission of the NLCA, 1943-. v. 23 cm. Contents.--vol. i. no. 1. Centennial address at old Muskego, by T. F. Gullixson. no. 2. Now thank we all our God, by J. R. Hestenes. [BX8054.A45] 44-822
1. Norwegian Lutheran church of America—Hist. 2. Norwegians in the U.S. I. Title.

VOGT, Volrath i.e. Henrik
Ludwig Volrath 1817-1889.
Illustrated Bible history and brief outlines of church history, by Volrath Vogt ... Revised according to the new translation of the Bible by the Publishing committee of the United Norwegian Lutheran church. From the Norwegian by N. C. Brun. Minneapolis, Minn., Augsburg publishing house, 1905. 140 p., 1 l. incl. front., illus. double map. 20 cm. 5-39860
I. Brun, N. C., tr. II. United, Norwegian Lutheran church of America. Publishing committee. III. Title.

Norwegians in the United States

ROHNE, John Magnus.
Norwegian American Lutheranism up to 1872, by J. Magnus Rohne... New York, The Macmillan company, 1926. xxiv p., 1 l., 271 p. 22 1/2 cm. Bibliography: p. 245-252. [BX8050.R6] 26-18377
1. Norwegians in the U.S. 2. Lutheran church in the U.S. I. Title.

WHO'S who among pastors in all the Norwegian Lutheran synods of America, 1843-1927. 3d ed. of Norsk lutherske prester i Amerika, Minneapolis, Minn., Augsburg publishing house, 1928. 662 p. illus. (ports.) 24 cm. [BX8050.N66] 28-21029
1. Norwegians in the U.S. 2. Lutheran church in the U.S.—Clergy. I. Malmin, Rasmus, 1865- II. Norlie, Olaf Morgan, 1876- III. Tingelstad, Oscar Adolf, 1882-

Norwegians, Lutheran.

NELSON, E Clifford, 1911- 284.773
The Lutheran Church among Norwegian-Americans; a history of the Evangelical Lutheran Church by E. Clifford Nelson and Eugene L. Fevold. Minneapolis. Augsburg Pub. House [1960] 2v. illus. 23cm. Based on E. C. Nelson's 'doctoral dissertation. 'The union movement among Norwegian-American Lutherans, 1880-1917' (Yale University, 1952) ... and Eugene L. Fevold's Norwegian- American Lutheranism, 1870-1890' (Ph. D. dissertation, University of Chicago, 1951) Includes bibliography. [BX8050.N4] 60-6438
1. Norwegians, Lutheran. 2. Norwegians in the U. S. 3. Evangelical Lutheran Church—Hist. I. Fevold, Eugene L., joint author. II. Title.

Norwich Cathedral.

THURLOW, A G G *726.5 726.6
Norwich Cathedral. Photographed by S. J. Brown. Norwich, Jarrold [1951] unpaged. illus. 18 cm. [NA5471.N8T48] 52-43398
1. Norwich Cathedral. I. Title.

THURLOW, Gilbert. 726'.6'094261
Norwich Cathedral. Norwich, Jarrold [1966] [25] p. front. (col. plan) illus. (some col.) 25 cm. (A Jarrold "Sandringham" book) [NA5471.N8T49] 67-80840
1. Norwich Cathedral.

Norwich, Conn.—Churches, Methodist Episcopal.

CLARK, Edgar Frederick, 287.
1835-1914.
The Methodist Episcopal churches of Norwich, Conn. By Rev. Edgar F. Clark, A.M. Norwich, 1867. xii, 270 p. 3 port. (incl. front.) 19 1/2 cm. [BX8249.N9C5] 24-10699
1. Norwich, Conn.—Churches, Methodist Episcopal. I. Title.

Norwich, Eng. (Diocese)—History

JESSOPP, Augustus, 1824-1914.
... Norwich. By the Rev. Augustus Jessopp ... Pub. under the direction of the Tract committee. London, Society for promoting Christian knowledge; New York, E. & J. B. Young & co., 1884. xii, 254 p. front. (fold. map) 17 cm. (Diocesan histories) [BX5107.N8J5] 4-204
1. Norwich, Eng. (Diocese)—Hist. I. Title.

Norwich Priory—History—Sources.

FERNIE, E. C. 914.26'1'008 s
The early communar and pitancer rolls of Norwich Cathedral Priory with an account of the building of the cloister / by E. C. Fernie and A. B. Whittingham. [Norwich, Eng.] : Norfolk Record Society, 1972. 128 p., [1] leaf of plates : ill. ; 26 cm. (Publications - Norfolk Record Society ; v. 41) Includes bibliographical references and indexes. [DA670.N59N863 vol. 41] [BX4631.N6] 283'.426'15 75-324048
1. Norwich Priory—History—Sources. I. Whittingham, Arthur Bensly, joint author. II. Title. III. Series: Norfolk Record Society. Publications ; v. 41.

Norwich, Vt. Congregational Church.

JOHNSON, Louise Coleman.
The Congregational heritage, 1770-1961, in Norwich, Vermont, by Louise Coleman Johnson. Pastors, music & musicians, by Fred E. Metcalf. A catalogue of members, statement of faith, convenant, bylaws, form of admission. [Woodstock, Vt., Elm Tree Press, 1961] 58 p. plates. 24 cm. 64-14187
1. Norwich, Vt. Congregational Church. 2. Norwich, Vt. — History. I. Metcalf, Fred E. II. Title.

Noth, Martin, 1902-1968.

GEUS, C. H. J., de. 309.1'33
The tribes of Israel : an investigation into some of the presuppositions of Martin Noth's amphictyony hypothesis / C. H. J. de Geus. Assen : Van Gorcum, 1977. xii, 258 p. ; 25 cm. (Studia Semitica Neerlandica ; 18) A revision of the author's thesis, Groningen. Includes indexes. Bibliography: p. 213-248. [BS1197.G47 1976] 76-359513 ISBN 9-02-321337-8 : 28.75
1. Noth, Martin, 1902-1968. 2. Bible. O.T.—Criticism, interpretation, etc. 3. Twelve tribes of Israel. I. Title. II. Series.
Distributed by Humanities Press

Notre Dame, Ind. University—Students.

NOTRE Dame, Ind. University.
... Survey of fifteen religious surveys, 1921-1936. Notre Dame, Ind. [The University press] 1939. 128 p. 23 cm. (Its Bulletin, vol. XXXIV, no. 1) Edited by John J. Cavanaugh, CSC. cf. Introd. A42
1. Notre Dame, Ind. University—Students. 2. Youth—Religious life. I. Cavanaugh, John Joseph, 1899- II. Title.

NOTRE Dame, Ind. University.
... Survey of fifteen religious surveys, 1921-1936. Notre Dame, Ind. [The University press] 1939. 128 p. 23 cm. (Its Bulletin, vol. xxxiv, no. 1) Edited by John J. Cavanagh, C. S. C. cf. Introd. A 42
1. Notre Dame, Ind. University—Students. 2. Youth—Religious life. I. Cavanaugh, John Joseph, 1899- II. Title.

Notredame, Michel de, 1503-1566.

ALLEN, Hugh Anthony, 1892- 133.3
Window in Provence, by Hugh Allen. Boston, B. Humphries, inc. [1943] xvi p., 1 l. 686 p. front. (port.) 24 1/2 cm. "First edition." "French reference works consulted": p. 685-686. [BF1815.N8A6] 43-4836
1. Notredame, Michel de, 1503-1566. I. Title.

CAVANAGH, John W. 133.
Notre Dame; or, Michael de Nostradamus. He wrote the history of the world divinely 2279 years in advance from the year 1555 to the year 3797, the end of the world without making a mistake to date, nearly 400 years. By John W. Cavanagh ... New York, Maria R. Cavanagh, c1923. 60 p. 17 cm. Portrait on cover. [BF1815.N8C3] 24-474
1. Notredame, Michael de, 1503-1566. I. Title.

CRISWELL, Jeron. 133.3
Criswell's forbidden predictions; based on Nostradamus and the Tarot, by Criswell. [1st ed.] Atlanta, Droke House/Hallux [1972] 128 p. illus. 22 cm. [BF1815.N8C75] 72-83125 ISBN 0-8375-6769-6 4.95
1. Notredame, Michel de, 1503-1566. 2. Prophecies (Occult sciences) 3. Tarot. I. Title. II. Title: Forbidden reflections.

IRWIN, Frank. 133.3'2'0924
The centuries of Nostradamus. Franklin, N.H., Hillside Press, 1964. ix, 74 p. port. 60 mm. "Limited to 375 numbered copies ... Number 26." Bibliography: p. 69-74. [BF1815.N817] 65-6990
1. Notredame, Michel de, 1503-1506. Les propheties. 2. Bibliography — Microscopic and miniature editions — Specimens I. Title.

KING, Bruce. 133.3
Everything you want to know about nature's mysteries, the prophets, Nostradamus, tea leaf readings, herbs, candle burning, by Zolar. New York, Arco Pub. Co. [1973, c1972] 203 p. 18 cm. On spine: Nature's mysteries, the prophets, Nostradamus. [BF1791.K56] 72-3137 ISBN 0-668-02661-8 0.95 (pbk.)
1. Notredame, Michel de, 1503-1566. 2. Prophecies. 3. Fortune-telling by tea leaves. 4. Herbs (in religion, folk-lore, etc.) 5. Candles (in religion, folk-lore, etc.) I. Title. II. Title: Nature's mysteries, the prophets, Nostradamus.

MURRAY, Richard D., 133.3'2'0924
1921-
The key to Nostradamus / by Richard D. Murray. Cleveland : Scorcap Pub. Co., 1975. xiii, 523 p. : ill. ; 21 cm. Errata leaf inserted. [BF1815.N8M85] 75-319955 15.95
1. Notredame, Michel de, 1503-1566. I. Title.
Publisher's address: Superior Bldg., Suite 1111, 815 Superior, N.E., Cleveland, Oh 44114.

PRIEDITIS, Arthur, 1909- 133.3'2
The fate of the nations [by] Arthur Prieditis. [1st ed.] Saint Paul, Llewellyn Publications, 1974 [i.e. 1975] xiii, 428 p. 24 cm. Bibliography: p. 425-428. [BF1815.N8P7] 73-20450 ISBN 0-87542-624-7
1. Notredame, Michel de, 1503-1566. 2. Prophecies. I. Title.

PRIEDITIS, Arthur A., 133.3'2
1909-
The fate of the nations [by] Arthur A. Prieditis. [1st ed.] Saint Paul, Minn., Llewellyn Publications, 1973. p. [BF1815.N8P7] 73-20450 ISBN 0-87542-624-7 12.95
1. Notredame, Michel de, 1503-1566. 2. Prophecies. I. Title.

ROBB, Stewart. 133.3
Letters on Nostradamus and miscellaneous writings. [New York, Maranatha Publishers, 1945?] 128 p. 19 cm. [AC8.R532] 50-36977
1. Notredame, Michel de, 1506-1566. 2. Prophecies. I. Title.

ROBB, Stewart 133.5
Prophecies on world events by Nostradamus Tr. and interpreted by Stewart Robb [Kew Gardens] New York, Box 142, Oracle Pr., [c.1961] 144p. illus. p1.00 pap., 61-2912
1. Notredame, Michel de, 1503-1566. 2. Prophecies. I. Title.

ROBB, Stewart 133.5
Prophecies on world events by Nostradamus. Tr., interpreted by Stewart Robb. New York, Liveright [1964, c.1961] 144p. illus. 21cm. 1.95 pap.,
1. Notredame, Michel de, 1503-1566. 2. Prophecies. I. Title.

VOLDBEN, A. 133.32
After Nostradamus [by] A. Voldben. Translated from the Italian by Gavin Gibbons Secaucus, N.J., Citadel Press, 1974 xiii., 183 p. 22 cm. Bibliography: 184-186 [BF1815.N8V64] 74-80821 ISBN 0-8065-0431-5 6.95
1. Notredame, Michel de, 1503-1566. 2. Prophecies. I. Title.

WARD, Charles A. 133.3'2
Oracles of Nostradamus / by Chas. A. Ward. New York : Gordon Press, 1975. xxix, 375 p. ; 24 cm. Originally published in 1891 by Leadenhall Press, London. Includes index. [BF1815.N8W2 1975] 75-16676 ISBN 0-87968-232-9
1. Notredame, Michel de, 1503-1566. 2. Prophecies (Occult sciences) I. Title.

WARD, Charles A. 133.3
Oracles of Nostradamus, by Chas. A. Ward... New York, C. Scribner's sons, 1940. 2 p. l., [vii]-xxix, [3], 375, 50 p. 1

illus. 19 1/2 cm. A reprint of the edition of 1891, with a supplement containing translations from the French text of Nostradamus which seem to have a bearing on twentieth century events. [RF1815. N8W2 1940] 40-31305
1. Notredame, Michel de, 1508-1566. I. Title.

WARD, Charles A. 133.3
Oracles of Nostradamus, by Charles A. Ward ... New York, The Modern library [1942] xxiv, [4], 3-366 p. 18 1/2 cm. (Half-title: The Modern library of the world's best books) "First Modern library edition 1942." [BF1815.N8W2 1942] (159.9613) 42-36139
1. Notredame, Michel de, 1503-1566 I. Title.

Nott, Abner Kingman, 1834-1859.

[NOTT, Richard Means] 922.673
1831-1880.
Memoirs of Abner Kingman Nott, late pastor of the First Baptist church in the city of New York; with copious extracts from his correspondence. By his brother ... New York, Sheldon and company, 1860. v, [13]-395 p. front. (port.) 20 cm. [BX6495.N65N6] 35-24715
1. Nott, Abner Kingman, 1834-1859. I. Title.

Nouwen, Henri J. M.

NOUWEN, Henri J. 248'.48'20924 B
M.
The Genesee diary : report from a Trappist monastery / Henri J. M. Nouwen. 1st ed. Garden City, N.Y. : Doubleday, 1976. xiv, 195 p. ; 22 cm. Includes bibliographical references. [BX4705.N87A33] 75-38169 ISBN 0-385-11368-4 : 6.95
1. Nouwen, Henri J. M. 2. Spiritual life—Catholic authors. I. Title.

NOUWEN, Henri J. M. 248.4
The Genesee diary : report from a Trappist monastery / Henri J. M. Nouwen. Garden City, N.Y. : Image Books, 1981, c1976. p. cm. "Complete and unabridged." Includes bibliographical references. [BX4705.N87A33 1981] 19 80-23632 ISBN 0-385-17446-2 : 3.95 (pbk.)
1. Nouwen, Henri J. M. 2. Spiritual life—Catholic authors. I. Title.

NOUWEN, Henri J. M. 248.2
In memoriam / Henri J. M. Nouwen. Notre Dame, Ind. : Ave Maria Press, c1980. 62 p. ; 20 cm. [BT825.N68] 79-56690 ISBN 0-87793-197-6 pbk. : 2.50
1. Nouwen, Henri J. M. 2. Death. 3. Grief. I. Title.

Nova Scotia—Emigration and immigration

BELL, Winthrop 325.34209716
Pickard.
The foreign Protestants and the settlement of Nova Scotia; the history of a piece of arrested British colonial policy in the eighteenth century. [Toronto] University of Toronto Press [1961] xiv, 673p. illus., maps (1 fold.) diagrs., facsims., tables. 26cm. Bibliography: p. [638]-646. [F1038.B42] 61-4799
1. Nova Scotia—Emig. & immig. 2. Lunenburg Co., N. S.—Hist. I. Title.

Novak, Frank, 1884-

ALLEE, George Franklin, 1897- 922
Beyond prison walls; the story of Frank Novak, once a desperate criminal and convict, now national prison chaplain no. 1 by the grace of God. Kansas City, Mo., Beacon Hill Press [1960] 96p. 20cm. [BV4465.A4] 60-12063
1. Novak, Frank, 1884- 2. Prisons—Missions and charities. I. Title.

Novenas.

CASSIDY, Norma Cronin, 242'.802
comp.
Favorite novenas and prayers. New York, Paulist Press [1972] x, 134 p. 18 cm. (Paulist Press/Deus books) [BX2170.N7C27] 72-91456 ISBN 0-8091-1761-4
1. Novenas. 2. Prayers. I. Title.

THE Catholic family book 264.025
of novenas. New York, J. J. Crawley, 1956. o71p. illus. 16cm. [BX2170,N7C3] 57-18418
1. Novenas.

HABIG, Marion 282'.092'4 B
Alphonse, 1901- comp.
A modern Saint Anthony; a novena in honor of the servant of God Brother Jordan Mai, with a sketch of the saintly American Brother Simon Van Ackeren, and a novena prayer to obtain his help [compiled by] Marion A. Habig. Chicago, Franciscan Herald Press [1974] p. cm. [BX4705.M2614H3] 74-18313 ISBN 0-8199-0553-4 0.65 (pbk.)
1. Mai, Jordan, 1866-1922. 2. Van Ackeren, Simon, 1918-1938. 3. Novenas. I. Title.

LINGS, Albert Ad. 1915. 264.025
Our favorite novenas prayerbook; includes indulgenced novenas and prayers from The raccolta, the book of indulgenced prayers authorized by the Sovereign Pontiff. New York, Benziger Bros. [1956] x, 569p. 17cm. [BX2170.N7L52] 59-33497
1. Novenas. 2. Indulgences. I. Title.

Novitiate.

COLIN, Louis. 1884- 271.069
The novitiate. Tr. from the French by Una Morrissy. Westminster. Md., Newman [c.] 1961. 447p. Bibl. 61-16566 4.95
1. Novitiate. I. Title.

DUFFEY, Felix D 1903- 271
Manual for novices. St. Louis, Herder [1957] 232p. 21cm. [BX2438.D79] 57-10689
1. Novitlate. I. Title.

FARRELL, Ambrose. 271.9
The education of the novice [by] Ambrose Farrell, Henry St. John [and] F. B. Elkisch. With an introd. by Conrad Pepler. Westminster, Md., Newman Press [1956] 73p. 19cm. 'The essays in this volume represent some of the papers read to ... novice mistresses gathered at Spode House in Staffordshire in January 1955.' [BX4213.F34] 56-43424
1. Novitiate. 2. Monastic and religious life of women. I. Title.

PHILIPPE, Paul, 1905- 271.9069
The movitiate. [Notre Dame, Ind.] Univ. of Notre Dame Pr. [c.]1961 169p. (Religious life in the modern world; selections from the Notre Dame Insts. of Spirituality, v.2; NDP4) 61-65517 1.95 pap.,
1. Novitiate. 2. Spiritual direction. I. Title.

PHILIPPE, Paul, 1905- 271.9069
The novitiate. [Notre Dame, Ind.] University of Notre Dame Press, 1961. 169p. 21cm. (Religious life in the modern world; selections from the Notre Dame Institutes of Spirituallty, v. 2) 'Articles ... previously published in the Proceedings of the Sisters' Institute of Spirituality, 1953, 1954, and 1955 respectively.' [BX4213.P5] 61-65517
1. Novitiate. 2. Spiritual direction. I. Title.

THEOLOGICAL Institute 271.9069
for local Superiors, University of Notre Dame
The novitiate, by Paul Philippe. [Notre Dame] University of Notre Dame Press, 1961. 169 p. 21 cm. (Religious life in the modern world, v. 2) "Articles ... previously published in the Proceedings of the Sisters' Institute of Spirituality, 1953, 1954, and 1955 respectively." [BX4213.T45] 61-65517
1. Novitiate. 2. Spiritual direction. I. Philippe, Paul, 1905- . II. Notre Dame, Ind. University. III. Title. IV. Series.

Nowell, Alexander, 1507?-1602.

CHURTON, Ralph, 1754-1831. 922.
The life of Alexander Nowell, dean of St. Paul's, chiefly compiled from registers, letters, and other authentic evidences. By Ralph Churton ... Oxford, The University press for the author; sold by F. C. and J. Rivington, London; [etc., etc.] 1809. xxix, 387 p., 1 l., 391-448 (i.e. 452) p. front., fold. plates, ports. (part fold.) facsim., fold. geneal. tab. 22 1/2 cm. On spine: Nowell's life, by Churton. [BX5199.N75C5] 44-37438
1. Nowell, Alexander, 1507?-1602. I. Title.

Noyes, John Humphrey, 1811-1886.

NOYES, George 289.9 922.89
Wallingford, ed.
John Humphrey Noyes, the Putney community; compiled and edited by George Wallingford Noyes; with twenty-four illustrations. Oneida, N. Y., 1931. xii p., 1 l., 393 p. front., plates, ports. 23 cm. [BX8795.P4N65] 289.9 31-17286
1. Noyes, John Humphrey, 1811-1886. 2. Oneida community. I. Title.

NOYES, George 289.9 B
Wallingford, ed.
Religious experience of John Humphrey Noyes, founder of the Oneida Community. Freeport, N.Y., Books for Libraries Press [1971] xiii, 416 p. illus., ports. 23 cm. Reprint of the 1923 ed. [BX8795.P4N8 1971] 72-152998 ISBN 0-8369-5750-4
1. Noyes, John Humphrey, 1811-1886.

Noyon, France. Notre-Dame (Cathedral)

SEYMOUR, Charles, 726'.6'094435
1912-
Notre-Dame of Noyon in the twelfth century; a study in the early development of gothic architecture New York, Norton [1968] xx, 202 p. illus., plans. 20 cm. (The Norton library, N464) Reprint of the 1939 ed. Includes bibliographical references. [NA5551.N6S4 1968] 77-683 2.95
1. Noyon, France. Notre-Dame (Cathedral) 2. Architecture, Gothic—Noyon, France. I. Title.

SEYMOUR, Charles, 726.6094435
1912-
Notre-Dame of Noyon in the twelfth century; a study in the early development of Gothic architecture, by Charles Seymour, jr... New Haven, Yale university press. London, H. Milford, Oxford university press, 1939. xx p., 1 l., 202 p. front., illus., plates (part fold.) plans (1 fold.) diagrs. 27 1/2 cm. (Half-title: Yale historical publications...History of art. 1) "Bibliographical note": p. [179]-187. [NA5551.N6S4] 39-24917
1. Noyon, France. Notre-Dame (Cathedral) 2. Architecture, Gothic. I. Title.

Ntlakyapamuk Indians—Religion and mythology.

TEIT, James Alexander, 299'.7
1864-
Mythology of the Thompson Indians / by James Teit. New York : AMS Press, [1975] 199-416 p. ; 24 cm. Reprint of the 1912 ed. published by E. J. Brill, Leiden, and G. E. Stechert, New York, which was issued as v. 12 of the Memoirs of the American Museum of Natural History, and as v. 8, pt. 2 of the Publications of the Jesup North Pacific Expedition. Includes bibliographical references. [E99.N96T23 1975] 73-3529 ISBN 0-404-58125-0 : 27.50
1. Ntlakyapamuk Indians—Religion and mythology. 2. Ntlakyapamuk Indians—Legends. 3. Indians of North America—Religion and mythology. 4. Indians of North America—Legends. I. Title. II. Series: American Museum of Natural History, New York. Memoirs ; v. 12. III. Series: The Jesup North Pacific Expedition. Publications ; v. 8, pt. 2.

Nubia—Archaeology.

WEEKS, Kent R
The classic christian townsite at Arminna West. Based on field work, notes, and plans by the author and the director, and Peter Mayer [and others] New Haven, Peabody Museum of Natural History of Yale University, 1967. xv, 73 p. illus., plates. 35 cm (Pennsylvania--Yale Expedition to Egypt, 1961-1962. Publications. no. 3) Bibliography, p. xi-xii. 68-76334
1. Nubia—Archaeology. 2. Christian archaeology and antiquities—Nubia. I. Yale University. Peabody Museum of Natural History. Arminna West. II. Title. III. Series.

Nuer (African tribe)

MCFALL, Ernest A. 261
Approaching the Nuer of Africa through the Old Testament [by Ernest A. McFall. South Pasadena, Calif., William Carey Library, c1970] iv, 99 l. 28 cm. Bibliography: leaves 95-98. [DT132.M27] 72-136099 ISBN 0-87808-104-6
1. Jews—Social life and customs. 2. Nuer (African tribe) 3. Sociology, Biblical. I. Title.

Nuer (African tribe)—Religion.

EVANS-PRITCHARD, Edward 299'.6
Evan, 1902-
Nuer religion. Oxford, Clarendon Press, 1956. xii, 335p. illus. 23cm. Errata slip inserted. Bibliographical footnotes. [BL2480.N7E9] 56-58065
1. Nuer (African tribe)—Religion. I. Title.

Nuestra Sefiora de la Soledad mission.

ENGELHARDT, 266.20979476
Zephyrin, father, 1851-1934.
Mission Nuestra Senora de la Soledad, by Fr. Zephyrin Engelhardt... Santa Barbara, Calif., Mission Santa Barbara, 1929. 1 p. l., [iv]-v p., 2 l., [3]-88 p. front., illus. (incl. map. facsims.) 22 1/2 cm. (Missions and missionaries of California. New series. Local history) [F869.S67E5] [2779.476] 30-10454
1. Nuestra Sefiora de la Soledad mission. I. Title.

Nuestra Senora de la Purisima Concepcion de Acuna Mission.

GUIDELINES for a 266'.2'764351
Texas Mission : instructions for the missionary of Mission Concepcion in San Antonio, ca. 1760 : transcript of the Spanish original and English translation, with notes / by Benedict Leutenegger. San Antonio, Tex. : Old Spanish Missions Historical Research Library at San Jose Mission, 1976. 61 leaves ; 29 cm. ([Documentary series] - Old Spanish Missions Historical Research Library ; 1) English and Spanish. [F394.S2G93] 76-379353
1. Nuestra Senora de la Purisima Concepcion de Acuna Mission. 2. San Antonio—History—Sources. 3. Indians of North America—Missions. 4. Missions—San Antonio. I. Leutenegger, Benedict. II. Series: Old Spanish Missions Historical Research Library. Documentary series — Old Spanish Missions Historical Research Library ; 1.

Numa Pompilius, king of Rome.

CARTER, Jesse Benedict, 1872- 292
1917.
The religion of Numa, and other essays on the religion of ancient Rome; by Jesse Benedict Carter. London, Macmillan and co., limited; New York, The Macmillan company, 1906. viii p., 1 l., 189 p. 20 cm. "References to the more recent literature ... have been given in connection with the appropriate topics in ... [the] index." Contents.The religion of Numa.--The reorganization of Servius.--The coming of the sibyl.--The decline of faith.--The Augustan renaissance. [BL801.C3] 6-16617
1. Numa Pompilius, king of Rome. 2. Augustus, emperor of Rome, B.C. 63-A.D. 14. 3. Rome—Religion. I. Title.

Numbers in the Bible.

DAVIS, John James, 1936- 220.6'8
Biblical numerology, by John J. Davis. Grand Rapids, Baker Book House [1968] 174 p. 20 cm. Bibliography: p. 157-167. [BS680.N8D3] 68-19207 3.95
1. Numbers in the Bible. I. Title.

LUCAS, Jerry. 220.6
Theomatics : God's best kept secret revealed / Jerry Lucas, Del Washburn. Briarcliff Manor, N.Y. : Stein and Day, c1977. 347 p. ; 24 cm. [BS534.L84] 76-49958 ISBN 0-8128-2181-5 : 8.95
1. Bible—Miscellanea. 2. Numbers in the Bible. I. Washburn, Del, joint author. II. Title.

Numbers, Theory of.

ELLIS, Keith. 133.3'35
Numberpower : in nature, art, and everyday life / Keith Ellis. [1st American ed.] New York : St. Martin's Press, 1978. xv, 236 p. : ill. ; 23 cm. Includes bibliographical references and index. [QA241.E44 1978] 78-3124 ISBN 0-312-57988-8 : 10.00
1. Numbers, Theory of. 2. Cycles. 3. Symbolism of numbers. I. Title.

Numerology.

*KNIGHT, Alva, 1934- 133.3'35
Find happiness in your name [by] Alva Knight. Cartoons by Steve Mitchell. New York, Vantage Press [1973] 239 p. illus. 21 cm. [BF1623] ISBN 0-533-00465-9. 5.95
1. Numerology. I. Title.

Nuns.

AUGUSTA, Mary Sister 1878- 265.
Dear Jesus; child's first communion prayer book, by Sister M. Augusta. Chicago, Ill., John P. Daleiden co. [c1929] 166 p. incl. illus., col. plates. 11 cm. [BX2217.A8] 29-12723
I. Title.

BERNSTEIN, Marcelle. 271'.9
The nuns / Marcelle Bernstein. 1st ed. Philadelphia : Lippincott, c1976. 326 p. ; 24 cm. Includes index. [BX4210.B377] 76-14794 ISBN 0-397-01135-0 : 9.95
1. Nuns. 2. Monastic and religious life of women. I. Title.

BERNSTEIN, Marcelle. 271'.9
Nuns / Marcelle Bernstein. London : Collins, 1976. 361 p. ; 22 cm. Includes index. [BX4210.B377 1976b] 76-365019 ISBN 0-00-215579-6 : £4.95
1. Nuns. 2. Monastic and religious life of women. I. Title.

CATHERINE, Thomas of Divine Providence, Mother. 922.273
My beloved; the story of a Carmelite nun. New York, McGraw-Hill [1955] 252 p. illus. 21 cm. [BX4705.C346A3] 55-6175
I. Title.

CECILIA, Sister, 1911- 922.2437
The deliverance of Sister Cecilia, as told to William Brinkley. New York, Farrar, Straus and Young [1954] 360p. 22cm. [BX4705.C347A3] 54-11973
I. Brinkley, William W., 1913- II. Title.

CECILIA, Sister, 1911- 922.2437
The deliverance of Sister Cecilia, as told to William Brinkley. London, New York, Longmans, Green [1955] 344p. 19cm. [BX4705.C347A3 1955] 56-33592
I. Brinkley, William, 1917- II. Title.

CODE, Joseph Bernard, 1899- 248.8'943'0922
Great American foundresses, by Joseph B. Code. Freeport, N.Y., Books for Libraries Press [1968] xviii, 512 p. ports. 22 cm. (Essay index reprint series) "First published 1929." Contents.Contents.—Mother D'Youville, of the Grey Nuns of Montreal.—Mother Clare Joseph Dickinson, of the Carmelites of Maryland.—Mother Elizabeth Ann Seton, of the Sisters of Charity of St. Vincent de Paul.—Mother Mary Rhodes, of the Sisters of Loretto at the Foot of the Cross.—Mother Catherine Spalding, of the Sisters of Charity of Nazareth.—Mother Teresa Lalor, of the Nuns of the Visitation of Georgetown.—Mother Philippine Duchesne, of the Religious of the Sacred Heart.—Mother Angela Sansbury, of the Dominicans of Kentucky.—Mother Mary Francis Clarke, of the Sisters of Charity of the Blessed Virgin Mary.—Mother Theodore Guerin, of the Sisters of Providence of St. Mary-of-the-Woods.—Mother Gamelin, of the Sisters of Charity of Providence.—Mother Mary Xavier Warde, of the Sisters of Mercy.—Mother Mary Rose Durocher, of the Sisters of the Holy Names of Jesus and Mary.—Mother Cornelia Connelly, of the Religious of the Holy Child Jesus.—Mother Mary Amadeus of the Heart of Jesus, of the Ursulines of Montana and Alaska.—Mother Alphonsa Lathrop, of the Dominican Sisters, Servants of Relief for Incurable Cancer. [BX4225.C6 1968] 68-20291
1. Nuns. 2. Women—United States—Biography. I. Title.

DEEDY, John G. 255'.9
The new nuns : serving where the spirit leads / John Deedy. Chicago, IL : Fides/Claretian, 1982. p. cm. [BX4210.D35 1982] 19 82-11895 ISBN 0-8190-0649-1 : 7.95
1. Nuns. 2. Monastic and religious life of women. I. Title.

THE life of an enclosed nun, by a mother superior ... New York, The John Lane company; [etc., etc.] 1911. 124 p. front. (port.) 18 cm. [BX4210.L5] 11-4459 1.00 271.
I. A mother superior.

LOWNDES, Mary E.
The nuns of Port Royal, as seen in their own narratives, by M. E. Lowndes ... London, New York [etc.] H. Frowde, 1909. xiii p., 1 l., 400 p. 17 pl. (incl. front., ports., plan) 24 cm. "Sources": p. vi-vii. 10-35756
I. Title.

RITA Agnes, Sister 1890- 271.9069
Dear atoms; [story-essays] Boston, Humphries [c.1962] 139p. 22cm. 62-51417 3.75
I. Title.

SMITH, T. Stratton. 271.98
The rebel nun; the moving story of Mother Maria of Paris. Springfield, Ill., Templegate [c.1965] 252p. illus., ports. 23cm. First pub. in England by Souvenir Pr. in 1965 [BX597.S53S6] 65-29349 4.95
I. Skobtsova, Evgeniia Iur'evna (Pilenko) d. 1945. II. Title.

WALSH, James Joseph, 1865-1942, comp. 271'.9 B
These splendid Sisters, compiled by James Joseph Walsh with introd. Freeport, N.Y., Books for Libraries Press [1970] 252 p. 23 cm. (Essay index reprint series) Reprint of the 1927 ed. Contents.—St. Bridget: pioneer feminine educator.—St. Hilda: abbess of streoneshalh (Whitby).—St. Scholastica and her Benedictine nuns. By J. J. Walsh.—St. Clare: founder of the Franciscan nuns, by Friar Thomas of Celano.—Mother Marie de L'Incarnation, by F. Parkman and W. Wood.—Mother Seton: founder of the American Sisters of Charity, by C. I. White.—The Irish Sisters of Charity and Mercy, by J. J. Walsh.—Sisters in the Crimean War, by Sister Mary Aloysius.—Mother Angela and the Sisters of the Civil War, by J. J. Walsh.—The nuns of the battlefield, by A. Kennedy.—Mother Cabrini: an apostle of the Italians, by J. J. Walsh.—Mother Mary, of the sick poor, by T. M. Schwertner.—Mother Alphonsa Lathrop, by J. J. Walsh.—Twenty five years among New York's cancerous poor, by H. A. Gillis. [BX4225.W3 1970] 75-128326 ISBN 0-8369-1856-8
1. Nuns. I. Title.

Nuns—Australia—Biography.

WORDLEY, Dick. 271'.97 B
No one dies alone / [by] Dick Wordley, with assisted creative research by Sister Jeanne Hyland and Frank S. Greenop. [Sydney] : Australian Creative Workshop for The Little Company of Mary, 1976. 244 p., [16] p. of col. plates : ill. ; 25 cm. [BX4390.Z8W67] 77-373919 ISBN 0-909246-33-5 : 14.95
1. Potter, Mary, 1847-1913. 2. Little Company of Mary—History. 3. Nuns—Australia—Biography. I. Hyland, Jeanne, joint author. II. Greenop, Frank Sydney, joint author. III. Title.

Nuns—Correspondence, reminiscences, etc.

AGNES Martha, Sister, S.C.H. 248.8'943'0924
Nothing on earth. Milwaukee, Bruce [1967] ix, 148 p. 21 cm. [BX4210.A4] 67-21494
1. Nuns—Correspondence, reminiscences, etc. I. Title.

MARYANNA, Sister 922.273
With love and laughter: reflections of a Dominican nun. Garden City, N. Y., Doubleday [1964, c.1960] 199p. 18cm. (Image bk., D172) .95 pap.,
I. Title.

MARYANNA, Sister. 922.273
With love and laughter: reflections of a Dominican nun. [1st ed.] Garden City, City, N. Y., Hanover House, 1960. 213p. 22cm. [BX4705.M4244A3] 60-7879
I. Title.

QUIN, Eleanor. 271'.976'0924 B
Last on the menu, by Sister Eleanor Quin (Sister M. Vincent dePaul, C.S.J.) Englewood Cliffs, N.J., Prentice-Hall [1969] 182 p. 22 cm. Autobiographical. [BX4210.Q5] 78-80997 ISBN 0-13-524033-6 4.95
1. Nuns—Correspondence, reminiscences, etc. I. Title.

Nuns—England—Correspondence.

GYSI, Lydia. 271'.98 B
Mother Maria, her life in letters / selected, edited, and introduced with a brief biography by Sister Thekla. New York : Paulist Press, c1979. xlviii, 144 p. : port. ; 23 cm. [BX395.G94A35 1979] 79-63455 ISBN 0-8091-0286-2 : 12.95
1. Gysi, Lydia. 2. Nuns—England—Correspondence. I. Thekla, Sister. II. Title.

Nuns—Fiction.

NUNSUCH : FIC
stories about sisters / collected by Candida Lund. Chicago, Ill. : T. More Press, c1982. 235 p. ; 22 cm. The surgeon and the nun / Paul Horgan — The bees / Joan Vatsek — Meditation / Katharine West — The Lord's day / J.F. Powers — The Corkerys / Frank O'Connor — Minutes of the meeting / Rose Tillemans — In the region of ice / Joyce Carol Oates — Round trip / Charles Healy — The model chapel / Madeline De Frees — Mother Coakley's reform / Brendan Gill — The song at the scaffold / Gertrud von Le Fort. [PS648.N68N86 1982] 813'.01'0835222 19 82-139374 ISBN 0-88347-139-6 : 12.95
1. Nuns—Fiction. 2. Short stories, American. I. Lund, Candida.

Nuns—Florida—Biography.

QUINN, Jane, 1916- 271'.976'024 B
The story of a nun : Jeanie Gordon Brown / Jane Quinn. St Augustine, Fla. : Villa Flora Press, c1978. xii, 469 p. : ill. ; 24 cm. Includes bibliographical references. [BX4705.B84653Q56] 78-60323 15.00
1. Brown, Jeanie Gordon, 1886-1960. 2. Nuns—Florida—Biography. 3. Florida—Biography. I. Title.

Nuns in campus ministry—Statistics.

DAVIS, Martin Winfrid. 253
The sister as campus minister; a survey-study of the religious sister's role and status in the campus ministry. Washington, Center for Applied Research in the Apostolate, 1970. xvi, 124 p. illus. 22 cm. [BV4376.D38] 76-23062
1. Nuns in campus ministry—Statistics. I. Title.

Nuns—India—Biography.

DOIG, Desmond. 266'.2'0924 B
Mother Teresa, her people and her work / Desmond Doig. 1st paperback ed. San Francisco : Harper & Row, [1980], c1976. p. cm. [BX4406.5.Z8D65 1980] 19 80-19610 ISBN 0-06-061941-4 : 9.95
1. Teresa, Mother, 1910- 2. Nuns—India—Biography. I. Title.

Nuns—India—Biography—Juvenile literature.

LEE, Betsy, 1949- 266'.2'0924 B
Mother Teresa : caring for all God's children / by Betsy Lee ; illustrated by Robert Kilbride. Minneapolis, Minn. : Dillon Press, c1981. 47 p. : col. ill. ; 24 cm. (Taking part books) A biography of the nun whose many years of working with poor and outcast people has been recognized with the 1980 Nobel Peace Prize. [BX4406.5.Z8L43] 92 19 80-20286 ISBN 0-87518-205-4 : 6.95
1. Teresa, Mother, 1910- —Juvenile literature. 2. Missionaries of Charity—Juvenile literature. 3. [Teresa, Mother, 1910-] 4. Nuns—India—Biography—Juvenile literature. 5. [Nuns.] I. Kilbride, Robert. II. Title.

Nuns—India—Calcutta—Biography.

GONZALEZ-BALADO, Jose Luis. 266'.2'0924 B
Always the poor : Mother Teresa, her life and message / Jose Luis Gonzalez-Balado. Liguori, Mo. : Liguori Publications, c1980. 112 p. : ill. ; 18 cm. Revised translation of Madre Teresa de los pobres mas pobres. "Resources: film and cassette tapes": p. 112. [BX4406.5.Z8G6513] 19 80-83484 ISBN 0-89243-134-2 (pbk.) : 2.50
1. Teresa, Mother, 1910- 2. Nuns—India—Calcutta—Biography. 3. Calcutta—Biography. I. Title.

MCGOVERN, James. 266'.2'0924 B
To give the love of Christ : a portrait of Mother Teresa and the Missionaries of Charity / by James McGovern. New York : Paulist Press, c1978. 109 p. ; 19 cm. (Emmaus books) [BX4406.5.T4455M32] 77-14832 ISBN 0-8091-2076-3 pbk. : 1.95
1. Teresa, Mother, 1910- 2. Missionaries of Charity—History. 3. Nuns—India—Calcutta—Biography. 4. Calcutta—Biography. I. Title.

SERROU, Robert. 266'.2'0924 B
Teresa of Calcutta : a pictorial biography / Robert Serrou ; with a foreword by Malcolm Muggeridge. New York : McGraw-Hill, [1980] p. cm. [BX4406.5.Z8S47] 80-18477 ISBN 0-07-056319-5 : 14.95 ISBN 0-07-056318-7 (pbk.) : 9.95
1. Teresa, Mother, 1910- 2. Nuns—India—Calcutta—Biography. 3. Calcutta—Biography. I. Title.

Nuns—Italy—Biography.

ZAPPULLI, Cesare. 271'.9
The power of goodness : the life of blessed Clelia Barbieri / by Cesare Zappulli ; translated by David Giddings. Boston, MA : Daughters of St. Paul, c1980. 84 p. : ill. ; 22 cm. Translation of La forza del bene. "St. Paul editions." [BX4405.5.Z8Z3613] 19 80-26836 ISBN 0-8198-5800-5 : 3.00 ISBN 0-8198-5801-3 pbk. : 2.00
1. Barbieri, Clelia, 1847-1870. 2. Minim Sisters of the Sorrowful Mother—Biography. 3. Nuns—Italy—Biography. I. Title.

Nuns—Italy—Biography—Juvenile literature.

DAUGHTERS of St. Paul. 271'.9 B
Yes is forever / by the Daughters of St. Paul. Boston : St. Paul Editions, c1979. p. cm. A biography of Mother Thecla Merlo, the Italian nun who was a co-founder of the Daughters of St. Paul. [BX4334.Z8D38 1979] 92 79-22266 ISBN 0-8198-8700-5 : 2.25 ISBN 0-8198-8702-1 pbk. : 1.25
1. Merlo, Thecla, 1894-1964—Juvenile literature. 2. Daughters of St. Paul—Biography—Juvenile literature. 3. [Merlo, Thecla, 1894-1964.] 4. [Daughters of St. Paul—Biography.] 5. Nuns—Italy—Biography—Juvenile literature. 6. [Nuns.] I. Title.

Nuns—Lebanon—Biography.

ZAYEK, Francis M. 271'.9 B
Rafka, the blind mystic of Lebanon / Francis M. Zayek. Still River, Mass. : St. Bede's Publications, c1980. viii, 83 p. : ill.

; 21 cm. [BX4713.595.R39Z39] 19 80-21176 ISBN 0-932506-02-X : 3.95
1. Rayyis, Rufqah, 1832-1914. 2. Nuns—Lebanon—Biography. I. Title.
Publisher's address P. O. Box 61, Still River, MA 01467.

Nuns—Quebec (Province)—Montreal—Biography.

MONK, Maria, d.ca.1850. 271'.97 B
Awful disclosures of the Hotel Dieu Nunnery of Montreal / Maria Monk. New York : Arno Press, 1977. 376 p. ; 21 cm. (Anti-movements in America) Maria Monk's personal narrative as related to T. Dwight. Has also been ascribed to J. J. Slocum and to W. K. Hoyte. Cf. New York herald, Aug. 12, 1836, p. 2, column 1; The Colophon, pt. 17, 1934; Sabin and Gagnon, P. Essai de bibl. can. Reprint of the rev. ed. published in 1836 for M. Monk by Hoisington & Trow, New York. [BX4216.M6A3 1977] 76-46089 ISBN 0-405-09962-2 : 21.00
1. Monk, Maria d. ca. 1850. 2. Nuns—Quebec (Province)—Montreal—Biography. 3. Montreal, Que.—Biography. I. Dwight, Theodore, 1796-1866. II. Slocum John Jay, 1803-1863. III. Hoyte, William K. IV. Title. V. Series.

Nuns—United States.

EWENS, Mary. 271'.9'073
The role of the nun in nineteenth century America / Mary Ewens. New York : Arno Press, 1978, c1971. 427 p. ; 24 cm. (The American Catholic tradition) Originally presented as the author's thesis, University of Minnesota. Bibliography: p. 392-425. [BX4220.U6E93 1978] 77-11285 ISBN 0-405-10828-1 : 27.00
1. Nuns—United States. 2. Monastic and religious life of women. I. Title. II. Series.

Nuns—United States—Biography.

MURPHY, Angelina. 271'.9 B
Mother Florence : a biographical history / Angelina Murphy ; foreword by Patrick F. Flores. 1st ed. Smithtown, N.Y. : Exposition Press, c1980. xiii, 258 p., [4] leaves of plates : ill. ; 22 cm. (An Exposition-testament book) Bibliography: p. 257-258. [BX4705.W263M87] 19 80-67314 ISBN 0-682-49625-1 : 15.00
1. Walter, Florence, 1858-1944. 2. Nuns—United States—Biography. I. Title.

TOBIN, Luke, 1908- 271'.9
Hope is an open door / Mary Luke Tobin. Nashville, Tenn. : Abingdon, c1981. 143 p. ; 21 cm. (Journeys in faith) Includes bibliographical references. [BX4705.T6722A33] 19 80-21414 ISBN 0-687-17410-4 : 7.95
1. Tobin, Luke, 1908- 2. Nuns—United States—Biography. 3. Church and social problems—Catholic Church. I. Title. II. Series.

Nupe (African people)—Religion.

NADEL, Siegfried Frederick, 1903- 299.65
Nupe religion. Glencoe, Ill., Free Press [1954] x, 288p. illus. 22cm. 'Intended as a sequel to ... [the author's] A black Byzantium.' Bibliographical footnotes. [BL2480] 55-14016
1. Nupe (African people)—Religion. I. Title.

NADEL, Siegfried Frederick, 1903-1956. 299'.6
Nupe religion; traditional beliefs and the influence of Islam in a West African chiefdom. New York, Schocken Books [1970] x, 288 p. illus. 23 cm. "Intended as a sequel to ... [the author's] first monograph on the Nupe people, a black Byzantium." Includes bibliographical references. [BL2480.N8N3 1970] 71-114163 10.00
1. Nupe (African people)—Religion. I. Title.

Nurculuk.

NURSi, Said, 1873-1960. 297'.23
Resurrection and the hereafter : a decisive proof of their reality / by Bediuzzaman Said Nursi ; [translated from the Turkish and Arabic by Hamid Algar]. [Berkeley, Calif.] : Risale-i Nur Institute of America, c1980. 174 p. ; 18 cm. [BP252.N8713] 19 79-65624 ISBN 0-933552-09-2 (pbk.) : 2.95
1. Nurculuk. I. Title.
Publisher's address: 2506 Shattuck Ave., Berkeley, CA 94704

Nuremberg—Church history.

EVANS, Austin Patterson. 261.7'2'094332
An episode in the struggle for religious freedom. New York, AMS Press [1970, c1924] xi, 235 p. 19 cm. Bibliography: p. 207-230. [BR359.N8E8 1970] 74-130618 ISBN 0-404-02357-6
1. Nuremberg—Church history. 2. Reformation—Germany—Nuremberg. 3. Religious liberty—Germany. I. Title.

EVANS, Austin Patterson.
An episode in the struggle for religious freedom; the sectaries of Nuremberg, 1524-1528, by Austin Patterson Evans ... New York, Columbia university press, 1924. xi, 235 p. 19 1/2 cm. The author's doctoral dissertation. Cornell university, 1916, but not published as a thesis. Bibliography: p. 207-230. [BR359.N8E8] 24-31307
1. Nuremberg—Church history. 2. Reformation—Germany—Nuremberg. 3. Religious liberty—Germany—Nuremberg. I. Title.

Nurse, Mrs. Rebecca (Towne) 1621-1692.

TAPLEY, Charles Sutherland, 1899- 272.8
Rebecca Nurse, saint but witch victim, by Charles Sutherland Tapley. Boston, Mass., Marshall Jones company [c1930] xiii, 105 p. front. (port.) plates. 20 cm. [BF1576.T23] 30-33553
1. Nurse, Mrs. Rebecca (Towne) 1621-1692. 2. Witchcraft—Salem, Mass. I. Title.

Nursery schools.

DANIELSON, Frances Weld. 268.432
Three years old; for the nursery class of the church school, by Frances W. Danielson and Jessie E. Moore. Boston, Chicago, The Pilgrim press [c1933] 4 p. l., [3]-214 p., 1 l. 20 cm. "The songs": p. [195]-205. [LB1140.D25] 33-5839
1. Nursery schools. 2. Religious education. 3. Object-teaching. I. Moore, Jessie Eleanor, joint author. II. Title.

DANIELSON, Frances Weld. 263.432
Three years old; for the nursey class of the church shcool, by Frances W. Danielson and Jesie E. Moore. Boston, Chicago, The Pilgrim press [c1936] vi, 214 p., 1 l. 20 cm. Blank pages for "Notes" (4 at end) "The songs": p. [195]-205. [LB1140.D25 1936] 36-21301
1. Nursery schools. 2. Religious education. 3. Object-teaching. I. Moore, Jessie Eleanor, joint author. II. Title.

Nurses and nursing.

CATHARINE De Jesus Christ Mother, 1869- 610.73069
At the bedside of the sick; precepts and counsels for hospital nurses. Translated by E. F. Peeler. Westminster, Md., Newman Press [1951] 150 p. 19 cm. [RT85.C315 1951] 174.2 52-8903
1. Nurses and nursing. 2. Nursing ethics. 3. Christian ethics—Catholic authors. I. Title.

CUSHING, Richard James, Cardinal 252.55
Hands that care, sermon delivered on the occasion of the capping ceremony, School of Nursing, Boston College, Sunday, January 31, 1960. Boston, Daughters of St. Paul, 1960. 16p. front. (port.) 16cm. .15 pap.,
I. Title.

GARESCHE, Edward Francis, 1876- 264.
A vade mecum for nurses and social workers, by Edward F. Garesche ... New and rev. ed. Milwaukee, Wis., The Bruce publishing company [c1926] 4 p. l., 5-184 p. front. 16 cm. [BX2373.N8G3 1926] 26-13144
I. Title.

LECLERCQ, Jacques, 1891- 248.8'8
The apostolic spirituality of the nursing sister. [Tr. by Norah Smaridge. Staten Island, N.Y., Alba, 1967] 138p. 20cm. Tr. of La soeur hospitaliere, [BX4240.L4] 67-15200 2.95
1. Nurses and nursing. 2. Hospitalers—Religious life. I. Title.

OSTLER, Daniel Eugene, father, 1894- 265.8
A nurse's manual [by] Fr. Daniel E. Ostler ... Paterson, N. J., St. Anthony guild press, Franciscan monastery, 1936. 1 p. l., 57 p. illus. 18 cm. On cover: Manual for nurses caring for Catholic patients. [Secular name: Eugene Ostler] "Bibliographical references used in preparing this material": p. 57. [BX2292.O8] 36-31246
1. Nurses and nursing. 2. Sacraments—Catholic church. I. Title.

Nurses and nursing—History

MURPHY, Denis G 610.7309
They did not pass by ; the story of the early pioneers of nursing. London, New York, Longmans, Greeen [1956] 208p. 20cm. Includes bibliography. [BX2825.M8] 56-14690
1. Nurses and nursing—Hist. 2. Monasticism and religious orders. 3. Monasticism and religious orders for women. I. Title.

Nursing ethics.

MESSAGES to Catholic nurses, by the late Pius XIX. [Washington, National Council of Catholic Nurses, 1957] 1v. (unpaged) 22cm.
1. Nursing ethics. I. Catholic Church. Pope, 1939-1958 (Pius XII)

Nursing ethics—Addresses, essays, lectures.

ETHICAL issues in nursing 174'.2
a proceedings adapted from nursing institutes held in Boston, Chicago, Houston and San Francisco during 1975-76 and sponsored by School of Nursing, Catholic University of America, Washington, D.C. and Department of Nursing Services, the Catholic Hospital Association, St. Louis, Missouri. St. Louis, Mo. : The Association, c1976. v, 99 p. ; 23 cm. Includes bibliographical references. [RT85.E83] 76-24218 ISBN 0-87125-033-0 pbk. : 6.00
1. Nursing ethics—Addresses, essays, lectures. 2. Christian ethics—Catholic authors—Addresses, essays, lectures. 3. Pastoral medicine—Catholic Church—Addresses, essays, lectures. I. Catholic University of America. School of Nursing. II. Catholic Hospital Association. Dept. of Nursing Services.

Nussbaum, Jean, 1888-1967.

LOEWEN, Gertrude. 286'.7'0924 B
Crusader for freedom; the story of Jean Nussbaum. Nashville, Southern Pub. Association [1969] 227 p. ports. 22 cm. [BX6193.N8L6] 77-86336
1. Nussbaum, Jean, 1888-1967. I. Title.

Nutrition.

CURTIS, Norah. 289.
Malnutrition (Quaker work in Austria 1919-24 and Spain 1936-39) by Norah Curtis & Cyril Gilbey. With a preface by Professor J. R. Marrack ... London, New York [etc.] H. Milford, Oxford university press, 1944. 87, [1] p. 18 cm. (On cover: Studies in relief problems] [BX7747.C8] A 45
1. Nutrition. 2. Reconstruction (1914-1939)—Austria. 3. Spain—Hist.—Civil war, 1936-1939—Hospitals, charities, etc. 4. Friends, Society of—Charities. I. Gilbey, Cyril, joint author. II. Title. III. Title: Quaker work in Austria 1919-24 and Spain 1936-39.

LANDERS, Lucille 289.9
Walking in obedience [the nutritional aspects of the Word of wisdom] Illus. by John Brlej. Salt Lake City, Bookcraft. [1963] 128p. illus. 24cm. 63-25377 price unreported
1. Nutrition. 2. Word of wisdom. I. Title.

SMITH, Mildred Nelson. 613.2
The Word of Wisdom : a principle with promise / by Mildred Nelson Smith. Independence, Mo. : Herald Pub. House, c1977. p. cm. Bibliography: p. [BX8643.D5S57] 76-46311 ISBN 0-8309-0175-2 : 12.00
1. Smith, Joseph, 1805-1844. 2. Nutrition. 3. Hygiene. 4. Mormons and Mormonism. I. Title.

Nuttall, Enos, abp., 1842-1916.

CUNDALL, Frank, 1858-
The life of Enos Nuttall, archbishop of the West Indies, by Frank [Cundall. With a foreword by the Archbishop of Canterbury. With maps and illustrations. London, Society for [promoting Christian knowledge; New York [etc.] Macmillan, 1922. xiv, 256 p. front. (port.) 6 pl., fold. map 23 cm. "Publications": p. 240-248. A 22
1. Nuttall, Enos, abp., 1842-1916. I. Title.

Nyaya.

KEITH, Arthur Berriedale, 1879- 181.
Indian logic and atomism; an exposition of the Nyaya and Vaicesika systems, by Arthur Berriedale Keith ... Oxford, The Clarendon press, 1921. 291, [1] p. 20 cm. [B132.N8K4] 22-6540
1. Nyaya. 2. Vaiceshika. I. Title.

Nyein Tha, Daw.

PROCTER, Marjorie. 286'.1'0924 B
The world my country : the story of Daw Nyein Tha of Burma / by Marjorie Procter. London : Grosvenor Books, 1976. 142 p., [8] p. of plates : ill., ports. ; 19 cm. (A Grosvenor biography) [BX6495.N88P76] 77-364619 ISBN 0-901269-22-0 : £1.25
1. Nyein Tha, Daw. 2. Baptists—Burma—Biography. I. Title.

Nygren, Anders Bp., 1890-

HALL, Thor, 1927- 230'.4'10924
Anders Nygren / by Thor Hall. Waco, Tex. : Word Books, c1978. 230 p. ; 23 cm. (Makers of the modern theological mind) Bibliography: p. 227-230. [BX8080.N8H34] 78-59427 ISBN 0-8499-0098-0 : 7.95
1. Nygren, Anders, 1890-

WINGREN, Gustaf, 1910- 230
Theology in conflict; Nygren, Barth, Bultmann. Translated by Eric H. Wahlstrom. Philadelphia, Muhlenberg Press [1958] 170 p. 21 cm. Translation of Teologiens metodfraga. [BT28.W573] 58-5750
1. Nygren, Anders Bp., 1890- 2. Barth, Karl, 1886- 3. Bultmann, Rudolf Karl, 1884- 4. Theology, Doctrinal — Hist. — 20th cent. 5. Law and gospel. I. Title.

Nygren, Anders, Bp., 1890- — Addresses, essays, lectures.

KEGLEY, Charles W., 1912- 200
The philosophy and theology of Anders Nygren. Edited by Charles W. Kegley. Carbondale, Southern Illinois University Press [1970] xiv, 434 p. 25 cm. "Bibliography of the publications of Anders Nygren to 1970 [by] Ulrich E. Mack": p. [379]-397. [BX8080.N8K4] 76-83670 ISBN 0-8093-0427-9 12.95
1. Nygren, Anders, Bp., 1890- — Addresses, essays, lectures. I. Title.

O-kee-pa (Religious ceremony)

CATLIN, George, 1796-1872. 299'.7
O-kee-pa, a religious ceremony, and other customs of the Mandans. Edited, and with an introd., by John C. Ewers. Centennial ed. New Haven, Yale University Press, 1967. 106 p. col. illus. 26 cm. Includes bibliographical references. [E99.M2C3 1967] 67-20336
1. O-kee-pa (Religious ceremony) 2. Mandan Indians. I. Ewers, John Canfield, ed.

CATLIN, George, 1796-1872. 299'.7
O-kee-pa, a religious ceremony, and other customs of the Mandans / by George Catlin ; edited, and with an introd. by John C. Ewers. Lincoln : University of Nebraska Press, [1976] c1967. p. cm. Reprint of the ed. published by Yale University Press, New Haven. Includes index. Bibliography: p. [E99.M2C3 1976] 76-4522 ISBN 0-8032-5845-3 pbk. : 7.95
1. O-kee-pa (Religious ceremony) 2. Mandan Indians. I. Ewers, John Canfield. II. Title.

Oak Grove Mennonite Church, Smithville, Ohio.

LEHMAN, James O. 289.7'771'61
Creative congregationalism : a history of the Oak Grove Mennonite Church in Wayne County, Ohio / James O. Lehman. Smithville, Ohio : Oak Grove Mennonite Church, 1978. 320 p. : ill. ; 22 cm. "Published in conjunction with the celebration on September 29-October 1, 1978, of 160 years of history in Wayne County, Ohio." Includes bibliographical references and index. [BX8131.S636L43] 78-111251 pbk. : 1.95
1. Oak Grove Mennonite Church, Smithville, Ohio. I. Title.
Publisher's address: 7843 Smucker Rd., Smithville, OH

Oakham Parish Church.

HADDELSEY, Stephen Andrew. 942.5'45
Oakham Parish Church / by Stephen Haddelsey. 5th ed. [Leicester] : The author, 1976. 3-25 p. : ill. ; 21 cm. [BX5195.R85O173 1976] 77-371976 ISBN 0-9505504-0-X : £0.25
1. Oakham Parish Church. I. Title.

Oakland, Calif. Church of the Ascension.

THE Greek Orthodox Church of the Ascension ... Architecture 2N, May 11, 1961 Berkeley, Calif., 1961] 1v. (unpaged, chiefly mounted plates)
1. Oakland, Calif. Church of the Ascension. I. Ruth, H Stuart.

SMITH, Brian.
The First Church of the Ascension. [Architecture 2N. Berkeley, Calif., 1962] 1 v. (unpaged, chiefly mounted plates) Cover title. "It was designed by John Lyon Reid and his partners, Tarks, Rockwell, and Banwell." 63-58549
1. Oakland, Calif. Church of the Ascension. I. Reid, John Lyon. II. Title.

Oakland, Calif. Church of the Ascension (Greek Orthodox)

OAKLAND, Calif. Church of the Ascension (Greek Orthodox)
Greek Orthodox Church of the Ascension, Hellenic community of Oakland and vicinity. [Oakland? Calif., 1961?] 1 v. (unpaged) illus., facsims., ports. 28 cm. 66-48761
1. Oakland, Calif. Church of the Ascension (Greek Orthodox) 2. Greeks in California. 3. Church history—California—Greek Orthodox. I. Title.

Oakland, Calif. First Methodist Church.

NORMAN, Albert E 287.679466
A steeple among the oaks, a centennial history of the First Methodist Church, Oakland, California, 1862-1962, by Albert E. Norman. Oakland, Calif., 1962. 73 p. illus., ports. 27 cm. Errata slip mounted on first leaf. [BX8481.O3F5] 64-5422
1. Oakland, Calif. First Methodist Church. I. Title.

Oakland, Calif. First Presbyterian Church.

EDWARDS, Ben F 1873- 285.1794
100 years of achievement and challenge; a brief history of the First Presbyterian Church of Oakland, California. Oakland, Centennial Committee of the First Presbyterian Church, 1953. 72p. illus. 24cm. [BX9211.O2E3] 53-23622
1. Oakland, Calif. First Presbyterian Church. I. Title.

Oaths (Canon law)

MORIARTY, Eugene James, 1907- 347.94
... *Oaths in ecclesiastical courts,* an historical synopsis and commentary ... by Eugene James Moriarty ... Washington, D.C., The Catholic university of America, 1937. x, 115 p. 23 cm. (The Catholic university of America. Canon law studies, no. 110) Thesis (J.C.D.)--Catholic university of America, 1937. Biographical note. Bibliography: p. 101-103. [BX1939.O2M6 1937] 37-16521
1. Oaths (Canon law) 2. Oaths—Hist. 3. Catholic church. Codex juris canonici. C. 1767-1769: De iurelurando testium. 4. Catholic church. Codex juris canonici. C. 1829-1936: De iurelurando partium. I. Title.

Oaths — Jews.

MOSES Ben Mainion, 1135-1204.
The book of asseverations, translated from the Hebrew by B. D. Klien. New Haven, Yale university press, 1962. xxv, 273 p. 23 cm. (Code of maimonides. Book 6) Yale Judaica series. v. 15. 65-34253
1. Oaths — Jews. 2. Oaths. I. Klien, B. D., tr. II. Title. III. Series.

Obedience.

CULLITON, Joseph T. 241'.4
Obedience : gateway to freedom / by Joseph T. Culliton ; [with a foreword by Bernard Cooke]. Plainfield, N.J. : Logos International, c1979. xi, 139 p. ; 21 cm. Includes bibliographical references. [BJ1459.C84] 78-71962 ISBN 0-88270-352-8 pbk. : 3.95
1. Obedience. I. Title.

ESPINOSA POLIT, Manuel Maria, father. 234.6
Perfect obedience; commentary on the letter on obedience of Saint Ignatius of Loyola, by Father Manuel Maria Espinosa Polit ... Westminster, Md., The Newman bookshop, 1947. xiii p., 1 l., 331 p. front. (port.) 2 facsim. on 1 l. 24 cm. Bibliography: p. 309-316. [BX3703.E8] 47-20379
1. Obedience. 2. Jesuits. I. Loyola, Ignacio de, Saint, 1491-1556. II. Title.

LEEMING, Bernard 271.0698
The mysticism of obedience. St. Paul Eds. [dist. Boston, Daughters of St. Paul, c.1964] 71p. 19cm. 64-16827 2.00; 1.00 pap.,
1. Obedience. I. Title.

LEEMING, Bernard. 271.0698
The mysticism of obedience. [Boston?] St. Paul Editions [1964] 71 p. 19 cm. [BX2435.L43] 64-16827
1. Obedience. I. Title.

MACDONALD, Hope. 248.4
Discovering the joy of obedience / Hope MacDonald. Grand Rapids : Zondervan Pub. House, c1980. 124 p. ; 21 cm. Includes bibliographical references. [BV4647.O2M32] 19 80-29 ISBN 0-310-28521-6 pbk. : 3.95
1. Obedience. I. Title.

MURRAY, Andrew, 1828-1917. 248
The school of obedience, by Rev. Andrew Murray ... Chicago, New York [etc.] Fleming H. Revell company [1899] 122 p. 19 cm. Addresses. [BV4501.M8S3] 99-1589
1. Obedience. I. Title.

OBEDIENCE;
being the English version of L'Obeissance et la religieuse d'aujourd'hui. Westminster, Md., Newman Press, 1953. viii, 289p. 22cm. (Religious life, 3) Bibliographical footnotes. A 53
1. Obedience. 2. Obedience (Vow) 3. Monasticism and religious orders.

SOLLE, Dorothee. 241
Beyond mere obedience; reflections on a Christian ethic for the future. Translated by Lawrence W. Denef. Minneapolis, Augsburg Pub. House [1970] 85 p. 20 cm. Translation of Phantasie und Gehorsam. Includes bibliographical references. [BJ1459.S5713] 70-121967
1. Obedience. 2. Christian ethics. I. Title.

VALENTINE, Ferdinand. 271.9
Religious obedience; a practical exposition for religious sisters. Westminster, Md., Newman Press, 1952. xiv, 128p. 19cm. [BX4210.V28] 51-13501
1. Obedience. 2. Monasticism and religious orders for women. I. Title.

Obedience—Collections.

.DAUGHTERS of St.Paul 234.608
Obedience, the greatest freedom, in the words of Albereone [others. Boston St. Paul Eds. 1966 363p. 22cm. [BX2435.D27] 66-28123 4.00; 3.00 pap.,
1. Obedience—Collections. I. Title.

Obedience—Juvenile literature.

BUERGER, Jane, 1922- 241'.4
Obedience / by Jane Buerger ; illustrated by Helen Endres. Elgin, Ill. : Child's World, [1980] p. cm. (What does the Bible say?) Illustrates ways to obey one's parents as God tells us to do. [BV4647.O2B83] 80-14590 ISBN 0-89565-164-5 : 4.95
1. Obedience—Juvenile literature. 2. [Obedience.] 3. [Conduct of life.] I. Endres, Helen. II. Title. III. Series.

CORIELL, Ron. 241'.4
His mind, his heart / Ron and Rebekah Coriell. Old Tappan, N.J. : Revell, 1980, c1979 p. cm. (Christian character reading program) Discusses, with examples, three desirable character traits, and how they may be attained. [BV4647.O2C66] 79-25021 ISBN 0-8007-7002-1 pbk. : 1.35
1. Obedience—Juvenile literature. 2. Wisdom—Juvenile literature. 3. Kindness—Juvenile literature. 4. [Christian life.] I. Coriell, Rebekah, joint author. II. Title. III. Series. IV. Spy glass series ; no. 2

CORIELL, Ron. 241'.4
Seeing and being like Him / Ron and Rebekah Coriell. Old Tappan, N.J. : Revell, 1980, c1979 p. cm. (Eye-glass series ; no. 1) (Christian character reading program) Short stories expound three Christian "character traits." [BV4647.O2C667 1980] 79-25016 ISBN 0-8007-7000-5 pbk. : 1.35
1. Obedience—Juvenile literature. 2. Wisdom—Juvenile literature. 3. Kindness—Juvenile literature. 4. [Christian life.] I. Coriell, Rebekah, joint author. II. Title. III. Series.

CORIELL, Ron. 241'.4
Walking his way / Ron and Rebekah Coriell. Old Tappan, N.J. : Revell, 1980, c1979 p. cm. (Christian character reading program) Short stories expound three Christian "character traits." [BV4647.O2C67] 79-25023 pbk. : 1.35
1. Obedience—Juvenile literature. 2. Wisdom—Juvenile literature. 3. Kindness—Juvenile literature. 4. [Christian life.] I. Coriell, Rebekah, joint author. II. Title. III. Series. IV. Spy glass series ; no. 1

Obedience—Religious aspects—Christianity.

SOLLE, Dorothee. 241'.4
Beyond mere obedience / by Dorothee Soelle ; translated by Lawrence W. Denef. New York : Pilgrim Press, c1982. xxii, 73 p. ; 21 cm. Translation of: Phantasie und Gehorsam. Includes bibliographical references. [BV4647.O2S5913 1982] 19 81-15431 ISBN 0-8298-0488-9 pbk. : 5.95
1. Obedience—Religious aspects—Christianity. 2. Christian ethics. 3. Woman (Christian theology) I. [Phantasie und Gehorsam.] English II. Title.

Oberammergau passion-play.

BACON, Eugenia (Jones) Mrs. 1840- 282.
The real stone face; or, Suffering depicted by nature, by Eugenia Jones Bacon ... Atlanta, Ga., The Fotte & Davies company, printers, 1899. 97 p. front. (port.) plates. 19 cm. Description of a natural likeness of the Saviour on a stone found at Oberamanergau. [BT309.B2] 6-559
1. Jesus Christ—Art. 2. Oberamanergau passion-play. I. Title.

CONKLING, Wallace Edmonds. 232.96
Darkness and light [by] Wallace Edmonds Conkling ... Milwaukee, Morehouse publishing co.; London, A. R. Mowbray & co., ltd. [c1931] 5 p. l., [3]-71, [1] p. 17 1/2 cm. [BT430.C55] 31-32931
1. Jesus Christ—Passion—Prayer-books and devotions. 2. Oberammergau passion-play. I. Title.

DAY, Ernest Hermitage, 1866-
Ober-Ammergan and the passion play; a practical and historical handbook for visitors, by the Rev. E. H. Day ... London, A. R. Mowbray & co., ltd., Milwaukee, The Young churchman co., 1910. 4 p. l., 96 p. front., 23 pl. 17 cm. "Books on the passion play": p. 94. A 10
1. Oberammergau. 2. Oberammergau passion-play. I. Title.

FULLER, Raymond Tifft, 1889- 792.1
The world's stage; Oberammergau, 1934; a book about the passion play: its history, its meaning and its people, by Raymond Tifft Fuller. New York, R. M. McBride & company, 1934. 3 p. l., 58 p. incl. front., illus. 17 cm. "First edition." "Further reading on the passion play": p. 58. [PN3235.F8] 34-11198
1. Oberammergau passion-play. 2. Oberammergau—Descr. I. Title.

GARBER, William Allen, 1878-
The Passion play graft; or, Oberammergau with the lid off. By Prof. W. A. Garber ... Dayton, Va., W. A. Garber [c1911] 63, [1] p. 19 1/2 cm. $0.15 [PN3238.G2] 11-20092
1. Oberammergau passion-play. I. Title.

LOCHEMES, M. J.
Recollections of Oberammergau. By M. J. Lochemes ... Dayton, O., G. A. Pflaum [1892] 64 p. incl. front., illus. 19 cm. [PN3238.L6] 11-15818
1. Oberammergau passion-play. I. Title.

MILLEN, William Arthur, 1896- 792.1
Opportunity at Oberammergau: the Passion play's potential [by] William A. Millen. [1st ed.] New York, Exposition Press [1971] 100 p. 21 cm. [PN3235.M5] 78-146913 ISBN 0-682-47237-9 3.50
1. Oberammergau passion-play. I. Title.

OBERAMMERGAU passion-play.
The passion play at Ober Ammergau, by Esse Esto Maplestone: with complete text from the German. New York, Broadway publishing co. [c1911] 226 p. 20 cm. "The text of the passion play from the German": p. 19-226. 11-10660 1.00
I. Maplestone, Esse Esto. II. Title.

OBERAMMERGAU passion-play.
The passion play at Ober Ammergau, by Esse Esto Maplestone; with complete text

from the German. New York, Broadway publishing co. [c1911] 226 p. 20 cm. "The text of the passion play from the German": p. 19-226. 11-10660 1.00
I. Maplestone, Esse Esto. II. Title.

OBERAMMERGAU passion-play. 792.1
The passion play of Oberammergau. Rev. ed. for the 1930 celebration, translated from the original German text, with an introduction, by Montrose J. Moses. New York city, Duffield & company, [c1930] ixxxvi p., 1 l., 222 p. front. (port.) 20 1/2 cm. Bibliography: p. 206-222. [PN3241.M6 1930] 30-14121
1. Oberammergau passion-play. I. Moses, Montrose Jonas, 1878-1934, tr. II. Title.

OBERAMMERGAU passion-play. 792.1
The passion play of Oberammergau. Rev. ed for the 1934 celebration, translated from the original German text, with an introduction, by Montrose J. Moses. New York city, Dodd, Mead & company [1934] lxxxvi p., 1 l., 221, [1] p. front., (port.) 20 1/2 cm. Bibliography: p. 205-[222] [PN3241.M6 1934] 34-27236
1. Oberammergau passion-play. I. Moses, Montrose Jonas, 1878-1934, tr. II. Title.

OBERAMMERGAU passion-play. 792.1
The passion play of Oberammergau. Rev. ed. for the 1930 celebration, translated from the original German text, with an introduction, by Montrose J. Moses. New York city, Duffield & company [c1930] ixxxvi p., 1 l., 222 p. front. (port.) 21 cm. Bibliography: p. 205-222. [PN3241.M6 1930] 30-14121
1. Oberammergau passion-play. I. Moses, Montrose Jonas, 1878-1934, tr. II. Title.

OBERAMMERGAU passion-play. 792.1
The passion play of Oberammergau. Rev. ed. for the 1934 celebration, translated from the original German text, with an introduction, by Montrose J. Moses. New York city, Dodd, Mead & company [1934] ixxxvi p., 1 l., 221, [1] p. front. (port.) 21 cm. Bibliography: p. 205-[222] [PN3241.M6 1934] 34-27236
1. Oberammergau passion-play. I. Moses, Montrose Jonas, 1878-1934, tr. II. Title.

UTTING, Mattie Johns. Mrs. 792.1
The passion play of Oberammergau, by Mattie Johns Utting. Philadelphia, Dorrance and company [c1937] 62 p. 19 cm. [PN3235.U6] 37-1572
1. Oberammagau passion-paly. I. Title.

Oberlin College.

FULLERTON, Kemper, 1865-1940. 208
Essays & sketches, Oberlin, 1904-1934. Freeport, N.Y., Books for Libraries Press [1971, c1938] x, 284 p. 23 cm. (Essay index reprint series) [BV4310.F8 1971] 70-156644 ISBN 0-8369-2361-8
1. Oberlin College. 2. Theology—Addresses, essays, lectures. I. Title.

Oberlin, Johann Friedrich, 1740-1826.

[ATKINS, Sarah] 230.
Memoirs of John Frederic Oberlin, pastor of Waldbach, in the Ban de La Roche. With an introduction by Henry Ware, jr. 2d American ed., with additions. Boston, J. Munroe & company, 1845. 3 p. l., [v]-xvi, 320 p. front. (port.) 18 1/2 cm. Added t.-p., engraved. [BX4827.03A7 1845] 42-44679
1. Oberlin, Johann Friedrich, 1740-1826. 2. Education—Alsace-Lorraine—Steinthal. I. Title.

BEARD, Augustus Field, 1833-1934. 230.
The story of John Frederic Oberlin, by Augustus Field Beard. Boston, New York [etc.] The Pilgrim press [c1909] xiii, 196 p. front., 3 pl. 21 1/2 cm. [BX4827.03B4] 9-13949
1. Oberlin Johann Fredrich, 1740-1826. I. Title.

DAWSON, Marshall, 1880- 922.444
Oberlin, a Protestant saint, by Marshall Dawson. Chicago, New York, Willett, Clark & company, 1934. ix, 166 p. 20 cm. Bibliography: p. 166. [BX4827.O3D3] 35-7299
1. Oberlin, Johann Friedrich, 1740-1826. I. Title.

KURTZ, John W. 284'.1'0924 B
John Frederic Oberlin / by John W. Kurtz. Boulder, Colo. : Westview Press, [1976] p. cm. Includes index. Bibliography: p. [BX4827.O3K87] 76-25211 ISBN 0-89158-118-9 : 15.00
1. Oberlin, Johann Friedrich, 1740-1826-

THE life of John Frederic 922.444
Oberlin. pastor of Waldbach, in the Ban de la Roche. Compiled for the American Sunday-school union, and revised by the Committee of publication. Philadelphia. American Sunday school union, 1830. 140 p. incl. front. pl. 18 cm. [BX4827.O3L5] 33-17056
1. Oberlin, Johann Friedrich, 1740-1836. I. American Sunday-school union.

Obituaries—Indexes.

SEDER, A. R., Mrs. 289.9
Index to the subjects of obituaries (Sterbfalle, Todesanzeigen) abstracted from Der Christliche Botschafter of the Evangelical Church, 1836-1866. Compiler: Mrs. A. R. Seder. [Naperville? Ill., 1967] iv, 295 p. 27 cm. Cover title. [BX7541.S4] 68-5168
1. Evangelical Association of North America—Biography. 2. Obituaries—Indexes. I. Der Christliche Botschafter. II. Title.

Object-teaching.

CRAFTS, Wilbur Fisk, 1850-1922. 016.
Through the eye to the heart; or, Eye-teaching in the Sunday-school. By Rev. W. F. Crafts. ["Callene Fisk.] With an introduction by J. H. Vincent, D. D. and an appendix for infant-class teachers by Miss Sara J. Timanus. New York, Nelson & Phillips; Cincinnati, Hitchcock & Walden [c1873] 224 p. front., illus. 20 cm. [BV1535.C73 1873] 15-22027
1. Object-teaching. 2. Sunday-schools—Exercises, reciations, etc. I. Crafts, Sara Jane (Timanus) "Mrs. W. F. Crafts." II. Title.

CRAFTS, Wilbur Fisk, 1850-1922. 268.
Through the eye to the heart; or, Eye-teaching in the Sunday-school. By Rev. W. F. Crafts. ["Callene Fisk."] With an introduction by J. H. Vincent, D.D., and an appendix for primary-class teachers by Mrs. W. F. Crafts. [Sara J. Timanus]... New York, Nelson & Phillips; Cincinnati, Hitchcock & Walden [1873?] 224 p. front., illus. 19 1/2 cm. [BV1535.C73 1873a] 15-22026
1. Object-teaching. 2. Sunday-schools. I. Crafts, Sara Jane (Timanus) "Mrs. W. F. Crafts," d. 1930. II. Title.

DANIELSON, Frances Weld. 016.
Object lessons for the cradle roll, by Frances Weld Danielson; blackboard illustrations by D. R. Augsburg, music by Grace Wilbur Conant ... Boston, New York [etc.] The Pilgrim press [c1915] 4 p. l., 106 p. plates. 22 cm. "The following series of lessons is an attempt to give a year's definite religious nurture preparatory to that of the Beginners' department" [of the sunday school] Bibliography: p. [96] [BV1535.D3] 15-26790
1. Object-teaching. I. Title.

FARIS, Lillie Anne, 1868- 268.684
The new sand-table (a revision of The sand table) a manual for Sunday school teachers, by Lillie A. Faris. Cincinnati, The Standard publishing company [c1931] 132 p. illus. 20 cm. [BV1536.F3 1931] 31-33877
1. Object-teaching. I. Title. II. Title: Sand-table, The new.

FARIS, Lillie Anne, 1868- 268.
The sand-table; a manual for Sunday school teachers by Lillie A. Faris. Cincinnati, The Standard publishing company [c1915] 86 p. l. ilus. (maps) plates. 20 cm. [BV1536.F3] 15-23092
1. Object-teaching. I. Title.

FOUSHEE, Clyde C 1900- 252
Animated object talks. [Westwood, N. J.] Revell [1956] 159p. 20cm. [BV4315.F617] 56-7440
1. Object teaching. 2. Children's sermons. I. Title.

FOUSHEE, Clyde C, 1900- 252
52 workable youth object lessons. Grand Rapids, Zondervan Pub. House [1951] 120 p. 20 cm. [BV4315.F62] 52-18160
1. Object-teaching. 2. Children's sermons. I. Title.

FOUSHEE, Clyde C., 1900- 252
Object lessons for youth, by Clyde C. Foushee ... Grand Rapids, Mich., Zondervan publishing house [1947] 121 p. 20 cm. [BV4315.F63] 47-24767
1. Object-teaching. 2. Children's sermons. I. Title.

FRANCIS, Dorothy Brenner. 268'.432
The boy with the blue ears and 49 other object lessons for children / Dorothy Brenner Francis. Nashville : Abingdon, c1979. 112 p. ; 20 cm. [BV4315.F638] 79-9899 ISBN 0-687-03908-8 pbk. : 3.95
1. Object-teaching. 2. Children's sermons. I. Title.

HEATON, Alma. 268'.432
Tools for teaching / Alma Heaton ; illustrated by Richard Holdaway. Salt Lake City, Utah : Bookcraft, c1979. vi, 58 p. : ill. ; 23 cm. [BV1536.5.H4] 19 79-53129 ISBN 0-88494-379-8 (pbk.) : 1.95
1. Object-teaching. 2. Christian education—Teaching methods. I. Title.

MILLER, Basil William, 1897- 252
Chemical illustrations; easy-to-do experiments for Christian workers, by Basil Miller ... Grand Rapids, Mich., Zondervan publishing house [1947] 115, [1] p. 20 cm. "Copyright MCMXLVI." [BV4315.M48] 47-24761
1. Object-teaching. 2. Children's sermons. I. Title.

MINOR, Nell Irene, 1878- 268.
Through the church school door; expressional activity--including handwork, by Nell I. Minor and Emily F. Bryant. A source book for teachers. For use with children between the ages of three and nine in the church school, the vacation school, the home. New York, Cincinnati [etc.] The Abingdon press [c1929] 2 p. l., [3]-73 p. illus. 25 x 32 1/2 cm. Music: p. 70-73. [BV1536.M5] 29-29225
1. Object-teaching. I. Bryant, Emily Frances, 1878- joint author. II. Title.

REICHEL, George Valentine, 1863-1914. 016.
Bible truth through eye and ear, [by] Rev. George V. Reichel ... New York, T. Whittaker [c1906] 437 p. 19 1/2 cm. [BV1535.R4] 6-45727
1. Object-teaching I. Title.

RICE, Rebecca, 1899- 268.68
Creative activities, with patterns and illus. by Verna Grisier McCully. Boston, Pilgrim Press [1947] viii, 148 p. illus., maps. 26 cm. [BV1536.R5] 47-12104
1. Object-teaching. I. Title.

SHETLER, Samuel Grant, 1871- 268.69
One hundred seventeen object lessons for boys and girls, by S. G. Shetler and Sanford G. Shetler ... Scottdale, Pa., Herald press, 1941. xii, 147 p. front. (ports.) illus. 20 1/2 cm. At head of title: Something different. Illustrated lining-papers. [BV1535.S45] 41-5083
1. Object-teaching. 2. Religious education—Teaching methods. I. Shetler, Sanford Grant, 1912- joint author. II. Title.

TYNDALL, Charles Herbert, 1857-1935. 252.
Object sermons in outline, with numerous illustrations, by Rev. C. H. Tyndall ... Introduction by Rev. A. F. Schauffler, D.D. New York, Chicago, Fleming H. Revell company [1891] x, [11]-254 p. illus. 19 cm. [BV4227.T9]
1. Object-teaching. 2. Sermons—Outlines. I. Title.

WOOD, Ella Nancy, 1862- 268.
Object lessons for junior work, with practical suggestions, by Ella N. Wood. New York, Chicago [etc.] F. H. Revell company [c1897] 113 p. illus. 19 cm. [BV1535.W55] 2-25506
1. Object-teaching. 2. Religious education—Teaching methods. I. Title.

WOOLSTON, Clarence Herbert. 268.635
Penny object lessons; 25 lessons for 25 cents, edited by Rev. C. H. Woolston, D.D., Homer A. Rodeheaver [and] Rev. Frank B. Lane ... Chicago, Philadelphia, The Rodeheaver company [c1916] 90 p. illus. (incl. ports.) 20 cm. [BX1535.W585] 34-15689
1. Object-teaching. 2. Religious education. I. Rodeheaver, Homer Alvan, 1880- II. Lane, Frank B. III. Title.

WOOLSTON, Clarence Herbert. 268.635
Penny object lessons; 25 lessons for 25 cents, edited by Rev. C. H. Woolston, D.D., Homer A. Rodeheaver [and] Rev. Frank B. Lane. 2d ed. ... Chicago, Philadelphia, The Rodeheaver company [c1917] 87 p. illus. (incl. ports.) 19 1/2 cm. [BV1535.W586] 34-15690
1. Object-teaching. 2. Religious education. I. Rodeheaver, Homer Alvan, 1890- II. Lane, Frank B. III. Title.

WOOLSTON, Clarence Herbert. 268.69
Seeing truth; a book of object lessons with magical and mechanical effects ... by Rev. C. Herbert Woolston ... Philadelphia, Boston [etc.] The Griffith & Rowland press [1914?] 208 p. front., illus. (incl. music) plates, ports., diagrs. 20 cm. [BV1535.W59] 34-15691
1. Object-teaching. 2. Religious education. I. Title.

ZOBELL, Albert L. 268'.6
Talks to see. Compiled by Albert L. Zobell, Jr. Salt Lake City, Deseret Book Co., 1971. 127 p. 20 cm. [BV4227.Z6] 77-155236 ISBN 0-87747-436-2 3.25
1. Object-teaching. 2. Homiletical illustrations. I. Title.

Object teaching (Religious education)

LINDGREN, Carl E
Teaching Bible truths with simple objects edited by Judith C. Kaiser. Rev. ed. Wheaton, Scripture Press [c1962] 64 p. illus. 65-78067
1. Object teaching (Religious education) I. Title.

*POGANSKI, Donald J. 268'.6
50 object lessons; the Gospel visualized for children St. Louis, Concordia [1967] 152p. illus. 18cm. 2.75 pap.,
I. Title.

Oblate sisters of providence.

[MARY Petra, sister] 1865- 271.
Blossoms gathered from the lower branches; or, A little work of an Oblate sister of providence ... [St. Louis, Con. P. Curran printing co., c1914] 4 p. l., 7-69 p., 1 l. incl. pl., ports. 20 cm. [Secular name: Mary Clopenia Boston] [BX4410.O2M3] 15-4659
1. Oblate sisters of providence. I. Title.

SHERWOOD, Grace (Hausmann) Mrs., 1873- 271.97
The Oblates' hundred and one years, by Grace H. Sherwood. New York, The Macmillan company, 1931. xi p., 2 l., 3-288 p. pl., ports. 19 1/2 cm. [Full name: Mrs. Mary Grace (Hausmann) Sherwood] Bibliography included in prefaces. [BX4410.O2S5] 31-13257
1. Joubert de la Muraille, Jacques Hector Nicholas, 1777-1843. 2. Oblate sisters of providence. 3. Negroes—Education. I. Title.

Oblates of Mary Immaculate.

LEFLON, Jean, 1893- 922.244
Eugene de Mazenod, Bishop of Marseilles, founder of the Oblates of Mary Immaculate, 1782-1861, v.2. Tr. [from French] by Francis D. Flanagan. New York, Fordham [c.1966] 702p. 24cm. Contents.v.2. Missions of Province, restoration of the Diocese of Marseilles; 1814-1837 Bibl. [BX4705.M4575L43] 61-13025 8.50
1. Mazenod, Charles Joseph Eugene de,

Bp., 1782-1861. 2. Oblates of Mary Immaculate. I. Title.

LEFLON, Jean, 1893- 922.244
Eugene de Mazenod, Bishop of Marseilles, founder of the Oblates of Mary Immaculate, 1782-1861. [v. 1] Tr. [from French] by Francis D. Flanagan. New York, Fordham Univ. Pr. [c.1961] 511p. Contents.v. 1. The steps of a vacation, 1782-1814. Bibl. 61-13025 7.50
1. Mazenod, Charles Joseph Eugene de, Bp., 1782-1861. 2. Oblates of Mary Immaculate. I. Title.

Oblates of Mary Immaculate—Missions.

DUCHAUSSOIS, Pierre Jean Baptiste, 1878-
Hidden apostles, our lay brother missionaries, by Father Pierre Duchaussois ... Translated from "Apotres inconnus" by Father Thomas Dawson, O.M.I. With portraits and many other illustrations ... Buffalo, N.Y., Missionary oblates of Mary Immaculate, 1937. 5 p. l., [13]-222 p., 1 l. illus., plates, ports., fold. map. 22 cm. "Printed in Belgium." A 39
1. Oblates of Mary Immaculate—Missions. 2. Missions—Canada. I. Dawson, Thomas, 1850- tr. II. Title.

LEISING, William A. 922.271
Arctic wings. [1st ed.] Garden City, N.Y., Doubleday [1959] 335 p. illus. 22 cm. [BV2815.N6L4] 59-13976
1. Oblates of Mary Immaculate—Missions. 2. Missions—Northwest, Canadian. I. Title.

Oblates of Mary Immaculate. Our Lady of Hope Province—History

WILD, Joseph Charles. 271'.76'09
Men of hope; the background and history of the Oblate Province of Our Lady of Hope (Eastern American Province), by JosephC. Wild. [Boston?] Missionary Oblates of Mary Immaculate, 1967. x,324 p. 21 cm. Includes bibliographical references. [BX3821.Z6088] 67-30024
1. Oblates of Mary Immaculate. Our Lady of Hope Province—Hist. I. Title.

Oblates of Mary Immaculate—Texas.

DOYON, Bernard. 271.76
The Cavalry of Christ on the Rio Grande, 1849-1883. Milwaukee, Bruce Press [1956] 252p. illus. 23cm. (Catholic life publications) [BX3820.M3D6] 56-4137
1. Oblates of Mary Immaculate—Texas. I. Title.

Oblates of St. Francis de Sales. Toledo-Detroit Province.

SOTTEK, James J. 255'.76
A star rose in the West; a short account of the Toledo foundations of the Oblates of St. Francis de Sales from 1943 to 1972, by James J. Sottek. [Toledo, Printed by Magers Print., 1972] v, 110 p. illus. 22 cm. Appendices (p. 102-110): A. Significant dates in the history of the Toledo foundations.—B. Necrology of the Oblates of St. Francis de Sales who have served in the Toledo-Detroit Province. [BX3825.Z6T67] 75-304180 2.95
1. Oblates of St. Francis de Sales. Toledo-Detroit Province. I. Title.

Obookiah, Henry, 1792?-1818.

DWIGHT, Edwin Welles, 1789-1841. 266'.022'0924
Memoirs of Henry Obookiah, a native of Owhyhee and a member of the Foreign Mission School, who died at Cornwall, Connecticut, February 17, 1818, aged 26 years. Honolulu [Woman's Board of Missions for the Pacific Islands] 1968. xiv, 112 p. illus., facsims., map, ports. 21 cm. "150th anniversary edition." [BV3680.H4O33 1968] 68-7300 1.50
1. Obookiah, Henry, 1792?-1818. I. Woman's Board of Missions for the Pacific Islands. II. Title.

[DWIGHT, Edwin Welles] 1789-1841.
Memoirs of Henry Obookiah, a native of Owhyhee, and a member of the Foreign mission school; who died at Cornwall, Conn. Feb. 17, 1818, aged 26 years. New-Haven: Published at the office of the Religious intelligencer, 1818. 109, 34, 34 p. front. (port.) 16 cm. Appended are two sermons with separate title-pages and pagination but with register continuous with the memoir: Beecher, Lyman. A sermon delivered at the funeral of Henry Obookiah ... New Haven, 1818.--Harvey, Joseph. The banner of Christ set up. A sermon, delivered at the inauguration of the Rev. Herman Daggett, as principal of the Foreign mission school in Cornwall, Connecticut, May 6, 1818 ... New-Haven, 1818. A22
1. Obookiah, Henry, 1792?-1818. I. Title.

O'Brien, James M., 1841-1928.

WASHINGTON, D.C. St. Peter's church. 282.753
... Centenary of St. Peter's church, and golden jubilee of Rt. Rev. Monsignor James M. O'Brien, pastor of St. Peter's church, Washington, D.C. [Washington, D.C., T. A. Cantwell, 1920] cover-title, 80 p. illus. (incl. ports.) 23 cm. At head of title: 1820, 1870, 1920. Edited by Andrew McGarraghy. [BX4603.W32S35] 34-8090
1. O'Brien, James M., 1841-1928. I. McGarraghy, Andrew, ed. II. Title.

O'Brien, Matthew Anthony, 1804-1871.

O'DANIEL, Victor Francis, 1868- 922.
An American apostle, the Very Reverend Matthew Anthony O'Brien, O.F., model priest and religious, promoter of Catholic education, tireless and fruitful harvester of souls in the United States and Canada, by Very Rev. Victor F. O'Daniel... Washington, D.C., The Dominicana [c1923] xvi, 341 p. incl. front., plates, ports. 22 1/2 cm. Bibliography: p. 329-332. [BX4705.O2O2] 23-13877
1. O'Brien, Matthew Anthony, 1804-1871. I. Title.

O'DANIEL, Victor Francis, 1868- 922
An American apostle, the Very Reverend Matthew Anthony O'Brien, O. P., model priest and religious, promoter of Catholic education, tireless and fruitful harvester of souls in the United States and Canada, by Very Rev. Victor F. O'Daniel ... Washington, D. C., The Dominicana [c1923] xvi, 341 p. incl. front., plates, ports. 23 cm. Bibliography: p. 329-332. [BX4705.O2O2] 28-13877
1. O'Brien, Matthew Anthony, 1804-1871. I. Title.

O'Callaghan, Eugene, 1831-1891.

CALLAHAN, Nelson J. 282'.0924 B
A case for due process in the church; Father Eugene O'Callaghan American pioneer of dissent [by] Nelson J. Callahan. Staten Island, N.Y., Alba House [1971] x, 133 p. illus. 22 cm. Includes bibliographical references. [BX4705.O25C33] 71-158570 ISBN 0-8189-0214-0 3.95
1. O'Callaghan, Eugene, 1831-1891. 2. Catholic Church—Government. I. Title.

O'Callaghan, Jose.

ESTRADA, David. 225.4'8
The first New Testament / by David Estrada and William White, Jr. Nashville : T. Nelson, c1978. 144 p. : ill. ; 21 cm. Bibliography: p. 141-144. [BM487.E84] 78-4057 5.95
1. O'Callaghan, Jose. 2. Dead Sea scrolls—Criticism, interpretation, etc. 3. Qumran. 4. Bible. N.T.—Manuscripts, Greek. I. White, William, 1934- joint author. II. Title.

Occasional sermons.

ALISON, Archibald, 1757-1839. 252.03
Sermons, chiefly on particular occasions. By Archibald Alison ... From the Edinburgh edition. Boston: Printed and published by Wells and Lilly. 1815-16. 2 v. 22 cm. (v. 2: 19 1/2 cm) Vol. [1] is without volume designation. Vol. 2 has title: Sermons, by Archibald Alison ... volume second. Boston: Published by Wells and Lilly; and by M. Carey, Philadelphia. [BX5330.A4S4 1815 a] 33-14918
1. Occasional sermons. 2. Sermons, English. 3. Episcopal church in Scotland—Sermons. I. Title.

ALISON, Archibald, 1757-1839. 252.03
Sermons, chiefly on particular occasions. By Archibald Alison ... 3d American ed. Georgetown, Col. Printed and published by W. A. Rind and co. 1815. xi, [18]-296 p. 17 1/2 cm. [BX5330.A4S4 1815 b] 33-14919
1. Occasional sermons. 2. Sermons, English. 3. Episcopal church in Scotland—Sermons. I. Title.

*ALLEN, R. Earl 252.6
Days to remember; sermons for special days [by] R. Earl Allen Grand Rapids, Baker Book House, [1975] 136 p. 20 cm. [BV4254.2] ISBN 0-8010-0077-7 2.95 (pbk.)
1. Occasional sermons. 2. Sermons, American. I. Title.

ANGELL, Charles Roy. 252
Rejoicing on great days [by] C. Roy Angell. Nashville, Broadman Press [1968] 126 p. 21 cm. Bibliographical footnotes. [BV4254.2.A54] 68-20665
1. Occasional sermons. 2. Baptists—Sermons. 3. Sermons, American. I. Title.

*APOSTOLON, Billy. 251.08
52 special-day invitation illustrations. Grand Rapids, Baker Book House, [1975] 107 p. 20 cm. [BV4225.2] ISBN 0-8010-0082-3 1.95 (pbk.)
1. Occasional, sermons. 2. Hamiletical illustrations. I. Title.

BAUMGAERTNER, John H. 252.6
Declaration of dependence; sermons for national holidays. St. Louis, Concordia [c.1965] 135p. 23cm. [BV4254.2.B3] 65-18456 2.00 pap.,
1. Occasional sermons. 2. Sermons. American. 3. Lutheran Church—Sermons. I. Title.

BLACKWOOD, Andrew Watterson, 1882- 252.051
This year of Our Lord; sermons for special occasions, by Andrew Watterson Blackwood. Philadelphia, The Westminster press [c1943] 244 p. 21 1/2 cm. [BX9178.B66T5] 44-3292
1. Occasional sermons. 2. Presbyterian church—Sermons. 3. Sermons, American. I. Title.

BUDDY, Charles Francis, Bp. 252.02
The thoughts of His heart, and selected writings. [Paterson? N. J.] 1954. 363p. illus. 21cm. [BX1756.B824T5] 54-30269
1. Occasional sermons. 2. Catholic Church—Sermons. 3. Sermons, American. I. Title.

CHAPPELL, Clovis Gillham, 1882- 252.6
Chappell's special day sermons [by] Clovis G. Chappell. Nashville, Cokesbury press [c1936] 204 p. 20 cm. [BX8333.C5C5] 36-5073
1. Occasional sermons. 2. Methodism—Sermons. 3. Sermons, American. I. Title.

CHAPPELL, Clovis Gillham, 1882- 252.6
Chappell's Special day sermons [by] Clovis G. Chappell. Nashville, Cokesbury press [1936] 204 p. 19 1/2 cm. [BX8333.C5C5] 36-5073
1. Occasional sermons. 2. Methodist church—Sermons. 3. Sermons, American. I. Title.

CROWE, Charles M. 252.07
Sermons for special days. Nashville, Abingdon Press [1961, c.1951] 171p. (Apex bk., F3) .95 pap.,
1. Occasional sermons. 2. Methodist Church—Sermons 3. Sermons, American. I. Title.

CROWE, Charles M. 252.07
Sermons for special days. New York, Abingdon-Cokesbury Press [1951] 171 p. 20 cm. [BV4254.2.C7] 51-10932
1. Occasional sermons. 2. Methodist Church—Sermons. 3. Sermons, American. I. Title.

DOWLING, Austin, abp., 1868-1930. 252.02
Occasional sermons and addresses of Archbishop Dowling, with a foreword by the Most Rev. John T. McNicholas ... Paterson, N.J., St. Anthony guild press, 1940. vii, 208 p. 25 1/2 cm. [BX1756.D66] 40-7180
1. Occasional sermons. 2. Catholic church—Sermons. 3. Sermons, American. I. McNicholas, John Timothy, abp., 1877- ed. II. Title.

DYKSTRA, John Albert, 1886- 252.057
Heavenly days, by John A. Dykstra, D.D. Grand Rapids, Mich., Wm. B. Eerdmans publishing company, 1944. 200 p. 20 cm. [BX9527.D9] 44-44914
1. Occasional sermons. 2. Reformed church in America—Sermons. 3. Sermons, American. I. Title.

EAVEY, Charles Benton, 1889- 252
Ninety-five brief talks for various occasions. Grand Rapids, Baker Book House, 1956. 103p. 21cm. [BV425.2.E3] 56-12748
1. Occasional sermons. I. Title.

EAVEY, Charles Benton, 1889- 252
Ninty-five brief talks for various occasions. Grand Rapids, Baker Bk. [1967, c.1956] 103p. 20cm. (Preaching helps ser.) [BV4254.2.E3] 56-12748 1.50 pap.,
1. Occasional sermons. I. Title.

FORD, William Herschel, 1900- 252.6
Simple sermons for special days and occasions. Introd. by Forrest C. Feezor. Grand Rapids, Zondervan Pub. House [c1956] 136p. 20cm. [BV4254.2.F6] 57-23347
1. Occasional sermons. 2. Baptists—Sermons. 3. Sermons, American. I. Title.

GRAF, Arthur E. 252.04'1
Sermons for special occasions; funerals, weddings, and various other occasions, by Arthur E. Graf. Giddings, Tex., Faith Publications [1972] 151 p. 20 cm. [BV4254.2.G69] 70-183106
1. Lutheran Church—Sermons. 2. Occasional sermons. 3. Sermons, American. I. Title.

GRANT, James Ralph, 1908- 252.6
The Word of the Lord for special days. Grand Rapids, Mich., Baker Bk., 1964. 174p. 20cm. 64-20451 2.95
1. Occasional sermons. 2. Sermons, American. 3. Baptists—Sermons. I. Title.

HALLOCK, Gerard Benjamin Fleet, 1856- 251
The minister's week-day manual; a handbook for the minister of whole-year help toward meeting the many demands for week-day addresses from innumerable organizations in both church and civic life, written and compiled by Rev. G. B. F. Hallock... New York and London, Harper & brothers, 1934. xv p., 1 l. 284 p. 22 cm. "First edition." [BV4241.H26] 34-13527
1. Occasional sermons. 2. Homiletical illustrations. I. Title.

HALLOCK, Gerard Benjamin Fleet, 1856 comp. 252
New sermons for special days and occasions, with a comprehensive collection of choice illustrations upon the themes, compiled and edited by G. B. F. Hallock ... New York [etc.] Fleming H. Revell company [c1933] 286 p. 22 1/2 cm. [BV4241.H27] 33-31104
1. Occasional sermons. 2. Sermons. American. 3. Homiletical illustrations. I. Title.

HOBBS, Herschel H 252.6
Welcome speeches, and emergency addresses for all occasions. Grand Rapids, Zondervan Pub. House [1960] 64p. 20cm. [BV4254.2.H6] 60-51664
1. Occasional sermons. I. Title.

JENKENS, Millard Alford, 1872- 252.6
Special day sermons, by Millard Alford Jenkens ... Nashville, Tenn., Broadman press [1942] 139 p. 20 cm. [BX6333.J4S6] 42-14976

1. Occasional sermons. 2. Baptists—Sermons. 3. Sermons, American. I. Title.

JONES, George Curtis, 1911- 252.6
March of the year; especial sermons for special days. St. Louis, Bethany Press [1959] 192p. 21cm. [BV4254.2.J6] 59-13167
1. Occasional sermons. 2. Disciples of Christ— Sermons. 3. Sermons, American. I. Title.

KERSHNER, Frederick Doyle, 1875- 252
Sermons for special days, by Frederick D. Kershner... New York, George H. Doran company [c1922] x, 11-223 p. 19 1/2 cm. [BX7327.K4S4] 22-8153
1. Occasional sermons. 2. Sermons, American. I. Title.

LANKENAU, Francis James, 1868-1939. 252.041
Occasional addresses, by F. J. Lankenau, D. D. Edited by F. Lankenau. St. Louis, Mo., Concordia publishing house, 1941. 100 p. 20 cm. [BX8066.L39O25] 41-12395
1. Occasional sermons. 2. Lutheran church—Sermons. 3. Sermons, American. I. Lankenau, Frank Clarence, 1897- ed. II. Title.

MARTIN, William Benjamin James. 252
Sermons for special days / W. B. J. Martin. Nashville : Abingdon Press, [1975] 157 p. ; 19 cm. [BV4254.2.M37] 74-34062 ISBN 0-687-37989-X pbk. : 3.95
1. Occasional sermons. 2. Sermons, American. I. Title.

MILLER, Calvin. 252.06
Sixteen days on the church calendar. Grand Rapids, Baker Book House [1968] 130 p. 21 cm. ([The New minister's handbook series]) [BV4254.2.M5] 68-31475 2.95
1. Occasional sermons. 2. Baptists—Sermons. 3. Sermons, American. I. Title.

MILLER, Charles Edward, 1929- 252'.02
Living in Christ; sacramental and occasional homilies [by] Charles E. Miller. New York, Alba House [1974] 121 p. 21 cm. Includes bibliographical references. [BV4254.2.M53] 73-22092 2.95 (pbk.)
1. Catholic Church—Sermons. 2. Occasional sermons. 3. Sermons, American. I. Title.

OBERMEIER, Arnold, 1915- 252.041
What shall I say? Devotional addresses for special occasions. Saint Louis, Concordia Pub. House [1954] 95p. 21cm. [BV4254.2.O2] 54-3555
1. Occasional sermons. 2. Lutheran Church—Sermons. 3. Sermons, American. I. Title.

PHELAN, Thomas Patrick, 1870- 252.02
Sermons for special occasions, by the Rev. Thomas P. Phelan ... New York, P. J. Kenedy & sons 53c1933] x p., 1 l., 243 p. 21 cm. [BX1756.P57S4] 33-11519
1. Occasional sermons. 2. Catholic church—Sermons. 3. Sermons, American. I. Title.

POOVEY, William Arthur, 1913- 264
Celebrate with drama : dramas and meditations for six special days, Easter, Ascension Day, Pentecost, Mission Sunday, Fellowship Sunday, Thanksgiving / W. A. Poovey. Minneapolis : Augsburg Pub. House, [1974] c1975. 128 p. ; 20 cm. [BV4254.2.P66] 74-14172 ISBN 0-8066-1456-0 pbk. : 2.95
1. Lutheran Church—Sermons. 2. Occasional sermons. 3. Sermons, American. 4. Christian drama, American. I. Title.

PREACHING on national holidays / edited by Alton M. Motter. Philadelphia : Fortress Press, c1976. viii, 120 p. ; 22 cm. Includes bibliographical references. [BV4254.2.P73] 75-36445 ISBN 0-8006-1222-1 pbk. : 2.95 252
1. Occasional sermons. 2. Sermons, American. I. Motter, Alton M.

SCHUETTE, Walter Erwin. 252.041
Keeping the faith; sermons for special occasions, by Walter E. Schuette ... Columbus, O., The Wartburg press [c1942] 227 p. pl. 20 cm. [BX8066.S37K4] 42-2532
1. Occasional sermons. 2. Lutheran church—Sermons. 3. Sermons, American. I. Title.

SERMONS for special occasions. St. Louis, Mo. : Concordia Pub. House, c1981. 99 p. ; 23 cm. Includes bibliographical references. [BV4254.2.S43] 19 80-25118 ISBN 0-570-03825-1 pbk. : 4.95 252'.6
1. Lutheran Church—Sermons. 2. Occasional sermons. 3. Sermons, American. I. Concordia Publishing House, St. Louis.

SMITH, Luther Wesley, 1897- 252.061
And so I preached this! By Luther Wesley Smith. Philadelphia, Boston [etc.] The Judson press [c1936] 7 p. l., 3-178 p. 20 cm. (Half-title: The Judson press sermons) "Sermons preached on...special occasions."--Foreword. Bibliography: p. 178. [BX6333.S54A5] 37-3837
1. Occasional sermons. 2. Baptists—Sermons. 3. Sermons, American. I. Title.

SWEETING, George, 1924- 252
Special sermons for special days : eighteen condensed sermons for the twentieth century / by George Sweeting. Chicago : Moody Press, c1977. 157 p. ; 22 cm. [BV4254.2.S93] 77-1218 ISBN 0-8024-8206-6 : 2.95
1. Occasional sermons. 2. Sermons, American. I. Title.

TERRA, Russell. 252
To see His face : homily themes for various occasions / Russell G. Terra. New York : Alba House, c1977. ix, 173 p. : ill. ; 21 cm. [BV4254.2.T47] 77-24083 ISBN 0-8189-0358-9 pbk. : 4.50
1. Catholic Church—Sermons. 2. Occasional sermons. 3. Sermons, American. I. Title.

TRUETT, George Washington, 1867-1944. 252.06
The inspiration of ideals; compiled and edited by Powhatan W. James. Grand Rapids, Eerdmans, 1950. 195 p. 20 cm. (Truett memorial series, v. 5) [BV4254.2.T7] 51-1114
1. Occasional sermons. 2. Baptists — Sermons. 3. Sermons, American. I. Title.

TRUETT, George Washington, 1867-1944. 252'.06
The inspiration of ideals, by George W. Truett. Compiled & edited by Powhatan W. James. Grand Rapids, Mich., Baker Book House [1973, c.1950] 195 p. 20 cm. (George W. Truett library) At head of title: Vol. V in the Truett Memorial series. [BV4254.2T7] ISBN 0-8010-8800-3 2.95 (pbk.)
1. Occasional sermons. 2. Baptists—Sermons. 3. Sermons, American. I. Title. L.C. card no. for the 1950 edition: 51-1114.

20 occasional sermons, by pastors of the Evangelical Lutheran Church Minneapolis, Augsburg Pub. House [1953] 234p. 21cm. [BV4254.2.T9] 53-12930 252.6
1. Occasional sermons. 2. Lutheran Church—Sermons. 3. Sermons, American. I. Evangelical Lutheran Church.

WILLIAMS, Lacey Kirk, 1871-1940. 252.061
"Lord! Lord!" Special occasion sermons and addresses of Dr. L. K. Williams, edited by Theodore S. Boone... [Fort Worth, Tex.] Historical commission, National Baptist convention, U.S.A., inc., 1942. 5 p. l., iv, 188 p. port. 20 cm. [BX6452.W45] 42-7725
1. Occasional sermons. 2. Baptists—Sermons. 3. Sermons, American. I. Boone, Theodore Sylvester, 1896- ed. II. National Baptist convention of the United States of America. Historical commission. III. Title.

Occasional sermons, Jewish.

RASKAS, Bernard S., ed. 296.42
Beacons of light; thoughts for special days and occasions. New York, Bloch [c.1965] viii, 263p. 24cm. [BM744.R3] 65-26712 6.50 bds.,
1. Occasional sermons, Jewish. I. Title.

RASKAS, Bernard S ed. 296.42
Beacons of light; thoughts for special days and occasions, compiled and edited by Bernard S. Raskas. New York, Bloch Pub. Co. [1965] viii, 263 p. 24 cm. [BM744.R3] 65-26712
1. Occasional sermons, Jewish. I. Title.

Occasional sermons—Outlines.

CAIN, Benjamin H. 251.027
The town and country pulpit; sermon blueprints for forty special days. Anderson, Ind., Warner Press [dist. by Gospel Trumpet Press] [c.1960] 112p. illus. 19cm. 60-6470 1.25 pap.,
1. Occasional sermons—Outlines. I. Title.

Occasional services.

O'GUIN, C. M. 264
Special occasion helps. Grand Rapids, Mich., Baker Book [c.]1965. 87p. 21cm. (Minister's handbk. ser.) [BV199.O3O35] 65-18265 1.95
1. Occasional services. I. Title.

PICKTHORN, William E., ed. 264
Minister's manual. Springfield, Mo., Gospel Pub. House [1965] 3v. 17cm. Contents.v.1. Services for special occasions.--v.2. Services for weddings and funerals.--v.3. Services for ministers and workers. [BV199.O3P5] 65-13222 price unreported
1. Occasional services. I. Title.

Occasional services. - Anglican.

HUNTER, Leslie Stannard, Bp. of Sheffield, 1890- ed. 264.035
A diocesan service book; services and prayers for various occasions. Ed., ordered by Leslie Stannard Hunter. New York, Oxford [c.]1965. xx, 203p. 20cm. [BX5147.O3H7] 65-1695 3.40
1. Occasional services—Anglican Communton. 2. Pastoral prayers. I. Title.

Occasional services—Catholic Church.

RIVERS, Clarence Joseph. 264.02'06
Celebration. Designed by William Schickel & Associates. New York, Herder and Herder [1969] 112 p. illus. 21 cm. Includes melodies with words. "Seven celebrations" (a collection of paraliturgical Catholic devotions): p. 41-109. [BV199.O3R58] 76-87767 4.95
1. Occasional services—Catholic Church. I. William Schickel & Associates. II. Title.

Occasional services — Methodist Church.

METHODIST Church (United States) Liturgy and ritual. 264.076
Ritual of the Methodist Church, the general services and occasional offices of the Church, adopted by the General Conference Conference, 1964. Nashville, Methodist Pub. House [c1964] 128 p. 16 cm. [BX8337.A2] 65-3890
1. Occasional services — Methodist Church. I. Title.

Occult sciences.

ALAMAH, Saundra, pseud.
Esdranalda; illumination on the essence of the spiritual realm: life everlasting. [1. ed.] New York, Exposition press [1961] 167 p. 21 cm. NUC63
1. Occult sciences. I. Title.

ALDER, Vera Stanley. 133
The finding of the 'third eye,' by Vera Stanley Alder. 3d thousand. London, New York [etc.] Rider & co. [194-?] x, 11-126, [2] p. illus. 19 cm. Bibliography: p. [128] [BF1031.A4] 44-49941
1. Occult sciences. I. Title.

[ATKINSON, William Walker] 1862- 181
Advanced course in Yogi philosophy and oriental occultism, by Yogi Ramacharaka [pseud.] ... Chicago, Ill., The Yogi publication society, 1905. 3 p. l., 337 p. 20 cm. (On back of cover: Yogi philosophy. vol. iii) "These lessons were intended as a contiminuation of or sequel to The fourteen lessons in Yogi philosophy and oriental occultism."--Publisher's notices. [BF1999.A7] 5-35582
1. Occult sciences. 2. Yoga. I. Title.

[ATKINSON, William Walker] 1862- 181.4
Advanced course in yogi philosophy and Oriental occultism, by Yogi Ramacharaka [pseud.] ... 30th ed. Chicago, Ill, The Yogi publication society [c1931] 3 p. l. 837 p. 19 cm. (On cover: Yogi philosophy. vol. ii) "These lessons were intended as a ... sequal to the fourteen lessons in yogi philosophy and Oriental occultism:"--Publisher's notice. [BF1999.A736 1931] 37-6450
1. Occult sciences. 2. Yogi. I. Title.

ATKINSON, William Walker, 1862- 133
Vril; or, Vital magnetism being volume six of the arcane teaching or secret doctrine of ancient Atlantis, Egypt, Chaldea and Greece. Chicago, A. C. McClurg & co., 19119. 123 p. 18 cm. [BF1623.V7A8] 11-28836 0.50
1. Occult sciences. I. Title.

ATKINSON, William Walker. 1862-1932.Practicalpsychomancyandcrystazing. 133
Psycho-magic: how to use the psychic powers of the astral plane. A course of lessons on: the psychic phenomena of distant sensing, clairvoyance, psychometry, crystal gazing. Astral and spirit. The wonders of the magic mirror. Interior focalization of the mind. State of introspection. Interior concentration. Astral auras. Reading in the astral light. Telepathy. The masterworks of William Walker Atkinson and L. W. de Laurence. [New York] Life Resources Institute [1967] 256 p. 21 cm. [BF1031.P8] 67-9349
1. Occult sciences. 2. Psychometry (Occult sciences). I. De Laurence, Lauron William, 1868- The mystic text book of The Hindu occult chambers. II. Title.

BAILEY, Alice A Mrs. 133
Initiation, human and solar, by Alice A. Bailey ... 1st ed. New York city, Lucifer publishing co.[c1922] 8 p. l., 225 p. diagrs. 24 cm. [BF1999.B3] 22-19241
1. Occult sciences. 2. Theosophy. I. Title.

BAILEY, Alice A Mrs. ed. 133
Letters on occult meditation, received and edited by Alice A. Bailey ... 1st ed. New York city, Lucifer publishing co. [c1922] 8 p. l., 357 p. diagrs. 24 cm. [BF1999.B35] 22-19242
1. Occult sciences. 2. Theosophy. I. Title.

BAILEY, Alice A. Mrs. 1881- 133
The consciousness of the atom, by Alice A. Bailey: a series of lectures delivered in New York city, winter of 1921-22... 1st ed. New York city, Lucifer publishing co. [c1922] 5 p. l., 104 p. 24 cm. [BF1999.B25] 22-20382
1. Occult sciences. I. Title.

BAILEY, Alice A. Mrs. 1881 ed. 133
Letters on occult meditation, received and edited by Alice A. Bailey ... 2d ed. New York city, Lucis publishing co [c1926] 8 p. l., 372 p. diagrs. 24 cm. [BF1999.B35 1826] 26-8569
1. Occult sciences. 2. Theosophy. I. Title.

BAILEY, Alice A. Mrs. 1881- 133.4
A treatise on white magic; or, The way of the disciple, by Alice A. Bailey. New York, Lucis publishing company [1934] xiii, 640 p. 24 cm. "First edition." [BF1611.B25] 159.9614 34-4815
1. Occult sciences. I. Title. II. Title: White magic, A treatise on. III. Title: The way of the disciple.

BAILEY, Alice A. Mrs. 1881- 133.4
A treatise on white magic; or, The way of the disciple, by Alice A. Bailey. New York, Lucis publishing company [1934] xiii, 640 p. 24 cm. "First edition." [BF1611.B25] 159.9614 34-4815
1. Occult sciences. I. Title. II. Title: White magic, A treatise on. III. Title: The way of the disciple.

BAILEY, Alice Anne (La Trobe-Bateman) 1880- 133
The destiny of the nations. New York, Lucis Pub. Co. [1949] 152 p. 23 cm. [BF1999.B257] 50-1813
1. Occult sciences. I. Title.

BAILEY, Alice Anne (La Trobe-Bateman) 1880-1949. 133
Discipleship in the new age. [1st ed.] New York, Lucis Pub. Co. [1944-55] 2v. 24cm. [BF1999.B26] 44-28587
1. Occult sciences. I. Title.

BAILEY, Alice Anne (La Trobe-Bateman) 1880-1949. 133
Initiation, human and solar. [6th ed.] New York, Lucis Pub. Co. [1951] 240 p. illus. 24 cm. [BF1999.B3 1951] 52-179
1. Occult sciences. 2. Theosophy. I. Title.

BAILEY, Alice Anne (La Trobe-Bateman), 1880-1949, ed. 133
Letters on occult meditation. 6th ed. New York, Lucis Pub. Co., 1950. 375 p. diagrs. 24 cm. [BF1999.B35 1950] 50-3343
1. Occult sciences. 2. Theosophy. I. Title.

BAILEY, Alice Anne (La Trobe-Bateman), 1880-1949. 133
A treatise on cosmic fire. 4th ed. New York, Lucis Pub. Co., 1951. 1316 p. illus. 24 cm. [BF1999.B37 1951] 51-6116
1. Occult sciences. I. Title. II. Title: Cosmic fire.

BAILEY, Alice Anne (La Trobe-Bateman), 1880-1949. 133.4
A treatise on white magic; or, The way of the disciple. [5th ed.] New York, Lucis Pub. Co. [1951] 675 p. 24 cm. [BF1611.B25 1951] 51-8401
1. Occult sciences. I. Title. II. Title: White magic. III. Title: The way of the disciple.

BAILEY, Alice Anne Latiobe Bateman 1880-1949
A treatise on cosmic fire. New York, Lucis Pub. Co. [1967, c1962] xxvi, 1367 p. illus. 22 cm. 68-29138
1. Occult sciences. I. Title. II. Title: Cosmic fire.

BAILEY, Alice Anne (LaTrobe-Bateman) 1880- 133
The consciousness of the atom, a series of lectures delivered in New York city, winter of 1921-22 ... by Alice A. Bailey; 1st ed. New York city, Lucifer publishing co. [c1922] 5 p. l., 104 p. 23 1/2 cm. [BF1999.B25] 22-20382
1. Occult sciences. I. Title.

BAILEY, Alice Anne (LaTrobe-Bateman) 1880- 133
Discipleship in the new age, by Alice A. Bailey. New York, Lucis publishing company [1944] xv, [1], 790 p. 1 l. 23 1/2 cm. "First edition." "The teachings of 'The Tibetan' as written down by Alice A. Bailey."--Leaf at end. [BF1999.B26] 44-28587
1. Occult sciences. 2. The Tibetan, pseud. I. Title.

BAILEY, Alice Anne (LaTrobe-Bateman) 1880-
Initiation, human and solar, by Alice A. Bailey ... 1st ed. New York city, Lucifer publishing co. [c1922] 8 p. l., 225 p. diagrs. 24 cm. [BF1999.B3] 22-19241
1. Occult sciences. 2. Theosophy. I. Title.

BAILEY, Alice Anne (LaTrobe-Bateman) 1880- ed. 133
Letters on occult meditation, received and edited by Alice A. Bailey ... 1st ed. New York city, Lucifer publishing co. [c1922] 8 p. l., 357 p. diagrs. 23 1/2 cm. [BF1999.B35 1922] 22-19242
1. Occult sciences. 2. Theosophy. I. Title.

BAILEY, Alice Anne (LaTrobe-Bateman) 1880- ed. 133
Letters on occult meditation, received and edited by Alice A. Bailey ... 2d ed. New York city, Lucis publishing co. [c1926] 8 p. l., 372 p. diagrs. 23 1/2 cm. [BF1999.B35 1926] 26-8569
1. Occult sciences. 2. Theosophy. I. Title.

BAILEY, Alice Anne (LaTrobe-Bateman) 1880- 133
A treatise on cosmic fire, by Alice A. Bailey ... 1st ed. New York, Lucis publishing company, 1925. 2 v. illus., diagrs. 23 1/2 cm. Paged continuously. [BF1999.B37] 25-9082
1. Occult sciences. I. Title. II. Title: Cosmic fire.

BAILEY, Alice Anne (LaTrobe-Bateman) 1880- 133.4
A treatise on white magic; or, The way of the disciple by Alice A. Bailey. New York, Lucis publishing company [1934] xiii, 640 p. 23 1/2 cm. "First edition." [BF1611.B25] [159.9614] 34-4815
1. Occult sciences. I. Title. II. Title: White magic. III. Title: The way of the disciple.

BAILEY, Alice Anne(LaTrobe-Bateman) 1880-1949.
Discipleship in the new age. New York, Lucis Pub. Ca. [1966] 2 v. 24 cm. 68-76810
1. Occult sciences. I. Title.

BAILEY, Alice Anne (LaTrobe-Bateman) 1880-1949.
Glamour; a world problem. New York, Lucis Pub. Co. [1967] xi, 290 p. 24 cm. 68-30024
1. Occult sciences. I. Title.

BAILEY, Alice Anne (LaTrobe-Bateman) 1880-1949, ed.
Letters on occult meditation, received and edited by Alice A. Bailey. New York, Lucis Pub. Co. [1966] 375 p. illus. 24 cm. 68-27814
1. Occult sciences. I. Title.

BAILEY, Alice Anne (LaTrobe-Bateman) 1880-1949.
The soul and its mechanism; the problem of psychology. New York, Lucis Pub. Co. [1965] 165 p. 24 cm. Bibliography: p. 158-160. 68-32373
1. Occult sciences. I. Title.

BAILEY, Foster. 133
Changing esoteric values. Tunbridge Wells, Kent, Lucis Press [1955, c1954] 92p. 22cm. [BF1999.B372 1955] 56-17622
1. Occult sciences. I. Title.

*BARCLAY, Glen. 133
Mind over matter; beyond the bounds of nature. Indianapolis, Bobbs-Merrill Co. [1973] 142 p. 22 cm. Bibliography: p. 135-139. [BF1999] 73-3908 ISBN 0-672-51867-8 5.95
1. Occult Sciences. I. Title.

BAZL, Frank M. 133
The conquest of mind. [1st ed.] Los Angeles, De Vorss [1951] 554 p. 24 cm. [BF1999.B385] 51-794
1. Occult sciences. I. Title.

BEATON-TROKER, Katherine 133.91
Psychic experiences. New York, Vantage [c.1962] 62p. 21cm. 2.50 bds.,
I. Title.

BENNETT, Alfred Gordon, 1901- 133
Focus on the unknown. [The story of unexplained mysteries] New York, Library Publishers [1954] 260 p. illus. 22 cm. [BF1411.B47] 54-12527
1. Occult sciences. I. Title.

BERGIER, Jacques, 1912- 133
Secret doors of the earth / Jacques Bergier ; translated by Nicole Taghert. Chicago : H. Regnery Co., 1975. 159 p., [4] leaves of plates : ill. ; 22 cm. Translation of Visa pour une autre terre. [BF1412.B3713 1975] 75-13213 ISBN 0-8092-8208-9 : 7.95
1. Occult sciences. I. Title.

BIRDSONG, Robert E. 133
The revelations of Hermes : an exposition of Adamic Christianity / by Robert E. Birdsong. 1st ed. San Francisco : Sirius Books, c1974. xviii, 278 p. : ill. ; 22 cm. [BF1999.B55] 74-84553
1. Occult sciences. 2. Christianity—Miscellanea. I. Title.

BLAIR, Lawrence. 133
Rhythms of vision : the changing patterns of belief / Lawrence Blair ; foreword by Lyall Watson. New York : Schocken Books, 1976, c1975. 234 p. : ill. ; 23 cm. Includes bibliographical references and index. [BF1999.B6514 1976] 75-34508 ISBN 0-8052-3610-4 : 8.95
1. Occult sciences. I. Title.

BLAIR, Lawrence. 133
Rhythms of vision / byLawrence Blair. New York : Warner Books, 1977c1975. 320p. : ill. ; 18 cm. Includes bibliographic references and index. [BF1999B65141976] ISBN 0-446-81232-3 pbk. : 2.50.
1. Occult sciences. I. Title.
L.C. card no. for 1976 Schocken ed.:75-34508.

BLAVATSKY, Helene Petrovna (Hahn-Hahn), 1831-1891. 133
Studies in occultism. Pasadena, Calif. Theosophical Univ. Pr. [1968] 212p. 20cm. Articles orig. pub. in the author's magazine Lucifer, 1887-1891. [BF1405.B6 1967] 67-18822 1.95 pap.,
1. Occult sciences. I. Title.
Contents Omitted. Publisher's address: P.O. Bin C, Pasadena, Calif. 91109.

BLAVATSKY, Helene Petrovna (Hahn-Hahn) 1831-1891. 133
Studies in occultism. Pasadena, Calif., Theosophical University Press [1967?] 212 p. 20 cm. Articles orginally published in the author's magazine Lucifer, 1887-1891. [BF1405.B6] 67-18822
1. Occult sciences. I. Title.
Contents Omitted

*BOLTON, Brett L. 133.3
The secret powers of plants [by] Brett L. Bolton. [New York] Berkley Pub. Co. [1974] 190 p. illus. 18 cm. (A Berkley medallion book) Bibliography: p. 180-183. [BF1411] ISBN 0-425-02567-5. 1.25 (pbk.)
1. Occult sciences. I. Title.

BOND, Helen Merrick. 133.9'3
The inner signature / Pensatia [i.e. H. M. Bond]. New York : Euclid Pub. Co., 1977, c1958. 76 p. ; 24 cm. First published as part of v. 1 of the author's A journey into the light. [BF1999.B65168 1977] 77-377302
1. Occult sciences. I. Title.

THE book of fate and fortune, an encyclopedia of the occult sciences ... New York, R. M. McBride & company, 1932. 496 p. illus., diagrs. 21 1/2 cm. [BF1411.B7] 32-24422 133
1. Occult sciences.

BOWEN, Patrick Gillman, 1877- 133
The occult way, by P. G. Bowen ... New York, E. P. Dutton & co., inc., 1939. ix p., 1 l., 13-224 p. 21 cm. "First edition." [BF1411.B75 1939] [159.961] 39-8045
1. Occult sciences. I. Title.

BOWMAN, Frank. 133
New horizons beyond the world. Los Angeles, DeVorss [1969] 368 p. illus. 22 cm. [BF1999.B6525] 70-89920
1. Occult sciences. I. Title.

BOYLE, John P., 1931- 133'.028
The psionic generator pattern book / by John P. Boyle. Englewood Cliffs, N.J. : Prentice-Hall, [1975] 89 p. : ill. ; 28 cm. (A Reward book) [BF1999.B654] 74-34292 ISBN 0-13-736975-1 pbk. : 4.95
1. Occult sciences. I. Title.

†BRASCH, Rudolf, 1912- 133
strange customs, how did they begin? : The origins of the unusual and occult customs, superstitions, and traditions / by R. Brasch. New York : McKay, c1976. xviii, 302 p. ; 22 cm. Includes index. [BF1411.B76] 77-3604 ISBN 0-679-50573-3 : 9.95
1. Occult sciences. 2. Superstition. I. Title.

BRASCH, Rudolph, 1912- 133
The supernatural and you! / [by] R. Brasch. Stanmore, N.S.W. : Cassell Australia, 1976. xii, 327 p. : ill. ; 24 cm. Includes index. [BF1411.B763] 77-369803 ISBN 0-7269-0442-2
1. Occult sciences. I. Title.

BRAUN, Peter 1864-
... *Occult traps and trappers.* By P. Braun. Omaha, Neb., New man publishing co. [1904?] cover-title, 67 p. 21 cm. (Higher self-culture library, no. 4) 6-22294
I. Title.

*BRENNAN, J. H. 133
Occult Reich. [by] J. H. Brennan [New York] New American Library [1974] 184 p. 18 cm. [BF1411] 1.50 (pbk.)
1. Occult sciences. I. Title.

*BRENNAN, J. H. 133.4
The ultimate elsewhere: an examination of fantastic reality [by] J. H. Brennan New York, New American Library, [1975] 189 p. 18 cm. [BF1411] 1.50 (pbk.)
1. Occult sciences. I. Title.

BUCKLAND, Raymond. 133.4
The anatomy of the occult / Raymond Buckdland. New York : S. Weiser, 1977. 151 p. : ill. ; 18 cm. Includes bibliographies. [BF1411.B79] 76-15541 ISBN 0-87728-304-4 : 2.95
1. Occult sciences. I. Title.

BUREN, R. 133
Occult experiences; a true narrative of experiences in the present time and deductions thereform, by R. Buren... San Francisco, Calif., Holmes book company, [c1919] 2 p. l., 7-62 p. 15 1/2 cm. [BF1040.B8] 19-9455
I. Title.

BURGOYNE, Thomas H. 133
The light of Egypt; or, The science of the soul and the stars, by Thomas H. Burgoyne. Denver, H. O. Wagner [1963] 2 v. illus. 22 cm. Reprint of the ed. published in Denver, 1889-1900. "Dictated by the author from the subjective plane of life" through Mrs. Belle M. Wagner—Pref., v. II. Supplement to the Light of Egypt volume II ... It was thought advisable to add two chapters, number XIV and XV, to the 1965 reprint edition of volume II. The 1963 reprint edition plus this supplement contains the same material as shown in the 1965 reprint edition. [BF1411.B832] 73-263877
1. Occult sciences. 2. Astrology. I. Wagner, Belle M. II. Title.

BURKE, May Morse, Mrs.
Key to the laws of the occult psyche science; or, Glimpses of Beulah land as viewed from earth through the psyche commune, of May Morse Burke. Jamestown, N.Y., Titus publishing company [c1910] xviii, 128 p. incl. front. (port.) port. 21 cm. 10-15222
I. Title.

BURNETT, Mary Weeks, ed.
The principles of occult healing, a working hypothesis which includes all cures; studies by a group of theosophical students, ed. by Mary Weeks Burnett, M. D. Chicago, The Health publishing co., 1916. 3 p. l., 5-134 p. 19 cm. 16-16291 0.75.
1. Occult sciences. I. Title.

BUTLER, Hiram Erastus, 1841- 133
The goal of life; or, Science and revelation, by H. E. Butler ... Applegate, Calif., Esoteric publishing company; [etc., etc.] 1908. xi, 363 p. 2 pl. port. 20 cm. [BF1999.B77] 8-6992
1. Occult sciences. I. Title.

CAVENDISH, Richard. 133'.03
The encyclopedia of the unexplained: magic, occultism, and parapsychology. Special consultant on parapsychology: J. B. Rhine. New York, McGraw-Hill [1974] 304 p. illus. 29 cm. Bibliography: p. 286-297. [BF1411.C32 1974] 73-7991 ISBN 0-07-010295-3 17.95
1. Occult sciences. 2. Psychical research. I. Title.

CHASE, Jo Anne 133
You can change your life through psychic power, by Jo Anne Chase as told to Constance Moon. New York, Permabooks [dist. Pocket Books, c.1960] 114p. e(Permabook original M4186) .35 pap.,
1. Occult science. I. Moon, Constance, jt. author. II. Title.

CHEW, Willa C. 291.2'11
The goddess faith : a religion of the mind / Willa C. Chew. 1st ed. Hicksville, N.Y. : Exposition Press, c1977. 222 p. ; 24 cm. (An Exposition-banner book) Includes index. Bibliography: p. 211-214. [BF1999.C53] 77-79628 ISBN 0-682-48773-2 : 10.00
1. Occult sciences. 2. Goddesses. 3. Sex and religion. I. Title.

CHRISTOPHER, Milbourne. 133
ESP, seers & psychics. New York, Crowell [1970] x, 268 p. illus., facsims., ports. 22 cm. Bibliography: p. 251-256. [BF1411.C45] 78-127607 ISBN 6-902681-57- 6.95
1. Occult sciences. I. Title.

CLYMER, Reuben Swinburne, 1878-
A compendium of occult laws; the selection, arrangement and application of the most important of occult and Arcane laws taught by the masters of the august fraternities of initiation, and the practice of the laws in the development of the fourfold nature of man... [2nd ed., rev.] Quakertown, Pa., Beverly Hall Corp.,[1966] 311 p. 24 cm. 68-16818
1. Occult sciences. I. Title.

CLYMER, Reuben Swinburne, 1878-
The philosophy of fire, arcanum of the spiritual light. [5th completely rev. ed.] Quakertown, Pa., Beverly Hall [c1964] 261 p. illus. 65-72010
1. Occult sciences. I. Title.

CLYMER, Reuben Swinburne, 1878- 133
The philosophy of fire... by Dr. R. Swinburne Clymer... Rev. ed. ... Allentown, Pa., The Philosophical publishing co. [c1907] 254 p. 19 1/2 cm. [BF1999.C66 1907] 7-36284
1. Occult sciences. I. Title.

CLYMER, Reuben Swinburne, 1878- 133
The philosophy of fire... by R. Swinburne Clymer, M.D. ... Quakertown, Pa., The Philosophical publishing co. [c1920] 2 p. l., [7]-210, [2] p. 25 1/2 cm. Third edition. [BF1999.C66 1920] 30-24930
1. Occult sciences. I. Title. II. Title: Fire, The philosophy of.

CLYMER, Reuben Swinburne, 1878- 133
The philosophy of fire... [by] R. Swinburne Clymer... Quakertown, Pa., The Philosophical publishing company [1942] xxvi, 267 p. incl. col. pl. 23 1/2 cm. "Completely revised edition." [BF1999.C66 1942] [[159.961]] 42-16119 ISBN 159.961
1. Occult sciences. I. Title.

CLYMER, Reuben Swinburne, 1878- 133
The teachings of the masters; the wisdom of the ages. Enl. and completely rev., together with many additions. Quakertown, Pa., Philosophical Pub. Co. [1952] 256 p. 24 cm. [BF1999.C666] 52-9991
1. Occult sciences. I. Title.

COBB, Eben. 133
The star of Endor, by Eben Cobb ... Hyde Park, Mass., E. Cobb [c1891] 311 p. front. (port.) 20 cm. [BF1999.C673] 32-16709
1. Occult sciences. I. Title.

COLTON, Ann Ree.
Draughts of remembrance. [1st ed.] Glendale, Calif., ARC Pub. Co., [c1959] iv, 177 p. 20 cm. 67-82437
1. Occult sciences. I. Title.

[COSGROVE, Eugene Milne] 133
1886-
The science of the initiates; a ready hand-book on the ageless wisdom; questions and answers, by a server. New York, Lucis publishing company, 1934. viii p., 2 l., 13-223 p. 24 cm. [BF1999.C697] 159.961 34-13523
1. Occult sciences. I. Title.

*CRAWFORD, Quantz. 133
Methods of psychic development. St. Paul, Minnesota, Llewellyn Pubns, 1973. 102 p. 21 cm. (A Llewellyn occult guide) [BF1411] 2.95 (pbk.)
1. Occult sciences. 2. Psychical research. I. Title.

CROWLEY, Aleister, 1875- 133.4
1947.
Golden twigs / by Aleister Crowley. Kings Beach, Calif. : Thelema Publications, c1978. p. cm. [BF1411.C86 1978] 78-16810 ISBN 0-913576-23-9 : 16.95 ISBN 0-913576-24-7 deluxe : 25.00 ISBN 0-913576-25-5 pbk. : 8.25
1. Occult sciences. I. Title.

CROWLEY, Aleister, 1875- 135.4
1947.
777; vel, prolegomena symbolica ad systeman sceptico-mysticae viae explicandae, fundamentcem lierogloy icum sanctissimorum sciential sunmac. New York, Gordon Press, 1974. xxvii, 154 p. illus. 24 cm. "First published, 1909." [BF1999.C745 1974] 73-21397 ISBN 0-87968-105-5
I. Title.

CROWLEY, Aleister, 1875-1947. 133
777 : vel prolegomena symbolica ad systemam sceptico-mysticae viae explicandae, fundamentum hieroglyphicum sanctissimorum scientiae summae / by Aleister Crowley. [Enlarged ed. Hastings : Metaphysical Research Group, 1977. xxviii, 155 p. : ill. ; 21 cm. Bibliography: p. xxviii. [BF1999.C745 1977] 77-373245 ISBN 0-900684-24-0 : £2.50
1. Occult sciences. I. Title.

CROWLEY, Aleister, 1875- 135.4
1947.
777 revised; vel, Prolegomena symbolica ad sceptico-mysticae viae explicandae, fundamentum hieroglyphicum sanctissimorum scientiae summae. A reprint of 777 with much additional matter New York, S. Weiser, 1970. xxvii, 155 p. illus. 22 cm. 1909 ed. published under title: 777. [BF1999.C745 1970] 77-16929 10.00
I. Title.

CULLING, Louis T. 133
Occult renaissance, 1972-2008; the great prophecy for the golden age of occultism, by Louis T. Culling with epilogue by Carl C. Weschcke. St. Paul, Minn., Llewellyn Publications, 1972. iii, 56 p. illus. 22 cm. Includes bibliographical references. [BF1791.C83] 72-188478 ISBN 0-87542-133-4 1.00
1. Occult sciences. 2. Prophecies (Occult sciences) I. Title.

CURTISS, Harriette Augusta, 133
Mrs. 1856?-1932.
The message of Aquaria; the significance and mission of the Aquarian age, by Harriette Augusta Curtiss and F. Homer Curtiss ... San Francisco, The Curtiss philosophic book co., 1921. ix, 11-487 p. 21 cm. [BF1999.C825] 22-4189
1. Occult sciences. I. Curtiss, Frank Homer, 1875- joint author. II. Title.

DAVIES, Thomas Witton, 1851-
1923.
"Magic," black and white; charms and counter charms. Divination and demonology among the Hindus, Hebrews, Arabs and Eygptions ... An epitome of "supernaturalism" magic, black, white and natural; conjuring and its relation to prophecy, including Biblical and Old Textament terms and words for magic ... Present ed. prepared for publication under the editorship of Dr. L. W. de Laurence, by T. Witton Davies ... Chicago, Ill., De Laurence, Scott & co., 1910. xvi, 130 p. incl. front. 20 cm. "This treatise was presented to the University of Leipzig [for the degree of doctor of philosophy] July, 1897."--Pref. Published in 1898 under the title; Magic, divination, and demonology among the Hebrews and their neighbors. "Books and editions consulted or referred to ...": p. [xi]-xvi. [BF1591.D27] 11-657 1.50
1. Occult sciences. 2. Magic. 3. Demonology. I. De Laurence, Lauron William, 1868- ed. II. Title.

DAVIES, Thomas Witton, 133.4
1851-1923.
Magic, divination, and demonology among the Hebrews and their neighbours; including an examination of Biblical references and of the Biblical terms. New York, Ktav Pub. House, 1969. xvi, 130 p. 24 cm. Thesis—University of Leipzig, 1897. Reprint of the 1898 ed. Bibliography: p. [xi]-xvi. [BF1591.D25 1969] 70-92695 6.95
1. Occult sciences. 2. Magic. 3. Demonology. I. Title.

[DEAMUDE, Jesse Ross] 1875- 133
Self mastery, by Froid Daniels [pseud.] The author's private edition for students of the occult, and especially for those who seek wisdom, happiness, health and success through self illumination and the great occult way. Cleveland, O., The author, c1913. 108 p. 19 cm. [BF1999.D34] 18-8943
1. Occult sciences. I. Title.

DEAMUDE, Jesse Ross, 1875- 133
Self mastery, by J. Ross Deamude. 3d ed. rev. ... Special ed. for students of applied psychology ... [Canton, O., Boyer printing co.] c1922. 95 p. 19 cm. [BF1999.D34 1922] 22-14291
1. Occult sciences. I. Title.

DE CAMP, Lyon Sprague, 1907- 133
Spirits, stars, and spells; the profits and perils of magic, by L. Sprague de Camp and Catherine C. de Camp. New York, Canaveral Press [1966] 348 p. illus., ports. 24 cm. Bibliography: p. 315-324. [BF1411.D4] 65-25470
1. Occult sciences. I. De Camp, Catherine C., joint author. II. Title.

DELANEY, Walter, 1930- 133
Ultra-psychonics: how to work miracles with the limitless power of psycho-atomic energy. West Nyack, N.Y., Parker Pub. Co. [1974, c1975] 237 p. illus. 24 cm. [BF1999.D347] 74-16232 ISBN 0-13-935635-5
1. Occult sciences. 2. Success. I. Title.

DE LAURENCE, Lauron William, 133
1868-
The book of magical art, Hindu magic and Indian occultism ... by Dr. L. W. de Laurence ... Chicago, Ill. [c1904] 2 v. in 1. fronts., illus., plats. ports. (part col.) 26 cm. Paged continuously. "Third edition." [BF1025.D3 1904] 159.961 34-13673
1. Occult science. I. Title.

DE LAURENCE, Lauron William, 133.
1868-
The cave of the oracle. The great white brotherhood. Persian and Chaldean magic. Talismanic magic. Occultism. Seals and talismans; their construction, powers and influence. Dreams, visions, omens and oracles. Healing. Telepathy, clairvoyance, spiritism and Bible contradictions. By Dr. L. W. De Laurence ... Chicago, Ill., De Laurence, Scott & co. [c1916] 2 p. l., 175 p. incl. front. (port.) illus. 20 cm. p. 174-75, advertising matter. [BF1031.D4] 16-24821 2.00
1. Occult sciences. 2. Spiritualism. I. Title.

DE LAURENCE, Lauron William, 133
1868-
The great book of magical art, Hindu magic and East Indian occultism now combined with The book of secret Hindu, ceremonial, and talismanic magic, by Dr. L. W. de Laurence. Rev. ed., limited ... Chicago, Ill., De Laurence, Scott, & co. [c1915] 6 p. l., 43-647 p. front., illus., plates, ports., tables. 26 cm. Two books in 1 v., each having special t.-p. [BF1025.D3 1915] 15-14583 6.75
1. Occult sciences. I. Title.

DE LAURENCE, Lauron William, 133
1868-
The great book of magical art, Hindu magic and East Indian occultism, now combined with The book of secret Hindu, ceremonial talismanic magic, by L. W. de Laurence. Rev. ed., limited ... Chicago, Ill., The de Laurence company [c1915] 6 p. l., 43-635 p. front., illus., plates. ports. 26 cm. Each "book" has also special t.-p. "Twelfth edition, revised, 1914." [BF1025.D3 1915 a] 159.961 34-13019
1. Occult sciences. I. Title.

DE LAURENCE, Lauron William, 133
1868-
The sacred book of death, Hindu spiritism, soul transition and soul reincarnation; exclusive instruction for the personal use of Dr. de laurence's chelas (disciples) in Hindu spiritism, soul transition, reincarnation, clairvoyancy and occultism ... by Dr. L. W. De. Laurence ... Chicago, Ill., The Benares India publishing co. [c1905] 400 p. front. (port.) pl. 21 cm. [BF1611.D3] 6-2999
1. Occult sciences. I. Title.

DE LAURENCE, Lauron William, 133
1868- ed.
The sixth and seventh books of Moses ... the wonderful magical and spirit arts of Moses and Aaron, and the old wise Hebrews, taken from the Mosaic books of the Cabala and the Talmud, for the good of mankind. Prepared for publication under the editorship of Dr. L. W. de Laurence ... Chicago, Ill., De Laurence, Scott & co., 1910. 190 p. front., illus. 20 cm. [BF1611.D32] 11-761 1.00
1. Occult sciences. I. Title.

DEWEY, John Hamlin. 225.
The New Testament occultism; or, Miracle working power interpreted as the basis of an occult and mystic science. By John Hamlin Dewey ... New York. The J. H. Dewey publishing co. [c1895] 256, [4] p. 20 cm. [BS2545.M5D4] 20-8469
1. Occult sciences. I. Title.

DODDS, James E. 133
The Gentleman from Heaven. Santa Barbara, Calif., Aquarian Ministry [1948] 123 p. 23 cm. [BF1999.D614] 49-1023
I. Title.

DOWER, William H., 1866- 133
Occultism for beginners, by William H. Dower, M.D. series no. 1- Halcyon, Cal., Halcyon book concern [c1917- v. illus. 16 cm. [BF1999.D7] 17-25992
1. Occult sciences. I. Title.

[DOWLING, Levi H.] 133.
Self culture; a course of lessons on developing the physical, unfolding the soul, attaining unto the spiritual, by Levi [pseud.] ... Los Angeles, Cal., E. S. Dowling, 1912. 92 p. 18 cm. $0.75. [BF1325.D6] 13-801
1. Occult sciences. I. Title.

DRILLINGER, Emma Ruder, 1865- 133
The Journey of the soul and the ethereal world [by] E. Ruder Drollinger. [Los Angeles, Occult pub. co., c1919] 3 p. l., 182 p. front. (port.) 19 1/2 cm. [BF1999.D8] 19-15407
I. Title.

DRURY, Nevill, 1947- 133.4
Inner visions : explorations in magical consciousness / Nevill Drury. London ; Boston : Routledge & K. Paul, 1979. 142 p., [12] leaves of plates : ill. ; 24 cm. Includes index. Bibliography: p. 133-138. [BF1411.D76] 79-40254 ISBN 0-7100-0257-2 : 15.95 ISBN 0-7100-0184-3 pbk. : 9.95
1. Occult sciences. 2. Magic. I. Title.

DUBIN, Reese P. 133.8'2
Telecult power; the amazing new way to psychic and occult wonders, by Reese P. Dubin. West Nyack, N.Y., Parker Pub. Co. [1970] 225 p. illus. 24 cm. Includes bibliographical references. [BF1411.D8] 78-97838 6.95
1. Occult sciences. 2. Success. I. Title.

EAGAN, Frances W 133.9
Traditions, Kabala, and Qabalah. [By] a seeker. Venice, Calif., F.W. Eagan Co., c1962. 2, 103 p. illus., map. 28 cm. On cover: Atlantean symbologies. With, as issued, the author's The path of recognition. "From . . . Keys to the bundle of wonderful things." [BF1999.E16 1962] 64-6464
I. Title. II. Title: Atlantean symbologies.

EBBRAUNON, Christilina. 133
Understanding the laws of life, by the spirit author Franciscolighte Ebbraunon, transcribed by Christilina Ebbraunon. Los Angeles, Calif., De Vorss & co. [1946] 1 p. l., 7-166 p. 20 1/2 cm. [BF1999.E23] 46-19984
I. Ebbraunon, Franciscolighte. II. Title.

ELWOOD, Roger. 133.4
Strange things are happening; satanism, witchcraft, and God. Elgin, IL, D. C. Cook Pub. Co. [1973] 127 p. 18 cm. Bibliography: p. 126-127. [BF1411.E43] 72-87051 ISBN 0-912692-10-3 0.95
1. Occult sciences. I. Title.

EMERSON,Charles Harris, 1843- 133
Psychocraft; being the art of following the lead of instinct which uses human organic mechanisms ... to avert disaster, create genius, prophetic insight, or verify faith with superorganic intuitions, incidentally introducing a new idea of the principle of onwardness ... with illustrations by the author, giving for the first time in over two thousand years a definite operative solution of the greatest mystery of ancient Hebrew literature: the oracle of Aaron's breastplate, carefully worked out and practically applied as herein presented in the elegant and infallible oracle of Ellu, by C.H. Emerson ... [Portland, Me., Press of Southworth printing company, c1911] 407, [6] p. incl. illus. (partly col.) chart, diagrs. 24cm. p $2.50 Accompanied by small tin box containing crystals and lettered: The oracle of Ellu. [BF1999.E6] 11-26648
1. Occult sciences. I. Title.

FARNSWORTH, Edward Clarence. 133
The heart of things, written down by Edward Clarence Fornsworth. Portland, Me., Smith & Sale, printers, 1914. xii, 256, [1] p. pl. 21 cm. [BF1999.F3] 14-19176
1. Occult sciences. I. Title.

FARNSWORTH, Edward Clarence. 133
Special teachings from the arcane science, written down by Edward Clarence Farnsworth. Portland, Me., Smith & Sale, printers, 1913. x, 188, [1] p. 20 cm. [BF1999.F34] 13-14801 1.00
1. Occult sciences. I. Title.

FIRTH, Violet Mary. 133.4
Psychic self-defence; a study in occult pathology and criminality, by Dion Fortune. New York, S. Weiser [1971, c1930] 209 p. 23 cm. [BF1411.F57 1971] 79-27453 ISBN 0-87728-150-5 6.00
1. Occult sciences. 2. Psychology, Pathological. I. Title.

FISICHELLA, Anthony J. 133
Echoes from eternity : a treatise on the ageless wisdom / by Anthony J. Fischella. Norfolk, Va. : Donning, c1982. p. cm. [BF1999.F57 1982] 19 82-9726 ISBN 0-89865-182-4 (pbk.) : 6.95
1. Occult sciences. I. Title.

[FLETCHER, Augusta W.] 133.
Man's spiritual possibilities; or, The triumph of the spirit over physical conditions ... New York, C. B. Reed, 1893. 302 p. 18 1/2 cm. (White cross literature, no. 2) Copyrighted by Augusta W. Fletcher, M.D. [BF1261.F63] 11-3143
1. Occult sciences. I. Title.

FRIEDMAN, Isidore. 133
Organics: the law of the breathing spiral; a primer of psycho-synthesis and creative education. Edited by Joseph Polansky. Illustrated by Nancy Dahlberg. New York, Society for the Study of Natural Order, 1973. 86 p. illus. 24 cm. [BF1411.F7] 73-89354
1. Occult sciences. 2. Conduct of life. I. Title.

GAFFIELD, Erastus Celley, 133.
1840-
The past revealed; a series of revelations concerning the early Scriptures, recorded by E. C. Gaffield ... Author's ed. Boston, Lothrop, Lee & Shepard co. [1905] 309 p. 20 cm. [BF1301.G23] 6-8
1. Occult sciences. I. Title.

GARDENER, Harry J. 133
Outwitting tomorrow, by Harry J. Gardener ... Los Angeles, Calif.. H. J. Gardener, c1939. 64 p. illus. 23 1/2 cm. [BF1999.G27 1939] 159.961 41-15885
1. Occult sciences. I. Title.

GARDENER, Harry J. 133
Outwitting tomorrow, by Harry J. Gardener ... Los Angeles, Calif., H. J. Gardener, c1941. 64 p. illus. 23 1/2 cm. [BF1999.G27 1941] [159.961] 41-15886
1. Occult sciences. I. Title.

GARRETT, Eileen Jeanette 133
(Lyttle), 1893-
The sense and nonsense of prophecy. [New York] Creative Age Press [1950] 279 p. illus. 21 cm. [BF1411.G3] 50-9904
1. Occult sciences. I. Title.

GARVIN, Richard M. 133
The world of the twilight believers, by Richard M. Garvin and Robert E. Burger. Los Angeles, Sherbourne Press [1970] xvii, 268 p. 22 cm. Includes bibliographical references. [BF1411.G33] 69-20139 6.50
1. Occult sciences. I. Burger, Robert E., joint author. II. Title. III. Title: The twilight believers.

GIBSON, Walter Brown, 1897- 133
The complete illustrated book of the psychic sciences [by] Walter B. Gibson and Litzka R. Gibson. Drawings by Murray Keshner. [1st ed.] Garden City, N.Y., Doubleday, 1966. xx, 403 p. illus. 22 cm. [BF1411.G5] 65-19872
1. Occult sciences. 2. Psychical research. I. Gibson, Litzka R., joint author. II. Title.

GITLIN, Murray. 133
Body and mind and their possibilities : especially in occult experience / Murray Gitlin. Philadelphia : Dorrance, [1975] c1974. 167 p. ; 22 cm. Includes index. [BF1411.G57 1975] 74-15156 ISBN 0-8059-2078-1 : 7.95
1. Occult sciences. 2. Psychical research. I. Title.

THE golden hoard,
gateway to synthesis. Houston, Texas, Texas Southern University [1959] 282p. 23cm.
1. Occult sciences. 2. Theosophy. I. Merchant, Francis.

GOODAVAGE, Joseph F. 133
Magic : science of the future New York : New American Library ,1976. 196 p. ; 18 cm. (Signet Book) Bibliography: pp. 195-196. [BF1429] pbk. : 1.50
1. Occult sciences. I. Title.

GRASSET, Joseph, 1849-1918. 133.
The marvels beyond science (L'occultisme hier et aujourd'hui; le merveilleux prescientifique) being a record of progress made in the reduction of occult phenomena to a scientific basis, by Joseph Grasset ... with a preface by Emile Faguet ... Authorized English translation of the 2d rev. and enl. French ed., by Rene Jacques Tubeuf ... New York and London, Funk & Wagnalls company, 1910. xxii, 387 p. diagr. 23 cm. [BF1031.G6] 10-23637
1. Occult sciences. I. Tubeuf, Rene Jacques, tr. II. Title.

GRAY, Mary (Tudor) 1886- 212
Echoes of the cosmic song; leaves from an occult notebook, by Mary Gray. New York, Margent press, 1945. 173 p. 21 cm. [BP605.G65] 45-2799
I. Title.

GRAY, William G. 135.4
The talking tree / by Wm. G. Gray. New York : S. Weiser, 1977. xvii, 556 p., [1] leaf of plates : ill. ; 24 cm. [BF1999.G715] 77-153606 ISBN 0-87728-190-4 : 17.50
1. Occult sciences. 2. Cabala. 3. Tarot. 4. Tree of life—Miscellanea. I. Title.

GRAY-COBB, Geof, 1928- 133
The miracle of new avatar power. West Nyack, N.Y., Parker Pub. Co. [1974] 199 p. 24 cm. [BF1999.G72] 74-1316 ISBN 0-13-585372-9 6.95
1. Occult sciences. 2. Success. I. Title.

GREENBURG, Dan. 133
Something's there / by Dan Greenburg. 1st ed. Garden City, N.Y. : Doubleday, 1976. xi, 320 p. ; 22 cm. Bibliography: p. 315-320. [BF1411.G76] 75-23928 ISBN 0-385-03898-4 : 8.95
1. Greenburg, Dan. 2. Occult sciences. I. Title.

GRILLOT de Givry, Emile 133
Angelo, 1870-1929.
The illustrated anthology of sorcery, magic, and alchemy / by Grillot de Givry ; translated by J. Courtenay Locke. Introd. to the Causeway ed. / by Charles Sen. New York : Causeway Books, c1973. 394 p., [10] leaves of plates : ill. ; 29 cm. Translation of Le musee des sorciers, mages, et alchimistes. Includes index. [BF1412.G82 1973] 73-85119 ISBN 0-88356-018-6 : 15.00
1. Occult sciences. I. Title.

GRILLOT de Givry, Emile 133
Angelo, 1870-1929.
A pictorial anthology of witchcraft, magic & alchemy. Translated by J. Courtenay Locke. Chicago, University Books [1958] 394 p. illus. 25 cm. Translation of Le musee des sorciers, mages, et alchimistes. [BF1412.G82 1958] 58-11782
1. Occult sciences. I. Title. II. Title: Witchcraft, magic & alchemy.

GRILLOT de Givry, Emile 133
Angelo 1870-1929.
Picture museum of sorcery, magic & alchemy. Translated by J. Courtenay Locke. New Hyde Park, N.Y., University Books [1963] 394 p. illus., ports. 25 cm. Translation of Le musee des sorciers, mages et alchimistes. [BF1412.G82] 63-11177
1. Occult sciences. I. Title.

GRILLOT de Givry, Emile 133
Angelo, 1870-1929.
Witchcraft, magic & alchemy. Translated by J. Courtenay Locke. New York, Dover [1971] 394 p. illus., facsims., ports. 24 cm. Translation of Le musee des sorciers, mages, et alchemistes. Reprint of 1931 ed. [BF1412.G82 1971] 78-142878 ISBN 0-486-22493-7 4.00
1. Occult sciences. I. Title.

GRILLOT DE GIVRY, Emile 133
Angelo, 1870-
Witchcraft, magic & alchemy, by Grillot de Givry, translated by J. Courtenay Locke: with 10 plates in colour and 366 illustrations in the text. Boston and New York, Houghton Mifflin company, 1930. 394, [1] p. col. front., illus., col. plates, diagrs. 30 x 23 cm. "A collection of the iconography of occultism."--Pref. [BF1412.G82] 32-4023
1. Occult sciences. I. Locke, J. Courtenay, tr. II. Title.

GRIMKE, Sarah Stanley. 133
Esoteric lessons, by Sarah Stanley Grimke, PH. D.; sequel to "First lessons in reality." Denver, Col., The Astro-philosophical publishing co., 1900. 3 p. l., [iii]-xvii, [19]-307 p. illus. 17 x 13 cm. [BF1611.G8] 0-4191
1. Occult sciences. I. Title.
Contents omitted.

GRUNWALD, Stefan. 133.9'3
The renderings of Stefanos / Stefan F. L. Grunwald. Virginia Beach : Donning, 1979- p. cm. (Unilaw library) Contents.Contents.—Book 1. Science and technology. [BF1999.G854] 79-10680 ISBN 0-915442-91-4 pbk. : 4.95
1. Occult sciences. I. Title.

HALL, Manly Palmer. 133
An essay on the fundamental principles of operative occultism, by Manly P. Hall, illustrated with three oil paintings by Mihran K. Serailian. 2d rev. ed. Los Angeles, Hall publishing company, 1929. 60 p. incl. illus., pl. 17 cm. Advertising matter p. 54-60. [BF1999.H325 1929] ca 30
1. Occult sciences. I. Title.

HALL, Manly Palmer. 133
Words to the wise; a practical guide to the occult sciences, by Manly P. Hall. 1st ed. Los Angeles, Calif., Philosophical research society press, 1936. 172 p. 24 cm. [BF1411.H36] 37-8118
1. Occult sciences. I. Title.

HALL, Manly Palmer, 1901- 133
Self-unfoldment by disciplines of realization; releasing and developing the inward perceptions; practical instruction in the philosophy of disciplined thinking and feeling, by Manly Palmer Hall. 1st ed. Twelve illustrations. Los Angeles, Philosophical research society, inc. [c1942] 221 p. illus. 24 cm. [BF1999.H3345] 43-5075
1. Occult sciences. I. Title.

HARRIS, William Richard, 133.
1847-1923.
Essays in occultism, spirtism, and demonology, by Dean W. R. Harris ... St. Louis, Mo. [etc.] B. Herder Book co., 1919. 3 p. l., vi, [2], 181 p. 20 cm. [BF1042.H26] 19-3410
1. Occult sciences. 2. Psychical research. I. Title.

HARTMANN, Franz. 133
Magic, white and black; the science of finite and infinite life, containing practical hints for students of occultism, by Franz Hartmann ... 7th American ed., rev. New York, Theosophical society, 1904. 292 p. incl. illus., pl. 20 cm. [BF1611.H36] 4-21745
1. Occult sciences. I. Title.

HARTMANN, Franz, d.1912. 133
Magic, white and black; or, The science of finite and infinite life, containing practical hints for students of occultism. New introd. by Leslie Shepard. 4th ed. rev. New Hyde Park, N.Y., University Books [1970] vii, 298 p. illus. 22 cm. (Library of the mystic arts) Includes bibliographical references. [BF1611.H33 1970] 75-118601 7.95
1. Occult sciences. I. Title. II. Title: The science of finite and infinite life.

HARTMANN, Franz, d.1912. 133
Magic white and black; or, The science of finite and infinite life; containing practical hints for students of occultism, by Franz Hartmann ... 3d ed. rev. and enl. Boston, Occult publishing company, 1888. 324 p. front., illus. 20 cm. [BF1611.H3 1888] 150.961 159.961 34-13669
1. Occult science. I. Title.

HARTMANN, Franz, d.1912. 133
Magic, white and black; or, The science of finate [!] and infinite life, containing practical hints for students of occultism, by Franz Hartmann ... 4th American ed. rev. New York, J. W. Lovell company [c1890] 281, x p. front. (port.) illus., pl. 20 cm. (On cover: Lovell's occult series. no. 4) [BF1611.H33] 11-14364
1. Occult sciences. I. Title.

HARTMANN, Franz, d.1912. 133
Magic, white and black; the science of finite and infinite life, containing practical hints for students of occultism, by Franz Hartmann ... 6th American ed., rev. New York, The Metaphysical publishing co. [1901] 292 p. incl. illus., pl. front. (port.) 21 cm. [BF1611.H35] 1-31448
1. Occult sciences. I. Title.

HATCH, David Patterson, 1846- 133
1912.
Scientific occultism, a hypothetical basis of life, by David P. Hatch. ... Los Angeles, Cal., Baumgardt pub. co., 1905. 4 p. l., [3]-95 p. 20 1/2 cm. [BF1999.H4] 5-23651
1. Occult sciences. I. Title.

HAYES, Christine. 133
Red tree: insight into lost continents, Mu and Atlantis, as revealed to Christine Hayes. San Antonio, Naylor Co. [1972] xviii, 176 p. illus. 21 cm. [BF1999.H435] 72-6829 ISBN 0-8111-0465-6
1. Occult sciences. 2. Lost continents. I. Title.

HELINE, Corinne (Smith) 133
Dunklee, 1882-
America's invisible guidance. Los Angeles, New Age Press [1949] 175 p. illus. 24 cm. Reprinted from the New age interpreter. Jan. 1944-Mar. 1946, with additional material. [BF1999.H44] 52-30628
1. Occult sciences. I. Title.

HELINE, Corinne (Smith) 133
Dunklee, 1882-
Occult anatomy and the Bible; the achetype or heavenly pattern of the human body, by Corinne D. Heline. [Los Angeles, New Age press, 1944] cover-title, 82 p. 15 1/2 cm. "First edition, 1937. Revised 1944." [BF1999.H45 1944] 45-2244
1. Occult sciences. I. Title.

HILL, Douglas 133
The supernatural [by] Douglas Hill and Pat Williams N.Y., New American Library, [1974, c1965] (351 p.) illus. (port col.) facsims., maps. 24 cm. (A plume book) [BF1411.H5 1974] 6.95 (pbk.)
1. Occult sciences. I. Williams, Pat II. Title.
L.C. card number for original ed.: 66-11502.

HILL, Douglas Arthur, 1935- 133
The supernatural [by] Douglas Hill, Pat Williams. [1st Amer. ed.] New York, Hawthorn [1966, c.1965] 350p. illus. (pt. col.) facsims., maps. 25cm. [BF1411.H5] 66-11502 12.50
1. Occult sciences. I. Williams, Patricia, 1931- joint author. II. Title.

HILL, Douglas Arthur, 1935- 133.
The supernatural [by] Douglas Hill, Pat Williams. New York, New Amer. Lib. [1967, c.1965] 240p. illus. 18cm. (Signet bk., Q3256) [BF1411.H5] .95 pap.,
1. Occult sciences. I. Williams, Patricia, 1931- joint author. II. Title.

HILLS, Christopher B. 133
Nuclear evolution : discovery of the rainbow body / by Christopher Hills ; edited by Norah Hills ... [et al.]. 2d ed. Boulder Creek, Calif. : University of the Trees Press, c1977. p. cm. Includes bibliographical references and index. [BF1999.H6133 1977] 76-53180 ISBN 0-916438-09-0 pbk. : 9.95.
1. Occult sciences. 2. Cosmology. I. Title.

HISEY, Lehmann. 133
Keys to inner space; an open-ended guide to occultism, metaphysics & the transcendental. New York, Julian Press [1974] xi, 250 p. illus. 22 cm. Bibliography: p. 247-248. [BF1411.H55] 73-88235 7.95

1. Occult sciences. 2. Spirit writings. I. Title.

H ITCHCOCK, Helyn. 133.8'8
The magic of psychograms : new way to power and prosperity / Helyn Hitchcock. New York : Barnes and Noble, 1977. 224p. ; 21 cm. [BF1999.H614] 06-464016 ISBN pbk. : 2.95 sychical research.
1. Occult sciences. 2. Success. I. Title.
L.C. card no. for 1975 Parker Pub. Co. ed.:75-31555.

HITCHCOCK, Helyn. 133.8'8
The magic of psychograms : new way to power and prosperity / by Helyn Hitchcock. West Nyack, N.Y. : Parker Pub. Co., 1975. p. cm. [BF1999.H614] 75-31555
1. Occult sciences. 2. Psychical research. 3. Success. I. Title.

HOLZER, Hans W., 1920- 133
The new pagans [by] Hans Holzer. [1st ed.] Garden City, N.Y., Doubleday, 1972. xiii, 197 p. 22 cm. [BF1429.H64] 71-173269 5.95
1. Occult sciences. 2. Sects. I. Title.

HOUSE, Elwin Lincoln, 1861- 133
Psychic phenomena, by Rev. Elwin L. House... [Toledo, O., The Toledo typesetting co., c1916] 49 p. 17 cm. $0.25 [BF1040.H6] 16-24938
1. Occult sciences. I. Title.
Contents omitted.

HUEBNER, Louise. 133'.0924
Never strike a happy medium. Los Angeles, Nash Pub. [1970] 334 p. illus., facsims., ports. 22 cm. [BF1408.2.H83A3] 75-127483 ISBN 0-8402-1161-9 5.95
1. Occult sciences. I. Title.

HUFFMAN, Robert W 133
Many wonderful things, by Robert W. Huffman and Irene Specht. Los Angeles, De Vorss [1957] 379p. 23cm. [BF1999.H87] 57-29438
1. Occult sciences. I. Specht, Irene, joint author. II. Title.

HUNT, Douglas 133
Exploring the occult. New York, Ballantine [1965, c.1964] 219p. 18cm. (U5025) [BF1031.H867] 65-5446 .60 pap.,
1. Occult sciences. I. Title.

HURWOOD, Bernhardt J., comp. 133'.08
The first Occult review reader, edited by Bernhardt J. Hurwood. New York, Award Books [1968] 188 p. 18 cm. [BF1023.H8 1968] 74-949 0.75
1. Occult sciences. 2. Psychical research. I. Rider's review. II. Title.

INGALESE, Richard. 133
From incarnation to re-incarnation, by Richard Ingalese and Isabella Ingalese ... New York city, The Occult book concern [c1903] 286 p. 21 cm. [BF1999.I 5 1903] 20-5337
1. Occult sciences. I. Ingalese, Isabella, joint author. II. Title.
Contents omitted.

INGALESE, Richard.
From incarnation to re-incarnation, by Richard Ingalese and Isabella Ingalese. Rev. ed. New York city, The Occult book concern [c1908] 311 p. 21 cm. [BF1994.I 5 1908] 8-17231
1. Occult sciences. I. Ingalese, Isabella, Mrs. joint author. II. Title.
Contents omitted.

INGALESE, Richard, 1863- 133
Fragments of truth, by Richard Ingalese and Isabella Ingalese. New York, Dodd, Mead and company, 1921. 5 p. l., 322 p. 21 cm. [BF1999.I 47] 21-4336 2.50
1. Occult sciences. I. Ingalese, Isabella Mrs. joint author. II. Title.

INGALESE, Richard, 1863- 133
From incarnation to re-incarnation, by Richard Ingalese and Isabella Ingalese. New York, The Occult book concern [1904] 3 p. l., 323 p. 21 cm. [BF1999.I 5 1904] 4-6243
1. Occult sciences. I. Ingalese, Isabella, Mrs. joint author. II. Title.
Contents omitted.

INGALESE, Richard, 1863- 133
The greater mysteries, by Richard Ingalese. New York, Dodd, Mead and company, 1923. xi p., 1 l., 330 p. 21 cm. "Some of these lessons ... were published under the title of 'Cosmogony and evolution' ... Isabella Ingalese is responsible for that portion of the text containing excerpts from the diary of a student of occultism."--Pref. [BF1999.I 52] 23-8168 2.50
1. Occult sciences. I. Ingalese, Isabella, Mrs. joint author. II. Title.

INGALESE, Richard, 1863- 133
The history and power of mind, by Richard Ingalese. New York, The Occult book concern [1902] 286 p. front. (port.) 21 cm. [BF1999.I 55 1902] 2-25430
1. Occult sciences. 2. Mind and body. 3. Mental suggestion. I. Title.

INGALESE, Richard, 1863- 133
The history and power of mind, by Richard Ingalese. 2d thousand. New York, the Occult book concern [1903] 284, xxiv p. front. (port.) 21 cm. [BF1999.I55 1903] 4-1015
1. Occult sciences. 2. Mind and body. 3. Mental suggestion. I. Title.

INGALESE, Richard, 1863- 133
The history and power of mind, by Richard Ingalese. 4th ed. New York city, The Occult book concern [1905] 284, xiviii p. front. (port.) 21 cm. [BF1999.I4 1905] 28-3267
1. Occult sciences. 2. Mind and body. 3. Mental suggestion. I. Title.

INGALESE, Richard, 1863- 133
The history and power of mind, by Richard Ingalese. New York, Dodd, Mead and company, 1920. 2 p. l., ix-xxiv p., 1 l., 329 p. 21 cm. [BF1999.I55 1920] 20-10777
1. Occult science. 2. Mind and body. 3. Mental suggestion. I. Title.

INGALESE, Richard, 1863- 133
The history and power of mind, by Richard Ingalese. New York, Dodd, Mead and company, 1940. 2 p. l., ix-xxiv p., 1 l., 329 p. 21 cm. "Copyright, 1902 ... Seventeenth printing, September, 1940." [BF1999.14 1940] 159.961 41-3763
1. Occult sciences. 2. Mind and body. 3. Mental suggestion. I. Title.

INGALESE, Richard, 1863- 133.8
The history and power of mind / by Richard Ingalese. San Bernardino, Calif. : Borgo Press, 1980, c1976. p. cm. Reprint of the ed. published by Newcastle Pub. Co., North Hollywood, Calif. Includes index. [BF1999.I4 1980] 19 80-19897 11.95
1. Occult sciences. 2. Mind and body. 3. Mental suggestion. I. Title.

[INGALESE, Richard] 1863- 133
Occult philosophy, by Isabella Ingalese. Rev. ed. New York, Dodd, Mead and company, 1920. ix p., 2 l., 321 p. 21 cm. Earlier editions have title: From incarnation to re-incarnation, by Richard Ingalese and Isabella Ingalese. [BF1999.I 5 1920] 20-18063
1. Occult sciences. I. Ingalese, Isabella, Mrs. joint author. II. Title.

INITIATION, human and solar.
[6th ed.] New York, Lucis Pub. Co. [1959] xv, 240p. diagrs. 24cm. The Lucis Publishing Company is the organ of the Arcane School.
1. Occult sciences. 2. Theosophy. I. Bailey, Alice Anne (La Trobe-Bateman) 1880-1949.

INTO the unknown / 001.9
Reader's digest ; editor, Will Bradbury. Pleasantville, N.Y. : Reader's Digest Association, c1981. 352 p. : ill. (some col.) ; 29 cm. Includes index. Bibliography: p. 342-343. [BF1411.I55 1981] 19 80-54189 ISBN 0-89577-098-9 : 20.50 20.50
1. Occult sciences. 2. Psychical research. I. Bradbury, Wilbur. II. Reader's Digest Association. III. Reader's digest.

THE Invisibles : 001.9
a dialectic / by Thibaut D'Amiens (?)/F. Borishinski (?) ; introd. by Hugh Fox. 1st ed. New York : The Smith : [distributed by Horizon Press], 1976. 105 p. : ill. ; 22 cm. Includes bibliographical references. [BF1999.I57] 76-3358 ISBN 0-912292-40-7 : 3.00
1. Occult sciences.

JACOLLIOT, Louis, 1837-1890. 133.
Occult science in India and among the ancients, with an account of their mystic initiations and the history of spiritism. By Louis Jacolliot ... Tr. from the French by Willard L. Felt ... New York, J. W. Lovell company [c1884] iv p., 4 l., [13]-274, [1] p. illus. 24 cm. [BF1434.I 4J2] 11-6879
1. Occult sciences. 2. Brahmanism. I. Felt, Willard L., tr. II. Title.

JACOLLIOT, Louis, 1837-1890. 133
Occult science in India and among the ancients, with an account of their mystic initiations, and the history of spiritism. By Louis Jacolliot ... translated from the French by Willard L. Felt. New York, Theosophical publishing co., 1908. iv p., 4 l., [13]-274 p., 1 l. illus. 24 cm. [BF1434.I 4J2 1908] 32-21742
1. Occult sciences. 2. Brahmanism. I. Felt, Willard L.; tr. II. Title.

JOHNSON, Josephine Lucas. 149.3
The mysteries of the space age; an exploration of the eternal truths. New York, William-Frederick Press, 1966. 157 p. 22 cm. Bibliography: p. 153-157. [BF1411.J6] 66-28148
1. Occult sciences. 2. Religion—Philosophy. I. Title.

JONES, Charles Robert Stansfeld, 1886- 135.4
The Egyptian revival; or, The evercoming son in the light of the tarot, by Frater Achad. New York, S. Weiser, 1969. xviii, 120 p. illus. 24 cm. Originally published in 1923. [BF1999.J6 1969] 73-16613 10.00
1. Occult sciences. 2. Tarot. I. Title.

*JONES, Jessie Shaver 133.8
Psychic vistas, by Jessie Shaver Jones, Ruth Shaver. New York, Vantage [1967] 119p. illus. 21cm. 2.95 bds.,
I. Title.

JONES, Marc Edmund. 133
Key truths of occult philosophy; an introduction to the codex occultus [by] Marc Edmund Jones ... Los Angeles, J. F. Rowny press, 1925. 4 p. l., 7-270 p. 21 cm. [BF1999.J65] 26-8
1. Occult sciences. I. Title.

JONES, Marc Edmund, 1888- 133
Occult philosophy : an introduction, the major concepts, and a glossary / Marc Edmund Jones. Stanwood, Wash. : Sabian Pub. Society, 1977, c1948. x, 436 p. ; 21 cm. Includes indexes. [BF1999.J65 1977] 76-55121 ISBN 0-394-73343-6 : 6.95
1. Occult sciences. I. Title.

JONES, Marc Edmund, 1888- 133
Occult philosophy: an introduction, the major concepts and a glossary. Key truths of occult philosophy, completely rewritten and expanded. Philadelphia, D. McKay Co., 1947 [i.e. 1948] x, 436 p. 21 cm. [BF1999.J65 1948] 48-5791
1. Occult sciences. I. Title.

*KARPEL, Craig, comp. 133
The rite of exorcism, [edited by] Craig Karpel. New York, Berkley [1975] 217 p. 18 cm. (Ae(A Berkley Medallion Book) [BF1411] ISBN 0-425-02848-8 1.50 (pbk.)
1. Occult sciences. I. Title.

KERR, John Stevens. 133
The mystery and magic of the occult. Philadelphia, Fortress Press [1971] 152 p. illus. 22 cm. Includes bibliographical references. [BF1411.K47] 79-154486 ISBN 0-8006-0157-2 3.50
1. Occult sciences. 2. Christianity and occult sciences. I. Title.

KING, Bruce. 133
The encyclopedia of ancient and forbidden knowledge [by] Zolar. Los Angeles, Nash [1970] 472 p. illus. 22 cm. [BF1411.K55] 77-103882 7.95
1. Occult sciences. I. Title.

KING, Francis. 133
Wisdom from afar / Francis King. Garden City, N.Y. : Doubleday, 1976, c1975. 144 p. : ill. ; 28 cm. (A New library of the supernatural) [BF1411.K555 1976] 75-16750 7.95
1. Occult sciences. 2. Sects. I. Title. II. Series.

KING, Henry Walter, 1872- 212
Out of the crucibles, by Henry W. King. Boston, Meador publishing company, 1932. 4 p. l., 7-274 p. incl. illus., plates. front. pl. 20 1/2 cm. [BF1623.R7K5] 33-18343
1. Occult sciences. 2. Rosicrucians. I. Title.

KINGSFORD, Anna (Bonus) Mrs., 1846-1888. 133
The perfect way; or, The finding of Christ, by Anna (Bonus) Kingsford ... and E. Maitland. 5th ed. New York, The Metaphysical pub. co., 1901. 1 p. l., xii, xxv, [1], 384 p. 21 cm. [BF1999.K55 1901] 1-31878
1. Occult sciences. I. Maitland, Edward, 1824-1897, joint author. II. Title.

KNIGHT, Anna A
The broken circle. Boston, Forum Pub. Co. [c1961] 224 p. illus. 20 cm. 65-5312
1. Occult sciences. I. Title.

KOCH, Kurt E. 133
Between Christ and Satan, by Kurt E. Koch. Grand Rapids, Mich., Kregel Publications [1971?] 192 p. 18 cm. [BF1411.K6] 79-160690 ISBN 0-8254-3003-8 1.25
1. Occult sciences. 2. Psychical research. 3. Faith-cure. I. Title.

KOCH, Kurt E. 253.5
Christian counseling and occultism; the Christian counseling of persons who are psychically vexed or ailing because of involvement in occultism. A practical theological and systematic investigation in consultation with medical and psychological bordering sciences. Tr. from German by Andrew Petter. Grand Rapids, Mich., Kregel [c.]1965. 299p. 24cm. Bibl. [BF1033.K573] 65-23118 4.95
1. Occult sciences. 2. Pastoral psychology. I. Title.

KOCH, Kurt E 253.5
Christian counseling and occultism; the Christian counseling of persons who are psychically vexed or ailing because of involvement in occultism. A practical theological and systematic investigation in consultation with medical and pyschological bordering sciences, by Kurt E. Koch. Translated from the German by Andrew Petter. Grand Rapids, Kregel Publications, 1965. 299 p. 24 cm. Translation of Seeisorge und Okkultismus. Bibliography: p. 293-299. [BF1033.K573 1965] 65-23118
1. Occult sciences. 2. Pastoral psychology. I. Title.

KOCH, Kurt E. 133
The devil's alphabet, by Kurt Koch. Grand Rapids, Mich., Kregel Publications [1971?] 156 p. 18 cm. [BF1411.K62] 76-160692 ISBN 0-8254-3004-6 1.25
1. Occult sciences. 2. Psychical research. I. Title.

KOCH, Kurt E. 133
Occult bondage and deliverance; advice for counselling the sick, the troubled, and the occultly oppressed, by Kurt Koch. Grand Rapids, Mich., Kregel Publications [1971?] 198 p. 18 cm. [BF1411.K63] 72-160691 ISBN 0-8254-3006-2 1.25
1. Occult sciences. 2. Psychical research. 3. Faith-cure. 4. Demonology. I. Title.

THE Kybalion; 133
a study of the hermetic philosophy of ancient Egypt and Greece, by three initiates ... Chicago, Ill., The Yogi publication society [c1908] 223 p. 19 cm. [BF1611.K9] 8-18560
1. Occult sciences.

LACHAPELLE, Dolores. 394
Earth festivals : seasonals celebrations for everyone young and old / Dolores LaChapelle and Janet Bourque ; ill. by Randy LaChapelle. Silverton, Colo. : Finn Hill Arts, c1976. 196 p., [4] leaves of col. plates : ill. ; 28 cm. Bibliography: p. 191-193. [BF1999.L15] 76-15321 ISBN 0-917270-00-2 : 10.95
1. Occult sciences. 2. Festivals. I. Bourque, Janet, joint author. II. Title.

[LA DUE, Francia A. Mrs.] 1849-1922. 133
Beacon fires. New York, E. B. Page & co., 1899. 100 p. 15 cm. Preface signed: B. S. [i. e. Blue star, pseud. of author] [BF1999.L17 1899] 99-4304
1. Occult sciences. I. Title.
Contents omitted.

[LA DUE, Francia A. Mrs.] 133
1849-1922.
Beacon fires. Halcyon, Cal., Published by the Temple of the people [c1927] 6 p. l., 70 p., 1 l. 16 cm. "Second edition." Preface signed: B. S. [i. e. Blue star, pseud. of author] Foreword signed: R. S. (G. in C.) [BF1999.L17 1927] 38-33158
1. Occult sciences. I. Title.
Contents omitted.

LEECH, Walter Stuart, 1868- 133
The most important thing in the world, by W. Stuart Leech ... Chicago, Occult publishing company, 1926. 4 p. l., 11-78 p. xi pl. (incl. front.) 24 cm. "First edition." "This edition is limited to one thousand signed and numbered copies." This copy neither numbered nor signed. [BF1999.L33] 27-23515
1. Occult sciences. I. Title.

LEEK, Sybil. 133
Sybil Leek's Book of the curious and the occult / Sybil Leek. 1st ed. New York : Ballantine Books, 1976. p. cm. [BF1411.L36] 76-21718 ISBN 0-345-25385-X pbk. : 1.75
1. Occult sciences. 2. Psychical research. I. Title. II. Title: Book of the curious and the occult.

LESTOCQ, Hubert. 133
Secret man, by Hubert Lestocq. New York, London [etc.] Rider & co. [1945] 112 p. 19 cm. "Books recommended to the reader": p. 112. [BF1999.L39] 47-15361
1. Occult sciences. I. Title.

LEWIS, Ralph M. 133
Along civilization's trail, by Ralph M. Lewis... San Jose, Calif., Supreme grand lodge of AMORC, Printing and publishing department [c1940] 216 p. illus. 23 1/2 cm. (Rosicrucian library. vol. xix) Pages 208-216, advertising matter. [BF1623.R7R65 vol. 19] [159.961] (133.062) [(159.961082)] 41-11764
1. Rosicrucians. 2. Occult sciences. 3. Voyages and travels. I. Title.

LIEB, Frederick George, 1888- 133
Sight unseen, a journalist visits the occult, by Frederick G. Lieb. New York, London, Harper & brothers [c1939] x p., 1 l., 257 p. 22 cm. "First edition." [BF1031.L47] 159.961 39-10231
1. Occult sciences. I. Title.

*LINHARES, Margaret. 133.4
I married a witch's love. New York, Vantage Press, [1974] 113 p. 21 cm. [BF1576] ISBN 0-533-01025-X. 4.50
1. Occult sciences. I. Title.

LOBSANG Rampa, Tuesday
You-forever. [1. ed. New York] Pageant Press [1966] 276 p. 21 cm. 68-14100
1. Occult sciences. I. Title.

LONG, Max. 133
The secret science at work: new light on prayer. Los Angeles, Huna Research Publications [1953] 336p. 22cm. [BF1999.L57] 53-30045
1. Occult sciences. I. Title.

LONG, Max Freedom, 1890- 133
The Huna code in religions. Vista, Calif., Huna Research Publications [1965] xiv, 306 p. 22 cm. Bound with Andrews, Lorrin. A dictionary of the Hawaiian language. Honolulu, 1865. [BF1999.L565] 67-6333
1. Occult sciences. I. Title.

LOOMIS, Ernest.
Concentration methods and helps; containing one hundred and eighty-one subjects, drills, etc., which show how to develop and use occult forces in all business and art. Chicago, E. Loomis & co. [1900] 1 p. l., 166 p. 23 cm. (Occult science library, v. 7) [BF1439.L] 0-3047
1. Occult sciences. I. Title.

LOOMIS, Ernest.
... Seven essays on the subject of force-massing methods. Showing how to use occult forces, etc., in all business and art. Chicago, E. Loomis & co. [1899] 1 p. l., 134 22 p. 8 degrees. (Occult science library) 99-1315
1. Occult sciences. I. Title. II. Title: Force massing methods.

LOOMIS, Ernest. 133
... Seven essays on the subject of your practical forces, showing how to use them in all business and art. By Ernest Loomis. Chicago, E. Loomis & company [c1897] 5 p. l., [iii]-124, p. 23 cm. (Occult science library) Reprinted from the Occult science library magazine. cf. Pref. [BF1999.L6] 12-36301
1. Ocult science. I. Title.

THE Lord God of truth 181.4
within; a posthumous sequel to The daysprint of youth, by M. Los Angeles, Calif., The Phoenix press, 1941. 6 p. l., 390 p. 24 cm. On cover: For western yogi. "First published 1941." [BF1999.L63 1941] 41-10313
1. Occult sciences. I. M.

LOVE, Jeff. 133
The quantum gods : the origin and nature of matter and consciousness / Jeff Love. [Salisbury, Eng.] : Compton Russell Element, 1976. 242 p. : ill. ; 24 cm. Includes bibliographical references. [BF1999.L64 1976] 76-379737 ISBN 0-85955-030-3 : £3.95
1. Occult sciences. I. Title.

LUNDSTROM, Emil Ferdinand. 131.3
Our deeper destiny, by Emil Ferdinand Lundstrom... Philadelphia, Dorrance & company, inc. [c1933] 154 p. 19 1/2 cm. [BF1999.L75] 159.913 33-18641
1. Occult sciences. 2. Future life. I. Title.

[MCDONALD, Jonathan S] 133
Hermetic philosophy. Including lessons, general discourses, and explications of "fragments" from the schools of Egypt, Chaldea, Greece, Italy, Scandinavia, etc. Designed for students of the hermetic, Pythagorean, and Platonic sciences, and western occultism. By an acolyte of the "H.B. of L." ... Philadelphia, J. B. Lippincott company, 1890-93. 3 v. 19 cm. Vol. ii by "Styx, of the 'H.B. of L.' [pseud.]" Vol. iii has title: Hermetic philosophy. Can virtue and science be taught? A comedy founded on Plato's "Meno," applied to modern discoveries in theosophy, Christian science, magic, etc., and to those who are making these discoveries. By Styx [pseud.] [BF1611.M2] 11-15008
1. Occult sciences. I. Title.

MCGILL, Ormond. 133
How to produce miracles / Ormond McGill. South Brunswick : A. S. Barnes, c1976. 118 p. : ill. ; 26 cm. Includes index. [BF1411.M15] 74-9288 ISBN 0-498-01553-X : 9.95
1. Occult sciences. 2. Hypnotism. 3. Mesmerism. 4. Entertaining. I. Title.

MCGILL, Ormond. 133
How to produce miracles / by Ormond McGill. New York : New American Library, 1977,c1976. 178p. : ill. ; 18 cm. (A Signet Book) Includes index. [BF1411.M15] ISBN 0-451-07618-4 pbk. : 1.50
1. Occult sciences. 2. Hypnotism. 3. Mesmerism. 4. Entertaining. I. Title.
L.C. card no. for 1976 A.S. Barnes ed.: 74-9288.

MACKAY, Charles H. 133
A new system of occult training. West gate philosophy. Book 1. By Charles H. Mackay, (founder.)... Boston, C. H. Mackay [c1900] 72 p. 15 1/2 cm. [BF1611.M3] 0-2848
1. Occult sciences. I. Title. II. Title: West gate philosophy.

MACKENZIE, Andrew. 133
The unexplained; some strange cases in psychical research. With an introd. by H. H. Price. London, New York, Abelard-Schuman [1970] xvii, 180 p. 22 cm. [BF1411.M17 1970] 68-14570 5.95
1. Society for Psychical Research, London. 2. Occult sciences. 3. Psychical research. I. Title.

*MACKLIN, John 133.3.
Case book of the unknown New York, Ace Books [1974] 207 p. 18 cm. [BF1411] 0.95 (pbk.)
1. Occult sciences. I. Title.

*MACKLIN, John. 133
Dimensions beyond the known. New York, Ace [1968] 158p. 18cm. (Star bk., H89) .60 pap.,
1. Occult sciences. I. Title.

*MACKLIN, John. 133
The enigma of the unknown. New York, Ace [1967] 192p. illus. 18cm. (Star bk., K292) .50 pap.,
1. Occult sciences. I. Title.

*MACKLIN, John. 133.3
A look through secret doors. New York, Ace Books [1974? c1969] 156 p. 18 cm. (The Exorcism series, book VI) [BF1411] 1.25 (pbk.)
1. Occult sciences. I. Title.

*MACKLIN, John. 133
Passport to the unknown. New York, Ace [1968] 158p. 18cm. (H81) .60 pap.,
1. Occult sciences. I. Title.

*MACKLIN, John. 133
The strange and uncanny. New York, Ace Books [1975, c1967] 192 p. 18 cm. [BF1411] 0.95 (pbk.)
1. Occult sciences. 2. Psychical research. I. Title.

MCMILLON, Lynn A., 1941 133
Doctrines of demons : a Christian response to the occult / Lynn A. McMillon. Nashville : Gospel Advocate Co., 1976 c1975 vii, 153 p. ; 20 cm. Includes index. [BF1411.M18] 75-27826 2.95
1. Occult sciences. 2. Spiritualism. 3. Christianity and occult sciences. I. Title.

MANNING, Al G. 133
The miracle of universal psychic power: how to pyramid your way to prosperity [by] Al G. Manning. West Nyack, N.Y., Parker Pub. Co. [1974] 228 p. 24 cm. [BF1411.M26] 73-13512 ISBN 0-13-585729-5 6.95
1. Occult sciences. 2. Psychical research. 3. Success. I. Title.

MASON, Frank L 133.93
Out of the unknown; or, Spooks and spirits in action. Boston, Christopher Pub. House [1950] viii, 124 p. 21 cm. [BF1031.M37] 50-3930
1. Occult sciences. I. Title. II. Title: Spooks and spirits in action.

METZNER, Ralph. 133
Maps of consciousness; I Ching, tantra, tarot, alchemy, astrology, actualism. New York, Macmillan [1971] 160 p. illus. 29 cm. Includes bibliographical references. [BF1411.M48 1971b] 72-30537 7.95
1. Occult sciences. I. Title.

METZNER, Ralph. 133
Maps of consciousness; I Ching, Tantra, Tarot, alchemy, astrology, actualism. New York, Collier Books [1971] 160 p. illus., facsims., plates. 28 cm. Includes bibliographical references. [BF1411.M48 1971] 78-142346
1. Occult sciences. I. Title.

MICHAEL, William. 133
A miracle a day, by William Michael. A course of instruction in 5 volumes, consisting of 54 lessons comprising telepathy, self betterment, health and astrology ... [Los Angeles, The Paty co., c1931] 5 v. 16 cm. On cover: 1932 edition. [BF1411.M5 1931] ca 32
1. Occult sciences. I. Title.

MONTANDON, Pat. 133
The intruders / Pat Montandon. New York : Coward, McCann & Geoghegan, [1975] 286 p. ; 22 cm. [BF1411.M59 1975] 74-16638 ISBN 0-698-10636-9 : 8.95
1. Montandon, Pat. 2. Occult sciences. I. Title.

MONTANDON, Pat. 133
The intruders / Pat Montandon. Greenwich, Conn : Fawcett Crest, 1976c1975. 288p. ; 18 cm. [BF1411M59] ISBN 0-449-22963-7 pbk. : 1.95
1. Montandon, Pat. 2. Occult sciences. I. Title.
L.C. card no. for 1975 Coward McCann and Geoghegan edition: 74-16638.

MONTGOMERY, John Warwick. 133
Principalities and powers; the world of the occult, including a ghost story by the author, a Reformation-era letter on demon possession, and hitherto unpublished cartoons on the occult by C. S. Lewis. Minneapolis, Bethany Fellowship [1973] 224 p. illus. 23 cm. Includes bibliographical references. [BF1411.M6] 73-3206 ISBN 0-87123-457-2 4.95
1. Occult sciences. 2. Psychical research. I. Title.

MONTGOMERY, John Warwick. 133
Principalities and powers : the world of the occult / John Warwick Montgomery. Newly rev. and enl. ed. Minneapolis, Minn. : Published by Pyramid Publications for Bethany Fellowship, 1975. 255 p. : ill. ; 18 cm. (Dimension books) Includes bibliographical references and indexes. [BF1411.M6 1975] 75-321523 ISBN 0-87123-460-2 pbk. : 1.75
1. Occult sciences. 2. Psychical research. I. Title.

MONTGOMERY, John Warwick. 133
Principalities and powers; a new look at the world of the occult. Newly revised and enlarged edition. New York, Pyramid Publications [1975 c1973] 255 p. 17 cm. (Dimension Books) Includes bibliographical references and index. [BF1411.M6] 74-29081 ISBN 0-87123-460-2 1.75 (pbk.)
1. Occult sciences. 2. Psychical research. I. Title.

MUSCAT, Jane Oliphant. 113
Letters from an occult student, by Jane Oliphant Muscat. Boston, The Christopher publishing house [c1922] 3 p. l., [9]-61 p. diagrs. 21 cm. [BF1999.M9] 22-17547 1.00
1. Occult sciences. 2. New thought. I. Title.

NEBEL, Long John
The way out world. Englewood Cliffs, N.J., Prentice-Hall [c.1961] 225p. p3.95 61-17882
1. Occult sciences. I. Title.

*NEWALL, Venetia 133.3
The encyclopedia of witchcraft & magic [by] Venetia Newall. Introduction by Richard M. Dorson. New York Dial Press 1974 192 p. illus. 30 cm. [BF1563] 73-17944 ISBN 0-8037-2343-1 17.50
1. Dorson, Richard M. 2. Occult sciences. I. Title.

NORTH, Gary. 133
None dare call it witchcraft / Gary North. New Rochelle, N.Y. : Arlington House, c1976. 253 p. ; 24 cm. Includes bibliographical references. [BF1411.N66] 76-12109 ISBN 0-87000-301-1 : 8.95
1. Occult sciences. 2. Psychical research. I. Title.

*OCCULT review 133
The first Occult review reader. Ed. by Bernhardt J. Hurwood. London, Tamdem; New York, Award Bks. [1968] 188p. 18cm. (A346S K) Excerpts from material pub. in Occult review, 1906-1955. .75 pap.,
1. Occult sciences. I. Hurwood, Bernhardt J. ed. II. Title.

[OLD, Walter Gorn] 1864- 133
A manual of occultism, by "Sepharial". Philadelphia, D. McKay [19-] xiii, 356 p. illus., diagrs. 19 cm. "Printed in England." [BF1411.O6] 159.961 33-20359
1. Occult sciences. I. Title.

OLIVER, Frederick Spencer, 133
1866-1899.
A dweller on two planets : or, The dividing of the way / by Phylos the Thibetan [i.e. F. S. Oliver]. Blauvelt, N.Y. : Multimedia Pub. Corp., c1974. 423 p., [7] leaves of plates : ill. ; 18 cm. (Steinerbooks) Includes index. [BF1999.O42 1974] 73-94420 ISBN 0-8334-1753-3 : 2.95
1. Occult sciences. I. Title.

OLIVER, Frederick Spencer] 133
1866-1899.
A dweller on two planets; or, The dividing of the way, by Phylos the Thibetan [pseud.] ... Los Angeles, Borden publishing company, 1940. 3 p. l., v. [2], x-xix, [2], 26-423 p. front., illus. (incl. map) plates. 20 cm. [BF1999.O42 1940] 159.961 41-2579
1. Occuit sciences. I. Title.

OLIVER, Frederick 133.9'3
Spencer, 1866-1899.
A dweller on two planets : the dividing of the way / by Phylos the Thibetan. San Francisco : Harper & Row, 1981, c1974. p. cm. Originally published by Multimedia Pub. Corp., Blauvelt, N.Y. [BF1999.O42

1981] 19 80-8896 ISBN 0-06-066565-3 pbk. : 6.95
1. Occult sciences. I. Phylos the Thibetan. II. Title.

[OLIVER, Frederick Spencer] 133
1866-1899.
... *A dweller on two planets; or, The dividing of the way,* by Phylos, the Thibetan [pseud.] ... Los Angeles, Cal., Baumgardt publishing company, 1905. 3 p. l., xix, [2], 26-423, [1] p. front., illus., plates. 20 cm. [BF1999.O42 1905] 5-9186
1. Occult sciences. I. Title.

[OLIVER, Frederick Spencer] 133
1866-1899.
... *A dweller on two planets; or, The dividing of the way,* by Phylos, the Thibetan [pseud.] ... Los Angeles, Calif., Poseid publishing company, 1920. 3 p. l., xix, [1], 25-423 p. front., illus., plates. 22 1/2 cm. [BF1999.O42 1920] 20-5581
1. Occult sciences. I. Title.

[OLIVER, Frederick Spencer] 133
1866-1899.
A dweller on two planets; or, The dividing of the way, by Phylos the Thibetan [pseud.] ... 4th ed. Los Angeles, Calif., Poseid publishing company, 1924. 3 p. l., xix, [2], 26-423 p. front., illus., plates. 21 1/2 cm. Title transliterated: Yehowah. [BF1999.O42 1924] 24-28667
1. Occult sciences. I. Title. II. Title: A dweller on two planets.

†OPHIEL. 135.4
The art and practice of Caballa magic / by Ophiel. New York : S. Weiser, 1977, c1976. 152 p., [4] leaves of plates : ill. ; 21 cm. Bibliography: p. 152. [BF1623.C2O63] 78-103573 ISBN 0-87728-303-6 : 5.00
1. Cabala. 2. Occult sciences. I. Title.

*OPHIEL. 133
The art and practice of the occult. St. Paul, Minn., Peach Pub. Co., 1968. 159p. illus. col. front.) 20cm. 4.95
1. Occult sciences. I. Title.
Distributed by Llewellyn Pubns., Box 3383, St. Paul, Minn. 55101

ORPHANUS. 133
Look within; a preliminary introduction to the recovery of the gnosis. Oroville, Calif., Point Dawn Foundation, 1968. 284 p. illus. 23 cm. Bibliography: p. 275-276. [BF1411.O7] 68-58831 3.75
1. Occult sciences. 2. Mind and body. I. Title.

OSBORN, Arthur Walter, 1891- 133
The meaning of personal existence in the light of paranormal phenomena, the doctrine of reincarnation, and mystical states of consciousness [by] Arthur W. Osborn. Forewordby Ian Stevenson. [1st ed. in U.S.A.] Wheaton, Ill., Theosophical Pub. [1967, c.1966] xviii, 232p. 22cm. Bibl. [BF1411.O8 1967] 67-8034 3.45
1. Occult sciences. I. Title.

PARACELSUS, 1493-1541. 133.
The Hermetic and alchemical writings of Aureolus Phillippus Theophrastus Bombast of Hohenheim, called Paracelsus, the Great, now for the first time faithfully and accurately translated into English. The present American, Oriental, Egyptian and Asiatic ed. prepared for publication under the editorship of Dr. L. W. de Laurence...Faithfully reproduced from the London ed. of 1894, which was edited, with a biographical preface, elucidatory notes, and a copious Hermetic vocabulary and accurate index, by Arthur Edward Waite... Limited ed. ... Chicago, Ill., De Laurence, Scott & co., 1910. 2 v. fronts. (ports.) 29 cm. $12.00 Contents.v. 1. Hermetic chemistry--v. 2. Hermetic medicine and hermetic philosophy. [BF1598.P23] 11-522
1. Occult sciences. I. Waite, Arthur Edward, ed. II. De Laurence, Lauron William, 1868- ed. III. Title.

PARCHMENT, Samuel Richard, 212
1881-
"The middle path--the safest", the religion of "head and heart", by S. R. Parchment; a labour of love in the cause of universal brotherhood. 1st ed. San Francisco, Calif., San Francisco center, Rosicrucian fellowship; Boston, New York [etc.] Pilot publishing co., San Francisco branch [1930] 1 p. l., 119 p. 1 illus., pl. 20 cm. "Sequel to [the author's] 'Step to self mastery'."--p. [6] [BF1429.P32] 30-15743
1. Occult sciences. 2. Buddha and Buddhism. 3. Christianity and other religious—Buddhism. 4. Rosicrucians. I. Title.

PARCHMENT, Samuel Richard, 212
1881-
Steps to self-mastery, by S. R. Parchment. Oceanside, Calif., Fellowship press [c1927] 223 p. fold. front., illus., diagr. 20 cm. [BF1429.P3] 27-14972
1. Occult sciences. I. Title.

PARCHMENT, Samuel Richard, 133
1881-
Steps to self-mastery, by S. R. Parchment. 3d ed. [San Francisco] The author, 1932. 242 p. fold. front., illus., diagr. 20 cm. [BF1429.P3 1932] 32-12095
1. Occult sciences. I. Title.

PAUWELS, Louis, 001.9
1920(Aug.2)-
The morning of the magicians / by Louis Pauwels and Jacques Bergier ; translated from the French by Rollo Myers. New York : Stein and Day, [1977] c1963. p. cm. "A Scarborough book." [BF1412.P3813 1977] 77-22874 ISBN 0-8128-2260-9 pbk. : 4.95
1. Occult sciences. I. Bergier, Jacques, 1912- joint author. II. Title.

PELLEY, William Dudley, 133.93
1890-
Star guests; design for mortality. [1st ed. Noblesville, Ind., Soulcraft Press, 1950] 318p. 22cm. [BF1999.P428] 51-20227
I. Title.

*PELTON, Robert W. 133
Your future, your fortune. Greenwich, Conn., Fawcett [1973] 176 p. 18 cm. [BF1411] 0.95 (pbk)
1. Occult Sciences. 2. Psychical Research. I. Title.

PENSATIA. 299'.93
The flame of white ; & The rose of life / by Pensatia. New York : Euclid Pub. Co. : Bond & Bacon [distributor], c1981. 86 p. : col. ill. ; 24 cm. [BF1999.P475 1981] 19 81-67515 ISBN 0-935490-02-7 : 7.95
1. Occult sciences. I. Pensatia. Rose of life. 1981. II. Title.
Publisher's address: P. O. Box 121, Cathedral Sta., New York, NY 10025.

PEREZ, Rene. 133
"Thy whisper", by Rene Perez ... Chicago, Ill., The "Master's books" publishing co. [c1922] [69] p. 16 cm. [BF1999.P5] 22-16338
I. Title.

PETERSEN, William J. 200.6
Those curious new cults [by] William J. Petersen. New Canaan, Conn., Keats [1973] vii, 214 p. 22 cm. Bibliography: p. 213-214. [BF1411.P47] 72-93700 ISBN 0-87983-031-X 4.95
1. Occult sciences. 2. Psychical research. 3. Sects. 4. Religions. I. Title.

PETERSEN, William J. 200'.6
Those curious new cults / William J. Petersen. New Canaan, Conn. : Keats Pub., 1975. 272 p. ; 18 cm. (A Pivot family reader) Bibliography: p. 271-272. [BF1411.P47 1975] 75-328425 pbk. : 1.95
1. Occult sciences. 2. Psychical research. 3. Sects. 4. Religions. I. Title.

PHILOSOPHY of science 001.9'01
and the occult / edited by Patrick Grim. Albany : State University of New York Press, c1982. 336 p. : ill. ; 24 cm. (SUNY series in Philosophy) Includes bibliographies and index. [BF1411.P49 1982] 19 81-13552 ISBN 0-87395-572-2 : 30.50 ISBN 0-87395-573-0 pbk . : 9.95
1. Occult sciences. 2. Psychical research. 3. Unidentified flying objects. 4. Science—Philosophy. I. Grim, Patrick. II. Title. III. Series.

A pictorial anthology of witchcraft, magic & alchemy. Translated by J. Courtenay Locke. [1st American ed.] New Hyde Park, N.Y., University Books [1958] 394p. illus. 25cm. Translation of Le musee des sorciers, mages, et alchimistes. 'Complete reproduction of the original printed in England in 1931.'
1. Occult sciences. I. Grillot de Givry, Emile Angelo, 1870- II. Title: Witchcraft, magic & alchemy.

PIERCE, Carl Horton. 133
Heal yourself; what to do and how to do it, by Carl Horton Pierce. New York, N.Y., J. Felsberg, inc., 1945. 192 p. 2 port. 21 cm. "Articles by Dr. Pierce reprinted from various magazines": p. [101]-185. [BF1999.P548] 45-8950
1. Occult sciences. I. Title.

[PILAI, M. Gnauapiakesam] 133
India's hood unveiled, astral and spirit sight at will. South India mysteries, Hindu hypnograph, ancient Hindu methods for Hindu clairvoyance. Hindu levitation (raising the human body in the air). Hindu method of burial alive, (suspended animation). Spirit sight at will. By a native Hindu of South India. Prepared for publication in the United States under the editorship of Dr. L. W. de Laurence ... Chicago, Ill., De Laurence, Scott & co. [c1910] 3 v. in 1. front. (port.) 19 1/2 cm. $2.00 [BF1141.P6] 11-758
1. Occult sciences. I. De Laurence, Lauron William, 1868- ed. II. Title.

PITTWOOD, Ann, 1890- 133
The power of your desire; the science of the word. [Hollywood? Calif., 1954] 123p. illus. 23cm. [BF1999.P557] 54-32585
1. Occult sciences. I. Title.

*PLAYFAIR, Guy Lyon 133
The unknown power by Guy Lyon Playfair New York Pocket Books [1975] xvi., 317 p. illus. 18 cm. Original British title: The Flying Cow [BF1411] ISBN 0-671-80080-9 1.95 (pbk.)
1. Occult sciences. I. Title.

PONCE, Charles. 133
The game of wizards : psyche, science, and symbol in the occult / by Charles Ponce. Harmondsworth, Eng. ; Baltimore : Penguin Books, 1975. 240 p. : ill. ; 19 cm. Includes bibliographical references. [BF1411.P66] 73-90932 ISBN 0-14-003864-7 pbk. : 2.50
1. Occult sciences. I. Title.

PSYCHOMAGIC; how to use the 133
psychic powers of the astral plane A course of lessons on: the psychic phenomena of distant sensing, clairvoyance, psychometry, crystal gazing. Astral and spirit. The wonders of the magic mirror. Interior focalization of the mind. State of introspection. Interior concentration. Astral auras. Reading in the astral light. Telepathy. The masterworks of William Walker Atkinson and L. W. de Laurence. [New York] Life Resources Institute [1967] 256 p. 21 cm. [BF1031.P8] 67-9349
1. Occult sciences. 2. Psychometry (Occult sciences) I. Atkinson, William Walker, 1862-1932. Practical psychomancy and crystal gazing. II. De Laurence, Lauron William, 1868- The mystic text book of the Hindu occult chambers.

RACHLEFF, Owen S. 133
The occult conceit; a new look at astrology, witchcraft & sorcery [by] Owen S. Rachleff. Chicago, Cowles Book Co. [1971] xvii, 235 p. 22 cm. Bibliography: p. 225-227. [BF1411.R18] 77-143489 6.95
1. Occult sciences. 2. Psychical research. I. Title.

RAINS, Clara Beatrice, 1890- 133
The spirit of man, by Clara Rains and Leon Rains. New York city, Lucifer publishing company [c1924] viii, 242 p. diagrs. 21 cm. [BF1999.R2] 24-24717
1. Occult sciences. I. Rains, Leon, 1870- joint author. II. Title.

RAKADAZAN, Guru, pseud. 133
Ritualistic occultism, true white magic; including full instruction in higher occult training, the making of tailsmans and amulets, the charging of waters and oils, invocations of the hierarchies and invisible potentates, and full instructions in the magnetic eye. By Guru Rakadazan, of the Aryan yoga society. Prepared only for the Imperialistic council ... Allentown, Pa., Priv. print. by the Philosophical publishing co., c1913. 3 p. l., 9-272 p. 24 cm. Printed on one side of leaf only. [BF1611.R2] 14-436 25.00
1. Occult sciences. I. Title.

RANSKE, Jutta (Mordt) Bell. 133
Mrs.
The revelation of man; a key to mystic science, by Jutta Bell-Ranske. Reading, Pa., New York, N. Y. [etc.] William S. Rhode company, inc. [c1924] 5 p. l., [viii] xvi p., 3 l., 196 p. illus., plates. 24 cm. Cover-title: The revelation of man, with key to invisible laws. "First limited edition, issued unde the auspices of the progressive forum. Autographed copy." [BF1999.R37] 24-29940
1. Occult sciences. I. Title.

REDDING, William A. 133
... *Mysteries unveiled;* the hoary past come forward with astonishing messages for the prophetic future. By William A. Redding. [Navarre? Kan.,] c1896. 4 p. l., 195 p. incl. front. (port.) illus., 2 diagr. 21 cm. At head of title: No. 9. No. 9 of a series of books by the author on "Our near future," cf. Advertisement at end. [BF1999.R4] 22-11416
1. Occult sciences. I. Title.

RHINE, Joseph Banks 133.8072
New world of the mind [New York, Apollo Eds., 1962, c.1953] 339p. (A42) Bibl. 1.95 pap.,
1. Occult sciences. I. Title.

RHINE, Joseph Banks, 133.8072
1895-
New world of the mind. New York, Sloane, 1953. 339 p. 22 cm. [BF1411.R47] 53-9339
1. Occult sciences. I. Title.

*RICHARDS, Eugene. 133
Satan, demons & dildoes. Chatsworth, Calif., Barclay House [1974] 158 p. 18 cm. Bibliography: p. 158 [BF1411] ISBN 0-87682-406-8 1.95 (pbk.)
1. Occult sciences. I. Title.

RICHARDSON, John Emmett, 133
1853-
The great message; the lineal key of the great school of the masters. Rev. ed. [Los Gatos, Calif.] Great School of Natural Science [1950] 388 p. 22 cm. (Harmonic series. v. 5) [BF1999.R46 1950] 50-57173
1. Occult sciences. I. Title. II. Title: Great school of the masters.

RICHARDSON, John Emmett, 133
1853-
The great message; a definite message from the great school of the masters to humanity... By J. E.Richardson... [Hollywood, Calif.] The Great school of natural science [c1927] 382 p. 21 cm. (Harmonic series, vol. V) [BF1999.H38 vol. 5] 27-15070
1. Occult sciences. I. Title. II. Title: Great school of the masters.

RICHARDSON, John Emmett, 133
1853-
The great message; the lineal key of the great school of the masters... By J. E. Richardson... Rev. ed. [Hollywood, Calif.] The Great school of natural science [c1928] 388 p. 21 cm. (Harmonic series, vol. V) [BF1999.H38 vol. 5 1928] 29-1599
1. Occult sciences. I. Title. II. Title: Great schol of the masters.

[RICHARDSON, John Emmett] 133
1853-
The great work, the constructive principle of nature in individual life, by the author of "The great psychological crime"... 6th ed. Chicago, Indo-American book co., 1908. 456 p., 2 l. front., illus., plates. 19 1/2 cm. (Harmonic series, vol. III) [BF1999.H38 vol. 3 1908] 32-19331
1. Occult sciences. I. Title.

[RICHARDSON, John Emmett] 133.
1853-
The reality of matter; a critical correspondence between Heinrich Hensoldt, PH.D. of Columbia university, and a member of the Order of the brotherhood of India. Republished in book form at request of students and friends of the great work, for the benefit of those who are confused by the fundamental teachings of Christian science and other cults and schools of mental therapeutics... 1st ed. Chicago, Indo-American book company, 1911. 172 p. plates. 18 1/2 cm. (Supplemental harmonic series, v. 6) Prelude signed: TK. [BF1031.R4] 12-924

1. *Occult sciences. 2. Theosophy. I. Hensoldt, Heinrich. II. Title.*

RICHMOND, Olney H. 133.
Temple lectures of the Order of the magi, delivered before the Grand temple of the order, at various times, by Olney H. Richmond... Chicago, [A. L. Fyfe, printer] 1892. 270 p. front. (port.) illus. 17 1/2 cm. [BF1701.R5] 11-9222
1. Occult sciences. I. Title.

ROGERS, Louis William, 1859- 212
Hints to young students of occultism, by L. W. Rogers 3d ed. Ridgewood, N.J., The Theosophical book co., 1911. 162 p. 17 1/2 cm. [BP565.R75] 11-8088
1. Occult sciences. I. Title.

*ROSE, Ronald. 133'.4
Primitive psychic power; the realities underlying the psychical practices and beliefs of Australian Aborigines [New York] New Amer. Lib. [1968, c.1956] 224p. 18cm. (Signet mystic, T3537) .75 pap.,
1. Occult Sciences. I. Title.

RUDHYAR, Dane, 1895- 133
Occult preparations for a new age / by Dane Rudhyar. Wheaton, Ill. : Theosophical Pub. House, 1975. 275 p. : ill. ; 21 cm. (A Quest book) Includes bibliographical references. [BF1411.R79] 74-19054 ISBN 0-8356-0460-8 pbk. : 3.25
1. Occult sciences. I. Title.

RUSH, John A. 133.4
Witchcraft and sorcery; an anthropological perspective of the occult, by John A. Rush. Springfield, Ill., Thomas [1974] ix, 166 p. illus. 24 cm. Bibliography: p. 153-159. [BF1411.R85 1974] 73-16066 ISBN 0-398-02981-4 10.50
1. Occult sciences. I. Title.
Pbk. 7.95, ISBN 0-398-03019-7

RUSSELL, Edward Wriothesley. 133
Design for destiny; science reveals the soul. New York, Ballantine [1973, c.1971] x, 213 p. 18 cm. Bibliography: p. 198-215. [BF1411.R87] ISBN 0-345-23405-7 1.25 (pbk.)
1. Occult sciences. I. Title.
L.C. card no. for the hardbound (London) edition: 76-165309.

RUSSELL, Walter Bowman, 1871- 133
The message of the divine Iliad. Limited, autographed edition de luxe. New York, [1948- v. col. port. 21 cm. [BF1999.R868] 48-11886
1. Occult sciences. I. Title.

SACRED order of the blue flame. 133
Authorized literature of the Sacred order of the blue flame, released for world distribution. 1st ed. Los Angeles, Calif., Department of publications of S.O.B.F., c1925. [3]-82 p. diagr. 23 1/2 cm. Cover-title: A key to blue flame science. [BF1999.S25 1925] 26-1650
1. Occult sciences. I. Title.

*SAGAN, Carl, 1934- 133.3
Other worlds, by Carl Sagan; produced by Jerome Agel. New York, Bantam Books [1975] 159 p. illus. 18 cm. [BF1701] 1.95 (pbk.)
1. Occult sciences. I. Title.

SALVERTE, Eusebe, 1771-1839. 133.4
The occult sciences. The philosophy of magic, prodigies, and apparent miracles. From the French of Eusebe Salverte. With notes illustrative, explanatory, and critical, by Anthony Todd Thomson... New York, Harper & brothers, 1847. 2 v. 18 1/2 cm. [Full name: Anne Joseph Eusebe Baconniere Salverte] [BF1612.S24 1847] [159.9614] 34-10923
1. Occult sciences. I. Thomson, Anthony Todd, 1778-1849, tr. II. Title.

SALVERTE, Eusebe, 1771-1839. 133.4
The occult sciences. The philosophy of magic, prodigies, and apparent miracles. From the French of Eusebe Salverte. With notes illustrative, explanatory, and critical, by Anthony Todd Thomson... New York, Harper & brothers, 1855. 2 v. 17 1/2 cm. [Full name: Anne Joseph Eusebe Baconniere Salverte] [BF1612.S24 1855] [159.9614] 34-10924
1. Occult sciences. I. Thomson, Anthony Todd, 1778-1849, tr. II. Title.

[SANDERSON, Florence Helen] 1896- 123
Your invisible self, by Sandra Sanderson [pseud.] illustrated by A. N. Merryman, jr. Los Angeles, Calif., De Vorss & co. [c1935] 2 p. l., 9-110 p. front. (port.) illus. 20 cm. "First edition." [BF1411.S3] (159.961) 35-13101
1. Occult sciences. 2. Fortune-telling. I. Title.
Contents omitted.

SANDERSON, Ivan Terence, 1911-
Things. New York, Pyramid Books [c1967] 188 p. 18 cm. 68-106116
1. Occult sciences. 2. Monsters. I. Title.

SARAYDARIAN, H. 133
The Hierarchy and the plan / by H. Saraydarian. Agoura, Calif. : Aquarian Educational Group, c1975. 58 p. : ill. ; 22 cm. Includes bibliographical references. [BF1999.S337] 75-39432
1. Occult sciences. I. Title.

SAVAGE, Helen. 133
... Psychic powers, by Helen Savage. Point Loma, Calif., Theosophical university press, 1940. 3 p. l., 125, [3] p. 15 cm. (Theosophical manual no. XI) [BF1031.S28] 44-44062
1. Occult sciences. 2. Theosophy. I. Title.

SAVOY, Gene. 001.9
Project X : the search for the secrets of immortality / by Gene Savoy ; ill. by Nicholas A. Nush. Indianapolis : Bobbs-Merrill, c1977. p. cm. [BF1999.S3423] 76-44670 ISBN 0-672-52181-4 : 11.95
1. Savoy, Gene. 2. Occult sciences. I. Nush, Nicholas A. II. Title.

SCHMIDT, Philipp, 1881- 133
Superstition and magic. [Tr. from German by Marie Heffernan, A. J. Peeler] Westminister, Md., Newman, 1963. 243p. 19cm. 62-9734 3.75
1. Occult sciences. I. Title.

SCHNEIDERFRANKEN, Joseph Anton, 1876-1943. 001.9
About by books, Concerning my name, and other texts / Bo Yin Ra (Joseph Anton Schneiderfranken) ; translated from the German by B. A. Reichenbach. Berkeley, Calif. : Kober Press, c1977. xiv, 73 p. ; 20 cm. "The works of Bo Yin Ra": p. 47-59. [BF1999.S348613] 76-27910 pbk. : 1.75
1. Occult sciences. I. Schneiderfranken, Joseph Anton, 1876-1943. Warum ich meinen Namen fuhre. English. 1977. II. Title. III. Title: Concerning my name.
Publisher's address : 2534 Chilton Way, Berkeley, CA 94704

SCHURE, Edouard, 1841-1929. 291
From Sphinx to Christ : an occult history / by Edouard Schure. 1st Harper & Row paperback ed. San Francisco : Harper & Row, 1982, c1970. p. cm. Translation of: L'evolution divine. Reprint. Originally published: Blauvelt, N.Y. : R. Steiner Publications, 1970. Includes bibliographical references. [BF1412.S3513 1982] 19 82-47754 ISBN 0-06-067124-6 : 7.95
1. Occult sciences. 2. Religions. I. [Evolution divine.] English II. Title.

SCOTT, Cyril Meir, 1879- 133
The greater awareness, by Cyril Scott ... New York, E. P. Dutton & co., inc., 1937. xii, 243 p. 20 cm. Sequel to An outline of modern occultism. "First printing." [BF411.S432] 159.961 37-3377
1. Occult sciences. I. Title.

SCOTT, Cyril Meir, 1879- 133
An outline of modern occultism. Enl. ed. New York, Dutton, 1950. x, 226 p. 20 cm. Sequel: The greater awareness. Bibliography: p. 225-226. [BF1411.S43 1950] 50-8556
1. Occult sciences. I. Title.

SCOTT, Cyril Meir, 1879- 133
An outline of modern occultism, by Cyril Scott. New York, E. P. Dutton & co., inc. [c1935] viii, 239, [1] p. 20 cm. "First edition." Bibliography: p. 289-[240] [BF1461.S35] 35-13087
1. Occult sciences. I. Title.

SHAH, Ikbel Ali sirder
Occultism; its theory and practice. New York, Castle Books [1956] 231 p. illus. 24 cm.
1. Occult sciences. I. Title.

SHEPARD, Leslie. 133.4
How to protect yourself against black magic and witchcraft / Leslie Shepard. 1st ed. Secaucus, N.J. : Citadel Press c1978. x, 162 p. ; 22 cm. Includes index. "Recordings": p. 157-159. [BF1411.S54] 78-12933 ISBN 0-8065-0646-6 : 7.95
1. Occult sciences. I. Title.

SLADEK, John Thomas. 001.9
The new Apocrypha : a guide to strange science and occult beliefs / John Sladek. New York : Stein and Day, 1974, c1973. 375 p. : ill. ; 24 cm. Includes index. Bibliography: p. [357]-362. [BF1411.S55 1974] 74-79418 ISBN 0-8128-1712-5 : 8.95
1. Occult sciences. 2. Psychical research. I. Title.

SLATER, Philip Elliot. 133
The wayward gate : science and the supernatural / Philip Slater. Boston : Beacon Press, [1977] p. cm. Bibliography: p. [BF1411.S57] 77-75445 ISBN 0-8070-2956-4 : 8.95
1. Occult sciences. I. Title.

SMITH, Richard Furnald. 133
Prelude to science / by Richard F. Smith. New York : Scribner, [1975] p. cm. Includes bibliographical references and index. [BF1411.S656] 75-17959 ISBN 0-684-14370-4 : 8.95
1. Occult sciences. I. Title.

SMITH, Robert Tighe, 1926- 200'.6
Cult & occult [by] Robert T. Smith. Minneapolis, Winston Press [1973] 142 p. 24 cm. [BF1411.S658] 72-93590 ISBN 0-03-007536-X 2.95
1. Occult sciences. 2. Psychical research. 3. Sects. I. Title.
Publisher's address: 25 Groveland Terrace.

*SMITH, Warren. 133
Strange powers of the mind. New York, Ace Books, [1974, c1968] 192 p., 18 cm. [BF1031] 0.95 (pbk.)
1. Occult sciences I. Title.

*SMITH, Warren. 133
Strange women of the occult. New York, Popular Lib. [1968] 128p. 18cm. (60-2342) Bibl. .60 pap.,
1. Occult. I. Title.

SNELLING, Christopher Hanbury William. 001.9
... and into the light / by C. H. W. Snelling. London ; New York : Regency Press, 1976. 307 p. : ill. ; 23 cm. [BF1999.S558] 77-369743 ISBN 0-7212-0447-3 : £3.00
1. Occult sciences. I. Title.

SOWDER, Zella Mae, 1902- 133
The best of luck. Los Angeles, Wetzel Pub. Co. [1947] 159 p. illus. 21 cm. [BF1031.S68] 47-11362
1. Occult sciences. I. Title.

*SPRAGGETT, Allen. 133
The world of the unexplained. [New York] New American Library [1974] 128 p. 18 cm. [BF1411] 1.25 (pbk.)
1. Occult sciences. I. Title.

STEARN, Jess. 133
Adventures into the psychic. New York, Coward-McCann [1969] 256 p. 22 cm. [BF1411.S8] 79-81004 4.95
1. Occult sciences. 2. Psychical research. I. Title.

*STEIGER, Brad. 133
The occult world of John Pendragon. New York, Ace [1968] 158p. 18cm. (Ace star bk., K307) .50 pap.,
1. Occult sciences. I. Title.

*STEIGER, Brad. 133
The unknown. New York, Popular Library [1974? c1966] 128 p. 18 cm. [BF1411] 0.95 (pbk.)
1. Occult sciences. I. Title.

STEINER, Rudolf 133
An outline of occult science. Tr. from German [into Russian] Steiner [dist. Stamford, Conn., Herman Pub. Serv., c.] 1962. 345p. 28cm. 6.00 pap.,
1. Occult science. I. Title.

STEINER, Rudolf, 1861- 133
Investigations in occultism, showing its practical value in daily life, based upon lectures by Rudolph Steiner ... New York and London, G. P. Putnam's sons, 1920. xii p., 1 l., 253 p. 20 cm. Preface signed: H. Collison. [BF1033.S79] 21-2328 2.00
1. Occult sciences. 2. Theosophy. I. Collison, Harry, ed. II. Title.

STEINER, Rudolf, 1861-1925. 133
The gates of knowledge; with an additional chapter entitled Philosophy and theosophy, by Rudolf Steiner ... Authorized translation from the German. New York and London, G. P. Putnam's sons, 1912. iii, 187 p. 20 cm. Max Gysi, editor. [BF1033.S78] 12-18074
1. Occult science. I. Gysi, Max, ed. II. Title.

STEINER, Rudolf, 1861-1925. 133
Occult science, an outline. Translated by Amud Breckenridge Monges and Henry Babad Monges. [2d ed.] New York, Anthroposophic Press, 1950. xxvi, 325 p. port. 24 cm. Translation of Die Geheimwissenschaft im Umriss. [BF1033.S712] 50-3555
1. Occult sciences. 2. Theosophy. I. Title.

STEINER, Rudolf, 1861-1925. 133
... Occult science--an outline; translated by Maud Breckenridge Monges and Henry Babad Monges. New York city, Anthroposophic press; London, Rudolf Steiner publishing co., 1939. xxx, 337 p. front. (port.) 24 cm. "This book ... formerly An outline of occult science, is an autorized, completely new translation of the latest original German text--Geheimwissenschaft im umriss--cotaining revisions and additions by the author, Dr. Rudolf Steiner: an entirely new preface; a completly rewritten fire chapter; considerable new matter not contained in previous English editions." [BF1033.S712 1939] 159.961 40-4020
1. Occult sciences. 2. Theosophy. I. Monges, Maude (Breckenridge) Mrs. 1874- tr. II. Monges, Henry Babad, joint tr. III. Title.

STEINER, Rudolf, 1861-1925. 133
An outline of occult science, by Rudolf Steiner, PH. D. Authorized translation from the 4th ed. Chicago, New York, Rand, McNally & company, 1914. xvi, 469 p. incl. front. (port.) 21 cm. "Max Gysi, editor." [BF1033.S73] 14-7733
1. Occult sciences. 2. Theosophy. I. Gysi, Max, ed. II. Title.

STONE, Robert B. 133
The power of miracle metaphysics / Robert B. Stone. West Nyack, N.Y. : Parker Pub. Co., c1976. 220 p. : ill. ; 24 cm. [BF1411.S85] 75-28309 ISBN 0-13-686683-2 : 8.95
1. Occult sciences. 2. Success. I. Title.

*STONELEY, Jack. 133
Is anyone out there? By Jack Stoneley with A. T. Lawton. [New York] Warner Paperback Library [1974] 288 p. 18 cm. Bibliography: p. 277-280. [BF1411] 1.25 (pbk.)
1. Occult sciences. I. Lawton, A. T. II. Title.

STOWE, Lyman E., 1843- 133.
Karmenia; or, What the spirit told me, "Truth stranger than fiction"; a series of short occult stories, real experiences during the life of a man 72 years of age, garnished in the clothes of faction ... by Lyman E. Stowe ... [Detroit, J. Bornman & son,] [c1918] [336] p. illus. (incl. port.) 20 cm. Various pagings. [BF1301.S8] 18-11293
I. Title.

TAIMNI, I. K. 1898- 133
Man, God and the universe, by I. K. Taimni. Wheaton, Ill. Theosophical Pub. House [1974, c1969] 447 p. illus. 21 cm. (A Quest book) [BF1429.T3] 71-906172 ISBN 0-8356-0447-0 3.45 (pbk.)
1. Occult sciences. I. Title.

TAIMNI, I. K., 1898- 133
Self-culture; the problem of self-discovery and self-realization in the light of occultism, by I. K. Taimni. Wheaton, Ill.,

Theosophical Pub. House [1970, c1967] xviii, 304 p. illus. 21 cm. (A Quest book) [BF1411.T13 1970] 70-104033 2.95
1. Occult sciences. 2. Yoga. I. Title.

TAIMNI, I. K., 1898- 133
Self-culture: the problem of self-discovery and self-realization in the light of occultism. By I. K. Taimni. [2d rev. ed.] Madras, Wheaton, Ill., Theosophical Pub. House, 1967. xviii, 304 p. illus. 21 cm. [BF1411.T13 1967] SA 68 12.00
1. Occult sciences. 2. Yoga. I. Title.

TAYLOR, C. Tousey. 133
Which? Impulse, instinct or intuition, by C. Tousey Taylor; applied psychology, geometry and astronomy. Seattle, Wash. [International printing co] 1919. 165 p. illus. (1 col.) 17 1/2 cm. [BF1999.T3] 19-19377
1. Occult sciences. I. Title.

THOMAS, Fred W., 1931- 239
Kingdom of darkness, by F. W. Thomas. Plainfield, N.J., Logos International [1973] xi, 158 p. 21 cm. Includes bibliographical references. [BF1411.T45] 73-75958 ISBN 0-88270-041-3 1.95
1. Occult sciences. 2. Spiritualism. I. Title.

TITUS, Justin E. 001.9
Alpha and omega : the beginning and end of the world / Justin E. Titus. [s.l.] : Titus, c1976. 104 p. ; 21 cm. [BF1999.T545] 75-44537
1. Occult sciences. I. Title.

TOFANI, Louise E 133
Cosmic revelations, by Theophany [pseud. 1st ed.] New York, Vantage Press [1957] 63p. 21cm. [BF1999.T6] 56-12772
1. Occult sciences. I. Title.

TOFANI, Louise E 133
Cosmic revelations, by Theophany [pseud. 1st ed.] New York, Vantage Press [1957] 63 p. 21 cm. [BF1999.T6] 56-12772
1. Occult sciences. I. Title.

*TRALINS, Robert. 133.3
Supernatural warnings. New York, Popular Library [1974] 192 p. 18 cm. [BF1411] 0.95 (pbk.)
1. Occult sciences. I. Title.

A treatise on white magic;
or, The way of the disciple. [6th ed.] New York, Lucis Pub. Co. [1956] 675p. 24cm.
1. Occult sciences. I. Bailey, Alice Anne (La Trobe-Bateman) 1880-1949. II. Title: White magic. III. Title: The way of the disciple.

TRITON, Pseud [Tibetan Dakini] 133.8
The magic of space. Larchmont, N.Y., P.O. Box 312, Triad Pub. Co., c.1962. 314p. 22cm. Bibl. 62-4472 7.50
1. Occult sciences. I. Title.

TRUETT, Jack R
The laws of cyclic motion; the link between physical and metaphysical science. [1st ed. York, Pa.] c1963. 169 l. diagrs. 28 cm. 64-45766
1. Occult sciences. 2. Metaphysics. 3. Astrology. I. Title.

TRYON, William Ernest, 1856- 133
Whither--Charon [By] William E. Tryon, M.D. Minneapolis, Minn. [c1925] 94, [1] p. diagrs. 15 1/2 cm. "Vital informaiton ...of philosophy, pschology, phsiology, religion and occultism; including explanations of after-death states, as given by those who are there." [BF1999.T7] 25-18795
1. Occult sciences. I. Title.

TUTTLE, Amber M. 133
The work of invisible helpers, by Amber M. Tuttle. New York, The Paebar company, 1945. 2 p. l., 635 p. 22 1/2 cm. [BF1999.T8] 45-6084
1. Occult sciences. I. Title.

USPENSKII, Petr Dem'ianovich, 1878- 197
A new model of the universe; principles of the psychological method in its application to problems of science, religion, and art, by P. D. Ouspensky. New York, A. A. Knopf, 1931. xv, 554 p. diagrs. 24 1/2 cm. Printed in Great Britain. "Translated from the ms. by R. R. Merton under the supervision of the author." [B4279.U73N43] [133] 31-32739
1. Occult sciences. 2. Fourth dimension. I. Merton, Reginald, tr. II. Title.
Contents omitted.

VADIS, John. 133
Adventures in consciousness; what happens when a man increases his conscious perception beyond normal limits. New York, Vantage Press [1953] 92p. 23cm. [BF1999.V28] 53-10312
1. Occult sciences. I. Title.

THE veritable black art:
a key to ... the occult sciences and ... witchcraft, being a ... historical elucidation of the theory and practice of magic, alchemy, necromancy, astrology, cartomancy, chiromancy, &c. together with directions for the making of gold; the raising of the dead; the calling up of spirits ... and laying bare the operations ... sorcerers, including an explanation of modern spiritualism, and all species of devination ... in vogue at the present day. By Merlin Secundus, (the living alchemist) New York, Hurst & co. [186-] 162 p. illus 16 cm. 1-20429

WAGNER, Belle M. Mrs. 133
Within the temple of Isis. By Belle M. Wagner. Denver Col., Astro-philosophical publishing co., 1899. 156 p. 17 cm. [BF1909.W2] 99-5907
1. Occult sciences. I. Title.

WAITE, Arthur Edward, 1857-1942. 133
The book of ceremonial magic; the secret tradition in Goetia, including the rites and mysteries of Goetic theurgy, sorcery, and infernal necromancy. New Hyde Park, N Y., University Books [c.1961] 336p. illus 61-9320 10.00
1. Occult sciences. 2. Magic. I. Title.

WAITE, Arthur Edward, 1857-1942. 133
The book of ceremonial magic; the secret tradition in Goetia, including the rites and mysteries of Goetic theurgy, sorcery, and infernal necromancy. New Hyde Park, N.Y., University Books [1961] 336 p. illus. 24 cm. A revision of the author's The book of black magic and of pacts, first published in 1898. [BF1611.W3 1961] 61-9320
1. Occult sciences. I. Title.

WARMAN, Edward Barrett, 1847-
Psychic science made plain, by Edward B. Warman ... Holyoke, Mass., Elizabeth Towne co. [c1914] 2 v. 20 cm. A 21
I. Title.

WATSON, Lyall. 133
Supernature. [1st ed. in U.S.] Garden City, N.Y., Anchor Press, 1973. xiv, 344 p. 22 cm. Bibliography: p. [317]-335. [BF1411.W35 1973] 72-92399 ISBN 0-385-00744-2 7.95
1. Occult sciences. 2. Psychical research. I. Title.

WATSON, Lyall. 133
Supernature. New York, Bantam Books [1974, c1973] 310 p. 18 cm. Bibliography: p. 283-300. [BF1411.W35 1974] 1.95 (pbk.)
1. Occult sciences. 2. Psychical research. I. Title.
L.C. card number for original ed.: 72-92399.

WE and the vague beyond.
[1st ed.] New York, Vantage Press [c1958] 60p. 21cm. d.]
1. Occult science. I. O58Toole, Edward J

WEDECK, Harry Ezekiel, 1894- 133.4
Treasury of witchcraft. New York, Philosophical Library [1960, c.1961] 271p. illus. p.265-270. Bibl.: 60-15919 10.00
1. Occult sciences. 2. Witchcraft. I. Title.

WEDECK, Harry Ezekiel, 1984- 133.4
Treasury of witchcraft. New York, Citadel [1966, c. 1961] 271p. illus. 21cm. (C-214) Bibl. [BF1411.W38] 2.25 pap.,
1. Occult sciences. 2. Witchcraft. I. Title.

WEED, Joseph J. 133
Psychic energy; how to change desires into realities [by] Joseph J. Weed. West Nyack, N.Y., Parker Pub. Co. [1970] 216 p. 24 cm. [BF1411.W39] 78-92527 6.95
1. Occult sciences. 2. Success. I. Title.

WELLESLEY, Gordon. 133
Sex and the occult. [New York] New American Library [1975, c1973] 222 p. 18 cm. (A Signet book) Bibliography: p. 217 [BF1411.W395] 1.50 (pbk.)
1. Occult sciences. 2. Sex. I. Title.
L.C. card number for original ed.: 73-175928

WHEATLEY, Dennis, 1897- 133
The devil and all his works. New York, American Heritage Press [1971] 302 p. illus. (part col.), maps, ports. 29 cm. [BF1411.W45 1971] 79-145620 ISBN 0-07-069501-6 14.95
1. Occult sciences. 2. Psychical research. I. Title.

WHITE, Theodore H.
...Dr. Theodore H. White's higher courses and complete system of occult science. A correspondence course in spiritualism, hypnotism, personal magnetism, mental healing, magnetic healing, planetary readings and white and black art, by Dr. Theodore H. White... 3d ed. Baltimore, Md., c1905. 208 p. illus. 38 cm. At head of title: Series A, B, D, E, F, G. [BF1439.W5] 11-9717
1. Occult sciences. I. Title.

[WHITNEY, Harvey Greene] 1891-
Initiation into occult consciousness, two minor and two major parts composing the final unity in one. Each part a complete, functioning unit in itself, yet a part in the ultimate five point, two aspect, seven plane, cosmic-unit. By: Dico Adrem [pseud.]... Los Angeles, Calif., The Austin publishing company [c1927] 123 p. diagrs. 20 cm. [BF1439.W65] 27-17834
1. Occult sciences. I. Title.

WIESINGER, Alois, 1885- 133
Occult phenomena in the light of theology. Westminster, Md., Newman Press, 1957. 294p. 22cm. 'Translated [from the German] by Brian Battershaw.'--Dust jacket. [BF1033.W512] 56-11423
1. Occult sciences. I. Title.

[WILLIAMS, Henry T.] 133
The secret book of the black arts. Containing all that is known upon the occult sciences of damonology, spirit rappings, witchcraft, sorcery, astrology, palmistry, mind reading, spiritualism, table turning, ghosts and apparitions, omens, lucky and unlucky signs and days, dreams, charms, divination, second sight, mesmerism, clairvoyance, psychological fascination, etc. ... New York, Hurst & co., c1878. 224 p. incl. front., illus. 16 1/2 cm. [BF1611.W75 1878 a] 15-22009
1. Occult sciences. 2. Magic. I. Title.

[WILLIAMS, Henry T.] (159.961)
The secret book of the black arts. Containing all that is known upon the occult sciences of daemonology, spirit rappings, witchcraft, sorcery, astrology, palmistry, mind reading, spiritualism, table turning, ghosts and apparitions, divination, second sight, mesmerism, clairvoyance, psychological fascination, etc. ... [New York?] 1878. 180 p. incl. front., illus. 20 cm. [BF1611.W75 1878] 133 (159.961) 34-15697
1. Occult sciences. 2. Magic. I. Title.

WILSON, Colin, 1931- 133
The occult; a history. New York, Vintage Books [1973, c1971] 601 p. 21 cm. Bibliography: p. [581]-586. [BF1411.W53 1973] 72-7474 ISBN 0-394-71813-5 3.95
1. Occult sciences. I. Title.

WILSON, Colin, 1931- 133
They had strange powers / by Colin Wilson. Garden City, N.Y. : Doubleday, 1975. 142 p. : ill. ; 27 cm. (A New library of the supernatural) British ed. published under title : Mysterious powers. [BF1411.W54 1975] 75-16748 7.95
1. Occult sciences. 2. Occult sciences—Biography. I. Title. II. Series.

WILSON, Colin, 1931- 133
The unexplained / Colin Wilson ; [edited by Robert Durand and Roberta Dyer]. Lake Oswego, OR : Lost Pleiade Press, 1975. 65 p. ; 20 cm. [BF1439.W68] 74-27923 ISBN 0-915270-00-5 : 3.50
1. Occult sciences. I. Title.

WILSON, Robert Anton, 1932- 001.9
Right where you are sitting now : further tales of the illuminati / Robert Anton Wilson. Berkeley, Calif. : And/Or Press, c1982. 207 p. : ill. ; 22 cm. [BF1999.W628 1982] 19 82-4084 ISBN 0-915904-71-3 pbk. : 6.95
1. Occult sciences. I. Title.
Publisher's address: P. O. Box 2246, Berkeley, CA 94702

WINSOR, Laura Ellen.
To eternity and back. [Chicago, Adams press; distributed by A. G. Winsor, San Francisco, 1960] 165 p. 23 cm. 65-9717
1. Occult sciences. I. Title.

WROUGHTON, Oliver Loraine. 270
Spiritual science, by Oliver Loraine Wroughton ... [Kansas City, Mo.] Franklin Hudson publishing co., 1918. 269 p. incl. front. (port.) 1 illus. 16 cm. [BR125.W85] 19-2789
I. Title.

Occult sciences—Addresses, essays, lectures.

BECKLEY, Timothy Green. 133
Witchcraft and occultism today. New York, Drake Publishers [1972] p. [BF1411.B43] 72-2422 ISBN 0-87749-286-7
1. Occult sciences—Addresses, essays, lectures. I. Title.

FUTURE science : 133.8
life energies and the physics of paranormal phenomena / edited by John White and Stanley Krippner. 1st ed. Garden City, N.Y. : Anchor Books, 1977. 598 p. : ill. ; 18 cm. Bibliography: p. [572]-581. [BF1411.F87] 76-23808 ISBN 0-385-11203-3 pbk. : 4.50
1. Occult sciences—Addresses, essays, lectures. 2. Psychical research—Addresses, essays, lectures. I. White, John Warren, 1939- II. Krippner, Stanley, 1932-

LEEK, Sybil. 133'.08
The best of Sybil Leek / edited by Glen A. Hilken. New York : Popular Library, c1974. 253 p. ; 18 cm. Includes bibliographical references. [BF1408.2.L44A29] 75-325035 1.50
1. Leek, Sybil. 2. Occult sciences—Addresses, essays, lectures. I. Title.

THE Satan trap : 133
dangers of the occult / edited by Martin Ebon. 1st ed. Garden City, N.Y. : Doubleday, 1976. xii, 276 p. ; 21 cm. [BF1411.S34] 75-14816 ISBN 0-385-07941-9 : 7.95
1. Occult sciences—Addresses, essays, lectures. 2. Psychical research—Addresses, essays, lectures. I. Ebon, Martin.

WILLIAMSON, John Jacob. 133
Metaphysical application, by J. J. Williamson. Hastings, Society of Metaphysicians Ltd., 1970. vi, 39 p. 21 cm. (New metaphysics, no. 3) (The Cranwell lectures, pt. 2) [BF1439.W54] 70-851799 ISBN 0-900684-12-7 10/6
1. Occult sciences—Addresses, essays, lectures. I. Title. II. Series.

Occult sciences—Biblical teaching.

BASHAM, Don, 1926- 220.8'133
The most dangerous game : a Biblical expose of occultism / Don Basham and Dick Leggatt. Greensburg, Pa. : Manna Christian Outreach, c1974. 128 p. ; 21 cm. Bibliography: p. 127-128. [BS680.O26B37] 74-23010 ISBN 0-8007-0726-5 pbk. : 1.95
1. Occult sciences—Biblical teaching. I. Leggatt, Dick, joint author. II. Title.

Occult sciences—Bibliography.

CLARIE, Thomas C., 1943- 016.133
Occult bibliography : an annotated list of books published in English, 1971 through 1975 / by Thomas C. Clarie. Metuchen, N.J. : Scarecrow Press, 1978. xxvii, 454 p. ; 23 cm. Includes indexes. [Z6876.C56] [BF1411] 78-17156 ISBN 0-8108-1152-9 : 20.00
1. Occult sciences—Bibliography. 2. Psychical research—Bibliography. I. Title.

HYRE, K. M. 016.133'029
Price guide to the occult and related subjects. Compiled by K. M. Hyre and Eli Goodman. Los Angeles, Reference Guides [1967] 380 p. 23 cm. [Z6876.H9] 67-7473
1. Occult sciences—Bibliography. 2. Books—Prices. I. Goodman, Eli, joint author. II. Title.

PHILLIPS, Leona. 133
The occult : hauntings, witchcraft, dreams, and all other avenues of paranormal phenomena : an annotated bibliography / by Leona and Jill Phillips. New York : Gordon Press, 1976. p. cm. (Gordon Press bibliographies for librarians series) [Z6876.P45] [BF1411] 76-55811 ISBN 0-8490-0748-8 lib. bdg. : 39.95
1. Occult sciences—Bibliography. 2. Psychical research—Bibliography. I. Phillips, Jill M., joint author. II. Title.

Occult sciences—Bibliography—Catalogs.

MACPHAIL, Ian, 1923- 016.133
Alchemy and the occult; a catalogue of books and manuscripts from the collection of Paul and Mary Mellon given to Yale University Library. With essays by R. P. Multhauf and Aniela Jaffe and additional notes by William McGuire. New Haven, Yale University Library, 1968- v. illus., facsims., ports. 32 cm. Vols. 1-2 issued in a case. 500 copies. Contents.—v. 1. Printed books, 1472-1623.—v. 2. Printed books, 1624-1790. Includes bibliographical references. [Z6880.M3] 68-11512
1. Jung, Carl Gustav, 1875-1961. 2. Occult sciences—Bibliography—Catalogs. 3. Alchemy—Bibliography—Catalogs. I. Yale University. Library. Beinecke Rare Book and Manuscript Library. II. Mellon, Paul. III. Mellon, Mary, 1905-1946. IV. Title.

Occult sciences—Biography.

COHEN, Daniel. 133'.0922
Masters of the occult. New York, Dodd, Mead [1971] x, 234 p. illus. 22 cm. Bibliography: p. 221-225. [BF1408.C63] 74-165669 ISBN 0-396-06407-8 5.95
1. Occult sciences—Biography. I. Title.

EYRE, John, 1918- 133.8'092'4 B
The god trip : the story of a mid-century man / John Eyre. 1st British Commonwealth ed. London : P. Owen, 1976. 155 p. ; 22 cm. [BF1997.E95A33 1976] 76-372181 ISBN 0-7206-0294-7 : £4.50
1. Eyre, John, 1918- 2. Occult sciences—Biography. I. Title.

INDEX to occult 133'.092'2 B
sciences. Garden City, N.Y. : Doubleday, 1977. 128 p. : ill. ; 27 cm. (A New library of the supernatural) Includes index to the 1st 19 volumes of the series. "Also published as guide to index." [BF1408.I5] 76-40569 ISBN 0-385-11326-9 : 8.95
1. A New library of the supernatural—Indexes. 2. Occult sciences—Biography. 3. Psychical research—Biography.

LILLIE, Arthur, 133'.092'2
b.1831.
Modern mystics and modern magic; containing a full biography of the Rev. William Stainton Moses, together with sketches of Swedenborg, Boehme, Madame Guyon, the Illuminati, the kabbalists, the theosophists, the French spiritists, the Society of Psychical Research, etc. Freeport, N.Y., Books for Libraries Press [1972] vii, 172 p. illus. 22 cm. (Essay index reprint series) Reprint of the 1894 ed. [BF1408.L53 1972] 72-5680 ISBN 0-8369-2996-9
1. Occult sciences—Biography. I. Title.

PETSCHEK, Joyce S. 133.9'3
The silver bird / Joyce S. Petschek. Millbrae, Calif. : Celestial Arts, c1981. p. cm. [BF1408.2.P47A37] 19 80-28074 ISBN 0-89087-284-8 : 8.95
1. Petschek, Joyce S. 2. Occult sciences—Biography. I. Title.

WILSON, Robert Anton, 1932- 133
Cosmic trigger : final secret of the illuminati / by Robert Anton Wilson ; illustrated by John Thompson. Berkeley, Calif. : And/Or Press, c1977. p. cm. Includes bibliographical references and index. [BF1408.2.W54A33] 77-89429 ISBN 0-915904-29-2 pbk. : 5.95
1. Wilson, Robert Anton, 1932- 2. Occult sciences—Biography. 3. Occult sciences. I. Title.

Occult sciences—California.

ST. Clair, David. 133'.09794
The psychic world of California. [1st ed.] Garden City, N.Y., Doubleday, 1972. x, 323 p. 22 cm. Bibliography: p. [317]-319. [BF1434.U6S23] 75-178834 7.95
1. Occult sciences—California. 2. Occult sciences—Biography. 3. Psychical research—California. 4. Psychical research—Biography. I. Title.

Occult sciences—Collections.

*CANNING, John, comp. 133
50 strange stories of the supernatural. New York, Bantam, [1975] ix., [470 p. 18 cm. [BF1031] 1.95 (pbk.)
1. Occult sciences—Collections. I. Title.

*EBON, Martin, comp. 133
The psychic scene, edited and with an introduction by Martin Ebon. [New York] New American Library [1974] 188 p. 18 cm. [BF1031] 1.25 (pbk.)
1. Occult sciences—Collections. I. Title.

Occult sciences—Dictionaries.

BASKIN, Wade. 133.4'2'03
Dictionary of Satanism. New York, Philosophical Library [1971, c1972] 351 p. illus. 22 cm. [BF1407.B37 1972] 75-155971 ISBN 0-8022-2056-8 12.50
1. Occult sciences—Dictionaries. I. Title.

BASKIN, Wade. 133'.03
The sorcerer's handbook. New York, Philosophical Library [1974] 635 p. illus. 22 cm. [BF1407.B39] 73-77399 ISBN 0-8022-2112-2 15.00
1. Occult sciences—Dictionaries. 2. Psychical research—Dictionaries. I. Title.

*BYFIELD, Barbara Ninde. 133
The book of the weird; being a most desirable lexicon of the fantastical, wherein kings and dragons, trolls and vampires, to say nothing of elves and gnomes, queens, knaves and werewolves are made manifest, and many, many further revelations of the mystical order of things are brought to light, by Barbara Ninde Byfield. Illus. by the author. Garden City, N.Y., Doubleday [1973, c.1967] 160 p. illus. 28 cm. (A Dolphin herald, C525) [BF1411] ISBN 0-385-06591-4 3.95 (pbk.)
1. Occult sciences—Dictionaries. 2. Supernatural—Dictionaries. I. Title.

CHAMBERS, Howard V., comp. 133
An occult dictionary for the millions. Los Angeles, Sherbourne Press [1966] 160 p. 21 cm. (For the millions series, FM-5) [BF1025.C5] 66-26077
1. Occult sciences—Dictionaries. I. Title.

*CHAPLIN, James P. 133.03
Dictionary of the occult and paranormal / J. P. Chaplin; illustrated by Aline Demers New York : Dell ,1976 xi, 176 p. : ill. ; 18 cm. [BF1407] pbk. : 1.95
1. Occult sciences—Dictionaries. I. Title.

THE Encyclopedia of occult 133
sciences. Introd. by M. C. Poinsot. New York, R. M. McBride. Detroit, Gale Research Co., 1972. 496 p. illus. 22 cm. Reprint of 1939 ed. Includes bibliographical references. [BF1407.E5 1972] 75-78148
1. Occult sciences—Dictionaries. I. Poinsot, Maffeo Charles, 1872-

THE encyclopedia of occult 133.03
sciences; introduction by M. C. Poinsot. New York, R. M. McBride and company [1939] 496 p. illus., diagrs. 24 1/2 cm. "The author has desired to remain annonymous."--p. 13. [BF1025.E5] 39-33585
1. Occult sciences—Dictionaries. I. Poinsot, Maffeo Charles, 1872-

ENCYCLOPEDIA of occultism 133'.03
& parapsychology / edited by Leslie Shepard ; editorial assistants, Claudia Dembinski, Susan Hutton. Detroit : Gale Research Co., c1977. p. cm. "Compiled from Encyclopaedia of the occult, by Lewis Spence, London, 1920, and Encyclopaedia of psychic science by Nandor Fodor, London, 1934, with additional material edited by Leslie Shepard." "A compendium of information on the occult sciences, magic, demonology, superstitions, spiritism, mysticism, metaphysics, psychical science, parapsychology, with biographical and bibliographical notes and comprehensive indexes." [BF1407.E52] 77-92 ISBN 0-8103-0185-7 : 48.00 (set)
1. Occult sciences—Dictionaries. 2. Psychical research—Dictionaries. I. Shepard, Leslie. II. Dembinski, Claudia. III. Hutton, Susan. IV. Spence, Lewis, 1874-1955. An encyclopaedia of occultism. V. Fodor, Nandor. Encyclopaedia of psychic science.

ENCYCLOPEDIA of 133'.03'21
occultism & parapsychology : a compendium of information on the occult sciences, magic, demonology, superstitions, spiritism, mysticism, metaphysics, physical science, and parapsychology, with biographical and bibliographical notes and comprehensive indexes. Supplement / edited by Leslie Shepard. Detroit, Mich. : Gale Research Co., c1982. vii, 231 p. ; 29 cm. "Cumulative index encompassing both the supplementary material [in Occultism update, 1978-1981] and the material in the basic Encyclopedia"—Pref. Includes index. [BF1407.E52 Suppl] 19 82-3077 ISBN 0-8103-0196-2 : 125.00
1. Occult sciences—Dictionaries. 2. Psychical research—Dictionaries. I. Shepard, Leslie. II. Encyclopedia of occultism & parapsychology. III. Title: Encyclopedia of occultism and parapsychology.

SPENCE, Lewis, 1874-1955. 133.03
An encyclopaedia of occultism; a compendium of information on the occult sciences, occult personalities, psychic science, magic, demonology, spiritism, mysticism, and metaphysics. New York, Strathmore Press [1960, c1959] xxiv, 440 p. illus., ports. 26 cm. "Originally published in 1920 ... Reprint ... now verbatim, except for an occasional correction of a misprint." Bibliography: p. xxiii-xxiv. [BF1025.S7 1960] 59-15875
1. Occult sciences—Dictionaries.

TELESTIC guild, Tampa, 133.03
Fla.
The students' dictionary; a glossary of extensively used metaphysical, philosophical, theurgic words; with an astrological supplement ... Tampa, Fla., The Telestic guild, 1936. 131 p. 22 1/2 cm. "Astrological supplement" (p. [97]-131) has special t.-p., with diagr. [BF1025.T4] [159.96103] 36-17606
1. Occult sciences—Dictionaries. 2. Astrology—Dictionaries. I. Title.

WALKER, George Benjamin, 001.9
1913-
Man and the beasts within : the encyclopedia of the occult, the esoteric, and the supernatural / Benjamin Walker. New York : Stein and Day, 1977. x, 343 p. ; 25 cm. Includes bibliographies and index. [BF1407.W34 1977] 76-42238 ISBN 0-8128-1900-4 : 24.25
1. Occult sciences—Dictionaries. 2. Body, Human—Dictionaries. I. Title.

Occult sciences—Directories

HARTMANN'S international directory of psychic science and spiritualism ... issued under the auspices of the Occult brotherhood ... 1930 Jamaica, N. Y., The Occult press [c1930- v. 24 cm. annual. Editor: 1930- W. C. Hartmann. Contains bibliographies. [BF1409.H25] 30-6076
1. Occult sciences—Direct. 2. Spiritualism-Direct. I. Hartman, William C., 1869- ed.

HARTMANN'S who's who in occult, psychic and spiritual realms ... in the United States and foreign countries, compiled and edited by William C. Hartman ... to be issued annually, about October first under the auspices of the Occult brotherhood ... Jamaica, N. Y., The Occult press [c1925- v. 24 cm. [BF1409.H3] 26-529
1. Occult sciences—Direct. 2. Spiritualism.—Direct. I. Hartman, William C., ed. II. Title: Who's who in occult, psychic and spiritual realms.

HOLZER, Hans W., 133'.025'73
1920-
The directory of the occult [by] Hans Holzer. Chicago, H. Regnery Co. [1974] x, 201 p. 22 cm. "Official publication of the New York Committee for the Investigation of Paranormal Occurrences." [BF1409.H6] 74-6895 ISBN 0-8092-8377-8 ISBN 0-8092-8377-8 8.95
1. Occult sciences—Directories. I. New York Committee for the Investigation of Paranormal Occurrences. II. Title.
Pbk. 3.95; ISBN 0-8092-8338-7.

Occult sciences—Early works to 1900.

AGRIPPA von Nettesheim, 133.4
Heinrich Cornelius, 1486?-1535.
The philosophy of natural magic : a complete work on natural magic, white magic, black magic, divination, occult binding, sorceries, and their power. Unctions, love medicines and their virtues .... / Henry Cornelius Agrippa von Nettesheim ; new forward [sic] to 1974 ed. by Leslie Shepard. Official ed. Secaucus, N.J. : University Books, [1974] 307 p. : ill. ; 22 cm. Translation of book 1 of De occulta philosophia. Reprint of p. [5]-307 of the 1913 ed. published by De Laurence, Scott, Chicago. [BF1598.A3D4313 1974] 74-196072 ISBN 0-8216-0218-7 : 8.95
1. Occult sciences—Early works to 1900. 2. Magic. I. Title.

AGRIPPA von Nettesheim, 133
Heinrich Cornelius, 1486?-1535.
Three books of occult philosophy or magic. Book one—Natural magic which includes the early life of Agrippa, his seventy-four chapters on natural magic, new notes, illustrations, index, and other original and selected matter. Edited by Willis F. Whitehead. By direction of the Brotherhood of Magic: The magic mirror, a message to mystics containing full instructions on its make and use. New York, S. Weiser, 1971. 288 p. illus. 24 cm. On spine: Occult philosophy or magic. Translation of Book 1 of De occulta philosophia. "First published 1897." The 2d and 3d books were not published. [BF1598.A3O533 1971] 70-166413
1. Occult sciences—Early works to 1900. I. Title. II. Title: Occult philosophy or magic.

BARRETT, Francis. 133
The magus. With a new introd. by Timothy d'Arch Smith. New Hyde Park, N.Y., University Books [1967] xxii, 198 p. port. 26 cm. Half title: The magus; or Celestial intelligence, being a complete system of occult philosophy. Reprint of the 1801 ed. [BF1611.B3 1967] 67-22946
1. Occult sciences—Earley works to 1900. 2. Alchemy. 3. Magic. I. Title. II. Title: Celestial intellignece, being a complete system of occult philosophy.

CIRUELO, Pedro, 1470(ca.)- 133.4
1560.
Pedro Ciruelo's A treatise reproving all superstitions and forms of witchcraft : very necessary and useful for all good Christians zealous for their salvation / translated by Eugene A. Maio and D'Orsay W. Pearson ; annotated and with an introd. by D'Orsay W. Pearson. Rutherford : Fairleigh Dickinson University Press, c1975. p. cm. Translation of Reprobacion da las supersticiones y hechicerias. Includes bibliographical references and index. [BF1410.C5713] 74-4979 ISBN 0-8386-1580-5 : 22.50
1. Occult sciences—Early works to 1900. 2. Superstition. I. Title. II. Title: A treatise reproving all superstitions and forms of witchcraft.

DENDY, Walter Cooper, 1794- 133
1871.
The philosophy of mystery. [Folcroft, Pa.] Folcroft Library Editions, 1974. 442 p. 24 cm. Reprint of the 1845 ed. published by Harper, New York. [BF1412.D4 1974] 74-2364 ISBN 0-8414-3723-8 (lib. bdg.)
1. Occult sciences—Early works to 1900. 2. Psychical research—Early works to 1900. 3. Dreams. I. Title.

KIESEWETTER, Karl, 1854-1895. 133 S
Die Geheimwissenschaften / Karl Kiesewetter. New York : Arno Press, 1976. (The Occult) (His Geschichte des neueren Occultismus ; v. 2) Reprint of the 1895 ed. published by W. Friedrich, Leipzig. [BF1429.K4 vol. 2] [BF1413] 133 76-74
1. Occult sciences—Early works to 1900. I. Title. II. Series. III. Series: The Occult (New York, 1976-)

KIESEWETTER, Karl, 1854-1895. 133
Geschichte des neueren Occultismus / Karl Kiesewetter. New York : Arno Press, 1976. p. cm. (The Occult) Vol. 2 has also special title: Die Geheimwissenschaften. Reprint of the 1891-95 ed. published by W. Friedrich, Leipzig. [BF1429.K4 1976] 75-36847 ISBN 0-405-07961-3
1. Occult sciences—Early works to 1900. I. Title. II. Series: The Occult (New York, 1976-)

KIESEWETTER, Karl, 1854-1895. 133
Der Occultismus des Altertums / Karl Kiesewetter. New York : Arno Press, 1976. p. cm. (The Occult) Continued after the author's death by L. Kuhlenbeck. Reprint of the 1895-96 ed. published by W. Friedrich, Leipzig. [BF1421.K4 1976] 75-36846 ISBN 0-405-07958-3
1. Occult sciences—Early works to 1900. I. Kuhlenbeck, Ludwig, 1857-1920. II. Title. III. Series: The Occult (New York, 1976-)

Occult sciences—Findhorn, Scot.

THE Findhorn garden 133'.09412'23
/ by the Findhorn community ; foreword by William Irwin Thompson. 1st ed. New York : Harper & Row, c1975. xi, 180 p. : ill. ; 25 cm. "A Lindisfarne book." [BF1434.G7F56] 75-6335 ISBN 0-06-011249-2 : 10.00.
1. Occult sciences—Findhorn, Scot. 2. Psychical research—Findhorn, Scot. 3. Gardening—Scotland—Findhorn.

THE Findhorn garden 133'.09412'23
/ by the Findhorn Community ; foreword by Sir George Trevelyan, bt. London : Turnstone Books : Wildwood House, 1976. xii, 180 p. : ill., ports. ; 24 cm. [BF1434.G7F56 1976] 76-372356 ISBN 0-7045-0230-5 £5.50. ISBN 0-7045-0231-3 pbk.
1. Occult sciences—Findhorn, Scot. 2. Psychical research—Findhorn, Scot. 3. Gardening—Scotland—Findhorn.

HAWKEN, Paul. 133'.09412'23
The magic of Findhorn / Paul Hawken. 1st ed. New York : Harper & Row, [1975] 216 p. ; 24 cm. [BF1434.S3H38 1975] 74-15831 ISBN 0-06-011787-7 : 8.95
1. Occult sciences—Findhorn, Scot. 2. Psychical research—Findhorn, Scot. I. Title.

Occult sciences—France—Rennes-le-Chateau.

FANTHORPE, P. A. 001.9'4
The Holy Grail revealed : the real secret of Rennes-le-Chateau / by Patricia and Lionel Fanthorpe ; edited by R. Reginald. San Bernardino, Calif. : Borgo Press, 1982. p. cm. [BF1434.F8F36 1982] 19 82-4303 ISBN 0-89370-660-4 : 12.95
1. Sauniere, Berenger, 1852-1917. 2. Occult sciences—France—Rennes-le-Chateau. 3. Rennes-le-Chateau (France)—Miscellanea. 4. Treasure-trove—France—Rennes-le-Chateau. I. Fanthorpe, R. Lionel. II. Reginald, R. III. Title.

FANTHORPE, P. A. 001.9'4
The Holy Grail revealed : the real secret of Rennes-le-Chateau / Patricia & Lional Fanthorpe ; edited and with an introduction by R. Reginald ; line drawings by Patrick Kirby. 1st ed. North Hollywood, Calif. : Newcastle Pub. Co., 1982. 143 p. : ill. ; 22 cm. [BF1434.F8F36 1982b] 19 82-6315 ISBN 0-87877-060-7 (pbk.) : 5.95
1. Sauniere, Berenger, 1852-1917. 2. Occult sciences—France—Rennes-le-Chateau. 3. Rennes-le-Chateau (France)—Miscellanea. 4. Treasure-trove—France—Rennes-le-Chateau. I. Fanthorpe, R. Lionel. II. Reginald, R. III. Title.

Occult sciences—Georgia.

CROY, Eugene. 299'.7'09758265
Spooks / Eugene Croy. Cumming, Ga. : Croy, c1976. viii, 118 p. : ill. ; 23 cm. [BF1434.U6C76] 77-350352
1. Occult sciences—Georgia. 2. Indians of North America—Georgia—Antiquities. 3. Georgia—Antiquities. I. Title.

Occult sciences—Germany.

ANGEBERT, Jean Michel. 135.4'0943
The occult and the Third Reich; the mystical origins of Nazism and the search for the Holy Grail. Translated by Lewis A. M. Sumberg. [1st American ed.] New York, Macmillan [1974] xix, 306 p. illus. 21 cm. Translation of Hitler et la tradition cathare. Bibliography: p. 283-289. [DD247.H5A81713 1974] 73-2748 ISBN 0-02-502150-8 7.95
1. Hitler, Adolf, 1889-1945. 2. Occult sciences—Germany. 3. National socialism—History. I. Title.

ANGEBERT, Jean Michel. 135.4'0943
The occult and the Third Reich : the mystical origins of Nazism and the search for the Holy Grail / Jean-Michel Angebert ; translated by Lewis A. M. Sumberg. New York : McGraw-Hill, 1975, c1974. p. cm. Translation of Hitler et la tradition cathare. Bibliography: p. [DD247.H5A81713 1975] 75-23473 ISBN 0-07-001850-2 pbk. : 3.95
1. Hitler, Adolf, 1889-1945. 2. Occult sciences—Germany. 3. National socialism—History. I. Title.

Occult sciences—Haiti.

HUXLEY, Francis. 133'.097294
The invisibles; Voodoo gods in Haiti. [1st U.S. ed.] New York, McGraw-Hill [1969, c1966] 247 p. 22 cm. [BF1434.H2H8 1969] 68-17506
1. Occult sciences—Haiti. 2. Voodooism. 3. Haiti—Social life and customs. I. Title.

Occult sciences—History

BURLAND, Cottie Arthur, 1905- 133.4
The magical arts; a short history [by] C. A. Burland. [1st American ed.] New York, Horizon Press [1966] viii, 196 p. illus. 23 cm. [BF1411.B85 1966a] 66-25192
1. Occult sciences—History. I. Title.

DODDS, Eric Robertson, 1893-
The Greeks and the irrational, [2d paperbounded ed.] Berkeley, University of California Press, 1963. 327 p. (Cal 74) Originally publsihed as v. 25 of the Sather classical lectures. Includes bibliography. 64-35808
1. Occult sciences — Hist. 2. Civilization, Greek. I. Title.

EDWARDES, Michael. 133.4
Dark side of history : magic in the making of man / Michael Edwardes. Briarcliff Manor, N.Y. : Stein and Day, [1977] p. cm. Includes index. Bibliography: p. [BF1411.E33] 76-44265 10.00
1. Occult sciences—History. I. Title.

THE Greeks and the irrational.
Berkeley, University of California Press, 1956. 327p. (Sather classical lectures, v. 25) Includes bibliographical notes.
1. Occult sciences—Hist. 2. Civilization—Greece. I. Dodds, Eric Robertson, 1893- II. Series.

HALL, Manly Palmer. 133
First principles of philosophy; the science of perfection, by Manly P. Hall. 1st ed. Los Angeles, Calif., The Phoenix press, 1935. 2 p. l., 3-165 p. 19 cm. [BF1999.H3243] 37-3063
1. Occult sciences—Hist. 2. Philosophy, Ancient. 3. Metaphysics. I. Title.

HALL, Manly Palmer. 133
Man, the grand symbol of the mysteries, by Manly Hall. [Los Angeles, Manly P. Hall publications, 1932] 254 p. illus. (incl. ports., facsim.) pl. 27 1/2 cm. "Essays in occult anatomy."--p. [1] "The lore of the human body ... [as found in the writings of] a wide diversity of old authorities."--pref. "Second edition." [BF1999.H3285 1932] 33-2303
1. Occult sciences—Hist. 2. Metaphysics. 3. Symbolism. 4. Human figure in literature. I. Title. II. Title: Theosophy.

HALL, Manly Palmer, 1901- 133
The adepts in the Western esoteric tradition. Los Angeles, Philosophical Research Society [1949- v. illus., ports. 24 cm. Contents.pt. 1. Orders of the Quest. [PF1999.H313] 50-230
1. Occult sciences—Hist. I. Title.

HALL, Manly Palmer, 1901- 135.4
An encyclopedic outline of Masonic, Hermetic, Qabbalistic, and Rosicrucian symbolical philosophy : being an interpretation of the secret teachings concealed within the rituals, allegories, and mysteries of all ages / by Manly P. Hall. Golden anniversary ed. Los Angeles : Philosophical Research Society, 1975 [c1928] ccxlv p., [48] col. leaves of plates (2 fold.) : ill. ; 48 cm. At head of title: The secret teachings of all ages. "The illustrations in color by J. Augustus Knapp." One port. accompanied by superposed transparent overlay. L.C. copy no. 428 signed by the author. Reprint of the subscriber's ed. (1928) printed by H. S. Crocker Co., San Francisco; with a new pref. and foreword. Includes index. Bibliography: p. ccv-ccxi. [BF1411.H3 1975] 76-356549
1. Occult sciences—History. 2. Symbolism. 3. Mysteries, Religious. 4. Secret societies. I. Knapp, J. Augustus. II. Title: An encyclopedic outline of ... III. Title: The secret teachings of all ages.

HALL, Manly Palmer, 1901- 133
First principles of philosophy; direction of mental activity in the science of perfection... 2d enl. ed. Los Angeles, Philosophical Research Society [1949] 199 p. illus. 24 cm. [[BF1999.H]] (159.961) A 51
1. Occult sciences—Hist. 2. Philosophy, Ancient. 3. Metaphysics. I. Title.

HALL, Manly Palmer, 1901- 133.09
The Phoenix; An illustrated review of occultism and philosophy. 4th ed. Los Angeles, Philosophical Research Society, 1960. 175 p. illus., ports. 35 cm. [BF1411.H35] 63-24640
1. Occult sciences—Hist. I. Title.

JASTROW, Joseph, 1863- 133.7
Wish and wisdon; episodes in the vagaries of belief, by Joseph Jastrow. New York, London, D. Appleton-Century company, incorporated, 1935. xiv p., 1 l., 394 p. illus., plates (1 col.) ports. 23 cm. [AZ999.J3] 159.9618 35-27176
1. Occult sciences—Hist. 2. Psychical research. 3. Credulity. I. Title.

JASTROW, Joseph, 1863-1944 133.7
Error and eccentricity in human belief [Orig. title: Wish and wisdom, episodes in the vagaries of belief] New York, Dover [1962, c.1935] 394p. illus. 22cm. (T986) 1.85 pap.,
1. Occult sciences—Hist. 2. Psychical research. 3. Credulity. I. Title.

JASTROW, Joseph, 1863-1944.
Error and eccentricity in human belief (formerly title: Wish and wisdom, episodes in the vagaries of belief) New York, Dover Publications [1962] xiv, 394 p. illus., plates, ports. "Unabridged republication of the work first published by D. Appleton-Century Company in 1935 under the former title." 63-22218
1. Occult sciences—Hist. 2. Psychical research. 3. Credulity. I. Title.

SHUMAKER, Wayne. 133'.09'024
The occult sciences in the Renaissance; a study in intellectual patterns. Berkeley, University of California Press [1972] xxi, 284 p. illus. 26 cm. Bibliography: p. 260-266. [BF1429.S58] 70-153552 ISBN 0-520-02021-9 15.00
1. Occult sciences—History. I. Title.

WEBB, James, 1946- 133'.09
The occult establishment / James Webb. La Salle, Ill. : Open Court Pub. Co., 1975. p. cm. "A Library Press book." [BF1429.W4] 75-22157 ISBN 0-912050-56-X : 12.50
1. Occult sciences—History. I. Title.

YATES, Frances Amelia 133
Giordano Bruno and the Hermetic tradition [Chicago] Univ. of Chic. Pr. [c.1964] xiv, 466p. illus. 23cm. Bibl. 64-10094 7.50
1. Bruno, Giordano, 1548-1600. 2. Occult sciences—Hist. I. Title.

Occult sciences—Hungary.

TABORI, Cornelius, 1879-1944. 133.0924
My occult diary. Translated and edited by Paul Tabori. New York, Living Books [1966] 251 p. ports. 23 cm. [BF1434.H8T3] 66-18472
1. Occult sciences — Hungary. I. Tabori, Paul, ed. and tr. II. Title.

Occult sciences—India.

JACOLLIOT, Louis, 1837-1890. 133'.0954
Occult science in India and among the ancients, with an account of their mystic initiations and the history of spiritism. New foreword by Omar V. Garrison. Translated from the French by William L. Felt. New Hyde Park, N.Y., University Books [1971] xvi, 274 p. 22 cm. First published in 1884. Translation of Le spiritisme dans le monde. [BF1434.I4J2 1971] 73-118606 5.95
1. Occult sciences—India. 2. Brahmanism. I. Title.

Occult sciences—Juvenile literature.

DICKINSON, Peter, 1927- 133
Chance, luck, & destiny / by Peter Dickinson. 1st American ed. Boston : Little, Brown, c1976. 254 p. : illus. ; 24 cm. "An Atlantic Monthly Press book." A collection of anecdotes, stories, facts, and activities relating to chance, luck, magic, witchcraft, and fortune-telling. [BF1411.D53 1976] 75-28403 ISBN 0-316-18428-4 : 9.95
1. Occult sciences—Juvenile literature. 2. Chance—Juvenile literature. 3. [Occult sciences.] 4. [Chance.] I. Title.

ESTERER, Arnulf K. 133.8
The occult world / Arnulf K. Esterer and Louise A. Esterer. New York : J. Messner, c1978. 223 p. ; 22 cm. Includes index. Bibliography: p. 216-218. Defines, gives the history, and provides examples of a variety of occult phenomena including ESP, ghosts, spirit possession, precognition, and others. [BF1411.E77] 78-18267 ISBN 0-671-32876-X : 7.79
1. Occult sciences—Juvenile literature. 2. Psychical research—Juvenile literature. 3. [Occult sciences.] 4. [Psychical research.] I. Esterer, Louise A., joint author. II. Title.

HAISLIP, Barbara. 133
Stars, spells, secrets, and sorcery / by Barbara Haislip. 1st ed. Boston : Little, Brown, c1975. p. cm. Bibliography: p. Examines the origins, uses, and meaning of astrology, graphology, palmistry, Tarot cards, ESP, and other ways of foretelling the future or divining individual fortunes. [BF1411.H27] 75-28360 ISBN 0-316-33820-6 : 7.95
1. Occult sciences—Juvenile literature. 2. [Occult sciences.] I. Title.

Occult sciences—Mexico.

ST. Clair, David. 133'.0972
Pagans, priests, and prophets : a personal investigation into the living traditions of occult Mexico / David St. Clair. Englewood Cliffs, N.J. : Prentice-Hall, c1976. 218 p., [4] leaves of plates : ill. ; 22 cm. Includes index. [BF1434.M6S24] 76-26457 ISBN 0-13-647727-5 : 8.95
1. Occult sciences—Mexico. 2. Mexico—Religion. I. Title.

Occult sciences—Miscellanea.

SARAYDARIAN, Torkom. 133
The psyche and psychism / by Torkom Saraydarian. Agoura, Calif. : Aquarian Educational Group, c1981. iv, 1214 p. : ill. ; 32 cm. Includes bibliographical references. [BF1999.S3377 1981] 19 80-67684 ISBN 0-911794-06-9 (set) : 50.00
1. Occult sciences—Miscellanea. 2. Psychical research—Miscellanea. I. Title.

Publisher's address: 30188 Mulholland Hwy., Agoura, CA 91301

SCHUTZ, Albert L. 135'.42
Call Adonoi : manual of practical Cabalah and Gestalt mysticism / Albert L. Schutz. 1st ed. Goleta, Calif. : Quantal, c1980. xvi, 100 p. : ill. ; 23 cm. [BF1999.S3614] 19 80-50264 ISBN 0-936596-00-7 (pbk.) : 8.95
1. Occult sciences—Miscellanea. 2. Cabala—Miscellanea. 3. Mysticism—Miscellanea. I. Title.

Occult sciences—New England.

MATHER, Increase, 1639-1723. 133
An essay for the recording of illustrious providences / Increase Mather. New York : Garland Pub., 1977. 372 p. ; 16 cm. (The Garland library of narratives of North American Indian captivities ; v. 2) Reprint of the 1684 ed. printed by S. Green for J. Browning, Boston. [E85.G2 vol. 2] [BF1434.U6] 75-7021 ISBN 0-8240-1626-2 lib.bdg. : 25.00
1. Occult sciences—New England. 2. Supernatural. 3. Indians of North America—Captivities. I. Title. II. Series.

Occult sciences—Oriental.

*DANE, Christopher. 133
The occult in the orient. New York, Popular Library [1974] 190 p. 18 cm. [BF1411] 0.95 (pbk.)
1. Occult sciences—Oriental. I. Title.

Occult sciences—Periodicals

THE Hidden world. 133'.05
[Editor: Ray Palmer. Mundelein, Ill., Palmer Publications, 1961- p. illus., facsims., ports. 24 cm. Cover title. Issued serially. Includes the Shaver mystery by R. S. Shaver. [BF1001.G54] 72-23672
1. Occult sciences—Periodicals. I. Palmer, Ray, 1910- ed. II. Shaver, Richard S.

THE Record 133.05
v.1-3, no.1; Sept./Oct. 1949-Jan./Feb. 1951 [New York, Philosophical Research] c3v. in 1. illus. (part col.) 29cm. 5 no. a year (irregular) No more published? [BF1995.R4] 59-31713
1. Occult sciences—Period. I. Philosophical Research, New York.

Occult sciences—Societies, etc.

CULLING, Louis T. 133.4'3
The complete magick curriculum of the secret order G. .B. .G. ., by Louis T. Culling. Being the entire study curriculum, magick rituals, and initiatory practices of the G. .B. .G. . (The Great Brotherhood of God) Saint Paul, Minn., Llewellyn Publications, 1969. 127 p. illus. (part col.), port. 26 cm. [BF1995.C8] 76-14668 ISBN 0-87542-102-4 10.00
1. Great Brotherhood of God (Secret order) 2. Occult sciences—Societies, etc. I. Title.

Occult sciences—Study and teaching.

COLVILLE, William J.
Spiritual science; an advanced course of lessons, by W. J. Colville. Part ii of "The people's hand-book." New York, The Alliance publishing company, 1903. 87 p. 19 cm. 3-9567
I. Title.

HALL, Manly Palmer. 133
Talks to students on occult philosophy, by Manly P. Hall. 2d ed. Los Angeles, Hall publishing company, 1929. 64 p. 17 cm. "Literature for the occult student": p. 48-56. Advertising matter: p. 58-64. [BF1999.H335 1929] ca 30
1. Occult sciences—Study and teaching. I. Title.

Occult sciences—United States.

COOPER, John Charles. 133'.0973
Religion in the age of Aquarius. Philadelphia, Westminster Press [1971] 175 p. 19 cm. [BF1434.U6C6] 77-133618 ISBN 0-664-24905-1 2.45
1. Occult sciences—U.S. 2. U.S.—Religion. I. Title.

FREEDLAND, Nat, 1936- 133'.0973
The occult explosion. New York, Putnam [1972] 270 p. 22 cm. [BF1434.U6F73] 74-175261 6.95
1. Occult sciences—U.S. 2. Psychical research—U.S. I. Title.

GODWIN, John, 1928- 133'.0973
Occult America. [1st ed.] Garden City, N.Y., Doubleday, 1972. xvii, 314 p. illus. 22 cm. [BF1434.U6G6] 79-168289 7.95
1. Occult sciences—U.S. 2. Psychical research—U.S. I. Title.

LEVENTHAL, Herbert, 1941- 133'.0973
In the shadow of the Enlightenment : occultism and Renaissance science in eighteenth century America / Herbert Leventhal. New York : New York University Press, 1976. 330 p. : ill. ; 24 cm. Includes index. Bibliography: p. 272-314. [BF1434.U6L38] 75-13762 ISBN 0-8147-4965-8 : 18.00
1. Occult sciences—United States. 2. United States—Intellectual life—18th century. I. Title.

LOGAN, Daniel, 1936- 133'.0973
America bewitched; the rise of black magic and spiritism. New York, Morrow 1974 [c1973] 187 p. 21 cm. Bibliography: p. 179. [BF1434.U6L63 1974] 73-12734 ISBN 0-688-00221-8 5.95
1. Logan, Daniel, 1936- 2. Occult sciences—United States. I. Title.

Occult sciences—United States—Biography.

FRANCIS, Anne, 1932- 133.8'092'4 B
Voices from home : an inner journey / Anne Francis ; drawings by Chris Nickens. Millbrae, Calif. : Celestial Arts, c1982. 153 p. : ill. ; 23 cm. [BF1408.2.F73A38 1982] 19 82-4308 ISBN 0-89087-340-2 (pbk.) : 9.95
1. Francis, Anne, 1932- 2. Occult sciences—United States—Biography. 3. Actors—United States—Biography. I. Title.

MANNING, Al G. 133'.092'4 B
Eye of newt in my martini : a certified public accountant turned occultist tells why and how / by Al G. Manning. Los Angeles, CA : Pan/Ishtar Unlimited, c1981. 192 p. ; 23 cm. [BF1408.2.M36A33 1981] 19 81-84169 ISBN 0-941698-01-7 : 12.95
1. Manning, Al G. 2. Occult sciences—United States—Biography. I. Title.
Publisher's address: 7559 Santa Monica Blvd., LA 90046

Occultism.

BLAND, Oliver.
The adventures of a modern occultist, by Oliver Bland. New York, Dodd, Mead and company, 1920. viii p., 3 l., 221 p. 19 cm. $2.00 [BF1261.B5] 20-17101
I. Title.

[MURRAY-FORD, Alice May (Harte-Potts) Mrs.] 1879- 133
The white-magic book, by Mrs. John Le Breton [pseud.] Philadelphia, G. W. Jacobs & co. [c1920] xxx, 5-100 p. illus. 19 cm. Lettered on cover: John Le Breton. [BF1611.M8] 21-9737
I. Title.

*SOLOMON, Paul. 133.8
Excerpts from the Paul Solomon tapes; [a sleeping man speaks on] Virginia Beach, Va., Heritage Publications, 1974. ix, 149 p. 24 cm. [BF1301] 4.95
1. Occultism. I. Title.
Publisher's address: Box 444 Virginia Beach Va., 23458.

WILTSE, May Barnard. 133
Who is God ... who is the devil? or, A scientific God, by May Barnard Wiltse. [Los Angeles 1930] 168 p. incl. front., illus. 17 1/2 cm. [X3.W53] 39-33990
I. Title.

Occultism in literature.

SAURAT, Denis, 1890-1958 809.933
Literature and occult tradition; studies in philosophical poetry. Tr. from French by Dorothy Bolton. Port Washington, N.Y., Kennikat [1966] 245p. 22cm. Bibl. [PN1077.S35] 65-27133 7.50
1. Occultism in literature. I. Bolton, Dorothy, tr. II. Title. III. Title: Philosophical poetry.

SAURAT, Denis, 1890-1958. 808.8038
Literature and occult tradition; studies in philosophical poetry. Translated from the French by Dorothy Bolton. New York, Haskell House, 1966. viii, 245 p. 22 cm. Bibliographical footnotes. [PN1077.S35 1966b] 809.1 68-759
1. Occultism in literature. I. Bolton, Dorothy, tr. II. Title.

SINNETT, Alfred Percy, 1840-1921. 821'.8
Tennyson, an occultist, as his writings prove. London, Theosophical Pub. House, 1920. New York, Haskell House Publishers, 1972. 89 p. 23 cm. [PR5592.O25S5 1972] 72-2102 ISBN 0-8383-1485-6
1. Tennyson, Alfred Tennyson, Baron, 1809-1892. 2. Occultism in literature. I. Title.

Occupations.

HALL, Douglas T., 1940- 253
Organizational climates and careers; the work lives of priests [by] Douglas T. Hall [and] Benjamin Schneider. New York, Seminar Press, 1973. xix, 291 p. illus. 24 cm. (Quantitative studies in social relations) Based on a survey conducted by the authors for the Archdiocese of Hartford, Conn. Bibliography: p. 281-288. [BX1912.H32] 78-187261 ISBN 0-12-842550-4 11.95
1. Catholic Church in the United States—Clergy. 2. Occupations. I. Schneider, Benjamin, joint author. II. Hartford (Archdiocese) III. Title.

Occupations—History.

COLEMAN, Arthur D. 220.8'331'7
Occupations: contemporary and Biblical; a review of job titles mentioned in the Bible and a comparison with their present day American counterparts. Complied by Arthur D. Coleman. Salt Lake City, Utah, 1969. ix, 164 l. 22 cm. [BS680.O3C6] 74-89853
1. Bible—Antiquities. 2. Occupations—History. 3. Occupations—Classification. I. Title.

DUCKAT, Walter B. 220.8'3317
Beggar to king; all the occupations of Biblical times, by Walter Duckat. [1st ed.] Garden City, N.Y., Doubleday, 1968. xxvii, 327 p. 22 cm. Bibliography: p. [325]-327. [BS680.O3D8] 67-19112
1. Bible—Antiquities. 2. Occupations—History. I. Title.

Occupations—Social aspects.

VERA, Hernan, 1937- 305'.922
The professionalization and professionalism of Catholic priests / Hernan Vera. Gainesville : University Presses of Florida, c1982. xii, 116 p. ; 22 cm. (University of Florida monographs. Social sciences ; no. 68) Includes index. Bibliography: p. 99-112. [BX1912.V46 1982] 19 82-6886 ISBN 0-8130-0713-5 pbk. : 7.00
1. Catholic Church—Clergy. 2. Occupations—Social aspects. 3. Professions—Social aspects. I. Title. II. Series.

Ocean Grove camp meeting association of the Methodist Episcopal church.

STOKES, Ellwood Haines, 1815-1897, comp.
Ocean Grove. Its origin and progress, as shown in the annual reports presented by the president, to which are added other papers of interest, including list of lot-holders, charter, by-laws, &c., &c. Compiled by Rev. E. H. Stokes. Published by order of the association. [Philadelphia, Press of Haddock & son] c1874. 88 p. front., illus., plates, map, fold. plan. 22 1/2 cm. On spine: Ten years by the sea. Ocean Grove, 1869-1879. Includes First-Fourth annual reports, 1870-73 (somewhat abridged) of the Ocean Grove camp meeting association of the Methodist Episcopal church. With this are bound, as issued, the association's Fifth-Tenth annual reports, 1875-79, each with title-page and separate paging. [BX8476.O2S75] 44-26535
1. Ocean Grove camp meeting association of the Methodist Episcopal church. I. Title. II. Title: Ten years by the sea.

Ocean Grove, N. J.—Description

DANIELS, Morris S.
... The story of Ocean Grove, related in the year of its golden jubilee, by Morris S. Daniels ... illustrations from his private collection of original photographs. New York, Cincinnati, The Methodist book concern [c1919] 288 p. incl. illus., ports. front. 23 cm. At head of title: 1869-1919. [BX8476.O2D3] 19-16109
1. Ocean Grove, N. J.—Descr. 2. Ocean Grove camp meeting association of the Methodist Episcopial church. I. Title.

Oceanica.

HUGENBERG, Joyce A., ed. 266.29
Oceania in five hours, a symposium. Contributors: Vincent I. Kennally [others] Cincinnati, CSMC [c.1963] 71p. illus. group ports., map. 22cm. (CSMC five-hour ser.) 63-24566 .75 pap.,
1. Oceanica. 2. Missions—Oceanica. I. Kennally, Vincent I. II. Title.

Oceanica—Description and travel

BANKS, Martha Burr.
Heroes of the South seas. By Martha Burr Banks ... New York, American tract society [c1896] 220 p. front., plates. 19 cm. [BV3670.B3] 4-16750
1. Oceanica—Descr. & trav. 2. Missions—Oceanica. I. Title.

MARY Rose de Lima, mother, 1893- 279.6
A mission tour in the southwest Pacific from the diary account of Rev. Mother Mary Rose, S.M.S.M. Edited by Rev. Charles F. Decker, S.M., with an introduction by His Excellency Most Reverend Richard J. Cushing, D.D. [Boston, The Society for the propagation of the faith, 1942] 3 p. l., 9-214 p. illus. (incl. ports., maps) 23 1/2 cm. [DU22.M3] [266.2] 42-22482
1. Oceanica—Descr. & trav. 2. Missions—Oceanica. 3. Catholics in Oceanica. I. Decker, Charles F., ed. II. Society for the propagation of the faith. III. Title.

PATON, James, Rev. 1843-1906. 922
The story of John G. Paton, told for young folks; or, Thirty years among South sea cannibals. By the Rev. James Paton, B. A. New copyright ed., with two new chapters and forty-five full-page illustrations by James Finnemore ... New York, A. C. Armstrong and son, 1898. 404 p. incl. front., plates. 21 cm. "Fifteenth thousand." [BV3680.N6P3] C-372
1. Paton, John Gibson, 1824-1907. 2. Oceanica—Descr. & trav. I. Title.

Oceanica—Religion.

MOSS, Rosalind Louisa Beaufort. 299.
The life after death in Oceania and the Malay archipelago. By Rosalind Moss ... [London, New York, etc.] Oxford university press, H. Milford, 1925. xii, 247, [1] p. 2 maps (1 fold.) 23 cm. Bibliography: p. [219]-224. [BL2600.M6] 25-20960
1. Oceanica—Religion. 2. Funeral rites and ceremonies—Oceanica. 3. Future life. I. Title.

Ochino, Bernardino, 1487-1564.

BENRATH, Karl, 1845-1924. 270.6
Bernardino Ochino, of Siena: a contribution towards the history of the reformation. By Karl Benrath. Translated from the German by Helen Zimmern. With an introductory preface by William Arthur, A. M. New York, R. Carter & brothers, 1877. xvi, vii, 304 p. front. (port.) 23 cm. [BR350.O3B4] 33-22668
1. Ochino, Bernardino, 1487-1564. I. Zimmern, Helen, 1846- tr. II. Title.

Ockbrook, Eng.

HARNAN, J. W. 283'.425'1
A history of All Saints' Church, Ockbrook: including a brief account of the early origins of the village and parish, by J. W. Harnan. Darby, J. W. Harnan, 1971. (4), 34 p. map, plans. 22 cm. [BX5370.O3A45] 72-183821 ISBN 0-9502209-0-6 £0.25
1. All Saints Church, Ockbrook, Eng. 2. Ockbrook, Eng. I. Title.

Ockenga, Harold John, 1905-

LINDSELL, Harold, 1913- 922.573
Park Street prophet, a life of Harold John Ockenga. Wheaton, Ill., Van Kampen Press [1951] 175 p. illus., ports. 20 cm. [BX7260.O3L5] 51-10787
1. Ockenga, Harold John, 1905- 2. National Association of Evangelicals for United Action. I. Title.

Ockham, William, d. ca. 1349.

RYAN, John Joseph. 262'.001
The nature, structure, and function of the Church in William of Ockham / by John Joseph Ryan. Missoula, Mont. : Scholars Press, [1978] p. cm. (AAR studies in religion ; no. 16 ISSN 0084-6287s) Includes bibliographical references. [BV598.R9] 78-2891 ISBN 0-89130-230-1 pbk. : 7.50
1. Ockham, William, d. ca. 1349. 2. Church—History of doctrines—Middle Ages, 600-1500. I. Title. II. Series: American Academy of Religion. AAR studies in religion ; no. 16.

TIERNEY, Brian. 262'.5'2
Ockham, the conciliar theory, and the Canonists. Philadelphia, Fortress Press [1971] xxi, 42 p. 20 cm. (Facet books. Historical series, 19 (Medieval)) Includes bibliographical references. [BV720.T53] 74-157547 ISBN 0-8006-3064-5 1.00
1. Ockham, William, d. ca. 1349. 2. Conciliar theory—History of doctrines. I. Title.

O'Connell, Eugene, 1815-1891.

DWYER, John T. 282'.092'4 B
Condemned to the mines : the life of Eugene O'Connell, 1815-1891, pioneer bishop of Northern California and Nevada / by John T. Dwyer. 1st ed. New York : Vantage Press, c1976. xxiii, 302 p. : ill., ports. ; 21 cm. Includes bibliographical references and index. [BX4705.O293D88] 76-150322 ISBN 0-533-02130-8 : 8.95
1. O'Connell, Eugene, 1815-1891. 2. Catholic Church—Bishops—Biography. 3. Bishops—California—Biography. I. Title.

O'Connell, William Henry, cardinal, 1859-1944.

O'CONNELL, William Henry, cardinal, 1859-
The letters of His Eminence, William cardinal O'Connell, archbishop of Boston... Cambridge, Printed at the Riverside press, 1915- v. front., plates, ports. 23 cm. 15-27985
I. Title.

O'CONNELL, William Henry, cardinal, 1859-
The letters of His Eminence, William cardinal O'Connell, archbishop of Boston ... Cambridge, Printed at the Riverside press, 1915- v. front., plates, ports. 23 cm. 15-27985
I. Title.

O'CONNELL, William Henry, 922 cardinal, 1859-1944.
The letters of His Eminence, William cardinal O'Connell, archbishop of Boston, Vol. I. From college days, 1876, to Bishop of Portland, 1901. Cambridge [Mass.] Printed at the Riverside press, 1915- vii p., 2 l., 280 p. front., plates, ports. 23 cm. No more published. [BX4705.O3A4] 15-27985
I. Title.

SEXTON, John E. 922.
Cardinal O'Connell; a biographical sketch, souvenir of the silver jubilee of his episcopate, by the Rev. John E. Sexton... Boston, Mass., The Pilot publishing company, 1926. 4 p. l., [3]-356 p. front. (port.) 21 1/2 cm. [BX4705.O3S4] 27-8834
1. O'Connell, William Henry, cardinal, 1859- I. Title.

SEXTON, John Edward. 922
Cardinal O'Connell; a biographical sketch, souvenir of the silver jubilee of his episcopate, by the Rev. John E. Sexton ... Boston, Mass., The Pilot publishing company, 1926. 4 p. l., [3]-356 p. front. (port.) 21 1/2 cm. [BX4705.O3S4] 27-8834
1. O'Connell, William Henry, cardinal, 1859-1944. I. Title.

WAYMAN, Dorothy (Godfrey) 922.273 1893-
Cardinal O'Connell of Boston; a biography of William Henry O'Connell, 1859-1944. New York, Farrar, Straus and Young [ci955] 307p*2cm. [BX4705.O3W3] 55-5834
1. O'Connell, William Henry, Cardinal, 1859-1944. I. Title.

O'Connor, Brian, 1945-

GOLD, Don. 282'.092'4 B
The priest / Don Gold. 1st ed. New York : Holt, Rinehart and Winston, c1981. 290 p. ; 24 cm. [BX4705.O33G64] 19 80-22752 ISBN 0-03-053981-1 : 13.95
1. O'Connor, Brian, 1945- 2. Catholic Church—Clergy—Biography. 3. Clergy—New York (City)—Biography. 4. New York (City)—Biography. I. Title.

O'Connor, Flannery.

EGGENSCHWILER, David, 211'.6 1936-
The Christian humanism of Flannery O'Connor. Detroit, Wayne State University Press, 1972. 148 p. 24 cm. Bibliography: p. 141-148. [PS3565.C57Z665] 79-179560 ISBN 0-8143-1463-5 8.95
1. O'Connor, Flannery. 2. Humanism, Religious. I. Title.

Odo, Abbot of Cluny, Saint 879 (ca.)-942.

JOANNES, monk of 922.244 Cluny,fl. 945.
St. Odo of Cluny; being the Life of St. Odo of Cluny by John of Salerno, and the Life of St. Gerald of Aurillac by St. Odo. Translated and edited by Gerard Sitwell. London, New York, Sheed and Ward [1958] xxix, 186p. 22cm. (The Makes of Christendom) 'Odo's writings': p. xxv-xxvi. Bibliography: p. [xxvii]-xxix. eraldus Aurillaechsis, Saint, 855 (ca.)-909. [BX4700.O35J63 1958] 59-793
1. Odo, Abbot of Cluny, Saint 879 (ca.)-942. I. Odo, Abbot of Cluny, Saint 879 (ca.)-942. Life of St. Gerald of Aurillac. II. Sitwell, Gerard, ed. and tr. III. Title. IV. Series.

Odors in the Bible.

ARMERDING, George 220.8'1521'66 D.
The fragrance of the Lord : toward a deeper appreciation of the Bible / George D. Armerding. 1st ed. San Francisco : Harper & Row, c1979. xiv, 141 p. ; 21 cm. Includes indexes. Bibliography: p. [135]-136. [BS680.O34A75 1979] 79-1774 6.95
1. Odors in the Bible. I. Title.

O'Driscoll, Richard.

O'DRISCOLL, Richard. 649
Pop's primer / by Richard O'Driscoll. Plainfield, N.J. : Bridge Pub., c1981. xv, 237 p., [12] p. of plates : ill. ; 21 cm. Includes references. [HQ769.O224] 19 81-82593 ISBN 0-88270-527-X : 4.95
1. O'Driscoll, Richard. 2. Father and child. 3. Parenting—Religious aspects—Christianity. 4. Christian life. 5. Cowboys—Biography. I. Title.

Oecolampadius, Joannes, 1482-1531.

RUPP, Ernest Gordon. 270.6'0922
Patterns of reformation, by Gordon Rupp. Philadelphia, Fortress Press [1969] xxiii, 427 p. illus. 26 cm. Contents.Contents.—Johannes Oecolampadius; the reformer as scholar.—Andrew Karlstadt; the reformer as Puritan.—Thomas Muntzer; the reformer as rebel.—A sixteenth-century Dr. Johnson and his Boswell; the reformer as layman. Bibliographical footnotes. [BR315.R86] 69-14626 9.50
1. Oecolampadius, Joannes, 1482-1531. 2. Karlstadt, Andreas Rudolf, 1480 (ca.)-1541. 3. Munzer, Thomas, 1490 (ca.)-1525. 4. Vadianus, Joachim, 1484-1551. 5. Kessler, Johannes, 1502?-1574. I. Title.

Oesterreicher, John M., 1904- — Addresses, essays, lectures.

STANDING before God : 230'.2
studies on prayer in Scriptures and in tradition with essays : in honor of John M. Oesterreicher / edited by Asher Finkel and Lawrence Frizzell. New York : Ktav Pub. House, 1981. 410 p., [1] leaf of plates : port. ; 24 cm. "Bibliography of Msgr. John M. Oesterreicher": p. 393-399. [BS1199.W73S72] 19 80-21102 ISBN 0-87068-708-5 : 29.50
1. Oesterreicher, John M., 1904- — Addresses, essays, lectures. 2. God—Worship and love—Biblical teaching—Addresses, essays, lectures. 3. Prayer—Biblical teaching—Addresses, essays, lectures. I. Oesterreicher, John M., 1904- II. Finkel, Asher. III. Frizzell, Lawrence.

Offenses against religion—Great Britain.

HAIR, Paul, comp. 262.9
Before the bawdy court; selections from church court and other records relating to the correction of moral offences in England, Scotland, and New England, 1300-1800. New York, Barnes & Noble Books [1972] 271 p. illus. 25 cm. Bibliography: p. [259]-266. [KD8760.H3 1972] 73-156599 ISBN 0-06-492646-X 13.75
1. Offenses against religion—Great Britain. 2. Court records—Great Britain. I. Title.

Office equipment and supplies.

LESSEL, William M 254
Duplicating and publicity manual for Christian workers. Chicago, Moody Press [1957] 94p. illus. 28cm. [BV653.L18] 57-37886
1. Office equipment and supplies. 2. Church work. I. Title.

Office practice in churches.

MCCARTT, Clara Anniss 254
How to organize your church office. [Westwood, N.J.] Revell [1962] 63p. 22cm. (Revell's better church res.) 62-17111 1.00 pap.,
1. Office practice in churches. I. Title.

O'Flynn, James Christopher, 1881-1962.

O'DONOGHUE, Richard. 282'.092'4 B
Like a tree planted. Dublin, Gill [1968] vii, 269 p. 21 cm. [BX4705.O39O36 1968] 75-300737 30/-
1. O'Flynn, James Christopher, 1881-1962. I. Title.

Ogdensburg, N.Y. (Diocese)

TAYLOR, Mary 282'.747'5 Christine.
A history of Catholicism in the north country. [Camden, N.Y., Printed by A. M. Farnsworth Sons, 1972] xii, 282 p. illus. 28 cm. On cover: Diocese of Ogdensburg centennial, 1872-1972. Includes bibliographical references. [BX1417.O3T38] 72-188926
1. Ogdensburg, N.Y. (Diocese) I. Title. II. Title: Diocese of Ogdensburg centennial, 1872-1972.

Oglala Indians—Religion and mythology.

POWERS, William K. 299.7
Oglala religion / William K. Powers. Lincoln : University of Nebraska Press, c1977. xxi, 233 p., [2] leaves of plates : ill. ; 23 cm. Includes index. Bibliography: p. [215]-222. [E99.O3P68] 76-30614 ISBN 0-8032-0910-X : 11.75
1. Oglala Indians—Religion and mythology. 2. Oglala Indians—Social life and customs. 3. Oglala Indians—Ethnic identity. 4. Indians of North America—Great Plains—Religion and mythology. 5. Indians of North America—Great Plains—Ethnic identity. I. Title.

Oglala Indians—Rites and ceremonies.

THE sacred pipe 970.1
Black Elk's account of the seven rites of the Oglala Sioux. Recorded and edited by Joseph Epes Brown. [1st ed.] Norman, University of Oklahoma Press [1953] xx, 144 p. ports. 24 cm. (The Civilization of the American Indian [v. 36]) [E99.O3B5] [E99.O3B5] [E99.O3B5] 299.7 970.62 53-8810 53-8810 53-8810
1. Oglala Indians—Rites and ceremonies. I. Clack Ellk, Oglala Indian, 1863-1950. II. Brown, Joseph Epes, ed. III. Series.

Ogle, George E., 1929-

OGLE, George E., 266'.009519'5 1929-
Liberty to the captives : the struggle against oppression in South Korea / George E. Ogle. Atlanta : John Knox Press, c1977. 188 p. ; 21 cm. Includes bibliographical references. [BV3462.O34A34] 76-48578 ISBN 0-8042-1494-8 pbk. : 5.95
1. Ogle, George E., 1929- 2. Missionaries—Korea—Biography. 3. Missionaries—United States—Biography. 4. Civil rights—Korea. 5. Christianity and democracy—Korea. 6. Korea—Politics and government—1960- I. Title.

Oglethrope, James Edward, 1696-1765.

MCCONNELL, Francis John, 922 bp., 1871-
Evangelicals, revolutionists and idealists; six English contributors to American thought and action, by Francis John McConnell. New York, Nashville, Abingdon-Cokesbury press [1942] 184 p. 19 1/2 cm. [Drew lectureship in biography. 1942] [BR758.M3] 43-849
1. Oglethrope, James Edward, 1696-1765. 2. Wesley, John, 1703-1791. 3. Whitefield, George, 1714-1770. 4. Paine, Thomas, 1737-1809. 5. Berkeley, George, bp. of Cloyne, 1685-1753. 6. Wilberforce, William, 1759-1883. 7. Religious thought—Gt. Brit. 8. Religious thought—U.S. I. Title.

MCCONNELL, Francis 201'.1'0922 B John, Bp., 1871-1953.
Evangelicals, revolutionists, and idealists; six English contributors to American thought and action. Port Washington, N.Y., Kennikat Press [1972, c1942] 184 p. 21 cm. (Essay and general literature index reprint series) Contents.Contents.—James Edward Oglethorpe.—John Wesley.—George Whitefield.—Thomas Paine.—George Berkeley.—William Wilberforce. [BR758.M3 1972] 75-153252 ISBN 0-8046-1505-5
1. Oglethorpe, James Edward, 1696-1785. 2. Wesley, John, 1706-1791. 3. Whitefield, George, 1714-1770. 4. Paine, Thomas,

1737-1809. 5. Berkeley, George, Bp. of Cloyne, 1685-1753. 6. Wilberforce, William, 1759-1833. 7. Religious thought—Gt. Brit. 8. Religious thought—U.S. I. Title.

O'Hanlon, Virginia—Juvenile literature.

[CHURCH, Francis Pharcellus] 1839-1906. 394.2'68282
Yes, Virginia. Illustrated by Suzanne Hausman. New York, Elizabeth Press [1972] [31] p. illus. (part col.) 22 x 24 cm. Contains chiefly the text of the editorial by F. P. Church which appeared in the New York Sun, September 21, 1897 under title: Is there a Santa Claus? The text of the well-known editorial explaining that Santa Claus exists despite rumors to the contrary. [GT4985.C545 1972] 72-87236 3.95
1. O'Hanlon, Virginia—Juvenile literature. 2. Santa Claus. 3. [Santa Claus.] 4. [Christmas.] I. O'Hanlon, Virginia. II. Hausman, Suzanne, illus. III. Title.

O'Hara, Edwin Vincent, Bp. 1881-

SHAW, James Gerard. 922.273
Edwin Vincent O'Hara: American prelate. Foreword by Matthew F. Brady. New York, Farrar, Straus and Cudahy [1957] 274p. illus. 22cm. [BX4705.O43S5] 57-6500
1. O'Hara, Edwin Vincent, Bp. 1881- I. Title.

SHAW, James Gerard. 922.273
Edwin Vincent O'Hara: American prelate. Foreword by Matthew F. Brady. New York, Farrar, Straus and Dudahy [1957] 274 p. illus. 22 cm. [BX4705.O43S5] 57-6500
1. O'Hara, Edwin Vincent, Bp., 1881- I. Title.

O'Hara, John Francis, 1888-1960.

MCAVOY, Thomas Timothy, 1903-1969. 271'.79
Father O'Hara of Notre Dame, the Cardinal-Archbishop of Philadelphia [by] Thomas T. McAvoy. Notre Dame, Ind., University of Notre Dame Press [1967] xi, 514 p. ports. 24 cm. "Footnotes": p. 492-505. [BX4705.O44M3] 66-14627
1. O'Hara, John Francis, 1888-1960. I. Title.

Ohio — Church history

KENNEDY, William Sloane, 1822-1861. 261.
The plan of union; or, A history of the Presbyterian and Congregational churches of the western Reserve, with biographical sketches of the early missionaries. Hudson, Ohio, Pentagon Steam Press, 1856. 202 p. 18 cm. [BR555.O4W4] 49-34954
1. Ohio—Church history. 2. Presbyterian Church in Ohio. 3. Congregational churches in Ohio. I. Title.

REGIONAL Church Planning Office, Cleveland.
The churches of Lakewood. Cleveland, Regional Church Planning Office, 1966. 101 p. charts, stat. 28 cm. (Basic Church Planning Studies, 31) Summary attached. 67-83877
1. Ohio — Church hist. 2. Lakewood, Ohio — Church hist. I. Title.

WARREN, Ohio. First Baptist Church. 286.177138
One hundred fifty years; history, First Baptist Church, Warren, Ohio 1803-1953, by Twila Coe Dilley, church historian. [Warren, 1953] 59p. illus. 23cm. [BX6480.W28F5] 55-24542
I. Dilley, Twila Coe II. Title.

Ohio Council of Churches.

SANDERSON, Ross Warren, 1884- 922.89
B. F. Lamb, ecumenical pioneer; a biography of Rev. B. F. Lamb, D. D., LL. D.; including the development of church cooperation in Ohio, the growth of the Ohio Council of Churches, and progress toward the Temple of Good Will, by Ross W. Sanderson. [Nashville] Printed by the Parthenon Press Manufacturing Division of the Methodist Pub. House [1964] 250 p. illus., ports. 23 cm. [BX6.8,L3S3] 65-1310
1. Lamb, Burley Frank, 1886- 2. Ohio Council of Churches. I. Title.

O'Kelly, James, 1735-1826.

MACCLENNY, Wilbur E. 922.
The life of Rev. James O'Kelly and the early history of the Christian church in the South, by W. E. MacClenny ... Raleigh, N.C., Edwards & Broughton printing company, 1910. 253 p. front., plates, ports. 22 cm. [BX6793.O6M3] 26-22115
1. O'Kelly, James, 1735-1826. I. Title. II. Title: Christian church in the South.

Okinawa Island—Religion.

LEBRA, William P. 299.56
Okinawan religion: belief, ritual, and social structure. [Honolulu] Univ. of Hawaii Pr. [c.1966] xiv, 241p. illus. 21cm. [BL2215.O4L4] 66-16506 4.75 pap.,
1. Okinawa Island—Religion. I. Title.

Oklahoma—Church history.

†BROWN, Thomas Elton. 282'.766
Bible belt Catholicism : a history of the Roman Catholic Church in Oklahoma, 1905-1945 / by Thomas Elton Brown. New York : United States Catholic Historical Society, 1977. vii, 230 p. ; 23 cm. (Monograph series - United States Catholic Historical Society ; 33) Bibliography: p. 224-227. [BX1415.O4B76] 77-368281 8.75
1. Catholic Church in Oklahoma—History. 2. Oklahoma—Church history. I. United States Catholic Historical Society. II. Title. III. Series: United States Catholic Historical Society. Monograph series ; 33. Publisher's address: St. Joseph's Seminary, Dunwoodie, Yonkers, NY 10704

Oklahoma City, First Baptist Church.

SAPP, Phyllis Woodruff, 1908- ed. 286.1766381
Lighthouse on the corner; a history of the First Baptist Church, Oklahoma City, Oklahoma. Malinda Brown, director of research. Oklahoma City, Century Press, 1964. xiv, 135, vii p. illus., ports. 24 cm. [BX6480.O4F5] 64-57876
1. Oklahoma City. First Baptist Church. I. Title.

Okumenische Marienschwesternschaft.

SCHLINK, Basilea 271.98
Realities; the miracles of God experienced today [by] M. Basilea Schlink. Tr. [from German] by Larry Christenson, William Castell. Grand Rapids, Mich Zondervan [c.1966] 128p. 21cm. [BX8071.5.S3313] 66-18951 1.50 pap.,
1. Okumenische Marienschwesternschaft. I. Title.

SCHLINK, Basilea [Secular name: Klara Schlink] 271.98
God is always greater. Foreword by Olive Wyon. Tr. from German by N. B. Cryer] London, Faith Pr. [dist. Westminister, M.D., Centerbury, c.1963 130p. illus. group port. 19cm. (Ecumenical Sisterhood of Mary, Darmstadt. Pub. 2) 63-4128 2.00 pap.,
1. Okumemsche Marienschwesternschaft. I. Title.

Olan, Levi Arthur, 1903- —Addresses, essays, lectures.

A Rational faith : 296
essays in honor of Levi A. Olan / edited by Jack Bemporad. New York : Ktav Pub. House, 1977. xi, 211 p. ; 24 cm. Contents.Contents.—Atlas, S. On the relation between subject and object.—Bamberger, B. Religion and the arts.—Bemporad, J. Man, God, and history.—Braude, W. C. The two lives of Hillel's sandwich.—Chapman, C. B. The health guilds, the public interest and the malpractice dilemma.—Feuer, L. Influence of Abba Hillel Silver on the evolution of Reform Judaism.—Hackerman, N. Ignorance, the motivation for understanding.—Hartshorne, C. Whitehead's metaphysical system.—Ogden, S. M. Prolegomena to a Christian theology of nature.—Sandmel, S. The rationalist denial of Jewish tradition in Philo.—Shakow, D. Educating the mental health researcher for potential development in man.—Turner, D. An Ashendene dozen from the Levi A. Olan collection of fine books.—Olan, L. A. A preliminary summing up. Includes bibliographical references. [BM42.R35] 77-13626 ISBN 0-87068-448-5 : 12.50
1. Olan, Levi Arthur, 1903- —Addresses, essays, lectures. 2. Judaism—History—Addresses, essays, lectures. 3. Philosophy—Addresses, essays, lectures. I. Olan, Levi Arthur, 1903- II. Bemporad, Jack.
Contents omitted

Olcott, Henry Steel, 1832-1907.

MURPHET, Howard. 212'.52'0924 B
Hammer on the mountain: life of Henry Steel Olcott (1832-1907) Wheaton, Ill., Theosophical Pub. House [1972] xii, 339 p. illus. 23 cm. "H. S. Olcott's works": p. [326]-327. [BP585.O4M8] 72-76427 ISBN 0-8356-0210-9 7.95
1. Olcott, Henry Steel, 1832-1907. I. Title.

Old age.

BAUNARD, Louis, 1826-1919. 248
The evening of life (compensations of old age) translated and condensed from the original French of monsignor Baunard by John L. Stoddard. Milwaukee, The Bruce publishing company [c1930] xvii, 304 p. 20 cm. Bibliography: p. 285-304. [BV4580.B35] 30-30121
1. Old age. I. Stoddard, John Lawson, 1850-1961, tr. II. Title.

CONGREVE, George, 1835-1918. 264.
Treasures of hope for the evening of life, by the late Rev. George Congreve ... London, New York [etc.] Longmans, Green and co., 1918. 223 p. 19 1/2 cm. [BX2170.C6C6] 19-15959
1. Old age. I. Title.

COURTENAY, Charles. 248
On growing old gracefully, by the Revd. Charles Courtenay ... New York, The Macmillan company, 1936. x p., 2 l., 3-285 p. 21 cm. [BV4580.C6 1936a] 36-33122
1. Old age. I. Title.

ESHBACH, Warren M., 1940- 261.8'34'35
A future with hope / Warren M. Eshbach, Harvey S. Kline ; drawings by Cindy Staub. Elgin, Ill. : Brethren Press, [1978] p. cm. Bibliography: p. [HV1451.E84] 78-17720 ISBN 0-87178-298-7 pbk. : 2.95
1. Old age. 2. Aged. 3. Church work with the aged. I. Kline, Harvey S., 1921- joint author. II. Title.

MAVES, Paul B. 248
The best is yet to be. Philadelphia, Westminster Press [1951] 96 p. 20 cm. (The Westminster pastoral aid books) [BV4580.M35] 51-9868
1. Old age. I. Title.

MOUNTFORD, William, 1816-1885. 248
Euthanasy; or, Happy talk towards the end of life. By William Mountford ... Boston, W. Crosby and H. P. Nichols; New York, D. Appleton and company, 1848. xii, 466 p. 18 cm. [BV4580.M6 1848] 15-3400
1. Old age. I. Title.

MOUNTFORD, William, 1816-1885. 236.1
Euthanasy; or, Happy talk towards the end of life, by William Mountford. Boston, J. R. Osgood and company, 1874. xviii, 511 p. 20 cm. [BV4580.M6 1874] 32-35939
1. Old age. I. Title.

WANG, Ch'ung-yu, 1879-
Old age, afterlife and the spirit; an anthology of great thoughts, comp. by Chung Yu Want. [1st ed.] New York, Vantage Press [c1958] 157 p. 21 cm. Includes bibliography.
1. Old age. 2. Future life. 3. Religion — Anecdotes, facetiae, satire, etc. I. Title.

Old age—Prayer-books and devotions—English.

BILLING, Gottfrid, bp., 1841-1925. 242
At eventide; meditations and prayers, by Bishop Gottfrid Billing; rendered from the ninth Swedish edition by E. W. Olson. Rock Island, Ill., Auglustana book concern [c1937] 158, [2] p. 23 cm. [Full name: Axel Gottfrid Leonard Billing] [BV4580.B3] 37-39203
1. Old age—Prayer-books and devotions—English. 2. Lutheran church—Prayer-books and devotion—English. I. Olson, Ernest William, 1870- tr. II. Title. III. Title: Translation of For de gamia.

DOERFFLER, Alfred, 1884- 264.041
Treasures of hope, by Alfred Doerffler. Saint Louis, Mo., Concordia publishing house, 1945. 4 p. l., 3-274 p. 22 cm. [BV4580.D6] 45-8523
1. Old age—Prayer-books and devotions—English. 2. Lutheran church—Prayer-books and devotions—English. I. Title.

Old age—Religious life.

HAWKES, Ernest William, 1883- 248
Paths of peace. [1st ed.] New York, Exposition Press [1952] 166 p. 22 cm. [BV4580.H3] 52-9819
1. Old age—Religious life. I. Title.

ROBINSON, George Livinstone, 1864- 248
Live out your years [1st ed.] New York, Abelard Press [1951] 114 p. 24 cm. [BV4580.R6] 51-14801
1. Old age — Religious life. I. Title.

Old Catholic Church.

DE VOIL, Walter Harry, 1893- 264.04815
Old Catholic eucharistic worship; with notes, and translations of the Dutch, German, and Swiss rites, by Rev. Walter H. De Voil, M.A., and H. D. Wynne-Bennett, D. sc. Foreword by the Most Rev. the Primus of the Episcopal church in Scotland. London, The Faith press, ltd.; New York & Milwaukee, Morehouse publishing co. [1936] 5 p. l., 85, [1] p. front. 17 cm. "First published, February, 1936." [BX4773.D4] 37-1318
I. Old Catholic church. Liturgy and ritual. II. Wynne-Bennett, Henry Douglas, joint author. III. Title.

HERZOG, Eduard, bp., 1841-1924.
... An Old-Catholic view of confession; being the pamphlet "Compulsory auricular confession, as practised in the church of Rome, a human invention," by Eduard Herzog ... Tr., with the author's permission, by G. C. Richards ... Pub. under the direction of the Tract committee. London [etc.] Society for promoting Christian knowledge; New York, E. S. Gorham, 1905. 59, [1] p. 22 cm. (The Church historical society. [Publications] lxxxiii) Translation of the author's "Die obligatorische romische obrenbeichte eine menschilche erfindung," which appeared first in the Katholik. June 8 and 15, 1901, as an answer to an address by Dr. Egger, bishop of St. Gall, entitled, "Die beichte keine menschiche erffindung". [BV845.H4] 20-16438
I. Richards, George Chatterton, 1867- tr. II. Title.

MOSS, Claude Beaufort, 1888-
The Old Catholic movement, its origins and history. 2d ed. New York, Morehouse-Barlow, 1964. 362 p. 23 cm. 65-43068
1. Old Catholic Church. I. Title.

THE Old Catholic missal and ritual. 264.02'3
Prepared for the use of English-speaking congregations of Old Catholics in communion with the ancient Catholic Archiepiscopal See of Utrecht. New York, AMS Press [1969] xvi, 326 p. 23 cm. "Prepared by ... Arnold H. Mathew." Reprint of the London ed., 1909. [BX4773.A3 1969] 73-84708
I. Mathew, Arnold Harris, 1852-1919.

Old Catholicism.

[DOLLINGER, Johann Joseph Ignaz von] 1799-1890. 262.
The pope and the council; by Janus [pseud.] Authorized translation from the German. Boston, Roberts brothers, 1870. xxviii, 346 p. 18 cm. [BX1806.D6 1870] 1-481
1. Old Catholicism. 2. Popes—Infallibility. I. Huber, Johannes, 1830-1879, joint author. II. Title.

Old Colony Mennonites.

REDEKOP, Calvin Wall, 1925- 289.7'3
The Old Colony Mennonites; dilemmas of ethnic minority life. Foreword by Everett C. Hughes. Baltimore, Johns Hopkins Press [1969] xiv, 302 p. illus., map. 23 cm. Bibliography: p. [287]-288. [BX8129.O4R4] 69-13192 10.00
1. Old Colony Mennonites.

Old Concord Presbyterian Church, Appomattox Co., Va.

CHILTON, Harriett A. 929'.3755'625
Register of Old Concord Presbyterian Church, Appomattox County, Virginia - 1826-1878; baptism 1826-1876, membership 1826-1878, obituary 1829-1854. Transcribed and edited by Harriett A. Chilton and Mitzi Chilton Wilkerson. [Falls Church? Va.] 1973. 51 p. illus. 23 cm. [BX9211.A6O42] 74-160732
1. Old Concord Presbyterian Church, Appomattox Co., Va. 2. Appomattox Co., Va.—Biography. 3. Registers of births, etc.—Appomattox Co., Va. I. Wilkerson, Mitzi Chilton, joint author. II. Title.

Old fashioned revival hour (Radio program)

FULLER, Grace (Payton) comp. 922
Heavenly sunshine; letters to the 'Old fashioned revival hour,'complied by Mrs. Charles E. Fuller. [Westwood, N. J.] Revell [1956] 156p. 20cm. [BV3785.F8A4] 56-13217
1. Fuller, Charles Edward, 1887- 2. Old fashioned revival hour (Radio program) I. Title.

Old hundredth tune.

HAVERGAL, William Henry, 1793-1870. 245.
A history of the old hundredth psalm tune, with specimens. By the Rev. W. H. Havergal ... With a prefatory note by Rt. Rev. J. M. Wainwright ... New York, Mason brothers, 1854. vii, [9]-74 p. 23 1/2 cm. [ML3186.H38] 9-6799
1. Old hundredth tune. I. Title.

Old North Reformed Church, Dumont, N.J.

THE Old North 285'.749'21
Reformed Church of Dumont, New Jersey, 1724-1974. Dumont, N.J. : The Church, [1976] c1974. p. cm. "This book is number of a limited edition of five hundred." Bibliography: p. [BX9531.D85O46 1976] 76-6085 7.95
1. Old North Reformed Church, Dumont, N.J.

Old Oxford Presbyterian Church.

DIEHL, George West. 285'.1755'852
Old Oxford and her families. [Verona, Va.] McClure Press [1971] ix, 217 p. illus. 24 cm. Includes bibliographical references. [BX9211.V38O433] 79-160702 7.50
1. Old Oxford Presbyterian Church. 2. Rockbridge Co., Va.—Genealogy. I. Title.

Old Paramus Reformed Church, Ridgewood, N.J.

OLD Paramus Reformed Church, Ridgewood, N.J. Historical Committee. 285'.7749'21
Old Paramus Reformed Church in Ridgewood, New Jersey, the years 1725-1975 / [prepared for the 250th anniversary of Old Paramus Reformed Church by the Historical Committee]. Ridgewood, N.J. : Old Paramus Reformed Church, c1975. 64 p. : ill., facsims. ; 29 cm. Cover title. [BX9531.R55O4 1975] 75-322483
1. Old Paramus Reformed Church, Ridgewood, N.J. 2. Ridgewood, N.J.—History.

Oldcastle, Sir John, styled Lord Cobham, d. 1417.

BALE, John, bp. of Ossory, 1495-1563. 208.1
Select works of John Bale ... Containing the examinations of Lord Cobham, William Thorpe, and Anne Askewe, and The image of both churches. Edited for the Parker society. [Publications. v. 7]) Cambridge [Eng.] Printed at the University press, 1849. xii, 647 p. 23 cm. (Half-title: The Parker society. [Publications. v. 1]) Includes reprints of original title-pages. [BX5065.P2 vol. 1] (283.082) AC 33
1. Oldcastle, Sir John, styled Lord Cobham, d. 1417. 2. Thorpe, William, d.1407? 3. Askew, Anne, 1521-1546 4. Bible. N.T. Revelation—Commentaries. 5. Theology—Collected works—16th cent. 6. Church of England—Collected works. 7. Bible—Commentaries—N.T. Revelation. I. Christmas, Henry, 1811-1868, ed. II. Title. Contents omitted.

FIEHLER, Rudolph 270.40924
The strange history of Sir John Oldcastle, [1st ed.] New York, American Pr. [c.1965] 243p. 21cm. Bibl. [BX4906.O6G5] 65-25021 3.50
1. Oldcastle, John, styled Lord Cobham, d. Sir 1417. I. Title.

FIEHLER, Rudolph. 270.50924 (B)
The strange history of Sir John Oldcastle. [1st ed.] New York, American Press [c1965] 243 p. 21 cm. "Notes on the sources": p. 239-243. [BX4906.O6F5] 65-25021
1. Oldcastle, Sir John, styled Lord Cobham, d. 1417. I. Title.

Oldham, Dale.

OLDHAM, Dale. 269'.2'0924 B
Giants along my path; my fifty years in the ministry. Anderson, Ind., Warner Press [1973] 288 p. illus. 21 cm. [BX7027.Z8O4] 73-16413 ISBN 0-87162-165-7 10.00
1. Oldham, Dale. I. Title.
Pbk. 3.95; ISBN 0-87162-162-2.

Oldham, Doug.

OLDHAM, Doug. 783'.092'4 B
I don't live there anymore [by] Doug Oldham with Fred Bauer. Nashville, Impact Books [1973] 190 p. illus. 23 cm. [BV4935.O46A3] 73-75986 4.95
1. Oldham, Doug. 2. Conversion. I. Bauer, Fred, fl. 1968- II. Title.

Oldham, Laura Lee, 1931-

OLDHAM, Laura Lee, 1931- 242'.64
Some things are priceless / Laura Lee Oldham. Nashville : Abingdon, c1981. p. cm. [GV4526.2.O42] 19 81-3498 ISBN 0-687-39060-5 : 14.95
1. Oldham, Laura Lee, 1931- 2. Family—Religious life—Meditations. I. Title.

Olds Hall, Daytona Beach, Fla.

PRINCE, John Conger.
Olds Hall, a residence for retired ministers and missionaries. Nashville, Parthenon Press, 1955. 94p. illus. 20cm. [BV4383.D3P7] 55-38898
1. Olds Hall, Daytona Beach, Fla. I. Title.

Olean. N. Y. First Baptist Church.

ANDERSON, Margaret Jobe. 286.1747
The widening way. [Olean? N. Y., 1950?] 65 p. illus., ports. 24 cm. [BX6480.O5F5] 51-21951
1. Olean. N. Y. First Baptist Church. I. Title.

Olier, Jean Jacques, 1608-1657.

POURRAT, Pierre, 1871- 922.244
Father Olier, founder of St. Sulpice; from the French of the Very Rev. Pierre Pourrat ... by the Rev. W. S. Reilly ... Roland park, Baltimore, Md., The Voice publishing company [c1932] 223 p. front., ports. 20 cm. [BX4705.O48P63] 33-3812
1. Olier, Jean Jacques, 1608-1657. 2. Sulpicians. I. Reilly, Wendell Stephen, 1875- tr. II. Title.

Olive Branch Mission.

WOODWORTH, Ralph. 266'.022'0977311
Light in a dark place : the story of Chicago's oldest rescue mission / by Ralph Woodworth. Winona Lake, Ind. : Light and Life Press, c1978. 127 p. : ill. ; 21 cm. [BV2805.C48W66] 78-104723 ISBN 0-89367-022-7 : 3.50
1. Olive Branch Mission. 2. City missions—Illinois—Chicago. I. Title.

Olive Chapel Baptist Church, Wake Co., N. C.

HENDRICKS, Garland A. 286.1756
Biography of a country church. Nashville, Broadman Press [1950] xiv, 137 p. illus., ports. 20 cm. [BX6480.W27O5] 50-58193
1. Olive Chapel Baptist Church, Wake Co., N. C. I. Title.

Oliver, Richard Weber, 1900-1980.

[OLIVER, Lillie F (Weber)] Mrs. 922
Richard Weber Oliver, a challenge to American youth, a biography by his mother. Providence, R. I., Challenge publishing company, 1932. 224 p. front., ports. 21 cm. Music: p. 197, 200-202. [BV3785.O6O6] 32-29523
1. Oliver, Richard Weber, 1900-1980. I. Title.

Olivetan Benedictine Sisters (U.S.)

VOTH, M. Agnes. 271'.97
Green olive branch, by M. Agnes Voth. Edited by M. Raymond. Illus. by M. Louise Frankenberger and M. Michelle Bullock. Chicago, Franciscan Herald Press [1973] xii, 351 p. illus. 21 cm. Includes bibliographical references. [BX4412.7.Z5U58] 74-166216
1. Olivetan Benedictine Sisters (U.S.) I. Title.

Olivi, Pierre Jean, 1248-1298.

BURR, David, 1934- 271'.3'024 B
The persecution of Peter Olivi / David Burr. Philadelphia : American Philosophical Society, 1976. 98 p. ; 30 cm. (Transactions of the American Philosophical Society ; new ser., v. 66, pt. 5 ISSN 0065-9746s) Includes index.IBibliography: p. 93-96.I[BX4705.O48543B87].76-24254 ISBN 0-87169-665-7 pbk. : 6.00
1. Olivi, Pierre Jean, 1248 or 9-1298. 2. Franciscans in France—Biography. I. Title. II. Series: American Philosophical Society, Philadelphia. Transactions ; new ser., v. 66, pt. 5.

Olivieri, Umberto, 1884-1973.

ABELOE, William N. 282'.092'4 B
To the top of the mountain : the life of Father Umberto Olivieri, "Padre of the Otomis" / William N. Abeloe ; with a foreword by Miguel Dario Cardinal Miranda. 1st ed. Hicksville, N.Y. : Exposition Press, c1976. 160 p., [11] leaves of plates : ill. ; 22 cm. [BX4705.O48545A63] 76-7187 ISBN 0-682-48558-6 : 8.00
1. Olivieri, Umberto, 1884-1973. 2. Catholic Church—Clergy—Biography. 3. Clergy—United States—Biography. I. Title.

Olmecs—Religion and mythology.

LUCKERT, Karl W., 1934- 299'.7
Olmec religion : a key to Middle America and beyond / by Karl W. Luckert. 1st ed. Norman : University of Oklahoma Press, [1975] p. cm. (The Civilization of the American Indian series ; v. 137) Includes index. Bibliography: p. [F1219.3.R38L8] 75-12869 ISBN 0-8061-1298-0 : 8.95 pbk. : 6.95
1. Olmecs—Religion and mythology. 2. Serpent-worship. 3. Indians of Mexico—Religion and mythology. 4. Indians of Central America—Religion and mythology. I. Title. II. Series.

Olson, Bruce.

KUNG, Andres, 1945- 266'.0092'4
Bruce Olson : missionary or American colonizer? / Andres Kung ; [translated by Frederic Love]. Chappaqua, N.Y. : Christian Herald Books, c1981. p. cm. Translation of: Bruce. [F2319.2.M6O43513] 19 80-69309 ISBN 0-915684-83-7 : 6.95
1. Olson, Bruce. 2. Kung, Andres, 1945- 3. Motilon Indians—Missions. 4. Indians of South America—Colombia—Missions. I. [Bruce.] English II. Title.
Publisher's address : 40 Overlook Dr., Chappaqua, NY 10514.

OLSON, Bruce. 266'.023'0987
Bruchko by Bruce Olson. Carol Stream, Ill. : Creation House, 1978. 208p. ; 18 cm. First ed. published in 1973 under title: For this cross I'll Kill you [F2319.2M6044 1978] 78-107540 ISBN 0-88419-133-8 pbk. : 1.95
1. Olson, Bruce. 2. Motilon Indians — Missions. 3. Yuko Indians — Missions. 4. Indians of South America — Venezuela — Missions. 5. Missionaries — Venezuela — Biography. 6. Missionaries — United States — Biography. I. Title.

OLSON, Bruce. 266'.023'0987
For this cross I'll kill you. [1st ed.] Carol Stream, Ill., Creation House [1973] 221 p. illus. 24 cm. [F2319.2.M6O44] 73-81494 ISBN 0-88419-038-2 4.95
1. Olson, Bruce. 2. Motilon Indians—Missions. 3. Yuko Indians—Missions. I. Title.

Olson, Lois Ellen, 1941-

OLSON, Lois Ellen, 1941- 287'.6'0924 B
Meeting Him in the wilderness : a true story of adventure and faith / Lois Ellen Olson. 1st ed. Garden City, N.Y. : Doubleday, 1980. p. cm. "A Doubleday-Galilee original." [BX8495.O47A35] 79-7504 ISBN 0-385-15132-2 : 9.95
1. Olson, Lois Ellen, 1941- 2. Olson, Tom. 3. Methodist Church—United States—Biography. I. Title.

Omaha. Presbyterian theological seminary.

HAWLEY, Charles Arthur, 1889- 207.782
Fifty years on the Nebraska frontier; the history of the Presbyterian theological seminary at Omaha, Nebraska, written for the semicentennial of the seminary, by Charles Arthur Hawley... Omaha, Ralph printing co., 1941. 152 p. front., plates, ports. 23 1/2 cm. "First edition." "Bibliography of those who have served on the faculty": p. 132-134. [BV4070.O686H3 1941] 41-8458
1. Omaha. Presbyterian theological seminary. 2. Presbyterian church in Nebraska. I. Title.

Omens.

SUMMA izbu. English & Akkadian. 133.3'34'0935
The omen series Summa izbu. By Erle Leichty. Locust Valley, N.Y., J. J. Augustin, 1970. viii, 242 p. 29 cm. (Texts from cuneiform sources, v. 4) "Contains a combined text with transliteration, translation, and philological notes based on the 146 fragments listed by von Soden, and almost as many new, unpublished fragments." Includes bibliographical references. [BF1777.S9] 74-21953
1. Omens. 2. Folk-lore, Assyro-Babylonian. 3. Birth (in religion, folk-lore, etc.) 4. Assyro-Babylonian language—Texts. I.

Leichty, Erle, 1933- ed. II. Soden, Wolfram, Freiherr von, 1908- III. Title. IV. Series.

Onahan, William James, 1836-1919.

GALLERY, Mary (Onahan) Mrs. 920
Life of William J. Onahan; stories of men who made Chicago, by Mary Onahan Gallery. [Chicago] Loyola university press [c 1929] xiii, 74 p. incl. front. plates, ports. 20 cm. [Full name: Mrs. Mary Josephine (Onahan) Gallery] [CT275.O55G3] 29-22411
1. Onahan, William James, 1836-1919. 2. Catholics in Chicago. I. Title.

Onderdonk, Benjamin Tredwell, bp., 1791-1861.

OBSEQUIES and obituary 922.
notices of the late Right Reverend Benj. Tredwell Onderdonk, D.D., bishop of New York: including the several applications for the removal of his sentence, and other documents, so arranged as to form a connected history of events, with introductory remarks. By a New-York churchman. New York, H. B. Price, 1862. vi, [7]-191 p. front. (port.) 23 cm. [BX5995.O6O3] 2-27132
1. Onderdonk, Benjamin Tredwell, bp., 1791-1861. I. New York churchman.

OBSEQUIES and obituary 922
notices of the late Right Reverend Benj. Tredwell Onderdonk, D. D., bishop of New York, Including the several applications for the removal of his sentence, and other documents, so arranged as to form a connected history of events, with introductory remarks. By a New-York churchman. New York, H. B. Price, 1862. vi, [7]-191 p. front. (port.) 23 cm. [BX5995.O6O3] 2-27132
1. Onderdonk, Benjamin Tredwell, bp., 1791-1861. I. New York churchman.

ONDERDONK, Benjamin Tredwell, bp., 1791-1861, respondent.
The proceedings of the court convened under the third canon of 1844, in the city of New York ... December 10, 1844, for the trial of the Right Rev. Benjamin T. Onderdonk, D.D., bishop of New York; on a presentment made by the bishops of Virginia, Tennessee, and Georgia ... New York, D. Appleton & co.; Philadelphia, G. S. Appleton, 1845. 333 p. 22 1/2 cm. [BX5960.O6A2] 45-33460
I. Protestant Episcopal church in the U.S.A. Court of trial of a bishop. II. Title.

Onderdonk, Henry Ustick, bp., 1789-1858. Episcopacy tested by Scripture.

EMORY, John. bp., 262.12
bp.,1789-1835.
The Episcopal controversy reviewed. By John Emory...Edited by his son, from an unfinished manuscript. New York, T. Mason and G. Lane, for the Methodist Episcopal church, 1838. vi, [7]-183 p. front. (port.) 24 cm. Preface signed: R. E. [i.e. Robert Emory] "The manuscript contained only a discussion of the subject of episcopacy in general, in a reply to 'An essay on the invalidity of Presbyterian ordination', by John Eaten Cooke...and a part of a reply to a tract entitled 'Episcopacy tested by Scripture', by Dr. H. U. Onderdonk".--p. iv. [BV670.E5] 39-3001
1. Onderdonk, Henry Ustick, bp., 1789-1858. Episcopacy tested by Scripture. 2. Cooke, John Esten, 1783-1853. An essay on the invalidity of Presbyterian ordination. 3. Episcopacy. 4. Apostolic succession. I. Emory, Robert, 1814-1848, ed. II. Title.

One (The One in philosophy)—Addresses, essays, lectures.

COPLESTON, Frederick 291.2
Charles.
Religion and the One : philosophies East and West / Frederick Copleston. New York : Crossroad, 1981. p. cm. (Gifford lectures ; 1980) Includes index. [BD395.C66] 19 81-5372 ISBN 0-8245-0092-X : 14.95
1. One (The One in philosophy)—Addresses, essays, lectures. 2. Many (Philosophy)—Addresses, essays, lectures. 3. Philosophy, Comparative—Addresses, essays, lectures. 4. Religion—Philosophy—Addresses, essays, lectures. 5. Mysticism—Addresses, essays, lectures. I. Title. II. Series.

Oneida community.

CARDEN, Maren 335'.9'74764
Lockwood.
Oneida: Utopian community to modern corporation. Baltimore, Johns Hopkins Press [1969] xx, 228 p. illus., ports., plan. 23 cm. Bibliography: p. 213-218. [HX656.O5C3] 73-75183 8.50
1. Oneida Community. 2. Oneida, ltd. I. Title.

ESTLAKE, Allan. 335'.9'74764
The Oneida community; a record of an attempt to carry out the principles of Christian unselfishness and scientific race-improvement. London, G. Redway, 1900. [New York, AMS Press, 1973] viii, 158 p. 23 cm. [HX656.O5E8 1973] 72-4179 ISBN 0-404-10758-3 9.50
1. Oneida Community.

NOYES, George 289.9 922.89
Wallingford, ed.
John Humphrey Noyes, the Putney community; compiled and edited by George Wallingford Noyes; with twenty-four illustrations. Oneida, N. Y., 1931. xii p., 1 l., 393 p. front., plates, ports. 23 cm. [BX8795.P4N65] 289.9 31-17286
1. Noyes, John Humphrey, 1811-1886. 2. Oneida community. I. Title.

NOYES, John Humphrey, 230.99
1811-1886.
The Berean: a manual for the help of those who seek the faith of the primitive church. By John H. Noyes ... Putney, Vt., Office of the Spiritual magazine, 1847. viii, [9]-504 p. 23 1/2 cm. [PX8795.P4A8] 33-5408
1. Oneida community. I. Title.

NOYES, John Humphrey, 230.99
1811-1886.
The Berean: a manual for the help of those who seek the faith of the primitive church. By John H. Noyes ... Putney, Vt., Office of the Spiritual magazine, 1847. viii, [9]-504 p. 24 cm. [BX8795.P4A8] 33-5408
1. Oneida community. I. Title.

NOYES, John Humphrey, 335.9'747'6
1811-1886.
Home-talks / by John Humphrey Noyes ; edited by Alfred Barron and George Noyes Miller. Vol. 1. New York : AMS Press, 1975. v, 358 p. : port. ; 19 cm. (Communal societies in America) No more published. Reprint of the 1875 ed. published by the Oneida Community, Oneida, N.Y. [HX656.O5N8 1975] 72-2974 ISBN 0-404-10738-9 : 18.00
1. Oneida Community. I. Barron, Alfred. II. Miller, George Noyes, 1845-1904. III. Title.

NOYES, John Humphrey, 1811- 289
1886.
Religious experience of John Humphrey Noyes, founder of the Oneida community; with seventeen illustrations, compiled and edited by George Wallingford Noyes. New York, The Macmillan company, 1923. xiii p., 1 l., 416 p. front., plates, ports. 19 1/2 cm. [BX8795.P4N8] 23-8624
1. Oneida community. I. Noyes, George Wallingford, ed. II. Title.

NOYES, John Humphrey, 1811- 922.
1886.
Religious experience of John Humphrey Noyes, founder of the Oneida community; with seventeen illustrations, compiled and edited by George Wallingford Noyes. New York, The Macmillan company, 1923. xiii p., 1 l., 416 p. front., plates. ports. 20 cm. [BX8795.P4N8] 23-8624
1. Oneida community. I. Noyes, George Wallingford, ed. II. Title.

ONEIDA Community. 335'.9'74764
Bible communism; a compilation from the annual reports and other publications of the Oneida Association and its branches; presenting, in connection with their history, a summary view of their religious and social theories. Brooklyn, N.Y., Office of the Circular, 1853. [New York, AMS Press, 1973] 128 p. illus. 23 cm. At head of title: A book for students of the higher law. On spine: COM. [HX656.O5O54 1973] 72-2978 ISBN 0-404-10742-7
1. Oneida Community. I. Title.

[ONEIDA Community] 335'.9'74764
Mutual criticism / introd. by Murray Levine and Barbara Benedict Bunker. Syracuse, N.Y. : Syracuse University Press, 1975. xxx, 96 p. ; 21 cm. "May most likely be attributed to John Humphrey Noyes." Reprint of the 1876 ed. published by the Office of the American Socialist, Oneida, N.Y. Bibliography: p. xxix-xxx. [HX656.O5O54 1975] 75-6236 ISBN 0-8156-2169-8 : 8.50 ISBN 0-8156-2170-1 pbk. 4.75
1. Oneida Community. 2. Socialism, Christian. I. Noyes, John Humphrey, 1811-1886. II. Levine, Murray, 1928- III. Bunker, Barbara Benedict. IV. Title.

ROBERTSON, Constance 335'.9'74764
(Noyes)
Oneida Community: the breakup, 1876-1881. [1st ed.] [Syracuse] Syracuse University Press, 1972. xv, 327 p. illus. 23 cm. (A York State book) Bibliography: p. 317-320. [HX656.O5R63] 72-38405 ISBN 0-8156-0086-0
1. Oneida Community.

ROBERTSON, Constance 335'.9'74764
Noyes.
Oneida Community profiles / Constance Noyes Robertson. Syracuse, N.Y. : Syracuse University Press, 1977. ix, 146 p. : ill. ; 24 cm. (A York state book) [HX656.O5R633] 77-8226 ISBN 0-8156-0140-9 : 10.00
1. Oneida Community. I. Title.

Oneida Community—History.

KERN, Louis J., 1943- 261.8'357
An ordered love : sex roles and sexuality in Victorian Utopias : the Shakers, the Mormons, and the Oneida Community / by Louis J. Kern. Chapel Hill : University of North Carolina Press, c1981. p. cm. Includes index. Bibliography: p. [BT708.K47] 80-10763 ISBN 0-8078-1443-1 : 24.00 ISBN 0-8078-4074-2 pbk. : 12.50
1. Oneida Community—History. 2. Sex (Theology)—History of doctrines. 3. Sex customs—United States—History—19th century. 4. Sex role. 5. Shakers—United States—History. 6. Mormons and mormonism in the United States—History. I. Title.

O'Neill, Eugene, 1888-1953—Criticism and interpretation.

ROBINSON, James A. 812'.52
A divided vision, Eugene O'Neill and Oriental thought / by James A. Robinson. Carbondale : Southern Illinois University Press, c1982. p. cm. Includes index. Bibliography: p. [PS3529.N5Z794] 19 81-14428 ISBN 0-8093-1035-X : 17.50
1. O'Neill, Eugene, 1888-1953—Criticism and interpretation. 2. O'Neill, Eugene, 1888-1953—Philosophy. 3. Philosophy, Oriental. 4. Asia—Religion. I. Title.

Onesimus, Saint, d. 109.

GOODSPEED, Edgar Johnson, 227.5
1871-1962.
The key to Ephesians. [Chicago] University of Chicago Press [1956] xvi, 75 p. 25 cm. Suggests that the author of Ephesians was Onesimus. [BS2695.G58] 56-6550
1. Onesimus, Saint, d. 109. 2. Bible. N. T. Ephesians—Criticism, interpretation, etc. I. Bible. N. T. Ephesians. English. American Revised. 1956 II. Title.

Ontology.

ATKINSON, William Walker, 111
1862-
The mastery of being; a study of the ultimate principle of reality, and the practical application thereof, by William Walker Atkinson ... Holyoke, Mass., The Elizabeth Towne company, 1911. 196 p. front. (port.) 19 cm. [BD331.A8] 11-25953 1.00
1. Ontology. 2. Reality. I. Title.

BANDTLOW, Peter. 111.8
Being and transcendental awareness. [Staten Island, N.Y.] League of the Morning Star [1970] 44 p. front. 23 cm. "Book one." [BD331.B265] 74-132994
1. Ontology. 2. Wisdom. I. Title.

BEING known and being revealed. Stockton, Calif., College of the Pacific, 1957. 55p. 20cm. (Pacific Philosophy Institute publication, v. 7) Tully Cleon Knoles lectures in philosophy, 1957.
1. Ontology. I. Hartt, Julian Norris. II. Series: Stockton, Calif. College of the Pacific. Pacific Philosophy Institute. Pacific Philosophy Institute publications, v. 7 III. Series: Tully Cleon Knoles lecture, 1957

BERGMENN, Gustar 1906- 111
Realism; a critique of Brentano and Meinong. Madison, University of Wisconsin Press, 1967. viii, 458 p. 22 cm. "Bibliographical note": p. 445-446. [B3212.Z7B4] 67-12003
1. Brentano, Franz Clemens, 1838-1917. 2. Meinong, Alexius, Ritter von Handschuchsheim. 1853-1920. 3. Ontology. I. Title.

BITTLE, Celestine Nicholas 111
Charles, 1884-
The domain of being, ontology [by] Celestine N. Bittle, O.M. CAP. New York, Milwaukee [etc.] The Bruce publishing company [c1939] x, 401 p. diagrs. 22 1/2 cm. "Readings" at end of each chapter. Bibliography: p. 391-394. [BD611.B5] 30-2581
1. ontology. I. Title.

BOBBE, Dorothie (De Bear) 111
1927
Aquinas On being and essence. A translation and interpretation by Joseph Bobik [Notre Dame, Ind.] Univ. of Notre Dame Pr. [c.1965] xv, 286p. 21cm. Bibl. [B765.T53D52] 65-23516 5.00
1. Ontology. 2. Subsatnce (Philosophy) I. Thomas Aquinas, Saint, 1222?-1274 II. Title.

BOBIK, Joseph, 1927- 111
Aquinas On being and essence. A translation and interpretation by Joseph Bobik. [Notre Dame, Ind.,] University of Notre Dame Press [1965] xv, 286 p. 21 cm. Bibliographical references included in "Notes" (p. 270-277) [B765.T53D52] 65-23516
1. Ontology. 2. Substance (Philosophy) I. Thomas Aquinas, Saint, 1225?-1274. On being and essence. II. Title.

CERNUSCHI, Alberto. 111
Theory of autodeism; evolutionary chain in ontological-metaphysical terms. New York, Philosophical Library [1969] xi, 59 p. 23 cm. Translation of Teoria del autodeismo; cadena de evolucion en terminos ontologico-metafisicos. [B1034.C43T43] 69-15948 3.50
1. Ontology. 2. Philosophical anthropology. I. Title.

CHASE, Warren, 1813-1891. 111
Essence and substance: a treatise on organic and inorganic matter: the finite and the infinite: transient and eternal life. By Warren Chase ... Boston, Colby & Rich, 1886. 126 p. 20 cm. [BD331.C5] 28-4984
1. Ontology. I. Title.

COCHRANE, Arthur C 111
The existentialists and God; being and the being of God in the thought of Soren Kierkegaard, Karl Jaspers, Martin Heidegger, Jean-Paul Sartre, Paul Tillich, Etienne Gilson [and] Karl Barth. Philadelphia, Westminster Press [c1956] 174p. 21cm. Includes bibliography. [BD331.C56] 56-5105
1. Ontology. 2. God. 3. Existentialism. I. Title.

COFFEY, Peter, 1876-
Ontology; or, The theory of being; an introduction to general metaphysics, by P. Coffey ... London, New York [etc.] Longmans, Green and co., 1914. xii, 439 p. 23 1/2 cm. A 15
1. Ontology. I. Title.

COFFEY, Peter, 1876- 111
Ontology, or the theory of being; an introduction to general metaphysics by P. Coffey New York, P. Smith, 1938. xii, 439 p. 24 cm. "First published, 1914; reprinted 1938." [BD311.C6 1938] 39-15568
1. Ontology. I. Title.

COLONNA, Egidio, Abp., d. 1316. 111
Theorems on existence and essence (Theoremata de esse et essentia) [By] Giles of Rome. Translated from the Latin with an introd. and pref. by Michael V. Murray. Milwaukee, Marquette University Press, 1952 [i. e. 1953] xiv, 112p. 23cm. (Mediaeval philosophical texts in translation, no. 7) Bibliography: p. 22-23. Bibliographical footnotes. [B765.C63T53] 53-1722
1. Ontology. I. Murray, Michael V., 1906- tr. II. Title.

CUNNINGHAM, Walter F. 111
Ontology, by Walter F. Cunningham ... New York, N. Y., Fordham university press [c1939] 68 p. 22 cm. "References": p. 68. [BD311.C8] 39-30169
1. Ontology. I. Title.

DAY, Henry Noble, 1808-1890. 111
Outlines of ontological science; or, A philosophy of knowledge and of being, by Henry N. Day ... New York, G. P. Putnam's sons, 1876. xi, 441 p. 20 cm. [BD311.D2] 11-22194
1. Ontology. 2. Knowledge, Theory of. I. Title.

DOUGHERTY, Kenneth Francis, 1917- 111
Metaphysics; an introduction to the philosophy of being Peekskill, N. Y., Graymoor Pr. 1965. 203p. illus. 24cm. Bibl. [BD311.D6] 65-14722 price unreported
1. Ontology. I. Title.

ESSER, Gerard, 1882- 111
Metaphysica generalis in usum scholarum. Ed. alters, emendata, et aucta. Techny, Ill., Typis Domus Missionum ad St. Mariam, 1952. 368 p. 24 cm. Includes bibliography. [BD318.L3E8 1952] 52-44594
1. Ontology. I. Title.

FARBER, Marvin, 1901- 111.
Phenomenology and existence; toward a philosophy within nature [Magnolia. Mass., P. Smith, 1967] 244p. 21cm. (Harper torch- bk., Acad. lib. rebound) Bibl. [BD311.F3] 4.50
1. Ontology. 2. Phenomenology. 3. Philosophical anthropology. I. Title.

FARBER, Marvin, 1901- 111.1
Phenomenology and existence; toward a philosophy within nature. [1st ed.] New York, Harper & Row [1967] 244 p. 21 cm. (Harper torchbooks) (The Academy library.) Bibliographical footnotes. [BD311.F3] 67-10673
1. Ontology. 2. Phenomenology. 3. Philosophical anthropology. I. Title.

FEIBLEMAN, James, 1904- 111
Ontology. Baltimore, Johns Hopkins Press, 1951. xix, 807 p. diagrs. 24 cm. [BD311.F45] 51-14817
1. Ontology. I. Title.

FEIBLEMAN, James Kern, 1904- 111
Ontology, by James K. Feibleman. New York, Greenwood Press, 1968 [c1951] xix, 807 p. 24 cm. [BD311.F45 1968] 68-8333
1. Ontology. I. Title.

FISK, Milton. 111
Nature and necessity; an essay in physical ontology. Bloomington, Indiana University Press [1974, c1973] xv, 301 p. illus. 24 cm. (Indiana University humanities series, no. 73) Bibliography: p. 281-292. [BD311.F57 1974] 72-85605 ISBN 0-253-33980-4 12.50
1. Ontology. 2. Philosophy of nature. 3. Necessity (Philosophy) I. Title. II. Series: Indiana. University. Indiana University humanities series, no. 73.

[GARRETSON, James Edmund] 1828-1895. 218
Man and his world; or, The oneness of now and eternity. A series of imaginary discourses between Socrates and Protagoras. By John Darby [pseud.]... Philadelphia, J. B. Lippincott company, 1889. xiv, [2], 13-259 p. front. (port.) 17 1/2 cm. Part 1, p. 1-106, first published in 1875, under title "Two thousand years after." Contents.--pt. i. Two thousand years after.--pt. ii. Philosophy of the eternal now. [BD431.D35] 20-6266
1. Ontology. 2. Soul. I. Title. II. Title: Socrates and Protagoras.

GAUGHAN, J. Anthony. 111
The metaphysical value and importance of the concept of being, by J. Anthony Gaughan. Dublin, Kamac Publications [1969] 102 p. 22 cm. Bibliography: p. 92-98. [BD331.G35] 79-263849 12/6
1. Ontology. 2. Metaphysics. I. Title.

GLENN, Paul Joseph, 1893- 111
Ontology, a class manual in fundamental metaphysics, by Robt. C. Cumming and Frank B. Gilbert St. Louis, Mo., and London, B. Herder book co., 1937. x, 340 p. 19 cm. [BD311.G5] 37-39097
1. Ontology. I. Title.

GOHEEN, John. 189.4
The problem of matter and form in the De ente et essentia of Thomas Aquinas, by John Goheon. Cambridge, Mass., Harvard university press, 1940. 5 p. l., [3]-137 p. 20 cm. [Full name: John David Maclay Goheen] Contents.--Aquinas and the problem of matter and form in the "Fons vitae."-- Augustine and the problem of matter and form--Aquinas answers Avicebron: the distinction between essence and existence.--Bibliography (p. [123]-127) [B765.T53D53] 40-6897
1. Thomas Aquinas, Saint, 1225?-1274. De ente et essentia. 2. Ibn Gabirol, Solomon ben Judah, known as Avicebron. 3. Ontology. 4. Substance (Philosophy) I. Title. II. Title: Matter and form in the De ente et essentia of Thomas Aquinas.

GREGG, Richard Bartlett, 1885- 111
What's it all about and what am I? [by] Richard B. Gregg. New York, Grossman Publishers, 1968. 189 p. 21 cm. Bibliographical references included in "Notes" (p. 165-179) [BD311.G69 1968] 68-30781 4.50
1. Ontology. I. Title.

[GREPPO, Claude]
The exegesis of life ... New York, The Minerva publishing company, 1889. 192 p. 20 cm. (On cover: Minerva series, no. 16) [BD811.G7] 15-13533
1. Ontology. I. Title.

GROSSMANN, Reinhardt, 1931- 111
Ontological reduction. Bloomington, Indiana University Press, 1973. vi, 215 p. 24 cm. (Indiana University humanities series, v. 72) Includes bibliographical references. [BD331.G76 1973] 72-85604 ISBN 0-253-34246-5 9.00
1. Frege, Gottlob, 1848-1925. 2. Ontology. 3. Categories (Philosophy) 4. Number concept. I. Title. II. Series: Indiana. University. Indiana University humanities series, v. 72.

HARDING, Michael J. 110
The science of metaphysics. Copyright...by Michael J. Harding... [Worcester, Mass., C. H. Rosseel, jr.] c1943. 126 p. 23 cm. [BD311.H26] 44-35813
1. Ontology. 2. Metaphysics I. Title.

HARRISON, Ross. 111
On what there must be / by Ross Harrison. Oxford [Eng.] : Clarendon Press, 1974. x, 210 p. ; 22 cm. Includes index. [BD331.H318] 74-189853 ISBN 0-19-824507-6 : 13.75
1. Ontology. 2. Space and time. 3. Perception. 4. Private language problem. 5. Act (Philosophy) I. Title.
Distributed by Oxford University Press, N.Y.

HARTMANN, Nicolai, 1882-1950. 111
New ways of ontology / by Nicolai Hartmann ; translated by Reinhard C. Kuhn. Westport, Conn. : Greenwood Press, 1975, c1952. 145 p. ; 22 cm. Translation of Neue Wege der Ontologie. Reprint of the 1953 ed. published by Regnery, Chicago. [BD331.H334 1975] 75-1112 ISBN 0-8371-7989-0 lib.bdg. : 9.75
1. Ontology. I. Title.

HARTMANN, Nicolai, 1882-1951. 111
New ways of ontology; translated by Reinhard C. Kuhn. Chicago, H. Regnery Co., 1953 [c1952] 145p. 22cm. [BD331.H334] 53-5776
1. Ontology. I. Title.

HASEROT, Francis Samuel, 1895- 111
Essays on the logic of being. Freeport, N.Y., Books for Libraries Press [1969] xiii, 641 p. 24 cm. (Essay index reprint series) Reprint of the 1932 ed. [BD311.H3 1969] 74-90643
1. Ontology. 2. Worth. I. Title. II. Title: Logic of being.

HASEROT, Francis Samuel, 1895- 111
Essays on the logic of being, by Francis S. Haserot. New York, The Macmillan company, 1932. xiii, 641 p. 24 cm. The second part of the essays is devoted to value as an ontological category. cf. Pref. [BD311.H3] 32-9768
1. Ontology. 2. Worth. I. Title. II. Title: Logic of being.

HEIDEGGER, Martin, 1889- 111.1
Being and time. Translated by John Macquarrie p Edward Robinson. New York, Harper [1962] 589 p. 23 cm. Bibliographical references included in "Author's notes" (p. [489]-501) [B3279.H48S43] 62-7289
1. Ontology. 2. Space and time. I. Title.

HEIDEGGER, Martin, 1889- 111.1
Being and time. Translated by John Macquarrie & Edward Robinson. New York, Harper [1962] 589 p. 23 cm. Bibliographical references included in "Author's notes" (p. [489]-501) [B3279.H48S43 1962a] 62-7289
1. Ontology. 2. Space and time. I. Title.

HEIDEGGER, Martin, 1889- 111
Discourse on thinking. Tr. of Gelassenheit, by John M. Anderson, E. Hans Freund. Introd. by John M. Anderson. New York, Harper [1966] 93p. 22cm. (His Works) Bibl. [B3279.H48G43] 66-15041 3.50 bds.,
1. Ontology. 2. Thought and thinking. I. Title.

HEIDEGGER, Martin, 1889- 111
Discourse on thinking. A translation of Gelassenheit, by John M. Anderson and E. Hans Freund. With an introd. by John M. Anderson. New York, Harper & Row [1969, c1966] 93 p. 21 cm. (Harper torchbooks, TB1459) [B3279] 70-7430 1.45
1. Ontology. 2. Thought and thinking. I. Title.

HEIDEGGER, Martin, 1889- 111
An introduction to metaphysics. Tr. [from German] by Ralph Manheim. GardenCity, N.Y., Doubleday, 1961, [c.1959] 182p. (Anchor bk. A251) .95 pap.,
1. Ontology. I. Title.

HEIDEGGER, Martin, 1889- 111
An introduction to metaphysics. Translated by Ralph Manheim. New Haven, Yale University Press, 1959. xi, 214 p. 22 cm. [BD331.H4313] 59-6796
1. Ontology.

HEIDEGGER, Martin, 1889- 111.8
On time and being. Translated by Joan Stambaugh. [1st ed.] New York, Harper & Row [1972] xi, 84 p. 22 cm. Translation of works collected in 1969 under title: Zur Sache des Denkens. Contents.Contents.—Time and being.—Summary of a seminar on the lecture "Time and being."—The end of philosophy and the task of thinking.—My way to phenomenology. Includes bibliographical references. [B3279.H48Z7813 1972] 72-78334 ISBN 0-06-063855-9 4.95
1. Ontology. 2. Space and time. 3. Phenomenology. I. Title.

HEIDEGGER, Martin, 1889- 111
The question of being. Translated with an introd. by William Kluback and Jean T. Wilde. New York, Twayne Publishers [1958] 109p. 23cm. Bibliography: p. 31. [B3279.H47E56] 59-382
1. German text and translation of the author's Uber die Linie, an article contributed to the publication issued in honor of Ernst Junger (1955) 2. Ontology. I. Title.

HERMANCE, William Ellsworth. 111
An unorthodox conception of being; a synthetic philosophy of ontology, by William Ellsworth Hermance. New York and London, G. P. Putnam's sons, 1912. x p., 1 l., 441 p. 22 cm. [BD331.H5] 13-611 2.50
1. Ontology. 2. Science—Philosophy. I. Title.

INGARDEN, Roman, 1893- 111
Time and modes of being. Tr. [from Polish] by Helen R. Michejda. Springfield, Ill., Thomas [c.1960, 1964] xi, 170p. 24cm. (Amer. lect. ser., pubn. no. 558. Amer. lects. in phil.) Bibl. 63-18518 6.75
1. Ontology. I. Title.

KAMINSKY, Jack, 1922- 111'.01'4
Language and ontology. Carbondale, Southern Illinois University Press [1969] xii, 318 p. 24 cm. Bibliography: p. [305]-312. [BD311.K3 1969] 69-11516 10.00
1. Ontology. 2. Languages—Philosophy. I. Title.

KENYON, Roger A. 111
Existential structure : an analytic enquiry / by Roger A. Kenyon. New York : Philosophical Library, c1976. 63 p. ; 22 cm. [BD331.K38] 76-4222 ISBN 0-8022-2181-5 : 6.00
1. Ontology. 2. Existentialism. 3. Languages—Philosophy. I. Title.

KLUBERTANZ, George Peter, 1912- 111
Being and God; an introduction to the philosophy of being and to natural theology [by] George P. Klubertanz, Maurice R. Holloway. New York, Appleton [c.1963] 382p. 22cm. Abridgment of the combined texts of Introduction to the philosophy of being, by G. P. Klubertanz, and An introduction to natural theology, by M. R. Holoway. Bibl. 63-15359 4.50
1. Ontology 2. Natural theology. I. Holloway, Maurice R. II. Title.

KLUBERTANZ, George Peter, 1912- 111
Being and God; an introduction to the philosophy of being and to natural theology [by] George P. Klubertanz [and] Maurice R. Holloway. New York, Appleton-Century-Crofts [1963] 382 p. 22 cm. An abridgment of the combined texts of Introduction to the philosophy of being, by G. P. Klubertans, and An introduction to natural theology, by M. R. Holloway. [BD125.K55] 63-15359
1. Ontology. 2. Natural theology. Holloway, Maurice R. I. Title.

LANGO, John W. 113
Whitehead's ontology, by John W. Lango. [1st ed.] Albany, State University of New York Press, 1972. 102 p. 24 cm. Includes bibliographical references. [B1674.W353P76] 78-171184 ISBN 0-87395-093-3 6.00
1. Whitehead, Alfred North, 1861-1947. Process and reality. 2. Ontology. I. Title.

LAVELLE, Louis, 1883-1951.
Introduction to ontology. Translated by Wesley Piersol Murphy. New York, Carlton Press [c1966] 111 p. 21 cm. (A Reflection book) Bibliography: p. 110-111. 68-55169
1. Ontology. 2. Worth. I. Title.

MCGLYNN, James V. 111
A metaphysics of being and God [by] James V. McGlynn, Sister Paul Mary Farley. Englewood Cliffs, N.J., Prentice [c.1966] viii, 312p. 22cm. Bibl. [BD331.M23] 66-12091 4.95
1. Ontology. 2. Natural theology. I. Farley, Paul Mary, Sister, joint author. II. Title.

MCTAGGART, John McTaggart Ellis, 1866-1925. 111
The nature of existence. Cambridge, University Press, 1921. Grosse Pointe, Mich., Scholarly Press, 1968. 2 v. 23 cm. Vol. 2 edited by C. D. Broad. Bibliographical footnotes. [BD331.M313 1968] 70-2985
1. Ontology. 2. Reality. I. Broad, Charlie Dunbar, 1887- ed. II. Title.

MCTAGGART, John McTaggart Ellis, 1866-1925. 111
The nature of existence, by John McTaggart Ellis McTaggart... Cambridge [Eng.] The University press, 1921-27. 2 v. 23 1/2 cm. Vol. 2 edited by C. D. Broad. [BD331.M3] 21-13018

1. Ontology. 2. Reality. I. Broad, Charlie Dunbar, 1887- ed. II. Title.

MARITAIN, Jacques, 1882- 111
A preface to metaphysics; seven lectures on being. [New York] New Amer. Lib. [1962] 142p. (Mentor omega bk., MP403) 60 pap.,
1. Ontology. I. Title.

MARITAIN, Jacques, 1882- 111
A preface to metaphysics; seven lectures on being. Freeport, N.Y., Books for Libraries Press [1971] v, 152 p. 23 cm. Reprint of the 1939 ed. Translation of Sept lecons sur l'etre et les premiers principes de la raison speculative. Includes bibliographical references. [BD312.M32 1971] 74-157346 ISBN 0-8369-5807-1
1. Ontology. I. Title.

MARITAIN, Jacques, 1882- 111
A preface to metaphysics; seven lectures on being, by Jacques Maritain. New York, Sheed and Ward, 1939. v, 152 p. diagr. 20 cm. Translation of Sept lecons sur l'etre et les premiers principes de la raison speculative. [BD312.M32] 40-6096
1. Ontology. I. Title.

MERLEAU-PONTY, Maurice, 1908- 111
1961.
The visible and the invisible; followed by working notes. Edited by Claude Lefort. Translated by Alphonso Lingis. Evanston [Ill.] Northwestern University Press, 1968. lvi, 282 p. 24 cm. (Northwestern University studies in phenomenology & existential philosophy) Bibliographical footnotes. [B2430.M379V513] 68-31025
1. Ontology. 2. Knowledge, Theory of. I. Lefort, Claude, ed. II. Title. III. Series.

MOORE, Jared Sparks, 1879- 111
Rifts in the universe; a study of the historic dichotomies and modalities of being, by Jared Sparks Moore ... New Haven, Yale university press; London, H. Milford, Oxford university press, 1927. xv, 130 p. illus. 21 cm. "Published on the foundation established in memory of James Wesley Cooper of the class of 1865, Yale college." [BD311.M6] 27-24606
1. Ontology. I. Yale university. James Wesley Cooper memorial publication fund. II. Title.

MULLER-THYM, Bernard Joseph, 111
1909-
...Establishment of the university of being in the doctrine of Meister Eckhart of Hochheim [by] Bernard J. Muller-Thym ... with a preface by Etienne Gilson ... New York, London, Pub. for the Institute of medieval studies by Sheed & Ward, 1939. xx, 140 p. 24 cm. (Saint Michael's mediaeval studies. Monograph series) "First printing." Bibliography: p. 117-137. [B765.E34M8] 39-31039
1. Eckhart, meister, d. 1327. 2. Ontology. I. Title.

MUNITZ, Milton Karl, 1913- 111
Existence and logic / Milton K. Munitz. New York : New York University Press, 1974. xvi, 221 p. ; 24 cm. Includes bibliographical references and index. [BD331.M86] 74-4740 ISBN 0-8147-5366-3 : 13.75
1. Ontology. 2. Logic. I. Title.

NEVILLE, Robert C. 111
God the Creator; on the transcendence and presence of God, by Robert C. Neville. Drawings by Beth Neville. Chicago, University of Chicago Press [1968] xi, 320 p. ports. 24 cm. Bibliographical footnotes. [BD331.N48] 68-13128
1. Ontology. 2. Creation. 3. God—Knowableness. 4. Religion—Philosophy. I. Title.

OWENS, Joseph. 111.1
An interpretation of existence. Milwaukee, Bruce Pub. Co. [1968] vii, 153 p. 22 cm. (Horizons in philosophy) Bibliographical footnotes. [BD331.O93] 68-25960
1. Ontology. I. Title.

THE philosophy of being 111
[by] Henri Renard ... Milwaukee, The Bruce publishing company [c1943] viii, 256 p. 20 1/2 cm. Bibliographical foot-notes. [BD331.R] A 45
1. Ontology. 2. Individuality. 3. Reality.

PONTIFEX, Mark, 1896- 111
The meaning of existence; a metaphysical enquiry, by Mark Pontifex and Illtyd Trethowan. London, New York, Longmans, Green [1953] 179p. 19cm. [BD311.P6] 53-9938
1. Ontology. I. Trethowan, Illtyd, 1907- II. Title.

A preface to metaphysics;
seven lectures on being. New York, Sheed & Ward [1958] 152p. diagr. 21cm. Translation of Sept. lecons sur l'etre et les premiers principes de la raison speculative.
1. Ontology. I. Maritain, Jacques, 1882-

RAEYMAEKER, Louis de, 1895- 111
The philosophy of being; a synthesis of metaphysics. Translated by Edmund H. Ziegelmeyer. St. Louis, B. Herder Book Co. [1954] xii, 360p. 22cm. [BD312.R33] 53-8704
1. Ontology. I. Title.

RENARD, Henri, 1894- 111
The philosophy of being [by] Henri Renard ... St. Louis, New York [etc.] Planographed by John S. Swift co., inc. [c1942] iv, 55, [1], 56-139 p. 28 x 22 cm. Bibliographical foot-notes. [BD331.R4] 44-28630
1. Ontology. 2. Individuality. 3. Reality. I. Title.

RENARD, Henri, 1894- 111
The philosophy of being [by] Henri Renard ... 2d ed., rev. and enl. Milwaukee, The Bruce publishing company [1946] x, 262 p. 20 1/2 cm. Bibliographical foot-notes. [BD331.R4 1946] 46-5932
1. Ontology. 2. Individuality. 3. Reality. I. Title.

ROTHER, Aloysius Joseph, 111
1859-
Being; a study in metaphysics, by Rev. Aloysius Rother ... St. Louis, Mo., B. Herder; [etc., etc.] 1911. viii, 127 p. 20 cm. [BD331.R7] 11-29050
1. Ontology. I. Title.

RUEFF, Jacques. 111
The gods and the kings; a glance at creative power. Translated by George Robinson and Roger Glemet. [1st American ed.] New York, Macmillan [1973] 247 p. 21 cm. Translation of Les Dieux et les rois. Includes bibliographical references. [BD312.R8313 1973] 72-94011 8.95
1. Broglie, Louis, prince de, 1892- 2. Ontology. 3. Individuation. 4. Order (Philosophy) 5. Quantum theory. I. Title.

SANTAYANA, George, 1863- 111.1
1952.
The realm of essence. Book first of Realms of being. Westport, Conn., Greenwood Press [1974] xxiii, 183 p. 22 cm. Reprint of the 1928 ed. published by Constable, London. [BD331.S3 1974] 72-11745 ISBN 0-8371-6700-0 9.75
1. Ontology. I. Title.

SANTAYANA, George, 1863-1952. 111
Realms of being. One-volume ed., with a new introd. by the author. New York, Cooper Square Publishers, 1972 [c1942] xxxii, 862 p. 24 cm. "Compact edition ... originally issued in four separate volumes at intervals of years." Contents.Contents.—The realm of essence.—The realm of matter.—The realm of truth.—The realm of spirit. [B945.S23R42 1972] 72-79638 ISBN 0-8154-0425-5
1. Ontology. 2. Matter. 3. Truth. 4. Consciousness. I. Title.

SCHELLING, Friedrich Wilhelm 111
Joseph von, 1775-1854.
The ages of the world. Translated with introd. and notes by Frederick De Wolfe Bolman, Jr. New York, AMS Press, 1967 [c1942] xi, 251 p. 23 cm. Translation of Die Weltalter. Bibliography: p. [241]-243. [B2894] 68-444
1. Ontology. I. Bolman, Frederick De Wolfe, 1912- tr. II. Title.

SCHELLING, Friedrich Wilhelm 111
Joseph von, 1775-1854.
... The ages of the world, translated with introduction and notes by Frederick de Wolfe Bolman, jr. New York, Columbia university press, 1942. xi p., 2 l., [3]-251 p. 22 1/2 cm. (Half-title: Columbia studies in philosophy, ed. under the Dept. of philosophy, Columbia university, no. 3) At head of title: Schelling. Translation of Die weltalter, begun in 1811 but published only after Schelling's death. cf. p. 5. Bibliography: p. [241]-248. [B2894.W43E52] 42-15925
1. Ontology. I. Bolman, Frederick De Wolfe, tr. II. Title.

SCHEU, Marina, sister. 111
...The categories of being in Aristotle and St. Thomas... by Sister M. Marina Scheu... Washington, D.C., The Catholic university of America press, 1944. xiii, 100 p. incl. tables. 23 cm. (The Catholic university of America. Philosophical studies, vol. lxxxviii) Thesis (Ph. D.)--Catholic university of America, 1944. Bibliography: p. 98-101. [BD311.S35] A 45
1. Aristoteles. 2. Thomas, Aquinas, Saint, 1225?-1274. 3. Ontology. I. Title.

SCHNEIDER, Herbert Wallace, 111
1892-
Ways of being elements of analytic ontology. New York, Columa [c.]1962. 116p. 21cm. (Woodbridge lecs., no. 7) 62-19907 4.50
1. Ontology. I. Title.

SCHNEIDER, Herbert Wallace, 111
1892-
Ways of being; elements of analytic ontology [by] Herbert W. Schneider. Westport, Conn., Greenwood Press [1974, c1962] x, 116 p. 22 cm. Reprint of the ed. published by Columbia University Press, New York, which was issued as no. 7 of Woodbridge lectures, Columbia University. Includes bibliographical references. [BD331.S394 1974] 72-9832 ISBN 0-8371-6149-5 7.75
1. Ontology. I. Title. II. Series: Woodbridge lectures, Columbia University, no. 7.

SIKORA, Joseph John. 110
Inquiry into being [by] Joseph J. Sikora. Chicago, Loyola University Press, 1965. ix, 296 p. illus. 23 cm. [BD331.S5] 65-26034
1. Ontology. I. Title.

SILBERSTEIN, Solomon Joseph, 113
1845-
The disclosures of the universal mysteries ... By Solomon J. Silberstein. New York, P. Cowen, 1896. viii, [5]-297, [1] p. diagrs. 19 cm. [BD701.S5] 11-24658
1. Ontology. 2. Cosmology. I. Title.
Contents omitted.

SMITH, Gerard. 111
The philosophy of being: Metaphysics [by] Gerard Smith [and] Lottie H. Kendzierski. New York, Macmillan [1961] 408 p. 22 cm. (Christian wisdom series) Includes bibliography. [BD311.S6] 61-5281
1. Ontology. I. Kendzierski, Lottie H, joint author. II. Title.

SNOWDEN, James Henry, 1852- 110
The world a spiritual system; an outline of metaphysics, by James H. Snowden ... New York, The Macmillan company, 1910. xiii, 316 p. 20 cm. [BD111.S6] 10-14642 1.50
1. Ontology. 2. Metaphysics. 3. Idealism. I. Title.

STEENBERGHEN, Fernand van, 111
1904-
Ontology; translated by Martin J. Flynn. New York, J. F. Wagner [c1952] 279p. 21cm. (The Philosophical series of the Higher Institute of Philosophy. University of Louvain, Belgium) [BD312.S813] 53-9294
1. Ontology. I. Title.

SUAREZ, Francisco, 1548-1617. 110
On the various kinds of distinctions (Disputationes metaphysicae, Disputatio VII, de variis distinctionum generibus) Translation from the Latin, with an introd. by Cyril Vollert. Milwaukee, Marquette Univ. Press, 1947. 67 p. 22 cm. (Mediaeval philosophical texts in translation, no. 4) Includes bibliographies. [BD331.S842] 47-6922
1. Ontology. I. Vollert, Cyril O., tr. II. Title. III. Series.

TALLET, Jorge. 111
The absolute being. [Translated by Beverly Thurman and the author] New York, Philosophical Library [1958] 74 p. 21 cm. [BD331.T343] 58-59470
1. Ontology. I. Title.

THALHEIMER, Alvin, 1894- 111.1
Existential metaphysics. New York, Philosophical Library [c.1960] viii, 632p. Bibl. notes: p.601-627 24cm. 60-15963 7.50
1. Ontology. 2. Reality. I. Title.

THALHEIMER, Alvin, 1894- 111.1
Existential metaphysics. New York, Philosophical Library [1960] 632 p. 24 cm. Includes bibliography. [BD331.T48] 60-15963
1. Ontology. 2. Reality. I. Title.

WELLS, Robert Dolling.
Fundamentals of new individualism; with the collaboration of Constance Rodger Emerson. Seattle, Plum Tree Press [c1963] 197 p. 22 cm. Includes bibliography. 67-24177
1. Ontology. 2. Individuality. 3. Consciousness. I. Emerson, Constance (Rodger) joint author. II. Title. III. Title: New individualism.

WYCLIFFE, John, d.1384. 111
Johannis Wyclif Summa de ente; libri primi tractatus primus et secundus. Now first edited with critical introduction and notes from the two extant manuscripts by S. Harrison Thomson ... Oxford, The Clarendon press, 1930. xxxvi, 119, [1] p. 24 cm. [BD300.W9] 30-31903
1. God. 2. Ontology. I. Thomson, Samuel Harrison, ed. II. Title.

WYSCHOGROD, Michael, 1928- 111
Kierkegaard and Heidegger; the ontology of existence. New York, Humanities Press, 1954. xii, 156p. 22cm. Bibliography: p.145-154. [B4377] 54-14647
1. Kierkegaard, Soren Aabye, 1813-1855. 2. Heidegger, Martin, 1889- 3. Ontology. I. Title.

Ontology — Addresses, essays, lectures.

ALLAIRE, Edwin B.
Essays in ontology [by] Edwin B. Allaire [and others] Iowa City, University of Iowa, 1963. 215 p. 24 cm. (Iowa publications in philosophy, v. 1)
1. Ontology — Addresses, essays, lectures. I. Title. II. Series.

LOGIC and ontology. 111.1
Edited by Milton K. Munitz. New York, New York University Press, 1973. viii, 302 p. 24 cm. "Contributions to a seminar on ontology held under the auspices of the New York University Institute of Philosophy for the year 1970-1971." Includes bibliographies. [BD331.L824] 72-96480 ISBN 0-8147-5363-9 13.75
1. Ontology—Addresses, essays, lectures. 2. Logic—Addresses, essays, lectures. I. Munitz, Milton Karl, 1913- ed. II. New York University. Dept. of Philosophy.

Ontology—Congresses.

PHILOSOPHY Conference, 3d, 111
University of Georgia, 1970
Ontological commitment / edited by Richard H. Severens. Athens : University of Georgia Press, [1974] x, 136 p. ; 22 cm. Sponsored by the Dept. of Philosophy of the University of Georgia. Papers of the 2d conference are entered under the title: Education and ethics. Includes bibliographical references and index. [BD311.P48 1970] 73-76785 ISBN 0-8203-0335-6 pbk. : 4.50
1. Ontology—Congresses. I. Severens, Richard H., ed. II. Georgia. University. Dept. of Philosophy and Religion. III. Title.

THE Question of being : 111
East-West perspectives / Mervyn Sprung, ed. University Park : Pennsylvania State University Press, [1977] p. cm. Papers read at a symposium at Brock University, St. Catherines, Ont. Includes index. [BD331.Q4] 76-41846 ISBN 0-271-01242-0 : 12.00
1. Ontology—Congresses. I. Sprung, Mervyn.

Ontology—History.

HARLE, Wilfried, 1941- 230
Sein und Gnade : die Ontologie in Karl

Barths kirchlicher Dogmatik / von Wilfried Harle. Berlin ; New York : De Gruyter, 1975. x, 428 p. ; 22 cm. (Theologische Bibliothek Topelmann ; Bd. 27) Habilitationsschrift—Kiel, 1973. Includes bibliographies and indexes. [BT75.B286H33 1975] 75-522676 ISBN 3-11-005706-9 : DM92.00
1. Barth, Karl, 1886-1968. Die kirchliche Dogmatik. 2. Ontology—History. I. Title.

THATCHER, Adrian. 111'.092'4
The ontology of Paul Tillich / by Adrian Thatcher. Oxford [Eng.] ; New York : Oxford University Press, 1978. vi, 196 p. ; 23 cm. (Oxford theological monographs) Originally presented as the author's thesis, Oxford. Includes index. Bibliography: p. [178]-187. [BX4827.T53T47 1978] 77-30288 ISBN 0-19-826715-0 : 19.50
1. Tillich, Paul, 1886-1965. 2. Ontology—History. I. Title. II. Series.

Oosterwal, Gottfried.

DAVIS, Thomas A. 266.6'7'0924
Island of forgotten men, by Thomas A. Davis. Photos by Gottfried Oosterwal. Washington, Review Herald [1967] 127p. illus., map (on lining papers), ports. 22cm. [BV3680.N52O6] 67-19717 3.95
1. Oosterwal, Gottfried. 2. Missions—New Guinea. I. Title.

Opie, Robert T.

OPIE, Robert T. 285'.1'0924 B
Rev'rund, get your gun / Robert T. Opie. Carol Stream, Ill. : Creation House, c1978. 182 p. ; 23 cm. [BX9225.O67A35] 77-78851 ISBN 0-88419-141-9 pbk. : 3.50
1. Opie, Robert T. 2. Presbyterian Church—Clergy—Biography. 3. Pentecostals—United States—Biography. 4. Clergy—United States—Biography. 5. Faith-cure. I. Title.

Oppel, Lloyd Dudley.

CLARK, Marjorie A. 959.704'38 B
Captive on the Ho Chi Minh Trail / by Marjorie A. Clark. Chicago : Moody Press, c1974. 160 p. : ill. ; 22 cm. [BV3325.L3O663] 75-327711 ISBN 0-8024-1170-3
1. Oppel, Lloyd Dudley. 2. Mattix, Sam. 3. Missions—Laos. 4. Vietnamese Conflict, 1961-1975—Prisoners and prisons, North Vietnamese. I. Title.

Optimism.

PENNIMAN, Alford Brown, 1858-1915. 252.
Studies in optimism; or, Subjects suggested by the humanism and hope of the times. By Alford Brown Penniman ... Adams, Mass., Freeman publishing co., 1902. 5 p. l., 3-172 p. 20 cm. "These studies ... have been presented to my people in substantially the form in which they here occur."--Pref. [BX7233.P445S7] 3-2971
1. Optimism. I. Title.
Contents omitted.

RICE, Merton Stacher, 1872- 287
A discontented optimist; ten sermons, by M. S. Rice ... Cincinnati, New York, The Abingdon press [c1929] 169 p. 19 1/2 cm. [BX8333.R5D5] 29-16325
I. Title.

Oracles.

COLTON, Ann Ree. 133.9'1
The lively oracles. [1st ed.] Glendale, Calif., Arc Pub. Co. [1962] 151 p. 24 cm. [BF1999.C6885] 67-9752
I. Title.

ORACULA sibyllina
The Sibylline oracles, tr. from the Greek into English blank verse, by Milton S. Terry ... New York, Hunt Eaton; Cincinnati. Cranston & Stowe, 1890. 267 p. 21 cm. [PA4253.O83E5 1890] 20-23355
1. Oracles. I. Terry, Milton Spencer, 1840-1914, tr. II. Title.

ORACULA sibyllina
The sibylline oracles, books iii-v, by the Rev. H. N. Bate, M. A. London, Society for promoting Christian knowledge; New York, The Macmillan company, 1918. v, [7]-118 p. 20 cm. (Half-title: Translations of early documents. ser. ii. Hellenistic-Jewish texts. [no. 2]) Bibliography: p. 41-43. [PA4253.Q83A3 1918] 19-7663
1. Oracles. I. Bate, Rev. Herbert Newell, 1871- tr. II. Society for promoting Christian knowledge, London. III. Title.

Oracles—Addresses, essays, lectures.

ORACLES and divination 291.3'2
/ edited by Michael Loewe and Carmen Blacker ; with contributions by Chime Radha ... [et al.]. Boulder : Shambhala ; [New York] : Distributed in the United States by Random House, 1981. p. cm. Includes index. Contents.Contents.—Tibet / Chime Radha — China / Michael Loewe — Japan / Carmen Blacker — The Classical world / J.S. Morrison — The Germanic world / Hilda Ellis Davidson — The Babylonians and Hittites / O.R. Gurney — Ancient Egypt / J.D. Ray — Ancient Israel / J.R. Porter — Islan / R.B. Serjeant. [BL613.O73] 19 81-50968 ISBN 0-87773-214-0 (pbk.) : 7.95 ISBN 0-394-74880-8 (Random House : pbk.) : 7.95
1. Oracles—Addresses, essays, lectures. 2. Divination—Addresses, essays, lectures. I. Loewe, Michael. II. Blacker, Carmen. III. Lama Chime Radha, Rinpoche.

Oracles, Greek.

FLACELIERE, Robert, 1904- 292.32
Greek oracles. Tr. [from French] by Douglas Garman. New York, Norton [1966, c.1965] ix, 92p. plan, 16 plates. 23cm. [BF1765.F5513] 65-25935 4.50 bds.,
1. Oracles, Greek. I. Title.

MANAS, John Helen, 1890- 133.3
The Delphic oracle; oracles through the ages. by John H. Manas. 1st ed. New York city, Pythagorean society, 1940. 63 p. incl. illus., plates. 16 1/2 cm. [BF1999.M24] [[159.9613]] 41-11081
1. Oracles, Greek. I. Title.

Oracula sibyllina.

COLLINS, John Joseph, 1946- 296.1
The Sibylline oracles of Egyptian Judaism / John J. Collins. Missoula, Mont. : Published by Society of Biblical Literature for the Pseudepigrapha Group, 1974, c1972. xiii, 238 p. ; 22 cm. (Dissertation series ; no. 13) Originally presented as the author's thesis, Harvard, 1972. Bibliography: p. 215-238. [BM485.C64 1974] 74-81099 ISBN 0-88414-039-3
1. Oracula sibyllina. 2. Judaism—Egypt. I. Title. II. Series: Society of Biblical Literature. Dissertation series ; no. 13.

Oral contraceptives—United States—History.

MCLAUGHLIN, Loretta. 613.9'432'0924 B
The pill, John Rock, and the church : the biography of a revolution / by Loretta McLaughlin. 1st ed. Boston : Little, Brown, c1982. p. cm. Includes index. [RG137.5.M38 1982] 19 82-16187 ISBN 0-316-56095-2 : 12.95
1. Rock, John Charles, 1890- 2. Oral contraceptives—United States—History. 3. Oral contraceptives—Religious aspects—Catholic Church. 4. Gynecologists—United States—Biography. 5. Medical research personnel—United States—Biography. I. Title.

Oral tradition.

NIELSEN, Eduard. 221.6
Oral tradition, a modern problem in Old Testament introduction; with a foreword by H. H. Fowley. Chicago, A. P. Allenson [1954] 108p. 22cm. (Studies in Biblical theology, no. 11) Translation of 'articles, published in Dansk teologisk tidsskrift, xiii (1950) and xv (1952) [BS1185.N5] 54-10022
1. Oral tradition. 2. Bible. O. T.—Criticism, interpretation, etc. I. Title. II. Series.

Orange, N. J. St. John's Catholic church.

CAREW, Paul T 1863- 282.74933
The story of a mother church, St. John's Orange, N. J., 1851-1934, by Rt. Rev. Mgr. Paul T. Carew ... [Orange, N. J.] The author, 1934. 1 p. l., 1, 164 p. front., plates, ports. 21 cm. "Sources": p. 162. [BX4603.O72S3] 35-2976
1. Orange, N. J. St. John's Catholic church. 2. Catholic church in Orange, N. J. 3. Catholics in Orange, N. J. I. Title.

Orangeville Evangelical and Reformed Church.

HENRIE, Rodney Arden. 285'.7748'38
A history of the Orangeville Evangelical and Reformed Church, Orangeville, Pennsylvania. Lancaster[?] Pa., [1957?] 48 p. illus., port. 23 cm. Thesis (B.D.)—Theological Seminary of the Evangelical and Reformed Church. Bibliography: p. 47. [BX7481.O7O75] 74-8206
1. Orangeville Evangelical and Reformed Church. I. Title.

Oratorians in England (Birmingham)

NEWMAN, John Henry, cardinal, 1801-1890. 248
Sermon notes of John Henry Newman, 1849-1878, ed. by Fathers of the Birmingham oratory ... London, New York [etc.] Longmans, Green, and co., 1913. xxiii, 344 p. front. (port.) 19 1/2 cm. [BX1756.N5 1913] 13-35655
1. Oratorians in England (Birmingham) I. Title.

Oratorians in England (London)

BOWDEN, John Edward, 1820-1874.
The life and letters of Frederick William Faber, D.D., priest of the Oratory of St. Philip Neri. By John Edward Bowden... With an introduction by an American clergyman... Baltimore, J. Murphy & co.; New York, Catholic publication society; [etc., etc.] 1869. xxiv, 25-487 p. front. (port.) 20 cm. [BN4705.F2B6] 30-22392
1. Faber, Frederick William, 1824-1863. 2. Oratorians in England (London) I. Title.

Oratorio.

DAVIES, Henry Walford, 1869-
The temple, an oratorio; words selected from the Bible and set to music for soprano, tenor and baritone soli, chorus, orchestra and organ, by H. Walford Davies. (Op. 14.) ... London, Novello and company, limited; New York, Novello, Ewer and co., 1902. viii, 193 p. 26 cm. (Novello's oroginal octavo edition) Composed for the Worcester musical festival, 1902. Vocal score with planoforte accompaniment. 2-26947
I. Title.

UPTON, George Putnam, 1834-1919. 783.3
The standard oratorios: their stories, their music, and their composers; a handbook, by George P. Upton ... Chicago, A. C. McClurg & company, 1887. 335 p. 18 cm. [MT110.U75] 4-11747
1. Oratorio. I. Title.

Oratorio Society of New York.

KREHBIEL, Henry Edward, 1854-1923. 783.4'062'7471
Notes on the cultivation of choral music and the Oratorio Society of New York. New York, AMS Press [1970] ix, 106 p. 23 cm. Reprint of the 1884 ed. [ML1511.8.N5K8 1970] 75-137315
1. Oratorio Society of New York. 2. Choral societies—New York (City) I. Title.

Oratorios—Scores.

LOHR, Ina 783.3'5
The greatest song; in critique of Solomon. Freshly, literally tr. from Hebrew and arr. for oratorio performance [by] Calvin Seerveld. Melody, music [by] Ina Lohr. Woodcuts [by] Flip van der Burgt. Design [by] Sypko Bosch. [Palos Heights, Ill.] Trinity Pennyasheet Pr. [1967] 104p. illus. 23cm. For voices and 2 unidentified treble instruments. [M2000.L74G7] 67-27706 5.00
1. Oratorios—Scores. 2. Song of Solomon (Music) I. Seerveld, Calvin. The greatest song. II. Burgt, Flip van der, illus. III. Title.
Contents omitted. Publisher's address: 12301 Cheyenne Dr., Palos Heights, Ill. 60463

Order (in religion, folklore, etc.)—Addresses, essays, lectures.

ORDER / 291.2
[editor, Vincent G. Stuart]. Boulder, CO : Shambhala ; [New York] : distributed by Random House, 1977. 103 p. : ill. ; 23 cm. (Maitreya ; 6) Includes bibliographical references. [BL325.O74O73] 76-55122 ISBN 0-87773-104-7 pbk. : 4.50
1. Order (in religion, folklore, etc.)—Addresses, essays, lectures. I. Stuart, Vincent. II. Series.
Contents omitted.

Order of Christian mystics.

CURTISS, Frank Homer, 1875- 212
Prayers of the Order of Christian mystics, selected from the writings of Dr. and Mrs. F. Homer Curtiss ... compiled by Emily B. Percival. Washington, D. C., The Curtiss philosophic book co., 1934. viii, 50 p. 14 cm. [The gems series] Advertising matter: p. [43]-50. [BF1999.C76] 34-39189
1. Order of Christian mystics. I. Curtiss, Harriette Augusta (Brown) Mrs. 1856?-1932, joint author. II. Percival, Emily Brownile, 1871- comp. III. Title.

CURTISS, Harriette Augusta. Mrs.
The key to the universe; or, A spiritual interpretation of numbers, by Harriette Augusta Curtiss ... and R. Homer Curtiss ... with portrait of Mrs. Curtiss and many illustrations, diagrams and tables. San Francisco, Cal., The Curtiss book company; [etc., etc.] 1915. xv, [17]-386 p. incl. front. (port.) illus., diagrs. 20 cm. Lettered on cover: Teachings of the Order of Christian mystics (Order of the 15) 16-2016 2.50
1. Curtiss, Frank Homer, 1875- joint author. II. Title.

CURTISS, Harriette Augusta (Brown) Mrs. 1856?-1932. 133
The inner radiance, by Harriette Augusta Curtiss and F. Homer Curtiss ... Washington, D. C., The Curtiss philosophic book co., 1935. vi p., 1 l., 369 p. 20 cm. [BF1999.C79] 159.961 35-8814
1. Order of Christian mystics. I. Curtiss, Frank Homer, 1875- joint author. II. Title.

CURTISS, Harriette Augusta (Brown) Mrs. 1856?-1932. 149.3
The mystic life; an introduction to practical Christian mysticism, by Harriette Augusta Curtiss and F. Homer Curtiss ... compiled by Arthur L. Champion. Washington, D. C., The Curtiss philosophic book co., 1934. v, 156 p. 13 cm. [The gems series] "Literature by Dr. and Mrs. F. Homer Curtiss": p. 140-143. Advertising matter: p. [149]-156. [BF1999.C827] 35-603
1. Order of Christian mystics. I. Curtiss, Frank Homer, 1875- joint author. II. Champion, Arthur Leslie, 1887- comp. III. Title.

Order of De Molay for boys.

BIBLE. English. 1928. 220.
... The Holy Bible, containing the Old and New Testaments according to the authorized or King James' version, together with frontispiece, presentation page and helps to the De Molay student. Philadelphia, A. J. Holman company, c1928. 16, 1164, 121 p. front., port., maps. 19 cm. At head of title: De Molay edition. Contains also title-pages of the Holman pronouncing editions of the Bible and of the New Testament. "Four thousand questions and answers on the Old and New Testaments, intended to open up the Scriptures for the use of students and Sunday- school teachers": 121 p. at end. [BS185.1928.P5] 28-30625

1. Order of De Molay for boys. I. Holman, A. J., & co., pub. II. Title.

Order of St. Elizabeth of Hungary.

INTO the deep, 271.
being the story of the first five years of the Confraternity of the divine love, by the author of "The vocation of the soul". With 10 illustrations. London, New York [etc.] Longmans, Green & co., 1917 [1918] v. (i.e. xv) 107 p. front., plates, ports. 19 1/2 cm. Imprint covered by label: London, The Confraternity of divine love, 1917. Pages xii to xv wrongly numbered. Vol. I of the author's Story of the Confraternity of the divine love and the Order of St.Elizabeth of Hungary. Vol. II is entitled: Letting down the acts. [BX4410.O85S7] 24-31310
1. Order of St. Elizabeth of Hungary. I. Vocation of the soul, Author of.

Order of the eastern star.

BIBLE. English. 1930. Authorised. 220.52
... The Holy Bible, containing the Old and New Testaments, translated out of the original tongues, and with the former translations diligently compared and revised; the text conformable to that of the edition of 1611, commonly known as the authorized or King James' version. Philadelphia, A. J. Holman co. [c1930] 1 p. l., 16, 916 p. maps. 16 cm. At head of title: Holman edition. Prefixed: History and facts concerning the Order of the eastern star with Scriptural quotations and references prepared by Rev. W. Mark Sexson ... Philadelphia, Pa., c1930. [BS198.E3H6 1930] 31-4277
1. Order of the eastern star. I. Sexson, W. Mark. II. Title.

VOORHIS, Harold Van Buren, 1894- 366'.18
The Eastern Star : the evolution from a rite to an order / by Harold Van Buren Voorhis. Richmond, Va. : Macoy Pub. and Masonic Supply Co., c1976. xvi, 137 p. : ill. ; 21 cm. Bibliography: p. 136-137. [HS853.3.V6 1976] 76-375124 4.50
1. Order of the Eastern Star. I. Title.

Order of the Eastern Star. Connecticut.

ORDER of the Eastern star. Grand chapter of New York.
The authorized standard ritual of the Order of Eastern star in the state of New York; a system of forms and ceremonies, with necessary instructions for chapters as revised by a committee appointed at the annual session of the Grand chapter, held in June, 1897. New York, The Grand chapter, 1901. 2 p. l., 226 pp. illus. 15 cm. 2-1436
I. Title.

RAINES, Ruth E., 1920- 366'.18
O.E.S. in Connecticut; a history in commemoration of the 100th anniversary of the Grand Chapter of Connecticut, Order of the Eastern Star [by] Ruth E. Raines, with assistance by Evelyn M. Estey [and] Lydia F. Lester. [New Haven] Grand Chapter of Connecticut, Order of the Eastern Star, 1974. vi, 362 p. illus. 23 cm. [HS853.7.C8R34] 74-171915
1. Order of the Eastern Star. Connecticut. I. Order of the Eastern Star. Grand Chapter of Connecticut. II. Title.

Order of the Eastern Star—Rituals.

ADAMS, Ruth (Holland) 1904- 366.18
Gathered memories. Eastern Star ceremonies; containing 30 programs for various occasions during the fraternal year, by Ruth Adams [and others] New York, Macoy Pub. and Masonic Supply Co. [1961] 142p. 21cm. [HS853.5.A63] 61-15946
1. Order of the Eastern Star—Rituals. I. Title.

ADAMS, Ruth (Holland) 1904- 366.18
One little candle. New York, 10001, Macoy Pub. Masonic Supply Co., 34 W. 33rd St. [c.1966] xii, 194p. 21cm. [HS853.5.A64] 65-29180 3.00
1. Order of the Eastern Star—Rituals. I. Title.

ORDER of the Eastern Star. 366.1
Adoptive rite ritual; a book of instruction in the organization, government and ceremonies of chapters of the Order of the Eastern Star; together with the Queen of the South. Arr. by Robert Macoy. Rev. ed. New York, Macoy Pub. and Masonic Supply Co. [1952] 301 p. illus. 15 cm. [HS853.5.A3] 52-64991
1. Order of the Eastern Star—Rituals. I. Macoy, Robert, 1815-1895. II. Title.

Order of the holy cross.

SCUDDER, Vida Dutton, 1861- 922.373
Father Huntington, founder of the Order of the holy cross, by Vida Dutton Scudder, with a preface by Alan Whittemore ... New York, E. P. Dutton & company, inc., 1940. 375 p. front. (port.) 22 cm. "First edition." [BX5995.H77S35 1940] 40-314778
1. Huntington, James Otis Sargent, 1854-1935. 2. Order of the holy cross. I. Title.

Order of the Incarnate word and blessed sacrament.

SAINT PIERRE OF JESUS, Mother. 922
Life of the Reverend Mother Jeanne Chezard de Matel, foundress of the order of the Incarnate word and the blessed sacrament according to original manuscripts by the Reverend Mother Saint Pierre of Jesus... Tr. from the original French by Henry Churchill Semple San Antonio, Tex., Convent of the Incarnate word [c1922] xix, [5], 661 p. front., illus. (incl. ports., facsims.) 20 1/2 cm. [BX4705.C47S3] 23-711
1. Order of the Incarnate word and blessed sacrament. I. Semple, Henry Churchill, 1853- tr. II. Title.

Order of the visitation.

FRANCOIS de Sales Saint,bp. of Geneva 1567-1622
An abridgment of the Interior spirit of the Religious of the visitation of the Blessed Virgin Mary. Explained by St. Francis, of Sale, bishop and prince of Geneva, and collected by the late Mr. Maupas, bishop of Evreux. Translated from the French. Washington, G. Templeman, 1834. 155, 7, [1] p. 15 cm. [BX4547.F8 1834] 28-16966
1. Order of the visitation. I. Maupas du Tour Henri Cauchon de, bp. of Puy, 1600-1680. II. Title. III. Title: Interior spirit of the Religious of the visitation of the Blessed Virgin Mary.

FRANCOIS desales Saint,bp. of Geneva 1567-1622
Abridgment of the Interior spirit of the Religious of the visitation of Holy Mary, explained by Saint Francis de Sales, bishop and prince of Geneva, their founder. Collected by the late Monsignor Maupas, bishop of Evreux. Rev. translation from the French ed. of 1914. Baltimore, Md., John Murphy company [c1927] 6 p. l., 146 p. 16 cm. [BX4547.F8 1927] 28-15198
1. Order of the visitation. I. Maupas du Tour, Henri Cauuchon de, bp. of Puy, 1600-1680. II. Title. III. Title: Interior spirit of the Religious of the visitation of Holy Mary.

Orders of knighthood and chivalry—Spain.

KING, Georgiana Goddard, 1871-1939. 271'.79
A brief account of the military orders in Spain / by Georgiana Goddard King. 1st AMS ed. New York : AMS Press, 1978, c1921. xii, 275 p., [6] leaves of plates : ill. ; 23 cm. Reprint of the ed. published by Hispanic Society of America, which was issued as the Peninsula series of Hispanic notes and monographs. Bibliography: p. 273-275. [CR5819.K5 1978] 76-29841 ISBN 0-404-15421-2 : 26.50
1. Orders of knighthood and chivalry—Spain. I. Title. II. Title: Military orders in Spain. III. Series: Hispanic notes & monographs : essays, studies, and brief biographies. Peninsular series.

Ordination.

BISKUPEK, Aloysius, 1884- 262.15
Deaconship; conferences on the rite of ordination, by Rev. Aloysius Biskupek, S.V.D. St. Louis, Mo., and London, B. Herder book co., 1944. v. 258 p. 22 cm. [BX2240.B5] 44-6335
1. Ordination. 2. Catholic church—Clergy. I. Title.

CLANCY, Walter Burroughs, 1926- 265.4
The rites and ceremonies of sacred ordination (canons 1002-1005); a historical conspectus and a canonical commentary. Washington, Catholic University of America Press, 1962. xi, 122 p. 23 cm. (Catholic University of America. Canon law studies, no. 394) Thesis—Catholic University of America. Vita. Bibliography: p. 113-118. [BX2240.C5] 68-7414
1. Ordination. I. Title. II. Series.

DADOLLE, Pierre, bp. of Dijon, 1857-1911. 265.
Ordination retreat, by Right Rev. Pierre Dadolle ... authorized translation from the French by Rev. S. A. Raemers, M. A. Baltimore, Md., John Murphy company [c1926] 95 p. front. 14 cm. [BX2240.D33] 26-11759
I. Raemers, Sydney Albert, 1892- tr. II. Title.

ELLARD, Gerald. 265.4
Ordination anointings in the western church before 1000 A.D. [by] Gerald Ellard ... Cambridge, Mass., The Mediaeval academy of America, 1933. xii, 123 p. vi pl. (facsims.) on 3 l. 26 cm. (Half-title: Monographs of the Mediaeval academy of America. no. 8) "Academy publications. no. 16." "Presented to the Ludwig-Maximilian university, Munich, as a requirement of candidacy for the degree of doctor of philosophy. November, 1930."--p. [iv] "Early sacramentaries, pontificals, and ordinals in which not ordination ritual is found": ,. 105-111. "Books most frequently cited": p. xi-xii; "Index of manuscripts cited": p. 112-118. [BX2240.E6] 33-6801
1. Ordination. 2. Unction. 3. Catholic church—Clergy. 4. Catholic church—Liturgy and ritual—Hist. I. Title.

MCEACHERN, Alton H. 262'.146
Set apart for service / Alton H. McEachern. Nashville, Tenn. : Broadman Press, c1980. 138 p. ; 20 cm. Includes bibliographical references. [BV664.5.M32] 19 79-51140 ISBN 0-8054-2537-3 : 4.95
1. Ordination. 2. Ordination—Baptists. 3. Baptists—Clergy. I. Title.

WARKENTIN, Marjorie, 1921- 234'.164
Ordination, a biblical-historical view / by Marjorie Warkentin. Grand Rapids, Mich. : Eerdmans, c1982. p. cm. Includes indexes. Bibliography: p. [BV664.5.W37 1982] 19 82-8908 ISBN 0-8028-1941-9 : 7.95
1. Ordination. I. Title.

WHITHAM, Arthur Richard, 1863-
Holy orders, by the Rev. A. R. Whitham ... London, New York [etc.] Longmans, Green & co., 1903. 6 p. l., 310 p. 19 1/2 cm. (Half-title: The Oxford library of practical theology ...) A 21
1. Ordination. 2. Theology, Pastoral. I. Title.

Ordination—Anniversary sermons.

FISK, Elisha, 1769-1851. 922.573
Wrentham jubilee. A sermon preached in Wrentham, Mass., June 12, 1849, by Rev. Elisha Fisk, on the fiftieth anniversary of his ordination, as pastor of the original Congregational church in said town. With an appendix. Boston, Printed by C. C. P. Moody, 1850. 64 p. 23 cm. [BX7260.F53W7] 36-2804
1. Ordination—Anniversary sermons. I. Title.

IDE, Jacob, 1785-1880. 922.573
A pastor's review. A discourse preached in Medway, Mass., Nov. 2, 1864, on the fiftieth anniversary of the author's ordination and settlement. By Jacob Ide ... Boston, Congregational board of publication, 1865. 72 p. 24 cm. [BX7260.I 3A3] 36-3225
1. Ordination—Anniversary sermons. I. Congregational board of publication, Boston. II. Title.

KIMBALL, David Tenney, 1782-1860. 922.
The pastor's jubilee. A discourse delivered in Ipswich, October 8, 1856, by David Tenney Kimball, senior pastor of the First church in that town on the fiftieth anniversary of his ordination. With an appendix. Published under the direction of the committee of arrangements. Boston, Press of J. B. Chisholm, 1857. 96 p. front. (port.) 29 cm. [BX7260.K48A5] 1-21022
1. Ordination—Anniversary sermons. I. Title.

PHILADELPHIA. First Unitarian church. 922.8173
Exercises at the meeting of the First Congregational Unitarian society. January 12, 1875, together with the discourse delivered by Rev. W. H. Furness, D. D., Sunday, Jan. 10, 1875, on the occasion of the fiftieth anniversary of his ordinatiion, January 12, 1825. Philadelphia, Sherman & co., printers, 1875. 110, [1] p. front., 2 pl. 24 cm. [BX9869.F9P5] 37-10037
1. Ordination—Anniversary sermons. I. Furness, William Henry, 1802-1896. II. Title.

Ordination (Canon law)

GALLAGHER, Thomas Raphael, 1914- 265
... The examination of the qualities of the ordinated; an historical synopsis and commentary, by Thomas Raphael Gallagher ... Washington, D.C., The Catholic university of America press, 1944. ix, 166 p. 28 cm. (The Catholic university of America. Canon law studies. No. 195) Thesis (J.C.D.)--Catholic university of America, 1944. "Biographical note": p. 151. Bibliography: p. 140-147. [BX1939.O82G3] A 45
1. Ordination (Canon law) I. Title.

GANNON, John Mark, 1916-
... The interstices required for the promotion to orders, by Rev. John Mark Gannon ... Washington, D.C., The Catholic university of America press, 1944. xi, 100 p. 23 cm. (The Catholic university of America. Canon law studies, no. 196) Thesis (J.C.D.)--Catholic university of America, 1944. "Biographical note": p. 88. Bibliography: p. 85-87. A 45
1. Ordination (Canon law) I. Title.

Ordination— Catholic Church.

BISKUPEK, Aloysius, 1884- 265.4
Priesthood; conferences on the rite of ordination, by Rev. Aloysius Biskupek, S.V.D. St. Louis, Mo., and London, B. Herder book co., 1945. vi, 398 p. 22 cm. [BX2240.B52] 45-2800
1. Ordination—Catholic church. 2. Catholic church—Clergy. I. Title.

BLIGH, John. 265.4
Ordination to the priesthood. London, New York, Sheed and Ward [1956] 189p. illus. 23cm. [BX2240.B56] 56-3627
1. Ordination—Catholic Church. 2. Catholic Church. Liturgy and Ritual. Pontifical. Ritus ordinum. I. Title.

CATHOLIC Church. Liturgy and ritual. 265'.4
The ordination of deacons, priests, and bishops : provisional text prepared by the International Committee on English in the Liturgy, approved for interim use by the Bishops' Committee on the Liturgy, National Conference of Catholic Bishops, and confirmed by the Apostolic See. Washington : National Conference of Catholic Bishops, Bishops' Committee on the Liturgy, 1969. 51 p. ; 28 cm. At head of title: The Roman pontifical; restored by decree of the Second Vatican Ecumenical Council and promulgated by authority of Pope Paul VI. Translation of De ordinatione diaconi, presbyteri, et episcopi. [BX2031.R5A4 1969] 75-306712
1. Ordination—Catholic Church. I. International Committee on English in the

Liturgy. II. Catholic Church. National Conference of Catholic Bishops. Bishops' Committee on the Liturgy. III. [Rite of ordination. English] IV. Title.

CENTRE DE PASTORALE LITURGIGUE, Strasbourg 265.4
The sacrament of holy orders; some papers and discussions concerning holy orders at a session of the Centre de pastorale liturgique, 1955. Collegeville, Minn., Liturgical Press [c1962] vi. 358 p. 23 cm. Bibliographical footnotes. [[BX2240]] 64-9052
1. Ordination — Catholic Church. I. Title.

GOEBEL, Bernardin 262.14
Seven steps to the altar; preparation for priesthood. [Tr. by A. V. Littledale, Geoffrey Stevens] New York, Sheed [c.1963] 182p. 21cm. 63-10675 3.50 bds.,
1. Ordination—Catholic Church. 2. Tonsure. I. Title.

HALLIGAN, Francis Nicholas, 1917- 264'.02'008 s
Sacraments of community renewal: holy orders, matrimony [by] Nicholas Halligan. New York, Alba House [1974] xvii, 217 p. 21 cm. (His The ministry of the celebration of the sacraments, v. 3) Includes bibliographical references. [BX2200.H25 vol. 3] [BX2240] 265'.4 74-3209 3.95 (pbk.)
1. Ordination—Catholic Church. 2. Marriage—Catholic Church. I. Title. II. Series.

LECUYER, Joseph. 253.2
What is a priest? Translated from the French by Lancelot C. Sheppard. [1st American ed.] New York, Hawthorn Books [1959] 125p. 22cm. (The Twentieth century encyclopedia of Catholicism, v. 53. Section 5: The life of faith) Translation of Pretres du Christ. [BX2240.L383] 59-6730
1. Ordination— Catholic Church. 2. Clergy—Office. I. Title.

ORZELL, Laurence. 265'.4
Rome and the validity of orders in the Polish National Catholic Church / Laurence Orzell. Scranton, Pa. : Savonarola Theological Seminary Alumni Association, 1977. 49 p. ; 24 cm. Bibliography: p. 46-49. [BX2240.O75] 77-75372
1. Polish National Catholic Church of America. 2. Ordination—Catholic Church. I. Title.

PLASSMANN, Thomas Bernard, 1879- 265.4
The priest's way to God. 2d ed. Paterson, N.J., St. Anthony Guild Press, 1945. xxii, 447 p. illus. 19 cm. "Ritus ordinationum": p. [401]-447. [BX2240.P45 1945] 47-24755
1. Ordination—Catholic Church. 2. Clergy—Minor orders. 3. Clergy—Religious life. 4. Catholic Church—Clergy. 5. Asceticism—Catholic Church. I. Catholic Church. Liturgy and ritual. Pontifical. Ritus ordinum. II. Title.

Ordination—History.

REYNOLDS, Roger E., 1936- 265'.4'09
The ordinals of Christ from their origins to the twelfth century / Roger E. Reynolds. Berlin ; New York : W. de Gruyter, 1978. xiv, 194 p. ; 25 cm. (Beitrage zur Geschichte und Quellekunde des Mittelalters ; Bd. 7) Includes bibliographical references. [BV664.5.R49] 78-1517 ISBN 3-11-007058-8 : 52.00
1. Ordination—History. I. Title. II. Series.

Ordination of women.

HEYER, Robert J. 253'.2
Women and orders, edited by Robert J. Heyer. New York, Paulist Press [1974] xi, 104 p. 19 cm. (Deus books) Includes bibliographical references. [BV676.H5] 74-80262 ISBN 0-8091-1841-6 1.65 (pbk.).
1. Ordination of women. I. Title.

HUNGATE, Jesse A.
The ordination of women to the pastorate in Baptist churches. Hamilton, N.Y., J. B. Grant [1899] xi, 172 p. 12 cm. Aug *I. Title.*

JEWETT, Paul King. 262'.14
The ordination of women ; an essay on the office of Christian ministry / by Paul K. Jewett. Grand Rapids, Mich. : Eerdmans, c1980. p. cm. [BV676.J48] 80-15644 ISBN 0-8028-1850-1 pbk. : 4.95
1. Ordination of women. I. Title.

STENDAHL, Krister. 220.830141
The Bible and the role of women; a case study in hermeneutics. Translated by Emilie T. Sander. Philadelphia, Fortress Press [1966] xiv, 48 p. 20 cm. (Facet books. Biblical series, 15) Translation of Bibelaynen och kvinnan, which was originally published in Kvinnan, Samballet, Kyrkan (Stockholm, Svenska Kyrkans Diakonistyreleses Bokforiag, 1958) p. 138-167. Bibliography: p. 44-47. [BV676.S713] 66-25262
1. Ordination of women. 2. Women in the Bible. I. Title. II. Series.

STENDAHL, Krister 220.830141
The Bible and the role of women; a case study in hermeneutics. Tr. by Emilie T. Sander. Philadelphia, Fortress [1966] xiv, 48 p. 20 cm. (Facet bks. Biblical ser., 15) Tr. of Bibelsynen och kvinnan, which was orig. pub. in Kvinnan, Samballet, Kyrkan (Stockholm, Svenska Kyrkans Diakonistyreleses Bokforlag, 1958) p. 138-167. Bibl. [BV676.S713] 66-25262 pap., .85
1. Ordination of woman. 2. Women in the Bible. I. Title. II. Series.

Ordination of women—Addresses, essays, lectures.

THE Ordination of women—pro and con / edited by Michael P. Hamilton and Nancy S. Montgomery. New York : Morehouse-Barlow Co., [1975] xi, 212 p. ; 22 cm. Includes bibliographical references. [BV676.O73] 76-350554 ISBN 0-8192-1203-2 pbk. : 4.95 253'.2
1. Ordination of women—Addresses, essays, lectures. I. Hamilton, Michael Pollock, 1927- II. Montgomery, Nancy S.

Ordination of women—Catholic Church.

MALONEY, David M. 262'.14
The Church cannot ordain women to the priesthood / David M. Maloney. Chicago : Franciscan Herald Press, c1978. 64 p. ; 18 cm. (Synthesis series) On cover: Declaration of the Congregation for Doctrine of the Faith. Includes bibliographical references. [BV676.M34] 77-27906 ISBN 0-8199-0724-3 : 0.65
1. Catholic Church—Clergy. 2. Ordination of women—Catholic Church. I. Title.

Ordination of women—Catholic Church—Addresses, essays, lectures.

WOMEN priests : 261'.14
a Catholic commentary on the Vatican declaration / edited by Leonard Swidler and Arlene Swidler. New York : Paulist Press, c1977. ix, 352 p. ; 23 cm. Includes bibliographical references. [BV676.W57] 77-83572 ISBN 0-8091-2062-3 pbk. : 9.95
1. Catholic Church—Clergy—Addresses, essays, lectures. 2. Ordination of women—Catholic Church—Addresses, essays, lectures. I. Swidler, Leonard J. II. Swidler, Arlene.

Ordination of women—Catholic Church—Congresses.

DETROIT Ordination Conference, 1975. 262'.14
Women and Catholic priesthood : an expanded vision : proceedings of the Detroit Ordination Conference / edited by Anne Marie Gardiner. New York : Paulist Press, c1976. vii, 259 p. ; 22 cm. Bibliography: p. 199-208. [BV676.D47 1975] 76-12653 ISBN 0-8091-1955-2 pbk. : 5.95
1. Ordination of women—Catholic Church—Congresses. 2. Women in Christianity—Congresses. I. Gardiner, Anne Marie. II. Title.

Ordination of women—Church of England.

RUTLER, George William. 253'.2
Priest and priestess. Ambler, Pa., Trinity Press [1973] xi, 99 p. 22 cm. Includes bibliographical references. [BV676.R87] 73-75334 ISBN 0-912046-09-0
1. Ordination of women—Church of England. I. Title.

Ordination of women—Church of England—Addresses, essays, lectures.

BRUCE, Michael. 262'.14
Why not? : priesthood & the ministry of women : a theological study / edited by Michael Bruce & G. E. Duffield. Revised & augmented ed. / prepared by R. T. Beckwith. Abingdon : Marcham Manor Press, 1976. 174 p. ; 22 cm. Includes bibliographical references. [BV676.B78 1976] 77-355557 ISBN 0-900531-28-2 : £3.50
1. Ordination of women—Church of England—Addresses, essays, lectures. 2. Women in Christianity—Addresses, essays, lectures. I. Duffield, Gervase E., joint author. II. Beckwith, Roger T. III. Title.

Ordination of women—History—20th century.

MARRETT, Michael McFarlene, 1935- 262'.53
The Lambeth Conferences and women priests : the historical background of the conferences and their impact on the Episcopal Church in America / Michael McFarlene Marrett. 1st ed. Smithtown, N.Y. : Exposition Press, c1981. xi, 188 p. ; 22 cm. (An Exposition-testament book) Includes index. Bibliography: p. 73-77. [BX5965.M28] 19 81-66739 ISBN 0-682-49765-7 : 12.50
1. Episcopal Church—Clergy—History—20th century. 2. Lambeth Conference—History—20th century. 3. Episcopal Church—History—20th century. 4. Ordination of women—History—20th century. I. Title.

Ordination of women—Protestant Episcopal Church.

HEWITT, Emily C. 253'.2
Women priests: yes or no? [By] Emily C. Hewitt [and] Suzanne R. Hiatt. New York, Seabury Press [1973] 128 p. 21 cm. Bibliography: p. 126-128. [BV676.H48] 72-81027 ISBN 0-8164-2076-9 2.95
1. Ordination of women—Protestant Episcopal Church. I. Hiatt, Suzanne R., joint author. II. Title.

Ordination of women—Protestant Episcopal Church in the U.S.A.

HEYWARD, Carter. 283'.092'4 B
A priest forever / Carter Heyward. 1st ed. New York : Harper & Row, c1976. 146 p. : ill. ; 21 cm. Includes bibliographical references. [BX5995.H46A34 1976] 75-36736 ISBN 0-06-063893-1 : 6.95
1. Heyward, Carter. 2. Ordination of women—Protestant Episcopal Church in the U.S.A. I. Title.

MOORE, Paul, 1919- 253'.2
Take a Bishop like me / Paul Moore, Jr. 1st ed. New York : Harper & Row, c1979. viii, 200 p. ; 22 cm. Includes index. [BX5695.M66 1979] 78-2148 ISBN 0-06-013018-0 : 8.95
1. Protestant Episcopal Church in the U.S.A.—Clergy. 2. Moore, Paul, 1919- 3. Ordination of women—Protestant Episcopal Church in the U.S.A. 4. Homosexuality and Christianity. I. Title.

Ordination sermons.

APPLETON, Nathaniel, 1693-1784. 252.
Superiour skill and wisdom necessary for winning souls, which is the grand design of the ministerial office, illustrated in a sermon preached at the ordination of the Reverend Mr. John Sparhawk, to the pastoral office over a Church of Christ in Salem; on the eighth day of December, 1736. By Nathanael Appleton ... Together with The charge given by the Reverend Mr. Holyoke: and The right hand of fellowship, by the Reverend Mr. Prescott ... Boston: Printed and sold by Kneeland and Green, in Queenstreet, mdccxxxvii. 2 p. l., 51 p. 18 cm. [BX7233.A62S8] 46-34171
1. Ordination sermons. I. Title.

CHANNING, William Ellery, 1780-1842. 252.
A sermon, delivered at the ordination of the Rev. Ezra Stiles Gannett, as colleague pastor of the Church of Christ, in Federal-street, Boston, June 30, 1824. By William Ellery Channing ... 3d ed. Boston, The Christian register office, 1824. 32 p. 24 x 14 cm. [BX9843.C5S5 1824 b] 40-25742
1. Gannett, Ezra Stiles, 1801-1871. 2. Ordination sermons. I. Title.

EELLS, Nathaniel, 1678-1750.
The ministers of the gospel, as ambassadors for Christ, should beseech men to be reconciled to God. A sermon preach'd at Taunton, Feb. 21, 1728, 9. At the ordination of the Reverend Mr. Thomas Clap. And new published (at the desire of many of the inhabitants of that town) with some inlargement. By Nathanael Eells, V. D. M. and pastor of the South church in Scituate ... Boston, Printed by B. Green, for J. Eliot, at his shop at the south end, 1729. 2 p. l., ii, 47 p. 17 cm. Imperfect: half-title? wanting. A34
1. Ordination sermons. I. Clap, Thomas, 1763-1767. II. Title.

FISH, Joseph, 1706-1781. 252.
Love to Christ a necessary qualification in a gospel minister. A sermon preached at the ordination of the Reverend Mr. William Vinal, to the pastoral charge of the First Congregational church of Christ in Newport on Rhode Island, October 29, 1746. With some enlargement and correction, by Joseph Fish...With the charge by the Rev. Mr. S. Checkley, and the right hand of fellowship by the Rev. Mr. J. Cotton... Newport, R. I., Printed by the Widow Franklin, at the town-school house, 1747. 55 p. 19 1/2 cm. [BX7233.F52L6] 22-2675
1. Vinal, William, 1718?-1781. 2. Ordination sermons. I. Title.

HAVEN, Jason, 1733-1803.
A sermon preached July 4, 1764. At the ordination of the Reverend Mr. Edward Brooks, to the pastoral care of the church in North-Yarmouth. By Jason Haven, A.M., pastor of the First church in Dedham. Boston, Printed by Richard and Samuel Draper, at the printing-office in Newbury-street, MDCCLXIV. 55 p. 20 1/2 cm. Half-title: Mr. Haven's sermon at the ordination of the Reverend Mr. Brooks. A 34
1. Brooks, Edward, d. 1781. 2. Ordination sermons. I. Title.

HOLMES, Abiel, 1763-1837.
A sermon, preached at the ordination of the Rev. Jonathan Whitaker to the pastoral care of the church and society in Sharon, Massachusetts. February 27, 1799. By Abiel Holmes. A.M., pastor of the First church in Cambridge. Dedham [Mass.]; Printed by Herman Mann. 1799. 49 p. 20 cm. Half-title: Mr. Holmes sermon. A 35
1. Whitaker, Jonathan, 1771?-1835. 2. Ordination sermons. I. Title.

MILLEDOLER, Philip, 1775-1852. 243
A sermon, preached in the Presbyterian church in Beekmanstreet, New-York, on Wednesday, August 8, 1810; at the ordination and installation of the Rev. Gardiner Spring, as pastor of said church. By Philip Milledoler...To which are added, the charge to the minister, and the exhortation to the people... New-York; Published by Williams & Whiting, at their theological and classical book-store, no. 118, Pearl-street. Printed by J. Seymour, 1810. 60 p. 21 1/2 cm. The charge to the minister is by Samuel Miller; the exhortation to the people by John B. Romeyn. [BX9178.M472S4] 42-26727
1. Ordination sermons. I. Miller, Samuel, 1769-1850. II. Romeyn, John Brodhead, 1777-1825. III. Title.

SPRING, Samuel, 1746-1819. 252.058

The nature and importance of rightly dividing the truth. A sermon, delivered at the ordination of the Rev. Benjamin Bell, A.M., to the pastoral care of the First church in Amesbury, Nov. 13, 1784. By Samuel Spring, A.M., pastor of the North church in Newbury-port. Published by desire. Newbury-port: Printed and sold by John Mycall, MDCCLXXXIV. 64 p. 19 1/2 cm. Half-title: Mr. Spring's sermon at the ordination of the Rev. Mr. Bell. [BX7233.S72N3] [252.7] 6-26898
1. Ordination sermons. I. Title.

SPRING, Samuel, 1746-1819.
A sermon, preached at the ordination of the Rev. Daniel Merril, in Sedgwick, Sept. 17, 1793. By Samuel Spring, A.M. pastor of the North church in Newburyport. Newburyport [Mass.]: Printed by Edmund M. Blunt, MDCCXCIV. 50 p. 19 1/2 cm. Half-title: Mr. Spring's sermon. A 33
1. Merrill, Daniel, 1765-1833 2. Ordination sermons. I. Title.

STILES, Isaac, 1697-1760. 252.
A sermon preached by the Reverend Isaac Stiles, A.M., pastor of the church in North-Haven, at the ordination of his son Ezra Stiles, A.M., to the pastoral charge of the church and congregation meeting in Clark street, Newport, October 22, 1755. [Four lines of Bible quotations] Newport, Rhode Island; Printed by J. Franklin, at the Town-school-house [1755] 2 p. l., 33 p. 20 cm. Signatures: 2 leaves (t.-p.: dedication) unsigned, A-H2, leaf, unsigned. [BX7233.S782S4] 31-4014
1. Stiles, Ezra, 1727-1795. 2. Ordination sermons. I. Title.

Oregon City, Or. First Congregational Society.

BACHELDER, Horace Lyman. 285'.8795'41

The liberal church at the end of the Oregon Trail; a history of the First Congregational Society of Oregon City and of the Atkinson Memorial Congregational Church, from the first meeting in 1844 to the 125th anniversary in 1969. [Portland, Or., Watson Print. Co., 1969] 137 p. illus., ports. 23 cm. Bibliography: p. 136-137. [BX7255.O76F5] 75-98940

1. Oregon City, Or. First Congregational Society. 2. Oregon City, Or. Atkinson Memorial Congregational Church. I. Title.

Organ—Instruction and study.

LOVELACE, Austin Cole. 783.1
The organist and hymn playing. New York, Abingdon Press [1962] 71p. illus. 19cm. (A Basic music book, 110) Includes bibliography. [MT180.L69] 62-4543
1. Organ—Instruction and study. 2. Hymns—Accompiment. I. Title.

Oriental literature—Translations into English.

PRITCHARD, James Bennett, 1909- ed. 221.93

The ancient Near East; an anthology of texts and pictures. Translators and annotators: W. F. Albright [and others. Princeton] Princeton University Press, 1958. 380 p. illus. 23 cm. Combined selections from, and condensation of, the editor's Ancient Near Eastern texts relating to the Old Testament, 2d ed., 1955, and The ancient Near East in pictures relating to the Old Testament, 1954. [BS1180.P82 1958] 58-10052
1. Bible. O.T.—History of contemporary events, etc. 2. Bible. O.T.—Anntiquities. 3. Oriental literature—Translations into English. 4. English literature—Translations from Oriental literature. I. Title.

VEDAS. Atharvaveda. 294.
Atharva-veda Samhita; translated with a critical and exegetical commentary, by William Dwight Whitney ... revised and brought nearer to completion and ed. by Charles Rockwell Lanman ... Cambridge, Mass., Harvard university, 1905. 2 v. port. double facism. 28 cm. (Added t.p.: Harvard oriental series ... vol. VII-VIII) "First edition, first issue, 1906. One thousand copies. Paged continuously: 1st half: cixi, [1], 470 p. ; 2d half: p. l., 471-1054 p. "Harvard oriental series": p. 1047-1052. "Books for the study of Indo-Iranian languages": p. 1058-1054. [PK2971.H3 vol. VII-VIII] [PK3406.E5 1905] 6-1899
I. Whitney, William Dwight, 1827-1894, tr. II. Lanman, Charles Rockwell, 1850- ed. III. Title.

Oriental Missionary Society—Biography.

ERNY, Edward. 266'.023'0922 B
No guarantee but God; the story of the founders of the Oriental Missionary Society, by Edward and Esther Erny. Greenwood, Ind., Oriental Missionary Society [1969] vii, 116 p. ports. 19 cm. Contents.Contents.—Charles Cowman.—Juji Nakada.—Ernest Kilbourne.—Lettie B. Cowman. [BV2360.O7E7] 78-16999
1. Oriental Missionary Society—Biography. I. Erny, Esther, joint author. II. Title.

Oriental philology—Collections.

ORIENTAL club of Philadelphia. 297
Oriental studies; a selection of the papers read before the Oriental club of Philadelphia 1888-1894. Boston, Ginn & company, 1894. 278 p., 1 l. plates. 24 cm. [PJ2.O8] 7-34460
1. Oriental philology—Collections. I. Title. Contents omitted.

Origenes.

BIGG, Charles, 1840-1908. 201
The Christian Platonists of Alexandria; eight lectures preached before the University of Oxford in the year 1886 of the foundation of the late Rev. John Bampton. New York, AMS Press [1970] xxvii, 304 p. 23 cm. Reprint of the 1886 ed. Includes bibliographical references. [BR1705.B5 1970] 75-123764
1. Philo Judaus. 2. Clemens, Titus Flavius, Alexandrinus. 3. Origenes. 4. Platonists. I. Title.

CADIOU, Rene, 1900- 189.2
Origen, his life at Alexandria, by Rene Cadiou, translated by John A. Southwell [pseud.] St. Louis, Mo. and London, B. Herder book co., 1944. xiii, 338 p. 23 1/2 cm. Translation of La jeunesse d'Origene. [BR1720.O7C32] 44-4645
1. Origines. 2. Alexandria, Egypt. Catechetical school. I. Ronayne, Charles F., 1894- tr. II. Title.

CASPARY, Gerard E. 230'.1'3
Politics and exegesis : Origen and the two swords / Gerard E. Caspary. Berkeley : University of California Press, c1979. xv, 215 p. ; 24 cm. English and Latin. Includes bibliographical references and indexes. [BR65.O68C37] 77-71058 ISBN 0-520-03445-7 : 20.00
1. Origenes. 2. Christianity and politics—History. 3. Church and state—History. I. Title.

DANIELOU, Jean. 281.3
Origen; translated by Walter Mitchell. New York, Sheed and Ward [1955] 343p. 22cm. [BR1720.O7D315] 55-7487
1. Origenks. I. Title.

DE LANGE, Nicholas Robert Michael, 1944- 261.2
Origen and the Jews : studies in Jewish-Christian relations in third-century Palestine / N. R. M. de Lange. Cambridge ; New York : Cambridge University Press, 1976. p. cm. (University of Cambridge oriental publications ; 25) Based on the author's thesis, Oxford University, 1970. Bibliography: p. [BM535.D44] 75-36293 ISBN 0-521-20542-5 : 14.95
1. Origenes. 2. Bible. O.T.—Criticism, interpretation, etc., Jewish. 3. Judaism—Relations—Christianity. 4. Christianity and other religions—Judaism. I. Title. II. Series: Cambridge. University. Oriental publications ; 25.

FAIRWEATHER, William. 922.
...Origen and Greek patristic theology, by Rev. William Fairweather, M. A. New York, C. Scribner's sons, 1901. xiv, 268 p. 19 cm. (Half-title: The world's epoch-makers, ed. by O. Smeaton. [v]) Series title also at head of t.-p. [BR1720.O7F3] 2-10318
1. Origenes. I. Title.

FAYE, Eugene de, 1860-1929. 230'.13'0924
Origen and his work / by Eugene de Faye ; authorised translation by Fred Rothwell. Folcroft, Pa. : Folcroft Library Editions, 1978. 192 p. ; 23 cm. Reprint of the 1929 ed. published by Columbia University Press, New York. Includes bibliographical references and index. [BR65.O68F3913 1978] 78-16959 ISBN 0-8414-3684-3 lib. bdg. : 27.50
1. Origenes. I. Title.

GREGORIUS THAUMATURGUS, Saint, bp. of Neocaesarea. 230
... Address to Origen, by W. Metcalfe, B. D. London, Society for promoting Christian knowledge; New York, The Macmillan company, 1920. 96 p. 19 cm. (Translations of Christian literature. ser. i: Greek texts [13]) At head of title: Gregory Thaumaturgus. "First published 1907 under the title of 'Origen the teacher.' Re-issue, 1920." "Origen's letter to Gregory": p. 89-96. Bibliographical foot-notes. [BR45.T6G7] 21-4248
1. Origenes. I. Metcalfe, William Charles, ed. and tr. II. Title.

HARRIS, Carl Vernon, 1922- 281'.3'0924
Origen of Alexandria's interpretation of the teacher's function in the early Christian hierarchy and community. [1st ed.] New York, American Press [c1966] 278 p. 22 cm. Bibliography: p. 267-278. [BR65.O68H32] 66-28803
1. Origenes. 2. Religious education—Hist.—Early church. I. Title.

ORIGENES. 265.
The Philocalia of Origen; the text revised, with a critical introduction and indices, by J. Armitage Robinson ... Cambridge [Eng.] University press, 1893. lii, 278 p. 2 tab. 20 cm. "The Philocalia ... is a compilation of selected passages from Origen's works made by SS. Gregory and Basil."--Pref. [BR65.O6] 19-465
I. Gregorius Narianzennus, Saint, patriarch of Constantinople. abp. II. Basilius, Saint, the Great, abp. of Caesarea, 330 (ca.)-379. III. Robinson, Joseph Armitage, 1858- ed. IV. Title.

RUST, George, bp. of Dromore, d.1670. 230
A letter of resolution concerning Origen and the chief of his opinions, by George Rust; reproduced from the edition of 1661, with a bibliographical note by Marjorie Hope Nicolson. New York, Published for the Facsimile text society by Columbia university press, 1933. 3 p. l., facsim: 4 p. l., 136 p. 20 cm. (Half-title: The Facsimile text society. Series III: Philosophy, v. 3) "Reproduced from the copy in the McAlpin collection in the Union theological seminary."--Bibliographical note. With facsimile of original t.-p.: A letter of resolution concerning Origen and the chief of his opinions. Written to the learned and most ingenious C. L. esquire; and by him published. London, MDCLXI. [BR1720.O7R8 1661 a] [189.2] 33-5726
1. Origenes. I. Nicolson, Marjorie Hope, 1894- II. Title.

SHIRLEY, Alfred.
In the days of Origen; a tale of the third century, by the Rev. A. Shirley. London, Society for promoting Christian knowledge; New York, Macmillan [1920?] 125 p. front., 4 pl. 19 cm. A 21

1. Origenes. I. Title.

Origin of species.

CLARK, Harold Willard, 1891- 213
Genesis and science, by Harold W. Clark. Nashville, Southern Pub. Association [1967] 124 p. illus. 20 cm. [BS651.C552 1967] 67-28546

1. Bible. O.T. Genesis—Criticism, interpretation, etc. 2. Origin of species. 3. Bible and science. 4. Bible and evolution. 5. Creation. I. Title.

Original Hebrew Israelite Nation in Jerusalem.

GERBER, Israel Joshua, 1918- 296.6'7

The heritage seekers : American Blacks in search of Jewish identity / by Israel J. Gerber. Middle Village, N.Y. : Jonathan David Publishers, c1977. 222 p. ; 23 cm. Includes index. Bibliography: p. 211-215. [BM205.G44] 77-2907 ISBN 0-8246-0214-5 : 9.95

1. Original Hebrew Israelite Nation in Jerusalem. 2. Afro-American Jews. 3. Israel—Emigration and immigration. 4. Lost tribes of Israel—Miscellanea. I. Title.

Orione, Luigi, 1872-1940.

HYDE, Douglas Arnold, 1911- 922.245
God's bandit, the story of Don Crione, Father of the Poor. Westminster, Md., Newman Press, 1957. 207p. illus. 21cm. [HV28.O7H9] 57-59081
1. Orione, Luigi, 1872-1940. I. Title.

O'Rourke, John H., 1856-1929.

NEVILS, Coleman, 1878- 922.273
A moulder of men, John H. O'Rourke, s. j.; a memoir. New York, Apostleship of Prayer, 1953. 284p. illus. 20cm. [BX4705.O67N4] 53-7495
1. O'Rourke, John H., 1856-1929. I. Title.

Orozco, Alonso de, 1500-1591.

CAMARA Y CASTRO, Tomas Jenaro, bp., 1847-1904. 922.246
Life of Blessed Alphonsus Orozco, O.S.A. Compiled from the Spanish of Rt. Rev. Thos. Camara ... By Rev. W. A. Jones, O.S.A. Philadelphia, H. L. Kilner & co. [1895] 326 p. front. (port.) 19 1/2 cm. [BX4705.068C31 37-17415

1. Orozco, Alonso de, 1500-1591. 2. Augustinians in Spain. I. Jones, William Ambrose, father, 1865-1921, ed. and tr. II. Title.

Orphans and orphan asylums—Taiwan.

COWIE, Vera. 266'.023'0924 B
Girl Friday to Gladys Aylward / [by] Vera Cowie. London : Lakeland, 1976. 156 p., [4] p. of plates : ports. ; 18 cm. [HV887.T28C68] 77-370365 ISBN 0-551-00763-X : £0.95

1. Aylward, Gladys. 2. Orphans and orphan asylums—Taiwan. 3. Missionaries—Biography. I. Title.

Orphans and orphan-asylums-Texas.

CHRISTIAN love in action;
a narrative of events that foreshadowed and culminated in the establishing of the Mexican Baptist Orphans Home, located in San Antonio, Texas. [Waco? Tex.] 1957. viii, 87p. illus., ports. 28cm. Part of the illustrative matter is mounted.

1. Orphans and orphan-asylums-Texas. 2. Mexican Baptist Orphans Home, San Antonio. I. Bailey, Nannie Lou Tynes.

Orpheus.

GUTHRIE, William Keith Chambers, 1906- 292
Orpheus and Greek religion; a study of the Orphic movement. [2d ed. rev.] New York, Norton [1966] xix, 291p. illus. 20cm. (Methuen's handbks. of archaeology;Norton lib. N377) [BL820.O7G8 1952] 1.95 pap.,
1. Orpheus. 2. Dionysia. 3. Mysteries, Religious. 4. Cultus, Greek. I. Title.

GUTHRIE, William Keith Chambers, 1906- 292
Orpheus and Greek religion; a study of the Orphic Movement [by] W. K. C. Guthrie. [Rev. ed.] New York, Norton [1966, i.e. 1967] x, 291p. illus. 21cm. Bibl. [BL820.O7G8 1967] 67-250 6.50
1. Orpheus. 2. Dionysia. 3. Mysteries, Religious. 4. Cultus, Greek. I. Title.

LINFORTH, Ivan Mortimer, 1879- 292'2'11
The arts of Orpheus, by Ivan M. Linforth. New York, Arno Press, 1973 [c1941] xviii, 370 p. 23 cm. (Philosophy of Plato and Aristotle) Reprint of the ed. published by University of California Press, Berkeley. [BL820.07L5 1973] 72-9296 ISBN 0-405-04847-5 18.00
1. Orpheus. 2. Dionysus. 3. Mysteries, Religions. I. Title. II. Series.

LINFORTH, Ivan Mortimer, 1879- 292
The arts of Orpheus, by Ivan M. Linforth. Berkeley and Los Angeles, University of California press, 1941. xviii p., 1 l., 370 p. 20 cm. Bibliographical foot-notes. [BL820.O7L5] 41-52443
1. Orpheus. 2. Dionysus. 3. Mysteries, Religious. I. Title.

MACCHIORO, Vittorio D., 1880- 292
From Orpheus to Paul; a history of Orphism, by Vittorio D. Macchioro. New York, H. Holt and company [c1930] 6 p. l., 3-262 p. front., plates (1 fold.) 22 1/2 cm. (Half-title: Studies in religion and culture) "Schermerhorn lectures, I." "Notes": p. 227-258. [BL795.07M3] 30-13999

1. Orpheus. 2. Paul, Saint, apostle. 3. Mysteries, Religious. 4. Christianity and other religions. I. Title. II. Title: Orphism.

MEAD, George Robert Stow, 1863-1933 292
Orpheus. New York, Barnes & Noble [1965] 208p. 21cm. Bibl. [BL795.Q7M4] 65-3755 6.50
1. Orpheus. I. Title.

SCHURE, Edouard, 1841-1929. 291.6
The mysteries of ancient Greece: Orpheus/Plato. Blauvelt, N.Y., Rudolf Steiner Publications, 1971. 11-134 p. illus. 18 cm. (Steinerbooks) Published also in 1961 as the 5th and 7th chapters of the author's The great initiates which was G. Rasberry's translation of Les grands inities. Includes bibliographical references. [BL795.O7S3813] 76-150261 1.45
1. Orpheus. 2. Plato. 3. Mysteries, Religious. I. Schure, Edouard, 1841-1929. Les grands inities. Plato. English. 1971. II. Title. III. Title: Orpheus/Plato.

WATMOUGH, Joseph Ronald. 292
Orphism, by J. R. Watmough ... Cambridge [Eng.] The University press, 1934. vii, 79, [1] p. 17 cm. "Cromer Greek prize 1934." "I wish to demonstrate that the tradition of mysticism, reform, and subjective morality associated with the name of 'Orpheus' is no less characteristic of Greek thought that is the cult of the Olympian gods. Second, I wish to draw what seems to me the obvious analogy between ancient 'Orphism' and modern Protestantism."--Pref. [BL820.O7W3] 35-4771
1. Orpheus. 2. Greece—Religion. 3. Protestantism. 4. Christianity and other religions. I. Title.

Orphir Church.

WORDEN, Ian P. 726'.5'0941132
The round church of Orphir, Orkney / by Ian P. Worden. Cambridge : Institute of Geomantic Research, 1976. 5 p., plate : ill., plan ; 30 cm. (Occasional paper - Institute of Geomantic Research ; no. 6 ISSN 0308-1966s) [NA5481.O74W67]177-373205.ISBN 0-905376-04-8
1. Orphir Church. 2. Symbolism in architecture—Scotland—Orkney. I. Title. II. Series: Institute of Geomantic Research. Occasional paper — Institute of Geomantic Research ; no. 6.

Orr, James Edwin, 1912-

ALBERTYN, Charles Murray. 922
Messenger of revival; the contribution of Dr. J. Edwin Orr to evangelical Christianity in the mid-twentieth-century. [Pasadena? Calif.] c1960. 144p. 19cm. 'Abridgment of a... thesis submitted to Pasadena College for the master of arts degree.; Includes bibliography. [BV3785.O7A6] 60-42660
1. Orr, James Edwin, 1912- I. Title.

Orsini, Joseph E.

ORSINI, Joseph E. 282'.092'4 B
The anvil / by Joseph E. Orsini. Plainfield, N.J. : Logos International, [1974] 111 p. ; 18 cm. [BX4705.O715A28] 73-93895 ISBN 0-88270-089-8 : 1.25
1. Orsini, Joseph E. 2. Pentecostalism. I. Title.

ORSINI, Joseph E. 282'.092'4 B
Hear my confession / Joseph Orsini. New and updated ed. Plainfield, N.J. : Logos International, c1977. 144 p. ; 21 cm. [BX4705.O715A3 1977] 77-73151 ISBN 0-88270-231-9 pbk. : 2.95
1. Orsini, Joseph E. 2. Catholic Church—Clergy—Biography. 3. Clergy—New Jersey—Biography. 4. Pentecostalism—Catholic Church. I. Title.

Orthodox Church of the British Isles.

NEWMAN-NORTON, Seraphim. 281.9'41
Fitly framed together : a summary of the history, beliefs, and mission of the Orthodox Church of the British Isles / by Seraphim Newman-Norton. Glastonbury : Metropolitical Press, 1976. 20 p. : ill., port. ; 22 cm. Bibliography: p. 19-20. [BX747.5.N48] 77-360456 ISBN 0-905146-02-6 : £0.50
1. Orthodox Church of the British Isles. I. Title.

Orthodox Eastern Church.

BENZ, Ernst, 1907-
The Eastern Orthodox Church, it's thought and life. Translated from the German by Richard and Clara Winston. Chicago, Aldine [c1963] 230 p. 18 cm. Translation of Geist und Leben Der Ostkirche. Bibliography: p. [218]-230. NUC64
1. Orthodox Eastern Church. I. Title.

BENZ, Ernst, 1907- 281.9
The Eastern Orthodox Church, its thought and life. Translated from the German by Richard and Clara Winston. [1st ed.] Garden City, N.Y., Anchor Books, 1963. 230 p. 18 cm. (Anchor, A332) Translation of Geist und Leben der Ostkirche. Bibliography: p. [218]-230. [BX320.2.B413] 63-7690
1. Orthodox Eastern Church.

CONSTANTELOS, Demetrios J. 281.9
The Greek Orthodox Church: faith, history, and practice [by] Demetrios J. Constantelos. Foreword by Archbishop Iakovos. New York, Seabury Press [1967] 127 p. 21 cm. (A Seabury paperback, SP38) Bibliography: p. 125-127. [BX320.2.C64] 67-11468
1. Orthodox Eastern Church. 2. Orthodox Eastern Church, Greek. I. Title.

CONSTANTELOS, Demetrios J. 281.9'3
Understanding the Greek Orthodox church : its faith, history, and practice / Demetrios J. Constantelos. New York, N.Y. : Seabury Press, 1982. xiii, 178 p. ; 22 cm. Includes indexes. Bibliography: p. 166-171. [BX320.2.C66 1982] 19 81-21313 ISBN 0-8164-0515-8 15.95
1. Orthodox Eastern Church. 2. Orthodoxos Ekklesia tes Hellados. I. Title.

ETTELDORF, Raymond. 281.9
The soul of Greece. Westminster, Md., Newman Press, 1963. xiv, 235 p. illus. 23 cm. Bibliography: p. 225-228. [BX320.2.E8] 63-23098
1. Orthodox Eastern Church. 2. Orthodox Eastern Church, Greek. I. Title.

FORTESCUE, Adrian, 1874-1923. 281.9
The Orthodox Eastern Church. Freeport, N.Y., Books for Libraries Press [1971] xxxiii, 451 p. illus. 23 cm. Reprint of the 1920 ed. Bibliography: p. xxi-xxxiii. [BX320.F6 1971] 70-179520 ISBN 0-8369-6649-X
1. Orthodox Eastern Church.

FORTESCUE, Adrian, 1874-1923. 281.9
The Orthodox Eastern Church. With illus. by the author. New York, B. Franklin [1969] xxvii, 451 p. illus., map. 22 cm. (Medieval & Byzantine series 2) (Burt Franklin research & source works series 380.) Reprint of the 1907 ed. Bibliography: p. xv-xxvii. [BX320.F6 1969] 79-80232
1. Orthodox Eastern Church.

LACEY, Thomas James, 1870-
A study of the Eastern orthodox church, by Rev. T. J. Lacey ... 2d ed., rev. New York, E. S. Gorham, 1912. 3 p. l., [9]-63 p. front., plates, ports. 17 cm. Contents.--Preface.--The ancient patriarchates.--The eastern communion.--The orthodox in America. [BX325.L3 1912] 18-20569
I. Title.

LE GUILLOU, M. J. 281.9
The spirit of Eastern Orthodoxy. Tr. from French by Donald Attwater. New York, Hawthorn [c.1962] 144p. (Twentieth cent. ency. of Catholicism, v. 135. Section 14: Outside the church) Bibl. 62-11413 3.50 bds.,
1. Orthodox Eastern Church. 2. Orthodox Easternern Church—Relations—Catholic Church. 3. Catholic Church—Relations—Orthodox Eastern Church. I. Title.

LE GUILLOU, M. J. 281.9
The spirit of Eastern Orthodoxy, Tr. from French by Donald Attwater. Glen Rock,N.J., Paulist [c.1964] 121p. 18cm. (Vol. of the 20th cent. ency. of Catholicism; Deus/Century bks.) Bibl. 1.00 pap.,
1. Orthodox Eastern Church. 2. Orthodox Eastern Church—Relations—Catholic Church. 3. Catholic Church—Relations—Orthodox Eastern Church. I. Title.

NEALE, John Mason, 1818-1866. 281.9'09
A history of the Holy Eastern Church. London, J. Masters, 1850-73. [New York, AMS Press, 1973] p. [BX320.2.N42 1973] 74-144662 ISBN 0-404-04670-3 (set)
1. Orthodox Eastern Church. I. Title.

NEALE, John Mason, 1818-1866, comp. 281.9
Voices from the East; documents on the present state and working of the Oriental Church. Translated from the original Russ, Slavonic, and French, with notes. London, J. Masters, 1859. [New York, AMS Press, 1974] xii, 215 p. 19 cm. Includes six essays and letters by Andrew Nicolaievitch Mouravieff and the Acathiston by Innocent, Archbishop of Odessa. [BX320.N4 1974] 75-173069 ISBN 0-404-04659-2 12.50
1. Orthodox Eastern Church. I. Murav'ev, Andrei Nikolaevich, 1806-1874. II. Innokentii, Abp. of Kherson, 1800-1857. III. Title.

SOROKA, Leonid, 1916- 281.9
Faith of our fathers; the Eastern Orthodox religion, by Leonid Soroka and Stan W. Carlson. Minneapolis, Olympic Press [1954] 160p. illus. 27cm. [BX325.S67] 55-21996
1. Orthodox Eastern Church. I. Carlson, Stanley Waldo, 1909- joint author. II. Title.

SOROKA, Leonid, 1916- 281.9
Faith of our fathers; the Eastern Orthodox religion, by Stan W. Carlson and Leonid Soroka. Rev. ed. Minneapolis, Olympic Press [1958] 176 p, illus. 27 cm. In the earlier ed. Soroka's name appeared first on t. p. [BX325.S67 1958] 58-42572
1. Orthodox Eastern Church. I. Carlson, Stanley Waldo, 1909- joint author. II. Title.

STEPHANOU, Eusebius A 230.19
Belief and practice in the Orthodox Church, by Eusebius A. Stephanou. [New York, Minos Pub. Co.] 1965. 124 p. 18 cm. [BX320.2.S8] 66-6801
1. Orthodox Eastern Church. I. Title.

TSANKOV, Stefan, 1881- 281.9
The Eastern Orthodox church [by] Stefan Zankov, translated and edited by Donald A. Lowrie. Milwaukee, Wis., Morehouse publishing company, 1930. 2 p. l., 168 p. 19 cm. Printed in Great Britain. "First published September 1929; second edition January 1980." The present book was produced in connection with six lectures delivered in the University of Berlin, 1927. cf. Pref to the original edition. Bibliography, p. 164-168. [BX320.T73 1930] 33-36222
1. Orthodox Eastern church. I. Lowrie, Donald Alexander, tr. II. Title.

TSANKOV, Stefan, 1881-
The Eastern orthodox church [by] Stefan Zankov, translated and edited by Donald A. Lowrie. Milwaukee, Wis., Morehouse publishing company, 1929. 2 p. l., 168 p. 19 cm. Printed in Great Britain. Translation of Das orthodoxe Christentum des Osterns. Bibliography, p. 164-168. [BX329.T73] 30-6827
1. Orthodox Eastern church. I. Lowrie, Donald Alexander, tr. II. Title.

WARE, Timothy, 1934- 281.9
The orthodox church [Gloucester, Mass., P. Smith, 1964, c.1963] 352p. 19cm. (Pelican bk., A592 rebound) Bibl. 3.25

1. Orthodox Eastern Church. I. Title.

WARE, Timothy, 1934- 281.9
The Orthodox Church. Baltimore, Penguin [c.1963] 352p. map. 18cm. (Pelican orig., A592) Bibl. 63-4018 1.25 pap.,
1. Orthodox Eastern Church. I. Title.

ZERNOV, Nicolas 281.9
Eastern Christendom, a study of the origin and development of the Eastern Orthodox Church. New York, Putnam [c.1961] 326p. illus. (Putnam hist. of religion) Bibl. 61-5715 7.50
1. Orthodox Eastern Church. I. Title.

ZERNOV, Nicolas. 281.9
Eastern Christendom, a study of the origin and development of the Eastern Orthodox Church, 1st American ed.,] New York, Putnam [1961] 326 p. illus. 24 cm. (The Putnam history of religion) Includes bibliography. [BX320.2.Z45 1961] 61-5715
1. Orthodox Eastern Church. I. Title.

Orthodox Eastern Church—Addresses, essays, lectures.

MEYENDORFF, John, 1926- 281.9
The Byzantine legacy in the Orthodox Church / by John Meyendorff. Crestwood, N.Y. : St. Vladimir's Seminary Press, 1982. 268 p. ; 22 cm. Includes index. Bibliography: p. 257-259. [BX325.M49 1982] 19 82-797 ISBN 0-913836-90-7 pbk. : 8.95
1. Orthodox Eastern Church—Addresses, essays, lectures. 2. Byzantine Empire—Civilization—Addresses, essays, lectures. I. Title.
Publisher's address : 575 Scarsdale Rd., Crestwood, NY 10707.

ORTHODOXY, life and freedom 281.9
: essays in honour of Archbishop Iakovos / edited by A. J. Philippou. San Bernardino, Calif. : Borgo Press, 1980, c1973. p. cm. Reprint of the ed. published by Studion Publications, Oxford. Includes bibliographical references. [BX325.O78 1980] 19 80-20616 ISBN 0-89370-089-4 : 15.95 pbk. : 11.95
1. Orthodox Eastern Church—Addresses, essays, lectures. 2. Iakovos, Abp. of the Greek Orthodox Archdiocese of North and South America—Addresses, essays, lectures. I. Iakovos, Abp. of the Greek Orthodox Archidocese of North and South America. II. Philippou, A. J.
Contents omitted.

VERHOVSKOY, Serge S., 1907- 281.9
The light of the World : Essays on Orthodox Christianity / Serge S. Verhovskoy ; [editor Theodore Bazil]. Crestwood, N.Y. : St. Vladimir's Seminary Press, c1982. p. cm. "The first three articles: 'Orthodoxy,' 'Christ,' 'Christianity' are translated from Russian." Includes bibliographical references. [BX325.V47 1982] 19 82-16963 ISBN 0-88141-004-7 pbk. : 6.95
1. Orthodox Eastern Church—Addresses, essays, lectures. 2. Theology, Eastern church—Addresses, essays, lectures. I. Title.

Orthodox Eastern Church—Bibliography

ANDREWS, Dean Timothy, 016.2819
1914-
The Eastern Orthodox Church, a bibliography. 2d ed. Brookline, Mass., Greek Archdiocese of North and South America, Holy Cross Orthodox Theological School [1957] 79p. 22cm. (Publications of the Greek Archdiocese of North and South America, 5) [Z7842.A3A6 1957] 57-41145
1. Orthodox Eastern Church—Bibl. I. Title.

Orthodox Eastern Church—Biography.

FOR the glory of 281.9'092'2 B
the Father, Son, and Holy Spirit: a history of Eastern Orthodox saints, by Michael James Fochios. Translations from [Megas synaxaristes and Vioi ton hagion (romanized form)] Edited by Aristides Isidoros Cederakis. Illustrated by Michael James Fochios [and] Harry Constantine Maistros. [Baltimore, Phanari Publications, 1974] 175 p. plates. 22 cm. [BX393.F67] 74-174410
1. Orthodox Eastern Church—Biography. 2. Christian saints. I. Fochios, Michael James, tr. II. Cederakis, Aristides Isidoros, ed. III. Doukakes, K. Megas synaxaristes. Selections. English. 1974. IV. Vioi ton hagion. Selections. English. 1974. V. Title: A history of Eastern Orthodox saints.

Orthodox Eastern Church, Bulgarian—History.

MEININGER, Thomas A. 281.9'0924
Ignatiev and the establishment of the Bulgarian Exarchate, 1864-1872; a study in personal diplomacy [by] Thomas A. Meininger. Madison [Prepared by] State Historical Society of Wisconsin for the Dept. of History, University of Wisconsin, 1970. xii, 251 p. 24 cm. Bibliography: p. 198-229. [BX653.M43] 70-630135
1. Ignat'ev, Nikolai Pavlovich, graf, 1832-1908. 2. Orthodox Eastern Church, Bulgarian—History. I. Title.

Orthodox Eastern Church—Catechisms and creeds.

ORTHODOX Eastern Church. 264.0192
Liturgy and ritual. Evangelion. English.
Gospel lectionary of the Eastern Orthodox Church. Translated by Bishop Fan Stylian Noli. Boston, Albanian Orthodox Church in America, 1956. 542p. (p.535-542 advertisements) 24cm. [BX375.E78A4] 57-45295
1. Noli, Fan Stylian, Bp., 1882- tr. II. Albanian Orthodox Church in America. III. Title.

POLYZOIDES, Germanos, Bp., 1897-
A catechism of the Eastern Orthodox Church; a Sunday school primer. 2d ed. New York, D. C. Divry [1956?] 99 p. illus. 23 cm. 68-1201
1. Orthodox Eastern Church—Catechisms and creeds. I. Title.

Orthodox Eastern church—Catechisms and creeds—England.

POLYZOIDES, Germanos, 238.19
1897-
A catechism of the Eastern orthodox church, a Sunday school primer, by Rev. Germonas Polizoides, D.D. New York, D.C. Divry [1939] 109, [1] p. incl. front., illus. 21 cm. [BX735.P6] 44-35141
1. Orthodox Eastern church—Catechisms and creeds—England. I. Title.

Orthodox Eastern Church. Catechisms and creeds—English.

BOULGARIS, Nikolaos, 1635-1684.
A holy catechism; or, Explanation of the divine and holy liturgy, and examination of candidates for ordination. Now revised after the purer style, and edited at the expense of Messrs. Andiades and Polytakes for the common benefit of the Orthodox. Constantinople, At the Patriarchal Press, 1861 [Maitland, Fla., Three Hierarchs Seminary, 1965?] xxviii, 300 p. 68-11211
1. Orthodox Eastern Church. Catechisms and creeds—English. I. Title.

DEMETRY CONSTAS HADZI, 238.19
1873-
Catechism of the Eastern orthodox church, with most essential differences of others principal churches scriptually criticized, by Rev. Constas H. Demetry ... Approved by the Holy synod 1929. [Detroit, Eagle printing company, 1935] 4 p. l., 116 p. 20 cm. On cover: Christian comparative and aploogetical catechism. [BX735.D4] 35-20700
1. Orthodox Eastern church—Catechisms and creeds—English. I. Title.

MIHALCESCU, Irineu, Metropolitan
of Moldava.
Beliefs of Orthodox Christians. [Translated by Father Vasile Halegan. Jackson, Mich.] Romanian Orthodox Episcopate of America [n.d.] 95 p. 16 cm. 66-7054
1. Orthodox Eastern Church — Catechisms and creeds — English. I. Romanian Orthodox Episcopate of America. II. Title.

NOLI, Fan Stylian, Abp., 238.19
1882- ed. and tr.
Eastern Orthodox catechism. Boston, Albanian Orthodox Church in America, 1954. 162p. 19cm. Based on the Catechism in Russian by Meteopolitan Phllaret, Moscow, 1840. [BX345.N6] 55-16568
1. Orthodox Eastern Church—Catechisms and creeds—English. I. Filaret, Metropolitan of Moscow, 1782-1867. II. Albanian Orthodox Church in America. III. Title.

ORTHODOX Eastern Church. 264.019
Liturgy and ritual. Euchologion. English.
Liturgy and Catechism of the Eastern Orthodox Church in Albanian and English; translated by Bishop F. S. Noli. Boston, Albanian Orthodox Church in America, 1955. 235p. 19cm. Translation of the Liturgy of St. John Chrysostom from the Euchologion in Greek, and of the Cathechism, Russian version by Metropolitan Philaret. [BX360.A5N6] 55-44675
1. Orthodox Eastern Church—Catechisms and creeds—English. I. Orthodox Eastern Church. Liturgy and ritual. Euchologion. Albanian. II. Filaret, Metropolitan of Moscow, 1782-1867. Catechism. III. Filaret, Metropolitan of Moscow, 1782-1867. Catechism. IV. Noll, Fan Stylian, Bp., 1882- tr. V. Albanian Orthodox Church in America. VI. Title.

VELIMIROVIC, Nikolaj, 238.19
bp., 1880-
The faith of the saints; a catechism of the Eastern Orthodox Church. [Pittsburgh, Serb National Federation, 1949] 115 p. illus. 22 cm. [BX735.V4] 49-26101
1. Orthodox Eastern Church—Catechisms and creeds—English. I. Title.

Orthodox Eastern Church—Collected works.

FLOROVSKII, Georgii 230'.193
Vasel'evich, 1893-
Ways of Russian theology / Georges Florovsky ; general editor, Richard S. Haugh ; translated by Robert L. Nichols. Belmont, Mass. : Nordland Pub. Co., c1979- v. ; 22 cm. (Collected works of Georges Florovsky ; v. 5) Translation of Puti russkogo bogosloviia. Includes bibliographical references. [BX260.F55 vol. 5] 19 78-78267 ISBN 0-913124-23-0 (v. 1) : 27.50
1. Orthodox Eastern Church—Collected works. 2. Theology—Collected works—20th century. I. Title.

FLOROVSKII, Georgii 230'.1'908
Vasil'evich, 1893-
Collected works of Georges Florovsky. Belmont, Mass., Nordland Pub. Co. [1972- v. 23 cm. Contents.Contents.—v. 1. Bible, church, tradition: an Eastern Orthodox view. [BX260.F55] 72-197090
1. Orthodox Eastern Church—Collected works. 2. Theology—Collected works—20th century. I. Title.

Orthodox Eastern Church—Congresses.

SAINT Nectarios Orthodox 281.9'3
Conference (2nd:1980: Seattle, Wash.)
Saint Nectarios Orthodox Conference, Seattle, Washington, July 22-25, 1980. Seattle, Wash. : St. Nectarios Press, 1981. xiv, 174 p. ; 27 cm. Sponsored by the Russian Orthodox Church outside of Russia. Contents.Contents. Parish life/home and family / Anthony Gavalas — The Western God / Michael Azkoul — Education of children / Rodion Laskowski — Old Testament heritage / Father Panteleimon — Monasticism / Father Ioannikios — The Canons and their significance / Panagiotes Carras — The isolated Orthodox / Lev Puhalo — The river of fire / Alexandre Kalomiros — Scholarship and faith / Michael Henning — The worship of the church / Father Ephraim. Includes bibliographical references. [BX215.S24 1980] 19 80-53258 ISBN 0-913026-14-X pbk. : 15.00
1. Orthodox Eastern Church—Congresses. 2. Russkaia pravoslavnaia tserkov zagranitsei—Congresses. I. Seattle, Wash. II. Russkaia pravoslavnaia tserkov zagranitsei. III. Title.
Publisher's address 10300 Ashworth Ave. N., Seattle, WA 98133.

Orthodox Eastern Church—Dictionaries.

DEMETRAKOPOULOS, George 281.903
H.
Dictionary of Orthodox theology: a summary of the beliefs, practices and history of the Eastern Orthodox Church. Introd. by John E. Rexine. New York, Philosophical [c.1964] xv, 187p. 21cm. 63-13346 5.00 bds.,
1. Orthodox Eastern Church—Dictionaries. 2. Theology, Dictionaries. I. Title.

LANGFORD-JAMES, Richard 281.9'03
Lloyd.
A dictionary of the Eastern Orthodox Church / by R. Ll. Langford-James ; with a pref. by Joannes Gennadius. New York : B. Franklin, [1976] p. cm. Reprint of the 1923 ed. published by the Faith Press, London. Bibliography: p. [BX230.L3 1975] 72-82261 ISBN 0-8337-4210-8 : 18.00
1. Orthodox Eastern Church—Dictionaries. I. Title.

Orthodox Eastern Church— Doctrinal and controversial works.

BULGAKOV, Sergel Nikolaevich,
1871-1944.
The Orthodox church. [Clayton, Wis., American Orthodox Press, 1964?] 224 p. 18 cm. Translated by Elizabeth S. Cram; edited by Donald A. Lowrie. 66-6441
1. Orthodox Eastern Church-Doctrinal and controversial works. I. Lowrie, Donald Alexander, ed. II. Title.

CABASILAS, Nicolaus, 234'.16
14thcent.
The life in Christ / Nicholas Cabasilas ; translated from the Greek by Carmino J. deCatanzaro ; with an introduction by Boris Bobrinskoy. Crestwood, N.Y. : St. Vladimir's Seminary Press, 1982, c1974. p. cm. Translation of: Peri tes en Christoi Zoes. Includes bibliographical references. [BT767.7.C313 1982] 19 82-16870 ISBN 0-913836-12-5 : 7.95
1. Orthodox Eastern Church—Doctrinal and controversial works. 2. Mystical union. 3. Sacraments—Orthodox Eastern Church. I. [Peri tes en Christoi Zoes.] English II. Title.
Publisher's address : 575 Scarsdale Rd., Crestwood, NY 10707.

THE City of Zion;
or, the church built upon the rock, i. e., the human society in Christ. Translated out of the original Greek by D. Cummings. [Chicago, Orthodox Christian Educational Society, 1958] ii, 106p.
1. Orthodox Eastern Church— Doctrinal and controversial works. I. Makrakes, Apostolos, 1831-1905.

CONCERNING our duties to God.
Chicago, Orthodox Christian Educational Society, 1958. ii, 170p. 'Reprinted from th Logos.'
1. Orthodox Eastern Church—Doctrinal and controversial works. 2. God—Worship and love. I. Makrakes, Apostolos, 1831-1905.

CONIARIS, Anthony M. 281'.9
Introducing the Orthodox Church, its faith and life / by Anthony M. Coniaris. Minneapolis, Minn. : Light and Life Pub. Co., c1982. vii, 214 p. : ill. ; 23 cm. Includes bibliographical references. [BX320.2.C63 1982] 19 81-81309 ISBN 0-937032-25-5 pbk. : 6.95
1. Orthodox Eastern Church—Doctrinal and controversial works. I. Title.
Publisher's address: 3450 Irving Ave. S., Minneapolis, MN 55408

CRONK, George, 1939- 220.6'1
The message of the Bible : an orthodox Christian perspective / by George Cronk. Crestwood, N.Y. : St. Vladimir's Seminary Press, 1982. 293 p. ; 22 cm. Bibliography: p. 291-293. [BS475.2.C76 1982] 19 82-7355 ISBN 0-913836-94-X : 8.95
1. Orthodox Eastern Church—Doctrinal and controversial works. 2. Bible—Introduction. 3. Bible—Criticism, interpretation, etc. I. Title.

Publisher's address : 575 Scarsdale Rd., Crestwood, NY 10707.

FOUYAS, Mathodios. 281.9
Orthodoxy, Roman Catholicism and Anglicanism. London, New York, Oxford University Press, 1972. xxi, 280 p. 23 cm. Bibliography: p. 260-272. [BX320.2.F68] 72-195672 ISBN 0-19-213947-9 £4.50
1. Orthodox Eastern Church—Doctrinal and controversial works. 2. Catholic Church—Doctrinal and controversial works—Orthodox Eastern authors. 3. Church of England—Doctrinal and controversial works. 4. Christian union. I. Title.

GAVIN, Frank Stanton Burns, 1890-1938.
Some aspects of contemporary Greek orthodox thought. New York, American Review of Eastern Orthodoxy, 1962. xxxiv, 430 p. 18 cm. Stamp on title page: Hialeah, Fla., Orthodox Book Center. Bibliography: p. [xxix]-xxxiv. 63-11699
1. Orthodox Eastern church — Doctrinal and controversial works. I. Title.

GAVIN, Frank Stanton Burns, 1890-1938. 20?
Some aspects of contemporary Greek Orthodox thought. New York, AMS Press [1970] xxxiv, 430 p. 23 cm. Reprint of the 1923 ed. Originally presented as lectures at the Western Theological Seminary, Chicago, on the invitation of the Committee of the Hale Lectureship Foundation. Bibliography: p. [xxix]-xxxiv. [BX320.G3 1970] 73-133818
1. Orthodox Eastern Church—Doctrinal and controversial works. I. Title.

KHERBAWI, Basil M. 230.19
The old church in the new world; or, The mother church, being a plain exposition and vindication of the true church founded and headed by Our Lord Jesus Christ, her doctrine, her sacraments, etc., etc., by Archpriest Basil M. Kherbawi ... Brooklyn, N.Y., The author [c1930] xviii, 353 p. front. (port.) 22 cm. [BX320.K5] [281.9] 32-23850
1. Orthodox Eastern church—Doctrinal and controversial works. I. Title.

KOHANIK, Peter G., 1880- 281.9
The mother church of Christendom is the Holy Apostolic Orthodox Greek-Catholic Church. Roman Catholicism and Protestantism. Wilkes-Barre, Pa., "SVIT"-- The Light, 1948 228 p. illus. 18 cm. [BX320.K6] 49-16360
1. Orthodox Eastern Church—Doctrinal and controversial works. I. Title.

MAKRAKES, Apostolos, 1831-1905. 230.19
Memoir on the nature of the church of Christ on its fundamental law and on Christian life, tr. from the 2d ed. by D. Cummings. New York, Christian Brotherhoods, Zealots of Orthodoxy and John the Baptist, 1947. 168 p. port. 24 cm. [BX320.M32] 49-13922
1. Orthodox Eastern Church—Doctrinal and controversial works. I. Title.

MAKRAKES, Apostolos, 1831-1905. 230'.1'9
Orthodox Christian meditations, by Apostolos Makrakis (1831-1905). Translated out of the original Greek by D. Cummings. [Chicago, Orthodox Christian Educational Society, 1965] 143 p. 21 cm. [BX320.2.M3313 1965] 74-172642
1. Orthodox Eastern Church—Doctrinal and controversial works. 2. Meditations. I. Cummings, Denver, 1889- tr. II. Title.

MAKRAKES, Apostolos, 1831-1905. 260.7
The political philosophy of the Orthodox Church, by Apostolos Makrakis. Translated from the Greek by D. Cummings. Chicago, Orthodox Christian Educational Society, 1965. 162 p. 21 cm. [BL51.M24813] 77-16996
1. Orthodox Eastern Church—Doctrinal and controversial works. 2. Philosophy and religion. 3. Political science. I. Title.

MPRATSIOTES, Panagiotes Ioannou, 1889- 230.1'9
The Greek Orthodox Church, by Panagiotis Bratsiotis. Translated by Joseph Blenkinsopp. Notre Dame [Ind.] University of Notre Dame Press [1968] xi, 120 p. 24 cm. Translation of Von der griechischen Orthodoxie. Includes bibliographies. [BX320.2.M6513] 68-27579
1. Orthodox Eastern Church—Doctrinal and controversial works. I. Title.

PAAVALI, Abp. of Karelia and All Finland, 1914- 230'.19
The faith we hold / Archbishop Paul of Finland ; translated from the Finnish by Marita Nykanen and Esther Williams. Crestwood, N.Y. : St. Vladimir's Seminary Press, 1980. p. cm. Translation of Miten uskomme. [BX320.2.P3313] 80-10404 ISBN 0-913836-61-3 pbk. : 3.95
1. Orthodox Eastern Church—Doctrinal and controversial works. 2. Spiritual life—Orthodox Eastern authors. I. Title.

PAPADOPOULOS, Gerasimos. 230'.19
Orthodoxy, faith and life / by Bishop Gerasimos Papadopoulos. Brookline, Mass. : Holy Cross Orthodox Press, 1980- v. <1> ; 22 cm. Includes index. Contents.Contents.—v. 1. Christ in the Gospels. [BX320.2.P333] 19 80-21101 ISBN 0-916586-37-5 pbk. : 4.95
1. Orthodox Eastern Church—Doctrinal and controversial works. I. Title.

PATRINACOS, Nicon D. 281.9
The individual and his Orthodox Church [by] Nicon D. Patrinacos. [New York] Orthodox Observer Press [1970] xii, 152 p. 22 cm. [BX320.2.P35] 73-128773
1. Orthodox Eastern Church—Doctrinal and controversial works. I. Title.

PLATON, Metropolitan of Moscow, 1737-1812. 230.1'9
The Orthodox doctrine of the Apostolic Eastern Church; or, A compendium of Christian theology. Translated from the Greek. To which is prefixed an Historical and expalnatory essay on general catechism; and appended, a Treatise on Melchisedec. New York, AMS Press [1969] vi, 239 p. 22 cm. Historical and explanatory essay on general catechism signed: A. Coray. Reprint of the London ed. published in 1857. Translation of Pravoslavnoe uchenie (romanized form); translated from the Greek translation of A. Koraes by G. Potessaro. [BX320.P5613 1969] 70-81772
1. Orthodox Eastern Church—Doctrinal and controversial works. I. Potessaro, G., tr. II. Koraes, Adamantios, 1748-1833, tr. III. Title. IV. Title: A compendium of Christian theology.

RYCAUT, Paul, Sir, 1628-1700. 281.9'3
The present state of the Greek and Armenian churches, anno Christi, 1678. Written at the command of His Majesty. London, J. Starkey, 1679. [New York, AMS Press, 1970] 452 p. 23 cm. [BX320.R9 1970] 75-133821 ISBN 0-404-05476-5
1. Orthodox Eastern Church—Doctrinal and controversial works. 2. Armenian Church—Doctrinal and controversial works. I. Title.

SAKKAS, Basile. 262.9'8'19
The calendar question, by Basile Sakkas. Translated from the French by Holy Transfiguration Monastery in Boston. Jordanville, N.Y., Holy Trinity Monastery, 1973. 94 p. illus. 24 cm. Bibliography; p. 80. [BX323.S213] 72-90868
1. Orthodox Eastern Church—Doctrinal and controversial works. 2. Church calendar. I. Title.

STRATMAN, Chrysostomos H
The Roman rite in Orthodoxy, by Chrysostomos H. Stratman; and additional testimonies, by Apostolos Makrakis. Chicago, Orthodox Christian Educational Society, 1957. 62 p.
1. Orthodox Eastern Church — Doctrinal and controversial works. I. Macrakis, Apostolos. 1831-1905. II. Title.

ZERNOV, Nicolas. 281.9
The church of the eastern Christians, by Nicolas Zernov ... Published for the Fellowship of St. Alban and St. Sergius. London, Society for promoting Christian knowledge; New York, The Macmillan company [1942] v, [1], 114 p. 18 1/2 cm. "First published in 1942." Bibliography: p. 113-114. [BX320.Z4] 43-17291
1. Orthodox Eastern church—Doctrinal and controversial works. 2. Orthodox Eastern church—Relations—Church of England. 3. Church of England—Relations—Orthodox Eastern church. I. Fellowship of St. Alban and St. Sergius. II. Title.

Orthodox Eastern Church—Doctrinal and controversial works—Addresses, essays, lectures.

CONTOS, Leonidas. 281.9'3
2001, the church in crisis / by Leonidas C. Cantos. Brookline, Mass. : Holy Cross Orthodox Press, 1981, c1982. 52 p. ; 22 cm. (Patriarch Athenagoras memorial lectures) [BX320.2.C67 1982] 19 81-7028 pbk : 12.50
1. Orthodox Eastern Church—Doctrinal and controversial works—Addresses, essays, lectures. 2. Greek Orthodox Archdiocese of North and South America—Doctrinal and controversial works—Addresses, essays, lectures. I. Title. II. Series.

EXETASTES. 230'.1'93
Contemporary issues : Orthodox Christian perspectives / by "Exetastes". New York : Greek Orthodox Archdiocese Press, 1976. 103 p. ; 23 cm. Articles republished from the Orthodox observer. [BX325.E86 1976] 76-151121
1. Orthodox Eastern Church—Doctrinal and controversial works—Addresses, essays, lectures. 2. Church and social problems—Orthodox Eastern Church—Addresses, essays, lectures. I. Title.

Orthodox Eastern Church—Doctrinal and controversial works—Orthodox Eastern authors—Collected works.

SCHMEMANN, Alexander, 1921- 281.9
Church, world, mission : reflections on orthodox in the West / Alexander Schmemann. Crestwood, N.Y. : St. Vladimir's Seminary Press, 1979. p. cm. [BX320.2.S29] 79-27597 ISBN 0-913836-49-4 : 5.95
1. Orthodox Eastern Church—Doctrinal and controversial works—Orthodox Eastern authors—Collected works. 2. Orthodox Eastern Church—Collected works. I. Title.
Publishers Address: 575 Scarsdale Rd., Crestwood, NY 10707

Orthodox Eastern Church—Doctrinal and controversial works—Protestant authors.

CALIAN, Carnegie Samuel. 281.9
Icon and pulpit; the Protestant-Orthodox encounter. Philadelphia, Westminster Press [1968] 220 p. 21 cm. Bibliography: p. 171-181. Bibliographical references included in "Notes" (p. 183-214) [BX324.5.C3] 68-23798 6.50
1. Orthodox Eastern Church—Doctrinal and controversial works—Protestant authors. 2. Orthodox Eastern Church—Relations—Protestant Churches. 3. Christian union—Orthodox Eastern Church. 4. Protestant churches—Relations—Orthodox Eastern Church. I. Title.

Orthodox Eastern Church—Education.

KOULOMZIN, Sophie. 268
Our church and our children / Sophie Koulomzin. [Crestwood, N.Y.] : St. Vladimir's Seminary Press, 1975. 158 p. ; 22 cm. Bibliography: p. 157-158. [BV1475.2.K68] 75-20215 ISBN 0-913836-25-7 pbk. : 4.50
1. Orthodox Eastern Church—Education. 2. Christian education of children. I. Title.

Orthodox Eastern Church—Europe.

LATOURETTE, Kenneth Scott, 1884-1968. 270.8 s
The nineteenth century in Europe: the Protestant and Eastern churches. Westport, Conn., Greenwood Press [1973, c1959] viii, 532 p. 23 cm. (His Christianity in a revolutionary age, v. 2) Bibliography: p. 495-512. [BR475.L33 vol. 2] [BX4837] 280'.4'094 72-11977 ISBN 0-8371-5702-1 95.00, 5 vol. set
1. Orthodox Eastern Church—Europe. 2. Protestant churches—Europe. I. Title. II. Series.

Orthodox Eastern Church, Greek.

ALLACCI, Leone, 1586-1669. 914.95'03'5
The newer temples of the Greeks. Translated, annotated, and with introd. by Anthony Cutler. University Park, Pennsylvania State University Press, 1969. xxviii, 47 p. plans. 23 cm. Translation of De templis Graecorum recentioribus. Bibliographical references included in "Notes" (p. [41]-47) [BX618.A413] 68-8177 5.00
1. Orthodox Eastern Church, Greek. 2. Liturgy and architecture. I. Cutler, Anthony, 1934- tr. II. Title.

THE evolution of the Greek Orthodox church in America and its present problems... New York [Printed by Cosmos Greek-American printing co.] 1959. 62p. 21cm.
I. Kourides, Peter T

PAPADOPOULLOS, Theodore H. 281.9'495
Studies and documents relating to the history of the Greek Church and people under Turkish domination, by Theodore H. Papadopoullos. Brussels, 1952. [New York, AMS Press, 1973] xxiv, 507 p. 23 cm. Original ed. issued as no. 1 of Bibliotheca Graeca aevi posterioris. "[Planosparaktes (romanized form)], a document in political verse, edited from British Museum manuscript Additional 10077" (summary, text, and notes): p. [265]-392. Bibliography: p. [xi]-xxiv. [BX613.P3 1973] 70-180302 ISBN 0-404-56314-7 27.50
1. Orthodox Eastern Church, Greek. 2. Orthodox Eastern Church—History—Sources. I. Planosparaktes. 1973. II. Title. III. Series: Bibliotheca Graeca aevi posterioris, 1.

RINVOLUCRI, Mario. 281.9495
Anatomy of a church; Greek Orthodoxy today. With a foreword by Peter Hammond. [Bronx, N.Y.] Fordham University Press [1966] 192 p. 21 cm. Bibliography: p. 187-188. [BX615.R5 1966] 66-30071
1. Orthodox Eastern Church, Greek. I. Title.

THE waters of Marah;
the present state of the Greek church. New York, Macmillan, 1956. ix, 186p. 21cm.
1. Orthodox Eastern Church, Greek. I. Hammond, Peter, 1921-

THE waters of Marah;
the present state of the Greek church. New York, Macmillan, 1956. ix, 186p. 21cm.
1. Orthodox Eastern Church, Greek. I. Hammond, Peter, 1921-

Orthodox Eastern Church, Greek—Addresses, essays, lectures.

MAKRAKES, Apostolos, 1831-1905. 252.019
A revelation of treasure hid, together with three important lectures ... and apostolical canons respecting baptism; translated out of the original Greek by D. Cummings. Chicago, Orthodox Christian Educational Society, 1952. 80p. illus. 23cm. [BX616.M3] 53-8789
1. Orthodox Eastern Church, Greek—Addresses, essays, lectures. I. Title.

Orthodox Eastern Church, Greek—History.

FRAZEE, Charles A. 322'.1'09495
The Orthodox Church and independent Greece, 1821-1852, by Charles A. Frazee. London, Cambridge U.P., 1969. viii, 220 p. 23 cm. Bibliography: p. 198-211. [BX613.F7] 69-10488 60/-($10.00)
1. Orthodox Eastern Church, Greek—History. 2. Church and state in Greece. I. Title.

Orthodox Eastern Church, Greek, in the United States—Catechisms and creeds—English.

CALLINICOS, Constantine N 238.19
The Greek Orthodox catechism; a manual of instruction on faith, morals, and worship. New York, Published under the auspices of Greek Archdiocese of No. and So. America, 1953. 119p. illus. 20cm. [BX735.C3] 53-39559
1. Orthodox Eastern Church, Greek, in the U. S.—Catechisms and creeds—English. I. Title.

Orthodox Eastern Church, Greek—United States—Membership.

SCOURBY, Alice. 306'.6
Third generation Greek Americans : a study of religious attitudes / Alice Scourby. New York : Arno Press, 1980. v, 93 p. ; 24 cm. (American ethnic groups) Originally presented as the author's thesis, New School for Social Research, 1967. Bibliography: p. 84-86. [BR563.G73S37 1980] 80-893 ISBN 0-405-13454-1 : 14.00
1. Orthodox Eastern Church, Greek—United States—Membership. 2. Greek Americans—Religion. 3. Greek Americans—Ethnic identity. I. Title. II. Series.

Orthodox Eastern Church—History.

CALLINICOS, Constantine. 281.9
A brief sketch of Greek church history by the Rev. Constantine Callinicos ... translated by Katherine Natzio ... with an introduction by the Most Rev. Archbishop of Thyateira, Germanos. D. D. London. The Faith press, ltd., Milwaukee, The Morehouse publishing co. [1931] viii, 159 p. front. 19 cm. [BX290.C3] 32-2578
1. Orthodox Eastern church—Hist. I. Natzio, Katherine. tr. II. Title.

EVERY, George 281.9
The Byzantine patriarchate, 451-1204. [2d ed., rev. dist. Greenwich, Conn., Seabury, c.]1962. 204p. illus. 22cm. Bibl. 62-51093 5.00
1. Orthodox Eastern Church—Hist. 2. Schism—Eaetern and Western Church. I. Title.

EVERY, George. 281.9
The Byzantine patriarchate, 451-1204 / [by George Every]. New York : AMS Press, 1980 [c1962] p. cm. Reprint of the 2d ed., rev. published by S.P.C.K., London. Includes index. [BX300.E8 1980] 78-63340 ISBN 0-404-17015-3 : 21.50
1. Orthodox Eastern Church—History. 2. Schism—Eastern and Western Church. I. Title.

FRENCH, Reginald Michael, 281.9
1884-
The Eastern Orthodox Church. London, New York, Hutchinson's University Library, 1951. 186 p. 19 cm. (Hutchinson's university library. Christian religion) [BX290.F7] 51-11318
1. Orthodox Eastern Church—Hist. I. Title.

FRENCH, Reginald Michael, 1884-
The Eastern Orthodox Church. London, New York, Hutchinson's University Library, 1961. 186 p. 19 cm. (Hutchinson's university library. Christian religion) 64-29008
1. Orthodox Eastern Church — Hist. I. Title. II. Series.

FRENCH, Reginald Michael, 1884-
The Eastern Orthodox Church. London, New York, Hutchinson's University Library, 1961. 186 p. 19 cm. (Hutchinson's university library. Christian religion) 64-29008
1. Orthodox Eastern Church — Hist. I. Title. II. Series.

THE history of the orthodox church; a brief sketch of the one holy orthodox Catholic and apostolic church; translated by Katherine Natzio; with an introduction by Germanos. [Rev. ed.] Los Angeles, Cal., Prothymos Press [1957] xiv, 146p. front.
1. Orthodox Eastern Church—History. I. Callinicos, Constantine N

KOULOMZIN, Sophie. 281.909
The Orthodox Christian Church through the ages. New York, Metropolitan Council Publications Committee, Russian Orthodox Greek Catholic Church of America, 1956. 239p. illus. 21cm. (The Advanced Sunday school series for teen-agers) [BX290.K65] 57-24411
1. Orthodox Eastern Church—Hist. 2. Orthodox Eastern Church, Russian—Hist. 3. Russian Orthodox Greek Catholic Church of North America—Hist. I. Title.

MAGOULIAS, Harry J. 281.9'3
Byzantine Christianity: emperor, church, and the West [by] Harry J. Magoulias. Chicago, Rand McNally [1970] x, 196 p. map. 21 cm. (The Rand McNally European history series) Bibliography: p. 181-185. [BX290.M3] 70-75615
1. Orthodox Eastern Church—History. I. Title.

MEYENDORFF, Jean, 1926- 281.9
The Orthodox Church, its past and its role in the world today. Translated from the French by John Chapin. [New York] Pantheon Books [1962] 244 p. 21 cm. Translation of L'Eglise orthodoxe: hier et aujourd'hui. Includes bibliographies. [BX290.M413] 62-14260
1. Orthodox Eastern Church—History. I. Title.

PARASKEVAS, John E. 281.9'09
The Eastern Orthodox Church; a brief history, including a church directory and prominent orthodox laymen, by John E. Paraskevas and Frederick Reinstein. [1st ed.] Washington, El Greco Press [1969] vii, 131 p., illus., map, ports. 21 cm. Bibliography: p. 127. [BX290.P36] 73-10983 5.95
1. Orthodox Eastern Church—History. I. Reinstein, Frederick, joint author. II. Title.

POLYZOIDES, Germanos, 281.9
1897-
The history and teachings of the Eastern Greek Orthodox church. New York, D. C. Divry [1969] 95 p. illus., ports. 23 cm. [BX290.P63 1969] 77-243091
1. Orthodox Eastern Church—History. I. Title.

POLYZOIDES, Germanos, 281.9'09
1897-
The history and teachings of the Eastern Greek Orthodox Church / by Germanos Polizoides. New York : D.C. Divry, c1977. 95 p. : ill. ; 23 cm. [BX732.5.P64 1977] 77-152803
1. Orthodox Eastern Church—History. 2. Christian education—Text-books—Orthodox Eastern. I. Title.

SCHMEMANN, Alexander, 1921- 281.
The historical road of Eastern Orthodoxy. Tr. by Lydia W. Kesich. Chicago, Regnery [1966, c.1963] viii, 343p. 18cm. (Logos ed., 51L-713) Bibl. [BX290.S373] 1.95 pap.,
1. Orthodox Eastern Church—Hist. I. Title.

SCHMEMANN, Alexander, 1921- 281.9
The historical road of Eastern Orthodoxy. Tr. by Lydia W. Kesich. New York, Holt [1963] viii, 343p. 22cm. Bibl. 63-11873 6.50
1. Orthodox Eastern Church—Hist. I. Title.

SCHMEMANN, Alexander, 1921-
The historical road of eastern orthodoxy. Trans. by Lydia W. Kesich. Chicago, Henry Regnery, [1966] viii, 342 p. 18 cm. 67-1068
1. Orthodox Eastern church—History. I. Title.

SCHMEMANN, Alexander, 1921- 281.9
The historical road of Eastern Orthodoxy / Alexander Schmemann ; translated by Lydia W. Kesich. Crestwood, N.Y. : St. Vladimir's Seminary Press, 1977, c1963. viii, 343 p. ; 24 cm. Translation of Istoricheskii put' pravoslaviia. Reprint of the 1963 ed. published by Holt, Rinehart and Winston, New York. Bibliography: p. 342-343. [BX290.S373 1977] 77-12074 ISBN 0-913836-47-8 pbk. : 6.95
1. Orthodox Eastern Church—History. I. Title.

SPINKA, Matthew, 1890- 209'.496
A history of Christianity in the Balkans; a study in the spread of Byzantine culture among the Slavs. [Hamden, Conn.] Archon Books, 1968 [c1933] 202 p. 23 cm. Bibliography: p. 189-191. [BR737.S6S6 1968] 68-20379
1. Orthodox Eastern Church—History. 2. Slavs, Southern—Church history. I. Title. II. Title: Christianity in the Balkans.

STANLEY, Arthur Penrhyn, 281.9
1815-1881.
Lectures on the history of the Eastern church, with an introduction on the study of ecclesiastical history, by Arthur Penrhyn Stanley ... New ed. ... New York, C. Scribner's sons, 1900. 79, 422 p. incl. plan, tables. fold. map. 19 1/2 cm. "Works for reference on the history of the Eastern church": p. [77]-79. [BX290.S7 1900] 4-4192
1. Orthodox Eastern church—Hist. 2. Church history—Study and teaching. I. Title.

STANLEY, Arthur Penrhyn, 281.9
1815-1881.
Lectures on the history of the Eastern church, by Arthur Penrhyn Stanley. London, J. M. Dent & sons, ltd. New York, E. P. Dutton & co. [1924] xx, 396 p. illus. (map, plan) 17 1/2 cm. (Half-title: Everyman's library, ed. by Ernest Rhys. History. [no. 251]) "First issue of this edition, 1907; reprinted, 1924." "Prefatory note by A. J. Grieve." Bibliographies interspersed. [AC1.E8 no. 251] 36-37430
1. Orthodox Eastern church—Hist. 2. Church history—Study and teaching. I. Title.

UPSON, Stephen H R 281.909
Orthodox church history, by Stephen H. R. Upson. 3d ed. [Batavia? N.Y., c1954] 96 p. 18 cm. [BX290.U6] 65-2714
1. Orthodox Eastern Church — Hist. I. Title.

Orthodox Eastern Church—History—Addresses, essays, lectures.

ORTHODOX theology and diakonia : essays in honor of His Eminence Archbishop Iakovos on the occasion of his seventieth birthday / edited by Demetrios J. Constantelos. Brookline, Mass. : Hellenic College Press, 1981. p. cm. Includes index. [BX320.2.O77] 19 81-6811 ISBN 0-916586-79-0 : Write for information. ISBN 0-916586-80-4 pbk. : Write for information. 281.9
1. Orthodox Eastern Church—History—Addresses, essays, lectures. 2. Orthodox Eastern Church—Relations—Addresses,essays, lectures. 3. Iakovos, Archbishop of the Greek Orthodox Archdiocese of North and South America—Addresses, essays, lectures. 4. Theology, Eastern Church—Addresses,essays, lectures. I. Iakovos, Archbishop of the Greek Orthodox Archdiocese of North and South America. II. Constantelos, Demetrios J.

Orthodox Eastern Church—History—Sources.

ORTHODOX Eastern Church. 262'.4
Synod of Jerusalem, 1672.
The acts and decrees of the Synod of Jerusalem, sometimes called the Council of Bethlehem, holden under Dositheus, Patriarch of Jerusalem in 1672. Translated from the Greek with an appendix containing the confession published with the name of Cyril Lucar condemned by the Synod and with notes by J. N. W. B. Robertson. New York, AMS Press [1969] vii, 215 p. 22 cm. Reprint of the London ed., 1899. Translation of Aspis orthodoxias e apologia kai elenchos pros tous diasyrontas ten Anatoliken Ekklesian (romanized form) [BX220.A4513 1969] 78-81769
1. Orthodox Eastern Church—History—Sources. 2. Councils and synods—Jerusalem. I. Dositheos, Patriarch of Jerusalem, 1641-1707. II. Kyrillos Loukaris, Patriarch of Constantinople, 1572-1638. The Eastern Confession of the Christian faith. III. Robertson, James Nathaniel William Beauchamp, ed. IV. Title.

WILLIAMS, George, 281.9'09'033
comp.
The Orthodox Church of the East in the eighteenth century, being the correspondence between the Eastern patriarchs and the Nonjuring bishops. With an introduction on various projects of reunion between the Eastern Church and the Anglican Communion. [1st AMS ed.] New York, AMS Press [1970] lxxi, 180 p. port. 23 cm. Reprint of the 1868 ed. [BX310.W54 1970] 73-131028 ISBN 0-404-06977-0
1. Orthodox Eastern Church—History—Sources. I. Title.

Orthodox Eastern church—Hymns.

BROWNLIE, John, tr.
Hymns of the Russian church, being translations, centos, and suggestions from the Greek office books, with an introduction, by John Brownlie ... London, New York [etc] H. Milford Oxford university press. 1920. xviii, 122, [1] p. 19 cm. [BV467.B83] 21-8001
1. Orthodox Eastern church—Hymns. I. Title.

GELSINGER, Michael George 783.9
Howard, 1890-
... *Orthodox hymns in English,* melodies adapted from the Russian and Greek traditions and their texts translated from the Greek by Michael G. H. Gelsinger ... Brooklyn, N. Y., Syrian Antiochian orthodox archdiocese of New York and all North America, 1939. 3 p. l., 9-124 p. 22 cm. (Orthodox Catholic religion series, v. 2) [M2157.G31O7] 40-15403
1. Orthodox Eastern church—Hymns. 2. Hymns, English—Translations from Greek. 3. Hymns, Greek—Translations into English. I. Orthodox Eastern church, Syrian, in the U. S. II. Title.

NEALE, John Mason, 264.01'9'02
1818-1866, comp.
Hymns of the Eastern Church. New York, AMS Press [1971] xii, 164 p. 19 cm. Reprint of the 1862 ed. [BV467.N52] 77-131029 ISBN 0-404-04666-5
1. Orthodox Eastern Church—Hymns. 2. Hymns, Greek—Translations into English. 3. Hymns, English—Translations from Greek. I. Title.

PICK, Bernhard, 1842-1917, comp.
Hymns and poetry of the Eastern church, collected and chronologically arranged by Bernhard Pick. New York, Eaton & Mains; Cincinnati, Jennings & Graham [c1908] 175 p. 20 cm. [BV467.P5] 8-6991
1. Orthodox Eastern church—Hymns. 2. Hymns, English—Translations from Greek. 3. Hymns, Greek—Translations into English. I. Title.

Orthodox Eastern Church — Hymns — History and criticism

BOGOLEPOV, Aleksandr 264.019
Aleksandrovich, 1886-
Orthodox hymns of Christmas, Holy Week, and Easter [by] Alexander A. Bogolepov. New York, Russian Orthodox Theological Fund [1965] 78 p. 23 cm. [BV467.B6] 65-16177
1. Orthodox Eastern Church — Hymns — Hist. & crit. I. Title.

Orthodox Eastern Church—Liturgy.

MAXIMUS, Confessor, 264'.014
Saint, ca.580-662.
The church, the liturgy, and the soul of man : the Mystagogia of St. Maximus the Confessor / translated with historical notes and commentaries by Dom Julian Stead, O.S.B. Still River, MA : St. Bede's Publications, c1982. 120 p. ; 21 cm. Translation of: Mystagogia. Includes index. [BR65.M413M9713 1982] 19 82-10545 ISBN 0-932506-23-2 : 6.95
1. Orthodox Eastern Church—Liturgy. 2. Catholic Church—Byzantine rite—Liturgy. 3. Lord's Supper—Orthodox Eastern Church—Liturgy. 4. Lord's Supper—Catholic Church—Liturgy. 5. Church—Early works to 1800. 6. Man (Christian theology)—Early works to 1800. I. Stead, Julian. II. [Mystagogia.] English III. Title.
Publisher's address : P. O. Box 61, Still River, MA 01467.

Orthodox, Eastern Church. Liturgy and ritual.

DABOVICH, Sebastin. 264.019
The holy Orthodox church; or, The ritual, services, and sacraments of the Eastern apostolic (Greek-Russian) church, by the Rev. Sebastian Dabovich ... Wilkesbarre, Pa., 1898. 85 p. 20 cm. [BX350.D3] 38-34608
1. Orthodox Eastern church. Liturgy and ritual. I. Title.

GOGOL', Nikolai Vasil'evich, 1809-1852
Meditations on the devine liturgy of the Holy Eastern Orthodox Catholic and Apostolic Church. [New York] American Review of Eastern Orthodoxy, 1964. 56 p. 23 cm. Translation of Razmyshleniia o bozhestvennoi liturgii. Reprint of 1960 edition of Orthodox Book Society. 68-46283
1. Orthodox, Eastern Church. Liturgy and ritual. I. Title.

GOGOL, Nikolai 264.019
Vasil'evich, 1809-1852.
Meditations on the divine liturgy of the Holy Eastern Orthodox Catholic and Apostolic Church. [New York 27, 537 W. 121 St., Orthodox Book Society, 1960] 56p. 23cm. Translation of (transliterated: Razmyshienii c bozhestvennoi liturgi) 60-2330 1.00
1. Orthodox, Eastern Church. Liturgy and ritual. I. Title.

KING, John Glen, 264'.01'947
1732-1787.
The rites and ceremonies of the Greek church, in Russia; containing an account of its doctrine, worship, and discipline. [1st AMS ed.] London, Printed for W. Owen, 1772. [New York, AMS Press, 1970] xix, 477 p. illus. 23 cm. [BX350.K5 1970] 73-126673 ISBN 0-404-03692-9
1. Orthodox Eastern Church. Liturgy and ritual. I. Title.

NEALE, John Mason, 1818- 264.01'9
1866, comp.
The liturgies of S. Mark, S. James, S. Clement, S. Chrysostom, and the Church of Malabar. Translated with introd. and appendices, by J. M. Neale. New York, AMS Press [1969] xxxvi, 224 p. illus., plan. 22 cm. Reprint of the London ed., 1859. Appendices (p. [175]-224):—1. The formulae of institution as they occur in every extant liturgy.—2. Prayers for the departed faithful. [BX375.L4N4 1969] 76-83374
I. Orthodox Eastern Church. Liturgy and ritual. Leitourgikon. English. II. Catholic Church. Liturgy and ritual. Malabar rite. English. III. Title.

OAKLEY, Austin. 264
The Orthodox liturgy. Alcuin Club ed. London, Mowbray; New York, Morehouse-Gorham [1958] 50p. 22cm. (Studies in Eucharistic faith and practice) Includes bibliography. [BX350.O2] 59-498
1. Orthodox Eastern Church. Liturgy and ritual. I. Title.

ORTHODOX Eastern 264'.019034
Church. Liturgy and ritual. Apostolos. English.
The Apostolos : the acts and letters of the holy apostles read in the Orthodox Church throughout the year / edited by Father Nomikos Michael Vaporis. Brookline, Mass. : Holy Cross Orthodox Press, 1980. p. cm. "The Apostolos follows the traditional order as used by the Ecumentical Patriarchate of Constantinople ... It is a complete edition, including the Prokeimena, Alleluaria, Antiphons, Entrance Hymns, and Koinonika." [BX375.A65A45 1980] 19 80-23557 ISBN 0-916586-39-1 : 56.00
I. Vaporis, Nomikos Michael. II. Title.

ORTHODOX Eastern Church. 264.01'9
Liturgy and ritual. Menaion. English
The ferial Menaion; or, The book of services for the twelve great festivals and the new-year's day. Translated from a Slavonian ed. of last century ... [by N. Orloff] New York, AMS Press [1969] 330 p. 22 cm. Reprint of the 1900 ed. [BX375.M37A4 1969] 72-79155
I. Orloff, Nicolas, tr. II. Title.

ORTHODOX Eastern 264'.01'9
Church. Liturgy and ritual.
The festal Menaion / translated from the original Greek by Mother Mary and Kallistos Ware ; with an introduction by Georges Florovsky. London : Faber, 1977. 3-564 p. ; 20 cm. (Service books of the Orthodox Church) (Faber paperbacks) Includes bibliographical references. [BX375.M37A45 1977] 78-322350 ISBN 0-571-11137-8 : 10.95
I. Mary, Mother. II. Ware, Kallistos, 1934- III. Title.
Distributed by Faber & Faber, Salem, NH

ORTHODOX Eastern Church. 264.01'9
Liturgy and ritual. Menaion. English.
The general Menaion; or, The book of services common to the festivals of our Lord Jesus of the Holy Virgin and of the different orders of saints. Translated from the Slavonian 16th ed. of 1862 [by N. Orloff] New York, AMS Press [1969] 287 p. 22 cm. Reprint of the 1899 ed. [BX375.M37A38 1969] 76-79156
I. Orloff, Nicolas, tr. II. Title.

ORTHODOX Eastern Church. 264.01'9
Liturgy and ritual. Horologion. English.
Horologion; a primer for elementary village schools. Translated from the Slavonian ed. of 1894 ... [by N. Orloff] New York, AMS Press [1969] xi, 151 p. 22 cm. Reprint of the 1897 ed. [BX375.H6A4 1969] 79-79154
I. Orloff, Nicolas, tr. II. Title.

ORTHODOX Eastern Church. 264.01'9
Liturgy and ritual. Oktoechos. English.
Octoechos; or, The book of eight tones; a primer containing the Sunday service in eight tones. Translated from the Slavonian 1st ed. of 1891 ... by N. Orloff. New York, AMS Press [1969] 169 p. 22 cm. Reprint of the 1898 ed. [BX375.O3A4 1969] 75-79153
I. Orloff, Nicolas, ed. II. Title.

ORTHODOX Eastern Church. 264.01'9
Liturgy and ritual.
Offices from the service-books of the Holy Eastern Church. With translation, notes, and glossary [by] Richard Frederick Littledale. [1st ed.] New York, AMS Press [1970] xii, 339 p. 23 cm. Reprint of the 1863 ed., London. English and Greek. [BX350.A2 1970] 77-133819 ISBN 0-404-03996-0
I. Title.

ORTHODOX Eastern 264'.01'9
Church. Liturgy and ritual. Euchologion. English & Greek.
An Orthodox prayer book / edited by N. M. Vaporis ; translated by John von Holzhausen and Michael Gelsinger. Brookline, Mass. : Holy Cross Orthodox Press, 1977. x, 160 p. ; 21 cm. Added t.p. in Greek (romanized: Mikron Euchologion. English and Greek. [BX360.A5V36] 77-77642 ISBN 0-916586-09-X : 10.95
I. Vaporis, Nomikos Michael. II. Title. III. Title: Mikron Euchologion.
Publihser's address : 50 Goddard Ave., Brookline, MA 02146

ORTHODOX Eastern 264'.01'9
Church. Liturgy and ritual.
An Orthodox prayer book / by Nomikos Michael Vaporis. Brookline, Mass. : Holy Cross Orthodox Press, [1977] p. cm. Translation of Mikron euchologion. [BX360.A5V36 1977b] 77-13874 ISBN 0-916586-11-1 pbk. : 5.00
I. Vaporis, Nomikos Michael. II. Title.

ORTHODOX Eastern Church. 264.0192
Liturgy and ritual. Apostolos. English.
Epistle lectionary of the Eastern Orthodox Church. Translated by Archbishop Fan Stylian Noli. Boston, Albanian Orthodox Church in America, 1957. 463p. 24cm. [BX375.A65A4 1957] 57-46679
I. Noli, Fan Stylian, Abp., 1882- tr. II. Albanian Orthodox Church in America. III. Title.

ORTHODOX Eastern Church. 264.01'9
: Liturgy and ritual. : Menaion. : English.
The festal Menaion / translated from the original Greek by Mother Mary and Archimandrite Kallistos Ware ; with an introd. by Georges Florovsky. London : Faber and Faber, 1977. 564p. ; 20 cm. (The Service Books of the Orthodox Church) [BX375.M37A44] ISBN 0-571-11137-8 : 10.95
I. Mary,Mother, tr. II. Ware, Kallistos, 1934- III. Title.
L.C. card no. for 1969 Faber and Faber ed. : 70-518366. Distributed by Faber and Fber, Salem, NH.

POLYZOIDES, Germanos, 264.019
Bp., 1897-
What we see and hear in an Eastern Orthodox Church. New York, D. C. Divry [1961] 92p. illus. 23cm. [BX350.P58] 61-31896
1. Orthodox Eastern Church. Liturgy and ritual. I. Title.

SCHMEMANN, Alexander, 264.019
1921-
Introduction to liturgical theology; tr. from Russian by Asheleigh E. Moorhouse. London, Faith Pr.; Portland (Maine), American Orthodox Pr., 1966. 170p. 23cm. (Lib. of Orthodox theol., no. 4) Bibl. [BX350.S35] 66-69197 6.50
1. Orthodox Eastern Church. Liturgy and ritual. I. Title. II. Series.
Publisher's address: Box 1096. Portland, Maine 04104.

SCHMEMANN, Alexander, 264.019
1921-
Introduction to liturgical theology; translated from the Russian by Asheleigh E. Moorhouse. London, Faith P.; Portland (Maine), American Orthodox P., 1966. 170 p. 22 1/2 cm. (Library of Orthodox theology, no. 4) 37/6 Includes bibliographical references. [BX350.S35] 66-69197
1. Orthodox Eastern Church. Liturgy and ritual. I. Title. II. Series.

SCHMEMANN, Alexander, 1921- 265
Sacraments and orthodoxy. [New York] Herder and Herder [1965] 142 p. 21 cm. [BX350.S36] 65-13482
1. Orthodox Eastern Church. Liturgy and ritual. 2. Sacraments—Orthodox Eastern Church. I. Title.

SWAINSON, Charles 264.01'9
Anthony, 1820-1887.
The Greek liturgies, chiefly from original authorities. With an appendix containing the Coptic ordinary canon of the mass from two manuscripts in the British Museum. Edited and translated by C. Bezold. Hildesheim, New York, G. Olms, 1971. lii, 395 p. 23 cm. Reprint of the ed. published in London in 1884. English, Latin, Greek, or Coptic. Coptic text has English translation. [BX350.S8 1971] 76-886448 ISBN 3-487-04054-9 (Hildesheim)
1. Orthodox Eastern Church. Liturgy and ritual. I. Bezold, Carl, 1859-1922, tr. II. Title.

Orthodox Eastern church—Liturgy and ritual— English.

THE Orthodox companion.
Bridgeville, Pa., Orthodox Catholic literature assoc., 1956. 237p. illus. 19cm.
1. Orthodox Eastern church—Liturgy and ritual— English. I. Abramtsov, David Feodor, 1924- II. Orthodox Catholic Literature Association.

ORTHODOX Eastern Church. 264.01'9
Liturgy and Ritual. Euchologion. English.
Book of needs of the Holy Orthodox Church, with an appendix containing offices for the laying on of hands. Done into English by G. V. Shann. New York, AMS Press [1969] xxxix, viii, 260, 28 p. 22 cm. "A translation, with some omissions, of the Slavonic service book entitled Trebnik [printed in Moscow, 1882] " Reprinted from the 1894 London ed. [BX375.E75A43] 77-82258
I. Shann, G. V., tr. II. Title.

ORTHODOX Eastern Church. 264.01'9
Liturgy and ritual. Molityoslov. English
Euchology; a manual of prayers of the Holy Orthodox Church done into English by G. V. Shann. New York, AMS Press [1969] xxxi, 524 p. 22 cm. Reprint of the Kidderminster, Eng., ed. of 1891. Bibliography: p. xxv-xxviii. [BX360.A5S5 1969] 75-82260
I. Shann, G. V., tr. II. Title.

ORTHODOX Eastern Church. 264.01'9
Liturgy and ritual. Molityoslov. English
Euchology; a manual of prayers of the Holy Orthodox Church done into English by G. V. Shann. New York, AMS Press [1969] xxxi, 524 p. 22 cm. Reprint of the Kidderminster, Eng., ed. of 1891. Bibliography: p. xxv-xxviii. [BX360.A5S5 1969] 75-82260
I. Shann, G. V., tr. II. Title.

ORTHODOX Eastern Church. 264.01'9
Liturgy and ritual. English.
The offices of the Oriental Church, with an historical introd. Edited by Nicholas Bjerring. New York, AMS Press [1969] xxxi, 189 p. 22 cm. Reprint of the 1884 ed. [BX350.A5B5 1969] 73-79805
I. Bjerring, Nicholas, 1831-1900, ed. II. Title.

ORTHODOX Eastern Church. 264.01'9
Liturgy and ritual. Menaion. English.
The twelve great feasts; or, Festival Menaion of the Holy Orthodox Catholic and Apostolic Church. Translated by the Archimandrite Lazarus. Edited by the American Orthodox Associates. Chicago, American Orthodox Associates, 1965. 187 l. 28 cm. [BX375.M37A47] 71-17875
I. Lazarus, Archimandrite, tr. II. American Orthodox Associates. III. Title. IV. Title: Festival Menaion.

ORTHODOX Eastern church. 264.
Liturgy and ritual. English.
The offices of the Oriental church, with an historical introduction. Edited by the Rev. Nicholas Bjerring. New York, A. D. F. Randolph & co. [c1884] 3 p. l., [v]-xxxi, 189 p. 24 cm. [BX350.A5B5] 38-34593
I. Bjerring, Nicholas, 1831-1900, ed. II. Title.

ORTHODOX Eastern church. Liturgy and ritual. Liturgy. English.
The liturgy of the Eastern Orthodox church; with an introduction & explanatory note by H. Hamilton Maughan ... London, The Faith press; Milwaukee, The Young churchman company, 1916. vi, 80 p. front., 5 pl. 22 cm. A 39
I. Orthodox Eastern church. Liturgy and ritual. English. II. Maughan, Herbert Hamilton, 1884- III. Title.

Orthodox Eastern Church. Liturgy and ritual. Leitourgikon.

HELIOPOULOS, Demetrius, 264.011
1902-
The morning sacrifice; a brief explanation of the divine liturgy of the Eastern Orthodox Church. Illustrated by Nicholas Nefos. [Pittsburgh? 1955, c1954] 148p. illus. 22cm. [BX350.H4] 55-24285
1. Orthodox Eastern Church. Liturgy and ritual. Leitourgikon. I. Title.

ORTHODOX Eastern Church. 264.01'9
Liturgy and ritual. Leitourgikon. English.
The divine liturgy of our father among the saints, John Chrysostom, of the Holy Orthodox Catholic and Apostolic Church. Translated by Archimandrite Lazarus. Edited and arranged by John Schneyder. [2d ed. New York?] Holy Orthodox Catholic Apostolic American Church (the Orthodox American Church) [1965] ii, 115 p. 16 cm. [BX375.L4A427 1965] 77-17717
I. Lazarus, Archimandrite, tr. II. Schneyder, John, ed. III. Title.

ORTHODOX Eastern Church. 264.01'9
Liturgy and ritual. Leitourgikon. English.
The divine liturgy of our father among the saints, John Chrysostom, of the Holy Orthodox Catholic and Apostolic Church. Translated by Archimandrite Lazarus. Edited and arranged by John Schneyder. [2d ed. New York?] Holy Orthodox Catholic Apostolic American Church (the Orthodox American Church) [1965] ii, 115 p. 16 cm. [BX375.L4A427 1965] 77-17717
I. Lazarus, Archimandrite, tr. II. Schneyder, John, ed. III. Title.

ORTHODOX Eastern 264'.01'9
Church. Liturgy and ritual. Leitourgikon.
The Orthodox liturgy : the Greek text of the Ecumenical Patriarchate / with a translation into English by the Liturgical Commission of the Greek Orthodox Archdiocese of North and South America. Together with a study of the development of the Orthodox liturgy from the 2nd century to this day / by Nicon D. Patrinacos. Garwood, N.J. : Graphic Arts Press, 1976. 336 p. ; 19 cm. "Authorized to be used within the Greek Orthodox

Church of the Americas." [BX350.A2 1976] 76-12252
I. Patrinacos, Nicon D. II. North and South America (Archdiocese, Orthodox). Liturgical Commission. III. Orthodox Eastern Church. Liturgy and ritual. Leitourgikon. English. 1975. IV. Title.

ORTHODOX Eastern Church. Liturgy and ritual. Leitourgikon. 264'.01'9
The Orthodox liturgy; the Greek text with a completely new translation followed by notes on the text, the Sunday Gospel and Apostolic readings, together with: tracing the development of the Orthodox liturgy from the 2nd century to this day, by Nicon D. Patrinacos. Foreword by Archbishop Iakovos. [Garwood, N.J., Graphic Arts Press, 1974] 352 p. 18 cm. Text of the divine liturgy of St. John Chrysostom in English and Greek. [BX350.A2 1974] 74-75002
I. Patrinacos, Nicon D., ed. II. Orthodox Eastern Church. Liturgy and ritual. Leitourgikon. English. III. Title.

ORTHODOX Eastern Church. Liturgy and ritual. Leitourgikon. 264.019
The divine liturgy of St. John Chrysostom of the Eastern Orthodox Church. Edited and arranged by George Mastrantonis] New York, Greek Orthodox Archdiocese of North and South America [1966] 148 p. illus. 16 cm. Text in English and Greek. [BX375.L4A43] 66-22700
I. Mastrantonis, George, 1906- ed. II. Orthodox Eastern Church. Liturgy and ritual. Leitourgikon. English. III. Title.

ORTHODOX Eastern Church. Liturgy and ritual. Leitourgikon. 264.019
The divine liturgy of St. John Chrysostom of the Eastern Orthodox Church. Edited and arranged by George Mastrantonis] New York, Greek Orthodox Archdiocese of North and South America [1966] 148 p. illus. 16 cm. Text in English and Greek. [BX375.L4A43] 66-22700
I. Mastrantonis, George, 1906- ed. II. Orthodox Eastern Church. Liturgy and ritual. Leitourgikon. English. III. Title.

ORTHODOX Eastern church. Liturgy and ritual. Leitourgikon. English.
The divine liturgies of our holy fathers John Chrysostom and Basil the Great. With the authorization of the Most holy governing synod of Russia. New York, E. P. Dutton & company, 1873. 66 p. 17 cm. [BX375.L4A42 1873] 46-35438
I. Chrysostomus, Joannes, Saint, patriarch of Constantinople, d. 407. II. Basilius, Saint, the Great, abp. of Caesarea, 330 (ca.)-379. III. Title.

ORTHODOX Eastern church. Liturgy and ritual. Leitourgikon. English.
The divine liturgies of our holy fathers John Chrysostom and Basil the Great. With the authorization of the Most holy governing synod of Russia. New York, E. P. Dutton & company, 1873. 66 p. 17 cm. [BX375.L4A42 1873] 46-35438
I. Chrysostomus, Joannes, Saint, patriarch of Constantinople, d. 407. II. Basilius, Saint, the Great, abp. of Caesarea, 330 (ca.)-379. III. Title.

ORTHODOX Eastern Church. Liturgy and ritual.. Leitourgkon. 264.019
The divine liturgy of St. Chrysostom of the Eastern Orthodox Church. [Ed., arranged by George Mastrantonis] New York, Greek Orthodox Archdiocese of North & South America [1966] 148p. illus. 16 cm. Text in English & Greek. [BX375.L4A43 1966] 66-22700 2.00
I. Mastrantonis, George, 1906- ed. II. Orthodox Eastern Church. Liturgy and ritual.. Leiturgikou English. III. Title.
Pub. address: 777 United Nations Plaza, New York, N.Y. 10017

ORTHODOX Eastern Church. Liturgy and ritual.. Leitourgkon. 264.019
The divine liturgy of St. Chrysostom of the Eastern Orthodox Church. [Ed., arranged by George Mastrantonis] New York, Greek Orthodox Archdiocese of North & South America [1966] 148p. illus. 16 cm. Text in English & Greek. [BX375.L4A43 1966] 66-22700 2.00
I. Mastrantonis, George, 1906- ed. II. Orthodox Eastern Church. Liturgy and ritual.. Leiturgikou English. III. Title.
Pub. address: 777 United Nations Plaza, New York, N.Y. 10017

Orthodox Eastern Church—North America.

SERAFIM, Archimandrite. 281.9'73
The quest for Orthodox Church unity in America; a history of the Orthodox Church in North America in the twentieth century. New York, Saints Boris and Gleb Press, 1973. 187 p. 24 cm. Errata slip inserted. Bibliography: p. 176-187. [BX735.S47] 73-82540
1. Orthodox Eastern Church—North America. 2. Christian union—Orthodox Eastern Church. I. Title.

Orthodox Eastern Church—Pennsylvania—Philadelphia.

TESKE, Robert Thomas. 265'.9
Votive offerings among Greek-Philadelphians : a ritual perspective / Robert Thomas Teske. New York : Arno Press, 1980. xxix, 326 p., [11] leaves of plates : ill. ; 24 cm. (Folklore of the world) Originally presented as the author's thesis, University of Pennsylvania, 1974. Includes index. Bibliography: p. ix-xxvi. [BX560.T47 1980] 80-735 ISBN 0-405-13325-1 : 29.00
1. Orthodox Eastern Church—Pennsylvania—Philadelphia. 2. Votive offerings—Pennsylvania—Philadelphia. 3. Philadelphia—Religious life and customs. 4. Greek Americans—Pennsylvania—Philadelphia—Religion. I. Title. II. Series. III. Series: Folklore of the world (New York

Orthodox Eastern Church—Prayer-books and devotions—English.

HORTON-BILLARD, Peter H. comp. 264.019
Prayer book for Eastern orthodox Christians, a collection of orthodox prayers and devotions, compiled by the Reverend Peter H. Horton-Billard ... and the Reverend Vasile Hategan ... including confessional and communion prayers, audible portions of the divine liturgy, and the small catechism, translated and edited by the Very Reverend Archpriest Michael G. H. Gelsinger ... New York, N.Y., Association press [1944] 176 p. col. front., illus. 13 cm. Table of contents on p. [2] of cover. [BX376.E5H6] 45-14643
1. Orthodox Eastern church—Prayer-books and devotions—English. I. Hategan, Vasile, joint comp. II. Gelsinger, Michael George Howard, 1890- tr. III. Title.

MIHALY, Joseph, 1907- comp. 264.019
Under the Cross, Pod Krestom. [Trumbull Conn., 1954] 319p. illus. 12cm. English and Ruthenian-Church Slavic. [BX376.E4M5] 54-27705
1. Orthodox Eastern Church—Prayer-books and devotions—English. I. Title. II. Title: Pod Krestom.

Orthodox Eastern Church—Relations—Anglican Communion.

SPOER, Hans Henry, 1873-1951. 264.01'9
An aid for churchmen, Episcopal and Orthodox, toward a mutual understanding, by means of a brief comparison of the rites and ceremonies of the Orthodox Church with those of the Episcopal (Anglican) Church. With a foreword by Frank Gavin. New York, AMSPress [1969] ix, 105 p. 6 illus. 22 cm. Reprint of the 1930 ed. Bibliography: p. 104-105. [BX5927.S7 1969] 71-79152
1. Orthodox Eastern Church—Relations—Anglican Communion. 2. Orthodox Eastern Church. Liturgy and ritual. 3. Anglican Communion—Relations—Orthodox Eastern Church. I. Title.

Orthodox Eastern Church—Relations—Catholic Church.

FINN, Edward E. 281.9
Brothers East and West : a Catholic examines for Catholics the proposed Pan-Orthodox Synod / by Edward Finn. Collegeville, Minn. : Liturgical Press, c1975. 172 p. : maps ; 18 cm. Includes index. Bibliography: p. 164-165. [BX324.3.F56] 76-353847 ISBN 0-8146-0876-0
1. Orthodox Eastern Church—Relations—Catholic Church. 2. Catholic Church—Relations—Orthodox Eastern Church. I. Title.

HALECKI, Oskar, 1891- 281.9
From Florence to Brest (1439-1596) [by] Oscar Halecki. 2d. ed. [Hamden, Conn.] Archon Books, 1968. 456 p. 25 cm. Includes bibliographical references. [BX830 1596.H3 1968] 68-26103 ISBN 0-208-00702-4
1. Orthodox Eastern Church—Relations—Catholic Church. 2. Ferrara-Florence, Council of, 1438-1439. 3. Brest-Litovsk, Council of, 1596. 4. Catholic Church—Relations—Orthodox Eastern Church. I. Title.

MEYENDORFF, Jean, 1926- 262'.001
Orthodoxy and catholicity [by] John Meyendorff. New York, Sheed & Ward [1966] vi, 180 p. 21 cm. Includes bibliographical references. [BX324.3.M4513] 66-22017
1. Orthodox Eastern Church—Relations—Catholic Church. 2. Catholic Church—Relations—Orthodox Eastern Church. I. Title.

Orthodox Eastern Church—Relations—Church of England.

OVERBECK, Julian Joseph, 1821-1905. 262.7'2
Catholic orthodoxy and Anglo-Catholicism, a word about intercommunion between the English and the Orthodox Churches. New York, AMS Press [1969] viii, 200 p. 22 cm. Reprint of the 1866 ed. Bibliographical footnotes. [BX324.5.O9 1969] 76-81771 10.00
1. Church of England—Relations—Orthodox Eastern Church. 2. Orthodox Eastern Church—Relations—Church of England. I. Title.

Orthodox Eastern Church—Relations—Protestant churches.

MAKRAKES, Apostolos, 1831-1905. 281.9
An Orthodox-Protestant dialogue. Translated from the Greek by Denver Cummings. [2d ed.] Chicago, Orthodox Christian Educational Society [1966] 127 p. 23 cm. [BX324.5.M313 1966] 67-9736
1. Orthodox Eastern Church—Relations—Protestant churches. 2. Protestant churches—Relations—Orthodox Eastern Church. I. Title.

Orthodox Eastern Church—Relations—Reformed Church.

THE New man: 281.9'3
an Orthodox and Reformed dialogue. Edited by John Meyendorff and Joseph McLelland. [New Brunswick, N.J.] Agora Books, 1973. 170 p. 22 cm. Papers and summaries from a 3-year cycle of theological conversations, 1968-70, between representatives of the Standing Conference of Canonical Orthodox Bishops in America and the World Alliance of Reformed Churches, North America Area. "A short Orthodox bibliography in English, prepared by Prof. Nomikos M. Vaporis ...": p. 167-170. [BX324.5.N48] 73-78229
1. Orthodox Eastern Church—Relations—Reformed Church. 2. Reformed Church—Relations—Orthodox Eastern Church. I. Meyendorff, Jean, 1926- ed. II. McLelland, Joseph C., ed. III. Standing Conference of Canonical Orthodox Bishops in America. IV. Alliance of Reformed Churches throughout the World Holding the Presbyterian System. North America Area.

Orthodox Eastern church—Rites and ceremonies.

ORTHODOX Eastern church. Liturgy and ritual.
A guide to the Divine liturgy in the East ... by Athelstan Riley ... London & Oxford, Mowbray; Milwaukee, Morehouse [1922] xvi, 93, [1] p. front. 15 cm. On opposite pages the liturgy of St. Chrysostom in English and the congregational parts of the same. A 23
1. Orthodox Eastern church—Rites and ceremonies. I. Riley, Athelstan, 1858- II. Title.

Orthodox Eastern Church, Romanian—Collected works.

STANILOAE, Dumitru. 230'.19498
Theology and the church / Dumitru Staniloae ; translated by Robert Barringer ; foreword by John Meyendorff. Crestwood, N.Y. : St. Vladimir's Seminary Press, 1980. p. cm. Collection of essays translated from various Romanian journals. Includes bibliographical references. [BX695.S7] 19 80-19313 ISBN 0-913836-69-9 pbk. : 7.95
1. Orthodox Eastern Church, Romanian—Collected works. 2. Theology—Collected works—20th century. I. Title.

Orthodox Eastern church, Russian.

ARSEN'EV, Nikolai Sergeevich 1888- 281.9473
Holy Moscow; chapters in the religious and spiritual life of Russia in the nineteenth century, by Nicholas Arseniev, London, Society for promoting Christian knowledge; New York, The Macmillan company, [1940] vii, 184 p. 19 cm. "First published 1940." [BX491.A7] 41-4455
1. Orthodox Eastern church, Russian. 2. Russia—Church history. I. Title. II. Title: Religious and spritual life of Russia.

BOURDEAUX, Michael. 272
Patriarch and prophets; persecution of the Russian Orthodox Church today. New York, Praeger [1970] 359 p. 23 cm. Includes bibliographical references. [BR1608.R8B67 1970] 79-106201 10.00
1. Orthodox Eastern Church, Russian. 2. Persecution—Russia. I. Title.

DANZAS, IUllia Nikolaeyna. 281.947
The Russian church, by J. N. Danzas; translated from the French by Countess Olga Bennigsen. New York, Sheed & Ward, 1936. viii, 164 p. 19 cm. "Printed in Great Britain." [BX485.D32] 37-4626
1. Orthodox Eastern church, Russian. 2. Russia—Church history. 3. Russia—Religion. I. Bennigsen, Olga, countess, 1879- tr. II. Title.

ESHLIMAN, Nikolai. 281.9'47
A cry of despair from Moscow churchmen [by Nicholas Eshliman and Gleb Yakunin] An open letter of two Moscow priests to Patriarch Alexis of Moscow and to the chairman of the Presidium of the Supreme Soviet of the USSR about the persecution of religion. With an introd. by George Grabbe. New York, Synod of Bishops of the Russian Orthodox Church Outside of Russia, 1966. 65 p. 23 cm. Cover title. [BX492.E8] 67-8584
1. Orthodox Eastern Church. Russian. 2. Church and state in Russia — 1917- 3. Persecution — Russia I. Iakunin, Gleb P., joint author. II. Title.

50TH anniversary, Holy Trinity Russian Orthodox Church, Brooklyn, New York. [New York? 1959;] 100p. illus. 27cm. Cover title. Articles in Russian or English, with English translation of some of the Russian articles.
1. Orthodox Eastern church, Russian. I. Brooklyn. Holy Trinity Church.

FIRESIDE, Harvey, 1929- 322'.1'0947
Icon and swastika; the Russian Orthodox Church under Nazi and Soviet control. Cambridge, Mass., Harvard University Press, 1971. xx, 242 p. 25 cm. (Russian Research Center Studies, 62) Bibliography: p. 195-205. [BX492.F47] 70-123567 ISBN 0-674-44160-5 8.00
1. Orthodox Eastern Church, Russian. 2. Church and state in Russia—1917- 3. Russia—History—German occupation, 1941-1944. I. Title. II. Series: Harvard University. Russian Research Center. Studies, 62

FLETCHER, William C. 281.9'3
The Russian Orthodox Church underground, 1917-1970, [by William C. Fletcher] London, New York, Oxford University Press, 1971. x, 314 p. 23 cm.

Bibliography: p. [293]-308. [BX492.F49] 70-868518 ISBN 0-19-213952-5 £3.75
1. Orthodox Eastern Church, Russian. 2. Church and state in Russia—1917- 3. Persecution—Russia. I. Title.

HEARD, Albert F. 281.9'47
The Russian church and Russian dissent, comprising orthodoxy, dissent, and erratic sects, by Albert F. Heard. New York, Harper, 1887. [New York, AMS Press, 1971] ix, 310 p. 23 cm. Bibliography: p. [vii]-ix. [BX510.H4 1971] 70-127909 ISBN 0-404-03198-6
1. Orthodox Eastern Church, Russian. 2. Raskolniks. 3. Sects—Russia. I. Title.

KORPER, Ruth. 281.9
The candlelight kingdom; a meeting with the Russian Church. New York, Macmillan, 1955. 83 p. 22 cm. [BX510.K65] 55-1152
1. Orthodox Eastern Church, Russian. I. Title.

ZERNOV, Nicolas. 281.9'47
Moscow, the third Rome. New York, AMS Press [1971] 94 p. 19 cm. Reprint of the 1938 ed. A history of the Russian Orthodox Eastern church. [BR932.Z4 1971] 76-149664 ISBN 0-404-07075-2
1. Orthodox Eastern Church. Russian. 2. Russia—Church history. I. Title.

Orthodox Eastern Church, Russian—Clergy—History.

FREEZE, Gregory L., 1945- 281.9'3
The Russian Levites : parish clergy in the eighteenth century / Gregory L. Freeze. Cambridge, Mass. : Harvard University Press, 1977. xi, 325 p. ; 25 cm. (Russian Research Center studies ; 78) Includes index. Bibliography: p. [298]-317. [BX540.F73] 76-30764 ISBN 0-674-78175-9 : 15.00
1. Orthodox Eastern Church, Russian—Clergy—History. 2. Clergy—Russia—History. I. Title. II. Series: Harvard University. Russian Research Center. Studies ; 78.

Orthodox Eastern Church, Russian—Collected works.

BULGAKOV, Sergei 230'.1'93
Nikolaevich, 1871-1944.
A Bulgakov anthology / Sergius Bulgakov ; edited by James Pain and Nicholas Zernov. Philadelphia : Westminster Press, 1976. p. cm. Bibliography: p. [BX480.B78 1976] 76-23245 ISBN 0-664-21338-3 : 12.50
1. Orthodox Eastern Church, Russian—Collected works. 2. Bulgakov, Sergei Nikilaevich, 1871-1944. 3. Theology—Collected works—20th century. I. Title.

BULGAKOV, Sergei 230'.1'93
Nikolaevich, 1871-1944.
A Bulgakov anthology / Sergius Bulgakov ; edited by James Pain and Nicolas Zernov. London : SPCK, 1976. xxv, 191, [2] p. ; 22 cm. Bibliography: p. [193] [BX480.B78 1976b] 76-379873 ISBN 0-281-02933-4 : £5.50
1. Orthodox Eastern Church, Russian—Collected works. 2. Bulgakov, Sergei Nikolaevich, 1871-1944. 3. Orthodox Eastern Church, Russian—Biography. 4. Theology—Collected works—20th century. I. Title.

SCHMEMANN, Alexander, 1921- 201
ed.
Ultimate questions; an anthology of modern Russian religious thought. [1st ed.] New York, Holt, Rinehart and Winston [1965] vii, 310 p. 22 cm. Includes bibliographies. [BX478.S3] 65-10132
1. Orthodox Eastern Church, Russian—Collected works. 2. Theology—Collected works. 3. Religious literature, Russian—Translations into English. I. Title.

Orthodox Eastern church, Russian—Doctrinal and controversial works.

PLATON, Metropolitan 230'.1'947
of Moscow, 1737-1812.
The present state of the Greek Church in Russia; or, A summary of Christian divinity. Translated from the Slavonian. With a preliminary memoir on the ecclesiastical establishment in Russia; and an appendix, containing an account of the origin and different sects of Russian dissenters. By Robert Pinkerton. New York, Printed and sold by Collins, 1815. [New York, AMS Press, 1973] xi, 276 p. 19 cm. [BX510.P6 1973] 75-131031 ISBN 0-404-05059-X 15.00
1. Orthodox Eastern Church, Russian—Doctrinal and controversial works. 2. Dissenters, Religious—Russia. I. Pinkerton, Robert. II. Title.

PLATON, Metropolitan of Moscow,
1737-1812.
The present state of the Greek church in Russia, or, A summary of Christian divinity; by Platon, late metropolitan of Moscow. Translated from the Slavonian. With a preliminary memoir on the ecclesiastical establishment in Russia; and an appendix, containing an account of the origin and different sects of Russian dissenters. By Robert Pinkerton. New-York: Printed and sold by Collins & co. No. 189, Pearl-street ... 1815. xi, 276 p. 19 cm. [BX510.P6 1815] 39-19568
1. Orthodox Eastern church, Russian—Doctrinal and controversial works. 2. Dissenters—Russia. I. Pinkerton, Robert. II. Title.

Orthodox Eastern Church, Russian—Doctrinal and controversial works—Miscellanea.

DUDKO, Dmitrii. 230'.1'9
Our hope / Dmitrii Dudko ; translated by Paul D. Garrett ; foreword by John Meyendorff. Crestwood, N.Y. : St. Vladimir's Seminary Press, 1977, c1975. 292 p. ; 22 cm. Translation of O nashem upovanii. Includes bibliographical references. [BX512.D8213] 77-1051 ISBN 0-913836-35-4 pbk. : 6.95
1. Orthodox Eastern Church, Russian—Doctrinal and controversial works—Miscellanea. 2. Theology—Miscellanea. I. Title.

Orthodox Eastern church, Russian—History

ALEKSEEV, Vasilii 322'.1'0947
Ivanovich, 1906-
The great revival : the Russian Church under German occupation / by Wassilij Alexeev and Theofanis G. Stavrou. Minneapolis : Burgess Pub. Co., c1976. xvi, 229 p. : ill. ; 23 cm. Includes index. Bibliography: p. 213-222. [BX492.A55] 76-683 ISBN 0-8087-0131-2 : 21.95
1. Orthodox Eastern Church, Russian—History. 2. Church and state in Russia—1917- I. Stavrou, Theofanis George, 1934- joint author. II. Title.

FEDOTOV, Georgii Petrovich, 281.9
1886-1951
The Russian religious mind; 2v. Cambridge, Mass., Harvard [c.1946, 1966] 2v. (431; 423) 24cm. Contents.v.1. Kievan Christianity.--v2. The Middle Ages. Bibl. [BX485.F4] A47 v.1, 10.00; v.2, 12.00
1. Orthodox Eastern church, Russian—Hist. 2. Religious thought—Russia. 3. Russia—Church history. 4. Spirituality. I. Title.

FLETCHER, William C 281.947
A study in survival: the church in Russia, 1927-1943 [by] William C. Fletcher [1st American ed.] New York, Macmillan [1965] 168 p. 21 cm. Bibliography: p. [158] -165. [BX492.F5] 65-28240
1. Orthodox Eastern Church, Russian — Hist. 2. Russia — Church history — 1917- I. Title.

ISWOLSKY, Helene. 281.947
Christ in Russia; the history, tradition, and life of the Russian Church. Includes bibliography. [BX485.I8] 60-12648
1. Orthodox Eastern Church, Russian—Hist. I. Title.

LOWRIE, Donald Alexander.
The light of Russia an introduction to the Russian church. By Donald A. Lowrie. Prague, The YMCA press, ltd., 1923. x, 241 p. front. (port.) 20 cm. Imprint covered by label: London, Student Christian movement, 1924. Bibliography: p. viii-x. [BX510.L6] 25-5228
1. Orthodox Eastern church, Russian—Hist. I. Title.

MURAV'EV, Andrei 281.9'47
Nikolaevich, 1806-1874.
A history of the Church of Russia, by A. N. Mouravieff. Tanslated by R. W. Blackmore. New York, AMS Press [1971] xix, 448 p. 24 cm. Translation of Istoriia Rossiiskoi tserkvi (romanized form) [BX485.M813 1971] 76-133816 ISBN 0-404-04541-3
1. Orthodox Eastern Church, Russian—History. I. Title.

REYBURN, Hugh Young. 281.
The story of the Russian church, by Hugh Y. Reyburn. London & New York, A. Melrose, ltd., 1924. vii, 323 p. 22 1/2 cm. Bibliography: p. 315-318. [BX485.R4] 25-7815
1. Orthodox Eastern church, Russian—Hist. 2. Church and state in Russia. 3. Russia—Church history. 4. Russia—Hist. I. Title.

SOLOVIEV, Alexandre V. 274.7
Holy Russia; the history of a religious-social idea [tr. from the Russian]. 's-Gaevenhage, Mouton. [dist. New York, Humanities Press, 1959, i.e., 1960] 61 p. 23 cm. (Musagets contributtions to the history of Slavic literature and culture 12) This article was written in 1927 and printed in the Sbornik Russkogo archeologiceskogo obscstva'v Korolevste SHS in Belgrade. Bibliographical footnotes A60 2.00 pap.,
1. Orthodox Eastern church, Russian—Hist. 2. Religious thought—Russia. 3. Russia—Church history. I. Title. II. Series.

STROYEN, William B. 322'.1'0947
Communist Russia and the Russian Orthodox Church, 1943-1962 Washington, Catholic University of America Press [1967] x, 161 p. 24 cm. Bibliography: p. 149-158. Bibliographical footnotes. [BR933.S75] 67-28340
1. Orthodox Eastern Church, Russian—History. 2. Church and state in Russia—1917- I. Title.

ZERNOV, Nicolas. 281.9
The Russians and their church, by Nicolas Zernov ... London, Society for promoting Christian knowledge; New York, The Macmillan company [1945] v, [1], 193, [1] p. 22 cm. "First published 1945." Bibliography: p. 188-189. [BX485.Z4] 46-3459
1. Orthodox Eastern church, Russian—Hist. 2. Russia—Church history. I. Title.

Orthodox Eastern church, Russian—Missions.

BOLSHAKOFF, Serge. 266.19
The foreign missions of the Russian orthodox church, by Serge Bokshakoff. London, Society for promoting Christian knowledge; New York, The Macmillan company, 1943. 120 p. 18 1/2 cm. "First published in 1943." Bibliography: p. 117-118. [BV2123.B6] 44-29710
1. Orthodox Eastern church, Russian—Missions. I. Title.

Orthodox Eastern Church, Russian. Pomestnyi sobor. Moscow, 1917-1918.

BOGOLEPOV, Aleksandr 281.947
Aleksandrovich, 1886-
Church reforms in Russia, 1905-1918, in commemoration of the 50th anniversary of the All-Russian Church Council of 1917-1918 [by] Alexander A. Bogolepov. [Translated by A. E. Moorhouse] Bridgeport, Conn., Publications Committee of the Metropolitan Council of the Russian Orthodox Church of America [1966] 59 p. 23 cm. Bibliography: p. 57-59. [BX491.B613] 66-28385
1. Orthodox Eastern Church, Russian. Pomestnyi sobor. Moscow, 1917-1918. 2. Councils and synods—Russia. I. Title.

Orthodox Eastern Church, Russian—Relations—Catholic Church.

MARY Just, Sister. 281.947
Rome and Russia, a tragedy of errors. Westminster, Md., Newman Press, 1954. 223p. 22cm. [BX323.M3] 54-12078
1. Orthodox Eastern Church, Russian—Relations—Catholic Church. 2. Catholic Church—Relations—Orthodox Eastern Church, Russian. I. Title.

Orthodox Eastern Church, Russian—Relations—Protestant churches.

NATIONAL Council of 280'.4'0973
the Churches of Christ in the United States of America.
American churchmen visit the Soviet Union; who went and what was achieved. [New York, 1956?] 24 p. illus., ports. 31 cm. [BX4817.N37] 73-253261
1. Orthodox Eastern Church, Russian—Relations—Protestant churches. 2. Protestant churches—Relations—Orthodox. I. Title.

Orthodox Eastern Church, Russian—Russia—History.

MEDLIN, William K. 322'.1'0947
Moscow and East Rome : a political study of the relations of church and state in Muscovite Russia / par William-Kenneth Medlin. Westport, CT : Hyperion Press, [1981] p. cm. Reprint of the ed. presented as the author's thesis, University of Geneva, 1952. Includes index. Bibliography: p. [BR933.M4 1981] 19 79-2913 ISBN 0-8305-0082-0 : 21.00
1. Orthodox Eastern Church, Russian—Russia—History. 2. Church and state in Russia—History. 3. Russia—Church history. I. Title.

Orthodox Eastern Church, Russian—Russia—History—20th century.

ANDERSON, Paul B., 322'.1'0947
1894-
People, church, and state in modern Russia / by Paul B. Anderson. Westport, CT. : Hyperion Press, [1981] c1944. p. cm. Reprint of the ed. published by Macmillan, New York. Includes bibliographical references and index. [BR936.A8 1981] 19 79-5204 ISBN 0-8305-0058-8 : 21.00
1. Orthodox Eastern Church, Russian—Russia—History—20th century. 2. Church and state in Russia—1917- 3. Russia—Church history—1917- I. Title.

SPINKA, Matthew, 322'.1'0947
1890-1972.
The church in Soviet Russia / by Matthew Spinka. Westport, Conn. : Greenwood Press, [1980] c1956. p. cm. Reprint of the ed. published by Oxford University Press, New York. Includes index. Bibliography: p. [BR936.S62 1980] 80-18191 ISBN 0-313-22658-X lib. bdg. : 19.75
1. Orthodox Eastern Church, Russian—Russia—History—20th century. 2. Church and state in Russia—1917- 3. Russia—Church history—1917- I. Title.

Orthodox Eastern Church, Russian—Russia—History—Congresses.

RUSSIAN Orthodoxy under 281.9'47
the old regime / edited by Robert L. Nichols and Theofanis George Stavrou. Minneapolis : University of Minnesota Press, c1978. xiv, 261 p., [4] leaves of plates : ill. ; 23 cm. Includes index. Bibliography: p. 229-237. [BX491.R87 1978] 78-3196 ISBN 0-8166-0846-6 : 16.50. ISBN 0-8166-0847-4 : 6.95
1. Orthodox Eastern Church, Russian—Russia—History—Congresses. 2. Church and state in Russia—History—Congresses. 3. Russia—Church history—Congresses. I. Nichols, Robert Lewis, 1942- II. Stavrou, Theofanis George, 1934-

Orthodox Eastern Church, Serbian, in the United States

GARY, Ind. St. Sava Serbian
Orthodox Church.
Our religious heritage in America; St. Sava Serbian Orthodox Church, fiftieth anniversary, 1914-1964, November 14, 15, 1964, Gary, Ind. [Gary? 1964] 317 p. illus., ports. 27 cm. Text in English and/or Serbian. 66-11917
1. Orthodox Eastern Church, Serbian, in

the U.S. 2. Gary, Ind. St. Sava Serbian Orthodox Church — Anniversaries, etc. I. Title.

ST. Sava (Serbian Orthodox Church) Gary Ind.
Our religious heritage in America. Gary, Ind., 1964. 317 p. illus. 26 cm. At head of title: St. Sava Serbian Orthodox Church fiftieth anniversary. Text in English and Serbian. 66-32556
1. Orthodox Eastern Church, Serbian, in the U.S. I. Title.

Orthodox Eastern Church—Sermons.

CONIARIS, Anthony M. 252'.01'9
Gems from the Sunday gospels in the Orthodox Church : talks based on the yearly cycle of Sunday Gospel lessons / by Anthony M. Coniaris. Minneapolis : Light and Life Pub. Co., [1975- v. ; 21 cm. Contents.Contents.—v. 1. January through June. [BX330.C62] 74-81199 ISBN pbk. : 3.95
1. Orthodox Eastern Church—Sermons. 2. Sermons, English. I. Title.

Orthodox Eastern Church, Ukrainian—History

OUTLINE history of the Ukrainian Orthodox Church. New York, Ukrainian Orthodox Church ofU.S.A., 1956- v. illus., ports. 25cm. Contents.v. 1, The baptism of Ukraine to the Union of Berestye (988-1596)
1. Orthodox Eastern Church, Ukrainian—Hist. I. Vlasovs'kyi, Ivan.

VLASOVS'KYI, Ivan.
Outline history of the Ukrainian Orthodox Church. New York, Ukrainian Orthodox Church of U.S.A., 1956- v. illus., ports. 25 cm. Contents.-- v. 1, The baptism of Ukraine to the Union of Berestyo (988-1596)
1. Orthodox Eastern Church Ukrainian — Hist. I. Title.

VLASOVS'KYI, Ivan.
Outline history of the Ukrainian Orthodox Church. New York, Ukrainian Orthodox Church of USA, 1956- v. illus. 25 cm. Contents.v. 1. The baptism of Ukraine to the union of Berestye (988-1596) [BX750.U4V563] 67-41021
1. Orthodox Eastern Church, Ukrainian—Hist. I. Title.

Orthodox Eastern Church—United States

ABRAMTSOV, David Feodor, 1924- 281.973
Complete directory of Orthodox Catholic churches in the United States. Philadelphia, Orthodox Cathllic Literature Association, 1953. unpaged. 10cm. [BX732.A6] 53-12476
1. Orthodox Eastern Church—U. S. 2. Churches—U. S.—Direct I. Title. II. Title: Orthodox Catholic churches in the United States.

BOGOLEPOV, Aleksandr Aleksandrovich, 1886- 281.973
Toward an American Orthodox Church; the establishment of an autocephalous Orthodox Church. New York, Morehouse [c.1963] 124p. 21cm. Bibl. 63-21703 3.00
1. Orthodox Eastern Church—U.S. 2. Orthodox Eastern Church, Russian, in the U.S. I. Title.

BOGOLEPOV, Aleksandr Aleksandrovich, 1886- 281.973
Toward an American Orthodox Church; the establishment of an autocephalous Orthodox Church. New York, Morehouse-Barlow Co. [c1963] 124 p. 21 cm. Bibliography: p. 105-108. [BX735.B6] 63-21703
1. Orthodox Eastern Church — U.S. 2. Orthodox Eastern Church, Russian, in the U.S. I. Title.

Orthodox Eastern Church—United States—Directories

BESPUDA, Anastasia.
Guide to Orthodox America. Pref. by Alexander Schmemann. [Tuckahoe, N. Y.] St. Vladimir's Seminary Press [1965] 150 p. illus. 23 cm. Includes bibliography. 68-26667
1. Orthodox Eastern Church—U. S.—Direct. 2. Orthodox Eastern Church—Canada—Direct. I. Title.

BESPUDA, Anastasia. 281.9*025*1812
Guide to Orthodox America. Pref. by Alexander Schmemann. [Tuckahoe, N.Y.] St. Vladimir's Seminary Press [1965] 150 p. illus. 23 cm. Bibliography: p. 8. [BX240.B47] 72-177219
1. Orthodox Eastern Church—United States—Directories. 2. Orthodox Eastern Church—Canada—Directories. 3. Orthodox Eastern Church—South America—Directories. I. Title.

ETEROVICH, Adam S. 281.9'73
Eastern Orthodox Church directory of the United States, 1968. Editor: Adam S. Eterovich. Saratoga, Calif., R & E Research Associates [1968?] 32 l. 29 cm. [BX731.E8] 73-23143
1. Orthodox Eastern Church—U.S.—Directories. I. Title.

Orthodox Eastern Church—United States—Yearbooks.

ALEUTIAN Islands and North America (Archdiooese) 281.9798
Yearbook. New York, Exarchal Council. v. illus. 21cm. [BX496.A5L55] 53-33367
1. Orthodox Eastern Church—U. S.—Yearbooks. 2. Orthodox Eastern Church, Russian—Yearbooks. I. Title.

Orthodox Judaism.

BROWN, Jonathan M. 296.1'8
Modern challenges to Halakhah, by Jonathan M. Brown. Chicago, Published for the Hebrew Union College-Jewish Institute of Religion by Whitehall Co. [1969] xv, 137 p. 24 cm. Originally presented as the author's thesis, Hebrew Union College-Jewish Institute of Religion. Bibliography: p. 129-137. [BM522.42.R6 1969] 78-83999
1. Hoffmann, David, 1843-1921. Melamed le-ho'il. 2. Orthodox Judaism. I. Hebrew Union College-Jewish Institute of Religion. II. Title.

RACKMAN, Emanuel. 296.8'32'08
One man's Judaism. New York, Philosophical Library [1970] 397 p. 23 cm. Includes bibliographical references. [BM565.R25] 73-100583 ISBN 8-02-223230- 8.95
1. Orthodox Judaism. I. Title.

SCHILLER, Mayer. 296
The road back : a discovery of Judaism without embellishments / Mayer Schiller ; foreword by Norman Lamm. Jerusalem ; New York : Feldheim Publishers, 1978. 251 p. ; 24 cm. Includes bibliographical references and index. [BM565.S34] 78-110299 ISBN 0-87306-164-0 : 8.95
1. Orthodox Judaism. I. Title.

SHAFRAN, Avi. 296.8'32
Jewthink : a guide to real Judaism for the thinking individual / by Avi Shafran. New York : Hermon Press, c1977. 94 p. ; 21 cm. Subtitle varies on cover: A manual of Jewish belief for the thinking individual. Bibliography: p. [90]-94. [BM580.S4] 77-79097 ISBN 0-87203-064-4 pbk. : 3.95
1. Orthodox Judaism. I. Title.
Publisher's address : 175 Fifth Ave., N.Y.10010

STITSKIN, Leon D., comp. 296'.08
Studies in Torah Judaism, edited by Leon D. Stitskin. [New York] Yeshiva University Press, 1969. xxi, 587 p. 24 cm. Originally published as separate monographs in the series Studies in Torah Judaism. Contents.—The philosophy of purpose, by S. Belkin.—Sabbath and festivals in the modern age, by E. Rackman.—Prayer, by E. Berkovits.—The Kaddish: man's reply to the problem of evil, by M. Luban.—The nature and history of Jewish law, by M. Lewittes.—Jewish law faces modern problems, by I. Jakobovits.—Knowledge and love in rabbinic lore, by L. Jung.—Science and religion, by S. Roth. Includes bibliographical references. [BM40.S72] 68-21858 12.50
1. Orthodox Judaism. 2. Jewish law—Addresses, essays, lectures. I. Title.

Orthodox Judaism—Addresses, essays, lectures.

LAMM, Norman. 296.8'32
Faith and doubt; studies in traditional Jewish thought. New York, Ktav Pub. House [1972, c1971] ix, 309 p. 24 cm. Includes bibliographical references. [BM601.L3 1972] 75-138852 ISBN 0-87068-138-9 10.00
1. Orthodox Judaism—Addresses, essays, lectures. I. Title.

LAMM, Norman, comp. 296.8'32'08
A treasury of "Tradition". A treasury of "Tradition." New York, Hebrew Pub. Co. [1967] ix, 462 p. 22 cm. "Sponsored by Rabbinical Council of America." Bibliographical footnotes. [BM40.L35] 67-24738
1. Orthodox Judaism—Addresses, essays, lectures. I. Wurzburger, Walter S., joint comp. II. Tradition; a journal of orthodox Jewish thought. III. Title.

POSNER, Zalman I. 296.3
Think Jewish : a contemporary view of Judaism, a Jewish view of today's world / Zalman I. Posner. [Nashville] : Kesher Press, 1979, c1978 191 p. ; 23 cm. [BM565.P57] 78-71323 ISBN 0-9602394-0-5 : 7.95 ISBN 0-9602394-1-3 pbk. :3.95
1. Orthodox Judaism—Addresses, essays, lectures. 2. Hasidism—Addresses, essays, lectures. I. Title.

PRAGER, Dennis, 1948- 296.7'4
Nine questions people ask about Judaism / by Dennis Prager and Joseph Telushkin ; foreword by Herman Wouk. New York, N.Y. : Simon and Schuster, c1981. 216 p. ; 22 cm. Previously published as: Eight questions people ask about Judaism. 1975. Bibliography: p. 198-200. Includes index. Includes bibliographical references. [BM565.P7 1981] 19 81-5694 ISBN 0-671-42594-3 : 11.95
1. Orthodox Judaism—Addresses, essays, lectures. 2. Jewish way of life—Addresses, essays, lectures. I. Telushkin, Joseph, 1948- II. Title.

Orthodox Judaism—Germany.

REICHEL, O. Asher, 1921- 296'.072'024 B
Isaac Halevy, 1847-1914: spokesman and historian of Jewish tradition, by O. Asher Reichel. New York, Yeshiva University Press, 1969. 176 p. facsims., port. 24 cm. Includes, in Hebrew, "Facsimiles of Halevy's letters" (p. 129-158) Bibliography: p. 160-170. Bibliographical footnotes. [BM755.H225R4] 70-85704
1. Halevy, Isaak, 1847-1914. 2. Orthodox Judaism—Germany.

Orthodox Judaism—Study and teaching.

HECHT, Michael. 296.8'32
Have you ever asked yourself these questions? A guide to traditional Jewish thought. New York, Shengold [1971] 267 p. 22 cm. "Teacher's guide."—Dust jacket. [BM105.H35] 75-163738 5.00
1. Orthodox Judaism—Study and teaching. I. Title.

Orthodox Judaism—United States.

HEILMAN, Samuel C. 296.6'5
Synagogue life : a study in symbolic interaction / Samuel C. Heilman. Chicago : University of Chicago Press, 1976. xiii, 306 p. : ill. ; 23 cm. Includes index. Bibliography: p. 291-296. [BM205.H44 1976] 75-36403 ISBN 0-226-32488-5 : 16.50
1. Orthodox Judaism—United States. 2. Jewish way of life—Case studies. 3. Jews in the United States—Social life and customs. I. Title.

Orthodox Judaism—United States—Addresses, essays, lectures.

PELCOVITZ, Ralph. 296.8'32
Danger and opportunity / by Ralph Pelcovitz. New York : Shengold Publishers, c1976. 189 p. ; 26 cm. [BM205.P38] 76-47304 ISBN 0-88400-047-8 : 6.95
1. Orthodox Judaism—United States—Addresses, essays, lectures. 2. Ethics, Jewish—Addresses, essays, lectures. 3. Israel—Addresses, essays, lectures. I. Title.

Orthodox Judaism—United States—Biography.

HELMREICH, William B. 974.7'1'04924024 B
Wake up, wake up, to do the work of the creator / William B. Helmreich. 1st ed. New York : Harper & Row, c1976. 210 p. ; 22 cm. [BM755.H33A33 1976] 76-5129 ISBN 0-06-011823-7 : 8.95
1. Helmreich, William B. 2. Orthodox Judaism—United States—Biography. 3. Jewish way of life. 4. New York (City)—Biography. I. Title.

Orthodox Judaism—United States—Pictorial works.

WARSHAW, Mal. 974.7'23'004924
Tradition : Orthodox Jewish life in America / Mal Warshaw. New York : Schocken Books, 1976. x, 118 p. : ill. ; 28 cm. [BM205.W26] 76-9130 ISBN 0-8052-3637-6 : 14.95
1. Jews—Rites and ceremonies—Pictorial works. 2. Orthodox Judaism—United States—Pictorial works. 3. Jews in Brooklyn—Pictorial works. 4. United States—Religious life and customs—Pictorial works. 5. Brooklyn—Description—Views. I. Title.

Orthodoxy.

BAIN, Foree, 1853- 211
Decadence of the orthodox church, by Foree Bain ... [Chicago, George Hornstein bros.] c1920. cover-title, 25 p. 26 cm. [BL2780.B2] 20-6673
I. Title.

BASS, William A. 1847- 220
The great conflict; divine love versus human orthodoxy, God versus Pope of Rome ... by Rev. Dr. W. A. Bass ... Los Angeles, Calif., 1925. 205 p., 1 l., incl. front. (mounted port.) 23 cm. [BR125.B367] 25-7032
I. Title.

CLARKE, James Freeman, 1810-1888. 230.
Orthodoxy: its truths and errors. By James Freeman Clarke ... 14th ed. Boston, American Unitarian association, 1880. xi, 512 p. 19 1/2 cm. [BX9841.C63] 15-24992
I. Title.

GRAY, Joseph M M 1877- 220
An adventure in oothodoxy, by Joseph M. M. Gray. New York, Cincinnati, The Abingdon press [c1923] 143 p. 20 cm. [BR125.G728] 23-11851
I. Title.

JONES, Edgar De Witt, 1876- 252
Ornamented orthodoxy; studies in Christian constancy, by Edgar De Witt Jones ... introduction by Prof. Arthur S. Hoyt ... New York, Chicago [etc.] Fleming H. Revell company [c1918] 221 p. 20 cm. [BX7327.J8O7] 19-2065
I. Title.

LIEBMAN, Charles S
Orthodoxy in American Jewish life. [New York, American Jewish Committee, 1966] 81 p. 22 cm. Reprinted from American Jewish Year Book, v. 66. 68-75113
1. Orthodoxy. I. Title.

Orthodoxy, Modern.

AMES, Edward Scribner, 1870- 225
The new orthodoxy, by Edward Scribner Ames ... Chicago, Ill., The University of Chicago press [c1918] ix, 127 p. 19 cm. [BR121.A5] 18-19384
I. Title.

AMES, Edward Scribner, 1870- 225
The new orthodoxy, by Edward Scribner Ames ... Chicago, Ill., the University of Chicago press [c1925 xxv, 127 p. 19 cm. "Second edition." [BR121.A5 1925] 25-3453
I. Title.

CARUS, Paul, 1852-
The dawn of a new religious era, and other essays, by Paul Carus. Rev. and enl. ed. Chicago, London, The Open court publishing company, 1916. vii p., 1 l., 128, [3] p., 1 l. 20 cm. Contents.--The dawn of a new religious era.--Science a religious revelation.--The new orthodoxy.--The late Professor Romanes's Thoughts on religion.--The revision of a creed.--Behold! I make all things new.--Definition of religion.--The clergy's duty of allegiance to dogma and the struggle between world-conceptions.--The work of the Open court. 17-10988
I. Title.

RACKMAN, Emanuel.
Jewish values for modern man; introduction by Leon A. Feldman. New York, Jewish Education Commitee, 1962. 134 p. Spiral bound. 65-22391
1. Orthodoxy, Modern. 2. Ethics, Jewish. 3. Jewish law. I. Title.

Osborn, Ethan. 1758-1858.

HOTCHKIN, Beriah Bishop, 1806?-1878. 922.573
The pastor of the old stone church. Mr. Hotchkin's memorial, Judge Elmer's eulogy, and Mr. Burt's address, commemorative of Rev. Ethan Osborn ... Philadelphia, W. S. and A. Martien, 1858. 143, [1] p. front. (port.) pl. 19 1/2 cm. [BX9225.O7H6] 33-24793
1. Osborn, Ethan. 1758-1858. 2. Osborn family. 3. Fairton, N.J. Presbyterian congregation at Fairfield. I. Elmer, Lucius Quintius Cincinnatus, 1793-1883. II. Burt, Nathaniel Clark, 1825-1874. III. Title.

Osborn, Mrs. Sarah (Haggar) 1714-1796.

HOPKINS, Samuel, 1721-1803. 922
Memoirs of the life of Mrs. Sarah Osborn, who died at Newport, Rhodeisland, on the second day of August, 1796. In the eighty third year of her age. By Samuel Hopkins, D.D., pastor of the First Congregational church in Newport. Printed at Worcester, Massachusetts, by Leonard Worcester. 1799. 380 p. 17 1/2 cm. [BR1725.O7H6] 38-3074
1. Osborn, Mrs. Sarah (Haggar) 1714-1796. I. Title.

OSBORN, Sarah (Haggar) Mrs. 1714-1796. 922
Familiar letters, written by Mrs. Sarah Osborn, and Miss Susanna Anthony, late of Newport, Rhode-Island ... Newport, (R. I.) Printed at the office of the Newport Mercury. 1807. 170 p. 19 cm. [BR1725.O7A4] 38-10388
I. Anthony, Susanna, 1726-1791. II. Title.

Osgood, Don.

OSGOOD, Don. 261.8'34'2
The family and the corporation man / Don Osgood. 1st ed. New York : Harper & Row, [1975] viii, 148 p. : ill. ; 21 cm. [HQ535.O75 1975] 74-25696 6.95
1. Osgood, Don. 2. Family—United States. 3. Executives—United States. 4. Family—Religious life. I. Title.

Osgood, Frances Sargent (Locke) 1811-1850.

HEWITT, Mary Elizabeth (Moore), b.1807,. 242
Laurel leaves: a chaplet woven by the friends of the late Mrs. Osgood. New York, Lamport, Blakeman & Law, 1854. 347p. illus. 24cm. 'Originally published as 'The memorial.'' 'Frances Sargent Osgood,' by R. W. Griswold: p. 13-30. [PS535.H4 1854] 10-20231
1. Osgood, Frances Sargent (Locke) 1811-1850. I. Griswold, Rufus Wilmot, 1815-1857. II. Title.

Osiris.

BUDGE, Ernest Alfred Thompson Wallis, Sir 1857-1934. 299.31
Osiris; the Egyptian religion of resurrection. New Hyde Park, N. Y., University Books [1961] 2v. in 1. illus., facsims. 24cm. First published in 1911 under title: Osiris and the Egyptian resurrection. Bibliographical footnotes. [BL2450.O7B8 1961] 61-10531
1. Osiris. 2. Eschatology, Egyptian. I. Title.

BUDGE, Ernest Alfred Thompson Wallis, Sir, 1857-1934. 299'.3'1
Osiris and the Egyptian resurrection / by E. A. Wallis Budge ; illustrated after drawings from Egyptian papyri and monuments. New York : Dover Publications, 1973. 2 v. : ill. ; 24 cm. "Originally published in 1911 by the Medici Society, ltd." Includes bibliographical references and index. [BL2450.O7B8 1973] 72-81534 ISBN 0-486-22780-4 (v. 1). ISBN 0-486-22781-2 (v. 2) : 4.00 per vol.
1. Osiris. 2. Eschatology, Egyptian. I. Title.

BUDGE, Ernest Alfred Thompson Wallis, Sir 1857-1934. 299.
Osiris and the Egyptian resurrection: by E. A. Wallis Budge ... illustrated after drawing from Egyptian papyri and monuments ... London, P. L. Warner: New York, G. P. Putnam's sons, [1911] 2 v. fold. col. fronts., illus., plates (part fold.) 26 cm. [BL2450.O7B8] 12-5172
1. Osiris. 2. Eschatology, Egyptian. I. Title.

Oss, John.

RUFFO, Vinnie. 266'.023'0922
Behind barbed wire. Mountain View, Calif., Pacific Press Pub. Association [1967] v, 121 p. 22 cm. [BV3427.O68R8] 67-27708
1. Oss, John. 2. Oss, Olga Bertine (Osnes) 1897- I. Title.

Ostraka.

RAY, J. D. 493'.1'17
The archive of Hor / by J. D. Ray. London : Egypt Exploration Society, 1976. xv, 192 p., [39] leaves of plates : ill. ; 32 cm. (Texts from excavations ; second memoir ISSN 0307-5125s) (Excavations at North Saqqara documentary series ; 1) Includes Egyptian texts in demotic script and Roman transcription, with English translation. Includes bibliographical references and index. [PJ1829.R3] 77-367940 ISBN 0-85698-061-7
1. Hor of Sebbenytos. 2. Ostraka. 3. Egyptian language—Inscriptions. 4. Egypt—History—332-30 B.C.—Sources. I. Hor of Sebbenytos. II. Egypt Exploration Society. III. Title. IV. Series. V. Series: Texts from excavations ; second memoir.

O'Sullivan, Francis Joseph, 1870- tr.

ARVISENET, Claude, 1755-1831. 262.
An epitome of the priestly life, by Canon Arvisenet; adapted from the Latin original Memoriale vitae sacerdotalis, by Rev. F. J. O'Sullivan. New York, Cincinnati [etc.] Benziger brothers, 1921. x, 428 p. front. 15 1/2 cm. [BX1912.A7] 21-20431
1. O'Sullivan, Francis Joseph, 1870- tr. I. Title.

O'Sullivan, Jeremiah Francis, 1903-

STUDIES in medieval 271'.12
Cistercian history. Presented to Jeremiah F. O'Sullivan. Spencer, Mass., Cistercian Publications, 1971. xi, 204, [1] p. 23 cm. (Cistercian studies series, no. 13) Contents.Contents.—O'Callaghan, J. F. Preface.—Donnelly, J. S. Dedication.—Lackner, B. K. The liturgy of early Citeaux.—Sommerfeldt, J. R. The social theory of Bernard of Clairvaux.—Constable, G. A report of a lost sermon by St. Bernard on the failure of the Second Crusade.—Brundage, J. A. A transformed angel (X 3.31.18): the problem of the crusading monk.—O'Callaghan, J. F. The Order of Calatrava and the archbishops of Toledo, 1147-1245.—Buczek, D. S. "Pro defendendis ordinis": the French Cistercians and their enemies.—Hays, R. W. The Welsh monasteries and the Edwardian conquest.—Desmond, L. A. The statute of Carlisle and the Cistercians, 1298-1369.—Telesca, W. J. The Cistercian dilemma at the close of the Middle Ages: Gallicanism or Rome.—Volz, C. Martin Luther's attitude toward Bernard of Clairvaux.—Bibliography of studies by Jeremiah F. O'Sullivan (p. [205]) [BX3402.2.S78 1971b] 77-152486 ISBN 0-87907-813-8 7.95
1. O'Sullivan, Jeremiah Francis, 1903- 2. O'Sullivan, Jeremiah Francis, 1903-—Bibliography. 3. Cistercians—Addresses, essays, lectures. I. O'Sullivan, Jeremiah Francis, 1903- II. Title. III. Series.

Oswald, Helen K.

OSWALD, Helen K. 286.7'3 B
Precious harvest : a sequel to That book in the attic / by Helen K. Oswald ; [cover photos by Howard Larkin and Henry Rasmussen]. Mountain View, Calif. : Pacific Press Pub. Association, c1979. 75 p. ; 22 cm. (A Destiny book) [BX6193.O7A36] 79-88027 pbk. : 3.95
1. Oswald, Helen K. 2. Seventh-Day Adventists—United States—Biography. I. Oswald, Helen K. That book in the attic. II. Title.

Oswald, Saint, abp. of York, d. 992.

ROBINSON, Joseph Armitage, 1858- 262
... *St. Oswald and the church of Worcester,* by J. Armitage Robinson ... London, Pub. for the British academy by H. Milford, Oxford university press [1919] 51 p. 25 cm. (The British academy. Supplemental papers. v) Bibliographical foot-notes. [DA154.9.O7R5] 20-22067
1. Oswald, Saint, abp. of York, d. 992. 2. Worcester cathedral. I. Title.

Otey, James Hervey, bp., 1800-1863.

GREEN, William Mercer, bp., 1798-1887. 922
Memoir of Rt. Rev. James Hervey Otey, D.D., LL.D., the first bishop of Tennessee. By Rt. Rev. William Mercer Green... New York, J. Pott and company, 1885. 3 p. l., 359 p. front. (port.) 24 cm. [BX5995.O7G8] 16-27492
1. Otey, James Hervey, bp., 1800-1863. I. Title.

Otey, William Wesley, 1867-1961.

WILLIS, Cecil. 922.673
W. W. Otey, contender for the faith; a history of controversies in the Church of Christ from 1860-1960. Akron, Ohio [c1964] xi, 425 p. illus. ports. 22 cm. "A compendlum of the writings of W. W. Otey": p. 393-416. Bibliography: p. 417-422. [BX7343.O8W5] 66-4455
1. Otey, William Wesley, 1867-1961. I. Title.

Otomi language—Texts.

AN Otomi catechism. 238
[Introd. by Gillett G. Griffin] Princeton [N.J.; Printed by the Meriden Gravure Co., Meriden, Conn.] 1968. [21], 51 p. illus. "Published under the sponsorship of the Friends of the Princeton University Library." Includes a facsimile (51 p.) of an early 19th century Testerian MS. in native picture writing, containing in addition to the catechism, the Ave Maria, the Credo, Articles of faith, the Ten commandments, and various practical instructions. The MS. was given to Princeton in 1949 by Robert Garrett. [PM4149.O8] 68-8966
1. Catholic Church—Cathechisms and creeds—Otomi. 2. Otomi language—Texts. I. Griffin, Gillett Good, 1928- II. Princeton University. Library. Friends of the Princeton University Library.

Otterbein, Philip William, Bp., 1726-1813.

CORE, Arthur C. 289.9 B
Philip William Otterbein; pastor ecumenist ... By Arthur C. Core. Dayton, Ohio, Board of Publication, Evangelical United Brethren Church [1968] 127 p. illus., facsims., port. 22 cm. Includes bibliographical references. [BX9877.O8C6] 68-22446
1. Otterbein, Philip William, Bp., 1726-1813. I. Title.

DRURY, Augustus Waldo, 1851- 922.89
The life of Rev. Philip William Otterbein, founder of the Church of the United brethren in Christ. By A. W. Drury, A.M. With an introduction by Bishop J. Weaver, D.D. Dayton, O., United brethren publishing house, 1884. xviii p., 1 l., 21-384 p. front., plates, port. 19 1/2 cm. [BX9677.O6D7] 37-8724
1. Otterbein, Philip William, bp., 1726-1813. I. Title.

MILHOUSE, Paul William, 1910- 289.9 B
Philip William Otterbein; pioneer pastor to Germans in America, by Paul W. Milhouse. Nashville, Upper Room [1968] 71 p. illus. 16 cm. Includes bibliographical references. [BX9877.O8M5] 68-19994
1. Otterbein, Philip William, Bp., 1726-1813.

Otto, bp. of Bamberg, ca. 1060-1139.

EBBO, d.1163. 230
...*The life of Otto, apostle of Pomerania,* 1060-1139, by Ebo and Herbordus [tr. by] Charles H. Robinson, D. D. London, Society for promoting Christian knowledge; New York, The Macmillan company, 1920. 2 p. o., 193 [1] p. 19 cm. (Translations of Christian literature, ser. ii, Latin texts) Bibliography: p. 14-15. [BR45.T62E3] 22-4586
1. Otto, bp. of Bamberg, ca. 1060-1139. I. Herbordus, d. 1168. II. Bobinson, Charles Henry, 1861-1925, tr. III. Title.

Otto, Rudolf, 1869-1937.

DAVIDSON, Robert Franklin, 1902- 201
Rudolf Otto's interpretation of religion. Princeton, Princeton Univ. Press, 1947. viii, 213 p. 21 cm. "The works of Rudolf Otto": p. 207-209. [BL43.O8D3] 47-30875
1. Otto, Rudolf, 1869-1937. 2. Religion—Philosophy. I. Title.

Oudersluys, Richard Cornelius, 1906- —Addresses, essays, lectures.

SAVED by hope : 225.6
essays in honor of Richard C. Oudersluys / edited by James I. Cook. Grand Rapids : Eerdmans, c1978. p. cm. Contents.Contents.—Hesselink, I. J. Richard C. Oudersluys: Biblical scholar for a new age.—Ridderbos, H. The Christology of the fourth Gospel.—Morris, L. Love in the fourth Gospel.—DeJonge M. The Son of God and the children of God in the fourth Gospel.—Kooy, V. H. The transfiguration motif in the Gospel of John.—Meye, R. P. Mark 8:15-a misunderstood warning.—Reicke, B. Jesus, Simeon, and Anna (Luke 2:21-40).—Van Elderen, B. Another look at the parable of the good Samaritan.—Schweizer, E. 1 Corinthians 15:20-28 as evidence of Pauline eschatology and its relation to the preaching of Jesus.—Cook, J. I. The conception of adoption in the theology of Paul.—Piper, O. A. The novelty of the Gospel.—Takemori, M. Canon and worship.—Kuyper, L. J. Covenant and history in the Bible. "A Bibliography of the writings of Richard C. Oudersluys": p. [BS540.S24] 78-5416 ISBN 0-8028-1736-X pbk. : 10.95
1. Oudersluys, Richard Cornelius, 1906- —Addresses, essays, lectures. 2. Oudersluys, Richard Cornelius, 1906- —Bibliography. 3. Bible—Criticism, interpretation, etc.—Addresses, essays, lectures. I. Oudersluys, Richard Cornelius, 1906- II. Cook, James I., 1925-

Ouija board.

COVINA, Gina. 133.9'3
The Ouija book / Gina Covina. New York : Simon and Schuster, c1978. p. cm.

[BF1343.C68] 78-24571 ISBN 0-671-22840-4 : 8.95
1. Ouija board. I. Title.

COVINA, Gina. 133.9'3
The Ouija book / Gina Covina. New York : Simon and Schuster, c1979. 158 p. : ill. ; 23 cm. [BF1343.C68] 78-24571 ISBN 0-671-22840-4 : 9.95
1. Ouija board. I. Title.

GRUSS, Edmond G. 133.9'3
The ouija board : doorway to the occult / by Edmond C. Gruss, with John G. Hotchkiss. Chicago : Moody Press, [1975] 191 p. ; 18 cm. Bibliography: p. 190-191. [BF1343.G77] 75-315859 ISBN 0-8024-6185-9 pbk. : 1.50
1. Ouija board. 2. Occult sciences—Biblical teaching. I. Hotchkiss, John G., joint author. II. Title.

Ouija board—Juvenile literature.

STADTMAUER, Saul A., 1929- 133.9'3
Visions of the future : magic boards / by Saul A. Stadtmauer. New York : Contemporary Perspectives ; Milwaukee : distributor, Raintree Publshers, c1977. 48 p. : ill. ; 24 cm. Discusses the use of magic boards and automatic writing and speaking to receive communications from spirits. [BF1343.S75] 77-10735 ISBN 0-8172-1040-7 lib. bdg. : 4.95
1. Ouija board—Juvenile literature. 2. Spiritualism—Juvenile literature. 3. [Ouija board.] 4. [Spiritualism.] I. Title.

Our Heritage Wesleyan Church, Scottsdale, Ariz.

RICHARDS, Lawrence O. 262'.001
Three churches in renewal / Lawrence O. Richards. Grand Rapids : Zondervan Pub. House, c1975. 128 p. ; 21 cm. [BV600.2.R48] 74-25345 pbk. : 2.95
1. Our Heritage Wesleyan Church, Scottsdale, Ariz. 2. Mariners Church, Newport Beach Calif. 3. Trinity Church, Seattle. 4. Church renewal—Case studies. I. Title.

Our Lady and St. Michael Catholic Church, Workington, Eng.

OUR Lady & St. Michael, Workington : centenary, 1876-1976. [Workington] : [The Priory], [1976] [2], 20, [1] p. : ill., ports. ; 25 cm. Cover title. [BX4631.W64O946] 77-359587 ISBN 0-9505428-0-6 : £0.30 282'.427'87
1. Our Lady & St. Michael Catholic Church, Workington, Eng.

Our Lady of Angels Parish, Bronx, New York.

OUR Lady of Angels Parish, Bronx, New York. 282'.747'275
Our Lady of Angels Parish, Bronx, New York. White Plains, N.Y. : Monarch Pub., c1974. [76] p. : ill. ; 28 cm. [BX1418.B78O9 1974] 74-14423
1. Our Lady of Angels Parish, Bronx, New York.

Our Lady of Mount Carmel Church, Baden, Mo.

BARRY, R. K. 282'.778'66
The history of Our Lady of Mount Carmel Parish, Baden, Missouri. Compiled by R. K. Barry. [Baden? Mo., 1972?] 48 p. illus. 28 cm. Cover title: Our Lady of Mt. Carmel centennial celebration, 1872-1972. [BX4603.B28O862] 74-152668
1. Our Lady of Mount Carmel Church, Baden, Mo. 2. Baden, Mo.—Biography. I. Title. II. Title: Our Lady of Mt. Carmel centennial celebration, 1872-1972.

Our Lady of Mount Carmel Church, Bayonne, N.J.

OUR Lady of Mount Carmel Church, Bayonne, N.J. Diamond Jubilee Book Committee. 282'.749'26
Our Lady of Mount Carmel Church, Bayonne, New Jersey, U.S.A. : seventy-five years, 1898-1973. [Bayonne, N.J. : Our Lady of Mt. Carmel Church Diamond Jubilee Book Committee], c1974. 623 p., [2] fold. leaves of plates : ill. ; 32 cm. English or Polish. [BX1418.B3O9 1974] 75-309828
1. Our Lady of Mount Carmel Church, Bayonne, N.J.

Outler, Albert Cook, 1908-

OUR common history as Christians : essays in honor of Albert C. Outler / edited by John Deschner, Leroy T. Howe, and Klaus Penzel. New York : Oxford University Press, 1975. xxi, 298 p. ; 22 cm. [BR50.O7] 74-83988 ISBN 0-19-501865-6 : 9.50 230
1. Outler, Albert Cook, 1908- 2. Outler, Albert Cook, 1908- —Bibliography. 3. Theology—Addresses, essays, lectures. I. Deschner, John. II. Howe, Leroy T., 1936- III. Penzel, Klaus.
Contents omitted

Ouvrard, Gabriel Julien,

WOLFF, Otto, 1881-
Ouvrard, speculator of genius, 1770-1846. Translated by Stewart Thomson. With an introd. and notes by T. A B. Corley. New York, D. McKay Co. [1963, c1962] 239 p. illus. 23 cm. Translation of Die geschafte des herrn Ouvrard. Includes bibliography. [HJ1085.W613] 63-13474
1. Ouvrard, Gabriel Julien, 1770-1846. 2. Finance, Public — France — Hist. I. Title.

Owen co., Ind.—Church history.

DEGROOT, Alfred Thomas, 1903- 286.677243
The Churches of Christ in Owen county, Indiana. Spencer, Ind., A. T. DeGroot [1935] 181 p. incl. map. plates, 2 port. on 1 pl. 22 cm. "Other books by the same author": p. [2] [BR555.I7O82] 36-824
1. Owen co., Ind.—Church history. 2. Churches of Christ—Indiana—Owen co. 3. Disciples of Christ—Indiana—Owen co. 4. General convention of the Christian church—Indiana—Owen co. I. Title.

Owen, John, 1616-1683.

ORME, William, 1787-1830. 922.542
The life of the Rev. John Owen, D. D., abridged from Orme's Life of Owen. Philadelphia, Presbyterian board of publication, 1840. 2 p. l., [9]-256 p. 16 cm. 2 p. l., [9]-256 p. 16 cm. "The life of the Rev. John Janeway" (p. [225]-256, with special t.-p.) is by James Janeway. [BX9225.O8O7] 32-28868
1. Owen, John, 1616-1683. 2. Janeway, John, 1633-1657. I. Janeway, James, 1636?-1674. II. Title.

TEMPTATION and sin.
Evansville (Ind.) Sovereign Grace Book Club, 1958. viii, 322p.
I. Owen, John, 1616-1683.

TOON, Peter, 1939- 285'.9'0924 B
God's statesman: the life and work of John Owen, pastor, educator, theologian. Grand Rapids, Mich., Zondervan Pub. House [1973, c1971] viii, 200 p. 23 cm. Bibliography: p. [188]-195. [BX5207.O88T66 1973] 72-95518 ISBN 0-85364-133-1 5.95
1. Owen, John, 1616-1683. I. Title.

Owen, Mrs. Louisa (Graves) 1841-1915.

[OWEN, Adeline W] 922
Louisa Graves Owen, a good steward of the manifold grace of God. [New York, J. J. Little & Ives co., c1916] 2 p. l., 64 p. 17 cm. [CT275.O85O8] 16-15653
1. Owen, Mrs. Louisa (Graves) 1841-1915. I. Title.

Owens, Claire Myers.

OWENS, Claire Myers. 289.9
Discovery of the self. Introd. by Anthony Sutich. Boston, Christopher Pub. [c.1963] 334p. 21cm. 63-22782 3.95
I. Title.

OWENS, Claire Myers. 289.9
Discovery of the self. Introd. by Anthony Sutich. Boston, Christopher Pub. [c.1963] 334p. 21cm. 63-22782 3.95
I. Title.

OWENS, Claire Myers. 294.3'927'0924 B
Zen and the lady : memoirs—personal and transpersonal in a world in transition / by Claire Myers Owens. New York : Baraka Books, c1979. v, 306 p. ; 23 cm. Includes index. Bibliography: p. 299-302. [BQ976.W457A35] 79-50288 ISBN 0-88238-996-3 : 5.95
1. Owens, Claire Myers. 2. Zen Buddhists—United States—Biography. 3. Spiritual life (Zen Buddhism) I. Title.

VOGT, Von Ogden, 1879- 246
Art & religion. With a new pref. and epilogue by the author. [Rev ed.] Boston, Beacon Press [1960] 269 p. illus. 21 cm. (Beacon series in liberal religion, LR5) [BV150.V6 1960] 61-479
1. Art and religion. 2. Church. 3. Church architecture. 4. Christian art and symbolism. I. Title.

VOGT, Von Ogden, 1879- 246
Art & religion. With a new pref. and epilogue by the author. [Rev ed.] Boston, Beacon Press [1960] 269 p. illus. 21 cm. (Beacon series in liberal religion, LR5) [BV150.V6 1960] 61-479
1. Art and religion. 2. Church. 3. Church architecture. 4. Christian art and symbolism. I. Title.

Owens, Virginia Stem.

OWENS, Virginia Stem. 242
A taste of creation / Virginia Stem Owens. Valley Forge, PA : Judson Press, c1980. 104 p. : ill. ; 22 cm. Includes bibliographical references. [BV4832.2.O93] 79-28076 ISBN 0-8170-0865-9 : 4.50
1. Owens, Virginia Stem. 2. Meditations. I. Title.

Oxenham, Frank Nutcombe. The validity of papal claims.

MERRY DEL VAL, Raphael, cardinal, 1865-1930. 262.
The truth of papal claims, by Raphael Merry del Val a realy to The validity of papal claims, by F. Nutcombe Oxenham ... St. Louis, Mo., B. Herder; London, Sands & company, 1902. xvi, 129, xv p. 19 cm. Printed in Great Britain. [BX1805.M5] 9-5554
1. Oxenham, Frank Nutcombe. The validity of papal claims. 2. Papacy. I. Title. II. Title: Papal claims, The truth of.

Oxford cathedral.

WARNER, Stephen Alfred. 726.
Oxford cathedral, by S. A. Warner ... Illustrations in line are by the author. London, Society for promoting Christian knowledge. New York and Toronto, The Macmillan co., 1924. xii p., 1 l., 258, vi p. front., illus. (incl. music) plates (1 col.) double plan. 19 1/2 cm. "Detachable guide": VI p. at end. Bibliography: p. [244]-251. [NA5471.O9W3] 25-4328
1. Oxford cathedral. I. Title.

Oxford, Conn. St. Peter's Church.

LITCHFIELD, Norman. 283.7467
History of St. Peter's Church in Oxford, Connecticut. [Ann Arbor Mich., 1958] 119p. illus. 23cm. [BX5980.O85S3] 59-29213
1. Oxford, Conn. St. Peter's Church. I. Title.

Oxford (Diocese)—History

MARSHALL, Edward, 1815-1899.
... Oxford. By the Rev. Edward Marshall ... Published under the direction of the Tract committee. London, Society for promoting Christian knowledge; New York, E. & J. B. Young & co., 1882. 1 p. l., iv, 301 p. front. (fold. map) 17 cm. (Diocesan histories) [BX5107.O8M4] 4-201
1. Oxford (Diocese)—Hist. I. Title.

Oxford group.

BENSON, Clarence Irving, 1897- 248
The eight points of the Oxford group; an exposition for Christians and pagans, by C. Irving Benson. London [etc.] H. Milford, Oxford university press, 1936. xviii p., 1 l., 163, [1] p. 19 cm. "First edition, 1936; reprinted ... 1936." [BV4915.B47 1936 c] 37-23818
1. Oxford group. I. Title.

CROSSMAN, Richard Howard Stafford, ed. 248
Oxford and the groups; the influence of the groups considered by Rev. G. F. Allen, John Maud, Miss B. E. Gweyer ... [and others] Edited by R. H. S. Crossman; preface by Dr. W. B. Selbie. Oxford, B. Blackwell, 1934. xiv, 208 p. 20 cm. "Published January, 1934: reprinted March, 1964." [BV4915.C7 1934 a] 34-13738
1. Oxford group. I. Title.

DU MAURIER, Daphne, 1907- 248
Come wind, come weather, by Daphne Du Maurier. New York, Doubleday, Doran and company, inc., 1941. xvi, 78 p., 1 l. 18 cm. "This book of true stories was written for the people of Britain in the hope that it would bring courage and strength to them in a time of crisis."--p. v. "First edition." [BV4915.D85 1941] 41-4435
1. Oxford group. 2. European war, 1939— Gt. Brit. I. Title.

FOOT, Stephen, 1887- 248
Life began yesterday, by Stephen Foot. New York and London, Harper & brothers, 1935. 4 p. l., 175 p. 19 1/2 cm. [Full name: Stephen Henry Foot] [BV4915.F6 1935a] 35-22948
1. Oxford group. 2. Conversion. I. Title.

HENSON, Herbert Hensley, bp. of Durham, 1863-
The group movement, being the first part of the charge delivered at the third quadrennial visitation of his diocese together with an introduction by Herbert Hensley Henson ... London Oxford university press, H. Milford 1933 2 p. l., 82 p. 19 cm. Published also under title: Oxford group movement. A33
1. Oxford group. I. Title.

HENSON, Herbert Hensley, bp. of Durham, 1863- 248
The Oxford group movement, by Herbert Hensley Henson ... 2d ed., with a new preface. New York, Oxford university press, 1934. xi, 82 p., 1 l. 19 cm. First edition published, 1933, under title: The Oxford groups: the charge delivered at the third quadrennial visitation of his diocese. The second edition does not include part 3 of the charge, nor the appendix. [BV4915.H47 1934] [283.42] 34-8547
1. Oxford group. I. Title.

HENSON, Herbert Hensley, bp. of Durham, 1863- 248
The Oxford groups: the charge delivered at the third quadrennial visitation of his diocese together with an introduction, by Herbert Hensley Henson ... London, H. Milford, Oxford university press, 1933. 3 p. l., 156 p. 19 cm. "First impression, March 1933; second impression, May 1933." [BV4915.H47 1933a] [283.42] 33-19918
1. Oxford group. I. Title.

HOWARD, Peter. 248
... Ideas have legs. New York, Coward-McCann, inc. [1946] viii, 184 p. 21 1/2 cm. [BV4915.H725 1946] 46-7228
1. Oxford group. I. Title.

HOYT, Marshall William. 248
Lessons in finding God, by Marshall W. Hoyt. Sault St. Marie, Mich., The Sault news printing company [c1939] 4 p. l., 117 p. 17 1/2 cm. [BV4915.H75] 39-25950
1. Oxford group. 2. Christian life. I. Title.

LEON, Philip. 248
The philosophy of courage: or, The Oxford group way, by Philip Leon. New York, Oxford university press, 1939. 3 p. l., [9]-222 p. 19 cm. [BV4915.L45] 39-21395
1. Oxford group. I. Title.

MACMILLAN, Ebenezer, 1881- 252.052
Seeking and finding, by Ebenezer

Macmillan... New York and London, Harper and brothers, 1933. xiii p., 1 l., 17-281 p. 19 1/2 cm. [BX9178.M293S4] 33-11235
1. Oxford group. 2. Presbyterian church—Sermons. 3. Sermons, English. I. Title.

MURRAY, Robert Henry, 1874- 270
1947.
Group movements throughout the ages. Freeport, N.Y., Books for Libraries Press [1972] 377 p. illus. 23 cm. (Essay index reprint series) Reprint of the 1935 ed. Contents.Contents.—The Montanists; or, The priest versus the prophet.—The Franciscans; or, The realisation of the ideal.—The Friends of God; or, The quest of the ideal under difficulties.—Port Royal; or, The group in miniature.—The Methodists; with a reference to the Evangelicals.—The Oxford group movement; with a reference to the Tractarians. Includes bibliographies. [BX4487.O9M87 1972] 72-301 ISBN 0-8369-2810-5
1. Oxford Group. 2. Sects. 3. Revivals—History. I. Title.

RICHARDSON, John Andrew, 248
abp., 1868-
The groups movement, by the Most Rev. John A. Richardson... Milwaukee, Wis., Morehouse publishing co. [c1935] vi, 82 p. 18 1/2 cm. "Acknowledgements": p. [ii] Bibliography: p. [81]-82. [BV4915.R5] 35-1731
1. Oxford group. I. Title.

ROSE, Cecil, 1896- 248
When man listens, by Cecil Rose ... New York, Oxford university press, 1937. 76, [1] p. 19 cm. [BV4915.R67] 38-21848
1. Oxford group. I. [Full name: Cecil Herbert Rose. II. Title.

SANGSTER, William Edwin, 248
1900-
God does guide us [by] W. E. Sangster. New York, Cincinnati [etc.] The Abingdon press [c1934] 147 p. 19 1/2 cm. [Full name: William Edwin Robert Sangster] [BV4915.S25 1934a] 34-39332
1. Oxford group. I. Title.

WEATHERHEAD, Leslie Dixon, 248
1893-
Discipleship [by] Leslie D. Weatherhead. New York, Cincinnati [etc.] The Abingdon press [1934] 152 p. 19 1/2 cm. [BV4915.W47] 34-2039
1. Oxford group. 2. Christian life. I. Title.

WHAT is the Oxford group? 248
By the layman with a notebook; with a foreword by L. W. Grensted ... New York, Oxford university press, 1933. 6 p. l., [3]-132 p. 19 cm. [BV4915.W48] 34-1736
1. Oxford group. I. The layman with a notebook. II. Grensted, Laurence William, 1884-

Oxford mission to Calcutta.

HOLMES, Walter Herbert Greame.
From a hostel veranda in Bengal, by W. H. G. Holmes ... With preface by Viscount Halifax, K.G. London and Oxford, A. R. Mowbray & co. limited; New York, Morehouse-Gorham co. [1945] 74 p. 19 cm. "First published in 1945." A 46
1. Oxford mission to Calcutta. 2. Missions—India. I. Title.

Oxford movement.

BATTISCOMBE, Georgina. 922.342
John Keble; a study in limitations. New York, Knopf, 1964 [c1963] xix, 395 p. illus., facsims., ports. 24 cm. Includes bibliographies. [BX5199.K3B3 1964] 64-12222
1. Keble, John, 1792-1866. 2. Oxford movement.

BRILIOTH, Yngve Torgny, 1891-
The Anglican revival, studies in the Oxford movement, by the Rev. Yngve Brilioth ... With a preface by the Right Rev. the Lord Biship of Gloucester. London, New York [etc.] Longmans, Green and co., 1925. xv, 357 p. 22 1/2 cm. [BX5096.B7] 25-6865
1. Oxford movement. I. Title.

BRILIOTH, Yngve Torgny, 1891- 283
Three lectures on evangelicalism and the Oxford movement, together with a lecture on the theological aspect of the Oxford movement, and a sermon preached in Fairford church on 11 July 1933, By Yngve Brilioth ... London, Oxford university press, H. Milford, 1934. vi p., 1 l., 77, [1] p. 19 1/2 cm. [BX5100.B7] 34-36614
1. Oxford movement. 2. Protestantism, Evangelical. I. Title. II. Title: Evangelicalism and the Oxford movement.

BRISCOE, John 922.342
Fetherstonhaugh, 1877-
A tractarian at work; a memoir of Dean Randall, by J.F. Briscoe... and H.F.B. Mackay...with a foreword by Viscount Halifax. London and Oxford, A.R. Mowbray & co., ltd.; Milwaukee, Morehouse publishing co. [1932] xi, 211, [1] p. front., plates, ports. 22 cm. "First published, September, 1932; second impression, December, 1932." [BX5199.R23B7 1932a] 33-9562
1. Randall, Richard William, 1824-1906. 2. Oxford movement. I. Mackay, Henry Falconer Barclay, joint author. II. Title.

CHADWICK, Owen, ed. 283.42
The mind of the Oxford movement. Stanford, Calif., Stanford University Press [c1960] 239p. 23cm. (A Library of modern religious thought) [BX5099.C45] 60-15256
1. Oxford movement. I. Title.

CHURCH, Richard William, 283.42
1815-1890
The Oxford movement; twelve years. 1833-1845. [Hamden, Conn.] Archon, 1966. xv, 416p. 18cm. Reprint of the 3d ed., 1892. [BX5100.C5 1966] 66-18647 11.00
1. Oxford movement. I. Title.

CHURCH, Richard William, 283'.42
1815-1890.
The Oxford movement; twelve years, 1833-1845. Edited and with an introd. by Geoffrey Best. Chicago, University of Chicago Press [1970] xxxi, 280 p. map. 23 cm. (Classics of British historical literature) [BX5100.C5 1970] 77-115873 ISBN 0-226-10618-7
1. Oxford movement.

CHURCH, Richard William, 1815-
1890.
The Oxford movement, twelve years, 1833-1845, by R. W. Church ... London and New York, Macmillan and co., 1891. xiii, 358 p. 23 cm. E 10
1. Oxford movement. I. Title.

CHURCH, Richard William, 1815-
1890.
The Oxford movement, twelve years, 1833-1845, by R. W. Church ... London, Macmillan and co., limited; New York, The Macmillan company, 1904. xv, 416 p. 18 1/2 cm. Third edition. [BN6098.C5 1904] 7-37991
1. Oxford movement. I. Title.

CHURCH, Richard William, 1815-
1890.
The Oxford movement, twelve years, 1833-1845, by R. W. Church ... London, Macmillan and co., limited; New York, The Macmillan company, 1897. xv, 416 p. 18 1/2 cm. "First edition ... March, 1891 ... Third edition ... January 1892; reprinted July 1892, 1897." Bibliographical foot-notes. [BX5098.C5 1897] 45-53089
1. Oxford movement. I. Title.

DAWSON, Christopher Henry, 283
1889-
The spirit of the Oxford movement, by Christopher Dawson. New York, Sheed & Ward, inc., 1933. xv, 144 p. 19 cm. "Printed in Great Britain." "First published, September 1933; second impression, November 1933." [BX5100D3 1963 a] 34-1851
1. Oxford movement. I. Title.

DAWSON, Christopher 283'.42
Henry, 1889-1970.
The spirit of the Oxford movement / by Christopher Dawson. New York : AMS Press, [1976] p. cm. Reprint of the 1934 ed. published by Sheed & Ward, London. [BX5100.D3 1976] 75-30020 ISBN 0-404-14025-4 : 9.50
1. Oxford movement. I. Title.

DILWORTH-HARRISON, Talbot. 283
Every man's story of the Oxford movement, by T. Dilworth-Harrison ... London and Oxford, A. R. Mowbray & co., ltd.; Milwaukee, Morehouse publishing co. [1933] vii, 154 p., 1 l. 19 cm. "First published in 1932, second impression, 1933." Bibliography: p. iv-v. [BX5093.D5 1933] 33-15489
1. Oxford movement. I. Title.

DONALD, Gertrude. 283'.43
Men who left the movement: John Henry Newman, Thomas W. Allies, Henry Edward Manning, Basil William Maturin. Freeport, N.Y., Books for Libraries Press [1967] viii, 422 p. 21 cm. (Essay index reprint series) Reprint of the 1933 ed. [BX5100.D6 1967] 67-23207
1. Newman, John Henry, Cardinal, 1801-1890. 2. Allies, Thomas William, 1813-1903. 3. Manning, Henry Edward, Cardinal, 1808-1892. 4. Maturin, Basil William, 1847-1915. 5. Oxford movement. I. Title.

FABER, Geoffrey 262'.135'0924 B
Cust, Sir, 1889-1961.
Oxford apostles : a character study of the Oxford movement / by Geoffrey Faber. New York : AMS Press, [1976] p. cm. Reprint of the 1936 ed. published by Faber and Faber, London. Includes index. Bibliography: p. [BX5100.F3 1976] 75-30022 ISBN 0-404-14027-0 : 32.50
1. Newman, John Henry, Cardinal, 1801-1890. 2. Church of England—Biography. 3. Oxford movement. I. Title.

GOODE, William, 1801-1868. 283
The case as it is: or, A reply to the letter of Dr. Pusey to His Grace the Archbishop of Canterbury; including a compendious statement of the doctrines and views of the tractors as expressed by themselves. By William Goode ... 1st American, from the 2d London ed. ... Philadelphia, H. Hooker, 1842. 1 p. l., [5]-57 p. 24 cm. [BX5099.P83G6 1842] 36-33989
1. Pusey, Edward Bouverie, 1800-1882. A letter to ... the Archbishop of Canterbury. 2. Oxford movement. I. Title.

HALL, Samuel, Sir, 1841-1907. 28
A short history of the Oxford movement, by Sir Samuel Hall ... London, New York [etc.] Longmans, Green, and co., 1906. x, 267 p. 20 1/2 cm. "Principal authorities used": p. ix-x. [BX5098.H3] 7-2068
1. Oxford movement. I. Title.

HUNTER, Aylmer Douglas T. 28
Englands' reawakening; a few words on the history of Anglo-Catholicism, and its attitude towards the prospect of a future reunion, by Aylmer Hunter...Preface by His Grace the Duke of Argyll. New York, E. P. Dutton and company [1924] 93 p. 17 1/2 cm. Printed in Great Britain. [BX5098.H8] 24-30401
1. Oxford movement. I. Title.

KNOX, Edmund Arbuthnott, 283.42
bp. of Manchester, 1847-
The tractarian movement, 1833-1845; a study of the Oxford movement as a phase of the religious revival in western Europe in the second quarter of the nineteenth century. By the Right Rev. E. A. Knox London, New York, Putnam, 1933. xix, 410 p. 22 cm. Bibliography: p. 398-403. [BX5100.K6] 33-19916
1. Oxford movement. I. Title.

LESLIE, Shane, 1885- 28
The Oxford movement, 1833-1933, by Shane Leslie... Milwaukee, The Bruce publishing company [c1933] xiii p., 1 l., 189, [2] p. ports. 22 cm. (Half-title: Science and culture series) [Full name: John Randolph Shane Leslie] "A select bibliography of the Oxford movement": p. 183-189. [BX5098.L4] 33-24059
1. Oxford movement. 2. Church of England—Hist. 3. Gt. Brit.—Church history. I. Title.

MAY, James Lewis, 1873- 283
The Oxford movement, its history and its future; a layman's estimate, by J. Lewis May. With 12 illustrations. New York, The Dial press, incorporated, 1933. xi, 301 p. front., 2 pl. ports. 22 1/2 cm. "Printed in Great Britain." [BX5098.M3] 38-82240
1. Oxford movement. I. Title.

MORSE-BOYCOTT, Desmond Lionel,
1892
They shine like stars. London, New York, Skeffington [1947] 380 p. illus., ports. 22 cm. Bibliography: p. 353-300. A 48
1. Oxford movement. I. Title.

MORSE-BOYCOTT, 283'.0922 B
Desmond Lionel, 1892-
Lead, kindly light; studies of the saints and heros of the Oxford movement. Freeport, N.Y., Books for Libraries Press [1970] 240 p. 23 cm. (Essay index reprint series) Reprint of the 1933 ed. Contents.Contents.—Introduction. The romance of the century.—John Henry Newman.—Hugh James Rose.—Richard Hurrell Froude.—Isaac Williams.—John Keble.—Edward Bouverie Pusey.—Charles Marriott.—Frederick William Faber.—Henry Edward Manning.—Christina Rossetti.—Charles Fuge Lowder.—Robert Radclyffe Dolling.—Henry Parry Liddon.—Father Ignatius.—Arthur Henry Stanton.—Mary Scharlieb.—Frank Weston.—Arthur Tooth.—Thomas Alexander Lacey.—Mother Kate. [BX5100.M6 1970] 70-107728 ISBN 8-369-15291-
1. Church of England—Biography. 2. Oxford movement. 3. Anglo-Catholicism. I. Title.

MORSE-BOYCOTT, Desmond 922.342
Lionel, 1892-
Lead, kindly light; studies of the saints and heroes of the Oxford movement, by the Rev. Desmond Morse-Boycott. New York, The Macmillan company, 1933. 240 p. 19cm. Printed in Great Britain. "A survey of a century of the Oxford movement better known now as Anglo-Catholicism."--P. 9. [BX5100.M6] 33-5725
1. Oxford movement. 2. Church of England—Biog. 3. Anglo-Catholicism. I. Title.
Contents omitted.

MOZLEY, Thomas, 1806-1893.
Reminiscences chiefly of Oriel college and the Oxford movement, by the Rev. T. Mozley ... in two volumes ... Boston, New York, Houghton, Miffilin and co, 1882. 2 v. 19 cm. E 10
1. Oxford movement. 2. Oxford. University. Oriel college. I. Title.

O'CONNELL, Marvin 283'.42
Richard.
The Oxford conspirators; a history of the Oxford movement 1833-45, by Marvin R. O'Connell. [New York] Macmillan [1969] x, 468 p. 24 cm. Bibliographical references included in "Notes" (p. 427-456) [BX5098.O25] 68-31279
1. Oxford movement. I. Title.

OLLARD, Sidney Leslie, 1875- 28
The Anglo-Catholic revival, some persons and principles; six lectures delivered at All Saints', Margaret street, by S. L. Ollard...with a preface by H. F. B. Mackay... London [etc.] A R. Mowbray & co., ltd.; Milwaukee, U. S. A., The Morehouse publishing co. [1925] xi, 98 p., 1 l. 23 cm. [BX5098.O6] 26-5190
1. Oxford movement. I. Title.

OLLARD, Sidney Leslie, 1875-
A short history of the Oxford movement, by S. L. Ollard ... London, A. R. Mowbray & co., ltd.; Milwaukee, The Young churchman co. [1915] xv, 288 p. front., plates (incl. ports.) 20 cm. A 16
1. Oxford movement. I. Title.

OLLARD, Sidney Leslie, 1875- 283
1949
A short history of the Oxford movement London, Faith Pr. Reprints. [dist. New York, Morehouse, 1964, c.1963] 194p. port. 19cm. (Faith pr. reprints, 1) Bibl. 64-1276 1.50 pap.,
1. Oxford movement. I. Title.

PECK, William George, 1883- 283
... The social implications of the Oxford movement, by William George Peck ... New York, London, C. Scribner's sons, 1933. x p., 2 l., 346 p. 21 cm. (The Hale lectures, 1933) "List of works consulted": p. 333-337. [BX5100.P4] 33-37439
1. Oxford movement. 2. Anglo-Catholicism. 3. Sociology, Christian—Anglican authors. I. Title.

PERRY, William. 283.41
The Oxford movement in Scotland, by W. Perry ... with a foreword by the Most Reverend the Primus of the Episcopal

church in Scotland. Cambridge [Eng.] The University press, 1933. xiv, 125, [1] p. 19 cm. [BX5300.P4] 33-14855
1. Oxford movement. 2. Episcopal church in Scotland—Hist. I. Title.

SHAW, Plato Ernest, 1883- 28
The early tractarians and the Eastern church, by P. E. Shaw ... with a foreword by Rev. Leighton Pullan ... Milwaukee, Morehouse publishing co.; London, A. R. Mowbray & co. [c1930] 5 p. l., 200 p., 1 l. 20 cm. Bibliography: p. [188]-196. [Full name: Plato Ernest Oliver Shaw] [BX5098.S5] 30-3802
1. Oxford movement. 2. Church of England—Relations—Orthodox Eastern church. 3. Orthodox Eastern church—Relations—Church of England. 4. Christian union. I. Title.

TAYLOR, Isaac, 1787-1865. 238.
Ancient Christianity, and the doctrines of the Oxford tracts. By Isaac Taylor ... Philadelphia, H. Hooker, 1840. xx, [21]-554 p. 19 1/2 cm. [BX5097.T3 1840a] 22-22537
I. Title.

WALSH, Walter, 1847-1912. 283'.42
The secret history of the Oxford Movement. 4th ed. London, S. Sonnenschein, 1898. [New York, AMS Press, 1973] xv, 424 p. 23 cm. Includes bibliographical references. [BX5098.W3 1973] 73-101915 ISBN 0-404-06819-7 25.00
1. Oxford movement. I. Title.

WALWORTH, Clarence Augustus, 283.
1820-1900.
The Oxford movement in America; or, Glimpses of life in an Anglician seminary. By Rev. Clarence E. [!] Walworth ... New York, The Catholic book exchange [1895] iv, 175 p. front., illus. (incl. ports.) pl. 23 cm. [BX5925.W3] 2-4373
1. Oxford movement. I. Title. II. Title: Glimpses of life in an Anglican seminary.

WARD, Wilfrid Philip, 1856-
The Oxford movement, by Wilfrid Ward. London [etc.] T. C. & E. C. Jack; New York, Dodge publishing co. [1912] v, 7-94 p. 16 1/2 cm. (Half-title: The people's books. [V. 33]) W 13
1. Oxford movement. I. Title.

WARD, Wilfrid Philip, 1856- 922.2
1916.
The life and times of Cardinal Wiseman, by Wilfrid Ward... 3d ed. London, New York and Bombay, Longmans, Green, and co., 1898. 2 v. 3 port. (incl. fronts.) 20 cm. [BX4705.W6W3 1898] 37-18671
1. Wiseman, Nicholas Patrick Stephen, cardinal, 1802-1865. 2. Oxford movement. I. Title.

WARD, Wilfrid Philip, 1856- 922.2
1916.
The life and times of Cardinal Wiseman, by Wilfrid Ward...New impression. London, New York [etc.] Longmans, Green and co., 1900. 2 v. 3 port. (incl. fronts.) 19 cm. [BX4705.W6W3] 4-16975
1. Wiseman, Nicholas Patrick Stephen, cardinal, 1802-1865. 2. Oxford movement. I. Title.

WARD, Wilfrid 283'.092'4 B
Philip, 1856-1916.
William George Ward and the Oxford movement / by Wilfrid Ward. New York : AMS Press, 1977. xxix, 462 p. : ill. ; 23 cm. Reprint of the 1889 ed. published by Macmillan, London, New York. [BX4705.W3W35 1977] 75-29625 ISBN 0-404-14043-2 : 31.50
1. Ward, William George, 1812-1882. 2. Catholics in England—Biography. 3. Oxford movement. I. Title.

WARD, Wilfrid Philip, 922.242
1856-1916.
William George Ward and the Oxford movement, by Wilfrid Ward. London and New York, Macmillan and co., 1889. xxix, 462 p. front. (port.) 23 cm. [BX4705.W3W35] 37-18688
1. Ward, William George, 1812-1882. 2. Oxford movement. I. Title.

WARD, Wilfrid Philip, 1856- 922.
1916.
William George Ward and the Oxford movement, by Wilfrid Ward. 2d ed. London and New York, Macmilland co., 1890. xxxi, 481 p. front. (port.) 22 1/2 cm. [BX5199.W2W2] E 10
1. Ward, William George, 1812-1882. 2. Oxford movement. I. Title.

WEBB, Clement Charles Julian, 283
1865-
Religious thought in the Oxford movement, by C. C. J. Webb ... London, Society for promoting Christian knowledge; New York and Toronto, The Macmillan co., 1928. viii, 9-156, [1] p. 19 cm. "The follwoing chapters contain the substance of a course of lectures delivered by me in 1925 as Oriel professor of the philosophy of the Christian religion [in the University of Oxford]"--Author's pref. [BX5100.W35] 28-22171
1. Oxford movement. I. Title.

WHATELY, Richard, abp. of 283
Dublin, 1787-1863.
Cautions for the times. Addressed to the parishioners of a parish in England, by their former rector, Richard Whately ... In three parts. pt. I-[II] New York, Stanford & Swords, 1853. 2 v. 23 cm. No more published? [BX5100.W5] CA 33
1. Oxford movement. 2. Catholic church—Doctrinal and controversial works—Protestant authors. I. Title.

WILLIAMS, Isaac, 1802-1865. 922.
The autobiography of Isaac Williams, B.D., fellow and tutor of Trinity college, Oxford, author of several of the "Tracts for the times"... Edited by his brother-in-law, the Ven. Sir George Prevost...as throwing further light on the history of the Oxford movement. London and New York, Longmans, Green, & co., 1892. vi p., 1 l., 186 p. 19 1/2 cm. [BX5199.W64A3] 1-28242
1. Oxford movement. I. Prevost, Sir George, 1804-1893, ed. II. Title.

WILLIAMS, Isaac, 1802-1865. 922.
The autobiography of Isaac Williams, B.D., fellow and tutor of Trinity college, Oxford, author of several of the "Tracts for the times"... Edited by his brother-in-law, the Ven. Sir George Prevost...as throwing further light on the history of the Oxford movement. London and New York, Longmans, Green, & co., 1892. vi p., 1 l., 186 p. 19 1/2 cm. [BX5199.W64A3] 1-28242
1. Oxford movement. I. Prevost, Sir George, 1804-1893, ed. II. Title.

WILLIAMS, Norman Powell, 283
1883- ed.
Northern Catholicism; centenary studies in the Oxford and parallel movements, edited by N. P. Williams...and Charles Harris...A publication of the Literature committee of the English church union. New York, The Macmillan comapny [1933] xvi, 554, [1] p. 22 cm. "First published in 1933; printed in Great Britain." [BX5100.W57] 34-1035
1. Oxford movement. 2. Catholicity. I. Harris, Charles, 1865- joint ed. II. English church union. Literature committee. III. Title.

WINDLE, Bertram Coghill Alan, 289
Sir 1858-1929.
Who's who of the Oxford movement, prefaced by a brief story of that movement [by] Bertram C. A. Windle ... New York & London, The Century co. [c1926] viii, 251 p. front. 20 1/2 cm. [BX5100.W6] 26-4287
1. Oxford movement. I. Title.

Oxford. St. Mary the Virgin, Church of.

JACKSON, Thomas Graham, 726.
bart., Sir. 1835-1924.
The church of St. Mary the Virgin, Oxford, by T. G. Jackson ... Oxford, Clarendon press, 1897. xiv, [2], 231, [1] p. illus., xxiv pl. (part fold., incl. front., plan) 30 x 25 cm. [NA5471.O95J2] 1-2902
1. Oxford. St. Mary the Virgin, Church of. I. Title.

Oxford. University. All Souls College.

EASON, R E. 378.1'98
The last of their line : the Bible Clerks of All Souls College, Oxford : some notes and reminiscences / by R. E. Eason and R. A. Snoxall. Oxford : All Souls College, 1976. vii, 24 p. : 1 ill. ; 25 cm. (All Souls College history series ; 1 ISSN 0308-6143s) Limited ed. of 450 copies. [BV677.E17] 77-352400 ISBN 0-9504374-1-7 : £0.60
1. Oxford. University. All Souls College. 2. Lay readers. I. Snoxall, R. A., joint author. II. Title. III. Title: Bible Clerks of All Souls College, Oxford. IV. Series: Oxford. University. All Souls College. All Souls College history series ; 1.

Oxford university press.

BIBLE, English. 1877. 220.52
The Holy Bible, containing the Old and New Testaments; translated out of the original tongues: and with the former translations diligently compared and revised, by His Majesty's special command. Appointed to be read in churches. Oxford, Printed at the University press; London, New York, H. Frowde [1877] 3 p. l., [1051] p. 17 cm. At head of added t.-p.: In memoriam Gul. Caxton. "Wholly printed and bound in twelve hours. on this 30th day of June, 1877. for the Caxton celebration. Only100 copies were printed. of which this is no. 56." "Presented to the Library of Congress by the delegates of the Oxford university press, through Henry Stevens of Vermont." On cover: Arms of the University of Oxford. In case. Title within engraved border. With reproduction of the t.-p. of the Memorial Bible. A list of the Oxford Caxton memorial Bibles allotted up to Easter, MDCCCLXXVIII": p.24-30 [Supplement] The history of the Oxford Caxton memorial Bible, printed and bound in twelve consecutive hours, June 30, 1877:by Henry Stevens London, H. Stevens, 1878. 30p. 1 [BS185.1877.08] 6-37733
1. Oxford university press. 2. Bible, English. 1877. Oxford Caxton memorial Bible I. Stevens, Henry 1819-1886. II. Title.

BIBLE. English. 1941. 220.52
Authorized.
The Bible for to-day, edited by John Stirling, illustrated by Rowland Hilder and other artists. London, New York [etc.] Oxford university press, 1941. xv, [1], 1255, [1] p. incl. front., illus., diagrs. 25 cm. [BS185.1941.L6] 41-19352
I. Stirling, John, ed. II. Title.

BIBLE. English. 1941. 220.52
Authorized.
The Bible for to-day, edited by John Stirling, illustrated by Rowland Hilder and other artists. London, New York [etc.] Oxford university press, 1941. xix, [1], 1255 p. incl. front., illus. 24 cm. [BS185.1941.L62] 41-23468
I. Sterling, John, ed. II. Title.

Oxford. University—Students.

WOODFORDE, James, 283'.0924 B
1740-1803.
Woodforde at Oxford, 1759-1776: [extracts from his diary] edited by W. N. Hargreaves-Mawdsley Oxford, Clarendon P. for the Oxford Historical Society, 1969. [1], xviii, 351 p. plate, port. 23 cm. (Oxford Historical Society. [Publications] new ser., v. 21) [LF517.W6 1969] 76-565426 ISBN 0-901775-01-0 4/4/-
1. Oxford. University—Students. I. Hargreaves-Mawdsley, W. N., ed. II. Title. III. Series.

Oxnam, Garfield Bromley, Bp., 1891-1963.

OXNAM, Garfield 287'.6'0924 B
Bromley, Bp., 1891-1963.
I protest / by G. Bromley Oxnam. Westport, Conn. : Greenwood Press, 1979, c1954. 186 p. ; 23 cm. Reprint of the ed. published by Harper, New York. [BX8495.O93A34 1979] 78-21506 ISBN 0-313-21154-X : 16.00
1. Oxnam, Garfield Bromley, Bp., 1891-1963. 2. Methodist Church—Bishops—Biography. 3. United States. Congress. House. Committee on Un-American Activities. 4. Bishops—United States—Biography. I. Title.

SMITH, Rembert Gilman, 922.773
1878-
Garfield Bromley Oxnam, revolutionist? Houston, Tex. [1953] 192p. illus. 21cm. [BX8495.O93S6] 54-16104
1. Oxnam, Garfield Bromley, Bp., 1891- I. Title.

Oxyrhychus papyrl.

BIBLE. N. T. Apocryphal books.
Logia Iesou. Greek. 1920.
The sayings of Jesus from Oxyrhynchus, ed. with introduction, critical apparatus and commentary, by Hugh G. Evelyn White ... Cambridge [Eng.] University press, 1920. lxxvi. 48 p. 20 cm. Bibliography: p. xi-xiii. [BS2970.W5] A 21
1. Oxyrhychus papyrl. 2. Bible. N. T. Gospels—Criticism, interpretation, etc. 3. Bible. N. T. Apocryphal books, Gospel according to the Hebrews—Criticism, interpretation, etc. I. Bible. N. T. Apocryphal books. Logia Iesou. English. 1920. II. Evelyn-White, Hugh Gerard, d. 1924, ed. III. Title.

Ozanam, Antoine Frederic, 1813-1853.

AUGE, Thomas E. 282.440924
Frederic Ozanam and his world. Milwaukee, Bruce [c.1966] xi, 148p. 21cm. [BX4705.O8A83] 66-15088 3.75
1. Ozanam, Antoine Frederic, 1813-1853. I. Title.

DERUM, James Patrick. 928.4
Apostle in a top hat; the life of Frederic Ozanam. 1st ed. Garden City, N.Y., Hanover House, 1960. 240 p. 22 cm. [BX4705.O8D4] 60-13515
1. Ozanam, Antoine Frederic, 1813-1853. I. Title.

O'MEARA, Kathleen, 1839- 922.
1888.
Frederic Ozanam, professor at the Sorbonne; his life and works, by Kathleen Omeara (Grace Ramsay) ... with a preface by His Eminence Cardinal Manning; preface to the present edition by Thomas M. Mulry ... New York, Christian press association publishing company [c1911] xx, iii-vii, 345 p. 19 cm. [BX4705.O8O6 1911] 11-9947
1. Ozanam, Antoine Frederic, 1813-1853. I. Title.

SCHIMBERG, Albert Paul, 928.4
1885-
...The great friend: Frederick Ozanam. Milwaukee, The Bruce publishing company [1946] vii, 344 p. 2 port. on 1 l. 20 cm. "A list of books": p. 336-339. [BX4705.O8S4] 46-1103
1. Ozanam, Antoine Frederic, 1813-1853. I. Title.

Ozark Mountains-Church history.

SECHLER, Earl Truman, 1890- 277.6
Our religious heritage; church history of the Ozarks, 1806-1906. Springfield, Mo., Westport Press; [stamped: c1961] 123p. 22cm. Includes bibliography. [BR540.S4] 62-1411
1. Ozark Mountains-Church history. 2. Ozark Mountains— Religion. I. Title.

Ozone Park, N.Y. St. James Lutheran church.

KREIDER, Harry Julius, 284.1747
1896-
The story of St. James; a quarter century of St. James Lutheran church, Ozone Park, New York city, by Harry Julius Kreider ... New York city [Ann Arbor, Mich., Lithoprinted by Edwards brothers, inc.] 1946. vii, 116 p. illus. (incl. ports., facsim., music) pl. 22 1/2 cm. [BX8076.O9S3] 46-20669
1. Ozone Park, N.Y. St. James Lutheran church. I. Title.

P document (Biblical criticism)

MILGROM, Jacob, 1923- 221.4'4
Studies in Levitical terminology. Berkeley, University of California Press, 1970- v. 27 cm. (University of California

publications. Near Eastern studies, v. 14) Contents.Contents.—1. The encroacher and the Levite. The term 'Aboda. Bibliography (p. 91-94) [PJ4801.M5] 76-626141 ISBN 0-520-09308-9 (v. 1) 5.50 (v. 1)
1. P document (Biblical criticism) 2. Tabernacle—Desecration. 3. Levites. 4. 'Avodah (The word) I. Title. II. Series: California. University. University of California publications. Near Eastern studies, v. 14

POLZIN, Robert. 222'.1'06
Late Biblical Hebrew : toward an historical typology of Biblical Hebrew prose / by Robert Polzin. Missoula, Mont. : Published by Scholars Press for the Harvard Semitic Museum, c1976. xii, 170 p. ; 21 cm. (Harvard Semitic monographs ; 12) Bibliography: p. 161-165. [BS1345.5.P64] 76-3559 ISBN 0-89130-101-1 : 6.00
1. Bible. O.T. Chronicles—Language, style. 2. Bible. O.T. Pentateuch—Language, style. 3. P document (Biblical criticism) 4. Hebrew language—Style. I. Title. II. Series.

Pache, Boris N.

PACHE, Boris N. 286.7'3 B
By ways I knew not / Boris N. Pache. Washington, D.C. : Review and Herald Pub. Association, 1980. p. cm. [BX6193.P23A33] 80-15003 pbk. : 4.95
1. Pache, Boris N. 2. Seventh-Day Adventists—Biography. I. Title.

Pacher, Michael, 15th cents.

*RONEN, Avraham. 755
The Peter and Paul altarpiece and Friedrich Pacher. New York, Humanities Press [1975] vi, 106 p. col. ill. 27 cm. Bibliography: p. 104-106. [NK2190] ISBN 0-391-00356-9 19.50.
1. Pacher, Michael, 15th cents. 2. Altarpieces. I. Title.

Pachomius, Saint.

THE life of 270.1'092'4 B
Pachomius : vita prima Graeca / translated by Apostolos N. Athanassakis ; introd. by Birger A. Pearson. Missoula, Mont. : Published by Scholars Press for the Society of Biblical Literature, c1975. xi, 201 p. : 24 cm. (Texts and translations - Society of Biblical Literature ; 7) (Early Christian literature series ; 2) English and Greek. "Contains the text of G1 [i.e. the Vita prima Graeca] as edited by F. Halkin." Bibliography: p. xi. [BR1720.P23V5613] 75-37766 ISBN 0-89130-065-1 : 2.80
1. Pachomius, Saint. I. Athanassakis, Apostolos N. II. Title. III. Series. IV. Series: Society of Biblical Literature. Texts and translations ; 7.

THE Life of Saint 281'.3 s
Pachomius and his disciples / translated and introduced by Armand Veilleux ; foreword by Adalbert de Vogue. Kalamazoo, Mich. : Cistercian Publications, 1981. xxx, 493 p. ; 23 cm. (Pachonian koinonia ; v. 1) Bibliography: p. 481-488. [BR1720.P23P3 vol. 1] 281'.3'0924 B 19 80-21796 ISBN 0-87907-945-2 pbk. : 12.95
1. Pachomius, Saint. 2. Christian saints—Egypt—Biography. 3. Monasticism and religious orders—Egypt. 4. Monasticism and religious orders—Early church, ca. 30-600. I. Veilleux, Armand. II. Title. III. Series. IV. Cistercian studies series ; 45

Pacianus, Saint, bp. of Barcelona, 4th century

MCAULIFFE, Clarence R. 922.
The penitential doctrine of Saint Pacianus [by] Rev. Clarence McAuliffe ... [n.p., 1941] 1 p. l., [365]-381, [20]-34 p. 22 1/2 cm. Summary of thesis (S.T.D.)--St. Louis university. "Reprinted from Theological studies, vol. 1, no. 4, 1940; vol. 2, no. 1, 1941." [BR1720.P25M3] 42-45628
1. Pacianus, Saint, bp. of Barcelona, 4th cent. 2. Penance—Hist. I. Title.

Pacific Garden Mission, Chicago.

ADAIR, James R., 267.10977311
1923-
The Old Lighthouse; the story of the Pacific Garden Mission, by James R. Adair. Chicago, Moody Press [1966] 157 p. 22 cm. [BV2656.C4P26] 66-9629
1. Pacific Garden Mission, Chicago. I. Title.

HENRY, Carl Ferdinand Howard, 269
1913-
The Pacific garden mission, a doorway to heaven, by Carl F. H. Henry; introduction by H. A. Ironside, LITT.D. Grand Rapids, Mich., Zondervan publishing house [1942] 9 p., 2 l., 13-142 p. 2 pl. on 1 l. 20 cm. [BV2656.C4P3] 42-24208
1. Pacific garden mission, Chicago. I. Title.

Pacifism.

CADOUX, Cecil John, 327'.172
1883-1947.
Christian pacifism re-examined. With a new introd. for the Garland ed. by John M. Swomley, Jr. New York, Garland Pub., 1972. 12, xx, 245 p. 22 cm. (The Garland library of war and peace) Reprint of the 1940 ed. [JX1953.C25 1972] 79-147668 ISBN 0-8240-0426-4
1. Pacifism. 2. World War, 1939-1945—Religious aspects. I. Title. II. Series.

THE dagger and the cross;
an examination of Christian pacifism...Foreword by John C. Bennett. Nyack, N. Y., Fellowship publications, 1958. 142p. 20cm. 'Fellowship paperback edition.'
I. Rutenber, Culbert Gerow, 1909-

FREEMAN, Ruth (St. John) 289.6
1901-
Quakers and peace, by Ruth Freeman, aided by Robert and Etta Vogle. Ithaca, N.Y., Pacifist Research Bureau [1947] 70 p. 21 cm. (Pacifism and government, ser. 5, no. 3. July 1947) "The first three-fourths of this pamphlet is a condensation of ... The Quakers in peace and war, by Margaret Hirst." Full name: Ruth Nimme (St. John) Freeman. [BX7748.W2F65] 47-30983
1. Pacifism. 2. Friends, Society of—Hist. I. Hirst, Margaret Esther. The Quakers in peace and war. II. Title. III. Series: Pacifist Research Bureau. Pacifism and government, ser. 5, no. 3. July 1947

FRIEDMAN, Maurice S. 296.38
The covenant of peace; a personal witness. Wallingford, Pa., Pendle Hill. [c.1960] 32p. 19cm. (Pendle Hill pamphlet 110) (Bibl.) 60-9785 .35 pap.,
1. Pacifism. I. Title.

FRIENDS, Society of. American Friends Service Committee.
Speak truth to power, a Quaker search for an alternative to violence; a study of international conflict. [Philadelphia, 1955] 71p. 23cm. Includes bibliography. A56
1. Pacifism. 2. U. S.—For. rel.—1945- I. Title.

HOYT, Herman Arthur, 230.992
1909-
Then would my servants fight. Winona Lake, Ind., Brethren Missionary Herald Co. [1956] 115p. 20cm. [BX7829.B64H6] 230.65 56-39520
1. Pacifism. 2. The Brethren Church (Progressive Dunkers)—Doctrinal and controversial works. I. Title.

LIND, Millard, 1918- 289.7
Answer to war; illustrated by Allan Eitzen. Scottdale, Pa., Mennonite Pub. House, 1952. 143 p. 20 cm. [BR115.P4L5] 52-30259
1. Pacifism. I. Title.

MAHAFFEY, Margaret M. 261
The cause and cure of war. Boston, Christopher Pub. House [1949] 64 p. port. 16 cm. [BR115.P4M32] 49-50087
1. Pacifism. I. Title.

RAVEN, Charles Earle, *261.6
1885-
The theological basis of Christian pacifism. New York, Fellowship Publications [1951] 87 p. 20 cm. (The Robert Treat Paine lectures, 1950) [BR115.P4R3] 52-6753
1. Pacifism. I. Title.

TOLSTOI, Lev 261.8'73
Nikolaevich, graf, 1828-1910.
The law of love and the law of violence [by] Leo Tolstoy. Translated by Mary Koutouzow Tolstoy. With a foreword by Baroness Budberg. [1st ed.] New York, Holt, Rinehart and Winston [1970] x, 101 p. 22 cm. Translation of La loi de l'amour et la loi de la violence. [HM278.T6313 1970] 73-105433 3.95
1. Pacifism. 2. Government, Resistance to. I. Title.

TOLSTOI, Lev Nikolaevich, 172.4
graf, 1828-1910.
The law of love and the law of violence, tr. by Mary Koutouzow Tolstoy. New York, R. Field [1948] 130 p. 21 cm. "Translated from the French."--Dust jacket. [BR115.P4T563] 48-9682
1. Pacifism. 2. Government, Resistance to. I. Tolstoy, Mary (Frothingham) Koutouzoff, comtesse. II. Title.

WENGER, John Christian, 261.8'73
1910-
Pacifism and Biblical nonresistance, by J. C. Wenger. Scottdale, Pa., Herald Press [1968] 28 p. 20 cm. (Focal pamphlet series, no. 15) "Papers ... read at the Peace Witness Seminar, Evangelicals in Social Action, Eastern Mennonite College, Harrisonburg, Virginia, November 30, 1968." [BT736.4.W4] 68-7991
1. Pacifism. 2. Evil, Non-resistance to. I. Title.

Pacifism—History.

BROCK, Peter, 1920- 261.8'73
Pacifism in Europe to 1914. Princeton, N.J., Princeton University Press, 1972. x, 556 p. 25 cm. (His A History of pacifism, v. 1) Bibliography: p. 505-544. [JX1938.B76] 75-166362 ISBN 0-691-04608-5 17.50
1. Pacifism—History. I. Title.

BROCK, Peter, 1920- 289.6'73
Pioneers of the peaceable kingdom. Princeton, N.J., Princeton University Press [1970, c1968] xvi, 382 p. 22 cm. "The chapters of the present volume are reprinted from a more extensive book: Pacifism in the United States: from the Colonial era to the First World War (Princeton University Press, 1968)." Bibliography: p. 359-373. [BX7635.B76] 70-123078 ISBN 0-691-00573-7 3.45
1. Friends, Society of—History. 2. Pacifism—History. I. Title.

HIRST, Margaret Esther. 289.6
The Quakers in peace and war; an account of their peace principles and practice, by Margaret E. Hirst. With an introd. by Rufus M. Jones. With a new introd. for the Garland ed. by Edwin B. Bronner. New York, Garland Pub., 1972. 560 p. 22 cm. (The Garland library of war and peace) Reprint of the 1923 ed. [BX7748.W2H5 1972] 70-147671 ISBN 0-8240-0429-9
1. Friends, Society of—History. 2. Pacifism—History. I. Title. II. Series.

Packard, Thomas Jones, 1854-1912, ed.

PACKARD, Joseph, 1812-1902. 922.
Recollections of a long life, by Joseph Packard ... Edited by Rev. Thomas J. Packard. Washington, D.C., B. S. Adams, 1902. 4 p. l., 5-364 p. plates, 2 port. (incl. front.) 23 1/2cm. [BX5995.P25A3] 3-844
1. Packard, Thomas Jones, 1854-1912, ed. I. Title.

Paddock, Benjamin Green, 1789-1872.

PADDOCK, Zachariah, 1798- 922.773
1879.
Memoir of Rev. Benjamin G. Paddock, with brief notices of early ministerial associates. Also, an appendix, containing more extended sketches of Rev. George Gary, Abner Chase, William Case, Seth Mattison, Isaac Puffer, Charles Giles, and others. By Rev. Z. Paddock, D.D. New York, Nelson & Phillips; Cincinnati, Hitchcock & Walden, 1875. 377 p. 2 port. (incl. front.) 19 1/2 cm. [BX8495.P2P3] 36-37390
1. Paddock, Benjamin Green, 1789-1872. 2. Gary, George, 1793-1855. 3. Chase, Abner, 1784-1854. 4. Case, William, 1780-1855. 5. Mattison, Seth, 1788-1843. 6. Puffer, Isaac, 1784-1853. 7. Giles, Charles, 1783-1867. I. Title.

Paddock, Robert Lewis, Bp. 1869-1939.

MINOR, Maria Sheerin. 922.373
Portrait of a rebel; the story of Robert Lewis Paddock, 1869-1939, by Maria Minor. New York, Seabury Press [1965] vii, 150 p. 22 cm. [BX5995.P26M5] 64-19628
1. Paddock, Robert Lewis, Bp., 1869-1939. I. Title.

Padgett's Creek Baptist Church.

SPARKS, Claude 286'.1757'41
Ezell.
A history of Padgett's Creek Baptist Church. [Union, S. C., Counts Print. Co., 1967] v, 172 [27] p. illus., map, ports. 22 cm. [BX6480.P26P34] 68-1836
1. Padgett's Creek Baptist Church. I. Title.

SPARKS, Claude 286'.1757'41
Ezell.
A history of Padgett's Creek Baptist Church. [Union, S.C., Counts Print. Co., 1967] v, 172, [27] p. illus., map, ports. 22 cm. [BX6480.P26P34] 68-1836
1. Padgett's Creek Baptist Church. I. Title.

Padma Sambhava, ca. 717-ca. 762.

YE-SES-MTSHO- 294.3'6'30924 B
RGYAL, 8thcent.
The life and liberation of Padmasambhava / as recorded by Yeshe Tsogyal [i.e. Ye-ses-mtsho-rgyal], rediscovered by Urgyan Linpa ; translated into French as de dict de Padma by Gustav-Charles Toussaint ; translated into English by Kenn Dougals and Gwendolyn Bays ; corrected with the original Tibetan manuscript and with an introduction by Tarthany Tulka. Berkeley, Calif. : Dharma Pub., 1978. 2 v. (xxxiv, 769 p. : ill. ; 26 cm. (Tibetan translation series) [BQ7950.P327Y4713] 78-17445 ISBN 0-913546-19-4 (v. 1) : 50.00. ISBN 0-913546-20-8 (vol. 2) : 50.00
1. Padma Sambhava, ca. 717-ca. 762. 2. Lamas—Tibet—Biography. I. O-rgyan-glin-pa, gter-ston, b. 1323. II. Tarthang Tulku. III. Title. IV. Series.

Paganism.

COMBES, Gustave, 1880- 201
Revival of paganism. Translated by Augustine Stock. St. Louis, Herder, 1950. v, 360 p. 25 cm. Translation of Le retour offensif du paganisme. Bibliographical footnotes. [BR127.C583] 50-3484
1. Paganism. 2. Religion—Philosophy. I. Title.

FARRER, James Anson, 1849-
Paganism and Christianity, by J. A. Farrer ... London, Watts & co., 1910. 112 p. 21 cm. (On cover: No. 43.--R. P. A. cheap reprints. Classical & Christian ideals) "Issued for the Rationalist press association, limited." Portrait of author on cover. A 22
1. Paganism. 2. Christianity. I. Rationalist press association, limited, London. II. Title.

FRANKE, Elmer E.
Pagan festivals in Christian worship, thoughts on the day of Christ's resurrection, by E. E. Franke. New York city, E. E. Franke [c1919] 79 p. illus. 19 cm. [BV35.F8] 19-16906
I. Title.

GEFFCKEN, Johannes, 1861- 291
1935.
The last days of Greco-Roman paganism / by Johannes Geffcken ; translated by Sabine MacCormack. Amsterdam ; New York : North Holland Pub. Co. ; New York : Distributors for the U.S.A. and Canada, Elsevier North-Holland, 1978 i.e. 1977. p. cm. (Europe in the Middle Ages ; v. 9) Translation of Der Ausgang des griechisch-romischen Heidentums. This

translation of the 1929 rev. ed. of the original 1920 ed. has up-dated references and index added by S. MacCormack. Includes index. Bibliography: p. [BR166.G4313] 77-23029 ISBN 0-444-85005-8 : 52.25
1. Paganism. 2. Church history—Primitive and early church, ca. 30-600. I. Title. II. Series.

HAYNES, Willard Calvin, 1875-
Twentieth century paganism; a review of the Old and New Testaments, showing their teachings, derived from pagan mythology, to be without truth, inspiration or authorship; together with a comparison of the six leading mythologies as affecting Christianity when applied to the teachings of Moses and Christ, by Willard C. Haynes, M.D. New York, Peter Eckler publishing company, 1915. 496 p. 20 cm. $2.50 15-24505
I. Title.

LEWIS, Abram Herbert, 1836-1908.
Paganism surviving in Christianity, by Abram Herbert Lewis... New York, London, G. P. Putnam's sons, 1892. xv, 309 p. 21 cm. [BR135.L4] 41-24294
1. Paganism. 2. Christianity and other religions. I. Title.

MAURIER, Henri. 234
The other covenant; a theology of paganism. Translated by Charles McGrath. Glen Rock, N.J., Newman Press [1968] xiii, 268 p. 21 cm. Translation of Essai d'une theologie du paganisme. Bibliographical footnotes. [BT759.M313] 68-55400 4.95
1. Paganism. 2. Salvation outside the church. I. Title.

Page, Harlan, 1791-1834.

HALLOCK, William Allen, 1794-1880. 922
Memoir of Harlan Page; or, The power of prayer and personal effort for the souls of individuals. By William A. Hallock ... New York, American tract society [1835] 2 p. l. [3]-230 p. front. (port.) pl. 15 cm. Added t. p., engraved, with vignette. Music: p. 221-222. [BV3785.P3H3 1835a] 1-955
1. Page, Harlan, 1791-1834. I. Title.

HALLOCK, William Allen, 1794-1880. 922
Memoir of Harlan Page; or, The power of prayer and personal effort for the souls of individuals. By William A. Hallock ... New York, Leavitt, Lord & co.; Boston, Crocker & Brewster, 1836. 2 p. l. [3]-230 p. front. (port.) 15 1/2 cm. Added t. p. engraved, with vignette. Music: p. 221-222. [BV3785.P3H3 1836] 1-956
1. Page, Harlan, 1791-1834. I. Title.

Page, Kirby, 1890-1957.

PAGE, Kirby. 225
Something more, a consideration of the vast, undeveloped resources of life [by] Kirby Page. New York, Association press, 1920. 5 p. l., 3-88 p. 20 cm. (On verse of half-title: New generation series) [BR121.P25] 20-11091
I. Title.

PAGE, Kirby, 1890-1957. 230
Kirby Page and the social gospel : an anthology / edited, with an introd., by Charles Chatfield and Charles DeBenedetti. New York : Garland Pub., 1976. p. cm. (The Garland library of war and peace) Bibliography: p. [BR85.P23 1976] 70-147695 ISBN 0-8240-0451-5 lib.bdg. : 25.00
1. Page, Kirby, 1890-1957. 2. Page, Kirby, 1890-1957—Bibliography. 3. Theology—Addresses, essays, lectures. 4. Church and social problems—Addresses, essays, lectures. I. Title. II. Series.

Page, Mrs. Anne Randolph (Meade) 1781-1838.

ANDREWS, Charles Wesley, 1807-1875. 920.7
Memoir of Mrs. Anne R. Page. By Rev. C. W. Andrews. Philadelphia, H. Hooker, 1844. 101 p. front. (port.) 16 cm. [BR1725.P2A6] 38-7491
1. Page, Mrs. Anne Randolph (Meade) 1781-1838. I. Title.

Pageants.

BOWAN, Harold Leonard, 1889-
Heroic faith of pioneers; a pageant written for the seventy-fifth anniversary of the First Presbyterian church, June 2-9, 1929, by Harold Leonard Bowman. [Portland, Or., 1929] 1 p. l., 65-100 p. 20 cm. [BX211.P75F5] 29-18429
1. Pageants. 2. Portland, Or. First Presbyterian church. I. Title.

BREWSTER, May M. 268.75
We would see Jesus, a Children's day pageant for younger children; book and lyrics by May M. Brewster; incidental music by Stewart Landon ... Dayton, O., New York [etc.] Lorenz publishing co., c1945. 20 p. 22 1/2 cm. [BV1572.C45B7] 45-17401
1. Pageants. I. Landon, Stewart. II. Title.

CLAUSEN, Bernard Chancellor, 1892-
Pilgrim's progress in pageant, by Rev. Bernard C. Clausen and Florence L. Purington. New York, American tract society [c1928] 5 p. l., 73 p. 21 cm. [PR3330.Z33C6] 29-22542
1. Bunyan, John. Pilgrim's progress-Dramatizations. 2. Pageants. I. Purington, Florence Lois, 1893- joint author. II. Title.

COPENHAVER, Laura Scherer. 268.
Short pageants for the Sunday school, by Laura S. Copenhaver. Garden City, N. Y., Doubleday, Doran & company, inc., 1929. xi, 152 p. illus. 20 cm. Contains music. [BV1575.C6] 29-20807
1. Pageants. 2. Sunday-schools. I. Title.

COPENHAVER, Laura Scherer. 266
The striking of America's hour; a pageant of Christian liberty, by Laura Scherer Copenhaver, Katherine Scherer Cronk, Mathilde A. Vossler ... Philadelphia, Pa., Literature headquarters, Women's missionary society, The United Lutheran church in America [c1925] 15 p. 1 illus. 23 cm. [BV2086.C55] ca 25
1. Pageants. I. Cronk, Katharine (Scherer) Mrs. 1877- joint author. II. Vossler, Mathilde A., joint author. III. Title.

COPENHAVER, Laura Scherer. 172.
The way of peace; a pageant, by Laura Scherer Copenhaver Katharine Scherer Cronk, Ruth Mougey Worrell. Philadelphia, Pa., Literature headquarters, Women's missionary society, The United Lutheran church in America [c1924] 19 p. 23 cm. [JX1936.5.C6] 24-29527
I. Cronk, Katharine (Scherer) Mrs. 1877- joint author. II. Worrell, Ruth Mougey, joint author. III. Title.

COX, Mabel Crampton. 791.6
Nobody's child, a Christmas pageant, by Mabel Crampton Cox ... Franklin, O., Denver, Colo., Eldridge entertainment house, incorporated, c1930. 16 p., 1 l. 19 cm. (On cover: Eldridge Christmas material) Includes music. [PN6120.C5C6718] 40-23621
1. Pageants. 2. Christmas plays. I. Title.

CREASMAN, Myrtle R. 791.6
Pageants of the kingdom [by] Myrtle R. Creasman. Nashville, Tenn., Broadman press [1943] 117 p.22 1/2 cm. Includes songs with music (piano accompaniment) [PN3205.C7] 43-3546
1. Pageants. I. Title.

DEMEREST, Ada Rose. 268.
Junior pageants; pageants and dramatic programs designed especially for junior groups, by Ada Rose Demerest ... Cincinnati, O., The Standard publishing company [c1927] 93 p. illus. 24 cm. Contains music. [BV1575.D4] 28-30
1. Pageants. 2. Children's plays. 3. Religious education. I. Title.

EDLAND, Elisabeth. 285.
The tercentenary pageant, 1628-1928, a dramatic representation of the history of the Reformed church in America, by Elisabeth Edland in collaboration with the Pageant committee. New York city, The Tercentenary committee, c1928. 106 p. 23 cm. [BX9515.E25] 28-10982
1. Pageants. 2. Reformed church in America—Hist. I. Title.

EMERSON, Elizabeth (Holaday) 922.
Life of George Fox in story and scene, by Elizabeth H. Emerson and Gladys May Hunt. Suggestions for stage setting and costuming by Eva Rae Marshall. Richmond, Ind., George Fox tercentenary committee of the five years meeting of Friends, 1924. 32 p. 20 cm. Bibliography: p. 32. [BX7795.F7E8] 27-9554
1. Fox, George, 1624-1691. 2. Pageants. I. Hunt, Gladys May, joint author. II. Title.

FERRIS, Anita Brockway, 1881- 266
The gift of light; a missionary pagenat, by Anita B. Ferris...prepared for the jubilee celebration of the Woman's board of missions, Nov. 12-16, 1917. [Burlington, Vt., Free press printing co., c1917] 56 p., 1 l. 23 cm. [BV2087.F4] 17-24677
1. Pagents. 2. Woman's board of missions. Boston. I. Title.

FIELD, Elliot, 1875- 791.6
Let there be light! A pageant-drama, by Elliot Field. New York, N.Y., American Bible society [c1933] 7 p. l., 17-87 p. 23 cm. Presented by the American Bible society for the use of churches which wish to present the Bible in dramatic form on universal Bible Sunday or other occasions. cf. Foreword. Music: p. 82-85. "Books on religious drama": p. 81. [PN6120.R4F47] 33-38216
1. Pageants. I. American Bible society. II. Title.

GITHENS, Harry Wright, 1895- 791.6
One rehearsal pageants for the church, by Harry W. Githens. Cincinnati, O., The Standard publishing company [c1935] 224 p. 20 cm. [PN3205.G5] 36-3121
1. Pageants. I. Title.

HERON, Henrietta, comp. 268.
Pageants for the year compiled by Henmetta Heron, chapter on costuming by J. H Shonkwiller Cincinnati, O., The Standard publishing company [c1928] 192 p. illus. (incl. music) 24 cm. Bibliography: p. 192. [BV1575.H4] 28-11738
1. Pageants. 2. Children's plays. 3. Religious education. I. Shonkweiler, James Harvey, 1877- II. Title.

JONES, Jessie Mae (Orton) 394.268
Pageant text for A little Child, the Christmas story told in Bible verses, with directions for presentation. New York, Viking Press, 1946. 15 p. 22 cm. [BT315.J62] 48-4272
1. Pageants. I. Jones, Jessie Mae (Orton) comp. A little Child. II. Title. III. Title: A little Child.

MCGROARTY, John Steven, 1862- 791.6
The mission play, a pageant play in three acts, by John S. McGroarty. [Los Angeles] c1911. 2 p. l., 3-40, [1] p. 24 1/2 x 12 cm. [PN3206.M3] 37-31811
1. Pageants. 2. Missions—California—Drama. I. Title.

MACNICKLE, Mary Donatus, sister, 1885- 791.6
The greater glory; a pageant of the English martyrs, Saints John Fisher and Thomas More, by Sister Mary Donatus... Immaculata, Pa., Immaculata college [1936] 87 p. 21 1/2 cm. [PN3206.M34] 37-32889
1. Fisher, John Saint bp. of Rochester, 1469?-1535—Drama. 2. More, Sir Thomas, Saint, 1478-1535—Drama. 3. Pageants. I. Title.

METHODIST Episcopal church. Board of education. 268.75
The new Children's day book, services of worship, dramatizations, and pageants for the observance of children's day in the church. New York, Cincinnati [etc.] The Methodist book concern [c1937] 88 p. illus. 23 cm. Music: p. 78-84. [BV1572.C45M4] 39-426
1. Pageants. I. Title. II. Title: Children's day book.

MILLER, Madeleine (Sweeney) Mrs., 1890- 792
Church pageantry, by Madeleine Sweeney Miller (Mrs. J. Lane Miller) introduction by Adna W. Leonard ... designed as a handbook for amateur producers of educational dramatics; and as a textbook for study classes in individual churches, at midwinter and summer institutes and conferences of young people. New York, Cincinnati, The Methodist book concern [c1924] 216 p. front., plates. 20 1/2 cm. "The fruits of peace; a pageant for young people, by Madeleine Sweeney Miller": p. [175]-200. [Full name: Mrs. Madeleine Georgeanna (Sweeney) Miller] Bibliography: p. [201]-216. [BV1472.M5] 24-21048
1. Pageants. 2. Religious drama. I. Title.

NIEDERMEYER, Frederick David, 1881- 244
The missing cross, a pageant, by Rev. Frederick D. Niedermeyer ... Perth Amboy, N. J., LaRoe press, c1933. 10 p. diagr. 21 x 12 cm. [PN6120.R4N55] 37-33587
1. Pageants. 2. International society of Christian endeavor—Drama. I. Title.

NIEDERMEYER, Frederick David, 1881- 791.6
To show the mind of Christ, a pageant, by the Rev. Frederick D.Niedermeyer ... Perth Amboy, N. J., La Roe press, c1931. 19 p. diagr. 21 cm. [PN3206.N43] 37-31820
1. Pageants. I. Title.

[SHANNON, Mattie Bayly] 1885- 791.6
A garden of praise; a pageant for children's day and general use, by Martha Bayly [pseud.]; music by Arthur Grantley. A pageant for the children with Scriptural truth ... New York, N.Y., Tullar-Meredith co., c1942. 17 p. 22 cm. The third page of cover is numbered as page 17. [PN6120.R4S453] 42-14108
I. Title.

SKINNER, Florence W. 791.6
The hope of the world, a pageant in one act, by Florence W. Skinner ... Franklin, O., Denver, Colo., Eldridge entertainment house, inc., c1926. 15 p. 19 cm. (On cover: Eldridge church entertainments) [PN3206.S437] 37-33022
1. Pageants. I. Title.

SMITH, Mary Brainerd, 1871- 791
The quest, a missionary pageant, by Mary Brainerd Smith. Philadelphia, The Union press, c1926. 8 p. diagr. 21 cm. [BV2086.S7] 46-30559
1. Pageants. I. Title.

SQUIRES, Beulah Greene. 244
The halo of the cross, a pageant for chuches which may be used for special days of Sunday night services; consists of a dialogue interspersed with twelve visions, by Beulah Greene Squires ... Indianapolis, Ind., Meigs publishing company [c1931] 19 p. 18 cm. (On cover: Meigs religious plays and pageants) [PN6120.R4S73] 37-33451
1. Pageants. I. Title.

STEVENS, Edmund Harding, 1882- 812.5
The Holy night; a mystery play for Christmas-tide, by the Rev. Edmund H. Stevens. Milwaukee, Wis., Morehouse publishing co. [c1930] 2 p. l., 16 p. 21 cm. [PN6120.C5S69] 394.268 30-21762
1. Pageants. 2. Christmas plays. I. Title.

WICKSER, Josephine Wilhelm, Mrs. 791.6
Three pageants ... by Josephine Wilhelm Wickser. New York, The H. W. Wilson company, 1936. 48 p. 19 1/2 cm. Contents.--A pageant of the library.--A pageant of Christmas.--A pageant of the garden. [PN3205.W5 1936] 36-14769
1. Pageants. I. Title.

WILLCOX, Helen Lida, 1883- 287
Along the years; a pageant of Methodism, in prologue, three episodes two interludes and finale, by Helen L. Willcox. New York, Cincinnati [etc.] The Methodist book concern [c1930] 60 p. 23 cm. [BX8232.W5] 30-6392
1. Pageants. 2. Methodism—Hist.—Drama. I. Title.

WILLCOX, Helen Lida, 1883- 266
El Dorado; a pageant of South American freedom, in a prelude, four episodes, and two interludes, by Helen L. Willcox... New York, Missionary education movement of

the United States and Canada [c1917] 48 p. 22 1/2 cm. "Aids to the study of South America": p. 48 and p. [3] of cover. [BV2087.W6] 17-11239
I. Title.

WILSON, Dorothy Clarke. 791.6
The sorrowful star; a Christmas pageant, by Dorothy Clarke Wilson ... Boston, Mass., and Los Angeles, Cal. [Walter H. Baker company, c1939] 27 p. 19 cm. [PN6120.C5W5458] 40-3392
1. Pageants. 2. Christmas plays. I. Title.

WILSON, Dorothy Clarke. 791.6
The straight white road; a pageant of Christian growth, by Dorothy Clarke Wilson ... Boston, Mass, and Los Angeles, Cal. [Walter H. Baker company, c1937] 26 p. 18 1/2 cm. [PN6120.R4W644] 37-32287
1. Pageants. I. Title.

WILSON, Louis, 1899- 268.75
The pageant of the helping hands, together with a service of worship for children's day [by] Louis Wilson; music selected by Violet Otto Wilson. New York, Cincinnati [etc.] The Methodist book concern, c1934. 16 p. illus., diagrs. 23 cm. Music: p. 5. [Full name: Louis LeRoy Wilson] [PN6120.R4W67] 37-32922
1. Pageants. I. Title.

WIRE, Edith. 791.6
The pageant of the nativity; the story of the first Christmas, by Edith Wire. Salt Lake City, Utah, Wire company, c1940. 20 p. 20 1/2 cm. [PN6120.C5W493] 41-23905
1. Pageants. 2. Christmas plays. I. Title.

Pageants—Auburn, N. Y.

LANGDON, William Chauncy, 1871- 016.
The centennial pageant of Auburn theological seminary, 1818-1918, by William Chauncy Langdon ... on the campus of the seminary at Auburn, New York, October 8-9-10, 1918. [Auburn, The Jacobs press, c1918] 60 p. 25 cm. "Motifs and themes of the music": p. [55]-60. [BV4070.A765 1918] 19-94
1. Pageants—Auburn, N. Y. 2. Auburn theological seminary. I. Title.

Pageants—St. Louis.

LONG, George, 1871-
Pageant of the church, given in honor of the General convention of the Protestant Episcopal church The pageant designed and produced by the Rev. George Long. [St. Louis, Woodward & Tiernan printing co., c1916] 59 p. illus. 23 cm. [BX5883.L6] 16-22923
1. Pageants—St. Louis. 2. Protestant Episcopal church in the U. S. A.—Hist. I. Title.

Paget, Henry Luke, bp. of Chester, 1853-1937.

PAGET, Elma Katie (Hoare) Mrs. 922.342
Henry Luke Paget; portrait and frame, by Elma K. Paget; with 4 illustrations. London, New York [etc.] Longmans, Green and co. [1939] ix, [1] 278 p. front., ports. 22 1/2 cm. "First published, 1939." [BX5199.P23P3] 39-18651 39-18651
1. Paget, Henry Luke, bp. of Chester, 1853-1937. I. Title.

Paige, Charlotte Brayton.

[JUDKINS, Mary Amelia] 922
"Child of gentleness." A memorial of Charlotte Brayton Paige. Written for the Massachusetts Sabbath school society, and approved by the Committee of publication. Boston, Massachusetts Sabbath school society [1855] 54 p. incl. front. 16 cm. [BR1725.P22J8] 38-7488
1. Paige, Charlotte Brayton. I. Massachusetts Sabbath school society. Committee of publication. II. Title.

Pain.

LEWIS, Clive Staples, 1898- 231.8
The problem of pain. New York, Macmillan [1962, c.1944] 160p. 18cm. (mp 120) .95 pap.,
1. Pain. 2. Good and evil. 3. Providence and government of God. I. Title.

LEWIS, Clive Staples, 1898-1963.
The problem of pain. New York, Macmillan [1962] 160 p. 18 cm. (Macmillan paperbacks, 120) 64-47644
1. Pain. 2. Good and evil. 3. Providence and government of God. I. Title.

LINDELL, Paul J., 1915-1974. 248'.86
The mystery of pain. Minneapolis, Augsburg Pub. House [1974] 80 p. 18 cm. [BJ1409.L5] 74-77676 ISBN 0-8066-1424-2 1.75 (pbk.)
1. Pain. I. Title.

PAIN and gladness;
a Biblical study, by a sister in an English community, with a preface by the Rev. J. Neville Figgis... London, New York [etc.] Longmans, Green, and co., 1911. x p., 2 l., 114 p. 19 1/2 cm. A 12
1. Pain. I. Figgis, John Neville, 1866-

THE problem of pain.
New York, Macmillan, 1959. viii, 148p.
1. Pain. 2. Good and evil. 3. Providence and government of God. I. Lewis, Clive Staples, 1898-

SARANO, Jacques, 1920- 111.8'4
The hidden face of pain. Translated by Dennis Pardee. Valley Forge, Judson Press [1970] 222 p. 23 cm. Translation of La douleur. Includes bibliographical references. [BJ1409.S3313] 74-116726 6.95
1. Pain. 2. Good and evil. I. Title.

WATON, Harry.
Pain and pleasure; a philosophy of life, by Harry Waton ... New York, Marx institute, 1919. 128 p. front. (port.) 23 1/2 cm. "Written in the months of July and August, 1909; first edition published by the Marx institute of America in December, 1913; revised in July, 1916." A 41
1. Pain. 2. Pleasure. I. Title.

Paine, Robert, bp., 1799-1882.

RIVERS, Richard Henderson, 1814-1894. 922.
The life of Robert Paine, D. D., bishop of the Methodist Episcopal church, South. By R. H. Rivers ... With an introduction by Rev. W. P. Harrison ... Nashville, Tenn., Southern Methodist publishing house, 1884. 314 p. front. (port.) 19 cm. [BX8495.P24R5] 12-38012
1. Paine, Robert, bp., 1799-1882. I. Title.

Paine, Thomas, 1737-1809.

AN Antidote for Tom Paine's theological and political poison; containing 1. Tom's life interspersed with remarks and reflections by P. Porcupine. 2. An apology for the Bible, in a series of letters addressed to Paine by the bishop of Landaff. 3. An apology for Christianity, by the same learned, elegant writer. 4. An answer to Paine's anarchical nonsense, commonly called, the Rights of man. Philadelphia, Printed for, and sold by, William Cobbett, North Second Street, opposite Christ church, Oct. 1796. 79 p. 1 l., 80, 56, vii, [9]-96 p. 22 1/2 cm. Four pamphlets bound together, with the addition of a general t.-p. No. 1 is Porcupine's political censor for September, 1896, and consists of an abstract of the "Life of Thomas Pain" by Francis Oldys (pseud. of George Chalmers) together with "Remarks on the pamphlets lately published against Peter Porcupine" (p. [54]-79). Bishop Watson's "Apology for the Bible" and "Apology for Christianity" have imprint: Philadelphia. Printed by J. Carey, 1796. Mackenzie's "Answer to Paine's Rights of man" has imprint: Philadelphia. Printed for and sold by William Cobbett, 1796. [BL2742.A6] 8-36468
1. Paine, Thomas, 1737-1809. 2. Paine, Thomas, 1737-1800. The age of reason. 3. Paine, Thomas, 1737-1809. Rights of man. I. Cobbett, William, 1763-1835. II. Porcupine's political censor. III. Chalmers, George, 1742-1825.

LEVI, David, 1740-1799.
A defence of the Old Testament, in a series of letters, addresed to Thomas Paine, author of a book entitled, The age of reason, part the second, being an investigation of true and of fabulous theology. By David Levi ... New York; Printed by William A. Davis, 26 Moore street, for Naphtali Judah, bookseller, no. 47. Water street. 1797. 240 p. 17 cm. 4-2002
I. Title.

MCCLURE, James Baird, 1832-1895, ed. 211
Mistakes of Ingersoll on Thomas Paine, as shown by E. P. Goodwin, D.D. Wm. M. Blackburn, D.D., Bishop Fallows, Rev. Simeon Gilbert, Pere Hyacinthe, Prof. Wilcox, Rev. James Maclaughlin, W. F. Hatfield, D.D., and others. Including also Ingersoll's lecture on Thomas Paine. Edited by J. B. McClure. Chicago, Rhodes & McClure, 1880. 158 p. incl. front., illus., port. 21 1/2 cm. [BL2727.M28] 4-16028
1. Paine, Thomas, 1737-1809. 2. Ingersoll, Robert Green, 1833-1899. Lecture on Thomas Paine, 1880. 3. Rationalism—Controversial literature. I. Title.

MUIR, James, 1757-1820. 211
An examination of the principles contained in the Age of reason. In ten discourses. By James Muir, D. D., minister of the Presbyterian church, Alexandria. Baltimore: Printed by S. & J. Adams, for the Author: and sold by Clarke and Keddie, booksellers, in Market-Street, 1795. v, [7]-166 p. 17 cm. [BL2740.M8] 9-1100
1. Paine, Thomas, 1737-1809. I. Title. II. Title: Age of reason.

PAINE, Thomas, pseud.
The religion of the sun, a posthumous poem of Thomas Paine [pseud.] with a preface, by the proprietor. Philadelphia, Published for the book-sellers, 1826. 1 p. l., 28 p., 1 l. 18 1/2 cm. By Samuel Yorke At Lee (the proprietor)? 4-16097
I. At Lee, Samuel Yorke. II. Title.

PAINE, Thomas, 1737-1809.
The age of reason: being an investigation of true and fabulous theology. By Thomas Paine... Edited by Moncure Daniel Conway... New York, London, G. P. Putnam's sons, 1896. vii, 208 p. 23 1/2 cm. Separate, from Conway's edition of Paine's Writings, with new t.-p., table of contents, and reprint of t.-p. and dedication of the original edition, Paris, printed for Barrois, 1794. "Letters concerning 'The age of reason'": p. 196-208. 4-1971
I. Title.

PAINE, Thomas, 1737-1809.
The age of reason. Being an investigation of true and of fabulous theolgoy. By Thomas Paine... [part I] Philadelphia: Printed, and sold by the booksellers, 1794. vi, [7]-196 p. 17 cm. "Epitome of Lequinio's Prejudice destroyed": p. 153-188. "Twenty-five precepts of reason," by J. Graset St. Sauveur: p. 189-192. "France. National convention...(8 May, 1793)" decrees concerning the institution of national festivals: p. 194-196. 4-1961
I. Lequinio, Joseph Marie, b. 1755 II. Grasset de Saint-Sauveur, Jaques, 1757-1810. III. Title.

PAINE, Thomas, 1737-1809.
The complete religious and theological works of Thomas Paine... Illustrated ed. New York, P. Eckler [1892] 4 p. l., [5]-432 p. front., pl., port. 21 cm. Parts I, III, and IV have special t.-p. [BL2735.A1 1892] 4-1953
I. Title.
Contents omitted.

PAINE, Thomas, 1737-1809.
The Simpson-Paine combination of facts, truths and reasons, the great moral way; Thomas Paine's Age of reason, rev., modernized, changed and harmonized with present state of enlightenment on invented false and fabulous theology, by Thomas Jefferson Simpson... St. Louis, Mo., Nixon-Jones printing co., 1912. 241, [7] p. 2 port. 20 1/2 cm. [With Simpson, Thomas Jefferson. Simpson's Bible; a comparison of science and religion... [St. Louis] 1912. 12-12700
I. Simpson, Thomas Jefferson. II. Title.

PAINE, Thomas, 1737-1809.
The theological works of Thomas Paine. To which are added the Profession of faith of a Savoyard vicar, by J. J. Rousseau; and other miscellaneous pieces. Boston, Printed for the advocates of common sense, 1840. 384 p. 20 cm. Title vignette. 16-24020
I. Rousseau, Jean Jacques, 1712-1778. II. Title.

PRIESTLEY, Joseph, 1733-1804. 192
A continuation of the Letters to the philosophers and politicians of France on the subject of religion, and of the Letters to a philosophical unbeliever in answer to Mr. Paine's Age of reason / by Joseph Priestley. Millwood, N.Y. : Kraus Reprint Co., 1977. vii, 96 p. ; 24 cm. Reprint of the 1794 ed. printed by A. Kennedy, Northumberland-Town. [BL2740.P7 1977] 77-2935 ISBN 0-527-72705-9 lib.bdg. : 30.00
1. Paine, Thomas, 1737-1809. The age of reason. 2. Rationalism. I. Priestley, Joseph, 1733-1804. Letters to a philosophical unbeliever. Pt. 3. 1977. II. Title: A continuation of the Letters to the philosophers and politicians of France on the subject of religion ...

WOOD, Horace G. 133.93
The philosophy of creation: unfolding the laws of the progressive development of nature, and embracing the philosophy of man, spirit, and the spirit world, by Thomas Paine, through the hand of Horace G. Wood, medium. 7th ed. Boston, Colby and Rich, 1882. iv, 5-120 p. incl. diagrs. 19 1/2 cm. Edited by H. A. Burbank. [BF1291.W8 1882] 33-20367
1. Paine, Thomas, 1737-1809. I. Burbank, H. A., ed. II. Title.

Paine, Thomas, 1737-1809. The age of reason.

BELKNAP, Jeremy, 1744-1798. 232.
Dissertations on the character, death & resurrection of Jesus Christ, and the evidence of His gospel; with remarks on some sentiments advanced in a book intitled "The age of reason." by Joseph Belknap, no. 8, Dock-square. mdccxcv. in boston From the Apollo press by Joseph Belknap, no.8, dock-square 1795 140 p., 1 l. 22 cm. Running title: Dissertaions on Christianity. [BT300.B4] 4-1960
1. Paine, Thomas, 1737-1809. The age of reason. 2. Jesus Christ—Character. 3. Jesus Christ—Crucifixion. 4. Jesus Christ—Resurrection. 5. Apologetics—18th cent. I. Title.

BOUDINOT, Elias, 1740-1821 211
The age of revelation. Or, The age of reason shown to be an age of infidelity. By Elias Boudinot... (Dickin's ed.) Philadelphia; Published by Asbury Dickins, opposite Christ-church. Hugh Maxwell, printer, Columbia-house... 1801. 2 p. l., (iii)-xxiii (25)-282 (i.e. 332) p. 1 l., 21 1/2 cm. A reply to Thomas Paine's Age of reason. Page 332 incorrectly numbered 232. [BL2740.B6] 4-1981
1. Paine, Thomas, 1737-1809. The age of reason. 2. Bible—Evidences authority, etc. I. Title.

BROADDUS, Andrew.
The age of reason & revelation; or, Animadversions on .. Thomas Paine's late piece, intitled "The age of reason &c"; containing a vindication of the sacred Scriptures, from the reasonings, objections and aspersions in that piece. Richmond, J. Dixon, 1795. 70 pp. 16° 1-3320
I. Title.

BROADDUS, Andrew, 1770-1848.
The age of reason & revelation; or, Animadversions of Mr. Thomas Paine's late piece, intitled "The age of reason, &c.;" containing a vindication of the sacred Scriptures, from the reasonings, objections and aspersions in that piece. By Andrew Broaddus ... Richmond [Va.] Printed by John Dixon, for an enquirer after the truth, 1795. 70+ p. 17 cm. 4-1982
I. Title.

THE examiners examined; 211
being a defence of The age of reason. [Line

from Leibnitz] New-York; Printed for the author; and sold by L. Wayland and J. Fellows.-- 1794.--(Copyright secured.) 82 + p. 17 cm. No. 2 in a volume of three pieces lettered: Doctrines of Christ. Signatures: 2 l. (t.-p.; contents) unsigned, A-F4. G3. Imperfect: p. 29-34, 37-40, 43-46, and all after p. 82 wanting. [BL2773.F4] 31-4599
1. Paine, Thomas, 1737-1809. Age of reason.
Contents omitted.

LESLIE, Charles, 1650-1722. 239.5
A short and easy method with the deists; wherein the certainty of the Christian religion is demonstrated; in a letter to a friend. By Mr. Charles Leslie. To which are added, An apology for Christianity, and an apology for the Bible. By R. Watson... Lancaster [Pa.] Printed and sold by W. & R. Dickson, in Queen street, and W. Hamilton, In Kingstreet, 1797. 32, 78, 118 p. 22 1/2 cm. "An apology for the Bible: [118 p.] has special t.-p., dated 1796. [BT1180.L45 1797] 34-5244
1. Paine, Thomas, 1737-1809. The age of reason. 2. Deism. 3. Christianity—Evidences. 4. Bible—Evidences, authority, etc. I. Title. II. Title: An apology for Christianity.

[NELSON, D.] fl.1800. 211
An investigation of that false, fabulous and blasphemous misrepresentation of truth, set forth by Thomas Paine, in his two volumes, entitled The age of reason, dedicated to the protection of the United States of America. By a Delaware waggoner: also dedicated to the protection of the United States of America: where the devil, Mahomet, and the heathen philosophers, are evidences against Paine's Age of reason. [n.p., 1800] 192 p. 18 cm. "To the impartial and candid lovers of truth" signed: D. Nelson. At the end is mounted a clipping from the Truth seeker (New York, Jan. 11, 1896) containing an advertisement copied from the Lancaster, Pa., Intelligencer & advertiser of October, 1800, in which this work is announced as "just published." [BL2740.N4] 4-2003
1. Paine, Thomas, 1737-1809. The age of reason. I. Title.

OBSERVATIONS on 1st. The chronology of Scripture. 2d. Strictures on The age of reason. 3d. The evidence which reason, unassisted by revelation, affords us with respect to the nature and properties of the soul of man. 4th. Arguments in support of the opinion, that the soul is inactive and unconscious from death to the resurrection, derived from Scripture. New-York-- Printed by Thomas Greenleaf, 1795. 141 p. tables (1 fold.) 21 x 12 cm. A 33
1. Paine, Thomas, 1737-1809. The age of reason. 2. Bible—Chronology. 3. Soul.

OBSERVATIONS on first. The chronology of Scripture. 2d. Scriptures on The age of reason 3d. The evidence which reason, unassisted by revelation, afford us with respect to the nature and properties of the soul of man. 4th Arguments in support of the opinion, that the soul is inactive and unconscious from death to the resurrection, derived from Scripture. New-York-- Printed by Thomas Greenleaf, 1795. 141 p. tables (1 fold.) 20 1/2 x 11 1/2 cm. A33
1. Paine, Thomas, 1737-1809. The age of reason. 2. Bible—Chronology. 3. Soul.

OGDEN, Uzal, 1744-1822. 211
Antidote to deism. The deist unmasked; or, An ample refutation of all the objections of Thomas Paine, against the Christian religion; as contained in a pamphlet, intitled, The age of reason; addressed to the citizens of these states. By the Reverend Uzal Ogden, rector of Trinity church, at Newark, in the state of New-Jersey. To which is prefixed, remarks on Boulanger's Christianity unveiled. And to The deist unmasked, is annexed A short method with the deists. By the Reverend Charles Leslie ... Newark, Printed by John Woods, m,dcc,xcv. 2 v. 17 cm. (Copyright secured, according to law) "Le christianisme devolle was published by Baron P. H. T. d'Holbach under the name of Nicolas Antoine Boulanger. "Appendix to The deist unmasked; containing the concessions and recantations of several deists in favor of Christianity": v. 2, p. [307]-318. "A short method with the deists Wherein the certainty of the Christian religion is demonstrated. In a letter to a friend. By the Reverend Charles Leslie": p. [319]-342. [BL2740.O5] 4-2005
1. Paine, Thomas, 1737-1809 The age of reason. 2. Holbach, Paul Henry Thirty baron d', 1723-1789. 3. Deism. I. Title.

PAINE, Thomas, 1737-1809. 211
The age of reason. Being an investigation of true and fabulous theology. By Thomas Paine... Boston, Printed by Thomas Hall, MDCCXCIV. 58 p. 21 cm. Signatures: A-E (last leaf blank) [BL2740.A] A 31
I. Title.

PAINE, Thomas, 1737-1809. 211
The age of reason: being an investigation of true and fabulous theology, by Thomas Paine... Chicago, G. E. Wilson [189-?] 154 p. 19 cm. [BL2740.A1 1893] 6-24780
I. Title.

PAINE, Thomas, 1737-1809.
Age of reason, being an investigation of true and fabulous theology. By Thomas Paine... In two parts... New York, P. Eckler [1892?] 186 p. 18 1/2 cm. 10-712
I. Title.

PATTEN, William, 1763-1839. 211
Christianity the true theology, and only perfect moral system; in answer to "The age of reason:" with an Appendix, in answer to "The examiners examined." By William Patten ... Warren (Rhode-Island): Printed by Nathaniel Phillips, m,dcc,xcv. viii, [9]-177 p., 1 l. 19 cm. [BL2740.P3] 35-31645
1. Paine, Thomas, 1737-1809. The age of reason. 2. Christianity—Apologetic works—18th cent. 3. The examiners examined. I. Title.

SCOTT, Thomas, 1747-1821. 230
A vindication of the divine inspiration of the Holy Scriptures, and of the doctrines contained in them: being an answer to the two parts of Mr. T. Paine's Age of reason. By Thomas Scott ... London, Printed: New-York, Re-printed by G. Forman, for C. Davis, book-seller, no. 94, Water-street, 1797. xii, [13]-202, [2] p. 18 cm. Signatures: A-R5. Advertising matter: 2 p. at end. [BL2740.S4 1797]
1. Paine, Thomas, 1737-1809. The age of reason. I. Title.

SIMPSON, David, 1745-1799. 239
A plea for religion and the Sacred Writings; addressed to the disciples of Thomas Paine, and wavering Christians of every persuasion. With an appendix, containing the author's determination to have relinquished his charge in the established church, and the reasons on which that determination was founded. By the late Rev. David Simpson ... From the ninth London edition. Saxton's Village, Vt., S. Taylor, 1824. xxii, 345, [8] p. 18 1/2 cm. [BT1100.S6 1824] 42-27976
1. Paine, Thomas, 1737-1809. Age of reason. 2. Apologetics—18th cent. I. Title.

SNYDER, G W.
The Age of reason unreasonable; or, The folly of rejecting revealed religion. In a series of letters to a friend. By G. W. Snyder, A. M. Philadelphia: Published by William Cobbett, opposite Christ church, May, 1798. 213 p. 19 cm. A remonstrance against Paine's Age of reason and the writings of other deists. 4-2022
I. Title.

TYTLER, James, 1747?-1805. 973
Paine's second part of The age of reason answered. By James Tytler, author of the Remarks on Paine's first part of The age of reason, by a citizen of the world, published at Belfast in Ireland, 1794 ... Salem [Mass.] Printed by Thomas C. Cushing, 1796. 107 p. 18 1/2 cm. [BL2740.T9] [AC901.M5 vol. 341] 4-2026
I. Paine, Thomas, 1737-1809. The age of reason. II. Title.

WATSON, Richard, bp. of Llandaff, 1737-1816. 211
An apology for the Bible, in a series of letters, addressed to Thomas Paine, author of a book entitled, The age of reason, part the second, being an investigation of true and of fabulous theology. By R. Watson, D.D.... [n.p.] Printed in the year 1796. 1 p. l., 102 p. 21 1/2 cm. [BL2740.W3 1796x] 4-2034
1. Paine, Thomas, 1737-1809. The age of reason. 2. Bible—Criticism, interpretation, etc. I. Title.

WATSON, Richard, bp. of Llandaff, 1737-1816. 211
An apology for the Bible, in a series of letters, addressed to Thomas Paine, author of a book entitled, The age of reason, part the second, being an investigation of true and of fabulous theology. By R. Watson... Albany, Printed and sold by Barber & Southwick, 1796. 192 p. 17 1/2 cm. [BL2740.W3 1796a] [BL2740.W] 211 A 32
1. Paine, Thomas, 1737-1809. The age of reason. 2. Bible—Evidences, authority, etc. I. Title.

WATSON, Richard, bp. of Llandaff, 1737-1816. 211
An apology for the Bible, in a series of letters, addressed to Thomas Paine, author of a book entitled, The age of reason, part the second, being an investigation of true and of fabulous theology. By R. Watson... Boston: Printed by Manning & Loring, For James White, at Franklin's Head, Court Street, 1796. 168 p. 18 1/2 cm. [BL2740.W3 1796b] 4-2038
1. Paine, Thomas, 1737-1809. The age of reason. 2. Bible—Evidences, authority, etc. I. Title.

WATSON, Richard, bp. of Llandaff, 1737-1816. 211
An apology for the Bible, in a series of letters, addressed to Thomas Paine, author of a book entitled, The age of reason, part the second, being an investigation of true and of fabulous theology. By R. Watson... New Brunswick [N.J.]: Printed by Abraham Blauvelt, 1796. 1 p. l., 201 p. 18 1/2 cm. [BL2740.W3 1796nb] 4-2040
1. Paine, Thomas, 1737-1809. The age of reason. I. Title.

WATSON, Richard, bp. of Llandaff, 1737-1816. 211
An apology for the Bible, in a series of letters, addressed to Thomas Paine, author of a book entitled, The age of reason, part the second, being an investigation of true and of fabulous theology. By R. Watson, D.D., F.R.S., lord bishop of Llandaff, and regius professor of divinity in the University of Cambridge. New York: Printed by John Bull, no. 115, Cherry-street, 1796. iv, 252 p. 17 cm. "Subcribers' names": p. [243]-252. [BL2740.W3 1796 N.Y.] [AC901.D8 vol. 117] 252. 4-2041
1. Paine, Thomas, 1737-1809. The age of reason. 2. Bible—Evidences, authority, etc. I. Title.

WATSON, Richard, bp. of Llandaff, 1737-1816. 211
An apology for the Bible, in a series of letters, addressed to Thomas Paine, author of a book entitled, The age of reason, part the second, being an investigation of true and of fabulous theology. By R. Watson... New York: Printed by T. & J. Swords, no. 99, Pearl-street, 1796. 178 p. 17 cm. [BL2740.W3 1796 N.Y.S.] 4-2042
1. Paine, Thomas, 1737-1809. The age of reason. 2. Bible—Evidences, authority, etc. I. Title.

WATSON, Richard, bp. of Llandaff, 1737-1816. 211
An apology for the Bible; in a series of letters, addressed to Thomas Paine, author of a book entitled The age of reason, part the second, being an investigation of true and of fabulous theology. By R. Watson, D.D.... Philadelphia; Printed for W. Young, Mills & Son, No. 52, corner of Second and Chesnut Streets, by W. Woodward, 1796. 206 p. 17 1/2 cm. [BL2740.W3 1796p] 4-2044
1. Paine, Thomas, 1737-1809. The age of reason. I. Title.

WATSON, Richard, bp. of Llandaff, 1737-1816. 211
An apology for the Bible, in a series of letters, addressed to Thomas Paine, author of a book entitled, The age of reason, part the second, being an investigation of true and of fabulous theology. By R. Watson, D.D. ... Carey's 3d Philadelphia ed. Philadelphia: Printed by James Carey, No. 83, North Second-Street. 1797. [Price three-eighths of a dollar] 1 p. l., 80 p. 21 1/2 cm. [BL2740.W3 1797] [JC177.A3 1797 vol. 2] 944. 4-2045
1. Paine, Thomas, 1737-1809. The age of reason. 2. Bible—Evidences, authority, etc. I. Title.

WATSON, Richard, bp. of Llandaff, 1737-1816.
An apology for the Bible, in a series of letters, addressed to Thomas Paine, author of a book entitled, The age of reason, part the second, being an investigation of true and of fabulous theology. By R. Watson... 2d Philadelphia ed. Philadelphia: Printed by James Carey, no. 83, North-Second street. 1796. [Price three-eighths of a dollar] 1 p. l., 80 p. 22 1/2 cm. (In An antidote for Tom Paine's theological and political poison... Philadelphia, 1796) Signatures: [A1], B-L4. [BL2742.A6] 31-907
1. Paine, Thomas, 1737-1809. The age of reason. 2. Bible—Evidences, authority, etc. I. Title.

Painters—Dictionaries.

KEIRSTEAD, C. Fraser. 704.948'5
Art studies in the life of Christ, and lives of the artists, by C. Fraser Keirstead. Needham Heights, Mass., Whittemore Associates [1967] 64 p. illus., ports. 19 cm. [N8050.K38] 68-771
1. Jesus Christ—Art. 2. Painters—Dictionaries. I. Title.

Painting, Islamic.

ARNOLD, Thomas Walker, Sir, 1864-1930. 759.956
Painting in Islam; a study of the place of pictorial art in Muslim culture. With a new introd. by B. W. Robinson. New York, Dover Publications [1965] xviii, 159 p. illus. 24 cm. Unabridged republication of the work first published in 1928, with a new introd. Bibliographical footnotes. [ND198.A7] 65-12451
1. Painting, Islamic. 2. Illumination of books and manuscripts. 3. Civilization, Islamic. I. Title.

ARNOLD, Thomas Walker, Sir 1864-1930 759.956
Painting in Islam: a study of the place of pictorial art in Muslim culture. New introd. by B. W. Robinson [Gloucester, Mass., P. Smith, c.1965] xviii, 159p. illus. 24cm. (Dover bk. T1310 rebound) [ND198.A7] 5.00
1. Painting, Islamic. 2. Illumination of books and manuscripts. 3. Civilization, Islamic. I. Title.

Painting, Medieval.

BROWN, Stephanie. 755'.4
Religious painting : Christ's passion and crucifixtion in the history of art / by Stephanie Brown. New York : Mayflower Books, [1979] p. cm. [ND1430.B76] 78-24454 ISBN 0-8317-7370-7 : 12.95 ISBN 0-8317-7371-5 pbk. : 6.95
1. Jesus Christ—Passion—Art. 2. Jesus Christ—Crucifixion—Art. 3. Painting, Medieval. 4. Painting, Renaissance. 5. Painting, Baroque. I. Title.

Painting, Mohammedan.

ETTINGHUSEN, Richard 759.956
Arab painting. Skira [dist. Cleveland, World, c.1962] 208p. mounted illus. (pt. col.) map. 29cm. (Treasures of Asia) Bibl. 62-10990 22.50, bxd.
1. Painting, Mohammedan. 2. Illusmination of books and manuscripts, Mohammedan. I. Title. II. Series.

Painting, Oriental.

EMERSON, James Christopher, 1913- 755'.5
The life of Christ in the conception & expression of Chinese and oriental artists : the mystery of Christ as conceived by the oriental mind / James Christopher Emerson. Albuquerque, N.M. : Gloucester Art Press, [1978] p. cm. Bibliography: p. [N8050.E45] 78-16581 ISBN 0-930582-13-6 : 39.75

1. Jesus Christ—Art. 2. Painting, Oriental. I. Title.
Publisher's address : P.O. Box 4526, Albuquerque, NM 87106

Painting, Renaissance.

HURLL, Estelle May, 1863-1924. 704.948'55
The Madonna in art. Boston, L. C. Page, 1898. Detroit, Gale Research Co., 1974. p. cm. Original ed. issued in series: Art lovers' series. Bibliography: p. [N8070.H9 1974] 78-159857 ISBN 0-8103-4083-6
1. Mary, Virgin—Art. 2. Painting, Renaissance. I. Title. II. Series: Art lovers' series.

Painting—Themes, motives.

BERNEN, Satia. 755'.094
Myth & religion in European painting, 1270-1700; the stories as the artists knew them [by] Satia & Robert Bernen. New York, G. Braziller [1973] 280 p. 19 cm. On spine: A guide to myth & religion in European painting, 1270-1700. [ND1288.B47 1973] 72-96070 ISBN 0-8076-0683-9 6.95
1. Painting—Themes, motives. 2. Art and mythology. 3. Art and religion. I. Bernen, Robert, joint author. II. Title. III. Title: A guide to myth & religion in European painting, 1270-1700.
pap. 3.95; ISBN 0-8067-0682-0.

Painting, Zen—Exhibitions.

FARRAR, Frederic William, 1831-1903.
... *Beautiful stories about Jesus;* the complete standard life of Christ, by Canon Farrar...A wonderful gallery of the greatest paintings, by a hundred of the most famous artists of world, including the celebrated engravings by Alexandre Bida, a pictorical interpreting of the most beautiful of stories, the story of Jesus... [Chicago, Printed by Cuneo binding co.] c1913. 723 p. incl. front., illus. 22 cm. At head of title: Authorized pictorial-interpreting self-pronouncing. Illustrated t.-p. Front. printed on both sides. 13-24473 2.00
I. Title.

FONTEIN, Jan. 759.952'074'014461
Zen painting & calligraphy; an exhibition of works of art lent by temples, private collectors, and public and private museums in Japan, organized in collaboration with the Agency for Cultural Affairs of the Japanese government [by] Jan Fontein & Money L. Hickman. Boston, Museum of Fine Arts; distributed by New York Graphic Society, Greenwich, Conn. [1971, c1970] liv, 173 p. illus. (part col.) 29 cm. Catalog of the exhibition held Nov. 5-Dec. 20, 1970, at the Boston Museum of Fine Arts. [ND197.F6 1971] 76-127853 ISBN 0-87846-000-4 18.50
1. Painting, Zen—Exhibitions. 2. Calligraphy, Zen—Exhibitions. I. Hickman, Money L., joint author. II. Japan. Bunkacho. III. Boston. Museum of Fine Arts. IV. Title.

Paintings.

BAILEY, Henry Turner, 1865- 704.
The great painters' gospel: pictures representing scenes and incidents in the life of Our Lord Jesus Christ,with Scriptural quotations, references and suggestions for comparative study, by Henry Turner. Bailey. Boston, Mass., W. A. Wilde company [c1900] xiv, 63, [3] p. incl. illus., pl. 29 cm. [N8080.B2] 1-29425
1. Paintings. 2. Jesus Christ—Biog. 3. Jesus Christ—Art. I. Title.

DRAPER, Bourne Hall. 220.
Bible illustrations; or, A description of manners and customs peculiar to the East, especially explanatory of the Holy Scriptures. By the Rev. B. H. Draper ... American ed. with many improvements ... Boston, Carter, Hendee & co., 1832. iv, [vii]-viii, [9]-215 p. front., illus. 15 x 12 1/2 cm. Another edition (Philadelphia, Thomas, Cowperthwait & co., 1832) has title: Bible stories ... by the author of "Peter Parley's tales", & c. Both editions contain the statement that they were copyrighted by Samuel G. Goodrich ("Peter Parley") but the work is not included in Goodrich's list of his works in his "Recollections of a lifetime". It is not the same work as "Peter Parley's Book of Bible stories". [BS620.D7 1832] 26-9072
I. Title.

HODGKIN, Eliot, comp. 704.9485
A pictorial Gospel; a life of Christ in the works of the old masters and the words of the Gospels. New York, Macmillan, 1950. 212 p. illus. 27 cm. [N8050.H68] 50-7054
1. Jesus Christ—Art. 2. Bible. N. T. Gospels—Pictorial illustrations. 3. Paintings. I. Bible. N. T. Gospels. English. Authorized. Selections. 1950. II. Title.

Paintings—Catalogs

ALINARI, Fratelli, Florence. 704.9485
Pitture di venti secoli; [catalogo] Peintures de vingt siecles. Paintings of twenty centuries. Firenze, Fratelli Alinari, Istituto di edizioni artistiche; U. S. distributors: International Art Pub. Co., Detroit [1964] 239 p. (chiefly illus.) 34 cm. "Le piccole illustrazioni monocrome ... presentano i primi mille e cinquecento dipinti che i'Istituto di edizioni artistiche Alinari ha riprodotto in fotografia diretta a colori." [ND1170.A45 1964] 68-44781
1. Paintings—Catalogs 2. Paintings of twenty centuries. I. Title. II. Title: Peintures de vingt siecles.

MASTERPIECES of Biblical art. 755'.4
St. Paul, Catholic Digest Edition, College of St. Thomas, 1973. xvi, 95 plates of col. illus. 29 cm. [ND1430.M33 1973] 74-176212 ISBN 0-8326-1802-0 14.95
1. Bible—Pictures, illustrations, etc. 2. Paintings—Catalogs.

OEHME, Julius. 755
Modern paintings and water colors by Dutch, French, and American artists, the property of Mr. Julius Oehme [by] Harpignies, Kaemmerer, Courtois [and others] ... also decorative portraits of the French school with some additions, consigned by private owners; which comprise the second session of the sale, to be sold without reserve at the Anderson galleries on ... February 29th and March 1st, 1912 ... New York, The Anderson auction company [1912] 123 items. L.C. copy imperfect: p. 57-58 wanting. [N8650.O4] 45-49707
1. Paintings—Catalogs. 2. Water colors—Catalogs. I. Anderson galleries, New York. II. Title.

Paintings—Ceylon.

DHANAPALA, D. B. 759.5488
Buddhist paintings from shrines and temples in Ceylon. Introd. by D. B. Dhanapala. [New York] Pub. by the New Maer. Lib. of World Lit. by arrangement with UNESCO [c.1957, 1964] 24p. [4]p. (on fold 1.) illus., 28 col. plates. (pt. fold.) 17cm. (Mentor-Unesco art bk., MQ585) Bibl. [ND1005.D5] 65-269 .95 pap.,
1. Paintings—Ceylon. 2. Art, Buddhist. I. United Nations Educational, Scientific and Cultural Organization. II. Title.

Paisii Velichkovskii, archimandrite, 1722-1794.

CHETVERIKOV, Sergii, 1867-1947. 271'.8 B
Starets Paisii Velichkovskii : his life, teachings, and influence on Orthodox monasticism / Sergii Chetverikov ; translated from the Russian by Vasily Lickwar and Alexander I. Lisenko. Belmont, Mass. : Nordland Pub. Co., 1980. 339 p. : port ; 22 cm. Bibliography: p. 323-327. [BX597.P26C4613] 19 75-29632 ISBN 0-913124-22-2 (pbk.) : 35.00
1. Paisii Velichkovskii, archimandrite, 1722-1794. 2. Orthodox Eastern Church, Russian—Clergy—Biography. 3. Monasticism and religious orders, Orthodox Eastern. 4. Clergy—Romania—Moldavia—Biography. I. Title.

Paisley Abbey.

ADAM, Isabel. 133.4'0941441
Witch hunt : a true story / Isabel Adam. New York : St. Martin's Press, c1978. 256 p. ; 22 cm. Includes index. Bibliography: p. 241-251. [BF1581.A37 1978b] 78-19427 ISBN 0-312-88429-X : 10.95
1. Paisley Abbey. 2. Witchcraft—Scotland—Paisley. I. Title.

Pakistanis in Great Britain—Education.

JORDANHILL College of Education. 371.9'7'91412041443
The immigrant school learner : a study of Pakistani pupils in Glasgow / [by] L. Dickinson ... [et al.] [for the] Jordanhill College of Education. Slough : NFER, 1975. 200 p. : ill., map ; 22 cm. "This book is the outcome of a study of the immigrant school pupils in Glasgow conducted by members of the staff of Jordanhill College of Education." Distributed in the U.S.A. by Humanities Press, Atlantic Highlands, N.J. Bibliography: p. [159]-162. [LC3485.S35J67 1975] 76-352166 ISBN 0-85633-062-0 : 13.25
1. Pakistanis in Great Britain—Education. 2. Children of immigrants—Education—Glasgow. 3. Elementary school students' socio-economic status—Glasgow. I. Dickinson, Leslie. II. Title.

Palamas, Gregorius, Saint, Abp. of Thessalonica, ca. 1296-ca. 1359.

PAPADEMETRIOU, George C. 281.9'092'4
Introduction to Saint Gregory Palamas, by George C. Papademetriou. New York, Philosophical Library [1973] 103 p. 22 cm. Bibliography: p. 81-83. [BX395.P3P36] 73-77406 ISBN 0-8022-2120-3 5.00
1. Palamas, Gregorius, Saint, Abp. of Thessalonica, ca. 1296-ca. 1359. I. Title.

Palau, Luis, 1934-

PALAU, Luis, 1934- 269'.2'0924 B
The Luis Palau story / Luis Palau as told to Jerry B. Jenkins. Old Tappan, N.J : Revell, c1980. p. cm. [BV3785.P32A34] 19 80-22400 ISBN 0-8007-1134-3 : 7.95
1. Palau, Luis, 1934- 2. Evangelists—Latin America—Biography. I. Jenkins, Jerry B. II. Title.

Paleography, Greek.

METZGER, Bruce Manning. 220.4'8
Manuscripts of the Greek Bible : an introduction to palaeography / Bruce M. Metzger. New York : Oxford University Press, 1981. p. cm. Includes index. Bibliography: p. [BS39.M47] 19 80-26205 ISBN 0-19-502924-0 : 17.95
1. Bible—Manuscripts, Greek. 2. Bible—Manuscripts, Greek—Facsimiles. 3. Paleography, Greek. 4. Greek language, Biblical. I. Title.

Palermo. Cattedrale.

BELLAFIORE, Giuseppe. 726'.6'0945823
The Cathedral of Palermo / Giuseppe Bellafiore. Palermo : S. F. Flaccovio, c1976. 418 p. : ill. (some col.) ; 33 cm. Includes indexes. Bibliography: p. 345-350. [NA5621.P3P44] 77-482111 L50000
1. Palermo. Cattedrale. I. Title.

Palermo, Louie.

PALERMO, Louie. 783.7'092'2 B
'Atsa Louie, I'ma Phil / Louie and Phil Palermo, with Bernard Palmer. Wheaton, Ill. : Victor Books, c1975. 135 p. : ill. ; 21 cm. [ML420.P15A3] 75-18082 ISBN 0-88207-650-7 : 2.95
1. Palermo, Louie. 2. Palermo, Phil. 3. Gospel musicians—Correspondence, reminiscences, etc. I. Palermo, Phil, joint author. II. Palmer, Bernard Alvin, 1914- joint author. III. Title.

Palestine.

BERRY, George Ricker, 1865- 915.69
Old and new in Palestine by George Ricker Berry. Hamilton, N.Y. The Republican press 1939. 128 p. 19 cm. [DS107.3B555] 39-24188
1. Palestine. I. Title.

COOPER, David Lipscomb, 1886- 915.69
... *Prophetic fulfillments in Palestine today,* by David L. Cooper ... Los Angeles, Calif., Bibical research society [c1940] 125 p. incl. illus. plates. 23 cm. Music: p. 19-20. [DS126.C56] 40-11480
1. Palestine. 2. Jews—Restoration. 3. Bible—Prophecies. I. Title.

DAVIS, George Thompson Brown, 1873- 915.69
Rebuilding Palestine according to prophecy, by George T. B. Davis ... Philadelphia, Pa., The Million testaments campaigns [c1935] 126 p. incl. front., illus., maps. 19 cm. [DS126.D3] 36-8732
1. Palestine. 2. Bible—Prophecies. 3. Jews in Palestine. 4. Jews—Restoration. I. Title.

KLOSE, Ellen. 915.69
With Jack and Jean in Bible lands. Washington, Review and Herald [1948] 384 p. illus. 23 cm. [DS107.3.K58] 49-1294
1. Palastine—Descr. & trav. I. Title.

RUSSELL, Michael, bp. of Glasgow and Gallaway, 1781-1848. 933
... *Palestine;* or, The Holy land. From the earliest period to the present time. By the Rev. Michael Russell ... With a map and nine engravings. New-York, J. & J. Harper, 1832. 2 p. l., [9]-330 p. incl. plates. front. (fold. map) illus. 16 cm. (On cover: Harper's family library. no. xxvii) At head of title: Harper's stereotype edition. Added t.-p., engraved, with vignette. Cover dated 1833. [DS118.R8] A 31
1. Palestine. I. Title.

SMITHER, Ethel Lisle. 915.69
A picture book of Palestine, by Ethel L. Smither, illustrated by Ruth King. New York, Nashville, Abingdon-Cokesbury press, c1947. 63, [1] p. illus. (part col.; incl. map) 25 cm. [DS107.3.S73] 47-30304
1. Palestine. I. King, Ruth, illus. II. Title.

Palestine—Antiquities

CHAVEZ, Moises. 220.9'3
Enfoque arqueologico del mundo de la Biblia / Moises Chavez. Miami, Fla. : Editorial Caribe, c1976. 138 p. : 21 cm. "Tabla arqueologica del mundo de la Biblia": fold. sheet inserted in pocket. Includes index. [DS111.C46] 76-25325
1. Bible. O.T.—Antiquities. 2. Palestine—Antiquities. 3. Man, Prehistoric—Palestine. I. Title.

COBERN, Camden McCormack, 1855-1920. 220.
Recent explorations in the Holy Land and Kadesh-Barnes, the "lost oasis" of the Sinaitic peninsula, by Camden M. Cobern ... Meadville, Pa., Pub. for the World's Bible conference by the Tribune publishing co. [1914] 126 p. front. (port.) plates. 19 1/2 cm. [DS111.C6] 15-3634
1. Palestine—Antiq. I. Title.

DUNCAN, John Garrow, 1872- 220.96
Digging up Biblical history; recent archaeology in Palestine and its bearing on the Old Testament, by J. Garrow Duncan ... New York, The Macmillan company [1931- v. fronts., illus. (incl. plans) plates. 22 cm. "Printed in Great Britain." Bibliography: v. 1, p. xi-xii; v. p. xi. [DS111.D8] 31-10665
1. Palestine—Antiq. 2. Bible. O. T.—Antiq. 3. Bible—Antiq.—O. T. I. Title.

LANDAY, Jerry M. 220.9'3
Silent cities, sacred stones: archaeological discovery in the land of the Bible [by] Jerry M. Landay. London, Weidenfeld and Nicolson, 1971. 272 p. illus. (some col.), maps, ports. 25 cm. Illus. on lining papers. American ed. (New York, McCalls) has title: Silent cities, sacred stones: archaeological discovery in Israel. [DS111.L35 1971b] 72-185212 ISBN 0-297-00426-3

1. Palestine—Antiquities. I. Title.
14.95, ISBN 0-8415-0112-2. Available from Saturday Review Press

MAGNUSSON, Magnus. 221.9
Archaeology of the Bible / Magnus Magnusson ; drawings and maps by Shirley Felts. New York : Simon and Schuster, [1978] c1977. 239 p., [16] leaves of plates : ill. ; 26 cm. First published in 1977 under title: BC, the archaeology of the Bible lands. Includes index. Bibliography: p. 234-235. [BS621.M33 1978] 78-9547 ISBN 0-671-24010-2 : 12.95
1. Bible. O.T.—Antiquities. 2. Palestine—Antiquities. 3. Excavations (Archaeology)—Palestine. I. Title.

NEGEV, Avraham. 933
Archaeology in the land of the Bible / Avraham Negev. New York : Schocken Books, 1977, c1976. p. cm. [DS111.N38 1977] 77-23213 ISBN 0-8052-3659-7 : 12.50
1. Bible—Antiquities. 2. Palestine—Antiquities. 3. Excavations (Archaeology)—Palestine. I. Title.

TIME-LIFE Books. 221.9'5
The Israelites / by the editors of Time-Life Books. New York : Time-Life Books, [1975] 159 p. : ill. ; 27 cm. (The Emergence of man) Includes index. Bibliography: p. 155. [BS1197.T53 1975] 75-4101 7.95
1. Jews—History—To 586 B.C. 2. Bible. O.T.—History of Biblical events. 3. Palestine—Antiquities. I. Title.

Palestine—Antiquities—Addresses, essays, lectures.

STUDIES on the ancient 221.9
Palestinian world; presented to Professor F. V. Winnett on the occasion of his retirement 1 July 1971. Edited by J. W. Wevers and D. B. Redford. [Toronto, Buffalo] University of Toronto Press [1972] 171 p. illus. 24 cm. (Toronto Semitic texts and studies) Contents.Contents.—An incense burner from Tell es-Sa'idiyeh, Jordan Valley, by J. B. Pritchard.—The archaeological history of Elealeh in Moab, by W. L. Reed.—Three Byzantine tombstones from Dhiban. Jordan, by A. D. Tushingham.—The placing of the accent signs in Biblical texts with Palestinian pointing, by E. J. Revell.—The textual affinities of the Arabic Genesis of Bib. Nat. Arab 9, by J. W. Wevers.—Energic verbal forms in Hebrew, by R. J. Williams.—Israel's eschatology from Amos to Daniel, by W. S. McCullough.—Oral tradition and historicity, by R. C. Culley.—Abraham and David? by N. E. Wagner.—Studies in relations between Palestine and Egypt during the first millennium B.C.: I. The taxation system of Solomon, by D. B. Redford.—Cylinder C of Sin-sarra-iskun, a new text from Baghdad, by A. K. Grayson.—Bibliography of Professor Winnett's publications, by A. Bembenek (p. [169]-171) [BS1192.S75] 79-151397 ISBN 0-8020-5254-1 ISBN 0-8020-0033-9 (microfiche) 10.00
1. Bible. O.T.—Addresses, essays, lectures. 2. Palestine—Antiquities—Addresses, essays, lectures. 3. Winnett, Frederick Victor—Bibliography. I. Winnett, Frederick Victor. II. Wevers, John William, ed. III. Redford, Donald B., ed.

Palestine—Antiquities—Dictionaries.

THE Encyclopedia of 220.9'3
archaeological excavations in the Holy Land. Michael Avi-Yonah, general editor. English-language ed. Englewood Cliffs, N.J., Prentice-Hall [1973- p. [DS111.A2E5] 73-14997 25.00
1. Bible—Antiquities—Dictionaries. 2. Palestine—Antiquities—Dictionaries. I. Avi-Yonah, Michael, 1904- ed.

ENCYCLOPEDIA of 933
archaeological excavations in the Holy Land. English ed. London : Oxford University Press, [1976- v. : ill. (some col.), col. maps, col. plans ; 29 cm. Rev. translation of Entsi.klopedyah la-.hafirot arkhe ologiyot be-Erets Yi.srael. Vol. 1 edited by M. Avi-Yonah. [DS111.A2E5313 1976] 76-371476 ISBN 0-19-647923-1 (v. 1) : £8.50 (v. 1)
1. Bible—Antiquities—Dictionaries. 2. Palestine—Antiquities—Dictionaries. 3. Excavations (Archaeology)—Palestine—Dictionaries. I. Avi-Yonah, Michael, 1904-1974.

NEGEV, Avraham. 220.9'5
Archaeological encyclopedia of the Holy Land / edited by Avraham Negev. Englewood, N.J. : SBS Pub., c1980. 354 p. : ill. ; 25 cm. Reprint of the 1972 ed. published by Putnam, New York. [DS111.A2N38 1980] 19 79-92775 ISBN 0-89961-004-8 : 14.95
1. Bible—Antiquities—Dictionaries. 2. Palestine—Antiquities—Dictionaries. I. Title.

Palestine—Boundaries

ISAACS, Samuel Hillel, 1825-1917.
The true boundaries of the Holy Land, as described in Numbers XXXIV: 1-12, solving the many diversified theories as to their location, by Samuel Hillel Isaacs; ed. by Jeanette Isaacs Davis. Chicago, 1917. 102 p. incl. VII maps. front. (port.) 28 1/2 cm. [DS108.9.17] 18-1356
1. Palestine—Bound. I. Davis, Mrs. Jeannette (Isaacs) ed. II. Title.

ISAACS, Samuel 222'.14'091
Hillel, 1825-1917.
The true boundaries of the Holy Land / Samuel Hillel Isaacs. New York : Arno Press, 1977, [c1917] 102 p. : ill. ; 23 cm. (America and the Holy Land) Reprint of the ed. published in Chicago. Includes index. [DS108.9.I7 1977] 77-70706 ISBN 0-405-10256-9 : 12.00
1. Bible. O.T. Numbers XXXIV, 1-12—Criticism, interpretation, etc. 2. Palestine—Boundaries. I. Title. II. Series.

Palestine—Description and travel

ALEXANDER, Walter 915.69
Richardson, 1889-
Holy hours in the Holy Land, by Walter R. Alexander, D.D. Grand Rapids, Mich., Wm. B. Eerdmans publishing company [1946] 160 p. plates. 20 cm. [DS107.3.A32] 47-16825
1. Palestine—Descr. & trav. I. Title.

ANSON, Peter Frederick, 915.69
1889-
A pilgram artist in Palestine, by Peter F. Anson ... New York, E. P. Dutton & co., inc. [c1932] 164 [1] p. incl. front., plates. 22 1/2 cm. "First edition." [DS107.3.A65] 32-28915
1. Palestine—Descr. & trav. 2. Palestine—Descr. & trav.—Views. I. Title.

BAILEY, Albert Edward, 1871- 282.
On Nazareth hill, by Albert Edward Bailey ... Boston, New York [etc.] The Pilgrim press [c1915] vii, 98 p., 1 l. front., illus., fold. map. 19 cm. Frontispiece accompanied by guard sheet with descriptive letterpress. [BT309.B23] 15-24221
1. Palestine—Descr. & trav. I. Title.

BARROWS, Elijah Porter, 1807-1888.
Sacred geography, and antiquities ... By Rev. E. P. Barrows, D. D. New York, American tract society [1872] 685 p. illus., plates, 5 maps (incl. front.) 21 cm. [DS114.B27] 4-13454
1. Palestine—Descr. & trav. 2. Bible—Geography. I. Title.

BERENSON, Mary. Mrs. 915.69
A modern pilgrimage, by Mary Berenson ... New York, London, D. Appleton and company, 1933. xiii, 354, [1] p. front., illus. (map) 23 cm. [DS107.3.B54] 33-14666
1. Palestine—Descr. & trav. 2. Syria—Descr. & trav. I. Title.

BERENSON, Mary (Smith) 915.69
A modern pilgrimage. New York, Appleton, 1933. xiii. 334 p. fron., map. 23 cm. [DS107.3.B54] 33-14666
1. Palestine—Descr. & trav. 2. Syria—Trav. I. Title.

BIBESCO, Marthe Lucie 915.69
(Lahovary) "Princesse G. V. Bibesco," 1887-
... *Crusade for the anemone;* letters from the Holy Land; translation by Thomas Kernan. New York, The Macmillan company, 1932. viii p., 2 l., 3-180 p. 20 cm. At head of title: Princess Marthe Bibesco. [DS107.3.B56] 32-12494
1. Palestine—Descr. & trav. I. Kernan, Thomas, tr. II. Title.

BLANCHARD, Raoul, 1877- 915.694
1965.
The Promised Land, by Raoul Blanchard and M. Du Buit. Translated from the French by Robert Hunt. [1st ed.] New York, Hawthorn Books [1966] 142, [1] p. illus., maps. 21 cm. (Twentieth century encyclopedia of Catholicism, v. 61. Section VI: The Word of God) Translation of La Terre de la promesse. Bibliography: p. [143] [DS107.4.B5513 1966a] 66-15245
1. Palestine—Description and travel. I. Du Buit, Michel, joint author. II. Title. III. Series: The Twentieth century encyclopedia of Catholicism, v. 61.

BLOOMFIELD, Bernard M. 915.69
Israel diary. New York, Crown Publishers [1950] x, 182 p. illus., map. 22 cm. [DS107.3.B575] 50-6294
1. Palestine—Descr. & trav. I. Title.

BOLITHO, Hector, 1898- 915.69
Beside Galilee; a diary in Palestine [by] Hector Bolitho ... New York, D. Appleton-Century company, incorporated, 1933. xv, 205, [1] p. front., plates 22 1/2 cm. [Full name: Henry Hector Bolitho] [DS107.3.D585 1933a] 33-29513
1. Palestine—Descr. & trav. 2. Jews in Palestine. 3. Arabs in Palestine. 4. Jews—Restoration. 5. Palestine—Pol. & govt. I. Title.

BONAR, Horatius, 1808- 915.69
1889.
The land of promise: notes of a spring-journey from Beersheba to Sidon, By Horatius Bonar ... New York, R. Carter & brothers, 1858. viii, 568 p. front., illus. (incl. plan, music) plates, fold. map. 19 cm. "Topographical works": p. [514]-525. [DS107.B6] 34-35558
1. Palestine—Dexcr. & trav. I. Title.

BUSHELL, Gerard, 1915- 915.694
Churches of the Holy Land. Photos. by Anna Riwkin-Brick. New York, Funk and Wagnalls [1969] 191 p. illus. (part col.) 31 cm. (A Sabra book) Bibliography: p. 186-188. [DS108.5.B83] 69-11714 12.50
1. Palestine—Description and travel. 2. Churches—Palestine. I. Riwkin-Brick, Anna, 1908- illus. II. Title.

BYFORD-JONES, W. 915.694
Quest in the Holy Land, by W. Byford-Jones. New York, Roy Publishers, [1967, c1961] 206 p. illus. 23 cm. [BT303.9.B9 1967] 67-11258
1. Jesus Christ—Journeys. 2. Palestine—Description and travel. I. Title.

CUNNINGHAM, Bessie 915.69
Mothersill.
In the shadow of the Mosque of Omar, by Bessie Mothersill Cunningham. Portland, Or., Printed by the Metropolitan press, 1932. 6 p. l., 97 p. 21 cm. Maps on lining-papers. [DS107.3.C85] 32-14685
1. Palestine—Descr. & trav. I. Title.

DALMAN, Gustaf Hermann, 915.69
1855-
Sacred sites and ways; studies in the topography of the Gospels, by Gustaf Dalman ... authorised translation by Paul P. Levertoff, D. D. New York, The Macmillan company [1935] xii, 397, [1] p. illus. (incl. maps, plans) 22 cm. "Made in Great Britain." "First published 1935." "List of church authorities": [1] p. at end. Translation of Orte and wege Jesu. [DS104.3.D32] 35-7147
1. Palestine—Descr. & trav. 2. Jesus Christ—Biog. 3. Bible. N. T. Gospels—Geography. 4. Bible—Geography—N. T. Gospels. I. Levertoff, Paul Philip, 1878- tr. II. Title.

DAVIS, George Thompson 915.69
Brown, 1873-
Seeing prophecy fulfilled in Palestine, by George T. B. Davis ... Philadelphia, Pa., The Million testaments campaigns [1937] 134 p. incl. front., illus., map. 19 cm. "First printing 25,000 copies. November 15, 1937." [DS107.3.D32] 38-3150
1. Palestine—Descr. & trav. 2. Jews in Palestine. 3. Jews—Restoration. 4. Bible—Prophecies. I. Title.

DEHASS, Frank S. 933
Buried cities recovered : or, Explorations in Bible lands / Frank S. DeHass. New York : Arno Press, 1977, c1882. p. cm. (America and the Holy Land) Originally published under title: Recent travels and explorations in Bible lands. Reprint of the ed. published by Bradley, Garretson, Philadelphia. Includes index. [DS107.D32 1977] 77-70674 ISBN 0-405-10242-9 lib.bdg. : 30.00
1. DeHass, Frank S. 2. Palestine—Description and travel. 3. Palestine—Antiquities. 4. Jordan—Description and travel. 5. Jordan—Antiquities. I. Title. II. Series.

-EVANS, Alice]Pickford: 915.69
Mrs. 1868-
Sunny lands and blue waters, by Alice Pickford Brockway ... Philadelphia, Boston [etc.] The Judson press [c1925] 7 p. l., 114 p. front., plates. 19 1/2 cm. [Full name: Mrs. Alice Tolman (Pickford) Evans] [DS107.3.E85] 26-1347
1. Palestine—Descr. & trav. 2. Egypt—Descr. & trav. I. Title.

FARAGO, Ladislas. 915.69
Palestine at the crossroads, by Ladislas Farago ... New York, G. P. Putnam's sons [c1937] x, 286 p. front., plates, ports. 22 cm. Maps on lining-papers. London edition (Putnam) has title: Palestine on the eve. [DS107.3.F26 1937] 37-2618
1. Palestine—Descr. & trav. 2. Jews—Restoration. 3. Jews in Palestine. 4. Arabs in Palestine. I. Title.

FLEG, Edmond, 1874- 915.69
The land of promise, by Edmond Fleg ... translated from the French by Louise Waterman Wise; with an introduction by Ludwig Lewisohn. New York, The Macaulay company [c1933] 256 p. fold. front. (map) plates. 21 1/2 cm. Translation of Ms. Palestine. [DS107.3.F632] 33-7175
1. Palestine—Descr. & trav. 2. Jews—Restoration. I. Wise, Mrs. Louise (Waterman) tr. II. Title.

FOSDICK, Harry Emerson, 915.69
1878-
A pilgrimage to Palestine. New York, Macmillan Co., 1949. xiii, 332 p. fold. col. map. 21 cm. "A selected bibliography for the traveler": p. 295-297. [DS107.3.F67 1949] 49-9154
1. Palestine—Descr. & trav. 2. Palestine—Historical geography. I. Title.

FOX, Winifred Lowe 915.69
(Baggett)
An observer in Palestine, by Winifred Lowe Fox ... New York [etc.] Fleming H. Revell company [1939] 253p. front., illus. (map) plates. 23cm. Illustrated lining-papers. [DS107.3.F68] 39-24581
1. Palestine—Descr. & trav. I. Title.

FRANKL, Ludwig August, 915.69'04
1810-1894.
The Jews in the East / by P. Beaton from the German of Dr. Frankl. Westport, Conn. : Greenwood Press, [1975] p. cm. Translation of Nach Jerusalem. Reprint of the 1859 ed. published by Hurst and Blackett, London. [DS107.F813 1975] 78-97278 ISBN 0-8371-2596-0 : 28.50
1. Frankl, Ludwig August, 1810-1894. 2. Palestine—Description and travel. 3. Jews in the Levant—Social life and customs. 4. Jews in Palestine—Social life and customs. I. Beaton, Patrick. II. Title.

FULTON, John, 1834- 915.694'04'3
1907.
The beautiful land, Palestine : historical, geographical, and pictorial / John Fulton. New York : Arno Press, 1977 [c1891] p. cm. (America and the Holy Land) Reprint of the ed. published by T. Whittaker, New York. [DS107.F97 1977] 77-70694 ISBN 0-405-10248-8 lib.bdg. : 39.00
1. Palestine—Description and travel. I. Title. II. Series.

FULTON, John, 1834- 915.694'04'3
1907.
The beautiful land, Palestine : historical, geographical, and pictorial / John Fulton. New York : Arno Press, 1977 [c1891] p. cm. (America and the Holy Land) Reprint of the ed. published by T. Whittaker, New

York. [DS107.F97 1977] 77-70694 ISBN 0-405-10248-8 lib.bdg. : 39.00
1. Palestine—Description and travel. I. Title. II. Series.

GAGE, William Leonard, 1832-1889. 296
The home of God's people. By Rev. William L. Gage ... Hartford [Conn.] Dustin, Gilman & co.; [etc., etc.] 1873. xxii, [23]-557 p. front., illus. (incl. plates, maps, facsims.) 23 cm. [DS118.G2] 5-7824
1. Palestine—Descr. & trav. 2. Bible—History of Biblical events. I. Title.

GAGE, William Leonard, 1832-1889. 296
Palestine, historical and descriptive; or, The home of God's people. By theRev. William L. Gage ... Boston, Estes & Lauriat, 1883. 557 p. incl. front., illus., plates, maps, facsims. plates, port. 23 cm. [DS118.G22] 5-7825
1. Palestine—Descr. & trav. 2. Bible—History of Biblical events. I. Title.

GALBRAITH, John Albert. 915.69
Pilgrims in Palestine, by J. A. Galbraith, D. D. Ridgway, Pa., 1930. 128 p. front. (port.) 18 cm. [DS107.3.G3] 31-13247
1. Palestine—Descr. & trav. I. Title.

GIBBONS, John, 1882- 915.694'04'4
The road to Nazareth : through Palestine today / by John Gibbons. New York : AMS Press, 1975. 320 p., [16] leaves of plates : ill. ; 18 cm. Reprint of the 1936 ed. published by R. Hale, London. [DS107.3.G48 1975] 77-180339 ISBN 0-404-56264-7 : 20.00
1. Gibbons, John, 1882- 2. Palestine—Description and travel. I. Title.

GODBEY, William B 1833-1920. 287.
The apocalyptic angel, by Rev. W. B. Godbey ... Cincinnati, O., God's revivalist press, 1914. iv p., 1 l., 7-509 p. 20 cm. [BX7990.H6G62] 14-11105
1. Palestine—Descr. & trav. I. Title.

GOLDBERG, Ruth L Polhemus. 915.694
I saw Israel, an American reports. [1st ed.] New York, Exposition Press [1955] 217p. 21cm. (A Banner book) [DS107.3.G56] 55-5717
1. Palestine—Descr. & trav. I. Title.

GOODSPEED, Frank Lincoln, 1861- 220.
Palestine "a fifth gospel," four lectures on the Christian evidence borne by the Holy Land as it is to-day, by Frank L. Goodspeed ... Springfield, Mass., The F. A. Bassette company [c1901] 139 p. 20 cm. [BS630.G55] 1-15203
1. Palestine—Descr. & trav. I. Title.

GRUBER, Ruth, 1911- 915.69
Israel without tears; with photos. by the author. New York, Current Books, inc. [and] A. A. Wyn, 1950. 240 p. illus., ports. 21 cm. [DS126.4.G76] 50-10924
1. Palestine—Descr. & trav. I. Title.

HADDAD, Anis Charles. 915.69
Palestine speaks, by Anis Charles Haddad... Anderson, Ind., The Warner press [c1936] v, 7-173 p. front., plates. 19 1/2 cm. [DS112.H25] 37-630
1. Palestine—Descr. & trav. 2. Palestine—Soc. life & cust. I. Title.

HAMILTON, Elizabeth, 1906- *915.694
Put off thy shoes; a journey through Palestine. New York, Scribner [c1957] 192p. 22cm. [DS107.4.H27 1957a] 57-12357
1. Palestine—Descr. & trav. I. Title.

HASWELL, John Hirst Winn. 915.694'04'5
An introduction to the Holy Land, based on modern tour routes [by] J. H. Winn Haswell. New York, St. Martin's Press [1971] xi, 140 p. illus. 23 cm. [DS107.4.H344 1971] 73-181300 4.95
1. Palestine—Description and travel. I. Title.

HEGLAND, Martin, 1880- 915.69
In the Holy Land with Dr. and Mrs. Martin Hegland. Minneapolis, Augsburg publishing house, 1938. 3 p. l, 158 p. front. (maps) 20 1/2 cm. [DS107.3.H355] 39-2336
1. Palestine—Descr. & trav. I. Hegland, Georgina Ellinora (Dieson) "Mrs. Martin Hegland." 1882- joint author. II. Title.

HOFFMAN, Gail 915.694
The land and people of Israel. [Rev. ed.] Philadelphia, Lippincott [c.1960] 119p. illus. (map) 22cm. (Portraits of the nations series) 60-11189 2.95
1. Palestine—Descr. & trav. I. Title.

HOFFMAN, Gail. 915.694
The land and people of Israel. [Rev. ed.] Philadelphia, Lippincott [1955] 119 p. illus. 22 cm. (Portraits of the nations series) J. B. Lippincott Company books for young people. [DS107.3.H753 1955] 55-7770
1. Palestine—Description and travel. I. Title.

HOFFMAN, Gail. 915.69
The land and people of Israel. [1st ed.] Philadelphia, Lippincott [1950] 119 p. illus., port., map. 22 cm. (Portraits of the nations series) [DS107.3.H753] 50-5947
1. Palestine—Description and travel. I. Title.

ISAC, Edouard Victor Michel, 1891- 915.69404
The Holy Land -- then and now, by Edouard Victor Izac. [1st ed.] New York, Vantage Press [1965] 243 p. maps (on lining papers) 22 cm. [DS107.4.I9] 66-1029
1. Palestine — Descr. & trav. 2. Pilgrims and pilgrimages — Palestine. I. Title.

KIRBAN, Doreen. 915.694'04'5
Stranger in tomorrow's land, by Doreen and Diane Kirban. Huntingdon Valley, Pa., S. Kirban, c1970. 96 p. col. illus. 22 cm. [DS107.4.K48] 70-124355 4.95
1. Palestine—Description and travel. I. Kirban, Diane, joint author. II. Title.

KNIGHT, William Allen, 1863-
On the way to Bethlehem, by William Allen Knight ... New York, Boston [etc.] The Pilgrim press, 1912. ix, 222 p. front., plates. 19 cm. Illustrated lining-papers. [D5107.3.K6] 12-24042 1.25
1. Palestine—Descr. & trav. I. Title.

LEETE, Frederick De Land, bp., 1866- 915.69
Palestine; land of the light, by Frederick De Land Leete ... Boston and New York, Houghton Mifflin company, 1932. x p., 1 l., 279 p. front., plates. 19 cm. Maps on front lining-paper. London edition (Skeffington & son, limited) has title: Palestine: its scenery, peoples and history. [DS107.3.L52] 32-33813
1. Palestine—Descr. & trav. I. Title.

LEGENDRE, Adolph Alphonse Francois, 1849-1928. 220.91
... The cradle of the Bible, by Mgr. Legendre ... translated by the Dominican sisters of Portobello road, London. St. Louis, Mo., B. Herder book co.; London, Sands & co. [1930] 255 p. incl. illus. (incl. maps) pl. 19 cm. (Catholic library of religions knowledge. ix) Foreword signed: Joseph Plessis. [BX880.C3 vol. 9] (282.082) 35-23970
1. Palestine—Descr. & trav. 2. Bible—Geography. I. Sisters of the Order of St. Dominic, Portobello road, London, tr. II. Plessis, Joseph, ed. III. Title.

LYNCH, William Francis, 1801-1865. 915.69
Narrative of the United States' expedition to the river Jordan and the Dead sea, by W. F. Lynch, U.S.N., commander of the expedition, with maps and numerous illustrations. 7th ed., rev. Philadelphia, Lea and Blanchard, 1850. xx, [13]-509 p. front., plates, fold. maps. 24 1/2 cm. [DS107.L98 1850] 31-405
1. Palestine—Descr. & trav. 2. U.S.—Exploring expeditions. I. Title.

MACCOUN, Townsend, 1845-1932. 296
The Holy Land in geography and in history, By Townsend MacCoun... New York, T. MacCoun, 1897. 2 v. maps, plans. 18 cm. Contents.v. 1. Geography.--v. 1. History. [DS118.M117] 4-14461
1. Palestine—Descr. & trav. 2. Bible—Geography. 3. Palestine—Hist. 4. Jews—Hist. I. Title.

MCGILL, Ralph Emerson, 1898- 915.69
Israel revisited; with a foreword by Billy Rose. Atlanta, Tupper and Love [1950] ix. 116 p. map (on lining papers) 22 cm. [DS107.3.M23] 50-12945
1. Palestine—Descr. & trav. I. Title.

MCLENNAN, William Etridge. 232.9
In His footsteps; a record of travel to and in the land of Christ, with an attempt to mark the Lord's journeyings in chronological order from His birth to His ascension, by William E. McLennan. Rev. ed. New York, Eaton & Mains; Cincinnati, Jennings & Graham [1911] xviii, 247 p. front., illus. (incl. maps) 20 1/2 cm. Maps on lining-papers. [BT590.J7M2 1896a] 11-26628
1. Jesus Christ—Journeys. 2. Palestine—Descr. & trav. I. Title.

MCLENNAN, William Etridge. 232.9
...In His steps; a record of travel to and in the land of Christ with an attempt to mark the Lord's journeyings in chronological order from His birth to His ascension, by William E. McLennan. New York, Eaton & Mains; Cincinnati, Curts & Jennings, 1896. 111 p. incl. front., illus. (incl. maps, plan) 20 cm. (The footsteps series) Maps on lining-papers. [BT590.J7M2 1896] 39-11840
1. Jesus Christ—Journeys. 2. Palestine—Descr. & trav. I. Title.

MELVILLE, Herman, 1819-1891.
Clarel, a poem and pilgrimage in the Holy Land. By Herman Melville. New York, G. P. Putnam's sons 1876. 2 v. 18 cm. Paged continously. Contents.--v. 1. Jerusalem. The wilderness--v. 2. Mar Saba. Bethlehem. [PS238405 1876] 22-9429
1. Palestine—Descr. & trav. 2. Poetry of places—Palestine. I. Title.

MEYER, Fulgence, father, 1876- 915.69
To Our Lord's country; a familiar narrative of a voyage from the United States of America to Palestine, Asia, by Rev. Fulgence Meyer, O. F. M. Cincinnati, O., The Mountel press company, 1935. 7 p. l., 213 p. illus. 21 cm. "The contents of this book appeared serially in St. Anthony messenger, Cincinnati, Ohio, from September, 1934, until August, 1935, included."--Foreword. [Secular name: Alphonse Meyer] [DS107.3.M4] 36-5228
1. Palestine—Descr. & trav. I. Title.

MILLER, Madeleine (Sweeny) Mrs. 915.69
Footprints in Palestine; where the East begins, by Madeleine Sweeny Miller (Mrs. J. Lane Miller) commendation by Viscount Allenby, F.M.; all photographs by J. Lane Miller. New York [etc.] Fleming H. Revell company [c1936] 223, [1] p. front., plates. 22 cm. Illustrated lining-papers. [Full name: Mrs. Madeleine Georgeanna (Sweeny) Miller] [DS107.3.M58] 36-7446
1. Palestine—Descr. & trav. I. Title.

MORTON, Henry Canova Vollam, 1892- 915.69
In the steps of the Master, by H. V. Morton with illustrations and maps. New York, Dodd, 1934. xiv, 448p. maps (on lining papers) 20cm. Bibl. [DS107.3.M7] 34-40301 6.00
1. Palestine—Descr. & trav. I. Title.

MYERS, Paul Revere, 1888- 915.694
Touring the Holy Land; illustrated with actual photos. taken while in the land. Greentown, Ohio, c1954. 308p. illus. 24cm. [DS107.3.M9] 54-33353
1. Palestine— Descr. & trav. I. Title.

NEWMAN, Paul S. 915.694'04'5
Land of the Bible, by Paul S. Newman. Photos. by Adrian Williams. Norwalk, Conn., C. R. Gibson Co. [1974] 57 p. illus. 21 cm. (C. R. Gibson gift books) [DS107.4.N45] 73-88090 ISBN 0-8378-1753-6 3.95
1. Bible—Geography. 2. Palestine—Description and travel. I. Title.

NIEDERMEYER, Frederick David. 252
Palestine pathways; sermons of travel in the Holy land, by FrederickDavid Niedermeyer ... with introduction by Charles R. Erdman ... New York, Chicago [etc.] Fleming H. Revell company [c1928] 190 p. 20 cm. [BX9178.N5P3] 28-12885
1. Palestine—Descr. & trav. I. Title.

O'CEALLAIGH, Sean S 915.694
From Liffey to Jordan. Ilfracombe, Devon, A. H. Stock-well [1959] 238p. illus. 19cm. [DS107.4.O25] 59-54081
1. Palestine—Descr. & trav. I. Title.

OLCOTT, Frances Jenkins. 915.69
In the bright Syrian land, by Frances Jenkins Olcott; photographs by the author. Washington, D.C., Review and herald [1946] 3 p. l., 5-96 (i.e. 132) p. incl. front., illus. 19 cm. [DS107.3.O4] 46-858
1. Palestine—Descr. & trav. I. Title.

OLIPHANT, Laurence, 1829-1888. 915.69
Haifa; or, Life in modern Palestine, by Laurence Oliphant ... Ed., with introduction, by Chales A. Dana. New York, Harper & brothers [190-?] iv p., 1 l., 369 p. 21 cm. First published as a series of letters to the New York sun. [DS107.O48] 4-17320
1. Palestine—Descr. & trav. I. Dana, Charles Anderson, 1819-1897. ed. II. Title.

O'SHEA, Denis. 915.694
Jerusalem, the golden. Milwaukee, Bruce Pub. Co. [1954] 145p. illus. 23cm. [DS107.3.O78] 54-10177
1. Palestine—Descr. & trav. I. Title.

OURSLER, Fulton, 1893- 915.69
A skeptic in the Holy Land, by Fulton Oursler ... New York, Farrar & Rinehart, incorporated [c1936] 4 p. l., 3-250 p. 21 cm. [DS107.3.O8] 36-28745
1. Palestine—Descr. & trav. I. Title.

PARROT, Andre, 1901- 226'.09
Land of Christ; archaeology, history, geography. Translated by James H. Farley. Philadelphia, Fortress Press [1968] ix, 166 p. illus., maps, plans. 22 cm. Translation of Terre du Christ, archeologie, histoire, geographie. Bibliography: p. 147-[150] [DS107.4.P2813] 68-15863 5.95
1. Bible. N.T. Gospels—Geography. 2. Palestine—Description and travel. I. Title.

PEALE, Norman Vincent, 1898- 915.69
Adventures in the Holy Land. Englewood Cliffs, N.J., Prentice-Hall [1963] 176 p. illus. (part col.) col. map (on lining papers) 26 cm. Bibliography: p. 167-168 [DS107.4.P3 8] 63-18112
1. Palestine—Descr. & trav. I. Title.

PEREGRINATIO, Aetheriae 230
... The pilgrimage of Etheria, by M. L. McClure and C. L. Feltoe, D. D. London, Society for promoting Christian knowledge; New York, The Macmillan company [1919] xiviii, 103, [1] p. 3 pl. 19 cm. (Half-titles: Translations of Christian literature. ser. iii, Liturgical texts) Series title also at head of t.-p. Quoted formerly as Peregrinatio Silviae, or Peregrinatio ad loca sancta, after Gamurrini's first edition ... S. Silvise peregination ad loa sana,Romae, 1887. [BR45.T63P5] 20-22335
1. Palestine—Descr. & trav. 2. Pilgrims and pilgrimages—Palestine. 3. Fasts and feasts. 4. Liturgies, Early Christian. I. McClure, M. L. (Herbert) Mrs. d., 1918, tr. II. Feltoe, Charles Lett., ed. III. Title.

PHILLIPS, Ordis E 1886- 915.69
Through Europe to the Promised Land, 1951 A.D. Philadelphia, Hebrew Christian Fellowship [1951] 134 p. illus. 19 cm. [DS107.3.P57] 51-8406
1. Palestine — Descr. & trav. I. Title.

POPE Paul VI in the Holy Land 262.13
[Tr.] from German by Aileen O'Brien. Photos. by Werner Schiller. New York] Herder & Herder [c.1964] 198p. illus. (pt. col.) col. maps, ports. (pt. col.) 31cm. 64-19604 7.50
1. Paulus VI, Pope, 1897- 2. Palestine—Descr. & trav. I. Schiller, Werner.

POWELL, Adam Clayton, 1865- 915.69
Palestine and saints in Caesar's household, by A. Clayton Powell, sr. New York, R. R. Smith, 1939. viii, p., 2 l., 13-217 p. 21 cm. [BX6452.P6] 39-25033
1. Palestine—Descr. & trav. 2. Baptists.—Sermons. 3. Sermons, American. I. Title.

POWYS, Llewelyn, 1884- 915.69
A pagan's pilgrimage [by] Llewelyn Powys. New York, Harcourt, Brace and company [c1931] 207 p. front., plates. 20 cm. A

description of a journey to the Holy Land. "First edition." [DS107.3.P75] 31-6177
1. Palestine—Descr. & trav. I. Title.

PRESCOTT, Hilda Frances 915.69
Margaret
Friar Felix at large; a fifteenth century pilgrimage to the Holy Land. New Haven [Conn.] Yale University Press [1960, c.1950] 254p. Bibl.; and Bibl. notes: p.[228] -244. illus., 21cm. (Yale paperbound Y-30) 1.25 pap.,
1. Fabri, Felix, 1441 or 2-1502. 2. Palestine—Descr. and trav. I. Title.

RICHARDS, Harold Marshall 915.69
Sylvester, 1894-
30,000 miles of miracles Los Angeles, Voice of Prophecy [c1950] 112 p. illus. 20 cm. [DS107.3.R45] 51-24625
1. Palestine — Descr. & trav. 2. Flights around the world. I. Title.

ROBINSON, Edward, 1794- 220.9'1
1863.
Biblical researches in Palestine, Mount Sinai, and Arabia Petraea / Edward Robinson. New York : Arno Press, 1977. p. cm. (America and the Holy Land) Also authored by E. Smith. Reprint of the 1841 ed. published by Crocker & Brewster, Boston. Includes bibliographical references. [DS107.R664 1977] 77-70738 ISBN 0-405-10281-Xlib.bdg. : 120.00
1. Robinson, Edward, 1794-1863. 2. Smith, Eli, 1801-1857. 3. Bible—Geography. 4. Palestine—Description and travel. 5. Sinaitic Peninsula—Description and travel. 6. Palestine—Antiquities. 7. Sinaitic Peninsula—Antiquities. I. Smith, Eli, 1801-1857, joint author. II. Title. III. Series.

ROBINSON, O. Preston, 915.694
1903-
Biblical sites in the Holy Land [by] O. Preston Robinson, Christine H. Robinson. Salt Lake City, Deseret [c.]1963. 209p. illus. (pt. col.) 24cm. 63-3402 3.95
1. Palestine—Descr. & trav. I. Robinson, Christine Hinckley, joint author. II. Title.

ROBINSON, O. Preston, 915.694
1903-
Biblical sites in the Holy Land [by] O. Preston Robinson and Christine H. Robinson. Salt Lake City, Desert Book Co., 1963. 209 p. illus. 24 cm. [DS107.4.R6] 63-3402
1. Palestine—Descr. & trav. I. Robinson, Christine Hinckley, joint author. II. Title.

ROBINSON, O. Preston, 915.694
1903-
Israel's Bible lands; a walk through the past [by] O. Preston Robinson and Christine H. Robinson. [Salt Lake City] Deseret Book Co., 1973. xi, 264 p. illus. 24 cm. [DS107.4.R62] 73-88233 ISBN 0-87747-023-5 6.95
1. Bible—Geography. 2. Palestine—Description and travel. I. Robinson, Christine Hinckley, joint author. II. Title.

ROMNEY, Thomas Cottam. 915.69
A visit to the Holy Land and other Mediterranean countries, by Dr. Thomas Cottam Romney ... Boston, The Christopher publishing house [c1940] 3 p. l., 9-242 p. 20 cm. [DS49.R65] 40-29990
1. Palestine—Descr. & trav. 2. Levant—Descr. & trav. I. Title.

ROSS, Emma Jewell. 915.69
Living where Jesus lived, by Emma Jewell Ross. New York, The Macmillan company, 1941. xi p., 1 l., 111 p. front., plates. 20 cm. Map on lining-papers. "First printing." Bibliography: p. 105. [DS107.3.R727] 41-3012
1. Palestine—Descr. & trav. I. Title.

SALE-HARRISON, Leonard, 915.69
1875-
Palestine: God's monument of prophecy; the wonders of a remarkable book in a remarkable land, by L. Sale-Harrison...illustrated with photographs by the author and his wife... Harrisburg, Penna., L. Sale-Harrison; London [etc.] Pickering & Inglis [c1933] xxi, 250 p. front. (map) plates, ports. 20 cm. [DS107.3.S17] 33-29512
1. Palestine—Descr. & trav. I. Title.

SAVERY, Christine, 915.694'04
1902-
Pilgrim's logbook, [a tour through the Holy Land] by Chris Savery. Anderson, Ind., Warner Press [1973] 96 p. maps (on p. [2]-[3] of cover 21 cm. Pages 94-96 blank. [DS107.4.S323] 73-7933 ISBN 0-87162-157-6 2.50 (pbk.)
1. Palestine—Description and travel. 2. Meditations. I. Title.

SCHARFSTEIN, Sol, 1921- 915.694
Rocket trip to Israel, story by Robert Sol [pseud.] Pictures by Gabe Josephson. [New York] Ktav Pub. House, c1953. unpaged. illus. 22cm. [DS107.3.S238] 53-38111
1. Palestine—Descr. & trav. I. Title.

SCHILLER, Werner. 262.13
Pope Paul VI in the Holy Land. [Translation by Aileen O'Brien. Photos. by Werner Schiller. New York] Herder and Herder [1964] 198 p. illus. (part col.) col. maps, ports, (part col.) 31 cm. [BX1378.3P6] 64-19604
1. Paulus vi, Pope, 1897- 2. Palestine—Descr. & trav. I. Title.

SERGEANT, George, 1881- 915.69
From Egypt to the Golden Horn, by George Sergeant; with photographs by J. Lane Miller. New York, London [etc.] Fleming H. Revell company [c1940] 4 p. l., 7-254 p. front., illus. (map) plates. 22 1/2 cm. [DS49.S45] 40-32516
1. Palestine—Descr. & trav. I. Title.

SHEPARD, Judy. *915.694
Ticket to Israel, an informative guide, by Judgy Shepard and Alvin Rosenfeld. New York, Rinehart [1952] 305 p. illus. 21 cm. [DS107.3.S33] 52-55668
1. Palestine—Descr. & trav. I. Title.

SIGLER, Pearl Nixon, 1870- 915.69
God speaks again in Palestine, by P. N. Sigler ... Published under the auspices of the City rescue mission, Dayton, Ohio. [Dayton, O., Modmir publishing company, c1935] 236 p. plates, port. 21 cm. Map on front end-paper. Bibliography: p. 183; "Biblical references": p. 235-236. [DS126.S5] 35-11752
1. Palestine—Descr. & trav. 2. Jews—Restoration. 3. Bible—Propheies. I. Title.

STANLEY, Arthur Penrhyn, 915.69
1815-1881.
Sinai and Palestine, in connection with their history. By Arthur Penrhyn Stanley ... New ed., with maps and plans. New York, A. C. Armstrong and son, 1903. 1 p. l., 641 p. incl. plans. front., maps (part fold.) 22 cm. [DS107.S789] 4-16624
1. Palestine—Descr. & trav. 2. Sinaitic peninsula—Descr. & trav. I. Title.

STEVENSON, Dwight 915.694
Eshelman, 1906-
On holy ground; meditations written in Jerusalem. St. Louis, Bethany [c.1963] 144p. 21cm. 62-22317 2.50
1. Palestine—Descr. & trav. I. Title.

STEVENSON, Dwight Eshelman, 242
1906-
A way in the wilderness; Holy Land meditations, by Dwight E. Stevenson. St. Louis, Bethany Press [1968] 128 p. 21 cm. Bibliographical footnotes. [DS107.4.S73] 68-4561
1. Palestine—Description and travel. 2. Meditations. I. Title. II. Title: Holy Land meditations.

THOMSON, William *915.694
McClure, 1806-1894.
The land and the Book; or, Biblical illustrations drawn from the manners and customs, the scenes and scenery of the Holy Land. Grand Rapids, Baker Book House, 1954. 718p. illus., maps (part fold.) plans. 22cm. Bibliographical footnotes. [DS107.T475 1954] 54-11081
1. Palestine—Descr. & trav. 2. Bible—Criticism, Interpretation, etc. 3. Bible—Geography. I. Title.

VAN DYKE, Henry, 1852-1933.
Out-of-doors inthe Holy Land; impressions of travel in body and spirit, by Henry Van Dyke. New York, C. Scribner's sons, 1920. x p., 2 l., 3-297 p. front. 21 1/2 cm. (Half-title: The works of Henry Van Dyke. Avalon ed. vol. IV. Outdoor essays IV) [PS3115.A2 1920 vol. 4] 20-8225
1. Palestine—Descr. & trav. I. Title.

WAGGETT, John Macphail, 915.69
1884-
Bible landmarks in a changing land, by J. MacPhail Waggett ... introduction by Prof. Ernest Trice Thompson ... New York, Chicago [etc.] Fleming H. Revell company [c1930] 1 p. l., 5-130 p. map. 19 1/2 cm. [DS107.3.W25] 30-12235
1. Palestine—Descr. & trav. I. Title.

WALLACE, Susan Arnold 232.92
(Elston) "Mrs. Lew Wallace," 1830-1907.
The city of the King; what the child Jesus saw and heard, by Mrs Lew Wallace... Indianapolis, The Bobbs-Merrill company [1903] 97 p. front., plates. 24 cm. [BT310.W2] [915.69] 3-29850
1. Jesus Christ—Childhood. 2. Palestine—Descr. & trav. I. Title.

WEATHERHEAD, Leslie Dixon, 232.9
1893-
It happened in Palestine [by] Leslie D. Weatherhead ... New York, Cincinnati [etc.] The Abingdon press [c1936] 325 p. front., plates. 19 1/2 cm. [BT303.W28 1966a] [915.69] 37-938
1. Palestine—Descr. & trav. 2. Jesus Christ—Biog. I. Title.

WHITTINGHAM, George 915.69
Napier, 1865-
The home of fadeless splendour; or, Palestine of to-day, by George Napier Whittingham. With a foreword by Major-General Sir Arthur Wigram Money ... Illustrated with 16 etchings and maps by B. C. Boulter, and 8 coloured plates by Stanley Inchbold. New York, E. P. Dutton & company [1921] xxiv, [2], 27-360 p. front., plates (part col.) group port., map, plan, 22 cm. Plan on lining-papers. Printed in Great Britain. "A short bibliography": p. 350-351. Imperfect: half-title, frontispiece and plan on lining-papers wanting. [DS107.3.W44 1921a] 41-31757
1. Palestine—Descr. & trav. I. Title. II. Title: Palestine of to-day.

WILD, Laura Hulda, 1870- 221.9'1
Geographic influences in Old Testament masterpieces / by Laura H. Wild. Folcroft, Pa. : Folcroft Library Editions, 1980, c1915. p. cm. Reprint of the ed. published by Ginn, Boston. Includes bibliographies and indexes. [DS107.3.W445 1980] 80-36850 ISBN 0-8414-9701-X (lib. bdg.) : 30.00
1. Bible. O.T.—Geography. 2. Bible. O.T.—Criticism, interpretation, etc. 3. Palestine—Description and travel. I. Title.

WILLCOX, 915.694'04'30924
Kathleen Mary.
With Kinglake in the Holy Land. by K. M. Willcox; illus. by Harry Toothill. London, Muller, 1967. 144p. illus., 4 plates, maps, diagr. 20cm. (Adventures in geog. ser. [26]) [DS107.4.W53] 67-111290 3.75 bds.,
1. Kinglake, Alexander William. 1809-1891. 2. Palestine—Descr. & trav. I. Title. Distributed by SportShelf, New Rochelle, N.Y.

WORLD'S Sunday-school
convention, 4th, Jerusalem, 1904. Central committee.
The cruise of the eight hundred to and through Palestine. Glimpses of Bible lands: two hundred and twelve full-page photo-engravings, two twelve-inch panoramic views of Jerusalem, four colored plates of Palestine wild flowers, and fifty-eight other photographs of persons and places connected with the World's fourth Sunday-school convention, Jerusalem, April, 1904. New York, The Christian herald [c1905] 386 p. incl. front., illus. 4 col. pl., map. 15 1/2 x 21 cm. Published also under the title: Glimpses of Bible lands. [DS44.5.W91] 5-35805
1. Palestine—Descr. & trav. 2. Levant—Descr. & trav. I. Title.

WORLD'S Sunday-school
convention, 4th, Jerusalem, 1904. Central committee.
Glimpses of Bible lands; being the cruise of the eight hundred to the World's fourth Sunday-school convention in Jerusalem, April 17, 18, 19, 1904. 212 full-page pictures, 24-inch panoramic view of Jerusalem, 4 colored plates of Palestine wild flowers, 58 other illustrations of persons and places connected with the cruise. Boston, The Central committee, E. K. Warren, W. N. Hartshorn, A. B. McCrillis, 1905. 388 p. incl. front., illus. 4 col. pl., map. 15 1/2 x 21 1/2 cm. [DS44.5.W9] 5-11345
1. Palestine—Descr. & trav. 2. Levant—Descr. & trav. I. Title.

ZELIGS, Dorothy Freda. 915.69
The story of modern Israel for young people. New York, Bloch Pub. Co., 1950. xvii, 370 p. illus., ports. 23 cm. "A completely revised edition of the writer's earlier book, The story of modern Palestine." [DS107.3.Z4 1950] 50-6304
1. Palestine — Descr. & crav. 2. Jews in Palestine. 3. Zionism. I. Title.

Palestine—Description and travel—Guide-books.

FUTTERER, Antonia 915.69
Fredrich.
Palestine speaks, by the pioneer golden ark explorer, A. F. Futterer; an up-to-date timely tour through all parts of the Holyland, with a thorough explanation of its past and photographs of its present of every essential place of interest to everybody interested in the most remarkable country in all the world. With some references to its more remarkable future. Los Angeles, Calif., A. F. Futterer [1931] 748 p. incl. col. front., illus. (incl. music) fold. pl. 25 cm. Maps on lining-papers. [DS103.F8] 32-1304
1. Palestine—Descr. & trav.—Guide-books. I. Title.

HOADE, Eugene. 915.694'04'5
Guide to the Holy Land / Eugene Hoade. 8th ed. Jerusalem : Franciscan Print. Press, [1976] xi, 823 p., [9] fold. leaves of plates : ill. ; 21 cm. [DS103.H57 1976] 77-363233 6.00
1. Palestine—Description and travel—Guide-books. 2. Israel—Description and travel—Guide-books. I. Title.

ISRAEL, 915.694
Paris, New York, Nagel [1954] viii, 304p. illus., maps (part fold., part col.) 16cm. (Nagel's travel guides) Cover title: Nagel's Israel travel guide. [DS103.I8] 54-10952
1. Palestine—Descr. & trav.—Guide-books.

Palestine—Description and travel—Juvenile literature.

WARREN, Mary Phraner. 226'.09'5
The land of Christmas / text by Mary Phraner Warren ; nineteenth-century engravings and drawings. 1st U.S.A. ed. Minneapolis : Augsburg Pub. House, 1979. 116, [5] p. : ill. ; 28 cm. Bibliography: p. [121] [DS112.W19 1979] 78-58241 ISBN 0-8066-1675-X : 12.95
1. Jews—Civilization—Juvenile literature. 2. Jesus Christ—Nativity—Juvenile literature. 3. Palestine—Description and travel—Juvenile literature. I. Title.

WITTER, Evelyn. 226'.09'5
In Jesus' day / written by Evelyn Witter. St. Louis : Concordia Pub. House, c1980. p. cm. Describes everyday life in Palestine in the time of Jesus Christ. [DS112.W53] 79-24142 ISBN 0-570-03485-X pbk. : 2.50
1. Jews—Social life and customs—Juvenile literature. 2. Jesus Christ—Biography—Juvenile literature. 3. [Jews—Social life and customs.] 4. [Jesus Christ—Biography.] 5. Palestine—Description and travel—Juvenile literature. 6. Christian biography—Palestine—Juvenile literature. 7. [Palestine—History—To 70 A.D.] I. Title.

Palestine—Description and travel—Maps.

SERAPHIN, Eugene William, 232.9
father, 1898-
Maps of the land of Christ; a book of maps of Palestine, by Eugene Seraphin O.F.M., and Jerome A. Kelly, O.F.M., based on "The life of Christ" by Isidore O'Brien, O.F.M. Paterson, N.J., St. Anthony's guild, 1938. vi, 62 p. incl. col. front. illus. (part col.) maps. 28 cm. "First edition." [Secular name: William Joseph Seraphin] [BT307.O36S4] 38-32776
1. Palestine—Descr. & trav.—Maps. 2. Bible—Geography—Maps. I. Kelly, Jerome Aemilian, father, 1910- joint author. II.

O'Brien, Isidore, father, 1895- The life of Christ. III. Title.

Palestine—Description and travel—Views.

ALEXANDER, David, 1937- 225.9'1
The New Testament in living pictures; a photo guide to the New Testament, by David S. Alexander. [2d ed.] Glendale, Calif., G/L Regal Books [1973, c1972] 155 p. col. illus. 25 cm. [BS630.A58 1973] 73-79755 ISBN 0-8307-0172-9 5.95
1. Bible. N.T.—Geography. 2. Palestine—Description and travel—Views. 3. Near East—Description and travel—Views. I. Bible. N.T. English. Selections. 1973. II. Title.

ALEXANDER, David S. 221.9'0222
The Old Testament in living pictures; a photo guide to the Old Testament, by David S. Alexander. [1st ed.] Glendale, Calif., G/L Regal Books [1973] 156 p. illus. 25 cm. [DS108.5.A67] 73-85490 ISBN 0-8307-0225-3 5.95
1. Bible. O.T.—Geography. 2. Palestine—Description and travel—Views. I. Title.

ARNDT, William, 1880- 915.69
From the Nile to the waters of Damascus. St. Louis, Concordia Pub. House [1949] [DS108.5.A76] 49-9738
1. Palestine—Descr. & trav.—Views. I. Title.

BUSHELL, Gerard, 1915- 232.9'01
Jesus: where it all began, by Gerald [i.e. Gerard] Bushell. Photography by David Harris. General editor, Mordecai Raanan. New York, Abelard-Schuman [1975] 223 p. illus. (part col.) 28 cm. Adaptation of In the footsteps of Jesus, by W. E. Pax. Details the life of Jesus using historical and literary allusions and photographs of the Holy Land. [BT301.2.P382B87 1975] 74-9373 ISBN 0-200-00144-2 8.95
1. Jesus Christ—Biography. 2. [Jesus Christ—Biography.] 3. Palestine—Description and travel—Views. 4. Shrines—Palestine. I. Pax, Wolfgang E. In the footsteps of Jesus. II. Harris, David, fl. 1967- illus. III. Title.

CONVERSE, Gordon N. 225.9'5
Fishers of men : the way of the Apostles / photos. by Gordon N. Converse ; text by Robert J. Bull and B. Cobbey Crisler. Englewood Cliffs, N.J. : Prentice-Hall, c1980. 140 p. : ill. ; 23 x 29 cm. Contains selections from the New Testament. [DS107.4.C666] 19 80-23760 ISBN 0-13-322610-7 : 14.95
1. Palestine—Description and travel—Views. 2. Mediterranean region—Description and travel—Views. 3. Apostles. I. Bull, Robert J. II. Crisler, B. Cobbey, 1933- III. Bible. N.T. English. Selections. 1980. IV. Title.

CRETEN, J. 915.694
The Holy Land. Tr. by G. A. Colville, Gladys Wheelhouse [Munich, W. Andermann] Dist. by Garden City N. Y. Doubleday [1963, c.1958] 60p. col. illus. 17cm. (Panorama-books) 64-9534 2.95 bds.,
1. Palestine—Descr. & trav.—Views. I. Title.

DURAN, Frederique 915.694
In the steps of Jesus. Introd. by Cardinal Lienart. Text and archaeologicalnotes by Rene Leconte. Photos. by Frederique Duran. [Translated from the French by Margaret Case] New York, Hastings House [1960, c.1953] 121p. (chiefly illus., part col.) map. 31cm. 60-1355 8.50
1. Palestine—Descr. & trav.—Views. I. Leconte, Rene II. Title.

HOLLEY, Jasper Elza, 1875- 915.694
Pictorial profile of the Holy Land, by J. E. Holley and Carolyn F. Holley. [Westwood, N. J.] F. H. Revell Co. [1959] 248p. (chiefly illus., maps) 26cm. [DS108.5.H68] 59-8727
1. Palestine—Descr. & trav.—Views. I. Holley, Carolyn Fizzell, joint author. II. Title.

PAX, Wolfgang E. 232.9'01
In the footsteps of Jesus [by] Wolfgang E. Pax. New York, Putnam [1970] 231 p. illus. (part col.), map (on lining papers) 29 cm. Bibliography: p. 229-231. [BT301.2.P38 1970] 78-90908 15.00
1. Jesus Christ—Biography. 2. Palestine—Description and travel—Views. 3. Shrines—Palestine. I. Title.

ROSENBERG, Stuart E. 200'.95694
Great religions of the Holy Land; an historical guide to sacred places and sites [by] Stuart E. Rosenberg. South Brunswick, A. S. Barnes [1971] 192 p. illus. 29 cm. [DS108.5.R68 1971] 70-159839 ISBN 0-498-07994-5 15.00
1. Palestine—Description and travel—Views. 2. Shrines—Palestine. I. Title.

ROSNER, Jakob, 1902- 915.69
A Palestine picture book; photographs by Jakob Rosner. New York, Schocken Books [1947] 141 p. (p. 11-141 illus.) 29 cm. [DS108.5.R85] 47-4326
1. Palestine—Descr. & trav.—Views. I. Title.

SHAW, Irwin, 1913- 915.69
Report on Israel, by Irwin Shaw and Robert Capa. (New York) Simon and Schuster [1950] 144 p. illus., ports. 27 cm. [DS108.5.S48] 50-3713
1. Palestine—Description and travel—Views. 2. Palestine—History—1948- I. Capa, Robert, 1913-1954, joint author. II. Title.

TAYLOR, Lawrence E *915.694
The Holy Land in pictures. San Antonio, Naylor Co. [1957] 76p. illus. 22cm. [DS108.5.T3] 57-4504
1. Palestine—Descr. & trav.—Views. I. Title.

Palestine—Foreign relations

GLICK, Edward Bernard. 327.569408
Latin America and the Palestine problem. New York, Theodor Herzl Foundation, 1958. viii, 199 p. 23 cm. Bibliography: p. 182-196. [DS126.4.G53] 58-3123
1. Palestine—For. rel. 2. Israel—For. rel. I. Title.

Palestine—Historical geography.

GARSTANG, John, 1876-1956. 222'.2'07
Joshua-Judges / by John Garstang. Grand Rapids : Kregel Publications, 1978. p. cm. (Kregel limited edition library series) Reprint of the 1931 ed. published by Constable, London, under title: The foundations of Bible history: Joshua, Judges. Includes index. [BS1295.G35 1978] 78-9518 ISBN 0-8254-2719-3 : 16.95
1. Jews—History—To 953 B.C. 2. Bible. O.T. Joshua—Criticism, interpretation, etc. 3. Bible. O.T. Judges—Criticism, interpretation, etc. 4. Palestine—Historical geography. I. Title.

LE STRANGE, Guy, 1854-1933 915.6903
Palestine under the Moslems; a description of Syria and the Holy Land from A. D. 650 to 1500. Tr. from works of medieval Arab geographers. New introd. by Walid Khalidy. Beirut, Khayats [Mystic, Conn., Verry] 1965. xxii, 604p. illus., maps. plans. 21cm. (Khayats oriental reprints, no. 14) [DS124.L6] 66-1063 9.00
1. Palestine—Historical geography. 2. Syria—Historical geography. I. Title.

NOTH, Martin, 1902- 221.9
The Old Testament world. Tr. [from German] by Victor I. Gruhn. Philadelphia, Fortress [c.1962-1966] xxii, 404p. illus., plans, maps. 24cm. [BS1197.N6513] 65-10061 8.00
1. Palestine — Historical geography. 2. Bibl. O. T. — Antiq. 3. Bible. O. T. — Criticism. Textual. I. Title.

OWEN, George Frederick, 1897- 220.9'1
The Holy Land / by G. Frederick Owen ; foreword by James B. Irwin. Kansas City : Beacon Hill Press of Kansas City, c1977. 327 p. : ill. ; 27 cm. Bibliography: p. 325-327. [DS108.9.Q94] 77-76289 ISBN 0-8341-0489-X : 9.95
1. Palestine—Historical geography. I. Title.

PEARLMAN, Moshe, 1911- 221.9'3
Digging up the Bible : the stories behind the great archaeological discoveries in the Holy Land / Moshe Pearlman. New York : Morrow, 1980. 240 p. : ill. ; 26 cm. Includes index. Bibliography: p. 230-232. [DS108.9.P4] 19 79-48063 ISBN 0-688-03677-5 : 19.95
1. Bible O.T.—Antiquities. 2. Palestine—Historical geography. 3. Palestine—Antiquities. I. Title.

SMITH, George Adam, Sir 1856- 915.69
The historical geography of the Holy land, especially in relation to the history of Israel and of the early church, by George Adam Smith ... With six maps. 9th ed. New York, A. C. Armstrong and son [etc., etc.] 1902. xxvii, 713, [1] p. vi maps (part fold., incl. fronts.) 22 1/2 cm. One of the maps in pocket and one in the text. "Appendix IV. The bibliography of eastern Palestine": p. 665-667. [DS107.S6 1902] 3-12955
1. Palestine—Historical geography. 2. Bible—Geography. 3. Jews—Hist. I. Title.

SMITH, George Adam, Sir 1856-1942 915.694/03
The historical geography of the Holy Land. Introd. by H. H. Rowley [Magnolia, Mass., P. Smith, 1968] 512p. maps. 20cm. (Harper torchbk., Cloister lib., rebound) Bibl. of Eastern Palestine: p. 446-447 [DS107.S6 1966] 6.00
1. Palestine—Historical geography. 2. Bible—Geography. I. Title.

SMITH, George Adam, Sir, 1856-1942 915.694'03
The historical geography of the Holy Land, by George Adam Smith. Introd. by H. H. Rowley. Gloucester, Mass., Peter Smith, 1972. 515 p. maps. 21 cm. Bibl. Index of authorities: p. 498-505. 66-19780 ISBN 0-8446-4006-9 7.50
1. Palestine—Historical geography. 2. Bible—Geography. I. Title.

SMITH, Sir George Adam, 1856-1942. 915.69403
The historical geography of the Holy Land. Introd. by H. H. Rowley. New York, Harper & Row [1966] 512 p. maps. 20 cm. (Harper torchbooks) The Cloister library. "Bibliography of eastern Palestine": p. 446-447. "Index of authorities": p. 498-505. [DS107.S6 1966] 66-19780
1. Palestine — Historical geography. 2. Bible — Geography. I. Title.

SMITH, William Walter, 1868-1942. 915.694
The students' historical geography of the Holy Land. Grand Rapids, Baker Book House, 1954. ix, 65p. illus., maps. 20cm. Published in 1912 under title: The students' illustrated historical geography of the Holy Land. [DS107.3.S72 1954] 54-11080
1. Palestine—Historical geography. I. Title.

Palestine—History

AVI-YONAH, Michael, 1904- 933
A history of the Holy Land, edited by Michael Avi-Yonah. [Translated by Charles Weiss and Pamela Fitton. 1st American ed. New York] Macmillan [1969] 323 p. illus. (part col.), maps, ports. 29 cm. [DS117.A9 1969] 70-84052 14.95
1. Palestine—History. I. Title.

AVI-YONAH, Michael, 1904- 709'.5694
The Holy Land. Special photography by Mario Carrieri. [1st ed.] New York, Holt, Rinehart and Winston [1973, c1972] 288 p. illus. 26 cm. (World cultural guides) [DS111.A88 1973] 72-83345 ISBN 0-03-003466-3 9.95
1. Palestine—History. 2. Palestine—Antiquities. 3. Art—Israel. I. Title.

BULFINCH, Stephen Greenleaf, 1809-1870. 296
The Holy Land and its inhabitants. By S. G. Bulfinch. Cambridge, J. Munroe and company, 1834. 1 p. l., iv, 298 p. front. (fold. map) 16 cm. (Added t.-p. The Sunday library for young persons. Ed. by the Rev. H. Ware, jr. v. 3) [DS118.B9] 5-7820
1. Palestine—Hist. 2. Jews—Antiq. I. Title.

JONES, Arnold Hugh Martin, 1904- 933
The Herods of Judaea, by A. H. M. Jones ... Oxford, The Clarendon press, 1938. xii, 271, [1] p. front., 7 pl., fold. maps, fold. geneal tab. 20 cm. Map on lining-paper. [DS122.J7] 38-16083
1. Herod, House of. 2. Palestine—Hist. I. Title.

KITTO, John, 1804-1854. 296
The Bible history of the Holy Land. By John Kitto ... New ed. London, New York, G. Routledge and sons, 1867. 2 p. l., 496 x p. illus., plates, 2 maps (incl. front.) 22 cm. Published in 1841 as part of the author's Palestine, the Bible history of the Holy Land. 2 vols. [DS118.K64 1867] 17-12795
1. Palestine—Hist. I. Title.

KITTO, John, 1804-1854. 933
The history of Palestine, from the patriarchal age to the present time, by John Kitto ... New York, R. Sears [etc.] 1851. 3 p. l., 223 p. front., illus., fold. map. 20 cm. Added t.-p., illustrated. [DS118.K62 1851 a] 33-32446
1. Palestine—Hist. 2. Jews—Hist.—To A. D. 70. I. Title.

KITTO, John, 1804-1854. 933
The history of Palestine, from the patriarchal age to the present time; with introductory chapters on the geography and natural history of country, and on the customs and institutions of the Hebrews. By John Kitto ... With upwards of 200 illustrations. Boston, Gould and Lincoln, 1852. iv p., 1 l., 426 p. illus. 20 cm. [DS118.K62 1852] 33-32447
1. Palestine—Hist. 2. Jews—Hist.—To A. D. 70. 3. Palestine—Descr. & trav. I. Title.

OLMSTEAD, Albert Ten Eyck, 1880- 933
History of Palestine and Syria to the Macedonian conquest, by A. T. Olmstead ... New York, London, C. Scribner's sons, 1931. xxxii p. 2 l., 664 p. col. front., illus., plates, maps (1 fold.) plans, facsims. 25 cm. Bibliographical foot-notes. [DS121.O4] 31-32522
1. Palestine—Hist. 2. Syria—Hist. I. Title.

OWEN, George Frederick, 1897- 933
Abraham to Allenby, by G. Frederick Owen ... Grand rapids, Mich., Wm. B. Eerdmans publishing company, 1939. 351 p. front., plates. 23 cm. Bibliography: p. 337-341. [DS118.O8] 39-9950
1. Palestine—Hist. I. Title.

OWEN, George Frederick, 1897- 933
Abraham to the Middle-East crisis. [4th ed., rev.] Grand Rapids, Eerdmans Pub. Co. [1957] 429p. illus., ports., map. 24cm. An enlarged ed. of the author's work first published in 1939 under title: Abraham to Allenby. Bibliography:p. 425-429. [DS118.O8 1957] 57-13039
1. Palestine—Hist. I. Title.

TALMAGE, Thomas DeWitt, 1832-1902. 232.9
From manger to throne, Embracing a new life of Jesus the Christ, and a history of Palestine and its people, by Rev. T. DeWitt Talmage, D.D. including Dr. Talmage's account of his journey to, through, and from the Christ-land. Illustrated with more than four hundred ... engravings ... Also a grand panorama of the crucifixion, in twelve colors, and ten feet in length ... Sold only by subscription. Philadelphia, Pa., Historical publishing company, [1890] 1 p. l., 656 p. front., illus. (incl. maps) plates (part col., double) ports. 26 1/2 cm. [BT301.T2 1890a] 33-33635
1. Jesus Christ—Biog. 2. Palestine—Hist. I. Title.

TALMAGE, Thomas DeWitt, 1832-1902. 232.9
From manger to throne; embracing a new life of Jesus the Christ and a history of Palestine and its people, by Rev. T. DeWitt Talmage ... Including an account of the author's journey to, through and from the Christ-land. Illustrated with more than two hundred ... engravings ... Philadelphia, Pa., Published by Historical publishing company for The Christian Herald, 1893. 3 p. l., 33-544 p. front., illus., ports. 23 cm. [BT301.T2 1893] 33-35167
1. Jesus Christ—Biog. 2. Palestine—Hist. I. Title.

Palestine—History—1917-1948.

FURLONGE, Geoffrey Warren, Sir, 1903- 915.694 B
Palestine is my country; the story of Musa Alami [by] Sir Geoffrey Furlonge. New York, Praeger [1969] viii, 244 p. illus., maps, ports. 22 cm. Bibliography: p. 240. [DS126.F83 1969b] 76-94116 6.95
1. al-'Alami, Musa, 1897- 2. Palestine—History—1917-1948. 3. Jewish-Arab relations. I. Title.

Palestine—History—Pictorial works.

THORBECKE, Ellen (Kolban) 915.69
Promised land, described and photographed by Ellen Thorbecke, with an introduction by Dr. W. J. R. Thorbecke ... Cover, diagrams and sketches designed by I. David. New York, London, Harper & brothers [1947] 171, [1] p. illus. (part col., incl. maps) diagrs. 23 1/2 x 19 1/2 cm. Errata slip inserted. [DS149.T52] 47-3298
1. Palestine—Hist.—Pictorial works. 2. Jews in Palestine. I. Title.

Palestine—History—To 70 A.D.

AVI-YONAH, Michael, 1904- 933
The Holy Land, from the Persian to the Arab conquests (536 B.C. to A.D. 640); a historical geography. Grand Rapids, Baker Bk. [1966] 231p. 24maps. 23cm. (transliterated: Ge'ografyah historit shel Erets-Yisrael) [DS118.A8713] 65-18260 5.95
1. Palestine—Hist.—To 70 A.D. 2. Palestine—Hist.—70-638. I. Title.

Palestine in Judaism.

HESCHEL, Abraham Joshua, 1907- 296'.095694
Israel: an echo of eternity. Drawings by Abraham Rattner. New York, Farrar, Straus and Giroux [1969] 233 p. illus. 21 cm. Bibliographical footnotes. [BM729.P3H37 1969] 69-11573 5.50
1. Palestine in Judaism. 2. Israel. I. Title.

Palestine in literature.

HALKIN, Abraham S., 1903- ed. 892.41093
Zion in Jewish literature. New York, Herzl Press [c.]1961. 135p. Bibl. 61-10026 2.00 pap.,
1. Palestine in literature. 2. Hebrew literature—Hist. & crit. I. Title.

Palestine in Mohammedanism.

MATTHEWS, Charles D 1901- 297
Palestine, Mohammedan Holy Land; with a foreword by Julian Obermann. New Haven, Yale University Press, 1949. xxx, 176 p. fold. map. 26 cm. (Yale oriental series. Researches, v. 24) Bibliography: p. 157-158. [BP163.M38] 49-50057
1. Palestine in Mohammedanism. 2. Mohammedanism—Relations. 3. Jerusalem. 4. Hebron, Palestine. I. Title. II. Series.

Palestine in the Bible.

DAVIES, William David, 1911- 236
The Gospel and the land; early Christianity and Jewish territorial doctrine, by W. D. Davies. Berkeley, University of California Press [1974] xiv, 521 p. illus. 24 cm. Bibliography: p. 439-471. [BS2545.P43D38] 72-82228 ISBN 0-520-02278-5 15.00
1. Palestine in the Bible. 2. Palestine in Judaism. I. Title.

DAVIES, William David, 1911- 296.3'877
The territorial dimension of Judaism / W. D. Davies. Berkeley : University of California Press, c1982. xviii, 169 p. ; 21 cm. Includes index. Bibliography: p. [149]-156. [BS1199.P26D38 1982] 19 81-53 ISBN 0-520-04331-6 : 14.95
1. Palestine in the Bible. 2. Palestine in Judaism. I. Title.

HONG, Christopher C. 236
To whom the land of Palestine belongs / Christopher C. Hong. 1st ed. Hicksville, N.Y. : Exposition Press, c1979. 178 p. ; 22 cm. Includes bibliographical references and indexes. [BS1199.P26H66] 78-69897 ISBN 0-682-49161-6 : 6.50
1. Bible—Criticism, interpretation, etc. 2. Palestine in the Bible. 3. Covenants (Theology)—Biblical teaching.

Palestine—Kings and rulers—Biography.

JORDEN, Paul J. 222'.40924 B
A man's man called by God / Paul J. Jorden, with Carole Sanderson Streeter ; [cover art by Joe Van Severen]. Wheaton, Ill. : Victor Books, c1980. 180 p. ; 21 cm. [BS580.D3J59] 19 80-50675 ISBN 0-88207-220-X (pbk.) : 3.50
1. David, King of Israel. 2. Bible. O.T.—Biography. 3. Palestine—Kings and rulers—Biography. I. Streeter, Carole Sanderson, joint author. II. Title.

NYSTROM, Carolyn. 222'.40924 B
A woman's workshop on David and his Psalms / with helps for leaders, Carolyn Nystrom. Grand Rapids, Mich. : Zondervan Pub. House, c1982. 159 p. : maps ; 21 cm. Includes index. Bibliography: p. 157-158. [BS580.D3N97 1982] 19 82-2703 ISBN 0-310-41931-X pbk. : 2.95
1. David, King of Israel. 2. Bible. O.T.—Biography. 3. Bible. O.T. Psalms—Textbooks. 4. Palestine—Kings and rulers—Biography. I. Title.

Palestine—Library resources.

GUIDE to America-Holy Land studies, 1620-1948 / edited by Nathan M. Kaganoff ; introduction by Moshe Davis ; foreword by Nathan M. Kaganoff. New York, N.Y. : Praeger, c1982. p. cm. Includes index. Contents.Contents. — v. 2. Political relations and American Zionism. [Z3476.G84 1982] 19 82-13322 ISBN 0-03-062812-1 (v. 2) : 26.95 016.95694
1. Palestine—Library resources. 2. United States—Relations—Palestine—Library resources. 3. Palestine—Relations—United States—Library resources. I. Kaganoff, Nathan M.

Palestine — Religion.

GRAHAM, William Creighton, 1887- 292.2
Culture and conscience; an archaeological study of the new religious past in ancient Palestine, by William Creighton Graham ... and Herbert Gordon May ... Chicago, Ill., The University of Chicago press [c1936] xxviii, 356 p. front. (map) illus. (incl. plans) 20 cm. (Half-title: The University of Chicago publications in religious education. Hand-books of ethics and religion) Maps on lining-papers. [BL1640. G7] 221.98 36-18281
1. Palestine—Religion. 2. Palestine—Antiq. 3. Bible. O. T.—History of contemporary events, etc. 4. Civilization, Semitic. 5. Bible—Antiq. 6. Excavations (Archaelogy)—Palestine. 7. Bible—History of contemporary events, etc.—O. T. I. May, Herbert Gordon. 1904- joint author. II. Title.

HABEL, Norman C 291
Yahweh versus Baal: a conflict of religious cultures; a study in the relevance of Ugaritic materials for the early faith of Israel, by Norman C. Habel. New York, Published for the School for Graduate Studies, Concordia Seminary, St. Louis [by] Bookman Associates, 1964. 128 p. 21 cm. (Concordia Theological Seminary, St. Louis Graduate study no. 6) Revised and shortened ed. of the author's thesis, Concordia Theological Seminary. Bibliography: p. 119-121. [BL1670.H3] 64-14448
1. Res Shamra. 2. Palestine — Religion. 3. Bible. O.T. — Criticism, interpretation, etc. I. Title. II. Series: Concordia Theological Seminary, St. Louis. School for Graduate Studies. Graduate study no. 6

HIGGENS, Elford. 296
Hebrew idolatry and superstition: its place in folk-lore. Port Washington, N.Y., Kennikat Press [1971] x, 80 p. 21 cm. Reprint of the 1893 ed. [BL1650.H6 1971] 73-118527 ISBN 0-8046-1150-5
1. Palestine—Religion. 2. Superstition. 3. Judaism—History—To 70 A.D. 4. Folk-lore. I. Title.

PALESTINE. Commission on the affairs of the orthodox patriarchate of Jerusalem.
Report of the Commission appointed by the Government of Palestine to inquire into the affairs of the orthodox patriarchate of Jerusalem, by the commissioners, Sir Anton Bertram...and Harry Charles Luke... London, New York [etc.] Oxford university press, H. Milford, 1921. vi p., 2 l., [3]-336 p. 22 1/2 cm. [BX440.A5 1921] 22-17985
I. Bertram, Sir Anton, 1869- II. Luke, Harry Charles Joseph, 1884- III. Title.

VIOLETT, Ebal Eleadah, 1880- 223.
In Palestine with the Twenty-third psalm, by E. E. Violette, Cincinnati, The Standard publishing company [c1918] 68 p. front. 18 cm. [BS1450.23d.V5] 18-20257
I. Title.

Palestine — Social life and customs

BAILEY, Albert Edward, 1871- 220.93
Daily life in Bible times, by Albert Edward Bailey. New York, C. Scribner's sons, 1943. xx p., 1 l., 360 (i.e. 362) p. illus. (incl. maps, plans, facsims.) diagr. 20 1/2 cm. "Bibliographical references": p. 329-333. [DS112.B27] 43-15531
1. Palestine—Soc. life & cust. 2. Bible—Antiq. I. Title.

BAR-DAVID, Molly (Lyons) 1910- 915.694
My Promised Land. New York, Putnam [1953] 307p. 22cm. [DS112.B313] 53-8155
1. Palestine—Soc. life & cust. I. Title.

BOUQUET, Alan Coates, 1884- 225.91
Everyday life in New Testament times; illustrated from drawings by Marjorie Quennell. New York, Scribner, 1954 [c1953] 235 p. illus. 24 cm. [DS112.B64 1954] 54-7082
1. Bible. N.T.—History of contemporary events, etc. 2. Palestine—Social life and customs. I. Title.

CASSANDRE. 232.9'2 B
Life when Jesus was a boy / written and illustrated by Cassandre. Valley Forge, Pa : Judson Press, c1981. [48] p. : ill. (some col.) ; 21 x 27 cm. Describes how Jesus might have lived as a boy, interweaving the customs and practices of the time. Includes explanatory material on terms in the story. [BT320.C37] 19 81-7283 ISBN 0-8170-0913-2 pbk. : 5.95
1. Jesus Christ—Childhood—Juvenile literature. 2. [Jesus Christ—Childhood.] 3. [Palestine—Social life and customs.] I. Title.

DANIEL-ROPS, Henry, 1901-
Daily life in the time of Jesus. Translated by Patrick O'Brian. New York, New American Library [1964, c1962] 448 p. map. 18 cm. (Mentor-Omega book, MQ570) 67-13578
1. Palestine — Soc. life & cust. 2. Bible. N. T. — History of contemporary events, etc. I. Title.

DANIEL-ROPS, Henry [Real name: Henry Jules Charles Petiot] 933
Daily life in the time of Jesus. Tr. by Patrick O'Brian. New York, Hawthorn [c.1962] 512p. 22cm. 62-9040 6.00
1. Palestine—Soc. life & cust. 2. Bible. N.T.—History of contemporary events, etc. I. Title.

GIL, Emma (Wiliams) Mrs. 1870- 220.93
Home life in the Bible, by Emma Williams Gill ... Nashville, Tenn., Broadman press [c1936] 6 p. l., 17-189 p. illus., 1 pl. 21 cm. [Full name: Mrs. Emma Geraldine (Williams) Gill] [BS620.G5] 37-2513
1. Palestine—Soc. life & cust. 2. Sociology, Biblical. I. Title.

HENDERSON, Robert J. 220.9 (j)
Life in Bible times, by Robert Henderson and Ian Gould. Consultant editor, Mary Alice Jones. [Chicago] Rand McNally [1967] 48 p. illus. (part col.) 28 cm. [BS621.H44 1967] 67-18286
1. Bible—Antiquities. 2. Palestine—Social life and customs. I. Gould, Ian, joint author. II. Title.

KLINCK, Arthur William, 1900- 220.93
Home life in Bible times; a study in Biblical antiquities, by Arthur W. Klinck ... illustrated by the author. St. Louis, Mo., Concordia publishing house, 1947. vi, 142 p. illus., diagrs. 19 cm. (Concordia teacher training series) [DS112.K5] 47-23888
1. Palestine—Soc. life & cust. 2. Bible—Antiq. I. Title.

VAN LENNEP, Henry John, 1815-1889. 296
Bible lands; their modern customs and manners illustrative of Scripture, by the Rev. Henry J. Van-Lennep ... New York, Harper & brothers, 1903. 832 p. incl. illus., pl. front., fold. maps. 24 cm. Title edition. [DS112.V26] 3-12262
1. Palestine—Soc. life & cust. 2. Syria—Soc. life & cust. I. Title.

VAN-LENNEP, Henry John, 1815-1889. 296
Bible lands; their modern customs and manners illustrative of Scripture. By the Rev. Henry J. Van-Lennep ... New York, Harper & brothers, 1875. 832 p. incl. illus., pl. front., fold. maps 24 cm. [DS112.V25] 3-12079
1. Palestine—Soc. life & cust. 2. Syria—Soc. life & cust. I. Title.

WEINGARTEN, Murray. 915.694
Life in a kibbutz. New York, Reconstructionist Press, 1955. 173 p. 21 cm. [DS112.W27] 55-7308
1. Palestine—Social life and customs. 2. Communistic settlements. I. Title.

Palestine—Social life and customs—Study and teaching.

RICE, Lillian (Moore) 220.91
In the land where Jesus lived. Illustrated by Don Fields. [Teacher's ed.] Nashville, Convention Press [1967] 104, [17] p. illus., forms. 20 cm. Map on p. [4] of cover. "Church study course [of the Sunday School Board of the Southern Baptist Convention] This book is number 95 in category 2, section for juniors." "Helps for the teacher": [17] p. (2d group) [BS621.R5] 67-27898
1. Bible—Antiquities—Study and teaching. 2. Palestine—Social life and customs—Study and teaching. I. Southern Baptist Convention. Sunday School Board. II. Title.

RICE, Lillian (Moore) 220.91
In the land where Jesus lived. Illustrated by Don Fields. [Teacher's ed.] Nashville, Convention Press [1967] 104, [17] p. illus., forms. 20 cm. Map on p. [4] of cover. "Church study course [of the Sunday School Board of the Southern Baptist Convention] This book is number 95 in category 2, section for juniors." "Helps for the teacher": [17] p. (2d group) A teacher's supplement to Sunday School teaching, which describes the social customs, geography, and climate of Palestine in Biblical times. [BS621.R5] AC 67
1. Bible—Antiquities—Study and teaching. 2. Palestine—Social life and customs—Study and teaching. I. Southern Baptist Convention. Sunday School Board. II. Fields, Don, illus. III. Title.

Palestrina, Giovanni Pierluigi da, 1525?-1594.

PALESTRINA, Giovanni Pierluigi, 1525?-1594. 783.2'2'54
Pope Marcellus Mass; an authoritative score, backgrounds and sources, history and analysis, views and comments. Edited by Lewis Lockwood. [1st ed.] New York, W. W. Norton [1975] ix, 142 p. music. 21 cm. (A Norton critical score) Bibliography: p. 141-142. [M2011.P25M38 1975] 74-17020 ISBN 0-393-02185-8 ISBN 0-393-09242-9 (pbk.)
1. Palestrina, Giovanni Pierluigi, 1525?-1594. Missa Papae Marcelli. 2. Masses—To 1800—Scores. I. Lockwood, Lewis, ed.

II. [Missa Papae Marcelli] III. Title. IV. Series.

PYNE, Zoe Kendrick. 783'.0924 B
Giovanni Pierluigi da Palestrina, his life and times. Westport, Conn., Greenwood Press [1970] xxv, 232 p. illus., music, port. 23 cm. Reprint of the 1922 ed. Includes bibliographical references. [ML410.P15P9 1970b] 74-100831 ISBN 0-8371-4002-1
1. Palestrina, Giovanni Pierluigi da, 1525?-1594.

PYNE, Zoe Kendrick. 783'.0924 B
Giovanni Pierluigi da Palestrina, his life and times. Freeport, N.Y., Books for Libraries Press [1970] xxv, 232 p. illus., port. 23 cm. "First published 1922." [ML410.P15P9 1970] 79-107828
1. Palestrina, Giovanni Pierluigi da, 1525?-1594.

ROCHE, Jerome. 783'.0924
Palestrina. London, New York, Oxford University Press, 1971. 60 p. music. 22 cm. (Oxford studies of composers, 7) "List of works": p. 54-60. [ML410.P15R5] 75-32091 ISBN 0-19-314117-5 £0.90
1. Palestrina, Giovanni Pierluigi da, 1525?-1594. Works. I. Title. II. Series.

Paley, William, 1743-1805.

CLARKE, Martin Lowther. 283'.092'4 B
Paley; evidences for the man [by] M. L. Clarke. [Toronto, Buffalo] University of Toronto Press [1974] viii, 161 p. 22 cm. Includes bibliographical references. [BX5199.P26C55 1974] 73-86991 ISBN 0-8020-2112-3 10.00
1. Paley, William, 1743-1805.

LEMAHIEU, D. L., 1945- 230'.3'0924
The mind of William Paley : a philosopher and his age / D. L. LeMahieu. Lincoln : University of Nebraska Press, c1976. xi, 215 p. ; 23 cm. Based on the author's thesis, Harvard University. Includes bibliographical references and index. [BL182.L45] 75-22547 ISBN 0-8032-0865-0 : 12.95
1. Paley, William, 1743-1805. Natural theology. 2. Paley, William, 1743-1805. 3. Natural theology—History of doctrines. I. Title.

PALEY, William, 1743-1805. 252.
The works of William Paley... containing his life, Moral and political philosophy, Evidences of Christianity, Natural theology, Tracts, Horae Paulinae, Clergyman's companion, and sermons, printed verbatim from the original editions. Complete in one volume. New ed. Philadelphia, J. J. Woodward, 1836. 2 p. l., xxvi, 27-604 p. front. 23 cm. Added t.-p., engraved, with vignette. [BR75.P3 1836] 27-9585
I. Title.

Palladino, Eusapia, 1854-1918.

CARRINGTON, Hereward, 1880- 133.9
The American seances with Eusapia Palladino. New York, Garrett Publications, 1954. 273p. 20cm. [BF1283.P3C28] 54-7143
1. Palladino, Eusapia, 1854-1918. I. Title.

CARRINGTON, Hereward, 1880- 133.
Eusapia Palladino and her phenomena, by Hereward Carrington ... New York, B. W. Dodge & company, 1909. xiv, 353 p. front. (port.) illus., plates. 21 cm. [BF1283.P3] 9-29965 2.00
1. Palladino, Eusapia, 1854- 2. Spiritualism. I. Title.

FEILDING, Everard, 1867-1936. 133.91072
Sittings with Eusapia Palladino & other studies. Introd. by E. J. Dingwall, New Hyde Park, N.Y., University Books [1963] 324 p. illus. 24 cm. [BF1030.P3F42] 63-18682
1. Palladino, Eusapia, 1854-1918. 2. Spiritualism. I. Title.

FEILDING, Everard [Francis Henry Everard Joseph Feilding] 133.91072
Sittings with Eusapia Palladino & other studies. Introd. by E. J. Dingwall. New Hyde Park, N.Y., University Bks. [c.1963] 324p. illus. 24cm. 63-18682 10.00
1. Palladino, Eusapia, 1854-1918. 2. Spiritualism. I. Title.

Pallotti, Vincenzo, Saint, 1795-1850.

BONIFAZI, Flavian. 282'.0924
Our Pallottine heritage; for the infinite glory of God. Baltimore, Pallottine Fathers & Brothers Press, 1968. x, 48 p. 23 cm. Bibliography: p. ix-x. [BX4700.P23B58] 68-29101
1. Pallotti, Vincenzo, Saint, 1795-1850. 2. Pallottines. I. Title.

BONIFAZI, Flavian. 922.22
Soul of a saint; St. Vincent Pallotti, pioneer of Catholic action. Staten Island, N. Y., Alba House [1963] 192 p. 21 cm. Bibliography: p. [185]-186. [BX4700.P23B6] 63-19455
1. Pallotti, Vincenzo, Saint, 1795-1850. I. Title.

BURTON, Katherine (Kurz) 1890- 922.245
In haven we shall rest; the life of Vincenzo Pallotti, founder of the Congregation of the Catholic Apostolate. Foreword by Francis Cardinal Spellman. New York, Benziger Bros. [1955] 214p. illus. 21cm. [BX4705.P36B8] 55-12726
1. Palloti, Vincenzo, 1795-1850. I. Title.

GREENE, Ellis 282'.0924(B)
Champion of the apostolate; the life of St. Vincent Pallotti. Illustrated by Dorothy Koch. North Easton, Mass., Holy Cross Pr., 1967. 111p. illus. 22cm. [BX4700.P23G7] 67-25215 2.50
1. Pallotti, Vincenzo, Saint, 1795-1850 I. Title.

HERBERT, Mary Elizabeth (A'Court) Herbert, baroness, 1822-1911. 922.245
Venerable Vincent Pallotti, apostle and mystic, by Lady Mary E. Herbert, revised and enlarged by the Rev. Nicholas M. Wilwers ... Milwaukee, The Pallottine fathers, 1942. 160 p. 8 fronts. (incl. port., facsim.) on 4 l. 19 cm. [BX4705.P36H4] 42-12991
1. Pallotti, Vincenzo, 1795-1850. I. Wilwers, Nicholas M., ed. II. Title.

PALLOTTI, Vincenzo, Saint, 1795-1850. 242
Spiritual thoughts and aspirations of St. Vincent Pallotti. Translated and edited under the supervision of Flavian Bonifazi. Baltimore, Pallottine Fathers Press, 1964. xix, 227 p. 21 cm. [BX4700.P23A33] 64-8852
I. Bonifazi, Flavian, ed. and tr. II. Title.

[WEBER, Eugen] 922.245
Vincent Pallotti an apostle and mystic [by] Eugene Weber. Tr. by Horst Vollmer. Staten Island, N. Y., Alba [c.1964] 460p. 23cm. 63-14572 5.95
1. Pallotti, Vincenzo, Saint, 1795-1850. I. Title.

WEBER, Eugene, 1890- 922.245
Vincent Pallotti; an apostle and mystic. Translated by Horst Vollner. Staten Island, N.Y., Alba House [1964] 460 p. 23 cm. [BX4700.P23W43] 63-14572
1. Pallotti, Vincenzo, Saint, 1795-1850. I. Title.

Pallottine Missionary Sisters.

MARY Bernadita, Sister, S.A.C., 1932- 271'.979
A house built on rock, by Sister Mary Bernadita [and] Sister Mary Anthony. Philadelphia, Dorrance [1967] 136 p. illus., ports. 21 cm. Bibliography: p. 134. [BX4415.8.M3] 67-13052
1. Pallottine Missionary Sisters. I. Mary Anthony, Sister, S.A.C., joint author. II. Title.

Pallottines.

BONIFAZI, Flavian. 282'.0924
Our Pallottine heritage; for the infinite glory of God. Baltimore, Pallottine Fathers & Brothers Press, 1968. x, 48 p. 23 cm. Bibliography: p. ix-x. [BX4700.P23B58] 68-29101
1. Pallotti, Vincenzo, Saint, 1795-1850. 2. Pallottines. I. Title.

PALLOTTI, Vincenzo, Saint, 1795-1850. 282'.0924
Pious Society of the Catholic Apostolate. Translated and edited under the supervision of Louis J. Lulli, from the Italian critical ed. published in Rome, Italy, by Francesco Moccia. Baltimore, Pallottine Fathers & Brothers Press, 1968. xviii, 177 p. 24 cm. (His Complete writings, v. 1) Bibliographical footnotes. [BX890.P25 vol. 1] 67-31436
1. Pallottines. I. Title. II. Series.

Palm Beach, Fla. Church of Bethesda-by-the-Sea.

HALL, Kathryn Evangeline, 1924- 283.75932
History of the Episcopal Church of Bethesda-by-the-Sea, documented from authentic and contemporary sources. By Kathryn E. Hall. [Palm Beach Fla.] 1964. 31-88 p. illus., ports. 30 cm. Caption title. [BX5980.P25B44] 64-56658
1. Palm Beach, Fla. Church of Bethesda-by-the-Sea. I. Title.

Palm, Johannes Heuricus van der, 1763-1840.

BEETS, Nicolaas, 1814-1903. 922-4492
Life and character of J. H. van der Palm ... Sketched by Nicolaas Beets, D.D. Translated from the Dutch by J. P. Westervelt. New York, Hurd and Houghton. Boston, F. P. Dutton and company, 1865. xii, 401 p. 19 1/2 cm. "Sermons of J. H. van der Palm ...": p. [175]-401. "Articles relating to van der Palm ...": p. 172-173. [BX9479.P3B42] 36-22145
1. Palm, Johannes Heuricus van der, 1763-1840. 2. Reformed church—Sermons. I. Westervelt, John P., 1816-1879, tr. II. Title.

Palmer, Albert Gallatin, 1813-1891.

HISCOX, Edward Thurston, 1814-1901 920.
A memorial of Albert Gallatin Palmer, D.D., preacher, pastor, poet, scholar ... Prepared by Edward T. Hiscox ... Philadelphia, American Baptist publication society, 1894. 348 p. front., plates, ports. 19 1/2 cm. [BX6495.P25H5] 2-4642
1. Palmer, Albert Gallatin, 1813-1891. I. American Baptist publication society. II. Title.

HISCOX, Edward Thurston, 1814-1901. 922.
A memorial of Albert Gallatin Palmer, D.D., preacher, pastor, poet, scholar ... Prepared by Edward T. Hiscox ... Philadelphia, American Baptist publication society, 1894. 348 p. front., plates, ports. 19 1/2 cm. [BX6495.P25H5] 2-4642
1. Palmer, Albert Gallatin, 1813-1891. I. American Baptist publication society. II. Title.
Contents omitted.

Palmer, Benjamin Morgan, 1818-1902.

JOHNSON, Thomas Cary, 1859- 285.
The life and letters of Benjamin Morgan Palmer, by Thomas Cary Johnson ... Richmond, Va., Presbyterian committee of publication [c1906] 3 p. l., [v]-x. 688 p. front., plates, ports., fold. geneal. tab. 24 cm. [BX9225.P27J6] 7-16777
1. Palmer, Benjamin Morgan, 1818-1902. I. Title.

Palmer, Mrs. Sarah A. (Worrall) Lankford, 1806-1896.

ROCHE, John Alexander, 1813-1898. 922.773
The life of Mrs. Sarah A. Lankford Palmer, who for sixty years was the able teacher of entire holiness. By John A. Roche ... With an introduction by John P. Newman ... New York, G. Hughes & co. [1898] 286 p. incl. front., port. 19 1/2 cm. [BX8495.P27R6] 36-37391
1. Palmer, Mrs. Sarah A. (Worrall) Lankford, 1806-1896. I. Title.

Palmer, William, 1803-1885. Letters to N. Wiseman.

SIBTHORP, Richard Waldo, 1792-1879. 230.
The true path for the true churchman wandering in the mazes of Protestantism, exemplified in two letters in answer to the enquiry: Why have you become a Catholic? Including a reply to Rev. Messrs. Palmer and Dodsworth, by Richard Waldo Sibthorp...From last rev. London ed. New York, Casserly & sons, 1843. 51 p. 24 cm. first published, 1842, in two letters, under the titles: Some answer to the enquiry; why are you become a Catholic? and A further answer to the enquiry: why have you becoma a Catholic? [BX1755.S55 1843] 36-3258
1. Palmer, William, 1803-1885. Letters to N. Wiseman. 2. Dodsworth, William, 1798-1861. Why have you become a Romanist? 3. Catholic church—Doctrinal and controversial works—Catholic authors. I. Title.

Palmistry.

HAMON, Louis, 1866-1936. 133.3'24
The Cheiro book of fate and fortune: palmistry, numerology, astrology. New York, Arco Pub. Co. [1971] xii, 339 p. illus. 23 cm. [BF921.H135 1971b] 72-164693 ISBN 0-668-02507-7 5.95
1. Palmistry. 2. Symbolism of numbers. 3. Astrology. I. Title.

HATHAWAY, [Evangeline] and Dunbar, [Mary Elizabeth]
The A B C of palmistry Boston, Banner of light pub. co., 1900. 86 p. illus. 16 degrees. Oct
I. Title.

HENDERSON, Elisa Easter.
A guide to palmistry; with supplement. Cambridge, Mass., The author, 1897. 132, 41 p. illus., pl. 16. Sep
I. Title.

Palmyra Church of the Brethren.

CARPER, Frank S. 286'.5
History of the Palmyra Church of the Brethren 1892-1967 Palmyra, Pa., Palmyra Church of the Brethren, 1967. xv, 340 p. illus., ports. (part col.) 24 cm. [BX7831.P3C3] 68-2375
1. Palmyra Church of the Brethren. I. Title.

CARPER, Frank S. 286'.5
History of the Palmyra Church of the Brethren, 1892-1967, by Frank S. Carper. Palmyra, Pa., Palmyra Church of the Brethren, 1967. xv, 340 p. illus., ports. (part col.) 24 cm. [BX7831.P3C3] 68-2375
1. Palmyra Church of the Brethren. I. Title.

Pancaratra—Bibliography—Catalogs.

SMITH, H. Daniel, 1928- 016.2945'9
The Smith Agama collection : Sanskrit books and manuscripts relating to Pancaratra studies : a descriptive catalog /

by H. Daniel Smith ; foreword by Agehananda Bharati. Syracuse, N.Y. : Maxwell School of Citizenship and Public Affairs, Syracuse University, 1978. p. cm. (Foreign and comparative studies : South Asian special publications ; 2) Bibliography: p. [Z7835.B8S6] [BL1135.P34] 78-9149 ISBN pbk. : 6.50
1. Pancaratra—Bibliography—Catalogs. 2. Pancaratra—Manuscripts—Catalogs. 3. Manuscripts, Sanskrit—Catalogs. I. Title. II. Series.

Panfili, Olimpia (Maldachini) 1594-1656.

[LETI, Gregorio] 1630-1701.
Biography of Donna Olimpia Maldachini the sister-in-law and bonne amie of Pope Innocent X, and who governed the church of Rome from the year 1644 to the year 1655, with unlimited sway by the Abbe pseud. Philadelphia, Barrett & Jones, printers, 1846. v, [7]-84 p. front., pl. 19 cm. The Italian original was first published, supposedly at Geneva, with imprint: Cosmopoli, Appresso Eugenio Migani, 1666. In the same year an English translation was published at London, of which this is a modernized version. 3-9521
1. Panfili, Olimpia (Maldachini) 1594-1656. 2. Innocent X, pope, d. 1655. I. Title.

Pankey family.

PANKEY, William Russell. 286'.1'73
Edge of paradise; fifty years in the pulpit. Parsons, W. Va., McClain Print. Co., 1972. x, 245 p. coat of arms. 23 cm. [BX6495.P26A3] 79-174564 ISBN 0-87012-111-1
1. Pankey family. I. Title.

Pannenberg, Wolfhart, 1928-

GALLOWAY, Allan Douglas, 1920- 230.0924
Wolfhart Pannenberg [by] Allan D. Galloway London, George Allen and Unwin [1975 c1973] 143 p. 22 cm. (Contemporary religious thinkers) Includes index. Bibliography: p. 139-140. [BX4827.P3G34] ISBN 0-04-230011-8
1. Pannenberg, Wolfhart, 1928- I. Title.
Distributed by Humanities Press for 9.75. L.C. card no. for original edition: 73-179423.

MCKENZIE, David, 1943- 230'.044
Wolfhart Pannenberg and religious philosophy / David McKenzie. Washington, D.C. : University Press of America, 1980. p. cm. A revision of the author's thesis, University of Texas, 1977. Includes index. Bibliography: p. [BX4827.P3M32 1980] 19 80-8171 ISBN 0-8191-1314-X lib. bdg. : 17.50 ISBN 0-8191-1315-8 (pbk.) : 9.00
1. Pannenberg, Wolfhart, 1928- 2. Religion—Philosophy—History. I. Title.

OLIVE, Don H. 230'.092'4 B
Wolfhart Pannenberg [by] Don H. Olive. Waco, Tex., Word Books [1973] 120 p. 23 cm. (Makers of the modern theological mind) Bibliography: p. 117-120. [BX4827.P3O44] 78-188068 4.95
1. Pannenberg, Wolfhart, 1928- I. Title.

ROBINSON, James McConkey, 1924- 230'.09'04
Theology as history, edited by James M. Robinson [and] John B. Cobb, Jr. [1st ed.] New York, Harper & Row [1967] x, 276 p. 22 cm. (New frontiers in theology: discussions among Continental and American theologians, v. 3) Contents.Revelation as word and as history, by J. M. Robinson. -- Focal essay: The revelation of God in Jesus of Nazareth, by W. Pannenberg. -- The meaning of history, by M. J. Buss -- Revelation and resurrection, by K. Grobel. -- The character of Pannenberg's theology, by W. Hamilton. -- Past, present, and future, by J. B. Cobb. -- Response to the discussion, by W. Pannenberg. Includes bibliographical references. [BT28.R58] 67-14936
1. Pannenberg, Wolfhart, 1928- 2. Theology, Doctrinal — Hist. — 20th cent. 3. History (Theology) — History of doctrines. I. Cobb, John B., joint author. II. Title. III. Series. IV. Series: New frontiers in theology. v. 3

TUPPER, Elgin Frank, 1941- 230'.4'10924
The theology of Wolfhart Pannenberg, by E. Frank Tupper. Postscript by Wolfhart Pannenberg. Philadelphia, Westminster Press [1973] 322 p. 25 cm. Based on the author's thesis, Southern Baptist Theological Seminary, 1971. Bibliography: p. 307-316. [BX4827.P3T86] 73-6662 ISBN 0-664-20973-4 10.95
1. Pannenberg, Wolfhart, 1928- I. Title.

Panos, Chris.

PANOS, Chris. 269'.2'0924 B
God's spy / by Chris Panos. 1st ed. Plainfield, N.J. : Logos International, 1976. xiii, 270 p. ; 22 cm. [BV3785.P33A33] 76-55451 ISBN 0-88270-213-0 : 6.95. pbk. : 3.50
1. Panos, Chris. 2. Evangelists—United States—Biography. I. Title.

Pantheism.

AIKEN, Alfred. 212
Now, a book on the Absolute. New York, Hillier Press [1956] 256p. 21cm. [BL220.A33] 57-17391
1. Pantheism. I. Title.

AIKEN, Alfred. 212
That which is, a book on the Absolute. New York, Hillier Press [1955] 249 p. 21 cm. [BL220.A35] 55-42628
1. Pantheism. I. Title.

AIKEN. ALFRED. 212
Now, a book on the Absolute. New York, Hillier Press [1956] 256p. 21cm. [BL220.A33] 57-17931
1. Pantheism. I. Title.

AMRYC, C.
Pantheism, the light and hope of modern reason ... [n. p.] 1898. 302 p. illus. 12 cm. 1-3731
I. Title.

DIX, Morgan, 1827-1908. 212
Lectures on the pantheistic idea of an impersonal-substance-deity, as contrasted with the Christian faith concerning Almighty God. By the Rev. Morgan Dix ... New York, Hurd and Houghton; Boston, E. P. Dutton and company, 1864. xv, 109 p. 20 cm. [BL220.D5] 30-28764
1. Pantheism. I. Title.

HITTELL, John Shertzer, 1825-1901. 212
A plea for pantheism. By John S. Hittell. New York, C. Blanchard, 1857. x, 56 p. 18 1/2 cm. [BL220.H5] 30-28768
1. Panthsism. I. Title.
Contents omitted.

HUNT, John, 1827-ca.1908. 261.2
Pantheism and Christianity. Port Washington, N.Y., Kennikat Press [1970] viii, 397 p. 23 cm. "First published in 1884." Based on the author's An essay on Pantheism. [BL220.H8 1970] 78-102573
1. Pantheism. 2. Christianity and the other religion. 3. Idealism. 4. Transcendentalism. I. Title.

LLOYD, John William.
Dawn-thought on the reconciliation; a volume of pantheistic impressions and glimpses of larger religion. Wellesley Hills, Mass., Maugus press [1900] xi, 197 p. front. (port.) sq. 16 degrees. Feb
I. Title.

LLOYD, John William, 1857- 212
Dawn thought on the reconciliation; a volume of pantheistic impressions and glimpses of larger religion, by J. Wm. Lloyd ... 2d ed., rev., with appendix. Westfield, N. J., The Lloyd group [1904] xi, 197, [2] p. front. (port.) 18 x 16 cm. [BL220.L6 1904] 4-13662
1. Pantheism. I. Title.

PICTON, James Allanson, 1832-1910. 212'.5
Pantheism; its story and significance. Freeport, N.Y., Books for Libraries Press [1973] p. Reprint of the 1905 ed. published by A. Constable, London, issued in series: Religions ancient and modern. Bibliography: p. [BL220.P5 1973] 73-4495 ISBN 0-518-19038-2
1. Pantheism. I. Title. II. Series: Religions ancient and modern.

REISER, Oliver Leslie, 1895- 147
Nature, man, and God; a synthesis of pantheism and scientific humanism. [Pittsburgh] University of Pittsburgh Press, 1951. ii, 152 p. illus. 23 cm. [BD558.R4] 51-2628
1. Pantheism. 2. Humanism. I. Title.

TOLAND, John, 1670-1722. 147
Pantheisticon / John Toland. New York : Garland Pub., 1976. 110 p. ; 19 cm. (British philosophers and theologians of the 17th and 18th centuries) Reprint of the 1751 ed. printed for Sam Paterson and sold by M. Cooper, London, under title: Pantheisticon: or, The form of celebrating the Socratic-society. Written originally in Latin. [BL220.T613 1976] 75-11260 ISBN 0-8240-1810-9 lib.bdg. : 25.00
1. Pantheism. I. Title. II. Series.

Paolo della Croce, Saint, 1694-1775.

ALMERAS, Charles. 922.245
St. Paul of the Corss, founder of the Passionists. Translated by M. Angeline Bouchard. [1st ed.] Garden City, N. Y., Hanover House, 1960. 286p. 22cm. Includes bibliography. [BX4700.P25A63] 60-15165
1. Paold della Croce, Saint, 1694-1775. I. Title.

ALMERAS, Charles 922.245
St. Paul of the Cross, founder of the Passionists. Translated [from the French] by M. Angeline Bouchard. Garden City, N. Y., Hanover House [c.] 1960. 286p. Bibl. notes: p.262-277. 22cm. 60-15165 3.95
1. Paolo della Croce, Saint, 1694-1775. I Title.

PAOLO della Croce, Saint, 1694-1775. 271'.62'024 B
Words from the heart : a selection from the personal letters of Saint Paul of the Cross / translated [from the Italian] and annotated by Edmund Burke ; [edited by] Roger Mercurio, Silvan Rouse. Dublin : Gill and Macmillan, 1976. viii, 168 p. ; 23 cm. Includes index. [BX4700.P25A4 1976] 77-363539 ISBN 0-7171-0806-6 : £7.00
1. Paolo della Croce, Saint, 1694-1775. I. Burke, Edmund, 1904-1975. II. Mercurio, Roger. III. Rouse, Silvan. IV. Title.

PIUS a Spiritu Sancto, Father. 922.
The life of S. Paul of the Cross: founder of the Congregation of discalced clerks of the Holy Cross and passion of Our Lord. Usually called Passionists. By the Rev. Father Pius a Sp. Sancio ... New York, Montreal, D. & J. Saddier & co.; [etc., etc.] 1868. xvi, 437 p. front. (port.) 19 cm. [BX4700.P25P5] 3-14301
1. Paolo delia Croce, Saint, 1694-1775. I. Title.

Paolo della Croce, Saint, 1694-1775—Juvenile literature.

ROBERTO, Brother, 1927- 922.245
A light on the mountain; a story of St. Paul of the Cross. Notre Dame, Ind., Dujarie Press [1960] 143p. illus. 22cm. [BX4700.P25R6] 60-52059
1. Paolo della Croce, Saint, 1694-1775—Juvenile literature. I. Title.

Paotinafu massacre, 1900.

KETLER, Isaac Conrad, 1853-1913.

The tragedy of Paotingfu; an authentic story of the lives, services and sacrifices of the Presbyterian, Congregational and China Inland missionaries who suffered martyrdom at Paotingfu, China, June 30th and July 1, 1900, by Isaac C. Ketler. New York, Chicago [etc.] F. H. Revell company, 1902. 16, [3] 19-400 p. front., pl., port. 21 1/2 cm. [DS772.K4] 2-17061
1. Paotingfu massacre, 1900. 2. Missions—China. I. Title.

Papacy.

BARROW, Isaac, 1630-1677. 262.13

The pope's supremacy. By Isaac Barrow ...

To which are added a Sypopsis [!] of the treatise; and two complete indexes. New York, J. C. Riker, 1845. 268 p. 24 cm. "To the reader" signed: J. Tillotson. "Synopsis of the treatise on the pope's supremacy ... compiled by Dr. Hughes": p. [244]-257. [BX1805.B3 1845] 35-38365
1. Papacy. 2. Catholic church—Doctrinal and controversial works—Protestant authors. I. Tillotson, John, abp. of Canterbury, 1630-1694, ed. II. Hughes, Thomas Smart, 1786-1874. III. Title.

BARROW, Isaac. 1630-1677. 262.13
A treatise of the pope's supremacy. By the Rev. Isaac Barrow, d. d. 2d American ed.

New-York, Stanford & Swords, 1844. xxxix, [13]-433 p. 23 cm. "Biographical memoir of Dr. Isaac Barrow [by T. S. Hughes]": p. [vii]-xxiv: "Summary of A treatise of the pope's supremacy [compiled by T. S. Hughes]": p. [xxv]-xxxix. [BX1805.B3 1844] 35-38362

1. Papacy. 2. Catholic church—Doctrinal and controversial works—Protestant authors. I. Hughes, Thomas Smart, 1736-1847. II. Title.

BELLARMINO, Roberto Francesco Romolo, Saint, 1542-1621. 262.132
Extracts on politics and government from the Supreme Pontiff from Third general controversy. [De Summo Pontifice] translated, edited, and published by George Albert Moore. Chevy Chase, Md., Country Dollar Press ['1951] xi, 134 p. port. 28 cm. (The Moore series of English translationsof source books) "Collector's edition ... limited to sixty copies, signed and numbered ... No. 4." [BX1805.B333] 52-27192
1. Papacy. 2. Popes—Temporal power. I. Title.

BELLARMINO, Roberto Francesco Romolo, Saint, 1542-1621. 262.132
Power of the Pope in temporal affairs, against William Barclay: Cologne, 1610. Translated and edited by George Albert Moore. Chevy Chase, Md., Country Dollar Press [1949] xxi. 239 p. port. 20 cm. (The Moore series of English translations of source books) Running title: Power of Pope in temporals. "Collector's edition ... limited to fifty (50) signed and numbered copies, of which this is no. 4" [BX1805.B373] 49-50126
1. Barclay, William, 1545 or 6-1608. De potestate Papae. 2. Papacy. 3. Church and state—Catholic Church. I. Moore, George Albert, 1893- ed. and tr. II. Title.

BERNARD de Clairvaux, Saint, 1091?-1153. 230'.2 s
Five books on consideration : advice to a Pope / translated by John D. Anderson & Elizabeth T. Kennan. Kalamazoo, Mich. : Cistercian Publications, 1976. 222 p. ; 22 cm. (Cistercian Fathers series ; no. 37) (His The works of Bernard of Clairvaux ; v. 13) Translation of De consideratione. Includes index. Bibliography: p. 211-215. [BX890.B5 1970 vol. 13] [BX953] 262'.13 75-27953 ISBN 0-87907-737-9 pbk. : 4.00
1. Papacy. I. Title. II. Series.

BREZZI, Paolo. 262.13
The papacy, its origins and historical evolution. Translated by Henry J. Yannone. Westminster, Md., Newman Press, 1958. 225p. 23cm. Includes bibliography. [BX1805.b713] 58-8747
1. Papacy. I. Title.

CATHOLIC Church. Pope.
The papal encyclicals in their historical context, by Anne Fremantle. With an introd. by Gustave Weigel. [New York] New American Library [1960, c1956] 317 p. (A Mentor book, MT256) A Mentor religious classic. Bibliography: p. [311]-[312] 65-88357
I. Fremantle, Anne (Jackson) 1909- ed. II. Title.

CLIFFORD, T. A., 1893- 225.9'24 B
Peter and the keys, by T. A. Clifford. Philadelphia, Dorrance [1972] 58 p. 22 cm. Includes bibliographical references. [BS2515.C54] 72-171930 ISBN 0-8059-1615-6 3.50
1. Peter, Saint, apostle. 2. Papacy. I. Title.

DALLMANN, William, 1862- 262.13
How Peter became pope [by William Dallmann. St. Louis, Mo., Concordia publishing house, 1931. 2 p. l., 113 p. 24 cm. "Orginaly these articles appeared in the Concordia theological monthly." [Full name: Charles Frederick William Dallmann] [BX1805.D3] 31-32328
1. Papacy. 2. Peter, Saint, apostle. I. Title.

DOLAN, Thomas Stanislaus, 1869-1918. 244
The See of Peter and the voice of antiquity; critical notes on Bishop Coxe's Ante-Nicene fathers, by Rev. Thomas S. Dolan ... with a preface by His Eminence James, cardinal Gibbons, D. D. St. Louis, Mo., and Freiburg (Baden) B. Herder, 1908. xi, 106 p. 20 cm. [BX980.D6] 8-29373
1. Coxe, Arthur Cleveland, bp, 1818-1806. 2. Papacy. 3. The ante-Nicene fathers. I. Title.

FULOP-MILLER, Rene, 1891- 262.13
... The power and secret of the papacy; translated by Conrad M. R. Bonacina. London, New York [etc.] Longmans, Green and co., 1937. 3 p. l., 202 p. front. (port.) 23 cm. "First edition." Bibliography: p. 187-197. [BX1397.F8] 39-19369
1. Papacy. 2. Sociology, Christian—Catholic authors. I. Bonacina, Conrad M. R., tr. II. Title.

GOHDES, Conrad Bruno, 1866- 282
Does the modern papacy require a new evaluation! By C. B. Gohdes ... Burlington, Ia., The Lutheran literary board, 1940. 263 p. 24 cm. "Literature": p. [260]-263. [BX1765.G56] 40-84299
1. Papacy. 2. Catholic church—Doctrinal and controversial works—Protestant authors. I. Title.

GRANFIELD, Patrick. 262'.13
The Papacy in transition / Patrick Grandfield. 1st ed. Garden City, N.Y. : Doubleday, 1980. xi, 228 p. ; 22 cm. Includes index. Bibliography: p. [204]-216. [BX1805.G66] 79-7049 ISBN 0-385-14327-3 : 8.95
1. Papacy. I. Title.

HARTE, Thomas Joseph, 1914-
Papal social principles; a guide and digest. Gloucester, Mass., Peter Smith, 1960. ix, 207 p. 21 cm. Includes bibliographical references. Bibliography: p. 193-196. 63-18506
I. Title.

MCKNIGHT, John P 262.13
The papacy, a new appraisal. New York Rinehart [1952] 487 p. 22 cm. Bibliography: p. 350-360. [BX957.M25] 52-5567
1. Papacy. I. Title.

MAJOR, Henry. 262.13
Reasons for acknowledging the authority of the Holy Roman see. By Henry Major ... Philadelphia, The author, 1846. viii, [9]-248 p. 19 1/2 cm. [BX1805.M35] 35-34412
1. Papacy. 2. Catholic church—Doctrinal and controversial works—Catholic authors. I. Title.

MARCELLO, Cristoford, d 1527; 262'13
Christophori Marcelli De avthoritate Svmmi Pontificis et his qvae ad illam pertinent. adversvs impia Martini Lvtherii dogmata. Ridgewood, N.J., Gregg Pr. 1966. 1451. 20cm. Reproduction of the 1521 Florentine ed. pub. by Haeredes Philippi Iunate. [BX1805.M37 151a] 67-3194 28.00
1. Luther. Martin, 1483-1546. 2. Papacy. I. Title. II. Title: De avthoritate Svmmi Pontificis.

MERRY DEL VAL, Raphael, cardinal, 1865-1930. 262.
The truth of papal claims, by Raphael Merry del Val a realy to The validity of papal claims, by F. Nutcombe Oxenham ... St. Louis, Mo., B. Herder; London, Sands & company, 1902. xvi, 129, xv p. 19 cm. Printed in Great Britain. [BX1805.M5] 9-5554
1. Oxenham, Frank Nutcombe. The validity of papal claims. 2. Papacy. I. Title. II. Title: Papal claims, The truth of.

MOURETT, Fernand, 1854- 262.13
... The papacv, by F. Mourret ... translated by Robert Eaton ... London, Sands & co.; St. Louis, Mo., B. Herder book co. [1931] xi, 238, [1] p. 19 cm. (Catholic library of religious knowledge. xix) Bibliography: p. 237-[239] [BX880.C3 vol. 19] 282.082 35-23980
1. Papacy. I. Eaton, Robert Ormston, 1866- tr. II. Title.

NATIONS, Gilbert O.
Papal sovereignty, the government within our government, by Gilbert O. Nations ... Cincinnati, The Standard publishing company [c1917] 183 p. 20 cm. [BX1810.N3] 17-29747
I. Title.

NELSON, Cleland Kinlock, 1814-1890.
Review of Major's Reasons for acknowledging the authority of the Roman see. With an appendix. By C. K. Nelson ... Upper Marlborn [Md.] G. W. Wilson, printer, 1847. 60 p. 21 cm. [BX1805.M36N4] 35-38396
1. Major. Henry. Reasons for acknowledging the authority of the Holy Roman see. 2. Papacy. 3. Catholic church—Doctrinal and controversial works—Protestant authors. I. Title.

ORMESSON, Wladimir, comte d', 1888- 262.1309
The papacy. Translated from the French by Michael Derrick. [1st ed.] New York, Hawthorn Books [1959] 142p. 21cm. (The Twentieth century encyclopedia of Catholicism, v.81. Section 8: The organization of the church) Bibliography: p.[141]-142. [BX1805.O713] 59-6740
1. Papacy. I. Title. II. Series: The Twentieth century encyclopedia of Catholicism, v.81

PIROLO, Nicholas. 220.1
Babylon, political and ecclesiastical, showing characteristics of anti-Christ and false prophet, considering Mussolini and the Pope with their respective, "Vv il Duce" and "Vicarius Filii Dei", 666, by Evangelist Nicholas Pirolo... Milwaukee, Wis., [Word and witness publishing company, c1937] 2 p. l., 7-109 p. 22 cm. On cover: The Pope, Mussolini, Babylon, 666. [BS647.P55] 37-23526
1. Mussolini, Benito, 1883- 2. Papacy. 3. Catholic church—Doctrinal and controversial works—Protestant authors. 4. Bible—Prophecies. I. Title. II. Title: The Pope, Mussolini, Babylon, 666.

PULLER, Frederick William, 1843-
The primitive saints and the see of Rome, by F. W. Puller ... with a preface by Edward, lord bishop of Lincoln. London and New York, Longmans, Green & co., 1893. xxxi, [1], 428 p. 20 cm. [BX970.P8] 25-23325
1. Papacy. 2. Church history—Primitive and early church. 3. Catholic church—Doctrinal and controversial works—Protestant authors. I. Title.

SELDES, George, 1890- 262.13
The Vatican: yesterday, today, tomorrow, by George Seldes... New York and London, Harper & brothers, 1934. vi p., 1 l., 439 p. 22 1/2 cm. Illustrated lining-papers. "First edition." [Full name: George Henry Seldes] [BX955.S35] 34-4556
1. Papacy. 2. Vatican. 3. Popes. 4. Catholic church—Government. 5. Catholic church—Relations (Diplomatic) I. Title.

STEVENS, Jesse C. 220.
The papacy in Bible prophecy, by Jesse C. Stevens ... Tacoma Park, Washington, D. C., South Bend, Ind. [etc.] Review and herald publishing association [c1928] 128 p. incl. front., illus. 19 cm. [BS649.R7S8] 28-13683
1. Papacy. 2. Bible—Prophecies. I. Title.

VAUGHAN, John Stephen, 1853-
The purpose of the papacy, by the Right Reverend John S. Vaughan ... London, [etc.] Sands & co.; St. Louis, Mo., U.S.A. B. Herder, 1910. xiii, p., 1 l., 3-158 p. 19 cm. 12-39783
I. Title.

WALL, Bernard, 1908- 262.132
The Vatican story. New York, Harper [1957, c1956] 247p. illus. 22cm. Published in London in 1956 under title: Report on the Vatican. [BX957.W3 1957] 56-6036
1. Papacy. 2. Catholic Church. 3. Vatican. I. Title.

WALL, Bernard, 1908- 262.132
The Vatican story. New York, Harper [1957, c1956] 247 p. illus. 22 cm. Published in London in 1956 under title: Report on the Vatican. [BX957.W3 1957] 56-6036
1. Papacy. 2. Catholic Church. 3. Vatican. I. Title.

WILKS, Michael 262.132
The problem of sovereignty in the later Middle Ages; the papal monarchy with Augustinus Triumphus and the publicists [New York] Cambridge [c.]1963. xiii, 619p. 23cm. (Cambridge studies in medieval life and thought, new ser., v.9) Bibl. 63-3163 12.50
1. Papacy. 2. Sovereignty. 3. Trionfo, Agostino, 1243-1328. 4. Political science—Hist. I. Title. II. Series.

Papacy—Addresses, essays, lectures.

OUR name is Peter 262'.13'0924
: an anthology of key teachings of Pope Paul VI / compiled by Sean O'Reilly. Chicago : Franciscan Herald Press, c1977. xi, 146, [1] p. ; 23 cm. Bibliography: p. [147]. [BX955.2.O95] 77-380 ISBN 0-8199-0666-2 : 6.95
1. Paulus VI, Pope, 1897- —Addresses, essays, lectures. 2. Papacy—Addresses, essays, lectures. I. O'Reilly, Sean, 1922-

PAPAL ministry in the Church. 262'.13
Edited by Hans Kung. [New York] Herder and Herder [1971] 158 p. 23 cm. (Concilium: religion in the seventies. Ecumenism, v. 64) On cover: The New concilium: religion in the seventies. Includes bibliographical references. [BX955.2.P35] 78-150303 2.95
1. Papacy—Addresses, essays, lectures. I. Kung, Hans, 1928- ed. II. Series: Concilium (New York) v. 64

A Pope for all Christians? : 262'.13
An inquiry into the role of Peter in the modern church / edited by Peter J. McCord. New York : Paulist Press, c1976. vi, 212 p. ; 23 cm. Includes bibliographical references. [BX1805.P66] 75-32859 ISBN 0-8091-1918-8 pbk. : 7.50
1. Papacy—Addresses, essays, lectures. 2. Authority (Religion)—Addresses, essays, lectures. 3. Church—Authority—Addresses, essays, lectures. I. McCord Peter J.

WE are Peter : 262'.13'0924
some key teachings of Pope Paul VI / edited by Sean O'Reilly. Chicago : Franciscan Herald Press, [1977] p. cm. [BX955.2.W4] 76-45573 ISBN 0-672-52288-8 : 5.95
1. Paulus VI, Pope, 1897- —Addresses, essays, lectures. 2. Papacy—Addresses, essays, lectures. I. O'Reilly, Sean, 1922-

Papacy—Controversial literature.

MARTIN, Malachi. 282
The decline and fall of the Roman church / by Malachi Martin. New York : Putnam, c1981. p. cm. Includes index. [BX1779.5.M275 1981] 19 81-7385 ISBN 0-399-12665-1 : 14.95
1. Catholic Church—Controversial literature. 2. Papacy—Controversial literature. I. Title.

Papacy—Documents.

THE popes and the priest of today; a selection of papal documents. Dublin, Clonmore and Reynolds [1957] 160p.
1. Papacy—Documents. 2. Catholic Church—Clergy. I. Catholic Church. Pope.

A voice from Rome, answered 265.
by an American citizen; or, A review of the encyclical letter of Pope Gregory XVI, A.D. 1832, The bishop's oath, and the pope's curse upon heretics, schismatics, and all infringers upon ecclesiastical liberties, as contained in the Bulla in coena Domini, pronounced annually on Maundy Thursday. Philadelphia, J. M. Campbell; New York, Saxton & Miles, 1844. 84 p. 19 cm. [BX1767.V6] 1-4177

Papacy — Documents, 1878-1903 (Leo XIII)

CATHOLIC Church. Pope. 1878-1903(LeoXIII)
The church speaks to the modern world; the social teachings of Leo XIII. Edited, annotated and with an introd. by Etienne Gilson. Garden City, Doubleday [1961] 348 p. (Image book, D7) 63-32346
1. Papacy — Documents, 1878-1903 (Leo XIII) I. Gilson, Etienne Henry, 1884- II. Title.

Papacy—History

ARETIN, Karl Otmar, Freiherr von, 1923- 262'.13'09034
The Papacy and the modern world. Translated by Roland Hill. New York, McGraw-Hill [1970] 256 p. illus. (part col.), facsims., col. maps, ports. (part col.) 20 cm. (World university library) Includes bibliographical references. [BX955.2.A73 1970b] 76-77021 4.95
1. Papacy—History. I. Title.

BALDWIN, Marshall Whithed, 1903- 262.130902
The medieval papacy in action, by Marshall W. Baldwin ... New York, The Macmillan company, 1940. xiii, 113 p. 20 cm. [The Christendom series] "First printing." "Bibliographical note": p. 110-111. [BX1068.B3 1940] 40-31208
1. Papacy—Hist. 2. Church history—Middle ages. I. Title.

BARRACLOUGH, Geoffrey, 1908- 262'.13'09
The medieval papacy. [1st American ed. New York] Harcourt, Brace & World [1968] 216 p. illus., facsims., maps, ports. 22 cm. ([History of European civilization library]) Part of illustrative matter colored. "Bibliographical notes": p. 197-205. [BX955.2.B3 1968b] 68-29667 5.95
1. Papacy—History. I. Title.

BARRY, William Francis, 1849-1930. 282
The papacy and modern times; a political sketch, 1303-1870, by William Barry ... New York, H. Holt and company; [etc., etc., c1911] ix, 11-256 p. 18 cm. (Half-title: Home university library of modern knowledge, no. 22) Bibliography: p. 253-254. [BX955.B3 1911a] 12-38
1. Papacy—Hist. 2. Europe—Politics. I. Title.

BELL, Mary I M (Ottley) Mrs. 282
A short history of the papacy, by Mary I. M. Bell, with two maps. New York, Dodd, Mead and company, 1921. xiii, 390 p., 1 l. ii maps. 23 cm. Printed in Great Britain. [BX955.B45] 21-20142
1. Catholic church—Hist. 2. Papacy—Hist. I. Title.

BERNHART, Joseph, 1881- 282
... The Vatican as a world power: translated by George N. Shuster. London, New York [etc.] Longmanns, Green and co., 1939. vii, 456 p. 22 cm. [BX955.B472 1939] 39-27170
1. Papacy—Hist. 2. Catholic church—Hist. I. Shuster, George Nauman, 1894- tr. II. Title.

BURDICK, Charles Rollin, 1826-1897.
Before the dawn; a poem; with introductory lectures on prophetic symbols:

portraying the last great conflicts which result in the downfall of papal domination, the destruction of political and ecclesiastical depotism, and the removal of other hindrances to Christianity in the nineteenth century. By Rev. C. R. Burdick, M.A. Buffalo, Breed, Lent and company, 1872. vi, [7]-311 p. 19 cm. [PS1206.B22B4 1872] 21-22138
I. Title.

BURN-MURDOCH, Hector, 1881- 282
The development of the papacy. New York, Praeger [1954] 432p. 23cm. (Books that matter) Bibliographical footnotes. [BX955.B88 1954a] 54-12063
1. Papacy—Hist. I. Title.

BURY, John Bagnell, 1861-1927.
History of the papacy in the 19th century (1864-1878) by the late J.B. Bury ... edited, with a memoir, by the Rev. R.H. Murray. New York, Schocken Books [1964] lxi, 175 p. 68-84162
1. Pius IX, Pope, 1792-1878. 2. Papacy—Hist. 3. Catholic Church—Hist. I. Murray, Robert Henry, 1874- II. Title.

CHADWICK, Owen. 282'.09
Catholicism and history : the opening of the Vatican Archives / Owen Chadwick. Cambridge ; New York : Cambridge University Press, 1978. vi, 174 p. ; 23 cm. (The Herbert Hensley Henson lectures in the University of Oxford ; 1976) Includes index. Bibliography: p. 163-165. [CD1581.C47] 77-77740 ISBN 0-521-21708-3 : 13.95
1. Vatican. Archivio vaticano. 2. Catholic Church—Historiography. 3. Papacy—History. 4. Freedom of information in the church. 5. Church history—Historiography. I. Title. II. Series.

CORBETT, James Arthur. 262.1309
The papacy, a brief history. Princeton, N.J., Van Nostrand [1956] 192p. 18cm. (An Anvil original, no. 12) [BX955.C66] 56-6881
1. Papacy—Hist. 2. Papacy—Hist.—Sources. I. Title.

CREIGHTON, Mandell, Bp. 282'.09
of London, 1843-1901.
A history of the papacy from the great schism to the sack of Rome. New ed. London, New York, Longmans, Green, 1897. [New York, AMS Press, 1969] 6 v. 22 cm. Includes bibliographical references. [BX955.C8 1969] 74-77897
1. Catholic Church—History. 2. Papacy—History. I. Title.

DOW, Earle Wilbur, 1868- 282
Short histories, I. II., by Earle W. Dow. New York, London, The Century co. [c1928] v, 97 p. 21 cm. $1.25. Contents.The papacy amidst rising states, till Avignon.--Monarchy and people in France, under Philip IV and sons.--Bibliographical note. [BX955.D6] 28-9870
1. Papacy—Hist. 2. France—Pol. & govt.—Capetians to 1328. I. Title.

ECKHARDT, Carl Conrad. 261.7
The papacy and world affairs as reflected in the seculaization of politics, by Carl Conrad Eckhardt... Chicago, Ill., The University of Chicago press, [c1937] xiv, 309, [1] p. 23 1/2 cm. "Bibliography : p. 270-290. [BX1790.E25] 37-2626
1. Papacy—Hist. 2. Popes—Temporal power. 3. Church and state—Hist. I. Title.

ELLIOTT-BINNS, Leonard 282'.09'02
Elliott, 1885-
The history of the decline and fall of the medieval Papacy, by L. Elliott Binns. [Hamden, Conn.] Archon Books, 1967. xv, 388 p. 22 cm. Reprint of the 1934 ed. Bibliographical footnotes. [BX1068.E5 1967] 67-19514
1. Papacy — Hist. 2. Catholic Church — Hist. 3. Church history — Middle Ages. I. Title.

FARROW, John, 1904- 262.1309
Pageant of the popes; a frank history of the papacy. St. Paul, Catechetical Guild Educational Society [1955, c1950] 464p. 17cm. Includes bibliography. [BX955] 56-628
1. Papacy—Hist. I. Title.

FARROW, John, 1904- 922.21
Pageant of the popes; illustrated by Jean Charlot. Holy Year [i. e. 2d] ed. New York, Sheed & Ward, 1950. v, 394 p. ports. 22 cm. Bibliography: p. 381. [BX955.F33 1950] 50-6234
1. Papacy—Hist. I. Title.

GONTARD, Friedrich. 262.1309
The Chair of Peter; a history of the papacy. Translated from the German by A. J. and E. F. Peeler. [1st ed.] New York, Holt, Rinehart and Winston [1964] 629 p. coat of arms, map, plates, ports. 25 cm. Translation of Die Papste. [BX955.2.G63] 64-14346
1. Papacy—History. I. Title.

GRANT, Frederick Clifton, 262.13
1891-
Rome and reunion [by] Frederick C. Grant. New York, Oxford University Press, 1965. ix, 196 p. 21 cm. [BX957.G7] 65-11525
1. Papacy—Hist. 2. Christian union—Catholic Church. 3. Vatican Council, 2d. I. Title.

THE growth of papal government in the Middle Ages; a study in the ideological relation of clerical to lay power. New York, Barnes & Noble, Inc. [1956] xviii, 482p. illus.
1. Papacy— Hist. 2. Popes—Temporal power. 3. Church and state—Hist. I. Ullmann, Walter, 1910-

THE history of the popes,
from the close of the middle ages. Drawn from the secret archives of the Vatican and other original sources. From the German. London, Routledge & K. Paul; St. Louis, Mo., B. Herder, 1938-1961. 40v. 23cm. Translation of Geschichte der papste seit dem ausgang des mittelalters. Bibliographies. Vols. 1-6 edited by F. I. Antrobus; v. 7-24 by R. F. Kerr; v. 25-34 by Ernest Graf; v. 35-40 by E. F. Peeler. Imprint varies: Vols. 1-9, 11-36, London, Routledge Kegan Paul St. Louis, Mo. B. Herder; vol. 10, London, K. Paul, Trench, Trubner; v. 37, St. Louis, Mo., B. Herder, v. 38-40, London, Routledge and K. Paul. Onspine of all vols.: Routledge & Kegan Paul. Vols. 7-8, 11-12: 3d ed.; vols. 9-10: 4th ed; vols. 3-6: 5th ed.; v. 1: 6th ed.; v. 2: 7th ed.; vols. 13-40 have no edition statment.
1. Papacy—Hist. 2. Catholic church—Hist. I. Pastor, Ludwig, Freiherr von, 1854-1928. II. Antrobus, Frederick Ignatius, 1837-1903, ed. III. Kerr, Ralph Francis, 1874-1932, ed.

HOLLIS, Christopher, 262.1309
1902- ed.
The Papacy; an illustrated history from St. Peter to Paul VI. New York, Macmillan [c.1964] 304p. illus. (pt. col.) facsims., col. maps, ports. (pt. col.) 33cm. 64-12539 25.00
1. Papacy—Hist. I. Title.

HOLLIS, Christopher, 262.1309
1902- ed.
The Papacy; an illustrated history from St Peter to Paul VI. New York, Macmillan [1964] 304 p. illus. (part col.) facsims., col. maps, ports. (part col.) 33 cm. [BX955.2.H6] 64-12539
1. Papacy — Hist. I. Title.

JALLAND, Trevor Gervase, 282
1898-
The church and the papacy, a historical study, being eight lectures delivered before the University of Oxford, in the year 1942, on the foundation of the Rev. John Bampton, canon of Salisbury, by Trevor Gervase Jalland ... London, Society for promoting Christian knowledge; New York, Morehouse-Gorham co., 1944. xi, 568 p. 22 cm. [Bampton lectures, 1942] [BX955.J35] 44-11244
1. Papacy—Hist. 2. Church history. 3. Church—Foundation. I. Title.

JAMES, Arthur Walter, 1912-
... The growth of the papacy, by A. W. James, B.A. Published for the International committee of the Church union. New York, Milwaukee, Morehouse publishing Co. [1936] cover-title, 24 p. 21 1/2 cm. (Union of Christendom ... The causes of disruption (section II. 1) Discusses project for "International convention, 1940." Bibliography: p. 24. 41-331
1. Papacy—Hist. 2. The Church union. International committee. I. Title.

JOHN of Salisbury, bp. of
Chartres, d.1180.
Ioannis Saresberiensis Historiae pontificalis quae supersunt, edited by Rginald L. Poole ... Oxford, The Clarendon press, 1927. c, 128 p. 23 cm. "All that remains to us comprises only the years from 1148 to 1152: but incidentally it throws a flood of light on the events of many years earlier ... The book is believed to be preserved only in a single copy in the town library at Bern [ms. 367]"-Pref., p. viii. "List of editions cited": p. [xcvii]-c. [BX953.J6] 20-591
1. Eugenius iii. pope, d. 1153. 2. Papacy—Hist. 3. Catholic church—Hist. I. Poole, Reginald Lane, 1857-ed. II. Title.

JOHN OF SALISBURY, Bp. of 270.3
Chapters(d.1180.
Memoirs of the Papal Court translated from the Latin with introd. and notes by Marjorie Chibnall. London, New York, Nelson [1956] 1, 89, 109p. 23cm. (Medieval texts) Added t. p.: Historia pontificalis. Paged, in part, in duplicate. Latin and English. Reginald L. Poole's edition of the text was used as a basis for this edition, the original ms., which came from the Monastery of Fleury, is now ms. 367 in the Library of Berne. [BX953.J613] 270.46 56-4947
1. Eugenius III, Pope, d. 153. 2. Papacy—Hist. 3. Catholic Church—Hist. I. Chibnall, Marjorie, ed. and tr. II. Title. III. Title: Historia pontificalis. IV. Series: Medieval classics (London)

KERR, Cecil, Lady, 1883- 922.21
The child's book of great popes, by Cecil Kerr; with illustrations by Doris Pailthorpe. London, New York [etc.] Longmans, Green and co., 1931. iv, 124 p. illus. 19 1/2 cm. [Full name: Lady Anne Cecil Kerr] [BX960.K4] 31-14643
1. Papacy—Hist. I. Title.

KORN, Frank J. 262'.13
From Peter to John Paul II : an informal study of the papacy / by Frank J. Korn. Canfield, Ohio : Alba Books, c1980. 282 p. : ill. ; 18 cm. Includes bibliographical references. [BX955.2.K64] 19 80-65721 ISBN 0-8189-1160-3 pbk. : 4.95
1. Papacy—History. 2. Popes—Biography. I. Title.

KUHNER, Hans. 262.13
Encyclopedia of the Papacy. [Translated from the German by Kenneth J. Northcott] New York, Philosophical Library [1958] 249p. 22cm. Bibliography: p. 249. [BX955.K853] 58-4521
1. Papacy—Hist. I. Title.

MCCABE, Joseph, 1867- 282
Crises in the history of the papacy; a study of twenty famous popes whose careers and whose influence were important in the development of the church and in the history of the world, by Joseph McCabe ... New York and London, G. P. Putnam's sons, 1916. xiv p., 1 l., 459 p. 22 1/2 cm. $2.50. [BX955.M2] 16-5965
1. Papacy—Hist. 2. Catholic church—Hist. I. Title.
Contents omitted.

MCCORMICK, Anne (O'Hare) 262.13
Vatican journal, 1921-1954. Compiled and edited by Marion Turner Sheehan; with an introd. by Clare Booth Luce. New York, Farrar, Straus and Cudahy [1957] 288p. 22cm. [BX1389.M32] 57-11490
1. Papacy—Hist. 2. Catholic Church—Relations (diplomatic) I. Title.

MACGREGOR-HASTIE, Roy 262.1309
The throne of Peter; a history of the papacy. New York, Criterion [1966] 192p. ports. 23cm. [BX955.2.M3] 66-15134 3.95
1. Papcy—Hist. I. Title.

MACGREGOR-HASTIE, Roy.
262'.13'09
The throne of Peter; a history of the Papacy. London, New York [etc.] Abelard Schuman, 1966. 192 p. ports. 22 cm. 18/- (B***) [BX955.2.M3] 68-86661
1. Papacy—Hist. I. Title.

MORGAN, Thomas Brynmor, 1886- 282
The listening post; eighteen years on Vatican hill, by Thomas B. Morgan. New York, G. P. Putnam's sons [1944] v. 242 p. 21 1/2 cm. [BX1389.M6] 44-3061
1. Papacy—Hist. 2. Popes—Court. 3. Catholic church—Relations (diplomatic) I. Title.

MURPHY, John Nicholas. 282
The chair of Peter, or, The papacy considered in its institution, development, and organization, and in the benefits, which, for over eighteen centuries, it has conferred on mankind. By John Nicholas Murphy ... 3d ed., with events and statistics brought down to the present time ... London, Burns and Oates, ld.; New York, Catholic publication society co., 1888. xvi, 720 p. 20 cm. [BX955.M8] 4-215
1. Papacy—Hist. I. Title.

PASTOR, Ludwig, freiherr von, 282
[Full name: Ludwig Friedrich August, freiherr von Pastor von Camperfelden], 1854-1928
The history of the popes, from the Middle Ages. Drawn from the secret archives of the Vatican and other orig. sources. From the German of Dr. Ludwig Pastor. London, J. Hodges. 1891. Nendeln, Liechtenstein, Kraus-Thomson. 1968. 40v. 1891-1961. 23 cm. Half-title: Catholic standard library. Vs. 1-6 ed. by F. I. Antrobus: v. 7-24 by R. F. Kerr; v. 25-34 by Ernest Graf; v. 35-40 by K. F. Peeler. Imprint varies . . . Bibl. 24-12249 600.00
1. Papacy—Hist. 2. Catholic church—Hist. I. Title.
Order from Kraus-Thomson Org., 9491 Nendeln, Liechtenstein.

POOLE, Reginald Lane, 1857- 270.5
Wycliffe and movements for reform, by Reginald Lane Poole ... New York, A. D. F. Randolph & company [1889] 1 p. l., [v]-xi, 204 p. 19 cm. (On cover: Epochs of church history) [BR295.P8 1889] 33-6270
1. Wycliffe, John, d. 1884. 2. Papacy—Hist. 3. Reformation—Early movements. I. Title.

POOLE, Reginald Lane, 1857- 270.
Wycliffe and movements for reform, by Reginald Lane Poole ... New ed. London, New York [etc.] Longmans, Green, and co., 1896. xi, 204 p. 18 cm. (Half-title: Epochs of church history ...) [BR295.P8 1896] 3-826
1. Wycliffe, John, d. 1884. 2. Papacy—Hist. 3. Reformation—Early movements. I. Title.

POOLE, Reginald 270'.5'0924 B
Lane, 1857-1939.
Wycliffe and movements for reform / by Reginald Lane Poole. New York : AMS Press, 1978. xi, 204 p. ; 19 cm. Reprint of the 1889 ed. published by A. D. F. Randolph, New York, in series: Epochs of church history. Includes bibliographical references and index. [BR295.P8 1978] 77-84729 ISBN 0-404-16129-4 : 19.00
1. Wycliffe, John, d. 1384. 2. Papacy—History. 3. Reformation—Early movements. I. Title. II. Series: Epochs of church history.

RANKE, Leopold von, 262'.13'09
1795-1886.
History of the Popes; their church and state. [Translated from the German by E. Fowler] New York, F. Ungar Pub. Co. [1966] 3 v. illus., facsims., ports. 22 cm. Translation of Die romischen Papste. Reprint of the 1901 ed. Includes bibliographical references. [BX955.R35 1966] 66-25109
1. Papacy—History. I. Title.

RIDLEY, Francis A., 1897- 262'.13
The Papacy and fascism; the crisis of the twentieth century, by F. A. Ridley. London, M. Secker, Warburg, 1937. [New York, AMS Press, 1973] 264 p. 19 cm. Includes bibliographical references. [BX1790.R5 1973] 72-180422 ISBN 0-404-56156-X 13.50
1. Catholic Church—Relations (diplomatic) 2. Papacy—History. 3. Socialism and Catholic Church. 4. Fascism and Catholic Church. I. Title.

SETTON, Kenneth Meyer, 081 s
1914-
The Papacy and the Levant, 1204-1571 / Kenneth M. Setton. Philadelphia : American Philosophical Society, 1976- v. ; 28 cm. (Memoirs of the American Philosophical Society ; v. 114 ISSN 0065-9738s) Contents.Contents.—v. 1. The thirteenth and fourteenth centuries.

Includes bibliographical references and index. [Q11.P612 vol. 114] [BX955.2] 270.5 75-25476 ISBN 0-87169-114-0 (v. 1)
1. Papacy—History. 2. Levant—History. 3. Crusades. I. Title. II. Series: American Philosophical Society, Philadelphia. Memoirs ; v. 114.

SHOTWELL, James Thompson, 1874- ed. 282
The see of Peter, by James T. Shotwell...and Louise Ropes Loomis... New York, Columbia university press, 1927. xxvi, 737 p. 23 cm. (Half-title: Records of civilization: Sources and studies, ed. by J. T. Shotwell) A documentary study containing extracts of essential texts relating to the history of the rise of the papacy. cf. General introd. [BX955.S5] 27-25032
1. Papacy—Hist. 2. Peter, Saint, apostle. 3. Catholic church—Hist. 4. Church history—Primitive and early church. 5. Popes—Hist. I. Loomis, Louise Ropes, 1874- joint ed. II. Title.

SHOTWELL, James Thomson, 1874-1965, ed. 262.13
The see of Peter [ed.] by James T. Shotwell, Louise Ropes Loomis. New York, Octagon, 1965[c.1927, 1955] xxvi, 737p. 24cm. (Records of civilization: sources and studies, no.7) Bibl. [BX955.S5] 65-25615 17.50
1. Peter, Saint, apostle. 2. Papacy—Hist. 3. Church history—Primitive and early church. I. Loomis, Louise Ropes, 1874-1958, ed. II. Title. III. Series.

THOMSON, John A. F. 262'.13'09024
Popes and princes, 1417-1517 : politics and polity in the late medieval church / John A.F. Thomson. London ; Boston : Allen & Unwin, 1980. xvii, 252 p. ; 23 cm. (Early modern Europe today) Includes index. Bibliography: p. [218]-236. [BX1270.T48] 19 80-40514 ISBN 0-04-901027-1 : 19.50
1. Papacy—History. 2. Popes—Temporal power—History. 3. Church and state—Europe—History. 4. Church history—Middle Ages, 600-1500. I. Title. II. Series.

ULLMAN, Walter, 1910- 282
The growth of papal government in the Middle Ages; a study in the ideological relation of clerical to lay power. New York, Barnes & Noble [1956] xviii, 482 p. front. 23 cm. [BX955.U] A59
1. Papacy — Hist. 2. Popes — Temporal power. 3. Church and state — Hist. I. Title.

ULLMANN, Walter, 1910- 282
The growth of papal government in the Middle Ages; a study in the ideological relation of clerical to lay power. [2 ed.] London, Methuen [dist. New York, Barnes & Noble, 1963] xxiv, 492p. 23cm. Bibl. 63-4507 8.50
1. Papacy—Hist. 2. Popes—Temporal power. 3. Church and state—Hist. I. Title.

ULLMANN, Walter, 1910-
The growth of papal government in the Middle Ages; a study in the ideological relation of clerical to lay power. New York, Barnes & Noble [1962] 24 + 492 p. front. 23 cm. Imprint on mounted label. 2d ed. 63-59477
1. Papacy — Hist. 2. Popes — Temporal power. 3. Church and state — Hist. I. Title.

VAILLANCOURT, Jean-Guy. 306'.6
Papal power : a study of Vatican control over lay Catholic elites / Jean-Guy Vaillancourt. Berkeley : University of California Press, c1980. p. cm. Includes index. Bibliography: p. [BX957.V36] 78-59443 ISBN 0-520-03733-2 : 16.95
1. Catholic Church—Teaching office. 2. Papaey—History. 3. Laity—Catholic church. I. Title.

VAN DYKE, Paul, 1859-1933. 270.
...The age of the renascence; an outline sketch of the history of the papacy from the return Avignon to the sack of Rome (1377-1527), by Paul Van Dyke. With an introduction by Henry Van Dyke. New York, The Christian literature co., 1897. xxii p., 1 l., 397 p. 19 1/2 cm. (Half-title: Ten epochs of church history, ed. by J. Fulton, vol. VII) Series title also at head of t.-p. [BR141.T4 vol. 7] 4-4197
1. Papacy—Hist. I. Title.

WALSH, Michael J. 262'.13'09
The illustrated history of the Popes / Michael Walsh. New York : St. Martin's Press, [1980] p. cm. [BX955.2.W28] 80-50818 ISBN 0-312-40817-X : 19.95
1. Papacy—History. I. Title.

WINTER, Michael M. 262.13
Saint Peter and the Popes. Baltimore, Helicon Press [1960] 236p. Bibl. footnotes. 60-13379 4.50 bds.,
1. Peter, Saint, apostle. 2. Papacy—Hist. I. Title.

WINTER, Michael M. 262'.13'09
Saint Peter and the Popes / Michael M. Winter. Westport, Conn. : Greenwood Press, 1979, c1960. p. cm. Reprint of the ed. published by Helicon Press, Baltimore. Includes index. Bibliography: p. [BX955.2.W5 1979] 78-21507 ISBN 0-313-21158-2 lib. bdg. : 18.75
1. Peter, Saint, Apostle. 2. Papacy—History. I. Title.

Papacy—History—1309-1378.

MOLLAT, Guillaume, 1877- 262.1309
The popes at Avignon, 1305-1378. Tr. from the 9th French ed., 1949 [by Janet Love] New York, Nelson [c.1963] xxii, 361p. 24cm. Bibl. 63-24639 9.25
1. Papacy—Hist.—1309-1378. 2. Avignon—Hist. I. Title.

MOLLAT, Guillaume, 1877- 262.1309
The popes at Avignon, 1305-1378. Translated from the 9th French ed., 1949 [by Janet Love] London, New York, T. Nelson [1963] xxii, 361 p. 24 cm. Bibliography: p. x. Bibliographical footnotes. [BX1300.M613 1963] 63-24639
1. Papacy — Hist. — 1309-1378. 2. Avignon — Hist. I. Title.

RENOUARD, Yves. 262'.13'09023
The Avignon papacy, 1305-1403. Translated by Denis Bethell. [Hamden, Conn.] Archon Books, 1970. 157 p. maps, port. 23 cm. Translation of La papaute a Avignon. Bibliography: p. 138-150. [BX1270.R413] 70-21164 ISBN 0-208-01156-0 7.50
1. Papacy—History—1309-1378. I. Title.

Papacy—History—1566-1799.

CHADWICK, Owen. 262'.13'09033
The Popes and European revolution / Owen Chadwick. Oxford : Clarendon Press ; New York : Oxford University Press, 1981. ix, 646 p. ; 25 cm. (Oxford history of the Christian Church) Includes index. Bibliography: p. [614]-631. [BX1361.C45] 19 80-40673 ISBN 0-19-826919-6 (Oxford University Press) : 84.00
1. Catholic Church in Europe—History. 2. Papacy—History—1566-1799. 3. Papacy—History—19th century. 4. Europe—Politics and government—18th century. 5. Europe—Politics and government—1789-1900. I. Title. II. Series.

Papacy—History—20th century

DELZELL, Charles F., comp. 262'.13'0904
The Papacy and totalitarianism between the two World Wars, edited by Charles F. Delzell. New York, Wiley [1974] viii, 179 p. 22 cm. (Major issues in history) Bibliography: p. 173-179. [BX1389.D44] 73-16419 ISBN 0-471-20638-5 4.50 (pbk)
1. Papacy—History—20th century. 2. Papal documents. I. Title.

FALCONI, Carlo. 262'.13'0904
The Popes in the twentieth century, from Pius X to John XXIII. Translated from the Italian by Muriel Grindrod. [1st American ed.] Boston, Little, Brown [1968, c1967] xvi, 400 p. illus., ports. 24 cm. Translation of I papi del ventesimo secolo. Bibliography: p. [370]-378. [BX1389.F313 1968b] 68-14744
1. Papacy—History—20th century. I. Title.

FALCONI, Carlo. 262'.13'0904
The Popes in the twentieth century, from Pius X to John XXIII. Translated from the Italian by Muriel Grindrod. [1st American ed.] Boston, Little, Brown [1968, c1967] xvi, 400 p. illus., ports. 24 cm. Translation of I papi del ventesimo secolo. Bibliography: p. [370]-378. [BX1389.F313 1968b] 68-1474
1. Papacy—Hist.—20th cent. I. Title.

HEBBLETHWAITE, Peter. 262'.13'09047
The year of the three popes / Peter Hebblethwaite. London : Collins, 1978. ix, 220 p. ; 22 cm. Includes index. Bibliography: p. 213-214. [BX1389.H36] 79-307264 ISBN 0-00-215047-6 : 8.95
1. Paulus VI, Pope, 1897- 2. John Paul I, Pope, 1912-1978. 3. John Paul II, Pope, 1920- 4. Papacy—History—20th century. 5. Popes—Biography. I. Title.
Distributed by Collins Publishers, Inc., Cleveland, OH 44111

MARTIN, Malachi. 282
Three Popes and the Cardinal. New York, Popular Lib. [1973? c.1972] 414 p. 18 cm. [BX1389.M37 1972] pap., 1.50
1. Papacy—History—20th century. 2. Catholic Church—History—1965- 3. Civilization, Modern—1950- I. Title.

MARTIN, Malachi. 282
Three Popes and the Cardinal. New York, Farrar, Straus and Giroux [1972] xiv, 300 p. 23 cm. [BX1389.M37 1972] 74-181756 ISBN 0-374-27675-7 7.95
1. Catholic Church—History—1965- 2. Papacy—History—20th century. 3. Civilization, Modern—1950- I. Title.

MURPHY, Francis Xavier, 1914- 262'.13'0904
The papacy today / Francis Xavier Murphy. 1st American ed. New York : Macmillan, 1981. p. cm. Includes index. Bibliography: p. [BX1389.M8 1981] 81-869 ISBN 0-02-588890-0 : 10.95 lib. bdg. : 10.95
1. Papacy—History—20th century. I. Title.

NICHOLS, Peter, 1928- 262'.13'0904
The politics of the Vatican. New York, Praeger [1968] ix, 373 p. 8 plates (incl. ports.) 22 cm. Bibliographical footnotes. [BX1389.N5 1968] 68-11321
1. Papacy—History—20th century. I. Title.

RHODES, Anthony Richard Ewart. 327'.45'634
The Vatican in the age of the dictators, 1922-1945 [by] Anthony Rhodes. New York, Holt, Rinehart and Winston [1974, c1973] 383 p. ports. 24 cm. Bibliography: p. [359]-368. [BX1389.R48 1974] 72-91593 ISBN 0-03-007736-2 12.50
1. Pius XI, Pope, 1857-1939. 2. Pius XII, Pope, 1876-1958. 3. Papacy—History—20th century. 4. Church and state in Europe. 5. World War, 1939-1945—Catholic Church. I. Title.

Papacy—History—Addresses, essays, lectures.

ULLMANN, Walter, 1910- 262'.13'0902
The papacy and political ideas in the Middle Ages / Walter Ullmann. London : Variorum Reprints, 1976. 406 p. in various pagings : port. ; 23 cm. (Variorum reprint ; CS44) Includes original pagings. Reprints of articles in English or German, originally published between 1952 and 1973. Contents.Contents.—1. Cardinal Humbert and the Roman Ecclesia.—2. Von Canossa nach Pavia.—3. The Pontificate of Adrian IV.—4. Cardinal Roland and Besancon.—5. The significance of Innocent III's decretal Vergentis.—6. Dies ortus imperii.—7. The decline of the Chancellor's authority in medieval Cambridge.—8. The curial exequies for Edward I and Edward III.—9. A decision of the Rota Romana on the benefit of clergy in England.—10. De Bartoli sententia.—11. The University of Cambridge and the Great Schism.—12. The recognition of St Bridget's Rule by Martin V.—13. Eugenius IV, Cardinal Kemp and Archibishop Chichele.—14. Thomas Becket's miraculous oil.—15. The legal validity of the papal electoral pacts.—16. Julius II and the schismatic cardinals.—17. The medieval papal court as an international tribunal.—18. The Papacy as an institution of government in the Middle Ages. Includes bibliographies and index. [BX1068.U44] 76-379934 ISBN 0-902089-87-0 : £13.50
1. Papacy—History—Addresses, essays, lectures. I. Title.

Papacy—History—Sources.

GILES, Edward, ed. 262'.13
Documents illustrating papal authority, A.D. 96-454 / edited and introduced by E. Giles. Westport, Conn. : Hyperion Press, 1979. xxi, 344 p. ; 22 cm. Reprint of the 1952 ed. published by S.P.C.K., London. Includes bibliographical references and indexes. [BX953.G5 1979] 78-59023 ISBN 0-88355-696-0 : lib.bdg. : 25.00
1. Papacy—History—Sources. 2. Church history—Primitive and early church, ca. 30-600—Sources. 3. Christian literature, Early. I. Title.

LIBER pontificalis 262.130922
The book of the Popes. Liber pontificalis. Translated with an introd. by Louise Ropes Loomis. New York, Octagon Books, 1965- v. 24 cm. (Records of civilization; sources and studies, no. 3 Contents.CONTEnTS. -- [1] To the pontificate of Gregory I. [BX950.E6L612] 65-9020
1. Papacy — Hist. — Sources. 2. Catholic Church — Hist. — Sources. 3. Popes. I. Loomis, Louis Ropes, 1874- tr. II. Title. III. Series.

LIBER PONTIFICALIS 262.1309
The book of the popes (Liber pontificalis) New York, Octagon, 1965 [c.1916, 1944] 169p. 24cm. (Records of civilization: sources and studies, no.3) Tr. is based upon the text ed. by Mommsen in the Monumenta Germaniae historica. [BX950.E6L6] 7.50
1. Papacy—Hist.—Sources. 2. Catholic church—Hist.—Sources. I. Liber pontificalis. tr. II. Title.
Contents omitted

Papacy—History—To 1309.

DUCHESNE, Louis Marie Olivier, 1843-1922. 945'.6
The beginnings of the temporal sovereignty of the popes, A.D. 754-1073. Authorised translation from the French by Arnold Harris Mathew. New York, B. Franklin [1972] xi, 312 p. 23 cm. (Burt Franklin research and source work series. Philosophy and religious history monographs, 121) Reprint of the 1908 ed., which was issued as v. 11 of International Catholic library. Translation of Les premiers temps de l'Etat pontifical. Includes bibliographical references. [BX1070.D83 1972] 73-185937 ISBN 0-8337-4079-2
1. Papacy—History—To 1309. 2. Popes—Temporal power. 3. Papal states—History. I. Title. II. Series: The International Catholic library, v. 11.

RICHARDS, Jeffrey. 262'.13'09021
The popes and the papacy in the early Middle Ages, 476-752 / Jeffrey Richards. London ; Boston : Routledge & Kegan Paul, 1979. viii, 422 p. ; 22 cm. Includes index. Bibliography: p. 398-409. [BX970.R48] 78-41023 ISBN 0-7100-0098-7 : 35.00
1. Papacy—History—To 1309. 2. Europe—Church history. I. Title.

SHANNON, Albert Clement, 1918- 272
The popes and heresy in the thirteenth century / [by Albert Clement Shannon]. New York : AMS Press, 1980. p. cm. Reprint of the author's thesis, Columbia, 1949, published by Augustinian Press, Villanova, Pa. Vita. Includes index. Bibliography: p. [BX1210.S5 1980] 78-63192 ISBN 0-404-16228-2 : 21.50
1. Papacy—History—To 1309. 2. Christian sects, Medieval. 3. Church history—Middle Ages, 600-1500. I. Title.

Papago Indians—Legends—Juvenile literature.

BAKER, Betty. 299'.7
At the center of the world. Based on Papago and Pima myths. Illustrated by Murray Tinkelman. New York, Macmillan [1973] 53 p. illus. 23 cm. Contents.Contents.—Earth magician.—Coyote drowns the world.—The killing pot.—The monster eagle.—The killing of Eetoi.—The first war. [PZ8.1.B1724At] 72-88820 ISBN 0-02-708290-3 4.95 (lib. bdg.)
1. Papago Indians—Legends—Juvenile literature. 2. Pima Indians—Legends—

Juvenile literature. 3. [Papago Indians—Legends.] 4. [Pima Indians—Legends.] 5. [Indians of North America—Legends.] I. Tinkelman, Murray, illus. II. Title.

Papago Indians—Music.

UNDERHILL, Ruth Murray, 1884- 299'.7
Singing for power : the song magic of the Papago Indians of southern Arizona / Ruth Murray Underhill. Berkeley : University of California Press, 1976, c1938. vii, 158 p. : ill. ; 21 cm. (California library reprint series) [ML3557.U53 1976] 77-354970 ISBN 0-520-03280-2 pbk. : 2.95
1. Papago Indians—Music. 2. Indians of North America—Arizona—Music. I. Title. II. Series.

Papago Indians—Religion and mythology.

UNDERHILL, Ruth Murray, 1884- 299'.7
Papago Indian religion [by] Ruth M. Underhill. New York, AMS Press [1969] vi, 359 p. 24 cm. (Columbia University contributions to anthropology, no. 33) Reprint of the 1946 ed. Sequel to Social organization of the Papago Indians. Bibliography: p. [341]-347. [E99.P25U518 1969] 74-82363
1. Papago Indians—Religion and mythology. I. Title. II. Series: Columbia University. Columbia University contributions to anthropology, v. 33

UNDERHILL, Ruth Murray, 1884- 970.62
Papago Indian religion. New York, Columbia university press, 1946. vi p., [4], [3]-359 p. diagrs. 23 1/2 cm. (Half-title: Columbia university contributions to anthropology, no. 33) At head of title: Ruth M. Underhill. "A sequel to a previous paper on Social organization."--Foreword. Bibliography: p. [341]-347. [E51.C7 no. 33] [E99.P25U518] [299.7] (572.97) A 47
1. Papago Indians—Religion and mythology. I. Title.

*UNDERHILL, Ruth Murray, 1884- 2991.7
Singing for power; the song magic of the Papago Indians of Southern Arizona. New York, Ballantine Books [1973, c1938] vii, 148 p. illus. 18 cm. (Walden Edition) [E99] ISBN 0-345-23615-7 1.50 (pbk.)
1. Papago Indians—Religion and mythology. I. Title.

Papal documents.

CATHOLIC Church Pope 262.82
Seven great encyclicals: labor, education, marriage, reconstructing the social order, atheistic communism, world social problems, world peace. Glen Rock, N.J. Paulist Press [c.1939,1963] vii, 344 p. 20 cm. 63-24169 1.50, pap.
1. Papal documents. I. Title.

CATHOLIC Church. Pope, 1963. (Paulus VI) 270
The apostolic letter, Sabaudiae gemma, of Pope Paul VI to the cardinals, archbishops, bishops, and other ordinaries of France, Switzerland and the Piedmont Region commemorating the four-hundredth anniversary of the birth of Saint Francis de Sales. Translated by Neil Kilty. Hyattsville, Md., Institute of Salesian Studies [1967] 15, [1] p. 19 cm. Bibliographical references included in "Notes" (p. [16]) [BX4700.F85C313] 68-6901
I. Francois de Sales, Saint, Bp. of Geneva, 1567-1622. II. [Sabaudiae gemma] III. Title. IV. Title: Sabaudiae gemma.

HAYES, James M. comp.
Chips of wisdom from the rock of Peter; a collection of brief papal utterances bearing on modern social questions ... ("St. Anthony truth guild" ed.) Chicago, J. J. Collins' sons, printers, 1900. xv, [1], 168 p. 16°. Aug
I. Title.

Papal documents—Indexes.

CARLEN, Mary Claudia, 1906- 262.82
Dictionary of papal pronouncements, Leo XIII to Pius xii, 1878-1957. Compiled by Sister M. Claudia New York, P. J. Kenedy [1958] 216p. 24cm. 'Papal document collections':p. 173-177. [BX873.7.C3] 58-12095
1. Papal documents—Indexes. 2. Papal documents—Bibl. I. Title.

Papal Volunteers for Latin America.

MCCARTHY, Dan B. 266'.00985
Mission to Peru; a story of papal volunteers [by] Dan B. McCarthy. Milwaukee, Bruce Pub. Co. [1967] xi, 164 p. illus., ports. 22 cm. [BV2300.P3M3] 67-28889
1. Papal Volunteers for Latin America. 2. Missions—Peru. I. Title.

MICHENFELDER, Joseph. 266.2'85
Gringo volunteers. Photos by Fred Albert [i.e. Allert] Maryknoll, N.Y., Maryknoll Publications, 1969. 96 p. illus., ports. 24 cm. [BV2300.P3M5] 72-11070 4.95
1. Papal Volunteers for Latin America. 2. Missions—Peru. I. Allert, Fred, illus. II. Title.

PEACE or violence in Latin America? 266'.2'8 Needed: competent personnel for Latin America. [Washington, Papal Volunteers for Latin America, 1968 or 9] 22 p. illus. 22 cm. Special issue of The Papal volunteer, vol. 8, no. 5. [BV2300.P3P4] 74-153076
1. Papal Volunteers for Latin America. I. Papal Volunteers for Latin America. II. The Papal volunteer.

Papias, Saint. bp. of Hierapolis, 2d century

HALL, Edward Henry, 1831-1912. 270.
Papias and his contemporaries; a study of religious thought in the second century, by Edward H. Hall. Boston and New York, Houghton, Mifflin and company, 1899. 2 p. l., 318 p., 1 l. 19 1/2 cm. [BR165.H25] 99-1298
1. Papias, Saint. bp. of Hierapolis, 2d cent. 2. Church history—Primitive and early church. I. Title.

Parables.

BIBLE. N. T. Selections. English. 1923
The parables and other sayings of Jesus. London [etc.] J. M. Dent & sons, ltd.; New York, E. P. Dutton & co., 1923. 2 p. l., vii-xix, iii, [1] p. front., plates. 16 cm. (Half-title: The bedside series) "This little book has been drawn from a collection entitled Verba Christi, which was made by the late Dr. Charles W. Stubbs ... The parables are illustrated from the woodcut drawings of Sir John Everett Millais."--Pref. W23
1. Jesus Christ. 2. Parables. I. Title.

EBERHART, Elvin T., 1925- 248'.4
Burnt offerings : parables for 20th-century Christians / Elvin T. Eberhart. Nashville : Abingdon, c1977. 96 p. ; 20 cm. [BV4515.2.E23] 77-23158 ISBN 0-687-04375-1 pbk. : 3.95
1. Parables. I. Title.

FREESE, Jacob R 1826-1885.
... Elizabeth's mission (faithful and true): a parable of what might have been; of what was; and of what will be. By Dr. Freese ... Philadelphia, Crombargar & co., 1882. 2 p. l., ix-xvii, 18-361 incl. front., illus., plates. 21 cm. "Illustrated edition." [PS1714.F4E5] 27-22276
I. Title.

GAMBRELL, James Bruton, 1841-1921. 252.
Parable and precept, a Baptist message, by J. B. Gambrell ... comp. by E. C. Routh ... New York, Chicago [etc.] Fleming H. Revell company [c1917] 183 p. 19 1/2 cm. $1.00. Reprinted from the Baptist standard. [BX6333.G29P3] 17-16713
I. Routh, Eugene C., 1874- comp. II. Title.

GOETHE, Johann Wolfgang von, 1749-1832. 212
The parable. Translated by Alice Raphael. [1st ed.] New York, Harcourt, Brace & World [1963] xiii, 73 p. 21 cm. Translation of Das Marchen. Bibliographical references included in "Notes" (p. 67-70) Bibliography: p. 71-73. [PT1971.M2E57] 63-17776
I. Raphael, Alice Pearl, 1887- tr. II. Title.

KIRK, Edward Norris, 1802-1874. 226.8
Lectures on the parables of Our Saviour. By Edward N. Kirk, D.D. New York, J. F. Trow, printer, 1856. xiv p., 2 l., [3]-506 p. 20 1/2 cm. [BT375.K5 1856] 35-30461
1. Jesus Christ—Parables. 2. Parables. I. Title.

KIRK, Edward Norris, 1802-1874. 226.8
Lectures on the parables of Our Saviour. By Edward N. Kirk, D.D. New York, R. Craighead, printer, 1857. xiv p., 1 l., [3]-368 p. 16 1/2 cm. [BT375.K5 1857] 35-21112
1. Jesus Christ—Parables. 2. Parables. I. Title.

*LANE, Thomas Clifford 226
The parables. New York, Vantage [c.1964] 127p. 21cm. 2.50
I. Title.

LINN, Samuel.
The seven parables of the kingdom, by Rev. Samuel Linn. [Osage, Ia., Press of the Woolvertn printing & publishing co., c1908] 108 p. 15 x 12 cm. 8-18055
I. Title.

MACARTNEY, Clarence Edward.
The parables of the Old Testament, by Clarence Edward Macartney ... New York, Chicago [etc.] Fleming H. Revell company [c1916] 122 p. 19 1/2 cm. $0.75 16-10812
I. Title.

MACARTNEY, Clarence Edward Noble, 1879- 221.
The parables of the Old Testament, by Clarence Edward Macartney ... New and enl. ed. New York, Chicago [etc.] Fleming H. Revell company [c1926] 4 p. l., 7-201 p. 19 1/2 cm. [BS1199.P3M3 1926] 26-22093
I. Title.

MARSH, Frederick Edward, 1858-
Pearls, points and parables, by F. E. Marsh. New York, Gospel publishing house [c1908] 1 p. l., xxviii p., 1 l., 269 p. 22 cm. 9-6854
I. Title.

PARK, John Edgar, 1879- 170
Parables of life, by J. Edgar Park ... Boston, New York [etc.] The Pilgrim press [c1912] 79 p. 20 cm. Cover-title: Parables of life; being timely treatises based upon human idiosyncrasies, interpreted by J. Edgar Park. [BJ1595.P3] 12-26698 0.75
I. Title.

*PAULSON, John F. 226.806
Parables of the kingdom, by John F. Paulson. Donald R. Pichaske. John Gretzer, illus. Philadelphia, Lutheran Church Pr. [c.1964] 112p. 21cm. 1.25; pap., teacher's ed., pap., 1.50
I. Title.

PRATER, Arnold 248.42
Parables from life. Grand Rapids, Mich., Zondervan [c.1963] 84p. 21cm. 1.95 bds.,
I. Title.

REY, Alfonso, fl.1973- 226'.8'09505
The lost sheep and other parables : The good Samaritan, The prodigal son / ill. Beaumont ; text Alfonso Rey ; [English translation by Albert J. Nevins]. [Huntington, Ind.] : Our Sunday Visitor, c1979. 60 p. : col. ill. ; 31 cm. Translation of Parabolas de Jesus: La oveja perdida. Presents three parables related by Jesus and recorded in the four Gospels. [BT378.L6R4813] 78-71329 ISBN 0-87973-712-3 : 5.95
1. Lost sheep (Parable)—Juvenile literature. 2. Good Samaritan (Parable)—Juvenile literature. 3. Prodigal son (Parable)—Juvenile literature. 4. [Lost sheep (Parable)] 5. [Good Samaritan (Parable)] 6. [Prodigal son (Parable)] 7. [Parables.] 8. [Bible stories—N.T.] I. Beaumont. II. Title.

REY, Alfonso, fl.1973- 226'.8'09505
Poor Lazarus and other parables : The parable of the sower, the good shepherd / ills. Beaumont ; text Alfonso Rey ; [English translation by Albert J. Nevins]. [Huntington, Ind.] : Our Sunday Visitor, c1979. 60 p. : col. ill. ; 31 cm. Translation of Parabolas de Jesus: El pobre Lazaro. Retells three parables which illustrate God's love. [BT378.D5R4913] 78-71328 ISBN 0-87973-711-5 : 5.95
1. Dives and Lazarus (Parable)—Juvenile literature. 2. Sower (Parable)—Juvenile literature. 3. Bible. N.T. John X, 1-18—Juvenile literature. 4. [Dives and Lazarus (Parable)] 5. [Sower (Parable)] 6. [Parables.] 7. [Bible stories—N.T.] I. Beaumont. II. Title.

ROBERTSON, Jenny. 226'.809505
Jesus, the storyteller / by Jenny Robertson ; illustrated by Alan Parry. Grand Rapids, Mich. : Zondervan Pub. House, 1980. p. cm. (Zondervan/Ladybird Bible series) Retells several of the parables of Jesus. [BT376.R6] 19 80-23031 ISBN 0-310-42840-8 : 1.95
1. Jesus Christ—Parables—Juvenile literature. 2. [Parables.] 3. [Bible stories—N.T.] I. Parry, Alan. II. Title. III. Series.

SCHINDLER, Regine. 226'.809505
The lost sheep / Regine Schindler ; illustrated by Hilde Heyduck-Huth. Nashville : Abingdon, c1981. p. cm. Translation of Das Verlorene Shaf. Retells the Bible story in which a shepherd leaves his entire flock to search for a little lost sheep. [BT378.L6S3513] 19 80-68546 ISBN 0-687-22780-1 : 5.95
1. Lost sheep (Parable)—Juvenile literature. 2. [Lost sheep (Parable)] 3. [Parables.] 4. [Bible stories—N.T.] I. Heyduck-Huth, Hilde. II. Title.

SMITH, Christopher.
The Gospel parables in verse, by Rev. Christopher Smith. New York, Washington [etc.] Broadway publishing co. [c1911] 89 p. 20 1/2 cm. $0.75 11-27067
I. Title.

STEINER, Edward Alfred, 1866- 244
The parable of the cherries, by Edward A. Steiner ... New York, Chicago [etc.] Fleming H. Revell company [1913] 64 p. col. plates. 19 1/2 cm. [BV4515.S62] 13-24812
I. Title.

STIRLING, James.
Christ's vision of the kingdom of heaven, by James Stirling ... Boston, The Pilgrim press; London, J. Clarke & co., 1913. 6 p. l., 7-459, [1] p. 22 cm. (Half-title: Christ's vision of the kingdom of heaven) A 16
1. Parables. I. Title.

THOMAS, J. B.
Some parables of nature in the light of to-day, by J. B. Thomas ... Cincinnati, Jennings and Graham; New York, Eaton and Mains [c1911] 95 p. 18 cm. $0.50 "This little gem of New Testament study is taken from the Methodist review."--Introd. 11-20315
I. Title.
Contents omitted.

TOLBERT, Mary Ann, 1947- 226'.8'06
Perspectives on the parables : an approach to multiple interpretations / Mary Ann Tolbert. Philadelphia : Fortress Press, c1978. p. cm. Includes indexes. [BT375.2.T65] 78-54563 ISBN 0-8006-0527-6 : 8.95
1. Parables. I. Title.

WARD, John William George. 252
Parables for little people; fifty-two sermonettes, by Rev. J. W. G. Ward... with an introduction by Rev. G. Campbell Morgan, D.D. New York, George H. Doran company [c1921] xiii p., 1 l., 15-219 p. illus. 19 1/2 cm. [BV4315.W3] 21-20764
I. Title.

WAY, Robert E., 1912- 226'.8'066
The garden of the beloved [by] Robert E. Way. Illus. by Laszlo Kubinyi. [1st ed.]

Garden City, N.Y., Doubleday, 1974. 71 p. illus. 24 cm. [BL624.W38] 74-8 ISBN 0-385-02117-8 5.95
1. Parables. I. Title.

*WELLS, Edmund E. 226.8
The gospel according to Mother Goose, [by] Edmund E. Wells. Anderson, Indiana, Warner Press [1973, c1969] 59 p. 18 cm. (A Portal book) [BT375.2] 0.75 (pbk.)
1. Parables. I. Title.

Parables,Biblical—Juvenile literature.

*LATOURETTE, Jane R. 226.8
The house on the rock; Matthew 7: 24-27 for children, Illus. by Sally Mathews. St. Louis, Concordia, [c.1966] 1v. (unpaged) col. illus. 21cm. (Arch bks., set 3, no. 59-1128) .35 pap.,
1. Parables,Biblical—Juvenile literature. 2. Bible stories, English—N.T.—Juvenile literature. I. Title.

THE parable book; 226.
Our Divine Lord's own stories, retold for you by children; illustrated with masterpieces from Dore, Bida, Hofmann, and other artists and with numerous pen sketches by B. E. Waddell and Bess Bethel Crank... Chicago, Ill., Extension press [c1921] xiv, 213 p. incl. front., illus. 24 cm. Dedication by the Sisters of Notre Dame de Namur. [BT376.P3] 21-21620
I. Sisters of Notre Dame de Namur.

Parables—Congresses.

†SEMIOLOGY and parables 226'.8'06
: exploration of the possibilities offered by structuralism for exegesis : papers of the conference sponsored by the Vanderbilt Interdisciplinary Project, "Semiology and Exegesis," and supported by a grant from the National Endowment for the Humanities, held at Vanderbilt University, Nashville, Tennessee, May 15-17, 1975 / edited by Daniel Patte. Pittsburgh : Pickwick Press, 1976. xx, 384 p. : diagrs. ; 22 cm. (Pittsburgh theological monograph series ; 9) Includes bibliographical references. [BT375.2.S45] 76-20686 ISBN 0-915138-11-5 pbk. : 7.50
1. Jesus Christ—Parables—Congresses. 2. Parables—Congresses. 3. Semiotics—Congresses. I. Patte, Daniel. II. Vanderbilt University, Nashville. III. Series.

Parables, Jewish.

FELDMAN, Asher, 1873-1950. 296.1'4
The parables and similes of the rabbis, agricultural and pastoral / by A. Feldman. Philadelphia : R. West, 1976. ix, 290 p. ; 23 cm. Reprint of the 1927 ed. published by the University Press, Cambridge, Eng. Includes bibliographical references and indexes. [BM518.P3F4 1976] 76-44204 ISBN 0-8492-0800-9 : 30.00
1. Parables, Jewish. 2. Agriculture in the Midrash. I. Title.

Parables of Christ.

CALKINS, Wolcott.
Parables for our times; a study of present-day questions in the light of Christ's illustrations. By Wolcott Calkins, D.D. 2nd ed. rev. Boston, New York [etc.] The Pilgrim press [c1910] 2 p. l., 122 p. 16 cm. 10-2138 0.50
I. Title.

DIGEST for Christ' s parables for preacher, teacher, and student. Techny, Ill. Divine Word Publications, 1956. viii, 92p.
I. Le Frois, Bernard J

LINNEMANN, Eta.
Parables of Jesus; introduction and exposition. New York, Harper & Row [1966] xv, 218 p. 22 cm. "Translated by John Sturdy from the third ed. (1964) of Gleichnisse Jesu, Einfuhrung und Auslegung." Bibliography: p. [199]-208. 68-56105
I. Title.

MINER, Edmund Bridges, 1829-
Parabolical teachings of Christ in Matthew xiii and Luke xv; or, Old truths found in new places, by E. B. Miner... Boston, The Gorham press; [etc., etc., c1915] 4 p. l., 7-138 p. 19 1/2cm. (Lettered on cover: Library of religious thought) $1.25. 16-367
I. Bible. N.T. Matthew xiii. English. II. Bible. N.T. Luke xv. English. III. Title.

THE Parables of Jesus.
New York, Scribner, 1956. 176p.
I. Jeremias, Joachim, 1900-

THE Parables of Jesus.
New York, Scribner, 1956. 176p.
I. Jeremias, Joachim, 1900-

PAULSON, John F.
Parables of the kingdom; by John F. Paulson and Donald R. Pichaske. Philadelphia, Lutheran Church Press [1964] 96 p. (Teacher's guide) 67-57200
1. Parables of Christ. I. Title.

RUSSELL, Elbert.
The parables of Jesus; a course of ten lessons arranged for daily study, by Elbert Russell ... New York, National board of the Young women's Christian associations of the United States of America [c1909] 93 p. 19 cm. 9-18016
I. Title.

RUSSELL, Elbert, 1871-
The parables of Jesus; a course of ten lessons arranged for daily study, by Elbert Russell ... New York, National board of the Young women's Christian associations of the United States of America [c1912] 94 p. 20 cm. 12-15242 0.40
I. Title.

SWANN, George Betts. 226.
The parables of Jesus, by George Swann ... Owensboro, Ky., Progress printing company, incorporated [c1918] 279 p. 20 cm. $1.00 [BT375.S9] 18-5308
I. Title.

WILLARD, Samuel, 1640-1707.
The barren fig trees doom; or, A brief discourse wherein is set forth the woful danger of all who abide unfruitful under gospel privileges, and Gods husbandry. Being the substance of sixteen sermons preached on Christ's parable of the fig-tree. By Samuel Willard, teacher of a church in Boston... Boston, Printed by Benjamin Harris, and John Allen, 1691. 3 p. l., 300 p. 15 1/2 cm. Signatures: 3 leaves unsigned, B-K8, L-M4, N-X3 (last 2 leaves blank) A 32
I. Title.

Paracelsus, 1493-1541.

PACHTER, Henry Maximilian, 1907- 921.9
Paracelsus; magic into science, being the true history of the troubled life, adventures, doctrines, miraculous cures, and prophecies of the most renowned, widely traveled, very learned and pious gentleman, scholar, and most highly experienced and illustrious physicus, the Honorable Philippus Theophrastus Aureolus Bombastus ab Hohenheim, Eremita, called Paracelsus. New York, Schuman [1951] x, 360 p. illus., ports., facsims. 22 cm. Bibliography: p. [341]-343. [B785.P24P3] 51-10192
1. Paracelsus, 1493-1541.

PAGEL. WALTER, 1898- 921.9
Paracelsus; an introduction to philosophical medicine in the era of the Renaissance. Basel, New York, S. Karger, 1958. xii, 368p. illus. ports., facsims. 25cm. Bibliographical footnotes. [R128.6.P33P3] 59-2446
1. Paracelsus, 1493-1541. I. Title.

PARACELSUS, 1493-1541. 133'.092'4
The prophecies of Paracelsus; occult symbols and magic figures with esoteric explanations, by Theophrastus Paracelsus of Hohenheim, and The life and teachings of Paracelsus, by Franz Hartmann. Introd. by Paul M. Allen. Blauvelt, N.Y., Rudolf Steiner Publications [1973] 86, xiii, 220 p. illus. 18 cm. (Steinerbooks, 1733) The prophecies of Paracelsus is a translation of Prognosticatio eximii doctoris Theophrasti Paracelsi. The life and teachings of Paracelsus is a reprint of the 1887 ed. published by G. Redway, London, under title: The life of Philippus Theophrastus, Bombast of Hohenheim known by the name Paracelsus. [BF1598.P19P7613] 72-81591 2.45 (pbk.)
1. Paracelsus, 1493-1541. 2. Prophecies. 3. Occult sciences. I. Hartmann, Franz, d. 1912. The life of Philippus Theophrastus, Bombast of Hohenheim. 1973. II. Title.

ROSEN, Sidney. 921.9
Doctor Paracelsus. Illustrated by Rafaello Busoni. [1st ed.] Boston, Little, Brown [1959] 214 p. illus. 22 cm. Includes bibliography. [R147.P2R6] 59-7359
1. Paracelsus, 1493-1541.

Paradise.

MCGAVIN, Elmer Cecil. 237.4
Paradise revisited, by E. Cecil McGavin. Boston, Meador publishing company, 1937. 88 p. 19 cm. [BT848.M25] 37-39469
1. Paradise. 2. Future life. 3. Future punishment. I. Title.

MARSELLA, Elena Maria 291.23
The quest for Eden. New York, Philosophical Lib. [c.1966] 275p. 22cm. Bibl. [BL540.M3] 66-16172 5.00
1. Paradise. I. Title.

MARY Sylvia, Sister 291.13
Nostalgia for paradise, by Sister Mary Sylvia. New York, Desclee [1966, c.1965] 230p. 22cm. Bibl. 4.75
I. Title.

MILLS, Philo Laos. 291.13
The Asiatic Arcadia or "Paradise lost" in Hebrew and Indo-Persian lore, in the light of modern discoveries and the unanimous tradition of the fathers, by Philo Laos Mills ... Washington, The Bengalese press, 1931. xxviii, 293 p. illus. (part col.) plates, maps, diagrs. 27 cm. [BL325.E4M5] 31-2872
1. Paradise. 2. Eden. 3. Literature, Comparative—Themes, motives. I. Title. II. Title: "Paradise lost."

VAN AMBURGH, William Edwin, 1863- 289.
The way to paradise; a brief history of the 7,000 years of sin ... brief Scriptural biographies of Michael who became the Christ, and of Lucifer who became the devil. In simple, pictorial language with many Scripture citations and quotations adapted to intermediate students of the Bible ... by W. E. Van Amburgh. Brooklyn, N.Y., London [etc.] International Bible students association, 1924. 1 p. l., iii, [1], 11-254 p. front., illus. 19 cm. "50,000 edition." [BX8526.V3] 24-13365
I. Title.

Paradise in literature.

CHAINEY, George. 211
Paradise; or, The garden of the Lord God, by George Chainey ... Boston, The Christopher publishing house [c1925] 121 p. front. (port.) plates. 21 cm. [BL390.C5] 25-17964
I. Title.

DUNCAN, Joseph Ellis, 1921- 821'.4
Milton's earthly paradise; a historical study of Eden [by] Joseph E. Duncan. Minneapolis, University of Minnesota Press [1972] viii, 329 p. illus. 23 cm. (Minnesota monographs in the humanities, v. 5) Bibliography: p. 291-315. [PR3562.D78] 71-187167 ISBN 0-8166-0633-1 12.50
1. Milton, John, 1608-1674. Paradise lost. 2. Paradise in literature. I. Title. II. Series.

SELFE, Rose E.
With Dante in paradise; readings from the "Paradiso," by Rose E. Selfe... London, Paris, New York & Melbourne, Cassell and company, limited, 1900. 3 p. l., 106 p. 6 pl. incl. front. 19 cm. The plates are copies of Dore's illustrations to the Paradisco. 2-29275
I. Title.

SELFE, Rose E.
With Dante in paradise; readings from the "Paradiso," by Rose E. Selfe... London, Paris, New York & Melbourne, Cassell and company, limited, 1900. 3 p. l., 106 p. 6 pl. incl. front. 19 cm. The plates are copies of Dore's illustrations to the Paradisco. 2-29275
I. Title.

Paradox.

KELLER, Edmund B. 227
Some paradoxes of Paul / by Edmund B. Keller. New York : Philosophical Library, [1974] xi, 263 p. ; 22 cm. Originally presented as the author's thesis, Boston University. Bibliography: p. 207-229. [BS2652.K44 1974] 74-75085 ISBN 0-8022-2144-0 : 8.50
1. Paul, Saint, apostle. 2. Bible. N.T. Epistles of Paul—Theology. 3. Paradox. I. Title.

SOCKMAN, Ralph Washington, 1889- 232.9
The paradoxes of Jesus. New York, Abingdon Press [c1936] 264 p. 21 cm. (Apex books, D4) Includes bibliography. [BT590.P3S6 1936a] 59-16378
1. Paradoxes. 2. Jesus Christ — Teachings. I. Title.

SOCKMAN, Ralph Washington, 1889- 232
The paradoxes of Jesus [by] Ralph W. Sockman. New York, Cincinnati [etc.] The Abingdon press [c1936] 264 p. 22 cm. [BT590.P3S6] 232 ISBN 37-27035
1. Jesus Christ—Teachings. 2. Paradoxes. I. Title.

Paraguay—History—To 1811.

GRAHAM, Robert Bontine Cunninghame, 1852-1936. 271.
A vanished Arcadia; being some account of the Jesuits in Paraguay, 1607 to 1767, by R. B. Cunninghame Graham ... New York, Lincoln MacVeagh, The Dial press incorporated, 1924. xvi, 294 p. fold. map. 23 cm. "Printed in Great Britain." [F2684.G74 1924] 42-29550
1. Paraguay—Hist.—To 1811. 2. Jesuits in Paraguay. I. Title.

Paramananda, swami, 1883-1940.

DEVAMATA, sister. 921.9
Swami Paramananda and his work, by Sister Devamata ... La Crescenta, Calif., Anada-ashrama [c1926-41] 2 v. fronts., plates, ports., facsim. 20 cm. Stamped above imprint, v. 1: Boston, Mass., The Vedanta centre. [B133.P32D4] 42-9206
1. Paramananda, swami, 1883-1940. 2. Hindus in the U. S. I. Title.

PARAMANANDA, swami.
The way of peaced and blessdness, by Swami Paramananda ... Boston, Mass., The Vedanta centre [c1913] 105 p. front. (port.) 18 cm. 13-19136 1.00
I. Title.

Paramus, N. J. Reformed Dutch church.

PARAMANANDA, swami.
Vedanta in practice, by Swami Paramananda ... New York, The Baker and Taylor company, 1909. 140 p. front. (port.) 18 cm. 9-961 1.00
I. Title.

PARAMUS, N. J. Reformed Dutch church. 289
Manual and record of the church of Paramus. 1859. Revised and enlarged. Published by order of Consistory. New York, Hosford & co. [1859] 105, [2] p. 24 cm. Additions and corrections in manuscript. Preface signed: E. T. C. [i. e. Edward Tanjore Corwin] [BX9531.P17R4 1859] 24-12266
1. Paramus, N. J. Reformed Dutch church. I. Corwin, Edward Tanjore, 1834-1914. II. Title.

Parapsychology and animals.

BAYLESS, Raymond. 133.1'4
Animal ghosts. With a foreword by Robert Crookall. New York, University Books [1970] 188 p. 22 cm. Includes bibliographical references. [BF1045.A6B37] 77-115778 5.95

1. Parapsychology and animals. I. Title.

Parapsychology and animals—Juvenile literature.

LAYCOCK, George. 133.8
Does your pet have a sixth sense? / George Laycock ; with photos. by the author. 1st ed. Garden City, N.Y. : Doubleday, c1980. 89 p. : ill. ; 22 cm. Includes index. Bibliography: p. [86]-87. Several accounts of amazing feats performed by animals using the "sixth" sense in many different ways including finding their way home across thousands of miles, knowing when a disaster is imminent, and many others. [BF1045.A6L39] 79-7690 ISBN 0-385-14997-2 : 6.95 ISBN 0-385-14998-0 lib. bdg. : 7.90
1. Parapsychology and animals—Juvenile literature. 2. Pets—Juvenile literature. 3. [Parapsychology and animals.] 4. [Extrasensory perception.] I. Title.

Parapsychology and archaeology.

JONES, David E. 133.8
Visions of time : experiments in psychic archeology / David E. Jones. Wheaton, Ill. : Theosophical Pub. House, c1979. ix, 404 p., [8] leaves of plates : ill. ; 22 cm. (A Quest book) Bibliography: p. 403-404. [BF1045.A74J66] 78-64909 ISBN 0-8356-0525-6 : 12.95. ISBN 0-8356-0523-X pbk. : 7.50 pbk. : 6.50
1. Parapsychology and archaeology. I. Title.

SCHWARTZ, Stephan A. 133.8'092'6
The secret vaults of time : psychic archaeology and the quest for man's beginnings / by Stephan A. Schwartz. New York : Grossett & Dunlap, c1978. xii, 370 p., [1] leaf of plates : ill. ; 24 cm. Includes index. Bibliography: p. 353-366. [BF1045.A74S38] 77-71742 ISBN 0-448-12717-2 : 12.95
1. Parapsychology and archaeology. 2. Man—Origin. I. Title.

Parapsychology and criminal investigation—Juvenile literature.

†WILCOX, Tamara, 1941- 133.8
Mysterious detectives : psychics / by Tamara Wilcox. New York : Contemporary Perspectives ; Milwaukee : distributor, Raintree Publishers, c1977. 48 p. : ill. (some col.) ; 24 cm. "A CPI book from Raintree Childrens Books." Discusses how some of the world's psychics have helped to solve crimes. [BF1045.C7W54] 77-14315 ISBN 0-8172-1061-X : 4.95 (lib. bdg.)
1. Parapsychology and criminal investigation—Juvenile literature. 2. [Parapsychology.] 3. [Criminal investigation.] I. Title.

Parapsychology and drugs.

DRUGS and magic / 133.4
edited by George Andrews. St. Albans : Panther, 1975. 591 p. : ill. ; 18 cm. Includes bibliographical references and index. [BF1045.D76D78] 75-317209 ISBN 0-586-03931-7 : £1.50
1. Parapsychology and drugs. 2. Magic and drugs. I. Andrews, George.

Parapsychology and philosophy.

PHILOSOPHERS in wonderland 133.8
: philosophy and psychical research / edited with an introd. and comments by Peter A. French. St. Paul, Minn. : Llewellyn Publications, 1975. xiii, 376 p. : ill. ; 25 cm. Includes bibliographical references. [BF1045.P5P47] 75-2318 ISBN 0-87542-242-X : 10.00
1. Parapsychology and philosophy. I. French, Peter A.

Parapsychology and philosophy—Addresses, essays, lectures.

PHILOSOPHY and 133.8
parapsychology / edited by Jan Ludwig. Buffalo : Prometheus Book, 1978. 454 p. ; 24 cm. Bibliography: p. 423-448. [BF1045.P5P48] 77-91852 ISBN 0-87975-075-8 : 16.95
1. Parapsychology and philosophy—Addresses, essays, lectures. I. Ludwig, Jan.

Pardow, William O'Brien, 1847-1900.

PARDOW, William O'Brien, 1847-1909.
Searchlights of eternity [by] William Pardow ... New York, The Encyclopedia press [c1916] 106 p. 20 cm. Preface signed: Justine Ward. "The following sketches are a mosaic made up of Father Pardow's thoughts as they were found scattered among his notes."--Pref. 16-24088 0.75.
I. Ward, Justine Bayard (Cutting) Mrs. 1879- comp. II. Title.

WARD, Justine Bayard 922.
(Cutting) Mrs., 1879-
William Pardow of the Company of Jesus, by Justine Ward. New York, London [etc.] Longmans, Green, and co., 1914. xiv, 274 p. front., ports. 21 cm. [BX4705.P375W3] 14-21189
1. Pardow, William O'Brien, 1847-1900. I. Title.

Parent and child.

BRANDT, Henry R. 261.8'342'7
I want to enjoy my children : a handbook on parenthood / Henry Brandt, Phil Landrum. Grand Rapids, Mich. : Zondervan Pub. House, [1975] 184 p. ; 21 cm. [HQ772.B6815] 75-21115 pbk. : 2.95
1. Parent and child. 2. Family—Religious life. I. Landrum, Phil, joint author. II. Title.

GEISSLER, Eugene S. 248.84
The meaning of parenthood. Discussion questions by Gerard Pottebaum. Notre Dame, Ind., Fides [c.1962] 159p. (Fides dome bk., D-16) At head of title: Sex, love, and life, 2. 62-1683 .95 pap.,
1. Parent and child. 2. Family,—Religious life. I. Title.

HILLIS, Newell Dwight, 1858-1929.
The school in the home; a study of the debt parents owe their children, by Newell Dwight Hillis; with a list of great chapters of the Bible and the twenty classic hymns, for memorizing. New York, Chicago [etc.] F. H. Revell company, 1902. 3 p. l., 9-126 p. 19 1/2 cm. 3-8450
I. Title.

KOHN, Jacob, 1881- 173.5
Modern problems of Jewish parents; a study in parental attitudes, by Jacob Kohn ... New York city, Women's league of the United synagogue of America, 1932. ix, 130 p. 19 cm. [HQ771.Z7K6] 266 296
1. Parent and child. 2. Children—Management. 3. Marriage—Jews. 4. Jews—Soc. life & cust. I. Title. II. Title: Jewish parents, Modern problems of.

MARVIN, Dwight Edwards, 649.1
1851-
Home and the children, by Dwight Edwards Marvin ... New York [etc.] Fleming H. Revell company [c1937] 88 p. 19 1/2 cm. [BV4526.M34] [249] 38-7717
1. Parent and child. 2. Children—Management. 3. Religious education. 4. Family—Prayer-books and devotions—English. I. Title.

MOW, Anna B. 249
Your teen-ager and you [by] Anna B. Mow. Grand Rapids, Zondervan [1967] 95, [1] p. 21cm. Bibl. [BV4526.2.M6] 67-14103 2.95 pap.,
1. Parent and child. 2. Family—Religious life. I. Title.

NORTON, Florence E.
Parent training in the church school, by Florence E. Norton ... Philadelphia, Board of Christian education of the Presbyterian church in the U. S. A., 1923. 96 p. front. 19 cm. Contains bibliographies. [BV1477.N6] 23-17705
1. Parent and child. I. Title.

STAPLES, Ethlyne Babcock. 249
Children in a Christian home, by Ethlyne Babcock Staples and Edward Daniel Staples. New York, Abingdon-Cokesbury Press [1948] 128 p. 18 cm. Bibliography: p. 126-128. [BV4529.S8] 48-3378
1. Parent and child. 2. Family—Religious life. 3. Religious education—Home training. I. Staples, Edward Daniel, joint author. II. Title.

Parent and child—Personal narratives.

WHAT they did right 261.8'34'27
: reflections on parents by their children / edited by Virginia Hearn. Wheaton, Ill. : Tyndale House Publishers, c1974. 294 p. ; 21 cm. [HQ772.W42] 74-23717 ISBN 0-8423-7920-7 : 3.95
1. Parent and child—Personal narratives. 2. Children—Religious life—Personal narratives. 3. Family—Religious life—Personal narratives. I. Hearn, Virginia.

Parent-teacher relationships—Addresses, essays, lectures.

AN Education handbook of 371.9
parents of handicapped children / edited by Stanley I. Mopsik, Judith Andrews Agard. Cambridge, Mass. : Abt Books, c1980. xiv, 287 p. ; 23 cm. Includes bibliographical references and index. [LC4019.E33] 78-67848 ISBN 0-89011-511-7 : 20.00
1. Parent-teacher relationships—Addresses, essays, lectures. 2. Handicapped children—Education—United States—Addresses, essays, lectures. 3. Handicapped children—Services for—United States—Addresses, essays, lectures. I. Mopsik, Stanley I., 1939- II. Agard, Judith Andrews, 1938-

Parenting.

BARBER, Cyril J. 248.8'4
The effective parent : Biblical principles of parenting, based upon the model of God the Father / Cyril J. Barber and Gary H. Strauss. San Bernardino, CA : Here's Life Publishers, c1980. xii, 147 p. ; 21 cm. ontents omitted. Includes bibliographical references. [BS1605.2.B37] 19 80-82669 ISBN 0-89840-012-0 (pbk.) : 4.95
1. Bible. O.T. Jonah—Criticism, interpretation, etc. 2. Bible. O.T. Nahum—Criticism, interpretation, etc. 3. Parenting. I. Strauss, Gary H., joint author. II. Title.

Parenting—Religious aspects—Christianity.

HOEK, Ann 248.84
Heart-to-heart talks with mothers. Grand Rapids, Mich., Zondervan [c.1962] 61p. 21cm. 1.00 pap.,
I. Title.

PREBLE, Jedidiah, 1765-1847. 922
Birth, parentage, life and experience of Jedidiah Preble, Written by himself 3d. ... Portland [Me.] J. and W. E. Edwards, 1830. 216 p. 19 cm. [BR1725.P67A3] 38-7493
I. Title.

WILSON, Earl D., 1939- 649'.125
You try being a teenager! : a challenge to parents to stay in touch / Earl D. Wilson. Portland, Or. : Multnomah Press, c1982. 191 p. ; 22 cm. Includes bibliographical references. [HQ755.8.W54 1982] 19 82-8314 ISBN 0-930014-97-9 pbk. : 6.95
1. Parenting—Religious aspects—Christianity. 2. Parent and child. 3. Adolescent psychology. 4. Conflict of generations. 5. Interpersonal communication. I. Title.
Publisher's address: 10209 S.E. Division St., Portland, OR 97266

Parenting—Religious aspects—Christianity—Dictionaries.

THE Encyclopedia of 649'.1'0321
Christian parenting. Old Tappan, N.J. : F.H. Revell, c1982. 464 p. ; 26 cm. Includes bibliographies and index. [HQ755.8.E52 1982] 19 82-562 ISBN 0-8007-1276-5 : 16.95
1. Parenting—Religious aspects—Christianity—Dictionaries.

Parenting—United States.

DRESCHER, John M. 261.8'342'7
What should parents expect? / John M. Drescher. Nashville : Abingdon, c1980. 96 p. ; 20 cm. Bibliography: p. 90-96. [HQ755.85.D73] 79-20949 ISBN 0-687-44909-X pbk. : 5.95
1. Parenting—United States. 2. Moral education—United States. I. Title.

KERN, Mary Margaret, 261.8'34'27
1906-
Be a better parent / Mary Margaret Kern. 1st ed. Philadelphia : Westminster Press, c1979. 160 p. ; 20 cm. [HQ755.8.K47] 79-9098 ISBN 0-664-24271-5 pbk. : 6.95
1. Parenting—United States. 2. Social values. 3. Socialization. 4. Family—Religious life. I. Title.

WHITE, John, 261.8'34'27
1924(Mar.5)-
Parents in pain : a book of comfort and counsel / John White. Downers Grove, Ill. : InterVarsity Press, c1979. 244 p. ; 21 cm. Includes bibliographical references. [HQ755.8.W48] 78-24760 ISBN 0-87784-582-4 : 4.95
1. Parenting—United States. 2. Parent and child—United States. 3. Adolescence. I. Title.

Parents—Prayer-books and devotions—English.

ADELSPERGER, Charlotte. 242'.4
When your child hurts / Charlotte Adelsperger. 1st ed. Chappaqua, NY : Christian Herald Books, 1981, c1982. p. cm. [BV4529.A32] 19 81-68639 ISBN 0-86693-000-0 : 4.95
1. Parents—Prayer-books and devotions—English. 2. Children—Diseases. I. Title.

Paris—Churches.

OLIVER, Alfred Cookman, 272.4
1885-
A Paris rosary, Boston, Christopher Pub. House [1952] 64 p. illus. 21 cm. [BR848.P304] 52-4810
1. Paris—Churches. I. Title.

Paris, Francois de, 1690-1727.

KREISER, B. Robert, 274.4'36
1943-
Miracles, convulsions, and ecclesiastical politics in early eighteenth-century Paris / B. Robert Kreiser. Princeton, N.J. : Princeton University Press, 1978. xvii, 485 p. ; 25 cm. Includes index. Bibliography: p. 403-467. [BT97.2.K73] 77-85546 ISBN 0-691-05262-X : 27.50
1. Paris, Francois de, 1690-1727. 2. Catholic Church. Pope, 1700-1721 (Clemens XI). Unigenitus (8 Sept. 1713) 3. Paris. Saint-Medard (Church) 4. Miracles. 5. Jansenists. 6. Church and state in France—History. 7. Paris—Church history. I. Title.

Paris. Notre-Dame (Cathedral)

ANDERSON, Robert Gordon, 282.44
1881-
The biography of a cathedral; the living story of man's most beautiful creation, with glimpses, through the centuries, of the pageant that led to Notre Dame, by Robert Gordon Anderson. New York, Toronto, Longmans, Green and co., 1944. xii p., 1 l., 496 p. col. front. 22 cm. "First edition." [BX4629.P3N62] 44-9848
1. Paris. Notre-Dame (Cathedral) 2. France—Church history. I. Title.

BOTTINEAU, Yves. 726'.6'094436
Notre-Dame de Paris and the Sainte-Chapelle. Translated by Lovett F. Edwards. [Chicago] Rand McNally [1967, c1965] 91 p. 108 illus. (part col.), plans. 24 cm. $9.95 Translation of Notre-Dame de Paris et la Sainte-Chapelle. [NA5550.N7B63] 67-11464
1. Paris. Notre Dame (Cathedral) 2. Paris. Sainte-Chapelle. I. Title.

GILLERMAN, Dorothy 730'.944'361
W.
The cloture of Notre-Dame and its role in the fourteenth century choir program /

Dorothy Gillerman. New York : Garland Pub., 1977. p. cm. (Outstanding dissertations in the fine arts) Originally prresented as the author's thesis, Harvard, 1973. Bibliography: p. [NK9749.P37G54 1977] 76-23623 ISBN 0-8240-2693-4 : 37.50
1. Paris. Notre-Dame (Cathedral). Cloture du chour. 2. Wood-carving, Gothic—France—Paris. 3. Wood-carving—France—Paris. I. Title. II. Series.

GILLERMAN, Dorothy W. 730'.944'361
The cloture of Notre-Dame and its role in the fourteenth century choir program / Dorothy Gillerman. New York : Garland Pub., 1977. p. cm. (Outstanding dissertations in the fine arts) Originally prresented as the author's thesis, Harvard, 1973. Bibliography: p. [NK9749.P37G54 1977] 76-23623 ISBN 0-8240-2693-4 : 37.50
1. Paris. Notre-Dame (Cathedral). Cloture du chour. 2. Wood-carving, Gothic—France—Paris. 3. Wood-carving—France—Paris. I. Title. II. Series.

SMITH, Katharine Lawrence, 1874- 282.44
People, pomp & circumstance in Saint Denis and Notre Dame, Paris. [1st ed.] New York, Blackmore Press [1955] 117p. 21cm. [BX4629.P3S55] 55-30111
1. Saint-Denis, France. Eglise abbatiale de Saint-Denis. 2. Paris. Notre-Dame (Cathedral) I. Title.

TEMKO, Allan. 726.6094436
Notre-Dame of Paris. Time reading program special ed. New York, Time Inc. [c1962] New York, Barnes & Noble [1966] 343 p. illus. 21 cm. xvi, 600 p. 24 cm. "First edition 1938." Bibliography: p. [xvii] [NA5550.N7T4] [Z2009.T28] 016.32742 63-1623 66-3780
1. Paris. Notre-Dame (Cathedral) 2. Gt. Brit. — Pol. & govt. — Bibl. 3. Gt. Brit. — For. rel. — Bibl. 4. Gt. Brit. — Government publications — Bibl. I. Temperley, Harold William Vazeille, 1879-1939, ed. II. Penson, Dame Lillian Margery, 1896-1963, joint ed. III. Title. IV. Title: A century of diplomatic blue books, 1814-1914;

TEMKO, Allan. 726.6 726.5*
Notre-Dame of Paris New York, Viking Press, 1955. viii, 341 p. illus., map, plans. 24 cm. Bibliography: p. [316]-319. [NA5550.N7T4] 55-9643
1. Paris. Notre-Dame (Cathedral) I. Title.

Parish councils.

BRODERICK, Robert C., 1913- 254
The parish council handbook; a handbook to bring the power of renewal to your parish, by Robert C. Broderick. Chicago, Franciscan Herald Press [1968] vii, 76 p. 21 cm. [BV652.9.B7] 68-21817
1. Parish councils. I. Title.

BRODERICK, Robert C., 1913- 254'.02
Your parish comes alive, by Robert C. Broderick. [Chicago] Franciscan Herald Press [1970] ix, 72 p. 21 cm. [BV652.9.B73] 76-130463 ISBN 8-19-904139- 1.95
1. Parish councils. I. Title.

LYONS, Bernard. 254
Parish councils; renewing the Christian community. Foreword by John J. Wright. Techny, Ill., Divine World [1967] xvii, 149p. 22cm. Bibl. [BV652.9.L9] 67-29363 2.25 pap.,
1. Parish councils. I. Title.

LYONS, Bernard. 254
Programs for parish councils; an action manual. Introd. by Mr. and Mrs. Patrick F. Crowley. Techny, Ill., Divine Word Publications [1969] xix, 124 p. illus. 22 cm. Includes bibliographies. [BV652.9.L92] 69-20417 1.50
1. Parish councils. I. Title.

O'NEILL, David P. 262'.22
The sharing community; parish councils and their meaning, by David P. O'Neill. Dayton, Ohio, Pflaum Press, 1968. vii, 88 p. 21 cm. [BV652.9.O54] 68-55964 1.50
1. Parish councils. I. Title.

RADEMACHER, William J., 1928- 254
Working with parish councils? / W. J. Rademacher. Canfield, Ohio : Alba Books, [1977?] 186 p. ; 18 cm. Bibliography: p. 185-186. [BV652.9.R3] 77-71024 ISBN 0-8189-1149-2 pbk. : 1.75
1. Parish councils. I. Title.

TIDWELL, Charles A. 254
Working together through the church council [by] Charles A. Tidwell. Nashville, Convention Press [1968] xii, 114 p. 19 cm. "Church study course [of the Sunday School Board of the Southern Baptist Convention] This book is number 1606 in category 16, section for adults and young people." [BV652.9.T5] 68-10608
1. Parish councils. I. Southern Baptist Convention. Sunday School Board. II. Title.

Parish councils—Handbooks, manuals, etc.

LYONS, Bernard. 262.1'5
Leaders for parish councils; a handbook of training techniques. Foreword by John P. Donnelly. [Techny, Ill., Divine Word Publications [1971] xv, 151 p. 22 cm. Cover title. [BV652.9.L89] 75-148029 ISBN 0-87298-141-X 2.95
1. Parish councils—Handbooks, manuals, etc. 2. Christian leadership—Handbooks, manuals, etc. I. Title. II. Title: A handbook of training techniques.

Parish missions.

A Dominican mission, 269
by a Dominican missionary. New York city, Holy name headquarters [c1938] 138 p., 1 l. 15 cm. [BX2375.D6] 44-48508
1. Parish missions. I. A Dominican missionary. II. Holy name society.

MOTTE, Jean Francois, 1913- 269
The new parish mission; the work of the church, by Jean-Francois Motte and Medard Dourmap. Translated by Paul J. Oligny. Chicago, Franciscan Herald Press [1962] 100 p. 19 cm. "Translated and condensed ... from Mission generale, oeuvre d'englise [sic]" [BX2375.M633] 62-15826
1. Parish missions. I. Dourmap, Medard, joint author. II. Title.

[O'NEIL, James Louis] 241
How to make the mission. By a Dominican father. Boston, T. B. Noonam & co., 1886. 137 p. 15 cm. [BX2375.O6] 34-28839
1. Parish missions. I. Title.

Parish missions—Anglican Communion.

WINCKLEY, Edward 264.035
The practice of healing evangelism; v.1. San Diego, Calif., 2243 Front St. St. Luke's Pr., [c.1963] 74p. 19cm. Contents.v.1. Preaching and healing. 63-21190 1.00
1. Parish missions—Anglican Communion. 2. Faith-cure. I. Title.

WINCKLEY, Edward. 264.035
The practice of healing evangelism. San Diego, Calif., St. Luke's Press [1963-] v, 19 cm. Contents.Contents. -- V. 1. Preaching and healing. [BX5969.W5] 63-21190
1. Parish missions — Anglican Communion. 2. Faith-cure. I. Title.

Parish missions—United States.

DOLAN, Jay P., 1936- 282'.73
Catholic revivalism in the United States, 1830-1900 / Jay P. Dolan. Notre Dame, Ind. : University of Notre Dame Press, c1977. p. cm. Includes index. Bibliography: p. [BX1406.2.D64] 77-89755 ISBN 0-268-00722-5 : 10.00
1. Catholic Church in the United States—History. 2. Parish missions—United States. 3. Revivals—United States. I. Title.

Parish of the templed hills, Oak Hill, O.

BICKSLER, Harry Edward, 1887- ed. 285.177185
The Parish of the templed hills; a study of the country church problem, edited by Rev. Harry E. Bicksler ... Philadelphia [The Magee press] 1938. 96 p. incl. front. plates. fold. map. 18 cm. [BX8999.C3B5] 38-17810
1. Parish of the templed hills, Oak Hill, O. 2. Cavinistic Methodist church in the U. S. A. 3. Presbyterian church in the U. S. A. Welsh synods. I. Title.

GOODWIN, William Archer Rutherfoord, 1869-
The parish; its life, its organization, its teaching mission, and its divine contacts; a handbook for the clergy and laity, by Rev. William A. R. Goodwin ... with introduction by Rt. Rev. Charles Henry Brent ... Milwaukee Wis., Morehouse publishing co., 1921. xiii, 136 p. 19 cm. [BV700.G6] 21-4246
I. Title.

Parishes.

BARRY, Joseph Gayle Hurd, 1858- 250
The parish priest, by J. G. H. Barry ... and Selden Peabody Delany ... New York, E. S. Gorham [1926] 271 p. 24 cm. [BX1912.B4] 26-5187
I. Delany, Selden Peabody, 1874- joint author. II. Title.

BLOCHLINGER, Alex, 1924- 262.2
The modern parish community. [Tr. from German by Geoffrey Stevens. Adaptation, abridgement by Hilda Graef] New York, Kenedy [c.1965] viii, 263p. 23cm. [BX1913.B553] 65-14809 4.95
1. Parishes. 2. Pastoral theology—Catholic Church. I. Title.

CHAMPLIN, Joseph M. 254
The living parish : a believing, caring, praying people / Joseph M. Champlin. Notre Dame, Ind. : Ave Maria Press, c1977. 156 p. : ill. ; 22 cm. [BV700.C47] 76-51887 ISBN 0-87793-129-1 pbk. : 2.95
1. Parishes. I. Title.

CURRIER, Richard. 262'.22
The future parish. Huntington, Ind., Our Sunday Visitor [1971] 74 p. 21 cm. Bibliography: p. 71-74. [BX1913.C87] 79-151291 0.95
1. Parishes. I. Title.

FLORISTAN, Casiano, 1926- 250
The parish, eucharistic community. Translated by John F. Byrne, with a foreword by Louis J. Putz. Notre Dame, Ind., Fides Publishers [1964] 240 p. 21 cm. Bibliography: p. 208-240. [BV700.F513] 64-23519
1. Parishes. 2. Pastoral theology — Catholic Church. I. Title.

GARESCHE, Edward Francis, 1876- 250
Modern parish problems, by Edward F. Garesche, S.J., with a preface by Most Rev. S. G. Messmer ... New York, J. f. Wagner, inc. London, B. Herder [c1928] vii, 239 p. 19 1/2 cm. [BX1912.G3] 29-663
I. Title. II. Title: Parish problems.

HAHN, Celia A. 254
Patterns for parish development, edited by Celia A. Hahn. Foreword by Martin E. Marty. New York, Seabury Press [1974] xviii, 169 p. 21 cm. "A Crossroad book." Includes bibliographical references. [BV700.H3] 74-11189 ISBN 0-8164-2098-X 3.95
1. Parishes. I. Title.

KILIAN, Sabbas J. 1916- 262'.22
Theological models for the parish / Sabbas J. Kilian. New York : Alba House, c1977. xi, 192 p. ; 22 cm. Bibliography: p. [177]-192. [BX1746.K49 1977] 76-42986 ISBN 0-8189-0337-6 : 5.95
1. Parishes. 2. Church. I. Title.

MCCUDDEN, John. 254
The parish in crisis, edited by John McCudden. Techny, Ill., Divine World Publications [1967] xiv, 193 p. 21 cm. Bibliographical footnotes. [BX1913.M3] 67-19034
1. Parishes. 2. Pastoral theology—Catholic Church. I. Title.

MILLS, Harlow Spencer, 1846- 261
The making of a country parish, a story by Harlow S. Mills ... New York, Missionary education movement of the United States and Canada, 1914. xviii, 126 p. front., illus. (map) plates. 19 1/2 cm. (Library of Christian progress) [BV638.M5] 14-16563
I. Title.

NEW York. Trinity Church. 283.747
Book of commemoration of the one hundredth anniversary of the consecration of the present church edifice and the two hundred and fiftieth anniversary of the founding of the parish of Trinity Church in the City of New York, 1946-1947. [New York? 1950] 80 p. mounted illus., plan. 23 cm. [BX5980.N5T76] 50-4952
I. Title.

NORTH American Liturgical Week. 25th, St. Louis, 1964.
The challenge of the council; person, parish, world ... Washington, Liturgical Conference, 1964. xiv, 287 p. 23 cm. 67-61470
I. Liturgical Conference, inc. II. Title.

NOYCE, Gaylord B. 260
New perspectives on parish ministry : a view from the third world / Gaylord Noyce. Valley Forge, PA : Judson Press, c1981. 124 p. ; 22 cm. Includes bibliographical references. [BV700.N69] 19 81-8385 ISBN 0-8170-0926-4 : 5.95
1. Parishes. 2. Christianity—20th century. I. Title.

NUESSE, Celestine Joseph, 1913- ed. 262.2
The sociology of the parish; an introductory symposium, edited by C. J. Nuesse and Thomas J. Harte. Milwaukee, Bruce Pub. Co. [1951] xii, 354 p. illus. 23 cm. Includes bibliographies. [BX1912.N77] 52-86
1. Parishes. 2. Theology, Pastoral—Catholic Church. 3. Church work. 4. Church and social problems—Catholic Church. I. Harte, Thomas Joseph, 1914- joint ed. II. Title.

OWENSBORO, Ky. St. Stephen's cathedral. 282.769
The centennial celebration of the parish of St. Stephen's cathedral, 1839-1939, celebrated August 31-September 1, 1941. Owensboro, Ky. [1941?] 3 p. l., 13-127 p. illus., fold. plates, ports. 23 cm. Pages 103-127, advertising matter. [BX4603.O82A3] 42-22952
I. Title.

PARISH, priest & people : 253
new leadership for the local church / by Andrew Greeley ... [et al.]. Chicago, Ill. : Thomas More Press, c1981. 262 p. ; 21 cm. Bibliography: p. 261-262. [BX1913.P287] 19 81-178109 ISBN 0-88347-131-0 : 14.95
1. Parishes. 2. Sociology, Christian (Catholic) 3. Pastoral theology—Catholic Church. 4. Christian leadership. I. Greeley, Andrew M., 1928- II. Title: Parish, priest, and people.

PHILADELPHIA (ARCHDIOCESE) SUPERINTENDENT OF PARISH SCHOOLS. 377'.82'77311
Report. Philadelphia, Published by the Diocesan School Board. v. illus. 23 cm. annual. Report year ends June 30. [LC503.P5A5] 51-39651
I. Title.

PRESCRIPTIONS for parishes, 254
by Jean M. Haldane [and others] New York, Seabury Press [1973] 123 p. 21 cm. (An Original Seabury paperback, 81) [BV700.P74] 73-76062 ISBN 0-8164-2080-7 2.95
1. Parishes. 2. Church renewal. I. Haldane, Jean M.

RAHNER, Hugo, 1900- ed. 262.2
The parish, from theology to practice. Translated by Robert Kress. Westminster, Md., Newman Press, 1958. 142p. 23cm. Includes bibliography. [BV700.R213] 58-13640
1. Parishes. 2. Pastoral theology—Catholic Church. I. Title.

TONNE, Arthur J., Rt. Rev. Msgr. 242
Five-minute parish talks. [Emporia, Kans., Didde, c.1962] 60p. 23cm. 1.50 pap.,
I. Title.

TONNE, Arthur J., Rt. Rev. Msgr. 242
Five-minute parish talks. [Emporia, Kans., Didde, c.1962] 60p. 23cm. 1.50 pap.,
I. Title.

Parishes—Addresses, essays, lectures.

MONEY, Walter Baptist. 250
Humours of a parish and other quaintnesses, by the Rev. W. B. Money, with a preface by Walter Herries Pollock. London, John Lane; New York, John Lane company, 1920. xiii p., 1 l., 203 p. front., ports. 20 cm. [BV4015.M6] 20-16287
I. Title.

THE Parish in community and ministry 254'.02 / [with contributions by Albert Ottenweller, et al.] ; edited and introduced by Evelyn Eaton Whitehead. New York : Paulist Press, c1978. vii, 118 p. ; 21 cm. "Edited for the Notre Dame Center for Pastoral and Social Ministry." Includes bibliographical references. [BX1913.P28] 78-58960 ISBN 0-8091-2133-6 pbk. : 3.95
1. Parishes—Addresses, essays, lectures. 2. Pastoral theology—Catholic Church—Addresses, essays, lectures. I. Ottenweller, Albert. II. Whitehead, Evelyn Eaton. III. Notre Dame, Ind. University. Center for Pastoral and Social Ministry.

Parishes (Canon law)

[BACHOFEN, Charles Augustine] 1872- 271.
The canonical and civil status of Catholic parishes in the United States, by the Rev. Charles Augustin ... St. Louis, Mo. and London, B. Herder book co., 1926. v, 334 p. 20 cm. [BX1407.P3B3] 26-19634
1. Parishes (Canon law). 2. Catholic church in the U.S. I. Title. II. Title: Catholic parishes in the United States, The canonical and civil status of.

MUNDY, Thomas Maurice, 1914- 262.2
... The union of parishes; an historical synopsis and commentary, by Rev. Thomas M. Mundy ... Washington, D.C., The Catholic university of America press, inc., 1945. x, 164 p. 23 cm. (The Catholic university of America. Canon law studies, no. 204) Thesis (J.C.D.)--Catholic university of America, 1944. "Biographical note": p. 153. Bibliography: p. 145-149. [BX1939.P27M8] A 46
1. Parishes (Canon law) 2. Catholic church. Codex juris canonici. C. 1419-1428. De unione, translatione, dismembratione, conversione et suppressione beneficiorum. I. Title.

Parishes—Chicago metropolitan area—Case studies.

SWEETSER, Thomas P. 282'.773'11
The Catholic parish : shifting membership in a changing church / by Thomas P. Sweetser. Chicago : Center for the Scientific Study of Religion, [1974] x, 134 p. : ill. ; 23 cm. (Studies in religion and society) Includes index. Bibliography: p. 98-100. [BX1418.C4S93] 74-84543 ISBN 0-913348-06-6 : 3.95
1. Catholic Church in Chicago metropolitan area—Case studies. 2. Parishes—Chicago metropolitan area—Case studies. I. Title. II. Series: Studies in religion and society series.

Parishes—Congresses.

PARISH, a place for worship : 264'.02 papers from the Ninth Annual Conference of the Notre Dame Center for Pastoral Liturgy, University of Notre Dame, June 16-19, 1980 / edited by Mark Searle. Collegeville, Minn. : Liturgical Press, 1981. p. cm. [BX1970.A1P35] 19 81-13655 ISBN 0-8146-1236-9 pbk. : 5.95
1. Catholic Church—Liturgy—Congresses. 2. Parishes—Congresses. I. Searle, Mark, 1941- II. Notre Dame Center for Pastoral Liturgy.

Parishes—England.

BETTEY, J. H. 274.2
Church & community : the parish church in English life / J. H. Bettey. New York : Barnes & Noble, 1979. p. cm. Includes index. Bibliography: p. [BR744.B443] 79-14739 ISBN 0-06-490381-8 : 17.00
1. Parishes—England. 2. England—Religious life and customs. 3. England—Church history. I. Title.

Parishes—Great Britain.

GARBETT, Cyril Forster, ed.
The work of a great parish. By nine Portsea men, edited by the Rev. C. F. Garbett ... With an introduction by the Archbishop of York ... London, New York [etc.] Longmans, Green, and co., 1915. xiv p., 1 l., 291 p. front., plates. 20 cm. A 15
I. Title.
Contents omitted.

WARE, Sedley Lynch, 1868- 320.9'73 s
The Elizabethan parish in its ecclesiastical and financial aspects. Baltimore, Johns Hopkins Press, 1908. [New York, Johnson Reprint Corp., 1973] p. Original ed. issued as no. 7-8 of Administrative and political history, which forms the 26th series of Johns Hopkins University studies in historical and political science. Originally presented as the author's thesis, Johns Hopkins University, 1908. Includes bibliographical references. [JA37.A45 no. 7-8] [BX5150] 254'.03'42 73-3212 ISBN 0-384-65802-4 pap. 4.50
1. Church of England—Finance. 2. Parishes—Great Britain. I. Title. II. Series: Johns Hopkins University. Studies in historical and political science, 26th ser., 7-8. III. Series: Administrative and political history, no. 7-8.

Parishes—Maryland.

BALTIMORE. Church of the Redeemer. 283.7526
This parish under God, 1855-1955; a record of the people, the moments, and especially the high purposes that have, in its first century, made this parish a home for Christian worship and fellowship. Baltimore [1955] 123p. illus. 24cm. [BX5980.B2C52] 59-20261
I. Title.

INGLE, Edward, 1861-1924. 320.4 s
Parish institutions of Maryland, with illustrations from parish records. Baltimore, Johns Hopkins University, 1883. [New York, Johnson Reprint Corp., 1973] 48 p. illus. 22 cm. Original ed. issued as no. 6 of Local institutions, which forms the 1st series of Johns Hopkins University studies in historical and political science. Includes bibliographical references. [JS308.L57 no. 6] [BX5917.M3] 254'.03'752 72-13167 ISBN 0-384-25740-2 4.00 (pbk.)
1. Church of England in Maryland. 2. Parishes—Maryland. I. Title. II. Series: Johns Hopkins University. Studies in historical and political science, 1st ser., 6. III. Series: Local institutions, no. 6.

Parishes — United States

GRIFFIS, William Elliot, 1843- 922.
Sunny memories of three pastorates, with a selection of sermons and essays, byWilliam Elliot Griffis ... Ithaca, N. Y., Andrus & Church, 1903. 7 p. l., 3-310 p. 11 pl., 3 port. (incl. front.) 20 cm. (Half-title: Sunny memories of three pastorates: Schenectady (1877-1886); Boston (1886-1896); Ithaca (1893-1903) [BX7260.G78A2] 3-31931
I. Title.

GRIFFIS, William Elliot, 1843-1928. 922.
Sunny memories of three pastorates, with a selection of sermons and essays, by William Elliot Griffis ... Ithaca, N.Y., Andrus & Church, 1903. 7 p. l., 3-310 p. 11 pl., 3 port. (incl. front.) 20 cm. Half-title: Sunny memories of three pastorates: Schenectady (1877-1886); Boston (1886-1893); Ithaca (1893-1903) [BX7260.G78A3] 3-31931
I. Title.

NEW York. St. Anselm's church (Catholic) 282.747
... The story of the founding and growth of St. Anselm's parish ... New York city. Published on the occasion of the golden jubilee of the parish, November 24, 1942, by the Benedictine fathers. [New York, 1942] 59, [1] p., 1 l. incl. front., illus. (incl. ports.) 26 1/2 cm. At head of title: 1892-1942. [BX4603.N6S3] 44-26687
I. Title.

SCHREIBER, Albert M. 1901- 282.764
Mesquite does bloom; an historical account of the first fifty years of St. Mary's parish and community, Windthorst, Texas, 1892-1942, by Albert M. Schreiber... San Antonio, Tex., Standard printing company, 1942. 124 p., 1 l. incl. illus, ports. 23 1/2 cm. [BX4603.W572S3] 43-130
I. Windthorst, Tex. St. Mary's parish. II. Title.

THE story of St. Aloysius' church, Pottstown, Pennsylvania. [Boyertown, Pa., Gilbert Printing co., 1956] 103p. illus. 23cm. Cover-title: One hundred years of service.
I. Pickar, Charles H 1907-

WARD, Leo Richard, 1893- 254.2
The living parish. Notre Dame, Ind., Fides Publishers Association [1959] 191 p. 21 cm. [BX1913.W35] 59-14097
1. Parishes — U.S. 2. Pastoral theology — Catholic Church. I. Title.

WASHINGTON, D.C. St. Albans parish. 726.
The story of St. Albans parish, 1854-1929. Washington, D.C., St. Albans parish, 1929. 168 p. illus. (incl. ports.) 22 cm. "Edited by Mary Badger Wilson." [BX5980.W3A4] 30-1112
I. Wilson, Mary Badger, ed. II. Title.

Parishes—Virginia.

COCKE, Charles Francis. 283'.746
Parish lines, Diocese of Virginia. Richmond, Virginia State Library, 1967. xv, 321 p. col. maps. 23 cm. (Virginia State Library publications, no. 28) "Parish changes of 1967": p. 275-276. Bibliography: p. 271-274. [BX5918.V8C6] A 67
1. Protestant Episcopal Church in the U.S.A. Virginia (Diocese) 2. Parishes—Virginia. I. Title. II. Series: Virginia. State Library, Richmond. Publications, no. 28

Park college, Parkville, Mo.

SHERWOOD, Elisha Barber, 1810-1905. 922.573
Fifty years on the skirmish line. By Rev. Elisha B. Sherwood ... Introduction by Rev. Geo. P. Hays ... Chicago, New York, Fleming H. Revell company [1893] 264 p. incl. front. pl., ports. 20 cm. Autobiography. [BX9225.S39A3] 36-31465
1. Park college, Parkville, Mo. 2. Presbyterian church—Sermons. 3. Sermons, American. I. Title.

Park, Edwards Amasa, 1808-1900

FOSTER, Frank Hugh, 1851-1935. 922.573
The life of Edwards Amasa Park, (S. T. D., LL. D.) Abbot professor, Andover theological seminary, by Frank Hugh Foster ... foreword by Walter Marshall Horton. New York [etc.] Fleming H. Revell company [c1936] 275 p. front., plates, ports., facsim. 21 cm. [BX7260.P27F6] 37-1727
1. Park, Edwards Amasa, 1808-1900 I. Title.

PHELPS, Austin, 1820-1890. 264'.2
Hymns and choirs: or, The matter and the manner of the service of song in the house of the Lord, by Austin Phelps, Edwards A. Park, and Daniel L. Furber. Andover [Mass.] W. F. Draper, 1860. [New York, AMS Press, 1971] iv, 425 p. 23 cm. Includes bibliographical references. [BV310.P5 1971] 78-144671 ISBN 0-404-07207-0
1. Park, Edwards Amasa, 1808-1900, ed. The Sabbath hymn book. 2. Hymns—History and criticism. 3. Church music. I. Park, Edwards Amasa, 1808-1900. II. Furber, Daniel Little, 1820-1899. III. Title.

Parker, Albert George, 1863-1937.

PARKER, Donald Dean, 1899- 922.573
A goodly heritage; the life of Albert George Parker, sr., with notes on his family, by Donald Dean Parker. [Moberly, Mo.] 1941. 5 p. l., 221 (i. e. 223) numb. l., 4 l. pl. (ports.) maps, geneal, tables. 23 cm. Reproduced from type-written copy. Extra numbered leaves 177a, 177b. "Fifty copies of this book have been produced." [BX9225.P28P3] 41-21851
1. Parker, Albert George, 1863-1937. I. Title.

Parker, Edwin Wallace, bp., 1833-1901.

MESSMORE, J H. 922.
The life of Edwin Wallace Parker, D. D., missionary bishop of southern Asia, forty-one years a missionary in India, by J. H. Messmore; with an introduction by Bishop James M. Thoburn. New York, Eaton & Mains; Cincinnati, Jennings & Pye [1903] 333 p. 7 pl., 2 port. (incl. front.) 21 cm. [BV3269.P3M4] 3-31012
1. Parker, Edwin Wallace, bp., 1833-1901. I. Title.

Parker, James Alfred, 1880-1929.

WILLARD, Warren Wyeth, 1905- 922
Steeple Jim, by Warren Wyeth Willard, foreword by Robert Dick Wilson... Princeton, N.J., Princeton publishing house, 1929. xv, 301 p. front., ports. 21 cm. "The biography of James Alfred Parker."--Introd. Bibliography included in introduction. [BV4935.P3W5] 30-8277
1. Parker, James Alfred, 1880-1929. 2. Temperance. 3. Steeple-jacks. 4. Evangelistic work. I. Title.

Parker, Larry.

PARKER, Larry. 234'.2
We let our son die / by Larry Parker, as told to Don Tanner. Irvine, Calif. : Harvest House Publishers, c1980. 204 p. ; 21 cm. [KF224.P37P37] 19 80-80457 ISBN 0-89081-219-5 (pbk.) : 4.95
1. Parker, Larry. 2. Parker, Wesley, 1962-1973. 3. Trials (Homicide)—California. 4. Spiritual healing. 5. Christian life—1960- I. Tanner, Don. II. Title.

Parker, Matthew, Abp. of Canterbury, 1504-1575.

BROOK, Victor John Knight, 1887- 922.342
A life of Archbishop Parker. [New York] Oxford [c.]1962[ ] 358p. Bibl. 62-2860 5.60
1. Parker, Matthew, Abp. of Canterbury, 1504-1575. I. Title.

BROOK, Victor John Knight, 1887- 922.342
A life of Archbishop Parker. Oxford [Eng.] Clarendon Press, 1962. 358p. 23cm. Includes bibliography. [BX5199.P3B7] 62-2860
1. Parker, Matthew, Abp. of Canterbury, 1504-1575. I. Title.

MATTHEW Parker's legacy : 016.091 books and plate. Cambridge : Corpus Christi College, 1975. 61 p. : ill. (some col.) ; 24 cm. [BX5199.P3M37] 75-324603
1. Parker, Matthew, Abp. of Canterbury, 1504-1575. 2. Cambridge. University. Corpus Christi College. 3. Manuscripts, Latin—Catalogs. 4. Silverwork—Catalogs. I. Cambridge. University. Corpus Christi College.

PARKER, Matthew, adp. of Canterbury, 1504-1575. 289
Correspondence of Matthew Parker ... Comprising letters written by and to him, from A. D. 1535, to his death, A. D. 1575. Edited for the Parker society, by John Bruce, esq., and the Rev. Thomas Thomason Perowne ... Cambridge [Eng.] Printed at the University press, 1853. xxiv,

510 p., 1 l. 23 cm. [The Parker society. Publications. v. 33] [[BX5035.P2]] A C
I. Bruce, John, 1802-1869, ed. II. Perowne, Thomas Thomason, 1824-1913, joint ed. III. Title.

PARKER, Matthew, abp. of Canterbury, 1504-1575. 922.342
Correspondence of Matthew Parker ... Comprising letters written by and to him, from A.D. 1535, to his death, A.D. 1575. Edited for the Parker society, by John Bruce, esq., and the Rev. Thomas Thomason Perowne ... Cambridge [Eng.] Printed at the University press, 1853. xxiv, 510 p., 1 l. 23 cm. (Half-title: The Parker society. [Publications. v. 33]) [BX5035.P2] (283.082) AC 33
I. Bruce, John, 1802-1809, ed. II. Perowne, Thomas Thomason, 1824-1913, joint ed. III. Title.

Parker, Mrs. Lois Stiles (Lee) 1834-1925.

WARNE, Francis Wesley, bp., 1854-1932. 922.
A tribute to the triumphant, by Francis Wesley Warne ... introduction by Evelyn Riley Nicholson ... New York, Cincinnati, The Methodist book concern [c1926] 95 p. incl. front. (port.) illus. (incl. facsims.) 19 1/2 cm. [BV3269.P35W3] 26-11581
1. Parker, Mrs. Lois Stiles (Lee) 1834-1925. I. Title.

Parker, Nathan, 1783-1888.

WARE, Henry, 1794-1843. 922.
Memoir of the Rev. Nathan Parker, D.D., late pastor of the South church and parish in Portsmouth, N.Y. By Henry Ward, jr. ... Portsmouth, J. W. Foster and J. F. Shores; Boston, J. Munroe and company, 1835. 2 p. l., [ix]-xcii p. 20 1/2 cm. "Extracts from letters on various occasions": p. [xxix]-xcii. [BX9869.P28W3] 37-10045
1. Parker, Nathan, 1783-1888. I. Title.

Parker, Peter, 1804-1888.

GULICK, Edward Vose. 266'.0092'4 B
Peter Parker and the opening of China [by] Edward V. Gulick. Cambridge, Harvard University Press, 1973. xi, 282 p. illus. 25 cm. (Harvard studies in American-East Asian relations, no. 3) "Works by Peter Parker": p. [253]-256. [BV3427.P29G84] 73-82628 ISBN 0-674-66326-8 12.00
1. Parker, Peter, 1804-1888. 2. Missions—China. I. Title. II. Series.

STEVENS, George Barker, 1854-1906. 922
The life, letters, and journals of the Rev. and Hon. Peter Parker ... by the Rev. George B. Stevens ... with the co-operation of the Rev. W. Fisher Markwick ... Boston and Chicago, Congregational Sunday-school and publishing society [c1896] 3 p. l., [5]-362 p. front. (port.) 21 cm. Chapters vi-xviii relate to Rev. Parker's work in China and Japan. [R154.P253.S8] A 21
1. Parker, Peter, 1804-1888. I. Markwick, William Fisher, 1848-1911, joint author. II. Title.

STEVENS, George Barker, 1854-1906. 266'.0092'4 B
The life, letters, and journals of the Rev. and Hon. Peter Parker, M.D., missionary, physican, diplomatist ... by George B. Stevens, with the co-operation of W. Fisher Markwick. Wilmington, Del., Scholarly Resources [1972] 362 p. port. 23 cm. [R154.P253S8 1972] 72-79840 ISBN 0-8420-1357-1
1. Parker, Peter, 1804-1888. I. Markwick, William Fisher, 1848-1911, joint author.

Parker, Theodore, 1810-1860.

ALBRECHT, Robert C. 288'.0924 B
Theodore Parker by Robert C. Albrecht. New York, Twayne Publishers [1971] 160 p. 21 cm. (Twayne's United States authors series, 179) Bibliography: p. 150-155. [BX9869.P3A43] 76-120521
1. Parker, Theodore, 1810-1860.

CHADWICK, John White, 1840-1904. 922.
Theodore Parker, preacher and reformer, by John White Chadwick. Boston and New York, Houghton, Mifflin and company, 1900. xx, 422 p., p. l., 2 port. (incl. front.) 20 cm. Bibliography: p. [xi]-xx. [BX9869.P3C5] 0-4996
1. Parker, Theodore, 1810-1860. I. Title.

CHADWICK, John White, 1840-1904. 288'.0924 B
Theodore Parker, preacher and reformer. Boston, Houghton, Mifflin, 1900. St. Clair Shores, Mich., Scholarly Press, 1971. xx, 422 p., ports. 22 cm. Bibliography: p. [xi]-xx. [BX9869.P3C5 1971] 72-144939 ISBN 0-403-00925-1
1. Parker, Theodore, 1810-1860.

COBBE, Frances Power, 1822-1904. 204
The religious demands of the age: a reprint of the preface to the London edition of the collected works of Theodore Parker, By Frances Power Cobbe. Boston, Walker, Wise and company, 1863. 63 p. 19 1/2 cm. [BX9815.P3 1863 a] 43-48091
1. Parker, Theodore, 1810-1860. 2. Theism. I. Title.

COMMAGER, Henry Steele 922.8173
Theodore Parker. With a new introd. by the author. [Gloucester, Mass., Peter Smith, c.1947, 1960] xi, 339p. (Bibl. p.[311]-331) 21cm. (Beacon paperback LR4 rebound in cloth) 3.75
1. Parker, Theodore, 1810-1860. I. Title.

COMMAGER, Henry Steele 922.8173
Theodore Parker. With a new introd. by the author. Boston, Beacon Press [c.1947,1960]. 339p. Includes bibliography. 21cm. (Beacon series in liberal religion, LR4) 59-10731 1.75 pap.,
1. Parker, Theodore, 1810-1860. I. Title.

COMMAGER, Henry Steele, 1902- 922.8173
Theodore Parker. [2d ed.] Boston, Beacon Press, 1947. viii, 339 p. illus., ports. 22 cm. Bibliography: p. [311]-331. [BX9869.P3C] A 48
1. Parker, Theodore, 1810-1860. I. Title.

COMMAGER, Henry Steele, 1902- 922.8173
Theodore Parker, by Henry Steele Commager ... Boston, Little, Brown, and company, 1936. ix p., 3 l., [3]-339 p. front., plates. ports., facsim. 22 cm. Bibliography: p. [311]-331. [BN9869.P3C65] 36-27204
I. Parker, Theodore, 1810-1860. II. Title.

COOKE, Frances E.
Story of Theodore Parker, by Frances E. Cooke; to which is added an introduction and a bibliography of books and articles by and pertaining to him. Boston, Cupples and Hurd [c1889] 3 p. l., [iii]-xiviii, [7]-115, x p. front. (port.) 19 cm. (Half-title: The Algonquin press library; pictures of American life and character, past and present) Third edition. Introduction signed: G. A. O. [i. e. Grace A. Oliver] "Theodore Parker, bibliography: x p. at end. [BX9809.P3C7] 12-31654
1. Parker, Theodore, 1810-1860. I. Oliver, Grace Atkinson (Little) Mrs. 1844-1899. II. Title.

DIRKS, John Edward. 230.8
The critical theology of Theodore Parker. New York, Columbia Univ. Press, 1948. viii, 173 p. port. 21 cm. (Columbia studies in American culture, no. 19) Bibliography: p. [161]-164. [BX9869.P3D5] 48-7527
1. Parker, Theodore, 1810-1860. I. Title. II. Series.

DIRKS, John Edward, 1919- 230.8
The critical theology of Theodore Parker. Westport, Conn., Greenwood Press [1970, c1948] viii, 173 p. port. 23 cm. (Columbia studies in American culture, no. 19) Bibliography: p. [161]-164. [BX9869.P3D5 1970] 70-100156
1. Parker, Theodore, 1810-1860. I. Title. II. Series.

FROTHINGHAM, Octavius Brooks, 1822-1895. 922.8173
Theodore Parker: a biography. By Octavius Brooks Frothingham. Boston, J. R. Osgood and company, 1874. viii, 588 p. front. (port.) 21 cm. [BX9869.P3F8] 37-10044
1. Parker, Theodore, 1810-1860. I. Title.

JOHNSON, Samuel, 1822-1882. 922.8173
Theodore Parker; a lecture by Samuel Johnson. Edited by John H. Clifford and Horace L. Traubel. Chicago, C. H. Kerr & company, 1890. 4, [7]-78 p. 21 cm. [BX9869.P3J7] 37-10034
1. Parker, Theodore, 1810-1860. I. Clifford, John Herbert, 1848- ed. II. Traubel, Horace, 1858-1919, joint editor. III. Title.

PARKER, Theodore, 1810-1860. 204
Autobiography, poems and prayers, by Theodore Parker; ed. with notes by Rufus Leighton. Boston, American Unitarian association [1911] 9 p. l., 486 p. front. (port.) 22 cm. [His Works. Centenary ed. v. 13] [BX9815.P3 1907 vol. 13] [BX9869.P3A2] 922. 11-35311
I. Leighton, Rufus, jr., ed. II. Title.

PARKER, Theodore, 1810-1860. 204
A discourse of matters pertaining to religion, by Theodore Parker; ed., with a preface, by Thomas Wentworth Higginson ... Boston, American Unitarian association [c1907] xxiv, 451 p. front. (port.) 22 cm. [His works. Centenary ed. v. 1]) [BX9815.P3 1907 vol. 1] [BX9841.P3 1907] 230. 7-38887
I. Higginson, Thomas Wentworth, 1823-1911, ed. II. Title.

PARKER, Theodore, 1810-1860. 204
A discourse of matters pertaining to religion, by Theodore Parker; ed., with a preface, by Thomas Wentworth Higginson ... Boston, American Unitarian association [c1907] xxiv, 451 p. front. (port.) 22 cm. [His works. Centenary ed. v. 1]) [BX9815.P3 1907 vol. 1] [BX9841.P3 1907] 230. 7-38887
I. Higginson, Thomas Wentworth, 1823-1911, ed. II. Title.

PARKER, Theodore, 1810-1860. 204
Saint Bernard and other papers, by Theodore Parker; ed., with notes by Charles W. Wendte. Boston, American Unitarian association [c1911] 4 p. l., 483 p. front. (port.) 21 cm. [His Works. Centenaru ed. v. 14] [BX9815.P3 1907 vol. 14] [BX9815.P36] 204 12-1329
I. Wendte, Charles William, 1844- ed. II. Title.
Contents omitted.

PARKER, Theodore, 1810-1860. 288'.092'4 B
Theodore Parker: American transcendentalist; a critical essay and a collection of his writings, by Robert E. Collins. Metuchen, N.J., Scarecrow Press, 1973. v, 271 p. illus. 22 cm. Contents.Contents.—Essay: A forgotten American.—Selections from Theodore Parker: Transcendentalism. A discourse of the transient and permanent in Christianity. The position and duties of the American scholar. The political destination of America and the signs of the times. The writings of Ralph Waldo Emerson. A sermon of war.—Selected bibliography (p. 261-264) [BX9869.P3A25 1973] 73-9593 ISBN 0-8108-0641-X 7.50
1. Parker, Theodore, 1810-1860. 2. Emerson, Ralph Waldo, 1803-1882. 3. Transcendentalism—Collected works. I. Collins, Robert E., ed.

PARKERISM:
three discourses delivered on the occasion of the death Theodore Parker. By William F. Warren, Fales H. Newhall, Gilbert Haven ... New York, Carlton & Porter, 1860. 115 p. 19 cm. "The following discourses have been previously published."--Publishers' notice. Contents..--Theodore Parker: the good and evil in his opinions and influence, by W. F. Warren.--The life-work of Theodore Parker, by F. H. Newhall.--The character and career of Theodore Parker, by G. Haven. 16-24040
I. Warren, William Fairfield, 1833- II. Newhall, Fales Henry. III. Haven, Gilbert, bp., 1824-1880.

RADICALISM in religion, philosophy, and social life; four papers from the Boston courier for 1858. Freeport, N.Y., Books for Libraries Press, 1972 [c1858] 79 p. 22 cm. (The Black heritage library collection) Contents.Contents.—Revival sermons.—Mr. Ralph Waldo Emerson as a lecturer.—Fair play to women.—The philosophy of abolition. [BX9869.B3R3 1972] 72-1804 ISBN 0-8369-9052-8 081
1. Parker, Theodore, 1810-1860. 2. Emerson, Ralph Waldo, 1803-1882. 3. Woman—History and condition of women. 4. Slavery in the United States. I. Boston daily courier. II. Title. III. Series.

RAMSDELL, Sarah A. 133.93
Spirit life of Theodore Parker, through the inspiration of Sarah A. Ramsdell. Boston, Press of Rand, Avery & co., 1876. 84 p. 20 cm. [BF1311.P3R33] 159.96173 33-29418
1. Parker, Theodore, 1810-1860. 2. Spiritualism. I. Title.

TRIBUTES to Theodore Parker, comprising the exercises at the Music hall, on Sunday, June 17, 1860, with the Proceedings of the New England anti-slavery convention, at the Melodeon, May 31, and the resolutions of the Fraternity and the Twenty-eighth Congregational society. Boston, Published by the Fraternity, 1860. 60 p. 19 1/2 cm. [BX9869.P3T8] 37-10036 922.8173
1. Parker, Theodore, 1810-1860. I. New England anti-slavery convention. Boston, 1860.

WALKER, James Barr, 1805-1887. 922.8173
Philosophy of skepticism and ultraism, wherein the opinions of Rev. Theodore Parker, and other writers are shown to be inconsistent with sound reason and the Christian religion. By James B. Walker... New York, Derby & Jackson; Cincinnati, Rickey, Mallory & Webb; [etc., etc.] 1857. ix, [11]-286 p. 19 1/2 cm. [BX9869.P3W3] 38-3770
1. Parker, Theodore, 1810-1860. 2. Skepticism—Controversial literature. 3. Apologetics—19th cent. I. Title.

WEISS, John, 1818-1879. 288'.0924 B
Life and correspondence of Theodore Parker. New York, Bergman Publishers [1969] 2 v. illus., ports. 24 cm. Reprint of the 1864 ed. [BX9869.P3W4 1969b] 68-28772
1. Parker, Theodore, 1810-1860. I. Parker, Theodore, 1810-1860. Correspondence. II. Title.

WEISS, John, 1818-1879. 288'.0924 B
Life and correspondence of Theodore Parker, minister of the Twenty-eighth Congregational Society, Boston. New York, D. Appleton, 1864. Freeport, N.Y., Books for Libraries Press [1969] 2 v. illus., facsim., ports. 23 cm. (Select bibliographies reprint series) [BX9869.P3W4 1969] 69-16854
1. Parker, Theodore, 1810-1860. I. Title.

WEISS, John, 1818-1879. 288'.0924 B
Life and correspondence of Theodore Parker. New York, Arno Press, 1969. 2 v. in 1 illus., facsim., ports. 24 cm. (Religion in American) Reprint of the 1864 ed. [BX9869.P3W4 1969d] 70-83446
1. Parker, Theodore, 1810-1860. I. Parker, Theodore, 1810-1860. Correspondence. 1969. II. Title.

WEISS, John, 1818-1879. 288'.0924 B
Life and correspondence of Theodore Parker. New York, Da Capo Press, 1970. 2 v. illus., ports. 24 cm. Reprint of the 1864 ed. [BX9869.P3W4 1970] 76-106987
1. Parker, Theodore, 1810-1860. I. Parker, Theodore, 1810-1860. Correspondence. 1970. II. Title.

WEISS, John, 1818-1879. 922.8173
Life and correspondence of Theodore Parker, minister of the Twenty-eighth Congregational society, Boston. By John Weiss ... New York, D. Appleton & company, 1864. 2 v. fronts. (port.) illus., pl., facsim. (2 l.) 23 cm. [B 260.P24W] [BX9869.P3W4 1864] A 31
1. Parker, Theodore, 1810-1860. I. Title.

WEISS, John, 1818-1879. 288'.0924
Life and correspondence of Theodore Parker, minister of the Twenty-eighth Congregational Society, Boston. New York, Negro Universities Press [1969] 2 v. 23 cm. Reprint of the 1864 ed. [BX9869.P3W4 1969c] 74-97443
1. Parker, Theodore, 1810-1860. I. Parker,

Theodore, 1810-1860. Correspondence. 1969. II. Title.

WENDTE, Charles William, 1844- 208.
Bibliography and index to the works of Theodore Parker, ed., with a preface, by Charles W. Wendte. Boston, American Unitarian association, [1913?] 5 p. l., 166 p. 21 cm. [Parker, Theodore. Works. Centenary ed. v. 15] "Report to the trustees of the Boston public library on the Parker library by Thomas Wentworth Higginson": p. 1-10. "Index prepared by Arthur A. Brooks": p. [51]-166. [BX9815.P3 1907 vol. 15] 17-30244
1. Parker, Theodore, 1810-1860. II. Higginson, Thomas Wentworth, 1823-1911. III. Brooks, Arthur A. IV. Title.

Parkhurst, Daniel Bigelow, 1818-1842.

MEMORIALS of the Rev. Daniel B. Parkhurst, minister of the First Congregational society in Deerfield, comprising a sketch of his life and character, by Samuel Willard, two sermons selected from his manuscripts by a committee appointed by the parish, and a few paragraphs from other papers. Boston, Printed by D. Clapp, jr., 1842. 51 p. 24 cm. 5-14714
1. Parkhurst, Daniel Bigelow, 1818-1842. I. Willard, Samuel, 1775-1859. II. Deerfield, Mass. First Congregational society.

Parnel, James, 1638-1655.

BUDGE, Frances Anne. 922.
Annals of the earlyRiends. Third series. Philadelphia, H. Longstreth, 1883. 175-307 p. 18 cm. "Reprinted fromt 'the Friends' quarterly examiner, with slight additions." London ed. (S. Harris) has title: The Barclays of Ury and other sketches of the early Friends. Barclay family. Rigge, Ambrose, d. 1704. [BX7791.B85 1883] 49-34838
1. Parnel, James, 1638-1655. 2. Howgill Francis. 1618-1668. 3. Watson, Samuel, 1620?-1708. 4. Coale, Joseph, d. 1670. 5. Gwin, Thomas, 1656-1720. 6. Friends, Society of. England. I. ebden, Roger, 1620?-1695. II. Title.

Parry, Sir Charles Hubert Hastings, bart., 1848-1918.

GREENE, Gwendolen Maud (Parry) Mrs. 1878- 927.8
Two witnesses; a personal recollection of Hubert Parry and Friedrich von Hugel, by Gwendolen Greene. London and Toronto, J. M. Dent and sons, ltd.; New York, E. P. Dutton & co., inc. [1930] v. [1], 199 p. 2 port. (incl. front.) 20 cm. [BX4668.G7] 31-15891
1. Parry, Sir Charles Hubert Hastings, bart., 1848-1918. 2. Hugel, Friedrich, freiherr von, 1852-1925. 3. Spiritual life. I. Title.

PARRY, Charles Hubert Hastings, Sir. bart., 1848-1918. 783.
... Te Deum laudamus: set to music for soprano and bass soli, chorus and orchestra, by C. Hubert H. Parry ... London, Novello and company limited; New York, Novello, Ewer and co., c1900. 1 p. l., 81 p. 27 cm. At head of title: Novello's original octavo edition. "Composed for the Hereford musical festival, 1900." Publisher's plate no.: 8308. [M2023.P264T3] Mus
I. Title.

Parsees.

FLUEGEL, Maurice, 1831?-1911. 290
The Zend-Avesta and eastern religions; comparative legislations, doctrines, and rites of Parseeism, Brahmanism, and Buddhism; bearing upon Bible, Talmud, Gospel, Koran, their Messiah-ideals and social problems. By Maurice Fluegel... Baltimore, H. Fluegel & co., 1898. 1 p. l., iii, 244 p. 24 cm. [BL1031.F6] 98-1217
1. Parsees. 2. Avesta. 3. Buddha and Buddhism. 4. Brahmanism. 5. Asia—Religions. I. Title.

MODI, Jivanji Jamshedji, Sir, 1854-1933. 295'.3'8
The religious ceremonies and customs of the Parsees / Jivanji J. Modi. New York : Garland Pub., 1979. lii, 484 p., [1] fold. leaf of plates : ill. ; 23 cm. (Oriental religions ; 7) Reprint of the 1922 ed. published by British India Press, Bombay. Includes bibliographical references and index. [BL1570.M57 1979] 78-74280 ISBN 0-8240-3913-0 lib. bdg. : 55.00
1. Parsees. 2. Parsee cults—India. 3. Parsees—Rites and ceremonies. 4. India—Religion. I. Title. II. Series.

POSTON, Charles Dibrell, 1825-
The sun worshipers of Asia; by Charles D. Poston. Reprinted for the author from the London edition. San Francisco, A. Roman & co., 1877. 106 p. 16 cm. "The ruins of Persepolis. Copied by permission from 'Remains of lost empires' by P. V. N. Myers, pub. by Harper & brothers, 1875": p. 76-104. A 10
1. Parsees. 2. Sun worship. I. Myers, Philip Van Ness, 1846- II. Title.

Parsonages.

FELTON, Ralph Almon, 1882- 726.91
The home of the rural pastor. Madison, N. J., Dept of the Rural Church, Drew Theological Seminary [1948] 111 p. illus., lans. 23 cm. [BV4381.F4] 49-1301
1. Parsonages. I. Title.
Contents omitted

HOWELL, Elizabeth Dosher, 1872-1943. 244
Inside the parsonage, by Elizabeth Dosher Howell. New York, N.Y., The Hobson book press, 1946. ix p., 2 l., 199 p. incl. front. (port.) 22 cm. [BV4395.H6] 46-8557
I. Title.

METHODIST Church (United States) Dept. of Architecture.
Parsonage planning. [Philadelphia, Division of National Missions of the Methodist Church] 1962. 94 p. illus. Cover title. Bibliography: p. 94. 63-65265
1. Parsonages. I. Title.

Parsons, Levi, 1792-1822.

†MORTON, Daniel Oliver, 1788-1852. 226'.5'80924 B
Memoir of Rev. Levi Parsons / compiled by Daniel Oliver Morton. New York : Arno Press, 1977. 431 p. ; 22 cm. (America and the Holy Land) Reprint of the 1824 ed. published by Smith & Shute, Poultney, Vt. [BV3202.P3M6 1977] 77-70730 ISBN 0-405-10271-2 : 25.00
1. Parsons, Levi, 1792-1822. 2. Missionaries—Palestine—Biography. 3. Missionaries—United States—Biography. I. Parsons, Levi, 1792-1822. II. Title. III. Series.

Part-songs Sacred—To 1800.

MCPEEK, Gwynn S., d. 783.205
The British Museum manuscript Egerton 3307. The music, except for the carols, ed., transcribed, general commentary by Gwynn S. McPeek. Text ed., transcribed by Robert White Linker. London, Oxford Chapel Hill, Univ. of N.C. Pr. [1964, c.] 1963. vii, 34p., score (35-108p.) 29cm. For 2-5 voices; Latin words. Includes liturgical music, a drinking song and a motet. Commentary. The texts with notes and concordances by Robert White Linker. Critical notes on the musical transcriptions. 64-1810 7.50
1. Part-songs Sacred—To 1800. 2. Music—England —Hist. & crit. I. British Museum. MSS. (Egerton 3307) II. Title.

Partai Muslimin Indonesia.

WARD, Kenneth Egerton, 1948- 329.9'598
The foundation of the Partai Muslim in Indonesia, by K. E. Ward. Ithaca, N.Y., Modern Indonesia Project, Cornell University, 1970. v, 75 p. 28 cm. (Cornell University. Modern Indonesia Project. Interim reports series) Bibliography: p. 73-75. [JQ779.A555W36] 74-27433 3.00
1. Partai Muslimin Indonesia. I. Title. II. Series.

Partido Democrata-Cristiano (Chile)

PETRAS, James.
Chilean Christian Democracy: politics and social forces. Berkeley, Institute of International Studies, University of California [c1967] ix, 61 p. 23 cm. (Politics of modernization, no. 4) 68-104056
1. Partido Democrata-Cristiano (Chile) 2. Chile—Pol. & gov.—1920- I. Title. II. Series.

Partito della democrazia cristiana.

EINAUDI, Mario, 1904- 329.9'45
Christian democracy in Italy and France, by Mario Einaudi and Francois Goguel. [Hamden, Conn.] Archon Books, 1969 [c1952] viii, 229 p. 22 cm. Bibliographical footnotes. [JN5657.D43E54 1969] 69-19224
1. Partito della democrazia cristiana. 2. Mouvement republicain populaire. 3. Christian democracy. I. Goguel-Nyegaard, Francois. II. Title.

Partito popolare italiano.

EINAUDI, Mario, 1904- 329.945
Christian democracy in Italy and France, by Mario Einaudi and Francois Goguel. Notre Dame, Ind., University of Notre Dame Press [1952] x, 229 p. maps. 24 cm. (International studies of the Committee on International Relations, University of Notre Dame) Bibliography: p. 97-103, 225. [JN3007.P58E5] 52-2728
1. Partito popolare italiano. 2. Mouvement republicain populaire. I. Goguel, Francois. II. Title. III. Series: Notre Dame, Ind. University. Committee on International Relations. International studies

Pascal, Blaise, 1623-1662.

BISHOP, Morris, 1893- 194
Blaise Pascal. [New York, Dell Pub. Co., 1966] 256 p. 19 cm. (The Laurel great lives and thought) Bibliography: p. [6] [BX4735.P26B5] 66-996
1. Pascal, Blaise, 1623-1662. I. Title.

CAILLIET, Emile, 1894- 201
The clue to Pascal. Foreword by John A. Mackay. [Folcroft, Pa.] Folcroft Library Editions, 1973. 128 p. 20 cm. Reprint of the 1944 ed. published by S. C. M. Press, London. Includes bibliographical references. [BX4735.P26C3 1973] 73-15921 ISBN 0-8414-3504-9 (lib. bdg.)
1. Pascal, Blaise, 1623-1662. I. Title.

CAILLIET, Emile, 1894- 921.4
The clue to Pascal [by] Emile Cailliet ... foreword by John A. Mackay ... Philadelphia, The Westminster press [1943] 3 p. l., 5-187 p. 21 cm. Based on a series of lectures delivered at the Institute of theology at Princeton theological seminary during the summer of 1943. cf. Pref. Bibliographical references included in "Notes" (p. [167]-187) [BX4735.P26C3] 43-15816
1. Pascal, Blaise, 1623-1662. I. Title.

CAILLIET, Emile, 1894- 921.4
Pascal; genius in the light of Scripture [by] Emile Cailliet ... Philadelphia, The Westminster press [1945] 383 p. 23 1/2 cm. Bibliographical foot-notes. [BX4735.P26C32] 45-3607
1. Pascal, Blaise, 1623-1662. I. Title.

CAILLIET, Emile, 1894- 194
Pascal; the emergence of genius. 2d., with an appendix on recent research. Introd. by C. S. Duthie. New York, Greenwood Press [1969, c1961] 383 p. 23 cm. [BX4735.P26C32 1969] 75-94602
1. Pascal, Blaise, 1623-1662.

CAILLIET, Emile, 1894- 921.4
Pasoal: the emergence of geneus. 2d ed., wtih an appedix on recent research. Introd. by C. S. Duthie. New York, Harper [1961] 383p. 21cm. (Harper torchbooks, The Closter library, TB82) Includes bibliography. [BX4735.P26C32 1961] 61-3102
1. Pascal, Blaise, 1623-1662. I. Title.

DAVIDSON, Hugh McCullough, 1918- 271'.5
A concordance to Pascal's Les provinciales / Hugh M. Davidson, Pierre H. Dube. New York : Garland Pub., 1980. p. cm. (Garland reference library of the humanities ; v. 189) [PQ1876.P3P73 1980] 79-54323 ISBN 0-8240-9536-7 lib. bdg. : 100.00
1. Pascal, Blaise, 1623-1662. Provinciales—Concordances. I. Dube, Pierre H., joint author. II. Pascal, Blaise, 1623-1662. Provinciales. III. Title.

DAVIDSON, Hugh McCullough, 1918- 239'.7
The origins of certainty : means and meaning in Pascal's Pensees / Hugh M. Davidson. Chicago : University of Chicago Press, 1979. xi, 158 p. ; 22 cm. Includes bibliographical references and index. [B1901.P43D38] 78-12768 ISBN 0-226-13716-3 lib. bdg. : 13.50
1. Pascal, Blaise, 1623-1662. Pensees. 2. Catholic Church—Doctrinal and controversial works. 3. Apologetics—17th century. 4. Certainty. 5. Belief and doubt. I. Title.

HUBERT, Marie Louise, Sister. 239
Pascal's unfinished Apology; a study of his plan. Port Washington, N.Y., Kennikat Press [1973, c1952] ix, 165 p. 23 cm. Original ed. issued as 2d ser., 3 of Yale Romanic studies. A revision of the author's thesis, Yale University. Bibliography: p. 150-159. [B1901.P44H8 1973] 70-153272 ISBN 0-8046-1699-X 9.75
1. Pascal, Blaise, 1623-1662. Pensees. 2. Catholic Church—Doctrinal and controversial works—Catholic authors. 3. Apologetics—17th century. I. Title. II. Series: Yale Romanic studies, 2d ser., 3.

KRAILSHEIMER, A. J. 230'.2'0924
Pascal / by A. J. Krailsheimer. 1st American ed. New York : Hill and Wang, c1980. p. cm. (Past masters) Includes index. Bibliography: p. [B1903.K67 1980b] 79-27590 ISBN 0-8090-7550-4 : 7.95 ISBN 0-8090-1412-2 (pbk.) : 2.95
1. Pascal, Blaise, 1623-1662. I. Title. II. Series.

PASCAL, Blaise, 1623-1662. 230'.2
The heart of Pascal, being his meditations & prayers, notes for his anti-Jesuit campaign, remarks on language and style, etc. Drawn from the Pensees by H. F. Stewart. [Folcroft, Pa.] Folcroft Library Editions, 1973. p. Text in French; preface and notes in English. Reprint of the 1945 ed. published by the University Press, Cambridge. [B1901.P42S77 1973] 73-16024 17.50
I. Stewart, Hugh Fraser, 1863-1948, ed. II. Title.

PASCAL, Blaise, 1623-1662. 239.7
OEuvres completes. Pref. d'Henri Gouhier. Presentation et notes de Louis Lafuma. [New York] Macmillan [1963] 676 p. illus., diagrs. 23 cm. (L'Integrale) [PQ1876.P3 1963] 63-19624
I. Lafuma, Louis. ed. II. Title.

PASCAL, Blaise, 1623-1662. 239
Pensees [by] Blaise Pascal. London, J. M. Dent & sons, ltd.; New York, E. P. Dutton & co., inc. [1931] xix p., 1 l., 297, [1] p. 18 cm. (Half-title: Everyman's library, ed. by Ernest Rhys. Theology & philosophy. [no. 874]) "First published in this edition 1981." "Translated by W. F. Trotter; introduction by T. S. Eliot." Bibliography: p. xix. [AC1.E8 no. 874] 37-5568
I. Trotter, William Finlayson, 1871- tr. II. Title.

PASCAL, Blaise, 1623-1662. 239
... Thoughts, tr. by W. F. Trotter: letters, tr. by M. L. Booth; minor works, tr. by O. W. Wight; with introductions, notes and illustrations ... New York, P. F. Collier & son [c1910] 1 p. l., 451, [1] p. front. (port.) double facsim. 23 cm. (The Harvard classics, ed. by C. W. Eliot. [vol. xlviii]) [B1901.P43T7] [AC1.A4 vol. 48] 100 10-20506
I. Trotter, W. F. II. Booth, Mary Louise, 1831-1889, tr. III. Wight, Orlando Williams, 1824-1888, tr. IV. Title.

PASCAL, Blaise, 1623-1662.
Thoughts ... translated by C. K. Paul, with a critical and biographical introduction by J. F. Hurst. [Aldine ed.] New York, D. Appleton & co., 1899. xi, 247 p. pl., port. 8 degee. (The World's great books) With

[Imitatio Christl. English. 1890] Of the imitation of Christ, by Thomas a Kempis. New York, 1899. [BV4821.A]] 0-2447
I. Title.

REX, Walter E. 271'.5
Pascal's Provincial letters : an introduction / Walter E. Rex. London [etc.] : Hodder and Stoughton, 1977. 84 p. ; 22 cm. Label mounted on t.p.: Holmes & Meier Publishers, Inc., New York. Bibliography: p. 80-83. [BX4720.P4R43] 78-312159 ISBN 0-340-20203-3 : pbk. : 4.50
1. Pascal, Blaise, 1623-1662. Les provinciales. 2. Jesuits. 3. Port Royal. 4. Jansenists. I. Title.

WEBB, Clement Charles Julian, 1865-
Pascal's philosophy of religion, by Clement C. J. Webb ... Oxford, The Clarendon press, 1929. 4 p. l., 118 p., 1 l. 19 1/2 cm. [B1904.R4W4] 30-8112
1. Pascal, Blaise, 1623-1662. 2. Religion—Philosophy. I. Title.

WETSEL, David, 1949- 230'.2
L'Ecriture et le reste : the Pensees of Pascal in the exegetical tradition of Port-Royal / David Wetsel. Columbus, Ohio : Ohio State University Press, 1981. p. cm. Includes index. Bibliography: p. [B1901.P43W47] 19 81-9610 ISBN 0-8142-0324-8 : 22.50
1. Pascal, Blaise, 1623-1662. Pensees. 2. Catholic Church—Doctrinal and controversial works—Catholic authors. 3. Apologetics—17th century. I. Title.

Pascal, Blaise, 1623-1662—Concordances.

A Concordance to Pascal's 239'.7
Pensees / edited by Hugh M. Davidson and Pierre H. Dube. Ithaca : Cornell University Press, 1975. ix, 1476 p. ; 25 cm. (The Cornell concordances) [B1900.A16C65] 75-16808 ISBN 0-8014-0972-1 : 27.50
1. Pascal, Blaise, 1623-1662—Concordances. I. Pascal, Blaise, 1623-1662. Pensees. II. Davidson, Hugh McCullough, 1918- III. Dube, Pierre H. IV. Series.

Pascal, Blaise, 1623-1662—Ethics.

BAIRD, Alexander 170'.92'4
William Stewart.
Studies in Pascal's ethics / by A. W. S. Baird. The Hague : M. Nijhoff, 1975,i.e.1976 viii, 100 p. ; 24 cm. (International archives of the history of ideas : Series minor ; 16) Includes index. Bibliography: p. [95]-96. [B1904.E7B3] 75-31555 ISBN 90-247-1677-2 pbk. 11.00
1. Pascal, Blaise, 1623-1662—Ethics. I. Title. II. Series: Archives internationales d'histoire des idees : Series minor ; 16.
Distributed by Humanities

Pascal, Blaise, 1623-1662. Les provincials.

PASCAL, Blaise, 1623-1662. 271.
... Lettres ecrites a un provincial (i, iv, v, xiii) Cambridge [Eng.] The University press, 1923. viii, 64 p. 16 cm. (Half-title: Cambridge plain texts) At head of title: Pascal. "The text here adopted is that of the original issue, with the spelling modernized." [BX4720.P28 1923] 25-22597
I. Title.

TOPLISS, Patricia 239.7
The rhetoric of Pascal: a study of his art of persuasion in the 'Provinciales' and the 'Pensees.' Leicester, Leicester Univ. Pr., 1966. 342p. 23cm. Bibl. [PQ1876.P3P74] 66-78161 8.50
1. Pascal, Blaise, 1623-1662. Les provincials. 2. Pascal, Blaise, 1623-1662. Pensees. I. Title.
American distributor: Humanities, New York.

Pascal, Jacqueline, 1625-1661.

WOODGATE, Mildred Violet, 922.444
1904-
Pascal and his sister Jacqueline, by M. V. Woodgate. St. Louis, Mo. and London, B. Herder book co., 1945. vii, 207 p. 21 cm. Published also under title: Jacqueline Pascal and her brother. [BX4735.P3W6 1945] 45-10246
1. Pascal, Jacqueline, 1625-1661. 2. Pascal, Blaine, 1623-1662. I. Title.

Paschal mystery.

HAMMAN, Adalbert, 1910- 264.02'72
ed.
The paschal mystery; ancient liturgies and patristic texts. Editor: A. Hamman. English editorial supervisor: Thomas Halton. [Translated by Thomas Halton] Staten Island, N.Y., Alba House [1969] 230 p. 22 cm. (Alba patristic library, 3) Translation of Le mystere de Paques. Bibliography: p. [225]-227. [BV55.H313] 78-77646 4.95
1. Paschal mystery.

Paschalls II, Pope, d. 1118.

ROWE, John Gordon. 016.0941
Paschal II, Bohemund of Antioch and the Byzantine empire 25 cm. v. 49 (1966) p. 165-202) Bibliographical footnotes. [Z921.M18B vol. 49] A67
1. Paschalls II, Pope, d. 1118. 2. Bohemund I, Prince of Antioch, 1058?-1111. Byzantine Empire — Hist. I. Title.

Pascua passion-play.

PAINTER, Muriel Thayer. 809.2'51
A Yaqui Easter. Tucson, University of Arizona Press [1971] 40 p. illus. 22 cm. Second ed. published in 1960 under title: Easter at Pascua Village. [E99.Y3P3] 74-153706 ISBN 0-8165-0168-8
1. Pascua passion-play. 2. Yaqui Indians—Rites and ceremonies. I. Title.

Passavant, William Alfred, 1821-1894.

GERBERDING, George Henry, 922.
1847-1927.
Life and letters of W. A. Passavant, D. D., by G. H. Gerberding ... Greenville, Pa., The Young Luthereran co., 1906. 615 p. front., plates, ports. 24 cm. [BX8080.P3G4]
1. Passavant, William Alfred, 1821-1894. I. Title.

Passion-music—History and criticism.

SMALLMAN, Basil. 783.3
The background of Passion music; J. S. Bach and his predecessors. 2d rev. and enl. ed. New York, Dover Publications [1970] 180 p. facsims., music. 22 cm. Bibliography: p. 173-175. [ML3260.S6 1970] 69-19465 ISBN 0-486-22250-0 2.50
1. Bach, Johann Sebastian, 1685-1750. Passions. 2. Passion-music—History and criticism. I. Title.

Passion-plays.

CAUDWELL, Irene.
The Iscariot; a sacred drama, by Irene Caudwell. London, The Faith press, ltd. New York, Morehouse-Gorham co. [1944] viii, 56 p. 18 cm. "First published, November, 1944." A 45
1. Passion-plays. I. Title.

HILLERN, Wilhelmine (Birch) von, Frau, 1836-
On the cross; a romance of the Passion play at Oberammergau, by Wilhelmine von Hillern and Mary J. Safford. Philadelphia, D.Biddle [1902] 2 p. l., xiv, 442 p. front., pl. 19 1/2 cm. 2-23596
I. Title.

MAHR, August Carl, 1886-
The Cyprus passion cycle. Notre Dame, Ind., 1947. xvi, 225 p. illus. 23 cm. (Notre Dame, Ind. University. Publications in mediaeval studies) "This cyclical passion play [Greek and English, p. 124-217] was reconstructed from a scenario...contained in Codex palatious graecus 387, fol. 34-39, of the Vatican Library." Bibliography: p. xiii-xvi. [PA8395.P25 1947] 882 ISBN 48-3718
I. Passionis Dominicae ludus scenicus. II. Title. III. Series.

Passion-plays—History and criticism.

EDWARDS, Robert, 1947- 872'.03
The Montecassino Passion and the poetics of medieval drama / Robert Edwards. Berkeley : University of California Press, c1977. x, 204 p., [2] leaves of plates : ill. ; 22 cm. "The Montecassino Passion play: translation": p. 10-21. Includes bibliographical references and index. [PA8385.M643E3] 75-22655 ISBN 0-520-03102-4 : 12.50
1. Montecassino Passion play. 2. Passion-plays—History and criticism. I. Montecassino Passion play. English. c1977. II. Title.

FRANCISCANS in California.
Official program of the passion play, Colliseum, San Francisco, October 11-26, 1909. Given under the auspices of the Franciscan fathers. [San Francisco, Printed by the Stanley-Taylor company] c1909. 80 p. incl. illus. ports. 27 cm. Includes advertisements. 10-13469
I. Title.

Passionists.

WARD, Felix, 1854-1927. 271.6
The Passionists; sketches historical and personal, by Rev. Felix Ward, C.P., with a preface by the late Cardinal Gibbons. New York, Cincinnati [etc.] Benziger brothers, 1923. 478 p. front., pl., ports. 28 cm. [Name in religion: Felix of Saint Joseph, father] [BX3880.W3] 23-11847
1. Passionists. I. Title.

Passionists—Collected works.

PASSIONISTS. Province of 255'.62
St. Paul of the Cross. Research and Planning Project.
The Passionists / Research and Planning Project, St. Paul of the Cross Province ; [directors] Herbert E. Stotts ... [et al.]. [Union City, N.J. : Provincial Print. Office, 1974- v. ; 23 cm. Cover title. Contents.Contents.—v. 1. The religious. Includes bibliographies. [BX3880.A1P37 1974] 75-305489
1. Passionists—Collected works. I. Stotts, Herbert Edward, 1916- II. Title.

Passionists in China.

NORRIS, Ronald. 271.6
The Passionists in China, a series of articles by Rev. Ronald Norris ... [n.p.] 1942. 78, [2] p. illus. (incl. ports., maps) 17 cm. Text on p. [3] of cover. [BX3880.N6] 43-16560
1. Passionists in China. 2. Hongkong—Siege, 1941. 3. World war, 1939—Prisoners and prisons, Japanese. 4. World war, 1939—Personal narratives, American. I. Title.

Passionists in Lithuania—Biography.

VYTELL, Virginia 271'.62'024 B
Marie.
Praise the Lord, all you nations : Lithuania's historical and cultural development form a background for the life story of Rev. Alphonsus Maria, CP, missionary and founder of the Poor Sisters of Jesus Crucified and of the Sorrowful Mother / Virginia Marie Vytell. Eimhurst [i.e. Elmhurst] Pa. : Sisters of Jesus Crucified and the Sorrowful Mother, c1976. 351 p. : ill. ; 22 cm. Includes bibliographical references and index. [BX4705.A5554V95] 76-21454
1. Alphonsus Maria, Father, CP, 1884-1949. 2. Passionists in Lithuania—Biography. 3. Lithuania—History. I. Title.

Passionists in New Jersey.

SOUVENIR of the 271.609749
diamond jubilee of the Passionist fathers in the diocese of Newark and of the rededication of St. Michael's monastery church. September 29th, 1936, Union City, N.J. [Union City? 1936?] 2 p. l., 9-61, [1] p., 1 l. incl. illus., plates. front. 25 1/2 cm. Cover-title: The Passionists in New Jersey, 1861-1936. Historical data by Herbert McDevitt. "St Michael's monastery church, by Charles D. Maginnis": p. 45-53. [BX3880.S6] 37-23878
1. Passionists in New Jersey. 2. Union City, N.J. St. Michael's church. I. McDevitt, Herbert, father, 1881- II. Maginnis, Charles Donagh, 1867-

Passionists in the United States

YUHAUS, Cassian J. 271'.62
Compelled to speak; the Passionists in America, origin and apostolate, by Cassian J. Yuhaus. Pref. by John J. Wright. Westminster, Md., Newman [1967] xxii, 343p. illus., facsim., ports. 24cm. Centenary ed. canonization of St. Paul of the Cross. [BX3880.Y8] 67-23610 5.95
1. Passionists in the U.S. I. Title.
Publisher's new address: 21 Harristown Rd., Glen Rock, N.J. 07452.

Passive resistance to government.

REGAMEY, Raymond, 1900- 261.7
Non-violence and the Christian conscience [by] P. Regamey. With a Pref. by Thomas Merton and a foreword by Stanley Windass. [New York] Herder & Herder [1966] 272p. 22cm. Bibl. [BT736.6.R413 1966] 66-22610 5.95
1. Passive resistance to government. I. Title.

Passover.

[AGUDATH Israel Youth Council 296
of America]
The book of Passover; Passover in life and literature. New York, 1947. 72 p. illus. 17 cm. (Jewish pocket books, 4) [BM695.P3A37] 48-13394
1. Passover. I. Title. II. Series.

ALEXANDER, William Arnold, 296
ed.
A book for Passover and other holidays, adapted for young people, edited and collated by W. A. Alexander. [Chicago, Printed by the Lakeside press, c1937] 71. [1] p. illus. 23 cm. [BM690.A5] 37-4287
1. Passover. 2. Festivals—Jews. I. Bible. O. T. English. Selections, 1937. II. Bible. English. Selections. O. T. 1937. III. Title. IV. Title: A book for Passover and other holidays.

BIAL, Morrison David, 1917- 296.4
The Passover story. Pictures by Stephen Kraft. New York, Behrman House [1952] unpaged. illus. 23cm. [BM695.P3B5] 52-14826
1. Passover. I. Title.

GARVEY, Robert. 296.4
When it's Passover. Pictures by Laszlo Matulay. [New York] Ktav Pub. House [1954] unpaged. illus. 22cm. (A Two-in-one holiday book) Bound with the author's When it's Purim. [New York, 1954] [BM695.P3G33] 54-1800
1. Passover. I. Title.

GASTER, Theodor Herzl, 1906- 296
Passover: its history and traditions. Boston, Beacon [1962, c.1949] 102p. illus., map. (LR16) Bibl. 1.45 pap.,
1. Passover. I. Title.

GASTER, Theodor Herzl, 1906- 296
Passover; its history and traditions. New York, H. Schuman [1949] 102 p. illus., map. 23 cm. Bibliography: p. 95-97. [BM695.P3G36] 49-8641
1. Passover. I. Title.

GOODMAN, Philip, 1911- 296.437
ed.
The Passover anthology. Philadelphia, Jewish Pubn. Soc. of America [1962, c.1961] 496p. illus. (JPS holiday ser.) Bibl. 61-11706 5.00
1. Passover. I. Title.

GREENSTEIN, Joseph. 296
Let my people go! A Passover portfolio for the Zionist district, by Joseph Greenstein. [New York] Zionist organization of America, 1946. cover-title, 56 p. 21 1/2 cm. Illustration on cover. "Issued ... by National education department, Zionist organization of America." Includes bibliographies. [BM695.P3G7] 46-6033
1. Passover. 2. Zionism. I. Zionist

organization of America. National education dept. II. Title.

GUTSTEIN, Morris Aaron, 1905-
Passover Haggadah, for the family, school and community seder; edited, translated and arranged with explanations, readings and transliteration by Dr. Morris A. Gutstein. Chicago, Excello Press, 1963. 62 p. 68-104483
I. Jews. Liturgy and Ritual. Haggadah. 1963. II. Title.

HOWARD, Clifford, 1868-
The Passover (an interpretation) by Clifford Howard... New York, R. F. Fenno & company [c1910] 3 p. l., 9-260 p. 18 1/2 cm. 10-17591
I. Title.

JEWS. Liturgy and ritual. 296.4'37
A first Haggadah / by Shulamit E. Kustanowitz and Ronnie C. Foont ; illustrated by Ronnie C. Foont. New York : Bonim Books, c1979. 63 p. : ill. (some col.) ; 24 cm. English and/or Hebrew. Includes the ritual and text of the Passover service. [BM675.P4Z68424 1979] 78-11598 ISBN 0-88482-766-6 : 9.95
1. [Passover.] I. Kustanowitz, Shulamit E. II. Foont, Ronnie C. III. Jews. Liturgy and ritual. Children's services, Kustanowitz. IV. [Hagadah (Children's services, Kustanowitz)] V. Title.

JEWS. Liturgy and ritual. Hagadah. 1969. 296.4'37
The Passover Haggadah. With English translation, introd., and commentary based on the commentaries of E. D. Goldschmidt; edited by Nahum N. Glatzer. Rev. ed. New York, Schocken Books [1969] xxvii, 109 p. illus. 22 cm. Text in English and Hebrew on opposite pages. Translation of the Haggadah text by Jacob Sloan. [BM675.P4G55 1969] 69-10846 4.50
I. Goldschmidt, Ernst Daniel. II. Glatzer, Nahum Norbert, 1903- ed. III. Jews. Liturgy and ritual. Hagadah. English. 1969. IV. Title.

JEWS. Liturgy and ritual. 296.4'37
A Passover Haggadah : the new Union Haggadah / prepared by the Central Conference of American Rabbis ; edited by Herbert Bronstein ; drawings by Leonard Baskin. Rev. ed. Harmondsworth, Eng. ; New York : Penguin, 1978, c1975. 123 p. : col. ill. (1 fold.) ; 27 cm. On half title: Hagadah shel Pesah. One illustration inserted. English and/or Hebrew. Unacc. melodies (Hebrew text romanized): p. 97-122. [BM675.P4Z66313 1978] 78-952106 ISBN 0-14-004871-5 pbk. : 5.95
I. Bronstein, Herbert. II. Baskin, Leonard, 1922- III. Central Conference of American Rabbis. IV. Jews. Liturgy and ritual. Reform rite, Central Conference of American Rabbis. V. [Hagadah (Reform, Central Conference of American Rabbis). English and Hebrew] VI. Title.

JEWS. Liturgy and ritual. Hagadah. Selections. 1970. 296.4'37
The Passover Seder; pathways through the Haggadah, arranged by Arthur Gilbert. Illustrated by Ezekiel Schloss [and] Uri Shulevitz. Music arranged by Moshe Nathanson. [New York] Ktav Pub. House [1970] 64 p. col. illus. 26 cm. Partly in Hebrew. "Passover music" (melodies, part with words in English, part in Hebrew transliterated): p. 57-64. [BM675.P4G52 1970] 71-12643
I. Gilbert, Arthur, ed. II. Jews. Liturgy and ritual. Hagadah. English. Selections. 1970. III. Title.

JEWS. Liturgy and ritual. Hagadah. 296
The Union Haggadah. [New York, Sole selling agents, Bloch publishing co., c1907] ix, 10-106 p. incl. illus., pl., music. 19 cm. On cover: The: Union: Haggadah: Home service for the Passover Eve. "Edited and published by the Central conference of American rabbis." [BM675.P4A3 1907] 7-12268
1. Passover. I. Central conference of American rabbis. II. Title.

JEWS. Liturgy and ritual. Hagadah. 1850. 296
[Service for the two first nights of the Passover] In Hebrew and English. 2d American ed. ... New York, J. M. Jackson, 5610 [1850] 80 p. 15 cm. Text and translation on opposite pages. [BM675.P3A3 1850] 47-19899
I. Title.

JEWS. Liturgy and ritual. Hagadah. 1907. 296
The Union Haggadah, [New York, Sole selling agents, Bloch publishing co., 1907] ix, 10-106 p. incl. illus., pl., music. 19 cm. On cover: The: Union: Haggadah: Home service for the Passover eve. "Edited and published by the Central conference of American rabbis." [BM675.P4A3 1907] 7-12268
1. Passover. I. Central conference of American rabbis. II. Title.

JEWS. Liturgy and ritual. Hagadah. 1953. 296.4'37
The Passover Haggadah; with English translation [by Jacob Sloan] Introd. and commentary based on the commentaries of E. D. Goldschmidt; edited by Nahum N. Glatzer. [New York] Schocken Books and Farrap, Straus and Young [1953] 113p. illus. 24cm. Half title: [BM675.P4G55] 53-1493
I. Jews, Liturgy and ritual. Hagadah. English. 1953. II. Glatzer, Nahum Norbert, 1903- ed. III. Title.

JEWS Liturgy and ritual. Hagadah. Selections. 1965. 296.437
The Passover Seder; pathways through the Haggadah, arranged by Arthur Gilbert. Illustrated by Ezekiel Schloss [and] Uri Schulevitz Music arranged by Moshe Nathanson. [New York] Ktav Pub. House [1965] 64 p. col. illus. 26 cm. Partly in Hebrew. "Passover music" (unacc. melodies, part with words in English, part in Hebrew transliterated): p. 57-64. [BM675.P4G52] 65-17003
I. Gilbert, Arthur, ed. II. Jews. Liturgy and ritual. Hagadah. English. Selections. 1965. III. Title.

PESAH is coming!
With illustrations by Leonard Kessler. New York, United Synagogue Commission on Jewish Education, c1956. 1 v. col. illus. 27cm.
1. Passover. I. Chanover, Hyman. II. Chanover, Alice, joint author.

PESAH is coming!
With illustrations by Leonard Kessler. New York, United Synagogue Commission on Jewish Education, c1956. 1 v. col. illus. 27cm.
1. Passover. I. Chanover, Hyman. II. Chanover, Alice, joint author.

PESAH is here!
With illustrations by Leonard Kessler. New York, United Synagogue Commission on Jewish Education, c1956. v. col. illus. 27cm.
1. Passover. I. Chanover, Hyman. II. Chanover, Alice, joint author.

PESAH is here-
With illustrations by Leonard Kessler. New York, United Synagogue Commission on Jewish Education. c1956. 1 v. col. illus. 27cm.
1. Passover. I. Chanover, Hyman II. Chanover, Alioe, joint author.

ROSEN, Moishe. 296.4'37
Christ in the Passover : or, Why is this night different? / By Moishe and Ceil Rosen. Chicago : Moody Press, c1978. p. cm. Includes index. Bibliography: p. [BM695.P3R67] 77-10689 ISBN 0-8024-1392-7 pbk. : 2.95
1. Jesus Christ—Passion. 2. Passover. I. Rosen, Ceil, joint author. II. Title.

SCHARFSTEIN, Edythe, 1922- 296.4
The book of Passover ; by Edythe and Sol Scharfstein. Pictures by Siegmond Forst [New York] Ktav Pub. House, c1953. unpaged. illus. 26cm. [BM695.P3S33] 53-30194
1. Passover. I. Scharfastein, Sol, 1921- joint author. II. Title.

SEGAL, Judas Benzion, 1912- 296.437
The Hebrew Passover, from the earliest times to A.D. 70. New York, Oxford [c.] 1963. xiv, 294p. 26cm. (London oriental ser., v.12) Bibl. 63-3751 6.75
1. Passover. I. Title. II. Series.

WENGROV, Charles Rabbi 296.437
Passover in song and story; being a dramatic narrative account of the Hebrews in Egypt, from the days of Joseph to the great Exodus written and illustrated especially for children, together with a collection of best-loved melodies for the Passover seder. Illustrated by Emanuel Schary; music edited by Samuel Bugatch. New York3, 21 E. 4th St. Press of Shulsinger Bros., [c.1960] 64p. col. illus., map (on lining papers) 32cm. 'The songs of Passover' (unacc.): p.51-64. 60-1573 1.50 bds.,
1. Passover. I. Title.

Passover— Biblical teaching.

GRELOT, Pierre, 1917- 263.93
The Paschal feast in the Bible, by P. Grelot, J. Pierron. Baltimore, Helicon [1966] 127p. 18cm. (Living world ser., 3) Tr. of La nuit et les fetes de Paques. [BS680.P33G714] 66-9665 1.25 pap.,
1. Passover— Biblical teaching. I. Pierron, J., joint author. II. Title.
Available from Taplinger, New York.

Passover—Christian observance.

HYNES, Arleen. 296.4'37
The Passover meal; a ritual for Christian homes. New York, Paulist Press [1972] 63 p. illus. 17 cm. [BV199.P25H94] 76-187207 ISBN 0-8091-1653-7 0.75 (pbk.)
1. Jews. Liturgy and ritual. Hagadah. 2. Passover—Christian observance. 3. Family—Prayer-books and devotions—English. I. Title.

Passover—Juvenile literature.

ADLER, David A. 793.7
Passover fun book : puzzles, riddles, magic, and more / by David A. Adler. New York : Bonim Books, c1978. 48 p. : ill. ; 28 cm. (A Bonim fun-to-do book) A collection of puzzles, word games, riddles, magic tricks, and number games with Passover themes. [BM695.P3A33] 77-27422 ISBN 0-88482-759-3 pbk. : 1.95
1. Passover—Juvenile literature. 2. Games—Juvenile literature. 3. [Passover.] 4. [Games.] I. Title.

ADLER, David A. 296.4'37
A picture book of Passover / by David A. Adler ; illustrated by Linda Heller. 1st ed. New York : Holiday House, c1982. 32 p. : col. ill. ; 25 cm. Describes the events which led to the liberation of the children of Israel from slavery in Egypt, and explains some of the Passover traditions and customs. [BM695.P3A34 1982] 19 81-6983 ISBN 0-8234-0433-1 : 8.95
1. Passover—Juvenile literature. 2. [Passover.] I. Heller, Linda, ill. II. Title.

DRUCKER, Malka. 296.4'37
Passover, a season of freedom / by Malka Drucker ; drawings by Brom Hoban. New York : Holiday House, c1981. 95 p. : ill. ; 24 cm. (A Jewish holidays book) Includes index. Bibliography: p. 91. Retells the story of the Exodus and relates its meaning to the Seder meal and Passover preparations. Includes recipes, crafts, puzzles, and games for celebrating the oldest Jewish holiday. [BM695.P3D78] 19 80-8810 ISBN 0-8234-0389-0 (lib. bdg.) : 8.95
1. Passover—Juvenile literature. 2. [Passover.] I. Hoban, Amrom, ill. II. Title. III. Series.

GREENFELD, Howard. 296.4'37
Passover / by Howard Greenfeld ; illustated by Elaine Grove ; designed by Bea Feitler. New York : Holt, Rinehart and Winston, c1978. 32 p. : ill. ; 16 x 24 cm. A history of this 3000-year-old Jewish holiday and an explanation of the Seder which commemorates it. [BM695.P3G68] 77-13910 ISBN 0-03-039921-1 : 5.95
1. Passover—Juvenile literature. 2. [Passover.] I. Grove, Elaine. II. Title.

SALZMANN, Laurence. 296.4'37
A family Passover / photos. by Laurence Salzmann ; story by Anne, Jonathan & Norma Rosen. 1st ed. Philadelphia : Jewish Publication Society of America, c1980. [64] p. : ill. ; 23 cm. A 10-year-old girl describes how her family celebrates Passover. [BM695.P3S24] 79-89298 ISBN 0-8276-0169-7 : 6.95
1. Passover—Juvenile literature. 2. [Passover.] I. Rosen, Anne. II. Rosen, Jonathan, 1963- III. Rosen, Norma Stahl, 1925- IV. Title.

SIMON, Norma 296.4
Passover, Illus. by Symeon Shimin. New York, Crowell [c.1965.40] p. illus. (pt. col.) 22cm. (Crowell holiday bk.) [BM695.P3S53] 65-11644 2.95 bds.,
1. Passover—Juvenile literature. I. Shimin, Symeon, 1902-illus. II. Title.

SPECTOR, Shoshannah, 1908- 394.2'68296437
The Seder that almost wasn't. Illustrated by Raphael Wettenstein. [New York, Shengold Publishers, c1967] 1 v. (unpaged) illus. 26 cm. [PZ7.S74133Se] 67-31080
1. Passover—Juvenile literature. I. Wettenstein, Raphael, illus. II. Title.

Pastoral counseling.

*ADAMS, Jay E. 253.5
The Christian counselor's casebook, by Jay E. Adams. Grand Rapids, Baker Book House, [1974]. ix, 213 p. 22 cm. A workbook designed for individual or class use in conjunction with competent to counsel and the Christian counselor's manual. [BV4012.2] 74-81707 ISBN 0-8010-0075-0. 3.50 (pbk.).
1. Pastoral counselling. I. Title.

*ADAMS, Jay E. 235.5
Coping with counseling crises : first aid for Christian crises / Jay E. Adams. Grand Rapids : Baker Book House, 1976. v, 90p. : music ; 22 cm. [BV4012.2] ISBN 0-8010-0112-9 pbk. : 1.95
1. Pastoral counseling. I. Title.

*ADAMS, Jay E. 253.5
The use of the Scriptures in counseling, [by] Jay E. Adams. Grand Rapids, Baker Book House, [1975] vii, 105 p. 18 cm. (Direction books) Includes bibliographical references. [BV4012.2] ISBN 0-8010-0099-8 1.50 (pbk.)
1. Pastoral counseling. I. Title.

*ADAMS, Jay E. 253.5
Your place in the counseling revolution, [by] Jay E. Adams. Grand Rapids, Baker Book House, [1975] vii, 62 p. 18 cm. (Direction books) [BV4012.2] ISBN 0-8010-0100-5 0.95 (pbk.)
1. Pastoral counseling. I. Title.

ALDRICH, Clarence Knight, 1914- 253.5
A pastoral counseling casebook, by C. Knight Aldrich and Carl Nighswonger. Philadelphia, Westminster Press [1968] 224 p. illus. 21 cm. Bibliography: p. 215-220. [BV4012.2.A4] 68-24677 5.95
1. Pastoral counseling. I. Nighswonger, Carl, joint author. II. Title.

AUGSBURGER, David W. 253
Anger and assertiveness in pastoral care / David W. Augsburger. Philadelphia : Fortress Press, c1979. x, 86 p. ; 22 cm. (Creative pastoral care and counseling series) Bibliography: p. 85-86. [BV4012.2.A87] 78-14660 ISBN 0-8006-0562-4. pbk. : 2.95
1. Pastoral counseling. 2. Pastoral psychology. 3. Anger. 4. Aggressiveness (Psychology) I. Title.

BOBGAN, Martin, 1930- 253.5
The psychological way/the spiritual way / by Martin and Deirdre Bobgan. Minneapolis : Bethany Fellowship, c1979. p. cm. Bibliography: p. [BV4012.2.B56] 79-17884 ISBN 0-87123-026-7 pbk. : 5.95
1. Pastoral counseling. 2. Pastoral psychology. 3. Psychotherapy. I. Bobgan, Deidre, 1935- joint author. II. Title.

BONNELL, John Sutherland, 1893- 253.5
No escape form life. [1st ed.] New York, Harper [1958] 215p. 22cm. [BV4012.2.B6] [BV4012.2.B6] 258 57-12933 57-12933
1. Pastoral counselling. I. Title.

BONNELL, John Sutherland, 1893- 258
No escape from life. New York, Harper

[1965, c.1958] 215p. 21cm. (Harper chapel bk. CB14J) [BV4012.2.B6] 1.60 pap.,
1. Pastoral counseling. I. Title.

BRANDT, Henry R. 253.5
Christians have troubles, too; a psychologist finds the answers in the Bible [by] Henry R. Brandt & Homer E. Dowdy. Old Tappan, N.J., Revell [1968] 127 p. 22 cm. [BV4012.2.B7] 68-28436 3.50
1. Pastoral counseling. I. Dowdy, Homer E., joint author. II. Title.

BRISTER, C. W. 253.5
The promise of counseling / C. W. Brister. 1st ed. San Francisco : Harper & Row, c1978. xiii, 210 p. ; 21 cm. Includes bibliographical references and index. [BV4012.2.B74 1978] 77-20453 ISBN 0-06-061052-2 : 8.95
1. Pastoral counseling. 2. Counseling. I. Title.

CAPPS, Donald. 253.5
Biblical approaches to pastoral counseling / by Donald Capps. 1st ed. Philadelphia : Westminster Press, c1981. 214 p. ; 21 cm. Includes bibliographical references. [BV4012.2.C26 1981] 19 81-11473 ISBN 0-664-24388-6 pbk. : 9.95
1. Bible—Criticism, interpretation, etc. 2. Pastoral counseling. I. Title.

CAPPS, Donald. 253
Pastoral counseling and preaching : a quest for an integrated ministry / Donald Capps. 1st ed. Philadelphia : Westminster Press, c1980. 156 p. ; 20 cm. Includes bibliographical references. [BV4012.2.C27] 80-18502 ISBN 0-664-24342-8 pbk. : 8.95
1. Pastoral counseling. 2. Preaching. I. Title.

CAVANAGH, John R 1904- 253.5
Fundamental pastoral counseling; technic and psychology. Milwaukee, Bruce Pub. Co. [1962] 326p. 24cm. Includes bibliography. [BV4012.2.C3] 62-10437
1. Pastoral counseling. I. Title.

CHRISTENSEN, James L. 253.5
The pastor's counseling handbook. [Westwood, N. J.] Revell [c.1963] 181p. 22cm. 63-10394 3.95 bds.,
1. Pastoral counseling. I. Title.

CLINEBELL, Charlotte H. 253.5
Counseling for liberation / Charlotte Holt Clinebell. Philadelphia : Fortress Press, c1976. viii, 88 p. ; 22 cm. (Creative pastoral care and counseling series) Bibliography: p. 84-88. [BV4012.2.C52] 75-36447 ISBN 0-8006-0555-1 pbk. : 2.95
1. Pastoral counseling. 2. Pastoral psychology. I. Title.

CLINEBELL, Howard John, 253.5
1922-
Basic types of pastoral counseling [by] Howard Clinebell, Jr. Nashville, Abingdon [1966] 318p. 24cm.) Bibl. [BV4012.2.C53] 66-21187 6.00
1. Pastoral counseling. I. Title.

CLINEBELL, Howard John, 253.5
1922-
Growth counseling : hope-centered methods of actualizing wholeness / Howard Clinebell. Nashville : Abingdon, c1979. 204 p. ; 21 cm. Includes index. Bibliography: p. 198-199. [BV4012.2.C534] 79-14358 ISBN 0-687-15974-1 : 7.95
1. Pastoral counseling. 2. Self-actualization (Psychology) I. Title.

COBB, John B. 253.5
Theology and pastoral care / John B. Cobb, Jr. Philadelphia : Fortress Press, c1977. xii, 79 p. ; 22 cm. (Creative pastoral care and counseling series) Bibliography: p. 77-79. [BV4012.2.C55] 76-7862 ISBN 0-8006-0557-8 pbk. : 2.95
1. Pastoral counseling. 2. Pastoral theology. I. Title.

COLLINS, Gary R. 253.5
Christian counseling : a comprehensive guide / by Gary R. Collins. Waco, Tex. : Word Books, c1980. 477 p. ; 23 cm. Includes bibliographies and index. [BV4012.2.C56] 19 79-67361 ISBN 0-8499-2889-3 (pbk.) : 10.95
1. Pastoral counseling. I. Title.

COLSTON, Lowell G. 253.5
Judgment in pastoral counseling [by] Lowell G. Colston. Nashville, Abingdon Press [1969] 207 p. 23 cm. Bibliographical footnotes. [BV4012.2.C57] 77-84717 4.50
1. Pastoral counseling. 2. Judgment. I. Title.

CRANE, William E. 253.5
Where God comes in; the divine "plus" in counseling [by] William E. Crane. Waco, Tex., Word Books [1970] 147 p. 23 cm. Bibliography: p. 145-147. [BV4012.2.C7 1970] 79-111959 3.95
1. Pastoral counseling. I. Title.

CRYER, Newman S., ed. 253.5
Casebook in pastoral counseling, ed. by Newman S. Cryer, Jr., John Monroe Vayhinger. Nashville, Abingdon [c.1952-1962] 320p. 62-8105 4.95
1. Pastoral counseling. I. Vayhinger, John Monroe, joint ed. II. Title.

CURRAN, Charles Arthur. 253.5
Religious values in counseling and psychotherapy, by Charles A. Curran. New York, Sheed and Ward [1969] viii, 398 p. illus. 22 cm. Includes bibliographical references. [BV4012.2.C85] 69-16992 7.50
1. Pastoral counseling. I. Title.

DENTON, Wallace 253.5
The minister's wife as a counselor. Philadelphia, Westminster [1966, c.1965] 172p. 21cm. Bibl. [BV4012.2.D45] 66-10704 3.95
1. Pastoral counseling. 2. Clergymen's wives. I. Title.

DICKS, Russell Leslie, 235.5
1906-
Principles and practice of pastoral care. Philadelphia, Fortress [1966,c.1963] 143p. 21cm. (Successful pastoral counseling ser.) bBibl. 1.50 pap.,
1. Pastoral counsling. I. Title.

DICKS, Russell Leslie, 235.5
1906-
Principles and practices of pastoral care. Englewood Cliffs, N.J., Prentice [c.1963] 143p. 21cm. (Successful pastoral counseling ser.) Bibl. 63-8623 2.95 bds.,
1. Pastoral counseling. I. Title.

DOTY, James Edward, 1922-
The pastor as agape counselor. Foreword by Seward Hiltner. Indianapolis, John Woolman Press [1964] 147 p. 20 cm. 68-31905
1. Pastoral counseling. I. Title.

DRAKEFORD, John W. 253.5
Counseling for church leaders. Nashville, Broadman [c.1961] 150p. Bibl. 61-12412 2.95
1. Pastoral counseling. I. Title.

DUCKER, E. N. 253.5
A Christian therapy for a neurotic world. Foreword by Frank Lake. Introd. to the Amer. ed. by Charles Di Salvo. New York, Taplinger [1963, c.1961] 225p. 22cm. Bibl. 62-8355 4.95
1. Pastoral counseling. 2. Psychiatry and religion. I. Title.

DUCKER, E. N. 253.5
Psychotherapy: a Christian approach. Foreword by E. Graham Howe. London, Allen & Unwin [dist. New York, Hillary, 1965, c.1964] 126p. 23cm. [BV4012.2.D83] 64-6109 4.00 bds.,
1. Pastoral counseling. 2. Psychiatry and religion. I. Title.

FABER, Heije, 1907- 253.5
The art of pastoral conversation [by] Heije Faber, Ebel van der Schoot. Nashville, Abingdon [c.1965] 223p. 21cm. Bibl. [BV4012.2.F313] 65-21977 3.75
1. Pastoral counseling. I. Schoot, Ebel van der, joint author. II. Title.

FABER, Heije, 1907- 253.5
The art of pastoral conversation [by] Heije Faber and Ebel van der Schoot. [Translation by Abingdon Press] New York, Abingdon Press [1965] Arnhem, Van Loghum Slaterus, 1961. 223 p. 21 cm. 126 p. 21 cm. (The Church in a changing society, 1) Translation of Het pastorale gesprek. Bibliographical footnotes. [BV4012.2.F313] [BV4012.2.F3] 65-21977 63-44900
1. Pastoral counseling. 2. Pastoral psychology — Study and teaching. 3. Clergy — U.S. I. Schoot, Ebel van der, joint author. II. Faber, Heije, 1907- III. Title. IV. Title: Pastoral care and clinical training in America; V. Series.

GERKIN, Charles V., 1922- 253.5
Crisis experience in modern life : theory and theology for pastoral care / Charles V. Gerkin. Nashville : Abingdon, c1979. 352 p. ; 23 cm. Includes index. Bibliography: p. 340-346. [BV4012.2.G47] 79-892 ISBN 0-687-09905-6 : 12.95
1. Pastoral counseling. I. Title.

GODIN, André. 253.5
The pastor as counselor. Translated by Bernard Phillips. [1st ed.] New York, Holt, Rinehart and Winston [1965] vi, 182 p. 22 cm. Translation of La relation humaine dans le dialogue pastoral. "Notes and bibliography": p. [145]-182. [BV4012.2.G613] 65-15056
1. Pastoral counseling. I. Title.

GODIN, André. 253.5
The priest as counselor. Tr. by Bernard Phillips. Techny, Ill., Divine Word [1968, c.1965. 182p. 22cm. Tr. of La relation humaine dans le dialogue pastoral. Orig: pub. by Holt undertitle "The pastor as counselor. Notes & Bibl. [BV4012.2.G613] 1.85 pap.,
1. Pastoral counseling. I. Title.

HAGMAIER, George. 253.5
Counselling the Catholic; modern techniques and emtional conflicts [by] George Hagmaier and Robert W. Gleason. New York, Sheed & Ward [1959] 301p. 22cm. [BV4012.2.H3] 59-12094
1. Pastoral counseling. I. Gleason, Robert W., joint author. II. Title.

HAMILTON, James D., 1926- 253.5
The ministry of pastoral counseling [by] James D. Hamilton. Grand Rapids, Baker Book House [1972] 126 p. 19 cm. (Source books for ministers) Includes bibliographical references. [BV4012.2.H33 1972] 73-152922 ISBN 0-8010-4069-8 1.95 (pbk.)
1. Pastoral counseling. I. Title.

HAUCK, Paul A. 253.5
Reason in pastoral counseling, by Paul A. Hauck. Philadelphia, Westminster Press [1972] 236 p. 22 cm. Bibliography: p. [231] -233. [BV4012.2.H37] 72-76436 ISBN 0-664-20945-9 5.95
1. Pastoral counseling. 2. Pastoral psychology. I. Title.

*HEYMEN, Ralph. 248.4
The Christian home. Grand Rapids, Baker Book House, [1975] 79 p. 18 cm. (Contemporary discussion series) [BV4525] ISBN 0-8010-4109-0 1.25 (pbk.)
1. Pastoral counseling. 2. Marriage counseling. I. Title.

HILTNER, Seward, 1909- 253.5
The Christian shepherd; some aspects of pastoral care. New York, Abingdon Press [1959] 190p. 21cm. [BV4012.2.H48] 59-7246
1. Pastoral counseling. I. Title.

HILTNER, Seward, 1909- 253.5
The context of pastoral counseling [by] Seward Hiltner and Lowell G. Colston. New York, Abingdon Press [1961] 272p. 24cm. Includes bibliography. [BV4012.2.H49] 61-13193
1. Pastoral counseling. I. Colston, Lowell G., joint author. II. Title.

HOFFMAN, John Charles, 253.5
1931-
Ethical confrontation in counseling / John C. Hoffman. Chicago : University of Chicago Press, 1979. x, 125 p. ; 21 cm. Includes bibliographical references and index. [BV4012.2.H55] 78-11799 ISBN 0-226-34785-0 : 10.50
1. Pastoral counseling. 2. Ethics. 3. Psychotherapy. I. Title.

HOSTIE, Raymond, 1920- 253.5
Pastoral counseling, Tr. by Gilbert Barth. New York, Sheed [1966] xii, 243p. 22cm. First pub. in 1963 under title: L'entretien pastoral. Bibl. [BV4012.2H5713] 66-12275 5.00
1. Pastoral counseling. I. Title.

HUDSON, Robert Lofton. 253.5
Sir, I have a problem. New York, Crowell [1959] 148p. 21cm. [BV4012.2.H77] 59-7757
1. Pastoral counseling. 2. Questions and answers—Theology. I. Title.

HULME, William Edward, 253.5
1920-
Counseling and theology. Philadelphia, Fortress [1967, c.1956] 249p. 18cm. [BV4012.2.H8] 1.95 pap.,
1. Pastoral counseling. I. Title.

HULME, William Edward, 223'.1'07
1920-
Dialogue in despair; pastoral commentary on the Book of Job [by] William E. Hulme. Nashville, Abingdon Press [1968] 157 p. 21 cm. [BS1415.3.H84] 68-11476
1. Bible. O.T. Job—Commentaries. 2. Pastoral counseling. I. Title.

HULME, William Edward, 253.5
1920-
Pastoral care & counseling : using the unique resources of the Christian tradition / William E. Hulme. Minneapolis : Augsburg Pub. House, c1981. 176 p. ; 20 cm. Bibliography: p. 174-176. [BV4012.2.H825] 19 80-67806 ISBN 0-8066-1869-8 pbk. : 6.50
1. Pastoral counseling. I. Title. II. Title: Pastoral care and counseling.

HULME, William Edward, 253.5
1920-
Pastoral care come of age [by] William E. Hulme. Nashville, Abingdon Press [1970] 175 p. 23 cm. Includes bibliographical references. [BV4012.2.H827] 79-109680 4.50
1. Pastoral counseling. 2. Pastoral theology. I. Title.

HULME, William Edward, 253.5
1920-
The pastoral care of families, its theology and practice. Nashville, Abingdon [c.1962] 208p. Bibl. 61-11784 3.50
1. Pastoral counseling. 2. Pastoral theology. I. Title.

HUSKEY, Hyrum H. 253.3
Counseling skills for church leadership / by Hyrum H. Huskey, Jr. ; Pastoral Care Office. Independence, MO : Herald Pub. House, [1980] p. cm. Bibliography: p. [BV4012.2.H85] 19 80-20368 ISBN 0-8309-0295-3 : 5.75
1. Pastoral counseling. I. Reorganized Church of Jesus Christ of Latter-Day Saints. Pastoral Care Office. II. Title.

INSTITUTE of Pastoral Care,
Framingham, Mass., 1960.
Fall conference, chaplain supervisors. Framingham, Mass., 1960. 107 l. On cover: Objectives of clinical pastoral training. 64-14657
1. Pastoral counseling. 2. Pastoral theology. I. Title. II. Title: Objectives of clinical pastoral training.

JACKSON, Edgar Newman. 253.5
Parish counseling / by Edgar N. Jackson. New York : J. Aronson, c1975. xviii, 221 p. ; 24 cm. Includes index. Bibliography p. [212]-[216] [BV4012.2.J3] 75-29698 ISBN 0-87668-222-0 : 10.00
1. Pastoral counseling. I. Title.

JAMES, Donald H
The pastoral care of alcoholics and their families, a report on the clergy workshops on alcoholism sponsored by the North Conway Institute and the Division of Alcoholism, Massachusetts Department of Public Health. Concerning the four workshops held in Eastern Massachusetts, 1963. Written in consultation with Paul E. Johnson. Boston, North Conway Institute, 1965. v, 17 l. tables. 28 cm. 66-35725
1. Pastoral counseling. 2. Alcoholism and religion. I. Johnson, Paul E. II. North Conway Institute. III. Massachusetts. Dept. of Public Health. Division of Alcoholism. IV. Title.

JOHNSON, Paul Emanuel, 253.5
1898-
Person and counselor [by] Paul E. Johnson. Nashville, Abingdon Press [1967] 208 p. 21 cm. Bibliographical footnotes. [BV4012.2.J6] 67-11710
1. Pastoral counseling. I. Title.

KEMP, Charles F 1912- 253.5
The pastor and vocational counseling. St. Louis, Bethany Press [1961] 190p. 21cm.

Includes bibliography. [BV4012.2.K44] 61-8602
1. Pastoral counseling. 2. Vocational guidance. I. Title.

KERN COUNTY MENTAL HEALTH ASSOCIATION.
Basic principles in pastoral counseling; the proceedings of the seminar for the clergy held at the First Christian Church, Bakersfield, California, 1961, October 2, 9, 16, 23, 30, and November 2. Sponsored by the Kern County Mental Association and the Department of Mental Hygiene, State of California ... [Bakersfield, Calif., 1961] 50 p. 28 cm. 65-45448
I. Title.

KLINK, Thomas W. 253.5
Depth perspectives in pastoral work. Englewood Cliffs, N.J., Prentice [c.1965] 144p. 21cm. (Successful counseling ser.) Bibl. [BV4012.2.K5] 65-22190 2.95 bds.,
1. Pastoral counseling. I. Title. II. Series.

LAHAYE, Tim F 248.4'8'6
Spirit-controlled temperament, by Tim LaHaye. [2d ed.] Wheaton, Ill., Tyndale House [1967, c1966] 141 p. illus. 23 cm. Spiritual life -- Baptist authors. [BV4501.2.L315] 67-28429
1. Pastoral counseling. 2. Temperament. I. Title.

LAPLACE, Jean, S. J. 253.5
The direction of conscience. Translated by John C. Guinness. [New York] Herder and Herder [1967] 192 p. 21 cm. [BV4012.2.L2413] 67-13295
1. Pastoral counseling. 2. Spiritual direction. I. Title.

LAYCOCK, Samuel Ralph, 1891- 253.5
Pastoral counseling for mental health. [Nashville] Abingdon [c.1958, 1961] 96p. 61-17154 1.00 pap.,
1. Pastoral counseling. I. Title.

LEAS, Speed, 1937- 253
The pastoral counselor in social action / Speed Leas, Paul Kittlaus. Philadelphia : Fortress Press, c1981. xi, 84 p. ; 22 cm. (Creative pastoral care and counseling series) Bibliography: p. 82-84. [BV4012.2.L39] 19 80-8059 ISBN 0-8006-0565-9 pbk. : 3.25
1. Pastoral counseling. 2. Social action. I. Kittlaus, Paul, 1934- joint author. II. Title.

LONG, Louise, 1908- 253
Door of hope. Nashville, Abingdon Press [1972] 189 p. 22 cm. [BV4012.2.L65] 70-185545 ISBN 0-687-11179-X 2.95
1. Pastoral counseling. 2. Pastoral psychology. I. Title.

MCLEMORE, Clinton W., 1946- 253.5
Clergyman's psychological handbook; clinical information for pastoral counseling, by Clinton W. McLemore. Grand Rapids, Eerdmans [1974] 146 p. 22 cm. Includes bibliographies. [BV4012.2.M24] 74-2011 ISBN 0-8028-1576-6 2.45 (pbk.).
1. Pastoral counseling. I. Title.

MEET Joe Ross. 253.5
New York, Abingdon Press [1957] 159p. 21cm. [BV4012.2.D5] [BV4012.2.D5] 258 57-11008 57-11008
1. Pastoral counseling. I. Dicks, Russell Leslie, 1906-

MEIER, Paul D. 253'.5
Introduction to psychology and counseling : Christian perspectives and applications / Paul D. Meier, Frank B. Minirth, Frank B. Wichern. Grand Rapids, Mich. : Baker Book House, c1982. 433 p. : ill. ; 27 cm. Includes index. Bibliography: p. 407-426. [BV4012.2.M44 1982] 19 82-187856 ISBN 0-8010-6128-8 : 19.95
1. Pastoral counseling. 2. Psychology. I. Minirth, Frank B. II. Wichern, Frank B. III. Title.

MIKESELL, William Henry, 1887- 253.5
Counseling for ministers. Boston, Christopher Pub. House [1961] 190p. 21cm. [BV4012.2.M5] 61-15194
1. Pastoral counseling. I. Title.

MOSER, Leslie E 253.5
Counseling: a modern emphasis in religion. Englewood Cliffs, N. J., Prentice-Hall, 1962. 354p. 22cm. Includes bibliography. [BV4012.2.M6] 62-8569
1. Pastoral counselling. 2. Counseling. I. Title.

NARRAMORE, Clyde Maurice, 1916- 253.5
The psychology of counseling; professional techniques for pastors, teachers, youth leaders, and all who are engaged in the incomparable art of counseling. Grand Rapids, Zondervan Pub. House [1960] 303 p. 23 cm. Includes bibliography. [BV4012.2.N3] 60-10242
1. Pastoral counseling. 2. Psychology—Dictionaries. I. Title.

NATALE, Samuel. 253.5
Pastoral counselling : reflections and concerns / by Samuel M. Natale, in collaboration with Richard J. Wolff. New York : Paulist Press, c1977. v, 117 p. ; 21 cm. (An Exploration book) Includes bibliographical references. [BV4012.2.N34] 76-57341 ISBN 0-8091-2008-9 pbk. : 3.95
1. Pastoral counseling. I. Wolff, Richard, 1927- joint author. II. Title.

OATES, Wayne Edward, 1917- ed. 253.5
An introduction to pastoral counseling. Nashville, Broadman Press [1959] 331p. 22cm. [BV4012.2O22] 59-9688
1. Pastoral counselling. I. Title.

OATES, Wayne Edward, 1917- 253.5
Pastoral counseling, by Wayne E. Oates. Philadelphia, Westminster Press [1974] 240 p. 22 cm. [BV4012.2.O23] 73-19719 ISBN 0-664-20992-0 7.50
1. Pastoral counseling. I. Title.

OATES, Wayne Edward, 1917- 253.5
Pastoral counseling in social problems: extremism, race, sex, divorce, by Wayne E. Oates. Philadelphia, Westminster [1966] 128p. 21cm. Bibl. [BV4012.023] 66-15962 1.75
1. Pastoral counseling. 2. Church and social problems. I. Title.

OATES, Wayne Edward, 1917- 253.5
Pastoral counseling in social problems: extremism, race, sex, divorce, by Warren E. Oates. Grand Rapids, Mich., Baker Book House [1974, c1966] 128 p. 20 cm. (Source books for ministers) [BV4012.023] 66-15962 ISBN 0-8010-6656-5. 2.45 (pbk.)
1. Pastoral counseling. 2. Church and social problems. I. Title.

OATES, Wayne Edward, 1917- 253.5
Protestant pastoral counseling. Philadelphia, Westminster [c.1962] 256p. 21cm. 62-9228 4.50
1. Pastoral counseling. I. Title.

O'BRIEN, Michael J. 253.5
An introduction to pastoral counseling [by] Michael J. O'Brien. Staten Island, N.Y., Alba House [1968] 272 p. 22 cm. (Mental health series, 10) Includes bibliographical references. [BV4012.2.O27] 68-31511 4.95
1. Pastoral counseling. I. Title. II. Title: Pastoral counseling.

OGLESBY, William B. 253.5
Referral in pastoral counseling [by] William B. Oglesby, Jr. Englewood Cliffs, N.J., Prentice-Hall [1968] 139 p. 21 cm. (Successful pastoral counseling series) [BV4012.2.O35] 68-11945
1. Pastoral counseling. I. Title. II. Series.

OGLESBY, William B. 253.5
Referral in pastoral counseling / William B. Oglesby, Jr. Rev. ed. Nashville : Abingdon, [1978] p. cm. Includes index. [BV4012.2.O35 1978] 78-7976 ISBN 0-687-35887-6 pbk. : 6.95
1. Pastoral counseling. I. Title.

OGLESBY, William P. 253.5
Biblical themes for pastoral care / William B. Oglesby, Jr. Nashville : Abingdon, c1980. 240 p. ; 23 cm. [BV4012.2.O34] 19 79-26828 ISBN 0-687-03448-5 : 10.95
1. Bible—Use. 2. Pastoral counseling. I. Title.

PSYCHIATRY, the clergy, and pastoral counseling; 253.5 the St. John's story. Editors: Dana L. Farnsworth [and] Francis J. Braceland. Collegeville, Minn., Institute for Mental Health, St. John's University Press [1969] xviii, 356 p. 24 cm. Adapted from lectures given at the annual seminars of the psychiatric-pastoral workshops conducted by the Institute for Mental Health at St. John's University since 1954. Includes bibliographical references. [BV4012.2.P75] 73-83088 6.50
1. Pastoral counseling. 2. Psychiatry and religion. I. Farnsworth, Dana L., ed. II. Braceland, Francis James, 1900- ed. III. St. John's University, Collegeville, Minn. Institute for Mental Health.

RASSIEUR, Charles L., 1938- 253.5
The problem clergymen don't talk about / by Charles L. Rassieur. Philadelphia : Westminster Press, c1976. 157 p. ; 19 cm. Includes bibliographical references. [BV4012.2.R33] 75-40306 ISBN 0-664-24790-3 pbk. : 3.95
1. Pastoral counseling. 2. Clergy—Sexual behavior. I. Title.

RIGHTOR, Henry Haskell. 253.5
Pastoral counseling in work crises : an introduction for both lay and ordained ministers / Henry Haskell Rightor. Valley Forge, Pa. : Judson Press, c1979. 80 p. ; 22 cm. Includes index. Bibliography: p. 75-78. [BV4012.2.R53] 78-22007 ISBN 0-8170-0814-4 : 2.95
1. Pastoral counseling. 2. Vocational guidance. I. Title.

ROE, John E. 1945- (John Ed), 158'.3
A consumer's guide to Christian counseling / John E. Roe. Nashville, Tenn. : Abingdon, c1982. 143 p. ; 20 cm. [BV4012.2.R63] 19 81-12790 ISBN 0-687-09480-1 pbk. : 5.95
1. Pastoral counseling. 2. Counseling. I. Title.

SCHROEDER, Theodore W. 253.5
Pastors counseling manual for ministry to those who must sustain a loved one in crisis / Theodore W. Schroeder. St. Louis, Mo. : Concordia Pub. House, c1981. 43 p. ; 21 cm. Bibliography: p. 41. [BV4012.2.S36] 19 81-4706 ISBN 0-570-08250-1 pbk. : 2.95 2.95
1. Pastoral counseling. 2. Family—Religious life. I. Title. II. Title: Ministry to those who must sustain a loved one in crisis.

SCHURMAN, Paul G. 332.024'2
Money problems and pastoral care / Paul G. Schurman. Philadelphia : Fortress Press, c1982. x, 86 p. : ill. ; 22 cm. (Creative pastoral care and counseling series) Bibliography: p. 85-86. [BV4012.2.S37 1982] 19 81-70662 ISBN 0-8006-0568-3 : 3.95
1. Pastoral counseling. 2. Finance, Personal. 3. Clergy—Finance, Personal. I. Title. II. Series.

SEIFERT, Harvey. 253.5
Personal growth and social change; a guide for ministers and laymen as change agents, by Harvey Seifert and Howard J. Clinebell, Jr. Philadelphia, Westminster Press [1969] 240 p. 22 cm. Bibliographical references included in "Notes" (p. [220]-236) [BV4012.2.S4] 73-80977 6.95
1. Pastoral counseling. 2. Church and social problems. I. Clinebell, Howard John, 1915- joint author. II. Title.

SHRADER, Wesley. 253.5
Of men and angels. New York, Rinehart [1957] 184p. 21cm. [BV4012.2.S5] [BV4012.2.S5] 258 57-6574 57-6574
1. Pastroral counselling. I. Title.

SOLOMON, Charles R. 253.5
Counseling with the mind of Christ : the dynamics of spirituotherapy / Charles R. Solomon. Old Tappan, N.J. : F. H. Revell Co., c1977. 159 p. : ill. ; 21 cm. Bibliography: p. 157-159. [BV4012.2.S64] 77-12227 ISBN 0-8007-0889-X pbk. : 3.95
1. Pastoral counseling. 2. Counseling. I. Title.

STEIN, Calvert, 1903- 253.5
Practical pastoral counseling. Springfield, Ill., Thomas [1970] xiii, 283 p. illus. 24 cm. Includes bibliographies. [BV4012.2.S7] 76-97536
1. Pastoral counseling. I. Title.

STEWART, Charles William. 253.5
The minister as family counselor / Charles William Stewart. Nashville : Abingdon, c1979. 207 p. ; 21 cm. Includes index. Bibliography: p. 195-200. [BV4012.2.S73] 79-10854 ISBN 0-687-26955-5 : 8.95
1. Pastoral counseling. 2. Family psychotherapy. 3. Family—Religious life. I. Title.

STONE, Howard W. 253.5
Crisis counseling / Howard W. Stone. Philadelphia : Fortress Press, c1976. xiv, 81 p. ; 22 cm. (Creative pastoral care and counseling series) Bibliography: p. 79-81. [BV4012.2.S75] 75-13047 ISBN 0-8006-0553-5 pbk. : 2.95
1. Pastoral counseling. 2. Counseling. I. Title.

STONE, Howard W. 253.5
Using behavioral methods in pastoral counseling / Howard W. Stone. Philadelphia : Fortress Press, c1980. p. cm. (Creative pastoral care and counseling series) Bibliography: p. [BV4012.2.S753] 79-2287 ISBN 0-8006-0563-2 pbk. : 3.25
1. Pastoral counseling. 2. Behavior therapy. I. Title.

SWITZER, David K., 1925- 253.5
The minister as crisis counselor [by] David K. Switzer. Nashville, Abingdon Press [1974] 288 p. illus. 23 cm. Includes bibliographical references. [BV4012.2.S9] 73-13722 ISBN 0-687-26953-9 6.95
1. Pastoral counseling. I. Title.

THORNTON, Edward E. 253.5
Theology and pastoral counseling. Englewood Cliffs, N.J., Prentice [c.1964] 144p. 21cm. (Successful counseling ser.) 64-12847 2.95 bds.,
1. Pastoral counseling. I. Title. II. Series.

THORNTON, Edward E. 253.5
Theology and pastoral counseling. Philadelphia, Fortress [1967, c.1964] 144p. 21cm. (Successful pastoral counseling ser.) Bibl. [BV4012.2.T5] 1.50 pap.,
1. Pastoral counseling. I. Title. II. Series.

TSCHUDY, James Jay. 253.5
The art of counseling. Salt Lake City, Deseret Book Co., 1963. 242 p. illus. 24 cm. [BV4012.2.T8] 63-3392
1. Pastoral counseling. I. Title.

TURNER, F. Bernadette. 253.5
God-centered therapy; how to live abundantly, a scriptural approach to problem living [by] F. Bernadette Turner. New York, R. Speller [1968] xvii, 277 p. 23 cm. [BV4012.2.T9] 68-21749
1. Pastoral counseling. 2. Christian life. I. Title.

TYRRELL, Bernard, 1933- 615.8'52
Christotherapy II : the fasting and feasting heart / Bernard J. Tyrrell. Ramsey, N.J. : Paulist Press, c1982. xiii, 337 p. ; 23 cm. Includes bibliographical references and indexes. [BV4012.2.T96 1982] 19 82-60597 ISBN 0-8091-2482-3 (pbk.) : 8.95
1. Pastoral counseling. 2. Spiritual healing. I. Title.

VANDERPOOL, James A. 253.5
People in pain : a guide to pastoral care / by James A. Vanderpool. Springfield, Ill. : Thomas, c1979. xii, 190 p. ; 24 cm. Includes index. Bibliography: p. 179-185. [BV4012.2.V27] 78-13045 ISBN 0-398-03846-5 : 12.75
1. Pastoral counseling. 2. Church work with the mentally ill. I. Title.

VAN DEUSEN, Dayton G. 253.5
Redemptive counseling; relating psychotherapy to the personal meanings in redemption. Richmond, John Knox Press [1960] 191 p. 21 cm. Includes bibliography. [BV4012.2.V3] 60-14142
1. Pastoral counseling. I. Title.

VAUGHAN, Richard Patrick. 253.5
An introduction to religious counseling: a Christian humanistic approach [by] Richard P. Vaughan. Englewood Cliffs, N.J., Prentice-Hall [1969] x, 164 p. 22 cm. Includes bibliographical references. [BV4012.2.V38] 74-86957 ISBN 1-349-52839- 5.95
1. Pastoral counseling. I. Title.

WEITZEL, Eugene J. 253.5
Contemporary pastoral counseling. Eugene J. Weitzel, participating editor. New York, Bruce Pub. Co. [1969] xiii, 299 p. 24 cm. Includes bibliographical references. [BV4012.2.W4] 75-75032

1. Pastoral counseling. I. Title.

WHITLOCK, Glenn E. 253.5
Preventive psychology and the church, by Glenn E. Whitlock. Philadelphia, Westminster Press [1973] 74 p. 22 cm. Bibliography: p. [171]-174. [BV4012.2.W44] 72-8359 ISBN 0-664-20959-9 5.95
1. Pastoral counseling. 2. Pastoral psychology. 3. Mental hygiene. I. Title.

WILLIAMS, Daniel Day, 1910- 253.5
The minister and the care of souls. New York, Harper [c.1961] 157p. Bibl. 61-12936 3.50 bds.,
1. Pastoral counseling. I. Title.

WILLIAMS, Daniel Day, 1910- 253.5
The minister and the care of souls. [1st ed.] New York, Harper [1961] 157 p. 22 cm. Incudes bibliography. [BV4012.2.W48] 61-12836
1. Pastoral counseling. I. Title.

WIMBERLY, Edward P., 1943- 253.5'08996073
Pastoral counseling and spiritual values : a Black point of view / Edward P. Wimberly. Nashville : Abingdon, [1982] p. cm. Includes bibliographical references. [BV4012.2.W49] 19 81-10918 ISBN 0-687-30336-2 pbk. : 6.95
1. Pastoral counseling. I. Title.

WISE, Carroll Alonzo, 1903- 253.5
Pastoral counseling, its theory and practice. [1st ed.] New York, Harper [1951] xi, 231p. 22cm. 'Notes and references': p. 223-227. [BV4012.2.W5] 258 51-9232
1. Pastoral counseling. I. Title.

THE Workaholic and his 248.4
family : an inside look / Frank Minirth ... [et al.]. Grand Rapids, Mich. : Baker Book House, c1981. 159 p. ; 23 cm. Includes bibliographical references. [BV4012.2.W58] 19 81-148595 ISBN 0-8010-6111-3 : 7.95
1. Pastoral counseling. 2. Work (Theology) 3. Obsessive-compulsive neurosis. I. Minirth, Frank B.

WORKSHOP in Pastoral 253.5
Counseling, University of Florida, 1959. *Proceedings.* Edited by J. Milan Kolarik. [Gainesville, Fla., 1959] 85 p. 23 cm. Includes bibliographies. [BV4012.2.W6 1959] A60
1. Pastoral counseling. I. Kolarik J. Millan, ed. II. Title.

WYNN, John Charles, 1920- 616.89'156'0242
Family therapy in pastoral ministry / J.C. Wynn. 1st ed. San Francisco : Harper & Row, c1982. viii, 184 p. : ill. ; 22 cm. Includes index. Bibliography: p. [166]-171. [BV4012.2.W89 1982] 19 81-47840 ISBN 0-06-069703-2 : 12.25
1. Pastoral counseling. 2. Family psychotherapy. I. Title.

YOUNG, Richard K 253.5
Spiritual therapy; how the physician, psychiatrist and minister collaborate in healing [by] Richard K Young and Albert L. Meiburg. New York, Harper [1960] 184 p. 22 cm. Includes bibliography. [BV4012.2.Y6] 60-7958
1. Pastoral counseling. 2. Medicine, Psychosomatic — Cases, clinical reports, statistics. I. Meiburg, Albert L. joint author. II. Title.

Pastoral counseling—Addresses, essays, lectures.

CARE for the dying : 253.5
resources of theology / edited with an introd. by Richard N. Soulen. Atlanta : John Knox Press, [1975] x, 141 p. ; 22 cm. Includes bibliographical references. [BV4012.2.C28] 74-19968 ISBN 0-8042-1098-5 pbk. : 4.95
1. Pastoral counseling—Addresses, essays, lectures. 2. Death—Addresses, essays, lectures. I. Soulen, Richard N., 1933-

KELSEY, Morton T. 253.5
Prophetic ministry : the psychology and spirituality of pastoral care / Morton T. Kelsey. New York : Crossroad, 1982. xii, 210 p. ; 24 cm. Bibliography: p. 204-210. [BV4012.2.K435 1982] 19 81-17471 ISBN 0-8245-0441-0 : 12.95
1. Jung, C. G. (Carl Gustav), 1875-1961—Addresses, essays, lectures. 2. Pastoral counseling—Addresses, essays, lectures. I. Title.

PASTORAL care in the 253'.5
liberal churches. Edited by James Luther Adams and Seward Hiltner. Nashville, Abingdon Press [1970] 256 p. 21 cm. Includes bibliographical references. [BV4012.2.P28] 70-97572 4.75
1. Pastoral counseling—Addresses, essays, lectures. 2. Liberalism (Religion)—Addresses, essays, lectures. I. Adams, James Luther, 1901- ed. II. Hiltner, Seward, 1909- ed.

Pastoral counseling—Case studies.

AAEN, Bernhard, 1918- 253.5
No appointment needed : case histories from a counselor's file / Bernard Aaen. Washington, D.C. : Review and Hearld Publishing Association, c1980. 128 p. ; 21 cm. [BV4012.2.A15] 19 80-20249 pbk. : 4.95
1. Aaen, Bernhard, 1918- 2. Pastoral counseling—Case studies. I. Title.

ISHEE, John A. 253.5'0926
When trouble comes, compiled by John Ishee. Nashville, Tenn., Broadman Press [1970] 128 p. 20 cm. (A Broadman inner circle book) Includes bibliographical references. [BV4012.2.I8] 75-113211
1. Pastoral counseling—Case studies. I. Title.

MATTHEWS, Victor M. 253.5'01'86
Confessions to a counselor; responses to the plea, "Confidentially, I need help." Grand Rapids, Zondervan Pub. House [1969] 96 p. 21 cm. (A Zondervan paperback) [BV4012.2.M3] 69-11633 0.95
1. Pastoral counseling—Case studies. I. Title.

STROUP, Herbert W. 253.5
Sexuality and the counseling pastor [by] Herbert W. Stroup, Jr. & Norma Schweitzer Wood. Philadelphia, Fortress Press [1974] xi, 122 p. 23 cm. Bibliography: p. [119]-122. [BV4012.2.S8] 73-88344 ISBN 0-8006-0264-1 5.25
1. Pastoral counseling—Case studies. 2. Sex (Theology) I. Wood, Norma Schweitzer, joint author. II. Title.

Pastoral counseling centers—Addresses, essays, lectures.

THE Organization & 253.5
administration of pastoral counseling centers / [edited by] John C. Carr, John E. Hinkle, Jr., and David M. Moss III. Nashville : Abingdon, c1981. 304 p. ; 23 cm. Includes indexes. Bibliography: p. 294-297. [BV4012.25.074] 19 80-22416 ISBN 0-687-29430-4 : 15.95
1. Pastoral counseling centers—Addresses, essays, lectures. I. Carr, John, Crosby, 1938- II. Hinkle, John E. III. Moss, David M.

Pastoral counseling—Handbooks, manuals, etc.

VANDERPOOL, James A. 253.5
Person to person : a handbook for pastoral counseling / by James A. Vanderpool. 1st ed. Garden City, N.Y. : Doubleday, 1977. 156 p. ; 22 cm. Bibliography: p. [151]-156. [BV4012.2.V28] 76-20837 ISBN 0-385-12518-6 : 6.95
1. Pastoral counseling—Handbooks, manuals, etc. I. Title.

Pastoral counseling (Judaism)

GROLLMAN, Earl A. 296.6
Rabbinical counseling, ed. by Earl A. Grollman. Contributing authors: Irwin M. Blank [others] New York, Bloch [1967, c.1966] xvii, 190p. 24cm. Bibl. [BM652.5G715] 67-17827 6.50
1. Pastoral counseling (Judaism) I. Blank, Irwin M. II. Title.

SCHNITZER, Jeshaia. 296.6
New horizons for the synagogue; a counseling program for the rabbi and the synagogue. With a foreword by Harry Halpern. [1st ed.] New York, Bloch Pub. Co., 1956. 106p. 24cm. [BM652.5.S35] 56-10193
1. Pastoral counseling (Judaism) I. Title.

Pastoral literature—Addresses, essays, lectures.

CUSHING, Richard James, Cardinal 248.482
Pastoral letter: the Christian and the community. Boston, Daughters of St. Paul, 1960. 31p. 22cm. .15 pap.,
I. Title.

DAILEY, Edward Vincent, 1905-- 922.273
The pastor's cat, and other people. Illus. byEdward F. Johnson. Cat sketches by 'Shep.' Milwaukee, Bruce [1955] 146p. illus. 21cm. [BX4705.D183A3] 55-11515
I. Title.

KEMPTHORNE, John Augustine, bp. of Lichfield, 1864- 262.
Pastoral life and work to-day, by the Right Rev. J. A. Kempthorne ... London, New York [etc.] Longmans, Green and co., 1919. xvi, 176 p. 20 cm. [BX5175.K4] 19-14546
I. Title.

LINCOLN, Eleanor Terry, comp. 809.9'33
Pastoral and romance; modern essays in criticism. Englewood Cliffs, N.J., Prentice-Hall [1969] vii, 296 p. 22 cm. (Prentice-Hall English literature series) Bibliographical footnotes. [PN56.P3L5] 69-10869
1. Pastoral literature—Addresses, essays, lectures. 2. Romances—Addresses, essays, lectures. I. Title.

STEVENS, George Dewey 253
A pastor's diary; 'all in a day's work' for a Baptist minister. New York, Exposition Press [c.1960] 187p. 3.00
I. Title.

WHALLON, Edward Payson, 1849-
Pastoral memories; or, Reminiscences and reflections, by Rev. E. P. Whallon ... Cincinnati, Monfort & company, 1907. 256 p. 18 1/2 cm. 7-31426
I. Title.

Pastoral medicine.

FAIRCHILD, Roy W. 253.5
Finding hope again : a pastor's guide to counseling depressed persons / Roy W. Fairchild. 1st ed. San Francisco : Harper & Row, c1980. p. cm. Includes bibliographical references and index. [BV4335.F34 1980] 79-2988 ISBN 0-06-062325-X : 8.95
1. Pastoral medicine. 2. Depression, Mental. 3. Hope. I. Title.

PAZHAYATIL, Harshajan. 253.5
Counseling and health care / Harshajan Pazhayatil. 2d ed. Chicago : Franciscan Herald Press, c1977. xxviii, 357 p. ; 23 cm. Bibliography: p. 335-357. [BV4335.P39 1977] 76-29068 ISBN 0-8199-0623-9 : 10.95
1. Pastoral medicine. 2. Pastoral counseling. 3. Chaplains, Hospital. I. Title.

PLATT, Nancy Van Dyke. 253
Pastoral care to the cancer patient / by Nancy Van Dyke Platt ; foreword by Christian A. Hovde. Springfield, Ill. : Thomas, c1980. xiii, 84 p. ; 23 cm. Includes bibliographical references. [BV4335.P567] 80-15813 ISBN 0-398-04051-6 pbk. : 8.75
1. Pastoral medicine. 2. Cancer patients. I. Title.

RICHARDS, Lawrence O. 259'.4
Death & the caring community : ministering to the terminally ill / Larry Richards, Paul Johnson. Portland, Or. : Multnomah Press, c1980. 210 p. ; 23 cm. Includes indexes. Bibliography: p. 195-201. [BV4335.R52] 19 80-19752 ISBN 0-930014-45-6 : 8.95
1. Pastoral medicine. 2. Church work with the sick. 3. Terminal care—Moral and religious aspects. I. Johnson, Paul, 1915- joint author. II. Title.

THE Role of the minister in 253.5
caring for the dying patient and the bereaved / edited by Brian O'Connor, Daniel J. Cherico, Austin H. Kutscher, et al. ; with the editorial assistance of Lillian G. Kutscher. New York : MSS Information Corp., [1975] p. cm. (Continuing series on thanatology) [BT732.7.R64] 75-5716 ISBN 0-8422-7279-8 : 13.50
1. Pastoral medicine. 2. Church work with the bereaved. I. O'Connor, Brian. II. Cherico, Daniel J. III. Kutshcer, Austin H.

SAYLOR, Dennis E. 253
"... and you visited me" / by Dennis E. Saylor. Medford, Or. : Morse Press, c1979. x, 212 p. ; 22 cm. Bibliography: p. 205-212. [BV4335.S2] 79-88403 ISBN 0-933350-21-X pbk. : 5.95
1. Pastoral medicine. I. Title.

WHEELOCK, Robert D. 658'.91'2618321
Health care ministries : a guide to organization, management, evaluation / Robert D. Wheelock. St. Louis, : Catholic Hospital Association, [1975] x, 114 p. ; 23 cm. Bibliography: p. 111-113. [BV4335.W48] 74-18748 ISBN 0-87125-021-7 : 4.50
1. Pastoral medicine. 2. Chaplains, Hospital. I. Title.

Pastoral medicine—Addresses, essays, lectures.

PASTORAL care in health 253.5
facilities : a book of readings / edited by Ward A. Knights, Jr. St. Louis : Catholic Hospital Association, c1977. viii, 114 p. ; 23 cm. Includes bibliographical references. [BV4335.P37] 76-26994 1975. ISBN 0-87125-035-7 pbk. : 6.50
1. Pastoral medicine—Addresses, essays, lectures. I. Knights, Ward A., 1927-

Pastoral medicine—Catholic Church.

NIKLAS, Gerald R. 253
Ministry to the hospitalized / by Gerald R. Niklas and Charlotte Stefanics. New York : Paulist Press, c1975. v, 135 p. ; 21 cm. Includes bibliographies. [BX2347.8.S5N5] 75-22986 ISBN 0-8091-1899-8 : 3.95
1. Pastoral medicine—Catholic Church. 2. Church work with the sick. I. Stefanics, Charlotte, joint author. II. Title.

NIKLAS, Gerald R. 253
Ministry to the sick / Gerald R. Niklas and Charlotte Stefanics. [2nd ed.] Staten Island, N.Y. : Alba House, c1982. x, 143 p. ; 21 cm. First ed. published as: Ministry to the hospitalized. 1975. Includes bibliographies. [BX2347.8.S5N5 1982] 19 82-4083 pbk. : 6.95
1. Pastoral medicine—Catholic Church. 2. Church work with the sick. I. Stefanics, Charlotte. II. Title.

WHEELOCK, Robert D. 253
Policies and procedures for the pastoral care department / [Robert D. Wheelock]. St. Louis : Catholic Hospital Association, c1977. xiii, 65 p. ; 26 cm. [BX1914.W53] 76-9660 ISBN 0-87125-036-5 pbk. : 3.50
1. Pastoral medicine—Catholic Church. I. Catholic Hospital Association. II. Title.

Pastoral medicine—Catholic Church—Congresses.

INSTITUTE of Pastoral 261.8
Psychology, 10th, Fordham University, 1975.
Human life : problems of birth, of living, and of dying / edited by William C. Bier. New York : Fordham University Press, c1977. x, 295 p. ; 24 cm. (The Pastoral psychology series ; no. 9) Papers presented at the 10th Institute of Pastoral Psychology, sponsored by the Fordham University Dept. of Psychology. Includes bibliographies. [BX1759.5.M4157 1975] 77-71939 ISBN 0-8232-1025-1 : 12.50
1. Pastoral medicine—Catholic Church—Congresses. 2. Pastoral psychology—Congresses. 3. Medical ethics—Congresses. 4. Christian ethics—Catholic authors—Congresses. 5. Sociology, Christian (Catholic)—Congresses. I. Bier, William Christian, 1911- II. Fordham University. Dept. of Psychology. III. Title. IV. Series.

Pastoral medicine—Wisconsin—Milwaukee.

SCHROEDER, Arnold H. 253
Other sheep / Arnold H. Schroeder. Milwaukee, Wis. : Northwestern Pub. House, 1981. 168 p. ; 21 cm. [BV4335.S36] 19 81-80055 ISBN 0-8100-0140-3 pbk. : 6.95
1. Pastoral medicine—Wisconsin—Milwaukee. 2. Church work with prisoners—Wisconsin—Milwaukee. I. Title.

Pastoral prayers.

BARTH, Karl, 1886- 242.3
Selected prayers. Tr. [from German] by Keith R. Crim. Richmond, Va., Knox [c.1965] 72p. 19cm. (Chime paperbacks) [BV250.B37] 65-10144 1.00 pap.,
1. Pastoral prayers. I. Title.

CONTEMPORARY prayers for 264'.13 *public worship,* by Anthony Coates [and others]; edited by Caryl Micklem. [1st American ed.] Grand Rapids, W. B. Eerdmans Pub. Co. [1967] 141 p. 21 cm. [BV250.C6 1967b] 67-28374
1. Pastoral prayers. I. Micklem, Caryl, ed. II. Coates, Anthony.

CURRIE, David M., 1918- 242'.89'2
Come, let us worship God : a handbook of prayers for leaders of worship / by David M. Currie. Philadelphia : Westminster Press, c1977. p. cm. [BV250.C87] 77-6808 ISBN 0-664-24757-1 pbk. : 4.25
1. Pastoral prayers. I. Title.

CURRIE, David M., 1918- 242'.89'2
Come, let us worship God : a handbook of prayers for leaders of worship / by David M. Currie. Philadelphia : Westminster Press, c1977. p. cm. [BV250.C87] 77-6808 ISBN 0-664-24757-1 pbk. : 4.25
1. Pastoral prayers. I. Title.

GEFFEN, Roger, comp. 264.13
The handbook of public prayer. New York, Macmillan [1963] 204 p. 21 cm. [BV250.G4] 63-8185
1. Pastoral prayers. I. Title.

GRAY, Walter G 264.1
Prayers for the pulpit. [West wood, N. J.] F. H. Revell Co. [1957] 127p. 20cm. [BV250.G7] 57-6855
1. Pastoral prayers. I. Title.

GUPTILL, Nathanael M. 264.13
Contemporary pastoral prayers for the Christian year. Philadelphia, Christian Education Press [c.1960] 151p. 60-53182 2.50
1. Pastoral prayers. I. Title.

MICKLEM, Caryl, ed. 261'.13
Contemporary prayers for public worship, by Anthony Coates [and others]; edited by Caryl Micklem. [1st American ed.] Grand Rapids, W. B. Eerdmans Pub. Co. [1967] 141 p. 21 cm. [BV250.C6] 67-28374
1. Pastoral prayers. I. Coates, Anthony. II. Title.

ORCHARD, William Edwin, 1877- 264.13
The temple; a book of prayers. Ed., foreword by Marvin Halverson [Rev. ed.] New York, Seabury [1965] xvi, 120p. 17cm. [BV250.O8] 65-22864 3.50
1. Pastoral prayers. I. Halverson, Marvin, 1913- ed. II. Title.

PEARSON, Roy Messer, 1914- 264.1
Hear our prayer; prayers for public worship. [1st ed.] New York, McGraw-Hill [1961] 174p. 21cm. [BV250.P4] 60-53351
1. Pastoral prayers. I. Title.

PHILLIPS, E. Lee. 264'.13
Prayers for worship / E. Lee Phillips. Waco, Tex. : Word Books. c1979. 148 p. ; 20 cm. Bibliography: p. 144-148. [BV250.P47] 78-65814 ISBN 0-8499-0137-5 : 8.95
1. Pastoral prayers. I. Title.

PRAYERS for all 264.13 *occasions.* Grand Rapids, Baker Book House, 1960. 80p. 20cm. [BV250.P7] 60-16792
1. Pastoral prayers.

SANDLIN, John Lewis 264.13
Aprayer for every meeting [Westwood, N.J.] Revell [c.1964] 128p. 17cm. 64-16606 2.50 bds.,
1. Pastoral prayers. I. Title.

SANDLIN, John Lewis. 264.13
A prayer for every meeting. [Westwood, N. J.] Revell [1964] 128 p. 17 cm. [BV250.S2] 64-16606
1. Pastoral prayers. I. Title.

SCHMIECHEN, Samuel John. 264.1
Pastoral prayers for the church year. New York, Abingdon Press [1957] 144p. 20cm. [BV250.S35] 57-11015
1. Pastoral prayers. I. Title.

TYLER, Edward. 248'.8
Prayers in celebration of the turning year / Edward Tyler ; drawings by Gillian Tyler. Nashville : Abingdon, c1978. 95 p. : ill. ; 21 cm. [BV250.T9] 77-17067 ISBN 0-687-33650-3 : 5.95
1. Pastoral prayers. I. Title.

UEHLING, Carl T. 264'.13
Prayers for public worship, by Carl T. Uehling. Philadelphia, Fortress Press [1972] xi, 163 p. 27 cm. [BV250.U33] 72-75657 ISBN 0-8006-0234-X 10.95
1. Pastoral prayers. I. Title.

WILLIAMSON, Robert L. 264.1
Effective public prayer. Nashville, Broadman Press [1960] 152 p. 21 cm. Includes bibliography. [BV226.W5] 60-9535
1. Pastoral prayers. 2. Prayer. I. Title.

ZEIDLER, Clemens H. 264.13
Altar prayers for the church year. Minneapolis, Augsburg [c.1962] 200p. 27cm. 62-12925 6.50, bxd.
1. Pastoral prayers. I. Title.

Pastoral psychology.

ARNOLD, William V., 1941- 253.5
Introduction to pastoral care / William V. Arnold. 1st ed. Philadelphia : Westminster Press, c1982. 221 p. ; 21 cm. Includes index. Bibliography: p. [215]-216. [BV4012.A76] 19 81-16092 ISBN 0-664-24400-9 : 10.95
1. Pastoral psychology. 2. Pastoral theology. I. Title.

BELGUM, David Rudolph, 1922- 258
Clinical training for pastoral care. Philadelphia, Westminster Press [1956] 136 p. illus. 21 cm. [BV4012.B38] 56-5102
1. Pastoral Sychology. I. Title.

BELL, Walter Presley. 253.5
The case for pastoral clinical training. Boston, Christopher Pub. House [1967] 147 p. 21 cm. Bibliography: p. 143-146. [BV4012.B382] 66-28033
1. Council for the Clinical Training of Theological Students. 2. Pastoral psychology. I. Title.

BENNETT, George, 1931- 253
When they ask for bread : or, Pastoral care and counseling in everyday places / by George Bennett. Atlanta : John Knox Press, c1978. 124 p. ; 24 cm. Includes index. Bibliography: p. 118-124. [BV4012.B39] 77-15743 ISBN 0-8042-1159-0 : 6.95
1. Pastoral psychology. 2. Pastoral theology. I. Title.

BIBLICAL and psychological 253.5 *perspectives for Christian counselors.* Robert K. Bower, editor. [Contributions by] Kenneth B. Mulholland [and others. South Pasadena, Calif.] Publishers Services [1974] x, 310 p. illus. 23 cm. "Each presentation is based on a doctoral dissertation conducted by the respective author while in residence at the Fuller Theological Seminary." Includes bibliographical references. [BV4012.B45] 74-12239 ISBN 0-87808-951-9 5.45 (pbk. text ed.)
1. Pastoral psychology. 2. Pastoral counseling. I. Bower, Robert K., ed. II. Mulholland, Kenneth B.

BLAZER, Dan G. 248'.86
Healing the emotions / Dan G. Blazer, II. Nashville, Tenn. : Broadman Press, c1979. 112 p. ; 19 cm. Bibliography: p. 105-112. [BV4012.B56] 78-72278 ISBN 0-8054-6926-5 pbk. : 2.95
1. Pastoral psychology. 2. Mental health. I. Title.

BRANDT, Frans M. J. 248.4
The renewed mind : Christian re-educative therapy and self-counseling / Frans M.J. Brandt. Oscoda, Mich. : Wesselhoeft Associates, c1982. 251 p. ; 22 cm. Bibliography: p. 245-250. [BV4012.B67 1982] 19 81-51869 ISBN 0-941954-01-3 (pbk.) : 7.95
1. Pastoral psychology. 2. Christian life—Baptist authors. 3. Rational-emotive psychotherapy. I. Title.
Publisher's address: 3885 Lawrence, Oscoda, MI 48750

BRILLENBURG WURTH, Gerrit. 253.5
Christian counseling in the light of modern psychology. [Translation by H. de Jongste] Philadelphia, Presbyterian and Reformed Pub. Co., 1962. 307p. 22cm. [BV4012.B853] 61-16942
1. Pastoral psychology. 2. Pastoral theology. I. Title.

CAPLAN, Ruth B. 253
Helping the helpers to help; mental health consultation to aid clergymen in pastoral work, by Ruth B. Caplan in collaboration with Gerald Caplan [and others] New York, Seabury Press [1972] x, 241 p. 22 cm. Includes bibliographical references. [BV4012.C315] 72-81024 ISBN 0-8164-0239-6 6.95
1. Pastoral psychology. I. Title.

CAPPS, Donald. 253
Pastoral care : a thematic approach / by Donald Capps. 1st ed. Philadelphia : Westminster Press, c1979. 161 p. ; 21 cm. Includes bibliographical references. [BV4012.C317] 78-15093 ISBN 0-664-24222-7 pbk. : 5.95
1. Pastoral psychology. 2. Pastoral theology. I. Title.

CARRINGTON, William Langley. 253.5
Psychology, religion, and human need; a guide for ministers, doctors, teachers, and social workers. Great Neck, N. Y., Channel Press [1957] 315p. illus. 21cm. [BV4012.C32] 258 57-12036
1. Pastoral psychology. I. Title.

CLINEBELL, Howard John, 1922- 253
The mental health ministry of the local church [by] Howard J. Clinebell, Jr. Nashville, Abingdon Press [1972] 300 p. 23 cm. 1965 ed. published under title: Mental health through Christian community. Bibliography: p. 285-289. [BV4012.C56 1972] 73-185551 ISBN 0-687-24829-9 2.95
1. Pastoral psychology. 2. Mental hygiene. I. Title.

CLINEBELL, Howard John, 1922- 253.5
Mental health through Christian community; the local church's ministry of growth and healing. Nashville, Abingdon [c.1965] 300p. 24cm. Bibl. [BV4012.C56] 65-15230 4.75
1. Pastoral psychology. 2. Mental hygiene. I. Title.

CLINEBELL, Howard, John, 1922- 253.5
Mental health through Christian community; the local church's ministry of growth and healing [by] Howard J. Clinebell, Jr. New York, Abingdon Press [1965] 300 p. 24 cm. "Reading by chapters": p. 285-289. Bibliographical footnotes. [BV4012.C56] 65-15230
1. Pastoral psychology. 2. Mental hygiene. I. Title.

COLLINS, Gary R. 253
Man in transition; the psychology of human development [by] Gary R. Collins. [1st ed.] Carol Stream, Ill., Creation House [1971] 203 p. 22 cm. (Psychology for church leaders series) Bibliography: p. 189-198. [BV4012.C59] 79-163763 4.95
1. Pastoral psychology. 2. Christian leadership. I. Title.

CONLEY, Thomas H. 253.5
Pastoral care for personal growth / by Tom Conley. Valley Forge, Pa. : Judson Press, [1977] p. cm. Includes bibliographical references. [BV4012.C64] 77-79776 ISBN 0-8170-0754-7 pbk. : 3.50
1. Pastoral psychology. 2. Church group work. I. Title.

DAVIS, Creath. 248'.4
How to win in a crisis / by Creath Davis ; foreword by Gloria and Bill Gaither. Grand Rapids, Mich. : Zondervan, c1976. p. cm. Includes bibliographical references. [BV4012.D346] 76-4220 6.95
1. Pastoral psychology. 2. Interpersonal relations. I. Title.

DE LONG, Russell Victor, 1901-
Illnesses of the modern soul. Kansas City, Beacon Hill Press [1965] 111 p. 20 cm. 68-34568
1. Pastoral psychology. I. Title.

DEVLIN, William Joseph, 1905-1961 137
Psychodynamics of personality development. Staten Island, N. Y., Alba [c.1965] 324p. 22cm. (Mental health ser., 3) Bibl. [BV4012.D37] 64-15374 4.95
1. Pastoral psychology. 2. Genetic psychology. I. Title.

DRAPER, Edgar, 1926- 253.5
Psychiatry and pastoral care. Englewood Cliffs, N.J., Prentice [1966] 138p. 21cm. (Successful pastoral counseling ser.) Bibl. [BV4012.D7] 65-23861 2.95 pap.,
1. Pastoral psychology. 2. Pastoral counseling. I. Title. II. Series.

DRAPER, Edgar, 1926- 253.5
Psychiatry and pastoral care. Philadelphia, Fortress [1967, c.1965] 138p. 21cm.

(Successful pastoral counseling ser.) Bibl. [BV4012.D7] 65-23861 1.50 pap.,
1. Pastoral psychology. 2. Pastoral counseling. I. Title. II. Series.

DUCKER, E. N. 253.5
A Christian therapy for a neurotic world. Foreword by Frank Lake. London, Allen & Unwin [Mystic, Conn., Verry, 1964, c.1961] 225p. illus. 23cm. Bibl. 62-32733 4.50
1. Pastoral psychology. I. Title.

DUFFIE, David. 250'.1'9
Psychology and the Christian religion. Nashville, Southern Pub. [1967,c.1968] 160p. 22cm. Bibl. [BV4012.D84] 67-31387 4.50
1. Pastoral psychology. I. Title.

GOLDBRUNNER, Josef 253.5
Realization; anthropology of pastoral care. Tr. by Paul C. Bailey, Elisabeth Reinecke. [Notre Dame, Ind.] Univ. of Notre Dame Pr., 1966. ix, 221p. 24cm. (Liturgical studies, v.9) Bibl. [BV4012.G5513] 66-14629 6.00 bds.,
1. Pastoral psychology. I. Title. II. Series: Nortre Dame, Ind., University, Liturgical studies, v. 9

HARRIS, Charles D. 248'.4
Heaven? Yes! Hell? No! / By Charles D. Harris. [Waco? Tex.] : Harris, [1975] ix, 148 p. ; 24 cm. Bibliography: p. 147-148. [BV4012.H32] 75-15071
1. Pastoral psychology. 2. Christian life—1960- I. Title.

HILLMAN, James. 253.5'019
Insearch; psychology and religion. New York, Scribner [1968, c1967] 126 p. 22 cm. [BV4012.H5 1968] 67-24042
1. Pastoral psychology. 2. Soul. I. Title.

HOFMANN, Hans, 1923- 253.5
Religion and mental health; a casebook with commentary, and An essay on pertinent literature. [1st ed.] New York, Harper [1961] 333p. 22cm. Includes bibliography. [BV4012.H63] 61-5262
1. Pastroal psychology. 2. Psychotherapy—Cases, clinical reports, statistics. I. Title.

HOFMANN, Hans F., 1923- 253.5
Religion and mental health a casebook with commentary, and An essay on pertinent literature. [1st ed.] New York Harper [1961] 333 p. 22 cm. Includes bibliography. [BV4012.H63] 61-5262
1. Pastoral psychology. 2. Psychotherapy — Cases, clinical reports, statistics. I. Title.

HOUGH, Lynn Harold, 1877- 258
Twelve merry fishermen, by Lynn Harold Hough. New York, Cincinnati, The Abingdon press [c1923] 128 p. 19 cm. [BV4012.H7] 23-11654
I. Title.

INSTITUTE of Pastoral Care, Framingham, Mass., 1961.
Levels of clinical pastoral training. [Fall conference chaplain supervisors, October 16-20, 1961, Framingham, Massachusetts. n.p., 1961?] vii, 102 l. 29 cm. Cover title. 63-30616
1. Pastoral psychology. 2. Theological education. 3. Pastoral office and work. I. Title. II. Title: Levels of clinical pastoral training.

JACKSON, Edgar Newman. 253.5
The pastor and his people; a psychology for parish work. Introd. by James A. Knight. Manhasset, N.Y., Channel Press [c1963] 224 p. 21 cm. [BV4012.J25] 62-18046
1. Pastorial psychology. I. Title.

LEACH, Max, 1909- 253.5
Christianity and mental health. Dubuque, Iowa. W. C. Brown [1957] 135p. 23cm. [BV4012.L39] 258 57-2298
1. Pastoral psychology. 2. Mental hygiene. I. Title.

LEACH, Max, 1909-
Christianity and mental health. Dubuque, Iowa, W.C. Brown [1967] 163 p. 23 cm. Sixth printing 1967. 67-102059
1. Pastoral psychology. 2. Mental hygiene. I. Title.

LEE, Ronald R. 253.5
Clergy and clients : the practice of pastoral psychotherapy / Ronald R. Lee. New York : Seabury Press, 1980. 173 p. ; 24 cm. (A Crossroad book) Bibliography: p. [170]-173. [BV4012.L425] 80-50606 ISBN 0-8164-0115-2 : 10.95
1. Pastoral psychology. I. Title.

LELEN, Joseph Mary, Rev., 252.02 1873-
The gospel of a country pastor; sketches and sermons, by the Rev. J. M. Lelen. St. Louis, B. Herder [1962] xvi 179p. 20cm. 22-12182 2.95
I. Title.

MCCANN, Richard Vincent 253.5
The churches and mental health. A report to the staff director, Jack R. Ewalt, New York, Basic [c.]1962. x, 278p. 24cm. (Joint Comm. on Mental Illness and Health. Monograph ser., no. 8) Bibl. 62-11204 6.00
1. Pastoral psychology. I. Title. II. Series.

MASON, Robert Lee. 253.5
The clergyman and the psychiatrist—when to refer / Robert L. Mason, Jr., Carol B. Currier, John R. Curtis. Chicago : Nelson-Hall, c1978. xiv, 230 p. ; 23 cm. Includes bibliographical references and index. [BV4012.M35] 77-22597 ISBN 0-88229-260-9 : 11.95
1. Pastoral psychology. 2. Pastoral counseling. 3. Mental illness. I. Currier, Carol B., joint author. II. Curtis, John Russell, 1934- joint author. III. Title.

OATES, Wayne Edward, 1917- 253
New dimensions in pastoral care, by Wayne E. Oates. Philadelphia, Fortress Press [1970] 86 p. 19 cm. Based on lectures originally presented by the author as the Zimmerman lectures at the Lutheran Theological Seminary, Gettysburg, Pa., May 1-2, 1968. Bibliography: p. 84-86. [BV4012.O225] 73-122832 1.95
1. Pastoral psychology. 2. Clergy—Psychology. I. Title.

ODEN, Thomas C. 230'.09'04
Contemporary theology and psychotherapy, by Thomas C. Oden. Philadelphia, Westminster Press [1967] 158 p. 23 cm. Bibliographical references included in "Notes" (p. [143]-158) [BV4012.O26] 67-11798
1. Pastoral psychology. 2. Theology, Doctrinal—History—20th century. I. Title.

ODEN, Thomas C 253.5
Kerygma and counseling; toward a covenant ontology for secular psychotherapy, by Thomas C. Oden. Philadelphia, Westminster Press [1966] 186 p. 21 cm. Bibliographical references included in "Notes" (p. [171]-186) [BV4012.O27] 66-11516
1. Rogers, Carl Ransom, 1902- 2. Barth, Karl, 1886- 3. Pastoral psychology. 4. Psychotherapy. I. Title.

O'DOHERTY, Eamonn Feichin, 253.5 ed.
The priest and mental health, ed. by E. F. O'Doherty, S. Desmond McGrath. Staten Island, N.Y., St. Paul Pubns. [dist.] Alba House [c.1963] xi, 251p. 22cm. Bibl. 63-14316 4.95
1. Pastoral psychology. I. McGrath, Sean Desmond, joint ed. II. Title.

O'DOHERTY, Eamonn Feichin, 253.5 ed.
The priest and mental health, edited by E. F. O'Doherty [and] S. Desmond McGrath. Staten Island, N.Y., Alba House [1963] xi, 251 p. 22 cm. Papers presented at the first Stillorgan conference held in 1960. Includes bibliographies. [BV4012.O3] 63-14316
1. Pastoral psychology. I. McGrath, Sean Desmond, joint ed. II. Title.

OLSEN, Peder 253.5
Pastoral care and psychotherapy; a study in cooperation between physician and pastor. Tr. [From Norwegian] by Herman E. Jorgensen. Minneapolis. Augsburg Pub. House [c.1961] 144p. Bibl. 61-6997 3.50
1. Pastoral psychology. 2. Psychotherapy. I. Title.

PASTORAL care in crucial 253.5 *human situations.* [Edited by] Wayne E. Oates and Andrew D. Lester. Valley Forge [Pa.] Judson Press [1969] 206 p. 23 cm. Includes bibliographical references. [BV4012.P3] 70-81444 6.50
1. Pastoral psychology. 2. Pastoral counseling. I. Oates, Wayne Edward, 1917- ed. II. Lester, Andrew D., ed.

PROCEEDINGS.
Edited by William C. Bier, S. J. and Alexander A. Schneiders. Sponsored by the Department of Psychology of Fordham University, financed in part by a grant from the New York State Department of Mental Hygiene. [New York, 1958?] x,253p. 23cm. Bibliographies at ends of some chapters.
1. Pastoral psychology. I. Institute for the Clergy on Problems in Pastoral Psychology. 2d, Fordham University, 1957. II. Bier, William Christian, 1911- ed. III. Fordham University, New York. Dept. of Psychology.

PSYCHIATRY and religious 253.5 *experience,* by Louis Linn and Leo W. Schwarz. New York, Random House [1958] 307p. 22cm. [BV4012.L54] 258 58-9873
1. Pastoral psychology. 2. Psychology, Religious. I. Linn, Louis. II. Schwarz, Leo Walder, 1906- joint author.

RUNESTAM, Arvid, 1887- 253.5
Psychoanalysis and Christianity. Translated by Oscar Winfield. Rock Island, Ill., Augustana Press [1958] 194p. 21cm. [BV4012.R84] 258 58-6526
1. Pastoral psychology. 2. Psychoanalysis. I. Title.

ST. Clair, Robert James 253.2
Neurotics in the church. [Westwood, N.J.] Revell [1963] 251 p. 21 cm. [BV4011.S3] 63-13360
1. Pastoral psychology. 2. Pastoral theology—Anecdotes, facetiae, satire, etc. I. Title.

SEMINARS for Clergymen, 253.5 Cleveland, 1962.
Mental health problems confronting clergymen; proceedings of Seminars for Clergymen presented by the Cleveland Mental Health Association in cooperation with the Academy of Religion and Mental Health, Cleveland Metropolitan Group. Edward N. Hinko, editor. Gwen Converse, editorial assistant. Cleveland, Cleveland Mental Health Association, 1963. viii, 74 p. 28 cm. Organized by the Committee on Assistance to the Clergy, Cleveland Mental Health Association. Includes bibliographies. [BV4012.S4 1962] 63-25376
1. Pastoral psychology. I. Hinko, Edward N., ed. II. Cleveland Mental Health Association. Committee on Assistance to the Clergy. III. Title.

SHARPE, William Donald, 253.5 1927-
Medicine and the ministry; a medical basis for pastoral care [by] William D. Sharpe. Pref. by Lauriston. L. Scaife. [1st ed.] New York, Appleton-Century [1966] xix, 356p. 24cm. Bibl. [BV4012.S47] 66-19997 6.95
1. Pastoral psychology. 2. Pastoral medicine. I. Title.

THILO, Hans Joachim, 1914- 253.5
Unfragmented man; a study in pastoral psychology. Tr. from German by Arthur J. Seegers. Minneapolis, Augsburg [c.1964] 208p. 22cm. Bibl. 64-13433 5.00
1. Pastoral psychology. 2. Psychology, Religious. I. Title.

THILO, Hans Joachim, 1914- 253.5
.
Unfragmented man; a study in pastoral psychology. Translated from the German by Arthur J. Seegers. Minneapolis, Augsburg Pub. House [1964] 208 p. 22 cm. "Notes and references": p. 201-208. [BV4012.T483] 64-13433
1. Pastoral psychology. 2. Psychology, Religious. I. Title.

ULEYN, Arnold. 253'.01'9
The recognition of guilt; a study in pastoral psychology. Translated by Mary Ilford. [Dublin] Gill and Macmillan [1969] xiv, 240 p. 22 cm. Translation of Actualite de la fonction prophetique. Includes bibliographical references. [BV4012.U413] 71-254089 ISBN 0-7171-0266-1 36/-
1. Pastoral psychology. I. Title.

VAN DER VELDT, James 616.89 Herman, 1893-
Psychiatry and Catholicism [by] James H. Vander Veldt [and] Robert P. Odenwald. 2d ed. New York, Blakiston Division, 1957. 474p. 24cm. Includes bibliographies. [BX1759.V3 1957] 57-8633
1. Pastoral psychology. 2. Psychiatry. 3. Christian ethics—Catholic authors. I. Odenwald, Robert. p., 1899- joint author. II. Title.

WEBER, Carlo A., 1927- 253.5
Pastoral psychology; new trends in theory and practice [by] Carlo A. Weber. New York, Sheed and Ward [1970] 160 p. 21 cm. Includes bibliographical references. [BV4012.W37] 73-101548 ISBN 0-8362-1420-X 6.00
1. Pastoral psychology.

WESTBERG, Granger E. 253.5
Minister and doctor meet. New York, Harper [c.1961] 179p. 61-7352 3.50 bds.,
1. Pastoral psychology. 2. Medicine and religion. I. Title.

WESTBERG, Granger E. 253.5
Minister and doctor meet. [1st ed.] New York, Harper [1961] 179 p. 22 cm. [BV4012.W43] 61-7352
1. Pastoral psychology. 2. Medicine and religion. I. Title.

WITTKOFSKI, Joseph 253.5 Nicholas, 1912-
The pastoral use of hypnotic technique. Foreword by T. J. Freeborn, Jr., introd. by Austin Pardue. New York, Macmillan [c.] 1961. 111p. Bibl. 61-14715 2.50
1. Pastoral psychology. 2. Hypnotism—Therapeutic use. I. Title.

WITTKOFSKI, Joseph 253.5 Nicholas, 1912-
The pastoral use of hypnotic technique. With a foreword by T. J. Freeborn, Jr., and an introd. by Austin Pardue. New York, Macmillan, 1961. 111 p. 22 cm. Includes bibliography. [BV4012.W55] 61-14715
1. Pastoral psychology. 2. Hypnotism — Therapeutic use. I. Title.

WITTKOFSKI, Joseph Nicholas, 253 1912-
The pastoral use of hypnotic technique, by Joseph Wittkofski. With a foreword by T. J. Freeborn, Jr., and an introd. by Austin Pardue. Springfield, Ill., Thomas [1971] xvi, 111 p. 22 cm. Bibliography: p. 107. [BV4012.W55 1971] 74-21535
1. Pastoral psychology. 2. Hypnotism—Therapeutic use. I. Title.

WORKSHOP on Pastoral Problems and Clinical Understanding, Gearhart, Or., 1959.
Pastoral problems and clinical understanding [workshop on mental health for clergymen, sponsored by the Oregon Council of Churches, the Oregon Mental Health Association, and the Oregon State Board of Health] Hotel Gearhart, Oregon, May 4, 5, 6, and 7, 1959. [Gearhart, Or., 1959?] 110 p. 28 cm. Cover title.
I. Title.

Pastoral psychology—Addresses, essays, lectures.

DYNAMIC interpersonalism for 253 *ministry;* essays in honor of Paul E. Johnson. Edited by Orlo Strunk, Jr. Nashville, Abingdon Press [1973] 320 p. 23 cm. Includes bibliographical references. [BV4012.D96] 73-7813 11.95
1. Johnson, Paul Emanuel, 1898- 2. Pastoral psychology—Addresses, essays, lectures. 3. Pastoral theology—Addresses, essays, lectures. I. Johnson, Paul Emanuel, 1898- II. Strunk, Orlo, ed.
Contents omitted. Contents omitted.

HEALING: 253.5082
human and divine; man's search for health and wholeness through science, faith, and prayer. New York, Association Press [1957] 254p. 20cm. (Pastoral psychology series) [BV4012.D617] [BV4012.D617] 258 57-6889 57-6889
1. Pastoral psychology—Addresses, essays, lectures. I. Doniger, Simon, ed.

INSTITUTE of Pastoral 253.5082 Psychology, Fordham University. 1st, 1955.
Personality and sexual problems in pastoral psychology. Edited by William C. Bier. New York, Fordham University Press

[1964] xiii, 256 p. 24 cm. (The Pastoral psychology series, no. 1) Contains "papers...derived from the 1955 and 1957 institutes" sponsored by the Dept. of Psychology, Fordham University. Includes bibliographies. [BV4012.I 48] 62-16224
1. Pastoral psychology — Addresses, essays, lectures. I. Blier, William Christian, 1911- ed. II. Institute of Pastoral Psychology, Fordham University. 2d, 1957. III. Fordham University, New York. Dept. of Psychology. IV. Title. V. Series.

MCKENZIE, John Grant, 1882- 253.5
Nervous disorders and religion : a study of souls in the making / by John G. McKenzie. Westport, Conn. : Greenwood Press, 1981. p. cm. Reprint of the 1951 ed. published by G. Allen and Unwin, London, which was issued as Tate lectures, 1947. [BV4012.M293 1981] 19 79-8719 ISBN 0-313-22192-8 : 18.75
1. Pastoral psychology—Addresses, essays, lectures. 2. Psychotherapy—Addresses, essays, lectures. I. Title. II. Series: Tate lectures ; 1947.

NOUWEN, Henri J. M. 253.5
Intimacy; pastoral psychological essays [by] Henri J. M. Nouwen. Notre Dame, Ind., Fides Publishers [1969] ix, 164 p. 21 cm. Bibliographical footnotes. [BV4012.N63] 79-79241 2.50
1. Pastoral psychology—Addresses, essays, lectures. 2. Pastoral theology—Catholic Church—Addresses, essays, lectures. 3. Intimacy (Psychology)—Addresses, essays, lectures. I. Title.

Pastoral psychology-Bibliography

ANNOTATED bibliography in religion and psychology. New York, Academy of Religion and Mental Health, 1961. xi, 235p.
1. Pastoral psychology-Bibl. 2. Psychology, Religious-Bibl. I. Meissner, William W

Pastoral psychology — Congresses.

LEVY, Jerome, ed. 253.5
A clinical approach to the problems of pastoral care, edited by Jerome Levy [and] Roma K. McNickle. Boulder, Colo., Western Interstate Commission for Higher Education, 1964. vii, 106 p. 28 cm. "Report to two institutes on mental health, Anchorage, Alaska. September 9-10, 1963, and Fairbanks, Alaska, Septemper 12-13, 1963." Sponsored by the Western Interstate Commission for Higher Education. [BV4012.L48] 64-63497
1. Pastoral psychology — Congresses. 2. Psychiatry and religion. I. McNickle, Roma K., joint ed. II. Western Interstate Commission for Higher Education. III. Title.

Pastoral psychology (Judaism)

INSTITUTE on Religion and Psychiatry, Congregation Adath Israel, Boston, 1947. 150
Psychiatry and religion. Edited by Joshua Loth Liebman. Freeport, N.Y., Books for Libraries Press [1972, c1948] xix, 202 p. 23 cm. (Essay index reprint series) [BM652.5.16 1947b] 72-156666 ISBN 0-8369-2658-7
1. Pastoral psychology (Judaism) 2. Psychotherapy. I. Liebman, Joshua Loth, 1907-1948, ed. II. Title.

Pastoral psychology—Study and teaching.

SAINT Elizabeths Hospital, Washington, D. C. Chaplain Services Branch. 253.5
A survey of ten years of clinical pastoral training at Saint Elizabeth's Hospital, by Ernest E. Bruder and Marian L Barb. [Washington] 1956. iv, 98p. tables. 28cm. [BV4012.3.S3] 258 56-62388
1. Pastoral psychology—Study and teaching. I. Bruder, Ernest E. II. Barb, Marian L. III. Title.

Pastoral psychology—Study and teaching—History.

THORNTON, Edward E. 253.5
Professional education for ministry; a history of clinical pastoral education [by] Edward E. Thornton. Nashville, Abingdon Press [1970] 301 p. illus., ports. 24 cm. Bibliography: p. 265-293. [BV4012.T53] 79-97569 7.50
1. Pastoral psychology—Study and teaching—History. I. Title.

Pastoral theology.

*ADAMS, Jay E. 253
Shepherding God's flock / Jay E. Adams. Grand Rapids : Baker Book House, 1976c1975. v,199p. : ill., chart ; 22 cm. Contents.Contents: v.3.Pastoral leadership Includes bibliographical references. [BV 420] ISBN 0-8010-0091-2 pbk. : 3.75.
1. Pastoral theology. 2. Group ministry. 3. Clergy. I. Title.

BARR, Browne. 250
The ministering congregation, by Browne Barr and Mary Eakin. Philadelphia, United Church Press [1972] 127 p. 22 cm. "A Pilgrim Press book." Includes bibliographical references. [BV4011.B367] 72-5587 ISBN 0-8298-0243-6 4.95
1. Pastoral theology. 2. Church work. I. Eakin, Mary (Mulford) 1914- joint author. II. Title.

BARTLETT, Gene E. 253.2
The authentic pastor / Gene E. Bartlett. Valley Forge, PA : Judson Press, c1978. 111 p. ; 22 cm. Includes bibliographical references. [BV4011.B372] 78-2523 ISBN 0-8170-0777-6 pbk. : 3.95
1. Pastoral theology. I. Title.

BARTLETT, Gene E. 253
Postscript to preaching : after forty years, how will I preach today? / Gene E. Bartlett. Valley Forge, PA : Judson Press, c1981. 87 p. ; 22 cm. Includes bibliographical references. [BV4011.B373] 19 80-24394 ISBN 0-8170-0909-4 pbk. : 3.95
1. Pastoral theology. 2. Preaching. I. Title.

BEDELL, Gregory Thurston, bp., 1817-1892.
The pastor. Pastoral theology ... By Rt. Rev. Gregory Thurston Bedell ... Philadelphia [etc.] J. B. Lippincott & co., 1880. 607 p. 19 1/2 cm. 15-22796
I. Title.

BEDELL, Gregory Thurston, bp., 1817-1892.
The pastor. Pastoral theology ... By Rt. Rev. Gregory Thurston Bedell ... Cleveland, W.W. Williams, 1883. 607 p. 19 1/2 cm. 1st edition, Philadelphia, 1880. 15-24169
I. Title.

BEDSOLE, Adolph. 253.2
The pastor in profile. Grand Rapids, Baker Book House, 1960 [c1958] 163p. 21cm. [BV4011.B4] 58-10857
1. Pastoral theology. I. Title.

BLACKWOOD, Andrew Watterson 253
The growing minister, his opportunities and obstacles. Nashville, Abingdon Press [c.1960] 192p. 23cm. (bibl.:184-187; footnotes) 60-9194 3.00
1. Pastoral theology. I. Title.

BLACKWOOD, Andrew Watterson, 1882- 253
The growing minister : his opportunities and obstacles / Andrew W. Blackwood. Grand Rapids : Baker Book House, 1977,c1960. 192p. ; 20cm. Includes index. Bibliography:p.184-187. [BV4011.B55] ISBN 0-8010-0646-5 pbk. : 3.45
1. Pastoral theology. I. Title.
L.C. card no. for 1960 Abingdon ed.:60-9194.

BLACKWOOD, Andrew Watterson, 1882- 253
The growing minister, his opportunities and obstacles. New York, Abingdon Press [1960] 192p. 23cm. Includes bibliography. [BV4011.B55] 60-9194
1. Pastoral theology. I. Title.

BOVET, Theodore, 1900- 253.5
The road to salvation; a handbook on the Christian care of persons, by Theodor Bovet. Translated by F. A. Baker. [1st ed. in the U. S. A.] Garden City, N. Y., Doubleday, 1964. xiv, 249 p. 22 cm. Translation of Lebendige Seelsorge. Bibliography: p. 235-242. [BV4011.B613 1964a] 64-20575
1. Pastoral theology. I. Title.

BRISTER, C. W. 253.5
Take care / C. W. Brister. Nashville : Broadman Press, 1979, c1978. 164 p. ; 20 cm. Continues People who care. Includes bibliographical references. [BV4011.B685] 76-51022 ISBN 0-8054-5578-7 pbk. : 2.95
1. Pastoral theology. 2. Church work. I. Title.

BROWN, Jeff D 253
A handbook for the preacher at work. Grand Rapids, Baker Book House, 1958. 90p. 21cm. [Minister's handbook series] [BV4011.B7] 59-20730
1. Pastoral theology. I. Title. II. Title: The Preacher at work.

BYERS, Laurence P. 253
Christians in crossfire; the face of my parish, by Laurence P. Byers. Philadelphia, Westminster Press [1967] 151 p. 21 cm. Bibliography: p. 149-151. [BV4011.B9] 67-18726
1. Pastoral theology. I. Title.

CALIAN, Carnegie Samuel. 253
Today's pastor in tomorrow's world / Carnegie Samuel Calian. New York : Hawthorn Books, c1977. xii, 153 p. ; 22 cm. Includes index. Bibliography: p. 145-148. [BV4011.C24 1977] 76-15419 ISBN 0-8015-7761-6 : 6.95
1. Pastoral theology. I. Title.

CAMPBELL, Alastair V. 253
Rediscovering pastoral care / by Alastair V. Campbell. Philadelphia : Westminster Press, c1981. 131 p. ; 22 cm. Includes bibliographical references and index. [BV4011.C26] 19 81-7547 ISBN 0-664-24381-9 pbk. : 8.95
1. Pastoral theology. I. Title.

CEVETELLO, Joseph F X ed.
All things to all men. New York, Joseph F. Wagner, inc. [1965] ix, 438 p. 22 cm. (Pastoral Theology Today) 68-103120
1. Pastoral theology. I. Title.

CLARK, Wayne C 253.2
The minister looks at himself ... Philadelphia, Judson Press [1957] 135p. 21cm. [BV4010.C55] 57-7628
1. Pastoral theology. I. Title.

CLIFFORD, Paul Rowntree. 253
The pastoral calling. Great Neck, N. Y., Channel Press [1961] 144p. 21cm. Includes bibliography. [BV4011.C55 1961] 61-7570
1. Pastoral theology. I. Title.

COLTON, Clarence Eugene, 1914- 250
The minister's mission; a survey of ministerial responsibilities and relationships. [Rev. ed.] Grand Rapids, Zondervan Pub. House [1961, c.1951] 223p. Bibl. 61-4320 3.50
1. Pastoral theology. I. Title.

CURRY, William Melville. 248
The pastor's corner; an intimate discussion of moral and spiritual problems, by William Melville Curry ... with introduction by Charles R. Erdman ... New York, Chicago [etc.] Fleming H. Revell company [c1927] 208 p. 20 cm. [BV4501.C82] 27-5048
I. Title.

DICK, Russell Leslie, 1906-
Principles and practices of pastoral care. Englewood Cliffs, Prentice-Hall [c1963] 143 p. 21 cm. 68-19525
I. Title.

DITTES, James E. 250
The church in the way, by James E. Dittes. New York, Scribner [1967] xix, 358 p. 24 cm. [BV4011.D54] 67-24041
1. Pastoral theology. I. Title.

DOTY, Harry L., 1911- 253'.2
Letters to Ron / by Harry L. Doty. Independence, Mo. : Herald Pub. House, c1976. 98 p. ; 21 cm. [BV4011.D67] 74-28091 ISBN 0-8309-0142-6 : 5.00
1. Doty, Harry L., 1911- 2. Pastoral theology. I. Title.

FACKRE, Gabriel J. 253
The purpose and work of the ministry; a mission pastor's point of view. Philadelphia, Christian Education Press [c.1959] xi, 141p. 21cm. (bibl. footnotes) 59-14166 2.50
1. Pastoral theology. I. Title.

FENHAGEN, James C. 253
Ministry and solitude : the ministry of the laity and the clergy in church and society / James C. Fenhagen. New York : Seabury Press, 1981. p. cm. Includes bibliographical references. [BV4011.F43] 19 81-14398 ISBN 0-8164-0498-4 : 9.95
1. Pastoral theology. I. Title.

FENHAGEN, James C. 253'.2
Mutual ministry : new vitality in the local church / James C. Fenhagen. New York : Seabury Press, 1977. p. cm. "A Crossroad book." [BV4011.F45] 76-49997 ISBN 0-8164-0332-5 : 6.95
1. Pastoral theology. 2. Church. I. Title.

FORSYTH, Nathaniel Frederick, ed. 253
The minister and Christian nurture. New York, Abingdon Press [1957] 250p. 23cm. [BV4360.F57] 57-6755
1. Pastoral theology. 2. Religious education. I. Title.

FRAY, Harold R. 253'.2
The pain and joy of ministry [by] Harold R. Fray, Jr. Philadelphia, Pilgrim Press [1972] 127 p. 22 cm. Includes bibliographical references. [BV4011.F7] 72-182234 ISBN 0-8298-0221-5 4.95
1. Pastoral theology. 2. Christianity—20th century. I. Title.

GLASSE, James D. 253
Putting it together in the parish [by] James D. Glasse. Nashville, Abingdon Press [1972] 159 p. illus. 23 cm. (Currie lectures, 1970) [BV4011.G55] 71-185548 ISBN 0-687-34932-X 3.95
1. Pastoral theology. I. Title. II. Series.

GREY, J. D., 1906- 253'.2
Epitaphs for eager preachers [by] J. D. Grey. Nashville, Broadman Press [1972] 126 p. 21 cm. [BV4011.G73] 72-79167 ISBN 0-8054-7904-X
1. Pastoral theology. I. Title.

GRIFFITH, Earle Gordon. 253
The pastor as God's minister / Earle G. Griffith ; foreword by Charles H. Stevens. Schaumburg, Ill. : Regular Baptist Press, [1977] p. cm. [BV4011.G74] 76-50694 ISBN 0-87227-054-8 : 7.95
1. Pastoral theology. I. Title.

GUFFIN, Gilbert Lee 250
Pastor and church; a manual for pastoral leadership.4th ed. Birmingham, Ala., Banner Pr. [1963, c.1955] xii, 160p. 22cm. Bibl. 63-21959 2.65 pap.,
1. Pastoral theology. I. Title.

HEWITT, Arthur Wentworth, 1883- 258
Steeples among the hills, by Arthur Wentworth Hewitt ... New York, Cincinnati, The Abingdon press [c1926] 260 p. 20 cm. [BV4320.H4] 26-6521
I. Title.

HILTNER, Seward, 1909- 253
Ferment in the ministry. Nashville, Abingdon Press [1969] 222 p. 23 cm. [BV4011.H48] 69-18441 4.95
1. Pastoral theology. I. Title.

HILTNER, Seward, 1909- 250
Preface to pastoral theology. New York, Abingdon Press [1958] 240p. 24cm. (The Ayer lectures, 1954) Includes bibliography. [BV4011.H5] 58-5398
1. Pastoral theology. 2. Spencer, Ichabod, 1798-1854. A pastor's sketches. I. Title.

HOLMES, Urban Tigner, 1930- 250
The future shape of ministry; a theological projection [by] Urban T. Holmes III. New York, Seabury Press [1971] vi, 310 p. 21 cm. Includes bibliographical references. [BV4011.H58] 72-150697 4.50
1. Pastoral theology. I. Title.

HOLMES, Urban Tigner, 1930- 253
Ministry and imagination / Urban T.

Holmes III. New York : Seabury Press, c1976. 279 p. ; 24 cm. "A Crossroad book." Includes bibliographical references. [BV4011.H583] 76-1851 ISBN 0-8164-0292-2 : 10.95
1. Pastoral theology. 2. Experience (Religion) I. Title.

HOPKIN, Charles Edward, 1900- 250
The watchman. New York, Crowell [1960] 117p. 21cm. [BV4011.H6] 60-8253
1. Pastoral theology. 2. Apologetics—20th cent. I. Title.

HUDNUT, Robert K. 253
Surprised by God; what it means to be a minister in middle-class America today, by Robert K. Hudnut. New York, Association Press [1967] 127 p. 20 cm. [BV4011.H75] 67-21144
1. Pastoral theology. I. Title.

JACKSON, Gordon E. 253
Pastoral care and process theology / Gordon E. Jackson. Washington, D.C. : University Press of America, c1981. p. cm. [BV4011.J29] 19 81-40159 ISBN 0-8191-1710-2 : 22.00 ISBN 0-8191-1711-0 (pbk.) : 12.00
1. Pastoral theology. 2. Process theology. I. Title.

JACOBSEN, David C. 253
The positive use of the minister's role, by David C. Jacobsen. Philadelphia, Westminster [1967] 111, [1] p. 21cm. Bibl. [BV4011.J3] 67-15870 3.25
1. Pastoral theology. 2. Clergy. I. Title.

JOHNSON, Orien. 253
Recovery of ministry: a guide for the laity. Valley Forge [Pa.] Judson Press [1972] 62 p. 23 cm. Includes bibliographical references. [BV4011.J64] 72-433 ISBN 0-8170-0566-8 1.50
1. Pastoral theology. 2. Christian life—1960- I. Title.

JONES, George Curtis, 1911- 253
The naked shepherd : a pastor shares his private feelings about living, working, and growing together in the church / G. Curtis Jones. [Waco, Tex.] : Word Books, c1979. 167 p. ; 22 cm. [BV4011.J67] 79-63935 ISBN 0-8499-2870-2 pbk. : 5.95
1. Pastoral theology. I. Title.

KEAN, Charles Duell, 1910- 253
Christian faith and pastoral care. Greenwich, Conn., Seabury Press [c.]1961. 139p. Bibl. 61-5573 3.75
1. Pastoral theology. I. Title.

KEMP, Charles F. 253
The pastor and community resources. St. Louis, Bethany Press [c.1960] 96p. 'Published for the Department of Social Welfare, National Council of the Churches of Christ in the U.S.A.' 18cm. 59-10370 1.50, pap., spiral binding
1. Pastoral theology 2. Church and social problems. I. Title.

KENNEDY, Gerald Hamilton, Bp., 1907- 250
The seven worlds of the minister [by] Gerald Kennedy. [1st ed.] New York, Harper & Row [1968] xiii, 173 p. 21 cm. [BV4011.K44] 68-17580
1. Pastoral theology. I. Title.

KENNEDY, James William, 1905- 253
Minister's shop-talk. New York, Harper [c.1965] 211p. 22cm. Bibl. [BV4011.K43] 65-20454 3.95 bds.,
1. Pastoral theology. I. Title.

KENNEDY, James William, 1905- 253
Minister's shop-talk, by James W. Kennedy. [1st ed.] New York, Harper & Row [1965] 211 p. 22 cm. Bibliographical references included in "Notes" (p. [199]-206) [BV4011.K43] 65-20454
1. Pastoral theology. I. Title.

KENNEDY, John, 1897-
The minister's vocation. Edinburgh, Saint Andrew Press [1963] 139 p. (The McNeill-Fraser lectures) 65-3499
1. Pastoral theology. I. Title. II. Series.

KENT, Homer Austin, 1898- 250
The pastor and his work, by Homer A. Kent, Sr. Chicago, Moody Press [1963] 301 p. illus. 24 cm. Includes bibliographical references. [BV4011.K45] 63-14563
1. Pastoral theology. I. Title.

KENT, Homer Austin, 1926- 250
The pastor and his work. Chicago, Moody [c.1963] 301p. illus. 24cm. Bibl. 63-14563 4.50
1. Pastoral theology. I. Title.

KOLLER, Charles W., 1896- 253
Pointers for pastors / Charles W. Koller. Dallas : Crescendo Book Publications, [1974] 144 p. ; 20 cm. [BV4011.K63] 74-76738 ISBN 0-89038-016-3 : 2.95 2.95
1. Pastoral theology. I. Title.

KOSTYU, Frank A. 254'.6
Ways to spark your church program, by Frank A. Kostyu. Nashville, Abingdon Press [1974] 141 p. illus. 19 cm. [BV4011.K67] 73-12236 ISBN 0-687-44236-2 2.95 (pbk.)
1. Pastoral theology. I. Title.

KUNG, Hans, 1928- 262'.14
Why priests? A proposal for a new church ministry. Translated by Robert C. Collins. Garden City, N.Y., Doubleday, 1972. 118 p. 22 cm. Translation of Wozu Priester? (Eine Hilfe) [BV4011.K7913] 70-186656 5.95
1. Pastoral theology. I. Title.

LEACH, William Herman, 1888- 250
Handbook of church management. Englewood Cliffs, N. J., Prentice-Hall, 1958. 504 p. illus. 22 cm. [BV4011.L4] 58-12327
1. Pastoral theology. 2. Church work. I. Title: Church management.

LEE, Mark W. 253
The minister and his ministry. Grand Rapids, Mich., Zondervan Pub. House [c.1960] 280p. Includes bibliography. illus. 23cm. 60-1374 3.95
1. Pastoral theology. I. Title.

LINGER, O. Afton. 253
Church management guidelines [by] O. Afton Linger. Hendersonville, N.C., Fruitland Baptist Bible Institute [1972] v, 95, [7] p. illus. 29 cm. Bibliography: p. [100] [BV4011.L53] 72-87864
1. Pastoral theology. I. Title.

MCCABE, Joseph E., 1912- 253
How to find time for better preaching and better pastoring, by Joseph E. McCabe. Philadelphia, Westminster Press [1973] 112 p. 20 cm. [BV4011.M23] 73-10264 ISBN 0-664-20983-1 4.50
1. Pastoral theology. 2. Preaching. I. Title.

MCCUTCHEON, James N., 1929- 253'.2
The pastoral ministry / James N. McCutcheon. Nashville : Abingdon, c1978. 144 p. ; 23 cm. Includes bibliographical references. [BV4011.M24] 78-7253 ISBN 0-687-30088-6 : 6.95
1. Pastoral theology. 2. Clergy—Office. I. Title.

MCELVANEY, William K., 1928- 253
The people of God in ministry / William K. McElvaney. Nashville : Abingdon, c1981. 175 p. ; 21 cm. Includes bibliographical references. [BV4011.M25] 19 80-26077 ISBN 0-687-30660-4 pbk. : 6.95
1. McElvaney, William K., 1928- 2. Pastoral theology. 3. Laity. I. Title.

MCINTOSH, Ian F. 253.5
Pastoral care and pastoral theology, by Ian F. McIntosh. Philadelphia, Westminster Press [1972] 160 p. 21 cm. Includes bibliographical references. [BV4011.M26] 71-169599 ISBN 0-664-20924-6 5.50
1. Pastoral theology. 2. Pastoral counseling. I. Title.

MCLANE, Edwin D. 250
The 7:05 and the church alive; dynamic and successful programs in today's churches. Englewood Cliffs, N.J., Prentice [c.1963] xiv, 207p. 22cm. Bibl. 63-19619 4.95
1. Pastoral theology. I. Title.

MATTHEWS, DeWitt. 253
Capers of the clergy : the human side of the ministry / DeWitt Matthews. Grand Rapids : Baker Book House, c1976. 140 p. ; 22 cm. [BV4011.M39] 76-378854 ISBN 0-8010-5990-9 : 4.95
1. Pastoral theology. I. Title.

MICKEY, Paul A., 1937- 253
Pastoral assertiveness : a new model for pastoral care / Paul Mickey and Gary Gamble, with Paula Gilbert. Nashville : Abingdon, [1978] p. cm. [BV4011.M483] 78-9020 ISBN 0-687-30138-6 : 7.95
1. Pastoral theology. I. Gamble, Gary, 1943- joint author. II. Gilbert, Paula, 1952- joint author. III. Title.

MILLER, Paul M. 253
Leading the family of God / Paul M. Miller ; introduction by Lyle E. Schaller. Scottdale, Pa. : Herald Press, 1981. p. cm. Includes bibliographical references. [BV4011.M496] 19 81-2267 ISBN 0-8361-1950-9 (pbk.) : 7.95
1. Pastoral theology. I. Title.

MONDALE, Robert Lester, 1904- 250
Preachers in purgatory, with reference to accounts of more than a hundred ministers reporting on crisis situations, by Lester Mondale. Boston, Beacon Press [1966] xii, 243 p. 22 cm. Bibliographical references included in "Notes" (p. 240-243) [BV4011.M6] 66-15071
1. Pastoral theology. I. Title.

MORGAN, George Campbell, 1863-1945. 253
The ministry of the Word. Grand Rapids, Baker Book House [1970] 252 p. 20 cm. (Notable books on preaching) Reprint of the 1919 ed. with a new introd. by Ralph G. Turnbull. [BV4010.M6 1970] 73-129056 ISBN 8-01-058589- 2.95
1. Pastoral theology. I. Title.

MULLEN, Thomas James, 1934- 250
The renewal of the ministry. Introd. by D. Elton Trueblood. Nashville, Abingdon [c.1963] 143p. 21cm. 63-14596 3.00
1. Pastoral theology. I. Title.

MULLEN, Thomas James, 1934- 250
The renewal of the ministry. With an introd. by D. Elton Trueblood. New York, Abingdon Press [1963] 143 p. 21 cm. [BV4011.M8] 63-14596
1. Pastoral theology. I. Title.

MURPHEY, Cecil B. 253
When in doubt, hug 'em! : How to develop a caring church / Cecil B. Murphey. Atlanta : John Knox Press, c1978. 142 p. ; 21 cm. [BV4011.M84] 77-15751 ISBN 0-8042-1890-0 : 5.95
1. Pastoral theology. I. Title.

NOUWEN, Henri J. M. 250
Creative ministry [by] Henri J. M. Nouwen. [1st ed.] Garden City, N.Y., Doubleday, 1971. xxi, 119 p. 22 cm. [BV4011.N68] 73-139050 4.95
1. Pastoral theology. I. Title.

NOUWEN, Henri J.M. 250
Creative ministry / Henri J.M. Nouwen. Garden City, N.Y. : Doubleday, 1978, c1971. 123p. ; 18 cm. (Image Books) [BV4011.N68] ISBN 0-385-12616-6 pbk. : 2.45
1. Pastoral theology. I. Title.
L.C. card no. for 1971 Doubleday ed.: 73-139050.

NOUWEN, Henri J. M. 248.8'9
The way of the heart : desert spirituality and contemporary ministry / Henri J.M. Nouwen. New York : Seabury Press, 1981. 96 p. ; 21 cm. Includes bibliographical references. [BV4011.N682] 19 80-21790 ISBN 0-8164-0479-8 : 7.95
1. Pastoral theology. 2. Clergy—Office. 3. Christian life—1960- 4. Apophthegmata Patrum. 5. Christian literature, Early—Collected works. I. Title.

NOUWEN, Henri J. M. 253
The wounded healer; ministry in contemporary society [by] Henri J. M. Nouwen. Illus. by Roel de Jong. [1st ed.] Garden City, N.Y., Doubleday, 1972. xiv, 104 p. illus. 22 cm. [BV4011.N683] 72-186312 ISBN 0-385-02856-3 5.95
1. Pastoral theology. I. Title.

NOUWEN, Henri J.M. 253
The wounded healer : ministry in contemporary society / Henri J.M Nouwen. Garden City N.Y. : Image Books, 1979, c1972. xvi, 100p. ; 18 cm. [BV4011.N683] ISBN 0-385-14803-8 pbk. : 1.95
1. Pastoral theology. I. Title.
L.C. card no. for 1972 Doubleday ed.:72-186312.

NOYCE, Gaylord B. 253.5
The art of pastoral conversation / Gaylord Noyce. Atlanta : J. Knox Press, 1982, c1981. 140 p. ; 20 cm. Includes bibliographical references. [BV4013.N69 1982] 19 81-82350 ISBN 0-8042-1131-0 (pbk.) : 7.95
1. Pastoral theology. 2. Communication (Theology) 3. Conversation. I. Title.

OATES, Wayne Edward, 1917- 253
The Christian pastor. Rev. and enl. ed. Philadelphia, Westminster [c.1961, 1964] xii, 258p. 21cm. Bibl. 63-18553 5.00
1. Pastoral theology. 2. Pastoral psychology. I. Title.

OATES, Wayne Edward, 1917- 253
The Christian pastor. Rev. and enl. ed. Philadelphia, Westminster Press [1964] xii, 258 p. 21 cm. Bibliography: p. 247-253. [BV4011.O2] 63-18553
1. Pastoral theology. 2. Pastoral psychology. I. Title.

OATES, Wayne Edward, 1917- 253
The Christian pastor / by Wayne E. Oates. 3rd ed., rev. Philadelphia : Westminster Press, c1982. 298 p. ; 21 cm. Includes index. Bibliography: p. 285-291. [BV4011.O2 1982] 19 82-4933 ISBN 0-664-24372-X pbk. : 6.95
1. Pastoral theology. 2. Pastoral psychology. I. Title.

OATES, Wayne Edward, 1917- 253.5
Pastoral care and counseling in grief and separation / Wayne E. Oates. Philadelphia : Fortress Press, c1976. ix, 86 p. ; 22 cm. (Creative pastoral care and counseling series) Bibliography: p. 84-86. [BV4011.O25] 75-13048 ISBN 0-8006-0554-3 pbk. : 2.95
1. Pastoral theology. 2. Pastoral counseling. 3. Bereavement. I. Title.

PATTISON, E. Mansell, 1933- 253
Pastor and parish : a systems approach / E. Mansell Pattison. Philadelphia : Fortress Press, c1977. viii, 88 p. ; 22 cm. (Creative pastoral care and counseling series) Bibliography: p. 88. [BV4011.P35] 76-62619 ISBN 0-8006-0559-4 pbk. : 2.95
1. Pastoral theology. 2. System theory. 3. Pastoral psychology. I. Title.

PETERSON, Eugene H., 1932- 253
Five smooth stones for pastoral work / Eugene H. Peterson. Atlanta, : J. Knox Press, c1980. 201 p. ; 21 cm. Includes bibliographical references. [BV4011.P43] 79-87751 ISBN 0-8042-1103-5 : 10.00
1. Bible. O.T. Five Scrolls—Use. 2. Bible. O.T. Five Scrolls—Criticism, interpreation, etc. 3. Pastoral theology. I. Title.

PINSON, William M. 253
The local church in ministry [by] William M. Pinson, Jr. Nashville, Broadman Press [1973] 145 p. 22 cm. Bibliography: p. 132-138. [BV4011.P5] 73-75629 ISBN 0-8054-6304-6
1. Pastoral theology. I. Title.

PRATER, Arnold. 253
Seven keys to a more fruitful ministry. Foreword by Eugene M. Frank. Grand Rapids, Zondervan Pub. House [1960] 120p. 21cm. [BV4011.6.P7] 60-4356
1. Pastoral theology. I. Title.

PRUYSER, Paul W. 253
The minister as diagnostician : personal problems in pastoral perspective / Paul W. Pruyser. Philadelphia : Westminster Press, c1976. p. cm. Includes bibliographical references and index. [BV4011.P7] 76-8922 ISBN 0-664-24123-9 pbk. : 4.95
1. Pastoral theology. 2. Pastoral psychology. 3. Clergy—Office. I. Title.

RICHARDS, Lawrence O. 253
A theology of personal ministry : spiritual giftedness in the local church / Lawrence O. Richards and Gib Martin. Grand Rapids, Mich. : Zondervan Pub. House, 1981. 332 p. ; 24 cm. Includes indexes. [BV4011.R53] 19 81-2193 ISBN 0-310-31970-6 : 15.95
1. Pastoral theology. 2. People of God. 3. Priesthood, Universal. I. Martin, Gilbert R. II. Title. III. Title: Spiritual giftedness in the local church.

RILEY, William Bell, 1861- 1947. 250
Pastoral problems. [Westwood, N. J.] F. H. Revell Co. [1959] 192p. 21cm. (Revell's preaching and pastoral aid series) [BV4010.R5 1959] 59-5503
1. Pastoral theology. I. Title.

RODENMAYER, Robert N 250
We have this ministry. [1st ed.] New York, Harper [1959] 126p. 20cm. (The Kellogg lectures at the Episcopal Theological School, Cambridge, Massachusetts, 1958) Bibliographical references included in 'Notes' (p. 125-126) [BV4011.R6] 59-5548
1. Pastoral theology. I. Title. II. Series: The Kellogg lectures. 1958

ROGERS, Clement Francis, 1866-
An introduction to the study of pastoral theology, by the Rev. Clement F. Rogers... Oxford, The Clarendon press, 1912. 291 p. 22 1/2 cm. A 19
I. Title.

SCHALLER, Lyle E. 254
The pastor and the people; building a new partnership for effective ministry [by] Lyle E. Schaller. Nashville, Abingdon Press [1973] 176 p. 20 cm. Includes bibliographical references. [BV4011.S33] 72-8567 ISBN 0-687-30136-X pap. 2.45
1. Pastoral theology. 2. Theology, Practical. I. Title.

SCHALLER, Lyle E. 254
Survival tactics in the parish / Lyle E. Schaller. Nashville : Abingdon, c1977. 208 p. ; 21 cm. [BV4011.S34] 76-54751 ISBN 0-687-40757-5 pbk. : 4.95
1. Pastoral theology. 2. Parishes. I. Title.

SCHILLEBEECKX, Edward Cornelis Florentius Alfons, 1914- 253
Ministry, leadership in the community of Jesus Christ / Edward Schillebeeckx ; [translated by John Bowden from the Dutch]. New York : Crossroad, 1981. ix, 165 p. ; 24 cm. Translation of Kerkelijk ambt. Includes bibliographical references. [BV4011.S34713] 19 80-28402 12.95
1. Pastoral theology. I. [Kerkelijk ambt.] English II. Title.

SCHUETZE, Armin W. 253
The shepherd under Christ : a textbook for pastoral theology / Armin W. Schuetze, Irwin J. Habeck. Milwaukee : Northwestern Pub. House, 1974. xvi, 389 p. : forms ; 24 cm. Includes bibliographical references. [BV4011.S357] 74-81794 10.00
1. Pastoral theology. I. Habeck, Irwin J., joint author. II. Title.

SHANNON, Harper. 250
Trumpets in the morning. Nashville, Tenn., Broadman Press [1969] 156 p. 21 cm. (Broadman books) [BV4011.S46] 76-93912 3.50
1. Pastoral theology. I. Title.

SHIPMAN, Raymond M 253
We ordinary preachers, by one of them. [1st ed.] New York, Vantage Press [1957] 255p. 21cm. [BV4011.S48] 57-7816
1. Pastoral theology. I. Title.

SHIPMAN, Raymond M 253
We ordinary prechers, by one of them. [1st ed.] New York, Vantage Press [1957] 255 p. 21 cm. [BV4011.S48] 57-7816
1. Pastoral theology. I. Title.

SLUSSER, Gerald H. 230
The local church in transition: theology, education, and ministry. Philadelphia, Westminster [c.1964] 204p. 21cm. Bibl. 64-16351 4.75
1. Pastoral theology. I. Title.

SLUSSER, Gerald H 230
The local church in transition: theology, education, and ministry, by Gerald H. Slusser. Philadelphia, Westminster Press [1964] 204 p. 21 cm. Bibliographical references included in "Notes" (p. [199]-204) [BV4011.S57] 64-16351
1. Pastoral theology. I. Title.

SOUTHARD, Samuel. 253'.2
Comprehensive pastoral care / by Samuel Southard. Valley Forge, Pa. : Judson Press, [1975] p. cm. Includes bibliographical references. [BV4011.S59] 74-22518 ISBN 0-8170-0655-9 pbk. : 3.50 with cassette : 9.95
1. Pastoral theology. 2. Laity. 3. Church management. 4. Christian leadership. I. Title.

SPARKS, James Allen, 1933- 253'.2
Potshots at the preacher / James Allen Sparks. Nashville : Abingdon, c1977. 128 p. ; 19 cm. Bibliography: p. 126-128. [BV4011.S6] 76-30753 ISBN 0-687-33240-0 pbk. : 4.95
1. Pastoral theology. 2. Clergy—Psychology. 3. Church controversies. I. Title.

STAMM, Frederick Keller, 1883- 251
So you want to preach. New York, Abingdon Press [1958] 109 p. 20 cm. [BV4011.S8] 58-8124
1. Pastoral theology. 2. Preaching. I. Title.

STONE, Sam E. 253
The Christian minister : a practical approach to the preaching ministry / by Sam E. Stone. Cincinnati, Ohio : Standard Pub., c1980. p. cm. Includes index. Bibliography: p. [BV4011.S866] 79-63601 ISBN 0-87239-348-8 : 6.95
1. Pastoral theology. I. Title.

STOTT, John R. W. 253
One people [by] John R. W. Stott. Downers Grove, Ill., Inter-Varsity Press [1971] 93, [1] p. 20 cm. "Revision and expansion of the Pastoral theology lectures delivered in Durham University in February 1968." Bibliography: p. 93-[94] [BV4011.S87] 72-127931 ISBN 0-87784-694-4
1. Pastoral theology. I. Title.

SUGDEN, Howard F. 253
When pastors wonder how [by] Howard F. Sugden & Warren W. Wiersbe. Chicago, Moody Press [1973] 160 p. 22 cm. [BV4011.S93] 73-179180 ISBN 0-8024-9431-5 3.95
1. Pastoral theology. I. Wiersbe, Warren W., joint author. II. Title.

THIESSEN, John Caldwell 253
Pastoring the smaller church. Grand Rapids, Mich., Zondervan [c.1962] 168p. 23cm. 62-51429 2.95
1. Pastoral theology. I. Title.

THIESSEN, John Caldwell. 253
Pastoring the smaller church. Grand Rapids, Zondervan Pub. House [1962] 168 p. 23 cm. [BV4011.T43] 62-51429
1. Pastoral theology. I. Title.

THOMPSON, Murray Stewart, 1923- 253.5
Grace and forgiveness in ministry / Murray Stewart Thompson. Nashville : Abingdon, c1981. 174 p. ; 20 cm. Includes bibliographical references. [BV4011.T44] 19 80-23613 ISBN 0-687-15680-7 pbk. : 6.95
1. Thompson, Murray Stewart, 1923- 2. Pastoral theology. 3. Pastoral counseling. I. Title.

THURNEYSEN, Eduard, 1888- 253.5
A theology of pastoral care. Basic tr. by Jack A. Worthington, Thomas Wieser asst. by a panel of advisers. Richmond, John Knox [c.1962] 343p. 62-8614 5.50
1. Pastoral theology. I. Title.

TURNBULL, Ralph G. 248.8
A minister's obstacles. Westwood, N.J., Revell [1965, c.1964] 192p. 21cm. [BV4010.T75] 64-20189 2.95 bds.,
1. Pastoral theology. I. Title.

TURNBULL, Ralph G 253
A minister's obstacles. [Westwood, N. J.] F. H. Revell Co. [1959] 159 p. 21 cm. (Revell's preaching and pastoral aid series) [BV4010.T75] 59-5504
1. Pastoral theology. I. Title.

ULEYN, Arnold. 250'.1'9
Is it I, Lord? Pastoral psychology and the recognition of guilt. Translated by Mary Ilford. [1st ed.] New York, Holt, Rinehart and Winston [1969] xiv, 240 p. 22 cm. Translation of Actualite de la fonction prophetique. Includes bibliographical references. [BV4011.U413] 69-10763 5.95
1. Pastoral theology. I. Title.

WAGNER, Charles U. 253
The pastor, his life and work / Charles U. Wagner. Schaumburg, Ill. : Regular Baptist Press, c1976. xiii, 274 p. ; 24 cm. Includes bibliographical references and index. [BV4011.W27] 76-22402 ISBN 0-87227-001-7 : 7.95
1. Pastoral theology. I. Title.

WEATHERLY, Owen Milton 253
Help your minister to do his best. Illus. by Russell Keeter. Valley Forge [Pa.] Judson [c.1965] 156p. illus. 21cm. [BV4015.W4] 65-22000 3.95
1. Pastoral theology. I. Title.

WEED, Michael R., comp. 253
The minister and his work [compiled by] Michael R. Weed. Austin, Tex., Sweet Pub. Co. [1970] 192 p. 21 cm. "The essays contained in this volume formerly appeared in a column in the Christian chronicle entitled 'For the minister.'" Includes bibliographies. [BV4011.W36] 72-134689 ISBN 0-8344-0063-4
1. Pastoral theology. 2. Clergy—Office. I. Christian chronicle. II. Title.

WHITE, Reginald E. O. 253
A guide to pastoral care : a practical primer of pastoral theology / [by] R. E. O. White. London : Pickering and Inglis, 1976. ix, 325 p. ; 21 cm. Bibliography: p. 321-324. [BV4011.W45] 77-363285 ISBN 0-7208-0377-2 : £7.50
1. Pastoral theology. I. Title.

WIMBERLY, Edward P., 1943- 253
Pastoral care in the Black church / Edward P. Wimberly. Nashville : Abingdon, c1979. 127 p. : 20 cm. Includes bibliographical references. [BV4011.W49] 78-22011 ISBN 0-687-30289-7 pbk. : 3.95
1. Pastoral theology. 2. Afro-Americans—Religion. I. Title.

WISE, Carroll Alonzo, 1903- 230
The meaning of pastoral care. New York, Harper [c.1966] xi,144p. 21cm. Bibl. [BV4011.W55] 66-15048 3.50 bds.,
1. Pastoral theology. I. Title.

WISE, Carroll Alonzo, 1903- 230
The meaning of pastoral care, by Carroll A. Wise. [1st ed.] New York, Harper & Row [1966] xi, 144 p. 21 cm. Bibliographical references included in "Notes" (p. 137-142) [BV4011.W55] 66-15048
1. Pastoral theology. I. Title.

WYNN, John Charles. *253.5 258
Pastoral ministry to families. Philadelphia, Westminster Press [1957] 214 p. 21 cm. Includes bibliography. [BV4320.W9] 57-6553
1. Pastoral theology. 2. Family — Religious life. I. Title.

Pastoral theology—Addresses, essays, lectures.

BARR, Browne 250.81
Parish back talk. Nashville, Abingdon [c.1964] 127p. 20cm. (Lyman Beecher lects., 1963) Bibl. 64-16145 2.50
1. Pastoral theology—Addresses, essays, lectures. I. Title. II. Series: Lyman Beecher lectures on preaching, Yale University, 1963

BARR, Browne. 250.81
Parish back talk. New York, Abingdon Press [1964] 127 p. 20 cm. (Lyman Beecher lectures, 1963) Bibliographical footnotes. [BV4011.B37] 64-16145
1. Pastoral theology — Addresses, essays, lectures. I. Title. II. Series: Lyman Beecher lectures on preaching. Yale University, 1963

BROWNING, Don S. 253
The moral context of pastoral care / Don S. Browning. Philadelphia : Westminster Press, c1976. p. cm. Includes bibliographical references. [BV4011.5.B76] 76-5858 ISBN 0-664-20742-1
1. Pastoral theology—Addresses, essays, lectures. 2. Pastoral counseling—Addresses, essays, lectures. I. Title.

CREATING an intentional ministry / edited by John E. Biersdorf. Nashville : Abingdon, c1976. 237 p. ; 22 cm. Includes bibliographical references and index. [BV4011.C68] 75-40463 ISBN 0-687-09810-6 pbk. : 5.75 253'.2
1. Pastoral theology—Addresses, essays, lectures. I. Biersdorf, John E., 1930-

EUCHARIST & ministry / 262'.1
edited by Paul C. Empie and T. Austin Murphy. Minneapolis : Augsburg Pub. House, 1979. 326 p. ; 20 cm. (Lutherans and Catholics in dialogue ; 4) Includes bibliographical references. [BV4011.E77] 80-106920 ISBN 0-8066-1781-0 pbk. : 4.95
1. Lutheran Church—Relations—Catholic Church—Addresses, essays, lectures. 2. Catholic Church—Relations—Lutheran Church—Addresses, essays, lectures. 3. Pastoral theology—Addresses, essays, lectures. 4. Lord's Supper—Addresses, essays, lectures. I. Empie, Paul C. II. Murphy, Thomas Austin, 1911- III. Title. IV. Series.

GROWTH in ministry / 253
edited by Thomas E. Kadel. Philadelphia : Fortress Press, c1980. ix, 165 p. ; 22 cm. & study guide. Includes bibliographical references. [BV4011.G77] 19 79-8902 ISBN 0-8006-1383-X : 5.95
1. Pastoral theology—Addresses, essays, lectures. 2. Pastoral theology—Lutheran Church—Addresses, essays, lectures. I. Kadel, Thomas E.

HOLMES, Urban Tigner, 1930- 253
The priest in community : exploring the roots of ministry / Urban T. Holmes III. New York : Seabury Press, 1978. p. cm. "A Crossroad book." [BV4011.H584] 78-17645 ISBN 0-8164-0400-3 : 8.95
1. Pastoral theology—Addresses, essays, lectures. 2. Priests—Addresses, essays, lectures. I. Title.

NAPIER, Bunyan Davie. 222'.53'077
Word of God, word of earth / Davie Napier. Philadelphia : United Church Press, c1976. 105 p. ; 22 cm. "A Pilgrim Press book." Includes the author's edited translation of selected passages from the Old Testament book of 1st Kings. Includes bibliographical references. [BS580.E4N36] 75-45312 ISBN 0-8298-0304-1 : 4.95 ISBN 0-8298-0307-6 pbk. : 3.25
1. Elijah, the prophet—Addresses, essays, lectures. 2. Bible. O.T. 1 Kings XVII-XIX, XXI—Criticism, interpretation, etc.—Addresses, essays, lectures. 3. Pastoral theology—Addresses, essays, lectures. I. Bible. O.T. 1 Kings XVII-XIX, XXI. English. Napier. 1976. II. Title.

NAVY Supervisory Chaplains Conference, Washington, D.C., 1966. 253
Navy Supervisory Chaplains Conference; [proceedings] Washington, 1966. 245 p. port. 26 cm. Cover title. [BV4017.N34 1966] 76-10894
1. Pastoral theology—Addresses, essays, lectures. 2. Chaplains, Military—U.S.—Addresses, essays, lectures. I. Title.

THE New shape of pastoral theology; essays in honor of Seward Hiltner. Edited by William B. Oglesby, Jr. Nashville, Abingdon Press [1969] 383 p. port. 24 cm. Includes bibliographical references. [BV4017.N37] 72-84721 ISBN 6-87278-791- 7.95 250
1. Pastoral theology—Addresses, essays, lectures. I. Hiltner, Seward, 1909- II. Oglesby, William B., ed.

NEWBIGIN, James Edward Lesslie, Bp. 253
"The Good Shepherd" : meditations on Christian ministry in today's world / Lesslie Newbigin ; foreword by the Archbishop of Canterbury. Grand Rapids : Eerdmans, 1977. 158 p. ; 21 cm. "A revised edition; originally published by the Christian Literature Society, Madras." [BV4017.N38 1977] 77-740 ISBN 0-8028-1686-X pbk. : 2.95
1. Pastoral theology—Addresses, essays, lectures. I. Title.

THE Plurality of ministries. Edited by Hans Kung and Walter Kasper. [New York] Herder and Herder [1972] 152 p. 23 cm. (Concilium: religion in the seventies. Ecumenism, v. 74) On cover: The New concilium: religion in the seventies. Includes bibliographical references. [BV4011.P58] 76-185750 2.95 (pbk) 253
1. Pastoral theology—Addresses, essays, lectures. I. Kung, Hans, ed. II. Kasper, Walter, ed. III. Series: Concilium: theology in the age of renewal, v. 74.

RICHARDS, Herbert Forest. 261.8
The church for our time; the kind of

church needed for today's world, by H. F. Richards. [1st ed.] New York, Vantage Press [1964] 112 p. 21 cm. [BV4017.R52] 64-6060
1. Pastoral theology — Addresses, essays, lectures. I. Title.

Pastoral theology—African Methodist Episcopal Church—Handbooks, manuals, etc.

PASTOR'S manual of the A.M.E. Church / G. Lovelace Champion, editor. [Nashville] : H. Belin, c1976. 2 v. : ill. ; 23 cm. Contents.Contents.—v. 1. Toward deaconate orders.—v. 2. Toward elders orders. Includes bibliographies. [BX8447.P34] 76-360432 253
1. African Methodist Episcopal Church—Doctrinal and controversial works. 2. Pastoral theology—African Methodist Episcopal Church—Handbooks, manuals, etc. I. Champion, G. Lovelace.

Pastoral theology—Anecdotes, facetiae, satire, etc.

ASQUITH, Glenn H 817.54
Selected works of Ryters Krampe. [1st ed.] Valley Forge [Pa.] Judson Press [1962] 96p. 21cm. [BV4015.A8] 62-16997
1. Pastoral theology—Anecdotes, facetiae, satire, etc. I. Title.

BASSET, Bernard 253.0207
Priest in the presbytery; a psycho-ecclesiastical extravaganza. Illus. by Penelope Harter. [New York] Herder & Herder [1966, c.1964] 104p. illus. 21cm. [BV4015.B27] 65-29206 3.50
1. Pastoral theology—Anecdotes, facetiae, satire, etc. I. Title.

BOUSMAN, Gary. 253.088
The human side of the ministry. Fargo, N. D., Fireside Press [1959] 106p. illus. 22cm. [BV4015.B53] 60-18501
1. Pastoral theology—Ancedotes, facetiae, satire, etc. I. Title.

BRODE, Anthony. 253.088
Wayward vicarage. Illustrated by Fritz Kredel. Philadelphia, Lippincott, 1959. 190 p. illus. 21 cm. Autobiographical. "Published in England under the title, Picture a country vicarage." [BV4015.B6 1959] 59-7110
1. Pastoral theology—Anecdotes, facetiae, satire, etc. I. Title.

CLEVELAND, Philip Jerome, 1903- 250.8
It's bright in my valley. [Westwood, N. J.] Revell [1962] 192p. 21cm. [BV4015.C54] 62-10734
1. Pastoral theology—Anecdotes, facetiae, satire, etc. I. Title.

CLEVELAND, Philip Jerome, 1903- 250.88
Three churches and a Model T. [Westwood, N. J.] Revell [1960] 189p. 22cm. [BV4015.C55] 60-5504
1. Pastoral theology—Anecdotes, facetiae, satire, etc. I. Title.

FREEMAN, Gary. 253'.02'07
A funny thing happened on the way to heaven. Illustrated by Jim Crane. [1st ed.] New York, Harper & Row [1969] 126 p. illus. 22 cm. [PN6231.C5F7] 69-17012 3.95
1. Pastoral theology—Anecdotes, facetiae, satire, etc. I. Title.

LARGE, John Ellis 250.81
The small needle of Dr. Large. Englewood Cliffs, N. J., Prentice [c.1962] 177p. 22cm. 62-10175 3.50
1. Pastoral theology—Anecdotes, facetiae, satire, etc. I. Title.

MILHAM, Richard. 253'.02'07
Brother Fred Chicken, superpastor. Nashville, Broadman Press [1968] 96 p. illus. 20 cm. [BV4015.M5] 68-20682
1. Pastoral theology—Anecdotes, facetiae, satire, etc. I. Title.

SEGERHAMMAR, Robert E 253.088
Just call me Pastor; a Peter Pulpitpounder book. Illustrated by Donald J. Wallerstedt. Rock Island, Ill., Augustana Press [1959] 91p. illus. 20cm. [BV4015.S32] 59-9092
1. Pastoral theology—Anecdotes, facetiae, satire, etc. I. Title.

SEGERHAMMAR, Robert E 253.088
Peter Pulpitpounder, B. D. Rock Island, Ill., Augustana Press [1957] 54p. illus. 20cm. [BV4015.S33] 57-7761
1. Pastoral theology—Anecdotes, facetiae, satire, etc. I. Title.

SEGERHAMMAR, Robert E 523.088
Peter Pulpitpounder, B. D. Rock Island, Ill., Augustana Press [1957] 54p. illus. 20cm. [BV4015.S33] 57-7761
1. Pastoral theology—Anecdotes, facetiae, satire, etc. I. Title.

SMITH, Charles Merrill 817.54
How to become a bishop without being religious. New York, Pocket Bks. [1966, c.1965] 159p. 17cm. (50300) [BV4015.S58] .50 pap.,
1. Pastoral theology—Anecdotes, facetiae, satire, etc. I. Title.

SMITH, Charles Merrill. 817.54
How to become a bishop without being religious. [1st ed.] Garden City, N. Y., Doubleday, 1965. xii, 131 p. 22 cm. [BV4015.S58] 65-10623
1. Pastoral theology—Anecdotes, facetiae, satire, etc. I. Title.

STERLING, Chandler W. Bp., 1911- 262.1208
Little malice in Blunderland; being a not so fanciful account of the adventures of Alfred Chatworthy, D. D., Bishop of Blunderland, in the land of shining mountains and on the rolling plains of the great northwest during the early reign of the mass-man ... by Chandler W. Sterling. With illus. by Bolte Gibson. New York, Morehouse-Barlow [1965] 176 p. illus. 22 cm. [BV4015.S77] 65-27000
1. Pastoral theology—Anecdotes, facetiae, satire, etc. I. Title.

TRAYLOR, Melvin Alvah. 250'.2'07
The nomenclatural standing of clericus polydenominata [by] Melvin A. Traylor. Gurnee, Ill., Vanishing Press, 1967. 11 p. 14 cm. (Vanishing Press natural history references, no. 2) (A Vanishing Press monograph.) [PN6231.C5T7] 75-10256
1. Pastoral theology—Anecdotes, facetiae, satire, etc. I. Title.

Pastoral theology—Anglican Communion.

DE SATGE, John. 253'.2
Letters to an ordinand : a study in vocation / [by] John de Satge. London : S.P.C.K. : Advisory Council for the Church's Ministry, 1976. x, 45 p. ; 19 cm. [BX5175.D44] 77-350373 ISBN 0-281-02948-2 : £0.95
1. Pastoral theology—Anglican Communion. 2. Vocation, Ecclesiastical. I. Title.

LICHTENBERGER, Arthur. 260.81
The day is at hand. New York, Seabury Press [1964] 124 p. 22 cm. "Largely based on addresses, sermons, and seasonal messages." [BV4011.L5] 64-19625
1. Pastoral theology — Angilcan Crmmunion — Addresses, essays, lectures. I. Title.

STIRES, Ernest Van R. 253
Not as a man pleaser; John Doe & the church, by Ernest Van R. Stires. Darien, Ga., Printed for the author at the Ashantilly Press, 1965. 50 p. 25 cm. [BX5175.S7] 331.1'1 68-2180
1. Pastoral theology—Anglican communion. I. Title. II. Title: John Doe & the church.

THORNTON, Martin 250
Feed my lambs; essays in pastoral reconstruction. Greenwich, Conn., Seabury Press, 1961[ ] 142p. Bibl. 61-979 3.95
1. Pastoral theology—Anglican Communion. I. Title.

THORNTON, Martin. 250
Feed my lambs; essays in pastoral reconstruction. [American ed.] Greenwich, Conn., Seabury Press 1961. 142 p. 23 cm. Includes bibliography. [BV4011.T45] 61-979
1. Pastoral theology—Anglican Communion. I. Title.

Pastoral theology —Anglican Communion—Handbooks, manuals, etc.

LAWRENCE, William Appleton, Bp., 1889- 250
Parsons. vestries, and parishes: a manual. Greenwich, Conn., Seabury Pr. [c.]1961 304p. Bibl. 61-12427 6.00
1. Pastoral theology—Anglican Communion—Hand-books. manuals, etc. I. Title.

LAWRENCE, William Appleton, Bp., 1889- 250
Parsons, vestries, and parishes: a manual. New York, Seabury [1964, c.1961] 304p. 21cm. (SP12) Bibl. 1.95 pap.,
1. Pastoral theology—Anglican Communion—Hand-books, manuals, etc. I. Title.

LAWRENCE, William Appleton, Bp., 1889- 250
Parsons, vestries, and parishes: a manual. Greenwich, Conn., Seabury Press, 1961. 304p. 22cm. Includes bibliography. [BX5965.L3] 61-12427
1. Pastoral theology —Anglican Communion—Handbooks, manuals, etc. I. Title.

Pastoral theology—Baptist Church

*GORMAN, F. E. 253
Rocking the pulpit the pastor as biblical shepherd. New York, Exposition [1967] 80p. 21cm. [EP45683] 3.50
1. Pastoral theology—Baptist Church I. Title.

Pastoral theology—Baptists.

BEDSOLE, Adolph 248.8
Parson to parson. Grand Rapids, Mich., Baker Bk. [1965, c.1964] 149p. 20cm. [BV4011.B39] 64-8344 2.95 bds.,
1. Pastoral theology—Baptists. I. Title.

BRISTER, C. W. 253.5
Pastoral care in the church. New York, Harper [c.1964] xxiv, 262p. 22cm. Bibl. 64-19497 5.00
1. Pastoral theology—Baptists. I. Title.

BRISTER, C W 253.5
Pastoral care in the church [by] C. W. Brister. [1st ed.] New York, Harper & Row [1964] xxiv, 262 p. 22 cm. Includes bibliographical references. [BV4011.B7] 64-19497
1. Pastoral theology — Baptists. I. Title.

COTHENS, Joe. 253
Equipped for good work : a guide for pastors / Joe H. Cothen. Gretna, La. : Pelican Pub. Co., 1980, c1981. p. cm. Bibliography: p. [BV4011.C65 1981] 19 80-27964 ISBN 0-88289-271-1 : 14.95
1. Pastoral theology—Baptists. 2. Baptists—Clergy. I. Title.

CRISWELL, Wallie A. 253
Criswell's guidebook for pastors / W. A. Criswell. Nashville, Tenn. : Broadman Press, c1980. 385 p. : port. ; 24 cm. [BV4011.C74] 19 79-7735 ISBN 0-8054-2536-5 : 9.95
1. Pastoral theology—Baptists. 2. Baptists—Doctrinal and controversial works. I. Title. II. Title: Guidebook for pastors.

HINCHEY, Roy W. 253
Plain talk about the pastorate / Roy W. Hinchey. Nashville : : Broadman Press, c1975. 64 p. ; 19 cm. Includes bibliographical references. [BV4011.H53] 76-352205 ISBN 0-8054-2410-5 pbk. : 1.50
1. Pastoral theology—Baptists. I. Title.

Pastoral theology—Biblical teaching—Addresses, essays, lectures.

A Biblical basis for ministry / edited by Earl E. Shelp and Ronald Sunderland. 1st ed. Philadelphia : Westminster Press, c1981. p. cm. Contents.Contents.—Theology and ministry in the Hebrew scriptures / by James A. Wharton — Ministry in Judaism: reflections on suffering and caring / by Samuel E. Karff — Theology and ministry in the Pauline letters / by Victor Paul Furnish — Resources for pastoral ministry in the synoptic gospels / by Paul J. Achtemeier — Theology and ministry in John / by D. Moody Smith. Includes bibliographical references. [BS2545.P45B5] 19 81-920 ISBN 0-664-24371-1 pbk. : 9.50 253
1. Pastoral theology—Biblical teaching—Addresses, essays, lectures. 2. Pastoral theology (Judaism)—Addresses, essays, lectures. I. Shelp, Earl E., 1947- II. Sunderland, Ronald, 1929-

Pastoral Theology — Bibliography.

MIDWESTERN Baptist Tehological Seminary, Kansas City, Mo.
A selected bibliography for theological students. Prepared by the faculty. Kansas City, Mo., Midwestern Baptist Theological Seminary, 1964. 61 p. 23 cm. 66-52065
1. Pastoral Theology — Bibliography. I. Title.

PFNUR, Vinzenz. 254
Kirche und Amt : neuere Literatur zur okumenischen Diskussion um die Amtsfrage / zusammengestellt von Vinzenz Pfnur ; mit einem Geleitwort von Albert Brandenburg. Munster, Westfalen : Aschendorff, c1975. 32 p. ; 25 cm. (Catholica : Beiheft ; 1) Cover title. [Z7820.P43] [BV4011] 016.2621 75-518521 ISBN 3-402-07243-2
1. Pastoral theology—Bibliography. 2. Christian union—Bibliography. 3. Pastoral theology and Christian union—Bibliography. I. Title. II. Series.

Pastoral theology—Case studies.

BRISTER, C. W. 253
Beginning your ministry / C.W. Brister, James L. Cooper, J. David Fite. Nashville : Abingdon, c1981. 158 p. ; 21 cm. Findings from the Young ministers project, sponsored jointly by the Southwestern Baptist Theological Seminary and Baptist General Convention of Texas. Bibliography: p. 149-158. [BV4011.B67] 19 80-25763 ISBN 0-687-02780-2 pbk. : 6.95
1. Fort Worth, Tex. Southwestern Baptist Theological Seminary—Alumni—Case studies. 2. Pastoral theology—Case studies. 3. Clergy—United States—Case studies. 4. Baptists—Clergy—Case studies. I. Cooper, James L., 1924- joint author. II. Fite, David, joint author. III. Title.

MAYER, Herbert T. 253
Pastoral care : its roots and renewal / Herbert T. Mayer. Atlanta : John Knox Press, [1978] p. cm. [BV4011.M42] 78-52444 ISBN 0-8042-1130-2 : 14.00
1. Pastoral theology—Case studies. I. Title.

MICKEY, Paul A., 1937- 253
Conflict and resolution [by] Paul A. Mickey and Robert L. Wilson. Nashville, Abingdon Press [1973] 160 p. 20 cm. [BV4013.M5] 73-4974 ISBN 0-687-09400-3 4.50
1. Pastoral theology—Case studies. I. Wilson, Robert Leroy, 1925- joint author. II. Title.

PEALE, Norman Vincent, 1898- 248.4
The positive power of Jesus Christ / Norman Vincent Peale. Wheaton, Ill. : Tyndale House, c1980. 266 p. ; 22 cm. [BV4011.P39] 19 79-67855 ISBN 0-8423-4874-3 : 8.95
1. Peale, Norman Vincent. 2. Pastoral theology—Case studies. 3. Christian life—Reformed authors. I. Title.

Pastoral theology—Catholic Church.

BAUSCH, William J. 253
The Christian parish : whispers of the risen Christ / William J. Bausch. Notre Dame, Ind. : Fides/Claretian, [1980] p. cm. Includes bibliographical references. [BX1913.B38] 80-14765 ISBN 0-8190-0639-4 : 9.95
1. Pastoral theology—Catholic Church. 2. Pastoral theology. 3. Parishes. I. Title.

CASEY, Thomas Francis, 1923- 250
Pastoral manual for new priests. Foreword by Richard Cardinal Cushing. Milwaukee, Bruce Pub. Co. [1962] 164p. 23cm. [BX1913.C3] 62-12431

1. Pastoral theology—Catholic Church. I. Title.

CURRAN, Charles E. 253'.2
The crisis in priestly ministry [by] Charles E. Curran. Notre Dame, Ind., Fides Publishers [1972] vii, 146 p. 18 cm. (A Fides dome book, D-82) Includes bibliographical references. [BX1913.C86] 72-80236 ISBN 0-8190-0577-0 1.50
1. Pastoral theology—Catholic Church. I. Title.

GEANEY, Dennis J. 253
Emerging lay ministry / by Dennis Geaney. Kansas City : Andrews, and McMeel, c1979. xx, 136 p. ; 22 cm. Includes bibliographical references. [BX1913.G42] 78-13990 ISBN 0-8362-3305-0 pbk. : 4.95
1. Pastoral theology—Catholic Church. I. Title.

GREELEY, Andrew M., 1928- 250
The crucible of change; the social dynamics of pastoral practice [by] Andrew M. Greeley. New York, Sheed and Ward [1968] 188 p. 21 cm. [BV4011.G69] 68-26039 4.50
1. Pastoral theology—Catholic Church. I. Title.

GUERRETTE, Richard H. 253'.2
A new identity for the priest; toward an ecumenical ministry, by Richard H. Guerrette. Paramus, N.J., Paulist Press [1973] v, 100 p. 21 cm. Includes bibliographical references. [BX1912.G83] 72-95651 ISBN 0-8091-1764-9 2.95
1. Catholic Church—Clergy. 2. Pastoral theology—Catholic Church. I. Title.

HEENAN, John Carmel, Cardinal, 1905- 250
The people's priest. New York, Sheed and Ward, 1952 [c1951] 243 p. 21 cm. [BX1913.H36] 52-1489
1. Pastoral theology—Catholic Church. I. Title.

HOUTART, Francois, 1925- 250
Sociology and pastoral care. Tr. from French by Malachy Carroll. Chicago, Franciscan Herald [c.1965] vi, 77p. 21cm. [BX1913.H613] 65-25839 price unreported pap.,
1. Pastoral theology—Catholic Church. 2. Religion and sociology. I. Title.

JUNGMANN, Josef Andreas, 1889- 250
Announcing the word of God, by Josef A. Jungmann. [New York, Herder and Herder, 1967, c1968] 176 p. 22 cm. Translation of Glaubensverkundigung im Lichte der Frohbotschaft. Bibliographical footnotes. [BX1912.J8413] 68-17328
1. Pastoral Theology—Catholic Church. 2. Kerygma. I. Title.

KENNEDY, Eugene C. 253
Comfort my people; the pastoral presence of the church, by Eugene C. Kennedy. New York, Sheed and Ward [1968] xiii, 208 p. 21 cm. Includes bibliographies. [BX1913.K4] 68-26037 4.95
1. Catholic Church—Clergy. 2. Pastoral theology—Catholic Church. I. Title.

KEYES, Paul T., 1936- 253
Pastoral presence and the diocesan priest / Paul T. Keyes. 1st ed. Whitinsville, Mass. : Affirmation Books, c1978. p. cm. [BX1913.K44] 78-22009 ISBN 0-89571-004-8 : 4.95
1. Pastoral theology—Catholic Church. 2. Clergy—Office. I. Title.

KLOPPENBURG, Boaventura, 1919- 253'.2
The priest: living instrument and minister of Christ, the eternal priest, by Bonaventure Kloppenburg. Translated by Matthew J. O'Connell. Chicago, Franciscan Herald Press [1974] xiv, 233 p. 21 cm. Translation of O ser do padre. [BX1912.K54913] 73-23059 ISBN 0-8199-0495-3 5.95
1. Catholic Church—Clergy. 2. Pastoral theology—Catholic Church. I. Title.

LAVERDIERE, Eugene. 225.6
The New Testament in the life of the church : evangelization, prayer, catechetics, homiletics / by Eugene LaVerdiere. Notre Dame, Ind. : Ave Maria Press, c1980. 189 p. : port. ; 21 cm. Includes bibliographies. [BS2530.L38] 19 80-67403 ISBN 0-87793-213-1 (pbk.) : 4.95
1. Bible. N.T.—Study. 2. Bible. N.T.—Use. 3. Pastoral theology—Catholic Church. I. Title.

MAGNER, James Aloysius, 1901- 253
The Catholic priest in the modern world. Milwaukee, Bruce Pub. Co. [1957] 291p. 23cm. [BX1912.M22] 57-6319
1. Pastoral theology—Catholic Church. I. Title.

MATHIS, Marcian Joseph, 1918- ed. 348
The pastoral companion; a handbook of canon law. 12th ed., by Marcian J. Mathis and Nicholas W. Meyer. Chicago, Franciscan Herald Press, 1961. 474p. 19cm. New ed. of Honoratus Bonzelet's translation and adapation of Ludwig Anler's Comes pastoralis. [BX1913.M35 1961] 61-11199
1. Pastoral theology—Catholic Church. 2. Canon law. 3. Sacraments—Catholic Church. I. Meyer, Nicholas W., joint ed. II. Title.

MICHONNEAU, Georges, 1899- 253
My father's business; a priest in France. [English translation by Edmund Gilpin. New York] Herder and Herder [1959] 154p. 19cm. 'Based on the original version of Le cure.' [BX1913.M543 1959a] 59-10890
1. Pastoral theology—Catholic Church. 2. Catholic Church—Clergy. I. Title.

MULLIN, Joseph 250.96
The Catholic Church in modern Africa; a pastoral theology. London, G. Chapman [New York, Herder & Herder, 1966, c. 1965] ix, 256p. 23cm. Bibl. [BX1913.M8] 66-3287 4.95 bds.,
1. Pastoral theology—Catholic Church. 2. Missions—Africa. 3. Catholic Church in Africa. I. Title.

NIKLAS, Gerald R. 253
The making of a pastoral person / Gerald R. Niklas. New York, N.Y. : Alba House, c1981. ix, 159 p. ; 21 cm. Includes bibliographical references. [BX1913.N57] 19 80-26978 ISBN 0-8189-0409-7 : 5.95
1. Catholic Church—Clergy. 2. Pastoral theology—Catholic Church. 3. Lay ministry—Catholic Church. I. Title.

O'NEILL, Joseph H. 253
A pastor's point of view. Milwaukee, Bruce [c.1963] x, 267p. 22cm. Bibl. 63-17494 5.00
1. Pastoral theology—Catholic Church. I. Title.

OSTER, Henri. 250
The paschal mystery in parish life. Translated by Michael O'Brien. [New York] Herder and Herder [1967] 144 p. 22 cm. Translation of Le mystere pascal dans la pastorale. Bibliographical footnotes. [BX1913.O813] 66-13070
1. Pastoral theology—Catholic Church. 2. Paschal mystery. I. Title.

THE Pastoral mission of the church. 260.82
Glen Rock, N. J., Paulist Press [1965] vi, 186 p. 24 cm. (Concilium theology in the age of renewal: Pastoral theology, v. 3) Includes bibliographies. [BX1913.P3] 65-19634
1. Pastoral theology—Catholic Church. 2. Religion and sociology. I. Series.

PASTORAL mission of the church (The) 260.82
v.3. Glen Rock, N. J., Paulist Pr. [c.1965] vi, 186p. 24cm. (Concilium theology in the age of renewal: Pastoral theology, v.3) Bibl. [BX1913.P3] 65-19634 4.50
1. Pastoral theology—Catholic Church. 2. Religion and sociology. (Series)

PFLIEGLER, Michael, 1891- 250
Pastoral theology. Translated by John Drury. Westminster, Md., Newman Press 1966. x, 311 p. 23 cm. [BX1913.P413] 65-25981
1. Pastoral theology—Catholic Church. I. Title.

THE postconciliar parish 254
ed. by James OGara. New York, Kenedy [1967] xiii, 197p. 22cm. Bibl. [BX1913.P63] 67-18428 4.95
1. Pastoral theology—Catholic Church. 2. Parishes—U. S. I. O'Gara, James, ed.

QUINN, Bernard, 1928- 253
The small rural parish / Bernard Quinn. New York : Parish Project, National Conference of Catholic Bishops ; Washington, D.C. : Glenmary Research Center, 1980. xii, 118 p. ; 21 cm. Includes bibliographical references. [BX1913.Q56] 79-56508 ISBN 0-914422-11-1 pbk. : 3.50
1. Pastoral theology—Catholic Church. 2. Rural churches. 3. Small churches. I. Title.
Publisher's address: 4606 East-West Hwy., Washington, DC 20014

RAHNER, Karl, 1904- 250
Christian in the market place. Translated by Cecily Hastings. New York, Sheed & Ward [1966] 184 p. 21 cm. One of 3 vols., each with distinctive title, which together represent the English translation of the author's Sendung und Gnade, published in London under title: Mission and grace. Includes bibliographical references. [BX1913.R29] 66-22022
1. Pastoral theology—Catholic Church. I. Title.

RAHNER, Karl, 1904- 253
Mission and grace; essays in pastoral theology. Tranlated by Cecily Hastings. London, New York, Sheed and Ward [1963-66] 3 v. 18 cm. (Stagbooks) vol. 2 translated by Cecily Hastings and Richard Strachan. Includes bibliographies. [BX1913.R3132] 66-2860
1. Pastoral theology—Catholic Church. I. Title.

SECULAR priest in the new church, 253
edited by Gerard S. Sloyan. [New York] Herder and Herder [1967] 252 p. 22 cm. Contents.Contents.—Theology of the priesthood, by J. Powell.—Spirituality for the secular priesthood, by G. S. Sloyan.—Vatican II and the secular priest, by J. A. O'Donohoe.—Future laws for the secular priest, by P. M. Shannon.—The priest as liturgist, by J. T. Nolan.—The priest and his bishop, by J. K. Mussio.—The office of pastor, by J. G. Chatham.—The parish assistant, by A. M. Greeley.—The social mission of the secular priest, by J. V. Coffield.—The priest and the intellectual life, by J. T. Ellis.—The human side, by H. Fehren.—Ministry in the church of the future, by R. Ruether.—Notes on contributors. Bibliographical footnotes. [BX1913.S4] 67-25885
1. Catholic Church—Clergy. 2. Pastoral theology—Catholic Church. I. Sloyan, Gerard Stephen, 1919- ed.

SEGUNDO, Juan Luis. 261.8'098
The hidden motives of pastoral action : Latin American reflections / Juan Luis Segundo ; translated by John Drury. Maryknoll, N.Y. : Orbis Books, c1978. viii, 141 p. ; 22 cm. Translation of Accion pastoral latinoamericana. Includes bibliographical references. [BX1426.2.S4313] 77-13420 ISBN 0-88344-185-3 : 7.95 ISBN 0-88344-186-1 pbk. : 3.95
1. Catholic Church in Latin America. 2. Pastoral theology—Catholic Church. 3. Latin America—Social conditions—1945- I. Title.

TORMEY, John C. 253'.02'07
What's cooking in the priesthood? / John C. Tormey. Canfield, Ohio : Alba Books, [1975] 128 p. : ill. ; 18 cm. [BX1912.T6] 74-28963 pbk. : 1.25
1. Catholic Church—Clergy—Caricatures and cartoons. 2. Pastoral theology—Catholic Church. I. Title.

WALSH, John J., 1913- 253
Evangelization and justice : new insights for Christian ministry / John Walsh. Maryknoll, N.Y. : Orbis, c1982. p. cm. Bibliography: p. [BX1913.W28] 19 82-6279 ISBN 0-88344-109-8 pbk. : 5.95
1. Pastoral theology—Catholic Church. 2. Christianity—20th century. 3. Evangelistic work. 4. Justice. 5. Peace. I. Title.

Pastoral theology—Catholic Church—Addresses, essays, lectures.

BORDELON, Marvin. 254'.02
The parish in a time of change, edited by Marvin Bordelon. Notre Dame, Ind., Fides Publishers [1967] x, 227 p. 23 cm. Includes bibliographical references. [BX1912.B67] 66-30590
1. Pastoral theology—Catholic Church—Addresses, essays, lectures. I. Title.

CATHOLIC ministries in our time 262'.142
/ edited by George A. Kelly. Boston, MA : St. Paul Editions, c1980. p. cm. "These lectures were given by the faculty of the Institute for Advanced Studies in Catholic Doctrine at St. John's University during the Spring of 1979." Includes index. [BX1913.C38] 19 80-22927 ISBN 0-8198-1400-8 : 4.00 pbk. : 3.00
1. Catholic Church—Clergy—Addresses, essays, lectures. 2. Pastoral theology—Catholic Church—Addresses, essays, lectures. I. Kelly, George Anthony, 1916- II. St. John's University, New York. Institute for Advanced Studies in Catholic Doctrine.
Publisher's address: 50 St. Paul's Ave., Boston, MA 02130

PARISH ministry resources / 253
Maria Bruck, editor. New York : Paulist Press, c1979. v, 170 p. ; 28 cm. "These essays first appeared in Service." Includes bibliographies. [BX1913.P285] 79-63618 pbk. : 8.95
1. Pastoral theology—Catholic Church—Addresses, essays, lectures. I. Bruck, Maria. II. Service (New York, 1973-)

RAHNER, Karl, 1904- 250
The Christian commitment; essays in pastoral theology. Translated by Cecily Hastings. New York, Sheed and Ward [1963] vi, 218 p. 22 cm. One of 3 vols., each with distinctive title, which together represent the English translation of the author's Sendung und Gnade, published in London under title: Mission and grace. Bibliographical references included in "Notes" (p. 200-204, 217-218) [BX1913.R313] 63-17146
1. Pastoral theology—Catholic Church—Addresses, essays, lectures. I. Title.

THE Right of the community to a priest 262'.142
/ edited by Edward Schillebeeckx and Johann-Baptist Metz ; English language editor, Marcus Lefebure. Edinburgh : T. & T. Clark ; New York : Seabury Press, 1980. ix, 138 p. ; 22 cm. (Concilium ; 133, 3 : Dogma) Includes bibliographical references. [BX1913.R54] 19 80-50477 ISBN 0-567-30013-7 (pbk.) ISBN 0-8164-2275-3 (Seabury Press : pbk.) : 5.95
1. Catholic Church—Clergy—Addresses, essays, lectures. 2. Pastoral theology—Catholic Church—Addresses, essays, lectures. 3. Parishes—Addresses, essays, lectures. I. Schillebeeckx, Edward Cornelis Florentius Alfons. II. Metz, Johannes Baptist, 1928- III. Lefebure, Marcus. IV. Series: Concilium (New York) ; 133, 3.

WEITZEL, Eugene J., ed. 250
Pastoral ministry in a time of change. Eugene J. Weitzel, participating editor. Milwaukee, Bruce Pub. Co. [1966] xiv, 494 p. 23 cm. Bibliography: p. 447-478. [BX1913.W4] 66-29713
1. Pastoral theology—Catholic Church—Addresses, essays, lectures. I. Title.

Pastoral theology—Catholic Church—Bibliography.

MIERZWINSKI, Theophil T., 1924- 016.2621
What do you think of the priest? A bibliography on the Catholic priesthood. Compiled and edited by Theophil T. Mierzwinski. With a foreword by John F. Whealon. [1st ed.] New York, Exposition Press [1972] 95 p. 22 cm. (An Exposition-university book) [Z7820.M53] 72-86589 ISBN 0-682-47527-0 5.00
1. Catholic Church—Clergy—Bibliography. 2. Pastoral theology—Catholic Church—Bibliography. I. Title.

Pastoral theology—Catholic Church—Collections.

THE Dimensions of the priesthood: theological, Christological, liturgical, ecclesial, apostolic, Marian. 253'.2
Compiled by the Daughters of St. Paul. [Boston] St. Paul Editions [1973] 322 p. 22 cm. "A compilation of 325 selected passages from the documents of Vatican II; from postconciliar documents; from the writings and addresses of Popes Pius XII,

John XXIII, Paul VI, and the 1971 World Synod of Bishops." [BX1913.D53] 73-76310 5.00
1. Catholic Church—Clergy—Collections. 2. Pastoral theology—Catholic Church—Collections. I. Daughters of St. Paul.

Pastoral theology — Catholic Church — Congresses.

EVANGELIZATION in the 269'.2
American context / David B. Burrell and Franzita Kane, editors. Notre Dame, Ind. : University of Notre Dame, c1976. p. cm. Proceedings of a symposium held at the University of Notre Dame, Jan. 11-13, 1976. [BX1913.E9] 76-22403 ISBN 0-268-00901-5 : 7.95. ISBN 0-268-00902-3 pbk. : 2.95
1. Catholic Church in the United States—Congresses. 2. Pastoral theology—Catholic Church—Congresses. 3. Catholic learning and scholarship—Congresses. I. Burrell, David B. II. Kane, Franzita, 1909- III. Notre Dame, Ind. University.

MIDWESTERN Institute of 250
Pastoral Theology. 1st, Sacred Heart Seminary, 1961.
Sharing the Christian message. [Proceedings of the] first annual institute, August 27-30, 1961. Detroit, 1962. 120 p. illus. 22 cm. Sponsored by St. John's Provincial Seminary and Sacred Heart Seminary. Includes bibliographical references. [BX1913.A1M5] 63-3808
1. Pastoral theology — Catholic Church — Congresses. 2. Religious education — Congresses. I. St. John's Provincial Seminary. Plymouth, Mich. II. Detroit. Sacred Heart Seminary. III. Title.

MIDWESTERN Institute of 253.5
Pastoral Theology. 2d, Sacred Heart Seminary, 1962.
Pastoral counseling. [Proceedings of the] second annual institute, August 27-30, 1962. Detroit, 1962. 136 p. 22 cm. Sponsored by St. John's Provincial Seminary and Sacred Heart Seminary. Includes bibliographies. [BX1913.A1M5] 62-22108
1. Pastoral theology — Catholic Church — Congresses. 2. Pastoral psychology — Congresses. I. St. John's Provincial Seminary, Plymouth, Mich. II. Detroit. Sacred Heart Seminary. III. Title.

MIDWESTERN Institute of 250.07152
Pastoral Theology. 4th Sacred Heart Seminary,1964.
The priest: the teacher of morality. [Proceedings of the] fourth annual institute, August 24-27, 1964. Detroit, 1964 [i.e. 1965] 157 p. 22 cm. Sponsored by the faculties of St. John's Provincial Seminary and Sacred Heart Seminary. [BX1913.A1M5] 65-29265
1. Pastoral theology — Catholic Church — Congresses. 2. Christian ethics — Study and teaching — Congresses. I. St. John's Provincial Seminary, Plymouth, Mich. II. Detroit. Sacred Heart Seminary. III. Title.

MIDWESTERN Institute of 253.5
Pastoral Theology. Conference. 2d, Detroit, 1962.
Pastoral counseling; proceedings. Detroit, Midwestern Institute of Pastoral Theology, Sacred Heart Seminary, 1962. 136 p. 22 cm. Includes bibliographies. [BX1913.A1M5] 62-22108
1. Pastoral theology — Catholic Church — Congresses. 2. Pastoral psychology. I. Title.

Pastoral theology—Catholic Church—History.

MURNION, Philip J. 253'.2
The Catholic priest and the changing structure of pastoral ministry / Philip J. Murnion. New York : Arno Press, 1978. xi, 487 p. : ill. ; 24 cm. (The American Catholic tradition) Originally presented as the author's thesis, Columbia University, 1972, under title: Towards theopolitan ministry. Bibliography: p. 466-487. [BX1913.M83 1978] 77-11302 ISBN 0-405-10845-1 : 30.00
1. Catholic Church—Clergy. 2. Pastoral theology—Catholic Church—History. 3. Clergy—New York (City) I. Title. II. Series: American Catholic tradition.

Pastoral theology—Catholic Church—Research—Congresses.

TOWARD more effective 253'.07
research in the church : a national Catholic symposium / Joseph Fitzpatrick ... [et al.] ; sponsored by Foundations and Donors Interested in Catholic Activities ; co-sponsors, United States Catholic Conference ... [et al. ; edited by Frances F. Butler]. [Washington, D.C.] : FADICA, c1981. xiii, 117 p. ; 23 cm. "Proceedings of the National Catholic Symposium on Applied Research"—p. x. Bibliography: p. 109-117. [BX1913.T68] 19 81-181210 4.95 (pbk.)
1. Pastoral theology—Catholic Church—Research—Congresses. 2. Research—Congresses. I. Fitzpatrick, Joseph. II. Butler, Frances F. III. Foundations and Donors Interested in Catholic Activities, Inc. IV. Unites States Catholic Conference. V. National Catholic Symposium on Applied Research Catholic University of America) (1981 :
Distributed by Wm C Brown; 2460 Kerper Blvd., Dubuque, IA 52001

Pastoral theology—Christian Church (Disciples of Christ)

JOHNSON, H. Eugene. 253'.2
Duly and scripturally qualified : a study of the ministry of the Christian Church movement / by H. Eugene Johnson. Cincinnati : New Life Books, [1975] 176 p. ; 22 cm. Includes bibliographical references. [BX7326.J63] 75-12445 ISBN 0-87239-054-3 pbk. : 3.95
1. Pastoral theology—Christian Church (Disciples of Christ) 2. Pastoral theology—Churches of Christ. I. Title.

Pastoral theology—Church of God—Addresses, essays, lectures.

PASTORAL pointers / 253
[O. W. Polen, editor in chief]. Cleveland, Tenn. : Pathway Press, 1976c1975 92 p. : ill. ; 20 cm. [BV4017.P28] 75-18284 ISBN 0-87148-686-5 pbk. : 1.95
1. Pastoral theology—Church of God—Addresses, essays, lectures. I. Polen, O. W.

Pastoral theology—Church of the Nazarene.

SPRUCE, Fletcher Clarke. 253
Of grasshoppers and giants : a formula for achieving ministers / by Fletcher Spruce. Kansas City, Mo. : Beacon Hill Press of Kansas City, c1975. 160 p. ; 20 cm. Includes bibliographical references. [BV4011.S68] 76-356021 ISBN 0-8341-0357-5
1. Pastoral theology—Church of the Nazarene. I. Title.

Pastoral theology—Collected works.

AND he gave pastors : 253
pastoral theology in action / editor, Thomas F. Zimmerman, associate editors, G. Raymond Carlson, Zenas J. Bicket. Springfield, Mo. : Gospel Pub. House, c1979. 629 p. : forms ; 23 cm. Includes bibliographies. [BV4011.A48] 78-50485 ISBN 0-88243-460-8 : 12.95
1. Pastoral theology—Collected works. I. Zimmerman, Thomas F. II. Carlson, G. Raymond. III. Bicket, Zenas J.

Pastoral theology—Congresses.

MINISTRY and education in 253
conversation / edited by Mary C. Boys. Winona, Minn. : Saint Mary's Press, c1981. 133 p. ; 23 cm. Cover title: Ministry & education in conversation. Contents.Contents. Introduction / Mary C. Boys — The ministry of the Word and contemporary Catholic education / Sandra M. Schneiders — Ministry in education from a pastoral-theological perspective / Virgil P. Elizondo — Beyond professionalism in ministry and education / Sara Butler — Tradition and modernity / Robert Wood Lynn — Ministry and education / Richard P. McBrien. Includes bibliographical references and index. [BV4002.M57 1981] 19 80-53204 ISBN 0-88489-126-7 (pbk.) : 6.95
1. Pastoral theology—Congresses. 2. Christian education—Congresses. I. Boys, Mary C. II. Title: Ministry & education in conversation.

Pastoral theology—Early works to 1900.

BAXTER, Richard, 1615-1691 250
The reformed pastor. Ed. by Hugh Martin. Richmond, Va., Knox [1963] 125p. 19cm. Orig. pub. under title: Gildas Salvianus; or The reformed pastor. 63-16412 1.50 pap.,
1. Pastoral theology—Early works to 1900. I. Title.

BAXTER, Richard, 1615-1691. 253
The reformed pastor / Richard Baxter ; edited by William Brown. Edinburgh ; Carlisle, Pa. : The Banner of Truth Trust, 1974. 256 p. ; 19 cm. (Puritan paperbacks) Originally published under title: Gildas Salvianus. Includes bibliographical references. [BV4009.B3 1974] 74-189719 ISBN 0-85151-191-0 : £0.65
1. Pastoral theology—Early works to 1900. I. Title.

Pastoral theology—Friends, Society of.

STEERE, Douglas Van, 248'.48'96
1901-
On speaking out of the silence; vocal ministry in the unprogrammed meeting for worship, by Douglas V. Steere. [Wallingford, Pa., Pendle Hill Publications, 1972] 20 p. 20 cm. (Pendle Hill pamphlet, 182) [BX7745.S75] 72-182983 0.70
1. Pastoral theology—Friends, Society of. 2. Public worship. I. Title.

Pastoral theology—Handbooks, manuals, etc.

BOYNTON, George Mills, 1837-1908.
The pilgrim pastor's manual; a handbook of services and forms, by George M. Boynton ... Boston and Chicago, Congregational Sunday-school and publishing society [c1894] 2 p. l., 235 p. 17 cm. 16-22927
I. Title.

BOYNTON, George Mills, 1837-1908.
The pilgrim pastor's manual; a handbook of services and forms, by George M. Boynton. 10th ed., rev. and enl. by Parris Thaxter Farwell. Boston, New York, The Pilgrim press [c1916] v p., 3 l., 3-217 p. 18 cm. 16-22932 0.75
I. Farwell, Parris Thaxter, 1856- II. Title.

CHRISTENSEN, James L. 264
The minister's service handbook. [Westwood, N. J.] Revell [c.1960] 160p. 17cm. Bibl. notes: p. 157-160 60-13092 2.50
1. Pastoral theology—Handbooks, manuals, etc. 2. Liturgies. I. Title.

DRURY, M[arion] R[ichardson]
1849- comp.
The pastor's companion; a pocket manual of forms, services, and Scripture readings for special occasions, together with a brief summary of rules of order for deliberative assemblies, and suggestive outlines for revival and funeral sermons, adapted to the use of ministers of all Evangelical demoninations. Comp. and arranged by Rev. M. R. Drury... Dayton, O., W. J. Shuey, 1894. 2 p. l., vii-xii, 13-127 p. 19 cm. 9-90063
I. Title.

KOON, Warren L ed. 250.2
Ministers' manual and discipline. [1st ed.] New York, Vantage Press [1957] 86p. 21cm. Includes bibliography. [BV4016.K6] 56-12307
1. Pastoral theology—Handbooks, manuals, etc. I. Title.

MCNEIL, Jesse Jai. 250.2
Minister's service book for pulpit and parish. Grand Rapids, Eerdmans [1961] 212p. 18cm. [BV4016.M26] 61-10860
1. Pastoral theology—Handbooks, manuals, etc. I. Title.

MALLORY, Orson E[rskine] 1835-
Pastor's hand book with communion helps [by] O. E. Mallory ... Worcester? Mass., [c1905] 123 p. 19 cm. 6-34258
I. Title.

OATES, Wayne Edward, 1917- 253
Pastor's handbook / by Wayne E. Oates. 1st ed. Philadelphia : Westminster Press, c1980- v ; 20 cm. Ministerial supplement to the first six vols. of Christian care books. Includes bibliographies. [BV4016.O17] 79-28639 ISBN 0-664-24300-2 pbk. : 4.95
1. Pastoral theology—Handbooks, manuals, etc. 2. Pastoral psychology—Handbooks, manuals, etc. I. Christian care books. II. Title.

PERRY, Lloyd Merle. 253.02
A manual of pastoral problems and procedures, by Lloyd Merle Perry and Edward John Lias. Grand Rapids, Baker Book House, 1962. 171p. 29cm. Includes bibliography. [BV4016.P44] 62-4310
1. Pastoral theology—Handbooks, manuals, etc. I. Lias, Edward John, joint author. II. Title. III. Title: Pastoral problems and procedures.

PERRY, Lloyd Merle. 253.02
A manual of pastoral problems and procedures, by Lloyd Merle Perry and Edward John Lias. Grand Rapids, Mich., Baker BookHouse, 1964[c1962] 171 p. 29 cm. Includes bibliographies. [BV4016.P44] 65-4895
1. Pastoral theology—Handbooks, manuals, etc. I. Lias, Edward John joint author. II. Title.

SCHULZE, Frederick, 1855- 262.
A manual of pastoral theology; a practical guide for ecclesiastical students and newly ordained priest, by the Rev. Frederick Schulze ... 3d, rev. and enl. ed. adapted to the Code of canon law. St. Louis, Mo. [etc.] B. Herder book co., 1923. xvii, 564 p. 20 cm. [BX1912.S43 1923] 23-8326
I. Title.

SCHULZE, Frederick, 1855-
Manual of pastoral theology; a practical guide for ecclesiastical students and newly ordained priests, by Rev. Frederick Schulze ... 2d, rev. andts enl. ed. with supplement in accordance with the latest decrees. Milwaukee, Wis., Diederich-Schaefer co., 1914. 478 p. 21 cm. 14-15443 1.75
I. Title.

SEGLER, Franklin M. 250
The Broadman minister's manual [by] Franklin M. Segler. Nashville, Broadman Press [1968] iv, 154 p. 17 cm. [BV4016.S37] 68-26920
1. Pastoral theology—Handbooks, manuals, etc. I. Title. II. Title: Minister's manual.

Pastoral theology—History

BRAY, Allen F. 260
The return to self-concern. Philadelphia, Westminister Press [1964] 142 p. 21 cm. Bibliographical references included in "Notes" (p. 135-142) [BV4006.B7] 64-10517
1. Pastoral theology — Hist. 2. Identification (Religion) 3. Individuality. I. Title.

CLEBSCH, William A. 253.509
Pastoral care in historical perspective, an essay with exhibits, by William A. Clebsch, Charles R. Jaekle. Englewood Cliffs, N.J., Prentice [c.1964] x, 344p. 22cm. Bibl. 64-10746 7.95
1. Pastoral theology—Hist. 2. Pastoral theology—Collections. I. Jaekle, Charles R., joint author. II. Title.

CLEBSCH, William A 253.509
Pastoral care in historical perspective, an essay with exhibits, by William A. Clebsch and Charles R. Jackle. Englewood Cliffs, N.J., Prentice-Hall [1964] x, 344 p. 22 cm. "Twenty-one exhibits of the history of the pastoral art": p. 87-335. Bibliographical footnotes. [BV4005.C64] 64-10746
1. Pastoral theology — Hist. 2. Pastoral theology — Collections. I. Jackle, Charles R., joint author. II. Title.

Pastoral theology—History of doctrines.

COOKE, Bernard J. 253'.09
Ministry to word and sacraments : history and theology / Bernard Cooke. Philadelphia : Fortress Press, c1976. ix, 677 p. ; 27 cm. Includes bibliographies and indexes. [BV4006.C66] 75-36459 ISBN 0-8006-0440-7 : 25.00
1. Pastoral theology—History of doctrines. I. Title.

HALL, David D. 253
The faithful shepherd; a history of the New England ministry in the seventeenth century, by David D. Hall. Chapel Hill, Published for the Institute of Early American History and Culture, Williamsburg, Va., by the University of North Carolina Press [1972] xvi, 301 p. 24 cm. Includes bibliographical references. [BR520.H3] 72-81326 ISBN 0-8078-1193-9 11.95
1. Pastoral theology—History of doctrines. 2. Clergy—New England. 3. New England—Church history. I. Title.

HALL, David D. 253
The faithful shepherd; a history of the New England ministry in the seventeenth century, by David D. Hall. New York, Norton [1974, c1972] xvi, 301 p. 20 cm. (The Norton library, N719) Reprint of the ed. published by the University of North Carolina Press, Chapel Hill, for the Institute of Early American History and Culture, Williamsburg, Va. Bibliography: p. [279]-290. [BR520.H3 1974] 74-818 ISBN 0-393-00719-7 3.45 (pbk.)
1. Pastoral theology—History of doctrines. 2. Clergy—New England. 3. New England—Church history. I. Institute of Early American History and Culture, Williamsburg, Va. II. Title.

KARANT-NUNN, Susan C. 262'.1441
Luther's pastors : the reformation in the Ernestine countryside / Susan C. Karant-Nunn. Philadelphia : American Philosophical Society, 1979. 80 p. ; 29 cm. (Transactions of the American Philosophical Society ; v. 69 pt. 8 ISSN 0065-9746s) Includes index.IBibliography: p. 75-78.I[BV4006.K37] 79-51539 ISBN 0-87169-698-3 pbk. : 8.00
1. Lutheran Church—Clergy. 2. Pastoral theology—History of doctrines. 3. Clergy—Germany. I. Title. II. Series: American Philosophical Society, Philadelphia. Transactions ; v. 69, pt. 8.

PELLEGRINO, Michele. 250
The true priest; the priesthood as preached and practised by St. Augustine. Translated by Arthur Gibson. [New York] Philosophical Library [1968] 184 p. 23 cm. Translation of Verus sacerdos. Articles published between 1962 and 1965 in the Seminarium. Bibliographical footnotes. [BR1720.A9P363] 68-7498 6.00
1. Augustinus, Aurelius, Saint, Bp. of Hippo. 2. Pastoral theology—History of doctrines. I. Title.

Pastoral theology—History of doctrines—16th century—Addresses, essays, lectures.

HAENDLER, Gert. 253
Luther on ministerial office and congregational function / Gert Haendler ; translated by Ruth C. Gritsch ; edited by Eric W. Gritsch. Philadelphia : Fortress Press, c1981. p. cm. Translation of: Amt und Gemeinde bei Luther im Kontext der Kirchengeschichte. Bibliography: p. [BR333.5.P32H3313] 19 81-43075 ISBN 0-8006-0665-5 : 9.95
1. Luther, Martin, 1483-1546—Addresses, essays, lectures. 2. Pastoral theology—History of doctrines—16th century—Addresses, essays, lectures. 3. Church—History of doctrines—16th century—Addresses, essays, lectures. I. Gritsch, Eric W. II. [Amt und Gemeinde bei Luther im Kontext der Kirchengeschichte.] English III. Title.

Pastoral theology—Lutheran Church.

DAEHLIN, Reidar A. 253
Pastor to pastor; conversations with parish ministers. Minneapolis, Augsburg [c.1966] 124p. 19cm. [BV4011.D3] 66-13056 2.50 pap.,
1. Pastoral theology—Lutheran Church. I. Title.

DAEHLIN, Reidar A 253
Pastor to pastor; conversations with parish ministers, by Reidar R. Daehlin. Minneapolis, Augsburg Pub. House [1966] 124 p. 19 cm. [BV4011.D3] 66-13056
1. Pastoral theology — Lutheran Church. I. Title.

GRAF, Arthur E. 253.7
The church in the community; an effective evangelism program for the Christian congregation. Grand Rapids, Mich. Eerdmans [c.1965] 207p. forms. 23cm. Bibl. [BV4011.G67] 64-22019 3.95
1. Pastoral theology—Lutheran Church. I. Title.

LUTHERAN Church in America. Task Group for Long-Range Planning. 254'.6
Significant issues for the 1970's; report. [Philadelphia, Board of Publication of the Lutheran Church in America, 1968] 122 l. 28 cm. Includes bibliographies. [BV4011.L8] 68-5334
1. Pastoral theology—Lutheran Church. 2. Sociology, Christian (Lutheran) I. Title.

LUTHERAN Church in America. Task Group for Long-range Planning. 254'.6
Significant issues for the 1970's; report. Edward W. Uthe, director. Philadelphia, Fortress Press [1968] 172 p. 21 cm. Includes bibliographies. [BV4011.L8 1968b] 68-9485
1. Pastoral theology—Lutheran Church. 2. Sociology, Christian (Lutheran) I. Uthe, Edward W. II. Title.

MAILS, Thomas E. 284.173
The nature of heresy in our time, written, illus. by T. E. Mails. Hayfield, Minn., Hayfield Pub. Co. [1964, c.1963] 259p. illus. 24cm. 64-5676 4.95
1. Pastoral theology—Lutheran Church. I. Title.

MARTY, Martin., 1928- 262.2
Death and birth of the parish [by] Martin E. Marty, ed., author, with Paul R. Biegner, Roy Blumhorst, Kenneth R. Young. St. Louis, Concordia [c.1964] vii, 163p. 21cm. Bibl. 64-23370 3.00
1. Pastoral theology—Lutheran Church. 2. Parishes. I. Title.

THE Pastor at work. 253
Authors: Richard R. Caemmerer [and others] Saint Louis, Concordia Pub. House [1960] 414p. 24cm. Includes bibliography. [BV4011.P34] 59-11470
1. Pastoral theology— Lutheran Church. I. Caemmerer, Richard Rudolph, 1904-

PASTOR at work (The). 253
Authors: Richard R. Caemmerer [and others] Saint Louis, Concordia Pub. House [c.1960] viii, 414p. 24cm. (bibls.) 59-11470 6.50
1. Pastoral theology—Lutheran Church. I. Caemmerer, Richard Rudolph.

Pastoral theology—Mennonites.

MILLER, Paul M. 253
Servant of God's servants; the work of a Christian minister. Scottdale, Pa., Herald Pr. [c.1964] 236p. 20cm. (Conrad Grebel lectures, 1963) Bibl. 63-15499 4.50
1. Pastoral theology—Mennonites. I. Title. II. Series.

Pastoral theology—Methodist Church.

GERDES, Egon W. 253
Informed ministry : theological reflections on the practice of ministry in methodism / Egon W. Gerdes. Zurich : Publishing House of the United Methodist Church, 1976. 94 p. ; 21 cm. (Studies in Methodism and related movements : Series A, Monographs ; v. 1) [BV4011.G45] 76-370415 ISBN 3-85706-186-3 : 19.00F
1. Pastoral theology—Methodist Church. I. Title. II. Series.

GREEVES, Frederic, 1903- 250
Theology and the cure of souls; an introduction to pastoral theology. Manhasset, N.Y., Channel Press [1962] 180 p. 21 cm. (The Cato lecture of 1960) [[BV4011.G7]] 62-18047
1. Pastoral theology — Methodist Church. I. Title.

LOWDER, Paul D. 253
Feed whose sheep? [by] Paul D. Lowder. Waco, Tex., Word Books [1973] 127 p. 23 cm. Includes bibliographical references. [BV4011.L68] 72-96358 3.95
1. Lowder, Paul D. 2. Pastoral theology—Methodist Church. I. Title.

METHODIST Church (United States) Council of Bishops 253
Who is the parish minister? Ed. by T. Otto Nall. Nashville, Abingdon [c.1965] 128p. 19cm. [BV4011.M46] 65-26732 1.25 pap.,
1. Pastoral theology—Methodist Church. I. Nall, Torney Otto, 1900- ed. II. Title.

Pastoral theology—Mormon Church.

THE Priesthood manual. 262'.14933
An extensively rev. ed. Independence, MO : Herald Pub. House, c1982. 320 p. ; 21 cm. (Pastors' reference library) At head of title: Reorganized Church of Jesus Christ of Latter Day Saints. Compiled by Clifford A. Cole. Includes index. [BX8675.P74 1982] 19 81-7220 ISBN 0-8309-0334-8 : Write for information.
1. Pastoral theology—Mormon Church. I. Cole, Clifford Adair, 1915- II. Reorganized Church of Jesus Christ of Latter-Day Saints. III. Title. IV. Series.

REORGANIZED Church of Jesus Christ of Latter--Day Saints. 250
The priesthood manual. Prepared under the direction of the director of priesthood education. Rev. Independence, Mo., Herald House, 1957. 164p. 19cm. [BX8675.A45 1957] 57-1208
1. Pastoral theology—Mormon Church. I. Title.

REORGANIZED Church of Jesus Christ of Latter-Day Saints. 250
The priesthood manual. Prepared under the direction of the Office of Priesthood and Leadership Education, [New ed.] Independence, Mo., Herald House, 1964. 214 p. 18 cm. (Pastors' reference library) Bibliography: p. 209-210. [BX8675.A45] 64-25012
1. Pastoral theology — Mormon Church. I. Title.

Pastoral theology—Mormonism.

A Guide for good priesthood ministry, 253
edited by Norman D. Ruoff. [Independence, Mo., Herald Pub. House, 1971] 408 p. illus. 21 cm. Includes bibliographical references. [BV4011.G83] 75-150660 ISBN 0-8309-0044-6
1. Pastoral theology—Mormonism. I. Ruoff, Norman D., ed.

REORGANIZED Church of Jesus Christ of Latter-Day Saints. 250
The Priesthood manual, prepared by Alfred H. Yale. [Completely rev. ed.] [Independence, Mo., Herald Press, 1972] 317 p. 18 cm. (Pastor's reference library) Bibliography: p. 316-317. [BX8675.A45 1972] 72-177206 ISBN 0-8309-0065-9
1. Pastoral theology—Mormonism. I. Yale, Alfred H. II. Title.

REORGANIZED Church of Jesus Christ of Latter-Day Saints. Pastoral Care Office. 253
Empowered to care : pastoral care in the church / Pastoral Care Office. Independence, MO : Herald Pub. House, c1980. p. cm. [BV4011.R46 1980] 19 80-19335 ISBN 0-8309-0291-0 pbk. : 8.25
1. Pastoral theology—Mormonism. I. Title.

Pastoral theology—Presbyterian Church.

BAKER, Wesley C. 260
The split-level fellowship. Philadelphia, Westminster [1965] 151p. 21cm. Bibl. [BV4011.B33] 65-10080 4.50
1. Pastoral theology—Presbyterian Church. 2. Church membership. I. Title.

Pastoral theology — Research.

BAILEY, Ambrose Moody, 1875- 250
The pastor in action; tested ways to ministerial success, by Ambrose Moody Bailey ... New York, Round table press, inc., 1939. ix. 180 p. diagrs. 20 cm. Bibliography: p. 179-180. sTheology, Pastoral. [BV4010.B32] 39-25827
I. Title.

LITTLE, Lawrence Calvin, 1897-
Toward understanding the church and the clergy; contributions of selected doctoral dissertations. Pittsburgh, Dept. of Religious Education, University of Pittsburgh, 1963. ix, 218 p. 29 cm. Bibliography: p. 214-218.
1. Pastoral theology — Research. 2. Dissertations, Academic — U.S. — Abstracts. I. Title.

LITTLE, Lawrence Calvin, 1897- 253
Toward understanding the church and the clergy; contributions of selected doctoral dissertations. Pittsburgh, Dept. of Religious Education, University of Pittsburgh, 1963. ix, 218 p. 29 cm. Bibliography: p. 214-218. [BV4011.L55] 63-23863
1. Pastoral theology — Research. 2. Dissertations, Academic — U.S. — Abstracts. I. Title.

Pastoral theology—Seventh-Day Adventists.

BERG, Orley. 250
The work of the pastor. Nashville, Southern Pub. Association [1966] 180 p. 22 cm. [BV4011.B45] 66-4718
1. Pastroal theology — Seventh-Day Adventist. I. Title.

RHODES, John D 250
Success secrets for pastors, by John Rhodes. Mountain View, Calif., Pacific Press Pub. Association [1965] viii, 166 p. illus., facsims., forms. 26 cm. Bibliography: p. 160-162. [BV4011.R5] 64-8744
1. Pastoral theology — Seventh-Day Adventists. I. Title.

Pastoral theology—Study and teaching.

FALLAW, Wesner 250
The case method in pastoral and lay education. Philadelphia, Westminister [c.1963] 207p. 21cm. 63-7343 4.00
1. Pastoral theology—Study and teaching. I. Title.

Pastoral theology—United Church of Christ.

FACKRE, Gabriel J 250
The pastor and the world; the public sector witness of the parish minister [by] Gabriel J. Fackre. Philadelphia, United Church Press [1964] 126 p. 24 cm. Bibliographical references included in "Notes" (p. 119-126) [BV4011.F27] 64-25364
1. Pastoral theology — United Church of Christ. I. Title.

Patanjali.

DASGUPTA, Surendra Nath, 1885-1952. 181'.452
Yoga as philosophy and religion. Port Washington, N.Y., Kennikat Press [1970] x, 200 p. 21 cm. A brief exposition of the doctrines taught by Patanjali and elaborated by his commentators. [B132.Y6D27 1970] 75-102567
1. Patanjali. 2. Yoga. 3. Philosophy, Hindu. I. Title.

ELIADE, Mircea, 1907- 181'.452
Patanjali and yoga / Mircea Eliade ; translated by Charles Lam Markmann. New York : Schocken Books, 1975, c1969. viii, 216 p. : ill. ; 21 cm. Translation of Patanjali et le Yoga. Reprint of the ed. published by Funk & Wagnalls, New York. Includes index. Bibliography: p. [205]-209. [B132.Y6E493 1975] 75-10785 ISBN 0-8052-0491-1 pbk. : 2.95
1. Patanjali. 2. Yoga. I. Title.

ELIADE, Mircea, 1907- 181.45
Patanjali and Yoga. Translated by Charles Lam Markmann. New York, Funk &

Wagnalls [1969] viii, 216 p. illus. 21 cm. Bibliography: p. [205]-209. [B132.Y6E493] 69-18686 5.95
1. Patanjali. 2. Yoga.

RAJANEESH, Archarya, 1931- 181'.452
Yoga, the alpha and the omega : discourses on the yoga sutras of Patanjali / Rajneesh ; compilation, Swami Amrit Pathik ; editing, Ma Ananda Prem. 1st ed. Poona : Rajneesh Foundation, 1976- v. : ill. ; 23 cm. [B132.Y6R322] 76-902396 Rs65.00 (v. 1)
1. Patanjali. Yogasutra—Addresses, essays, lectures. 2. Yoga—Addresses, essays, lectures. I. Title.

SATYANANDA Saraswati, Swami, 1923- 181'.452
Four chapters on freedom : commentary on Yoga sutras of Patanjali / lectures delivered by Satyananda Paramahamsa ; editor, Swami Haripremananda Saraswati. Monghyr : Bihar School of Yoga, c1976. xxii, 288 p., [1] leaf of plates : ill. ; 22 cm. English and Sanskrit. Includes index. [B132.Y6S393] 76-904616 Rs35.00
1. Patanjali. Yogasutra. 2. Yoga. I. Title.

"Paths of life—Christian parenting program.

CHRISTIAN parenting, the adolescent. 649'.7 New York, N.Y. : Paulist Press, c1979. 121 p. : ill. ; 21 cm. [BX2351.C526] 79-90623 ISBN 0-8091-2265-0 pbk. : 2.45
1. "Paths of life—Christian parenting program. 2. Family—Religious life—Addresses, essays, lectures. 3. Youth—Religious life—Addresses, essays, lectures.

Patience.

LASANCE, Francis Xavier, 1860- ed. 242
Patience; thoughts on the patient endurance of sorrows and suffering; compiled and edited by Rev. F. X. Lasance ... New York, Cincinnati [etc.] Benziger brothers, 1937. vi, 148 p. incl. front., plates. 16 cm. [BX2170.S5L3] 37-17378
1. Patience. 2. Suffering. I. Title.

Patience—Addresses, essays, lectures.

THE Triumph of Patience 241'.4 : medieval and Renaissance studies / edited by Gerald J. Schiffhorst. Orlando : University Presses of Florida, 1977. p. cm. "A Florida Technological University book." Bibliography: p. [BJ1533.P3T74] 77-12732 ISBN 0-8130-0590-6 : 10.00
1. Patience (Middle English poem)—Addresses, essays, lectures. 2. Patience—Addresses, essays, lectures. 3. Patience in literature—Addresses, essays, lectures. I. Schiffhorst, Gerald J.

*WEDGE, Florence. 248.4
Watch it! Patience. Pulaski, Wis., Franciscan Pubs. [1968] 55p. 17cm. .25 pap.,
I. Title.

Patience (Middle English poem)—Addresses, essays, lectures.

THE Triumph of Patience 241'.4 : medieval and Renaissance studies / edited by Gerald J. Schiffhorst. Orlando : University Presses of Florida, 1977. p. cm. "A Florida Technological University book." Bibliography: p. [BJ1533.P3T74] 77-12732 ISBN 0-8130-0590-6 : 10.00
1. Patience (Middle English poem)—Addresses, essays, lectures. 2. Patience—Addresses, essays, lectures. 3. Patience in literature—Addresses, essays, lectures. I. Schiffhorst, Gerald J.

Patmore, Emily Honoria, 1853-1882.

A daughter of Coventry 922. *Patmore, Sister Mary Christina, S. H. C. J.,* by a religious of the Society of the Holy Child Jesus, with a foreword by the Right Reverend Dom Anscar Vonier ... London, New York [etc.] Longmans, Green and co., 1924. xv, 199, [1] p. incl. facsim. front., plates, ports. 20 cm. [BX4705.P38D3] 24-1985
1. Patmore, Emily Honoria, 1853-1882.

Paton, John Gibson, 1824-1907

BELL, Ralph R 922
John G. Paton, apostle to the New Hebrides. Butler, Ind., Higley Press [c1957] 240p. illus. 20cm. [BV3680.N6P35] 58-26406
1. Paton, John Gibson, 1824-1907 I. Title.

BYRUM, Bessie L. 922
John G. Paton, hero of the South Seas, by Bessie L. Byrum ... Anderson, Ind., Gospel trumpet company [c1924] 127 p. front. (port.) illus. 20 cm. [BV3680.N6P4] 24-9440
1. Paton, John Gibson, 1824-1907. I. Title.

LANGRIDGE, Albert Kent. 922
John G. Paton, later years and farewell; a sequel to John G. Paton-an autobiography. By his friend A. K. Langridge and his son Frank H. L. Paton, with an introduction by Lord Kinnaird. New York and London, Hodder and Stoughton [1910] xv, 286 p., 1 l. front., pl., ports. 20 1/2 cm. [BV3680.N6P6] 47-37657
1. Paton, John Gibson, 1824-1907. I. Paton, Frank Hume Lyall. II. Title.

MAXFIELD, Heln Adell, 1894- 268.61
The Tabernacle; director's manual. Grand Rapids, Zondervan [1950] 180 p. 20 cm. [BM654.M36] 50-4560
1. Paton, John Gibson, 2. Tabernacle—Study and teaching. I. Title.

MUELLER, John Theodore, 1885- 922
John G. Paton, missionary to the New Herbrides, 1824-1907, by Rev. J. Theodore Mueller ... Grand Rapids, Mich., Zondervan publishing house [c1941] 129 p. 20 cm. [BV3680.N6M8] 41-7846
1. Paton, John Gibson, 1824-1907. 2. Missions—New Hebrides. I. Title.

PATON, James, Rev. 1843-1906. 922
The story of John G. Paton, told for young folks; or, Thirty years among South sea cannibals. By the Rev. James Paton, B. A. New copyright ed., with two new chapters and forty-five full-page illustrations by James Finnemore ... New York, A. C. Armstrong and son, 1898. 404 p. incl. front., plates. 21 cm. "Fifteenth thousand." [BV3680.N6P3] C-372
1. Paton, John Gibson, 1824-1907. 2. Oceanica—Descr. & trav. I. Title.

Paton, John Gibson, 1824-1907—Juvenile literature.

ROBINSON, Virgil E. 266'.6'73 B
Curse of the cannibals / Virgil E. Robinson ; [ill., John Gourley]. Washington : Review and Herald Pub. Association, c1976. 125 p. : ill. ; 21 cm. (Penguin series) "Originally published in Guide magazine under the title King of the cannibals." A biography of the Scottish missionary with emphasis on his work in the New Hebrides. [BV3680.N6P67 1976] 92 76-23025
1. Paton, John Gibson, 1824-1907—Juvenile literature. 2. [Paton, John Gibson, 1824-1907.] 3. Missionaries—Scotland—Biography—Juvenile literature. 4. Missionaries—New Hebrides—Biography—Juvenile literature. 5. Missions—New Hebrides—Juvenile literature. 6. [Missionaries.] I. Title.

Patriarchs and patriarchate.

CLARKE, Boden, 1948- 280'.2
Lords temporal & lords spiritual : a chronological checklist of the popes, patriarchs, katholikoi, and independent archbishops and metropolitans of the autocephalous monarchical churches of the Christian East and West ... / Boden Clarke. San Bernardino, Calif. : Borgo Press, [1980] p. cm. [BX400.C55] 80-10979 ISBN 0-89370-800-3 : 8.95 ISBN 0-89370-900-X (pbk.) : 2.95
1. Patriarchs and patriarchate. 2. Patriarchs and patriarchate (Catholic Oriental) I. Title.

KANE, Thomas Aloysius, 1915-
The jurisdiction of the patriarchs of the major sees in antiquity and in the Middle Ages; a historical commentary. Washington, Catholic Univ. of America Press, 1949. xii, 111 p. 23 cm. (The Catholic University of America. Canon law studies, no. 276) Thesis--Catholic Univ. of America. Biographical note. Bibliography: p. 92-95. A 49
1. Patriarchs and patriarchate. I. Title. II. Series.

Patriarchs and patriarchate—Biography.

†TSAKONAS, Demetrios Gr. 281.9'092'4 B
A man sent by God : the life of Patriarch Athenagoras of Constantinople / Demetrios Tsakonas ; [translated from the Greek by George Angeloglou]. Brookline, Mass. : Holy Cross Orthodox Press, c1977. x, 99 p., [8] leaves of plates : ill. ; 22 cm. Translation of Athenagoras ho Oikoumenikos ton neon ideon. Includes bibliographical references and index. [BX395.A8T7613] 77-77669 ISBN 0-916586-07-3 pbk. : 3.95
1. Athenagoras I, Ecumenical Patriarch of Constantinople, 1886-1972. 2. Patriarchs and patriarchate—Biography. I. Title.
Publisher's address : 50 Goddard Ave., Brookline, MA 02146

Patriarchs and patriarchate (Catholic Oriental)—Congresses.

ARCHIEPISCOPAL and patriarchal autonomy; 262 a symposium held on July 15, 1972, at Lincoln Center Campus. Editors: Thomas E. Bird [and] Eva Piddubcheshen. New York, Fordham University, 1972. 74 p. 23 cm. Includes bibliographical references. [BX4711.62.A7] 72-11841
1. Catholic Church. Byzantine rite (Ukrainian)—Congresses. 2. Patriarchs and patriarchate (Catholic Oriental)—Congresses. I. Bird, Thomas E., 1888- ed. II. Piddubcheshen, Eva, ed. III. Fordham University, New York.

Patriarchs (Bible)

HOLT, John Marshall. 222.11095
The patriarchs of Israel. Nashville, Vanderbilt University Press, 1964. vii, 239 p. 23 cm. Bibliography: p. 219-224. [BS1235.2.H6] 64-13543
1. Bible. O. T. Genesis—Criticism, interpretation, etc. 2. Patriarchs (Bible) I. Title.

STORIES of the patriarchs, 221. from the days of our first parents in Eden to the time of the judges ... New York, World syndicate company [c1924] [100] p. illus. (part col.) 24 1/2 x 19 1/2 cm. [BS551.S78] 24-21701

STORIES of the prophets, 221. *warriors and kings,* from the invasion of and occupation of Canaan to the captivity in Babylon ... New York, World syndicate company, 1924. [100] p. illus. (part. col.) 24 x 19 1/2 cm. [BS551.S785] 24-21698

WESTERMANN, Claus. 222'.11'06
The promises to the fathers : studies on the patriarchal narratives / Claus Westermann ; translated by David E. Green. Philadelphia : Fortress Press, c1979. p. cm. Translation of Die Verheissungen an die Vater. Includes bibliographical references and index. [BS1235.2.W45413] 79-7395 ISBN 0-8006-0580-2 : 12.95
1. Bible. O.T. Genesis—Criticism, interpretation, etc. 2. Patriarchs (Bible) I. Title.

Patriarchs (Bible)—Biography.

COLE, C. Donald. 222'.11'0924 B
Abraham : God's man of faith / by C. Donald Cole. Chicago : Moody Press, c1977. 223 p. ; 22 cm. [BS580.A3C57] 77-1268 ISBN 0-8024-0033-7 pbk. : 3.95
1. Abraham, the patriarch. 2. Bible. O.T.—Biography. 3. Patriarchs (Bible)—Biography. I. Title.

FERGUSON, Ben. 222'.11'0924 B
The shaping of a man of faith / Ben E. Ferguson. Wheaton, Ill. : Victor Books, c1979. 95 p. ; 18 cm. [BS580.A3F47] 78-55178 ISBN 0-88207-516-0 pbk. : 1.75
1. Abraham, the patriarch. 2. Bible. O.T.—Biography. 3. Patriarchs (Bible)—Biography. 4. Christian life—1960- I. Title.

FLYNN, Leslie B. 222'.11'0924 B
Joseph, God's man in Egypt / Leslie B. Flynn. Wheaton, Ill. : Victor Books, c1979. 152 p. : ill. ; 18 cm. [BS580.J6F63] 79-64820 ISBN 0-88207-788-0 pbk. : 2.25
1. Joseph, the patriarch. 2. Bible. O.T.—Biography. 3. Patriarchs (Bible)—Biography. I. Title.

PETERSEN, Mark E. 222'.11'0924 B
Abraham, friend of God / Mark E. Petersen. Salt Lake City : Deseret Book Co., c1979. 161 p. ; 24 cm. Includes index. [BS580.A3P45] 79-17445 ISBN 0-87747-780-9 : 5.95
1. Abraham, the patriarch. 2. Bible. O.T.—Biography. 3. Patriarchs (Bible)—Biography. 4. Mormons and Mormonism—Doctrinal and controversial works. I. Title.

Patriarchs (Bible)—Biography—Juvenile literature.

COHEN, Barbara. 221.9'24 B
The binding of Isaac / Barbara Cohen ; illustrated by Charles Mikolaycak. 1st ed. New York : Lothrop Lee & Shepard, c1978. [32] p. : col. ill. ; 22 cm. An aged Isaac recounts to his grandchildren the story of how God tested Abraham by asking him to sacrifice his son. [BS580.I67C63] 77-90367 ISBN 0-688-41830-9. ISBN 0-688-51830-3 lib. bdg. : 6.67
1. Isaac, the patriarch—Juvenile literature. 2. Abraham, the patriarch—Juvenile literature. 3. [Isaac, the patriarch.] 4. [Abraham, the patriarch.] 5. Bible. O.T.—Biography—Juvenile literature. 6. Patriarchs (Bible)—Biography—Juvenile literature. 7. [Bible stories—O.T.] I. Mikolaycak, Charles. II. Title.

COHEN, Barbara. 222'.11'0924 B
I am Joseph / Barbara Cohen ; illustrated by Charles Mikolaycak. 1st ed. New York : Lothrop, Lee, & Shepard Books, c1980. [48] p. : col. ill. ; 26 cm. Retells the Biblical story of Joseph, from his viewpoint, relating how he was sold into slavery and became the Egyptian Pharaoh's adviser. [BS580.J6C64] 79-20001 ISBN 0-688-41933-X : 9.95 ISBN 0-688-51933-4 lib. bdg. : 9.55
1. Joseph, the patriarch—Juvenile literature. 2. [Joseph, the patriarch.] 3. Bible. O.T.—Biography—Juvenile literature. 4. Patriarchs (Bible)—Biography—Juvenile literature. 5. [Bible stories—O.T.] I. Mikolaycak, Charles. II. Title.

†GRIFFITHS, Kitty Anna. 222'.11'0924 B
Come, meet Abraham, God's friend : the story of Genesis 21-25 / Kitty Anna Griffiths. Grand Rapids : Zondervan Pub. House, 1977. 95 p. : ill. ; 21 cm. (Come, meet series) Retells the events in the life of Abraham. [BS580.A3G68] 76-54670 ISBN 0-310-25201-6 pbk : 1.95.
1. Abraham, the patriarch—Juvenile literature. 2. [Abraham, the patriarch.] 3. Bible. O.T.—Biography—Juvenile literature. 4. Patriarchs (Bible)—Biography—Juvenile literature. 5. [Bible stories—O.T.] I. Title.

†GRIFFITHS, Kitty Anna. 222'.11'0924 B
Come, meet Abraham, the pioneer : the story of Genesis 12-20 / Kitty Anna Griffiths. Grand Rapids : Zondervan Pub. House, 1977. 95 p. : ill. ; 21 cm. (Come, meet series) Discusses the life of Abraham and God's promise to him as found in Genesis 12-20. [BS580.A3G683] 76-54844 ISBN 0-310-25191-5 pbk : 1.95
1. Abraham, the patriarch—Juvenile literature. 2. [Abraham, the patriarch.] 3. Bible. O.T.—Biography—Juvenile literature. 4. Patriarchs (Bible)—Biography—Juvenile literature. 5. [Bible stories—O.T.] I. Title.

†GRIFFITHS, Kitty Anna. 222'.11'0924
Come, meet Isaac : the story of Genesis 25-28 / Kitty Anna Griffiths. Grand

Rapids : Zondervan Pub. House, 1977. 95 p. : ill. ; 21 cm. (Come, meet series) Retells the life of Isaac, as found in Genesis. [BS580.I67G74] 76-13173 ISBN 0-310-25211-3 pbk : 1.95
1. Isaac, the patriarch—Juvenile literature. 2. [Isaac, the patriarch.] 3. Bible. O.T.—Biography—Juvenile literature. 4. Patriarchs (Bible)—Biography—Juvenile literature. 5. [Bible stories—O.T.] I. Title.

RIVES, Elsie. 222'.11'0924 B
Abraham, man of faith / Elsie Rives ; illustrated by William N. McPheeters. Nashville : Broadman Press, c1976. 48 p. : col. ill. ; 24 cm. (Biblearn series) Discusses Abraham's efforts to obey God and establish a new nation in Canaan. [BS580.A3R58] 76-382767 3.95
1. Abraham, the patriarch—Juvenile literature. 2. [Abraham, the patriarch.] 3. Patriarchs (Bible)—Biography—Juvenile literature. 4. [Bible stories—O.T.] I. McPheeters, William N. II. Title.

Patriarchs (Bible)—Juvenile literature.

BORUCH, Behn. 221.92
The patriarchs; the story of Abraham, Isaac and Jacob. Illustrated by Bernard Spingsteel. New York, Hebrew Pub. Co., c1960. unpaged. illus. 23cm. [BS573.B6] 60-2150
1. Patriarchs (Bible)—Juvenile literature. I. Title.

Patriarchs (Bible)—Sermons.

ROUTLEY, Erik. 252'.05'8
Saul among the prophets. [Abridged ed. Nashville, Tenn.] The Upper Room [1972] vi, 91 p. 20 cm. Includes bibliographical references. [BS573.R682] 79-188604 1.25
1. Patriarchs (Bible)—Sermons. 2. Congregational churches—Sermons. 3. Sermons, English. I. Title.

Patriarchs (Mormonism)—Addresses, essays, lectures.

THE Patriarchs / 253.7
edited by Reed M. Holmes. Independence, Mo. : Herald Pub. House, 1978. p. cm. [BX8675.P37] 78-1895 ISBN 0-8309-0205-8 pbk. : 6.75
1. Reorganized Church of Jesus Christ of Latter-Day Saints—Government—Addresses, essays, lectures. 2. Patriarchs (Mormonism)—Addresses, essays, lectures. I. Holmes, Reed M.

Patrick, Saint, 373?-463?

BEEBE, Catherine, 270.20924 B
1898-
Saint Patrick, apostle of Ireland. Drawings by S. Ohrvel Carlson. Paterson, N.J., Saint Anthony Guild Press [1968] 40 p. col. illus. 23 cm. Relates what is known of St. Patrick, whose feast day is celebrated March 17th, describing his servitude in Ireland, his journey to England and freedom, and his return to Ireland to teach Christianity. [BX4700.P3B4] 92 AC 68
1. Patrick, Saint, 373?-463? I. Carlson, S. Ohrvel, illus. II. Title.

BIELER, Ludwig. 282.415 s
St. Patrick and the coming of Christianity. Dublin, Gill [1967] [8], 100 p. 22 cm. (A History of Irish Catholicism, v. 1, 1) Bibliography: 7th-8th prelim. pages. [BX1503.H55 vol. 1, no. 1] 74-17605 7/6
1. Patrick, Saint, 373?-463? I. Title. II. Series.

BUCK, Alan Michael. 922.2415
My Saint Patrick, by Alan Michael Buck; pictires by Richard Bennett. Boston, New York, Lothrop, Lee and Shepard company, 1937. xi, 13-243 p. incl. front., illus., plates. 21 cm. Bibliography: p. 241-243. [BX4700.P3B75] 37-21634
1. Patrick, Saint, 373?-468? I. Title.

BURY, John Bagnell, 270.20924 B
1861-1927.
The life of St. Patrick and his place in history. Freeport, N.Y., Books for Libraries Press [1971] xv, 404 p. maps. 23 cm. Reprint of the 1905 ed. Includes bibliographical references. [BX4700.P3B8 1971] 79-175691 ISBN 0-8369-6606-6
1. Patrick, Saint, 373?-463? I. Title.

BURY, John Bagnell, 1861- 922.
1927.
The life of St. Patrick and his place in history, by J. B. Bury... London, Macmillan and co., limited; New York, The Macmillan company, 1905. xv, 404 p. 2 maps. 23 cm. "Bibliographical note": p. 225. [BX4700.P3B8] 5-35681
1. Patrick, Saint, 373?-468? I. Title.
Contents omitted.

CONCANNON, Helena, Mrs. 922.2415
Saint Patrick: his life and mission [by] Mrs. Thomas Concannon ... London, New York [etc.] Longmans, Green and co., 1931. xxxiv, 269 p. illus. (map) plates, 2 port. (incl. front.) facsim. 20 cm. "The sources of St. Patrick's story": p. ix-xxxiii. [BX4700.P3C6] 31-34000
1. Patrick, Saint, 373?-463? I. Title.

CUSHING, Richard James 922.2415
Cardinal 1895-
Saint Patrick and the Irish. [Boston] St. Paul Eds. [dist Daughters of St. Paul, c.1963] 114p. illus. 22cm. 63-14892 2.50;1.50 pap.,
1. Patrick, Saint, 373?-463? I. Title.

CUSHING, Richard James, 922.2415
Cardinal, 1895-
Saint Patrick and the Irish. [Boston] St. Paul Editions [1963] 114 p. illus. 22 cm. [BX4700.P3C8] 63-14892
1. Patrick, Saint, 373?-463? I. Title.

CZARNOWSKI, Stefan. 282'.415
Le culte des heros et ses conditions sociales / Stefan Czarnowski. New York : Arno Press, 1975, c1919. p. cm. (European sociology) Reprint of the ed. published by F. Alcan, Paris, in series Travaux de l'Annee sociologique and Bibliotheque de philosophie contemporaine. Includes index. [BX4700.P3C9 1975] 74-25745 ISBN 0-405-06500-0
1. Patrick, Saint, 373?-463? 2. Heroes. I. Title. II. Series. III. Series: L'Annee sociologique. Travaux.

DE BLACAM, Aodh 922.2415
Sandrach.
Saint Patrick, apostle of Ireland, by Hugh De Blacam. Milwaukee, The Bruce publishing company [1941] xi p., 1 l., 176 p. 22 cm. (Half-title: Science and culture series; Joseph Husslein ... general editor) [BX4700.P3D4] 41-5093
1. Patrick, Saint, 373?-463? I. Title.

ERNEST, Brother, 1897- 922.2415
Saint of the fighting Irish; a story of St. Patrick. Illus. by Brother Bernard Howard. Notre Dame, Ind., Dujarie Press [1953] 95p. illus. 24cm. [BX4700.P3E7] 53-2906
1. Patrick, Saint, 373?—163? I. Title.

GOGARTY, Oliver St. 922.2415
John, 1878-
I follow Saint Patrick, [by] Oliver St. John Gogarty. New York, Reynal & Hitchcock, [c1938] xi, [1] 321 p. front. (map) illus., plates. (1 double) 23 cm. Illustrated lining-papers. [BX4700.P3G6 1938 a] 38-277267
1. Patrick, Saint, 373?-463? 2. Ireland—Descr. & trav. I. Title.

HANSON, Richard 270.2'0924
Patrick Crosland.
Saint Patrick, his origins and career, by R. P. C. Hanson. New York, Oxford University Press, 1968. 248 p. 22 cm. Bibliography: p. [230]-235. [BX4700.P3H27] 68-20360
1. Patrick, Saint, 373?-463? I. Title.

HARNEY, Martin 270.2'092'4 B
Patrick, 1896-
The legacy of Saint Patrick as found in his own writings [by] Martin P. Harney. [Boston] St. Paul Editions [1972] 144 p. illus. 22 cm. Includes bibliographical references. [BX4700.P3H29] 76-183441 3.00
1. Patrick, Saint, 373?-463? I. Title.

LESLIE, Shane, 1885- 922.
The story of St. Patrick's purgatory, by Shane Leslie. St. Louis, Mo., and London, B. Herder book co., 1917. 5 p. l., xv p., 1 l., 78 p. 19 1/2 cm. [Full name: John Randolph Shane Leslie] [BX4700.P31L5] 19-6220
1. Patrick, Saint, 373?-463? I. Title.

MARIE de France, 12thcent.
... *The Espurgatoire Saint Patriz* of Marie de France, with a text of the Latin original, by T. Atkinson Jenkins ... Chicago, The University of Chicago press, 1903. 95 p. 29 cm. Printed from First series. v. 7 (p. 235-327) of the Decennial publications of the University of Chicago. Supersedes the editor's earlier edition of the French text (Johns Hopkins dissertation, 1894) which made small use of the Latin Tractatus de Purgatorio Sancti Patricil of Henry of Saltrey. The revised text of Marie's version is given in parallel columns with the latin (mainly from Brit. mus. Harley ms. 3846, here printed for the first time) The appendix (p. 78-95) contains an additional latin text. Brit. mus. Royal ms. 13 B. viii, printed in full for the first time. [PQ1494.P3J52] 3-14274
I. Patrick, Saint. Legend. Purgatorium. II. Henry of Saltrey, fl. 1150. III. Jenkins, Thomas Atkinson, 1868- ed. IV. Title.

NEWELL, Ebenezer Josiah, 281.
1853-
... *St. Patrick;* his life and teaching; by the Rev. E. J. Newell ... 2d ed., rev., pub. under the direction of the Tract committee. London, Society for promoting Christian knowledge; New York, E. S. Gorham, 1907. viii, 237, [1] p. 17 cm. (The Fathers for English readers) [BR1705.F4P3] 20-17691
1. Patrick, Saint, 373?-463? I. Society for promoting Christian knowledge, London. Tract committee. II. Title.

PATRICK, Saint, 270.2'092'4 B
373?-463?
Patrick in his own words. [Translated and with commentary by] Joseph Duffy. [Dublin] Veritas Publications [1972] 97 p. 19 cm. English translation and Latin original of the author's Confessio. Includes bibliographical references. [BX4700.P3P3713] 74-152587 £0.50
1. Patrick, Saint, 373?-463? I. Duffy, Joseph A. II. Title.

PATRICK, Saint, 373?-463? 235
... *St. Patrick,* his writings and life, by Newport J. D. White, D. D. London, Society for promoting Christian knowledge; New York, The Macmillan company, 1920. v, 142 p. 19 cm. (Translations of Christian literature. series v: Lives of the Celtic saints) Contains a translation of Muirchu's Life of St. Patrick. [BR45.T65P3] 21-8934
I. Muirchu maccu Machtheni, fl. 697. II. White, Newport John Davis. 1860- ed. and tr. III. Title.

REYNOLDS, Quentin 270.2'0924 B
James, 1902-1965.
The life of Saint Patrick, by Quentin Reynolds. Illustrated by Douglas Gorsline. New York, Random House [1955] 182 p. illus. 22 cm. (World landmark books [W-17]) A biography of the British boy, captured by raiding Irish warriors at age sixteen, who performed miracles, ended the power of the Druid priests over the Irish people, and converted the Irish kings and their people to Christianity. [BX4700.P3R4] 92 AC 68
1. Patrick, Saint, 373?-463? I. Gorsline, Douglas W., 1913- illus. II. Title.

REYNOLDS, Quentin James, 922.2415
1902-1965.
The life of Saint Patrick; illustrated by Douglas Gorsline. New York, Random House [1955] 182 p. illus. 22 cm. (World landmark books [W-17]) [BX4700.P3R4] 55-5826
1. Patrick, Saint, 373-463?

RYAN, John, 1894- ed. 922.22
Saint Patrick. [Dublin] Published for Radio Eireann by the Stationery Off., 1958. 94p. 19cm. (Thomas Davis lectures, [4]) Added t. p., in Gaelic. [BX4700.P3R9] 58-46462
1. Patrick, Saint, 373?-463? I. Title. II. Series.

SANDERSON, Joseph, 1823-1915.
The story of Saint Patrick, with a sketch of Ireland's condition before and after Patrick's time, by Joseph Sanderson ... Ireland and the Irish; their Christianity, institutions, missions, mission fields and learning, from the earliest times, with an appendix by John Borland Finlay ... Boston, W. L. Richardson co.; New-York, [1894] 2 v. in 1. 24 1/2 cm. Two separate works, each with special t.-p. [DA932.2.P3S2] 4-3124
1. Patrick, Saint, 373?-463? 2. Catholic church in Ireland. I. Finlay, John Borland, 1826-1897. II. Title.

SHAHAN, Thomas Joseph, bp., 922.
1857-1932.
Saint Patrick in history, by the Very Rev. Thos. J. Shahan... New York, London [etc.] Longmans, Green, and co., 1904. 2 p. l., 77 p. 17 cm. Bibliography: p. 69-77. [BX4700.P3S5] 4-7336
1. Patrick Saint, 373?-463? I. Title.

Patrick, Saint, 373?-463?—Bibliography

CHICAGO. Public library.
St. Patrick; list of books and magazine articles in the Chicago Public library. [Chicago] The Chicago public library, 1910. 8 p. 16 cm. [Z8665.3C56] 13-10494
1. Patrick, Saint, 373?-463?—Bibl. I. Title.

Patrick, Saint, 373?-463?—Juvenile literature.

BEEBE, Catherine, 1898- 92 (j)
Saint Patrick, apostle of Ireland. Drawings by S. Ohrvel Carlson. Paterson, N.J., Saint Anthony Guild Press [1968] 40 p. col. illus. 23 cm. [BX4700.P3B4] 68-25401
1. Patrick, Saint, 373?-463?—Juvenile literature. I. Title.

CORFE, Thomas 270.2'092'4 B
Howell.
St. Patrick and Irish Christianity / Tom Corfe. Minneapolis : Lerner Publications Co., 1979, c1973. 51 p. : ill. ; 21 x 23 cm. (A Cambridge topic book) Includes index. Relates what is known about the life and times of Saint Patrick, how he brought the Christian religion to Ireland, and the work of Christian missionaries in Britain and Europe. [BX4700.P3C63 1979] 92 78-56811 ISBN 0-8225-1217-3 lib.bdg. : 4.95
1. Patrick, Saint, 373?-463?—Juvenile literature. 2. [Patrick, Saint, 373?-463?] 3. Missions—Europe—Juvenile literature. 4. [Saints.] 5. [Missions—Europe.] I. Title.

HAYS, Wilma 270.2'0924 B
Pitchford.
Patrick of Ireland. Illustrated by Peter Burchard. New York, Coward-McCann [1970] 64 p. illus. (part col.) 23 cm. A biography of the fifth-century monk who brought Christianity to Ireland. [BX4700.P3H36] 92 71-87885 3.29
1. Patrick, Saint, 373?-463?—Juvenile literature. 2. [Patrick, Saint, 373?-463?] I. Burchard, Peter, illus. II. Title.

HUNT, Marigold 92
Patrick. Drawings by Gareth Floyd. New York, Sheed [1965] 1v. (unpaged) illus. (pt. col.) 21cm. (Patron saint books) [BX4700.P3H8] 64-18775 2.50
1. Patrick, Saint, 373?-463?—Juvenile literature. I. Title.

ROQUITTE, Ruth. 270.2'092'4 B
Saint Patrick, the Irish saint / by Ruth Roquitte ; illustrated by Robert Kilbride. Minneapolis, Minn. : Dillon Press, c1981. 46 p. : col. ill. ; 26 cm. An easy-to-read biography of Ireland's patron saint. [BR1720.P26R66] 92 19 81-3152 ISBN 0-87518-218-6 : 7.95
1. Patrick, Saint, 373?-463?—Juvenile literature. 2. [Patrick, Saint, 373?-463?] 3. Christian saints—Ireland—Biography—Juvenile literature. 4. [Saints.] I. Kilbride, Robert. II. Title.

Patrick, Ted.

PATRICK, Ted. 200'.1'9 B
Let our children go! / By Ted Patrick, with Tom Dulack. 1st ed. New York : Dutton, 1976. 285 p. : ill. ; 22 cm. "Thomas Congdon books." [BP603.P37 1976] 75-45298 ISBN 0-525-14450-1 : 7.95
1. Patrick, Ted. 2. Sects—Controversial literature. 3. Youth—Religious life. I. Dulack, Tom, 1935- joint author. II. Title.

PATRICK, Ted. 200'.1'9
Let our children go! / by Ted Patrick, with Tom Dulack. New York : Ballantine Books, 1977c1976. vii, 176p. : ill. ; 18 cm.

[BP603.P37 1976] ISBN 0-345-25663-8 pbk. : 1.95
1. Patrick, Ted. 2. Sects-Controversial literature. 3. Youth-Religious life. I. Dulack, Tom., joint author. II. Title.
L.C. card no. for 1976 E.P. Dutton ed.: 75-45298.

Patriotism.

ALDEN, Joseph, 1807-1885. 221.92
The Jewish Washington; or, Lessons of patriotism and piety suggested by the history of Nehemiah. By Rev. Joseph Alden, D.D. Written for the Massachusetts Sabbath school society, and revised by the Committee of publication. Boston, Massachusetts Sabbath school society, 1846. 90 p. incl. front. 19 cm. Tall-pieces. [BS580.N45A6] 37-7012
1. Nehemiah. 2. Patriotism. I. Massachusetts Sabbath school society. Committee of publication. II. Title. III. Title: Lessons of patriotism and piety.

Patriotism—Moral and religious aspects.

MINEAR, Paul Sevier, 1906- 261.7
I pledge allegiance : patriotism and the Bible / by Paul S. Minear. Philadelphia : Geneva Press, [1975] 140 p. ; 21 cm. Includes bibliographies. Examines various national issues, such as civil disobedience, amnesty, and segregation, from Biblical perspectives. [BR115.P7M543] 74-31489 ISBN 0-664-24819-5 pbk. : 2.65
1. Patriotism—Moral and religious aspects. 2. [Patriotism.] 3. [Christian life.] I. Title.

SHAVER, Erwin L. 265.
A Christian's patriotism; a suggested plan for a project for young people's groups, by Erwin L. Shaver. Chicago, Ill., The University of Chicago press [c1927] ix, 58 [6] p. 19 1/2 cm. (Half-title: The University of Chicago publications in religious education ... Constructive studies) Blank pages for "Notes" between p. 26 and 27 and at end. "Reference and source material": p. 27-58. [BR115.P7S44] 27-24911
I. Title.

Patron saints.

MCLOUGHLIN, Helen 249
My nameday--come for dessert. Collegeville, Minn., Liturgical Pr. [1963, c.1962] 320p. illus., 21cm. 63-3393 2.75
1. Patron saints. 2. Desserts. 3. Saints—Prayerbooks and devotions—English. I. Title.

OUR patron saints, with prayers and indulgences. 263.98 New York, J. J. Crawley [1963] vii, 120 p. illus. (part col.) 23 cm. [BX4656.5.O8] 64-331
1. Patron saints.

STARR, Eliza Allen, 1824-1901. 922.2
Patron saints. By Eliza Allen Starr ... Baltimore, J. Murphy & co.; New York, Catholic publication society, 1871. 382 p. front., plates. 19 cm. The author published "Patron saints" (2d ser.) in 1881. [BX4058.S7 1st ser.] 38-11164
1. Patron saints. I. Title.
Contents omitted.

STARR, Eliza Allen, 1824-1901. 922.2
... Patron saints, by Eliza Allen Starr ... Baltimore, J. B. Piet, 1881. vi p., 1 l., [9]-489 p. front., plates. 20 cm. At head of title: Second series. The author's "Patron saints" (1st ser.) appeared in 1871. [BX4658.S7 2d ser.] 38-11163
1. Patron saints. I. Title.
Contents omitted.

Patronage, Ecclesiastical.

SMITH, Waldo Edward Lovel, 1901- 262.1
Episcopal appointments and patronage in the reign of Edward II, a study in the relations of church and state, by Waldo E. L. Smith ... Chicago, Ill., The American society of church history, 1938. xv, 144 p. incl. front. (facsim.) 25 cm. (Half-title: Studies in church history, vol. iii) "This essay was first submitted as a doctoral dissertation at the University of Edinburgh in 1931."--Foreword. Bibliography: p. 138-141. [BR750.S6] 38-25903
1. Patronage, Ecclesiastical. 2. Benefices, Ecclesiastical. 3. Church and state in Great Britain. 4. Catholic church in, England. 5. Gt. Brit.—Hist.—Edward II, 1307-1327. I. American society of church history. II. Title.

Patronage, Ecclesiastical—Great Britain

HOWELL, Margaret 262
Regalian right in medieval England. [Dist. New York, Oxford, c.]1962. xv, 264p. illus. 23cm. (Univ. of London historical studies, 9) Bibl. 62-6241 6.75
1. Patronage, Ecclesiastical—Gt. Brit. I. Title. II. Series: London. University. Historical studies, 9

Patronage, Ecclesiastical—Spain—Colonies.

SHIELS, William Eugene, 1897- 261.7
King and church; the rise and fall of the Patronato Real. Chicago, Loyola Univ. Press [c.]1961. xxiii, 399p (Jesuit studies; contributions to the arts and sciences by members of the Society of Jesus) Bibl. 61-11113 6.00
1. Patronage, Ecclesiastical—Spain—Colonies. 2. Church and state in Spain. I. Title.

Patten, David Wyman, 1800 (ca.)-1838.

WILSON, Lycurgus Arnold, 1856- 922.
Life of David W. Patten, the first apostolic martyr. [By] Lycurgus A. Wilson ... Salt Lake City, Utah, The Deseret news, 1904. viii, 72 p. 16 x 12 cm. [BX8695.P3W5] 44-13747
1. Patten, David Wyman, 1800 (ca.)-1838. I. Title.

Patterson, Frederic William, 1877-

MASON, Gwen. 286'.1'0924 B
Service from sea to sea: depicting the ministries of Frederic William Patterson, minister, denominational executive, and college president, in Canada, both west and east, 1895-1948. Compiled and written by Gwen and Merle H. Mason. [Ontario, Calif., Duplicated at the First Baptist Church, 1970- v. illus. 27 cm. Contents.Contents.—v. 1. A man of the cloth in the West. [BX6495.P28M3] 74-180514
1. Patterson, Frederic William, 1877- I. Mason, Merle H., joint author. II. Title.

Patterson, James, 1779-1837.

ADAIR, Robert. 285.
Memoir of Rev. James Patterson... by Robert Adair...With an introduction and chapter on field preaching, by Rev. D.L. Carroll... Philadelphia, H. Perkins, 1840. xxiii, (25)-324 p. 19 cm. Pages [1-11] (half-title) wanting. [BX9225.P37A4] 2-20199
1. Patterson, James, 1779-1837. I. Carroll, David L. 1787-1851. II. Title.

Patterson, John Coleridge, bp., 1827-1871.

DEBENHAM, Mary H. 266
Patteson of the isles, by Mary H. Debenham. With four illustrations by T. H. Robinson and other pictures and map. London, New York [etc.] H. Milford, Oxford university press, 1921. 159, [1] p. front. (port.) illus. (incl. map) plates. 19 cm. (Lettered on cover: The pathfinder series) [BV3640.P2D4] 22-13901
1. Patteson, John Cloeridge, bp., 1827-1871. I. Title.

TWICHELL, Joseph Hopkins, 1838-1918.
A modern knight, by Rev. Joseph Hopkins Twichell ... New Haven, Yale foreign missionary society, 1906. 1 p. l., 5-37 p. 2 port. (1 mounted) 15 1/2 x 13 1/2 cm. [BV3676.P3T9] 6-38353
1. Patterson, John Coleridge, bp., 1827-1871. 2. Yale foreign missionary society. I. Title.

Patterson, Virginia, 1931-

PATTERSON, Virginia, 1931- 242
A touch of God / Virginia Patterson. Nashville : Abingdon, c1979. 112 p. ; 21 cm. [BV4844.P34] 79-12283 ISBN 0-687-42399-6 : 6.95
1. Patterson, Virginia, 1931- 2. Women—Prayer-books and devotions—English. I. Title.

Pattison, George.

FOULDS, Elfrida Vipont (Brown), 1902- 922.8642
Blow the man down, by Charles Vipont [pseud.] With which is published The fighting sailor turn'd peaceable Christian of Thomas Lurting, first printed in 1710. Illustrated by Norman Hepple. Philadelphia, Lippincott [1952] 248 p. illus. 19 cm. [BX7795.P28F6] 52-11570
1. Pattison, George. I. Lurting, Thomas. II. Title. III. Title: The fighting sailor turn'd peaceable Christian.

Patton, William, 1796-1856.

MCANALLY, David Rice, 1810-1895. 922.773
Life and times of Rev. William Patton, and annals of the Missouri conference. By Rev. D. R. M'Anally. St. Louis, Printed at the Methodist book depository, 1858. vi, 347 p. 19 1/2 cm. [BX8495.P36M3] 36-37417
1. Patton, William, 1796-1856. 2. Methodist Episcopal church. Conferences. Missouri. I. Title.

Patton, William Weston, 1821-1889.

PATTON, Cornelius Howard, 1860- 922.573
Honour thy father. A sermon in memory of William Weston Patton by his son, Rev. Cornelius H. Patton. Congregational church of Christ, Westfield, N. J., April 13, mdcccxc. [n. p., 1890!] 3 p. l., [3]-75 p. front. (port.) 23 cm. Appendix includes: Testimonial from the faculty of Howard university; Resolution adopted by the First Congregational church of Chicago; The home life of Dr. Patton, by Caroline P. Hatch; How to make the next life seem real, by W. W. Patton. [BX7260.P38P3] 36-5001
1. Patton, William Weston, 1821-1889. I. Hatch, Caroline (Patton) Mrs. II. Title.

Paul, de Moll, pere. 1824-1896.

VAN SPEYBROUCK, Edouard. 922.2493
The Very Rev. Father Paul of Moll; a Flemish Benedictine and wonder worker of the nineteenth century, 1824-1896, by Edward Van Speybrouck: translated from the 2d French edition by a member of the Order of St. Benedict. Clyde, Mo., Benedictine convent, 1910. xiii, [3], 17-383 p. incl. front. (port.) plates. 20 cm. "Life of St. Benedict ... taken from the writings of Saint Gregory the Great": p. [306]-355. [BX4705.P384V3] 10-14340
1. Paul, de Moll, pere. 1824-1896. 2. Benedictus, Saint, abbot of Monte Cassino. 3. Miracles. I. Hetzinger, Ephrem, 1858-1911, tr. II. Title.

Paul James Francis, Father, 1863-1940.

ANGELL, Charles. 248'.242'0924 B
Prophet of reunion : the life of Paul of Graymoor / Charles Angell, Charles LaFontaine ; with an introd. by James Stuart Wetmore. New York : Seabury Press, [1975] xi, 224 p. : ill. ; 22 cm. "A Crossroad book." [BX4705.P3842A8] 74-32239 ISBN 0-8164-0281-7 : 6.95
1. Paul James Francis, Father, 1863-1940. I. LaFontaine, Charles, joint author. II. Title.

CRANNY, Titus, 1921- 922.273
Father Paul, apostle of unity; a biographical study of the unity vocation of Father Paul James Francis, S. A., founder of the Society of the Atonement and originator of the Chair of Unity Octave. Peekskill, N. Y., Graymoor Press [1955] 94p. 21cm. [BX4705.P3842C7] 55-3361
1. Paul James Francis, Father, 1863-1940. 2. Friars of the Atonement. I. Title.

GANNON, David, Father, 1904- 922.273
Father Paul of Graymoor. New York, Macmillan, 1951. x, 372 p. illus., ports. 22 cm. [BX4705.P3842G3] 51-5046
1. Paul James Francis, Father, 1863-1940. 2. Friars of the Atonement. 3. Franciscan Sisters of the Atonement. I. Title.

HANAHOE, Edward Francis, 1913- ed. 280.1
One fold; essays and documents to commemorate the golden jubilee of the Chair of Unity Octave, 1908-1958. Edited by Edward F. Hanahoe [and] Titus F. Cranny. Graymoor, Garrison, N. Y., Chair of Unity Apostolate, Franciscan Friars of the Atonement, 1959. 384p. illus. 22cm. Includes bibliography. [BX1786.H3] 50-15736
1. Paul James Francis, Father, 1863-1940. 2. Chair of Unity Octave. 3. Friars of the Atonement. I. Cranny, Titus F., 1921- joint ed. II. Title.

Paul, Saint, apostle.

ABBOTT, John Stevens Cabot, 1805-1877. 270
The history of Christianity; consisting of the life and teachings of Jesus of Nazareth; the adventures of Paul and the apostles; and the most interesting events in the progress of Christianity, from the earliest period to the present time. By John S. C. Abbott ... Boston, B. B. Russell; Philadelphia, Quaker-city-publishing-house; [etc., etc.] 1872. 504 p. front., plates, ports., maps. 21 cm. [BR145.A2 1872] 36-3229
1. Paul, Saint, apostle. 2. Church history. 3. Jesus Christ—Biog. I. Title.

ABBOTT, John Stevens Cabot, 1805-1877. 270
The history of Christianity: consisting of the life and teachings of Jesus of Nazareth; the adventures of Paul and the apostles; and the most interesting events in the progress of Christianity, from the earliest period to the present time. By John S. C. Abbott ... Boston, D. Lothrop and company [1881] 504 p. front., plates, map. 20 cm. [BR145.A2 1881] 36-3230
1. Paul, Saint, apostle. 2. Church history. 3. Jesus Christ—Biog. I. Title.

ABBOTT, John Stevens Cabot, 1805-1877. 270
The history of Christianity: consisting of the life and teachings of Jesus of Nazareth; the adventures of Paul and the apostles; and the most interesting events in the progress of Christianity, from the earliest period to the present time. By John S. C. Abbott ... Portland, G. Stinson & co. [c1883] 504 p. front., plates, ports., maps. 23 cm. [BR145.A2 1883] 36-3231
1. Paul, Saint, apostle. 2. Church history. 3. Jesus Christ—Biog. I. Title.

ABBOTT, Lyman, 1835-1922. 225.
The life and letters of Paul the apostle, by Lyman Abbott. Boston and New York, Houghton, Mifflin and company, 1898. xii, 882 p. 1 l., 20 1/2 cm. [BS2505.A35] 96-1915
1. Paul, Saint, apostle. 2. Bible. N.T. Epistles of Paul—Criticism, interpretation, etc. 3. Bible—Criticism, interpretations, etc.—N.T. Epistles of Paul. I. Title.

ACTON, Alexander Archibald, 1885- 922.1
O'er land and sea with the apostle Paul... by A. A. Action...introduction by Professor Ernest F. Scott... New York [etc.] Fleming H. Revell company [c1933] 222 p. 19 1/2 cm. [BS2505.A36] 225.92 33-7405
1. Paul, Saint, apostle. I. Title.

ADCOCK, Adam Kennedy. 227
At the feet of Paul; original outlines, by Adam Kennedy Adcock... Cincinnati, O., The Standard publishing company [c1927] 591 p. 20 cm. [BS2650.35] 28-2519
1. Paul, Saint, apostle. 2. Bible. N.T.

Epistles of Paul—Christian, interpretation, etc. I. Title.

ALCOTT, William Andrus, 1798-1859. 225.92
Paul at Ephesus. By William A. Alcott. Written for the Massachusetts Sabbath school society and revised by the Committee of publication. Boston, Massachusetts Sabbath school society, 1846. ix, [11]-198 p. incl. front., illus. 15 1/2 cm. [BS2505.A6] [922.1] 34-14838
1. Paul, Saint, apostle. I. Massachusetts Sabbath school society. II. Title.

ALCOTT, William Andrus, 1798-1859. 225.92
Paul's shipwreck. By William A. Alcott. Written for the Massachusetts Sabbath school society, and revised by the Committee of publication. Boston, Massachusetts Sabbath school society, 1842. viii, [9]-126 p. incl. front., 1 illus. 15 1/2 cm. [BS2505.A63] [922.1] 34-14837
1. Paul, Saint, apostle. I. Massachusetts Sabbath school society. II. Title.

ALLEN, Roland, 1869-1947 266
Missionary methods; St. Paul's or ours? Grand Rapids, Eerdmans [c.1962] 179p. 22cm. 62-5028 1.65 pap.,
1. Paul, Saint, apostle. 2. Missions, Foreign. I. Title.

ANDRY, Carl Franklin. 225.9'24 B
Paul and the early Christians / by Carl Franklin Andry. Dublin, Ind. : Prinit Press, 1978. xiii, 173 p. ill. ; 21 cm. Includes bibliographical references. [BS2650.2.A62] 78-71822 pbk. : 6.95
1. Paul, Saint, Apostle. 2. Bible. N.T. Epistles of Paul—Criticism, interpretation, etc. I. Title.

ANDRY, Carl Franklin. 225.9'24
Paul and the early Christians / Carl F. Andry. Washington, D.C. : University Press of America, c1981. 146 p. : maps ; 23 cm. Includes index. [BS2650.2.A62 1981] 19 81-40766 ISBN 0-8191-1935-0 : 18.50 ISBN 0-8191-1936-9 (pbk.) : 8.50
1. Paul, the Apostle, Saint. 2. Bible. N.T. Epistles of Paul—Criticism, interpretation, etc. I. Title.

ASHBROOK, James B., 1925- 230
Christianity for pious skeptics / James B. Ashbrook, Paul W. Walaskay. Nashville : Abingdon, c1977. 160 p. : ill. ; 21 cm. Includes bibliographical references. [BS2506.A83] 77-911 ISBN 0-687-07646-3 pbk. : 4.95
1. Paul, Saint, Apostle. 2. Bible. N.T.—Biography. 3. Christian saints—Turkey—Tarsus—Biography. 4. Tarsus, Turkey—Biography. 5. Faith and reason. 6. Christian life—1960- I. Walaskay, Paul W., 1939- II. Title.

ATKINSON, Louise Warren. 225.
The story of Paul of Tarsus; a manual for teachers, by Louise Warren Atkinson ... Chicago, The University of Chicago press, 1910. xxxiv, 194 p. 20 cm. (Constructive Bible studies. Elementary series) "Books recommended for reference": p. xxxiii-xxiv. [BS2507.A72] 10-1242
1. Paul, Saint, apostic. I. Title.

ATKINSON, Louise Warren. 225.
The story of Paul of Tarsus; a manual for teachers, by Louise Warren Atkinson ... Chicago, The University of Chicago press, 1910. xxxiv, 194 p. 20 cm. (Constructive Bible studies. Elementary series) "Books recommended for reference": p. xxxiii-xxiv. [BS2507.A72] 10-1242
1. Paul, Saint, apostle. I. Title.

ATKINSON, Louise Warren. 225.
The story of Paul of Tarsus; directions for home study, by Louise Warren Atkinson. Chicago, The University of Chicago press, 1910. viii, 76 p. front. (map) illus. 19 cm. [BS2507.A7] 10-1241 0.25
1. Paul, Saint, apostle I. Title.

BACON, Benjamin Wisner, 1860- 225.
The story of St. Paul; a comparison of Acts and Epistles, by Benjamin Wisner Bacon ... Boston and New York, Houghton, Mifflin and company, 1904. x, 392 p., 1 l., 20 cm. [BS2505.B23] 4-31300
1. Paul, Saint, apostle. I. Title.

BAIRD, William, 1924- 227.06
Paul's message and mission. New York, Abingdon Press [1960] 176p. 21cm. Includes bibliography. [BS2506.B3] 60-12066
1. Paul, Saint, apostle. 2. Bible. N. T. Epistles of Paul—Theology. I. Title.

BAIRD, William [Robb] 227.06
Paul's message and mission. Nashville, Abingdon Press [c.1960] 176p. 21cm. (Bibl. footnotes) 60-12066 3.00
1. Paul, Saint, apostle. 2. Bible. N. T. Epistles of Paul—Theology. I. Title.

BALL, Charles Ferguson. [922.1]
The life and journeys of Paul Illus. by Francis Mason Holt Chicago, Moody Press ['1951] 315 p. illus. 21 cm. [BS2505.B232] 225.92 52-6727
1. Paul, Saint, apostle. I. Title.

BALLARD, Frank Hewett. 225.92
The spiritual pilgrimage of St. Paul, by Frank H. Ballard ... New York and London, Harper & brothers [1931] 158 p. 19 cm. [BS2505.B233] (922.1) 32-25002
1. Paul, Saint, apostle. I. Title.

BARCLAY, William, 225.9'24 B lecturer in the University of Glasgow.
Ambassador for Christ; the life and teaching of Paul. Valley Forge, [Pa.] Judson Press [1974, c1973] 183 p. 22 cm. "Originally published in 1951 by the Church of Scotland Youth Committee." [BS2506.B34 1974] 73-9762 ISBN 0-8170-0631-1 1.95 (pbk)
1. Paul, Saint, apostle. I. Title.

BARNES, Albert, 1798-1870. 225.92
Scenes and incidents in the life the apostle Paul, viewed as illustrating the nature and influence of the Christian religion. By Albert Barnes. Philadelphia, Pa., Cincinnati, O. [etc.] Zeigler, McCurdy & co. [1869] v, [4], [3]-196 p. front. (port.) illus. (incl. plan) plates., fold. map. 21 cm. [BS2505.B25] [[922.1]] 34-17920
1. Paul, Saint, apostle. I. Title.

BARTON, Bruce, 1886- 225.92
He upset the world, by Bruce Barton. Indianapolis, The Bobbs-Merrill company [c1932] 6 p. l., 11-186 p. 21 cm. Maps on lining-papers. "First edition." [BS2505.B26] 922.1 32-5734 aul, Saint, Apostle.
I. Title.

BAUMANN, Emile, 1868- 225.
Saint Paul, by Emile Baumann; translated from the French by Kenneth Burke; with a frontispiece by Emile Bernard and decorations by Rene Pottier. New York, Harcourt, Brace and company [c1929] xxviii, 316 p. front., illus. 23 cm. [BS2505.B28] 29-9128
1. Paul, Saint, apostle. I. Burke, Kenneth, 1897- tr. II. Title.

BEACH, Harlan Page, 1854-1933. 268.
New Testament studies in missions. Part 1.--Missions in the light of the Gospels. Part 2.--St. Paul and the Gentile world. By Harlan P. Beach ... New York, Student volunteer movement for foreign missions, 1899. 69, [1] p. illus. (map) 18 cm. With few exceptions printed on one side of leaf only; blank pages "for manuscript notes." [BV2090.B3] 99-1931
1. Paul, Saint, apostle. 2. Missions, Foreign. I. Title.

BEDELL, Gregory Townsend, 1793-1834. 225.
The life and travels of St. Paul. Written for the American Sunday School Union. Rev. by the Committee of Publication. Philadelphia, American Sunday School Union, 1830. 197 p. 14 cm. [BS2505.B398] 49-33256
1. Paul, Saint, apostle. I. Title.

BESSER, Wilhelm Friedrich, 1816-1884. 225.92
St. Paul the apostle; a Biblical portrait and a mirror of the manifold grace of God. By W. F. Besser, D. D. Translated by Frederic Bultmann ... With an introductory notice by Rev. J. S. Howson, D. D. New York, R. Carter & brothers, 1864. xiv p., 1 l., 210 p. 20 cm. Printed in Great Britain. [BS2505.B45] 922.1 34-17156
1. Paul, Saint, apostle. I. Bultmann, Friedrich, tr. II. Title.

BIBLE. N.T. 1 220.6'6 s Corinthians. English. Orr-Walther. 1976.
I Corinthians : a new translation / introd., with a study of the life of Paul, notes, and commentary by William F. Orr and James Arthur Walther. 1st ed. Garden City, N.Y. : Doubleday, 1976. xv, 391 p. ; 24 cm. (The Anchor Bible ; 32) Includes indexes. Bibliography: p. [133]-138. [BS192.2.A1 1964.G3 vol. 32] [BS2673] 227'.2'07 75-42441 ISBN 0-385-02853-9 : 9.00
1. Paul, Saint, Apostle. 2. Bible. N.T. 1 Corinthians—Commentaries. I. Orr, William Fridell, 1907- II. Walther, James Arthur, 1918- III. Title. IV. Series.

BIBLE. N. T. Acts and 225.92 Epistles. English. Harmonies. 1895.
The life and epistles of Saint Paul, harmonized and chronologically arranged in Scripture language by Rev. S. W. Pratt ... New York, A. D. F. Randolph and company [1895] viii, [3]-239 p. fold. map. 18 cm. [BS2505.A3P7] 922.1 34-17160
1. Paul, Saint, apostle. I. Bible. English. Harmonies. N. T. Acts and Epistles. 1895. II. Pratt, Samuel Wheeler, 1838-1910, ed. III. Title.

BIBLE. N. T. Acts and 225.92 Epistles. English. Harmonies. 1906. American revised.
His great apostle; the life and letters of Paul, using the text of the American standard revised Bible. Prepared by Sydney Strong, William E. Barton, Theodore G. Soares ... Chicago, New York, Hope publishing company [1906] 4, v-xii, 212 p. 16 cm. [BS2505.A3S8] 922.1 6-34262
1. Paul, Saint, apostle. I. Strong, Sydney Dix, 1860- II. Barton, William Eleazar, 1861-1930. III. Soares, Theodore Gerald, 1869- IV. Bible. English. Harmonies. N. T. Acts and Epistles. 1906. American revised. V. Title.

BIBLE. N.T. Acts and 225.92 Epistles. English. Harmonies. 1964. Authorized.
A harmony of the life of St. Paul according to the Acts of the Apostles and the Pauline Epistles, by Frank J. Goodwin. Grand Rapids, Baker Book House, 1964. 240 p. maps. 23 cm. First ed. published in 1895. [BS2505.A3] 65-7472
1. Paul, Saint, apostle. I. Goodwin, Frank Judson, 1862-1953. II. Title.

BIBLE. N. T. Acts and 225.92 Epistles. English Harmonies. 1964. Authorized
A harmony of the life of St. Paul according to the Acts of the Apostles and the Pauline Epistles, by Frank J. Goodwin. Grand Rapids, Mich., Baker Bk. [1965] 240p. maps. 23cm. [BS2505.A3] 65-7472 3.95
1. Paul, Saint, apostle. I. Goodwin, Frank Judson, 1861-1953. II. Title.

BIBLE. N. T. Epistles of 227 Paul. English. Selections. 1911.
The living thoughts of Saint Paul, presented by Jacques Maritain ... New York, Toronto, Longmans, Green and co., 1941. 8 p. l., 161, [1] p. 19 cm. (The Living thoughts library, ed. by A. O. Mendel) Text and illustrations on lining-papers. "Translation by Harry Lorin Binsse." "First edition." [BS2651.M36] 41-24700
1. Paul, Saint, apostle. 2. Bible. N. T. Epistles of Paul—Theology. I. Maritain, Jacques, 1882- ed. II. Binsse, Harry Lorin, 1905- tr. III. Title.

BIBLE. N.T. Epistles of Paul. 227 English. Selections. 1941.
The living thoughts of Saint Paul, presented by Jacques Maritain ... New York, Toronto, Longmans, Green and co., 1941. 3 p. l., 161, [1] p. 19 cm. (The living thoughts library, ed. by A. O. Mendel) Text and illustrations on lining-papers. "Translation by Harry Lorin binase." "First edition." [BS2651.M36] 41-24700
1. Paul, Saint, apostle. 2. Bible. N.T. Epistles of Paul—Theology. 3. Bible—Theology—N.T. Epistles of Paul. I. Bible. English. Selections. N.T. Epistles of Paul. 1941. II. Maritain, Jacques, 1882- ed. III. Binsse, Harry Lorin, tr. IV. Title.

BIBLE. N.T. Acts and 227.07 Epistles. English. Knox. 1959.
It is Paul who writes, based on the translation of the Epistles of Saint Paul & of the Acts of the Apostles by Ronald Knox, arranged in a continuous narrative with explanations by Ronald Cox. New York, Sheed and Ward [1959, c1944] x, 487 p. maps. 22 cm. [BS2617.5.A3K6] 59-10654
1. Paul, Saint, apostle. 2. Bible. N. T. Acts and Epistles—Commentaries. 3. Bible—Harmonies. I. Knox, Ronald Arbuthnott, 1888-1957, tr. II. Cox, Ronald. III. Title.

BLACKWELDER, Boyce W. 225.92
Toward understanding Paul. Anderson, Ind., Warner Press [dist. Gospel Trumpet Press, c.1961] 127p. Bibl. 61-9720 2.95
1. Paul, Saint, apostle. I. Title.

BLENKINSOPP, Joseph, 1927- 225.92'4
Jesus is Lord; Paul's life in Christ. New York, Paulist Press [1967] 126 p. 19 cm. (Deus books) Bibliography: p. 119-121. [BS2506.B57] 67-23602
1. Paul, Saint, Apostle. I. Title.

BORNKAMM, Gunther. 225.9'24 B
Paul, Paulus. Translated by D. M. G. Stalker. [1st U.S. ed.] New York, Harper & Row [1971] xxviii, 259 p. 22 cm. [BS2506.B6213] 75-22728 7.50
1. Paul, Saint, apostle. 2. Bible. N.T. Epistles of Paul—Theology.

BRADFORD, Ernle 225.9'24 B Dusgate Selby.
Paul the traveller / Ernle Bradford. 1st American ed. New York : Macmillan, 1976, c1974. vii, 246 p., [6] leaves of plates : ill. ; 22 cm. Includes index. [BS2506.B7 1976] 75-28451 ISBN 0-02-514390-5 : 9.95
1. Paul, Saint, Apostle. I. Title.

BRUCE, Frederick 225.9'2'4 B Fyvie, 1910-
Paul, apostle of the heart set free / F. F. Bruce. 1st American ed. Grand Rapids : Eerdmans, 1977. 491 p., [8] leaves of plates : ill. ; 24 cm. Includes index. Bibliography: p. 476-479. [BS2506.B755 1977] 77-26127 ISBN 0-8028-3501-5 : 9.95
1. Paul, Saint, Apostle. 2. Bible. N.T.—Biography. 3. Bible. N.T. Epistles of Paul—Theology. 4. Christian saints—Turkey—Tarsus—Biography. 5. Tarsus, Turkey—Biography. I. Title.

BRUNOT, Amedee. 225.92
Saint Paul and his message. Translated from the French by Ronald Matthews. [1st ed.] New York, Hawthorne Books [1959] 140p. 21cm. (The Twentieth century encyclopedia of Catholicism, v. 70. Section 6: The word of God) Includes bibliography. [BS2505.B773] 59-8204
1. Paul, Saint, apostle. I. Title.

BUCK, Charles Henry, 1915- 225.92'4
Saint Paul; a study of the development of his thought, by Charles Buck and Greer Taylor. New York, Scribner [1969] x, 278 p. 24 cm. Bibliographical footnotes. [BS2506.B78 1969] 69-17054 7.95
1. Paul, Saint, apostle. I. Taylor, Greer, 1917- joint author. II. Title.

BUCKMASTER, Henrietta, pseud. 225.924
Paul, a man who changed the world. New York, McGraw [c.1965] ix, [1] 213p. maps. 21cm. Bibl. [BS2506.B8] 65-24889 4.95
1. Paul, Saint, apostle. I. Title.

BUCKMASTER, Henrietta, pseud 225.924 (B)
Paul, a man who changed the world. New York, McGraw-Hill [1965] ix, [1], 213 p. maps. 21 cm. Bibliography: p. [x] [BS2506.B8] 65-24889
1. Paul, Saint, apostle. I. Title.

BUELL, Marcus Darius, 1851-
The autographs of Saint Paul, by Marcus D. Buell ... New York, Eaton & Mains; Cincinnati, Jennings & Graham [c1912] 95 p. 18 cm. 12-25378 0.35
I. Title.

BURR, Alexander George, 1871- 225.
The Apostle Paul and the Roman law, by A. G. Burr ... foreword by Chief Justice Birdzell ... [Bismarck, N.D., Quick print, inc., c1928] c.88 [4] p. 20 cm.

Bibliography: p. [3] at end. [BS2505.B785] 28-8825
1. Paul, Saint, apostle. 2. Roman law. I. Title.

BURRELL, David James, 1844- 225.
Life and letters of St. Paul, by David James Burrell ... New York, American tract society [c1925] 4 p. l., 7-527 p. front. (port.) 19 cm. Each part also published separately. Contents.pt. i. Saul of Tarsus.--pt. ii. Paul's campaign.--pt. iii. Paul's compassions.--pt. iv. Paul's letters. [BS2505.B79] 25-15855
1. Paul, Saint, apostle. I. Title.

BURRELL, David James, 1844- 227
Paul's letters, by David James Burrell ... New York, American tract society [c;921) viii, 167 p. 19 cm. [BS2650.B8] 21-11794
I. Title.

BURTON, Ernest DeWitt, 1856-1925. 225.
A handbook of the life of the apostle Paul; an outline for class room and private study. By Ernest DeWitt Burton...2d ed. Chicago, The American institute of sacred literature, 1900. 100 p. front. (map) illus. 21 cm. "Books recommended": p. 33-34. [BS2507.B8 1900] 0-826
1. Paul, Saint, apostle. I. Title.

BUTLER, Clement Moore, 1810-1890. 225.92
St. Paul in Rome: lectures delivered in the legation of the United States of America, in Rome. By the Rev. C. M. Butler ... Philadelphia, J. B. Lippincott & co., 1865. xi, 13-293 p. 19 cm. [BS2505.B85] [922.1] 34-14836
1. Paul, Saint, apostle. I. Title.

CARTER, Thomas. 225.
Life and letters of Paul, by Thomas Carter ... introduction by Mrs. Hume R. Steele ... Nashville, Dallas [etc.] Publishing house of the M. E. church, South, 1921. 231 p. 18 cm. [BS2505.C36] 21-11795
1. Paul, Saint, apostle I. Title.

THE cities of St. Paul,
their influence on his life and thought: the cities of Eastern Asia Minor. Grand Rapids, Baker Book House, 1960. xv, 452p. illus., maps. 22cm. 'Reprinted ... from the 1907 edition by Hodder and Stoughton, London.' Bibliographical references included in Notes' (p. 437-452)
1. Paul, Saint, apostle. I. Ramsay, William Mitchell, Sir 1851-1939.

CLARKE, E. P. ed. 225.
Six orations of Paul; introduction and comments on text, by E. P. Clarke... San Francisco, Calif., Harx Wagner publishing co., 1922. 3 p. l., [9]-56 p. 18 cm. [BS2505.C5] 22-16631
1. Paul, Satin, apostle. I. Bible. N.t. Selctions. English. II. Title.

CLARKE, James Freeman, 1810-1888. 227
The ideas of the apostle Paul translated into their modern equivalents, by James Freeman Clarke ... Boston, J. R. Osgood and company, 1884. xiv, 436 p. 19 1/2 cm. [BS2651.C5] 39-34098
1. Paul, Saint, apostle. 2. Bible, N.T. Epistles of Paul—Theology. 3. Bible—Theology—N.T. Epistles of Paul. I. Title.

COHAUSZ, Otto, 1872- 250
The priest and Saint Paul; an interpretation of Saint Paul's writings bearing on the priesthood, by Rev. Otto Cohausz, S.J. translated by Rev. Laurence P. Emery, M.A. New York, Cincinnati [etc.] Benziger brothers, 1927. 311 p. 19 cm. Translation of Paulus, eln buch fur prieater [BX1912.C6] 28-31
I. Emery, Laurence Peter Ernest, tr. II. Title.

CONYBEARE, William John, 1815-1857. 225.92
The life and epistles of St. Paul. By the Rev. W. J. Conybeare ... and the Rev. J. S. Howson ... 6th ed. New York, C. Scribner, 1856-58. 2 v. illus., plates, maps (incl. front.; 2 fold.) plans (1 fold.) 23 1/2 cm. "While Mr. Conybeare and Mr. Howson have undertaken the joint revision of the whole work, the translation of the epistles and speeches of St. Paul is contributed by the former, and the historical and geographical portion of the work principally by the latter."--Introd. [BS2505.C65 1856] [[922.1]] 32-22498
1. Paul, Saint, apostle. I. Howson, John Saul, 1816-1885, joint author. II. Title. III. Title: Bible, N.T. Epistles of Paul. English. 1856. IV. Title: Bible. English. N.T. Epistles of Paul, 1856.

CONYBEARE, William John, 1815-1857. 225.
The life and epistles of St. Paul. By the Rev. W. J. Conybeare ... and the Rev. J. S. Howson ... 6th ed. New York, C. Scribner, 1858. 2 v. illus., plates, maps (incl. fronts, 1 fold.) plans (1 fold.) 23 1/2 cm. [BS2505.C65 1858] 22-21659
1. Paul, Saint, apostle. I. Howson, John Saul, 1816-1885, joint author. II. Bible. N.T. Epistles of Paul. English. 1858. III. Bible. English. N.T. Epistles of Paul, 1858. IV. Title.

CONYBEARE, William John, 1815-1857. 255.92
The life and epistles of St. Paul, By the Rev. W. J. Conybeare ... and the Rev. J. S. Howson ... The only complete and unabridged ed ... New York, Scribner, Armstrong & co., 1877. 2 v. in 1. illus., plates maps. (incl. fold. front.) plans (2 double) 23 1/2 cm. "While Mr. Conybeare and Mr. Howson have undertaken the joint revision of the whole work, the translation of the epistles and speeches of St. Paul is contributed by the former, and the historical and geographical portion of the work principally by the latter."--Introd. [BS2505.C65 1877] [922.1] 17-20203
1. Paul, Saint, apostle. I. Howson, John Saul, 1816-1885. II. Bible. N.T. Epistles of Paul. English. 1877. III. Bible. English. N.T. Epistles of Paul. 1877. IV. Title.

CONYBEARE, William John, 1815-1857. 225.92
The life and epistles of St. Paul. By the Rev. W. J. Conybeare ... and the Rev. J. S. Howson ... The only complete and unabridged edition ... New York, C. Scribner's sons, 1906. 2 v. in 1. fold. front., illus., plates, maps, plans (part double) 23 1/2 cm. First published London, 1852. "While Mr. Conybeare and Mr. Howson have undertaken the joint revision of the whole work, the translation of the epistles and speeches of St. Paul is contributed by the former, and the historical and geographical portion of the work principally by the latter."--Introd. [BS2505.C65 1906] [922.1] 8-22306
1. Paul, Saint, apostle. I. Howson, John Paul, 1816-1885. II. Bible. N.T. Epistles of Paul. English. 1906. III. Bible. English. N.T. Epistles of Paul. 1906. IV. Title.

CONYBEARE, William John, 1815-1857. 225.92
... The life and epistles of the apostle Paul ... By the Rev. W. J. Conybeare ... and the Rev. J. S. Howson ... With maps, chronological table, and appendix ... New York, G. Munro [c1880] 2 v. in 1. illus. (maps, plans) 31 1/2 cm. (The Seaside library ... v. 35, no. 730) [922.1] 32-28849
1. Paul, Saint, apostle. I. Howson, John Saul, 1816-1885, joint author. II. Bible. N.T. Epistles of Paul. English. 1880. III. Bible. English, N.T. Epistles of Paul. 1880. IV. Title.

CONYBEARE, William John, 1815-1857. 225.92
The life, times and travels of St. Paul. By the Rev. W. J. Conybeare ... and the Rev. J. S. Howson ... With introduction by Mathew [!] Simpson ... New York, E. B. Treat & co.; Chicago, Ill., C. W. Lilley; [etc., etc.] 1869. 2 v. in 1. fold. front., illus., plates, maps. plans (1 double) diagr. 23 1/2 cm. "While Mr. Conybeare and Mr. Howson have undertaken the joint revision of the whole work, the translation of the epistles and speeches of St. Paul is contributed by the former, and the historical and geographical portion of the work principally by the latter."--Introd. [BS2505.C65 1869] [922.1] A 23
1. Paul, Saint, apostle. I. Bible. N.T. Epistles of Paul. English. 1869. II. Howson, John Saul, joint author, 1816-1885. III. Bible. English. N.T. Epistles of Paul. 1869. IV. Title.

COOKE, Richard Joseph, bp., 1853-1931. 232.
Did Paul know of the virgin birth? An historical study, by the Rev. Bishop Richard J. Cooke ... New York, The Macmillan company, 1926. 152 p. 20 cm. [BT317.C65] 26-10614
1. Paul, Saint, apostle. 2. Virgin birth. I. Title.

DALLMANN, William, 1862- 225.
Paul; life and letters [by] William Dallmann. St. Louis, Mo., Concordia publishing house, 1929. x, 356 p. incl. front. (port.) illus. col. plates, fold. map. 26 cm. [Full name: Charles Frederick William Dallmann] "Works consulted": p. [351]-354. [BS2505.D3] 29-10652
1. Paul, Saint, apostle. I. Title.

DANA, Harvey Eugene, 1888- 225.92
The life and literature of Paul [by] H. E. Dana ... Chicago, Blessing book stores, inc., 1936. 198 p. 24 cm. [BS2505.D32] 922.1 37-14427
1. Paul, Saint, apostle. 2. Bible. N. T. Epistles of Paul—Commentaries. 3. Bible. N. T. Acts—Commentaries. 4. Bible—Commentaries—N. T. Epistles of Paul. 5. Bible—Commentaries—N. T. Acts. I. Title.

DANIEL-ROPS, Henry, 1901-
Saint Paul, apostle of nations; translated by Jex Martin. Notre Dame, Ind., Fides Publishers, Inc. [1964] 163 p. 21 cm. (A Fides Dome book D-29) Translation of Saint Paul, conquerant du Christ. "Dome book edition 1963." 68-81171
1. Paul, Saint, apostle. I. Title.

DAVIES, Arthur Powell.
The first Christian; a study of St. Paul and Christian origins. [New York] New American. Library [1959, c1957] 240 p. maps. 18 cm. (A Mentor book) Bibliography: p. 223-228. 65-10555
1. Paul, Saint, Apostle. 2. Christianity — Origin. I. Title.

DEISSMAN, Gustav Adolf, 1866- 225.
St. Paul; a study in social and religious history, by Adolf Deissmann ... translated by Lionel R. M. Strachan ... London, New York [etc.] Hodder and Stoughton, 1912. xix, 316 p. incl. front. plates, fold. map (in pocket) 23 cm. "Founded on eight lectures ... delivered in German by invitation of the Olaus Petri trustees at the University of Upsala in March, 1910, and which were immediately published in a Swedish translation."--Pref. [BS2505.D42] 13-269
1. Paul, Saint, apostle. I. Strachan, Lionel Richard Mortimer, 1876- tr. II. Title.

DEISSMANN, Gustav Adolf, 1866-1937. 225.92
Paul; a study in social and religious history. Translated by William E. Wilson. [1st Harper torchbook ed.] New York, Harper [1957] 323 p. illus. 21 cm. (Harper torchbooks, TB15) [BS2505.D42 1957] 922.1 57-7533
1. Paul, Saint, apostle.

DE WITT, Norman Wentworth, 1876- 227
St. Paul and Epicurus. Minneapolis, University of Minnesota Press [1954] 201p. 24cm. Sequel to Epicurus and his philosophy. [BS2651.D4] 54-12314
1. Paul, Saint, apostle. 2. Epicurus. 3. Bible. N. T. Epistles of Paul—Theology. I. Title.

DOTY, Brant Lee.
The apostle Paul; study course for youth and adults. Cincinnati, Standard Pub. [c1964] Includes bibliography. 65-43114
1. Paul, Saint, apostle. I. Title.

DOTY, Brant Lee.
The apostle Paul; study course for youth and adults. Cincinnati, Standard Pub. [c1964] 112 p. maps. "Based in part upon an earlier book, Paul, his life and teaching." Includes bibliography. 65-43114
1. Paul, Saint, apostle. I. Title.

DRANE, John William. 225.9'24 B
Paul : [an illustrated documentary on the life and writings of a key figure in the beginnings of Christianity] / John W. Drane. Berkhamsted : Lion Publishing, 1976. 127 p. : ill., facsims., maps ; 24 cm. Includes index. Bibliography: p. 123-125. [BS2506.D7] 77-373988 ISBN 0-85648-043-6 : £1.75
1. Paul, Saint, Apostle. 2. Bible. N.T. Epistles of Paul—Criticism, interpretation, etc. 3. Christian saints—Turkey—Tarsus—Biography. 4. Tarsus, Turkey—Biography.

DROWN, Lessie Mae. 225.
Out of the dark; the life story of Paul, by Mrs. Lessie M. Drown ... Mountain View, Calif., Omaha, Neb. [etc.] Pacific press publishing association [c1929] 176 p. incl. front., illus. (incl. maps) 22 1/2 cm. [BS2505.D7] 29-12633
1. Paul, Saint, apostle. I. Title.

DUDLEY, Carl Hermon. 225.
St. Paul's friendships and his friends, by Carl Hermon Dudley ... Boston, R. G. Badger, 1911. 287 p. 20 cm. [BS2505.D8] 11-8290 1.50
1. Paul, Saint, apostle. I. Title.

EASTVOLD, Seth Clarence, 1895- 225.92
Paul and Luther, by S. C. Eastvold. Minneapolis, Minn., Augsburg publishing house, 1937. xii, 206 p. 20 1/2 cm. "First edition." [BS2505.E47] 37-8557
1. Paul, Saint, apostle. 2. Luther, Martin, 1483-1546. I. Title.

EDMAN, Irwin, 1896- 225.92
The mind of Paul, by Irwin Edman. New York, H. Holt and company [c1935] 5 p. l., 3-187 p. 21 cm. (Half title: Studies in religion and culture) Schermerhorn lecture III. Bibliography: p. 183-184. [BS2651.E4] 35-33561
1. Paul, Saint, apostle. I. Title.

EICKMANN, Walther, 1872- 225.92
Pilgrim Paul; the adventurous journeys of a wandering apostle, with timely annotations, by Walther Eickmann. West New York,N.J., W. Eickmann [c1934] 5 p. l., 459 p. pl. 23 cm. [BS2505.E5] [[922.1]] 922.1 34-41826
1. Paul, Saint, apostle. I. Title.

ELLIS. EDWARD EARLE 227.06
Paul and his recent interpreters. Grand Rapids, Mich., Eerdmans [c.1961] 63p. Bibl. 61-10853 1.75 pap.,
1. Paul, Saint, apostle. 2. Eschatology—Biblical teaching. 3. Bible. N. T. Pastoral epistles—Criticism, interpretaion, etc. I. Title.

ENSLEY, Francis Gerald, Bp. 227
Paul's letters to local churches. [New York, 1956] 175p. illus. 29 cm. [BS2650.E65] 56-7572
1. Paul, Saint, apostle. 2. Bible. N. T. Epistles of Paul—Criticism, interpretation, etc. 3. Bible, N. T. Epistles of Paul—Theology. I. Title.

ENSLIN, Morton Scott, 1897- 225.92
The ethics of Paul. Nashville, Abingdon [1962, c.1957] 335p. 21cm. (Apex Bks. K 1) 2.25 pap.,
1. Paul, Saint, apostle. I. Title.

ENSLIN, Morton Scott, 1897-
The ethics of Paul. New York, Abington Press [c1957] 335 p. (Apex books K1225) First published 1930. 63-21258
1. Paul, Saint, apostle. I. Title.

ENSLIN, Morton Scott, 1897- 225.92
The ethics of Paul, by Morton Scott Enslin... New York and London, Harper & brothers, 1930. xix p., 1 l., 335 p. 22 1/2 cm. "First edition." [BS2655.E8E6] [171.1] 30-12630
1. Paul, Saint, apostle. I. Title.

ENSLIN, Morton Scott, 1897- 225.9'24 B
Reapproaching Paul. Philadelphia, Westminster Press [1972] 159 p. 21 cm. Includes bibliographical references. [BS2506.E57] 72-4941 ISBN 0-664-20951-3 5.95
1. Paul, Saint, apostle. I. Title.

EPPINGA, Jacob D. 265'.3
For sinners only; perspectives on the Lord's Supper drawn from the life of St. Paul, by J. D. Eppinga. Grand Rapids, Eerdmans [1970] 142 p. 19 cm. [BV825.2.E65] 74-127630 3.95
1. Paul, Saint, apostle. 2. Lord's Supper. I. Title.

FARRAR, Frederic William, 1831-1903. 225.
The life and work of St. Paul. By F. W.

Farrar ... London, New York [etc.] Cassell, Petter, Galpin & co. [1879-80] 2 v. 4 fold. maps (incl. fronts.) 22 cm. "Passages of Scripture quoted or referred to": v. 2, p. [651]-668. [BS2505.F3] 5-3751
1. Paul, Saint, apostle. I. Title.

FARRAR, Frederic William, 1831-1903. 225.
The life and work of St. Paul, by F. W. Farrar ... New York, E. P. Dutton and company, 1902. 2 p. l., [vii]-xx, 781 p. illus., fold. maps (incl. front.) 21 cm. First published in 1879. [BS2505.F3 1902] 4-10391
1. Paul, Saint, apostle. I. Title.

FINK, Leo Gregory, 1886-. 225.
Paul, hero and saint; an apostolic story of Roman battles and catholic victories, by Leo Gregory Fink ... New York, The Paulist press, 1921. xv, 239 p. front., plates, fold. map. 20cm. Bibliography: p. 230. [BS2505.F45] 21-21395
1. Paul, Saint, apostle. I. Title.

FIRMAGE, Edwin Brown. 266'.0092'4
Paul and the expansion of the Church today / Edwin Brown Firmage. Salt Lake City : Deseret Book Co., 1979. v, 71 p. ; 24 cm. Includes index. Bibliography: p. 65-68. [BS2506.F54] 79-21235 ISBN 0-87747-789-2 : 6.95
1. Paul, Saint, Apostle. 2. Church of Jesus Christ of Latter-Day Saints—Missions. 3. Missions—Biblical teaching. I. Title.

THE first Christian; 922.1
a study of St. Paul and Christian origins. New York, Farrar,Straus and Cudahy [1957] 275p. illus. 22cm. [BS2505.D36] [BS2505.D36] 225.92 57-14507 57-14507
1. Paul, Saint, apostle. 2. Christinaity-Origin. I. Davies, Arthur Powell.

FISHER, Fred L. 227'.06'6
Paul and his teachings [by] Fred L. Fisher. Nashville, Broadman Press [1974] 160 p. 22 cm. Includes bibliographical references. [BS2506.F55] 73-83829 ISBN 0-8054-1339-1 5.25
1. Paul, Saint, apostle. 2. Bible. N.T. Epistles of Paul—Theology. I. Title.

FLETCHER, John William, 1729-1785. 225.92
The portrait of Saint Paul: or, The true model for Christians and pastors. Translated from a French manuscript of the late Rev. John William de La Flechere ... by the Rev. Joshua Gilpin ... New York, Printed by Kirk & Robinson, for the Methodist society, and sold by E. Cooper, and J. Wilson at the book room, 1804. 426 p., 1 l 17 cm. Colophon: Published by E. Cooper & J. Wilson for the Methodist connexion: N. York, March 1, 1805. William C. Robinson, printer. [BS2505.F55 1804] (922.1) 34-19434
1. Paul, Saint, apostle. I. Gilpin, Joshua, vicar of Wrockwardine, tr. II. Title.

FLETCHER, John William, 1729-1785. 225.92
The portrait of St. Paul; or, The true model for Christians and pastors translated from a French manuscript of the late Rev. John William De La Flechere ... By the Rev. John [!] Gilpin ... New York, B. Waugh and T. Mason, for the Methodist Episcopal church, 1834. 1 p. l., [5]-241 p. 22 1/2 cm. [BS2505.F55 1834] 39-22842
1. Paul, Saint, apostle. I. Gilpin, Joshua, vicar of Wrockwardine, tr. II. Title.

FOAKES-JACKSON, Frederick John, 1855- 225.
The life of Saint Paul, the man and the apostle, by F. J. Foakes-Jackson. New York, Boni & Liveright, 1926. 292, [1] p. front., illus. (maps) 23 cm. [BS2505.F58] 26-8838
1. Paul, Saint, apostle. I. Title.

FOUARD, Constant Henri, 1837-1904 225.
The last years of Saint Paul, by the Abbe Constant Fouard; translated with the author's sanction and cooperation by George F. X. Griffith. New York and London, Longmans, Green and co., 1900. xiii, 326 p. 3 fold. maps (incl. front.) 2 plans 20 cm. [BS2505.F6] 1-29307
1. Paul, Saint, apostle. I. Griffith, George Francis Xavier, tr. II. Title.

FOUARD, Constant Henri, 1837-1904. 225.
Saint Paul and his missions, by the Abbe Constant Fouard. Tr. with the author's sanction and cooperation by George F. X. Griffith. New York and London, Longmans, Green, and co., 1894. xvi, 431 p. 2 fold. maps (incl. front.) 20 cm. [BS2505.F63] 4-4640
1. Paul, Saint, apostle. I. Griffith, George Francis Xavier, tr. II. Title.

FRANCISCUS, Brother, 1922- [922.1]
The tentmaker from Tarsus, a story of St. Paul. Illus. by Rosemary Donatino. Natre Dame, Ind., Dujarie Press [1950] 95 p. illus. 24 cm. [BS2505.F7] 225.92 50-2575
1. Paul, Saint, apostle. I. Title.

GAEBELEIN, Arno Clemens, 1861- 236
The prophet St. Paul; the eschatology of the apostle to the Gentiles, by Arno Clemens Gaebelein ... New York, N. Y., Publication office "Our hope"; London [etc.] Pickering & Inglis; [etc., etc., c1939] 181 p. 21 cm. [BS2655.E7G3] 39-34007
1. Paul, Saint, apostle. 2. Eschatology—Biblical teaching. 3. Bible. N. T. Epistles of Paul—Theology. 4. Bible—Theology—N. T. Epistles of Paul. I. Title.

GARDNER, Percy, 1846- 225.
The religious experience of Saint Paul, by Percy Gardner ... London, Williams & Norgate. New York, G. P. Putnam's sons, 1911. xvi, 263 p. 19 cm. (Half-title: Crown theological library. Vol. XXXIV) [BS2505.G3] 12-9637
1. Paul, Saint, apostle. I. Title.

[GEORGE, Robert Esmonde Gordon] 1894- 922.1 225.92
Saint Paul, envoy of grace, by Robert Sencourt [pseud.] New York, Sheed & Ward, 1948. x, 378 p. illus. 22 cm. (Great writers of the world) "General authorities": p. 318-320. "Notes" (bibliographical): p. 321-341. [BS2505.G38] 49-7216
1. Paul, Saint. apostle. I. Title. II. Series.

GIBBES, Emily Oliver. 225.92
Reflections on Paul according to the Acts in the New Testament; reflections on: Darwin's Origin of the species; Darwin's Descent of man; Cain--Chico, the chimpanzee; Bourget--The disciple; Moses--Egyptian religion; Electricity--the works of Jesus. By Emily Oliver Gibbes. New York, C. T. Dillingham & co., 1895. iii, 5-7, ix p., 1 l., 13-271 p. 19 cm. [BS2505.G45] 922.1 34-17154
1. Paul, Saint, apostle. 2. Religion and science—1860-1899. I. Title.

GIBBS, Paul T. 225.9'24 B
Paul the Conqueror [by] Paul T. Gibbs. Washington, Review and Herald Pub. Association [1972] 124 p. 22 cm. (Discovery paperbacks) [BS2506.G5] 75-178160
1. Paul, Saint, apostle. I. Title.

GILBERT, George Holley, 1854-1930. 225.
A short history of Christianity in the apostolic age, by George Holley Gilbert ... Chicago, The University of Chicago press, 1906. vi, 239 p. front. (map) illus. 23 cm. (Half-title: Constructive Bible studies, ed. by E. D. Burton. [College and academy series]) Series title also on t.-p. [BS2410.G6] 6-41055
1. Paul, Saint, apostle. 2. Church history—Primitive and early church. I. Title.

GILBERT, George Holley, 1854-1930. 225.
The student's life of Paul. New York and London, The Macmillan co., 1899. x, 279 p. 12 degrees. Index of literature cited: p. 279 [BS2505.G5] 99-1430
1. Paul, Saint, apostle. I. Title.

GILBERT, George Holley, 1854-1930. 225.
The student's life of Paul, by George Holley Gilbert ... New York, The Macmillan company; London, Macmillan & co., ltd., 1909. x, 279 p. 20 cm. "Set up and electrotyped March, 1899. Reprinted February 1902; May 1907, September, 1909." "Index of literature cited": p. 279. [BS2505.G5] 10-3628
1. Paul, Saint, apostle. I. Title.

GIORDANI, Igino, 1894- 225.92
St. Paul, apostle and martyr. Tr. from Italian by Clelia Maranzana, Mary Paula Williamson. Foreword by Richard Cardinal Cushing. [Boston] St. Paul Eds. [dist. Daughters of St.Paul, c.1961] 277p. illus. 61-11836 6.50; 5.00 pap.,
1. Paul, Saint, apostle. I. Title.

GIORDANI, Igino, 1894- 225.92
St. Paul, apostle and martyr, by Igino Giordani; translated from the Italian by Mother Clelia Maranzana and Mother Mary Paula Williamson ... New York, The Macmillan company, 1946. xviii, 286 p. 21 cm. "First printing." [BS2505.G532] 922.1 46-1836
1. Paul, Saint, apostle. I. Maranzana, Clelia, mother, tr. II. Williamson, Mary Paul, mother, joint tr. III. Title.

GLOVER, Terrot Reaveley, 1869- 225.
Paul of Tarsus, by T. R. Glover. New York, George H. Doran company [1925] 5 p. l., 256 p. 21 cm. [BS2505.G55] 25-25018
1. Paul, Saint, apostle. I. Title.

GOODMAN, Frederic Simeon, 1858- 225.92
... *Life and letters of Paul.* Prepared by Fred S. Goodman ... New York, The International committee of Young men's Christian associations [c1895] viii, [9]-96 p. 16 cm. (Progressive Bible studies. Course no. 2) Published in 1911 under title: Elementary studies in the life and letters of Paul. "Helps for Bible study": p. viii. [BS2507.G615] 922.1 39-11829
1. Paul, Saint, apostle. I. Young men's Christian associations. International committee. II. Title.

GOODSPEED, Edgar Johnson, 1871- 225.92
Paul. [1st ed.] Philadelphia, J. C. Winston Co. [1947] ix, 246 p. map (on lining-papers) 22 cm. "Books about Paul": p. 240. [BS2505.G58] [922.1] 47-12367
1. Paul, Saint, apostle. I. Title.

GOODSPEED, Edgar Johnson, 1871- 225.
Paul, by Edgar J. Goodspeed; an outline Bible-study course of the American institute of sacred literature. Chicago, Ill., The University of Chicago press [1922] v, 78 p. front. (map) 20 cm. (On cover: Outline Bible-study courses of the American institute of sacred literature) [BS2507.G63] 23-2473
1. Paul, Saint, apostle. I. Title.

GOODSPEED, Edgar Johnson, 1871-1962. 225.92
Paul; [a biography drawn from the evidence in the apostle's writings] Nashville, Abingdon Press [1962, c1947] 246 p. 21 cm. (Apex books, D2) Includes bibliography. [BS2505] A62
1. Paul, Saint, apostle. I. Title.

GOODWIN, Frank Judson, 1862- 225.924
A harmony and commentary on the life of St. Paul according to the Acts of the Apostles and the Pauline Epistles. Grand Rapids, Baker Book House, 1951. 240p. 20cm. 'In issuing this third edition ... the original edition has been reprinted without change.' First ed. published in 1895 under title: A harmony of the life of St. Paul. [BS2505.G] A53
1. Paul, Saint, apostle. I. Title.

GOODWIN, Frank Judson, 1862- 225.92
A harmony of the life of St. Paul according to the Acts of the apostles and the Pauline epistles. by Rev. Frank J. Goodwin. New York, American tract society [c1895] 240 p. incl. 4 double maps. 23 cm. [BS2505.G6] 922.1 34-19431
1. Paul, Saint, apostle. I. American tract society. II. Title.

GRANT, Michael, 1914- 225.9'24 B
Saint Paul / Michael Grant. New York : Scribner, c1976. 250 p. : maps ; 25 cm. Includes index. Bibliography: p. 242-244. [BS2506.G68 1976b] 76-6024 ISBN 0-684-14682-7 : 14.95
1. Paul, Saint, Apostle. 2. Bible. N.T.—Biography. I. Title.

GRANT, Michael, 1914- 225.9'24 B
Saint Paul / Michael Grant. London : Weidenfeld and Nicolson, c1976. 250 p. : maps ; 24 cm. Includes index. Bibliography: p. 242-244. [BS2506.G68] 76-364100 ISBN 0-297-77082-9 : £5.95
1. Paul, Saint, Apostle.

GRANT, Michael, 1914- 225.9'24 B
Saint Paul / Michael Grant. New York : Crossroad, 1982, c1976. 250 p. : ill. ; 23 cm. Includes index. Bibliography: p. 242-244. [BS2506.G68 1982] 19 81-70381 ISBN 0-8245-0434-8 (pbk.) : 8.95
1. Paul, Saint, Apostle. 2. Bible. N.T.—Biography. 3. Christian Saints—Turkey—Tarsus. 4. Tarsus (Turkey)—Biography. I. Title.

GRASSI, Joseph A. 225.9'2'4 B
The secret of Paul the Apostle / Joseph A. Grassi. Maryknoll, N.Y. : Orbis Books, c1978. 170 p. ; 21 cm. [BS2506.G693] 77-29045 ISBN 0-88344-454-2 pbk. : 7.95
1. Paul, Saint, Apostle. 2. Christian saints—Turkey—Tarsus—Biography. 3. Tarsus, Turkey—Biography. 4. Missions—History—Early church, ca. 30-600. I. Title.

GRASSI, Joseph A 266
A world to win; the missionary methods of Paul the Apostle, by Joseph A. Grassi. Maryknoll, N.Y., Maryknoll Publications, 1965. viii, 184 p. 21 cm. [BS2506.G7] 65-18543
1. Paul, Saint, apostle. 2. Missions—Hist.—Early church. I. Title.

GREENE, George Francis, 1858-
The many-sided Paul; a study of the character of the great apostle as unfolded in the Acts and Pauline epistles. By George Francis Greene ... Philadelphia, The Westminster press, 1901. 270 p. 19 cm. (Lettered on cover: Westminster handbooks) [BS2505] 1-10349
1. Paul, Saint, apostle. I. Title.

GRIFFITH, Gwilym Oswald, 1882- 227
St. Paul's life of Christ, by Gwilym O. Griffith. New York, George H. Doran company [1925] 2 p. l., vii-viii, [9]-288 p. 20 cm. Printed in Great Britain. [BS2651.G7] 26-3630
1. Paul, Saint, apostle. 2. Jesus Christ. I. Title.

GROLLENBERG, Lucas Hendricus, 1916- 225.9'2'4 B
Paul / Lucas Grollenberg. Philadelphia : Westminster Press, c1978. 179 p. ; 20 cm. Translation of Die moeilijk Paulus. [BS2506.G7713] 78-14372 ISBN 0-664-24234-0 pbk. : 4.50
1. Paul, Saint, Apostle. 2. Bible. N.T.—Biography. 3. Bible. N.T. Epistles of Paul—Theology. 4. Christian saints—Turkey—Tarsus—Biography. 5. Tarsus, Turkey—Biography.

GUNTHER, John J. 225.9'2'4 B
Paul: messenger and exile; a study in the chronology of his life and letters [by] John J. Gunther. Valley Forge, Judson Press [1972] 190 p. map. 23 cm. Includes bibliographical references. [BS2506.G85] 70-181022 ISBN 0-8170-0504-8 6.95
1. Paul, Saint, apostle. I. Title.

HALL, Asa Zadel 225.92
A cloud of witnesses; pen portraits and character sketches of people around Paulthe great apostle: his friends and enemies. Grand Rapids, Mich., Zondervan [c.1961] 88p. illus. 61-66713 1.95
1. Paul, Saint, apostle. 2. Bible. N. T.—Biog. I. Title.

HAUGHTON, Rosemary. 225.924 B
Paul and the world's most famous letters. [Nashville, Abingdon Press, 1970] 110 p. illus., maps. 27 cm. 1969 ed., London, published under title: Why the Epistles were written. Bibliography: p. 107. [BS2506.H3 1970] 72-105063 3.75
1. Paul, Saint, apostle. 2. Bible. N.T. Epistles of Paul—Criticism, interpretation, etc. I. Title.

HAYES, Doremus Almy, 1863-
... *Paul and his epistles,* by D. A. Hayes ... New York, Cincinnati, The Methodist book concern [c1915] 508 p. 21 1/2 cm. (Biblical introduction series) Bibliography: p. [489]-499. 15-18637
I. Title.

HEADLAM, Arthur Cayley, bp. of Gloucester, 1862- 227
St. Paul and Christianity, by Arthur C. Headlam ... New York, Longmans, Green & co., 1913. xv, 214 p. 19 1/2 cm. [BS2651.H4] A 14
1. Paul, Saint, apostle. 2. Bible. N.T. Epistles of Paul—Theology. I. Title.

HEADLAM, Arthur Cayley, bp. of Gloucester, 1862-
St. Paul and Christianity, by Arthur C. Headlam ... New York, Longmans, Green & co., 1913. xv, 214 p. 19 cm. A 14
1. Paul, Saint, apostle. 2. Christianity. I. Title.

HENDERLITE, Rachel. 922.1
Paul, Christian and world traveler. Student's book. With illus. by Dawn Kyoko Aoto. Richmond, Published for the Cooperative Publication Association by John Knox Press [1957] 66p. illus. 23cm. [BS2507.H4] 225.92 57-23346
1. Paul, Saint, apostle. I. Title.

HENRY, Lyman I. 225.
Paul, son of Kish, by Lyman I. Henry. Chicago, Ill., The University of Chicago press [1923] ix, 356 p. col. front., plates, map. 20 cm. (Half title: The University of Chicago publications in religious education ... Constructive studies) [BS2505.H4] 23-14371
1. Paul, Saint, apostle. I. Title.

HEUSER, Herman Joseph, 1851-1933. 225.
From Tarsus to Rome, the story of the first Christian hierarchy, by Herman J. Heuser ... London, New York [etc.] Longmans, Green and co., 1929. vii p., 2 l., 167 p. 19 cm. "'From Tarsus to Rome' completes the trilogy, begun in 'In the workshop of Saint Joseph' and continued in 'The house of Martha at Bethany'."--Publisher's announcement. [BS2505.H45] 29-20814
1. Paul, Saint, apostle. I. Title.

HILDE, Reuben. 225.9'24 B
In search of twentieth-century Pauls / by Reuben Hilde ; [artist, Paul Ricchiuti]. Mountain View, Calif. : Pacific Press Pub. Association, c1980. 112 p. ; 18 cm. (A Redwood paperback ; 121) Bibliography: p. 112. [BS2506.H54] 19 79-88822 pbk. : 3.95
1. Paul, Saint, apostle. I. Title.

HOLMBERG, Bengt, 1942- 262'.012
Paul and power : the structure of authority in the primitive church as reflected in the Pauline epistles / Bengt Holmberg. 1st Fortress Press ed. Philadelphia : Fortress Press, 1980, c1978. p. cm. Originally presented as the author's thesis, Lund University. Includes indexes. Bibliography: p. [BV648.H64 1980] 79-8905 ISBN 0-8006-0634-5 : 14.95
1. Paul, Saint, apostle. 2. Church polity—Early church, ca. 30-600. I. Title.

HOLMES, Arhtur, 1872- 225.
The mind of St. Paul; a psychological study, by Arhtur Holmes... New York, The Macmillan company, 1929. 263 p. diagr. 20 1/2 cm. [BS2505.H55] 29-21156
1. Paul, Saint, apostle. I. Title.

HOLZNER, Josef, 1875- 225.92
Paul of Tarsus, by Rt. Rev. Joseph Holzner, translated by Rev. Frederic C. Eckhoff. St. Louis, Mo., and London, B. Herder book co., 1944. vi, 502 p. maps. 24 1/2 cm. "A translation of Paulus, sein leben and seine briefe."--Publisher's note. [BS2505.H58] [922.1] 44-29984
1. Paul, Saint, apostle. I. Eckhoff. Frederic Clement, 1899- tr. II. Title.

HOSFORD, Benjamin Franklin, 1817-1864. 225.92
Paul, and the chief cities of his labors. By Rev. B. F. Hosford. Written for the Massachusetts Sabbath school society, and approved by the Committee of publication. Boston, Massachusetts Sabbath school society, 1857. xviii, 257 p. incl. front., illus., plates. pl. 20 1/2 cm. [BS2505.H6] [922.1] 34-17172
1. Paul, Saint, apostle. I. Massachusetts Sabbath school society. Committee of publication. II. Title.

HUGHES, Albert. 225.92
Paul, the faithful witness [by] Albert Hughes ... Grand Rapids, Mich., Zondervan publishing house [c1939] 2 p. l., 7-97 p. 20 cm. [BS2505.H78] [[922.1]] 39-23879
1. Paul, Saint, apostle. I. Title.

HUGHES, Albert. 225.92
Renamed; Saul becomes Paul, by Albert Hughes ... Philadelphia, Pa., The American Bible conference association [c1935] 6 p., 1 l., 7-128 p. 19 1/2 cm. [BS2505.H8] [[922.1]] 35-14989
1. Paul, Saint, apostle. 2. Conversion. I. Title. II. Title: Saul becomes Paul.

HUTTON, John Alexander, 1868- 225.92
Finally; with Paul to the end, by John A. Hutton, D. D. New York and London, Harper and brothers [1935] 302 p. 22 cm. "Printed in Great Britain." [BS2505.H9] [922.1] 35-7149
1. Paul, Saint, apostle. I. Title.

IN Christ;
a sketch of the theology of St. Paul. Translated and edited from the 2d rev. Dutch ed. by Martin W. Schoenberg. Westminster, Md., Newman Press, 1959. 138p. 19cm.
I. Grossouw, William Karel Maria, 1906-

IVERACH, James, 1839-1922.
... *St. Paul:* his life and times, by James Iverach ... New York, Chicago [etc.] Fleming H. Revell company [1900?] viii, 216 p. 19 cm. (Men of the Bible.) [BS205.I 9] 39-19534
1. Paul, Saint, apostle. I. Title.

JAMISON, Leland 226.606
Light for the Gentiles; Paul and the growing church. Philadelphia, Westminster Pr. [c.1961] 91p. (Westminster guides to the Bible) 62-7483 1.50
1. Paul, Saint, apostle. 2. Bible. N. T. Acts—Criticism, interpretation, etc. 3. Bible. N. T. Epistles of Paul—Criticism, interpretation, etc. I. Title.

JEFFERSON, Charles Edward, 1860-1937. 225.
The character of Paul, by Charles Edward Jefferson ... New York, The Macmillan company, 1923. vii2, 381 p. 21 cm. [BS2505.J4] 23-18001
1. Paul, Saint, apostle. I. Title.

JOHNSEN, Erik Kristian, 1863- 225.
Paul of Tarsus; i. Paul--a character sketch, ii. Paul's epistles. By E. Kr. Johnsen ... Minneapolis, Minn., Augsburg publishing house, 1919. 375, [1] p. front. (port.) 20 cm. [BS2505.J65] 20-1501
1. Paul, Saint, apostle. I. Title.

JOHNSON, Hubert Rex. 225.9'24 B
Who then is Paul? / By Hubert Rex Johnson. Lanham, MD : University Press of America, 1981. p. cm. Includes index. [BS2506.J63] 19 80-1406 ISBN 0-8191-1364-6 : 19.75 ISBN 0-8191-1365-4 (pbk.) : 10.75
1. Paul, Saint, apostle. 2. Christian saints—Turkey—Tarsus—Biography. 3. Tarsus, Turkey—Biography. I. Title.

JONES, Rufus Matthew, 1863- 225.
St. Paul, the hero, by Rufus M. Jones ... New York, The Macmillan company, 1917. 5 p. l., 172 p. front., plates, maps. 21 cm. [BS2505.J67] 17-10430
1. Paul, Saint apostle. I. Title.

KALLAS, James G 225.924 (B)
The story of Paul, by James G. Kallas. Minneapolis, Augsburg Pub. House [1966] 151 p. 22 cm. Includes bibliographies. [BS2506.K3] 66-19206
1. Paul, Saint, apostle. I. Title.

KECK, Leander E. 227'.06
Paul and his letters / Leander E. Keck. Philadelphia : Fortress Press, c1979. viii, 135 p. ; 22 cm. (Proclamation commentaries : The New Testament witnesses for preaching) Includes index. Bibliography: p. 131-132. [BS2651.K42] 78-54554 ISBN 0-8006-0587-X : pbk. : 3.50
1. Paul, Saint, Apostle. 2. Bible. N.T. Epistles of Paul—Theology. I. Title.

KELLER, Edmund B. 227
Some paradoxes of Paul / by Edmund B. Keller. New York : Philosophical Library, [1974] xi, 263 p. ; 22 cm. Originally presented as the author's thesis, Boston University. Bibliography: p. 207-229. [BS2652.K44 1974] 74-75085 ISBN 0-8022-2144-0 : 8.50
1. Paul, Saint, apostle. 2. Bible. N.T. Epistles of Paul—Theology. 3. Paradox. I. Title.

KELSO, James Leon, 1892- 225.92'4 B
An archaeologist follows the Apostle Paul [by] James L. Kelso. Waco, Tex., Word Books [1970] 142 p. illus., map. 23 cm. Includes bibliographical references. [BS2506.K44] 78-128446 3.95
1. Paul, Saint, apostle. 2. Bible. N.T. Epistles of Paul—Antiquities. I. Title.

KENNEDY, Harry Angus Alexander, 1866-
St. Paul and the mystery religions. London, New York [etc.] Hodder and Stoughton [pref. 1913] xviii, 311 p. 21 cm. A 14
I. Title.

KEPLER, Thomas Samuel, 1897- comp. 227
Contemporary thinking about Paul, an anthology. New York, Abingdon-Cokesbury Press [1950] 442 p. 24 cm. Bibliography: p. 419-422. [BS2505.K37] 50-5469
1. Paul, Saint, apostle. 2. Bible. N. T. Epistles of Paul—Criticism, interpretation, etc. I. Title.

KEPLER, Thomas Samuel, 1897- 242
A spiritual journey with Paul. Nashville, Abingdon-Cokesbury Press [1953] 157p. 20cm. [BV4832.K445] 52-12421
1. Paul, Saint, apostle. 2. Meditations. I. Title.

KERR, Mary Starck. 225.92
Paul, by Mary Starck Kerr ... Compton, Calif., Moore brothers printing co., c1931. 2 p. l., 7-80 p. 19 1/2 cm. [BS2505.K4] [922.1] 31-32814
1. Paul, Saint, apostle. I. Title.

KIM, Seyoon. 227'.06
The origin of Paul's gospel / by Seyoon Kim. American ed. Grand Rapids, Mich. : W.B. Eerdmans Pub. Co., 1982, c1981. p. cm. Revision of thesis (Ph.D.)—University of Manchester, 1977. Includes indexes. Bibliography: p. [BS2651.K55 1982] 19 82-5121 ISBN 0-8028-1933-8 pbk. : 13.95
1. Paul, the Apostle, Saint. 2. Bible. N.T. Epistles of Paul—Theology. I. Title.

KINSEY, Robert S 227
With Paul in Greece. Nashville, Parthenon Press [1957] 208p. illus. 21cm. Includes bibliography. [BS2505.K48] 57-59249
1. Paul, Saint, apostle. 2. Bible. N. T. Epistles of Paul—Criticism, 3. Greece, Modern—Descr. & trav.—1951- I. Title.

KLAUSNER, Joseph, 1874- 296
From Jesus to Paul, by Joseph Klausner ... translated from the Hebrew by William F. Stinespring ... New York, The Macmillan company, 1943. xvi, 624 p. 21 cm. "First printing." Bibliographical foot-notes. [BM535.K55] 43-8434
1. Paul, Saint, apostle. 2. Jews—Religion—Relations—Christianity. 3. Bible. N.T. Epistles of Paul—Theology. 4. Bible—Theology—N.T. Epistles of Paul. I. Stinespring, William Franklin, 1901- tr. II. Title.

KNOWLING, Richard John, 1851-1919. 227
The testimony of St. Paul to Christ viewed in some of its aspects by R. J. Knowling ... New York, C. Scribner's sons 1905. viii, 533 p. 24 cm. On verso of half-title: Boyle lectures, 1903-5. "Recent literature": p. 496-528. [BS2651.K6] 6-11301
1. Paul. Saint, opostle. 2. Bible. N. T. Gospels—Evidences, authority, etc. 3. Church history—Primitive and early church. 4. Bible—Evidences, authority, etc.—N. T. Gospels. I. Boyle lectures, 1903-1925. II. Title.
Contents omitted.

KNOX, John, 1900- 225.92
Chapters in a life of Paul. Nashville, Abingdon [1964, c.1950] 168p. 23cm. (Apex bks., P2) 1.25 pap.,
1. Paul, Saint, apostle. I. Title.

KNOX, John, 1900- [922.1]
Chapters in a life of Paul. New York, Abingdon-Cokesbury Press [1950] 168 p. 24 cm. [BS2505.K56] 225.92 50-5882
1. Paul, Saint, apostle. I. Title.

KNOX, Wilfred Lawrence, 1886- 225.92
St. Paul, by Wilfred Knox. New York, D. Appleton and company, 1932. 3 p. l., 153, [1] p. front. 20 cm. [Appleton biographies] "Bibliographical note": p. 151. [BS2505.K57 1932 a] 922.1 32-22106
1. Paul, Saint. apostle. I. Title.

KNOX, Wilfred Lawrence, 1886- 225.
St. Paul and the Church of Jerusalem, by the Reverend Wilfred L. Knox ... Cambridge [Eng.] The University press, 1925. xxvi (i. e. xxvii) 396 p. 25 cm. [BS2505.K6] 25-14536
1. Paul, Saint, apostle. 2. Church history—Primitive and early church. I. Title.

KNOX, Wilfred Lawrence, 1886- 227
St. Paul and the church of the gentiles, by the Reverend Wilfred L. Knox ... Cambridge [Eng.] The University press, 1939. x p., 1 l., 261, [1] p. 24 cm. [BS2651.K65] 39-25281
1. Paul, Saint, apostle. 2. Bible. N. T. Epistles of Paul—Theology. 3. Jews—Religion—Relations—Christianity. 4. Bible—Theology—N. T. Epistles of Paul. I. Title.

KRAELING, Emil Gottlieb Heinrich, 1892- 225.924 (B)
I have kept the faith; the life of the apostle Paul, by Emil G. Kraeling. Chicago, Rand McNally [1965] 320 p. maps (on lining papers) 22 cm. "Notes and references": p. 276-307. [BS2506.K7] 65-15357
1. Paul, Saint, apostle. I. Title.

KUIST, Howard Tillman. 227
The pedagogy of St. Paul, by Howard Tillman Kuist ... New York, George H. Doran company [c1925] xiii p., 3 l. 21-169 p. front., plates, diagrs. 19 cm. Thesis (PH. D.)--New York university, 1924. Published also without thesis note. Bibliography: p. 151-161. [BS2655.E3K8 1924] 25-9450
1. Paul, Saint, apostle. I. Title.

LAKE, Kirsopp, 1872- 225.92
Paul, his heritage and legacy, by Kirsopp Lake ... New York, Oxford university press, 1934. xix p., 1 l., [23]-153 p. 23 cm. (Half-title: The Mary Flexner lectures on the humanities. i) "Printed in Great Britain." [BS2651.L3] 922.1 34-24117
1. Paul, Saint, apostle. I. Title.

LAPIDE, Cornelius A, 1567-1637. 225.92
The personality of St. Paul. Translated by the Daughters of St. Paul. [Boston] St. Paul Editions [1959] 153p. illus. 22cm. [BS2505.L27] 59-33736
1. Paul, Saint, apostle. I. Title.

LARRIMER, Mary. 225.
The life of Paul of Tarsus, by Mary Larrimer ... Boston, Lothrop, Lee & Shepard co. [c1929] 242 p. 23 cm. [BS2505.L3] 30-542
1. Paul, Saint, apostle. I. Title.

LEAVELL, Roland Quinche, 1891- 225.92
The Apostle Paul, Christ's supreme trophy. Grand Rapids, Mich., Baker Bk. [1964, c.] 1963. 128p. illus. 23cm. 63-14400 1.50 pap.,
1. Paul, Saint, Apostle. I. Title.

LEAVELL, Roland Quinche, 1891-1963 225.92
The Apostle Paul, Christ's supreme trophy. Grand Rapids, Mich., Baker Bk. [c.]1963. 128p. illus. 23cm. 63-14400 2.95
1. Paul, Saint, Apostle. I. Title.

LECROY, Ruth Brooks. 225.9'24
Sunrise in Syria; a fact and fiction story about Saul of Tarsus who became Paul the Apostle. Little Rock, Ark., Pioneer Books [1972] ix, 250 p. 24 cm. [BS2506.L43] 74-189490 5.95
1. Paul, Saint, apostle. I. Title.

LEVY, Rosalie Marie, 1889- 225.92
The man in chain; Saint Paul, vessel of election. [n.p.] St. Paul Editions [c1957] 248p. illus. 22cm. [BS2505.L38] 59-23935

1. Paul, Saint, aposite. 2. Devotional calendars—Catholic Church. I. Title.

LIDDON, Henry Parry, 1829- 1890. 208.
Essays and addresses, by H. P. Liddon ... London and New York, Longmans, Green, and co., 1892. 4 p. l., 212 p. 20 cm. Contents.--Lectures on Buddhism.--Lectures on the life of St. Paul.--Papers on Dante. [BR85.L7] 10-12689
1. Paul, Saint, apostle. 2. Dante Alighieri, 1265-1321. 3. Buddha and Buddhism. I. Title.

THE life and epistles of St. Paul. 922.1
By W. J. Conybeare and J. S. Howson. New ed. Grand Rapids, W.B. Eerdmans Pub. Co., 1953. xxi, 850p. illus., maps. 22cm. Bibliographical footnotes. [BS2505.C65 1953] [BS2505.C65 1953] 225.92 53-1496 53-1496
1. Paul, Saint, apostle. I. Conybeare, William John, 1815-1857. II. Howson: John Saul, 1816-1885. III. Bible. N.T. Epistles of Paul. English. 1953.

THE life and travels of the apostle Paul. 225.92
Prepared with questions for the use of Sunday schools ... Boston, Lilly, Wait, Colman, and Holden, 1833. 1 p. l., [vii]-xi, [13]-272 p. front. (fold. map) 17 cm. [BS2505.L5] 922.1 39-10468
1. Paul, Saint, apostle.

THE life of Paul. 922.1
Philadelphia, Published for the Cooperative Publication Association by the Christian Education Press [1956, c1955] 81p. illus. 19cm. (The Cooperative series leadership training textbooks) [BS2507.M6] 225.92 56-7714
1. Paul, Saint, apostle. I. Moss, Robert V

LIGON, John Washington, 1865-
Paul the apostle, pioneer missionary to the heathen world, by John W. Ligon. New York, Chicago [etc.] Fleming H. Revell company [c1916] 240 p. map. 20 cm. 16-21209 1.00
I. Title.

LINEBERGER, Lawrence Otto, 1897- 225.92
The man from Tarsus, his world, personality and religious genius, by Lawrence Otto Lineberger. ... New York [etc.] Fleming H. Revell company [c1933] 240 p. 20 cm. [BS2505.L57] 922.1 33-6344
1. Paul. Saint. apostle. I. Title.

LOHFINK, Gerhard, 1934- 225.9'24 B
The conversion of St. Paul : narrative and history in Acts / by Gerhard Lohfink; translated and edited by Bruce J. Malina Chicago : Franciscan Herald Press, [1975] p. cm. (Herald scriptural library) Translation of Paulus vor Damaskus, 3d. ed. (1967) Bibliography: p. [BS2506.L5713] 75-12796 ISBN 0-8199-0572-0 : 5.95
1. Paul, Saint, apostle. 2. Bible. N.T. Acts—Criticism, interpretation, etc. I. Title.

LONGENECKER, Richard N. 225.92'4 B
The ministry and message of Paul [by] Richard Longenecker. Grand Rapids, Mich., Zondervan Pub. House [1971] 130 p. 21 cm. (Contemporary evangelical perspectives) Bibliography: p. 113-122. [BS2506.L598] 77-159661
1. Paul, Saint, apostle. I. Title.

LONGENECKER, Richard N. 227.06
Paul, apostle of liberty, by Richard N. Longenecker. [1st ed.] New York, Harper & Row [1964] x. 310 p. 22 cm. Bibliographical footnotes. [BS2506.L6] 64-19500
1. Paul, Saint, apostle. I. Title.

LUCE, Harry Kenneth, 1897- 922.1
St. Paul. Illustrated by G. S. Ronalds. [1st American ed.] New York, Putnam [1958] 118p. illus. 21cm. (Lives to remember) [BS2505.L7] 225.92 58-7445
1. Paul, Saint, apostle. I. Title.

LYMAN, Mary Redington (Ely) Mrs., 1887- 225.92
Paul the Conqueror, by Mary Redington Ely. New York, The Womans press, 1919. 112 p. 18 cm. "Suggested reading" at end of most of the chapters. [BS2505.L75] [922.1] 19-18855
1. Paul, Saint, apostle. I. Title.

MACARTNEY, Clarence Edward Noble, 1879- 225.
Paul the man, his life, his message and his ministry, by Clarence Edward Macartney ... New York, Chicago [etc.] Fleming H. Revell company [c1928] 221 p. front. (map) 21 cm. [BS2505.M23] 28-12565
1. Paul, Saint, apostle. I. Title.

MACCHIORO, Vittorio D., 1880- 292
From Orpheus to Paul; a history of Orphism, by Vittorio D. Macchioro. New York, H. Holt and company [c1930] 6 p. l., 3-262 p. front., plates (1 fold.) 22 1/2 cm. (Half-title: Studies in religion and culture. Schermerhorn lectures. I) "Notes": p. 227-258. [BL795.O7M3] 30-13999
1. Paul, Saint, apostle. 2. Orpheus. 3. Mysteries, Religious. 4. Christianity and other religions. I. Title. II. Title: Orphism, A history of.

MCCORRY, Vincent P., 1909- 227.07
Everyman's St. Paul. New York, Farrar, Straus and Cudahy [c.1961] 215p. 61-5898 3.95 half cloth,
1. Paul, Saint, apostle. 2. Bible. N.T. Epistles and Gospels, Liturgical—Commentaries. I. Title.

MACGREGOR, William Malcolm. 204
Christian freedom, by William Malcolm Macgregor ... New ed., with new introduction. New York and London, Harper & brothers [1931] 392 p. 23 cm. (Half-title: The Baird lecture for 1913) "Printed in Great Britain." [BR121.M32 1931] 31-28153
1. Paul, Saint, apostle. 2. Christianity—Addresses, essays, lectures. 3. Christian life. 4. Bible. N.T. Galatians—Criticism, interpretation, etc. 5. Bible—Criticism, interpretation, etc.—N. T. Galatians I. Title.

MACGREGOR, William Malcolm, 1861- 204
Christian freedom; the Baird lecture for 1913, by William Malcolm Macgregor ... London, New York [etc.] Hodder and Stoughton, 1914. xii, 428 p. 19 cm. (Half-title: The Baird lecture, 1913) [BR121.M32] A 15
1. Paul, Saint, apostle. 2. Christianity—Addresses, essays, lectures. 3. Christian life. 4. Bible. N.T. Galatians—Criticism, interpretation, etc. 5. Bible—Criticism, interpretation, etc.—N.T. Galatians. I. Title.

MACHEN, John Gresham, 1881- 1937 230
The origin of Paul's religion. Grand Rapids, Mich., Eerdmans [1966, c.1925] 239p. 20cm. (James Sprunt lects., 9th ser.) Bibl. [BS2651.M3] 66-2845 1.95 pap.,
1. Paul, Saint, apostle. 2. Bible. N. T. Epistles of Paul — Theology. I. Title.

MACKAY, Henry Falconar Barclay, 1864-1936. 225.92
The adventure of Paul of Tarsus [by] H. F. B. Mackay... Milwaukee, Wis., Morehouse publishing co. [1931] 3 p. l., 279 p. 21 1/2 cm. "First published in the United States of America, January, 1931. Second American edition, March, 1931." [BS2505.M27 1931a] (922.1) 31-12040
1. Paul, Saint, apostle. I. Title.

MACKINNON, James, 1860- 225.7
The gospel in the early church; a study of the early development of Christian thought, by James Mackinnon... London, New York [etc.] Longmans, Green, and co., 1933. xii, 339 p. 22 1/2 cm. "Note on the sources": p. 34-37, 56-57. [BS2361.M33] 33-16335
1. Paul, Saint, apostle. 2. Bible. N. T.—Theology. 3. Bible—Theology—N. T. 4. Apostolic fathers. 5. Fathers of the church—Hist. & crit. 6. Theology, Doctrinal—Hist.—Early church. I. Title.

MCNEILE, Alan Hugh, 1871- 1933. 225.
St. Paul; his life, letters, and Christian doctrine, by A. H. McNeile... Cambridge. The University press. 1920. xix, 319 p. iii maps (1 fold.) 20 cm. "Literature": p. [308]-311. [BS2505.M3] 20-11702
1. Paul, Saint, apostle. I. Title.

MCRAE, Glenn, 1887- 225.92
A man who wrote Scripture; Glenn McRae, author, Ronald E. Osborn, editor ... St. Louis, Mo., Christian board of publication, c1945. 96 p. illus. (map) 19 cm. (A Bethany course in Christian living) "Aids to study": p. 96. [BS2505.M315] [922.1] 45-1747
1. Paul, Saint, apostle. I. Osborn, Ronald E., ed. II. Title.

THE man from Tarsus. 922.1
With an introd. by A. Victor Murray. Newtown, Montgomeryshire Print. Co., 1956. 375p. 22cm. [BS2505.E8] [BS2505.E8] 225.92 57-39876 57-398768
1. Paul, Saint, apostle. I. Eurich, H F A

MARTIN, Ira Jay, 1911- 225.92
The faith of Paul, a study for inquiring Christians. NewYork, Pageant [1965, c.1964] 350p. 21cm. [BS2506.M37] 64-66331 6.00
1. Paul, Saint, apostle. I. Title.

MARY Eleanor, Mother, 1903- 225.924
The last apostle. Illustrated by George Pollard. Milwaukee, Bruce Pub. Co. [1956] 150p. illus. 22cm. (Catholic treasury books) [BS2505.M318] 56-11154
1. Paul, Saint, apostie—Juvenile literature. I. Title.

MATHEWS, Basil Joseph, 1879- 225.92
Paul the dauntless; the course of a great adventure, by Basil Mathews, M.A. Philadelphia, The Blakiston company, distributed by Fleming H. Revell company, New York and London [c1943] 6, 9-375 p. 19 1/2 cm. Bibliography: p. 367. [BS2505.M35 1943] [(922.1)] 44-4555
1. Paul, Saint, apostle. I. Title.

MATHEWS, Basil Joseph, 1879- 225.
Paul the dauntless, the course of a great adventure, by Basil Mathews, M.A. Illustrated in colour and black-and-white from drawings by Ernest Prater and with reproductions from photographs by the author and maps. New York, Chicago [etc.] Fleming H. Revell company [c1916] 375 p. col. front., illus., plates (part col.) 3 maps (1 fold.) 21 1/2 cm. Bibliography: p. 367. [BS2505.M35] 17-58
1. Paul, Saint, Apostle. I. Title.

MATHEWS, Basil Joseph, 1879-1951. 225.92
Paul the dauntless. [Westwood, N. J.] Revell [1959] 375p. 21cm. Includes bibliography. [BS2505.M35 1959] 59-4741
1. Paul, Saint, apostle. I. Title.

MEYER, Frederick Brotherton, 1847-1929. 225.92
Paul, a servant of Jesus Christ. By the Rev. F. B. Meyer ... New York, Chicago [etc.] Fleming H. Revell company [1897] 3 p. l., 9-208 p. 19 cm. [BS2505.M43] 922.1 34-17166
1. Paul, Saint, apostle. I. Title.

MEYER, Frederick Brotherton, 1847-1929. 922.1
Paul, a servant of Jesus Christ. Grand Rapids, Zondervan Pub. House [1953] 155p. 20cm. [BS2505.M43 1953] [BS2505.M43 1953] 225.92 53-13075 53-13075
1. Paul, Saint, apostle. I. Title.

MILLER, Donald G. 225.92
Conqueror in chains, a story of the apostle Paul; illustrated by Albert De Mee Jousset. Philadelphia, Westminster Press [1951] 271 p. illus. 22 cm. [BS2505.M52] 922.1 51-12690
1. Paul, Saint, apostle. I. Title.

MINEAR, Paul Sevier, 1906- 225.92
An introduction to Paul [by] Paul Sevier Minear ... New York, Cincinnati [etc.] The Abingdon press [c1937] 82 p. illus. (map) diagrs. 16 1/2cm. "Selected biographies": p. 78; "References and suggestions for study": p. 79-82. [BS2507.M5] 37-7828
1. Paul, Saint, apostle. I. Title.

MOE, Olaf Edvard, 1876- 225.92
The apostle Paul. Translated by L. A. Vigness. Minneapolis, Augsburg Pub. House [1950-54] 2 v. maps. 22 cm. Contents.Contents.—1. His life and his work.—2. His message and doctrine. Includes bibliographies. [BS2505.M5494] 922.1 50-7291
1. Paul, Saint, apostle.

MOFFATT, James, 1870- 225.
Paul and Paulinism, by James Moffatt ... Boston and New York, Houghton Mifflin company, 1910. 2 p. l., 76, [2] p. 17 1/2 cm. (Half-title: Modern religious problems) "Selected list of recent works on the criticism of Paul and Paulinism": p. 75-76, [1] [BS2505.M55] 10-7919
1. Paul, Saint, apostle. I. Title.

MONOD, Adolphe, 1802-1856. 225.92
Saint Paul: five discourses. By Adolphe Monod. Translated from the French by Rev. J. H. Myers, D. D. Andover, W. F. Draper; Boston, Gould and Lincoln; [etc., etc.] 1860. viii p., 1 l., [11]-191 p. 20 cm. [Full name: Adolphe Louis Frederic Theodore Monod] [BS2505.M6] 922.1 34-19430
1. Paul, Saint, apostle. I. Myers, J. H., tr. II. Title.

MONTAGUE, George T. 248'.4
Building Christ's body : the dynamics of Christian living according to St. Paul / by George T. Montague. Chicago : Franciscan Herald Press, [1975] p. cm. (Herald scriptural library) Bibliography: p. [BS2655.C4M66] 75-14100 ISBN 0-8199-0573-9 : 4.95
1. Paul, Saint, apostle. 2. Christian life—Biblical teaching. I. Title.

MONTEFIORE, Claude Joseph Goldsmid, 1858-1938. 296.3
Judaism and St. Paul: two essays. New York, Arno Press, 1973. 240 p. 21 cm. (The Jewish people: history, religion, literature) Reprint of the 1914 ed. published by M. Goschen, London. Includes bibliographical references. [BS2652.M6 1973] 73-2222 ISBN 0-405-05284-7 15.00
1. Paul, Saint, apostle. 2. Bible. N.T. Epistles of Paul—Theology. 3. Rabbinical literature—Relation to the New Testament. 4. Reform Judaism. I. Title. II. Series.

MONTIZAMBERT, Eric St. Lucian Percy, 1888- 227
The thought of St. Paul in the light of the modern world, by Eric Montizambert ... New York, Morehouse-Gorham co., 1941. xi p., 2 l., [3]-325 p. 21 cm. Bibliography: p. 308-304. [BS2651.M65] 42-773
1. Paul, Saint, apostle. 2. Bible. N. T. Epistles of Paul—Theology. 3. Bible—Theology—N. T. Epistles of Paul. I. Title.

MOORE, Hight C 1871- 225.92
From Pentecost to Patmos [by] Hight C. Moore ... Nashville, Tenn., The Sunday school board of the Southern Baptist convention [c1934] 132 p. illus. (map) 19 cm. (On cover: Bible biography, book 5) [BS571.B5 book 5] 922.1 35-315
1. Paul, Saint, apostle. 2. Bible. N. T. Acts and Epistles—Study—Text-books. 3. Bible—Study—Text-books—N. T. Acts and Epistles. I. Title.

MOORE, Hight C, 1871- 1957. 227.007
From Pentecost to Patmos. Nashville, Convention Press [1959, c1934]•145p. illus. 19cm. [BS2619.M65 1959] 59-9311
1. Paul, Saint, apostle. 2. Bible. N. T. Acts and Epistles—Study—Text-books. I. Title.

MORTON, Andrew Queen. 227'.01'4
Paul, the man and the myth; a study in the authorship of Greek prose, by A. Q. Morton and James McLeman. New York, Harper & Row [1966] 217 p. 22 cm. [BS2650.2.M6 1966] 67-10053
1. Paul, Saint, apostle. 2. Bible. N.T. Epistles of Paul—Authorship. 3. Greek language—Word frequency. 4. Greek language—Sentences. I. McLeman, James, joint author. II. Title.

MUGGERIDGE, Malcolm, 1903- 225.9'24 B
Paul, envoy extraordinary [by] Malcolm Muggeridge & Alec Vidler. [1st U.S. ed.] New York, Harper & Row [1972] 159 p. illus. 23 cm. [BS2506.M84 1972] 73-184408 5.95
1. Paul, Saint, apostle. I. Vidler, Alexander Roper, 1899- II. Title.

MUNCK, Johannes, 1904- 225.92
Paul and the salvation of mankind. [Translated by Frank Clarke from the German Paulus und die Heilsgeschichte. 1st English ed.] Richmond, John Knox Press [1959] 351 p. 24 cm. Includes

bibliography. [BS2505.M933 1959] 60-5412
1. Paul, Saint, apostle.

NEFF, Lawrence Wilson. 227
The final failure of Christianity [by] Lawrence W. Neff ... Emory University, Atlanta, Banner press [c1935] 76 p. 21 cm. On the "essential incompatibility [of the Pauline epistles] with the authentic teaching of Jesus".--Foreword. [BS2651.N4] 35-10614
1. Paul, Saint, apostle. 2. Christianity—Orgin. 3. Bible, N. T. Epistles of Paul—Theology. 4. Bible—Theology—N. T. Epistles of Paul. I. Title.

NELSON, Peter Christopher, 1868- 225.92
The life and letters of Paul, by P. C. Nelson ... Enid, Okl., The Southewestern press [c1939] 297, [1] p., 5 l., 5-300 p. incl. front., illus. (maps) 22 cm. Includes bibliographies. [BS2505.N4] 922.1 40-1921
1. Paul, Saint, apostle. 2. Bible, N. T. Epistles of Paul—Study—Outlines, syllabi, etc. 3. Bible—Study—Outlines, syllabi. etc.—N. T. Epistles of Paul. I. Title.
Contents omitted.

NOCK, Arthur Darby, 1902- 922.1
St. Paul. New York, Harper [1963] 255p. 18cm. (Harper torchbk.; Cloister Lib., TB104) Bibl. 1.45 pap.,
1. Paul, Saint, apostle. I. Title.

NOCK, Arthur Darby, 1902- 225.92
St. Paul. New York, Harper & Row [1963] 255 p. 21 cm. (Harper torchbooks. The Cloister library) "TB 104." Bibliography: p. 249-251. [[BS2506]]
1. Paul, Saint, apostle.

NORWOOD, Robert Winkworth, 1874- 225.
The heresy of Antioch, an interpretation, by Robert Norwood ... Garden City, N.Y., Doubleday, Doran & company, inc., 1928. xx p., 1 l., 303 p. 21 1/2 cm. [BS2505.N6] 28-8149
1. Paul, Saint, apostle. I. Title.

OLMSTEAD, Benjamin Luce, 1886- 225.92
A brief life of Paul, with a chart and six maps, by Benjamin L. Olmstead ... Winona Lake, Ind., Light and life press [c1938] 80 p. illus. (maps) 17 cm. [BS2507.O4] 922.1 40-2213
1. Paul, Saint, apostle. I. Title.

PARKER, Jane (Marsh) Mrs. 1836-1913. 225.92
The soldier of the cross; or, Life of St. Paul. Written for the lambs of the flock. By Jenny Marsh Parker. New York, Stanford & Delisser, 1858. 64 p. 15 cm. Initials. [BS2505.P3] [922.1] 34-17158
1. Paul, Saint, apostles. I. Title.

PARKS, William J. 225.92
Paul, his Master's champion. New York, Vantage [c.1961] 300p. 4.50 bds.,
I. Title.

PARKS, William J 225.92
Paul, his Master's champion. [1st ed.] New York, Vantage Press [1961] 330p. 21cm. [BS2506.P36] 61-66797
1. Paul, Saint, apostle. I. Title.

PAUL, 922.1
the tent maker. Foreword byAbram Woodard. Boston, Christopher Pub. House [1957] 109p. illus. 21cm. [BS2505.D37] [BS2505.D37] 225.92 57-28030 57-28030
1. Paul, Saint, apostle. I. Day, Bertram, 1871-

PAUL. 922.1
Edited and completed by Werner Georg Kummel. Translated by Frank Clarke. Philadelphia, Westminster Press [1953] 172p. illus. 19cm. [BS2505.D495] [BS2505.D495] 225.92 53-1574 53-1574
1. Paul, Saint, apostle. I. Dibelius, Martin, 1883-1947. II. Kummel, Werner Georg, 1905- ed.

PAUL and his interpreters, a critical history, [Translated from the German by W. Montgomery] New York, Macmillan, 1956. 252p. 22cm. Includes bibliographies.
1. Paul, Saint, apostle. 2. Bible. N. T. Epistles of Paul—Crit., interpretation, etc.—Hist. I. Schweitzer, Albert, 1875-

PAUL as a leader; 922.1
a study of the apostle's role and influence in the field of religious education. Foreword by W. L. Howse. [1st ed.] New York, Exposition Press [1955] 144p. 21cm. (Exposition--university book) [BS2505.C58] [BS2505.C58] 225.92 55-9397 55-9397
1. Paul, Saint, apostle. 2. Religious education. I. Collins, Carl A 1915-

PAUL of Tarsus; 225.
an inquiry into the times and the gospel of the apostle of the Gentiles. By a graduate. Boston, Roberts brothers 1872. viii, [9]-401 p. 18 cm. [BS2505.P35] 34-19436
1. Paul, Saint, apostle. I. A graduate.

PAUL'S life and letters. 922.1
[1st ed.] Salt Lake City, Bookcraft, 1955. 314p. illus. 24cm. [BS2505.S65] [BS2505.S65] 225.92 56-18630 56-18630
1. Paul, Saint, apostle. 2. Bible. N. T . Epsitles of Paul— Introductions. I. Sperry, Sidney Branton, 1895-

PEABODY, Francis Greenwood, 1847-1936. 227
The apostle Paul and the modern world; an examination of the teaching of Paul in its relation to some of the religious problems of modern life, by Francis Greenwood Peabody ... New York, The Macmillan company, 1923. xi p., 1 l., 285 p. 20 cm. [BS2651.P35] 23-6760
1. Paul, Saint, apostle. 2. Bible. N. T. Epistles of Paul—Theology. 3. Bible—Theology—N. T. Epistles of Paul. I. Title.

PEARCY, Henri Reubelt, 1894- 225.92
A vindication of Paul, by Henri Reubelt Pearcy, TH. D. New York, T. Nelson & sons, 1936. xi p., 1 l., 254 p. 20 cm. Bibliography: p. 248-254. [BS2651.P37] 922.1 36-21328
1. Paul, Saint, apostle. 2. Bible. N. T. Epistles of Paul—Theology. 3. Bible—Theology—N. T. Epistles of Paul. I. Title.

PELL, Edward Leigh, 1861- 225.
The story of Paul, as told by himself, by Edward Leigh Pell ... New York, Chicago [etc.] Fleming H. Revell company [c1920] 66 p. incl. front. (port.) plates. 20 cm. (Lettered on cover: Pell's Bible stories) [BS2505.P4] 21-3691
1. Paul, Saint, apostle. I. Title.

PETERSEN, William J. 227'.83'0924
The discipling of Timothy / William J. Petersen. Wheaton, Ill. : Victor Books, c1980. 186 p. ; 18 cm. [BS2520.T5P47] 19 80-50002 ISBN 0-88207-217-X (pbk.) : 2.95
1. Paul, Saint, apostle. 2. Timothy (Biblical character) I. Title.

PFLEIDERER, Otto, 1839-1908. 225.
The influence of the apostle Paul on the development of Christianity, by Otto Pfleiderer ... Translated by J. Frederick Smith ... New York, C. Scribner's sons, 1885. vii, 238 p. 22 cm. (The Hibbert lectures, 1885) [BS2505.P531] A 32
1. Paul, Saint, apostle. 2. Church history—Primitive and early church. I. Smith, John Frederick, tr. II. Title.

PFLEIDERER, Otto, 1839-1908. 225.9'24
Lectures on the influence of the apostle Paul on the development of Christianity : delivered in London and Oxford in April and May, 1885 / by Otto Pfleiderer ; translated by J. Frederick Smith. [1st AMS ed.] [New York : AMS Press, 1979] vii, 292 p. ; 18 cm. Reprint of the 1885 ed. published by Williams and Norgate, London, which was issued as the 1885 Hibbert lectures. [BS2651.P4 1979] 77-27166 ISBN 0-404-60406-4 : 22.50
1. Paul, Smith, apostle. 2. Bible. N.T. Epistles of Paul—Theology. 3. Theology, Doctrinal—History—Early church, ca. 30-600. I. Title. II. Series: Hibbert lectures (London) ; 1885.

PHILLIPS, Harold L 922.1
A man of Tarsus; life and work of Paul. Anderson, Ind., Warner Press [1955] 104p. 20cm. [BS2505.P46] [BS2505.P46] 225.92 55-35795 55-35795
1. Paul, Saint, apostle. I. Title.

PITTENGER, William Norman, 1905- 225.92'4
The life of Saint Paul [by] W. Norman Pittenger. New York, F. Watts [1968] ix, 141 p. map. 22 cm. (Immortals of philosophy and religion) Bibliography: p. 137-138. [BS2506.P5] 68-22145 3.95
1. Paul, Saint, apostle.

PITTENGER, William Norman, 1905- 225.92
The life of Saint Paul [by] W. Norman Pittenger. New York, F. Watts [1968] ix, 141 p. map. 22 cm. (Immortals of philosophy and religion) Bibliography: p. 137-138. A biography of the man known as "the first Christian missionary and theologian," including discussions of the world he lived in, other religions of the time, our sources of information about him, his teachings, and his influence on religious history. [BS2506.P5] AC 68
1. Paul, Saint, apostle. I. Title.

PLUMPTRE, Edward Hayes, 1821-1891. 225.
The heathen world and St. Paul. St. Paul in Asia Minor, and at the Syrian Antioch. By the late Rev. E. H. Plumptre ... Published under the direction of the General literature committee. London [etc.] Society for promoting Christian knowledge; New York, E. & J. B. Young & co., 1896. 190 p. front. (col. map) 17 cm. [BS2505.P5] 20-19096
1. Paul, Saint, apostle. I. Society for promoting Christian knowledge, London. General literature committee. II. Title. III. Title: St. Paul in Asia Minor, and at the Syrian Antioch.

POLLOCK, John Charles. 225.9'24
The apostle: a life of Paul, by John Pollock. [1st ed.] Garden City, N.Y., Doubleday, 1969. xiv, 244 p. maps (on lining papers) 22 cm. Bibliographical references included in "Notes" (p. [239]-244) [BS2506.P58] 69-15194 4.95
1. Paul, Saint, apostle. I. Title.

POSITIVE thinking is not enough. 922.1
New York, Vantage Press [1955] 124p. 23cm. [BS2505.B234] [BS2505.B234] 225.92 54-12650 54-12650
1. Paul, Saint, apostle. I. Barbour, Eve.

POWEL, Harford Willing Hare, 1887- 225.92
The invincible Jew [by] Harford Powel, Jr. ... Indianapolis, The Bobbs-Merrill company [c1930] xi p., 1 l., 15-275 p. 21 cm. "First edition." "Books": p. 273-275. [BS2505.P6] 30-12039
1. Paul, Saint apostle. 2. Bible. N. T. Epistles of Paul—Criscism, interpretation, etc. 3. Jews in the U. S. I. Title.

PRAT, Ferdinand, 1857-1938.
The theology of Saint Paul. Translated from the 11th French ed. by John L. Stoddard. Westminster, Md., Newman Bookshop [1946] 2 v. 22 cm. Vol. 2 translated from the 10th French ed. Appendix of corrections and alternatives in translation, based on the latest French ed.: v. 2, p. 477-484. Full name: Antoine Ferdinand Prat. Bibliography: v. 2, p. 485-497. A 52
1. Paul, Saint, apostle. 2. Bible, N.T. Epistles of Paul—Theology. 3. Bible, N.T. Epistles of Paul—Introduction. I. Title.

PRINCETON theological seminary. 207.
... Inauguration of George Tybout Purves, D.D., as professor of New Testament literature and exegesis. New York, A. D. F. Randolph & company (incorporated) 1892. 57 p. 24 1/2 cm. Cover-title: St. Paul and inspiration. Inaugural address. ... [BV4070.P735 1892] 45-26974
1. Paul, Saint, apostle. 2. Bible—Inspiration. I. Purves, George Tybout, 1852-1901. II. Baker, George Danielson, 1840-1903. III. Title. IV. Title: St. Paul and inspiration.
Contents omitted.

PRIOR, Kenneth Francis William. 253.7
The Gospel in a pagan society : a book for modern evangelists / Kenneth F. W. Prior. Downers Grove, Ill. : InterVarsity Press, 1975. 126 p. ; 18 cm. Includes bibliographical references. [BV3793.P7 1975] 75-7248 ISBN 0-87784-484-4 pbk. : 2.25
1. Paul, Saint, apostle. 2. Bible. N.T. Acts XVII, 16-34—Criticism, interpretation, etc. 3. Evangelistic work. I. Title.

QUIMBY, Chester Warren. 225.92
Paul for everyone, by Chester Warren Quimby. New York, The Macmillan company, 1944. xv, 176 p. diagrs. 19 1/2 cm. Maps on lining-papers. "First printing." [BS2505.Q5] [[922.1]] 44-9995
1. Paul, Saint, apostle. I. Title.

RAMSAY, William Mitchell, Sir 1851- 225.92
St. Paul the traveller and the Roman citizen, by W. M. Ramsay ... 3d ed. New York, G. P. Putnam's sons; London, Hodder & Stoughton, 1898. xvi, 394 p. fold. map (in pocket) 24 cm. "The Morgan lectures for 1894 in the Auburn theological seminary. and Mansfield college lectures, 1895." [BS2505.R3 1898] 922.1 2-11695
1. Paul, Saint, apostle. I. Title.

RAMSAY, William Mitchell, Sir 1851- 227
The teaching of Paul in terms of the present day; the Deems lectures in New York university, by Sir W. M. Ramsay. 2d ed. London, New York [etc.] Hodder and Stoughton [1914] xiii, 457 p. 23 cm. [BS2651.R3 1914] 14-22008
1. Paul, Saint, apostle. I. Deems, lectures, New York university. II. Title.

RAMSAY, William Mitchell, Sir 1851-1939. 225.92
St. Paul the traveller and the Roman citizen, by W. M. Ramsay ... New York, G. P. Putnam's sons; London, Hodder & Stoughton, 1896. xvi, 394 p. fold. map. 24 cm. Folded map mounted on lining-paper. "The Morgan lectures for 1894 in the Auburn theological seminary, and Mansfield college lectures, 1865." [BS2505.R3] 922.1 34-17914
1. Paul, Saint, apostle. I. Title.

RATTENBURY, John Ernest, 1870-
The religious experience of St. Paul; studies in doctrines born of evangelical experience, by J. Ernest Rattenbury. Nashville, Tenn., Cokesbury press, 1931. 313 p. 22 cm. Printed in Great Britain. A 31
1. Paul, Saint, apostle. I. Title.

RAWLINSON, George, 1812-1902. 225.
The heathen world and St. Paul. St. Paul in Damascus and Arabia. By the Rev. George Rawlinson ... Pub. under the direction of the Committee of general literature and education appointed by the Society for promoting Christian knowledge. London, Society for promoting Christian knowledge; New York, E. & J. B. Young & co. [1877] xii, 180 p. front. (col. map) illus. 17 cm. [BS2505.R35] 20-19085
1. Paul, Saint, apostle. 2. Damascus. I. Society for promoting Christian knowledge, London. General literature committee. II. Title. III. Title: St. Paul in Damascus and Arabia.

RENAN, Ernest, 1823-1892. 225.92
Saint Paul. By Ernest Renan ... Translated from the original French by Ingersoll Lockwood. New York, G. W. Carleton; Paris, Michel Levy freres, 1869. 1 p. l., v-vii, 8-422 p. 18 1/2 cm. [Full name: Joseph Ernest Renan] [BS2505.R4] [922.1] 34-14841
1. Paul, Saint, apostle. I. Lockwood, Ingersoll, 1841- tr. II. Title.

RENAN, Ernest, 1823-1892. 225.92
Saint Paul. By Ernest Renan. Translated from the original French by Ingersoll Lockwood. New York, G. W. Dillingham; Paris, Michel Levy freres, 1887. 1 p. l., v-vii, 8-422 p. 19 cm. [Full name: Joseph Ernest Renan] [BS2505.R36 1887] [922.1] 33-39261
1. Paul, Saint, apostle. I. Lockwood, Ingersoll, 1841- tr. II. Title.

RICCIOTTI, Giuseppe, 1890- 922.1
Paul the apostle; translated by Alba I. Zizzamia. Milwaukee, Bruce Pub. Co. [1953] 540p. illus. 25cm. [BS2505.R5132] [BS2505.R5132] 225.92 53-13257 53-13257
1. Paul, Saint, apostle. I. Title.

RICHARDS, Hubert J., 1921- 227'.06
Reading Paul today : a new introduction to the man and his letters / Hubert Richards. Atlanta : John Knox Press, 1980, c1979. 152 p. ; 22 cm. First published under title: St. Paul and his epistles. [BS2650.2.R48 1980] 79-26287 ISBN 0-8042-0392-X pbk. : 4.95
1. Paul, Saint, apostle. 2. Bible. N.T. Epistles of Paul—Criticism, interpretation, etc. I. Title.

RIDDLE, Donald Wayne, 1894- 225.92
Paul, man of conflict, a modern biographical sketch, by Donald W. Riddle ... Nashville, Cokesbury press [c1940] 244 p. 21 cm. Bibliographical references in "Notes" (p. 225-236) "Suggestions to further reading": p. 237-239. [BS2505.R52] 922.1 40-4825
1. Paul, Saint, apostle. I. Title.

RIGAUX, Beda. 227
The letters of St. Paul; modern studies. Editor and translator Stephen Yonick. Chicago, Franciscan Herald Press [1968] xviii, 272 p. 21 cm. ([Herald scriptural library]) Translation of Saint Paul et ses lettres. Bibliographical references included in "Notes" (p. 182-261) [BS2650.2.R513] 68-54395 6.95
1. Paul, Saint, apostle. 2. Bible. N.T. Epistles of Paul—Criticism, interpretation, etc. I. Title.

*ROBERTSON, A. T. 227.' 06
Paul the interpreter of Christ / By A. T. Robertson. Grand Rapids : Baker Book House, 1976c1921. 155p. ; 20 cm. (His Library II) [BS2651] ISBN 0-8010-7638-2 pbk. : 2.95.
1. Paul, Saint, apostle. 2. Bible. N. T. Epistles of Paul-Theology. I. Title.

ROBERTSON, Archibald Thomas, 1863-1934. 225.9'24
Epochs in the life of Paul : a study of development in Paul's career / A. T. Robertson. Nashville : Broadman Press, 1974. xi, 337 p. ; 20 cm. (A. T. Robertson library) Reprint of the 1909 ed. published by Scribner, New York. Includes indexes. Bibliography: p. 321-327. [BS2505.R57 1974] 74-192551 ISBN 0-8054-1348-0 : pbk. 3.45
1. Paul, Saint, apostle. I. Title.

ROBERTSON, Archibald Thomas, 1863-1934. 225.
Epochs in the life of Paul; a study of development in Paul's career, by A. T. Robertson ... New York, C. Scribner's sons, 1909. xi, 337 p. 20 cm. "A brief bibliography": p. 321-327. [BS2505.R57] 9-10139
1. Paul, Saint, apostle. I. Title.

ROBINSON, Benjamin Willard, 1883- 225.
The life of Paul, by Benjamin Willard Robinson... Chicago, Ill., The University of Chicago press [c1918] xiii, 250 p. front. (map) 20 cm. (Half-title: The University of Chicago publications in religious education, ed. by E. D. Burton, Shaller Mathews, T. G. Soares. Handbooks of ethics and religion) "Supplementary reading" at end of each chapter. Appendix II (p. 223-225): A reference library; appendix III (p. 226-228): Topics for special study. [BS2505.R6] 18-19810
1. Paul, Saint, apostle. I. Title.

ROBINSON, Benjamin Willard, 1883- 225.
The life of Paul, by Benjamin Willard Robinson... Chicago, Ill., The University of Chicago press [c1928] xiii, 268 p. front. (map) 20 cm. (Half-title: The University of Chicago publications in religious education...Handbooks of ethics and religion) "Supplementary reading" at end of each chapter. "Appendix II. A reference library": p. 242-244. [BS2505.R6 1928] 28-8772
1. Paul, Saint, apostle. I. Title.

ROETZEL, Calvin J. 227'.06'6
The letters of Paul : conversations in context / by Calvin J. Roetzel. Atlanta : John Knox Press, [1975] viii, 114 p. ; 23 cm. Includes bibliographical references and index. [BS2650.2.R63] 74-21901 ISBN 0-8042-0208-7 pbk. : 4.95
1. Paul, Saint, apostle. 2. Bible. N.T. Epistles of Paul—Criticism, interpretation, etc. I. Title.

ROLSTON, Holmes, 1900- 227'.06
The Apostle Paul speaks to us today / Holmes Rolston, Jr. Atlanta : John Knox Press, 1979, c1951. 188 p. ; 21 cm. Originally published under title: Consider Paul. Includes bibliographical references and index. [BS2651.R63 1979] 79-87735 ISBN 0-8042-0787-9 pbk. : 4.25
1. Paul, Saint, apostle. 2. Bible. N.T. Epistles of Paul—Theology. I. Title.

ROSSER, John Leonidas.
Paul, the preacher, by John L. Rosser ... New York, American tract society [c1916] 4 p. l., 3-106 p. 20 cm. 16-21956 0.60
I. Title.

RUBENSTEIN, Richard L. 225.9'24 B
My brother Paul [by] Richard L. Rubenstein. [1st ed.] New York, Harper & Row [1972] x, 209 p. 22 cm. Includes bibliographical references. [BS2506.R8 1972] 72-124704 ISBN 0-06-067014-2 5.95
1. Paul, Saint, apostle. I. Title.

SABATIER, Auguste, 1839-1901. 225.
The apostle Paul: a sketch of the development of his doctrine. By A. Sabatier ... Translated from the French. Edited, with an additional essay on the Pastoral epistles, by George G. Findlay ... New York, J. Pott & co., 1891. xix, 402 p. 20 1/2 cm. Translated by A. M. Hellier. "Besides the appendix, the English editor has thought fit to insert brief foot-notes, inclosed in square brackets."--Note (signed G. G. F.) [Full name: Louis Auguste Sabatier] [BS2505.S3 1891] 39-3983
1. Paul, Saint, apostle. I. Findlay, George Gillanders, 1849-1919, ed. II. Hellier, A. M., tr. III. Title.

SAINT Paul, 922.1
apostle of nations; translated by Jex Martin. Chicago, Fides Publishers Association [1953] 163p. 21cm. Translation of Saint Paul, conquerant du Christ. [BS2505.D3413] [BS2505.D3413] 225.92 53-11075 53-11075
1. Paul, Saint, apostle. I. Daniel- Rops, Henry, 1901-

SAINT Paul, the apostle of 922.1
the Gentiles. Translated from the Spanish by Paul Barrett. Westminster, Md., Newman Press, 1956. 430p. 23cm. [BS2505.P432] [BS2505.P432] 225.92 56-11428 56-11428
1. Paul, Saint, apostle. I. Perez de Urbel, Justo, 1895-

ST. Paul the traveller and the Roman citizen. [3d ed.] Grand Rapids, Mich., Baker Book House, 1960. xxviii, 402p. 22cm.
I. Ramsay, William Mitchell, Sir 1851-1939. II. Paul, Saint, apostle.

ST. Paul's journeys in the 922.1
Greek Orient [Translated by S. H. Hooke from the French] New York, Philosophical Library [1955*C75p. illus. 19cm. 75p. illus. 19cm. (Studies in biblical archaeology. no. 4) [BS2505.M423] [BS2505.M423] 225.92 56-2402 56-2402
1. Paul, Saint, apostle. I. Metzger. Benri.

SALLMON, William Henry, 1866- 225.
Studies in the life of Paul for Bible classes and private use, by William H. Sallmon, M.A. Rev. ed. 14th thousand. New York, The International commmittee of Young men's Christian associations, 1903. 2 p. l., 9-130 p. incl. maps. 17 1/2 x 9 cm. Bibliography: p. 11-14. [BS2505.S3 1903] 3-3226
1. Paul, Saint, apostle. I. Title.

SANDMEL, Samuel. 225.924
The genius of Paul; a study in history. With a new introd. by the author. New York, Schocken Books [1970, c1958] xvi, 239 p. 21 cm. Includes bibliographical references. [BS2506.S15 1970] 76-111287
1. Paul, Saint, apostle. I. Title.

SANDMEL, Samuel. 225.92
The genius of Paul, a study in history. New York, Farrar, Straus & Cudahy [1958] 239 p. 22 cm. Includes bibliography. [BS2505.S38] 58-12485
1. Paul, Saint, apostle. I. Title.

SANDMEL, Samuel. 225.9'2'4 B
The genius of Paul : a study in history / by Samuel Sandmel. 1st Fortress Press ed. Philadelphia : Fortress Press, 1979. xx, 236 p. ; 21 cm. Includes bibliographical references and indexes. [BS2506.S15 1979] 79-7392 ISBN 0-8006-1370-8 : 5.95
1. Paul, Saint, apostle. I. Title.

SANNESS, Palmer. 225.924
The incomparable Paul. Boston, Branden Press [1969] 39 p. 22 cm. [BS2506.S17] 78-83704 1.00
1. Paul, Saint, apostle. I. Title.

SATTERFIELD, Lawrence 225.92
Paul, soldier of the cross. Philadelphia, Dorrance [c.1963] 340p. 21cm. 63-16011 3.95
1. Paul, Saint, Apostle. I. Title.

SATTERFIELD, Lawrence. 225.92
Paul, soldier of the cross. Philadelphia, Dorrance [1963] 340 p. 21 cm. [BS2506.S2] 63-16011
1. Paul, Saint, Apostle. I. Title.

SCHERER, James Augustin Brown, 1870- 922
Four princes; or, The growth of a kingdom; a story of the Christian church centred around four types, by James A. B. Scherer... Philadelphia and London, J. B. Lippincott company, 1903. 276 p. 19 cm. [BR150.S4 1903] 2-29606
1. Paul, Saint, apostle. 2. Constantinus I, the Great, emperor of Rome, d. 337. 3. Bernard de Clairvaux, Saint, 1091?-1153. 4. Luther, Martin, 1483-1546. I. Title.
Contents omitted.

SCHERER, James Augustin Brown, 1870- 922
Four princes; or, The growth of a kingdom; a story of the Christian church centred around four types, by James A. B. Scherer... Philadelphia, The Sunday school times co., 1906. 276 p. plates. 19 cm. [BR150.S4 1906] 6-42945
1. Paul, Saint, apostle. 2. Constantinus I, the Great, emperor of Rome, d. 337. 3. Bernard de Clairvaux, Saint, 1091-1153. 4. Luther, Martin, 1483-1546. I. Title.
Contents omitted.

SCHMITHALS, Walter. 262'.1
The office of apostle in the early church. Translated by John E. Steely. Nashville, Abingdon Press [1969] 288 p. 24 cm. Translation of Das kirchliche Apostelamt. Bibliography: p. 11-15. [BS2618.S3513] 73-84724 ISBN 0-687-28399-X 6.50
1. Paul, Saint, apostle. 2. Apostles. 3. Christianity—Early church, ca. 30-600. I. Steely, John E., ed. II. Title.

SCHONFIELD, Hugh Joseph, 1901- 225.92
The Jew of Tarsus, an unorthodox portrait of Paul. New York, Macmillan Co., 1947. 255 p. 22 cm. [BS2505.S42 1947] 922.1 47-7212
1. Paul, Saint, apostle. I. Title.

SCHWEITZER, Albert, 1875- 227
The mysticism of Paul the apostle, by Albert Schweitzer ... translated into English by William Montgomery ... with a prefatory note by F. C. Burkitt ... New York, H. Holt and company [c1931] xv, 411 p. 22 cm. [BS2655.M9S43 1931 a] 32-1464
1. Paul, Saint, apostle. 2. Mysticism. 3. Bible. N. T. Epistles of Paul—Theology. 4. Bible—Theology—N. T. Epistles of Paul. I. Montgomery, William, 1871-1930- tr. II. Title.

SCHWEITZER, Albert, 1875- 227.007
Paul and his interpreters, a critical history [Tr. from German by W. Montgomery] New York, Schocken [1964] xiii, 255p. 21cm. (SB79) Bibl. 64-16461 1.95 pap.,
1. Paul, Saint, apostle. 2. Bible. N.T. Epistles of Paul—Criticism, interpretation, etc.—Hist. I. Title.

SCHWEITZER, Albert, 1875- 227
Paul and his interpreters; a critical history. [Translated from the German by W. Montgomery] New York, Macmillan, 1951. xii, 252 p. 22 cm. Includes bibliographies. [BS2651.S3 1951] 51-10193
1. Paul, Saint, apostle. 2. Bible. N.T. Epistles of Paul — Criticism, interpretation, etc. — Hist. I. Title.

SCHWEITZER, Albert, 1875-1965. 227'.08'24822
The mysticism of Paul the apostle. With a prefatory note by F. C. Burkitt. [Translated from the German by William Montgomery] New York, Seabury Press [1968, c1931] xv, 411 p. 21 cm. (A Seabury paperback, SP51) Translation of Die Mystik des Apostels Paulus. Bibliographical footnotes. [BS2655.M9S43 1968] 68-28707 2.95
1. Paul, Saint, apostle. 2. Bible. N.T. Epistles of Paul—Theology. 3. Mysticism—Biblical teaching. I. Title.

SCHWEITZER, Albert, 1875-1965. 227
The mysticism of Paul the apostle. Translated into English by William Montgomery. With a prefatory note by F. C. Burkitt. New York, Macmillan, 1955 [c1931] xv, 411 p. 22 cm. [BS2655.M9S43 1955] 56-967
1. Paul, Saint, apostle. 2. Bible. N. T. Epistles of Paul—Theology. 3. Mysticism. I. Title.

SCHWEITZER, Albert, 1875-1965.
Paul and his interpreters; a critical history. [Translated from the German by W. Montgomery] London, A. & C. Black [1956] xii, 252 p. 22 cm. "First English edition 1912; reprinted...1956." Translation of Geschichte der paulinischen Forschung. 66-22880
1. Paul, Saint, apostle. 2. Bible. N. T. Epistles of Paul—Criticism, interpretation, etc.—Hist. I. Title.

SCOTT, Charles Archibald Anderson, 1859- 227
Christianity according to St. Paul, by Charles A. Anderson Scott ... Cambridge [Eng.] The University press, 1927. xiii, [1], 288, [1] 23 cm. [BS2651.S35] 23-5574
1. Paul, Saint, apostle. 2. Bible, N. T. Epistles of Paul—Theology. 3. Christianity. 4. Salvation—Biblical teaching. 5. Bible—Theology—N. T. Epistles of Paul. I. Title.

SCOTT, Charles Archibald Anderson, 1859- 225.92
Saint Paul, the man & the teacher, by C. A. Anderson Scott, D. D. Cambridge [Eng.] The University press, 1936. vi p., 1 l., 264 p. 20 cm. [BS2505.S43] 922.1 36-19970
1. Paul, Saint, apostle. I. Bible, N. T. Acts and Epistices. English. Selections. 1936. Revised. II. Bible. English. Selections. N. T. Acts and Epistles. 1936. Revised. III. Title.

SCOTT, Charles Archibald Anderson, 1859-1941 227
Christianity according to St. Paul. by Charles A. Anderson Scott. Cambridge [Eng. The Univ. Pr. 1966. xiii, 283p. 19cm. (CAM405) Bibl. [BS2651.S35] 28-5574 5.00 1.95 pap.,
1. Paul, Saint. apostle. 2. Bible. N. T. Epistles of Paul—Theology. 3. Christianity. 4. Salvation—Biblical teaching. I. Title.
Available from Cambridge Univ. Pr., New York.

SCOTT, Charles Archibald Anderson, 1859-1941.
Christianity according to St. Paul, by Charles A. Anderson Scott ... Cambridge [Eng.] University Press, 1966. xiii, [1], 283, [1] p. 23 cm. 68-9683
1. Paul, Saint, apostle. 2. Bible. N.T. Epistles of Paul—Theology. 3. Christianity. 4. Salvation—Biblical teaching. I. Title.

SELBY, Donald Joseph. 225.92
Toward the understanding of St. Paul. Englewood Cliffs, N. J., Prentice-Hall, 1962. 355 p. 22 cm. [BS2506.S4] 62-8561
1. Paul, Saint, apostle. I. Title.

SELDEN, Edward Griffin, 1847-1904.
In the time of Paul; how Christianity entered into and modified life in the Roman empire. By Rev. Edward G. Selden... Chicago, New York [etc.] Fleming H. Revell company [1900] 4 p. l., 13-151 p. 19 cm. [BV170.S5] 0-6836
1. Paul, Saint, apostle. 2. Church history—Primitive and early church. 3. Rome—Civilization. I. Title.

SELL, Henry Thorne, 1854-1928. 225.92
Bible studies in the life of Paul; historical

and constructive, by Rev. Henry T. Sell... Chicago, New York [etc.] Fleming H. Revell company [c1935] 1 p. l., 5-129 p. illus. (maps) 18 cm. (On cover: Sell's new method for Bible classes) [BS2507.S4 1935] [922.1] 36-1896
1. Paul, Saint, apostle. I. Title.

SELL, Henry Thorne, 1854- 225.
1928.
Bible studies in the life of Paul, historical and constructive, by Rev. Henry T. Sell... Chicago, New York [etc.] Fleming H. Revell company [1904] 129 p., 1 l. illus. (maps) 19 cm. (Lettered on cover: Sell's Bible study text books] [BS2507.S4] 4-11217
1. Paul, Saint, apostle. I. Title.

SHEPARD, John Watson, 1879- 227
The life and letters of St. Paul; an exegetical study. 1st ed. Grand Rapids, Eerdmans, 1950. 605 p. 24 cm. Bibliography: p. [601]-605. Bibliographical footnotes. [BS2650.s55] 50-11380
1. Paul, Saint, apostle. 2. Bible. N. T. Epistles of Paul—Commentaries. I. Title.

SMITH, Daniel, 1806-1852. 225.92
The life of St. Paul. By Rev. Daniel Smith... New York, Pub. by T. Mason and G. Lane, for the Sunday school union of the Methodist Episcopal church, 1839. 175 p. incl. front. map. 14 1/2 cm. [BS2505.S45] 922.1 34-16733
1. Paul, Saint, apostle. 2. Sunday school union of the Methodist Episcopal church. I. Title.

SMITH, David, 1866-1932. 225.92
The life and letters of St. Paul. With a foreword by Otto A. Piper. New York, Harper [19-] xv, 704 p. fold. col. maps. 25 cm. [BS2505.S52] 922.1 48-10042
1. Paul, Saint, apostle. 2. Bible. N. T. Epistles of Paul—Criticism, interpretation, etc. I. Title.

SMITH, David, 1866-1932. 225.
The life and letters of St. Paul, by the Rev. David Smith... New York, George H. Doran company [1920] xv, 704 p. 3 fold. maps. 24 1/2 cm. [BS2505.S5] 20-9032
1. Paul, Saint, apostle. 2. Bible. N.T. Epistles of Paul—Criticism, interpretation, etc. 3. Bible—Criticism, interpretation, etc.—N.T. Epistles of Paul. I. Title.

SMITH, Egbert Watson, 225.92
1862-
Paul's ways in Christ, illustrated and applied, by Egbert W. Smith ... New York [etc.] Fleming H. Revell company [1942] 152 p. 19 1/2 cm. [BV4501.S647] [922.1] 42-20931
1. Paul, Saint, apostle. 2. Christian life. I. Title.

SMITH, Roy Lemon, 1887- 225.9'24
From Saul to Paul; the making of an apostle. Nashville, Tidings [1962] 104 p. 19 cm. [BS2506.S5] 62-20562
1. Paul, Saint, apostle. I. Title.

SMYTH, Bernard T. 225.9'24
Paul, mystic and missionary / Bernard T. Smyth. U.S. ed. Maryknoll, N.Y. : Orbis Books, 1980. xviii, 166 p. ; 21 cm. Includes index. [BS2506.S58 1980] 19 80-14041 ISBN 0-88344-380-5 pbk. : 7.95
1. Paul, Saint, apostle. 2. Bible. N.T. Epistles of Paul—Theology. I. Title.

SMYTH, John Paterson, 225.
d.1932.
The story of St. Paul's life and letters, by J. Paterson Smyth ... New York, J. Pott & co., 1917. viii p., 1 l., 223 p. incl. front. (map) 20 cm. [BS2505.S55] 17-12163
1. Paul, Saint, apostle. I. Title.

SOARES, Theodore Gerald, 225.92
1869-
The story of Paul for boys and girls of junior high school age; a teacher's manual, to be used in connection with the pupil's textbook, by Theodore Gerald Soares. Chicago, Ill., The University of Chicago press [c1930] xviii, 139 p. 20 cm. (Half-title: The University of Chicago publications in religious education ... Constructive studies) Bibliography included in Foreword. [BS2507.S6] 31-6185
1. Paul, Saint, apostle. I. Title.

SOARES, Theodore Gerald, 225.92
1869-
The story of Paul for boys and girls of junior high school age; the pupil's book, by Theodore Gerald Soares. Chicago, Ill., The University of Chicago press [c1930] xvii, 171 p. front. (map) 19 cm. (Half-title: The University of Chicago publications in religious education ... Constructive studies) [BS2507.S6] 31-6062
1. Paul, Saint, apostle. I. Title.

SPEER, Robert Elliott, 225.92
1867-
Studies of the man Paul, by Robert E. Speer ... New York, Chicago [etc.] Fleming H. Revell company [1900] 2 p. l., 9-303 p. 18 x 10 cm. [BS2505.S6] [922.1] 1-29584
1. Paul, Saint, apostle. I. Title.

SPENCER, Floyd Albert. 225.92
Beyond Damascus; a biography of Paul the Tarsian, by F. A. Spencer. New York and London, Harper & brothers, 1934. xiii, 466 p. fold. map. 22 1/2 cm. "First edition." Bibliography: p. 415. [BS2505.S63] [922.1] 34-28587
1. Paul, Saint, apostle. I. Title.

STALKER, James 225.92
Life of St. Paul; handbook for Bible classes. Grand Rapids, Mich., Zondervan [1960] 160p. Bibliographical references included in 'Hints to teachers and questions for pupils (p. 145-160)20cm. 1.25 bds.,
1. Paul, Saint, apostle. I. Title.

STALKER, James, [922.1] 225.92
1848-1927.
The life of St. Paul. New York, Revell [1950] 100 p. 20 cm. Bibliographical references included in "Hints to teachers and questions for pupils" (p. 145-160) [BS2505.S7 1950] 50-4996
1. Paul, Saint, apostle. I. Title.

STALKER, James, 1848-1927. 225.92
The life of St. Paul. By Rev. James Stalker ... New York, American tract society [1888?] 183 p. map. 19 1/2 cm. "Hints to teachers and questions for Bible students": p. 168-183. [BS2505.S7 1888] [922.1] 4-15350
1. Paul, Saint, apostle. I. Title.

STALKER, James, 1848-1927. 225.92
The life of St. Paul, by Prof. James Stalker ... with Foreword by Wilbert W. White ... New and rev. ed. New York, American tract society [1914?] 160 p. front. (map) 19 1/2 cm. "Hints to teachers and questions for pupils": p. 145-160. [BS2505.S7 1914] [922.1] 33-4898
1. Paul, Saint, apostle. I. American tract society. II. Title.

STALKER, James, 1848-1927. 225.92
The life of St. Paul, by Prof. James Stalker ... with foreword by Wilbert W. White ... New and rev. ed. New York, Chicago [etc.] Fleming H. Revell [192-] 160 p. front. (map) 19 1/2 cm. (On cover: Hand-book for Bible classes) "Hints to teachers and questions for pupils": p. 145-160. [BS2505.S7] [922.1] 37-23966
1. Paul, Saint, apostle. I. Title.

STEVENSON, John Gilchrist. 225.
The children's Paul, a life of St. Paul for young people, by J. G. Stevenson ... New York, George H. Doran company [1924] x p., 2 l., 15-188 p. front., plates. 21 cm. [BS2505.S78] 25-7967
1. Paul, Saint, apostle. I. Title.

STEWART, James Stuart, 225.92
1896-
A man in Christ: the vital elements of St. Paul's religion. New York, Harper [1963?] xv, 331 p. 21 cm. Bibliographical footnotes. [BS2651.S85] 63-6330
1. Paul, Saint, apostle. 2. Bible. N. T. Epistles of Paul — Theology. I. Title.

STILL, James Ironside, 1854- 225.
St. Paul on trial, a new reading of the history in the book of Acts and the Pauline epistles, by J. Ironside Still ... New York, George H. Doran company [1924] viii, 9-300 p. 19 1/2 cm. Printed in Great Britain. [BS2505.S8] 25-2864
1. Paul, Saint, apostle. 2. Bible, N.T. Acts—Criticism, interpretation, etc. 3. Bible, N.T. Epistles of Paul—Criticism, interpretation, etc. I. Title.

STONEHOUSE, Ned Bernard, 225.04
1902-
Paul before the Areopagus, and other New Testament studies. Grand Rapids, Eerdmans, 1957. 197p. 23cm. [BS2393.S8] PP13683
1. Paul, Saint, apostle. 2. Bible. N. T.—Addresses, essays, lectures. I. Title.

STONEHOUSE, Ned Bernard, 225.04
1902-
Paul before the Areopagus, and other New Testament studies. Grand Rapids, Eerdmans, 1957. 197 p. 23 cm. [BS2393.S8] HP13683
1. Paul, Saint, apostle. 2. Bible. N.T. — Addresses, essays, lectures. I. Title.

STOWE, William McFerrin, 252.07
1913-
Power of Paul. New York, Abingdon Press [1963] 128 p. 20 cm. [BS2506.S78] 63-11382
1. Paul, Saint, Apostle. 2. Methodist Church — Sermons. 3. Sermons, American. I. Title.

TALLMADGE, Alfred S.
Handbook of St. Paul. St. Paul, Minn. Chamber of Commerce, 1900. 116 p. illus., port. 8 cm. (St. Paul. Chamber of commerce. Thirty-second annual) 2-11234
I. Title.

TAYLOR, David Henry, 1847- 225.92
1890.
The life of Paul. By D. H. Taylor ... Boston, D. Lothrop and company, 1884. 367 p. incl. front., 1 illus., plates, fold. map. 19 cm. "List of books": p. 363-364. [BS2505.T35] [922.1] 34-19081
1. Paul, Saint, apostle. I. Title.

TAYLOR, William Mackergo, 225.92
1829-1895
Paul, the missionary. Grand Rapids, Mich., Baker Bk-House, 1962. 570p. 21cm. (Bible biographies) 62-21707 3.95
1. Paul, Saint, apostle. I. Title.

TAYLOR, William Mackergo, 225.92
1829-1895.
Paul, the missionary. Grand Rapids, Baker Book House, 1962. 570 p. 21 cm. (Bible biographies) [BX2505.T37 1962] 62-21707
1. Paul, Saint, apostle. I. Title.

TAYLOR, William Mackergo, 225.92
1829-1895.
Paul, the missionary, by the Rev. William M. Taylor ... New York, Harper & brothers, 1882. viii p., 1 l., [7]-570 p. incl. front., plates (incl. maps) 19 1/2 cm. [BS2505.T37] [922.1] 34-16721
1. Paul, Saint, apostle. I. Title.

TAYLOR, William Mackergo, 225.92
1829-1895.
Paul the missionary, by Rev. William M. Taylor ... New York, R. R. Smith, inc., 1930. viii p., 1 l., [7]-570 p. 19 1/2 cm. (Half-title: Bible biographies) Maps listed in contents not included in this edition. [BS2505.T37 1930] [922.1] 34-13007
1. Paul, Saint, apostle. I. Title.

THACKERAY, Henry St. John, 227
1869?-1930.
The relation of St. Paul to contemporary Jewish thought. An essay to which was awarded the Kaye prize for 1899. London, New York, Macmillan & co., 1900. xvii, 260 p. 19 1/2 cm. "Principal authorities consulted": p. [xv]-xvii. [BS2655.J4T5] 1-25085
1. Paul, Saint, apostle. 2. Christianity and other religions—Judaism. I. Title.

THE theology of Saint Paul.
Translated from the eleventh French edition by John L. Stoddard. Westminster, Md., Newman Bookshop, 1958. 2 v. 21cm. Vol. 2 'translated from the tenth French edition.' Bibliography: v. 2, p. 485-497.
1. Paul, Saint, apostle. I. Prat, Ferdinand, 1857-1938.

TRENT, Robbie, 1894- 225.9'24 B
Paul, God's adventurer / Robbie Trent ; [ill. by Ron Adair]. Waco, Tex. : Word Books, c1975. 224 p. : ill. ; 23 cm. Includes bibliographical references. [BS2506.T73] 75-10089 ISBN 0-87680-381-8 : 6.95
1. Paul, Saint, apostle. I. Title.

TRESMONTANT, [922.1] 225.92
Claude.
Saint Paul and the mystery of Christ. Translated by Donald Attwater. New York, Harper Torchbooks [c1957] 190 p. illus., maps (on cover, 1 fold.) facsims. 18 cm. (Men of wisdom, 1) "Bibliographical note": p. 188-189. [BS2505.T673] 58-5220
1. Paul, Saint, apostle. I. Title.

TRICOT, Alphonse, Elis, 225.92
1884-
... St. Paul, The apostle of the gentiles, by Abbe Tricot; translated by the Rev. W. Rees. London and Edinburgh, Sands & company; St. Louis, Mo., B. Herder book company [1930] 2 p. l., vii-x, 215, [1] p. 19 cm. (Catholic library of religious knowldge. x) [BX880.C3 vol. 10] (282.082) [922.1] 35-23972
1. Paul, Saint, apostle. I. Rees, William, tr. II. Title.

TROUPE, John Franklin. 227
St. Paul and the mystery religions, by John Franklin Troupe, M.A. Boston, The Gorham press; [etc., etc., c1917] 90 p. 19 1/2 cm. (Lettered on cover: Library of religious thought) $1.00 [BS2650.T8] 17-28784
I. Title.

VAN ETTEN, Isabel Upton. 225.92
Who was Saul of Tarsus. Los Angeles, Cole-Holmquist Press, 1957. 92p. 24cm. [BS2505.V3 922.1] [BS2505.V3] 57-28029 57-28029
1. Paul, Saint, apostle. I. Title.

VAN ETTEN, Isabel [922.1] 225.92
Upton.
Who was Saul of Tarsus. Los Angeles, Cole-Holmquist Press, 1957. 92 p. 24 cm. [BS2505.V3] 57-28029
1. Paul, Saint, apostle. I. Title.

VOS, Geerhardus, 1862-1949.
The Pauline eschatology. Grand Rapids, Wm. B. Eerdmans, 1952. vii,365p. 23cm. Pref. dated 1930 photolithoprinted ed., 1952. Appendix (p. [321]-305): Eschatology of the Psalter. Bibliography: p. [317]-319. A53
1. Paul, Saint, apostle. 2. Eschatology—Biblical teaching. I. Title.

WALKER, Rollin Hough, 225.92
1865-
Paul's secret of power, [by] Rollin H. Walker. New York, Cincinnati [etc.] The Abingdon press [c1935] 181 p. 19 1/2 cm. [BS2505.W23] [922.1] 35-16931
1. Paul, Saint, apostle. I. Title.

*WALSTON, Marie 225.92
Paul from Tarsus to Rome. New York, Vantage [c.1964] 101p. 21cm 2.75
I. Title.

WAND, John William Charles, 227
Bp. of London, 1885-
What St. Paul really said [by] J. W. C. Wand. New York, Schocken Books [1969, c1968] 173 p. 21 cm. (What they really said series) "Suggestions for further reading": p. 165-166. [BS2651.W33 1969b] 69-11188 4.00
1. Paul, Saint, apostle. 2. Bible. N.T. Epistles of Paul—Theology. I. Title.

WAYLAND, John Walter, 225.92
1872-
Paul, the herald of the cross, by John Walter Wayland. Elgin, Ill., Brethren publishing house, 1901. 105, [1] p. front., plates, map. 18 cm. [BS2505.W3] [922.1] 1-27371
1. Paul, Saint, apostle. I. Title.

WAYLAND, John Walter, 225.92
1872-
Paul, the herald of the cross, by John Walter Wayland. Elgin, Ill., Brethren publishing house, 1901. 105, [1] p. front., plates, map. 18 cm. [BS2505.W3] [922.1] 1-27371
1. Paul, Saint, apostle. I. Title.

WHITE, Reginald E O 225.92
Apostle extraordinary, a modern portrait of St. Paul. Grand Rapids, W. B. Eerdmans Pub. Co. [1962] 200 p. 22 cm. [BS2506.W5] 62-18955
1. Paul, Saint, apostle. I. Title.

WILFLEY, Xenophon Pierce, 1871-1931. 225.92
St. Paul, the herald of Christianity, by Xenophon P. Wilfley ... Nashville, Cokesbury press [c1931] 267 p. illus. (map) 19 1/2 cm. [BS2505.W47] [922.1] 31-18412
1. Paul, Saint, apostle. I. Title.

WILKINSON, William Cleaver, 1833-
The epic of Paul, by William Cleaver Wilkinson... New York and London, Funk & Wagnalls company [1910?] 2 p. l., [iii]-iv, [5], 12-722 p. 21 1/2 cm. 10-24051
I. Title.

WILKINSON, William Cleaver, 1833-1920. 225.
Paul and the revolt against him, by William Cleaver Wilkinson... Philadelphia, Boston [etc.] The Griffith & Rowland press [c1914] x, 258 p. 21 1/2 cm. [BS2505.W48] 14-9931
1. Paul, Saint, apostle. I. Title.

WILLIAMS, Albert Nathaniel, 1914- 922.1
Paul, the world's first missionary; a biography of the Apostle Paul. New York, Association Press [1954] 157p. illus. 20cm. (Heroes of God series) [BS2505.W49] 225.92 54-8251
1. Paul, Saint, apostle. I. Title.

WILSON, Alpheus Waters, bp., 1834-
The life and mind of Paul; lectures to the students of Vanderbilt university, delivered in March, 1910, on the Cole foundation, by the Rev. Alpheus W. Wilson ... Nashville, Tenn., Dallas, Tex. [etc.] Publishing house of the M. E. church, South, Smith & Lamar, agents, 1912. vii, 175 p. 19 1/2 cm. 13-1310
I. Title.

WINDEATT, Mary Fabyan, 1910- 225.92
The man on fire; the story of Saint Paul. Illustrated by Paul A. Grout. [St. Meinrad, Ind., 1949] 193 p. illus. 22 cm. "A Grall publication." [BS2505.W538] 922.1. 49-50264
1. Paul, Saint, apostle I. Title.

WINDHAM, Joan. 225.92
The adventures of Saint Paul, by Joan Windham; with illustrations by Francois Bisson. New York, Sheed & Ward, 1936. ix, 107 p. incl. front. (map) illus., plates. 22 1/2 cm. "Printed in Great Britain." [BS2505.W54] [922.1] 37-8571
1. Paul, Saint, apostle. I. Title.

WINROD, Gerald Burton. 225.
With Paul in Macedonia, by Gerald B. Winrod ... Wichita, Kan., Defender publishers [1935] 2 p. l., 7-49 p. illus. (incl. ports., map) 21 cm. [BS2505.W55] 42-39882
1. Paul, Saint, apostle. I. Title.

WREDE, William, 1859-1906.
Paul. Translated by Edward Lummis; with a preface by J. Estlin Carpenter. Lexington, Ky., American Theological Library Association, Committee on Reprinting, 1962. xvi, 183 p. 18 cm. Originally published in Boston by the American Unitarian Association, 1908.
1. Paul, Saint, apostle. I. Title.

WRIGHT, William Burnet, 1838- 225.
Cities of Paul; beacons of the past rekindled for the present, by William Burnet Wright ... Boston and New York, Houghton, Mifflin & company, 1905. ix p., 1 l., 237, [1] p. 18 cm. [BS2505.W7] 5-35799
1. Paul, Saint, apostle. I. Title.
Contents omitted.

YALE, Alfred H. 225.92
Life and letters of Paul; a study course for adults. [Independence? Mo.] Dept. of Religious Education, Reorganized Church of Jesus Christ of Latter Day Saints [1959] 304 p. illus. 21 cm. Includes bibliography. [BS2505.Y3] 59-8360
1. Paul, Saint, apostle. 2. Bible. N.T. Epistles of Paul — Study — Text-books. I. Title.

YOUNG, Howard Palmer, 1870- 225.92
The travels and adventures of St. Paul. Boston, W. A. Wilde Co. [1948] 246 p. illus., col. map. 21 cm. [BS2505.Y6] 922.1 48-9010
1. Paul, Saint, apostle. I. Title.

Paul, Saint, Apostle—Addresses, essays, lectures.

BAILEY, John William.
... Does Hellenism contribute constituent elements to Paul's Christology ... Chicago, Press of G. K. Hazlitt & co., 1905. 90 p. 24 cm. Thesis (PH. D.)--University of Chicago. 6-46343
I. Title.

FEINE, Paul i.e. Karl Eduard Paul, 1859-
St. Paul as a theologian, by Paul Feine ... New York, Eaton & Mains; Cincinnati, Jennings & Graham [c1908] 2 v. 17 1/2 cm. (On cover: Foreign religious series) 8-7867
I. Title.

PAULINE studies: 225.9'24
essays presented to Professor F.F. Bruce on his 70th birthday / edited by Donald A. Hagner and Murray J. Harris. Exeter [Eng] : Paternoster Press ; Grand Rapids, Mich. : W. B. Eerdmans Pub. Co., 1980. xli, 293 p. : port. ; 23 cm. Includes indexes. Bibliography: p. xxii-xxxvi. [BS2506.P37 1980] 80-16146 ISBN 0-8028-3531-7 : 19.95
1. Paul, Saint, apostle—Addresses, essays, lectures. 2. Bruce, Frederick Fyvie, 1910- —Addresses, essays, lectures. 3. Bible. N.T. Epistles of Paul—Criticism, interpretation, etc.—Addresses, essays, lectures. I. Bruce, Frederick Fyvie, 1910- II. Hagner, Donald Alfred. III. Harris, Murray J.
Distributor's address: 255 Jefferson Ave., S.E., Grand Rapids, MI 49503

SCROGGIE, William Graham, 1877-1958. 242'.5
Paul's prison prayers / by W. Graham Scroggie. Grand Rapids, Mich. : Kregel Publications, 1981. p. cm. Reprint of the 1921 ed. published by Pickering & Inglis, London. [BV235.S35 1981] 19 80-8077 ISBN 0-8254-3737-7 pbk. : 2.95
1. Paul, Saint, apostle—Addresses, essays, lectures. 2. Bible—Prayers—Addresses, essays, lectures. I. Title.

STENDAHL, Krister. 225.9'2'4
Paul among Jews and Gentiles, and other essays / Krister Stendahl. Philadelphia : Fortress Press, c1976. ix, 133 p. ; 22 cm. Includes bibliographical references. [BS2506.S76] 75-36450 ISBN 0-8006-1224-8 : 3.75
1. Paul, Saint, Apostle—Addresses, essays, lectures. 2. Bible. N.T. Epistles of Paul—Theology—Addresses, essays, lectures. 3. Christian saints—Turkey—Tarsus—Addresses, essays, lectures. 4. Tarsus, Turkey—Biography—Addresses, essays, lectures. I. Title.

Paul, Saint, apostle—Art.

SCHULTZE, Jurgen 704.9486
Paul [by] Jurgen Schultze. Text of story and legend by Leonhard Kuppers. [Tr. from German by Hans Hermann Rosenwald] Reckl inghausen 153Ger.] A. Bongers dist. Taplinger [New York, c.1964] 60p. col. illus. 18cm. (Saints in legend and art, v.3) (Saints in legend and art, v.3) [N8080.S3813] 67-16586 2.50 bds.,
1. Paul, Saint, apostle—Art. I. Kuppers, Leonhard, 1903- II. Title.

Paul, Saint, apostle—Bibliography

METZGER, Bruce Manning, ed. 016.22592
Index to periodical literature on the Apostle Paul. Grand Rapids, Mich., Eerdmans [1960] xv, 183p. 25cm. (New Testament tools and studies, v.1) 60-16310 4.00
1. Paul, Saint, apostle—Bibl. 2. Theology—Period.—Indexes. I. Title. II. Series.

Paul, Saint, Apostle—Chronology.

JEWETT, Robert. 225.9'2'4 B
A chronology of Paul's life / by Robert Jewett. Philadelphia : Fortress Press, c1979. viii, 160 p., [1] fold. leaf of plates : graph ; 24 cm. "Submitted as part of a dissertation at the Eberhard-Karls-University in Tubingen," 1964. Includes bibliographical references and indexes. [BS2506.J49] 78-54553 ISBN 0-8006-0522-5 : 10.95
1. Paul, Saint, Apostle—Chronology. I. Title.

Paul, Saint, apostle—Collections.

DALY, Emily Joseph, comp. 225.92
Paul, trumpet of the spirit; an anthology. With a foreword by Edward J. Maginn. Paterson, N.J., St. Anthony Guild Press [1963] 249 p. illus. 20 cm. [BS2506.D3] 63-15296
1. Paul, Saint, Apostle — Collections. I. Title.

MEEKS, Wayne A., comp. 227'.06'6
The writings of St. Paul. Edited by Wayne A. Meeks. [1st ed.] New York, Norton [1972] xvii, 454 p. 22 cm. (A Norton critical edition) Bibliography: p. 445-446. [BS2505.A3M43] 77-95542 ISBN 0-393-04338-X ISBN 0-393-09979-2 (pbk.) 4.95
1. Paul, Saint, apostle—Collections. 2. Bible. N.T. Epistles of Paul—Theology—Collections. I. Title.

MERIVALE, Charles, 1808-1893. 225.
The heathen world and St. Paul. St. Paul at Rome. By the late Very Rev. Charles Merivale ... Pub. under the direction of the Committee of general literature and education. Appointed by the Society for promoting Christian knowledge. London, Society for promoting Christian knowledge: New York, E. & J. B. Young & co. [1877] viii, 180 p. front., (col. map) 17 cm. [BS2505.M4] 20-19095
I. Title.

*PAUL, Saint 227
Saint Paul [selections from his writings. Introd. by] Jacques Maritain. New York, McGraw [1965, c.1941] 161p. 19cm. 1.95 pap.,
I. Title.

Paul, Saint, apostle — Conversion — Juvenile literature.

ARMSTRONG, April (Oursler) 225.9'24
The conversion of St. Paul. Sponsored by the Benedictine monks of Belmont Abbey. Garden City, N.Y. [N. Doubleday, 1963] 64 p. illus. (part col.) fold. map. 21 cm. (The Catholic know-your-Bible program) Full name: Grace April (Oursler) Armstrong. [BS2506.5.A7] 63-25273
1. Paul, Saint, apostle — Conversion — Juvenile literature. I. Title.

REITZEL, Charles Francis, 1869-
Paul's conversion; told in couplets, by Chas. F. Reitzel ... Pottsville, Pa., Seiders' book and job rooms, 1911. 100 p. 21 cm. $0.50. 11-26190
I. Title.

Paul, Saint, apostle—Fiction.

ASCH, Shalom, 1880- FIC
... The apostle, translated by Maurice Samuel. New York, G. P. Putnam's sons [1943] vii, 804 p. 22 cm. At head of title: Sholam Asch. A novel based on the life of Saint Paul. [PZ3.A798Ap] 892.493 43-51252
1. Paul, Saint, Apostle—Fiction. I. Samuel, Maurice, 1895- tr. II. Title.

BENSON, Ginny, 1923- JUV
According to Amos / by Ginny Benson ; illustrated by Barbara Williams-McKenna. Oakland, Calif. : A & P Books, c1981. iii, 134 p. : ill. ; 26 cm. Bibliography: p. 131-133. Amos, a little dog given to Saul of Tarsus to teach him about love and compassion, recounts the experiences of the many journeys on which he accompanied his master who was to become the Apostle Paul. [PZ7.B44723Ac 1981] [Fic] 19 81-10775 ISBN 0-86550-026-6 (pbk.) : 8.95
1. Paul, Saint, Apostle—Fiction. I. Williams-McKenna, Barbara, ill. II. Title.

MILLER, Rex. 813.5
I, Paul; an "autobiography" of the apostle to the gentiles, by Rex Miller. New York, Duell, Sloan and Pearce [c1940] ix p., 1 l., 210 p. 21 cm. Maps on lining-papers. "First edition." [BS2505.M53 1940] 40-29541
1. Paul, Saint, apostle—Fiction. I. Title.

SLAUGHTER, Frank Gill, 1908- 189.4
God's warrior [by] Frank G. Slaughter. [1st ed.] Garden City, N.Y., Doubleday, 1967. 371 p. 22 cm. (The Pathway of faith series [2]) [PZ3.S63165Gn] 67-10379
1. Paul, Saint, apostle—Fiction. I. Title.

SMITH, Roy Lemon, 1887- 225.9'24
The tentmakers, a story. New York, Abingdon Press [1963] 112 p. illus. 19 cm. [BS2506.5.S4] 63-7332
1. Paul, Saint, apostle — Fiction. I. Title.

Paul, Saint, apostle—Friends and associates.

BURRELL, David James, 1844- 262.
Paul's companions, by David James Burrell ... New York, American tract society [c1921] v p., 1 l., 196 p. 19 cm. [BS2430.B8] 21-10190
I. Title.

HIEBERT, David Edmond, 1910- 225.9'24 B
Personalities around Paul [by] D. Edmond Hiebert. Chicago, Moody Press [1973] 270 p. 24 cm. Bibliography: p. 252-266. [BS2430.H48] 72-95028 ISBN 0-8024-6473-4 5.95
1. Paul, Saint, apostle—Friends and associates. I. Title.

WEISS, Johannes, 1863-1914.
Paul and Jesus; by Johannes Weiss ... Tr. by Rev. H. J. Chaytor ... London and New York, Harper & brothers, 1909. 3 p. l., 130, 2 p. 17 1/2 cm. (Half-title: Harper's library of living thought) Added t.-p., illustrated. W 10
I. Chaytor, Henry John, 1871- tr. II. Title.

Paul, Saint, apostle—Journeys.

BURRELL, David James, 1844- 225.
Paul's campaigns, by David James Burrell ... New York, American tract society [c1918] viii, 118 p. charts. 20 cm. $0.75 [BS2505.B8] 18-19583
I. Title.

JACKSON, Melvin. 225.
Travels of Paul; a course of study for boys' Bible classes, by Melvin Jackson; introduction by Professor W. G. Ballantine. Teachers' ed. New York, International committee of Young men's Christian associations, 1903. 59 p. 17 cm. Bibliography: p. 10-11. [BS2507.J3] 3-20381
I. Title.

MEINARDUS, Otto Friedrich August. 915.61
St. Paul in Ephesus and the cities of Galatia and Cyprus / Otto F. A. Meinardus. New Rochelle, N.Y. : Caratzas Bros., 1979. vii, 141 p. : ill. ; 21 cm. (In the footsteps of the saints) Includes index. Bibliography: p. 139-141. [BS2506.M397 1979] 78-51246 ISBN 0-89241-071-X : 7.50 ISBN 0-89241-044-2 (pbk.) : 4.95
1. Paul, Saint, apostle—Journeys. 2. Turkey—Description and travel—1960- —Guide-books. 3. Cyprus—Description and travel—Guide-books. I. Title. II. Series.

MEINARDUS, Otto Friedrich August. 914.95
St. Paul in Greece / Otto F. A. Meinardus. New Rochelle, N.Y. : Caratzas Bros., 1979. xiii, 127 p., [1] leaf of plates : ill. ; 21 cm. (In the footsteps of the saints) Includes index. Bibliography: p. 119-121. [BS2506.M4 1979] 78-51244 ISBN 0-89241-072-8 : 7.50 ISBN 0-89241-045-0 (pbk.) : 4.95
1. Paul, Saint, apostle—Journeys. 2. Greece, Modern—Description and travel—1951- I. Title. II. Series.

MEINARDUS, Otto Friedrich August. 914.5
St. Paul's last journey / Otto F. A. Meinardus. New Rochelle, N.Y. : Caratzas Bros., 1979. xiv, 159 p., [1] leaf of plates : ill. ; 21 cm. (In the footsteps of the saints) Includes index. Bibliography: p. 149-151. [BS2506.M42] 78-51247 ISBN 0-89241-073-6 : 7.50 ISBN 0-89241-046-9 (pbk.) : 4.95
1. Paul, Saint, apostle—Journeys. 2. Near East—Description and travel—Guide-books. 3. Italy—Description and travel—1945- —Guide-books. 4. Spain—Description and travel—1951- —Guide-books. 5. Malta—Description and travel—Guide-books. I. Title. II. Series.

PEROWNE, Stewart, 1901- 225.9'24 B
The journeys of St. Paul. London, New York, Hamlyn, 1973. 144 p. illus. (some col.), col. maps (on lining papers), ports. 29 cm. Bibliography: p. 142. [BS2506.P45 1973] 73-162279 £2.25
1. Paul, Saint, apostle—Journeys. I. Title.

Paul, Saint, apostle—Journeys—Juvenile literature.

ROBERTSON, Jenny. 225.9'24
Paul the traveler / by Jenny Robertson ; illustrated by Alan Parry. Grand Rapids, MI : Zondervan Pub. House, 1980, c1978. p. cm. (Zondervan/Ladybird Bible series) [BS2506.5.R62 1980] 19 80-22482 ISBN 0-310-42890-4 : 1.95
1. Paul, Saint, apostle—Journeys—Juvenile literature. I. Perry, Alan. II. Title. III. Series.

Paul, Saint, apostle—Juvenile literature.

BRUCE, Janet 225.92
The life of Saint Paul. Pictures by Emile Probst. London, Burns & Oates; New York, Herder & Herder [c.1965] [27]p. col. illus. 19cm. (Men of God 4) [BS2506.5.B7] 65-21948 1.50 bds.
1. Paul, Saint, apostle—Juvenile literature. I. Probst, Emile, illus. II. Title. III. Series.

DAUGHTERS of St. Paul. 225.9
The great hero, St. Paul the apostle. Written and illustrated by the Daughters of St. Paul. [Boston] St. Paul Editions [1963] 170 p. illus. 22 cm. [BS2506.5.D38] 63-15968
1. Paul, Saint, apostle — Juvenile literature. I. Title.

DAUGHTERS OF ST. PAUL. 225.9
The great hero, St. Paul the apostle. Written, illus. by the Daughters of St. Paul. [Boston] St. Paul Eds. [dist. Author, c.1963] 170p. col. illus. 22cm. 63-15968 2.50
1. Paul, Saint, apostle—Juvenile literature. I. Title.

FOSDICK, Harry Emerson, 1878- 225.9
The life of Saint Paul. Illus. by Leonard Everett Fisher. New York, Random [c.1962] 175p. col. illus. 22cm. (World landmark bks., W-53) 62-7881 1.95
1. Paul, Saint, apostle—Juvenile literature. I. Title.

HARINGTON, Joy 270.1
Paul of Tarsus. Cleveland, World [1965, c.1961] 216p. illus. (pt. col.) fold. map. 23cm. (Shepherd Bks.) [BS2506.5.H3] 65-15121 3.95
1. Paul, Saint, Apostle—Juvenile literature. I. Title.

LIBBEY, Scott 222.1095
Rebels and God. Illus. by Shirley Hirsch. [Philadelphia] United Church [1964] 89p. illus. (pt. col.) 22cm. Pt. of the United Church curriculum, prepared, pub by the Div. of Christian Educ. and the Div. of Pubn. of the United Church Bd. for Homeland Ministries. 64-14494 1.50
1. Paul, Saint, apostle—Juvenile literature. 2. Moses—Juvenile literature. I. United Church for Homeland Ministries. Division of Christian Education. II. United Church of Christ. III. United Church Board Division of Publication. IV. Title.

PRIESTER, Gertrude Ann. 225.92'4 B
Who are you, Lord? [By] Gertrude Priester. Illustrated by Shannon Stirnweis. Richmond, CLC Press [1969] 126 p. col. illus. 21 cm. (The Covenant life curriculum) A biography of the Apostle Paul based largely on the Book of Acts telling how he traveled throughout the Biblical world preaching about Jesus Christ. [BS2506.5.P73] 92 70-13550
1. Paul, Saint, apostle—Juvenile literature. 2. [Paul, Saint, apostle.] I. Stirnweis, Shannon, illus. II. Title.

ROBERTSON, Jenny. 225.9'24
Paul meets Jesus / by Jenny Robertson ; illustrated by Alan Parry. Grand Rapids, MI : Zondervan Pub. House, 1980, c1978. p. cm. (Zondervan/Ladybird Bible series) Traces the events leading up to and following Paul's conversion on the road to Damascus, including Stephen's martyrdom, Paul's baptism, and his subsequent missionary journeys with first Barnabas and then Silas. [BS2506.5.R6 1980] 19 80-22808 ISBN 0-310-42880-7 : 1.95
1. Paul, Saint, apostle—Juvenile literature. 2. [Paul, Saint, apostle.] 3. Christian saints—Turkey—Tarsus—Juvenile literature. 4. Tarsus, Turkey—Biography—Juvenile literature. 5. [Saints.] 6. [Bible stories—N.T.] I. Parry, Alan. II. Title. III. Series.

TUCKER, Iva Jewel. 225.9'24 B
Paul, the missionary / Iva Jewel Tucker ; illustrated by Ron Hester. Nashville : Broadman Press, c1976. 46 p. : col. ill. ; 24 cm. (Biblearn series) Discusses the conversion and ministry of Paul the missionary. [BS2506.5.T82] 76-382994 ISBN 0-8054-4228-6 : 3.95
1. Paul, Saint, Apostle—Juvenile literature. 2. [Paul, Saint, Apostle.] 3. Evangelists (Bible)—Biography—Juvenile literature. 4. Bible. N.T.—Biography—Juvenile literature. 5. [Bible stories—N.T.] I. Hester, Ronald. II. Title.

WILLETT, Franciscus. j225.9
The tentmaker from Tarsus, a story of St. Paul, by Brother Franciscus. Illus. by Rosemary Donatino. Notre Dame, Ind., Dujarie Press [1950] 95 p. illus. 24 cm. [BS2505.W486] 50-2575
1. Paul, Saint, apostle — Juvenile literature. I. Title.

Paul, Saint,apostle—Meditations.

ALBERIONE, Giacomo Giuseppe, 1884-1971. 242
Meditation notes on Paul the Apostle, model of the spiritual life. [Translated by Aloysius Milella. Boston] St. Paul Editions [1972] 100 p. facsims. 20 cm. [BS2506.A4 1972] 72-83471 2.00
1. Paul, Saint, apostle—Meditations. 2. Spiritual exercises. I. Title.

FULTON, Mary Beth. 227.06
This love on which I speak; worship with St. Paul. Valley Forge [Pa.] Judson [c.1962] 129p. 21cm. 62-12902 2.50
1. Paul, Saint, apostle—Meditations. 2. Worship programs. I. Title.

RATZLAFF, Ruby. 225.9'24
"A good fight" : lessons from the life of Paul / by Ruby Ratzlaff. Mountain View, Calif. : Pacific Press Pub. Association, c1979. 127 p. ; 18 cm. (A Redwood paperback ; 112) [BS2506.R36] 78-57356 pbk. : 2.95
1. Paul, Saint,apostle—Meditations. I. Title.

Paul, Saint, Apostle—Sermons.

*ADAMS, Jay E. 226.'6
Audience adaptations in the sermons and speeches of Paul / Jay E. Adams Grand Rapids : Baker Book House, c1976. [vii], 107 p. ; 22 cm. (Studies in preaching ; 2). Bibliography: pp. [72] - 77, [103] - 107. [BS2655.A6] ISBN 0-8010-0104-8 pbk. : 2.95
1. Paul, Saint, Apostle—Sermons. 2. Bible—Homiletical use. I. Title.

BOSLEY, Harold Augustus, 1907- 252'.07
Men who build churches; interpretations of the life of Paul [by] Harold A. Bosley. Nashville, Abingdon Press [1972] 158 p. 19 cm. [BS2506.B65] 72-701 ISBN 0-687-24801-9
1. Paul, Saint, apostle—Sermons. 2. Methodist Church—Sermons. 3. Sermons, American. I. Title.

CHRYSOSTOMUS, Joannes, Saint, Patriarch of Constantinople, d. 407. 225.92
In praise of Saint Paul. Tr. [from Greek] by Thomas Halton. [Boston] St. Paul Eds. [dist. Daughters of St. Paul, c.1963] 123p. 20cm. 63-14467 2.00; 1.00 pap.,
1. Paul, Saint, Apostle—Sermons. 2. Sermons, Greek—Translations into English. 3. Sermons, English—Translations from Greek. I. Halton, Thomas, tr. II. Title.

*TRUETT, George Washington, 1867-1944. 227
Sermons from Paul, by George W. Truett. Edited by Powhatan W. James. Grand Rapids, Mich., Baker Book House [1973, c.1947] 213 p. 20 cm. (George W. Truett library) At head of title: Vol. 11 in the Truett memorial series [BS2765.3] ISBN 0-8010-8796-1 2.95 (pbk.)
1. Paul, Saint, apostle—Sermons. I. James, Powhatan W., ed. II. Title. III. Series: Truett memorial series, v. 11

Paul, Saint, apostle—Study.

*BURNSIDE, L. Brooks 227.06
The Apostle Paul speaks to this age. New York, Exposition [c.1965] 173p. 22cm. 4.00
I. Title.

BURNSIDE, L Brooks.
The Apostle Paul speaks to this age. New York, Exposition Press [1965] 713 p. (An Exposition-Testament book) 67-4684
I. Title.

*DOTY, Brant Lee 227
The apostle Paul: study course for youth and adults. Cincinnati, Ohio, Standard c.1964 112p. 22cm. (Training for service ser.) 1.25 pap.,
I. Title.

GARVIE, Alfred Ernest, 1861-
Studies of Paul and his gospel, by Alfred E. Garvie ... London, New York [etc.] Hodder and Stoughton [1911] xi p., 1 l., 312 p. 20 cm. "These studies have appeared in the pages of the Expositor."--Pref. A 15
I. Title.

HALL, Edward Henry, 1831-1912. 225.92
Lessons on the life of St. Paul, drawn from the Acts and the Epistles. By Edward H. Hall. Boston, Unitarian Sunday-School society, 1885. iv p., 1 l., [7]-114 p., 1 l., 17 1/2 cm. "References" at end of chapters. [BS2507.H3] [[922.1]] 39-11831
1. Paul, Saint, apostle—Study. 2. Unitarian Sunday-school society. I. Title.

KNOX, Charles Eugene, 1833-1900. 225.92
A year with St. Paul; or, Fifty-two lessons for the Sundays of the year. By Charles E. Knox. New York, A. D. F. Randolph, 1863. viii, 319, 104 p. front., illus. (incl. maps, plans) 20 cm. "Questions" at end of each are paged consecutively (104 p.) [BS2507.K6 1863] 922.1 39-11835
1. Paul, Saint, apostle—Study. I. Title.

KNOX, Charles Eugene, 1833-1900. 225.92
A year with St. Paul; or, Fifty-two lessons, for the Sundays of the year, By Charles E. Knox. New and rev. ed. New York, A. D. F. Randolph & company, 1877. iv, [4], 349 104 p. front., illus. (incl. maps, plans) 18 cm. "Questions" at end of each chapter are paged consecutively (104 p.) [BS2507.K6 1877] 922.1 39-11836
1. Paul, Saint, apostle—Study. I. Title.

LEACOCK, Arthur Gordner, 1868- 225.92
Studies in the life of St. Paul, by Arthur Gordner Leacock ... New York, The International committee of young men's Christian associations, 1906. xiv, 192 p. fold. maps. 21 cm. [BS2507.L4] 922.1 6-41772
1. Paul, Saint, apostle—Study. I. Young men's Christian associations. International committee II. Title.

LESSONS on the life of the apostle Paul for Bible classes. 225.92 Philadelphia, American Sunday-school union [1872?] 132 p. front. (fold. map) 15 cm. "List of works on the life and writings of the apostle Paul": p. 119-128. Advertising matter: p. 129-132. [BS2507.L45] [922.1] 39-10926
1. Paul, Saint, apostle—Study. I. American Sunday-school union.

PERRY, William Stevens, bp., 1832-1898. 225.92
Questions on the life and labors of the great apostle. For Sunday and parishschools, and Bible classes. By William Stevens Perry ... Boston, New York, E. P. Dutton and company, 1869. vii, [3], 133 p. 17 cm. [BS2507.P4] 922.1 39-10934
1. Paul, Saint, apostle—Study. I. Title.

PROTESTANT Episcopal church in the U. S. A. New York (Diocese) Sunday school commission. 225.92
Teacher's notes on S. Paul and the first Christian missionaries. Prepared by the Sunday school commission, diocese of New York ... 2d ed., rev. Milwaukee, The Young churchman co., 1904- v. front., illus. (maps, plan) 19 cm. On cover: 3d thousand. "Suggested books of reference": v. 1. p. 14. [BS2507.P7 1904] 922.1 4-31060
1. Paul Saint, apostle—Study. I. Title.

PROTESTANT Episcopal church in the U. S. A. New York (Diocese) Sunday school commission. 225.92
Teacher's notes on St. Paul and the first Christian missionaries, prepared by the Sunday school commission, diocese of New York Milwaukee, The Young churchman co., 1903. 134 p. front., illus. (maps, plan) 19 cm. "Suggested books of reference": p. 14. Advertising matter: p. 130-134. [BS2507.P7 1903] 39-16030
1. Paul, Saint, apostle—Study. I. Title.

SALLMON, William Henry, 1866- 225.92
Studies in the life of Paul. For Bible classes and private use. By Wm. H. Sallmon. New York, The International committee of Young men's Christian associations [1896] ix, [11]-74 p. 15 1/2 cm. [Young men's Christian associations. International committee. College series. 325] Bibliography: p. [vii]-ix. [BS2507.S3 1896] [[922.1]] 39-10940
1. Paul, Saint, apostle—Study. I. Young men's Christian associations. International committee. II. Title.

STALKER, James, 1848-1927. 225.92
The life of St. Paul, by Prof. James Stalker ... with forword by Wilbert W. White ... New and rev. ed. New York, American tract society [c1912] 160 p. front. (double map) 19 1/2 cm. "Hints to teachers and questions for pupils": p. 145-160. Paul, Saint, apostle. [BS2505.S7 1912] [922.1] 12-27453
I. Title.

STEVENS, George Barker, 1854-1906. 227
The Pauline theology, a study of the origin and correlation of the doctrinal teachings of the apostle Paul, by George B. Stevens ... New York, C. Scribner's sons, 1892. xi p., 1 l., 383 p. 21 cm. [BS2651.S8 1892] 22-5769
I. Title.

WAHLSTROM, Eric Herbert 225.92
Let's look at Paul; studies in the life and teachings of St. Paul. Rock Island, Ill.. Augustana Press [c.1960] ix, 90p. Includes bibl. 20cm. 60-16831 1.50 pap.,
1. Paul, Saint, apostle—Study. I. Title.

WOODS, Matthew, 1848-
Was the apostle Paul an epileptic? By Matthew Woods ... New York, The Cosmopolitan press, 1913. 131 p. 19 1/2 cm. $1.25. 13-18977
I. Title.

Paul, Saint, apostle—Trial.

RODDY, Irving Gaines. 225.92
Paul before Caesar from the legal

viewpoint [by] Irving Gaines Roddy... Philadelphia, Boston [etc.] The Judson press [c1936] 6 p. l., 3-148 p. 20 cm. Bibliography: p. [145]-148. [BS2505.R62] 922.1 36-18290
1. Paul, Saint, apostle—Trial. 2. Roman law. I. Title.

Paul, Thomas Cooke, 1831-1845.

SANDERS, Ephraim D. 248
Sketch of the life and character of Thomas Cooke Paul, son of D'Arcy Paul, of Petersburg, Va. Written for the American Sunday-school union, by Rev. E. D. Sanders. Philadelphia, New York [etc.] American Sunday-school union [1849] 230 p. front. (port.) illus. 15 1/2 cm. [BR1715.P3S3] 2-9849
1. Paul, Thomas Cooke, 1831-1845. I. American Sunday-school union. II. Title.

Paulicians.

GARSOIAN, Nina G., 1923- 273'.9
The Paulician heresy. A study of the origin and development of Paulicianism in Armenia and the eastern provinces of the Byzantine empire. By Nina G. Garsoian. The Hague, Paris, Mouton, 1967 [1968] 296p. fold. map. 24cm. (Columbia Univ. Pubns. in Near & Middle East studies. Ser. A, 6) Bibl. [BT1445. G3] 67-24377 15.50
1. Paulicians. I. Title. II. Series.
Distributed by Humanities, New York.

PAULICIANS. Liturgy and ritual. 273.9
The key of truth, a manual of the Paulician church of Armenia. The Armenian text edited and translated with illustrative documents and introduction by Fred C. Conybeare ... Oxford, Clarendon press, 1898. cxcvi, 201, [2] p. 23 cm. "List of works consulted": Pecto of last leaf. [BT1445.A4 1898] 34-28841
1. Paulicians. I. Conybeare, Frederick Cornwallis, 1856-1924. II. Title.

Pauline, mother, 1854-1935.

FRANCIS, Jerome, sister. 922.273
This is Mother Pauline, by Sister Francis Jerome, C.S.C. ... [Paterson, N.J., St. Anthony guild press] 1945. x p., 1 l., 250 p. 2 port. (incl. front.) 21 1/2 cm. (Centenary chronicles of the Sisters of the holy cross, vol. VII) [BX4705.P3845F7] 45-9609
1. Pauline, mother, 1854-1935. I. Title.

Paulist fathers

FOR one hundred years active with voice and with pen to crusade for the Church in our land: Paulist Fathers centennial year, 1958. [San Francisco, 1958] 49p. illus., ports., map. 26cm. Cover title.
I. Paulist Fathers.

GILLIS, James Martin, 1876- 271.79
The Paulists, by James M. Gillis, C. S. P. New York, The Macmillan company, 1932. vi p., 2 l., 67 p. 17 cm. [BX3885.G5] 32-14688
1. Paulist fathers I. Title.

MERRICK, Mary Virginia. 265.
The altar of God: a story of books of the mass of children ... by Mary Virginia Merrick; with a preface by Rev. John J. Burke, C. S. P. New York city, The Paulist press [c1920] 127 p. incl. illus., plates, 23 cm. [BX2230.M5] 21-296
I. Title.

Paulist Fathers—United States—Biography.

HECKER, Isaac Thomas, 1819-1888. 230'.2
Questions of the soul / Isaac Thomas Hecker ; with an introd. by Joseph F. Gower. New York : Arno Press, 1978. 294 p. ; 21 cm. (The American Catholic tradition) Reprint of the 1855 ed. published by D. Appleton, New York. [BX1752.H35 1978] 77-11290 ISBN 0-405-10834-6 : 18.00
1. Catholic Church—Apologetic works. 2. Hecker, Isaac Thomas, 1819-1888. 3. Paulist Fathers—United States—Biography. I. Title. II. Series.

Paulsen, Norman, 1929-

PAULSEN, Norman, 1929- 299'.93 B
Sunburst : return of the ancients : an autobiography / by Norman Paulsen. Goleta, CA : Sunburst Farms Pub. Co., c1980. 610 p., [6] leaves of plates : ill. ; 23 cm. Includes index. Bibliography: p. 599-600. [BP605.S74P38] 19 79-66005 7.95
1. Paulsen, Norman, 1929- 2. Sunburst Communities—Biography. I. Title.
Publisher's address: 1400 Calle Real, Rte. 1, Goleta, CA 93017

Paulson, Hank.

PAULSON, Hank. 272'.9 B
Beyond the wall : the people communism can't conquer / by Hank Paulson, with Don Richardson. Ventura, CA : Regal Books, c1982. 173 p. ; 21 cm. Includes bibliographical references. [BV2372.P38A33 1982] 19 81-84567 ISBN 0-8307-0806-5 pbk. : 4.95
1. Paulson, Hank. 2. Bible—Publication and distribution—Communist countries. 3. Evangelists—United States—Biography. 4. Persecution—Communist countries—History—20th century. 5. Communism and Christianity. 6. Communist countries—Church history. I. Richardson, Don. II. Title.

Paulus, Thebaeus, Saint.

HIERONYMUS, Saint. 270.1'0924 B
The first desert hero: St. Jerome's Vita Pauli. With introd., notes, and vocabulary by Ignatius S. Kozik. Mount Vernon, N.Y., King Lithographers [1968] x, 67 p. illus. 22 cm. Text in Latin. "The Migne edition is the one mainly followed ... The following sections of the Vita have been omitted: Prologue (PL 23. 17-18), the story of the two martyrs (ibid. 19-20), and Anthony's journey through the desert (ibid. 22-24)." Bibliography: p. 12-14. Bibliographical footnotes. [BR1720.P28H5] 68-56001
1. Paulus, Thebaeus, Saint. I. Kozik, Ignatius S., ed. II. Title. III. Title: Vita Pauli.

Paulus VI, Pope 1897-

ADLER, Bill 262.130924
Pope Paul in the United States: his mission for peace on earth, October 4, 1965, by Bill Adler with Sayre Ross. New York, Hawthorn [c.1965] 97p. illus., ports. 29cm. [BX1378.3.A6] 65-28438 2.95
1. Paulus VI, Pope, 1897- I. Title.

ADLER, Bill. 262.130924
Pope Paul in the Unites States: his mission for peace on earth, October 4, 1965, by Bill Adler with Sayre Ross. [1st ed.] New York, Hawthorn Books [1965] 97 p. illus., ports. 29 cm. [BX1378.3.A6] 65-28438
1. Paulus vi, Pope, 1897- I. Title.

BARRETT, William Edmund, 1900- 922.21
Shepherd of mankind a biography of Pope Paul VI. Garden City, N. Y., Doubleday [c.]1964. 288p. illus., ports. 24cm. 64-16869 4.95
1. Paulus VI, Pope, 1897- I. Title.

BARRETT, William Edmund, 1900- 262.130924
Shepherd of mankind; a biography of Pope Paul VI. [1st ed.] Garden City, N.Y., Doubleday, 1964. 288 p. illus., ports. 24 cm. [BX1378.3.B6] 64-16869
1. Paulus VI, Pope, 1897- I. Title.

*CATHOLIC CHURCH, Pope (Paul VI) 262.82
Ecclesiam suam; encyclical letter of His Holiness Pope Paul VI: the paths of the church, commentary by Gregory Baum, with study-club outline. Glen Rock, N. J., Paulist [c.1964] 80p. 18cm. .50 pap.,
I. Title.

CIOFALO, Andrew C 262.13
The pilgrimage for peace [written by Andrew C. Ciofalo. South Hackensack, N.J. Custombook, inc., 1965] 72 p. illus. (part col.) ports. (part col.) 28 cm. Published to commemorate Pope Paul's visit to the United States, Oct. 4, 1965; includes the texts of his speeches made during the visit. [BX1378.3C52] 65-28655
1. Paulus vi, Pope, 1897- I. Title.

CLANCY, John G. 922.21
Apostle for our time, Pope Paul VI. Introd. by Richard Cardinal Cushing. [New York] Avon [1964, c.1963] 239p. 18cm. (S159) Bibl. .60 pap.,
1. Paulus VI, Pope, 1897- I. Title.

CLANCY, John Gregory. 922.21
Apostle for our time, Pope Paul VI New York, P. J. Kenedy [1963] xiv, 238 p. illus., ports. 22 cm. Bibliographical footnotes. [BX1378.3.C55] 63-21413
1. Paulus VI, Pope, 1897- I. Title.

COLUMBIA Broadcasting System, inc. CBS News. 262'.13'0924 B
Pope Paul VI, by the staff CBS News Project editor William E. Shapiro New York, F. Watts [1967] 66 p. illus., ports. 23 cm. (The Twentieth century) "Based on the CBS News television series, the Twentieth century." [BX1378.3.C6] 67-25099
1. Paulus VI, Pope, 1897- I. Title.

CORNELL, George W. 262.001
Voyage of faith; the Catholic Church in transition New York, Odyssey [c.1966] 250p. 24cm. [BX8.2.C6] 65-27074 5.00 bds.,
1. Paulus VI, 1897- 2. Christian union—Catholic Church. I. Title.

FOURTEEN hours; 262.13
a picture story of the Pope's historic first visit to America. Introd. by Francis Cardinal Spellman. New York, Dell [c.1965] 1v. (unpaged) illus., ports. 24cm. (8756) [BX1378.3.F6] 65-9199 1.00 pap.,
1. Paulus VI, Pope, 1897-

FOURTEEN hours; 262.13
a picture story of the Pope's historic first visit to America. With an introd. by Francis Cardinal Spellman. New York, Dell Pub. Co. [1965] 1 v. (unpaged) illus., ports. 24 cm. [BX1378.3.F6] 65-9199
1. Paulus VI, Pope, 1897-

GONZALEZ, James L. 922.21
Paul VI, by J. A. Gonzalez. English version by Edward L. Heston. [Boston] St. Paul Eds. [dist. Daughters of St. Paul, c.1964] 338p. illus., ports. 22cm. [BX1378.3.G613] 64-7923 5.00; 4.00 pap.,
1. Paulus, VI, Pope, 1897- I. Perez, Thomas, joint author. II. Title.

GONZALEZ, Jose Luis. 262.13 (B)
Chats with Pope Paul by J. L. Gonzalez. Translated by Mary F. Ingoldsby. [Boston] St. Paul Editions [c1965] 217 p. illus. ports. 22 cm. Bibliographical footnotes. [BX1378.3.G5813] 65-28756
1. Paulus vi, Pope, 1897- I. Title.

GUITTON, Jean. 208
The Pope speaks: dialogues of Paul VI with Jean Guitton. English tr. by Anne and Christopher Fremantle. [1st U. S. ed.] New York, Meredith [1968] xiv, 306p. 24cm. Tr. of dialogues avec Paul VI. [BX1378.3.G813] 68-15204 5.95
1. Paulus VI, Pope 1897- I. Title.

GUITTON, Jean. 262'.13'0924
The Pope speaks: dialogues of Paul VI with Jean Guitton. English translation by Anne and Christopher Fremantle. [1st U.S. ed.] New York, Meredith Press [1968] xiv, 306 p. 24 cm. Translation of Dialogues avec Paul VI. [BX1378.3.G813] 68-15204
1. Paulus VI, Pope, 1897- I. Title.

HATCH, Alden, 1898- 262.13
Pope Paul VI New York. Random [1966] 279p. ports. 22cm. Bibl. [BX1378.3.H3] 66-12006 5.95 bds.,
1. Paulus VI, Pope, 1897- I. Title.

HATCH, Alden, 1898- 262.13
Pope Paul VI New York, Random House [1966] 279 p. ports. 22 cm. Bibliography: p. 267. [BX1378.3.H3] 66-12006
1. Paulus VI, Pope, 1897- I. Title.

HEBBLETHWAITE, Peter. 262'.13'09047
The year of the three popes / Peter Hebblethwaite. London : Collins, 1978. ix, 220 p. ; 22 cm. Includes index. Bibliography: p. 213-214. [BX1389.H36] 79-307264 ISBN 0-00-215047-6 : 8.95
1. Paulus VI, Pope, 1897- 2. John Paul I, Pope, 1912-1978. 3. John Paul II, Pope, 1920- 4. Papacy—History—20th century. 5. Popes—Biography. I. Title.
Distributed by Collins Publishers, Inc., Cleveland, OH 44111

INSTRUMENT of Your peace (An); 262.13
the mission for peace by Pope Paul VI and his momentous visit to America [Ed.: Edward T. Fleming. New York, N.Y. 10017, Commemorative Pubns., 400 Madison Av., 1966, c.1965] 223p. illus. (pt. col.) 29cm. Official documentary report of the visit of His Holiness, Pope Paul VI, to the United Nations and New York. Pub. by Commemorative Pubns. in conjunction with the Archdiocese of New York [BX1378.3.I5] 66-1589 7.95
1. Paulus VI, Pope, 1897- I. Fleming, Edward T., ed. II. Commemorative Publications, inc., New York.

MACGREGOR-HASTIE, Roy 922.21
Pope Paul VI. New York, Criterion [c. 1965] 162p. illus., ports. 22cm. (Criterion bk. for young people) [BX1378.3.M2] 64-22139 3.50
1. Paulus VI, Pope, 1897- I. Title.

MORLEY, Hugh M. 262'.13'0924
The Pope and the press [by] Hugh Morley. With an introd. by James Doyle. Notre Dame [Ind.] University of Notre Dame Press [1968] xi, 143 p. 21 cm. Bibliographical references included in "Notes" (p. 137-143) [BX1378.3.M6] 68-25116 2.45
1. Paulus VI, Pope, 1897- 2. Press. I. Title.

NEW York times. 262.13
The Pope's journey to the United States, written by staff members of the New York times. Edited by A. M. Rosenthal and Arthur Gelb. New York, Bantam Books [1965] 120 p. illus., map, ports. 18 cm. (A Bantam extra, SZ3224) [BX1378.3.N4] 65-28642
1. Paulus VI, Pope, 1897- I. Rosenthal, Abraham Michael, 1922- ed. II. Gelb, Arthur, 1924- ed. III. Title.

O'CONNOR, Edward Dennis. 231'.3
Pope Paul and the Spirit : charisms and church renewal in the teaching of Paul VI / Edward D. O'Connor. Notre Dame, Ind. : Ave Maria Press, c1978. xiii, 258 p. : ill. ; 23 cm. Bibliography: p. 253-258. [BT119.O26] 78-55013 ISBN 0-87793-157-7 : 7.95 ISBN 0-87793-151-8 pbk. : 4.95
1. Paulus VI, Pope, 1897- 2. Holy Spirit—History of doctrines. 3. Gifts, Spiritual—History of doctrines. 4. Pentecostalism—Catholic Church. 5. Church renewal—Catholic Church. I. Paulus VI, Pope, 1897- II. Title.

PALLENBERG, Corrado, 1912- 922.21
The making of a Pope. [New York, Macfadden, c1964] 176p. 18cm. (60-188) Bibl. 64-55963 .60 pap.,
1. Paulus VI, Pope, 1897- I. Title.

PALLENBERG, Corrado, 1912- 922.21
The making of a Pope. [New York, Macfadden-Bartell Corp., 1964] 176 p. 18 cm. "A Macfadden original." "60-188." Bibliography: p. 175-176. [BX1378.3.P3] 64-55963
1. Paulus VI, Pope, 1897- I. Title.

PALLENBERG, Corrado, 1912- 262'.13'0924
Pope Paul VI. [Rev. ed.] New York, Putnam [1968] 224p. 22cm. (Lives to remember). First pub. in 1964 under title: The making of a Pope. Bibl. [BX1378.3.P3 1968] (B) 67-14795 3.49 lib. ed.,
1. Paulus VI, Pope, 1897- I. Title.

PALLENBERG, Corrado, 1912- 262'.13'0924 B
Pope Paul VI. [Rev. ed] New York, Putnam [1968] 224 p. 22 cm. (Lives to remember) First published in 1964 under title: The making of a Pope. Bibliography: p. 221-222. A biography of Pope Paul VI, covering his boyhood, education, the positions he held leading to his election as Pope, and the reform movements of his reign. [BX1378.3.P3 1968] 92 AC 68
1. Paulus VI, Pope, 1897- I. Title.

POPE Paul VI in the Holy Land 262.13
[Tr.] from German by Aileen

O'Brien. Photos. by Werner Schiller. New York] Herder & Herder [c.1964] 198p. illus. (pt. col.) col. maps, ports. (pt. col.) 31cm. 64-19604 7.50
1. Paulus VI, Pope, 1897- 2. Palestine—Descr. & trav. I. Schiller, Werner.

POZO, Candido. 238'.2
The Credo of the People of God : a theological commentary / by Candido Pozo ; translated and edited by Mark A. Pilon. 2d ed. Chicago : Franciscan Herald Press, [1979] p. cm. Translation of El credo del pueblo de dios. Appendices (p.): Latin text of the Credo of the People of God.—English version of the Credo by the translator.—Allocution of Pope Paul on the Credo, June 3, 1968.—Allocution of Pope Paul on the Credo, July 10, 1968.—Allocution of Pope Paul on the Credo, October 30, 1968. Bibliography: p. [BX1755.P6913 1979] 79-1401 10.95
1. Paulus VI, Pope, 1897- Credimus. 2. Catholic Church—Doctrinal and controversial works—Catholic authors. I. Pilon, Mark A. II. Paulus VI, Pope, 1897- Credimus. English & Latin. 1979. III. Title.

SCHILLER, Werner. 262.13
Pope Paul VI in the Holy Land. [Translation by Aileen O'Brien. Photos. by Werner Schiller. New York] Herder and Herder [1964] 198 p. illus. (part col.) col. maps, ports, (part col.) 31 cm. [BX1378.3P6] 64-19604
1. Paulus vi, Pope, 1897- 2. Palestine—Descr. & trav. I. Title.

SERAFIAN, Michael, pseud. 282
The pilgrim. New York, Farrar, Straus [1964] xix, 281 p. 22 cm. [BX1378.3.S4] 64-19805
1. Paulus VI, Pope, 1897- 2. Vatican Council, 2d. I. Title.

SHAW, Mark, ed. 262.130924
Messenger of peace; the visit of Pope Paul VI to the United Nations and the United States in the cause of peace. October 4, 1965. Photographed by Magnum. Trinity House; dist. Garden City, N.Y., Doubleday [1965] 63p. (chiefly illus., ports.) 29cm. [BX1378.3.S5] 65-28806 3.30
1. Paulus VI, Pope, 1897- I. Magnum Photos, inc. II. Title.

SLONIM, Reuben. 282
In the steps of Pope Paul; a rabbi's impression of the Pope in the Holy Land. Introd. by Archibishop Philip F. Pocock. Baltimore, Helicon [1965] 126 p. 23 cm. [BX1378.3.S55] 65-18648
1. Paulus VI, Pope, 1897- I. Title.

TIME, inc. 262.13
The Pope's visit. New York, Author [1966, c.1965] 96p. Illus. (pt. col.) ports. (pt. col.) 29cm. (Time-Life special report bks.) [BX1378.3.T5] 65-28741 1.95 pap.,
1. Paulus VI, Pope, 1897- I. Title.

UNITED Nations. Office of Public Information. 261.873
Never again war! A documented account of the visit to the United Nations of His Holiness Pope Paul VI, with texts of the encyclical letter of Pope John XXIII, Pacem in terris, and the United Nations Universal declaration of human rights. New York 1965. 134 p. illus., facsims. (1 col.) ports. (1 mounted col.) 28 cm. "Sales no.: 65.I.27." Bibliographical references included in "Footnotes" (p. 125-126). [BX1378.3.U48] 66-995
1. Paulus VI, Pope, 1897- 2. Peace. I. Paulus VI, Pope, 1897- II. Catholic Church. Pope, 1958-1963 (Joannes XXIII) Pacem in terris (11 Apr. 1963) III. Title.

Paulus VI, Pope, 1897- —Addresses, essays, lectures.

ANDREWS, James F., 1936- 262'.13'0924
Paul VI, critical appraisals. Edited by James F. Andrews. New York, Bruce Pub. Co. [1970] 160 p. 22 cm. Includes bibliographical references. [BX1378.3.A75] 78-131474 6.95
1. Paulus VI, Pope, 1897- —Addresses, essays, lectures.

OUR name is Peter 262'.13'0924
: an anthology of key teachings of Pope Paul VI / compiled by Sean O'Reilly. Chicago : Franciscan Herald Press, c1977. xi, 146, [1] p. ; 23 cm. Bibliography: p. [147]. [BX955.2.O95] 77-380 ISBN 0-8199-0666-2 : 6.95
1. Paulus VI, Pope, 1897- —Addresses, essays, lectures. 2. Papacy—Addresses, essays, lectures. I. O'Reilly, Sean, 1922-

WE are Peter : 262'.13'0924
some key teachings of Pope Paul VI / edited by Sean O'Reilly. Chicago : Franciscan Herald Press, [1977] p. cm. [BX955.2.W4] 76-45573 ISBN 0-672-52288-8 : 5.95
1. Paulus VI, Pope, 1897- —Addresses, essays, lectures. 2. Papacy—Addresses, essays, lectures. I. O'Reilly, Sean, 1922-

Paulus VI, Pope, 1897—Portraits, etc.

PALMER, Russell, 1917- 262'.13'0924
You could not come to me ... so I have come to you : a salute to Pope Paul VI / by Russell Palmer ; [graphics by Eric Nesheim]. Huntington, Ind. : Our Sunday Visitor, c1977. 100 p. : chiefly ill. ; 24 x 29 cm. [BX1378.3.P325] 77-82346 ISBN 0-87973-885-5 : 9.95
1. Paulus VI, Pope, 1897—Portraits, etc. I. Title.

Pax (Organization)

BENDER, Urie A. 267'.23
Soldiers of compassion, by Urie A. Bender. Scottdale, Pa., Herald Press [1969] 319 p. illus., ports. 21 cm. [BX8128.W4B4] 71-76623 4.95
1. Pax (Organization) 2. Conscientious objectors. I. Title.

Payne, Daniel Alexander, 1811-1893.

SMITH, Charles Spencer, 1852- 922
A monograph. The life of Daniel Alexander Payne, D.D., LL.D., by Rev. C. S. Smith, D.D., with an introduction by Bishop Abram Grant, D.D., and a poem, "In memoriam," by Bishop Jas. A. Handy, D.D. Nashville, Tenn., Publishing house A. M. E. church Sunday school union, 1894. 57 p. 7 pl., 2 port. (incl. front.) 17 1/2 cm. [E185.97.P37] 1-19551
1. Payne, Daniel Alexander, 1811-1893. I. Title.

Payne, Squier, 1676?-1751.

HART, Arthur Tindal 253.0942
Country counting house; the story of two eighteenthcentury clerical account books. London, Phoenix House [dist. Hollywood-by-the-Sea, Fla., Transatlantic, c.1962] xxix, 142p. illus. 23cm. Bibl. 63-1753 6.25
1. Payne, Squier, 1676?-1751. 2. Mease, Henry, 1680 or 81-1746. 3. Clergy—England. 4. Church finance—England—Hist.—Sources. I. Title.

Payson, Edward, 1783-1827.

CUMMINGS, Asa, 1791-1856. 922.573
Memoir and select thoughts, of the late Rev. Edward Payson, D. D. pastor of the Second church in Portland. By Rev. Asa Cummings, D. D. A new ed., much enl. New York, W. H. Hyde, 1849. xiii, [13]-606 p. front. (port.) 24 cm. Half-title: The complete works of Edward Payson, D. D. [BX7260.P4C82 1849] 36-23984
1. Payson, Edward, 1783-1827. I. Title.

[CUMMINGS, Asa] 1791-1856. 922.573
A memoir of the Rev. Edward Payson, [D. D., late pastor of the Second church in Portland ... Portland [Me.] Ann L. Payson, Shirley & Hyde,[printers, 1830. xii, [13]-444 p. front. (port.) 21 cm. [BX7260.P4C8 1830] 37-21279
1. Payson, Edward, 1783-1827. I. Title.

CUMMINGS, Asa, 1791-1856. 922.573
A memoir of the Rev. Edward Payson, D. D., late pastor of the second church in Portland. By Asa Cummings ... 3d ed. Boston, Crocker and Brewster; New York, J. Leavitt, 1830. vii, 400 p. 20 cm. [BX720.P4C8 1830 b] 36-2674
1. Payson, Edward, 1783-1827. I. Title.

[WESTON, Isaac] 1787-1870. 922.573
Our pastor; or, Reminiscences of Rev. Edward Payson, D.D., pastor of the Second Congregational church in Portland, Me. By one of his flock ... Boston, Tappan & Whittemore; Portland, Sanborn & Carter [etc.] 1855. xv, [v]-vii, [9]-360 p. incl. front. 19 1/2 cm. [BX7260.P4W4] 36-6875
1. Payson, Edward, 1783-1827. I. Title.

Payton, Everett Lee.

PAYTON, Everett J. 248'.86 B
I won't be crippled when I see Jesus / Everett J. Payton. Minneapolis, Minn. : Augsburg Pub. House, c1979. 158 p. ; 20 cm. [BR1725.P33P39] 79-50084 ISBN 0-8066-1716-0 pbk. : 3.95
1. Payton, Everett Lee. 2. Payton, Everett J. 3. Christian biography—United States. 4. Blind—Biography. 5. Hydrocephalus—Biography. 6. Cerebral palsy—United States—Biography. I. Title.

Paz, Nestor, 1945-1970.

PAZ, Nestor, 1945-1970. 322.4'2'0984
My life for my friends : the guerrilla journal of Nestor Paz, Christian / translated and edited by Ed Garcia and John Eagleson. Maryknoll, N.Y. : Orbis Books, [1975] viii, 103 p. : ill. ; 20 cm. "Originally published in various sources, including Los cristianos y la revolucion, Quimantu, Santiago de Chile, 1972, and Suplemento de Pastoral popular (Santiago de Chile) no. 125." [F3326.P275] 74-21107 4.95
1. Paz, Nestor, 1945-1970. 2. Guerrillas—Bolivia. I. Title.

Peabody, Ephraim, 1807-1856.

[PEABODY, Robert Swain] 1845-1917. 922.8173
A New England romance; the story of Ephraim and Mary Jane Peabody [1807-1892] told by their sons ... Boston and New York, Houghton Mifflin company, 1920. xi, [1] p., 1 l., 163, [1] p., 1 l. front., plates, ports. 21 cm. [BX9869.P355P4] 20-19929
1. Peabody, Ephraim, 1807-1856. 2. Peabody, Mrs. Mary Jane (Derby) 1807-1892. I. Peabody, Francis Greenwood, 1847- joint author. II. Title.

Peabody, Oliver William Bourn, 1799-1848.

PEABODY, William Bourn Oliver, 1799-1847. 252.
Sermons by the late William B. O. Peabody, D. D., with a memoir, by his brother. 2d ed. Boston, B. H. Greene, 1849. vi p., 1 l., 393 p. 20 cm. "Memoir" by O. W. B. Peabody: p. 1-110; "Notices of the Rev. Oliver W. B. Peabody": p. [111]-132. [BX9843.P68S5] 6-39850
1. Peabody, Oliver William Bourn, 1799-1848. I. Title.

Peace.

AINSLIE, Peter, 1867-1934. 172.
Christ or Napoleon--which? A study of the cure for world militarism and the church's scandal of division, by Peter Ainslie ... New York, Chicago [etc.] Fleming H. Revell company [c1915] 96 p. 19 1/2 cm. [JX1953.A5] 15-7406
1. Peace. I. Title.

APPLEWHITE, Harry. 261.87'3
Waging peace: a way out of war. Philadelphia, Published for Joint Educational Development [by] United Church Press [1974] 190 p. 22 cm. (A Shalom resource) Includes bibliographies. [JX1953.A6463] 73-20080 ISBN 0-8298-0266-5 2.95 (pbk.)
1. Peace. 2. War and religion. I. Joint Educational Development. II. Title.

ASHER, Percy Frank, 1898- 172.4
Can Christians preserve peace? [By] Percy F. Asher. With an introduction by Dr. Ralph W. Sockman. Boston, Chapmans & Grimes [c1935] 94 p. illus. (map) 20 cm. Bibliography: p. 11-12. [BR115.P4A8] 35-10461
1. Peace. I. Title.

BELDEN, Albert David, 1883- 261
Pax Christi, the peace of Christ, a new policy of Christendom today. [American rev. ed.] Elgin, Ill., Brethren Pub. House [1947] 155 p. 20 cm. [BR115.P4B4 1947] 48-213
1. A Peace. 2. World War, 1939-1945—Religious aspects. I. Title.

BOYER, Laura F. 265.
The search for peace; an outline for the study of methods toward peace, to be used by leaders of forums and discussion groups, by Laura F. Boyer ... New York, N. Y., The National council, 1925. 71, [1] p. 19 cm. "Books recommended": p. 6-8. [BR115.P4B6] 25-10957
1. Peace. I. Protestant Episcopal church in the U. S. A, National council. II. Title.

CADMAN, Samuel Parkes, 1864-1936. 248
Peace, by S. Parkes Cadman. New York, E. P. Dutton & co., inc., [c1929] 3 p. l., 3-71 p. 17 cm. "First edition." [BV4510.C25] 29-21687
1. Peace. I. Title.

CALL, Arthur Deerin, 1869- 172.
Our country and world peace, by Arthur Deerin Call ... Denver, The Estes Park conference of Young men's Christian associations [1926] 169 p., 1 l. 20 cm. The main portions of six lectures delivered before the Estes Park summer school of the Young men's association, at the Estes Park conference, Association camp, Colorado, in July, 1926. Much of this material has appeared elsewhere and in a variety of forms. "--Introd. [JX1961.U6C25] 26-19148
1. Peace. 2. International cooperations. 3. Arbitration, International. I. Title.
Contents omitted

CAMAERTS, Emile. 261
The peace that is left [by] Emile Cammserts. New York and London, Harper & brothers [c1945] x, 150 p. 19 1/2 cm. London edition (The Cresent press) has title: The peace that was left. [BR115.P4C25 1945a] 46-3833
1. Peace. 2. Christianity—20th cent. I. Title.

CATHOLIC church. Pope. 261
Principles for peace; selections from papal documents, Leo XIII to Pius XII, edited for the Bishop's committee on the Pope's peace points by the Reverend Harry C. Koenig ... With a preface by the Most Reverend Samuel A. Stritch ... Washington, National Catholic welfare conference, 1943. xxv, 894 p. 23 1/2 cm. Bibliography: p. 821-827. [BX850.A48] 43-9841
1. Peace. 2. Sociology, Christian—Catholic authors. I. Koenig, Harry Corcoran, 1909- ed. II. National Catholic welfare conference. Bishops' committee on the Pope's peace points. III. Title.

COOKE, Richard Joseph, bp., 1853- 172.
The church and world peace, by Richard J. Cooke ... New York, Cincinnati, The Abingdon press [c1920] 178 p. 20 cm. [JX1953.C6] 20-8653
1. Peace. 2. League of nations. I. Title.

DAVIS, Jerome, 1891- 265.
Christian fellowship among the nations; a discussion course which will help groups of young people and adults to do straight thinking on our greatest problem [by] Jerome Davis ... and Roy B. Chamberlin ... Boston, Chicago, The Pilgrim press [c1925] 2 p. l., iii-vi, 116 p. 20 cm. "Bibliography on war and the peace movement": p. 114-116. [BR115.P4D3] 25-8227
1. Peace. 2. War. I. Chamberlin, Roy Bullard, 1887- joint author. II. Title.

FORWARD, Carnice E. 261
If one be lifted up; the nucleus of peace. New York, Carlton [dist. Comet, c.]1962. 21p. (Reflection bk.) 1.95
I. Title.

FUCHS, Harald. 239'.3
Augustin und der antike Friedensgedanke. With a new introd. for the Garland ed. by Walter F. Bense. New York, Garland Pub.,

1973. 26, 258 p. 22 cm. (The Garland library of war and peace) Originally presented as the author's thesis, Berlin, 1925. Reprint of the 1926 ed., issued as Heft 3 of Neue philologische Untersuchungen. Bibliography: p. 20-26. [BR65.A65F8 1973] 72-147669 ISBN 0-8240-0337-3 15.00
1. Augustinus, Aurelius, Saint, Bp. of Hippo. De civitate Dei. 2. Peace. I. Title. II. Series. III. Series: Neue philologische Untersuchungen, Heft 3.

[GARDNER, Milton Bliss] 1889- 261
The fall of great Babylon; or, The prevalence and perversity of Babylonish militaristic religion in the present world crisis, by M. B. G. Presenting the whole case of Christian militarists vs. Christian objectors to war. Babylon politically considered, seasonable warning and appeal to the nation. "The great decision", by John Bunyan. [Philadelphia, 1943] 128 p. incl. front. 18 1/2 cm. Signed: M. B. Gardner. [BR115.P4G3] 43-14130
1. Peace. 2. War and religion. I. Title.

GREENE, Theodore Ainsworth, 1890- 172.4
What can Christians do for peace? A syllabus prepared for the use of church discussion groups on peace problems, by Theodore Ainsworth Greene ... Boston, Chicago, The Pilgrim press [c1935] 2 p. l., 3-61 p. 20 cm. (Adult education series) "Books of reference" at end of each chapter. [BR115.P4G7] 261 ISBN 35-4350
1. Peace. 2. War and religion. I. Title.

GULICK, Sidney Lewis, 1860- 172.
The Christian crusade for a warless world, by Sidney L. Gulick ... New York, The Macmillan company, 1922. xiv p., 2 l., 3-197 p. 18 cm. "The Federal council of the churches of Christ in America, through its Commission on international justice and goodwill, issues this appeal for a 'Christian crusade for a warless world.'"--Foreword. [JX1953.G72] 22-18681
1. Peace. I. Federal council of the churches of Christ in America. Commission on international justice and goodwill. II. Title.

GULICK, Sidney Lewis, 1860- 172.
The Christian crusade for a warless world, by Sidney L. Gulick ... New York city, Federal council of the churches of Christ in America, 1923. xiv p., 2 l., 3-197 p. 20 cm. "Published September, 1922. Reprinted November, 1923." "The Federal council of the churches of Christ in America, through its Commission on international justice and goodwill, issues this appeal for a 'Christian crusade for a warless world'"--Foreword. Bibliography: p. 194-197. [JX1953.G72 1923] 24-2259
1. Peace. I. Federal council of the churches of Christ in America. Commission on international justice and goodwill. II. Title.

HASTINGS, James, 1852-1922, ed. 265.
The Christian doctrine of peace, edited by James Hastings, D.D. New York, C. Scribner's sons; Edinburgh, T. & T. Clark, 1922. ix, 300 p. 23 cm. (Half-title: The great Christian doctrines) "Literature" preceding each chapter. [BR115.P4H3] 24-5750
I. Title.

HERSHBERGER, Guy Franklin, 1896- 261.6
War, peace, and nonresistance. [Rev. ed.] Scottdale, Pa., Herald Press, 1953. 375p. 24cm. [BR115.P4H4 1953] 53-7586
1. Peace. 2. Mennonites—Hist. 3. Facifism. I. Title.

[HOLMES, Arthur David] 1876- 172.4
The only way out, by The Hermit of Willow beach, author and publisher. [Los Angeles, 1945] 156 p. 21 cm. [BR115.P4H63] 45-6088
1. Peace. 2. Providence and government of God. I. Title.

JEFFERSON, Charles Edward, 1860-1937. 172.
Christianity and international peace; six lectures at Grinnell college, Grinnell, Iowa, in February, 1915, on the George A. Gates memorial foundation, by Charles Edward Jefferson ... New York, Thomas Y. Crowell company [c1915] 2 p. l., 9-287 p. 20 cm. [JX1953.J4] 15-11255
1. Peace. I. Title.
Contents omitted.

KING, Rufus Gunn. 172.4
You and I, by Rufus Gunn King, jr. Washington, D.C., National home library foundation [c1940] 5 p. l., 81 p. 16 cm. [Jacket library. 12] [BR115.P4K5] 41-8451
1. Peace. 2. Civilization. I. Title.

LAWSON, James Gilchrist, 1874- ed. 252.6
Great sermons on world peace. compiled by James Gilchrist Lawson ... New York, Round table press, inc., 1937. vi, 200 p. 21 cm. [BR115.P4L3] 172.4 37-23521
1. Peace. 2. Sermons, English. I. Title.
Contents omitted.

LOFQUIST, Henry Victor, 1897- 261
An uncommon commonplace, a collection of sermons and articles, by Henry V. Lofquist ... [Brookhaven, Miss.] 1942. 140 p. pl. 23 cm. [BR115.P4L6] 43-4446
1. Peace. 2. Stewardship, Christian. 3. Sociology, Christian. I. Title.

LYNCH, Frederick Henry, 1867- 172.
The last war: a study of things present and things to come, by Frederick Lynch ... New York, Chicago [etc.] Fleming H. Revell company [c1915] 118 p. 19 1/2 cm. [JX1953.L77] 15-13202
1. Peace. 2. European war, 1914-1918. 3. Christianity. I. Title.

MCFEETERS, James Calvin, 1848- 265.
Peace on earth versus another world-war, by J. C. McFeeters... Boston, The Christopher publishing house [c1926] viii, 178 p. 19 1/2 cm. [BR115.P4M3] 26-14280
I. Title.

MUSTE, Abraham John, 1885- 261
Not by might; Christianity, the way to human decency. New York, Harper [1947] xii, 227 p. 21 cm. [BR115.P4M8] 47-12403
1. Peace. I. Title.

NEILL, Thomas Patrick, 1915- 261
Weapons for peace, by Thomas P. Neill ... Milwaukee, The Bruce publishing company [1945] ix, 234 p. 22 1/2 cm. "A note on books": p. 221-224. Bibliographical references included in "Footnotes" (p. 225-229) [BX961.P4N4] 45-5565
1. Peace. 2. Church and state—Catholic church. 3. World politics. I. Title.

NICHOLSON, Evelyn Carrie (Riley) Mrs. 172.
... Thinking it through, a discussion on world peace (Epworth league ed.) By Evelyn Riley Nicholson ... New York, Cincinnati, The Methodist book concern [c1928] 135 p. 20 cm. (Christian comradeship series, W. E. J. Gratz, editor) "Approved by the Committee on curriculum of the Board of education of the Methodist Episcopal church." [JX1953.N5] 28-14811
1. Peace. I. Title.

NOLDE, Otto Frederick, 1899-. 261
Christian world action; the Christian citizen builds for tomorrow [by] O. Frederick Nolde. Philadelphia, Muhlenberg press [1942] xi, 113 p. incl. tab. 17 1/2 cm. "References":p. 110-113. [BR115.P4N6] 42-22748
1. Peace. I. Title.

NOLDE, Otto Frederick, 1899-. 261
Christian world action; the Christian citizen builds for tomorrow [by] O. Frederick Nolde. Philadelphia, Muhlenberg press [1943] xi, 127 p. 18 cm. "Revised ... September 1943." "References": p. 124-127. [BR115.P4N6 1943] 43-22885
1. Peace. 2. World war, 1939—Peace. I. Title.

PAGET, Henry Luke, bp. of Chester, 1853- 220
Peace & happiness, by the Right Rev. H. L. Paget ... With an introduction by the Bishop of London. London, New York, [etc.] Longmans, Green and co., 1922. 128 p. 19 cm. [BR125.P17] 22-7457
I. Title.
Contents omitted.

PEARL, Reuben. 261.7
The road to peace. New York, Philosophical Library [1957] 189p. 22cm. [BR115.P4P42] 57-13953
1. Peace. I. Title.

PEARSON, Margaret (Crawford) Mrs. 248
Peace, perfect peace; an earnest appeal to Christians to so live that they may enjoy fully the rich blessings of God ... by Mrs. Margaret Crawford Pearson. Hartford, Conn., The S. S. Scranton co., 1924. 63 p. 24 cm. [BV4501.P43] 24-10061
I. Title.

[QUILLIBET] pseud. 204
The peace parliament, or, The reconstruction creed of Christendom. Boston, Houghton, Osgood and company [1879] 49 p. 18 cm. [BR126.Q66p] A 31
I. Title.

REED, Edward, ed. 261.873
Peace on earth: Pacem in terris. Proceedings of an Intl. Convocation on the requirements of peace. Sponsored by the Center for the Study of Democratic Institutions. New York, Pocket Bks. [c.1965] 260p. 18cm. (95019) .95 pap.,
I. Title.

ROGERS, W. Henry 261.873
There shall be no peace unless. 2nd ed. New York, Vantage [c.1955, 1966] 79p. 20cm. 2.50 bds.,
I. Title.

RUST, John Benjamin. 261.4
The great peace motto, "In essentials unity, in non-essentials liberty, in both charity", by John Benjamin Rust... Cleveland, O., Central publishing house [c1929] 1 p. l., 5-96 p. 20 1/2 cm. This motto, which in its Latin form reads: In necessariis unitas, in non necessariis libertas, in utrisque caritas, was originally published in a treatise entitled: Paraenesis votiva pro pace ecclesiae ad theologos Augustanae confessionis. Actore Ruperto Meldenio theologo. "This volume grew out of a series of articles which appeared in the Christian world during the year 1927."--Pref. [BR115.P4R8] 30-20134
1. Meldenius, Rupertus. Paraenesis votiva pro pace ecclesiae ad theologos Augustanae confessionis. 2. Peace. 3. Christian union. 4. Mottoes. I. Title. II. Title: In necessariis unitas, in non necessariis libertas, in utrisque caritas.

[SATTERLEE, Henry Yates] bp., 1843-1908, comp.
The peace cross book; cathedral of SS. Peter and Paul, Washington. New York, R. H. Russell, 1899. 75 p. pl., facsim. 8°. 99-2154
I. Title.

SHRIGLEY, George Andrew Cleveland, 1902- comp. 264.1
101 prayers for peace, compiled by G. A. Cleveland Shrigley... Philadelphia, The Westminister press, 1941. 144 p. 19 cm. [BV283.P4S5] 41-9701
1. Peace. 2. Prayers. I. Title.

SILVER, Benno 248.42
Toward peace. New York, Vantage [c. 1962] 94p. 21cm. 2.50
I. Title.

SMITH, Fred Burton, 1865-1936. 172.
Must we have war? [By] Fred W. Smith ... with a foreword by Owen D. Young. New York and London, Harper & brothers, 1929. xxi p., 1 l., 318 p., 1 l. plates. 19 1/2 cm. "First edition." Recognition is given the executive staff of the World alliance for international friendship in editing the manuscript. cf. Introd. "Edited by Charles Stelzle."--Publisher's note. [JX1953.S58] 29-25927
1. Peace. 2. War. 3. War and religion. I. World alliance for promoting international friendship through the churches. II. Stelzle, Charles, 1869- ed. III. Title.

SMITH, Fred Burton, 1865-1936. 172.
On the trail of the peacemakers, by Fred B. Smith. New York, The Macmillan company, 1922. 3 p. l., 239 p. front. (port.) plates. 19 1/2 cm. "I was invited to go forth as a messenger of the 'World alliance for international friendship through the churches' and under the joint auspices of that organization and the 'Federal council of the churches of Christ in America'." [JX1953.S6] 22-17763
1. Peace. I. Title.

SNYDER, William Cloyd. 261
Would Christ wear khaki? By W. Cloyd Snyder. Boston, The Christopher publishing house [c1937] xii, 15-220 p. 21 cm. "A protest against extreme and unwarranted declarations ... of clergymen ... on social questions."--Pref. [BR517.S5] 37-20987
1. Peace. 2. Clergy—U. S. 3. Communism—U. S.—1917- I. Title.

SOLOV'EV, Vladimir Sergieevich, 1853-1900. 256
War and Christianity, from the Russian point of view. Three conversations by Vladimir Solovyof, with an introduction by Stephen Graham. New York, G. P. Putnam's sons, 1915. x, 188 p. 21 cm. Printed in Great Britain. "Solovyof issued 'War and Christianity' on Easter day, 1900."--Pref. "Mr. Edward Cazalet ... translated conversation ii ... Mr. W. J. Barnes and Mr. H. H. Haynes ... translated conversation iii."--Pref. [JX1952.S7] 15-20905 1.50
1. Peace. I. Graham, Stephen, 1884- II. Cazalet, Edward Alexander, tr. III. Barnes, W. J., tr. IV. Haynes, H. H., joint tr. V. Title. VI. Title: Three conversations.

UNITED Nations. Office of Public Information. 261.873
Never again war! A documented account of the visit to the United Nations of His Holiness Pope Paul VI, with texts of the encyclical letter of Pope John XXIII, Pacem in terris, and the United Nations Universal declaration of human rights. New York 1965. 134 p. illus., facsims. (1 col.) ports. (1 mounted col.) 28 cm. "Sales no.: 65.I.27." Bibliographical references included in "Footnotes" (p. 125-126). [BX1378.3.U48] 66-995
1. Paulus VI, Pope, 1897- 2. Peace. I. Paulus VI, Pope, 1897- II. Catholic Church. Pope, 1958-1963 (Joannes XXIII) Pacem in terris (11 Apr. 1963) III. Title.

WALD, Marcus, 1905- 296
Jewish teaching on peace, by M. Wald ... New York, Bloch publishing company, 1944. xx, 296 p. 20 1/2 cm. Title transliterated. Shalom. "List of extracts and references": p. [213]-291. [BM538.P3W3] 44-4539
1. Peace. 2. Jews—Religion. I. Title.

YODER, Edward, 1893-1945. 261
Must Christians fight, a Scriptural inquiry by Edward Yoder, in collaboration with Jesse W. Hoover and Harold S. Bender. [2d ed.] Akron Pa., Mennonite Central Committee, 1943. 68 p. 20 cm. "A short bibliography on non-resistance": p. [3] of cover. [BR115.P4Y6 1943] 48-31913
1. Peace. 2. Evil, Non-resistance to. 3. Mennonites—Doctrinal and controversial works. I. Hoover, Jesse W., joint author. II. Bender, Harold Stauffer, 1897- joint author. III. Mennonite Central Committee. IV. Title.

Peace—Addresses, essays, lectures.

CENTRAL Conference of American Rabbis.
Summary of proceedings: Washington conference on disarmament and world peace, conducted by Religious Action Center, Union of American Hebrew Congregations. February 4-5, 1964. [Washington, D.C., 1964] xi, 76 p. illus. 28 cm. 68-44543
I. Union of American Hebrew Congregations. Religious Action Center. II. Conference on Disarmament and World Peace, Washington, D.C., 1964. III. Title. IV. Title: Washington conference on disarmament and world peace.

THE First American peace movement; comprising War inconsistent with the religion of Jesus Christ, by David Low Dodge, with an introd. by Edwin D. Mead; The lawfulness of war for Christians, examined, by James Mott [and] A solemn review of the custom of war, by Noah Worcester. With a new introd. for the Garland ed. by Peter Brock. New York, Garland Pub., 1972. 11, xx [i.e. xxiv] 261.8'73

, 168, 33, 23 p. 22 cm. (The Garland library of war and peace) Reprint of three works originally published in 1905, 1814, and 1815, respectively. [JX1949.F57 1972] 73-147428 ISBN 0-8240-0220-2
1. Peace—Addresses, essays, lectures. 2. War—Addresses, essays, lectures. I. Dodge, David Low, 1774-1852. War inconsistent with the religion of Jesus Christ. 1972. II. Mott, James, 1788-1868. The lawfulness of war for Christians, examined. 1972. III. Worcester, Noah, 1758-1837. A solemn review of the custom of war. 1972. IV. Title. V. Series.

HOOKER, James, 1864- 218
The road to universal peace; the way that leads to a state of harmonious existence through individual freedom, by James Hooker. Indianapolis, Ind., The Peace publishing co. [c1924] xi p., 1 l., 344 p. 19 1/2 cm. [BD431.H55] 24-29201
I. Title.

INTERNATIONAL Inter-Religious Symposium on Peace, New Delhi, 1968. 261.8'73
World religions and world peace. Edited by Homer A. Jack. Pref. by Zakir Husain. Introd. by Dana McLean Greeley. Boston, Beacon Press [1968] xvi, 208 p. 21 cm. Bibliography: p. 206. [JX1963.I65 1968] 68-54849 4.95
1. Peace—Addresses, essays, lectures. 2. Religions—Addresses, essays, lectures. I. Jack, Homer Alexander, ed. II. Title.

MERTON, Thomas, 1915-1968. 261.8'73
The nonviolent alternative / Thomas Merton ; edited, and with an introd. by Gordon C. Zahn. New York, N.Y. : Farrar, Straus & Giroux, c1980. xli, 270 p. ; 22 cm. Rev. ed. of Thomas Merton on peace, originally published in 1971. [JX1963.M549 1980] 80-12960 ISBN 0-374-22312-2 : 12.95
1. Peace—Addresses, essays, lectures. 2. Nonviolence—Addresses, essays, lectures. 3. Christianity and international affairs—Addresses, essays, lectures. I. Zahn, Gordon Charles, 1918-

MERTON, Thomas, 1915-1968. 261.8'73
Thomas Merton on peace / [by] Thomas Merton. London : Mowbrays, 1976. 156 p. ; 22 cm. [JX1963.M549 1976] 77-358970 ISBN 0-264-66339-X : £2.25
1. Peace—Addresses, essays, lectures. 2. Nonviolence—Addresses, essays, lectures. 3. Christianity and international affairs—Addresses, essays, lectures. I. Title.

MERTON, Thomas, 1915-1968. 261.8'73
Thomas Merton on peace. With an introd. by Gordon C. Zahn. New York, McCall Pub. Co. [1971] xli, 269 p. 22 cm. [JX1963.M549 1971] 75-122148 ISBN 0-8415-0060-6 7.95
1. Peace—Addresses, essays, lectures. 2. Nonviolence—Addresses, essays, lectures. 3. Christianity and international affairs—Addresses, essays, lectures. I. Title.

NATIONAL Inter-Religious Conference on Peace Washington, D.C., 1966. 261.87'3
Religion and peace; papers from the National Inter-Religious Conference on Peace. Edited by Homer A. Jack. Indianapolis, Bobbs-Merrill [1966] xvi, 137 p. 21 cm. [JX1963.N24 1966aa] 66-27885
1. Peace—Addresses, essays, lectures. 2. Christianity and international affairs—Addresses, essays, lectures. I. Jack, Homer Alexander, ed. II. Title.

PEACE, on not leaving it to the pacifists / edited by Gerald O. Pedersen ; with contributions by William Lesher ... [et al.] ; and a foreword by Gerhard L. Belgum. Philadelphia : Fortress Press, [1975] viii, 88 p. ; 19 cm. Bibliography: p. 85-87. [JX1963.P334] 74-26328 ISBN 0-8006-1092-X pbk. : 2.95 261.8'73
1. Peace—Addresses, essays, lectures. I. Pedersen, Gerald O. II. Lesher, William.

ROAD to peace (The); Christian approaches to defence and disarmament [by] John C. Bennett [others] Philadelphia, Fortress [1966] 54, [1] p. 20cm. (Facet bks. Soc. ethics ser., 10) Bibl. [JX1963.R62 1966] 66-14795 .85 pap., 261.873
1. Peace—Addresses, essays, lectures. 2. Christianity and international affairs—Addresses, essays, lectures. I. Bennett, John Coleman, 1902-(Series)
Contents omitted

Peace—Biblical arguments.

MACGREGOR, George Hogarth Carnaby, 1892- 225.81724
The New Testament basis of pacifism and The relevance of an impossible ideal. Nyack, N. Y., Fellowship Publications, 1956. 160p. 22cm. Includes bibliography. [BS2545.P4M32] 60-7634
1. Peace—Biblical arguments. 2. Pacifism. 3. War and religion. I. Niebuhr, Reinhold, 1892- II. Macgregor, George Hogarth Carnaby, 1892- The relevance of an impossible ideal. III. Title. IV. Title: The relevance of an impossible ideal.

Peace of mind.

ALLEN, James, 1864-1912. 291.4'3
The gift of inner peace; inspirational writings. Edited by Marianne Wilson. [Kansas City, Mo.] Hallmark Editions [1971] 61 p. illus. 20 cm. [BF637.P3A43 1971] 73-127741 ISBN 0-87529-168-6 3.00
1. Peace of mind. I. Title.

BRANDT, Henry R. 248
The struggle for peace. Wheaton, Ill., Scripture [c.1965] 79p. illus. 21cm. Bibl. [BV4908.B7] 65-11930 1.00 pap.,
1. Peace of mind. I. Title.

FINEGAN, Jack, 1908- 248.86
At wit's end. Richmond, John Knox Press [1963] 125 p. 21 cm. [BV4908.5.F5] 63-13831
1. Peace of mind. I. Title.

GOCKEL, Herman William, 1906- 242
Answer to anxiety. St. Louis, Concordia [c.1961] 179p. 61-13455 3.00
1. Peace of mind. I. Title.

GUIDEPOSTS. 248
Guideposts to a stronger faith, edited by Norman Vincent Peale. Carmel, N. Y., Guideposts Associates [1959] 308p. 22cm. [BV4908.5.G83] 59-4153
1. Peace of mind. 2. Christian biography. I. Peale, Norman Vincent, ed. II. Title.

HAGGAI, John Edmund 248
How to win over worry; a practical formula for successful living. New York, Pyramid [1967, c. 1959] 157p. 18cm. (X1674) [BV4908.5.H3] .60 pap.,
1. Peace of mind. I. Title.

HAGGAI, John Edmund. 248
How to win over worry; a practical formula for victorious living. Grand Rapids, Zondervan Pub. House [1959] 179p. 21cm. [BV4908.5.H3] 59-4286
1. Peace of mind. I. Title.

HERTZ, Richard C 296
Prescription for heartache. [1st ed.] New York, Pageant Press [1958] 138p. 21cm. [BM723.H4] 58-14132
1. Peace of mind. I. Title.

IRALA, Narciso. 248'.48'2
Achieving peace of heart. Translated by Lewis Delmage. Rev. and enl. St. Meinrad, Ind., Abbey Press, 1973 [c1969] 254 p. illus. 18 cm. (A Priority edition) Translation of Control cerebral y emocional. Includes bibliographical references. [BF637.P3I713 1973] 73-157907 1.95 (pbk.)
1. Peace of mind. I. Title.

MANN, Stella Terrill 248
How to analyze and overcome your fears. New York [Apollo Eds., 1965, c.1962] vii, 179p. 20cm. (A113) [BV4908.5.M33] 1.50 pap.,
1. Peace of mind. I. Title.

MANN, Stella Terrill. 248
How to analyze and overcome your fears. New York, Dodd, Mead [1962] 179p. 21cm. [BV4908.5.M33] 61-15984
1. Peace of mind. I. Title.

MAX, Peter, 1937- 210
Peace. [With the words of Swami Sivananda, Himalayas]. Editorial assistance by Arjuna (Victor Zurbel). New York, Morrow, 1970. [31] p. col., illus., 15 cm. [BV4908.5.M34] 75-118293 1.95
1. Peace of mind. 2. Peace (Theology) I. Sivananda, Swami. II. Title.

MAX, Peter, 1937- 210
Thought. [With the words of Swami Sivananda, Himalayas]. Editorial assistance by Arjuna (Victor Zurbel). New York, Morrow, 1970. [31] p. col. illus. 15 cm. [BF637.P3S55] 78-118291 1.95
1. Peace of mind. I. Sivananda, Swami. II. Title.

MAXWELL, Arthur Stanley, 1896- 248.42
Courage for the crisis: strength for today, hope for tomorrow; how to find peace of mind and fortitude of spirit for the dangerous days ahead. Mountain View, Calif., Pacific Press Pub. Association [1962] 258p. illus. 18cm. [BV4908.5.M35] 62-7223
1. Peace of mind. I. Title.

MESERVE, Harry C 248
No peace of mind. [1st ed.] New York, Harcourt, Brace [1958] 181p. 21cm. [BV4908.5.M4] 58-10902
1. Peace of mind. I. Title.

MURRAY, Andrew, 1828-1917. 248
The inner chamber and the inner life, by the Rev. Andrew Murray, D. D. New York, Chicago [etc.] Fleming H. Revell company [c1905] 170 p. 20 cm. "The most of these chapters have already appeared in the South African pioneer."--Pref. [BV4501.M8 I 5] 5-29967
I. Title.

PEALE, Norman Vincent, 1898- 248
The power of positive thinking. Designed by Gene Galasso. Norwalk, Conn., C. R. Gibson Co. [1970, c1956] 105 p. 22 cm. "Especially condensed for this Gift Edition." [BF637.P3P42 1970] 75-130444 ISBN 0-8378-1786-2 3.50
1. Peace of mind. I. Title.

PENTECOST, Dorothy Harrison. 242
My pursuit of peace. Chicago, Moody Press [1962] 253p. 22cm. [BV4908.5.P45] 62-52075
1. Peace of mind. I. Title.

ROBERTS, Oral 248.2
God is a good God; believe it and come alive. Indianapolis, Bobbs-Merrill [c.1960] 188p. (col front.) 23cm. 60-7419 2.95 bds.,
1. Peace of mind. I. Title.

ROSENFIELD, Joe. 248
Have no fear, [1st ed.] New York, Citadel Press [1959] 102p. illus. 21cm. [BV4908.5.R6] 59-11133
1. Peace of mind. 2. Happiness exchange (Radio program) I. Title.

SAMUEL, William. 131.3'2
A guide to awareness and tranquillity; a practical blueprint for immediate peace of mind and sufficiency. [1st ed.] Mountain Brook, Ala., Mountain Brook [1967] ix, 290p. 21cm. [BV4908.5.S2] 67-29799 6.95
1. Peace of mind. 2. Awareness. 3. Quietude. I. Title.
Distributed by Banner Pr., Brimingham, Ala.

SCHULLER, Robert H. 248'.3
Peace of mind through possibility thinking / Robert H. Schuller. 1st ed. Garden City, N.Y. : Doubleday, 1977. 168 p. ; 22 cm. [BV4908.5.S37] 72-76203 ISBN 0-385-00673-X : 6.95
1. Peace of mind. I. Title.

SCHULLER, Robert H. 248'.3
Peace of mind through possibility thinking / Robert H. Schuller. 1st ed. New York : Harcourt Brace Jovanovich 191p. ; 18 cm. (A jove HBJ Book) [BV4908.5.S37] ISBN 0-515-04784-8 pbk. : 1.95
1. Peace of mind I. Title.
L.C. card no. for 1977 Doubleday ed.: 72-76203

SCHULLER, Robert H. 248'.3
Peace of mind through possibility thinking / Robert H. Schuller. New York : Jove Pubns., 1979,c1977. 191p. ; 18 cm. (A Jove/HBJ book) [Bv4908.5.S37] ISBN 0-515-04784-8 pbk. : 1.95
1. Peace of mind. I. Title.
L.C. card no. 1977 Doubleday ed.:72-76203.

SELECMAN, Charles C. 220
Christ or chaos, by Charles C. Selecman... Nashville, Tenn., Cokesbury press, 1923. 88 p. 20 1/2 cm. [BR125.S38] 23-15366
I. Title.

WHEELER, Joseph Clyde. 242
Light for dark days. St. Louis, Bethany Press [1961] 124 p. 17 cm. [BV4908.5.W48] 61-11932
1. Peace of mind. I. Title.

WHEELER, Joseph Clyde. 248
Winning what you want. St. Louis, Bethany Press [1960] 156 p. 21 cm. [BV4908.5.W5] 60-6229
1. Peace of mind. I. Title.

WOODS, Bobby W. 242.4
God's answer to anxiety [by] B. W. Woods. Nashville, Broadman Press [1968] 127 p. 20 cm. Bibliographical references included in "Notes" (p. 124-127) [BV4908.5.W66] 68-20687
1. Peace of mind. I. Title.

Peace—Societies, etc.—History—20th century.

MCNEAL, Patricia F. 261.8'73'06273
The American Catholic peace movement, 1928-1972 / Patricia F. McNeal. New York : Arno Press, 1978, c1974. 326 p. ; 24 cm. (The American Catholic tradition) Originally presented as the author's thesis, Temple University, 1974. Bibliography: p. 313-320. [JX1952.M184 1978] 77-11297 ISBN 0-405-10840-0 : 20.00
1. Peace—Societies, etc.—History—20th century. 2. Catholic Church and world politics—History—20th century. I. Title. II. Series.

Peace—Study and teaching.

FENWICK, Charles Ghequiere, 1880-
A catholic primer on world peace, prepared by Charles G. Fenwick... Washington, D.C., National council of Catholic women, 1937. cover-title, 58, [2] p. 19 cm. Published also by the Catholic association for international peace, 1937, under title: A primer of peace. "Suggested readings for further study": p. 56-58. [JX196.1.F34] A 40
1. Peace—Study and teaching. 2. Peace—[Handbooks] I. Title.

MCPHERSON, Imogene McCrary, Mrs. 172.4
Educating children for peace, [by] Imogene M. McPherson... New York, Cincinnati [etc.] The Abingdon press [c1936] 109 p. incl. front. illus. 21 1/2 cm. Frontispiece accompanied by leaf with descriptive letterpress. An account of the experiment in peace education conducted in the daily vacation Bible schools of New York by the Peace action committee of the Greater New York federation of churches at the request of the Carnegie endowment for international peace. cf. Pref. Includes hymns (words and music) "The dramatic peace festivals": p. 72-136. "Sources": p. 187-190. [JX1936.25] 36-1154
1. Peace—Study and teaching. 2. Peace—Drama. 3. Pageants-New York (City) 4. Vacation schools, Religious. I. Greater New York federation of churches. II. Title.

MCPHERSON, Imogene McCrary, Mrs. 268.61
Learning about war and peace, a textbook for juniors in vacation chruch schools, by Imogene M. McPherson... St. Louis, Mo., Pub. for the Interdenominational committee on co- operative publication of vacation church school curiculum by the Bethany press [c1937] 183 p. 22 cm. (The co-operative series of church school texts) Includes music. "Book lists": p. 179-183. [JX1953.M335] [172.404714] 37-13360
1. Peace—Study and teaching. 2. War. 3. Vacation schools, Religious—Text-books. I. Title.

Peace (Theology)

CATHOLIC Church. Pope, 1958-1963 261.7
Peace on earth; an encyclical letter of His Holiness Pope John XXIII. Photos. by

Magnum. [Editors: Jerry Mason and Fred R. Sammis] New York, Ridge Press/Odyssey Press [1964] 159 p. illus. 30 cm. "Footnotes": p. 158-159. [BX1793.A253 1964] 64-25011
1. Peace (Theology) 2. Christianity—20th century. 3. Christianity and politics. I. Mason, Jerry, ed. II. Sammis, Fred R., ed. III. Magnum Photos, Inc.

CATHOLIC Church. Pope, 1958- 261.7 1963(Joannesxxiii)Pacem,interris(11Apr.1 963)English
Pacem in terris. Peace on earth; encyclical letter of Pope John xxiii. Ed. for class and study-group use, with topical outline, selected reading list, commentary, and questions for discussion. [New York] America Pr. [1963] 80p. 19cm. Cover title. Text in English. 63-4376 .50 pap.,
1. Peace (Theology) 2. Christianity—20th cent. 3. Christianity and politics. I. Title.

CATHOLIC Church. Pope 261.7 (Joannes XXIII), 1958-1963(Joannesxxiii)P minterris(11Apr.1963)English. Pacem Terris (11 Apr. 1963) English
Pacem in terris. Peace on Earth; encyclical letter of His Holiness Pope John xxiii. [English tr. from Latin] Ed. by William J. Gibbons. With study-club outline. New York, Paulist Pr. [c.1963] 80p. 18cm. (Deus bk.) Bibl. 63-4423 .35 pap.,
1. Peace (Theology) 2. Christianity—20th cent. 3. Christianity and politics. I. Gibbons, William Joseph. 1912- ed. II. Title.

CATHOLIC Church. Pope 261.7 (Joannes XXIII), 1958-1963(JoannesXXII aceminterris(11Apr.1963)English. Pacem In Terris (11 Apr 1963) English
Pacem in terris. Peace on earth; encyclical letter of His Holiness Pope John XXIII. Edited by William J. Gibbons. With study-club outline. New York, Paulist Press [1963] 80 p. 18 cm. Text in English. "Selected references": p. 78-80. [BX1793.A253 1963a] 63-4423
1. Peace (Theology) 2. Christianity — 20th cent. 3. Christianity and politics. I. Gibbons, William Joseph, 1912- ed. II. Title.

CATHOLIC Church, Pope (Joannes XXIII) 1958-1963(JoannesXXIII)Pacemin ris(11Apr.1963)English. Pacem In Terris (11 Apr. 1963) English
Peace on earth. Pacem in terris; encyclical letter of His Holiness Pope John XXIII,addressed to all mankind. [Boston, Daughters of St. Paul, 1963] 61 p. 18 cm. (St. Paul editions) "N.C.W.C. translation." Includes bibliographical references. 64-65899
1. Peace (Theology) 2. Christianity — 20th cent. 3. Christianity and politics. I. Title.

CHURCH Peace Mission. 241.6'24
Church Peace Mission pamphlet. 1- Washington, 1963- v. 21 cm. Vol. 1 is a reissue; first published in 1950. [BT736.4.C5] 65-5754
1. Peace (Theology) I. Title.

CRAWFORD, Florence Gloria. 265.
The Christ ideal for world peace, by Florence Gloris Crawford. San Francisco, Calif., The Comforter league of light [c1925] 7 p. l., 11-289 p. 21 cm. [BR115.P4C7] 25-5629
I. Title.

DOUGLASS, James W. 261.8'73
The non-violent cross; a theology of revolution and peace, by James W. Douglass. New York, Macmillan [1968] xv, 301 p. 21 cm. Includes bibliographical references. [BT736.4.D6 1968] 68-31276
1. Peace (Theology) I. Title.

DRESCHER, John M. 261.8'73
Why I am a conscientious objector / John M. Drescher ; introdcution by Myron S. Augsburger. Scottdale, Pa. : Herald Press, 1982. 73 p. ; 20 cm. (A Christian peace shelf selection) Bibliography: p. 65-73. [BT736.4.D66 1982] 19 82-894 ISBN 0-8361-1993-2 (pbk.) : 3.55
1. Peace (Theology) I. Title. II. Series.

EPP, Frank H., 1929- 261.8'73
A strategy for peace: reflections of a Christian pacifist, by Frank H. Epp. Grand Rapids, Eerdmans [1973] 128 p. 21 cm. Includes bibliographical references. [BT736.4.E66] 73-2290 ISBN 0-8028-1516-2 2.45 (pbk.)
1. Peace (Theology) I. Title. II. Title: Reflections of a Christian pacifist.
Contents omitted.

FRANCK, Sebastian, 1499- 241.6'24 1542.
Krieg Buchlin des Friedes / Sebastian Franck. Hildesheim ; New York : G. Olms, 1975. 307 leaves ; 15 cm. Reprint of the 1550 ed. by C. Jacob, Frankfurt. [BT736.4.F68 1975] 75-507198 ISBN 3-487-05381-0
1. Peace (Theology) 2. War and religion. 3. Alcoholism. I. Title.

GRAY, Arthur Herbert, 1868- 248
The secret of inward peace. New York, Macmillan Co., 1948. 159 p. 20 cm. [BR115.P4G68 1948] 48-4586
1. Peace (Theology) I. Title.

GUILD, Daniel R 248.42
We can have peace; victorious living in tumultuous times. Mountain View, Calif., Pacific Press Pub. Association [1960] 170p. 23cm. [BV4908.5.G84] 60-16413
1. Peace (Theology) I. Title.

HERSHBERGER, Guy 261.8'73 Franklin, 1896-
War, peace, and nonresistance. [3d ed., rev.] Scottdale, Pa., Herald Press [1969] xvi, 382 p. 23 cm. Includes bibliographical references. [BT736.4.H47 1969] 72-8199 5.00
1. Peace (Theology) 2. Mennonites—History. 3. Pacifism. I. Title.

IRONSIDE, Henry Allan, 1876- 248
The way of peace, by Harry A. Ironside ... New York, American tract society [c1940] 202 p. 20 1/2 cm. [BV4647.P35 I 7] 40-13567
1. Peace (Theology) I. Title.

JOHNS, Hazel T., 1920- 261.8
Peaceworld / Hazel T. Johns, Michael McIntyre, Sister Luke Tobin ; cartoons by Claudius. New York : Friendship Press, 1976. p. cm. Includes bibliographical references. [BT736.4.J63] 76-12410 ISBN 0-377-00054-X pbk. : 2.50
1. Peace (Theology) 2. Violence—Moral and religious aspects. 3. Nonviolence—Moral and religious aspects. 4. Peace. I. McIntyre, Michael, 1942- joint author. II. Tobin, Luke, 1908- joint author. III. Title.

LASANCE, Francis Xavier, 242 1860-
Peace; reflections on a Christian's peace with God, with every neighbor, and within himself, consoling thoughts on divine providence and conformity to the will of God, compiled and edited by Rev. F. X. Lasance ... New York, Cincinnati [etc.] Benziger brothers, 1938. viii, 9-128 p. incl. front., illus. 16 cm. [BX2182.L33] 38-11597
1. Peace (Theology) 2. Providence and government of God. 3. Devotional literature. I. Title.

LEE, Frederick. 248
Thoughts of peace. Washington, Review and Herald Pub. Association [1950] 95 p. 20 cm. [BV4647.P35L4] 50-4999
1. Peace (Theology) I. Title.

MACQUARRIE, John. 261.8'73
The concept of peace. [1st U.S. ed.] New York, Harper & Row [1973] 82 p. 21 cm. Includes bibliographical references. [BT736.4.M25 1973] 73-6325 ISBN 0-06-065365-5 4.95
1. Peace (Theology) I. Title.

MILLER, Ella May. 248'.48'97
The peacemakers : how to find peace and share it / Ella May Miller. Old Tappen, N.J. : F. H. Revell, c1977. 179 p. ; 21 cm. [BT736.4.M5] 77-1625 ISBN 0-8007-0865-2 : 6.95
1. Peace (Theology) 2. Christian life—Mennonite authors. I. Title.

MUSTE, Abraham John, 261.8'73 1885-1967.
Not by might; Christianity: the way to human decency, and Of holy disobedience. With a new introd. for the Garland ed. by Jo Ann Robinson. New York, Garland Pub., 1971 [i.e. 1972, c1947] 15, xiii, 227, 34 p. 23 cm. (The Garland library of war and peace) Reprint of 2 works first published in 1947 and 1952 respectively. [BT736.4.M88] 70-147628 ISBN 0-8240-0403-5
1. Peace (Theology) 2. Conscientious objectors. 3. Pacifism. I. Muste, Abraham John, 1885-1967. Of holy disobedience. 1971. II. Title. III. Title: Of holy disobedience. IV. Series.

[REES, Janet Emily (Meagens) Ruutz] Mrs., 1842-
The threefold path to peace, written down by Xena and dedicated to disciples. New York, The Grafton press [1904] 60 p. 19 cm. 4-30178
I. Title.

RUSSELL, Chester. 261.8'73
Was Jesus a pacifist? Nashville, Tenn., Broadman Press [1971] 96 p. 21 cm. Includes bibliographies. [BT736.4.R87] 72-145987 ISBN 0-8054-5511-6 2.95
1. Peace (Theology) I. Title.

SNOW, Michael. 261.8'73
Christian pacifism : fruit of the narrow way / Michael Snow. Richmond, Ind. : Friends United Press, c1981. xiii, 96 p. : ill. ; 22 cm. Includes bibliographical references. [BT736.4.S65] 19 81-69724 ISBN 0-913408-67-0 (pbk.) : 6.95
1. Snow, Michael. 2. Peace (Theology) I. Title.

STOTTS, Jack L. 261.8'73
Shalom: the search for a peaceable city. Nashville, Abingdon [1973] 224 p. 21 cm. Includes bibliographical references. [BT736.4.S85] 72-6970 ISBN 0-687-38324-2 5.95
1. Peace (Theology) I. Title.

WENGER, John Christian, 261.8'73 1910-
The way of peace / J. C. Wenger. Scottdale, Pa. : Herald Press, [1977] 70 p. ; 18 cm. (Mennonite faith series ; 4) Bibliography: p. 69-70. [BT736.4.W42] 77-86349 ISBN 0-8361-1835-9 pbk. : 0.75
1. Peace (Theology) I. Title. II. Series.

THE Witness of U.S. 261.8'73
Lutherans on peace, war, conscience : prepared for the Division for Parish Services of the Lutheran Church in America, the Division for Life and Mission in the Congregation of the American Lutheran Church, and the Board of Parish Education of the Lutheran Church—Missouri Synod / John E. Schramm, consultant ; Hartland H. Gifford, editor .... [Minneapolis] : Augsburg Pub. House, [1975] 32 p. : ill. ; 28 cm. Cover title: Peace, war, conscience. Caption title. Bibliography: p. 32. [BT736.4.W55] 75-308067
1. Lutheran Church—Doctrinal and controversial works. 2. Peace (Theology) 3. War and religion. 4. Conscience. I. Schramm, John, 1931- II. Gifford, Hartland H. III. Lutheran Church in America. Division for Parish Services. IV. American Lutheran Church (1961-) Division for Life and Mission. V. Lutheran Church—Missouri Synod. Board of Parish Education.

Peace (Theology)—Addresses, essays, lectures.

ON earth peace : 261.8'73
discussions on war/peace issues between Friends, Mennonites, Brethren, and European churches, 1935-75 / edited by Donald F. Durnbaugh. Elgin, Ill. : Brethren Press, c1978. 412 p. : ill. ; 22 cm. Includes bibliographical references and index. [BT736.4.O5] 78-538 ISBN 0-87178-660-5 : 9.95
1. Peace (Theology)—Addresses, essays, lectures. I. Durnbaugh, Donald F.

PEACE! Peace! 261.8'73
Waco, Tex., Word Books [1967] 162 p. 21 cm. Chapters were first presented at conferences sponsored by the Christian Life Commission of the Southern Baptist Convention, and held in Glorieta, N.M., and Ridgecrest, N.C. Bibliographical footnotes. [BT736.4.P4] 67-23975
1. Peace (Theology)—Addresses, essays, lectures. I. Valentine, Foy, ed. II. Southern Baptist Convention. Christian Life Commission.

Peace (Theology)—Biblical teaching.

ENZ, Jacob J. 261.8'73
The Christian and warfare; the roots of pacifism in the Old Testament, by Jacob J. Enz. Scottdale, Pa., Herald Press [1972] 95 p. 18 cm. (Christian peace shelf series, 3) "Substance of the Menno Simons Lectures as originally delivered at Bethel College, North Newton, Kansas, in 1957." Includes bibliographical references. [BS680.P4E59] 72-192756 ISBN 0-8361-1684-4
1. Peace (Theology)—Biblical teaching. I. Title.

Peace (Theology)—Caricatures and cartoons.

CAGIATI, Annie. 248'.4
Peace-where is it? / by Annie Cagiati ; illustrated by C. Piccinni. Boston : St. Paul Editions, [1974] ca. 100 p. : chiefly ill. ; 18 cm. [BT736.4.C3] 73-91996
1. Peace (Theology)—Caricatures and cartoons. I. Piccinni, C., ill. II. Title.

Peace (Theology)—Prayer-books and devotions—English.

RANDOLPH, David James, 1934- 264 comp.
Peace plus : worship resources for peace and justice / edited by David James Randolph. Nashville : Tidings, [1974] 68 p. ; 21 cm. [BT736.4.R35] 74-80891 pbk. : 1.25
1. Peace (Theology)—Prayer-books and devotions—English. 2. Worship programs. I. Title.

Peace (Theology)—Study and teaching.

GRANNIS, J. Christopher. 261.8'73
The risk of the cross : Christian discipleship in the nuclear age / J. Christopher Grannis, Arthur J. Laffin, Elin Schade. New York : Seabury Press, 1981. xiv, 110 p. : ill. ; 21 cm. Bibliography: p. 108-109. [BT736.4.G69] 19 80-29281 ISBN 0-8164-2305-9 (pbk.) : 5.95
1. Bible. N.T. Mark—Study. 2. Peace (Theology)—Study and teaching. 3. Atomic warfare—Moral and religious aspects. I. Laffin, Arthur J., joint author. II. Schade, Elin, joint author. III. Title.

Peacock, Aubrey Eckert Lawrence, 1882-1924.

LAWRENCE, Ida (Eckert) Mrs. 133. 1864- ed.
Aubrey messages; evidence of life, memory, affection after the change called death ... Los Angeles, Calif., The Austin publishing company, 1928. 212 p. front., ports. 21 cm. [BF1311.P4L3] 29-4338
1. Peacock, Aubrey Eckert Lawrence, 1882-1924. 2. Spiritualism. I. Title.

Peale, Norman Vincent, 1898-

BROADHURST, Allan R. 201
He speaks the word of God; a study of the sermons of Norman Vincent Peale. Englewood Cliffs, N.J., Prentice-Hall [1963] 106 p. 24 cm. Includes bibliography. [BX9543.P4B7] 63-8280
1. Peale, Norman Vincent, 1898- I. Title.

GORDON, Arthur. 287'.1'0924 B
One man's way; the story and message of Norman Vincent Peale, a biography. Rev. and enl. ed. of Minister to millions. Englewood Cliffs, N.J., Prentice-Hall [1972] 324 p. illus. 21 cm. Published in 1958 under title: Norman Vincent Peale; minister to millions. [BX9543.P4G6 1972] 72-3311 ISBN 0-13-636084-X 5.95
1. Peale, Norman Vincent, 1898- I. Title.

PEALE, Norman Vincent, 248.4 1898-
The positive power of Jesus Christ / Norman Vincent Peale. Wheaton, Ill. : Tyndale House, c1980. 266 p. ; 22 cm. [BV4011.P39] 19 79-67855 ISBN 0-8423-4874-3 : 8.95
1. Peale, Norman Vincent. 2. Pastoral theology—Case studies. 3. Christian life—Reformed authors. I. Title.

WESTPHAL, Clarence 922.573
Norman Vincent Peale, Christian crusader, a biography. Minneapolis, Denison [c.1964] 141p. 22cm. (Men of achievement ser.) [BX9543.P4W4] 64-7703 3.00
1. Peale, Norman Vincent, 1898- I. Title.

WESTPHAL, Clarence. 922.573
Norman Vincent Peale, Christian crusador, a biography. Minneapolis, Denison [1964] 141 p. 22 cm. (Men of achievement series) [BX9543.P4W4] 64-7703
1. Peale, Norman Vincent, 1898- I. Title.

Peapack, N.J. Reformed church.

[THOMPSON, Henry Post] 1831- 1891. 285.
History of the Reformed church at Peapack, N.J., with biographical sketches. Trenton, N.J., W. S. Sharp, printer, 1881. 68 p. 23 cm. "Introduction" signed: Henry P. Thompson. Publication transferred 1881 to Board of publication of the Reformed church in America, New York, whose label covers the imprint. [BX9531.P27T5] 2-849
1. Peapack, N.J. Reformed church. I. Anderson, Charles Thomas, 1849-1932. II. Title.
Contents omitted.

Pearce, Samuel, 1766-1799.

FULLER, Andrew, 1754- 1815. 922.642
Memoirs of the late Rev. Samuel Pearce, A. M., with extracts from some of his most interesting letters. Compiled by Andrew fuller, D. D. To which are added. An oration, delivered at the grave by the Rev. J. Brewer. A funeral sermon on his death, by J. Ryland, D. D. An elegy, by Benjamin Francis, A. M.; together with The memoirs of Mrs. Pearce. and extracts from letters. 3d American ed. ... Philadelphia: Published by John Hellings, 1809. Dickinson, printer- -Whitehall. 3 p. l., [x]-xi [13]-288 p. front. (port.) 18 cm. "A funeral sermon on his death" (p. [209]-251) has special t.-p. Imperfect: p. 193-194 mutilated. [BX6495.P4F8 1809] 33-19155
1. Pearce, Samuel, 1766-1799. 2. Pearce, Mrs. Sarah (Hopkins) 1771-1804. 3. Funeral sermons. I. Ryland, John, 1753-1825. II. Brewer, Jehoiada, 1752?-1817. III. Francis, Benjamin, 1734-1799. IV. Title.

FULLER, Andrew, 1754-1815. 920.
Memoirs of the late Rev. Samuel Pearce, A. M., with extracts from some of his most interesting letters. To which is added, a brief memoir of Mrs. Pearce. Comp. by Andrew Fuller, D. D. Philadelphia, American Sunday school union, 1829. iv, [5]-162 p. front. (port.) 14 cm. [BX6495.P4F8] 5-12583
1. Pearce, Samuel, 1766-1799. 2. Pearce, Mrs. Sarah (Hopkins) d. 1804. I. Title.

FULLER, Andrew, 1754- 1815. 922.642
Memoirs of the late Rev. Samuel Pearce ... with extracts from some of his most interesting letters. Compiled by Andrew Fuller d. d. To which is added an oration, delivered at the grave: a sermon, occasioned by the death of the Rev. Samuel Pearce, A. M., and three occasional sermons ... 3d American ed. Newark. N. J., Printed by E. B. Gould. 1809. vi, [7]-180, 124 p. 18 cm. "A sermon, occassioned by the death of the Rev. Samuel Pearce", by John Ryland, has special t.-p. and separate paging. [BX6495.P4F8 1809 a] 33-20032
1. Pearce, Samuel, 1766-1799. 2. Funeral sermons. 3. Baptists—Sermons. I. Ryland, John, 1753-1835. II. Title.

Pearl of great price (Parable)— Sermons.

PRICE, Daniel, 1581-1631. 226'.8
The marchant : a sermon / Daniel Price. Amsterdam : Theatrum Orbis Terrarum ; Norwood, N.J. : W. J. Johnson, 1979. 38 p. ; 21 cm. (The English experience, its record in early printed books published in facsimile ; no. 951) Photoreprint of the 1608 ed. printed by J. Barnes, Oxford. STC 20296. [BT378.P4P74 1979] 19 79-84133 ISBN 90-221-0951-8 pbk. : 6.00
1. Church of England—Sermons. 2. Pearl of great price (Parable)—Sermons. 3. Merchants—Religious life—Sermons. 4. Sermons, English. I. Title. II. Series: English experience, its record in early printed books published in facsimile ; no. 951.

Pearse, Joseph, 1837-1911.

MOSS, Charles Frederick Arrowsmith. 266'.023'0924 B
A pioneer in Madagascar, Joseph Pearse of the L.M.S., by C. F. A. Moss. New York, Negro Universities Press [1969] xvi, 261 p. illus., map, ports. 23 cm. Reprint of the 1913 ed. [BV3625.M22P4 1969] 70-98738
1. Pearse, Joseph, 1837-1911. 2. Missions—Madagascar. I. Title.

Pearson, Carol Lynn.

PEARSON, Carol Lynn. 289.3'3 B
Will I ever forget this day? : Excerpts / from the diaries of Carol Lynn Pearson ; edited by Elouise M. Bell. Salt Lake City, Utah : Bookcraft, c1980. 130 p. : ill. ; 24 cm. [BX8695.P42A38] 79-54897 ISBN 0-88494-390-9 pbk. : 5.50
1. Pearson, Carol Lynn. 2. Mormons and Mormonism in the United States—Biography. I. Bell, Elouise M. II. Title.

Peasants' War, 1524-1525.

CROSSLEY, Robert N., 1924- 943'.031
Luther and the peasants' war; Luther's actions and reactions [by] Robert N. Crossley. New York, Exposition Press [1974] xii, 164 p. 21 cm. (An Exposition-university book) Bibliography: p. 155-162. [BR326.6.C76] 73-92849 ISBN 0-682-47890-3 8.00
1. Luther, Martin, 1483-1546. 2. Peasants' War, 1524-1525. I. Title.

KIRCHNER, Hubert. 943'.031
Luther and the Peasants' War. Translated by Darrell Jodock. Philadelphia, Fortress Press [1972] vii, 40 p. (p. 37-40 advertisement) 20 cm. (Facet books. Historical series (Reformation) 22) Originally appeared in the 1967 Lutheran World Federation conference proceedings which were published under title: Reformation heute. Bibliography: p. 35-36. [BR326.6.K57] 73-171507 ISBN 0-8006-3068-8 1.00
1. Luther, Martin, 1483-1546. 2. Peasants' War, 1524-1525. I. Title.

Pebbles, James Martin, 1822-1922.

BARRETT, Joseph O. 920.9
The spiritual pilgrim: a biography of James M. Pebbles By J. O. Barrett ... 2d ed. Boston, W. White and company, 1872. 303 p. front. (port.) 22 cm. [BF1283.P4B3 1872] 32-5794
1. Pebbles, James Martin, 1822-1922. 2. Spiritualism. I. Title.

BARRETT, Joseph O. 133.
The spiritual pilgrim: a biography of James M. Pebbles. By J. O. Barrett ... 3d ed. Boston, W. White and company, 1872. 303 p. front. (port.) 22 cm. [BF1283.P4B] A 23
1. Pebbles, James Martin, 1822-1922. 2. Spiritualism. I. Title.

BARRETT, Joseph O. 920.9
The spiritual pilgrim: a biography of James M. Pebbles. By J. O. Barrett ... 4th ed. Boston. Colby & Rich. 1872. 303 p. front. (port.) 22 cm. [BF1283.P4 B3 1878] 32-4056
1. Pebbles, James Martin, 1822-1922. 2. Spiritualism. I. Title.

Peck, Edmund James, 1850-

LEWIS, Arthur
Life and work of the Rev. E. J. Peck among the Eskimos, by the Rev. Arthur Lewis... New York, A. C. Armstrong & son, 1904. xvi, 349, [1] p. front. (port.) plates. 20 cm. A22
1. Peck, Edmund James, 1850- 2. Eskimos. I. Title.

Peck, John Mason, 1789-1858.

HAYNE, Coe Smith, 1875- 922.673
Vanguard of the caravans; a life-story of John Mason Peck, by Coe Hayne ... Edited by the Department of missionary education, Board of education of the Northern Baptist convention ... Philadelphia, Boston [etc.] The Judson press [1931] 5 p. l., 157 p. front., plates, ports. 20 1/2 cm. Bibliography: p. [153]-157. [F353.P38] 31-19630
1. Peck, John Mason, 1789-1858. 2. Missions—Mississippi valley. 3. Baptists—Missions. 4. Frontier and pioneer life—Mississippi valley. I. Northern Baptist convention. Board of education. II. Title.

Peck, William Jay, 1853-1920.

MOORE, Helen (Peck) 1899- 922.573
William Jay Peck, a shepherd's heart. Narberth, Pa., Livingston Pub. Co., 1957. 84p. illus. 24cm. [BX7260.P46M6] 57-14828
1. Peck, William Jay, 1853-1920. I. Title.

Peckham, John. Abp. of Canterbury. d. 1292.

DOUIE, Decima Langworthy, 1901- 922.342
Archbishop Pecham. Oxford, Clarendon Press, 1952. 362p. 23cm. [BR754.P4D67] 53-546
1. Peckham, John. Abp. of Canterbury. d. 1292. I. Title.

Pecock, Reginald, 1305?-1400?

GREEN, Vivian Hubert Howard. 922.242
Bishop Reginald Pecock; a study in ecclesiastical history and thought, by V. H. H. Green ... Cambridge [Eng.] The University press, 1945. viii, 261, [1] p. 19 1/2 cm. (Thirlwall prize, 1941) Bibliography: p. [250]-254. [BX4705.P4G7] 45-10018
1. Pecock, Reginald, 1305?-1400? I. Title.

LEWIS, John, 1675-1747. 922.
The life of the learned and Right Reverend Reynold Pecock, S.T.P., local bishop of St. Asaph, and Chichester, in the reign of King Henry VI. Faithfully collected from records and mss. Being a sequel of The Life of Dr. John Wielif, in order to an introduction to the history of the English reformation. By John Lewis ... A new ed. Oxford, The Clarendon press, 1820. 1 p. l., vii, 235, [2] p. pl. 21 1/2 cm. [BX4705.P4L4 1820] 12-36174
1. Pecock, Reginald, 1395?-1400? I. Title.

Peden, Alexander, 1626?-1686.

[WALKER, Patrick] 1666?- 1745? 922.
Some remarkable passages of the life and death of Mr. Alexander Peden ... From the 4th Aberdeen ed. ... Pittsburgh, Printed for Alexander M'Queen, by Robert Ferguson and co. 1815. xxx, [33]-276 p. 17 1/2 cm. Includes also the lives of John Semple, James Welwood, Richard Cameron, John Welsh and Robert Bruce. [BX9220.W33] 42-33825
1. Peden, Alexander, 1626?-1686. 2. Semple, John, d. 1677? 3. Welwood, John, 1649?-1679. 4. Cameron, Richard, 1655?-1680. 5. Welsh, John, 1568?-1622. 6. Bruce, Robert, 1554-1631. I. Title.

Pedro de Alcantara, Saint, 1499-1562.

ROBERTO, Brother, 1927- 922.246
Peter laughed at pain; a story of St. Peter of Alcantara. Illus. by William Pero. Notre Dame, Ind., Dujarie Press1[1956] 96p. illus. 24cm. [BX4700.P362R6] 56-42844
1. Pedro de Alcantara, Saint, 1499-1562. I. Title.

Peer counseling in the church.

BURCHETT, Harold Ewing. 248'.07
People helping people / by Harold Ewing Burchett. Chicago : Moody Press, c1979. 127 p. (p. 123-127 blank for "Notes") : ill. ; 22 cm. [BV4409.B87] 78-21546 ISBN 0-8024-6457-2 : 6.95
1. Peer counseling in the church. 2. Christian life—Baptist authors. I. Title.

HART, Thomas N. 253.5
The art of Christian listening / by Thomas N. Hart. New York : Paulist Press, c1980. 128 p. ; 21 cm. Includes bibliographies. [BV4409.H37] 19 80-82810 ISBN 0-8091-2345-2 (pbk.) : 4.95
1. Peer counseling in the church. 2. Helping behavior. 3. Listening. I. Title.

MILLER, Paul M. 259
Peer counseling in the church / Paul M. Miller ; introd. by Wayne W. Oates. Scottdale, Pa. : Herald Press, 1978. 166 p. ; 20 cm. Bibliography: p. 163-166. [BV4409.M54] 78-9299 ISBN 0-8361-1854-5 : pbk. : 4.95
1. Peer counseling in the church. I. Title.

Peerman, Frank.

PEERMAN, Frank. 248'.86 B
See you in the morning / Frank Peerman. Nashville : Broadman Press, c1976. 94 p. ; 20 cm. [BJ1487.P4] 76-5296 ISBN 0-8054-5237-0 : 3.50
1. Peerman, Frank. 2. Grief. 3. Baptists—Biography. I. Title.

Peet, Josiah. 1780-1852.

SHEPLEY, David, 1804- 1881. 922.573
Memoir, with sermons, of Rev. Josiah Peet. By Rev. David Shepley ... New York, J. F. Trow, printer, 1854. 5 p. l., [7]-344 p. front. (port.) plates. 28 1/2 cm. [BX7260.P4785] 36-28601
1. Peet, Josiah. 1780-1852. 2. Congregational churches—Sermons. 3. Sermons, American. I. Title.

Pegasus—Juvenile literature.

HAWTHORNE, Nathaniel, 1804- 1864 292
Pegasus, the winged horse; a Greek myth retold by Nathaniel Hawthorne. Introd. by Robert Lowell. Illus. by Herschel Levit. New York, Macmillan, 1963. 39p. col. illus. 34cm. Orig. pub. in the author's A wonder book, under title: The Chimaera. 63-24867 1.95 bds.,
1. Pegasus—Juvenile literature. I. Title.

Peguy, Charles Pierre, 1873-1914.

FOWLIE, Wallace, 1908- 920.044
Jacob's night; the religious renascence in France. New York, Sheed & Ward, 1947. 6 l., 3-116 p. front. 21 cm. Full name: Wallace Adams Fowlie. [DC365.F6] 47-4849
1. Peguy, Charles Pierre, 1873-1914. 2. Rouault, Georges, 1871- 3. Maritain, Jacques, 1882- 4. France—Civilization. I. Title.
Contents omitted.

Peirce, Charles Santiago Sanders, 1839-1914.

BOLER, John Francis. 149.2
Charles Peirce and scholastic realism, a study of Peirce's relation to John Duns Scotus. Seattle, University of Washington Press, 1963. xi, 177 p. 24 cm. Bibliography: p. 167-171. [B945.P44B6] 63-10794
1. Peirce, Charles Santiago Sanders, 1839-1914. 2. Duns, Joannes, Scotus, 1265?-1308? I. Title.

Pelagianism.

LEFF, Gordon. 273.5
Bradwardine and the Pelagians; a study of his 'De causa Dei' and its opponents. Cambridge [Eng.] University Press, 1957. 282p. 23cm. (Cambridge studies in medieval life and thought, new ser., v. 5) Bibliography: p. [269]-273. [BT1450.B73L4] 57-2511
1. Bradwardine, Thomas, Abp. of Canterbury, 1290-1349. De causa Dei. 2. Pelagianism. I. Title. II. Series.

WIGGERS, Gustav Friedrich, 1777-1860.
An historical presentation of Augustinism and Pelagianism from the original sources, by G. F. Wiggers ... Translated from the German, with notes and additions, by Rev. Ralph Emerson ... Andover, New York, Gould, Newman & Saxton, 1840. 383 p. 22 cm Translation of Versuch einer pragmatischen darstellung. [BT1450.W54] 30-14959
1. Pelagianism. 2. Augustinus, Aurelius, Saint, bp. of Hippo. I. Emerson, Ralph, 1787-1863, tr. II. Title. III. Title: Augustinism and Pelagianism.

Pelagius.

EVANS, Robert F. 273'.5
Four letters of Pelagius [by] Robert F. Evans. New York, Seabury Press [1968] 134 p. 24 cm. (Studies in Pelagius) Bibliographical references included in ""Notes" (p. 120-132) [BT1450.E88] 68-11594
1. Pelagius. I. Pelagius. II. Title.

EVANS, Robert F 273'.5
Pelagius; inquiries and reappraisals [by] Robert F. Evans. New York, Seabury Press [1968] xvi, 171 p. 22 cm. Bibliographical references included in ""Notes" (p. [123]-167) [BT1450.E9] 67-20939
1. Pelagius. I. Title.

EVANS, Robert F. 273'.5
Pelagius; inquiries and reappraisals [by] Robert F. Evans. New York, Seabury Press [1968] xvi, 171 p. 22 cm. Bibliographical references included in "Notes" (p. [123]-167) [BT1450.E9 1968] 67-20939
1. Pelagius.

FERGUSON, John, 1921- 273.5
Pelagius; a historical and theological study. Cambridge [Eng.] W. Heffer, 1956. 206p. 22cm. Includes bibliography. [BT1450.F4] 57-4262
1. Pelagius. I. Title.

FERGUSON, John, 1921- 273'.5
Pelagius : a historical and theological study / by John Ferguson. 1st AMS ed. New York : AMS Press, 1978. ix 206 p. ; 23 cm. Reprint of the 1956 ed. published by W. Heffer, Cambridge, Eng. "The writings of Pelagius": p. 186-187. Includes indexes. Bibliography: p.188-192. [BT1450.F4 1978] 77-84700 ISBN 0-404-16107-3 : 20.00
1. Pelagins. 2. Pelagianism.

Pelagius. Commentarii in epistolas States Pauli.

SOUTER, Alexander, 1873- 227
... The character and history of Pelagius' Commentary on the Epistles of St. Paul, by Alexander Souter ... (From the Proceedings of the British academy, vol. VII) London, Pub. for the British academy by H. Milford, Oxford university press [1916] cover-title, 36 p. 3 facsim., diagr. 24 1/2 cm. At head of title: The British academy. "Read March 15, 1916." [BS2635.P4] 19-75
1. Pelagius. Commentarii in epistolas S. Pauli. I. British academy for the promotion of historical, philosophical and philological studies. II. Title.

Pelendo, Isaac.

ANDERSON, Alpha E. 276.75
(Almquist)
Pelendo, God's prophet in the Congo. Minneapolis, 1515 E. 66 St. Free Church Pubns., [c.1964] 175p. illus., ports., maps. 21cm. 64-2732 3.45; 1.95 pap.,
1. Pelendo, Isaac. 2. Missions—Congo (Leopoldville) I. Title.

ANDERSON, Alpha E. 276.75
(Almquist)
Pelendo, God's prophet in the Congo. Chicago, Moody [1967, c.1964] 160p. 18cm. [BV3625.C36P4] .59 pap.,
1. Pelendo, Isaac. 2. Missions—Congo (Leopoldville) I. Title.

ANDERSON, Alpha E 266'.023'
(Almquist)
Pelendo, God's prophet in the Congo. Minneapolis, Free Church Publications [1964] 175 p. illus., ports., maps. 21 cm. [BV3625.C63P4] 64-2732
1. Pelendo, Isaac. 2. Missions — Congo (Leopoldville) I. Title.

Pelletier, Marie de Sainte Euphrasie, Saint, 1796-1868.

BERNOVILLE, Gaetan [Marie Joseph] 922.244
Saint Mary Euphasia Pelletier, foundress of the Good Shepherd Sisters. [Translation from the French] Westminster, Md., Newman Press [1959] 196p. illus. 22cm. 60-47 3.50
1. Pelletier, Marie de Sainte Euphrasie, Saint, 1796-1868. 2. Sisters of Our Lady of Charity of the Good Shepherd. I. Title.

BOARDMAN, Anne (Cawley) 922.244
Good Shepherd's fold; a biography of St. Mary Euphrasia Pelletier, R. G. S., foundress of the Congregation of Our Lady of Charity of the Good Shepherd of Angers. [1st ed.] New York, Harper [c1955] 292p. illus. 22cm. [BX4700.P38B6] 54-12327
1. Pelletler, Arie de Sainte Euphrasie, Saint, 1796-1868. 2. Sisters of Our Lady of Charity of the Good Shepherd. I. Title.

MARY of our lady of the Angels, Sister. 922.244
The little white shepherdess, the story of the life of St. Mary Euphrasia: illustrated by Clifford Hickox, Milwaukee, Tower Press [1950] xviii, 220 p. illus. (part col.) 24 cm. [BX4700.P38M3] 50-11975
1. Pelletier, Marie de Sainte Euphrasie, Saint, I. Title.

Penance.

ANCIAUX, Paul. 265.6
The sacrament of penance. New York, Sheed Ward [1962] 190p. 21cm. [BX2265.A513] 62-52076
1. Penance I. Title.

BARRY, David W. 265'.6
Ministry of reconciliation : modern lessons from scripture and sacrament / David W. Barry. New York : Alba House, [1975] xii, 129 p. ; 21 cm. Includes bibliographical references. [BX2260.B28] 75-4630 ISBN 0-8189-0317-1 pbk. : 2.95
1. Penance. I. Title.

BARTON, John Mackintosh Tilney, 1898- 265.6
Penance and absolution. [1st ed.] New York, Hawthorn Books [1961] 159p. 21cm. (The Twentieth century encylopedia of Catholicism, v. 51. Section 5: The life of Faith) Includes bibilography. [BX2260.B3] 61-12987
1. Penance. I. Title.

BELTON, Francis George. 265.6
A manual for confessors; being a guide to the administration of the sacrament of penance for the use of priests of the English church, by Francis George Belton ... London and Oxford, A. R. Mowbray & co., ltd.; Milwaukee, Morehouse publishing co. [1931] xii, 331, [1] p. 22 cm. "First printed in June, 1916; 2d impression, August, 1916 ... New and revised edition, September, 1931." [BX5149.C6B4 1931] 33-10292
1. Penance. 2. Church of England—Discipline. 3. Confession. I. Title. II. Title: Confessors, A manual for.
Contents omitted.

BUCKLEY, Francis J. 234'.166
"I confess"; the sacrament of Penance today [by] Francis J. Buckley. Notre Dame, Ind., Ave Maria Press [1972] 95 p. illus. 21 cm. Bibliography: p. 95. [BX2260.B8] 72-80971 ISBN 0-87793-048-1 1.25
1. Penance. 2. Confession. I. Title.

CATHOLIC Theological Society of America. Committee on the Renewal of the Sacrament of Penance. 265'.6
Committee report : the renewal of the sacrament of penance / [CTSA Committee on the Renewal of the Sacrament of Penance]. [Washington] : The Society, 1975. 106 p. ; 23 cm. On spine: CTSA committee report. Bibliography: p. 49-95. [BX2260.C28 1975] 76-354199
1. Penance. I. Title. II. Title: The renewal of the sacrament of penance.

DARCY-BERUBE, Francoise. 265'.6
Sacrament of peace, by Francoise Darcy Berube [and] John Paul Berube. [New York, Paulist Press, 1974] 4 v. illus. (part col.) 22 cm. Contents.Contents.—[1] Book 1, for 7 and 8 year old children.—[2] Book 2, for 9 to 12 year old children.—[3] Director's guide.—[4] Parent guide. Discusses the significance of the Sacrament of Penance. [BX2260.D3] 73-92894 4.00 (pbk.)
1. Penance. 2. Penance—Juvenile literature. 3. [Penance.] 4. [Christian life.] I. Berube, John Paul, joint author. II. Title.

DOYLE, Charles Hugo 265.6
Go in peace. Garden City, N. Y., Hanover House [c.1961] 141p. 61-12514 2.95
1. Penance. I. Title.

GUILLOIS, Ambroise, 1796-1856. 265.
The history of confession; or, The dogma of confession vindicated from the attacks of heretics and infidels. Translated from the French of Rev. Ambroise Guillois. By Louis de Goesbriand ... New York, Cincinnati [etc.] Benziger brothers, 1889. 1 p. l., 190 p. 18 cm. Translation of Le dogme de la confession venge. [BX2265.G85] 38-35195
1. Penance. 2. Catholic church.—Discipline. I. De Goesbriand, Louis, bp., 1816-1899, tr. II. Title.

GUNSTONE, John Thomas Arthur.
The liturgy of penance. London, Faith Press; New York, Morehouse-Barlow [1966] 83 p. 19 cm. (Studies in Christian worship, 7) 67-96098
1. Penance. I. Title. II. Series.

GUZIE, Tad W. 265'.6
The forgiveness of sin / by Tad Guzie and John McIlhon. Chicago : Thomas More Press, c1979. viii, 180 p. ; 21 cm. Includes bibliographical references. [BX2260.G85] 79-113331 ISBN 0-88347-103-5 : 9.95
1. Penance. I. McIlhon, John, joint author. II. Title.

HALLIGAN, Francis Nicholas, 1917- 264'.02'008 s
Sacraments of reconciliation: penance, anointing of the sick [by] Nicholas Halligan. Staten Island, N.Y., Alba House [1973] xii, 209 p. 21 cm. (His The ministry of the celebration of the sacraments, v. 2) On spine: Penance, anointing of the sick. Includes bibliographical references. [BX2200.H25 vol. 2] [BX2260] 265'.6 73-9604 ISBN 0-8189-0279-5 3.95
1. Penance. 2. Unction. I. Title. II. Title: Penance, anointing of the sick. III. Series.

HAMELIN, Leonce. 234'.166
Reconciliation in the Church : a theological and pastoral essay on the sacrament of penance / by Leonce Hamelin ; translated by Matthew J. O'Connell. Collegeville, Minn. : Liturgical Press, c1980. p. cm. Translation of La reconciliation en Eglise. Bibliography: p. [BS2260.H18713] 19 80-29328 ISBN 0-8146-1215-6 pbk. : 5.50
1. Penance. 2. Reconciliation. I. Title.

HARING, Bernhard, 1912- 265'.6
Shalom: peace; the sacrament of reconciliation [by] Bernard Haring. New York, Farrar, Straus and Giroux [1968] xii, 308 p. 22 cm. [BX2260.H18] 68-11424
1. Penance. I. Title.

HARING, Bernhard, 1912- 265'.6
Shalom: peace; the sacrament of reconciliation [by] Bernhard Haring. New York, Farrar, Straus and Giroux [1968] xii, 308 p. 22 cm. [BX2260.H18 1968] 68-11424
1. Penance. I. Title.

HARING, Bernhard, 1912- 265'.6
Shalom: peace; the sacrament of reconciliation [by] Bernhard Haring. Rev. ed. Garden City, N.Y., Image Books [1969] 354 p. 19 cm. [BX2260.H18 1969] 72-78750 1.35
1. Penance. I. Title.

HARRINGTON, Henry. 265.
The sacrament of penance, by the Reverend H. Harrington, M. A.; introduction by Very Reverend John F. Fenlon ... New York, The Macmillan company, 1929. vii p., 1 l., 87 p. 17 cm. (Half-title: The treasury of the faith series: 27) [BX2260.H2 1929 a] 29-12638
1. Penance. I. Title.

HEENAN, John Carmel, Bp., 1905- 265.62
Confession. New York, Sheed and Ward [1957?] 95p. 18cm. (Canterbury books) 'An abridged version [i. e. all that is directly on the sacrament of penance from] . . . the same author's Priest and penitent.' [BX2265.H42] 57-4544
1. Penance. I. Title.

HEENAN, John Carmel, Cardinal, 1905- 265.62
Confession. New York, Sheed and Ward [1957?] 95 p. 18 cm. (Canterbury books) "An abridged version [i.e. all that is directly of the sacrament of penance from] ... the same author's Priest and penitent." [BX2265.H42] 57-4544
1. Penance. I. Title.

HEGGEN, Franz J. 265'.62
Confession and the service of penance [by] F. J. Heggen. Translated by Peter Tomlinson. [1st American ed.] Notre Dame [Ind.] University of Notre Dame Press [1968, c1967] 176 p. 21 cm. Translation of Boeteviering en private biecht. Bibliographical footnotes. [BX2260.H413 1968] 67-31394
1. Penance. I. Title.

HUNOLT, Franz, 1691-1746. 265.6
The penitent Christian; or, Sermons on the virture and sacrament of penance, and on everything required for Christian repentance and amendment of life, and also on doing penance during the time of a jubilee, and during public calamities. In seventy-six sermons, adapted for all the Sundays and most of the holy days of the year. With a full index of all the sermons, an alphabetical index of the principal subjects treated, and copious marginal notes. By the Rev. Father Francis Hunolt...Translated from the original German edition of Cologne, 1740, by the Rev. J. Allen... New York, Cincinnati [etc.] Benziger brothers, 1889. 2 v. 23 cm. (Half-title: Hunolt's sermons, vol. v-vi) Published, 1897, under title: Sermons on penance. [BX1756.H8 vol. 5-6] [(252.02)] 37-19947
1. Penance. 2. Confession. 3. Catholic church—Sermons. 4. Sermons, English—Translations from German. 5. Sermons, German—Translations into English. I. Allen, J., tr. II. Title.

HUNOLT, Franz, 1691-1746. 265.6
Sermons on penance, and on everything required for Christian repentance and amendment of life. Adapted for all the Sundays and most of the holydays of the year. By the Rev. Father Francis Hunolt...Translated by the Rev. J. Allen... New York, Cincinnati [etc.] Benziger brothers, 1897. 2 v. 23 cm. Published, 1889, under title: The penitent Christian. [BX1756.H812] 37-23876
1. Penance. 2. Confession. 3. Catholic church—Sermons. 4. Sermons, English—Translations from German. 5. Sermons, German—Translations into English. I. Allen, J., tr. II. Title.

KANE, John A. 265.6
The school of repentance, by John A. Kane ... Paterson, N.J., St. Anthony guild press, 1943. xxvi, 126 p. 20 cm. [BX2260.K3] 43-6708
1. Penance. I. Title.

KELLY, George Anthony, 1916- 234'.166
The sacrament of penance and reconciliation / [George A. Kelly]. Chicago : Franciscan Herald Press, c1975. 55 p. ; 18 cm. (Synthesis series) Includes bibliographical references. [BX2260.K4] 75-35596 ISBN 0-8199-0701-4 : 0.65
1. Penance. 2. Sociology, Christian (Catholic) I. Title.

KELLY, James Patrick, 1901- 265.
The jurisdiction of the confessor according the Code of canon law, by Rev. James P. Kelly, J. C. D., with a preface by Rt. Rev. Msgr. Philip Bernardini ... New York, Cincinnati [etc.] Benziger brothers, 1929. xiii, 273 p. 19 cm. Published as author's

thesis (D. C. L.) Catholic university, 1927, as Catholic university of America, Canon law studies, no. 43, under title: The jurisdiction of the simple confessor. [BX2260.K4 1929] 29-4796
1. Penance. 2. Absolution. 3. Canon law. I. Title.

LEHMEIER, Ludwig.
The ecclesial dimension of the sacrament of Penance from a catechetical point of view. Washington, 1965. xiv, 316 l. 28 cm. (Catholic University of America. Studies in sacred theology. 2d ser., no. 169) Typescript of thesis (S.T.D.) -- Catholic University of America. Bibliography: leaves 304-316. 67-37813
1. Penance. I. Title.

MANNING, Henry Edward, Cardinal, 1808-1892. 265.62
The love of Jesus to penitents. Westminster, Md., Newman Press, 1950. 122 p. 16 cm. [[BX2265.M]] A51
1. [Penance] 2. [Jesus Christ—Devotional literature] 3. Confession. I. Title.

MORTIMER, Robert Cecil.
The origins of private penance in the Western church, by Rev. R. C. Mortimer ... Oxford, The Clarendon press, 1939. 3 p. l., 194 p., 1 l. 23 cm. Bibliographical foot-notes. A 42
1. Penance. I. Title.

MORTIMER, Robert Cecil, Bp. of Exeter, 1902-
The origins of private penance in the Western churcn, by Rev. R. C. Mortimer... Oxford, The Clarendon press, 1939. 3 p. 1., 194 p., 1 l. 23 cm. Bibliographical foot-notes. A 42
1. Penance. I. Title.

ORSY, Ladislas M., 1921- 265'.6
The evolving church and the Sacrament of Penance / Ladislas Orsy. Denville, N.J. : Dimension Books, c1978. 211 p. ; 22 cm. In part, a discussion of the Roman Catholic post-Vatican II Ordo paenitentiae. Bibliography: p. [191]-211. [BX2260.O47] 78-65538 ISBN 0-87193-072-2 : 11.95
1. Catholic Church. Liturgy and ritual. Ordo paenitentiae. 2. Penance. I. Title.

PARIS. Saint-Severin (Church) Clergy. 265.6
Confession: meaning and practice, by the community of Saint-Severin Translated [from the French] by A. V. Littledale. Chicago, Fides Publishers Association [1960] 128p. 19cm. 60-863 3.25 bds.,
1. Penance. I. Title.

PARIS. Saint-Severin (Church) Clergy. 265'.6
Confession; meaning and practice, by the community of Saint-Severin. Translated by A. V. Littledale. With and introd. by John E. Corrigan. Notre Dame, Ind., Fides Publishers [1967] 127 p. 18 cm. (A Fides dome book, D-60) [BX2260.P313 1967] 67-24815
1. Penance. I. Title.

RICHTER, Stephan. 265'.6
Metanoia: Christian penance and confession. Translated by Raymond T. Kelly. New York, Sheed and Ward [1966] 126 p. 21 cm. Bibliography: p. 124-126. Bibliographical references included in "Notes". [BX2260.R513] 66-22024
1. Penance. 2. Confession. I. Title.

SACRAMENT of penance, (The) 265.6 by M. B. Carra de Vaux Saint-Cyr. others.[Tr. by R. L. Sullivant. St. Agnes Cunningham. M. Renelle] Glen Rock, N.J. Paulist [1966] v, 122p. 19cm. (Deus bk.) Bibl. [BX2260.S213] 66-22054 .95 pup.,
1. Penance. 2. Confession I. Cana de Vaux Saint-Cyr. M. B.

SPEYR, Adrie 265.6
Confession, the encounter with Christ in penance [tr. from german by a. v. littledale. New York] Herder & Herder [c.1964] 234 p. 22 cm. 64-15376 4.75
1. Penance. 2. Confession. I. Title.

SPEYR, Adrienne von. 265.6
Confession, the encounter with Christ in penance. [Translated by A. V. Littledale. New York] Herder and Herder [1964] 234 p. 22 cm. Translation of Die Reichte. [BX2260.S613 1964] 64-15376
1. Penance. 2. Confession. I. Title.

TERTULLIANUS, Quintus Septimius Florens. 265.6
Treatises on penance: On penitence and On purity. Translated and annotated by William P. LeSaint. Westminster, Md., Newman Press, 1959. vi, 330 p. 23 cm. (Ancient Christian writers; the works of the Fathers in translation, no. 28) Bibliographical references includes in "Notes" (p. [129]-298) [BR60.A35 no.28] 58-10746
1. Penance. 2. Chastity. I. Le Saint, William P., ed. and tr. II. Title. III. Series.

VAN ZELLER, Hubert, 1905- 265.6
Approach to penance. New York, Sheed & Ward [1958] 103 p. 21 cm. Secular name: Claude Van Zeller. [BX2260.V36] 58-5882
1. Penance. I. Title. II. Series.

WEILAND, Duane. 265'.6
Resistance; the sacrament of penance. Dayton, Ohio, G. A. Pflaum, 1969. 128 p. illus. 18 cm. (Christian identity series) (Witness book, CI 1.) Bibliography: p. 123-124. [BX2260.W43] 71-97043 0.95
1. Penance. I. Title.

WHARTON, Charles Henry, 1748-1833.
A short answer to "A true exposition of the doctrine of the Catholic church touching the sacrament of penance, with the grounds on which this doctrine is founded," contained in an appendix to the Catholic question decided in the city of New York, in July, 1813. By Charles H. Wharton ... Philadelphia, Moses Thomas J. Maxwell, printer, 1814. 130, [1] p. 23 cm. [BX2267.W4] A 32
1. Penance. I. Title.

Penance—Addresses, essays, lectures.

†THE Sacrament of penance in our time 234'.166 / edited by George A. Kelley. Boston : St. Paul Editions, c1976. 165 p. ; 21 cm. Includes bibliographical references and index. [BX2260.S23] 76-18719 4.00 pbk. : 3.00
1. Penance—Addresses, essays, lectures. I. Kelly, George Anthony, 1916-

Penance (Canon law)

MORIARTY, Francis Edwin, 1909- 265.6
... The extraordinary absolution from censures; an historical synopsis and commentary ... by the Rev. Francis E. Moriarty ... Washington, D.C., The Catholic university of America, 1938. xv, 334 p. 23 cm. (The Catholic university of America. Canon law studies, no. 113) Thesis (J.C.D.)--Catholic university of America, Bibliography: p. 305-313. [BX1939.P45M6] 42-8518
1. Penance (Canon law) 2. Absolution. 3. Censures, Ecclesiastical. 4. Catholic church. Codex juris canonici. I. Title.

Penance — History

HASLEHURST, Richard Stafford Tyndale.
Some account of the penitential discipline of the early church in the first four centuries, by R. S. T. Haslehurst... London, Society for promoting Christian knowledge; New York, Macmillan, 1921. ix, 162 p. 22 cm. A21
1. Penance—History. I. Title. II. Title: The penitential discipline of the early church.

MCAULIFFE, Clarence R. 922.
The penitential doctrine of Saint Pacianus [by] Rev. Clarence McAuliffe ... [n.p., 1941] 1 p. l., [365]-381, [20]-34 p. 22 1/2 cm. Summary of thesis (S.T.D.)--St. Louis university. "Reprinted from Theological studies, vol. 1, no. 4, 1940; vol. 2, no. 1, 1941." [BR1720.P25M3] 42-45628
1. Pacianus, Saint, bp. of Barcelona, 4th cent. 2. Penance—Hist. I. Title.

POSCHMANN, Bernhard. 1878-1955. 265.609
Penance and the anointing of the sick. Translated and rev. by Francis Courtney. [New York] Herder and Herder [1961] cxi, 257 p. 23 cm. (The Herder history of dogma) Includes bibliographies. [BX2262.P613] 64-11976
1. Penance—Hist. 2. Extreme unction—Hist. I. Title.

TENTLER, Thomas N., 1932- 234'.166
Sin and confession on the eve of the Reformation / Thomas N. Tentler. Princeton, N.J. : Princeton University Press, c1977. xxiv, 395 p. ; 25 cm. Includes index. Bibliography: p. 371-389. [BV840.T43] 76-3022 ISBN 0-691-07219-1 : 25.00
1. Penance—History. I. Title.

WATKINS, Oscar Daniel, 1848-
A history of penance, being a study of authorities (A) for the whole church to A.D. 450 (B) for the Western church from A.D. 450 (B) for the Western church from A.D. 450 to A.D. 1215. New York, B. Franklin, 1961. 2 v. (xxix, 775 p.) (Burt Franklin research & source work series, 16) "Originally published in London -- 1920." Bibliographical footnotes.
1. Penance — Hist. 2. Penance — Hist. — Early Church. I. Title.

WATKINS, Oscar Daniel, 1848-
A history of penance, being a study of authorities (A) for the whole church to A.D. 450 (B) for the Western church from A.D. 450 to A.D. 1215, by Oscar D. Watkins ... London, New York [etc.] Longmans, Green and co., 1920. 2 v. 23 1/2 cm. [BV840.W3] 20-11907
I. Title.

Penance—History—Sources.

WATKINS, Oscar Daniel, 1848-1926. 265'.6'09
A history of penance; being a study of the authorities. New York, B. Franklin, 1961. 2 v. (xxix, 775 p.) 24 cm. (Burt Franklin research & source works series, #16) Reprint of the 1920 ed. Contents.Contents.—v. 1. The whole church to A.D. 450.—v. 2. The Western church from A.D. 450 to A.D. 1215. Bibliographical footnotes. [BV840.W3 1961] 72-6537
1. Penance—History—Sources. I. Title.

Penance—Prayer-books and devotions—English.

RABALAIS, Maria. 265'.6
Come, be reconciled! : Penance celebrations for young Christians / by Maria Rabalais, Howard Hall, David Vavasseur ; [ill., Gloria Ortiz]. New York : Paulist Press, 1975. 148 p. : ill. ; 25 cm. Bibliography: p. 144-148. Devotions on both the elementary and high school level designed to raise one's consciousness of the spirit of forgiveness and prepare one for the sacrament of Penance. [BX2150.R3] 74-33576 ISBN 0-8091-1876-9 pbk. : 4.95
1. Penance—Prayer-books and devotions—English. 2. Children—Prayer-books and devotions—English—1961- 3. Youth—Prayer-books and devotions—English. 4. [Penance.] 5. [Prayer books and devotions.] I. Hall, Howard, 1936- joint author. II. Vavasseur, David, joint author. III. Title.

Pencille, Bill.

WAGNER, C. Peter. 266'.023'0924 B
Defeat of the bird god / C. Peter Wagner. South Pasadena, Calif. : William Carey Library, c1975. 256 p. : ill. ; 22 cm. [F3320.2.Z3W3 1975] 75-331578 ISBN 0-87808-721-4 pbk. : 4.95
1. Pencille, Bill. 2. Zamucoan Indians—Missions. 3. Indians of South America—Bolivia—Missions. I. Title.

WAGNER, C. Peter. 266'.023'0924
Defeat of the bird god; the story of missionary Bill Pencille, who risked his life to reach the Ayores of Bolivia [by] C. Peter Wagner. Foreword by Paul S. Rees. Grand Rapids, Zondervan Pub. House [1967] 256 p. illus., map (on lining papers), ports. 23 cm. [F3320.2.Z3W3] 67-11615
1. Pencille, Bill. 2. Zamucoan Indians—Missions. 3. Santa Cruz, Bolivia (Dept.)—Description and travel. I. Title.

Pendleton, S.C. Presbyterian Church.

BOGGS, Annie Lee. 285'.1757'25
Pendleton Presbyterian Church, 1789-1966; church history. [Pendleton? S.C., 1966] 117 p. illus., facsims., ports. 23 cm. Cover title. Bibliography: p. 117. [BX9211.P28P4] 77-261778 3.00
1. Pendleton, S.C. Presbyterian Church. I. Title.

Peng, Fu, 1888-

BURGESS, Andrew Severance, 1897- 922.451
Peng Fu; a biography by Andrew Burgess. Minneapolis, Minn., Augsburg publishing house, [c1939] 128 p. inc. plates, ports, map facsim. 19 1/2 cm. Cover-title: Peng Fu from Junan. "The Lutheran church in China": p. 125-128. [BV3427.P4B8] 39-34141
1. Peng, Fu, 1888- 2. Lutherans in China. I. Title.

Peninsula Bible Church.

STEDMAN, Ray C. 200
Body life, by Ray C. Stedman. [2d ed.] Glendale, Calif., G/L Regal Books [1972] 149 p. illus. 18 cm. [BV600.2.S75 1972] 74-181764 ISBN 0-8307-0143-5 0.95
1. Peninsula Bible Church. 2. Church. I. Title.

Penitential Psalms.

PISAN, Christian de, ca.1363-ca.1431. 242.1
Les sept psaumes allegorises. A critical ed. from the Brussels and Paris manuscripts; by Ruth Ringland Rains. Washington. D.C., Catholic Univ. of Amer. Pr. [c.1965] ix, 181p. geneal. table. 28cm. Introd. material in English; the author's text written in 1409 in Old French, includes O.F. tr. of the 7 penitential Psalms. The Brussels ms. (Bib. roy. 10987) has been used as the basic text, except where the Paris reading (B. n. nouv. acq. fr. 4792) is obviously superior. Bibl. [BS1445.P4P55] 65-17049 5.00 pap.,
1. Penitential Psalms. I. Rains, Ruth Rea Ringland, 1927- ed. II. Bible. O.T. Psalms. French (Old French) Selections. 1965. Pisan. III. Title.

SWANK, Calvin Peter, 1880- 223.306
Sermons from the Psalms. Grand Rapids, Mich., Baker [c.]1962. 122p. 20cm. (Evangelical pulpit lib.) 62-12670 2.50
1. Penitential Psalms. 2. Sermons, American. 3. Lutheran Church—Sermons. 4. Evangelistic sermons. I. Title.

Penitentials.

MCNEILL, John Thomas, 1885- tr. 265.60902
Medieval handbooks of penance; a translation of the principal libri poenitentiales and selections from related documents, by John T. McNeill, Helena M. Gamer. New York, Octagon, 1965[c.1938] xiv, 476p. facsims. 24cm. (Records of civilization: sources and studies, no. 29) Bibl. [BX2260.M3] 65-20970 12.50
1. Penitentials. I. Gamer, Helena Margaret, 1900- joint tr. II. Title. III. Series.

MCNEILL, John Thomas, 1885- tr. 265.6
Medieval handbooks of penance; a translation of the principal libri poenitentiales and selections from related documents, by John T. McNeill and Helena M. Gamer. New York city, Columbia university press, 1938. xiv, 476, [2] p. facsims. 23 1/2 cm. (Half=title: Records of civilization: sources and studies, ed. under the auspices of the Dept. of history, Columbia university ... no. xxix) "On documents omitted": p. [427]-431: "The manuscripts of the penitentials": p. [432]-450; Selected bibliography": p. [451]-454. [BX2260.M3] 38-32774
1. Penitentials. I. Gamer, Helena Margaret, 1900- joint tr. II. Title.

MOREY, Adrian, father, 1901- 922.242
Bartholomew of Exeter, bishop and canonist; a study in the twelfth century, by Dom Adrian Morey...with the text of Bartholomew's Penitential, from the Cotton ms. Vitellius A. xii. Cambridge [Eng.] The University press, 1937. xi, [1], 320, [2] p. 22 cm. "Select bibliography": p. [301]-305. [BX4705.B235M6] 38-7157
1. Bartholomew, bp. of Exeter, d. 1184. 2. Penitentials. I. Bartholomew, bp. of Exeter, d. 1184. Penitentiale. II. British museum. Mss. (Cotton Vitellius. A xii) III. [Secular name: Richard Morey] IV. Title.

OAKLEY, Thomas Pollock, 1884-1943. 262.9
English penitential discipline and Anglo-Saxon law in their joint influence. [1st AMS ed.] New York, AMS Press [1969] 226 p. 23 cm. (Studies in history, economics and public law, v. 107, no. 2; whole no. 242) Series statement also appears as: Columbia University studies in the social sciences, 242. Originally presented as the author's thesis, Columbia, 1923. Reprint of the 1923 ed. Bibliography: p. 201-213. [LAW] 71-82243
1. Penitentials. I. Title. II. Series: Columbia studies in the social sciences, 242.

Penitents.

BLUNT, Hugh Francis, 1877- 922
Great penitents, by Reverend Hugh Francis Blunt, LL.D. New York, The Macmillan company, 1921. 7 p. l., 245 p. 20 cm. [BX4668.B5] 21-18941
I. Title.

MEEHAN, Thomas A 922
Now is the acceptable time; timely thoughts from the lives of great penitents. Pref. by Samuel Cardinal Stritch. New York, Benziger Bros. [c1957] 211p. 19cm. [BX4669.M367] 58-400
1. Penitents. I. Title.

Penn, William, 1644-1718.

ENDY, Melvin B. 289.6'092'4 B
William Penn and early Quakerism [by] Melvin B. Endy, Jr. [Princeton, N.J.] Princeton University Press [1973] viii, 410 p. 24 cm. Based on the author's thesis. Bibliography: p. 378-395. [F152.2.E52] 72-7798 ISBN 0-691-07190-X 17.50
1. Penn, William, 1644-1718. 2. Friends, Society of—History. I. Title.

SMYTH, Clifford, 1866- 923.273
William Penn, Quaker courtier and founder of colonies, by Clifford Smyth ... New York and London, Funk & Wagnalls company, 1931. 175 p. 19 cm. (His Builders of America, v. 7) [E178.S68 vol. 7] [F152.2.S64] 920.073 31-35720
1. Penn, William, 1644-1718. I. Title.

VINING, Elizabeth (Gray) 1902- 248.2'2
William Penn: mystic, as reflected in his writings. [Wallingford, Pa., Pendle Hill Publications, 1969] 31 p. 19 cm. (Pendle Hill pamphlet 167) [F152.2.V79] 74-95891 0.55
1. Penn, William, 1644-1718. I. Title.

Penn, William, 1644-1718—Bibliography

MASON, Wilmer G 016.2896'0924
Penn bibliography, by Wilmer G. Mason. Columbus, Ohio, 1967- v. illus., facsims. 28 cm. Contents.Contents.--1, pt. a. A letter of love. [Z8672.M3] 68-3410
1. Penn, William, 1644-1718—Bibl. I. Title.

MASON, Wilmer G. 016.2896'0924
Penn bibliography, by Wilmer G. Mason. Columbus, Ohio, 1967- v. illus., facsims. 28 cm. Contents.Contents.—1, pt. a. A letter of love. [Z8672.M3] 68-3410
1. Penn, William, 1644-1718—Bibliography. I. Title.

Pennell, Theodore Leighton, 1867-1912.

PENNELL, Alice Maud (Sorabji) Mrs. 922
Pennell of the Afghan frontier; the life of Theodore Leighton Pennell, M. D., B. SC., F. R. C. S. Kaisar-i-Hind medal for public service in India, by Alice M. Pennell ... with an introduction by Field-Marshal Earl Roberts ... with 20 illustrations & 2 maps. New York, E. P. Dutton & company; London, Seeley, Service & co., ltd., 1914. xv, [1] 464 p. incl. map. front., plates, ports., fold. map. 23 cm. Printed in Great Britain. Glossary: p. 455-459. [DS479.1.P4P4] 14-30912
1. Pennell, Theodore Leighton, 1867-1912. 2. Missions—India. 3. Missions, Medical. I. Title.

Penney, Thomas C., 1909 or 10-1943.

RAYMOND, Father, 1903- 248
God goes to murderer's row. Milwaukee, Bruce Pub. Co. [1951] 211 p. illus. 21 cm. [HV6248.P38R3] 51-14888
1. Penney, Thomas C., 1909 or 10-1943. I. Title.

Pennington, M. Basil.

PENNINGTON, M. Basil. 271'.125'024 B
Monastic journey to India / M. Basil Pennington. New York : Seabury Press, 1982. 162 p. ; 21 cm. [BX4705.P423A35 1982] 19 81-14422 ISBN 0-8164-2367-9 : 9.95
1. Pennington, M. Basil. 2. Monks—United States—Biography. 3. India—Description and travel—1947- 4. Sri Lanka—Description and travel. 5. Nepal—Description and travel. I. Title.

Pennsylvania—Biography

CENTURY cyclopedia of history and biography of Pennsylvania. 289.
George Irving Reed, a. m., editor-in-chief: Rev. Andrew A. Lambing ... Eli Sheldon Glover, associate editors. Daniel Carhart ... James D. Moffat ... John A. Brashear ... William J. Holland ... authors and contributors. Chicago, The Century publishing and engraving company, 1906. 2 v. ports. 30 cm. Running title: History of western Pennsylvania. [F149.C39] 5-5087
1. Pennsylvania—Biog. 2. Pittsburgh, Pa.—Biog. I. Reed George Irving, ed. II. Lambing, Andrew Arnold, 1842-1918, joint ed. III. Glover, Eli Sheldon, joint ed.

Pennsylvania—Church history—Sources.

HEIDELBERG union church (Reformed and Lutheran) Heidelberg township, Lehigh co., Pa. 289
Two hundredth anniversary of Heidelberg union church Reformed and Lutheran, Heidelberg township, Lehigh co., Pennsylvania, Sunday, August 4, 1940. [New Tripoli, Pa., New Tripoli print shop, 1940] 112 p. illus. (incl. ports.) 23 cm. On cover: Heidelberg church history and records, 1740, 1940. "This history was written by Mr. Raymond E. Hollenbach."--p. 3. [BX9581.H4A5] 43-31080
1. Hollenbach, Raymond E. II. Title.

THE Keithian controversy in early Pennsylvania / 289.6'092'4
[compiled] by J. William Frost. Norwood, Pa. : Norwood Editions, 1979. p. cm. Reprints or transcriptions of 19 tracts and documents originally issued 1691-1692. Bibliography: p. [BX7743.K4K43] 79-14836 ISBN 0-8482-0847-1 lib. bdg. : 15.00
1. Keith, George, 1639?-1716. 2. Friends, Society of—Pennsylvania—History—Sources. 3. Pennsylvania—Church history—Sources. I. Frost, Jerry William.

Pennsylvania—History—Colonial periodicals

APPLEGARTH, Albert Clayton. 973'.08 S
Quakers in Pennsylvania, by Albert C. Applegarth. Baltimore, Johns Hopkins Press, 1892. [New York, Johnson Reprint Corp., 1973] 84 p. 22 cm. Pages also numbered 386-464. Original ed. issued as no. 8-9 of Church and state—Columbus and America, which forms the 10th series of Johns Hopkins University studies in historical and political science. Includes bibliographical references. [E18.C54 no. 8-9] [F152] 289.6'748 72-14272 ISBN 0-384-01765-7 pap 4.00
1. Friends, Society of. Pennsylvania. 2. Pennsylvania—History—Colonial period. I. Title. II. Series: Johns Hopkins University. Studies in historical and political science, 10th ser., 8-9. III. Series: Church and state—Columbus and America, no. 8-9.

Penry, John, 1563-1593.

MCGINN, Donald Joseph 274.2
John Penry and the Marprelate controversy. New Brunswick, N.J., Rutgers [c.1966] xi, 274p. facsims. 22cm. Bibl. [BR757.M16] 65-28212 9.00
1. Penry, John, 1563-1593. 2. Marprelate controversy. I. Title.

Pensacola, Fla. Christ church.

YONGE, Julia J. 283.759991
Christ church parish, Pensacola, Florida, 1827-1927 [by] Julia J. Yonge. [Pensacola? 1927?] 3 p. l., 80 p. illus. (incl. ports.) 22 1/2 cm. [BX5980.P35C5] 31-933
1. Pensacola, Fla. Christ church. I. Title.

Pensacola, Fla.—Church history.

HOSKINS, Frank W. 287.
The history of Methodism in Pensacola, Florida; its rise and progress, by F. W. Hoskins ... Nashville, Dallas [etc.] Publishing house M. E. church, South [c1928] 120 p. front., plates, ports. 19 cm. [BX8249.P25H6] 29-1033
1. Pensacola, Fla.—Church history. 2. Methodist Episcopal church in Florida. I. Title.

Pentecost.

BENNETT, Willis G. 287.9
Pentecost, its scope, power and perpetuation, by W. G. Bennett ... Kansas City, Mo., Printed for W. G. Bennett by Nazarene publishing house [1936] 7 p. l., 17-158 p. 22 cm. [BX8699.N3B4] 36-17859
1. Pentecost. 2. Revivals. 3. Evangelistic work. I. Title.

BRUNER, Benjamin Harrison, 1888- 220
Pentecost: a renewal of power, by B. H. Brummer. Garden City, N.Y., Doubleday, Doran & company, inc., 1928. xii p., 1 l., 162 p. 19 1/2 cm. [BR125.B817] 28-28524
I. Title.

FOWLER, Charles J.
Back to Pentecost. Philadelphia, Christian standard co. [1900] 144 p. incl. front. (port.) 16 cm. Oct
I. Title.

HUGHES, Ray H. 231.3
What is Pentecost? [Cleveland, Tenn., Pathway, c.1963] 108p. 19cm. 63-14593 1.50 pap.,
1. Pentecost. 2. Holy Spirit. I. Title.

JONES, Eli Stanley, 1884- 220
The Christ of every road; a study in Pentecost, by E. Stanley Jones. New York, Cincinnati [etc.] The Abingdon press [c1930] 271 p. 20 cm. [BR125.J565] 30-1407
I. Title. II. Title: Pentecost, A study in.

SCARBOROUGH, Lee Rutland, 1870- 231.3
Products of Pentecost, by L. R. Scarborough ... New York [etc.] Fleming H. Revell company [c1934] 127 p. front. (port.) 19 1/2 cm. [BT122.S26] 35-503
1. Pentecost. I. Title.

SMITH, Oswald J.
Back to Pentecost, by Oswald J. Smith... New York, N.Y., The Christian alliance publishing co. [c1926] 1 p. l., 5-124 p. 18 cm. [BT780.S6] 26-13337
I. Title.

STEWART, James Alexander, 1910-
The phenomena of Pentecost. Philadelphia, Revival Literature [1960] 82 p. 21 cm.
I. Title.

THOBURN, James Mills, bp., 1836-1922. 230
The church of Pentecost. By Bishop J. M. Thoburn. Rev. ed. Cincinnati, Jennings & Pye; New York, Eaton & Main [c1901] 392 p. 19 cm. [BV600.T45 1901] 1-31069
1. Pentecost. 2. Holy Spirit. I. Title.

VERSTEEG, John Marinus, 1888- 261.
Perpetuating Pentecost, by John M. Versteeg. Chicago,New York, Willett, Clark & Colby, 1930. 6 p. l., 207 p. 19 1/2 cm. [BT121.V4] 30-8388
I. Title.

YORK, Raymond. 282'.0924 B
Pentecost comes to Central Park. [New York] Herder and Herder [1969] 160 p. 22 cm. Autobiographical. [BX4705.Y56A3] 69-11391 4.95
I. Title.

Pentecost festival.

FLICOTEAUX, Emmanuel, 1882- 264.02
The splendor of Pentecost. Tr. from French by Mary Louise Helmer. Baltimore, Helicon Press, [c.]1961 112p. Bibl. 61-11759 3.50
1. Pentecost festival. I. Title.

POOVEY, William Arthur, 1913- 242'.37
The days of Pentecost : devotions, customs, and summertime activities to celebrate the season of the Spirit / W. A. Poovey. Minneapolis : Augsburg Pub. House, c1979. 141 p. ; 20 cm. [BV60.P66] 78-66953 ISBN 0-8066-1678-4 pbk. : 3.50
1. Pentecost festival. I. Title.

Pentecost, George Frederick, 1842-1920.

HEADLEY, Phineas Camp, 1819-1903. 922.573
George F. Pentecost: life, labor, and Bible studies. By Rev. P. C. Headley ... 4th ed. Boston, J. H. Earle, 1880. 456 p. incl. facsim. front. (port.) 19 1/2 cm. [BX9225.P47H4 1880] 36-25402
1. Pentecost, George Frederick, 1842-1920. I. Title.

PENTECOST, George Frederick, 1842- 243
Fighting for faith, the justice of our fight, the reasons for our faith, by George F. Pentecost ... New York, George H. Doran company [c1918] 1 p. l., v-xiii p., 1 l., 17-306 p. 20 cm. [BX9178.P4F5] 18-21561 1.50
I. Title.

Pentecost—Sermons.

HOLMES, Nickels J. 1847-1919. 287.
Life sketches and sermons, by Reverend N. J. Holmes and wife. Royston, Ga., Press of the Pentecostal holiness church [c1920] 310 p. front., port. 20 cm. [BX7990.H6H6] 20-23006
I. Holmes, Lucy Elizabeth (Simpson) "Mrs. N. J. Holmes" joint author. II. Title.

MOTTER, Alton M., ed. 252.67
Preaching on Pentecost and Christian unity; thirty outstanding sermons dealing with theme of Pentecost and the ecumenical movement. Philadelphia, Fortress [1966, c.1965] viii, 248p. 19cm. Bibl. [BV4300.5.M6] 66-10157 2.48 pap.,
1. Pentecost—Sermons. 2. Christian union—Sermons. 3. Sermons, English. I. Title.

Pentecostal assemblies of the world.

FRODSHAM, Stanley Howard. 269
With signs following; the story of the pentecostal revival in the twentieth century. Rev. ed. By Stanley Howard Frodsham. Springfield, Mo., Gospel publishing house, 1941. 279 p. 20 cm. [BX8795.P25F6 1941] 42-10098
1. Pentecostal assemblies of the world. I. Title.

Pentecostal Assemblies of the World. Foreign Missionary Department

REEDER, Hilda. 266.99
A brief history of the Foreign Missionary Department of the Pentecostal Assemblies of the World. [Indianapolis?] Foreign Missionary Dept. [1951] 76 p. illus., ports. 20 cm. [BV2595.P4R4] 51-40440
1. Pentecostal Assemblies of the World. Foreign Missionary Dept. I. Title.

Pentecostal churches.

CHURCH of the Nazarene. General assembly. 287.
Manual of the Pentecostal church of the Nazarene, published by authority of the General assembly held at Nashville, Tenn. 1911; E. F. Walker, H. B. Hosley, E. A. Girvin, editors. Kansas City, Mo., Publishing house of the Pentecostal church of the Nazarene [1911] 96 p. 14 cm. "Course of study for preachers looking forward to ordination": p. [89]-91; "Course of study for deaconesses": p. 91 [BX8699.N3A5 1911] 18-5834
I. Walker, E. F., ed. II. Title.

CONN, Charles W 289.9
Pillars of Pentecost. [1st ed.] Cleveland, Tenn., Pathway Press, 1956. 141p. 21cm. [BX8795.P25C6] 56-6820
1. Pentecostal churches. I. Title.

HALL, Burton Allen, 1879- 200
The promise of the Father; or, This is that, by Burton & Hall... [Franklin Springs, Ga., Printed by Publishing house, P.H. church, c 1926] 169 p. port. 20 1/2 cm. [BX8795.P25H3] 26-11390
I. Title.

NICHOL, John Thomas. 289.9
Pentecostalism. [1st ed.] New York, Harper & Row [1966] xv, 264 p. 22 cm. "Much of this material was originally submitted to satisfy the doctoral requirements at the Boston University Graduate School." Bibliography: p. 247-255 [BX8763.N5] 66-20782
1. Pentecostal churches. 2. Pentecostalism. I. Title.

**PERSPECTIVES on the new* 289.9
Pentecostalism / Russell P. Spittler, Editor. Grand Rapids : Baker Book House, c1976. 268p. ; 23 cm. Includes bibliographical references. [BX8762] ISBN 0-8010-8076-2 : 7.95
1. Pentecostal churches. I. Spittler, Russell P., ed.

SHERRILL, John L. 289.9
They speak with other tongues, by John L. Sherrill. [1st ed.] New York, McGraw Hill [1964] vii, 165 p. 21 cm. Bibliography: p. 163-165. [BX8763.S5] 64-25003
1. Pentecostal churches. 2. Glossolalia. I. Title.

WOMACK, David A. 289.9
The wellsprings of the Pentecostal movement, by David A. Womack. Written in cooperation with the Committee on Advance for the General Council of the Assemblies of God. Springfield, Mo., Gospel Pub. House [1968] 96 p. 21 cm. Bibliographical footnotes. [BX8763.W65] 68-7288
1. Pentecostal churches. 2. Church. I. Assemblies of God, General Council. Committee on Advance. II. Title.

WOOD, William W. 289.9
Culture and personality aspects of the Pentecostal Holiness religion. The Hague, Mouton, [New York, Humanities, 1966, c.1965] 125p. illus., maps. 24cm. Bibl. [BX8764.W6] 66-518 7.75
1. Pentecostal churches. 2. Psychology, Religious. I. Title.

Pentecostal churches—Clergy—Biography.

HUIE, William Bradford, 1910- 289.9 B
It's me O Lord! / William Bradford Huie. Nashville : T. Nelson, c1979. 189 p., [4] leaves of plates : ill. ; 21 cm. [BX8762.Z8R653] 79-403 ISBN 0-8407-5141-9 7.95
1. Ronsisvalle, Daniel. 2. Pentecostal churches—Clergy—Biography. 3. Clergy—United States—Biography. I. Title.

KENNEDY, Nell L. 289.9 B
Dream your way to success : the story of Dr. Yonggi Cho and Korea / by Nell L. Kennedy. Plainfield, N.J. : Logos International, c1980. xiii, 248 p., [12] leaves of plates ; 21 cm. Includes bibliographical references. [BX8762.Z8C484] 19 79-93290 ISBN 0-88270-407-9 pbk. : 4.95
1. Cho, Yong-gi, 1936- 2. Pentecostal churches—Clergy—Biography. 3. Clergy—Korea—Biography. I. Title.

Pentecostal churches—Colombia.

FLORA, Cornelia Butler, 1943- 278'.61
Pentecostalism in Colombia : baptism by fire and spirit / Cornelia Butler Flora. Rutherford, [N.J.] : Fairleigh Dickinson University Press, c1976. 288 p. : ill. ; 22 cm. Includes index. Bibliography: p. 263-282. [BX8762.Z7C643 1976] 74-4974 ISBN 0-8386-1578-3 : 13.50
1. Pentecostal churches—Colombia. 2. Sociology, Christian—Colombia. 3. Social classes—Colombia. I. Title.

PALMER, Donald C. 289.9
Explosion of people evangelism, by Donald C. Palmer. Chicago, Moody Press [1974] 191 p. illus. 22 cm. Bibliography: p. 186-191. [BX8762.Z7C646] 73-15087 ISBN 0-8024-2413-9 2.95 (pbk.)
1. Pentecostal churches—Colombia. 2. Church growth. I. Title.

Pentecostal churches—Doctrinal and controversial works.

PAULK, Earl P 230.99
Your Pentecostal neighbor. [1st ed.] Cleveland, Tenn., Pathway Press, 1958. 237p. 21cm. [BX8795.P25P3] 58-13662
1. Pentecostal churches—Doctrinal and controversial works. I. Title.

Pentecostal churches—Education—Canada.

PETERS, Erna Alma, 1914- 377'.8'99
The contribution to education by the Pentecostal Assemblies of Canada. [Homewood, Man.] 1970 [c1971] vi, 205 p. 23 cm. Originally presented as the author's thesis, University of Manitoba. Bibliography: p. 203-205. [LC586.P4P47 1971] 74-163110 ISBN 0-919212-09-3 3.75
1. Pentecostal churches—Education—Canada. I. Title.

Pentecostal churches—Europe, Eastern.

DURASOFF, Steve. 266'.023'0947
Pentecost behind the Iron Curtain. Plainfield, N.J., Logos International, 1972. x, 128 p. 21 cm. [BX8762.Z7E82] 72-93080 ISBN 0-88270-018-9 1.50
1. Pentecostal churches—Europe, Eastern. I. Title.

Pentecostal churches—Great Britain

CALLEY, Malcolm J. C. 289.9
God's people: West Indian Pentecostal sects in England New York, Oxford [c.] 1965. xiv, 182p. illus. 23cm. Issued under the auspices of the Inst. of Race Relations, London. Bibl. [BX8762.Z7G73] 66-536 5.60
1. Pentecostal churches—Gt. Brit. 2. West Indians in Gt. Brit. I. Title.

CALLEY, Malcolm J C 289.9
God's people; West Indian Pentecostal sects in England [by] Malcolm J. C. Calley. London, New York, Oxford University Press, 1965. xiv, 182 p. illus. 23 cm. "Issued under the auspices of the Institute of Race Relations, London." Bibliography: p. [170]-173. [BX8762.Z7G73] 66-536
1. Pentecostal churches—Gt. Brit. 2. West Indians in Gt. Brit. I. Title.

Pentecostal churches—History

KENDRCK, Klaude. 289.9
The promise fulfilled; a history of the modern Pentecostal movement. Springfield, Mo., Gospel Pub. House [1961] 237p. 23cm. 'Outgrowth of a dissertation presented ... [at] the University of Texas ...for the degree of doctor of philosophy in history.' Includes bibliography. [BX8762.K4] 61-28191
1. Pentecostal churches—Hist. I. Title.

Pentecostal churches—Latin America.

WAGNER, C. Peter. 289.9
Look out! The Pentecostals are coming [by] C. Peter Wagner. [1st ed.] Carol Stream, Ill., Creation House [1973] 196 p. 22 cm. Bibliography: p. 183-186. [BX8762.Z7L38] 73-77528 ISBN 0-88419-040-4 4.95
1. Pentecostal churches—Latin America. I. Title.

Pentecostal churches—Norway.

BLOCH-HOELL, Nils 289.9
The Pentecostal movement; its origin, development, and distinctive character [Oslo] Universite forlaget [dist. New York, Humanities, 1965, c.1964] 255p. 24cm. (Scandinavian univ. bks.) Bibl. [BX8795.P25B553] 65-3204 6.00 bds.,
1. Pentecostal churches—Norway. I. Title.

Pentecostal churches—South Africa—East London—Case studies.

DUBB, Allie A. 289.9
Community of the saved : an African revivalist church in the East Cape / Allie A. Dubb. Johannesburg : Witwatersrand University Press for African Studies Institute, 1976. xvii, 175 p., [10] p. of plates : ill. ; 22 cm. Bibliography: p. 173-175. [BX8762.Z6E173] 76-375918 ISBN 0-85494-292-0 : R7.00
1. Bhengu, Nicholas B. H., 1909- 2. Pentecostal churches—South Africa—East London—Case studies. 3. East London—Church history. I. Title.

Pentecostal Holiness Church—Doctrinal and controversial works.

KING, Joseph Hillery(1869- 230.99
From Passover to Pentecost. 3d ed., rev. and enl. Franklin Springs, Ga., Pub. House of the Pentecostal Holiness Church [1955] 208p. 21cm. [BX8795.P25K5 1955] 58-42355
1. Pentecostal Holiness Church—Doctrinal and controversial works. I. Title.

KING, Joseph Hillery, 1869- 230.99
From Passover to Pentecost, by Rev. J. H. King... 2d ed., rev. and enl. Franklin Springs, Ga., The Publishing house of the Pentecostal holiness church [c1934] 219 p. 24 cm. [BX8795.P25K5 1934] 35-683
1. Pentecostal holiness church—Doctrinal and controversial works. I. Title.

Pentecostal holiness church—Hymns.

PENTECOSTAL holiness church. Board of education and publication. 783.9
Pentecostal holiness hymnal, for use in all services of the church, compiled and edited by Rev. I. H. Presley. Published by Board of educatior and publication of the Pentecostal holiness church ... Franklin Springs, Ga., Publishing house P. H. church, c1938. [192] p. 21 cm. [M2131.P4H9] 38-9555
1. Pentecostal holiness church—Hymns. 2. Hymns, English. I. Presley, I. H., ed. II. Title.

PENTECOSTAL holiness church. Board of education and publication. 783.9
Pentecostal holiness hymnal no. 2, compiled and edited by Rev. I. H. Presley. Published by Board of publication of the Pentecostal holiness church ... Franklin Springs, Ga., Publishing house P. H. church, c1941. [240], 12, [4] p. 21 cm. With music (shaped notes) [M2131.P4H92] 41-24279
1. Pentecostal holiness church—Hymns. 2. Hymns, English. I. Presley, I. H., ed. II. Title.

Pentecostalism.

AGRIMSON, J. Elmo. 270.8'2
Gifts of the spirit and the body of Christ; perspectives on the charismatic movement. Edited by J. Elmo Agrimson. Minneapolis, Augsburg Pub. House [1974] 112 p. 20 cm. Includes bibliographies. [BX8763.A15] 73-88608 ISBN 0-8066-1411-0 2.95 (pbk.)
1. Pentecostalism. I. Title.

BYRNE, James E. 248'.29
Living in the spirit : a handbook on Catholic charismatic Christianity / by James E. Byrne. New York : Paulist Press, c1975. viii, 184 p. ; 21 cm. Bibliography: p. 177-178. [BX2350.57.B9] 75-28628 ISBN 0-8091-1902-1 pbk. : 2.95
1. Pentecostalism. I. Title.

CHANTRY, Walter J., 1938- 234'.1
Signs of the apostles : observations on Pentecostalism old and new / Walter J. Chantry. 2d rev. ed. Edinburgh ; Carlisle, Pa. : Banner of Truth Trust, 1976. viii, 147 p. ; 18 cm. Bibliography: p. 147. [BR1644.C42 1976] 77-366357 £0.60
1. Pentecostalism. I. Title.

CHRISTENSON, Laurence. 261.8'3
A charismatic approach to social action, by Larry Christenson. Minneapolis, Bethany Fellowship [inc., 1974] 122 p. 22 cm. Includes bibliographical references. [BX8763.C48] 74-1326 ISBN 0-87123-389-4 3.95
1. Pentecostalism. 2. Church and social problems. I. Title.

CHRISTENSON, Laurence. 261.8'3
Social action, Jesus style / Larry Christenson. 2d ed. Minneapolis : Bethany Fellowship, 1976, c1974. 112 p. ; 18 cm. (Dimension books) First ed. published in 1976 under title: A charismatic approach to social action. Includes bibliographical references. [BX8763.C48 1976] 75-44927 ISBN 0-87123-504-8 pbk. : 1.50
1. Pentecostalism. 2. Church and social problems. I. Title.

CULPEPPER, Robert H. 270.8'2
Evaluating the charismatic movement : a theological and Biblical appraisal / by Robert H. Culpepper. Valley Forge, Pa. : Judson Press, c1977. 192 p. ; 22 cm. Includes index. Bibliography: p. 185-189. [BR1644.C84] 77-1197 ISBN 0-8170-0743-1 pbk. : 6.95
1. Pentecostalism. I. Title.

DURASOFF, Steve. 289.9
Bright wind of the spirit: Pentecostalism today. Englewood Cliffs, N.J., Prentice-Hall [1972] 277 p. 22 cm. Bibliography: p. 271-272. [BX8763.D87] 72-6536 ISBN 0-13-083089-5 6.95
1. Pentecostalism. I. Title.

ERVIN, Howard M. 234'.1
This which ye see and hear, by Howard M. Ervin. Plainfield, N.J., Logos International [1972] 112 p. 21 cm. [BX8763.E78] 79-186153 ISBN 0-912106-27-1 1.95
1. Pentecostalism. I. Title.

FAHEY, Sheila Macmanus. 261.8
Charismatic social action : reflection/resource manual / by Sheila Macmanus Fahey. New York : Paulist Press, c1977. xvii, 174 p. ; 21 cm. (An Exploration book) Includes bibliographies. [BR1644.F34] 77-70633 ISBN 0-8091-2014-3 pbk. : 4.95
1. Pentecostalism. 2. Church and social problems. I. Title.

FICHTER, Joseph Henry, 1908- 301.5'8
The Catholic cult of the Paraclete / by Joseph H. Fichter ; with a foreword by Donald L. Gelpi. New York : Sheed and Ward, [1975] xv, 183 p. ; 21 cm. Includes bibliographical references and index. [BX2350.57.F5] 74-10163 ISBN 0-8362-0599-5 : 6.95
1. Pentecostalism. I. Title.

FORD, Josephine Massyngberde. 248.2
The pentecostal experience, by J. Massingberd Ford. Paramus, N.J., Paulist Press [1970] 60 p. 17 cm. [BX8763.F66] 72-116869 0.75
1. Pentecostalism. I. Title.

FORD, Josephine Massyngberde. 262'.001
Which way for Catholic pentecostals? / J. Massyngberde Ford. 1st ed. New York : Harper & Row, c1976. x, 143 p. ; 21 cm. Bibliography: p. [137]-143. [BX2350.57.F67 1976] 75-36757 ISBN 0-06-062672-0 : 6.95
1. Pentecostalism. I. Title.

FRODSHAM, Stanley H. 200
"With signs following"; the story of the latter-day Pentecostal revival, by Stanley H. Frodsham ... Springfield, Mo., Gospel publishing house [c1926] 3 p. l., 9-254 p. 20 cm. [BX8795.P3F] 27-1733
I. Title.

GATES, Helen Litchfield (Kolb) 1895-1961. 922.8773
Bless the Lord, O my soul; a biography of Bishop John Fretz Funk, 1835-1930, creative pioneer for Christ and Mennonite leader, by Helen Kolb Gates [others] Ed. by J. C. Wenger. Scottdale, Pa., Herald Pr. [c.1964] 261p. illus., ports. 23cm Bibl. [BX8143.F8G3] 64-23375 4.75
1. Funk, John Fretz, Bp., 1835-1930. I. Title.

*GEE, Donald. 231.6
The fruit of the spirit. Springfield, Mo., Gospel Publishing House, [1975 c1928] 79 p. 18 cm. (Radiant books) [BT130] ISBN 0-88243-501-9 0.95 (pbk.)
1. Pentecostalism. 2. Holy Spirit. I. Title.

GELPI, Donald L., 1934- 248.2'9
Pentecostalism, a theological viewpoint, by Donald L. Gelpi. New York, Paulist Press [1971] v, 234 p. 19 cm. [BX8763.G45] 73-158489 1.95
1. Pentecostalism. I. Title.

HEALEY, John B. 282
Charismatic renewal : reflections of a pastor / by John B. Healey. New York : Paulist Press, c1976. vi, 109 p. ; 18 cm. (Deus book) [BX2350.57.H4] 76-9368 ISBN 0-8091-1948-X pbk. : 1.95
1. Pentecostalism. I. Title.

HEGSTAD, Roland R. 270.8'2
Rattling the gates [by] Roland R. Hegstad. Washington, Review and Herald Pub. Association [1974] 253 p. illus. 21 cm. Includes bibliographical references. [BX8763.H43] 73-87488 4.95; 3.50 (pbk.).
1. Pentecostalism. I. Title.

*HEYER, Robert, comp. 248.2
Pentecostal Catholics. New York, Paulist Press [1975 c1974] 75 p. ill. 18 cm. [BT767.3] 75-10114 ISBN 0-8091-1879-3 1.45 (pbk.)
1. Pentecostalism. I. Title.

HOLLENWEGER, Walter J., 1927- 289.9
The Pentecostals; the charismatic movement in the churches [by] W. J. Hollenweger. [Translated by R. A. Wilson with revisions by the author. 1st U.S. ed.] Minneapolis, Augsburg Pub. House [1972] xx, 572 p. illus. 25 cm. Translation of Enthusiastisches Christentum. Bibliography: p. [523]-557. [BX8763.H613] 70-176103 ISBN 0-8066-1210-X
1. Pentecostalism. I. Title.

THE Holy Spirit and power : the Catholic charismatic renewal / Kilian McDonnell, editor. 1st ed. Garden City, N.Y. : Doubleday, 1975. 186 p. ; 21 cm. Includes bibliographical references. [BX2350.57.H64] 74-32573 ISBN 0-385-09909-6 pbk. : 2.95 262'.001
1. Pentecostalism. I. McDonnell, Kilian.

HUMMEL, Charles E. 270.8'2
Fire in the fireplace : contemporary charismatic renewal / Charles E. Hummel. Downers Grove, Ill. : InterVarsity Press, c1978. 275 p. ; 21 cm. Includes bibliographical references and indexes. [BR1644.H85] 77-6031 ISBN 0-87784-742-8 : 4.95
1. Pentecostalism. I. Title.

ISENHOUR, Walter E. 1889- 248
Life's beautiful way heavenward, by Rev. Walter E. Isenhour. Louisville, Ky., Pentecostal publishing company [c1919] 292 p. 20 cm. Reprinted from the Union republican. [BV4501.17] 19-12300
I. Title.

JONES, James William, 1943- 262'.001
Filled with new wine; the charismatic renewal of the church [by] James W. Jones. [1st ed.] New York, Harper & Row [1974] xiii, 141 p. 21 cm. Includes bibliographical references. [BX8763.J65] 73-6342 5.95
1. Pentecostalism. 2. Church renewal. I. Title.

JORSTAD, Erling, 1930- 248'.173
Bold in the spirit; Lutheran charismatic renewal in America today. Minneapolis, Augsburg Pub. House [1974] 128 p. 20 cm. Bibliography: p. 127-128. [BX8065.2.J67] 74-77681 ISBN 0-8066-1432-3 2.95 (pbk.)
1. Lutheran Church—Doctrinal and controversial works. 2. Pentecostalism. I. Title.

JORSTAD, Erling, 1930- comp. 269'.2
The Holy Spirit in today's church; a handbook of the new pentecostalism. Nashville, Abingdon Press [1973] 160 p. 20 cm. Bibliography: p. 157-160. [BX8763.J67] 73-8691 ISBN 0-687-17293-4 2.75
1. Pentecostalism. I. Title.

KERR, John Stevens. 234'.1
The fire flares anew; a look at the new Pentecostalism. Philadelphia, Fortress Press [1974] 107 p. illus. 18 cm. [BX8763.K47] 73-89061 ISBN 0-8006-1074-1 2.95 (pbk.)
1. Pentecostalism. I. Title.

KIRKPATRICK, William J
Pentecostal edition of songs of praise and victory by Wm. J. Kirkpatrick and Dr. H. L. Gilmour assisted by Rev. Chas. A. Tushingham. Epworth heights camp meeting ed. Philadelphia, Pepper pub. co. [c1900] 154 pp. 12 degree. Suitable for evangelical meetings and gospel services. 1-309
I. Title.

MACARTHUR, John F. 234'.1
The charismatics : a doctrinal perspective / John F. MacArthur, Jr. Grand Rapids : Zondervan Pub. House, c1978. 224 p. ; 23 cm. Bibliography: p. 217-224. [BR1644.M27] 78-5297 ISBN 0-310-28490-2 : 7.95
1. Pentecostalism. I. Title.

MCDONNELL, Kilian. 270.8'2
Charismatic renewal / Kilian McDonnell. New York : Seabury Press, c1976. p. cm. "A Crossroad book." Includes index. Bibliography: p. [BX8763.M28] 76-896 ISBN 0-8164-0293-0 : 6.95
1. Pentecostalism. 2. Glossolalia—Psychology. I. Title.

MARTIN, Ralph, 1942- 248'.9'2
Hungry for God; practical help in personal prayer. [1st ed.] Garden City, N.Y., Doubleday 1974. 168 p. 21 cm. Includes bibliographical references. [BX2350.57.M37] 74-4830 ISBN 0-385-09535-X 5.95
1. Pentecostalism. 2. Spiritual life—Catholic authors. 3. Prayer. I. Title.

MURRAY, Andrew. Rev.
The full blessing of Pentecost; the one thing needful, by Andrew Murray ... New York, Chicago [etc.] F. H. Revell company [c1908] 158 p. 20 cm. 8-14320
I. Title.

O'CONNOR, Edward Dennis. 282
The pentecostal movement in the Catholic Church, by Edward D. O'Connor. Notre Dame, Ind., Ave Maria Press [1971] 301 p. 22 cm. Bibliography: p. 295-301. [BX8763.O25] 70-153878 5.95
1. Catholic Church. 2. Pentecostalism. I. Title.

OLSON, William George. 262'.001
The charismatic church. Minneapolis, Bethany Fellowship, 1974. 152 p. 21 cm. Includes bibliographical references. [BX8763.O43] 74-10600 ISBN 0-87123-080-1 2.25 (pbk.)
1. Pentecostalism. 2. Church polity. I. Title.

ORSINI, Joseph E. 282'.092'4 B
The anvil / by Joseph E. Orsini. Plainfield, N.J. : Logos International, [1974] 111 p. ; 18 cm. [BX4705.O715A28] 73-93895 ISBN 0-88270-089-8 : 1.25
1. Orsini, Joseph E. 2. Pentecostalism. I. Title.

ORSINI, Joseph E. 248.2
Hear my confession, by Joseph E. Orsini. Plainfield, N.J., Logos International [1971] 90 p. 18 cm. [BX4705.O715A3] 73-173430 ISBN 0-912106-25-5 1.00
1. Pentecostalism. I. Title.

OTTERLAND, Anders, 1920- 248'.2
Upwinds : a short report on spiritual upwinds in our time / by Anders Otterland and Lennart Sunnergren. Nashville : Nelson, [1975] p. cm. Translation of Uppvindar. [BX8763.O8713] 75-14367 ISBN 0-8407-5599-6 : 3.50
1. Pentecostalism. I. Sunnergren, Lennart, 1930- joint author. II. Title.

PALMER, Bernard Alvin, 1914- 262'.001
The winds of God are blowing [by] Bernard and Marjorie Palmer. Wheaton, Ill., Tyndale House Publishers [1973] 186 p. 22 cm. [BX8763.P34] 72-97654 ISBN 0-8423-8220-8 ISBN 0-8423-8221-6 (pbk.) 3.95
1. Pentecostalism. I. Palmer, Marjorie, joint author. II. Title.

RANAGHAN, Kevin. 282
Catholic pentecostals, by Kevin and Dorothy Ranaghan. Paramus, N.J., Paulist Press [1969] v, 266 p. 18 cm. (Deus books) Bibliography: p. 263-266. [BX8763.R3] 73-79919
1. Pentecostalism. I. Ranaghan, Dorothy, joint author. II. Title.

ROEBLING, Karl. 270.8'2
Pentecostals around the world / Karl Roebling ; photos by the author. 1st ed. Hicksville, N.Y. : Exposition Press, c1978. 120 p., [6] leaves of plates : ill. ; 21 cm. [BR1644.R63] 78-108185 ISBN 0-682-49109-8 : 6.00
1. Pentecostalism. I. Title.

ROUNER, Arthur Acy. 248.2
Receiving the spirit at Old First Church / Arthur A. Rouner, Jr. New York : Pilgrim Press, c1982. viii, 86 p. ; 21 cm. [BR1644.R68] 19 81-19959 ISBN 0-8298-0492-7 pbk. : 5.95
1. Rouner, Arthur Acy. 2. Colonial Church of Edina (Minneapolis, Minn.) 3. Pentecostalism. I. Title.

RUTH, Christian Wismer, 1865-
The Pentecostal experience, by Rev. C. W. Ruth... Chicago and Boston, Christian witness co., 1909. 75 p. 20 cm. 9-16213
I. Title.

SEYER, Herman D. 234'.1
The stewardship of spiritual gifts : a study of First Corinthians, chapters twelve, thirteen, and fourteen, and the charismatic movement / by Herman D. Seyer. Madison, Wis. : Published for Herman D. Seyer by Fleetwood Art Studios, [1974] 103 p. ; 22 cm. [BS2675.2.S47] 74-18872 2.95
1. Bible. N.T. 1 Corinthians. XII-XIV—Criticism, interpretation, etc. 2. Pentecostalism. 3. Holy Spirit. I. Title.

SHEPARD, William Edward.
The palm tree blessing; a discourse on the various characteristics of the palm tree, illustrating the many features of the sanctified, Christian life. By Evangelist W. E. Shepard ... Kansas City, Mo., Publishing house of the Pentecostal church of the Nazarene, 1913. 167 p. 20 cm. $0.50. 14-9520
I. Title.

SHIBLEY, David. 270.8'2
A charismatic truce / David Shibley. Nashville : T. Nelson, c1978. 116 p. ; 21 cm. Includes bibliographical references. [BR1644.S53] 78-10469 ISBN 0-8407-5663-1 pbk. : 4.95
1. Pentecostalism. I. Title.

STARKES, M. Thomas. 270.8'2
A search for common ground / [M. Thomas Starkes]. Nashville : Broadman Press, c1977. 94 p. ; 19 cm. Bibliography: p. 92-94. [BR1644.S73] 77-79608 ISBN 0-8054-6533-2 pbk. : 1.95
1. Pentecostalism. I. Title.

SYNAN, Vinson. 289.9
The Holiness-Pentecostal movement in the United States. Grand Rapids, Mich., Eerdmans [1971] 248 p. 23 cm. Bibliography: p. 225-239. [BX8763.S96] 79-162033 5.95
1. Pentecostalism. I. Title.

TUGWELL, Simon. 234'.1
Did you receive the Spirit? New York, Paulist Press [1972] 143 p. 19 cm. (Deus books) Includes bibliographical references. [BX2350.T76 1972b] 72-93023 ISBN 0-8091-1760-6 1.25
1. Pentecostalism. I. Title.

URQUHART, Colin. 248'.2'0924 B
When the Spirit comes / Colin Urquhart. 1st U.S. ed. Minneapolis : Bethany Fellowship, 1975, c1974. 127 p. ; 18 cm. (Dimension books) [BX5195.L44S348 1975] 75-21165 ISBN 0-87123-645-1 pbk. : 1.50
1. St. Hugh's Church, Lewsey, Eng. 2. Urquhart, Colin. 3. Pentecostalism. I. Title.

VOIGT, Robert J. 234'.1
Go to the mountain : an insight into charismatic renewal / by Robert J. Voigt; with a foreword by Larry Christenson. St. Meinrad, IN : Abbey Press, 1975. xi, 143 p. ; 21 cm. (A Priority edition) Bibliography: p. 141-143. [BX2350.57.V64] 75-205 ISBN 0-87029-040-1 pbk. : 2.95
1. Pentecostalism. I. Title.

WALSH, Vincent M. 234'.1
A key to charismatic renewal in the Catholic Church / by Vincent M. Walsh. St. Meinrad, Ind. : Abbey Press, 1974. xi, 286 p. ; 20 cm. (A Priority edition) Bibliography: p. 285-286. [BX2350.57.W34] 74-82238 ISBN 0-87029-033-9 : 4.95
1. Pentecostalism. I. Title.

WEAD, Doug. 282'.73
Catholic charismatics: are they for real? Carol Stream, Ill., Creation House [1973] 120 p. 22 cm. First published in 1972 under title: Father McCarthy smokes a pipe and speaks in tongues. [BX2350.57.W42 1973] 73-82862 ISBN 0-88419-044-7 3.95
1. Pentecostalism. I. Title.

WHITAKER, Robert C. 248'.4
Hang in there : counsel for charismatics / by Robert C. Whitaker. Plainfield, N.J. : Logos International, c1974. 49, [5] p. ; 18 cm. Bibliography: p. [51]-[54] [BX8763.W44] 77-179364 ISBN 0-88270-106-1 : 0.75
1. Pentecostalism. I. Title.

WILD, Robert, 1936- 248'.2
Enthusiasm in the Spirit / Robert Wild. Notre Dame, Ind. : Ave Maria Press, c1975. 176 p. ; 21 cm. Includes bibliographical references. [BX2350.57.W54] 75-14742 ISBN 0-87793-101-1 : 4.95 ISBN 0-87793-102-X pbk. : 2.45
1. Pentecostalism. I. Title.

WOGEN, Norris L. 284'.1'0924 B
The shadow of His hand : the dramatic account of one man's quest for fulness of life in the Spirit / Norris L. Wogen. Minneapolis : Bethany Fellowship, [1974] 127 p. ; 21 cm. [BX8080.W65A37] 74-21059 ISBN 0-87123-533-1 pbk. : 2.25
1. Wogen, Norris L. 2. Pentecostalism. I. Title.

Pentecostalism—Addresses, essays, lectures.

FORD, Josephine Massyngberde. 248.2
Baptism of the Spirit; three essays on the Pentecostal experience [by] J. Massingberd Ford. Techny, Ill., Divine Word Publications [1971] xv, 133 p. 18 cm. Contents.Contents.—Charismatic renewal.—Pentecostal blueprint.—Speaking in tongues. Includes bibliographical references. [BX8764.Z6F67] 76-164738 2.95

1. Pentecostalism—Addresses, essays, lectures. I. Title.

HAMILTON, Michael Pollock, 1927- 270.8'2
The charismatic movement, edited by Michael P. Hamilton. Grand Rapids, Eerdmans [1975] 196 p. 23 cm. and phonodisc (2 s. 5 1/2 in. 33 1/3 rpm. microgroove) in pocket. Bibliography: p. 195-196. [BX8764.Z6A2] 74-14865 ISBN 0-8028-3453-1 ISBN 0-8028-1589-8 (pbk.) 6.95
1. Pentecostalism—Addresses, essays, lectures. I. Title.

NEW heaven? New earth? : 230
an encounter with Pentecostalism / [by] Simon Tugwell ... [et al.] ; preface by Walter Hollenweger. London : Darton, Longman and Todd, 1976. 206 p. ; 22 cm. Includes bibliographical references. [BR1644.N48] 77-353539 ISBN 0-232-51350-3 : £2.25
1. Pentecostalism—Addresses, essays, lectures. I. Tugwell, Simon.

PRESENCE, power, praise : 269
documents on the charismatic renewal / Kilian McDonnell, editor. Collegeville, Minn. : Liturgical Press, [1980] p. cm. Includes index. Contents.Contents.—v. 1. National documents.—v. 2. International documents. [BR1644.P73] 79-26080 ISBN 0-8146-1126-5 (set) : 35.00
1. Pentecostalism—Addresses, essays, lectures. I. McDonnell, Kilian.

THE Spirit and the church : 282
a personal and documentary record of the charismatic renewal and the ways it is bursting to life in the Catholic Church / compiled by Ralph Martin. New York : Paulist Press, c1976. viii, 341 p. ; 18 cm. [BX2350.57.S64] 76-9366 ISBN 0-8091-1947-1 pbk. : 2.95
1. Pentecostalism—Addresses, essays, lectures. 2. Church renewal—Catholic Church—Addresses, essays, lectures. I. Martin, Ralph, 1942-

TELFER, William.
A message for you. By William Telfer ... Louisville, Ky., Pentecostal publishing company, c1910. 319 p. front. (port.) 20 cm. 10-11382
I. Title.

Pentecostalism and Christian union.

SUENENS, Leon Joseph, Cardinal, 1904- 261'.001
Ecumenism and charismatic renewal : theological and pastoral orientations / Leon Joseph Cardinal Suenens. Ann Arbor, Mich. : Servant Books ; South Bend, Ind. : available from Servant Books Distribution Center, c1978. ix, 109 p. ; 22 cm. (Malines document ; 2) Translation of Ocumenisme et renouveau charismatique. Includes bibliographical references. [BX9.5.P45S913] 78-108563 ISBN 0-89283-059-X pbk. : 3.00
1. Pentecostalism and Christian union. 2. Pentecostalism—Catholic Church. I. Title. II. Series.

Pentecostalism—Caribbean area—Case studies—Addresses, essays, lectures.

PERSPECTIVES on 278'.082
Pentecostalism : case studies from the Caribbean and Latin America / [edited by] Stephen D. Glazier. Washington, D.C. : University Press of America, c1980. viii, 197 p. ; 22 cm. Includes bibliographies and indexes. [BR1644.5.C37P47] 80-7815 ISBN 0-8191-1071-X lib. bdg. : 16.75 ISBN 0-8191-1072-8 pbk. : 9.00
1. Pentecostalism—Caribbean area—Case studies—Addresses, essays, lectures. 2. Pentecostalism—Latin America—Case studies—Addresses, essays, lectures. I. Glazier, Stephen D.

Pentecostalism—Catholic Church.

BRECKENRIDGE, James F. 230'.2
The theological self-understanding of the Catholic charismatic movement / James F. Breckenridge. Washington, D.C. : University Press of America, c1980. x, 144 p. ; 21 cm. Bibliography: p. 133-144. [BX2350.57.B73] 79-6198 ISBN 0-8191-1006-X pbk. : 7.75
1. Pentecostalism—Catholic Church. I. Title.

CHERVIN, Ronda. 248'.2
Why I am a charismatic, a Catholic explains : reflections on charismatic prayer and the longings of the human heart / Ronda Chervin. Liguori, MO : Liguori Publications, 1978. 123 p. : ill. ; 18 cm. [BX2350.57.C48] 78-62167 ISBN 0-89243-089-3 pbk. : 2.95
1. Chervin, Ronda. 2. Pentecostalism—Catholic Church. I. Title.

LAURENTIN, Rene. 282
Catholic pentecostalism / Rene Laurentin ; translated by Matthew J. O'Connell. 1st ed. Garden City, N.Y. : Doubleday, 1977. 239 p. ; 22 cm. Translation of Pentecotisme chez les catholiques. Bibliography: p. [204]-222. [BX2350.57.L3613] 76-18358 ISBN 0-385-12129-6 : 6.95
1. Pentecostalism—Catholic Church. I. Title.

LAURENTIN, Rene. FIC
Catholic pentecostalism / Rene Laurentin ; translated by Matthew J. O'Connell. Garden City, N.Y : Doubleday, 1978, c1977. 272p. ; 18 cm. (Image Books) Translation of Pentecotisme chez les Catholiques: risques el auenir. Includes bibliographical references. [BX2350.57.L3613] 282 ISBN 0-385-12165-2 pbk. : 3.50
1. Pentecostalism — Catholic Church. I. Title.
L.C. card no. for 1977 Doubleday ed.: 76-18358.

MCDONNELL, Kilian. 262'.001
Charismatic renewal and ecumenism / by Kilian McDonnell. New York : Paulist Press, c1978. ix, 125 p. ; 21 cm. (An Exploration book) Includes bibliographical references. [BX2350.57.M24] 78-58314 ISBN 0-8091-2124-7 pbk. : 4.95
1. Pentecostalism—Catholic Church. 2. Christian union—Catholic Chruch. I. Title.

MCGUIRE, Meredith B. 306'.6
Pentecostal Catholics : power, charisma, and order in a religious movement / Meredith B. McGuire. Philadelphia : Temple University Press, c1982. 270 p. ; 24 cm. Includes bibliographical references and index. [BX2350.57.M39 1982] 19 81-14434 ISBN 0-87722-235-5 : 22.50
1. Catholic Church—United States. 2. Pentecostalism—Catholic Church. I. Title.

PETTEY, Richard J. 253
In His footsteps : the priest and the Catholic charismatic renewal / by Richard J. Pettey. New York : Paulist Press, c1977. 106 p. ; 19 cm. (A Deus book) Bibliography: p. 93-106. [BX2350.57.P48] 76-45274 ISBN 0-8091-2007-0 pbk. : 2.45
1. Pentecostalism—Catholic Church. 2. Pastoral theology—Catholic Church. I. Title.

THERRIEN, Vincent. 248'.48'2
Reaching out : together through the Holy Spirit / Vincent Therrien. 1st ed. Hicksville, N.Y. : Exposition Press, c1978. xi, 107 p. ; 22 cm. (An Exposition-testament book) [BX2350.57.T47] 78-59371 ISBN 0-682-49162-4 : 6.00
1. Pentecostalism—Catholic Church. I. Title.

Pentecostalism—Catholic Church—Addresses, essays, lectures.

SUENENS, Leon-Joseph, Cardinal, 1904- 261.8
Charismatic renewal and social action : a dialogue / Cardinal Leon-Joseph Suenens, Dom Helder Camara. Ann Arbor, Mich. : Servant Books, c1979. 98 p. ; 21 cm. (Malines document ; 3) Includes bibliographical references. [BX2350.57.S93] 79-124023 ISBN 0-89283-074-3 : 3.00
1. Pentecostalism—Catholic Church—Addresses, essays, lectures. 2. Church and social problems—Catholic Church—Addresses, essays, lectures. I. Camara, Helder, 1909- joint author. II. Title. III. Series.

Pentecostalism—Catholic Church—Congresses.

SCRIPTURE and the charismatic 220
renewal : proceedings of the Milwaukee symposium, December 1-3, 1978 / [Avery Dulles ... et al.] ; edited by George Martin. Ann Arbor, Mich. : Servant Books, c1979. 127 p. ; 21 cm. Includes bibliographical references. [BS587.S36] 79-118786 ISBN 0-89283-070-0 pbk. : 4.00
1. Bible—Study—Catholic Church—Congresses. 2. Bible—Criticism, interpretation, etc.—Congresses. 3. Pentecostalism—Catholic Church—Congresses. I. Dulles, Avery Robert, 1918- II. Martin, George, 1939-

THEOLOGICAL reflections 262'.001
on the charismatic renewal : proceedings of the Chicago conference, October 1-2, 1976 / edited by John C. Haughey. Ann Arbor : Servant Books ; South Bend, Ind. : available from Servant Publications Distribution Center, c1978. viii, 129 p. ; 21 cm. "Sponsored by the National Service Committee of the Catholic Charismatic Renewal." Includes bibliographical references. [BX2350.57.T45] 78-105558 ISBN 0-89283-048-4 pbk. : 4.00
1. Pentecostalism—Catholic Church—Congresses. I. Haughey, John C. II. National Service Committee of the Catholic Charismatic Renewal.

Pentecostalism—Church of England.

†GUNSTONE, John Thomas Arthur. 283'.092'4 B
Living together : the warm and candid story of one man's experience in a Christian community / John Gunstone ; drawings by Sylvia Lawton. 1st American ed. Minneapolis : Bethany Fellowship, 1976. 125 p. : ill. ; 18 cm. (Dimension books) [BX5186.B37G86 1976] 76-57794 ISBN 0-87123-325-8 pbk. : 1.95
1. Barnabas Fellowship. 2. Gunstone, John Thomas Arthur. 3. Church of England—Clergy—Biography. 4. Pentecostalism—Church of England. 5. Clergy—England—Biography. I. Title.

Pentecostalism—Congresses.

WHAT the Spirit is saying 234'.1
to the churches : essays / by Krister Stendahl ... [et al.] ; edited by Theodore Runyon. New York : Hawthorn Books, c1975. viii, 142 p. ; 21 cm. Includes bibliographical references. [BX8762.A2A5 1975] 75-2563 ISBN 0-8015-8546-5 : 3.95
1. Pentecostalism—Congresses. 2. Holy Spirit—Congresses. I. Stendahl, Krister. II. Runyon, Theodore.

Pentecostalism—Controversial literature.

GARDINER, George E. 234'.1
The Corinthian catastrophe / George E. Gardiner. Grand Rapids, MI : Kregel Publications, [1974] 56 p. ; 18 cm. [BX8763.G37] 74-75106 ISBN 0-8254-2708-8 pbk. : 0.95
1. Pentecostalism—Controversial literature. I. Title.

†REYMOND, Robert L. 248'.29
"What about continuing revelations and miracles in the Presbyterian Church today?" : A study of the doctrine of the sufficiency of Scripture / by Robert L. Reymond. [Nutley, N.J.] : Presbyterian and Reformed Pub. Co., 1977. 64 p. ; 22 cm. Bibliography: p. 54. [BX9177.R48] 78-104353 pbk. : 1.95
1. Presbyterian Church—Doctrinal and controversial works. 2. Bible—Inspiration. 3. Pentecostalism—Controversial literature. 4. Authority (Religion) I. Title.

Pentecostalism—History.

QUEBEDEAUX, Richard. 270.8'2
The new charismatics : the origins, development, and significance of neo-pentecostalism / Richard Quebedeaux. 1st ed. Garden City, N.Y. : Doubleday, 1976. xii, 252 p. ; 22 cm. A revision of the author's thesis, Oxford University, 1975. Includes index. Bibliography: p. [233]-242. [BX8762.Q4 1976] 75-21242 ISBN 0-385-11007-3 : 7.95
1. Pentecostalism—History. I. Title.

Pentecostalism—History—Congresses.

ASPECTS of pentecostal- 270.8'2
charismatic origins / Vinson Synan, editor. Plainfield, N.J. : Logos International, c1975. iv, 252 p. ; 21 cm. Papers delivered at the 3d annual meeting of the Society for Pentecostal Studies at Lee College, Cleveland, Tenn., in 1973. Includes bibliographical references and index. [BX8762.A72] 75-2802 ISBN 0-88270-110-X : 5.95. ISBN 0-88270-111-8 pbk. : 3.50
1. Pentecostalism—History—Congresses. I. Synan, Vinson. II. Society for Pentecostal Studies.

Pentecostalism—History—Sources.

TOUCHED by the fire : 269
eyewitness accounts of the early twentieth-century Pentecostal revival / edited by Wayne E. Warner. Plainfield, N.J. : Logos International, c1978. xiv, 163 p. ; 20 cm. [BR1644.T68] 77-99206 ISBN 0-88270-270-X pbk. : 2.95
1. Pentecostalism—History—Sources. I. Warner, Wayne E.

Pentecostalism—Lutheran Church.

CHRISTENSON, Laurence. 234'.1
The charismatic renewal among Lutherans : a pastoral and theological perspective / Larry Christenson. [Minneapolis] : Lutheran Charismatic Renewal Services : distributed by Bethany Fellowship, c1976. 160 p. ; 21 cm. Bibliography: p. [141]-151. [BX8065.5.C47] 76-377263 pbk. : 2.95
1. Pentecostalism—Lutheran Church. I. Title.

Pentecostalism—Mennonites—Addresses, essays, lectures.

MY personal Pentecost 230'.9'7
/ edited by Roy S. and Martha Koch ; foreword by Kevin Ranaghan. Scottdale, Pa. : Herald Press, c1977. 275 p. : port. ; 20 cm. Includes bibliographical references. [BX8128.C47M9] 77-79229 ISBN 0-8361-1816-2 pbk. : 3.95
1. Pentecostalism—Mennonites—Addresses, essays, lectures. 2. Mennonites—United States—Biography—Addresses, essays, lectures. I. Koch, Roy S., 1913- II. Koch, Martha.

Pentecostalism—Periodicals—Bibliography.

ORAL Roberts University. Pentecostal Collection. 016.2482'05
A bibliography of the pentecostal periodical holdings in the Oral Roberts University Pentecostal Collection. S. Juanita Walker, compiler. Tulsa, Okla. [1971] 27 l. 28 cm. [Z7845.P4O7] 73-31387
1. Pentecostalism—Periodicals—Bibliography. I. Walker, S. Juanita, comp. II. Title.

Pentecostalism—Personal narratives.

NEW wine, new skins : 248'.5
twenty-five people tell how they encountered the transforming power of the Spirit in the charismatic renewal / compiled by Ralph Martin. New York : Paulist Press, c1976. viii, 174 p. ; 19 cm. [BX2350.57.N48] 76-2855 ISBN 0-8091-1942-0 pbk. : 2.25
1. Pentecostalism—Personal narratives. I. Martin, Ralph, 1942-
Contents omitted

Pentecostalism—United States.

ANDERSON, Robert Mapes. 289.9
Vision of the disinherited : the making of American Pentecostalism / Robert Mapes Anderson. New York : Oxford University Press, 1979. 334 p. ; 22 cm. Includes index. Bibliography: p. 297-326.

[BR1644.5.U6A5] 78-12905 ISBN 0-19-502502-4 : 14.95
1. Pentecostalism—United States. I. Title.

POLOMA, Margaret M. 306'.6'0973
The charismatic movement : is there a new pentecost? / Margaret M. Poloma. Boston, Mass. : Twayne Publishers, c1982. p. cm. (Social movements past and present) Includes index. Bibliography: p. [BR1644.5.U6P64 1982] 19 82-11983 ISBN 0-8057-9701-7 : 16.95
1. Pentecostalism—United States. I. Title. II. Series.

Pentecostalism—United States—History.

BRUMBACK, Carl, 1917- 270.8'2
A sound from heaven / Carl Brumback. Springfield, Mo. : Gospel Pub. House, c1977. iii, 153 p. : ill. ; 22 cm. Includes index. Bibliography: p. 147-149. [BR1644.5.U6B76] 76-58781 ISBN 0-88243-560-4 : 2.95
1. Pentecostalism—United States—History. I. Title.

Pentecostals—Bulgaria—Biography.

POPOV, Ladin, 1915- 272'.9 B
The fugitive / Ladin Popov, with Phil Streeter. Grand Rapids, Mich. : Zondervan Pub. House, c1981. 127 p. ; 18 cm. [BX8762.Z8P666] 19 81-16014 ISBN 0-310-44612-0 pbk. : 2.95
1. Popov, Ladin, 1915- 2. Pentecostals—Bulgaria—Biography. 3. Clergy—Bulgaria—Biography. I. Streeter, Phil. II. Title.

Pentecostals—Clergy—Biography.

CAROTHERS, Merlin R. 289'.9 B
Victory on Praise Mountain / Merlin Carothers. Plainfield, N.J. : Logos International, c1979. viii, 177 p. ; 21 cm. [BX8762.Z8C373] 79-88266 ISBN 0-88270-378-1 pbk. : 2.95
1. Carothers, Merlin R. 2. Pentecostals—Clergy—Biography. 3. Clergy—United States—Biography. I. Title.

CHAMBERS, Catherine, 1920- 289.9 B
The measure of a man : the biography of Stanley Warren Chambers / by Catherine Chambers. Hazelwood, Mo. : Word Aflame Press, c1978. 191 p., [16] leaves of plates : ill. ; 22 cm. [BX8780.Z8C463] 78-111263 7.94
1. Chambers, Stanley Warren, 1915- 2. Pentecostals—Clergy—Biography. 3. Clergy—United States—Biography. I. Title.
Pub. Address: 8855 Dunn Rd., Hazelwood MO 63042

MAINSE, David. 289.9'4'0924
100 Huntley Street : the exciting success story from the host of Canada's popular television program / by David Mainse with David Manuel Plainfield, NJ : Logos International, c1979. xi, 158 p., [7] leaves of plates : ill. ; 21 cm. [BX8762.Z8M374] ISBN 0-88270-383-8 pbk. : 3.95 3.95
1. Mainse, David. 2. 100 Huntley Street (Television program) 3. Pentecostals—Clergy—Biography. 4. Clergy—Canada—Biography. I. Manuel, David, joint author. II. 100 Huntley Street (Television program)

SMITH, Malcolm, 1938- 248'.3
How I learned to meditate / Malcolm Smith. Plainfield, N.J. : Logos International, c1977. viii, 127 p. ; 21 cm. [BX8762.Z8S637] 77-18482 ISBN 0-88270-253-X pbk. : 2.95
1. Smith, Malcolm, 1938- 2. Pentecostals—Clergy—Biography. 3. Clergy—United States—Biography. 4. Clergy—England—Biography. 5. Meditation. I. Title.

Pentecostals—United States—Biography.

ASHCRAFT, Tom. 289.9 B
Prodigal husband / by Tom Ashcraft, with Max Call. Costa Mesa, Calif. : Gift Publications, 1980, c1981. ii, 172 p. ; 22 cm. [BX8762.Z8A852] 19 80-67300 ISBN 0-86595-002-4 pbk. : Price unreported.
1. Ashcraft, Tom. 2. Pentecostals—United States—Biography. I. Call, Max, joint author. II. Title.

BARTLEMAN, Frank, 1871-1935. 289.9 B
Azusa Street / by Frank Bartleman ; with foreword by Vinson Synan. Plainfield, N.J.: Logos International, c1980. xxvi, 184 p. ; 21 cm. Reprint of the 1925 ed. published under title: How Pentecost came to Los Angeles. [BX8762.Z8B373 1980] 19 80-82806 ISBN 0-88270-439-7 pbk. : 4.95
1. Bartleman, Frank, 1871-1935. 2. Pentecostals—United States—Biography. 3. Pentecostalism—History. 4. Revivals—California—Los Angeles. 5. Los Angeles—Church history. I. Title.

BROWNELL, Ada. 289.9 B
Confessions of a pentecostal / Ada Brownell. Springfield, Mo. : Gospel Pub. House, c1978. 96 p. ; 18 cm. (Radiant books) [BX8762.Z8B763] 77-92887 ISBN 0-88243-476-4 : pbk. : 1.25
1. Brownell, Ada. 2. Pentecostals—United States—Biography. I. Title.

CLARK, Donna, 1932- 289.9 B
Christ's people / by Donna Clark. Westminster, Calif. : New World Cup Press, c1980. 139 p., [5] leaves of plates : ill. ; 22 cm. [BX8762.Z8A17] 19 80-81940 ISBN 0-9604636-0-7 (pbk.) : 5.95
1. Clark family. 2. Pentecostals—United States—Biography. I. Title.

GODMAN, Henry C. 289.9 B
Supreme Commander / by Henry C. Godman, with Cliff Dudley. 1st ed. Harrison, Ark. : New Leaf Press, 1980. 125 p. : ill. ; 22 cm. [BX8762.Z8G63] 19 80-80658 ISBN 0-89221-076-1 pbk. : 3.95
1. Godman, Henry C. 2. United States. Air Force—Biography. 3. Pentecostals—United States—Biography. 4. Air pilots, Military—United States—Biography. I. Dudley, Cliff, joint author. II. Title.

VALDEZ, A. C. 269'.2'0924 B
Fire on Azusa Street / by A.C. Valdez, Sr. with James F. Scheer. Costa Mesa, Calif. : Gift Publications, c1980, 1981. 139 p. ; 22 cm. [BX8762.Z8V348] 19 80-67301 ISBN 0-86595-003-2 pbk. : Price unreported.
1. Valdez, A. C. 2. Pentecostals—United States—Biography. 3. Pentecostalism—History. 4. Revivals—California—Los Angeles. 5. Los Angeles (Calif.)—Church history. I. Scheer, James F. II. Title. III. Title: Azusa Street.

Peoples Temple.

FEINSOD, Ethan. 289.9
Awake in a nightmare : Jonestown, the only eyewitness account / Ethan Feinsod. 1st ed. New York : Norton, c1981. 222 p. ; 22 cm. Based on interviews with Odell Rhodes. Includes bibliographical references. [BP605.P46F44 1981] 19 80-20229 ISBN 0-393-01431-2 : 14.95
1. Peoples Temple. 2. Jones, Jim, 1931-1978. 3. Rhodes, Odell. I. Rhodes, Odell. II. Title. III. Title: Jonestown, the only eyewitness account.

KERNS, Phil. 289.9
People's Temple, people's tomb / by Phil Kerns, with Doug Wead. Plainfield, N.J. : Logos International, c1979. xi, 288 p. : ill. ; 18 cm. [BP605.P46K47] 78-71992 ISBN 0-88270-349-8 pbk. : 2.25
1. Peoples Temple. 2. Jones, Jim, 1931-1978. I. Wead, Doug, joint author. II. Title.

LANE, Mark. 988'.11
The strongest poison / Mark Lane. New York : Hawthorn Books, c1980. x, 494 p. ; 25 cm. Includes bibliographical references and index. [BP605.P46L36 1980] 79-87777 ISBN 0-8015-3206-X : 12.95
1. Peoples Temple. 2. Jones, Jim, 1931-1978. I. Title.

MILLS, Jeannie. 289.9
Six years with God : life inside Reverend Jim Jones's Peoples Temple / by Jeannie Mills. New York : A & W Publishers, c1979. 319 p. : ill. ; 24 cm. [BP605.P46M54] 79-50356 ISBN 0-89479-046-3 : 12.95
1. Peoples Temple. 2. Jones, Jim, 1931-1978. 3. Mills, Jeannie. I. Title.

NAIPAUL, Shiva, 1945- 289.9
Journey to nowhere : a New World tragedy / by Shiva Naipaul. New York : Simon and Schuster, c1981. 336 p. ; 22 cm. First published in 1980 under title: Black and white. Includes index. Bibliography: p. 317-320. [BP605.P46N34 1981] 19 80-28138 ISBN 0-671-42471-8 : 13.95
1. Peoples Temple. 2. Jones, Jim, 1931-1978. I. [Black and white] II. Title.

NAIPAUL, Shiva, 1945- 289.9
Journey to nowhere : a New World tragedy / by Shiva Naipaul. New York, N.Y. : Penguin, 1982. 336 p. ; 20 cm. Previously published as: Black and white. New York : Simon and Schuster, 1981. Includes index. Bibliography: p. 317-320. [BP605.P46N34 1982] 19 81-19228 pbk. : 5.95
1. Peoples Temple. 2. Jones, Jim, 1931-1978. I. [Black and white] II. Title.

WOODEN, Kenneth. 362.7'044
The children of Jonestown / by Kenneth Wooden. 1st McGraw-Hill paperback ed. New York : McGraw-Hill, 1980, c1981. p. cm. Bibliography: p. [BP605.P46W66] 80-16663 ISBN 0-07-071641-2 (pbk.) : 4.95
1. Peoples Temple. 2. Children—Guyana. 3. Children—United States. I. Title.

YEE, Min S. 973.92092'2 B
In my father's house : the story of the Layton family and the Reverend Jim Jones / by Min S. Yee, Thomas N. Layton [et al54. 1st ed. New York : Berkley Books, 1982, c1981. 335 p. ; 18 cm. [CT274. L38 Y43] ISBN 0-425-05387-3 pbk. : 2.95
1. Layton Family. 2. Jones Jim, 1931-1978. 3. People's Temple. I. Layton, Thomas N. joint author. II. Title.
L.C. card number for 1981 Holt Rinehart and Winston edition: 80-26349

Peoples Temple—Addresses, essays, lectures.

VIOLENCE and religous 289.9
commitment : implications of Jim Jones's People's Temple movement / edited by Ken Levi. University Park : Pennsylvania State University Press, [1981] p. cm. Includes index. Bibliography: p. [BP605.P46V56] 19 81-83147 ISBN 0-271-00296-4 : 17.50
1. Peoples Temple—Addresses, essays, lectures. 2. Jones, Jim, 1931-1978—Addresses, essays, lectures. 3. Cults—Addresses, essays, lectures. 4. Violence—Moral and religious aspects—Addresses, essays, lectures. I. Levi, Ken, 1946-

People's Temple—History.

MAGUIRE, John. 289.9
Hold hands and die! : The incredibly true story of the People's Temple and the Reverend Jim Jones / by John Maguire and Mary Lee Dunn. New York : Dale Books, c1978. 271 p. : ill. ; 18 cm. [BP605.P46M33] 78-74721 ISBN 0-89559-190-1 : 2.50
1. People's Temple—History. 2. Jones, Jim, 1931-1978. I. Dunn, Mary Lee, joint author. II. Title.

Pepys, Samuel, 1633-1703—Addresses, essays, lectures.

MATTHEWS, Arnold Gwynne. 280'.4'0941
Mr. Pepys and Nonconformity / A. G. Matthews. Folcroft, Pa. : Folcroft Library Editions, 1979. p. cm. Reprint of the 1954 ed. published by Independent Press, London. Includes bibliographical references. [DA447.P4M38 1979] 79-1353 ISBN 0-8414-6335-2 lib. bdg. : 12.50
1. Pepys, Samuel, 1633-1703—Addresses, essays, lectures. 2. Dissenters, Religious—England—Addresses, essays, lectures. 3. Puritans—Addresses, essays, lectures. I. Title.

Perboyre, Jean Gabriel, 1802-1840.

LIFE of the blessed 922.251
servant of God, the heroic martyr, John Gabriel Perboyre, priest of the Congregation of the mission. Translated from the French by Lady Clare Feilding. Appendix specially prepared for American edition. New Orleans, Finney brothers, 1894. x p., 1 l., [13]-177 p. front. (port.) pl. 18 cm. [BX4705.P425V52 1894] 37-14652
1. Perboyre, Jean Gabriel, 1802-1840. 2. Congregation of priests of the mission in China. I. Feilding, Clara. Lady r.

Perceval, Arthur Philip, 1799-1853.

POWELL, Thomas. 262.
An essay on apostolical succession; being a defence of a genuine protestant ministry, against the exclusive and intolerant schemes of papists and high churchmen: and supplying a general antidote to poperly: also a critique on the Apology for apostolical succession, by the Hon. and Rev. A. P. Perceval ... and a review of Dr. W. F. Hook's sermon on "Hear the church," preached before the Queen, June 17, 1838: by Thomas Powell ... New York, G. Lane & P. P. Sandford, 1842. 354 p. 19 cm. Second edition, London, 1840. [BV665.P7 1842] 17-31585
1. Perceval, Arthur Philip, 1799-1853. 2. An apology for the doctrine of apostolical succession. 3. Hook, Walter Farquhar, 1798-1875. Hear the church. 4. Apostolic succession. I. Title.

Perfection.

ALGER, Simeon. 232
The Scripture doctrines of the pre-existence of the humanity of Jesus Christ, before His birth in Bethlehem of Judea. And the nature of His kingdom that was promised to Him: also, in part second, Christian perfection and purity as found in the Scriptures. By Rev. Simeon Alger. Des Moines, Ia., Mills & company, printers, 1884. 94 p. 21 1/2 cm. [BT201.A35] 37-15219
1. Jesus Christ—Pre-existence. 2. Perfection. I. Title.

ANDREWS, W P. 234
Two epistles: I. To professors of perfect love. II. To opposers of the "second blessing". By Rev. W. P. Andrews ... Edited by Jno. J. Tigert ... Nashville, Tenn., Publishing house of the M.E. church, South, Barbee & Smith, agents, 1897. vi p., 1 l., 144 p. 19 cm. [BT766.A5] 41-31263
1. Perfection. I. Tigert, John James, 1856-1906. II. Title.

BIDDLE, Jacob Albert.
The perfect life, by Rev. Jacob Albert Biddle. Boston, The Roxburgh publishing company, incorporated [c1915] 192 p. 20 cm. 15-18638 1.25
I. Title.

[CALDWELL, Merritt] 1806-1848. 234
The philosophy of Christian perfection; embracing a psychological statement of some of the principles of Christianity on which this doctrine rests: together with a practical examination of the peculiar views of several recent writers on this subject. Philadelphia, Sorin and Ball, 1848. v, 7-159 p. 19 cm. [BT766.C2 1848] 41-32816
1. Perfection. I. Title.

CALDWELL, Merritt, 1806-1848. 234.
The philosophy of Christian perfection: embracing a psychological statement of some of the principles of Christianity on which this doctrine rests: together with a practical examination of the peculiar views of several recent writers on this subject. By Merritt Caldwell ... Introduction by Rev. Wm. Hosmer. Auburn, Derby and Miller; Buffalo, Derby, Orton and Mulligan, 1853. ix, [ii]-v, 7-164 p. 19 cm. First published 1847? [BT760.C2] 7-30192
1. Perfection. I. Title.

CARTER, Thomas, 1817-1888. 234
All for Christ; or, How the Christian may obtain, by a renewed consecration of his heart, the fullness of joy referred to by the Saviour just previous to His crucifixion. With illustrations from the lives of those who have made this consecrations By Rev. Thomas Carter ... New York, Nelson & Phillips; Cincinnati, Hitchcock & Walden, 1875. 192 p. 17 cm. [BT766.C3] 41-31264
1. Perfection. 2. Title. I. Title.

CHADWICK, Samuel, 1860-1932. 234
... *The call to Christian perfection.* United States ed. Kansas City, Mo., Beacon hill press, 1943. 110 p. 20 1/2 cm. [BT766.C5 1943] 44-7792
1. Perfection. I. Title.

DAMPHOUX, Edward, 1788-1860. 234
The practice of Christian perfection; from Rodriguez, and other Catholic authors. By the Rev. D. Damphoux ... 2d ed., rev. and enl. Baltimore, F. Lucas, jr. [1836] viii, [13]-634 p. 19 cm. [BT766.D3 1836] 38-20560
1. Perfection. I. Rodriguez, alonso, 1526-1616. II. Title.

DUNN, Lewis Romaine, 1822-1898.
A manual of holiness and review of Dr. James B. Mudge. By Rev. Lewis R. Dunn ... Cincinnati, Cranston & Curts; New York, Hunt & Eaton, 1895. 152 p. 20 cm. [BT67.M9D8] 41-35230
1. Mudge, James, 1844-1918. Growth in holiness toward perfection. 2. Perfection. I. Title.

FLEW, Robert Newton. 234
The idea of perfection in Christian theology; an historical study of the Christian ideal for the present life, by R. Newton Flew ... London, H. Milford, Oxford university press, 1934. xv, 422 p., 1 l 22 1/2 cm. [BT766.F5] 34-24116
1. Perfection. I. Title.

FOWLER, Charles J. 234
Chair-talks on perfection, by Rev. Charles J. Fowler ... Chicago, Ill., The Christian witness co. [c1918] 1 p. l., 75 p. 17 cm. [BT766.F6] 18-15891
I. Title.

FRANKLIN, Samuel, 1820-1887. 234
A critical review of Wesleyan perfection, in twenty-four consecutive arguments, in which the doctrine of sin in believers is discussed, and the proof-texts of Scripture advocating entire sanctification, as a second and distinct blessing in the soul after regeneration, fairly debated. By Rev. S. Franklin ... Cincinnati, Printed at the Methodist book concern, for the author, 1866. 614 p. 21 cm. [BT766.F8] 41-82881
1. Perfection. 2. Methodist church—Doctrinal and controversial works. I. Title. II. Title: Wesleyan perfection.

GODBEY, William B 1833-1920. 234
Christian perfection. By Rev. W. B. Godbey ... Nashville, Southern Methodist publishing house, printed for the author, 1886. 128 p. 16 cm. [BT766.G5] 41-31266
1. Perfection. I. Title.

MCDONALD, William, 1820-1901. 234
The New Testament standard of piety; or, Our love made perfect. By Rev. W. McDonald ... Rev. ed. Boston, McDonald & Gill, 1882. 287 p. front. (port.) 17 1/2 cm. [BT766.M2] 41-31267
1. Perfection. I. Title.

MAHAN, Asa, 1800-1889. 234.8
Scripture doctrine of Christian perfection; with other kindred subjects, illustrated and confirmed in a series of discourses designed to throw light on the way of holiness. By Rev. Asa Mahan ... Boston, D. S. King, 1839. 237 p. 18 cm. [BT766.M3 1839] 18-174
1. Perfection. I. Title.

MAHAN, Asa, 1800-1889. 234.8
Scripture doctrine of Christian perfection; with other kindred subjects illustrated and confirmed in a series of discourses designed to throw light on the way of holiness. By Rev. Asa Mahan ... 4th ed. Boston, D. S. King, 1840. 198 p. 16 cm. [BT766.M3] 41-31269
1. Perfection. I. Title.

MAHAN, Asa, 1800-1889. 234.8
Scripture doctrine of Christian perfection; with other kindred subjects, illustrated and confirmed in a series of discourses designed to throw light on the way of holiness. By Rev. Asa Mahan ... 7th ed. Boston, Waite, Peirce & co., 1844. 193 p. 16 cm. [BT766.M3 1844] 18-173
1. Perfection. I. Title.

MASSON, Thomas Lansing, 1866-1934. 218
The city of perfection, by Thomas L. Masson. New York, and London, The Century co. [c1927] xii, 406 p. front. (port.) 19 cm. Bibliography: p. 391-400. [BD431.M38] 27-3657
I. Title.

MERRITT, Timothy, 1775-1845 comp. 234
The Christian's manual, a treatise on Christian perfection; with directions for obtaining that state. Compiled principally from the works of the Rev. John Wesley. By the Rev. T. Merritt. 4th ed. New-York, Pub. by N. Bangs and J. Emory for the Methodist Episcopal church, 1827. viii, [9]-160 p. 11 cm. [BT766.M4 1827] 8-6828
1. Perfection. I. Wesley, John, 1703-1791. II. Title.

MUDGE, James, 1844-
The perfect life in experience and doctrine; a restatement, by Rev. James Mudge, D. D. With an introduction by Rev. William F. Warren ... Cincinnati, Jennings and Graham; New York, Eaton and Mains [c1911] 311 p., 1 l. 21 cm. 11-22152 1.25
I. Warren, William Fairfield, 1833- II. Title.

MURRAY, Andrew, 1828-1917 240
Be perfect! A message from the Father in heaven to His children on earth; Meditations. Minneapolis, Bethany [c.1965] 171p. 19cm. [BT766.M78] 1.50 pap.,
1. Perfection. I. Title.

MURRAY, Andrew, 1828-1917. 240
Be perfect; "Be perfect as your Heavenly Father is perfect": a devotional study of Christ's Command. Minneapolis, Minn., Bethany Fellowship [1973, c.1966] 171 p. 18 cm. (Dimension Books) [BT766.M78] ISBN 0-87123-031-3 pap., 1.25
1. Perfection. I. Title.

MURRAY, Andrew, 1828-1917. 234
"Love made perfect." By the Rev. Andrew Murray ... Chicago, New York [etc.] Fleming H. Revell company [1894] 73 p. incl. front. (port.) 16 cm. "The substance of addresses delivered at the South African Keswick of 1893." First published in the South African pioneer. cf. Pref. [BT766.M8] 40-25519
1. Perfection. 2. Love (Theology) I. Title.

PECK, George, 1797-1876. 234
The Scripture doctrine of Christian perfection stated and defended; with a critical and historical examination of the controversy, both ancient and modern. Also practical illustrations and advices. In a series of lectures. By Rev. George Peck, D. D. New-York, G. Lane & P. P. Sandford, 1842. 474 p. 20 cm. [BT766.P3 1842] 33-25838
1. Perfection. I. Title.

PECK, George, 1797-1876. 234
The Scripture doctrine of Christian perfection stated and defended: with a critical and historical examination of the controversy, ancient and modern. Also practical illustrations and advices. By George Peck, D. D. 3d ed., rev. New-York, Lane & Scott, 1848. 470 p. 19 cm. [BT766.P3 1848] 15-24160
1. Perfection. I. Title.

PECK, George, 1797-1876. 234
The Scripture doctrine of Christian perfection stated and defended: with practical illustrations and advices. In a series of lectures. By Rev. George Peck, D. D. Abridged from the author's larger work. New-York, Lane & Scott, 1851. xiv, [7]-332 p. 16 cm. [BT766.P34 1851] 15-16199
1. Perfection. I. Title.

PECK, George, 1797-1876. 234
The Scripture doctrine of Christian perfection stated and defended; with a critical and historical examination of the controversy, ancient and modern. Also practical illustrations and advices, by George Peck, D. D. 10th ed., rev. New York, Carlton & Porter [186-?] 470 p. 19 cm. [BT766.P32] 33-35171
1. Perfection. I. Title.

PECK, George, 1797-1876. 234
The Scripture doctrine of Christian perfection stated and defended: withpractical illustrations and advices. In a series of lectures. By Rev.George Peck, D. D. Abridged from the author's larger work. New-York, Lane and Tippett, 1845. xiv, [7]-332 p. 16 cm. [BT766.P34 1845.] 33-25833
1. Perfection. I. Title.

PERFECT love; 234
or, The speeches of Rev. E. L. Janes, Rev. H. Mattison, D. D., Rev. D. Curry, D. D., Rev. J. M. Buckley, and Rev. S. D. Brown, in the New York preachers' meeting, in March and April, 1867, upon the subject of sanctification. Also, Bishop Janes' sermon, on sin and salvation, at the Newark conference camp-meeting, Morristown, Aug. 18, 1867. New York, N. Tibbals & co., 1868. 129 p. 20 cm. [BT766.P4] 41-33833
1. Perfection. I. Janes, Edmund Storer, bp., 1807-1876. II. Mattison, Hiram, 1811-1868. III. Janes, Edwin Lines, 1807-1875.

PRESBYTERIAN church in the U. S. A. (New school) Presbyterian of Cleveland. 234
An exposition of the peculiarities, difficulties and tendencies of Oberlin perfercionism. Prepared by a committee of the presbytery of Cleveland; and by the presbytery ordered to be published under the direction of said committee, October 8th, 1840. Cleveland, Printed by T. H. Smead, 1841. 84 p. 21 cm. [BT766.P8] 5-3207
1. Perfection. I. Title.

REED, Marshall Russell, B p., 1891- 248.42
Achieving Christian perfection. Nashville, Methodist Evangelistic Materials [c1962] 63 p. 29 cm. [BT766.R4] 62-20645
1. Perfection. I. Title.

STEEL, Daniel, 1824-1914. 234.
A defense of Christian perfection; or, A criticism of Dr. James Mudge's "Growth in holiness toward pefection," by Daniel Steele ... New York, Hunt & Eaton; Cincinnati, Cranston & Curtis, 1896. 136 p. 19 cm. [BT767.M9S8] 41-25231
1. Mudge, James, 1844-1918. Growth in holiness toward perfection. 2. Perfection. I. Title.

STEELE, Daniel, 1824-1914. 234
Love enthroned: essays on evangelical perfection. By Daniel Steele ... New York, Nelson & Phillips; Cincinnati, Hitchcock & Walden, 1875. 416 p. 18 cm. [BT66.S8] 41-32833
1. Perfection. I. Title.

STEELE, Daniel, 1824-1914. 234
Love enthroned; essays on evangelical perfection, by Daniel Steele ... 12th thousand. New York, Eaton & Mains; Cincinnati, Jennings & Pye [c1903] 416 p. 19 cm. Original copyright, 1875. [BT766.S8 1903] 3-17551
1. Perfection. I. Title.

STEELE, Daniel, 1824-1914. 234
Love enthroned; essays on evangelical perfection, by Daniel Steele ... 13th thousand. Rev. ed. New York, Eaton & Mains; Cincinnati, Jennings & Graham [c1908] 427 p. 19 cm. [BT766.S8 1908] 8-31646
1. Perfection. I. Title.

TREFFRY, Richard. 234
A treatise on Christian perfection. By Richard Treffry ... Boston, Mass., McDonald, Gill & co., 1888. 215 p. 19 cm. [BT766.T7] 41-32834
1. Perfection. I. Title.

TRUE method of promoting perfect love. 234
From debates in the New-York preachers' meeting of the Methodist-Episcopal church, on the question, What are the best methods of promoting the experience of perfect love? 3d ed. New York, Foster & Palmer, jr., 1867. iv, 5-136 p. 18 1/2 cm. [BT766.T8 1867] 41-33064
1. Perfection. I. Inskip, John Swanel, 1816-1884. II. Title: Perfect love, True method of promoting.
Contents omitted.

WARFIELD, Benjamin Breckinridge, 1851-1921. 234
Perfectionism ... by Benjamin Breckinridge Warfield ... New York [etc.] Oxford university press, 1931- v. 24 cm. Lettered on cover: Studies in perfectionism. "Prefatory note" signed: Ethelbert D. Warfield, William Park Armstrong, Caspar Winstar Hodge, committee. [BT766.W3] 32-1171
1. Perfection. I. Warfield, Ethelbert Dudley, 1861- ed. II. Title.

WESLEY, John, 1703-1791. 234
Christian perfection, as believed and taught by John Wesley; edited and with an introd. by Thomas S. Kepler. Cleveland, World Pub. Co. [1954] xviii, 144p. 17cm. (World devotional classics) [BT766.W515 1954] 52-8445
1. Perfection. I. Title.

WESLEY, John, 1703-1791. 234
Christian perfection as taught by John Wesley. Compiled by Rev. J. A. Wood ... Introduction by Bishop W. F. Mallalieu ... Chicago and Boston, The Christian witness co. [c1921] 288 p. front. (port.) 19 cm. [BT766.W5 1921] 22-1726
1. Perfection. I. Wood, John Allen, b. 1828, comp. II. Title.

WESLEY, John, 1703-1791. 234
Christian perfection as taught by John Wesley, by Josiah Henry Barr. [Apollo, Pa.] The American holiness journal [1946] 2 p. l., 119, [1] p. 19 1/2 cm. [BT766.W515] 46-20755
1. Perfection. I. Barr, Josiah Henry, ed. II. Title.

WESLEY, John, 1703-1791. 234'.8
Christian perfection; selections, edited by David A. MacLennan. New York, World Pub. Co. [1969] 63 p. 17 cm. (World inspirational books) [BT766.W522 1969] 71-90925 1.25
1. Perfection. I. Title.

WESLEY, John, 1703-1791. 234
A plain account of Christian perfection, as believed and taught by Rev. John Wesley, from 1725 to 1777. 36th ed. New York, Carlton & Lanahan; Cincinnati, Hitchcock & Walden [187-?] 175 p. 12 1/2 cm. [BT766.W52] 34-28851
1. Perfection. I. Title.

WOODS, Leonard, 1774-1854. 234
An examination of the doctrine of perfection, as held by Rev. Asa Mahan ... and others. By Rev. Leonard Woods ... New York, W. R. Peters; London, Wiley & Putnam, 1841. viii, [9]-140 p. 15 1/2 cm. "First published in the 'American Biblical repository' for January and April, 1841." [BT766.W8] 34-7196
1. Perfection. I. Mahan, Asa, 1800-1889. Scripture doctrine of Christian perfection. II. Title.

WRIGHT, Thomas, 1874-
Living faith, the Catholic layman instructed in the way of Christian perfection, by the Very Rev. Canon Thomas Wright; foreword by the Rt. Rev. Bishop of Middlesbrough. London, Burns, Oates & Washbourne, ltd.; New York, P. J. Kenedy & sons [1934] viii, 196 p. 19 cm. A 40
1. Perfection. I. Title.

Perfection—Addresses, essays, lectures.

PERFECTION : 234'.1
the impossible possibility / by Herbert E. Douglass ... [et al.]. Nashville : Southern Pub. Association, [1975] 200 p. : ports. ; 22 cm. (Anvil series) [BT766.P42] 75-10350 ISBN 0-8127-0097-X
1. Perfection—Addresses, essays, lectures. 2. Seventh-Day Adventists—Doctrinal and controversial works—Addresses, essays, lectures. I. Douglass, Herbert E.

Perfection—Biblical teaching.

PURKISER, W T 234.8
Sanctification and its synonyms; studies in the Biblical theology of holiness. Kansas City, Mo., Beacon Hill Press [c1961] 96p. 20cm. (Aycock lectures, 1959) Includes bibliography. [BT766.P9] 61-5118
1. Perfection—Biblical teaching. 2. Church of the Nazarene— Doctrinal and controversial works. I. Title.

Perfection (Buddhism)

PRAJNAPARAMITAS. 294.3'8
Astasahasrika. English.
The perfection of wisdom in eight thousand lines & its verse summary. Translated by Edward Conze. Bolinas, Four Seasons Foundation; distributed by Book People, Berkeley, 1973. xxii, 325 p. 23 cm. (Wheel series, 1) Contains some sections of the Ratnagunasancayagatha. Includes bibliographical references. [BQ1912.E5C66 1973] 72-76540 ISBN 0-87704-048-6 ISBN 0-87704-049-4 (pbk.) 5.00
I. Conze, Edward, 1904- tr. II. Prajnaparamitas. Ratnagunasancayagatha. English. Selections. 1973. III. Title. IV. Series.

RINPOCHE, Namgyal. 294.3'444
The path of victory : discourses on the Paramita / Namgyal Rinpoche ; edited by Karma Sonam Senge Gelong, assistant editor, Pannananda. Boise, Idaho (703 North 18th Street, Boise, Idaho 83702) : Open Path, c1980. 75 p. : ill. ; 22 cm. Limited ed. of 500 copies. [BQ4336.R56] 19 80-84669 ISBN 0-9602722-1-6 pbk. : 5.00
1. Perfection (Buddhism) 2. Spiritual life (Buddhism) I. Karma Sonam Senge Gelong. II. Pannananda. III. Title.

Perfection (Catholic)

BONAVENTURA, Saint, Cardinal, 1221-1274. 248.4
The way of perfection, based on the Rule for novices of St. Bonaventure. [Translated by] Anselm Romb. Edited by Method C. Billy and Salvator Pantano. Chicago, Franciscan Herald Press [c1958] 96p. 19cm. (FHP text series) [B2350.5] 58-13683
1. Perfection (Catholic) I. Romb, Anselm M., tr. II. Title.

DOYLE, Charles Hugo 248.2
Bitter waters; helps in the pursuit of perfection. New York, Kenedy [c.1961] 175p. 61-15822 3.95
1. Perfection (Catholic) I. Title.

HERIS, Charles Vincent, 1885- 241.4
Perfection and charity [by] C. V. Heris. Translated by Lillian M. McCarthy. St. Louis, Herder, 1969. vii, 118 p. 18 cm. (An Intex selection) Bibliographical footnotes. [BX2350.5.H413] 70-83698 1.35
1. Perfection (Catholic) I. Title.

ROYO MARIN, Antonio 234
The theology of Christian perfection [by] Antonio Royo, Jordan Aumann. [Tr. from Spanish, adapted by Jordan Aumann] Dubuque, Iowa, Priory Pr. [1962] 692p. 25cm. 62-17314 10.95
1. Perfection (Catholic) I. Aumann, Jordan. II. Title.

Perfection — Catholic authors.

BUCKLER, Henry Reginald, 1840- 234
The perfection of man by charity. St. Louis, Herder [1954] 235p. 23cm. [BX2350.5] 54-14435
1. Perfection—Catholic authors. I. Title.

COLIN, Louis, 1884- 234
Striving for perfection; the fundamental obligation of the religious state. Translated from the French by Kathryn Day Wyatt. Westminster, Md., Newman Press [c1956] 272p. 22cm. Translation of Tendance a la perfection. [BX2350.5.C63] 55-12403
1. Perfection—Catholic authors. I. Title.

DOYLE, Charles Hugo. 234
In pursuit of perfection; conferences for religious. 214p. 21cm. [BX2350.5.D6] 56-1029
1. Perfection—Catholic authors. I. Title. II. Title: Tarrytown, N. Y.,

DUKEHART, Claude Henry, 1917- 234
State of perfection and the secular priest; a theological study. St. Meinrad, Ind. [1952] x, 186 p. 23 cm. "A Grail publication." Issued also as thesis, Catholic University of America, in microcardform. Bibliography: p. 174-180. [BX1912.D883] 52-4011
1. Perfection—Catholic authors. 2. Clergy—Religious life. 3. Clergy (Canon law) I. Title.

GARRIGOU-LAGRANGE, Reginald, Father, 1877- 253.2
The priesthood and perfection. Translated by E. Hayden. Westminster, Md., Newman Press, 1955. 208p. 22cm. [BX2350.5.G355] 55-7046
1. Perfection—Catholic authors. 2. Clergy—Religions life. I. Title.

GREENSTOCK, David L. 234
Be ye perfect. St. Louis, Herder, 1952. 362 p. 21 cm. [BX2350.5.G7] 52-9323
1. Perfection—Catholic authors. I. Title.

PERRIN, Joseph Marie, 1905- 234
Christian perfection and married life. Translated by P.D.Gilbert. Westminister, Md., Newman Press, 1958. 92p. 19cm. [BX2350.5.P413] 58-14896
1. Perfection—Catholic authors. 2. Marriage—Catholic Church. I. Title.

PETITOT, Hyacinthe, 1870-1934.
An introduction to holiness. Translated from the French by Malanchy Gerald Carroll. Westminster, Md., Newman Press, 1950. 176 p. 19 cm. Based on the spirituality of St. Therese of Lisieux. A51
1. Therese, Saint, 1873-1897. 2. Perfection — Catholic authors. I. Title.

SCUPOLI, Lorenzo, 1530-1610. 248
The spiritual combat, and a Treatise on peace of the soul. A translation, rev. by William Lester [and] Robert Mohan. With an introd. by B. F. Marcetteau. Westminister, Md., Newman Press, 1950 [c1945] xv, 240 p. 19 cm. [BX2349.S372 1950] 51-4565
1. Perfection—Catholic authors. I. Title. II. Title: Treatise on peace of the soul.

SCUPOLI, Lorenzo, 1530-1610. 248
The spiritual combat, and a Treatise on peace of the soul, by Lawrence Scupoli; a translation, revised by William Lester, M. A. [and] Robert Mohan, M. A., with an introduction by B. F. Marcetteau ... Westminster, Md., The Newman bookshop, 1945. xv, 240 p. 19 cm. [BX2349.S372 1945] 45-11303
1. Perfection—Catholic authors. I. Lester, James William, 1919- tr. II. Mohan, Robert Paul, 1920- joint tr. III. Title. IV. Title: Treatise on peace of the soul.

TERESA Saint 1515-1582.
The way of perfection, by St. Teresa of Avila. Translated & edited by E. Allison Peers, from the critical ed. of P. Silverio de Santa Teresa. Garden City, N.Y., Image Books [1964] 280 p. 19 cm. 65-99548
1. Perfection — Catholic authors. 2. God-Worship and love. I. Title.

TERESA, Saint, 1515-1582. 242
Way of perfection; tr. from the Spanish by Alice Alexander. With an introd. by Angelus M. Kopp. Westminister, Md., Newman Bookshop, 1948 [c1946] xxx, 274 p. 21 cm. [BX2179.T4C32 1948] 49-4780
1. Perfection—Catholic authors. 2. God—Worship and love. I. Title.

TERESA, Saint 1515-1582. 242
The way of perfection, and Conceptions of divine love. By Saint Teresa. Translated from the Spanish by the Rev. John Dalton. New York, E. Dunigan and brother, 1852. xxi, 274 p. 19 1/2cm. "Conceptions of divine love "is a translation of four chapters of the author's Conceptos del amor de Dios sobre algunas palabras de los Cantares de Salomon." [BX2179.T3E5 1852] 41-39790
1. Perfection—Catholic authors. 2. God—Worship and love. I. Dalton, John, 1814-1874, tr. II. Title. III. Title: Conceptions of divine love.

Perfection — Catholic Church.

THOMAS Aquines Saint 1225?-1274. 248
The religious state; the episcopate and the priestly office. A translation of the minor work of the Saint, On the perfection of the spiritual life. Edited with prefatory notice by Father Proctor. Westminster, Md., Newman Press, 1950. viii, 166 p. 20 cm. [BX2350.5.T52] 50-12499
1. Perfection — Catholic Church. 2. Clergy — Religious life. 3. Bishops. I. Title.

Perfection (Catholic)—History of doctrines.

MASON, Mary Elizabeth 271.069
Active life and contemplative life, a study of the concepts from Plato to the present. Ed., foreword by George E. Ganss. Milwaukee, Marquette Univ. Pr. [c.]1961. 137p. Bibl. 60-16598 2.50 pap.,
1. Perfection (Catholic)—History of doctrines. I. Title.

MASON, Mary Elizabeth. 271.069
Active life and contemplative life, a study of the concepts from Plato to the present. Edited, with a foreword by George E. Ganss. Milwaukee, Marquette University Press, 1961. 137p. 23cm. Includes bibliography. [BX2350.5.M3] 60-165984
1. Perfection (Catholic)—History of doctrines. I. Title.

Perfection, Christian.

HOGE, Moses Drury, 1818-1899. 243
The perfection of beauty, and other sermons, by the Rev. Moses D. Hoge...with a lecture on "The success of Christianity an evidence of its divine origin", delivered at the University of Virginia. Richmond, Va., The Presbyterian committee of publication, 1904. 335 p. front. (port.) pl. 21 cm. [BX9178.H54P4] 4-27968
I. Title.

KRIEBEL, Oscar Schultz, 1863-
A discourse on sanctification versus Christian perfection, by Rev. Oscar S. Kriebel ... Pennsburg, Pa. [1905?] 60 p. 23 cm. Preached in the Washington Schwenkfelder church, on Sunday morning, March 12th, 1905 ... 7-39353
I. Title.

KRIEBEL, Oscar Schultz, 1863-
A discourse on sanctification versus Christian perfection, by Rev. Oscar S. Kriebel ... Pennsburg, Pa. [1905?] 60 p. 23 cm. Preached in the Washington Schwenkfelder church, on Sunday morning, March 12th, 1905 ... 7-39353
I. Title.

THE meaning of Christian perfection, by Jordan Aumann and David L. Greenstock. St. Louis, Herder [1956] 162p. 23cm.
1. Perfection, Christian. 2. Spiritual life. I. Aumann, Jordan, 1916- II. Groonstock, David L joint author.

A new creation;
towards a theology of the Christian life. New York, Philosophical Library [1956] 143p. 28cm. Translation of: Eine neue Sohopfung: ein Beitrag sur Theologie des christliohen Lebens.
1. Perfection, Christian. 2. Christian life. I. Brunner, August, 1894-

A new creation;
towards a theology of the Christian life. New York, Philosophical Library [1956] 143p. 23cm. Translation of: Eine neue Schopfung: ein Beitrag zur Theologie des christlichen Lebens.
1. Perfection, Christian. 2. Christian life. I. Brunner, August, 1894-

SIMON Peter.
Chicago, Scepter [1959] xiii, 246p. 20cm.
1. Perfection, Christian. 2. Peter, Saint, Apostle. I. Chevrot, Georges.

[TAULER, Johannes] ca., 1300-1361.
The plain path to Christian perfection ... Translated from the French ... Philadelphia, Printed by J. Crukshank, 1772. xi, 124 p. 16 1/2 cm. Translated by Anthony Benezet. CA 10
I. Benezet, Anthony, 1713-1784, tr. II. Title.

WESLEY, John, 1703-1791. 234
Christian Perfection, as taught by John Wesley. Comp. by Rev. J. A. Wood ... Introduction by Bishop W. F. Mallalieu ... Chicago and Boston, The Christian witness co. [c1921] 288 p. front. (port.) 19 cm. [BT766.W5] 22-1726
I. Wood, John Allen, 1828- comp. II. Title.

Perfection—History of doctrines.

FLEW, Robert Newton, 1886- 234
The idea of perfection in Christian theology; an historical study of the Christian ideal for the present life, by R. Newton Flew. Oxford, Clarendon Press, 1968. xv, 422 p. 23 cm. Bibliographical footnotes. [BT766.F5 1968] 68-121493 ISBN 0-19-826620-0
1. Perfection—History of doctrines. I. Title.

PETERS, John Leland. 234
Christian perfection and American Methodism. New York, Abingdon Press [1956] 252p. 23cm. [BT766.P43] 56-7764
1. Perfection—History of doctrines. 2. Methodist Church in the U. S. I. Title.

TURNER, George Allen. 287.10924
The vision which transforms; is Christian perfection scriptural? Kansas City, Mo., Beacon Hill Press [1964] 348 p. 23 cm. "A through revision under ... new title' of the author's thesis, first published in 1952 under title: The more excellent way; the MS. Thesis (Harvard University) has title: A comparative study of the Biblical and Wesleyan ideas of perfection. Bibliography: p. 329-345. [BX8495.W5T67 1964] 64-18588
1. Wesley, John, 1703-1791. 2. Perfection — History of doctrines. I. Title.

Performance—Biblical teaching.

GUNNEWEG, Antonius H. J. 241
Achievement / Antonius H.J. Gunneweg and Walter Schmithals ; translated by David Smith. Nashville : Abingdon, c1981. 204 p. ; 22 cm. (Biblical encounters series) Translation of: Leistung. Includes bibliographical references. [BS680.P44G8615] 19 80-26977 ISBN 0-687-00690-2 pbk. : 7.95
1. Performance—Biblical teaching. I. Schmithals, Walter. II. [Leistung.] English III. Title. IV. Series.

Periodicals — Bibliography Periodicals — Indexes.

SHETTER, Claire b comp.
A list of periodicals and other serial publications which have been indexed in current indexes or bibliographies, pertinent to theological or philosophical research. Rev. ed. Compiled by Claire B. Shetter and Stillson Judah. Rev. ed. Berkeley, Calif. [Pacific school of religion] 1956. iii, 25 1. 34 cm. Cover title.
1. Periodicals — Bibl. Periodicals — Indexes. I. Judah, Stillson, joint comp. II. Berkeley, Calif. Pacific School of Religion. III. Title.

Periodicals—Bibliography—Union lists.

SUDWEEKS, Joseph, 1883- 016.05
Discontinued L.D.S. periodicals / by Joseph Sudweeks. Provo, Utah : Brigham Young University, 1955. 55 p. ; 22 cm. "Contribution of the Department of Graduate Studies in Religion, Brigham Young University." [Z7845.M8S9] [BX8601] 75-314495
1. Church of Jesus Christ of Latter-Day Saints—Periodicals—Bibliography. 2. Periodicals—Bibliography—Union lists. I. Title.

Periodicity.

ROSS, Lydia, 1859- 212
... The doctrine of cycles, by Lydia Ross, M.D. Covina, Calif., Theosophical university press, 1944. 3 p. l., 150, [2] p. 15 cm. (Theosophical manual no. VIII) "First edition, 1939. Second edition, 1940." [BP573.P4R6 1944] 44-44877
1. Periodicity. 2. Theosophy. I. Title.

VAN PELT, Gertrude Wyckoff, 1856- 212
... Rounds and races; man's divine parentage and destiny, by Gertrude W. Van Pelt, M.D. Point Loma, Calif., Theosophical university press, 1940. 3 p. l., 84 p., 1 l. diagrs. 15 cm. (Theosophical manual no. VII) "Second edition, revised." Bibliography: p. [85] [BP573.P4V3 1940] 44-52889

1. Periodicity. 2. Theosophy. I. Title.

Perkins, Justin, 1805-1869.

PERKINS, Henry Martyn. 266
... Life of Rev. Justin Perkins, D. D., pioneer missionary to Persia. By his son, Rev. Henry Martyn Perkins. Chicago, Woman's Presbyterian board of missions of the Northwest, [c1887] 96 p. 20 cm. (Missionary annals. [4]) [BV3217.P4P4] 12-37572
1. Perkins, Justin, 1805-1869. I. Title.

Pernet, Etienne Claude, 1824- 1899.

BURTON, Katherine (Kurz) 922.244
1890-
The stars beyond the storms: Father Etienne Pernet, founder of the Congregation of the Little Sisters of the Assumption. With a pref. by Francis Cardinal Spellman. New York, Benziger Bros. [1954] 204p. illus. 21cm. [BX4705.P429B8] 54-4346
1. Pernet, Etienne Claude, 1824- 1899. 2. Little Sisters of the Assumption. I. Title.

Perrella, Robert.

PERRELLA, Robert. 282'.092'4 B
They call me the showbiz priest, by Robert Perrella ("Father Bob"). New York, Trident Press [1973] 287 p. ports. 22 cm. [BX4705.P4325A33] 73-82874 ISBN 0-671-27112-1 7.95
1. Perrella, Robert. I. Title.

Perrin, Norman—Addresses, essays, lectures.

CHRISTOLOGY and a modern 232
pilgrimage; a discussion with Norman Perrin. Edited by Hans Dieter Betz. [Missoula, Mont.] Society of Biblical Literature, 1971 [reprinted 1973, c1971] vi, 157 p. 22 cm. Published to honor N. Perrin on the occasion of his 50th birthday. Contents.Contents.—Perrin, N. Towards an interpretation of the Gospel of Mark.—Hobbs, E. C. Norman Perrin on methodology in the interpretation of Mark: a critique of "The christology of Mark" and "Toward an interpretation of the Gospel of Mark."—Furnish, V. P. Notes on a pilgrimage: Norman Perrin and New Testament christology.—Epp, E. J. Norman Perrin on the Kingdom of God: an appreciation and an assessment from the perspective of 1970.—Koester, H. The historical Jesus: some comments and thoughts on Norman Perrin's Rediscovering the teaching of Jesus.—Wilder, A. Norman Perrin, What is redaction criticism?—Robinson, J. M. The promise of Bultmann.—Bibliography of the works of Norman Perrin (p. [153]-157) [BS2585.2.C45 1973] 74-181526 ISBN 0-88414-000-8
1. Perrin, Norman—Addresses, essays, lectures. 2. Perrin, Norman—Bibliography. 3. Bible. N.T. Mark—Criticism, interpretation, etc. I. Perrin, Norman. II. Betz, Hans Dieter, ed.

Perry, Charies, 1807-1891.

ROBIN, Arthur de 283'.0924
Quettevillef.
Charles Perry, Bishop of Melbourne; the challenges of a colonal episcopate, 1847-76 [by] A. de Q. Robin. [Nedlands, Perth] Univ. of Western Australia Pr. [1967] x, 229p. illus., facsim, maps (on lining-papers) ports. 25cm. Bibl. [BX5720.P4R6] (B) 67-27319 8.50 bds.,
1. Perry, Charies, 1807-1891. I. Title.
Distributed by Verry, Mystic, Conn.

Perry, James H., 1811-1862. Reply to Professor Mattison's Calm review.

MATTISON, Hiram, 1811-1868. 922.
An answer to Dr. Perry's Reply to the Calm review. By H. Mattison ... New-York, 1856. ix, [3]-96 p. 22 1/2 cm. [BX8495.P26P38] 38-20509
1. Perry, James H., 1811-1862. Reply to Professor Mattison's Calm review. 2. Palmer, Mrs. Phoebe (Worrell) 1807-1874. 3. Sanctification. 4. Methodist Episcopal church—Doctrinal and controversial works. I. Title.

Perry, May, 1890-

ANDERSON, Susan, 266'.023'09669
1892-
May Perry of Africa. Nashville, Broadman Press [1966] 60 p. illus., ports. 19 cm. [BV3625.N6P43] 66-27945
1. Perry, May, 1890- 2. Missions—Nigeria. I. Title.

Perry, Oliver Hazard, 1785-1819.

BANCROFT, George, 1800-1891. 295
Oliver Hazard Perry and the battle of lake Erie, by George Bancroft. Together with the addresses of Dr. Usher Parsons, fleet surgeon under Commodore Perry, and of Governor William Sprague of Rhode Island, delivered in Cleveland, Sept. 10, 1860, and other papers of interest. Newport, R.I., Printed by The Mercury publishing company, 1912. 55 p. 23 cm. (On cover: Rhode Island education circulars. Historical series--VI ...) [F76.R32 no. 6] [E356.E6B22] 973. 13-33141
1. Perry, Oliver Hazard, 1785-1819. 2. Erie, Lake, Battle of, 1813. I. Parsons, Usher, 1788-1868. II. Sprague, William, 1830-1915. III. Title.

Perry, Roswell Park, 1852-1867.

[PERRY, Thomas W.] 922
Little Rossie ... Written for the Mass. Sabbath school society, and approved by the Committee of publication. Boston, Mass. Sabbath school society [1868] 158 p. front. (mounted phot.) 18 cm. [BR1715.P4P4] 37-19952
1. Perry, Roswell Park, 1852-1867. I. Perry, Thomas W., Mrs. joint author. II. Massachusetts Sabbath school society. Committee of publication. III. Title.

Persatuan Islam.

FEDERSPIEL, Howard M. 297'.8
Persatuan Islam; Islamic reform in twentieth century Indonesia, by Howard M. Federspiel. Ithaca, N.Y., Modern Indonesia Project, Cornell University, 1970. vii, 247 p. 28 cm. (Cornell University. Modern Indonesia Project. Monograph series) Bibliography: p. 213-247. [BP10.P48F4] 72-632241 7.50
1. Persatuan Islam. 2. Islam—Indonesia. I. Title. II. Series.

Perse Grammar School, Cambridge, Eng.

MITCHELL, S. John D. 261
Perse : a history of the Perse School, 1615-1976 / [by] S. J. D. Mitchell. Cambridge : Oleander Press, 1976. viii, 263 p. : ill., coat of arms, map, plans, ports. ; 22 cm. Includes bibliographical references and index. [LF795.C185M57] 77-357892 ISBN 0-902675-71-0 : £4.95
1. Perse Grammar School, Cambridge, Eng. 2. Cambridge, Eng.—Schools—History. I. Title.

Persecution.

CRAIG, Asa Hollister, 1847- 272
Christian persecutions; being a historical exposition of the principal Catholic events from the Christian era to the present time. Written from an unprejudiced standpoint. By Asa H. Craig ... Burlington, Wis., The Burlington publishing company [c1899] 2 p. l., 7-503 p. 22 cm. "Works consulted": 1 p. preceding p. 7. [BR1601.C8] 5-13954
1. Persecution. I. Title.

GALTER, Alberte. 282.0904
The red book of the persecuted church. Westminster, Md., Newman Press, 1957. 491p. 22cm. 'Translation ... published by arrangement with the proprictors, Editions Fleurus, Paris.' [BX1378.G312] 57-14025
1. Persecution. 2. Catholic Church—Hist.—20th cent. 3. Communism and religion. I. Title.

GARRISON, Winfred Ernest, 272
1874-
Intolerance, by Winfred Ernest Garrison. New York, Round table press, inc., 1934. xv, 270 p. 23 1/2 cm. [BR1601.G3] 34-33082
1. Persecution. 2. Toleration. 3. Religious liberty. 4. Race problems. I. Title.

HARRIS, James Coffee, 1858- 272
The persecution of progressives, by James Coffee Harris ... Cave Spring, Ga., 1933. 2 p. l., [3]-99 p. 23 cm. Additional material on labels mounted on p. 9. 30, 74. [BR1601.H36] 33-11525
1. Persecution. 2. Religion and Science—History of controversy. I. Title.

HEALY, Patrick Joseph, 1872- 272.
The Valerian persecution; a study of the relations between church and state in the third century A.D., by the Reverend Patrick J. Healy ... Boston and New York, Houghton, Mifflin and company, 1905. xv, 285 [1] p. 20 1/2 cm. Bibliography: p. [273]-281. [BR1604.H4] 5-25388
1. Persectuion. 2. Church and state. 3. Church history—Primitive and early church. I. Title.

HUNTER, Allan Armstrong, 272
1893-
Christians in the arena. Nyack, N. Y., Fellowship Publications, 1958. 108p. 19cm. [BR1601.H8] 58-2873
1. Persecution. I. Title.

MCCABE, James Dabney, 1842- 272
1883.
Cross and crown; or, The sufferings and triumphs of the heroic men and women who were persecuted for the religion of Jesus Christ. With illus. on steel by Sartain and Illman. Cincinnati, National Pub. Co., 1874. 619 p. plates. 24 cm. [E687.M11 1881a] 48-30271
1. Persecution. 2. Waldeness. 3. Huguenots in France. 4. Reformation—England. I. Title.

MEYER, F[rederick] B[rotherton]
1847-
Cheer for life's pilgrimage, by the Rev F. B. Meyer ... New York, Chicago [etc.] F. H. Revell company [c1897] 159 p. 16 cm. 3-22865
I. Title.

PARSONS, Robert, 1546- 230'.2 s
1610.
A treatise of three conversions, 1603-1604 / Robert Persons. Ilkley [Eng.] : Scolar Press, 1976. 3 v. ; 20 cm. (English recusant literature, 1558-1640 ; v. 304-306) (Series: Rogers, David Morrison, comp. English recusant literature, 1558-1640 ; v. 304-306.) Reprint of the 1603-1604 ed. from a copy in the library of Stonyhurst College. [BX1750.A1E5 vol. 304-306] [BX1492] 282'.42 76-374618 ISBN 0-85967-316-2 (v. 1)
1. Catholic Church in England. 2. Catholic Church—Doctrinal and controversial works—Catholic authors. 3. Foxe, John, 1516-1587. Actes and monuments. 4. Persecution. 5. Church history. I. Title. II. Series.

PHILLIPS, John Bertram, 1906- 266
The church under the Cross. New York, Macmillan, 1956. 111 p. 22 cm. [BV2064.P44 1956a] 56-10964
1. Persecution. 2. Suffering. 3. Missions, Foreign. I. Title.

RUTHERFORD, Joseph F., 1869- 289.
Oppression, when will it end? Written by Judge J. F. Rutherford... Brooklyn, N.Y. [etc.] International Bible students association, c1929. 63 p. illus. 19 cm. Includes advertising matter. [BX8526.R873] 29-8639
I. Title.

SPAULDING, Jonah. 272
A summary history of persecution, from the crucifixion of our Savior to the present time. Containing an account of the rise and progress of several respective churches: viz.--the Papal, the Waldensean, the Baptist, the Protestant, Friends and Methodist. By Jonah Spaulding ... Hallowell, Printed by S. K. Gilman, 1819. 182, [4] p. 18 cm. [BR1601.S6] 22-11395
1. Persecution. I. Title.

WHITTLESEY, John. 922.773
An authentic account of the persecutions and trials of the Rev. John Whittlesey, of Salem, Connecticut, late ordained elder of the Methodist Episcopal church, holden at Salem, Conn., on the second and third days of May, 1845, and at Montville on the fifth day of the said month, before the Quarterly conference. With appropriate remarks. New York, 1845. 72 p. 18 1/2 cm. [BX8495.W586A3] [AC901.M5 vol. 354] 37-12148
I. Title.

WORKMAN, Herbert Brook 272.1
Persecutions in the early church. Nashville, Abingdon [1961, c.1960] 155p. (Apex bks., G4) 1.00 pap.,
1. Persecution. 2. Church history—Primitive and early church. I. Title.

Persecution—Albania—Miscellanea.

SINISHTA, Gjon, 1929- 272
The fulfilled promise : a documentary account of religious persecution in Albania / by Gjon Sinishta. Santa Clara, Calif. : Sinishta, 1976. 248 p. : ill. ; 22 cm. Bibliography: p. 242-247. [BR1608.A38S57] 76-57433 7.95
1. Persecution—Albania—Miscellanea. 2. Martyrs—Albania—Miscellanea. 3. Albania—Church history—Miscellanea. I. Title.

Persecution—Brazil.

WOOD, Miriam. 272'.9'0924
Imprison him! / by Miriam Wood. Mountain View, Calif. : Pacific Press Pub. Association, c1980. 175 p. : ill. ; 22 cm. (A Destiny book ; D-194) [BR1608.B6W66] 19 79-90083 pbk. : 4.95
1. Persecution—Brazil. I. Title.

Persecution—Bulgaria.

POPOFF, Haralan, 1907- 289.9 B
Tortured for his faith : an epic of Christian courage and heroism in our day / by Haralan Popov. Rev. ed. Grand Rapids, Mich. : Zondervan Pub. House, 1975. 140 p. ; 18 cm. [BX8764.Z8P62 1975] 76-360631 1.50
1. Popoff, Haralan, 1907- 2. Persecution—Bulgaria. 3. Prisoners—Bulgaria—Personal narratives. I. Title.

POPOFF, Haralan, 1907- 289.9 B
Tortured for his faith; an epic of Christian courage and heroism in our day, by Haralan Popov. Grand Rapids, Zondervan Pub. House [1970] 156 p. 18 cm. [BR1608.B8P6] 77-102834 0.75
1. Persecution—Bulgaria. 2. Prisoners—Bulgaria—Personal narratives. I. Title.

Persecution—China (People's Republic of China, 1949-)

BULL, Geoffrey T. 1921- 248.2
The sky is red. Chicago, Moody [1966, c.1965] 254p. 22cm. Bibl. [BV3427.B79A33] 66-4124 3.95
1. Persecution—China (People's Republic of China, 1949-) 2. Missions—China (People's Republic of China, 1949-) I. Title.

NORTHROP, Henry Davenport.
Chinese horrors and persecutions of the Christians containing a full account of the great insurrection in China; atrocities of the "Boxers" ... together with the complete history of China down to the present time ... Philadelphia, National pub. co. [1900] vi, 17-430 p. front., illus., pl., maps. 8 degree. Feb
I. Title.

Persecution—Colombia.

WALL, Martha. 248
In crossfire of hate. Chicago, Moody Press [1970] 288 p. facsim. 22 cm. [BR1608.C66W3] 72-104827 4.95
1. Franco, Marco. 2. Persecution—Colombia. I. Title.

Persecution—Communist countries—Collected works.

GROSSU, Sergiu, comp. 272
The church in today's catacombs / edited by Sergiu Grossu ; translated from the French by Janet L. Johnson. New Rochelle, N.Y. : Arlington House Publishers, [1975] 224 p. ; 24 cm. "Originally published in France in 1973 as a supplement to the journal Catacombes." Bibliography: p. 224. [BR1608.C7G7613] 74-32251 ISBN 0-87000-260-0 : 8.95
1. Persecution—Communist countries—Collected works. 2. Communism and Christianity—Communist countries—Collected works. I. Title.

Persecution—Cuba.

CRAWFORD, Don, 1929- 272'.097291
Red star over Cuba, by Don Crawford and Brother Andrew. Wheaton, Ill., Tyndale House Publishers [1971] 112 p. illus. 18 cm. [BR1608.C9C7] 76-123286 ISBN 0-8423-5350-X
1. Persecution—Cuba. 2. Refugees, Religious. I. Andrew, Brother, joint author. II. Title.

Persecution—Early church.

CANFIELD, Leon Hardy, 1886- 272'.1
The early persecutions of the Christians. New York, AMS Press [1968] 215 p. 22 cm. (Studies in history, economics, and public law, v. 55, no. 2, whole no. 136) Reprint of the 1913 ed. Bibliography: p. 210-215. [BR1604.C32 1968] 68-54259
1. Persecution—Early church. I. Title. II. Series: Columbia studies in the social sciences, no. 136

FREND, W. H. C. 272'.1
Martvrdom and persecution in the early church; a study of a conflict from the Maccabees to Donatus. by W. H. C. Frend [New York] N.Y.U. Pr., 1967. xviii, 577p. 24cm. Bibl. [BR1604.2.F7 1967] 8.00
1. Persecution—Early church. I. Title.

FREND, W H C
Martyrdom and persecution in the early church; a study of a conflict from the Maccabees to Donatus, by W.H.C. Frend. [New York] New York University Press, 1967. [c1965] xviii, 577 p. 24 cm. Bibliography: p. [527]-557. 68-16773
1. Persecution—Early church. I. Title.

FREND, W. H. C. 272'.1
Martyrdom and persecution in the early church; a study of a conflict from the Maccabees to Donatus, by W. H. C. Frend. Garden City, N.Y., Anchor Books, 1967 [c1965] xviii, 577 p. 18 cm. Bibliography: p. [527]-557. [BR1604.2.F7 1967] 66-24325
1. Persecution—Early church. I. Title.

FREND, W. H. C. 272.1
Martyrdom and persecution in the early church : a study of a conflict from Maccabees to Donatus / by W. H. C. Frend. Grand Rapids, MI : Baker Book House, 1981, c1965. 625 p. ; 21 cm. Includes index. Reprint of the 1965 edition published by Blackwell, Oxford. Bibliography : p. 572-604. [BR1604.2F7 1965] 66-8610 ISBN 0-8010-3502-3 pbk. : 12.95
1. Persecution — Early church. I. Title.

WORKMAN, Herbert Brook, 1862- 272'.1
Persecution in the early church. New York, Abingdon Press [1960] 155 p. 17 cm. [Apex books, G4) [BR1604.W8 1960] 62-762
1. Persecution — Early church. I. Title.

Persecution—Early church, ca. 30-600.

WORKMAN, Herbert Brook, 1862- 272'1
Persecution in the early church / by Herbert B. Workman ; with a foreword by Michael Bourdeaux. Oxford ; New York : Oxford University Press, 1980. p. cm. Bibliography: p. [BR1604.2.W67 1980] 79-42765 ISBN 0-19-283025-2 : 10.95
1. Persecution—Early church, ca. 30-600. I. Title.

Persecution —Europe, Eastern.

BRUNELLO, Aristide. 274.7
The silent church; facts and documents concerning religious persecution behind the Iron Curtain, by Lino Gussoni and Aristede Brunello. [1st ed. in English] New York, Veritas [1954] 391p. illus. 21cm. A translation of Brunello's La chiesa del silenzio. Includes bibliography. [BR738.6.B73] 54-10337
1. Persecution —Europe, Eastern. 2. Europe, Eastern—Religion. I. Gussoni, Lino, 1920- tr. II. Title.

PASTOR Nicoli. 274.7
Persecuted but not forsaken : the story of a church behind the iron curtain / by Pastor Nicoli. Valley Forge, Pa. : Judson Press, c1977. 172 p. ; 22 cm. [BR1608.E8P37] 77-7114 ISBN 0-8170-0749-0 pbk. : 3.95
1. Persecution—Europe, Eastern. I. Title.

Persecution—History.

NORWOOD, Frederick Abbott. 272'.09
Strangers and exiles; a history of religious refugees [by] Frederick A. Norwood. Nashville, Abingdon Press [1969] 2 v. illus., maps. 25 cm. Bibliography: v. 2, p. 479-511. [BR1601.2.N6] 75-86164 25.00
1. Persecution—History. 2. Refugees, Religious. 3. Dissenters, Religious. I. Title.

Persecution—Korea (Democratic People's Republic)

AWE, Chulho. 951.9042
Decision at dawn; the underground Christian witness in Red Korea [by] Chulho Awe as told to Herbert F. Webster. [1st ed.] New York, Harper & Row [1965] x, 180 p. illus., maps (on lining paper) 22 cm. [BR1725.A9A3] 65-10964
1. Persecution—Korea (Democratic People's Republic) I. Webster, Herbert F. II. Title.

Persecution—Latin America.

LERNOUX, Penny, 1940- 261.8
Cry of the people : United States involvement in the rise of fascism, torture, and murder and the persecution of the Catholic Church in Latin America / Penny Lernoux. 1st ed. Garden City, N.Y. : Doubleday, 1980. xiv, 535 p. ; 22 cm. Includes index. [BX1426.2.L43] 19 78-55841 ISBN 0-385-13150-X : 12.95
1. Catholic Church in Latin America. 2. Persecution—Latin America. 3. United States—Foreign relations—Latin America. 4. Latin America—Foreign relations—United States. I. Title.

Persecution—Latin America—Addresses, essays, lectures.

CHRISTENVERFOLGUNG in Sudamerika. 272'.9'098
Witnesses of hope : the persecution of Christians in Latin America / edited by Martin Lange and Reinhold Iblacker ; foreword by Karl Rahner ; translated from the German by William E. Jerman. Maryknoll, N.Y. : Orbis Books, c1981. xx, 156 p. ; 21 cm. Translation of: Christenverfolgung in Sudamerika. Includes bibliographical references and index. [BR1608.L37C4713] 19 81-38378 ISBN 0-88344-759-2 pbk. : 6.95
1. Persecution—Latin America—Addresses, essays, lectures. 2. Christian martyrs—Latin America—Addresses, essays, lectures. 3. Church and state—Latin America—Addresses, essays, lectures. I. Lange, Martin. II. Iblacker, Reinhold.

WITNESSES of hope : 272'.9'098
the persecution of Christians in Latin America : a tract on martyrdom in the theology of liberation / edited by Martin Lange, Reinhold Iblacker ; preface by Georg Moser ; epilogue by Karl Rahner ; translated by William E. Jerman. Maryknoll, N.Y. : Orbis Books, c1981. p. cm. Translation Christenverfolgung in Sudamerika. Includes bibliographical references. [BR1608.L37C4713] 19 81-38378 ISBN 0-88344-759-2 pbk. : 6.95
1. Persecution—Latin America—Addresses, essays, lectures. 2. Christian martyrs—Latin America—Addresses, essays, lectures. 3. Church and state—Latin America—Addresses, essays, lectures. I. Lange, Martin. II. Iblacker, Reinhold. III. [Christenverfolgung in Sudamerika.] English

Persecution—Latin America—History—20th century.

LERNOUX, Penny, 1940- 261.8
Cry of the people : the struggle for human rights in Latin America—the Catholic Church in conflict with U.S. policy / Penny Lernoux. New York, N.Y. : Penguin Books, 1982. xxiv, 535 p. ; 20 cm. Reprint. Originally published: Garden City, N.Y. : Doubleday, 1980. Includes bibliographical references and index. [BX1426.2.L43 1982] 19 81-13843 pbk. : 6.95
1. Catholic Church—Latin America. 2. Persecution—Latin America—History—20th century. 3. United States—Foreign—Latin America. 4. Latin America—Foreign relations—United States. 5. Latin America—Church history. I. Title.

Persecution—Lithuania.

VARDYS, Vytas Stanley, 1924- 282'.47'5
The Catholic Church, dissent, and nationality in Soviet Lithuania / V. Stanley Vardys. Boulder [Colo.] : East European quarterly ; New York : distributed by Columbia University Press, 1978. xiii, 336 p. : map ; 23 cm. (East European monographs ; no. 43) Includes index. Bibliography: p. [320]-332. [BX1559.L5V36] 78-50546 ISBN -914710-36-2 : 18.00
1. Catholic Church in Lithuania. 2. Persecution—Lithuania. 3. Dissent—Lithuania. 4. Nationalism—Lithuania. 5. Nationalism and religion—Lithuania. I. Title. II. Series.

Persecution—Rumania.

UNITED States. Congress. Senate. Committee on the Judiciary. Subcommittee to Investigate the Administration of the Internal Security Act and Other Internal Security Laws. 272'.9
Communist exploitation of religion. Hearing, Eighty-ninth Congress, second session, May 6, 1966: testimony of Rev. Richard Wurmbrand. Washington, U.S. Govt. Print. Off., 1966. ii, 42, ii p. 24 cm. [BR1608.R8U5] 66-61649
1. Persecution—Rumania. 2. Communism and religion. I. Wurmbrand, Richard. II. Title.

WURMBRAND, Richard. 272'.9
Christ in the communist prisons. Edited by Charles Foley. [1st American ed.] New York, Coward-McCann [1968] 255 p. 22 cm. [BR1608.R8W8 1968] 68-11879
1. Persecution—Romania. 2. Prisoners—Romania—Personal narratives. I. Title.

*WURMBRAND, Richard. 252.04'1
The Wurmbrand letters. Glendale, Calif., Diane Books [1973? c.1972] 157 p. 18 cm. [BR1608] 1.95 (pbk.)
1. Persecution—Rumania. 2. Prisoners—Rumania—Personal narratives. I. Title.
Publisher's address: Box 488, Glendale, CA 91209.

WURMBRAND, Sabina. 272
The pastor's wife. Edited by Charles Foley. [1st American ed.] New York, John Day Co. [1971, c1970] 218 p. 24 cm. [BR1608.R8W85 1971] 79-143216 5.95
1. Persecution—Romania. I. Title.

Persecution—Russia.

AIDA of Leningrad: 272 B
the story of Aida Skripnikova; edited by Xenia Howard-Johnston and Michael Bourdeaux. [Reading, Eng.] Gateway Outreach [1972] [8], 121 p. port. 23 cm. [BX6495.S52A75 1972] 73-160416 ISBN 0-901644-09-9 £1.50
1. Skripnikova, Aida Mikhailovna, 1942- 2. Persecution—Russia. I. Howard-Johnston, Xenia, ed. II. Bourdeaux, Michael, ed.

BOURDEAUX, Michael. 272
Faith on trial in Russia. [1st U.S. ed.] New York, Harper & Row [1971] 192 p. 22 cm. Bibliography: p. 190. [BR1608.R85B68 1971] 70-160642 ISBN 0-06-060985-0 5.95
1. Persecution—Russia. 2. Baptists—Russia. I. Title.

BOURDEAUX, Michael. 272
Patriarch and prophets; persecution of the Russian Orthodox Church today. New York, Praeger [1970] 359 p. 23 cm. Includes bibliographical references. [BR1608.R8B67 1970] 79-106201 10.00
1. Orthodox Eastern Church, Russian. 2. Persecution—Russia. I. Title.

THE Evidence that convicted 272 B
Aida Skripnikova [edited] by [Xenia Howard-Johnson and] Michael Bourdeaux. Elgin, Il[l.] D. C. Cook [1973, c1972] 154 p. 18 cm. First published under title: Aida of Leningrad. [BX6495.S52A75 1973] 73-78712 ISBN 0-912692-22-7 1.25 (pbk.)
1. Skripnikova, Aida Mikhailovna, 1942- 2. Persecution—Russia. I. Howard-Johnson, Xenia, ed. II. Bourdeaux, Michael, ed.

GRANT, Myrna. 286.1'092'4 B
Vanya. Carol Stream, Ill., Creation House [1974] 222 p. ports. 22 cm. Map on lining-paper. [BX6495.M53G72] 73-89729 ISBN 0-88419-071-4 4.95
1. Moiseev, Ivan Vasil'evich, 1952-1972. 2. Persecution—Russia. I. Title.

POLLOCK, John Charles. 272'.9
The Siberian seven / John Pollock. Waco, Tex. : Word Books, c1980. 267 p. : ill. ; 23 cm. [BR1608.R85P64 1980] 79-57352 ISBN 0-8499-0262-2 : 8.95
1. Persecution—Russia. 2. Pentecostals—Russia—Biography. I. Title.

Persecution—Russia—Barnaul, Siberia.

DEYNEKA, Anita. 272
A song in Siberia : [the true story of a Russian church that could not be silenced] / Anita and Peter Deyneka, Jr. Elgin, Ill. : D. C. Cook Pub. Co., c1977. 235 p., [4] leaves of plates : ill. ; 22 cm. [BR1608.R8D49] 77-70790 ISBN 0-89191-065-4 pbk. : 3.95
1. Persecution—Russia—Barnaul, Siberia. 2. Baptists—Russia—Barnaul, Siberia. I. Deyneka, Peter, 1931- joint author. II. Title.

Persecution—Russia—History—Sources.

SCHEFFBUCH, Winrich. 209'.47
Christians under the hammer & sickle. Translated from the German by Mark A. Noll. Grand Rapids, Zondervan Pub. House [1974] 214 p. illus. 21 cm. [BR1608.R85S3413] 73-13077 2.95 (pbk.).
1. Persecution—Russia—History—Sources. 2. Sects—Russia—History—Sources. I. Title.

Persecution—Uganda.

WOODING, Dan. 272'.9'096761
Uganda holocaust / Dan Wooding and Ray Barnett. Grand Rapids, MI : Zondervan Pub. House, c1980. 253 p., [8] leaves of plates : ill. ; 23 cm. Includes index. [BR1608.U45W66] 80-434 ISBN 0-310-41800-3 : 7.95
1. Amin, Idi, 1925- 2. Persecution—Uganda. 3. Uganda—Church history. I. Barnett, Ray, joint author. II. Title.

Persephone—Juvenile literature.

FARMER, Penelope, 1939- JUV
The story of Persephone. Illustrated by Graham McCallum. New York, Morrow, 1973. [48] p. col. illus. 25 cm. A retelling of the Greek myth in which Persephone returns from the underworld each year to bring spring to the earth. [PZ8.1.F223St3] 292'.2'11 73-4923 ISBN 0-688-20084-2 4.50
1. Persephone—Juvenile literature. 2. [Persephone.] 3. [Mythology, Greek.] I. McCallum, Graham, 1943- illus. II. Title.
Library binding; 5.25, ISBN 0-688-30084-7.

PRODDOW, Penelope. JUV
Demeter and Persephone; Homeric hymn number two. Translated and adapted by Penelope Proddow. Illustrated by Barbara Cooney. [1st ed.] Garden City, N.Y., Doubleday [1972] [48] p. col. illus. 29 cm. Demeter grieves when her daughter Persephone is carried off by Hades to his underworld kingdom and punishes the world until an agreement is made to share the girl. [PZ8.1.P9346De] 292'.2'11 76-155852 5.95
1. Persephone—Juvenile literature. 2. Demeter—Juvenile literature. 3. [Demeter.] 4. [Persephone.] 5. [Mythology, Greek.] I. Cooney, Barbara, 1917- illus. II. Homerus. Hymnus in Cererem. III. Title.

TOMAINO, Sarah F. 292'.2'11
Persephone, bringer of spring [by] Sarah F. Tomaino. Pictures by Ati Forberg. New York, Crowell [1971] [40] p. illus. (part col.) 26 cm. A retelling of the Greek myth in which Persephone returns from the underworld each year to bring spring to the earth. [PZ8.1.T58Pe] 71-87160 ISBN 0-690-61448-9 4.50
1. Persephone—Juvenile literature. 2. [Persephone.] 3. [Mythology, Greek.] I. Forberg, Ati, illus. II. Title.

Perseus.

HARTLAND, Edwin Sidney, 1848-1927. 200'.4
The legend of Perseus; a study of tradition in story, custom, and belief. [Folcroft, Pa.] Folcroft Library Editions, 1973. p. Reprint of the 1894-96 ed. published by D. Nutt, London, which was issued as no. 2, 3, and 5 of Grimm library. Contents.Contents.—v. 1. The supernatural birth.—v. 2. The life-token.—v. 3. Andromeda. Medusa. Bibliography: v. 1, p. xiii-xxxiv; v. 3, p. [xiii]-xxxvii. [GR75.P53H37 1973] 73-11485 45.00
1. Perseus. 2. Folk-lore—Classification. 3. Rites and ceremonies. I. Title.

HULST, Cornelia (Steketee) 1865- 292
Perseus and the Gorgon, by Cornelia Steketee Hulst ... La Salle, Ill., The Open court publishing co. [1946] xvii, [1], 221, [1] p. front., illus. 22 cm. Map on lining-papers. Bibliography: p. [219]-221. [BL820.P5H8] 47-20880
1. Perseus. 2. Gorgons. I. Title.

LE GALLIENNE, Richard, 1866- 292
Perseus and Andromeda; the story retold, by Richard Le Gallienne. New York, R.H. Russell, 1902. 4 p. l., 7-53, [1] p. front., 5 pl. 21 1/2 cm. [BL820.P5L4] 2-26877
1. Perseus. I. Title.

Perseus (Greek mythology)—Juvenile fiction.

PEMSTEEN, Hans. JUV
Clash of the Titans / [illustrations by Mike Eagle ; story adaptation by Hans Pemsteen ; based on the original screenplay by Beverley Cross]. New York : Golden Press, c1981. 35 p. : col. ill. ; 29 cm. With the aid of his father Zeus, Prince Perseus rescues Andromeda from the curse of Calibos, then sets out to destroy the sea monster Kraken. [PZ7.P372Cl 1981] [Fic] 19 80-84679 ISBN 0-307-16801-8 : 5.95
1. Perseus (Greek mythology)—Juvenile fiction. 2. [Perseus (Greek mythology)—Fiction.] 3. [Mythology, Greek—Fiction.] I. Eagle, Michael, ill. II. Cross, Beverley, 1931- III. Title.

Perseverance.

OLIVERS, Thomas, 1725-1799. 234.9
A full refutation of the doctrine of unconditional perservance: in a discourse on Heb. ii, 3. By Thomas Olivers ... New-York; Published by D. Hitt and T. Ware, for the Methodist connexion in the U. States. J. C. Totten, printer. 1815. viii, [9]-214 p. 12 cm. [BT768.O4] 33-28652
1. Perseverance. I. Title.

POTTER, Ray, 1795-1858. 234.9
A vindication of the doctrine of the final perseverance of the saints ... By Ray Potter ... To which is prefixed, introductory comprising a brief sketch of the author's life, so far as it relates to his change of sentiments on this subject ... Pawtucket [R. I.] Printed for the author, 1827. 119, [1] p. 18 cm. [BT768.P6] 33-25258
1. Perseverance. I. Title.

Perseverance (Ethics)

OATES, Wayne Edward, 1917- 248'.4
Life's detours [by] Wayne E. Oates. [Nashville] The Upper Room [1974] 86 p. 21 cm. [BJ1533.P4O2] 74-75221
1. Perseverance (Ethics) I. Title.

SWINDOLL, Charles R. 248.4
Three steps forward, two steps back : persevering through pressure / by Charles R. Swindoll. Nashville : T. Nelson, 1980. 191 p. ; 21 cm. Includes bibliographical references. [BV4647.P45S94] 80-11892 ISBN 0-8407-5187-7 : 8.95 ISBN 0-8407-5723-9 pbk. : 4.95
1. Perseverance (Ethics) 2. Christian life—1960- I. Title.

Perseverance (Theology)

BALCH, Stephen Bloomer, 1747-1833. 234.1
Two sermons on the certain and final perseverance of the saints. By Stephen Bloomer Balch, A.M., pastor of the Presbyterian congregation, George-town ... Georgetown, Printed, for the author, by M. Day and W. Hancock, 1791. [Philadelphia, Reprinted 1907?] p. 125-176, 2 pl. (incl. front., port.) 27 cm. Reprinted from "Balch genealogica, by Thomas Willing Balch. Philadelphia, Allen, Lane and Scott, 1907." "Said to be the first book printed in the District of Columbia." [BT768.B3 1907] 10-19576
1. Perseverance (Theology) I. Title.

BERKOUWER, Gerrit Cornelis, 1903- 234.9
Faith and perseverance. [Translated by Robert D. Knudsen from the Dutch] Grand Rapids, Eerdmans [1958] 256p. 23cm. (His Studies in dogmatics) Includes bibliography. [BT68.B413] 57-11583
1. Perseverance (Theology) 2. Reformed Church—Doctrinal and controversial works. I. Title.

LASSITER, Perry. 234
Once saved ... always saved / Perry Lassiter. Nashville : Broadman Press, [1975] 96 p. ; 18 cm. Includes bibliographical references. [BT768.L37] 74-15289 ISBN 0-8054-1931-4 pbk. : 1.50
1. Perseverance (Theology) I. Title.

MCELLIGOTT, C. J. 241
The crown of life; a study of perseverance [St. Louis] B. Herder [c.1963] xiv, 268p. 22cm. Bibl. 63-23155 4.50
1. Perseverance (Theology) I. Title.

MARSHALL, I. Howard. 234
Kept by the power of God : a study of perseverance and falling away / I. Howard Marshall. [2d ed.] Minneapolis : Bethany Fellowship, [1974] c1969. 281 p. ; 22 cm. Based on thesis, University of Aberdeen, 1963. Includes indexes. Bibliography: p. 259. [BT768.M34 1974] 74-23996 ISBN 0-87123-304-5 : 3.95
1. Perseverance (Theology) I. Title.

SHANK, Robert, 1918- 230.6
Life in the Son; a study of the doctrine of perseverance. Introd. by William W. Adams. Springfield, Mo. Westcott Publishers [1960] 380 p. 23 cm. Includes bibliography. [BT768.S5] 59-15488
1. Perseverance (Theology) I. Title.

SHANK, Robert [Lee] 230.6
Life in the Son: a study of the doctrine of perseverance. Introd. by William W. Adams. Springfield, Mo., [P.O. Box 803, Westcott Publishers c.1960] xix 3,80p. (3p. bibl.) 23cm. 50-15488 4.95
1. Perseverance (Theology) I. Title.

STRINGFELLOW, William 241
Free in obedience. New York, Seabury [1967, c.1964] 128p. 21cm. (SP30) Cover title: Free in obedience; the Radical Christian life. 1.45 pap.,
1. Perseverance (Theology) I. Title.

Persia—History—Ancient to A. D. 640.

HIRSCHY, Noah Calvin.
Artaxerxes iii Ochus and his reign, with special consideration of the Old Testament sources bearing upon the period ... Chicago, The University of Chicago press, 1909. v, 85 p. 26 cm. Inaug.-diss.--Bern. Contains bibliographies. [DS285.H5] 9-18446 0.75
1. Artaxerxes iii, Ochus, king of Persia, 358-338 B. C. 2. Persia—Hist.—Ancient to A. D. 640. 3. Bible. O. T.—Criticism, interpretation, etc. I. Title.

Persia—Religion.

DINKARD. Books 6. English & Pahlavi. 295
The wisdom of the Sasanian sages (Denkard VI) / [compiled] by Aturpat-e Emetan ; translated by Shaul Shaked. Boulder, Colo. : Westview Press, 1979. p. cm. (Persian heritage series ; no. 34) Text in Pahlavi and English; introd. and commentary in English. Includes bibliographical references and indexes. [PK6197.D5213 1979] 79-2957 ISBN 0-89158-376-9 lib. bdg. : 42.00
I. Aturpat-e Emetan. II. Shaked, Shaul. III. Title. IV. Series: UNESCO collection of representative works : Persian heritage series ; no. 34.

JOHNSON, Samuel, 1822-1882. 290.
Oriental religions and their relation to universal religion, by Samuel Johnson. With an introduction by O. B. Frothingham. Persia. Boston, New York, Houghton, Mifflin, and company, 1885. xliv, 782 p., 1 l. 23 cm. Note at end signed: A. M. Haskell, editor. [BL2270.J6] 8-17089
1. Persia—Religion. I. Haskell, Augustus Mellen, 1832-1893, ed. II. Frothingham, Octavius Brooks, 1822-1895. III. Title.

NAKOSTEEN, Mahdi Khan, 1904- 290.955
Religions of Iran, by Mehdi Nakosteen ... Denver, Col., Charles Mapes publishing co., 1943. 106 p. 22 1/2 cm. "225 copies ... printed." "First edition." [BL2270.N3] 43-7480
1. Persia—Religion. 2. Religion. I. Title.

Personalism.

BAKER, Rannie Belle, 1889- 141
The concept of a limited God; a study in the philosophy of personalism, by Rannie Belle Baker ... Washington, D. C., Strasburg, Va., Shenandoah publishing house, inc. [1934] xx, 234 p. 24 cm. Bibliography: p. [229]-234. [R828.5.R3] 34-2087
1. Personalism. 2. Goal. I. Title.

BRIGHTMAN, Edgar Sheffield, 1884- 141
Nature and values, by Edgar Sheffield Brightman ... New York, Nashville, Abingdon-Cokesbury press [1945] 171 p. 19 1/2 cm. (The Fondren lectures for 1945, Southern Methodist university) [B828.5.B7] 46-278
1. Personalism. I. Title.

BRIGHTMAN, Edgar Sheffield, 1884- 201
Personality and religion [by] Edgar Sheffield Brightman... New York, Cincinnati [etc.] The Abingdon press [c1934] 160 p. 21 1/2 cm. "Lowell institute lectures delivered at King's chapel in Boston in the month of April, 1934."--Pref. [BL51.B688] 34-31082
1. Personalism. 2. Religion—Philosophy. 3. Theism. I. Lowell institute lectures, 1934. II. Title.

BUCKHAM, John Wright, 1864- 201
Christianity and personality, by John Wright Buckham ... New York, Round table press, inc., 1936. xi, 192 p. 20 cm. [BF698.B78] 36-7347
1. Personalism. 2. Christianity—20th cent. I. Title.

KNUDSON, Albert Cornelius, 1873- 141
The philosophy of personalism. Boston, Boston University Press, 1949[c1927] 438 p. 21 cm. Bibliographical footnotes. [(B828.5K)] 51-8993
1. Personalism. 2. Philosophy and religion. I. Title.

KNUDSON, Albert Cornelius, 1873- 141
The philosophy of personalism. A study in the metaphysics of religion. By Albert C. Knudson ... New York [etc.] The Abingdon press [1927] 438 p. 22 cm. [B828.5.K6] 27-21477
1. Personalism. 2. Philosophy and religion. I. Title. II. Title: Metaphysics of religion.

VAUGHAN, Richard Miner, 1870- 201
The significance of personality, by Richard M. Vaughan ... New York, The Macmillan company, 1930. viii, p. 21, 302 p. 19 1/2 cm. [B828.5V3] 30-11522
1. Personalism. 2. Philosophy and religion. I. Title.

WESTOW, Theodore L 261
The variety of Catholic attitudes. [New York] Herder and Herder [1963] 159 p. 21 cm. Bibliographical footnotes. [BX1793.W45] 63-18160
1. Personalism. 2. Individualism. 3. Sociology, Christian (Catholic) 4. Man (Theology) 5. Christianity — 20th cent. I. Title.

Personalism—Addresses, essays, lectures.

PERSONALISM in theology : 230
a symposium in honor of Albert Cornelius Knudson / by associates and former students ; edited by Edgar Sheffield Brightman. New York : AMS Press, 1979. x, 257 p., [1] leaf of plates : port. ; 23 cm. Reprint of the 1943 ed. published by Boston University Press, Boston. Contents.Contents.—Leslie, E. A. Albert Cornelius Knudson, the man.—McConnell, F. J. Bowne and personalism.—Brightman, E. S. Personality as a metaphysical principle.—Hildebrand, C. D. Personalism and nature.—Ramsdell, E. T. The cultural integration of science and religion.—Ensley, F. G. The personality of God.—Harkness, G. Divine sovereignity and human freedom.—Pfeiffer, R. H. Personalistic elements in the Old Testament.—Flewelling, R. T. Personalism and the trend of history.—Mueller, W. G. Personality and Christian ethics.—King, W. J. Personalism and race.—Marlatt, E. B. Personalism and religious education. "Bibliography of Albert Cornelius Knudson, compiled by Carroll DeWitt Hildebrand": p. 249-257. [BR828.5.K63P4 1979] 75-3088 ISBN 0-404-59086-1 : 18.00
1. Knudson, Albert Cornelius, 1873- — Addresses, essays, lectures. 2. Personalism—Addresses, essays, lectures. 3. Theology—Addresses, essays, lectures. I. Knudson, Albert Cornelius, 1873- II. Brightman, Edgar Sheffield, 1884-1953.
Contents omitted

Personality.

BISHOP, William Samuel, 1865- 230
Spirit and personality, an essay in theological interpretation, by William Samuel Bishop... New York [etc.] Longmans, Green and co., 1923. xi, 188 p. 20 cm. [BT78.B5] 23-8161
1. Personality. 2. God. I. Title.

BISHOP, William Samuel, 1865- 230
The theology of personality, by William Samuel Bishop... New York [etc.] Longmans, Green and co., 1926. xi, 231 p. 20 cm. "In this volume the positions taken up in 'Spirit and personality' are amplified, illustrated and reaffirmed."--Pref. [BT78.B53] 26-8360
1. Personality. 2. God. I. Title.

BRUCE, Henry Addington Bayley, 1874- 133.07
The riddle of personality, by H. Addington Bruce. New York, Moffat, Yard & company, 1909. xiii, 247 p. 19 cm. "Reprinted August 1908; third printing, March 1909." "A large part of the present work appeared originally in the pages of Appleton's magazine."--Pref. to 1st ed. [BF1031.B86 1909] 32-6513
1. Personality. 2. Mental healing. 3. Spiritualism. I. Title.

BRUCE, Henry Addington Bayley, 1874- 133.
The riddle of personality, by H. Addington Bruce. New and rev. ed. New York, Moffat, Yard & company, 1915. xviii, 289 p. 19 1/2 cm. Fourth edition. "A large part of the present work appeared originally in the pages of Appleton's magazine."--Pref. to 1st edition. [BF1031.B86 1915] 16-26316 1.50.
1. Personality. 2. Mental healing. 3. Spiritualism. I. Title.

BURKART, Anna Driver. 201
The person in religion; an examination of Christianity's contribution to the history of thought... [by] Anna Driver Burkart. Philadelphia, 1930. 82 p. 23 cm. Thesis (P.H.D.)--University of Pennsylvania, 1930. Bibliography: p. 81-82. [BL51.B85 1930] 31-1842
1. Personality. 2. Religion—Philosophy. I. Title.

BURKE, Henry Robert, 1911- 207
... Personality traits of successful minor seminarians ... by Henry R. Burke ... Washington, D.C., The Catholic university of America press, 1947. vii, 65 p. incl. tables, diagrs. 23 cm. Thesis (PH.D.)--Catholic university of America, 1947. "References": p. 47-48. [BF698.B85] A 47
1. Personality. 2. Seminarians. I. Title.

DAY, Albert Edward, 1884- 232.9
Jesus and human personality [by] Albert Edward Day. New York, Cincinnati [etc.] The Abingdon press [c1934] 269 p. 21 cm. "Lectures given under the auspices of the Lyman Beecher foundation at Yale university in April, 1934."--Foreword. "References": p. 265-269. [BT590.P4D3] 248 34-32141
1. Personality. 2. Psychology, Religious. 3. Preaching. I. Title.

HENRY, Paul 126
Saint Augustine on personality. New York, Macmillan, [c.]1960. 44p. (bibl. footnotes) 20cm. (The Saint Augustine lecture series: Saint Augustine and the Augustinian tradition, 1959) 60-8123 2.25
1. Augustinus, Aurelius, Saint, Bp. of Hippo—Philosophy. 2. Personality. I. Title.

ILLINGWORTH, John Richardson, 1848-1915. 230
Personality, human and divine; being the Bampton lectures for the year 1894, by J. R. Illingworth ... London and New York, Macmillan and co., 1894. xv, 274 p. 23 cm. (On cover: Bampton lectures, 1894) [BR45.B3 1894] 12-84529
1. Personality. 2. God. I. Title.

JOHNSON, Paul E. 248
Who are you? [By] Paul E. Johnson. New York, Cincinnati [etc.] The Abingdon press [c1937] 3 p. l., 3-204 p. 20 cm. (Half-title: The Abingdon religious education texts, J. W. Langdale, general editor; Guides to Christian leadership, P. H. Vieth, editor) "For further reading" at end of each chapter. [BV4531.J6] 37-24786
1. Personality. 2. Character. 3. Christian life. I. Title.

MYERS, Frederic William Henry, 1843-1901. 133.
Human personality and its survival of bodily death, by Frederic W. H. Myers ... New York [etc.] Longmans, Green, and co., 1903. 2 v. illus. 24 cm. Edited after the author's death by Richard Hodgson and Alice Johnson. [BF1031.M85] 3-3539
1. Personality. 2. Immortality. 3. Psychical research. I. Hodgson, Richard, 1855-1905, ed. II. John, Alice, ed. III. Title.

MYERS, Frederic William Henry, 1843-1901. 133.
Human personality and its survival of bodily death, by Frederic W. H. Myers; ed. and abridged by his son Leopold Hamilton Myers ... New York [etc.] Longmans, Green, and co., 1907. 3 p. l., v-xviii, 470 p. 23 cm. [BF1031.M88] 7-1302
1. Personality. 2. Immortality. 3. Psychical research. I. Myers, Leopold Hamilton, 1882- ed. II. Title.

MYERS, Frederic William Henry, 1843-1901. 133.
Human personality and its survival of bodily death, by Frederic W. H. Myers ... New impression. London, New York, [etc.] Longmans, Green, and co., 1920. 2 v. illus. 24 cm. Edited after the author's death by Richard Hodgson and Alice Johnson. [BF1031.M85 1920] 21-8598
1. Personality. 2. Immortality. 3. Psychical research. I. Hodgson, Richard, 1855-1905, ed. II. Johnson, Alice, ed. III. Title.

MYERS, Frederic William Henry, 1843-1901. 133.027
Human personality and its survival of bodily death, by Frederic W. H. Myers; edited and abridged by S. B. and L. H. M. London, New York [etc.] Longmans, Green and co., [1936] xi, [1], 307 p. front. (port.) 18 cm. (Half-title: The swan library, v. 28) "Swan library edition, January 1935;. new impression, May 1936." [BF1931.M88 1936] 159.961 37-8549
1. Personality. 2. Immortality. 3. Psychical research. I. Myers, Leopold Hamilton, 1882- ed. II. Blennerhassett, Silvia (Myers) Mrs. joint ed. III. Title.

THIRKIELD, Wilbur Patterson, 1854-
The personality and message of the preacher, by Wilbur Patterson Thirkield ... New York, Cincinnati, The Abingdon press [c1914] 56 p. 19 cm. $0.35. 14-18411
I. Title.

TOURNIER, Paul. 155.2
The meaning of persons / Paul Tournier. San Francisco : Harper & Row, 1982, c1957. p. cm. Translation of: Le personnage et la personne. Reprint. Originally published: New York : Harper, 1957. Includes index. [BF698.T63 1982] 19 82-9296 ISBN 0-06-068369-4 : 9.95
1. Personality. 2. Social role. 3. Interpersonal relations. 4. Man (Christian theology) I. [Personnage et la personne.] English II. Title.

WEATHERFORD, Willis Duke, 1875- 243
Personal elements in religious life, by W. D. Weatherford, PH.D. Nashville, Tenn., Dallas, Tex. [etc.] Publishing house Methodist Episcopal church, South, Smith & Lamar, agents, 1916. 159 p. 20 1/2 cm. Reprinted in part from the Methodist review. Bibilography: p. 159. [BV4915.W45] 16-14466
1. Personality. 2. Theism. I. Title.

WEST, William, 1890- 922.773
Personality in retrospection-introspection; My God and I. [Denver? 1962] 182 p. illus. 20 cm. Autobiographical. [BX8495.W56A3] 63-38377
I. Title.

WHAT religion does for personality, by Shailer Matthews, Forrest A. Kingsbury, Charles T. Holman [and others] ... An outline study course for young people and adults. Chicago, Ill., The American institute of sacred literature [1932] viii, 148 p. 19 1/2 cm. (On cover: Outline study courses of the American institute of sacred literature) "References" at end of study IV (p. 68) [BS645.W5] 33-12269 220.95
1. Personality. 2. Psychology, Religious. 3. Bible—Psychology. I. Matthews, Shailer, 1863-

Personality and culture—India.

KAKAR, Sudhir. 305.2'3'0954
The inner world : a psycho-analytic study of childhood and society in India / Sudhir Kakar. 2nd ed., rev. and enl. Delhi ; New York : Oxford University Press, 1981. 241 p. : ill. ; 23 cm. Includes index. Bibliography: p. 231-237. [BF698.9.C8K34 1981] 19 81-902910 ISBN 0-19-561305-8 : 14.95
1. Personality and culture—India. 2. Child psychology—India. 3. Psychoanalysis—India. 4. Hinduism—Psychology. I. Title.

Personality assessment.

ROWE, Dorothy. 150'.1
The construction of life and death / Dorothy Rowe. Chichester [Eng.] ; New York : John Wiley, c1982. p. cm. Includes index. Bibliography: p. [BF698.4.R68] 19 81-13056 ISBN 0-471-10064-1 : 29.95
1. Personality assessment. 2. Faith—Psychological aspects. 3. Life—Philosophy. 4. Death—Philosophy. I. Title.

Personality—Biblical teaching.

YATES, David O. 220.8'1552
What the Bible says about your personality / David O. Yates. 1st ed. San Francisco : Harper & Row, c1980. p. cm. Bibliography: p. [BS645.Y37 1980] 80-7759 ISBN 0-06-069711-3 pbk. : 5.95
1. Bible—Psychology. 2. Personality—Biblical teaching. I. Title.

Personality, Disorders of.

EATON, Joseph W 1919- 616.8
Culture and mental disorders; a comparative study of the Hutterites and other populations, by Joseph W. Eaton in collaboration with Robert J. Weil. Glencoe, Ill., Free Press [1955] 254p. illus. 22cm. [BX8129.H8E2] 55-7336
1. Hutterite Brethren. 2. Personality, Disorders of. I. Title.

WILKERSON, David R. 253'.5
The untapped generation, by David & Don Wilkerson. Grand Rapids, Zondervan Pub. House [1971] 256 p. illus. 22 cm. [RC554.W54] 75-146572 4.95
1. Personality, Disorders of. 2. Youth. 3. Counseling. 4. Psychology, Religious. I. Wilkerson, Don, joint author. II. Title.

Personality—Religious Interpretation.

POWELL, Robert Richard.
Choose life; finding Christian answers to teen-age questions. New York; Abingdon Press [1959] 135 p. 17 cm. 66-94555
1. Personality—Religious Interpretation. 2. Vocation. 3. Christian life. 4. Youth. I. Title.

SANDAY, William.
Personality in Christ and in ourselves, by William Sanday ... New York Oxford university press, American branch 1911 iii, 75 p. 21 1/2 cm. $0.50 11-18190
I. Title.

SANDAY, William, 1843-
Personality in Christ and in ourselves, by William Sanday ... Oxford, The Calrendon press, 1911. 3 p. l., [3]-75, [1] p. 23 cm. 11-29688
I. Title.

Personnel service in education.

YOUNG men's Christian associations. International committee. Educational council.
...Guidance in associations with limited staff. Lancaster, Pa., The Educational council of the Young men's Christian associations of the United States of America [1931] 112 p. fold. tab. 23 cm. (The Educational council bulletin, vol. II, no. 2) [LC589.Y49 vol. 2, no. 2] E 32
1. Personnel service in education. 2. Profession, Choce of. 3. Vocational guidance—Young men's Christian associations] I. Title.

YOUNG men's Christian associations. International committee. Educational council.
...Personnel and guidance in Y.M.C.A. schools. Lancaster Pa., The Educational council of the Young men's Christian associations of the United States of America [1931] Lancaster, Pa., The Educational council of the Young men's Christian associations of the United States of America [1931] 122 p. 23 cm. 27 p. 23 cm. (The Educational council bulletin. vol. II, no. 1) (The Educational council bulletin. Supplement I, vol. II, no. 1) [LC589.Y49 vol. 2, no. 1] E 32
1. Personnel service in education. 2. Profession, Choice of. 3. Interest (Psychology) 4. Occupations. I. Herring, John Peabody, 1882- II. Title. III. Title: — A point of view and practical technique for evaluating activity,

Persons (Canon law)

MULDOON, James, 1935- 262.9'32
Popes, lawyers, and infidels : the church and the non-Christian world, 1250-1550/ James Muldoon. [Philadelphia] : University of Pennsylvania Press, 1979. xi, 212 p. ; 24 cm. (The Middle Ages) Includes index. Bibliography: p. [197]-208. [LAW] 79-5049 ISBN 0-8122-7770-8 : 15.00
1. Persons (Canon law) I. Title. II. Title: The church and the non-Christian world, 1250-1550. III. Series: Middle Ages.

Perth Amboy, N. J. Presbyterian church.

MENDENHALL, Harlan George, 1851- 285.
Presbyterianism in Perth Amboy, New Jersey, by Harlan G. Mendenhall. Perth Amboy, N. J., The Perth Amboy publishing company, 1903. 3 p. l., 92 p., 1 l., [8] p. front., illus. (incl. ports., map) 24 cm. Authorities consulted: verso of 2d prelim. leaf. "Program for the feast of dedication and one hundredth anniversary celebration held January 25 to February 1, 1903": 8 p. at end of volume. [BX8949.P4M4] 3-2970
1. Perth Amboy, N. J. Presbyterian church. 2. Presbyterian church in New Jersey. I. Title.

Perth Amboy, N. J. St. Peter's Church.

HISTORY of St. Peter's Church in Perth Amboy, New Jersey, 1685-1956; this being an extension of A brief history of St. Peter's Church in Perth Amboy, 1635-1945. [Perth Amboy, N. J., 1956] 99p. 23cm.
1. Perth Amboy, N. J. St. Peter's Church. I. McGinnis, William Carroll, 1884-

JONES, William Northey, 1866- 283.
The history of St. Peter's church in Perth Amboy, New Jersey, the oldest congregation of the church in 1698 to the year of Our Lord 1923, and the celebration of the 225th anniversary of the parish; also a genealogy of the families buried in the churchyard, by the Rev. W. Northey Jones ... [New York, Patterson press, 1925] 1 p. l., 5-519 p. illus., plates, ports., diagr. 25 cm. [BX5980.P4P5] 25-1036
1. Perth Amboy, N. J. St. Peter's church. 2. Perth Amboy, N. J.—Geneal. 3. Registers of births, etc.—Perth Amboy, N. J. 4. Epitaphs—Perth Amboy, N. J. I. Title.

Peru—Politics and government—1829-

KLAIBER, Jeffrey L. 322'.1'0985
Religion and revolution in Peru, 1824-1976 / Jeffry L. Klaiber. Notre Dame, Ind. : University of Notre Dame Press, c1977. p. cm. [F3446.5.K55] 76-51616 ISBN 0-268-01599-6 : 14.95
1. Catholic Church in Peru. 2. Peru—Politics and government—1829- 3. Church and state—Peru. 4. Poor—Peru. I. Title.

MCGINNIS, William Carroll, 1884- 283.74941
History of St. Peter's Church in Perth Amboy, New Jersey, 1685-1956. [Perth Amboy, N. J., 1956] 99p. illus. 24cm. Includes bibliography. [BX5980.P4P53] 59-41581
1. Perth Amboy, N. J., St. Peter's Episcopal Church. I. Title.

Pesch, Heinrich, 1854-1926.

MUELLER, Franz, 1900- 261
Heinrich Pesch and his theory of Christian solidarism, by Franz H. Mueller ... St. Paul, Minn., The College of St. Thomas [1941] 50 p. 19 1/2 cm. (Aquin papers: no. 7) [Full name: Franz Hermann Joseph Mueller] Bibliographical references included in "Notes" (p. 47-50) [HN37.C3M8] 43-6931
1. Pesch, Heinrich, 1854-1926. 2. Sociology, Christian—Catholic authors. 3.

Economics. I. St. Paul. College of St. Thomas. II. Title.

Pestana, Ken.

MCLEAN, Gordon R. 248'.246'0924 B
Devil at the wheel / Gordon McLean with Ken Pestana. Minneapolis : Bethany Fellowship, [1975] 142 p. : ill. ; 18 cm. (Dimension books) [BV4935.P44M3] 74-28547 ISBN 0-87123-101-8 pbk. : 1.50
1. Pestana, Ken. 2. Conversion. I. Pestana, Ken, joint author. II. Title.

Peter, Carrie 1868-1937.

STERLING, Tamar (Wright) 922
Mrs. 1895-
Miss Carrie Peter and trophies in India, by Tamar Wright Sterling ... Findlay, O., Fundamental truth publishers [c1938] 159 p. illus. (port.) 19 cm. [Full name: Tamar Elizabeth (Wright) Sterling] [BV3265.S72] 38-19987
1. Peter, Carrie 1868-1937. 2. Missions—India. I. Title.

Peter Chrysologus, Saint, ca. 400—ca.450.

THE Incarnation in the sermons of Saint Peter Chrysologus. Mundelein, Ill., Saint Mary of the Lake Seminary, 1956. 150p. 23cm. (Pontificia Facultas Theologica Seminarii Sanctae Mariae ad Lacum. Dissertationes ad lauream, 25) Bibliography: p.146-150.
1. Peter Chrysologus, Saint, ca. 400—ca.450. 2. Incarnation—History ofdoctrines—Early Church. I. McGlynn, Robert H

THE Incarnation in the sermons of Saint Peter Chrysologus. Mundelein, Ill., Saint Mary of the Lake Seminary, 1956. 150p. 23cm. (Pontificia Facultas Theologica Seminarii Sanctae Mar iae ad Lacum. Dissertationes ad lauream, 25) Bibliography: p. 146-150.
1. Peter Chrysologus, Saint, ca. 400—ca. 450. 2. Incarnation—History of doctrines—Early Church. I. McGlynn, Robert H

Peter I, the Great, Emperor of Russia, 1672-1725.

CRACRAFT, James. 281.9'47
The church reform of Peter the Great. Stanford, Calif., Stanford University Press, 1971. xii, 336 p. 23 cm. Based on the author's thesis, University of Oxford. Bibliography: p. [308]-322. [BR935.C7 1971] 70-130823 ISBN 0-8047-0747-2 13.50
1. Peter I, the Great, Emperor of Russia, 1672-1725. 2. Church and state in Russia. 3. Russia—Church history. I. Title.

Peter, Saint, apostle.

ALCOTT, William Andrus, 225.92
1798-1859.
The life of Peter the apostle. By William A. Alcott. Written for the Massachusetts Sabbath school society, and revised by the Committee of publication. Boston, Massachusetts Sabbath school society, 1836. 188 p. front. 15 cm. [BS2515.A6] [922.1] 84-14839
1. Peter, Saint, apostle. I. Massachusetts Sabbath school society. II. Title.

AUCHINCLOSS, William Stuart, 922.
1842-
Saint Peter, the apostle of Asia, by W. S. Auchincloss. Philadelphia, 1901. 129 p. front. (fold. map) 14 cm. [BS2515.A8] 1-14650
1. Peter, Saint, apostle. I. Title.

BARNES, Arthur Stapylton, 270.1
1861-1936.
Christianity at Rome in the apostolic age; an attempt at reconstruction of history. Westport, Conn., Greenwood Press [1971] xiii, 222 p. 23 cm. Reprint of the 1938 ed. Includes bibliographical references. [BR165.B285 1971] 72-114462 ISBN 0-8371-4760-3
1. Peter, Saint, apostle. 2. Paul, Saint, apostle. 3. John, Saint, apostle. 4. Rome (City)—Church history. 5. Church history—Primitive and early church, ca. 30-600. I. Title.

BARRETT, Ethel. 225.9'24 B
Peter, the story of a deserter who became a forceful leader / Ethel Barrett. Ventura, CA : Regal Books, c1982. 123 p., [2] p. of plates : 1 map ; 18 cm. "Book 9"—Cover. [BS2515.B36] 19 81-52941 ISBN 0-8307-0768-9 (pbk.) : 1.95
1. Peter, The Apostle, Saint. 2. Bible. N.T.—Biography. 3. Apostles—Biography. I. Title.

BENNET, James E. 225.92
God and Peter, by James E. Bennet ... Grand Rapids, Mich., Zondervan publishing house [c1939] 70 p. 20 cm. [BS2515.B4] 922.1 39-13841
1. Peter, Saint, apostle I. Title.

BENOIT, Pierre, 226'.06'6
Aug.3,1906-
Jesus and the gospel. Translated by Benet Weatherhead. [New York] Herder and Herder [1973-74] 2 v. 23 cm. "A translation of selected articles from ... Exegese et theologie." Vol. 2 published by Seabury Press, New York, as A Crossroad book. Includes bibliographical references. [BS2555.2.B4613] 72-94303 ISBN 0-07-073770-3 (v. 1) 9.75 (v. 1) varies
1. Peter, Saint, apostle. 2. Bible. N.T Gospels—Addresses, essays, lectures. 3. Bible. N.T. Epistles of Paul—Theology. I. Title.

BYRUM, Enoch Edwin, 1861- 225.92
Peter the fisherman preacher, by E. E. Byrum ... Anderson, Ind., The Warner press [c1931] x, 11-141 p. incl. front. pl. 19 cm. [BS2515.B8] 31-8055 922
1. Peter, Saint apostle. I. Title.

CLIFFORD, T. A., 1893- 225.9'24 B
Peter and the keys, by T. A. Clifford. Philadelphia, Dorrance [1972] 58 p. 22 cm. Includes bibliographical references. [BS2515.C54] 72-171930 ISBN 0-8059-1615-6 3.50
1. Peter, Saint, apostle. 2. Papacy. I. Title.

CRISCOE, Arthur H. 225.9'24 B
Original : Peter was one of a kind, so are you! / Arthur H. Criscoe. Kalamazoo, Mich. : Master's Press, c1977. xi, 52 p. : ill. ; 18 cm. (Master's moments) Includes bibliographical references. [BS2515.C68] 77-70113 ISBN 0-89251-021-8 pbk. : 1.50
1. Peter, Saint, apostle. 2. Bible. N.T.—Biography. 3. Apostles—Biography. 4. Christian live—Baptist authors. I. Title.

CULLMANN, Oscar 225.92
Peter; disciple, apostle, martyr: a historical and theological study. Tr from German by Floyd V. Filson. 2d rev.,)expanded ed. Philadelphia, Westminster [c.1962] 252p. 22cm. (Lib of hist. and doctrine) Bibl. 62-10169 5.00
1. Peter, Saint, apostle. I. Title.

DALLMANN, William, 1862- 225.92
Peter; life and letters [by] William Dallmann ... St. Louis, Mo., Concordia publishing house, 1930. x, 222 p. incl. front. (port.) illus. col. plates, 26 cm. Pages vii and ix wrongly numbered 7 and 9 respectively. [Full name: Charles Frederick William Dallmann] [BS2515.D25] 922.1 30-15285
1. Peter, Saint, apostle. I. Title.

DAVIDSON, John, 1870-
St. Peter and his training, by the Rev. John Davidson ... London, J. M. Dent & co.; Philadelphia, J. B. Lippincott co. [1905] viii, 120 p. front., map. 14 cm. (Half-title: The Temple series of Bible handbooks, ed. by O. Smeaton) Lettered on cover: The Temple series of Bible characters & scripture handbooks. Title within ornamental border. 16-19298
I. Title.

ELTON, Godfrey Elton, 226.0905
baron, 1892-
Simon Peter [by] Lord Elton. [1st ed. in the U.S.A.] Garden City, N.Y., Doubleday, 1966 [c1965] xvii, 236 p. 22 cm. Bibliographical footnotes. [BS2515.E45 1966] 66-10918
1. Peter, Saint, apostle. I. Title.

ELTON, Godfrey Elton, 226.0905
baron, 1892-
Simon Peter [1st ed. in the U.S.A.] Garden City, N.Y., Doubleday, 1966 [c.1965] xvii, 236p. 22cm. Bibl. [BS2515.E45] 66-10918 4.50
1. Peter, Saint, apostle. I. Title.

ENGLISH, Eugene Schuyler, 922.1
1899-
The life and letters of Saint Peter, containing landmarks in the life and expositions of the epistles of the fisherman-apostle, by E. Schuyler English... New York, N.Y., Publication office "Our hope," A. C. Gaebelein, inc. [c1941] xiv p. 1 l., 17-271 p. 21 cm. [BS2515.E5]
1. Peter, Saint, apostle. 2. Bible N.T. Peter—Commentaries. 3. Bible—Commentaries—N. T. Peter. I. Title.

FILSON, Floyd Vivian, 225.92
1896-
Pioneers of the primitive church [by] Floyd V. Filson... New York, Cincinnati [etc.] The Abingdon press [c1940] 194 p. 20 cm. "Selected books on the apostolic age": p. 15-18; "Selected references." at end of each chapter. [BS2440.F5] 40-5742
1. Peter Saint apostle. 2. Stephen, Saint, martyr. 3. Barnabas, Saint, apostle. 4. Paul, Saint, apostle. 5. James, brother of the Lord. I. Title.
Contents omitted.

FINDLAY, James Alexander, 225.92
1880-
A portrait of Peter [by] J. Alexander Findlay. New York, Cincinnati [etc.] The Abingdon press [c1935] 214 p. 18 1/2 cm. [BS3515.F5 1935] (982.1) 36-730
1. Peter, Saint, apostle. I. Title.

FLYNN, Leslie B. 226'.092'4 B
From clay to rock : personal insights into life from Simon Peter / Leslie B. Flynn. 1st ed. Chappaqua, N.Y. : Christian Herald Books, c1981. 158 p. ; 21 cm. [BS2515.F56] 19 80-69307 ISBN 0-915684-79-9 pbk. : 5.95
1. Peter, Saint, apostle. 2. Bible. N.T.—Biography. 3. Apostles—Biography. I. Title.

FOAKES-JACKSON, Frederick 922.
John, 1855-
Peter: prince of apostles; a study in the history and tradition of Christianity, by F. J. Foakes-Jackson... New York, George H. Doran company [c1927] xviii p., 2 l., 23-320 p. front., illus. (maps) 21 cm. [BS2515.F6] 27-24402
1. Peter, Saint, apostle. 2. Church history—Primitive and early church. I. Title.

FOUARD, Constant Henri, 270.
1837-1904.
Saint Peter and the first years of Christianity, by the Abbe Constant Fouard; tr. from the 2d ed. with the author's sanction by George F. X. Griffith; with an introduction by Cardinal Gibbons. New York and London, Longmans, Green, and co., 1892. xxv, 422 p. 3 fold. maps (incl. front.) 20 cm. [BR165.F7] 12-85571
1. Peter, Saint, apostle. I. Griffith, George Francis Xavier, tr. II. Title.

GREENE, Joseph Nelson.
The exalted fisherman; a practical and devotional study in the life and experience of the apostle St. Peter, by Joseph Nelson Greene ... New York, Cincinnati, The Methodist book concern [c1914] 329 p. 19 1/2 cm. $1.00. 14-14517
I. Title.

GREENE, Richard Arnold.
Saint Peter, by Richard Arnold Greene. Boston, Sherman, French & company, 1909. 3 p. l., 47 p. 18 cm. In verse. 9-13611
I. Title.

JAKI, Stanley L. 262.001
And on this rock : the witness of one land and two covenants / Stanley L. Jaki. Notre Dame, Ind. : Ave Maria Press, c1978. 125 p. : ill. ; 21 cm. Includes bibliographical references. [BS2515.J28] 78-59925 ISBN 0-87793-161-5 : 2.95
1. Peter, Saint, apostle. 2. Popes—Infallibility. 3. Baniyas, Syria. I. Title.

KARRER, Otto, 1888- 262.11
Peter and the church; an examination of Cullmann's thesis. [Tr. from German by Ronald Walls. New York] Herder & Herder [1963] 141p. 22cm. (Quaestiones disputatae, 8) 63-10690 2.25 pap.,
1. Peter, Saint, apostle. 2. Church—Foundation. 3. Church—Foundation. I. Title.

KNIGHT, William Allen, 1863- 922.
Peter in the firelight, by William Allen Knight ... Boston, New York [etc.] The Pilgrim press, 1911. ix, 102 p., 1 l. front., plates. 19 cm. [BS2515.K6] 11-25687
1. Peter, Saint, Apostle. I. Title.

THE life and writings of 225.92
the apostle Peter. Written for the American Sunday-school union, and revised by the Committee of publication. Philadelphia, American Sunday-school union [1836] 323 p. front., illus. 15 cm. "Letters of the apostle Peter. Written about A. D. 64 and 65.": p. 211-232. [BS2515.L5] 922.1 34-19078
1. Peter, Saint, Apostle. I. Bible, N. T. Peter. English. 1836. II. American Sunday-school union.

LIPSCOMB, Andrew Adgate, 225.92
1816-1890.
Lessons from the life of Saint Peter. Six essays. By A. A. Lipscomb ... [Macon, Ga., J. W. Burke & co., 1882] 120 p. 22 cm. [BS2515.L54] 922.1 39-11838
1. Peter, Saint, apostle. I. Title.

LIVIUS, Thomas Stiverd, 262.
1829?-1903.
S. Peter, bishop of Rome; or, The Roman episcopate of the prince of the apostles. Proved from the fathers, history, and archaeology, and illustrated by arguments from other sources. By the Rev. T. Livius ... London, Burns & Oates, limited; New York, Catholic publication society co., 1888. xxii, 560 p. 22 cm. [BV665.L5] 25-15263
1. Peter, Saint, apostle. 2. Apostolic succession. I. Title.

LOWE, John, 1899- 922.1
Saint Peter. New York, Oxford University Press, 1956. 65p. 20cm. [BS2515.L7] 225.92 56-8573
1. Peter, Saint, apostle. I. Title.

LOWRIE, Walter, 1868-
SS. Peter and Paul in Rome, an archaeological rhapsody, by Walter Lowrie ... London, New York [etc.] Oxford university press, 1940. 9 p. l., [3]-164 p. front., plates. 19 cm. A 41
1. Peter, Saint, apostle. 2. Paul, Saint, apostle. 3. Christian antiquities—Rome. I. Title.

MACARTNEY, Clarence Edward 225.92
Noble, 1879-
Peter and his Lord; sermons on the life of Peter, by Clarence Edward Macartney ... Nashville, Cokesbury press [c1937] 247 p. 19 1/2 cm. [BS2515.M25] [922.1] 37-16013
1. Peter, Saint, apostle. 2. Presbyterian church—Sermons. 3. Sermons, American. I. Title.

MACINNIS, John Murdoch, 225.92
1871-
Peter, the fisherman philosopher; a study in higher fundamentalism, by John Murdoch MacInnis ... New York and London, Harper & brothers, 1930. xiii p., 1 l., 150 p. 19 1/2 cm. [BS2515.M3 1930] 30-22552
1. Peter, Saint, apostle. I. Title.

MACINNIS, John Murdoch, 922.
1871-
Peter the fisherman philosopher; a study in higher fundamentalism, by John Murdoch MacInnis ... Los Angeles, Calif., The Biola book room [c1927] 214 p. 19 1/2 cm. [BS2515.M3] 28-19670
1. Peter, Saint, apostle. I. Title.

MARY Simeon, Mother, 225.92
Simon called Peter. Decorations by John F. Kelly. Westminster, Md., Newman Press, 1959[i.e., 1960] 111p. illus. 19cm. 60-1823 2.25 bds.,
1. Peter, Saint, apostle. I. Title.

MEYER, Frederick Brotherton, 922.
1847-
Peter: fisherman, disciple, apostle, by F. B. Meyer ... New York, Chicago [etc.] Fleming H. Revell company [c1920] viii, 224 p. 20 cm. [BS2515.M4] 20-2354

I. Title.

MEYER, Frederick Brotherton, 1847-1929.
Peter, fisherman, disciple, apostle. [New ed.] Fort Washington, Pa., Christian Literature Crusade [1961] 190 p. This edition first published 1950. 66-51410
1. Peter, Saint, apostle. I. Title.

NOLAND, Cora Mabel (Shaw) 225. "Mrs. H. B. Noland," 1882-
Peter the fisherman, by Mrs. H. B. Noland. Washington, D. C. [etc.] Review and herald publishing assn [c1926] 143 p. incl. front., illus. 20 cm. [BS2515.N6] 26-9933
1. Peter, Saint, apostle. I. Title.

O'CONNOR, Daniel 225.92'4 William, 1925-
Peter in Rome: the literary, liturgical, and archeological evidence. New York, Columbia University Press, 1969. xiv, 242 p. illus., plans. 29 cm. Bibliography: p. 214-226. [BS2515.O28] 68-17552 20.00
1. Peter, Saint, apostle. I. Title.

PALAU, Luis. 248'.4
Walk on water, Pete! / By Luis Palau. Glendale, Calif. : G/L Regal Books, [1974] 87 p. ; 18 cm. [BV4501.2.P27] 74-79563 ISBN 0-8307-0286-5 pbk. 1.25
1. Peter, Saint, apostle. 2. Christian life—1960- I. Title.

PETER, disciple, apostle, 922.1 *martyr;* a historical and theological study. Translated from the German by Floyd V. Filson. Philadelphia, Westminster Press [1953] 252p. illus. 24cm. Bibliographical footnotes. [BS2515.C813] [BS2515.C813] 225.92 53-13084 53-13084
1. Peter, Saint, apostle. I. Cullmann, Oscar.

PETER in the New 225.9'24 B *Testament;* a collaborative assessment by Protestant and Roman Catholic scholars. Edited by Raymond E. Brown, Karl P. Donfried, and John Reumann, from discussions by Paul J. Achtemeier [and others] Minneapolis, Augsburg Pub. House, 1973. ix, 181 p. 21 cm. Bibliography: p. 169-177. [BS2615.P47] 73-83787 ISBN 0-8066-1401-3 1.95 (pbk.)
1. Peter, Saint, apostle. 2. Bible. N.T.—Criticism, interpretation, etc. I. Brown, Raymond Edward, ed. II. Donfried, Karl P., ed. III. Reumann, John Henry Paul, ed.

PITTENGER, William 225.9'24 B Norman, 1905-
The life of Saint Peter, by W. Norman Pittenger. New York, Watts [1971] x, 116 p. 22 cm. (Immortals of philosophy and religion) Includes bibliographical references. The life of the disciple who founded the Christian Church. [BS2515.P58] 92 70-134659 ISBN 0-531-00963-7
1. Peter, Saint, apostle. 2. [Peter, Saint, apostle.] 3. [Apostles.] I. Title.

PRIMACY of Peter (The) 262.13 [by] J. Meyendorff, N. Afanassieff [others. Tr. from French] London, Faith Pr. [dist. Westminster, Md., Canterbury, c.1963] 134p. 23cm. (Lib. of Orthodox theology, no. 1) Bibl. 63-5439 2.50
1. Peter, Saint, apostle. 2. Popes—Primacy. 3. Church—History of doctrines. I. Meyendorff, Jean, 1926- II. Afanas'ev, Nikolai III. Series.

RENICH, Fred. 226'.092'4
When the chisel hits the rock / Fred C. Renich ; [photo by Wayne Hanna]. Wheaton, Ill. : Victor Books, c1980. 132 p. ; 21 cm. [BS2515.R46] 19 80-51394 ISBN 0-88207-218-8 (pbk.) : 3.50
1. Peter, Saint, apostle. 2. Christian life—1960- I. Title.
Publisher's address 1825 College Ave., Wheaton, IL 60187.

ROBERTSON, Archibald 225.92 Thomas, 1863-1934.
Epochs in the life of Simon Peter, by A. T. Robertson ... New York, London, C. Scribner's sons, 1933. xvi p., 1 l., 342 p. 20 cm. "A brief bibliography on Peter and his Epistles": p. 323-326. [BS2515.R57] 922.1 33-24711
1. Peter, Saint, apostle. I. Title.

ROBINSON, Charles Seymour, 225.92 1829-1899.
Simon Peter: his early life and times. By Chas. S. Robinson, D.D. New York, American tract society 1889 3 p. l., [5]-309 p. 19 1/2 cm. [PS2515.R6] [922.1] 34-16737
1. Peter, Saint, apostle. I. American tract society. II. Title.

ROBINSON, Charles Seymour, 225.92 1829-1899.
Simon Peter; his later life and labours, by Chas. S. Robinson, D.D. New York, London and Edinburgh, T. Nelson and sons, 1894. viii, 9-325 p. incl. front. plates. 20 cm. [BS2515.R62] [922.1] 34-16738
1. Peter, Saint, apostle. I. Title.

SAINT Peter.
Oxford, Clarendon Press, 1956. 65p. 20cm.
1. Peter, Saint, apostle. I. Lowe, John, 1899-

SHOTWELL, James Thomson, 262.13 1874-1965, ed.
The see of Peter [ed.] by James T. Shotwell, Louise Ropes Loomis. New York, Octagon, 1965[c.1927, 1955] xxvi, 737p. 24cm. (Records of civilization: sources and studies, no.7) Bibl. [BX955.S5] 65-25615 17.50
1. Peter, Saint, apostle. 2. Papacy—Hist. 3. Church history—Primitive and early church. I. Loomis, Louise Ropes, 1874-1958, ed. II. Title. III. Series.

SIMON Peter, 922.1 sinner and saint. Grand Rapids, Zondervan Pub. House [1954] 185p. 20cm. [BS2515.D4] [BS2515.D4] 225.92 54-11935 54-11935
1. Peter. Saint, apostle. I. De Haan, Martin Ralph, 1891-

SMITH, Daniel, 1806-1852. 225.92
The life of St. Peter. By Rev. Daniel Smith... New York, Pub. by T. Mason and G. Lane, for the Sunday school union of the Methodist Episcopal church, 1840. 132 p. incl. front. double map. 14 1/2 cm. [BS2515.S40] [(922.1)] 34-16734
1. Peter, Saint, apostle. I. Sunday school union of the Methodist Episcopal church. II. Title.

STRATON, Hillyer 225.92 Hawthorne.
Peter, the man Jesus made, by Hillyer Hawthorne Straton ... introduction by Austen K. deBlois. Grand Rapids, Mich., Zondervan publishing house [c1938] viii, [8] 11-147 p. 19 1/2 cm. [BS2515.S8] [922.1] 38-39121
1. Peter, Saint, apostle. I. Title.

TAYLOR, William Mackergo, 225.92 1829-1895.
Peter, the apostle. By the Rev. William M. Taylor ... New York, Harper & brothers, 1877. 371 p. 19 1/2 cm. [BS2515.T3 1877] [922.1] 34-16720
1. Peter, Saint, apostle. I. Title.

TAYLOR, William Mackergo, 922. 1829-1895.
Peter the apostle. By the Rev. William M. Taylor ... New York, Harper & brothers [c1904] 371 p. 19 1/2 cm. "Selected bibliography": p. 195-196. [BS2515.T3 1904] 4-34135
1. Peter, Saint, apostle. I. Title.

THOMAS, William Henry 225.92 Griffith, 1861-1924.
The apostle Peter, outline studies of his life, character, and writings, by W. H. Griffith Thomas ... Grand Rapids, Mich., Wm. B. Eerdmans publishing company [1946] 4 p. l., 296 p. 20 cm. Bibliography: p. 293-294. [BS2515.T47] [922.1] 46-18621
1. Peter, Saint, apostle. 2. Bible. N.T Peter—Commentaries. I. Title.

WALSH, John Evangelist, 225.9'24 1927-
The bones of St. Peter : a first full account of the search for the Apostle's body / John Evangelist Walsh. 1st ed. Garden City, N.Y. : Doubleday, 1982. xvi, 195 p., [16] p. of plates : ill. ; 22 cm. Includes index. Bibliography: p. [179]-183. [BS2515.W28 1982] 19 80-2883 ISBN 0-385-15039-3 : 13.95
1. Peter, the Apostle, Saint—Relics. I. Title.

WALSH, William Thomas, 225.92 1891-
Saint Peter, the apostle. New York, Macmillan Co., 1948. viii, 307 p. 21 cm. [BS2515.W3] 922.1 922.1 922.1 48-10557
1. Peter, Saint, apostle. I. Title.

WINTER, Michael M. 262.13
Saint Peter and the Popes. Baltimore, Helicon Press [1960] 236p. Bibl. footnotes. 60-13379 4.50 bds.,
1. Peter, Saint, apostle. 2. Papacy—Hist. I. Title.

WINTER, Michael M. 262'.13'09
Saint Peter and the Popes / Michael M. Winter. Westport, Conn. : Greenwood Press, 1979, c1960. p. cm. Reprint of the ed. published by Helicon Press, Baltimore. Includes index. Bibliography: p. [BX955.2.W5 1979] 78-21507 ISBN 0-313-21158-2 lib. bdg. : 18.75
1. Peter, Saint, Apostle. 2. Papacy—History. I. Title.

Peter, Saint, Apostle— Art.

EMMINGHAUS, Johannes H. 704.9486
Peter [by] Joh. H. Emminghaus. Text of story and legend by Leonhard Kuppers. [Translated from the German by Hans Hermann Rosenwald] Recklinghausen [Ger.] A. Bongers; distributed by Taplinger Pub. Co. [New York, c1964] 69 p. col. illus. 18 cm. (The Saints in legend and art, v. 2) [N8080.E4513] 67-4500
1. Peter, Saint, apostle — Art. I. Kuppers, Leonhard, 1903- II. Title.

Peter, Saint, apostle—Drama.

CLINTON, Inez Funk.
The resurrection of Peter; a short drama for Easter, by Inez Funk Clinton...with an order of worship to be used when the drama is presented. Boston, Chicago, The Pilgrim press [1925] 1 p. l., 17 p. 18 1/2 cm. "Written for the young people of the Pilgrim Congregational church, Oak Park Illinois." [PN6120K2C5] 26-1048
1. Peter, Saint, apostle—Drama. 2. Peter, Saint, apostle—Drama. I. Title.

Peter, Saint, Apostle — Fiction.

DOUGLAS, Lloyd Cassel, 1877-1951.
The Big Fisherman. New York, Pocket Books [1959, c1948] 597 p. map. 17 cm. (Cardinal giant) Cardinal edition. 64-35514
1. Peter, Saint, Apostle — Fiction. I. Title.

Peter, Saint, apostle — Juvenile literature.

BLACKWELL, Muriel 225.9'24 B Fontenot.
Peter, the prince of apostles / Muriel F. Blackwell ; illustrated by Paul Karch. Nashville : Broadman Press, c1976. 48 p. : col. ill. ; 24 cm. (Biblearn series) Discusses the conversion and ministry of Peter, the apostle chosen to lead Jesus' followers after the crucifixion. [BS2515.B52] 76-382762 ISBN 0-8054-4227-8 : 3.95
1. Peter, Saint, apostle—Juvenile literature. 2. [Peter, Saint, apostle.] 3. Bible. N.T.—Biography—Juvenile literature. 4. Apostles—Biography—Juvenile literature. 5. [Bible stories—N.T.] I. Karch, Paul. II. Title.

DAUGHTERS of St. Paul. 225.92 (j)
The fisher prince; the story of St. Peter, Apostle, written and illustrated by the Daughters of St. Paul. [Boston] St. Paul Editions [1966] 69 p. illus. 22 cm. (Their Encounter books) [BS2515.D29] 66-29163
1. Peter, Saint, apostle—Juvenile literature. I. Title.

SCHRAFF, Francis. 225.9'22 B
The adventures of Peter and Paul : Acts of the Apostles for the young / Francis and Anne Schraff ; with 17 playlets by Suzanne Hockel ; [ill., Linda Harris]. Liguori, Mo. : Liguori Publications, c1978. 79 p. : col. ill. ; 28 cm. Brief stories and plays recount the deeds of Christ's apostles. [BS2515.S3] 78-64755 ISBN 0-89243-094-X : 2.95
1. Peter, Saint, apostle—Juvenile literature. 2. Paul, Saint, Apostle—Juvenile literature. 3. Apostles—Biography—Juvenile literature. 4. Christian saints—Turkey—Tarsus—Juvenile literature. 5. Tarsus, Turkey—Biography—Juvenile literature. 6. [Apostles.] 7. [Bible stories—N.T.] 8. [Bible plays.] 9. [Plays] I. Schraff, Anne E., joint author. II. Hockel, Suzanne. III. Harris, Linda. IV. Title.

THOMPSON, Blanche 225.92 Jennings, 1887-.
Peter and Paul; the rock and the sword. Illustrated by Harry Barton. New York, Vision Books [1964] 177 p. illus. 22 cm. "62." [BS2515.T48] 64-11634
1. Peter, Saint, apostle — Juvenile literature. 2. Paul, Saint, apostle — Juvenile literature. I. Title.

WILLETT, Franciscus. j225.9
The fisherman saint, a story of Saint Peter, by Brother Franciscus. Illustrations by Rita McCann. Notre Dame, Ind., Dujarie Press [1947] 89 p. illus. 24 cm. [BS2515.W48] 47-23431
1. Peter, Saint, apostle — Juvenile literature. I. Title.

WOOD, Katharine Marie, 225.92 1910-
The holy apostles: Peter and Paul. Story and pictures by Katharine Wood. New York, P. J. Kenedy [c.1960] unpaged. 29cm. 60-13883 2.50
1. Peter, Saint, apostle—Juvenile literature. 2. Paul, Saint, apostle—Juvenile literature. I. Title.

Peter, Saint, apostle—Meditations.

RUSTAD, Richard L., 225.9'24 1936-
The struggling disciple : meditations on Peter, the fisherman / Richard L. Rustad. Cleveland : Collins, 1979. 96 p. : ill. ; 22 cm. [BS2515.R87] 79-16992 ISBN 0-529-05670-4 pbk. : 3.95
1. Peter, Saint, apostle—Meditations. I. Title.

Peter, Saint, apostle—Sermons.

CHAPPELL, Clovis Gillham, 225.92 1882-
Sermons on Simon Peter. New York, Abingdon Press [1959] 128p. 20cm. [BS2515.C5] 59-10357
1. Peter, Saint, apostle—Sermons. 2. Methodist Church—Sermons. 3. Sermons, American. I. Title.

Peter, Saint, apostle—Study.

MORRILL, Madge (Haines) 225.92
The child's storybook of Peter and Paul, by Madge Haines Morrill, M.A. Mountain View, Calif., Portland, Or. [etc.] Pacific press publishing association [1944] 128 p. col. illus. 20 1/2 cm. Cover-title: Peter and Paul. [Full name: Madge Arty (Haines) Morrill] [BS2515.M6] [922.1] 44-47811
1. Peter, Saint, apostle—Study. 2. Paul, Saint, apostle—Study. I. Title.

Peter, Saint, apostle—Tomb.

GUARDUCCI, Margherita. 225.92
The tomb of St. Peter; the new discoveries in the sacred grottoes of the Vatican. With an introd. by H. V. Morton. Translated from the Italian by Joseph McLellan. [1st ed.] New York, Hawthorn Books [1960] 198 p. illus. 24 cm. [BS2515.G813] 60-5898
1. Peter, Saint, apostle—Tomb. 2. Vatican City. San Pietro in Vaticano (Basilica) I. Title.

GUARDUCCI, Margherita. 226'.09224
The tomb of St. Peter : the new discoveries in the sacred grottoes of the Vatican / by Margherita Guarducci ; with an introd. by H. V. Morton ; translated from the Italian by Joseph McLellan. New York : AMS Press, 1980. p. cm. Includes index. Bibliography: p. [BS2515.G813 1980] 78-63462 ISBN 0-404-16534-6 : 27.50
1. Peter, Saint, apostle—Tomb. 2. Vatican City. San Pietro in Vaticano (Basilica) I. Title.

KIRSCHBAUM, Engelbert, 225.93 1902-
The tombs of St. Peter & St. Paul.

Translated from the German by John Murray. New York, St. Martin's Press [1959] 247 p. illus. 24 cm. Translation of Die Graeber der Apostelfuersten. Includes bibliography. [BS2515.K513 1959] 59-11406
1. Peter, Saint, apostle—Tomb. 2. Paul, Saint, apostle. 3. Vatican (City) San Pietro in Vaticano (Basilica) I. Title.

PETERSON, Finis Paul. 225.92
Peter's tomb recently discovered in Jerusalem. McKeesport, Pa. [1960] 87p. illus. 20cm. [BS2515.P48] 61-23402
1. Peter, Saint, apostle—Tomb. 2. Catholic Church— Doctrinal and controversial works—Protestant authors. I. Title.

TOYNBEE, Jocelyn M C 726.82
The shrine of St. Peter and the Vatican excavations, by Jocelyn Toynbee and John Ward Perkins. London, New York, Longmans, Green [1956] xxii, 293 p. plates, plans. 26 cm. [NA5620.S9T6] 56-1914
1. Peter, Saint, apostle — Tomb. 2. Vatican City. San Pietro in Vaticano (Basilica) I. Ward-Perkins, John Bryan, 1912- joint author. II. Title.

TOYNBEE, Jocelyn M C 726.82
The shrine of St. Peter and the Vatican excavations, by Jocelyn Toynbee and John Ward Perkins. New York, Pantheon Books [1957] xxii, 293 p. plates, plans. 26 cm. Includes bibliographical references. [NA5620.S9T6] 56-13363
1. Peter, Saint, apostle — Tomb. 2. Vatican City. San Pietro in Vaticano (Basilica) I. Ward-Perkins, John Bryan, 1912- joint author. II. Title.

Peter, Saint, apostle—Tomb—Bibliography

DE MARCO, Angelus A. 016.27010924
The tomb of Saint Peter; a representative and annotated bibliography of the excavations. Leiden, E. J. Brill [New York, Humanities, 1965, c.1964] x, 261p. 25cm. (Supplements to Novum Testamentum, v. 8) Title. (Series: Novum Testamentum. Supplements, v.8) [Z8675.65.D45] 66-1271 11.00
1. Peter, Saint, apostle—Tomb—Bibl. I. Title. II. Series.

Peterborough cathedral.

SWAIN, Edmund Gill, 1861- 942.55
The story of Peterborough cathedral, by E. G. Swain ... With a foreword by the Lord Bishop of Peterborough (the Right Reverend Claude Martin Blagden, D.D.) London, New York [etc.] R. Tuck & sons, ltd, 1932. viii, 9-80 p. front., plates, plan. 19 cm. "A list of the books used in compiling the story of the cathedral": p. 79. [NA5471.P5S8] 36-13951
1. Peterborough cathedral. I. Title.

Peterborough, Eng.

POOLE, George Ayliffe, 1809-1883.
... Peterborough. By Geo. Ayliffe Poole ... Pub. under the direction of the Tract committee. London, Society for promoting Christian knowledge; New York, E. & J. B. Young & co. [1881] viii, 247 p. front. (fold. map) 17 cm. (Diocesan histories) [BX5107.P4P8] 4-210
1. Peterborough, Eng. 2. Gt. Brit.—Church history. I. Title.

Peterkin, George William, bp., 1841-1916.

STRIDER, Robert Edward Lee, bp., 1887- 922.
The life and work of George William Peterkin, by Robert Edward Lee Strider ... Philadelphia, G. W. Jacobs & company [c1929] xiii p., 1 l., 331 p. front., ports. 21 1/2 cm. [BX5995.P45S8] 29-20805
1. Peterkin, George William, bp., 1841-1916. 2. Protestant Episcopal church in the U.S.A.—West Virginia. I. Title.

Peters, Anzonetta Rebecca, 1815-1838.

CLARK, John Alonzo, 1801-1843. 922.378
The young disciple; or, A memoir of Anzonetta R. Peters, By Rev. John A. Clark... Abridged from the 5th ed. New York, American tract society [1849] 230 p. 16 cm. [BR1725.P46C6 1849] 38-7484
1. Peters, Anzonetta Rebecca, 1815-1838. I. American tract society. II. Title.

CLARK, John Alonzo, 1801-1843. 922.373
The young disciple; or, A memoir of Anzonetta R. Peters. By Rev. John A. Clark... New York, R. Carter & brothers, 1860. 328 p. 19 1/2 cm. [BR1725.P46C6 1860] 33-3190
1. Peters, Anzonetta Rebecca, 1815-1838. I. Title.

Peters, Hugh 1598-1660.

STEARNS, Raymond Phineas, 1904- 922.542
The strenous Puritan: Hugh Peters, 1598-1660. Urbana, University of Illinois, 1954. x, 463p. illus., ports. 27cm. Bibliographical footnotes. [DA407.P4S8] 53-9765
1. Peters, Hugh 1598-1660. 2. Gt. Brit.—Hist.—Puritan Revolution, 1642-1660. I. Title.

Petersburg, Va.—Biography.

STEVENSON, Arthur Linwood, 1891- 287'.1'0922 B
Natives of Petersburg, Virginia, and vicinity in the Methodist ministry, by Arthur L. Stevenson. Brevard, N.C., 1973. 44 p. 22 cm. (His Native Methodist minister series, 4th) [BX8491.S7] 74-150410
1. Methodist Church—Biography. 2. Petersburg, Va.—Biography. I. Title.

Petersburg, Va. Washington street church.

DREWRY, Patrick Henry, 1875- 287.
The story of a church; a history of Washington street church (Methodist Episcopal church, South) at Petersburg, Virginia, 1773-1923, by P. H. Drewry, B.A. [Petersburg, Va., Plummer printing co., inc., c1923] 240 p. incl. front., illus., plates. 23 cm. [BX8481.P4W3] 24-4912
1. Petersburg, Va. Washington street church. 2. Petersburg, Va.—Biog. I. Title.

Peterson, Gladys.

PETERSON, Gladys. 274.7
The undying flame / by Gladys Peterson. Westchester, Ill. : Good News Publishers, c1979. 144 p. : ill. ; 21 cm. Translation of Zwischen Kreuz und rotem Stern. [BR936.P4413] 79-53991 ISBN 0-89107-173-3 pbk. : 2.95
1. Peterson, Gladys. 2. Christianity—Russia. 3. Russia—Description and travel—1970. I. Title.

Peterson, John W.

PETERSON, John W. 783.7
The miracle goes on / by John W. Peterson, with Richard Engquist. Grand Rapids : Zondervan Pub. House, c1976. p. cm. [ML410.P2957A3] 76-4976
1. Peterson, John W. 2. Gospel musicians—Correspondence, reminiscences, etc. I. Engquist, Richard, joint author. II. Title.

Petit, Adolphe, 1822-1914.

ENRODY, Ladislas J 922.2493
Hope unlimited; little stories from the life of the saintly Father Petit. S. J. English translation by Sister Teresa Clare. [Boston] St Paul Editions [c1962] 113 p. illus. 22 cm. [BX4705.P435E5] 62-21100
1. Petit, Adolphe, 1822-1914. I. Title.

MAXWELL, Joseph Raymond Nonnatus, 1899- 922.2493
The happy ascetic. Adolph Petit of the Society of Jesus, by Joseph R. N. Maxwell, S.J. New York, Chicago [etc.] Benziger brothers, 1936. xi, 212 p. front. (port.) 2 pl. on 1 l. 19 cm. [BX4705.P435M3] 36-10369
1. Petit, Adolphe, 1822-1914. I. Title.

Petri, Olavus, 1493-1552.

BERGENDOFF, Conrad John Immanuel, 1895- 274.85
Olavus Petri and the ecclesiastical transformation in Sweden, 1521-1552; a study in the Swedish Reformation [New introd. by the author] Philadelphia, Fortress [c.1965] xvi, 267p. 20cm. Orig. pub. in 1928. Bibl. [BR350.P4B4] 3.75
1. Petri, Olavus, 1493-1552. 2. Reformation—Sweden. 3. Sweden—Church history. 4. Church and state in Sweden. I. Title.

BERGENDOFF, Conrad John Immanuel, 1895- 922.
Olavus Petri and the ecclesiastical transformation in Sweden [1521-1552]; a study in the Swedish reformation, by Conrad Bergendoff. New York, The Macmillan company, 1928. 6 p. l., 264 p. 20 cm. Bibliography: p. 252-257. [BR350.P4B4] 28-14024
1. Petrl. Olavus, 1493-1552. 2. Reformation-Sweden 3. Sweden—Church history. 4. Church and state in Sweden. I. Title.

Petrie, Irene Eleanora Verita, d. 1897.

CARUSWILSON, Mary Louisa Georgina]Petrie: Mrs. 922.354
A woman's life for Kashmir; Irene Petrie, a biography, Mrs. Ashley Carus-Wilson, B. A. with an introduction by Robert E. Spear... Chicago, New York [etc.] Fleming H. Revell company, 1901. 4 p. l., vii-xxii, 343 p. front., plates, ports., fold. map. 22 cm. Published in Great Britain under title: Irene Petrie, missionary to Kashmir. [BV3280.K3C3 1901] 34-34682
1. Petrie, Irene Eleanora Verita, d. 1897. 2. Missions—Kashmir. I. Title.

Petrus Lombardus, Bp of Paris, 12th century

ROGERS, Elizabeth Frances, 1892- 234'.16'09
Peter Lombard and the sacramental system / Elizabeth Frances Rogers. Merrick, N.Y. : Richwood Pub. Co., 1976. 250 p. ; 24 cm. Reprint of the 1917 ed. published in New York. Originally presented as the author's thesis, Columbia University, 1917. Vita. Bibliography: p. 247-250. [BX2200.R6 1976] 76-20688 ISBN 0-915172-22-4 lib.bdg. : 18.50
1. Petrus Lombardus, Bp of Paris, 12th cent. 2. Sacraments—History of doctrines. I. Title.

Petrus Lombardus, Bp. of Paris, 12th century Sententiarum libri quattuor.

BIEL, Gabriel, d. 1495 230.20902
Epitome et collectorium ex Occamo circa quatuor Sententiarum libros. Tübingen, 1501 [i.e. Basel, 1508] Frankfurt/ Maim, Minerva, New York, Johnson Reprint, 1965 iv. (unpaged) 27cm. Facsim. reprod. of the 1508 ed. printed by Jacob de Pfortzen. Based on Ockham's commentary on Sententiarum libri quattuor of Petrus Lombardus, ed. by V. Steinbach, the work first pub. in 1501 in Tübingen, with title generally quoted as Collectorium super IV libros Sententiarum. Cf. Goff. 3d census. [BX1749.P4B5] 65-7869 43.75
1. Petrus Lombardus, Bp. of Paris, 12th cent. Sententiarum libri quattuor. I. Steinbach, Vendelinus, fl. 1490-1515, ed. II. Ockham, William, d. ca. 1349. Quaestiones et decisiones in quattuor libros Sententiarum. III. Title. IV. Title: Collectorium super quattuor libros Sententiarum.

THOMAS of Strassburg 1357. 282
Thomae ab Argentina . . . Commentaria in IIII libros sententiarvm, hac postrema editione a mendis . . . repurgata. Vna cvm avctoris vita. Venetiis, Ex Officina Stellae, 1564. 202, 217 l. Commentary on Petrus Lombarous Sententiarum libri quattuor, edited by Simon Brazzolato. Photooffset. Ridgewood, N. J., Gregg Pr., 1966. 34cm. [BX1749.P4T5 1564a] 67-3777 84.00
1. Petrus Lombardus, Bp. of Parts, 12th cent. Sententiarum libri quattuor. I. Brazzolato, Simon, 16th cent., ed. II. Title.

Petrus Pictaviensis, chancellor of Paris, 1130 (ca.)—1205.

MOORE, Philip Samuel, 1900- 208.1
... The works of Peter of Poitiers, master in theology and chancellor of Paris (1193-1205) by Philip S. Moore ... Notre Dame, Ind. [University of Notre Dame] 1936. ix, [1], 218 p. 23 cm. (Publications in mediaeval studies, the University of Notre Dame; editor: P. S. Moore. i) "Presented in November, 1932, as dissertation to the faculty of the Ecole nationale des chartes, Paris"; in 1936 (translated into English and in large part revised) as thesis (PH. D.) to the faculty of the Catholic university of America. cf. p. vi. Bibliography: p. 211-214. [BX4705.P4415M6 1936 a] 39-25425
1. Petrus Pictaviensis, chancellor of Paris, 1130 (ca.)—1205. I. Title.

Petrus Thomae, ca. 1280-ca. 1340.

BRIDGES, Geoffrey G. 111
Identity and distinction in Petrus Thomae, O.F.M., by Geoffrey G. Bridges. St. Bonaventure, N.Y., Franciscan Institute, 1959. ix, 186 p. 24 cm. (Franciscan Institute publications. Philosophy series, no. 14) Bibliography: p. 181-182. [B765.P48B7] 77-277260
1. Petrus Thomae, ca. 1280-ca. 1340. 2. Duns, Joannes Scotus, 1265?-1308? 3. Identity. I. Title. II. Series: St. Bonaventure University, St. Bonaventure, N.Y. Franciscan Institute. Philosophy series, no. 14.

Petrus Thomasius, Saint, 1305-1366.

BOEHLKE, Frederick J 1926- 271.9710924 (B)
Pierre de Thomas, scholar, diplomat, and crusader [by] Frederick J. Boehlke, Jr. Philadelphia, University of Pennsylvania Press [1966] 360 p. 22 cm. Based on thesis, University of Pennsylvania. Bibliography: p. 328-352. [BX4700.P466B6 1966] 65-23579
1. Petrus Thomasius, Saint, 1305-1306. I. Title.

BOEHLKE, Frederick J., Jr., 1926- 271.9710924
Pierre de Thomas, scholar, diplomat, and crusader. Philadelphia, Univ. of Pa. Pr. [c.1966] 360p. 22cm. Bibl. [BX4700.P466B6] 65-23579 7.50
1. Petrus Thomasius, Saint, 1305-1366. I. Title.

Petry, Ray C.

CONTEMPORARY reflections 209'.02
on the medieval Christian tradition; essays in honor of Ray C. Petry. Edited by George H. Shriver. Durham, N.C., Duke University Press, 1974. xv, 279 p. 25 cm. Includes bibliographical references. [BR252.C58] 73-77639 ISBN 0-8223-0304-3 9.75
1. Petry, Ray C. 2. Petry, Ray C.—Bibliography. 3. Christianity—Middle Ages, 600-1500—Addresses, essays, lectures. I. Petry, Ray C., 1903- II. Shriver, George H., ed.
Contents omitted.

CONTEMPORARY reflections 209'.02
on the medieval Christian tradition; essays in honor of Ray C. Petry. Edited by George H. Shriver. Durham, N.C., Duke University Press, 1974. xv, 279 p. 25 cm. Contents.Contents.—Henry, S. C. Ray C. Petry: an appreciation.—Ritchie, B. M. Preaching and pastoral care in John Tauler.—Mallard, W. Clarity and dilemma: the Forty sermons of John Wyclif.—White, J. F. Durandus and the interpretation of Christian worship.—Shinn, G. H. The eschatological function of the iconography in the Dresden manuscript of the Sachsenspiegel.—Shriver, G. H. Images of catharism and the historian's task.—Bond, H. L. Nicholas of Cusa and the reconstruction of theology.—Jordan, J.

Jacques Lefevre d'Etaples: principles and practice of reform at Meaux.—Ray, R. D. Orderic vitalis on Henry I.—Zinn, G. A., Jr. Historia fundamentum est: the role of history in the contemplative life according to Hugh of St. Victor.—McNeill, J. T. Perspectives on Celtic church history.—Burr, D. Olivi and the limits of intellectual freedom.—Cannon, W. R. The genesis of the university.—Farris, J. L. and D. M. Ray C. Petry: a bibliography (p. [223]-225)—Three addresses by Ray C. Petry selected and introduced by George H. Shriver: The church and church history, in classroom and parish. Christ and the Gospels in worship and the arts. The historic university and the divinity school. Includes bibliographical references. [BR252.C58] 73-77639 ISBN 0-8223-0304-3 9.75
1. Petry, Ray C. 2. Petry, Ray C.—Bibliography. 3. Christianity—Middle Ages, 600-1500—Addresses, essays, lectures. I. Petry, Ray C., 1903- II. Shriver, George H., ed.

Petschek, Joyce States

PETSCHEK, Joyce S. 133.9'3
The silver bird / Joyce S. Petschek. Millbrae, Calif. : Celestial Arts, c1981. p. cm. [BF1408.2.P47A37] 19 80-28074 ISBN 0-89087-284-8 : 8.95
1. Petschek, Joyce S. 2. Occult sciences—Biography. I. Title.

Pettigrew, Charles, 1744-1807.

LEMMON, Sarah McCulloh. 283'.0924 B
Parson Pettigrew of the "Old Church", 1744-1807. Chapel Hill, University of North Carolina Press, 1970. 168 p. 23 cm. (The James Sprunt studies in history and political science, v. 52) Bibliography: p. [149]-155. [F251.J28 vol. 52] 76-132259 ISBN 0-8078-5052-7
1. Pettigrew, Charles, 1744-1807. I. Title. II. Series.

Pettit, Hermon, 1894-

PETTIT, Hermon, 1894- 269'.2'0924 B
Jubilee! : Autobiography of Hermon Pettit / Hermon Pettit and Helen Wessel ; [cover photo, Jim Morgenstern]. Fresno, Calif. : Bookmates International, c1979. 177 p. : ill. ; 21 cm. [BV3785.P48A34] 78-73580 ISBN 0-933082-00-2 pbk. : 3.95
1. Pettit, Hermon, 1894- 2. Evangelists—United States—Biography. I. Wessel, Helen Strain, 1924- joint author. II. Title.

Pews and pew rights.

BENNETT, Robinson Potter Dunn, 1869-
The pew and the pupil, by Robinson P. D. Bennett ... Philadelphia, The Westminister press, 1914. 165 p. 19 cm. 15-5866 0.75
I. Title.

COX, John Charles, 1843-1919.
Bench-ends in English churches, by J. Charles Cox ... with 164 illustrations. London, New York [etc.] H. Milford, Oxford university press, 1916. vii, 208 p. incl. front., illus. 23 cm. Bibliography: p. 191. [NA5075.C7] 17-27913
1. Pews and pew rights. 2. Church furniture. 3. Wood-carving. I. Title.

[NEALE, John Mason] 1818-1866. 254
The history of pues, being the substance of a paper read before the Cambridge Camden society on Monday, November 22, 1841, with an appendix containing a report presented to the society on the statistics of pues, on Monday, December 6, 1841 ... 3d ed., containing the "Supplement." with additions. Cambridge [Eng.] Stevenson; [etc., etc.] 1843. viii, 108 p. 22 cm. On cover: Published by the Cambridge Camden society. [BV604.N4 1843] 35-34766
1. Pews and pew rights. I. Ecclesiological society, Cambridge. II. Title. III. Title: Pues, The history of.

STIDGER, William Le Roy, 1886- 204
The pew preaches; edited with an introduction, by William L. Stidger. Nashville, Tenn., Cokesbury press, 1930. 251 p. 22 1/2 cm. With brief notices of the authors. [BR50.S75] 30-7911
I. Title.
Contents omitted.

Peyote.

ABERLE, David Friend, 1918- [299.7]
Navaho and Ute peyotism: a chronological and distributional study, by David F. Aberle and Omer C. Stewart. Boulder, Univ. of Colorado Press, 1957. ix, 129p. maps, tables 26 cm. (University of Colorado studies. Series in anthropology, no. 6) (Colorado. University. University of Colorado studies. Series in anthropology, 6) [E98.R3Az] 970.62 57-63108
1. Peyote. 2. Navaho Indians—Religion and mythology. 3. Ute Indians—Religion and mythology. 4. Navaho Indians—Rites and ceremonies. 5. Ute Indians—Rites and ceremonies I. Stewart, Omer Call, 1908- joint author. II. Title. III. Series.

LA BARRE, Weston 299.7
The peyote cult. Hamden, Conn., Reprinted by Shoe String Press, [c.]1959. 188p. illus. 25cm. (bibl. notes: p. 175-188) 60-572 4.00
1. Peyote. 2. Indians of North America—Religion and mythology. 3. Indians of North America—Rites and ceremonies. I. Title.

LA BARRE, Weston. 299.7
... *The peyote cult* [by] Weston La Barre. New Haven, Published for the Department of anthropology, Yale university, by the Yale university press; London, H. Milford, Oxford university press, 1938. 188, [2] p. illus., 2 pl. on 1 l. 25 cm. (Yale university publications in anthropology. no. 19) Bibliography: p. 175-188. [GN2.Y3 no. 10] 572.082 39-775
1. Peyote. 2. Indians of North America—Religion and mythology. 3. Rites and ceremonies. I. Title.

LA BARRE, Weston, 1911- 299.7
The peyote cult. Hamden, Conn., Reprinted by Shoe String Press, 1959. 188p. illus. 25cm. 'Originally published [in 1938] as Yale University publications in anthropology, number 19. Bibliography: p. 175-188. [E98.R3L3 1959] 60-572
1. Peyote. 2. Indians of North America—Religion and mythology. 3. Indians of North America—Rites and ceremonies. I. Title.

NAVAHE and Ute peyotism: 299.7
a chronological and distributional study. by David F. Aberle and Omer C. Stewart. Boulder, University of Colorado Press, 1957. ix, 129p. maps, tables, 26cm. (University of Colorado studies, Series in anthropology, no. 6) Bibliography: p. 126-120. [E9S.R3A2] [E9S.R3A2] 970.62 57-63108 57-63108
1. Peyote. 2. Navaho Indians—Religion and mythology. 3. Ute Indians—Religion and mythology. 4. Navaho Indians—Rites and ceremonies. 5. Ute Indians— Rites and ceremonies. I. Aberle, David Friend, 1918- II. Stewart, Omer Call, 1908- joint author. III. Series: Colorado, University, University of Colorado studies. Series in anthropology, no. 6

TSA TO KE, Monroe, 1904-1937. [299.7] 970.62
The peyote ritual; visions and descriptions. San Francisco, Grabhorn Press [1957] xvii, 66 p. col. illus. 40 cm. "Three hundred and twenty-five copies printed at the Grabhorn Press." [E98.R3T8] 58-16338
1. Peyote. 2. Indians of North America — Rites and ceremonies. 3. Indians of North America — Art. 4. Klowa Indians. I. Title.

Peyotism.

ABERLE, David Friend, 1918-
The peyote religion among the Navaho, by David F. Aberle. With field assistance by Harvey C. Moore and with an appendix on Navaho population and education by Denis F. Johnston. Chicago, Aldine Pub. Co. [1966] xxvi, 454 p. illus., maps. 27 cm. (Viking Fund publications in anthropology, no. 42) Bibliography: p. 423-436. 68-61574
I. Title.

ANDERSON, Edward F., 1932- 299'.7
Peyote, the divine cactus / Edward F. Anderson. Tucson : University of Arizona Press, c1979. p. cm. Bibliography: p. [E98.R3A5] 79-20173 ISBN 0-8165-0680-9 : 14.95 ISBN 0-8165-0613-2 pbk. : 6.95
1. Peyotism. 2. Indians of North America—Religion and mythology. 3. Indians of North America—Rites and ceremonies. 4. Peyote. I. Title.

LABARRE, Weston, 1911- 299.7
The Pevote cult. New enl. ed. [Hamden, Conn.] Shoe String Press, 1964. 260 p. illus. 25 cm. Includes bibliographies. [E98.R3L3] 64-19133
1. Peyotism. 2. Indians of North America — Religion and mythology. 3. Indians of North America — Rites and ceremonies. I. Title.

LA BARRE, Weston, 1911- 299.7
The Peyote cult. New enl. ed. [Hamden, Conn.] Shoe String [c.1959, 1964] 260p. illus. 25cm. Bibl. 64-19133 7.50
1. Peyotism. 2. Indians of North America—Religion and mythology. 3. Indians of North America—Rites and ceremonies. I. Title.

LA BARRE, Weston, 1911- 299'.7
The peyote cult. With a new pref. by the author. Enl. ed. New York, Schocken Books [1969] xvii, 260 p. illus. 21 cm. Includes bibliographies. [E98.R3L3 1969] 78-91546 2.45
1. Peyotism. 2. Indians of North America—Religion and mythology. 3. Indians of North America—Rites and ceremonies. I. Title.

LA BARRE, Weston, 1911- 299'.7
The peyote cult / Weston La Barre. 4th ed. enl. Hamden, Conn. : Archon Books, 1975. p. cm. Includes index. Bibliography: p. [E98.R3L3 1975] 75-19425 ISBN 0-208-01456-X : 10.00
1. Peyotism. 2. Indians of North America—Religion and mythology. 3. Indians of North America—Rites and ceremonies. I. Title.

LA BARRE, Weston, 1911- 299'.7
The peyote cult / Weston La Barre. 2d enl. ed. New York : Schocken Books, [1975] p. cm. Includes index. Bibliography: p. [E98.R3L3 1975b] 75-10608 ISBN 0-8052-0493-8 pbk. : 4.95
1. Peyotism. 2. Indians of North America—Religion and mythology. 3. Indians of North America—Rites and ceremonies. I. Title.

MARRIOTT, Alice Lee, 1910- 299'.7
Peyote [by] Alice Marriott and Carol K. Rachlin. New York, Crowell [1971] x, 111 p. illus. 22 cm. Bibliography: p. 99-102. [E98.R3M3 1971] 75-146284 ISBN 0-690-61697-X 6.95
1. Native American Church of North America. 2. Peyotism. I. Rachlin, Carol K., joint author. II. Title.

ROSEMAN, Bernard 299.7
The peyote story. 1966 ed. Hollywood, Calif., Wilshire [1966, c.1963] 67p. illus., port. 22 cm. [E98.R3R6] 66-2260 1.00 pap.,
1. Peyotisim. 2. Native American Church of North America. I. Title.

SLOTKIN, James Sydney, 1913-1958. 299'.7
The peyote religion : a study in Indian-white relations / J. S. Slotkin. New York : Octagon Books, 1975, c1956. vii, 195 p. : ill. ; 24 cm. Reprint of the ed. published by the Free Press, Glencoe, Ill. Bibliography: p. 143-187. [E98.R3S5 1975] 74-23409 ISBN 0-374-97480-2 : 10.50
1. Native American Church of North America. 2. Peyotism. 3. Indians of North America—Government relations. I. Title.

Peyton, Patrick J.

PEYTON, Patrick J. 282'.092'4 B
All for her; the autobiography of Father Patrick Peyton. [Rev. ed.] Hollywood, Calif., Family Theater Publications [1973] viii, 241 p. illus. 18 cm. [BX4705.P4458A3 1973] 73-181329 1.50
1. Peyton, Patrick J. I. Title.

PEYTON, Patrick J. 282.0924
All for her; the autobiography of Father Patrick Peyton, C.S.C. Garden City, N.Y., Doubleday [1967] 286 p. illus., ports. 22 cm. [BX4705.P4458A3] 67-22441
I. Title.

Pfafftown, N. C. Christian Church.

WARE, Charles Crossfield, 1886- 284.675667
Star in Wachovia; centennial history of the Christian Church Disciples of Christ, Pfafftown, N. C. Wilson, N. C., 1965. 151 p. illus., ports. 24 cm. [BX7331.P4C75] 66-2172
1. Pfafftown, N. C. Christian Church. I. Title.

Phallicism.

BERGER, Charles G. 291.212
Our phallic heritage, by C. G. Berger. [1st ed.] New York, Greenwich Book Publishers [1966] 216 p. illus. 23 cm. Bibliographical footnotes. [BL460.B4] 66-12676
1. Phallicism. I. Title.

BROWN, Sanger, 1884- 291.2'12
Sex worship and symbolism / Sanger Brown II. New York : AMS Press, 1975. 149 p. : ill. ; 19 cm. Reprint of the 1922 ed. published by R. G. Badger, Boston. Includes index. Bibliography: p. 139-142. [BL460.B7 1975] 72-9624 ISBN 0-404-57419-X : 10.95
1. Phallicism. 2. Sex and religion. 3. Symbolism. I. Title.

BROWN, Sanger, 1884- 291.
Sex worship and symbolism [by] Sanger Brown II... Boston, R. G. Badger [1922] 3 p. l., 3-149 p. xiv pl. (incl. front.) 24 1/2 cm. "The greater part of the first three chapters of this book appeared in the Journal of abnormal psychology."--Pref. first published, without plates, 1916. Bibliography: p. 139-142. [BL460.B7 1922] 22-20143
1. Phalicism. I. Title.

CZAJA, Michael. 299'.56
Gods of myth and stone; phallicism in Japanese folk religion. With a foreword by George De Vos. [1st ed.] New York, Weatherhill [1974] 294 p. illus. 27 cm. Bibliography: p. 279-288. [BL460.C9 1974] 73-88468 ISBN 0-8348-0095-0 20.00
1. Phallicism. 2. Gods, Japanese. 3. Husband and wife (in religion, folklore, etc.) I. Title.

DAUGHERTY, Mason, 1893- 176
Sex worship and disease (phallic worship) a scientific teatise on sex worship and its influence on religion and symbolism, with special reference to disease of the sexual organs, by Mason Daugherty ... Cleveland, O., The author [c1935] 240 p. illus. 19 cm. Bibliography: p. 232-233. [HQ21.D27] 35-7468
1. Phallicism. 2. Sex and religion. 3. Venereal diseases 4. Sexual ethics. I. Title.

DULAURE, Jacques-Antoine, 1755-1835. 291.2'12
The gods of generation : a history of phallic cults among ancients & moderns / Jacques-Antoine Dulaure ; translated from the French by A. F. N. New York : AMS Press, 1975. 280 p. ; 19 cm. Translation of Des divinites generatrices. Reprint of the 1934 ed. priv. print. by Panurge Press, New York. Includes bibliographical references and index. [BL460.D82 1975] 72-9635 ISBN 0-404-57433-5 : 24.50
1. Phallicism. 2. Sex and religion. 3. Religion, Primitive. I. Title.

THE gods of love;
the creative process in early religion. With a preface by Edward Podolsky. Westport, Conn., Associated Booksellers [c1960] 273p. illus.
1. Phallicism. 2. Sex and religion. I. Longworth, T Clifton.

HOWARD, Clifford, 1868- 291.21291
Sex worship; an exposition of the phallic origin of religion. By Clifford Howard.

Washington, D.C., The author, 1897. 195 p. 19 cm. [BL460.H7] 12-34528
1. Phallicism. 2. Sex and religion. I. Title.

HOWARD, Clifford, 1868- 291.21291
Sex worship; an exposition of the phallic origin of religion. by Clifford Howard. 2d ed. Washington, D.C., The author, 1898. 1 p. l., 5-215 p. 19 1/2 cm. "List of principal works on phallicism": p. 213-215. [BL460.H7 1898] 33-6027
1. Phallicism. 2. Sex and religion. I. Title.

KNIGHT, Richard Payne, 1750-1824 291.212
Sexual symbolism; a history of phallic workship, 2v. in 1 byRichard Payne Knight, Thomas Wright. Introd. by Ashley Montagu. [New York, N.Y., 10003, Matrix House, 119 Fifth Ave.] 1966[c.1957] 2v. in 1 (217; 196p.) illus. 21cm. (Agora softback, A-12) Contents.v.1. A discourse on the worship of Priapus and its connection with the mystic theology of the ancients, by R. P. Knight.--v.2. The worship of the generative powers during the Middle Ages of western Europe, by T. Wright. Bibl. [BL460.K6] 2.25 pap.,
1. Phallicism. 2. Priapus. I. Wright, Thomas, 1810-1877. II. Knight, Richard Payne, 1750-1824. A discourse on the worship of Priapus. III. Wright, Thomas, 1810-1877. The worship of the generative powers. IV. Title. V. Title: A discourse on the worship of Priapus. VI. Title: The worship of the generative power.

PHALLIC worship;
a history of sex and sex rites in relation to the religions of all races from antiquity to the present day . . . Westport, Conn., Mental Health Press [1958?] xx, 299p. illus., xxiv plates. 22cm. Bibliography: p. 280-288.
1. Phallicism. 2. Sex and religion. I. Scott, George Ryley, 1886- II. Title: Sex rites in relation to the religions of all races.

STONE, Lee Alexander, 1879- 291.212
The power of a symbol, by Lee Alexander Stone, M.D., to which is added The worship of Priapus, by Hargrave Jennings, Phallicism in Japan, by Edmund Buckley, Prostitution in antiquity, by Dr. Edmund Dupouy [translated by Thos. Minor, M.D.] Chicago, P. Covici, 1925. 7 p. l., 301 p., 1 l., front. 24 1/2 cm. "This edition is limited to 1100 numbered copies, 1000 sold by subscription and this is no. 1042." Bibliography: p. [89]-99. [BL460.S8] 25-63318
1. Phallicism. 2. Prostitution. I. Jennings, Hargrave, 1817?-1890. The worship of Priapus. II. Buckley, Edmund, 1855- Phallicism in Japan. III. Dupouy, Edmond, 1838- La prostitution dans l'antiquite. IV. Minor, Thomas, tr. V. Title.

STONE, Lee Alexander, 1879- 291.
The story of phallicism, by Lee Alexander Stone, M.D., with other essays on related subjects by eminent authorities; introduction by Frederick Starr ... Chicago, P. Covici, 1927. 2 v. 23 cm. Paged continuously. "Of this edition there have been issued by Pascal Covici, for subscribers only, one thousand and fifty copies. Printed by the Cuneo press, inc., in June, 1927. Typography by Douglas C. McMurtrie. This is no. 630." Contents.v. 1.--Introduction. The story of phallicism, by L. A. Stone. Sex, the foundation of the God idea, by Eliza B. Gambie. Religious ideas in Japanese phallicism, by G. Kato. Phallicism in Japan, by E. Buckley.--v. 2. The worship of Priapus, by H. Jennings. Prostitution in antiquity, by E. Dupouy. Sacred prostitution, by C. S. Wake. Prostitution in Japan, by D. C. McMurtrie. Prostitution in China, by D. C. McMurtrie. Phallic worship to a secularized sex, by T. Schroeder. [BL460.S85A] 28-1074
1. Phallicism. 2. Prostitution. I. Title.

TALBOT, Percy Amaury, 1877-
Some Nigerian fertility cults, by P. Amaury Talbot ... London, Oxford university press, H. Milford, 1927. xi, 140 p. front., illus., plates. 23 cm. [BL2470.N5T3] 28-1077
1. Phallicism. 2. Nigeria—Religion. 3. Cultus—Nigeria. I. Title. II. Title: Fertility cults.

TALBOT, Percy Amaury, 1877-1945. 291.2'12
Some Nigerian fertility cults. New York, Barnes & Noble [1967] xi, 140 p. illus. 22 cm. Reprint of the 1927 ed. Bibliographical footnotes. [BL2470.N5T3 1967a] 67-6629
1. Phallicism. 2. Nigeria—Religion. 3. Cultus—Nigeria. I. Title.

WALL, Otto Augustus, 1846-1922. 291.212
Sex and sex worship (phallic worship) a scientific treatise on sex, its nature and function, and its influence on art, science, architecture, and religion--with special reference to sex worship and symbolism, by O. A. Wall... St. Louis, C. V. Mosby company, 1919. 2 p. l., vii-xv, 607 p. illus. 25 1/2 cm. Title vignette. [BL460.W2] 19-7090
1. Phallicism. 2. Sex. I. Title.

WALL, Otto Augustus, 1846-1922. 291.212
Sex and sex worship (phallic worship); a scientific treatise on sex, its nature and function, and its influence on art, science, architecture, and religion--with special reference to sex worship and symbolism, by O. A. Wall...Three hundred seventy-two illustrations. St. Louis, C. V. Mosby company, 1922. 2 p. l., vii-xv, 608 p. illus. 25 1/2 cm. Title vignette. Bibliography: p. 599-603. [BL460.W2 1922] 25-22611
1. Phallicism. 2. Sex. I. Title.

WALL, Otto Augustus, 1846-1922. 291.2'12
Sex and sex worship (phallic worship); a scientific treatise on sex, its nature and function, and its influence on art, science, architecture, and religion— with special reference to sex worship and symbolism. College Park, Md., McGrath Pub. Co., 1970 [c1922] xv, 608 p. illus. 24 cm. Bibliography: p. 599-603. [BL460.W2 1970] 73-119244 ISBN 0-8434-0091-9
1. Phallicism. I. Title.

WESTROPP, Hodder Michael, d.1884. 291.212
Ancient symbol worship. Influence of the phallic idea in the religions of antiquity. By Hodder M. Westropp and C. Staniland Wake. With an introduction, additional notes, and an appendix. By Alexander Wilder, M.D. New York, J. W. Bouton; London, Trubner & co., 1874. viii, [9]-98 p. 23 cm. Two papers, read before the Anthropological society of London, April 5th, 1870. [BL460.W4] 31-7891
1. Phallicism. 2. Religion, Primitive. I. Wake, Charles Staniland, 1835-1910. II. Wilder, Alexander, 1823-1908, ed. III. Title.

WESTROPP, Hodder Michael, d.1884. 291.21291
Ancient symbol worship. Influence of the phallic idea in the religions of antiquity. By Hodder M. Westropp and C. Staniland Wake. With an introduction, additional notes, and an appendix. By Alexander Wilder, M.D. 2d ed. ... New York, J. W. Bouton, 1875. viii, [9]-98 p. front., plates, plan. 25 cm. Two papers, read before the Anthropological society of London, April 5th, 1870. [BL460.W4 1875] 31-33802
1. Phallicism. 2. Religion, Primitive. I. Wake, Charles Staniland, 1835-1910. II. Wilder, Alexander, 1823-1908, ed. III. Title.

Phallicism—Addresses, essays, lectures.

STONE, Lee Alexander, 1879- 291.2'12
The story of phallicism / by Lee Alexander Stone ; with other essays on related subjects by eminent authorities ; introd. by Frederick Starr. New York : Ams Press, 1976. xvi, 652 p. ; 19 cm. Reprint of the 1927 ed. published by P. Covici, Chicago. [BL460.S85 1976] 72-9682 34.50
1. Phallicism—Addresses, essays, lectures. 2. Prostitution—Addresses, essays, lectures. I. Title.
Contents omitted

Phallicism—Bibliography.

GOODLAND, Roger, 1880- 016.392'6
A bibliography of sex rites and customs : an annotated record of books, articles, and illustrations in all languages / by Roger Goodland. Boston : Longwood Press, 1977. p. cm. Reprint of the 1931 ed. published by G. Routledge, London. [Z7833.G65 1977] [BL460] 77-11605 ISBN 0-89341-193-0 lib.bdg. : 60.00
1. Phallicism—Bibliography. 2. Sex and religion—Bibliography. 3. Religion, Primitive—Bibliography. I. Title.

Phallicism—Miscellanea.

SPINK, Walter M. 291
The axis of Eros [by] Walter M. Spink. New York, Schocken Books [1973] 191 p. illus. 25 cm. [BL460.S67] 73-79055 ISBN 0-8052-3512-4 10.00
1. Phallicism—Miscellanea. 2. Sin—Miscellanea. I. Title.

SPINK, Walter M. 291
The axis of Eros [by] Walter M. Spink. Baltimore, Penguin Books [1975, c1973] 191 p. illus. 24 cm. [BL460.S67] ISBN 0-14-004017-X 3.95 (pbk.)
1. Phallicism—Miscellanea. 2. Sin—Miscellanea I. Title.
L.C. card number for original ed.: 73-79055

Pharisees.

ABRAHAMS, Israel, 1858-1925. 226'.06
Studies in Pharisaism and the Gospels. First and second series. [Prolegomenon by Morton S. Enslin. New York, Ktav Pub. House, 1967] 2 v. in 1. 24 cm. (Library of Biblical studies) Half title; each vol. has also special t.p. Includes bibliographical references. [BS2555.A32] 67-11899
1. Bible. N.T. Gospels—Criticism, interpretation, etc. 2. Pharisees. I. Title. II. Title: Pharisaism and the Gospels. III. Series.

ABRAHAMS, Israel, 1858-1925. 225.
Studies in Pharisaism and the Gospels, by I. Abrahams...First series. Cambridge [Eng.] University press, 1917. xiii, [2], 178 p. 22 1/2 cm. Originally designed as an appendix to C. G. Montefiore's commentary on the synoptic gospels cf. Pref., p. [v] [BS2555.A3 1st series] 19-15726
1. Pharisees. I. Title. II. Title: Pharisaism and the Gospels.

ABRAHAMS, Israel, 1858-1925. 226
Studies in Pharisaism and the Gospels, by I. Abrahams...Second series. Cambridge [Eng.] The University press, 1924. x, 226 p. 22 1/2 cm. The "first series" appeared in 1917. [BS2555.A3 2d ser.] 24-11341
1. Pharisees. 2. Bible N.T. Gospels—Criticism, interpretation, etc. 3. Bible—Criticisms, Interpretation, etc.—N.T. Gospels. I. Title. II. Title: Pharisaism and the Gospels.

BAECK, Leo, 1873- 296.04
The Pharisees, and other essays [tr. from the German] New York, Schocken Books [1947] vii, 164 p. 24 cm. [BM175.P4B33] 47-6559
1. Pharisees. 2. Jews—Addresses, essays, lectures. I. Title.

BAECK, Leo, 1873-1956. 296.08
The Pharisees, and other essays. [Translated from the German] Introd. by Krister Stendahl. New York, Schocken Books [1966] xxv, 164 p. 21 cm. (Schocken paperbacks, SB122) Includes bibliographical references. [BM175.P4B33 1966] 66-15818
1. Pharisees. 2. Judaism—Addresses, essays, lectures. I. Title.

BOWKER, John Westerdale. 232.9'5
Jesus and the Pharisees [by] John Bowker. Cambridge [Eng.] University Press, 1973. 192 p. 23 cm. Bibliography: p. [180]-181. [BM175.P4B69] 72-87439 ISBN 0-521-20055-5
1. Jesus Christ—Trial. 2. Pharisees. 3. Rabbinical literature—Translations into English. I. Title.
Distributed by Cambridge University Press, N.Y. 13.50

COLEMAN, William L. 296.8'12
The Pharisees' guide to total holiness / William L. Coleman. Minneapolis, Minn. : Bethany House, [1982], c1977. 147 p. ; 20 cm. Reprint. Originally published: Those Pharisees. New York : Hawthorn Books, c1977. Includes index. Bibliography: p. 139-141. [BM175.P4C64 1982] 19 82-4551 ISBN 0-87123-472-6 pbk. : 3.95
1. Jesus Christ—Attitude toward Pharisees. 2. Pharisees. I. [Those Pharisees] II. Title.

COLEMAN, William L. 296.8'1
Those Pharisees / William L. Coleman. New York : Hawthorn Books, c1977. 147 p. ; 21 cm. Includes index. Bibliography: p. 139-141. [BM175.P4C64 1977] 77-150046 3.95
1. Jesus Christ—Relation to Judaism. 2. Pharisees. I. Title.

DAVIES, William David, 1911- 296.8'1
Introduction to Pharisaism, by W. D. Davies. Philadelphia, Fortress Press [1967] xxi, 34 p. 19 cm. (Facet books. Biblical series, 16) "Originally published as the W. M. Llewelyn lecture for 1954." Bibliography: p. 29-32. Bibliographical footnotes. [BM175.P4D3 1967] 67-10503
1. Pharisees. I. Title.

FINKELSTEIN, Louis, 1895- 296.81
The Pharisees, the sociological background of their faith. [3d ed.] Philadelphia, Jewish Publication Society of America, 1962. 2 v. illus. 22 cm. (The Morris Loeb series) [BM175.P4F5 1962] 61-11709
1. Jews—History—To 70 A.D. 2. Pharisees.

FINKELSTEIN, Louis, 1895-. 933
The Pharisees, the sociological background of their faith, by Louis Finkelstein ... Philadelphia, The Jewish publication society of America, 1938. 2 v. diagr. 22cm. (The Morris Loeb series) "Notes": v. 2, p. [647]-710; Bibliography: v. 2, p. 711-751. [BM175.P4F5] 38-36491
1. Pharisees. 2. Jews—Hist.—To a.d. 70. I. Title.

HERFORD, Robert Travers, 1860- 296
Pharisaism, its aim and its method, by R. Travers Herford ... London, Williams & Norgate; New York, G. P. Putnam's sons, 1912. ix, 340 p. 19 cm. (Half-title: Crown theological library, vol. xxxv) "Most of the contents of the following pages were given as lectures in Manchester college, Oxford, in the autumn of 1911." [BM175.P4H35] 12-16937
1. Pharisees. I. Title.

HERFORD, Robert Travers, 1860- 296
The Pharisees, by R. Travers Herford ... New York, The Macmillan company, 1924. 2 p. l., 7-248 p. 23 cm. [BM175.P4H37 1924 a] 24-10493
1. Pharisees. I. Title.

HERFORD, Robert Travers, 1860-1950. 296.81
The Pharisees [new foreword by Nahum N. Glatzer] Boston, Beacon Pr. [1962, c.1924, 1952] 248p. (Beacon BP134) 62-1314 1.75 pap.,
1. Pharisees. I. Title.

NEUSNER, Jacob, 1932- 296.8'1
From politics to piety; the emergence of Pharisaic Judaism. Englewood Cliffs, N.J., Prentice-Hall [1972, c1973] xxiii, 168 p. 24 cm. Bibliography: p. 155-156. [BM175.P4N44 1973] 72-3822 ISBN 0-13-331447-2 7.95
1. Pharisees. I. Title.
Pap. 3.95

NEUSNER, Jacob, 1932- 296.8'1
From politics to piety : the emergence of Pharisaic Judaism / by Jacob Neusner. New York : Ktav Pub. House, 1979. p. cm. Reprint of the 1973 ed. published by Prentice-Hall, Englewood Cliffs, N.J., with new pref. Includes indexes. Bibliography: p. [BM175.P4N44 1979] 78-23521 4.95
1. Pharisees. I. Title.

RIDDLE, Donald Wayne, 1894- 290
Jesus and the Pharisees, a study in Christian tradition, by Donald W. Riddle ... Chicago, Ill., The University of Chicago press [c1928] ix, 103 p. 21 cm. [BM175.P4R5] 28-23814
1. Jesus Christ. 2. Pharisees. I. Title.

RIVKIN, Ellis, 1918- 296.8'1
A hidden revolution : the Pharisees' search for the kingdom within / Ellis Rivkin. Nashville : Abingdon, c1978. p. cm. Includes index. [BM175.P4R58] 78-17180 ISBN 0-687-16970-4 : 15.00
1. Pharisees. I. Title.

UMEN, Samuel. 296.81
Pharisaism and Jesus. New York, Philosophical Library [1963] 145 p. 23 cm. Includes bibliography. [BM175.P4U4] 62-20875
1. Pharisees. 2. Jesus Christ — Jewish interpretations. I. Title.

WHITELOCKE, Lester T. 296'.09'01
The development of Jewish religious thought in the inter-testamental period / Lester T. Whitelocke. 1st ed. New York : Vantage Press, c1976. 143 p. ; 22 cm. Includes index. Bibliography: p. 129-139. [BM175.P4W47] 76-380362 ISBN 0-533-02215-0 : 7.50
1. Pharisees. 2. Judaism—History—Post-exilic period, 586 B.C.-210 A.D. I. Title.

WOMAN of the Pharisees.
Translated by Gerard Hopkins. Garden City, N. Y., Image books, A division of Doubleday & co. [1959, c1946] 200p. 18cm. (Image book D82) Translation of La pharisienne.
I. Mauriac, Francois, 1885-

Pharisees—Historiography—Addresses, essays, lectures.

NEUSNER, Jacob, 1932- 296.1'2306
Method and meaning in ancient Judaism, third series / by Jacob Neusner. Chico, CA : Scholars Press, c1981. 247 p. ; 23 cm. (Brown Judaic studies ; no. 16) Includes bibliographical references and index. [BM497.8.N4783] 19 80-19449 ISBN 0-89130-417-7 ISBN 0-89130-418-5 pbk. : 27.50
1. Mishnah—Criticism, interpretation, etc.—Addresses, essays, lectures. 2. Pharisees—Historiography—Addresses, essays, lectures. I. Title. II. Series.

Phelps, Albert H., 1839-1890.

PHELPS, Albert H. Mrs. 922.7931
Gathering jewels; or, Life and labors of Mr. and Mrs. A. H. Phelps in New Zealand, Norfolk island and their native land. By Mrs. A. H. Phelps. Meriden, Conn., Journal publishing co., 1896. vi, 394 p. front., plates, ports. 19 cm. [BV3785.P5A3] 37-36753
1. Phelps, Albert H., 1839-1890. 2. Evangelistic work. 3. Methodist church—Missions. I. Title.

Phelps, Davenport, 1755-1813.

NORTON, John Nicholas, 1820- 922
1881.
Pioneer missionaries; or, The lives of Phelps and Nash. By John N. Norton ... New York, General Protestant Episcopal S. school union and church book society, 1859. 4 p. l., [11]-193 p. 16 cm. [BX5995.P5N6] 22-20247
1. Phelps, Davenport, 1755-1813. 2. Nash, Daniel, 1763-1836. I. Title.

Phi Beta Kappa.

HASTINGS, William Thomson, 1881-
Phi Beta Kappa as a secret society, with its relations to Freemasonry and antimasonry; some supplementary documents. Washington, United Chapters of Phi Beta Kappa, 1965. 104 p. illus. (front.) 24 cm. 67-29547
1. Phi Beta Kappa. 2. Freemasons. I. Phi Beta Kappa. II. Title.

Philadelphia. Almshouse.

PEARSON, Francis Calhoun. 248
Sparks among the ashes: including reminiscences of nineteen years of labor in the Philadelphia almshouse. By Rev. F. C. Pearson. With an introduction by Mrs. Dr. Bell. Philadelphia, J. B. Lippincott & co., 1873. 327 p. 20 cm. Account of religious work under the auspices of the Female domestic missionary society for the support of the gospel in the almshouse. [BV4930.P4] 9-22959
1. Philadelphia. Almshouse. I. Female domestic missionary society for the support of the gospel in the almshouse, Philadelphia. II. Title.

Philadelphia, Christ Church.

WASHBURN, Louis Cope, 1860- 283.
comp.
Christ church, Philadelphia; a symposium compiled in connection with the two hundred and twenty-fifth anniversary, by Louis C. Washburn. Philadelphia, Macrae Smith company [c1925] 317, [1] p. front., illus., plates, ports., plan, facsims. 23 1/2 cm. Illustrated lining-papers. [BX5980.P5C64] 25-27647
1. Philadelphia, Christ Church. I. Title.

Philadelphia—Church history.

WILLIAMS, Richard 289'.8'0924 B
E., 1951-
Called and chosen : the story of Mother Rebecca Jackson and the Philadelphia Shakers / Richard E. Williams ; edited by Cheryl Dorschner. Metuchen, N.J. : Scarecrow Press, 1981. xiii, 179 p. : ill. ; 23 cm. (ATLA monograph series ; no. 17) Includes index. Bibliography: p. 173-175. [BX9793.J33W54] 19 80-25498 ISBN 0-8108-1382-3 : 11.00
1. Jackson, Rebecca, 1795-1871. 2. Shakers—United States—Biography. 3. Shakers—Pennsylvania—Philadelphia. 4. Philadelphia—Church history. I. Dorschner, Cheryl. II. Title. III. Series: American Theological Library Association. ATLA monograph series ; no. 17.

Philadelphia. Church of the covenant (Protestant Episcopal)

TYNG, Dudley Atkins, 283.74811
1825-1858.
The Church of the covenant. A memorial volume, by Rev. Dudley A. Tyng. Philadelphia, Printed by H. B. Ashmead, 1858. 82 p. 15 cm. [BX5980.P5C67] 38-18184
1. Philadelphia. Church of the covenant (Protestant Episcopal) I. Title.

Philadelphia. Church of the Holy Trinity (Protestant Episcopal)

ASPINWALL, Marguerite. 283.748
A hundred years in His house; the story of the Church of the Holy Trinity on Rittenhouse Square, Philadelphia, 1857-1957. Decorated by Jack Bowling. [Philadelphia? 1956] 72p. illus. 24cm. [BX5980.P5H6] 57-21737
1. Philadelphia. Church of the Holy Trinity (Protestant Episcopal) I. Title.

ASPINWALL, Marguerite. 283.748
*A hundred years *in house;* the story of the Church of the Holy Trinity on Rittenhouse Square. Philadelphia, 1857-1957. Decorated by Jack Bowling. [Philadelphia? 1956] 72p. illus. 24cm. [BX5980.P5H6] 57-21737
1. Philadelphia. Church of the Holy Trinity (Protestant Episcopal) I. Title.

Philadelphia. Congregation Rodeph Shalom.

DAVIS, Edward. 296.
The history of Rodeph Shalom Congregation, Philadelphia, 1802-1926, with an introd. by Louis Wolsey. Commemorating theone hundred and twenty-fifth anniversary. [Philadelphia, 1926] 155 p. 21 cm. [BM225.P5R65] 49-33223
1. Philadelphia. Congregation Rodeph Shalom. I. Title.

Philadelphia. Eastern Baptist Theological Seminary.

DE BLOIS, Austen 207.74811
Kennedy, 1866-
The making of ministers; the drama of a decade at the Eastern Baptist theological seminary, by Austen Kennedy De Blois; with a concluding chapter by Harry Watson Barras. [Philadelphia] The Judson press, 1936. 6 p. l., 3-279 p. 20 cm. [BV4070.P546D4] 36-19216
1. Philadelphia. Eastern Baptist theological seminary. I. Barras, Harry Watson, 1868. II. Title.

GUFFIN, Gilbert Lee, 207.74811
ed.
What God hath wrought; Eastern's first thirty-five years. Chicago, Judson Press [1960] 179p. 24cm. [BV4070.P546G8] 60-9653
1. Philadelphia. Eastern Baptist Theological Seminary. I. Title.

Philadelphia. Episcopal church of St. Paul.

BARRATT, Norris Stanley, 283.
1862-
... Outline of the history of old St. Paul's church, Philadelphia, Pennsylvania, with an appeal for its preservation, together with articles of agreement, abstract of title, list of rectors, vestrymen, and inscriptions of tombstones and vaults. By Norris Stanley Barratt ... [Philadelphia] The Colonial society of Pennsylvania, 1917. vi, 327, [7] p. front., plates, ports., fold. plan, facsims. 26 cm. At head of title: 1760. 1898. [BX5980.P5P3] 18-22035
1. Philadelphia. Episcopal church of St. Paul. I. Title.

Philadelphia. First African Baptist church.

BROOKS, Charles H. 1861- 286.
Official history of the First African Baptist church, Philadelphia, Pa., by Charles H. Brooks. Philadelphia, Pa., 1922. 167 p. incl. plates, ports. 21 1/2cm. [BX6445.P5B7] 23-8814
1. Philadelphia. First African Baptist church. I. Title.

Philadelphia. First African Presbyterian church.

CATTO, William T. 285.1'748'11
A semi-centenary discourse, delivered in the First African Presbyterian Church, Philadelphia, May, 1857, by William T. Catto. Freeport, N.Y., Books for Libraries Press, 1971. 111 p. 23 cm. (The Black heritage library collection) Reprint of the 1857 ed. [BX9211.P5F53 1971] 78-154073 ISBN 0-8369-8784-5
1. Philadelphia. First African Presbyterian Church. 2. Gloucester, John, 1776 or 7-1822. I. Title. II. Series.

CATTO, William T. 285.
A semi-centenary discourse, delivered in the First African Presbyterian church. Philadelphia, on the fourth Sabbath of May, 1857: with a history of the church from its first organization: including a brief notice of Rev. John Gloucester, its first pastor. By Rev. William T. Catto, pastor. Also, an appendix. containing sketches of all the colored churches in Philadelphia. Philadelphia, J. M. Wilson. 1857. 111 p. 23 cm. [BX9211.P5A3] 13-14590
1. Gloucester, John, 1776 or 7-1822. 2. Philadelphia. First African Presbyterian church. I. Title.

Philadelphia. First Baptist church.

KEEN, William Williams, 286.
1837- ed.
... The bi-centennial celebration of the founding of the First Baptist church of the city of Philadelphia, 1898, edited by William Williams Keen ... Philadelphia, American Baptist publication society, 1899. 1 p. l., 5-511 p. illus., pl., double facsim. 23 cm. At head of title: 1698. Title vignette: Seal of the church in red. [BX6480.P5F5] 99-1567
1. Philadelphia. First Baptist church. I. Title.

Philadelphia. First Moravian church.

RITTER, Abraham, 1792- 284.674811
1860.
History of the Moravian church in Philadelphia, from its foundation in 1742 to the present time. Comprising notices, defensive of its founder and patron, Count Nicholas Ludwig von Zinzendorff. Together with an appendix. By Abraham Ritter. Philadelphia, Hayes & Zell, 1857. xx, [17]-281 p., 1 l. front., plates (1 col.) ports. (1 col.) plan. 23 cm. [BX8581.P5R5] 35-36632
1. Zinzendorf, Nicolaus Ludwig, graf von, 1700-1760. 2. Philadelphia. First Moravian church. I. Title.

Philadelphia. Free Quaker Meeting House.

PETERSON, 726'.58'96074014811
Charles Emil, 1906-
Notes on the Free Quaker Meeting House, Fifth and Arch Streets, Philadelphia, built 1783-4. Compiled for Harbeson, Hough, Livingston and Larson, architects to the Commonwealth of Pennsylvania, from a study of the documents and of the fabric, by Charles E. Peterson. [Philadelphia] 1966. 1 v. (various pagings) illus., facsims., plans. 28 cm. Bibliographical references included in foreword. [F158.8.F7P4] 68-22779
1. Philadelphia. Free Quaker Meeting House. I. Harbeson, Hough, Livingston and Larson. II. Title.

PETERSON, 726'.58'96074014811
Charles Emil, 1906-
Notes on the Free Quaker Meeting House, Fifth and Arch Streets, Philadelphia, built 1783-4. Compiled for Harbeson, Hough, Livingston and Larson, architects to the Commonwealth of Pennsylvania, from a study of the documents and of the fabric, by Charles E. Peterson. [Philadelphia] 1966. 1 v. (various pagings) illus., facsims., plans. 28 cm. Bibliographical references included in foreword. [F158.8.F7P4] 68-22779
1. Philadelphia. Free Quaker Meeting House. I. Harbeson, Hough, Livingston and Larson. II. Title.

Philadelphia. Friends' meeting house (Fourth and Arch streets)

[FRIENDS' historical 289.
association]
The Friends' meeting-house, Fourth and Arch streets, Philadelphia; a centennial celebration, sixth month fourth, 1904; illustrated by numerous interesting and rare portraits and pictures of early meeting-houses. Philadelphia, Pa., The John C. Winston company [1904] 141 p. front., illus., plates, ports. 21 cm. Each plate accompanied by guard sheet with descriptive letterpress. "Papers ... by the Friends' historical society."--Introd. "Limited to five hundred copies ... Number 449." [BX7780.P5F62] 45-51994
1. Philadelphia. Friends' meeting house (Fourth and Arch streets) 2. Friends, Society of. Philadelphia. I. Title.

NELSON, Lee H. 726'.9
An architectural study of Arch Street Meeting House, Fourth and Arch Streets, Philadelphia, Pennsylvania. Prepared for Philadelphia Yearly Meeting of the Religious Society of Friends, October 1968 [by] Lee H. Nelson [and] Penelope Hartshorne Batcheler. [Philadelphia? 1968 or 9] 1 v. (various pagings) illus., facsims., plates (incl. plans) 29 cm. "Copy no. 5 of thirteen copies." Includes bibliography. [NA5235.P45N4] 77-12481
1. Philadelphia. Friends' Meeting House (Fourth and Arch Streets) I. Batcheler, Penelope Hartshorne, joint author. II. Friends, Society of. Philadelphia Yearly Meeting. III. Title.

Philadelphia. Grace Baptist temple.

ELLIOTT, Edward O. 286.1748
Tent to temple, a history of the Grace Baptist church, Philadelphia, Pa., 1870 to 1895 ... By Edward O. Elliott. [Jenkintown, Pa., Printed by Times chronicle company, c1946. 107 p. illus. (incl. ports.) 23 cm. On cover ... The founding by Russell H. Conwell of the Baptist temple, the Temple college [and] Samaritan hospital. Bibliography: p. 107. [BX6480.P5G7] 46-20693
1. Conwell, Russell Herman, 1843-1925. 2. Philadelphia. Grace Baptist temple. 3. Philadelphia. Temple university. I. Title.

Philadelphia. Holy Trinity church.

BAKER, William Deal, 1812-1876.
Speech of William D. Baker in the German Roman Catholic Holy Trinity church case. Reported by Albert L. Gihon ... Philadelphia, T. K. and P. G. Collins, printers, 1852. 57 p. 23 cm. "The parties on the record are the Commonwealth ex relatione John George Fisher [et al.] ... vs. Francis Juker [et al.] ... It was a feigned issue upon a quo warranto issued against the defendants, to show cause by what authority they claim to exercise the office of "Trustees of the German religious society of Roman Catholics of the Holy Trinity church in the city of Philadelphia." --Introd. 42-26861
1. Philadelphia. Holy Trinity church. I. Fisher, John George, relator. II. Gihon, Albert L., reporter. III. Title.

Philadelphia. Lutheran Theological Seminary.

TAPPERT, Theodore Gerhardt, 1904- 207.4811
History of the Lutheran Theological Seminary at Philadelphia, 1864-1964. Philadelphia, Lutheran Theological Seminary. 1964. 168p. illus., facsims., ports. 24cm. Bibl. 64-22501 2.25
1. Philadelphia. Lutheran Theological Seminary. I. Title.

Philadelphia. Parish of the Holy Apostles.

THE first ninety years of the Parish of the Holy Apostles, 1868-1958. [Philadelphia? c1958] 74p. illus.
1. Philadelphia. Parish of the Holy Apostles. I. MacAfee, John Curtin.

Philadelphia—Poor.

SEWELL, Benjamin T. 266
Sorrow's circuit, or Five years' experience in the Bedford street mission, Philadelphia. By Rev. Benjamin T. Sewell...Revised by Rev. J. B. McCullough... Philadelphia, Pub. for the support of the gospel in the Bedford street mission, and sold at the Philadelphia conference tract depository, 1859. 416 p. front., plates. 19 cm. [HV4046.P5S5] 10-2364
1. Philadelphia—Poor. 2. Philadelphia. Bedford street mission. I. McCullough, John B., ed. II. Title.

Philadelphia. St. Agatha's Church.

PHILADELPHIA. St. Agatha's Church. 282.74811
Saint Agatha's Church, Philadelphia, Pennsylvania. South Hackensack, N.J., Custombook [1966] 1v. (unpaged) illus. (part col.) ports. 28 cm. Addenda slip inserted. [BX4603.P52S24] 66-6777
1. Philadelphia. St. Agatha's Church. I. Title.

Philadelphia, St. Augustine's church.

TOURSCHER, Francis Edward, 1870- 282.74811
Old Saint Augustine's in Philadelphia, with some records of the work of the Austin friars in the United States, prepared by one of the friars at Villanova, Pennsylvania, Fr. Francis Edward Tourscher, S.T.M. Philadelphia, The Peter Reilly company, 1937. vi, 261 p. 20 1/2 cm. "A list of the Augustinian friars, members of the Province of St. Thomas of Vilianova, who have departed this life since...1796": p. 171-231. [Name in religion: Joseph Tourscher, father] [BX4603.P52S27] 38-11521
1. Augustinians. Province of St. Thomas of Villanova. 2. Augustinians—Biog. 3. Philadelphia, St. Augustine's church. I. Title.

Philadelphia. St. George's church (Methodist)

TEES, Francis Harrison, 1875- 287.6748
The story of old St. George's, American Methodism's oldest and most historic church [by] Francis H. Tees ... [Philadelphia, The Message publishing co., c1941] 159 p. incl. front., illus. (incl. ports., facsims.) 20 1/2 cm. [BX8481.P5O4] 43-11765
1. Philadelphia. St. George's church (Methodist) I. Title.

Philadelphia. St. Joan of Arc parish.

HAWKS, Edward, 1878- 282.74811
History of the parish of St. Joan of Arc, Harrowgate, Philadelphia, by Monsignor Edward Hawks... Philadelphia, The Peter Reilly company, 1937. vii, 172 p. front., plates, maps. 21 cm. [BX1418.P5H35] 38-2324
1. Philadelphia. St. Joan of Arc parish. I. Title.

Philadelphia. Saint Martin of Tours parish.

MAIER, Eugene F. J. 282.74811
A history of Saint Martin of Tours parish, 1923-[1943] ... by the Reverend Eugene F. J. Maier, M.A. [Philadelphia, Printed by Bradley brothers, inc., 1933-43] 2 v. illus. (incl. ports., map, plan) 25 1/2 cm. [BX4603.P52S43] 46-521
1. Philadelphia. Saint Martin of Tours parish. I. Title.

Philadelphia. St. Mary's church.

[CAREY, Mathew] 1760-1839. 922.
... A desultory examination of the reply of the Rev. W. V. Harold to a Catholic layman's rejoinder. By a Catholic layman. To which is annexed an appendix, containing the above reply verbatin ... Philadelphia, H. C. Carey & I. Lea, 1822. viii, [9]-72 p. 23 cm. At head of title: No. 7. No. 15 in a volume lettered: Hogan pamphlets ... Philadelphia, 1821-24. [BX4705.H7A5 no. 15] [BX4795.H7C3] 36-38759
1. Harold, William Vincent. Reply to the Catholic layman's rejoinder. 2. Hogan, William, d. 1848. 3. Philadelphia. St. Mary's church. 4. Catholic church in Philadelphia. I. Title.

TOURSCHER, Francis Edward, 1870- 282.74811
The Hogan schism and trustee troubles in St. Mary's church, Philadelphia, 1820-1829, by Francis E. Tourscher... Philadelphia, The Peter Reilly company [c1930] 3 p. l., Ix-xxii, 234 p. illus. (map) 20 1/2 cm. "Sources of information": p. 2. [BX4608.P52S45] 30-33236
1. Hogan, William, d. 1848. 2. Conwell, Henry, bp., 1745 (ca.)-1842. 3. Philadelphia. St. Mary's church. 4. Catholic church in Philadelphia. I. Title.

Philadelphia. St. Matthew's church.

EDMONDS, Franklin Spencer, 1874- 283.
History of St. Matthew's church, Francisville, Philadelphia, 1822-1925, by Franklin Spencer Edmonds ... Philadelphia, St. Matthew's church, Francisville, 1925. xii, 323 p. front., plates, ports., facsim, fold. tab. 21 cm. [BX5980.F75E5] 26-14779
1. Philadelphia. St. Matthew's church. I. Title.

Philadelphia. St. Patrick's Church.

CAMPBELL, William Edward, 1898- 282.74811
... how unsearchable His ways; one hundred twenty-fifth anniversary, Saint Patrick's Church [by] William E. Campbell. [Lebanon? Pa., 1965] xxxii, 208 p. illus. (part col.) plans, ports. 26 cm. [BX4603.P52S49] 64-66418
1. Philadelphia. St. Patrick's Church. I. Title.

Philadelphia. St. Peter's church.

DE LANCEY, William Heathcote, bp., 1797-1865. 288.74811
A sermon preached at the centennial celebration of the opening of St. Peter's church, Philadelphia, September 4th, 1861, by William Heathcote DeLancey ... Punblished by Request of the vestry. Philadelphia, King & Baird, printers, 1862. 3 p. l., [3]-78 p. 23 cm. [BX5980.P5P4] 40-682
1. Philadelphia. St. Peter's church. I. Title.

Philadelphia. Temple Presbyterian church.

MITCHELL, James Young, 1832-1908. 285.
History and directory of Temple Presbyterian church formerly Central Presbyterian church in the Northern Liberties, Philadelphia. By James Y. Mitchell... Philadelphia, J. W. Daughaday & co., 1873. 241,vi p. front., plates ports. 18 1/2 cm. [BX9211.P5T4] 42-26094
1. Philadelphia. Temple Presbyterian church. I. Title.

Philadelphia Theological Seminary of Saint Charles Borromeo.

O'DONNELL, George Edward, 1896-
St. Charles Seminary, Philadelphia; a history of the Theological Seminary of Saint Charles Borromeo, Overbrook, Philadelphia, Pennsylvania, 1832-1964, with a chronological record of ordinations and pictures of the living alumni, by George E. O'Donnell. Foreword by John J. Krol. [Philadelphia, American Catholic Historical Society, 1964] x, 604 p. illus., coats of arms, ports. 24 cm. Published in 2 v., 1943-53 under title: Saint Charles Seminary, Overbrook. Bibliography: p. 559-560.
1. Philadelphia Theological Seminary of Saint Charles Borromeo. I. Title.

Philadelphia. Third Presbyterian church.

ALLEN, Richard Howe, 1820?-1892, ed.
Leaves from a century plant. Report of the Centennial celebration of Old Pine street church, (Third Presbyterian,) Philadelphia, Pa. May 29,1868. Edited by Rev. R. H. Allen, pastor. Philadelphia, H. B. Ashmead, printer, 1870. 2 p. l., vii-xi, [13]-215, [1] p. incl. pl. front., plates, ports. 21 1/2 cm. [BN9211.P5P6] 1-17525
1. Philadelphia. Third Presbyterian church. I. Title.

Philadelphia. Third Presbyterian church—History

GIBBONS, Hughes Oliphant, 1843- 285.
A history of old Pine street; being the record of an hundred and forty years in the life of a colonial church, with seventy-two full-page illustrations, by Hughes Oliphant Gibbons ... Philadelphia, The John C. Winston company, 1905. 3 p. l., 3-366 p. front., illus., plates, ports., facsims. (1 double) 21 cm. Most of the plates accompanied by guard sheet with descriptive letterpress. [BX9211.P5P65] 5-30560
1. Philadelphia. Third Presbyterian church—Hist. I. Title.

Philadelphia. Trinity Lutheran church, Germantown.

HOCKER, Edward W., 1878- 284.174811
History of Trinity Lutheran church, Germantown, Philadelphia, 1836-1936, by Edward W. Hocker ... with a preface by the Rev. Harry F. Baughman ... Germantown, Philadelphia, Pa., Trinity Lutheran church, 1936. 240 p. front., plates, ports. 19 1/2 cm. "Errata" (1 leaf) inserted. "Sources of information": p. 179. [BX8076.G4H6] 36-30345
1. Philadelphia. Trinity Lutheran church, Germantown. I. Title.

Philadelphia. Wakefield Presbyterian church.

REEVES, Francis Brewster, 1836- 285.
A brief historical sketch of Wakefield Presbyterian church and Sunday school, Germantown avenue below Fisher's lane, Philadelphia, 1856-1910, by Francis B. Reeves. [Philadelphia? 1910?] 52 p. front. 20 cm. [BX9211.P5W3] 19-10942
1. Philadelphia. Wakefield Presbyterian church. I. Title.

Philadelphia., Wharton street Methodist Episcopal church.

CLARK, William H.
Gleanings from my scrap book. By Wm. H. Clark. Philadelphia, Press of W. F. Fell & co., 1889. ix p., 1 l., 212 p. 2 port. (incl. front.) 18 1/2 cm. Poems. [PS1299.C25G5] 26-23621
1. Philadelphia., Wharton street Methodist Episcopal church. I. Title.

Philip, Metropolitan.

ORTHODOX synthesis : 230'.19
the unity of theological thought : an anthology published in commemoration of the fifteenth anniversary of Metropolitan Philip as Primate of the Antiochian Orthodox Christian Archdiocese of North America / Joseph J. Allen, editor. Crestwood, N.Y. : St. Vladimir's Seminary Press, 1981. p. cm. Includes bibliographical references. [BX320.2.O76] 19 81-5674 ISBN 0-913836-84-2 pbk. : 8.95
1. Philip, Metropolitan. 2. Theology, Eastern church—Addresses, essays, lectures. I. Allen, Joseph J. II. Philip, Metropolitan.
Publisher' address 575 Scrasdale Rd., Crestwood, NY 10707. Publisher's address: 575 Scarsdale Rd., Crestwood, NY 10707

Philip the evangelist, deacon—Juvenile literature.

NAISH, Jack. 226'.6'0924 B
Philip : traveling preacher / Jack Naish ; illustrated by Ron Hester. Nashville : Broadman Press, c1978. 48 p. : col. ill. ; 24 cm. (Biblearn series) Tells how a Jewish man converted to Christianity and spread the mission of the early church. [BS2520.P5N34] 78-105146 ISBN 0-8054-4241-3 : 3.95
1. Philip the evangelist, deacon—Juvenile literature. 2. [Philip the evangelist, deacon.] 3. Bible. N.T.—Biography—Juvenile literature. 4. [Bible stories—N.T.] I. Hester, Ronald. II. Title.

Philippine Islands—Church history—Addresses, essays, lectures.

ANDERSON, Gerald H. 279.14
Studies in Philippine church history. Edited by Gerald H. Anderson. Ithaca [N.Y.] Cornell University Press [1969] xiv, 421 p. 24 cm. [BR1260.A5] 69-18208 14.50
1. Philippine Islands—Church history—Addresses, essays, lectures. I. Title.

CLAVER, Francisco F. 282'.599
The stones will cry out : letters to the churches / Francisco F. Claver. Maryknoll, N.Y. : Orbis Books, c1978. p. cm. [BX874.C54S77] ISBN 0-88344-471-2 pbk. : 7.95
1. Catholic Church—Pastoral letters and charges. 2. Claver, Francisco F. 3. Catholic Church in the Philippine Islands—Addresses, essays, lectures. 4. Philippine Islands—Church history—Addresses, essays, lectures. I. Title.

Philippine Islands—History

THE hour before sunset. 266
Butler, Ind., Higley Press [c1957] 204p. illus. 20cm. The author's experiences as a pastor in the Philippines. [DS669.M3] 279.14 58-17207
1. Philippine Islands—Hist. 2. Philippine Islands—Church history. I. Mandoriao, Jose N

Philippine islands—Religion.

LAUBACH, Frank Charles, 1884- 279.
The people of the Philippines, their religious progress and preparation for spiritual leadership in the Far East, by

Frank Charles Laubach, PH. D.; with a foreword by Daniel Johnson Fleming ... New York, George H. Doran company [c1925] xx p., 1 l., 23-515 p. front., plates, ports., maps, facsim., diagr. 22 cm. Bibliography: p. 467-473. [BV3380.L3] 25-4216
1. Philippine island—Religion. 2. Missions—Philippine islands. I. Title.

OSIAS, Camilo, 1889- 279.14
Evangelical Christianity in the Philippines, by Camilo Osias and Avelina Lorenzana. Dayton, O., The United brethren publishing house [c1931] xx, 240 p. 20 cm. "References" at end of most of the chapters. [BR120.O8] 31-3090
1. Philippine islands—Religion. 2. Missions—Philippine islands. 3. Philippine islands. I. Lorenzana, Avelina, joint author. II. Title.

Philistines.

HINDSON, Edward E. 220.9'3
The Philistines and the Old Testament, by Edward E. Hindson. Grand Rapids, Baker Book House [1972, c1971] 184 p. illus. 22 cm. (Baker studies in Biblical archaeology) Bibliography: p. 175-181. [DS90.H56] 72-182084 ISBN 0-8010-4034-5 3.95
1. Bible. O.T.—History of Biblical events. 2. Philistines. I. Title.

Phillips, Bertha Wilson.

PHILLIPS, Bertha Wilson. 286'.1'0924 B
A time for everything. [North Newton, Kan., Mennonite Press, 1974] 218 p. 24 cm. [BX6495.P47A36] 73-93113
1. Phillips, Bertha Wilson. 2. Christian life—Baptist authors. I. Title.

Phillips, Margaret I.

PHILLIPS, Margaret I. 242
Songs of the good Earth / by Margaret Phillips. Gretna, La. : Pelican Pub. Co., 1979. p. cm. [BV4832.2.P498] 79-10731 ISBN 0-88289-221-5 : 3.50
1. Phillips, Margaret I. 2. Meditations. I. Title.

Phillips, Thomas, 1904-

BECKER, Kurt, 1915- 922.273
I met a traveller; the triumph of Father Phillips. New York, Farrar, Straus and Cudahy, 1958. 208p. 22cm. [BV3427.P47B4] 58-9448
1. Phillips, Thomas, 1904- I. Title.

Phillips, William Wirt, 1796-1865.

NEW York. First Presbyterian church. 922.573
Memorial of Rev. William W. Phillips, D.D. Printed by request of the session, and of the Board of trustees of the First Presbyterian church. New York, C. Scribner & company, 1865. 66 p., 1 l. front. (mounted phot.) port. 24 1/2 cm. "Address of Rev. Dr. Krebs": p. [7]-25. "Discourse ... commemorative of...Rev. William Wirt Phillips...April 30th, 1865. By Rev. Richard W. Dickinson, D.D.": p. [33]-66. [BX9225.P5N4] 36-24302
1. Phillips, William Wirt, 1796-1865. 2. Funeral sermons. 3. Presbyterian church—Sermons. 4. Krebs, John Michael, 1804-1867. I. Dickinson, Richard William, 1804-1874. II. Title.

Phillips, Ze Barney Thorpe.

MCCLENAHAN, Sallie Hews (Phillips) 922.373
"So live"; Ze Barney Thorne Phillips, D.D., L.L. D., S.T.D., 1875-1942. [Hyannis Mass., 1950] 127 p. illus., ports. 24 cm. [BX5995.P52M3] 50-547360
1. Phillips, Ze Barney Thorpe. I. Title.

Philo Judaeus.

ASPECTS of wisdom in Judaism and early Christianity / Robert L. Wilken, editor. Notre Dame, Ind. : University of Notre Dame Press, [1975] xxii, 218 p. ; 21 cm. ([Studies in Judaism and Christianity in antiquity] ; no. 1) Papers presented at a seminar sponsored by the Dept. of theology, University of Notre Dame in 1973. Includes indexes. Bibliography: p. 201-210. [BS1455.A8] 74-27888 ISBN 0-268-00577-X : 13.95 223
1. Philo Judaeus. 2. Bible. N.T.—Relation to Old Testament—Addresses, essays, lectures. 3. Midrash—History and criticism. 4. Wisdom literature—Criticism, interpretation, etc.—Addresses, essays, lectures. 5. Christianity—Early church, ca. 30-600—Addresses, essays, lectures. I. Wilken, Robert Louis, 1936- II. Notre Dame, Ind. University. Dept. of Theology. III. Title. IV. Series.

BELKIN, Samuel. 296
Philo and the oral law; the Philonic interpretation of Biblical law in relation to the Palestinian Halakah, by Samuel Belkin ... Cambridge, Mass, Harvard university press, 1940. xiv, 292 p. 23 cm. (Half-title: Harvard Semitic series, vol. xi) Bibliography: p. [271]-280. [BM646.B48] 41-2968
1. Philo Judaeus. 2. Jews—Law. 3. Ethics, Jewish. 4. Jews in Alexandria. 5. Halacha. I. Title. II. Title: Biblical law in relation to Halakah.

BENTWICH, Norman De Mattos, 1883- 181.
Philo-Judaeus of Alexandria, by Norman Bentwich ... Philadelphia, The Jewish publication society of America, 1910. 273 p. 19 cm. [B689.Z9B4] 10-7808
1. Philo Judaeus. I. Title.

BIGG, Charles, 1840-1908. 201
The Christian Platonists of Alexandria; eight lectures preached before the University of Oxford in the year 1886 of the foundation of the late Rev. John Bampton. New York, AMS Press [1970] xxvii, 304 p. 23 cm. Reprint of the 1886 ed. Includes bibliographical references. [BR1705.B5 1970] 75-123764
1. Philo Judaus. 2. Clemens, Titus Flavius, Alexandrinus. 3. Origenes. 4. Platonists. I. Title.

BIGG, Charles, 1840-1908. 201
The Christian Platonists of Alexandria; the 1886 Bampton lectures. Oxford, Clarendon P., 1968. 386 p. 23 cm. "First published 1913." Bibliographical footnotes. [BR1705.B5 1968] 76-370393 unpriced
1. Philo Judaus. 2. Clemens, Titus Flavius, Alexandrinus. 3. Origenes. 4. Platonists. I. Title.

BIGG, Charles, 1840-1908. 231.1
The Christian Platonists of Alexandria. Eight lectures preached before the University of Oxford in the year 1886 on the foundation of the late Rev. John Bampton ... by Charles Bigg ... Oxford, The Clarendon press, 1886. xxvii, 304 p. 23 cm. (On cover: Bampton lectures. 1886) Contents.--i. Introduction. Philo and the Gnostics.--ii-iii. Clement.-- iv-vi. Origen.--vii. The reformed paganism.--viii. Summary. [BR45.B3 1886] 230.062 38-16290
1. Philo Judeaeus. 2. Clemens, Titus Flavius, Alexandrinus. 3. Origenes. 4. Platonists. I. Title.

BIGG, Charles, 1840-1908. 231.1
The Christian Platonists of Alexandria; being the Bampton lectures of the year 1886, by the late Charles Bigg ... Reprinted with some additions and corrections. Oxford, The Clarendon press, 1913. 386 p. 1 l., 23 cm. On cover: Second edition. Edited by F. E. Brightman. Contents.--i. Introduction. Philo and the Gnostics.--ii. iii. Clement.--iv-vi. Origen.--vii. The reformed paganism.--viii. Summary. [BR1705.B5 1913] 230.082 14-1994
1. Philo Judeaus. 2. Clemens, Titus Flavius, Alexandrinus. 3. Origenes. 4. Platonists. I. Brightman, Frank Edward, 1856-1982, ed. II. Title.

CENTER for Hermeneutical Studies in Hellenistic and Modern Culture. 231'.7
The transcendence of God in Philo : some possible sources : protocol of the sixteenth colloquy, 20 April 1975 / the Center for Hermeneutical Studies in Hellenistic and Modern Culture, the Graduate Theological Union & the University of California, Berkeley, California ; John M. Dillon ; W. Wuellner, editor. Berkeley, CA : The Center, c1975. 44 p. ; 21 cm. (Colloquy - the Center for Hermeneutical Studies in Hellenistic and Modern Culture ; nr. 16) Includes bibliographical references. [BT100.C34 1975] 75-38047 ISBN 0-89242-015-4
1. Philo Judaeus. 2. Transcendence of God—History of doctrines. I. Dillon, John M. II. Wuellner, Wilhelm H., 1927- III. Title. IV. Series: Center for Hermeneutical Studies in Hellenistic and Modern Culture. Protocol series of the colloquies ; nr. 16.

GOODENOUGH, Erwin Ramsdell, 1893- 181.3
An introduction to Philo Judaeus. 2d ed. [rev.] New York, Barnes & Noble [1963] 167p. 20cm. Bibl. 63-5863 4.00
1. Philo Judaeus. I. Title.

KENNEDY, Harry Angus Alexander, 1866-
Philo's contribution to religion, by H. A. A. Kennedy ... London, New York [etc.] Hodder and Stoughton, 1919. xi, 245, [1] p. 20 cm. A 20
1. Philo Judaeus. I. Title.

SANDMEL, Samuel. 181.3
Philo's place in Judaism; a study of conceptions of Abraham in Jewish literature. Cincinnati, Hebrew Union College Press, 1956. vii, 218p. 24cm. 'Initially published in two installments of the Hebrew Union College annual, vols. XXV and XXVI. Bibliographical footnotes. [B689.Z7S3] 56-8999
1. Philo Judseus. 2. Abraham, the patriarch. I. Title.

SANDMEL, Samuel. 181'.3
Philo's place in Judaism: a study of conceptions of Abraham in Jewish literature. Augm. ed. New York, Ktav Pub. House, 1971 [i.e. 1972, c1956] xxix, 232 p. 24 cm. Based on the author's thesis, Yale, entitled Abraham in normative and Hellenistic Jewish tradition. First published in 2 installments of the Hebrew Union College Annual, v. 25 and 26. Includes a new introd. and Subject index of Public passages. Bibliography: p. ix-xxvii. [B689.Z7S3 1972] 79-149603 ISBN 0-87068-135-4 14.95
1. Philo Judaeus. 2. Abraham, the patriarch, in the Midrash. I. Title.

SOWERS, Sidney G. 220.6
The hermeneutics of Philo and Hebrews; a comparison of the interpretation of the Old Testament in Philo Judaeus and the Epistle to the Hebrews. Richmond, Va., Knox [c.1965] 154p. 21cm. (Basel studies of theology, no.1) Bibl. [BS1160.S64] 65-10146 2.75 pap.,
1. Philo Judaeus 2. Bible. O. T.—Criticism, interpretation, etc.—Hist. 3. Bible. N. T. Hebrews—Relation to O. T. 4. Allegory. I. Title. II. Series.

VAN TIL, Cornelius, 1895- 261.2
Christ and the Jews. [Philadelphia] Presbyterian and Reformed Pub. Co., 1968. v, 99 p. 23 cm. (International library of philosophy and theology: Biblical and theological studies) Includes bibliographical references. [BM535.V3] 68-25835
1. Philo Judaeus. 2. Buber, Martin, 1878-1965. 3. Judaism—Relations—Christianity. 4. Christianity and other religions—Judaism. I. Title. II. Series: International library of philosophy and theology: Biblical and theological studies series.

WOLFSON, Harry Austryn, 1887-
Philo: foundations of religious philosophy in Judaism, Christianity, and Islam. Rev. Cambridge, Mas., Harvard University Press, 1962 [c1947] 2 v. 23 cm. (His Structure and growth of philosophic systems from Plato to Spinoza, 2) 67-14904
1. Philo Judaeus. I. Title.

WOLFSON, Harry Austryn, 1887- 181.3
Philo; foundations of religious philosophy in Judaism, Christianity, and Islam. Cambridge, Harvard Univ. Press, 1947. 2 v. 23 cm. (His Structure and growth of philosophic systems from Plato to Spinoza, 2) [B689.Z7W83] 47-30635
1. Philo, Judaeus. I. Title.

WOLFSON, Harry Austryn, 1887-1974. 200'.1
From Philo to Spinoza : two studies in religious philosophy / by Harry Austryn Wolfson ; introd. by Isadore Twersky. New York : Behrman House, c1977. p. cm. Contents.—What is new in Philo?—Spinoza and the religion of the past. Includes bibliographical references. [B689.Z7W685 1977] 77-1909 ISBN 0-87441-262-5 pbk. : 3.95
1. Philo Judaus. 2. Spinoza, Benedictus de, 1632-1677. 3. Religion—Philosophy—History. I. Wolfson, Harry Austryn, 1887-1974. Spinoza and the religion of the past. 1977. II. Title.

Philo Judaeus—Congresses.

CENTER for Hermeneutical Studies in Hellenistic and Modern Culture. 296.3'2
Philo and the gnostics on man and salvation : protocol of the twenty-ninth colloquy, 17 April, 1977 / the Center for Hermeneutical Studies in Hellenistic and Modern Culture, the Graduate Theological Union & the University of California Berkeley, California ; Birger A. Pearson. Berkeley, CA : The Center, c1977. 60 p. ; 21 cm. (Protocol series of the colloquies of the Center ; 29 ISSN 0098-0900s) "Select bibliography of Birger A. Pearson": p. 59-60. [B689.Z7C4 1977] 77-14930 ISBN 0-89242-028-6 pbk. : 4.00
1. Philo Judaeus—Congresses. 2. Man (Jewish theology)—Congresses. 3. Gnosticism—Congresses. I. Pearson, Birger Albert. II. Title. III. Series: Center for Hermeneutical Studies in Hellenistic and Modern Culture. Protocol series of the colloquies ; 29.

CENTER for Hermeneutical Studies in Hellenistic and Modern Culture. 296.4'4
Philo's description of Jewish practices : protocol of the thirteenth colloquy, 5 June, 1977 / the Center for Hermeneutical Studies in Hellenistic and Modern Culture, the Graduate Theological Union & the University of California, Berkeley, California ; Baruch Bokser. Berkeley, CA : The Center, c1977. 41 p. ; 21 cm. (Protocol series of the colloquies of the Center ; 30 ISSN 0098-0900s) "Bibliography of Baruch M. Bokser": p. 41. [B689.Z7C4 1977b] 77-14931 ISBN 0-89242-029-4 pbk. : 4.00
1. Philo Judaeus—Congresses. 2. Jews—Rites and cermonies—Congresses. 3. Therapeutae—Congresses. 4. Qumran community—Congresses. I. Bokser, Baruch M. II. Title. III. Series: Center for Hermeneutical Studies in Hellenistic and Modern Culture. Protocol series of the colloquies ; 30.

Philomena, Saint.

THE life and miracles of 922.
Saint Philomena, virgin and martyr, whose sacred body was lately discovered in the catacombs at Rome, and from thence transferred to Mugnano, in the kingdom of Naples. Translated from the French ... New York, P. O'Shea, 1865. xi, 135 p. front. 16 cm. For a discussion of the correct identification of the body referred to in the title see Marucchl: Studio archeologico sulla celebre iscrizlone di Filumena scoperta nel cimitero di Priscilla (Nuovo bullettino di archeol, crist. xii, 1906) and Butler: Lives of the saints, vol. viii (1933) [BX4700.P75L5] 41-12181
1. Philomena, Saint.

MOHR, Marie Helene, Sister. 922.245
Saint Philomena, powerful with God. Milwaukee, Bruce Pub. Co. [1956] 186p. illus. 23cm. [BX4700.P75M6 1956] 57-644
1. Philomena, Saint. I. Title.

MOHR, Marie Helene, Sister. 922.245
Saint Philomena, powerful with God. Milwaukee, Bruce [1953] 136p. illus. 23cm. [BX4700.P75M6] 53-2859
1. Philomena, Saint. I. Title.

Philosophers.

DUNHAM, James Henry, 1870- 180
The religion of philosophers. Philadelphia, Univ of Pennsylvania Press for Temple Univ. publications, 1947. 314 p. 24 cm. Bibliography: p. 304-307. [B56.D8] 48-408
1. Philosophers. 2. Philosophy and religion. I. Title.

NETTLESHIP, Richard Lewis, 1846-1892.
Philosophical lectures and remains of Richard Lewis Nettleship ... Ed., with a biographical sketch, by A. C. Bradley ... and G. R. Benson ... London, New York, Macmillan and co., ltd., 1897. 2 v. front. (port.) 21 cm. [B1648.P5 1897] A 14
I. Bradley, Andrew Cecil, 1851- ed. II. Charnwood, Godfrey Rathbone, Benson, 1st baron, 1864- joint ed. III. Title.

PALEY, Alan L. 299'.5126'4
Confucius, ancient Chinese philosopher, by Alan L. Paley. Charlotteville, N.Y., SamHar Press, 1973. 32 p. 22 cm. (Outstanding personalities, no. 59) Bibliography: p. 31-32. A brief biography of the Chinese teacher and sage whose teachings, though largely ignored during his lifetime, influenced all aspects of Chinese life for many centuries after his death. [B128.C8P33] 92 73-77600 ISBN 0-87157-559-0. 1.98 (lib. bdg.)
1. Confucius—Juvenile literature. 2. [Confucius.] 3. [Philosophers.] I. Title.
Pbk., 0.98, ISBN 0-87157-059-9.

RUFFIN, John Demosthenes N.
Great logicians, by J. N. Ruffin, B. A. New York city, E. S. Werner & co. [c1926] 2 p. l., 151 p. 1 illus., diagrs. 22 cm. [BC15.R8] 26-24171
1. Philosophers. 2. Logic. I. Title.

RUNES, Dagobert David, 1902- ed.
Treasury of world philosophy. Paterson, N.J., Littlefield, Adams, 1959. xxiv, 1270 [1271-1280] p. 21 cm. First published under title: Treasury of philosophy. 65-84280
1. Philosophers. 2. Philosophy. I. Title.

SIMS, Bennett B. 299'.5146'3 B
Lao-Tzu and the Tao te Ching, by Bennett B. Sims. New York, F. Watts [1971] 122 p. 22 cm. (Immortals of philosophy and religion) A brief introduction to and commentary on the life of the Chinese philosopher Lao-tzu is followed by an interpretative text of his teachings. [BL1900.L35S47] 92 73-142996 ISBN 0-531-00961-0
1. Lao-tzu. Tao te ching.—Juvenile literature. 2. [Lao-tzu.] Tao te ching. 3. [Philosophers.] 4. [Philosophy.] I. Title.

Philosophers, Ancient.

FENELON, Francois de Salignac de La Mothe-, abp., 1651-1715.
Lives of the ancient philosophers; translated from the French of Fenelon, with notes, and a life of the author. By the Rev. John Cormack. New-York, Harper & brothers, 1841. vi p., 1 l., [9]-299 p. 16 cm. (On cover: Harper's family library; no. CXL.) [PQ1795.A5E] A 31
1. Philosophers, Ancient. I. Cormack, John, tr. II. Title.

MORE, Paul Elmer, 1864-1937. 180
Hellenistic philosophies, by Paul Elmer More... Princeton, Princeton university press; [etc., etc.] 1923. 3 p. l., 385 p. 21 1/2 cm. (His The Greek tradition, vol. II) [B171.M75] 24-2328
1. Philosophers, Ancient. 2. Philosophy, Ancient. I. Title.
Contents omitted.

RANDOLPH, Vance.
... *Ancient philosophers* [by] Vance Randolph ... Girard, Kan., Haldeman-Julius company [c1924] 60 p. 15 cm. (Little blue book no. 613, ed. by E. Haldeman-Julius) [B111.R3] ca 26
1. Philosophers, Ancient. I. Title.

THE theology of the early Greek philosophers. [Translated for the Gifford lectures from the German manuscript by E. S. Robinson] Oxford, Clarendon Press [1960] 259p. (The Gifford lectures, 1936)
I. Jaeger, Werner Wilhelm, 1888-

Philosophers. Arabic.

[MUBASHSHIR IBN FATIK, Abu al-Wafa] 11thcent.
The dictes and sayings of the philosophers. [Detroit, Mich., The Cranbrook press, 1901] 124 [2] p. illus. 29 cm. Lord Rivers' translation of Tignonville's French version of the Dicta philosophorum, a collection of sayings of wise men, originally compiled in Arabic. Colophon: Here ends the book which is called the Dictes and sayings of the philosophers, first printed in the English language by William Caxton in the year mcccclxxvii. now emprinted anew by ancient process by me, George G. Booth, at the Cranbrook press ... Detroit, Michigan, U. S. A., and finished this xix day of January, in the first year of the twentieth century, the same being anno Domini mdcccci. The total number of copies, printed is ccxliv, of which this is no. 61. The thanks of the printer are especially due to Henry M. Utley for permission to use the facsimile copy of this rare book owned by the Detroit Public library, and to James E. Scripps and Edgar B. Whitcomb for assistance in the preparation of the work for the press. "Wood-cut initials, borders, head and tail pieces from designs by George G. Booth, including two original engravings on copper, from drawings by De Voss W. Driscoll." The second, third, sixth, seventh and last pages of text within ornamental border. Autograph presenttion copy: To Wilberforce Eames with the sincere regards of the printer George G. Booth. July 5, 1901. [B745.D5M8] 6-19107
1. Philosophers. Arabic. I. Tignonville, Guillamme de, d. 1414. II. Caxton, William, 1422 (ca.)-1491. III. Rivers, Anthony Woodville, 2d early, 1442?-1483, tr. IV. Title.

Philosophers—China—Biography—Juvenile literature.

JOHNSON, Spencer. 299'.5126'3 B
The value of honesty : the story of Confucius / by Spencer Johnson ; illustrated by Pileggi. 1st ed. La Jolla, Calif. : Value Communications, c1979. 63 p. : col. ill. ; 29 cm. (ValueTales) A biography of the Chinese philosopher and teacher emphasizing his ideas about the value of honesty. [B128.C8J63] 92 79-4351 ISBN 0-916392-36-8 : 5.95
1. Confucius—Juvenile literature. 2. [Confucius.] 3. Philosophers—China—Biography—Juvenile literature. 4. Honesty—Juvenile literature. 5. [Philosophers.] 6. [Honesty.] I. Pileggi, Steve. II. Title.

Philosophers—India—Biography.

BELFRAGE, Sally, 1936- 291.4
Flowers of emptiness : reflections on an ashram / Sally Belfrage. 1st ed. New York : Dial Press, c1981. 240 p. ; 22 cm. [B5134.R3464B44] 19 80-25283 ISBN 0-8037-2523-X : 9.95
1. Rajaneesh, Acharya, 1931- 2. Belfrage, Sally, 1936- 3. Philosophers—India—Biography. 4. Life. I. Title.

Philosophers, Jewish.

BERGMAN, Shmuel Hugo, 1883- 181.3
Faith and reason: an introduction to modern Jewish thought, by Samuel H. Bergman. Translated and edited by Alfred Jospe. Washington, b'nai B'rith Hillel Foundations, 1961. 158 p. 19 cm. (The Hillel little books, v. t) "The translation is based on the original German text of the lectures as well as on ... Bergman's ... Hogim u-maaminim." Includes bibliography. [B159.B45] 61-10414
1. Philosophers, Jewish. I. Title. II. Series.

BERGMAN, Shmuel Hugo, 1883-
Faith and reason: an introduction to modern Jewish thought, by Samuel H. Bergman. Translated and edited by Alfred Jospe. [1st ed.] New York, Schocken Books [1963] 158 p. 19 cm. (Schocken Paperbacks, SB 56) "The translation is based on the original German text of the lectures as well as on ... Bergman's ... Hogim u-maaminim." Includes bibliography. NUC64
1. Philosophers, Jewish. I. Title.

BERGMANN, Samuel Hugo, 1883- 181.3
Faith and reason; an introduction to modern Jewish thought. Tr., ed. by Alfred Jospe. New York, Schocken [1963, c.1961] 158p. 21cm. (SB56) Bibl. 1.45 pap.,
1. Philosophers, Jewish. I. Title.

Philosophers, Jewish—Germany—Biography.

FRIEDMAN, Maurice S. 296.3'092'4 B
Martin Buber's life and work : the early years, 1878-1923 / by Maurice Friedman. 1st ed. New York : Dutton, c1980. p. cm. [B3213.B84F69 1980] 19 79-17868 ISBN 0-525-15325-X : 25.00
1. Buber, Martin, 1878-1965. 2. Philosophers, Jewish—Germany—Biography. 3. Philosophers—Germany—Biography. 4. Zionists—Germany—Biography. I. Title.

Philosophers-United States-Biography.

RYAN, Thomas Richard, 1898- 282'.092'4 B
Orestes A. Brownson : a definitive biography / Thomas R. Ryan. Huntington, Ind. : Our Sunday Visitor, c1976. 872p. ; 27 cm. Includes index. Biography:p. 851-763. [B908.B64R78] 76-29141 ISBN 087973-884-7 : 29.95
1. Brownson, Orestes Augustus, 1803-1876. 2. Philosophers-United States-Biography.

Philosophical anthropology.

MEHL, Roger 128
Images of man. Tr. [from French] by James H. Farley. Richmond, Va., Knox [c.1965] 64p. 19cm. (Chime paperbacks) Bibl. [BT703.M383] 65-12189 1.00 pap.,
1. Philosophical anthropology. 2. Man (Theology) I. Title.

Philosophical theology.

BAX, Ernest Belfort, 1854-
The roots of reality; being suggestions for a philosophical reconstruction, by Ernest Belfort Bax ... New York, B. W. Dodge & company, 1908. 3 p. l., ix-xi, 331 p. 21 cm. Printed in Great Britain. 8-8287
I. Title.
Contents omitted.

BRUMMER, Vincent. 230'.01
Theology and philosophical inquiry : an introduction / by Vincent Brummer. Philadelphia : Westminster Press, c1982. 306 p. ; 22 cm. Includes bibliographical references and index. [BT40.B69 1982] 19 81-11557 ISBN 0-664-24398-3 pbk. : 16.95
1. Philosophical theology. 2. Philosophy and religion. I. Title.

BURI, Fritz, 1907- 230'.01
Thinking faith; steps on the way to a philosophical theology. Translated by Harold H. Oliver. Philadelphia, Fortress Press [1968] xii, 100 p. 22 cm. Translation of Denkender Glaube. Bibliographical footnotes. [BT40.B8513] 68-10984
1. Philosophical theology. I. Title.

CUPITT, Don. 210
Christ and the hiddenness of God. Philadelphia, Westminster Press [1971] 219 p. 21 cm. "Based on the Stanton Lectures delivered at Cambridge in the Lent Terms of 1969 and 1970." Includes bibliographical references. [BT40.C78] 75-144038 ISBN 0-664-20905-X 6.00
1. Philosophical theology. I. Title.

CURTIS, Charles J. 230'.01
The task of philosophical theology [by] C. J. Curtis. New York, Philosophical Lib. [1967] xxvi, 165p. 23cm. Bibl. [BT40.C8] 67-17634 4.50
1. Philosophical theology. 2. Process theology. I. Title.

FARRER, Austin Marsden 230'.01
Faith and speculation; an essay in philosophical theology, by Austin Farrer. New York, N.Y.U. Pr., 1967. vii, 175p. 23cm. (Deems lects., 1964) [BT40.F35] 67-16975 5.00
1. Philosophical theology. I. Title. II. Series: The Deems lectures, 1964

FARRER, Austin Marsden. 230'.3
Reflective faith; essays in philosophical theology. Edited by Charles C. Conti. Grand Rapids, Eerdmans [1974, c1972] xv, 234 p. 21 cm. "Chronological list of published writings: 1933-1973": p. [227]-234. [BT40.F36 1974] 73-14737 ISBN 0-8028-1519-7 3.45 (pbk.)
1. Philosophical theology. I. Title.

FLEW, Antony Garrard Newton, 1923- ed. 230.01
New essays in philosophical theology. Edited by Antony Flew [and] Alasdair MacIntyre. New York, Macmillan [1964] x, 274 p. 22 cm. (Macmillan paperback edition) "MP184." [BT40.F54 1964] 64-57338
1. Philosophical theology. I. MacIntyre, Alasdair O., joint ed. II. Title.

FOSTER, Michael Beresford. 230
Mystery and philosophy / Michael B. Foster. Westport, Conn. : Greenwood Press, 1980. p. cm. Reprint of the 1957 ed. published by SCM Press, London, in series: The Library of philosophy and theology. Includes index. [BT40.F56 1980] 19 79-8721 ISBN 0-313-20792-5 lib. bdg. : 18.75
1. Philosophical theology. 2. Mystery. I. Title.

HARTSHORNE, Charles, 1897- 210
Whitehead's view of reality / Charles Hartshorne, Creighton Peden. New York : Pilgrim Press, c1981. 106 p. ; 23 cm. Includes bibliographical references. [B1674.W354H38] 19 80-23532 ISBN 0-8298-0381-5 pbk. : 6.95
1. Whitehead, Alfred North, 1861-1947. 2. Whitehead, Alfred North, 1861-1947—Theology. 3. Philosophical theology. 4. Methodology. I. Peden, Creighton, 1935- joint author. II. Title.

HERBERT, Robert T., 1928- 230'.01
Paradox and identity in theology / R. T. Herbert. Ithaca, N.Y. : Cornell Uiversity Press, 1979. 197 p. ; 23 cm. Includes index. Bibliography: p. 191-193. [BT55.H47 1979] 78-20784 ISBN 0-8014-1222-6 : 12.50
1. Philosophical theology. I. Title.

ROSS, James F., 1931- 230'.01
Philosophical theology, by James F. Ross. Indianapolis, Bobbs-Merrill [1969] x, 326 p. 24 cm. Bibliographical footnotes. [BT40.R6] 68-17707 8.50
1. Philosophical theology.

ROSS, James F., 1931- 231
Philosophical theology / James F. Ross. [Rev. ed.] Indianapolis : Hackett Pub. Co., c1981. p. cm. Includes index. [BT40.R6 1981] 19 80-22024 ISBN 0-915144-67-0 : 17.50 ISBN 0-915144-68-9 (pbk.) : 6.95
1. Philosophical theology. I. Title.

ROUSSEAU, Richard W. 230
Disclosure of the ultimate : fundamental theology reconsidered / Richard W. Rousseau. Washington, D.C. : University Press of America, [1980] p. cm. [BT40.R64] 80-8259 ISBN 0-8191-1284-4 lib. bdg. : 21.50
1. Philosophical theology. I. Title.

TORRANCE, Thomas Forsyth, 1913- 230'.01
Theological science [by] Thomas F. Torrance. London, New York [etc.] Oxford U.P., 1969. xx, 368 p. 23 cm. "Based on the Hewett lectures for 1959." Bibliographical footnotes. [BT40.T65 1969] 76-413012 84/-
1. Philosophical theology. I. Title.

Philosophical theology—Addresses, essays, lectures.

CONSULTATION on the Future of Philosophical Theology, McCormick Theological Seminary, 1970. 201
The future of philosophical theology. Edited by Robert A. Evans. Philadelphia, Westminster Press [1971] 190 p. 21 cm. [BT40.C65 1970] 77-141196 ISBN 0-664-20902-5 6.95
1. Philosophical theology—Addresses, essays, lectures. I. Evans, Robert A., 1937- ed. II. Title.

KANT, Immanuel, 1724-1804. 200'.1
Lectures on philosophical theology / Immanuel Kant ; translated by Allen W. Wood and Gertrude M. Clark ; with introd. and notes by Allen W. Wood. Ithaca : Cornell University Press, 1978. 175 p. ; 23 cm. Translation of Vorlesungen uber die philosophische Religionslehre. Includes bibliographical references and index. [B2794.V642E54 1978] 78-58034 ISBN 0-8014-1199-8 : 12.50
1. Philosophical theology—Addresses, essays, lectures. I. Wood, Allen W. II. Clark, Gertrude M. III. Title.

THE Philosophical 230'.01
frontiers of Christian theology : essays presented to D.M. MacKinnon / edited by Brian Hebblethwaite and Stewart Sutherland. Cambridge [Cambridgeshire] ; New York : Cambridge University Press, 1982. ix, 252 p. : port. ; 23 cm. Includes index. Contents.Contents.—The borderlands of ontology in the New Testament / C.F.D. Moule — Athens and Jerusalem / G.W.H. Lampe — The concept of mind and the concept of God in the Christian fathers / Christopher Stead — Kant and the negative theology / Don Cupitt — Ideology, metaphor, and analogy / Nicholas Lash — Theological study / S.W. Sykes — Optimism, finitude, and the meaning of life / R.W. Hepburn — Practical necessity / Bernard Williams — Religion, ethics, and action / Stewart Sutherland — Theological realism / T.F. Torrance — Notes on analogical predication, and speaking about God / Roger White — 'True' and 'false' in Christology / Brian Hebblethwaite. "Donald MacKinnon's published writings, 1937-1980" / compiled by Paul Wignall: p. 239-248. [BT40.P44] 19 81-10132 ISBN 0-521-24012-3 : 29.50
1. Mackinnon, Donald Mackenzie, 1913- 2. Philosophical theology—Addresses, essays, lectures. 3. Philosophy and religion—Addresses, essays, lectures. I. MacKinnon, Donald MacKenzie, 1913- II. Hebblethwaite, Brian. III. Sutherland, Stewart R.
Contents omitted.

Philosophy.

ALDEN, Joseph, 1807-1885.
Elements of intellectual philosophy. By Rev. Joseph Alden... New York, D. Appleton and company, 1873. 292 p. 19 cm. A 11
1. Philosophy. I. Title.

AMERICAN philosophical society, Philadelphia.
The record of the celebration of the two hundredth anniversary of the founding of the American philosophical society held at Philadelphia for promoting useful knowledge, April 27 to April 30, 1927 ... Philadelphia, American philosophical society, 1927. xiii, 750 p. incl. illus., plates, facsims, tables, diagrs. 26 cm. (Its Proceedings. v. 66) [Q11.P5 vol. 66] 28-13343
I. Title.

BENNETT, Charles T.
A new system of orificial philosophy, embracing all the latest improvements in orificial surgery, by C. T. Bennett ... [Flint, Mich., Werkheiser & sons, printers, 1891] 80 p. 18 cm. [RD78.B46] 8-1888
I. Title.

BIERBOWER, Austin, 1844-
Principles of a system of philosophy, in accordance with which it is sought to reconcile the more difficult questions of metaphysics and religion with themselves, and with the sciences and common sense. 2d ed. New York, Eaton & Mains; Cincinnati, Jennings & Pye [1898] 240 p. 12 cm. Title edition. 1-15119
I. Title.

BOWEN, Horace.
The overshadowing power of God. A synopsis of a new philosophy concerning the nature of the soul of man, its union with the animal soul, and its gradual creation through successive acts of overshadowing and the insertion of shoots, to its perfection in Jesus the Christ...by Horace Bowen, M.D. ... Transcribed in verse by Sheridan Wait, with chart and illustrations by M. W. Fairchild. New York, New life publishing company, 1883. i., 499 p. 2 pl (incl. front.) col. fold. chart. 22 cm. 15-3367
I. Wait, Sheridan. II. Title.

*CAMPBELL, Anthony. 135
Seven states of consciousness; a vision of possibilities suggested by the teaching of Marharishi Mahesh Yogi. New York, Harper & Row [1974] vi, 181 p. 18 cm. (Perennial library) Bibliography: p. [171]-173. [B132] 73-9078 ISBN 0-06-080289-8 1.50 (pbk.)
1. Philosophy. 2. Psychology. I. Title.

CARTER, W H 1909- 208.8
The philosopher's stone, by the Inkhorn. Boston, Meador Pub. Co. [1955] 69p. 22cm. [BR126.C28] 55-28915
I. Title.

DAVIS, Andrew Jackson, 1826- 133.
1910.
The great harmonia; being a philosophical revelation of the natural, spiritual, and celestial universe. By Andrew Jackson Davis ... Boston, Sanborn, Carter & Bazin; Portland, Blake & Carter, 1855-60. 5 v. front. (v. 5) illus. 19 cm. Title varies slightly. Imprint of v. 5; New York, A. J. Davis; Boston, B. Marsh, 1860. Vol. 1, 4th edition. Contents.v. 1. The physician.--v. 2. The teacher.--v. 3. The seer.--v. 4. The reformer.--v. 5. The thinker. [BF1291.D27 1855] 11-3617
I. Title.

DAVIS, Charles Gilbert, 1849-
The philosophy of life, by Charles Gilbert Davis, M. D. Chicago [Garner-Taylor press] 1906. 128, [2] p. 18 x 14 cm. 6-8280
I. Title.

DE BOER, Annie M Long, Mrs. 212
The philosophy of a novitiate; poems and essays of Annie M. L. De Boer ... Los Angeles, Cal., The Ideal publishing co. [c1920] 142 p. 23 cm. [BP567.D4] 20-14131
I. Title.

FISCHER, Bela. 128'.5
The human exile / by Bela Fischer. New York : Philosophical Library, [1974] 185 p. ; 22 cm. [BM755.F496A53] 74-75081 ISBN 0-8022-2139-4 : 6.00
I. Title.

GORDIN, Harry Mann, 1854- 218
1923.
Science, truth, religion and ethics as foundations of a rational philosophy of life, by Harry Mann Gordin. Chicago, C. H. Kerr & company [c1924] 467 p. front. (port.) diagr. 20 cm. [BD431.G6] 24-27690
1. Philosophy. 2. Life. I. Title.

GRABO, Carl Henry, 1881- 218
The amateur philosopher, by Carl H. Grabo. New York, C. Scribner's sons, 1917. xv p., 1 l., 290 p. 20 cm. [BD431.G7] 17-7480
1. Philosophy. 2. Life. 3. Religion. I. Title.

GROTE, John, 1813-1866.
Exploratio philosophica ... By John Grote ... Cambridge [Eng.] The University press, 1900. 2 v. front. (v. 2: port.) 23 1/2 cm. A reissue of pt. I (first published in 1865) and first edition of pt. II, edited by J. B. Mayor. "Pamphlets and essays [by Prof. Grote] printed before the publication of the Exploratio": pt. II, p. xi-xii. Contents.I. Phenomenalism. Philosophy and consciousness. Sensation, intelligence, and will. Ferrier's Institutes of metaphysic. Sir William Hamilton's Lectures on metaphysics. The scale of sensation or knowledge. Sir William Hamilton--consciousness of matter. Logic--Mr. Mill. Dr. Wherwell's philosophy of science. The fundamental antithesis of philosophy. The interpretation of nature. Substance and medium.--II. The author's views compared with those of other philosophers. Immediateness and reflection. What is materialism? Idealism and positivism. [B1589.G83E8 1900] 43-33562
I. Mayor, Joseph Bickersteth, 1828-1916, ed. II. Title.

GUIDE to philosophy.
New York, Dover Publications [1956] 592p. 20cm. (Dover books, T297)
1. Philosophy. I. Joad, Cyril Edwin Mitchinson, 1891-1953.

HAWKINS, Denis John Bernard, 1906-
Approach to philosophy, by D. J. B. Hawkins. Albany, Magi Books [1964] 116 p. 18 cm. "First published 1938". 66-8358
1. Philosophy. I. Title.

HUDSON, Jay William, 1874- 218
The truths we live by, by Jay William Hudson ... New York, London, D. Appleton and company, 1921. ix, [1] p., 1 l., 307, [1] p. 21 cm. [BD431.H7] 21-9622
1. Philosophy. 2. Ethics. I. Title.

HUTCHISON, John Alexander, 190
1912-
Living options in world philosophy / John A. Hutchison. Honolulu : University Press of Hawaii, c1977. vii, 316 p. ; 25 cm. Includes bibliographies and index. [B74.H85] 76-46489 ISBN 0-8248-0455-4 : 15.00
1. Philosophy. 2. Philosophy, Comparative. 3. Philosophy and religion. I. Title.

HYSLOP, James Hervey, 1854- 110
1920.
Problems of philosophy; or, Principles of epistemology and metaphysics, by James Hervey Hyslop ... New York, The Macmillan company; London, Macmillan & co. ltd., 1905. xiv, 647 p. 24 cm. [BD21.H8] 5-28654
1. Philosophy. 2. Knowledge, Theory of. 3. Metaphysics. I. Title.
Contents omitted.

KIERKEGAARD, Soren Aabye, 1813-
1855.
... Selections from the writings of Kierkegaard, translated by L. M. Hollander ... Austin, Tex., The University [1923] 239 p. incl. 2 port. 22 cm. (University of Texas bulletin. no. 2326: July 8, 1923. Comparative literature series, no. 3) Bibliography: p. 42. [PT8142.A25] 23-27325
I. Hollander, Lee Milton, 1890-tr. II. Title.
Contents omitted.

KINNEY, Bruce, 1865-1936.
Mormonism; the Islam of America, by Bruce Kinney ... New York, Chicago [etc.] Fleming H. Revell company [c1912] 3 p. l., 5-189 p. front., plates. 20 cm. (On verso of half-title: Interdenominational home mission study course. 9) At head of title: Issued under the direction of the Council of women for home missions. [Full name: Edwin Bruce Kinney] Bibliography: p. 183-185. [BN8635.K5] 12-18075
1. Mormons and Mormonism. I. Title.

LEIBNIZ, Gottfried Wilhelm, freiherr von, 1646-1716.
The philosophical works of Leibnitz ... tr. from the original Latin and French. With notes by George Martin Duncan ... New Haven, Tuttle, Morehouse & Taylor, 1890. 4 p. l., 392 p., 1 l. 23 1/2 cm. Notes (largely bibliographical): p. [366]-392. [B2558.D8] 11-19544
I. Duncan, George Martin, 1857- ed. II. Title.

LEIBNIZ, Gottfried Wilhelm freiherr von, 1646-1716.
The philosophical works of Leibnitz ... tr. from the original Latin and French, with notes by George Martin Duncan ... 2d ed. New Haven, The Tuttle, Morehouse & Taylor company, 1908. ix, 409 p. 23 1/2 cm. Notes (largely bibliographical): p. [381]-409. [B2558.D9] 8-7163
I. Duncan, George Martin, 1857- ed. II. Title.

LODGE, Oliver Joseph Sir 218
1851-
Science and human progress ... by Sir Oliver Lodge, F. R. S. New York, George H. Doran company [c1927] viii p., 1 l., 11-243 p. 21 cm. (Halley Stewart lectures, 1926) [BD431.L65 1927 a] 27-18884
1. Philosphy. 2. Religion and science—1900- 3. Progress. I. Title.

LOVELAND, E Winchester. 248
The philosophy of life. By E. Winchester Loveland. Boston, B. Marsh; New York, S. T. Munson, 1859. xi, 532 p. 20 cm. [BV4501.L6] 18-178
I. Title.

LUTHER, Martin, 1483- 230'.4'1
1546.
The wisdom of Martin Luther. [Compiled by N. Alfred Balmer] St. Louis [Published by Pyramid Publications for] Concordia Pub. House [1973] 62 p. 18 cm. [BR331.E5B34 1973] 73-78850 ISBN 0-570-03166-4 0.75 (pbk.)
I. Title.

LUTHER, Martin, 1483- 230'.4'1
1546.
The wisdom of Martin Luther. [Compiled by N. Alfred Balmer] St. Louis [Published by Pyramid Publications for] Concordia Pub. House [1973] 62 p. 18 cm. [BR331.E5B34 1973] 73-78850 ISBN 0-570-03166-4 0.75 (pbk.)
I. Title.

MCDANIEL, Ivan G., 1891- 212
Lamp of the soul; the cosmic purpose of man, as disclosed by the fundamental wisdom of all races, is to develop a conscious soul. The factors, methods, and causal means involved in realizing this state, and the findings of modern sciences and philosophy connected therewith, are herein discussed. By Ivan G. McDaniel ... Quakerstown, Pa., Philosophical publishing co., 1942. 2 p. l., [vii]-xxii, x, 513 ii p. 23 1/2 cm. (On cover: Rosicrucian series) Bibliographical foot-notes. [B945.M237L3 1942 a] 44-1323
I. Title.

MCLELLAN, George William, 201
1874-
Meaning without expression; a philosophy which includes but goes beyond the brotherhood of man, by G. W. McLellan and Nelle Irene Henry. Los Angeles, Calif., Wetzel publishing company, inc. [c1937] 5 p. l., [13]-115 p. 19 1/2 cm. [BR126.M356] 37-23955
I. Henry, Mrs. Nelle Irene (Johnson) 1889- joint author. II. Title.

MACLENNAN, Simon Fraser.
...The impersonal judgment; its nature, origin, and significance, by Simon Fraser Mac Lennan. Chicago, The University of Chicago press, 1897. 49 p. 23 1/2 cm. (University of Chicago Contributions to philosophy [v. 1] no. iv) Appeared first as the author's thesis (PH.D) University of Chicago, 1897. 5-34193
I. Title.

A manual of modern scholastic philosophy by Cardinal Mercier and professors of the Higher Institute of Philosophy, Louvain. Authorized translation, and 3d English ed. by T. L. Parker and S. A. Parker, with a preface by P. Coffey. London, Routledge & Paul; St. Louis, Mo., B. Herder Book Co. 1952-60 [v. 1, 1960] 2 v. 23cm. Vol. 2 has imprint: St. Louis, Mo., B. Herder Book Co. Translation of Traite elementaire de philosophie, made from the 4th French ed., with the aid of the 2d Italian ed.
1. Philosophy. I. Louvain. Universite catholique. Institut superieur de philosophie (Ecole Saint Thomas d'Aquin) II. Mercier, Desire Felicien Francois Joseph, Cardinal, 1851-1926.

MASSON-OURSEL, Paul.
Comparative philosophy, by Paul Masson-Oursel...with an introduction by F. G. Crookshank... London, K. Paul, Trench, Trubner & co., ltd.; New York, Harcourt, Brace & company, inc., 1926. 4 p. l., 212 p. 22 1/2 cm. (Half-title: International library of psychology, philosophy and scientific method) "Part II has been translated by V. C. C. Collum." Contains bibliographies. [B79.M37] 27-13401
1. Philosophy. I. Collum Vera Christian Chute 1883 II. Title.

MIDDLETON, George W. 1866- 218
After twenty years; a dissertation on the philosophy of life in narrative form, by Geo. W. Middleton, M.D. Salt Lake City, Press of the Deseret news, 1914. vii, 295 p. 19 cm. $1.25. [BD431.M55] 15-2078
I. Title.

NEW Mexico. University.
Philosophical series. v. 1, no. 1-2; Dec. 1918-Oct. 1, 1936. Albuquerque, University of New Mexico press [etc.] 1918-36. 1 v. in 2. 22 1/2 cm. Issued as the University of New Mexico bulletin (formerly Bulletin) whole no. 96, 295. No more published. 20-27126
I. Title.
Contents omitted.

NEWCOMB, Charles Benjamin, 1845-
Principles of psychic philosophy, by Charles B. Newcomb ... Boston, Lothrop, Lee & Shepard co., 1908. xi, 199 p. 21 cm. 8-10430
I. Title.

NEWCOMB, Charles Benjamin, 1845-1922. 218
All's right with the world, by Charles B. Newcomb ... Boston, The Philosophical publishing company, 1897. 261 p. 20 cm. [BD431.N4] 12-37256
I. Title.

NIETZSCHE, Friedrich Wilhelm, 1844-1900.
The will to power in science, nature, society & art. [Translated by Anthony M. Ludivici] New York, Frederick Publications c1960] 288 p. 66-94237
1. Philosophy. I. Title.

PALMER, Louis Philander, 1856- 133
A philosophical pot pourri or miscellany, embracing many new scientific and theological hypotheses both tentative and insistent, by Louis P. Palmer. [Rev. ed.] Paducah, Ky., Billings printing company, incorporated [c1915] 5 p. l., 270 p. front. (port.) illus. 19 1/2 cm. $1.50 [X3.P2 1915a] 16-10474
I. Title.

[PALUMBO, Anthony] 1879- 232
Who and what is Christ? An practical philosophy. By A Dove (Colombo Palumbo) [pseud.]... [Gulfport, Miss., c1933] viii, 128 p. incl. col. pl. 19 cm. [BT295.P3] 84-1738
I. Title.

PEARSON, Peter, 1848- 133.
Psycho-harmonial philosophy, by P. Pearson ... Illustrated in colors. 1st ed. Ponca City, Okla., The Harmonial publishing company, 1910. x, 13-269 p. incl. 4 col. pl., port. plates (partly col.) 24 cm. [BF1261.P3] 10-20834 3.50
I. Title.

PHILOSOPHIC inquiry;
an introduction to philosophy. Englewood Cliffs, N. J., Prentice-Hall [1958] xvi, 470p. (Prentice-Hall Philosophy series)
1. Philosophy. I. Beck, Lewis White.

PLATO.
... Selections, edited by Raphael Demos ... New York, Chicago [etc.] C. Scribner's sons [c1927] xxxviii p., 3 l., 448 p. 17 cm. (Half-title: The modern student's library. [Philosophy series]) "The text of this volume is that of the Jowett translation." "Short "Short bibliography": p. [xxxix] [B355 1927 a] 27-21482
I. Demos, Raphael, ed. II. Title.

PLUTARCHUS.
Plutarch's Morals Tr. from the Greek by several hands. Cor. and rev. by William W. Goodwin ... With an introduction by Ralph Waldo Emerson ... Boston, Little, Brown, and company, 1871. 5 v. 23 cm. "The translation of Plutarch's Morals by 'several hands' was first published in London in 1634-1694." "The name 'Morals' is used by tradition to include all the works of Plutarch except the Lives."--Editor's pref. [PA4374.M6G6 1871] 8-882
I. Goodwin, William Watson, 1831-1912, ed. II. Title.

PRINCIPLE:
the great creator. [An inquiry concerning the spiritual laws of the universe] A reflection book. New York, Comet Press, 1958. 57p. (Comet Press books)
1. Philosophy. I. Keller, Jacob Anton, 1879-

REILEY, Katharine C.
Studies in the philosophical terminology of Lucretius and Cicero, by Katharine C. Reiley, PH.D. New York, The Columbia university press, 1909. ix, 133 p. 18 1/2 cm. (Half-title: Columbia university studies in classical philology) Bibliography: p. 127-128. 9-20120
I. Title.

SCHLEIER, Sylvester Theron, 1897- 201
An analysis of man and his philosophy, by S. T. Schleier. [St. Louis, Audrey publishing co., c1935] xiii, 256 p. 24 cm. [BD21.S35] 35-8886
1. Philosophy. 2. Religion—Philosophy. 3. Religion and science—1900- I. Title.

SPINOZA, Benedictus de, 1632-1677.
... Selections, edited by John Wild ... New York, Chicago [etc.] C. Scribner's sons [c1930] ixi, [2], 479 p. illus., diagrs. 18 cm. (Half-title: The modern student's library. [Philosophy series]) At head of title: Spinoza. Bibliography: p. ix-ixi. [B3958.W5] 30-7009
I. Wild, John, 1902- ed. II. Title.

USHENKO, Andrew Paul, 1901- 110
Power and events; an essay on dynamics in philiosophy, by Andrew Paul Ushenko. Princeton, Princeton university press, 1946. xxi p., 1 l., 301 p. pl., diagrs. 22 1/2 cm. Errata slip inserted. [BD21.U8] A 46
1. Philosophy. 2. Metaphysics. 3. Perception. I. Title.

WEAVER, Richard M. 1910-
Ideas have consequences. [Chicago] University of Chicago Press [1960, c1948] vii, 189 p. 20 cm. (Phoenix books)
1. Philosophy. I. Title.

[WILLIAMS, Thomas] Calvinist preacher.
The age of infidelity; in answer to Thomas Paine's Age of reason. By a layman ... [Part I] London printed: Philadelphia, Reprinted for Stephen C. Ustick, n. 278, South Front street, 1794. 70 p. 21 cm. 4-2071
I. Title.

[WILLIAMS, Thomas] Calvinist preacher.
The age of infidelity; in answer to Thomas Paine's Age of reason. By a layman ... [Part I] The 3d ed. Worcester, (Massachusetts) Printed by Isaiah Thomas, jun. for Isaiah Thomas; sold by him at the Worcester bookstore, 1794. 50 p. 17 1/2 cm. 4-2072
I. Title.

WISE, Isaac Mayer, 1819-1900. 110
The cosmic God. A fundamental philosophy in popular lectures. By Isaac M. Wise ... Cincinnati, Office American Israelite and Deborah, 1876. 181 p. front. (port.) 21 1/2 cm. [BD701.W8] 11-24665
1. Philosophy. I. Title.

YOUNG, Warren Cameron, 1913-
A Christian approach to philosophy. Grand Rapids, Baker Book House, 1962 [c1954] 252 p. illus. 22 cm. Includes bibliographies. 63-39224
1. Philosophy. I. Title.

Philosophy—Addresses, essays, lectures.

ALDER, Mortimer Jerome, 1902-
The conditions of philosophhy; its checkered past, its present disorder, and its future promise [by] Mortimer J. Alder. [1st ed.] New York, Athencum, 1965. xi, 303 p. 22 cm. Bibliographical footnotes. NUC66
1. Hilosophy-Addresses, essays, lectures. I. Title.

BERGSON, Henri Louis, 1859-1941.
The creative mind; an introduction to metaphysics. [Translated by Mabell L. Andison] New York, Wisdom Library [196-] 252 p. NUC65
1. Bernard, Claude, 1813-1878. 2. James, William, 1842-1910. 3. Ravaisson-Mollien, Felix, 1813-1900. 4. Philosophy — Addresses, essays, lectures. 5. Metaphysics — Addresses, essays, lectures. I. Title.

BUBER, Martin, 1878-
Pointing the way; collected essays. Edited and translated with an introd. by Maurice S. Friedman. [1st Harper torchbook ed.] New York, Harper & Row [1963] xvi, 239 p. 21 cm. (Harper torchbooks. The Cloister library, TB103) 64-59309
1. Philosophy — Addresses, essays, lectures. 2. Dialectic. I. Title.

HOERNLE, Reinhold Friedrich Alfred, 1880- 110
Studies in contemporary metaphysics, by R. F. Alfred Hoernle... New York, Harcourt, Brace and Howe, 1920. viii p., 2 l., 3-314 p. 21 cm. Bibliographical footnotes. [BD111.H75] 20-4123
1. Philosophy—Addresses, essays, lectures. I. Title.

HUME, David, 1711-1776.
Essays, moral, political, and literary. [London] Oxford University Press, 1963. vii, 616 p. 65-53634
1. Philosophy—Addresses, essays, lectures. 2. Political science—Addresses, essays, lectures. I. Title.

LOGIC and knowledge;
essays, 1901-1950. Edited by Robert Charles Marsh. New York, Macmillan [1956] xi, 382p. Bibliographical footnotes.
1. Philosophy—Addresses, essays, lectures. 2. Logic, Symbolic and mathematical—Addresses, essays, lectures. I. Russell, Betrand Russell, 3d earl, 1872-

LOGIC and knowledge;
essays, 1901-1950. Edited by Robert Charles Marsh. New York, Macmillan [1956] xi, 382p. Bibliographical footnotes.
1. Philosophy—Addresses, essays, lectures. 2. Logic, symbolic and mathematical—Addresses, essays, lectures. I. Russell, Bertrand Russell, 3d earl, 1872-

MARCEL, Gabriel, 1887-
Homo vistor; introduction to a metaphysic of hope. Translated by Emma Craufurd. Chicago, H. Regnery Co., 1951. 270 p. 20 cm. A 52
1. Philosophy—Addresses, essays, lectures. I. Title.

MATSON, Howard, 1907- 252.08
The fourth wise man; a quest for reasonable certainties. [Laguna Beach, Calif.] Carlborg Blades [1954] 139p. illus. 25cm. [B29.M37] 54-13393
1. Philosophy—Addresses, essays, lectures. I. Title.

MYERS, Gerald E ed. 110.82
Self, religion, and metaphysics; essays in memory of James Bissett Pratt. New York, Macmillan, 1961. viii, 241p. port. 25cm. 'Bibliography of the works of James B. Pratt':p.235-241. Bibliographical references included in 'Notes' (p. 229-233) [B29.M94] 61-7062
1. Pratt, James Bissett, 1875-1944. 2. Philosophy—Addresses, essays, lectures. 3. Self. 4. Religion—Philosophy. 5. Metaphysics. I. Title.

NEWMAN, John Henry, Cardinal 1801-1890. 192
Philosophical readings in Cardinal Newman, edited by James Collins. Chicago, H. Regnery Co., 1961. 436p. 25cm. Includes bibliography. [BX890.N454] 61-14727
1. Philosophy—Addresses, essays, lectures. I. Collins, James Daniel., ed. II. Title.

NISHIDA, Kitaro, 1870-1945. 181'.12
Intelligibility and the philosophy of nothingness; three philosophical essays. Translated and introduced by Robert Schinzinger, in collaboration with I. Koyama and T. Kojima. Westport, Conn., Greenwood Press [1973, c1958] 251 p. illus. 22 cm. These essays were published in 1943 in German translation under title: Die intelligible Welt. Includes bibliographical references. [B5244.N55A313 1973] 72-12319 ISBN 0-8371-6689-6 10.95
1. Philosophy—Addresses, essays, lectures. 2. Philosophy, Buddhist. I. Title.

POST, Charles Cyrel, 1846- 110
Metaphysical essays. By C. C. Post. Boston, Freedom publishing company, 1895. 130 p. 17 cm. Contents.--The First Cause.--Life.--Individual life, universal energy.--Of matter, life, mind and spirit.--Thought.--Of the will.--Of matter.--Understanding, faith, desire.--God and the devil, or good and evil.--Influence of fear upon individuals.--Love; selfishness.--The value of the new faith. [BD701.P8] 11-24665
1. Philosophy—Addresses, essays, lectures. I. Title.

RATNER, Sidney, 1908- ed. 190
Vision & action; essays in honor of Horace M. Kallen on his 70th birthday. Port Washington, N.Y., Kennikat Press [1969, c1953] xvii, 277 p. port. 22 cm. (Essay and general literature index reprint series) Contents.Contents.—Academic freedom revisited, by T. V. Smith.—Human rights under the United Nations Charter, by B. V. Cohen.—The absolute, the experimental method, and Horace Kallen, by P. H. Douglas.—Some tame reflections on some wild facts, by J. Frank.—Some central themes in Horace Kallen's philosophy, by S. Ratner.—Cultural relativism and standards, by G. Boas.—The philosophy of democracy as a philosophy of history, by S. Hook.—The rational imperatives, by C. I. Lewis.—From Poe to Valery, by T. S. Eliot.—Events and the future, by J. Dewey.—Teleological explanation and teleological systems, by E. Nagel.—Ch'an (Zen) Buddhism in China: its history and method, by H. Shih.—Reconsideration of the origin and nature of perception, by A. Ames.—Horace M. Kallen: A bibliography (p. 275-277) Bibliographical footnotes. [B29.R35 1969] 68-8195
1. Philosophy—Addresses, essays, lectures. I. Kallen, Horace Meyer, 1882- II. Title.

RICHARD, James, 1767-1843. 124
Lectures on mental philosophy and theology. By James Richards... With a sketch of his life, by Samuel Gridley... New York, M. W. Dodd, 1846. viii, [9]-501 p. front. (port.) 23 1/2 cm. [BD541.R5] 11-23107
1. Philosophy—Addresses, essays, lectures. 2. Theology—Addresses, essays, lectures. I. Gridley, Samuel H. II. Title.
Contents omitted.

RICHARDS, Lysander Salmon, 1835- 110
New propositions in speculative and practical philosophy, by Lysander Salmon Richards... [Plymouth, Mass., The Memorial press, c1903] 190 p. 20 1/2 cm. [BD701.R5] 3-29610
1. Philosophy—Addresses, essays, lectures. I. Title.

SHELDON, Henry Clay, 1845-1928. 180
Pantheistic dilemmas and other essays in philosophy and religion, by Henry C. Sheldon ... New York, Cincinnati, The Methodist book concern [c1920] 358 p. 19 1/2 cm. Bibliographical foot-notes. [B56.S4] 20-8601
1. Philosophy—Addresses, essays, lectures. 2. Religion—Addresses, essays, lectures. I. Title.
Contents omitted.

SUNDELL, Albert F[rank] Oscar, 1873-
Sundell's system of philosophy. Essays and speeches, by Albert F. O. Sundell. Shelby, Mich., The Oceana herald print, 1895. 106 p. 16 1/2 cm. 3-17120
I. Title.

WHITEHEAD, Alfred North, 1861-1947.
Modes of thought. Six lectures delivered in Wellesley College, Massachusetts, and two lectures in the University of Chicago. New York, Macmillan [1956, c1938] viii, 241 p. 20 cm.
1. Philosophy — Addresses, essays, lectures. I. Title.

WHITEHEAD, Alfred North, 1861-1947.
Modes of thought; six lectures delivered in Wellesley College, Massachusetts, and two lectures in the University of Chicago. Cambridge [Eng.] University Press, 1956. 241 p. 20 cm. First published 1938. 67-32890
1. Philosophy — Addresses, essays, lectures. I. Title.

Philosophy, Ancient.

CAIRD, Edward, 1835-1908. 210'.38
The evolution of theology in the Greek philosophers. Glasgow, J. MacLahose, 1904. Grosse Pointe, Mich., Scholarly Press, 1968. 2 v. 22 cm. (Gifford lectures, 1900-1902) "Delivered in the University of Glasgow in sessions 1900-1 and 1901-2." [B187.T5C3 1968] 72-3480
1. Philosophy, Ancient. 2. Theology. 3. God (Greek religion) I. Title. II. Series.

COCKER, Benjamin Franklin, 1821-1883. 180
Christianity and Greek philosophy; or, The

relation between spontaneous and reflective thought in Greece and the positive teaching of Christ and his apostles. By B. F. Cocker ... New York, Harper & brothers, 1870. x p., 1 l., [13]-531 p. 21 cm. [B171.C66] 10-21490
1. Philosophy, Ancient. 2. Christianity. 3. Church history—Primitive and early church. I. Title.

CORNFORD, Francis MacDonald, 1874- 180
From religion to philosophy; a study in the origins of western speculations. By Francis Macdonald Cornford ... New York, Longmans, Green and co.: [etc., etc.] 1912. 2 p. l., vii-xx, 276 p. 23 cm. Printed in Great Britain. [B188.C6] 13-891
1. Philosophy, Ancient. 2. Greece—Religion. I. Title.

[CORNWALLIS, Caroline Frances] 1786-1858. 180
A brief view of Greek philosophy, from the age of Socrates to the coming of Christ. Philadelphia, Lea and Blanchard, 1846. 87 p. 17 cm. (Half-title: Small books on great subjects...No. VI) With her A brief view of Greek philosophy up to the age of Pericles. Philadelphia, 1846. [B171.C8 1846] [AC1.S6 no. 6] 878. 43-49197
1. Philosophy, Ancient. I. Title.

[CORNWALLIS, Caroline Frances] 1786-1858. 180
A brief view of Greek philosophy up to the age of Pericles. Philadelphia, Lea and Blanchard, 1846. 81 p. 17 cm. (Half-title: Small books on great subjects...No. V) With this are bound, as issued, the author's A brief view of Greek philosophy, from the age of Socrates to the coming of Christ. Philadelphia, 1846; [Clemens, Titus Flavius, Alexandrinus] Christian doctrine and practice in the second century. Philadelphia, 1846 and the author's An exposition of vulgar and common errors adapted to the year of grace MDCCCXLV. By Thomas Brown Redivivus [pseud.] Philadelphia, 1846. [B171.C8 1846] [AC1.S6 no. 5a] [AC1.M5 no. 2] 878. 878. 11-21408
1. Philosophy, Ancient. I. Title.

HACK, Roy Kenneth. 211'.0922
God in Greek philosophy to the time of Socrates. New York, B. Franklin [1970] vii, 157 p. 23 cm. (Burt Franklin research & source works series, 455) (Philosophy monograph series, 28.) Reprint of the 1931 ed. Bibliography: p. 155-157. [B188.H17 1970] 76-118174
1. Philosophy, Ancient. 2. Greece—Religion. 3. Gods. 4. Monotheism. 5. Religious thought—To 600. 6. Religious thought—Greece. I. Title.

HACK, Roy Kenneth. 180
God in Greek philosophy to the time of Socrates, by Roy Kenneth Hack... Princeton, Princeton university press for the University of Cincinnati, 1931. vii p., 1 l., 157, [2] p. 23 cm. Half-title: Published with the aid of the Charles Phelps Taft memorial fund and the Graduate school. "Select bibliography": p. 155-157. [B188.H17] 31-19555
1. Philosophy, Ancient. 2. Greece—Religion. 3. Gods. 4. Monotheism. 5. Religious thought. I. Cincinnati. University. Charles Phelps Taft memorial fund. II. Cincinnati. University. Graduate school. III. Title.

HAVELOCK, Eric Alfred.
Preface to Plato. New York, Grosset & Dunlap [1967, c1963] 328 p. 20 cm. (Universal library) Includes bibliography. 68-90156
1. Plato. 2. Phiiosophy, Ancient. 3. Greek poetry—Hist. & crit. I. Title.

METAPHYSICS in process; an introduction to the philosophy of being through its primitive history. Florham Park, N. J., Florham Park Press [c1958] iv, 211p.
1. Philosophy, Ancient. I. Papay, Joseph L

PAPAY, Joseph L
Metaphysics in process; a selected history of ancient philosophy as an introduction to the philosophy of being. Madison, N.J., Florham Park Press [c1963] xiv, 347 p. illus. 23 cm. Bibliography: p. 315-334. 65-47977
1. Philosophy, Ancient. 2. Metaphysics. I. Title.

PARTEE, Charles. 230'.4'20924
Calvin and classical philosophy / by Charles Partee. Leiden : E. J. Brill, 1977, i.e.1978 163 p. ; 25 cm. (Studies in the history of Christian thought ; v. 14) Includes indexes. Bibliography: p. [148]-158. [BX9418.P374] 77-359582 ISBN 9-00-404839-1 : 25.00
1. Calvin, Jean, 1509-1564. 2. Philosophy, Ancient. 3. Christianity—Philosophy—History. I. Title. II. Series.
Distributed by Heinman, 1966, Broadway, New York 10023

RALEIGH, Albert Sidney.
The stanzas of dzjn. Theogenesis, with commentary by Dr. A. S. Raleigh ... San Diego, Calif., Hermetic publishing company, c1915. 3 p. l., 5-189 p. 24 cm. "Theogenesis. Part two. The foundation of hermetic philosophy p. [129]-189. 15-5751 2.50
I. Title.

VEGA, Angel Custodio, 1894- 189.2
Saint Augustine, his philosophy, by Angel C. Vega ... authorized translation from the Spanish by Denis J. Kavanagh ... Philadelphia, The Peter Reilly company, 1931. xi, 264 p. 20 1/2 cm. "Authentic works of St. Augustine": p. 229-241. Translation of introduction a la flosofia de san Augustin. Bibliography: p. 242-256. [B655.27V4] 31-8778
1. Augustinus, Aurelius, Saint, bp. of Hippo. 2. Philosophy, Ancient. I. Kavanagh, Denis Joseph, 1886- tr. II. Title.

Philosophy, Ancient—Addresses, essays, lectures.

JOSEPH, Horace William Brindley, 1867- 180.4
Essays in ancient & modern philosophy, b H. W. B. Joseph ... Oxford, The Clarendon press, 1935. 4 p. l., 340 p. 23 cm. Contents.--Plato's Republic: the argument with Polemarchus.--Plato's Republic: the argument with Thrasymachus.--Plato's Republic: the nature of the soul.--Plato's Republic: the comparison between the soul and the state.--Plato's Republic: the proof that the most just man is the happiest.--Aristotle's definition of moral virtue and Plato's account of justice in the soul.--Purposive action.--A comparison of Kant's idealism with that of Berkeley.--The syntheses of sense and understanding in Kant's Kritik of pure reason.--The schematism of the categories in Kant's Kritik of pure reason.--The concept of evolution. [B29.J6] 36-4486
1. Philosophy, Ancient—Addresses, essays, lectures. 2. Philosophy Modern—Addresses, essays, lectures. I. Title.

Philosophy and religion.

ANSELM, Saint, abp. of Canterbury 1033-1109. 189.
Proslogium; Monologium; and appendix, In behalf of the fool, by Gaunilon; and Cur Deus homo; tr. from the Latin by Sidney Norton Deane, B.S., with an introduction, bibliography, and reprints of the opinions of leading philosophers and writers on the ontological argument. Chicago, The Open court publishing company; [etc., etc.] 1903. xxxv, 288 p. 20 1/2 cm. (On cover: Philosophical classics, Religion of science library, no. 54) Bibliography: p. xxv-xxvi. [B765.A88P73] 3-25305
I. Deane, Sidney Norton, tr. II. Gaunilon, 11th cent. III. Title.

BASCOM, John, 1827-1911. 180
Science, philosophy and religion. Lectures delivered before the Lowell institute, Boston. By John Bascom ... New York, G. P. Putnam & sons, 1871. iv, 311 p. 19 cm. [B56.B3 1871] 10-21502
1. Philosophy and religion. 2. Religion and science—1860-1899. I. Title.

BECK, Lewis White 190
Six secular philosophers. New York, Free Pr. [1966, c.1960] 126p. 20cm. Bibl. [BD573.B4] 1.95 pap.,
1. Philosophy and religion. 2. Secularism. I. Title.

BECK, Lewis White.
Six secular philosophers, [1st Free Press paperbacked.] New York, Free Press [1966, c1960] 126 p. 21 cm. (Free Press paperback, 90212) Includes bibliography. NUC67
1. Philosophy and religion. 2. Secularism. I. Title.

BECK, Lewis White. 190
Six secular philosophers. [1st ed.] New York, Harper [1960] 126 p. 20 cm. Includes bibliography. [BD573.B4] 60-11769
1. Philosophy and religion. 2. Secularism. I. Title.

[BELL, William Mara]
The rise of man; an interlude in philosophy, by William Marabell [pseud.] ... 2d ed. [San Francisco] The author [c1906] 562 p. 20 cm. Contents.--On life and literature.--On law and government.--On marriage and morals.--On science and religion.--On race, creed and color. 6-42962
I. Title.

BEWKES, Eugene Garrett, 1895- 201
The Western heritage of faith and reason [by] Eugene G. Bewkes [and others. Rev. ed. by] J. Calvin Keene. New York, Harper & Row [1963] 703 p. illus. 25 cm. First ed. published in 1940 under title: Experience, reason and faith: a survey in philosophy and religion. [BL51.B55] 63-9052
1. Philosophy and religion. 2. Religious thought — Hist. 3. Judaism. I. Keene, James Calvin. II. Title.

BLOESCH, Donald G., 1928- 230.5'7
The ground of certainty; toward an evangelical theology of revelation, by Donald G. Bloesch. Grand Rapids, Eerdmans [1971] 212 p. 21 cm. Includes bibliographical references. [BR100.B517] 76-142899 3.25
1. Philosophy and religion. I. Title.

BLONDEL, Maurice, 1861-1949. 239
The letter on apologetics, and History and dogma. Texts presented and translated by Alexander Dru and Illtyd Trethowan. [1st ed.] New York, Holt, Rinehart and Winston [1965, c1964] 301 p. port. 22 cm. Translation of Lettre sur les exigences de la pensee contemporaine en matiere d'apologetique et sur la methode de la philosophie dans l'etude du probleme reliqieux, and Historie et dogme. Bibliography: p. [289]-293. [B2430.B584L43] 65-12073
1. Philosophy and religion. 2. Apologetics—Methodology. 3. Tradition (Theology) 4. History—Philosophy. I. Dru, Alexander, ed. and tr. II. Trethowan, Illtyd, 1907- ed. and tr. III. Blondel, Maurice, 1861-1949. History and dogma. IV. Title.

BOETHIUS, d.524. 189'.4
The consolation of philosophy. Translated with an introd. by V. E. Watts. Baltimore, Penguin Books [1969] 187 p. 19 cm. (The Penguin classics, L208) Bibliography: p. 171-[174] [B659.C2E59 1969] 71-4931 1.45
1. Philosophy and religion. 2. Happiness. I. Watts, V. E., tr. II. Title.

BOETHIUS, d.524. 100
The consolation of philosophy / by Boethius ; translated by W.V. Cooper. Chicago, Ill. : Regnery Gateway, 1981. 120 p. ; 18 cm. Translation of: De consolatione philosophiae. [B659.D472E5 1981] 19 81-52212 ISBN 0-89526-885-X (pbk.) : 3.95
1. Philosophy and religion. 2. Happiness. I. Cooper, W. V. 1876- (Wilbraham Villiers), II. [De consolatione philosophiae.] English III. Title.

BOETHIUS, d. 524. 189.4
The consolation of philosophy. [From the Latin] tr. of I. T. Ed., introd. by William Anderson. Carbondale, Southern Ill. Univ. Pr. [1964, c.1963] 118p. 26cm. (Centaur classics) 63-8903 12.00
1. Philosophy and religion. 2. Happiness. I. Title.

BOETHIUS, d. 524. 189.4
The consolation of philosophy. Tr. [from Latin] introd., notes, by Richard Green. Indianapolis, Bobbs [1963, c.1962] 134p. 21cm. (Lib. of liberal arts, 86) 62-11788 1.25 pap.,
1. Philosophy and religion. 2. Happiness. I. Title.

BONAVENTURA, Saint, cardinal, 1221-1274. 201
Saint Bonaventure's De reductione artium ad theologiam; a commentary with an introduction and translation ... by Sister Emma Therese Healy ... Saint Bonaventure, N.Y., Saint Bonaventure college, 1939. xi p., 1 l., 212 p. 23 cm. Thesis (PH. D)--Saint Bonaventure college, 1939. "Principal dated works": p. 25 "Less important or not dated works": p. 25,26. Bibliography: p. [203]-208. [BX890.B67316] 40-35356
1. Philosophy and religion. I. Healy, Emma Therese, sister, 1892- II. Title.
contents omitted.

BROWN, Colin. 201
Philosophy and the Christian faith; a historical sketch from the Middle Ages to the present day. [1st ed.] Chicago, Inter-varsity Press [1969] 319 p. 20 cm. (A Tyndale paperback) "A note on books": p. [291]-309. [BR100.B65] 68-58083 12/-
1. Philosophy and religion. 2. Christianity—Philosophy. I. Title.

CARR, Herbert Wildon 1857- 201
Changing backgrounds in religion and ethics; a metaphysical meditation, by Herbert Wildon Carr ... New York, The Macmillan company, 1927. 224 p. 20 cm. [BL51.C35] 27-2868
1. Philosophy and religion. 2. Ethics. 3. Metaphysics. I. Title.

CATHOLIC University of America. Workshop on Christian Philosophy and Religious Renewal, 1964. 201
Christian philosophy in the college and seminary; [proceedings] Edited by George F. McLean. Washington, Catholic University of America Press, 1966. vii, 193 p. 23 cm. Bibliographical footnotes. [B52.C34] 66-9148
1. Philosophy and religion. 2. Philosophy — Study and teaching. I. McLean, George F., ed. II. Title.

CATHOLIC University of America. Workshop on Philosophy and the Integration of Contemporary Catholic Education, 1961. 377.82
Philosophy and the integration of contemporary Catholic education; the proceedings. Edited by George F. McLean. Washington, Catholic University of America Press, 1962. x, 366 p. 22 cm. Bibliography: p. 327-353. Bibliographical footnotes. [B52.C35] 62-53243
1. Philosophy and religion. 2. Philosophy — Study and teaching. 3. Catholic Church — Education. I. McLean, George F., ed. II. Title.

CLARKE, John Caldwell Calhoun. 201
Man and his divine father, by John C. C. Clarke, D.D. Chicago, A. C. McClurg & co., 1900. 364 p. 20 cm. [BL51.C55] 0-2599
1. Philosophy and religion. 2. God. 3. Christianity—Evidences. 4. Man. I. Title.

COPLESTON, Frederick Charles. 110
Religion and philosophy / Frederick C. Copleston. New York : Barnes & Noble, 1974. x, 195 p. ; 23 cm. Includes bibliographical references and index. [B56.C62 1974] 73-21365 ISBN 0-06-491282-5 : 16.00
1. Philosophy and religion. I. Title.

ECLIPSE of God; studies in the relation between religion and philosophy. New York, Harper [1957, c1952] 152p. 21cm. (Harper torchbooks)
1. Philosophy and religion. I. Buber, Martin, 1878- II. Series.

[EDGERLY, Webster] 370
The Shaftesbury school of philosophy known as the story of our existences or the doctrine of diversity, by Edmund Shaftesbury [pseud.] ... Washington, D.C., Shaftesbury college [c1894] 1 p. l., 541 p. incl. port. front. 25 cm. [LC6001.S5E4] 12-32075
I. Title.

FISKE, John, 1842-1901.
... The historical writings of John Fiske.

Illustrated with many photogravures, maps, charts, facsimiles, etc. [Standard library ed. Boston and New York, Houghton, Mifflin and company, 1902] 12 v. fronts., plates, ports, maps, plans, facsims. 23 cm. Half-title. Another issue of v. 1-12 of The writings of John Fiske. Contents.--v. 1-3. The discovery of America.--v. 4-5. Old Virginia and her neighbours.--v. 6. The beginnings of New England.--v. 7-8. The Dutch and Quaker colonies in America.--v. 9. New France and New England.--v. 10-11. The American revolution.--v. 12. The critical period of American history, 1783-1789. Bibliographical note: v. 6, p. 349-[361]; v. 12, p. 421-429. A 13
I. Title.

FISKE, John, 1842-1901.
... The historical writings of John Fiske. Illustrated with many photogravures, maps, charts, facsimiles, etc. [Standard library ed. Boston and New York, Houghton, Mifflin and company, 1902] 12 v. fronts., plates, ports, maps, plans, facsims. 23 cm. Half-title. Another issue of v. 1-12 of The writings of John Fiske. Contents.--v. 1-3. The discovery of America.--v. 4-5. Old Virginia and her neighbours.--v. 6. The beginnings of New England.--v. 7-8. The Dutch and Quaker colonies in America.--v. 9. New France and New England.--v. 10-11. The American revolution.--v. 12. The critical period of American history, 1783-1789. Bibliographical note: v. 6, p. 349-[361]; v. 12, p. 421-429. A 13
I. Title.

FRANK, Erich, 1883- 201
Philosophical understanding and religious truth [by] Erich Frank. New York, Oxford, 1966[c.1945] xii, 209p. 21cm. (Galaxy bk. GB174) Bibl. Rev. of the Mary E. Flexner lects. delivered at Bryn Mawr in 1943. [BL51.F68] 45-1882 1.50 pap.,
1. Philosophy and religion. I. Title.

FRANK, Erich, 1883- 201
Philosophical understanding and religious truth [by] Erich Frank. London, New York [etc.] Oxford university press, 1945. x, 209 p. 22 cm. A revision of the Mary E. Flexner lectures delivered at Bryn Mawr in 1943. cf. Pref. "First edition." Bibliographical references included in "Notes" at end of each chapter. [BL51.F68] 45-1882
1. Philosophy and religion. I. Title.

GILSON, Etienne Henry, 1884- 201
Christianity and philosophy [by] Etienne Gilson ... translated by Ralph MacDonald, C. S. B. New York, London, Pub. for the Institute of mediaeval studies by Sheed & Ward, 1939. xxvi, 134 p. 24 cm. Bibliographical references in "Notes" (p. 127-132) [BR100.G54] 40-4537
1. Philosophy and religion. 2. Apologetics—20th cent. I. MacDonald, Ralph, 1915- tr. II. Title.

GILSON, Etienne Henry, 1884--
Elements of Christian philosophy. [New York] New American Library [1963] 380 p. 18 cm. (A Mentor-omega book) 64-24603
I. Title.

GILSON, Etienne Henry, 1884- 921.4
The philosopher and theology. Tr. from French by Cecile Gilson. New York, Random [c.1962] 236p. 24cm. 62-8440 3.75
1. Philosophy and religion. I. Title.

GILSON, Etienne Henry, 1884- 189
Reason and revelation in the middle ages, by Etienne Gilson. New York, Scribners [1961, c.1938] 114p. (Scribner lib. SL37) Bibl. 1.25 pap.,
1. Philosophy and religion. 2. Philosophy, Medieval. I. Title.

GROVER, Delo Corydon.
The volitional element in knowledge and belief; and other essays in philosophy and religion, by Delo Corydon Grover ... introduction by Francis J. McConnell ... Boston, Sherman, French & company, 1911. 3 p. l., ix, 168 p. 21 cm. 11-13723 1.20
I. Title.

GUGGENHEIMER, Samuel H. 211
The need of a new Bible and a creedless church, by Samuel H. Guggenheimer ... New York, Greenberg [c1929] xvii p., 1 l., 388 p. 22 cm. [BL2775.G79] 29-2618
I. Title.

GURNHILL, James. 201
Interpretation of the spiritual philosophy, by Rev. Canon J. Gurnhill ... London, New York [etc.] Longmans, Green and co., 1920. xi, 179, [1] p. 23 cm. [BL51.G9] 20-20214 3.40
I. Title. II. Title: Spiritual philosophy.

GURNHILL, James, 1836-
Christian philosophy discussed under the topics of absolute values, creative evolution and religion, by Rev. Canon J. Gurnhill ... London, New York [etc.] Longmans, Green and co., 1921. xi, 100 p. 23 cm. [B1641.G53C5] 22-209
I. Title.

HEPBURN, Ronald W. 201
Christianity and paradox; critical studies in twentieth-century theology [by] Ronald W. Hepburn. New York, Pegasus [1968, c1958] ix, 210 p. 21 cm. "A Pegasus original." [BD573.H4 1968] 68-17550
1. Philosophy and religion. 2. Theology, Doctrinal—History—20th century. I. Title.

HICK, John, ed.
Faith and the philosophers. Edited by John Hick. London, New York, Macmillan & Co., 1964. viii, 255 p. 23 cm. "This...is the product of a two-day conference...held at the Princeton Theological Seminary, Princeton, New Jersey". 65-80033
1. Barth, Karl, 1886- 2. Philosophy and religion. I. Title.

HODGES, Herbert Arthur, 1905-
Languages, standpoints and attitudes. London, New York, Oxford University Press, 1953. 68p. 23cm. (Riddell memorial lectures, 24th ser.) At head of title: University of Durham. A56
1. Philosophy and religion. 2. Semantics (Philosophy) I. Title. II. Series.

HYDE, William De Witt, 1858- 1917. 113
Practical idealism, by William De Witt Hyde ... New York, The Macmillan company; London, Macmillan & co., ltd., 1905. xi, 335 p. 20 cm. Contents.--pt. i. The natural world.--pt. ii. The spiritual world. [BD523.H9 1905] 34-41708
1. Philosophy and religion. 2. Idealism. I. Title.

IINO, Norimoto, 1908- 201
A seven-hued rainbow. New York, Philosophical Library [1967] 127 p. 22 cm. Bibliography: p. 126-127. [BL51.I58] 66-26966
1. Philosophy and religion. 2. Philosophy, Japanese. 3. Christianity—Japan. I. Title.

INGE, William Ralph, 1860- 201
Science and ultimate truth, Fison memorial lecture, 1926, delivered at Guy's hospital medical school, March 25, 1926, by the Very Rev. W. R. Inge ... New York, London [etc.] Longmans, Green and co., 1926. 82 p. 22 cm. Printed in Great Britain. [BL51.I 6] 26-27495
1. Philosophy and religion. 2. Religion and sciences. I. Title.

JAMISON, David Lee, 1867- 201
Philosophy studies religion, by David Lee Jamison ... New York [etc.] Fleming H. Revell company [c1937] 192 p. 20 cm. Bibliography: p. 188-189. [BL51.J3] 37-5964
1. Philosophy and religion. 2. Christianity—Philosophy. I. Title.

JONES, William Tudor, 1865- 180
The spiritual ascent of man, by W. Tudor Jones, D. PHIL., with an introduction by A. L. Smith ... New York and London, G. P. Putnam's sons, 1917. x p., 1 l., 247 p. 20 cm. [B56.J6 1917] 17-5700 1.50
1. Philosophy and religion. 2. Religion and science. I. Title.

KANT, Immanuel, 1724-1804. 198.2
Religion within the limits of reason alone, by Immanuel Kant; translated with an introduction and notes by Theodore M. Green ... and Hoyt H. Hudson ... Chicago, London, The Open court publishing company [c1934] lxxxv, 200 p. 24 cm. "The content of this introduction has been taken largely from ... [t. M. Green's] doctoral dissertation ... presented in 1924 at the University of Edinburg ... Professor Hudson ... [assisted] in the selection, condensation, and extensive rewriting of this material."--Foot-note, p. ix. [B2789.E5G7] 34-22775
1. Philosophy and religion. I. Greene, Theodore, Mever, 1897- tr. II. Hudson, Hoyt Hopewell, joint tr. III. Title.

KAUFMANN, Walter Arnold 201
The faith of a heretic. Garden City, N.Y., Doubleday, 1961 [c.1959-1961] 432p. Bibl. 61-9523 4.95
1. Philosophy and religion. I. Title.

KAUFMANN, Walter Arnold 201
The faith of a heretic. Garden City, N.Y., Doubleday [1963, c.1959-1961] 414p. 18cm. (Anchor bk., A336) Bibl. 1.45 pap.,
1. Philosophy and religion. I. Title.

KAUFMANN, Walter Arnold. 201
The faith of a heretic / by Walter Kaufmann. New York : New American Library, c1978. xiii, 414 p. ; 21 cm. "A Meridian book." Bibliography: p. [407]-414. [BL51.K34 1978] 78-103407 ISBN 0-452-00482-9 pbk. : 4.95
1. Philosophy and religion. I. Title.

LEGANT, William 110
Metaphysical teachings; how they differ from orthodox theology. New York, Exposition [c.1963] 93p. 22cm. 63-6332 3.50
1. Philosophy and religion. I. Title.

LEGANT, William. 110
Metaphysical teachings; how they differ from orthodox theology. [1st. ed.) New York, Exposition Press [1963] 93 p. 23 cm. [BD573.L4] 63-6332
1. Hilosophy and religion. I. Title.

THE Literary and philosophical repertory: embracing discoveries and improvements in the physical sciences; the liberal and fine arts; essays moral and religious; occasional notices and reviews of new publications; and articles of miscellaneous intelligence. Ed. by a number of gentlemen. v. 1-2; Apr. 1812-May 1817. Middlebury, Vt., Printed for S. Swift by T. C. Strong [etc., 1812-17] 2 v. 22 cm. Vol. 2 has imprint: Middlebury, Vt., Printed and published by T. C. Strong. [AP2.L559] 7-22278 051

LOUX, Du Bois Henry, 1867- 232.
Reform philosophy to the mind of Christ, by Du Bois H. Loux, PH. D. Jackson, Mich., Palestine endowment travel fund, 1929. 1 p. l., xi, [1], 91 p. 20 cm. Blank pages for "Reader's notes" (91) [BT590.P5L6] 29-11899
1. Jesus Christ. 2. Philosophy and religion. I. Title.

LOWBER, James William, 1847-
Thought and religion; or, The mutual contributions of philosophy and theology [by] James William Lowber ... Boston [etc.] R. G. Badger [c1912] 4 p. l., 5-250 p. 20 cm. 12-18076 1.50
I. Title.

MACQUARRIE, John.
An existentialist theology; a comparison of Heidegger and Bultmann. New York, Harper & Row [1960] x, 252 p. 21 cm. Includes bibliographical references. 68-62834
1. Heidegger, Martin, 1889- 2. Bultmann, Rudolf Karl, 1884- 3. Philosophy and religion. 4. Christianity—Philosophy. 5. Existentialism. I. Title.

MAKRAKES, Apostolos, 1831- 1905. 260.7
The political philosophy of the Orthodox Church, by Apostolos Makrakis. Translated from the Greek by D. Cummings. Chicago, Orthodox Christian Educational Society, 1965. 162 p. 21 cm. [BL51.M24813] 77-16996
1. Orthodox Eastern Church—Doctrinal and controversial works. 2. Philosophy and religion. 3. Political science. I. Title.

MAN, Myth and maturity.
Boston, The Minns Lecturship Committee, 1958. 67p. (The Minns Lectures for 1958)
1. Philosophy and religion. I. Ross, Floyd Hiatt.

MASARYK, Tomas Garrigue, 200'.1
Pres. Czechoslovak Republic, 1850-1937.
Modern man and religion [by] Thomas Garrigue Masaryk. Translated by Ann Bibza and Vacla[v] Benes. Translation rev. by H. E. Kennedy. With a pref. by Vasil K. Skrach. Freeport, N.Y., Books for Libraries Press [1970] viii, 320 p. 23 cm. Translations of Moderni clovek a nabozenstvi, Jak pracovat, and Idealy humanitni. Reprint of the 1938 ed. [BL51.M47 1970] 74-107816
1. Philosophy and religion. I. Title.

MASARYK, Tomas Garrigue, 200'.1
Pres. Czechoslovak Republic, 1850-1937.
Modern man and religion. Translated by Ann Bibza and Vaclar Benes. Translation rev. by H. E. Kennedy. With a pref. by Vasil K. Skrach. Westport, Conn., Greenwood Press [1970] viii, 320 p. 23 cm. Translations of Moderni clovek a nabozenstvi, Jak pracovat, and Idealy humanitni. Includes bibliographical references. [BL51.M47 1970b] 78-109783 ISBN 0-8371-4273-3
1. Philosophy and religion. I. Title.

MASCALL, Eric Lionel, 1905-
Words and images, a study in cxi, 132p. 20cm. New York, Longmans, Green [1957]
1. Philosophy and religion. 2. Christianity—Philosophy. 3. Knowledge, Theory of (Religion). I. Title. II. Title: heological discourse.

MATHER, Cotton, 1663-1728. 204
Selections from Cotton Mather, edited with an introduction and notes by Kenneth B. Murdock. New York, Harcourt, Brace and company [c1926] ixiii, 377 p. 17 1/2 cm. (Half-title: American authors series, general editor, S. T. Williams) "Selected reading list": p. ixi-ixiii. [BX7117.M25] 26-12606
I. Murdock, Kenneth Ballard, 1895- ed. II. Title.

MEAKIN, Frederick, 1848-1923. 201
Nature and deity; a study of religion as a quest of the ideal, by Frederick Meakin... Chicago, C. H. Kerr & company [1895) 1 p. l., 5-136 p. 20 1/2 cm. [BL51.M48] 34-30344
1. Philosophy and religion. 2. Natural theology. 3. Idealism. I. Title.

MILLER, Theodore Augustus, 1885- 201
The mind behind the universe; a book of faith for the modern mind, by Theodore A. Miller. New York, Frederick A. Stokes company, 1928. x, 201 p. 19 1/2 cm. [BL51.M64] 28-12453
1. Philosophy and religion. 2. God. I. Title.

MILTNER, Charles Christopher, 1886- 218
Progressive ignorance; a little book of familiar essays, by Charles C. Miltner ... St. Louis, Mo. [etc.] B. Herder book co., 1925. 3 p. l., 96 p. 19 1/2 cm. [BD431.M68] 25-17355
I. Title.

MOORE, Edward Caldwell, 1857-
An outline of the history of Christian thought since Kant, by Edward Caldwell Moore ... New York, C. Scribner's sons, 1912. x p., 1 l., 249 p. 19 cm. (On verso of half-title: Studies in theology) Bibliography: p. 243-246. [BR450.M7] 12-29045
1. Philosophy and religion. 2. Philosophy, Modern—Hist. 3. Church history—19th cent. I. Title.

MORRISON, Bakewell. 110
Think & live [by] Bakewell Morrison ... and Stephen J. Rueve ... New York, Milwaukee [etc.] The Bruce publishing company [c1937] vii, 183 p. diagr. 22 1/2 cm. (Half-title: Science and culture series. J. Husslein ... general editor) "This volume is a presentation of part of Scholastic philsophy."--Author's pref. [BD125.M6] 37-31474
1. Philosophy and religion. I. Rueve, Stephen J., joint author. II. Title.

NEW York University Institute of Philosophy, 4th, 1960. 201
Religious experience and truth; a symposium, edited by Sidney Hook. [New York] New York University Press, 1961. xiii, 333 p. 21 cm. "Proceedings of the fourth annual New York University

Institute of Philosophy ... New York, October 21-22, 1960." Includes bibliographical references. [BL51.N47 1960] 61-15886
1. Philosophy and religion. 2. Symbolism. 3. Faith. 4. Knowledge, Theory of (Religion) I. Hook, Sidney, 1902- ed. II. New York University. III. Title.

*OBERFIELD, William J., 1921- 211
The conflict within; a heretic's views. New York. Exposition [1968] 106p. 21cm. (EP 46802) 4.00
1. Philosophy and religion. I. Title.

PHILLIPS, Dewi Zephaniah. 200'.1
Faith and philosophical enquiry [by] D. Z. Phillips. New York, Schocken Books [1971, c1970] viii, 277 p. 20 cm. Bibliography: p. 273-277. [B56.P48 1971] 79-135520 ISBN 0-8052-3366-0
1. Philosophy and religion. 2. Belief and doubt. I. Title.

RASHDALL, Hastings, 1858-1924. 201
Philosophy and religion; six lectures delivered at Cambridge. Westport, Conn., Greenwood Press [1970] xvi, 189 p. 23 cm. Reprint of the 1910 ed. Contents.Contents.—Mind and matter.—The universal cause.—God and the moral consciousness.—Difficulties and objections.—Revelation.—Christianity. Includes bibliographical references. [B56.R3 1970] 79-98791
1. Philosophy and religion. 2. Christianity.

RASHDALL, Hastings, 1858-1924. 201
Philosophy and religion; six lectures delivered at Cambridge by Hastings Rashdall ... New York, C. Scribner's sons, 1910. xvi, 189 p. 19 cm. (On cover: Studies in theology) "Literature" at end of each lecture except no. iv. [B56.R3 1910] 35-22147
1. Philosophy and religion. 2. Christianity. I. Title.
Contents omitted.

ROHRBAUGH, Lewis Guy. 180
Religious philosophy, by Lewis Guy Rohrbaugh... New York, George H. Doran company [c1923] ix p., 2 l., 15-183 p. 19 1/2 cm. $1.60 [B56.R6] 23-11204
1. Philosophy and religion. I. Title.

ROSMARIN, Trude (Weiss) Mrs. 201
Religion of reason; Hermann Cohen's system of religious philosophy, by Trude Weiss Rosmarin. New York, Bloch publishing company, 1936. xi, 195 p. 21 cm. Bibliography: p. [177]-195. [BL51.C58R6] 36-6092
1. Cohen, Hermann, 1842-1918. 2. Philosophy and religion. I. Title.

RYAN, John Kenneth, 1897- ed.
John Duns Scotus, 1265-1965. Edited by John K. Ryan and Bernardine M. Bonansea. Washington, D.C., Catholic University of America, Press, 1965. vii, 387 p. 23 cm. (Studies in philosophy and the history of philosophy, v. 3) Bibliographical footnotes. 66-46540
I. Title.

SCHELER, Max Ferdinand, 1874-1928. 100
On the eternal in man. Translated by Bernard Noble. [Hamden, Conn.] Archon Books, 1972 [c1960] 480 p. 23 cm. Translation of Vom Ewigen im Menschen. "Bibliography of Scheler's published works": p. [457]-461. [BL51.S423 1972] 72-6599 ISBN 0-208-01280-X 15.00
1. Philosophy and religion. 2. Religion—Philosophy. I. Title.

SCHELER, Max Ferdinand, 1874-1928. 201
On the eternal in man; translated by Bernard Noble. New York, Harper [1961, c1960] 480 p. 23 cm. "Bibliography of Scheler's published works": p. [457]-461. Bibliographical footnotes. [BL51.S423 1961] 61-7349
1. Philosophy and religion. 2. Religion—Philosophy. I. Title.

SMART, Ninian, 1927- 200'.1
Philosophers and religious truth. [2d ed. 1st American ed. New York] Macmillan [1970, c1969] xii, 211 p. 18 cm. Includes bibliographical references. [BL51.S569 1970] 74-102974 1.95
1. Philosophy and religion. I. Title.

SMITH, Alan Gordon. 124
The Western dilemma. London, New York, Longmans, Green [1954] 186p. 19cm. [BD573.S56] 54-27383
1. Philosophy and religion. 2. Philosophy, Modern. I. Title.

SMITH, John Edwin 211
Reason and God; encounters of philosophy and religion. New Haven, Yale Univ. Pr. [1967, c.1961] xv, 274p. 21cm. (Y181) 1.75 pap.,
1. Philosophy and religion. I. Title.

SMITH, John Edwin. 211
Reason and God; encounters of philosophy with religion. New Haven, Yale University Press, 1961. 274 p. 23 cm. [BL51.S577] 61-15002
1. Philosophy and religion. I. Title.

SPARSHOTT, F. E.
An enquiry into goodness and related concepts; with some remarks on the nature and scope of such enquiries. [Toronto] University of Toronto Press, 1958. xiv, 304 p. Bibliographical footnotes.
I. Title.

SPIER, J M 1902-
An introduction to Christian philosophy; translated by David Hugh Freeman. 2d ed. Philadelphia, Presbyterian and Reformed Pub. Co., 1966 [c1954] 269 p. 21 cm. Translation of Een inleiding tot de wijsbegeerte der wetsidee. 68-72174
1. Philosophy and religion. 2. Christianity—Philosophy. 3. Knowledge, Theory of. 4. Sociology. I. Title.

SPIER, J.M., 1902-
An introduction to Christian philosophy. Translated by David Hugh Freeman. 2d ed. Nutley, N.J., Craig Press, 1966. vii, 269 p. 20 cm. (University series: philosophical studies) 67-57882
1. Philosophy and religion. 2. Christianity — Philosophy. 3. Knowledge, Theory of. I. Title.

STRONG, Augustus Hopkins, 1836- 180
Philosophy and religion; a series of addresses, essays and sermons designed to set forth great truths in popular form, by Augustus Hopkins Strong ... 2d ed. Philadelphia, Griffith and Rowland press, 1912. xv, 637 p. 22 cm. $1.00. [B56.S8 1912] 12-11754
1. Philosophy and religion. I. Title.

STRONG, Augustus Hopkins, 1836-1921. 201
Philosophy and religion; a series of addresses, essays and sermons designed to set forth great truths in popular form, by Augustus Hopkin Strong ... New York, A. C. Armstrong and son, 1888. xv, [1], 632 p. 25 cm. [BR85.S83 1888] 30-31433
1. Philosophy and religion. I. Title.

TEMPLE, William, abp. of York, 1881- 204
Christianity in thought and practice; three lectures delivered at Mandel hall, University of Chicago, by William Temple, archbishop of York. New York, Milwaukee, Morehouse publishing co., 1936. 112 p. 22 1/2 cm. [Moody lectures, University of Chicago] [BR85.T385] 36-11180
1. Philosophy and religion. 2. Christian ethics—Anglican authors. I. Title.
Contents omitted.

TEMPLE, William, abp. of Canterbury, 1881- 204
Christianity in thought and practice; three lectures delivered at Mandel hall, University of Chicago, by William Temple, archbishop of York. New York, Milwaukee, Morehouse publishing co., 1936. 112 p. 22 1/2 cm. [Moody lectures, University of Chicago] [BR85.T385] 36-11180
1. Philosophy and religion. 2. Christian ethics—Anglican-authors. I. Title.
Contents omitted.

TEMPLE, William, Abp. of Canterbury, 1881-1944.
Mens creatrix; an essay. London, Macmillan; New York, St. Martin's Press, 1961 [1917] xiii, 367, [1] p. 22 cm. 68-22303
1. Philosophy and religion. 2. Knowledge, Theory of. 3. Aesthetics. 4. Ethics. I. Title.

TOULMIN, Stephen Edelston. 200'.1
Metaphysical beliefs; three essays by Stephen Toulmin, Ronald W. Hepburn [and] Alasdair Macintyre. With a pref. by Alasdair MacIntyre. New York, Schocken Books [1970] xii, 206 p. 23 cm. Includes bibliographical references. [BD573.T6 1970b] 75-13956 5.95
1. Philosophy and religion. I. Hepburn, Ronald W. II. MacIntyre, Alasdair C. III. Title.

VAN TIL, Cornelius, 1895- 201
Christianity and idealism. Philadelphia, Presbyterian and Reformed Pub. Co., 1955. 139p. 23cm. [BR100.V3] 55-9041
1. Philosophy and religion. 2. Idealism. I. Title.

WAGERS, Charles Herndon, 1910-
Christian faith and philosophical inquiry. Lexington, Ky., The College of the Bible, 1961. 80 p. 23 cm. (The College of the Bible. Spring lectures, 1959)
1. Philosophy and religion. I. Title. II. Series.

WAGERS, Herndon 234.2
Christian faith and philosophical inquiry. Lexington, Ky., College of the Bible, 1961. 80p. (Coll. of the Bible spring lectures, 1959) 61-66146 1.50 pap.,
1. Philosophy and religion. 2. Christianity—Philosophy. I. Title.

WEBB, Clement Charles Julian, 1865- 231
Divine personality and human life; being the Gifford lectures delivered in the years 1918 & 1919, second course, by Clement C. J. Webb ... Aberdeen, The University, 1920. 291 p. 22 1/2 cm. (Half-title: Aberdeen university studies, no. 80) [BT101.W18 1920] 23-832
1. Philosophy and religion. 2. God. 3. Personality. 4. Gifford lectures, 1918-1919. I. Title.

WEBB, Clement Charles Julian, 1865- 231
Divine personality and human life; being the Gifford lectures delivered in the University of Aberdeen in the years 1918 & 1919, second course, by Clement C. J. Webb ... London G. Allen and Unwin ltd. New York The Macmillan company 1920 291 p. 22 cm. (Half-title: Library of philosophy, ed. by J. H. Muirhead) [BT101.W18] 20-12837
1. Philosophy and religion. 2. God. 3. Personality. I. Title.

WEBB, Clement Charles Julian, 1865-1954. 211
Divine personality and human life. Freeport, N.Y., Books for Libraries Press [1972] 291 p. 23 cm. Reprint of the 1920 ed., issued in series: Gifford lectures, 1918-19 and Library of philosophy. Includes bibliographical references. [BT101.W18 1972] 77-37917 ISBN 0-8369-6754-2
1. Philosophy and religion. 2. God. 3. Personality. I. Title. II. Series: Gifford lectures, 1918-1919. III. Series: Library of philosophy.

WILSON, John, 1928- 201
Philosophy and religion; the logic of religious belief. London, New York, Oxford University Press, 1961. 119 p. 19 cm. Includes bibliography. [BL51.W62 1961] 61-19355
1. Philosophy and religion. I. Title.

WILSON, John, 1928- 200'.1
Philosophy and religion : the logic of religious belief / John Wilson. Westport, Conn. : Greenwood Press, 1979, c1961. vii, 119 p. ; 23 cm. Reprint of the ed. published by Oxford University Press, London. Includes index. Bibliography: p. 118. [BL51.W62 1979] 78-14000 ISBN 0-313-20738-0 lib. bdg. : 14.00
1. Philosophy and religion. I. Title.

WILSON, John Boyd, 1928- 201
Philosophy and religion; the logic of religious belief. New York, Oxford [c.] 1961. 119p. Bibl. 61-19355 2.00 bds.,
1. Philosophy and religion. I. Title.

WOLFSON, Harry Austryn 201
Religious philosophy; a group of essays. New York, Atheneum, 1965 [c.1947-1961] xii, 278p. 18cm. (Atheneum 75) Bibl. 1.95 pap.,
1. Philosophy and religion. I. Title.

WOLFSON, Harry Austryn, 1887- 201
Religious philosophy, a group of essays. Cambridge, Mass., Belknap Pr. of Harvard [c.1947-1961] 278p. 61-16696 6.00
1. Philosophy and religion. I. Title.

WOLFSON, Harry Austryn, 1887- 201
Religious philosophy, a group of essays. Cambridge, Belknap Press of Harvard University Press, 1961. 278 p. 23 cm. [BL51.W757 1961] 61-16696
1. Philosophy and religion. I. Title.

WOODFIN, Yandall, 1929- 230
With all your mind : a Christian philosophy / Yandall Woodfin. Nashville, Tenn. : Abingdon, c1980. 272 p. ; 22 cm. Includes bibliographical references and indexes. [BT40.W66] 19 80-24453 ISBN 0-687-45839-0 pbk. : 8.95
1. Philosophy and religion. 2. Philosophical theology. I. Title.

Philosophy and religion—Addresses, essays, lectures.

FRANK, Erich, 1883-1949. 200'.1
Philosophical understanding and religious truth / Erich Frank. Washington, D.C. : University Press of America, [1982], c1945. p. cm. Reprint. Originally published: 1st ed. : London, New York : Oxford University Press, 1945. Includes bibliographical references and index. [BL51.F68 1982] 19 82-8476 ISBN 0-8191-2510-5 (pbk.) : 10.25
1. Philosophy and religion—Addresses, essays, lectures. 2. Faith and reason—Addresses, essays, lectures. I. Title.

GILL, Jerry H., comp. 200'.1
Philosophy and religion; some contemporary perspectives, edited by Jerry H. Gill. Minneapolis, Burgess Pub. Co. [1968] vii, 372 p. 23 cm. Contents.Contents.—Reason and quest for revelation, by P. Tillich.—On the ontological mystery, by G. Marcel.—The problem of non-objectifying thinking and speaking, by M. Heidegger.—The problem of natural theology, by J. Macquarrie.—Metaphysical rebellion, by A. Camus.—Psychoanalysis and religion by E. Fromm.—Why I am not a Christian, by B. Russell.—The quest for being, by S. Hook.—The sacred and the profane; a dialectical understanding of Christianity, by T. J. J. Altizer.—Three strata of meaning in religious discourse by C. Hartshorne.—The theological task, by J. B. Cobb.—Theology and objectivity, by S. A. Ogden.—Can faith validate God-talk? by K. Nielsen.—The logic of God, by J. Wisdom.—Mapping the logic of models in science and theology, by F. Ferre.—On understanding mystery, by I. T. Ramsey.—Teilhard de Chardin; a philosophy of precession, by E. R. Baltazar.—The nature of apologetics, by H. Bouillard.—Metaphysics as horizon, by B. Lonergan.—Deciding whether to believe, by M. Novak. Includes bibliographical references. [B56.G5] 68-54894
1. Philosophy and religion—Addresses, essays, lectures. I. Title.

GUTKIND, Eric, 1877-1965. 215
The body of God; first steps toward an anti-theology; the collected papers of Eric Gutkind. Edited by Lucie B. Gutkind and Henry Le Roy Finch. Introd. by Henry Le Roy Finch. New York, Horizon Press [1969] 237 p. 25 cm. [B56.G8] 70-92718 6.95
1. Philosophy and religion—Addresses, essays, lectures. 2. Judaism—Addresses, essays, lectures. I. Title.

MACGREGOR, Geddes, comp. 208.2
Readings in religious philosophy [by] Geddes MacGregor [and] J. Wesley Robb. [Under the editorship of Lucius Garvin] Boston, Houghton Mifflin [1962] 424p. 24cm. [BL51.M215] 62-4425
1. Philosophy and religion—Addresses, essays, lectures. I. Robb, John Wesley, joint comp. II. Title.

MACGREGOR, Geddes [John Geddes MacGregor] comp. 208.2
Readings in religious philosophy [by] Geddes MacGregor, Boston, Houghton

[c.1962] 424p. 24cm. Bibl. 62-4425 3.95 pap.,
1. Philosophy and religion—Addresses, essays, lectures. I. Robb, John Wesley, joint comp. II. Title.

MITCHELL, Basil. 200'.1
Neutrality and commitment: an inaugural lecture delivered before the University of Oxford on 13 May 1968. Oxford, Clarendon P., 1968. 22 p. 22 cm. [BL51.M655] 79-362880 5/-
1. Philosophy and religion—Addresses, essays, lectures. I. Title.

PATTERSON, David. 200'.1
Faith and philosophy / David Patterson. Washington, D.C. : University Press of America, c1982. x, 151 p. ; 21 cm. Includes bibliographical references and index. [BL51.P317 1982] 19 81-43469 ISBN 0-8191-2651-9 : 8.75
1. Philosophy and religion—Addresses, essays, lectures. 2. Faith—Addresses, essays, lectures. I. Title.

RAMSEY, Ian T. 201
Christian empiricism / Ian Ramsey ; edited by Jerry H. Gill. Grand Rapids : Eerdmans, [1974] 260 p. ; 21 cm. (Studies in philosophy and religion) Bibliography: p. [258]-260. [BR100.R34 1974] 74-182340 pbk. : 4.95
1. Philosophy and religion—Addresses, essays, lectures. I. Title.

ROSE, Mary Carman. 201
Essays in Christian philosophy. Boston, Christopher Pub. House [1963] 200 p. 21 cm. [BR100.R65] 63-11504
1. Philosophy and religion — Addresses, essays, lectures. I. Title.

SMITH, John Edwin. 200'.1
Reason and God : encounters of philosophy with religion / by John E. Smith. Westport, Conn. : Greenwood Press, 1978, c1961. xv, 274 p. ; 23 cm. Reprint of the ed. published by Yale University Press, New Haven. Includes bibliographical references index. [BL51.S577 1978] 77-13887 ISBN 0-8371-9867-4 lib.bdg. : 18.75
1. Philosophy and religion—Addresses, essays, lectures. I. Title.

TRAP, William Martin, 1887- 231
Divine personality; a study in the philosophy of religion, by William M. Trap ... Ann Arbor, Mich., G. Wahr [1925] 83 p. 23 cm. Thesis (PH.D.)--University of Michigan, 1925. Published also without thesis note. Bibliography: p. 81-83. [BT101.T7 1925 a] 26-8215
I. Title.

TRAP, William Martin, 1887- 231
Divine personality; a study in the philosophy of religion, by William M. Trap ... Ann Arbor, Mich., G. Wahr [1925] 83 p. 23 cm. Thesis (PH.D.)--University of Michigan, 1925. Published also without thesis note. Bibliography: p. 81-83. [BT101.T7 1925 a] 26-8215
I. Title.

Philosophy, Arabic.

AFFIFI, Abul Ela. 189.3
The mystical philosophy of Mubyid Din-ibnul 'Arabi, by A. E. Affifi... Cambridge [Eng.] The University press, 1939. xx p. 1 l., 213, [1] p. diagrs. 22 cm. Bibliography: p. [195]-201. [B758.I24A35] 40-138
1. Ibn al-'Arabi, Muhammad ibn 'alf, Muhyl al-Din, called, 1165-1240. 2. Philosophy, Arabic. 3. Mysticism—Mohammedanism. I. Title.

Philosophy, Buddhist.

DAUER, Dorothea W., 1917- 181'.04'3
Schopenhauer as transmitter of Buddhist ideas. By Dorothea W. Dauer. Berne, Lang, 1969. 39 p. 21 cm. (European University papers. Series 1: German language and literature, v. 15) Bibliographical footnotes. [B3148.D3] 76-427548 10.00
1. Schopenhauer, Arthur, 1788-1860. 2. Philosophy, Buddhist. I. Title. II. Series: Europaische Hochschulschriften. Reihe 1: Deutsche Literatur und germanistik, Bd. 15

KEITH, Arthur Berriedale, 1879-1944. 181'.04'30954
Buddhist philosophy in India and Ceylon / by A. Berriedale Keith. New York : Gordon Press, 1974. 339 p. ; 24 cm. Reprint of the 1923 ed. published by the Clarendon Press, Oxford. Includes bibliographical references and indexes. [B162.K4 1974] 74-24530 ISBN 0-87968-181-0 : 30.00
1. Philosophy, Buddhist. 2. Buddhist doctrines. I. Title.

Philosophy, Buddhist—History.

GUENTHER, Herbert V. 181'.04'3
Buddhist philosophy in theory and practice [by] Herbert V. Guenther. Baltimore, Penguin Books [1972, c1971] 240 p. illus. 18 cm. Bibliography: p. 210-212. [B162.G79] 72-181092 ISBN 0-14-021392-9 2.45
1. Philosophy, Buddhist—History. I. Title.

Philosophy, Chinese.

CHUANG-TZU. 181'.11
Chuang tzu: mystic, moralist, and social reformer. Translated from the Chinese by Herbert A. Giles. 2d ed. rev. Shanghai, Kelly & Walsh, 1926. [New York, AMS Press, 1974] xxviii, 466 p. 23 cm. [BL1900.C5G4 1974] 70-38059 ISBN 0-404-56915-3 25.00
1. Philosophy, Chinese. 2. Ethics, Chinese. I. Giles, Herbert Allen, 1845-1935, tr.

CONFUCIUS. 181.1
The basic thoughts of Confucius; the conduct of life [by] Miles Menander Dawson. New York, Garden City publishing co., inc. [1939] 3 p. 1., v-xxi, 323 p. 21 1/2 cm. First published, 1915, under title: The ethics of Confucius. "The 'Great principle' of Confucius. By Dr. Chen Huan Chang": p. 299-305. [B128.C7D3] 39-32736
1. Philosophy, Chinese. 2. Ethics, Chinese. I. Dawson, Miles Menander, 1863- II. Title.

CONFUCIUS. 181.1
The conduct of life; the basic teachings of Confucius arranged for easy reading by Miles Menander Dawson. New York, The New home library [1942] 3 p. l., v-xxi, 323 p. 21 cm. Cover-title: The basic teachings of Confucius. First published, 1915, under title: The ethics of Confucius. Also published under title: The basic thoughts of confucius. "The 'great principle' of Confucius," by Dr. Chen Huan Chang: p. 299-305. [B128.C7D3 1942] 43-134
1. Philosophy, Chinese. 2. Ethics, Chinese. I. Dawson, Miles Menander, 1863- II. Title.

CONFUCIUS. 181.
the ethics of Confucius; the sayings of the master and his disciples upon the conduct of "the superior man", arranged according to the plan of Confucius, with running commentary by Miles Menander Dawson ... with a foreword by Wu Ting Fang ... prepared under the auspices of the American institute for scientific reasearch. New York and London, G. P. Putnam's sons, 1915. xxi, 323 p. front. (port.) 20 cm. Appendix: The "great principle" of Confucius [by Chen Huan Chang]: p. 299-305. [B128.C7D3] 15-24506
1. Philosophy, Chinese. 2. Ethics, Chinese. I. Dawson, Miles Menander, 1863- II. American institute for scientific research. III. Title.

CONFUCIUS.
The philosophy of Confucius in the translation of James Legge. With illus. by Jeanyee Wong. Mount Vernon, N. Y., Peter Pauper Press [1953?] 220p. illus. 25cm. A56
1. Philosophy, Chinese. 2. Ethics, Chinese. I. Legge, James, 1815- 1897, tr. II. Title.

CONFUCIUS 181.11
The wisdom of Confucius. Decorated by Paul McPharlin. Mount Vernon, N.Y., PeterPauper [c.1963] 61p. col. illus. 19cm. 63-25472 1.00 bds.,
1. Philosophy, Chinese. 2. Ethics, Chinese. I. Title.

CONFUCIUS. 181'.11
The wisdom of Confucius. New York, Philosophical Library; [distributed by Book Sales, inc., 1968] 128 p. 19 cm. Translation of Lun yu (romanized form) "The present selection is taken from The Confucian analects, translated by William Jennings ... [published in] 1895." [PL2478.L4 1968] 68-56192 3.00
1. Philosophy, Chinese. 2. Ethics, Chinese. I. Jennings, William, 1847-1927, tr. II. Title.

CONFUCIUS. 181.1
The wisdom of Confucius; a collection of the ethical sayings of Confucius and of his disciples. Edited by Miles Menander Dawson ... Boston, International pocket library [c1932] 63 p. 15 cm. Illustrated lining--papers. [B128.C7D35] 34-1385
1. Philosophy, Chinese. 2. Ethics, Chinese. I. Dawson, Miles Menander, 1863- ed. II. Title.

CONFUCIUS. 181.1
The wisdom of Confucius, edited and translated with notes by Lin Yutang. New York, The Modern library [c1938] xviii, 290 p. illus. (map) 17 cm. (Half-title: The modern library of the world's best books) "First Modern library edition." "The life of Confucius (by Szema Ch'ien)": p. 53-100. Chapter iii, Central harmony "is the only chapter in which I have not made my own translation, the one used being by the late Ku Hungming". cf. p. 102. [B128.C7L5] 38-27366
1. Philosophy, Chinese. 2. Ethics, Chinese. I. Lin, Yu-t'ang, 1895- ed. and tr. II. Ssuma Ch'ien B. C. 145 (ca)-86(-74) III. Ku, Hungming. IV. Title.

CONFUCIUS. 181.1
The wisdom of Confucius, edited and translated with notes by Lin Yutang; illustrated by Jeanyee Wong. New York, The Modern library [1943] xvii, [1], 265, [1] p. illus. (incl. map) col. plates. 19 cm. (Half-title: Illustrated modern library) "The life of Confucius (by Szema Ch'ien)": p. 18-91. Chapter iii. Central harmony "is the only chapter in which I have not made my own translation, the one used being by the late Ku Hungming." cf. p. 93. [B128.C7L5 1943] 43-51329
1. Philosophy, Chinese. 2. Ethics, Chinese. I. Lin, Yu-t'ang, 1895- ed. and tr. II. Ssu-ma, Ch'ien, ca. 145-ca. 86 B. C. III. Ku, Bung-ming, tr. IV. Wong, Jeanyee, illus. V. Title.

CREEL, Herrlee Glessner, 1905- 181'.11
Sinism : a study of the evolution of the Chinese world-view / by Herrlee Glessner Creel. Westport, Conn. : Hyperion Press, 1974. p. cm. Reprint of the 1929 ed. published by Open Court Pub. Co., Chicago. [B126.C7 1974] 74-2904 ISBN 0-88355-165-9 : 12.00
1. Philosophy, Chinese. 2. China—Religion. I. Title.

FENG, Yu-lan, 1895-
The spirit of Chinese philosophy. Boston, Beacon Press [1962] xiv, 224 p. 21 cm. (BP 148) "First English edition published in 1947. First Chinese edition published in 1947 under the title Hsin Ylian Tao." Bibliographical footnotes. 64-31588
1. Philosophy, Chinese. I. Title.

LAO-TZU. 299.
Lao tze's Tao teh king, the Bible of Taoism; English version by Sum Nung Au-Young ... With an introduction by Merton S. Yewdale ... New York, March & Greenwood [1938] 15 p. l., 15-123 p. 24 cm. "Author's edition." Title in red and blue, with Chinese characters in red. Printed on one side of double leaves, folded once in Chinese style. [BL1900.L] A 40
1. Philosophy, Chinese. I. Au-Young, Sum Nung, tr. II. Yewdale, Merton Stark. III. Title.

LAO-TZU 299.51
The way and its power; a study of the Tao te ching and its place in Chinese thought, by Arthur Waley [Tr. from Chinese] New York, Barnes & Noble [1963] 262p. 21cm. Bibl. 2.50
1. Philosophy, Chinese. I. Waley, Arthur. II. Title.

LAO-TZU. 181.1
The way and its power; a study of the Tao te ching and its place in Chinese thought, by Arthur Waley. New York, Grove Press [1958] 262p. 21cm. (Evergreen books, E-84) [BL1900.L3W3 1958] 58-5092
1. Philosophy, Chinese. I. Waley, Arthur, ed. and tr. II. Title.

LIU, Wu-chi, 1907- 181.11
A short history of Confucian philosophy [New York, Dell] 1964[c.1955] 226p. 21cm. (Delta bk., 7854) Bibl. 64-55947 1.75 pap.,
1. Philosophy, Chinese. 2. Confucius and Confucianism. I. Title.

WANG, Kung-hsing. 181.1
... The Chinese mind ... New York, The John Day company [1946] viii, 192 p. 19 1/2 cm. At head of title: Gung-Hsing Wang. "An Asia press book." [B126.W34] 46-4685
1. Confucius and Confucianism. 2. Philosophy, Chinese. I. Title.

THE way and its power;
a study of the Tao te ching and its place in Chinese thought, by Arthur Waley. London, G. Allen Unwin; New York, MacMilan [1956] 262p. 21cm. 'First published 1934.' 'Translation of Tao te ching': p. 141-243.
1. Philosophy, Chinese. I. Lao-tzu. II. Waley, Arthur.

THE way and its power,
a study of the Tao te ching and its place in Chinese thought, by Arthur Waley. London, g. Allen Unwin' New York, MacMillan [1956] 262p. 21cm. First published 1934.' 'Translation of Tao te ching': p. 141-243.
1. Philosophy, Chinese. I. Lao-tzu. II. Waley, Arthur.

WRIGHT, Marcenus Rodolphus Kilpatrick, 1830- 181.
The moral aphorisms and terseological teachings of confucius ... To which is added a correct likeness of the great philosopher, and a short sketch of his life. By M. R. K. Wright. Battle Creek, Mich., Pub. for the author, 1870. 62 p. front. (port.) 17 1/2 cm. [B128.C8W8] 10-33819
1. Philosophy, Chinese. 2. Ethics, Chinese. I. Confucius. II. Title.

Philosophy, Chinese—Bibliography

CHAN, Wing-tsit, 1901-
An outline and an annotated bibliography of Chinese philosophy. [New Haven] Far Eastern Publications, Yale University, 1959. vi, 127p. 22cm. Previous editions published under title: An outline and a bibliography of Chinese philosophy.
1. Philosophy, Chinese—Bibl. 2. 7129.C5C5 1959 016.1811 I. Title.

Philosophy—Collected works.

BERKELEY, George, Bp. of Cloyne, 1685-1753.
Principles, dialogues, and philosophical correspondence. Edited, with an introd., by Colin Murray Turbayne. Indianapolis, Bobbs-Merril [1965] xivi, 247 p. 21 cm. (The Library of liberal arts, 208) Bibliography: p. xiii-xiv.
1. Philosophy — Collected works. I. Title.

EDWARDS, Jonathan, 1703-1758. 285'.8 s
Scientific and philosophical writings / Jonathan Edwards ; edited by Wallace E. Anderson. New Haven : Yale University Press, 1980. p. cm. (The works of Jonathan Edwards ; v. 6) Includes index. Contents.Contents.—The spider papers.—Natural philosophy.—The mind.—Short scientific and philosophical papers. [BX7117.E3 1957 vol. 6] [B870.A5] 191 78-26663 ISBN 0-300-02282-4 : 40.00
1. Philosophy—Collected works. 2. Science—Collected works. I. Anderson, Wallace Earl, 1931-

HAGERSTROM, Axel Anders Theodor, 1868-1939. 198.5
Philosophy and religion. Translated by Robert T. Sandin. New York, Humanities Press, 1964. 320 p. port. 23 cm. (Muirhead library of philosophy) "Bibliography of the published writings of Hagerstrom": p. [317]-318. [B4495.H32E57 1964] 64-25430
1. Philosophy — Collected works. 2. Religion — Philosophy. I. Title.

HOBBES, Thomas, 1588-1679.
Selections edited by Frederick J. E. Woodbridge. New York, Scribner [1958] xxx, 418 p. 17 cm. Based on the editor's The philosophy of Hobbes in extracts and notes collated from his writings, published in 1903. 63-19953
I. Woodbridge, Frederick James Eugene, 1867-1940. II. Title.

OCKHAM, William, d.ca.1349.
Philosophical writings; a selection edited and translated by Philotheus Boehner. [Edinburgh, New York] Nelson, 1957. lix, 147, 154p. facsim. 19cm. (The Nelson philosophical texts) Latin and English. Bibliography: p. lii-lix. A58
1. Philosophy—Collected works. I. Bohner, Philotheus, Father, ed. II. Title.

PHILO, of Alexandria. 296.3
The contemplative life ; The giants ; and, Selections / Philo of Alexandria ; translation and introduction by David Winston ; preface by John Dillon ; [cover art, Liam Roberts]. New York : Paulist Press, c1981. xxi, 425 p. ; 23 cm. (Classics of Western spirituality) Includes bibliographical references and index. [B689.A4E5 1981] 19 80-84499 ISBN 0-8091-2333-9 (pbk.) : 7.95
1. Philosophy—Collected works. I. Winston, David. II. [Selections.] English. 1981 III. Title. IV. Series.

SMITH, Roy L. 252.
Sentence sermons; five hundred seven-fold illustrations of philosophy and humor, by Roy L. Smith ... New York, Chicago [etc.] Fleming H. Revell company [c1925] 3 p. l., 5-188 p. 20 cm. [BX8333.S575S4] 25-9223
I. Title.

TEILHARD de Chardin, Pierre. 201
Writings in time of war. Translated by Rene Hague. [1st U.S. ed.] New York, Harper & Row [1968] 315 p. 22 cm. Essays translated from Ecrits du temps de la guerre. Bibliographical footnotes. [B2430.T372E5 1968] 68-17597
1. Philosophy—Collected works. I. Title.

THOMAS Aquinas Saint, 189'.4
1225?-1274.
Saint Thomas Aquinas; selections from his works made by George N. Shuster. Wood engravings by Reynolds Stone. New York, Heritage Press [1971] xiv, 112 p. illus. 27 cm. [B765.T52E53] 76-28322
1. Philosophy—Collected works. I. Shuster, George Nauman, 1894- ed.

Philosophy — Collections.

JOAD, Cyril Edwin Mitchinson, 1891-1953.
Classics in philosophy and ethics; a course of selected reading by authorities. Introductory reading guide by C. E. M. Joad. [New York] Philosophical Library [1960] xxvi, 313 p. 24 cm. Cover title. British ed. published in 1958 by International University Society has title: Philosophy and ethics: a course of selected reading by authorities.
1. Philosophy — Collections. 2. Ethics — Collections. I. International University Society. II. Title.

Philosophy, Comparative.

SAHER, P. J. 200'.1
Eastern wisdom and Western thought; a comparative study in the modern philosophy of religion, by P. J. Saher. New York, N.Y., Barnes and Noble [1970] 292 p. 23 cm. Includes bibliographical references. [B799.S32 1970] 73-16605
1. Philosophy, Comparative. 2. Religion—Philosophy. I. Title.

SIU, Ralph Gun Hoy, 1917-
The Tao of science; an essay on Western knowledge and Eastern wisdom. Cambridge, Mass., M.I.T. Press [1966, c1957] xii, 180 p. 21 cm. (M.I.T. Paperback series, 17) Bibliography: p. 167-170. 68-64547
1. Philosophy, Comparative. 2. Science—Philosophy. I. Title.

Philosophy, Comparative—Addresses, essays, lectures.

SPIRITUAL perspectives : 181'.4
essays in mysticism and metaphysics / edited by T. M. P. Mahadevan. New Delhi : Arnold Heinemann Publishers (India), 1975. 303 p., [2] leaves of plates : ill. ; 22 cm. Volume commemmorating Chandrasekharendra Saraswati, Jagatguru Sankaracharya of Kamakoti, on his 81st birthday. [B799.S67] 75-903650 ISBN 0-89253-021-9 lib.bdg.: 15.00
1. Chandrasekharendra Saraswati, Jagatguru Sankaracharya of Kamakoti, 1893- —Addresses, essays, lectures. 2. Philosophy, Comparative—Addresses, essays, lectures. 3. Philosophy, Indic—Addresses, essays, lectures. I. Chandrasekharendra Saraswati, Jagatguru Sankaracharya of Kamakoti, 1893- II. Mahadevan, Telliyavaram Mahadevan Ponnambalam, 1911-
Distributed by InterCulture Distributed by Inter-Culture, Thompson Conn.

Philosophy, Confucian.

CHAI, Ch'u. 181'.09'512
Confucianism [by] Ch'u Chai [and] Winberg Chai. Woodbury, N.Y. Barron's Educational Series [1973] vi, 202 p. 21 cm. Bibliography: p. 185-191. [B128.C8C38] 73-3977 ISBN 0-8120-0303-9 1.95 (pbk.)
1. Philosophy, Confucian. 2. Neo-Confucianism. I. Chai, Winberg, joint author. II. Title.

CREEL, Herrlee Glessner, 921.9
1905-
Confucius and the Chinese way. New York, Harper [1960] 363 p. illus. 21 cm. (Harper torchbooks, TB63. The Cloister library) First published in 1949 under title: Confucius, the man and the myth. Includes bibliography. [B128.C8C65 1960] 60-5492
1. Philosophy, Confucian.

WILHELM, Richard, 181'.09'512
1873-1930.
Confucius and Confucianism. Translated into English by George H. Danton and Annina Periam Danton. Port Washington, N.Y., Kennikat Press [1970] x, 181 p. 20 cm. Reprint of the 1931 ed. Translation of K'ungtse und der konfuzianismus. Bibliography: p. 177-181. [B128.C8W55 1970] 70-86073 ISBN 0-8046-0643-9
1. Philosophy, Confucian.

Philosophy—Congresses.

OBERLIN Colloquium in 190
Philosophy, 6th, Oberlin College, 1965.
Art, mind, and religion; proceedings. Ed. by W. H. Capitan, D. D. Merrill. [Pittsburgh] Univ. of Pittsburgh Pr. [1967] 158p. 23cm. Sponsored by the Oberlin College Dept. of Phil. Bibl. footnotes. [B20.O22 1965] 67-13924 5.00
1. Philosophy—Congresses. I. Capitan W. H. ed. II. Merrill, Daniel Davy. ed. III. Oberlin College. Dept. of Philosophy. IV. Title.

OBERLIN Colloquium in 190
Philosophy, 6th Oberlin College, 1965.
Art, mind, and religion; proceedings. Edited by W. H. Capitan and D. D. Merrill. [Pittsburgh] University of Pittsburgh Press [1967] 158 p. 23 cm. Sponsored by the Oberlin College Dept. of Philosophy. Bibliographical footnotes. [B20.O22 1965] 67-13924
1. Philosophy — Congresses. I. Capitan, W. H., ed. II. Merrill, Daniel Davy, ed. III. Oberlin College. Dept. of Philosophy. IV. Title.

Philosophy—Dictionaries—Hebrew.

EFROS, Israel Isaac, 181'.3'03
1890-
Philosophical terms in the Moreh nebukim, by Israel Efros. New York, AMS Press, 1966 [c1924] xi, 157 p. 23 cm. A glossary of Hebrew terms, names, and titles occuring in the translations of Moses ben Maimon's Dalalat al-ha'irin, made by Ibn Tibbon and al-Harizi, with the equivalent terms in the Arabic original, and explanatory matter in English. Original ed. issued as v. 22 of Columbia University oriental studies. "Notes by Prof. Louis Ginzberg": p. [127]-144. [BM545.D35E33 1966] 72-185386
1. Moses ben Maimon, 1135-1204. Dalalat al-ha'irin. 2. Philosophy—Dictionaries—Hebrew. I. Ginzberg, Louis, 1873-1953. II. Title. III. Series: Columbia University oriental studies, v. 22.

Philosophy. — Epistemology.

BRADLEY, Francis Herbert, 1846-1924.
Appearance and reality; a metaphysical essay. Oxford, Clarendon Press [1959] xix, 570 p. 22 cm. 63-25589
1. Philosophy. — Epistemology. 2. Philosophy. — Metaphysics. I. Title.

Philosophy, French.

ABERCROMBIE, Nigel. 189.2
Saint Augustine and French classical thought, by Nigel Abercrombie ... Oxford, The Clarendon press, 1938. 3 p. l., 123, [1] p. 22 1/2 cm. "Summary bibliography": p. [118] [B655.Z7A2] 39-12132
1. Augustinus, Aurelius, Saint, bp. of Hippe. 2. Philosophy, French. I. Title.

ROUSSEAU, Jean Jacques, 1712-1778.
Selections from the works of Jean-Jacques Rousseau, edited for the use of college classes, with an introduction and notes, by Christian Gauss ... Princeton, Princeton university press; [etc., etc.] 1914. 70 p. 21 cm. [PQ2033.G2] 14-19149 0.65
I. Gauss, Christian Frederick, 1878- ed. II. Title.

SPINK, John 211'.4'0944
Stephenson.
French free-thought from Gassendi to Voltaire, by J. S. Spink. New York, Greenwood Press [1969, c1960] ix, 345 p. 23 cm. Bibliography: p. [329]-330. [B1815.S68 1969] 69-14089
1. Philosophy, French. 2. Philosophy—History—France. 3. Free thought—History. I. Title.

Philosophy — Hindu.

[ATKINSON, William Walker] 181.
1862-
The inner teachings of the philosophies and religions of India, by Yogi Ramacharaka [pseud.] ... Chicago, The Yogi publication society; [etc., etc., c1909] 2 p. l., 359 p. 21 cm. Lettered: vol. v. [B131.A8] 9-4923
1. Philosophy, Hindu. 2. India—Religion. 3. Buddha and Buddhism. 4. Sufism. I. Title.

BECK, Lily (Moresby) Adams, 181
Mrs. d.1931.
The story of oriental philosophy, by L. Adams Beck, (E. Barrington) New York, Cosmopolitan book corporation, 1928. viii p., 2 l., 429 p. front., plates (1 fold. col.) 24 1/2 cm. Illustrated lining-papers. "Books recommended": p. 427-429. [B121.B4] 28-21510
1. Philosophy, Hindu. 2. Buddha and Buddhism. 3. Philosophy, Chinese. 4. Confucius and Confucianism. 5. Philosophy, Persian. 6. Philosophy, Japanese. I. Title. II. Title: Oriental philosophy.

BERNARD, Theos, 1908- 181'.4
Hindu philosophy. New York, Greenwood Press, 1968 [c1947] xi, 207 p. illus. 23 cm. Bibliography: p. 146-156. [B131.B45 1968] 68-21323
1. Philosophy, Hindu.

BERNARD, Theos, 1908- 181.4
Hindu philosophy. New York, Philosophical Library [1947] xi, 207 p. diagrs. 23 cm. "General works': p. 146-156. [B131.B45] 47-11335
1. Philosophy, Hindu. I. Title.

BERNARD, Theos, 1908- 181.4
Philosophical foundations of India. London, New York, Rider, [1945] 168 p. diagr. 24 cm. Bibliography: p. 117-125. [B131.B46] 48-19592
1. Philosophy, Hindu. I. Title.

BRUNTON, Paul. 181.4
Indian philosophy and modern culture, by Paul Brunton. New York, E. P. Dutton & co., inc., 1939. 92 p. 20 cm. "First edition." Contents.Indian monism and western thought--Indian idealist metaphysics and western culture. [B131.B7] 39-28886
1. Philosophy, Hindu. 2. Religious thought—India. 3. Monism. 4. Idealism. I. Title.

CHATTERJI, Jagadish 294'.1
Chandra.
The wisdom of the Vedas / Jagadish Chandra Chatterji. Wheaton, Ill. : Theosophical Pub. House, 1980, c1973. 102 p. ; 21 cm. (Quest books) Published in 1931 under title: India's outlook on life. Includes bibliographical references. [BL1115.C45 1980] 19 80-51550 ISBN 0-8356-0538-8 pbk. : 3.95
1. Vedas. 2. Philosophy, Hindu. I. Title.

DASGUPTA, Surendra Nath, 181.4
1887-
A history of Indian philosophy, by Surendranth Dasgupta ... Cambridge, The University press, 1922- v. 24 cm. [B131.D3] 22-18463
1. Philosophy, Hindu. 2. India—Religion. I. Title.

DASGUPTA, Surendra Nath, 181.4
1887-
A history of Indian philosophy, by Surendranath Dasgupta ... Cambridge [eng.] The University press, 1932- v. 24 cm. Vol. 1, "First edition 1922, reprinted 1962." [B131.D3 1932] 33-1595
1. Philosophy, Hindu. 2. India—Religion. I. Title.

GARBE, Richard von, 1857- 181.
1927.
The philosophy of ancient India, by Richard Garbe ... Chicago [etc.] The Open court publishing company, 1897. 3 p. l., 89 p. 20 cm. [B131.G3] 12-32383
1. Philosophy, Hindu. I. Title.

GOKHALE, Balkrishna Govind 181.4
Indian thought through the ages; a study of some dominant concepts. New York, Asia Pub. House [dist. Taplinger, c.1961] 236p. Bibl. 61-4646 5.50
1. Philosophy, Hindu. 2. Civilization, Hindu. 3. Religious thought—India. I. Title.

GOKHALE, Balkrishna Govind. 181.4
Indian thought through the ages; a study of some dominant concepts. Bombay, New York. Asia Pub. House [1961] 236 p. 23 cm. Includes bibliographies. [B131.G6 1961a] 61-66184
1. Philsophy, Hindu. 2. Civilization, Hindu. 3. Religious thought — India. I. Title.

GRANT, Frances Ruth. 181
Oriental philosophy; the story of the teachers of the East, by Francis [!] Grant ... New York, The Dial press [c1936] xi p., l., 3-308 p. plates. 25 cm. Bibliography: p. 301-308. [B121.G7] 36-8800
1. Philosophy, Hindu. 2. Philosophy, Chinese. 3. Philosophy, Japanese. 4. Philosophy, Persian. 5. Buddha and Buddhism. 6. Mohammedanism 7. Asia—Religion. I. Title.

GRISWOLD, Hervey De Witt, 181.
1860-
... *Brahman;* a study in the history of Indian philosophy, by Hervey De Witt Griswold ... New York, The Macmillan company, 1900. viii, 89 p. 25 cm. (Cornell studies in philosophy, no. 2) Thesis (PH. D.)--Cronell university, 1900. [B21.C8 no. 2] [B132.B7G7] 108. 7-21436
1. Philosophy, Hindu. 2. Brahmanism. I. Title.

KEITH, Arthur Berriedale, 294'.1
1879-1944.
The religion and philosophy of the Veda and Upanishads. Westport, Conn., Greenwood Press [1971] 2 v. (xviii, 683 p.) 27 cm. Reprint of the 1925 ed. Includes bibliographical references. [BL1150.K43 1971] 71-109969 ISBN 0-8371-4475-2
1. Vedas. 2. Upanishads. 3. Philosophy, Hindu. 4. India—Religion. I. Title.

MANDAL, Sant Ram, comp. 181.4
Gems of Aryan wisdom, extracted and compiled by Sant Ram Mandal... San Francisco, Calif., Universal brotherhood temple and school of Eastern philosophy,

inc. [c1931] 161 p. incl. port. plates. 19 cm. [B130.M3] 32-129
1. Philosophy, Hindu. 2. Sanskrit literature (Selections: Extracts, etc.) I. Title. II. Title: Aryan wisdom, Gems of.

MULLER, Friedrich Max, 1823-1900. 181.
The six systems of Indian philosophy, by the Right Hon. F. Max Muller ... New York [etc.] Longmans, Green, and co., 1899. xxxi, 618 p. 23 cm. [B131.M9] 12-36949
1. Philosophy, Hindu. I. Title.
Contents omitted.

PRABHAVANADA, Swami, 1893- 181.4
The spiritual heritage of India [by] Swami Prabhavananda, with the assistance of Frederick Manchester. Garden City, N.Y., Doubleday, 1963. 374 p. 22 cm. Bibliography: p. [357]-361. [B131.P7 1963] 63-10517
1. Philosophy, Hindu. 2. Religious thought—India. I. Title.

RADHAKRISHNAN, Sarvepalli Sir 1888- 181.
Indian philosophy; by S. Radhakrishnan ... London, G. Allen & Unwin. ltd.; New York, The Macmillan company [1923-27] 2 v. 23 cm. (Half-title: Library of philosophy, ed by J. H. Muirhead) [B131.R3] 23-15076
1. Philosophy, Hindu. 2. Veins. 3. Upanishads. 4. Buddha and Buddhism. 5. Jainism. 6. Brahmanism. I. Title.

RADHAKRISHNAN, Sarvepalli, Sir 1888- ed. 181.4
A source book in Indian philosophy, edited by Sarvepalli Radhakrishnan and Chalrles A. Moore. Princeton, N. J., Princeton University Press, 1957. xxix, 688p. 24cm. Bibliography: p.643-669. [B130.R3] 55-6698
1. Philosophy, Hindu. I. Moore, Charles Alexander, 1901- joint ed. II. Title.

RADHAKRISHNAN, Sarvepalli, Pres. India, 1888- 181.4
A source book in Indian philosophy, edited by Sarvepalli Radhakrishnan and Charles A. Moore. Princeton, N. J., Princeton University Press, 1957. xxix, 683p. 24cm. Bibliography: p. 643-669. [B130.R3] 55-6698
1. Philosophy, Hindu. I. Moore, Charles Alexander, 1901- joint ed. II. Title.

RADHARKRISHNAN, Sir Sarvepalli, 1888- ed. 181.4
A source book in Indian philosophy, ed. by Sarvepalli Radhakrishnan, Charles A. Moore. Princeton, N.J., Princeton [1967, c.1957] xxxi, 683p. 21cm. (Princeton paperbacks 82) Bibl. [B130.R3] 3.45 pap.,
1. Philosophy, Hindu. I. Moore, Charles Alexander, 1901- joint ed. II. Title.

RAJU, Poolla Tirupati, 1902- 181.48
Idealistic thought of India. Cambridge, Harvard University Press, 1953. 454p. facsim. 22cm. Bibliographical footnotes. [B131.R] A53
1. Philosophy, Hindu. I. Title.

RAMA-PRASADA. 181.
The science of breath and the philosophy of the tattvas; translated from the Sanskrit, with introductory and explanatory essays on nature's finer forces. Reprinted from "The Theosophist," with modifications and additions. By Rama Prasad ... 2d and rev. ed. London, Theosophical publishing society; New York, The Path; [etc., etc.] 1894. vi p., 1 l., 251 p. diagrs. 19 cm. "Preface to the second and revised edition" signed: G. R. S. M. [i.e. G. R. S. Mead] Cover-title: Nature's finer forces. [B131.R35 1894] 44-52285
1. Philosophy. Hindu. 2. Breath and breathing (in religion, folklore, etc.) I. Mead, George Robert Stow, 1863-1933, ed. II. Title. III. Title: Nature's finer forces.

ROLLAND, Romain, 1866- 181.4
...Prophets of the new India. New York, A. & C. Boni, 1930. xxxiv p., 2 l., 3-683 p. 22 1/2 cm. "Translated from the French by E. F. Malcolm-Smith." Translation of Essal sur la mystique et l'action de l'Indevivante. Bibliography on Ramakrishna: p. 270-275. [B131.R62] 30-25250
1. Ramakrishna, 1836-1886. 2. Vivekananda, swami, 1863-1902. 3. Philosophy, Hindu. I. Malcolm-Smith, Elizabeth Frances, 1891- tr. II. Title.

ROY, Robindra Lal, 1904-
Aesthetic philosophy of peace. [Calcutta, Ranjan Roy, 1964] 125 p. 67-7796
1. Philosophy — Hindu. I. Title.

SAMRAS, Kharaiti Ram. 181.4
Mind made visible, a message from India; the pursuit of happiness according to the teachings of Vedic lore, by Kharaiti Ram Samras, P.H.D. New York, The William-Frederick press, 1944. 160 p. incl. front., illus. (ports.) 20 1/2 cm. [B131.S3] 44-12526
1. Philosophy, Hindu. 2. Realism. I. Title.

SHARMA, Chandradhar. 181.4
Indian philosophy: a critical survey. [New York] Barnes & Noble [1962] 405 p. 21 cm. (University paperbacks, UP-40) Includes bibliography. [B131.S48 1962] 62-18222
1. Philosophy, Hindu. I. Title.

*SINHA, Jadunath, 1894- 181.4
Indian realism. Delhi, [India], Motilal Banarsidas, [1972, c1938] xvi, 287 p., 22 cm. [B131]
1. Philosophy, Hindu. I. Title.
Distributed by Verry, 9.00

STEPHEN, Dorothea Jane. 181.
Studies in early Indian thought, by Dorothea Jane Stephen, S. TH. Cambridge, The University press, 1918. 4 p. l., 176 p. 20 cm. [B131.S7] 20-6886
1. Philosophy, Hindu. 2. India—Religion. 3. Sanskrit literature—Hist. & crit. I. Title.

TAGORE, Rabindranath, Sir, 1861-1941. 181.
Creative unity, by Rabindranath Tagore. New York, The Macmillan company, 1922. 3 p. l., v-vi p., 2 l., 3-195 p. 19 cm. [B133.T3C7] 22-4932
1. Philosophy, Hindu. I. Title.
Contents omitted.

UPANISHADS. English. 294.5'921
The thirteen principal Upanishads. Translated from the Sanskrit with an outline of the philosophy of the Upanishads. 2d ed., rev. London, New York, Oxford University Press [1971] xvi, 587 p. 21 cm. (A Galaxy book, GB365) Bibliography: p. 459-515. [BL1120.A3H8 1971] 71-30455 ISBN 0-19-501490-1 3.50 (U.S.)
1. Upanishads—Bibliography. 2. Philosophy, Hindu. I. Hume, Robert Ernest, 1877-1948, tr. II. Title.

UPANISHADS. English. 294.1
The thirteen principal Upanishads, translated from the Sanskrit with an outline of the philosophy of the Upanishads and an annotated bibliography, by Robert Ernest Hume... London, New York [etc.] H. Milford, Oxford university press, 1921. xvi, 539 p. 22 1/2 cm. "A bibliography of the Upanishads": p. 459-508. [BL1120.A3H8] 21-21402
1. Philosophy, Hindu. 2. Upanishads—Bibl. I. Hume, Robert Ernest, 1877- tr. II. Title.

UPANISHADS. English. 294.1
The thirteen principal Upanishads, translated from the Sanskrit, with an outline of the philosophy of the Upanishads and annotated bibliography, by Robert Ernest Hume... 2d ed., rev., with a list of recurrent and parallel passages, by George C. O. Haas, PH.D. London, New York [etc.] Oxford university press, H. Milford, 1931. xvi, 587, [1] p. 23 cm. "A bibliogrpahy of the Upanishads": p. 459-515. [BL1120.A3H8 1931] 32-8958
1. Philosophy, Hindu. 2. Upanishads—Bibl. I. Hume, Robert Ernest, 1877- tr. II. Haas, George Christian Otto, 1883- ed. III. Title.

VIVEKANANDA, Swami, 1863-1902. 181.45
Vivekananda: the yogas and other works, including the Chicago addresses, Janana-yoga, Bhakti-yoga, Karma-yoga, Raja-yoga, Inspired talks, and lectures, poems,and letters. Chosen and with a biography by Swami Nikhilananda. Rev. ed. New York, Ramakrishna-Vivekananda Center, 1953. xii, 978p. illus., ports. 25cm. [B133.V4A27 1953] 53-7534
1. Philosophy, Hindu. 2. Yoga. I. Nikhilananda, Swami, ed. II. Title.

ZIMMER, Heinrich Robert, 1890-1943. 181.4
Philosophies of India. Edited by Joseph Campbell. New York, Meridian Books, 1956. 687 p. illus. 21 cm. (Meridian books, MG6) Includes bibliography. [B131.Z52 1956] 56-10022
1. Philosophy, Hindu. I. Title.

ZIMMER, Heinrich Robert, 1890-1943. 181.4
Philosophies of India. Edited by Joseph Campbell. New York, Meridian Books, 1956. 687 p. illus. 21 cm. (Meridian books, MG6) Includes bibliography. [B131.Z52 1956] 56-10022
1. Philosophy, Hindu. I. Title.

ZIMMER, Heinrich Robert, 1890-1943. 181.4
Philosophies of India; edited by Joseph Campbell. [New York] Pantheon Books [1951] xvii, 687 p. illus. 24 cm. (Bollingen series, 26) Bibliography: p. [619]-631. [B131.Z52] 51-13167
1. Philosophy, Hindu. I. Title. II. Series.

Philosophy, Hindu—Addresses, essays, lectures.

MURTY, K. Satchidananda 181.4
Metaphysics, man and freedom. Foreword by S. Radhakrishnan. New York, Asia Pub. [dist. Taplinger, c.1963] 80p. 23cm. (Andhra Univ. ser., no. 70, Annamalai Univ. special lects., 1960) 63-2895 3.50 bds.,
1. Philosophy, Hindu—Addressess essays, lectures. I. Title.

RAMASWAMI Aiyar, Chetpat Pattabhirama Sir 181.4
Fundamentals of Hindu faith and culture; a collection of essays and addresses. madras, Ganesh, [label: Hollywood, Calif., Vedanta Press, 1959[ ] 160p. illus. 25cm. 60-1346 3.00
1. Philosophy, Hindu—Addresses, essays, lectures. 2. Hinduism—Addresses, essays, lectures. I. Title.

Philosophy—History

DE NICOLAS, Antonio T. 294.5'924
Avatara, the humanization of philosophy through the Bhagavad Gita : a philosophic journey through Greek philosophy, contemporary philosophy and the Bhagavad Gita on Ortega yGassett's intercultural theme, Man and circumstance: including a new translation with critical notes of the Bhagavad Gita / Antonio T. de Nicolas ; with prologue by Raimundo Panikkar. New York : N. Hayes, c1976. xv, 465 p. : ill. ; 24 cm. Includes bibliographical references and index. [BL1130.D46] 76-152 ISBN 0-89254-001-X : 18.00 ISBN 0-89254-002-8 pbk. :
1. Mahabharata. Bhagavadgita. 2. Philosophy—History. I. Mahabharata. Bhagavadgita. II. Title.

EUCKEN, Rudolf Christof, 1846-1926. 218
The problem of human life as viewed by the great thinkers from Plato to the present time, by Rudolf Eucken ... tr. from the German by Williston S. Hough ... and W. R. Boyce Gibson ... New York, C. Scribner's sons, 1909. xxv, 582 p. 23 cm. [BD431.E8 1900] 9-24685
1. Philosophy—Hist. 2. Ethics—Hist. I. Hough, Williston Samuel, 1860-1912, tr. II. Gibson, William Ralph Boyce, 1869- joint tr. III. Title.

EUCKEN, Rudolf Christof, 1846-1926. 218
The problem of human life as viewed by the great thinkers from Plato to the present time, by Rudolf Eucken ... tr. from the German by Williston S. Hough and W. R. Boyce Gibson ... Rev. and enl. ed. New York, C. Scribner's sons, 1914. xxv, 614 p. 21 1/2 cm. [BD431.E8 1914] 14-9293
1. Philosophy—Hist. 2. Ethics—Hist. I. Hough, Williston Samuel, 1860-1912, tr. II. Gibson, William Ralph Boyce, joint tr. III. Title.

FULLER, Benjamin Apthorp Gould, 1879-
A history of philosophy, by B. A. G. Fuller ... New York, H. Holt and company [c1938] 2 v. in 1. 22 cm. Contents.--v. 1. Ancient and medieval philosophy.--v. 2. Modern philosophy. Bibliography: v. 2, p. 629-635. A 38
I. Title.

FULLER, Benjamin Apthorp Gould, 1879-
A history of philosophy, by B. A. G. Fuller ... New York, H. Holt and company [c1938] 2 v. in 1. 22 cm. Contents.--v. 1. Ancient and medieval philosophy.--v. 2. Modern philosophy. Bibliography: v. 2, p. 629-635. A 38
I. Title.

GILSON, Etienne Henry, 1884- 189.09
History of Christian philosophy in the Middle Ages. New York, Random House [c1955] 829p. 24cm. (The Random House lifetime library) [B72.G48] 54-7802
1. Philosophy—Hist. 2. Philosophy, Medieval. 3. Christianity—Philosophy. I. Title.

SPECULATION and revelation in the history of philosophy. Philadelphia, Westminster Press [1956-61] 3v. 24cm. Contents.1. Speculation in pre--Christian philosophy.--2. Speculation and revelation in the age of Christian philosophy.--3. Speculation and revelation in modern philosophy.
I. Kroner, Richard, 1884-

Philosophy, India.

CHETHIMATTAM, John B. 200'.954
Patterns of Indian thought [by] John B. Chethimattam. Maryknoll, N.Y., Orbis Books [1971] viii, 172 p. 23 cm. (Indian religions and philosophies) Bibliography: p. 155-157. [B131.C5824 1971b] 77-164418 4.95
1. Philosophy, Indic. I. Title. II. Series.

Philosophy—Introductions.

BUSWELL, James Oliver, 1895- 110
A Christian view of being and knowing; an introduction to philosophy. Grand Rapids, Zondervan Pub. House [1960] 214p. illus. 23cm. Includes bibliography. [BD21.B85] 60-4639
1. Philosophy—Introductions. I. Title.

Philosophy, Islamic.

BOER, Tjitze J. De, 1866- 181'.07
The history of philosophy in Islam. Tr. by Edward R. Jones [Magnolia, Mass., P. Smith, 1967] xiii, 216p. 22cm. (Dover bk. rebound) Orig. pub. in 1903. Tr. of Geschichte der Philosophie im Islam [B741.B7 1967] 4.00
1. Philosophy, Islamic. I. Title.

BOER, Tjitze J. de, 1866- 181'.07
The history of philosophy in Islam, by T. J. de Boer. Translated by Edward R. Jones. New York, Dover Publications [1967] xiii, 216 p. 22 cm. "Unabridged and unaltered republication of the work originally published ... in 1903." Translation of Geschichte der Philosophie im Islam. [B741.B7 1967] 66-30424
1. Philosophy, Islamic. I. Title.

WALZER, Richard, 1900- 181'.9'47
Greek into Arabic; essays on Islamic philosophy. Columbia, University of South Carolina Press [1970, c1962] 256 p. 24 cm. (Oriental studies, 1) Includes bibliographical references. [B741.W3 1970] 70-93305 ISBN 0-87249-176-5 9.95
1. Philosophy, Islamic. 2. Philosophy, Ancient. 3. Philosophy, Comparative. I. Title. II. Series.

Philosophy, Islamic—Addresses, essays, lectures.

HOURANI, George Fadlo, comp. 181'.07
Essays on Islamic philosophy and science, edited by George F. Hourani. [1st ed.] Albany, State University of New York Press, 1975. viii, 261 p. 24 cm. (Studies in

Islamic philosophy and science) A collection of papers originally presented at two conferences sponsored by State University of New York and Society for the Study of Islamic Philosophy and Science; held at S.U.N.Y., Binghamton, Apr. 30-May 1, 1970, and Columbia University, Apr. 23-25, 1971, respectively. Includes bibliographical references. [B741.H68] 74-13493 ISBN 0-87395-225-1 (microfiche)
1. Philosophy, Islamic—Addresses, essays, lectures. 2. Islam and science—Addresses, essays, lectures. I. Title. II. Series.

ISLAMIC philosophy and 181'.07
mysticism / edited by Parviz Morewedge. 1st ed. Delmar, N.Y. : Caravan Books, 1981. viii, 245 p. ; 22 cm. Includes bibliographies. [B741.I83] 80-14364 ISBN 0-88206-302-2 : 35.00
1. Philosophy, Islamic—Addresses, essays, lectures. 2. Mysticism—Islam—Addresses, essays, lectures. 3. Islamic ethics—Addresses, essays, lectures. I. Morewedge, Parviz.

ISLAMIC philosophy and 181'.07
the classical tradition; essays presented by his friends and pupils to Richard Walzer on his seventieth birthday. Editors: S. M. Stern, Albert Hourani and Vivian Brown. Columbia, University of South Carolina Press [1972] viii, 549 p. illus. 24 cm. (Oriental studies, 5) Chiefly in English, some in French, or German. Includes bibliographical references. [B740.I74 1972] 72-2497 ISBN 0-87249-271-0 25.00
1. Walzer, Richard, 1900- 2. Philosophy, Islamic—Addresses, essays, lectures. 3. Philosophy, Ancient—Addresses, essays, lectures. I. Walzer, Richard, 1900- II. Stern, Samuel Miklos, 1920-1969, ed. III. Hourani, Albert Habib, ed. IV. Brown, Vivian, ed. V. Title. VI. Series.

RESCHER, Nicholas. 181'.9'47
Studies in Arabic philosophy. [Pittsburgh] University of Pittsburgh Press [1967 or 8] vii, 162 p. illus. 24 cm. Bibliographical footnotes. [B740.R4] 67-18690
1. Philosophy, Islamic—Addresses, essays, lectures. I. Title.

Philosophy, Islamic—Early works to 1800.

IBN Tufayl, Muhammed ibn 181
'Abd al-Malik, d.1185or6.
Ibn Tufayl's Hayy ibn Yaqzan; a philosophical tale translated with introd. and notes, by Lenn Evan Goodman. New York, Twayne Publishers [1972] ix, 246 p. 22 cm. (Library of classical Arabic literature, v. 1) Translation of Risalat Hayy ibn Yaqzan. Includes bibliographical references. [B753.I53R53 1972] 74-169633
1. Philosophy, Islamic—Early works to 1800. I. Goodman, Lenn Evan, 1944- tr. II. Title. III. Title: Hayy ibn Yaqzan.

Philosophy, Islamic—Greek influences.

PETERS, Francis E. 181'.07
Aristotle and the Arabs; the Aristotelian tradition in Islam [by] F. E. Peters. New York, New York University Press, 1968. xxiv, 303 p. 24 cm. (New York University studies in Near Eastern civilization, no. 1) Includes bibliographical references. [B744.3.P43] 68-29431 9.50
1. Philosophy, Islamic—Greek influences. I. Title. II. Series: New York University. Studies in Near Eastern civilization, no. 1

Philosophy, Islamic—History.

FAKHRY, Majid. 181'.07
A history of Islamic philosophy. New York, Columbia University Press, 1970. xv, 427 p. 23 cm. (Studies in Oriental culture, no. 5) Bibliography: p. 401-408. [B741.F23 1970] 71-110144 ISBN 0-231-03231-5 15.00
1. Philosophy, Islamic—History. I. Title. II. Series.

Philosophy, Jaina.

BHATTACHARYYA, Narendra 181'.04'4
Nath, 1934-
Jain philosophy : historical outline / by Narendra Nath Bhattacharyya. New Delhi : Munshiram Manoharlal Publishers, 1976. xix, 220 p. ; 23 cm. Running title: Jain philosophy in historical outline. Includes index. Bibliography: p. [207]-211. [B162.5.B483] 76-902152 11.00
1. Philosophy, Jaina. I. Title.
Distributed by South Asia Books

Philosophy, Japanese.

FUJISAWA, Chikao 181.12
Zen and Shinto; the story of Japanese philosophy. New York, Philosophical Library [c.1959] 92p. 19cm. 59-65330 2.75
1. Philosophy, Japanese. 2. Zen (Sect) 3. Shinto. I. Title.

FUJISAWA, Chikao, 1893- 181'.12
Zen and Shinto; the story of Japanese philosophy. Westport, Conn., Greenwood Press [1971, c1959] 92 p. 23 cm. [B136.F83 1971] 78-139133 ISBN 0-8371-5749-8
1. Philosophy, Japanese. 2. Zen Buddhism—Japan. 3. Shinto. I. Title.

Philosophy, Jewish.

ADLER, Joshua. 181.3
Philosophy of Judaism. New York, Philosophical Library [1960] 160p. 20cm. [B154.A3] 60-2640
1. Philosophy, Jewish. I. Title.

BOMAN, Thorleif 181.3
Hebrew thought compared with Greek. [Translated [from the German] by Jules L. Moreau] Philadelphia, Westminster Press [1961] 224p. bBibl.: p.209-216. (Library of history and doctrine) 60-10167 4.50
1. Philosophy, Jewish. 2. Philosophy, Ancient. I. Title.

BOOKSTABER, Philip David, 181.3
1892-
The idea of development of the soul in medieval Jewish Philosophy. Philadelphia, M. Jacobs, 1950. 104 p. 24 cm. Bibliographical footnotes. [B757.P8B6] 50-10850
1. Philosophy, Jewish. 2. Soul. I. Title.

EFROS, Israel Isaac, 1890- 181.3
Ancient Jewish philosophy; a study in metaphysics and ethics [by] Israel I. Efros. Detroit, Wayne State University Press, 1964. 199 p. 24 cm. Bibliographical references included in "Notes" (p. 165-182) [B156.E3] 64-11361
1. Philosophy, Jewish. 2. Judaism—History of doctrines. 3. Ethics, Jewish—Hist. I. Title.

EFROS, Israel Isaac, 1890- 181'.3
Studies in medieval Jewish philosophy, [by] Israel Efros. New York, Columbia University Press, 1974. 269 p. 23 cm. Substantially the same material as originally published in the author's ha-Filosofyah ha-yehudit bi-yeme ha-benayim. Contents.Contents.—The philosophy of Saadia Gaon.—Three essays.—Studies in pre-Tibbonian philosophical terminology. Includes bibliographical references. [B755.E33] 73-12512 ISBN 0-231-03194-7
1. Saadiah ben Joseph, gaon, 892?-942. al-Amanat wa-al-i'tiqadat. 2. Judah, ha-Levi, 12th cent. Kitab al-Hujjah. 3. Moses ben Maimon, 1135-1204. Dalalat al-ha'irin. 4. Abraham bar Hiyya, ha-Nasi, 12th cent. 5. Philosophy, Jewish. 6. Philosophy, Medieval. I. Title.

GOLDMAN, Solomon, 1893- 181.3
The Jew and the universe, by Solomon Goldman. New York and London, Harper & brothers, 1936. xi p., 1 l., 184 p., 1 l., 185-257 p. 21 cm. [B755.G6] 36-21330
1. Moses ben Maimon, 1135-1204. 2. Philosophy, Jewish. I. Title.

GOLDMAN, Solomon, 1893- 181'.3
1953.
The Jew and the universe. New York, Arno Press, 1973 [c1936] xi, 257 p. 23 cm. (The Jewish people: history, religion, literature) Reprint of the ed. published by Harper, New York. Includes bibliographical references. [B755.G6 1973] 73-2200 ISBN 0-405-05265-0 15.00
1. Moses ben Maimon, 1135-1204. 2. Philosophy, Jewish. I. Title. II. Series.

GUTTMANN, Julius, 1880-1950 181.3
Philosophies of Judaism; the history of Jewish philosophy from Biblical times to Franz Rosenzweig. Introd. by R. J. Zwi Werblowsky. Tr. [from the Hebrew ed.] by David W. Silverman. Garden City, N.Y., Doubleday [1966, c.1964] 546p. 18cm. (Anchor bk., A509) Bibl. [B154.G813] 1.95 pap.,
1. Philosophy, Jewish. 2. Judaism. I. Title.

GUTTMANN, Julius, 1880-1950.
Philosophies of Judaism; the history of Jewish philosophy from Biblical times to Franz Rosenzweig. Introd. by R. J. Zwi Werblowsky. Translated by David W. Silverman. Philadelphia, Jewish Publication Society of America, 1964. x, 464 p. 24 cm. 64-20239
I. Title.

GUTTMANN, Julius, 1880- 181.3
1950.
Philosophies of Judaism; the history of Jewish philosophy from Biblical times to Franz Rosenzweig. Introd. by R. J. Zwi Werblowsky. Translated by David W. Silverman. [1st ed.] New York, Holt, Rinehart and Winston [1964] x, 464 p. 24 cm. Bibliography: p. [399]-411. [B154.G813] 63-11875
1. Philosophy, Jewish. 2. Judaism. I. Title.

HARTMAN, David. 181'.3
Maimonides : Torah and philosophic quest / David Hartman ; foreword by Shlomo Pines. 1st ed. Philadelphia : Jewish Publication Society of America, 1976. xv, 296 p. ; 22 cm. Includes index. Bibliography: p. 269-288. [B759.M34H36] 76-6305 ISBN 0-8276-0083-6 : 7.95
1. Moses ben Maimon, 1135-1204. 2. Philosophy, Jewish. 3. Philosophy, Medieval. 4. Jewish law—Philosophy. I. Title.

HERRING, Basil. 221.6
Joseph ibn Kaspi's Gevia' kesef : a study in medieval Jewish philosophic Bible commentary / by Basil Herring. New York : Ktav Pub. House, 1981. p. cm. Added t.p.: Sefer Gevi'a kesef. Includes Hebrew text and translation of Gevi'a kesef. Includes index. Bibliography: p. [B759.C374H47] 19 81-2536 ISBN 0-87068-716-6 : 20.00
1. Caspi, Joseph, ca. 1280-ca. 1340. 2. Bible O.T.—Criticism, interpretation, etc., Jewish. 3. Bible. O.T. Genesis—Criticism, interpretation, etc. 4. Philosophy, Jewish. 5. Philosophy, Medieval. I. Caspi, Joseph, ca. 1280-ca. 1340. Gevi'a kesef. English & Hebrew. 1981. II. Title. III. Title: Gevi'a kesef.

MACDONALD, Duncan Black, 181.3
1863-
The Hebrew philosophical genius; a vindication, by Duncan Black Macdonald ... Princeton, Princeton university press, 1936. x, [2], 155 p. 23 1/2 cm. "This book, considered on one side, is a supplement to my The Hebrew literary genius, expanding the two chapters there on Philosophy and on Ecclesiastes."--Pref. [B156.M25] 36-12667
1. Philosophy, Jewish. 2. Bible. O.T. Wisdom literature—Criticism, interpretation, etc. 3. Bible—Criticism, interpretation, etc.—O.T. Wisdom literature. I. Title.

MACDONALD, Duncan Black, 181.3
1863-1943
The Hebrew philosophical genius; a vindication. New York, Russell & Russell, 1965[c.1936] x, 155p. 23cm. Cover title: The Hebrew philosophic genius. Supplement to my The Hebrew literary genius, expanding the two chapters there on philosophy and on Ecclesiastes [B156.M25] 65-18819 6.50
1. Philosophy, Jewish. 2. Bible. O. T. Wisdom literature—Criticism, interpretation, etc. I. Macdonald, Duncan Black, 1863-1943. The Hebrew literary genius. II. Title.

MINKIN, Jacob Samuel, 1885- 181.3
1962.
The shaping of the modern mind; the life and thought of the great Jewish philosophers. Introductory appreciation by Fanny R. Minkin. New York, Yoseloff [c.1963] 488p. 24cm. Bibl. 63-18240 6.00
1. Philosophy, Jewish. 2. Philosophers, Jewish. I. Title.

MINKIN, Jacob Samuel, 1885- 181.3
1962.
The shaping of the modern mind; the life and thought of the great Jewish philosophers. With an introductory appreciation by Fanny R. Minkin. New York, T. Yoseloff [1963] 488 p. 24 cm. Bibliography: p. 483-488. [B154.M5] 63-18240
1. Philosophy, Jewish. 2. Philosophers, Jewish. I. Title.

MOSES Ben Maiman, 1135- 181.3
1204.
The guide for the preplexed. Translated from the Arabic text, by M. Friedlander. 2d ed., rev. throughout. [New York] Dover Publications [1961] 414 p. 21 cm. [BM545] 62-226
1. Philosophy, Jewish. 2. Philosophy, Medieval. 3. Judaism — Works to 1900. I. Title.

MOSES Ben Maiman, 1135- 181.3
1204.
The guide of the preplexed. Translated with an introd. and notes by Shlomo Pines. With an introductory essay by Leo Strauss. [Chicago] University of Chicago Press [1963] cxxxiv, 658 p. 26 cm. [BM545.D33P5] 62-18113
1. Philosophy, Jewish. 2. Philosophy, Medieval. 3. Judaism — Works to 1900. I. Pines, Salomon, ed. and tr. II. Title.

MOSES ben Maimon, 1135- 181'.3
1204.
Rambam : readings in the philosophy of Moses Maimonides / selected and translated, with introduction and commentary, by Lenn Evan Goodman. New York : Viking Press, [1975] p. cm. (The Jewish heritage classics) Includes index. Bibliography: p. [B759.M32E5 1975] 75-14476 ISBN 0-670-58964-0 : 12.50
1. Moses ben Maimon, 1135-1204. 2. Philosophy, Jewish. 3. Philosophy, Medieval. 4. Ethics, Jewish. I. Goodman, Lenn Evan, 1944- II. Title. III. Series.

MOSES ben Maimon, 1135- 181'.3
1204.
Rambam : readings in the philosophy of Moses Maimonides / selected and translated with introd. and commentary by Lenn Evan Goodman. New York : Schocken Books, 1977, c1976. xiv, 444 p. ; 21 cm. Selections from the author's Dalalat al-ha'irin and Thamaniyat fusul. Includes index. Bibliography: p. [B759.M33D3132 1977] 76-48856 ISBN 0-8052-0569-1 pbk. : 5.95
1. Moses ben Maimon, 1135-1204. 2. Philosophy, Jewish. 3. Philosophy, Medieval. 4. Ethics, Jewish. I. Goodman, Lenn Evan, 1944- II. Moses ben Maimon, 1135-1204. Thamaniyat fusul. English. Selections. 1977. III. Title. IV. Title: Readings in the philosophy of Moses Maimonides.

MOSES Ben Mainion, 1135- 181.3
1204
The guide of the perplexed [by] Moses Maimonides. Tr. from Arabic by M. Friedlander. 2d ed., rev. [Gloucester, Mass., Peter Smith, 1962] 414p. 21cm. (Dover bk. rebound) 3.85
1. Philosophy, Jewish. 2. Philosophy, Medieval. 3. Judaism—Works to 1900. I. Title.

MOSES BEN MAIMON, 1135- 181.3
1204.
The guide for the perplexed, by Moses Maimonides; translated from the original Arabic text by M. Friedlander, PH.D. 2d ed. rev. throughout (3d impression) London, G. Routledge & co., 1919. lix, 414 p. 22 cm. [BM545.G8 1919] 22-17636
1. Philosophy, Jewish. 2. Philosophy, Medieval. 3. Jews—Religion. I. Friedlander, Michael, 1833-1910, tr. II. Title.

MOSES BEN MAIMON, 1135- 181.3
1204.
The guide for the perplexed, by Moses Maimonides; translated from the original Arabic text by M. Friedlander, PH.D. [New York] Pardes publishing house, inc. [1946] lix, 414 p. 23 1/2 cm. Illustrated t.-p. "American edition." [BM545.D3 1946] 47-26090
1. Philosophy, Jewish. 2. Philosophy,

Medieval. 3. Jews—Religion. I. Friedlander, Michael, 1833-1910, tr. II. Title.

ROTH, Leon, 1896- 181.3
The guide for the perplexed [by] Moses Maimonides. London, New York, Hutchinson's University Library [1948] 141 p. 19 cm. (Hutchinson's university library: Jewish religion, 11) Bibliography: p. 135. [BM545.D35R6] 50-13601
1. Moses ben Maimon, 1135-1204. Dalalat al-ha'irin. 2. Philosophy, Jewish. 3. Philosophy, Medieval. 4. Jews—Religion. I. Title.

SARACHEK, Joseph, 1892- 181.3
... Faith and reason: the conflict over the rationalism of Maimonides, by Joseph Sarachek ... Williamsport, Pa., The Bayard press, 1935- v. 21 cm. (Oriental series) Vol. I issued also as thesis (PH. D.) Columbia university. Bibliography: vol. I, p. 275-278. [BM755.M6S3] 36-9650
1. Moses ben Maimon, 1135-1204. 2. Jews—Religion. 3. Philosophy, Jewish. 4. Philosophy, Medieval. 5. Philosophy and religion. 6. Religion and science—1900- I. Title. II. Title: The rationalism of Maimonides.

SIMON, Leon, 1881- ed. 296
Aspects of the Hebrew genius, a volume of essays on Jewish literature and thought, ed. by Leon Simon ... London, G. Routledge & sons, limited. New York, Bloch publishing co., 1910. xxviii, 210 p., 1 l. 19 1/2 cm. [B755.S5] 12-14498
1. Philosophy, Jewish. 2. Jewish literature—Hist. & crit. 3. Hebrew literature—Hist. & crit. I. Title.
Contents omitted.

THREE Jewish 181.3
philosophers. Philo: Selections, edited by Hans Lewy. Saadya Gaon: Book of doctrines and beliefs, edited by Alexander Altmann. Jehuda Halevi: Kuzari, edited by Isaak Heinemann. New York, Meridian Books [1960] 112, 190, 147p. Bibl. footnotes (JP13) 60-9081 1.65 pap.,
1. Philosophy, Jewish. I. Philo Judaus. II. Saadiah ben Joseph, gaon, 892?-942. Book of doctrines and beliefs. III. Judah, ha-Levi, 12th cent. Kuzari.

TRESMONTANT, Claude. 181.3
A study of Hebrew thought. Translated by Michael Francis Gibson. New York, Desclee Co., 1960. 178 p. 22 cm. Translation of Essal sur la pensee hebraique. Includes bibliography. [B154.T713] 60-6516
1. Philosophy, Jewish. 2. Creation. 3. Man (Theology) I. Title.

UNTERMAN, Isaac, 1889- 181.3
A light amid the darkness; medieval Jewish philosophy. New York, Twayne Publishers [1959] 208 p. 23 cm. Includes bibliography. [B755.U5] 59-8384
1. Philosophy, Jewish. 2. Philosophers, Jewish. I. Title.

Philosophy, Jewish—Addresses, essays, lectures.

ALTMANN, Alexander, 1906- 296'.01
Studies in religious philosophy and mysticism / by Alexander Altmann. Plainview, N.Y. : Books for Libraries Press, 1975, c1969. p. cm. (Essay index reprint series) Reprint of the ed. published by Cornell University Press, Ithaca. Includes bibliographical references and indexes. [B154.A4 1975] 75-14347 ISBN 0-518-10194-0 : 19.50
1. Philosophy, Jewish—Addresses, essays, lectures. 2. Mysticism—Judaism—Addresses, essays, lectures. I. Title.

MYSTICS, philosophers, and 296
politicians : essays in Jewish intellectual history in honor of Alexander Altmann / edited by Jehuda Reinharz and Daniel Swetschinski with the collaboration of Kalman P. Bland. Durham, N.C. : Duke University Press, c1982. xii, 372 p. : port. ; 25 cm. (Duke monographs in medieval and Renaissance studies ; no. 5) "Bibliography of Alexander Altmann's writings": p. [343]-354. [B755.M95] 19 81-5540 ISBN 0-8223-0446-5 : 32.75
1. Herzl, Theodor, 1860-1904—Addresses, essays, lectures. 2. Altmann, Alexander, 1906- —Addresses, essays, lectures. 3. Philosophy, Jewish—Addresses, essays, lectures. 4. Philosophy, Medieval—Addresses, essays, lectures. 5. Mysticism—Judaism—Addresses, essays, lectures. 6. Jews—France—Identity—Addresses, essays, lectures. I. Altmann, Alexander, 1906- II. Reinharz, Jehuda. III. Swetschinski, Daniel, 1944- IV. Bland, Kalman P., 1942- V. Title. VI. Series.

RAWIDOWICZ, Simon, 1897- 181'.3
1957.
Studies in Jewish thought / by Simon Rawidowicz ; foreword by Abram L. Sachar ; biographical introd. by Benjamin C. I. Ravid ; edited by Nahum N. Glatzer. 1st ed. Philadelphia : Jewish Publication Society of America, [1974] ix, 449 p. ; 22 cm. Includes bibliographical references. [DS102.5.R37 1974] 74-15462 ISBN 0-8276-0057-7 : 6.95
1. Jews—History—Philosophy. 2. Rawidowicz, Simon, 1897-1957. 3. Philosophy, Jewish—Addresses, essays, lectures. I. Title.

ROSENTHAL, Erwin Isak 296'.08
Jakob, 1904-
Studia Semitica [by] Erwin I. J. Rosenthal. Cambridge, University Press, 1971. 2 v. 24 cm. (University of Cambridge. Oriental publications, no. 16-17) One essay in German. Contents.Contents.—v. 1. Jewish themes.—v. 2. Islamic themes. Includes bibliographical references. [BS1186.R68 1971] 70-116836 ISBN 0-521-07958-6 (v. 1) ISBN 0-521-07959-4 (v. 2) £6.20 ($22.00 U.S.)
1. Bible. O.T.—Criticism, interpretation, etc., Jewish—Addresses, essays, lectures. 2. Philosophy, Jewish—Addresses, essays, lectures. 3. Political science—History—Islamic Empire—Addresses, essays, lectures. 4. Islam and politics. I. Title. II. Series: Cambridge. University. Oriental publications, no. 16-17

Philosophy, Jewish—Collections.

MARTIN, Bernard, 1928- comp. 190
Great twentieth century Jewish philosophers: Shestov, Rosenzweig, Buber, with selections from their writings. Edited and with introductions by Bernard Martin. [New York] Macmillan [1969, c1970] xi, 336 p. 22 cm. Bibliography: p. [335]-336. [B158.7.M3] 79-85787
1. Philosophy, Jewish—Collections. 2. Philosophy, Modern—20th century—Collections. I. Shestov, Lev, 1866-1938. II. Rosenzweig, Franz, 1886-1929. III. Buber, Martin, 1878-1965. IV. Title.

Philosophy, Jewish—History.

BLAU, Joseph Leon, 1909- 181.309
The story of Jewish philosophy. New York, Random House [1962] 322p. 22cm. Includes bibliography. [B154.B55] 62-8451
1. Philosophy, Jewish—Hist. I. Title.

BLAU, Joseph Leon, 1909- 181.3'09
The story of Jewish philosophy, by Joseph L. Blau. New York, Ktav Pub. House, 1971 [c1962] x, 322 p. 23 cm. Bibliography: p. 314-317. [B154.B55 1971] 76-31070 ISBN 0-87068-174-5 5.95
1. Philosophy, Jewish—History. I. Title.

JEWISH philosophers / 181'.3
edited by Steven T. Katz. New York : Bloch Pub. Co., c1975. xvi, 299 p. : ill. ; 25 cm. "Based for the most part on entries that appeared in the Encyclopaedia Judaica." Includes index. Bibliography: p. 280-293. [B154.J48] 75-7590 ISBN 0-8197-0387-7 : 10.95
1. Philosophy, Jewish—History. I. Katz, Steven T., 1944- II. Encyclopaedia Judaica.

Philosophy, Medieval.

DELHAYE, Philippe 189
Medieval Christian philosophy; translated from the French by S. J. Tester. New York, Hawthorn Books [c.1960] 126p. Bibl.: p.[125]-126. 21cm. (The Twentieth century encyclopedia of Catholicism, v.12. Section 1: Knowledge and faith) 60-8787 2.95 half cloth,
1. Philosophy, Medieval. I. Title.

FREMANTLE, Anne (Jackson) 1909-
ed.
The age of belief; the medieval philosophers. Selected, with introd. and interpretive commentary. [New York] New American Library [1961] xii, 218 p. (Mentor philosophers, MD 126) 63-17296
I. Title.

FREMANTLE, Anne (Jackson) 1909-
ed.
The age of belief; the medieval philosophers. Selected, with introd. and interpretive commentary. [New York] New American Library [1961] xii, 218 p. (Mentor philosophers, MD 126) 63-17296
I. Title.

GILSON, Etienne Henry, 189'.4
1884-
The philosophy of St. Thomas Aquinas. Authorised translation from the 3d. rev. and enl. ed. of 'Le thomisme', by [Etienne Gilson. Translated by Edward Bullough. Edited by G. A. Elrington.] Freeport, N.Y., Books for Libraries Press [1971] xv, 372 p. 23 cm. Reprint of the 1937 ed. [B765.T54G5 1971] 70-157337 ISBN 0-8369-5797-0
1. Thomas Aquinas, Saint, 1225?-1274—Philosophy. 2. Philosophy, Medieval. I. Title.

GILSON, Etienne Henry, 189'.4
1884-
The philosophy of St. Thomas Aquinas; authorised translation from the 3d rev. ed. of "Le thomisme", by Etienne Gilson. [Translated by Edward Bullogh. Edited by G. A. Elrington.] Folcroft, Pa.] Folcroft Library Editions, 1972. xv, 287 p. 24 cm. "Limited to 150 copies." Translation of Le thomisme. Reprint of the 1924 ed., issued in series: The Mediaeval scholastic series. Includes bibliographical references. [B765.T54G5 1972] 72-190713
1. Thomas Aquinas, Saint, 1225?-1274—Philosophy. 2. Philosophy, Medieval. I. Elrington, G. Aidan, ed. II. Title. III. Series: The Mediaeval scholastic series.

GILSON, Etienne Henry, 189.4
1884-
The philosophy of St. Thomas Aquinas; authorized translation from the 3d rev. and enl. ed. of Le thomisme' by Etienne Gilson ... Translated by Edward Bullough ... edited by Rev. G. A. Elrington ... St. Louis, Mo., and London, B. Herder book co., 1937. xv, 372 p. 19 cm. (The mediaeval scholastic series) "Second edition, revised 1937." [B765.T54G5 1937] 39-4162
1. Thomas Aquinas, Saint, 1225?-1274. 2. Philosophy, Medieval. I. Bullough, Edward, 1880-1934, tr. II. Elrington, G. Aldan, ed. III. Title.

GILSON, Etienne Henry, 1884-
Reason and revelation in the Middle Ages. New York, Scribner [1962, c1938] 114 p. 21 cm. (The Scribner library. SL 37) Bibliography included in "Notes," p. 103-110. 63-12457
1. Philosophy, Medieval. 2. Philosophy and religion. I. Title.

GILSON, Etienne Henry, 1884- 189
The spirit of mediaeval philosophy [Reissue] Tr. by H. C. Downes. New York, Scribners [1965, c.1936] ix, 490p. 21cm. (Gifford lect., 1931-1932) Bibl. Reissue of the 1940 ed. [B721.G433] 36-16204 3.50 pap.,
1. Philosophy, Medieval. 2. Christianity—Philosophy. 3. Religion—Philosophy. 4. Scholasticism. I. Downes, Alfred Howard Campbell, 1882- tr. II. Title.

GILSON, Etienne Henry, 1884- 189
The spirit of mediaeval philosophy ... by Etienne Gilson; translated by A. H. C. Downes. New York, C. Scribner's sons, 1936. ix, 490 p. 23 cm. (Gifford lectures, 1931-1932) Bibliographical references in "Notes" (p. 427-485) [B721.G433 1936 a] 36-16204
1. Philosophy, Medieval. 2. Christianity—Philosophy. 3. Religion—Philosophy. 4. Scholasticism. I. Downes, Alfred Howard Campbell, 1882- tr. II. Title.

HYMAN, Arthur, comp., 1921- 189
Philosophy in the Middle Ages; the Christian, Islamic, and Jewish traditions, edited by Arthur Hyman [and] James J. Walsh. New York, Harper & Row [1967] vii, 747 p. 24 cm. Includes bibliographies. [B721.H8] 67-18445
1. Philosophy, Medieval. I. Walsh, James Jerome, joint comp. II. Title.

HYMAN, Arthur, 1921- comp. 189
Philosophy in the Middle Ages; the Christian, Islamic, and Jewish traditions. Edited by Arthur Hyman [and] James J. Walsh. Indianapolis, Hackett Pub. Co. [1973] vii, 747 p. 24 cm. Bibliography: p. [723]-728. [B721.H8 1973] 73-179309 15.00
1. Philosophy, Medieval. I. Walsh, James Jerome, joint comp. II. Title.
Pbk. 5.95.

HYMAN, Arthur, 1921- comp. 189
Philosophy in the Middle Ages; the Christian, Islamic, and Jewish traditions, edited by Arthur Hyman [and] James J. Walsh. New York, Harper & Row [1967] vii, 747 p. 24 cm. Includes bibliographies. [B721.H8] 67-18445
1. Philosophy, Medieval. I. Walsh, James Jerome, joint comp. II. Title.

LEFF, Gordon: 189
Medieval thought: St. Augustine to Ockham. [Harmondworth, Middlesex] Penguin Books [1958] 316p. 19cm. (Pelican books, A424) Includes bibliography. [B 21.L4] 58-5848
1. Philosophy, Medieval. I. Title.

PEGIS, Anton Charles. 189.4
... Saint Thomas and the Greeks; under the auspices of the Aristelian society of Marquette university, by Anton C. Pegis ... Milwaukee, Marquette university press, 1939. 4 p. l., 107 p. 19 cm. (The Aquinas lecture, 1939) Bibliographical references in "Notes": p. 88-107. [B765.T54P35] 39-23515
1. Thomas Aquinas, Saint, 1225?-1274. 2. Philosophy, Medieval. 3. Philosophy, Ancient. I. Title.

POOLE, Reginald Lane, 1857- 189
Illustrations of the history of medieval thought and learning, by Reginald Lane Poole. 2d ed., rev. London, Society for promoting Christian knowledge; New York, The Macmillan company, 1920. xiii, 327, [1] p. 23 cm. First edition published in 1864 under title: Illustrations of the history of medieval thought in the departments of theology and ecclesiastical politics. [B721.P6 1920] 21-17882
1. Philosophy, Medieval. 2. Church polity. I. Title.

POOLE, Reginald Lane, 1857- 189
1939.
Illustrations of the history of medieval thought and learning, 2nd ed. rev. [Gloucester, Mass., Peter Smith, 1961] 327p. First pub. in 1884 under title: Illustrations of the history of medieval thought in the departments of theology and ecclesiastical politics. (Dover bk. rebound) 4.00
1. Philosophy, Medieval. 2. Church polity. I. Title.

POOLE, Reginald Lane, 1857- 189
1939
Illustrations of the history of medieval thought and learning. 2d ed., rev. New York, Dover Publications [1960] 327p. First ed. published in 1884 under title: Illustrations of the history of medieval thought in the departments of theology and ecclesiastical politics. (Dover T674) Bibl. footnotes & bibl. marginal notes. 60-51887 1.85 pap.,
1. Philosophy, Medieval. 2. Church polity. I. Title.

SHARP, Dorothea Elizabeth 189.4
Franciscan philosophy at Oxford in the thirteenth century New York, Russell & Russell, 1964. viii, 419p. facsim. 23cm. Bibl. 64-10707 8.50
1. Philosophy, Medieval. 2. Philosophy, English—13th cent. 3. Franciscans in England. 4. Oxford, University. I. Title.

SHARP, Dorothea Elizabeth. 189
Franciscan philosophy at Oxford in the thirteenth century, by D. E. Sharp ... London, Oxford university press, H. Milford, 1930. viii, 419 [1] p. front. (facsim.) 23 cm. (Half-title: British society of Franciscan studies. [Publications] vol. XVI) [BX3601.B7 vol. 16] (271.3) 31-4957
1. Philosophy, Medieval. 2. Philosophy,

English. 3. Franciscans. 4. Oxford. University. I. Title.
Contents omitted.

VIGNAUX, Paul. 189
Philosophy in the Middle Ages; an introduction. Translated from the French by E. C. Hall. Westport, Conn., Greenwood Press [1973, c1959] 223 p. 20 cm. Translated from the third French ed. with title: Philosophie au moyen age, which was originally published under title: La pensee au moyen age. Bibliography: p. [215]-218. [B721.V513 1973] 72-8244 ISBN 0-8371-6546-6
1. Philosophy, Medieval. 2. Religious thought—Middle Ages. I. Title.

VIGNAUX, Paul. 189
Philosophy in the Middle Ages, an introduction. Translated from the French by E. C. Hall. New York, Meridian Books [1959] 223 p. 18 cm. (Meridian books, M81) Translated from the third French ed. with title: Philosophie au moyen age; previous editions published under title: La pensee au moyen age. Includes bibliography. [B721.V513 1959] 59-12915
1. Philosophy, Medieval. 2. Religious thought—Middle Ages, 600-1500. I. Title.

WAUTIER d'Aygalliers, 248.2'2
Alfred.
Ruysbroeck the Admirable, by A. Wautier d'Aygalliers. Port Washington, N.Y., Kennikat Press [1969] xliii, 326 p. 22 cm. First published in 1923, as thesis, University of Paris. Bibliographical footnotes. [BV5095.J3W32 1969] 68-26207
1. Jan van Ruysbroeck, 1293-1381. 2. Philosophy, Medieval.

WAUTIER d'Aygalliers, Alfred. 922
Ruysbroeck the Admirable, by A. Wautier d'Aygalliers; authorized translation by Fred Rothwell. London & Toronto, J. M. Dent & sons ltd.; New York, E. P. Dutton & co., 1925. xiii, 326 p. 23 1/2 cm. [BV5095.J3W32] 26-3635
1. Jan van Ruysbroeck, 1298-1381. 2. Philosophy, Medieval. I. Rothwell, Fred, 1869- tr. II. Title.

WULF, Maurice Marie Charles 189
Joseph de, 1867-
History of mediaeval philosophy, by Maurice de Wulf ... Translated by Ernest C. Messenger ... London, New York [etc.] Longmans, Green and co., 1925-26. 2 v. 22 1/2 cm. Contents.I. From the beginnings to Albert the Great.--II. From St. Thomas Aquinas to the end of the sixteenth century. Contains bibliographies. [B721.W93 1925] 26-10825
1. Philosophy, Medieval. I. Messenger, Ernest Charles, 1888- tr. II. Title.

WULF, Maurice Marie Charles 189.
Joseph de, 1867-
Mediaeval philosophy illustrated from the system of Thomas Aquinas, by Maurice de Wulf ... Cambrige, Harvard university press; [etc., etc.] 1922. 6 p. l., 3-153, [1] p. 22 cm. Bibliography: p. 153. [B734.W8] 22-19416
1. Thomas Aquinas, Saint, 1225?-1274. 2. Philosophy, Medieval. I. Title.

WULF, Maurice Marie Charles 189.4
Joseph de, 1867-1947
The system of Thomas Aquinas. Formerly titled: Mediaeval philosophy illustrated from the system of Thomas Aquinas [Gloucester, Mass., Peter Smith, 1961] 151p. (Dover bk. rebound) Bibl. 3.25
1. Thomas Aquinas, Saint—Philosophy. 2. Philosophy, Medieval. I. Title.

WULF, Maurice Marie Charles 189.4
Joseph de, 1867-1947.
The system of Thomas Aquinas. Formerly titled: Mediaeval philosophy illustrated from the system of Thomas Aquinas. New York, Dover Publications [1959] 151 p. 21 cm. Includes bibliography. [B734.W8 1959] 59-65175
1. Thomas Aquinas, Saint, 1225?-1274—Philosophy. 2. Philosophy, Medieval. I. Title.

Philosophy, Medieval—History

MACDONALD, Allan John 189
Macdonald, 1887-
Authority and reason in the early middle ages, being the Hulsean lectures, 1931-1932, delivered in the University of Cambridge in Michaelmas term, 1931, by A. J. Macdonald ... London, Oxford university press, H. Milford, 1933. vi p., 1 l., 136 p. 23 cm. "List of abbreviations": p. [viii] [B721.M3] 33-24327
1. Philosophy, Medieval—Hist. 2. Authority (Religion) 3. Reason. I. Hulsean lectures, 1931-1932. II. Title.

Philosophy—Miscellanea.

HALLOCK, Charles, 1834- 110
Luminous bodies here and hereafter (the shining ones) Being an attempt to explain the interrelation of the intellectual, celestial and terrestial(!) kingdoms, and of man to his Maker, by Charles Hallock ... New York, The Metaphysical publishing co. [c1906] 110 p. incl. front. 19 1/2 cm. [BD701.H36] 6-17856
1. Philosophy—Miscellanea. I. Title.

SWANDER, John I. 1833-1925. 110
The invisible world. Thoughts upon the reality of immaterial entities in the universe of God. By John I. Swander ... Dayton, O., Press Reformed publishing co., 1891. 3 p. l., 9-333 p. 20 1/2 cm. [BD701.S9] 11-24744
1. Philosophy—Miscellanea. I. Title.

Philosophy, Modern.

ADLER, Felix, 1851-1933. 218
An ethical philosophy of life presented in its main outlines, by Felix Adler. New York, London, D. Appleton and company, 1918. viii, 380 p. 22 1/2 cm. [BD431.A4] 18-10283
1. Philosophy, Modern. 2. Ethics. I. Title.

BREYFOGLE, William La Martine,
1845-
Sense and satire based upon nineteenth century philosophy, by Wm. L. Breyfogle ... Illustrations by J. W. Breyfogle. Chicago and New York, Rand, McNally & co. [1899] xv p. 1 l., 237 p. plates. 19 cm. [PS1122.B8S4] 99-4522
I. Title.

BURKILL, T. Alec 190
God and reality in modern thought. Englewood Cliffs, N.J., Prentice-Hall, 1963. 272 p. 22 cm. Includes bibliography. [B791.B78] 63-9833
1. Philosophy, Modern. 2. Religion — Philosophy. I. Title.

COUSE, Adam, comp.
The new philosophy of being and existence, taken from the sayings of Pythagoras, Parmenides, Soorates ... and others ... Ed. and pub. by Adam Couse. Detroit, Mich. [c1883] 2 p. l., 234 p. 20 cm. [BD555.C84] 11-23113
I. Title.

HODDER, Alfred, 1866-1907. 149.
The adversaries of the sceptic; or, The specious present, a new inquiry into human knowledge, by Alfred Hodder, PH.D. London, S. Sonnenschein & co., ltd. New York, The Macmillan company, 1901. 339 p. 20 cm. For the most part reprinted from the Philosophical review, International journal of ethics, and the Nation. "The first four chapters ... and a portion of the sixth were accepted by the Faculty of Harvard college as a thesis for the degree of doctor of philosophy."--Pref. [B837.H6] 2-12252
I. Title.
Contents omitted.

KLOCKER, Harry R. 189.4
Thomism and modern thought. New York, Appleton [c.1962] 320p. 22cm. Bibl. 62-9414 4.00 bds.,
1. Thomas Aquinas, Saint—Philosophy. 2. Philosophy, Modern. I. Title.

LOWITH, Karl, 1897- 190.9
From Hegel to Nietzche; the revolution in nineteenth-century thought, by Karl Lowith. Tr. from German by David E. Green. Garden City, N. Y., Doubleday [1967, c.1964] xii, 468p. 19cm. (Anchor bk., A553] Bibl. 1.75 pap.,
1. Hegel, Georg Wilhelm Friedrich, 1770-1831. 2. Philosophy, Modern. 3. Sociology. 4. Religious thought-19th cent. I. Title. II. Title: The revolution in nineteenth-century thought.

LOWITH, Karl, 1897- 190.9
From Hegel to Nietzsche: the revolution in nineteenth-century thought. Translated from the German by David E. Green. [1st ed.] New York, Holt, Rinehart and Winston [1964] xiii, 464 p. 24 cm. Bibliography: p. 389-395. [B803.L623] 64-11274
1. Hegel, Georg Wilhelm Friedrich, 1770-1831. 2. Philosphy, Modern. 3. Sociology. 4. Religious thought—19th century. I. Title. II. Title: The revolution in nineteenth-century thought.

MACRAKIS, Apostolos, 199.495
1831-1905.
A new philosophy, and the philosophical sciences, by Apostolos Makrakis... New York, G. P. Putnam's sons, 1940. 2 v. fronts (ports.) 24 1/2 cm. Each volume has added t.-p: A new original philosophical system. Edited by Peter Vassilakos and Kostas Andronis. Vol. 1 translated by Denver Cummings; v. 2 by Albert George Alexander. Contents.--v. 1. Introduction to philosophy. Psychology. Logic. Theology. Philosophy.--v. 2. Ethics. [BS515.M33N4 1940] 40-12143
I. Vassilakos, Peter, 1877- ed. II. Andronis, Kostas, 1908-joint ed. III. Cummings, Denver, tr. IV. Alexander, Albert George, tr. V. Title.

MAHONY, Michael Joseph, 1860- 190
History of modern thought, the English, Irish and Scoth schools, by Michael J. Mahony ... New York, Fordham university press, 1933. 4 p. l., [7]-188 p. 22 cm. An exposition of the philosophy of Locke, Berkeley, Hume and Kant. [B791.M3] 33-16987
1. Locke, John, 1632-1704. 2. Berkeley, George, bp. of Cloyne, 1685-1753. 3. Hume, David, 1711-1776. 4. Kant, Immanuel, 1724-1804. 5. Philosophy, Modern. I. Title.

NEBORAK, Sonja. 270.8
Thoughts in the atomic age. New York, Philosophical Library [1951] 157 p. 21 cm. [BR126.N37] 52-6324
I. Title.

SANTAYANA, George, 1863-1952. 190
Winds of doctrine, and Platonism and the spiritual life. Gloucester, Mass., P. Smith, 1971. v, 312 p. 21 cm. "First published 1913 and 1927." [B945.S23W7 1971] 73-27989
1. Philosophy, Modern. 2. Spiritual life. I. Santayana, George, 1863-1952. Platonism and the spiritual life. 1971. II. Title.

SHEEN, Fulton John, 1895- 204
Old errors and new labels. Garden City, N.Y., Garden City Pub. Co. [1950, c1931] ix, 336 p. 21 cm. [B804.S5 1950] 51-2078
1. Philosophy, Modern. 2. Philosophy and religion. I. Title.

SHEEN, Fulton John, 1895- 204
Old errors and new labels, by Fulton J. Sheen ... New York, The Century co. [c1931] ix, 336 p. 19 1/2 cm. $2.00 Critical essays on contemporary ideas. cf. Pref. [B804.S5] 31-12475
1. Philosophy, Modern,. 2. Philosophy and religion. I. Title.

SMITH, Thomas Vernor, 1890- ed.
Berkeley, Hume and Kant; ed. by T. V. Smith and Marjorie Grene. [Chicago] University of Chicago press [1957] v, 377 p. 21 cm. (Philosophers speak for themselves; Phoenix books, P18)
1. Philosophy, Modern. I. Grene, Marjorie (Glicksman) 1910- joint ed. II. Title.

SMITH, Thomas Vernor, 190.822
1890- ed.
From Descartes to Kant; readings in the philosophy of the renaissance and enlightenment, by T. V. Smith and Majorie Grene. Chicago, Ill., The University of Chicago press [1940] viii, 899 p. diagrs. 24 cm. Includes bibliographies. [B790.S55] 40-34132
1. Philosophy, Modern. I. Grene, Majorie, joint ed. II. Title.

STOUT, George Frederick, 190
1860-1944.
God & nature. The second of two volumes (the first being 'Mind & matter') based on the Gifford lectures delivered in the University of Edinburgh in 1919 and 1921. Edited by A. K. Stout, with a memoir by J. A. Passmore. Cambridge [Eng.] University Press, 1952. liv, 339 p. port. 22 cm. "List of Stout's works": p. L-iiv. [B1667.S373G6] 52-9148
1. Philosophy, Modern. 2. Religion — Philosophy. 3. Knowledge, Theory of. 4. Mind and body. I. Title.

Philosophy, Modern—20th century

EDMAN, Irwin, 1896-1954.
The contemporary and his soul. Port Washington, N. Y., Kennikat Press [1967, c1959] vii, 191 p. 21 cm. 68-85471
1. Philosophy, Modern—20th cent. 2. Philosophy and religion. 3. Salvation I. Title.

MACQUARRIE, John 190
Twentieth-century religious thought; the frontiers of philosophy and theology, 1900-1960. New York, Harper [c.1963]. 415p. 22cm. (Lib. of religion and culture) Bibl. 63-12166 5.00
1. Philosophy, Modern—20th cent. 2. Religious thought—20th cent. I. Title.

MACQUARRIE, John. 200'.9'04
Twentieth-century religious thought : the frontiers of philosophy and theology, 1900-1980 / John Macquarrie. New York : Scribner, c1981. 429 p. ; 23 cm. Includes bibliographical references and index. [B804.M25 1981] 19 81-9349 ISBN 0-684-17333-6 : 17.95 ISBN 0-684-17334-4 (pbk.) : 12.00
1. Philosophy, Modern—20th century. 2. Religious thought—20th century. I. Title.

SHEEN, Fulton John, Bp., 190
1895-
Old errors and new labels, by Fulton J. Sheen. Port Washington, N.Y., Kennikat Press [1970, c1931] ix, 336 p. 22 cm. (Essay and general literature index reprint series) [B804.S5 1970] 72-93071
1. Philosophy, Modern—20th century. 2. Philosophy and religion. I. Title.

Philosophy, Modern—Addresses, essays, lectures.

BIBLICAL errancy : 190
an analysis of its philosophical roots / Norman L. Geisler, editor. Grand Rapids, Mich. : Zondervan Pub. House, c1981. 270 p. ; 22 cm. Includes bibliographical references and indexes. [BS480.B4753] 19 80-28486 ISBN 0-310-39291-8 pbk. : 7.95
1. Bible—Evidences, authority, etc.—Addresses, essays, lectures. 2. Philosophy, Modern—Addresses, essays, lectures. I. Geisler, Norman L.

SHESTOV, Lev, 1866-1938. 190
Speculation and revelation / Lev Shestov ; translated by Bernard Martin. Athens : Ohio University Press, c1982. x, 312 p. ; 24 cm. Translation of Umozrenie i otkrovenie. Includes bibliographical references and index. [B803.S513] 19 81-38425 ISBN 0-8214-0422-9 : 32.95
1. Philosophy, Modern—Addresses, essays, lectures. 2. Philosophy and religion—Addresses, essays, lectures. I. [Umozrenie i otkrovenie.] English II. Title.

Philosophy, Modern—Collections.

KUYKENDALL, Eleanor, 1938- 190
comp.
Philosophy in the age of crisis. New York, Harper & Row [1970] xi, 498 p. 25 cm. (Harper's philosophy series) Includes bibliographies. [B790.K88] 71-113489
1. Philosophy, Modern—Collections. 2. Man—Addresses, essays, lectures. 3. Violence—Addresses, essays, lectures. 4. Religion—Philosophy—Addresses, essays, lectures. I. Title.

Philosophy of nature.

BONIFAZI, Conrad 1912- 210
A theology of things; a study of man in his physical environment [1st ed.] Philadelphia, Lippincott [1967] 237 p. 21 cm. Bibliographical footnotes. [BD581.B587] 67-20168
1. Philosophy of nature. 2. Christian ethics. I. Title.

BONIFAZI, Conrad, 1912- 210
A theology of things : a study of man in his physical environment / Conrad Bonifazi. Westport, Conn. : Greenwood Press, 1976, c1967. 237 p. ; 23 cm. Reprint of the ed. published by Lippincott, Philadelphia. Includes bibliographical references and index. [BD581.B587 1976] 76-7549 ISBN 0-8371-8838-5 lib.bdg. : 14.00
1. Philosophy of nature. 2. Nature (Theology) I. Title.

BONIFAZI, Conrad, 1912- 210
A theology of things; a study of man in his physical environment. [1st ed.] Philadelphia, Lippincott [1967] 237 p. 21 cm. Bibliographical footnotes. [BD581.B587] 67-20168
1. Philosophy of nature. 2. Christian ethics. I. Title.

KOHN, Harold E 248.42
Reflections on the nature of the world and man, life's values and its destiny. Illustrated by the author. Grand Rapids Eerdmans [1963] 190 p. illus. 24 cm. [BD581.K55] 62-18953
1. Philosophy of nature. 2. Religion and science—1946- I. Title.

Philosophy, Oriental.

ADAM, Michael. 181
Wandering in Eden : three ways to the East within us / Michael Adam. 1st ed. New York : Knopf : distributed by Random House, 1976. 108 p. : ill. ; 29 cm. Includes bibliographical references. [B121.A3 1976] 75-34287 ISBN 0-394-49980-8 : 10.00
1. Philosophy, Oriental. 2. East and West. 3. Zen Buddhism. 4. Art, Oriental. 5. Religions. I. Title.

ADAM, Michael. 181
Wandering in Eden : three ways to the East within us / Michael Adam. 1st ed. New York : Vintage Books, 1976. p. cm. [B121.A3 1976b] 75-34303 ISBN 0-394-73141-7
1. Philosophy, Oriental. 2. East and West. 3. Zen Buddhism. 4. Art, Oriental. 5. Religions. I. Title.

KIM, Yong Choon. 291'.095
Oriental thought : an introduction to the philosophical and religious thought of Asia / by Yong Choon Kim ; with a foreword by David H. Freeman. Totowa, N.J. : Littlefield, Adams, 1981. p. cm. (Littlefield, Adams quality paperback series ; 365) Reprint of the 1973 ed. published by Thomas, Springfield, Ill. Includes bibliographical references and index. [B121.K5 1981] 19 80-39680 ISBN 0-8226-0365-9 pbk. : 8.95
1. Philosophy, Oriental. 2. Civilization, Oriental. I. Title.

ROBINSON, James A. 812'.52
A divided vision, Eugene O'Neill and Oriental thought / by James A. Robinson. Carbondale : Southern Illinois University Press, c1982. p. cm. Includes index. Bibliography: p. [PS3529.N5Z794] 19 81-14428 ISBN 0-8093-1035-X : 17.50
1. O'Neill, Eugene, 1888-1953—Criticism and interpretation. 2. O'Neill, Eugene, 1888-1953—Philosophy. 3. Philosophy, Oriental. 4. Asia—Religion. I. Title.

Philosophy, Renaissance.

DE SANTILLANA, Giorgio, 1902- ed.
The age of adventure; the Renaissance philosophers, selected, with introd. and interpretive commentary. Boston, Houghton Mifflin, 1962. 2 v. 24 cm. 66-23266
1. Philosophy, Renaissance. I. Title.

Philpot, Ford.

BOWDOIN, Herbert L. 922.773
It took a miracle! [By] Herbert L. Bowdoin. Westwood, N. J., F. H. Revell Co. [1964] 126 p. 21 cm. [BX8495.P53B6] 64-25010
1. Philpot, Ford. I. Title.

Phinehas ben Abraham, of Korets, 1726 or 8-1791.

WIESEL, Elie, 1928- 296.8'33
Four Hasidic masters and their struggle against melancholy / by Elie Wiesel ; foreword, Theodore M. Hesburgh. Notre Dame [Ind.] : University of Notre Dame Press, c1978. xix, 131 p., [1] leaf of plates : ill. ; 21 cm. (Ward-Phillips lectures in English language and literature ; v. 9) [BM198.W5125] 78-1419 ISBN 0-268-00944-9 : 7.95
1. Phinehas ben Abraham, of Korets, 1726 or 8-1791. 2. Baruch, of Tul'chin, 1757 (ca.)-1811. 3. Horowitz, Jacob Isaac, d. 1815. 4. Horowitz, Naphtali Zebi, 1760-1827. 5. Hasidim—Biography. I. Title. II. Series.

Phinney, Clement, 1780-1855.

GRAHAM, Daniel McBride, 1817- 922 1889.
The life of Clement Phinney. By D. M. Graham ... Dover, N. H., W. Burr, printer, 1851. x p., 1 l., [13]-190 p. front. (port.) 17 cm. [F24.G73] 5-158
1. Phinney, Clement, 1780-1855. 2. Free Baptists—Maine. I. Title.

Phonorecords in missionary work.

BARLOW, Sanna Morrison. 266.0847
Arrows of His bow. Chicago, Moody Press [1960] 208p. illus. 22cm. [BV2082.A8B3] 60-16877
1. Richter, Don. 2. Phonorecords in missionary work. 3. Gospel Recordings, inc. I. Title.

Phonotapes in church work.

SoGAARD, Viggo B. 266'.0028
Everything you need to know for a cassette ministry : cassettes in the context of a total Christian communication program / by Viggo B. Sogaard. Minneapolis : Bethany Fellowship, inc., [1975] 221 p. : ill. ; 21 cm. Bibliography: p. 211-214. [BV652.83.S63] 74-20915 ISBN 0-87123-125-5 : 3.95
1. Phonotapes in church work. I. Title.

Photius I, Saint, Patriarch of Constantinople, ca. 820-ca. 891.

GEROSTERGIOS, Asterios. 281'.4'0924 B
St. Photios the Great / by Asterios Gerostergios. Belmont, Mass. : Institute for Byzantine and Modern Greek Studies, c1980. 125 p. : ill. ; 21 cm. Includes index. Bibliography: p. 113-116. [BX395.P5G47] 19 80-82285 ISBN 0-914744-50-X : 7.00 ISBN 0-914744-51-8 pbk. : 5.00
1. Photius I, Saint, Patriarch of Constantinople, ca. 820-ca. 891. 2. Christian saints—Turkey—Istanbul—Biography. 3. Istanbul—Biography. I. Title.

HAUGH, Richard. 231
Photius and the Carolingians : the Trinitarian controversy / Richard Haugh. Belmont, Mass. : Nordland Pub. Co., [1975] 230 p. ; 23 cm. Includes index. Bibliography: p. 207-214. [BT109.H35] 74-22859 ISBN 0-913124-05-2 : 15.00
1. Photius I, Saint, Patriarch of Constantinople, ca. 820-ca. 891. 2. Trinity—History of doctrines. I. Title.

PHOTIUS, Patriarch of Constantinople. 270
... The library of Photius ... By J. H. Freese. London, Society for promoting Christian knowledge; New York, The Macmillan company, 1920. v. 19 cm. (Translations of Christian literature. ser. i: Greek texts. [2]) "Alphabetical list of authors criticised": v. 1, p. vii-x. [BR45.T6P5] 21-3789
I. Freese, John Henry, d. 1930, ed. and tr. II. Title.

WHITE, Despina Stratoudaki. 270.3'092'4 B
Patriarch Photios of Constantinople : his life, scholarly contributions, and correspondence together with a translation of fifty-two of his letters / by Despina Stratoudaki White. Brookline, Mass. : Holy Cross Orthodox Press, 1981, c1982. 234 p. ; 23 cm. (The Archbishop Iakovos library of ecclesiastical and historical sources ; no. 5) Includes index. Bibliography: p. 204-222. [BX395.P5W48 1982] 19 82-1004 ISBN 0-916586-26-X pbk. : 4.95 ISBN 0-916586-21-9 : 9.95
1. Photios I, Saint, Patriarch of Constantinople, ca. 820-ca. 891. 2. Christian saints—Turkey—Biography. I. Photius I, Saint, Patriarch of Constantinople, ca. 820-ca. 891. II. Title. III. Series.

Photography of the invisible.

COATES, James. 133.
Photographing the invisible; practical studies in spirit photography, spirit portraiture, and other rare but allied phenomena, by James Coates... with 90 photographs. Chicago, Ill., Advanced thought publishing co.: [etc., etc.] 1911. vi, [2], vii-xxi, 394 p. front. (port.) illus. (incl. ports.) 20 cm. [BF1381.C6] 11-29051 2.00
1. Photography of the invisible. 2. Spiritualism. I. Title.

Phrenology.

BURTON, Warren, 1800-1866.
Uncle Sam's recommendation of phrenology to his millions of friends in the United States. In a series of not very dull letters. New York, Harper and brothers, 1842. iv, [5]-302 [1] p. illus. 16 cm. [BP870.B9] 10-27084
1. Phrenology. I. Title.

EMERY, Philip Alfred, 1830- 133
Landscapes of history. A manual explanatory of chart, Religion and science: and the twelve axioms of history. By P. A. Emery...The twin rivers, a poem by J. T. C. Appendix containing a brief biographical sketch of the author and a written delineation of his phrenological character. Chicago, Mrs. M. A. Emery, 1875. 115 p. incl. front. (port.) 15 1/2 cm. Some sections preceded by half-titles (4. l.) not included in the pagination. [X3.E5] 33-3665
I. C., J. T. II. J. T. C., III. Title. IV. Title: The twin rivers.

FOWLER, Orson Squire, 1809-1887.
Religion; natural and revealed or, The natural theology and moral bearings of phrenology and physiology: including the doctrines taught and duties inculcated thereby, compared with those enjoined in the Scriptures. Together with the phrenological exposition of the doctrines of a future state ... By O. S. Fowler ... 2d ed., enl. and improved. New York, O. S. Fowler; [etc., etc.] 1844. iv, [vii]-xiv, [15]-174 p. illus. (diagr.) 23 cm. [BF885.R3F7] 18-12147
1. Phrenology. I. Title.

VAUGHT, Louis Allen, 1859-
Vaught's practical character reader, by L. A. Vaught ... Chicago, L. A. Vaught, 1902. 257 p. front., illus. (incl. ports.) 19 1/2 cm. Advertising matter: p. 256-257. [BV871.V3] 3-18663
1. Phrenology. 2. Physiognomy. I. Title.

WICKES, Edward Zeus Franklin.
Improved phreno-chart and compass of life, a new, true, mental and spiritual science ... All rights reserved by the author E. Z. Franklin Wickes ... New York, Mutual benefit publishing co., 1882. 190 p. illus. 17 1/2 cm. Published 1865 under title: Illustrated phreno-chart and compass of life. CA 9
I. Title.

Phrygia—History

RAMSAY, William Mitchell, Sir 1851-
The cities and bishoprics of Phrygia; being an essay of the local history of Phrygia from the earliest times to the Turkish conquest, by W. M. Ramsay ... Oxford, The Clarendon press, 1895. v. illus., plates, maps (3 fold.) 25 cm. General map in pocket. Most of the chapters have appendices containing inscriptions, list of bishops, etc. [DS156.P5R18] 1-3404
1. Phrygia—Hist. 2. Incriptions, Greek—Phrygia. 3. Bishops—Phrygia. 4. Asia Minor—Historical geography. I. Title.
Contents omitted.

Phylacteries.

KAPLAN, Aryeh. 296.7'2
Tefillin : G-d, man and tefillin / by Aryeh Kaplan. New York : National Conference of Synagogue Youth, c1973. 80 p. : ill. ; 21 cm. Includes bibliographical references. [BM657.P5K3] 74-193351 2.50
1. Phylacteries. I. Title.

Physical education and training.

PANZER, Henry, 1867-
A teacher's manual of physical education; general gymnastics for boys, by Henry Panzer...with one hundred and forty-one illustrations. New York, A. S. Barnes and company, 1928. xvii, 237 p. illus. 24 cm. [BV363.P3] 28-15559
1. Physical education and training. 2. Gymnastics. I. Title.

YOUNG men's Christian Associations. 267.355
The new physical education in the Young men's Christian associations; a contribution to understanding and planning, by a special committee under the chairmanship of John R. McCurdy, appointed by the Program services committee of the National council. New York, Association press, 1938 ix, 160 p. diagrs. 22 cm. Includes bibliographies. [GV341.Y6] 40-13218
1. Physical education and training. I. McCurdy, John R. II. Title.

Physical research.

ADLEMAN, Robert H., 1919- 133
The black box; an excursion into inner sensory perception, by Robert H. Adleman. Los Angeles, Nash Pub. [1973] 170 p. 23 cm. Bibliography: p. 161-170. [BF1031.A24] 72-95249 ISBN 0-8402-1299-2 7.95
1. Physical research. I. Title.

BENNETT, Ernest Nathaniel, Sir 1868- 133
Apollonius; or, The present and future of psychical research, by E. N. Bennett ... London, K. Paul, Trench, Trubner & co., ltd.; New York, E. P. Dutton & co., ltd. [1927] 95 p. 16 1/2 cm. [To-day and to-morrow] [BF1031.B4 1927a] 42-49753
1. Physical research. I. Title.

CARRINGTON, Hereward, 1880- 133
The world of psychic research. [New ed.] No. Hollywood, Calif., Wilshire Book Co. [1973] 190 p. 21 cm. (Self-improvement library) Published in 1946 under title: The invisible world. [BF1031.C32193] ISBN 0-87980-254-5 2.00 (pbk.)
1. Physical research. I. Title.
L.C. card no. for the hardbound edition: 72-6371

CLARKE, John Bertrum. 133.
The chart of mind, and Winning health and great aims with waves of mind power, by John Bertrum Clarke. Los Angeles, Calif., J. B. Clarke; [etc., etc. 1923]. xi, 12-154 p. fold. front. (tab.) plates. 20 cm. [BF1301.C55] 23-11539
1. Physical research. I. Title.

DUBOR, Georges de, 1848- 133.072
The mysteries of hypnosis (Les mysteres de l'hypnose) by Georges de Dubor; translated by G. M. Hort. New York, Moffat, Yard & co., 1923. xi, 235 p. 19 cm. Printed in Great Britain. [BF1062.D62] [159.961] 41-37846
1. Physical research. 2. Hypnotism. I. Hort, G. M., tr. II. Title.

IRWIN, Frank 133.4
The Blocksberg tryst. Franklin, N.H., Hillside Pr. Box 204 [c.] 1963. 70 p. illus. 60mm. 63-3827 lim. ed. 3.50
1. Physical research. 2. Witchcraft. I. Title.
Contents omitted.

PERSINGER, Michael A. 133'.01'8
The paranormal, by Michael A. Persinger. New York, MSS Information Corp. [1974- p. cm. Contents.Contents.— —pt. 2. Mechanisms and models. Includes bibliographical references. [BF1031.P47] 74-19227 11.00; 5.00 (pbk.).
1. Physical research. I. Title.

SEYMOUR, Charles J. 133.072
Curiosities of physical research, by Charles J. Seymour. London, New York [etc.] Rider [1944] 64 p. front. (port.) illus. (incl. facsims) 19 cm. Bibliographical foot-notes. [BF1031.S445] 44-47850
1. Physical research. I. Title.

SMITH, Alson Jesse. 130.072
Religion and the new psychology. [1st ed.] Garden City, N.Y., Doubleday, 1951. 192 p. 21 cm. [BF1031.S6] 51-9915
1. Physical research. I. Title.

SPRAGGETT, Allen. 133
The unexplained. Foreword by James A. Pike. [New York] New American Library [1967] xiii, 232 p. 21 cm. Bibliography: p. 231-232. [BF1031.S76] 67-26236
1. Physical research. I. Title.

TRUMAN, Olivia M. 133.
The A. B. C. of occultism, the answer to life's riddles, by Olivia M. Truman. London, K. Paul, Trench, Trubner & co. ltd.; New York, E. P. Dutton & co., 1920. xii, 100 p. 18 1/2 cm. Bibliography: p. 98-100. [BF1031.T7] 21-18518
1. Physical research. 2. Occult sciences. I. Title.

Physical research — Dictionaries.

FODOR, Nandor. 133.903
Encyclopedia of psychic science. [New Hyde Park, N.Y.] University Books [1966] xxxix, 415 p. 26 cm. Includes bibliographical references. [BF1025.F6] 66-16316
1. Physical research — Dictionaries. 2. Spiritualism — Dictionaries. I. Title.

Physically handicapped—Rehabilitation—Korea.

STEENSMA, Juliana. 266.5'1519
The quality of mercy. Richmond, John Knox Press [1969] 143 p. illus., ports. 21 cm. [HV1559.K8S73] 69-13271 3.95
1. Steensma, John. 2. Physically handicapped—Rehabilitation—Korea. 3. Missions—Korea. I. Title.

[Physicians.]

MONTGOMERY, Elizabeth Rider. 266'.025'0924 B
Albert Schweitzer, great humanitarian. Illustrated by William Hutchinson. Champaign, Ill., Garrard Pub. Co. [1971] 144 p. illus., ports. 22 cm. ([A People in the arts and sciences book]) A biography of the musician, minister, and teacher who gave up a comfortable teaching career to become a missionary doctor in the African jungle. [CT1098.S45M63] 92 70-132035 ISBN 0-8116-4510-X 2.59
1. Schweitzer, Albert, 1875-1965—Juvenile literature. 2. [Schweitzer, Albert, 1875-1965.] 3. [Physicians.] I. Hutchinson, William M., illus. II. Title.

STEPHENS, James T 610.69
The Christian as a doctor, by James T. Stephens and Edward LeRoy Long. New York, Association Press,[1960] 126 p. 20 cm. (Series on the Christian in his vocation) A Haddam House book. [BL265.M4S8] 60-12714
1. Physicians. 2. Medicine and religion. I. Long, Edward Le Roy, joint author. II. Title.

Physicians—Correspondence, reminiscences, etc.

SEEL, David John, 1925- 248.8'6
Does my father know I'm hurt? Illustrated by Peggy Bradford Long. Wheaton, Ill., Tyndale House Publishers [1971] 96 p. illus. 18 cm. [R630.S4A3] 70-155975 ISBN 0-8423-0670-6(pbk)
1. Physicians—Correspondence, reminiscences, etc. 2. Cancer—Korea. 3. Missions, Medical—Korea. I. Title.

Physics—Early works to 1800.

SWEDENBORG, Emanuel, 1688-1772. 530
Miscellaneous observations connected with the physical sciences. By Emanuel Swedenborg ... translated from the Latin by Charles Edward Strutt ... London, W. Newbery; Boston, U.S., O. Clapp, 1847. xvi, 168 p. ix pl. 22 1/2 cm. [With his Some specimens of a work on the principles of chemistry ... London, 1847. Copy 3] Binder's title: Swedenborg [Works] v. 7. [BX8711.A2 1819 vol. 7] (230.94) 36-29683
1. Physics—Early works to 1800. 2. Mineralogy—Early works to 1800. I. Strutt, Charles Edward, tr. II. Title.

Physics—Philosophy.

JAKI, Stanley L
The role of faith in physics. Chicago, 1967. 187-202 p. 23 cm. "Reprinted from Zygon: Journal of religion and science, vol. 2, no. 2, June 1967." 68-96453
1. Physics—Philosophy. I. Title.

Physiology—Early works to 1800.

SWEDENBORG, Emanuel, 1688-1772. 612
The animal kingdom, considered anatomically, physically, and philosophically. By Emanuel Swedenborg ... Translated from the Latin, by James John Garth Wilkinson ... London, W. Newbery [etc.]; Boston, U.S., O. Clapp, 1843-44. 2 v. 22 1/2 cm. [Works. London. 1819-50. v. 32-33] John Spurgin cooperated in the revision of this work. cf. J. Hyde. A bibliography of the works of Emanuel Swedenborg (nos. 439-440) "Index of subjects": v. 2, p. [609]-652; "Appendix": v. 2, p. [653]- 658: "Corrections in the work": v. 2, p. 658. "Bibliographical notices respecting certain authors cited": v. 2, p. [599]-608: [BX8711.A2 1819 vol. 32-33] (230.94) 36-30565
1. Physiology—Early works to 1800. I. Wilkinson, James John Garth, 1812-1899, tr. II. Spurgin, John, 1797-1866, ed. III. Title.

SWEDENBORG, Emanuel, 1688-1772. 612
The economy of the animal kingdom, considered anatomically, physically, and philosophically. By Emanuel Swedenborg ... Translated from the Latin by the Rev. Augustus Clissold ... London, W. Newberry [etc.]; Boston, U.S., O. Clapp, 1846. 2 v. illus., pl. 22 1/2 cm. [Works. London, 1819-50. v. 30-31] "Edited by Mr. Wilkinson."--Pref. "Introduction to rational psychology": v. 2, p. [1]-56. "The human soul": v. 2, p. [201]-357. With v. 2 is bound the author's ... CEconomia regni animails ... nunc primum edidit Jae, Joh. Garth Wilkinson ... Londini, 1847. "Bibliographical notices of authors cited": v. 2, p. [363]-369. [BX8711.A2 1819 vol. 30-31] (230.94) 36-29685
1. Physiology—Early works to 1800. 2. Science—Philosophy. 3. Soul. 4. Psychology—Early works to 1850. I. Clissold, Augustus, 1797?-1882, tr. II. Wilkinson, James John Garth, 1812-1899, ed. III. Title.

Pichaske, Donald R., ed.

MULLINS, Terence.
The Old Testament for us. Term 1. and 2. Youth's real life problems Term 3 Philadelphia, Lutheran Church Press [c1965] 320 p., illus. 23 cm. (Lutheran church in America. Sunday church school ser. Teacher's guide, grade 8, terms 1-3) 67-57663
1. Pichaske, Donald R., ed. I. Title. II. Series.

Pickard, Mrs. Hannah Maynard (Thompson) 1812-1844.

OTHEMAN, Edward. 922.773
Memoir and writings of Mrs. Hannah Maynard Pickard; late wife of Rev. Humphrey Pickard ... By Edward Otheman ... Boston, D. H. Ela, printer, 1845. 1 p. l., [v]-xii, [13]-311 p. 22 cm. [BX8495.P54O7] 36-37394
1. Pickard, Mrs. Hannah Maynard (Thompson) 1812-1844. I. Title.

Pickett, Aaron, 1792-1866.

[ALLEN, George], 1792-1883. 922.
A review of the Reverend Aaron Pickett's "Reply" and "Defense" By Vindex [pseud.] ... Boston, W. Crosby and H. P. Nichols, 1848. 57 p. 23 cm. In vindication of Dr. Edward Bescher. "Appendix. Resolutions of the South church in Reading, adopted December 15, 1847": p. [53]-57. "The "Reply" and "Defense" appeared in the Boston "Reporder", Oct. 7, 1867, and in the Boston "Reporter", Nov. 25, 1847."--J. Sabin, Bibl. Amer., v. 15. [BX7260.P6A6] 12-18341
1. Pickett, Aaron, 1792-1866. 2. Beecher, Edward, 1803-1895. I. Title.

Pickett, Clarence Evan, 1884-1965.

KAHOE, Walter, ed. 289.60924(B)
Clarence Pickett, a memoir, [Moylan? Penn.] 1966. v, 52p. mounted ports. 23cm. Bibl. [BX7795.P55K3] 66-21720 2.00 bds.,
1. Pickett, Clarence Evan, 1884-1965. I. Title.
Available from the editor at the Rose Valley Pr., Moylan, Pa., 19065.

Pickett, Joseph Worthy, 1832-1879.

SALTER, William, 1821-1910. 922.573
Memoirs of Joseph W. Pickett, Missionary superintendent in southern Iowa and in the Rocky mountains for the American home missionary society. By William Salter... Burlington, Ia., J. Love; Colorado Springs, Col., Mrs. S. B. Pickett, 1880. 1 p. l., [5]-150 p. 19 1/2 cm. [BX7260.P62S3] 36-25683
1. Pickett, Joseph Worthy, 1832-1879. I. Title.

Picture dictionaries, Hebrew—Juvenile literature.

MESHI, Ita. 492.4'09 E
A child's picture Hebrew dictionary. Illustrated by Ita Meshi. New York, Sabra Books [1970?] [40] p. col. illus. 28 cm. Words in English and Hebrew. Words for each letter of the Hebrew alphabet are accompanied by illustrations. [PZ7.M549Ch] 70-124122 ISBN 0-87631-041-2 4.95
1. Picture dictionaries, Hebrew—Juvenile literature. 2. Hebrew language—Dictionaries—English. 3. [Picture dictionaries, Hebrew.] 4. [Alphabet books, Hebrew.] I. Title.

Pictures.

SMITH, Jean Louise. 268.6354
Great art and children's worship, with twenty-four examples of programs interpreting art masterpieces in the church school. New York, Abingdon-Cokesbury Press [1948] 200 p. illus. 21 cm. "Suggested books on art": p. 193-195. [BV1535.S57] 48-10046
1. Pictures. 2. Worship (Religious education. I. Title.

Pierce Lusanna T., 1828-1836.

GOULD, William. 922
Memoir of Susanna T. Pierce, who died in Freetown. Mass., Sept. 24th, 1836. Aged 7 years and 10 months. By Rev. William Gould ... Written for the Massachusetts Sabbath school society, and revised by the Committee of publication. Boston, Massachusetts Sabbath school society, 1837. 72 p. 16 cm. "The name should have been Lusanna T. Pierce, instead of Susanna T. Pierce."--Slip mounted on lining-paper. [BR1715.P44G6] 37-20251
1. Pierce Lusanna T., 1828-1836. I. Massachusetts Sabbath school society. Committee of publication. II. Title.

Pierce, Robert Willard, 1914-

DUNKER, Marilee Pierce. 269'.2'0924 B
Man of vision, woman of prayer / Marilee Pierce Dunker. Nashville : T. Nelson, c1980. 254 p., [8] leaves of plates : ill. ; 21 cm. [BV3785.P53D86] 19 80-19698 ISBN 0-8407-5220-2 : 9.95
1. Pierce, Robert Willard, 1914- 2. Pierce, Lorraine. 3. Evangelists—East Asia—Biography. I. Title.

GEHMAN, Richard 275
Let my heart be broken with the things that break the heart of God. Photos. by Richard Reinhold. Grand Rapids, Mich., Zondervan [1966, c.1960] 245p. illus. 21cm. [BV2360.W88G4] .98 pap.,
1. Pierce, Robert Willard, 1914- 2. World Vision, Inc. 3. Missions—Asia. I. Title.

Pierpont, John, 1786-1808.

WASHBURN, Emory, 1800- 1877. 922.8173
Argument of Hon. Emory Washburn, before an ecclesiastical council, convened in Hollis street meeting house, July, 1841: with the charges preferred by the proprietors of said meeting house against the Rev. John Pierpont, and the result of said council. Boston, Printed by S. N. Dickinson, 1841. vi, [7]-120 p. 24 cm. [BX9869.P6W3] 37-9302
1. Pierpont, John, 1786-1808. I. Boston. Hollis street church. II. Title.

Pierre le Venerable, 1092 (ca.)-1156.

KRITZECK, James. 297
Peter the Venerable and Islam. Princeton, N.J., Princeton University Press, 1964. xiv, 301 p. 25 cm. (Princeton oriental studies, no 23) An analysis and new annotated edition of the following texts:Summa totius haeresis Saracenorum. Epistola Petrl Cluniacensis ad Bernardum Claravaevallis. Epistola Petrl Pictavensis. Capitula Petrl Pictavensis. Liber contra sectam sive haeresim Saracenorum. Bibliographical footnotes. [PJ25.P7] [BX4705.P478K7] 63-18646
1. Pierre ie Venerable, 1092 (ca.)-1156. 2. Christianity and other religions — Mohammedanism. 3. Mohammedianism — Relations — Christianity. I. Title. II. Series: Oriental studies series, no. 23

Pierz, Minn. St. Joseph's Church.

VOIGT, Robert J 282.77669
Pierzana: 1865-1965; the religious and secular history of the community at Pierz, Minnesota by Robert T. Voight [Saint Cloud, Minn., Mills Creative Printing, 1965] 197 p. illus., map. ports. 24 cm. [BX4603.P53S4] 65-6684
1. Pierz, Minn. St. Joseph's Church. I. Title.

Pietism.

NAGLER, Arthur Wilford. 287.
Pietism and Methodism; or, The significance of German pietism in the origin and early development of Methodism, by Arthur Wilford Nagler ... Nashville, Tenn., Dallas, Tex. [etc.] Publishing house M. E. Church, South, Smith & Lamas, agents, 1918. 3 p. l., 3-200 p. 20 cm. Bibliography: p. 186-199. [BX8231.N3] 19-1047
I. Title.

PINSON, Koppel Shub, 1904- 273.7
Pietism as a factor in the rise of German nationalism, by Koppel S. Pinson, PH.D. New York, Columbia university press; London, P. S. King & son, ltd., 1934. 227 p. 23 cm. (Half-title: Studies in history, economics and public law, ed. by the Faculty of political science of Columbia university, no. 308) Issued also as thesis (PH.D.) Columbia university. Bibliography: p. 207-223. [H31.C7 no. 308] [BX4982.G3P5 1934 a] (308.2) 34-23478
1. Pietism. 2. Sociology, Christian—Germany. 3. Germany—Nationality. 4. Germany—Religion. 5. Germany—Civilization—Hist. 6. Germany—Church history. I. Title.

RITSCHL, Albrecht Benjamin, 1822-1889. 230'.4
Three essays. Translated and with an introd. by Philip Hefner. Philadelphia, Fortress Press [1972] 301 p. 24 cm. Contents.Contents.—Theology and metaphysics.—"Prolegomena" to The history of pietism.—Instruction in the Christian religion. Includes bibliographical references. [B85.R58] 72-75654 ISBN 0-8006-0224-2 10.50
1. Ritschl, Albrecht Benjamin, 1822-1889. 2. Pietism. 3. Christianity—Philosophy. 4. Theological, Doctrinal. I. Title.

SPENER, Philipp Jakob, 1635-1705 284.143
Pia desideria, by Philip Jacob Spener. Tr. [from German] introd. by Theodore G. Tappert. Philadelphia, Fortress [c.1964] vii, 131p. 21cm. (Seminar eds.) Bibl. 64-12995 1.75 pap.,
1. Pietism. 2. Germany—Religion—17th cent. I. Title.

Pietism—Addresses, essays, lectures.

PIETISM / 274'.06
G. Thomas Halbrooks, editor. Nashville, Tenn. : Broadman Press, c1981. 414 p. ; 24 cm. (Christian classics) Includes bibliographical references. [BR1650.2.P49] 19 79-55536 ISBN 0-8054-6546-4 : price unreported.
1. Pietism—Addresses, essays, lectures. I. Halbrooks, G. Thomas. II. Title. III. Series.

Pietism—Baltic States.

MEZEZERS, Valdis. 274.7'4
The Herrnhutian pietism in the Baltic, and its outreach into America and elsewhere in the world / by Valdis Mezezers. North Quincy, Mass. : Christopher Pub. House, c1975. 151 p., [1] leaf of plates : ill. ; 20 cm. Bibliography: p. 147-151. [BR1652.B34M49] 74-28646 ISBN 0-8158-0322-2 : 6.95
1. Zinzendorf, Nicolaus Ludwig, Graf von, 1700-1760. 2. Pietism—Baltic States. I. Title: The Herrnhuterian pietism in the Baltic ...

Pietism—Germany.

PINSON, Koppel Shub, 1904-1961. 320.1'58'0943
Pietism as a factor in the rise of German nationalism. New York, Octagon Books, 1968 [c1934] 227 p. 24 cm. (Studies in history, economics, and public law, no. 398) Bibliography: p. 207-223. [BR1652.G3P5 1968] 68-15888
1. Pietism—Germany. 2. Church and social problems—Germany. 3. Nationalism—Germany. I. Title. II. Series: Columbia studies in the social sciences, no. 398

Pietism—History.

BROWN, Dale W., 1926- 273'.7
Understanding Pietism / by Dale W. Brown. Grand Rapids : W. B. Eerdmans Pub. Co., c1978. 182 p. ; 20 cm. Includes bibliographical references and index. [BR1650.2.B76] 77-29104 ISBN 0-8028-1710-6 pbk. : 4.95
1. Pietism—History. I. Title.
Distributed by Halsted.

O'MALLEY, John Steven. 284'.2
Pilgrimage of faith: the legacy of the Otterbeins, by J. Steven O'Malley. Metuchen, N.J., Scarecrow Press, 1973. xiii, 212 p. 22 cm. (ATLA monograph series, no. 4) Thesis—Drew University, 1970. Bibliography: p. 197-207. [BX9422.2.O4 1973] 73-5684 ISBN 0-8108-0626-6 6.50
1. Reformed Church—Doctrinal and controversial works. 2. Otterbein, Georg Gottfried, 1731-1800. 3. Otterbein, Johann Daniel, 1736-1804. 4. Otterbein, Philip William, Bp., 1726-1813. 5. Pietism—History. I. Title. II. Series: American Theological Library Association. ATLA monograph series, no. 4.

Pietism—United States

EISENACH, George John, 1900- 273.7
Pietism and the Russian Germans in the United States. Berne, Ind., Berne Publishers, 1948 [i.e. 1949] 218 p. 21 cm. Bibliography: p. 210-215. [BX4982.U55E4] 49-24491
1. Pietism—U.S. 2. Russian German Brotherhood in America. 3. Russian Germans in the U.S. I. Title.

HALE, Frederick. 289.9
Trans-Atlantic conservative Protestantism in the evangelical free and mission covenant traditions / Frederick Hale. New York : Arno Press, 1979. p. cm. (Scandinavians in America) Originally presented as the author's thesis, Johns Hopkins University, 1976. Bibliography: p. [BX7548.A4H34 1979] 78-15183 ISBN 0-405-11638-1 : 26.00
1. Evangelical Free Church of America—History. 2. Evangelical Covenant Church of America—History. 3. Pietism—United States. 4. Pietism—Scandinavia. 5. Revivals—United States. 6. Revivals—Scandinavia. 7. United States—Church history. 8. Scandinavia—Church history. 9. Disserters, Religious—Scandinavia. I. Title. II. Series.

Pietism—United States—Addresses, essays, lectures.

CONTINENTAL pietism and early American Christianity / edited by F. Ernest Stoeffler. 280'.0973 Grand Rapids : Eerdmans, c1976. 276 p. ; 21 cm. Includes bibliographies and index. [BR1652.U6C66] 75-46511 ISBN 0-8028-1641-X pbk. : 4.50
1. Pietism—United States—Addresses, essays, lectures. 2. Sects—United States—Addresses, essays, lectures. I. Stoeffler, F. Ernest.

Piety.

BUCHLER, Adolf, 1867-1939. 296.7'4
Types of Jewish-Palestinian piety from 70 B.C.E. to 70 C.E.; the ancient pious men, by Adolph Buchler. New York, Ktav Pub. House, 1968. 264 p. 24 cm. Reprint of the 1922 ed. Contents.Contents.—Hillel the Hasid.—The ancient pious men.—The pious men in the Psalms of Solomon.—Honi the Hasid and his prayer for rain. Bibliographical footnotes. [BM723.B8 1968] 68-56292
1. Hillel, the elder, d. ca. 10. 2. Honi ha-Meaggel, 1st century B.C. 3. Bible. O.T. Apocryphal books. Psalms of Solomon—Criticism, interpretation, etc. 4. Piety. I. Title. II. Title: Jewish-Palestinian piety.

A course of sermons on early piety. 252. By the eight ministers who carry on the Thursday-lecture in Boston. With a preface by the Reverend Dr. Increase Mather, and also clos'd with a discourse lately had by him to young people ... Boston: in N. E. Printed by S. Kneeland, for N. Buttolph, B. Eliot, and D. Henchman, and sold at their shops, 1721. [336] p. 17 cm. Various pagings. Head and tail pieces; initials. [BX7233.A1C6] 5-21277
1. Piety. 2. Youth-Religious life. 3. Congregational churches—Sermons. 4. Sermons, American. I. Mather, Cotton, 1663-1728. II. Wadsworth, Benjamin, 1669-1737. III. Colman, Benjamin, 1673-1747. IV. Sewall, Joseph, 1688-1769. V. Prince, Thomas, 1687-1758. VI. Webb, John, 1682-1750. VII. Cooper, William, 1694-1743. VIII. Foxcroft, Thomas, 1697-1769. IX. Mather, Increase, 1639-1723. X. Thursday lecture, Boston.
Contents omitted.

GUIDE to piety: 248
a memento of affection from Christian pastors. Newburyport, C. Whipple, 1832. 96 p. 8 x 6 cm. [BV4520.G8] 33-4912
1. Piety. 2. Christian life. I. Whipple, Charles, Newburyport, pub.

HORN, Henry E. 248.4'8'41
The Christian in modern style [by] Henry E. Horn. Philadelphia, Fortress Press [1968] viii, 184 p. 18 cm. (A Fortress paperback original) Bibliographical references included in "Notes" (p. 170-184) [BV4647.P5H63] 68-29462 2.50
1. Piety. 2. Christian life—Lutheran authors. I. Title.

HUGHES, Henry Trevor 922.342
The piety of Jeremy Taylor. New York, St. Martin's Press, 1960[ ] 183p. Bibl.: p.178-180 and bibl. notes. 60-50586 5.75
1. Taylor, Jeremy, Bp. of Down and Conner, 1613-1667. 2. Piety. I. Title.

Piety—Addresses, essays, lectures.

SHELLEY, Bruce Leon, 1927- 248.4
A call to Christian character; toward a recovery of Biblical piety [by] Earl S. Kalland [and others] Edited by Bruce L. Shelley. Grand Rapids, Zondervan [1970] 186 p. 22 cm. Includes bibliographical references. [BV4647.P5S46] 74-106441 4.95
1. Piety—Addresses, essays, lectures. I. Kalland, Earl S., 1910- II. Title.

Piety—History.

VERSENYI, Laszlo. 179'.9
Holiness and justice : an interpretation of Plato's Euthyphro / Laszlo Versenyi. Washington, D.C. : University Press of America, c1982. p. cm. Bibliography: p. [B370.V47] 19 81-43830 ISBN 0-8191-2316-1 : 19.75 ISBN 0-8191-2317-X (pbk.) : 9.50
1. Plato. Euthyphro. 2. Piety—History. I. Title.

Pignatelli, Jose Maria, 1737-1811.

HANLY, Daniel Aloysius, 1873 922.246
Blessed Joseph Pignatelli (of the Society of Jesus) a great leader in a great crists, by Monsignor D. A. Hanly, P. A. New York, Cincinnati [etc.] Benziger brothers, 1937. xii, 269 p. 23 cm. [BX4705.P48H35] 38-3709
1. Pignatelli, Jose Maria, 1737-1811. 2. Jesuits. I. Title.

Pike, Diane Kennedy.

PIKE, Diane Kennedy. 242'.4
Life is victorious! : How to grow through grief : a personal experience / Diane Kennedy Pike. New York : Simon and Schuster, c1976. 209 p., [4] leaves of plates : ill. ; 23 cm. [BR1725.P54A34] 76-17328 ISBN 0-671-22335-6 : 7.95
1. Pike, Diane Kennedy. 2. Pike, James Albert, Bp., 1913-1969. 3. Grief. I. Title.

PIKE, Diane Kennedy. 242'.4
Life is victorious!: How to grow through grief ; a personal experience / Diane Kennedy Pike. New York : Pocket Books, 1977,c1976. 238p. : ill. ; 18 cm. (A Kangaroo Book) [BR1725.P54A34] ISBN 0-671-81241-6 pbk. : 1.95
1. Pike, Diane Kennedy. 2. Pike, James Albert, Bp. 1913-1969. 3. Grief. I. Title.
L.C. card no. for 1976 Simon & schuster ed.:76-17328.

Pike, James Albert, Bp., 1913-1969.

HOLZER, Hans W., 1920- 133.9'0924
The psychic world of Bishop Pike [by] Hans Holzer. New York, Crown Publishers [1970] 224 p. 22 cm. [BX5995.P54H6 1970] 70-119164 5.95
1. Pike, James Albert, Bp., 1913-1969. 2. Psychical research. I. Title.

PIKE, Diane Kennedy. 283'.0924 B
Search: the personal story of a wilderness journey. [1st ed.] Garden City, N.Y., Doubleday, 1970, [c1969] xii, 198 p. col. map (on lining papers) 22 cm. [BX5995.P54P5] 74-108620 4.95
1. Pike, James Albert, Bp., 1913-1969. I. Title.

STRINGFELLOW, William. 230'.0924
The Bishop Pike affair; scandals of conscience and heresy, relevance and solemnity in the contemporary church [by] William Stringfellow [and] Anthony Towne. [1st ed.] New York, Harper & Row [1967] xxii, 266 p. 21 cm. Bibliographical references included in "Notes" (p. 251-266) [BX5995.P54S8] 67-21554
1. Pike, James Albert, Bp., 1913- I. Towne, Anthony, joint author. II. Title.

STRINGFELLOW, William. 283'.092'4 B
The death and life of Bishop Pike / William Stringfellow and Anthony Towne. 1st ed. Garden City, N.Y. : Doubleday, 1976. xxxii, 446 p., [8] leaves of plates : ill. ; 22 cm. "Books by James A. Pike": [445]-446. [BX5995.P54S83] 75-32721 ISBN 0-385-07455-7 : 10.00
1. Pike, James Albert, Bp., 1913-1969. I. Towne, Anthony, joint author. II. Title.

UNGER, Merrill Frederick, 1909- 133.9
The haunting of Bishop Pike; a Christian view of The other side [by] Merrill F. Unger. Wheaton, Ill., Tyndale House Publishers [1971] 115 p. 22 cm. Includes bibliographical references. [BF1042.U5 1971] 76-144329 ISBN 0-8423-1340-0 2.95
1. Pike, James Albert, Bp., 1913-1969. 2. Pike, James Albert, Bp., 1913-1969. The

other side. 3. Spiritualism—Controversial literature. I. Title.

Pike, Robert, 1616-1706.

PIKE, James Shepherd, 1811- 1882. 922
The new Puritan: New England two hundred years ago; some account of the life of Robert Pike, the Puritan who defended the Quakers, resisted clerical domination, and opposed the witchcraft prosecution. By James S. Pike. New York, Harper & brothers, 1879. 237 p. 19 cm. [F67.P63] 3-18837
1. Pike, Robert, 1616-1706. 2. Massachusetts—Hist.—Colonial period. 3. Friends, Society of. New England. 4. Witchcraft—New England. I. Title.

Pilate, Pontius, 1st century

CAILLOIS, Roger, 1913- 923.233
Pontius Pilate. Translated by Charles Lam Markmann. New York,Macmillan [1963] 111 p. 21 cm. [BS2520.P55C33] 63-13184
1. Pilate, Pontius, 1st cent. I. Title.

CROZIER, William Percival, 1879- 232.
Letters of Pontius Pilate written during his governorship of Judea to his friend Sencea in Rome; edited by W. P. Crozier. New York, J. H. Sears & company, inc. [c1928] 172 p. 20 cm. [BT430.C6 1928 a] 28-22163
1. Pilate, Pontius, 1st cent. 2. Jesus Christ—Passion. I. Title.

FOX, Gresham George, 1888- 296.3
Jesus, Pilate, and Paul; an amazingly new interpretation of the trial of Jesus under Pontius Pilate, with a study of little known facts in the life of Paul before his conversion. Based upon the author's 'The Jews, Jesus, and Christ.' Chicago, Isaacs, 1955 [i. e. 1956] 159p. 20cm. [BM620.F6] 56-20605
1. Pilate, Pontius, 1st cent. 2. Jesus Christ—Jewish interpretations. 3. Jesus Christ— Trial. 4. Paul, Saint, apostle. I. Title.

Pilate, Pontius, 1st century—Drama.

STABLEY, Rhodes R. 812.5
So Pilate washed his hands, a Biblical play in one act, by Rhodes R. Stabley. Philadelphia, The Penn publishing company [c1934] 31 p. diagrs. 18 1/2 cm. [PN6120.R4S746] [232.992] 37-32534
1. Pilate, Pontius, 1st cent.—Drama. I. Title.

Pilate, Pontius, 1st century—Fiction.

SHEHADI, Beshara, 1871- 232.962
The confession of Pontius Pilate, first written, as alleged, in Latin, by Fabrieius Albinus, a playmate of Pilate; translated into Arabic by Jerasimus Jared, late bishop of Zahleh, in Lebannon and rendered from the Arabic into English by Beshara Shehadi ... 3d ed. East Orange, N.J. The translator, 1943. 63 p. 21 cm. Title in Arabic characters on cover. [PR6037.H4C7 1943] 44-21087
1. Pilate, Pontius, 1st cent.—Fiction. I. Title.

Pilcher, Elijah Holmes, 1810-1887.

PILCHER, James Elijah, 1857-1911. 922.773
Life and labors of Elijah H. Pilcher, of Michigan. Fifty-nine years a minister of the Methodist Episcopal church. Edited by his son, James E. Pilcher, M.D. New York, Hunt & Eaton, 1892. 142 p. 3 port. (incl. front.) facsim. 23 x 20 cm. [BX8495.P547P5] 36-37396
1. Pilcher, Elijah Holmes, 1810-1887. I. Title.

Pilgrim fathers.

SAWYER, Joseph Dillaway, 1849- 922
History of the Pilgrims and Puritans, their ancestry and descendants; basis of Americanization, by Joseph Dillaway Sawyer ... William Elliot Griffs ... editor ... New York city, The Century history company, inc. [c1922] 3 v. front., illus. (incl. ports., maps, facsims.) 26 cm. [F67.S27] 22-19063
1. Pilgrim fathers. 2. Puritans. 3. Massachusetts—Hist.—Colonial period. 4. Massachusetts—Hist.—Colonial period (New Plymouth) I. Griffs, William Elliot, 1843-1928, ed. II. Title.

WEBSTER, Daniel, 1782-1852. 252.
A discourse, delivered at Plymouth, December 22, 1820. In commemoration of the first settlement of New-England. By Daniel Webster. 2d ed. Boston, Wells and Lilly, 1821. 55, [1] p. 20 1/2 cm. [F68.W38] [AC901.M2 vol. 31] 923. 1-12108
1. Pilgrim fathers. I. Title.

Pilgrim Fathers—Bibliography

BOSTON. Public library. 016.
...The Pilgrims; a selected list of works in the Public library of the city of Boston. A contribution to the tercentenary celebration comp. by Mary Alice Tenney, Catalogue department. Boston, The Trustees, 1920. 2 p. l., 43, [1] p. 18 1/2 cm. (Brief reading lists no. 15. June 1920) [Z1295.B74] [Z881.B751 no. 15] 016. 20-14310
1. Pilgrim fathers—Bibl. I. Tenney, Mary Alice. II. Title.

PITTSBURGH. Carnegie library. 016.
The Pilgrims; selected material for use in connection with the Pilgrim tercentenary celebration. [Pittsburgh] Carnegie library of Pittsburgh, 1920. 13 p. 18 cm. [Z1295.P69] 20-18746
1. Pilgrim fathers—Bibl. I. Title.

SANFORD, Edwin G. 016.91744'03'1
The Pilgrim Fathers and Plymouth Colony: a bibliographical survey of books and articles published during the past fifty years. A contribution to the 350th anniversary observance of the landing of the Pilgrims at Plymouth, Massachusetts, in 1620. Compiled by Edwin G. Sanford. [Boston] Boston Public Library, 1970. 29 p. 23 cm. Intended to supplement The Pilgrims, issued by the Boston Public Library in 1920. [Z1295.S25] 74-160696
1. Pilgrim fathers—Bibliography. I. Boston. Public Library. II. Boston. Public Library. The Pilgrims. III. Title.

SPRINGFIELD, Mass. City library association. 016.
The Pilgrim tercentenary, the Puritans, and the New England spirit ... Springfield, Mass., The City library [1921] [8] p. 20 cm. A bibliography. [Z881.S763S] 21-2085
1. Pilgrim fathers—Bibl. I. Title.

U.S. Library of Congress. Division of Bibliography. 016.
List of references on the Pilgrim Fathers. [Washington] 1920. 5 l. 27 cm. Caption title. [Z1295.A53] 51-62848
1. Pilgrim Fathers—Bibl. I. Title.

Pilgrim holiness church—Doctrinal and controversial works.

MOURER, Charles Calvin, 1882- 230.99
Twelve [t]heological [t]ornadoes, by Chas. C. Mourer ... Cincinnati, c1935] 271 p. front. (port.) 20 cm. Title within lined border stating the doctrines of the church. [BX7990.H6M6] 36-11119
1. Pilgrim holiness church—Doctrinal and controversial works. I. Title.

Pilgrim Holiness Church—History.

NEWTON, John, 1725-1807.
The aged pilgrim's triumph over sin and the grave; illustrated in a series of letters never before published. By the Rev. John Newton... Written during the decline of life, to some of his most intimate friends. From the 2d London ed., New York, Wilder & Campbell, 1825. v, [7]-271 p. 19 1/2 cm. 11-2594
I. Title.

THOMAS, Paul Westphal. 287'.173
The days of our pilgrimage : the history of the Pilgrim Holiness Church / by Paul Westphal Thomas, Paul William Thomas ; edited by Melvin E. Dieter, Lee M. Haines, Jr. Marion, Ind. : Wesley Press, 1976. xviii, 382 p. : ill. ; 23 cm. (Wesleyan history series ; 2) Includes index. Bibliography: p. 357-361. [BX8795.P453T47] 76-374750
1. Pilgrim Holiness Church--History. I. Thomas, Paul William, joint author. II. Title. III. Series.

Pilgrim holiness church—Sermons.

WOODS, John Franklin, 1865- 252.099
God's marvelous grace to me, by Rev. J. F. Woods ... A short history of the life of the author, with a few Bible readings and sermons. With an introduction by Rev. W. L. Surbrook ... [Huntington, W.Va., c1936] 175 p. front., plates, ports. 19 1/2 cm. [BX7990.H62W65] 37-4483
1. Pilgrim holiness church—Sermons. 2. Sermons, American. I. Title.

Pilgrim Society, Plymouth, Mass.

BARR, Lillie E.
Coral and Christian; or, The children's Pilgrim's progress. By Lillie E. Barr. New York, W. B. Mucklow. 1877. 109 p. 18 cm. Extracts with running commentary in form of a story. [PR3330.A25B4] 26-9285
I. Bunyan John. The pilgrim's progress II. Title.

GELLER, Lawrence D. 016.09
The books of the Pilgrims / by Lawrence D. Geller and Peter J. Gomes. New York : Garland Pub., 1975. xv, 91 p. : ill. ; 22 cm. (Garland reference library of the humanities ; v. 13) [Z997.A1G44] 74-30056 ISBN 0-8240-1065-5: 10.00
1. Pilgrim Society, Plymouth, Mass. 2. Bibliography—Rare books—Catalogs. 3. Pilgrim Fathers—Libraries. I. Gomes, Peter J., joint author. II. Title.

Pilgrims and pilgrimages.

ATWOOD, John, 1811. 220
The pilgrimage of a pilgrim eighty years. By John Atwood ... Boston, The author, 1892. 215 p. incl . front. (port.) 21 cm. [BR125.A8] 5-6445
I. Title.

BENSON, Samuel Benney, 1884- 923.573
Up from a sod hut; a preacher's pilgrimage, by S. Benney Benson ... Grand Rapids, Mich., Zondervan publishing house, [1936] 256 p. 21 cm. [Full name: Samuel Cranston Benny Benson] [BX9543.B36A3] 37-7833
I. Title.

DE JONG, Jerome 251.027
Sermon outlines on a spiritual pilgrimage [Based on Israel's journey from Egypt to Canaan] Grand Rapids, Mich., Baker Bk. [c.]1962. 90p. 22cm. 1.00 pap.,
I. Title.

FEALY, Lawrence Augustus. 133
The pilgrim, prophet and me, by Bishop L. A. Fealy ... Birmingham, Ala., Altrurian society [c1938] 2 p. l., vii-xi p., 1 l., 422 p. 22 cm. (His I am I series, vol. I) [BF1999.F36 vol. 1] (159.961) (133) [159.961] 39-3203
I. Altrurian society, Birmingham, Ala. II. Title.

FRENCH, Reginald Michael, 1884- tr. 248.3
The way of a pilgrim; and, The pilgrim continues his way. Translated from the Russian by R. M. French. New York, Seabury Press [1965] x, 242 p. maps, 21 cm. (A Seabury paperback, SP18) [BX597.Z9O732 1965] 65-4899
1. Pilgrims and Pilgramages. I. The pilgrim continues his way. II. Title.

GITELSON-KAMAIKO Foundation.
Eight hundred years of journeys to the Holy Land, from Benjamin of Tudela to the present. [New York, Tarbuth Press, 1964] 1 reel. (Its Tarbuth chrestomathy) The Gitelson collection. Originally appeared in The chronicle, 1964, III. Microfilm (positive) 68-60952
I. Title.

KEABLE, Robert, 1887- 220
Pilgrim papers from the writings of Francis Thomas Wilfrid, priest, by Robert Keable. New York, E. P. Dutton & company [c1921] xiv, p., 1 l., 234 p. 20 cm. [BR125.K35 1921] 21-7199
I. Title.

KELLEY, William Valentine, 1843- 218
A pilgrim of the infinite, by William Valentine Kelley ... New York, Cincinnati, The Methodist book concern [c1914] 84 p. 19 cm. [BD431.K35] 14-16954
I. Title.

KHAN, Gazanfar Ali.
With the pilgrims to Mecca; the great pilgrimage of A.H. 1319; A.D. 1902, by Hadji Khan ... and Wilfrid Sparroy ... With an introduction by Professor A. Vambery. London and New York, J. Lane, 1905. 314 p. incl. front., plates, ports. 23 cm. The greater part of the work appeared first in the London Morning post. [DS248.M4K3] 5-21048
1. Pilgrims and pilgrimages. 2. Mecca. I. Sparroy, Wilfrid. II. Vambery, Armin, 1832?-1913. III. Title.

PALMER, Blanche 266.673
Pilgrim of the night by Blanche Palmer. Illus. by Don Fields. Nashville, Southern Pub. [c.1966] 157p. illus. 21cm. 3.75 bds.,
I. Title.

PILGRIMAGE to Palestine,
by George & Letha Ledbetter. Indianapolis, Ind., Church Members publishers [1956?] 1v.
I. Ledbetter, George H

A Pilgrim's guide to planet Earth : 910'.202
traveler's handbook & spiritual directory. San Rafael, Calif. : Spiritual Community Publications, [1974] 287 p. : ill. ; 22 cm. Bibliography: p. 283-286. [BL619.P5P54 1974] 73-83144 ISBN 0-913852-07-4 pbk. : 4.50
1. Pilgrims and pilgrimages.

RANSOM, Reverdy Cassius, Bp., 1861- 922.773
The pilgrimage of Harriet Ransom's son. Nashville, Sunday School Union [1949] 336 p. port. 23 cm. Autobiography. [BX8473.R25A3] 51-27687
I. Title.

THOMAS, Joseph, b.1791. 922.
The life of the pilgrim Joseph Thomas, Containing an accurate account of his trials, travels and gospel labours, up to the present date. Winchester, Va. J. Foster, printer ... 1817. 372 p. 18 cm. [BX6793.T5A3] 1-21324
I. Title.

THOMAS, Joseph, 1791- 1835. 922.673
The life, travels, and gospel labors of Eld. Joseph Thomas, more widely known as the "White pilgrim:" to which are added his poems: religious, moral, and satirical. New York, M. Cummings, 1861. vi, [7]-266 p., 1 l. incl. front. (port.) pl. 15 1/2 cm. On cover: The White pilgrim. [BX6793.T5A2 1861] 36-31068
I. Title. II. Title: The White pilgrim.

THE way of a pilgrim, 248.3
and the pilgrim continues his way. Translated from the Russian, by R. M. French. New York, Ballantine Books [1974] ix, 180 p. maps. 18 cm. [BX597.Z90732 1974] ISBN 0-345-24254-8 1.50 (pbk.)
1. Pilgrims and pilgrimages. I. French, Reginald Michael, 1884-, tr. II. Title: The pilgrim continues his way.
L.C. card no. for original ed.: 65-4899.

WAY of a pilgrim (The); 248.3
and, The pilgrim continues his way. Tr. from Russian by R. M. French. New York, Seabury [1965] x. 242p. maps. 21cm. (SP18) Orig. pub. in two separate eds. [BX597.Z90732] 65-4899 1.95 pap.,
1. Pilgrims and pilgrimages. I. French. Reginald Michael, 1884- tr. II. Title: Athe pilgrim continues his way.

Pilgrims and Pilgrimages—Europe.

KRAMER, Helen Mary, 1892- 231.73
When we were there. Rockford, Ill.,

Bellevue Books [1954] 246p. illus. 23cm. [BX2323.K7] 54-22116
1. Pilgrims and Pilgrimages—Europe. I. Title.

SMITH, John Talbot, 1855-
A pilgrimage to see the Holy Father through the stereoscope, conducted by Rev. John Talbot Smith ... New York [etc.] Underwood & Underwood [c1907] 140 p. front., pl., fold. plans, facsims. 18 cm. 7-24026
I. Underwood & Underwood. II. Title.

Pilgrims and pilgrimages—India.

BHARDWAJ, Surinder Mohan. 294.5'3'8
Hindu places of pilgrimage in India; a study in cultural geography. Berkeley, University of California Press [1973] xviii, 258 p. illus. 24 cm. Bibliography: p. 233-247. [BL1227.A1B495] 73-174454 ISBN 0-520-02135-5 12.00
1. Pilgrims and pilgrimages—India. 2. Hindu shrines—India. I. Title.

Pilgrims and pilgrimages—Levant.

WEATHERSPOOL, William W. 248.2'9
This big world, by W. W. Weatherspool. [1st ed.] New York, Greenwich Book Publishers [1967] xiv, 120 p. 22 cm. [DS49.7.W35] 66-23418
1. Pilgrims and pilgrimages—Levant. I. Title.

Pilgrims and pilgrimages—Mecca.

KAMAL, Ahmad, 1914- 297.38
The sacred journey, being pilgrimage to Makkah; the traditions, dogma and Islamic ritual that govern the lives and the destiny of more than five hundred million who call themselves Muslim: one seventh of mankind. New York, Duell, Sloan and Pearce [1961] xx, 108, 115, 9 p. 22 cm. Added t.-p. English and Arabic. [BP181.K3] 61-6920
1. Pilgrims and pilgrimages—Mecca. I. Title. II. Title: al-Rihlah al-muqaddasah.

RUTTER, Owen, 1889- 297
Triumphant pilgrimage; an English Muslim's journey from Sarawak to Mecca, by Owen Rutter. Philadelphia, London, J. B. Lippincott company [c1937] 7 p. l., 13-296 p. incl. map. 2 port. (incl. front.) 22 cm. [BP175.M4R8] 37-19498
1. Chale, David, pseud. 2. Pilgrims and pilgrimages—Mecca. 3. Mohammedanism. 4. Sarawak. 5. Arabia—Soc. life & cust. I. Title.

Pilgrims and pilgrimages—Palestine.

MORTON, Henry Canova Vollam, 1892- 915.694
This is the Holy Land, a pilgrimage in words and pictures, conducted by Fulton J. Sheen, photographed by Yousuf Karsh, described by H. V. Morton. Foreword by Bishop Sheen. Garden City, N.Y., Doubleday [1962, c.1960, 1961] 160p. 18cm. (Image bk.) .95 pap.,
1. Pilgrims and pilgrimages—Palestine. I. Sheen, Fulton John, Bp., 1895- II. Karsh, Yousuf, 1908-illus. III. Title.

MORTON, Henry Canova Vollam, 1892- 915.694
This is the Holy Land, a pilgrimage in words and pictures, conducted by Fulton J. Sheen, photographed by Yousuf Karsh [and] described by H. V. Morton. With a foreword by Bishop Sheen. [1st ed.] New York, Hawthorn Books [1961] 143p. illus. 27cm. [DS107.4.M63] 61-6706
1. Pilgrims and pilgrimages— Palestine. I. Sheen, Fulton John, Bp., 1895- II. Karsh, Yousuf, 1908- illus. III. Title.

THE Pylgrymage of Sir Richard Guylforde to the Holy Land, A.D. 1506, from a copy believed to be unique, from the press of Richard Pynson. Edited by Sir Henry Ellis. [London] Printed for the Camden Society, 1851. New York, AMS Press [1968] xvi, 92 p. 24 cm. Original ed. issued as no. 51 of Publications of Camden Society, London. On spine: Pilgrimage of Sir Richard Guylforde. [DS106.P95 1968] 72-187218 915.694'04'3
1. Guildford, Richard, Sir, 1455?-1506. 2. Pilgrims and pilgrimages—Palestine. 3. Palestine—Description and travel. I. Ellis, Henry, Sir, 1777-1869, ed. II. Title: Pilgrimage of Sir Richard Guylforde. III. Series: Camden Society, London. Publications, no. 51.

ROBINSON, Godfrey Clive. 915.694'04'5
In the Holy Land; a journey along the King's highways, with Godfrey C. Robinson and Stephen F. Winward. Photos. by the authors and Carol Acworth, and maps and drawings by L. F. Lupton. [1st U.S. ed.] Grand Rapids, W. B. Eerdmans Pub. Co. [1968, c1963] 128 p. illus. (part col.), maps. 22 cm. [DS107.4.R59 1968] 68-18840 1.95
1. Bible—Geography. 2. Pilgrims and pilgrimages—Palestine. I. Winward, Stephen F., joint author. II. Title.

VAN PAASSEN, Pierre, 1895- *915.694
A pilgrim's vow. New York, Dial Press, 1956. 344 p. 21 cm. Autobiographical. [DS107.3.V33] 56-12131
1. Pilgrims and pilgrimages — Palestine. I. Title.

WEIBEL, Johann Eugen, 1853-
My voyage to Europe and the Holy Land in 1913, by John Eugene Weibel ... Hot Springs, Ark., Sentinel-record print [1915!] 2 p. l. 184 [2] p. front., illus., pl. port. group. 24 1/2 cm. [BX2323.W4] 45-44713
1. Pilgrims and pilgrimages—Palestine. I. Title.

Pilgrims and pilgrimages—Palestine—History.

KOLLEK, Teddy, 1911- 291.4'2
Pilgrims to the Holy Land; the story of pilgrimage through the ages [by] Teddy Kollek and Moshe Pearlman. [1st U.S. ed.] New York, Harper and Row [1970] 204 p. illus. 29 cm. [DS108.9.K63 1970b] 74-123946 15.00
1. Pilgrims and pilgrimages—Palestine—History. I. Pearlman, Moshe, 1911- joint author. II. Title.

Pilgrims and pilgrimages—Rome.

MEYER, Louis Joseph, 1897- ed. 215
Anno santo, Holy year, 1925; the story of the pilgrimage sailing April twenty-seventh, nineteen hundred and twenty-five from Philadelphia to Rome on the steamship "Ohio", edited by Reverend Louis J. Meyer. Philadelphia, Madeira Islands, gibraltar, Algiers, Naples, Amalfi Sorento, Capri to Rome. Philadelphia, The Peter Reilly company [c1927] xvi, 17-162 p. front., plates. 21 cm. [BX961.H6M8] 27-16445
I. Title. II. Title: Holy year, 1925.

MEYERS, Bertrande, Sister. 231.73
Devotedly yours. Westminster, Md., Newman Press, 1951. 400 p. 23 cm. [BX2323.M4] 51-12465
1. Pilgrims and pilgrimages — Rome. 2. Pilgrims and pilgrimages — Palestine. 3. Daughters of Charity of St. Vincent de Paul. I. Title.

Pilgrims and pilgrimages—Santiago de Compostela.

HELL, Vera 248.29
The great pilgrimage of the Middle Ages: the road to St. James of Compostela [by] Vera and Hellmut Hell; tr. [from German] by Alisa Jaffa. Introd. by Sir Thomas Kendrick. New York, Potter [1966] 275p. col. front., illus. (6 col. plates) maps. 33cm. Bibl. [DC20.H413] 66-22138 17.50
1. Pilgrims and pilgrimages—Santiago de Commpostela. 2. France—Descr. & trav.—Views. 3. Spain—Descr. & trav.—Views. I. Hell, Hellmut, joint author. II. Title.

MULLINS, Edwin B. 914.6'1'0482
The pilgrimage to Santiago [by] Edwin Mullins. New York, Taplinger [1974] x, 222 p. illus. 24 cm. Bibliography: p. [214]-216. [BX2321.S3M84 1974] 74-5820 ISBN 0-8008-6249-X 12.95
1. Pilgrims and pilgrimages—Santiago de Compostela. 2. Santiago de Compostela—History. I. Title.

The Pilgrims, London.

BRITTAIN, Harry Ernest, Sir, 1873-
Pilgrim partners; forty years of British-American fellowship, by Sir Harry Brittain ... With 17 illustrations. London, New York [etc., Hutchinson & co., ltd. 1942] 3 p. l., 5-156 p. front., plates, ports. 22 1/2 cm. "This edition is limited to one hundred numbered copies." A 42
1. The Pilgrims, London. I. The Pilgrims, New York II. Title.

Pilkington, George Lawrence, 1865-1897.

HARFORD, Charles Forbes, 1864- 922.
Pilkington of Uganda, by Charles F. Harford-Battersby ... with introductory chapters by A. T. Pierson ... and J. H. Shrine ... New York, Chicago [etc.] Fleming H. Revell company [1899] 1 p. l., xvi, 346, v p. illus., 2 port. (incl. front.) 2 fold. maps. 21 cm. [BV3625.U4P5] 99-2872
1. Pilkington, George Lawrence, 1865-1897. 2. Missions—Uganda. I. Title.

Pillar of fire church.

PAIGE, Clara R. 1869- comp. 269
Alma White's evangelism; press reports, compiled by C. R. Paige [and] C. K. Ingler ... Zarephath, N.J., Pillar of fire, 1939-40. 2 v. fronts. (ports.) illus. 19 cm. "Drawings by Branford Clarke." Includes advertising matter. [BX8795.P5P3] 42-44306
1. White, Alma (Bridwell) 1862- 2. Pillar of fire church. I. Ingler, Clifford Knowlton, 1876- joint comp. II. Clarke, Branford, illus. III. Title.

PILLAR of fire church. 289
Doctrines and discipline of the Pillar of fire church. 1918. Written and comp. by Rev. Ray B. White, A.B. Zarephath, N.J., Pillar of fire [c1918] 1 p. l., [5]-234 p. 15 cm. [BX8795.P5A5] 18-14870
I. White, Ray Bridwell, 1892- comp. II. Title.

WHITE, Alma (Briduell) Mrs., 1862- 289.9
Demons and tongues, by Alma White. Zarephath, N.J., Pillar of fire [c1936] 1 p. l., v-vi, 7-128 p. 18 1/2 cm. Advertising matter: p. 121-123. [Full name: Mrs. Mollie Alma (Bridwell) White] [BX8795.P5W45 1936] 36-7427
1. Pillar of fire church. 2. Demoniac possession. 3. Glossolatia. I. Title.

WHITE, Alma (Bridwell) 1862- 252.099
Everlasting life [by] Alma White. Zarephath, N.J., Pillar of fire, 1944. 341 p. front (port.) plates. 19 cm. [BX8795.P5W453] 45-83
1. Pillar of fire church. I. Title.

WHITE, Alma (Bridwell) Mrs., 1862- 922.89
Modern miracles and ansuers to prayer, by Alma White. Zarephath, N.J., Pillar of fire, 1939. vi-i p., 1 l., 11-248 p. incl. front. (port.) plates. 19 1/2 cm. Advertising matter: p. 245-248. [Full name: Mrs. Mollie Alma (Bridwell) White] [BX8795.P5W455] 39-10084
1. Pillar of fire church. I. Title.

WHITE, Alma (Bridwell) Mrs., 1862- 922.
The New Testament church, by Mrs. Alma White ... Denver, Col., Pillar of fire, c1907. 174 p. front. (port.) 18 1/2 cm. [Full name: Mrs. Mollie Alma (Bridwell) White] [BX8795.P5W48 1907] 7-26324
1. Pillar of fire church. I. Title.

WHITE, Alma (Bridwell) Mrs., 1862- 289.9
Truth stranger than fiction, by Alma White. Rev. ed. Zarephath, N.J., Pillar of fire, 1936. viii p., 1 l., 11-256 p. incl. front. (port.) illus. 19 1/2 cm. Advertising matter: p. 249-256. [Full name: Mrs. Mollie Alma (Bridwell) White] [BX8795.P5W62 1936] 36-15997
1. Pillar of fire church. I. Title.

Pillar of Fire Church—Catechisms and creeds—English.

PILLAR of Fire Church. 238.99
Catechism. Denver, Pillar of Fire [1948] 208 p. illus. 16 cm. [BX8795.P5A45] 49-15997
1. Pillar of Fire Church—Catechisms and creeds—English. I. Title.

Pillar of Fire Church—History

WOLFRAM, Gertrude (Metlen) 1888- 289.9
The widow of Zarephath, a church in the making. Zarephath, N.J., Pillar of Fire, 1954. 244p. illus. 24cm. [BX8795.P5W74] 55-16559
1. Pillar of Fire Church—Hist. I. Title.

Pillar of fire church—Hymns.

WHITE, Alma (Bridwell) Mrs., 1862- ed. 783.9
Cross & crown hymnal, Church of the Pillar of fire, edited by Bishop Alma White ... [and] Rev. Arthur K. White ... Zarephath, N.J., Pillar of fire, 1939. [516] p. 2 port. (incl. front.) 23 cm. With music. [Full name: Mrs. Mollie Alma (Bridwell) White] [M2117.W58C7] 40-3496
1. Pillar of fire church—Hymns. 2. Hymns, English. I. White, Arthur Kent, 1889- joint ed. II. Title.

Pillar of fire church—Sermons.

WHITE, Alma (Bridwell) 1862- 922.
Gospel truth, by Alma White. Zarephath, N.J., Pillar of fire, 1945. vi p., 1 l., 9-261 p. front. (port.) 19 1/2 cm. [Full name: Mollie Alma (Bridwell) White] [BX8795.P5W454] 46-12278
1. Pillar of fire church—Sermons. 2. Sermons, American. I. Title.

WHITE, Alma (Bridwell) Mrs., 1862- 252.099
Radio sermons and lectures, by Alma White ... Denver, Colo., Pillar of fire, 1936. ix, 11-300 p. front. (port.) plates. 19 1/2 cm. "A collection of sermons given over the two Pillar of fire radio stations, viz., KPOF at Denver, Colorado, and WAWZ at Zarephath, New Jersey."--Foreword. [Full name: Mrs. Mollie Alma (Bridwell) White] [BX8795.P5W49] 36-29587
1. Pillar of fire church—Sermons. 2. Sermons, American. I. Title.

WHITE, Alma (Bridwell) Mrs., 1862- 252.099
Short sermons, by Alma White ... Zarephath, N.J., Pillar of fire, 1932. ix, 11-416 p. incl. front. (port.) plates. 20 cm. Advertising matter: p. 408-416. [Full name: Mrs. Mollie Alma (Bridwell) White] [BX8795.P5W55] 33-430
1. Pillar of fire church—Sermons. 2. Sermons, American. I. Title.

WHITE, Alma (Bridwell) Mrs., 1862- 252.099
The sword of the spirit, by Alma White ... Zarephath, N.J., Pillar of fire, 1937. ix, 11-375 p. front. (port.) plates. 19 1/2 cm. Advertising matter: p. 370-375. [Full name: Mrs. Mollie Alma Bridwell White] [BX8795.P5W614] 37-12270
1. Pillar of fire church—Sermons. 2. Sermons, American. I. Title.

WHITE, Arthur Kent, 1889- 252.099
The boys made good and other sermons, by Arthur K. White. Zarephath, N.J., Pillar of fire, 1936. x, 11-352 p. front. (port.) illus., plates. 19 1/2 cm. Advertising matter: p. 349-352.. [BX8795.P5W64] 37-1388
1. Pillar of fire church—Sermons. 2. Sermons, American. I. Title.

WHITE, Ray Bridwell, 1892- 252.099
Pulpit and pen [by]Rev. Ray B. White, A.M. Zarephath, N.J., Pillar of fire, 1938. xii, 13-404, [2] p. front. (port.) illus., plates (part col.) 19 cm. Advertising matter: p. 401-404. [BX8795.P5W72] 38-5480

1. Pillar of fire church—Sermons. 2. Sermons, American. I. Title.

Pimeria Alta.

KINO, Eusebio Francisco, 1644-1711. 266.2'79
Kino's Historical memoir of Pimeria Alta : a contemporary account of the beginnings of California, Sonora, and Arizona / by Eusebio Francisco Kino ; published for the first time from the original manuscript in the Archives of Mexico translated into English, edited, and annotated by Herbert Eugene Bolton. New York : AMS Press, 1976. 2 v. in 1 : ill. ; 23 cm. Translation of the ms. entitled: Favores celestiales. Reprint of the 1919 ed. published by A. H. Clark Co., Cleveland. Bibliography: p. v. 2, p. 279-296. [F799.K56 1976] 74-7975 ISBN 0-404-11863-1 : 52.50 (2 vols in one)
1. Kino, Eusebio Francisco, 1644-1711. 2. Pimeria Alta. 3. Jesuits in Pimeria Alta. 4. Missions—Pimeria Alta. 5. Pima Indians. I. Title.

Pingree, Enoch Merrill, 1817-1849.

JEWELL, Henry. 922.
Life and writings of Rev. Enoch M. Pingree, who died in Louisville, Kentucky, January 6, 1849, aged 32 years. By Rev. Henry Jewell ... Cincinnati, Longley & brother, 1850. vi, [9]-385 p. front. (port.) 19 cm. [BX9969.P5J4] 8-25317
1. Pingree, Enoch Merrill, 1817-1849. I. Title.
Contents omitted.

Pink, Arthur Walkington, 1886-1952.

PINK, Arthur W. 220.
The divine inspiration of the Bible [by] Arthur W. Pink. Swengel, Pa., Bible truth depot [c1917] 145 p. 18 1/2 cm. $0.50 [BS480.P6] 17-29230
I. Title.

PINK, Arthur W. 220.
The divine inspiration of the Bible [by] Arthur W. Pink. Swengel, Pa., Bible truth depot [c1917] 145 p. 18 1/2 cm. $0.50 [BS480.P6] 17-29230
I. Title.

PINK, Arthur W. 232.
The Redeemer's return, by Arthur W. Pink ... Swengel, Pa., Bible truth depot [c1918] 405 p. 20 cm. $1.35 [BT885.P5] 18-9286
I. Title.

PINK, Arthur W. 225.
Why four gospels? [By] Arthur W. Pink. Swengel, Pa., Bible truth depot [c1921] 184 p. 18 1/2 cm. [BS2555.P5] 22-287
I. Title.

PINK, Arthur Walkington, 1886-1952. 230
Letters of Arthur W. Pink. Edinburgh ; Carlisle, Pa. : Banner of Truth Trust, 1978. 135 p. ; 18 cm. [BS501.P56A34] 79-315829 ISBN 0-85151-285-2 pbk. : 2.50
1. Pink, Arthur Walkington, 1886-1952. 2. Biblical scholars—Correspondence. I. Title.
Publisher's Address : P.O. Box 621, Carlisle, PA 17013

Pinkham, Mrs. Rebekah (Porter) 1792-1839.

GARRISON, Edwin William, 1804-1840. 922.673
Memoir of Mrs. Rebekah P. Pinkham, late consort of Rev. E. Pinkham, of Sedgwick, Me., containing an account of her conversion; interesting letters to her friends; her writings for the promotion of missionary objects, &c. By E. W. Garrison ... Portland [Me] Printed at the office of Zion's advocate, 1840. vi, [7]-160 p. front. (port.) 15 1/2 cm. [BX6495.P54G3] 36-24283
1. Pinkham, Mrs. Rebekah (Porter) 1792-1839. I. Title.

Pinkney, William, bp., 1810-1883.

HUTTON, Orlando.
Life of the Right Reverend William Pinkney, D. D., LL. D., fifth bishop of Maryland. By O. Hutton, D. D. Washington, D. C., Gibson bros., printers, 1890. viii, 388 p. 2 port. (incl. front.) 24 cm. 15-10373
1. Pinkney, William, bp., 1810-1883. I. Title.

Pio da Pietrelcina, father.

CARROLL, Malachy Gerard, 1918- 922.245
Padre Pio. Chicago, H. Regnery Co., 1955. 80p. 18cm. (Angelus books) [BX4705.P49C34] 55-4768
1. Pio da Pietrelcina, Father. I. Title.

DE LISO, Oscar 922.245
Padre Pio. New York, All Saints Pr. [1962,c.1960] 183p. (AS-218) .50 pap.,
1. Pio da Pietralcina, Father. I. Title.

DE LISO, Oscar 922.245
Padre Pio, the priest who bears the wounds of Christ. New York, McGraw-Hill [c.1960] 233p. 21cm. 60-15686 4.95 half cloth,
1. Pio da Pietrelcina, Father. I. Title.

DE LISO, Oscar 922.245
Padre Pio. New York, All Saints Pr. [1962,c.1960] 183p. (AS-218) .50 pap.,
1. Pio da Pietralcina, Father. I. Title.

GAUDIOSE, Dorothy M., 1920- 271'.36'024 B
Prophet of the people; a biography of Padre Pio, by Dorothy M. Gaudiose. Illustrated by George Lallas. New York, Alba House [1974] xviii, 237 p. illus. 22 cm. [BX4705.P49G38] 74-7123 ISBN 0-8189-0290-6
1. Pio da Pietrelcina, Father. I. Title.

GIGLIOZZI, Giovanni. 271.360924 B
Padre Pio; a pictorial biography. Translation by Oscar DeLiso. [New York] Phaedra, 1965. 84 p. illus., map, ports. 23 cm. Translation of I monilli dello sposo. [BX4705.P49G53] 65-23441
1. Pio da Pietrelcina, Father. I. Title.

MCCAFFERY, John. 271'.36'024
Tales of Padre Pio : the friar of San Giovanni / John McCaffery. Kansas City : Andrews and McMeel, [1979] c1978. vi, 143 p., [3] leaves of plates : ill. ; 23 cm. First published in London under title: The friar of San Giovanni. [BX4705.P49M23 1979] 79-52811 ISBN 0-8362-3500-2 : 9.95
1. Pio da Pietrelcina, Father. 2. Miracles. I. Title.

PARENTE, Pascal P 1890- 922.245
A city on a mountain: Padre Pio of Pietrelcina, O.F.M. CAP. [St. Meinrad, Ind., 1952] 148 p. illus. 22 cm. "A Grall publication." [BX4705.P49P3] 52-12557
1. Plo da Pietralcina, Father. I. Title.

SCHUG, John A. 271'.36'024 B
Padre Pio / John A. Schug. Huntington, Ind. : Our Sunday Visitor, 1976. 256 p. : port. ; 21 cm. [BX4705.P49S38] 76-17953 ISBN 0-87973-856-1 pbk. : 4.95
1. Pio da Pietrelcina, father. 2. Capuchins—Biography. I. Title.

THREE studies in 282'.092'2 B
simplicity, by Malachy Carroll and Pol de Leon Albaret. [Pol de Leon Albaret's Sainte Benedict l'Africain translated from the French by Malachy Carroll] Chicago, Franciscan Herald Press [1974] vii, 201 p. 21 cm. [BX4655.2.T45] 74-8284 ISBN 0-8199-0533-X 5.95
1. Pio da Pietrelcina, Father. 2. Martin de Porres, Saint, 1579-1639. 3. Benedetto da San Filadelfo, Saint, 1526-1589. I. Carroll, Malachy Gerard, 1918- Padre Pio. 1974. II. Carroll, Malachy Gerard, 1918- St. Martin de Porres. 1974. III. Albaret, Pol de Leon, Father, 1906- Benedict l'Africain. English. 1974.
Contents omitted.

Pio, padre, 1887-1968.

RUFFIN, Bernard, 1947- 271'.36'024 B
Padre Pio, the true story / C. Bernard Ruffin. Huntington, Ind. : Our Sunday Visitor, c1982. x, 324 p., [12] p. of plates : ill. ; 23 cm. Includes bibliographical references and index. [BX4705.P49R83 1982] 19 81-81525 ISBN 0-87973-673-9 (pbk.) : 8.95
1. Pio, padre, 1887-1968. 2. Catholic Church—Clergy—Biography. 3. Clergy—Italy—Biography. 4. Stigmatization—Case studies. I. Title.

Pioneers—North America.

CAMPBELL, Thomas Joseph, 1848-1925.
Pioneer laymen of North America, by the Rev. T. J. Campbell, S. J. ... New York, The America press, 1915. 2 v. front. plates, ports., maps. 24 cm. "Books consulted": v. 1, p. xv. Contents.--i. Jacques Cartier. Pedro Menendez. Samuel Champlain. Charles de la Tour. Maisonneuve Charles Le Moyne. Pierre Esprit Radisson.--ii. Le Moyne de Longueuil. Nicolas Perrot. Le Moyne d'Iberville. Frontenac. La Salle. Le Moyne de Blenville. Pierre Gaultier de Verendrye. John McLoughlin. [E36.C18] 15-10062
1. Pioneers—North America. 2. New France—Biog. I. Title.

CHRISTIAN Miller, an American pioneer; his descrndants through the families of David A. Miller and Samuel P. Miller, 1738-1956. By David A. Miller and Frederick C. Miller. With a memorial supplement in tribute to David A. Miller. [Allentown, Pa., 1959] 174p.
I. Miller, David Aaron, 1869-1958.

MURRAY, John O'Kane, 1847-1885.
The Catholic pioneers of America. By John O'Kane Murray ... New York, P. J. Kenedy, 1882. xv, 433 p. front. 18 cm. 12-36941
I. Title.

Piper, Leonora E. Mrs.

BELL. CLARK, 1832-1918, ed. 133.
Spiritism, hypmotism and telepathy, as involved in the case of Mrs. Leonora E. Piper and the Society of psychical research, by Clark Bell ... and the discussion thereon by Thompson day Hudson, LL. D., and more than twenty observers ... 2d ed. ... New York, Medico-legal journal, 1904. 3 p. l., 191 p. front., illus. (ports.) 23 cm. [BF1283.P6B3 1904] 4-29369
1. Piper, Leonora E. Mrs. 2. Spiritualism. 3. Hypnotism. 4. Thought-transference. I. Hudson, Thomson Jay, 1834-1903. II. Title.

ROBBINS, Anne Manning. 133
Both sides of the veil; a personal experience, by Anne Manning Robbins. Boston, Sherman, French & company, 1909. 4 p. l., vii-xii p., 1 l., 15-258 p. ports., facsims. 20 cm. [BF1283.P6R6] 9-26326 1.25
1. Piper, Mrs. Leonora E. 2. Spiritualism. I. Title.

ROBBINS, Anne Manning. 133
... Past and present with Mrs. Piper, by Anne Manning Robbins ... New York, H. Holt and company, 1922. 2 p. l., iii-iv, 280 p. front., ports. 20 cm. (The psychic series) Part i is rewritten, with great abbreviation and some trifling expansion from the author's Both sides of the veil. cf. Pref. [BF1283.P6R65] 22-19729
1. Piper, Mrs. Leonora E. 2. Spiritualism. I. Title.

SAGE, Michel, 1863-1931. 920.
Mrs. Piper & the Society for psychical research; translated & slightly abridged from the French of M. Sage by Noralie Robertson, with a preface by Sir Oliver Lodge. New York, Scott-Thaw co., 1904. xxiv 187, [1] p. 19 cm. [BF1283.P6S2] 4-16274
1. Piper, Lenora E. 2. Spiritualism. I. Robertson, Noralie, tr. II. Title.

Piper, Otto A., 1891-

KLASSEN, William, ed. 225.6
Current issues in New Testament interpretation; essays in honor of Otto A. Piper. Ed. by William Klassen, Graydon F. Snyder. New York, Harper [c.1962] xiv, 302p. 22cm. front. port. 62-11132 5.00
1. Piper, Otto A., 1891- 2. Bible. N.T.—Addresses, essays, lectures. I. Snyder, Graydon F., joint ed. II. Title.

Pirc, Franc, 1785-1880.

FURLAN, William P. 922.273
In charity unfeigned; the life of Father Francis Xavier Pierz. [St. Cloud? Minn.] Diocese of St. Cloud, 1952. 270 p. illus. 23 cm. [BX4705.P496F8] 52-12087
1. Pirc, Franc, 1785-1880. I. Title.

Pisa. Battistero.

SMITH, Christine. 726'.4
The Baptistery of Pisa / Christine Smith. New York : Garland Pub., 1978. p. cm. (Outstanding dissertations in the fine arts) Originally presented as the author's thesis, New York University, 1975. Bibliography: p. [NA1121.P6S44 1978] 77-94715 ISBN 0-8240-3249-7 : lib.bdg. : 36.00
1. Pisa. Battistero. I. Title. II. Series.

Piscataqua association of ministers.

SPALDING, George Burley, 1835-1914. 285.
Historical discourse delivered on the one hundredth anniversary of the Piscatagua association of ministers, at the North church, Portsmouth, N.H., October 26, 1881, by George B. Spalding...with reminiscences and remarks by Edward Robin, D.D., Alonzo H. Quint, D.D., Rev. Josiah H. Stearns, Rev. Thomas V. Haines, Rev. Israel T. Otis, Deacon Marcellus Bufford, and Rev. William A. McGinley. With an appendix. Dover, N.H., Morning star job printing office, 1881. 83 p. 25 cm. [BX7108.P5S6] 26-8391
1. Piscataqua association of ministers. 2. Congregational church in New Hampshire. I. Title.

Pitkin, Horace Tracy, 1869-1900.

SPEER, Robert Elliott, 1867- 922.
A memorial of Horace Tracy Pitkin, by Robert E. Speer. New York, Chicago [etc.] Fleming H. Revell company [1903] 1 p. l., 310 p. front. (port.) 20 cm. [BV3427.P5S6] 3-31447
1. Pitkin, Horace Tracy, 1869-1900. I. Title.

Pitman, Charles, 1796-1854.

MALMSBURY, Caleb A. 922.
The life, labors and sermons of Rev. Charles Pitman, D.D., of the New Jersey conference, by C. A. Malmsbury. With an introduction by Rev. Charles H. Whitecar, D.D. Philadelphia, Methodist Episcopal book rooms [c1887] xvi, 352 p. front. (port.) 23 cm. [BX8495.P55M3] 1-13562
1. Pitman, Charles, 1796-1854. I. Title.

Pittsboro, N. C. St. Bartholomew's church.

[JAMES, Joshua Marion] 1884 comp. 283.756
St. Bartholomew's parish, Pittsboro, N. C., eighteen thirty three to nineteen thirty three... [Pittsboro, N. C., R. G. Shannonhouse] 1933. 54 p. 24 cm. "Compiled by J. Marion James."--p. 3 On cover: Edited by Rev. R G. Shannonhouse. [BX5980.P58S3] 34-1023
1. Pittsboro, N. C. St. Bartholomew's church. I. Shannonhouse, Royal Graham, 1875- ed. II. Title.

Pittsburgh (Diocese, Catholic)

CATHOLIC historical society of western Pennsylvania. 282.748
Catholic Pittsburgh's one hundred years, a symposium prepared by the Catholic historical society of western Pennsylvania. Published under the patronage of His Excellency the Most Reverend Hugh C. Boyle, D.D., in commemoration of the one hundredth anniversary of the establishment of the diocese. Chicago, Ill., Loyola university press, 1943. xvi, 271 p. front., plates, ports. 23 1/2 cm. [BX1417.P6C3] 43-17532
1. Pittsburgh (Diocese, Catholic) I. Title.

Contents omitted.

PITTSBURGH Catholic. 282.748
Centenary edition, the Pittsburgh Catholic, commemorating the completion of 100 years of the diocese of Pittsburgh ... published on the 100th anniversary of the first issue of the Pittsburgh Catholic, March 16, 1944. [Pittsburgh, 1944] cover-title, 58 p. incl. illus. (incl. maps, facsims.) ports. (1 col.) 41 1/2 cm. "Supplement to the Pittsburgh Catholic, March 16, 1944." Includes advertising matter. [BX1417.P6P5] 44-7056
1. Pittsburgh (Diocese, Catholic) I. Title.

Pittsburgh (Diocese, Catholic)—Directories

ST. Regis association's 282.
Catholic year book and directory of Pittsburgh diocese. 1st- ed., 1908/09- Pittsburgh, Pa. [c1908- v. port. 23 1/2 cm. "Published by and for the benefit of St. Regis association." Title varies: 1908, Catholic year book of Pittsburgh diocese. 1910- St. Regis association's Catholic year book and directory of Pittsburgh diocese. [BX1418.P53S3] 8-34259
1. Pittsburgh (Diocese, Catholic)—Direct. 2. Catholic church in Pittsburgh—Direct.

Pittsburgh (diocese)—History

LAMBING, Andrew Arnold, 1842-1918. 282.
A history of the Catholic church in the dioceses of Pittsburg and Allegheny from its establishment to the present time. By Rev. A. A. Lambing ... New York, Cincinnati [etc.] Benziger brothers, 1880. 531 p. front., ports. 24 cm. [BX1417.P6L3] 20-16452
1. Pittsburgh (diocese)—Hist. 2. Catholic church in Pennsylvania—Hist. 3. Catholic church in Pennsylvania—Biog. I. Title.

Pittsburgh. First Presbyterian church.

DUFF, Joseph M. 285.174886
A record of twenty-five years of the pastorate of Maitland Alexander ... in the First Presbyterian church in the city of Pittsburgh. By J. M. Duff. [Pittsburgh 1924] 6 p. l., 11-133 p. front., plates, ports., facsim. 25 cm. [BX9225.A615D8] 40-25740
1. Alexander, Maitland 1857-1940. 2. Pittsburgh. First Presbyterian church. I. Title.

Pittsburgh. First Unitarian Church.

PITTSBURGH'S First 288.74886
Unitarian Church, by George Swetnam [and others] Pittsburgh, Boxwood Press [1961] 125p. 22cm. Includes bibliography. [BX9861.P55F5] 61-19849
1. Pittsburgh. First Unitarian Church. I. Swetnam, George.

Pittsburgh. Shadyside Presbyterian Church.

BELFOUR, Stanton. 285.10974886
Centennial history of the Shadyside Presbyterian Church. Pittsburgh [1966] xii, 154 p. illus., ports. 24 cm. Bibliography: p. 153. [BX9211.P6S53] 66-9034
1. Pittsburgh. Shadyside Presbyterian Church. I. Title.

Pittsburgh—Social conditions

MARSH, Daniel Lash, 1880- 277.
The challenge of Pittsburgh, by Daniel L. Marsh ... New York, Missionary education movement of the United States and Canada, 1917. viii, 311 p. front., illus. (map) plates, charts. 20 cm. [The challenge of the cities series] "Issued under the auspices of the Pittsburgh council of churches of Christ."--Pref. [BV2805.P6M3] 17-20430
1. Pittsburgh—Soc. condit. I. Title.

Pittsburgh Synod of the Evangelical Lutheran Church.

HEISSENBUTTEL, Ernest G 284.1748
Pittsburgh Synod congregational histories. Warren, Ohio, Studio of Printcraft, 1959. 434p. illus. 24cm. The first of a two-volume synodical history, prepared under authorization of the Executive Committee of the Pittsburgh Synod of the Evangelical Lutheran Church. [BX8061.P6H4] 59-2372
1. Pittsburgh Synod of the Evangelical Lutheran Church. 2. Churches—Pennsylvania. I. Title.

Pittsburgh synod of the Evangelical Lutheran church (General council) Conferences, Southern.

ULERY, William Frederick, 1829-1903. 284.1748
History of the Southern conference of the Pittsburg synod of the Evangelical Lutheran church, by Rev. William F. Ulery, A.M. Edited and published by Rev. W. F. Ulery, A.M., and A. L. Young ... Greensburg, Pa., Church register company, 1902. xv, [1], 416 p. front., plates, ports., map. 23 cm. [BX8061.P667U6] 3-34
1. Pittsburgh synod of the Evangelical Lutheran church (General council) Conferences, Southern. I. Yount, Adolphus Le Roy, 1851-joint author II. Title.

Pittsburgh Synod of the Evangelical Lutheran Church — History

HEISSENBUTTEL, Ernest G 284.10974886
Pittsburgh Synod history; its auxiliaries and institutions, 1845-1962 by Ernest G. Heissenbuttel and Roy H. Johnson. Warren, Ohio, Published by the Pittsburgh Synod of the United Lutheran Church at Studio of Printcraft,inc. [1963] 483 p. illus. 24 cm. The 2d of a two-volume synodical history, the 1st appeared in 1959 under title: Pittsburgh Synod congregational histories. Includes bibliography. [BX8061.P6H42] 63-5777
1. Pittsburgh Synod of the Evangelical Lutheran Church — Hist. 2. Pittsburgh Synod of the United Lutheran Church in America — Hist. I. Johnson, Roy H., joint author. II. Title.

Pittsburgh. Trinity Cathedral.

MANTLE, Eric. 283'.748'86
Trinity and Pittsburgh. [Pittsburgh, 1969] 32 p. illus. (part col.), ports. 24 cm. Cover title. Bibliography: p. 31-32. [BX5980.P6T755] 79-279390
1. Pittsburgh. Trinity Cathedral. I. Title.

Pittsburgh. Western theological seminary—Biography

PITTSBURGH. Western theological seminary. 207.74886
General biographical catalogue, the Western theological seminary of the Presbyterian church, Pittsburgh, Pennsylvania, 1827-1927. [Pittsburgh, 1927] 2 p. l., 429 p. 23 1/2 cm. [BV4070.P689442] 37-16277
1. Pittsburgh. Western theological seminary—Biog. I. Title.

Pius II, Pope, 1405-1464.

MITCHELL, Rosamond Joscelyne, 1902- 922.21
The laurels and the tiara; Pope Pius II, 1458-1464. [1st ed. in the U.S.A.] Garden City, N.Y., Doubleday [1963, c1962] 286 p. 22 cm. [BX1308.M5 1963] 63-14329
1. Pius II, Pope, 1405-1464. I. Title.

PIUS I I, pope, 1405-1464 922.21
... *The Commentaries of Pius II;* translation by Florence Alder Gragg, with historical introduction and notes by Leona C. Gabel. Northampton, Mass., The Department of history of Smith college [1937] 114 p. 23 cm. (Smith college studies in history. vol. XXII, nos. 1-2. October, 1936-January, 1937) Memoirs. Bibliography: p. 108-110. [BX1308.A37] 39-14024
I. Gragg, Florence Alden, 1877- tr. II. Gabel, Leona Christine, 1895- ed. III. Title.

PIUS II Pope, 1405-1464 922.21
Memoirs of a Renaissance Pope; the commentaries of Pius II, an abridgement. Tranlslated by Florence A. Gragg. Edited with introd. by Leona C. Gabel. Illus. selected by Ruth Olitzky Rubinstein. New York, Putnam [1959] 381 p. illus., ports., map (on lining papers) 22 cm. [BX1308.A38] 59-5680
I. Title.

Pius IX, Pope, 1792-1878.

BRENNAN, Richard, 1833?-1893. 922.21
A popular life of our Holy Father, Pope Pius the Ninth drawn from the most reliable authorities. By Rev. Richard Brennan... New York, Cincinnati and St. Louis Benziger brothers, 1877. xii [7]-279 p. incl. front., illus. (incl. ports.) 21 cm. [BX1373.B7] 39-32766
1. Pius IX, pope, 1792-1878. I. Title.

BRENNAN, Richard, 1833?-1893. 922.21
A popular life of our Holy Father, Pope Pius the Ninth drawn from the most reliable authorities. By Rev. Richard Brennan ... 6th ed. New York, Cincinnati, and St. Louis, Benziger brothers, 1877. xii [7]-282 p. incl. front., illus. (incl. ports.) 21 cm. [BX1373.B7 1877 f] 39-32767
1. Pius IX, pope, 1792-1878. I. Title.

BURY, John Bagnell, 1861-1927.
History of the papacy in the 19th century (1864-1878) by the late J.B. Bury ... edited, with a memoir, by the Rev. R.H. Murray. New York, Schocken Books [1964] lxi, 175 p. 68-84162
1. Pius IX, Pope, 1792-1878. 2. Papacy—Hist. 3. Catholic Church—Hist. I. Murray, Robert Henry, 1874- II. Title.

BURY, John Bagnell, 1861-1927. 262.130903
History of the papacy in the 19th century liberty and authority in the Roman Catholic Church [by] J. B. Bury. Edited by R. H. Murray. Augm. ed.: Vatican Countil I, Vatican Council II. Introd., epilogue, and bibliographical notes by Frederick C. Grant. New York, Schocken Books [1964] xxxiv, 217 p. 23 cm. "First appeared in 1960." Bibliography: p. 199-207. [BX1386.B8] 64-22610
1. Pius IX, Pope, 1792-1878. 2. Papacu — Hist. 3. Catholic Church — Hist. I. Title.

ERNEST, Brother, 1897- 922.21
The prisoner in the Vatican; a story of Pope Pius IX. Illus. by Brother Bernard Howard. Notre Dame, Ind., Dujarie Press [1953] 102p. illus. 24cm. [BX1373.E7] 53-3992
1. Plus ix, Pope, 1792-1878. I. Title.

HALES, Edward Elton Young, 1908- 282
Pio Nono, a study in European politics and religion in the nineteenth century. Garden City, N.Y., Doubleday [1962, c.1954] 402p. map. (Image bk., D133) Bibl. 1.25 pap.,
1. Pius IX, Pope, 1792-1878. 2. Europe—Politics—1848-1871. I. Title.

HASLER, August. 262'.131
How the Pope became infallible : Pius IX and the politics of persuasion / August Bernhard Hasler ; introd. by Hans Kung ; translated by Peter Heinegg. 1st ed. Garden City, N.Y. : Doubleday, 1981. xi, 383 p. : ill. ; 22 cm. Translation of Wie der Papst unfehlbar wurde. Includes index. Bibliography: p. [355]-359. [BX1806.H3813] 19 79-6851 ISBN 0-385-15851-3 : 14.95
1. Pius IX, Pope 1792-1878. 2. Popes—Infallibility—History. I. Title.

HASSARD, John Rose Greene, 1836-1888.
A life of Pope Pius ix... New York, The Catholic publication co., 1878. 242 p. 12 cm. 1-10259
I. Title.

MONTALEMBERT, Charles Forbes Rene de Tryon, comte de, 1810-1870. 922.
Pius ix. and France, in 1849 and 1859, by the Count de Montalembert ... Translated from the second French edition, by Madelaine V. Goddard. To which is added A. biographical sketch of the late Duke of Norfolk, by the same author. Boston, P. Donahoe, 1861. 70 p. 19 cm. The sketch of the Duke of Norfolk was translated from the Correspondent, for the Liverpool Northern press. [BX1373.M7] 3-32473
1. Plus ix, pope, 1792-1878. 2. Norfolk, Henry Granville Fitzalan-Howard, 14th duke of, 1815-1860. 3. Popes—Temporal power. I. Dahlgren, Madeleine (Vinton) Mrs. 1825-1898, tr. II. Title.

THORNTON, Francis Beauchesne, 1898- 922.21
Cross upon cross; the life of Pope Pius IX. New York, Benziger Bros. [1955] 263p. 21cm. Includes bibliography. [BX1373.T47] 55-3892
1. Plus IX, Pope, 1792-1878. I. Title.

Pius V, Saint, pope, 1504-1572.

ANDERSON, Robin, 1913- 262'.13'0924 B
St. Pius V, a brief account of his life, times, virtues & miracles / by Robin Anderson ; foreword by Alfredo Ottaviani. Rockford, Ill. : Tan Books and Publishers, 1978. 111 p. : ill. ; 18 cm. [BX1323.A52] 78-55637 ISBN 0-89555-068-7 : 2.00
1. Pius V, Saint, Pope, 1504-1572. 2. Popes—Biography. 3. Christian saints—Italy—Biography. I. Title.

MCCARTHY, Gerontius, 1920- 922.21
Who is like to God; a story of Pope St. Pius v. Illus. by Frances Sheeran. Notre Dame, Ind., Dujarie Press [1955] 95p. illus. 24cm. [BX1323.M25] 55-3408
1. Plus v, Saint, Pope, 1504-1572. I. Title.

OLF, Lillian (Browne) 1880- 922.21
The sword of Saint Michael; Saint Pius V, 1504-1572 [by] Lillian Browne-Olf. Milwaukee, The Bruce publishing company [1943] x p., 1 l., 284 p. front. (port.) 21 cm. (Half-title: The Science and culture series; Joseph Husslein ... editor) Bibliography: p. 282-284. [BX1323.O4] 43-13066
1. Pius V, Saint, pope, 1504-1572. I. Title.

[WOODCOCK, Catherine Mary Antony]
Saint Pius V. pope of the holy rosary, by C. M. Antony [pseud.] With a preface by the Very Rev. Monsignor Benson ... With four illustrations. New York, London [etc.] Longmans. Green and co., 1911. xiii, [1], 114 p. front. (port.) 3 pl. 17 1/2 cm. (Half-title: The friar saints series) On cover and on verso of half-title: Lives of the friar saints. Bibliography: p. 112-114. A 12
1. Pius V, Saint, pope, 1504-1572. I. Title.

[Pius VI, Pope, 1717-1799.]

OLF, Lillian (Browne) 1880- 262'.13'0922 B
Their name is Pius; portraits of five great modern popes [by] Lillian Browne-Olf. Freeport, N.Y., Books for Libraries Press [1970] xv, 382 p. ports. 23 cm. (Essay index reprint series) Reprint of the 1941 ed. Bibliography: p. 371-374. [BX1365.O4 1970] 74-107729
1. [Pius VI, Pope, 1717-1799.] 2. [Pius VII, Pope, 1742-1823.] 3. [Pius IX, Pope, 1792-1878.] 4. [Pius X, Saint, Pope, 1835-1914.] 5. [Pius XI, Pope, 1857-1939.] I. Title.

OLF, Lillian (Browne) Mrs. 1880- 922.21
Their name is Pius; portraits of five great modern popes [by] Lillian Browne-Olf. Milwaukee, The Bruce publishing company [c1941] xv p., 2 l., 3-382 p. front., ports. 22 cm. (Half-title: Science and culture series: Joseph Husslein ... general editor) Bibliography: p. 371-374. [BX1365.O4] 41-17718
1. Plus vi, pope, 1717-1799. 2. Plus vii, pope, 1742-1923. 3. Plus ix, pope, 1792-1878. 4. Plus x, pope, 1835-1914. 5. Plus xi, pope, 1857-1939. I. Title.

Pius VII, Pope, 1742-1823.

HALES, Edward Elton Young, 1908- 262'.13'0924 B
The Emperor and the Pope : the story of Napoleon and Pius VII / E. E. Y. Hales. New York : Octagon Books, 1978, c1961. p. cm. Reprint of the ed. published by

Doubleday, Garden City, N.Y. [BX1369.H34 1978] 78-14767 ISBN 0-374-93375-8 lib.bdg. : 12.00
1. Pius VII, Pope, 1742-1823. 2. Napoleon I, Emperor of the French, 1769-1821. 3. Popes—Biography. 4. France—Kings and rulers—Biography. I. Title.

WISEMAN, Nicholas 262'.13'0922
Patrick Stephen, Cardinal, 1802-1865.
Recollections of the last four popes and of Rome in their times. New and rev. ed. Freeport, N.Y., Books for Libraries Press [1973] p. (Essay index reprint series) "First published 1858." [BX1386.W5 1973] 72-14111 ISBN 0-518-10032-4
1. Pius VII, Pope, 1742-1823. 2. Leo XII, Pope, 1760-1829. 3. Pius VIII, Pope, 1761-1830. 4. Gregorius XVI, Pope, 1765-1846. I. Title. II. Title: The last four popes.

WISEMAN, Nicholas Patrick 922.21
Stephen, cardinal, 1802-1865.
Recollections of the last four popes and of Rome in their times. [By] H. E. Cardinal Wiseman ... Boston, P. Donahoe, 1858. 474 p. 19 1/2 cm. [BX1386.W5 1858 a] 36-29973
1. Pius VII, pope, 1742-1823. 2. Leo XII, pope, 1760-1829. 3. Pius VIII, pope, 1761-1830. 4. Gregorius XVI, pope, 1765-1846. I. Title. II. Title: The last four popes.

Pius x, pope, 1835-1914.

BURTON, Katherine (Kurz), 922.21
1890-
The great mantle; the life of Giuseppe Melchiore Sarto, Pope Pius x. [1st ed.] New York, Longmans, Green, 1950. xiv, 238 p. port. 22 cm. Bibliography: p. 225-226. [BX1375.B8 1950] 50-6259
1. Plus x, Pope, 1835-1914. I. Title.

CATHOLIC Church. Pope, 1903- 208.1
1914(Piusx)
All things in Christ; encyclical letters and selected documents of Blessed Pius x, edited by Vincent A. Yzermans. Introd. by Peter W. Bartholome. [Saint Paul?] '1952. xxviii, 231 p. 28 cm. Bibliography: p. 229-231. [BX870 1903] 52-4099
I. Title.

CATHOLIC church. Pope, 1903- 238.2
1914 (Piusx)
Catechetical documents of Pope Pius X, translated and edited, with a biographical note, by Joseph B. Collins ... Introduction by Most Reverend Edwin V. O'Hara ... Paterson, N.J., Saint Anthony guild press, 1946. ixviii, 204 p. front. (port.) 24 cm. English and Latin. Bibliographical references included in "Biographical note" (p. xiii-ixviii) [BX1968.C35] 47-50
1. Pius x, pope, 1835-1914. 2. Catechetics—Catholic church. I. Collins, Joseph Burns, 1897- ed. and tr. II. Title.

CATHOLIC Church Pope (Pius 208.1
x), 1903-1914
All things in Christ; encyclicals and selected documents of Saint Pius x. Edited by Vincent A. Yzermans. Westminster, Md., Newman Press, 1954. xviii, 275p. 24cm. Bibliography: p. 261-269. [BX870 1903a] 54-7544
I. Yzermans, Vincent Arthur, 1925- ed. II. Title.

CONFRATERNITY of Christian 922.21
doctrine.
A symposium on the life and work of Pope Pius X, commemorating the fortieth anniversary of his encyclical "Acerbonimis" ... prepared under the direction of the Episcopal committee of the Confraternity of Christian doctrine. Preface by Most Reverend Amleto Giovanni Cicognani ... Washington, D.C., Confraternity of Christian doctrine, 1946. xiii p., 1 l., 304 p. col. front. (port.) 24 cm. "References" at end of each chapter except one. Contents.Biographical sketch of Pope Pius X, by R. M. Huber.--Pius X and the integrity of doctrine, by J. M. Egan.--Sacred Scripture, by W. L. Newton.--The diffusion of Christian teaching, by J. B. Collins.--Catholic action--lay apostolate, by J. V. Sommers.--Lay participation in the liturgy of the church, by Godfrey Diekmann.--The eucharistic banquet: frequent and daily communion, by Gerald Ellard.--The eucharistic formation of children, by R. G. Bandas.--Church music, B. A. G. Ehmann.--The revision of the Roman breviary and the reform of the curia, by B. A. Finn--Ecclesiastical discipline, by J. D. Hannon.--The priesthood, by Thomas Plassman.--The causes of Pius X, by J. S. Mix. In the cause for the beautification and canonization of Pius X, by Benedetto Pierami. "Acerbo nimis." 1905-1945.--"Pius X--servant of God," by E. V. O'Hara. "Bibliography, arranged by R. M. Huber": p. 297-300. [BX1375.C65] 47-16114
1. Pius X, pope, 1835-1914. 2. Catholic church. Pope, 1903-1914. (Pius X) Acerbo nimis (15 Apr. 1905) I. Title.

DAL-GAL, Girolamo. 922.21
Pius x, the life-story of the Beatus: the new Italian life of Pius x, translated and adapted by Thomas F. Murray. Westminster, Md., Newman Press, 1954. 246 p. illus. 22 cm. [BX1375.D323] 54-5661
1. Pius x, Pope, 1835-1914. I. Title.

DIETHELM, Walther. 922.21
Saint Pius X, the farm boy who became Pope. Illustrated by G.W. Thompson. New York, Vision Books [1956] 189p. illus. 22cm. (Vision books, 8) [BX1375.D52] 56-5990
1. Plus x. Saint. Pope, 1835-1914. I. Title.

ERNEST, Brother, 1897- 922.21
A story of Saint Pius x. Pictures by Joan Roytek Notre Dame, Ind., Dujarie Press [1957] unpaged. illus. 21cm. [BX1375.E7] 57-4989
1. Plus x, Saint, Pope, 1835-1914. I. Title.

FARNUM, Mabel Adelaide, 922.21
1887-
The White Knight, a biography of Pope Pius x for children, by Mabel A. Farnum ... illustrated by Rose de Lima Arsenault. Saint Paul, Minn., Catholic library service [c1937] 6 p. l., 19-219 p., 1 l. illus., pl. 19 cm. [BX1375.F35] 38-8788
1. Pius x, pope, 1835-1914. I. Title.

FITCH, Lawrence, 1930- 922.21
The song of the shoemaker's son; a story of Blessed Pius X. Illus. by Harold Ruplinger. Notre Dame, Ind., Dujarie Press [1951] 92 p. illus. 24 cm. [BX1375.F5] 52-18159
1. Pius x, Pope, 1835-1914. I. Title.

GIORDANI, Igino, 1894- 922.21
Pius x, a country priest; translated by Thomas J. Tobin. Milwaukee, Bruce Pub. Co. [1954] 205p. illus. 21cm. [BX1375.G52] 54-7602
1. Plus x, Pope, 1835-1914. I. Title.

GRASHOFF, Raphael. 922.21
'A good shepherd he was; the life of Blessed Pius x. St. Meinrad, Ind, [1952] 79p. illus. 20cm. 'A Grail publication.; [BX1375.G7] 53-28243
1. Pius x, Pope, 1835-1914. I. Title.

HUNERMANN, Wilhelm. 922.21
Flame of white, a life of Saint Pius x. Translated from the German by M. Ida Adler. Chicago, Franciscan Herald Press [1959] 269p. 22cm. Translation of Brennendes Feuer. [BX1375.H813] 59-9332
1. Pius x, Saint, Pope, 1855-1914. I. Title.

LIFE of His Holiness Pope 922.
Pius x, together with a sketch of the life of his venerable predecessor, His Holiness Pope Leo xiii, also a history of the conclave, giving a full account of the rites and ceremonies connected with the election of a successor to th see of St. Peter. With a preface by His Eminence James, cardinal Gibbons ... New York, Cincinnati [etc.] Benziger brothers, 1904. 401 p. incl. front. (port.) illus. 21 cm. "The life of Plus x has been largely taken from the sketch by Rev. Dr. Joseph Sschmidlin ... and also from the more comprehensive life, byMonsignor Anton de Waal." [BX1375.L5] 4-14161
1. Plus x, pope, 1835-1914. 2. Leo xiii, pope, 1810-1908. I. Schmidlin, Joseph, 1876- II. Waal, Anton de, 1836-1917.

MARTINI, Teri. 922.21
The Fisherman's ring; the life of Giuseppe Sarto, the children's Pope. Pref, by Edwin V. O Hara. Illustrated by June Roberts. Paterson, N. J., St. Anthony Guild Press, 1954. 117p. illus. 24cm. [BX1375.N37] 54-27102
1. Pius x, 1835-1914. I. Title.

MARYGROVE College, 922.21
Detroit.
St. Pius X. Detroit, 1954. 78p. illus. 31cm. A reprint of the commencement number of the Campus reporter.' [BX1375.M38] 55-22512
1. Pius x, Saint, Pope, 1835-1914. I. Title.

MATT, Leonard von 922.245
Pope Pius X [by] Leonard von Matt, Nello Vian. Tr. from German. New York, Universe [c.1963] 48p. 75illus., (incl. ports.) 18cm. [Orbis bks., 1) Summary of St. Pius X, a pictorial biography, orig. pub. in German under title: Pius X. 63-18342 1.75 pap.,
1. Pius X, Saint, Pope, 1835-1914. I. Vian, Nello. II. Title.

MATT, Leonard von. 922.21
St. Pius X, a pictorial biography, by Leonard von Matt and Nello Vian. Translated from the German by Sebastian Bullough. Chicago, H. Regnery Co. [1955] 90p. illus. 25cm. [BX1375.M3915] 55-13810
1. Plus x, Saint, Pope, 1835-1914. I. Vian, Nello. II. Title.

MERRY DEL VAL, Raphael, 922.21
Cardinal, 1865-1930.
Memories of Pope Pius X. Forewords by Cardinal Hinsley and Cardinal Hayes. Westminster, Md., Newman Press, 1951. 81 p. 19 cm. [BX1375.M43] 52-6152
1. Pius x, Pope, 1835-1914. I. Title.

O'BRIEN, Felicity. 262'.13'0924 B
St Pius X / by Felicity O'Brien. London : Catholic Truth Society, 1976. 20 p. ; 19 cm. Includes bibliographical references. [BX1375.O18] 77-359057 ISBN 0-85183-183-4 : £0.15
1. Pius X, Saint, Pope, 1835-1914. 2. Popes—Biography. I. Title.

SCHMITZ, Emil i. e. William
Emil Schmitz-Didier, 1857-
Life of Pius x, by Monsignor E. Canon Schmitz ... New York, The American Catholic publication society [c1907] xv, 443 p. col. front., illus., ports. 27 cm. "By special arrangement the royalty accuring from the sale of this work shall be presented to His Holiness Pope Piux x as Peter's pence." Title within ornamental border. 8-26512
I. Title.

SMIT, Jan Olav, Bp., 262.130924
D.D., 1883-
St. Pius X, Pope. Tr. by James H. Van der Veldt. Foreword by Richard Cardinal Cushing,Archbishop of Boston. [Boston] St. Paul Eds. [dist. Daughters of St. Paul, c.1965] 185p. illus., facsim., ports. 22cm. [BX1375.S64] 64-7924 4.00; 3.00 pap.,
1. Pius X, Saint, Pope, 1835-1914. I. Title.

SMIT, Jan Olay, 262.130924 (B)
Bp., 1883-
St. Pius x, Pope. Translated by James H. Van der Veldt. With a foreword by Richard Cardinal Cushing, Archbishop of Boston. [Boston] St. Paul Editions [1965] 185 p. illus., facsim, ports. 22 cm. [BX1375.S64] 64-7924
1. Plus x, Saint, Pope, 1835-1914. I. Title.

SMITH, John Talbot, 1855- 922.
1923.
A pilgrimage to see the Holy Father, through the stereoscope, through the stereoscope, conducted by Rev. John Talbot Smith ... New York [etc.] Underwood & Underwood [1907] 140 p. front., illus. (facsims.) pl., fold. plans. 18 cm. [BX1375.S65] 7-24026
1. Pius X, pope, 1835-1914. 2. Popes—Court. I. Underwood & Underwood. II. Title.

UNDERWOOD & Underwood. 922.
A pilgrimage to see the Holy Father, Pope Pius x, and members of his household in the Vatican and St. Peter's, with a message from His Holiness and letters of approval from distinguished officials. Through the stereoscope. New York and London [etc.] Underwood & Underwood [1904] 71 p. front., facsims., fold. map. 17 1/2 cm. [BX1375.U6] 4-35751
1. Pius x, pope, 1835-1914. 2. Popes—Court. I. Title.

Pius X, Saint, Pope, 1835-1914—Juvenile literature.

DIETHELM, Walther. 92
St. Pius x, the farm boy who became Pope. Illustrated by Charles Dolesch. Condensed for very young readers from the original Vision book. New York, Guild Press [1963] 76 p. illus. (port. col.) 24 cm. (A Junior Vision book) Condensed from translation of Ein Bauernbub wird Papst. [BX1375.D533] 63-24996
1. Pius x, Saint, Pope, 1835-1914 — Juvenile literature. I. Title.

FITCH, Lawrence, 1930- 92
The song of the shoemaker's son; a story of Saint Pius X. Illus. by Harold Ruplinger. Notre Dame, Ind., Dujarie, 1966[c.1951] 94p. illus. 24cm. [BX1375.F5] 66-3448 2.25
1. Pius X, Saint, Pope, 1835-1914—Juvenile literature. I. Title.

Pius xi, pope, 1857-1939.

ANDERSON, Robin, 262'.13'0924 B
1913-
Between two wars : the story of Pope Pius XI (Achille Ratti, 1922-1939) / by Robin Anderson. Chicago : Franciscan Herald Press, 1977. xxix, 154 p., [4] leaves of plates : ill. ; 23 cm. Includes index. Bibliography: p. 147-148. [BX1377.A5] 77-14365 ISBN 0-8199-0687-5 : 7.95
1. Pius XI, Pope, 1857-1939. 2. Popes—Biography. I. Title.

ARADI, Zsolt. 922.21
Pius XI, the Pope and the man. [1st ed. Garden City, N. Y., Hanover House, 1958. 262 p. illus. 22 cm. Includes bibliography. [BX1377.A7] 58-6628
1. Pius XI, Pope, 1857-1939.

BRUEHL, Charles Paul, 1876- 261
The Pope's plan for social reconstruction; a commentary on the social encyclicals of Pius xi, by Charles P. Bruehl ... New York, The Devin-adair co. [c1939] xii, 356 p. 22 cm. Bibliography: p. 349-353. [HN37.C38687] 39-27779
1. Pius xi, pope, 1857-1939. 2. Sociology, Christian—Catholic authors. I. Title.

CLONMORE, William Cecil 922.21
James Phillop John Paul Howard, lord, 1902.
Pope Pius XI and world peace, by Lord Clonmore. New York, E. P. Dutton & co., incl., 1938. xi, 15-308 p. incl. front. (port) 22 1/2 cm. "First edition." [BX1377.C5] 38-27495
1. Pius XI pope, 1857- 2. Catholic church—Relations (diplomatic) I. Title.

CUDDIHY, Robert Joseph, 922.21
1862- ed.
Pope Pius xi and American public opinion, edited by Robert J. Cuddihy and George N. Shuster. New York, and London, Funk & Wagnalls company, 1939. [BX1377.C8] 39-10628
1. Pius xi, pope, 1857-1939. I. Shuster, George Nauman, 1894- joint ed. II. Title.

CURRAN, Edward Lodge, 922.21
1898-
Pope of peace; the story of Pope Pius xi. The peace of Christ in the reign of Christ, by Rev. Edward Lodge Curran ... Brooklyn, N. Y., International Catholic truth society [c1939] 63 p. illus. (incl. ports.) 16 cm. "Encyclicals of Pope Pius xi": p. 55. [BX1377.C84] 39-13202
1. Pius xi, pope, 1857-1939. I. Title.

DAILEY, Edward Vincent. 922.21
Pius ofxI, pope of the people [by] Reverend of Edward V. Dailey ... preface by His Excellency of the Most Reverend Ameleventh Chicago, Ill., Photopress. inc. [c1937] 3 p. l., 79 p. front., illus., plates, ports., map, facsims. 24 cm. "First published in the 'Chicago evening American.'"--Pref. [BX1377.D3] 38-3716
1. Pius XI, pope, 1857- I. Title.

HUGHES, Philip, 1895- 922.21
Pope Pius the Eleventh, by Philip Hughes... New York, Sheed & Ward, 1937. x, 318 p. front., ports. 22 1/2 cm. "Printed in Great Britain." "Bibliographical note": p. ix-x. [BX1377.H8] 38-9011
1. Pius xi, pope, 1857- I. Title.

KENT, Peter C., 1938- 322'.1'0945
The Pope and the Duce : the international impact of the Lateran agreements / Peter C. Kent. New York : St. Martin's Press, 1981. ix, 248 p., [4] leaves of plates : ill. ; 23 cm. Originally presented as the author's thesis, London, under title: The implications for Italian foreign policy of the 1929 Lateran Agreements. Includes index. Bibliography: p. [227]-236. [BX1545.K46 1981] 19 80-26277 ISBN 0-312-63024-7 : 19.95
1. Pius XI Pope, 1857-1939. 2. Mussolini, Benito, 1883-1945. 3. Concordat of 1929 (Italy) 4. Church and state in Italy—History—20th century. 5. Catholic Church in Italy—History—20th century. I. Title.

MORGAN, Thomas Brynmor, 1886- 922.21
A reporter at the Papal court; a narrative of the reign of Pope Pius XI, by Thomas B. Morgan. New York, Toronto, Longmans, Green and co., 1937. vi 302 p. front., plates, ports. 22 cm. "First edition." [BX1377.M6] 37-28738
1. Pius XI, pope, 1857-1939. 2. Popes—Court. I. Title.

NOVELLI, Angelo. 282
The life of Pius xi, by Rev. A. Novelli, translated from the Italian by Rev. p. T. Lambardo, with the addition of two new chapters: "Pius xi and America "and" the Holy year." Yonkers, N. Y., Mt. Carmel press [c1925] 3 p. l., [11]-303 p. front., plates, ports. 21 cm. [BX1377.N6] 25-8081
1. Pius xi, pope, 1857- I. Lombardo, Pasquale Thomas, 1889- tr. II. Title.

OLF, Lillian (Browne) Mrs. 1880.- 922.21
Pius XI, apostle of peace, by Lillian Browne-Olf. New York, The Macmillan company, 1938. xiv, 257 p. front. (port.) 21 cm. "First printing." Bibliograpy: p. 241-244. [BX1377.O55] 38-9244
1. Plus xi, pope, 1857-1930. I. Title.

RHODES, Anthony Richard Ewart. 327'.45'634
The Vatican in the age of the dictators, 1922-1945 [by] Anthony Rhodes. New York, Holt, Rinehart and Winston [1974, c1973] 383 p. ports. 24 cm. Bibliography: p. [359]-368. [BX1389.R48 1974] 72-91593 ISBN 0-03-007736-2 12.50
1. Pius XI, Pope, 1857-1939. 2. Pius XII, Pope, 1876-1958. 3. Papacy—History—20th century. 4. Church and state in Europe. 5. World War, 1939-1945—Catholic Church. I. Title.

TEELING, William, 1903- 282
Pope Pius XI and world affairs, by William Teeling ... New York, Frederick A. Stokes company, 1937. viii, 312 p. front. (port.) 21 1/2 cm. London edition (L. Dickson) has title: The Pope in politics. [BX1377.T4 1937 a] 37-28735
1. Pius XI, pope, 1857- 2. Catholic church—Relations (diplomatic) 3. World politics. I. Title.

WICKLOW, William Cecil James Philip John Paul Howard, 8th earl of, 1902- 922.21
Pope Pius XI and world peace. [1st ed. [New York, Dutton, 1938. 306 p. port. 23 cm. [BX1377.W47 1938] 38-27495
1. Pius XI, pope, 1857-1939. 2. Catholic Church—Relations (diplomatic) I. Title.

Pius XII, Pope 1876-1958.

BARGELLINI, Piero, 1897- 922.21
Pius XII, the angelic shepherd. English translation. New York, Good Shepherd Pub. Corp. [1950] 181 p. illus., ports. 23 cm. [BX1378.B314] 50-11205
1. Pius XII, Pope, 1876- I. Title.

BURTON, Katherine (Kurz) 1890- 922.21
Witness of the light; the life of Pope Pius XII. [1st ed.] New York, Longmuns, Green, 1958. 248p. 22cm. Includes bibliography. [BX1378.B8] 58-7680
1. Plus XII, Pope, 1876- I. Title.

CATHOLIC church. Pope. 1939- (Pius xii) 282
The Pope speaks: the words of Pius xii: with biography by Charles Rankin, and a preface by the Most Reverend Edwin V. O'Hara, D. D. ... New York, Harcourt, Brace and company [1940] xi, 337 p. front. (port.) 21 cm. "First American edition." [BX870 1939 a] 40-27790
I. Rankin Charles. II. Title.

CIANFARRA, Camille Maximilian, 1907- 940.531522
The Vatican and the war, by Camile M. Cianfarra. New York, Literary classics, inc. distributed by E. P. Dutton & company, inc., 1944. 344 p. 21 cm. "First edition." [BX1378.C5] 44-860
1. Pius xii, pope, 1876- 2. World war, 1939- Catholic church. I. Title.

CODE *of international ethics;* translated and edited with a commentary by John Eppstein. Westminster, Md., Newman Press, 1953. xiv, 256p. 23cm. Appendixes (p. 184-248): [JX1952.U543 1953] 172.4 52-10392 177
1. Pope Pius XII and international morality—SCharter of the United Nations.—SA declaration of rights (National Catholic Welfare Conference) 2. International relations. 3. Peace. I. Union internationale d etudes sociales.

CONNIFF, James C G 922.21
Pope Pius XII; the holy life of Eugenio Pacelli. Greenwich, Conn., Fawcett Publications, c1955. 32p. illus. 29cm. [BX1378.C6] 55-1739
1. Plus xii, Pope, 1876- I. Title.

DINNEEN, Joseph Francis, 1897- 922.21
Pius xii, pope of peace, by Joseph F. Dinneen. New York, R. M. McBride and company [c1939] viii p., 3 l., 3-281 p. plates, ports 22 cm. "First edition." [BX1378.D5] 39-27312
1. Pius xii, pope, 1876- I. Title.

DOYLE, Charles Hugo. 262.131
A day with the Pope. Format by Heyworth. [1st ed.] Garden City, N. Y., Doubleday, 1950. 64 p. illus., ports. 26 cm. [BX1378.D575]
1. Pius XII, Pope, 1876- I. Title.

DOYLE, Charles Hugo. 922.21
The life of Pope Pius XII [by] Charles Hugo Doyle. New York, Didier [1945] x, 258 p. col. front. 21 cm. "References": p. 249-252. [BX1378.D58] 45-4244
1. Pius XII, pope, 1876- I. Title.

DOYLE, Charles Hugo. 922.21
We have a pope; the life of Pope Pius XII, by Rev. Charles Hugo Doyle. Paterson, N.J., St. Anthony guild press, 1942. viii, [2], 118 p. illus. (incl. ports.) 20 cm. Bibliographical foot-notes. [BX1378.D6] 42-16430
1. Pius XII, pope, 1876- I. Title.

FALCONI, Carlo. 940.532'5'45634
The silence of Plus XII. Translated by Bernard Wall. [1st American ed.] Boston, Little, Brown [1970] 430 p. 25 cm. Translation of Il silenzio di Pio XII. Includes bibliographical references. [BX1378.F313 1970] 78-79360 10.00
1. Pius XII, Pope, 1876-1958. I. Title.

FITCH, Lawrence, 1930-- 922.21
The world and the white prince; a story of Pope Pius XII.Illus. by Harold Ruplinger. Notre Dame, Ind., Dujarie Press [1954] 98p. illus. 24cm. [BX1378.F5] 54-3699
1. Plus XII, Pope, 1876— I. Title.

FRIEDLANDER, Saul, 1932- 262.130924
Pius XII and the Third Reich; a documentation. Tr. from French and German by Charles Fullman. [1st Amer. ed] New York, Knopf, 1966. xxiv, 238p. 22cm. Bibl. [BX1378.F713] 66-10029 4.95
1. Pius XII, Pope, 1876-1958. 2. Catholic Church—Relations (diplomatic) with Germany. 3. Germany —For. rel.—Catholic Church. I. Title.

FRIEDLANDER, Saul, 1932- 940.53'25
Pius XII and the Third Reich : a documentation / Saul Friedlander ; translated from the French and German by Charles Fullman. New York : Octagon Books, 1980, c1966. xxiv, 238 v. p. ; 23 cm. Translation of Pie XII et le IIIe Reich. Reprint of the ed. published by Knopf, New York. Includes bibliographical references and index. [BX1378.F713 1980] 19 80-12830 ISBN 0-374-92930-0 lib. bdg. : 16.00
1. Pius XII, Pope, 1876-1958. 2. Catholic Church—Relations (diplomatic) with Germany. 3. Germany—Foreign relations—Catholic Church. I. Title.

HALECKI, Oskar, 1891- 922.21
Eugenio Pacelli, Pope of peace, by Oscar Halecki in collaboration with James F. Murray, Jr. New York, Creative Age Press, 1951. viii, 355 p. 22 cm. Bibliography: p. 347-349. [BX1378.H3] 51-9673
1. Plus xii, Pope, 1876- I. Title.

HATCH, Alden, 1898- 922.21
Crown of glory; the life of Pope Pius xii, by Alden Hatch, Seamus Walshe. Drawings by Louis Priscilla. Garden City, N. Y., Doubleday [c.1957-1965] 273p. illus. 18cm. (Echo bk. E1) [BX1378.H35] .85 pap.,
1. Pius xii, Pope, 1876-1958. I. Walshe, Seamus, 1918- joint author. II. Title.

HATCH, Alden, 1898- 922.21
Crown of glory the life of Pope Pius XII by Alden Hatch and Seamus Walshe. Illustrated with drawings by Louis Priscilla [Memorial ed., rev. and enl.] New York, Hawthorn Books [1957] 251p. illus. 24cm. [BX1378.H35] 57-6362
1. Pius XII, Pope, 1876- I. Walshe, Seamus, 1918- joint author. II. Title.

HATCH, Alden, 1898- 922.21
Crown of glory the life of Pope Pius XII by Alden Hatch and Seamus Walshe. Illustrated with drawings by Louis Priscilla. [Memorial ed., rev. and enl.] New York, Hawthorn Books [1958] 271p. illus. 24cm. [BX1378.H35 1958] 58-59703
1. Pius XII, Pope, 1876-1958. I. Walshe, Seamus, 1918- joint author. II. Title.

HATCH, Alden, 1898- 922.21
Crown of glory; the life of Pope Pius XII, by Alden Hatch and Seamus Walshe. Illustrated with drawings by Louis Priscilla. Garden City, Echo Books [1965] 273 p. illus. 19 cm. 67-30090
1. 1. Pius XII, Pope, 1876-1958. I. Walshe, Seamus, 1918- joint author. II. Title.

KONSTANTIN, Prince of Bavaria, 1920- 922.21
The Pope : a portrait from life. Translated by Diana Pyke. New York, Roy Publishers [1955?] 307p. illus. 23cm. [BX1378] 56-5048
1. Pius XII, Pope, 1876- I. Title.

LAVELLE, Elise. 922.21
The man who was chosen; the story of Pope Pius XII. New York, Whittlesey House [1957] 156p. illus. 21cm. [BX1378.L3] 57-6401
1. Pius XII, Pope, 1876- I. Title.

LENN, Lottie Helen, 1908- 922.21
Pope Pius XII, Rock of Peace, by Lottie H. Lenn and Mary A. Reardon; illustrated by Mary A. Reardon. Foreword by Richard J. Cushing. [1st ed.] New York, Dutton, 1950. 152 p. illus. 21 cm. Bibliography: p. 147-148. [BX1378.L39] 50-5908
1. Pius XII, Pope, 1876-1958. I. Reardon, Mary A., joint author.

MCDERMOTT, Thomas. 922.21
Keeper of the keys, a life of Pope Pius XII, by Thomas McDermott. Milwaukee, The Bruce publishing [1946] x p., 1 l., 267 p. plates, ports. 20 1/2 cm. [BX1378.M3] 46-6685
1. Pius XII, pope, 1876- I. Title.

MCGURN, Barrett 282
A reporter looks at the Vatican. New York, Coward [c.1962] 316p. 22cm. 62-10952 5.00
1. Pius XX, Pope, 1876-1958. 2. Joannes XXIII, Pope, 1881- 3. Popes—Court. I. Title.

MURPHY, Thomas J 265.5
The supernatural perfection of conjugal life according to Pope Pius XII. Mundelein, Ill., Saint Mary of the Lake Seminary, 1960. 154p. 23cm. (Pontifica Facultas Theologica Seminaril Sanctae Mariae ad Lacum. Dissertationes ad lauream, 33) Bibliography: p. 138-154. [BX2250.M84] 61-1795
1. Pius XII, Pope, 1876-1958. 2. Marriage—Catholic Church. I. Title. II. Series: St. Mary of the Lake Seminary, Mundele, Ill. Dissertationes ad lauream, 33

NAUGHTON, James W. 261
Pius XII on world problems, by James W. Naughton, S. J. New York, The America press [c1943] xx1v 199 p. 21 cm. "Second edition." "Short bibliography on the pontificate of Pius XII": p. [147]-178. "Index of papal documents": p. 179-181. [BX1378.N3 1943 a] 44-3712
1. Pius XII, pope, 1876- 2. World war, 1939—Catholic church. 3. Sociology, Christian—Catholic authors. I. Title.

O'CONNELL, William Henry, cardinal, 1859- 262.135
A memorable voyage [by] William cardinal O'Connell. [Brighton, Mass., c1939] 3 p. l., 5-51 p. front., plates, ports. 23 1/2 cm. "I have attempted...to describe my historic journey to the conclave of 1939."--p. 51. [BX1378.O3] 39-25690
1. Pius XII, pope, 1876- 2. Popes—Election. I. Title.

O'CONNOR, Daniel A. 261.8
Catholic social doctrine. Westminster, Md., Newman Press, 1956. 204p. 23cm. [BX1753.O27] 55-10551
1. Pius XII, Pope, 1876- 2. Sociology, Christian (Catholic) I. Title.

O'CONNOR, Daniel A 261.8
Catholic social Locke [a critical introduction] London, Baltimore, Christian (Catholic) [BX1753.O27] 55-10551
1. Pius XII, Pope, 1876- I. Title.

O'MIKLE, Stephen, ed. 922.21
Pope Pius XII, his voice and life. New York, Wilson Pub. Co. [1958] 64p. (chiefly illus.) 25cm. and phonodisc (2 s. 6 in. 78 rpm) in pocket. [BX1378.O5] 59-291
1. Pius XII, Pope, 1876-1958. I. Title.

PADELLARO, Nazareno 1892- 922.21
Portrait of Pius XII. Translated by Michael Derrick. Foreword by Daniel-Rops. [1st American ed.] New York, Dutton, 1957 [c1956] 274 p. illus. 22 cm. Translation of Pio XII. [BX1378.P312 1957] 56-6317
1. Pius XII, Pope, 1876-

PFISTER, Pierre, 1895- 922.21
Pius xii; the life and work of a great Pope. New York, Studio Publications [1955] 159p. illus. 26cm. [BX1378.P49] 55-7828
1. Pius xii, Pope, 1876- I. Title.

PURDY, William Arthur, 1911- 262.130922
The Church on the move; the characters and politics of Pius XII and John XXIII [by] W. A. Purdy. Techny, Ill., Divine Word [1968,c.1966] 352p. 22cm. Bibl. [BX1378.P8 1966] 2.95 pap.,
1. Pius XII, Pope 1876-1958. 2. Joannes XXIII, Pope, 1881-1963. I. Title.

PURDY, William Arthur, 1911- 262.130922
The Church on the move; the characters and policies of Pius XII and John XXIII [by] W. A. Purdy. New York, John Day Co. [1966] 352 p. 22 cm. Bibliography: p. [343]-346. [BX1378.P8 1966] 66-25867
1. Pius XII, Pope, 1876-1958. 2. Joannes XXIII, Pope, 1881-1963. I. Title.

SMIT, Jan Olva, Bp., 1883- 922.21
Angelic shepherd; the life of Pope Pius XII. Adapted into English by James H. Vanderveldt. New York, Dodd, Mead, 1950. x, 326 p. illus., ports. 22 cm. "References": p. 295-310. "Pius XII ... A checklist of published biographies and biographical notes, compiled by Elizabeth J. Barham": p. 311-318. [BX1378.S533] 50-6532
1. Pius XII, Pope, 1876- I. Title.

SMYTH, J Hilton LeBaron. 922.21
His Holiness Pope Pius XII; a memorial picture history of the Pope of Peace, with texts and notes [Stamped: New Rochelle, N.Y., Distributed by Sportshelf, 1958] 128 p. illus. 23 cm. [BX1378.S55] 58-4975
1. Pius XII, Pope, 1876-1958. I. Title.

TARDINI, Domenico, Cardinal. 922.21
Memories of Pius XII. Tr. by Rosemary Goldie. Goldie. Westminster, Md., Newman [c.]1961. 175p. ports. (col.) 60-53377 2.75
I. Title.

VAN HOCK, Kees, 1902- 922.21
Pope Pius XII, priest and statesman, a biography by Kees Van Hock; foreword by the Most Rev. Dr. Browne ... New York, Philosophical library [c1944] 3 p. l., 3-106 p. front. (port.) 22 cm. [BX1378.V3 1944] 45-9081
1. Pius XII, pope, 1876- I. Title.

Pius XII, Pope, 1876-1958—Juvenile literature.

DE WOHL, Louis, 1903- 922.21
Pope Pius XII, the world's shepherd. Illus. by Harry Barton. New York, Farrar, Straus & Cudahy [c.1961] 190p. (Vision books, 50) 61-5897 1.95
1. Pius, XII, Pope, 1876-1958—Juvenile literature. I. Title.

HATCH, Alden, 1898- 92
Apostle of peace; the story of Pope Pius XII. Illustrated by Jo Polseno. New York, Hawthorn Books [1965] 191 p. illus. 22 cm. Bibliography: p. [175] [BX1378.H34] 65-12735
1. Pius XII, Pope, 1876-1958 — Juvenile literature. I. Title.

Pius XII, Pope, 1876- —Dictionaries, indexes, etc.

PIUS XII, Pope, 1876- 204
The mind of Pius XII. Edited by Robert C. Pollock New York, Crown Publishers [1955] xix, 234p. port. 22cm. Excerpts from communications of His Holiness. Bibliography: p. 231-234. [BX890.P5818] 55-7235
1. Pius XII, Pope, 1876- —Dictionaries, indexes, etc. I. Title.

Piyutim.

PETUCHOWSKI, Jakob Josef, 1925- 296.4
Theology and poetry : studies in the medieval piyyut / Jakob J. Petuchowski. London ; Boston : Routledge and K. Paul, 1977. 153 p. ; 22 cm. (Littman library of Jewish civilization) Includes poems in English and Hebrew. Includes bibliographical references and index. [BM670.P5P47] 78-316120 ISBN 0-7100-8334-3 : 12.00
1. Piyutim. I. Title.

PL Kyodan.

BACH, Marcus, 1906- 299'.56
The power of perfect liberty; out of Japan: a creative breakthrough in humanity's quest for a new man in a new age. Englewood Cliffs, N.J., Prentice-Hall [1971] 163 p. 22 cm. [BL2228.P2B3] 78-161916 ISBN 0-13-686832-0 5.95
1. PL Kyodan. I. Title.

Placidus, Saint, ca. 515-ca. 550.

GALLOIS, Genevieve. 922.2
The life of little Saint Placid. Foreword by Marcelle Auclair. [Translated by the monks of Mount Saviour Monanstery. New York] Pantheon [1956] unpaged. illus. 20cm. [BX4700.P78G32] 56-6121
1. Placidus, Saint, ca. 515-ca. 550. I. Title.

Plague—England—London, 1625—Poetry.

WITHER, George, 1588-1667. 223'.06
Britain's remembrancer. (cl' I[reverse c] cxxviii). New York, B. Franklin [1967] 580 p. 25 cm. (Burt Franklin research & source works series, no. 150) Reprint of the 1880 ed., which was issued as no. 28-29 of The Spenser Society. [PR2392.B6 1967] 72-184254
1. Plague—England—London, 1625—Poetry. I. Title. II. Series: Spenser Society, Manchester. Publication no. 28-29.

Plagues of Egypt—Miscellanea.

BEN-DAVID, Eliezer. 222'.12
Out of the iron furnace : the Jewish redemption from ancient Egypt and the delivery from spiritual bondage / by Eliezer Ben-David ; translated and adapted by Yaakov Feitman. New York : Shengold Publishers, c1975. 144 p. ; 23 cm. An expanded translation of Mateh haElohim. Includes bibliographical references and index. [BS1245.5.B4513] 74-84829 ISBN 0-88400-040-0 : 5.95
1. Plagues of Egypt—Miscellanea. I. Feitman, Yaakov. II. Title.

Plainfield, N.J. Crescent avenue Presbyterian church.

COCKHRAN, Jean Carter, 1876- 285.1749
A world-wide church, Cresent avenue Presbyterian, Plainfield New Jersey [by] Jean Carter Cochran. Plainfield, N.J., Interstate printing corporation, 1944. viii, 172 p. front., illus., plates (part col.) ports. 20 cm. [BX9211.P7C7] 44-13188
1. Plainfield, N.J. Crescent avenue Presbyterian church. I. Title.

Plant lore.

DAVIDSON, Peter.
The mistletoe and its philosophy; shewing its history, the origin of its mystical and religious rites ... its legendary connection with the great world-reformer, Rama, along with a description of several rare plants and herbs that possess mystical properties. By P. Davidson ... Loudsville, Ga., P. Davidson; Glasgow. B. Goodwin, 1892. x, 55 p. front. 22 cm. [BL444.D3] 31-7894
1. Plant lore. 2. Mistletoe. I. Title.

Plants in the Bible.

LERNER, Carol. 220.9'1
A Biblical garden / Carol Lerner ; translations from the Hebrew Bible by Ralph Lerner. New York : Morrow, 1982. 46 p. : ill. (some col.) ; 27 cm. Descriptions and pictures of twenty plants mentioned in the Old Testament, including fig, lentil, olive, papyrus, and pomegranate. [BS665.L46 1982] 19 81-16886 ISBN 0-688-01071-7 : 10.00
1. Plants in the Bible. 2. [Plants in the Bible.] I. Title.

Plato.

CAVENGH, Francis A.
The ethical end of Plato's theory of ideas ... by Francis A. Cavenagh. London, New York [etc.] Henry Frowde, 1909. 89 p. 23 cm. Thesis (M. A.)--University of London. List of books consulted: p. 3-4. A 10
1. Plato. 2. Ideals. 3. Ethics. I. Title.

CHERNISS, Harold Fredrik, 1904- 292
The Platonism of Gregory of Nyssa, by Harold Fredrik Cherniss ... Berkeley, Calif., University of California press, 1930. cover-title, 2 p. l., 92 p. 25 cm. (University of California publications in classical philology. v. 11. no. 1) "Bibliographical note": p. 65. [PA25.C3 vol. 11, no. 1] A 30
1. Gregorius, Saint, bp. of Nyssa. 2. Plato. I. Title.

COLLINS, Clifton Wilbraham, 1845?- 281
Plato; by Clifton W. Collins ... Philadelphia, J. B. Lippincott & co., 1880. vi p., 1 l., 197 p. 18 cm. (Half-title: Ancient classics for English readers, ed. by W. L. Collins. [vol. xix]) [PA3606.A6P7] 16-25522
1. Plato. I. Title.

FEIBLEMAN, James Kern, 1904- 201
Religious Platonism; the influence of religion on Plato and the influence of Plato on religion. New York, Barnes & Noble [1962, c.1959] 236p. 23cm. Bibl. 60-1560 5.00
1. Plato. 2. Plato—Influence. I. Title.

HAVELOCK, Eric Alfred.
Preface to Plato. New York, Grosset & Dunlap [1967, c1963] 328 p. 20 cm. (Universal library) Includes bibliography. 68-90156
1. Plato. 2. Philiosophy, Ancient. 3. Greek poetry—Hist. & crit. I. Title.

HERSHBELL, Jackson P., 1935- 128'.5
Pseudo-Plato, Axiochus / by Jackson P. Hershbell. Chico, Calif. : Scholars Press, c1981. viii, 90 p. ; 23 cm. (Texts and translations ; 21 ISSN 0145-3203s) (Graeco-Roman religion series ; 6) ISSN 0145-3211) English and Greek. Includes indexes. Bibliography: p. 71-73. [B391.A85H47] 79-20127 ISBN 0-89130-354-5 pbk. : 13.50
1. Plato. Spurious and doubtful works. Axiochus. 2. Death—Early works to 1800. I. Plato. Spurious and doubtful works. Axiochus. English. 1980. II. Title. III. Series. IV. Series: Society of Biblical Literature. Texts and translations ; 21.
Publisher's address: 101 Salem St. P.O. Box 2268, Chico, CA 95927

MARTIN, Thomas Henri, 1813-1884. 113
Etudes sur le Timee de Plato / Thomas Henri Martin. New York : Arno Press, 1975. p. cm. (History of ideas in ancient Greece) Reprint of the 1841 ed. published by Ladrange, Paris. "Texte et traduction du Timee": Bibliography: p. [B387.M3 1975] 75-13279 ISBN 0-405-07319-4
1. Plato. Timaeus. I. Plato. Timaeus. French and Greek. 1975. II. Title. III. Series.

MILLER, Irving Elgar, 1869-
... The significance of the mathematical element in the philosophy of Plato ... By Irving Elgar Miller. Chicago, The University of Chicago press, 1904. 95 p. 24 cm. Thesis (PH.D.)--University of Chicago, 1904. Bibliography: p. 93. [BS398.M3M6] 5-8078
1. Plato. 2. Mathematics—Philosophy. I. Title.

MOORS, Kent F. 184
Platonic myth : an introductory study / Kent F. Moors. Washington, D.C. : University Press of America, c1982. x, 137 p. ; 23 cm. Based on the author's thesis (Ph.D.)—Northern Illinois University. Includes bibliographical references. [B398.M8M66 1982] 19 81-43816 ISBN 0-8191-2314-5 : 18.25 ISBN 0-8191-2315-3 (pbk.) : 7.75
1. Plato. 2. Mythology—History. I. Title.

PLATO.
Dialogues of Plato, tr. by Benjamin Jowett, with a biographical and critical introduction by Josiah Royce ... [Aldime ed.] New York, D. Appleton and company, 1898. 2 p. l., iii-xxiii, 476 p. front., 5 pl., 2 facsim. (1 col.) 24 cm. (Half-title: The world's great books) [B355 1898] 11-6885
I. Jowett, Benjamin, 1817-1893, tr. II. Royce, Josiah, 1855-1916. III. Title.
Contents omitted.

PLATO.
The dialogues of Plato, selections from the translation of Benjamin Jowett ... edited with an introduction by William Chase Greene ... New York, Boni & Liveright [c1927] xxxix, 535 p. 22 1/2 cm. "List of books": p. 535. [B355 1927] 27-14313
I. Jowett, Benjamin, 1817-1893, tr. II. Greene, William Chase, 1890-ed. III. Title.

PLATO.
The Menexenus of Plato; ed. with introduction and notes, by J. A. Shawyer. Oxford, Clarendon press, 1906. xxxi, [1, 49] p. 19 cm. A 11
I. Shawyer, James Anderson, ed. II. Title.

PLATO.
The Meno of Plato, ed. with introduction, notes, and excursuses, by E. Seymer Thompson ... London, New York, Macmillan company, 1901. lxvi, 319 p. 17 cm. (Half-title: Classical series) A 15
I. Thompson, E. Seymer, ed. II. Title.

PLATO.
The Theaetetus of Plato, with translation and notes, by Benjamin Hall Kennedy ... Ed. for the syndics of the University press. Cambridge [Eng.] University press, 1894. xvi, 235, [1] p. 18 1/2 cm. A 15
I. Kennedy, Benjamin Hall, 1804-1889, ed. II. Title.

VERSENYI, Laszlo. 179'.9
Holiness and justice : an interpretation of Plato's Euthyphro / Laszlo Versenyi. Washington, D.C. : University Press of America, c1982. p. cm. Bibliography: p. [B370.V47] 19 81-43830 ISBN 0-8191-2316-1 : 19.75 ISBN 0-8191-2317-X (pbk.) : 9.50
1. Plato. Euthyphro. 2. Piety—History. I. Title.

WA SAID, Dibinga. 212'.5
Theosophies of Plato, Aristotle and Plotinus. New York, Philosophical Library [1970] 205 p. 22 cm. Bibliography: p. 199-205. [B398.G6W2] 72-81817 6.25
1. Plato. 2. Aristoteles. 3. Plotinus. 4. God (Greek religion) 5. Theosophy—History. I. Title.

Plato—Aesthetics.

CAVARNOS, Constantine. 111.8'5
Plato's theory of fine art. Athens, Astir Pub. Co. [1973] 98 p. 21 cm. Includes bibliographical references. [B398.A4C38] 73-164473
1. Plato—Aesthetics. I. Title.
Distributed by Institute for Byzantine and Modern Greek Studies, 115 Gilbert Road, Belmont, Mass. 02178; 1.95 (pbk.)

LODGE, Rupert Clendon, 1886- 111.8'5
Plato's theory of art / by Rupert C. Lodge. New York : Russell & Russell, 1975. 316 p. ; 23 cm. Reprint of the 1953 ed. published by Routledge & Paul, London, in series: International library of psychology, philosophy, and scientific method. Includes indexes. Bibliography: p. 305-307. [B398.A4L6 1975] 73-84756 ISBN 0-8462-1737-6 : 20.00
1. Plato—Aesthetics. 2. Art—Philosophy. I. Title. II. Series: International library of psychology, philosophy, and scientific method.

OATES, Whitney Jennings, 1904- 111.8'5
Plato's view of art [by] Whitney J. Oates. New York, Scribner [1972] 81 p. 21 cm. Includes bibliographical references. [B398.A4O2] 74-37202 ISBN 0-684-12751-2 ISBN 0-684-12839-X (pbk) 4.95
1. Plato—Aesthetics. I. Title.

Plato—Ethics.

HUBY, Pamela M. 170
Plato and modern morality. London, Macmillan, 1972. ix, 80 p. 23 cm. (New studies in practical philosophy) Includes bibliographical references. [B398.E8H83 1972] 73-154915 ISBN 0-333-12053-1
1. Plato—Ethics. I. Title.
Distributed by Humanities Press, 6.50.

Plato. Laches.

O'BRIEN, Michael John. 292.211
The unity of the Laches. (In Yale classical studiės. New Haven. 24 cm. v. 18 (1963) p. [131]-147) Bibliographical footnotes. [[PA25.Y3 vol. 18]] 63-5847
1. Plato. Laches. I. Title.

Plato—Manuscripts.

POST, Levi Arnold, 1889-
The Vatican Plato and its relations, by Levi Arnold Post ... Middletown, Conn., The American philological association, 1934. xi, 116 p. 24 cm. (Added t.-p.: Philological monographs ... no. iv) [PA1279.L4P6]
1. Plato—Manuscripts. 2. Vatican. Bibliothecs Vatican. Mass. vat. gr. 1) I. Title.

Plato—Religion.

FEIBLEMAN, James Kern, 1904- 200'.1
Religious Platonism; the influence of religion on Plato and the influence of Plato on religion [by] James K. Feibleman. Westport, Conn., Greenwood Press [1971, c1959] 236 p. 22 cm. Includes bibliographical references. [B398.R4F4 1971] 78-161628 ISBN 0-8371-6184-3
1. Plato—Religion. 2. Plato—Influence. I. Title.

Platonists.

BEACH, Alligood.
A disciple of Plato, by Alligood Beach; illustrated by John Ward Dunsmore. Boston, Roberts publishing co., 1902. 4 p. l., 353 p. front., pl. 20 1/2 cm. 2-25034
I. Title.

BIGG, Charles, 1840-1908. 201
The Christian Platonists of Alexandria; the 1886 Bampton lectures. Oxford, Clarendon P., 1968. 386 p. 23 cm. "First published 1913." Bibliographical footnotes. [BR1705.B5 1968] 76-370393 unpriced
1. Philo Judaus. 2. Clemens, Titus Flavius, Alexandrinus. 3. Origenes. 4. Platonists. I. Title.

BIGG, Charles, 1840-1908. 231.1
The Christian Platonists of Alexandria. Eight lectures preached before the University of Oxford in the year 1886 on the foundation of the late Rev. John Bampton ... by Charles Bigg ... Oxford, The Clarendon press, 1886. xxvii, 304 p. 23 cm. (On cover: Bampton lectures. 1886) Contents.--i. Introduction. Philo and the Gnostics.--ii-iii. Clement.-- iv-vi. Origen.--vii. The reformed paganism.--viii. Summary. [BR45.B3 1886] 230.062 38-16290
1. Philo Judeaeus. 2. Clemens, Titus Flavius, Alexandrinus. 3. Origenes. 4. Platonists. I. Title.

BIGG, Charles, 1840-1908. 231.1
The Christian Platonists of Alexandria; being the Bampton lectures of the year 1886, by the late Charles Bigg ... Reprinted with some additions and corrections. Oxford, The Clarendon press, 1913. 386 p. 1 l., 23 cm. On cover: Second edition. Edited by F. E. Brightman. Contents.--i. Introduction. Philo and the Gnostics.--ii. iii. Clement.--iv-vi. Origen.--vii. The reformed paganism.--viii. Summary. [BR1705.B5 1913] 230.082 14-1994
1. Philo Judeaus. 2. Clemens, Titus Flavius, Alexandrinus. 3. Origenes. 4. Platonists. I. Brightman, Frank Edward, 1856-1982, ed. II. Title.

INGE, William Ralph, 1860-
The Platonic tradition in English religious thought; the Hulsean lectures at Cambridge, 1925-1926, by William Ralph Inge ... London, New York [etc.] Longmans, Green and co., ltd., 1926. vii, 117 p. 20 cm. [B517.I6 1926] 26-13598
I. Hulsean lectures, 1925-1926. II. Title.

INGE, William Ralph, 1860-
The Platonic tradition in English religious thought; the Hulsean lectures at Cambridge, 1925-1926, by William Ralph Inge ... New York [etc.] Longmans, Green and co., 1926. vii, 124 p. 20 cm. [B517.I 6] 26-9936
I. Hulsean lectures 1925-1926 II. Title.

MASSON, Thomas Lansing, 1866-
The new Plato; or, Socrates redivivus, by Thomas L. Masson. New York, Moffat, Yard & company, 1908. 3 p. l., v-viii p., 1 l., 121 p. 20 cm. [PS2367.M6N4] 8-10888
I. Title.
Contents omitted.

MILES, Leland. 141
John Colet and the Platonic tradition. La Salle, Ill., Open Court, 1961. xix, 239p. 21cm. (His Fishers with Platonic nets, v. 1) Open Court classics, P86. Bibliography: p. [217]-230. [BR754.C6M5] 60-16716
1. Colet, John, 1467?-1519. 2. Platonists. I. Title.

SCHOPENHAUER, Arthur, 1788-1860.
... Selections, edited by De Witt H. Parker ... New York Chicago [etc.] C. Scribner's sons [c1928] xxxii, 447 p. 17 cm. (Half-title: The modern student's library. [Philosophy series]) At head of title: Schopenhauer. "Dated list of Schopenhauer's works": p. xxxii. [B3108.P3] 28-12566
I. Parker, De Witt Henry, 1885- ed. II. Title.

SELECTIONS, edited by D. H.
Parker. New York, Scribner [1956] xxxii, 447p. (The modern student's library)
I. Schopenhauer, Arthur, 1788-1860.

Plattsburg, N. Y. St. Peter's Church.

HOGUE, Roswell A 1890- 282.747
Centennial, 1853-1953: St.Peter's Roman Catholic Church Plattsburgh, N. Y. [Plattsburg? 1953] 182p. illus. 22cm. [BX4603.P6H6] 54-20985
1. Plattsburg, N. Y. St. Peter's Church. I. Title.

Play.

MILLER, David LeRoy. 200.1
Gods and games; toward a theology of play [by] David L. Miller. New York, World Pub. Co. [1970] xiii, 209 p. 22 cm. Bibliography: p. [197]-206. [BF717.M53 1970] 74-90923 5.95
1. Play. 2. Psycology, Religious. I. Title.

POWELL, Warren Thomson, 1884- ed. 790
Recreation in church and community, the values and theory of play, its influence upon character, its objectives and programs [by] Charles D. Gianuque, Raymond W. Porter, H. D. Edgreen, edited by Warren T. Powell ... New York, Cincinnati [etc.] The Abingdon press [c1938] 136 p. 18 cm. "Approved by the Committee on curriculum of the Board of education of the Methodist Episcopal church." Bibliography: p. 127-136. [BV1640.P58] 259 38-7151
1. Play. 2. Church entertainments. 3. Games. I. Giauque, Charles Dickens, 1891- II. Porter, Raymond Willis, 1889- III. Edgren, Harry Daniel, 1899- IV. Title.

RAHNER, Hugo. 1900- 233
Man at plav. [Tr. by Brian Battershaw. Edward Quinn. New York] Herder & Herder [1967, c.1965] xiv, 105p. 22cm. Tr. of Der Spielende Mensch. Bibl. [BT745.R313] 67-141470 3.50
1. Play. 2. Man (Theology) 3. Recreation. I. Title.

SHAVER, Erwin Leander, 1890- 261.4
A Christian's recreation; a suggested plan for a project for young people's groups, by Erwin L. Shaver. Chicago, Ill., The University of Chicago press [c1925] ix, 54 p. 19 1/2 cm. (Half-title: The University of Chicago publications in religious education ... Constructive studies) Blank pages for "Notes" inserted. Contains bibliographies. [BV1620.S5] 25-23308
1. Play. 2. Amusements—Moral and religious aspects. I. Title.

STONE, Phyllis. 791.6
The singing shepherd; a nativity play in four scenes, by Phyllis Stone ... London [etc.] S. French, ltd.; New York, Los Angeles, Cal., S. French, inc.; [etc., etc.] c1935. 18 p. 18 1/2 cm. (On cover: French's acting edition, no.30) [PN6120.C5S735] CA 36
I. Title.

Playboy.

RIDENOUR, Fritz. 241
It all depends; a comparison of Situation ethics and the Playboy philosophy with what the Bible teaches about morality. Illustrated by Joyce Thimsen. Research by Georgiana Walker. Glendale, Calif., G/L Regal Books [1969] 234 p. illus. 18 cm. Includes bibliographical references. [BJ1251.R5] 68-8388
1. Fletcher, Joseph Francis, 1905- Situation ethics. 2. Playboy. 3. Christian ethics. I. Title.

Plays—Presentation, etc.

JONES, Elizabeth Orton, 1910- 232.92
How far is it to Bethlehem? Boston, Horn Book, 1955. 38 p. illus. 18 cm. Describes a nativty play presented by crippled children at a rehabilitation center, telling how each participant achieved a small miracle as he sought to overcome physical disability and perform his role. [PN3157.J6] AC 68
1. Plays—Presentation, etc. 2. Christmas plays. 3. Handicapped. I. Title.

Pleasant Hill Church of the Brethren, Macoupin Co., Ill.

PLEASANT Hill. 289.92
Elgin, Ill., Brethren Pub. House c[1956] 259p. illus. 21cm. [BX7831.P56W4] 286.5 57-20881
1. Pleasant Hill Church of the Brethren, Macoupin Co., Ill. I. Weddle, Ethel Harshbarger.

WEDDLE, Ethel Harshbarger. *289.92
Pleasant Hill. Elgin, Ill., Brethren Pub. House [c1956] 250 p. illus. 21 cm. [BX7831.P56W4] 286.5 57-20881
1. Pleasant Hill Church of the Brethren, Macoupia Co., Ill. I. Title.

Pleasant Union Baptist Church, Gainesville, Ga.

GOOCH, Betty. 286'.1758'272
To the glory of God : the history of Pleasant Union Baptist Church, 1942-1976 / compiled and written by Betty Gooch and Shelby Dorsey. [s.l. : s.n., 1977], 1977. 181 p. : ill. ; 23 cm. Cover title: To God be the glory. Bibliography: p. 181. [BX6476.G34P583] 77-151701
1. Pleasant Union Baptist Church, Gainesville, Ga. I. Dorsey, Shelby, joint author. II. Title. III. Title: To God be the glory.

Pleasure.

APULEIUS Madaurensis.
The birth of pleasure. The story of Cupid and Psyche. From Apuleius. New York, Publication office, Bible House, 1867. 110 p. 17 cm. In prose, copyrighted by L.A. Osborn. [PA6209.M5 1867] 26-4528
I. Osborn, L.A. II. Title.

MOLTMANN, Jurgen. 218
Theology of play. Translated by Reinhard Ulrich. [1st ed.] New York, Harper & Row [1972] vii, 113 p. 22 cm. The first liberated men in creation was originally published in German under title: Die ersten Freigelassenen der Schopfung. Contents.Contents.—Moltmann, J. The first liberated men in Creation.—Responses: Neale, R. E. The Crucifixion as play.—Keen, S. godsong.—Miller, D. L. Playing the game to lose.—Moltmann, J. Are there no rules of the game? Includes bibliographical references. [BJ1483.M65] 73-160635 ISBN 0-06-065902-5 4.95
1. Pleasure. 2. Freedom (Theology) I. Neale, Robert E. II. Keen, Sam. III. Miller, David LeRoy. IV. Moltmann, Jurgen. Die ersten Freigelassenen der Schopfung. English. 1972. V. Title.

Plett, Jake, 1936-

PLETT, Jake, 1936- 248'.86'0924 B
Valley of shadows / by Jake Plett. Beaverlodge, Alta. : Horizon House, c1976. 168 p. ; 18 cm. (Horizon books) [BR1725.P555A33] 77-366234 ISBN 0-88965-004-7 : 1.75
1. Plett, Jake, 1936- 2. Plett, MaryAnn, 1942-1971. 3. Christian life—1960- 4. Murder—Alberta—Edmonton. 5. Christian biography—Alberta—Edmonton. 6. Edmonton, Alta.—Biography. I. Title.

Plockhoy, Pieter Corneliszoon, fl.1659.

HARDER, Leland, 1926- 922.87492
Plockhoy from Zurik-Zee; the study of a Dutch reformer in Puritan England and colonial America [by] Leland Harder and Marvin Harder. Newton, Kan., Board of Education and Publication [General Conference Mennonite Church] 1952. x, 255p. illus., map. facsims. 20cm. The writings of Plockhoy;: p 108-205. (Mennonite historical series, no.2) Includes bibliographical references. [BX8129.G4M4 vol.2] A54
1. Plockhoy, Pieter Corneliszoon, fl.1659. I. Harder, Marvin Andrew, 1921- joint author. II. Title. III. Series.

Plotinus.

ELSAS, Christoph. 126
Neuplatonische und gnostische Weltablehnung in der Schule Plotins / von Christoph Elsas. Berlin ; New York : de Gruyter, 1975. xv, 356 p. ; 23 cm. (Religionsgeschichtliche Versuche und Vorarbeiten ; Bd. 34) Based on the author's thesis, Gottingen, 1971. Bibliography: p. 301-317. [BL25.R37 Bd. 34] [B693.Z7] 301.15 75-515676 ISBN 3-11-003941-9 : DM92.00
1. Plotinus. 2. Gnosticism. 3. Neoplatonism. I. Title. II. Series.

THE essence of Plotinus;
extracts from the six Enneads and Porphyry's life of Plotinus, based on the translation by Stephen Mackenna; with an appendix giving some of the most important Platonic and Aristotelian sources on which Plotinus drew, and an annotated bibliography, comp. by Grace H. Turnbull. Foreword by W. R. Inge. New York, Oxford University Press, 1948 [i. e. 1957] xx, 303p. 20cm.
I. Plotinus.

Plumbe, Samuel Rolls, 1821-1832.

REED, Andrew, 1787-1862. 922
Samuel R. Plumbe: an authentic memoir of a child; in a series of letters to a child. By Rev. Andrew Reed, d. d. From the London edition. Revised by the Committee of publication. Boston, Massachusetts Sabbath school society, 1837. viii, [9]-92 p. incl. front., illus. 16 cm. English edition, 1832, has title: Rolls Plumbe: a narrative for children. [BR1715.P47R4 1837] 37-20262
1. Plumbe, Samuel Rolls, 1821-1832. I. Massachusetts Sabbath school society. Committee of publication. II. Title.

Plummer, Adam Francis, 1819-1905.

PLUMMER, Nellie Arnold, 1860- 922.
Out of the depths; or, The triumph of the cross, by Nellie Arnold Plummer ... Hyattsville, Md., 1927. 412 p. illus. (incl. ports.) 22cm. "The story of a colored American ... Adam Francis Plummer." [BX6455.P6P6] 28-3324
1. Plummer, Adam Francis, 1819-1905. 2. Plummer family. I. Title.

Plunket, Oliver. Abp., 1629-1681.

CURTAYNE, Alice. 922.2415
The trial of Oliver Plunkett. London, New York, Sheed and Ward [1953] 239p. illus. 23cm. [BX4705.P6515C8 1953] 53-12997
1. Plunket, Oliver. Abp., 1629-1681. I. Title.

ROBERTO, Brother, 1927- 922.2415
Now comes the hangman; a story of Blessed Oliver Plunkett. Illus. by Brother Eagan. Notre Dame, Ind., Dujarie Press [1956] 95p. illus. 24cm. [BX4705.P6515R6] 56-25349
1. Plunket, Oliver, Abp., 1629-1681. I. Title.

Pluralism.

BLOOD, Benjamin Paul, 1832-1919.
Pluriverse; an essay in the philosophy of pluralism, by Benjamin Paul Blood; with an introduction by Horace Meyer Kallen, Ph.D. Boston, Marshall Jones company, 1920. xiiv, 263 p. front. (port.) 19 1/2 cm. [B830.B6] 20-9219
1. Pluralism. I. Title.

RICHARDSON, Cyril Albert.
Spiritual pluralism and recent philosophy, by C. A. Richardson... Cambridge, The University press, 1919. xxi, 335 p. 22 cm. "The first essay...and the substance of the fourth were published in...the Philosophical review for May 1918 and Jan. 1919 respectively, while the third essay was published in Mind of Jan. 1919."--Pref. [BD394.R5] 20-7073
1. Pluralism. 2. Mind and body. I. Title.
Contents omitted.

Plurality of worlds.

GAVERLUK, Emil. 222'.11'066
Did Genesis man conquer space? Illustrated by Jack Hamm. Nashville, T.

Nelson [1974] 192 p. illus. 21 cm. Includes bibliographical references. [BS1235.5.G34] 74-1262 ISBN 0-8407-5553-8 2.95 (pbk.)
1. Bible. O.T. Genesis—Miscellanea. 2. Plurality of worlds. 3. Civilization, Ancient. I. Title.

VAN TASSEL, George W 1910-
Into this world and out again; a modern proof of the origin of humanity and its retrogression from the original creation of man. Verified by the Holy Bible. Revelations received through thought communication. 1st ed. [n.p., The Author, 1956] 94 p. 22 cm. The Author is director of the College of Universal Wisdom.
1. Plurality of worlds. 2. Supernatural. 3. Bible and science. 4. Man-Origin. 5. Cosmology. I. College of Universal Wisdom. II. Title.

Plutarchus. De superstitione.

MOELLERING, Howard Armin 292.21
Plutarch on superstition; Plutarch's De superstitione, its place in the changing meaning of deisidaimonia and in the context of his theological writings [Rev. ed.] Boston, Christopher Pub. [c.1963] 188p. 21cm. Bibl. 63-14334 4.00
1. Plutarchus. De superstitione. 2. Fear of God. 3. Superstition. I. Title.

Plymire, Victor Guy, 1881-1956.

PLYMIRE, David, 1921- 922.89
High adventure in Tibet. Springfield, Mo., Gospel Pub. House [c1959] 235p. illus. 20cm. [BV3420.T5P5] 60-26936
1. Plymire, Victor Guy, 1881-1956. I. Title.

Plymouth brethren.

COAD, Frederick Roy. 289.9
A history of the Brethren movement; its origins, its worldwide development, and its significance for the present day, by F. Roy Coad. Grand Rapids, Eerdmans [1968] 327 p. 23 cm. Bibliography: p. 307-316. [BX8800.C6 1968b] 76-1653 6.95
1. Plymouth Brethren. I. Title.

IRONSIDE, Henry Allan, 1876- 286.7
A historical sketch of the Brethren movement; an account of its inception, progress, principles and failures, and its lessons for present day believers, by H. A. Ironside, LITT. D. Grand Rapids, Mich., Zondervan publishing house [1942] 4 p. l., 7-219 p. 20 cm. Papers originally published as a series of articles in Serving and waiting, now re-edited, with more and later material. cf. Pref. [BX8800.I7] 42-18412
1. Plymouth brethren. I. Title.

NOEL, Napoleon, 1853-1932. 286.7
The history of the Brethren, by Napoleon Noel; edited by William F. Knapp. Denver, Col., W. F. Knapp, 1936. 2 v. fronts., illus., ports., fold. map, diagrs. 22 cm. Paged continuously. Includes bibliographies. [BX8800.N6] 37-23652
1. Plymouth brethren. I. Knapp, William Franklin, 1874- ed. II. Title.

STEELE, Daniel, 1824-
A substitute for holiness; or, Antinomianism revived; or, The theology of the so-called Plymouth Brethren examined and refuted. 2d ed., with index, and appendix by ... C. Munger. Boston and Chicago, The Christian witness co., 1899. 1 p. l., 370 p. port. 16 degree. May
I. Title.

STEELE, Daniel, 1824-1914. 248
A substitute for holiness; or, Antinomianism revived; or, The theology of the so-called Plymouth brethren examined and refuted. By Daniel Steele ... 2d ed., with index, and appendix by the late Rev. C. Munger. Boston and Chicago, The Christian witness co., 1899. 2 p. l., [3] -370 p. front. (port.) 17 cm. [BX8800.S7 1899] 99-1758
1. Plymouth brethren. 2. Antinomianism. I. Munger, Charles, ed. II. Title.

Plymouth Brethren—Bibliography.

EHLERT, Arnold D. 016.2899
Brethren writers; a checklist with an introduction to Brethren literature and additional lists, by Arnold D. Ehlert. Grand Rapids, Mich., Baker Book House [1969] 83 p. 23 cm. (BCH bibliographic series, no. 3) "Originally published in the Proceedings of the American Theological Library Association for 1957. The descriptive essay has been updated and the lists are greatly expanded." [Z7845.P5E4] 78-76779
1. Plymouth Brethren—Bibliography. I. Title. II. Series.

Plymouth Brethren—Biography.

WOOD, Christine. 283'.092'4 B
Exclusive by-path : the autobiography of a pilgrim / by Christine Wood. Evesham : James, 1976. 141 p. ; 19 cm. [BX5179.W74A33] 76-373348 ISBN 0-85305-183-6 : £2.80
1. Wood, Christine. 2. Church of England—Biography. 3. Plymouth Brethren—Biography. I. Title.

Plymouth Brethren in New York (City)—Biography.

MULLINGS, Gwendolyn Lydia, 1928- 209'.2'4 B
My pilgrim journey : the making of an evangelist / by Gwendolyn Lydia Mullings. New York : William-Frederick Press, 1976. 91 p. ; 22 cm. [BX8809.M84A35] 76-47764 ISBN 0-87164-035-X : 3.50
1. Mullings, Gwedolyn Lydia, 1928- 2. Plymouth Brethren in New York (City)—Biography. 3. New York (City)—Biography. I. Title.

Plymouth Brethren—Sermons.

SMITH, Daniel, 1907- 252
Worship and remembrance / by Daniel Smith. Neptune, N.J. : Loizeaux Brothers, [1975] p. cm. [BX8800.S55] 75-23215 ISBN 0-87213-790-2
1. Plymouth Brethren—Sermons. 2. Sermons, American. I. Title.

Plymouth, Mass.—Church history—Sources.

[PLYMOUTH, Mass. First Church] 929'.3744'82
Plymouth Church records, 1620-1859. Baltimore, Genealogical Pub. Co., 1975. 2 v. (lxii, 848 p.) illus. 22 cm. Reprint of the 1920-23 ed. published by the New England Society, in the City of New York, New York. Includes bibliographical references. [BX7255.P65F56 1975] 74-18426 ISBN 0-8063-0638-6
1. Plymouth, Mass.—Church history—Sources. 2. Registers of births, etc.—Plymouth, Mass. I. New England Society in the City of New York. II. Title.

Plymouth, Mass. First Church

MARSHALL, George N ed. 288.744
The church of the Pilgrim Fathers, selected and edited by George N. Marshall from the writings of John Cuckson [and others] Boston, Beacon Press, 1950. xx, 143 p. illus. 21 cm. Contents.--Foreword: "Old First."--Genesis of the Pilgrim church, by J. Cuckson.--John Robinson; two modern studies: Seventeenth-century liberal, by F. J. Taylor. The man who taught the Pilgrims, by J. E. Kalas.--The Pilgrims and early Plymouth, by H. W. Royal.--The Pilgrim's church in Plymouth, by A. Lord.--The historical Pilgrim church and the modern witness, by G. N. Marshall.--The National Memorial Pilgrim Church, by A. B. Whitney and G. N. Marshall.--Why a Unitarian church? by A. R. Hussey.--Appendix: Some historical notes on the First Church, by F. A. Jenks.--Suggested reading list. [BX9861.P65F55] 50-58120
1. Plymouth, Mass. First Church 2. Congregationalism—Hist. 3. Unitarianism—Hist. I. Title.

Pneuma (The word)

BULLINGER, Ethelbert William. 231'.3
The giver and his gifts : or, The Holy Spirit and his work : being the use and usage of [pneuma (romanized form)]"spirit" in the New Testament : with complete expository list of its 385 occurrences, appendixes of classified lists of passages and usages, and three indexes / by E. W. Bullinger. Grand Rapids : Kregel Publications, [1979] p. cm. Reprint of the 1905 ed. published by Eyre & Spottiswoode, London. [PA878.P5B8 1979] 79-14338 ISBN 0-8254-2234-5 : 5.95
1. Bible. N.T.—Criticism, interpretation, etc. 2. Pneuma (The word) 3. Holy Spirit—Biblical teaching. I. Title.

Pocatello, Id. First Congregational church.

HOWARD, Minnie Frances, 1872- 285.
Early life and times of the First Congregational church of Pocatello, by Minnie F. Howard ... [Pocatello, Id., Printed by Tribune publishing co., 1928] 65, [5] p., 1 l. illus. (incl. ports.) 23 1/2 cm. "Written for the dedication of the new church extension in Pocatello, Idaho, November 11, 1928." "Re-dedication services": p. [67-70] [BX7255.P685H6] 29-6366
1. Pocatello, Id. First Congregational church. I. Title.

Pocket Testament League,

LIU, Ling-pi. 922
Chinaman's chance; the story of Harry Liu of the Pocket Testament League, by Harry Liu and Ellen Drummond. Chicago, Moody Press [1956] 143p. illus. 22cm. [BV2370.P6L5] 56-1611
1. Pocket Testament League, I. Drummond, Ellen L. II. Title.

Poe, Edgar Allan, 1809-1849.

POE, Edgar Allan, 1809-1849. 27-287
The poems of Edgar Allan Poe; with a selection of essays. London & Toronto, J. M. Dent & sons, ltd.; New York. E. P. Dutton & co. [1927] xx, 340 p., 1 l. 18 cm. (Half-title: Everyman's library, ed. by Ernest Rhys. Poetry and the drama. [no. 791]) "First issue of this edition, 1927." Introduction by Andrew Lang. "List of the works of Edgar Allan Poe": p. xvi-xviii. [811.32]
I. Lang, Andrew, 1844-1912 II. Title.

STRICKLAND, Walter William, Sir bart., 1851- 133.335
The great divide, by W. W. Strickland ... New York, B. Westermann co., inc., 1931. 374, [1] p. plates, ports. 19 cm. [BF1623.P9S85] [159.961335] 32-33249
1. Poe, Edgar Allan, 1809-1849. 2. Symbolism of numbers. 3. Platenists. 4. Mysticism. I. Title.
Contents omitted.

Poe, Edgar Allan, 1809-1849 — Bibliography

KEGERREIS, Robert B 280.4
[Catalogue of the Poe collection of Robert B. Kegerreis. Richland, Pa., 1965] New York, Harper & Row [1965] 1 v. (various pagings) 36 cm. v. 282 p. 22 cm. Bibliographical footnotes. [BX4811.K35] 66-81401 65-20453
1. Poe, Edgar Allan, 1809-1849 — Bibl. 2. Protestantism — 20th cent. I. Kegley, Charles W II. Title. III. Title: Protestantism in transition

Poetry.

[ALLEN, Benjamin] 1789-1829.
Miscellaneous poems, on moral and religious subjects: by Osander [pseud.]... Hudson [N.Y.] Printed by Wm. E. Norman, 1811. 180 p. 17 x 10 cm. Page 5 numbered 7. [PS1029.A5M5 1811] 18-16223
I. Title.

[ALLEN, Benjamin] 1789-1829.
Miscellaneous poems, on moral and religious subjects. By Osander [pseud.]... New York, Printed by J. Seymour, and sold by Griffin and Rudd, agents for the publisher. 1812. 180 p. 14 cm. [PS1029.A5M5 1812] 1-2544
I. Title.

ALVAREZ Quintero Serafin, 1871-1938. 22-18566
The fountain of youth (La flor de la vida) a poetic drama in three acts, by Serafin & Joaquin Alvarez-Quintero; tr. by Samuel N. Baker. Cincinnati, Stewart Kidd company [c1922] 71 p. 19 cm. (Half-title: Riewart Kidd modern plays, ed. by F. Shay) [PQ6601.L6F5 1922]
I. Alvarez Quintero, Joaquin, 1873- joint author. II. Baker, Samuel N., tr. III. Title.

BARCLAY, Kate, ed.
The Odd Fellow's token: devoted to friendship, love, and truth. Geneva [N.Y.] G. H. Derby, 1846. 124 p. 12 cm. Poems. [HS995.B3 1846] 14-7816
I. Title.

BARCLAY, Kate, ed.
The Odd Fellow's token: devoted to friendship, love and truth. Auburn [N.Y.] Alden, Beardsley, 1852. [4] l., [7]-124 p. 12 cm. Poems. [HS995.B3 1852] 47-41350
I. Title.

BINYON, Laurence, Sir. 1869- 22-12646
Selected poems of Laurence Binyon. New York, The Macmillan company, 1922. xi p., 1 l., 184 p. 20 cm. [Full name: Robert Lawrence Binyon] Bibliography: p. 184. [PRG003.1 75A6 1922]
I. Title.

*BLAKE, William FIC
Selected poetry / William Blake; edited by David V. Erdman New York : New American Library ,1976 xxix, 303 p. ; 18 cm. (Signet book) (Signet Classic poetry series) Bibliography: pp. xvii-xviii. 75-29627 pbk. : 2.50
I. Title.

BLAKE, William, 1757-1827. 821'.7
The selected poetry of Blake / edited by David V. Erdman. New York : New American Library, c1981. xxix, 303 p. : ill. ; 21 cm. "A Meridian book." Reprint. Originally published: New York : New American Library, c1976. (Signet classic poetry series) (Signet classic ; CE878) Bibliography: p. xvii-xviii. [PR4142.E7 1981] 19 81-184270 ISBN 0-452-00569-8 (pbk.) : 6.95 ($7.95 Can.)
I. Erdman, David V. II. [Poems.] Selections III. Title.

BRADSTREET, Anne, 1612?-1672. 811'.1
A woman's inner world : selected poetry and prose of Anne Bradstreet / edited with an introduction by Adelaide P. Amore. Washington, D.C. : University Press of America, c1982. xli, 109 p. ; 23 cm. Includes bibliographies. [PS711.A4 1982] 19 82-40198 ISBN 0-8191-2639-X : 18.25 ISBN 0-8191-2640-3 (pbk.) : 7.75
I. Amore, Adelaide P. II. Title.

CAMPBELL, Thomas 1777-1844.
The complete poetical works of Thomas Campbell. With a memoir of his life, and an essay, on his genius and writings... New York, D. Appleton & co., 1852. llll, 329 p. front. (port.) 5 pl. 16 1/2 cm. The following...account of the life of Thomas Campbell, appeared in Fraser's magazine for November [i.e. September] 1844. Essay on the genius and character of Campbell, by George Glifillan: p. [xxxv]-xiix. [PR4410.A2 1852] 17-11662
I. Glifillan, George, 1813-1878. II. Title.

CAMPBELL, Thomas, 1777-1844.
The complete poetical works of Thomas Campbell; with an original biography, and notes. Ed. by Epes Sargent. Boston, Crosby, Nichols, Lee & co., 1854. xii, 479 p. 2 port. (incl. front.) [PR4410.A5S3 1854] 15-
I. Sargent, Epes, 1813-18880, ed. II. Title.

CAMPBELL, Thomas, 1777-1844.
The complete poetical works of Thomas Campbell; with an original biography, and notes. Ed. by Epes Sargent. Boston, Crosby, Nichols, Lee & co., 1860. xii, 479

p. 2 port. (incl. front.) 19 1/2 cm. [PR4410.A5S3 1860] 12-
I. Sargent, Epes, 1813-1880, ed. II. Title.

CAMPBELL, Thomas, 1777-1844.
The complete poetical works of Thomas Campbell, with a memoir of his life. New York, J. W. Lovell company [1885] 1 p. l., [35]-386 p. 18 1/2 cm. (On cover: Lovell's library, no. 10, no. 526) Imperfect: Memoir wanting. [PR4410.A2 1885] 25-2112
I. Title.

CAMPBELL, Thomas, 1777-1844.
...The complete poetical works of Thomas Campbell, ed. with notes, by J. Logie Robertson, M.A. London, New York [etc.] H. Frowde, Oxford university press, 1907. xxiv, 376 p. front. (port.) 19 cm. At head of title: Oxford edition. Genealogy of Thomas Campbell: p. [xix]-xx. [PR4410.A5R6] 26-
I. Robertson, James Logie, 1846-1922, ed. II. Title.

CHUANG-TZU. 181'.09514
The complete works of Chuang Tzu. Translated by Burton Watson. New York, Columbia University Press, 1968. 397 p. 21 cm. (Unesco collection of representative works: Chinese series) "Prepared for the Columbia College program of translations from the Oriental classics." Translation of Nan-hua ching (romanized form) [BL1900.C5W34] 68-19000 10.00
I. Columbia University. Columbia College. II. Title. III. Series. IV. Records of civilization: sources and studies, no. 80.

COOK, William, d.1876.
The euclea; works by the Rev. William Cook. [Salem, Mass., 1852-61] 10 v. in 1. illus., plates. 19 cm. Cover-title. Poems printed, bound, and illustrated by author. cf. ins. note. [PS1378.C7E8 1852] 22-23674
I. Title.
Contents omitted.

COOK, William, d.1876.
The euclea; works by the Rev. William Cook. [Salem, Mass., 1852-61] 10 v. in 1. illus., plates. 19 cm. Cover-title. Poems printed, bound, and illustrated by author. cf. ins. note. [PS1378.C7E8 1852] 22-23674
I. Title.
Contents omitted.

COWPER, William, 1731-1800.
The complete poetical works of William Cowper, esq., including the hymns and translations from Madame Guion, Milton, etc., and Adam; a sacred drama; from the Italian of Gio, Battista Andreini, with a Memoir of the author, by the Rev. H. Stebbing ... New York, D. Appleton & co., 1852. 2 v. in 1. fronts., plates. 17 cm. [PR3380.A2 1852] 16-17780
I. Stebbing, Henry, 1799-1883. II. Andreini, Giovanni Battista, b. 1578. III. Title.

[CRAFTS, William] 1787-1826.
Sullivan's island. The raciad, and other poems, reprinted ... Charleston, T. B. Stephens, 1820. 100 p. 8 degree. [BS1449.C675S8] 1-2162
I. Title.

DANNELLY, Elizabeth Otis (Marshall) Mrs. 1838-1896.
Cactus or, Thorns and blossoms: a collection of satirical and miscellaneous, embracing religious, temperance, and memorial poems, by Mrs. Elizabeth O. Dannelly. New York, Atlantic publishing & engraving co., 1879. xix, 21-378 p. 20 cm. [PS1510.D72] 25-309
I. Title.

DICKENS, Charles, 1812-1870.
... The complete works of Charles Dickens (in sixteen volumes) with steel photogravure illustrations from original designs by F. Barnard and others ... Philadelphia, Gebbie & co. [1892-94] 16 v. fronts., illus., plates. 24 cm. At head of title: Gebbie's choice edition. Contents--[v. 1] American notes, Pictures from Italy, and A child's history of England. [1894]--[v. 2] Barnaby Rudge. Illus. [1892]--[v. 3] Bleak house. [1894]--[v. 4] Christmas books and Hard times. illus. [1894]--[v. 5] Christmas stories. Master Humphrey's clock, and other stories. [1894]--[v. 6] David Copperfield. [1892]--[v. 7] Dombey and son. [1894]--[v. 8] Great expectations and the Uncommercial traveller. [1898]--[v. 9] Little Dorrit. [1894]--[v. 10] Martin Chuzzlewit. [1898]--[v. 11] Nicholas Nickieby. [1892]--[v. 12] Old curiosity shop and Reprinted pieces. [1893]--[v. 13] Oliver Twist and Tale of two cities. [1894]--[v. 14] Our mutual friend. [1893]--[v. 15] Pickwick papers. [1893]--[v. 16] Sketches by Boz and Edwin Drood. [1894] [PR4550.E92] 26-6904
I. Barnard, Frederick, 1846-1896, illus. II. Title.

DICKENS, Charles, 1812-1870.
The complete writings of Charles Dickens including his novels and tales, letters and speeches, plays and poems, miscellanies, etc., and Forester's Life of Charles Dickens, in forty volumes ... Boston, C. E. Lauriat company, 192o. 40 v. fronts. (ports. v. 37,38,40) plates. 22 cm. National library edition. 24-2855
I. Title.

[ENO, Joel Nelson] 1852-
The inner circles, and glimpses of the beyond. Poems. by J. N. E. Hartford, Case, Lockwood & Brainard, printers, 1873. 50 p. 15 cm. [PS1654.E2] 24-30035
I. Title.

[ENO, Joel Nelson] 1852-
The inner circles, and glimpses of the beyond. Poems. by J. N. E. Hartford, Case, Lockwood & Brainard, printers, 1873. 50 p. 15 cm. [PS1654.E2] 24-30035
I. Title.

FRANCIS d'assisi mother. 245.2
My candle and other poems, by Mother Francis d'Assisi ... New York, Cincinnati [etc.] Benziger brother, 1931. 66 p. 20 cm. [PS3511.R243M8] 31-35297
I. Title.

GERNES, Sonia. 811'.54
Brief lives : poems / by Sonia Gernes. Notre Dame, Ind. : University of Notre Dame Press, c1981. x, 79 p. ; 22 cm. [PS3557.E685B7] 19 81-40454 ISBN 0-268-00666-0 (pbk.) : 6.95
I. Title.

HARTLEY, Elizabeth Lyman, Mrs.
Cords with heaven; poems by Elizabeth Lyman Hartley ... New York city, Mrs. E. L. Hartley [c1927] 6 p. l., 15-138 p. 20 cm. [PS515.A7948C6 1927] 27-24013
I. Title.

HAWTHORNE, Nathaniel, 1804-1864.
...The complete works of Nathaniel Hawthorne, with introductory notes by George Parson Lathrop and illustrated with etchings by Blum, Church, Dielman, Gifford, Shirlaw, and Turner. In thirteen volumes. [Riverside ed. Boston and New York, Houghton Mifflin company, 1914] 13 v. fronts., facsims. 20 cm. Half-title. Each volume has also special t.-p. with title vignette. "Order of arrangement...in this edition with a list of frontispieces and vignettes" and "Index to titles": vol. xiii, p. [369-376] Contents.i. Twice-told tales.--ii. Mosses from an old manse.--iii. The house of the seven gables and The snow-image, and other Twice-told tales.--iv. A wonder-book, Tanglewood tales, and Grandfather's chair.--v. The scarlet letter, and the Blithedale romance.--vi. The marble faun.--vii-viii. Our old house, and English note-books. v. 1-2.--ix. Passages from the American note-books.--x. Passages from the French and Italian note-books.--xi. The Dolliver romance, Fanshawe, and SeptimusFelton, with an appendix containing The ancestral footstep.--xii. Tales, sketches, and other papers...with a biographical sketch by George Parsons Lathrop.--xiii. Doctor Grimshawe's secret...ed. with preface and notes by Julian Hawthorne. [PS1850.E98a] 15-4480
I. Lathrop, George Parsons, 1851-1898, ed. II. Hawthorne, Julian, 1846-1934, ed. III. Title.

HUBBARD, Elbert, 1856-1915.
The complete writings of Elbert Hubbard. Author's ed. [v. 1-20] East Aurora, N.Y., The Roycroft shop [1908-1915] 20 v. fronts., plates, ports., facsim. 30 cm. Edition of 1000 sets. This set not numbered; signed by the author, except v. 1, 6, and 10. Colored initials, title and text decorated in colors. [PS2040.A2 1908] 8-13365
I. Title.

JENKINS, Daphne Smith (Giles) Mrs.] b.1812.
A collectioon of Scriptural and miscellaneous poems. By Miss Daphne S. Giles. Ann. Arbor [Mich.] Cole & Arnold, 1845. 172 p. 15 cm. Includes some prose. Bibliographical preface by W. A. Bronson. [PS2129.J725 1845] 25-299
I. Title.

LOWELL, James Russell, 1819-1891.
The complete poetical works of James Russell Lowell. Library ed.; illustrated with pgotogravures ... Boston and New York, Houghton, Mifflin and company, 1900. 4 p. l., [v]-xvii p., 2 l., 515 p. front., plates, ports. 23 cm. [PS2305.A1 1900] 1-21933
I. Title.

MCDERMOTT, Hugh Farrar, 22-17110 1833-1890.
The blind canary, by Hugh Farrar McDermott, 2d ed. (rev. with additions) New York, G. P. Putnam's sons, 1883. 2 p. l., 149 p. front. (port.) 18 cm. Poems. [PS2356.M55]
I. Title.

NUNES, Joseph A.
"Let us have peace." A poem by Joseph A. Nunes. Philadelphia, King & Baird, printers, 1869. 9 p. 19 1/2 cm. [PS2480.N4] 5-40052
I. Title.

NUNES, Joseph A.
"Let us have peace." A poem by Joseph A. Nunes. Philadelphia, King & Baird, printers, 1869. 9 p. 20 cm. [PS2480.N4] 5-40052
I. Title.

THE Odd fellow's token:
devoted to friendship, love and truth. Ed. by Kate Barclay. Geneva [N.Y.] G. H. Derby & co. [etc.] 1846. 124 p. 12 cm. [HS995.O4 1846] 14-7816
I. Barclay, Kate, ed.

THE Odd fellow's token:
Devoted to friendship, love and truth. Ed. by Kate Barclay. Auburn, N.Y., J. M. Alden, 1850. 124 p. 12 cm. [HS995.O4 1850] 14-13079
I. Barclay, Kate, ed.

PIKE, Kenneth Lee, 1912- 248.8'8
Stir, change, create; [poems and essays in contemporary mood for concerned students] by Kenneth L. Pike. Grand Rapids, Eerdmans [1967] 164 p. illus. 21 cm. [PS3566.I45S7] 67-30962
I. Title.

REED, Ruth Bendure.
The book of Ruth, simple songs and other poems. [1st ed.] New York, Vantage Press [c1962] 42 p. 21 cm. 63-47485
I. Title.

SELECTED poems.
With an introd. by Basil de Selincourt. London, Oxford University Press [1957] xxvi, 309p. 16cm. (The World's classics, 324)
I. Blake, William, 1757-1827.

SELECTED poems;
edited with an introd. and explanatory notes by F. W. Bateson. New York, Macmillan [1957] xxx, 143p. col. front. (The poetry bookshelf)
I. Blake, William, 1757-1827. II. Bateson, Frederick Wilse, 1901- ed.

SHILLITO, Edward, 1872- 809.1
Poetry and prayer, by Edward Shillito ... New York, C. Scribner's sons, 1932. 125 p. 17 cm. "Printed in Great Britain." [PN1077.S5] [248] 32-14144
1. Poetry. 2. Prayer. I. Title.

SMITH, May (Riley) Mrs., 245. 1842?-
Sometime. By May Riley Smith. New York, A. D. F. Randolph & company, c1885. 6 numb. l. 9 1/2 x 12 cm. Poem. [Full name: Mrs. Mary Louise (Riley) Smith] [PS2869.S3S6 1885] 12-38762
I. Title.

SMITH, May (Riley) Mrs., 245. 1842?-
Sometime, and other poems, by May Riley Smith. New York, A. D. F. Randolph and company [1893] 167, [1] p. 17 1/2 cm. [Full name: Mrs. Mary Louise (Riley) Smith] [PS2869.S3S6 1893] 30-29687
I. Title.

THACHER, Delia Tudor. 235
Separation, and other poems, by Delia Tudor Thacher. New York, Duffield & company, 1922. 4 p. l., 3-56 p. 18 cm. $1.25 [PS 3539.H12S4 1922] 22-13484
I. Title.

TOLSTOI, Lev Nikolaevich, graf, 1828-1910.
The complete works of Count Tolstoy ... [Limited ed. Translated from the original Russian and edited by Leo Wiener] [Boston, D. Estes & company, 1904-05] 24 v. fronts., plates, ports., facsims. 23 1/2 cm. Half-title: each volume has special title. Contents.v. 1. Childhood, boyhood, youth. The incursion.--v. 2. A landed proprietor. The Cossacks. Sevastopol.--v. 3. A Moscow acquaintance. The snow-storm. Domestic happiness. Miscellanies.--v. 4. Prdagogical articles. Linen-measurer.--v. 5-8. War and peace.--v. 9-11. Anna Karenina.--v. 12. Fables for children. Stories for children. Natural science stories. Popular education. Decembrists. Moral tales.--v. 13. My confession. Critque of dogmatic theology.--v. 14-15. The four gospels harmonized and translated.--v. 16. My religion. On life. Thoughts on God. On the meaning of life.--v. 17. What shall we do then? On the Moscow census. Collected articles.--v. 18. Death of Ivan Ulich. Dramatic works. The Kreutzer sonata.--v. 19. Walk in the light while ye have light. Thoughts and aphorisms. Letters. Miscellanies.--v. 20. The kingdom of God is within you. Christianity and patriotism. Miscellanies.--v. 21. Resurrection. v. 1.--v. 22. Resurrection, v. 2. What is art? The Christian teaching.--v. 23. Miscellaneous letters and essays.--v. 24. Latest works. Life. General index. Bibliography: (p. 401-405) [PG3366.A1 1904] 4-24594
I. Wiener, Lee, 1882-1930, ed. and tr. II. Title.

TOLSTOI, Lev Nikolaevich, graf. 1828-1910.
The complete works of Count Tolstoy. [Limited edition. Translated from the original Russian and edited by Leo Wiener] [Boston, D. Estes & company, 1904-05] 24 v. fronts, plates, ports, facsims. 23 1/2 cm. "Edition de luxe, limited to one thousand copies." This set not numbered. Contents.--v. 1. Childhood, boyhood, youth; The incursion.--v. 2. A landed proprietor; The Cozencks; Sevastopol.--v. 3. A Moscow acquantance; The snow-storm; Domestic happiness; Miscellanies.--v. 4. Pedagogical articles; Linen-measurer.--v. 5.-8. War and peace.--v. 9.-11. Anna Karenin.--v. 12. Fables for children: Stories for children; Natural science stories; Popular education; Decembrists; Moral tales.--v. 13. My confession; Critique of dogmatic theology.--v. 14-15. The four gospels harmonized and translated.--v. 16. My religion; On life; Thoughts on God; On the meaning of live.--v. 17. What shall we do then? On the Moscow census; Collected articles.--v. 18. Death of Ivan flich; Dramatic works; The Kreutzer sonats.--v. 19. Walk in the light while ye have light; Thoughts and aphorsms; Letters; Miscellanies.--v. 20. The kingdom of God is within you; Christianity and patriolism; Miscellanies.--v. 21. Resurrection, v. 1.--v. 22. Resurrection, v. 2; What is art? The Christian teaching.--v. 22. Miscellaneous letters and essays.--v. 24. Latest works; Life; General index; Bibliography. 4-24594
I. Wiener, Leo, 1862- ed. and tr. II. Title.

[WARFIELD, Catherine Ann 245 (Ware) Mrs.] 1816-1877.
The wife of Leon, and other poems. By two sisters of the West. New-York, D. Appleton and company. Philadelphia, G. S. Appleton, 1844. viii, 256 p. 19 1/2 cm. [PS3149.W3W5 1844] 28-16098
I. Lee, Mrs. Eleanor Percy (Ware) 1820-1849, joint author. II. Title.

[WARFIELD, Catherine Ann (Ware) Mrs.] 1816-1877. 245
The wife of Leon, and other poems. By two sisters of the West. New-York, D. Appleton and company. Philadelphia, G. S. Appleton, 1844. viii, 256 p. 19 1/2 cm. [PS3149.W3W5 1844] 28-16098
I. Lee, Mrs. Eleanor Percy (Ware) 1820-1849, joint author. II. Title.

WESLEY, Chalres, 1707-1788. 245
Charles Wesley seen in his finer and less familiar poems. New York, Hurd and Houghton, 1867. xvi, 398 p. 17 cm. Edited by Frederic M. Bird. [PR3763.W4 1867] 14-17394
I. Bird, Frederic Mayer, 1838-1908, ed. II. Title.

WHITTIER, John Greenleaf, 1807-1892.
The complete poetical works of John Greenleaf Whittier. Household ed. Boston, J. R. Osgood and company, 1873. xii, 395 p. 19 1/2 cm. [PS3250.E73] 7-22869
I. Title.

WHITTIER, John Greenleaf, 1807-1892.
The complete poetical works of John Greenleaf Whittier. Household ed. Boston, J. R. Osgood and company, 1876. xii, 413 p. 19 1/2 cm. [PS3250.E76a] 7-22868
I. Title.

WHITTIER, John Greenleaf, 1807-1892.
The complete poetical works of John Greenleaf Whittier ... [Centennial ed.] Boston, J.R. Osgood and company, 1876. x, [11]-297 p. incl. front., illus. 24 1/2 cm. Title vignette (portrait) "Poems by Elizabeth H. Whittier": p. 281-284. [PS3250.E76] 7-22883
I. Whittier, Elizabeth Hussey, 1815-1864. II. Title.

WHITTIER, John Greenleaf, 1807-1892.
The complete poetical works of John Greenleaf Whittier. Household ed. Boston, Houghton, Mifflin and company, 1884. xiv, 466 p. front. (port.) 19 1/2 cm. [(PS3250.E84)] 7-22867
I. Title.

WHITTIER, John Greenleaf, 1807-1892.
The complete poetical works of John Greenleaf Whittier ... Boston, Houghton, Mifflin and company, 1884. x, [11]-326 p. incl. front., illus. 25 1/2 cm. Title vignette (portrait) [PS3250.E84] 40-37215
I. Title.

WHITTIER, John Greenleaf, 1807-1892.
The complete poetical works of John Greenleaf Whittier. Students' Cambridge ed. Boston, New York [etc.] Houghton, Mifflin company [c1894] xxii, 542 p. front. (port.) 20 cm. Biographical sketch signed: H. E. S. [i.e. Horace E. Scudder] [PS3250.E94] 41-33136
I. Scudder, Horace Elisha, 1838-1902, ed. II. Title.

WHITTIER, John Greenleaf, 1807-1892.
The complete poetical works of John Greenleaf Whittier. Handy volume ed. ... Boston and New York, Houghton, Mifflin and company, 1895. 4 v. fronts. (ports.) 15 cm. Engraved t.-p. "Biographical sketch," v. 1, p. [vii]-xxxv, signed: H. E. S. [i.e. Horace E. Scudder] Contents.I. Narrative and legendary poems.--II. Poems of nature. Personal poems. Occasional poems. The tent on the beach.--III. Anti-slavery poems. Songs of labor and reform.--IV. Poems subjective and reminiscent. Religious poems. At sundown. Poems by Elizabeth H. Whittier. Appendix: I. Early and uncollected verses; II. Poems printed in the "Life of Whittier"; III. A chronological list of Mr. Whittier's poems (p. 443-457) Index of first lines. Index of titles. [PS3250.E95] 7-22148
I. Scudder, Horace Elisha, 1838-1902, ed. II. Whittier, Elizabeth Hussey, 1815-1864. III. Title.

WHITTIER, John Greenleaf, 1807-1892. 252.
Legends of New-England ... By John G. Whittier. Hartford, Hanmer and Phelps; Boston, Carter, Hendee & Babcock; [etc., etc.] 1831. iv p., 1 l., [7]-142 p. 18 cm. [Miscellaneous pamphlets, v. 47, no. 2] In prose and verse. First book published by the author. [AC901.M5 vol. 47] 7-21871 ISBN rev.
I. Title.

WORDSWORTH, William, 1770-1850.
Intimations of immortality: and ode, by William Wordsworth. Portland, Me., T. B. Mosher, 1908. vii, [1], 13, [1] p., 1 l. 15 x 14 1/2 cm. "Nine hundred and twenty-five copies of this book printed on Van Gelder hand-made paper." [PR5860.A1 1908] 8-30145
I. Title.

WORDSWORTH, William, 1770-1850.
Intimations of immortality: and ode, by William Wordsworth. Portland, Me., T. B. Mosher, 1908. vii, [1], 13, [1] p., 1 l. 15 x 14 1/2 cm. "Nine hundred and twenty-five copies of this book printed on Van Gelder hand-made paper." [PR5860.A1 1908] 8-30145
I. Title.

WORDSWORTH, William, 1770-1850.
Intimations of immortality from recollections of early childhood and other poems, by William Wordsworth, with biographical sketch and notes. Boston, New York [etc.] Houghton, Mifflin and company [c1895] iv, [5]-95 p. 18 cm. (The Riverside literature series. [no. 76]). [PR5852.H6] 12-40126
I. Title.

WORDSWORTH, William, 1770-1850.
Intimations of immortality from recollections of early childhood and other poems, by William Wordsworth, with biographical sketch and notes. Boston, New York [etc.] Houghton, Mifflin and company [c1895] iv, [5]-95 p. 18 cm. (The Riverside literature series. [no. 76]). [PR5852.H6] 12-40126
I. Title.

Poets.

BIBLE. O. T. Psalms. English. Paraphrases. 1940. 223.5
The lyric Psalter; the modern reader's book of Psalms, edited by Harry H. Mayer. New York, Liveright publishing corporation [c1940] ix, 370 p. 25 cm. "Bibliographical index of authors": p. [301]-350. [BS1440.M35] 40-10008
1. Poets. I. Mayer, Harry Hubert, 1874- ed. II. Bible. English. Paraphrases. O. T. Psalms. 1940. III. Title.

BIBLE. OT. Psalms. English. Paraphrases. 1944. 223.5
The modern reader's book of Psalms, edited by Harry H. Mayer. New York, Liveright publishing corporation [1944] ix, 370 p. 22 1/2 cm. First published, 1940, under title: The lyric Psalter. "Bibliographical index": p. [301]-350. [BS1440.M35 1944] 44-51174
1. Poets. I. Mayer, Harry Hubert, 1874- ed. II. Title.

WALLIN, Johan Olof, 1779-1839.
The angel of death. A religious poem. Tr. from the Swedish of J. O. Wallin, by O. T. Richmond, jr., of Iowa... Chicago, Ill., J. C. W. Bailey, 1868. 15 p. 22 1/2 cm. [PT9845.D6A36] 17-25319
I. Richmond, O. T., jr., tr. II. Title.

Poets, English—19th century—Biography.

HODGSON, James Thomas, 1845-1880. 821'.6 B
Memoir of the Rev. Francis Hodgson, B. D., scholar, poet, and divine : with numerous letters from Lord Byron and others / by James T. Hodgson. New York : AMS Press, 1977. 2 v. ; 19 cm. Reprint of the 1878 ed. published by Macmillan, London. Includes bibliographical references and index. [PR4790.H65Z7 1977] 76-169470 ISBN 0-404-07374-3 : 57.50
1. Hodgson, Francis, 1781-1852. 2. Byron, George Gordon Noel Byron, Baron, 1788-1824—Correspondence. 3. Poets, English—19th century—Biography. 4. Authors, English—19th century—Correspondence. I. Byron, George Gordon Noel Byron, Baron, 1788-1824. II. Title.

Point Reyes light.

MITCHELL, Dave. 071'.9462
The Light on Synanon : how a country weekly exposed a corporate cult—and won the Pulitzer Prize / Dave Mitchell, Cathy Mitchell, and Richard Ofshe. 1st Wideview Books ed. [S.l.] : Wideview Books, 1982, c1980. viii, 307 p., [8] p. of plates : ill. ; 21 cm. Includes index. [PN4899.P575P65 1982] 19 81-68437 ISBN 0-87223-761-3 pbk. : 7.50
1. Synanon (Foundation) 2. Point Reyes light. I. Mitchell, Cathy. II. Ofshe, Richard. III. Title.

Poissy, Colloquy of, 1561.

NUGENT, Donald, 1930- 274.4
Ecumenism in the age of the Reformation: the Colloquy of Poissy. Cambridge, Mass., Harvard University Press, 1974. xi, 258 p. front. 22 cm. (Harvard historical studies, v. 89) Originally presented as the author's thesis, University of Iowa, 1965. Bibliography: p. 241-254. [BR355.P64N8 1974] 73-80026 ISBN 0-674-23725-0 14.00
1. Poissy, Colloquy of, 1561. 2. Christian union—History. I. Title. II. Series.

Poland—History—Jagellons, 1386-1572—Fiction.

SIENKIEWICZ, Henryk, 1846- FIC
Knights of the cross (Krzyzacy) historical novel, by Henry K. Sienkiewicz ... Tr. by S. C. de Soissons. New York, R. F. Fenno & company, 1897- xx, 7-406 p. front., plates, ports. 20 1/2 cm. Afterwards pub. as v. 1 of complete work. [PZ3.S57K] 276
1. Poland—Hist.—Jagellons, 1386-1572—Fiction. 2. Crusades. 3. Teutonic knights—Hist.—Fiction. I. Soissons, S. C. de. tr. II. Title.

Polanyi, Michael, 1891-

APCZYNSKI, John V. 191
Doers of the word : toward a foundational theology based on the thought of Michael Polanyi / by John V. Apczynski. Missoula, Mont. : Published by Scholars Press for the American Academy of Religion, c1977. xii, 202 p. ; 22 cm. (American Academy of Religion dissertation series ; no. 18) Originally presented as the author's thesis, McGill University, 1972. Bibliography: p. 193-202. [BL51.A62 1977] 76-51640 ISBN 0-89130-128-3 : 4.50
1. Polanyi, Michael, 1891- 2. Knowledge, Theory of (Religion) I. Title. II. Series: American Academy of Religion. Dissertation series — American Academy of Religion ; no. 18.

Polarity (in religion, folk-lore, etc.)

WATTS, Alan Wilson, 1915- 398.3
The two hands of God; the myths of polarity. New York, G. Braziller, 1963. xx, 261 p. illus., plates., diagrs. 22 cm. (Patterns of myth. I. Myth and experience) Bibliography: p. 249-253. [BL325.P7W3] 63-18190
1. Polarity (in religion, folk-lore, etc.) I. Title. II. Series: Patterns of myth.

Pole, Reginald, Cardinal, 1500-1558.

FENLON, Dermot. 262'.135'0924 B
Heresy and obedience in Tridentine Italy; Cardinal Pole and the counter reformation. Cambridge [Eng.] University Press, 1972. xiii, 300 p. 23 cm. Bibliography: p. 286-296. [DA317.8.P6F46] 72-87177 ISBN 0-521-20005-9 19.50
1. Pole, Reginald, Cardinal, 1500-1558. 2. Trent, Council of, 1545-1563. 3. Counter-Reformation. I. Title.

SCHENK, Wilhelm. 922.242
Reginal Pole, Cardinal of England. London, New York, Longmans, Green [1950] xvi, 176 p. plates, ports., geneal. table. 23 cm. Includes bibliographical references. [DA317.8.P6S3] 50-6816
1. Pole, Reginald, Cardinal, 1500-1558. I. Title.

Poles in Texas.

DWORACZYK, Edward J. 1906- comp. 325.243809764
The first Polish colonies of America in Texas; containing also the general history of the Polish people in Texas, compiled by Rev. Edward J. Dworaczyk. San Antonio, Tex., The Naylor company [c1936] xix, 201 p. incl. front., illus., ports., plan. 23 cm. "References": p. 201. [F395.P7D9] [BX1415.T4D9] 36-20431
1. Poles in Texas. 2. Catholic church in Texas. I. Title.

Poling, Clark Vandersall, 1910-1934.

POLING, Daniel Alfred, 1884- 922.573
Your daddy did not die, by Daniel A. Poling. New York, Greenberg [1944] 7 p. l., 3-148 p. 21 cm. [BX9543.P62P6] 44-8320
1. Poling, Clark Vandersall, 1910-1934. I. Title.

Poliomyelitis—Patients—United States—Biography.

FROST, Wally, 1925- 280'.4 B
Yes we can! / by Wally Frost. Ventura, Calif. : Regal Books, c1981. p. cm. [RC180.2.F76] 19 81-51743 ISBN 0-8307-0799-9 : 7.95
1. Frost, Wally, 1925- 2. Poliomyelitis—Patients—United States—Biography. I. Title.

Polish Americans—Illinois—Chicago region—Religion.

PAROT, Joseph John, 1940- 282'.0899185077311
Polish Catholics in Chicago, 1850-1920 : a religious history / Joseph John Parot. DeKalb : Northern Illinois University Press, c1981. p. cm. Includes bibliographical references and index. [BX1418.C4P37] 19 81-11297 ISBN 0-87580-081-5 : 22.50 ISBN 0-87580-527-2 pbk. : 10.00
1. Catholic Church—Illinois—Chicago region—History. 2. Polish National Catholic Church of America—Illinois—Chicago region—History. 3. Polish Americans—Illinois—Chicago region—Religion. 4. Chicago region (Ill.)—Church history. I. Title.

Polish National Catholic Church of America.

FOX, Paul, 1874- 274.38
The polish National Catholic Church. Scranton, School of Christian Living [1961?] 144 p. col. illus., ports. 23 cm. Includes bibliographical references. [BX4795.P63F6] 66-53641
1. Polish National Catholic Church of America. I. Title.

ORZELL, Laurence. 265'.4
Rome and the validity of orders in the Polish National Catholic Church / Laurence Orzell. Scranton, Pa. : Savonarola Theological Seminary Alumni Association, 1977. 49 p. ; 24 cm. Bibliography: p. 46-49. [BX2240.O75] 77-75372
1. Polish National Catholic Church of America. 2. Ordination—Catholic Church. I. Title.

Political ethics.

DEALEY, James Quayle, 1861-
... Ethical and religious significance of the state, by James Quayle Dealey ... Published for the Social service committee of the Northern Baptist convention. Philadelphia, Chicago [etc.] American Baptist publication society [c1909] 48 p. 21 cm. (Social service series.--no. ii, division 4) [JC514.D4] 9-17443 0.10.
1. Political ethics. I. Title.

JONES, Orville Davis.
Politics of the Nazarene, or, What Jesus said to do ... The Mount Vernon league. By O. D. Jones ... [Girard, Kan., Press of Appeal to reason, 1901] 2 p. l., [3]-288 p. 22 cm. Includes the author's proposal for

the establishment of a "Mount Vernon league," for moral and social betterment. [JC341.J6] 1-31456
1. Political ethics. I. Title. II. Title: The Mount Vernon league.

SIMON, Yves, 1903- 172
Community of the free; tr. from the French by Willard R. Trask. New York, H. Holt [1947] xi, 172 p. 21 cm. "Chapter II of this book first appeared, in another English translation, in the Reivew of politics; chapter IV, in the American Catholic Philosophical Association: Proceedings for the year of 1945." Full name: Yves Rene Marie Simon. [JA79.S55] 47-11183
1. Political ethics. 2. Race problems. 3. Totalitarianism. I. Trask, Willard Ropes, 1900- tr. II. Title.

VOORHIS, Horace Jeremiah, 1901- 172.1
The Christian in politics. New York, Association Press, 1951. 136 p. 21 cm. (A Haddam House book) [JA79.V6] 51-10834
1. Political ethics. 2. Democracy. 3. Church and social problems. I. Title.

Political parties.

STAHL, Friedrich Julius, 1802-1861. 329'.02
The present-day parties in the state and church : twenty-nine academic lectures / by Friedrich Julius Stahl ; translated and with an introduction by Timothy David Taylor. State College, Pa. : Blenheim Pub. House, 1976. xl, 502 p. ; 28 cm. Translation of Die gegenwartigen Parteien in Staat und Kirche. Includes bibliographical references. [JF2051.S713] 76-54054 ISBN 0-918288-01-0 : 35.75 ISBN 0-918288-08-8 pbk.(limited edition) : 26.75
1. Political parties. 2. Sects. I. Title.

Political parties—Germany—History.

LEVY, Richard S. 329'.02'0943
The downfall of the anti-Semitic political parties in imperial Germany / Richard S. Levy New Haven : Yale University Press, 1975. vii, 335 p. ; 24 cm. (Yale historical publications : Miscellany ; 106) Includes index. Bibliography: p. 309-323. [JN3933.L48 1975] 74-20083 ISBN 0-300-01803-7 : 18.50
1. Political parties—Germany—History. 2. Antisemitism—Germany—History. I. Title. II. Series.

Political parties—U.S.—History.

MCMILLAN, Joseph J., 1929- 329'.02'0973
Catholic principles and our political parties [by] Joseph J. McMillan. [1st ed.] New York, Vantage Press [1971] 327 p. 21 cm. Bibliography: p. 327. [JK2261.M19] 79-27410 6.50
1. Political parties—U.S.—History. 2. Catholic Church in the United States—History.

Political science.

CALVIN, Jean, 1509-1964.
John Calvin on God and political duty. Edited with an introd. by John T. McNeill. [2d ed.] Indianapolis, Bobbs-Merrill [1956] xxvi, 102 p. 21 cm. (The Library of liberal arts, no. 23) Selections from the author's Institutes of the Christian religion, Commentaries on Romans, and Commentaries on Daniel. Bibliography: p. vi. Bibliographical footnotes. 63-1920
1. Political science. I. Title. II. Title: God and political duty. III. Series.

CALVIN, Jean, 1509-1964.
On God and political duty. Edited, with an introd. by John T. McNeill. [2d rev. ed.] Indianapolis, Bobbs-Merrill [1956] xxv, 102 p. (Library of liberal arts, 23) Includes bibliography. 66-11236
1. Political science. I. McNeill, John Thomas, 1885- ed. II. Title.

CONFERENCE on Christian politics, economics and citizenship. Commission on politics and citizenship. 261
Politics and citizenship, being the report presented to the Conference on Christian politics, economics and citizenship at Birmingham, April 5-12, 1924. London, New York [etc.] Published for the conference committee by Longmans, Green and co., 1924. xiii, lll. [1] p. 18 1/2 cm. (Half-title: C.O.P.E.C. commission reports, vol. K) "Second impression, September 1924." Sir WyndhamDcedes, chairman [HN30.C6 vol. X] 25-6840
1. Political science. 2. Citizenship. 3. Sociology, Christian. I. Title.

JC139.C3A3 1956 320 57-799
John Calvin on God and political duty. Edited with an introd. by John T. McNeil. ,532d ed.] New York, Liberal Arts Press [1956] xxvi, 102p. 21cm. (The Liberary of liberal arts, no. 23) Selections from the authors Institutes of the Christian religion. Commentaries on Romans, and Commentaries on Daniel. Bibliography: p. Vi. Bibliographical footnotes.
1. Political science. I. Calvin, Jean, 1509-1564. II. Title. III. Title: God and political duty.

ON God and society;
essay on the generative principle of political constitutions and other human institutions. Edited by Elisha Greifer, and translated with the assistance of Laurence M. Porter. Chicago, H. Regnery [c1959] xxxiii, 92p. 18cm. (A Gateway edition, 6052) Translation of Essai sur principe generateur des constitutions politiques et des autres institutions.
1. Political science. I. Maistre, Joseph Marie, comte de, 1753-1821.

Political science—Early works to 1700.

BELLARMINO, Roberto Francesco Romolo, Saint, 1542-1621. 261.7
De laicis : or, The treatise on civil government / by Robert Bellarmoine ; translated by Kathleen E. Murphy. Westport, Conn. : Hyperion Press, [1979] c1928. p. cm. Translation of De laicis. Reprint of the ed. published by Fordham University Press, New York. [JC143.B3D4 1979] 78-20450 ISBN 0-88355-927-7 : 10.00
1. Political science—Early works to 1700. 2. Church and state—Catholic Church. I. Title.

DANTE Alighieri, 1265-1321. 261.7
Monarchy, and Three political letters / Dante ; with an introd. by Donald Nicholl and a note on the chronology of Dante's political works by Colin Hardie. Westport, Conn. : Hyperion Press, [1979] p. cm. Reprint of the 1954 ed. published by the Noonday Press, New York, in series: Library of ideas. Bibliography: p. [PQ4315.62.N5 1979] 78-20461 ISBN 0-88355-840-8 : 15.00
1. Political science—Early works to 1700. 2. Italy—Politics and government—1268-1559. 3. Church and state. I. Dante Alighieri, 1265-1321. Epistolae. English. 1979. II. Title. III. Title: Three political letters. IV. Series: Library of ideas.

Political science—History

WARING, Luther Hess, 1865-1941.
The political theories of Martin Luther, by Luther Hess Waring ... New York and London, G. P. Putnam's sons, 1910. vi p., 1 l., 298 p. 20 cm. "Bibliography of works consulted and cited": p. 288-289. [JC141.L8W3] 10-22435
1. Luther, Martin, 1483-1546. 2. Political science—Hist. 3. Church and state. 4. State, The. I. Title.

Polk, Leonidas, Bp., 1806-1864.

PARKS, Joseph Howard. 922.375
General Leonidas Polk, C.S.A., the fighting bishop. [Baton Rouge] Louisiana State University Press [1962] 408 p. illus., maps, ports. 24 cm. (Southern biography series) "Critical essay on authorities.": p. [387]-395. [E467.1.P7P3] 62-15028
1. Polk, Leonidas, Bp., 1806-1864. I. Title. II. Series.

Poltergeists.

ROGO, D. Scott. 133.1'4
The poltergeist experience / D. Scott Rogo. New York : Harmondsworth, Eng. ; Penguin Books, 1979. 301 p. ; 19 cm. Includes index. Bibliography: p. [285]-291. [BF1483.R63] 78-31465 ISBN 0-14-004995-9 pbk. : 2.95
1. Rogo, D. Scott. 2. Poltergeists. I. Title.

Poltergeists—Bibliography.

GOSS, Michael. 016.1331'4
Poltergeists : an annotated bibliography of works in English, circa 1880-1975 / compiled and introduced by Michael Goss. Metuchen, N.J. : Scarecrow Press, 1978. p. cm. Includes indexes. [Z6878.G5G67] [BF1483] 78-11492 ISBN 0-8108-1181-2 : 15.00
1. Poltergeists—Bibliography. I. Title.

Poltergeists—Case studies.

GAULD, Alan. 133.1'4
Poltergeists / Alan Gauld and A. D. Cornell. London ; Boston : Routledge & Kegan Paul, 1979. xii, 406 p., [4] leaves of plates : ill. ; 23 cm. Includes indexes. Bibliography: p. 363-398. [BF1483.G38] 79-321311 ISBN 0-7100-0185-1 : 20.00
1. Poltergeists—Case studies. I. Cornell, A. D., joint author. II. Title.

ROLL, William George, 1926- 133.1'4
The poltergeist / by William G. Roll. Metuchen, N.J. : Scarecrow Press, 1976, c1972. xvi, 208 p. ; 22 cm. Reprint of the ed. published by New American Library, New York. Includes index. Bibliography: p. 199-202. [BF1483.R64 1976] 76-25880 ISBN 0-8108-0984-2 : 7.50
1. Poltergeists—Case studies. I. Title.

WILSON, Colin, 1931- 133.1'4
Poltergeist! : a study in destructive haunting / Colin Wilson. 1st American ed. New York : Putnam, 1982, c1981. 382 p. ; 22 cm. Originally published: London : New English Library, 1981. Includes index. Bibliography: p. [365]-369. [BF1483.W54 1982] 19 81-48199 ISBN 0-399-12716-X : 13.95
1. Poltergeists—Case studies. I. Title.

Poltergeists—England—Enfield—Case studies.

PLAYFAIR, Guy Lyon. 133.1'4
This house is haunted : the true story of a poltergeist / [Guy Lyon Playfair]. New York : Stein and Day, 1980. 290 p., [8] leaves of plates : ill. ; 24 cm. [BF1473.H37P55 1980] 19 80-5387 ISBN 0-8128-2732-5 : 11.95
1. Harper family. 2. Poltergeists—England—Enfield—Case studies. 3. Enfield, Eng.—History. I. Title.

Poltergeists—Juvenile literature.

KETTELKAMP, Larry. 133.1'4
Mischievous ghosts : the poltergeist and PK / Larry Kettlekamp ; illustrated with photos. New York : Morrow, 1980. 127 p. : ill. ; 22 cm. Includes index. Discusses cases of psychokinetic activity caused by poltergeists, laboratory research which has been done in this area, and theories to explain PK. [BF1483.K47] 80-17138 ISBN 0-688-22243-9 : 6.95 ISBN 0-688-32243-3 lib. bdg. : 6.67
1. Poltergeists—Juvenile literature. 2. [Psychokinesis—Juvenile literature.] 3. [Poltergeists.] I. Title.

KNIGHT, David C. 133.1'4
Poltergeists: hauntings and the haunted [by] David C. Knight. [1st ed.] Philadelphia, Lippincott [1972] 160 p. illus. 21 cm. (The Weird and horrible library) Accounts of eleven famous poltergeists of the last few centuries, theories about them, studies of where, who, and why they haunt, and suggestions on what to do if you encounter one. [BF1483.K58] 72-2445 ISBN 0-397-31416-7 (pbk.) ISBN 0-397-31274-1 (lib. bdg.)
1. Poltergeists—Juvenile literature. 2. [Poltergeists.] 3. [Ghosts.] I. Title.

Polycarpus, Saint, bp. of Smyrna. Epistola ad Philippenses.

HARRISON, Percy Neale. 281.3
Polycarp's two epistles to the Philippians, by P. N. Harrison ... Cambridge [Eng.] The University press, 1936. xii, 356 p. 22 cm. "Dr. Harrison's theory ... is that ... the Epistle of Polycarp really consists of two letters."--Prefatory note. Appendices: Translation of Polycarp's two epistles. Greek text with parallels. Bibliography: p. [337]-351. [BR65.P62] 37-796
1. Polycarpus, Saint, bp. of Smyrna. Epistola ad Philippenses. I. Title.

POLYCARPUS, Saint, bp. of Smyrna. 281.
... St. Polycarp, bishop of Smyrna, by the Rev. Blomfield Jackson ... Pub. under the direction of the Tract committee. London [etc.] Society for promoting Christian knowledge; New York, E. & J. B. Young & co., 1898. vi, [7]-78 p., 1 l. 17 cm. (Early church classics) "Translation of the one extant letter of St. Polycarp [the Epistle to the Phillippians] and of the Smyrnsans narrating his marrtyrdon."--Pref. [BR60.E3P6] 22-6498
I. Jackson, Blomfield, 1839-1906, ed. II. Title.

Polygamy.

ANDERSON, J. Max. 234'.165
The polygamy story : fiction and fact / J. Max Anderson. Salt Lake City : Publishers Press, c1979. x, 166 p. : facsims. ; 24 cm. Includes bibliographical references and index. [BX8641.A52] 79-116699 pbk. : 4.95
1. Polygamy. 2. Mormons and Mormonism. I. Title.

CANNON, Angus Munn, b.1834, defendant.
The Edmunds law. "Unlawful cohabitation," as defined by Chief Justice Chas. S. Zane, of the territory of Utah, in the trial of Angus M. Cannon, esq., in the third District court, Salt Lake City, April 27, 28, 29, 1885. Full report of the arguments as to ther term "cohabitation" in the above law. Reported by John Irvine. Salt Lake City, Utah, Juvenile instructor office, 1885. iv, [5]-118 p. 17 1/2 cm. "Appendix. The Munner case": p. 107-118. [HQ994.C3] 41-38266
1. Polygamy. 2. Mormons and Mormonism. I. Zane, Charles Schuster, 1861-1915. II. Irvine, John, reporter. III. Munser, Amoe Milton b. 1890, defendant. IV. Utah (Ter.) District court (3d district) V. Title.

CANNON, George, Quayle, 1827-1901.
A review of the decision of the Supreme court of the United States, in the case of Geo. Reynolds vs. the United States. by George Q.Cannon. Salt Lake City, Utah, Deseret news printing and publishing establishment, 1879. v, 57 p. 24 cm. [BX8641.R4] 9-8716
1. Reynolds, George. 2. Polygamy. 3. Mormons and Mormonism. I. Title.

[JENCKS, E N]
The history and philosophy of marriage; or, Polygamy and monogamy compared. By a Christian philanthropist ... Boston, J. Campbell, 1869. 256 p. 18 cm. [HQ988.J5] 9-7269
1. Polygamy. 2. Marriage. I. Title.

LAWS, Samuel Spahr, 1824-1921.
Polygamy and citizenship in church and state, by Samuel Spahr Laws ... Washington, D. C., Judd & Detweiler (inc.) printers, 1906. 227 p. 23 cm. [HQ988.L42] 6-34874
1. Polygamy. 2. Utah—Pol. & govt. I. Title.

MERRILL, Melissa. 289.3'3 B
Polygamist's wife / by Melissa Merrill. Salt Lake City : Olympus Pub. Co., c1975. 167 p. : ill. ; 24 cm. [BX8695.M37A36] 74-29659 ISBN 0-913420-52-2 : 7.95
1. Merrill, Melissa. 2. Polygamy. I. Title.

MERRILL, Melissa. 289.3'3
Polygamist's wife / by Melissa Merrill. New York : Pocket Books, 1977c1975. 176p. ; 18 cm. (A Kangaroo Book)

[BX8695.M37A36] ISBN 0-671-81053-7 pbk.: 1.75
1. Merrill, Melissa. 2. Polygamy. I. Title.
L.C. card no. for c1975 Olympus Pub. Co., ed.: 74-29659.

PRATT, Orson, 1811-1881.
The Bible & polygamy. Does the Bible sanction polygamy? A discussion between Professor Orson Pratt ... and Rev. Doctor J. P. Newman ... in the new Tabernacle, Salt Lake City, August 12, 13, and 14, 1870. To which is added three sermons on the same subject, by Prest. George A. Smith, and elders Orson Pratt and George Q. Cannon. Salt Lake City, Utah. Desert news steam printing establishment, 1874. 1 p. l., 99 p. 24 cm. [BX8641.P8] 9-8715
1. Polygamy. 2. Mormons and mormonism. I. Newman, John Phillip, bp., 1826-1899, joint author. II. Smith, George Albert, 1817-1875. III. Cannon, George Quayle, 1827-1901. IV. Title.

PRATT, Orson, 1811-1881.
The Bible & polygamy. Does the Bible sanction polygamy? A discussion between Professor Orson Pratt ... and Rev. Doctor J. P. Newman ... in the new Tabernacle, Salt Lake City, August 12, 13, and 14, 1870. To which are added three sermons on the same subject, by Presi. George A. Smith and elders Orson Pratt and George Q. Cannon. Salt Lake City, Utah, Deseret news steam printing establishment, 1877. 105 p. 23 cm. [BX8641.P8 1877] 45-44903
1. Polygamy. 2. Mormons and Mormonism. I. Newman, John Philip, bp., 1826-1899, joint author. II. Smith, George Albert, 1817-1875. III. Cannon, George Quayle, 1827-1901. IV. Title.

SNOW, Lorenzo, 1814-1901, defendant.
His ten wives. The travels, trial and conviction of the Mormon apostle, Lorenzo Snow. From Nauvoo to the penitentiary. From the record. Butte, Mont., M. Koch, 1887. 104 p. front., ports. 20 cm. "Lorenzo Snow ... was indicted by the grand jury of the First judicial district of Utah, under the act of Congress of March 22d, 1882, commonly known as the Edmunds law."--Note. 24-18391
1. Polygamy. 2. Mormons and Mormonism. I. Utah, Supreme court. II. Title.

TAYLOR, Samuel Woolley, 1907- 289.3
I have six wives; a true story of present-day plural marriage. New York, Greenberg [1956] 275 p. 22 cm. [BX8641.T3] 56-7978
1. Polygamy. 2. Mormons and Mormonism. I. Title.

YOUNG, Kimball, 1893- 301.42'2
Isn't one wife enough? Illustrated with photos. Westport, Conn., Greenwood Press [1970, c1954] xiv, 476 p. illus. 23 cm. [BX8641.Y8 1970] 76-104233
1. Polygamy. 2. Mormons and Mormonism. I. Title.

YOUNG, Kimball, 1893- 289.3
Isn't one wife enough? Illustrated with photos. [1st ed.] New York, Holt [1954] 476 p. illus. 22 cm. [BX8641.Y8] 54-5461
1. Polygamy. 2. Mormons and Mormonism. I. Title.

Polyglot texts, selections, quotations, etc.

AVE Maria, 232.931
Ave Maria. Washington, Commisariat of the Holy Land, Franciscan monastery [c 1936] 4 p. l., 202 p. 1 l., 27 cm. Ornamental borders in color. Issued in box. "This book contains fifteen translations of the Lord's prayer, followed by the Hall Mary in one hundred fifty languages."--p. 186. [BX2175.A8 A1] 37-659
1. Polygiot texts selections, quotations, etc. 2. Printing—Specimens. 3. Washington, D. C. Mt St. Sepuichre (Frascican monastery) I. Lord's prayer Polyglot. II. Ave Maria. Polyglot. III. Title.

LORD'S prayer. Polyglot. 226.9
Pater Hemon ("Our Father"); 63 versions of the Lord's prayer in 41 languages, ancient and modern; with historical and linguistic notes by Paul D. Hugon ... Los Angeles, Calif., L. R. Ervin, 1936. 4 p. l., 7-53, [2] p. 16 cm. [P351.H8] 38-21128
1. Polyglot texts, selections, quotations, etc. I. Hugon, Paul Desdemaines, 1882- ed. II. Title.

NORTH, Eric McCoy, 1888- 220.5
The Book of a thousand tongues; being some account of the translation and publication of all or part of the Holy Scriptures into more than a thousand languages and dialects with over 1100 examples from the text, edited by Eric M. North. New York, Published for the American Bible Society [by] Harper, 1938 [c1939] Detroit, Tower Books, 1971. 386 p. ports. 29 cm. [P352.A2N6 1971] 73-174087
1. Bible—Versions. 2. Polyglot texts, selections, quotations, etc. 3. Printing—Specimens. I. American Bible Society. II. Title.

Polynesia—Religion.

BUCK, Peter Henry, 1880- 299.9
Anthrology and religion, by Peter Henry Buck (Te Rangi Hiroa) ... New Haven, Yale university press; London, H. Milford, Oxford university press, 1939. viii, 96 p. fold. map. 21 cm. (Half-title: The Terry lectures) [BI.2600.B8] 40-488
1. Polynesia—Religion. 2. Mythology, Polynesian. 3. Ethnology—Polynesia. 4. Polynesia—Soc. life & cust. 5. Religion, Primitive. I. Title.

BUCK, Peter Henry, Sir, 1880-1951. 301.2'4
Anthropology and religion, by Peter Henry Buck (Te Rangi Hiroa). [Hamden, Conn.] Archon Books, 1970 [c1939] viii, 96 p. fold. map. 22 cm. [BL2600.B8 1970] 72-121753 4.25
1. Polynesia—Religion. I. Title.

=HANDY, Edward Smith Craighill, 1892- 572
Polynesian religion, by E. S. Craighill Handy... Honolulu, Hawaii, The Museum, 1927. 2 p. l., [3]-342 p. 25 1/2 cm. (Bernice P. Bishop museum. Bulletin 34) Bayard Dominick expedition. Publication number 12. Bibliography: p. 331-336. [GN670.B4 no. 34] [BL2600.H3] 27-24080
1. Polynesia—Religion. I. Title.

WILLIAMSON, Robert Wood, 1856-1932. 301.5'8
Religion and social organization in central Polynesia / by Robert W. Williamson ; edited by Ralph Piddington ; with a pref. by Raymond Firth. New York : AMS Press, 1977. xxix, [1], 340 p. ; 23 cm. Reprint of the 1937 ed. published at the University Press, Cambridge, Eng. Includes index. Bibliography: p. [xvii]-[1]. [BL2600.W52 1977] 75-35218 ISBN 0-404-14241-9 27.50
1. Polynesia—Religion. 2. Ethnology—Polynesia. 3. Polynesia—Social life and customs. 4. Mythology, Polynesian. I. Title.

WILLIAMSON, Robert Wood, 1856-1932. 299'.9
Religious and cosmic beliefs of central Polynesia / by Robert W. Williamson. New York : AMS Press, [1977] p. cm. Reprint of the 1933 ed. published by The University Press, Cambridge. Includes index. Bibliography: v. 1, p. [BL2600.W53 1977] 75-35220 ISBN 0-404-14300-8 : 72.00
1. Polynesia—Religion. 2. Mythology, Polynesian. I. Title.

WILLIAMSON, Robert Wood, 1856-1932. 299.9
Religious and cosmic beliefs of central Polynesia, by Robert W. Williamson ... Cambridge [Eng.] The University press, 1933. 2 v. 1 illus., fold. map, fold. tables. 24 1/2 cm. Bibliography: vol. I, p. [ix]-[xxi] [BL2600.W5] 34-22783
1. Polynesia—Religion. 2. Mythology, Polynesian. I. Title.

WILLIAMSON ROBERT WOOD, 1856-1932. 299.9
Religion and social organization in central Polynesia, by Robert W. Williamson ... Edited by Ralph Piddington ... with a preface by Raymond Firth ... Cambridge [Eng.] The University press, 1937. xxix p., 1 l., 340 p. 24 1/2 cm. Bibliography: p. [xvii]-[xxxi] [BL2600.W52] 38-10069
1. Polynesia—Religion. 2. Ethnology—Polynesia. 3. Polynesia—Soc. life & cust. 4. Mythology, Polynesian. I. Piddington, Ralph, ed. II. Title.

Polyradiculitis—Personal narratives.

WILSON, Yvonne M. 248'.2 B
Sifted gold / Yvonne M. Wilson. St. Louis : Concordia Pub. House, [1974] 126 p. ; 20 cm. [RC416.W54] 74-4743 ISBN 0-570-03235-0 : 4.95
1. Polyradiculitis—Personal narratives. I. Title.

Polytheism.

MILLER, David LeRoy. 212'.2
The new polytheism; rebirth of the gods and goddesses [by] David L. Miller. [1st ed.] New York, Harper & Row [1974] x, 86 p. 21 cm. Includes bibliographical references. [BL355.M54 1974] 73-6345 ISBN 0-06-065751-0 4.95
1. Polytheism. 2. Gods, Greek. I. Title.

ZAKATARIOUS. 291.1'4
The secret of the golden calf; towards the foundation of a polytheistic psychology and the reawakening of the polytheistic faith. Berkeley, Calif., House of Zwillingsbruder Press, 1974. 80 p. illus. 24 cm. [BL355.Z34] 74-177232 10.00
1. Polytheism. 2. Psychology, Religious. 3. Golden calf (Bible) I. Title.

Pomo Indians—Religion and mythology.

WILSON, Birbeck. 299'.7
Ukiah Valley Pomo religious life, supernatural doctoring, and beliefs: observations of 1939-1941. Edited by Caroline L. Hills. Berkeley, University of California Archaeological Research Facility, Dept. of Anthropology, 1968. 92 p. 28 cm. (Reports of the University of California Archaeological Survey, no. 72) Bibliography: p. 91-92. [F863.C255 no. 72] 68-66244
1. Pomo Indians—Religion and mythology. I. Hills, Caroline L., ed. II. Title. III. Series: California. University. California Archaeological Survey. Reports, no. 72

Pomona, Calif. First Christian church.

POMONA, Calif. First Christian church. Historical committee. 286.6794
History of the First Christian church of Pomona, California, 1883-1943 by Pearl K. Baughman and Donald F. West, for the sixtieth anniversary of the church, October 31-November 7, 1943. Historical committee: Mrs. Pearl K. Baughman, chairman; Miss Minnie Joos, secretary [and others] ... [Pomona, c1943] 94 p. incl. front., illus. (ports.) 23 cm. [BX7331.P6A3] 44-26696
1. Pomona, Calif. First Christian church. I. Baughman, Pearl K. II. West, Donald F. III. Title.

Pontifical Association of the Holy Childhood.

ROYER, Fanchon, 1902- 922.244
The power of title children ... the story of Charles Conte de Forbin-Janson, primate of Lorraine, and the beginning of the Association of the Holy Childhood. Fresno, Calif., Academy Library Guild, 1954 [i. e. 1956] 112p. illus. 22cm. [BX4705.F63R6] 56-2247
1. Forbin-Janson, Charles August Marie Joseph de, Bp., 1785-1844. 2. Pontifical Association of the Holy Childhood. I. Title.

Pontificia Universita Gregoriana—History.

CARAMAN, Philip, 1911- 207'.45632
University of the nations : the story of the Gregorian University with its associated institutes, the Biblical and Oriental, 1551-1962 / by Philip Caraman. New York : Paulist Press, c1981. 157 p., [10] p. of plates : ill. ; 21 cm. Bibliography: p. 150-154. [BX920.R8848C37] 19 80-84513 ISBN 0-8091-2355-X (pbk.) : 6.95
1. Pontificia Universita Gregoriana—History. 2. Pontificio Istituio biblico—History. 3. Pontificium Institutum Orientalium Studiorum—History. I. Title.

Pontmain, Notre-Dame de.

ERNEST, Brother, 1897- 232.931
Our Lady comes to Pontmain. Illus. by Brother Etienne Cooper. Notre Dame, Ind., Dujarie Press [1954] 86p. illus. 24cm. [BT660.P7E7] 54-43125
1. Pontmain, Notre-Dame de. I. Title.

Poole Church of Christ.

WILLIAMS, Irene Aldridge, 1904- 286'.6769'883
A record of Poole Church of Christ, Poole, Webster County, Kentucky. Evansville, Ind., 1969. v, 97 l. 28 cm. Cover title: Poole Church of Christ. Typescript. [F459.P65W5] 74-275312
1. Poole Church of Christ. 2. Registers of births, etc.—Poole, Ky. I. Title.

Poomaihealani, Joseph.

WALKER, Gail. 286.7'3 B
Spirits in his parlor / by Gail Walker ; [cover art by Ron Stout]. Mountain View, Calif. : Pacific Press Pub. Association, c1980. 141 p. ; 22 cm. (A Destiny book ; D-184) [BX6189.P66W34] 79-87733 pbk. : 4.95
1. Poomaihealani, Joseph. 2. Converts, Seventh-Day Adventist—Hawaii—Biography. 3. Hawaii—Biography. 4. Spirits. 5. Spirit possession—Hawaii. I. Title.

Poor.

KEMP, Charles F., 1912- 362.5
Pastoral care with the poor [by] Charles Kemp. Nashville, Abingdon Press [1972] 128 p. illus. 20 cm. Bibliography: p. 124-128. [BV639.P6K44] 72-926 ISBN 0-687-30295-1
1. Poor. 2. Church and the poor. 3. Pastoral theology. I. Title.

MCKENNA, Mary J. 296
Our brethren of the tenements and ghetto, by M. J. McKenna. New York, J. S. Ogilvie publishing company [c1899] 1 p. l., [7]-99 p. 19 cm. [DS143.M15] 99-5103
1. Poor. 2. Jews in the U.S. 3. Tenement-houses. I. Title.

Poor—Biblical teaching.

PILGRIM, Walter E. 261.8'34569
Good news to the poor : wealth and poverty in Luke-Acts / Walter E. Pilgrim. Minneapolis, Minn. : Augsburg Pub. House, c1981. 198 p. ; 21 cm. Bibliography: p. 193-198. [BS2545.P65P54] 19 81-65653 ISBN 0-8066-1889-2 pbk. : 7.95
1. Bible. N.T. Luke—Criticism, interpretation, etc. 2. Bible. N.T. Acts—Criticism, interpretation, etc. 3. Poor—Biblical teaching. 4. Wealth—Biblical teaching. I. Title.

Poor Clares—Congresses.

FRANCISCAN women : 271'.973
the dynamics of Christian fidelity. Chicago : Franciscan Herald Press, c1975. 57 p. ; 18 cm. [BX4361.F7] 75-41389 ISBN 0-8199-0593-3 : 0.65
1. Poor Clares—Congresses.

Poor Handmaids of Jesus Christ.

MEAGHER, George T 922.243
With attentive ear and courageous heart; a biography of Mother Mary Kasper, foundress of the Poor Handmaids of Jesus Christ. Milwaukee, Bruce Press [c1957] xii, 258p. illus., port. 23cm. (Catholic life publications) [BX4705.K3M38] 58-562
1. Kasper, Maria, 1820-1898. 2. Poor Handmaids of Jesus Christ. I. Title.

Poor People's Campaign.

BRYANT, M. Darrol. 322'.4
To whom it may concern: poverty, humanity, community [by] M. Darrol Bryant. Philadelphia, Fortress Press [1969] vii, 54 p. illus. 22 cm. Bibliography: p. 51-54. [E185.615.B75] 72-77221 1.25
1. Poor People's Campaign. 2. Church and social problems—U.S. I. Title.

Poor School Sisters de Notre Dame.

MARY Charitas, Sister, 271.97
1893-
A new superior generation. Boston, Bruce Humphries [c1951] 143p. 21cm. [BX4410.P58M3] 53-11992
1. Poor School Sisters de Notre Dame. 2. Education of woman. I. Title.

Poor—Southern States—Addresses, essays, lectures.

THE Church and the 261.8'5'0975
rural poor / edited by James A. Cogswell. Atlanta : John Knox Press, [1975] p. cm. Includes bibliographical references. [HC107.A133P613] 74-7616 ISBN 0-8042-0797-6 : 1.95
1. Poor—Southern States—Addresses, essays, lectures. 2. Church and Social problems—Southern States—Addresses, essays, lectures. I. Cogswell, James A.

Poor—United States

KLEMME, Huber F. 261.83
Poverty and plenty in our time; a coursebook for leaders of adults [by] Huber F. Klemme. Boston, United Church Press [1966] 122 p. illus. 21 cm. "Part of the United Church curriculum, prepared and published by the Division of Christian Education and the Division of Publication of the United Church Board for Homeland Ministries." Bibliography: p. 24-27. [HC110.P6K55] 66-20543
1. Poor—U.S. 2. Church and social problems. 3. Social work education. I. United Church Board for Homeland Ministries. Division of Christian Education. II. United Church Board for Homeland Ministries. Division of Publication. III. Title.

Poor—United States—History.

MAGNUSON, Norris, 361.7'5'0973
1932-
Salvation in the slums : evangelical social work, 1865-1920 / by Norris Magnuson. Metuchen, N.J. : Scarecrow Press, 1977. xvi, 299 p. ; 23 cm. (ATLA monograph series ; no. 10) Includes index. Bibliography: p. 273-281. [HV4044.M34] 76-54890 ISBN 0-8108-0975-3 : 12.00
1. Poor—United States—History. 2. Church charities—History. 3. Evangelicalism—United States. 4. Urbanization—United States—History. 5. United States—Economic conditions—1865-1918. I. Title. II. Series: American Theological Library Association. ATLA monograph series ; no. 10.

Pope, Alexander, 1688-1744.

CARLSON, Leland Henry, 274.2
1908-
English satire; papers read at a Clark Library Seminar, January 15, 1972, by Leland H. Carlson and Ronald Paulson. Los Angeles, William Andrews Clark Memorial Library, University of California, 1972. v, 112 p. facsims. 24 cm. (William Andrews Clark Memorial Library seminar papers) Includes bibliographical references. [BR757.C26] 73-161452
1. Pope, Alexander, 1688-1744. 2. Marprelate controversy. 3. Satire, English. I. Paulson, Roland. II. California. University. University at Los Angeles. William Andrews Clark Memorial Library. III. Title. IV. Series.

HOMERUS.
... Four books of Pope's Iliad I, VI, XXII, XXIV. With an introduction, the story of the Iliad, and notes. Boston, Houghton, Mifflin and company, [c1896] xvi, 102 p. 19 cm. (The Riverside literature series. No. 101) [PA4025.A3P] A 41
I. Pope, Alexander, 1688-1744, tr. II. Title.

POPE, Alexander, 1688-1744.
An essay on man. By Alexander Pope, esq., enl. and improved by the author. With notes by William Warberton, M. A. London, Printed; Philadelphia, Re-printed by W. Dunlap, at the Newest-printing-office, in Market-street, for G. Noel, bookseller, in New-York, 1760. iv, 5-68 p. 19 cm. Contains also "The universal prayer": p. [65]-68. [PR3627.A1 1760] 12-39773
I. Warburton, William, bp., of Gloucester, 1698-1779. II. Title.

POPE, Alexander, 1688-1744.
An essay on man; in four epistles to H. St. John, lord Bolingbroke. To which is added, The universal prayer. By Alexander Pope, esq. Pinted at Worcester, Massachusetts: by Thomas, son & Thomas, sold by them,and the booksellers in Boston, 1797. 59 p. 15 cm. [PR3627.A] A 33
I. Title.

POPE, Alexander, 1688-1744.
An essay on man, by Alexander Pope, esq. To which is added, The universal prayer ... Canadaigua [N. Y.]: Published by J. D. Bemis, 1814. iv, [5]-54 p. 15 cm. Imperfect: p. 33-54 wanting. [PR3627.A1 1814] A 34
I. Title. II. Title: The universal prayer.

POPE, Alexander, 1688-1744.
An essay on man, by Alexander Pope, esq. To which are added, The universal prayer, and other valuable pieces, selected from his works ... New-York, Published by Evert Duyckinck, 1817. vi, [7]-106 p. incl. front. 14 cm. [PR3627.A1 1817] [PR3627.A] A 33
I. Title.
Contents omitted.

POPE, Alexander, 1688-1744.
An essay on man. In four epistles to H. St. John, lord Bloinbroke. To which is added, The universal prayer, Messiah, &c. By Alexander Pope, esq. Brattleborough, Published by John Holbrook, 1819. 52, [2] p. 16 cm. [PR3627.A1 1819] 4-19724
I. Title.

POPE, Alexander, 1688-1744.
An essay on man, by Alexander Pope, esq., to which is added, The universal prayer, and other valuable pieces, selected from his works ... Philadelphia, M'Carty & Davis, 1821. iv, [5]-72 p. 14 cm. [PR3627.A1 1821] 12-39792
I. Title.

POPE, Alexander, 1688-1744.
An essay on man: in four epistles to H. St. John, lord Bolingbroke. To which is added, The universal prayer. By Alexander Pope, esq. Hartford, S. Andrus, 1824. 2 p. l., [iii]-ix, [10]-67 p. 16 cm. Added t.-p., engraved. Notes: p. [57]-67. [PR3627.A1 1824] 12-39803
I. Title.

POPE, Alexander, 1688-1744.
Essay on man, tr. from the English by Charles Le Brun ... 3d ed. Philadelphia, 1834. 127 p. incl. pl. 23 cm. Added t.-p. in French. Text and French prose translation on opposite pages. 6-30134
I. Le Brun, Charles Francois Eugene, d. 1844, tr. II. Title.

[POPE, Alexander] 1688-1744.
Essay on man, tr. from the English by Charles Le Brun ... 6th ed. Philadelphia, 1836. 7 p. l., [17]-127 p. front. (port.) pl. 23 cm. Added t.-p. in French. Text and French prose translation on opposite pages. [PR3627.A45 1836] 13-4249
I. Le Brun, Charles Francois Eugene, d. 1844, tr. II. Title.

POPE, Alexander, 1688-1744.
An essay on man: in four epistles to Henry St. John, lord Bolingbroke. By Alexander Pope. With notes, explanatory of the grammatical construction and meaning of the author. By Charles Emerson, A. B. West Brookfield, C. A. Mirick & co., 1841. 60 p. 16 cm. [PR3627.A13] 13-4247
I. Emerson, Charles, 1817-1845, ed. II. Title.

POPE, Alexander, 1688-1744.
... An essay on man, in four epistles to Lord Bolingbroke, by Alexander Pope. Favorite poems, by Alexander Pope and Thomas Moore. Illustrated. Boston, Houghton, Mifflin, 1882. viii, [9]-96 p., 4 l., 12-96 p., 4 l., 12-112 p. plates. 14 cm. (Modern classics) [PR3627.A1 1882] A 32
I. Moore, Thomas, 1779-1852. II. Title.

POPE, Alexander, 1688-1744.
... An essay on man, by Alexander Pope; biographical and explanatory notes, including Clarke's grammatical notes. New York, Maynard, Merrill, & co. [1890] 64 p. front. (port.) 17 cm. (On cover: Maynard's English classic series. 83-84) Series title in part at head of t.-p. [PR3627.A1 1890] A 35
I. Title.

POPE, Alexander, 1688-1744.
... Essay on man, ed. by Mark Pattison, B. D. Oxford, The Clarendon press, 1904. 122 p. 17 cm. Clarendon press series. [PR3627.A1 1904] 15-22881
I. Pattison, Mark, 1813-1884, ed. II. Title.

POPE, Alexander, 1688-1744.
... Essay on man; edited by A. Hamilton Thompson ... Cambridge [Eng.] University press, 1913. xi, 92 p. front. (port.) 17 cm. (Half-title: Pitt press series) A 40
I. Thompson, Alexander Hamilton, 1873- ed. II. Title.

POPE, Alexander, 1688-1744.
An essay on man, in four epistles; to Henry St. John, lord Bolingbroke. Written in the year 1732. By A. Pope, esq. To which are added, the Recommendatory poems, notes and variations, the Universal prayer, and letters relating to the Essay on man. Richmond, Printed for and sold by William Prichard, 1805. 81 p. 15 cm. Contains no "letters on the Essay on man." 10-11016
I. Title.

POPE, Alexander, 1688-1744.
An essay on man, in four epistles, to Henry St. John, lord Bolingbroke. To which is added, The universal prayer, with other poems. By Alexander Pope, esq. Albany, Printed by G. J. Loomis & co., 1823. iv, [5]-72 p. 15 cm. [PR3627.A1 1823] 41-38041
I. Title.

Pope, William Kenneth, 1901-

POPE, William 287'.6'0924 B
Kenneth, 1901-
A Pope at roam : the confessions of a bishop / by W. Kenneth Pope. [s.l. : s.n.], c1976 (Nashville : Parthenon Press) 176 p. : port. ; 23 cm. [BX8495.P58A35] 76-354196
1. Pope, William Kenneth, 1901- I. Title.

Popes.

BAYER, Franz Joseph. 282
The book of the popes, by Dr. F. J. Bayer, translated from the German by E. M. Lamond, with a preface by Herbert Thurston, S.J. With 686 illustrations. New York and London, Harper & brothers, 1925. ii, 132 p. incl. front., illus., ports., plans. 26 cm. Printed in Great Britain. [BX955.B38 1925a] 26-26131
I. Lamond, E. M., tr. II. Title.

BRUSHER, Joseph 922.21
Stanislaus, 1906-
Popes through the ages. Photos. collected and edited by Emanuel Borden. Princeton, N. J., Van Nostrand [1959] xiii, 530p. illus., ports. (part col.) 29cm. [BX955.B77] 59-14622
1. Popes. I. Title.

BRUSHER, Joseph 922.21
Stanislaus, 1906-
Popes through the ages, by Joseph S. Brusher. Photos. collected and edited by Emanuel Borden. Rev. ed. Princeton, N. J., Van Nostrand [1964] 530 p. illus., ports (part col.) 29 cm. [BX955.B77 1964] 64-54692
1. Popes. I. Title.

CATHOLIC Church Pope, 262.13
(Gregorius VII), 1073-1085.
The correspondence of Pope Gregory VII; selected letters from the Registrum. tr. from Latin with introd. by Ephraim Emerton New York, Octagon, 1966[c.1932, 1966] xxxi, 212p. 24cm. (Records of civilization: sources and studies, no. 14) Bibl. [BX1187.A4] 66-16001 8.00
I. Title.

CATHOLIC Church 262'.13'0924
Pope,(Gregorius VII), 1073-1085
The correspondence of Pope Gregory VII; selected letters from the Registrum. Translated with an introd. by Ephraim Emerton New York, Norton [1969, c1932] xxxi, 212 p. 21 cm. (Records of civilization: sources and studies [14]) Bibliography: p. [196]-197. [BX1187.A4 1969] 70-8470
I. Title. II. Series.

CHAMBERLIN, Eric 262'.13'0922
Russell.
The bad Popes [by] E. R. Chamberlin. New York, Dial Press, 1969. 310 p. illus. (part col.) 25 cm. "A Brahmin book." Bibliography: p. 291-296. [BX955.2.C45] 78-83475 12.50
1. Popes. I. Title.

THE correspondence of Pope 922.21
Gregory vii, selected letters from the registrum; translated with an introduction by Ephraim Emerton ... New York, Columbia university press, 1932. xxi, 212 p. 24 cm. (Half-title: Records of civilization: sources and studies, edited under the auspices of the Dept. of history, Columbia university ... Vol. xiv) Bibliography: p. [196]-197. [BX1187.A4] 32-7802
I. Emerton, Ephraim, 1851-1935, tr. II. Catholic church. Pope, 1073-1085 (Gregorius vii)

*COSGROVE, John. 282'.092'4
Upon this rock : a tale of Peter / John Cosgrove. Huntington, IN : Our Sunday Visitor 1978. 298p. ; 20 cm. [BS2575] 77-94404 ISBN 0-87973-775-1 pbk. : 4.95
1. Saint Peter. 2. Popes. I. Title.

GAY, Jules, 1867- 262'.13
Les papes du XIe [i.e. onzieme] siecle et la chretiente. 2. ed. New York, B. Franklin [1974] xvii, 428 p. 21 cm. (Burt Franklin research and source works series. Selected studies in history, economics and social science: n.s. 39 (b) Medieval, Renaissance & Reformation studies.) Reprint of the 1926 ed. published by V. Lecoffre, Paris, in series: Bibliotheque de l'enseignement de l'histoire ecclesiastique. Includes bibliographical references. [BX1178.G3 1974] 74-12220 ISBN 0-8337-1302-7
1. Popes. 2. Church history—Middle Ages, 600-1500. I. Title. II. Series: Bibliotheque de l'enseignement de l'histoire ecclesiastique.

HORNER, James M. 920.
Popery stripped of its garb: or, The work of iniquity checked in its progress. By Rev. J. M. Horner ... [New York, 1836] xxiii, [25]-279 p. 20cm. [BX6495.H6A3] 1-10361
I. Title.

JOHN, Eric, ed. 262.1309
The Popes, a concise biographical history. Historical surveys by Douglas Woodruff. Biographical articles by J. M. W. Bean [others] New York, Hawthorn [c.1964] 496p. illus., plates (pt. col.) ports. 26cm. Bibl. 64-12422 15.00
1. Popes. I. Title.

JOHN, Eric, ed. 262.1309
The Popes, a concise biographical history, Historical surveys by Douglas Woodruff. Biographical articles by J. M. W. Bean [and others. 1st ed.] New York, Hawthorn Books [1964] 496 p. illus., plates (part col.) Ports. 26 cm. Bibliography: p. 481-482. [BX955.2.J58] 64-12422
1. Popes. I. Title.

LIBER pontificalis.
... The book of the popes (Liber pontificalis) i- New York, Columbia university press, 1916- v. 23 1/2 cm. (Added t.-p.: Records of civilization: sources and studies, ed. by J. T. Shotwell) "The following translation is based upon the text edited by Monnusen in the Monumenta Germaniae histories."--Introd. to v. 1. Contents.I. To the pontificate of Gregory I. tr., with an introduction by

Louise R. Loomis. [BX950.E6L6] 16-20523
1. Popes. 2. Catholic church—Hist. I. Loomis, Louise Ropes, 1874- tr. II. Title.

MAISTRE, Joseph Marie, comte de, 1753-1821. 262'.13
The Pope, considered in his relations with the church, temporal sovereignties, separated churches, and the cause of civilization / by Joseph de Maistre ; translated by Aeneas McD. Dawson ; with an introd. by Richard A. Lebrun. New York : H. Fertig, 1975. xli, 369 p. ; 21 cm. Translation of Du pape. Reprint of the 1850 ed. published by C. Dolman, London. Includes bibliographical references. [BX1805.M3213 1975] 75-5690 16.00
I. Title: The Pope, considered in his relations with the church ...

MANN, Horace Kinder, 1859-1928 922.21
The lives of the popes in the early Middle Ages, by the Rev. Horace K. Mann ... London, K. Paul, Trech, Trubner & Co., 1902-1932. Nendeln, Liechtenstein, Kraus-Thomson Org., 1968. 18v. in 19. fronts., illus., plates, maps (pt. fold.) plan, facsims. fold. geneal. tab. 23cm. Vols. vi- have title: The lives of the popes in the middle ages. V. 16, pt. 2 prepd. by Johannes Hollnsteiner. Bibl. ... [BX1070.M3] 4-16966 198.00
1. Popes. I. Hollnsteiner, Johannes, 1865- II. Title.
Order from Kraus-Thomson Org., 9491 Nendeln, Liechtenstein.

MATT, Leonard von 922.21
The popes; papal history in picture and word, by Leonard. von Matt, Hans Kuhner. [Tr. from German by Salvator Attnaasio.] New York, Universe Bks. [c.1963] 239p. illus., ports., coats of arms. 20cm. 63-18341 10.50
1. Popes. 2. Papacy—Hist.—Pictures, illustrations, etc. I. Kuhner, Hans, joint author. II. Title.

MOLLAT, Guillaume, 1877-
The popes at Avignon, 1305-1378. [Translated by Janet Love from the ninth French edition] New York, Harper & Row [1965] xx, 361 p. (Harper torchbooks, TB 308. The Cathedral library) Bibliography: p. viii. Bibliographical footnotes. 67-18882
I. Title.

PIUS II, Pope, 1405-1464. 876'.04
Selected letters of Aeneas Silvius Piccolomini. Translated and edited by Albert R. Baca. Northridge, Calif., San Fernando Valley State College, 1969. xiv, 167 p. 23 cm. (San Fernando Valley State College Renaissance editions, no. 2) On spine: Piccolomini letters. Bibliography: p. 163-167. [BX1308.A4 1969] 77-632462
I. Baca, Albert R., ed. II. Title. III. Title: Piccolomini letters. IV. Series: The Renaissance editions, no. 2

PRATI, Carlo.
Popes & cardinals in modern Rome, by Carlo Prati. Translated by E. I. Watkin, with an introduction by Jean Carrere. New York, L. MacVeagh, The Dial press, 1927. 233, [1] p. front. (port.) 23 cm. "The Italian original being unpublished, this translation has been made from the French adaptation by Nelly Carrere, to which when published the Italian text will itself conform, and which is therefore the authorized and original text of this work." [BX957.P6] 27-15042
1. Popes. 2. Cardinals. I. Carrere, Nelly. II. Watkin, Edward Ingram, 1888- tr. III. Title.

PRINZ, Joachim, 1902- 262.130922
Popes from the ghetto; a view of medieval Christendom. New York, Schocken [1968, c.1966] 256p. 20cm. (SB174) Bibl. [BX1178.P7] 1.95 pap.,
1. Popes. 2. Pierleoni family. I. Title.

PRINZ, Joachim, 1902- 262.130922
Popes from the ghetto; a view of medieval Christendom. New York, Horizon Press [1966] 256 p. illus. 25 cm. Bibliography: p. 251-256. [BX1178.P7] 66-16301
1. Popes. 2. Pierieoni family. I. Title.

REYNOLDS, Robert L. 262.13
The Story of the Pope. v. 1- [New York, Dell Pub. Co.] 1957- v. illus., ports. 28 cm. Compiler: 1957- R. L. Reynolds. [BX955.S8] 57-3980
1. Popes. I. Title.

SUGRUE, Francis. 922.21
Popes in the modern world. New York, Crowell [1961] 274 p. illus. 24 cm. Includes bibliography. [BX1365.S8] 61-9118
1. Popes. I. Title.

WELTIN, Edward George, 1911- 262.13
The ancient Popes, by E. G. Weltin. Westminster, Md., Newman Press, 1964. xv. 369 p. illus., map (on lining papers) 23 cm. (The Popes through history, v. 2) Bibliography: p. 355. [BX970.W4] 64-66033
1. Popes. I. Title. II. Series.

WOLFE, Rinna. 282'.092'4 B
The singing Pope ; the story of Pope John Paul II / Rinna Wolfe. New York : Seabury Press, c1980. vii, 120 p. : ill. ; 24 cm. "A Crossroad book." A biography of the former Polish cardinal who was the first non-Italian to be elected Pope since 1523. [BX1378.5.W64] 92 80-17531 ISBN 0-8164-0472-0 : 8.95
1. John Paul II, Pope, 1920- —Juvenile literature. 2. Popes—Biography—Juvenile literature. 3. [John Paul II, Pope, 1920-] 4. [Popes.] I. Title.

Popes—Biography.

ANDERSON, Robin, 1913- 262'.13'0924 B
Between two wars : the story of Pope Pius XI (Achille Ratti, 1922-1939) / by Robin Anderson. Chicago : Franciscan Herald Press, 1977. xxix, 154 p., [4] leaves of plates : ill. ; 23 cm. Includes index. Bibliography: p. 147-148. [BX1377.A5] 77-14365 ISBN 0-8199-0687-5 : 7.95
1. Pius XI, Pope, 1857-1939. 2. Popes—Biography. I. Title.

ANDERSON, Robin, 1913- 262'.13'0924 B
St. Pius V, a brief account of his life, times, virtues & miracles / by Robin Anderson ; foreword by Alfredo Ottaviani. Rockford, Ill. : Tan Books and Publishers, 1978. 111 p. : ill. ; 18 cm. [BX1323.A52] 78-55637 ISBN 0-89555-068-7 : 2.00
1. Pius V, Saint, Pope, 1504-1572. 2. Popes—Biography. 3. Christian saints—Italy—Biography. I. Title.

BONNOT, Bernard R. 262'.13'0924 B
Pope John XXIII : an astute, pastoral leader / by Bernard R. Bonnot. New York : Alba House, c1979. xxii, 315 p. ; 22 cm. Bibliography: p. [311]-315. [BX1378.2.B64] 79-17700 ISBN 0-8189-0388-0 : 9.95
1. Joannes XXIII, Pope, 1881-1963. 2. Popes—Biography. I. Title.

BRUSHER, Joseph Stanislaus, 1906- 282'.092'2 B
Popes through the ages / by Joseph S. Brusher ; photos. collected and edited by Emanuel Borden. 3d ed. San Rafael, Calif. : Neff-Kane, c1980. xiii, 536 p. : ill. ; 29 cm. Includes index. [BX955.2.B78 1980] 19 80-19450 ISBN 0-89141-110-0 : 30.00
1. Popes—Biography. I. Title.

FARROW, John, 1904- 922.21
Pageant of the popes, by John Farrow. New York, Sheed & Ward, 1942. 4 p. l., 420 p. ports. 22 cm. [Full name: John Neville Villiers Farrow] [BX955.F33] 42-36375
1. Popes—Biog. I. Title.

HALES, Edward Elton Young, 1908- 262'.13'0924 B
The Emperor and the Pope : the story of Napoleon and Pius VII / E. E. Y. Hales. New York : Octagon Books, 1978, c1961. p. cm. Reprint of the ed. published by Doubleday, Garden City, N.Y. [BX1369.H34 1978] 78-14767 ISBN 0-374-93375-8 lib.bdg. : 12.00
1. Pius VII, Pope, 1742-1823. 2. Napoleon I, Emperor of the French, 1769-1821. 3. Popes—Biography. 4. France—Kings and rulers—Biography. I. Title.

JOANNES XXIII, Pope, 1881-1963. 282'.092'4 B
Journal of a soul / Pope John XXIII ; translated by Dorothy White. Rev. ed. with new introd. Garden City, N.Y. : Image Books, 1980. lxii, 441 p., [16] leaves of plates : ill. ; 21 cm. Revised translation of the work published in 1967 under title: Il giornale dell'anima e altri scritti di pieta. Includes bibliographical references. [BX1378.2.A383 1980] 19 79-7786 ISBN 0-385-14842-9 (pbk.) : 5.95
1. Joannes XXIII, Pope, 1881-1963. 2. Popes—Biography. I. Title.

JOHN Paul II : 262'.13'0924 B
a pictorial biography / by Peter Hebblethwaite and Ludwig Kaufmann. 1st ed. New York : McGraw-Hill, 1979. p. cm. Includes index. [BX1378.5.J63] 79-9169 ISBN 0-07-033327-0 : 14.95 ISBN 0-07-033328-9 pbk. 7.95
1. John Paul II, Pope, 1920- 2. Popes—Biography. I. Hebblethwaithe, Peter. II. Kaufmann, Ludwig.

KERR, Cecil, 1883- 922.21
The child's book of great popes, by Cecil Kerr; with illustrations by Doris Pailthrope. London, New York [etc.] Longmans, Green and co., 1931. iv, 124 p. illus. 19 1/2 cm. [Full name: anne Cecil Kerr] [BX960.K4] 31-14643
1. Popes—Biog. I. [Full name: Anne Cecil Kerr] II. Title.

MACDONALD, Allan John Macdonald, 1887- 262'.13'0924 B
Hildebrand : a life of Gregory VII / by A. J. Macdonald. Merrick, N.Y. : Richwood Pub. Co., 1976. ix, 254 p. ; 23 cm. Reprint of the 1932 ed. published by Methuen, London, in series: Great medieval churchmen. Includes bibliographical references and index. [BX1187.M25 1976] 76-30354 ISBN 0-915172-26-7 : 15.00
1. Gregorius VII, Saint, Pope, 1015 (ca.)-1085. 2. Popes—Biography. I. Title. II. Series: Great medieval churchmen.

MALINSKI, Mieczyslaw. 262'.13'0924 B
Pope John Paul II, the life of Karol Wojtyla / by Miecyslaw Malinski. New York : Seabury Press, 1979. 64 p. : ill. ; 22 cm. "A Crossroad book." Includes index. [BX1378.5.M34] 79-4906 ISBN 0-8164-0434-8 : 10.95
1. John Paul II, Pope, 1920- 2. Popes—Biography. I. Title.

MURPHY, Francis Xavier, 1914- 922.21
John XXIII, the story of the Pope. Orig. title: John XXIII comes to the Vatican New York, Avon [1961, c.1959] 159p. illus. (G-1093) .50 pap.,
I. Title.

MURPHY, Francis Xavier, 1914-
John XXIII; the story of the pope. [New York, Hearst Corp. c1959] 159 p. illus. Original title: John XXIII comes to the Vatican. 68-49293
I. Title.

NEMEC, Ludvik. 262'.13'0924 B
Pope John Paul II : a festive profile / by Ludvik Nemec ; with a foreword by John Cardinal Krol. New York : Catholic Book Pub. Co., c1979. xiii, 242 p., [6] leaves of plates : ill. ; 23 cm. Includes index. Bibliography: p. [212]-235. [BX1368.5.N45] 79-117898 ISBN 0-89942-000-1 : 7.95 pbk. : 4.95
1. John Paul II, Pope, 1920- 2. Popes—Biography.

O'BRIEN, Felicity. 262'.13'0924 B
St Pius X / by Felicity O'Brien. London : Catholic Truth Society, 1976. 20 p. ; 19 cm. Includes bibliographical references. [BX1375.O18] 77-359057 ISBN 0-85183-183-4 : £0.15
1. Pius X, Saint, Pope, 1835-1914. 2. Popes—Biography. I. Title.

ORAM, James, 1936- 262'.13'0924 B
The people's Pope : the story of Karol Wojtyla of Poland / James Oram ; [photos of contemporary Poland by Neil Duncan]. San Francisco : Chronicle Books, c1979. 244 p. : ill. ; 25 cm. Bibliography: p. 224. [BX1378.5.O7] 79-120102 ISBN 0-87701-159-1 pbk. : 7.95
1. John Paul II, Pope, 1920- 2. Popes—Biography. I. Title.

RICHARDS, Jeffrey. 262'.13'0924 B
Consul of God : the life and times of Gregory the Great / Jeffrey Richards. London ; Boston : Routledge & Kegan Paul, 1980. x, 309 p., [12] leaves of plates : ill. ; 24 cm. Includes index. Bibliography: pp. 293-302. [BX1076.R52] 19 79-42757 ISBN 0-7100-0346-3 : 25.00
1. Gregorius I, the Great, Saint, Pope, 540 (ca.)-604. 2. Popes—Biography. I. Title.

SOMERVILLE, Robert, 1940- 262'.5'2
Pope Alexander III and the Council of Tours (1163) : a study of ecclesiastical politics and institutions in the twelfth century / Robert Somerville Berkeley : University of California Press, c1977. xi, 110 p. ; 24 cm. Includes indexes. Bibliography: p. 69-75. [BX1226.S65] 75-46043 ISBN 0-520-03184-9 : 8.50
1. Alexander III, Pope, d. 1181. 2. Council of Tours, 1163—History. 3. Popes—Biography. 4. Tours—Church history. I. Title.

SZOSTAK, John M., 1942- 282'.092'4 B
In the footsteps of Pope John Paul II : an intimate personal portrait / by his American friend, John M. Szostak, with Frances Spatz Leighton. Englewood Cliffs, N.J. : Prentice-Hall, c1980. p. cm. Includes index. [BX1378.5.S95] 19 80-20258 ISBN 0-13-476002-6 : 11.95
1. John Paul II, Pope, 1920- 2. Szostak, John M., 1942- 3. Popes—Biography. I. Leighton, Frances Spatz, joint author. II. Title.

TILLMAN, Helene, 1896- 282'.092'4 B
Pope Innocent III / by Helene Tillman ; translated by Walter Sax. Amsterdam ; New York : North-Holland ; New York, N.Y. : distributed by Elsevier North-Holland, 1980. xviii, 374 p. ; 23 cm. (Europe in the Middle Ages ; v. 12) Translation of: Papst Innocenz III. Includes index. Bibliography: p. [xi]-xviii. [BX1236.T513] 19 81-123984 ISBN 0-444-85137-2 : 53.75
1. Innocent III, Pope, 1160 or 61-1216. 2. Popes—Biography. I. [Papst Innocenz III.] English II. Title. III. Series.

ZIZOLA, Giancarlo, 1936- 282'.13'0924 B
The utopia of Pope John XXIII / Giancarlo Zizola; translated by Helen Barolini. Maryknoll, N.Y. : Orbis Books, c1979. p. cm. Translation of the 2d ed. of L'utopia di papa Giovanni. Includes bibliographical references. [BX1378.2.Z5913] 79-4347 ISBN 0-88344-520-4 pbk. : 9.95
1. Joannes XXIII, Pope, 1881-1963. 2. Popes—Biography. I. Title.

Popes—Biography—Juvenile literature.

DOUGLAS, Robert W., 1947- 262'.13'0924 B
John Paul II, the Pilgrim Pope / words by Robert W. Douglas. Chicago : Childrens Press, 1979. p. cm. Describes the life of Karol Cardinal Wojtyla of Poland, including his election as Pope John Paul II, his travels as a pastoral pope, and his effect on people around the world. [BX1378.5.D68] 92 79-24930 ISBN 0-516-03563-0 : 7.95
1. John Paul II, Pope, 1920- —Juvenile literature. 2. [John Paul II, Pope, 1920-] 3. Popes—Biography—Juvenile literature. 4. [Popes.] I. Title.

Popes—Court.

MCGURN, Barrett 282
A reporter looks at the Vatican. New York, Coward [c.1962] 316p. 22cm. 62-10952 5.00
1. Pius XX, Pope, 1876-1958. 2. Joannes XXIII, Pope, 1881- 3. Popes—Court. I. Title.

MACNUTT, Francis Augustus, 1863-1927. 922.273
A papal chamberlain, the personal chronicle of Francis Augustus MacNutt; edited by Rev. John J. Donovan ... foreword by His Eminence Cardinal Hayes; preface by G. K. Chesterton. London, New York [etc.] Longmans, Green and co., 1936. xvi p., 1 l., 398 p. col. front., plates. ports. (part col.) 22 1/2

cm. "First edition." [BX4705.M2545A3] 36-33928
1. Popes—Court. I. Donovan, John Joseph, 1881- ed. II. Title.

MORGAN, Thomas Brynmor, 1886- 922.21
A reporter at the Papal court; a narrative of the reign of Pope Pius XI, by Thomas B. Morgan. New York, Toronto, Longmans, Green and co., 1937. vi 302 p. front., plates, ports. 22 cm. "First edition." [BX1377.M6] 37-28738
1. Pius XI, pope, 1857-1939. 2. Popes—Court. I. Title.

SMITH, John Talbot, 1855-1923. 922.
A pilgrimage to see the Holy Father, through the stereoscope, through the stereoscope, conducted by Rev. John Talbot Smith ... New York [etc.] Underwood & Underwood [1907] 140 p. front., illus. (facsims.) pl., fold. plans. 18 cm. [BX1375.S65] 7-24026
1. Pius X, pope, 1835-1914. 2. Popes—Court. I. Underwood & Underwood. II. Title.

Popes—Election.

ARADI, Zsolt 262.13
The popes; the history of how they are chosen. elected, and crowned. New York, Chilton [1962, c.1955] 128p. 18cm. (AS175) Bibl. .95 pap.,
1. Popes—Election. I. Title.

ARADI, Zsolt. 262.13
The popes; the history of how they are chosen, elected, and crowned. New York, Farrar, Straus and Cudahy [1955] 192 p. illus. 22 cm. [BX1805.A7] 55-12206
1. Popes—Election.

GREELEY, Andrew M., 1928- 262'.136
The making of the Popes 1978 : the politics of intrigue in the Vatican / Andrew M. Greeley. Kansas City, Kan. : Andrews and McMeel, c1979. 302 p., [20] leaves of plates : ill. ; 24 cm. Includes bibliographical references and index. [BX1378.4.G73] 79-14714 ISBN 0-8362-3100-7 : 12.95
1. John Paul I, Pope, 1912-1978. 2. John Paul II, Pope, 1920- 3. Popes—Election. I. Title.

MARTIN, Malachi. 262'.13
The final conclave / Malachi Martin. New York : Stein and Day, 1978. ix, 354 p. ; 24 cm. Includes index. [BX1805.M39] 77-16145 ISBN 0-8128-2434-2 : 9.95
1. Popes—Election. I. Title.

O'CONNELL, William Henry, cardinal, 1859- 262.135
A memorable voyage [by] William cardinal O'Connell. [Brighton, Mass., c1939] 3 p. l., 5-51 p. front., plates, ports. 23 1/2 cm. "I have attempted...to describe my historic journey to the conclave of 1939."--p. 51. [BX1378.O3] 39-25690
1. Pius XII, pope, 1876- 2. Popes—Election. I. Title.

PIRIE, Valerie. 262'.135
The triple crown : an account of the papal conclaves from the fifteenth century to the present day / by Valerie Pirie. [Wilmington, N.C.] : Consortium Books, [1976?] xiii, 346 p., [27] leaves of plates : ill. ; 23 cm. Bibliography: p. 345-346. [BX1805.P5 1976] 76-375210 12.00
1. Popes—Election. 2. Papacy—History. I. Title.

Popes—History

ARFAUD de Montor, Alexis Francois, 1772-1849. 253
The lives and times of the popes, including the complete gallery of the portraits of the pontiffs reproduced from "Effigies pontificum romanorum Dominci Basae"; being a series of volumes giving the history of the world during the Christian era, retranslated, rev. and writted up to date from Les vies des papes, by the Chevalier Artaud de Montor... [Lateran ed.] New York, The Catholic publication society of America [c1910-11] 10 v. ports. 26 cm. "Limited to one thousand numbered, registered and signed sets." This was not numbered. [BX955.A7 1910] 10-7488
1. Popes—Hist. 2. Catholic church—Hist. I. Title.

CREIGHTON, Mandell, bp. of London, 1843-1901. 282
A history of the papacy from the great schism to the sack of Rome, by M. Creighton ... New ed. ... London, New York [etc.] Longmans, Green, and co., 1897. 6 v. 20 cm. [BX955.C8] 12-31846
1. Popes—Hist. 2. Catholic church—Hist. I. Title.

HAYWARD, Fernand. 282
A history of the popes, by Fernand Hayward; translated from the French by monks of St. Augustine's abbey, Ramagate; with sixteen illustrations. New York, E. P. Dutton & co., inc. [c1931] xvii, 405 p. plates, ports. 23 1/2 cm. "First edition." [BX955.H33] 31-25796
1. Popes—Hist. I. St. Augustine's abbey, Ramagate. II. Title.

PASTOR, Ludwig, freiherr von, 1854-1928. 253
The history of the popes, from the close of the middle ages. Drawn from the secret archives of the Vatican and other original sources. From the German of Dr. Ludwig Pastor ... Ed. by Frederick Ignatius Antrobus ... St. Louis, Mo., B. Herder, 1898- v. 23 cm. "Complete titles of books frequently quoted in vol. i and ii": p. vol. i, p. xi-xiv. [Full name: Ludwig Friedrich August freiherr Pastor von Camperfelen] [BX955.P35 1898] 15-13996
1. Popes—Hist. I. Antrobus, Frederick Ignatius, 1837-1903, ed. II. Title.

RANKE, Leopold von, 1795-1886. 253
The ecclesiastical and political history of the popes of Rome during the sixteenth and seventeenth centuries. By Leopold Ranke ... Translated from the German by Sarah Austin ... Philadelphia, Lea & Blanchard, 1841. 2 v. 24 cm. [BX955.R3 1841] 16-24732
1. Popes—Hist. I. Austin, Sarah (Taylor) Mrs. 1793-1867, tr. II. Title. III. Title: Translation of Die romischen papste, lhre kirche und lhr staat im 16, und 17, jahrhundert.

RANKE, Leopold von, 1795-1886. 289
History of the popes; their church and state, by Leopold von Ranke ... tr. by E. Fowler; with a special introduction by William Clark ... Rev. ed. ... New York, The Colonial press [1901] 3 v. fronts., plates, ports., facsims. (part col.) 24 cm. (Added t.-p.: The World's great classics) [BX955.R35] [PN6013.W8 vol. 48-50] 253 1-15121
1. Popes—Hist. I. Fowler, E., tr. II. Title.

SEPPELT, Franz Xaver, 1883- 282
A short history of the popes, based on the latest researches, by Professor Francis X. Seppelt, D.D. and Professor Clement Loffler, PH.D.: authorized adaptation from the German by Horace A. Frommelt, edited by Arthur Preuss. St. Louis, Mo. and London, B. Herder book co., 1932. vi, 567 p. 23 1/2 cm. Adapted from F. X. Seppelt's "Papatgeschichte von den anfangen bis zur franzoslachan revolution" and Klemens Loffler's "Papstegeschichte von der franzusischen revolution his zur gegenwart." "Presents...the results of the researchers of Mann, Pastor, and other learned modern historians."--Pref. [BX955.S4] 32-10203
1. Popes—Hist. I. Loffler, Klemeus, 1881-1933 II. Frommelt, Horace Aloysius, 1891- tr. III. Preuss, Arthur, 1871-1934, ed. IV. Title.

Popes—Infallibility.

CHIRICO, Peter. 262'.131
Infallibility : the crossroads of doctrine / by Peter Chirico. Kansas City, [Kan.] : Sheed and Ward, c1977. p. cm. Includes index. [BX1806.C45] 77-3694 ISBN 0-8362-0704-1 : 20.00. ISBN 0-8362-0706-8 pbk. : 6.95
1. Popes—Infallibility. I. Title.

COULTON, George Gordon, 1858- 262.131
Papal infallibility, by G. G. Coulton ... London, The Faith press, ltd.; Milwaukee, The Morehouse publishing co. [1932] xix, 306 p. 19 cm. "First published, May, 1932." [BX1806.C6] 33-18087
1. Popes—Infallibility I. Title.

DOLLINGER, Johann Joseph Ignaz von, 1799-1890. 262.5'2
Letters from Rome on the Council, by Quirinus. New York, Da Capo Press, 1973. 2 v. 21 cm. (Europe, 1815-1945) Reprint of the 1870 ed. Translation of Romische Briefe vom Concil. [BX830 1869.D63] 78-127193 ISBN 0-306-70040-9 29.50 (Lib. ed.)
1. Vatican Council, 1869-1870. 2. Popes—Infallibility. I. Title. II. Series.

[DOLLINGER, Johann Joseph Ignaz von] 1799-1890. 262.131
The pope and the council. By Janus [pseud.] Authorized translation from the German. 2d ed. London [etc.] Rivingtons; New York, Scribner, Welford and co., 1869. xxix, 425, [1] p. 20 cm. "The substance of the earlier portion of this volume appeared in a series of articles ... in the Allgemeine seitung ... March 10-15, 1869."--Notice by the translator. Written by Dollinger in collaboration with J. Huber. [BX1806.D6 1869] 34-24396
1. Popes—Infallibility. 2. Papacy—Hist. 3. Old Catholicism. I. Huber, Johannes, 1830-1879, joint author. II. Title.

JAKI, Stanley L. 262.001
And on this rock : the witness of one land and two covenants / Stanley L. Jaki. Notre Dame, Ind. : Ave Maria Press, c1978. 125 p. : ill. ; 21 cm. Includes bibliographical references. [BS2515.J28] 78-59925 ISBN 0-87793-161-5 : 2.95
1. Peter, Saint, apostle. 2. Popes—Infallibility. 3. Baniyas, Syria. I. Title.

KIRIEEV, Aleksandr Aleksieevich, 1833-1910. 262.131
Correspondence on infallability [!] between a father Jesuit and General Alexander Kireeff. (An eastern Orthodox) [New York] 1896. 96 p. 18 1/2 cm. [BX1806.K5] 38-19321
1. Popes—Infallibility. I. Title.

MACGREGOR, Geddes. 262.13
The Vatican revolution. Boston, Beacon Press [1957] xiv, 226p. 22cm. 'The text of the Vatican decrees, with an English translation and notes': p.[163]-197. Bibliography: p.205-216. [BX1806.M25] 57-6524
1. Popes—Infalilbility. I. Vatican Council, 1869-1870. Acta et decreta. II. Title.

Popes—Infallibility—Collected works.

NEWMAN, John Henry, Cardinal, 1801-1890. 220.1'3'08
The theological papers of John Henry Newman on Biblical inspiration and on infallibility / selected, edited, and introduced by J. Derek Holmes. Oxford : Clarendon Press ; New York : Oxford University Press, 1979. p. cm. Includes indexes. Bibliography: p. [BS480.N424 1979] 78-41118 ISBN 0-19-920081-5 : 17.95
1. Catholic Church—Infallibility—Collected works. 2. Bible—Inspiration—Collected works. 3. Popes—Infallibility—Collected works. I. Holmes, J. Derek. II. Title.

Popes—Infallibility—History.

HASLER, August. 262'.131
How the Pope became infallible : Pius IX and the politics of persuasion / August Bernhard Hasler ; introd. by Hans Kung ; translated by Peter Heinegg. 1st ed. Garden City, N.Y. : Doubleday, 1981. xi, 383 p. : ill. ; 22 cm. Translation of Wie der Papst unfehlbar wurde. Includes index. Bibliography: p. [355]-359. [BX1806.H3813] 19 79-6851 ISBN 0-385-15851-3 : 14.95
1. Pius IX, Pope 1792-1878. 2. Popes—Infallibility—History. I. Title.

Popes—Primacy.

BIEL, Gabriel, d.1495. 262'.13
Defensorium obedientiae apostolicae et alia documenta. Edited and translated by Heiko A. Oberman, Daniel E. Zerfoss, and William J. Courtenay. Cambridge, Belknap Press of Harvard University Press, 1968. vii, 387 p. 24 cm. Original Latin text and English translation on facing pages. Bibliography: p. 63-64. [BX1805.B513 1968] 68-14269
1. Popes—Primacy. 2. Conciliar theory. 3. Catholic Church in Germany. I. Oberman, Heiko Augustinus, ed. II. Zerfoss, Daniel E., ed. III. Courtenay, William J., ed. IV. Title.

COUGHLIN, Charles Edward, 1891- 262'.12
Bishops versus Pope, by Charles E. Coughlin. [Bloomfield Hills, Mich., Helmet and Sword, [1969] viii, 220 p. 24 cm. Cover title: Bishops versus the Pope. [BX1751.2.C68] 74-12617
1. Catholic Church—Doctrinal and controversial works—Catholic authors. 2. Popes—Primacy. 3. Bishops. I. Title.

DVORNIK, Francis, 1893- 262.131
Byzantium and the Roman primacy. New York, Fordham University Press [1966] 176 p. 22 cm. Includes bibliographical references. [BX324.3.D813] 66-14187
1. Catholic Church—Relations—Orthodox Eastern Church—History. 2. Orthodox Eastern Church—Relations—Catholic Church History. 3. Popes—Primacy. I. Title.

JOURNET, Charles. 262.11
The primacy of Peter from the Protestant and from the Catholic point of view; translated from the French by John Chapin. Westminster, Md., Newman Press, 1954. 144p. 22cm. [BX1805.J68] 54-12533
1. Popes—Primacy. 2. Apostolic succession. 3. Catholic Church—Relations—Protestant churches. 4. Protestant churches—Relations— Catholic Church. 5. Cullmann, Oscar. Petrus. I. Title.

PAPAL primacy and the universal church / edited by Paul C. Empie and T. Austin Murphy. Minneapolis : Augsburg Pub. House, [1974] 255 p. ; 18 cm. (Lutherans and Catholics in dialogue ; 5) Includes bibliographical references. [BX1805.P24] 74-83329 ISBN 0-8066-1450-1 : 1.95 262'.13
1. Lutheran Church—Relations—Catholic Church. 2. Catholic Church—Relations—Lutheran Church. 3. Popes—Primacy. I. Empie, Paul C., ed. II. Murphy, Thomas Austin, 1911- ed. III. Title. IV. Series.

PRIMACY of Peter (The) 262.13
[by] J. Meyendorff, N. Afanassieff [others. Tr. from French] London, Faith Pr. [dist. Westminster, Md., Canterbury, c.1963] 134p. 23cm. (Lib. of Orthodox theology, no. 1) Bibl. 63-5439 2.50
1. Peter, Saint, apostle. 2. Popes—Primacy. 3. Church—History of doctrines. I. Meyendorff, Jean, 1926- II. Afanas'ev, Nikolai III. Series.

SHARROCK, David John. 262.132
The theological defense of papal power by St. Alphonsus de Liguori. Washington, Catholic University of America Press, 1961. viii, 137 p. 23 cm. (Catholic University of America. Studies in sacred theology, no. 119) Abstract of thesis -- Catholic University of America. Bibliography: p. 128-135. [BX1805.S5] 62-2305
1. Popes — Primacy. 2. Liguori, Alfonso Maria de', Saint, 1696-1787. I. Title. II. Series: Catholic University of America. School of Sacred Theology. Studies in sacred theology, 2d ser., no. 119

Popes—Primacy—Controversial literature.

LAMPING, A. J. 262'.13
Ulrichus Velenus (Oldrich Velensky) and his treatise against the papacy / by A. J. Lamping. Leiden : Brill, 1976. viii, 291 p. ; 24 cm. (Studies in medieval and Reformation thought : v. 19) Thesis—Leiden. "In hoc libello ... ": p. [219]-276. Includes indexes. Bibliography: p. [277]-284. [BX1805.V363L35] 76-462277 ISBN 9-00-404397-7 : fl 94.00
1. Velenus, Ulrichus. Petrum Romam non venisse. 2. Popes—Primacy—Controversial literature. I. Velenus, Ulrichus. Petrum

Romam non venisse. 1976. II. Title. III. Series.

Popes—Primacy—History.

OHLIG, Karl-Heinz, 1938- 262'.13
Why we need the Pope : the necessity and limits of Papal primacy / Karl-Heinz Ohlig ; translated by Robert C. Ware. St. Meinrad, Ind. : Abbey Press, 1975. x, 152 p. ; 21 cm. (A Priority edition) Translation of Braucht die Kirche einen Papst? Includes bibliographical references. [BX1805.O3613] 75-19924 ISBN 0-87029-053-3 pbk. : 3.95
1. Popes—Primacy—History. I. Title.

Popes—Prophecies.

BANDER, Peter. 262'.13
The prophecies of St. Malachy. Introd. and commentary by Peter Bander. Foreword by Joel Wells. Pref. by Archbishop H. E. Cardinale. Staten Island, N.Y., Alba House [1970, c1969] 96 p. illus. 22 cm. [BX957.B3 1970] 74-125419 ISBN 0-8189-0189-6 2.95
1. Popes—Prophecies. I. Malachy O'Morgair, Saint, 1094?-1148. Prophetia Sancti Malachiae Archipiescopi de summis pontificibus. English and Latin. 1970. II. Title.

Popes—Temporal power.

CARRERE, Jean, 1868-1932.
The pope, by Jean Carrere, translated by Arthur Chambers. New York, H. Holt and company [1926] 265 p. 23 cm. [BX1810.C33 1926] 26-16615
1. Popes—Temporal power. 2. Roman question. I. Chambers, arthur, tr. II. Title.

DAWSON, AEneas MacDonell, 1810-1894.
The temporal sovereignty of the pope, with relation to the state of Italy; a lecture delivered in St. Andrew's Catholic church, Ottawa, with additional facts and observations, by the Rev. AEn. McD. Dawson. London, Baltimore [etc.] Catholic publishing and book-selling company, 1860. vi p., 2 l., [3]-227 p., 1 l. 19 cm. [BX1810.D43] 44-11912
1. Popes—Temporal power. 2. Church and state in Italy. I. Title.

GOSSELIN, Jean Edme Auguste, 1787-1858.
The power of the pope during the middle ages; or, An historical inquiry into the orgin of the temporal power of the Holy see, and the constitutional laws of the middle ages relating to the deposition of sovereigns. With an introduction, on the honours and temporal privileges conferred on religion and on its ministers by the nations of antiquity, especially by the first Christian emperors. By M. Gosselin ... Translated by the Rev. Matthew Kelly ... Baltimore, J. Murphy & co.; London, C. Dolman, 1853. 2 v. 23 cm. (Half-title: Library of translations from select foreign literature. v. 1-2) Vol. ii has imprint: London, C. Dolhan, 1853. [BX1810.G6 1853a] 39-3710
1. Popes—Temporal power. 2. Church history—Middle ages. I. Kelly, Matthew, 1814-1858, tr. II. Title.

JEAN de Paris, 1240?-1306. 262'.132
On royal and papal power. A translation, with introd., of the De potestate regia et papali of John of Paris [by] Arthur P. Monahan. New York, Columbia University Press, 1974. xlix, 197 p. 23 cm. (Records of civilization: sources and studies, no. 90) At head of title: John of Paris. Includes bibliographical references. [BX1810.J413 1974] 73-16302 ISBN 0-231-03690-6 9.00
1. Popes—Temporal power. 2. Church and state. I. Monahan, Arthur P., 1928- ed. II. Title. III. Series.

MONTALEMBERT, Charles Forbes 922. Rene de Tryon, comte de, 1810-1870.
Pius ix. and France, in 1849 and 1859, by the Count de Montalembert ... Translated from the second French edition, by Madelaine V. Goddard. To which is added A. biographical sketch of the late Duke of Norfolk, by the same author. Boston, P. Donahoe, 1861. 70 p. 19 cm. The sketch of the Duke of Norfolk was translated from the Correspondent, for the Liverpool Northern press. [BX1373.M7] 3-32473
1. Plus ix, pope, 1792-1878. 2. Norfolk, Henry Granville Fitzalan-Howard, 14th duke of, 1815-1860. 3. Popes—Temporal power. I. Dahigren, Madeleine (Vinton) Mrs. 1825-1898, tr. II. Title.

ULLMANN, Walter, 1910- 262'.132
Medieval papalism : the political theories of the medieval canonists / by Walter Ullmann. Westport, Conn. : Hyperion Press, [1979] p. cm. Reprint of the 1949 ed. published by Methuen, London, which was issued as the 1948 Maitland Memorial lecture. Bibliography: p. [JC513.U5 1979] 79-1644 ISBN 0-88355-946-3 : 19.50
1. Popes—Temporal power. 2. Church and state in the Holy Roman Empire. I. Title. II. Series: Maitland memorial lectures ; 1948.

WATT, John A. 262.132
The theory of papal monarchy in the thirteenth century; the contribution of the canonists. New York, Fordham [1966. c. 1965] viii, 160p. 25cm. Bibl. [BX1810.W3] 65-12886 5.00
1. Popes—Temporal power. I. Title.

WIDDRINGTON, Roger, 1563-1640. 230'.2 s
Roger Widdrington last reioynder, 1619 / Thomas Preston. Ilkley : Scolar Press, 1976. 645, [35] p. ; 26 cm. (English recusant literature, 1558-1640 ; v. 280) (Series: Rogers, David Morrison, comp. English recusant literature, 1580-1640 ; v. 280.) Photoreprint ed. Includes original t.p.: Roger Widdringtons last reioynder to Mr. Thomas Fitz-Herberts reply concerning to oath of allegiance, and the Popes power to depose princes. [BX1750.A1E5 vol. 280] [BX1810] 262'.132 76-359810 ISBN 0-85967-281-6
1. Catholic Church—Doctrinal and controversial works—Catholic authors. 2. Popes—Temporal power. 3. Oaths. I. Title. II. Series.

[ZURCHER, George] 1852-
The apple of discord; or, Temporal power in the Catholic church, by a Roman Catholic ... Buffalo, N.Y., The Apple of discord co., 1905. 3 p. l., [9]-495 p. 20 1/2 cm. [BX1810.Z8] 5-33907
1. Popes—Temporal power. 2. Church and state in the U.S. I. Title.

Popes—Voyages and travels.

PALMER, Russell, 1917- 282'.092'4
John Paul II, a pictorial celebration / Russell Palmer. Huntington, Ind. : Our Sunday Visitor, c1980. 128 p. : ill. ; 29 cm. Bibliography: p. 128. [BX1378.5.P34] 79-92691 ISBN 0-87973-835-9 : 12.95
1. John Paul II, Pope, 1920- 2. Popes—Voyages and travels. 3. Papacy. I. Title.

UNITED Press International. 262.13
The pilgrim Pope in the New World, the Holy Land, and India. Text and pictures by United Press International. New York, Pocket Books, 1965. 1 v. (unpaged) illus. (part col.) ports. (part col.) 28 cm. (A Pocket book special) Paulus VI, Pope, 1897- [BX1378.3.U5] 65-29641
I. Title.

Popes—Voyages and travels—United States.

JOHN Paul II, 262'.13'0924 B
pilgrimage of faith : the first year in the life of the new Pope and the story of his visit to the United States / edited and illustrated by the National Catholic News Service ; with a foreword by Fulton J. Sheen. New York : Seabury Press, 1979. p. cm. "A Crossroad book." [BX1378.5.J65] 79-23105 ISBN 0-8164-2014-9 pbk. : 8.95 ISBN 0-8164-0109-8 : 17.50
1. Popes—Voyages and travels—United States. I. John Paul II, Pope, 1920- II. National Catholic News Service.

POPE John Paul II—he 262'.13'0924
came to us as a father ; pastoral visit to the United States / by the Daughters of Saint Paul. Boston, MA : St. Paul Editions, c1979. ca. 250 p. : chiefly ill. ; 25 cm. [BX1378.5.P66] 79-26624 ISBN 0-8198-0628-5 : 14.95
1. John Paul II, Pope, 1920- 2. Popes—Voyages and travels—United States. I. Daughters of St. Paul.

Popes—Voyages and travels—Washington, D.C.—Pictorial works.

MITCHELL, Mike, 1945- 282'.092'4
John Paul II in our Nation's Capital : a pastoral visit / photos. by Mike Mitchell ; written by Lee Edwards. [Washington, D.C.] : Archdiocese of Washington, c1979. 64 p. : col. ill. ; 31 cm. [BX1378.5.M57] 79-92209 pbk. : 10.45 20.95 9.95 20.95
1. John Paul II, Pope, 1920- — Iconography. 2. Popes—Voyages and travels—Washington, D.C.—Pictorial works. 3. Popes—Iconography. I. Edwards, Lee. II. Title.
Publisher's Address : 1721 Rhode Island Ave., N.W., Washington, DC 20036

Popoff, Haralan, 1907-

POPOFF, Haralan, 1907- 289.9 B
Tortured for his faith : an epic of Christian courage and heroism in our day / by Haralan Popov. Rev. ed. Grand Rapids, Mich. : Zondervan Pub. House, 1975. 140 p. ; 18 cm. [BX8764.Z8P62 1975] 76-360631 1.50
1. Popoff, Haralan, 1907- 2. Persecution—Bulgaria. 3. Prisoners—Bulgaria—Personal narratives. I. Title.

Popoff, Peter.

POPOFF, Peter. 269'.2'0924 B
Behind curtains of darkness a new fire is blazing / Peter Popoff. Upland, Calif. : Faith Messenger Publications, c1980. 194 p. : ill., [4] leaves of plates ; 21 cm. On spine: A new fire is blazing. [BV3785.P625A36] 19 80-126454 ISBN 0-938544-02-0 pbk. : 4.95
1. Popoff, Peter. 2. Bible—Publication and distribution—Communist countries. 3. Evangelists—United States—Biography. I. Title. II. Title: A new fire is blazing.

Popol vuh.

GIRARD, Rafael. 299'.7
Esotericism of the Popol Vuh / Raphael Girard ; translated from the Spanish with a foreword by Blair A. Moffett. 1st English ed. Pasadena, Calif. : Theosophical University Press, 1979. xiv, 359 p. : ill. ; 22 cm. Translation of Esoterismo del Popol-vuh. Includes index. [F1465.P84513] 78-74712 ISBN 0-911500-13-8 : 12.50 ISBN 0-911500-14-6 pbk. : 7.50
1. Popul-vuh. 2. Quiches—Religion and mythology. 3. Indians of Central America—Guatemala—Religion and mythology. I. Title.

JACKSON, Donald, 1895- 299'.7
Religious concepts in ancient America and in the Holy Land : as illustrated by the Sacred book of the Quiche Mayans and by the Bible : quotes, notes, and notions / Donald Jackson. 1st ed. Hicksville, N.Y. : Exposition Press, c1976. viii, 142 p. ; 22 cm. (An Exposition-university book) Bibliography: p. 141-142. [F1465.P8466] 76-363012 ISBN 0-682-48503-9 : 8.00
1. Popol vuh. 2. Bible—Criticism, interpretation, etc. 3. Quiches—Religion and mythology. I. Title.

SPENCE, Lewis, 1874-1955. 299'.7
The Popol vuh; the mythic and heroic sagas of the Kiches of Central America. New York, AMS Press [1972] 63 p. 19 cm. Reprint of the 1908 ed., which was issued as no. 16 of Popular studies in mythology, romance and folklore. Bibliography: p. [57]-59. [F1465.P875 1972] 75-139178 ISBN 0-404-53516-X 5.50
1. Popol vuh. 2. Quiches—Religion and mythology. I. Title. II. Series: Popular studies in mythology, romance and folklore, no. 16.

Popov, Ladin, 1915-

POPOV, Ladin, 1915- 272'.9 B
The fugitive / Ladin Popov, with Phil Streeter. Grand Rapids, Mich. : Zondervan Pub. House, c1981. 127 p. ; 18 cm. [BX8762.Z8P666] 19 81-16014 ISBN 0-310-44612-0 pbk. : 2.95
1. Popov, Ladin, 1915- 2. Pentecostals—Bulgaria—Biography. 3. Clergy—Bulgaria—Biography. I. Streeter, Phil. II. Title.

Population.

MEYER, Frederick Brotherton, 1847-
Religion and race-regeneration, by Rev. F. B. Meyer, B. A. ... London, New York [etc.] Cassell and company, limited, 1912. 61, [1] p. 17 cm. (New tracts for the times) [HB993.M4] 15-5779
1. Population. 2. Religion. 3. Eugenics. I. Title. II. Title: Raceregeneration.

Population transfers—Jews.

SCHECHTMAN, Joseph B. 1891- 325.5694
On wings of eagles; the plight, exodus, and homecoming of oriental Jewry. New York, T. Yoseloff [1961] 429 p. illus. 24 cm. Includes bibliography. [JV6348.J4S35] 61-6156
1. Population transfers—Jews. 2. Jews in the Levant. 3. Israel—Emigration and immigration I. Title.

Pornography.

WILLIAMS, Tom M. 241'.6'6
See no evil : Christian attitudes toward sex in art and entertainment / T. M. Williams. Grand Rapids, Mich. : Zondervan Pub. House, c1976. 102, [1] p. ; 18 cm. "Zondervan books." Bibliography: p. [103] [BV4597.6.W54] 75-21125 pbk. : 1.50
1. Pornography. 2. Sex in the arts—Moral and religious aspects. 3. Censorship. I. Title.

Pornography—Moral and religious aspects—Christianity.

COURT, John Hugh. 261.8
Pornography, a Christian critique / John H. Court. Downers Grove, Ill. : InterVarsity Press ; Exeter, Eng. : Paternoster Press, c1980. 96 p. ; 21 cm. (Outreach and identity ; no. 5) Includes bibliographical references. [BV4597.6.C68 1980] 19 80-7668 ISBN 0-87784-494-1 (InterVarsity Press : pbk.) : 2.95 ISBN 0-85364-293-1 (Paternoster Press : pbk.) : £1.50
1. Pornography—Moral and religious aspects—Christianity. I. Title. II. Series.

Porphyrius.

HULEN, Amos Berry. 921.9
... Porphyry's work against the Christians: an interpretation, by Amos Berry Hulen ... Scottdale, Pa., Printed by the Mennonite press, 1933. 54, [2] p. 25 1/2 cm. (Yale studies in religion. no. 1) "An essay based upon a dissertation submitted to the faculty of the Graduate school of Yale university ... for the degree of doctor of philosophy [1930]" Bibliography: p. [56] [BR164.P6H8 1930] 33-28786
1. Porphyrius. 2. Christianity. I. Title.

Port Elizabeth, Cape of Good Hope. St. Mary's collegiate church.

WIRGMAN, Augustus Theodore, 1846-1917.
The Collegiate church and parish of S. Mary, Port Elizabeth; a record of parochial history; A.D. 1825 to A.D. 1892. by the late Archdeacon Wirgman, D.D.; A.D. 1893 to A.D. 1924, by Canon Cuthbert Edward May ... London, New York [etc.] Longmans, Green and co., 1925. viii, 196 p. front., illus. (double facsim.) plates, ports. 22 cm. $2.00. [BX5693.P6W5] 25-4942
1. Port Elizabeth, Cape of Good Hope. St. Mary's collegiate church. I. Mayo, Cuthbert Edward, 1860- II. Title.

Port Keats Mission.

PYE, John. 266'.2'9429
The Port Keats story / by Bro. John Pye. Kensington, N.S.W. : J. Pye, 1973. 52 p. : ill. ; 21 cm. Cover title. [BV3660.N6P93] 75-330136 ISBN 0-9598787-0-X : 1.00
1. Port Keats Mission. 2. Missions to Australian aborigines—Northern Territory, Australia. 3. Missions, Catholic. I. Title.

Port Republic, N. J. Methodist Episcopal church.

COLLINS, Anna C. 287.
History of the Methodist Episcopal church on Port Republic and Smithville charge. Also, a sketch of the Presbyterian church at Port Republic, and the Friends' at Leeds' Point. Prepared by Anna C. Collins. [Camden, N. J., Printed at the Gazette printing house] 1892. 56 p. 19 cm. [BX8481.P75C6] 24-24510
1. Port Republic, N. J. Methodist Episcopal church. 2. Smithville, N. J. Methodist Episcopal church. 3. Port Republic, N. J. Presbyterian church. 4. Friends, Society of. Leeds Point, N. J. I. Title.

Port Royal.

CLARK, Ruth. 284'.84'0942
Strangers & sojourners at Port Royal; being an account of the connections between the British Isles and the Jansenists of France and Holland. New York, Octagon Books, 1972. xviii, 360 p. illus. 23 cm. Reprint of the 1932 ed. Bibliography: p. 278-304. [BX4730.C55 1972] 72-6953 ISBN 0-374-91664-0
1. Port Royal. 2. Jansenists. 3. Great Britain—Church history—Modern period, 1485- 4. Jansenists—Bibliography. I. Title.

ESCHOLIER, Marc, 1906- 284'.84
Port-Royal; the drama of the Jansenists. [1st American ed.] New York, Hawthorn Books [1968] 343 p. illus. 24 cm. Bibliography: p. 323-332. [BX4730.E67 1968] 68-19111
1. Port-Royal.

REA, Lilian.
The enthusiasts of Port-Royal, by Lilian Rea; with twelve illustrations. New York, C. Scribner's sons, 1912. xiv p., 2 l., 3-354 p., 1 l. front., pl., ports., plan 23 cm. "List of authorities": p. 339-345. [BX4730.R3] 13-10623
1. Port Royal. 2. Jansenista. I. Title.

REX, Walter E. 271'.5
Pascal's Provincial letters : an introduction / Walter E. Rex. London [etc.] : Hodder and Stoughton, 1977. 84 p. ; 22 cm. Label mounted on t.p.: Holmes & Meier Publishers, Inc., New York. Bibliography: p. 80-83. [BX4720.P4R43] 78-312159 ISBN 0-340-20203-3 : pbk. : 4.50
1. Pascal, Blaise, 1623-1662. Les provinciales. 2. Jesuits. 3. Port Royal. 4. Jansenists. I. Title.

Port-Royal des Champs (Abbey of Ciatercian nuns)

SANDERS, Ella Katharine. 922
Angelique of Port Royal, 1591-1661, by E. K. Sanders ... London, Society for promoting Christian knowledge; New York and Toronto, The Macmillan co., [1928] xxxviii, 408 p. 2 port. (incl. front.) 22 1/2 cm. "First published 1905." "Authorities for the life of Angelique Arnauld": p. 402-408. [BX4735.A8S3] 44-49627
1. Arnauld, Jacqueline Marie Angelique, 1591-1661. 2. Port-Royal des Champs (Abbey of Ciatercian nuns) I. Title.

Portal, Fernand, 1855-1926.

HEMMER, H., ed. 922.244
Fernand Portal (1855-1926); apostle of unity. From the French Monsieur Portal. Tr. and ed. by Arthur T. Macmillan. New York, St. Martin's Press [c.]1961[ ] 181p. illus. Bibl. 61-3680 5.75 bds.,
1. Portal, Fernand, 1855-1926. 2. Malines conversations, 1921-1925. 3. Christian I. Title.

Porter, Charles Henry, 1811-1841.

SMITH, Elizur Goodrich, 1802- 1873. 922
Memoir of Charles Henry Porter, a student in theology. By E. Goodrich Smith ... New York, American tract society [1849] 168 p. 16 cm. [BR1715.P5S6] 7-23354
1. Porter, Charles Henry, 1811-1841. I. Title.

Porter, Ebenezer, 1772-1834.

MATTHEWS, Lyman, 1801- 1866. 922.573
Memoir of the life and character of Ebenezer Porter, D.D., late president of the Theological seminary, Andover. By Lyman Matthews ... Boston, Perkins & Marvin; Philadelphia, H. Perkins, 1837. 396 p. front. (port.) 19 1/2 cm. [BX7260.P68M3] 35-35746
1. Porter, Ebenezer, 1772-1834. I. Title.

Porter, Frank Chamberlin, 1859-1946.

HARRISVILLE, Roy A. 220.6'092'4 B
Frank C. Porter, pioneer in American Biblical interpretation / Roy A. Harrisville. [Missoula, Mont.] : Scholars Press for the Society of Biblical Literature, [1976] p. cm. (SBL studies in American Biblical scholarship ; 1) "Part one." Bibliography: p. [BS501.P67H37] 76-4498 ISBN 0-89130-104-6
1. Porter, Frank Chamberlin, 1859-1946. I. Title. II. Series: Society of Biblical Literature. SBL studies in American Biblical scholarship ; 1.

STUDIES in early Christianity, edited by Sherley Jackson Case, presented to Frank Chamberlin Porter and Benjamin Wisner Bacon by friends and fellow-teachers in America and Europe. New York & London, The Century co. [c1928] ix. 467 p. front. (2 port.) 23 cm. "Publications of Frank Chamberlin Porter": p. 440-443: "Publications of Benjamin Wisner Bacon": 443-457. [BR50.S83] 28-10979 204
1. Porter, Frank Chamberlin, 1859- 2. Bacon, Benjamin Wisner, 1860-1932. 3. Christianity—Addresses, essays, lectures. 4. Bible. N.T.—Criticism, Interpretation, etc. 5. Church history—Primitive and early church. 6. Bible—Criticism, interpretation, etc.—N.T. I. Case, Shirley Jackson, 1872- ed.
Contents omitted.

Porter, Josias Leslie, 1823-1889.

PORTER, Josias Leslie, 1823-1889. 915.694'4'0450925
Jerusalem, Bethany and Bethlehem / by J. L. Porter. Jerusalem : Ariel Pub. House, [1976] xxii, 168 p. : ill. ; 28 cm. Reprint of the 1886 ed. Includes index. [DS109.P65 1976] 77-366140
1. Porter, Josias Leslie, 1823-1889. 2. Jerusalem—Description. 3. Palestine—Description and travel. I. Title.

Porter, Mrs. Deborah H. (Cushing) 1809-1847.

DRINKWATER, Anne T. 922
Memoir of Mrs. Deborah H. Porter, wife of Rev. C. G. Porter, of Bangor. By Anne T. Drinkwater ... Portland, Me., Sanborn & Carter, 1848. 269 p. 19 cm. [BR1725.P57D7] 38-29411
1. Porter, Mrs. Deborah H. (Cushing) 1809-1847. I. Title.

Porter, Mrs. Eliza Emily (Chappell) 1807-1888.

PORTER, Mary Harriet, 1846- 920.7
Eliza Chappell Porter, a memoir by Mary H. Porter. Published for the benefit of the Oberlin missionary home association, Oberlin. Ohio. Chicago, New York, Fleming H. Revell company [1893] 4 p. l., v-ix, [1], 9-366 p. front., ports. 20 cm. [BX7260.P69P6] 36-23983
1. Porter, Mrs. Eliza Emily (Chappell) 1807-1888. I. Title.

Portiuncula indulgence.

HUBER, Raphael M. father, 1883 265.66
The portiuncula indulgence from Honorius III to Pius XI, by Raphael M. Huber ... New York, J. W. Wagner, inc., 1938. xxii, 207 p. front. 23 1/2 cm. (Franciscus studies, vol. XIX) "Abbreviations and bibliography": p. xviii-xxii. "Chronological list of pontifical bulls, decrees (1) etc., quoted in this treatise": p. 195-197. [Secular name: Louis Thomas Huber] [BX3601.F7 no. 19] [BX2282.H8] (271.3082 38-34975
1. Portiuncula indulgence. I. Title.

Portland, Conn. Trinity church.

MCLEAN, Julia Norton. 283.7466
History of Trinity church, Portland, Connecticut, 1788-1938 [by] Julia Norton McLean. Portland, Conn. [Middlesex county printery] 1938. 197, [1] p. illus. (incl. ports.) 23 cm. [BX5980.P68T715] 39-12137
1. Portland, Conn. Trinity church. I. Title.

Portland, Me. Cathedral Church of Saint Luke—History

BRINKLER, Alfred, 1880- 283'.741'9
The Cathedral Church of Saint Luke, Portland, Maine; a history of its first century. Portland, Me., House of Falmouth [1967] 86 p. illus. 22 cm. [BX5980.P7C3] 67-9452
1. Portland, Me. Cathedral Church of Saint Luke — Hist. I. Title.

Portland. Me. (Diocese)—Directories

ANNUAL Catholic information guide and business directory, complete; listing clergy, parishes, missions, schools and hospitals, Diocese of Portland, Maine. [Portland. Church World Pub. Co.] v. 28cm. [BX1417.P63A5] 59-47667 282.7419
1. Portland. Me. (Diocese)—Direct.

PORTLAND, Me. High street Congregational church. 285.
Covenant, articles of faith, and rules of High street Congregational church, Portland, Me., with a catalogue of its members. January, 1858. Printed for the use of the members. Portland, B. Thurston's steam press, 1855. 68 p. 18 cm. [BX7255.P7H5] 18-10321
I. Title.

Portland, Or. Congregation Beth Israel.

NODEL, Julius J 1915- 296.0979549
The ties between; a century of Judaism on America's last frontier; the human story of Congregation Beth Israel, Portland, Oregon, the oldest Jewish congregation in the Pacific Northwest, by Julius J. Nodel in association with Alfred Apsler. Portland, Or., Temple Beth Israel, 1959. 194p. illus. 24cm. [BM225.P63B42] 59-65510
1. Portland, Or. Congregation Beth Israel. I. Title.

Portland, Or. First Unitarian church.

WILBUR, Earl Morse, 1866- 288.
A history of the First Unitarian church, of Portland, Oregon. 1867-1892. Together with a sketch of the life of Rev. Thomas Lamb Eliot, its first pastor. And an account of the exercises of the twenty-fifth anniversary. By Earl Morse Wilbur. Portland, First Unitarian church, 1893. 95, [1] p. front., plates, ports. 19 1/2 cm. [BX9861.P8F5] 26-12131
1. Portland, Or. First Unitarian church. 2. Eliot, Thomas Lamb, 1841- I. Title.

Portland, Or.—Religion.

GUSTAFSON, Cloyd V 209.79549
A doctrinal survey of selected Protestant groups in Portland Oregon and vicinity. [Portland? 1956] unpaged. 28cm. [BR560.P82G8] 56-40844
1. Portland, Or.—Religion. 2. Sects—Oregon—Portland. I. Title.

Portraits, Israeli.

FREULICH, Roman. 915.694'03'5
The faces of Israel; a photographic commentary on the words of Koheleth [by] Roman Freulich and Joan Abramson. New York, T. Yoseloff [1972] 203 p. illus. 29 cm. Picture captions in English, French, and Hebrew from the Book of Ecclesiastes. [DS108.5.F69] 77-124200 ISBN 0-498-07639-3 12.50
1. Portraits, Israeli. 2. Israel—Description and travel—Views. I. Abramson, Joan, joint author. II. Title.

Portsmouth, Va. Emanuel African Methodist Episcopal church.

STEWART, Charles E. of Portsmouth, Va. 287.8755
... The African society becomes Emmanuel African Methodist Episcopal church, Portsmouth, Virginia; one hundred and seventy-two long years ... [By] Charles E. Stewart ... [Norfolk, Va., Guide quality press, 1944] 76 p. front. (ports.) 22 1/2 cm. At head of title: 1772-1944. "Bibliographical": p. 75. [BX8481.P76E58] 45-16718
1. Portsmouth, Va. Emanuel African Methodist Episcopal church. I. Title.

Portsmouth, Va. Monumental Methodist Church.

MONROE, Dorothy Fleet.
History of Monumental Methodist Church, 1772-1966. [Portsmouth, Va., 1966] 49 p. 22 cm. Bibliography: p. 49. 68-106955
1. Portsmouth, Va. Monumental Methodist Church. I. Title.

Positivism.

BRIDGES, John Henry, 1832- 1906. 146
Illustrations of positivism: a selection of articles from the "Positivist review" in science, philosophy, religion, and politics. By John Henry Bridges ... With a preface by Edward Spencer Beesly. New ed., enl. and classified, ed. by H. Gordon Jones. Chicago, The Open court publishing co., 1915. xiii, 480 p. 23 cm. [B831.B7] 16-15074
1. Positivism. I. Jones, Hedley Gordon, ed. II. Title.

COMTE, Auguste, 1798-1857.
The Positive philosophy of Auguste Comte. Translated by Harriet Martineau. New York, W. Gowans, 1868. 838 p. 25 cm. [Full name: Isidore Auguste Marie Francois Xavier Comte] [B2208.M2] E 16
1. Positivism. I. Martineau, Harriet, 1802-1876, tr. II. Title.

COMTE, Auguste, 1798-1857.
The Positive philosophy of Auguste Comte. Tr. by Harriet Martineau. Chicago, New York [etc.] Belford, Clarke & co. [1880-] 838 p. 25 cm. [Full name: Isidore Auguste Marie Francois Xavier Comte] [B2223.E5M3 1880] 17-14863
1. Positivism. I. Martineau, Harriet, 1802-1876, tr. II. Title.

HARRISON, Frederic, 1831- 1923. 201
The positive evolution of religion, its moral and social reaction. Freeport, N.Y., Books for Libraries Press [1971] xx, 267 p. 23 cm. (Essay index reprint series) Reprint of

the 1913 ed. [B831.H5 1971] 74-142641 ISBN 0-8369-2053-8
1. Positivism. 2. Religion. I. Title.

HARRISON, Frederic, 1831-1923. 146
The positive evolution of religion, its moral and social reaction, by Frederic Harrison, D.C.L. New York, G. P. Putnam's sons, 1913. xx p., 1 l., 267 p. 21 1/2 cm. (On cover: The Science series. [32]) "The substance of a series of public discourses given by me at different times at Newton hall ... The first four essays ... have never been published, the succeeding essays appeared in the Positivist review June, 1911 to June, 1912."--Note. [B831.H5] 13-1729
1. Positivism. 2. Religion. I. Title.

MILL, John Stuart, 1806-1873.
The positive philosophy of Auguste Comte, by John Stuart Mill. Boston, William V. Spencer, 1866. 182 p. 20 1/2 cm. A 34
1. Comte, Auguste, 1798-1857. 2. Positivism. I. Title.

SELLARS, Roy Wood, 1880-
Evolutionary naturalism, by Roy Wood Sellars... Chicago, London, The Open court publishing company, 1922. xiii, 343, [5] p. 21 cm. [BD581.S4] 22-1392
1. Positivism. I. Title.

*SVANCARA-HLOSKOVA, Katarina 248.42
The philosophy of positive life. New York, Carlton [c.1963] 291p. 21cm. (Reflection bk.) 3.95
I. Title.

Pospishil, Victor J. The quest for an Ukrainian Catholic Patriarchate.

MALONEY, George A., 1924- 262'.13
Critique of Msgr. Pospishil's The quest for an Ukrainian Catholic Patriarchate, by George A. Maloney and Eva Piddubcheshen. Philadelphia, Society for the Promotion of the Patriarchal System in the Ukrainian Catholic Church, 1972. 17 p. ports. 26 cm. [BX4711.634.M35] 74-151189
1. Catholic Church. Byzantine rite (Ukranian)—Doctrinal and controversial works. 2. Pospishil, Victor J. The quest for an Ukrainian Catholic Patriarchate. I. Piddubcheshen, Eva, joint author. II. Title.

Post-communion prayers.

KROSNICKI, Thomas A. 264'.0201
Ancient patterns in modern prayer, by Thomas A. Krosnicki. Washington, Catholic University of America Press, 1973. viii, 309 p. 24 cm. (Catholic University of America. Studies in Christian antiquity, no. 19) Originally presented as the author's thesis, Pontificium Institutum Liturgicum. "Postcommunion prayers and their sources" (p. 151-272) consists of the Latin text of the Postcommunion prayers from the Roman Missal of Paul VI (1970) Bibliography: p. 281-288. [BX2015.74.K76 1973] 74-172790 20.00
1. Post-communion prayers. I. Catholic Church. Liturgy and ritual. Post-Communion. 1973. II. Title. III. Series.

Post, Truman Marcellus, 1810-1886.

POST, Truman Augustus. 922.573
Truman Marcellus Post, D. D., a biography, personal and literary, by T. A. Post. Boston and Chicago, Congregational Sunday-school and publishing society [1891] xv, 507 p. front., plates, port. 22 cm. [BX7260.P7P6] 36-16654
1. Post, Truman Marcellus, 1810-1886. I. Congregational Sunday-school and publishing society. II. Title.

Posture in worship—Early works to 1800.

BRADSHAW, William, 1571-1618. 264
A proposition concerning kneeling : (Amsterdam?), 1605 / William Bradshaw. Norwood, N.J. : W.J. Johnson ; Amsterdam : Theatrum Orbis Terrarum, 1979. 29 p. ; 15 cm. (The English experience, its record in early printed books published in facsimile ; no. 912) Reprint of the 1605 ed. Reproduction of STC 3524. [BV197.K58B7 1979] 19 79-84092 ISBN 90-221-0912-7 pbk. : 4.00
1. Posture in worship—Early works to 1800. I. Title. II. Series: English experience, its record in early printed books published in facsimile ; no. 912.

Potawatomi Indians—Missions.

BAROUX, Louis, 1817-1897. 266'.2'7745
Correspondence of Rev. Louis Baroux, missionary apostolic of Michigan, to Rev. M. J. De Neve, superior of the American College at Louvain / translated from the French by E. D. Kelly. [Berrien Springs, Mich. : Hardscrabble Books, 1976] 95 p. : ill. ; 19 cm. Translation of Lettre de M. l'abbe Baroux, missionnaire apostolique du Michigan, a M. J. Deneve. Half-title: An early Indian mission. Added title: History of the Pottawatomies. Photoreprint ed. of the 1913 ed. published by E. D. Kelly, Ann Arbor, Mich. [E99.P8B313 1976] 75-28671 ISBN 0-915056-04-6 : 4.50
1. Catholic Church—Missions. 2. Baroux, Louis, 1817-1897. 3. Deneve, Jean, d. 1898? 4. Potawatomi Indians—Missions. 5. Missions—Michigan. I. Deneve, Jean, d. 1898? II. Title: An early Indian mission. III. Title: History of the Pottawatomies.

Potter, Alonzo, bp., 1800-1865.

HOWE, Mark Antony DeWolfe, bp., 1808-1895. 922.373
Memoirs of the life and services of the Rt. Rev. Alonzo Potter, D.D., LL.D., bishop of the Protestant Episcopal church in the diocese of Pennsylvania. By M. A. DeWolfe Howe ... Philadelphia, J. B. Lippincott & co., 1871. 427 p. incl. front. port. 22 cm. [BX5995.P64H6] 35-29963
1. Potter, Alonzo, bp., 1800-1865. I. Title.

Potter, Andrew, 1886-1951.

SCANTLAN, Sam W 922.673
Andrew Potter, Baptist builder. [Oklahoma City c1955] 204p. illus. 21cm. [BX6495.P55S35] 58-25951
1. Potter, Andrew, 1886-1951. I. Title.

Potter, Henry Codman, bp., 1834-1908.

HODGES, George, 1856-1919. 922.
Henry Codman Potter, seventh bishop of New York, by George Hodges ... New York, The Macmillan Company, 1915. xiii, 386 p. front., ports. 22 1/2 cm. [BX5995.P7H6] 15-20949
1. Potter, Henry Codman, bp., 1834-1908. I. Title.

POTTER, Henry Codman, bp., 1834-1908. 286.
Reminiscences of bishops and archbishops, by Henry Codman Potter, bishop of New York ... New York and London, G. P. Putnam's sons, 1906. xii, 225 p. 13 port. (incl. front.) 23 cm. [BX5990.P6] 6-33595
I. Title.
Contents omitted.

POTTER, Henry Codman, bp., 1834-1908. 252.
Waymarks, 1870-1891; being discourses, with some account of their occasions, by Henry C. Potter ... New York, E. P. Dutton and company, 1892. viii, 383 p. 19 cm. [BX5937.P7W3] 12-37805
I. Title.

SHEERIN, James, 1865- 922.373
Henry Codman Potter, an American metropolitan, by James Sheerin ... foreword by Ernest Milmore Stires ... New York [etc.] Fleming H. Revell company [c1933] xvi, 17-196 p. front. (port.) 21 cm. [BX5995.P7S5] 34-5198
1. Potter, Henry Codman, bp., 1834-1908. I. Title.

Potter, John, 1803-1878.

BREED, William Pratt, 1816-1889. 922.573
The model Christian worker, John Potter. By the Rev. Wm. P. Breed ... Philadelphia, Presbyterian board of publication [1879] 80 p. 18 cm. [BX9225.P6B7] 36-24295
1. Potter, John, 1803-1878. I. Presbyterian church in the U. S. A. Board of publication. II. Title.

Potter, Mary, 1847-1913.

WORDLEY, Dick. 271'.97 B
No one dies alone / [by] Dick Wordley, with assisted creative research by Sister Jeanne Hyland and Frank S. Greenop. [Sydney] : Australian Creative Workshop for The Little Company of Mary, 1976. 244 p., [16] p. of col. plates : ill. ; 25 cm. [BX4390.Z8W67] 77-373919 ISBN 0-909246-33-5 : 14.95
1. Potter, Mary, 1847-1913. 2. Little Company of Mary—History. 3. Nuns—Australia—Biography. I. Hyland, Jeanne, joint author. II. Greenop, Frank Sydney, joint author. III. Title.

Potter, Philip.

GENTZ, William H., 1918- 262'.001 B
The world of Philip Potter [by] William H. Gentz. New York, Friendship Press [1974] 96 p. illus. 20 cm. Includes excerpts from P. Potter's speeches. Includes bibliographical references. [BX6.8.P67G46] 74-9918 ISBN 0-377-00006-X 2.95 (pbk.)
1. Potter, Philip. I. Potter, Philip. The world of Philip Potter. 1974. II. Title.

Potter, Rockwell Harmon, 1874-

HARTFORD theological seminary, Hartford, Conn. Alumni association. 252.058
Sermons for today, a tribute to Rockwell Harmon Potter, edited by the Alumni association of Hartford theological seminary. Boston, The Pilgrim press, 1946. viii, 247 p. front. (port.) 22 cm. [BX7233.A1P6] 46-8693
1. Potter, Rockwell Harmon, 1874- 2. Congregational churches—Sermons 3. Sermons, English. I. Title.
Contents omitted.

Potterbaum, Charlene.

POTTERBAUM, Charlene. 248'.2'0924 B
His eye is on the sparrow so ... this is really for the birds / Charlene Potterbaum. Plainfield, N.J. : Logos International, c1979. ix, 190 p. ; 21 cm. On spine: This is really for the birds. [BR1725.P63A34] 79-83788 ISBN 0-88270-354-4 pbk. : 3.50
1. Potterbaum, Charlene. 2. Christian biography—United States. 3. Christian life—1960- I. Title. II. Title: This is really for the birds.

POTTERBAUM, Charlene. 248'.4
Thanks, Lord, I needed that! / By Charlene Potterbaum. Plainfield, N.J. : Logos International, c1977. ix, 155 p. : ill. ; 20 cm. [BR725.P63A35] 77-86470 ISBN 0-88270-248-3 pbk. : 2.95
1. Potterbaum, Charlene. 2. Christian biography—United States. 3. Christian life—1960- I. Title.

Potts, Arthur Ninde, 1889-1895.

[POTTS, James Henry] 1848- 242
Little Arthur; or, The ministry of a child. A tribute to the memory of Arthur Ninde Potts. By his father. Cincinnati, Cranston & Curts; New York, Hunt & Eaton, 1895. 96 p. 3 port. (incl. front.) 1 illus. 16 cm. [BR1715.P6P6] 12-37794
1. Potts, Arthur Ninde, 1889-1895. I. Title.

Pottsville, Pa. First Methodist Episcopal church.

POTTSVILLE republican, Pottsville, Pa. 287.674817
History compiled for First Methodist Episcopal church, Pottsville, Penna., on the occasion of its centennial anniversary, May eleventh to eighteenth, nineteen hundred and thirty, by the "Pottsville evening republican"and "Pottsvill morning paper", Pottsville, Pennsylvania. [Pottsville] The J. H. Zerbey newspapers, inc. [1930] 128 p. incl. front., illus. 24 cm. [BX8481.P77A5] 32-3240
1. Pottsville, Pa. First Methodist Episcopal church. I. Pottsville morning paper, Pottsville, Pa. II. Title.

Potwin Christian Church.

SMITH, Elsie Higdon. 286'.6'78188
Potwin Christian Church. [North Newton, Kan., Printed by the Mennonite Press] 1969. 163 p. map, plates, ports. 24 cm. [BX6781.P6C5] 78-99962
1. Potwin Christian Church.

Poudhon, Pierre Joseph, 1809-1865. Systeme des contradictions economiques.

MARX, Karl, 1818-1883.
The poverty of philosophy, by Karl Marx, with an introduction by Frederick Engels. New York, International publishers [1936] 214 p. 22 cm. "Edited by C. P. Dutt and V. Chattopadbyaya." "Printed in the Union of Soviet Socialist Republics." A 36
1. Poudhon, Pierre Joseph, 1809-1865. Systeme des contradictions economiques. 2. Economics. I. Engels, Friedrich, 1820-1895. II. Dutt, C. P., ed. III. Chattopadhyaya, V., joint ed. IV. Title.

Pouget, Guillaume, 1847-1933.

GUITTON, Jean. 922.244
Abbee Pouget discourses. Translated from the French by Fergus Murphy with a biographical note by the Earl of Wicklow. Baltimore, Helicon Press [1959] 163p. 22cm. Translation of Portrait de m. Pouget. [BX4705.P658G83] 59-6711
1. Pouget, Guillaume, 1847-1933. I. Title.

Poughkeepsie, N.Y. Reformed Dutch Church—History

COON, Edwin C 917.47'33
Old First; a history of the Reformed Church of Poughkeepsie New York, by Edwin C. Coon. New York, William-Frederick Press, 1967. 81 p. illus. 21 cm. Bibliographical footnotes. [BX9531.P67R4] 67-30054
1. Poughkeepsie, N.Y. Reformed Dutch Church—Hist. I. Title.

Poverty.

BRETON, Valentin Marie 1877- 271.3
Lady poverty. Tr. from French by Paul J. Oligny. Chicago, Franciscan Herald [c.1963] 104p. 21cm. 63-12855 2.50
1. Poverty. 2. Franciscans. I. Title.

BRETON, Valentin Marie, 1877- 271.3
Lady poverty. Translated from the French by Paul J. Oligny. Chicago, Franciscan Herald Press [1963] 104 p. 21 cm. Translation of La pauvrete. Secular name: Henri Breton. [BX3603.B713] 63-12855
1. Poverty. 2. Franciscans. I. Title.

GODBEY, Samuel Macginis, 1850-
The Bible and the problem of poverty, by Samuel M. Godbey. New York, Chicago etc., F. H. Revell company [c1908] 1 p. l., [5]-193 p. 20 cm. "Two of the following chapters have appeared in the Methodist review."--Pref. [HX31.G7] 8-29265
1. Poverty. 2. Sociology, Christian. I. Title.

HENSEY, James Andrew, 1866-
Poverty and preaching; the truth about it, by James A. Hensey; introduction by George Cleaton Wilding. New York, Cincinnati, The Methodist book concern [c1916] 88 p. 17 cm. 16-6913 0.20
I. Title.

MCCORMACK, Arthur 261.8
World poverty and the Christian. New York, Hawthorn [c.1963] 158p. 22cm. (Twentieth cent. ency. of Catholicism, v.132. Section 13: Catholicism and science) Bibl. 63-13108 3.50 bds.,
1. Poverty. 2. Population. 3. Food supply. 4. Church and social problems—Catholic Church. I. Title.

POVERTY. 271
Translated by Lancelot C. Sheppard. Westminster, Md., Newman Press [1954] viii, 253p. 22cm. (Religious life, 4) 'Papers read at the ... annual conference held in Paris to consider the needs of French nuns.' Bibliographical footnotes. [BX2435.P313] 54-4812
1. Poverty. 2. Monasticism and religious orders. I. Sheppard, Lancelot Capel, 1906- tr.

RICHMOND, Legh, 1772-1827. 244
Annals of the poor. Containing The dairyman's daughter, (with considerable additions) The negro servant, and The young cottager by the Reverend Legh Richmond... New Haven, Whiting and Tiffany, Sign of Franklin's head, corner of College green, 1815. 288 p. 14 1/2 cm. [[BV4515.R]] A 31
I. Title. II. Title: Dairyman's daughter. III. Title: Negro servant. IV. Title: Young cottager.

TURNER, Sidney Joseph, 1899- 271
The vow of poverty... by Sidney Joseph Turner ... Washington, D.C., The Catholic university of America, 1929. xxxiv, 217, xxxv-xii, [1] p., 1 l., xiii-xiix p. 28 cm. (The Catholic university of America. Cannon [7] law studies. no. 54) Series note covered by label; The Catholic university of America. Studies in canon law, no. 54. Thesis (J.U.D.)--Catholic university of America, 1929. Biographical note. Bibliography: p. ix-xxx. [BX2435.T8 1929] 29-19218
1. Poverty. 2. Monasticism and religious orders. I. Title. II. Title: Poverty, The vow of.

Poverty in the Bible.

BOERMA, Conrad. 261.8'5
The rich, the poor—and the Bible / by Conrad Boerma ; [translated by John Bowden from the Dutch]. Philadelphia, Pa. : Westminister Press, [1980] c1979. 112 p. ; 21 cm. Translation of Kan ook een rijke zalig worden? British ed. published in 1979 under title: Rich man, poor man—and the Bible. Includes bibliographical references and index. [BS680.P47B6313 1980] 80-15337 ISBN 0-664-24349-5 : 5.95
1. Poverty in the Bible. 2. Wealth—Biblical teaching. I. Title.

Poverty (Virtue)

GOBRY, Ivan 248.2'7
hrough the needle's eye. Tr. by Edmond Bonin. Westminster, Md., Newman 1967. x. 175p. 22cm. Tr. of La pauvrete du laic. [BV4647.P6G63] 66-30459 5.50 bds.,
1. Poverty (Virtur) I. Title.

GOBRY, Ivan. 248.27
Through the needle's eye. Translated by Edmund Bonin. Westminster, Md., Newman Press, 1967. x, 175 p. 22 cm. Translation of La pauvrete du laic. [BV4647.P6G63] 66-30459
1. Poverty (Virtue) I. Title.

METZ, Johannes Baptist, 1928- 241.4
Poverty of spirit. Translated by John Drury. Glen Rock, N.J., Newman Press [1968] 53 p. 19 cm. Translation of Armut im Geiste. [BV4647.P6M43] 68-31045
1. Poverty (Virtue) I. Title.

PAULUS VI, Pope. 1897- 241
The Christian in the material world, by Giovanni Battista Cardinal Montini. [Translated by Michael M. McManus. 1st ed.] Baltimore, Helicon Press [1964, c1963] 71 p. 20 cm. Translation of Il Cristiano e il benessere temporale. [BV4647.P6P313] 64-14666
1. Poverty (Virtue) 2. Charity. I. Title.

PAULUS VI, Pope, 1897- 241
The Christian in the material world, by Giovanni Battista Cardinal Montini [Tr. from Italian by Michael M. McManus] Helicon [dist. New York, Taplinger, 1964, c.1963] 71p. 20cm. 64-14666 1.95
1. Poverty (Virtue) 2. Charity. I. Title.

Poverty (Virtue)—Biblical teaching.

GELIN, Albert. 220.8241
The poor of Yahweh. Translated by Mother Kathryn Sullivan. Collegeville, Minn., Liturgical Press [1964] 125 p. 20 cm. Bibliographical footnotes. [BS680.P47G4] 65-547
1. Poverty (Virtue)—Biblical teaching. I. Title.

Poverty (Virtue)—Biblical teaching—Addresses, essays, lectures.

GOSPEL poverty : 241'.6'99
essays in biblical theology / A. George ... [et al.] ; pref. by C. Koser ; translated and with a pref. by Michael D. Guinan. Chicago : Franciscan Herald Press, [1976] p. cm. Translation of La Pauvrete evangelique. Papers presented at a symposium on poverty held in Rome, June 23-25, 1970. Includes bibliographical references. [BS680.P47P3813] 76-44548 ISBN 0-8199-0610-7 : 6.95
1. Poverty (Virtue)—Biblical teaching—Addresses, essays, lectures. I. George, Augustin.

Poverty (Virtue)—History of doctrines.

LITTLE, Lester K. 241'.4
Religious poverty and the profit economy in medieval Europe / Lester K. Little. Ithaca, NY : Cornell University Press, 1978. xi, 267 p. ; 25 cm. Includes bibliographical references and index. [BV4647.P6L57 1978] 78-58630 ISBN 0-8014-1213-7 : 27.50
1. Poverty (Virtue)—History of doctrines. 2. Monastic and religious life—History of doctrines. 3. Civilization, Medieval. 4. Economic history—Medieval, 500-1500. I. Title.

MULHERN, Philip F. 301.44'1
Dedicated poverty: its history and theology [by] Philip F. Mulhern. Staten Island, N.Y., Alba House [1973] xiii, 246 p. 22 cm. Bibliography: p. [229]-240. [BV4647.P6M8] 77-86825 ISBN 0-8189-0250-7 5.95
1. Poverty (Virtue)—History of doctrines. I. Title.

Poverty (Virtue)—Quotations, maxims, etc.

LESS is more : 179'.9
the art of voluntary poverty / selected and edited by Goldian VandenBroeck ; with a pref. by E. F. Schumacher. New York : Harper & Row, 1978. xvi, 316 p. ; 20 cm. (Harper colophon books ; CN 581) [BV4647.P6L47] 77-2417 ISBN 0-06-090581-6 : pbk. : 4.95
1. Poverty (Virtue)—Quotations, maxims, etc. I. VandenBroeck, Goldian.

Powell, Adam Clayton, 1865-1953.

POWELL, Adam Clayton, 1865-1953. 286'.133 B
Against the tide : an autobiography / A(dam) Clayton Powell. New York : Arno Press, 1980 [c1938] x, 327 p. ; 21 cm. (The Baptist tradition) Reprint of the ed. published by R. R. Smith, New York. [BX6455.P63A3 1980] 79-52603 ISBN 0-405-12468-6 : 24.00
1. Powell, Adam Clayton, 1865-1953. 2. Baptists—Clergy—Biography. 3. Clergy—United States—Biography. I. Title. II. Series: Baptist tradition.

Powell, Joab, 1790-1873.

NICHOLS, Marie Leona (Hobbs) Mrs., 1880- 922.673
Joab Powell: homespun missionary, by M. Leona Nichols. Portland, Or., Metropolitan press, 1935. 6 p. l., 3-116 p. incl. front. (mounted port.) 21 1/2 cm. "Authorities": p. 115-116. [BX6495.P56N5] 36-7784
1. Powell, Joab, 1790-1873. I. Title.

Powell, Lyman Pierson, 1866-1946.

MACFARLAND, Charles Stedman, 1866- 922.373
Lyman Pierson Powell, pathfinder in education and religion, by Charles S. Macfarland; introduction by Albert Shaw. New York, Philosophical library [1947] 299 p. front. (port.) 22 1/2 cm. "Books and brochures [by Lyman Pierson Powell]": p. 293-294. [BX5995.P72M3] 47-3417
1. Powell, Lyman Pierson, 1866-1946. I. Title.

Powelson, Mrs, Julia Anne (Buell) 1854-1925.

HUESTON, Ethel (Powelson) Mrs., 1887- 922.773
Preacher's wife, by Ethel Hueston. Indianapolis, New York, The Bobbs-Merrill company [c1941] 308 p. 22 cm. "First edition." [BX8495.P64H8] 41-9453
1. Powelson, Mrs, Julia Anne (Buell) 1854-1925. I. Title.

Power, Emily, Mother, 1844-1909.

SYNON, Mary. 922.273
Mother Emily of Sinsinawa, American pioneer. Milwaukee, Bruce Pub. Co. [c1955] 279p. illus. 23cm. [BX4705.P6595S9] 55-1260
1. Power, Emily, Mother, 1844-1909. 2. Sisters of the Order of St. Dominic. Sinsinawa, Wis. I. Title.

Power resources—United States—Moral and religious aspects.

ENERGY ethics, a 261.8'5
Christian response / Dieter T. Hessel, editor. New York : Friendship Press, 1980. 170 p. ; 22 cm. Outgrowth of a seminar of the Energy Study Panel of the National Council of Churches of Christ in the U.S.A. held at Abiquiu, N.M., summer 1978. Bibliography: p. 156-165. [TJ163.25.U6E476] 79-19345 ISBN 0-377-00095-7 : 4.29
1. Power resources—United States—Moral and religious aspects. 2. Energy policy—United States—Moral and religious aspects. I. Hessel, Dieter T. II. National Council of the Churches of Christ in the United States of America. Energy Study Panel.

The Power (Society)

BAINBRIDGE, William Sims. 301.5'8
Satan's power : a deviant psychotherapy cult / William Sims Bainbridge. Berkeley : University of California Press, c1978. vii, 312 p. : ill. ; 24 cm. Includes index. Bibliography: p. 291-305. [BP605.P68B34] 77-80466 ISBN 0-520-03546-1 : 14.95
1. The Power (Society) I. Title.

Power (Theology)

LEVINGTON, John, Rev.
Power with God and with men. By Rev. John Levington... Philadelphia, Methodist book room, 1868. 333 p. 19 cm. 3-25946
I. Title.

MCCARTHY, Estelle, 1931- 248'.4
The power picture, by Estelle and Charles McCarthy. New York, Friendship Press [1973] 175 p. 18 cm. Includes bibliographical references. [BT745.M23] 72-14310 ISBN 0-377-03031-7 1.95 (pbk.)
1. Power (Theology) I. McCarthy, Charles, 1926- joint author. II. Title.

POWELL, Cyril H. 220.82314
The Biblical concept of power. London, Epworth Pr. [dist. Mystic, Conn., Verry, 1964, c.1963] vii, 222p. 23cm. Bibl. 64-5207 6.00
1. Power (Theology) I. Title.

WIRT, Sherwood Eliot. 232
Jesus power. [1st ed.] New York, Harper & Row [1972] xi, 132 p. 22 cm. Bibliography: p. 125-128. [BT769.W57] 72-78059 ISBN 0-06-069603-6 4.95
1. Power (Theology) I. Title.

Power (Theology)—History of doctrines.

HENGEL, Martin. 232
Christ and power / Martin Hengel ; translated by Everett R. Kalin. Philadelphia : Fortress Press, c1977. vii, 82 p. ; 22 cm. Translation of Christus und die Macht. Includes bibliographical references. [BT745.H4613] 76-62608 ISBN 0-8006-1256-6 pbk. : 3.25
1. Jesus Christ—Person and offices. 2. Power (Theology)—History of doctrines. I. Title.

Powers (Christian theology) Biblical teaching.

BERKHOF, Hendrikus. 235
Christ and the powers / Hendrik Berkhof ; translated from the Dutch by John H. Yoder. [2d ed.]. Scottdale, Pa. : Herald Press, c1977. 79 p. ; 20 cm. Translation of Christus en de machten. Includes bibliographical references. [BS2655.P66B4713 1977] 77-378727 ISBN 0-8361-1820-0 pbk. : 2.95
1. Bible. N.T. Epistles of Paul—Theology. 2. Powers (Christian theology) Biblical teaching. I. Title.

CARR, Wesley. 235'.3
Angels and principalities : the background, meaning, and development of the Pauline phrase hai archai kai hai exousiai / Wesley Carr. Cambridge [Eng.] ; New York : Cambridge University Press, 1982. p. cm. (Monograph series - Society for New Testament Studies ; 42) A revision of the author's thesis, University of Sheffield, 1974. Includes index. Bibliography: p. [BS2655.P66C37 1981] 19 80-41242 ISBN 0-521-23429-8 : 27.95
1. Bible. N.T. Epistles of Paul—Theology. 2. Powers (Christian theology)—Biblical teaching. 3. Powers (Christian theology)—History of doctrines—Early church, ca. 30-600. I. Title. II. Series: Novi Testamenti Societas. Monograph series ; 42.

ROSSELOT, F. P.
The Christian's power, by Rev. F. P. Rosselot. Dayton, O., United Brethren publishing house [1904] 71 p. 17 cm. (On verso of half-title: The devotional series) 9-20234
I. Title.

Powers, John R.

POWERS, John R. 282'.092'4 B
Do black patent-leather shoes really reflect up? / John Powers. Chicago : Regnery, [1975] p. cm. [BX4705.P664A32 1975] 75-13247 ISBN 0-8092-8177-5 : 7.95
1. Powers, John R. I. Title.

POWERS, John R. FIC
Do black patent leather shoes really reflect up? / John R. Powers. New York : Popular Library, 1976c1975. 256p. ; 18 cm. [BX4705.P664A32] 282.0924 pbk. : 1.75
1. Powers, John R. I. Title.
L.C. card no. for for 1975 Henry Regnery edition: 75-13247.

Powers, Walter Ellis, 1824-1916.

WHITE, Alexander Newton, 1844- 922.
The life of Rev. Walter Ellis Powers, by A. N. White. Pub. under the auspices of the Kentucky Baptist historical society. Louisville, Ky., Baptist book concern [1917] vii, 9-236 p. front., pl., ports. 19 1/2 cm. [BX6495.P6W5] 19-15258
1. Powers, Walter Ellis, 1824-1916. I. Kentucky Baptist historical society. II. Title.

Pragmatism.

GEIGER, Joseph Roy. 141
Some religious implications of pragmatism, by Joseph Roy Geiger. Chicago, Ill., The University of Chicago press [1919] v. 54 p. 25 cm. (On cover: Philosophic studies, issued under the direction of the Department of philosophy of the University of Chicago, number 9) Published also as thesis (PH. D.) University of Chicago, 1916. [B832.G36] 19-17588
1. Pragmatism. I. Title.

Pragmatism (Philosophy)

HUIZINGA, Arnold van Couthen Piccardt, 1874- 141
The American philosophy pragmatism critically considered in relation to present day theology, by A. v. C. P. Huizinga ... Boston Sherman, French & company 1911 64 p. 20 cm. $0.60 [B832.H8] 11-18102
1. Pragmatism (Philosophy) I. Title.

Prahlada—Juvenile literature.

BHATIVEDANTA, A.C. Swami 1896- JUV
Prahlad : a story for children from the ancient Vedas of India / A. C. Bhaktivedanta Swami Prabhupada ; publisher and editor, Mohanananda das Adhikari ; [ill. by Goursundar das and Govinda devi dasi]. Dallas, Tex. : Iskcon Children's Press, c1973. [32] p. : col. ill. ; 28 cm. Relates the tale of the child Prahlad whose devotion for and love of Krishna helped him endure severe tortures and win for his father liberation from a curse. [PZ8.1.B48Pr] 294'.1 75-319632
1. Prahlada—Juvenile literature. 2. [Prahlada.] 3. [Mythology, Hindu.] I. Das, Goursundar. II. Govinda Devi. III. Title.

Praise.

OLSON, Charles, 1886- 241
It pays to praise spiritual praise. [1st ed.] New York, Pageant Press [1957] 63p. 21cm. [BV4520.O4] 58-293
1. Praise. I. Title.

REFORMED Episcopal church.
Book of common praise. Hymnal companion to the prayer book. Words only. Comp. and rev. by the trustees of the Sustenation fund of the Reformed Episcopal church, by authority of the General council, May. 1912. Philadelphia, Treasurer's office, 1915. 523 p. 15 1/2 cm. $0.50. 15-9580
I. Title.

SURSUM corda;
a book of praise. E. H. Johnson, editor. E. E. Ayres, associate editor. Philadelphia. American Baptist pub. soc. [1898] vii, 654 p. 22 1/2 cm. 100

Praise of God.

ALLEN, Ronald Barclay. 223'.206
Praise! A matter of life and breath / by Ronald Barclay Allen. Nashville : T. Nelson, c1980. 246 p. ; 21 cm. Bibliography: p. 245-246. [BS1430.2.A35] 19 80-23894 ISBN 0-8407-5733-6 pbk. : 5.95
1. Bible. O.T. Psalms—Criticism, interpretation, etc. 2. Praise of God. I. Title.

BLACKBURN, Joyce. 242
A book of praises / by Joyce Blackburn ; ill. by Martha Bentley ; [edited by Judith E. Markham.] Grand Rapids, Mich. : Zondervan Pub. House, c1980. 128 p. : ill. ; 22 cm. [BV4817.B53] 19 80-21787 ISBN 0-310-42061-X pbk. : 3.95
1. Praise of God. 2. Meditations. I. Markham, Judith E. II. Title.

CORNWALL, E. Judson. 231'.4
Let us praise [by] E. Judson Cornwall. [1st ed.] Plainfield, N.J., Logos International [1973] 148 p. 21 cm. [BV4817.C65] 73-75957 ISBN 0-88270-039-1 2.50
1. Praise of God. I. Title.

MURCHISON, Anne Ferrell. 248.3
Praise and worship : in earth as it is in heaven / Anne Murchison. Waco, Tex. : Word Books, c1981. 140 p. ; 22 cm. Bibliography: p. 140. [BV4817.M87] 19 81-51008 ISBN 0-8499-2938-5 (pbk.) : 5.95
1. Praise of God. 2. Worship. 3. God—Worship and love. I. Title.

PRIME, Derek. 248.3
Created to praise / Derek Prime. Downers Grove, Ill. : InterVarsity Press, c1981. 125 p. ; 18 cm. [BV4817.P74 1981] 19 81-4525 ISBN 0-87784-825-4 pbk. : 2.95
1. Praise of God. I. Title.

Praise of God—Biblical teaching.

CRENSHAW, James L. 224'.8'06
Hymnic affirmation of divine justice : the doxologies of Amos and related texts in the Old Testament / by James L. Crenshaw. Missoula, Mont. : Published by Scholars Press for the Society of Biblical Literature, c1975. xii, 178 p. ; 22 cm. (Dissertation series ; no. 24) Originally presented as the author's thesis, Vanderbilt University, 1964. Bibliography: p. 159-178. [BS1585.2.C73 1975] 75-22349 ISBN 0-89130-016-3 pbk. : 4.20 4.20
1. Bible. O.T. Amos—Criticism, interpretation, etc. 2. Praise of God—Biblical teaching. 3. Doxology. I. Title. II. Series: Society of Biblical Literature. Dissertation series ; no. 24.

VAN BUREN, James G. 231.7
What the Bible says about praise and promise / by James G. VanBuren and Don DeWelt. Joplin, Mo. : College Press Pub. Co., c1980. x, 457 p. ; 23 cm. (What the Bible says series) Spine title: Praise and promise. Includes indexes. [BS680.P63V36] 19 80-66127 ISBN 0-89900-078-9 : 14.50
1. Praise of God—Biblical teaching. 2. God—Promises—Biblical teaching. I. De Welt, Don. II. Title. III. Title: Praise and promise. IV. Series.

WESTERMANN, Claus. 223'.206
Praise and lament in the Psalms / Claus Westermann ; translated by Keith R. Crim and Richard N. Soulen. Atlanta, Ga. : J. Knox Press, c1981. p. cm. Translation of: Lob und Klagen in den Psalmen. Includes index. Bibliography: p. [BS1430.2.W3913] 19 81-13753 ISBN 0-8042-1791-2 : 16.95 ISBN 0-8042-1792-0 pbk. : 9.50
1. Bible. O.T. Psalms—Criticism, interpretation, etc. 2. Praise of God—Biblical teaching. 3. Laments in the Bible. I. [Lob und Klage in den Psalmen.] English II. Title.

Prajnaparamitas

NAGARJUNA, Siddha 294.392
Nagarjuna's philosophy as presented in the Mahaprajnaparamita-sastra, by K. Venkata Ramanan, [1st ed.] Rutland, Vt. Pub. for the Harvard-Yenching Inst. [by] Tuttle [1966] 409p. 22cm. Thesis--Visva-Bharati. Bibl. [BL1411.P66N33] 656 10.00 lim. ed.,
1. Prajnaparamitas I. Venkata, Ramanan, Krishniah, ed. II. Title. III. Title: Maha-prajnaparamita-sastra.

PRAJNAPARAMITAS. Ratnagunasancayagatha. 294.3'8
Prajna-paramita-ratna-guna-samcaya-gatha : Sanskrit recension A / edited with an introd., bibliographical notes, and a Tibetan version from Tunhuang by Akira Yuyama. Cambridge ; New York : Cambridge University Press, 1976. lxxii, 214 p. ; 23 cm. Revision of the author's Australian National University at Canberra, 1970, with title: A study of the Prajna-paramita-ratna-guna-samcaya-gatha. Bibliography: p. [199]-214. [BQ1920.Y86 1976] 75-32910 ISBN 0-521-21081-X : 25.00
I. Yuyama, Akira.

SUZUKI, Daisetz Teitaro, 1870-1966. 294.3'92
On Indian Mahayana Buddhism. Edited with an introd. by Edward Conze. [1st ed.] New York, Harper & Row [1968] 284 p. 21 cm. (Harper torchbooks, TB1403) Includes bibliographical references. [BL1483.S818] 68-26896 2.45
1. Prajnaparamitas. 2. Gandavyuha. 3. Mahayana Buddhism. I. Conze, Edward, 1904- ed. II. Title.

Prajnaparamitas. Hrdaya—Addresses, essays, lectures.

HASEGAWA, Seikan, 1945- 294.3'8
The cave of poison grass : essays on the Hannya sutra / by Seikan Hasegawa. Arlington, Va. : Great Ocean Publishers, [1975] 182 p. : ill. ; 21 cm. (Companions of Zen training) Includes the Hannya sutra in Chinese romanization and an English translation. Includes bibliographical references and indexes. [BQ1887.H37] 75-6600 ISBN 0-915556-00-6 10.00 ISBN 0-915556-01-4 pbk. : 3.95
1. Prajnaparamitas. Hrdaya—Addresses, essays, lectures. I. Prajnaparamitas. Hrdaya. English & Chinese. 1975. II. Title. III. Series.

Prather, Hugh.

PRATHER, Hugh. 291.4'48
There is a place where you are not alone / Hugh Prather. Garden City, N.Y. : Doubleday, 1980. p. cm. (A Dolphin book) [BL624.P72] 19 80-912 ISBN 0-385-14778-3 : 5.95
1. Prather, Hugh. 2. Spiritual life. I. Title.

Pratityasamutpada.

JOHANNSON, Rune Edvin Anders, 1918- 294.3'01'9
The dynamic psychology of early Buddhism / [by] Rune E. A. Johansson. London : Curzon Press, 1979. 236 p. : ill. ; 23 cm. (Monograph series - Scandinavian Institute of Asian Studies ; no. 37 ISSN 0069-1712s) Includes indexes. Bibliography: p. 223-225.V[BQ4245.J63] 79-318997 ISBN 0-7007-0114-1 : 12.00
1. Pratityasamutpada. 2. Buddhism—Psychology. I. Title. II. Series: Centralinstitut for nordisk Asienforskning. Monograph series ; no. 37.
Distributed by Humanities Press, Atlantic Highlands, NJ

Pratt, James Bissett, 1875-1944.

MYERS, Gerald E ed. 110.82
Self, religion, and metaphysics; essays in memory of James Bissett Pratt. New York, Macmillan, 1961. viii, 241p. port. 25cm. 'Bibliography of the works of James B. Pratt':p.235-241. Bibliographical references included in 'Notes' (p. 229-233) [B29.M94] 61-7062
1. Pratt, James Bissett, 1875-1944. 2. Philosophy—Addresses, essays, lectures. 3. Self. 4. Religion—Philosophy. 5. Metaphysics. I. Title.

Pratt, Lewellyn, 1832-1913.

IN affectionate memory of the Reverend Doctor Lewellyn Pratt of Norwich, Connecticut, who in the fullness of his years passed into the eternal light, onJune the fourteenth in the year nineteen hundred and thirteen. 922. [Norwich, Conn., 1914] [102] p. front. (mounted phot.) 24 cm. "The instinctive impulse to frame such a memorial arose at once after the death of Dr. Lewellyn Pratt ... especially on the part of the officers of theNorwich free academy and of the Broadway Congregational church, as well as within the circle of his family friends. It seemed best for these three interests to unite in gathering the more accessible materials for a memorial."--p. [5] [BX7260.P74 I 6] 14-11450
1. Pratt, Lewellyn, 1832-1913. I. Norwich free academy, Norwich, Conn. II. Norwich, Conn. Broadway Congregational church.

Pratt, Orson, 1811-1881.

PRATT, Orson, 1811-1881. 289.3'3 B
The Orson Pratt journals / compiled and arranged by Elden J. Watson. Salt Lake City : E. J. Watson, 1975. xii, 583 p. : port. ; 24 cm. Includes index. Bibliography: p. 563-567. [BX8695.P69A36 1975] 76-354771
1. Pratt, Orson, 1811-1881. I. Watson, Elden Jay. II. Title.

Pratt, Parley Parker, 1807-1857.

PRATT, Parley Parker, 1807-1857. 922.8373
The autobiography of Parley Parker Pratt, one of the twelve apostles of the Church of Jesus Christ of latter-day saints, embracing his life, ministry and travels, with extracts ... from his miscellaneous writings. Editedby his son, Parley P. Pratt ... New York, Published for the editor and proprietor by Russell brothers, 1874. 502, x p., front., illus., plates, ports. 23 cm. [BX8695.P7A3] 36-30781
I. Pratt, Parley P., 1837- ed. II. Title.

PRATT, Parley Parker, 1807-1857. 922.8373
Autobiography of Parley Parker Pratt, one of the twelve apostles of the Church of Jesus Christ of latter-day saints, embracing his life, ministry and travels, with extracts, in prose and verse, from his miscellaneous writings. Edited by his son, Parley P. Pratt ... 3d ed. Salt Lake City, Utah, Desert book company, 1938. 471 p. front., illus., plates, ports. 24 cm. On cover: Life and travels of Parley P. Pratt. "Genealogy": p. [457]-[465] [BX8695.P7A3 1938] 38-16150
I. Pratt, Parley Parker, 1837-1897, ed. II. Title.

SCOTT, Reva Lucile (Holdaway) 1900- 922.8373
A biography of Parley P. Pratt, the Archer of Paradise [by] Reva Stanley [pseud.] Illustrated with rare photographs. Caldwell, Id., The Caxton printers, ltd., 1937. 349 p. front., plates, ports., facsims. 23 1/2 cm. Cover-title: The Archer of Paradise. "First printing." Bibliographical references included in "Notes" (p. [334]-337) Bibliography: p. [338]-340. [BX8695.P7S35] 37-34656
1. Pratt, Parley Parker, 1807-1857. 2. Mormons and Mormonism. I. Title.

STANLEY, Reva. 922.8373
A biography of Parley P. Pratt, the archer of paradise [by] Reva Stanley; illustrated with rare photographs. Caldwell, Id., The Caxton printers, ltd., 1937. 349 p. front., plates, ports., facsims., geneal. tables. 23 1/2 cm. "Notes": p. [334]-337. Bibliography: p. [338]-340. [BX8695.P7S7] 37-34656
1. Pratt, Parley Parker, 1807-1857. 2. Mormons and Mormonism. I. Title.

Praxedes Mother.

PATRICIA Jean, Sister 922.273
Only one heart; the story of a pioneer nun in America. Garden City, N.Y., Doubleday [c.]1963. 312p. 22cm. Bibl. 63-10262 4.50
1. Praxedes Mother. I. Title.

Prayer.

ACKER, Julius William. 248.32
Teach us to pray. Saint Louis, Concordia Pub. House [1961] 135p. 20cm. (Concord books) Includes bibliography. [BV2102.A3] 60-11414
1. Prayer. I. Title.

ADAMS, Henry W. ed. 248
"I cried, He answered"; a faithful record of remarkable answers to prayer, compiled and edited by Henry W. Adams, Norman H. Camp, William Norton and F. A. Steven, with introduction by Charles Gallaudet Trumbull. Chicago, The Bible institute colportage ass'n [c1918] 127 p. 19 1/2 cm. [BV220.A3] 19-4344
1. Prayer. I. Camp. Norman Harvey, 1867- joint ed. II. Norton, William, joint ed. III. Steven, Frederick Arthur, 1859- joint ed. IV. Title.

AINSLIE, Peter, 1867- 248
The way of prayer, by Peter Ainslie. New York, Chicago [etc.] Fleming H. Revell company [c1924] 205 p. 16 1/2 cm. [BV210.A5] 24-13484
1. Prayer. I. Title.

ALBERIONE, Giacomo Giuseppe, 1884- 248.2
Pray always, by James Alberione. Translation by the Daughters of St. Paul. [Boston] St. Paul Editions [1966] 265 p. 19 cm. [BV210.2.A413] 65-29136
1. Prayer. I. Title.

ALLEN, Charles Livingstone, 1913- 264.1
All things are possible through prayer. [Westwood, N. J.] F. H. Revell Co. [1958] 127p. 21cm. [BV220.A4] 58-11022
1. Prayer. I. Title.

ALLEN, Charles Livingstone, 1913- 248.3
The prayerful heart / by Charles L. Allen ; with poems by Helen Steiner Rice. Old Tappan, N.J. : F.H. Revell, c1982. p. cm. [BV215.A44] 19 81-12068 ISBN 0-8007-5073-X pbk. : 4.95
1. Prayer. I. Rice, Helen Steiner. II. Title.

ALLEN, Nancy (Armistead) Mrs. 248
...*Prayer,* by Nancy Armistead Allen... New York, Chicago [etc.] Fleming H. Revell company [c1928] 127 p. 17 1/2 cm. (Little studies on great themes). Bibliography: p. 127. [BV210.A55] 28-29345
1. Prayer. I. Title.

ANDREASEN, Millian Lauritz, 264.1 1876-
Prayer. Mountain View, Calif., Pacific Press Pub. Association [1957] 246p. 18cm. (Christian home library) [BV210.A577] 57-7779
1. Prayer. I. Title.

ANDREW, Father, 1869-1946.
The adventure of prayer. London, A. R. Mowbray; New York, Morehouse-Gorham [1958] vii, 59 p. "First published...1928." NUC63
I. Title.

ANDREWS, Charles Freer, 264.1 1871-
Christ and prayer, by C. F. Andrews ... New York and London, Harper & brothers, 1937. 160 p. 19 cm. "First edition." [BV210.A58 1937a] 37-20455
1. Prayer. 2. Jesus Christ—Prayers. 3. Lord's prayer. I. Title.

APPERE, Guy. 248.3'2
Dialogue with God / Guy Appere. Scottdale, Pa. : Herald Press, 1982, c1979. 68 p. ; 18 cm. Translation of: Pour un dialogue avec Dieu. [BV213.A6613] 19 81-83729 ISBN 0-8361-1984-3 (pbk.) : 1.95
1. Prayer. I. [Pour un dialogue avec Dieu.] English II. Title.

APPLETON, Nathaniel, 1693-1784.
The right method of addressing the Divine Majesty in prayer; so as to support and strengthen our faith in dark and troublesome times, set forth in two discourses on April 5, 1770. Being the day of general fasting and prayer through the province: and in the time of the session of the General court at Cambridge. By Nathaniel Appleton, M.A., pastor of the First church in Cambridge ... Boston: Printed by Edes and Gill, Printers to the Honorable House of Representatives, 1770. 56 p. 21 cm. [BV4270.A6] 6-46126
1. Prayer. I. Title.

ARINTERO, Juan Gonzalez, 264.1 1860-1928.
Stages in prayer. Translated by Kathleen Pond. St. Louis, Herder [1957] 178p. 23cm. [BV210.A683] 58-187
1. Prayer. 2. Meditation. I. Title.

ARNDT, William, 1880- 264.1
Christian prayer, by W. Arndt... St. Louis, Mo., Concordia publishing house, 1937. viii, 67 p. 19 1/2 cm. [Full name: William Frederick Arndt] [BV210.A7] 38-4871
1. Prayer. I. Title.

*ASH, Anthony Lee 232
Prayer [by] Anthony Lee Ash. Austin, Tex., R. B. Sweet [1967] 100p. 21cm. (Living word ser.) .75 pap.,
I. Title.

AUSTIN, Bill R. 231.7
The back of God : signs of his presence / Bill Austin. Wheaton, Ill. : Tyndale House, c1980. 155 p. ; 21 cm. [BV215.A95] 19 79-67160 ISBN 0-8423-0115-1 (pbk.) : 3.95
1. Prayer. 2. God—Will. 3. God—Knowableness. I. Title.

AUSTIN, Mary (Hunter) Mrs. 264.1 1868-1934.
... *Can prayer be answered?* New York, Farrar & Rinehart, 1934. 4 p. l., 3-55 p. illus. 21 cm. At head of title: Mary Austin. [BV220.A8] 34-22377
1. Prayer. I. Title.

BAELZ, Peter R. 248.3
Prayer and providence; a background study [by] Peter R. Baelz. New York, Seabury Press [1968] 141 p. 23 cm. Bibliographical footnotes. [BV210.2.B27 1968b] 68-6128 3.25
1. Prayer. 2. Providence and government of God. I. Title.

BARKER, William Pierson. 248'.3
To pray is to live / William P. Barker. Old Tappan, N.J. : F. H. Revel Co., c1977. 122 p. ; 21 cm. [BV210.2.B298] 76-54315 ISBN 0-531-01214-X lib.bdg. : 4.95
1. Prayer. I. Title.

BARREAU, Jean Claude. 248'.3
Drugs and the life of prayer / Jean-Claude Barreau ; translated by Jeremy Moiser. Grand Rapids, Mich. : W. B. Eerdmans Pub. Co., 1975. 95 p. ; 18 cm. Translation of La priere et la drogue. Includes indexes. [BV210.2.B29913] 74-28249 ISBN 0-8028-1599-5 pbk. : 1.65
1. Prayer. 2. Hallucinogenic drugs and religious experience. I. Title.

BARRY, Joseph Gayle Hurd, 1858-
On prayers to the dead, by Rev. J. G. H. Barry, D.D. New York, E. S. Gorham, 1919. 162 p. 19 cm. "Book-list": p. 161-162. [BV227.B3] 19-7937
I. Title.

BARTH, Karl, 1886- 264.1
Prayer according to the catechisms of the Reformation; stenographic records of three seminars, adapted by A. Roulin. Translated by Sara F. Terrien. Philadelphia, Westminster Press [1952] 78 p. 20 cm. [BV210.B333] 52-9381
1. Prayer. 2. Lord's prayer. I. Title.

BASSET, Bernard. 264'.1
Let's start praying again. Garden City, N.Y., Doubleday [1973, c.1972] 118 p. 18 cm. (Image Book, D327) Bibliography: p. [118]-119. [BV210.2.B33] ISBN 0-385-05091-7 1.25 (pbk.)
1. Prayer. I. Title.
L.C. card no. for the hardbound edition: 78-176365.

BASSET, Bernard. 264'.1
Let's start praying again; field work in meditation. [New York] Herder and Herder [1972] 152 p. 21 cm. [BV210.2.B33] 78-176365 ISBN 0-665-00003-0 4.95
1. Prayer. I. Title.

BAUMAN, Edward W 264.1
Intercessory prayer. Philadelphia, Westminster Press [1958] 112p. 20cm. Includes bibliography. [BV210.B336] 58-5621
1. Prayer. I. Title.

BELDEN, Albert David, 1883- 248
The practice of prayer. New York, Harper [1954?] 96p. 20cm. [BV210] 54-3658
1. Prayer. I. Title.

BEWES, Richard. 248.3'2
Talking about prayer / Richard Bewes. Downers Grove, Ill. : Inter-Varsity Press, 1980, c1979. 127 p. ; 18 cm. [BV215.B43 1980] 80-7781 ISBN 0-87784-465-8 (pbk.) : 2.95
1. Prayer.

BICKERSTETH, Edward, 1786- 248 1850.
A treatise on prayer: designed to assist in the devout discharge of that duty: with a few forms of prayer. By the Rev. Edward Bickersteth ... From the 9th London ed. ... New-York, J. Leavitt; [etc., etc.] 1828. 2 p. l., [iii]-vi, [2], 302 p. 19 cm. Added t.-p. Bickersteth on prayer. Richmond, Va., A. Works, 1828. [BV210.B43] 42-9441
1. Prayer. I. Title.

BICKNELL, Edward John, 1882- 248
In defence of Christian prayer; a consideration of some of the intellectual difficulties that surround petition, by E. J. Bicknell ... London, New York [etc.] Longmans, Green and co., 1925. vi p. 1 l., 120 p. 19 cm. [BV210.B45] 25-9593 1.25
1. Prayer. I. Title.

BIEDERWOLF, William Edward, 248 1867-
How can God answer prayer? Being an exhaustive treatise on the nature, conditions and difficulties of prayer, by William Edward Beiderwolf ... Chicago, Ill., The Winona publishing company [c1906] 287 p. port. 19 cm. [BV210.B5 1906] 7-1944
1. Prayer. I. Title.

*BISAGNO, John R. 264.1
The power of positive praying. Grand Rapids, Mich., Zondervan [c.1965] 95p. 21cm. (6900 ser.) .69 pap.,
I. Title.

BISHOP, Shelton Hale. 264.1
The wonder of prayer. Greenwich, Conn., Seabury Press, 1959. 95p. 20cm. [BV210.2.B57] 59-5700
1. Prayer. I. Title.

*BLAIKLOCK, E. M. 226.906
Our Lord's teaching on prayer. Grand Rapids, Mich., Zondervan [c.1964] 60p. 19cm. (49) 1.25 pap.,
I. Title.

BLANCHARD, Charles Albert, 248 1848-1925.
Getting things from God; a study of the prayer life, by Charles A. Blanchard ... Chicago, The Bible institute colportage association [1915] 3 p. l., 5-270 p. 20 cm. [BV210.B55] 15-15285
1. Prayer. I. Title.

BLEGEN, Allen Raymond, 264.1 1905- ed.
The Prayer conference book; an edited digest of the messages brought at the Prayer conference sponsored by the Lutheran gospel hour, at the Park View Lutheran church, Chicago, Sept. 3-4, edited by Allen R. Blegen ... Elgin, Ill., The Lutheran gospel hour [c1940] 72 p. 19 cm. [BV205.B55] 40-11352
1. Prayer. I. Title.

BLOCKER, Simon, 1881- 264.1
How to achieve personality through prayer. [1st ed.] Grand Rapids, W. B. Eerdmans Pub. Co., 1954. 121p. 23cm. [BV210.B555] 54-14434
1. Prayer. I. Title.

BLOESCH, Donald G., 1928- 248.3'2
The struggle of prayer / Donald G. Bloesch. 1st ed. San Francisco : Harper & Row, c1980. p. cm. Includes index. [BV210.2.B576] 79-3589 ISBN 0-06-060797-1 : 9.95
1. Prayer. I. Title.

BLOOM, Anthony, 1914- 248'.3
Courage to pray / Anthony Bloom and Georges LeFebvre ; translated by Dinah Livingstone. New York : Paulist Press, [1974] c1973 122 p. ; 22 cm. Translation of pts. 2-3 of La priere, by A. de Robert, G. Lefebvre, and A. Bloom. Bibliography: p. [63] [BV210.2.R58213] 74-190392 ISBN 0-8091-0190-4 : 3.95
1. Prayer. I. Lefebvre, Georges, 1908- II. Title.

BOASE, Leonard 248.32
The prayer of faith. St. Louis, B. Herder [1963, c.1962] 147p. 22cm. 63-1370 3.25
1. Prayer. I. Title.

BOASE, Leonard. 248'.3
The prayer of faith / Leonard Boase. Huntington, Ind. : Our Sunday Visitor, c1976. 126 p. ; 21 cm. Bibliography: p. 125-126. [BV210.2.B6 1976] 76-5152 ISBN 0-87973-683-6 pbk. : 2.95
1. Prayer. I. Title.

BONNELL, John Sutherland, 264.1 1893-
The practice and power of prayer. Philadelphia, Westminster Press [1954] 93p. 20cm. [BV210.B56] 54-5654
1. Prayer. I. Title.

BOONE, Charles Eugene. 248.3'2
Pray to win : God wants you to succeed / by Pat Boone [i.e. C. E. Boone] New York : Putnam, c1980. 237 p. ; 21 cm. [BV210.2B645 1980] 79-25553 8.95
1. Prayer. 2. Success. I. Title.

BOROS, Ladislaus, 1927- 248'.3
Christian prayer / Ladislaus Boros ; translated by David Smith. New York : Seabury Press, c1976. p. cm. Translation of Uber das christliche Beten. "A Crossroad book." [BV210.2.B6513 1976] 76-7353 ISBN 0-8164-1199-9 : 6.95
1. Prayer. I. Title.

BOSTON.KING'S chapel. 223.
Book of common prayer, according to the use of King's chapel, Boston. Boston [Ticknor, Reed, and Fields] 1850. xii, [4], [3]-407 p. 25 1/2 cm. An adaptation, Unitarian in spirit, of the Book of common prayer for the use of King's chapel, done chiefly under the direction of F. W. P. Greenwood. Published also under title: A liturgy for the use of the church at King's chapel. [BX5943.A4B6 1850] 39-18054
I. Greenwood, Francis William Pitt, 1797-1843, ed. II. Title.

*BOUNDS, Edward M. 242
The necessity of prayer / Edward M. Bounds. Grand Rapids : Baker Book House, 1976. 144p. ; 18 cm. (Direction books) [BV210.2] ISBN 0-8010-0659-7 pbk. : 1.45.
1. Prayer. I. Title.

BOUNDS, Edward McKendree, 248 1835-1913.
The essentials of prayer, by Edward M. Bounds ... edited by Homer W. Hodge. New York, Chicago [etc.] Fleming H. Revell company [c1925] 143 p. front. (port.) 19 1/2 cm. [BV210.B575] 25-9228
1. Prayer. I. Hodge, Homer W., ed. II. Title.

BOUNDS, Edward McKendree, 248 1835-1913.
The necessity of prayer, by Edward M. Bounds ... edited by Rev. Homer W. Hodge. New York, Chicago [etc.] Fleming H. Revell company [c1929] 144 p. front. (2 port.) 19 1/2 cm. [BV210.B576] 29-14033
1. Prayer. I. Hodge, Homer W., ed. II. Title.

BOUNDS, Edward McKendree, 248 1835-1913.
The possibilities of prayer, by Edward M. Bounds ... edited by Homer W. Hodge. New York, Chicago [etc.] Fleming H. Revell company [c1923] 159 p. 19 1/2 cm. [BV210.B58] 23-6040
1. Prayer. I. Hodge, Homer W., ed. II. Title.

BOUNDS, Edward McKendree, 248 1835-1913.
Prayer and praying men, by Rev. Edward M. Bounds ... with an introduction by Rev. Homer W. Hodge. New York, George H. Doran company [c1921] ix p., 1 l., 13-160 p. 19 1/2 cm. [BV210.B59] 21-15355 1.25.
1. Prayer. I. Title.

BOUNDS, Edward McKendree, 248 1835-1913.
Purpose in prayer, by E. M. Bounds ... New York, Chicago [etc.] Fleming H. Revell company [c1920] 160 p. front. (port.) 19 1/2 cm. [BV210.B6] 29-20540
I. Title.

BOUNDS, Edward McKendree, 248 1835-1913.
The reality of prayer, by Edward M. Bounds ... edited by Homer W. Hodge. New York, Chicago [etc.] Fleming H. Revell company [c1924] 155 p. 19 1/2 cm. [BV210.B63] 24-13485
1. Prayer. I. Hodge, Homer W., ed. II. Title.

BOUNDS, Edward McKendree, 248 1835-1913.
The weapon of prayer; a study in Christian warfare, by Edward M. Bounds ... edited by Homer W. Hodge. New York, Chicago, [etc.] Fleming H. Revell company [c1931] 157 p. illus. (facsims) 19 1/2 cm. [BV210.B64] 31-20757
1. Prayer. I. Hodge, Homer Werle, 1859- ed. II. Title.

BOWDEN, Guy A G.
The dazzling darkness, an essay on the experience of prayer. With a forword by Bishop Walter Carey. London, New York, Longmans, Green [1950] vii, 200 p. 18 cm. A 51
1. Prayer. I. Title.

BOWDON, Boyce A., 248'.2'0922 B 1935-
Empowered! : Living experiences of talking with God / Boyce A. Bowdon. Atlanta : John Knox Press, c1978. 127 p. ; 20 cm. [BV210.2.B68] 77-15744 ISBN 0-8042-2318-1 pbk. : 3.95
1. Prayer. 2. Christian biography—United States. I. Title.

BOWMAN, Clarice Margurette, 264.1 1910-
Power through prayer [by] Clarice Bowman and George Harper. Nashville, Source [1947] v. 117 p. 20 cm. [BV215.B62] 48-1505
1. Prayer. I. Harper, George, joint author. II. Title.

BRANDT, Priscilla. 248'.3
Two-way prayer / Priscilla Brandt ; foreword by Joyce Landorf. Waco, Tex. : Word Books, c1979. 151 p. ; 23 cm. Bibliography: p. 147-151. [BV210.2.B685] 78-65802 ISBN 0-8499-0022-0 : 6.95
1. Prayer. 2. Christian life—1960- I. Title.

BRANDT, R. L. 227
Praying with Paul, by R. L. Brandt. Grand Rapids, Baker Book House [1966] 106 p. 20 cm. [BV210.2.B7] 66-18316
1. Prayer. I. Title.

BREAULT, William.
Under the fig tree : stories of prayer-filled moments / William Breault. Notre Dame, Ind. : Ave Maria Press, c1980. 95 p. : ill. ; 21 cm. [BV210.2.B686] 79-56689 ISBN 0-87793-199-2 (pbk.) : 2.75
1. Prayer. I. Title.

*BRINGMAN, Dale S. 248.3
Prayer and the devotional life, by Dale S. Bringman, Frank W. Klos. Philadelphia, Lutheran Church [c.1964] 121p. illus. 20cm. (LCA sch. of rel. ser.) 1.25; 1.25 teacher's guide, pap.,
I. Title.

BRINGMAN, Dale S
Prayer and the devotional life, by Dale S. Bringman and Frank W. Klos. Philadelphia, Lutheran Church Press [c1964] 121 p. illus. 20 cm. 68-69573
1. Prayer. 2. Devotion. I. Klos, Frank W. II. Title.

BRINGS, Lawrence Martin, 1897- comp. 264.1
We believe in prayer; a compilation of personal statements by American and world leaders about the value and efficacy of prayer. Minneapolis, T. S. Denison [1958] 616p. 23cm. [BV205.B7] 58-13126
1. Prayer. I. Title.

BRISCOE, D. Stuart. 248'.4
Getting into God : practical guidelines to the Christian life / D. Stuart Briscoe. Grand Rapids : Zondervan Pub. House, c1975. 156 p. ; 18 cm. [BS600.2.B73] 75-11016 pbk. : 1.50
1. Bible—Study. 2. Prayer. 3. Witness bearing (Christianity) I. Title.

BRISCOE, Jill. 248'.3
Hush! hush! / Jill Briscoe. Grand Rapids : Zondervan Pub. House, c1978. 160 p. ; 21 cm. Bibliography: p. 159-160. [BV210.2.B69] 77-27895 ISBN 0-310-21831-4 pbk. : 3.95
1. Prayer. I. Title.

BRIST, Gladys Z 264.1
The privilege and power of prayer, an inspirational handbook with material adaptable for devotional talks. [1st ed.] New York, Exposition Press [1957] 108p. 21cm. (A Testament book) [BV210.B72] 57-10655
1. Prayer. I. Title.

BRO, Bernard 248.3
Learning to pray. Tr. [from French] by John Morris. Staten Island, N. Y., Alba [c.1966] 176p. 22cm. [BV210.2.B713] 66-17217 3.95
1. Prayer. I. Title.

BRO, Margueritte (Harmon) 1894- 264.1
More than we are. Rev., enl. ed. New York, Harper [c.1948, 1965] 177p. 21cm. (Harper chapel bks. CB7) [BV210.B73] 64-20798 1.50 pap.,
1. Prayer. I. Title.

BRO, Margueritte (Harmon) 1894- 264.1
More than we are. Rev. and enl. ed. New York, Harper & Row [1965] 177 p. 21 cm. (Harper chapel books, CB7) [BV210.B73 1965] 64-20798
1. Prayer. I. Title.

BRO, Margueritte (Harmon) 1894- 264.1
More than we are. [1st ed.] New York, Harper [1948] 144 p. 20 cm. [BV210.B73] 48-3312
1. Prayer. I. Title.

BROADHURST, Cyrus Napoleon, 1856-
Wireless messages, possibilities through prayer, by C.N. Broadhurst. New York, Chicago [etc.] Fleming H. Revell company [c1910] 234 p. 19 1/2 cm. $1.00. 10-20835
I. Title.

BROADHURST, Cyrus Napoleon, 1856-
Wireless messages, possibilities through prayer, by C.N. Broadhurst. New York, Chicago [etc.] Fleming H. Revell company [c1910] 234 p. 19 1/2 cm. $1.00. 10-20835
I. Title.

BROWN, Charles Ewing, 1883- 264.1
The way of prayer, by Charles Ewing Brown, D.D. Anderson, Ind., The Warner press [c1940] vii, 9-192 p. 19 cm. [BV210.B77] 40-10019
1. Prayer. I. Title.

BROWN, William Adams, 1865- 248
The life of prayer in a world of science, by William Adams Brown... New York, C. Scribner's sons, 1927. x, 194 p. 19 1/2 cm. Bibliography: p. 183-188. [BV210.B78] 27-9589
1. Prayer. I. Title.

BRUCE, Michael. 264.1
The science of prayer, by Michael Bruce, B. SC. London, Society for promoting Christian knowledge. New York, The Macmillan company [1937] xiv, 15-134 p. 17 cm. "First published, 1937." [BV210.B782] 39-18003
1. Prayer. I. Society for promoting Christian knowledge, London. II. Title.

*BRUCKBERGER, Raymond Leopold, 1907- 248
The secret ways of prayer. Glen Rock, N.J., Paulist [1965, c.1964] 86p. 18cm. (Deus bk.) .75 pap.,
I. Title.

BUISSINK, P J.
Twenty-five exercises of the Way of the cross, followed by an exercise of the Way of the cross in the form of prayer, by Rev. P. J. Buissink ... New Orleans, La., Standard printing works, inc. [1916] 122 p., 1 l. 20 cm. 16-5964 0.50
I. Title. II. Title: Way of the cross.

BUNCH, Taylor Grant. 264.1
Prevailing prayer, by Taylor G. Bunch ... Washington, D. C., Review and herald, 1946. 124 p. 19 1/2 cm. [BV210.B784] 46-20667
1. Prayer. I. Title.

BUNDY, Walter Ernest, 1889- 232.9
Jesus prays, by Walter E. Bundy ... Indianapolis, The Bobbs-Merrill company [c1930] ix p. 1 l., 13-121 p. 19 cm. "First edition." "Revised extracts from the author's recent books, "The religion of Jesus", and 'Our recovery of Jesus'."--Pref. [BV229.B8] 30-24105
1. Jesus Christ—Prayers. 2. Prayer. I. Title.

BUSWELL, James Oliver, 1895- 248
Problems in the prayer life, from a pastor's question box, by James Oliver Buswell, jr. ... Chicago, The Bible institute colportage ass'n [c1928] 127 p. 19 cm. [BV210.B785] 28-7706
1. Prayer. I. Title.

BUTLER, Basil Christopher 248.32
Prayer in practice. Pref. by Gilbert Hess. Baltimore, Helicon [1962, c.1961] 118p. (Benedictine studies, 3) 61-16856 2.95
1. Prayer. I. Title.

BUTTRICK, George Arthur, 1892- 248.3
The power of prayer today. New York, World Pub. Co. [1970] 61 p. 21 cm. (World inspirational books) Includes bibliographical references. [BV210.2.B87] 71-131562
1. Prayer. I. Title.

BUTTRICK, George Arthur, 1892- 264.1
Prayer [by] George Arthur Buttrick ... New York, Nashville, Abingdon-Cokesbury press [1942] 333 p. 24 cm. Bibliographical references included in "Notes" (p. 305-322) [BV210.B788] 42-36028
1. Prayer. I. Title.

BYRUM, Enoch Edwin, 1861-
The secret of prayer; how and why we pray, by E. E. Byrum. New York, Chicago [etc.] Fleming H. Revell company [c1912] 1 p. l., 5-209 p. 20 cm. 12-17526 1.00
I. Title.

CAMPBELL, Dortch, 1880- 264.1
How to solve your problems by prayer, by Dorothy Campbell. New York, J. Felsberg, inc., 1946. 206 p. 22 cm. [BV210.C27] 47-15402
1. Prayer. I. Title.

CAMPBELL, Frank G 1879- 264.1
Prayer--it works. Washington [1953] 89p. illus. 20cm. [BV220.C3] 53-31154
1. Prayer. I. Title.

CAMPBELL, James Mann, 1840-
The place of prayer in the Christian religion, by James M. Campbell. New York, Cincinnati, The Methodist book concern [c1915] 303 p. 19 1/2 cm. 15-7266 1.00
I. Title.

CANT, Reginald 248.32
Heart in pilgrimage; a study in Christian prayer. New York, Harper [c.1961] 147p. Bibl. 61-5257 2.50
1. Prayer. I. Title.

CARREL, Alexis, 1873-1944. 264.1
Prayer; tr. by Dulcie de Ste. Croix Wright. New York, Morehouse-Gorham Co., 1948. 54 p. 20 cm. [BV210.C335] 48-5941
1. Prayer. I. Wright, Dulcie de Ste. Croix tr. II. Title.

CARROLL, James. 248.3
Prayer from where we are; suggestions about the possibility and practice of prayer today. Dayton, Ohio, G. A. Pflaum [1970] 120 p. illus. 17 cm. (Christian experience series. Witness book 13) Bibliography: p. 119-120. [BV210.2.C34] 71-133402 0.85
1. Prayer. I. Title.

CARRUTH, Thomas A. 248.32
Total prayer for total living. Grand Rapids, Zondervan Pub. House [c1962] 116 p. 22 cm. [BV210.2.C35] 63-1759
1. Prayer. I. Title.

CARRUTH, Thomas Albert. 264'.1
Prayer, a Christian ministry. Nashville, Tenn., Tidings [1971] 48 p. 19 cm. [BV213.C37] 71-159421
1. Prayer. I. Title.

CARTER, Edward, 1929- 248'.3
Prayer is love. St. Meinrad, Ind., Abbey Press, 1974. vii, 99 p. 21 cm. (A Priority edition) Includes bibliographical references. [BV210.2.C36] 74-78722 ISBN 0-87029-030-4 4.95
1. Prayer. I. Title.

CARVER, William Owen, 1868- 248
Thou when thou prayest, by William Owen Carver ... Garden City, N. Y., Doubleday, Doran & company, inc., 1928. 5 p. l., 3-76 p. 19 cm. [BV210.C35] 28-4632
1. Prayer. I. Title.

CASSIDY, Sheila, 1937- 248.3'2
Prayer for pilgrims : a book about prayer for ordinary people / Sheila Cassidy. New York : Crossroad, 1982, c1980. 134 p. : ill. ; 21 cm. [BV215.C37 1982] 19 81-70878 ISBN 0-8245-0420-8 (pbk.) : 6.95
1. Cassidy, Sheila, 1937- 2. Prayer. 3. Spiritual life—Catholic authors. I. Title.

CASTEEL, John Laurence, 1903- 264.1
The promise of prayer. New York, Association Press [1957] 125p. 16cm. (An Association Press reflection book) 'Based on the author's full length book, Rediscovering prayer.' [BV210.C358] 57-11606
1. Prayer. I. Title.

CASTEEL, John Laurence, 1903- 264.1
Rediscovering prayer. New York, Association Press [1955] 242p. 21cm. [BV210.C36] 55-7410
1. Prayer. I. Title.

CAULFIELD, Sean. 248.3
The experience of praying / Sean Caulfield. New York : Paulist Press, c1980. v, 82 p. ; 23 cm. [BV215.C38] 79-92428 ISBN 0-8091-0307-9 pbk. : 4.95
1. Prayer. I. Title.

CAUSSADE, Jean Pierre de, d.1751.
On prayer; spiritual instructions on the various states of prayer according to the doctrine of Bossuet, bishop of Meaux. Translated into English by Algar Thorold, with an introduction by John Chapman. Springfield, Ill., Templegate [1960] xxxvii, 273 p. 22 cm. The original, "Instructions spirituelles", appeared first in an anonymous edition, Perpignan, 1741. 65-13587
1. Prayer. 2. Meditation. I. Bossuet, Jacques Benigne, Bp. of Meaux, 1627-1704. Instruction sur les etats d'oraison. II. Title.

CAUSSADE, Jean Pierre de, d.1751. 248
Progress in prayer. Translated from Instructions spirituelles par le r. p. Caussade, S. J., by L. V. Sheehan. Adapted and edited, with an introduction, by Joseph McSorley, C. S. P. St. Louis, Mo., B. Herder, 1904. 178 p. 20 cm. Dialogues based on Bossuet's "Instructions sur les etas d'oraison." [BV209.C3] 5-1987
1. Prayer. 2. Meditation. I. Bossuet, Jacques Benigne, bp. of Meaux. Instruction sur les etats d'oraison. II. Sheehan, L. V., tr. III. McSorley, Joseph, 1874- ed. IV. Title.

CHADWICK, Samuel, 1860-1932. 246
The path of prayer [by] Samuel Chadwick. New York, Cincinnati [etc.] The Abingdon press [c1931] 3 p. l., 5-138 p. 20 cm. "These chapters written as devotional meditations for 'Joyful news." [BV210.C46] 31-32015
1. Prayer. I. Title.

CHALMERS, Allan Knight, 1897- 264.1
The commonplace prodigal; the tragedy of ineffective prayer, by Allan Knight Chalmers ... New York, H. Holt and company [c1934] xii p., 2 l., 3-229 p. 20 cm. "Prayers in the tabernacle": p. [207]-229. "Acknowledgments": leaf 1, following p. xii. [BV210.C28] 34-8969
1. Prayer. 2. Prayers. I. Title.

CHAMBERLAIN, Leander Trowbridge, 1837-1913. 248
The true doctrine of prayer, by Leander Chamberlain ... with foreword by the Rev. William R. Huntington, D. D. New York, The Baker & Taylor co., 1906. 5 p. l., v-xvi, 179 p. 19 cm. [BV210.C5] 6-1538
1. Prayer. I. Title.

CHAMBERLAIN, William Douglas, 1890- 264.1
The manner of prayer [by] William Douglas Chamberlain ... Philadelphia, The Westminster press [c1943] 163 p. 20 1/2 cm. Bibliographical references included in "Notes" (p. [147]-163) [BV215.C5] 44-3778
1. Prayer. I. Title.

CHAMBERS, Oswald, 1874-1917. 264.1
If ye shall ask ... by Oswald Chambers ... New York, Dodd, Mead & company, 1938. vii p., 1 l., 123 p. 19 cm. [BV210.C53] 39-3112
1. Prayer. I. Title.

CHANNELS, Lloyd V 264.1
The layman learns to pray. St. Louis, Bethany Press [1957] 96p. 21cm. [BV215.C52] 57-12726
1. Prayer. I. Title.

CHESTER, Ann E., 1901- 248'.3
Prayer, now : a response to the needs for prayer renewal / Ann E. Chester. Albany, N.Y. : Clarity Pub., [1975] 62 p. ; 28 cm. Includes bibliographical references. [BV210.2.C49] 75-3907 ISBN 0-915488-01-9 : 2.00
1. Prayer. 2. House of Prayer Movement. I. Title.

CHILSON, Richard. 248'.3
I can pray, you can pray : a worldly approach to spirituality / Richard W. Chilson. New York : McKay, c1978. vi, 152 p. ; 22 cm. Includes index. Bibliography: p. 144-147. [BV210.2.C5] 78-6553 ISBN 0-679-50860-0 : 7.95
1. Prayer. I. Title.

CHRISTENSON, Evelyn. 248.4
Two by Evelyn / Evelyn Christenson ; assisted editorially by Viola Blake. Wheaton, Ill. : Victor Books, c1979. 280 p. : ill. ; 24 cm. Contents.Contents.—What happens when women pray.—"Lord,

change me!" [BV210.2.C53 1979] 79-65289 ISBN 0-88207-791-0 : 8.95
1. Christenson, Evelyn. 2. Prayer. 3. Christian life—1960- I. Blake, Viola, 1921- II. Christenson, Evelyn. "Lord, change me!" 1979. III. Title.
Publishers Address: P. O. Box 1825, Wheaton IL, 60187

CHRISTENSON, Evelyn. 248'.3
What happens when women pray / Evelyn Christenson, with Viola Blake. Wheaton, Ill. : Victor Books, c1975. 144 p. ; 18 cm. (An input book) [BV210.2.C53] 75-171 ISBN 0-88207-715-5 pbk. : 1.75
1. Prayer. I. Blake, Viola, 1921- joint author. II. Title.

CHURCH of England. Book of common prayer. 264'.03
The Book of common prayer, 1559 : the Elizabethan prayer book / edited by John E. Booty. Charlottesville : Published for the Folger Shakespeare Library by the University Press of Virginia, 1976. x, 427 p. ; 23 cm. ([Folger documents of Tudor and Stuart civilization ; no. 22]) Includes index. Bibliography: p. 417-419. [BX5145.A4 1559b] 75-29330 ISBN 0-8139-0503-6 : 15.00 ISBN 0-8139-0696-2 pbk. : 5.95
I. Booty, John E. II. Title. III. Series.

CHURCH of England. Book of common prayer. 264.
The annotated Book of common prayer, being an historical, ritual, and theological commentary on the devotional system of the Church of England, edited by the Rev. John Henry Blunt ... with an introductory notice on the American Book of common prayer by the Rev. Frederick Gibson ... Rev. and enl. ed. New York, E. P. Dutton & co., 1884. xx, 8, 730 p. illus., ii pl. 28 1/2 x 22 1/2 cm. "A list of the principal liturgical and historical authorities used, quoted, or referred to, in this work": p. [xv]-xviii. [BX5145.B6 1884a] 29-24796
I. Blunt, John Henry, 1823-1884, ed. II. Title.

CHURCH of England. Book of common prayer. 264.
The annotated Book of common prayer, forming a concise commentary on the devotional system of the Church of England, edited by the Rev. John Henry Blunt ... Compendious ed. With a monograph on the American prayer book by the Rev. Samuel Hart ... New York, E. & J. B. Young & company, 1888. xxiii, 3-731 p. 18 1/2 cm. [BX5145.B6 1888] 29-24795
I. Blunt, John Henry, 1823-1884, ed. II. Title.

CHURCH of England. Book of common prayer. 264.
The annotated Book of common prayer, being an historical, ritual, and theological commentary on the devotional system of the Church of England, edited by the Rev. John Henry Blunt ... with an introductory notice by the Rev. Frederick Gibson ... Rev. and enl. ed., new impression (1899) New York, E. P. Dutton and company, 1903. xx, 8, 732 p. illus., 17 pl. 28 1/2 x 22 1/2 cm. "A list of the principal liturgical and historical authorities used, quoted, or referred to, in this work": p. [xv]-xviii. [BX5145.B6 1903] 29-24797
I. Blunt, John Henry, 1823-1884, ed. II. Title.

CHURCH of England. Book of common prayer. 264.03
The Book of common prayer, and administration of the sacraments, and other rites and ceremonies of the church, according to the use of the Church of England: together with the Psalter, or Psalms of David, pointed as they are to be sung or said in churches: and the form and manner of making, ordaining, and consecreating of bishops, priests, and deacons. Oxford, Printed at the University press; London, H. Frowde [1889?] 204 p. 18 cm. With this is bound: Helps to the study of the Book of common prayer, being a companion to church worship. Oxford [etc. 1889?] [BX5145.A4 1889] 35-31614
I. Title.

CHURCH of England. Book of common prayer. 264.06
The Book of common prayer, and administration of the sacraments, and other rites and ceremonies of the church according to the use of the Church of England: together with the Psalter, or Psalms of David, pointed as they are to be sung or said in churches; and the form and manner of making, ordaining and consecrating of bishops, priests, and deacons. Oxford, Printed at the University press; London, H. Frowde [19-] ix, 2-542 p. 10 cm. [BX5145.A4 1900] 33-6289
I. Title.

CHURCH of England. Book of common prayer. 264.
The Book of common prayer, and administration of the sacraments, & other rites & ceremonies of the church, according to the use of the Church of England: together with the Psalter or Psalms of David, pointed as they are to be sung or said in churches: & the form & manner of making, ordaining, and consecrating of bishops, pirests, and deacons. [New York, M. Walter Dunne, 1904] 7 p. l., 386 p., 1 l. incl. front., illus. 37 x 28 1/2 cm. Initials: title and table of contents within ornamental borders; rubrics in red. Binder's lettering: Prayer book of Edward vii. 1903. "Authorised American edition ... The designs and the type throughout are those of the English edition ... and are the work of C. R. Ashbee, of the Essex house press ... The proofs were corrected by the house of M. Walter Dunne ... and the printing was done at the Plumpton press, Norwood, Massachusetts ... The bindings are from designs drawn and executed at the bindery of M. Walter Dunne. Exclusive authority for the publication of this American edition ... was issued to M. Walter Dunne in March MDCCCIV, by the Essex house-press, of Camden, Gloucestershire, England, by the Guild of handicraft of London, England, and by Messrs. Eyre and Spottswoode, printers to His Majesty King Edward VII." Bound in purple cloth over boards with an armorial designed stamped in colors within a gift ornamental border; gift flet. [BX5145.A] A 34
I. Title.

CLARK, Glenn, 1882- 264.1
I will lift up mine eyes, by Glenn Clark... New York and London, Harper & brothers, 1937. ix p., 1 l., 178 p. diagrs. 19 1/2 cm. "First edition." [BV210.C54] 37-39204
1. Prayer. I. Title.

CLARK, Glenn, 1882- 264.1
On wings of prayer. [1st ed.] Saint Paul, Macalester ParkPub. Co. [1955] 258p. illus. 21cm. [BV220.C54] 55-57984
1. Prayer. 2. Voyages around the world. I. Title.

CLARK, Glenn, 1882- 248
The soul's sincere desire. Silver anniversary ed. Boston, Little, Brown, 1950 ['1925] 113 p. 20 cm. [BV210.C55 1950] 50-13727
1. Prayer. I. Title.

CLARK, Glenn, 1882- 248
The soul's sincere desire, by Glenn Clark. Boston, The Atlantic monthly press [1925] 6 p. l., 3-114 p. 20 1/2 cm. [BV210.C55] 25-7083
1. Prayer. I. Title.

CLARK, Glenn, 1882- 248
The soul's sincere desire, by Glenn Clark. Boston, Little, Brown, and company, 1931. 6 p. l., 3-114 p. 20 1/2 cm. "Tenth impression, March, 1931." [BV210.C55 1931] 33-14913
1. Prayer. I. Title.

CLARK, Glenn, 1882- 248
Two or three gathered together, by Glenn Clark. New York and London, Harper & brothers [1942] v. 154 p. 19 1/2 cm. "fIrst edition." [BV210.C56] 42-15288
1. Prayer. I. Title.

CLARK, Keith. 248'.3
Make space, make symbols : a personal journey into prayer / Keith Clark. Notre Dame, Ind. : Ave Maria Press, c1979. 112 p. : ill. ; 21 cm. [BV215.C56] 78-73826 ISBN 0-87793-173-9 pbk. : 2.45
1. Prayer. 2. Spiritual life—Catholic authors. I. Title.

CLARKE, James Freeman, 1810-1888. 248
The Christian doctrine of prayer. An essay. By James Freeman Clarke ... 6th ed. Boston, American Unitarian association, 1867. xviii, 313 p. 17 1/2 cm. [BV210.C6 1867] 44-53533
1. Prayer. I. American Unitarian association. II. Title.

CLAUDEL, Paul, 1868- 264.1
Lord, teach us to pray, tr. by Ruth Bethell. [1st American ed.] New York, Longmans, Green, 1948. 95 p. illus. 20 cm. Full name: Paul Louis Charles Marie Claudel. [BV215.C58 1948] 48-2915
1. Prayer. I. Bethell, Ruth, tr. II. Title.

CLEAVER, Solomon. 248
Life's great adventure--prayer, by Solomon Cleaver. New York, R. R. Smith, inc., 1931. 6 p. l., 3-163 p. 19 1/2 cm. [BV210.C63] 31-22921
1. Prayer. I. Title.

COBURN, John B. 248'.3
A life to live—a way to pray [by] John B. Coburn. New York, Seabury Press [1973] x, 143 p. 21 cm. (An Original Seabury paperback, SP 80) Includes bibliographical references. [BV210.2.C57] 72-96340 ISBN 0-8164-2079-3 2.95
1. Prayer. 2. Prayers. I. Title.

COBURN, John B 264.1
Prayer and personal religion. Philadelphia, Westminster Press [1957] 96p. 20cm. (Layman's theological library) [BV210.C686] 57-5397
1. Prayer. I. Title.

COLEMAN, George William, 1867-
The people's prayers, voiced by a layman, written by George W. Coleman ... Philadelphia, Boston, [etc.] The Griffith & Rowland press [c1914] 7 p. l., 93 p. 17 1/2 cm. Part of the pages blank. 15-1907 0.50.
I. Title.

COLIN, Louis, 1884- 248.32
The meaning of prayer. Tr. by Francis X. Moan. Westminster, Md., Newman [c.] 1962. 302p. 23cm. 62-15997 4.25
1. Prayer. 2. Catholic Church. Liturgy and ritual. I. Title.

CONN, Charles Gerard, 1844- 248
... The sixth sense, prayer; brain cell reformation, by Charles Gerard Conn. [2d ed.] Los Angeles, G. Rice & sons, 1916. xii, 203 p. 2 pl. 19 cm. Plates accompanied by guard sheet with descriptive letterpress. [BV210.C7 1906 a] 16-24939
1. Prayer. I. Title.

CONWELL, Russell Herman, 1843-1925. 248
Effective prayer, by Russell H. Conwell ... New York and London, Harper & brothers, 1921. 5 p. l., 221 p. 17 cm. [BV220.C6] 21-4241
1. Prayer. I. Title.

COOK, Charles Augustus, 1856- comp. 248
Practical portions for the prayer life; selected thoughts on prayer for each day of the year, by Chas. A. Cook. New York, Chicago [etc.] Fleming H. Revell company [1900] 377 p. 18 cm. [BV210.C77] 1-29286
1. Prayer. I. Title.

COOK, David Caleb, 1850-1927. 264.
Prayer, and some mistakes about it. By David C. Cook. Chicago, David C. Cook publishing company [1898] 63 p. 13 x 13 cm. [His The christian life series] [BV213.C6] 98-1005
1. Prayer. I. Title.

CORBISHLEY, Thomas. 248'.3
The prayer of Jesus / Thomas Corbishley. 1st ed. in the United States of America. Garden City, N.Y. : Doubleday, 1977, c1976. 119 p. ; 22 cm. [BV229.C67 1977] 76-23755 ISBN 0-385-12545-3 : 5.95
1. Jesus Christ—Prayers. 2. Jesus Christ—Spiritual life. 3. Prayer. I. Title.

CORNET, N E.
Prayer, a means of spiritual growth, by N. E. Cornetet ... Dayton, O., United Brethren publishing house [1904] 89 p. 17 cm. (On verso of half-title: The devotional series) 9-20232
I. Title.

COX, Enos Kincheloe. 248
"Where is the Lord God of Elijah?" by Enos Kincheloe Cox, D. D., with introduction by Byron Hoover De Ment ... Chicago, The Bible institute colportage association [c1929] 127 p. 19 cm. [BV210.C78] 20-20532
1. Prayer. I. Title.

CRANE, Aaron Martin, 1839-1914. 248
Ask and receive, by Aaron Martin Crane ... Boston, Lothrop, Lee & Shepard co. [c1920] xv, 194 p. 20 cm. [BV210.C8] 20-22091
I. Title.

CULLUMBER, Norman L. 264'.1
Please lead us in prayer / Norman L. Cullumber. St. Louis, Mo. : Bethany Press, c1980. 94 p. : ill. ; 23 cm. [BV226.C84] 80-10531 ISBN 0-8272-2928-3 pbk. : 4.95
1. Prayer. 2. Prayers. I. Title.

DABNEY, Elizabeth J. 264.1
What it means to pray through, by E. J. Dabney. Philadelphia, Pa., c1945. 215 p. 19 1/2 cm. [BV220.D3] 45-22161
1. Prayer. I. Title.

DAUJAT, Jean 264.1
Prayer. Tr. from French by Martin Murphy. New York, Hawthorn [c.1964] 159[1]p. 21cm. (Twentieth cent. ency. of Catholicism, v.37. Sec. 4: The means of redemption) Bibl. [BV210.2.D3513] 64-25386 3.50 bds.,
1. Prayer. (Series: The Twentieth century encyclopedia of Catholicism, v. 37) I. Title.

DAUJAT, Jean. 264.1
Prayer. Tranlsated from the French by Martin Murphy. [1st ed.] New York, Hawthorn Books [1964] 159 [1] p. 21 cm. (The Twentieth century encyclopedia of Catholicism, v. 37. Section 4: The means of redemption) Bibliography: p. [160] [BV210.2.D3513] 64-25386
1. Prayer. I. Title. II. Series. III. Series: The Twentieth century encyclopedia of Catholicism, v. 37

DAWSON, John B. 248.32
People of prayer. Nashville, Upper Room [c.1963] 64p. 19cm. .35 pap.,
I. Title.

DAWSON, William James, 1854-1928. 226.
The forgotten secret, by W. J. Dawson ... New York, Chicago [etc.] Fleming H. Revell company [c1906] 3 p. l., 5-64 p. 19 cm. [BV213.D3] 6-13321
1. Prayer. I. Title.

DAY, Albert Edward, 1884- 264.1
An autobiography of prayer. [1st ed.] New York, Harper [1952] 223 p. 22 cm. Includes bibliography. [BV210.D38] 52-8044
1. Prayer. I. Title.

DAY, Bertram, 1871- 264.1
The power of prayer, the only hope of mankind. Boston, Christopher Pub. House [1954] 376p. 21cm. [BV220.D35] 54-8657
1. Prayer. I. Title.

DAY by day;
short prayers for daily use. Cleveland, O., Central publishing house, 1916. 273 p. front. 13 cm. 16-12547 0.50

DE BARDELEBEN, Mary Christine, 1881- 248
Great souls at prayer, by Mary De Bardeleben. Nashville, Tenn., Cokebury press, 1930. 49 p. 19 cm. [BV214.D] 30-20135
1. Prayer. I. Title.
Contents omitted.

DEERE, George Henry, 1827-1910. 264.1
... Prayer. By Rev. George H. Deere ... Boston, Universalist publishing house, 1893. 3 p. l., [5]-101 p. 18 cm. (Added t.-p.: Manuals of faith and duty. Ed. by J. S. Cantwell, no. xi) Series title in part at head of t.-p. [BV210.D4] 38-11185
1. Prayer. I. Title.

DEHAAN, Richard W. 248.3'2
Pray, God is listening / Richard DeHaan. Grand Rapids, MI : Zondervan Pub.

House, 1981, c1980. p. cm. [BV215.D38 1981] 19 80-27857 ISBN 0-310-23542-1 (pbk.) : 2.50
1. Prayer. I. Title.

DEMARAY, Donald E 248.3
Alive to God through prayer; a manual on the practices of prayer, by Donald E. Demaray. Grand Rapids, Baker Book House, 1965. 156 p. 20 cm. Includes bibliographies. [BV210.2.D43] 64-8346
1. Prayer. I. Title.

DE PIERREFEU, Elsa (tudor) 291.3
Unity in the spirit. Rindge, N. H., R. R. Smith, 1955. 167p. 23cm. [BL560.D4] 55-9047
1. Prayer. I. Title.

DICKSON, Louis Klaer, 1890- 264.1
Key in the hand. Mountain View, Calif., Pacific Press Pub. Association [1956] 75p. 19cm. [BV210.D5] 56-35991
1. Prayer. I. Title.

DODD, Monroe Elmon, 1878- 232.
The prayer life of Jesus, by Rev. M. E. Dodd ... New York, George H. Doran company [c1923] xii p., 1 l., 15-173 p. 20 cm. [BT590.P6D6] 24-29783
1. Prayer. 2. Jesus Christ. I. Title.

DONNE, John, 1573-1631 264.1
Prayers; selected, ed. from the earliest sources, with an essay on Donne's idea of prayer, by Herbert H. Umbach. College & Univ. Pr. [dist. New York, Twayne, 1962, c.1961] 109p. 21cm. (L3) 1.25 pap.,
1. Prayers. Prayer. I. Umbach, Herbert Herman, 1908- ed. II. Title.

DOPPELT, Frederic Aubrey. 264.1
Dialogue with God, being a series of studies on the principle of prayer in human life, by Frederic A. Doppelt; with a foreword by Dr. Solomon B. Freehof. Philadelphia, Dorrance & company [1943] xiii, [1], 15-230 p. 19 1/2 cm. Bibliography: p. 226-230. [BV210.D65] 44-747
1. Prayer. I. Title.

DOTY, William Lodewick, 248'.3
1919-
Prayer in the spirit, by William L. Doty. Staten Island, N.Y., Alba House [1973] 154 p. 22 cm. [BV210.2.D65] 73-9580 ISBN 0-8189-0278-7 4.95
1. Prayer. 2. Pentecostalism. I. Title.

DOWKONTT, George H 1869- 264.1
Marvel mantel that caused a sweet mother to suffer in silence, and a strong father to sob out a prayer , and other true stories, and a strong father to sob out a prayer, and other true stories, written and edited by George H. Dowkontt. Jacket by F. Sands Brunner. New York, Loizeaux Bros. [194-] 160p. 20cm. Autobiographical. [BV220.D67] 57-15243
1. Prayer. I. Title.

DRAUN, Dorothy Jones, 1915-
My cares and prayers. Boston, Forum Pub. co. [c1963] 105 p. 21 cm. Poems. 64-63789
I. Title.

DRUMWRIGHT, Huber L. 248'.3
Prayer rediscovered / Huber L. Drumwright. Nashville : Broadman Press, c1978. 213 p. ; 21 cm. Includes bibliographical references. [BV210.2.D72] 76-57502 pbk. : 3.95
1. Prayer. I. Title.

DUBAY, Thomas. 242'.8
Pilgrims pray. New York, Alba House [1974] vi, 272 p. 22 cm. Includes bibliographical references. [BV210.2.D76] 74-533 ISBN 0-8189-0286-8 4.95
1. Prayer. I. Title.

DUNNAM, Maxie D. 248'.3
The workbook of intercessory prayer / Maxie Dunnam. Nashville : The Upper Room, c1979. 155 p. : ill. ; 28 cm. Includes bibliographical references. [BV215.D85] 78-65617 ISBN 0-8358-0382-1 pbk. : 3.50
1. Prayer. I. Title.

DUQUOC, Christian. 248'.3
The prayer life. Edited by Christian Duquoc and Claude Geffre. [New York] Herder and Herder [1972] 126 p. 23 cm. (Concilium: religion in the seventies. Spirituality, v. 79) On cover: The New concilium: religion in the seventies. Includes bibliographical references. [BV210.2.D85] 72-3944 ISBN 0-07-073609-X Pap. 2.95
1. Prayer. I. Geffre, Claude, joint author. II. Title. III. Series: Concilium: theology in the age of renewal, v. 79.

EASTMAN, Dick. 248.3
No easy road; inspirational thoughts on prayer. Grand Rapids, Mich., Baker Book House [1973, c.1971] 126 p. 18 cm. (Direction Books) Bibliography: p. 126. [BV210.2E28] 70-155861 ISBN 0-8010-3259-8 0.95 (pbk.)
1. Prayer. I. Title.

EATON, Kenneth Oxner 248.3
Men who talked with God. Nashville, Abingdon [c.1964] 95p. 20cm. 64-10105 2.25 bds.,
1. Prayer. 2. Prophets. I. Title.

EATON, Kenneth Oxner. 248.3
Men who talked with God. New York, Abingdon Press [1964] 95 p. 20 cm. [BV210.2.E3] 64-10105
1. Prayer. 2. Prophets. I. Title.

ECCLESTONE, Alan. 248'.3
Yes to God / Alan Ecclestone. St. Meinrad, Ind. : Abbey Press, 1975. 133 p. ; 21 cm. (A Priority edition) [BV210.2.E33 1975] 75-19923 ISBN 0-87029-050-9 pbk. : 3.95
1. Prayer. 2. Spirituality. I. Title.

EDNA MARY, Sister 248.3
This world and prayer. London, S.P.C.K. [New York, Morehouse, c.]1965. x, 85p. 19cm. (Here & now ser. Seraph bk.) Bibl. [BV213.E3] 65-6441 1.50 pap.,
1. Prayer. I. Title.

EDWARDS, Francis Henry, 248'.3
1897-
Meditation & prayer / by F. Henry Edwards. Independence, Mo. : Herald Pub. House, c1980. 272 p. ; 20 cm. Includes bibliographical references. [BV215.E4] 79-23708 ISBN 0-8309-0271-6 pbk. : 9.75
1. Prayer. 2. Meditation. I. Title.

ELBERT, John Aloysius, 264.1
1895-
Prayer in a modern age, by Rev. John A. Elbert ... Ozone Park, N.Y., Catholic literary guild [c1941] 3 p., l., 135 p. 18 1/2 cm. [BV210.E4] 41-26023
1. Prayer. I. Catholic literary guild, Ozone Park, N.Y. II. Title.

ELLIFF, Thomas D. 248'.3
Praying for others / Thomas D. Elliff. Nashville, Tenn. : Broadman Press, c1979. 97 p. ; 20 cm. [BV210.2.E38] 79-52341 ISBN 0-8054-5273-7 pbk. : 2.75
1. Elliff, Thomas D. 2. Prayer. I. Title.

ELLUL, Jacques. 248.3
Prayer and modern man. Translated by C. Edward Hopkin. New York, Seabury Press [1970] xi, 178 p. 22 cm. [BV210.2.E43] 79-103845 4.95
1. Prayer. I. Title.

EMERY, Pierre Yves. 248'.3
Prayer at the heart of life / Pierre-Yves Emery ; translated by William J. Nottingham. Maryknoll, N.Y. : Orbis Books, c1975. xxi, 168 p. ; 20 cm. Translation of La priere au coeur de la vie. Includes bibliographical references. [BV210.2.E4713] 74-17870 ISBN 0-88344-393-7 : 4.95
1. Prayer. I. Title.

ERPESTAD, Emil, 1912- 248
Ten studies in prayer. Minneapolis, Augsburg Pub. House [1951] 89 p. 20 cm. (Ten-week teacher-training course books) "Published under the auspices of the Board of Christian Educationof the Evangelical Lutheran Church." [BV215.E7] 51-4502
1. Prayer. I. Title.

ESSAYS on prayer; 264'.1
a His reader on conversing with God, by A. W. Tozer and others. Chicago, Inter-Varsity Press [1968] 89, [3] p. illus. 22 cm. A collection of articles that had originally appeared in His magazine. Bibliography: p. [92] [BV205.E8] 68-57740
1. Prayer. I. Tozer, Aiden Wilson, 1897-1963. II. His.

EVANS, Colleen Townsend. 248.3'2
Give us this day our daily bread : asking for and sharing life's necessitites / Collen Townsend Evans. 1st ed. Garden City, N.Y. : Doubleday, 1981. 160 p. ; 22 cm. "A Doubleday-Galilee original." [BV215.E9] 19 78-20070 ISBN 0-385-14091-6 : 7.95
1. Prayer. 2. Sharing. I. Title.

EVANS, Colleen Townsend. 248'.3
Teaching your child to pray / Colleen Townsend Evans ; photos. by Walter Bredel. 1st ed. Garden City, N.Y. : Doubleday, 1978. [64] p. : ill. ; 20 x 24 cm. "A Doubleday-Galilee original." [BV213.E88] 77-12847 ISBN 0-385-13249-2 : 6.95
1. Prayer. 2. Prayer—Juvenile literature. I. Title.

EVANS, Colleen Townsend. 248.3'2
Teaching your child to pray / by Colleen Townsend Evans. Garden City, N.Y. : Doubleday, 1982. p. cm. "A Doubleday-Galilee book." Includes separate discussions for parents and children about the essentials of personal prayer, including the meaning and application of the "Lord's Prayer." [BV213.E88 1982] 19 82-1434 ISBN 0-385-15045-8 (pbk.) : 6.95
1. Prayer. 2. Prayer—Juvenile literature. 3. [Prayer.] I. Title.

EVANS, Louis Hadley, 248.3'2
1897-
Can you really talk to God? / Louis H. Evans, Sr. Waco, Tex. : Word Books, c1982. 116 p. ; 22 cm. [BV210.2.E86] 19 81-52525 ISBN 0-8499-2940-7 (pbk.) : 5.95
1. Prayer. I. Title.

EVELY, Louis, 1910- 264'.1
Our prayer. [Tr. by Paul Burns.] Garden City, N.Y., Doubleday [1974, c1970] 112 p. 18 cm. (Image books) [BV210.2E8813 1974] ISBN 0-385-03072-X 1.45 (pbk.)
1. Prayer. I. Title.
L.C. card number for original ed.: 75-110078.

EVELY, Louis, 1910- 264'.1
Our prayer. [Translated by Paul Burns. New York] Herder and Herder [1970] 143 p. 22 cm. Translation of La priere d'un homme moderne. [BV210.2.E8813 1970] 75-110078 4.50
1. Prayer. I. Title.

EVELY, Louis, 1910- 248.3
Teach us how to pray. Translated by Edmond Bonin. Westminster, Md., Newman Press [1967] 90 p. 22 cm. Translation of the author's Apprenez-nous a prier, and Sur la priere. [BV210.2.E9] 67-26074
1. Prayer. I. Title.

EVERETT, Oliver P. 264.1
Morning and evening, by Oliver Everette. [Minneapolis, Augsburg publishing house, 1936] v, [3], 52 p. 29 1/2 cm. "Prayer meditations."--Foreword. [BV210.E84] 42-44303
1. Prayer. I. Title.

EVERETTE, 264.142-44303 rev
Oliver Page, 1912-
Morning and evening, by Oliver Everette. [Minneapolis, Augsburg publishing house, 1936] Chicago, Rand McNally, c1948. v. [3], 52 p. 20 1/2 cm. 40 p. col. illus. 21 cm. (A Rand McNally book-elf book) "Prayer meditations."--Foreword. [BV210.E84] [PZ10.3E8525Day] 48-7985
1. Prayer. I. Evers, Alf. II. Title. III. Title: A day on the farm;

FARICY, Robert L., 1926- 248.3'2
Praying / by Robert Faricy. Minneapolis, Minn. : Winston Press, 1980, c1979. 121 p. ; 22 cm. Includes bibliographical references. [BV215.F37 1979] 19 79-56631 ISBN 0-03-056661-4 pbk. : 3.50
1. Prayer. I. Title.

[FARIS, William Wallce] 1843- 248
1925.
How to talk with God, by a veteran pastor. Philadelphia, The Sunday school times company [1908] 97 p., 1 l., 17 cm. [BV210.F3] 9-2780
1. Prayer. 2. Prayers. I. Title.

FENTON, Joseph Clifford. 264.1
The theology of prayer [by] Joseph Clifford Fenton... Milwaukee, The Bruce publishing company [c1939] xii p., 1 l., 257 p. 22 1/2 cm. Bibliographical references in "Footnotes": p. 248-250. [BV210.F37] 39-20420
1. Prayer. I. Title.

FERRE, Nels Fredrick 248.3
Solomon, 1908-
A theology for Christian prayer. Nashville, Tenn., Tidings [1963] 71 p. illus. 19 cm. [BV210.2.F4] 63-21518
1. Prayer. I. Title.

*FERRIER, Christine M. 248.3
Guide to prayer. Chicago, Moody [1966, i.e. 1967] 127p. 18cm. (Lion ser.) Adapted from How to pray, by R. A. Torrey. .49 pap.,
1. Prayer. I. Torrev, R. A. How to pray. II. Title. III. Title: How to pray.

FIFE, Eric S. 248'.3
Prayer : common sense and the Bible / by Eric Fife. Grand Rapids : Zondervan Pub. House, c1976. 91 p. ; 18 cm. [BV210.2.F5] 76-43017 3.95 pbk. : 1.25
1. Prayer. I. Title.

FITTIPALDI, Silvio. 248'.3
How to pray always without always praying / Silvio Fittipaldi. Notre Dame : Fides/Claretian, c1978. viii, 111 p. ; 20 cm. Includes bibliographical references. [BV210.2.F56] 77-25970 ISBN 0-8190-0623-8 pbk. : 2.95
1. Prayer. I. Title.

FLEMING, G. Granger 264.1
The dynamic of all-prayer. Introd. by Andrew Murray, D.D. Chicago, Moody [1964] 157p. 18cm. (88) .59 pap.,
I. Title.

FLEMING, G Granger.
The dynamic of all-prayer; an essay in analysis by G.G. Fleming with an introduction by Rev. Andrew Murray. New York, Hodder & Stoughton, George Doran Company [n.d.] 215 p. 68-59511
I. Title.

FORRESTER, David. 248'.3
Listening with the heart / David Forrester ; introd. by Michael Hollings. New York : Paulist Press, c1978. 95 p. ; 21 cm. Bibliography: p. 95. [BV210.2.F67 1978] 78-70822 ISBN 0-8091-2183-2 pbk. : 2.95
1. Prayer. 2. Christian life—Catholic authors. I. Title.

FORSYTH, Peter Taylor, 264.1
1848-1921.
The soul of prayer. London, Independent Press [1951; label: Chicago, A. R. Allenson] 92p. 21cm. [BV210.F56] 53-33155
1. Prayer. I. Title.

FOSDICK, Harry Emerson, 248.32
1878-
The meaning of prayer. [New York] Association [c.1949, 1962] 186p. 18cm. (Giant reflection bk. 703) 62-5499 1.50 pap.,
1. Prayer. 2. Devotional exercises. I. Title.

FOSDICK, Harry Emerson, 1878- 248
The meaning of prayer [by] Harry Emerson Fosdick, with introduction by John R. Mott. New York [etc.] Association press, 1915. xii, 196 p. 17 cm. "Selected bibliography": p. 195-196. [BV210.F57] 15-13345
1. Prayer. I. Title.

FOSDICK, Harry Emerson, 1878- 248
The meaning of prayer, [by] Harry Emerson Fosdick ... with introduction by John R. Mott. New York, Cincinnati, The Abingdon press [c1915] xii, 196 p. 17 cm. "Selected bibliography": p. 195-196. [BV210.F57 1915a] 17-25646
1. Prayer. 2. Devotional exercises. I. Title.

FOSDICK, Harry Emerson, 248'.3
1878-1969.
The meaning of prayer / Harry Emerson Fosdick ; with introduction by John R. Mott. Folcroft, Pa : Folcroft Library Editions, 1976. xii, 196 p. ; 24 cm. Reprint of the 1946 ed. published by Association Press, New York. Bibliography: p. 195-196. [BV210.F57 1976] 76-50560 ISBN 0-8414-4159-6 lib. bdg. : 15.00
1. Prayer. 2. Devotional exercises. I. Title.

FOX, Matthew, 1940- 248'.4
On becoming a musical, mystical bear; spirituality American style [1st ed.] New York, Harper & Row [1972] xvi, 156 p. 22 cm. Includes bibliographical references. [BV210.2.F69 1972] 72-78053 ISBN 0-06-062912-6 5.95
1. Prayer. 2. Spirituality. I. Title.

FOX, Matthew, 1940- 248'.4
On becoming a musical, mystical bear : spirituality American style / Matthew Fox. New York : Paulist Press/Deus Book, c1976. xxxiv, 156 p. ; 18 cm. Includes bibliographical references. [BV210.2.F69 1976] 75-34842 ISBN 0-8091-1913-7 : 2.25
1. Prayer. 2. Spirituality. I. Title.

FREEMAN, James Dillet. 264'.1
Prayer, the master key. [1st ed.] Garden City, N.Y., Doubleday, 1968. 261 p. 22 cm. [BV210.2.F7] 68-11793
1. Prayer. I. Title.

FREER, Harold Wiley 248.3
Growing in the life of prayer. Nashville, Abingdon [c.1962] 176p. 21cm. Bibl. 62-9384 3.00
1. Prayer. I. Title.

FROST, Bede, father, 1877- 242
Prayer for all Christians, by Bede Frost. London and Oxford, A. R. Mowbray & co., ltd.; New York, Morehouse-Gorham co. [1939] 120 p. 19 cm. Printed in Great Britain. "First published in 1939." [Secular name: Albert Ernest Frost.] [BV215.F9] A40
1. Prayer. I. Title.

FROST, Henry Weston, 1858- 248
Effective praying, meditations upon the subject of prevailing prayer, by Henry W. Frost ... Philadelphia, The Sunday school times company [c1925] 4 p. l., 11-162 p. 19 cm. [BV220.F7] 26-1280
1. Prayer. I. Title.

GALLAGHER, Edwin, 1949- 248'.3
Yours for the asking : a guide to a dynamic and fulfilling prayer life / Edwin Gallagher. Washington : Review and Herald Pub. Association, c1978. 95 p. ; 21 cm. Includes bibliographical references. [BV210.2.G24] 77-80112 pbk. : 3.95
1. Prayer. I. Title.

GARNER, Kathryn F. 242'.9
My prayer diary / Kathryn F. Garner, Christa G. Young ; introd. by D. James Kennedy. 1st ed. Nashville : Nelson, c1978. p. cm. Includes index. [BV215.G37 1978] 78-17345 ISBN 0-8407-5657-7 pbk. : 4.95
1. Prayer. I. Young, Christa G., joint author. II. Title.

GARRETT, Constance, 1894- 264.1
Growth in prayer. New York, Macmillan, 1950. viii, 156 p. 21 cm. [BV210.G33] 50-5677
1. Prayer. I. Title.

GARRONE, Gabriel Marie, Abp., 1901- 264
Pourquoi prier? [Toulouse] Privat [dist. Philadelphia, Chilton, 1964, c.1962] 153p. 19cm. (Questions posees aux catholiques) 64-9073 1.50 pap.,
1. Prayer. I. Title.

GATLIN, Dana. 248
Prayer changes things. Lee's Summit, Mo., Unity School of Christianity, 1951. 186 p. 17 cm. [BV210.G35] 52-25950
1. Prayer. 2. Unity School of Christianity—Doctrinal and controversial works. I. Title.

GERTRUDE, Sister O. M. S. H 248.32
Christian prayer. New York, Association Press [c1959] 79 p. 19 cm. (World Christian books, 2d ser., no. 27) [BV210.2.G4] 59-14238
1. Prayer. I. Title.

GIBBARD, Mark. 248.3
Why pray? Valley Forge, Judson Press [1971, c1970] 125 p. 19 cm. Bibliography: p. 121. [BV210.2.G5 1971] 72-132999 ISBN 0-8170-0517-X 1.95
1. Prayer. I. Title.

GIBBS, Elsie. 226.
Silent prayer, by Elsie Gibbs. Chicago, Ill., Payne's school of metaphysics [c1923] 122 p. 19 cm. [BV213.G55] 23-6911
I. Title.

GIBSON, Elsie. 248.3'2
Honest prayer / by Elsie Gibson. 1st ed. Philadelphia : Westminster Press, c1981. 120 p. ; 21 cm. [BV210.2.G53] 19 80-39570 ISBN 0-664-24348-7 pbk. : 7.95
1. Prayer. I. Title.

GIRARDEY, Ferrol, 1839- 248
Popular instructions on prayer. By Very Rev. Ferrol Girardey, C. SS. R. New York, Cincinnati [etc.] Benziger brothers, printers, 1898. 224 p. 13 cm. [BV210.G54] 98-588
1. Prayer. I. Title.

[GODDARD, Neville Lancelot] 1905- 264.1
Prayer--the art of believing [by] Neville [pseud.] New York city, Goddard publications [1945] 5 p. l., 13-82 p. 14 1/2 cm. "First edition, 1945." [BF1999.G59] 46-13486
1. Prayer. I. Title.

GOFORTH, Rosalind (Bellsmith) Mrs. 1864- 248
How I know God answers prayer; the personal testimony of one life-time, by Rosalind Goforth (Mrs. Jonathan Goforth) ... Philadelphia, The Sunday school times company, [c1921] xi (i. e. ix), 142 p. 20 cm. [Full name: Mrs. Florence Rosalind (Bellsmith) Goforth] [BV220.G6] 22-547
1. Prayer. I. Title.

GOLDSMITH, Joel S., 1892- 248'.3
The altitude of prayer / Joel S. Goldsmith ; edited by Lorraine Sinkler. 1st ed. New York : Harper & Row, [1975] vii, 147 p. ; 20 cm. Includes bibliographical references. [BV210.2.G64 1975] 74-25685 ISBN 0-06-063171-6 : 5.95
1. Prayer. I. Title.

GOOD business. 248
Prayer in the market place; a collection from Good business. Lee's Summit, Mo., Unity School of Christianity, 1950. 188 p. 17 cm. [BV210.G58] 51-30189
1. Prayer. 2. Unity School of Christianity—Doctrinal and controversial works. I. Title.

GOODWIN, Conrad Harrison, 1887- 248
The force of intercession, by Conrad H. Goodwin ... Boston, Mass., Stratford publishing company, 1922. 4 p. l., 182 p. 19 cm. [BV210.G6] 22-14139
1. Prayer. I. Title.

GORDON, Samuel Dickey, 1859- 248
Five laws that govern prayer, by S. D. Gordon ... New York, Chicago [etc.] Fleming H. Revell company [c1925] 95 p. 20 cm. "Five addresses delivered at the School of foreign missions, Woman's foreign missionary society, Methodist Episcopal church at Lakeside, Ohio." [BV210.G64] 25-24786
1. Prayer. I. Title.

GORDON, Samuel Dickey, 1859- 264.1
Prayer and the Bible, by S. D. Gordon ... New York [etc.] Fleming H. Revell company [c1935] 3 p. l., 5-126 p. 19 cm. [BV210.G645] 35-18955
1. Prayer. I. Title.

GORDON, Samuel Dickey, 1859- 248
Quiet talks on how to pray, by S. D. Gordon ... New York, Chicago [etc.] Fleming H. Revell company [c1929] 162 p. 19 cm. [BV210.G68] 29-8550
1. Prayer. I. Title.

GORDON, Samuel Dickey, 1859- 248
Quiet talks on prayer, by S. D. Gordon ... New York, Chicago [etc.] Fleming H. Revell company [1904] 234 p. 19 cm. [BV210.G65] 4-26236
1. Prayer. I. Title.

GORDON, Samuel Dickey, 1859-1936 242
Quiet talks on prayer, by S. D. Gordon. Westwood, N. J., Revell [1967] 159p. 18cm. (Spire bk.) [BV210.G65] .60 pap.,
1. Prayer. I. Title.

GORE, Charles, Bp. of Oxford, 1853-1932. 264.1
Prayer and the Lord's prayer; with an introd. by Angus Dun. [1st ed.] New York, Harper [1947] xv, 124 p. 14 cm. "A reprint of papers published in Commonwealth, mostly in 1896." [BV210.G684] 47-31401
1. Prayer. 2. Lord's Prayer. I. Title.

GOSSIP, Arthur John, 1873- 264.1
In the secret place of the Most High, being some studies in prayer, by Arthur John Gossip ... New York, C. Scribner's sons, 1947. 5 p. l., 9-210 p. 19 1/2 cm. [BV210.G69] 47-3918
1. Prayer. I. Title.

GOTTEMOLLER, Bartholomew. 248.3
How to find happiness : a simple, yet comprehensive treatment of Christian prayer / Bartholomew Gottemoller. Huntington, Ind. : Our Sunday Visitor, c1979. 184 p. ; 18 cm. [BV210.2.G67] 79-88324 ISBN 0-87973-529-5 pbk. : 1.95
1. Prayer. 2. Contemplation. I. Title.

GRAEF, Richard, 1899- 248
Lord, teach us how to pray; translated from the German of Richard Graf by Sister Mary Hildegard Windecker. New York, F. Pustet Co., 1952. 193 p. 20 cm. [BV210.G6963] 52-38624
1. Prayer. I. Title.

GRAEF, Richard, 1899- 248.32
The power of prayer. Tr. from German by John J. Coyne. Westminster, Md., Newman [c.]1961. 139p. 61-65791 2.95
1. Prayer. I. Title.

GREEN, Thomas Henry, 1932- 248'.3
Opening to God : a guide to prayer / Thomas H. Green. Notre Dame, Ind. : Ave Maria Press, c1977. 110 p. ; 21 cm. Includes bibliographical references. [BV210.2.G73] 77-83197 ISBN 0-87793-135-6 : 4.95 ISBN 0-87793-136-4 pbk. : 2.45
1. Prayer. I. Title.

GREEN, Thomas Henry, 1932- 248.3
When the well runs dry / Thomas H. Green. Notre Dame, Ind. : Ave Maria Press, c1979. 175 p. ; 21 cm. Includes bibliographical references. [BV215.G7] 79-52404 ISBN 0-87793-181-X ISBN 0-87793-182-8 (pbk.) : 3.50
1. Prayer. 2. Spiritual life—Catholic authors. I. Title.

GREENE, Wade, ed. 264.1
The importance of prayer; a compilation of the views and experiences of people in all walks of life who confirm the value of prayer in managing their affairs and solving human problems as well as creating a more moral and spiritual world. Minneapolis, T. S. Denison [1958] 284p. 22cm. [BV205.G7] 57-14985
1. Prayer. I. Title.

GREENLEAF, Jonathan, 1785-1865. 264.1
Thoughts on prayer: its duty: its form: its subjects: its encouragements: its blessings. By Jonathan Greenleaf ... Philadelphia, Presbyterian board of publication [c1857] 156 p. 18 cm. [BV210.G7 1857 a] 39-1468
1. Prayer. I. Presbyterian church in the U. S. A. [Old school] Board of publication. II. Title.

GREENWALD, Emanuel, 1811-1885. 249
Jesus our table guest: an order of family prayer. By Rev. Emanuel Greenwald ... Philadelphia, Lutheran book store, 1883. iv, 5-317 p. 21 cm. [BV255.G65] 23-1360
I. Title.

GREGG, David, 1846-1919. 248
Individual prayer as a working force, by Rev. David Gregg ... Chicago, London [etc.] Fleming H. Revell company [c1903] 147 p. 19 cm. [BV210.G73] 3-13943
1. Prayer. I. Title.

GRIFFEN, Jonathan. 248'.3
Tranquility through prayer / Jonathan Griffen. New York : Simon and Schuster, c1977. 118 p. ; 21 cm. [BV210.2.G74] 77-24226 ISBN 0-671-22918-4 : 5.95
1. Prayer. 2. Prayers. I. Title.

GRIFFISS, James E., 1928- 264'.1
A silent path to God / James E. Griffiss. Philadelphia : Fortress Press, c1980. 110 p. ; 22 cm. Includes bibliographical references. [BV210.2.G744] 19 79-8903 ISBN 0-8006-1384-8 : 4.50
1. Jesus Christ—Temptation—Meditation. 2. Prayer. I. Title.

GROU, Jean Nicolas, 1731-1803. 264.1
How to pray; the chapters on prayer from The school of Jesus Christ translated by Joseph Dalby. New York, Harper [1955] 154p. 20cm. [BV210.G752] 55-8523
1. Prayer. I. Title.

GROU, Jean Nicolas, 1731-1803. 248'.3
How to pray; nine chapters on prayer from The school of Jesus Christ. Translated by Joseph Dalby. [Nashville] Upper Room [1973] 96 p. 19 cm. Translated from L'ecole de Jesus Christ. [BV210.G752 1973] 72-97118 1.00
1. Prayer. I. Title.

GRUSA, Jiri. FIC
The questionnaire, or, Prayer for a town & a friend / Jiri Grusa ; translated from the Czech by Peter Kussi. New York, N.Y. : Farrar, Straus & Giroux, c1982. 278 p. : ill., geneal. table ; 22 cm. Translation of: Dotaznik. "Published simultaneously in Canada by McGraw-Hill Ryerson Ltd., Toronto"—T.p. verso. [PG5039.17.R87D613 1982] 891.8'635 19 82-5042 ISBN 0-374-24010-8 : 15.95
I. [Dotaznik.] English II. Title. III. Title: Prayer for a town & a friend.

GUARDINI, Romano, 1885- 264.1
Prayer in practice. Tr. from German by Prince Leopold of Loewenstein-Wertheim. Garden City, N.Y., Doubleday [1963, c.1957] 159p. 18cm. (Image D157) .75 pap.,
1. Prayer. I. Title.

GUARDINI, Romano, 1885- 264.1
Prayer in practice. Translated from the German by Prince Leopold of Loewenstein-Wertheim. [New York] Pantheon Books [c1957] 228p. 22cm. Translation of Vorschule des Betens. [BV210.G813] 57-10243
1. Prayer. I. Title.

GUIDEPOSTS. 264.1
What prayer can do, by the editors of Guideposts; with photographic commentary by Lucien Aigner. Introd. by Norman Vincent Peale. [1st ed.] Garden City, N. Y., Doubleday, 1953. 95p. illus. 24cm. [BV220.G8] 53-7976
1. Prayer. I. Aigner, Lucien, illus. II. Title.

GUILLERAND, Augustin, 1877-1945. 248.3
The prayer of the presence of God. Translated from the French by a monk of Parkminster. [1st English ed.] Wilkes-Barre, Pa., Dimension Books [1966] 191 p. 21 cm. Translation of Face a Dieu. Bibliographical footnotes. [BV4813.G813] 66-22876
1. Prayer. 2. Meditation. I. Title.

*GUTZKE, Manford George. 264.1
Plain talk on prayer. Grand Rapids, Mich., Baker Book House [1973] 182 p, 21 cm. [BV215] ISBN 0-8010-3674-7 2.95 (pbk.)
1. Prayer. I. Title.

HACKNEY, Vivian. 264.1
Invitation to prayer. Nashville, Broadman Press [1965] 96 p. 19 cm. Bibliographical footnotes. [BV210.2.H3] 65-10340
1. Prayer. I. Title.

HALL, Arthur Crawshay Alliston, bp., 1847- 248
The Christian doctrine of prayer, by the Rt. Rev. A. C. A. Hall... 'new York, London [etc.] Longmans, Green, and co., 1904. xii, 120 p. 19 1/2 cm. (Half-title: The Bohlen lectures, 1904) [BV210.H3] 4-7795
1. Prayer. I. Title.

HALLESBY, Ole Christian, 1879- 248
Prayer, by O. Hallesby ... translated by Clarence J. Carlsen. Minneapolis, Minn., Augusburg publishing house [1931] 189 p. 20 cm. "First edition, November, 1931." [BV210.H34] 31-34725
1. Prayer. I. Carlsen, Clarence Johannes, 1894- tr. II. Title.

HALLIMOND, John G.
The miracle of answered prayer, by J. G. Hallimond, D.D. New York, The Christian

herald [c1916] vii, 248 p. 19 1/2 cm. 17-1168
I. Title.

HALLOCK, Edgar Francis, 1888- 248.3
Always in prayer [by] E. F. Hallock. Nashville, Broadman Press [1966] 128 p. 20 cm. [BV210.2.H35] 66-12572
1. Prayer. 2. Christian life—Baptist authors. I. Title.

HALLOCK, Edgar Francis, 1888- 264.1
Prayer and meditation [by] E. F. Hallock ... Nashville, Tenn., The Broadman press [c1940] viii, [1], 10-95 p. 19 1/2 cm. (My covenant series. book 4) [BV210.H343] 40-12952
1. Prayer. I. Title.

HANCOCK, Laurice Hicks. 248
Prayer in every day living. Dallas, Story Book Press [1950] 71 p. 20 cm. [BV210.H344] 50-4256
1. Prayer. I. Title.

HANNE, John Anthony. 248'.3
Prayer—or pretense? Grand Rapids, Zondervan Pub. House [1974] 96 p. 18 cm. [BV210.2.H354] 73-13066 0.95 (pbk.)
1. Prayer. I. Title.

HAPPOLD, Frederick Crossfield, 1893- 200
Prayer and meditation: their nature and practice [by] F. C. Happold. Harmondsworth, Penguin, 1971. 381 p. music. 19 cm. (Pelican books, A1257) Includes bibliographical references. [BV210.2.H36] 72-176065 ISBN 0-14-021257-4 £0.50
1. Prayer. 2. Prayers. 3. Devotional literature. I. Title.

HARDON, John A. 248'.3
Theology of prayer / John A. Hardon. Boston : St. Paul Editions, c1979. 172 p. : ill. ; 19 cm. [BV210.2.H364] 79-1400
1. Prayer. I. Title.

HARDY, Ruth (Bocock) Mrs. 1902- 264.1
Worship & intercession, by Ruth Hardy ... with a foreword by the Bishop of Bradford. London, New York [etc.] Longmans, Green and co. [c1936] xv, 95, [1] p. 18 cm. "First published, January, 1986." [BV210.H345] 36-25273
1. Prayer. 2. Worship. I. Title.

HARING, Bernhard, 1912- 248'.3
Prayer : the integration of faith and life / Bernard Haring. Notre Dame, Ind. : Fides Publishers, c1975. xi, 145 p. ; 23 cm. [BV210.2.H363] 75-330725 ISBN 0-8190-0609-2 : 5.95
1. Prayer. 2. Prayers. I. Title.

HARKNESS, Georgia Elma, 1891- 264.1
Prayer and the common life. Nashville, Abingdon [1962, c.1948] 224 p. (Apex bk. H4) 1.25, pap.
1. Prayer. I. Title.

HARKNESS, Georgia Elma, 1891- 264.1
Prayer and the common life. New York, Abingdon-Cokesbury Press [1948] 224 p. 22 cm. [BV210.H347] 48-7078
1. Prayer. I. Title.

HARRAH, Allegra. 248'.48'61
Prayer weapons / Allegra Harrah. Old Tappan, N.J. : F. H. Revell Co., c1975. p. cm. [BV210.2.H365] 75-29426 ISBN 0-8007-0773-7 : 4.95
1. Prayer. 2. Christian life—Baptist authors. I. Title.

HARRISON, Norman B. 248
His in a life of prayer, by Norman B. Harrison ... Chicago, The Bible institute colportage association [c1927] 96 p. 20 cm. [BV210.H36] 28-3814
1. Prayer. I. Title.

*HARTON, Sibyl 264.1
To make intercession [New rev. ed.] New York, Morehouse [c.1964] 125p. 18cm. Previously pub. under title: The Practice of Intercession. 1.00 pap.,
I. Title.

HARTWELL, Ray. 264.1
Prayer: an interpretation, by Ray Hartwell. Boston, Meador publishing company, 1933. 169 p. 21 cm. [BV210.H37] 33-23234
1. Prayer. 2. Prayers. I. Title.

HASKIN, Dorothy (Clark), 1905- 264.1
A practical primer on prayer. Chicago, Moody Press [1950] 127 p. 17 cm. (Colportage library, 206) [BV210.H372] 51-30535
1. Prayer. I. Title.

HASTINGS, James, 1852-1922, ed.
The Christian doctrine of prayer, ed. by James Hastings, D. D. New York, C. Scribner's sons; Edinburgh, T. & T. Clark, 1915. xi, 448 p. 23 cm. (Half-title: The great Christian doctrines, ed. by James Hastings. [v. 1]) Printed at Aberdeen, The University press. "Literature" preceding each chapter. A 15
1. Prayer. I. Title.

HASTINGS, James, 1852-1922, ed.
The Christina doctrine of prayer, ed. by James Hastings, D.D. New York, C. Scribner's sons; Edinburgh, T. & T. Clark, 1915. xi, 448 p. 23 cm. (Half-title: The great Christian doctrines, ed. by James Hastings. [v. 1*4 Printed at Aberdeen, The University press. "Literature" preceding each chapter. A15
1. Prayer. I. Title.

HAUSHERR, Irenee, 1891- 232.9'01
The name of Jesus / by Irenee Hausherr ; translated by Charles Cummings. Kalamazoo, Mich. : Cistercian Publications, 1978. p. cm. (Cistercian studies series ; no. 44) Translation of Noms du Christ et voies d'oraison. Includes index. Bibliography: p. [BT590.N2H3813] 77-10559 ISBN 0-87907-844-8 : 15.95
1. Jesus Christ—Name. 2. Prayer. 3. Jesus prayer. I. Title. II. Series.

*HAVERGAL, Frances Ridley, 1836-1878. 264.1
Kept for the master's use. New Canaan, Conn., Keats Publ. Co. [1973] 133 p. 18 cm. (A Pivot family reader) [BV220] 0.95 (pbk)
1. Prayer. 2. Meditations. I. Title.

HAYFORD, Jack W. 248'.3
Prayer is invading the impossible / Jack W. Hayford. Plainfield, N.J. : Logos International, c1977. 150 p. ; 21 cm. [BV210.2.H39] 77-71684 ISBN 0-88270-218-1 : 2.95
1. Prayer. I. Title.

HAZELTON, Roger, 1909- 264.1
The root and flower of prayer, by Roger Hazelton ... New York, The Macmillan company, 1943. ix p. 1 l., 137 p. 19 1/2 cm. "First printing." [BV210.H375] 43-3692
1. Prayer. I. Title.

HE sent leanness;
a book of prayers for the natural man. New York, Macmillan, 1959. 62p. 17cm.
1. Prayer. 2. Prayers. I. Head, David.

HEAD, David 264
Countdown, the launching of prayer in the space age. New York, Macmillan [1964, c.1963] 184p. 22cm. First pub. in London in 1963 under title: Three, two, one, zero. 64-14970 2.75 bds.,
1. Prayer. I. Title.

HEARD, Gerald, 1889- 248
A preface to prayer, by Gerald Heard. New York and London, Harper and brothers [1944] xvi p., 1 l., 250 p. fold. tab. 19 1/2 cm. "First edition." "Bibliography of practical works on prayer": p. 249-250. [BV210.H378] 44-3299
1. Prayer. I. Title.

HEILER, Friedrich, 1892- 264.1
Prayer; a study in the history and psychology of religion, by Friedrich Heiler ... translated and edited by Samuel McComb ... with the assistance of J. Edgar Park ... London, New York [etc.] Oxford university press [c1932] xxvii, 376 p. 21 cm. "Printed in the United States of America. "Select bibilography": p. [365]-372. [BV210.H38] 32-12970
1. Prayer. I. McComb, Samuel, 1864- ed. and tr. II. Park, John Edgar, 1879- joint ed. and tr. III. Title.

HEILER, Friedrich, 1892- 264.1
Prayer; a study in the history and psychology of religion. Translated and edited by Samuel McComb with the assistance of J. Edgar Park. New York, Oxford University Press, 1958 [c1932] 376p. 21cm. (A Galaxy book, GB16) Includes bibliography. [BV210.H38 1958] 58-3427
1. Prayer. I. Title.

HENAGHAN, John. 248
Pathways to God, by John Henaghan ... St. Columbans', Neb. [etc.] St. Columban's foreign mission society [c1939] 6 p. l., 8-147 p. 19 1/2 cm. [BV210.H44] 40-14744
1. Prayer. 2. Lord's prayer. I. Title.

HENRY, Matthew, 1662-1714. 248
A method for prayer. With Scripture expressions, proper to be used under each head. By Matthew Henry, minister of the gospel at Chester. Morristown, (N.J.) Published by Peter A. Johnson, Jacob Mann, printer, 1818. ix, [11]-202 p., 1 l. 18 1/2 cm. [BV209.H5 1818] 38-11191
1. Prayer. 2. Prayers. I. Title.

HENRY, Matthew, 1662-1714. 264.1
The secret of communion with God. Edited by Elisabeth Elliot. [Westwood, N. J.] Revell [1963] 120 p. 21 cm. [BV213.H4] 63-10397
1. "Originally entitled Directions for daily communion with God." 2. Prayer — Sermons. I. Elliot, Elisabeth, ed. II. Title.

HERMAN, Emily, Mrs. 1876-1923. 264.1
Creative prayer, by E. Herman ... New York and London, Harper & brothers [1934] ix, 13-218 p. 20 cm. [BV210.H47] 35-6686
1. Prayer. I. Title.

HERRING, Ralph A. 242
The cycle of prayer [by] Ralph A. Herring. Nashville, Brodman [1966] 80p. 21cm. [BV210.2H43] 67-12170 2.50 bds.,
1. Prayer. I. Title.

HESCHEL, Abraham Joshua, 1907-1972. 296.43
Man's quest for God; studies in prayer and symbolism. New York, Scribner, 1954. 151 p. 22 cm. [BM669.H45] 54-10371
1. Prayer. 2. Symbolism. I. Title.

HETTINGER, E D 248.32
Miracles through prayer. Plymouth, Pa., Helmbold Press, 1960. 166p. 20cm. Prose and poems. [BV220.H45] 60-37314
1. Prayer. 2. Miracles. I. Title.

HEYER, Robert J., comp. 242.8'3
Discovery in prayer [by] Robert J. Heyer [and] Richard J. Payne. Photographed by Edward Rice. New York, Paulist Press [1969] 144 p. illus. 21 cm. [BV210.2.H47] 78-104882
1. Prayer. 2. Prayers. 3. Meditations. I. Payne, Richard J., joint comp. II. Title.

HILL, Jeanne. 248.3'2
Secrets of prayer joy / Jeanne Hill. Valley Forge : Judson Press, c1981. 63 p. ; 22 cm. [BV215.H54] 19 80-27626 ISBN 0-8170-0910-8 : 2.95
1. Prayer. I. Title.

HINNEBUSCH, Paul. 264'.1
Prayer, the search for authenticity. New York, Sheed and Ward [1969] xiii, 271 p. 22 cm. [BV210.2.H55] 77-89476 5.95
1. Prayer. 2. Spiritual life—Catholic authors. I. Title.

HINSON, E. Glenn. 264'.1
The reaffirmation of prayer / E. Glenn Hinson. Nashville : Broadman Press, c1979. 149 p. ; 20 cm. Includes bibliographical references. [BV215.H56] 78-66775 ISBN 0-8054-1947-0 : 4.95
1. Prayer. I. Title.

HOCKEN, Peter. 248'.3
Prayer, a gift of life / Peter Hocken. New York : Paulist Press, [1975 c1974] 126 p. ; 22 cm. [BV210.2.H6 1974] 75-328472 ISBN 0-8091-0199-8 : 3.95
1. Prayer. I. Title.

HOLLINGS, Michael. 248'.3
Day by day; an encouragement to pray. New York, Morehouse-Barlow Co. [1973, c1972] 125 p. 18 cm. Includes bibliographical references. [BV210.2.H63 1973] 73-84095 ISBN 0-8192-1161-3 1.95 (pbk.)
1. Prayer. I. Title.

HOLLINGS, Michael. 264.1
Hey, you! A call to prayer. Westminster, Md., New-man Press [1955] 127p. 19cm. [BV210.H574] 55-8641
1. Prayer. I. Title.

HORNE, John, writer on prayer. 264.1
Prayer promptings; an aid in public prayer. Grand Rapids, Baker Book House, 1955. 154p. 21cm. (Minister's hand book series) 'Orginally printed in 1906 under the title: Promptings to devotion.' [BV226.H6 1955] 55-10555
1. Prayer. I. Title.

HORNER, William Wallace. 264.1
"Let us pray, by William Wallace Horner ... Montgomery, Ala., The Paragon press [1945] 182 p. 19 1/2 cm. [BV210.H58] 45-22089
1. Prayer. I. Title.

HORTON, Thomas Corwin, 1848- 248
The potency of prayer; a handbook on prayer for the everyday Christian, by Rev. Thomas C. Horton ... with an introduction by W. B. Riley ... New York, Chicago [etc.] Fleming H. Revell company [c1928] 192 p. 19 1/2 cm. [BV210.H6] 28-8942
1. Prayer. I. Title.

*HOTSINPILLER, Stanley T. 242.8
Cluster of church prayers. New York, Carlton [1966] 254p. 22cm. (Hearthstone bk.) 3.50
I. Title.

HOWE, Leroy T., 1936- 248'.3
Prayer in a secular world [by] Leroy T. Howe. Philadelphia, United Church Press [1973] 159 p. 23 cm. "A Pilgrim Press book." [BV210.2.H67] 73-321 ISBN 0-8298-0248-7 5.25
1. Prayer. I. Title.

HUBBARD, David Allan. 248'.3
The problem with prayer is ... [By] David A. Hubbard. Wheaton, Ill., Tyndale House Publishers [1972] 91 p. 18 cm. [BV210.2.H77] 72-75964 ISBN 0-8423-4880-8 (pbk) 0.95 (pbk)
1. Prayer. I. Title.

HUEBSCHMANN, John Simon, 1881- 264.1
Alone with God; the shut door. Nashville, Parthenon Press [1956] 95p. illus. 20cm. [BV210.H76] 56-44103
1. Prayer. I. Title.

HUEGEL, Frederick Julius, 1889- 248'.3
The ministry of intercession / by F. J. Huegel. 2d ed. Minneapolis : Bethany Fellowship, 1976, c1971. 74 p. ; 18 cm. (Dimension books) [BV213.H77 1976] 76-15861 ISBN 0-87123-365-7 pbk. : 1.25
1. Jesus Christ—Intercession. 2. Prayer. I. Title.

HUEGEL, Frederick Julius, 1889- 248.3
Prayer's deeper secrets. Grand Rapids, Zondervan Pub. House [1959] 96p. 20cm. [BV210.2.H8] 59-38174
1. Prayer. I. Title.

HUGEL, Friedrich, freiherr von, 1852-1925. 248
The life of prayer, by Baron Friedrich von Hugel. New York, E. P. Dutton & co., inc. [c1929] 63 p. 17 cm. [BV213.H78] 31-4543
1. Prayer. I. Title.

HUGHSON, Shirley Carter, 1867- 248
Contemplative prayer, by Shirley C. Hughson, O.H.C. London, Society for promoting Christian knowledge; New York, The Macmillan company [1935] xii, 294 p. 19 1/2 cm. "First published, 1935." [BV210.H8] 36-10701
1. Prayer. 2. Meditation. I. Society for promoting Christian knowledge, London. II. Title.

HULTSTRAND, Donald M., 1927- 248'.3
The praying church : with study guide / Donald M. Hultstrand. New York : Seabury Press, 1977. p. cm.

[BV210.2.H83] 77-8337 ISBN 0-8164-2159-5 pbk. : 3.95
1. Prayer. I. Title.

HUMPHREYS, Fisher. 248.3'2
The heart of prayer / Fisher Humphreys. Nashville, Tenn. : Broadman Press, c1980. 96 p. ; 20 cm. [BV210.2.H84] 19 80-122218 ISBN 0-8054-1619-6 pbk. : 3.50
1. Prayer. I. Title.

HUNTER, Frances Gardner, 1916- 248.3
Hot line to heaven, by Frances E. Gardner. Anderson, Ind., Warner Press [1970] 111 p. 19 cm. [BV210.2.H85] 72-21749
1. Prayer. I. Title.

HUNTLEY, Florence (Chance), d.1912, ed. 133
Who answers? Rev. ed. by RA, PO [and] TK. [Los Gatos, Calif.] Great School of Natural Science [1954] unpaged. 21cm. Cover title: Who answers prayer? [BF1999.H93 1954] 8-37353
1. Prayer. I. Title. II. Title: Who answers prayer?

IKERMAN, Ruth C. 248'.3
Let prayer help you / by Ruth C. Ikerman. Philadelphia, Pa. : Farm Journal ; Chappaqua, N.Y. : distributed to the trade by Christian Herald Books, c1980. vii, 135 p. : ill. ; 22 cm. (A Farm journal inspiration book) [BV210.2.136] 79-24320 ISBN 0-89795-009-7 : 5.95
1. Prayer. I. Title.

IMMACULATA, Sister, O.C.D. 248'.3
The pathways of prayer : communion with God / Sister Immaculata, O.C.D. Huntington, Ind. : Our Sunday Visitor, c1978. 147 p. ; 18 cm. [BV210.2.I47] 78-60487 ISBN 0-87973-639-9 pbk. : 2.50
1. Prayer. I. Title. II. Title: Communion with God.

IRONSIDE, Henry Allan, 1876-1951. 248.3
The mission of the Holy Spirit; and, Praying in the Holy Spirit. [Combined ed.] New York, Loizeaux Bros. [1950] 61, 64p. 20cm. [BV210.I7] 55-41750
1. Prayer. 2. Holy Spirit. I. Title. II. Title: Praying in the Holy Spirit.

JACKSON, Edgar Newman. 264'.1
Understanding prayer; an exploration of the nature, disciplines, and growth of the spiritual life [by] Edgar N. Jackson. Cleveland, World Pub. Co. [1968] ix, 212 p. 22 cm. [BV210.2.J3 1968] 68-26842 4.95
1. Prayer. I. Title.

JACKSON, Edgar Newman. 248.3
Understanding prayer : an exploration of the nature, disciplines, and growth of the spiritual life / Edgar N. Jackson. 1st Harper & Row pbk. ed. San Francisco : Harper & Row, [1982] c1968. p. cm. [BV210.2.J3 1982] 19 81-47845 ISBN 0-06-064112-6 pbk. : 6.68
1. Prayer. I. Title.

JACOBSEN, David C. 248'.3
Clarity in prayer : telling the small t truth / David C. Jacobsen. Corte Madera, CA : Omega Books, 1976. 94, [9] p. : ill. ; 22 cm. Bibliography: p. [101]-[102] [BV210.2.J32] 76-24101 ISBN 0-89353-015-8 pbk. : 4.00
1. Prayer. I. Title.

JEFFERY, H. B. 264.1
The spirit of prayer, by H. B. Jeffery ... Cambridge, Mass., Ruth Laighton [c1938] 2 p. l., 190 p. 21 cm. [BV210.J37] 40-12953
1. Prayer. I. Title.

JENKINS, Daniel Thomas, 1914- 248
Prayer and the service of God, by Daniel T. Jenkins. New York, Morehouse-Gorham co., 1945. vii, 135 p. 16 cm. [BV210.J39] 45-2239
1. Prayer. I. Title.

JENNINGS, Theodore W. 248.3'2
Life as worship : prayer and praise in Jesus' name / by Theodore W. Jennings, Jr. Grand Rapids, Mich. : W.B. Eerdmans Pub. Co., c1982. xi, 139 p. ; 21 cm. Includes bibliographical references. [BV210.2.J46 1982] 19 82-7283 ISBN 0-8028-1913-3 : 5.95
1. Prayer. 2. Praise of God. I. Title.

JESSOP, Harry Edward, 1884- 264.1
The ministry of prevailing prayer, heart-talks to prayer warriors, by Harry E. Jessop ... Berne, Ind., Light and hope publications [1941] 128 p. 20 cm. "First edition, June, 1941." [BV210.J45 1941] 41-11836
1. Prayer. I. Title.

JESSOP, Harry Edward, 1884- 248
When prayer seems not to work ... by Harry E. Jessop ... Chicago, Ill., Chicago evangelistic institute, 1945. 117 p. 19 1/2 cm. "Companion volume to The ministry of prevailing prayer." [BV210.J452] 46-1539
1. Prayer. I. Chicago evangelistic institute. II. Title.

JEWS. Liturgy and ritual.
The daily prayers. Pt 1, rev, and comp. by the Committee of the Cleveland Conference; translated by Isaac M. Wise. Cincinnati, Bloch, 5617 (1857) 120 p. 17 cm. No more published? Bound with as issued, Jews. Liturgy and ritual. Cincinnati, 1857. [BM665.W48] 51-54553
I. Wise, Isaac Mayer, 1819-1900, ed. and tr. II. Title.

JEWS. Liturgy and ritual.
Pulpit and public prayers, / comp. and ed. by Jacob Bosniak... New York, Reznick, Meenschel & co., 1927. 3 p.l., ix-xvii, 19-1690 p. 18 1 4 cm. [BM665.B6] 27-23828
I. Bosniak, Jacob, 1887-comp. II. Title. III. Title: (trnsliterated); Lekute tefiloth

JEWS. Liturgy and ritual. Daily prayers.
Daily prayer with English direction, rev. and arranged by A. Hyman. New York, Hebrew publishing company, 1916. 1 p. l., vi, 312 p. 23 cm. 22-4094
I. Hyman, Abraham, 1862- comp. II. Title.

JOERS, Lawrence Eugene Claire, 1900- 248.3
Call collect / by Lawrence Joers. Mountain View, Calif. : Pacific Press Pub. Association, c1982. p. cm. [BV220.J63] 19 81-16774 ISBN 0-8163-0458-0 pbk. : 3.95
1. Joers, Lawrence Eugene Claire, 1900- 2. Prayer. 3. Christian life—Seventh-Day Adventist authors. I. Title.

JOHNSON, Ben Campbell.
An adventure in prayer; a guide for groups and individuals. Nashville, The Upper Room [c1962] 64 p. 17 cm. 68-2634
1. Prayer. I. Title.

JOHNSON, Ben Campbell.
New life for prayer groups. Nashville, The Upper Room [c1964] 64 p. 17 cm. 68-4386
1. Prayer. I. Title.

JOHNSON, Merle Allison. 248'.3
Religious roulette & other dangerous games Christians play. Nashville, Abingdon Press [1975] 143 p. 19 cm. [BV210.2.J63] 74-17453 ISBN 0-687-36109-5 2.95 (pbk.)
1. Prayer. 2. Faith-cure. I. Title.

JONES, George Curtis, 1911- 264.13
Patterns of prayer, by G. Curtis Jones. St. Louis, Bethany Press [1964] 140 p. 23 cm. Bibliographical footnotes. [BV215.J6] 64-20803
1. Prayer. I. Title.

JORDAN, Gerald Ray, 1896- 264.1
Prayer that prevails. New York, Macmillan, 1958. 157p. 21cm. [BV220.J65] 58-7138
1. Prayer. I. Title.

JOWETT, J. H.
Yet another day; a prayer for every day in the year [by] J. H. Jowett. [New York, Chicago, etc.] F. H. Revell company [c1906] [191] p. 17 cm. 6-41052
I. Title.

KANE, Thomas S., 1942- 242'.5
Journey of the heart : a way of praying on the Gospels / Thomas S. Kane. Still River, Mass. : St. Bede's, c1981. xi, 89 p. ; 21 cm. [BV210.2.K33] 19 81-5278 ISBN 0-932506-13-5 : 4.95
1. Bible. N.T. Gospels—Criticism, interpretation, etc. 2. Prayer. I. Title.
Publisher's address P. O. Box 61, Still River, MA 04167.

KELPIUS, John, 1673-1708. 264.1
A method of prayer; edited, with an introd., by E. Gordon Alderfer. [1st ed.] New York, Published in association with Pendle Hill by Harper [1951] 127 p. 14 cm. Originally published under title: Eine kurtze und begreifilge Anleitung zum stillen Gebet: previous editions in English published under title: A short, easy and comprehensive method of prayer. [BV209.K315 1951] 51-10649
1. Prayer. I. Title.

KENSINGTON, J J. 242
Talking with God: some suggestions for the practice of private prayer, by J. J. Kensington, with an introduction by the Very Rev. Edmund S. Rousmaniere ... Milwaukee, Morehouse publishing co. [c1918] viii, 49 p. 15 cm. [BV215.K3] 19-652 0.60
I. Title.

KENSINGTON, J. J. 248
Talking with God; some suggestions for the practice of private prayer, by J. J. Kensington; with an introduction by the late Very Rev. Edmund S. Rousmaniere ... Milwaukee, Morehouse publishing co. [c1930] viii, 50 p. 15 cm. "Second edition, revised." [BV215.K3 1930] 30-19368
I. Title.

KENYON, Essek William, 1867-1948. 264.1
In His presence; the secret of prayer. A revelation of what we are in Christ... [Seattle, c1944] 188 p. port. 22cm. [BV210.K4] 48-37776
1. Prayer. 2. Agricultural extension work==Kentucky. I. Title.

KILLINGER, John. 248'.3
Bread for the wilderness, wine for the journey : the miracle of prayer and meditation / John Killinger. Waco, Tex. : Word Books, c1976. 133 p. ; 23 cm. [BV210.2.K48] 75-38049 ISBN 0-87680-443-1 : 5.95
1. Prayer. I. Title.

KILLINGER, John. 248.3'2
Prayer, the act of being with God / John Killinger. Waco, Tex. : Word Books, c1981. 90 p. ; 23 cm. [BV215.K48] 19 81-52524 ISBN 0-8499-0121-9 : 6.95
1. Prayer. I. Title.

KIMMEL, Jo, 1931- 248'.3
Steps to prayer power. Nashville [Tenn.] Abingdon Press [1972] 112 p. 19 cm. Bibliography: p. 110-112. [BV210.2.K5] 72-702 ISBN 0-687-39341-8
1. Prayer. I. Title.

KINNE, Clarence James, 1869-
Prayer, by C. J. Kinne. Kansas City, Mo., Publishing house of the Pentecostal church of the Nazarene, 1913. 85, [1] p. 17 cm. $0.15. 13-8048
I. Title.

KINSLEY, William Wirt, 1837-1923.
Science and prayer, by W. W. Kinsley ... Meadville, Pa. [etc.] Flood and Vincent, 1893. 111 p. 20 cm. (Chautauqua reading circle literature) E 16
1. Prayer. 2. Religion and science. I. Title.

KIRKLAND, Winifred Margaretta, 1872- 264.1
Let us pray, by Winifred Kirkland. New York and London, Harper & brothers, 1938. 4 p. l., 3-101 p. 17 cm. "First edition." [BV215.K5] 38-6569
1. Prayer. I. Title.

THE Kneeling Christian / 248'.3
by an unknown Christian. Grand Rapids : Zondervan, 1979, c1971. 155 p. ; 24 cm. "A Zondervan large print book." [BV210.2.K55 1979] 79-209 ISBN 0-310-33492-6 pbk. : 1.50
1. Prayer. 2. Large type books. I. An unknown Christian.

KOLB, Erwin J. 264'.1
A prayer primer : a guide on how to pray in public / Erwin J. Kolb. St. Louis : Concordia Pub. House, c1982. 90 p. : ill. ; 22 cm. Bibliography: p. 89-90. [BV226.K64] 19 81-14358 ISBN 0-570-03843-X pbk. : 3.95
1. Prayer. I. Title.

KUPFERLE, Mary L. 248'.3
The light will dawn ... through prayer / by Mary L. Kupferele. Unity Village, Mo. : Unity Books, c1978. 213 p. ; 20 cm. [BV210.2.K79] 77-91310 3.95
1. Lord's prayer. 2. Prayer. I. Title.

LAKE, Alexander. 264.1
You need never walk alone [stories] New York, Messner [1959] 192 p. 22 cm. [BV220.L34] 59-7585
1. Prayer. I. Title.

LAKE, Alexander. 264.1
Your prayers are always answered. [New York] Gilbert Press; distributed by J. Messner [c1956] 248p. 21cm. 'Prayer stories.' [BV220.L35] 56-6791
1. Prayer. I. Title.

LANDSTROM, Elsie H. 248.3
Friends, let us pray [by] Elsie H. Landstrom. [Wallingford, Pa., Pendle Hill Publications, 1970] 32 p. 20 cm. (Pendle Hill pamphlet, 174) Includes bibliographical references. [BV213.L35] 79-146679 0.70
1. Prayer. I. Title.

LANIER, John Jabez.
Prayer; the soul's sincere desire, by Rev. John J. Lanier ... Fredericksburg, Va., J. J. Lanier [c1914] 5 p. l., 3-149 p. 19 cm. (Lettered on cover: Kinship of God and man. vol. v) "Selections from poems: The lost pearl": p. [137]-149. 15-1657 1.00
I. Title.

LAUBACH, Frank Charles, 1884- 264.1
Prayer, the mightiest force in the world, by Frank C. Laubach, D.D. New York, London [etc.] Fleming H. Revell company [1946] 95 p. 19 1/2 cm. [BV210.L37] 46-2457
1. Prayer. I. Title.

LAUBACH, Frank Charles, 1884-1970. 264.1
Prayer, the mightiest force in the world. [Westwood, N. J.] Revell [1959] 127 p. 17 cm. (A Revell inspirational classic) [BV210.L37 1959] 59-11524
1. Prayer.

LAVENDER, John Allan 248.3
Why prayers are unanswered. Vally Forge [Pa.] Judson [1967] 77p. 21cm. [BV220.L38] 67-14361 2.95
1. Prayer. I. Title.

LAW, William, 1686-1761. 248.3
The spirit of prayer; and, The spirit of love. The full text, edited by Sidney Spencer. Cambridge, James Clarke, 1969. 301 p. 23 cm. The spirit of prayer originally published, London, 1749-50; The spirit of love originally published, London, 1752-54. Bibliography: p. [297]-298. [BV209.L3 1969] 75-882813 ISBN 0-227-67720-X £1.75
1. Prayer. 2. Theology. 3. Mysticism. I. Law, William, 1686-1761. The spirit of love. 1969. II. Title. III. Title: The spirit of love.

LEECH, Kenneth. 248.3'2
True prayer : an invitation to Christian spirituality / Kenneth Leech. 1st U.S. ed. New York : Harper & Row, c1980. p. cm. [BV215.L38 1980] 19 80-8358 ISBN 0-06-065227-6 : 9.95
1. Prayer. I. Title.

*LEFEBURE, Georges 248.3
Simplicity the heart of prayer translated by Dinah Livingstone. Foreword by Simon Tugwell New York, Paulist Press, [1975] 73 p. 21 cm. [BV210] ISBN 0-8091-1881-5 2.45 (pbk.)
1. Prayer. I. Title.

LEFEBVRE, Georges, 1908- 248'.3
Simplicity, the heart of prayer / Georges Lefebvre ; translated by Dinah Livingstone ; foreword by Simon Tugwell. New York : Paulist Press, [1975] 73 p. ; 21 cm. Translation of Simplicite de la priere. [BV210.2.L3813] 75-314214 ISBN 0-8091-1881-5 : 2.45
1. Prayer. I. Title.

LEFEBVRE, Georges, 1908- 242
The well-springs of prayer [Tr. from French by Kathleen Pond.] NewYork 7, 280 Broadway, Desclee Co., 1961[c.1960] 79p. 61-7440 1.75

1. Prayer. I. Title.

LEITCH, Flavia Gaines, Mrs. 248
"Ask what ye will"; His written promises your personal guarantee, by Flavia Gaines Leitch; one of a series of books serving as guides to a happy life. Los Angeles, Calif., The Pilot press, 1931. 4 p. l., 62 p. 18 1/2 cm. [BV215.L4] 31-34996
1. Prayer. I. Title.

LEITCH, Flavia Gaines, Mrs. 248
Praying through, by Flavia Gaines Leitch. New York and Los Angeles, The Pilot press [c1932] 68 p. 18 1/2 cm. [BV215.L42] 33-825
1. Prayer. I. Title.

LEKEUX, Martial, 1884- 248.3
The art of prayer. Translated by Paul Joseph Oligny. Chicago, Franciscan Herald Press [1959] 306p. 20cm. [BV210.2.L413] 59-14706
1. Prayer. I. Title.

LERRIGO, Peter Hugh James, 1875- 266
God's dynamite; or, Changing a world by prayer, by P. H. J. Lerrigo... a mission study book for adults and young people; edited by the Department of missionary education, Board of education of the Northern Baptist convention... Philadelphia, Boston [etc.] The Judson press [c1925] 5 p. l., 3-184 p. plates. 20 cm. [BV2063.L35] 25-10403
1. Prayer. 2. Missions. I. Northern Baptist convention. Board of education. II. Title.

LESTER, Muriel, 1883- 248.3
Praying: how, when, where, why. [Westwood, N. J.] F. H. Revell Co. [1960] 64p. 17cm. [BV215.L445] 60-13096
1. Prayer. I. Title.

LEWIS, Clive Staples, 1898-1963. 248.3
Letters to Malcolm; chiefly on prayer. [1st American ed.] New York, Harcourt, Brace & World [1964] 124 p. 22 cm. [BV210.2.L44] 64-11536
1. Prayer. 2. Christian life — Anglican authors. I. Title.

LEWIS, Clive Staples, 1898-1963. 248'.3
Letters to Malcolm: chiefly on prayer [by] C. S. Lewis. New York, Harcourt [1973? c.1964] 124 p. 21 cm. (Harvest Book, HB250) [BV210.2.L44] 64-11536 ISBN 0-15-650880-X pap., 1.85
1. Prayer. 2. Christian life—Anglican authors. I. Title.

LIGUORI, Alfonso Maria de', Saint, 1696-1787. 242
The great means of salvation and of perfection, Prayer--mental prayer--the exercises of a retreat--choice of a state of life, and the vocation to the religious state and to the priesthood. By St. Alphonsus de Liguori ... edited by Rev. Eugene Grimm ... Brooklyn, St. Louis [etc.] Redemptorist fathers [1927] 4 p. l., [13]-516 p. 19 cm. (Half-title: The complete works of Saint Alphonsus de Liguori ... tr. from the Italian. Ed. by ... E. Grimm ... The ascetical works. vol. iii) [BX890.L5 1926 vol. iii] 27-12059
1. Prayer. 2. Monasticism and religious orders. I. Grimm, Eugene, ed. II. Title.

LIND, Jayne, 1937- 248'.3
Talk with us, Lord / Jayne Lind. Nashville : Abingdon, c1979. 142 p. ; 21 cm. [BV215.L54] 78-12008 ISBN 0-687-41000-2 : 6.95
1. Prayer. I. Title.

LINDBLAD, Frank V. 264.
A few notes on prayer, by Frank Lindblad. Springfield, Mo., Gospel publishing house [c1927] 64 p. 19 cm. [BV213.L5] 28-13686
1. Prayer. I. Title.

LINDSELL, Harold, 1913 248.3
When you pray. Grand Rapids, Baker Book House [1975 c1969] 182 p. 20 cm. [BV210.2.L5] 78-79466 ISBN 0-8010-5554-7 2.95 (pbk.)
1. Prayer. I. Title.

LINDSELL, Harold, 1913- 248.3
When you pray. Wheaton, Ill., Tyndale House [1969] 182 p. 22 cm. Includes bibliographical references. [BV210.2.L5] 78-79466

1. Prayer. I. Title.

THE listening heart.
[1st ed.] New York, Pageant Press [c1958] 72p. 21cm.
1. Prayer. I. Baugher, Ruby Dell.

LOAVASIK, Lawrence George, 1913- 248.32
Prayer in Catholic life. New York, Macmillan, 1961. 197p. 22cm. [BV210.2.L65] 61-10341
1. Prayer. I. Title.

LOCKE, Charles Edward, bp., 1858- 248
Pray; a manual on prayer, by Charles Edaward Locke ... New York. Cincinnati [etc.] The Methodist book concern [c1929] 5 p. l., 13-186 p. 18 cm. [BV210.L6] 29-15066
1. Prayer. I. Title.

LOCKYER, Herbert. 264.1
How I can make prayer more effective. Grand Rapids, Zondervan Pub. House [1953] 125p. 19cm. [BV220.L6] 53-13072
1. Prayer. I. Title.

LOUF, Andre. 248'.3
Lord, teach us to pray. Translated by a Sister of the Anglican community of St. Clare, Oxford. Chicago, Franciscan Herald Press [1974] p. cm. Translation of Heer, leer ons bidden. [BV210.2.L6313] 74-7309 ISBN 0-8199-0532-1
1. Prayer. I. Title.

LUNN, Henry Simpson, Sir, 1859- 248
The secret of the saints; studies in prayer, meditation and self-discipline, by Sir Henry S. Lunn... New York, The Macmillan company, 1933. xi p., 1 l., 229 p. 15 1/2 cm. Bibliography: p. 219-223. [BV210.L8 1933a] 33-25960
1. Prayer. 2. Meditation. 3. Meditations. I. Title.

LYNCH, Etta. 248'.4
Help is only a prayer away. Old Tappan, N.J., F. H. Revell Co. [1972] 158 p. 21 cm. [BV220.L94] 72-172682 ISBN 0-8007-0496-7 3.95
1. Prayer. I. Title.

MCBIRNEY, Allegra. 264.1
A compass for prayer. Columbus, Ohio, Wartburg Press [1955] 72p. 18cm. [BV210.M234] 55-4429
1. Prayer. 2. Lutheran Church—Prayer-books and devotions—English. I. Title.

MCCLURE, James Gore King, 1848-1932. 248
A mighty means of usefulness; a plea for intercessory prayer, by Rev. James G. K. McClure. Chicago, New York [etc.] Fleming H. Revell company [c1902] 127 p. 19 1/2 cm. [BV210.M253] 2-11885
1. Prayer. I. Title.

MCCOY, Samuel Duff, 1882- ed. 264.1
How prayer helps me. New York, Dial Press, 1955. 143p. 19cm. [BV220.M25] 55-5441
1. Prayer. I. Title.

MCCRAW, Louis Harrison, 1893- 264.1
Does God answer prayer? By Louise Harrison McCraw... Grand Rapids, Mich., Zondervan publishing house [c1941] 6 p. l., 11-219 p. 19 1/2 cm. [BV210.M255] 41-19444
1. Prayer. I. Title.

MACDONALD, Hope. 248'.3
Discovering how to pray / Hope MacDonald. Grand Rapids : Zondervan Pub. House, c1976. 120 p. ; 18 cm. [BV210.2.M28] 75-37741 pbk. : 1.75
1. Prayer. I. Title.

MACFARLANE, Claire, 1906- 264.1
Prayer for moderns. Jersey City, Mann Publishers, 1956. 64p. illus. 22cm. [BV210.M264] 56-10027
1. Prayer. I. Title.

MCFATRIDGE, Forrest Vernon, 1892- 264.1
Lord, teach us to pray; with Jesus in the school of prayer. Nashville. Broadman Press [1956] 113p. 20cm. [BV215.M25] 56-8674

1. Prayer. 2. Lord's prayer. I. Title.

MCGEACHY, Pat, 1929- 248'.3
Help, Lord! : a guide to public and private prayer / Pat McGeachy. Atlanta : John Knox Press, c1978. 120 p. ; 24 cm. Bibliography: p. [119]-120. [BV210.2.M3] 77-79592 ISBN 0-8042-2358-0 : 5.95
1. Prayer. 2. Prayers. I. Title.

MACGREGOR, George Hogarth Carnaby, 1864-1900. 248
... Praying in the Holy Ghost, by Rev. G. H. C. Macgregor ... New York, Chicago [etc.] Fleming H. Revell company [1898] 139 p. 17 cm. (Little books for life's guidance) [BV210.M27] 44-29215
1. Prayer. I. Title.

MCKNIGHT, Ozro. 264.1
He prayed, by Rev. Ozro McKnight. Kansas City, Mo., Printed by the Western Baptist publishing co. [c1933] 154 p. incl. front. (port.) 20 cm. Bibliography: p. [7] [BV229.M3] 33-23038
1. Jesus Christ. 2. Prayer. I. Title.

MACLACHLAN, Lewis. 248'.3
21 steps to positive prayer / Lewis Maclachlan. Valley Forge, PA : Judson Press, 1978, c1965. 94 p. ; 22 cm. [BV215.M27 1978] 78-103582 ISBN 0-8170-0773-3 : 2.95
1. Prayer. I. Title.

MCLAREN, William Edward, 1831-1905.
The essence of prayer ... Milwaukee, The Young churchman co. [1901] 55 p. 16 cm. 1-30501
I. Title.

MCNEILE, Alan Hugh, 1871- 242
Self-training in prayer, by A. H. McNeile... New York, D. Appleton and company, 1926. vii, 78 p. 17 cm. [BV215.M3] 26-11001
1. Prayer. I. Title.

MCNEILL, Charles James, 1912- 264.1
Prayers; a study of prayers in common use in the church, by Charles J. McNeill...with an introduction by Rev. Leon A. McNeill... Wichita, Kan., Catholic action committee, 1939. 56 p. 23 cm. (The Catholic aciton series of discussion club textbooks) "Reference list" on p. [3] of cover. [Full name: Charles James Stanislaus McNeill] [BV214.M3] 42-2351
1. Prayer. I. Catholic action committee of the diocese of Wichita. II. Title.

MCSORLEY, Joseph, Rev., 1874- 248.3
A primer of prayer. New York, Deus Books, Paulist Press [1961, c.1934, 1961] 120p. Bibl. 61-8815 .75 pap.,
1. Prayer. 2. Meditation. I. Title.

MCSORLEY, Joseph, 1874- 264.1
A primer of prayer, by Joseph McSorley... London, New York [etc.] Longmans, Green, and co., 1934. viii, 120 p. 19 1/2 cm. "Printed in the United States of America." "First edition." "Books on prayer": p. 119-120. [BV210.M287] 35-3901
1. Prayer. 2. Meditation. I. Title.

MAGEE, John Benjamin, 1917- 264.1
Reality and prayer; a guide to the meaning and practice of prayer. [1st ed.] New York, Harper [1957] 239 p. 22 cm. [BV210.M288] 57-7350
1. Prayer. I. Title.

MAHONEY, Carl K. 248
The philosophy of prayer, by C. K. Mahoney. New York, Cincinnati, The Abingdon press [c1922] 124 p. 19 1/2 cm. "Selected bibliography": p. 121-122. [BV210.M29] 22-18795
I. Title.

MALZ, Betty. 248'.3
Prayers that are answered / Betty Malz. Lincoln, Va. : Chosen Books ; Waco, Texas : distributed by Word Books, c1980. 168 p. ; 23 cm. [BV210.2.M32] 79-24532 ISBN 0-912376-50-3 : 7.95
1. Malz, Betty. 2. Prayer. I. Title.

MANN, Stella Terrill.
How to live in the circle of prayer and make your dreams come true. New York, Dodd, Mead [1959] 180p. 21cm. [BV215M35]
1. Prayer. I. Title.

MARSHALL, Catherine Wood, 1914- 248'.3
Adventures in prayer / Catherine Marshall ; ill. by Ned Glattauer. Boston : G. K. Hall, 1975. p. cm. Large print ed. [BV210.2.M35 1975b] 75-17978 ISBN 0-8161-6317-0 lib.bdg. : 9.95
1. Prayer. 2. Prayers. 3. Sight-saving books. I. Title.

MARTIN, Fay C. 248
Availing prayer, by Fay C. Martin ... Anderson, Ind., Gospel trumpet company [c1929] ix, 11-160 p. 19 cm. [BV220.M3] 29-10039
1. Prayer. I. Title.

MARY Gertrude,
Sister, C. S. U., 1899- New York, Association Press [1959] 79p. 18cm. (World Christian books. 2d series, no.27)
1. Prayer. I. Title: Christian prayer ...

MASSEY, James Earl. 248.32
'When thou prayest'; an interpretation of Christian prayer according to the teachings of Jesus. Anderson, Ind., Warner Press [1960] 64p. 19cm. [BV215.M37] 60-11403
1. Prayer I. Title.

MATHER, Increase, 1639-1723. 248
A discourse concerning faith and fervency in prayer, and the glorious Kingdom of the Lord Jesus Christ, on earth, now approaching. Delivered in several sermons, in which the signs of the present times are considered, with a true account of the late wonderful and astonishing success of the gospel in Ceilon, Amboina, and Malabar. By I. Mather. Boston, In N.E. Printed by B. Green, for Benj. Eliot at his shop in King street, 1710. 1 p. l., xix, [1] 112, [6] p. 14 cm. Title within double line border. Signatures: A, aa, B-L (leaf preceding sig. A wanting; sig. L blank) [BV209.M3 1710] 5-26714
1. Prayer. 2. Millennium. 3. Sermons, American. I. Title.

MATHER, Increase, 1639-1723. 217
A discourse concerning faith and fervency in prayer, and the glroious kingdom of the Lord Jesus Christ, on earth, now approaching. Delivered in several sermons, in which the signs of the present times are considered, with a true account of the late wonderful and astonishing success of the gospel in Ceilon, Amboina, and Malabar. By I.Mather... Boston in N.E. Printed by B. Green, for Eleazer Phillips at his shop in King street. 1710. 1 p. l., xix, [1] 112, [6] p. 14 cm. Signatures: A, aa, B-L (leaf preceding sig. A wanting; Sig. L blank) Title within double line border. [BV209.M3 1710a] 31-18377
1. Prayer. 2. Millennium. 3. Sermons, Americna. I. Title.

MAUMIGNY, Rene de, 1837- 248
The practice of mental prayer, by Father Rene de Maumigny ... First treatise, ordinary prayer, translated from the 4th ed. with the author's corrections and additions. Translation revised by Father Elder Mullan, S.J. New York, P. J. Kenedy & sons [1913] 327 p. 19 1/2 cm. "Principal editions cited": p. [6] [BV210.M4] 14-7007
1. Prayer. 2. Meditation. I. Mullan, Elder, 1865-1925. II. Title.

MILLER, Basil William, 1897- 264.1
Remarkable answers to prayer. Kansas City, Mo., Beacon Hill Press [1950] 159 p. 20 cm. [BV220.M5] 50-3937
1. Prayer. I. Title.

MILLER, Joseph Hillis, 1899- 264.1
The practice of public prayer, by J. Hillis Miller ... New York, Columbia university press, 1934. xvi, 196 p. 21 cm. Issued also as thesis (PH.D.) Columbia university. Bibliography: p. [189]-193. [BV226.M5 1934a] 34-39334
1. Prayer. 2. Public worship. I. Title.

MILLER, Lew, 1917- 248'.3
Your divine connection : prayer through mental imagery / Lew Miller. Millbrae, Calif. : Celestial Arts, 1977 printing. 63 p. ; 22 cm. [BV215.M5] 77-79884 ISBN 0-89087-203-1 pbk. : 2.95

1. Prayer. I. Title.

MILLER, Osborne Theodore, comp. 248
The path of prayer, an anthology. Foreword by William E. Wilson. New York, Harper [1954] 159p. 21cm. [BV205] 54-8467
1. Prayer. I. Title.

MILLER, Samuel, 1769-1850. 264.1
Thoughts on public prayer. By Samuel Miller ... Philadelphia, Presbyterian board of publication, 1849. 306 p. front. (port.) 20 cm. [BV210.M6 1849] 33-23857
1. Prayer. 2. Public worship. I. Presbyterian church in the U.S.A. Board of publication. II. Title.

MILLER, Samuel, 1769-1850. 264.1
Thoughts on public prayer. By Samuel Miller ... Philadelphia, Presbyterian board of publication [185-?] 245 p. front. (port.) 20 cm. [BV210.M6 1850] 33-23856
1. Prayer. 2. Public worship. I. Presbyterian church in the U.S.A. Board of publication. II. Title.

MILLER, Samuel Martin, 1890- 264.1
Have faith in God; He answers prayer. Rock Island, Ill., Augustana Book Concern [1952] 156 p. 19 cm. [BV210.M62] 52-14451
1. Prayer. I. Title.

MINUTE of prayer (Radio program) 264.1
A minute of prayer, a prayer for every day in the year submitted by Protestant ministers, Catholic priests and Jewish rabbis, compiled from the Mutual network's "Minute of prayer." Garden City, N.Y., Blue ribbon books [1943] ix, 373 p. 17 1/2 cm. "First edition." [BV245.M565] 44-1051
1. Prayer. I. Title.

MISKOTTE, Kornelis Heiko, 1894- 248.3
The roads of prayer [by] Kornelis H. Miskotte. Translated by John W. Doberstein. New York, Sheed and Ward [1968] 175 p. 21 cm. Translation of De weg van het gebed. [BV210.2.M5513] 68-26032 4.50
1. Prayer. I. Title.

MITCHELL, Charles Anderson, 1864- 225
The model prayer, and other New Testament studies, expository and devotional, by C. A. Mitchell... Boston, The Gorham press, 1918. 9 p. 1 l., 11-154 p. 19 1/2 cm. (Lettered on cover: Library of religious thought) $1.25. "A few special reading references": p. 7. [BS2361.M6] 18-22369
I. Title.

MITCHELL, Curtis C., 1927- 248'.3
Praying Jesus' way : a new approach to personal prayer / Curtis C. Mitchell. Old Tappan, N.J. : Revell, c1977. 156 p. ; 21 cm. [BV229.M57] 76-49879 ISBN 0-8007-0843-1 : 5.95
1. Jesus Christ—Prayers. 2. Prayer. I. Title.

MONTGOMERY, Helen (Barrett) Mrs. 1861-1934. 248
Prayer and missions, by Helen Barrett Montgomery. West Medford, Mass., The Central committee on the United study of foreign missions [c1924] 224 p. front., ports. 20 cm. Contains bibliographies. [BV210.M67] 25-9321
1. Prayer. 2. Missions. I. Title.

MONTGOMERY, Richmond Ames.
The secret place; studies of prayer, by R. Ames Montgomery, B. A. Chicago, New York [etc.] F. H. Revell co. [1901] 135 p. 20 cm. 1-26889
1. Prayer. I. Title.

MOORE, Thomas Hendrick, 1898- 248
The morning offering. New York, Apostleship of Prayer, 1952. 162 p. 21 cm. [BV210.M755] 52-8062
1. Prayer. 2. Apostleship of prayer. I. Title.

MORE, Hannah, 1745-1833. 264.1
The spirit of prayer. By Hannah More. To which is added, Pietas quotidiana, or, Prayers and meditations for every day in the week, and on various occasions. Also, hymns suited to the subjects. New-York, Stanford & Swords; Philadelphia, G. S. Appleton, 1844. viii, [9]-256 p. front. 12 cm. "Lyrica sacra": p. [245]-256. [BV210.M76] 34-2697
1. Prayer. I. Title.

MORGAN, George Campbell, 1863- 248
The practice of prayer, by G. Campbell Morgan... New York, Chicago [etc.] Fleming H. Revell company [c1906] 128 p. 20 cm. [BV210.M77] 7-520
1. Prayer. I. Title.

MORTON, Clement Manly. 248.3
Adventures, in prayer [by] C. Manly Morton. Westwood, N. J., F. H. Revell Co. [1966] 115 p. 21 cm. [BV210.2.M6] 66-12438
1. Prayer. I. Title.

MOSCHNER, Franz Maria, 1896- 248.3
Christian prayer. Translated by Elisabeth Plettenberg. St. Louis, Herder [1962] 297p. 21cm. (Cross and crown series of spirituality, no. 23) [BV210.M783] 62-15402
1. Prayer. I. Title.

MULLER, George, 1805-1898. 362.730942
Trusting in God for five million dollars; personal methods and experiences of Rev. George Mueller as recorded in his diary, in his own words. Condensedand edited by William E. Towne from Mueller's autobiographical material in "The life of trust". London, L. N. Fowler & co.; Holyoke, Mass., The Elizabeth Towne co., inc. [c1934] 3 p. l., 9-83 p. 18 cm. [Full name: George (Georg) Friedrich Muller] [HV247.M8A3 1934] 264.1 34-5576
1. Prayer. 2. Orphans and orphan-asylums—Gt. Brit. I. Towne, William Elmer, 1874- ed. II. Title.

MUMFORD, Edith Emily Read. Mrs. 264.1
How we can help children to pray, by Edith E. Read Mumford ... 3d impression (8th thousand) London, New York [etc.] Longmans, Green and co., 1933. 3 p. l., 52 p. 19 cm. [BV215.M8 1933] 39-7596
1. Prayer. 2. Children—Religious life. I. Title.

MURCH, James DeForest, 1892- 264.1
Teach me to pray. Cincinnati, Standard Pub. Foundation [1958] 186p. 21cm. [BV215.M84] 58-40063
1. Prayer. I. Title.

MURPHEY, Cecil B. 248'.3
Prayer : pitfalls & possibilities / Cecil B. Murphey. New York : Hawthorn Books, [1975] vi, 153 p. ; 21 cm. Bibliography: p. 153. [BV210.2.M8] 74-22916 ISBN 0-8015-6016-0 : 3.50
1. Prayer.

MURPHEY, Cecil B. 248'.3
Prayerobics, getting started and staying going / Cecil Murphey. Waco, Tex. : Word Books, c1979. 187 p. ; 23 cm. [BV215.M85] 79-63934 ISBN 0-8499-0146-4 : 7.95
1. Prayer. I. Title.

MURPHY, Miriam. 248'.3
Prayer in action / Miriam Murphy. Nashville : Abingdon, [1979] p. cm. Includes index. Bibliography: p. [BV215.M36] 79-983 ISBN 0-687-34942-7 pbk. : 5.95
1. Prayer. 2. Spiritual life—Catholic authors. I. Title.

MURRAY, Andrew, 1828-1917. 248.3'2
The believer's school of prayer / Andrew Murray. Minneapolis, Minn. : Bethany House, c1982. 201 p. ; 21 cm. (The Andrew Murray prayer library) Rev. ed. of: With Christ in the school of prayer. 1895. [BV210.M85 1982] 19 82-4401 ISBN 0-87123-195-6 (pbk.) : 3.95
1. Prayer. I. Title. II. Series.

MURRAY, Andrew, 1828-1917. 248.3'2
The ministry of intercessory prayer / Andrew Murray. Edited ed. Minneapolis, Minn. : Bethany House Publishers, 1981. 155 p. ; 21 cm. Previously published in 1877 as: The ministry of intercession. [BV210.M83 1981] 19 81-18011 ISBN 0-87123-353-3 (pbk.) : 3.95
1. Prayer. I. [Ministry of intercession] II. Title.

MURRAY, Andrew, 1828-1917. 264.1
With Christ in the school of prayer; thoughts on our training for the ministry of intercession, by the Rev. Andrew Murray ... Philadelphia, H. Altemus, 1895. 307 p. 15 cm. Added t.-p. in colors. [BV210.M85] 40-23861
1. Prayer. I. Title.

MYERS, Cortland, 1864-
Real prayer, by Cortland Myers ... New York, Chicago [etc.] Fleming H. Revell company [c1911] 1 p. l., 7-100 p. 20 cm $0.50 11-15597 0.50
I. Title.

NEDONCELLE, Maurice 264.1
God's encounter with man; a contemporary approach to prayer. [Tr. from French by A. Manson] New York, Sheed [c.1962, 1964] viii, 183p. 22cm. Bibl. 64-19898 3.95
1. Prayer. I. Title.

NEDONCELLE, Maurice. 264.1
God's encounter with man; a contemporary approach to prayer. [Translation by A. Manson] New York, Sheed and Ward [1964] viii, 183 p. 22 cm. Translation of Priere humaine priere divine. Bibliographical footnotes. [BV210.N413] 64-19898
1. Prayer. I. Title.

NESPERLING, Delilah Ann. 244
The miracle power of prayer, its magic secret, by Delilah Ann Nesperling. Boston, R. G. Badger [c1929] 114 p. front. (port.) 20 cm. [BV220.N4] 29-11491
1. Prayer. 2. Faith-cure. I. Title.

NICOLL, William Robertson, Sir, 1851- 248
Prayer in war time. by W. Robertson Nicoll. London, New York [etc.] Hodder and Stoughton, 1916. viii, 187 p. 19 cm. "Articles ... published in the British weekly during the war."--Pref. [BV210.N5] 18-19137
1. Prayer. I. Title.

NOUWEN, Henri J. M. 248.3'2
Prayer and the priest / by Henri J. M. Nouwen. Chicago, Ill. : Franciscan Herald Press, [1980] p. cm. (Synthesis series) [BX1912.5.N68] 80-13861 ISBN 0-8199-0749-9 pbk. : 0.75
1. Prayer. 2. Priests—Religious life. I. Title.

OECHSLIN, Raphael Louis, 1907- 248.32
Louis of Granada. St. Louis, B. Herder [1963, c.1962] 142p. 23cm. Bibl. 63-3129 4.20
1. Luis, de Granada, 1504-1588. 2. Prayer. I. Title.

OLSEN, Kermit Robert, 1914- 264.1
First steps in prayer. New York, F. H. Revell Co. [1947] 118 p. 20 cm. [BV215.O4] 47-11457
1. Prayer. I. Title.

OLSEN, Kermit Robert, 1914- 248.3
The magnitude of prayer. [Westwood, N.J.] Revell [c.1962] 94p. 62-10737 2.00 bds.,
1. Prayer. I. Title.

O'MALLEY, William J. 248'.3
A book about praying / by William J. O'Malley. New York : Paulist Press, c1976. v, 127 p. : ill. ; 19 cm. [BV210.2.O45] 76-20954 ISBN 0-8091-1979-X pbk. : 1.95
1. Prayer. I. Title.

ORCHARD, William Edwin, 1877- 248
Prayer, its philosophy, practice and power, by the Reverend W. E. Orchard ... New York and London, Harper & brothers, 1930. vii p., 1 l., 135 p. 17 cm. [BV210.O68] 30-21518
1. Prayer. I. Title.

O'REAR, Arthur T. 248
The most dynamic thing in the world; a study of prayer, by Arthur T. O'Rear. Nashville, Tenn., Cokesbury press, 1925. 175 p. 19 cm. [BV210.O65] 26-3367 1.00
1. Prayer. I. Title.

ORSO, Kathryn Wickey. 248'.3
It's great to pray. New York, Morehouse-Barlow Co. [1974] 96 p. illus. 22 cm. [BV210.2.O77] 74-80379 ISBN 0-8192-1177-X 4.95
1. Prayer. 2. Christian life—Lutheran authors. I. Title.

OSBORNE, Cecil G. 248'.3
Prayer and you / Cecil G. Osborne. Waco, Tex. : Word Books, [1974] 106 p. ; 22 cm. Includes bibliographical references. [BV210.2.O8] 74-78043 3.95
1. Prayer. I. Title.

OSTROM, Henry, 1862-
The law of prayer, by Henry Ostrom ... Philadelphia, Chicago, The Praise publishing co. [c1910] 154 p., 1 l. 19 cm. 10-21033 0.50
I. Title.

PARDUE, Austin, Bp., 1899- 264.1
Prayer works. New York, Morehouse-Gorham Co., 1949. x, 127 p. 19 cm. "Broadcasts...published substantially as they were given over station WCAE in Pittsburgh." [BV220.P23] 49-50239
1. Prayer. I. Title.

PARKER, William R 248
Prayer can change your life; experiments and techniques in prayer therapy, by William R. Parker and Elaine St. Johns Dare. Englewood Cliffs, N. J., Prentice-Hall [1957] 270p. 22cm. [BV220.P24] 57-6777
1. Prayer. I. Dare, Elaine St. Johns, joint author. II. Title.

PARSONS, John W. 289.
A sign; instruction in the scientific method of right thinking, the principle of true prayer, by John W. Parsons ... Portland, Or., Anderson printing company [c1921] 3 p. l., 151, [1] p. 18 cm. [BX6997.P3] 21-10602
I. Title.

PATERSON, William Paterson, 1860-1938, ed. 248
The power of prayer; being a selection of Walker trust essays, with a study of the essays as a religious and theological document, ed. by the Right Rev. W. P. Paterson ... and David Russell ... New York, The Macmillan company, 1920. xiii, 528 p. 23 cm. Bibliography: p. 475-492. [BV205.P3] 20-15946
1. Prayer. I. Russell, David, joint ed. II. Title. III. Title: Walker trust essays.

PATTON, Cornelius Howard, 1860-1939. 291.
The rosary; a study in the prayer-life of the nations, by Cornelius Howard Patton ... New York, Chicago [etc.] Fleming H. Revell company [c1927] 160 p. front., illus., plates. 20 cm. [BL560.P3] 27-20141
1. Prayer. 2. Rosary. I. Title.

PATTON, William Weston, 1821-1889. 248
Prayer and its remarkable answers: being a statement of facts in the light of reason and revelation. By William W. Patton ... Chicago, J. S. Goodman; Cincinnati, C. F. Vent; [etc., etc.] 1876. 408 p. front. 19 1/2 cm. [BV210.P3 1876] 45-34459
1. Prayer. I. Title.

PATTON, William Weston, 1821-1889. 248
Prayer and its remarkable answers: being a statement of facts in the light of reason and revelation. By William W. Patton ... 20th ed. Enlarged by two supplementary chapters, on "The credulity of skepticism" and "The relations of science to revealed religion." Hartford, Conn., J. Betts & co.; Chicago, Ill., J. S. Goodman, 1880. 456 p. front. (port.) 19 1/2 cm. [BV210.P3 1880] 45-34920
1. Prayer. I. Title.

PATTON, William Weston, 1821-1889. 248
Prayer and its remarkable answers: being a statement of facts in the light of reason and revelation. By William W. Patton ... 20th ed., enlarged by two supplementary chapters, on "The credulity of skepticism" and "The relations of science to revealed religion." New York, London, Funk & Wagnalls, 1885. 456 p. 19 cm. (On cover: Standard library. No. 133, Supplement) [BV210.P3 1885] 46-30558

1. Prayer. I. Title.

*PAULUS VI, Pope, 1897- 248.3
16 Papal documents on the Rosary: Pope Paul vi, Pope John xxiii, Pope Leo xiii. [Boston] St. Paul Eds. [1966, i.e.1967] 96p. 18cm. .50 pap.,
1. Prayer. 2. Rosary. I. Title.
Available from Daughters of St. Paul, Boston.

PEDRO de Alcantara, Saint 242
1499-1562.
Treatise on prayer and meditation. Translated, with an introd. and sketch of the Saint's life, by Dominic Devas, O.F.M. Together with a complete English version of Pax animae by John of Bonilla. Westminster, Md., Newman Press, 1949. xix, 211 p. 16 cm. The authorship of Pax animae is generally ascribed to John of Bonilla, but in the English editions edited by Dom Jerome Vaughan the author is given as Saint Peter of Alcantara. Cf. Introd. to Pax animae. [BV4837.P] A50
1. Prayer. 2. Meditation. 3. Spiritual life. I. Bonilla, Juan de, 16th cent. supposed author. Tratado de quan necesaria sea la paz de l'alma. II. Pedro de Alcantara, Saint, 1499-1562, supposed author. Tratado de quan necesaria sea la paz de l'alma. III. Devas, Dominic, 1888- tr. IV. Title. V. Title: Paxanimae

PENNING de Vries, Piet. 248'.3
Prayer and life / Piet Penning de Vries ; translated by W. Dudok van Heel ; foreword by Theodore Zwartkruis. 1st ed. Hicksville, N.Y. : Exposition Press, [1974] x, 221 p. ; 21 cm. (An Exposition-testament book) Translation of Gebed en leven. [BV210.2.P4313] 73-91091 ISBN 0-682-47985-3 : 8.50
1. Bible. N.T. Gospels—Commentaries. 2. Prayer. I. Title.

PENNINGTON, M. Basil. 248'.3
Daily we touch Him : practical religious experiences / M. Basil Pennington. 1st ed. Garden City, N.Y. : Doubleday, 1977. 115 p. ; 22 cm. [BV210.2.P44] 76-20836 ISBN 0-385-12478-3 : 5.95
1. Prayer. 2. Spiritual life—Catholic authors. I. Title.

PERKINS, Mary, 1912- 264.1
Speaking of how to pray, by Mary Perkins. New York, Sheed & Ward, 1944. xii, 276 p. 19 1/2 cm. [Full name: Mary Elizabeth Perkins] [BV210.P44] 44-40282
1. Prayer. I. Title.

PERRIN, Joseph Marie, 248.32
1905-
Living with God. St. Louis, B. Herder Book Co. [1961] 165p. 20cm. [BV210.2.P453] 61-2915
1. Prayer I. Title.

PEYTON, Patrick J 264.1
The ear of God. [1st ed.] Garden City, N.Y., Doubleday, 1951. 226 p. 21 cm. Bibliographical references included in "Notes" (p. [217]-226) [BV210.P47] 51-10036
1. Prayer. 2. Catholic Church — Prayer-books and devotions — English. I. Title.

PHELPS, Austin, 1820-1890. 248
The still hour; or, Communion with God. By Austin Phelps ... Boston, Gould and Lincoln; New York, Sheldon and company; [etc., etc.] 1860. vi, [7]-136 p. 18 cm. [BV210.P5] 12-37723
1. Prayer. I. Title.

PHELPS, Austin, 1820-1890. 264.1
The still hour; or, Communion with God. By Austin Phelps ... Boston, Gould and Lincoln; New York, Sheldon and company; [etc., etc.] 1869. vi, [7]-136 p. 18 cm. [BV210.P5 1869] 38-13611
1. Prayer. I. Title.

PHELPS, Austin, 1820-1890. 248
The still hour; or, Communion with God, by Austin Phelps ... Boston, D. Lothrop company, 1893. 4 p. l., [v]-vi, [7]-143 p. front. (port.) 17 x 13 cm. First edition, Boston, 1859. [BV210.P5 1893 a] 12-37850
1. Prayer. I. Title.

PHILLIPS, D. Z. (Dewi 248.3'2
Zephaniah)
The concept of prayer / D.Z. Phillips. New York : Seabury Press, 1981, c1965. p. cm. Includes index. Bibliography: [BV210.2.P5 1981] 19 81-2883 ISBN 0-8164-0500-X pbk. : 7.95
1. Prayer. I. Title.

PHILLIPS, Dewi Zephaniah 248.3
The concept of prayer. New York, Schocken [c.1966] vii, 167p. 23cm. Bibl. [BV210.2.P5] 66-14086 4.95
1. Prayer. I. Title.

PHILLIPS, Dewi Zephaniah. 249.3
The concept of prayer, by D. Z. Phillips. New York, Schocken Books [1966] vii, 167 p. 23 cm. Bibliography: p. 161-164. [BV210.2.P5] 66-14086
1. Prayer. I. Title.

PITTENGER, William Norman, 248'.3
1905-
Praying today: practical thoughts on prayer, by Norman Pittenger. Grand Rapids, Eerdmans [1974] 107 p. 18 cm. [BV210.2.P53] 73-20146 ISBN 0-8028-1566-9
1. Prayer. I. Title.

PLUS, Raoul, 1882-
How to pray well. From the French. Westminster, Md., Newman Press, 1948. viii, 133 p. 16 cm. A 50
1. Prayer. I. Title.

POINSETT, Brenda. 248'.3
Prayerfully yours / Brenda Poinsett. Nashville : Broadman Press, c1979. 125 p. ; 20 cm. [BV210.2.P59] 78-54776 ISBN 0-8054-5265-6 pbk. : 2.95
1. Prayer. I. Title.

POLING, Daniel Alfred, 264.1
1884-
Faith is power for you. [Scranton 1962] 212 p. 22 cm. [BV220.P6] 62-50600
1. Prayer. I. Title.

POLING, Daniel Alfred, 264.1
1884-
Faith is power for you. New York, Greenberg [1950] viii, 212 p. 21 cm. [BV220.P6] 50-6842
1. Prayer. I. Title.

PORTER, David Richard, 1882- 264.
comp.
The enrichment of prayer, comp. by David R. Porter. New York, Association press, 1918. 4 p. l., 3-224 p. 17 cm. [BV245.P7] 18-9759
I. Title.

POST, Harry Grant, 1899- 264.1
Prayer for these times [by] Harry G. Post. New York, Coward-McCann, inc. [1943] vii p., 1 l., 166 p. 19 1/2 cm. [BV210.P65] 43-13889
1. Prayer. I. Title.

POWELL, Cyril H. 264.1
Secrets of answered prayer. New York, T. Y. Crowell [1960, c.1958] 192p. 21cm. (4p. bibl.) 60-5497 3.00 bds.,
1. Prayer. I. Title.

*POWELL, John 264.1
He touched me my pilgrimage of prayer. Niles, Ill., Argus Communications, 1974 95 p. col. illus. 19 cm. [BV215] ISBN 0-913592-47-1 1.50 (pbk.)
1. Prayer. I. Title.

POWERS, Isaias, 1928- 248'.3
Stereoscopic prayer : putting together scripture and self / by Isaias Powers ; photography by Philip Dattilo. New York : Alba House, [1975] viii, 176 p. : ill. ; 18 cm. [BV210.2.P63] 74-22409 ISBN 0-8189-0298-1 pbk. : 2.50
1. Prayer. I. Title.

PRANGE, Erwin E. 248'.3
How to pray for your children / Erwin E. Prange. Minneapolis : Bethany Fellowship, c1979. 91 p. ; 21 cm. Bibliography: p. [89]-91. [BV210.2.P636] 79-17382 ISBN 0-87123-162-X pbk. : 2.95
1. Prayer. 2. Family—Religious life. I. Title.

PRANGE, Erwin E. 264'.1
A time for intercession / Erwin Prange. Carol Stream, Ill. : Creation House, c1976. 160 p. ; 22 cm. Bibliography: p. 153-160. [BV210.2.P64] 76-20085 ISBN 0-88419-004-8 pbk. : 2.95
1. Prayer. I. Title.

PRATER, Arnold. 248'.3
You can pray as you ought! / By Arnold Prater. Nashville : T. Nelson, c1977. 128 p. : ill. ; 21 cm. [BV210.2.P75 1977] 77-8883 ISBN 0-8407-5631-3 pbk. : 2.95
1. Prayer. I. Title.

THE prayer-gauge debate. 248
By Prof. Tyndall, Francis Galton, and others, against Dr. Littledale, President McCosh, the Duke of Argyll, Canon Liddon, and "The Spectator." Boston, Congregational publishing society, 1876. 311 p. 20 cm. "Introductory" note signed: John O. Means. [BV220.P7] 39-18081
1. Prayer. I. Tyndall, John, 1820-1893. II. Galton, Francis, Sir 1822-1911. III. Littledale, Richard Frederick, 1833-1890. IV. McCosh, James, 1811-1894. V. Means, John Oliver, 1822-1883, ed. VI. Congregational publishing society.

PRAYER in my life; 248'.3
witnesses by persons in various vocations. Edited by Sulon G. Ferree. Nashville, The Upper Room [1967] 80 p. ports. 16 cm. Messages delivered at The Upper Room, Nashville, Tenn., during the 1967 Easter weekend as a part of the international prayer fellowship. [BV205.P7] 67-30661
1. Prayer. I. Ferree, Sulon G., ed.

PRICE, E. W. 248'.3
Acts in prayer / E. W. Price, Jr. Nashville : Broadman Press, [1974] 31 p. ; 14 cm. [BV213.P74] 74-15278 ISBN 0-8054-9209-7 pbk. : 0.50
1. Prayer. I. Title.

PRIME, Derek 248.3
A Christian's guide to prayer [Westwood, N. J.] Revell [1964, c.1963] 63p. 18cm. 64-583 .75 pap.,
1. Prayer. I. Title.

PRIME, Derek.
A Christian's guide to prayer. [Boston] Hodder and Stoughton [c1963] 63 p. 65-96425
1. Prayer. I. Title.

PRINCE, Derek. 248'.4
Shaping history through prayer & fasting; how Christians can change world events through the simple, yet powerful tools of prayer and fasting. Old Tappan, N.J., F. H. Revell Co. [1973] 160 p. facsim. 21 cm. [BV210.2.P72] 73-8973 ISBN 0-8007-0616-1 4.95
1. Prayer. 2. Fasting. I. Title.

PROTESTANT Episcopal 264.03
church in the Confederate States of America. Book of common prayer.
The Book of common prayer, and administration of the sacraments: and other rites and ceremonies of the church, according to the use of the Protestant Episcopal church in the Confederate States of America; together with the Psalter, or Psalms of David. Richmond, Va., J. W. Randolph, 1863. [592] p. 15 cm. "Longprimer 24mo." Printed in England. With this is bound: Bible. O. T. Psalms, English. Paraphrases, 1863. Selections from the Psalms of David in metre; with hymns suited to the feasts and fasts of the church ... Richmond, Va., 1863. [BX5943.A1 1863] 37-31957
I. Title.

PROTESTANT Episcopal church 223.
in the U. S. A. Book of common prayer.
The Book of common prayer, and administration of the sacraments, and other rites and cermonies, as revised and proposed to the use of the Protestant Episcopal church, at a convention of the said church in the states of New-York, New-Jersey, Pennsylvania, Delaware, Maryland, Virginia, and South-Carolina, held in Philadelphia, from September 27th to October 7th, 1785. Philadelphia, Printed by Hall and Sellers and sold for the benefit of sundry corporations and societies, instituted for the support of the widows and children of deceased clergymen, 1786. [361] p., 1 l., 8 p. 17 cm. Tunes suited to the Psalms and hymns of the Book of common prayer: 1 l., 8 p. at end. This edition contains the alterations which were intended to adapt the Book of common prayer to the changed political conditions in this country. The proposed Prayer book, owing to its radical changes was never adopted. It was reprinted in London in 1789, in an edition of 50 copies without the 8 engraved pages of music. cf. Evans. [BX5943.A1 1786] 5-5276
I. Title.

PROTESTANT Episcopal Church 223.
in the U. S. A. Book of common prayer.
The Book of common prayer and administration of the sacraments and other rites and ceremonies of the church according to the use of the Protestant Episcopal Church in the United States of America, together with the Psalter, or Psalms of David. Philadelphia, A. Dickinson, 1809. vii, 428 p. 11 cm. L. C. Copy imperfect: t. p. mutilated. With this is bound, as issued: Bible. O. T, Psalms. English. Paraphrases. 1809. The whole book of Psalms in metre, with Hymns suited to the feasts and fasts of the church and other occasions of public worship. Philadelphia,1809. [BX5943.A1 1809b] 49-32019
I. Title.

PROTESTANT Episcopal church 264.
in the U. S. A. Book of common prayer.
The Book of common prayer, and administration of the sacraments, and other rites and ceremonies, as revised and proposed to the use of the Protestant Episcopal church, at a convention of the said church in the states of New-York, New Jersey, Pennsylvania, Delaware, Maryland, Virginia, and Sokuth-Carolina, held in Philadelphia, from September 27th to October 7th, 1785. Philadelphia, Printed by Hall and Sellers and sold for the benefit of sundry corporations and societies, instituted for the support of the widows and children of deceased clergymen, 1786. [361] p., 1 l., 8 p. 17 cm. Tunes suited to the Psalms and hymns of the Book of common prayer: 1 l., 8 p. at end. This edition contains the alterations which were intended to adapt the Book of common prayer to the changed political conditions in this country. The proposed Prayer book, owing to its radical changes was never adopted. It was reprinted in London in 1789, in an edition of 50 copies without the 8 engraved pages of music. cf. Evans. [BX5943.A1 1786] 5-5276
I. Title.

PROTESTANT Episcopal church 264.
in the U. S. A. Book of common prayer.
The Book of common prayer, and aministration of the sacraments, and other rites and ceremonies, as revised and proposed to the use of the Protestant Episcopal church, at a convention of the said church in the states of New-York, New-Jersey, Pennsylvania, Delaware, Maryland, Virginia, and South-Carolina, held in Philadelphia, from September 27th to October 7th, 1785. Philadelphia, Printed: London, Re-printed for J. Debrett, opposite Burlington house, Piccadilly. 1789. [362] p. 19 cm. An edition of 50 copies, reprinted from the American edition of 1758, without the music. "The psalter selected from the Psalms of David": p. [182-247] "Psalms fitted to the tunes used in churches, selected from the Psalms of David ...": [248-361] [BX5943.A1 1789] 26-19055
I. Title.

PROTESTANT Episcopal church 264.
in the U. S. A. Book of common prayer.
The Book of common prayer, and administration of the sacraments, and other rites and ceremonies of the church, according to the use of the Protestant Episcopal church in the United States of America; together with the Psalter, or Psalms of David. Philadelhia: Printed by Hall & Sellers, in Market-Street, 1790. [327] p. 17 cm. With this is bound: The whole Book of Psalms, in metre, with hymns suited to the feasts and fasts of the church ... Philadelphia, 1790. [BX5943.A1 1790] 8-25627
I. Title.

PROTESTANT Episcopal church 264.
in the U. S. A. Book of common prayer.
The Book of common prayer, and administration of the sacraments and other rites and ceremonies of the church, according to the use of the Protestant Episcopal church in the United States of American; together with the Psalter or Psalms of David. Philadelphia; By permission of the General convention, printed by W. Young and J. Ormrod, 1795. [372] p. 15 cm. With this is bound: Bible.

O. T. Psalms. English. Paraphrases. 801. The whole book of Psalms, in metre; with hymns suited to the feasts and fasts of the church ... Philadelphia, 1801 [BX5943.A1] 5-31225
I. Title.

PROTESTANT Episcopal church 264. in the U. S. A. Book of common prayer. *The Book of common prayer,* and administration of the sacraments, and other rites and ceremonies of the church, according to the use of the Protestant Episcopal church, in the United States of America; together with the Psalter, or Psalms of David. Wilmington [Del.] Printed by Peter Brynberg. 1800. [370] p. 15 cm. With this is bound: Bible. O. T. Psalms. English. Paraphrases. [1800?] The whole book of psalms ... Wilmington [Del., 1800?] [BX5943.A] A 31
I. Title.

PROTESTANT Episcopal 264.03 church in the U. S. A. Book of common prayer. *The Book of common prayer,* and administration of the sacraments, and other rites and ceremonies of the church, according to the use of the Protestant Episcopal church in the United States of America. The whole calculated for private as well as public devotion. Printed at Worcester, By Isaiah Thomas, jun. June--1802. [228] p. 18 cm. "Facsims for holy days": 3 p. at end. [BX5943.A1 1802] 31-11683
I. Title.

PROTESTANT Episcopal 264.03 church in the U. S. A. Book of common prayer. *The Book of common prayer,* and administration of the sacraments and other rites and ceremonies of the church, according to the use of the Protestant Episcopal church in the United States of America: together with the Psalter, or Psalms of David. Philadelphia: Printed by John Bioren, no. 88, Chesnut-street, 1809. [324] p. 14 cm. With this is bound: Bible. O. T. Psalms. English. Paraphrases. 1809. The whole book of Psalms, in metre: with hymns, suited to the feasts and fasts of the church ... Philadelphia, 1809. [BX5943.A1 1809 a] 36-33238
I. Title.

PROTESTANT Episcopal church 264. in the U. S. A. Book of common prayer. *The Book of common prayer,* and administration of the sacraments, and other rites and ceremonies of the church, according to the use of the Protestant Episcopal church in the United States of America: together with the Psalter, or Psalms of David. New-York, Printed and sold by T. & J. Swords, 1813. 307 p. 14 cm. With this is bound: Bible. O. T. Psalms. English. Paraphrases. 1813. The whole book of Psalms, in metre ... New York, 1813. [BX5943.A1 1813] [BX5943.A] 264. A 32
I. Title.

PROTESTANT Episcopal 264.03 church in the U. S. A. Book of common prayer. *The Book of common prayer,* and administration of the sacraments, and other rites and ceremonies of the church, according to the use of the Protestant Episcopal church in the United States of America. Together with the Psalter, or Psalms of David. Hudson [N. Y.] Published by William E. Norman, 1814. 338 p. 19 cm. With this is bound Bible. O. T. Psalms. English. Paraphrases. 1814. The whole book of Psalms, in metre: with hymns ... Hudson [N. Y.] 1814. [BX5943.A1 1814] 34-28599
I. Title.

PROTESTANT Episcopal church 264. in the U. S. A. Book of common prayer. *The book of common prayer,* and administration of the sacraments, and other rites and ceremonies of the church, according to the use of the Protestant Episcopal church in the United States of America. Together with the Psalter, or Psalms of David. Stereotype ed. New-York, W. B. Gilley, 1817. 10 p. l., 377 p. 12 cm. Added t.-p., engr. "The Psalter, or Psalms of David", p. 220-322, has half-title engraved. With this is bound: The whole book of Psalms in metre, with hymns, suited to the feasts and fasts of the church and other occasions of public worship. Stereotype ed. New York, 1817. [BX5943.A1 1817] 22-5779
I. Title.

PROTESTANT Episcopal 264.03 church in the U. S. A. Book of common prayer. *The Book of common prayer,* and administration of the sacraments, and other rites and ceremonies of the church, according to the use of the Protestant Episcopal church, in the United States of America: together with the Psalter, or, Psalms of David. Philadelphia, W. Stavely, 1829. vi, 7-371 p. 16 cm. "The whole book of Psalms, in metre: with Hymns ..." (p. [289]-364) has special t.-p. with imprint: Philadelphia, The church missionary house, 1828. With this is bound: Protestant Episcopal church in the U. S. A. Hymnal. Hymns ... Philadelphia, 1829. [BX5943.A1 1829 b] 33-37104
I. Bible. O. T. Psalms. English. Paraphrases. 1828. II. Bible. English. Paraphrases. O. T. Psalms. 1828. III. Title.

PROTESTANT Episcopal church 264. in the U. S. A. Book of common prayer. *The Book of common prayer,* and administration of the sacraments, and other rites and ceremonies of the church, according to the use of the Protestant Episcopal church in the United States of America; together with the Psalter or Psalms of David. New York, Auxiliary New-York Bible and Common prayer book society, 1835. 296 p. 15 cm. Seal of "Aux. N. Y. Bible & Common prayer book soc." on verso of t.-p. With this is bound: Bible. O. T. Psalms. English. Paraphrases. 1835 Psalms, in metre, selected from the Psalms of David. New York, 1835. [BX5943.A1 1835 a] 27-4886
I. Title.

PROTESTANT Episcopal 264.03 church in the U. S. A. Book of common prayer. *The Book of common prayer,* and administration of the sacraments, and other rites and ceremonies of the church, according to the use of the Protestant Episcopal church in the United States of America; together with the Psalter, or, Psalms of David. New York, New York Bible and Common prayer book society, [1841. 296 p. 15 cm. With this is bound: Bible. O. T. Psalms. English. Paraphrases. 1840. Psalms, in metre, selected from the Psalms of David. New-York, 1840. [BX5943.A1 1841 a] 33-36474
I. Title.

PROTESTANT Episcopal 264.03 church in the U. S. A. Book of common prayer. *The Book of common prayer,* and administration of the sacraments, and other rites and ceremonies of the church, according to the use of the Protestant Episcopal church in the United States of America; together with the Psalter or Psalms of David. Hartford, S. Andrus & son, 1844. 309 p. front., plates. 24 cm. With this is bound: Bible. O. T. Psalms. English. Paraphrases. 1844. Psalms, in metre, selected from the Psalms of David ... Hartford, 1844. [BX5943.A1 1844 a] 33-20571
I. Title.

PROTESTANT Episcopal 264.03 church in the U. S. A. Book of common prayer. *The Book of common prayer,* and administration of the sacraments, and other rites and ceremonies of the church, according to the use of the Protestant Episcopal church in the United States of America. Together with the Psalter, or Psalms of David. Hartford, Ct. S. Andrus & son, 1844. 283 p. front. 16 cm. With this are bound: Bible. O. T. Psalms. English. Paraphrases. 1844. Psalms, in metre, selected from the Psalms of David ... Philadelphia [184-?] and Hymns of the Protestant Episcopal church ... Philadelphia [184-?] [BX5943.A1 1844 b] 34-38104
I. Title.

PROTESTANT Episcopal 264.03 church in the U. S. A. Book of common prayer. *The Book of common prayer,* and administration of the sacraments, and other rites and ceremonies of the church, according to the use of the Protestant Episcopal church in the United States of America; together with the Psalter, or Psalms of David. Buffalo, W. B. & C. E. Peck, 1845. 286 p. 16 cm. With this is bound: Bible. O. T. Psalms. English. Paraphrases. 1845. Psalms, in metre, selected from the Psalms of David: with hymns, suited to the feasts and fasts of the church ... Buffalo, 1845. [BX5943.A1 1845 a] 38-10389
I. Title.

PROTESTANT Episcopal 264.03 church in the U. S. A. Book of common prayer. *The Book of common prayer,* and administration of the sacraments; and other rites and ceremonies of the church, according to the use of the Protestant Episcopal church in the United States of America: together with the Psalter, or Psalms of David. New York, Harper & brothers, 1845. xx, 267 p. 16 cm. With this is bound: Selections from the Psalms of David in metre; with Hymns ... New-York, 1845. [BX5943.A1] 32-5062
I. Title.

PROTESTANT Episcopal 264.03 church in the U. S. A. Book of common prayer. *The Book of common prayer,* and administration of the sacraments; and other rites and ceremonies of the church, according to the use of the Protestant Eposcopal church in the United States of America: together with the Psalter, or Psalms of David. New York, D. Appleton & co.; Philadelphia G. S. Appleton, 1848. 670 p. front., plates, 15 cm. Added t.-p., illustrated in colors. With this is bound: Bible. O. T. Psalms, English. Paraphrases. 1848. Selections from the Psalms of David in meter: with Hymns, suited to the feasts and fasts of the church ... New York, 1848. [BX5943.A1 1848 b] 33-24575
I. Title.

PROTESTANT Episcopal 264.03 church in the U. S. A. Book of common prayer. ... *The Book of common prayer,* and administration of the sacraments; and other rites and ceremonies of the church, according to the use of the Protestant Episcopal church in the United States of America; together with the Psalter, or Psalms of David. Philadelphia, King & Baird [1848!] xx, 266 p. 16 cm. At head of title: By the standard. "Edition published for the Bishop White prayer book society." With this is bound: Bible. O. T. Psalms. English. Paraphrases, 1848? Selections from the Psalms of David in metre; with Hymns, suited to the feast and fasts of the church ... New York, 1848? [BX5943.A1 1848a] 33-6277
I. Bishop White prayer book society. II. Title.

PROTESTANT Episcopal 264.03 church in the U. S. A. Book of common prayer. *The Book of common prayer,* and administration of the sacraments; and other rites and ceremonies of the church, according to the use of the Protestant Episcopal church in the United States of America: together with the Psalter, or Psalms of David. New-York, Stanford and Swords, 1850. xxiii, 504 p. 13 cm. With this are bound: Bible. O. T. Psalms. English. Paraphrases. 1850. Selections from the Psalms of David in metre: with Hymns ... New York, 1850; and Bible. English. Lessons, Liturgical. 1850. Proper lessons for the Sunday and holidays ... New York, 1850. [BX5943.A1 1850 b] 33-16670
I. Title.

PROTESTANT Episcopal church 264. in the U. S. A. Book of common prayer. *The Book of common prayer,* and administration of the sacraments and other rites and ceremonies of the church, according to the use of the Protestant Episcopal church in the United States of America; together with the Psalter, or Psalms of David. New York, Stanford & Swords, 1850. 302, 51, 50 p. 16 cm. "The whole book of Psalms, in metre; with Hymns, suited to the feasts and fasts of the church, and other occasions of public worship": 51, 50 p. at end. [BX5943 1850] 18-4897
I. Bible. O. T. Psalms, English Paraphrases. II. Title.

PROTESTANT Episcopal 264.03 church in the U. S. A. Book of common prayer. *The Book of common prayer,* and administration of the sacraments, and other rites and ceremonies of the church, according to the use of the Protestant Episcopal church in the United States of America: together with the Psalter, or Psalms of David. Standard ed. Buffalo, G. H. Derby and co.; [etc., etc.] 1851. 286, 124 p. 15 cm. "Psalms in metre" (53 p.) and "Hymns suited to the feasts and fasts of the church" ([55-106] p. at end) have special title-pages. [BX5943.A1 1851] 30-33491
I. Bible. O. T. Psalms. English. Paraphrases. II. Title.

PROTESTANT Episcopal 264.03 church in the U. S. A. Book of common prayer. *The Book of common prayer,* and administration of the sacraments, and other rites and ceremonies of the church, according to the use of the Protestant Episcopal church in the United States of America, together with the Psalter, or Psalms of David. Philadelphia, Lippincott, Grambo & co., 1854. 1 p. l., 680, 286 p. front. 16 cm. Added t.-p., illustrated. With this is bound: Selections from the Psalms of David in metre; with Hymns. Philadelphia, 1854. Without music. [BX5943.A1 1854] 31-8487
I. Title.

PROTESTANT Episcopal 264.03 church in the U. S. A. Book of common prayer. *The Book of common prayer,* and administration of the sacraments, and other rites and ceremonies of the church, according to the use of the Protestant Episcopal church in the United States of America: together with the Psalter, or Psalms of David. Philadelphia, C. G. Henderson & co., 1857. 670 p. front. 16 cm. With this is bound: Bible. O. T. Psalms. English. Paraphrases. 1857. Selections from the Psalms of David in metre; with Hymns ... Philadelphia, 1857. [BX5943.A1 1857] 33-16673
I. Title.

PROTESTANT Episcopal 264.03 church in the U. S. A. Book of common prayer. ... *The Book of common prayer,* and administration of the sacraments, and other rites and ceremonies of the church, according to the use of the Protestant Episcopal church in the United States of America. Together with the Psalter, or Psalms of David. Philadelphia, C. G. Henderson & co., 1857. vi, [7]-327 p. front. (port.) 14 cm. Half-title, illustrated. At head of title: Revised edition. With this is bound Bible. O. T. Psalms. English. Paraphrases. 1857. Selections. from the Psalms of David, in metre; with Hymns ... Philadelphia, 1857. [BX5943.A1 1857 a] 33-24559
I. Title.

PROTESTANT Episcopal 264.03 church in the U. S. A. Book of common prayer. *The Book of common prayer,* and administration of the sacraments; and other rites and ceremonies of the church, according to the use of the Protestant Episcopal church in the United States of America: together with the Psalter, or Psalms of David. New York, T. Nelson and sons, 1862. vi, [14], 561, 243, [1] p. 15 cm. "Selections from the Psalms of David, in metre: with hymns, suited to the feasts and fasts of the church, and other occasions of public worship. New York, 1862": 243, [1] p. at end. [BX5943.A1 1862] 30-33489
I. Bible. O. T. Psalms. English. Paraphrases. II. Title.

PROTESTANT Episcopal church 264. in the U. S. A. Book of common prayer. *The Book of common prayer,* and administration of the sacraments, and other rites and ceremonies of the church, according to the use of the Protestant Episcopal church in the United States of America: together with the Psalter, or Psalms of David. New York, New York

Bible and Common prayer book society, 1865. 2 p. l., iii-xx, 21-402 p. 16 cm. With this is bound: Selections from the Psalms of David, in metre; with hymns, suited to the feasts and fasts of the church ... New York, 1863. [BX5943.A1 1865] 11-21981
I. Title.

PROTESTANT Episcopal church 264.
in the U. S. A. Book of common prayer.
... *The Book of common prayer,* and administration of the sacraments; and other rites and ceremonies of the church, according to the use of the Protestant Episcopal church in the United States of America: together with the Psalter, or Psalms of David. New York, The New York Bible and Common prayer book society [1869?] 12 p. l., 580 p. 19 cm. At head of title: From the standard edition. [BX5943.A1] 41-31778
I. New York Bible and Common prayer book society. II. Title.

PROTESTANT Episcopal 264.03
church in the U. S. A. Book of common prayer.
The Book of common prayer, and administration of the sacraments; and other rites and ceremonies of the church, according to the use of the Protestant Episcopal church in the United States of America: together with the Psalter, or Psalms of David. Oxford, Printed at the University press, 1869. 452 p. 11 cm. With this is bound: Selections from the Pslams of David in metre, with Hymns. Oxford, 1869. [BX5943.A1 1869] 31-11236
I. Bible. O. T. Psalms. English. Paraphrases. 1869. II. Title.

PROTESTANT Episcopal 264.03
church in the U. S. A. Book of common prayer.
The Book of common prayer, and administration of the sacraments; and other rites and ceremonies of the church, according to the use of the Protestant Episcopal church in the United States of America: together with the Psalter, or Psalms of David. Philadelphia, Pub. for the Bishop White prayer-book society by Claxton, Remsen & Haffelfinger [1873?] 440 p. 16 cm. [BX5943.A1 1873] 33-35604
I. Bishop White prayer book society. II. Title.

PROTESTANT Episcopal church 264.
in the U. S. A. Book of common prayer.
The Book of common prayer, and administration of the sacraments; and other rites and ceremonies of the church, according to the use of the Protestant Episcopal church in the United States of America: together with the Psalter, or Psalms of David. Philadelphia, J. B. Lippincott & co., 1875. 564 p. 13 cm. [BX5943.A1 1875] 27-4879
I. Title.

PROTESTANT Episcopal 264.03
church in the U. S. A. Book of common prayer.
The Book of common prayer, and administration of the sacraments, and other rites and ceremonies of the church according to the use of the Protestant Episcopal church in the United States of America; together with the Psalter, or Psalms of David. Oxford, Printed at the University press, New York, T. Nelson & sons [1892?] xxxii, 604 p. 13 cm. [BX5943.A1 1892 b] 33-6273
I. Title.

PROTESTANT Episcopal 264.03
church in the U. S. A. Book of common prayer.
The Book of common prayer, and administration of the sacraments, and other rites and ceremonies of the church according to the use of the Protestant Episcopal church in the United States of America; together with the Psalter, or Psalms of David. New York, J. Pott & co. [1892?] 2 p. l., iii-xxviii, 566 p. 15 cm. [BX5943.A1 1892 a] 33-6278
I. Title.

PROTESTANT Episcopal 264.03
church in the U. S. A. Book of common prayer.
The Book of common prayer, and administration of the sacraments, and other rites and ceremonies of the church according to the use of the Protestant Episcopal church in the United States of America; together with the Psalter, or Pslams of David. Cambridge [Eng.] Printed by C. J. Clay & sons at the University press, for J. Pott & co., New York [1893] xxxv, 432 p. 10 cm. [BX5943.A1 1893 b] 33-6272
I. Title.

PROTESTANT Episcopal church 264.
in the U. S. A. Book of common prayer.
The Book of common prayer, and administration of the sacraments and other rites and ceremonies of the church, according to the use of the Protestant Episcopal chruch in the United States of America: together with the Psalter, or Psalms of David. New York: By direction of the General convention, printed by Hugh Gaine, at the Bible, Pearl-street, m,dcc,xcviii. [350] p. 16 cm. With this is bound: Bible. O. T. Pslms. English. Paraphrases. 1798. The whole book of Psalms, in metre: with hymns ... New-York, m,dcc,xcviii. [BX5943.A] A 31
I. Title.

PROTESTANT Episcopal church in
the U. S. A. Book of common prayer.
The Book of common prayer, and administration of the sacraments and other rites and ceremonies of the church, according to the use of the Protestant Episcopal church in the United States of America: Together with the Psalter or Psalms of David. Philadelphia, Printed by Hall and Sellers, 1791. [327] p. 15 cm. With this is bound the "Whole book of Psalms in metre ..." Philadelphia, 1791. 6-26908
I. Title.

PROTESTANT Episcopal 264.03
church in the U. S. A. Book of common prayer.
The Book of common prayer and administration of the sacraments, and other rites and ceremonies of the church, according to the use of the Protestant Episcopal church in the United States of America; together with the Psalter, or Psalms of David. Philadelhia, J. B. Lippincott & co., 1847. 1 p. l., 680 p. 16 cm. Added t.-p., in colors. With this is bound: Selections from the Psalms of David in metre; with hymns ... Philadelphia, 1847. [BX5943.A1 1847] 31-13882
I. Title.

PROTESTANT Episcopal church 264.
in the U.S.A. Book of common prayer.
The Book of common prayer, and administration of the sacraments, and other rites and ceremonies of the church, according to the use of the Protestant Episcopal church in the United States of America: together with the Psalter, or Psalms of David. New-York, W. B. Gilley, 1819. vi, [7]-304 p. 22 1/2 cm. With this is bound: Bible. O.T. Psalms. English. Paraphrases. 1819. The whole book of Psalms, in metre; with hymns, suited to the feasts and fasts of the church ... New-York, 1819. [BX5943.A1 1819] 42-47979
I. Title.

PROTESTANT Episcopal church 264.
in the U.S.A. Book of common prayer.
The Book of common prayer, and administration of the sacraments and other rites and ceremonies of the church, according to the use of the Protestant Episcopal church in the United State of America, together with the Psalter or Psalms of David. London, Printed by Eyre and Spottiswoode for E. & J. B. Young & co., New York [1893?] xxviii, 566 p., 1 l. 15 1/2 cm. [BX5943.A1 1893 d] 42-51721
I. Title.

PROTESTANT Episcopal church in
the U. S. Book of common prayer.
The Book of common prayer, and administration of the sacraments and other rites and ceremonies of the church, according to the use of the Protestant Episcopal church in the United States of America: together with the Psalter, or Psalms of David. New York, Printed for T. Allen, 1797. 185 l. 15 cm. Appended with continuous signatures, but separate paging: The whole book of Psalms, in metre, with hymns, suited to the feasts and fasts of the church and other occasions of public worship. New-York, Printed for T. Allen, 1797. 6-39859
I. Title.

PROTESTANT Episcopal church in
the U. S. Book of common prayer.
The book of common prayer, and administration of the sacraments; and other rites and ceremonies of the church, according to the use of the Protestant Episcopal church in the United States of America; together with the Psalter, or Psalms of David. Philadelphia, H. F. Anners, 1850. 670 p. front., 2 pl. 15 cm. 8-6840
I. Title.

PROTESTANT Episcopal church in
the U. S. Book of Common prayer.
The Book of common prayer, and administration of the sacraments and other rites and ceremonies of the church, according to the use of the Protestant Episcopal church in the United States of America: together with the Psalter, or Psalms of David. Charleston, Printed for W. P. Young, 1799. [370] p. 17 cm. With this is bound "A selection of Psalms with occasional hymns. Charleston, Printed for W. P. Young ... [1792?]" 5-5275
I. Title.

PROTESTANT Episcopal church in
the U. S. Book of common prayer.
The Book of common prayer, and administration of the sacraments, and other rites and ceremonies of the church, according to the use of the Protestant Episcopal church in the United States of America: together with the Psalter, or Psalms of David. Philadelphia, M. Thomas, 1812. 19 p. l., 37-323, [1] p. front., plates, 18 cm. Added t.-p., engr.: M. Thomas' edition of the Book of common prayer ... With is this bound: The whole Book of Psalms, in metre; with hymns ... Philadelphia, M. Thomas, 1812. 1-14595
I. Bible. O. T. Psalms. Paraphrases. II. Thomas, Moses, pub. III. Title.

PROTESTANT Episcopal Church in
the U.S.A. National Council.
A calendar of prayer for missions, 1961-1962. [New York, 1961] 79 p. 63-36636
I. Title.

PRUGH, Marcella. 268.6
We talk with God; a Christian education unit for grade I and II, by Marcella Prugh ... New York, N.Y., The Nations council, Protestant Episcopal church [1942] 40 p. 21 1/2 cm. [Christian education units] "Source materials": p. 16-29. [BV214.P7] 42-19743
1. Prayer. 2. Religious education—Textbooks for children. I. Title.

PUGLISI PICO, Mario, 1867- 248
Prayer, by Mario Puglisi; translated by Bernard M. Allen ... New York, The Macmillan company, 1929. viii p., 2 l., 3-296 p. 21 cm. "Bibliographical appendix": p. [257]-296. [BV210.P85] 29-22399
1. Prayer. I. Allen, Bernard Meredith, 1864- tr. II. Title.

PULLEN, John Turner, 1852- 264.1
1913.
Prayer and its answer from the Word of God and Scripture comments, by John T. Pullen ... (4th ed.) Raleigh, N.C., C. E. Mitchell, 1936. 151, [1] p. illus. (ports.) 18 1/2 cm. [BV220.P8 1936] 43-191
1. Prayer. I. Title.

QUAYLE, William Alfred, 264.
bp., 1860-
The throne of grace; a volume of personal prayers, with a prelude, by William A. Quayle. New York, Cincinnati, The Methodist book concern [c1919] 117 p. 15 cm. [BV245.Q3] 19-3301
I. Title.

RADCLIFFE, Lynn James 264.1
Making prayer real. Nashville, Abingdon Press [1961, c.1952] 254p. (Apex Bks. E6) 1.25 pap.,
1. Prayer. I. Title.

RADCLIFFE, Lynn James. 264.1
Making prayer real. New York, Abingdon-Cokesbury [1952] 254 p. 23 cm. [BV210.R3] 52-8839
1. Prayer. I. Title.

RADCLIFFE, Lynn James. 248.3
With Christ in the Garden. New York, Abingdon Press [1959] 80p. 20cm. [BV210.R32] 59-5247
1. Prayer. I. Title.

RAGUIN, Yves, 1912- 248'.3
How to pray today. Translated by John Beevers. St. Meinrad, Ind., Abbey Press, 1974. 60 p. 21 cm. (Religious experience series, v. 4) Translation of Prier a l'heure qu'il est. [BV210.2.R2513] 73-85334 ISBN 0-87029-028-2 1.50 (pbk.)
1. Prayer. I. Title.

*RAHNER, Karl. 248.3
On prayer. Glen Rock, Paulist [1968, c.1958] 109p. 18cm. (Deus bks.) .95 pap.,
1. Prayer. I. Title.

RAHNER, Karl, 1904- 264.1
Happiness through prayer. Translated from the German. Westminster [sic] Md., Newman Press [1958] 109p. 19cm. [BV210.R333] 58-2283
1. Prayer. I. Title.

RAWSON, Frederick Lawrence, 264.
1859-
The nature of true prayer, by F. L. Rawson ... 3d ed. London, Eng., and New York city, U. S. A., The Crystal press limited [192-] 1 p. l., 83, viii, [1] p. 19 cm. First published 1919. [BV215.R25 1920] 28-15475
1. Prayer. I. Title.

RAWSON, Frederick Lawrence, 264.
1859-
True prayer for teachers; being one of the series of articles on right thinking (true prayer) appearing in "Active service" from October 19th to November 2nd, 1918, and from January 4th to February 15th, 1919, revised and enlarged. By F. L. Rawson ... 2d ed. ... London, New York city, The Crystal press, limited [1921] 1 p. l., 100 p. 19 cm. (On cover: Divine protection series. no. 7) [BV213.R3 1921] 28-16955
1. Prayer. I. Title.

REDWOOD, Hugh, 1883- 264.1
Practical prayer, by Hugh Redwood. New York, London and Edinburgh, Fleming H. Revell company [1938] 2 p. l., 7-128 p. 19 cm. "First printed, 1937; reprinted, 1938." [BV210.R37 1938] 39-18652
1. Prayer. I. Title.

*REES, Jean A. 248.3
Challenge to pray. Foreword by Ruth Graham. Grand Rapids, Mich., Zondervan [1967.c.1966] 96p. 21cm. Pub. in England in 1966 by Oliphants. 1.50 pap.,
1. Prayer. I. Title.

REIDHEAD, Paris. 248'.3
Beyond petition; six steps to successful praying. Minneapolis, Dimension Books [1974] 84 p. 18 cm. [BV210.2.R35] 74-3684 ISBN 0-87123-037-2 0.95
1. Prayer. I. Title.

REINBERGER, Francis E. 248.3
How to pray, by Francis E. Reinberger. [Rev. ed.] Philadelphia, Fortress Press [1967] 138 p. illus. 22 cm. Bibliographical footnotes. [BV210.2.R37 1967] 67-10247
1. Prayer. I. Title.

RHYMES, Douglas A. 264'.1
Prayer in the secular city, by Douglas Rhymes. Philadelphia, Westminister [c.1967] 140p. 21cm. Bibl. [BV210.2.R48 1967b] 68-15778 1.65
1. Prayer. I. Title.

RHYMES, Douglas A. 248'.3
Through prayer to reality [by] Douglas A. Rhymes. [Nashville] Upper Room [1974] 88 p. 22 cm. Continues the author's Prayer in the secular city. Includes bibliographical references. [BV210.2.R483] 74-81813 1.25
1. Prayer. I. Title.

RICE, John R., 1895- 264.1
Prayer, asking and receiving, by Evangelist John R. Rice ... with introduction by Rev. Oswald J. Smith ... Wheaton, Ill., Sword of the Lord publishers [1942] 328 p. 21 cm. "First printing, October, 1942." [BV210.R47] 43-16328
1. Prayer. I. Title.

RICHARDS, Thomas Cole, 1866- 248
Young men and prayer, by Thomas C. Richards. Boston, Chicago, The Pilgrim press [c1918] 4 p. l., [3]-81 p. 17 cm. [BV210.R5] 18-21557

1. Title.

RINKER, Rosalind 248.3
Communicating love through prayer. Grand Rapids, Mich., Zondervan [c.1966] 125p. 21cm. [BV210.2.R49] 66-18940 2.50 bds.,
1. Prayer. I. Title.

RINKER, Rosalind. 248.3
Communicating love through prayer. Grand Rapids, Zondervan Pub. House [1966] 125 p. 21 cm. [BV210.2.R49] 66-18940
1. Prayer. I. Title.

RINKER, Rosalind. 248.3
Prayer; conversing with God. Grand Rapids, Zondervan Pub. House [1959] 116 p. illus. 20 cm. Includes bibliography. [BV210.2.R5] 59-4291
1. Prayer.

ROBERTS, William. 248'.3
Teach us to pray. Liguori, Mo., Liguori Publications [1972] 71 p. 18 cm. (A Liguorian combination book) With, as issued, Herlong, T. L. Maturity revisited. Liguori, Mo. [1972] [BV213.R553] 72-81175 1.50 (pbk.)
1. Prayer. I. Title.

ROBINSON, Charles Elmo, 1867- 242
Praying to change things, being a presentation of rules, principles and warnings; intended to teach lowly and commonplace men how to pray effectively. By Chas. E. Robinson... Dayton, O., J. J. Scruby [c1925] 117 p. 19 cm. [BV215.R6] 25-21029
1. Prayer. I. Title.

ROCHE, William, 1856- 264.
Daybreak in the soul; the second part of The children's bread, by Father W. Roche, S.J. ... London, New York [etc.] Longmans, Green and co., 1929. ix, [1], 118 p. front., plates. 19 cm. $1.25 [BV212.R6] 29-29859
1. Prayer. I. Title.

ROCKWOOD, Elizabeth. 248'.3
A wide place for my steps : the realities of prayer / Elizabeth Rockwood. Waco, Tex. : Word Books, c1979. 123 p. ; 21 cm. Includes bibliographical references. [BV210.2.R59] 79-63929 ISBN 0-8499-0168-5 : 6.95
1. Prayer. I. Title.

ROGERS, Harold, 1907- 248'.3
Learning to listen, Lord. Waco, Tex., Word Books [1974] 104 p. 21 cm. [BV210.2.R63] 73-91689 1.95 (pbk.)
1. Prayer. 2. Prayers. I. Title.

ROUNER, Arthur A 264.1
When a man prays. Westwood, N. J., Revell [1953] 160p. 22cm. [BV210.R64] 53-10753
1. Prayer. I. Title.

ROYDEN, Agnes Maude, 1876- 248
Prayer as a force, by A. Maude Royden ... New York & London, G. P. Putnam's sons, 1923. vii, 132 p. 20 cm. "Published, January 1923. Reprinted, April, 1923." [BV210.R65 1923 a] 23-26241
1. Prayer. 2. God. I. Title.

RUNBECK, Margaret Lee, 264.1
1905-
Answer without ceasing. Boston, Houghton Miffin Co., 1949. xii, 333 p. 21 cm. [BV220.R8] 49-11207
1. Prayer. I. Title.

RYAN, Mary Perkins, 1915- 242
Psalms '70: a new approach to old prayers. Design: Wm. Schickel & Assoc. Dayton, Ohio, Pflaum Press, 1969. 109 p. illus. 13 cm. [BV210.2.R9] 73-93007 2.75
1. Bible. O.T. Psalms—Liturgical use. 2. Prayer. I. Title.

RYLE, John Charles, bp. of 264.
Liverpool, 1816-1900.
A call to prayer. By the Rev. J. C. Ryle ... [New York, American tract society, 185-] 54 p. 15 cm. Caption title. [BV213.R9 1850] 28-14355
1. Prayer. I. Title.

SALOFF-ASTAKHOFF, Nikita
Ignatievich, 1893-
Touching heaven by prayer. Westchester, Ill., Good News Publishers, 1960. 64 p. (A "one evening" condensed book) 63-53789
1. Prayer. I. Title. II. Series.

SANDERS, John Oswald, 248'.3
1902-
Prayer power unlimited / by J. Oswald Sanders. Chicago : Moody Press, c1977. p. cm. Includes bibliographical references and index. [BV210.2.S26] 77-23472 ISBN 0-8024-6808-X : 5.95
1. Prayer. I. Title.

SANGSTER, William Edwin, 248.32
1900-
Teach me to pray. Nashville, The Upper room [1959] 64p. 19cm. 'Previously published in [three booklets] ... under the titles: Teach us to pray, How to form a prayer cell [and] How to live in Christ.' [BV215.S25] 59-15667
1. Prayer. I. Sangster, William Edwin, 1900- Teach us to pray. II. Sangster, William Edwin, 1900- How to form a prayer cell. III. Sangster, aSangster, William Edwin, 1900- How to live in Christ. IV. Title.

SAVON, Herve 248.3
The church and Christian prayer, v.3. Notre Dame, Ind., Fides [1966, c.1965] 168p. 21cm. (Saint Severin ser. for adult Christians, v.3; Fides paperback textbks., PBT-19) Orig. pub. in France in 1963. [BV210.2.S313] 66-3237 1.75 pap.,
1. Prayer. I. Title.

SCHUH, Charles Gottlob, 1856- 244
God's treasure-house unlocked. Authentic accounts of providential assistance, and how it may be obtained by all. Original and compiled by Charles G. Schuh... Cincinnati, Cranston & Stowe; New York, Phillips & Hunt, 1887. 480 p. front., plates, ports, 19 cm. [BV220.S28] 46-32571
1. Prayer. I. Title.

SCROGGIE, William Graham, 248.3'2
1877-1958.
How to pray : an exposition and exhortation / by W. Graham Scroggie ; pref. by H. C. G. Moule. Grand Rapids, Mich. : Kregel Publications, 1981. p. cm. Reprint of the 1955 ed. published by Pickering & Inglis, London, under title: Method in prayer. [BV210.S3 1981] 19 80-8076 ISBN 0-8254-3736-9 : 2.95
1. Prayer. I. Title.

SEDDING, Edward Douglas. 264.1
The flame of prayer; a study of the life of prayer in the English church; with extracts from the devotional works of representative churchmen, by Edward D. Sedding ... London and Oxford, A. R. Mowbray & co., ltd; Milwaukee, Morehouse publishing co. [1934] xii, 155, [1] p. 18 cm. "First published in 1934." [BX210.S38] 35-5424
1. Prayer. 2. Church of England—Prayer-books and devotions. I. Title.

SELF, Carolyn Shealy. 248'.3
Learning to pray / Carloyn Shealy Self & William L. Self. Waco, Tex. : Word Books, c1978. 159 p. ; 21 cm. [BV215.S44] 77-83317 ISBN 0-8499-0054-9 : 5.95
1. Lord's Prayer—Meditations. 2. Prayer. I. Self, William L., joint author. II. Title.

SHAW, Solomon Benjamin, 1854- 244
The power of prayer; or, Touching incidents and remarkable answers to prayer. Reprinted and enl. by Teunis Oldenburger. [Grand Rapids, Calvin Press, 1945] 374 p. 20 cm. Cover title: Touching incidents; or, The power of prayer. Previous editions published under title: Touching incidents and remarkable answers to prayer. [BV220.S5 1945] 50-30413
I. Title.

SHAW, Solomon Benjamin, 1854- 244
Touching incidents and remarkable answers to prayer. Children's ed., compiled by Rev. S. B. Shaw ... Reprinted and enlarged by Rev. Teunis Oldenburger ... Grand Rapids, Mich., Calvin press, 1944. 142 p. illus. 19 cm. [BV220.S5 1944] 46-2028
1. Prayer. I. Oldenburger, Teunis, 1878- ed. II. Title.

SHEDD, Charlie W. 254'.6
The exciting church : where people really pray / Charlie W. Shedd. Waco, Tex. : Word Books, [1974] 105 p. ; 22 cm. [BX9211.J43J447] 74-78039 3.95
1. Jekyll Presbyterian Community Church, Jekyll Island. 2. Prayer. I. Title.

SHEDD, Charlie W. 248'.3
Getting through to the wonderful you : a Christian alternative to transcendental meditation / Charlie W. Shedd. Old Tappan, N.J. : Revell, c1976. 128 p. ; 21 cm. Includes index. [BV210.2.S48] 75-43875 ISBN 0-8007-0780-X : 4.95
1. Prayer. 2. Meditation. 3. Devotional exercises. I. Title.

SHEDD, Charlie W. 264.1
How to develop a praying church. Nashville, Abingdon [1964] 111p. 119cm. Bibl. 64-15761 1.25 pap.,
1. Prayer. I. Title.

SHEEHY, John F. 248.32
When you pray. Notre Dame, Ind., Fides [c.1961] 167p. Bibl. 61-10365 2.95 bds.,
1. Prayer. I. Title.

SHERMAN, Harold Morrow, 1898-
How to use the power of prayer. New York, Anthony, c1958. 144 p.
1. Prayer. I. Title.

SHOEMAKER, Helen Smith. 248'.3
Prayer and evangelism. Waco, Tex., Word Books [1974] 119 p. 23 cm. [BV210.2.S518] 73-91552 3.95, 2.25 (pbk.)
1. Prayer. 2. Evangelistic work. I. Title.

SHOEMAKER, Helen Smith. 264.1
Prayer and you. With introd. by E. Stanley Jones. New York, F. H. Revell Co. [1948] 157 p. 20 cm. [BV210.S47] 48-6175
1. Prayer. I. Title.

SHOEMAKER, Helen (Smith) 242
Prayer is action. New York, Morehouse-Barlow Co. [1969] 128 p. 21 cm. Bibliography: p. 125-128. [BV210.2.S52] 70-88122
1. Prayer. I. Title.

SHOEMAKER, Helen (Smith) 264.1
The secret of effective prayer. [Westwood, N. J.] Revell [1955] 158p. 22cm. [BV220.S66] 55-6624
1. Prayer. I. Title.

SHOEMAKER, Helen (Smith) 264'.1
The secret of effective prayer. [2d ed.] Waco, Tex., Word Books [1967] 171 p. 22 cm. Bibliography: p. 170-171. [BV220.S66 1967] 67-19306
1. Prayer. I. Title.

SIMMS, George Otto, 1910- 242
In my understanding / George Simms. 1st Fortress Press ed. Philadelphia : Fortress Press, 1982. 150 p. ; 22 cm. [BV215.S47 1982] 19 81-70555 ISBN 0-8006-0674-4 : 8.95
1. Prayer. I. Title.

SINCLAIR, Ronald Sutherland
Brook, 1894-
When we pray; a method of prayer taught by G. A. Studdert Kennedy. [New ed.] Lindon Mowbray; New York, Morehouse-Gorham [1957] 76 p. "First published ... 1935. New Edition ... 1957." 63-69718
1. Prayer. I. Studdert-Kennedy, Geoffrey Anketell, 1883-1929. II. Title.

SKELTON, Frederic. 240
Pray in the daylight too! [by] Frederic Skelton. [Yardley, Pa., F. S. Cook & son, c1927] 154, [2] p. 18 1/2 cm. [X3.S46] 27-20490
I. Title.

SLATTERY, Charles Lewis, 248
bp., 1867-1930.
Why men pray, by Charles Lewis Slattery... New York, The Macmillan company, 1916. 5 p. l., 5-118 p. 18 cm. (Half-title: Church principles for lay people) [BV210.S65] 16-3928
1. Prayer. I. Title.

SMITH, Bernie, 1920- 264.1
Meditations on prayer. Introd. by Robert G. Lee. Grand Rapids. Baker Bk. [1966] 81p. 20cm. [BV210.2.S6] 66-25396 1.95
1. Prayer. I. Title.

SMITH, Chuck, 1927- 248'.3
Effective prayer life / Chuck Smith. Costa Mesa, Calif. : Maranatha House Publishers, c1979. 95 p. ; 18 cm. Contents.Contents.—What is prayer?—The purpose of prayer.—Privilege of prayer.—Effective prayer.—Strength in prayer.—Pray, and I will answer.—Sin of prayerlessness. [BV210.2.S625] 78-27511 ISBN 0-89337-008-8 pbk. : 1.95
1. Prayer. I. Title.

SMITH, Herbert Booth, 1883- 248
Science and prayer: studies in communion and intercession, by Herbert Booth Smith... New York, Chicago [etc.] Fleming H. Revell company [c1924] 160 p. 19 1/2 cm. [BV210.S67] 24-23746
1. Prayer. I. Title.

[SMITH, William Goodhugh] 248
comp.
The way the preachers pray, with notes by one of them. Minneapolis, Minn., W. G. Smith & company, 1900. 103 p. 16 x 12 cm. [BV210.S7] 0-4508
1. Prayer. I. Title.

SOCIETY of retreat 264.1082
conductors.
Direction in prayer; studies in ascetic method, edited by Patrick Thompson for the Society of retreat conductors; with an introduction by Samuel Babcock Booth ... Milwaukee, Morehouse publishing co., 1933. xv, 215, [1] p. 19 cm. Bibliography: p. [213]-215. [BV210.S73 1933 a] 33-33473
1. Prayer. I. Thompson, Patrick, ed. II. Title.

SPALINK, Benjamin H. 242
The incense of prayer, by Rev. Benjamin H. Spalink... Grand Rapids, Mich., Smitter book company [c1928] iv, 5-157 p. 19 cm. [BV215.S65] 29-13464
1. Prayer. I. Title.

SPALINK, Benjamin Henry, 264.1
1890-
The inner chamber. by Benjamin H. Spalink... Grand Rapids, Mich., Zondervan publishing house [c1938] 142 p. 19 1/2 cm. [BV210.S74] 38-30637
1. Prayer. I. Title.

SPONG, John Shelby. 248'.3
Honest prayer. New York, Seabury Press [1972, c1973] 126 p. 22 cm. Bibliography: p. [125]-126. [BV210.2.S66] 72-90474 ISBN 0-8164-0245-0 4.50
1. Prayer. 2. Christian life—Anglican authors. I. Title.

STEDMAN, Ray C. 248'.3
Jesus teaches on prayer / Ray C. Stedman. Waco, Tex. : Word Books, c1975. 184 p. ; 21 cm. (Discovery books) [BV210.2.S69] 75-14710 4.95
1. Jesus Christ—Prayers. 2. Prayer. I. Title.

STEERE, Douglas Van, 1901- 248.32
Dimensions of prayer. New York, Harper [c.1962, 1963] 126p. 19cm. Bibl. 62-11822 2.50
1. Prayer. I. Title.

STEERE, Douglas Van, 1901- 248.32
Dimensions of prayer. [New York], 475 Riverside Dr., Women's Division of Christian Service Bd. of Missions, Methodist Church, [c.1962] 126p. 19cm. Bibl. 62-11822 1.00 pap.,
1. Prayer. I. Title.

STEERE, Douglas Van, 1901- 226
Dimensions of prayer. [New York] Woman's Division of Christian Service Board of Missions, Methodist Church [1962] 126 p. 19 cm. Includes bibliography. [BV210.2.S7] 62-11822
1. Prayer. I. Title.

STEERE, Douglas Van, 1901- 248.3
Dimensions of prayer. [1st ed.] New York, Harper & Row [1963] ix, 130 p. 20 cm. Bibliographical footnotes. [BV210.2.S7 1963] 63-6334
1. Prayer. I. Title.

STEINGRAEBER, John. 242
Love is prayer, prayer is love. Selected writings of St. Alphonsus, adapted for moderns by John Steingraeber. Liguori, Mo., Liguori Publications [1973] 191 p. 18 cm. [BV213.S7] 72-97592 1.50 (pbk.)
1. Jesus Christ—Meditations. 2. Mary, Virgin. 3. Prayer. 4. Christian life—Catholic authors. I. Liguori, Alfonso Maria de', Saint, 1696-1787. II. Title.

STEPHENS, John Underwood, 1901- 264.1
A simple guide to prayer. New York, Abingdon Press [1957] 124 p. 20 cm. Includes bibliography. [BV215.S75] 57-5281
1. Prayer. I. Title.

STEPHENSON, Virginia. 248'.3
Agreement : an attitude of prayer / by Virginia Stephenson. 1st ed. Redlands, CA : Allen-Greendale Publishers, c1977. 92 p. ; 15 cm. [BV213.S72] 77-81161
1. Prayer. I. Title.

STEWART, George Shaw. 264.1
The lower levels of prayer, by George S. Stewart ... Nashville, Cokesbury press [c1939] 189 p. 20 cm. "First published ... January, 1940." [BV210.S78 1939 a] 40-4799
1. Prayer. I. Title.

STOLZ, Karl Ruf, 1884-
... The Psychology of prayer, by Karl R. Stolz ... New York, Cincinnati, The Abingdon press [c1923] 247 p. 20 cm. (The Abingdon religious education texts; D. G. Downey, general editor, N. E. Richardson, associate editor) Revised and enlarged edition of Auto-suggestion in private prayer, published 1913. "A selected bibliography": p. 239-242. [BV225.S72] 28-7114
1. Prayer. I. Title.

STRABO, Mikhail. 264.1
The magic formula for successful prayer, by Mikhail Strabo. New York, N.Y., Guidance house, [1942] 61 p. 21 1/3 cm. [BV213.S75] 42-13230
1. Prayer. I. Title.

STRAUSS, Lehman. 248'.3
Sense and nonsense about prayer / by Lehman Strauss. Chicago : Moody Press, [1974] 123 p. ; 22 cm. [BV210.2.S77] 74-15324 ISBN 0-8024-7700-3 : 3.95
1. Prayer. I. Title.

STRONG, Anna Louise, 1885-
The psychology of prayer, by Anna Louise Strong. Chicago, The University of Chicago press, 1909. 122 p. 20 cm. Also published as thesis (PH.D) University of Chicago, 1908, with title: A consideration of prayer from the standpoint of social psychology. "A selected bibliography": p. 120-122. [BV225.S8] 9-31495
1. Prayer. I. Title.

STRONG, John Henry. 264.1
Jesus the man of prayer, by John Henry Strong. Philadelphia, Los Angeles [etc.] The Judson press [1945] 125 p. front. (port.) 19 1/2 cm. [BV210.S83] 45-11404
1. Prayer. I. Title.

STRONG, Sydney Dix, 1860- ed. 248
We believe in prayer; affirmations by one hundred men and women of many lands, edited by Sydney Strong. New York, Coward-McCann, inc., 1930. x, 210 p. 19 1/2 cm. "Acknowledgements": p. 210. [BV205.S7] 30-9620
1. Prayer. I. Title.

STURGIS, William Codman, 1862- 248
The practice of prayer, by William C. Sturgis, PH.D.: with preface by the Right Reverend Philip M. Rhinelander ... Milwaukee, Morehouse publishing co.; London, A. R. Mowbray & co, [c1930] viii, 120 p. 17 1/2 cm. (Half-title: Washington cathedral series) [BV210.S85] 30-7513
1. Prayer. I. Title.

SULZBERGER, Cyrus Leo, 1912- 242
Go gentle into the night / C. L. Sulzberger. Englewood Cliffs, N.J. : Prentice-Hall, c1976. 152 p. ; 22 cm. Includes index. [BL560.S94] 75-42344 ISBN 0-13-357293-5 : 6.95
1. Sulzberger, Cyrus Leo, 1912- 2. Prayer. 3. Prayers. 4. Religion. 5. Death. I. Title.

SUTTON, Joseph Wilson, 1881- 264.1
Our life of prayer, by the Rev. J. Wilson Sutton ... New York, Milwaukee, Morehouse-Gorham co., 1938. 141 p. 19 1/2 cm. [BV210.S92] 38-8435
1. Prayer. I. Title.

SWANSON, Neil H.
Dear Fiyon. Wauwatosa, Wisconsin, Swannet Press [n. d.] 112 p. 18 cm. Record of correspondence between a group of college-age young people and their minister. 67-54836
1. Prayer. I. Title.

SWIFT, Judson. 249
Prayer and meditation, by Judson Swift... New York, The Meridian press [c1917] 2 p. l., 89 p. 14 cm. $0.75. [BV255.S9] 17-30908
I. Title.

TALLING, Marshal P., 1857- 242
Communion with God; extemporte prayer, its principles, preparation, and practices, by the Rev. Marshall P. Talling ... Chicago, New York [etc.] Fleming H. Revell company [c1902] 4 p. l., 7-9 13-302 p. 19 1/2 cm. On cover: Extempors prayer. [BV215.T5] 2-17466
1. Prayer. I. Title.

TALLING, Marshall P., 1857- 248
Inter-communion with God; an exploration of spiritual power as manifested in intercourse and co-operation between God and man, by the Rev. Marshall P. Talling ... New York, Chicago [etc.] Fleming H. Revell company [1905] 206 p. 19 1/2 cm. [BV210.T3] 5-9044
1. Prayer. I. Title.

TAYLOR, Jack R. 248'.3
Prayer : life's limitless reach / Jack R. Taylor. Nashville : Broadman Press, c1977. 168 p. : ill. ; 22 cm. Bibliography: p. 167-168. [BV210.2.T39] 77-73984 ISBN 0-8054-5258-3 : 5.95
1. Prayer. I. Title.

THOMAS, George Ernest, 1907- 248'.3
The power of prayer in business and the professions / G. Ernest Thomas. Nashville : Tidings, [1975] viii, 67 p. ; 19 cm. [BV210.2.T45] 74-27907
1. Prayer. 2. Businessmen—Religious life. I. Title.

THOMAS, James Moulton, 1903- 248'.3
Prayer power / by J. Moulton Thomas. Waco, Tex. : Word Books, c1976. 146 p. ; 22 cm. Includes bibliographical references. [BV210.2.T46] 75-36195 ISBN 0-87680-876-3 pbk. : pbk. : 3.50
1. Prayer. I. Title.

THOMAS, Nancy White 248.3
On bended knee. Illus. by Charlene Miller. Richmond, Va., Knox [c.1966] 61p. illus. 21cm. [BV210.2.T47] 65-14513 2.00 bds.,
1. Prayer. I. Title.

THOMAS, Roy Wallace. 264.1
We pray Thee, Lord; studies in positive and creative prayer, by Roy Wallace Thomas. Nashville, Tenn., Cokesbury press [c1937] 170 p. 19 1/2 cm. "Selected bibliography": p. 163. [BV210.T38] 37-1962
1. Prayer. I. Title.

THOMPSON, Augustus Charles, 1812-1901. 248
The mercy-seat; or, Thoughts on prayer. By Augustus C. Thompson ... Boston, Gould and Lincoln; New York, Sheldon and company; [etc., etc.] 1864. xii, 13-345 p. 20 cm. [BV210.T4 1864] 39-3008
1. Prayer. I. Title. II. Title: Thoughts on prayer.

THURSTON, Mabel Nelson, 1869- 248
The adventure of prayer, by Mabel N. Thurston ... New York, Chicago [etc.] Fleming H. Revell company [c1927] 8 p. l., 5-149 p. 17 cm. [BV210.T57] 27-13838
1. Prayer. I. Title.

THURSTON, Mabel Nelson, 1869- 248
The open gate to prayer, by Mabel Nelson Thurston ... introduction by Helen B. Montgomery. New York, Chicago [etc.] Fleming H. Revell company [c1925] 3 p. l., 5-60 p. 19 cm. [BV210.T58] 26-3600
1. Prayer. I. Title.

TOLSON, Chester L 248.32
Peace and power through prayer [by] Chester L. Tolson and Clarence W. Lieb. With an introd. by Norman Vincent Peale. Englewood Cliffs, N.J., Prentice-Hall [1962?] 103 p. 21 cm. [BV210.2.T6] 62-17783
1. Prayer. 2. Prayers. I. Lieb, Clarence William, 1885- joint author. II. Title.

TOMPKINS, Iverna. 248'.3
God and I : a book about faith and prayer / by Iverna Tompkins ; edited by Irene Burk Harrell. Plainfield, N.J. : Logos International, c1978. 175 p. ; 21 cm. [BV215.T58] 78-52396 ISBN 0-88270-274-2 : 3.50
1. Prayer. I. Harrell, Irene Burk. II. Title.

TORKINGTON, Rayner. 248.3'2
Peter Calvay, hermit : a personal rediscovery of prayer / Rayner Torkington. New York, N.Y. : Alba House, 1980, c1978. p. cm. First published in 1977 under title: Peter Calvey, hermit. [BV210.2.T64 1980] 80-13188 ISBN 0-8189-0404-6 pbk. : 3.95
1. Calvay, Peter. 2. Torkington, Rayner. 3. Prayer. 4. Spiritual life—Catholic authors. I. Title.

TORREY, Reuben, Archer D.D. 1856- 264.1
The power of prayer and the prayer of power, by R. A. Torrey, D.D. Grand Rapids, Mich., Zondervan [1964, c.1924] 246p. 21cm. 2.50 pap.,
1. Prayer. I. Title.

TORREY, Reuben Archer, 1856- 248
The power of prayer and the prayer of power, by R. A. Torrey, D.D. New York, Chicago [etc.] Fleming H. Revell company [c1924] 246 p. 19 1/2 cm. [BV210.T6] 25-1672
1. Prayer. I. Title.

TORREY, Reuben Archer, 1856-1928. 242
How to pray, by R. A. Torrey... Chicago, New York [etc.] Fleming H. Revell company [1900] 130 p. 19 cm. [BV215.T6] 0-4124
1. Prayer. I. Title.

TORREY, Reuben Archer, 1856-1928. 242
The power of prayer and the prayer of power. Grand Rapids, Zondervan Pub. House [1972, c1924] 191 p. 18 cm. (Zondervan books) [BV210.T6 1972] 74-156243 1.25 (pbk)
1. Prayer. I. Title.

TREMAINE, Guy Everton. 232.9
The prayer life of Jesus; a devotional study of the prayer life of Jesus consisting of forty essays with Scripture references and a prelude and postlude. Philadelphia, Dorrance [1954] 160p. illus. 20cm. [BV210.T63] 54-6759
1. Prayer. 2. Jesus Christ—Prayers. I. Title.

TRESCH, John W. 264'.13
A prayer for all seasons [by] John W. Tresch. Nashville, Broadman Press [1971] 128 p. 21 cm. [BV210.2.T73] 78-155681 ISBN 0-8054-8220-2
1. Prayer. 2. Prayers. I. Title.

TROEGER, Thomas H., 1945- 248'.3
Rage! Reflect. Rejoice! : Praying with the psalmists / Thomas H. Troeger. 1st ed. Philadelphia : Westminster Press, c1977. p. cm. [BV210.2.T76] 77-22755 ISBN 0-664-24293-6 pbk. : 3.95
1. Bible. O.T. Psalms—Criticism, interpretation, etc. 2. Prayer. I. Title.

TROUPE, John Franklin. 248
Interviewing God; a study in spiritual questing, by John Franklin Troupe ... New York, Chicago [etc.] Fleming H. Revell company [c1930] 192 p. 19 1/2 cm. [BV210.T7] 30-12042
1. Prayer. I. Title.

TRUMBULL, Henry Clay, 1830-1903.
Illustrative answers to prayer, a record of personal experiences, by H. Clay Trumbull ... New York, Chicago [etc.] Fleming H. Revell company [c1900] vi, 140 p. 17 1/2 cm. 10-9127
I. Title.

TRUMBULL, Henry Clay, 1830-1903. 248
Prayer, its nature and scope, by H. Clay Trumbull. Philadelphia, J. D. Wattles & co., 1896. vi, 160 p. 17 1/2 cm. [BV210.T73 1896] 45-53467
1. Prayer. I. Title.

TYLER, Frances Landrum. 264.1
Pray ye, a study of prayer and missions, by Frances Landrum Tyler ... [Nashville, Broadman press, 1944] ix p., 2 l., 140 p.19 cm. Bibliography: p. 140. [BV210.T9] 44-10004
1. Prayer. I. Title.

TYLER, William Seymour, 1810-1897. 264.1
Prayer for colleges. A premium essay. Written for "the Society for the promotion of collegiate and theological education at the West". By W. S. Tyler ... New York, M. W. Dodd, for the Society, 1855. xii, [7] -214 p. 19 1/2 cm. [BV283.C7T8] [BV283.C7T8 1855] E 11
1. Prayer. 2. Church and college. 3. Universities and colleges—Religious life. I. Society for the promotion of collegiate and theological education. II. Title.

UNDERHILL, Francis Lees, 1878-
Prayer in modern life, by Francis Underhill ... London, A. R. Mowbray & co., ltd. Milwaukee, The Morehouse pub. co. [1929] xi, 224 p. 19 cm. Printed in England. A 30
1. Prayer. I. Title.

VAN DOOREN, L. A. T. 248.32
Prayer, the Christian's vital breath. Grand Rapids, Mich., Zondervan [1963] 88p. 21cm. 63-25418 1.00 pap.,
1. Prayer. I. Title.

*VAN ZELLER, Dom Hubert, 1905- 264.1
Approach to prayer & approach to penance. New York, All Saints [dist. Guild, 1966,c.1958] 288p. 17cm. (AS-251) .75 pap.,
1. Prayer. I. Title.

VAN ZELLER, Hubert, 1905- 264.1
Approach to prayer. New York, Sheed & Ward [1959, c1958] 128 p. 21 cm. Secular name: Claude Van Zeller. [BV210.2.V3] 58-14450
1. Prayer. I. Title. II. Series.

VAN ZELLER, Hubert 248.32
[Secular name: Claude Van Zeller] 1905-
Prayer in other words; a presentation for beginners. Springfield, Ill., Templegate [c.1963] 94p. 20cm. (In other words ser.) 63-25224 2.95
1. Prayer. I. Title.

VINCENT, Thomas, 1634-1678. 238.
An explicatory catechism; or, An explanation of the Assembly's Shorter catechism ... By Thomas Vincent ... Northampton, Printed by William Butler, 1805. vi, 7-265, 35 p. 17 1/2 cm. "An address on the subjects of prayer and family religion, by Benjamin Trumbull": 35 p. at end. [BX9184-A5V6 1805] 25-18753
1. Prayer. 2. Westminster assembly of divines. Shorter catechism. I. Trumbull, Benjamin, 1735-1820. II. Title.

VINCENT, Thomas, 1634-1678. 238.
An explicatory catechism: or, An explanation of the Assembly's Shorter catechism... By Thomas Vincent ... New Haven: Published by Walter, Austin and co. O. Steele & co. Printers. 1810. 276, 29 p. 17 1/2 cm. "Dr. Trumbull's Address on the subjects of prayer and family religion. 4th ed.": 29 p. at end. [BX9184.A5V6 1810] 25-18755
1. Westminster assembly of divines. Shorter catechism. 2. Trumbull, Benjamin, 1735-1820. 3. Prayer. I. Title.

WALKER, Lucille. 248'.3
What to do when you pray / by Lucille Settle Walker. Plainfield, N.J. : Logos International, c1978. xix, 181 p. ; 21 cm. Bibliography: p. 179-181. [BV215.W34] 78-60948 ISBN 0-88270-279-3 : 2.95
1. Prayer. I. Title. II. Title: When you pray.

WALKER, William Bruce. 264.1
The art of prayer, by Rev. William Bruce Walker... New York, American tract society [c1940] 272 p. 20 1/2 cm. [BV210.W25] 40-11840
1. Prayer. I. American tract society. II. Title.

WALKER, William Bruce. 264.1
The power of prayer. Butler, Ind., Higley Press [c1955] 167p. 20cm. [BV210.W22] 56-29296

1. Prayer. I. Title.

WALTERS, Annette, Sister, 1910- 248'.3
Prayer-who needs it? Camden [N.J.] T. Nelson [1970] vii, 92 p. 21 cm. (A Youth forum book, YF 12) Includes bibliographical references. Discusses how, why, when and where one prays. [BV210.2.W27] 73-127078 1.95
1. Prayer. 2. Youth—Religious life. 3. [Prayer.] I. Title. II. Series: Youth forum series, YF 12

WALTERS, Marvin Martin, 1882- 264.1
The unexplored land of prayer, by Marvin M. Walters ... Green Bay, Wis., Reliance publishing company [c1941] 6 p. l., [3]-139 p. 21 cm. [BV210.W27] 41-12014
1. Prayer. I. Title.

WARD, William Arthur, 1921- comp. 248.3
Prayer is— Compiled and edited by William Arthur Ward. [1st ed.] Anderson, S.C., Droke House: distributed by Grosset & Dunlap, New York [1969] 120 p. port. 23 cm. [BV205.W3] 72-79400
1. Prayer. 2. Prayers. I. Title.

WATTS, Isaac, 1674-1748.
A guide to prayer; or, A free and rational account of the gift, grace, and spirit of prayer; with plain directions how every Christian may attain them. By I. Watts ... Elizabethtown: Printed and sold by Shepard Kollock, M,DCC,XCVII. 1 p. l., ix, [13]-235, [3] p. 17 cm. [BV209.W3 1797] 9-17947
1. Prayer. I. Title.

WEBB, Lance 248.32
The art of personal prayer. Nashville, Abingdon [c.1962] 160p. 20cm. Bibl. 62-16255 2.50
1. Prayer. I. Title.

WEBB, Lance. 248.32
The art of personal prayer. New York, Abingdon press [1962] 100 p. 20 cm. [BV215.W4] 62-16255
1. Prayer. I. Title.

WEDGE, Florence. 264.1
Prayer without headaches. Pulaski, Wis., Franciscan Printery, 1956. 173 p. 22 cm. [BV210.W38] 57-37132
1. Prayer. I. Title.

WESTWOOD, Horace, 1884- 264.1
And so you never pray! Prayer is a human technique. Boston, Beacon Press, 1948. viii, 148 p. 19 cm. [BV210.W4] 48-7156
1. Prayer. I. Title.

WHELAN, Joseph P. 248'.3
Benjamin; essays in prayer [by] Joseph P. Whelan. New York, Newman Press [1972] 122 p. illus. 24 cm. Includes bibliographical references. [BV210.2.W45] 72-184543 4.95
1. Prayer. 2. Contemplation. 3. Christian life—Catholic authors. I. Title.

WHISTON, Charles Francis, 1900- 248'.3
Pray: a study of distinctively Christian praying. Grand Rapids, Eerdmans [1972] 154 p. 22 cm. [BV210.2.W475] 70-162036 2.95
1. Prayer. I. Title.

WHISTON, Charles Francis, 1900- 264.1
Teach us to pray; a study of distinctively Christian praying. With an introd. by Nels F. S. Ferre. Boston, Pilgrim Press [1949] xx, 243 p. 20 cm. [BV210.W43] 49-8170
1. Prayer. I. Title.

WHITMAN, Allen, 1925- 248.3
Pray for your life. Design by Donald Wallerstedt. Minneapolis, Augsburg Pub. House [1971] 91 p. 21 cm. Bibliography: p. 87-91. [BV210.2.W48] 78-159010 ISBN 0-8066-1133-2 3.50
1. Prayer. I. Title.

WHITMAN, Virginia. 248'.3
Mustard; the excitement of prayer answered. Wheaton, Ill., Tyndale House [1973] 160 p. 18 cm. [BV220.W48] 73-81012 ISBN 0-8423-4640-6 1.25
1. Prayer. I. Title.

WIEAND, Albert Cassel, 1871- 232.9
The gospel of prayer, its practice and psychology as revealed in the life and teachings of Jesus. Grand Rapids, W. B. Eerdmans Pub. Co., 1953. 245p. 23cm. [BV215.W47] 248 53-9295
1. Prayer. I. Title.

WIEAND, Albert Cassel, 1871- 248
The prayer life and teachings of Jesus, by Albert C. Wieand ... New York, Chicago [etc.] Fleming H. Revell company [c1932] 172 p. 19 1/2 cm. [BV210.W47] [232.9] 32-6910
1. Jesus Christ—Teachings. 2. Prayer. 3. Bible. N.T. Gospels—Study. 4. Bible—Study—N.T. Gospels. I. Title.

WILLIAMS, Harry Abbott. 248'.3
The simplicity of prayer / H. A. Williams. 1st American ed. Philadelphia : Fortress Press, 1977. p. cm. [BV210.2.W49 1977] 77-78649 ISBN 0-8006-1315-5 : 2.50
1. Prayer. I. Title.

WILLIS, Edward David. 248'.3
Daring prayer / David Willis. Atlanta : John Knox Press, c1977. 157 p. ; 21 cm. Bibliography: p. [152]-157. [BV210.2.W495] 76-44975 ISBN 0-8042-2249-5 : 6.95
1. Prayer. I. Title.

WILSON, Frank Elmer, bp., 1885- 248
An outline of personal prayer, by the Rt. Rev. Frank E. Wilson ... New York, Milwaukee, Morehouse publishing co., 1937. xiv p., 1 l., 79 p. incl. front., illus. 15 cm. [BV210.W53] 37-5075
1. Prayer. I. Title.

*WILSON, William Croft, 1931-1963 248'3
Pastoral prayers. With a foreword by Raymond E. Gibson. New York, Exposition Press [1973] 55 p. 21 cm. [BV4832.2] ISBN 0-682-47689-7. 3.00
1. Prayer. I. Title.

WINROD, Gerald Burton.
Prayer in the atomic age. Wichita, Kan., Defender Publishers [c1957] 61 p. illus. 22 cm. 65-69757
1. Prayer. 2. Religion and science. I. Title.

WINWARD, Stephen F. 248.3
Teach yourself to pray. New York, Harper & Row [1962, c.1961] 191p. 20cm. 62-11137 2.75 bds.,
1. Prayer. 2. Prayers. I. Title.

WISHART, John Elliott, 1866- 248
The fact of prayer, its problems and possibilities, by John Elliott Wishart ... with introduction by Melvin G. Kyle ... New York, Chicago [etc.] Fleming H. Revell company [c1927] 1 p. l., 5-225 p. 19 1/2 cm. [BV210.W55] 27-13843
1. Prayer. I. Title.

WITSELL, William Postell, 1874- 264.1
Two vital questions: Why pray? and After death -- what? Boston, Christopher Pub. House [1952] 172 p. 21 cm. [BV210.W56] 52-4878
1. Prayer. 2. Eschatology. I. Title.

WORLLEDGE, Arthur John, 1848-
Prayer, by the Rev. A. J. Worlledge ... London, New York [etc.] Longmans, Green & co., 1902. xvi, 378 p. 19 1/2 cm. (Half-title: The Oxford library of practical theology ...) A 21
1.. Prayer. I. Title.

WORTH, Grant A., 1943- 248.3'2
Do your prayers bounce off the ceiling? / Grant A. Worth. Salt Lake City, Utah : Deseret Book Co., c1982. x, 68 p. : ill. ; 24 cm. Includes index. [BV215.W63] 19 81-17411 ISBN 0-87747-895-3 : 6.95
1. Prayer. 2. Spiritual life—Mormon authors. I. Title.

WORTMAN, Arthur, comp. 248'.3
Springs of devotion : writings about the joy and power of prayer / selected by Arthur Wortman ; calligraphy by Rick Cusick. Kansas City, Mo. : Hallmark, c1975. 44 p., [1] leaf of plates : ill. ; 11 x 16 cm. (Hallmark editions) [BV205.W66 1975] 74-83759 ISBN 0-87529-408-1 : 3.00
1. Prayer. 2. Prayers. I. Title.

WORTMAN, Arthur, comp. 248.3
Springs of devotion; inspiring writings about the meaning and joy of prayer. Illustrated by William Gilmore. [Kansas City, Mo.] Hallmark Editions [1969] 61 p. 20 cm. [BV205.W66] 70-79741 ISBN 8-7529-0094- 2.50
1. Prayer. 2. Prayers. I. Title.

WRIGHT, John H. 248.3'2
A theology of Christian prayer / John H. Wright. New York : Pueblo Pub. Co., c1979. xvi, 174 p. ; 22 cm. Bibliography: p. 173-174. [BV210.2.W75] 80-109901 ISBN 0-916134-38-5 : 7.95
1. Prayer. I. Title.
Publisher's address: 1860 Broadway, NY, NY 10023

WUELLNER, Flora Slosson. 264'.1
Prayer and the living Christ. Nashville, Abingdon Press [1968, c1969] 144 p. 20 cm. Bibliography: p. 142-144. [BV210.2.W8] 69-12015 3.00
1. Prayer. I. Title.

WUELLNER, Flora Slosson. 248'.4
Release for trapped Christians. Nashville, Abingdon Press [1974] 94 p. 20 cm. [BV210.2.W815] 73-20034 3.75
1. Prayer. 2. Spiritual life. I. Title.

WUELLNER, Flora Slosson. 248.3
To pray and to grow. Nashville, Abingdon Press [1970] 159 p. 20 cm. Bibliography: p. 157-159. [BV210.2.W82] 70-124757 4.25
1. Prayer. I. Title.

WYON, Olive 248.32
Prayer. Philadelphia, Muhlenberg Press [c.1960] 68p. (bibl. footnotes) 20cm. (Fortress books) 60-3754 1.00 bds.,
1. Prayer. I. Title.

WYON, Olive. 264.1
The school of prayer, by Olive Wyon; foreword by Robert E. Speer. Philadelphia, The Westminster press [1944] 160 p. 16 cm. Bibliographical foot-notes. [BV210.W88 1944] 44-7442
1. Prayer. I. Title.

WYON, Olive 248.32
The school of prayers. New York, Macmillan [1963] 192p. 18cm. (mp 132) Bibl. .95 pap.,
1. Prayer. I. Title.

WYON, Olive, 1890- 248.32
Prayer. Philadelphia, Muhlenberg Press [1960] Includes bibliography. [BV215.W9] 60-3754
1. Prayer. I. Title.

WYON, Olive, 1890- 248'.3
Prayer / by Olive Wyon. Philadelphia : Fortress Press, 1978, c1960. 72 p. ; 19 cm. Includes bibliographical references. [BV215.W9 1978] 78-2965 ISBN 0-8006-1335-X pbk. : 1.75
1. Prayer. I. Title.

YUNGBLUT, John R. 248'.3
Rediscovering prayer [by] John R. Yungblut. New York, Seabury Press [1972] xii, 180 p. 22 cm. Includes bibliographical references. [BV210.2.Y85] 72-76349 ISBN 0-8164-0238-8 5.95
1. Prayer. I. Title.

ZWEMER, Samuel Marinus, 1867- 264.1
Taking hold of God: studies on the nature, need and power of prayer, by Samuel M. Zwemer ... Grand Rapids, Mich., Zondervan publishing house [c1936] 7 p. l., 13-188, [2] p. 20 cm. Blank pages for "Answered prayers" ([2] at end) "Selected list of books on prayer": p. 185-188. [BV210.Z9] 36-10848
1. Prayer. I. Title.

Prayer—Addresses, essays, lectures.

BIEDERWOLF, William Edward.
How can God answer prayer? Being an exhaustive treatise on the nature, conditions and difficulties of prayer, by William Edward Biederwolf ... New York, Chicago [etc.] F. H. Revell company [c1910] 287 p. front. (port.) 23 cm. 10-1429 1.25
I. Title.

CHRISTIANS at prayer / 248'.3
edited by John Gallen. Notre Dame, Ind. : University of Notre Dame Press, c1977. xii, 160 p. ; 24 cm. (Liturgical studies) Includes bibliographical references and index. [BV213.C46] 76-22407 ISBN 0-268-00718-7 : 9.95.
1. Prayer—Addresses, essays, lectures. I. Gallen, John. II. Series: Notre Dame, Ind. University. Liturgical studies.

THE courage to pray / 248.3'2
by Johann B. Metz and Karl Rahner. New York : Seabury Press, c1980. p. cm. Translation of Ermutigung zum Gebet. "A Crossroad book." Contents.Contents.—Metz, J. B. The courage to pray.—Rahner, K. Prayer to the saints. [BV213.E7513] 80-18594 ISBN 0-8164-2024-6 pbk. : 3.95
1. Prayer—Addresses, essays, lectures. 2. Christian saints—Cult—Addresses, essays, lectures. I. Rahner, Karl, 1904- Gebet zu den Heiligen. English. 1980. II. Metz, Johannes Baptist, 1928- Ermutigung zum Gebet. English. 1980.

DELIVERANCE prayer : 264'.94
experiential, psychological, and theological approaches / Matthew & Dennis Linn. New York : Paulist Press, c1981. iv, 267 p. ; 21 cm. Includes bibliographical references. [BV227.D44 1981] 19 81-82334 ISBN 0-8091-2385-1 (pbk.) : 5.95
1. Prayer—Addresses, essays, lectures. 2. Exorcism—Addresses, essays, lectures. 3. Spiritual healing—Addresses, essays, lectures. I. Linn, Matthew. II. Linn, Dennis.

EVANS, William, 1870- 264.1
Why pray? By William Evans ... Philadelphia, Pa., Pinebrook book press [c1937] iv p., 1 l., 7-158 p. 20 cm. sPrayer. [BV210.E8] 37-2813
I. Title.

EVANS, William, 1870- 264.1
Why pray? By William Evans ... Philadelphia, Pa., Pinebrook book press [c1937] iv p., 1 l., 7-158 p. 20 cm. sPrayer. [BV210.E8] 37-2813
I. Title.

GEARON, Patrick J. 232.9318
In praise of Mary; an explanation of the Hail Mary, the Angelus, the Hail Holy Queen, the Magnificat. [dist. Downers Grove, Ill., Aylesford, Madden at Route 66, The Carmelite Third Order Press, 1961] 186p. 2.50
I. Title.

HOW do I pray? / 248'.3
Edited by Robert Heyer. New York : Paulist Press, c1977. 101 p. : ill. ; 18 cm. "Articles in this book originally appeared in New Catholic world." "A New Catholic world book." [BV213.H67] 77-80808 ISBN 0-8091-2041-0 : 1.75
1. Prayer—Addresses, essays, lectures. I. Heyer, Robert J. II. New Catholic world.

KINSLEY, William Wirt, 1837-
Does prayer avail? By William W. Kinsley ... Boston, Sherman, French & company, 1911. 2 p. l., 157 p. 21 1/2 cm. $1.20 11-26189
I. Title.

MOUZON, Edwin Du Bose, bp. 1869- 214
Does God care? An answer to certain questions touching providence and prayer, by Edwin D. Mouzon ... New York, Chicago [etc.] Fleming H. Revell company [c1919] 88 p. 20 cm. [BT135.M6] 19-15712
I. Title.

PRAYER / 248'.3
Spencer W. Kimball ... [et al.]. Salt Lake City : Deseret Book Co., 1977. 141 p. ; 24 cm. Includes index. [BV210.2.P647] 77-15521 ISBN 0-87747-657-8 : 5.95
1. Prayer—Addresses, essays, lectures. 2. Mormons and Mormonism—Doctrinal and controversial works—Mormon authors—Addresses, essays, lectures. I. Kimball, Spencer W., 1895-

PRAYER and community. 248.3
Edited by Herman Schmidt. [New York] Herder and Herder [1970] 153 p. 23 cm. (Concilium: theology in the age of renewal, v. 52. Liturgy) Includes bibliographical references. [BV213.P7] 70-98257 2.95
1. Prayer—Addresses, essays, lectures. I. Schmidt, Herman, ed. II. Series: Concilium (New York) v. 52

SANDERS, J. Oswald 248.32
Effective prayer. Chicago, Moody [1963, c.1961] 59p. 18cm. (China Inland mission bk.; compact bks., 28) .29 pap.,
I. Title.

SYMPOSIUM on Prayer, Shrub Oak, N.Y., 1968. 264'.1
Prayer: the problem of dialogue with God. Edited by Christopher F. Mooney. Paramus, N.J., Paulist Press [1969] v, 138 p. 21 cm. (Exploration books) "Papers of the 1968 Bea Institute Symposium." Includes bibliographical references. [BV213.S94 1968] 78-92220 2.95
1. Prayer—Addresses, essays, lectures. I. Mooney, Christopher F., 1925- ed. II. Cardinal Bea Institute. III. Title.

TOWNSEND, Anne J. 248'.3
Prayer without pretending / Anne J. Townsend. Chicago : Moody Press, 1976, c1973. 96 p. ; 18 cm. [BV213.T63 1976] 76-1961 ISBN 0-8024-6807-1 pbk. : 0.95
1. Prayer—Addresses, essays, lectures. I. Title.

THE Unlimited power of prayer. 248.3'2 Carmel, N.Y. : Guideposts, c1980. 321 p. ; 22 cm. "A Guideposts anthology." [BV220.U54] 80-108234 ISBN 0-385-17235-4 : 13.95
1. Prayer—Addresses, essays, lectures. I. Guideposts.

THE Unlimited power of prayer. 248.3'2 Garden City, N.Y. : Doubleday, 1982, c1980. 321 p. ; 22 cm. Originally published: Carmel, N.Y. : Guideposts, 1980. [BV220.U54 1982] 19 81-43448 ISBN 0-385-17235-4 : 13.95
1. Prayer—Addresses, essays, lectures.

VINCENT, Mary Clare, 1925- 248.3'2
The life of prayer and the way to God / by Mary Clare Vincent, O.S.B. Still River, Mass. : St. Bede's Publications, c1982. p. cm. Includes index. Bibliography: p. [BV213.V52] 19 81-21257 ISBN 0-932506-11-9 pbk. : 3.50
1. Prayer—Addresses, essays, lectures. I. Title.

Prayer — Biblical teaching.

ALLEN, R. Earl. 248'.3
Prayers that changed history / R. Earl Allen. Nashville : Broadman Press, 1978,c1977. 127 p. ; 18 cm. [BV228.A44] 77-71728 ISBN 0-8054-5257-5 pbk. : 2.25
1. Bible—Prayers. 2. Prayer—Biblical teaching. I. Title.

FISHER, Fred L. 264.1
Prayer in the New Testament. Philadelphia, Westminster [c.1964] 192p. 21cm. Bibl. 64-11362 4.50
1. Prayer—Biblical teaching. I. Title.

FISHER, Fred L
Prayer in the New Testament. Philadelphia, Westminster Press [1964] 192 p. 21 cm. Bibliographical references included in "Notes" (p. 189-192)
1. Prayer — Biblical teaching. I. Title.

HAMMAN, Adalbert, 1910- 248.3
Prayer; the New Testament [by] A. Hamman. [Chicago] Franciscan Herald Press [1971] x, 238 p. 22 cm. Includes bibliographical references. [BV228.H2413] 74-85507 ISBN 0-8199-0424-4
1. Prayer—Biblical teaching. I. Title.

LOEW, Jacques, 1908- 248'.3
Face to face with God : the Bible's way to prayer / Jacques Loew ; translated by Alan Neame. New York : Paulist Press, 1978,c1977 xii, 191 p. ; 21 cm. Translation of La priere a l'ecole des grands priants. [BV228.L6313 1977b] 77-88179 ISBN 0-8091-0227-7 : 6.50
1. Prayer—Biblical teaching. 2. Spiritual life—Biblical teaching. I. Title.

MILLER, C. Leslie. 220.6
They talked with God / C. Leslie Miller. Burbank, Calif. : Manna Books, c1975. 110 p. ; 18 cm. Includes bibliographical references. [BV228.M54] 74-33130
1. Prayer—Biblical teaching. I. Title.

STANLEY, David Michael, 1914- 248'.3
Boasting in the Lord; the phenomenon of prayer in Saint Paul, by David M. Stanley. New York, Paulist Press [1973] vi, 192 p. 21 cm. Includes bibliographical references. [BV228.S76] 73-84361 ISBN 0-8091-1793-2 2.95 (pbk.).
1. Bible. N.T. Epistles of Paul—Criticism, interpretation, etc. 2. Prayer—Biblical teaching. I. Title.

THOMSON, James G S S 264.1
The praying Christ; a study of Jesus' doctrine and practice of prayer. Grand Rapids, Eerdmans [1959] 155 p. 21 cm. Includes bibliography. [BV229.T5] 58-59780
1. Prayer—Biblical teaching. 2. Jesus Christ—Teachings. 3. Lord's prayer. I. Title.

WENHE, Mary B. 248'.3
How to pray for healing / Mary B. Wenhe. Old Tappan, N.J. : Revell, [1975] 96 p. ; 18 cm. [BV228.W46] 74-34299 ISBN 0-8007-0741-9 : 1.50
1. Bible—Prayers. 2. Prayer—Biblical teaching. I. Title.

WHITE, John, 1924(Mar.5)- 248'.3
Daring to draw near : people in prayer / John White. Downers Grove, Ill. : Inter-Varsity Press, c1977. 162 p. ; 21 cm. [BV228.W48] 77-6554 ISBN 0-87784-788-6 pbk. : 3.95
1. Prayer—Biblical teaching. I. Title.

WHITE, Reginald E O 264.1
Prayer is the secret; the prayer experience of the apostles and church fathers. New York, Harper [1959, c1958] 143 p. 21 cm. [BV235.W46 1959] 59-7166
1. Prayer — Biblical teaching. I. Title.

Prayer-books.

ARMITAGE, William James, 1860-
The story of the Canadian revision of the prayer book, by W. J. Armitage ... with a foreword by the Most Rev. S. P. Matheson ... Cambridge [Eng.] The University press; [etc., etc.] 1922. xvii, 442 p., 1 l. front. (facsim.) 19 cm. [BX5616.A8] 22-21021
I. Title. II. Title: The Canadian revision of the prayer book.

BECQUET, Thomas 264
Missal for young Catholics [by] Thomas Becquet, Alfonso Pereira, Harold Winstone. Glen Rock, N.J., Paulist Pr. [c.1963] 224p. illus. 15cm. price unreported pap.,
I. Title.

CARPENTER, William Boyd, bp. of Ripon, 1841- ed.
The communion of prayer. A manual of private prayers and devotions; ed. by William Boyd Carpenter ... Philadelphia, G. W. Jacobs & co. [1911] xvi, [17]-318 p. 18 cm. "List of authors or sources": p. [ix]-xi. A 12
1. Prayer-books. I. Title.

CARRUTH, Thomas A. 248.32
Total prayer for living. Grand Rapids, Mich., Zondervan [c.1962] 116p. 21cm. Bibl. 1.95 bds.,
I. Title.

CATHOLIC church. Liturgy and ritual. Missal. 264.
The missal of St. Augustine's abbey, Canterbury, with excerpts from the Antiphonary and Lectionary of the same monastery. Ed. with an introductory monograph, from a manusceipt in the Library of Corpus Christi college, Cambridge, by Martin Rule, M. A. Cambridge, University press, 1896. 2 p. l., [iii]-clxxxiv, 174 p. 2 facsim. (incl. front.) 28 cm. Rubricated. [BX2015.A3S3 1896] 10-12700
I. Rule, Martin, ed. II. St. Augustine's abbey, Canterbury. III. Title.

CATHOLIC church. Liturgy and ritual. Missal.
The Sunday Missal, for all the Sundays and the principal feasts of the year, with introduction, notes, and a book of prayer; comp. by Rev. F. X. Lasance ... New York, Cincinnati [etc.] Benziger brothers, 1916. 675 p. front., pl. 14 cm. 16-22463 0.75
I. Lasance, Francis Xavier, 1860- II. Title.

CATHOLIC church. Liturgy and ritual. Missal. 264.
The Sunday missal for all the Sundays and the principal feasts of the year, with introduction, notes, and a book of prayer, compiled by Rev. F. X. Lasance ... rev. in conformity with the Vatican typical edition of the Missale Romanum (the book used by the priest when saying mass) New York, Cincinnati [etc.] Benziger brothers, 1928. 2 p. l., 27 degrees, v-xxxv, 417 p. incl. front. 14 cm. [BX2015.A4L35 1928] 28-29790
I. Lasance, Francis Xavier, 1860- II. Title.

CATHOLIC Church. Liturgy and ritual. Missal. English. 264.025
The cathedral daily missal; the Roman missal adapted to everyday life in conformity with the new decree on the rubrics of the missal and the Ordinationes ad librorum liturgicorum editores, issued by the Sacred Congregation of Rites, January 1, 1961, by Rudolph G. Bandas. Pref. by Pietro C. van Lierde. St. Paul, E. M. Lohmann Co. [1961] 2319 p. illus. (part col.) 16 cm. [BX2015.A4B3] 63-27413
I. Bandas, Rudolph George, 1896- II. Title.

CATHOLIC church. Liturgy and ritual. Missal. English. 264.025
The Catholic missal: being a translation of the Missale romanum, arranged for daily use by Rev. Charles J. Callan ... and Rev. John A. McHugh ... New York, P. J. Kenedy & sons [c1934] 1247 p. incl. front., illus. 16 cm. [BX2015.A4C26] 34-38173
I. Catholic church. Liturgy and ritual. English. II. Callan, Charles Jerome, father, 1877- tr. III. McHugh, John Ambrose, father, 1880- joint tr. IV. Title.

CATHOLIC church. Liturgy and ritual. Missal. English. 264.025
The Catholic missal; being a translation of the Missale romanum arranged for daily use by Rev. Charles J. Callan ... and Rev. John A. McHugh ... Plain ed. New York, P. J. Kenedy & sons [1935] 1247 p. incl. front., illus. 16 cm. "Third printing." [BX2015.A4C26 1935] 36-8241
I. Catholic church. Liturgy and ritual. English. II. Callan, Charles Jerome, father, 1877- tr. III. McHugh, John Ambrose, father, 1880- joint tr. IV. Title.

CATHOLIC church. Liturgy and ritual. Missal. English. 264.025
The Catholic missal; being a translation of the new Missale romanum arranged for daily use by Very Rev. Charles J. Callan ... and Very Rev. John A. McHugh ... New York, P. J. Kenedy and sons [c1943] 1252 p. incl. front., illus. 15 1/2 cm. [BX2015.A4C26 1943] 44-1322
I. Catholic church. Liturgy and ritual. English. II. Calan, Charles Jerome, father, 1877- tr. III. McHugh, John Ambrose, father, 1880- joint tr. IV. Title.

CATHOLIC Church. Liturgy and ritual. Missal. English. 264.025
The missal; containing all the Masses for Sundays and for holy days of obligation. Edited by John P. O'Connell and Jex Martin. Chicago, Catholic Press [c1954] 944p. illus. 18cm. [BX2015.ea4O34] 55-1076
I. O Connell, John P., ed. II. Martin, Jex., ed. III. Title.

CATHOLIC Church. Liturgy and ritual. Missal. English.
The Sunday missal ... In conformity with the Vatican typical edition of the Missale Romanum. With supplement "Read mass with the priest" (A study plan) by Rt. Rev. Msgr. W. R. Kelly. With new order of holy week. New York, Benziger brothers [1958] 747 p. front., illus. 15 cm. 65-31006
I. Lasance, Francis Xavier, 1860- ed. II. Title.

CATHOLIC church. Liturgy and ritual. Missal. English. 264.025
The Sunday missal: the masses for Sundays and principal feasts, the masses for the dead with burial service, the nuptial mass and marriage service and the masses and ceremonies for the forty hours', in conformity with the Vatican typical edition of the Missale Romanum (the book used by the priest when saying mass) by Rev. F. X. Lasance ... with supplement "Read mass with priest" (a study plan) by Rev. W. R. Kelly ... with mass pictures according to the liturgy and other illustrations. New York, Cincinnati [etc.] Benziger brothers, 1937. 704 p. incl. front., illus. 15 cm. [BX2015.A4L35 1937] 37-1545
I. Catholic church. Liturgy and ritual. English. II. Lasance, Francis Xavier, 1860- ed. III. Kelly, William Roswell, 1891- IV. Title. V. Title: Read mass with the priest.

CATHOLIC Church. Liturgy Putie, Walter, ed. 264.025
The Sunday missal; the Masses for illus. New York, Benziger Bros. [c1953,54 708p. illus. 15cm. [BD2015.A4L35 1953] 56-339
1. asses and ceremonies for the Forty Hours, in comformity Kelly, with Mass pictures according to te liturgy, and other aLasance(Francis Xavier, 1860-1946, I. Catholic Church. Liturgy and Ritual. Sunday and principal feasts, the Masses for the dead with burial service, the nuptial Mass and marriage service and the English. with the Vatican typical edition of the Missale Romanum (the book used by the priest when saying Massp By F. X. Lasance. With supplement 'Read Mass with the priest' (a study plan) by W. R. and ritual. Missal. English. II. Catholic Church. Liturgy and ritual. English. III. Title.

CHRISTIAN year (The); 264.036
the prayer book collects, with epistles and gospels as tr. by J. B. Phillips, notes by H. W. Dobson. New York, Macmillan [1963, c.1961] 311p. 21cm. (130) 1.45 pap.,

CHURCH of England. Book of common prayer. 783.2
The cathedral prayer book; being the Book of common prayer with the music necessary for the use of choirs, together with the canticles and Psalter pointed for chanting and set to appropriate chants, edited by Sir John Stainer ... and William Russell ... London & New York, Novello, Ewer and co. [etc.] 1891. [514], 86 p. 20 1/2 cm. [M2167.C35 1801] 39-15426
I. Stainer, Sir John, 1840-1901, ed. II. Russell, William, 1846?-1931, joint ed. III. Title.

CHURCH of England. Book of common prayer.
The cathedral prayer book; being the Book of common prayer with the music necessary for the use of choirs, together with the canticles and Psalter pointed for chanting and set to appropriate chants, ed. by Sir John Stainer ... and William Russell ... London, Novello and company, limited; New York, The H. W. Gray co. [pref. 1891] [514], 86 p. 20 cm. [M2167C35 1891] 19-7356
I. Stainer, Sir John, 1840-1901, ed. II. Russell, William, joint ed. III. Title.

CHURCH of England. Book of common prayer.
The cathedral prayer book; being the Book of common prayer with the music necessary for the use of choirs, together with the canticles and Psalter pointed for chanting, ed. by Sir John Stainer ... and William Russell ... London, Novello and company, limited; New York, The H. W. Gray co. [pref. 1891] [542], 86 p. 20 cm. [M2167.C35A] 19-7355
I. Stainer, Sir John, 1840-1901, ed. II. Russell, William, Joint ed. III. Title.

CHURCH of England. Book of common prayer. 264.
... A survey of the proposals for the alternative prayer book ... London [etc.] A. R. Mowbray & co., ltd.; Milwaukee, U.S.A., The Morehouse publishing co. [1923] v. 20 cm. (Alcuin club. Prayer book revision pamphlets. xii.) "This survey is the work of a group of members of the Alcuin club." [BX5145.A8 no. xii] 23-10958
I. Title. II. Title: Alternative prayer book.

DAVIS, Elisabeth Hamill, ed. 264.
For each day a prayer, selected and arranged by Elizabeth Hamill Davis. New York, Dodge publishing company [c1905] 271 p. 20 cm. [BV260.D3] 5-26244
1. Prayer-books. I. Title.

DIFFENDORFER, Ralph Eugene, comp.
Thy kingdom come, a book of social prayers for public and private worship, comp. by Ralph E. Diffendorfer. New York, Missionary education movement of

the United States and Canada, 1914. 62 p. 16 cm. 14-18408 0.25
I. Title.

FARIS, John Thomson, 1871-
The book of answered prayer, by John T. Faris...with an introductory chapter by a veteran pastor. New York Hodder & Stoughton, George H. Doran Company c[1914] 294 p. 20 cm. 14-15425 1.00
I. Title.

HERTZ, Joseph Herman, 1872- 1946 296
The authorised daily prayer book. Rev. ed. Hebrew text, English translation, with commentary and notes, by Joseph H. Hertz. New York Bloch Pub. Co., 1948. xxiii, 1119 p. 24 cm. [BM675.D3H4 1948] 48-24170
I. Title.

JEWS. Liturgy and ritual. 296
Abridged prayer book for Jews in the Armed Forces of the United States New York city, Jewish welfare board [c1941] [281] p. 14 cm. Various pagings. Hebrew and English on opposite pages. "First impression." [BM667.S6A5 1941] 42-6475
I. Jewish welfare board. II. Title.

JEWS. Liturgy and ritual. 296
Abridged prayer book for Jews in the armed forces of the United States. Philadelphia, The Jewish publication society of America, 3 p. l., 80, [2]-80, 81-85 p. 16 cm. Hebrew and English on opposite pages, numbered in duplicate. [BM667.S6A5] 18-3823
I. Title.

JEWS. Liturgy and ritual. 296.4
Children's services.
A prayer book for Jewish children. Text prepd. by Abraham Shusterman. Baltimore [1966] 87p. 21cm. [BM666.S46] 66-3129 3.95
I. Shusterman, Abraham, ed. II. Title.
Available from Har Sinai Congregation, 6300 Park Heights Ave., Baltimore, Md., 21215.

JEWS. Liturgy and ritual High 296
holy day prayers
High holiday prayer book, with supplementary prayers and readings and with a new English translation. Ed. by M. M. Kaplan, Eugene Kohn and Ira Eisenstein. New York, Jewish Reconstructionist Foundation, 1948. v. 19 cm. Hebrew and English; added t.-p. in Hebrew. Contents.v.1. Prayers for Rosh Hashanah--v.2. Prayers for Yom Kippur. [BM675.H5K3] 48-25384
I. Kaplan, Mordecal Menahem, 1881- ed. II. Title.

THE key of heaven;
or, A manual of prayer for the use of the faithful. New rev., and improved ed. New York, Cincinnati [etc.] Benziger bros., 1899. 750 p. 32°. 99-629

LASANCE, Francis Xavier, 1860- 264.
Let us pray; a simple prayer book adapted for the needs of all classes on all ordinary occasions of devotion, by Rev. F. X. Lasance ... New York, Cincinnati [etc.] Benziger brothers, 1925. 144 p. incl. front. 13 x 7 cm. [BX2110.L27] 25-10605
I. Title.

LEFFINGWELL, Charles Wesley, 1840- comp. 264.
A book of prayers, together with psalms and hymns and spiritual songs, ancient and modern, comp. by Charles W. Leffingwell ... Milwaukee, Wis., Morehouse publishing co., 1922. v, 206 p. 15 1/2 cm. [BV260.L4] 22-283
I. Title.

MCCOMB, Samuel, 1864- 264.
A book of prayers for public and personal use, by Samuel McComb ... Rev. and enl. ed. New York, Dodd, Mead and company, 1917. xvi, 244 p. 19 1/2 cm. [BV245.M3 1917] 17-29546
I. Title.

MCCOMB, Samuel, 1864-
A book of prayers, for public and personal use, by Samuel McComb ... New York, Dodd, Mead and company, 1912. xiii, 230 p. 19 1/2 cm. $1.00 12-7024
I. Title.

MCGRATH, Thomas Sylvester, 1878-
The prayer book for boy scouts, by Rev. Thomas S. McGrath ... New York, P. J. Kenedy & sons [c1916] 142 p. 11 cm. 16-15280 0.35.
I. Title.

THE missal in Latin and English, being the Missale Romanum with English rubrics and a new translation [by Ronald A. Knox] Westminster, Md., Newman Press, 1958. New York, Sheed & Ward, 1958. xlvi, 1240, 275p. 19p. Edited by J. O'Connell and H. P. R. Finberg. [With the preceding]
I. Catholic Church. Liturgy and ritual. Missal. II. Title: —Supplement. Masses proper to certain dioceses in the United States ofAmerica.

THE Missal in Latin and English, being the text of the Missale romanum with English rubrics and a new translation. [Edited by J. O'Connell and H. P. R. Finberg, the translation of the prayers is the work of the joint editors, the scriptural passages by R. A. Knox. 2d ed.] Westminster, Md., Newman Press, 1959. 1240, 275, 19p. 'Supplement... Masses proper to certain dioceses in the United States of America' (with special t. p.): 20p. at end.
I. Catholic Church. Liturgy and ritual. Missal.

MURCH, Artemas Allerton.
The story of the prayer book, its origin, sources and growth. Popular ed. Rev. By the Rev. A. Allerton Murch ... Newport, Vt., W. B. Bullock, printer, 1909. 118 p. 20 cm. "Works consulted": p. [7] p. 117-118, advertising matter. 9-26329 0.50
I. Title.

PICTORIAL prayer-book.
With hymns. Specially prepared for the scholars of Catholic schools ... New York, Christian press association publishing company [1910?] 175 p. illus. 13 cm. 12-27466
I. Catholic church. Liturgy and ritual.

POWELL, Lyman Pierson, 1866- 249
Family prayers, by Lyman P. Powell, with an introduction by Rt. Rev. O. W. Whitaker ... Philadelphia, G. W. Jacobs & co. [c1905] 112 p. double tab. 18 cm. [BV255.P6] 5-18300
1. Prayer-books. I. Title.

A prayer book for the use of families; prepared by the Association of ministers on Piscataqua-river, and recommended by them as an assistant to the social devotions of families. 3d ed. enl. Portsmouth, N. H., Printed for Charles Peirce, 1807. 87, [1] p. 18 cm. A 34
1. Prayer-books.

SIMPSON, Hubert Louis, 1880- 264
Let us worship God; a book of prayers for divine service, prepared by Hubert L. Simpson ... New York, Doubleday, Doran & co., inc.; London, J. Clarke & co., limited [1929] x, 11-191, [1] p. 20 1/2 cm. Printed in Great Britain. Blank pages for "Ms. prayers" (188-[192]) [BV198.S5] 29-4481
1. Prayer-books. I. Title.

SMITH, John Talbot, 1855- 264.
The wayfarer's prayer book, prepared by Rev. John Talbot Smith ... New York, The Catholic actors guild of America, 1917. 63 p. 14 cm. [BX2110.S6] 18-4360
I. Title.

TOMKINS, Floyd William, 1850- 264.
Prayers for the quiet hour, by Floyd W. Tomkins... Boston and Chicago, United society of Christian endeavor [c1910] 222 p. 16 cm. $1.00 [BV260.T6] 10-20508
1. Prayer-books. I. Title.

UNITY school of Christianity, Kansas City, Mo. 289
Book of silent prayer. Kansas City, Mo., Unity school of Christianity, 1940. 60, [1] p. 16 1/2 cm. [BX9890.U5A63] 42-44120
I. Title.

VAUGHAN, Herbert, cardinal, 1832
The people's manual.-- The holy sacrifice of the mass by ... Herbert Vaughan, bishop of Salford. [St. Louis] P. Fox, 1881. 127 (1) pp. 13 cm. 2-5623
I. Title.

WORTHINGTON, Edward William.
A study of the occasional offices of the prayer book, by Edw. Wm. Worthington ... Milwaukee, The Young churchman co., 1903. 96 p. 15 1/2 cm. 3-21024
I. Title.
Contents omitted.

WOTHERSPOON, Henry Johnstone, 1850- 264.
Kyrie eleison ("Lord, have mercy"); a manual of private prayers with notes and additional matter, by H. J. Wotherspoon ... Philadelphia, The Westminster press, 1905. 6 p. l., 5-168 p. 14 cm. [BV260.W6] 28-7143
1. Prayer-books. I. Title.

Prayer-books and devotions.

BISHOP, Bette, comp. 242.8
A child's prayers; beautiful prayers for every occasion. With color illus. by Vivian Smith. [Kansas City, Mo., Hallmark Editions, 1968] 60 p. col. illus. 20 cm. Seventy-eight prayers in verse for loved ones, meals, and special occasions, as well as morning and evening prayers. [BV265.B57] AC 68
1. Prayer-books and devotions. I. Smith, Vivian, illus. II. Title.

EXCELL, Edwin Othello,221851- 1921. ed.
Make His praise glorious; for the Sunday school and church. Practical ed. Chicago, E. O. Excell [1900] [233] p. 16 degree. 0-2402
I. Title.

FIRST graces. 242.8
Illustrated by Tasha Tudor. New York, H. Z. Walck, 1955 [i.e. 1959] 47 p. illus. 14 cm. Twenty-one short graces, including several for meals, and ones for the New Year, Easter, springtime, school, the Fourth of July, United Nations Day, Thanksgiving, and Christmas. [BV265.F54 1959] AC 68
1. Prayer books and devotions. 2. Grace at meals. I. Tudor, Tasha, illus.

FIRST prayers. 242.8
Illustrated by Tasha Tudor. [New York] H. Z. Walck [1959, c1952] 48 p. illus. 14 cm. Catholic edition. Twenty-six prayers for Catholic children, including ones for morning and evening, graces, and such familiar ones as The Lord's Prayer or the Twenty-Second Psalm. [BX2150.F56 1959] AC 68
1. Catholic Church—Prayer books and devotions. 2. Prayer books and devotions. I. Tudor, Tasha, illus.

[HUNGERFORD, Edward]
The common order of morning worship. Burlington, Vt., Free press association [1902] vi, [2], 67 p. 17 1/2 cm. Preface signed: Edward Hungerford. 5-39277
I. Title.

KIDDER, Daniel P[arish] 1815- 1891.
Helps to prayer: a manual, designed to aid Christians believers in acquiring the gift, and in maintaining the practice and spirit, of prayer, in the closet, the family, the social gathering, and the public congregation. Prepared by Daniel P. Kidder. New York, Hunt & Eaton. Cincinnati, Cranston & Curts [c1901] 379 p. 19 cm. Original copyright, 1874. 3-16911
I. Title.

LEVY, J. Leonard.
A book of prayer, by Dr. J. Leonard Levy... 2d ed. Pittsburgh, Publicity press, 1902. 1 p. l., 5-281 p., 1 l., a-v p. 19 1/2 cm. 3-3102
I. Title.

LEVY, Rosalie Marie, comp. 248
Heart talks with Jesus, compiled by Rosalie Marie Levy... 2d ed. New York, Rosalie M. Levy [c1926] xii, 175 p. illus. 14 cm. Advertising matter: p. 171-175. [BX2158.L4 1926] 26-1297
I. Title.

LEVY, Rosalie Marie, comp. 248
Heart talks with Jesus. 2d series. Compiled by Rosalie Marie Levy... New York, Rosalie M. Levy [c1929] ix, [2], 177 p. illus. 13 1/2 cm. Advertising matter: p. 174-177. [BX2158.L4 2d ser.] 29-10806
I. Title.

LEVY, Rosalie Marie, comp. 248
Heart talks with Jesus. Third series. Compiled by Rosalie Marie Levy. New York, N.Y., Rosalie M. Levy [c1930] 6 p. l., 177 p. illus. 13 1/2 cm. [BX2158.L4 3d ser.] 30-7006
I. Title.

SANDLIN, John Lewis. 242.8
A boy's book of prayers. Westwood, N.J., Revell [1966] 64 p. 17 cm. Prayers for all occasions especially written for young boys. [BV283.B7S2] AC 67
1. Prayer-books and devotions. I. Title.

SANDLIN, John Lewis. 242.8
A girl's book of prayers. Westwood, N.J., F. H. Revell [1966] 63 p. 17 cm. Prayers for various occasions especially written for young girls. [BV283.G5S2] AC 67
1. Prayer-books and devotions. I. Title.

[STELKENS, Mary Tehresa Mother] 1857- 264.
"Draw me after Thee, O Lord." A prayer book for persons who wish to make progress in the interior life. Suited to the adoration of the Blessed sacrament, for confession and communion. By A Poor Clare. West Park, O., Monastery of Poor Clares; Chicago, Ill., D. B. Hansen & sons [c1917] 2 p. l, 9-142 p. front., illus. 14 cm. [BX2060.S8] 19-242 0.15
I. Title.

Prayer-books and devotions—Episcopal.

**PRAYER BOOK for the Armed Forces (A).* 242.8'03
1967. Pub. for the Bishop for the Armed Forces, the Episcopal Church. New York, Seabury [1967] 168p. music. 15cm. 2.50
1. Prayer-books and devotions—Episcopal. 2. Armed Forces—Prayer-books and devotions—Episcopal.

Prayer-books—Bibliography

BOSTON. Public library.
Catalogue of selected editions of the Book of common prayer both English and American, together with illuminated missals in manuscript, early printed Books of hours and other books of devotion, in the possession of private collectors in Boston or owned by the Boston public and Harvard college libraries, on exhibition at the Boston public library from August 1906 until February 1907. Boston, The Trustees of the Public library, 1907. 52 p. 22 cm. [Z7813.B73] 7-40264
1. Prayer-books—Bibl. I. Title.

WRIGHT, John, 1836-1919.
Early prayer books of America; being a descriptive account of prayer books published in the United States, Mexico and Canada. By Rev. John Wright ... St. Paul, Minn., Priv. print. [Press of Evans & Bissell] 1896. xv, 492 p. front., 1 illus., pl., facsims. 22 cm. [Z7813.W95] 1-7536
1. Prayer-books—Bibl. 2. Printing—Hist.—America. I. Title.

Prayer-books—England.

THE book of common prayer,
and administration of the Sacraments and other rites and ceremonies of the church, according to the use of the Church of England. Together with the Psalter or Psalms of David, pointed as they are to be sung or said in churches; and the form and manner of making, ordaining, and consecrating of bishops, priests, and deacons. Oxford, University Press [1960?] 714p. tables.
1. Prayer-books—England. 2. Psalters. 3. Sacraments. I. Church of England. Book of common prayer.

GEE, Henry, 1858- 264.
The Elizabethan prayer-book & ornaments, with an appendix of documents, by Henry Gee ... London, Macmillan and co., limited; New York. The Macmillan company, 1902. xxiii, 288 p. 20 cm. The substance of this volume was delivered in

three "lectures to clergy held in Oxford in July 1901. I have in the interval revised my opinions, and have partly recast what I had written." cf. Pref. [BX5147.G4] 2-22044
I. Title.
Contents omitted.

Prayer-books, English.

BRING, Sven Libert, 1826-1905. 245
The Man of suffering; meditations and prayers for every day in Lent, by Prof. S. L. Bring, translated by Rev. B. G. Holmes. Rock Island, Ill., Augustana book concern [c1929] 362 p. 19 cm. [BV85.B67] 29-6480
I. Holmes, Bernt Gunnar, 1887- tr. II. Title. III. Title: Meditations and prayers for every day in Lent.

*CARTY, James W., Jr. 248.3
Communicating with God. Nashville, Upper Room [c.1964] 64p. 19cm. .35 pap.,
I. Title.

CATHOLIC Church. Liturgy and ritual. Breviary. English.
A short breviary for religious and the laity [complete edition] edited by William G. Heidt, O. S. B. 3d ed. Collegeville, Minn., Liturgical Press [1962] 1568 p. col. illus., music. 17 cm. 63-32333
1. Prayerbooks, English. I. Heidt, William George, 1913- ed. II. Title.

COLLINS, Joseph Burns, 1897-
Priest's daily manual; devotions, meditations, and aids for the spiritual life, by Joseph B. Collins and Raphael J. Collins. New York, Catholic Book Publishing Co. [c1964] 512 p. 16 cm. 67-81083
1. Prayer-books, English. 2. Priests — Prayer-books. I. Title.

FEDER, J ed.
The layman's missal, prayer book & ritual. Baltimore, Md., Helicon Press [1962] lxx, 1326 [18] p. illus., music. 16 cm. English version prepared by J. D. Crichton, S. Bullough, O.P., Clifford Howell, S.J., Herald Winstone and Donald Attwater (general editor). Basically a Sunday missal, but contains propers of daily masses for more important feasts and for Lent, with texts of Holy Week services. 63-15402
1. Prayer-books, English. I. Catholic Church. Liturgy and ritual, Missal. II. Title.

LASANCE, Francis Xavier, 1860- comp. 264.
... Manna of the soul; a little book of prayer for men and women, comp. by Rev. F. X. Lasance ... New York, Cincinnati [etc.] Benziger brothers, 1917. ix, 3-375 p. front. 12 cm. At head of title: Vest-pocket edition. [BX2110.L3] 17-24117 0.40
I. Title.

SEND forth thy Spirit;
a prayerbook. A book of prayers including a brief explanation before each part of Holy Mass. [4th ed. San Diego, Calif., University of San Diego, 1958] 340p. illus. 14cm. (St. Paul editions)
1. Prayer-books, English. I. Buddy, Charles Francis, Bp.

Prayer-books, Lithuanian.

MARY save us;
prayers written by Lithuanian prisoners in Northern Siberia. Translated by Kestutis A. Trimakas, S. J. New York, Paulist press [1959, c1960] 71p. 16cm. Facsimiles of the original Lithuanian text with English translation on opposite pages.
1. Prayer-books, Lithuanian. I. Trimakas, Kestutis A., tr.

Prayer—Collections.

*HOLLINGS, Michael. 248.3
The One who listens; a book of prayer [by] Michael Hollings and Etta Gullick. New York, Morehouse-Barlow [1971, c.1972] ix, 194 p. 18 cm. [BV4832] ISBN 0-8192-4037-0 pap., 2.75
1. Prayer—Collections. I. Gullick, Etta, joint author. II. Title.

LASANCE, Francis Xavier.
Prayer-book for religious: a complete manual of prayers and devotions for the use of the members of all religious communities. A practical guide to the particular examen and to the methods of meditation. By Rev. F. X. Lasance ... New York, Cincinnati [etc.] Benziger brothers, 1904- 1155 p. front., pl. 17 cm. 4-17236
I. Title.

LASANCE, Francis Xavier, 1860- 264.
Prayer-book for religious; prayers and devotions for the use of the members of all religious communities; a practical guide to the particular examen and to the methods of meditation, by Rev. F. X. Lasance ... New York, Cincinnati [etc.] Benziger brothers [c1921] xiv, 1200 p. front., pl. 17 cm. [BX2060.A1L3 1921] 21-19598
I. Title. II. Title: Prayers and devotions for ... religious communities.

LASANCE, Francis Xavier, 1860-
Prayer-book for religious: a complete manual of prayers and devotions for the use of the members of all religious communities. A practical guide to the particular examen and to the methods of meditation, by Rev. F. X. Lasance ... New, rev. ed. New York, Cincinnati [etc.] Benziger brothers, 1914. xiv, 1200 p. front., pl. 17 cm. 14-9777 1.50
I. Title.

Prayer—Comparative studies.

CRAGG, Kenneth, comp. 242.8
Alive to God: Muslim and Christian prayer; compiled with an introductory essay by the author. London, New York, Oxford U.P., 1970. xiv, 194 p. 20 cm. Bibliography: p. 173-183. [BL560.C7 1970] 72-525790 ISBN 1-921322-02- 30/-
1. Prayer—Comparative studies. 2. Prayers. 3. Islamic prayers. I. Title.

LE SAUX, Henri, 1910- 248'.3
Prayer [by] Abhishiktananda. Philadelphia, Westminster Press [1973, c1967] 81 p. 19 cm. Includes bibliographical references. [BL560.L47 1973] 73-600 ISBN 0-664-24973-6 1.95 (pbk.)
1. Prayer—Comparative studies. I. Title.

Prayer—Early works to 1800.

CHANTAL, Jeanne Francoise (Fremiot) de Rabutin, Baronne de, Saint, 1572-1641 248.3
St. Chantal on prayer; a translation of her writings on praver [by] A. Durand. [Boston] St. Paul Eds. [1968] 63p. 19cm. With one exception, all the extracts are to be found in vol. III of the official ed. of . . . [the author's] complete works: [Sainte Jeanne-Francoise Fremyot de Chantal, sa vie et ses oeuvres. Paris, 1876] [BV209.C48] 67-31593 1.00 pap.,
1. Prayer—Early works to 1800. 2. Meditation. I. Durand, A. comp. II. Title.

ORIGENES. 264.1
Prayer. Exhortation to martyrdom. Translated and annotated by John J. O'Meara. Westminster, Md., Newman Press, 1954. vii, 253p. 23cm. (Ancient Christian writers; the works of the Fathers in translation, no. 19) Bibliographical references included in 'Notes' (p. [197]-240) [BR60.A35 no.19] 54-13520
1. Prayer—Early works to 1800. 2. Prayer—Hist. 3. Martyrdom. I. O'Meara, John Joseph, ed. and tr. II. Title. III. Title: Exhortation to martyrdom.

RODRIGUEZ, Alonso, 1526-1616. 230'.2 s
A treatise of mentall prayer ; [A treatise of the presence of God] / [by] Alfonso Rodriguez ; [translated from the Spanish by T. B.]. Ilkley : Scolar Press, 1976. [21], 303 p. ; 20 cm. (English recusant literature, 1558-1640 ; v. 291) (Series: Rogers, David Morrison, comp. English recusant literature, 1558-1640 ; v. 291.) Translation of Tratados 5-6 of the author's Ejercicio de perfeccion y virtudes cristianas. Reprint of the 1st ed. of the translation, Douai, 1627. [BX1750.A1E5 vol. 291] [BV209] 248'.3 76-380514 ISBN 0-85967-292-1 : £10.00
1. Prayer—Early works to 1800. 2. Spiritual life—Catholic authors. I. Rodriguez, Alonso, 1526-1616. Ejercicio de perfeccion y virtudes cristianas. Tratado 6. English. 1976. II. Title. III. Series.

Prayer groups.

GUNSTOEE, John Thomas Arthur. 264'.7
The charismatic prayer group / John Gunstone. Minneapolis : Bethany Fellowship, 1976, c1975. 159 p. ; 18 cm. (Dimension books) [BV287.G86 1976] 76-6615 ISBN 0-87123-057-7 pbk. : 1.95
1. Prayer groups. 2. Pentecostalism. I. Title.

*JOHNSON, Ben C. 264.1
New life for prayer groups. Nashville, Upper Room [c.1964] 64p. 17cm. .35 pap.,
I. Title.

PRAYER and prayer groups.
West Port, N.Y., Holy Cross Press, 1956. 54p.
I. Garrett, Constance, 1894-

PRAYER group workshop / 264'.7
edited by Bert Ghezzi and John Blattner. Ann Arbor, Mich. : Servant Books, c1979. 138 p. ; 21 cm. Articles previously appeared in New covenant magazine in the monthly column Prayer group workshop. [BV287.P7] 79-115574 ISBN 0-89283-066-2 pbk. : 3.90
1. Prayer groups. I. Ghezzi, Bert. II. Blattner, John. III. New covenant.

SHOEMAKER, Helen (Smith) 264.7
Power through prayer groups their why and how. [Westwood, N.J., Revell [1958] 124 p. 21 cm. Includes bibliography. [BV287.S47] 58-8606
1. Prayer groups. 2. Prayer — Bibl. I. Title.

Prayer—History.

HAND, Thomas A 248.32
St. Augustine on prayer. Westminster, Md., Newman Press [1963] x. 133 p. 23 cm. Bibliography: p. 131. [BR65.A9H3] 63-24343
1. Augustinus, Aurelius, Saint, Bp. of Hippo. 2. Prayer—Hist. I. Title.

HIGGINS, John J. 248'.3
Thomas Merton on prayer [by] John J. Higgins. Garden City, N.Y., Image Books, 1975 [c1971] p. cm. Reprint of the ed. published by Cistercian Publications, Spencer, Mass. as v. 18 of the Cistercian studies series, under title: Merton's theology of prayer. Bibliography: p. [BV207.H53 1975] 74-8585 ISBN 0-385-02813-X 1.75 (pbk.)
1. Merton, Thomas, 1915-1968. 2. Prayer—History. I. Title. II. Series: Cistercian studies series, no. 18.

JUNGMANN, Josef Andreas, 1889-1975. 248'.3
Christian prayer through the centuries / by Joseph A. Jungmann ; translated by John Coyne. New York : Paulist Press, c1978. v, 169 p. ; 19 cm. (A Deus book) Translation of Christliches Beten in Wandel und Bestand. [BV207.J813] 78-61729 ISBN 0-8091-2167-0 pbk. : 2.45
1. Prayer—History. I. Title.

PROCTER, Francis, 1812-1905.
A history of the Book of common prayer, with a rationale of its offices. By Francis Procter ... 18th ed. London and New York, Macmillan and co., 1889. xiii p., 1 l., 528 p. 20 cm. 15-16188
I. Title.

SCOFIELD, William Campbell.
The Bible history of answered prayer. Chicago, New York [etc.] F. H. Revell co. [1899] 1 p. l., 235 p. 12 degrees. Oct
I. Title.

SIMPSON, Robert L. 264.1
The interpretation of prayer in the early church. Philadelphia, Westminster [c.1965] 189p. 23cm. (Lib. of hist. and doctrine)BBibl. [BV207.S5] 65-16147 5.00
1. Prayer—Hist. 2. Lord's prayer. I. Title.

SIMPSON, Robert L 264.1
The interpretation of prayer in the early church [by] Robert L. Simpson. Philadelphia, Westminster Press [1965] 189 p. 23 cm. (The Library of history and doctrine) Bibliography: p. [179]-183. [BV207.S5] 65-16147
1. Prayer — Hist. 2. Lord's prayer. I. Title.

Prayer—History—20th century.

LEFEVRE, Perry D. 248.3'2'0904
Understandings of prayer / by Perry LeFevre. 1st ed. Philadelphia : Westminster Press, c1981. p. cm. Includes bibliographical references. [BV207.L44] 19 81-11622 ISBN 0-664-32683-8 pbk. : 10.95
1. Prayer—History—20th century. I. Title.

Prayer (Islam)

KHAN, Naseer Ahmad. 297'.4'3
Muslim basic prayer book : Namaz, illustrated and romanized / Naseer Ahmad Khan. Lahore : Islamic Book Centre, [1976] 147 p., [14] leaves of plates : ill. ; 18 cm. [BP184.3.K49] 77-930094 Rs7.50 ($0.80 U.S.)
1. Prayer (Islam) I. Title.

Prayer (Judaism)

BAUMGARD, Herbert M. 296.7
Judaism and prayer; growing towards God. New York, Union of Amer. Hebrew Cong. [c.1964] xiii, 113p. 20cm. (Issues of faith) Bibl. 64-24341 1.50 bds.,
1. Prayer (Judaism) I. Title. II. Series.

BAUMGARD, Herbert M 296.7
Judaism and prayer; growing towards God [by] Herbert M. Baumgard. New York, Union of American Hebrew Congregations [1964] xiii, 113 p. 20 cm. (Issues of faith) Bibliography: p. 100-102. [BM669.B3] 64-24341
1. Prayer (Judaism) I. Title. II. Series.

BERKOVITS, Eliezer, 1908- 296.43
Prayer. New York, Yeshiva University, Dept. of Special Publications, 1962. 112 p. 23 cm. (Studies in Torah Judaism, 8) "Fifth in a series." Bibliographical references included in "Notes" (p. 105-110) [BM669.B44] 223.1 75-212123
1. Prayer (Judaism) I. Title. II. Series.

DONIN, Hayim. 296.4
To pray as a Jew : a guide to the prayer book and the synagogue service / Hayim Halevy Donin. New York : Basic Books, c1980. p. cm. [BM675.D3Z75] 80-86292 ISBN 0-465-08628-4 : 15.00
1. Jews. Liturgy and ritual. Daily prayers—Commentaries. 2. Jews—Rites and ceremonies. 3. Prayer (Judaism) I. Title.

HEINEMANN, Joseph. 296.4
Prayer in the Talmud : forms and patterns / by Joseph Heinemann. Berlin ; New York : de Gruyter, 1977. x, 320 p. : ill. ; 24 cm. (Studia judaica ; Bd. 9) A revision of the work originally published in Hebrew under title: ha-Tefilah bi-tekufat ha-Tana'im veha-Amora'im. Includes indexes. Bibliography: [302]-304. [BM660.H4613 1977] 77-1906 ISBN 3-11-004289-4 : 42.70
1. Jews. Liturgy and ritual—History. 2. Prayer (Judaism) 3. Rabbinical literature—History and criticism. I. Title. II. Series.

HESCHEL, Abraham Joshua, 1907- 296.4
Man's quest for God; studies in prayer and symbolism. New York, Scribners [1966, c.1954] xiv, 151p. 21cm. (Scribner lib., SL127) Bibl. [BM669] 66-6070 ISBN CD 1.45 pap.,
1. Prayer (Judaism) 2. Jewish art and symbolism. I. Title.

HOFFMAN, Lawrence A., 1942- 296.4
The canonization of the synagogue service / Lawrence A. Hoffman. Notre Dame [Ind.] : University of Notre Dame Press, c1979. p. cm. (Studies in Judaism and Christianity in antiquity ; no. 4) Includes index. Bibliography: p. [BM660.H63] 78-62972 ISBN 0-268-00727-6 : 13.95
1. Jews. Liturgy and ritual—History. 2. Prayer (Judaism) 3. Geonic literature—History and criticism. I. Title. II. Series.

JACOBS, Louis. 296.7'2
Hasidic prayer. New York, Schocken Books [1973, c1972] ix, 195 p. 22 cm. (The Littman library of Jewish civilization)

Bibliography: p. 183-186. [BM669.J3 1973] 72-86765 10.00
1. Prayer (Judaism) 2. Hasidism. I. Title.

JACOBS, Louis. 296.7'2
Hasidic prayer / Louis Jacobs. New York : Schocken Books, 1978, c1972. ix, 195p. ; 21 cm. (The littman library of Jewish Civilization) Includes index. Bibliography: p. 183-186. [BM669.J3 1973] ISBN 0-8052-0604-3 pbk. : 3.95
1. Prayer (Judaism) 2. Hasidism. I. Title.
L.C. card no. for 1972 Schocken Books ed.: 72-86765.

KON, Abraham Israel. 296.7'2
Prayer [by] Abraham Kon. Translated by the author from his book Si'ah Tefillah. London, New York, Soncino, 1971. xxii, 277 p. 24 cm. [BM660.K613] 73-156483 ISBN 0-900689-05-6 £2.50
1. Prayer (Judaism) 2. Synagogues—History. 3. Tallith. 4. Fringes (Jewish cultus) 5. Phylacteries.

NATIONAL council of Jewish women. New York section. 296
A book of prayer for Jewish girls ... compiled by the Committee on religion of the New York section of the Council of Jewish women. [2d ed.] [New York] 1923. 2 p. l., 51 p., 1 l. 18 cm. [BM667.G5N3 1923] 23-13414
I. Title.

ROTH, Tobias. 296.4
A Jewish view of prayer and worship. [1st ed.] Washington, B'nai B'rith Youth Organization [1969] 61 p. col. illus. 18 cm. (Judaism pamphlet series) Cover title. Bibliography: p. 59-61. [BM669.R67] 75-19479
1. Prayer (Judaism) I. Title. II. Series.

SIMPSON, William Wynn.
Jewish prayer and worship; an introduction for Christians. Naperville, Ill., SCM Book Club [c1965] 128 p. 19 cm. (SCM Book Club, 167) Includes bibliography. 66-52554
1. Prayer (Judaism) 2. Jews — Liturgy and ritual. I. Title.

UNION of American Hebrew Congregations. 296.4
The theological foundations of prayer; a Reform Jewish perspective. Edited with introductions by Jack Bemporad. [New York] Commission on Worship, Union of American Hebrew Congregations [1967] 126 p. 23 cm. "Papers presented at the UAHC 48th Biennial." [BM669.U5] 68-1817
1. Prayer (Judaism) 2. Reform Judaism—Addresses, essays, lectures. I. Bemporad, Jack, ed. II. Title.

Prayer (Judaism)—Addresses, essays, lectures.

PETUCHOWSKI, Jakob Josef, 1925- comp. 296.4
Understanding Jewish prayer, by Jakob J. Petuchowski. New York, Ktav Pub. House, 1972. xiv, 175 p. 24 cm. Includes bibliographical references. [BM669.P47] 71-155169 ISBN 0-87068-186-9 6.95
1. Prayer (Judaism)—Addresses, essays, lectures. I. Title.
Contents Omitted.

YOUR word is fire : 296.4
the Hasidic masters on contemplative prayer / edited and translated by Arthur Green and Barry W. Holtz. New York : Paulist Press, c1977. v, 133 p. ; 18 cm. (The Spiritual masters) Bibliography: p. 133. [BM669.Y68] 77-83589 ISBN 0-8091-2047-X pbk. : 1.95
1. Prayer (Judaism)—Addresses, essays, lectures. 2. Hasidism—Addresses, essays, lectures. I. Green, Arthur, 1941- II. Holtz, Barry W.

Prayer (Judaism)—Juvenile literature.

EPSTEIN, Morris, 1922- 296.43
Tell me about God and prayer; illustrated by Lawrence Dresser. New York, Ktav Pub. House [1953] 64 p. illus. 26 cm. [BM669.E6] 53-28740
1. Prayer (Judaism)—Juvenile literature. I. Title.

Prayer — Juvenile literature.

BICKERSTAFF, George. 248'.3
The gift of prayer / written by George Bickerstaff ; illustrated by Keith Christensen. Salt Lake City : Bookcraft, [1975] [24] p. : col. ill. ; 30 cm. A little girl learns the meaning of prayer. [BV212.B5] 74-33178 ISBN 0-88494-276-7
1. Prayer—Juvenile literature. 2. [Prayer.] I. Christensen, Keith. II. Title.

COUSINS, Mary 248
Tell me about prayer. Illus. by Thelma Lambert. New York, Kenedy [c.1963] 127p. illus. 23cm. 62-22116 2.95 bds.,
1. Prayer-Juvenile literature. I. Title.

CRANOR, Phoebe. 248.3'2
Is anybody listning when I pray? / Phoebe Cranor. Minneapolis, Minn. : Bethany Fellowship, c1980. p. cm. Twenty essays on various aspects of prayer. [BV212.C73] 79-27475 ISBN 0-87123-200-6 pbk. : 3.50
1. Prayer—Juvenile literature. 2. [Prayer.] I. Title.

GOLISCH, John 242'.6'2
It's time to talk to God, by John and Joan Golisch. Minneapolis, Augsburg Pub. House [1965] 1 v. (unpaged) col. illus. 22 x 28 cm. [BV212.G6] 65-12139
1. Prayer — Juvenile literature. I. Golisch, Joan, joint author. II. Title.

HEIN, Lucille E. 242'.6'2
I can make my own prayers [by] Lucille E. Hein. Illustrated by Joan Orfe. Valley Forge, Judson Press [1971] 31 p. col. illus. 25 cm. Discusses God's presence in the world and encourages the reader to make up his own prayers. [BV212.H4] 72-154026 ISBN 0-8170-0528-5 2.95
1. Prayer—Juvenile literature. 2. [Prayers.] I. Orfe, Joan, illus. II. Title.

KELLING, Furn. 248'.3
Prayer is ... / Furn L. Kelling ; illustrated by Ronnie Hester. Nashville : Broadman Press, c1978. 32 p. : col. ill. ; 24 cm. Defines the many aspects of prayer in simple terms. [BV212.K44] 78-113091 pbk. : 2.95
1. Prayer—Juvenile literature. 2. [Prayer.] I. Hester, Ronald. II. Title.

KUHLMANN, Edward, 1882- 264.1
God's children at prayer; narratives for children in interpretation of the Lord's prayer. Columbus, Ohio, Wartburg Press [c1946] 64 p. illus. 24 cm. "Fourth edition." [BV212.K8 1946] 48-16724
1. Prayer—Juvenile literature. I. Title.

LE GRICE, Edwin 248.3
Pattern for prayer [a work book for children] Illus. by David Pepin. New York, Morehouse [c.1963] 40p. illus. 25cm. 63-19477 .75 pap.,
1. Prayer—Juvenile literature. I. Title.

LLOYD, Ernest, ed. 264.1
Prayer stories for boys and girls, retold and comp. by Ernest Lloyd; illus. by Luis Chavarria. Mountain View, Calif., Pacific Press Pub. Assn. [1948] 96 p. illus. 23 cm. [BV212.L5] 48-6238
1. Prayer—Juvenile literature. I. Title.

RICHARDS, Jean H. 248.3
Why do people pray? Illustrated by June Goldsborough. Chicago, Rand McNally [c.1965] 1 v. (unpaged) col. illus. 24cm. [BV212.R5] 65-23976 2.00 bds.,
1. Prayer—Juvenile literature. I. Goldsborough, June, illus. II. Title.

WIMBERLY, Vera L. 242'.82
Please listen, God! / Vera L. Wimberly. St. Louis : Concordia Pub. House, c1977. p. cm. A selection of simple prayers accompanied by notes to help parents and teachers teach young children to pray. [BV212.W5] 77-8892 ISBN 0-570-03467-1 pbk. : 2.50
1. Prayer—Juvenile literature. 2. [Prayer.] I. Title.

WOLCOTT, Carolyn Muller. j264.1
I can talk with God. Pictures by Meg Wohlberg. New York, Abingdon Press, c1962. unpaged. illus. 19 x 23 cm. [BV212.W6] 62-7868
1. Prayer — Juvenile literature. I. Title.

Prayer—Lutheran Church.

**LEARNING to pray* 248.3
[teacher's guide: grades 7-9] Minneapolis, Augsburg [1967] 80p. 21cm. Prepd. for the Bd. of Parish Educ., and the Bd. of Pubn. of the Amer. Lutheran Church from the 1967 Vacation Church Sch., Ser., based on material prepd. by Clara M. Kemler, Cecelia Huglen. .95 pap.,
1. Prayer—Lutheran Church.

Prayer—Meditations.

FINNEY, Charles Grandison, 1792-1875. 248.3'2
Principles of prayer / Charles G. Finney ; compiled and edited by Louis Gifford Parkhurst, Jr. Minneapolis, Minn. : Bethany Fellowship, c1980. p. cm. Bibliography: p. [BV213.F56 1980] 80-17856 ISBN 0-87123-468-8 pbk. : 3.95
1. Prayer—Meditations. I. Parkhurst, Louis Gifford, 1946- II. Title.

MCCOMB, Samuel, 1864- ed. 264.
Prayers for today, with a series of meditations from modern writers, comp. and ed. by Samuel McComb... New York and London, Harper & brothers [c1918] xxiii, [1] p., 1 l., 179, [1] p. 17 1/2 cm. [BV245.M4] 18-6531
I. Title.

Prayer-meetings.

AHRENDT, Vivian. 264.7
More prayer meeting topics. Anderson, Ind., Warner Press [1953] 128p. 19cm. [BV285.A34] 53-7375
1. Prayer-meetings. I. Title.

AHRENDT, Vivian. 264.7
Prayer meeting topics, by Vivian Ahrendt. Anderson, Ind., The Warner press [1944] v, 6-135 p. 19 cm. [BV285.A35] 44-25997
1. Prayer—meetings. I. Title.

BANKS, Louis Albert, 1855-
Unused rainbows; prayer meeting talks. Chicago, New York [etc.] F. H. Revell co., 1901. [3]-194 p. 12° Apr
I. Title.

[BARTON, Frederick M] comp. 264.
One hundred prayer meeting talks and plans, including 1200 illustration ... 100 suggestions and tested plans for successful prayer meetings, introduction by Rev. F. B. Meyer ... Cleveland, O., F. M. Barton, 1911. 1 p. l., 544 p. 23 cm. "Foreword" signed: Frederick Barton. [BV285.B8] 11-31481
1. Prayer-meetings. I. Title. II. Title: Prayer meeting talks.

CHAPMAN, James Archer, 1885- 264.7
The neglected service, by J. A. Chapman ... Richmond, Garrett & Massie [c1935] xvii p., 1 l., 202 p. 20 cm. Messages on the parables and miracles of Jesus. [BV285.C57] 36-633
1. Jesus Christ—Miracles—Sermons. 2. Jesus Christ—Parables—Sermons. 3. Prayer-meetings. I. Title.

COWAN, John Franklin, 1854- 252
New life in the old prayer-meeting, by John F. Cowan, D.D. New York, Chicago [etc.] Fleming H. Revell company [1906] 237, [4] p. 20 cm. [BV285.C6] 6-42938
1. Prayer-meetings. I. Title.

COWAN JOHN FRANKLIN 1854-
New life in the old prayer-meeting, by John F. Cowan, D. D. New York, Chicago [etc.] F. H. Revell company [c1906] 237, [4] p. 20 cm. 6-42938
I. Title.

DOTY, Harry L., 1911- 264'.7
Prayer meetings : helps for priesthood / by Harry L. Doty. [Independence? Mo.] : Reorganized Church of Jesus Christ of Latter Day Saints, c1979. 150 p. ; 28 cm. [BV285.D67] 78-10622 ISBN 0-8309-0228-7 pbk. : 5.25
1. Prayer-meetings. I. Title.

ENGSTROM, Theodore Wilhelm, 1916- 264.7
Workable prayer meeting programs. Grand Rapids, Zondervan Pub. House [1955] 150 p. 20 cm. [BV285.E5] 55-1345
1. Prayer-meetings. I. Title.

HALLER, John George, 1858- 252
The redemption of the prayer-meeting, by J. George Haller, PH.D. Cincinnati, Jennings and Graham; New York, Eaton and Mains; [etc., etc., 1911] 222 p.19 cm. [BV285.H3] 11-18485
1. Prayer-meetings. I. Title.

HUSS, John Ervin, 1910- 264.7
The Hour of power; how a young pastor makes the spiritual pre-eminent in his church, by John Ervin Huss... Grand Rapids; Mich., Zondervan publishing house [1945] 98 p. 20 cm. Discussion of the author's midweek prayer service, "The Hour of power," at the Latonia Baptist church, Covington, Ky. [BV285.H8] 45-19110
1. Prayer-meetings. I. Title.

HUSS, John Ervin, 1910- 264.1
Paths to power; a guide to dynamic mid-week prayer meetings. Foreword by Roy O. McClain. Grand Rapids, Zondervan Pub. House [1958] 151p. 20cm. [BV285.H83] 58-42581
1. Prayer-meetings. I. Title.

LUCCOCK, Halford Edward, 1885- 264.
The mid-week service, by Halford E. Luccock and Warren F. Cook. New York, Cincinnati, The Methodist book concern [c1916] 109 p. 18 cm. [BV285.L8] 16-15866 0.35
1. Prayer-meetings. I. Cook, Warren F., joint author. II. Title.

MCGINTY, Claudius Lamar 264.7
Sermon outlines for prayer meetings. [Westwood, N. J.] Revell [c.1960] 64p. 21cm. (Revell's sermon outline series) 60-8461 1.00 pap.,
1. Prayer-meetings. I. Title.

MILLER, Basil William, 1897- 264.7
Prayer meetings that made history, by Basil Miller... Anderson, Ind., The Warner press [c1938] vi, 7-104 p. 19 cm. [BV285.M5] 38-30639
1. Prayer-meetings. I. Title.

MILLER, Milburn H 264.7
Ideas for the midweek service. Anderson, Ind., Warner Press [1956] 128p. 19cm. [BV285.M53] 57-4347
1. Prayer-meetings. 2. Sermons—Outlines. I. Title.

PRAYER-MEETING talks;
one hundred selections from Scripture with explanations. Cleveland, O., Publishing house of the Evangelical association [c1910] 428 p. 20 cm. 10-3016 1.25

PRAYER meeting talks and outlines by David Thomas, Charles Simeon, Charles H. Spurgeon, F. B. Meyer, and others. Grand Rapids, Baker Book House, 1954. 96p. 21cm. (Minister's handbook series) [BV285.P82] 54-3030 264.7
1. Prayer-meetings. I. Thomas, David, minister.

PRAYER meeting talks and outlines by David Thomas, Charles Simeon, Charles H. Spurgeon, F. B. Meyer. others. Grand Rapids, Baker Bk. [1968,c.1954] 96p. 21cm. (Minister's handbk. ser.) [BV285.P82] 54-3030 1.50 pap., 246.7
1. Prayer-meetings. I. Thomas, David, minister.

RICHARDSON, Norman Egbert, 1878- ed.
Present-day prayer-meeting helps for laymen and minister, by alumni of Boston university school of theology; ed. by Norman E. Richardson. New York, Eaton & Mains; Cincinnati, Jennings & Graham [c1910] 139 p. 17 1/2 cm. 10-15945 0.50
I. Title.

RINKER, Rosalind. 264'.7
Praying together. [1st ed.] Grand Rapids, Zondervan [1968] 128 p. 21 cm. [BV285.R55] 68-19841
1. Prayer-meetings. 2. Prayer groups. I. Title.

SELL, Henry Thorne, 1854-1928. 252
Prayer-meeting talks, by Henry T. Sell...

New York, Chicago [etc.] Fleming H. Revell company [c1931] 150 p. 19 1/2 cm. [BV285.S4] 31-19564
1. Prayer-meetings. I. Title.

SHULTZ, James Earl, 1884- 264.7
Fifty-two prayer meetings, J. E. Shultz. Takoma Park, Washington, D.C., Peekskill, N.Y. [etc.] Review and herald publishing association [c1936] 186 p. 19 1/2 cm. [BV285.S45] 36-8853
1. Prayer-meetings. 2. Seventh-day Adventists. I. Title.

STIDGER, William Le Roy, 1886- 264.
Building up the mid-week service, by William L. Stidger, D.D. New York, George H. Doran company [c1926] xiii p., 1 l., 17-134 p. 19 1/2. [BV285.S7] 26-12751
1. Prayer-meetings. I. Title.

WARD, William Thurman, 1871- 264.
Variety in the prayer meeting; a manual for leaders, by William T. Ward, introduction by Bishop William O. Shepard. New York, Cincinnati, The Methodist book concern [c1915] 192 p. 19 cm. "Prayer meeting bibliography": p. 189-192. [BV285.W3] 15-7835
1. Prayer-meeting. I. Title.

WELLS, Amos Russel, 1862-
Prayer-meeting methods, how to prepare for and conduct Christian endeavor prayer meeting and similar gatherings, by Amos R. Wells ... Boston and Chicago, United society of Christian endeavor, 1896. 174 p. 15 1/2 cm. Lettered on cover: A book of plans for young people's religious gatherings. 17-2321
I. Title.

WELLS, Amos Russel, 1862-
Prayer-meeting methods, how to prepare for and conduct Christian endeavor prayer meetings and similar gatherings, by Amos R. Wells ... Boston and Chicago, United society of Christian endeavor [c1916] 184 p. 15 1/2 cm. $0.35. Lettered on cover: A book of plans for young people's religious gatherings. 16-15865
I. Title.

Prayer, Mental.

MAUMIGNY, Rene de.
The practice of mental prayer, by Father Rene de Maumigny ... Second treatise, extraordinary prayer, tr. from the 4th ed. with the author's corrections and additions. Translation rev. by Father Elder Mullen, S.J. New York, P. J. Kenedy & sons [c1915] 293 p. 19 1/2 cm. $1.25 16-885
I. Mullan, Elder. II. Title. III. Title: Extraordinary prayer.

WITH Mary in mind;
a guide to mental prayer. Chicago, Carmelite Third Order Press [1959] 183p. front. 17cm.
1. Prayer, Mental. I. Rafferty, Howard, ed.

Prayer of St. Francis—Meditations.

GARRISON, R. Benjamin. 264'.13
Worldly holiness [by] R. Benjamin Garrison. Nashville, Abingdon Press [1971, c1972] 96 p. 19 cm. Includes bibliographical references. [BV284.F7G37 1972] 72-172808 ISBN 0-687-46336-X
1. Prayer of St. Francis—Meditations. I. Title.

PATON, Alan. 242'.726
Instrument of Thy peace : the Prayer of St. Francis / Alan Paton ; photos. by Ray Ellis. New York : Seabury Press, c1975. 128 p. : ill. ; 23 cm. "A Crossroad book." [BV284.F7P37 1975] 75-13522 ISBN 0-8164-2596-5 : 4.95
1. Prayer of St. Francis—Meditations. I. Title.

Prayer, Private—Collections.

LITTLE book of prayers. 248.37
Illus. by Jeff Hill. Mount Vernon, N.Y., Peter Pauper Press [1961, c.1960] 60p. col. illus. 1.00 bds.,
1. Prayer, Private—Collections. I. Peter Pauper Press, Mt. Vernon, N.Y.

Prayer—Psychology.

DAWSON, Marshall, comp. 264.
Prayer that prevails, a psychological approach to the practice of personal and public prayer, with examples, compiled and composed, by Marshall Dawson ... New York, The Macmillan company, 1924. xxviii, 162, [1] p. 20 cm. [BV245.D3] 24-24484
I. Title.

DONIGER, Simon, ed. 264.1082
Psychological aspects of prayer. Great Neck, N. Y., Pastoral Psychology Press [1954] 63p. 19cm. [BV225.D6] 54-32017
1. Prayer—Psychology. I. Title.

PARKER, William R. 248
Prayer can change your life; experiments and techniques in prayer theraphy by William R. Parker and Elaine St. Johns. New York, Cornerstone Library [1974, c1957] 224 p. 21 cm. [BV220.P24] 1.95 (pbk.)
I. St. Johns, Elaine, joint author. II. Title. L.C. card number for hardbound ed.: 57-6777.

SALIERS, Don E., 1937- 248.3'2'019
The soul in paraphrase : prayer and the religious affections / Don E. Saliers. New York : Seabury Press, 1980. x, 131 p. ; 22 cm. "A Crossroad book." Includes bibliographical references. [BV225.S2] 79-25325 ISBN 0-8164-0121-7 : 8.95
1. Prayer—Psychology. I. Title.

Prayer (Roman religion)

APPEL, Georg. 200'.8 s
De Romanorum precationibus / Georgius Appel. New York : Arno Press, 1975. 222 p. ; 23 cm. (Ancient religion and mythology) Reprint of the 1909 ed. (Gissae, Impensis A. Toepelmanni), which was issued as vol. 7, part 2 of Religionsgeschichtliche Versuche und Vorarbeiten. Includes bibliographical references and index. [BL25.R37 Bd. 7, Heft 2] [BL815.P68] 292'.3'8 75-10628 ISBN 0-405-07004-7
1. Prayer (Roman religion) I. Title. II. Series. III. Series: Religionsgeschichliche Versuche und Vorarbeiten ; 7 Bd., 2 Heft.

Prayer—Sermons.

CARROLL, Benajah Harvey, 1843-1914 264.1
Messages on prayer, by B. H. Carroll. Com. by J. W. Crowder, ed. J. B. Cranfill. Nashville, Tenn., Broadman press [1961, c.1942] 167p. (Broadman Starbooks) 1.25 pap.,
1. Prayer—Sermons. 2. Baptists—Sermons. 3. Sermons, American. I. Crowder, Joseph Wade, 1873- comp. II. Cranfill, James Britton, 1858- ed. III. Title.

CARROLL, Benajah Harvey, 1843-1914. 264.1
Messages on prayer, comprising pungent and penetrating sermons on a subject perennially vital to every Christian, by B. H. Carroll ... compiled by J. W. Crowder ... edited by J. B. Cranfill ... Nashville, Tenn., Broadman press [1942] 167 p. 20 cm. [BV210.S34] 42-23298
1. Prayer—Sermons. 2. Baptists—Sermons. 3. Sermons, American. I. Crowder, Joseph Wade, 1873- comp. II. Cranfill, James Britton, 1858- ed. III. Title.

FINNEY, Charles Grandison, 1792-1875 248.3
Prevailing prayer; sermons on prayer. Grand Rapids, Mich., Kregel [c.1965] 64p. 20cm. Sermons selected from the author's Sermons on the way of salvation. [BV210.F5] 65-25846 1.95; 1.00 pap.,
1. Prayer—Sermons. 2. Sermons, American. 3. Congregational churches—Sermons. I. Title.

FINNEY, Charles Grandison, 1792-1875. 248.3
Prevailing prayer; sermons on prayer. Grand Rapids, Kregel Publications [1965] 64 p. 20 cm. Sermons selected from the author's Sermons on the way of salvation. [BV210.F5 1965] 65-25846
1. Prayer — Sermons. 2. Sermons, American. 3. Congregational churches — Sermons. I. Title.

FORD, William Herschel, 1900- 242
Simple sermons on prayer, by W. Herschel Ford. Grand Rapids, Zondervan Pub. House [1969] 88 p. 21 cm. [BV213.F67] 72-95017 2.95
1. Prayer—Sermons. 2. Baptists—Sermons. 3. Sermons, American. I. Title.

FOWLER, Charles J.
Thoughts on prayer, from sermon talks, by Rev. Charles J. Fowler ... Chicago and Boston, The Christian witness co. [c1912] 112 p. 17 cm. 12-16932 0.30
I. Title.

HENRY, Matthew, 1662-1714. 264.1
The quest for communion with God. Containing the great English Bible commentator's personal and deeply spiritual directions for beginning, spending and closing each day with God. Grand Rapids, Eerdmans, 1954. 110p. 23cm. First published in 1712 in 'Works of Puritan divines' under title: Directions for daily communion with God. [BV213.H4] 54-1601
1. Prayer—Sermons. I. Title.

HENRY, Matthew, 1662-1714 264.1
The secret of communion with God. Ed. by Elisabeth Elliot. [Westwood, N.J.] Revell [c.1963] 120p. 21cm. 63-10397 2.50 bds.,
1. Prayer—Sermons. I. Elliot, Elisabeth, ed. II. Title.

HENRY, Matthew, 1662-1714. 264.1
The secret of communion with God. Edited by Elisabeth Elliot. [Westwood, N. J.] Revell [1963] 120 p. 21 cm. [BV213.H4] 63-10397
1. "Originally entitled Directions for daily communion with God." 2. Prayer — Sermons. I. Elliot, Elisabeth, ed. II. Title.

HENRY, Matthew, 1662-1714. 248.3'2
The secret of communion with God / Matthew Henry ; introduction by Sherwood Wirt ; illustrations by Ron McCarty. Shepherd illustrated classic ed. New Canaan, Conn. : Keats Pub., 1981. 123 p., [5] leaves of plates : ill. ; 21 cm. (A Shepherd illustrated classic) Originally published as: Directions for daily communion with God. [BV213.H4 1981] 19 79-93431 ISBN 0-87983-220-7 (pbk.) : 5.95
1. Prayer—Sermons. I. [Directions for daily communion with God] II. Title. III. Series.

MACARTNEY, Clarence Edward Noble, 1879- 264.1
Prayer at the golden altar, by Clarence Edward Macartney ... Grand Rapids, Mich., Zondervan publishing house [1944] 99, [1] p. 20 cm. [BV210.M23] 45-12324
1. Prayer—Sermons. 2. Presbyterian church—Sermons. 3. Sermons, American. I. Title.

REES, Paul Stromberg. 264.1
Prayer and life's highest. Grand Rapids, Eerdmans, 1956. 128p. 21cm. [BV213] 57-13637
1. Prayer—Sermons. 2. Evangelical Mission Covenant Church of America—Sermons. 3. Sermons, American. I. Title.

WEBB, John Henry, 1893- 264.1
At the gates of mercy, New Testament sermons on short texts, by John H. Webb ... Grand Rapids, Mich., Zondervan publishing house [c1938] 7 p. l., 11-96 p. 19 1/2 cm. "Ten sermons on prayer."--Introd. [BV210.W37] 38-30648
1. Prayer—Sermons. 2. Baptists—Sermons. 3. Sermons, American. I. Title.

WHYTE, Alexander, 1837-1921. 252
Lord, teach us to pray; sermons on prayer, by Alexander Whyte ... New York, George H. Doran company [1923] xx, 292 p. 19 1/2 cm. Printed in Great Britain. "Prepared for the press by J. M. E. Ross, with the assistance of Margaret Macadam Ross." [BV210.W45] 23-9558
1. Prayer—Sermons. 2. Free church of Scotland—Sermons. 3. Sermons, English—Scotland. I. Title.

Prayer—Study and teaching.

CHRISTIANSEN, Elmer E. 264.1
A study in prayer [2v.] for home fellowship meetings, organization Bible studies, individual Bible study, by Elmer E. Christiansen, Raymond A. Vogeley. Minneapolis, Augsburg [1963] 2v. (various p.) 20cm. Contents.[1] Leader's guide.--[2] Study guide. 63-16603 .50; .30 v.1, v.2,
1. Prayer—Study and teaching. I. Title.

COMMUNION with God. 248.3
Mountain View, Calif., Pacific Pr. Pub. [c.1964] 107p. 22cm. Devotional guide for the school of prayer, comprised of materials drawn from the Bible and the writings of Ellen G. White, and issued under auspices of the Ministerial Assn. of the Seventh-Day Adventists. 64-8715 1.25 pap.,
1. Prayer—Study and teaching. I. White, Ellen Gould (Harmon) 1827-1915. II. Seventh-Day Adventists. Ministerial Association.

COON, Glenn A. 248.4
Getting through to God : a book about communicating with God—for yourself, but mostly for others / Glenn A. Coon. Washington, D.C. : Review and Herald Pub. Association, c1980. 126 p. ; 21 cm. [BV214.C66] 80-16899 pbk. : 4.95
1. Prayer—Study and teaching. 2. Witness hearing (Christianity)—Study and teaching. 3. Evangelistic work—Study and teaching. I. Title.

DAWSON, David Miles, 1885- 264.1
More power in prayer; how to pray effectively, by David M. Dawson ... Grand Rapids, Mich., Zondervan publishing house [1942] 162 p. 20 cm. [BV210.D37] 42-18411
I. Title.

HUELSMAN, Richard J. 248'.3
Pray : [an introduction to the spiritual life for busy people] : moderator's manual / Richard J. Huelsman. New York : Paulist Press, c1976. 163 p. : ill. ; 28 cm. [BV214.H8] 76-24449 pbk. : 7.95
1. Prayer—Study and teaching. 2. Spiritual life—Catholic authors—Study and teaching. I. Title.

LEE, Robert Greene, 1886- 264.1
The Bible and prayer. Nashville, Broadman Press ['1950] x, 132 p. 20 cm. [BV214.L4] 51-1504
1. Prayer—Study and teaching. I. Title.

MORGAN, George Campbell 1863-
The morning message; a selection for daily meditation, from the works of Rev. G. Campbell Morgan, D.D. Comp. by William Ross. East Northfield, Mass., The Bookstore [c1906] [196] p. front. (port.) 18 1/2 cm. 6-28419
I. Ross, William, 1859- comp. II. Title.

*REINBERGER, Francis E. 264.1
How to pray. Ed.: Frank K. Klos. Artist: William H. Campbell. Philadelphia, Lutheran Church Pr. [c.1964] 138p. illus. 21cm. (LCA School of religion ser.) 1.50; 1.25 pap., teacher's guide;
I. Title.

RHEA, Carolyn. 248'.3'07
Come pray with me : the power of praying together / by Carolyn Rhea. Grand Rapids : Zondervan Pub. House, c1977. 129 p. ; 21 cm. [BV214.R43] 77-4951 ISBN 0-310-35601-6 pbk. : 2.95
1. Prayer—Study and teaching. I. Title.

RINKER, Rosalind. 264'.1'07
Teaching conversational prayer; a handbook for groups. Waco, Tex., Word Books [1970] 140 p. 23 cm. Bibliography: p. 125-133. [BV214.R5 1970] 70-91946 3.95
1. Prayer—Study and teaching. 2. Church group work. I. Title.

SKENE, George, 1845-
Morning prayers for home worship, by George Skene, with introduction by Edwin H. Hughes ... New York, Cincinnati, The Methodist book concern [c1913] v, 373 p. 21 1/2 cm. $1.50 13-19683
I. Title.

WHITE, Ellen Gould (Harmon) 18271915 248.3
Communion with God. 107 p. 22 cm. "A

devotional guide for the school of prayer, comprosed of materials drawn from the Bible and the writings of Ellen G. White, and issued under auspices of the Ministerial Association [of the Seventh-day Adventists]" [BV214.C6] 64-8716
1. Prayer — Study and teaching. I. Seventh-Day Adventists. Ministerial Association. II. Title. III. Title: How cities grew;

YOUNG, Fred L. 248.3
The Saints at prayer, by Fred L. Young. [Independence, Mo., Herald Pub. House, 1967] 176 p. 18 cm. Bibliographical footnotes. [BV214.Y6] 67-24546
1. Prayer — Study and teaching. I. Title.

Prayers.

[ABBETMEYER, Charles Dietrich August Frederick] 1867- comp.
The pastor in the sickroom; a handbook of lessons and prayers for the visitation of the sick, comp. by C.A. St. Louis, Mo., Concordia publishing house, 1912. iv p., 1 l., 58 p. 18 1/2 cm. 12-15753
I. Title.

ADDISON, Charles, 1856- comp. 264.1
...Prayers for the Christian year, compiled by the Rev. Charles Morris Addison, D.D. New York, London, The Century co. [c1931] xi, 258 p. 18 cm. (The Century devotional library) $1.50 [BV255.A3] 249 31-18838
1. Prayers. 2. Protestant Episcopal church in the U.S.A.—Prayer-books and devotions. I. Title.

ALBERTSON, Charles Carroll, 1865- ed. 264.1
The minister's book of prayers, edited by Charles Carroll Albertson. New York [etc.] Fleming H. Revell company [c1941] 112 p. 19 1/2 cm. Bibliography: p. 10-11. [BX250.A4] 41-19445
1. Prayers. I. Title.

ALDERMAN, Joy. 242'.8
Renewed in strength. Valley Forge [Pa.] Judson Press [1975] [28] p. illus. 18 cm. Prayers. [BV245.A38] 74-18108 ISBN 0-8170-0660-5 1.00 (pbk.)
1. Prayers. I. Title.

ALDRICH, Donald Bradshaw, 1892- ed. 264.1
The golden book of prayer; an anthology of prayer, edited by Donald B. Aldrich in collaboration with William Oliver Stevens. New York, Dodd, Mead & company, 1941. xvi p., 2 l., 3-275 p. col. front. 22 cm. "First edition." [BV245.A4] 41-26726
1. Prayers. I. Stevens, William Oliver, 1876- joint ed. II. Title.

ALDRICH, Donald Bradshaw, 1892- ed. 264.1
The golden book of prayer; an anthology of prayer, edited by Donald B. Aldrich in collaboration with William Oliver Stevens. New York, Permabooks [1949, c1941] xvi. 234 p. 17 cm. (Permabooks, P 45) [BV245.A4 1949] 49-53521
1. Prayers. I. Title.

ANDERSON, Andrew Gustaf, 1857- 248
Teach us to pray; a book of prayers for children, called in many fields, by A. G. Anderson. Rock Island, Ill., Augustana book concern [1925] 61, [1] p. front., illus. 14 cm. [BV265.A5] 25-24368
1. Prayers. I. Title.

ANSELM, Saint, Abp. of Canterbury, 1033-1109. 242'.802
The prayers and meditations of St. Anselm; translated [from the Latin] and with an introduction by Sister Benedicta Ward; with a foreword by R. W. Southern. Harmondsworth, Penguin, 1973. 287 p. 18 cm. (Penguin classics) [BV245.A5] 73-178518 ISBN 0-14-044278-2 £0.60
1. Prayers. 2. Meditations. I. Ward, Benedicta, tr. II. Title.

ARIAS, Juan. 242'.802
Prayer without frills / by Juan Arias ; translated by Paul Barrett. St. Meinrad, Ind. : Abbey Press, 1974. viii, 196 p. ; 20 cm. (A Priority edition) Translation of Preghiera nuda. [BV245.A7] 74-83340 ISBN 0-87029-037-1 : 3.95
1. Prayers. I. Title.

ARMSTRONG, Richard G. 242'.8
Christopher prayers for today [by] Richard Armstrong. Introd. by James Keller. New York, Paulist Press [1972] 64 p. illus. 17 cm. [BV245.A74] 72-86745 ISBN 0-8091-1735-5 0.75 (pbk.)
1. Prayers. I. Title.

BAILLIE, John, 1886- 248
A diary of private prayer. New York, Scribner's Sons, 1949. 135 p. 18 cm. Alternate pages left blank for "further petitions and intercessions." [BB260.B3 1949] 49-48692
1. Prayers. I. Title.

BAILLIE, John, 1886-1960.
A diary of private prayer, [Rev. ed.] New York, Scribner's Sons [1958] 135 p. 18 cm. Alternate pages left blank for "further petitions and intercessions." NUC67
1. Prayers. I. Title.

BAKER, Charles Richard, 1842-1898. 264.
Prayers for the Christian year and for special occasions, by Charles R. Baker, D.D. New York, T. Whittaker, 1897. xii, 210 p. 19 cm. [BV245.B3] 46-42450
1. Prayers. I. Title.

BARCLAY, William, lecturer in the University of Glasgow. 248.37
A book of everyday prayers. New York, Harper [1960, c.1959] 128p. 20cm. 60-5326 2.50
1. Prayers. I. Title.

BARCLAY, William, 1907-1978. 242'.8
Everyday prayers / William Barclay. San Francisco : Harper & Row, [1981], c1959. p. cm. Originally published as: The plain man's book of prayers. 1959. [BV245.B32 1981] 19 81-4236 ISBN 0-06-060411-5 pbk. : 5.95
1. Prayers. I. [Plain man's book of prayers] II. Title.

BARTLETT, Robert Merrill, 1898- 264.
A boy's book of prayers [by] Robert Merrill Bartlett ... Boston, Chicago, The Pilgrim press [c1930] 6 p. l., 71 p. 14 cm. [BV283.B7B3] 30-7008
1. Prayers. I. Title.

BARTLETT, Robert Merrill, 1898- 248.37
With one voice; prayers from around the world. New York, Crowell [1961] 181 p. 21 cm. [BL560.B3] 61-14530
1. Prayers. I. Title.

[BAUR, William] 1869- 249
Prayers for general use and for special occasions. St. Louis, Mo., Chicago, Ill., Eden publishing house [c1930] 136 p. 12 cm. [BV245.B35] 31-1889
1. Prayers. I. Title.

BECKER, August, comp. 264.
Daily inspiration, a book of prayers by ministers of the gospel and Christian workers, compiled by August Becker. Cleveland, O., Central publishing house [c1925] xi, 286 p. 19 1/2 cm. [BV245.B5] 25-16152
1. Prayers. I. Title.

BEECHER, Henry Ward, 1813-1887. 264.
Prayers from Plymouth pulpit. By Henry Ward Beecher. phonographically reported. 5th ed. New York, C. Scribner & company, 1867. vii, [1], 332 p. 19 1/2 cm. [BV250.B45 1867 a] 9-29951
1. Prayers. I. Title.

BEIMFOHR, Herman N. 242.8
Prayers for today [by] Herman N. Beimfohr. Westwood, N.J., F. H. Revell Co. [1967] 128 p. 17 cm. [BV245.B54] 67-22567
1. Prayers. I. Title.

BEL Geddes, Joan. 242
To Barbara with love; prayers and reflections by a believer for a skeptic. [1st ed.] Garden City, N.Y., Doubleday, 1974. xiv, 151 p. 22 cm. [BV260.B37] 73-14039 ISBN 0-385-09614-3 4.95
1. Prayers. 2. Meditations. I. Title.

BERG, Roger J. 242'.8
The roses are grinning / by Roger Berg. Corona Del Mar, Calif. : Emerson House Publishers, c1974. 142 p. ; 23 cm. [BV245.B544] 74-32585
1. Prayers. I. Title.

BERNARDIN, Joseph Buchanan, 1899- comp. 264.1
Prayers for schools and colleges. compiled by Joseph Buchanan Bernardin. New York. E. S. Gorham, inc., 1933. x p., 2 l., 3-133 p. 17 cm. [BV283.S3B4] 33-11969
1. Prayers. I. Title.

BERTHIER, Rene. 242'.8 s
Prayers for everyday life / Rene Berthier, Jean Puyo, Paul Gilles Trebossen ; [translated by Jerome J. DuCharme]. Notre Dame, Ind. : Fides Publishers, [1974] vii, 86 p. ; 20 cm. (Contemporary prayer ; v. 2) Includes indexes. [BV246.L5813 vol. 2] 242'.8 74-194398
1. Prayers. I. Puyo, Jean, joint author. II. Trebossen, Paul Gilles, joint author. III. Title. IV. Series: Livre de la priere. English. vol. 2.

BIMLER, Richard. 248'.3
Pray, praise, and hooray. St. Louis, Concordia Pub. House [1972] 113 p. illus. 21 cm. [BV245.B55] 77-175306 ISBN 0-570-03130-3
1. Prayers. I. Title.

BISHOP, James Alonzo, ed. 291.3
Go with God [ed. by] Jim Bishop. A treasury of the great prayers of alltime and all faiths, plus a moving personal narrative of prayer by the author. Derby, Conn., Monarch Books [1960, c.1958] 349p. 19cm. (Monarch human behavior bk. MB504) .50 pap.,
1. Prayers. I. Title.

BISHOP, James Alonzo, 1907- ed. 292.3
Go with God. [1st ed.] New York, McGraw-Hill [1958] 410 p. 22 cm. [BL560.B5] 58-13856
1. Prayers. I. Title.

BITTINGER, Lucy Forney, 1859- comp.
Prayers and thoughts for the use of the sick; selected by Lucy Forney Bittinger. Philadelphia & London, J. B. Lippincott company, 1902. 161 p. front. 16 1/2 cm. 2-00650
I. Title.

BLACKWOOD, Andrew Watterson, 1915- 242
We need you here, Lord; prayers from the city [by] Andrew W. Blackwood, Jr. Grand Rapids, Mich., Baker Book House [1969] 124 p. illus. 23 cm. [BV245.B57] 73-82127 3.95
1. Prayers. I. Title.

BLUMHARDT, Christoph, 1842-1919. 242.2
Evening prayers for every day of the year. Rifton, N.Y., Plough Pub. House [1971] xiii, 234 p. 15 cm. Translation of Abendgebete fur alle Tage des Jahres. [BV245.B5813 1971] 73-141948 ISBN 0-87486-204-3 2.95
1. Prayers. I. Title.

THE Book of prayers : 242'.8
compiled for everyday worship / edited by Leon and Elfr[i]eda McCauley ; introduction by Harry Emerson Fosdick. Avenel 1981 ed. New York : Avenel Books : Distributed by Crown, [1981] c1954. viii, 184 p. ; 18 cm. Includes index. [BV245.B614 1981] 19 81-3548 ISBN 0-517-34738-5 : 2.98
1. Prayers. I. McCauley, Leon. II. McCauley, Elfrieda.

BOUNDS, Edward McKendnee, 1835-1913. 248.32
A treasury of prayer, from the writings of E. M. Bounds. Compiled by Leonard Ravenhill. With foreword by David Otis Fuller. Minneapolis, Bethany Fellowship [1961] 192p. sPrayer. [BV210.B635] 69-27219
I. Title.

BOWIE, Walter Russell, 1882- 264.1
Lift up your hearts. Enl. ed. Nashville, Abingdon [1966, c.1939, 1956] 128p. 18cm. [BV245.B62] 56-5370 .95 pap.,
1. Prayers. 2. Liturgies. I. Title.

BOWIE, Walter Russell, 1882- 264.1
Lift up your hearts [by] Walter Russell Bowie. New York, The Macmillan company, 1939. viii p., 2 l., 3-118 p. 16 cm. "First printing." [BV245.B62] 39-34143
1. Prayers. 2. Liturgies. I. Title.

BOYD, Malcolm 242.8
Are you running with me, Jesus? Prayers by Malcolm Boyd. [New York] Avon [1967, c.1965] 158p. 18cm. (VS17) [BV425.B63] .75 pap.,
1. Prayers. I. Title.

BOYD, Malcolm. 242.8
Are You running with me, Jesus? Prayers. [1st ed.] New York, Holt, Rinehart and Winston [1965] 119 p. 21 cm. The personal prayers of a modern Episcopalian priest who believes that prayer is a direct response, offered freely by an individual man thinking as he usually speaks, and that prayer concerns the everyday events and concerns of man. Organized by topics, such as racial freedom, the campus, films, and sexual freedom. [BV245.B63] AC 68
1. Prayers. I. Title.

BOYD, Malcolm, 1923- 242
Am I running with you, God? / Malcolm Boyd. Boston : G. K. Hall, 1978, c1977. 155 p. ; 25 cm. Large print ed. [BV245.B628 1978] 78-981 ISBN 0-8161-6577-7 lib.bdg. : 8.95
1. Prayers. 2. Meditations. 3. Large type books. I. Title.

BOYD, Malcolm, 1923- 242.8
Are Your running with me, Jesus? Prayers. [1st ed.] New York, Holt, Rinehart and Winston [1965] 119 p. 21 cm. [BV245.B63] 65-22473
1. Prayers. I. Title.

BOYD, Malcolm, 1923- 248.3
Human like me, Jesus. [by] Malcolm Boyd. With a new introduction to the paperback edition. Revised and abridged. New York, Pyramid Family Library [1973, c1971] 141 p. 18 cm. [BV245.B634 1973] 71-159125 ISBN 0-515-03107-0. 1.25 (pbk.)
1. Prayers. I. Title.

BOYD, Malcolm, 1923- 242'.8
When in the course of human events [by] Malcolm Boyd and Paul Conrad. [New York] Sheed and Ward [1973] 155 p. illus. 23 cm. Prayers. [BV245.B636] 73-11507 ISBN 0-8362-0558-8 5.95
1. Prayers. 2. Editorial cartoons—United States. I. Conrad, Paul, 1924- illus. II. Title.

BRADLEY, Preston, 1888- 264.1
Meditations, by Preston Bradley. [Chicago] The Peoples church of Chicago, 1941. 4 p. l., 69, [1] p. 21 cm. "Fifteen hundred copies." [BV250.B67] 41-6825
1. Prayers. I. Title.

BRAINERD, David, 1718-1747. 266'.5'10924 B
Journey with David Brainerd : forty days or forty nights with David Brainerd. Downers Grove, Ill. : InterVarsity Press, [1975] 120 p. : ill. ; 21 cm. Selections from the author's An account of the life of the late Reverend Mr. David Brainerd; with a prayer by R. A. Hasler following each selection. Includes bibliographical references. [E98.M6M7864 1975] 74-20100 ISBN 0-87784-640-5 pbk. : 2.50
1. Brainerd, David, 1718-1747. 2. Prayers. I. Hasler, Richard A. II. Title.

BRANDT, Leslie F. 242'.8
Book of Christian prayer [by] Leslie F. Brandt. Minneapolis, Augsburg Pub. House [1974] 96 p. 18 cm. [BV245.B638] 73-88603 ISBN 0-8066-1406-4 1.95 (pbk.)
1. Prayers. I. Title.

BRANDT, Leslie F. 242'.8
Book of Christian prayer / Leslie F. Brandt. Minneapolis, Minn. : Augsburg Pub. House, c1980. 160 p. ; 17 cm. [BV245.B638 1980] 80-112089 ISBN 0-8066-1751-9 : 6.00
1. Prayers. I. Title.

BREAULT, William. 242'.802
Power & weakness; a book of honest prayers. [Boston] St. Paul Editions [1973]

119 p. illus. 20 cm. [BV245.B64] 73-86209 3.95
1. Prayers. I. Title.

BRENT, Charles Henry, bp., 1862-
With God in prayer, by the Right Rev. Chas. H. Brent. Philadelphia and London, G. W. Jacobs & company [1907] 73 p. 17 1/2 x 10 1/2 cm. 7-11202
I. Title.

BRENT, Charles Henry, bp., 1862-
With God in prayer, by the Right Rev. Chas. H. Brent. Philadelphia and London, G. W. Jacobs & company [1907] 73 p. 17 1/2 x 10 1/2 cm. 7-11202
I. Title.

BRENT, Charles Henry bp, 1862-1929. 248
Adventures in prayer, by Charles Henry Brent; arranged with an introduction by S. S. Drury. New York and London, Harper & brothers, 1932. xii, 104 p. illus. (facsims.) 17 1/2 cm. "First edition." [BV245.B65] 32-11675
1. Prayers. I. Drury, Samuel Smith, 1878- ed. II. Title.

BRENT, Charles Henry, Bp., 1862-1929. 252.03
No other wealth; the prayers of a modern-day saint, ed. by Frederick Ward Kates. Biographical memoir by Malcolm Endicott Peabody. Nashville, Upper Room [c.1965] 143p. 18cm. [BV245.B66] 65-18870 1.00 bds.,
1. Prayers. I. Kates, Frederick Ward, 1910- ed. II. Title.

BROKERING, Herbert F. 242.8
Lord, be with, by Herbert Brokering. Saint Louis, Concordia Pub. House [1969] 155 p. facsims. 22 cm. [BV245.B67] 74-88060 1.95
1. Prayers. I. Title.

BROOKE, Avery. 242'.8
Plain prayers for a complicated world / by Avery Brooke ; illustrated by Ronald Kuriloff. New York : Reader's Digest Press : distributed by Crowell, 1975. 95 p. : ill. ; 22 cm. [BV245.B673 1975] 75-10614 ISBN 0-88349-060-9 : 4.95 ISBN 0-88349-061-7 pbk. : 2.95
1. Prayers. I. Title.

BROWN, Annice Harris, 1897- 242'.8
Thank you, Lord, for little things. Illustrated by Eleanor Troth Lewis. Richmond, John Knox Press [1973] 39 p. illus. 16 cm. Poems. [BV245.B674] 72-11166 ISBN 0-8042-2580-X 2.95
1. Prayers. I. Title.

BROWN, James Good. 264.1
I came here to pray. Boston, Christopher Pub. House [1957] 123p. 21cm. [BV260.B83] 57-25844
1. Prayers. I. Title.

BROWN, William Adams, 1865- 264.
The quiet hour; experiences of fellowship in worship, recorded by William Adams Brown. New York, Association press, 1926. viii, 148 p. 17 cm. [BV250.B7] 26-13975
1. Prayers. I. Title.

[BUCKLEY, Annie L] comp.
Closet and altar; a collection of meditations and prayers upon various themes and for special occasions suitable for individual use and for family worship. Boston, W. L. Greene & co. [1899] 209 p. 12 cm. 99-5191
I. Title.

BULL, Henry, d.1575?, comp. A C 38-4579
Christian prayers and holy meditations, as well for private as public exercise. Collected by Henry Bull [A. D. 1566] ... Reprinted for the Parker society ... Cambridge [Eng.] Printed at the University press, 1842. xxxii, 209, [1] p. 16 cm. [The Parker society. Publications. v. 38] Contains reprint of t.-p. of the edition of 1570. [BX5035.P2 2]
1. Prayers. 2. Meditations. I. Title.

BULL, Henry, d.1575? comp. 264.1
Christian prayers and holy meditations, as well for private as public exercise. Collected by Henry Bull [A.D. 1566] ... Reprinted for the Parker society ... Cambridge [Eng.] Printed at the University press, 1842. xxxii, 209, [1] p. 16 cm. [The Parker society. Publications. v. 36) Includes reprint of t.-p. of the edition of 1570. [BX5035.P2] A C
1. Prayers. 2. Meditations. I. Title.

BUNTING, John Summerfield. 264.
Prayers for the way, by Rev. John S. Bunting... Philadelphia, G.W. Jacobs & company [c1928] 55 p. front. 17 cm. [BV260.B85] 28-29259
1. Prayers. I. Title.

BUSH, Roger. 242.8'07
Prayers for pagans. Dayton, Ohio, Pflaum Press, 1969 [c1968] vii, 63 p. illus. 21 cm. Poems. [BV245.B685 1969] 75-93002 1.50
1. Prayers. I. Title.

CALVIN, Jean, 1509-1564. 242
Devotions and prayers. Compiled by Charles E. Edwards. Grand Rapids, Baker Book House, 1954. 120p. 16cm. 'Originally published under the title Scripture texts, with expositions and sentence prayers from Calvin's Commentaries on the minor prophets.' [BV262] 54-10083
1. Prayers. I. Title.

CAMPBELL, Ernest T. 242'.8
Where cross the crowded ways: prayers of a city pastor [by] Ernest T. Campbell. New York, Association Press [1973] 96 p. 22 cm. [BV245.C26] 73-9792 ISBN 0-8096-1861-3 2.95
1. Prayers. I. Title.

CARR, Edwin Hamlin. 264.
"Let us give thanks"; prayers for the home, the school and the church, by Edwin Hamlin Carr ... New York, Chicago [etc.] Fleming H. Revell company [c1929] 96 p. front. 20 cm. Blank pages for records (94-96) [BV245.C3] 29-13460
1. Prayers. I. Title.

CARR, Jo. 248'.3
Bless this mess, & other prayers [by] Jo Carr and Imogene Sorley. Nashville, Abingdon Press [1969] 112 p. 21 cm. [BV245.C32] 69-12018 ISBN 0-687-03617-8 2.50
1. Prayers. I. Sorley, Imogene, joint author. II. Title.

CARR, Jo. 242'.8
Mockingbirds and angel songs & other prayers / Jo Carr and Imogene Sorley. Nashville : Abingdon Press, [1975] 109 p. ; 21 cm. [BV245.C324] 75-11847 ISBN 0-687-27099-5 : 3.50
1. Prayers. I. Sorley, Imogene, joint author. II. Title.

CARR, Jo. 242'.8
Plum jelly and stained glass & other prayers [by] Jo Carr & Imogene Sorley. Nashville [Tenn.] Abingdon Press [1973] 110 p. 21 cm. [BV245.C325] 72-14163 ISBN 0-687-31659-6 2.75
1. Prayers. I. Sorley, Imogene, joint author. II. Title.

CARROLL, James. 242
Tender of wishes; the prayers of a young priest. Paramus, N.J., Newman Press [1969] 138 p. illus. 23 cm. [BV245.C35] 73-92219 1.75
1. Prayers. I. Title.

CELTIC prayers / 242'.8
selected by Avery Brooke from the collection of Alexander Carmichael ; with calligraphy by Laurel Casazza. New York : Seabury Press, 1981. 95 p. : ill. ; 23 cm. "Selections from Carmina gadelica, volume III"—Verso t.p. [BV245.C4] 19 81-5693 ISBN 0-8164-2333-4 pbk. : 6.95
1. Prayers. I. Brooke, Avery. II. Carmichael, Alexander, 1832-1912.

CHAGNEAU, Francois. 264.02'01'3
Stay with us. Translated by John Drury. New York, Newman Press [1971] xii, 104 p. illus. 23 cm. Translation of Reste avec nous. [BV245.C4313] 70-152311 1.75
1. Prayers. I. Title.

CHAPMAN, Rex. 242
A kind of praying. Philadelphia, Westminster Press [1971, c1970] 121 p. 21 cm. Bibliography: p. 117. [BT306.4.C48 1971] 76-159476 ISBN 0-664-24934-5 1.95
1. Jesus Christ—Meditations. 2. Prayers. I. Title.

CHAPMAN J. WILBUR, 1859- andothers.
Answered! Remarkable instances of answered prayers. Boston and Chicago, United society of Christian endeavor [1899] 60 p. pl. 12 degree (Temple series) Aug
I. Title.

CHURCH of England. Liturgy and ritual. Primer. 264.1
Private prayers, put forth by authority during the reign of Queen Elizabeth. The Primer of 1559. The Orarium of 1560. The Preces private of 1564. The Book of Christian prayers of 1578. With an appendix, containing The Litany of 1544. Edited for the Parker society, by the Rev. William Keatinge Clay ... Cambridge [Eng.] Printed at the University press, 1851. xxvi, 576 p. 23 cm. (Half-title: The Parker society. [Publications, v. 37 54) Contains reprints of original title-pages. [BX5035.P2] (283.082) A C
1. Prayers. I. Clay, William Keatinge, 1797-1867, ed. II. Title.

CHURCH Service League of the Diocese of Massachusetts. 242'.803
Prayers for the Church Service League of the Diocese of Massachusetts. 7th ed. rev. and enl. Boston [Riverside Press] 1952. 146 p. 18 cm. [BV245.C46 1952] 75-313520
1. Prayers. I. Title.

CIHIAR, Many, 1888- comp. 264.1
Mystics of prayer, compiled by Fr. Many Cihlar ... with introduction by Dr. H. Spencer Lewis ... San Jose, Calif., Rosicrucian press [1932] 50, [6] p. 20 1/2cm. (Rosicrucian library, vol. ix) "First edition, March 1934; second edition, Mary 1932." [BF1623.R7R65 vol. 9a] [([159.961082]) [(133.082)] 36-17108
1. Prayers. 2. Mysticism. I. Title.

CIHLAR, Many, 1888-comp.
Mystics at prayer; with introd. by H. Spencer Lewis. [9th ed.] San Jose, Calif., Supreme Grand Lodge of AMORC [1960] 52 p. 21 cm. (Rosicrucian library, v. 9) 64-65452
1. Prayers. 2. Mysticism. I. Title. II. Series.

CLARK, Vivian Vreeland. 242'.8
If only I could fly : one woman's battle with depression / by Vivian Clark ; [original art by Linda Wolf]. Kalamazoo, Mich. : Master's Press, c1979. xii, 84 p. : ill. ; 18 cm. (Master's moments) [BV245.C53] 77-88385 ISBN 0-89251-040-4 pbk. : 1.50
1. Prayers. I. Title.
Publisher's address: 20 Mills St., Kalamazoo, MI 49001

CLOUD, Fred, comp. 242.8
Prayers for reconciliation. [Nashville, Tenn.] Upper Room [1970] 87 p. 13 cm. [BV245.C54] 71-103397
1. Prayers. I. Title.

COBURN, John B. 242'.8
A diary of prayers, personal and public / by John B. Coburn. Philadelphia : Westminster Press, [1975] 155 p. ; 21 cm. [BV245.C55] 75-12824 pbk. : 4.95
1. Prayers. I. Title.

COE, Albert Buckner, 1888- 264.1
Let us pray. [New York] G. W. Stewart [1952] 157 p. 18 cm. [BV245.C56] 52-1924
1. Prayers. I. Title.

A Companion of prayer for daily living / 242'.8
prepared and edited by Massey H. Shepherd, Jr. Wilton, Conn. : Morehouse Barlow Co., c1978. x, 107 p. ; 18 cm. Includes index. [BV245.C627] 78-62062 ISBN 0-8192-1230-X pbk. : 2.95
1. Prayers. I. Shepherd, Massey Hamilton, 1913-

CONRAD, Donald Williams, 1903 264.1
The golden censer, prayers for all ocassions, by Donald W. Conrad ... introduction by the Rt. Rev. J. Kenneth Pfohl, D.D. New York [etc.] Fleming H. Revell company [c1932] 106 p. 17 cm. [BV245.C63] 33-1754
1. Prayers. 2. Moravians—Prayer-books and devotions. I. Title.

CONTEMPORARY prayer / 242'.8
Thierry Maertens ... [et al. ; translated by Jerome J. DuCharme]. Notre Dame, Ind. : Fides Publishers, [1974] 2 v. ; 20 cm. Translation of 1-v. work: Livre de la priere. [BV246.L5813] 74-194400 ISBN 0-8190-0446-4(v.1) pbk. : 2.95
1. Prayers. I. Maertens, Thierry, 1921-

COSTELLO, Don. 242'.8
For inner peace and strength / by Don Costello. [Boston] : St. Paul Editions, c1978. 140 p. : ill. ; 22 cm. [BV245.C65] 78-315665 4.00
1. Prayers. 2. Meditations. I. Title.
Publisher's address; Saint Paul's Catholic Book and Film Center, 172 Tremont St., Boston, MA

COXE, Arthur Cleveland, bp. 1818-1896. 249
Covenant prayers. Short forms for family prayer, with special reference to the Christian covenant and the promises of our Saviour. By A. Cleveland Coxe ... Buffalo, M. Taylor, 1876. xx, [21]-143 p. 19 cm. [BV255.C75] 31-13883
1. Prayers. I. Title.

CRONBACH, Abraham, 1882- 296
Prayers of the Jewish advance, by Abraham Cronbach. New York, N. Y., Bloch publishing company, 1924. vii, 135 p. 21 cm. [BM565.C7] 25-8226
I. Title.
Contents omitted.

CROPPER, Margaret. comp. 248
A prayer book for boys, compiled by Margaret Cropper. New York, The Macmillan company, 1932. 64 p. 18 cm. London edition (Student Christian movement press) has title: A prayer book for boys and girls. [BV265.C7 1932] 32-5125
1. Prayers. I. Title.

CROSS, Christopher. 242'.8
Faces of prayer / by Christopher Cross. New York : Grosset & Dunlap, c1978. ca. 100 p. : ill. ; 28 cm. [BV245.C74] 77-94846 ISBN 0-448-14301-1 pbk. : 3.95
1. Prayers. I. Title.

CROSS, Christopher, ed. 264.1
A minute of prayer: prayers of all faiths for every purpose and every occasion. New York, Pocket Books [1954] 339 p. 17 cm. (A Cardinal edition, C-155) [BL560.C75] 54-42575
1. Prayers. I. Title.

CROTHERS, Samuel McChord, 1857-1927. 264.
Prayers, by Samuel McChord Crothers, with an z introductory note by Francis G. Peabody. Boston, Mass., The Beacon press, inc., 1928. 3 p. l., v-vi p., 1 l., 9-75 p. 17 cm. [BV250.C7] 28-9872
1. Prayers. I. Title.

CULLY, Kendig Brubaker, ed. 248.37
Prayers for church workers. Philadelphia, Westminster Press [c.1961] 109p. 61-5076 2.00
1. Prayers. I. Title.

CUNNINGHAM, Gail Harano. 242'.8
The little book of prayer, with inspiration from the Psalms. Selected and written by Gail Harano Cunningham. Illustrated by Linda Welty. [Kansas City, Mo., Hallmark, 1974] [48] p. col. illus. 16 cm. (Hallmark editions) [BV245.C83] 73-78223 ISBN 0-87529-348-4 2.50
1. Prayers. I. Welty, Linda, illus. II. Bible. O.T. Psalms. English. Revised Standard. Selections. 1974. III. Title.

CUNNINGHAM, Gail Harano. 242'.8
The little book of prayer : with inspiration from the Psalms / by Gail Harano Cunningham ; illustrated by Linda Welty. Kansas City, Mo. : Hallmark, c1975. [32] p. : ill. (some col.) ; 11 cm. (Hallmark editions) [BV245.C83 1975] 74-21915 ISBN 0-87529-435-9 : 2.00
1. Prayers. I. Welty, Linda. II. Bible. O.T. Psalms. English. Revised Standard. Selections. 1975. III. Title.

CURTIS, Muriel Anne (Streibert) ed.
Parents' prayers; for use by individuals or groups. New York, Morehouse-Gorham,

1953. 80p. 18cm. Includes bibliographical references. A57
1. Prayers. I. Title.

CUSHMAN, Ralph Spaulding, bp., 1879- comp. 264.1
A pocket prayer book and devotional guide, compiled by Ralph Spaulding Cushman. Nashville, Tenn., The Upper room press [c1941] 148 p. 12 cm. [BV260.C8] 41-11838
1. Prayers. 2. Devotional exercises. I. Title.

DAEHLIN, Marlene. 242
Hearts aglow. [Enl. and rev. ed.] San Antonio, Naylor Co. [1969] xi, 92 p. illus. 20 cm. [BV260.D23 1969] 75-110662 3.50
1. Prayers. I. Title.

DAEHLIN, Marlene. 242
Hearts aglow. San Antonio, Naylor Co. [1968] xi, 88 p. illus. 20 cm. [BV260.D23] 68-25398 3.50
1. Prayers. I. Title.

DANIELOU, Madeleine (Clamorgan) 248.32
How to pray. Tr. from French by Miriam Hederman. Westminster, Md., Newman [c.1963] 129p. 19cm. 63-122502 2.50
1. Prayers. 2. Church year—Meditations. I. Title.

DANIELOU, Madeline (Clamorgan) 248.32
How to pray. Translated from the French by Miriam Hederman. Westminster, Md., Newman Press [1963] 129 p. 19 cm. Translation of Vous prierez ainsi. [BV245.D273] 63-12250
1. Prayers. 2. Church year — Meditations. I. Title.

DAVIES, Arthur Powell. 264.1
The language of the heart; a book of prayers. New York, Farrar, Straus and Cudahy [1956] 117p. 21cm. [BV245.D29] 56-7859
1. Prayers. I. Title.

DAVIS, Elisabeth Hamill, comp. 264.1
Fellowship with the Father: a prayer for each day, selected and arranged by Elisabeth Hamill Davis. Grand Rapids, Mich., Wm. B. Eerdmans publishing company, 1936. 269, [5] p. 20 cm. Prose and verse. [BV260.D28] 38-7896
1. Prayers. 2. Calendars. I. Title.

DAVIS, Elisabeth Hamill, ed. 264.
For each day a prayer, selected and arranged by Elizabeth Hamill Davis. New York, Dodge publishing company [1905] 271 p. 19 1/2 cm. [BV260.D3] 5-26244
1. Prayers. 2. Calendars. I. Title.

DEANE, Elisabeth, comp. 242.8
Gift of prayer; a selection of prayers designed to make the burdens lighter and the hours less lonely. Mount Vernon, N.Y., Peter Pauper Press [1971] 62 p. 17 cm. (Gifts of gold) [BV245.D4] 79-25081 1.95
1. Prayers. I. Title.

DEVOTIONAL somnium;
or, A collection of prayers and exhortations, uttered by Miss Rachel Baker, in the city of New-York, in the winter of 1815, during her abstracted and unconscious state; to which ... is prefixed an account of her life ... together with a view of that faculty of the human mind which is intermediate between sleeping and waking ... By several medical gentlemen. New-York; Printed for the proprietor, by S. Marks, 63 Anthony-street, 1815. 298 (i.e. 288) p. front. (port.) 18 1/2 cm. Introduction signed: John H. Douglass. Second edition. "Exercises of Miss Baker, performed during her unconscious state": p. 180-292. [BF1352.D4] 2-23456
I. Baker, Rachel, b. 1794. II. Douglass, John H., ed.

[DICKINSON, Sarah (Truslow) Mrs. 1863- comp. 264.
Fellowship prayers. New York, The Womans press [c1928] 8 p. l., 15-126 p. 15 cm. "Revised edition." [BV245 D5 1928] 28-18229
1. Prayers. I. Title.

[DOERFFLER, Alfred] 1887- ed. 264.1
Open the meeting with prayer. Saint Louis, Concordia Pub. House [1955] 94p. 20cm. [BV250.D6] 55-7442
1. Prayers. I. Title.

DONNE, John, 1573-1631. 264.1
Prayers; selected and edited from the earliest sources, with an essay on Donne's idea of prayer, by Herbert H. Umbach. New York, Bookman Associates [1951] 109 p. 22 cm. Bibliography: p. 93. [BV245.D65] 51-5368
1. Prayers. 2. Prayer. I. Umbach, Herbert Herman, 1908- ed. II. Title.

DRAKE, Alice Hutchins. 264.1
Little prayers for stressful times, by Alice Hutchins Drake ... New York, Grosset & Dunlap [1943] 7 p. l., 3-84 p. 19 1/2 cm. [BV245.D68] 43-16647
1. Prayers. I. Title.

DRESCHER, John M. 242.8
Heartbeats; emerging from encounters in prayer [by] John M. Drescher. Grand Rapids, Zondervan Pub. House [1970] 158 p. 21 cm. [BV245.D73] 71-106443 3.50
1. Prayers. I. Title.

DU BOIS, William Edward Burghardt, 1868-1963. 242'.8
Prayers for dark people / W. E. B. Du Bois ; edited by Herbert Aptheker. Amherst : University of Massachusetts Press, 1980. xi, 75 p. ; 22 cm. [BV245.D8 1980] 80-12234 ISBN 0-87023-302-5 lib. bdg. 10.00 ISBN 0-87023-303-3 pbk. : 4.50
1. Prayers. 2. Afro-American students—Prayer-books and devotions—English. 3. Pastoral prayers. I. Aptheker, Herbert, 1915- II. Title.

EDMONDS, Henry M.
Sermonettes and prayers, by Henry M. Edmonds. [Birmingham, Ala., Dispatch printing co.] 1916. 2 p. l., 108 p. 15 1/2 cm. Reprinted from the Birmingham age-herald. 16-23970
I. Title.

EDMONDS, Henry Morris, 1878- 242
Beginning the day. New York, Abingdon-Cokesbury Press [1951] unpaged. 18 cm. [BV245.E3] 51-14216
1. Prayers. 2. Calendars. I. Title.

FERRIS, Theodore Parker, 1908- 248.374
Book of prayer for everyman. Greenwich, Conn., Seabury [c.]1962. 150p. 18cm. 62-17081 2.75 bds.,
1. Prayers. I. Title.

FERRIS, Theodore Parker, 1908- 242'.8
Prayers / Theodore Parker Ferris. New York : Seabury Press, 1981. p. cm. [BV245.F423] 19 80-26320 ISBN 0-8164-0483-6 : 6.95
1. Prayers. 2. Prayer. I. Title.

FIEDLER, Lois. 242.8'05'1
The many faces of love. Westwood, N.J., Revell [1968] 127 p. 21 cm. [BV260.F5] 68-17089
1. Prayers. 2. Meditations. I. Title.

FIELDS, William H. 242'.806'1
Lord, let them know I care : prayers for people where they are / William H. Fields. Waco, Tex. : Word Books, c1979. 102 p. ; 21 cm. [BV245.F45] 78-65811 ISBN 0-8499-2854-0 pbk. : 3.95
1. Prayers. I. Title.

FLEMING, Daniel Johnson, 1877- ed. 264.1
The world at one in prayer, edited by Daniel J. Fleming ... New York and London, Harper & brothers [1942] xi, 204 p. illus. 21 cm. "First edition." "An ecumenical series ... the fourth by the same author ... The others are: Heritage of beauty ... Each with his own brush ... Christian symbols in a world community." Bibliographical references included in "Acknowledgments" (p. 195-200) [BV245.F5] 42-13947
1. Prayers. I. Title.

FORD, Agnes Gibbs, comp. 242.8
Prayers for everyone. Illus. by Joyce D. May. Grand Rapids, Baker Book House [1967] 94 p. illus. 23 cm. [BV245.F65] 67-18175
1. Prayers. I. Title.

FOUST, Leila Atwood, Mrs. 264
With God and the colors; prayers by a mother for her soldier boy, by Mrs. Leila Atwood Foust. Philadelphia, Pa., The Vir publishing company; [etc., etc., c1918. 64 p. 18 cm. Ornamental borders; most of alternating pages blank. [BV273.F7] 18-9362
I. Title.

FOUST, Leila Atwood, Mrs. 264
With God and the colors; prayers by a mother for her soldier boy, by Mrs. Leila Atwood Foust. Philadelphia, Pa., The Vir publishing company; [etc., etc., c1918. 64 p. 18 cm. Ornamental borders; most of alternating pages blank. [BV273.F7] 18-9362
I. Title.

FOX, Selina Fitzherbert, comp. 264.1
A chain of prayer across the ages; forty centuries of prayer, from 2000 B.C., Compiled and arranged fro daily use by Selina Fitzherbert Fox ... With index of subjects and authors; introduction by the Rt. Rev. Ernest Milmore Stires ... New York, E. P. Dutton and company, inc. [1943] xxviii p., 1 l., 319, [1] p. 19 1/2 cm. "First edition January, 1913 ... Sixth edition June, 1941 ... [New American edition] January, 1943." [BV255.F65 1943] 43-51099
1. Prayers. 2. Calendars. I. Title. II. Title: Forty centuries of prayer.

FOX, Selina Fitzherbert, comp.
A chain of prayer across the ages: forty centuries of prayer, 2000 B. C.--A. D. 1912, comp. and arranged for daily use by Selina Fitzherbert Fox ... with index of subjects and authors. New York, E. P. Dutton and company, 1913. xvi, 231, [1] p. 22 cm. A14
1. Prayers. I. Title.

FRANCESCO d'Assisi, Saint, 1182-1226. 242'.802
Heaven on earth; the inspirational writings of Saint Francis of Assisi, selected by Karen Hill. Illustrated by Noreen Bonker. [Kansas City, Mo., Hallmark Cards, 1973] [48] p. illus. 16 cm. (Hallmark editions) [BV245.F67] 72-84373 ISBN 0-87529-322-0 2.50
1. Prayers. 2. Meditations. I. Title.

FRANCESCO d'Assisi, Saint, 1182-1226. 242'.802
Heaven on earth : inspirational writings of Saint Francis of Assisi / illustrated by Noreen Bonker. Kansas City, Mo. : Hallmark, c1975. [48] p. : col. ill. ; 11 x 16 cm. (Hallmark editions) [BV245.F67 1975] 74-83541 ISBN 0-87529-402-2 : 3.00
1. Prayers. 2. Meditations. I. Bonker, Noreen. II. Title.

FRANCESCO d'Assisi, Saint, 1182-1226. 242'.802
Saint Francis prayer book : compiled from the writings and early biographies of St. Francis of Assisi / by A. van Corstanje. Chicago : Franciscan Herald Press, c1978. 110 p. ; 13 cm. (Tau series) Includes bibliographical references. [BV245.F67 1978] 77-28014 ISBN 0-8199-0693-X pbk. : 1.75
1. Prayers. I. Corstanje, Auspicius van. II. Title.

FRANKE, Merle G. 242'.8
New life and other joys; prayers for today, by Merle G. Franke. Philadelphia, Fortress Press [1974] 127 p. illus. 22 cm. [BV245.F675] 73-88342 ISBN 0-8006-0263-3 4.95
1. Prayers. I. Title.

FRIDY, Wallace. 242'.8
Everyday prayers for all sorts of needs. Nashville, Abingdon Press [1974] 112 p. 16 cm. [BV245.F695] 73-14745 ISBN 0-687-12332-1 3.50
1. Prayers. I. Title.

FRITCHMAN, Stephen Hole, 1902- ed. 264.1
Prayers of the free spirit, edited by Stephen Hole Fritchman ... New York, N.Y., The Woman's press, c1945. 64 p. 1 illus. 20 1/2 cm. "Copyright ... by the National board of the Young women's Christian associations of the United States of America." [BV245.F7] 46-12270
1. Prayers. I. Young women's Christian associations. U.S. National board II. Title.

FRIZZELL, John Henry, 1881- 264.1
For days of crisis, a book of prayers. Boston, Christopher Pub. House [1952] 75 p. 21 cm. [BV245.F74] 52-25947
1. Prayers. I. Title.

GARDEN of prayer / 242'.8
[Ray Schafer, compiler ; Pat Pratt, designer ; Cathy Stanton, illustrator]. Santa Ana, CA. : Vision House, c1976. 85 p. : ill. ; 22 cm. [BV245.G35] 75-42851 ISBN 0-88449-052-1
1. Prayers. I. Schafer, Ray.

GARESCHE, Edward Francis, 1876- 264.02
Moments with God, by Rev. Edward F. Garesche, S.J. Milwaukee, The Bruce publishing company [c1931] xii p. 1 l., 414, 207 p. front., illus. 14 cm. [BX2110.G25] 32-1650
1. Prayers. 2. Catholic church—Prayer-books and devotions. I. Title.

GESCH, Roy G. 242.8'4'2
Man at prayer [by] Roy Gesch. St. Louis, Concordia Pub. House [1970] 113 p. 19 cm. [BV245.G45] 79-108884
1. Prayers. I. Title.

*GINGER, Helen, comp. 264.1
God still answers prayer; 36 true-life experiences with prayer on the mission field. Cincinnati, Standard Pub. [c.1964] 127p. illus. 22cm. 1.95, pap., plastic bdg.
I. Title.

GLOVER, Carl Archibald, 1891- 264.1
The lectern; a book of public prayers, by Carl A. Glover. New York, Nashville, Abingdon-Cokesbury press [1946] 224 p. 16 cm. [BV250.G5] 47-993
1. Prayers. I. Title.

A Golden treasury of Psalms and prayers for all faiths. 264.1 [Decorations and cover design by Fritz Kredel] Mount Vernon, N. Y., Peter Pauper Press [1952?] 61 p. illus. 18 cm. [BV245.G6] 52-43410
1. Prayers. I. Peter Pauper Press, Mount Vernon, N. Y.

GOODELL, Charles Le Roy, 1854- 264.1
Prayer of Sabbath reveries, presented to America by the National broadcasting company and associated radio stations from coast to coast [by] Charles L. Goodell ... New York, The Knickerbocker press [c1931] 4 p. l., 3-84 p. 20 cm. [BV250.G6] 32-875
1. Prayers. I. National broadcasting company, inc. II. Title. III. Title: Sabbath reveries, Prayers of.

GORDON, Samuel Dickey, 1859- 264.
The bent-knee time: a bit for every day of the year, by S. D. Gordon ... Philadelphia, American Sunday-school union [c1918] 186 p. 13 cm. [BV260.G6] 19-9321 0.75
I. Title.

GREENE, Barbara, comp. 248.37
God of a hundred names; prayers of many peoples and creeds collected and arranged by Barbara Greene and Victor Gollancz. [1st ed. in the U. S. A.] Garden City, N. Y., Doubleday, 1963 [c1962] 297 p. 22 cm. [BV245.G66 1963] 63-12347
1. Prayers. I. Gollancz, Victor, 1893-1967, joint comp. II. Title.

GRIOLET, Pierre. 242'.8
You call us together. Translated by Edmond Bonin. New York, Paulist Press [1973] x, 198 p. 23 cm. Poems. Translation of Tu viens nous rassembler. [BV245.G6813] 73-82650 ISBN 0-8091-1783-5 3.95 (pbk.)
1. Prayers. I. Title.

GRISWOLD, Alexander Viets, bp., 1766-1843. 264.
Prayers adapted to various occasions of social worship, for which provision is not made in the Book of common prayer. By Alexander V. Griswold ... Philadelphia, W. Marshall & co.; Providence, Marshall, Brown & co., 1835. xii, 13-190 p., 1 l. 18 1/2 cm. [BV245.G7 1835] 46-42449
1. Prayers. 2. Protestant Episcopal church in the U.S.A.—Prayer-books and devotions—English. I. Protestant Episcopal

church in the U.S.A. Liturgy and ritual. II. Title.

GRISWOLD, Alexander Viets, bp., 1766-1843. 264.
Prayers adapted to various occasions of social worship, for which provision is not made in the Book of common prayer. By Alexander V. Griswold ... Philadelphia, W. Marshall & co.; Providence, Marshall, Brown & co., 1836. xiv, [15]-271 p. 19 cm. "Second edition." [BV245.G7 1836] 46-34498
1. Prayers. 2. Protestant Episcopal church in the U.S.A.—Prayer-books and devotions—English. I. Protestant Episcopal church in the U.S.A. Liturgy and ritual. II. Title.

GUARDINI, Romano, 1885- 264.13
Prayers from theology. Translated by Richard Newham. [New York] Herder and Herder [1959] 61p. 19cm. Translation of Theologische Gebete. [BV260.G813 1959a] 58-13656
1. Prayers. I. Title.

GUHSE, Herman Paul. 264.
A book of invocations for use throughout the year, by Herman Paul Guhse ... with introduction by Harry Emerson Foskick ... New York, Fleming H. Revell company [c1928] 94 p. 20 cm. [BV250.G75] 28-9082
1. Prayers. I. Title.

GUILD, Caroline Snowden (Whitmarsh) 1827-1898, comp. 264.
Prayers of the ages, compiled by Caroline S. Whitmarsh ... Boston, Ticknor and Field, 1868. xvii, 335 p. 18 cm. [BV245.G8] 45-34922
1. Prayers. I. Title.

GUNSAULUS, Frank Wakeley, 1856-1921. 264.
Prayers of Frank W. Gunsaulus. New York, Chicago [etc.] Fleming H. Revell company [c1922] 160 p. front. (port.) 20 cm. [BV250.G8] 22-11672
I. Title.

HACKETT, Allen, 1905-
Pilgrim prayers and meditations, shared with the congregation of Pilgrim Congregational Church, St. Louis, Missouri: selected and edited, with a foreword by J. Martin and Betty Jane Bailey. [St. Louis, Eden Publishing House, c1962] 75 p. port. 63-17752
1. Prayers. I. Title.

HACKMAN, Jenny. 242'.6'8
Jenny's prayer diary. Old Tappan, N.J., F. H. Revell Co. [1971] 128 p. 19 cm. [BV245.H22] 70-160275 ISBN 0-8007-0469-X
1. Prayers. I. Title.

HALE, Edward Everett, 1822-1909. 264.
Prayers in the Senate. Prayers offered in the Senate of the United States in the winter session of 1904, by Edward E. Hale, chaplain. Boston, Little, Brown, and company, 1904. 2 p. l., [v]-ix, 136 numb. l. 18 1/2 cm. Printed on one side of leaf only. [BV280.H3] 5-9377
1. Prayers. 2. U.S. Congress. Senate. I. Title.

HALL, Asa Zadel 248.32
Prayers in the space age. Grand Rapids, Mich., Zondervan [c.1963] 64p. 21cm. 1.00 pap.,
I. Title.

HALLOCK, Gerard Benjamin Fleet, 1856- comp. 250.
Cyclopedia of pastoral methods ... compiled and edited by Rev. G. B. F. Hallock ... New York, George H. Doran company [c1924] xii, p., 1 l. 15-270 p. 22 cm. [BV4016.H25] 24-23388
1. Prayers. 2. Liturgies. I. Title.
Contents omitted.

HALLOCK, Gerard Benjamin Fleet, 1856- 264.1
Prayers for special days and occasions; a treasure of prayers, evangelical and interdenominational, for all occasions, both special and regularly recurring, and also for various dedicatory and other ceremonies, for certain times and seasons, special objects and persons, etc., etc.; for voluntary use, written and compiled by Rev. G. B. F. Hallock ... New York, R. R. Smith, inc., 1930. xi, 182 p. 15 cm. [BV250.H3] 30-24526
1. Prayers. I. Title.

HAMILTON, Herbert Alfred 248.3
Conversation with God; learning to pray. Nashville, Abingdon Press [1961] 93p. 61-8408 1.75
1. Prayers. 2. Meditations. I. Title.

HAMMAN, Gauthier Adalbert ed. 248.37
Early Christian prayers. Tr. [from French] by Walter Mitchell. Chicago, Regnery. [c.1961] xiii, 320p. Bibl. 61-65675 7.50
1. Prayers. 2. Christian literature, Early (Selections: Extracts, etc.) I. Title.

HAMMARBERG, Melvin A comp. 264.1
My book of prayers; a personal prayer book, compiled by Melvin A. Hammarberg [and] Clifford Ansgar Nelson. Rock Island, Ill., Augustana Press [1956] 172p. 13cm. [BV260.H25] 56-10134
1. Prayers. 2. Lord's prayer. I. Nelson, Clifford Ansgar, joint comp. II. Title.

HANEY, Thomas R. 242'.8
That nothing may be wasted, by T. R. Haney. New York, Sheed and Ward [1972] ix, 170 p. 21 cm. [BV245.H27] 72-5842 ISBN 0-8362-0501-4 5.95
1. Prayers. I. Title.

HARLOW, Samuel Ralph, 1885- 264.1
Prayers for times like these, by S. Ralph Harlow. New York, Association press, 1942. ix, 108 p. 19 1/2 cm. [BV245.H3] 43-1037
1. Prayers. I. Title.

HARMS, John W 264.1
Prayer in the market place. St. Louis, Mo., Bethany Press [1958] 96p. 21cm. [BV250.H37] 58-10867
1. Prayers. I. Title.

HARRELL, Costen J. 264.
In the school of prayer; a book of private devotions for young people, by Costen J. Harrell ... Nashville, Tenn., Cokesbury press, 1929. ix, 132 p. 20 cm. "Devotional books of highest merit": p. 131-132. [BV260.H3] 29-2927
1. Prayers. I. Title.

HAVEN, Robert Marshall, 1926- 242.4
Look at us, Lord. Photos. by James R. Finney. Design by Nancy R. Bozeman. Nashville, Abingdon Press [1969] [96] p. illus. 24 cm. [BV245.H34] 69-19736 4.95
1. Prayers. I. Finney, James R., illus. II. Title.

HEAD, David. 248.37
Shout for joy; a book of prayers faintly echoing the voices of seraphim and cherubim and thrones, dominions, virtues and powers, principalities, angels and archangels, the saints in light, and the great High Priest that is passed into the heavens. New York, Macmillan, 1962 [c1961] 156 p. 28 cm. [[BV260]] A62
1. Prayers. I. Title.

HEDGES, Sidney George, 1897- 200
Prayers and thoughts from world religions [by] Sid G. Hedges. Richmond, Va., John Knox Press [1972, c1970] 181 p. 21 cm. First published in 1970 under title: With one voice. [BL560.H4 1972] 72-1875 ISBN 0-8042-2500-1 4.95
1. Prayers. 2. Meditations. I. Title.

HENRY, Matthew, 1662-1714. 249
Prayers in Scripture expressions; for the use of families. To which are annexed, a number of prayers in other language, upon most occasions. By the Rev. Matthew Henry ... Wilmington [Del.] Printed by James Adams, 1786. x, 11-204 p. 17 cm. [BV255.H45] 32-15463
1. Prayers. I. Title.

*HERHOLD, Robert M. 248.3
Freewheeling; ----meditations [by] Robert M. Herhold. Design by Jan Herhold [and] introduction [by] Joseph Sittler. Palo Alto, Calif. New Being, [1974]. 124 p. illus 21 cm. [BV284] 3.95 (pbk.)
1. Prayers. I. Title.

HERZEL, Catherine B., comp. 242.8
Prayers of the people of God, by Catherine Herzel. Philadelphia, Fortress Press [1967] 90 p. 18 cm. [BV245.H4] 67-19038
1. Prayers. I. Title.

HEUSS, John, 1908- comp. 264.1
A book of prayers. New York, Morehouse-Gorham Co. [1957] 96p. 19cm. [BV260.H45] 57-5622
1. Prayers. I. Title.

HILBURN, May Stafford 248.37
One hundred short prayers. New York, 34 W. 33 St., Macoy Pub. & Masonic Supply Co. [1963] unpaged. 16cm. 63-15810 1.50 bds.,
1. Prayers. I. Title.

HILLIS, Newell Dwight, 1858-1929. 264.1
After-sermon prayers of Newell Dwight Hillis. New York, Chicago [etc.] Fleming H. Revell company [c1930] 109 p. 18 1/2 cm. [BV250.H5] 30-11049
1. Prayers. I. Title.

HOH, Paul J. 248
Little children, come unto me [by] Paul J. Hoh. Philadelphia, Pa., The United Lutheran publication house [c1927] 63 p. 15 1/2 cm. Prayers for children. [BV265.H6] 27-6826
1. Prayers. I. Title.

HOLLINGS, Michael. 242'.8
It's me, O Lord! New prayers for every day, by Michael Hollings and Etta Gullick. Illustrated by Paul Shuttleworth. [1st ed.] Garden City, N.Y., Doubleday, 1973. 159 p. illus. 22 cm. [BV245.H57 1973] 73-79069 ISBN 0-385-04141-1 4.95
1. Prayers. I. Gullick, Etta, joint author. II. Title.

*HOLLINGS, Michael. 242'.8
The one who listens; a book of prayers [compiled by] Michael Hollings & Etta Gullick. New York, Morehouse-Barlow [1973? c.1971] ix, 194 p. 18 cm. [BV245] ISBN 0-8192-4037-0 pap., 2.75
1. Prayers. I. Gullick, Etta, joint comp. II. Title.

HOWARD, Philip Eugene, 1870-
A prayer before the lesson, for superintendents and teachers in the Sunday-school and in the quiet hour at home, by Philip E. Howard. Philadelphia, The Sunday school times company [c1911] iv, 153 p. 16 cm. $0.50. 11-10356
I. Title.

HOWELL, Alexander, Rutherford, comp. 264.1
Church prayers for war-time, for use in Presbyterian and other churches, adapted and composed by the Rev. A. R. Howell ... London, Oxford university press, H. Milford [1941] viii, 83, [1] p. 17 cm. "Published 1940. Reprinted 1941." "Sources": p. [vi] [BV283.W3H6] 44-38733
1. Prayers. I. Title.

HOYLAND, John Somervill, 1887- 264.1
A book of prayers for youth, by J. S. Hoyland. New York, Association press 1939. 122 p. 19 1/2 cm. "Originally published in Great Britain under the title: A book of prayers written for use in an Indian college." "First American edition, November, 1939." [BV283.C7H6] 40-9267
1. Prayers. I. Title.

HUMPHREYS, George W. 264.1
To a listening heart, by George W. Humphreys, D.D. Sunbury, Pa., Item publishing company, 1940. 80 p. 24 cm. "First edition printed, January, 1940." [BV250.H8] 40-8896
1. Prayers. I. Title.

HUNT, Cecil, 1902- comp. 264.1
Uncommon prayers. American ed. arr, by John Wallace Suter. Greenwich, Conn., Seabury Press, 1955. 182p. 20cm. [BV245.H78] 55-6633
1. Prayers. I. Suter, John Wallace, 1890- II. Title.

[HUSTON, Martha Elizabeth] 264.
Guidance in prayer; suggestive forms of prayer for young people's societies, prepared by M. E. H., with an introduction by J. R. Miller, D.D. Philadelphia, Presbyterian board of publication and Sabbath school work, 1895. 96 p. 16 cm. [BV245.H8] 46-43314
1. Prayers. I. Title.

HUXHOLD, Harry N. 264'.1
Open the meeting with prayer. Rev. by Harry N. Huxhold. St. Louis, Concordia Pub. House [1973] 136 p. 16 cm. First ed. by A. Doerffler. [BV250.H85 1973] 73-156263 ISBN 0-570-03147-8
1. Prayers. I. Doerffler, Alfred, 1884- ed. Open the meeting with prayer. II. Title.

INTERNATIONAL Consultation on English Texts. 264'.1
Prayers we have in common : agreed liturgical texts / prepared by the International Consultation on English Texts. 2d rev. ed. Philadelphia : Fortress Press, 1975. 28 p. ; 22 cm. [BV236.I57 1975] 75-311125 ISBN 0-8006-1207-8 pbk. : 1.25
1. Prayers. 2. Creeds. I. Title.

[JARVIS, Mary Caroline] 1840- comp. 264.08
The services of the Protestant Episcopal church in the United States of America, as ordered by the bishops, during the civil war ... New York, Hatch & co., 1864. [136] p. 22 x 19 cm. Text lithographed from manuscript. Edited by Rev. A. H. Vinton from material compiled by Mary Caroline Jarvis. "For the benefit of the U. S. Sanitary commission." [BX5940.J3] 38-29425
1. Prayers. 2. U. S.—Hist.—Civil war—Religious life, etc. I. Protestant Episcopal church in the U. S. A. Liturgy and ritual. II. Vinton, Alexander Hamilton, 1807-1881, ed. III. Title.

JERPHAGNON, Lucien, 1921- 242'.8
Prayers for impossible days / Paul Geres [i.e. L. Jerphagnon] ; [translated by Ingalill H. Hjelm]. Philadelphia : Fortress Press, c1976. vi, 58 p. ; 17 cm. A translation of selections from the author's Prieres pour les jours intenables. [BV260.J35213] 75-36442 ISBN 0-8006-1214-0 pbk. : 1.95
1. Prayers. I. Title.

JOHN Paul II, Pope, 1920- 264'.02013
Prayers of Pope John Paul II / Karol Wojtyla ; edited by John F. McDonald. New York : Crossroad, 1982. 104 p. ; 21 cm. Includes index. [BV245.J62 1982] 19 82-72495 ISBN 0-8245-0537-9 (pbk.) : 5.95
1. Prayers. I. McDonald, John F. II. Title.

JOHNSON, Lois Walfrid. 242
Songs for silent moments : prayers for daily living / Lois Walfrid Johnson. Minneapolis : Augsburg Pub. House, c1980. 128 p. : ill. ; 18 cm. [BV245.J63] 19 79-54115 ISBN 0-8066-1765-9 (pbk.) : 2.50
1. Prayers. I. Title.

JOHNSON, Samuel, 1709-1784. 264'.1
Doctor Johnson's prayers / edited by Elton Trueblood. Folcroft, Pa. : Folcroft Library Editions, 1976. p. cm. Reprint of the 1947 ed. published by SCM Press, London. [BV260.J55 1976] 76-25954 ISBN 0-8414-8580-1 lib.bdg. : 10.00
1. Prayers. I. Trueblood, David Elton, 1900- II. Title. III. Title: Prayers.

JOHNSON, Samuel, 1709-1784. 264.1
Doctor Johnson's prayers; introduction by Elton Trueblood. Stanford University, Calif., J. L. Delkin [c1945] 2 p. l., vii-xxxii, 68 p., 1 l. 18 1/2 cm. "350 copies." [BV260.J55] 46-1831
1. Prayers. I. Trueblood, David Elton, 1900- ed. II. Title.

JOHNSON, Samuel, 1709-1784. 264.1
Doctor Johnson's prayers; ed. by Elton Trueblood. New York, Harper [1947] xxxv, 66 p. 16 cm. [BV260.J55 1947] 47-5956
1. Prayers. I. Trueblood, David Elton, 1900- ed. II. Title.

JONES, James Archibald, 1911-1966 264.05
Prayers for the people; a memorial collection of pulpit prayers [by] Jomes A. Jones. Richmond, Knox [1968, c1967] 127p. port. 24cm. [BV250.J59] 67-31322 4.00 bds.,
1. Prayers. I. Title.

JONES, Jenkin Lloyd, 1843- 264.
1918.
Prayers, by Jenkin Lloyd Jones. Boston, Mass., The Beacon press, inc. [c1927] xii, 120 p. 20 cm. [BV250.J6] 28-313
1. Prayers. I. Title.

JONES, Jessie Mae (Orton). 290.82
comp.
This is the way; prayers and precepts from world religions. Illustrated by Elizabeth Orton Jones. New York, Viking Press, 1951. 62 p. illus. 23 x 26 cm. [BL560.J6] 51-13305
1. Prayers. 2. Religious literature (Selections: Extracts, etc.) I. Title.

JOWETT, John Henry, 1864- 264.
1923.
Yet another day; a prayer for every day in the year [by] J. H. Jowett. [New York, Chicago, etc.] F. H. Revell company [1906] [191] p. 16 1/2 cm. [BV260.J7] 6-41052
1. Prayers. 2. Calendars. I. Title.

KADEL, William H 264.1
Prayers for every need. Richmond, John Knox Press [1957] 167p. 16cm. [BV260.K2] 57-11747
1. Prayers. I. Title.

KANABAY, Donald. 242
Prayers for the self-sufficient; the negative approach to God [by] Don Kanabay. Chicago, Regnery [1968] vi, 39 p. 22 cm. [BL2777.P7K3] 68-31465 1.95
1. Prayers. I. Title.

KAUFFMAN, Donald T ed. 248.37
A treasury of great prayers. Donald T. Kauffman, editor. Westwood, N.J., Revell [1964] 62 p. 17 cm. (A Revell inspirational classic) [BV245.K3] 64-20191
1. Prayers. I. Title.

KENSETH, Arnold. 248'.8
Prayers for worship leaders / Arnold Kenseth and Richard P. Unsworth. Philadelphia : Fortress Press, c1978. 128 p. ; 22 cm. [BV250.K46] 77-15249 ISBN 0-8006-1331-7 pbk. : 3.95
1. Prayers. I. Unsworth, Richard P., joint author. II. Title.

KIERKEGAARD, Soren Aabye, 264.1
1813-1855
The prayers of Kierkegaard, ed., new interpretation of his life and thought, by Perry D. LeFevre. Chicago, Univ. of Chic. Pr. [1963, c.1956] ix, 244p. 21cm. (Phoenix bks. P131) Bibl. 1.75 pap.,
1. Prayers. I. Title.

KIERKEGAARD, Soren Aabye, 264.1
1813-1855.
The prayers of Kierkegaard, edited and with a new interpretation of his life and thought, by Perry D. LeFevre. Chicago, University of Chicago Press [1956] ix, 244p. 23cm. Bibliography: p. 243-[245] [BV260.K5] 56-11000
1. Prayers. I. Title.

KIERKEGAARD, Soren Aabye, 1813-
1855.
The prayers of Kierkegaard. Edited and with a new interpretation of his life and thought, by Perry D. LeFevre. Chicago, University of Chicago Press [1963] ix, 244 p. (Phoenix books, P131) Includes bibliography. 68-336
1. Prayers. I. LeFevre, Perry D., ed. II. Title.

KIERKEGAARD, Soren Aabye, 1813-
1855.
The prayers of Kierkegaard. Edited and with a new interpretation of his life and thought, by Perry D. LeFevre. Chicago, University of Chicago Press [1963] ix, 244 p. (Phoenix books, P131) Includes bibliography. 68-336
1. Prayers. I. LeFevre, Perry D., ed. II. Title.

KLOS, Sarah. 264'.13
Prayers alone/together. Philadelphia, Fortress Press [1970] vii, 87 p. 21 cm. [BV245.K55 1970] 71-117977 2.95
1. Prayers. I. Title.

KLUG, Ron. 242'.8
Following Christ : prayers from the Imitation of Christ in the language of today / Ronald Klug ; illustrated by Kathy Counts. St. Louis, Mo. : Concordia Pub. House, c1981. 63 p. : ill. ; 21 cm. [BV237.K58] 19 80-25260 ISBN 0-570-03826-X (pbk.) : 3.50
1. Prayers. I. Imitatio Christi. II. Title.

KREBS, Joseph Aloysius.
Devotions and prayers for the sick room; with an appendix containing prayers and devotional exercises for the use of religious sick-nurses ... New York, Cincinnati [etc.[Benziger bros., 1900 [1899] 247 p. 16 degree Feb
I. Title.

LARSSON, Flora. 242'.8
Between you & me, Lord : prayer-conversations with God / Flora Larsson. Wheaton, Ill. : H. Shaw Publishers, 1976, c1975. 105 p. : ill. ; 18 cm. [BV245.L27] 76-1341 ISBN 0-87788-062-X pbk. : 1.45
1. Prayers. I. Title.

LARSSON, Raymond Ellsworth, 264.1
1901- ed.
Saints at prayer; a chronological collection of prayers since the birth of theLord Jesus Christ by the saints, with extracts from their writings on prayer, compiled and edited by Raymond E. F. [!] Larsson. New York, Coward-McCann, inc., 1942. xvii, 283, [1] p. 21 cm. [Full name: Raymond Edward Ellsworth Larsson] [BV245.L3] 42-3562
1. Prayers. I. Title.

LASANCE, Francis Xavier.
With God; a book of prayers and reflections, by Rev. F. X. Lasance ... New York, Cincinnati [etc.] Benziger brothers, 1911. 911 p. front., plates. 15 cm. 11-30334 1.25
I. Title.

LASANCE, Francis Xavier.
With God; a book of prayers and reflections, by Rev. F. X. Lasance ... New York, Cincinnati [etc.] Benziger brothers, 1911. 911 p. front., plates. 15 cm. 11-30334 1.25
I. Title.

LASANCE, Francis Xavier, 242
1860- ed.
With saints and sages; a book of reflections and prayers, compiled and edited by Rev. F. X. Lasance ... New York, Cincinnati [etc.] Benziger brothers, 1928. xxxix, 796 p. front., pl. 16 cm. [BX2177.L33] 29-1307
I. Title.

LAW, Virginia W., comp. 242'.8
Come on, let's pray! Prayers for personal and family worship. Compiled by Virginia Law. Edited by Ronald Patterson. [Nashville] Upper Room [1973] 96 p. 16 cm. [BV245.L33] 72-96026
1. Prayers. I. Title.

LAZ, Medard. 242'.8
Lift up my spirit, Lord! / By Medard Laz. N[ew] Y[ork] : Paulist Press, c1977. vi, 89 p. ; 18 cm. (Emmaus books) [BV245.L36] 76-24444 ISBN 0-8091-1991-9 pbk. : 1.45
1. Prayers. I. Title.

LEAVENS, Robert French, 264.1
1878-
Let us pray [by] Robert French Leavens ... Mills College. Calif. Eucalypus press 1939 [58] p., 1 l. 19 cm. "A limited edition of 350 copies." [BV283.C7L4] 39-19530
1. Prayers. 2. Universities and colleges—Prayers. I. Title.

LEWIS, Frederick White, 248.37
1873-
Prayers that are different, Grand Rapids, Eerdmans [1964] 166 p. 22 cm. [BV245.L47] 64-16583
1. Prayers. 2. Pastoral prayers. I. Title.

LUTHER, Martin, 1483- 242.8'04'1
1546.
Luther's prayers. Edited by Herbert F. Brokering. Minneapolis, Augsburg Pub. House [1967] 120 p. 17 cm. [BV260.L76] 67-25366
1. Prayers. 2. Lutheran Church — Prayer-books and devotions. I. Brokering, Herbert F., ed. II. Title.

LUTZE, Karl E. 242
Forgive our forgettings, Lord! Reflections on gifts and promises [by] Karl E. Lutze. St. Louis, Concordia Pub. House [1972] 94 p. illus. 21 cm. [BV245.L87] 72-81921 pap. 1.50
1. Prayers. I. Title.

MCCARTER, Neely Dixon, 242'.8
1929-
Help me understand, Lord : prayer responses to the Gospel of Mark / by Neely Dixon McCarter. 1st ed. Philadelphia : Westminster Press, c1978. 121 p. ; 19 cm. [BS2585.4.M25] 77-14511 ISBN 0-664-24180-8 pbk. : 4.95
1. Bible. N.T. Mark—Devotional literature. 2. Prayers. I. Bible. N.T. Mark. English. New English. 1978. II. Title.

MCCAULEY, Leon, ed. 264.1
The book of prayers, compiled for Protestant worship. Edited by Leon and Elfrieda McCauley. Introd. by Harry Emerson Fosdick. New York, Crown Publishers [1954] viii, 184p. 18cm. [BV245.M22] 54-12401
1. Prayers. I. McCauley, Elfrieda, joint ed. II. Title.

MCCAULEY, Leon, ed. 264.1
The book of prayers, compiled for Protestant worship. Edited by Leon and Elfrieda McCauley. Introd. by Harry Emrson Fosdick. [New York, Dell Pub. Co., 1954] 184p. 17cm. (A Dell first edition, 38) [BV245.M22 1954a] 54-8870
1. Prayers. I. McCauley, Elfrieda, joint ed. II. Title.

MCCOMB, Samuel, 1864- ed. 264.
A book of modern prayers; a collection of prayers and readings by modern writers, with an introductory essay on the meaning and value of prayer, compiled and edited by Samuel McComb, D.D. New York, London [etc.] Longmans, Green and co., 1926. xiii, 158 p. 19 1/2 cm. [BV245.M25] 27-268
1. Prayers. I. Title.

MACDUFF, John Ross, 1818- 249
1895.
Family prayers. By John R. Macduff... New York, R. Carter and brothers, 1878. 202 2 l., [0]-66 p. 17 1/2 cm. "The faithful promiser": 2 l., [0]-68 p. at end. [BV255.M2] 30-31443
1. Prayers. I. Title.

[MACDUFF, John Ross, 1818- 264.1
1895.
The morning watches, and Night watches. By the author of "The faithful promiser." New York, R. Carter & brothers, 1853. viii, [0]-132, 130 p. 17 1/2 cm. [BV260.M2 1853] 39-32780
1. Prayers. I. Title. II. Title: Night watches.

[MACDUFF, John Ross,] 1818- 264.
1895.
The morning watches and night watches. By the author of "The faithful promiser." New York, R. Carter & brothers, 1856. viii, [9]-132, 130 p. 17 1/2 cm. [BV260.M2 1856] 35-37808
1. Prayers. I. Title.

MACDUFF, John Ross, 1818- 264.
1895.
The morning watches and night watches. By the Rev. J. R. Macduff... New York, R. Carter & brothers, 1873. 128, 127 p. 13 1/2 cm. Preface dated 1851. [BV260.M2] 10-28390
1. Prayers. I. Title.

MCELROY, Paul Simpson, 242.8
1902- comp.
Prayers and graces of thanksgiving. With illus. by Stanley Clough. Mount Vernon, N.Y., Peter Pauper Press [1966] 62 p. illus. 19 cm. [BV245.M43] 67-2283
1. Prayers. 2. Grace at meals. I. Title.

MACGREGOR, Geddes. 242.2
So help me God; a calendar of quick prayers for half-skeptics. New York, Morehouse-Barlow Co. [1970] 95 p. 19 cm. [BV245.M44] 72-97263 ISBN 0-8192-1104-4
1. Prayers. I. Title.

MCKEE, Elmore McNeill, 264.1
1896- comp.
Communion with God; prayers of reality for chapel, pastoral and private use, compiled by Elmore McNeill McKee...with an introduction by Ernest Fremont Tittle... New York, R. Long & R. R. Smith, inc., 1932. xiv, 198 p. 18 1/2 cm. [BV245.M45] 32-3574
1. Prayers. I. Title.

MACLEOD, Earle Henry. 248.37
Prayers for everyone, to meet every need. Grand Rapids, Zondervan Pub. House [1962] 84p. 18cm. [BV260.M25] 62-16806
1. Prayers. I. Title.

MACLEOD, Flora Abigail.
The vigil of hope; thoughts and prayers for mothers during the months of expectation, by Flora Abigail Macleod... London, New York [etc.] Longmans, Green and co., 1923. xi, 77, [1] p. front. 17 cm. $1.25. [BV4847.M25] 23-11766
I. Title.

MAERTENS, Thierry, 1921- 242'.8 s
Prayers in community / Thierry Maertens, Marguerite DeBilde ; [translated by Jerome J. DuCharme]. Notre Dame, Ind. : Fides Publishers, [1974] x, 145 p. ; 20 cm. (Contemporary prayer ; v. 1) [BV246.L5813 vol. 1] 264'.13 74-194397 ISBN 0-8190-0446-4 : 2.95
1. Prayers. I. DeBilde, Marguerite, joint author. II. Title. III. Series: Livre de la priere. English. ; vol. 1.

MANK, Charles, 1902- comp. 264.1
My favorite prayer; collected from notables chiefly of screen, radio, and television, by Chaw Mank. Introd. by Leo Louis Martello. [1st ed.] New York, Exposition Press [1956] 76p. 21cm. [BV245.M46] 56-9561
1. Prayers. I. Title.

MANSCHRECK, Clyde Leonard, 264.1
1917- comp.
Prayers of the Reformers. [Philadelphia] Muhlenberg Press [1958] 183p. 18cm. [BV245.M465] 58-8944
1. Prayers. I. Title.

MARKOWITZ, Sidney L., 248.37
1905- comp.
Prayer for a day; prayers for all occasions and for people of all denominations. Based upon the Psalms, the Prophets, and ancient supplications. New York, Citadel [c.1964] xiii, 81p. 21cm. (C174) 64-21893 1.00 pap.,
1. Prayers. I. Title.

MARSHALL, Peter, 1902-1949. 264.1
Prayers; edited and with prefaces by Catherine Marshall. New York, McGraw-Hill [1954] 243 p. illus. 21 cm. [BV245.M48] 54-11762
1. Prayers.

MARTIN, Francis A. 242'.8
Prayers from where you are / Francis A. Martin. Waco, Tex. : Word Books, [1975] 96 p. : ill. ; 23 cm. [BV245.M482] 75-10084 2.95
1. Prayers. I. Title.

MARTINEAU, James, 1805-1900.
Home prayers, with two services for public worship, by James Martineau. 4th impression ... London, New York [etc.] Longmans, Green, and co., 1913. ix p., 1 l., 139, [1] p. 20 cm. A 22
1. Prayers. I. Title.

MARTINEAU, James, 1805-1900.
Prayers in the congregation and in college, by James Martineau. London, New York [etc.] Longmans, Green & co., 1911. 64 p. 19 1/2 cm. A 22
1. Prayers. I. Title.

MARVIN, Dwight Edwards. 264.
Fireside prayers, by Dwight E. Marvin. Summit, N.J., 1921. 68 p. 19 cm. [BV260.M35] 21-15197
I. Title.

MARVIN, Dwight Edwards. 264.
Fireside prayers, by Dwight E. Marvin. Summit, N.J., 1921. 68 p. 19 cm. [BV260.M35] 21-15197
I. Title.

MARVIN, Dwight Edwards, 1851- 248
Abba, Father, a book of prayers for private devotion. Rev. and enl. ed. [By] Dwight Edwards Marvin. Norwell, Mass., The Ross bookmakers, 1938. 7 p. l., 5-183 p. front. 25 cm. "This edition is limited to three hundred and thirty copies of which this is number 169." Published previously, 1932, under title: Alone with God; a book of prayers for private devotion. [BV260.M345 1938] 39-2586

1. Prayers. I. Title.

MARVIN, Dwight Edwards, 1851- 248
Alone with God: a book of prayers for private devotion [by] Dwight Edwards Marvin. Norwell, Mass., The Ross bookmakers, 1932. 145 p. front. 22 1/2 cm. "Four hundred copies of this book have been printed of which this is number 376." [BV260.M345] 33-1601
1. Prayers. I. Title.

MARY Loretta, Sister, A.P.B. 242.8'02
My thing. Liguori, Mo., Liguorian Pamphlets and Books [1970] 95 p. illus. 18 cm. Poem. [BV245.M483] 75-130661 1.50
1. Prayers. I. Title.

MARY save us, 232.9318
prayers written by Lithuanian prisoners in Northern Siberia; tr. by Kestutis A. Trimakas. New York, Paulist Press [c.1960] 71p. facsims. 15cm. .50 pap.,

MATHENY, E. Stacy. 264.
Patriotic devotion, Prayers offered at the opening of the daily sessions of the Senate during the 85th General assembly of the state of Ohio, 1923 by the Rev. E. Stacy Matheny, chaplain. Columbus, The F. J. Heer printing company, 1923. 86 p. illus. 15 x 8 cm. [BV280.M35] 24-15956
I. Title.

MBITI, John S. 299'.6
The prayers of African religion / John S. Mbiti. Maryknoll, N.Y. : Orbis Books, 1976, c1975. p. cm. [BV245.M484 1976] 75-42519 ISBN 0-88344-394-5
1. Prayers. 2. Africa—Religion. I. Title.

MEAD, Frank Spencer, 1898- 242'.8
Talking with God : prayers for today / edited by Frank S. Mead. 1st ed. Philadelphia : A. J. Holman Co., c1976. 96 p. ; 19 cm. [BV245.T26] 75-37620 ISBN 0-87981-052-1 : 3.95
1. Prayers. I. Mead, Frank Spencer, 1898- II. Title.

MERCHANT, Jane. 242
Think about these things. New York, Abingdon Press [1956] 96p. 16cm. Meditations in poetry and prayer, with selections from the Bible. [BV260.M38] 56-8742
1. Prayers. I. Title.

MEYER, Frederick Brotherton, 1847-1929. 242
My daily prayer; a short supplication for every day in the year. [Westwood, N. J.] Revell [1957] 63p. 17cm. (Revell's inspirational classics) [BV260.M4 1957] 57-12366
1. Prayers. 2. Devotional calendars. I. Title.

MEYER, Lucy Jane (Rider) 1849-1922, comp.
Some little prayers, by Lucy Rider Meyer. Cincinnati, Jennings and Graham; New York, Eaton and Mains [c1907] 106 p. 16 1/2 cm. [BV260.M43] 8-6096
1. Prayers. I. Title.

MICKLEM, Caryl. 248'.8
As good as your word : a third book of contemporary prayers / by Caryl Micklem and Roger Tomes ; edited by Caryl Micklem. Grand Rapids : Eerdmans, c1975. p. cm. Includes index. [BV245.M489] 76-9048 ISBN 0-8028-1644-4
1. Prayers. I. Tomes, Roger, joint author. II. Title.

MILES, O. Thomas 242.8
Dialogues with God; prayers for day-to-day living, by O. Thomas Miles. Grand Rapids, Eerdmans [1966] 185p. 21cm. [BV245.M49] 66-22947 2.25
1. Prayers. I. Title.

[MILLER, Daniel] b.1843. 264.
Sweet incense: prayers for various occasions in life ... Reading, Pa., D. Miller, 1894. 84 p. front. (form) 15 cm. [BV245.M5] 46-42440
1. Prayers. I. Title.

MILLER, Samuel Howard, 1900- 264.1
Prayers for daily use. [1st ed.] New York, Harper [1957] 128p. 18cm. [BV260.M49] 57-9880
1. Prayers. I. Title.

MILNER-WHITE, Eric, 1884- ed. 264.1
Daily prayer, compiled by Eric Milner-White ... and G. W. Briggs ... London, Oxford university press, H. Milford, 1941. viii, 188 p. 19 cm. [BV245.M56] 43-199
1. Prayers. I. Briggs, George Wallace, 1875- joint ed. II. Title.

MOLTON, Warren Lane. 242
Bruised reeds. Photos. by David Mark Breed. Valley Forge [Pa.] Judson Press [1970] 112 p. illus. 21 cm. [BV245.M58] 70-103391 2.50
1. Prayers. I. Breed, David Mark, illus. II. Title.

MOONEY, Patrick. 242'.802
Praise to the Lord of the morning! : Three prayer experiences / Patrick Mooney ; with photography by the author. Notre Dame, Ind. : Ave Maria Press, c1976. 127 p. : ill. ; 21 cm. [BV260.M64] 76-16673 ISBN 0-87793-116-X pbk. : 2.95
1. Prayers. I. Title.

MORE contemporary 242.8'03
prayers; prayers on fifty-two themes, by Anthony Coates [and others] Edited by Caryl Micklem. [1st U.S. ed.] Grand Rapids, Eerdmans [1970] ix, 117 p. 22 cm. [BV245.M595] 79-127634 3.50
1. Prayers. I. Micklem, Caryl, ed. II. Coates, Anthony.

MORROW, Abbie Clemens.
Prayers for public worship, private devotion, personal ministry, by Abbie C. Morrow ... New York, M. E. Munson [1902] 195 p. 19 1/2cm. 2-11637
1. Prayers. I. Title.

MORTIMER, Frederic Edward, comp. 264.
The pilgrim's path; a book of prayers for busy people, with instructions and illustrations, comp. by Frederic E. Mortimer ... Jersey City, N.J., Guild of St. Mark [c1922] iii, [1], 122 p. incl. front., illus. 12 cm. "105th to 125th thousand." [BX5947.P7M6 1922] 22-24885
I. Title.

MORTIMER, Frederic Edward, comp.
The pilgrim's path. A book of prayers for busy people. With instructions ... New York, R. W. Crothers. Jersey City, N.J., St. Mark's guild [1901] 2 p. l., 104 p. illus. 24°. 13th to 23d thousand. 1-31647
I. Title.

MORTON, Richard Knowles, 1904- 264.1
A book of prayers for young people and all who are interested in them (by] Rev. Richard K. Morton ... Nashville, Cokesbury press [c1935] 146 p., 1 l. 16 cm. [BV283.Y6M6] 35-38288
1. Prayers. 2. Youth—Prayer-books and devotions—English. I. Title.

MYERS, Ernest W 1906- 248.37
Prayers for laymen by a layman. [1st ed.] New York, Greenwich Book Publishers [1959] 85p. 21cm. [BV260.M9] 59-8652
1. Prayers. I. Title.

NEW Manual of private 264.
devotions ... The 3d American ed. New-York: Printed and sold by T. & J. Swords, no. 160 Pearl-street. 1817. 371 p. 18 1/2 cm. "The first American edition ... appeared in Charleston, South-Carolina, in 1810, from the press of Mr. John Hoff."--Advertisement. [BV245.M47 1817] 46-43312
1. Prayers.
Contents omitted.

NEW manual of private 264.
devotions in three parts. Containing prayers for families and private persons: offices, of humiliation, for the sick, for women, for the holy communion: with occasional prayers. Corrected and enlarged by the Right Reverend Levi Silliman Ives ... The 3d New York ed. To which is added, A friendly visit to the house of mourning. By the Rev. Richard Cecil ... New-York, T. and J. Swords, 1831. xv, [13]-368 p. front. 19 cm. "The first American edition ... appeared in Charleston, South-Carolina, in 1810, from the press of Mr. John Hoff."--Advertisement to the 2d New-York ed. [BV245.M47 1831] 46-43323
1. Prayers. I. Ives, Levi Silliman, 1797-1867, ed. II. Cecil, Richard, 1748-1810.

NEWTON, Joseph Fort, 1876- 264.
Altar stairs; a little book of prayer, by Joseph Fort Newton. New York, The Macmillan company, 1928. xi p., 1 l., 205 p. 15 1/2 cm. [BV245.N5] 28-23567
1. Prayers. I. Title.

NEWTON, Joseph Fort, 1876- 264.1
Altar stairs; a little book of prayer, by Joseph Fort Newton. New ed. New York, The Macmillan company, 1937. xii, p., 1 l., 209 p. 15 1/2 cm. [BV245.N5 1937] 37-20297
1. Prayers. I. Title.

NOLA, Alfonso Maria di, comp. 291.3
The prayers of man, from primitive peoples to present times. Ed. by Patrick O'Connor. Tr. by Rex Benedict. New York, I. Obolensky [c.1961] 544p. 25cm. 60-13420 8.50
1. Prayers. 2. Cultus. I. O'Connor, Patrick, 1925- ed. II. Title.

NOLA, Alfonso Maria di, comp. 291.3
The prayers of man, from primitive peoples to present times. Edited by Patrick O'Connor. Translations by Rex Benedict. New York, I. Obolensky [1961] 544p. 25cm. [BL560.N6] 60-13420
1. Prayers. 2. Cultus. I. O'Connor, Patrick, 1925- ed. II. Title.

NOYES, Morgan Phelps, 1891- comp. 264.1
Prayers for services; a manual for leaders of worship, compiled and edited by Morgan Phelps Noyes. New York, London, C. Scribner's sons, 1934. xvi p., 3 l., 5-297 p. 21 cm. Blank page "For the insertion of additional prayers" (297) "Sources": p. 273-276. [BV250.N6] 34-4557
1. Prayers. I. Title.

OGLESBY, Stuart Roscoe, 1888- 264.1
Prayers for all occasions; a book of short prayers for everyday life, by Stuart R. Oglesby. Richmond, Va., John Knox press [c1940] 187 p. 16 cm. [BV245.O35] 40-10369
1. Prayers. I. Title.

OOSTERHUIS, Huub. 242.8
Your word is near; contemporary Christian prayers. Translated by N. D. Smith. Westminster, Md., Newman Press [1968] xii, 152 p. 22 cm. Translation of Bid om vrede. [BV260.O613] 68-20848
1. Prayers. I. Title.

ORCHARD, William Edwin, 1877- 264.
The temple; a book of prayers, by the Rev. W. E. Orchard, D. D., with an introduction by Dr. Frank Crane. New York, E. P. Dutton & co. [c1918] xviii, 167, [1] p. 16 cm. [BV260.O8] 18-6037
I. Title.

ORLEANS, Ilo. 248.373
Within Thy hand; my poem book of prayers. Illustrated by Siegmund Forst. New York, Union of American Hebrew Congregations [1961] 70p. illus. 24cm. [PS3529.R475W5] 61-15353
I. Title.

ORLEANS, Ilo Louis 248.373
Within Thy hand; my poem book of prayers. Illus. by Siegmund Forst. NewYork, Union of Amer. Hebrew Congregations [c.1961] 70p. illus. (pt. col.) 61-15353 2.95
I. Title.

OXENDEN, Ashton, bp., 1808-1892. 264.
Prayers for private use. By the Rev. Ashton Oxenden ... New York, A. D. F. Randolph, 1867. 77 p. 13 cm. On cover: A book of private prayers. [BV260.O9] 35-37807
1. Prayers. I. Title.

OXENHAM, John, pseud. 248
First prayers for children; a manual of help for parents, by John Oxenham ... and Roderic Dunkerley ... New York, Chicago [etc.] Fleming H. Revell company [c1929] 80 p. 16 1/2 cm. [Real name: William Arthur Dunkerley] [BV265.O9] 30-3801
1. Prayers. I. Dunkerley, Roderic, joint author. II. Title.

PAGE, Herman, bp., 1866- 264.
Prayers, comp. and adapted from ancient and modern sources, by Herman Page ... Gilbert W. Laidlaw ... 5th ed.--rev. and enl. New York, E. S. Gorham, 1918. 70 p. 17 cm. [BV245.P3 1918] 18-6180
I. Laidlaw, Gilbert W., joint author. II. Title.

PAINE, Howard, comp. 248.37
Book of prayers for church and home [comp. by] Howard Paine, Bard Thompson. Philadelphia, Christian Educ. Pr. [dist. United Church, c.1962] 195p. 21cm. Bibl. 62-15845 3.00
1. Prayers. I. Thompson, Bard, 1925- joint comp. II. Title.

PARK, Charles Edwards, 1873- 264.1
Prayers. Boston. The Starr King Press [1955] 71p. 16cm. 'More than half of these prayers are taken from ... [the authors] Beginning the day, which was first published in 1922.' [BV260.P3] 55-11593
1. Prayers. I. Title.

PARKER, Theodore, 1810-1860. 264.
Prayers, by Theodore Parker. Boston, Walker, Wise and company, 1862. 2 p. l., [iii]-iv, [5]-200 p. front. (port.) 19 cm. [BV250.P3] 12-37479
1. Prayers. I. Title.

PARROTT, Bob W 242.8'07
A man talks with God, by Bob W. Parrott. [1st ed.] Dallas, Printed by Southern Methodist University Print. Dept. [1967] xi, 66 p. 20 cm. [BV260.P33] 67-30888
1. Prayers. I. Title.

PAWELZIK, Fritz, comp. 242
I lie on my mat and pray; prayers by young Africans. Illustrated by Georg Lemke. Translated by Robbins Strong. New York, Friendship Press [1964] 63 p. illus. 20 cm. A collection originally translated into German by Fritz Pawelzik and published in Wuppertal. [BV245.P34] 64-20103
1. Prayers. I. Title.

PEABODY, Francis Greenwood, 1847- 264.1
Prayers for various occasions and needs, by Francis Greenwood Peabody ... Boston and New York, Houghton Mifflin company, 1930. xi, 127 p. 18 cm. [BV245.P35] 31-3667
1. Prayers. I. Title.

PELL, Edward Leigh, 1861-
Prayers, by Edward Leigh Pell. Richmond, Va., The Harding press [c1910] 3 p. l., 9-63 p. 16 cm. 11-763 0.25
I. Title.

PELL, Edward Leigh, 1861- comp.
Prayers we love to pray, including the world's greatest prayers suitable for private devotion, selected and arranged by Edward Leigh Pell. Richmond, Va., Robert Harding company [c1909] 224 p. 20 cm. 9-31489 1.00
I. Title.

PETER Pauper Press, Mount Vernon, N. Y. 248.37
Little book of prayers. Illustrated by Jeff Hill. Mount Vernon [1960] 60p. illus. 19cm. [BV260.P45] 60-36295
1. Prayers. I. Title.

PETTY, Jo. 242'.8
Golden prayers / Jo Petty ; drawings by Martha Linbdo Heath. 1st ed. Garden City, N.Y. : Doubleday, 1980. p. cm. "A Doubleday-Galilee original." [BV245.P43] 79-7505 ISBN 0-385-15364-3 : 6.95
1. Prayers. I. Title.

PETTY, Jo. 242'.8
Golden prayers / by Jo Petty. Garden City, N.Y. : Doubleday, 1982. p. cm. "A Doubleday-Galilee book." [BV245.P43 1982] 19 82-1374 ISBN 0-385-18127-2 (pbk.) : 5.95
1. Prayers. I. Title.

PHILLIPS, E. Lee. 242'.2
Prayers for our day : morning, midday,

evening / E. Lee Phillips. Atlanta : John Knox Press, c1982. 103 p. : ill. ; 23 cm. [BV245.P46 1982] 19 81-82349 ISBN 0-8042-2583-4 (pbk.) : 7.95
1. Prayers. I. Title.

PIUS XII, Pope, 1876-1958. 248.37
Complete prayers. Translated from the original texts by Alastair Guinan. New York, Desclee Co. [1959] 175p. illus. 22cm. [BV245.P5] 59-12713
1. Prayers. I. Title.

PIUS XII, Pope, 1876-1958 264.1
Prayers. Translated from the Italian by Martin W. Schoenberg. Westminster, Md., Newman Press, 1957. 115p. 22cm. [BV264.I8P5] 57-5577
1. Prayers. I. Title.

A Pocketful of prayers for 242'.8
today's needs, moods, and circumstances / edited by Ralph L. Woods. New York : Pillar Books, 1976. 126 p. ; 18 cm. [BV245.P64] 76-16661 ISBN 0-89129-217-9 pbk. : 1.50
1. Prayers. I. Woods, Ralph Louis, 1904-

POTTEBAUM, Gerard A. 248.3
1,029 private prayers for worldly Christians [by] Gerard A. Pottebaum and Joyce Winkel. Dayton, Ohio, Pflaum Press [1968] 58 p. illus. 26 cm. (A Tree house production) [BV260.P65] 68-55960
1. Prayers. I. Winkel, Joyce, joint author. II. Title.

PRAYER and power in the 242'.88
capital / compiled by Pauline Innis. Washington, D.C. : Devon Pub. Co. ; Aurora, Ill. : Distributed by Caroline House, c1982. viii, 109 p. : ill. ; 22 cm. Includes index. [BV245.P78 1982] 19 82-156801 ISBN 0-941402-02-9 : 10.00
1. Prayers. 2. Presidents—United States—Religious life. I. Innis, Pauline B.
Publisher's address: 2700 Virginia Ave., N.W., Washington, D.C. 20037.

PRAYERS and other 264'.1
resources for public worship / [compiled by] Horton Davies, Morris D. Slifer. Nashville : Abingdon, [1976] p. cm. [BV245.P82] 76-23251 ISBN 0-687-33495-0 : 4.95
1. Prayers. I. Davies, Horton. II. Slifer, Morris D., 1904-

PRAYERS for all seasons 242'.8
/ edited by Paul S. McElroy ; with decorations by Ruth McCrea. Mount Vernon, N.Y. : Peter Pauper Press, [1975] 62 p. : ill. ; 20 cm. [BV245.P83] 75-307242 1.95
1. Prayers. I. McElroy, Paul Simpson, 1902-

PRAYERS for everyone : 242'.8
anthology compiled over thirty years / [by] Pat Lawlor. Melbourne : Hawthorn Press, 1975. 66 p. ; 22 cm. [BV245.P84] 75-317079 ISBN 0-7256-0117-5
1. Prayers. I. Lawlor, Patrick Anthony.

PRAYERS for our times / 242'.8
edited by John Cumming and Paul Burns. New York : Crossroad, 1981. p. cm. [BV245.P846 1981] 19 81-67829 ISBN 0-8245-0071-7 : 10.95 ISBN 0-8245-0107-1 (pbk.) : 4.95
1. Prayers. I. Cumming, John. II. Burns, Paul.

PRAYERS for today's 264'.13
church / edited by Dick Williams ; [foreword by Alvin N. Rogness]. 1st U.S. ed. Minneapolis : Augsburg Pub. House, 1977, c1972. 210 p. ; 22 cm. Includes index. [BV245.P85 1977] 76-27081 ISBN 0-8066-1565-6 : 4.95
1. Prayers. I. Williams, Dick, 1931-

THE Prayers I love / 242'.8
selected by David A. Redding ; cal[l]igraphy by Alice Girand ; illustrated by Sarah Blue. San Francisco, Calif. : Strawberry Hill Press, [1978] p. cm. Bibliography: p. [BV245.P853] 78-17798 ISBN 0-89407-025-8 pbk. : 5.95
1. Prayers. I. Redding, David A. II. Girand, Alice, 1938-

PRAYERS of faith / 242'.8
edited by Richard Newman. Boston : G. K. Hall, 1976. xxi, 165 p. : ill. ; 24 cm. Large print ed. [BV245.P86 1976] 76-7386 ISBN 0-8161-6368-5 lib.bdg. : 8.95
1. Prayers. 2. Sight-saving books. I. Newman, Richard.

THE prayers of the church,
a connected series of reflections on the liturgy. 1st American ed., adapted to the liturgy of the Protestant Episcopal church in the United States, with a prefatory address and occasional notes, &c. by Joseph R. Walker ... Philadelphia, W. Stavely and co.; New York, Swords, Stanford and co.; [etc., etc.] 1839. 1 p. l., xii, 215 p. 19 cm. Added t.-p., engr. 7-28734
1. Walker, Joseph R., ed.

...PRAYERS offered at daily sessions of the Assembly. [Sacramento? Calif.] California State printing office [1957] 104p. front. (port.) 15cm. At head of title: California legislature. 1957 regular session.
1. Romeis, Robert S

PUNGENT prayers / 242'.8
[edited] by Phil E. Pierce. Nashville : Abingdon, c1977. 124 p. : ill. ; 19 cm. [BV245.P93] 77-4936 ISBN 0-687-34909-5 pbk. : 3.95
1. Prayers. I. Pierce, Phil E., 1912-

QUALYLE, William Alfred, bp., 1860-
The climb to God; being a collection of pulpit and private prayers which are meant to grid the spiritual life. By William A. Quayle ... Cincinnati, Jennings and Graham; New York, Eaton and Mains [c1913] 281 p. 20 cm. 13-6299 1.00
I. Title.

QUAYLE, William Alfred, 264.
bp., 1860-1925.
The throne of grace; a volume of personal prayers, with a prelude, by William A. Quayle. New York, Cincinnati, The Methodist book concern [1919] 117 p. 15 cm. [BV245.Q3] 19-3301
1. Prayers. I. Title.

RANKIN, Isaac Ogden, 1852- 264.
Prayers and thanksgivings for a Christian year, by Isaac Ogden Rankin ... Boston, Chicago, The Pilgrim press [c1918] ix, 306 p. 18 cm. Reprinted in part from the Congregationalist and Christian world. [BV245.R3] 18-21768
I. Title.

RAUSCHENBUSCH, Walter, 242'.8
1861-1918.
For God and the people : prayers of the social awakening / by Walter Rauschenbusch. Folcroft, Pa. : Folcroft Library Editions, 1977. p. cm. Originally published in 1910 also under title: Prayers of the social awakening. Reprint of the 1910 ed. published by the Pilgrim Press, Boston. [BV245.R35 1977] 77-8615 ISBN 0-8414-7332-3 lib. bdg. : 10.00
1. Prayers. I. Title.

RAUSCHENBUSCH, Walter, 1861- 240
1918.
For God and the people; prayers of the social awakening, by Walter Rauschenbusch ... Boston, New York [etc.] The Pilgrim press [1910] 126 p. 21 cm. Ornamental borders. Published also under title: Prayers of the social awakening. [BR115.S6R37] 10-28335
1. Prayers. I. Title. II. Title: Prayers oif the social awakening.

RAUSCHENBUSCH, Walter, 1861- 240
1918.
Prayers of the social awakening, by Walter Rauschenbusch ... Boston, Chicago, The Pilgrim press [1910] 126 p. 17 cm. Published also under title: For God and the people; prayers of the social awakening. [BR115.S6R38] 21-20448
1. Prayers. I. Title.

REDDING, David A. 242
If I could pray again / David A. Redding. New rev. ed. Millbrae, Calif. : Celestial Arts, 1975. p. cm. Includes index. [BV245.R4 1975] 75-9084 ISBN 0-89087-060-8 pbk. : 3.95
1. Prayers. I. Title.

REISNER, Christian Fichthorne, 1872-
Prayers for eventide, by Christian F. Reisner. New York, Cincinnati, The Abingdon press [c1916] 79 p. 13 1/2 cm. $0.25. Printed on one side of leaf only. 16-16694
I. Title.

RHEA, Carolyn 242
My heart kneels too. New York, Grosset [c.1965] 113p. 17cm. (Family inspirational lib., 1665) [BV245.R5] 65-16921 1.50 bds.,
1. Prayers. I. Title.

ROBISON, Charles D. 242.8
Look deeply; prayers and photos., by Charles D. Robison. Valley Forge [Pa.] Judson Press [1971] 1 v. (unpaged) illus. 26 cm. [BV245.R6] 77-144084 ISBN 0-8170-0511-0
1. Prayers. I. Title.

ROSENBERGER, Mary Sue, 242'.8
1940-
"Sacraments in my refrigerator" / by Mary Sue Rosenberger. Elgin, IL : Brethren Press, [1979] p. cm. [BV245.R67] 79-502 ISBN 0-87178-769-5 pbk. : 3.95
1. Prayers. 2. Meditations. I. Title.

ROUNER, Arthur Acy. 242.8
Someone's praying, Lord [by] Arthur A. Rouner, Jr. With a foreword by James S. Stewart. Englewood Cliffs, N.J., Prentice-Hall [1970] xiii, 257 p. 25 cm. [BV245.R68] 74-105716 7.95
1. Prayers. I. Title.

ROWLINGSON, Edna V.
Leading in prayer, new prayers for women's meetings. London, Henry E. Walter [1957] 56 p. 19 cm. 67-489 '9
1. Prayers. I. Title.

RYAN, Marah Ellis (Martin) 291.8
Mrs., 1860- comp.
Pagan prayers, collected by Marah Ellis Ryan... Chicago, A. C. McClurg & co., 1913. [120] p. 18 cm. Bibliography: p. [120] [BL560.R8] 13-9783
1. Prayers. I. Title.

*SALLEE, Lynn. 242. '2
Coffee-time prayers. Grand Rapids : Baker Book House, 1976. 64p. : ill. ; 20 cm. [BV283.M7] ISBN 0-8010-8083-5 : 2.95.
1. Prayers I. Title.

SANBORN, Ruth. 242.8
Do you hear me, God? [by] Ruth and Arthayer Sanborn. Valley Forge [Pa.] Judson Press [1968] 80 p. 20 cm. [BV260.S29] 68-13605
1. Prayers. I. Sanborn, Arthayer, joint author. II. Title.

SANDLIN, John Lewis. 248.37
Graces and prayers. [Westwood, N. J.] Revell [1959] 125 p. 17 cm. [BV260.S28] 59-14957
1. Prayers. 2. Grace at meals. I. Title.

SANFORD, Don, comp. 264.1
Prayers for every occasion. Grand Rapids, Zondervan Pub. House [c1957] 121p. 16cm. [BV260.S3] 58-20214
1. Prayers. I. Title.

SCHAFFER, Ulrich, 1942- 242'.8
Greater than our hearts : prayers and reflections / Ulrich Schaffer. 1st ed. San Francisco, Calif. : Harper & Row, c1981. p. cm. [BV245.S3 1981] 19 81-47434 ISBN 0-06-067088-6 : 7.95
1. Prayers. 2. Meditations. I. Title.

SCHULLER, Robert Harold. 242'.8
Positive prayers for power-filled living / Robert H. Schuller. New York : Hawthorn Books, c1976. ix, 117 p. ; 22 cm. [BV245.S33 1976] 75-20901 ISBN 0-8015-5950-2 : 4.95
1. Prayers. I. Title.

SCOTT, John, 1921- comp. 242
Treasured volume of prayers; an anthology collected by John Scott. New York, Oak Tree Press [1970] 155 p. 22 cm. [BV245.S36] 76-104722
1. Prayers. I. Title.

SCOVIL, Elisabeth Robinson, 249
1849-
Prayers for girls, by Elisabeth Robinson Scovil ... Philadelphia, Henry Altemus company [c1924] 1 p. l., 5-64 p. 10 cm. [BV283.G5S4] 25-1738
I. Title.

SCUDDER, Delton Levis, 242'.8
1906-
A larger view; Delton L. Scudder's prayers and addresses. Edited by Austin B. Creel. Gainsville, University of Florida Foundation, 1973. xii, 131 p. 24 cm. [BV245.S38] 74-159912
1. Prayers. 2. Memorial service. I. Title.

SEAMAN, William R. 242.8'04'1
Daily prayer for family and private use, by William R. Seaman. Philadelphia, Fortress Press [1967] vi, 57 p. 18 cm. [BX8067.P7S4] 67-31233
1. Lutheran Church—Prayer-books and devotions. 2. Prayers. I. Title.

SERGIO, Lisa, 1905- ed. 248.374
Prayers of women. [1st ed.] New York, Harper & Row [1965] [BV283.W6S4] 65-10705
I. Title.

[SHEPARD, Morgan] 1865- 248
Prayers for little men & women (and other helpful verses) by "John Martin" [pseud.] with illustrations by John Rae, Harold Sichel, and Henry C. Pitz. New York, John Martin's book house, 1923. 96 p. incl. col. front., illus., plates. 19 1/2 cm. Title-page illustrated. [BV265.S5] 23-13757
I. Title.

[SHEPARD, Morgan] 1865- 248
Prayers for little men and women (and other helpful verses) by "John Martin" [pseud.] with illustrations by John Rae, Harold Sichel and Henry C. Pitz. Garden City, N.Y., Doubleday, Doran & company, inc., 1929. 96 p. incl col. front., illus., plates. 19 1/2 cm. [BV265.S5 1929] 29-6485
I. Title.

SHEPHERD, J. Barrie. 242'.2
Diary of daily prayer / J. Barrie Shepherd. Minneapolis : Augsburg Pub. House, [1975] 127 p. ; 18 cm. [BV245.S5] 74-14176 ISBN 0-8066-1459-5 pbk. : 2.95
1. Prayers. I. Title.

SHEPHERD, J. Barrie. 226'.806
A diary of prayer : daily meditations on the parables of Jesus / by J. Barrie Shepherd. 1st ed. Philadelphia : Westminster Press, c1981. 131 p. ; 21 cm. [BT375.2.S5] 19 80-27037 ISBN 0-664-24352-5 pbk. : 5.95
1. Jesus Christ—Parables—Meditations. 2. Prayers. I. Title.

SHRIGLEY, George Andrew 264.1
Cleveland, 1902- ed.
Daily prayer companion, a prayer for every day in the year, written by 366 religious leaders, compiled and edited by G. A. Cleveland Shrigley. Buffalo, Foster & Stewart Pub. Corp. [1947] xi, 371 p. 20 cm. [BV255.S53] 47-24108
1. Prayers. 2. Calendars. I. Title.

SHRIGLEY, George Andrew 264.1
Cleveland, 1902-
In His name; a prayer for every day, by G. A. Cleveland Shrigley ... Great Neck, N.Y., The Pulpit press, 1945. 3 p. l., 143 p. 17 1/2 cm. [BV260.S48] 45-21435
1. Prayers. I. Title.

SMALLWOOD, Kathleen Ann, 248.374
1909-
Spilled milk; litanies for living [by] Kay Smallzried. New York, Oxford University Press, 1964. 85 p. 21 cm. [BV245.S6] 64-18339
1. Prayers. 2. Christian life. I. Title. II. Title: Litanies for living.

SMALLZRIED, Kathleen Ann, 248.374
1909-
Spilled milk: litanies for living. New York, Oxford [c.]1964. 85p. 21cm. 64-18339 2.95
1. Prayers. 2. Christian life. I. Title. II. Title: Litanies for living.

SMITH, Alfred Franklin, 264.
1869- comp.
Talking with God, edited by Alfred Franklin Smith... Nashville, Tenn., Cokesbury press, 1929. 151 p. 15 cm. [BV260.S53] 29-27642
1. Prayers. I. Title.

SOULSBY, Lucy Helen Muriel.
The old world and the new; prayers, collected by L. H. M. Soulsby ... London, New York [etc.] Longmans, Green and co.,

1922. iv, 43, [1] p. 16 cm. "Largely taken from Short prayers and Prayers for to-day."--Pref. A 23
1. Prayers. I. Title.

[SPERRY, Willard Learoyd] 264.1 1882- ed.
Prayers for private devotions in war-time. [Cambridge] The Memorial church Harvard university [1942] 66 p. 19 1/2 cm. "Sources": p. 53-62. [BV283.W3S65 1942] 43-11434
1. Prayers. I. Harvard university. Memorial church. II. Title.

SPERRY, Willard Learoyd, 264.1 1882- ed.
Prayers for private devotions in war-time, compiled, edited, and in part written by Willard L. Sperry ... New York and London, Harper & brothers [1943] 3 p. l., ix-x p., 1 l., 64 p. 20 cm. "First edition." "Sources": p. 55-63. [BV283.W3S65] 43-7259
1. Prayers. I. Title.

SPRINGSTEEN, Anne. 242.8
It's me, O Lord. photography by Edward Bock III. St. Louis, Concordia [1975] 47 p. ill. 14 cm. by 21 cm. [BV245.S63] 75-8467 ISBN 0-570-03242-3 3.95.
1. Prayers. I. Title.

SPRINGSTEEN, Anne. 242.8
It's me, O Lord. St. Louis, Concordia Pub. House [1970] 71 p. illus. 16 cm. Poems. [BV245.S63] 75-128866
1. Prayers. I. Title.

STARKEY, Lycurgus Monroe, 242.8 ed.
Prayers of the modern era, edited by Lycurgus M. Starkey, Jr. Nashville, Upper room [1966] 80 p. 15 cm. [BV245.S65] 66-28997
1. Prayers. I. The Upper room. II. Title.

STEPHENS, John Underwood, 264.1 1901-
Prayers of the Christian life, for private and public worship. New York, Oxford University Press, 1952. 154 p. 19 cm. [BV245.S67] 52-6171
1. Prayers. I. Title.

STEWART, George, 1892- 240
A face to the sky; a book of prayers, by George Stewart ... New York, Association press [c1940] 3 p. l., 3-96 p. 20 cm. Title vignette. [BV260.S83] 40-10021
1. Prayers. I. Title.

STIDGER, William Le Roy, 220 1886-
Pulpit prayers and paragraphs, editorials, commandments and beatitudes, by William L. Stidger, D.D. New York, George H. Doran company [c1926] xvi p., 1 l., 19-208 p. 19 1/2 cm. [BR125.S837] 27-2262
I. Title.

STOCKDALE, Allen A 264.1
Unconventional prayers. [1st ed.] New York, Comet Press Books, 1955. 64p. illus. 22cm. [BV260.S84] 55-11740
1. Prayers. I. Title.

STRATON, Hillyer 248.37 Hawthorne, 1905-
Prayers in public. Valley Forge [Pa.] Judson Press [1963] 128 p. 16 cm. [BV245.S78] 63-17863
1. Prayers. I. Title.

STRAYER, Paul Moore, 1871- 264.
A sheaf of prayers by Paul Moore Strayer; with a sketch of his life and work by Hattie L. Webber. [Rochester, N.Y., 1926] 3 p. l., 11-123 p. front. (port.) 22 1/2 cm. [BV245.S8] 26-23088
1. Prayers. I. Webber, Hattie L. II. Title.

STREUFERT, Frank Charles, 264.04 1874- comp.
Songs and prayers for various occasions, selected and adapted by F. C. Streufert. St. Louis, Mo., Concordia publishing house [c1933] 94 p. 12 1/2 cm. [BV4805.S62] 34-1848
1. Prayers. 2. Lutheran church—Prayer books and devotions. I. Title.

STROUP, Herbert Hewitt, 264.1 comp.
A symphony of prayer, compiled by Herbert Hewitt Stroup. Philadelphia, Chicago [etc.] The Judson press [1944] 247 p. 22 1/2 cm. [BV245.S83] 44-32416
1. Prayers. I. Title.

STRUCHEN, Jeanette. 242.8
Prayers to pray wherever you are. [1st ed.] Philadelphia, Lippincott [1969] 64 p. 19 cm. [BV245.S83] 69-14498 2.50
1. Prayers. I. Title.

STRUCHEN, Jeanette. 242.8'07
Prayers to pray without really trying. [1st ed.] Philadelphia, Lippincott [1967] New York, Friendship Press [1966] 62 p. 19 cm. 32 p. illus. 26 cm. [BV245.S84] [HC110.P6S84] 339.46 67-16922 66-5820
1. Prayers. 2. Poverty. 3. Poor — U.S. I. Struchen, Jeanette. II. Title. III. Title: This is the puzzle of poverty.

STRUCHEN, Jeanette. 242.7'2
Thank God for the red, white, and black. [1st ed.] Philadelphia, J. B. Lippincott Co. [1970] 57 p. 19 cm. [BV245.S843] 75-105550
1. Prayers. I. Title.

STRUCHEN, Jeanette. 242.8'3
Zapped by Jesus. Photos. by Richard Lerner. [1st ed.] Philadelphia, Holman [1972] 91 p. illus. 24 cm. Conversational prayers of young people who have turned from drugs to God. Appropriate quotations from Scripture and a photograph of each individual accompany the conversations. [BV245.S846] 73-38739 ISBN 0-87981-004-1 (pbk) 2.95
1. Prayers. 2. [Prayers.] I. Title.

STUHLMUELLER, Carroll. 224'.1'06
Isaiah / by Carroll Stuhlmueller. Chicago : Franciscan Herald Press, [1976] p. cm. (Read and pray) [BS1515.3.S88] 76-879 ISBN 0-8199-0628-X pbk. : 0.95
1. Bible. O.T. Isaiah—Commentaries. 2. Bible. O.T. Isaiah—Meditations. 3. Prayers. I. Bible. O.T. Isaiah. English. Selections. 1976. II. Title. III. Series.

SUERKEN, Ernst Henry, ed. 248
Prayers for the week. New York, Exposition Press [1949] 64 p. 23 cm. [BV260.S87] 49-8627
1. Prayers. I. Title.

SUTER, John Wallace, 248.374 1890- ed.
Prayers for a new world. New York, Scribners [c.1964] xxxvi, 244p. 21cm. Bibl. [BV245.S85] 64-22754 4.95
1. Prayers. I. Title.

SWEENEY, Nelly K., Mrs. 248
Prayers, healing prayers and exhortations, given by William T. Stead through the mediumship of Nelly K. Sweeney ... [Kensington, Md., The Burleigh press, c1931] 2 p. l., 57, [1] p. 17 1/2 cm. [BF1311.P67S8] 32-1173
1. Prayers. I. Stead, William Thomas, 1849-1912. II. Title.

SWICHKOW, Louis J 296
Invocations. [Milwaukee] Bloch Pub. Co., 1951. 184 p. 18 cm. [BM675.O25S8 1951] 51-2743
I. Jews. Liturgy and ritual. Occasional prayers. II. Title.

SWICHKOW, Louis J. 296.4
Invocations and "D'var Torah" supplement. New York, Bloch [1964] xv, 231p. 18cm. [BM675.O25S8] 64-57861 3.50
I. Jews. Liturgy and ritual. Occasional prayers. II. Title.

TABLE prayer league, South 249 Bend, Ind.
Table prayers for daily bread; a collection of prayers appropriate for all table occasions. South Bend, In., Table prayer league [c1917] 64 p. 16 cm. [BV255.T2] 17-22309
I. Title.

TALEC, Pierre. 242'.8
Bread in the desert. Translated by Edmond Bonin. New York, Newman Press [1973] vi, 216 p. 23 cm. Translation of Un grand desir. [BV246.T3313] 72-95650 ISBN 0-8091-0178-5 5.95
1. Prayers. I. Title.
pap. 3.95; ISBN 0-8091-1763-0.

TANGHE, Omer, 1928- 242.8
Prayers from life. Translated from the Flemish by Annalies Nieuwenhuis. New York, P. J. Kenedy [1968] xii, 156 p. 21 cm. Translation of Wonderen vraag ik U niet. [BV260.T313] 68-22878
1. Prayers. I. Title.

THOMPSON, Ken, 1926- 242'.2
Bless this desk : prayers 9 to 5 / Ken Thompson. Nashville : Abingdon Press, c1976. 76 p. ; 21 cm. [BV245.T43] 75-33818 ISBN 0-687-33599-X : 3.95
1. Prayers. I. Title.

TIBBETTS, Orlando L. 242'.8
More sidewalk prayers [by] Orlando L. Tibbetts. Valley Forge [Pa.] Judson Press [1973] 96 p. 22 cm. [BV245.T46] 72-11222 ISBN 0-8170-0590-0 pap. 1.95
1. Prayers. 2. Prayer. I. Title.

TIBBETTS, Orlando L. 242.8
Sidewalk prayers [by] Orlando L. Tibbetts. Valley Forge [Pa.] Judson Press [1971] 94 p. 22 cm. [BV245.T47] 71-139501 ISBN 0-8170-0489-0 1.95
1. Prayers. I. Title.

TILESTON, Mary Wilder 264. (Foote) Mrs., 1843-1934, comp.
Prayers ancient and modern, selected by Mary Wilder Tileston. New and rev. ed. Boston, Little, Brown, and company, 1928. x p., 1 l., 380 p. 15 1/2 cm. [BV245.T5 1928] 28-25929
1. Prayers. I. Title.

TO his neighbors, on the 'Holy Cause of Freedom'; a prayer on Christmas Eve for the spread of reason and liberty over the face of the earth ... he expresses gratitude and pleasure at the welcome tendered by the citizens of Albemarle County, Virginia ... 24 December 1789. Charlottesville, Va., Thomas Jefferson Memorial Foundation, 1956. broadside (facsim.) 31 x 23cm. From the original manuscript in the Library of Congress.
I. Jefferson, Thomas, Pres, U. S., 1743-1826.

TONER, Helen L 248
Little prayers for personal poise. St. Louis, Bethany Press [1953] 64p. 18cm. [BV260.T65] 53-36753
1. Prayers. I. Title.

TOPPING, Frank. 242'.8
Lord of the morning / Frank Topping. 1st American ed. Philadelphia : Fortress Press, 1978. p. cm. [BV260.T663 1978] 77-78646 ISBN 0-8006-1313-9 pbk. : 1.95
1. Prayers. I. Title.

TREVELYAN, William Bouverie, 264. 1853-
Prayers for church and nation, by Rev. W. B. Trevelyan, with a preface by D. C. Lathbury. London, New York [etc.] Longmans, Green and co., 1921. x, [11]-96 p. 17 1/2 cm. $1.50 [BV245.T7] 21-1298
I. Title.

TRUMBULL, Henry Clay, 1830-1903.
Personal prayer; its nature and scope, with Illustrative answers to prayer, by H. Clay Trumbull. New York, Chicago [etc.] Fleming H. Revell company [c1915] 4 p. l., 160, [6] 139, [1] p. 19 1/2 cm. $0.50. "Illustrative answers to prayer" has special pagination. 15-14584
I. Title.

[TRUST, Josephine] 264.1
Three hundred golden name heart prayers, for various occasions and needs ... [Los Angeles, Superet press, c1939] xv, 90 p. 3 l., incl. front. 19 cm. "Copyright by Josephine Trust." [BV260.T7] 40-7578
1. Prayers. I. Title.

[TRUST, Josephine de 264.1 Croix] 1886-
Three hundred golden name heart prayers, for various occasions and needs ... [Los Angeles, Superet press, c1939] xv, 90 p., 3 l. incl. front. 18 cm. "Copyright by Josephine Trust." [BV260.T7] 40-7578
1. Prayers. I. Title.

VAN DYKE, Vonda Kay. 242'.8
Your love is here [by] Vonda Van Dyke. [1st ed.] Garden City, N.Y., Doubleday, 1974. viii, 117 p. illus. 22 cm. [BV245.V36] 74-3699 ISBN 0-385-09539-2 4.95
1. Prayers. I. Title.

WALDRON, Daniel Wingate, 264. 1840-1918.
The chaplain's prayers. Prayers offered in the Massachusetts House of representatives for twelve weeks of the session of 1892, by the chaplain, Rev. Daniel Wingate Waldron. [Boston] Beacon press, 1892. [64] p. front. (port.) 20 cm. [BV280.W3] 27-12430
1. Prayers. I. Title.

WALKER, George Bilby. 264.1
The quiet time; a collection of prayer-poems. [1st ed.] New York, Vantage Press [1957] 107 p. 21 cm. [BV260.W27] 56-14383
1. Prayers. I. Title.

WALKER, Michael, 1932- 242.8
Hear me, Lord; prayers from life. [1st ed.] Old Tappan, N.J., Revell [1971, c1969] 128 p. illus. 20 cm. [BV245.W27 1971] 76-138260 ISBN 0-8007-0438-X
1. Prayers. I. Title.

WALLACE, Betty Dollar. 242.8'2
Prayers for mother & child; beautiful prayers and inspirations for all occasions. Nashville, Impact Books [1970] 80 p. 15 cm. [BV245.W28] 78-141645 1.95
1. Prayers. I. Title.

WANAMAKER, John, 1838-1922. 264.
Prayers at Bethany chapel, by John Wanamaker, edited by A. Gordon MacLennan ... New York, Chicago [etc.] Fleming H. Revell company [c1925] 144 p. front. (port.) 19 cm. [BV260.W32] 25-9418
I. MacLennan, Alexander Gordon, 1889- ed. II. Title.

WANAMAKER, John, 1838-1922. 264.
Prayers of John Wanamaker, with an introduction by A. Gordon MacLennan ... New York, Chicago [etc.] Fleming H. Revell company [c1923] 159 p. front. (port.) 1 illus. (facsim.) 19 1/2 cm. [BV260.W3] 23-11002
I. Title.

WANAMAKER, John, 1838-1922. 264.
Prayers of John Wanamaker; with an introduction by A. Gordon MacLennan ... New York, Chicago [etc.] Fleming H. Revell company [c1927] 160 p. front. (port.) illus. (facsim.) 19 1/2 cm. [BV260.W3 1927] 27-23398
I. MacLennan, Alexander Gordon, 1889- ed. II. Title.

WEGENER, William E., comp. 242.8
Prayers for Protestants [Philadelphia] Fortress [1966, c.1946-1965] vi, 122p. 12cm. Bibl. [BV245.W36] 66-10158 1.95
1. Prayers. I. Title.

WEISHEIT, Eldon. 242.8
Excuse me, Sir ... St. Louis, Concordia Pub. House [1971] 117 p. 20 cm. Poems. [BV245.W38] 78-139996 ISBN 0-570-03009-9
1. Prayers. I. Title.

WERSELL, Thomas W. 242
Spiritual thoughts and prayers [by] Thomas W. Wersell. Philadelphia, Fortress Press [1974] 76 p. 18 cm. [BV245.W395] 74-76920 ISBN 0-8006-1305-8 1.95 (pbk.).
1. Prayers. 2. Meditations. I. Title.

WESLEY, John, 1703-1791. 264.1
Prayers, edited by Frederick C. Gill. New York, Abingdon-Cokesbury Press [1952, c1951] 124 p. 16 cm. [BV245.W4] 52-5381
1. Prayers. I. Title.

WEST, Herbert B. 242'.8
Stay with me Lord : a man's prayers. [by] Herbert B. West. New York, Seabury Press [1974] 127 p. 21 cm. "A Crossroad book." [BV245.W44] 73-17914 ISBN 0-8164-0255-8 4.95
1. Prayers. I. Title.

WHEELER, Francis L.
The unfolding year; devotions for the liturgical seasons for public and private use... London, The Faith Press. New York, Morehouse-Gorham [1958] x, 128 p. 18 cm.
1. Prayers. 2. Devotional calendars. I. Title.

WILLIAMS, Ronald Colvin 248.374
Prayers for every occasion. New York, Exposition [c.1962] 87p. 21cm. (Exposition-testament bk.) 3.00

I. Title.

WILSON, Alton H. 242'.8
Lord, it's me again / Alton H. Wilson. 1st ed. Garden City, N.Y. : Doubleday, 1975. 102 p. ; 22 cm. [BV245.W49] 74-22842 ISBN 0-385-09626-7 : 5.95
1. Prayers. I. Title.

WILSON, Bruce M. 242'.8
I'm glad you called [by] Bruce M. Wilson. [Jesup, Ga., Printed by Sentinel Press, c1973] 1 v. (unpaged) 19 cm. [BV245.W5] 74-168200
1. Prayers. I. Title.

WILSON, Hazel Thorne, comp. 264.1
Prayers for living. With an introd. by Georgia Harkness. New York, Abingdon Press [1955] 128p. 12cm. [BV260.W45] 55-8613
1. Prayers. I. Title.

WONG, Richard. 242.8'05'834
Prayers from an island. Pref. by J. Akuhead Pupule. Richmond, John Knox Press [1968] 79 p. 21 cm. First delivered daily on J. A. Pupule's radio program over Radio Station KGMB, Honolulu. [BV245.W6] 68-25014 3.00
1. Prayers. I. Title.

WYMAN, Charles A. ed. 264.1
At Thine altar, compiled and edited by Rev. Charles A. Wyman ... Boston, The Murray press [1946] 95 p. 18 cm. [BV245.W85] 47-543
1. Prayers. I. Title.

YATES, Elizabeth McGreal, 264.1
1905- comp.
Your prayers and mine. Decorations by Nora S. Unwin. Boston, Houghton Mifflin, 1954. 64 p. 20 cm. [BV260.Y3] 53-10987
1. Prayers. I. Title.

ZDENEK, Marilee. 242'.8
God is a verb! / Words by Marilee Zdenek ; action by Marge Champion. Waco, Tex. : Word Books, [1974] 91 p. : ill. ; 19 x 22 cm. [BV245.Z34] 74-82663 5.95
1. Prayers. I. Champion, Marge Belcher, ill. II. Title.

ZEOLI, Billy. 242'.8
God's got a better idea / Billy Zeoli. Old Tappan, N.J. : Revell, c1978. p. cm. Includes index. [BV245.Z46] 78-64373 ISBN 0-8007-0933-0 : 5.95
1. Ford, Gerald R., 1913- —Religion. 2. Prayers. I. Title.

ZIMMERMAN, Leander M., 264.1
1860-
Prayers, for all people, for all occasions, by Leander M. Zimmerman. Philadelphia, Pa., Pub. for the author, The United Lutheran publication house [c1939] vi p., 1 l., 9-68 p. 16 cm. "First printing, October 1, 1939." [BV245.Z5] 39-31037
1. Prayers. 2. Lutheran church—Prayer-books and devotions—English. I. Title.

Prayers—Collections—Juvenile literature.

*HARDIE, Katherine Johnson 242.08
Praise God! Hymns, prayers, and Bible passages selected for boys, girls, their families and friends. Illus. by Mary Alice Bahler. Richmond, Va., CLC Pr. 1966. 32p. illus. (pt. col.) 22cm. 1.45 bds.,
1. Prayers—Collections—Juvenile literature. I. Title.
Young readers. Available from Knox.

Prayers, Early Christian.

POTTS, James Manning, 1895- 264.1
ed.
Prayers of the early church. Nashville, The Upper Room [1953] 96p. 15cm. [BX236.P6] 53-39478
1. Prayers, Early Christian. I. Title.

Prayers for peace.

JOHNSON, William Samuel, 1859-
Prayer for peace, and other poems, by William Samuel Johnson. New York, M. Kennerley, 1915. 6 p. l., 3-113 p. 19 cm. Reprinted in part from various sources. [LS3519.O287P 1915] 15-14825 1.25
I. Title.

NOYES, Alfred, 1880-
The prayer for peace [a poem] by Alfred Noyes. Cleveland, O. [Jamaica, N.Y., Printed at the Marion press] 1911. [12] p. 20 cm. Printed from the author's manuscript, for copyright purposes and for strictly private distribution. One hundred copies. 11-10657
I. Title.

NOYES, Alfred, 1880-
The prayer for peace [a poem] by Alfred Noyes. Cleveland, O. [Jamaica, N. Y., Printed at the Marion press] 1911. [12] p. 20 cm. Printed from the author's manuscript, for copyright purposes and for strictly private distribution. One hundred copies. 11-10657
I. Title.

PETER Pauper Press, Mount 1264.13
Vernon, N.Y.
Prayers for peace. Illustrated by Ruth McCrea. Mount Vernon, N.Y. [1962] 60 p. illus. 19 cm. [BV283.P4P4] 62-53635
1. Prayers for peace. I. Title.

Prayers for the dead—November devotions.

ALBERIONE, Giacomo Giuseppe, 242
1884-
Lest we forget, by James Alberione. [Boston] St. Paul Editions [1967] 252 p. 19 cm. [BX2170.D5A5] 65-29135
1. Prayers for the dead—November devotions. I. Title.

MARY Emmanuel, sister, 264.021
1873-
The month of the holy souls; pious reflections for every day in November, by Sister M. Emmanuel, O.S.B. St. Louis, Mo. and London, B. Herder book co., 1929. viii, 215 p. 19 cm. [Secular name: Mary Josephine Irwin] [BX2170.D5M35] 29-16870
I. Title.

Prayers—Juvenile literature.

HAYWARD, Percy R. 248.373
Young people's prayers: religion at work in life. Illus. by Chester Bratten. New York, Association [1962, c.1945] 122p. (Keen-age reflection bk.) .50 pap.,
I. Title.

PRAYERS to grow by. 242'.82
1st American ed. Chappaqua, N.Y. : Christian Herald Books, 1977. 93 p. : ill. (some col.) ; 25 cm. Old and new prayers relating to children's experiences. [BV265.P764 1977] 76-41630 ISBN 0-915684-12-8 : 6.95
1. Prayers—Juvenile literature. 2. [Prayers.]

Prayers, Medieval.

POTTS, James Manning, 1895- 264.1
ed.
Prayers of the Middle Ages: light from a thousand years. Nashville, Upper room [c1954] 96p. 15cm. [BV237.P6] 57-3096
1. Prayers, Medieval. I. Title.

Prayers, Pastoral.

THOMAS a Kempis, 1380-1471. 242
Moments with the consoling Christ, prayers selected from Thomas a Kempis, by Rev. John A. Dillon, LL.D., with foreword by Right Rev. John J. O'Connor ... New York, Schwartz, Kirwin & Fauss [c1918] 5 p. l., 159 p. 15 cm. [BV4830.T5] 19-4881
I. Dillon, John A., comp. II. Imitatio Christi. III. Title.

TITTLE, Ernest Fremont, 264.1
1885-1949.
A book of pastoral prayers; with an essay on the pastoral prayer. New York, Abingdon-Cokesbury Press [1951] 108 p. 18 cm. "The essay 'The pastoral prayer' is reprinted from Religion in life, summer, 1946." [BV250.T5] 51-3220
1. Prayers, Pastoral. I. Title. II. Title: Pastoral prayers.

Prayers—Private—Collections.

HOFFMAN, Hazel 248.37
The greatest of these is love; God's holy words mingled with roses, by Hazel Hoffman; Verses and affectionate sentiments, by Audrey McDaniel. Norwalk, Conn., Knight St. C. R. Gibson Co., [c.1962] 40p. 22cm. illus. (pt. col.) 2.50; 3.50 deluxe ed.
1. Prayers—Private—Collections. I. McDaniel, Audrey, Verses and affectionate sentiments. II. Title.

WASHINGTON, George, pres. U.S., 1732-1799.
Washington's prayers, by W. Herbert Burk ... Published for the benefit of the Washington memorial chapel. Norristown, Pa., 1907. 95 p. incl. facsims. 25 cm. "The following account of Washington's prayers was read before the Clerical brotherhood of the diocese of Pennsylvania, May, 13, 1907."--Pref. "Five hundred copies of this book have been printed, of which this is no. 101." Contents.Washington's prayers.--The daily sacrifice: Fac-simile of manuscript prayer-book written by George Washington. First published by Stan. V. Henkels, Philadelphia, 1891. A transcript of "The daily sacrifice." 8-299
I. Burk, William Herbert, ed. II. Title.

Pre-existence.

BROUGH, Robert Clayton. 233
Our first estate : the doctrine of man's pre-mortal existence / R. Clayton Brough. Bountiful, Utah : Horizon Publishers, c1977. 174 p. ; 24 cm. Includes index. Bibliography: p. 167-169. [BX8643.P67B76] 77-79753 ISBN 0-88290-084-6 : 5.95
1. Pre-existence. 2. Mormons and Mormonism—Doctrinal and controversial works. I. Title.

Pre-existence—Biblical teaching.

HAMERTON-KELLY, R. G. 225.8'232
Pre-existence, wisdom, and the Son of Man; a study of the idea of pre-existence in the New Testament, by R. G. Hamerton-Kelly. Cambridge [Eng.] University Press, 1973. xii, 310 p. 23 cm. (Society for New Testament Studies. Monograph series, 21) Bibliography: p. 281-294. [BS2545.P684H35] 72-78890 ISBN 0-521-08629-9 23.50
1. Son of Man. 2. Pre-existence—Biblical teaching. I. Title. II. Series: Studiorum Novi Testamenti Societas. Monograph series, 21.
Distributed by Cambridge University Press N.Y.

Pre-Raphaelitism.

[PHYTHIAN, J Ernest]
The Pre-Raphaelite brotherhood. London, G. Newnes, limited; New York, F. Warne & co. [1905] xx p. front., 56 pl. 24 cm. (Half-title: Newnes' art library) W-6
1. Pre-Raphaelitism. I. Title.
Contents omitted.

Preaching.

ABBEY, Merrill R. 251
Living doctrine in a vital pulpit [by] Merrill R. Abbey. New York, Abingdon Press [1964] 208 p. 21 cm. Bibliographical footnotes. [BV4211.2.A18] 64-21129
1. Preaching. I. Title.

ABBEY, Merrill R. 251
Preaching to the contemporary mind. Nashville, Abingdon [c.1963] 192p. 23cm. 63-7763 4.00
1. Preaching. I. Title.

ABBEY, Merrill R. 251
Preaching to the contemporary mind. New York, Abingdon Press [1963] 192 p. 23 cm. [BV4211.2.A2] 63-7763
I. Title. II. Title: Preaching.

ABBEY, Merrill R. 251
The word interprets us [by] Merrill Abbey. New York, Abingdon Press [1967] 208 p. 21 cm. Bibliographical footnotes. [BV4211.2.A23] 67-11008
1. Bible—Homiletical use. 2. Preaching. I. Title.

ACHTEMEIER, Elizabeth Rice, 251
1926-
Creative preaching : finding the words / Elizabeth Achtemeier. Nashville : Abingdon, c1980. p. cm. (Abingdon preacher's library) Includes index. Bibliography: p. [BV4211.2.A27] 80-16890 ISBN 0-687-09831-9 pbk. : 4.95
1. Preaching. 2. Creation (Literary, artistic, etc.) I. Title.

*ADAMS, Jay E. 251
Sense appeal in the sermons of Charles Haddon Spurgeon / Jay E. Adams. Grand Rapids : Baker Book House, 1976 c1975. [viii], 62 p. ; 22 cm. (Studies in preaching ; 1) Bibliography: pp. 60-62. [BV4222] ISBN 0-8010-0102-1 pbk. : 1.95
1. Spurgeon, Charles Haddon—Sermons. 2. Preaching. I. Title.

ALEXANDER, James Waddel, 251
1804-1859.
Thoughts on preaching, being contributions to homiletics. By James w. Alexander, D. D. New York, C. Scribner, 1861. xii, 514 p. 20 1/2 cm. [BV4211.A5] 88-8174
1. Preaching. I. Title.

ALLAN, Arthur. 251
The art of preaching, by Arthur Allen [i. e. Allan] New York, Philosophical library, 1943. 96 p. 19 cm. [BV4211.A55 1943] 43-9849
1. Preaching. I. Title.

ALLEN, Chester L
Pentecostal preaching is different. Los Angeles, L. I. F. E. Bible College Alumni Association, 1961. 104p. (L. I. F. E. Bible College Alumni Association lectureship on preaching, 1961)
1. Preaching. I. Title. II. Series.

ALLMEN, Jean Jacques von. 251
Preaching and congregation. Tr. [from French] by B. L. Nicholas. Richmond, Va. Knox [1962] 67p. 22cm. (Ecumenical studies in worship, no. 10) 62-16769 1.50 pap.,
1. Preaching. I. Title.

ANDERSON, George Smith. 251
Bible student's primer in the science of truth, and The student's course in Scripture exposition, by Rev. G. S. Anderson ... Atlanta, Ga., Foote & Davies company, 1906. xvi, 17-221 p. illus. 20 cm. [BV4211.A6] 6-28420
1. Preaching. I. Title.

ANDERSON, Tony Marshall, 1888-
How to build expository sermons, by T.M. Anderson, with word and study by J. Harold Greenlee. Kansas City, Mo., Beacon hill Press [1965] 158 p. 20 cm. NUC67
1. Preaching. I. Greenlee, Jacob Harold, 1918- II. Title.

ARMITAGE, Thomas, 1819-1896. 251
Preaching: its ideal and inner life. By Thomas Armitage, D.D. Philadelphia, American Baptist publication society, 1880. 263 p. 19 1/2 cm. "These lectures were prepared at the request of the faculty of the Hamilton theological seminary, N.Y. ... delivered before that institution in February, 1880." Contents.The origin of preaching.--Jesus: the preacher's great model.--Apostolic copies of Christ.--The Holy Spirit in preaching.--The preaching for our times.--Preparation for the pulpit.--True pastoral work.--Personal experiences in preaching. [BV4211.A75] 42-43675
I. Title.

ASQUITH, Glenn H. 251'.01
Preaching according to plan [by] Glenn H. Asquith. Valley Forge, Pa., Judson Press [1968] 79 p. 20 cm. [BV4211.2.A8] 68-13606
1. Preaching. I. Title.

ATKINS, Gaius Glenn, 1868- 251
Preaching and the mind of today, by Gaius Glenn Atkins. New York, Round table press, inc., 1934. xvi p., 1 l., 227 p. 20 cm. [BV4211.A88] 34-27286
1. Preaching. I. Title.

ATKINSON, O'Brien, 1871- 251
How to make us want your sermon, by a listener, O'Brien Atkinson ... New York

city, J. F. Wagner, inc.; London, B. Herder [1942] 1 p. l., v-xiii, 179 p. 22 cm. [BV4211.A85] 42-25386
1. Preaching. I. Title.

BAAB, Otto Justice. 251
Prophetic preaching: a new approach. Nashville, Abingdon Press [1958] 159p. 21cm. [BV4211.2.B22] 58-6590
1. Preaching. I. Title.

BABIN, David E. 251
Week in, week out : a new look at liturgical preaching / David E. Babin. New York : Seabury Press, c1976. x, 130 p. ; 22 cm. "A Crossroad book." Includes bibliographical references. [BV4211.2.B224] 75-37814 ISBN 0-8164-0287-6 : 5.95
1. Preaching. I. Title.

*BACH, T. J. 200.8
710 pointed quotations and illustrations. Grand Rapids, Mich., Baker Bk. 1965[c.1951] 104p. 20cm. (Preaching helps ser.) Previously printed under title Pearls from many seas. 1.00 pap.,
I. Title.

BAILEY, Ambrose Moody, 1875- 250
Stand up and preach: a formual for better preaching, by Ambrose Moody Bailey ... New York, Round table press, inc., 1937. ix 141 p. 20 cm. [BV4211.B28] 37-25196
1. Preaching. I. Title.

BAILEY, Augustus Caesar. 251
Pastoral preaching, by Rev. Augustus Caesar Bailey ... Printed for author. [Forrest City, Ark., Times-Herald print.] 1924. 102 p. 17 cm. [BV4211.B3] 24-21352
1. Preaching. I. Title.

BAILLARGEON, Anatole O ed. 251.08
Handbook for special preaching, edited by Anatole O. Baillargeon. [New York] Herder and Herder [1965] 192 p. 22 cm. Includes bibliographies. [BV4211.2.B23] 65-21942
1. Preaching I. Title.

BAILLARGEON, Anatole O. 251
New media: new forms; contemporary forms of preaching. Anatole Baillargeon, editor. Chicago, Franciscan Herald Press [1968] vii, 230 p. 21 cm. Companion volume to the author's Handbook for special preaching. Includes bibliographies. [BV4211.2.B32] 67-28207
1. Preaching. I. Title.

BAIRD, John Edward. 251'.03
Preparing for platform and pulpit [by] John E. Baird. Nashville, Abingdon Press [1968] 222 p. 23 cm. Bibliography: p. 215-220. [BV4211.2.B24] 68-11468
1. Preaching. I. Title.

BANKS, Louis Albert, 1855- 251
Fresh bait for fishers of men. By Louis Albert Banks ... Containing six hundred ... illustrations from current events; suitable for sermons, Sunday-school lessons or young peoples' meeting topics. Cleveland, O., F. M. Barton, 1900. 251 p. 21 cm. [BV4225.B25] 0-4963
I. Title.

BARRY, Clara (Reasoner) 920.7
1880-
Preachers' progeny. New York, Vantage Press [1954] 144p. illus. 23cm. Autobiographical. [CT275.B465A3] 53-12121
I. Title.

BARTH, Karl, 1886- 251
The preaching of the gospel. Translated by B. E. Hooke. Philadelphia, Westminister Press [1963] 94 p. 20 cm. "The French text ... published on the occasion of the author's seventy-fifth birthday, was prepared by the Rev. A. Roulin from notes taken by students." [BV4211.2.B253] 63-7926
1. Preaching. I. Title.

BARTLETT, Gene E 251
The audacity of preaching. [1st ed.] New York, Harper [1962] 159p. 22cm. (The Lyman Beecher lectures, Yale Divinity School, 1961) Includes bibliography. [BV4211.2.B26] 62-11123
1. Preaching. I. Title.

BASS, George M 251
The renewal of liturgical preaching, by George M. Bass. Minneapolis, Augsburg Pub. House,[1967] xi, 155 p. 22 cm. Bibliograph p. 153-155. [BV4221.B3] 67-25364
1. Preaching. 2. Church year. I. Title.

BATLEY, Ernest Lawson. 248
The preacher of the law and testimony: the second book of the principalians. [1st ed.] New York, Exposition Press [1954, c1953] 174p. 21cm. [BR126.B33] 53-11253
I. Title. II. Title: Principalians.

BAUGHMAN, Harry Fridley, 251
1892-
Preaching from the Propers. Philadelphia, Board of Publication of the United Lutheran Church in America [1949] 120 p. 21 cm. (United Lutheran Church in America. Knubel-Miller Foundation Lectures, 4th ser.) [BV4211.B34] 50-140
1. Preaching. 2. Lutheran Church. Liturgy and ritual. I. Title. II. Series.

BAUMANN, J. Daniel. 251
An introduction to contemporary preaching [by] J. Daniel Baumann. Grand Rapids, Baker Book House [1972] 302 p. 24 cm. Includes bibliographical references. [BV4211.2.B29] 72-76649 ISBN 0-8010-0572-8 6.95
1. Preaching. I. Title.

BAXTER, Batsell Barrett, 251
1916-
The heart of the Yale lectures. New York, Macmillan Co., 1947. xiii, 332 p. 21 cm. A study of homiletics based on, and with many quotations from, the Lyman Beecher lectures on preaching, Yale Univ. Bibliography: p. [309]-315. [BV4211.B35] 47-30918
1. Preaching. 2. Lyman Beecher lectures on preaching, Yale University. I. Title.

BAYBROOK, Gar 251
Will you be the speaker? Mountain View, Calif., Pacific Press Pub. Association [c.1961] 162p. illus. 61-6480 3.50
1. Preaching. 2. Seventh-Day Adventists. I. Title.

BEECHER, Henry Ward, 1813- 251
1887.
Yale lectures on preaching. By Henry Ward Beecher. Delivered before the Theological department of Yale college ... From phonographic reports. Second series. New York, J.B. Ford and company, 1873. viii, 330 p. 19 1/2 cm. Lyman Beecher lectures on preaching for 1872-73. [BV4211.B42] 32-33643
1. Preaching. I. Title.

BEECHER, Henry Ward, 1813- 251
1887.
Yale lectures on preaching. By Henry Ward Beecher. Delivered before the Theological department of Yale college ... From phonographic reports by T.J. Ellinwood. Third series. New York, J.B. /ford and company, 1871. x, 326 p. 19 1/2 cm. Lyman Beecher lectures on preaching for 1873-74. [BV4211.B43] 32-33642
1. Preaching. I. Title.

BEECHER, Henry Ward, 1813- 251
1887.
Yale lectures on preaching. By Henry Ward Beecher. Delivered before the Theological department of Yale college. New Haven, Conn., in the regular course of the "Lyman Beecher lectureship on preaching". First, second, and third series ... Boston, Chicago, The Pilgrim press, [1902] 3 v, in 1. 19 cm. The lectures were delivered 1872-74. [BX4211.B39] 4-10405
1. Preaching. I. Title.

BEHRENDS, Adolphus Julius 251
Frederick, 1839-1900.
The philosophy of preaching, by A. J. F. Behrends ... New York, C. Scribner's sons, 1890. viii p., 1 l., 234 p. 18 cm. "Lectures given ... before the Divinity school of Yale university, on the Lyman Beecher foundation."--Prefatory note. [BV4211.B45] 13-18907
1. Preaching. I. Title.

[BENNETT, Ambrose Allen] 251
1884-
The preacher's weapon ... Nashville, Tenn., Preacher's weapon office [c1921- v. 20 cm. [BV4223.B4] 21-8389
I. Title.

BEST, Ernest. 251
From text to sermon : responsible use of the New Testament in preaching / by Ernest Best. Atlanta : John Knox Press, c1978. 117 p. ; 22 cm. Includes bibliographical references. [BV4211.2.B46] 77-79584 ISBN 0-8042-0245-1 : 5.95
1. Bible. N.T.—Hermeneutics. 2. Bible. N.T.—Theology. 3. Preaching. I. Title.

BLACK, James Macdougall, 251
1879-
... The mystery of preaching, by James Black ... New York, Chicago [etc.] Fleming H. Revell company [c1924] x p., 1 l., 13-277 p. 19 1/2 cm. (James Sprunt lectures, 1924. Union theological seminary, Richmond, Virginia) [BV4211.B5] 24-17964
1. Preaching. I. Title.

BLACK, James Macdougall, 251
1879-
... The mystery of preaching, by James Black ... New York, Chicago [etc.] Fleming H. Revell company [c1935] x p., 1 l., 13-277 p. 19 1/2 cm. (James Sprunt lectures, 1924. Union Theological seminary, Richmond, Virginia) [BV4211.B5 1935] 35-9996
1. Preaching. I. Title.

*BLACKWOOD, Andrew W. 251
Leading in public prayer [by] Andrew W. Blackwood. Grand Rapids: Baker Book, 1975 c1957. 207 p.; 20 cm. Bibliography, p. 197-202. [BV42112B55] ISBN 0-8010-0642-2 2.95 (pbk.)
1. Preaching. I. Title.

*BLACKWOOD, Andrew W. 251
Preaching from the Bible [by] Andrew W. Blackwood. Grand Rapids, Baker Book House [1974, c1969] 224 p. 20 cm. (Notable books on preaching.) Bibliography: 227-239. [BV4223] ISBN 0-8010-0619-8 2.95 (pbk.)
1. Preaching. I. Title.

BLACKWOOD, Andrew Watterson, 251
1882-
Biographical preaching for today; the pulpit use of Bible cases. Nashville, Abingdon Press [1954] 224 p. 21cm. [BV4211.B515] 54-8237
1. Preaching. I. Title.

BLACKWOOD, Andrew Watterson, 251
1882-
Doctrinal preaching for today; case studies of Bible teachings. New York, Abingdon Press [1956] 224p. 21cm. [BV4211.2.B55] 56-8739
1. Preaching. I. Title.

BLACKWOOD, Andrew Watterson, 251
1882-
Doctrinal preaching for today: case studies of Bible teachings. Grand Rapids: Baker Book House, [1975 c1956] 224 p.; 20 cm. (Andrew W. Blackwood library) Bibliography: p. 209-215. [BV4211.2.B55] 56-8739 ISBN 0-8010-0638-4 2.95 (pbk.)
1. Preaching. I. Title.

BLACKWOOD, Andrew 251.8
Watterson, 1882-
Expository preaching for today; case studies of Bible passages. Nashville, Abingdon-Cokesbury Press [1953] 224p. 21cm. Includes bibliography. [BV4211.B518] 53-5392
1. Preaching. I. Title.

BLACKWOOD, Andrew 251.8
Watterson, 1882-
Expository preaching for today: case studies of Bible passages. Grand Rapids: Baker Book House, [1975 c1943] 224 p. 20 cm. (Andrew W. Blackwood library) Bibliography: p. 209-214. [BV4211.B518] 53-5392 ISBN 0-8010-0639-2 2.95 (pbk.)
1. Preaching. I. Title.

BLACKWOOD, Andrew Watterson, 251
1882-
The fine art of preaching [by] Andrew Watterson Blackwood ... New York, The Macmillan company, 1937. ix p., 1 l., 108 p. 20 1/2 cm. [BV4211.B52] 37-39207
1. Preaching. I. Title.

BLACKWOOD, Andrew Watterson, 251
1882-
Planning a year's pulpit work [by] Andrew W. Blackwood ... New York, Nashville, Abingdon-Cokesbury press [1942] 240 p. 20 1/2 cm. Bibliographical foot-notes. [BV4211.B523] 43-4033
1. Preaching. I. Title.

BLACKWOOD, Andrew Watterson, 251
1882-
Preaching from the Bible. Nashville, Abingdon [1961, c.1941] 247p. (Apex bk. H1) 1.25 pap.,
1. Preaching. I. Title.

BLACKWOOD, Andrew Watterson, 251
1882-
Preaching from the Bible [by] Andrew W. Blackwood ... New York, Nashville, Abingdon-Cokesbury press [c1941] 247 p. 20 1/2 cm. "The preacher's library": p. 227-239. [BV4211.B525] 41-2887
1. Preaching. I. Title.

BLACKWOOD, Andrew Watterson, 251
1882-
The preparation of sermons. New York, Abingdon-Cokesbury Press [1948] 272 p. 24 cm. Includes bibliographies. [BV4211.B526] 48-10392
1. Preaching. I. Title.

BLOCKER, Simon, 1881- 251
The secret of pulpit power through thematic Christian preaching. Grand Rapids, W. B. Eerdmans Pub. Co., 1951. 209 p. 23 cm. [BV4211.B533] 51-8686
1. Preaching. I. Title.

BOHREN, Rudolf 253
Preaching and community. Tr. [from German] by David E. Green. Richmond, Va., Knox [1966, c.1965] 238p. 21cm. Bibl. [HV4214.B613] 65-12284 4.95 bds.,
1. Preaching. I. Title.

BOOTH, John Nicholls, 1912- 251
The quest for preaching power, by John Nicholls Booth ... New York, The Macmillan company, 1943. xviii p. 1 l., 240 p. 19 1/2 cm. "First printing." Bibliography: p. [237]-240. [BV4211.B585] 48-3137
1. Preaching. I. Title.

BOSCH, Paul. 251
The sermon as part of the liturgy / Paul Bosch. St. Louis : Concordia Pub. House, c1977. 48 p. ; 23 cm. (The Preacher's workshop series ; book 6) [BV4211.2.B65] 77-10879 ISBN 0-570-07405-3 pbk. : 1.95
1. Preaching. 2. Public worship. I. Title. II. Series.

BOSTON university. School of 251
theology. Conference on preaching, 1928.
Effective preaching; a series of lectures delivered before the Boston university School of theology, October 15, 16, and 17, 1928, edited by G. Bromley Oxnam... New York, Cincinnati [etc.] The Abingdon peess [c1929] 260 p. 20 cm. [BV4205.B6 1928] 29-11728
1. Preaching. I. Oxnam, Garfield Bromley, 1891- ed. II. Title.

BOSTON university. School of 251
theology. Conference on preaching, 1929.
Creative preaching; a series of lectures delivered before the Boston university school of theology, October 14, 15, and 16, 1929, edited by G. Bromley Oxnam... New York, Cincinnati [etc.] The Abingdon press [c1930] 347 p. 20 cm. [BV4205.B6 1929] 30-15411
1. Preaching. I. Oxnam, Garfield Bromley, 1891- ed. II. Title.

BOSTON university. School 251.08
of theology. Conference on preaching, 1930.
Contemporary preaching, a study in trends; lectures delivered before the Boston university school of theology, October, 13, 14, and 15, 1930; edited by G. Bromley Oxnam... New York, Cincinnati [etc.] The Abingdon press [c1931] 256 p. 20 cm. [BV4205.B6 1930] 31-6495
1. Preaching. I. Oxnam, Garfield Bromley, 1891- ed. II. Title.

BOSTON university. School 251.08
of theology. Conference on preaching, 1931.
The varieties of present-day preaching; a series of lectures delivered before the Boston university School of theology, edited by G. Bromley Oxnam... New York, Cincinnati [etc.] The Abingdon press

[c1932] 244 p. 20 cm. "The fourth Conference on preaching of Boston university School of theology...held October 12, 13, 14, 1931".--Introd. [BV4205.B6 1931] 32-11677
1. Preaching. I. Oxnam, Garfield Bromley, 1891- ed. II. Title.

BOUNDS, Edward McKendree, 1835-1913. 258
Preacher and prayer, [by] E. M. Bounds ... Nashville, Tenn., Dallas, Tex., Publishing house of the M. E. church, South, Smith & Lamar, agents, 1907. 128 p. 15 1/2 cm. (Prayer series) [BV4012.B6] 7-23283
I. Title.

BOWIE, Walter Russell, 1882- 251
Preachings Nashville, Abingdon Press [1954] 224p. 21cm. [BV4211.B538] 54-5508
1. Preaching. I. Title.

BOWIE, Walter Russell, 1882- 251
... The renewing gospel [by] Walter Russell Bowie. New York, London, C. Scribner's sons, 1935. viii p., 2 l., 296 p. 20 cm. (The Yale lectures on preaching) [BV4211.B54] 35-24910
1. Preaching. 2. Christianity—20th cent. I. Title.

BRACK, Harold Arthur, 1923- 251
Public speaking and discussion for religious leaders [by] Harold A. Brack, Kenneth G. Hance. Englewood Cliffs, N. J., Prentice-Hall [c.]1961. 259p. illus. 61-14151 6.35
1. Preaching. 2. Discussion. I. Hance, Kenneth Gordon, 1903- joint author. II. Title.

BRADFORD, Charles E. 251
Preaching to the times : the preaching ministry in the Seventh-day Adventist Church / Charles E. Bradford. Washington : Review and Herald Pub. Association, [1975] 144 p. ; 21 cm. (Discovery paperbacks) Bibliography: p. 143-144. [BV4211.2.B672] 75-318950 3.25
1. Seventh-Day Adventists—Doctrinal and controversial works. 2. Preaching. I. Title.

BRAGA, James. 251'.01
How to prepare Bible messages; a manual on homiletics for Bible students. Portland, Or., Multnomah Press [1971, c1969] xv, 216 p. 22 cm. Bibliography: p. 207-208. [BV4211.2.B674] 75-88213 4.95
1. Preaching. I. Title.

BRAGA, James. 251'.01
How to prepare Bible messages / by James Braga. Rev. ed. Portland, Or. : Multnomah Press, 1981. 257 p. ; 21 cm. Includes bibliographies and indexes. [BV4211.2.B674 1981] 19 81-14132 ISBN 0-930014-71-5 pbk. : 6.95
1. Preaching. I. Title.
Publisher's address: 10209 S.E. Division St., Portland, OR 97266

BRASTOW, Lewis Orsmond, 1834-1912. 251.
The modern pulpit; a study of homiletic sources and characteristics, by Lewis O. Brastow ... New York, The Macmillan company; London, Macmillan & co., ltd., 1906. xxii p., 1 l., 451 p. 20 cm. [BV4207.B65] 6-35521
1. Preaching. I. Title.

BREED, David Riddle, 1848- 251
Preparing to preach, by David R. Breed ... New York, Hodder & Stoughton, George H. Doran company [c1911] 11 p. l., 21-155 p. 22 cm. [BV4211.B63] 11-24986
1. Preaching. I. Title.

BROADUS, John Albert, 1827-1895. 231
On the preparation and delivery of sermons, by John A. Broadus. New and rev. ed. by Jesse Burton Weatherspoon ... New York, London, Harper & brothers [1944] xviii p. 1 l., 392 p. 21 1/2 cm. First edition, 1870, published under title: A treatise on the preparation and delivery of sermons. Bibliography: p. 379-388. [BV4211.B67 1944] 44-5786
1. Preaching. I. Weatherspoon, Jesse Burton, 1886- ed. II. Title.

BROADUS, John Albert, 1827-1895. 251
On the preparation and delivery of sermons / by John A. Broadus. New York : Harper & Row, c1979. p. cm. First ed. published in 1870 under title: A treatise on the preparation and delivery of sermons. Includes index. Bibliography: p. [BV4211.2.B678 1979] 79-15005 ISBN 0-06-061112-X. : 8.95
1. Preaching. I. Stanfield, Vernon L.

BROADUS, John Albert, 1827-1895. 251
A treatise on the preparation and delivery of sermons. by John A. Broadus ... Philadelphia, Smith, English & co.; New York, Sheldon & co. [1870] xv, 17-514 p. 19 cm. [BV4211.B67 1870] 38-3768
1. Preaching. I. Title.

BROADUS, John Albert, 1827-1895. 251
A treatise on the preparation and delivery of sermons, by John A. Broadus ... New [23d] ed., edited by Edwin Charles Dargan. New York, A.C. Armstrong and son, 1898. xxi, 562 p. 20 cm. Bibliography: p. 548-553. [BV4211.B67 1898] 10-7062
1. Preaching. I. Dargan, Edwin Charles, 1852-1900, ed. II. Title.

BROOKS, Phillips, Bp., 1835-1893. 251
The excellence of our calling; an abridgment of Phillips Brooks' Lectures on preaching, by Thomas F. Chilcote, Jr. [1st ed.] New York, Dutton, 1954. 192p. 22cm. [BV4211.B7 1954] 54-10919
1. Preaching. I. Chilcote, Thomas F. II. Title.

BROOKS, Phillips, bp., 1835-1893. 251
Lectures on preaching, delivered before the Divinity school of Yale college in January and Februray, 1877, by the Rev. Phillips Brooks ... New York, E. P. Dutton and company, 1877. 3 p. l., 281 p. 19 1/2 cm. [BV4211.B7 1877] 38-823
1. Preaching. I. Title.

BROOKS. PHILLIPS, Bp., 1835-1893. 251
On preaching. Introd. by Theodore Parker Ferris. New York, Seabury [c.1964] vi, 281p. 21cm. (SP14) First pub. in 1877 under title: Lectures on preaching. 64-23901 1.95 pap.,
1. Preaching. I. Title.

BROWN, Charles Reynolds, 1862- 251
The art of preaching, by Charles Reynolds Brown... New York, The Macmillan company, 1922. ix, 250 p. 19 1/2 cm. (The forty-eight series of Lyman Beecher lectures on preaching in Yale University) [BV4211.B73] 22-22071
1. Preaching. I. Title.

BROWN, Elijah P. 1842-
Point and purpose in preaching, by Elijah P. Brown... New York, Chicago [etc.] Fleming H. Revell company [c1917] 192 p. 19 1/2 cm. 17-11237
I. Title.

BROWN, Henry Clifton, ed. 251
Messages for men; for laymen and ministers. Grand Rapids, Zondervan Pub. House [1960] 150p. 21cm. [BV4205.B7] 61-712
1. Preaching. 2. Laity. I. Title.

BROWN, Henry Clifton. 251
A quest for reformation in preaching, by H. C. Brown, Jr. Waco, Tex., Word Bks. [1968] 251p. forms. 23cm. Annotated texts of 10 sermons by Karl Barth, others. Bibl. footnotes. [BV4211.2.B68] 67-26938 5.95
1. Preaching. I. Title.

BROWN, Henry Clifton. 251'.01
Sermon analysis for pulpit power [by] H. C. Brown, Jr. Nashville, Broadman Press [1971] 61 p. 19 cm. [BV4211.2.B686] 72-145979 ISBN 0-8054-2105-X
1. Preaching. I. Title.

BROWN, Henry Clifton. 251
Steps to the sermon; a plan for sermon preparation, by H. C. Brown, Jr., H. Gordon Clinard and Jesse J. Northcutt. Nashville, Broadman Press [1963] ix, 202 p. 22 cm. Bibliography: p. 197-202. [BV4211.1.B69] 63-19068
1. Preaching. I. Title.

BROWNE, Benjamin P 251
Let there be light; the art of sermon illustration. [Westwood, N. J.] Revell [1956] 157p. 21cm. [BV4211.2.B7] 56-7443
1. Preaching. 2. Homiletical illustrations. I. Title.

BROWNE, Robert Eric Charles. 251
The ministry of the word / Robert E. C. Browne. 1st American ed. Philadelphia : Fortress Press, 1976, c1975. 128 p. ; 22 cm. Includes bibliographical references and index. [BV4211.2.B73 1976] 76-1310 ISBN 0-8006-1229-9 pbk. : 3.50
1. Preaching. I. Title.

BRUNER, Benjamin Harrison, 1888- 251
Which gospel shall I preach! By B. H. Bruner ... New York, R. R. Smith, inc., 1930. 6 p. l., 2-239 p. 20 cm [BV4211.B76] 30-29121
1. Preaching. 2. Christianity. I. Title.

BRYAN, Dawson Charles, 1900- 251
The art of illustrating sermons, by Dawson C. Bryan. Nashville, Cokesbury press [c1938] 272 p. 21 cm. "References and notes": p. 261-272. [BV4226.B75] 38-5770
1. Preaching. 2. Homiletical illustrations I. Title.

BRYSON, Harold T. 251
Building sermons to meet people's needs / Harold T. Bryson, James C. Taylor. Nashville, Tenn. : Broadman Press, c1980. 138 p. ; 20 cm. Bibliography: p. 135-138. [BV4211.2.B76] 19 78-74962 ISBN 0-8054-2109-2 : 5.95
1. Preaching. I. Taylor, James Carter, 1912- joint author. II. Title.

BUCKNER, James Dysart Monroe, 1855- 922.
How I lost my job as a preacher [by] J. D. M. Buckner ... [Aurora, Neb., 1922] 63 p. port. 20 cm. [BX8495.B88A3] 23-2755
I. Title.

BUECHNER, Frederick, 1926- 251
Telling the truth : the Gospel as tragedy, comedy, and fairy tale / Frederick Buechner. San Francisco : Harper & Row, [1977] p. cm. [BV4211.2.B78] 77-10586 ISBN 0-06-061156-1 : 5.95
1. Preaching. 2. Communication (Theology) I. Title.

BULL, Paul Bertie, 1864-
Lectures on preaching and sermon construction, by Paul B. Bull ... London, Society for promoting Christian knowledge; New York [etc.] Macmillian, 1922. xiii, 328 p. 21 cm. A 23
1. Preaching. I. Title.

BULL, Paul Bertie, 1864- 251
Preaching and sermon construction, by Paul B. Bull ... New York, The Macmillan company, 1922. xiii, 315 p. 23 cm. [BV4211.B78] 22-16986
I. Title.

BURKE, John, 1928- 251
Gospel power : toward the revitalization of preaching / John Burke. New York : Alba House, c1978. xiv, 117 p. ; 21 cm. [BV4211.2.B85] 77-14517 ISBN 0-8189-0359-7 pbk. : 4.95
1. Preaching. I. Title.

BURRELL, David James, 1844-1926. 251
The sermon, its construction and delivery, by David James Burrell ... New York,Chicago [etc.] Fleming H. Revell company, [c1913] 4 p. l., 7-329 p. 21 cm. (The James Sprunt lectures, delivered at Union theological seminary in Virginia) [BV4211.B8] 13-13562
1. Preaching. I. Title.

BURTON, Nathaniel Judson, 1822-1887. 252
In pulpit and parish; Yale lectures on preaching, by Nathaniel J. Burton... Edited by Richard E. Burton. New York, The Macmillan company, 1925. 4 p. l., 376 p. 19 1/2 cm. [TT185.B8] 15-15199
1. Preaching. I. Burton, Richard, 1861- ed. II. Title.
Contents omitted.

BUTT, D. Gregory Claiborne, 1848- 922.
From saddle to city by buggy, boat and railway, by D. Gregory Claiborne Butts ... being the personal recollections and observations of fifty years service in the itinerancy, with pen portraits of leaders and places and times. [Richmond, 1922] 549 p. front. plates, ports. 19 cm. [BX8495.B9A3] 23-6589
I. Title.

BUTTRICK, George Arthur, 1892- 251
... Jesus came preaching; Christian preaching in the new age [by] George A. Buttrick ... New York, C. Scribner's sons, 1931. xii, p., 2 l., 3-239 p. 21 cm. (The Yale lectures on preaching) [BV4211.B85] 31-33420
1. Preaching. I. Title.

BYINGTON, Edwin Hallock, 1861- 251
Pulpit mirrors, by Edwin H. Byington ... New York, George H. Doran company [c1927] viii p., 1 l., 11-203 p. 20 cm. [BV4211.B86] 27-22730
1. Preaching. I. Title.

CADMAN, Samuel Parkes, 1864-1936. 251
Ambassadors of God, by S. Parkes Cadman. New York, The Macmillan company, 1920. 6 p. l., 3-353 p. 23 cm. Bibliography: p. 341-343. [BV4211.C25] 20-19175
1. Preaching. I. Title.

CAEMMERER, Richard Rudolph, 1904- 251
Preaching for the church. Saint Louis, Concordia Pub. House [1959] 353p. 24cm. Includes bibliography. [BV4211.2.C2] 58-13260
1. Preaching. I. Title.

CAIRNS, Frank. 251
The prophet of the heart; being the Warrack lectures on preaching for 1934 by Frank Cairns; with a friendly foreword by Charles Reynolds Brown. New York and London, Harper & brothers, 1935. xii p., 1 l., 149 p. 20 cm. "First edition." Contents.--A friendly foreword--Preaching, a chivalrous adventure.--The sermon as a act of worship.--The sermon as the prophet of the heart.--Technique.--The preacher himself. [BV4211.C26 1935] 35-5800
1. Preaching. 2. Theology, Pastoral. I. Title.

CALDWELL, Frank H 251
Preaching angles. Nashville, Abingdon Press [1954] 126p. 20cm. [BV4211.C265] 54-5228
1. Preaching. I. Title.

CALKINS, Raymond, 1869- 251
The eloquence of Christian experience, by Raymond Calkins. New York, The Macmillan company, 1927. xi p., 2 l., 232 p. 20 cm. Given as the Lyman Beecher lectures at Yale in April, 1926. Chapters i, iii, v-vii were used by the author in the George Shepard lectures on preaching, delivered at Bangor theological seminary in February, 1926. cf. Pref. [BV4211.C27] 27-3109
1. Preaching. 2. Clergy. I. Title.

CARNEY, Thomas A. 251
A primer of homiletics, by Reverend Thomas A. Carney ... Houston, Tex., Standard printing & lithographing company [c1943] 7 p. l., 143, [22] p. 23 1/2 cm. [BV4211.C3] 44-33892
1. Preaching. I. Title.

CARTER, Francis Edward, 1851-
Preaching, by F. E. Carter ... London, New York [etc.] Longmans, Green & co., 1909. vi, 180 p. 18 cm. (Handbooks for the clergy, ed. by Arthur W. Robinson) A 22
1. Preaching. I. Title.

*CHAPPELL, Clovis G. 251
The village tragedy and other sermons / Clovis G. Chappell. Grand Rapids : Baker Book House, 1976. ix, 182 p. ; 20 cm. (Clovis G. Chappell library.) [BV4211.2] ISBN 0-8010-2386-6 pbk. : 2.95
1. Preaching. I. Title.

CHAPPELL, Clovis Gillham, 1882- 251
Anointed to preach. Nashville, Abingdon-Cokesbury Press [1951] 124 p. 20 cm. [BV4211.C43] 51-9215
1. Preaching. I. Title.

CHARTIER, Myron Raymond. 251
Preaching as communication : an

interpersonal perspective / Myron R. Chartier. Nashville : Abingdon, c1981. 127 p. ; 20 cm. (Abingdon preacher's library) Includes index. Bibliography: p. 119-121. [BV4211.2.C46] 19 80-21304 ISBN 0-687-33826-3 pbk. : 4.95
1. Preaching. 2. Communication. I. Title.

CLARKE, James W 251
Dynamic preaching. [Westwood, N. J.] F. H. Revell Co. [1960] 128p. 21cm. Includes bibliography. [BV4211.2.C5] 60-8457
1. Preaching. I. Title.

CLAUDE, Jean, 1619-1687.
An essay on the composition of a sermon. By Rev. John Claude. Edited by Rev. Charles Simeon ... New-York, Lane & Scott, 1849. 252 p. 15 1/2 cm. [BV4213.C53] 7-28568
1. Preaching. I. Simeon, Charles, 1759-1836. ed. II. Title.

CLAUSEN, Bernard Chancellor, 1892- 251
"Preach it again"; the sermon test, by Bernard C. Clausen, D.D. Philadelphia, Boston [etc.] The Judson press [1922] 5 p. l., 3-130 p. 20 cm. [BV4211.C5] 22-17983
1. Preaching. I. Title.

CLELAND, James T 251
The true and lively Word. New York, Scribner, 1954. 120p. 20cm. [BV4211.C52] 54-6304
1. Preaching. I. Title.

CLEM, Paul L
Filing your sermon ideas. New York, Abingdon Press [1964] 80 p. illus. 18 cm. Bibliography: p. 80. 65-37131
1. Preaching. I. Title.

CLOWNEY, Edmund P 251
Preaching and Biblical theology. Grand Rapids, Eerdmans [1961] 124p. 21cm. Includes bibliography. [BV4211.2.C53] 60-53094
1. Preaching. 2. Bible—Homiletical use. I. Title.

COFFIN, Henry Sloane, 1877- 251
Communion through preaching; the monstrance of the Gospel. New York, Scribner, 1952. 124 p. 20 cm. (The George Craig Stewart lectures on preaching) [BV4211.C54] 52-14246
1. Preaching. 2. Lord's Supper. I. Title.

COFFIN, Henry Sloane, 1877- 251
What to preach, by Henry Sloane Coffin ... New York, George H. Doran company [c1926] 189 p. 20 1/2 cm. "The Warrack lectures for 1926 in New college, Edinburgh, and in the colleges of the United free church of Scotland in Glasgow and Aberdeen. These lectures were also given as the Russell lectures at Auburn seminary, and as the Swander lectures in the Theological seminary of the Reformed church in the United States at Lancaster, Penna." [BV4211.C55] 26-21366
1. Preaching. I. Title.

COLQUHOUN, Frank. 251
Christ's ambassadors; the priority of preaching. Philadelphia, Westminster Press [c1965] 93 p. 19 cm. (Christian foundations) Bibliographical footnotes. [BV1211.2.C58] 67-10471
1. Preaching. I. Title.

COLQUHOUN, Frank. 251
Christ's ambassadors : the priority of preaching / Frank Colquhoun. Grand Rapids : Baker Book House, 1979, c1965. 93p. ; 19 cm. (A Canterbury Book) [BV4211.2C58] ISBN 0-8010-2428-5 pbk. : 2.50
1. Preaching. I. Title.
L.C. card no. for 1967 Westminster ed.: 67-10471.

CONWAY, John Placid, 1855-1913. 251
Principles of sacred eloquence, by John Placid Conway ... New York, J. F. Wagner [c1904] 2 p. l., 54 p. 20 cm. [BV4211.C6] 4-34571
1. Preaching. I. Title.

COOKE, John Blair Deaver, 1901- 251
The Carpenter's method of preaching. Philadelphia, Seaboard Press [1953] 96p. illus. 20cm. [BV4211.C63] 53-32884
1. Preaching. I. Title.

COWAN, Arthur Aitken. 251
The primacy of preaching today. New York, Scribner [1955] 128p. 19cm. (The Warrack lectures for 1954) [BV4211.2.C6] 56-13730
1. Preaching. I. Title.

COX, James William, 1923- 251
A guide to biblical preaching / James W. Cox. Nashville : Abingdon, [1976] p. cm. Includes bibliographical references and index. [BV4211.2.C64] 76-13491 ISBN 0-687-16229-7 : 6.50
1. Bible—Homiletical use. 2. Preaching. I. Title.

CRADDOCK, Fred B. 251
As one without authority; essays on inductive preaching [by] Fred B. Craddock. Enid, Okla., Phillips University Press [1971] ix, 159 p. 21 cm. Includes bibliographical references. [BV4211.2.C7] 75-152003
1. Preaching. I. Title.

CRADDOCK, Fred B. 251
As one without authority / Fred B. Craddock. 3d ed. Nashville : Abingdon, c1979. 168 p. ; 21 cm. [BV4211.2.C7 1979] 79-4363 ISBN 0-687-01930-3 pbk. : 5.25
1. Preaching. I. Title.

CRADDOCK, Fred B. 251
Overhearing the gospel / Fred B. Craddock. Nashville : Abingdon, c1978. 144 p. ; 22 cm. ([Lyman Beecher lecturer, 1978]) Includes bibliographical references. [BV4211.2.C75] 77-19106 ISBN 0-687-29938-1 : 6.95
1. Preaching. 2. Communication (Theology) I. Title. II. Series. III. Series: Lyman Beecher lectures.

CRAIG, Archibald C 251
Preaching in a scientific age. New York, Scribner 1954 119p. 20cm. (The Warrack lectures for 1953) [BV4211.C67 1954a] 54-3863
1. Preaching. I. Title.

CROCKER, Lionel George. 251
Henry Ward Beecher's art of preaching, by Lionel George Crocker ... Chicago, Ill., The University of Chicago press [1934] ix, 145 p. 21 cm. "Published works of Beecher": p. 119; Bibliography: p. 132-138. [BV4211.B44C7] 34-1930
1. Beecher, Henry Ward, 1813-1887. 2. Preaching. I. Title.

CROSBY, Howard, 1826-1891. 254
The Christian preacher. Yale lectures for 1879-80. By Howard Crosby. New York, A. D. F. Randolph & company, [1880] 195 p. 20 cm. [Lyman Beecher lectures on preaching, Yale university, 1879-80] [BV4211.C7] 38-8175
1. Preaching. I. Title.

CRUM, Milton. 251
Manual on preaching / Milton Crum, Jr. Valley Forge, Pa. : Judson Press, [1977] p. cm. Includes bibliographical references and index. [BV4211.2.C78] 77-79775 ISBN 0-8170-0744-X : 8.95
1. Preaching. I. Title.

CUYLER, Theodore Ledyard, 1822-1909. 250
The young preacher. By Theodore L. Cuyler ... New York, Chicago, Fleming H. Revell company [1893] 5 p. l., 111 p. 18 cm. [BV4211.C8] 38-3765
1. Preaching. I. Title.

DAANE, James. 251
Preaching with confidence : a theological essay of the power of the pulpit / by James Daane. Grand Rapids, Mich. : Eerdmans, c1980. viii, 80 p. ; 21 cm. [BV4211.2.D3] 19 79-26862 ISBN 0-8028-1825-0 pbk. : 2.95
1. Preaching. I. Title.

DABNEY, Robert Lewis, 1820-1898. 251
Sacred rhetoric; or A course of lectures on preaching. Delivered in the Union theological seminary of the General assembly of the Presbyterian church in the U. S., in Prince Edward, Va. By Robert L. Dabney ... Printed for the use of his students. Richmond, Presbyterian Committee of publication, 1870. 361 p. 19 cm. [BV4211.D2] 38-636
1. Preaching. I. Presbyterian church in the U. S. Executive committee of publication. II. Title.

DABOVICH, Sebastian.
Preaching in the Russian church; or, Lectures and sermons by a priest of the holy orthodox church. San Francisco, Cubery & co., 1899. 172 p. 16 degree. Mar *I. Title.*

DALE, Robert William, 1829-1895. 251
Nine lectures on preaching. Delivered at Yale college, New Haven, Conn. By R. W. Dale ... New York, Chicago [etc.] A. S. Barnes and company, 1878. viii, 302 p. 20 cm. [Lyman Beecher lectures on preaching. Yale university. 1877-78] [BV4211.D25] 38-8173
1. Preaching. I. Title.

DARGAN, Edwin Charles, 1852-1930.
The art of preaching in the light of its history, by Edwin Charles Dargan ... New York, Doran [c1922] viii, [9]-247 p. 20 cm. (Half-title: The Holland lectures ... 1921) A 23
1. Preaching. 2. Preaching—History. I. Title.

DAVIS, Ozora Stearns, 1866-1931. 251
Principles of preaching, a textbook, based on the inductive method, for class use and private study, by Ozora S. Davis ... Chicago, Ill., The University of Chicago press [1924] xvii, 270 p. 20 cm. (Half-title: University of Chicago publications in religious education, ed. by E. D. Burton, Shaller Mathews [and] T. G. Soares. Handbooks of ethics and religion) [BV4211.D3] 24-24721
1. Preaching. I. Title.

DEFFNER, Donald L. 251
The real word for the real world : applying the word to the needs of people / Donald Deffner. St. Louis : Concordia Pub. House, c1977. 40 p. ; 23 cm. (The Preacher's workshop series ; book 3) Includes bibliographical references. [BV4211.2.D37] 77-11079 ISBN 0-570-07402-9 pbk. : 1.95
1. Preaching. I. Title. II. Series.

DEMARAY, Donald E. 251
An introduction to homiletics [by] Donald E. Demaray. Grand Rapids, Mich., Baker Book House [1974] 156 p. 23 cm. Bibliography: p. 149-152. [BV4211.2.D38] 74-176239 4.95
1. Preaching. I. Title.

DENNIE, Joseph, 1768-1812.
The lay preacher, by Joseph Dennie; edited with an introduction and a bibliographical note by Milton Ellis ... New York, Scholars' facsimiles & reprints, 1943. x, [2], 184 p. incl. facsims. 23 1/2 cm. [Scholars' facsimiles & reprints] Reprint of the author's essays, originally published in two collections, 1796 and 1817, the latter edited by John E. Hall. With reproductions of original title-pages. [PS1534.D6L3 1943] 43-9749
I. Hall, John Elihu, 1783-1829. II. Ellis, Harold Milton, 1885-ed. III. Title.

DIRKS, Marvin J. 251
Laymen look at preaching; lay expectation factors in relation to the preaching of Helmut Thielicke, by Marvin J. Dirks. North Quincy, Mass., Christopher Pub. House [1972] 326 p. port. 21 cm. Bibliography: p. 317-326. [BV4211.2.D5] 79-189364 6.50
1. Thielicke, Helmut, 1908- 2. Preaching. I. Title.

DIXON, Helen (Cadbury) Alexander. Mrs. 922.673
A. C. Dixon, romance of preaching, by Helen C. A. Dixon: with 70 illustrations. New York, London, G. P. Putnam's sons, 1931. xi, 324 p. front., plates, ports., facsim. 24 cm. Maps on lining-papers. [BX6495.D55D5] 31-34619
I. Dixon Amzi Clarence, 1854-1925. II. Title.

DONNELLY, Francis Patrick, 1869-
The art of interesting; its theory and practice for speakers and writers, by Francis P. Donnelly, S. J. New York, P. J. Kenedy & sons, 1920. ix, 321 p. 20 cm. [PN41274.D7] 20-18519
1. Preaching. 2. Authorship. I. Title.

DOUGLASS, Truman B 251
Preaching and the new reformation. [1st ed.] New York, Harper [1956] 142p. 22cm. (The Lyman Beecher lectures) [BV4211.2.D6] 56-7032
1. Preaching. I. Title.

DRAWBRIDGE, Cyprian Leycester, 1868- ed. 251
Futile sermons; opinions of the primate & the press, edited by the Rev. C. L. Drawbridge... London, New York [etc.] Longmans, Green and co., ltd., 1928. viii, 9-126 p. 19 1/2 cm. $1.80 [BV4211.D7] 26-5398
1. Davidson, Randall Thomas, abp. of Canterbury, 1848- 2. Preaching. I. Title.

DUFFEY, William Richard, 1892- 251
Preaching well; the rhetoric and delivery of sacred discourse. Milwaukee, Bruce [1950] xvii, 284 p. 23 cm. [BV4211.D8] 50-13438
1. Preaching. I. Title.

DUNCAN, Walter Wofford T 1869-
The preacher and politics; a study in ministerial relation to public life, by W. Wofford T. Duncan. New York Cincinnati [etc.] The Abingdon press [c1930] 151 p. 19 cm. [BV4327.D8] 30-6632
I. Title.

EDWARDS, Otis Carl, 1928- 251'.08
The living and active word : one way to preach from the Bible today / by O. C. Edwards, Jr. New York : Seabury Press, [1975] 178 p. ; 22 cm. "A Crossroad book." Bibliography: p. [173]-178. [BS534.5.E38] 74-30038 ISBN 0-8164-0265-5 : 6.95
1. Protestant Episcopal Church in the U.S.A.—Sermons. 2. Bible—Homiletical use. 3. Preaching. 4. Sermons, American. I. Title.

ELLIS, J. comp.
Gospel seed for busy sowers; furnishing materials for preachers, evangelists, Sabbath-school teachers, and layworkers. Comp. by J. Ellis ... New York, Chicago [etc.] F. H. Revell company, [1899] 127 p. 18 cm. 99-2089
I. Title.

ELLISON, John Malcus, 1889- 251
They who preach. Nashville, Broadman Press [1956] 180 p. 21 cm. [BV4211.2.E4] 56-13821
1. Preaching. I. Title.

ELLISON, John Malcus, 1892- 251
They who preach. Nashville, Broadman Press [1956] 180p. 21cm. [BV4211.2.E4] 56-13821
1. Preaching. I. Title.

ENGLISH, John Mahan, 1845-1927. 251
For pulpit and platform; a handbook on preparation, by John Mahan English... New York, The Macmillan company, 1919. vii, 143 p. 18 cm. [BV4211.E6] 19-15255
1. Preaching. I. Title.

ERDAHL, Lowell O. 251
Better preaching / by Lowell Erdahl. St. Louis : Concordia Pub. House, c1977. p. cm. (The Preacher's workshop series ; 9) [BV4211.2.E69] 77-21826 ISBN 0-570-07408-8 pbk. : 1.95
1. Preaching. I. Title. II. Series.

ERDAHL, Lowell O. 251
Better preaching / by Lowell Erdahl. St. Louis : Concordia Pub. House, c1977. p. cm. (The Preacher's workshop series ; 9) [BV4211.2.E69] 77-21826 ISBN 0-570-07408-8 pbk. : 1.95
1. Preaching. I. Title. II. Series.

ERDAHL, Lowell O. 251
Preaching for the people / Lowell O. Erdahl. Nashville : Abingdon, c1976. 127 p. ; 20 cm. Includes bibliographical references. [BV4211.2.E7] 75-43934 ISBN 0-687-33865-4 : 5.95
1. Preaching. I. Title.

ETTER, John W 1846-1895. 251
The preacher and his sermon; a treatise on homiletics, by Rev. John W. Etter ... Dayton, O., United Brethren publishing house, 1883. 2 p. l., xiv p., 1 l., 17-581 p. 23 1/2 cm. [BV4211.E7] 38-3762
1. Preaching. I. Title.

EVANS, Irwin Henry, 1862- 251
The preacher and his preaching [by] I. H. Evans. Mountain View, Cal., Portland, Or. [etc.] Pacific press pub. assn. [c1915] 383 p. front. 23 1/2 cm. [BV4211.E77] 38-23573
1. Preaching. I. Title.

EVANS, William, 1870-1950.
How to prepare sermons, by William Evans. Rev. [ed.] Chicago, Moody Press [1964] 158 p. 22 cm. 68-30940
1. Preaching. I. Title.

FANT, Clyde E. 251
Preaching for today / Clyde E. Fant. 1st ed. New York : Harper & Row, [1975] xvi, 196 p. ; 21 cm. Includes bibliographical references. [BV4211.2.F36 1975] 74-4640 ISBN 0-06-062331-4 : 8.95
1. Preaching. I. Title.

FARMER, Herbert Henry, 1892- 251
The servant of the Word. Philadelphia, Fortress [1964, c.1942] ix, 115p. 18cm. (Preacher's paperback lib., v.1) 64-20405 2.45 pap.,
1. Preaching. I. Title.

FARMER, Herbert Henry, 1892- 251
The servant of the Word, by Herbert H. Farmer, D.D. New York, C. Scribner's sons, 1942. vii p., 1 l., 9-152 p. 19 1/2 cm. [BV4211.F3] 42-24527
1. Preaching. I. Title.

FEENEY, Bernard, 1843or4-1919. 251
Manual of sacred rhetoric; or, How to prepare a sermon. By Rev. Bernard Feeney ... St. Louis, Mo., B. Herder, 1901. 1 p. l., x p., 1 l., 5-336 p. 20 cm. [BV4211.F4] 1-10338
1. Preaching. I. Title. II. Title: How to prepare a sermon.

FERRIS, Theodore Parker, 1908- 251
Go tell the people. New York, Scribner, 1951. 116 p. 20 cm. (George Craig Stewart lectures on preaching) [BV4211.F45] 51-3166
1. Preaching. I. Title. II. Series.

FEWLER, Willis Hadley, 1908- 922
I preached in those hills. [Rev. ed.] Oklahoma City, Bond Lithographing and Print. Co. [1950, '1949] 162 p. port. 19 cm. [BV3785.F65A3 1950] 50-35184
I. Title.

FISHER, Wallace E. 251
Who dares to preach? : The challenge of Biblical preaching / Wallace E. Fisher. Minneapolis : Augsburg Pub. House, c1979. 199 p. ; 20 cm. Bibliography: p. 194-199. [BV4211.2.F57] 79-54112 ISBN 0-8066-1769-1 pbk. : 4.95
1. Preaching. I. Title.

FISK, Franklin Woodbury, 1820-1901. 251
Manual of preaching. Lectures on homiletics. By Franklin W. Fisk ... New York, A. C. Armstrong and son, 1884. xv, 337 p. 21 1/2 cm. [BV4211.F5] 38-3763
1. Preaching. I. Title.

FITCH, Albert Parker, 1877- 251
Preaching and paganism, by Albert Parker Fitch ... New Haven, Yale university press, 1920. 229, [1] p. 19 1/2 cm. (Lyman Beecher lectureship on preaching in Yale university. 46th series) "Published on the foundation established in memory of James Wesley Cooper of the class of 1865, Yale college." [BV4211.F55] 20-19512
1. Preaching. 2. Theology, Pastoral. I. Title.

FITZGERALD, George R. 251
A practical guide to preaching / George R. Fitzgerald. New York : Paulist Press, c1980. 156 p. ; 21 cm. Bibliography: 148-156. [BV4211.2.F58] 79-67742 pbk. : 4.95
1. Preaching. I. Title.

FORD, Douglas William Cleverley. 251
The ministry of the Word / D. W. Cleverley Ford. Grand Rapids, Mich. : Eerdmans, c1979. p. cm. Includes indexes. Bibliography: p. [BV4211.2.F66 1979] 79-13172 ISBN 0-8028-3524-4 : 13.95
1. Preaching. I. Title.

*FORSYTH, P. T. 251
Positive preaching and the modern mind. Grand Rapids, Mich., Eerdmans [1964] 258p. 20cm. 1.95 pap.,
I. Title.

FREEMAN, James Edward, bp., 1866- 251
The ambassador; the Lyman Beecher lectures on preaching, delivered at Yale university in the month of April, 1928. "We are ambassadors for Christ." By the Rev. James Edward Freeman ... New York, The Macmillan company, 1928. 3 p. l., 5-212 p. 20 cm. [BV4211.F65] 28-23573
1. Preaching. I. Title.

FRITZ, John Henry Charles, 1874- 251
The essentials of preaching; a refresher course in homiletics for pastors. St. Louis, Concordia Pub. House [1948] xiv, 73 p. 20 cm. [BV4211.F667] 48-6345
1. Preaching. I. Title.

FRITZ, John Henry Charles, 1874- 251
The preacher's manual; a study in homiletics, with the addition of a brief history of preaching, sermon material, texts for various occasions, and pericopic systems, by John H. C. Fritz ... St. Louis, Mo., Concordia publishing house, 1941. xi, 390 p. 24 cm. (On cover: Concordia pulpit, 1942, vol xiii) Bibliography: p. 381. [BV4211.F67] 42-776
1. Preaching. I. Title.

FRY, Jacob, 1834-1920. 251
Elementary homiletics: or, Rules and principles in the preparation and preaching of sermons. By the Rev. Jacob Fry ... New York, The Christian literature co., 1897. 145 p. 20 cm. [BV4211.F7] 38-838
1. Preaching. I. Title.

FULLER, Reginald Horace. 251
The use of the Bible in preaching / Reginald H. Fuller. Philadelphia : Fortress Press, c1981. 79 p. ; 22 cm. Bibliography: p. 75-79. [BS534.5.F84 1981] 19 80-2377 ISBN 0-8006-1447-X : 3.50
1. Bible—Homiletical use. 2. Preaching. I. Title.

GARDNER, Charles Spurgeon, 1859- 251
Psychology and preaching, by Charles S. Gardner ... New York, The Macmillan company, 1918. 7 p. l., 389 p. 20 1/2 cm. $2.00 "Two of the chapters have been previously published,--that on Belief in the Review and expositor, and that on Assemblies in the American journal of sociology."--Pref. [BV4211.G3] 18-9359
1. Preaching. 2. Psychology. I. Title.

GARRISON, Webb B. 251
Creative imagination in preaching. Nashville, Abingdon Press [c.1960] 175p. 21cm. (bibl. notes: p.163-166) 60-9197 3.00
1. Preaching. 2. Creation (Literary, artistic, etc.) I. Title.

GARRISON, Webb B 251
The preacher and his audience. [Westwood, N.J.] Revell [1954] 285p. illus. 22cm. Includes bibliography. [BV4211.G33] 54-8003
1. Preaching. I. Title.

GARVIE, Alfred Ernest, 1861- 251
... The Christian preacher, by Alfred Ernest Garvie ... New York, C. Scribner's sons, 1921. xxviii, 490 p. 21 cm. (Half-title: International theological library) [BV4211.G35 1921] 28-26502
1. Preaching. I. Title.

GIBSON, George Miles, 1896- 251
Planned preaching. Philadelphia, Westminster Press [1954] 140p. 21cm. [BV4211.G5] 54-5653
1. Preaching. I. Title.

GILMORE, Alec. 251
Tomorrow's pulpit. Valley Forge, Pa., Judson Press [1975] 95 p. 22 cm. Originally presented as the Edwin Griffith Memorial lectures, Cardiff Baptist College, June 12-13, 1973. Bibliography: p. 89-92. [BV4211.2.G5] 74-13494 ISBN 0-8170-0641-9 3.50 (pbk.)
1. Preaching. I. Title.

GONZALEZ, Justo L. 251
Liberation preaching : the pulpit and the oppressed / Justo L. Gonzalez and Catherine Gunsalus Gonzalez. Nashville : Abingdon, c1980. 127 p. ; 20 cm. (Abingdon preacher's library) Includes indexes. Bibliography: p. 119-120. [BV4211.2.G65] 19 79-27858 ISBN 0-687-14850-2 pbk. : 4.95
1. Bible—Criticism, interpretation, etc. 2. Preaching. 3. Liberation theology. I. Gunsalus Gonzalez, Catherine, joint author. II. Title.

GRAHAM, Henry, 1841-
The preacher and his work, by Rev. Henry Graham, D. D. New York, Eaton & Mains; Cincinnati, Jennings & Graham [c1906] 294 p. 20 cm. 6-27986
I. Title.

GRASSO, Domenico, 1917- 251
Proclaiming God's message: a study in the theology of preaching. [Notre Dame, Ind.] Univ. of Notre Dame Pr. [c.]1965. xxxiii, 272p. 24cm. (Notre Dame Univ. Liturgical studies, v. 8) Bibl. [BV4211.2.G7] 65-14739 bds., 6.00; text ed., 4.00
1. Kerygma. 2. Preaching. I. Title. II. Series.

GRAY, Joseph M M 1877- 250
Sufficient ministers, by Joseph M. M. Gray, introduction by Bishop William F. McDowell. New York, Cincinnati, The Abingdon press [c1925] 134 p. 20 cm. Lectures delivered at De Pauw university, on the Matter Simpson foundation for lectures on preaching. cf. Foreword. [BV4010.G74] 25-8451
I. Title.

GREER, David Hummell, bp., 1844-1919. 251
The preacher and his place; the Lyman Beecher lectures on preaching, delivered at Yale university in the month of February, 1895. By Rev. David, H. Greer ... New York, C. Scribner's sons, 1895. 2 p. l., 263 p. 20 cm. [BV4211.G73] 38-839
1. Preaching. I. Title.

GRENNAN, Stanislaus, father, 1860- 251
The ministry of preaching, treating of the composition and delivery of religious discourse, by Rev. Stanislaus Grennan ... [Baltimore, Md., Printed by the Hess printing company, pref. 1936] 124 p. 19 cm. "This work ... is a revision of my 'Lessons in homiletics'."--Pref. [Secular name: Joseph Grennan] Bibliography: p. 124. [BV4211.G785] 40-36616
1. Preaching. I. Title.

GRESLEY, William, 1801-1876. 251
Ecclesiastes anglicanus; being a treatise on preaching, as adapted to a Church of England congregation: in a series of letters to a young clergyman. By the Rev. W. Greseley ... 1st American, from the second English ed., with supplementary notes collected and arranged by the Rev. Benjamin I. Haight ... New York, Appleton and co.; Philadelphia, G. S. Appleton, 1843. xvi, 340 p. 20 cm. [BV4211.G74] 38-635
1. Preaching. I. Title.

GRITTI, Jules 251
Precher aux hommes de notre temps [Toulouse] Privat [dist. Philadelphia, Chilton, 1964] 159p. 19cm. (Question posees aux catholiques) Bibl. 64-9075 1.00 pap.,
1. Preaching. I. Title.

GUNSAULUS, Frank Wakeley, 1856-1921. 251
... The minister and the spiritual life, by Frank W. Gunsaulus ... New York, Chicago [etc.] Fleming H. Revell company [c1911] 3 p. l., 9-397 p. 22 cm. (Yale lectures on preaching) [BV4211.G8] 12-850
1. Preaching. 2. Spiritual life. I. Title.

HALL, John, 1829-1898. 251
God's word through preaching. The Lyman Beecher lectures before the theological department of Yale college. (Fourth series.) By John Hall,D.D. New York, Dodd & Mead [1875] 2 p. l., 274 p. 19 1/2 cm. [BV4211.H3] 36-8172
1. Preaching. I. Title.

HALL, Thor, 1927- 251
The future shape of preaching. Philadelphia, Fortress Press [1971] xx, 140 p. 22 cm. Includes bibliographical references. [BV4211.2.H25] 77-157537 ISBN 0-8006-0019-3 3.50
1. Preaching. I. Title.

HALVORSON, Arndt L., 1915- 251
Authentic preaching / Arndt L. Halvorson. Minneapolis : Augsburg Pub. House, c1982. 188 p. ; 20 cm. [BV4211.2.H26] 19 81-52269 ISBN 0-8066-1901-5 pbk. : 7.95
1. Preaching. I. Title.

HARMS, Paul W. F. 251
Power from the pulpit : delivering the good news / Paul Harms. St. Louis : Concordia Pub. House, c1977. 54 p. ; 23 cm. (The Preacher's workshop series ; book 7) Bibliography: p. 52-55. [BV4211.2.H28] 77-11080 ISBN 0-570-07406-1 pbk. : 1.95
1. Preaching. I. Title. II. Series.

HARRIS, James, 1709-1780. 251
An essay on the action proper for the pulpit. New York, Garland Pub., 1971. 86 p. 21 cm. Bound with the author's Upon the rise and progress of criticism. New York, 1971. Facsim. of the 1753 ed. [B809.3.H37 1752a] [BV4210] [BV4210] 224 016.329 78-112117
1. Preaching. I. Title.

HASELDEN, Kyle. 251
The urgency of preaching. [1st ed.] New York, Harper & Row [1963] 121 p. 20 cm. [BV2311.2.H3] 63-10751
1. Preaching. I. Title.

HATCHER, Eldridge Burwell, 1865- 251
Christ in the marvelous Book, by Eldridge B. Hatcher... Grand Rapids, Mich., Zondervan publishing house [c1940] 125 p. 19 1/2 cm. "This book...makes its plea for more Christ-centered and less mancentered preaching."--Pref. [BV4211.H316] 40-10258
1. Preaching. I. Title.

HAYNES, Carlyle Boynton, 1882- 251
The divine art of preaching, by Carlyle B. Haynes ... Takoma Park, Washington, D.C., Review and herald publishing association [c1939] 256 p. 20 1/2 cm. (Ministerial reading course selection for 1940, Ministerial association of Seventh-day Adventists) Bibliography: p. 246-248. [BV4211.H317] 39-31044
1. Preaching. I. Title.

HENRY, Hugh Thomas, 1862- 251
Hints to preachers, by Rt. Rev. Msgr. Hugh T. Henry ... New York, Cincinnati [etc.] Benziger brothers, 1924. 299 p. 19 cm. "Reference works quoted": p. 287-289. [BV4211.H32] 24-6986
I. Title.

HENRY, Hugh Thomas, 1862- 251
Hints to preachers, by Rt. Rev. Msgr. Hugh T. Henry ... New York, Cincinnati [etc.] Benziger brothers, 1924. 299 p. 19 cm. "Reference works quoted": p. 287-289. [BV4211.H32] 24-6986
I. Title.

HENRY, Hugh Thomas, 1862- 251
Papers on preaching, by the Right Reverend Monsignor Hugh T. Henry ... Philadelphia, The Peter Reilly company; [etc., etc.] 1925. v, 254 p. 22 cm. "Thirteen of the Papers included in this volume were contributed to the Ecclesiastical review. The others are now printed for the first time." "Works quoted": p. 252-254. [BV4211.H325] 26-8109
1. Preaching. I. Title.

HENRY, Hugh Thomas, 1862- 251
Preaching, by the Right Rev. Msgr. Hugh T. Henry ... New York city, J. F. Wagner, inc.; London, B. Herder [c1941] vi, 282 p. 22 cm. "List of authors and works cited": p. 271-272. [BV4211.H326] 41-26529
1. Preaching. I. Title.

HENSON, Herbert Hensley, bp. of Durham, 1863- 251
The liberty of prophesying, with its just limits and temper considered with reference to the circumstances of the modern church; Lyman Beecher lectures delivered 1909, before the Yale divinity school, and three sermons, by H. Hensley

Henson ... New Haven, Conn., Yale university press, 1910. 3 p. l., v-xi, 293 p. 20 cm. [BV4211.H33] 9-31072
1. Preaching. 2. Christianity. I. Title.

HERVEY, George Winfred. 251
A system of Christian rhetoric, for the use of preachers and other speakers. By George Winfred Hervey ... New York, Harper & brothers, 1873. 5 p. l., 632 p. 24 cm. [BV4211.H35] 38-3761
1. Preaching. I. Title.

HIGDON, Barbara McFarlane. 251
Good news for today / by Barbara McFarlane Higdon. [Independence, Mo.] : H[erald] H[ouse] c1981. 172 p. : ill. ; 20 cm. Includes bibliographical references. [BV4211.2.H46] 19 80-25324 ISBN 0-8309-0298-8 : Price Unreported
1. Preaching. I. Title.

HITZ, Paul. 251
To preach the gospel. Translated by Rosemary Sheed. New York, Sheed and Ward [1963] 209 p. 21 cm. Translation of L'annonce missionaire de l'evangile. [BV4211.2.H513] 63-11552
1. Preaching. 2. Kerygma. I. Title.

HOEFLER, Richard Carl. 251
Oral writing; the art of effective manuscript preaching. Introd. by E. Eppling Reinartz. [Columbia, S.C.? 1964] 118 p. 21 cm. Bibliographical references included in "Notes" (p. 117-118) [BV4211.2.H6] 65-461
1. Preaching. I. Title.

HOLMES, George. 251
Toward an effective pulpit ministry. Springfield, Mo., Gospel Pub. House [1971] 176 p. 20 cm. [BV4211.2.H63] 72-152056
1. Preaching. I. Title.

HOMILETICAL and pastoral lectures. 251 Delivered in St. Paul's cathedral before the Church homiletical society. With a preface by the Right Rev. C. J. Ellicott, D.D., lord bishop of Gloucester and Bristol. New York, A. C. Armstrong & son, 1880. xv, 530 p. 19 cm. [BV4211.H44] 42-47753
1. Preaching. 2. Theology, Pastoral. I. Ellicott, Charles John, bp. of Gloucester, 1819-1905, ed.

HOOD, Edwin Paxton, 1820-1885. 251
Lamps, pitchers and trumpets; lectures on the vocation of the preacher. Illustrated by anecdotes, biographical, historical, and elucidatory, of every order of pulpit eloquence, from the great preachers of all ages. By Edwin Paxton Hood ...2d ser. New York, M. W. Dood, 1869. 4 p. l., 11-308 p. 20 cm. [BV4211.H45] 1-1732
1. Preaching. 2. Theology, Pastoral. I. Title.

HOPPIN, James Mason, 1820-1906. 251
Homiletics, by James M. Hoppin ... New York, Dodd, Mead & company [1882] 2 p. l., [iii]-xxxv, 809 p. 21 1/2 cm. "Literature of homiletics": p. [1]-6. [BV4211.H5] 38-3743
1. Preaching. I. Title.

HORNE, Charles Silvester, 1865-1914. 251.
The romance of preaching, by Charles Silvester Horne, with an introduction by Charles R. Brown, D. D., and a biographical sketch by Howard A. Bridgman, D. D. New York, Chicago [etc.] Fleming H. Revell company [c1914] 302 p. front. (port.) 21cm. (Yale lectures on preaching) [BV4207.H6] 14-16564
1. Preaching. 2. Orators. 3. Evangelistic work. I. Title.

HORNE, Chevis F. 251
Crisis in the pulpit : the pulpit faces future shock / Chevis F. Horne. Grand Rapids : Baker Book House, [1975] 144 p. ; 23 cm. Includes bibliographical references. [BV4211.2.H66] 74-20203 ISBN 0-8010-4108-2 : 4.95
1. Preaching. I. Title.

HORTON, Robert Forman, 1855-1934. 251
Verbum Dei. The Yale lectures on preaching, 1893. By Robert F. Horton ... New York and London, Macmillan & co., 1893. 300 p. 20 cm. [PV4211.H55] 38-3211
1. Preaching. I. Title.

HOUGH, Lynn Harold.
The theology of a preacher, by Lynn Harold Hough. New York, Eaton & Mains; Cincinnati, Jennings & Graham [c1912] 269 p. 19 1/2 cm. $1.00 12-5820
I. Title.

HOWE, Reuel L. 251
Partners in preaching; clergy and laity in dialogue [by] Reuel L. Howe. New York, Seaburv [1967] 127p. 22cm. In an earlier form these chapters were the Princeton Seminarv Alumni lects., delivered in Sept. 1965. [BV4221.H6] 67-20937 3.50
1. Preaching. 2. Communication (Theology) I. Title.

HOYT, Arthur Stephen, 1851-1924. 251
The preacher; his person, message, and method; a book for the class-room and study, by Arthur S. Hoyt ... New York, The Macmillan company, 1909. x, [2], 380 p. 19 1/2 cm. Contains bibliographies. [BV4211.H6] 9-4142
1. Preaching. I. Title.

HOYT, Arthur Stephen, 1851-1924. 251
Vital elements of preaching, by Arthur S. Hoyt ... New York, The Macmillan company, 1914. ix, 326 p. 20 cm. $1.50 "These lectures were given at the University of Chicago, in the summer term of nineteen hundred and twelve, and for three years to senior science at Auburn seminary."--Pref. [BV4211.H65] 14-16566
1. Preaching. I. Title.

HOYT, Arthur Stephen, 1851-1924. 251
The work of preaching; a book for the class-room and study, by Arthur S. Hoyt ... New York, The Macmillan company; London, Macmillan and co., ltd., 1905. ix, 355 p. 20 cm. [BV4211.H7 1905] 5-41737
1. Preaching. I. Title.

HUBERT de Romans 1194?-1277. 251
Treatise on preaching. Translated by the Dominican students, Province of St. Joseph; edited by Walter M. Conlon. Westminster, Md., Newman Press, 1951. xiii, 160 p. 21 cm. Translation of Liber de eruditione praedicationis. [BV4209.H83] 51-10275
1. Preaching. I. Title.

HUMPSTONE, John. 251
Man and message, eminent preachers who exemplify chief principles of ministerial efficiency; the Samuel A. Crozer lectures for 1926, by John Humpstone ... Philadelphia, Boston [etc.] The Judson press [c1926] 6 p. l., 3-245 p. 19 1/2 cm. [BV4211.H8] 27-3108
1. Preaching. 2. Clergy. I. Title.
Contents omitted.

HUNT, Ernest Edward. 251'.01
Sermon struggles : four methods of sermon preparation / Ernest Edward Hunt, III. New York : Seabury Press, 1982. xviii, 133 p. ; 21 cm. Bibliography: p. 131-133. [BV4211.2.H86 1982] 19 81-18344 ISBN 0-8164-2375-X pbk. : 8.95
1. Episcopal Church—Sermons. 2. Preaching. 3. Sermons, American. I. Title.

HUTCHINS, William James, 1871- 250
... *The preacher's ideals and inspirations,* by William J. Hutchins ... New York, Chicago [etc.] Fleming H. Revell company [c1917] 187 p. 20 cm. (Lectures on the George Shepard foundation, Bangor convocation, 1916) [BV4010.H9] 17-16186 1.00
I. Title.

JABUSCH, Willard. 251
The person in the pulpit : preaching as caring / Willard Francis Jabusch. Nashville : Abingdon, c1980. 127 p. ; 20 cm. (Abingdon preacher's library) Includes bibliographical references and index. [BV4211.2.J28] 19 79-28812 ISBN 0-687-30784-8 pbk. : 4.95
1. Preaching. I. Title.

JACKSON, Edgar Newman. 261
How to preach to people's needs. New York, Abingdon Press [c1956] 191p. 21cm. [BV4211.J25] 55-10269
1. Preaching. 2. Psychology, Pastoral. I. Title.

JACKSON, Edgar Newman 251
A psychology for preaching. Pref. by Harry Emerson Fosdick. Great Neck, N. Y., Channel Press [c.1961] 191p. Bibl. 61-7573 3.50 bds.,
1. Preaching. I. Title.

JACKSON, Edgar Newman. 251
A psychology for preaching Pref. by Harry Emerson Fosdick. Great Neck, N. Y., Channel Press [1961] 191p. 21cm. [BV4211.2.J3] 61-7573
1. Preaching. I. Title.

JACKSON, Edgar Newman. 251
A psychology for preaching / Edgar N. Jackson. San Francisco : Harper & Row, 1981. p. cm. (Harper's ministers paperback library) [BV4211.2.J3 1981] 19 81-47430 ISBN 0-06-064111-8 pbk. : 5.95
1. Preaching. I. Title. II. Series.

JEFFERSON, Charles Edward, 1860-1937. 251
The minister as prophet, by Charles Edward Jefferson ... New York, T. Y. Crowell & co. [c1905] v. 187 p. 18 cm. (Half-title: The George Shepard lectures on preaching, at Bengor theological seminary, 1904-1905) [BV4211.J38] 5-9712
1. Preaching. I. Title.

JENSEN, Richard A. 251
Telling the story : variety and imagination in preaching / Richard A. Jensen. Minneapolis : Augsburg Pub. House, c1980. 189 p. ; 20 cm. [BV4211.2.J45] 79-54113 ISBN 0-8066-1766-7 pbk. : 5.95
1. Lutheran Church—Sermons. 2. Preaching. 3. Sermons, American. I. Title.

JOHNSON, Howard Albert, 1915- ed. 251
Preaching the Christian year [by] Hughell E. W. Fosbroke [and others] Edited for the Dean and Chapter of the Cathedral Church of St. John the Divine. With a foreword by James A. Pike. New York, Scribner [1957] 243p. 22cm. Includes bibliography. [BV4211.2.J57] 57-12061
1. Preaching. 2. Church year. I. Fosbroke, Hughell E. W. II. Title.

JOHNSON, Howard Albert, 1915- ed. 251
Preaching the Christian year [by] Hughell E.W. Fosbroke [and others] Edited for the Dean and Chapter of the Cathedral Church of St. John the Divine. With a foreword by James A. Pike. New York, Scribner [1957] 243p. 22cm. Includes bibliography. [BV4211.2.J57] 57-12061
1. Preaching. 2. Church year. I. Fosbroke, Hughell E.W. II. Title.

JONES, Bob 251
How to improve your preaching. New enl. ed. Grand Rapids, Kregel Publication [c.1945, 1960] 151p. 20cm. (bibl.: p.148-151) 59-14905 2.50
1. Preaching. I. Title.

JONES, Bob, 1911- 251
How to improve your preaching. New enl. ed. Grand Rapids, Kregel Publications [1960] 151p. 20cm. Includes bibliography. [BV4211.J6 1960] 59-14905
1. Preaching. I. Title.

JONES, Bob, 1911- 251
How to improve your preaching, by Bob Jones, jr. ... New York, London [etc.] Fleming H. Revell company [1945] 126 p. 19 cm. Bibliography: p. 123-126. [BV4211.J6] 45-5005
1. Preaching. I. Title.

JONES, E. Winston. 251
Preaching and the dramatic arts. New York, Macmillan Co., 1948. ix, 123 p. 21 cm. Bibliographical footnotes. [BV4211.J615] 48-9572
1. Preaching. I. Title.

JONES, Ilion Tingnal, 1889- 251
Principles and practice of preaching. New York, Abingdon Press [1956] 272p. 23cm. [BV4211.2.J6] 56-7761
1. Preaching. I. Title.

JORDAN, Gerald Ray, 1896- 251
Preaching during a revolution: patterns of procedure. Anderson, Ind., Warner Press [1962] 192p. 22cm. [BV4211.2.J62] 62-11773
1. Preaching. I. Title.

JORDAN, Gerald Ray, 1896- 251
You can preach! Building and delivering the sermon. [Westwood, N. J.] Revell [c1958] 256p. 21cm. (Revell's preaching and pastoral aid series) [BV4211.2.J63 1958] 59-5501
1. Preaching. I. Title.

JORDAN, Gerald Ray, 1896- 251
You can preach! Building and delivering the sermon. New York, Revell [1951] 256 p. 22 cm. [BV4211.J63] 51-11399
1. Preaching. I. Title.

KEIGHTON, Robert Elwood, 1896- 251
The man who would preach. New York, Abingdon Press [1956] 128p. 20cm. [BV4211.2.K38] 56-7762
1. Preaching. I. Title.

KELMAN, John, 1864-1929. 250
... *The war and preaching,* by John Kelman ... New Haven, Yale university press, 1919. 4 p. l., 216 p. 21 cm. (Lyman Beecher lectureship on preaching, Yale university, 45 series [1918-19]) [BV4010.K4] 19-15030
1. Preaching. 2. European war, 1914-1918—Addresses, sermons, etc. 3. European war, 1914-1918—Religious aspects. I. Title.

KEMP, Charles F., 1912- ed. 251
Pastoral preaching. St. Louis, Bethany [c.1963] 252p. 22cm. 63-13913 4.00
1. Preaching. 2. Sermons, American. I. Title.

KEMP, Charles F. 1912- ed. 251
The preaching pastor, by Charles F. Kemp. St. Louis, Bethany Press [1966] 251 p. 21 cm. Bibliographical footnotes. [BV4211.2.K393] 66-22922
1. Preaching. 2. Sermons, American — Collections. I. Title.

KENNEDY, Gerald Hamilton, Bp., 1907- 251
God's good news. [1st ed.] New York, Harper [1955] 182p. 22cm. [BV4211.2.K4] 54-11662
1. Preaching. I. Title.

KENNEDY, Gerald Hamilton, Bp., 1907- 251
His word through preaching. New York, Harper [1947] x, 234 p. 22 cm. [BV4211.K415] 47-2123
1. Preaching. I. Title.

KENNEDY, Gerald Hamilton, 1907- 251
His word through preaching [by] Gerald Kennedy. New York, London, Harper & brothers [1947] x, 234 p. 21 1/2 cm. [BV4211.K415] 47-2123
1. Preaching. I. Title.

KENNEDY, Gerald Hamilton, Bp., 1907- 251
Who speaks for God? Nashville, Abingdon Press [1954] 139 p. 23 cm. [BV4211.K417] 54-9196
1. Preaching. I. Title.

KENNEDY, James William, 1905- 251
Parson's sampler, patterns whereby words become the language of power. Boston, Pilgrim Press [1948] xvi, 230 p. 22 cm. [BV4211.K42] 48-8115
1. Preaching. 2. Theology, Pastoral. I. Title.

KERN, John Adam, 1846-1926. 251
The ministry to the congregation; lectures on homiletics, by John A. Kern ... Nashville, Tenn., Publishing house of the Methodist Episcopal church, South, Barbee & Smith, agents [1897?] xvii, 551 p. 21 cm. [BV4211.K45 1897a] 35-22523
1. Preaching. 2. Public worship. I. Title.

KERN, John Adam, 1846-1926. 251
The ministry to the congregation; lectures on homiletics, by John A. Kern ... New York, W. B. Ketcham [1897] xvii, 551 p. 21 cm. [BV4211.K45 1897] 35-32548
1. Preaching. 2. Public worship. I. Title.

KERN, John Adam, 1846-1926. 251
Vision and power; a study in the ministry

of preaching, by John A. Kern ... New York, Chicago [etc.] Fleming H. Revell company [c1915] 395 p. 21 cm. [BV4211.K47] 15-24013
1. Preaching. I. Title.

KIDDER, Daniel Parish, 1815-1891. 251
A treatise on homiletics: designed to illustrate the true theory and practice of preaching the gospel. By Daniel P. Kidder ... New York, Carlton & Porter, 1834. 495 p. 19 1/2 cm. [BV4211.K5 1864] 38-3759
1. Preaching. I. Title.

KIDDER, Daniel Parish, 1815-1891. 251
A treatise on homiletics, designed to illustrate the true theory and practice of preaching the gospel. By Daniel P. Kidder ... Rev. ed. New York, Hunt & Eaton. Cincinnati, Cranston & Curts, 1894. 394 p. 29 cm. First published in 1866. [BV4211.K5 1894] 38-8176
1. Preaching. I. Title.

KILLINGER, John. 251
The centrality of preaching in the total task of the ministry. Waco, Tex., Word Books [1969] 123 p. 23 cm. [BV4211.2.K5] 69-12817 3.95
1. Preaching. 2. Clergy—Office. I. Title.

KIRKPATRICK, Robert White, 1908- 251
The creative delivery of sermons [by] Robert White Kirkpatrick ... with a foreword by Dr. Ralph W. Sockman. New York, The Macmillan company, 1944. xxii p., 1 l., 235 p. incl. form., diagr. 19 1/2 cm. "First printing." Bibliography: p. 233-235. [BV4211.K54] 44-2165
1. Preaching. I. Title.

KLEISER, Grenville, 1868- ed. 232.
Christ, the master speaker, by Grenville Kleiser ... New York and London, Funk & Wagnalls company, 1920. vii, 9-205 p. 18 cm. [BT590.P7K5] 20-7277
1. Jesus Christ—Preaching. 2. Preaching. I. Bible, N. T. English. Selections. 1920. II. Bible. English. Selections, N. T. 1920. III. Title.
Contents omitted.

†KNOCHE, H. Gerard. 251
The creative task : writing the sermon / H. Gerard Knoche. St. Louis : Concordia Pub. House, c1977. 46 p. ; 23 cm. (The Preacher's workshop series ; book 5) Includes bibliographical references. [BV4211.2.K54] 77-10787 ISBN 0-570-07404-5 : 1.95
1. Preaching. I. Title. II. Series.

KNOTT, Harold Elkin. 251
How to prepare an expository sermon, by Harold E. Knott ... Cincinnati, O., The Standard publishing company [c1930] 138 p. 20 cm. [BV4211.K58] 252.8 30-19600
1. Preaching. I. Title.

KNOX, John, 1900- 251
The integrity of preaching. New York, Abingdon Press [1957] 96p. 20cm. (Lectures on the James A. Gray Fund of the Divinity School of Duke University, Durham, North Carolina) [BV4211.2.K56] 57-5279
1. Preaching. I. Title.

KNOX, John, 1900- 251
The intergrity of preaching. New York, Abingdon Press [1957] 96p. 20cm. (Lectures on the James A. Gray Fund of the Divinity School of Duke University, Durham, North Carolina) [BV4211.2.K56] 57-5279
1. Preaching. I. Title.

KOLLER, Charles W., 1886- 251
Expository preaching without notes. Grand Rapids, Mich., Baker Bk. [c.]1962. 132p. 20cm. (Evangelical pulpit lib.) 62-21703 2.50
1. Preaching. I. Title.

KRAUS, Hans Joachim. 251
The threat and the power. Translated by Keith Crim. Richmond, Va., John Knox Press [1971] 107 p. 21 cm. Translation of Predigt aus Vollmacht. Bibliography: p. [105]-107. [BV4214.K713] 73-93827 3.95
1. Preaching. I. Title.

KROLL, Woodrow Michael, 1944- 251
Prescription for preaching / Woodrow Michael Kroll. Grand Rapids, Mich. : Baker Book House, c1980. xiii, 278 p. ; 23 cm. Includes index. Bibliography: p. 257-269. [BV4211.2.K73] 19 80-142663 ISBN 0-8010-5409-5 : 9.95
1. Preaching. I. Title.

LANGHORNE, John, 1735-1779. 251
Letters on the eloquence of the pulpit. New York, Garland Pub., 1970. 75, [1] p. 22 cm. Facsim. of a Yale University Library copy with imprint: London, Printed for T. Becket and P. A. de Hondt, 1765. "Books written by Mr. Langhorne": p. [76] Bound with Webb, Daniel. Literary amusements, in verse and prose. New York, 1970; Whally, Peter. An essay on the manner of writing history. New York, 1970; and Manwaring, Edward. Harmony and numbers in Latin and English. New York, 1970. [BV4210.L34 1765a] 70-112174
1. Preaching. I. Title.

LEAVELL, Roland Quinche, 1891-1963. 224
Prophetic preaching, then and now. Grand Rapids Mich., Baker Bk. [c.]1963. 96p. 20cm. 63-19098 2.25
1. Preaching. 2. Bible. O. T. Prophets—Homiletical use. I. Title.

LEAVELL, Roland Quinche, 1891-1963. 224
Prophetic preaching, then and now. Grand Rapios, Baker Book House, 1963. 96 p. 20 cm. [BV4211.2.L4] 63-19098
1. Preaching. 2. Bible. O.T. Prophets — Homiletical use. I. Title.

LEHMAN, H. T. 251
Heralds of the Gospel. Philadelphia, Muhlenberg Press [1953] 76p. 20cm. [BV4211.L43] 53-9215
1. Preaching. I. Title.

LEHMANN, Helmut T 251
Heralds of the Gospel. Philadelphia, Muhlenberg Press [1953] 76 p. 20 cm. [BV4211.2.L44] 53-9215
1. Preaching. I. Title.

LENSKI, Richard Charles Henry, 1864-1936. 251
The sermon; its homiletical construction. Introd. by Ralph G. Turnbull. Grand Rapids, Baker Book House [1968] 314 p. 20 cm. (Notable books on preaching) First published in 1927. [BV4211.L425 1968] 68-3995
1. Preaching. I. Title.

LEWIS, Ralph Loren, 1919- 251
Speech for persuasive preaching [by] Ralph L. Lewis. Wilmore, Ky. [1968] x, 276 p. 23 cm. Bibliography: p. 266-270. [BV4211.2.L48] 68-3037
1. Preaching. I. Title.

LINN, Edmund Holt. 251.01
Preaching as counseling; the unique method of Harry Emerson Fosdick. Valley Forge [Pa.] Judson Press [1966] 159 p. 23 cm. Bibliographical references included in "Notes" (p. 157-159) [BV4211.2.L52] 66-28296
1. Fosdick, Harry Emerson, 1878- 2. Preaching. I. Title.

LISCHER, Richard. 251
A theology of preaching : the dynamics of the Gospel / Richard Lischer. Nashville, Tenn. : Abingdon, c1981. 112 p. ; 20 cm. Includes bibliographical references and indexes. [BV4211.2.L536] 19 81-1470 ISBN 0-687-41570-5 : 4.95
1. Preaching. I. Title.

LISKE, Thomas V 251
Effective preaching. 2d ed. New York, Macmillan, 1960. 349p. 21cm. Includes bibliography. [BV4211.2.L54 1960] 60-15046
1. Preaching. I. Title.

LISKE, Thomas V. 251
Effective preaching. New York, Macmillan, 1951. 293 p. 21 cm. [BV4211.L5] 51-14326
1. Preaching. I. Title.

LITTORIN, Frank T 1900- 251.8
How to preach the Word with variety. Grand Rapids, Baker Book House, 1953. 157p. 21cm. [BV4211.L55] 53-3411
1. Preaching. I. Title.

*LOCKYER, Herbert. 251
The art and craft of preaching. Grand Rapids, Baker Book House [1975] 118 p. 19 cm. [BV4211.2] ISBN 0-8010-5556-3 2.95 (pbk.)
1. Preaching. I. Title.

LOWRY, Eugene L. 251
The homiletical plot : the sermon as narrative art form / Eugene L. Lowry. Atlanta : John Knox Press, c1980. p. cm. Includes bibliographical references. [BV4211.2.L68] 80-15811 ISBN 0-8042-1652-5 (pbk.) : 3.95
1. Preaching. I. Title.

LUCCOCK, Halford Edward, 1885- 251
Communicating the Gospel. [1st ed.] New York, Harper [c1954] 183p. 22cm. (The Lyman Beecher lectures on preaching, Yale University. 1958) [BV4211.L78] 53-10974
1. Preaching. I. Title.

LUCCOCK, Halford Edward, 1885- 250
In the minister's workshop, by Halford E. Luccock. New York, Nashville, Abingdon-Cokesbury press [1944] 254 p. 20 1/2 cm. "References": p. 241-246. [BV4211.L8] 44-6948
1. Preaching. I. Title.

LUTHI, Walter 251
Preaching. Confession. The Lord's Supper. [By] Walter Luthi [and] Eduard Thurneysen. Translated [from the German] by Francis J. Brooke, III. Richmond, Va., John Knox Press [c.1960] 121p. 21cm. 60-9291 2.50
1. Preaching. 2. Confession. 3. Lord's Supper. I. Thurneysen, Eduard Evangelical confession. II. Title.

LUTHI, Walter, 1901- 251
Preaching. Confession. The Lord's Supper. [By] Walter Luthi [and] Eduard. Thurneysen. Translated by Francis J. Brooke, III. Richmond. John Knox Press [1960] 121p. 21cm. [BV4211.2.L813] 60-9291
1. Preaching. 2. Confession. 3. Lord's Supper. I. Thurneysen, Eduard, 1888- Evangelical confession. II. Title.

LYMAN, Albert Josiah, 1845-1915. 251
Preaching in the new age; an art and an incarnation; a series of six lectures delivered in the Hartford theological seminary upon the "Carew" foundation in the spring of 1900 by Albert J. Lyman, D.D. New York, Chicago [etc.] Fleming H. Revell company, 1902. 7 p. l., 13-147 p. 19 1/2 cm. Contents.Introductory.--Preaching an art.--Preaching an incarnation.--The new age and its relation to preaching.--The preacher of to-day preparing his sermon.--The preacher of to-day before his congregation. [BV4211.L9] 2-16085
1. Preaching. I. Title.

*MACARTNEY, Clarence Edward. 251
Preaching without notes / by Clarence Edward Macartney. Grand Rapids : Baker Book House, 1976c1946. 186p. ; 20 cm. (Notable books on preaching) [BV4211.2] ISBN 0-8010-5992-5 pbk. : 2.95
1. Preaching. I. Title.

MACARTNEY, Clarence Edward Noble, 1879- 251
Preaching without notes, by Clarence Edward Macartney ... New York, Nashville, Abingdon-Cokesbury press [1946] 186 p. 19 1/2 cm. [BV4211.M14] 46-7141
1. Preaching. I. Title.

MCCALL, Oswald Walter Samuel, 1885- 251
The uses of literature in the pulpit, by Oswald W. S. McCall ... New York and London, Harper & brothers, 1932. vii p., 1 l., 127 p. 19 1/2 cm. "First edition." [BV4211.M13] 32-11676
1. Preaching. 2. Literature. 3. Homiletical illustrations. I. Title.

MCCOMB, Samuel, 1864- 251
Preaching in theory and practice, by the Rev. Smauel McComb, D.D., with an introduction by the Rev. Harry Emerson Fosdick, D.D. New York, London [etc.] Oxford university press, 1926. xiii, 231 p. 19 1/2 cm. "Selected bibliography": p. [229]-231. [BV4211.M15] 26-14929
1. Preaching. I. Title.

MCCONNELL, Francis John, bp., 1871. 251
The preacher and the people, [by] Francis John McConnell... New York, Cincinnati, The Abingdon press [c1922] 166 p. 19 cm. "The substance of three lectures delivered at De Pauw university, Greencastle, Indiana, in April, 1921, on the Matthew Simpson foundation for lectures on preaching."--Pref. [BV4211.M2] 22-18793
I. Title.

MCCONNELL, Francis John, bp., 1871- 251
The preacher and the people [by] Francis John McConnell ... New York, Cincinnati, The Abingdon press [c1922] 166 p. 19 cm. "The substance of three lectures delivered at De Pauw university, Greencastle, Indiana, in April, 1921, on the Matthew Simpson foundation for lectures on preaching."--Pref. [BV4211.M2] 22-18793
1. Preaching. I. Title.

MCCRACKEN, Robert James. 251
The making of the sermon. [1st ed.] New York, Harper [c1956] 104p. 20cm. [BV4211.M22] 55-11481
1. Preaching. I. Title.

MACGREGOR, William Malcolm, 1861-1944. 251
The making of a preacher ... by W. M. Macgregor; with an appreciation by A. J. Gossip. Philadelphia, The Westminster press [1946] 96 p. 19 1/2 cm. (The Warrack lectures) [BV4211.M23 1946] 46-20761
1. Preaching. I. Title.
Contents omitted.

MCILVAINE, Charles Pettit, bp., 1799-1873. 251
The work of preaching Christ. A charge; delivered to the clergy of the diocese of Ohio, at its forty-sixth annual convention, in St. Paul's church, Akron, on the 3d of June, 1863. By Charles Pettit McIlvaine ... 2d ed. New York, A. D. F. Randolph, 1864. 72 p. 17 cm. [BV4211.M25 1864] 38-3760
1. Preaching. I. Title.

MCILVAINE, Charles Pettit, bp., 1799-1873. 251
The work of preaching Christ. By Charles Pettit McIlvaine ... Boston, Gospel book and tract depository, 1871. 72 p. 17 1/2 cm. First published in 1863. [BV4211.M25 1871] 38-3758
1. Preaching. I. Title.

MCLAUGHLIN, Raymond W. 241'.6'41
The ethics of persuasive preaching / Raymond W. McLaughlin. Grand Rapids : Baker Book House, c1979. 215 p. ; 23 cm. Includes indexes. Bibliography: p. 195-206. [BV4235.E75M23] 78-59311 ISBN 0-8010-6051-6 : 9.95
1. Preaching. 2. Christian ethics—Baptist authors. I. Title.

MACLENNAN, David Alexander, 1903- 251
Entrusted with the gospel. Philadelphia, Westminster Press [1956] 128p. 20cm. (Warrack lectures on preaching) [BV4211.2.M17] 56-8426
1. Preaching. I. Title.

MACLENNAN, David Alexander, 1903- 251
Pastoral preaching. Philadelphia, Westminister Press. [c1955] 157p. 21cm. [BV4211.M263] 55-5176
1. Preaching. I. Title.

MACLENNAN, David Alexander, 1903-
A preacher's primer. New York, Oxford University Press, 1950. ix, 113 p. 18 cm. Bibliographical footnotes. A51
1. Preaching. 2. Theology. Pastoral. I. Title.

MACLEOD, Donald, 1914- ed. 251
Here is my method; the art of sermon construction. Westwood, N. J., F. H. Revell Co. [1952] 191 p. 21 cm. [BV4211.M265] 52-14107
1. Preaching. I. Title.

MCNEIL, Jesse Jai. 251
The preacher-prophet in mass society. Grand Rapids, Eerdmans [1961] 116p. 21cm. Includes bibliography. [BV4211.2.M176] 61-18335
1. Prenching. 2. Pastoral theology. I. Title.

MACNUTT, Sylvester F 251
Ganging sermon effectiveness. Dubuque, Iowa, Priory Press [c1960] 139p. illus. 21cm. [BV4211.2.M18] 61-9450
1. Preaching. I. Title.

MACPHERSON, Ian, 1912- 251
The art of illustrating sermons. Nashville, Abingdon [c.1964] 219p. 23cm. Bibl. 64-15759 3.50
1. Preaching. 2. Homiletical illustrations. I. Title.

MACPHERSON, Ian, 1912- 251
The art of illustrating sermons. Grand Rapids : Baker Book House, 1976c1966. 219p. ; 20 cm. (Minister's paperback library) Includes bibliographical references and index. [BV4211.2M19] ISBN 0-8010-5987-9 pbk. : 3.95
1. Preaching. 2. Homiletical illustrations. I. Title.
L. C. card no. for original ed. 64-15759.

MACPHERSON, Ian, 1912- 251
The burden of the Lord. New York, Abingdon Press [1955] 157p. 21cm. [BV4211.2.M2 1955a] 56-5126
1. Preaching. I. Title.

MAHAFFY, John Pentland, Sir, 251
1839-1919.
The decay of modern preaching. An essay by J. P. Mahaffy. New York, Macmillan and co., 1882. 4 p. l., 160 p. 19 1/2 cm. [BV4211.M3] 38-3210
1. Preaching. I. Title.

MALCOMSON, William L. 251
The preaching event [by] William L. Malcomson. Philadelphia, Westminister Press [1968] 144 p. 20 cm. [BV4211.2.M25] 68-23449 3.95
1. Preaching. I. Title.

MANNEBACH, Wayne C. 251
Speaking from the pulpit [by] Wayne C. Mannebach [and] Joseph M. Mazza. Valley Forge [Pa.] Judson Press [1969] 128 p. 23 cm. Includes bibliographical references. [BV4211.2.M26] 74-81445 ISBN 0-8170-0437-8 4.95
1. Preaching. I. Mazza, Joseph M., joint author. II. Title.

MANTON, Joseph E., 1904- 251
Ten responsible minutes : a pleasant approach to homily headache / Joseph E. Manton. Huntington, Ind. : Our Sunday Visitor, c1978. 232 p. ; 24 cm. Includes index. [BV4211.2.M27] 77-90976 ISBN 0-87973-862-6 : 6.95
1. Preaching. I. Title.

MARCEL, Pierre Charles 251
Raymond
The relevance of preaching. Tr. from French by Rob Roy McGregor. Grand Rapids, Mich., Baker Bk. [c.]1963. 110p. 23cm. 63-15823 2.95
1. Preaching. I. Title.

MARK, Harry Thiselton.
The pedagogics of preaching; being the substance of lectures given at the Hartley college, Manchester, in 1910 and in 1911, by Thiselton Mark ... New York, Chicago [etc.] Fleming H. Revell company [c1911] 92 p. 20 cm. 11-28833 0.50
I. Title.

MASSEY, James Earl. 251
Designing the sermon : order and movement in preaching / James Earl Massey ; [William D. Thompson, editor]. Nashville : Abingdon, c1980. 127 p. ; 20 cm. (Abingdon preacher's library) Includes index. Bibliography: p. 121-124. [BV4211.2.M277] 80-17920 ISBN 0-687-10490-4 pbk. : 4.95
1. Preaching. I. Thompson, William D. II. Title.

MASSEY, James Earl. 251
The responsible pulpit. Anderson, Ind., Warner Press [1974] 115 p. 22 cm. Includes bibliographical references. [BV4211.2.M28] 74-939 ISBN 0-87162-169-X 5.95
1. Preaching. 2. Clergy—Religious life. I. Title.

MERRILL, William Pierson, 251
1867-
The freedom of the preacher, by William Pierson Merrill ... New York, The Macmillan company, 1922. 5 p. l., 147 p. 20 cm. (The Lyman Beecher lectures on preaching, 1922) [BV4211.M38] 22-19727
I. Title.

*MEYER, F. B. 251.01
Expository preaching: plans and methods. Grand Rapids, Baker Book House [1974] 127 p. 20 cm. [BV4211] ISBN 0-8010-5945-3 1.25 (pbk.)
1. Preaching. I. Title.

MEYER, Frederick 251.8
Brotherton, 1847-1929.
Expository preaching; plans and methods, by Rev. F. B. Meyer, B. A. New York, Hodder & Stoughton, George H. Doran company [1912] vi p., 2 l., 3-141 p. 21 cm. [BV4211.M4] 12-27615
1. Preaching. I. Title.

MICHONNEAU, Georges, 1899- 251
From pulpit to people; thoughts on dynamic preaching, by Georges Michonneau, Francois Varillon. Tr. [from French] by Edmond Bonin. Westminster, Md, Newman [c.]1965. vii, 224p. 22cm. Bibl. [BV4211.2.M4413] 65-25982 3.95
1. Preaching. I. Varillon, Francois, 1905- joint author. II. Title.

MICHONNEAU, Georges, 1899- 251
.
From pulpit to people; thoughts on dynamic preaching, by Georges Michonneau and Francois Varillon. Translated by Edmond Bonin. Westminister, Md., Newman Press, 1965. vii, 224 p. 22 cm. Tranlsation of Propos sur ia predication. Bibliographical footnotes. [BV4211.2.M4413] 65-25982
1. Preaching. I. Varillon, Francois, 1905- joint author. II. Title.

MILLER, Donald G 251
Fire in thy mouth. Nashville, Abingdon Press [c1954] 160p. 21cm. [BV4211.M48] 54-5229
1. Preaching. I. Title.

MILLER, Donald G. 251
Fire in thy mouth / Donald G. Miller. Grand Rapids : Baker Book House, 1976c1954. 160p. ; 20 cm. (Notable books on preaching) Includes bibliographical references and index. [BV4211.M48] ISBN 0-8010-5986-0 pbk. : 2.95.
1. Preaching. I. Title.
L. C. card no. for original ed.54-5229.

MILLER, Donald G 251
The way to Biblical preaching. New York, Abingdon Press [1957] 160p. 21cm. [BV4211.2.M5] 57-11012
1. Preaching. I. Title.

MISSETT, Luke, father, 1913- 251
The pews talk back [essays on effective preaching] Westminster, Md., Newman Bookshop [1946] viii, 83 p. 20 cm. Contains material which first appeared in the American ecclesiastical review and The priest. Secular name: Robert Missett. [BV4211.M5] 47-26333
1. Preaching. I. Title.

MITCHELL, William Fraser, 251
1900-
English pulpit oratory from Andrewes to Tillotson; a study of its literary aspects, by W. Fraser Mitchell ... London, Society for promoting Christian knowledge; New York and Toronto, The Macmillan co. [1932] xii, 516 p. 22 1/2 cm. "First published 1932." "Select bibliography": p. [406]-473. [BV4208.G7M5] 32-19615
1. Preaching. 2. Church of England—Clergy. 3. Clergy—England. I. Title.

MOESLEIN, Mark, 1851- 251
The mechanism of discourses, by Rev. Mark Moeslein, C.P. Chicago, Ill., D. B. Hansen & sons [c1915] 220 p. 19 1/2 cm. Bibliography: p. 219. [BV4211.M6] 16-3140
1. Preaching. I. Title.

MONTGOMERY, Richmond Ames, 251
1870-
Expository preaching, by R. Ames Montgomery ... New York [etc.] Fleming H. Revell company [c1939] 90 p. 20 cm. [BV4211.M617] 39-24409
1. Preaching. I. Title.

MONTGOMERY, Richmond Ames, 251
1870-
Preparing preachers to preach, by R. Ames Montgomery ... Grand Rapids, Mich., Zondervan publishing house [c1939] 6 p. l., 11-249, [5] p. 20 cm. Blank pages for "Notes" ([5] at end) Bibliographical references in "Notes" (p. [245]-249) [BV4211.M62] 39-16396
1. Preaching. I. Title.

MOOREHEAD, Lee C 251
Freedom of the pulpit. New York, Abingdon Press [1961] 94p. 20cm. Includes bibliography. [BV4211.2.M65] 61-5558
1. Preaching. I. Title.

*MORGAN, Campbell G. 251.01
Preaching [by] G. Campbell Morgan. Grand Rapids, Baker Book House [1974] 90 p. 18 cm. (G. Campbell Morgan library) [BV4226] ISBN 0-8010-5953-4 1.95 (pbk.)
1. Preaching. I. Title.

MORGAN, George Campbell, 251
1863-
Preaching, by G. Campbell Morgan, D.D. New York [etc.] Fleming H. Revell company [c1937] 99 p. 19 1/2 cm. [BV4211.M63 1937a] 38-880
1. Preaching. I. Title.

MORLAN, George Kolmer, 1904- 251
Laymen speaking, by George K. Morlan ... New York, R. R. Smith, 1938. 6 p. l., 242 p. 22 1/2 cm. [BV4211.M64] 38-15164
1. Preaching. 2. Church attendance. I. Title.

MORRIS, Colin M. 251
The Word and the words / Colin Morris. Nashville : Abingdon Press, 1975. 174 p. ; 22 cm. Includes bibliographical references. [BV4211.2.M67 1975] 75-15955 ISBN 0-687-46045-X pbk. : 3.95
1. Preaching. I. Title.

MORRIS, Frederick M 251
Preach the Word of God. Foreword by Alden Drew Kelley. New York, Morehouse- Gorham Co., 1954. 157p. 21cm. [BV4211.M645] 54-3982
1. Preaching. I. Title.

MOUZON, Edwin Du Bose, bp., 251
1869-
Preaching with authority; the Lyman Beecher lectures on preaching, delivered at Yale in April, 1929, by Edwin Du Bose Mouzon ... Garden City, N. Y., Doubleday, Doran & company, inc., 1929. xiii, 245 p. 20 cm. [BV4211.M65] 29-18908
1. Preaching. I. Title.

NEELY, Thomas Benjamin, bp.
The minister in the itinerant system, by Bishop Thomas B. Neely ... New York, Chicago [etc.] Fleming H. Revell company [c1914] 206 p. 20 cm. 14-7736 1.00
I. Title.

NES, William Hamilton, 1895- 251
The excellency of the word, by William H. Nes, together with A survey of homiletics education, by Noah E. Fehl. New York, Morehouse- Gorham Co. [1956] 158p. 19cm. (The George Craig Stewart memorial lectures in preaching. 1954) [BV4211.2.N4] 56-5286
1. Preaching. I. Title.

NEWPORT, David.
Eudemon, spiritual and rational; the apology of a preacher for preaching. Philadelphia & London, J. B. Lippincott co., 1901. 527 p. front. (port.) 8 cm. Feb
I. Title.

NEWPORT, David.
Eudemon, spiritual and rational; the apology of a preacher for preaching. Philadelphia & London, J. B. Lippincott co., 1901. 527 p. front. (port.) 8 cm. Feb
I. Title.

NEWTON, Joseph Fort, 1876 251.06
ed.
If I had only one sermon to prepare, edited by Joseph Fort Newton. New York and London, Harper & brothers, 1932. x p., 1 l., 233 p. 21 cm. "First edition." [BV4205.N4] 32-11678
1. Preaching. I. Title.

NEWTON, Joseph Fort, 1876- 251
The new preaching; a little book about a great art, by Joseph Fort Newton... Nashville, Tenn., Cokesbury press, 1930. 187 p. 19 1/2 cm. [BV4211.N4] 30-3789
1. Preaching. I. Title.

NEWTON, Joseph Fort, 1876- 922.
Preaching in London; a diary of Anglo-American friendship, by Joseph Fort Newton... New York, George H. Doran company [c1922] viii p., 2 l., 13-140 p. 19 1/2 cm. [BX9969.N4A3] 22-8151
I. Title.

NEWTON, Joseph Fort, 1876- 922.
Preaching in New York; diaries and papers, by Joseph Fort Newton ... New York, George H. Doran company [c1924] ix p., 2 l., 15-206 p. 19 1/2 cm. [BX9969.N4A4] 24-4872
I. Title.
Contents omitted.

NICHOLS, J. Randall. 251
Building the word : the dynamics of communication and preaching / J. Randall Nichols. 1st ed. San Francisco : Harper & Row, c1980. xi, 174 p. ; 22 cm. Includes bibliographical references and index. [BV4211.2.N48 1980] 79-3590 ISBN 0-06-066109-7 : 8.95
1. Preaching. I. Title.

NICHOLS, Thomas McBride. 251
Preaching; a series of brief chapters, by Thomas McBride Nichols ... Philadelphia, Presbyterian board of publication, 1904. 74 p. 17 1/2 cm. [BV4211.N5] 4-5437
1. Preaching. I. Title.

NILES, Daniel T 251
Preaching the gospel of the resurrection. Philadelphia, Westminster Press [1954] 93p. 20cm. (The Bevan memorial lectures) [BV4211.N55 1954] 54-6325
1. Preaching. I. Title.

NILES, Daniel Thambyrajah. 251
The preacher's task and the stone of stumbling. [1st ed.] New York, Harper [1958] 125p. 20cm. (The Lyman Beecher lectures, 1957) [BV4211.2.N5] 57-12986
1. Preaching. I. Title.

NILES, Daniel Thambyrajah. 251
Preaching the gospel of the resurrection. Philadelphia, Westminster Press [1954] 93p. 20cm. (The Bevan memorial lectures) [BV4211.2.N52 1954] 54-6325
1. Preaching. I. Title.

NOTT, Samuel, 1788-1869.
Sixteen years' preaching and procedure, at Wareham, Ms., by Rev. Samuel Nott, jr. With a reprint of the memorial, legal opinion, and result of Ex parte council, laid before the Mutual council, Sept. 23, 1845. Boston, C. Tappan, 1845. iv, [5]-192 p. 24 1/2 cm. 12-40163
I. Title.

NOTT, Samuel, 1788-1869.
Sixteen years' preaching and procedure, at Wareham, Ms., by Rev. Samuel Nott, jr. With a reprint of the memorial, legal opinion, and result of Ex parte council, laid before the Mutual council, Sept. 23, 1845. Boston, C. Tappan, 1845. iv, [5]-192 p. 25 cm. 12-40163
I. Title.

NOYES, Morgan Phelps, 1891- 251
Preaching the word of God, by Morgan Phelps Noyes ... New York, C. Scribner's sons, 1943. ix, [2],219 p. 19 1/2 cm. (Lyman Beecher lectures on preaching in Yale university. 66th ser.) Bibliographical foot-notes. [BV4211.N6] 43-9599
1. Preaching. I. Title.

O'DOWD, William Bernard.
Preaching, by the Rev. W. B. O'Dowd. London, New York [etc.] Longmans, Green and co., 1919. xi, 235 p. 19 1/2 cm. (Half-title: The Westminster library) Bibliography: p. 234-235. A 21
1. Preaching. I. Title.

O'DOWD, William Bernard.
Preaching, by the Rev. W. B. O'Dowd. London, New York [etc.] Longmans, Green and co., 1919. xi, 235 p. 20 cm.

(Half-title: The Westminster library) Bibliography: p. 234-235. A 21
1. Preaching. I. Title.

OMAN, John Wood, 1860- 250
Concerning the ministry, by John Oman ... New York, London, Harper & brothers, 1937. viii p., 1 l., 180 p. 23 cm. [BV4010.O6 1937] 37-2093
1. Preaching. I. Title.

OMAN, John Wood, 1860-1939 250
Concerning the ministry. Richmond, Va., John Knox [1963] 248p. 22cm. 63-8126 2.50 pap.,
1. Preaching. I. Title.

OTT, Heinrich. 251
Theology and preaching; a programme of work in dogmatics, arranged with reference to Questions I-II of the Heidelberg catechism. Translated by Harold Knight. Philadelphia, Westminster Press [1965] 158 p. 23 cm. Translation of Dogmatik und Verkundigung. [BV4214.O813] 65-12513
1. Preaching. 2. Kerygma. 3. Sin. I. Heidelberg catechism. II. Title.

OXNAM, Garfield Bromley, 1891- ed. 251
Preaching and the social crisis; a series of lectures delivered before the Boston university School of theology, edited by G. Bromley Oxnam ... New York, Cincinnati [etc.] The Abingdon press [c1932] 234 p. 20 1/2 cm. [BV4235.S6O85] 33-10568
1. Preaching. 2. Sociology, Christian—Addresses, essays, lectures. 3. Social problems. I. Boston university. School of theology. II. Title.

OXNAM, Garfield Bromley, bp., 1891- 252
Preaching in a revolutionary age [by] G. Bromley Oxnam ... New York, Nashville, Abingdon-Cokesbury press [1944] 207 p. 20 1/2 cm. [Lyman Beecher lectures on preaching, Yale university] Bibliographical foot-notes. [BV4211.O9] 44-47053
1. Preaching. 2. Clergy. 3. Church and social problems. I. Title.

OXNAM, Garfield Bromley, Bp., 1891-1963. 251
Preaching in a revolutionary age. Freeport, N.Y., Books for Libraries Press [1971, c1944] 207 p. 23 cm. (Lyman Beecher lectures on preaching, 1943-44) (Essay index reprint series) Includes bibliographical references. [BV4211.O9 1971] 75-142687 ISBN 0-8369-2421-5
1. Preaching. 2. Clergy. 3. Church and social problems. I. Title. II. Series: Lyman Beecher lectures, 1944.

PARK, John Edgar, 1879- 251
The miracle of preaching. by John Edgar Park. New York, The Macmillan company. 1936. 4 p. l., 184 p. 20 cm. "The Lyman Beecher lectures delivered at Yale University in 1936." "Notes and references": p. 171-176. [BV4211.P25] 36-16375
1. Preaching. I. Title.

PATTISON, Thomas Harwood, 1838-1904. 251
The making of the sermon; for the class-room and the study, by T. Harwood Pattison ... Philadelphia, American Baptist publication society, 1898. x, 392 p. 20 cm. [BV4211.P3] 98-931
1. Preaching. I. Title.

PATTON, Carl Safford, 1866-1939. 251
The preparation and delivery of sermons, by Carl S. Patton ... Chicago, New York, Willett, Clark & company, 1938. xi p., 1 l., 191 p., 1 l. 21 cm. [The minister's professional library] "Acknowledgments": 1 leaf at end. [BV4211.P33] 38-10064
1. Preaching. I. Title.

PEARCE, J. Winston. 251'.01
Planning your preaching [by] J. Winston Pearce. Nashville, Broadman Press [1967] vii, 197 p. 22 cm. Bibliography: p. 189-194. [BV4211.2.P38] 67-19398
1. Preaching. I. Title.

PEARSON, Roy Messer, 1914- 251
The ministry of preaching. [1st ed.] New York, Harper [1959] 127p. 20cm. Includes bibliography. [BV4211.2.P4] 59-7158
1. Preaching. I. Title.

PEARSON, Roy Messer, 1914- 251
The preacher: his purpose and practice. Philadelphia,Westminister Press, [1962] 224 p. 21 cm. [BV660.2.P4] 62-15163
1. Preaching. I. Title.

PENNINGTON, Chester A. 251
God has a communication problem / Chester Pennington. New York : Hawthorn Books, c1976. viii, 136 p. ; 22 cm. Bibliography: p. 134-136. [BV4211.2.P42 1976] 75-28692 ISBN 0-8015-3044-X : 6.95
1. Preaching. I. Title.

PEPPER, George Wharton, 1867- 251
A voice from the crowd, by George Wharton Pepper. New Haven, Yale university press; London, H. Milford; [etc., etc., 1915. 6 p. l., 297 p. 21 cm. (Half-title: The forty-first series of Lyman Beecher lectures on preaching, delivered at Yale university in 1915) [BV4211.P4] 15-18738
1. Preaching. I. Title.

PERRY, Lloyd Merle. 251
Biblical preaching for today's world, by Lloyd M. Perry. Chicago, Moody Press [1973] 208 p. 22 cm. Based on the Lyman Stewart memorial lectures for 1971-72, delivered at Talbot Theological Seminary, La Mirada, Calif. Bibliography: p. 201-205. [BV4211.2.P433] 73-7471 ISBN 0-8024-0707-2 4.95
1. Preaching. I. Title.

PERRY, Lloyd Merle. 251
Biblical sermon guide; a step-by-step procedure for the preparation and presentation, by Lloyd M. Perry. Grand Rapids, Baker Book House [1970] 131 p. illus. 23 cm. Bibliography: p. 125-128. [BV4211.2.P435] 75-115642 4.95
1. Preaching. 2. Sermons—Outlines. I. Title.

PERRY, Lloyd Merle. 253
Evangelistic preaching / by Lloyd M. Perry and John R. Strubhar. Chicago : Moody Press, c1979. 215 p. ; 22 cm. Includes index. Bibliography: p. 199-212. [BV4211.2.P437] 79-13312 ISBN 0-8024-5989-7 pbk. : 4.95
1. Preaching. 2. Evangelistic work. I. Strubhar, John R., joint author. II. Title.

PERRY, Lloyd Merle. 251
A manual for Biblical preaching. Grand Rapids, Mich., Baker Book House, 1965. 215 p. 29 cm. Bibliography: p. 207-215. [CBV1211.2.P44] 65-9730
1. Preaching, I. Title. II. Title: Biblical preaching.

PHELPS, Austin, 1820-1890. 251
Men and books; or, Studies in homiletics; lectures introductory to The theory of preaching, by Austin Phelps ... New York, C. Scribner's sons, 1882. xi, 354 p. 21 cm. [BV4211.P43] 12-37603
1. Preaching. I. Title.

PHELPS, Austin, 1820-1890. 251
The theory of preaching; lectures on homiletics, by Austin Phelps ... New York, C. Scribner's sons, 1881. xvi p., 1 l., 610 p. 22 cm. [BV4211.P45] 12-37601
1. Preaching. I. Title.

PHILIBERT, Michel Andre Jean 253.7
Christ's preaching, and ours. [Tr. from French by David Lewis. American ed.] Richmond, Va., Knox [1964, c.1963] 55p. 22cm. (World Council of Churches. Commission on World Mission and Evangelism. Study pamph., no. 1) Bibl. 64-12262 1.00 pap.,
1. Preaching. I. Title.

PHILLIPS, Harold Cooke, 1892- 251
Bearing witness to the truth. New York, Abingdon-Cokesbury Press [1949] 219 p. 21 cm. (The Lyman Beecher Yale lectures on preaching) Bibliographical footonores. [BV4211.P47] 49-7598
1. Preaching. I. Title. II. Series: The Lyman Beecher lectures on preaching, Yale University

PICKELL, Charles N 1927- 251
Preaching to meet men's needs; the meaning of the Acts as a guide for preaching today. [1st ed.] New York, Exposition Press [1958] 82p. 21cm. Includes bibliography. [BV4211.2.P5] 58-3691
1. Preaching. 2. Bible. N. T. Acts—Criticism, interpretation,etc. I. Title.

PIERSON, Arthur Tappan, 1837-1911. 251
The divine art of preaching. Lectures delivered at the "Pastor's college," connected with the Metropolitan tabernacle, London, England, from January to June, 1892. By Arthur T. Pierson. New York, The Baker and Taylor co. [1892] xvi, 156 p. 17 1/2 cm. [BV4211.P5]
1. Preaching. I. Title.

PIKE, James Albert, Bp., 1913-1969. 251
A new look in preaching. New York, Scribner [1961] 107 p. 19 cm. (The George Craig Stewart memorial lectures) [BV4211.P53] 61-13607
1. Preaching. I. Title.

PITTENGER, William Norman, 1905- 251
Proclaiming Christ today. Greenwich, Conn., Seabury Press, 1962. 148p. 20cm. Includes bibliography. [BV4211.2.P56] 62-9616
1. Preaching. I. Title.

PORTER, Ebenezer, 1772-1834. 251
Lectures on homiletics and preaching, and on public prayer; together with sermons and letters. By Ebenezer Porter ... Andover [Mass.] Flagg, Gould and Newman; New York, J. Leavitt, 1834. iv, [5]-428 p. 25 cm. "Books and reading": p. [399]-414. [BV4211.P57] 36-2151
1. Preaching. 2. Prayer. 3. Congregational churches—Sermons. 4. Sermons, American. I. Title.

PORTER, Ebenezer, 1772-1834, comp. 251.082
The young preacher's manual, or, A collection of treatises on preaching: comprising Brown's Address to students in divinity. Fenelon's Dialogues on the eloquence of the pulpit. Claude's Essay on the composition of a sermon, abridged. Gregory on the composition and delivery of a sermon, Reybaz on the art of preaching. With a list of books. Selected and revised by Ebenezer Porter ... Boston: Published by Charles Ewer, and for sale at his bookstore no. 51 Cornhill. Flagg and Gould. Printers, 1819. vi p., 1 l., [9]-428 p. 23 cm. "A list of books": p. [423]-426 [BV4205.P6] 34-23727
1. Preaching. I. Brown, John, 1722-1787. II. Fenelon, Francois de Salignac de La Mothe, abp., 1651-1715. III. Claude, Jean, 1619-1687. IV. Gregory, George, 1754-1808. V. Reybaz, Etienne Salomon, 1737-1804 VI. Title.

POTTER, Thomas Joseph, 1828-1873. 251
Sacred eloquence; or, The theory and practice of preaching. By Rev. Thomas J. Potter ... 5th ed. ... New York, Cincinnati, F. Pustet & co., 1891. 350 p. 20 cm. [BV4211.P6 1891] 38-3755
1. Preaching. I. Title.

THE preacher and his work;
college lectures to student preachers. Rev. and enl. ed. Athens, Alabama, E. E. I., 1960. 230p.
I. Meyer, Jack.

PREACHING in these times; 251.04
Lyman Beecher lectures, delivered before the Divinity school of Yale university, by George Arthur Buttrick, Edwin McNeil Poteat, Arthur Howe Bradford [and other] ... New York, C. Scribner's sons, 1940. viii, 179 p. 21 cm. [BV4205.P7] 40-34450
1. Preaching. I. Buttrick, George Arthur, 1892-
Contents omitted.

PRICHARD, Harold Adye, 1882- 251
The minister, the method, and the message, suggestions on preaching [by] Harold Adye Prichard ... New York, London, C. Scribner's sons, 1932. x p., 2 l., 3-303 p. 19 cm. [BV4211.P67] 32-8289
1. Preaching. I. Title.

PROUDFOOT, John J A. 251
Systematic homiletics, by Rev. J. J. A. Proudfoot ... ed. by Rev. J. A. Turnbull ... and Rev. A. J. MacGillivray, M. A. Chicago, New York [etc.] Fleming H. Revell company, 1903. 1 p. l., 7-320 p. front. (port.) 20 cm. [BV4211.P7] 4-35757
1. Preaching. I. Turnbull, John A., ed. II. MacGillivray, Alexander James, joint ed. III. Title.

QUAYLE, William Alfred, bp., 1860-1925. 251
The pastor-preacher. By William A. Quayle ... Cincinnati, Jennings & Graham; New York, Eaton & Mains [c1910] 411 p. 21 cm. [BV4211.Q8] 10-6538
1. Preaching. I. Title.

PITT-WATSON, Ian, 1881-1955. 251
Preaching : a kind of folly / by Ian Pitt-Watson. Philadelphia : Westminster Press, [1978] c1976. ix, 109 p. ; 21 cm. First published in 1976 under title: A kind of folly. Based on the Warrack lectures delivered by the author between 1972 and 1975 at the universities of St. Andrews, Edinburgh, Aberdeen, and Glasgow. [BV4211.2.P55 1978] 77-21983 ISBN 0-664-24181-6 pbk. : 4.95
1. Preaching. I. Title.

RAINSFORD, William Stephen, 1850-1933. 922.373
A preacher's story of his work, by W. S. Rainsford ... New York, The Outlook company, 1904. x, 244 [1] p. front. (port.) 20 cm. [BX5995.R3A3] 4-1666
I. Title.

RANDOLPH, David James, 1934- 251
The renewal of preaching. Philadelphia, Fortress Press [1969] xi, 137 p. 23 cm. Bibliographical footnotes. [BV4211.2.R3] 69-14623 3.95
1. Bible—Hermeneutics. 2. Bible—Homiletical use. 3. Preaching. I. Title.

RAY, Jefferson Davis, 1860- 251.8
Expository preaching, by Jeff D. Ray ... Grand Rapids, Mich., Zondervan publishing house [c1940] 123, [5] p. 20 cm. Five pages at end blank for "Notes". [BV4211.R3] 40-11842
1. Preaching. I. Title.

READ, David Haxton Carswell. 251
The communication of the gospel. London, SCM press [label: Chicago, A. R. Alienson, 1952] 96p. 19cm. (The Warrack lectures for 1951) [BV4211.R33] 53-37774
1. Preaching. I. Title.

READ, David Haxton Carswell. 251
Sent from God; the enduring power and mystery of preaching [by] David H. C. Read. Nashville, Abingdon Press [1974] 112 p. 20 cm. [BV4211.2.R36] 73-18241 3.95
1. Preaching. I. Title.

REALITY in preaching 251
[by] Russell D. Snyder, Otto A. Piper, Oscar F. Blackwelder [and] Fred C. Wiegman ... Philadelphia, Muhlenberg press [1942] vii, 168 p. 20 cm. (The Kessler lectures) [BV4211.R34] 42-12807
1. Preaching. I. Snyder, Russell Dewey, 1898- II. Piper, Otto, 1891- III. Blackwelder, Oscar Fisher, 1898- IV. Wiegman, Fred Conrad, 1899-
Contents omitted.

REID, Clyde H. 251'.03
The empty pulpit; a study in preaching as communication [by] Clyde Reid. [1st ed.] New York, Harper & Row [1967] 122 p. 22 cm. Bibliographical footnotes. [BV4211.2.R4] 67-21552
1. Preaching. 2. Communication (Theology) I. Title.

REISNER, Christian Fichthorne, 1872-
The preacher-persuader, by Christian F. Reisner ... Cincinnati, Jennings and Graham. New York, Eaton and Mains [c1910] 67 p. 16 cm. $0.50. 10-22428
I. Title.

THE Renewal of preaching: 251
theory and practice, edited by Karl Rahner. New York, Paulist Press [1968] ix, 195 p. 24 cm. (Concilium: theology in the age of renewal: Pastoral theology, v. 33) Includes articles translated from several languages by various persons. Bibliographical footnotes. [BV4211.2.R43] 68-22795
1. Preaching. I. Rahner, Karl, 1904- ed. II. Series: Concilium (New York) v. 33

REU, Johann Michael, 1869- 251
1943.
Homiletics; a manual of the theory and practice of preaching. Translated into English by Albert Steinhaeuser. Grand Rapids, Baker Book House [1967, c1924] 639 p. 23 cm. (Limited editions library) [BV4211.R4 1967] 67-4175
1. Preaching. I. Title.

RHOADES, Ezra. 251
Case work in preaching, by Ezra Rhoades, D.D. New York [etc.] Fleming H. Revell company [1942] 159 p. 19 cm. [BV4211.R47] 42-20929
1. Preaching. I. Title.

RICE, Charles Lynvel, 1936- 251
Interpretation and imagination; the preacher and contemporary literature [by] Charles L. Rice. Philadelphia, Fortress Press [1970] xiv, 158 p. 18 cm. (The Preacher's paperback library) Includes bibliographical references. [BV4211.2.R48] 78-116463 3.50 (pbk)
1. Preaching. 2. Religion and literature. 3. Sermons, American. I. Title.

RICHARDS, Harold Marshall 251
Sylvester, 1894-
Feed my sheep. Washington, Review and Herald Pub. Association [c1958] 446p. 22cm. [BV4211.2.R5] 59-20241
1. Preaching. I. Title.

RIGELL, William Richard, 225.92
1887-
Prophetic preaching; a study of the ministry of John the Baptist for modern prophets, by William R. Rigell ... Nashville, Tenn., Broadman press [c1936] 5 p. l., 9-139 p. 20 cm. [BS2456.R5] 36-13333
1. John, the Baptist. 2. Preaching. I. Title.

RILEY, William Bell, 1861- 251
1947.
The preacher & hs preaching. Wheaton, Ill., Sword of the Lord Publishers [1948] 146 p. 21 cm. [BV4211.R53] 49-53
1. Preaching. I. Title.

RIPLEY, Henry Jones, 1798- 251
1875.
Sacred rhetoric; or, Composition and delivery of sermons. By Henry J. Ripley ... To which are added hints on extemporaneous preaching, by Henry Ware. jr. D. D. Boston, Gould, Kendall and Lincoln, 1849. 259 p. 20 cm. [BV4211.R55] 38-8168
1. Preaching. I. Ware, Henry, 1794-1843. II. Title.

RITSCHL, Dietrich 251
A theology of proclamation. Richmond, Va. John Knox Press [c.1960] 190p. 60-15296 3.50
1. Preaching. I. Title.

ROBBINS, Howard Chandler, 251
1876-
Preaching the gospel, by Howard Chandler Robbins ... New York, London, Harper & brothers, 1939. x p., 1 l., 151 p. 20 cm. (The John Bohlen lectures, 1938) "First edition." [BV4211.R57] 39-22332
1. Preaching. I. Title.

ROBERTS, Richard, 1874- 251
The Preacher as a man of letters [By Richard Roberts. New York, Cincinnati [etc.] The Abingdon press [c1931] 216 p. 20 cm. Bibliography: p. 215-216. [BV4211.R58] 31-22328
1. Preaching. 2. Theology, Pastoral. 3. Books and reading. I. Title.

ROBERTSON, Archibald Thomas, 251
1863-1934.
The glory of the ministry; Paul's exultation in preaching. Introd. by Ralph G. Turnbull. Grand Rapids, Baker Book House [1967] 243 p. 20 cm. First published 1911. Bibliographical footnotes. [BV4010.R63 1967] 67-18193
1. Preaching. 2. Pastoral theology. I. Title.

ROBERTSON, Archibald Thomas, 250
1863-1934.
The glory of the ministry; Paul's exultation in preaching, by A. T. Robertson ... New York, Chicago [etc.] Fleming H. Revell company [c1911] 243 p. 21 cm. [BV4010.R63] 11-27064
1. Preaching. 2. Theology, Pastoral. I. Title.

ROBINSON, Ezekiel Gilman, 251
1815-1894.
Lectures on preaching, delivered to the students of theology at Yale college, January and February, 1882, by E. G. Robinson... New York, H. Holt and company, 1883. 3 p. l., 214 p. 19 1/2 cm. [Lyman Beecher lectures on preaching. Yale university, 1881-82] [BV4211.R6] 38-3767
1. Preaching. I. Title.

ROBINSON, Haddon W. 251
Biblical preaching : the development and delivery of expository messages / Haddon W. Robinson. Grand Rapids, Mich. : Baker Book House, c1980. 230 p. ; 24 cm. Includes indexes. Bibliography: p. 221-224. [BV4211.2.R59] 19 80-66776 ISBN 0-8010-7700-1 : 9.95
1. Preaching. I. Title.

ROBINSON, James Herman. 251
Adventurous preaching. [1st ed.] Great Neck, N. Y., Channel Press [1956] 186p. 21cm. (The Lyman Beecher lectures at Yale, 1955 [BV4211.2.R6] 56-13819
1. Preaching. 2. Theology. Postoral. I. Title.

ROCHE, Aloysius. 251
Practical hints on preaching; a simple handbook for beginners, by Aloysius Roche. New York, P. J. Kenedy & sons [1933] xii, 191, [1] p. 19 cm. "Printed in Great Britain." [BV4211.R64] 35-3636
1. Preaching. I. Title.

ROCK, Augustine. 251
Unless they be sent; a theological study of the nature and purpose of preaching. Dubuque, W. C. Brown Co. [1953] 208p. 21cm. (Dominican Fathers, Province of St. Albert the Great. The Aquinas library. Doctrinal studies, 4) [BV4211.R65] 53-1632
1. Preaching. I. Title.

RODDY, Clarence 251.082
Stonelynn, ed.
We prepare and preach; the practice of sermon construction and delivery. Chicago, Moody Press [1959] 190p. 22cm. [BV4211.2.R63] 59-1089
1. Preaching. I. Title.

ROGERS, Clement Francis, 1866-
The parson preaching. New York, Macmillan [1947] xiv, 130 p. plate. 22 cm. A50
1. Preaching. I. Title.

ROHRBACH, Peter Thomas. 251
The art of dynamic preaching; a practical guide to better preaching. [1st ed.] Garden City, N.Y., Doubleday, 1965. 190 p. 22 cm. [BV4211.2.R65] 65-23781
1. Preaching. I. Title.

ROHRBAUGH, Richard L., 220.6'3
1936-
The Biblical interpreter : an agrarian Bible in an industrial age / Richard L. Rohrbaugh. Philadelphia : Fortress Press, c1978. 125 p. ; 22 cm. Includes bibliographical references. [BS476.R64] 78-54560 ISBN 0-8006-1346-5 pbk. : 4.95
1. Bible—Hermeneutics. 2. Preaching. I. Title.

RUST, Eric Charles. 251
The word and words : towards a theology of preaching / by Eric C. Rust. Macon, Ga. : Mercer University Press, c1982. xi, 130 p. ; 24 cm. Includes bibliographical references and index. [BV4211.2.R87 1982] 19 82-8032 ISBN 0-86554-055-1 : 10.95
1. Preaching. 2. Word of God (Theology) I. Title.

SANDERS, J. Pilant. 251
Preaching in the twentieth century, by J. Pilant Sanders [and others] ... [Los Angeles 1945] 208 p. 23 1/2 cm. [BV4205.S3] 45-6323
1. Preaching. I. Norred, C. Arthur. II. Tant, Fanning Yater. III. Cogdill, Roy E. IV. Title.
Contents omitted.

SANFORD, Jack D. 251
Make your preaching relevant. Nashville, Broadman [c.1963] 93p. 20cm. 63-11167 1.50 pap.,
1. Preaching. I. Title.

SANFORD, Jack D 251
Make your preaching relevant. Nashville, Broadman Press [1963] 93 p. 20 cm.SPreaching. [BV4211.2.S28] 63-11167
I. Title.

SANGSTER, P E 251
Speech in the pulpit. New York, Philosophical Library [1958] 84 p. illus. 20cm. [PN4173.S3] 58-59644
1. Preaching. 2. Oratory. I. Title.

*SANGSTER, W. E. 1900-1960 251
Power in preaching W. E. Sangster. Grand Rapids. : Baker Book House, 1976 c1958. 110 p. ; 20 cm. (Notable books on preaching) Includes index. [BV4211.2] ISBN 0-8010-8075-4 pbk. : 1.95
1. Preaching. I. Title.
L.C. card no. for 1958 Epworth Press ed.: 58-10462.

SANGSTER, William Edwin, 251
1900-
The craft of sermon construction. [A source book for ministers] Philadelphia, Westminster Press [1951] 208 p. 21 cm. (The Westminster source books) [BV4211.S24] 51-7833
1. Preaching. I. Title. II. Title: Sermon construction.

SANGSTER, William Edwin, 251
1900-
Power in preaching. New York, Abingdon Press [1958] 110p. 20cm. (The Fondren lectures, 39) [BV4211.2.S3] 58-10462
1. Preaching. I. Title.

SAYRES, Alfred Nevin. 251
That one good sermon. Philadelphia, United Church Press [1963] 95 p. 20 cm. [BV4211.2.S34] 63-21519
1. Preaching. I. Title.

*SCHERER, Paul. 251
For we have this treasure : the Yale lectures on preaching, 1943. Grand Rapids : Baker Book House, 1976c1944. 212p. ; 20 cm. (Notable books on preaching) Includes bibliographical references. [BV4211] ISBN 0-8010-8073-8 pbk. : 2.95.
1. Preaching. 2. Communication (Theology) I. Title.

SCHERER, Paul, 1892- 251
For we have this treasure ... [by] Paul Scherer ... New York and London, Harper & brothers [1944] xii, 212 p. 19 1/2 cm. (The Yale lectures on preaching, 1943) "First edition." [Full name: Paul Ehrman Scherer] Bibliographical references included in "Notes" (p. 207-212) [BV4211.S26] 44-6180
1. Preaching. 2. Clergy—Office. I. Title.

SCHERER, Paul, 1892- 251
The word God sent / Paul Scherer. Grand Rapids, Mich. : Baker Book House, 1977,c1965. 272p. ; 20 cm. Includes index. [BV4211.2S36] ISBN 0-8010-8102-5 pbk. : 3.95
1. Preaching. 2. Sermons, American. 3. Lutheran Church-Sermons. I. Title.
L.C. card no. for 1965 Harper & Row ed.: 65-20457.

SCHERER, Paul, 1892- 251
The work God sent. New York. Harper [c.1965] xiii, 272p. 22cm. Bibl. [BV4211.2.S36] 65-20457 4.95
1. Preaching. 2. Sermons, American. 3. Lutheran Church—Sermons. I. Title.

SCHLOERB, Rolland Walter, 251
1893-
The preaching ministry today, by Rolland W. Schloerb. New York and London, Harper & brothers [1946] viii p., 1 l. 113 p. 19 1/2 cm. [BV4211.S27] 46-7534
1. Preaching. I. Title.

SCHMAUS, Michael, 1897- 251
Preaching as a saving encounter. [Translated by J. Holland Smith] Staten Island, N.Y., Alba House [1966] 151 p. 20 cm. Translation of: Wahrheit als Heilsbegegnung. Bibliographical references included in "Annotations" (p. [137]-151) [BV4214.S5213] 66-21814
1. Preaching. I. Title.

SCHNEIDER, Stanley D. 251
As one who speaks for God; the why and how of preaching. Minneapolis, Augsburg [c.1965] vi, 114p. 22cm. Bibl. [BV4211.2.S38] 65-22842 3.50
1. Preaching. I. Title.

SCHROEDER, Frederick W 251
Preaching the Word with authority. Philadelphia, Westminister Press [1954] 128p. 20cm. [BV4211.S28] 54-8838
1. Preaching. I. Title.

SCHUCH, Ignaz, 1823-1893. 251
The priest in the pulpit: a manual of homiletics and catechetics. Adapted from the German of Rev. Ignaz Schuech, O. S. B., by Rev. Boniface Luebbermann ... With a preface by Most Rev. Wm. H. Elder ... New York, Cincinnati [etc.] Benziger brothers, 1894. 317 p. 21 cm. [BV4010.S3] 38-837
1. Preaching. 2. Catechetics—Catholic church. I. Luebbermann, Boniface, ed. and tr. II. Title.

*SCOFIELD, C.I. 252.05832
In many pulpits. Grand Rapids, Mich., Baker Bk. 1966 [c.1922] 317p. 22cm. 3.95
I. Title.

SCOFIELD, Cyrus Ingerson, 252.
1843-1921.
In many pulpits with Dr. C. I. Scofield ... New York [etc.] Oxford university press, 1922. 5 p. l., 3-317 p. front. (port.) 22 cm. [BX7233.S4 I 6] 22-15529
I. Title.

SCOTT, Andrew Boyd. 251
Preaching week by week; the Warrack lectures on preaching, 1928, by A. Boyd Scott ... New York, R. R. Smith, inc., 1929. 256 p. 19 cm. Printed in Great Britain. [BV4211.S33] 30-17009
1. Preaching. I. Title.

SEMMELROTH, Otto. 251
The preaching word; on the theology of proclamation. [Translated by John Jay Hughes. New York] Herder and Herder [1965] 256 p. 22 cm. Translation of Wirkendes Wort. Bibliographical references included in "Footnotes" (p. 247-252) [BV4211.2.S413] 64-19737
1. Kerygma. 2. Preaching. I. Title.

SHARP, John K. 251
Our preaching; characteristics of the sermon types: and the church law on the ceremonial of preaching [by] John K. Sharp ... foreword by the Most Reverend Thomas E. Molloy ... Philadelphia, Pa., The Dolphin press, 1936. xiv, 279 p. 23 cm. [BV4211.S45] 36-21475
1. Preaching. 2. Preaching (Canon law) 3. Catholic church. Codex juris canonici. C. 1322-1351. I. Title.

SHARP, John Kean, 1892- 251
Next Sunday's sermon; suggestions on sermon composition and delivery, by the Rev. John K. Sharp ... Philadelphia, Pa., The Dolphin press, 1937. xiii, 324 p. illus. 23 cm. [Full name: John Joseph Kean Sharp] [BV4211.S44] 37-29954
1. Preaching. 2. Oratory. I. Title.

SHEDD, William Greenough 250
Thayer, 1820-1894.
Homiletics, and pastoral theology. By William G. T. Shedd ... New York, C. Scribner & co., 1867. vi, 429 p. 23 1/2 cm. [BV4010.S5] 38-822
1. Preaching. 2. Theology, Pastoral. I. Title.

SIMPSON, Matthew, 1811-1884. 251
Lectures on preaching, delivered before the Theological department of Yale college. By Matthew Simpson ... New York, Nelson & Phillips; Cincinnati, Hitchcock & Walden, 1879. 336 p. 19 1/2 cm. [Lyman Beecher lectures on preaching. Yale university. 1878-79] [BV4211.S5 1879] 38-3756
1. Preaching. I. Title.

SIMPSON, Matthew, bp., 1811- 251
1884.
Lectures on preaching delivered before the Theological department of Yale college ... By Matthew Simpson ... New York, Eaton & Mains; Cincinnati, Jennings & Graham [c1906] 336 p. 19 cm. The Lyman Beecher lectures on preaching for 1878-79. [BV4211.S5 1906] 7-9615
1. Preaching. I. Title.

SITTLER, Joseph. 251
The ecology of faith. Philadelphia, Muhlenberg Press [1961] 104 p. 21 cm. [BV4211.2.S5] 61-10278

1. Preaching. I. Title.

SIZOO, Joseph Richard, 1884- 251
Preaching unashamed. New York, Abingdon-Cokesbury Press [1949] 132 p. 20 cm. [BV4211.S52] 49-8453
1. Preaching. I. Title.

SKINNER, Craig. 251
The teaching ministry of the pulpit; its history, theology, psychology, and practice for today. Grand Rapids, Mich., Baker Book House [1973] 255 p. illus. 23 cm. Bibliography: p. 237-246. [BV4211.2.S533] 72-93334 ISBN 0-8010-7981-0 5.95
1. Preaching. I. Title.

SKINNER, Thomas Harvey, 1791- 251
1871.
Aids to preaching and hearing. By Thomas Harvey Skinner ... New-York, J. S. Taylor, 1839. xii, [13]-305 p. 20 cm. [BV4211.S53] 38-8167
1. Preaching. I. Title.

SKUDLAREK, William. 264'.6
The word in worship : preaching in a liturgical context / William Skudlarek. Nashville : Abingdon, c1981. 128 p. ; 20 cm. (Abingdon preacher's library) Includes index. Bibliography: p. 119-120. [BV4211.2.S538] 19 80-25525 ISBN 0-687-46131-6 (pbk.) : 4.95
1. Preaching. 2. Liturgics. 3. Lectionaries. I. Title.

SLATTERY, Charles Lewis, 251
bp., 1867-1930.
Present-day preaching, by Charles Lewis Slattery... New York [etc.] Longmans, Green, and co., 1910. viii, 198 p. 20 cm. [BV4211.S55] 9-29967
1. Preaching. I. Title.

SLEETH, Ronald Eugene. 251
Persuasive preaching. [1st ed.] New York, Harper [1956] 96 p. 20 cm. [BV4211.2.S55] 55-85273
1. Preaching. I. Title.

SLEETH, Ronald Eugene 251
Proclaiming the Word. Nashville, Abingdon [c.1964] 142p. 20cm. Bibl. 64-10605 2.75 bds.,
1. Preaching. I. Title.

SMITH, Arthur Harms, 1867- 251
Preachers and preaching, by Arthur H. Smith... Philadelphia, Pa., The United Lutheran publication house [c1925] 2 p. l., 3-145 p. 20 1/2 cm. "Originally prepared as lectures and delivered in the spring of 1923, in accordance with the provisions of the Kessler foundation, before the faculty, students and friends of Hamma divinity school." [BV4211.S57] 25-7956
1. Preaching. I. Title.

SMITH, Charles William 251
Frederick, 1905-
Biblical authority for modern preaching. Philadelphia, Westminster Press [1960] 176 p. 21 cm. Includes bibliography. [BV4211.2.S6] 60-7190
1. Preaching. I. Title.

SMITH, Roland Cotton, 1860- 251
1934.
Preaching as a fine art, by Roland Cotton Smith ... New York, The Macmillan company, 1922. xvi, 46 p. 18 cm. "Lectures, delivered before the faculty and students of divinity schools in Alexandria, Cambridge and New York."--Pref. Introduction by Gerald Stanley Lee. [BV4211.S6] 22-19306
1. Preaching. I. Title.

SMITH, Roy Lemon, 1887- 251
... Preach the word [by] Roy L. Smith. New York, Nashville, Abingdon-Cokesbury press [1947] 128 p. 19 1/2 cm. (The first annual Peyton lectures, Perkins school of theology, Southern Methodist university) [BV4211.S62] 47-3589
1. Preaching. I. Title.

SMYTH, John Paterson. 251
The preacher and his sermon, by Rev. J. Paterson Smyth ... New York, George H. Doran company [c1922] 143 p. 20 cm. [BV4211.S65] 22-19415 1.50
I. Title.

SOCKMAN, Ralph Washington, 251
1889-
The highway of God, by Ralph W. Sockman ... New York, The Macmillan company, 1942. xiv, 228 p. 21 cm. (The Lyman Beecher lectures) "First printing." [BV4211.S66] 42-36164
1. Preaching. 2. Christianity—20th cent. I. Title.

SOPER, Donald Oliver, 1903- 251
The advocacy of the Gospel. Nashville, Abingdon [c.1961] 119p. 61-66124 2.50 bds.,
1. Preaching. I. Title.

SOPER, Donald Oliver, 1903- 251
The advocacy of the Gospel. New York, Abingdon Press [1961] 119 p. 18 cm. [BV4211,2.S65] 61-66124
1. Preaching. I. Title.

SPENCE, Hartzell, 1908- 920.5
Get thee behind me; my life as a preacher's son, by Hartzell Spence ... illustrated by Donald McKay. London, New York [etc.] Jarrolds limited [1943] 184 p. illus. 22 cm. [PS3537.P435Z5 1943] 44-34461
I. Title.

SPERRY, Willard Learoyd, 251
1882-
We prophesy in part; a re-examination of the liberty of prophesying, by Willard L. Sperry ... Lyman Beecher lectures delivered 1938, before the Yale divinity school. New York, London, Harper & brothers [c1938] ix p., 1 l., 201 p. 19 1/2 cm. "First edition." [BV4211.S68] 38-12277
1. Preaching. I. Title.

SPURGEON, Charles Haddon, 251
1834-1892.
Encounter with Spurgeon [by] Helmut Thielicke. Translated by John W. Doberstein. Grand Rapids: Baker Book House, [1975 c1963] [ix,] 283 p.; 20 cm. Translation of Vom geistlichen Reden: Begegnung mit Spurgeon. [BV4211.S6943] 63-12536 ISBN 0-8010-8825-9 3.95 (pbk.)
1. Preaching. I. Thielicke, Helmut, 1908- II. Title.

SPURGEON, Charles Haddon, 1834-
1892
Lectures to my students. Grand Rapids, Mich., Zondervan Pub. House [1958] 443 p. 22 cm.
1. Preaching. I. Title.

SPURGEON, Charles Haddon, 251'.02
1834-1892.
Lectures to my students : a selection from addresses delivered to the students of the Pastors' college, Metropolitan Tabernacle. / by C.H. Spurgeon. Grand Rapids, MI : Baker Book House, 1977. vi, 200p. : ill. ; 22 cm. This one-volume paperback edition includes 1st, 2nd, and 3rd series of Lecture to My Students. [BV4211.S688] ISBN 0-8010-8097-5 pbk. : 4.95
1. Preaching. I. Title.

SPURGEON, Charles Haddon, 251
1834-1892.
Spurgeon's lectures to his students; a condensation of the addresses delivered to the students of the Pastors' college, Metropolitan tabernacle, by Charles H. Spurgeon ... condensed and abridged by David Otis Fuller ... Grand Rapids, Mich., Zondervan publishing house [1945] 422 p. illus. 20 cm. [BV4211.S69] 46-239
1. Preaching. I. Fuller, David Otis, 1903- ed. II. Title.

STALKER, James, 1848-1927. 251
The preacher and his models. Introd. by Ralph G. Turnbull. Grand Rapids, Baker Book House [1967] 284 p. 20 cm. (Notable books on preaching) (The Yale lectures on preaching, 1891.) Bibliographical footnotes. [BV4211.S7 1967] 67-18196
1. Preaching. I. Title. II. Series: Lyman Beecher lectures, 1891.

STALKER, James, 1848-1927. 251
The preacher and his models. The Yale lectures on preaching, 1891. By the Rev. James Stalker ... New York, A. C. Armstrong and son, 1891. 4 p. l., [ix]-xii, 284 p. 19 cm. [BV4211.S7] 38-8165
1. Preaching. I. Title.

STANFIELD, Vernon L. 251
Effective evangelistic preaching. Grand Rapids, Mich., Baker Bk. [c.]1965. 78p. 23cm. [BV4211.2.S72] 65-29537 2.00
1. Preaching. 2. Evangelistic sermons. I. Title.

STEEL, David, 1910- 251
Preaching through the year / David Steel. Atlanta : John Knox Press, c1980. 170 p. ; 20 cm. [BV4211.2.S725] 19 80-82191 ISBN 0-8042-1801-3 pbk. : 6.50
1. Preaching. 2. Church year. I. Title.

STEVENSON, Dwight Eshelman, 253
1906-
The false prophet. Nashville, Abingdon [c.1965] 142p. 21cm. Bibl. [BV4211.2.S74] 65-13058 2.75
1. Preaching. I. Title.

STEVENSON, Dwight Eshelman, 253
1906-
The false prophet [by] Dwight E. Stevenson. New York, Abingdon Press [1965] 142 p. 21 cm. Bibliographical footnotes. [BV4211.2.S74] 65-13058
1. Preaching. I. Title.

STEVENSON, Dwight Eshelman, 251
1906-
Reaching people from the pulpit; a guide to effective sermon delivery, by Dwight E. Stevenson and Charles F. Diehl. [1st ed.] New York, Harper [1958] 172 p. illus. 22 cm. Includes bibliography. [BV4211.2.S75] 58-7104
1. Preaching. 2. Elocution. I. Diehl, Charles F., joint author. II. Title.

STEVENSON, Dwight Eshelman, 251
1906-
Reaching people from the pulpit : a guide to effective sermon delivery / by Dwight E. Stevenson and Charles F. Diehl. Grand Rapids : Baker Book House, 1978, c1958. x, 172p. ; 20 cm. [BV4211.2S75] ISBN 0-8010-8133-5 pbk. : 3.95
1. Preaching. 2. Elocution. I. Diehl, Charles F., joint author. II. Title.
L.C. card no. for 1958 Harper & Row ed.: 58-7104.

*STEWART, James Stuart, 251.01
1896-
Heralds of God [by] James S. Stewart. Grand Rapids, Mich., Baker Book House [1972, c.1946] 221 p. 20 cm. (James S. Stewart library) [BV4211] ISBN 0-8010-7976-4 pap., 1.95
1. Preaching. I. Title.

STIDGER, William Le Roy, 251
1886-
Planning your preaching, by William L. Stidger ... New York and London, Harper & brothers, 1932. xvi p., 1 l., 289 p. 22 1/2 cm. "First edition." Includes bibliographies. [BV4211.S748] 32-28934 82-26094
1. Preaching. 2. Sermons—Outlines. I. Title.

STIDGER, William Le Roy, 251
1886-
Preaching out of the overflow, by William L. Stidger ... Nashville, Tenn., Cokesbury press, 1929. 238 p. 20 cm. [BV4211.S75] 29-22815
1. Preaching. I. Title.

STUEMPFLE, Herman G. 251
Preaching law and gospel / Herman G. Stuempfle, Jr. Philadelphia : Fortress Press, c1978. 95 p. ; 22 cm. Includes bibliographical references. [BV4211.2.S85] 77-15247 ISBN 0-8006-1329-5 pbk. : 3.50
1. Preaching. I. Title.

SWANK, George W. 251
Dialogic style in preaching / George W. Swank. Valley Forge, PA : Judson Press, c1981. 96 p. ; 22 cm. (More effective preaching series) Includes bibliographical references. [BV4211.2.S9] 19 81-11778 ISBN 0-8170-0922-1 pbk. : 4.95
1. Preaching. 2. Communication (Theology) I. Title. II. Series.

SWEAZEY, George Edgar, 1905- 251
Preaching the good news / George E. Sweazey. Englewood Cliffs, N.J. : Prentice-Hall, [1976] viii, 339 p. ; 24 cm. Includes index. Bibliography: p. 319-326. [BV4211.2.S93] 75-4997 ISBN 0-13-694802-2 : 10.95
1. Preaching. I. Title.

TAYLOR, Richard Shelley, 251
1912-
Preaching holiness today, by Richard S. Taylor. Kansas City, Mo., Beacon Hill Press [1968] 216 p. 21 cm. Bibliography: p. 206-210. [BV4221.T3] 68-3324
1. Preaching. 2. Holiness. I. Title.

TAYLOR, William, bp., 1821- 251
1902.
The model preacher; comprised in a series of letters illustrating the best mode of preaching the gospel. By Rev. William Taylor ... Cincinnati, Swormstedt & Poe, for the author, 1859. 403 p. front. (port.) 19 1/2 cm. [BV4211.T3] 38-8106
1. Preaching. I. Title.

TEIKMANIS, Arthur L., 1914- 251
Preaching and pastoral care. Englewood Cliffs, N.J., Prentice [c.1964] 144p. 21cm. (Successful pastoral counseling ser.) 64-23551 2.95
1. Preaching. I. Title. II. Series.

THIELICKE, Helmut, 1908- 251
The trouble with the church; a call for renewal. Translated and edited by John W. Doberstein. [1st ed.] New York, Harper & Row [1965] xvi, 136 p. 21 cm. Translation of Leiden an der Kirche; ein personliches Wort. [BV4214.T473] 65-20458
1. Preaching. 2. Kerygma. I. Title.

THOMPSON, William D. 251
A listener's guide to preaching. Nashville, Abingdon [c.1966] 110p. illus. 18cm. [BV4211.2.T5] 66-14996 1.25 pap.,
1. Preaching. I. Title.

THOMPSON, William D
A listener's guide to preaching [by] William D. Thompson. Nashville, Abingdon Press [1966] 110 p. illus. 18 cm.
1. Preaching. I. Title.

THOMPSON, William D. 251
Preaching biblically : exegesis and interpretation / William D. Thompson. Nashville : Abingdon, c1981. 128 p. ; 21 cm. (Abingdon preachers library) Includes indexes. Bibliography: p. 120-123. [BS534.5.T48] 19 80-28096 ISBN 0-687-33840-9 : 4.95
1. Bible—Homiletical use. 2. Preaching. I. Title.

TITZARD, Leslie James.
Preaching; the art of communication; foreword by Leslie E. Cooke. New York, Oxford University Press, 1959. 106 p. 23 cm.
I. Title.

TIZARD, Leslie James.
Preaching; the art of communication. Foreword by Dr. Leslie E. Cooke. New York, Oxford University Press, 1959. 106 p. 23 cm.
1. Preaching. 2. Communication. I. Title.

TIZZARD, Leslie James.
Preaching, the art of communication. New York, Oxford, 1959. 107 p.
1. Preaching. I. Title.

TROEGER, Thomas H., 1945- 251
Creating fresh images for preaching : new rungs for Jacob's ladder / Thomas H. Troeger. Valley Forge, PA : Judson Press, c1982. 141 p. ; 22 cm. (More effective preaching series) Includes bibliographical references. [BV4211.2.T76] 19 81-13674 ISBN 0-8170-0937-X : 7.95
1. Preaching. I. Title. II. Series.

TUCKER, William Jewett, 1839- 251
1926.
The making and the unmaking of the preacher; lectures on the Lyman Beecher foundation, Yale university, 1898. Boston and New York, Houghton, Mifflin and company, 1898. 3 p. l., 224 p. 1 l. 19 1/2 cm. [BV4211.T8] 98-1685
1. Preaching. I. Title.

TURNBULL, Ralph G. 200.6
The preacher's heritage, task, and resources, by Ralph G. Turnbull. Grand Rapids, Baker Book House [1968] 178 p. 20 cm. Bibliography: p. 169-178. [BV4211.2.T87] 68-19215 2.95
1. Preaching. I. Title.

UNGER, Merrill Frederick, 252.6
1909-
Principles of expository preaching, by Merrill F. Unger. Grand Rapids, Mich., Zondervan Pub. House [1973, c1953] 267

p. 21 cm. Includes bibliographies. [BV4211.2.U5] 55-42014 4.95 (pbk.)
1. Preaching. I. Title.

UNGER, Merrill Frederick, 1909- 251.8
Principles of expository preaching. Grand Rapids, Zondervan Pub. House [1955] 267p. 22cm. Includes bibliographies. [BV4211.2.U5] 55-42014
1. Preaching. I. Title.

UTLEY, Uldine Mabelle, 1912- 269
Why I am a preacher; a plain answer to an oft-repeated question, by Uldine Utley, introduction by Bishop Edwin H. Hughes ... New York, Chicago [etc.] Fleming H. Revell company [c1931] 3 p. l., 3-152 p. front., plates, ports. 21 cm. [BV3785.U7W5] 31-8060
I. Title.

UTLEY, Uldine Mabelle, 1912- 269
Why I am a preacher; a plain answer to an oft-repeated question, by Uldine Utley, introduction by Bishop Edwin H. Hughes ... New York, Chicago [etc.] Fleming H. Revell company [c1931] 3 p. l., 3-152 p. front., plates, ports. 21 cm. [BV3785.U7W5] 31-8060
I. Title.

VALENTINE, Ferdinand. 251
The art of preaching; a practical guide. Westminster, Md., Newman Press, 1952. 224p. 22cm. [BV4211.V2 1952] 52-9506
1. Preaching. I. Title.

VAN DYKE, Henry, 1852-1933. 270
The gospel for an age of doubt, by Henry Van Dyke... 6th ed. rev., with a new preface... New York, The Macmillan company. London, Macmillan & co., ltd., 1902. 2 p. l., xiii-xxvi p., 2 l., 3-329 p. 20 cm. Originally "written in the form of a course of lectures on preaching on the "Lyman Beecher foundation." and delivered before the divinity students of Yale university."--Pref. [BR121.V32 1902] 4-11277
1. Preaching. 2. Christianity—Evidences. I. Title.

VINET, Alexandre Rodolphe, 1797-1847.
Homiletics; or, The theory of preaching, by A. Vinet ... Translated and edited by Thomas H. Skinner ... New York and Chicago, Ivison, Blakeman, Taylor & co., 1880 xviii, [19]-524 p. 20 cm. [BV4213.V53] 42-43803
1. Preaching. I. Skinner, Thomas Harvey, 1791-1871, ed. and tr. II. Title.

VOLBEDA, Samuel, 1881-1953. 251
The pastoral genius of preaching. Compiled and edited by Robert Evenhuis. Grand Rapids, Zondervan Pub. House [1960] 85 p. 21 cm. [BV4211.2.V6] 60-3430
1. Preaching. I. Title.

WALLIS, John Eyre Winstanley, 1886- 251
Verbi ministerium; an introduction to Anglican preaching, with appendices on extemporary prayer, &c. By John Eyre Winstanley Wallis...With a foreword by the Right Rev. the Lord Bishop of Blackburn. London, The Faith press, ltd.; Milwaukee, U.S.A., The Morehouse publishing co. [1930] xvi, 172 p. 19 cm. Bibliographies interspersed. [BV4211.W3] 31-14837
1. Preaching. I. Title. II. Title: Anglican preaching.

WATSON, John, 1850-1907. 250
The cure of souls; lyman Beecher lectures on preaching at Yale university 1896, by John Watson... New York, Dodd, Mead & company, 1896. x, 301 p. 19 1/2 cm. [BV4010.W3] CA 12
1. Preaching. 2. Theology, Pastoral. I. Title.

WEATHERSPOON, Jesse Burton, 1886- 251
Sent forth to preach; studies in apositolic preaching. [1st ed.] New York, Harper [1954] 182p. 21cm. Bibliography: p. 181-182. [BV4211.W38] 54-5855
1. Preaching. I. Title.

WEDEL, Alton F. 251
The mighty word / by Alton Wedel. St. Louis : Concordia Pub. House, c1977. p. cm. (The Preacher's workshop series ; book 1) Includes bibliographical references. [BV4211.2.W38] 77-21778 ISBN 0-570-07400-2 pbk. : 1.95
1. Preaching. I. Title. II. Series.

WEDEL, Theodore Otto, 1892- 251
The pulpit rediscovers theology. Greenwich, Conn., Seabury Press, 1956. 181p. 22cm. [BV4211.2.W4] 56-7969
1. Preaching. I. Title.

WELSH, Clement, 1913- 251
Preaching in a new key: Studies in the psychology of thinking and listening. Philadelphia, United Church Press [1974] 128 p. 22 cm. "A Pilgrim Press book." Includes bibliographical references. [BV4211.2.W42] 74-5268 ISBN 0-8298-0273-8 5.95
1. Preaching. 2. Perception. 3. Cognition. I. Title.

WEST, Emerson Roy 251
When you speak in church: purpose, preparation, presentation. Salt Lake City, Deseret, 1966 [c.1965] 196p. illus. 24cm. Bibl. [BV4211.2.W43] 65-28866 price unreported
1. Preaching. I. Title.

WHITE, Douglas Malcolm, 1909- 251
The excellence of exposition / by Douglas M. White ; foreword by Stephen F. Olford. Neptune, N.J. : Loizeaux Bros., c1977. 191 p. ; 21 cm. Includes indexes. Bibliography: p. 179-184. [BV4211.2.W433] 77-6807 ISBN 0-87213-938-7 : 4.25
1. Preaching. I. Title.

WHITE, Douglas Malcolm, 1909- 251
"He ezpounded"; a guide to ezpository preaching. Chicago, Moody Press [1952] 159 p. 20 cm. [BV4211.W43] 52-1588
1. Preaching. I. Title.

WHITE, Reginald E. O. 251
A guide to preaching; a practical primer of homiletics [by] R. E. O. White. [1st American ed.] Grand Rapids, W. B. Eerdmans Pub. Co. [1973] vii, 244 p. 21 cm. Bibliography: p. 241-244. [BV4211.2.W435 1973] 73-76535 ISBN 0-8028-1540-5 3.95
1. Preaching. I. Title.

WHITESELL, Faris Daniel, 1895- 251
Power in expository preaching. [Westwood, N.J.] Revell [1963] 174 p. 21 cm. [BV4211.2.W44] 63-10393
1. Preaching. I. Title.

WHITESELL, Faris Daniel, 1895- 251
Preaching on Bible characters. [1st ed.] Grand Rapids, Barker Book House, 1955. 150p. 20cm. Includes bibliography. [BV4211.2.W45] 55-6506
1. Preaching. 2. Preaching—Hist. 3. Bible—Biog.—Bibl. I. Title.

WHITESELL, Faris Daniel, 1895- 251
Variety in your preaching [by] Faris D. Whitesell [and] Lloyd M. Perry. [Westwood, N. J.], F. H. Revell Co. [1954] 219p. 22cm. [BV4211.W46] 54-5437
1. Preaching. I. Perry, Lloyd M., joint author. II. Title.

WILLIAMS, Jerome Oscar, 1885- 251
The gospel preacher and his preaching. Nashville, Broadman Press [1949] xi, 84 p. 20 cm. "Books to read" at ends of chapters. [BV4211.W5] 50-710
1. Preaching. I. Title.

WILLIMON, William H. 251
Integrative preaching : the pulpit at the center / William H. Willimon.. Nashville : Abingdon, c1981. 110 p. ; 21 cm. (Abingdon preacher's library) Includes indexes. Bibliography: p. 107. [BV4211.2.W5] 19 80-39628 ISBN 0-687-19129-7 pbk. : 4.95
1. Preaching. I. Title.

WINGREN, Gustaf, 1910- 230.41
The living word; a theological study of preaching and the church. [Tr. from Swedish by Victor C. Pogue] Philadelphia, Fortress [1965, c.1960] 223p. 18cm. (Preacher's paperback lib., 5) [BV4216.W513] 65-21821 3.00 pap.,
1. Preaching. 2. Lutheran Church—Doctrinal and controversial works. I. Title.

WINGREN, Gustaf [Fredrik] 1910- 230.41
The living word; a theological study of preaching and the church. [Translated by Victor C. Pogue from the Swedish] Philadelphia, Muhlenberg Press [1960] 223p. 23cm. Bibl. footnotes 60-51230 3.75 bds.,
1. Preaching. 2. Lutheran Church—Doctrinal and controversial works. I. Title.

WOOD, Arthur Skevington. 251
The art of preaching; message, method, and motive in preaching. [American ed.] Grand Rapids, Zondervan Pub. House [1964, c1963] 126 p. 22 cm. Published in London in 1963 under title: Heralds of the gospel. [BV4211.2.W6 1964] 64-11954
1. Preaching. I. Title.

YOHN, David Waite. 251
The contemporary preacher and his task. Grand Rapids, Mich., W. B. Eerdmans [1969] 159 p. 21 cm. Bibliography: p. 154-159. [BV4211.2.Y6] 67-28379 2.95
1. Preaching. 2. Clergy—Office. I. Title.

YOUNG, William Henry, 1853- 251
How to preach with power. by Rev. William Henry Young, PH.D. Athens, Ga., The How publishing co.; London, E. Stock, 1896. viii, 319, [1] p. front. (port.) illus. (incl. map. form) 20 1/2 cm. [BV4211.Y6 1896] 38-7515
1. Preaching. I. Title.

YOUNG, William Henry, 1853- 251
How to preach with power, by Rev. William Henry Young, PH.D. Rev. ed. Athens, Ga., The How publishing co.; London, E. Stock, 1897. 365 p. front. (port.) illus. (incl. map, form) 20 1/2 cm. [BV4211.Y6 1897] 38-7514
1. Preaching. I. Title.

ZIEGLER, Edward Krusen, 1903- 251
Rural preaching. [Westwood, N. J.] F. H. Revell Co. [1954] 158p. 21cm. [BV4211.2.Z5] 54-8002
1. Preaching. 2. Rural churches. I. Title.

Preaching—Addresses, essays, lectures.

ANDERSON, Roy Allan. 251.081
Preachers of righteousness. Nashville, Tenn., Southern Pub. Association [1963] 212 p. illus. 22 cm. [BV4211.2.A44] 63-12808
1. Preaching — Addresses, essays, lectures. I. Title.

ARMSTRONG, James, 1924- 251
Telling truth : the foolishness of preaching in a real world / James Armstrong. Waco, Tex. : Word Books, c1977. 114 p. ; 23 cm. [BV4222.A75] 76-53986 ISBN 0-87680-501-2 : 5.95
1. Preaching—Addresses, essays, lectures. I. Title.

BOYNTON, Nehemiah.
Real preaching; three addresses to the theological students of Oberlin ... Boston, The Pilgrim press [1897] 2 p. l., 123 p. 12 degrees. 1-4111
I. Title.
Contents omitted.

CLAYPOOL, John. 251
The preaching event / John R. Claypool. Waco, Tex. : Word Books, c1980. 139 p. ; 21 cm. (Lyman Beecher lectures) Includes bibliographical references. [BV4222.C54] 19 79-67669 ISBN 0-8499-0131-6 : 5.95
1. Preaching—Addresses, essays, lectures. I. Title. II. Series: Lyman Beecher lectures ; 1980.

CLELAND, James T. 251
Preaching to be understood. Nashville, Abingdon [1965] 126p. 20cm. (Warrack lects. on preaching, 1964) Bibl. [BV4222.C55] 65-13145 2.75
1. Preaching—Addresses, essays, lectures. I. Title. II. Series.

DRURY, Ronan, ed. 251
Preaching. New York, Sheed [1963, c.1962] 149p. 22cm. 63-8543 3.50
1. Preaching—Addresses, essays, lectures. I. Title.

GOD demands doctrinal preaching / edited by Thomas B. Warren, Garland Elkins. Jonesboro, Ark. : National Christian Press, c1978. 332 p. ; 22 cm. (Spiritual sword lectureship ; 3) Includes bibliographical references. [BV4222.G6] 78-113413 9.95 pbk. : 7.95 251
1. Bible—Biography—Addresses, essays, lectures. 2. Bible—Criticism, interpretation, etc.—Addresses, essays, lectures. 3. Preaching—Addresses, essays, lectures. I. Warren, Thomas B. II. Elkins, Garland. III. Title. IV. Series.

HALDEMAN, Isaac Massey, 1845- 232.
Why I preached the second coming, by I. M. Haldeman... New York, Chicago [etc.] Fleming H. Revell company [c1919] 2 p. l., 7-160 p. 19 1/2 cm. [BT885.H265] 19-18655
I. Title.

HALDEMAN, Isaac Massey, 1845- 232.
Why I preached the second coming, by I. M. Haldeman... New York, Chicago [etc.] Fleming H. Revell company [c1919] 2 p. l., 7-160 p. 19 1/2 cm. [BT885.H265] 19-18655
I. Title.

KECK, Leander E. 251'.08
The Bible in the pulpit : the renewal of biblical preaching / Leander E. Keck. Nashville : Abingdon, c1978. 172 p. ; 20 cm. Includes bibliographical references. [BS534.5.K42] 77-12015 ISBN 0-687-03160-5 pbk. : 4.95
1. Bible—Homiletical use—Addresses, essays, lectures. 2. Preaching—Addresses, essays, lectures. 3. Sermons, American. I. Title.

KENNEDY, Gerald Hamilton, Bp., 1907- 248.8
For preachers and other sinners. [1st ed.] New York, Harper & Row [1964] x, 110 p. 22 cm. [BV4221.K4] 64-14379
1. Preaching — Addresses, essays, lectures. 2. Christianity — 20th cent. — Addresses, essays, lectures. I. Title.

LOUTTIT, Henry Irving, Bp., 1903- 251
Commanded to preach, by Henry I. Louttit. New York, Seabury Press [1965] 111 p. 19cm. (George Craig Stewart Memorial lectures) Bibliography: p. 109-111. [BV4222.L6] 64-19632
1. Preaching — Addresses, essays, lectures. I. Title. II. Series: George Craig Stewart lectures on preaching

MASSEY, James Earl. 251
The sermon in perspective : a study of communication and charisma / James Earl Massey. Grand Rapids : Baker Book House, c1976. 116 p. ; 23 cm. Delivered in part as the Mary Claire Gautschi Lectures at Fuller Theological Seminary, Pasadena, Calif., in 1975, as the 1975 Fall Lectures at Ashland Theological Seminary, Ashland, Ohio, and at Gulf-Coast Bible College, Houston, Tex. in Feb. 1976 during the Fourteenth Annual Ministers' Refresher Institute. Includes bibliographical references and index. [BV4222.M28] 76-150073 ISBN 0-8010-6003-6 : 4.95
1. Preaching—Addresses, essays, lectures. I. Title.

MAST, Russell L. 251
Preach the word [by] Russell L. Mast. Newton, Kan., Faith and Life Press [1968] 90 p. 20 cm. Includes bibliographical references. [BV4222.M3] 68-28782
1. Preaching—Addresses, essays, lectures. I. Title.

MIDDLETON, Robert G. 251
Tensions in modern faith. Valley Forge [Pa.] Judson [c.1965] 158p. 21cm. [BV4211.2.M46] 65-22001 3.95
1. Preaching—Addresses, essays, lectures. 2. Christianity—20th cent.—Addresses, essays, lectures. I. Title.

MIDDLETON, Robert G. 251
Tensions in modern faith [by] Robert G. Middleton. Valley Forge [Pa.] Judson Press [1965] 158 p. 21 cm. [BV4211.2.M46] 65-22001
1. Preaching — Addresses, essays, lectures. 2. Christianity — 20th cent. — Addresses, essays, lectures. I. Title.

MILLER, Donald G. 230'.58'0924
P.T. Forsyth—the man, the preachers' theologian, prophet for the 20th century : a

contemporary assessment / by Donald G. Miller, Browne Barr, Robert S. Paul. Pittsburgh, Pa. : Pickwick Press, 1981. p. cm. (The Pittsburgh theological monograph series ; 36) "Containing a reprint of P.T. Forsyth, Positive preaching and modern mind." Includes indexes. Bibliography: p. [BX7260.F583M54] 19 81-10668 ISBN 0-915138-48-4 : Price unreported
1. Forsyth, Peter Taylor, 1848-1921—Addresses, essays, lectures. 2. Preaching—Addresses, essays, lectures. I. Barr, Browne. II. Paul, Robert S. III. Forsyth, Peter Taylor, 1848-1921. Positive preaching and modern mind. 1981. IV. Title. V. Series.
Publisher's address: 5001 Baum Blvd., Pittsburgh, PA 15213

MITCHELL, Henry H. 251
The recovery of preaching / by Henry H. Mitchell. New York : Harper & Row, [1977] p. cm. Includes bibliographical references. [BV4222.M5] 76-62959 ISBN 0-06-065763-4 : pbk. : 3.95
1. Preaching—Addresses, essays, lectures. I. Title.

PACK, Frank, 1916- 251
Preaching to modern man [by] Frank Pack and Prentice Meador, Jr. Abilene, Tex., Biblical Research Press [1969] vii, 173 p. 23 cm. Bibliography: p. 172-173. [BV4222.P28] 73-75928 3.95
1. Preaching—Addresses, essays, lectures. I. Meador, Prentice, 1938- joint author. II. Title.

PREACHING the story / 251
[edited by] Edmund A. Steimle, Morris J. Niedenthal, Charles L. Rice. Philadelphia : Fortress Press, c1980. p. cm. Includes bibliographical references. [BV4211.2.P73] 78-14675 ISBN 0-8006-0538-1 : 9.95
1. Preaching—Addresses, essays, lectures. 2. Sermons, American. I. Steimle, Edmund A. II. Niedenthal, Morris J., 1931- III. Rice, Charles Lynvel, 1936-

PREACHING with purpose and 251
power : selected E.Y. Mullins Lectures on Preaching / compiled and edited by Don M. Aycock. Macon, Ga. : Mercer University Press, c1982. 314 p. ; 24 cm. Includes index. [BV4211.2.P74] 19 81-22388 ISBN 0-86554-027-6 : 15.95
1. Preaching—Addresses, essays, lectures. I. Aycock, Don M.

ROSS, George Alexander 208.
Johnston, 1865-
Why preach Christ? A plea for the holy ministry; being the William Belden Noble lectures delivered in Harvard university, 1928, by G. A. Johnston Ross ... Cambridge, Harvard university press; London, H. Milford, Oxford university press, 1929. 6 p. l., [3]-114 p. 20 cm. [BR85.R73] 29-27801
I. Title.

ROSS, George Alexander 208.
Johnston, 1865-
Why preach Christ? A plea for the holy ministry; being the William Belden Noble lectures delivered in Harvard university, 1928, by G. A. Johnston Ross ... Cambridge, Harvard university press; London, H. Milford, Oxford university press, 1929. 6 p. l., [3]-114 p. 20 cm. [BR85.R73] 29-27801
I. Title.

SITTLER, Joseph. 251
The anguish of preaching. Philadelphia, Fortress Press [1966] vii, 70 p. 22 cm. [BV4222.S53] 66-25261
1. Preaching—Addresses, essays, lectures. I. Title.

TAYLOR, Gardner C. 252'.62
How shall they preach / by Gardner C. Taylor. Elgin, IL : Progressive Baptist Pub. House, c1977. 148 p. ; 22 cm. Includes bibliographical references. [BV4211.2.T38] 77-76732 ISBN 0-89191-097-2 : 7.50
1. Preaching—Addresses, essays, lectures. 2. Lenten sermons. I. Title.

Preaching—Audio-visual aids.

WEISHEIT, Eldon. 251
A sermon is more than words / by Eldon Weisheit. St. Louis : Concordia Pub. House, c1977. p. cm. (The Preacher's workshop series ; book 8) [BV4227.W43] 77-21557 ISBN 0-570-07407-X pbk. : 1.95
1. Preaching—Audio-visual aids. I. Title. II. Series.

Preaching—Biblical teaching.

KAHMANN, J 251
The Bible on the preaching of the World, by J. Kahmann. Translated by T. J. Holmes. De Pere, Wis., St. Norbert Abbey Press, 1965. 117 p. 17 cm. [BV4207.K313] 65-29090
1. Preaching — Biblical teaching. 2. Kerygma. I. Title.

LAYMON, Charles M. 220.6'6
They dared to speak for God [by] Charles M. Laymon. Nashville, Abingdon Press [1974] 176 p. 22 cm. Includes bibliographical references. [BS511.2.L4] 73-17196 ISBN 0-687-41649-3 5.95
1. Bible—Criticism, interpretation, etc. 2. Bible—Biography. 3. Preaching—Biblical teaching. I. Title.

MURPHY-O'CONNOR, 227.08251
Jerome, 1935-
Paul on preaching. New York, Sheed and Ward [1964] xx, 314 p. 20 cm. Bibliography: p. [303]-305. [BS2655.P8M8] 64-19908
1. Preaching — Biblical teaching. 2. Bible. N.T. Epistles of Paul — Criticism, interpretation, etc. I. Title.

STOTT, John R. W 251
The preacher's portrait; some New Testament word studies. Grand Rapids, Eerdmans [1961] 124 p. 21 cm. Includes bibliography. [BV4221.S8] 61-17392
1. Preaching — Biblical teaching. I. Title.

Preaching—Bibliography

CAPLAN, Harry, 1896- 016.251
Mediaeval artes praedicandi; a hand-list, by Harry Caplan... Ithaca, N.Y., Cornell university press; London, H. Milford, Oxford university press, 1934. 5 p. l., 42 p. 23 1/2 cm. (Half-title: Cornell studies in classical philology...vol. xxiv) "The expense of publishing this volume was borne by a grant from the Charles Edwin Bennett fund for research in the classical languages."--Verse of 3d prelim. leaf. """"A supplementary hand-list, by Harry Caplan...Ithaca, N.Y., Cornell university press; London, H. Milford, Oxford university press, 1936. 5 p. l., 36 p. 23 1/2 cm. (Half-Title: Cornell stuides in classical philology ...vol. xxv) [PA25.C7] [Z7751.C24] (480.82) 31-31424
1. Preaching—Bibl. 2. Preaching—Hist.—Middle ages. 3. Manuscripts. Latin—Bibl. I. Title. II. Title: Artes praedicandi.

PULPIT eloquence;
a list of doctrinal and historical studies in German. By Harry Caplan and Henry H. King. [Baton Rouge, La., Speech Association of America, 1956] 160p. 25cm. Issued as a special number of the Speech monographs, vol. 23, no. 5, 1956.
1. Preaching—Bibl. 2. Sermon, German—Bibl. I. Caplan, Harry, 1896- comp.

TOOHEY, William 016.251
Recent homiletical thought; a bibliography, 1935-1965, ed. by William Toohey, William D. Thompson. Nashville, Abingdon [1967] 303p. 23cm. [Z7826.T6] 67-15948 4.75
1. Preaching—Bibl. I. Thompson, William D., joint author. II. Title.

Preaching (Canon law)

ALLGEIER, Joseph L 1913-
The canonical obligation of preaching in parish churches; a historical synopsis and a commentary. Washington, Catholic University of America Press, 1949 [c1950] ix. 115 p. 23 cm. (The Catholic University of America. Canon law studies, no. 291) Thesis--Catholic University of America. Vita. Bibliography: p. 91-97. A 50
1. Preaching (Canon law) I. Title. II. Series.

MCVANN, James, 1902- 251
... *The canon law on sermon preaching,* by James McVann ... New York, The Paulist press, 1940. vii, 190 p. 25 cm. At head of title: Pontificia universitas Gregoriana. "A doctoral dissertation in the Faculty of canon law of the Pontifical Gregorian university, Rome." Bibliography: p. 175-180. [BX1939.P53M3] 44-26457
1. Preaching (Canon law) I. Catholic church. Codex juris canonici. C. 1327-1351: De divini verbi praedicatione. II. Rome (City) Pontificia universita gregoriana. III. Title.

Preaching—Congresses.

CATHOLIC University of 251.08
America. Workshop on the Renewal in Scriptural and Liturgical Preaching, 1965. *The Sunday homily;* scriptural and liturgical renewal. Edited by John Burke. [Washington, D.C., Thomist Press, 1966] iv, 141 p. 22 cm. Papers delivered at the 1965 Workshop on the Renewal in Scriptural and Liturgical Preaching conducted at the Catholic University of America. Includes bibliographies. [BV4211.2.C3] 66-26068
1. Preaching — Congresses. I. Burke, John, 1928- ed. II. Title.

Preaching—Early works to 1800.

ALANUS DE INSULIS, d.1202. 251
The art of preaching / by Alan of Lille ; translated, with an introd., by Gillian R. Evans. Kalamazoo, Mich. : Cistercian Publications, 1981. p. cm. (Cistercian Fathers series ; no. 23) Translation of Ars praedicandi, which was issued in v. 210 of Patrologiae cursus completus, series Latina. [BV4209.A4213 1981] 19 80-24611 ISBN 0-87907-923-1 pbk. : 13.95
1. Preaching—Early works to 1800. I. Title.

FRANCOIS DE SALES, Saint, 251
Bp. of Geneva, 1567-1622
On the preacher and preaching. Tr., introd., notes, by John K. Ryan [Chicago] Regnery [c.1964] 110p. 22cm. Tr. of a letter to Andre Fremyot, archbishop of Bourges, dated Oct. 5, 1604. Bibl. 64-14601 2.95
1. Preaching—Early works to 1800. I. Ryan, John Kenneth, 1887- ed. and tr. II. Title.

Preaching—England—History.

KNAPP, Peggy Ann. 252'.02
The style of John Wyclif's English sermons / by Peggy Ann Knapp. The Hague : Mouton, 1977. 116 p. : diagrs. ; 24 cm. (De proprietatibus litterarum : Series practica ; 16) Bibliography: p. [111]-116. [BX4905.K62] 77-369497 ISBN 9-02-793156-9 : 19.00
1. Wycliffe, John, d. 1384. 2. Preaching—England—History. I. Title. II. Series.
Available from Mouton, 3 Westchester Plaza, Elmsford, NY 10523

OWEN, Trevor A. 251'.00942
Lancelot Andrewes / Trevor A. Owen. Boston : Twayne, 1981. p. cm. (Twayne's English author series ; TEAS 325) Includes index. Bibliography: p. [BV4208.G7O79] 19 81-2154 ISBN 0-8057-6769-X : 13.95
1. Preaching—England—History. I. Andrewes, Lancelot, 1555-1626. II. Title. III. Series.

OWST, Gerald Robert. 250.
Preaching in medieval England; an introduction to sermon manuscripts of the the period c. 1350-1450, by G. R. Owst ... Cambridge [Eng.] The University press, 1926. xviii, 381, [1] p. illus. (incl. facsims.) ii pl. (incl. front.) 23 cm. (Half-title: Cambridge studies in medieval life and thought) [BV4208.G7O8] 26-15646
I. Title.

TRACY, Wesley. 251'.0092'4
When Adam Clarke preached, people listened : studies in the message and method of Adam Clarke's preaching / by Wesley Tracy. Kansas City, Mo. : Beacon Hill Press of Kansas City, [c1981] 238 p. : ill. ; 19 cm. Includes bibliographical references. [BX8495.C57T7] 19 81-146122 ISBN 0-8341-0714-7 pbk. : 4.95
1. Clarke, Adam, 1760?-1832. 2. Preaching—England—History. I. Title.

Preaching, Expository.

STIBBS, Alan Marshall.
Expounding God's word; some principles and methods. Grand Rapids, Wm. B. Eerdmans [1961] 112 p.
1. Preaching, Expository. I. Title.

Preaching, Extemporaneous.

SMITH, Wilder, 1835-1891. 251
Extempore preaching, by Wilder Smith. Hartford, Brown & Gross, 1884. 2 p. l., 170 p. 19 cm. [BV4235.E8S6] 38-24314
1. Preaching, Extemporaneous. I. Title.

STORRS, Richard Salter, 1821- 251
1900.
Conditions of success in preaching without notes. Three lectures delivered before the students of the Union theological seminary, New York: January 13, 20, 27: 1875; with an appendix. By Richard S. Storrs ... N[ew] Y[ork] Dodd and Mead, 1875. 233 p. 19 1/2 cm. [BV4235.E8S7] 38-19296
1. Preaching, Extemporaneous. I. Title.

WARE, Henry, 1794-1843.
Hints on extemporaneous preaching. By Henry Ware, jr.... 3d ed. Boston, Hilliard, Gray, Little and Wilkins, 1831. vii, 98 p. 15 cm. 16-24744
I. Title.

ZINCKE, Foster Barham, 1817- 251
1893.
The duty and the discipline of extemporary preaching. By F. Barham Zincke ... The 1st American from the 2d London edition. New York, C. Scribner & co., 1867. xxiii, 262 p. 19 1/2 cm. "Six short studies for sermons": p. 244-262. [BV4235.E8Z5] 38-24315
1. Preaching, Extemporaneous. 2. Sermons—Outlines. I. Title.

Preaching—France—History.

BAYLEY, Peter, 1944- 808.5'1
French pulpit oratory, 1598-1650 : a study in themes and styles, with a catalogue of printed French pulpit oratory / Peter Bayley. Cambridge [Eng.] ; New York : Cambridge University Press, 1980. x, 323 p. ; 24 cm. Includes index. Bibliography: p. [305]-316. [BV4208.F8B35] 79-50175 ISBN 0-521-22765-8 : 44.50
1. Preaching—France—History. 2. French prose literature—17th century—History and criticism. 3. Rhetoric—1500-1800. 4. Sermons, French—Bibliography. I. Title.

Preaching—History.

BRASTOW, Lewis 251'.00922
Orsmond, 1834-1912.
Representative modern preachers. Freeport, N.Y., Books for Libraries Press [1968] xv, 423 p. 23 cm. (Essay index reprint series) Reprint of the 1904 ed. Contents.Contents.—Friedrich Daniel Ernst Schleiermacher.—Fredrick William Robertson.—Henry Ward Beecher.—Horace Bushnell.—Phillips Brooks.—John Henry Newman.—James Bowling Mozley.—Thomas Guthrie.—Charles Haddon Spurgeon. [BV4207.B7 1968] 68-57306
1. Preaching—History. I. Title.

BRILIOTH, Yngve Torgny, 251.09
Abp. 1891-1959.
A brief history of preaching. Translated by Karl E. Mattson. Philadelphia, Fortress Press [1965] x. 229 p. 18 cm. (The Preacher's paperback library) "Translated from Predikans historia." Bibliography: p. 217-223. [BV4207.B7313] 65-13256
1. Preaching — Hist. I. Title.

BRILIOTH, Yngve Torgny, 251.09
Abp., 1891-1959
A brief history of preaching. Tr. by Karl E. Mattson. Philadelphia, Fortress [c.1965] x, 229p. 18cm. (Preacher's paperback lib.) Bibl. [BV4207.B7313] 65-13256 2.95 pap.,
1. Preaching—Hist. I. Title.

BROADUS, John Albert, 1827- 251
1895.
Lectures on the history of preaching. By John A. Broadus ... New York, Sheldon & company, 1876. xi, [5]-241 p. 19 1/2 cm. [BV4207.B75] 44-35146

1. Preaching—Hist. I. Title.

BROADUS, John Albert, 1827-1895. 251
Lectures on the history of preaching, by John A. Broadus ... New ed. New York, A. C. Armstrong & son, 1893. xi, [5]-241 p. 19 cm. Delivered at the Newton theological institution, May, 1876. [BV4207.B75 1893] 44-45497
1. Preaching—Hist. I. Title.

CHAMBERLIN, John S. 252'.03
Increase and multiply : arts-of-discourse procedure in the preaching of Donne / by John S. Chamberlin. Chapel Hill : University of North Carolina Press, c1976. p. cm. Based on the author's thesis, University of Toronto, 1970. Includes bibliographical references. [PR2248.C48] 76-6998 ISBN 0-8078-1266-8 : 12.95
1. Donne, John, 1572-1631—Prose. 2. Preaching—History. I. Title.

DARGAN, Edwin Charles, 1852-1930. 251.09
A history of preaching. Introd. by J. B. Weatherspoon. Grand Rapids, Baker Book House, 1954. 2v. in 1. 23cm. Includes bibliographical references. [BV4207.D3 1954] 54-2653
1. Preaching-Hist. I. Title.

DARGAN, Edwin Charles, 1852-1930. 251'.009
A history of preaching. New York, B. Franklin [1968] 2 v. 24 cm. (Burt Franklin: research and source works series, no. 177) (Art history and reference series, no. 19.) Reprint of the 1905-1912 ed. Contents.Contents.—v. 1. From the apostolic fathers to the great reformers, A.D. 70-1572.—v. 2. From the close of the Reformation period to the end of the nineteenth century, 1572-1900. Includes bibliographies. [BV4207] 68-4837
1. Preaching—History. I. Title.

DARGAN, Edwin Charles, 1852-1930. 251.
A history of preaching ... by Edwin Charles Dargan ... New York, A. C. Armstrong & son, 1905-[c12] 2 v. 21 cm. Vol. 2 has imprint: New York, Hodder & stoughton [etc.] No more published? Contents.[i] From the apostolic fathers to the great reference, A. D. 70-1572. --ii. From the close of the reformation period to the end of the nineteenth century, 1572-1900. Bibliography: v. 1, p. [565]-567: v. 2, p. [579-561. [BV4207.D3] 5-2103
1. Preaching—Hist. I. Title.

DEMARAY, Donald E. 251'.009'22 B
Pulpit giants; what made them great, by Donald E. Demaray. Chicago, Moody Press [1973] 174 p. ports. 22 cm. [BV4207.D38] 72-95026 ISBN 0-8024-6950-7 3.95
1. Preaching—History. 2. Christian biography. I. Title.
Contents Omitted.

ECHLIN, Edward P. 251'.009
The priest as preacher, past and future, by Edward P. Echlin. Notre Dame, Ind., Fides Publishers [1973] 91 p. 18 cm. (Theology today, no. 33) Bibliography: p. 88-90. [BV4207.E25] 73-176542 ISBN 0-85342-322-9 0.95 (pbk.)
1. Catholic Church—Clergy. 2. Preaching—History. I. Title.

FANT, Clyde E. 230'.092'4
Bonhoeffer : worldly preaching / Clyde E. Fant. Nashville : T. Nelson, [1975] xi, 180 p. ; 21 cm. Includes 10 lectures delivered by D. Bonhoeffer (p. 123-180). Includes bibliographical references. [BV4207.F36] 74-26806 ISBN 0-8407-5087-0 : 6.95 ISBN 0-8407-5586-4 pbk. :
1. Bonhoeffer, Dietrich, 1906-1945. 2. Preaching—History. I. Bonhoeffer, Dietrich, 1906-1945.

JONES, Edgar De Witt, 1876- 251.09
The royalty of the pulpit; a survey and appreciation of the Lyman Beecher lectures on preaching founded at Yale Divinity School 1871 and given annually (with four exceptions) since 1872. [1st ed.] New York, Harper [1951] xxx, 447 p. 22 cm. Bibliography: p. 432-439. [BV4207.J65] 51-9797
1. Preaching—Hist. 2. Lyman Beecher lectures on preaching, Yale University. I. Title.

JONES, Edgar De Witt, 1876-1956. 251'.009
The royalty of the pulpit; a survey and appreciation of the Lyman Beecher lectures on preaching founded at Yale Divinity School 1871 and given annually (with four exceptions) since 1872. Freeport, N.Y., Books for Libraries Press [1970, c1951] xxx, 447 p. 23 cm. (Essay index reprint series) Bibliography: p. 432-439. [BV4207.J65 1970] 79-134105 ISBN 0-8369-1979-3
1. Preaching—History. 2. Lyman Beecher lectures. I. Title.

KER, John, 1819-1886. 251.
Lectures on the history of preaching, by the late Rev. John Ker ... Edited by Rev. A. R. Macewen ... Introduction by Rev. Wm. M. Taylor ... New York, A. C. Armstrong & son, 1889. 3 p. l., v-xi, [3], 407 p. 22 cm. [BV4207.K4 1889] 10-19597
1. Preaching—Hist. I. Macewen, Alexander Robertson, 1851-1916, ed. II. Taylor, William Mackergo, 1829-1895. III. Title.

MCGRAW, James 251.09
Great evangelical preachers of yesterday. Nashville, Abingdon [c.1961] 159p. Bibl. 61-11785 2.75 bds.,
1. Preaching—Hist. I. Title.

PATTISON, Thomas Harwood, 1838-1904. 251.
The history of Christian preaching, by T. Harwood Pattison ... Philadelphia, American Baptist publication society, 1903. xvi, 412 p. 20 port. (incl. front.) 21 cm. "A chronology of preachers": p. 407-409. [BV4207.P3] 3-23508
1. Preaching—Hist. I. Title.

PETRY, Ray C., 1903- 251.09
Preaching in the great tradition, neglected chapters in the history of preaching. Philadelphia, Westminster Press [1950] 122 p. 20 cm. (The Samuel A. Crozer lectures for 1949) [BV4207.P4] 50-7643
1. Preaching — Hist. I. Title. II. Series.

WEBBER, Frederick Roth, 1887-
A history of preaching in Britain and America, including the biographies of many princes of the pulpit and the men who influenced them. Milwaukee, Northwestern Pub. House [c1952-1957] 3v. 24 cm. Bibliographical footnotes. NUC68
I. Title.

WILKINSON, William Cleaver, 1833-1920. 251
Modern masters of pulpit discourse, by William Cleaver Wilkinson... New York and London, Funk & Wagnalls company, 1905. viii, 526 p. 21 1/2 cm. "Most of the criticisms in this volume were written during the lifetime of their several subjects and then published anonymously as a series under a common title in "The Homiletic review"'--Pref. [BV4207.W5] 5-12383
1. Preaching—Hist. I. Title.
Contents omitted.

Preaching—History—20th century.

CROCKER, Lionel George, 1897- comp. 251'.00924
Harry Emerson Fosdick's art of preaching; an anthology. Compiled and edited by Lionel Crocker. Springfield, Ill., Thomas [1971] xii, 283 p. 24 cm. Contents.Contents.—Essays on preaching, by H. E. Fosdick: Learning to preach. What is the matter with preaching? How I prepare my sermons. Animated conversation. Personal counseling and preaching. The Christian ministry. To those interested in the profession of the ministry.—A young preacher listens to Fosdick, by S. H. Miller.—How Dr. Fosdick uses the Bible in preaching, by E. May.—Harry Emerson Fosdick and Reinhold Niebuhr: a contrast in the methods of the teaching preacher, by E. Harris.—Harry Emerson Fosdick: realist and idealist, by E. D. Jones.—Harry Emerson Fosdick: titan of the pulpit, by E. D. Jones.—Harry Emerson Fosdick: a study in sources of effectiveness, by R. C. McCall.—Harry Emerson Fosdick: the growth of a great preacher, by R. D. Clark.—Selected bibliography: (p. 181-185)—Harry Emerson Fosdick and the techniques of organization, by E. H. Linn.—Structural analysis of the sermons of Dr. Harry Emerson Fosdick, by G. S. Macvaugh.—Harry Emerson Fosdick: the methods of a master, by C. F. Kemp.—The rhetorical theory of Harry Emerson Fosdick, by L. Crocker.—Henry Ward Beecher and Harry Emerson Fosdick, by L. Crocker.—Phillips Brooks and Harry Emerson Fosdick, by L. Crocker.—A rhetorical analysis of Harry Emerson Fosdick's sermon, "The power to see it through," by L. Crocker.—Studies in the preaching of Harry Emerson Fosdick (bibliographical: p. 274-275) [BV4207.C75] 74-130922
1. Fosdick, Harry Emerson, 1878-1969. 2. Preaching—History—20th century. I. Fosdick, Harry Emerson, 1878-1969. II. Title.

DUKE, Robert W. 230'.044
The sermon as God's word : theologies for preaching / Robert W. Duke. Nashville : Abingdon, [1980] p. cm. (Abingdon preacher's library) Includes index. Bibliography: p. [BV4207.D84] 80-18094 ISBN 0-687-37520-7 pbk. : 4.95
1. Preaching—History—20th century. 2. Theology, Doctrinal—History—20th century. I. Title.

GERICKE, Paul. 251
The preaching of Robert G. Lee; adorning the doctrine of God. Orlando, Fla., Christ for the World Publishers [1967] 180 p. 22 cm. Bibliography: p. 176-180. [BX6495.L39G4] 66-30553
1. Lee, Robert Greene, 1886- 2. Preaching—History—20th century. I. Title.

Preaching—History—Early church.

KERR, Hugh Thomson, 1871- 251.0901
Preaching in the early church... by Hugh Thomson Kerr. New York [etc.] Fleming H. Revell company [1942] 238 p. 20 1/2 cm. (The Moore lectures) "Books of reference": p. 231-235. [BV4207.K42] 42-12803
1. Preaching—Hist.—Early church. I. Title.

WORLEY, Robert C. 251'.00924
Preaching and teaching in the earliest church, by Robert C. Worley. Philadelphia, Westminster Press [1967] 199 p. 21 cm. Based on the author's doctoral study. Bibliographical references included in "Notes" (p. [153]-194) [BX4827.D6W6] 67-20613
1. Dodd, Charles Harold, 1884- 2. Preaching—History—Early church. 3. Religious education—History—Early church. 4. Kerygma. I. Title.

Preaching—History—England.

BLENCH, J. W. 251.0942
Preaching in England in the late fifteenth and sixteenth centuries: a study of English sermons 1450-c. 1600, by J. W. Blench. New York, Barnes & Noble [c.]1964. xv, 378p. front. 23cm. Bibl. 64-4249 10.00
1. Preaching—Hist.—England. 2. Sermons, English—16th cent.—Hist. & crit. I. Title.

BLENCH, J. W. 251.0942
Preaching in England in the late fifteenth and sixteenth centuries; a study of English sermons 1450-c. 1600, by J. W. Blench. New York, Barnes & Noble, 1964. xv, 378 p. front. 23 cm. Bibliography: p. [350]-368. [BV4208.B7B55] 64-4249
1. Preaching — Hist. — England. 2. Sermons, English — 16th cent. — Hist. & crit. I. Title.

CARRITHERS, Gale H., 1932- 252'.03
Donne at sermons; a Christian existential world [by] Gale H. Carrithers, Jr. [1st ed.] Albany, State University of New York Press, 1972. x, 319 p. 24 cm. Includes the complete texts of four sermons by Donne: The sermon of valediction. The third sermon on John 1.8. The sermon on Psalm 63.7. The two-part sermon on fishers of men. Includes bibliographical references. [PR2248.C35] 74-171183 ISBN 0-87395-122-0 ISBN 0-87395-161-1 (microfiche) 10.00
1. Donne, John, 1572-1631. 2. Church of England—Sermons. 3. Preaching—History—England. 4. Sermons, English. I. Donne, John, 1572-1631. Selected works. 1972. II. Title.

DAVIES, Horton 251.0942
Varieties of English preaching, 1900-1960. London, SCM Pr.; Englewood Cliffs, N. J., Prentice [c.1963] 276p. illus. 23cm. Bibl. 63-11791 6.60
1. Preaching—Hist.—England. I. Title.

DAVIES, Horton. 251.0942
Varieties of English preaching,1900-1960 London, SCM Press; Englewood Cliffs, N.J., Prentice-Hall [1963] 276 p. illus. 23 cm. Includes bibliography. [BV4208.G7D3] 63-11791
1. Preaching — Hist. — England. I. Title.

DOWNEY, James. 251'.00942
The eighteenth century pulpit. A study of the sermons of Butler, Berkeley, Secker, Sterne, Whitefield and Wesley. Oxford, Clarendon Press, 1969. ix, 254 p. ports. 22 cm. Bibliography: p. [234]-247. [BV4208.G7D6] 75-438031 unpriced
1. Preaching—History—England. I. Title.

GATCH, Milton McC. 251'.00942
Preaching and theology in Anglo-Saxon England : Aelfric and Wulfstan / Milton McC. Gatch. Toronto ; Buffalo : University of Toronto Press, c1977. p. cm. "Aelfric's excerpts from Julian of Toledo, Prognosticon futuri saeculi": p. Includes indexes. Bibliography: p. [BV4208.G7G37] 77-3277 ISBN 0-8020-5347-5 : 15.00
1. Aelfric, Abbot of Eynsham. 2. Wulfstan II, Abp. of York, d. 1023. 3. Preaching—History—England. 4. Eschatology—History of doctrines—Middle Ages, 600-1500. I. Julianus, Saint, Bp. of Toledo, d. 690. Prognosticon futuri seculi. Selections. 1977.

MACLURE, Millar. 252
The Paul's Cross sermons, 1534-1642. [Toronto] University of Toronto Press [1958] 261p. illus. 24cm. (University of Toronto. Dept. of English. Studies and texts, no. 6) Includes bibliography. [BV4208.E5M2] 58-2173
1. Preaching—Hist.—England. 2. London. St. Paul's Cathedral. I. Title.

MITCHELL, William Fraser, 1900- 251.0942
English pulpit oratory, from Andrewes to Tillotson: a study of its literary aspects. New York, Russell, 1962. xii, 516p. Bibl. 61-17196 10.00
1. Preaching—Hist.—England. 2. Church of England—Clergy. 3. Clergy—England. I. Title.

OWST, Gerald Robert, 1894- 251.00942
Preaching in medieval England; an introduction to sermon manuscripts of the period c. 1350-1450. New York, Russell & Russell, 1965. xviii, 381p. illus., facsim. 23cm. (Cambridge studies in medieval life and thought) Bibl. [BV4208.G708] 65-18825 8.50
1. Preaching—Hist.—England. I. Title. II. Series.

OWST, Gerald Robert, 1894- 251.00942
Preaching in medieval England; an introduction to sermon manuscripts of the period c. 1350-1450, by G. R. Owst. New York, Russell & Russell, 1965. xviii, 381 p. illus., facsim. 23 cm. (Cambridge studies in medieval life and thought) "First published in 1926." Based on thesis, University of London. Bibliographical footnotes. [BV4208.G7O8] 65-18825
1. Preaching — Hist. — England. I. Title. II. Series.

SALA, John Robert, 1905- 251.0942
...Preaching in the Anglo-Saxon church... By John Robert Sala... Chicago, Ill., 1934. 1 p. l., p. 80-118, 125-144. 24 cm. Part of thesis (PH.D.)--University of Chicago, 1934. Lithographed. "Private edition, distributed by the University of Chicago libraries." "Summary of the contents of the Vercelli homilies": p. 125-144. [BV4208.G7S3 1934] 34-37031
1. Preaching—Hist.—England. 2. Anglo-Saxon literature—Hist. & crit. I. Vercelli book. II. Title. III. Title: Anglo-Saxon church, Preaching in the.

SMYTH, Charles Hugh Egerton, 1903- 251
The art of preaching; a practical survey of preaching in the Church of England, 747-1939, by Charles Smyth ... London, Society for promoting Christian knowledge; New York, The Macmillan company [1940] viii p., 2 l., 257, [1] p. 22 cm. "First published in 1940." "Select bibliography": p. 250-251. [BV4208.G7S55] A 42
1. Preaching—Hist.—England. 2. Society for promoting Christian knowledge, London. I. Title.

Preaching—History—France.

GOTAAS, Mary C., 1907- 251'.00922
Bossuet and Vieira; [a study in national, epochal, and individual style, by Mary C. Gotaas] New York, AMS Press [1970, c1953] xix, 136 p. 23 cm. (Catholic University of America. Studies in Romance languages and literatures, v. 46) Part of the author's thesis, Catholic University of America, 1953. Bibliography: p. [131]-136. [BV4207.G68 1970] 75-128929 ISBN 0-404-50346-2
1. Bossuet, Jacques Benigne, Bp. of Meaux, 1627-1704. 2. Vieira, Antonio, 1608-1697. 3. Preaching—History—France. 4. Preaching—History—Portugal. I. Title. II. Series.

Preaching—History—Germany.

IANNUCCI, Remo Joseph, 1914- 241.3
The treatment of the capital sins and the Decalogue in the German sermons of Berthold von Regensburg. New York, AMS Press [1970, c1942] xvii, 128 p. 23 cm. (Catholic University of America. Studies in German, v. 17) Originally presented as the author's thesis, Catholic University of America, 1942. Bibliography: p. 117-123. [BV4208.G3I3 1970] 70-140024 ISBN 0-404-50237-7
1. Berthold von Regensburg, d. 1272. 2. Preaching—History—Germany. 3. Commandments, Ten. 4. Deadly sins. I. Title. II. Series.

KIESSLING, Elmer Carl, 1895- 251'.009'02
The early sermons of Luther and their relation to the pre-reformation sermon. Grand Rapids, Zondervan Pub. House, 1935. [New York, AMS Press, 1971] 157 p. 18 cm. Thesis (Ph.D.)—University of Chicago, 1935. Bibliography: p. 151-157. [BR332.S75K5 1971] 75-171064 ISBN 0-404-03669-4 5.00
1. Luther, Martin, 1483-1546. 2. Preaching—History—Germany. 3. Preaching—History—Middle Ages, 600-1500. I. Title.

Preaching— History—Great Britain

CALKINS, Harold L 251.09
Master preachers: their study and devotional habits. Washington, Review and Heaald Pub. Association [c1960] 128p. 21cm. Includes bibliography. [BV4208.G7C3] 60-15509
1. Preaching— Hist.—Gt. Brit. 2. Preaching—Hist.—U. S. I. Title.

Preaching—History—Middle Ages, 600-1500.

BONAVENTURA, Saint, Cardinal, 1221-1274. 232.9
What manner of man? Sermons on Christ by St. Bonaventure. A translation with introd. and commentary by Zachary Hayes. Chicago, Franciscan Herald Press [1974] vi, 135 p. 21 cm. Contents.Contents.—Christ, the one teacher of all.—Sermon II on the nativity of the Lord.—Sermon II on the third Sunday of Advent. Includes bibliographical references. [BT198.B64] 74-1426 ISBN 0-8199-0497-X 4.95
1. Jesus Christ—History of doctrines—Middle Ages, 600-1500. 2. Catholic Church—Sermons. 3. Preaching—History—Middle Ages, 600-1500. 4. Sermons, English—Translations from Latin. 5. Sermons, Latin—Translations into English. I. Hayes, Zachary, ed. II. Title.

Preaching—History—New England.

ELLIOTT, Emory, 1942- 285'.9'0974
Power and the pulpit in Puritan New England / Emory Elliott. Princeton, N.J. : Princeton University Press, [1975] xi, 240 p. ; 23 cm. Includes index. Bibliography: p. 205-234. [BV4208.U6E43] 74-29093 ISBN 0-691-07206-X : 10.00
1. Preaching—History—New England. 2. Puritans—New England. I. Title.

LEVY, Babette May, 1907- 251'.00974
Preaching in the first half century of New England history. New York, Russell & Russell [1967], c1945] vii, 215 p. 24 cm. (Studies in church history, v. 6) Reprint of thesis, Columbia University. Bibliography: p. 177-207. [BV4208.U6L4] 66-27116
1. Preaching — Hist. — New England. 2. Theology, Doctrinal — Hist. — New England 3. New England — Church history. 4. Puritans. I. American Society of Church History. II. Title. III. Series.

Preaching—History—United States

BRISTOL, Sherlock, 1815-1906. 922.573
The pioneer preacher; incidents of interest, and experiences in the author's life. Revival labors in the frontier settlements. A perilous trip across the plains in time of Indian wars, and before the railroads. Three years in the mining camps of California and Idaho, twenty-one years' residence in southern California, etc., by Rev. S. Bristol ... Illustrated by Isabelle Blood. Chicago, New York, Fleming H. Revell [c1887] viii, 9-330 p. front. (port.) plates. 19 1/2 cm. [BX7200.B67A3] 35-37064
I. Title.

GERSTNER, John H. 234
Steps to salvation; the evangelistic message of Jonathan Edwards. Philadelphia, Westminster Press [c.1959] 192p. 22cm. 60-5118 3.95
1. Edwards, Jonathan, 1703-1758. 2. Preaching—Hist.—U.S. I. Title.

HIGGINS, Paul Lambourne. 922
Preachers of power; Henry Ward Beecher, Phillips Books, [and] Walter Rauschenbusch. New York, Vantage Press ['1950] 72 p. ports. 23 cm. [BV4208.U6H5] 51-787
1. Beecher, Henry Ward, 1813-1887. 2. Brooks, Phillips, 1835-1898 3. Rauschenbusch, Walter, 1861-1918. 4. Preaching—U. S.—Hist. I. Title.

HOLLAND, Dewitte Talmage, 1923- 251'.00973
The preaching tradition : a brief history / DeWitte T. Holland. Nashville : Abingdon, 1980. p. cm. (Abingdon preacher's library series) Includes index. Bibliography: p. [BV4208.U6H57] 80-16339 ISBN 0-687-33875-1 pbk. : 4.95
1. Preaching—United States—History. 2. Preaching—History. I. Title.

HOYT, Arthur Stephen, 1851-1924. 250.
The pulpit and Americanl life, by Arthur S. Hoyt ... New York, The Macmillan company, 1921. ix p., 1 l. 286 p. 19 1/2 cm. [BV4208.U6H6] 21-1297
1. Preaching—Hist.—U.S. I. Title.
Contents omitted.

JONES, Edgar De Witt, 1876- 922
American preachers of to-day; intimate appraisals of thirty-two leaders, by Edgar De Witt Jones ... Indianapolis, The Bobbs-Merrill company [c1933] 6 p. l., 11-317 p. 21 cm. "First edition." [BR525.J56] 33-29523
1. Preaching—Hist.—U. S. I. Title.

JONES, Edgar De Witt, 1876-1956. 251'.0922 B
American preachers of to-day; intimate appraisals of thirty-two leaders. Freeport, N.Y., Books for Libraries Press [1971, 1933] 317 p. 23 cm. (Essay index reprint series) [BV4208.U6J65] 76-156667 ISBN 0-8369-2279-4
1. Preaching—History—U.S. I. Title.

KULANDRAN, Sabapathy, Bp. 250.973
The message and the silence of the American pulpit. Foreword by Douglas Horton. Boston, Pilgrim Press [1949] xvii, 203 p. 22 cm. [BV4208.U6K8] 49-6334
1. Preaching—Hist.—U.S. 2. U.S.—Religion. 3. Christianity—Essence, genius, nature. 4. Christianity and other religions—Hinduism. I. Title.

MACARTNEY, Clarence Edward Noble, 1879- 922
Six kings of the American pulpit, by Clarence Edward Macartney ... Philadelphia, The Westminster press, 1942. 210 p. 21 cm. [BV4208.U6M3] 42-23295
1. Preaching—Hist.—U.S. I. Title.
Contents omitted.

MACARTNEY, Clarence Edward Noble, 1879-1957. 251'.00922
Six kings of the American pulpit. Freeport, N.Y., Books for Libraries Press [1971, c1942] 210 p. 23 cm. (The Smyth lectures, 1939) (Essay index reprint series) [BV4208.U6M3 1971] 75-152192 ISBN 0-8369-2323-5
1. Preaching—History—U.S. I. Title. II. Series: Thomas Smyth lectures, Columbia Theological Seminary, Decatur, Ga., 1939.

MCNAMARA, Robert Francis, 1910- 251
Catholic Sunday preaching : the American guidelines, 1791-1975 / by Robert F. McNamara. 1st ed. Washington : Word of God Institute, 1975. 62 p. ; 22 cm. (Special studies series - Word of God Institute) Includes bibliographical references. [BV4208.U6M34] 75-36695 1.95
1. Catholic Church in the United States—Clergy. 2. Preaching—History—United States. I. Title. II. Series: Word of God Institute. Special studies series — Word of God Institute.

MITCHELL, Henry H. 251'.00973
Black preaching [by] Henry H. Mitchell. [1st ed.] Philadelphia, Lippincott [1970] 248 p. 21 cm. (C. Eric Lincoln series on Black religion) Includes bibliographical references. [BV4208.U6M57 1970] 72-124546 5.50
1. Preaching—History—United States. 2. Negroes—Religion. I. Title.

ROSENBERG, Bruce A. 251'.00973
The art of the American folk preacher [by] Bruce A. Rosenberg. New York, Oxford University Press, 1970. x, 265 p. 24 cm. Includes bibliographical references. [BV4208.U6R67] 77-111649 8.50
1. Preaching—History—U.S. I. Title.

STASHEFF, Edward.
Methodist research project in preaching: a study of current developments in the teaching of preaching in America and the United Kingdom, by Edward Stasheff and Kenneth E. Andersen. Indianapolis, Indiana Area of the Methodist Church, 1963. 117 p. diagrs., forms, tables. 28 cm. 66-57803
1. Preaching—History—U.S. 2. Preaching—History—Gt. Brit. I. Andersen, Kenneth E., joint author. II. Title.

STEVENSON, Dwight Eshelman, 1906- 251'.00973
Disciple preaching in the first generation; an ecological study, by Dwight E. Stevenson. Nashville, Disciples of Christ Historical Society, 1969. 109 p. 23 cm. (The Forrest F. Reed lectures for 1969) Includes bibliographical references. [BV4208.U6S73] 70-22610
1. Disciples of Christ. 2. Preaching—History—U.S. I. Title. II. Series: The Reed lectures for 1969

THOMPSON, Ernest Trice, 1894- 251.09
Changing emphases in American preaching ... by Ernest Trice Thompson ... Philadelphia, The Westminster press [1943] 6 p. l., 9-234 p. 21 cm. (The Stone lectures for 1943) Bibliographical references included in "Notes" (p. [223]-234) [BV4208.U6T45] 43-15974
1. Preaching—Hist.—U.S. I. Title.

WAGENKNECHT, Edward Charles, 1900- 280'.092'2 B
Ambassadors for Christ; seven American preachers [by] Edward Wagenknecht. New York, Oxford University Press, 1972. 310 p. illus. 22 cm. Contents.Contents.—Lyman Beecher: great by his religion.—William Ellery Channing: messages from the Spirit.—Henry Ward Beecher: God was in Christ.—Phillips Brooks: the Lord our God is a sun.—D. L. Moody: whosoever will may come.—Washington Gladden: where does the sky begin?—Lyman Abbott: the life of God in the soul of man.—Appendix: a postscript on the Beecher-Tilton scandal (p. [249]-254) Includes bibliographical references. [BV4208.U6W34 1972] 76-179361 8.50
1. Preaching—History—U.S. I. Title.

WALKER, Granville T 251
Preaching in the thought of Alexander Campbell. St. Louis, Bethany Press [1954] 271p. 23cm. [Bethany history series] 'The original work ... was submitted as a doctoral dissertation to the Yale faculty in 1948.' [BX7343.C2W3] 54-14505
1. Campbell, Alexander, 1788-1866. 2. Preaching—Hist.—U. S. I. Title.

Preaching—History—U.S.—Addresses, essays, lectures.

MORRIS, Leon.
The apostolic preaching of the cross. [2d ed.] Grand Rapids, Mich., Eerdmans [1960] 296 p. 23 cm. 65-37600
I. Title.

PREACHING in American history; selected issues in the American pulpit, 1630-1967. Prepared under the auspices of the Speech Association of America. DeWitte Holland, editor. Jess Yoder and Hubert Vance Taylor, associate editors. Nashville, Abingdon Press [1969] 436 p. 25 cm. Includes bibliographical references. [BV4208.U6P7] 69-18453 8.95 261
1. Preaching—History—U.S.—Addresses, essays, lectures. I. Holland, DeWitte Talmadge, 1923- ed. II. Speech Association of America.

Preaching—Italy—Rome (City)—History.

O'MALLEY, John W. 251
Praise and blame in Renaissance Rome : rhetoric, doctrine, and reform in the sacred orators of the papal court, c. 1450-1521 / by John W. O'Malley. Durham, N.C. : Duke University Press, 1979. xii, 276 p. ; 25 cm. (Duke monographs in medieval and Renaissance studies ; no. 3.) Includes bibliographical references and indexes. [BV4208.I8O45] 79-51220 ISBN 0-8223-0428-7 : 17.75
1. Preaching—Italy—Rome (City)—History. 2. Rome (City)—Church history. I. Title. II. Series.

Preaching, Jewish.

BETTAN, Israel, 1889- 296
Studies in Jewish preaching ... by Israel Bettan ... Cincinnati Hebrew union college press, 1939- v. 24 cm. [The Henry and Ida Krolik memorial publications. [BM730.B4] 40-4533
1. Preaching, Jewish. I. Title.

CENTRAL Conference of American Rabbis. 296
Israel Bettan memorial volume. New York, 1961. 164p. port. 22cm. 'Some sermons of Israel Bettan : p. 63-62. 'Bibliography of Israel Bettan's writings, compiled by Theodore Wiener : p. 52-62. [BM730.A2C4] 61-14334
1. Bettan, Israel, 1889-1957. 2. Preaching, Jewish. I. Title.
Contents omitted.

FREEHOF, Solomon Bennett, 1892- 296
Modern Jewish preaching [by] Solomon B. Freehof. Based upon the Alumni lectures given at Hebrew union college, March, 1941. New York, Bloch publishing company, 1941. 171 p. 21 cm. [BM730.F7] 42-596
1. Preaching, Jewish. I. Hebrew union college, Cincinnati. II. Title.

Preaching, Lay.

BODEN, Evan H. 251
Guide for the lay preacher : helps for sermon preparation and delivery / Evan H. Boden. Valley Forge, PA : Judson Press,

c1979. 70 p. : ill. ; 22 cm. [BV4235.L3B6] 78-31748 ISBN 0-8170-0836-5 : 2.95
1. Preaching, Lay. I. Title.

BROWN, Henry Clifton. 251
A Christian layman's guide to public speaking [by] H. C. Brown, Jr. Nashville, Broadman Press [1966] 76 p. 20 cm. [BV4235.L3B7] 67-12167
1. Preaching, Lay. I. Title.

SEVENTH-DAY adventists. 250
General conference. Home mission department.
The lay preacher and his work. Principles and methods of lay evangelism [by] Home missionary department, General conference of Seventh-day Adventists ... Nashville, Tenn., Southern publishing association [c1940] 134 p. 20 cm. [BX6154.A55 1940] 40-29597
1. Preaching, Lay. 2. Seventh-day Adventists. I. Title.

VITRANO, Steven P. 251
So you're not a preacher! : A lay leader's guide for sermon preparation / Steven P. Vitrano. Washington : Review and Herald Pub. Association, 1978. 64 p. ; 21 cm. Bibliography: p. 62-64. [BV4235.L3V57] 76-17731 pbk. : 1.95
1. Preaching, Lay. I. Title.

Preaching—Spain—History—17th century.

SMITH, Hilary Dansey. 252'.02'46
Preaching in the Spanish golden age : a study of some preachers of the reign of Philip III / Hilary Dansey Smith. Oxford ; New York : Oxford University Press, 1978. ix, 190 p. ; 23 cm. (Oxford modern languages and literature monographs) A revision of the author's thesis, Oxford. Includes index. Bibliography: p. [160]-186. [BV4208.S6S58 1978] 78-40246 ISBN 0-19-815532-8 : 19.95
1. Preaching—Spain—History—17th century. I. Title.

Preaching-Study and teaching.

HOYT, Arthur Stephen, 1851-1924. 251
The work of preaching; a book for the class-room and study, by Arthur S. Hoyt ... New ed., with new chapters. New York, The Macmillan company, 1917. xiii, 389 p. 19 1/2 cm. "References" at the beginning of each chapter. [BV4211.H7 1917] 17-24302
I. Title.

THE teaching of preaching in Baptist theological seminaries of the United States. St. Paul, Minn., Bethel College & Seminary, 1960. xviii, 365 l. diagrs. 28cm. Includes bibliography.
1. Preaching-Study and teaching. 2. Theological education- Baptist. I. Lundquist, Carl Harold, 1916-

YOUNG, William Henry.
How to preach with power, by W. Harry Young... 3d revision. Decatur, Ga., The How publishing co.; [etc., etc. c1909] 276 p. 20 cm. $1.00. 9-27105
I. Title.

Preaching to children.

COLEMAN, Richard J. 251
Gospel-telling : the art and theology of children's sermons / by Richard J. Coleman. Grand Rapids, Mich. : Eerdmans, c1982. p. cm. Bibliography: p. [BV4235.C4C64 1982] 19 82-11435 ISBN 0-8028-1927-3 pbk. : 5.95
1. Preaching to children. 2. Children's sermons. I. Title.

DANN, Bucky, 1951- 251
Creating children's sermons : 51 visual lessons / by Bucky Dann. 1st ed. Philadelphia : Westminster Press, c1981. 132 p. ; 21 cm. Includes index. [BV4235.C4D36] 19 81-10493 pbk. : 7.95
1. Preaching to children. 2. Children's sermons—Outlines. I. Title.

Precept (Canon law)

PRECEPTS. 262.9
Paterson, N. J., St. Anthony Guild Press, 1955. 251p. 24cm. 348 55-14418
1. Precept (Canon law) I. Roelker, Edward George, 1897-

Precocity.

LAMSON, Edna Emma, 1883- 371.955
A study of young gifted children in senior high school, by Edna Emma Lamson ... New York city, Teachers college, Columbia university, 1930. viii, 117 p. 24 cm. (Teachers college, Columbia university. Contributions to education, no. 424) Published also as thesis (PH. D.) Columbia university. "This study is a continuation of the work of a joint committee ... for three years in charge of special opportunity classes for gifted children at Public school no. 165, Manhattan, New York city."--Introd. "Books which gifted group reported having read": p. 97-101; "Bibliographical references": p. 113-117. [LC3981.L3] [LB5.C8 no. 424] 30-20834
1. Precocity. 2. Ability. 3. Students. I. Title. II. Title: Gifted children in senior high school, A study of young.

Predestination.

BLAIR, Samuel, 1712-1751. 234.
The doctrine of predestination truly and fairly stated: confirmed from clear Scripture-evidence, and defended against all the material arguments and objections advanced against it. By Samuel Blair, late minister of the gospel at Shrewsbury in New Jersey, now at London-derry in Pennsylvania. Philadelphia: Printed by B. Franklin for the author M,DCC,XLII 79 p. 15 1/2 cm. Signatures: A-K. [BT810.B62] 6-1772
1. Predestination. I. Title.

BOETTNER, Loraine. 234.9
The Reformed doctrine of predestination [by] Loraine Boettner ... Grand Rapids, Mich., Wm. B. Berdmans publishing company, 1932. 5 p. l., 431 p. port. 23 1/2 cm. Bibliography: p. 431. [BT810.B66] 32-1086
1. Predestination. 2. Calvinism. I. Title.

CUSTANCE, Arthur C. 234
The sovereignty of grace / Arthur C. Custance. Phillipsburg, N.J. : Presbyterian and Reformed Pub. Co., c1979. xvi, 398 p. ; 24 cm. Includes index. Bibliography: p. 365-367. [BT810.2.C85] 19 80-125441 12.95
1. Predestination. 2. Calvinism. I. Title.

FARRELLY, Mark John. 234.9
Predestination, grace, and free will, by Dom M. John Farrelly. Westminster, Md., Newman Press, 1964. xiv, 317 p. 24 cm. Originally written as the author's thesis, Catholic University of America, under title: Predestination and grace: a re-examination in the light of modern Biblical and philosophical developments. Bibliographical footnotes. [BT810.2.F3] 64-15405
1. Predestination. 2. Free will and determinism. I. Title.

FOREMAN, Kenneth Joseph, 1891- 234.9
God's will and ours; an introduction to the problem of freedom, foreordination and faith. [1st ed.] Richmond, Outlook Publishers [1954] 63p. 19cm. [BT810.F6] 54-10449
1. Predestination. I. Title.

GARRIGOU-LAGRANGE, Reginald, pere, 1877- 234.9
Predestination, by the Rev R. Garrigou-Lagrange ... translated by Dom Bede Rose ... St. Louis, Mo., and London, B. Herder book co., 1939. xiv, 882 p. 22 1/2 cm. [Secular name: Gontran Garrigou-Lagrange] [BT810.G32] 30-31176
1. Predestination. 2. Grace (Theology) I. Rose, Bede, father, 1880- tr. II. Title.

GERSTNER, John H. 239.4
A predestination primer. Grand Rapids, Baker Book House [c.]1960. 51p. 22cm. 60-2958 .85 pap.,
1. Predestination. I. Title.

HAGEMAN, Howard G. 234.9
Predestination. Philadelphia, Fortress [c.1963] 74p. 20cm. (Fortress bk.) 63-12533 1.00 bds.,
1. Predestination. I. Title.

HUMBERGER, John. 234
The conquest and triumph of divine wisdom and love in predestination, by John Humberger ... Columbus, O., J. L. Trauger, printer, 1885. vi, 120 p. 20 cm. In verse. [PS2044.H36] 27-11472
1. Predestination. I. Title.

MAURY, Pierre, 1890-1956. 234.9
Predestination, and other papers. [Translated by Edwin Hudson from the French] With a memoir by Robert Mackie, and a foreword by Karl Barth. Richmond, John Knox Press [1960] 109p. 23cm. [BT810.M423 1960] 60-6369
1. Predestination. 2. Christmas sermons. I. Title.

MOODY, Samuel, 1676?-1747. 234.
The doleful state of the damned; especially such as go to hell from under the gospel; aggravated from their apprehensions of the saints happiness in heaven. Being the substance of several sermons, preached at York, in the province of Main [sic]. By Samuel Moodey ... iBoston: Printed & sold by Timothy Green in Middle Street. Also sold by Benj. Eliot in King Street, 1710 1 p. l., vi, 181 p. 16 cm. [BT810.M65] 41-36241
1. Predestination. 2. Future punishment. 3. Calvinism. I. Title.

RICE, Nathan Lewis, 1807-1877. 234.
God sovereign and man free: or, The doctrine of divine foreordination and man's free agency, stated, illustrated, and proved from the Scriptures. By N. L. Rice ... Cincinnati, J. D. Thorpe, 1850. viii, [9]-225 p. 18 cm. [BT810.R45] 42-27243
1. Predestination. I. Title.

SELLON, Walter. 234.9
Arguments against the doctrine of general redemption, considered. By the Rev. Walter Sellon... New-York, Published by D. Hitt and T. Ware, for the Methodist connexion in the United States, J. C. Totten. Printer, 1814. xxvi, [27]-252 p. 14 cm. [BT810.S4] 33-32109
1. Predestination. I. Title.

SMALL, John B.
A cordial and dispassionate discussion on predestination: its scriptural import... With introduction by E. Moore... York, Pa., Dispatch pub.co., 1901. 2 p. l., vi, 7-230 p. front. (port.) 8° 1-14658
I. Title.

SMALL, John Bryan, op., 1845- 234.
A cordial and dispassionate discussion on predestination: its Scriptural import. By Bishop John B. Small ... With introduction by E. Moore ... York, Pa., Dispatch publishing co., 1901. 2 p. l., vi, 7-230 p. front. (port.) 23 cm. [BT810.S6] 1-14658
1. Predestination. I. Title.

THORNWELL, James Henley, 1812-1862. 234.9
Election and reprobation. Philadelphia, Presbyterian and Reformed Pub. Co., 1961. 97 p. 23 cm. (Biblical and theological studies) International library of philosophy and theology. [BT810.T48 1961] 61-11745
1. Predestination. 2. Election (Theology) I. Title.

TWISSE, William, 1578?-1646. 234.9
The riches of God's love unto the vessells of mercy, consistent with his absolute hatred or reprobation of the vessells of wrath. Or An answer unto a book entituled: God's love unto mankind, manifested by disproving his absolute decree for their damnation. In two bookes. The first being a refutation of the said booke, as it was presented in manuscript by M'Hord unto Sir Nath: Rich. The second being an examination of certain passages inserted into M. Hord's discourse, (formerly answered) by an author that conceales his name, but was supposed to be M'Mason ... By that great and famous light of God's church, William Twisse ... Whereunto are annexed two tractates of the same author in answer unto D. H., the one concerning God's decrees definite or indefinite. The other about the object of predestination. Together with A vindiciation of D. Twisse from the exceptions of M'John Goodwin in his Redemption redeemed. By Henry Jeanes ... Oxford, Printed by L[eonard] L[ichfield] and H. H[all] printers to the University, for Tho: Robinson. M.DC.LIII. 2 v. in 1. 29 1/2 cm. The first book is in two parts, each having special t.-p.; the second book has also special t.-p. Each special t.-p. has vignette (printer's mark) "A vindication of D. Twisse ... by Henry Jeanes", is wanting in the Library of Congress copy. [BT810.T8] 30-34016
1. Hoard, Samuel, 1599-1658. God's love to mankind. 2. Mason, Henry, 1573?-1647. Certain passages in Mr. Sam. Hoard's book, entit. God's love to mankind. 3. Hammond, Henry, 1605-1660. 4. Predestination. I. Title.

ZANCHI, Giorolamo, 1516-1590. 234.9
The doctrine of absolute predestination stated and asserted: with a preliminary discourse on the divine attributes. Translated, in great measure, from the Latin of Jerom Zanchius. By Augustus Toplady... Wilmington. Delaware state, Printed at Adam's press, 1793. xii, 13-148 p. 19 1/2 cm. [BT810.Z3 1793] 33-19160
1. Predestination. 2. Calvinism. I. Toplady, Augustus Montague, 1740-1778. II. Title.

ZANCHI, Girolamo, 1516-1590. 234.9
The doctrine of absolute predestination stated and asserted: with a preliminary discourse on the divine attributes. Translated, in great measure, from the Latin of Jerom Zanchius. By Augustus Toplady... Philadelphia: Printed and sold by Stewart & Cochran, no. 34, South second-street, M,DCC,XCIII. xiv, [15]-148 p. 17 cm. [BT810.Z3 1796 a] 33-19159
1. Predestination. 2. Calvinism. I. Toplady, Augustus Montague. 1740-1778. II. Title.

ZANCHI, Girolamo, 1516-1590. 234.
The doctrine of absolute predestination stated and asserted: with a preliminary discourse on the divine attributes. Translated, in great measure, from the Latin of Jerom Zanchius, and An appendix concerning the fate of the ancients. To which is affixed, A letter to the Rev. John Wesley, relative to his pretended abridgment of Zanchius on predestination. By Augustus Toplady... Johnstown [N.Y.]: Printed by Abraham Romyen, 1804. 3 p. l., [iii]-xviii, [19]-189 p. 18 cm. "Appendix concerning the fate of the ancients" (p. [147]-153) is from the Latin of Justus Lipsius. [BT810, Z3 1804] 38-10409
1. Predestination. 2. Calvinism. 3. Wesley, John, 1703-1791. I. Toplady, Augustus Montague, 1740-1778. II. Lipsius, Justus, 1547-1606. III. Title.

ZANCHI, Girolamo, 1516-1590. 234.9
The doctrine of absolute predestination stated and asserted: translated in great measure from the Latin of Jerom Zanchius: with some account of his life prefixed: and An appendix concerning the fate of the ancients. Also, A caveat against unsound doctrines. To which is added, A letter to the Rev. John Wesley, By Augustus Toplady... New-York: Published by George Lindsay. Paul & Thomas, printers. 1811. 299 p. 18 cm. "An appendix concerning the fate of the ancients" (p. [200]-208) is from the Latin of Justus Lipsius." "A caveat against unsound doctrine" and "A letter to the Rev. John Wesley" (both by Toplady) have each special t.-p. [BT810.Z3 1811] 33-20052
1. Predestination. 2. Calvinism. 3. Wesley, John 1763-1791. I. Toplady, Augustus Montague, 1740-1778. II. Lipsius, Justus, 1547-1606. III. Title.

Predestination—Biblical teaching.

CLARK, Gordon Haddon. 234'.9
Biblical predestination, by Gordon H. Clark. Nutley, N.J., Presbyterian and Reformed Pub. Co., 1969. 155 p. 21 cm. (An International library of philosophy and theology. Biblical and theological studies) [BS680.P65C57] 74-92699
1. Predestination—Biblical teaching. I. Title. II. Series.

Predestination—Early works to 1800.

BLACKWELL, Thomas, 1660?- 230
1728.
Forms sacra, or, A sacred platform of natural and revealed religion; exhibiting, a Scriptural and rational account of these three important heads, 1 st. Of creation ... 2dly. Of the whole complex external plan of divine predestination ... 3dly. Of the wise divine procedure in accomplishing each part ... By the pious and learned Thomas Blackwell, to which is now added, an introduction ... By Simon Williams ... Boston, Printed and sold by William M'Alpine, at his printing-office in Marlborough-street, 1774. xvii, [1], xviii, vi [i.e. vii], [8]339 p. 16 cm. Includes "list of subscribers" [xviii p.] First published in Edinburg in 1710, with title, Shema sacrum; or A sacred scheme or natural and revealed religion... [BT70.B6 1774] 22-820
1. Williams, Simon, 1729-1793, ed. II. Title.

CALVIN, Jean, 1509-1564. 231
On God and man; selections from Institutes of the Christian religion. Edited by F. W. Strothmann. New York, F. Ungar Pub. Co. [1956] 54p. 21cm. (Milestones of thought) [BT810.C23] 56-7500
1. Predestination—Early works to 1800. 2. Reformed Church—Doctrinal and controversial works. I. Title.

GERMANUS I, Saint, 234'.9
Patriarch of Constantinople, d.ca.733.
On predestined terms of life / Germanus ; Greek text and English translation by Charles Garton and Leendert G. Westerink. Buffalo : Dept. of Classics, State University of N.Y. at Buffalow, c1979. xxix, 82 p. ; 23 cm. (Arethusa monographs ; 7) Includes index. [BT810.G3913] 79-121363 pbk. : 5.00
1. Predestination—Early works to 1800. I. Garton, Charles. II. Westerink, Leendert Gerrit. III. Title. IV. Series.

OCKHAM, William, 234'.9
d.ca.1349.
Predestination, God's foreknowledge, and future contingents. Translated with an introd., notes, and appendices by Marilyn McCord Adams [and] Norman Kretzmann. New York, Appleton-Century-Crofts [1969] ix, 136 p. 21 cm. (Century philosophy sourcebooks) Translation of Tractatus de praedestinatione et de praescientia Die et de futuris contigentibus. Bibliography: p. 115-128. [B765.O33T73] 69-19995 ISBN 0-390-67500-8
1. Predestination—Early works to 1800. 2. Logic—Early works to 1800. I. Adams, Marilyn McCord, ed. II. Kretzmann, Norman, ed. III. Title.

SIMOCATTA, Theophylactus. 234'.9
On predestined terms of life / Theophylactus Simocates ; Greek text and English translation by Charles Garton and Leendert G. Westerink. Buffalo : Dept. of Classics, State University of N.Y. at Buffalo, c1978. xv, 42 p. ; 24 cm. (Arethusa monographs ; 6) Includes index. [BT810.S5313] 79-121402 pbk. : 3.00
1. Predestination—Early works to 1800. I. Garton, Charles. II. Westerink, Leendert Gerrit. III. Title. IV. Series.

Predestination—History of doctrines.

BUIS, Harry. 234.9
Historic Protestantism and predestination. Philadelphia, Presbyterian and Reformed Pub. Co. [c1958] 142p. 21cm. Includes bibliography. [BT810.B8] 58-59920
1. Predestination—History of doctrines. I. Title.

KLOOSTER, Fred H. 234'.9
Calvin's doctrine of predestination / Fred H. Klooster. 2d ed. Grand Rapids, Mich. : Baker Book House, c1977. 98 p. ; 22 cm. (Baker Biblical monograph) Includes indexes. Bibliography: p. 89-93. [BT810.2.K57 1977] 77-88699 ISBN 0-8010-5385-4 pbk. : 3.95
1. Calvin, Jean, 1509-1564—Theology. 2. Predestination—History of doctrines. I. Title. II. Series.

Prefaces.

LE FEVRE, Jacques, 201'.1
d'Etaples, d.1537.
The prefatory epistles of Jacques Lefevre d'Etaples and related texts. Edited by Eugene F. Rice, Jr. New York, Columbia University Press, 1972. xl, 629 p. 24 cm. Texts chiefly in Latin, some in French; editorial matter in English. Bibliography: p. 535-568. [BR1725.L28A4 1972] 77-123577 ISBN 0-231-03163-7 15.00
1. Prefaces. I. Rice, Eugene F., ed. II. Title.

Prefaces (Liturgy)

CATHOLIC Church. 264.02'09
National Conference of Catholic Bishops. Bishops' Committee on the Liturgy.
The new eucharistic prayers and prefaces. Washington, 1968. 72 p. 23 cm. "The extensive notes to the four eucharistic prayers ... were prepared by the translating body, the International Committee on English in the Liturgy (ICEL)." Bibliography: p. 72. [BX2045.P65A5] 79-4460
1. Prefaces (Liturgy) I. Catholic Church. Liturgy and ritual. Eucharistic prayer II-IV. English. 1968. II. International Committee on English in the Liturgy. III. Title.

Pregnancy, Unwanted—Great Britain.

BARRELL, Dilys. 261.8'32
You don't need to have an abortion / by Dilys Barrell. London : Catholic Truth Society, 1976. 12 p. ; 19 cm. "S 318" [HV700.G7B29] 77-363541 ISBN 0-85183-186-9 : £0.15
1. Pregnancy, Unwanted—Great Britain. 2. Child welfare—Great Britain. I. Title.

Prejudices and antipathies.

KIMP, Bobbie. 241.675
Prejudice : the big sin / by Bobbie Kimp. Columbus,OH : Bobbie Kimp,1978. [BF575.D9] pbk. : 1.50
1. Prejudices and antipathies. 2. Christianity. I. Title.
Publisher's address 2483Edsel Ave., Columbus, OH 45707.

MARNEY, Carlyle, 1916- 241
Structures of prejudice. New York, Abingdon Press [1961] 256p. 24cm. Includes bibliography. [BF575.P9M3] 61-8411
1. Prejudices and antipathies. I. Title.

PAWLIKOWSKI, John. 377'.8'2
Catechetics and prejudice; how Catholic teaching materials view Jews, Protestants, and racial minorities, by John T. Pawlikowski. New York, Paulist Press [1973] vi, 154 p. 23 cm. Includes bibliographies. [BX1784.P38] 72-94109 ISBN 0-8091-1758-4 4.50
1. Catholic Church—Relations. 2. Prejudices and antipathies. 3. Religious education. I. Title.

SUNDAY school fights 301.45
prejudice [by] Mildred Moody Eakin and Frank Eakin. New York, Macmillan, 1953. 168p. 22cm. [BV1523.E2] [BV1523.E2] 323.173 53-915 38-915
1. Prejudices and antipathies. 2. Sunday-schools. I. Eakin, Mildred Olivia (Moody) 1890- II. Eakin. Frank, 1885- joint author.

Premonstrants.

KIRKFLEET, Cornelius James, 922.
1881-
History of Saint Norbert, Founder of the Norbertine (Premonstratensian) order, apostle of the blessed sacrament, archbishop of Magdeburg, by the Rev. Cornelius J. Kirkfleet ... (With twelve illustrations) St. Louis, Mo., and London, B. Herder, 1916. xvii p., 1 l., 364 p. front., plates, ports. 20 1/2 cm. "A list of biographies of St. Norbert": p. vi-ix. [BX4700.N8K5] 16-18298
1. Norbert, Saint, abp. of Magdeburg, d. 1134. 2. Premonstrants. I. Title.

KIRKFLEET, Cornelius James, 922.
1881-
History of Saint Norbert, founder of the Norbertine (Premonstratensian) order, apostle of the blessed sacrament, archbishop of Magdeburg, by the Rev. Cornelius J. Kirkfleet ... (With twelve illustrations) St. Louis, Mo., and London, B. Herder, 1916. xvii p., 1 l., 364 p. front., plates, ports. 21 cm. "A list of biographies of St. Norbert": p. vi-ix. [BX4700.N8K5] 16-18298
1. Norbert, Saint, abp. of Magdeburg. d. 1134. 2. Premonstrants. I. Title.

Premonstrants in Great Britain

KIRKFLEET, Cornelius 271.79
James, 1881-
The white canons of St. Norbert, a history of the Premonstratensian order in the British isles and America, by the Rev. Cornelius James Kirkfleet, O.PRAEM. West De Pere, Wis., St. Norbert abbey [1943] xxvi p., 1 l., 307 p. front. (map) plates, ports., plan. 23 1/2 cm. Bibliography: p. 295-297. [BX3916.K5] 43-13277
1. Premonstrants in Gt. Brit. 2. Premonstrants in the U.S. 3. St. Norbert abbey, West De Pere, Wis. I. Title.

Premonstratensians in Great Britain

COLVIN, Howard Montagu. 271.4
The White Canons in England. Oxford, Clarendon Press, 1951. viii, 459 p. front., fold. map. 23 cm. Bibliography: p. [369]-388. [BX3916.C6] 52-2460
1. Premonstratensians in Gt. Brit. I. Title.

Prerogative, Royal—France.

WEILL, Georges 328.44'07'4
Jacques, 1865-
Les theories sur le pouvoir royal en France pendant les guerres de religion, par Georges Weill. New York, Burt Franklin [1967?] 315p. 25cm. (Burt Franklin res. & source works ser., no. 191) Thesis--Paris. Orig. pub., Paris, 1891. Bibl. [JN2369] 68-5807 16.50
1. Prerogative, Royal—France. 2. France—Pol. & govt.—1562-1598. I. Title.

A presbyter.

A book of prayer for use in 264.
the churches of Jesus Christ, comp. by a presbyter. Boston, Sherman, French & company, 1917. 4 p. l., 299 p. 15 1/2 cm. [BV245.B6] 18-2729
1. A presbyter.

WHITE, Henry Alexander, 922.
1861-
Southern Presbyterian leaders, by Henry Alexander White...with portrait illustrations. New York, The Neale publishing company, 1911. 3 p. l., 476 p. front., ports. 22 1/2 cm. "Principal sources" p. 463-469. [BX9220.W5] 12-19
I. Title.

Presbyterian.

ROBINSON, George 922.573
Livingstone, 1864-
Autobiography of George L. Robinson, a short story of a long life. Grand Rapids, Baker Book House, 1957. 142p. illus. 23cm. [BX9225.R713A3] 57-12192
1. Presbyterian I. Title.

SMITH, William D d.1848. 230.5
What is Calvinism? or, The confession of faith, in harmony with the Bible and common sense, in a series of dialogues between a Presbyterian minister and a young convert. By the Rev. William D. Smith, D. D. Philadelphia, Presbyterian board of publication [1854] v, 7-260 p. 16 cm. [BX9183.S6] 238.5 33-37782
1. Presbyterian. I. Presbyterian church in the U. S. A. Board of publication. II. Title. III. Title: The confession of faith.

Presbyterian church.

AUGUSTA, Ga. First 285.
Presbyterian church.
Memorial of the centennial anniversary of the First Presbyterian church, Augusta, Georgia. The anniversary exercises May fifteenth to eighteenth, 1904. [Philadelphia, Press of Allen, Lane & Scott, 1904] 178 p. front. (port.) 4 pl. (1 col.) 25 cm. "This edition is limited to six hundred copies, signed by the pastor. This copy id no. 93." Chairman of the editorial committee. Mrs. Mary C. Wadley. [BX9211.A9F5 1904] 5-5279
I. Wadley, Mary C., Mrs. ed. II. Title.

BACON, Amos N.
A sketch of the Presbyterian and other churches in Princeton and vicinity, and the birth and progress of thought and knowledge. By Amos N. Bacon. Princeton, Ill., 1885. 100 p. 21 cm. 16-23737
I. Title.

FRANKLIN, Ind. First 285.1772
Presbyterian Church.
The First Presbyterian Church of Franklin, Indiana; one hundred and twenty years, 1824-1944, By Herriott C. Palmer, church historian, 1919-1944. Franklin, Ind., 1946. xv, 545 p. plates, ports. 25 cm. Errata slip mounted on p. xii. "Bibliography and acknowledgement": p. 509-510. [BX9211.F8F45] 47-26503
I. Palmer, Herriott Clare, 1866- II. Title.

FRY, John R. 252'.051
Fire and blackstone [by] John R. Fry. [1st ed.] Philadelphia, Lippincott [1969] vi, 248 p. 22 cm. [BX9178.F79F5] 73-91672 5.95
1. Presbyterian Chruch—Sermons. 2. Sermons, American. I. Title.

HOGE, Arista, ed.
The First Presbyterian church, Staunton, Virginia; material gathered and arranged by Arista Hoge. Staunton, Va., Press of Caldwell-Sites company, 1908. 336 p. front., illus., ports. 24 cm. 9-7429
I. Title.

MACARTNEY, Clarence 252.051
Edward Noble, 1879-
Sermons from life, by Clarence Edward Macartney ... Nashville, Cokesbury press [c1933] 292 p. 19 1/2 cm. [BX9178.M172S4] 33-3814
1. Presbyterian chruch—Sermons. 2. Sermons, American. I. Title.

MACLEOD, Donald, 1913- 264'.05
Presbyterian worship : its meaning and method / Donald Macleod. New rev. ed. Atlanta : John Knox Press, c1980. 186 p. ; 21 cm. Bibliography: p. [182]-186. [BX9185.M23 1981] 19 80-82226 ISBN 0-8042-1813-7 : 12.50
1. Presbyterian Church. 2. Liturgies—Presbyterian Church. 3. Public worship. I. Title.

M'CHORD, James, 1785-1820. 285
A last appeal to the "Market-street Presbyterian church and congregation": in a series of seven sermons, predicated on sketches of the dispensations of God toward his people. To which are added (in an appendix to sermon V.) strictures on "The fiend of the reformation detected":-- by James Gray ... By James M'Chord ... Lexington, Ky., Printed and published by T. T. Skillman, 1818. viii, [9]-332 p. 20 1/2 cm. "Subscribers' names": p. [329]-332. [BX9175.M3] 22-21899
I. Gray, James, 1770-1824. The fiend of the reformation detected. II. Title.

MILLER, Park Hays, 1879- 285.1
Why I am a Presbyterian. New York, T. Nelson [1956] 200 p. 21 cm. [BX9175.M5] 56-12396
1. Presbyterian Church. I. Title.

MILLER, Samuel, 1769-1850. 262.
An essay on the warrant, nature, and duties of the office of the ruling elder, in the Presbyterian church. By Samuel Miller ... 3d ed. Philadelphia, Presbyterian board of publication, 1840. 324 p. 15 cm. [BX9195.M5 1840] 22-23440
1. Presbyterian church. I. Title.

MOFFATT, James, 1870- 285
The Presbyterian churches, by James Moffatt ... Garden City, N.Y., Doubleday, Doran & company, inc., 1928. xi, 187, [1] p. 19 1/2 cm. (Half-title: The faiths: varieties of Christian expression) Printed in Great Britain. [BX9175.M55] 28-23320
1. Presbyterian church. I. Title.

MOSS, William Dyghum, 1866-1932. 252.051
Sermons and prayers, by William Dygnum Moss ... A memorial volume. Chapel Hill, The University of North Carolina press, 1940. xiii p., 1 l., 207 p. front. (port.) facsim. 21 cm. Selections made by an editorial committee. [BX9178.M64S4] 41-1157
1. Prebyterian church—Sermons. 2. Sermons, American. 3. Prayers. I. Harrer, Gustave Adolphus, 1886- ed. II. Title.

OTIS, Philo Adams, 1846-
The First Presbyterian church, 1833-1913; a history of the oldest organization in Chicago, with biographical sketches of the ministers and extracts from the choir records, by Philo Adams Otis ... 2d and rev. ed. Chicago, F. H. Revell co., 1913. ix p., 1 l., [13]-320 p. incl. front. plates, ports. 25 cm. 14-254 1.50
I. Title.

PITTSBURGH. East Liberty Presbyterian church. 285.174886
East Liberty Presbyterian church, with historical setting and a narrative of the centennial celebration, April 12-20, 1919. Compiled by Georgina G. Negley, A. M., for the East Liberty Presbyterian church ... Pittsburgh, Murdoch, Kerr & co. press, 1919. 7 p. l., 3-257 p. front., illus., plates, ports., facsims. 24 cm. [BX9211.P6E27] 37-6747
I. Negley, Georgina G., 1865- II. Title.

PITTSBURGH. East Liberty Presbyterian church. 285.174886
The East Liberty Presbyterian church. Pittsburgh, Pa., 1935. [132] p. incl. col. front., plates, plans. 34 cm. Descriptive letterpress on versos facing the plates. [BX9211.P6E28] 35-8242
I. Title.

PITTSBURGH. First Presbyterian church. 285.174886
Centennial volume of the First Presbyterian church of Pittsburgh, Pa. 1784-1884. Pittsburgh, W. G. Johnston & co., printers, 1884. 259 p. front., illus. (incl. plan) ports., 23 cm. Preface signed: Sylvester F. Scovel. "Sources of information": p. 259. [BX9211.P6F5] 35-37804
I. Scovel, Sylvester Fithian, 1835-1910, ed. II. Title.

THE plan of union of the Presbyterian Church in the United States of America and the United Presbyterian Church of North America to form the United Presbyterian Church in the United States of America. [n. p.] 1956. 308p. paper.
I. Presbyterian Church in the U. S. A.

PRESBYTERIAN church in the U. S. General assembly.
Calvin memorial addresses, delivered before the General assembly of the Presbyterian church in the United States at Savannah Ga., May, 1909. Richmond, Va., Presbyterian committee of publication [1909] 286 p. front., plates, ports. 21 cm. 10-11652
I. Title.

SMITH, Reba S
The First Presbyterian Church of Claremore, Oklahoma 1889-1964. . . [n.p.] Published in the Church Office, 1964. xi, 155 p. illus. 22 cm. 65-60021
I. Title.

WASHINGTON, D. C. New York avenue Presbyterian church.
The centennial of the New York avenue Presbyterian church, Washington, D.C., 1803-1903. [Washington? 1904?] 172 p. front., plates, ports. 23 cm. On cover: One hundredth anniversary New York avenue Presbyterian church, Washington, D.C. Memorial volume, 1803-1903. [BX922.W3N5 1903] 4-22474
I. Title.

WASHINTON, D. C. Metropolitan Presbyterian church.
Annual report. [Washington, D.C., v. 16 1/2 cm. Report year ends March 31. Full title of report for : Annual report of the Metropolitan Presbyterian church, Washington, D.C. CA 11
I. Title.

Presbyterian church—Addresses, essays, lectures.

CHALMERS, Thomas, 1780-1847. 208.1
... *Miscellanies;* embracing reviews, essays, and addresses. By the late Thomas Chalmers ... New York, Pittsburg, R. Carter, 1847. xxiv, [25]-544 p. 24 cm. At head of title: Chalmer's miscellanies. [BX8915.C53] 16-3277
1. Presbyterian church—Addresses, essays, lectures. 2. Theology—Addresses, essays, lectures. I. Title.

KNOX, Hugh, d.1790. 244
The moral and religious miscellany; or, Sixty-one aphoretical essays on some of the most important Christian doctrines and virtues. New York, Printed by Hodge and Shober, 1775. 360 p. 20 cm. [BX8915.K58 1775] 51-49547
1. Presbyterian Church—Addresses, essays, lectures. 2. Theology, Doctrinal—Addresses, essays, lectures. 3. Virtue. I. Title.

KNOX, Hugh, d.1790. 208.
The moral and religious miscellany; or, Sixty-one aphoretical essays, on some of the most Christian doctrines and virtues. By Hugh Knox ... Hartford: Re-printed by Hudson and Goodwin, M.DCC.XC. viii, [9]-352 p. 20 1/2 cm. [BX8915.K58] 46-41576
1. Presbyterian church—Addresses, essays, lectures. 2. Theology, Doctrinal—Addresses, essays, lectures. 3. Virtue. I. Title.

MILLER, James Russell, 1840-1912. 208.
Woman's ministry, and other papers. By Rev. J. R. Miller ... Philadelphia, J. B. Lippincott & co., 1875. 160 p. front. (prot.) 17 1/2 cm. [BX8915.M53] 45-33462
1. Presbyterian church—Addresses, essays, lectures. I. Title.

NEW York. Brick Presbyterian church. 285.
Brick church memorial, containing the discourse delivered by Dr. Spring on the closing of the old church in Beekman st., and the opening of the new church on Murray Hill; the discourse delivered on the fiftienth anniversary of his installation as pastor of the Brick church; with the proceedings of the memorial meeting, and the discourse preached on the occasion of Mrs. Spring's decease. New York, M. W. Dodd, 1861. 248 p. front., plates, port. 23 1/2 cm. [BX9211.N5B8] 20-15441
I. Spring, Gardiner, 1785-1878. II. Title.

SHEDD, William Greenough Thayer, 1820-1894. 208.
Orthodoxy and heterodoxy, a miscellany, by William G. T. Shedd, D.D. New York, C. Scribner's sons, 1893. xii, 297 p. 21 cm. [BX8915.S47] 45-34435
1. Presbyterian church—Addresses, essays, lectures. I. Title.

Presbyterian Church—Biography

HALL, Ralph J., 1891- 266.5'0924 B
The main trail, by Ralph J. Hall. Edited by Vic Jameson. San Antonio, Tex., Naylor [1971] xiii, 193 p. illus. 22 cm. Autobiographical. [BX9225.H312A3] 76-185994 ISBN 0-8111-0448-6 7.95
I. Title.

MOORE, Walter William, 1857-1926. 922.573
Appreciations and historical addresses, by Walter W. Moore ... [Richmond, Presbyterian committee of publication, 1914?] 167, [6] p. front., ports. 21 cm. [BX9220.M6] 15-12372
1. Presbyterian church—Biog. 2. Presbyterian church in North Carolina. I. Presbyterian church in the U. S. Executive committee of publication. II. Title.
Contents omitted.

PRESBYTERIAN Church in the U.S. 285'.133'02573
Ministerial directory of the Presbyterian Church, U.S., 1861-1967. Compiled by E. D. Witherspoon, Jr. Published by order of the General Assembly. Doraville, Ga., Foote & Davies, 1967. vii, 648 p. 24 cm. Supplements Ministerial directory of 1941 and of 1951. Bibliography: p. 648. [BX9220.P7 1967] 68-3645
1. Presbyterian Church—Biography. 2. Presbyterian Church in the U.S.—Biography. I. Witherspoon, Eugene Daniel, 1932- II. Title.

SCOTT, Eugene Crampton, 1889- comp. 922.573
Ministerial directory of the Presbyterian church, U.S., 1861-1941. Compiled by Rev. E. C. Scott ... Published by order of the General assembly. Austin, Tex., Press of Von Boeckmann-Jones co., 1942. viii, 826 p. 24 cm. Bibliography: p. 825-826. [BX9220.S35] 42-21661
1. Presbyterian church—Biog. 2. Presbyterian church in the U.S.—Biog. I. Presbyterian church in the U.S. General assembly. II. Title.

[SPAULDING, John] 1800-1889. 922.573
From the plow to the pulpit ... New York, R. Carter and brothers, 1874. viii p., 1 l., [11]-121 p. front. 17 1/2 cm. Autobiography. [BX9225.S64A3] 36-22138
I. Title.

Presbyterian Church—California—History—19th century.

WOODS, James L., 1846-1918. 285'.1794
California pioneer decade of 1849 : the Presbyterian Church, with some mention of other churches, and incidental reference to current events and civil affairs of early and later date / by James L. Woods. Fresno, Cal[if] : Pioneer Pub. Co. ; Reedley, CA : Additional copies m[a]y be obtained from L.K. Brown, 1981. 181 p., [2] p. of plates : ill. ; 24 cm. Reprint. Originally published: San Francisco, Calif. : Press of the Hansen Co., c1922. "An historical contribution supplemental to the synod's official history by Rev. James S. McDonald, D.D., including recollections of pioneer work in California by James Woods, a pioneer minister formerly of Stockton, Los Angeles, and Santa Rosa, combined with annals and memories of pioneer times by James L. Woods his son, formerly minister at Lakeport and Mendocino." Includes indexes. Bibliography: p. 176-178. [BX8947.C2W7 1981] 19 82-114335 ISBN 0-914330-44-6 : 10.00
1. Presbyterian Church—California—History—19th century. 2. California—Church history. I. Woods, James, 1814 or 15-1886. II. Title.
Publisher's address: Eight E. Olive Ave., Fresno, CA 93728

Presbyterian Church—Catechisms and creeds.

*DAUGHTERS of St. Paul 238.2
Christ lives in me; grade 2. Prep. by the Daughters of St. Paul under the direction of Rev. James Alberione, following the Concentric method and the Kerygmatic approach to Catechetics [Boston] St. Paul Catechetical Ctr. [dist. Daughters of St. Paul, c.1965] Richmond, Va., Author [c.1965] 60p. illus. (pt. col.) 21cm. 336p. 21cm. (St. Paul way, truth, and life ser. 2) Ea. lesson contains Sacred scripture; catechism; liturgy. With teacher's gd., and activity sheets. [BX9183.P7] 238.5 65-3898 2.10 pap., set, n3 1.50 pap.,
1. Presbyterian Church—Catechisms and creeds. I. Presbyterian Church in the U.S. General Assembly. II. Westminster Assembly of Divines. The Confession of Faith. III. Westminster Assembly of Divines. Larger catechism. IV. Westminster Assembly of Divines. Shorter catechism. V. Title. VI. Title: The Confession of Faith of the Presbyterian Church in the United States;

PRESBYTERIAN Church in the U.S. General Assembly. 238.5
The Confession of Faith of the Presbyterian Church in the United States; together with the Larger catechism and the Shorter catechism, declared by the General Assembly at Augusta, Georgia. December 1861. With amendments that were enacted by the General Assemblies of 1886, 1939, 1942, 1944, 1959, and 1963. [Rev. ed. with amendments] Richmond, Printed by the Board of Christian Education [1965] 336 p. 21 cm. [BX9183.P7] 65-3898
1. Presbyterian Church—Catechisms and creeds. I. Westminster Assembly of Divines. The Confession of Faith. II. Westminster Assembly of Divines. Larger catechism. III. Westminster Assembly of Divines. Shorter Catechism. IV. Title.

THE Westminster confession of faith : a new edition / edited by Douglas Kelly, Hugh McClure, and Philip B. Rollinson. 1st ed. Greenwood, S.C. : Attic Press, 1981, c1979. viii, 94 p. ; 21 cm. [BX9183.W47] 19 81-108413 ISBN 0-87921-065-6 pbk. : 5.95 238'.5
1. Presbyterian Church—Catechisms and creeds. I. Kelly, Douglas, 1943- II. McClure, Hugh. III. Rollinson, Philip B.

Presbyterian church—Catechisms and creeds—English.

WESTMINSTER Assembly of Divines 238.5
A harmony of the Westminster Presbyterian standards, with explanatory notes, by James Benjamin Green. Richmond, John Knox Press [1951] 231 p. 28 cm. [BX9183.A38] 51-2866
1. Presbyterian Church—Catechisms and creeds—English. I. Green, James Benjamin, 1871- II. Title. III. Title: Westminster Presbyterian standards.

WESTMINSTER assembly of divines. 238.
The larger catechism, agreed upon by the Assembly of divines at Westminster, with the assistance of commissioners from the Church of Scotland, and received by the several Presbyterian churches in America; with the proofs from the Scripture, revised by Alexander M'Leod ... New-York: Stereotyped and printed by J. Watts & co., for Whiting & Watson, theological and classical booksellers, June 1813. 1 p. l., 142 p. 17 1/2 cm. "The first book ever stereotyped in America." [BX9184.A2 1813] [BX9184.A2 1813] 238. A 35
1. Presbyterian church—Catechisms and creeds—English. I. McLeod, Alexander, 1774-1833, ed. II. Title.

Presbyterian Church — Clergy — Correspondence, reminiscences, etc.

BENJAMIN, Mooshie Sargis, 1889- 922.573
The Persian Yankee. [1st ed.] New York, Vantage Press [1957, c1956] 114p. illus. 21cm. Autobiographical. [BX9225.B534A3] 56-10558
1. Presbyterian Church—Clergy—Correspondence, reminiscences, etc. I. Title.

BROWN, Arthur Judson, 1856- 922.573
Memoirs of a centenarian; edited by William N. Wysham. New York, World Horizons, 1957. 174p. illus. 24cm. [BX9225.B758A3] 58-15906
1. Presbyterian Church— Clergy—Correspondence, reminiscences, etc. I. Title.

LEWIS, John, 1878- 922.573
The strange story of a minister's life. Boston, Christopher Pub. House [1956] 171p. illus. 21cm. [BX9225.L47A3] 57-177
1. Presbyterian Church—Clergy—Correspondence, reminiscences, etc. I. Title.

MCLEES, Richard Gustavus, 1864- 922.573
Opening doors my life's story. Weaverville, N. C., Southern Presbyterian journal, 1954. 87p. illus. 23cm. [BX9225.M2555A3] 54-24792
1. Presbyterian Church—Clergy—Correspondence, reminiscences, etc. I. Title.

OHAN, William Joseph, 1881-1964.
A backward look -- with a forward hope. [Chicago, 1964?] 22 l. port. 29 cm. Autobiography. 65-44489
1. Presbyterian Church — Clergy — Correspondence, reminiscences, etc. I. Title.

SEGESVARY, Lewis. 285.0922
I give you a new land. [Minneapolis, Osterhus Pub. House, 1953 or 4] 143p. 20cm. [BX9225.S36.A3] 56-26565
1. Presbyterian Church—Clergy—Correspondence, reminiscences, etc. I. Title.

YOUNG, Loyal, 1806-1890? 922.573
From dawn to dusk; a pastor's panorama; by the Rev. Loyal Young, D.D. ... Claremont, N.H., Claremont manufacturing co., 1884. x, 256 p. 19 1/2 cm. [BX9225.Y6A3] 36-31915
I. Title. II. Title: A pastor's panorama.

Presbyterian church—Collected works.

CHALMERS, Thomas, 1780-1847. 208.1
Posthumous works of the Rev. Thomas Chalmer ... edited by the Rev. William Hanna ... New York, Harper & brothers, 1848-50 [v. i, '49] 9 v. 20 cm. Each volume has also special t.-p. Contents.iii. Horae biblicae quotidianae.--iv-v. Horae biblicae sabbaticae.--vi. Sermons ... 1798-1847.--vii-viii. Institute of theology.--ix. Lectures and addresses. [BX8915.C55 1848a] 33-16026
1. Presbyterian church—Collected works. 2. Theology—Collected works—19 cent. I. Hanna, William, 1808-1882, ed. II. Title.

CHALMERS, Thomas, 1780-1847. 208.1
The work of Thomas Chalmers ... Hartford, Printed by G. Goodwin and sons, 1822. 3 v. 19 cm. [BX8915.C5 1822] 32-25197
1. Presbyterian church—Collected works. 2. Theology—Collected works—19th cent. I. Title.

GRIMKE, Francis James, 1850-1937. 208.1
The works of Francis J. Grimke, edited by Carter G. Woodson ... Washington, D.C., The Associated publishers, inc. [1942] 4 v. 23 1/2 cm. Contents.I.--Addresses mainly personal and racial.--II. Special sermons.--III. Stray thoughts and meditations.--IV. Letters. [BX8915.G73] 42-18902
1. Presbyterian church—Collected works. 2. Theology—Collected works—20th cent. 3. U.S.—Race question. I. Woodson, Carter Godwin, 1875- ed. II. Title.

MURRAY, John, 1898-1975. 285'.2'0924
Collected writings of John Murray : professor of systematic theology, Westminster Theological Seminary, Philadelphia, Pennsylvania, 1937-1966. Edinburgh ; Carlisle, Pa. : Banner of Truth Trust, 1976- v. ; 24 cm. Contents.Contents.—v. 1. The claims of truth.—v. 2. Select lectures in systematic theology. [BX8915.M87 1976] 77-376336 ISBN 0-85151-241-0 (v. 1) : write for information
1. Presbyterian Church—Collected works. 2. Theology—Collected works—20th century.

NOTT, Eliphalet, 1773-1866. 204
Miscellaneous works. By Eliphalet Nott ... With an appendix. Schenectady: Published by Wm. J. M'Cartee, bookseller. Ryer Schermerhorn, printer. 1810. viii p., 1 l., [11]-280 p. 22 cm. "The star in the east: a sermon ... By the Rev. Claudius Buchanan": p. [241]-280. [BX8915.N6] 36-30785
1. Presbyterian church—Collected works. 2. Theology—Collected works—19th cent. I. Buchanan, Claudius, 1766-1815. The star in the east. II. Title.

WARFIELD, Benjamin Breckinridge, 1851-1921. 230.5'1
Selected shorter writings of Benjamin B. Warfield, edited by John E. Meeter. Nutley, N.J., Presbyterian and Reformed Pub. Co., 1970-73. 2 v. 23 cm. Includes bibliographical references. [BX8915.W3] 76-110499 7.50 (v. 1) 8.95 (v. 2)
1. Presbyterian Church—Collected works. 2. Theology—Collected works—20th century.

WITHERSPOON, John, 1723-1794. 244
The works of the Rev. John Witherspoon ... To which is prefixed an account of the author's life, in a sermon occasioned by his death, by the Rev. Dr. John Rodgers ... 2d ed., rev. and cor. Philadelphia: Printed and published by William W. Woodward, n°. 52, South second street, 1802. 4 v. 21 1/2 cm. [BX8915.W5 1802] 36-4371
1. Presbyterian church—Collected works. 2. Theology—Collected works—18th cent. I. Rodgers, John, 1727-1811. II. Title.

Presbyterian Church—Discipline.

KENNEDY, John, 1897- 262.05
Presbyterian authority and discipline. Richmond, Va., Knox [1965, c.1960] viii, 118p. 21cm. (Church officer's lib.) Delivered as the Chalmers lects. Bibl. [BX9190.K4] 65-26743 1.50 pap.,
1. Presbyterian Church—Discipline. 2. Church—Authority. I. Title. II. Series.

PRESBYTERIAN church in the U.S.A. General assembly. 377.
Report of the Committee of the General assembly, appointed to draught a plan for disciplining baptized children. New-York: Published by Whiting and Watson, no. 96, Broadway. J. Seymour, printer. 1812. 56 p. 23 1/2 cm. James Richards, Samuel Miller, John B. Romeyn, committee. Listed among the works of John B. Romeyn by Sprague, W. B. Annals of the American pulpit, v. 4, p. 220. [BX8950.A5 1812] A 33
1. Presbyterian church—Discipline. 2. Presbyterian church—Education. I. Romeyn, John Brodhead, 1777-1825. II. Title.

Presbyterian Church—Doctrinal and controversial works.

CHEESEMAN, Lewis. 285
Differences between old and new school Presbyterians; by Rev. Lewis Cheeseman ... With an introductory chapter, by John C. Lord ... Rochester, E. Darrow, 1848. 224 p. 21 cm. [BX9175.C5] 12-22761
1. Presbyterian church—Doctrinal and controversial works. 2. Presbyterian church in the U. S. A. (Old school) 3. Presbyterian church in the U. S. A. (New school) I. Title.

DABNEY, Robert Lewis, 1820-1898. 230'.5'1
Lectures in systematic theology. Grand Rapids, Zondervan Pub. House [1972] 903 p. 25 cm. Reprint of the 1878 ed. published under title: Syllabus and notes of the course of systematic and polemic theology taught in Union Theological Seminary, Virginia. [BT75.D2 1972] 73-171200 12.95
1. Presbyterian Church—Doctrinal and controversial works. 2. Theology, Doctrinal. I. Title.

DICKINSON, Jonathan, 1688-1747. 230.
The true Scripture-doctrine concerning some important points of Christian faith; particularly, eternal election, original sin, grace in conversion, justification by faith, and the saint's perseverance. Represented and applied in five discourses. By Jonathan Dickinson, A. M., formerly minister of the gospel at Elizabeth-town, N. Jersey. With a preface, and some sketches of the life of the author, by Mr. Austin. Chambersburg [Pa.]: Printed by Robert & Geo. K. Harper, m.dccc. ix, [1], [11]-216 p. 17 cm. [BX9174.D] A35
1. Presbyterian church—Doctrinal and controversial works. 2. Calvinism. I. Austin, David, 1760-1831. II. Title.

DICKINSON, Jonathan, 1688-1747. 230.5
The true Scripture-doctrine concerning some important points of Christian faith, particularly eternal election, original sin, grace in conversion, justification by Faith, and the saints perseverance. Represented and apply'd in five discourses, By Jonathan Dickinson, A. M., minister of the gospel at Elizabeth-Town, N. Jersey. With a preface by Mr. Foxcroft. Boston, Printed by D. Fowle, for S. Kneeland & T. Green in Queen-street, 1741. 1 p. l., xiii, [1], 253 p. 10 cm. [BX9174.D53 1741] 32-21452
1. Presbyterian church—Doctrinal and controversial works. 2. Calvinism. I. Foxcroft, Thomas, 1697-1769. II. Title.

DICKINSON, Jonathan, 1688-1747. 230.5
The true Scripture-doctrine concerning some important points of Christian faith; particularly, eternal election, original sin, grace in conversion, justification by faith, and the saint's preseverance. represented and applied in five discourses. by Jonathan Dickinson, A. M. formerly minister of the gospel at Elizabeth Town, N. Jersey. With a preface, and some sketches of the life of the author, by Mr. Austin. Elizabeth Town; Printed by Shepard Kollock, at his book-store. and printing-office, 1793. ix, [1], [11]-208 p. 18 cm. [BX9174.D53 1798] 25-2742
1. Presbyterian church—Doctrinal and controversial works. 2. Calvinism I. Austin David, 1760-1861. II. Title.

DICKINSON, Jonathan, 1688-1747. 230.5
The true scripture doctrine concerning some important points of Christian faith; particularly, eternal election, original sin, grace in conversion, justification by faith, and the saints' perseverance. Represented and applied in five discourses. By Jonathan. Dickinson ... Philadelphia, Presbyterian board of publication, 1841. 292 p. 16 cm. Binder's title: Dickinson's Five points. [BX9174.D53 1841] 33-20574
1. Presbyterian church—Doctrinal and controversial works. 2. Calvinism. I. Presbyterian church. Board of publication. II. Title.

DIDIER, Ralph H. 230'.5'1
Hang on to your heritage / by Ralph H. Didier. Orange, Calif. : Covenant Press, c1977. viii, 140 p. : ill. ; 22 cm. [BX9175.2.D53] 77-608289
1. Presbyterian Church—Doctrinal and controversial works. I. Title.

DUNCAN, John Mason, 1790-1851. 922.573
A reply to Dr. Miller's letter to a gentleman of Baltimore, in reference to the case of the Rev. Mr. Duncan. By John M. Duncan ... Baltimore, Cushing & Jewett, 1826. 143 p. 20 cm. [BX9225.D83A3] 36-23695
1. Miller Samuel, 1769-1850. Letter to a gentleman of Baltimore. 2. Presbyterian church—Doctrinal and controversial works. 3. Creeds. I. Title.

GEAR, Felix B. 230.5
Basic beliefs of the reformed faith; a Biblical study of Presbyterian doctrine. Richmond, Va., John Knox Press [c.1960] 80p. (bibls.) 21cm. 60-9774 .60 pap.,
1. Presbyterian Church—Doctrinal and controversial works. I. Title.

HODGE, Archibald Alexander, 1823-1886. 230
Outlines of theology. Grand Rapids, Mich., Zondervan Pub. House [1972] 678 p. 23 cm. Reprint of the rewritten and enl. ed. of 1879. [BT75.H6 1972] 73-150624 9.95
1. Presbyterian Church—Doctrinal and controversial works. 2. Theology, Doctrinal. I. Title.

KERR, Hugh Thomson, 1871- 285
A God-centered faith; studies in the Reformed faith, by Hugh Thomson Kerr... New York [etc.] Fleming H. Revell company [c1935] 189, [1] p. 19 1/2 cm. "These five lectures were delivered at Princeton theological seminary under the L. P. Stone foundation."--Pref. "Source of materials quoted" at end of each chapter. [BX9175.K4] 35-18661
1. Presbyterian church—Doctrinal and controversial works. I. Title.

KLUBER, George Kendall.
On holy ground, by George K. Kluber. Illus.by Thomas E. Mails. [Hayfield, Minn., Hayfield Pub. Co., 1964, c1962] 168 p. illus. 28 cm. "A one-year communicant course designed for Presbyterian churches." [ICMcC] 66-92472
1. Presbyterian Church—Doctrinal and controversial works. 2. Presbyterian Church—Membership. 3. Church membership—Study and teaching. I. Title.

LEITCH, Addison H. 230.51
A layman's guide to Prebyterian beliefs. by Addison H. Leitch. Added feature: an analysis of the Confession of 1967. [1st ed.] Grand Rapids, Zondervan [1967] 158p. 21cm. [BX9175.2.L4] 66-11617 1.95 pap.,
1. Presbyterian Church —Doctrinal and controversial works. I. Title.

LEITCH, Addison H. 230.51
A layman's guide to Presbyterian beliefs, by Addison H. Leitch. Added feature: an analysis of the Confession of 1967. [1st ed.] Grand Rapids, Zondervan Pub. House [1967] 158 p. 21 cm. [BX9175.2.L4] 67-11617
1. Presbyterian Church—Doctrinal and controversial works. I. Title.

MOSELEY, John Watkins, jr. 230.5
Pan-Presbyterian principles, by Rev. John Watkins Moseley, jr. Grand Rapids, Mich., Wm. B. Eerdmans publishing company [c1935] 103 p. 20 cm. [BX9175.M65] 36-16368
1. Presbyterian church—Doctrinal and controversial works. I. Title.

[NELSON, John] 1738?-1766.
A letter to the Protestant-dissenters in the parish of Bally-kelly, in Ireland; occasioned by their objections against their late minister. In this letter there is an attempt, upon Scriptural and Protestant principles, to show what regard is due to human articles of faith; and also, to explain severalparticulars relative to the doctrines of original sin and election, &c. ... The 2d Salem ed. Belfast, in Ireland: Printed, 1766. Salem, New-England: Reprinted and sold by Samuel and Ebenezer Hall, nearthe exchange, 1772. 111 p. 18 cm. Signed: John Nelson. [BX9174.N4 1772] 9-15643
1. Presbyterian church—Doctrinal and controversial works. I. Title.

PRESBYTERIAN church in the U. S. A. Board of Christian education. 230.51
A manual of faith and life; a guide for individual Christians or communicant classes; authorised by the General assembly. Philadelphia, Presbyterian board of Christian education, 1937. iv p., 2 l., 112 p. 18 cm. Manual interpretive of the Brief statement of the Reformed faith for which Hugh Thomson Kerr war requested to prepare the manuscript by a committee of five, appointed to prepare a communicant's manual. This manuscript has been carefully reviewed by the committee, approved by it and by the Board of Christian education. cf. Foreword. [BX9175.P7] 37-21924
1. Presbyterian church—Doctrinal and controversial works. I. Kerr, Hugh Thomson, 1871- II. Title.

PRESBYTERIAN Church in the U. S. A. Board of Christian Education. 230.51
The way of discipleship; the meaning of membership in the Presbyterian Church. [Philadelphia, c1957] 91p. 19cm. [BX9177.A4] 57-5027
1. Presbyterian Church—Doctrinal and controversial works. I. Title.

†REYMOND, Robert L. 248'.29
"What about continuing revelations and miracles in the Presbyterian Church today?" : A study of the doctrine of the sufficiency of Scripture / by Robert L. Reymond. [Nutley, N.J.] : Presbyterian and Reformed Pub. Co., 1977. 64 p. ; 22 cm. Bibliography: p. 54. [BX9177.R48] 78-104353 pbk. : 1.95
1. Presbyterian Church—Doctrinal and controversial works. 2. Bible—Inspiration. 3. Pentecostalism—Controversial literature. 4. Authority (Religion) I. Title.

SMITH, Egbert Watson, 1862- 238.
The creed of Presbyterians, by Rev. Egbert Watson Smith, D.D. New York, The Baker and Taylor co. [c1901] viii, [9]-223 p. 18 1/2 cm. [BX9183.S55] 1-31923
1. Presbyterian church—Doctrinal and controversial works. I. Title.

SMITH, Egbert Watson, 1862- 238.5
The creed of Presbyterians. Rev. ed. By Rev. Egbert Watson Smith, D.D. Richmond, Va., John Knox press [c1941] 214 p. 18 1/2 cm. On cover: Revised and enlarged edition. [BX9183.S55 1941] 41-22307
1. Presbyterian church—Doctrinal and controversial works. I. Title.

UNITED Presbyterian Church in the U.S.A. Board of Christian Education.
The way of discipleship; the meaning of membership in the United Presbyterian Church. Philadelphia, c1959 91 p. 19 cm. Earlier ed. (1957) published by the board under the earlier name of the church:

Presbyterian Church in the U.S.A. 63-59694
1. Presbyterian Church-Doctrinal and controversial works. 2. Presbyterian Church-Membership. 3. Church membership-Study and teaching. I. Title.

UNITED Presbyterian church of North America.
The confessional statement and The book of government and worship [of] the United Presbyterian church of North America. [Pittsburgh, United Presbyterian board of publication and Bible school work, c1926] 195 p. 16 cm. Title from cover. Each part has special title-page. [BX8986.A3 1926] 26-11760
I. Title.

WARD, William B 230.5
Toward responsible discipleship. Richmond, John Knox Press [c1960] 86 p. 20 cm. [BX9175.2.W3] 61-7078
1. Presbyterian Church — Doctrinal and controversial works. I. Title.

Presbyterian Church—Doctrinal and controversial works—Presbyterian authors.

LEITH, John H. 230'.5133
The church, a believing fellowship / John H. Leith. Atlanta, Ga. : John Knox Press, 1980. p. cm. Bibliography: p. [BX9175.2.L44] 19 80-82192 ISBN 0-8042-0518-3 pbk. : 6.95
1. Presbyterian Church—Doctrinal and controversial works—Presbyterian authors. 2. Church. I. Title.

Presbyterian Church-Education.

LITTLE Eppie,
and other tales. Comp. for the Presbyterian board of publication. Philadelphia, Presbyterian board of publication [1865] 216 p. front., 2 pl. 16 cm. [PZ5.L72] [jUV] 7-16061

MCIVOR, John A. 377'.8'52415
Popular education in the Irish Presbyterian Church [by] John A. McIvor. Dublin, Scepter Books [1969] 166 p. 19 cm. (Legal and technical information) Bibliography: p. 158-162. [LC625.G7M3] 70-259748 ISBN 0-85415-002-1
1. Presbyterian Church—Education. 2. Education—Ireland. I. Title.

UNITED Presbyterian Church in the U.S.A. Commission on Ecumenical Mission and Relations. Office of Education.
Educational instructions overseas; directory. 1963 ed. New York, 1963. 70 p. 28 cm. 65-72907
1. Presbyterian Church-Education. I. Title.

Presbyterian church—Education—United States

PRESBYTERIAN church in the U. S. A. College board. 377.
Our Presbyterian colleges. [Philadelphia] The College board of the Presbyterian church in the U. S. A., 1907. 134 p. illus. (incl. ports., maps) 26 cm. [LC580.P9] E 9
1. Presbyterian church—Education—U. S. 2. Universities and colleges—U. S. I. Title.

PRESBYTERIAN church in the U. S. A. College board. 377.
Presbyterian colleges; the colleges cooperating with the College board of the Presbyterian church in the United States of America. New York, The College board of the Presbyterian church in the U. S. A., 1913. 128 p. illus., ports. 23 cm. [LC580.P9 1913] E 13
1. Presbyterian church—Education—U. S. 2. Universities and colleges—U. S. I. Title.

PRINCETON theological seminary.
A brief account of the rise progress and present state of the Theological seminary of the Presbyterian church in the United States at Princeton; including the constitution of the said seminary; a Catalogue of those who have been members, and a list of the present officers and students. Philadelphia, A. Finley, 1822. 87 p. 20 cm. E 9
I. Title.

Presbyterian Church, Fredericksburg, Va.

ALVEY, Edward. 285'.2'755366
History of the Presbyterian Church of Fredericksburg, Virginia, 1808-1976 / Edward Alvey, Jr. Fredericksburg, Va. : Session of The Presbyterian Church, 1976. xiv, 204 p., [8] leaves of plates : ill. ; 24 cm. Includes bibliographical references and index. [BX9211.F84P733] 76-45001 7.50
1. Presbyterian Church, Fredericksburg, Va. I. Title.

Presbyterian church—Government.

BEATTY, Frank M. 262.4
The office of clerk of session. [Rev. ed.] Richmond, Va., John Knox [c.1956, 1963] 99p. 21cm. 63-13185 1.50 pap.,
1. Presbyterian Church—Government. I. Title. II. Title: Clerk of session.

BEATTY, Frank M 262.4
The office of clerk of session. Richmond, John Knox Press [1956] 78p. 23cm. [BX9195.B4] 56-9342
1. Presbyterian Church—Government. I. Title. II. Title: Clerk of session.

BURNEY, Le Roy P 262.14
Presbyterian elders and deacons serving Christ in the church; a study course for church officers. Richmond, John Knox Press [1954] 59p. 22cm. [BX9195.B84 1954] 262.15 54-3698
1. Presbyterian Church—Government. 2. Church officers. I. Title.

THE divine right of church government: 285. wherein it is proved that the Presbyterian government, by preaching and ruling elders, in sessional, presbyterial and synodical assemblies, may lay the only lawful claim to a divine right according to the Holy Scriptures. A new ed., cor. and amended by sundry ministers of Christ within the city of London. To which is added an appendix containing extracts from some of the best authors who have written on church government ... together with an abstract of the arguments of the great Dr. Owen ... in favor of the divine right of the office of the ruling elder. New York, R. Martin & co., 1844. 276 p. 19 cm. Editor's preface signed: T. H. [BX9190.D5] 22-24308
1. Presbyterian church —Government. I. H. T., ed. II. Editor's preface signed: T. H. T. H. ed.

HAWTHORNE, Joseph M[atthew] 1859-
Proposed constitution for the Presbyterian church, which divides the government of the church universal and synodical into legislative, executive and judicial departments, and which naturally includes provisions for the election of a chief executive for a term of years, etc., etc. With a prefix giving reasons for the proposed constitution. By Joseph M. Hawthorne... St. Paul, Minn., West Saint Paul times press, 1905. xi, 62 p. 22 1/2 cm. 6-3630
I. Title.

HODGE, John Aspinwall, 1831-1901.
What is Presbyterian law as defined by the church courts? By the Rev. J. Aspinwall Hodge, D.D. Philadelphia, Presbyterian board of publication [c1882] 545 p. 18 1/2 cm. "List of authorities": p. 6. [BX9191.H6 1882] 15-3391
1. Presbyterian church—Government. I. Title.

HODGE, John Aspinwall, 1831-1901
What is Presbyterian law as defined by the church courts? With an appendix, containing the decisions of the general assemblies of 1882 and 1883, By the Rev. J. Aspinwall Hodge, D.D. 3d ed. Philadelphia Presbyterian board of publication [c1884] 575 p. 18 1/2 cm. "List of authorities": p. 6. [BX9191.H6 1884] 15-3390
1. Presbyterian church—Government. I. Title.

HODGE, John Aspinwall, 1831-1901.
What is Presbyterian law as defined by the church courts? Containing the decisions of the general assemblies to 1898 inclusive. By the Rev. J. Aspinwall Hodge. D.D. 8th ed. Rev. and enl. Philadelphia, Presbyterian board of publication and Sabbath school work, 1899. 606 p. 19cm. [BX9191.H6 1899] 99-2928
1. Presbyterian church—Government. I. Title.

HOUGH, H D 1922- 285
Churchmanship, a primer for Presbyterian churchmen. Charleroi, Pa., Courier and digest [1955] 105p. illus. 21cm. [BX9190.H66] 56-19292
1. Presbyterian Church—Government. I. Title.

PRESBYTERIAN Church in the U. S. Board of Christian Education. Division of Men's Work. 262
The work of the church--whose responsibility? Church officer's guide and notebook. [Rev.] Richmond, John Knox Press [1956] 88p. illus. col. maps, diagrs. (part col.) 28cm. 'Originally prepared in 1949 by Cameron D. Deans for the Division of Men's Work.' [BX8966.A44 1956] 56-9759
1. Presbyterian Church— Government. 2. Church officers. I. Title.

ROSE, Benjamin Lacy, 1914- 262'.18
Confirming your call in church, home, and vocation, by Ben Lacy Rose. Richmond, John Knox Press [1967] 72 p. 21 cm. [BX9190.R6] 67-12594
1. Presbyterian Church—Government. 2. Christian life—Presbyterian authors. I. Title.

WRIGHT, Paul S. 262'.15
The duties of the ruling elder, by Paul S. Wright. Rev. ed. Philadelphia, Westminster Press [1972] 87 p. 19 cm. [BX9195.W7 1972] 72-181899 ISBN 0-664-24952-3 1.50
1. Presbyterian Church—Government. 2. Elders (Church officers) I. Title.

Presbyterian Church-Handbooks, manuals, etc.

FREEHOLD, N. J. First Presbyterian church. 285 174946
Manual of the First Presbyterian church of Freehold. New Jersey. Containing a history of the church; the constitution and by-laws: the by-laws of the Sunday-school, adopted March 25, 1897 ... a list of members from March 11, 1871, to April 1, 1894 ... No. 3. Prepared and printed by order of the session. Freehold, N. J., Transcript printing house, 1900. 61 p. 1 l., 15-25. [1] p. 18 cm. Preface signed: Hugh B. MacCauley. "The following sheets were taken from the Manual prepared by Rev. Frank Chandler, D. D., and referred to in note at top of page 48": p. [13]-[26] at end. [BX9211.F85F7] 34-14196
I. MacCauley, Hugh B., ed. II. Title.

GLEN Moore, Pa. Fairview Presbyterian church. 285.
Directory and church register ... Fairview Presbyterian church, Glen Moore, Pa. [Glen Moore, 19 v. illus. (incl. port.) 23 cm. Foreword of 1929 issue signed: David Rankin Stewart. [BX9211.G64F3] 38-37378
I. Stewart, David Rankin, 1897- II. Title.

MILLER, James Russell, 1840-
The Presbyterian Christian endeavor manual for 1908, by J. R. Miller and Amos R. Wells ... Philadelphia, The Westminster press, 1907. 109 p. 14 1/2 x 7 1/2 cm. 7-33949
I. Wells, Amos Russel, 1862- joint author. II. Title.

PRESBYTERIAN church in the U. S. A. General assembly.
Manual of law and usage, comp. from the standards and the acts and deliverances of the General assembly of the Presbyterian church in the United States of America, by Benjamin F. Bittinger, D. D. Rev. ed., containing an appendix, 1895-1912., by the Rev. William H. Roberts ... Philadelphia, Presbyterian board of publication and Sabbath-school work, 1913. 286 p. 16 cm. Publisher's lettering: Presbyterian law and usage. 13-17327
I. Bittinger, Benjamin Franklin, 1824- II. Roberts, William Henry, 1844-1920. III. Title.

THE Presbyterian handbook 377. *containing facts respecting the history statistics and work of the Presbyterian church in the U. S. A.* Together with the international Sabbath-school lessons, daily Bible readings, and weekly prayer meeting topics, edited by Rev. Wm. H. Roberts ... Philadelphia, Presbyterian board of publication and Sabbath school work. v. 13 cm. [BX8950.P8] 15-14585
I. Roberts, William Henry, 1844-1920. II. Presbyterian church in the U. S. A. Board of publication.

UNITED Presbyterian Church in the U.S.A. Dept. of Stewardship and Promotion.
Plan book; a handbook for Presbyterians, edited by Marvin C. Wilbur. New York, 1961. 262 p. illus. 23 cm. 63-59699
1. Presbyterian Church-Handbooks, manuals, etc. I. Wilbur, Marvin C., ed. II. Title.

Presbyterian church—History

ASSOCIATE Reformed synod of the South.
The centennial history of the Associate Reformed Presbyterian church. 1803-1903. Prepared and pub. by order of the Synod. Charleston, S.C., Presses of Walker, Evans & Cogswell co., 1905. x, 750 p. incl. front., illus., ports. 23 1/2 cm. 5-11081
I. Title.

BALFOUR, Alexander Hugh Bruce, baron, 1849-1921.
An historical account of the rise and development of Presbyterianism in Scotland, by the Right Hon. Lord Balfour of Burleigh ... Cambridge, Eng., The University press, 1911. vi p., 1 l., 172 p. 17 cm. (Half-title: The Cambridge manuals of science and literature) Title within ornamental border. Books suggested for further study": p. 166-167. A 11
I. Title. II. Title: Presbyterianism in Scotland.

BALFOUR, Alexander Hugh Bruce, baron, 1849-1921.
An historical account of the rise and development of Presbyterianism in Scotland, by the Right Hon. Lord Balfour of Burleigh ... Cambridge, Eng., The University press, 1911. vi p., 1 l., 172 p. 17 cm. (Half-title: The Cambridge manuals of science and literature) Title within ornamental border. Books suggested for further study": p. 166-167. A 11
I. Title. II. Title: Presbyterianism in Scotland.

BRIDGEPORT, Conn. First Presbyterian church. 285.
1853 1903; anniversary services of the first Presbyterian church Bridgeport, Connecticut, October 25th-November 1st. [Bridgeport? 1903?] cover title, 2 p. l., 158 p. plates, ports. 26 cm. [BX9211.B76F5 1903] 23-4504
I. Title.

CRAIGHEAD, James Geddes, 1823-1895.
Scotch and Irish seeds in American soil: the early history of the Scotch and Irish churches, and their relations to the Presbyterian church of America. By the Rev. J. G. Craighead, D. D. Philadelphia, Presbyterian board of publication [c1878] 348 p. 18 cm. [BX8936.C8] 10-13345
1. Presbyterian church—Hist. 2. Presbyterian church in the U. S. A. 3. Presbyterian church in the U. S. I. Title.

DAVIES, Alfred Mervyn 285
Presbyterian heritage. Richmond, Va., Knox [c.1965] 141p. 21cm. [BX8931.2.D3] 65-10136 1.95 pap.,
1. Presbyterian Church—Hist. I. Title.

DI STASI, Anthony, 1893-1964.
The miracle of Trinity: a concise history of the Trinity Presbyterian Church. [n.p. 1964] 90 p. illus. 21 cm. 65-112328
1. Title.

HANZSCHE, William Thomson, 1891- 285
The Presbyterians; the story of a stanch and sturdy people, by Wm. Thomson Hanzsche ... Philadelphia, The Westminister press, 1934. 194 p. front. 19

1/2 cm. Bibliography: p. 192-194. [BX8931.H34] 34-39734
1. Presbyterian church—Hist. 2. Presbyterian church in the U.S. (General) I. Title.

HARDEN, Margaret G comp.
A brief history of the Bible Presbyterian Church and its agencies. [Collingswood (N.J.), Christian Beacon Press, 1967] 157 p. 68-95558
I. Title.

HENDERSON, George David, 1888- 285.09
Presbyterianism. Aberdeen, University Press [1955] 179p. 23cm. (Chalmers lectures) [BX8931.H4] 55-4298
1. Presbyterian Church—Hist. 2. Presbyterianism. I. Title.

JESSUP, Henry Wynans.
History of the Fifth avenue Presbyterian church of New York city, New York, from 1808 to 1908, together with an account of its centennial anniversary celebration, December 18-23, 1908; prepared by Henry W. Jessup ... under direction of the Centennial committee. [New York] 1909. 283 p. front., plates, ports., fold. tab. 25 cm. 9-10257
I. New York. Fifth avenue Presbyterian church. Centennial committee. II. Title.

KUGLER, John Backer.
The history of the First English Presbyterian church in Amwell, by John Backer Kugler ... Somerville, N. J., The Unionist-gazette association, 1912. x, 354 p. front. (port.) plates. 19 cm. 13-5682
I. Title.

LINGLE, Walter Lee, 1868-1956. 285
Presbyterians, their history and beliefs / by Walter L. Lingle and John W. Kuykendall. [4th rev. ed.]. Atlanta : John Knox Press, c1978. 110 p. : port. ; 21 cm. Includes index. [BX8931.2.L56 1978] 77-15750 ISBN 0-8042-0985-5 pbk. : 3.50
1. Presbyterian Church—History. 2. Presbyterianism. I. Kuykendall, John W., joint author. II. Title.

LOETSCHER, Lefferts Augustine, 1904- 285.09
A brief history of the Presbyterians. Rev. and enl. Philadelphia, Westminster Press [1958] 125p. 20cm. [BX8932.L6 1958] 58-5963
1. Presbyterian Church— Hist. I. Title.

LOETSCHER, Lefferts Augustine, 1904- 285
A brief history of the Presbyterians / Lefferts A. Loetscher. 3d ed. Philadelphia : Westminister Press, c1978. 205 p. ; 19 cm. Includes index. Bibliography: p. [197]-199. [BX8931.2.L64 1978] 78-1724 ISBN 0-664-24197-2 pbk. : 3.95
1. Presbyterian Church—History. I. Title.

MONTGOMERY, Ala. First Presbyterian church.
History and directory of the First Presbyterian church ... Montgomery, Alabama ... 1824-1914. [Montgomery? Ala.] Pub. by order of the Session, 1914. 76 p. incl. front., illus., ports. 22 cm. 15-590
I. Title.

MONTGOMERY, Ala. First Presbyterian church.
History and directory of the First Presbyterian church ... Montgomery, Alabama ... 1824-1914. [Montgomery? Ala.] Pub. by order of the Session, 1914. 76 p. incl. front., illus., ports. 22 cm. 15-590
I. Title.

MOORE, Robert Braden, 1835-1906. 266.
History of Huron presbytery, showing the working of the plan of union from its inception in 1801 till after the reunion in 1870; also the spirit of the presbytery regarding religious, general, and national interests; with biographical notice of some ministers, and sketches of the churches. Comp. and written by Rev. R. Braden Moore, D. D. Philadelphia, Press of W. F. Fell & co., 1892. ix, 486 p. 23 cm. [BX8958.H85M6] 22-22544
I. Title. II. Title: Huron presbytery, History of.

MOORE, Robert Braden, 1835-1906. 266.
History of Huron presbytery, showing the working of the plan of union from its inception in 1801 till after the reunion in 1870; also the spirit of the presbytery regarding religious, general, and national interests; with biographical notice of some ministers, and sketches of the churches. Comp. and written by Rev. R. Braden Moore, D. D. Philadelphia, Press of W. F. Fell & co., 1892. ix, 486 p. 23 cm. [BX8958.H85M6] 22-22544
I. Title. II. Title: Huron presbytery, History of.

PATTON, Jacob Harris, 1812-1903. 285.
A popular history of the Presbyterian church in the United States of America, by Jacob Harris Patton ... New York, D. Appleton and company, 1903. xxiii, 570 p. 20 port. incl. front. 25 cm. ... Authorities ... consulted": p. [vii] [BX8935.P3 1903] 3-27908
1. Presbyterian church—Hist. 2. Presbyterian church in the U. S. A.—Hist. I. Title.

[PLUMLEY, Gardiner Spring] 1827-1894 ed. 285
The Presbyterian church throughout the world: from the earliest to the present times, in a series of biographical and historical sketches. New York, D. W. C. Lent & company, 1875. 1 p. l., [vii]-xiii, 792 p. incl. illus., plates, facsims. front., ports. 23 1/2cm. Sketches drawn from various sources. "Authorities consulted in the preparation of this work": p. xiii. [BX8931.P6 1875] 37-25874
1. Presbyterian church—Hist. I. Title.

REED, Richard Clark, 1851- 285
History of the Presbyterian churches of the world, adapted for use in the class room, by R. C. Reed ... Philadelphia, The Westminster press, 1905. iii, 403 p. 20 1/2 cm. [BX8931.R4] 5-16622
1. Presbyterian church—Hist. I. Title.

ROBINSON, Charles Mulford, 1869-
First church chronicles, 1815-1915; centennial history of the First Presbyterian church, Rochester, New York, by Charles Mulford Robinson. Rochester, The Craftsman press, 1915. 206 p. front., plates, port. 20 cm. 15-9001
I. Title.

WARNER, Sydney Yantis.
History of the First Presbyterian Church, 1846-1960, including Fort Smith and the early churches, by Sydney Yantis Warner [and] Virginia Louise Foster. [n.p., 1960] 167 p. illus. 24 cm.
I. Title.

WOOD, James Edward.
Bound in the Spirit... A history of the First Presbyterian church of Morrisville, Pa. Compiled and ed. by James E. Wood, Clifford G. Pollock [and] Donald R. Zobler. In commemoration of the 100th anniversary of the Church. [Morrisville, Pa., First Presbyterian church, 1959] 77 p. illus., ports. 24 cm.
I. Pollock, Clifford Given, 1912- II. Title.

Presbyterian Church—Hymns.

THE army hymn-book.
2d ed. Richmond, Va., Presbyterian committee of publication, 1864. 128 p. 11 1/2 cm. [BV463.A7 1864] 15-10794
1. Presbyterian church—Hymns. 2. Hymns, English. I. Presbyterian church in the U.S. Executive committee of publication.

[HATFIELD, Edwin Francis] 1807-1883, comp.
The chapel hymn book, with tunes, for the worship of God... New York and Chicago, Ivison, Blakeman, Taylor & company, 1873. 292 p. 20 cm. Preface signed: Edwin F. Hatfield. "Abridged edition of the Church hymn book." [M2130.H38C5 1873 a] 45-46623
1. Presbyterian church—Hymns. 2. Hymns, English. I. Title.

[HATFIELD, Edwin Francis] 1807-1883, comp.
The church hymn book, with tunes, for the worship of God... New York and Chicago, Ivison, Blakeman, Taylor & company, 1873. 585, [1] p. 22 cm. Preface signed: Edwin F. Hatfield. With this is bound, as issued: Bible. O.T. Psalms. English. 1873. The Psalter: or, The book of Psalms ... New-York, 1873. [M2130.H38C5 1873] 45-46622
1. Presbyterian church—Hymns. 2. Hymns, English. I. Title.

[HATFIELD, Edwin Francis] 1807-1883, comp.
The church hymn book, with tunes, for the worship of God... New York and Chicago, Ivison, Blakeman, Taylor and company, 1874. 584, [1] p. 22 cm. Preface signed: Edwin F. Hatfield. [M2130.H38C5 1874] 45-47256
1. Presbyterian church—Hymns. 2. Hymns, English. I. Title.

NEW York. Brick Presbyterian church.
The sacrifice of praise, with tunes. Psalms, hymns, and spiritual songs designed for public worship and private devotion. With notes on the origin of hymns ... New York. A. D. F. Randolph & co. [1872] ixxi p., 1 l., 525 p. 20 cm. "Made by a committee of the session of the Brick Presbyterian church in the city of New York."--p. ix. [M2130.N57S3] 45-46647
1. Presbyterian church—Hymns. 2. Hymns, English. I. Title.

PHILADELPHIA. Woodland Presbyterian church.
The church-book of the Woodland Presbyterian church, Philadelphia. Containing the customary order of public worship and of the ministration of the sacraments, together with a hymnal. New York, D. Appleton & co., 1884. 11, [3]-4, xxiv, [5]-437 p. 19 1/2 cm. With music. [M2130.P5C5] 45-46649
1. Presbyterian church—Hymns. 2. Hymns, English. I. Title.

PRESBYTERIAN church in the U.S.A.
The chapel hymnal. Philadelphia, The Westminster press, 1898. xvii, [239] p. 21 1/2 cm. Edited by L. F. Benson. cf. p. iii. With this is bound, as issued: Bible. O.T. Psalms. English. Selections. 1898. Selections from the Psalter ... arranged by the Rev. Elijah R. Craven ... and the Rev. Louis F. Benson ... Philadelpha, 1898. [M2130.P7C5 1898] 45-46809
1. Presbyterian church—Hymns. 2. Hymns, English. I. Benson, Louis FitzGerald, 1855-1930, ed. II. Title.

PRESBYTERIAN church in the U.S.A. 245.
The hymnal, published by authority of the General assembly of the Presbyterian church in the United States of America. Philadelphia, The Presbyterian board of publication and Sabbath-school work, 1896. xxxv, 660 p. 18 1/2 cm. Edited by Rev. Louis F. Benson. of. p. iii. Without music. --Selections from the Psalter, for use in the services of the churches; arranged by the Rev. Elijah R. Craven ... and the Rev. Louis F. Benson. Philadelphia, The Presbyterian board of publication and Sabbath-school work, 1896. 109 p. 18 1/2 cm. With the main work, as issued. [BV430.A3 1896] 45-49062
1. Presbyterian church—Hymns. 2. Hymns, English. I. Benson, Louis FitzGerald, 1855-1930, ed. II. Craven, Elijah Richardson, 1824-1908, arr. III. Bible. O.T. Psalms. English. Selections. 1896. Authorized. IV. Title.

PRESBYTERIAN church in the U.S.A. 245.
The Presbyterian hymnal. Philadelphia, Presbyterian board of publication [c1878] 719, 72 p. 19 cm. "Compiled and edited by the Rev. Joseph T. Duryea." Without music. "The forms of government and forms of process of the Presbyterian church in the United States of America": p. 1-61 at end. [BV430.A3 1878] 45-47074
1. Presbyterian church—Hymns. 2. Hymns, English. I. Duryea, Joseph Tuthill, 1832-1898, ed. II. Title.

PRESBYTERIAN church in the U. S. A. Hymnal. 245.
The hymnal, published in 1895 and revised in 1911, by authority of the General assembly of the Presbyterian church in the United States of America. Philadelphia, The Presbyterian board of publication and Sabbath-school work, 1912. xxiv, 657 p. 19 cm. Cover-title: The humnal, revised; word edition. Edited by Rev. Louis F. Benson. cf. p. [ii] Without music. [BV430.A3 1912] 12-26370
1. Presbyterian church—Hymns. 2. Hymns, English. I. Presbsyterian church in the U. S. A. General assembly. II. Benson, Louis Fitzgerald, 1855-1980, ed. III. Presbyterian church in the U. S. A. Board of publication. IV. Title.

PRESBYTERIAN church in the U. S. A. 245.
Psalms and hymns adapted to public worship, and approved by the General assembly of the Presbyterian church in the United States of America. Philadelphia, Presbyterian board of publication [1830?] 596 p. 14 cm. [BV430.A3 1830] 20-13259
1. Presbyterian church—Hymns. I. Bible. O. T. Psalms. English. Paraphrases. 1830? II. Bible. English., Paraphrases. O. T. Psalms. 1830? III. Title.

PRESBYTERIAN church in the U. S. A. 245.2051
Psalms and hymns adapted to public worship, and approved by the General assembly of the Presbyterian church in the United States of America. Philadelphia, Pub. for the General assembly, by S. Allen, 1831. 669 p. 18 cm. [BV430.A3 1831] 35-33482
1. Presbyterian church—Hymns. 2. Hymns, English. I. Bible. O. T. Psalms. English. Paraphrases. 1831. II. Bible. English. Paraphrases. O. T. Psalms. 1831. III. Title.

PRESBYTERIAN church in the U. S. A. (Old school) Hymnal. 245.2051
Psalms and hymns adapted to social, private, and public worship in the Presbyterian church in the United States of America. Approved and authorized by the General assembly ... Philadelphia, Presbyterian board of publication [1843] 254, 36, [5]-481 p. 82 p. 14 cm. Without music. "Selections from the book of Paslms, in metre, according to the version used in the Church of Scotland" (36 p.) has special t.-p. and separate paging. "Form of government of the Presbyterian church, Directory for worship, Shorter catechism" [etc.]: 82 p. at end. [BV430.A3 1843 c] 40-1667
1. Presbyterian church—Hymns. 2. Hymns, English. I. Bible. O. T. Psalms. English. Paraphrases. 1843. II. Presbyterian church in the U. S. A. (Old school) General assembly. III. Presbyterian in the U. S. A. (Old school) Board of publication. IV. Bible. English. Paraphrases. O. T. Psalms. 1843. V. Title.

PRESBYTERIAN church in the U. S. A. Old school Hymnal. 285
Psalms and hymns adapted to social, private, and public worship in the Presbyterian church in the United States of America. Approved and authorized by the General assembly ... With a new index of subjects. Philadelphia, Presbyterian board of publication [c1860] 784, 776-864 p. 14 cm. Without music. First published 1843. "Forms of government of the Presbyterian church, Directory for the worship of God, The Shorter catechism [etc.]": p. 776-864. [BV430.A3 1860] 41-36245
1. Presbyterian church—Hymns. 2. Hymns. English. I. Bible. O. T. Psalms. English. Paraphrases. 1860. II. Presbyterian church in the U. S. A. (Old school) General assembly. III. Presbyterian church in the U. S. A. (Old school) Board of publication. IV. Bible. English. Paraphrases, O. T. Psalms. 1860. V. Title.

SOCIAL hymn and tune book;
for the lecture room, prayer meeting, family circle, and mission church. Philadelphia, Presbyterian publication committee; New York, A. D. F. Randolph [c1865] 510 p. 17 1/2 cm. "Hymns are mainly drawn from the 'Church psalmist'."--Pref. [M2130.S65 1865] 45-44988
1. Presbyterian church—Hymns. 2. Hymns, English.

SOCIAL hymn book, 245.
being the hymns of the Social hymn and tune book. For the lecture room, prayer meeting, family, and congregation. Philadelphia, Presbyterian publication committee; New York, A. D. F. Randolph

[1866] 395 p. 15 1/2 cm. Without music. [BV430.S6] 45-47075
1. Presbyterian church—Hymns. 2. Hymns, English. I. Social hymn and tune book.

SPRING, Gardiner, 1785-1873, comp.
The Brick church hymns, designed for the use of social prayer meetings and families, selected from the most approved authors and recommended by Gardner Spring, D.D., pastor of said church. New York, H. C. Sleight, printer, 1823. 170, [9] p. 14 cm. 15-3396
I. New York. Brick Presbyterian church. II. Title.

SYNOD of the Reformed 783.9
Presbyterian Church of North America.
The Book of Psalms ; rendered in metre and set to music Authoried by the Synod of the Reformed Presbyterian Church of North America. Chicago, 1950. vii, 359 p. 22 cm. [M2130.S9B6 1950] 51-38302
1. Presbyterian Church — Hymns. 2. Hymns, English. 3. Psalms (Music) I. Title.

SYNOD of the Reformed
Presbyterian Church of North Amrica.
The book of Psalms, rendered in metre and set to music, authorized by the Synod of the Reformed Presbyterian Church of North America. Philadelphia, 1929. vii, 376 p. 22 cm. [M2130.S9B6 1929] 51-54401
1. Presbyterian Church—Hymns. 2. Hymns, English. 3. Psalms (Music) I. Title.

Presbyterian Church in Arizona.

SMITH, Richard Knox. 285'.1791
Datelines and by-lines; a sketchbook of Presbyterian beginnings and growth in Arizona. Line drawings by Caroline Lansing. [Phoenix, Synod of Arizona, United Presbyterian Church in the U.S.A., 1969] 90 p. illus., ports. 23 cm. Prepared on the occasion of the centennial year of the Presbyterian Church in Arizona. Contents.Contents.—Dateline: Arizona Territory, by R. K. Smith.—By-lines: a synod grows, by J. M. Nelson. Includes bibliographical references. [BX8947.A7S6] 78-259829
1. Presbyterian Church in Arizona. I. Nelson, James Melvin. II. United Presbyterian Church in the U.S.A. Synods. Arizona. III. Title.

Presbyterian church in Baltimore.

BALTIMORE. First Presbyterian church.
A brief history of the First Presbyterian church of Baltimore, comp. under direction of its session and committee for publication on its one hundred and fiftieth anniversary, by William Reynolds ... Baltimore [Printed by Williams & Wilkins company] 1913. vii, 124 p. 4 pl. (incl. front.) 21 cm. 13-2618
I. Reynolds, William, comp. II. Title.

BOULDEN, James E. P. 285.
The Presbyterians of Baltimore; their churches and historic grave-yards. By J. E. P. Boulden ... Baltimore, W. J. Boyle & son, 1875. 134 p. illus. 23 1/2 cm. [BX8949.B2B7] 43-29662
1. Presbyterian church in Baltimore. 2. Baltimore—Churches, Presbyterian. I. Title.

SMITH, Joseph Tate, 1819?- 285.
1906.
Eighty years; embracing a history of Presbyterianism in Baltimore; with an appendix. By Joseph T. Smith ... Philadelphia, Pa., The Westminster press, 1899. x, 279 p. front. (port.) 19 cm. [BX8949.B2S6] 99-5000
1. Presbyterian church in Baltimore. 2. Baltimore—Churches, Presbyterian. I. Title.

Presbyterian church in California.

WICHER, Edward Arthur, 1872- 285.
The Presbyterian church in California, 1849-1927 [by] Edward Arthur Wicher ... New York, F. H. Hitchcock, 1927. xi p., 1 l., 360 p. front., plates, ports. 21 cm. [BX8947.C2W5] 28-8087
1. Presbyterian church in California. I. Title.

WILLEY, Samuel H[opkins]
The history of the first pastorate of the Howard Presbyterian church. San Francisco, California. 1850-1862... San Francisco, The Whitaker & Ray co., 1900. 171 pp. 12°. Dec
I. Title.

WOODS, James L., 1846-1918. 285.
California pioneer decade of 1849; the Presbyterian church with some mention of other churches, and incidental reference to current events and civil affairs of early and later date. An historical contribution; supplemental to the Synod's official history by Rev. James S. McDonald ... Including recollections of pioneer work in California, by James Woods ... Combined with annals and memories of pioneer times by James L. Woods ... By James L. Woods ... San Francisco, Calif., Press of the Hansen co., c1922. 5 p. l., 181, [3] p. 23 cm. "Authorities consulted": p. 176-178. [BX8947.C2W7] 22-16463
1. Presbyterian church in California. I. Woods, James, 1814 or 15-1886, joint author. II. Title.

Presbyterian Church in Canada.

BAILEY, Thomas Melville, 285'.271
1912-
The covenant in Canada / by T. M. Bailey. Hamilton, Ont. : Macnab, 1975. 160 p. : ill. ; 19 x 24 cm. Cover title. [BX9001.B34] 76-357174 ISBN 0-919874-02-9
1. Presbyterian Church in Canada. 2. Presbyterian Church in Canada—Biography. I. Title.

Presbyterian Church in Canada—History.

MOIR, John S. 285'.271
Enduring witness : a history of the Presbyterian Church in Canada / by John S. Moir. Hamilton, Ont. : Presbyterian Church in Canada, [1974?] xiii, 311 p., [16] leaves of plates : ill. ; 24 cm. Includes bibliographical references and index. [BX9002.C2M64] 75-312621
1. Presbyterian Church in Canada—History. I. Title.

Presbyterian church in Canada—Missions.

[MACGREGOR, Mary Esther (Miller) Mrs.] 1876-
The black bearded barbarian; the life of George Leslie Mackay of Formosa, by Marian Keith [pseud.] New York, Missionary education movement of the United States and Canada, 1912. x, 307 p. incl. front. plates, ports., fold. map. 19 1/2 cm. [BV3450.F7M3] 12-16914
1. Mackay, George Leslie, 1844-1901. 2. Missions—Formosa. 3. Presbyterian church in Canada—Missions. I. Title.

Presbyterian Church in Canada. Presbyteries. Hamilton, Ont.

PRESBYTERIAN Church 285'.09713'52
in Canada. Presbyteries. Hamilton, Ont.
The Presbytery of Hamilton, 1836-1967. Hamilton, Ont., 1967. 148 p. illus., map, plates, ports. 28 cm. Cover title. [BX9003.H3P7] 71-460079 1.00
1. Presbyterian Church in Canada. Presbyteries. Hamilton, Ont. I. Title.

Presbyterian church in Cleveland.

LUDLOW, Arthur Clyde, 1861- 285.
1927.
History of Cleveland Presbyterianism with directory of all the churches By Rev. and Mrs. Arthur Clyde Ludlow. Cleveland, O., W. M. Bayne printing co., 1896. 5 p. l., [9] -280 p. illus. (incl. ports.) 23 cm. [BX8949.C6L8] 21-13273
1. Presbyterian church in Cleveland. I. Ludlow, Rosa Elizabeth (Roeder) "Mrs. Arthur Clyde", d. 1918, joint author. II. Title.

Presbyterian Church in Colorado.

MURRAY, Andrew E. 282'.1788
The skyline synod; Presbyterianism in Colorado and Utah [by] Andrew E. Murrav [sic] Denver, Golden Bell Press [1971] 151 p. illus. 23 cm. (Presbyterian Historical Society. Publications, v. 10) Bibliography: p. 129-133. [BX8947.C6M87] 72-180975 2.95
1. Presbyterian Church in Colorado. 2. Presbyterian Church in Utah. 3. United Presbyterian Church in the U.S.A. Synods. Colorado-Utah. I. Title. II. Series.

Presbyterian church in Dubuque, Ia.

RUSTON, William O.
The presbytery of Dubuque. A history. By Rev. W. O. Ruston... [Dubuque] Pub. by the presbytery, 1889. 58 p. incl. tables. 23 cm. A 11
1. Presbyterian church in Dubuque, Ia. I. Title.

RUSTON, William Otis, 1852-
The presbytery of Dubuque. A history. By Rev. W. O. Ruston ... [Dubuque] Pub. by the presbytery, 1889. 58 p. incl. tables. 23 cm. A 11
1. Presbyterian church in Dubuque, Ia. I. Title.

Presbyterian church in England.

THE English 285'.242
Presbyterians, from Elizabeth Puritanism to modern Unitarianism, by C. Gordon Bolam [and others] Boston, Beacon Press [1968] 297 p. 23 cm. Bibliographical footnotes. [BX9055.E5 1968b] 67-22137 10.00
1. Presbyterian Church in England. I. Bolam, Charles Gordon.

GRIFFITHS, Olive M. 285.2
Religion and learning; a study in English Presbyterian thought from the Bartholomew ejections (1662) to the foundation of the Unitarian movement, by Olive M. Griffiths. Cambridge [Eng.] The University press, 1935. viii, 202 p., 1 l. 22 cm. Bibliography: p. 189-197. [BX9056.G7] 36-13141
1. Presbyterian church in England. 2. Unitarian churches in England. 3. Religious thought—Gt. Brit. I. Title.

Presbyterian church in Georgia.

CARTLEDGE, Groves 285.175811
Harrison, 1820-1899.
Historical sketches; Presbyterian Churches and early settlers in northeast Georgia. Compiled by Jessie Julia Mize and Virginia Louise Newton. Athens, Ga., 1960. 208p. illus. 24cm. [BX8947.G4C3] 60-15929
1. Presbyterian Church in Georgia. 2. Madison Co., Ga.—Hist. 3. Cartledge family. I. Mize, Jessie Julia, 1910- II. Title. III. Title: Presbyterian Churches and early settlers in northeast Georgia.

PRESBYTERIAN Church in the U.S. Synods. Georgia.
Minutes of . . . annual sessions. Milledgeville. v. 23 cm. [BX8967.G4A3] 50-45674
I. Title.

STACY, James, 1830-1912. 285.
A history of the Presbyterian church in Georgia, by Rev. James Stacy ... [Elberton, Ga., Press of the Star, 1912] 4 p. l., 404 p. plates, 2 port. (incl. front.) 19 1/2 cm. Completed and edited, after the author's death, by C. I. Stacy. cf. "Editor's explanation." [BX8947.G4S8] 18-10694
1. Presbyterian church in Georgia. I. Stacy, Carlton Ingersoll, 1866- II. Title.

Presbyterian Church in Ghana.

SMITH, Noel. 285'.2'09667
The Presbyterian Church of Ghana, 1835-1960: a younger Church in a changing society; maps by Brian Watson. Accra, Ghana Universities P.; London, Oxford U. P., 1966. [8], 304 p. 4 plates (incl. ports.), 9 maps, tables, 22 1/2 cm. 45/- (B 67-14562) Maps on endpapers. Bibliography: p. 281-285. [BX9162.G5S6] 68-100261
1. Presbyterian Church in Ghana. I. Title.

Presbyterian church in Illinois—History

CHICAGO Heights, Ill. 285.1773
First Presbyterian church.
A Christian century, 1843-1943, a history of the First Presbyterian church, Chicago Heights, Illinois. Rev. Clarence E. Showalter, TH. D., minister ... [Chicago Heights? Williams press, 1943] 51, [1] p. illus. (incl. ports.) 25 1/2 cm. [BX9211.C42F5] 44-11814
I. Showalter, Clarence Ernest, 1900-. II. Title.

JERSEYVILLE, Ill. Presbyterian church.
... Seventy-fifth anniversary of the organization of the Presbyterian church; twenty-fifth anniversary of the dedication of the present building, anniversary celebration, Feb. 14-16, 1909, Jerseyville, Illinois. [Jerseyville, Ill.] Perrin & Smith printing co. [1909?] 77 p. front., plates. 25 cm. At head of title: 1834-1909. 11-29689
I. Title.

NORTON, Augustus Theodore, 1808-12884.
History of the Presbyterian church, in the state of Illinois. By A. T. Norton. vol. i. St. Louis, W. S. Bryan, publisher, for the author, 1879. xiii, 735 p. front., ports. 23 cm. No more published. "The Rev. Aratus Kent of Galena. Contributed by Rev. D. W. Evans, of Litchfield, Illinois": p. [709]-726. [BX8974.I 3N7] 3-4877
1. Presbyterian church in Illinois—Hist. I. Evans, David Williams, 1838- II. Title.

Presbyterian Church in Indiana.

INDIANAPOLIS. Second 285.177252
Presbyterian church.
The Second Presbyterian church of Indianapolis. One hundred years, 1838-1938. Indianapolis, Ind., The Second Presbyterian church, 1939. xiii p., 1 l., 302 p. front., plates, ports. 25 cm. "Arthur C. Moore, chairman of the committee appointed to prepare this book."--Foreword. Bibilography: p. 301-302. [BX9211.I 5S4] 40-8929
I. Moore, Arthur C. II. Title.

RUDOLPH, L. 285.1772
Hoosier Zion; the Presbyterians in early Indiana. New Haven, Yale University Press, 1963. 218 p. illus. 23 cm. (Yale publications in religion) Presbyterian Historical Society publications, 4. [BX8947.I6R8] 62-8261
1. Presbyterian Church in Indiana. I. Title.

Presbyterian church in Ireland—History.

BECKETT, James 280'.4'09415
Camlin, 1912-
Protestant dissent in Ireland, 1687-1780 / by J. C. Beckett. Westport, Conn. : Hyperion Press, [1979] p. cm. Reprint of the 1948 ed. published by Faber and Faber, London, which was issued as no. 2 of Studies in Irish history. Includes index. Bibliography: p. [BX5203.7.B4 1979] 78-20448 ISBN 0-88355-828-9 : 16.00
1. Presbyterian church in Ireland—History. 2. Dissenters, Religious—Ireland. 3. Ireland—Church history. I. Title. II. Series: Studies in Irish history ; no. 2.

Presbyterian church in Kentucky.

DAVIDSON, Robert, 1808- 285.09769
1876.
History of the Presbyterian church in the state of Kentucky; with a preliminary sketch of the churches in the valley of Virginia. By the Rev. Robert Davidson ... New York, Pittsburgh, R. Carter; [etc., etc.] 1847. xii, [13]-371 p. 24 cm. [BX8947.K4D3] 33-25267
1. Presbyterian church in Kentucky. 2. Presbyterian church in Virginia. I. Title.

A Presbyterian celebration:
the 175th anniversary, First Presbyterian Church, Lexington, Kentucky, 1784-1959. [Lexington, Ky., 1959] 64p. illus. 20cm.
I. Lexington, Ky. First Presbyterian Church.

Presbyterian Church in Louisiana.

ST. Amant, Penrose, 1915- 285.1763

A history of the Presbyterian Church in Louisiana. [New Orleans] Synod of Louisiana [1961] 303p. illus. 22cm. Includes bibliography. [BX8947.L8S23] 60-16815
1. Presbyterian Church in Louisiana. 2. Presbyterian Church in the U. S. Synods. Louisiana. I. Title.

VOSS, Louis, 1856- comp. 285.1763
Presbyterianism in New Orleans and adjacent points; Its semi-centennial held in 1873; seventy-fifth anniversary of the organization of New Orleans presbytery, 1930. Sketches of individual churches, ministers and ruling elders. Compiled by Rev. Louis Voss ... [New Orleans!] The Presbyterian board of publications of the Synod of Louisiana, 1931. 416 p. incl. front., illus. (incl. ports.) 23 cm. With this is bound the author's History of the First street Presbyterian church. [New Orleans!] 1929. [BX8947.L8V6] 35-35431
1. Presbyterian church in Louisiana. 2. Presbyterian church in Louisiana—Clergy. I. Title.

VOSS, Louis, 1856-1936. 285.1763
The beginnings of Presbyterianism in the Southwest, by Louis Voss ... New Orleans, La., Presbyterian board of publications of the Synod of Louisiana, 1923. 50 p. 28 cm. [BX8947.L8V57] 40-704
1. Presbyterian church in Louisiana. 2. Southern states—Church history. I. Title.

Presbyterian church in Maryland.

SIMPSON, John Francis 285.17527
Minor.
Monocacy valley, Maryland, Presbyterianism; a history of the Frederick, Emmitsburg, Piney Creek, Taneytown and New Windsor Presbyterian congregations, by Rev. J. F. Minor Simpson. Frederick, Md. [The Great southern ptg. & mfg. co., c1936] 4 p. l., 3-58 p. illus. (incl. ports.) 23 cm. [BX8947.M3S55] 36-13849
1. Presbyterian church in Maryland. 2. Presbyterians in Maryland. I. Title.

Presbyterian Church in Michigan.

COMIN, John, 1869-1947. 285.1774
History of the Presbyterian Church in Michigan, by John Comin and Harold F. Fredsell. Ann Arbor, Ann Arbor Press, 1950. x, 215 p. ports. 24 cm. "Summer camp edition."--Dust jacket. Bibliography: p. 198-202. [BX8947.M5C6] 51-5324
1. Presbyterian Church in Michigan. I. Fredsell, Harold F. II. Title.

COMIN, John, 1869-1947.
History of the Presbyterian Church in Michigan, by John Comin and Harold F. Fredsell, [2d ed.] Ann Arbor, Mich., Ann Arbor Press, 1950 [i.e. 1961] 215 p. port. Includes bibliography. 63-4508
1. Presbyterian Church in Michigan. I. Fredsell, Harold F. II. Title.

DEARBORN, Mich. First 975
Presbyterian church.
Records of the Presbyterian church in Dearbornville, M. T. [Dearborn, 194-?] 1 p. l., 3-131 numb. l. 28 cm. Type-written (carbon copy) [BX9211.D3F5] 43-19223
I. Title.

DETROIT. Fort street 285.177434
Presbyterian church.
Records of the services connected with the twenty-fifth anniversary of the organization of the Fort street Presbyterian church, Detroit, Mich. Compiled under direction of the Session. Detroit, O. S. Gulley's steam printing house, 1874. 126 p. 23 cm. [BX9211.D4F6] 33-24791
I. Title.

GROSSE, Pointe, Mich. 285.177433
Grosse Pointe Memorial Church. 1965 Centennial Committee.
The Grosse Pointe Memorial Church (the United Presbyterian Church in the U.S.A.) history 1865-1965. [Grosse Pointe? Mich., 1965] ix, 110 p. illus., facsims., maps (on lining papers) 26 cm. [BX9211.G87G7] 65-26426
I. Title.

Presbyterian church in Montana.

EDWARDS, George, 1855- 285.1786
ed.
The pioneer work of the Presbyterian church in Montana, edited by Rev. George Edwards ... Helena, Mont., "Independent publishing company" [1907] 213 p. illus. (incl. ports., facsims.) 24 cm. "Reprinted from volume vi. of the Montana state historical society." [BX8947.M7E3] 33-33641
1. Presbyterian church in Montana. 2. Presbyterian church in the U.S.A.—Missions. I. Title.

Presbyterian church in Nebraska—Education.

WEYER, Frank Elmer, 377.85782
1890-
Presbyterian colleges and academies in Nebraska, by Frank E. Weyer ... Hastings, Neb. [Printed by Democrat printing co.] 1940. 2 p. l., [vii]-xi, 242 p. 23 1/2 cm. Bibliography: p. [185]-198. [LA322.W4] 41-1488
1. Presbyterian church in Nebraska—Education. 2. Education, Higher. 3. Education—Nebraska. 4. Hastings college, Hastings, Neb. I. Title.

Presbyterian church in New York.

ALEXANDER, Samuel Davies.
The presbytery of New York 1738 to 1888... New York, A. D. F. Randolph and company [1887] [iii]-viii, 198 p. 8°. 1-5121
I. Title.

ONEIDA, N. Y. Presbyterian 285.
church.
...The semi-centennial of the Presbyterian church of Oneida, N. Y., June 13, 1894. Published by the church. [Rahway, N. J., The Mershon company press, c1894] 88 p. front., plates, ports. 19 cm. At head of title: 1844-1894. [BX9211.O6A5 1894] 30-34015
I. Title.

PRESBYTERIAN church in the 266.
U. S. A. Presbytery of Westchester.
The Presbyterian church within the field of the Presbytery of Westchester, synod of New York. 1660-1889. By William J. Cumming ... Hartford, Conn., Press of the Case, Lockwood & Brainard company, 1889. ix, 229 p. 23 cm. [BX8958.W4A5] 26-22928
1. Presbyterian church in New York. I. Cumming, William James, 1847- II. Title.

TROY, N.Y. First 285.
Presbyterian church.
Proceedings of the centennial anniversary of the First Presbyterian church, Troy, N.Y., December 30 and 31, 1891. Troy, N.Y., Troy times printing house, 1892. 136 p. 5 pl., 7 port. 23 cm. [BX9211.T7F4] 24-2830
I. Title.

Presbyterian church in North Carolina—Clergy.

MCELROY, Isaac Stuart. 922.573
Some pioneer Presbyterian preachers of the Piedmont North Carolina, [by] Rev. I. S. McElroy, D.D. [Gastonia, N.C., Loftin & co., printers, 1928] 50 p. 22 cm. [BX8947.N8M3] 36-3159
1. Presbyterian church in North Carolina—Clergy. I. Title.

Presbyterian Church in North Carolina—History.

RUMPLE, Jethro. 285'.1756
The history of Presbyterianism in North Carolina. Richmond, Library of Union Theological Seminary in Virginia, 1966. xvii, 349 p. 28 cm. (Library of Union Theological Seminary in Virginia. Historical transcripts, no. 3) "Reprinted from the North Carolina Presbyterian, 1878-1887." [BX8947.N8R8] 71-3331
1. Presbyterian Church in North Carolina—History. I. Title. II. Series: Richmond. Union Theological Seminary. Library. Historical transcripts, no. 3

RUMPLE, Jethro, 1827-1906.
The history of presbyterianism in North Carolina, by Jethro Rumple. Reprinted from the North Carolina Presbyterian,1878-1887. With appendixes. Richmond, Va., Library of Union TheologicalSeminary in Va., 1966. xvii, 349 p. 28 cm. (Historical transcripts, No. 3) 67-75078
I. Title.

Presbyterian church in Ohio.

DAYTON, O. First 285.
Presbyterian church.
Centenary souvenir commemorative of the completion of a century by the First Presbyterian church of Dayton, Ohio, containing an account of the proceedings and the addresses delivered during the celebration, December 10, 11, and 12, 1899. Dayton, O., United brethren publishing house, 1900. iv, 5-112 p. front., plates, ports. 19 1/2 cm. [BX9211.D28F5] 45-44694
I. Title.

MCCUNE, William C., 285.
defendant.
The process, testimony and opening argument of the prosecution, vote and final minute, in the judicial trial of Rev. W. C. McCune by the Presbytery of Cincinnati, from March 5 to March 27, 1877. Cincinnati, R. Clarke & co., printers, 1877. 179 p. 23 cm. "Action brought by Common Fame, for disloyalty to the Presbyterian church." [BX9193.M3A3] 22-21663
I. Presbyterian church in the U.S.A. Prebytery of Cincinnati. II. Title.

PRESBYTERIAN church in 285.1771
the U. S. A. Presbytery of Cincinnati.
One hundred and fifty years of Presbyterianism in the Ohio valley, 1790-1940. Cincinnati, 1941. xiv p., 1 l., 308 p. illus. (incl. ports.) 22 cm. Prepared by the Committee on history of the Cincinnati presbytery, Earl R. North, chairman. "Individual church histories": p. 230-292. Bibliography: p. 301-306. [BX8958.C53A5] 42-15407
1. Presbyterian church in Ohio. 2. Churches—Ohio. I. North, Earl Roswell, 1880- ed. II. Title.

Presbyterian Church in Pennsylvania.

CORAOPOLIS. Pa. First 285.174885
Presbyterian church.
Semi-centennial of the First Presbyterian church of Coraopolis, Pennayvania ... Year of the jubilee December 21 1932 [Pittsburgh? 1933] 56 p. illus. (incl. ports.) 23 cm. The ... task of compiling the record here presented ... was laid upon Mr. Junius D. McCabe.--Foreword. [BX9211.C69F5] 34-12486
I. McCabe, Junius Dallas. II. Title.

DAWSON, Pa. Presbyterian Church.
The new church register 1874-1961, and minutes of the session, Jan. 15, 1956 -- Oct. 7, 1962. [n.p., 1962?] 1 v. Church dissolved by act of Redstone Presbytery Oct. 31, 1962. 64-37381
I. Title.

MORRIS, A Wayne. 285.1748
The Octorara family of churches. Sketches by the author. Honey Brook, Pa., Herald Pub. Co. [c1960] unpaged. illus. 21x24cm. [BX8947.P4M6] 61-2322
1. Presbyterian Church in Pennsylvania. 2. Churches—Pennsylvania. I. Title.

PITTSBURGH. Third 285.
Presbyterian church.
Dedicatory services of the new edifice of the Third Presbyterian church, of Pittsburgh, Penn'a. With some account of the history of the church from its organization, together with a full description of the present building, and its appointments. Pittsburgh, W. G. Johnston & co., printers, 1869. 96 p. front., plates, plan. 24 cm. "Historical address, by Rev. D. H. Riddle", "Prayer, by Rev. Henry Kendall", and "Sermon, by Rev. Herrick Johnson" are each preceded by half-title not included in the paging. [BX9211.P6T45] 40-25739
I. Riddle, David Hunter, 1805-1888. II. Johnson, Herrick, 1832-1913. III. Title.

PRESBYTERIAN church in the U. S.
A. Presbytery of Pennsylvania.
An act of the Associate presbytery of Pennsylvania, concerning public convenanting, unanimously agreed to at Philadelphia, April 29, 1791 ... To which is added an act concerning the admission of church members to communion. Philadelphia, Printed by W. Young, 1792. 1 p. l., [5]-53 p. 17 cm. 16-1202
I. Title.

PRESBYTERIAN church in the U. S.
A. Synod of Pennsylvania.
Minutes of the ... annual session of the Synod of Pennsylvania of the Presbyterian church in the United States of America ... Philadelphia, v. front. (port.) 23 cm. At head of title: Volume no. 10-34232
I. Title.

SILVER Spring, Cumberland Co.,
Pa. Presbyterian church.
... Exercises in commemoration of the one hundred and seventy-fifth anniversary of the Silver Spring Presbyterian church, Cumberland County, Pennsylvania. Thursday, August 5, 1909, 2:00 P.M. [n. p.,] 1909?] 2 p. l., 3-69 p. front., diagrs. 24 cm. At head to t.-p.: 1734, 1909. 15-28238
I. Title.

SILVER Spring, Cumberland Co.,
Pa. Presbyterian church.
... Exercises in commemoration of the one hundred and seventy-fifth anniversary of the Silver Spring Presbyterian church, Cumberland County, Pennsylvania. Thursday, August 5, 1909, 2:00 P.M. [n. p.,] 1909?] 2 p. l., 3-69 p. front., diagrs. 24 cm. At head to t.-p.: 1734, 1909. 15-28238
I. Title.

Presbyterian church in Philadelphia.

FORD, Harry Pringle.
A history of the Harriet Hollond memorial Presbyterian church of Philadelphia, Pa., by Harry Pringle Ford. Philadelphia, Castle & Heilman, printers, 1899. 3 p. l., 283 p. front., pl., port. 18 cm. 2-26886
I. Title.

WHITE, William Prescott, 285.
1840- ed.
The Presbyterian church in Philadelphia. A camera and pen sketch of each Presbyterian church and institution in the city, compiled and edited by Rev. Wm. P. White, D.D., and William H. Scott, with a prefatory note by Rev. William C. Cattell...and an introduction by Rev. Willard M. Rice... Philadelphia, Allen, Lane & Scott, 1895. xxiv, 311 p. incl. front. (ports.) illus. 24 1/2 x 19 1/2 cm. [BX8949.P5W4] 1-10650
1. Presbyterian church in Philadelphia. I. Scott, William H., joint ed. II. Title.

Presbyterian church in Prince Edward Island.

MACLEOD, John M., 1825-
History of Presbyterianism on Prince Edward Island. by Rev. John MacLeod. Presbyterian colleges, sermons by pioneer ministers on P. E. Island nearly a century ago. Chicago, Ill., Winona Lake, Ind., The Winona publishing company, 1904. 279 p. front. (port.) 20 1/2 cm. [BX9002.P8M3] 4-21685
1. Presbyterian church in Prince Edward Island. I. Title.

Presbyterian Church in Punjab, Pakistan (Province)

STOCK, Frederick, 266'.51'54914
1929-
People movements in the Punjab; with special reference to the United Presbyterian Church, [by] Frederick and Margaret Stock. South Pasadena, Calif., William Carey Library [1974, c1975] xxii, 364 p. illus. 23 cm. Bibliography: p. [341]-357. [BX9151.P18S76] 74-18408 ISBN 0-87808-417-7
1. Presbyterian Church in Punjab, Pakistan (Province) 2. Missions—Punjab, Pakistan (Province) 3. Sects—Pakistan—Punjab (Province) I. Stock, Margaret, 1929- joint author. II. Title.

Presbyterian church in Roanoke, Virginia.

HOFFER, Frank William. 285.1755
Presbyterian churches of Roanoke, Virginia [by] Frank William Hoffer ... Roanoke, Va., Economy printing company [1937?] 2 p. l., 65 p. plates, ports. 22 1/2 cm. [BX8949.R58H6] 45-45408
1. Presbyterian church in Roanoke, Virginia. 2. Roanoke, Va.—Churches, Presbyterian. I. Title.

Presbyterian church in South Carolina.

CHARLESTON, S.C. Second Presbyterian Church. 285.
Manual for the use of the members of the Second Presbyterian Church, Charleston, S.C., prepared under the direction of the Church by Thomas Smyth, pastor. Charleston. Printed by Jenkins & Hussey, 1838. 236 p. 18 cm. [BX9211.C26S4] 49-58257
I. Smyth, Thomas, 1808-1873. II. Title.

GIST, Margaret Adams. 285.
Presbyterian women of South Carolina ... Margaret A. Gist, editor; published by Woman's auxiliary of the Synod of South Carolina. [Greenville, S. C., c1929] xx p., 1 l., 785, [1] p. front., plates, ports. 24 cm. [BX8947.S6G5] 30-811
1. Presbyterian church in South Carolina. 2. Women in South Carolina. I. Title.

HOWE, George, 1802-1883. 285.
History of the Presbyterian church in South Carolina. By George Howe ... Prepared by order of the Synod of South Carolina. Columbia, Duffie & Chapman, 1870-83. 2 v. 23 cm. Vol. 2 published by W. J. Duffie [BX8947.S6H8] 7-39377
1. Presbyterian church in South Carolina. I. Title.

JONES, Frank Dudley, 1874- ed. 285.
History of the Presbyterian church in South Carolina since 1850, edited by F. D. Jones, D. D. and W. H. Mills, D. D.; published by the Synod of South Carolina Columbia, S. C., The R. L. Bryan company, 1926. xi, 1094 p. 24 cm. [BX8947.S6J6] 27-8216
1. Presbyterian church in South Carolina. I. Mills, William Hayne, joint ed. II. Presbyterian church in the U. S. Synod of South Carolina. III. Title.

Presbyterian church in Tennessee.

PIONEER Presbyterianism in Tennessee. 285. Addresses delivered at the Tennessee exposition on Presbyterian day, October 28, 1897. Richmond, Va., The Presbyterian committee of publication [1898] 83 p. 19 cm. [BX8947.T2P5] 98-179
1. Presbyterian church in Tennessee. I. Heiskell, Carrick White, 1836- II. Bachman, Jonathan Waverly, 1837-1924. III. Moore, Walter William, 1857-1926.
Contents omitted.

PRESBYTERIAN church in the U. S. Presbytery of Holston. 285.175
Minutes of the ... meeting of Holston presbytery ... [Pulaski, Va., B. D. Smith & bros., printers, 1931- v. 22 cm. [BX8968.H6A3] 31-20478
I. Title.

Presbyterian church in Texas.

RED, William Stuart, 1857-1933. 285.1764
A history of the Presbyterian church in Texas, by William Stuart Red. [Austin, Tex., Steck co., c1936] xiii p., 1 l., 433 p. incl. front., illus., plates, ports. 24 cm. "The history of the Southern Presbyterian [church] and ... of the Northern church prior to 1866-67."--Introd. Edited by Mrs. W. S. Red and Rev. M. L. Purcell. [BX8947.T3R4] 37-554
1. Presbyterian church in Texas. 2. Presbyterians in Texas. I. Red, Rizpah C. (Bowers) Mrs. 1866- ed. II. Purcell, Malcolm Lee. 1893- ed. III. Title.

Presbyterian Church in the New Southwest.

BRACKENRIDGE, R. Douglas. 285'.179
Iglesia Presbiteriana : a history of Presbyterians and Mexican Americans in the Southwest / by R. Douglas Brackenridge and Francisco O. Garcia-Treto. San Antonio : Trinity University Press, [1974] xiv, 262 p : ill. ; 25 cm. (Presbyterian Historical Society publication series ; 15) Includes index. Bibliography: p. [249]-255. [BV2788.M4B7 1974] 74-76777 ISBN 0-911536-53-1 : 8.00
1. Presbyterian Church in the New Southwest. 2. Missions to Mexican Americans—Southwest, New. 3. Mexican Americans—Southwest, New. I. Garcia-Treto, Francisco O., joint author. II. Title. III. Series: Presbyterian Historical Society. Publications ; no. 15.

Presbyterian Church in the Ohio Valley.

MCKINNEY, William Wilson, 1893- ed. 285.177
The Presbyterian Valley Foreword by Eugene Carson Blake. Pittsburgh, Davis & Warde, 1958. 639p. illus. 22cm. 'Published as a religious feature of the Pittsburgh Bicentennial Year 1958-1959 in recognition of the continued influence of Presbyterianism throughout the two hundred years of Pittsburgh's growth and expansion.' Includes bibliography. [BX8935.M2] 58-14156
1. Presbyterian Church in the Ohio Valley. I. Title.

Presbyterian Church in the Old Southwest — History

POSEY, Walter Brownlow, 1900- 285.176
The Presbyterian Church in the Old Southwest, 1778-1838. Richmond, John Knox Press, 1952. 192 p. map (on lining papers) 25 cm. Bibliographical references included in "Notes" (p. [139]-185) [BX8941.P65] 52-14324
1. Presbyterian Church in the Old Southwest — Hist. I. Title.

Presbyterian Church in the United States

ALEXANDER, William Addison. 285.
Supplement to the Digest of the acts and proceedings of the General assembly of the Presbyterian church in the United States, published in 1888, bringing the same down to date. By Rev. W. A. Alexander, D. D. Richmond, Va., Presbyterian committee of publication, 1898. x, 201 p. 24 1/2 cm. [BX8966.A7] 96-116
I. Presbyterian church in the U.S. General assembly. II. Title.

ALEXANDER, William Addison. 285.
Supplement to the Digest of the acts and proceedings of the General assembly of the Presbyterian church in the United States, published in 1888, bringing the same down to date. By Rev. W. A. Alexander, D. D. Richmond, Va., Presbyterian committee of publication, 1898. x, 201 p. 24 1/2 cm. [BX8966.A7] 96-116
I. Presbyterian church in the U.S. General assembly. II. Title.

ASSOCIATED presbyteries. 284.
A brief account of Associated presbyteries; and a general view of their sentiments concerning religion and ecclesiastical order. By a convention of said presbyteries [!] ... Printed in Catskill, by M. Croswell-- 1796. 2 p. l., 102, [6] p. 17 1/2 cm. "An act, to incorporate sundry persons as trustees of the society, insituted in Morris-county, for the promotion of learning and religion": [6] p. at end. [BX8009.A9A45] 3-16604
I. New Jersey. Laws, statutes, etc. II. Title.

BAIRD, Samuel John, 1817-1893, comp. 285.173
A collection of the acts, deliverances, and testimonies of the supreme judicatory of the Presbyterian church from its origin in America to the present time. With notes and documents, explanatory and historical: constituting a complete illustration of her polity, faith, and History. Compiled for the Board of publication by the Rev. Samuel L. Baird. Philadelphia, Presbyterian board of publication, 1856. xxiii, [1], 856 p. 24 cm. [BX9190.B3] 33-19151
1. Presbyterian church in the U. S. A. I. Presbyterian church in the U. S. A. Board of publication. II. Title.

BUNYAN, John, 1628-1688.
The pilgrims's progress from this world to that which is to come. Delivered under the similitude of a dream. In two parts. By John Bunyan. Philadelphia, U. Hunt, 1829. 249 p. front., pl. 15 cm. [PR3330.A1 1829] 26-1729
I. Title.

BUNYAN, John, 1628-1688. 230'.08 s
The poems / John Bunyan ; edited by Graham Midgley. Oxford : Clarendon Press ; New York : Oxford University Press, 1980. lxii, 345 p. : ill. ; 23 cm. (The miscellaneous works of John Bunyan ; v. 6) (Oxford English texts) Includes bibliographical references. [BR75.B73 1976 vol. 6] 821'.4 79-40422 ISBN 0-19-812734-0 pbk. : 8.95
I. Midgley, Graham.

BUNYAN, John, 1628-1688. 252.
The practical works of John Bunyan. Arranged and classified in natural order, with introductions and notes. By J. Newton Brown ... Philadelphia, The American Baptist publication society, 1852. 8 v. front. (port.) 19 1/2 cm. Imperfect: t.-p. of v. 6 wanting. [BR75.B7 1852] [BR75.B7 1852] [BR75.B7 1852] 252. 252. 26-8411 26-8411 26-8411
I. Brown, John Newton, 1803-1868, ed. II. American Baptist publication society. III. Title.

CUMBERLAND Presbyterian church in the U. S. 235.
The constitution of the Cumberland Presbyterian church, in the United States of America. Containing the Confession of faith; the Catechism; and a Directory for the worship of God. Together with the Form of government and discipline. Revised and adopted by the General assembly, at Princeton, Ky., May, 1829. Pittsburgh, Printed by A. A. Anderson, 1843. iv, [5]-186, [4] p. 15 cm. [BX8975.A3 1843] 5-42803
I. Title.

CUMMING, William James, 1847-1922. 266.
The Presbyterian church within the field [of the Presbytery of Westchester, synod of New York, 1660-1889. By William J. Cumming ... Hartford, Conn., Press of the Case, Lockwood & Brainard company, 1889. ix, 229 p. 24 cm. [BX8958.W4C8] 27-21567
1. Presbyterian church in the [U. S. A. Presbytery of Westchester, N. Y. I. Title.

DAYTON, Charles Henry, 1892- 285.173
A brief history of the Presbytery of Geneva and a tribute to some early ministers, by Charles H. Dayton and John Garth Coleman. Sesquicentennial of the Presbytery of Geneva, 1805-1955. [Shortsville? N. Y.] Geneva-Lyons c67p. illus. 28cm. On cover: Growth of the church on the 'Northwestern Frontier.' [BX8958.G4D3] 55-32281
1. Presbyterian Church in the U. S. A. Presbyteries. Geneva-lyons. I. Coleman, John Garth, joint author. II. Title. III. Title: Growth of the church on the 'Northwestern Frontier.'

DONNELLY, Harold I.
Manual for leaders of Presbyterian pioneers, by Harold I. Donnelly ... Philadelphia, The Westminster press, 1923. 64 p. diagrs. 18 cm. "Selected list of books on boys' work": 48-49. [BV1615.D6] 23-11351
I. Title.

DORT, Synod of, 1618-1619. 284.2
The articles of the Synod of Dort. Translated from the Latin, with notes, by the Rev. Thomas Scott, D.D. To which is added an introductory essay, by the Rev. Samuel Miller ... Philadelphia, Presbyterian board of publication, 1841. 371 p. 16 cm. Contents.Preface to the Reformed churches; in which the rise and progress of those controversies in Belgium, for the removal of which this Synod was especially held, are ... related.--The judgment of the National synod.--Articles of the Synod of Dort, &c.--The approbation of the lords the States-general. [BX9478.A2 1841] 17-14839
I. Scott, Thomas, 1747-1821, tr. II. Miller, Samuel, 1769-1850. III. Presbyterian church in the U.S.A. (Old school) Board of publication. IV. Title.

DORT, Synod of, 1618-1619. 284.2
The articles of the Synod of Dort. Translated from the Latin, with notes, by the Rev. Thomas Scott, D.D., with an introductory essay. By the Rev. Samuel Miller ... Philadelphia, Presbyterian board of publication [c1856] iv, 5-260 p. 17 1/2 cm. Contents.Preface to the Reformed churches; in which the rise and progress of those controversies in Belgium, for the removal of which this Synod was especially held, are ... related.--The judgment of the National synod.--Articles of the Synod of Dort, &c.--The approbation of the States general. [BX9478.A4 1856] 38-18178
I. Scott, Thomas, 1747-1821, tr. II. Miller, Samuel, 1760-1850. III. Presbyterian church in the U.S.A. (Old school) Board of publication. IV. Title.

DORT, Synod of, 1618-1619. 284.2
The articles of the Synod of Dort and its rejection of errors; with the history of events which made way for that Synod, as published by the authority of the States-general; and the documents confirming its decisions. Translated from the Latin, with notes, remarks, and references. By Thomas Scott ... Utica, W. Williams. New York, Collins & Hannay; [etc., etc.] 1831. xi, 304 p. 20 1/2 cm. [BX9478.A4 1831] 38-18177
I. Scott, Thomas, 1747-1821, tr. II. Title.

GALBRAITH, Robert Christy, 1832- 266.
The history of the Chillicothe presbytery, from its organization in 1799 to 1889. Prepared with the order of presbytery, by the Rev. R. C. Galbraith ... Published by H. W. Guthrie, Hugh Bell and Peter Platter, committee on publication appointed by the presbyterian. Chillicothe, O., Scioto gazette book and job office, 1889. iv, [5]-431 p. front., illus., ports. 24 cm. [BX8958.C5G3] 26-22919
1. Presbyterian church in the U. S. A. Presbytery of Chillicothe. I. Title.

[GREEN, Ashbel] 1762-1848, defendant.
The case of the General assembly of the Presbyterian church in the United States of America, before the Supreme court of the commonwealth of Pennsylvania, impartially reported by disinterested stenographers: including all the proceedings, testimony, and arguments at nisi prius, and before the court in bank, with the charge of Judge Rogers, the verdict of the jury, and the opinion of Chief Justice Gibson. The whole compiled and prepared for the press by the Rev. D. W. Lathrop. Philadelphia, A. M'Elroy, 1839. 2 p. l., [3]-628 p. 24 cm. Caption title (p. [13]): The case of "the General assembly of the Presbyterian church in the United States of America", before the Supreme court of the commonwealth of Pennsylvania. Quo warranto ... The commonwealth at the suggestion of James Todd [and others] ... vs. Ashbel Green [and others] ... Lettered on cover: A. McElroy's report of the Presbyterian church case. "The question at issue is, are the respondents in the case entitled to hold the office of trustees of the General assembly of the Presbyterian church in the United States of America? ... The secondary issue ... is, whether that body which elected these relatiors, was truly the General assembly of the Presbyterian church."--p. 268. 7-8912
1. Presbyterian church in the U. S. A. General assembly, 1833. I. Todd, James, relator. II. Lathrop, Daniel Whiting, 1798-1883, ed. III. Rogers, Molton Cropper, d. 1863. IV. Gibson, John Bannister, 1780-1833. V. Pennsylvania. Supreme court. VI. Title. VII. Title: Presbyterian church case.

GREEN, Ashbel, 1762-1848, defendant.
Report of the Presbyterian church case: The commonwealth of Pennsylvania, at the suggestion of James Todd and others, VS. Ashbel Green and others. By Samuel Miller, jr. ... Philadelphia, W. S. Martien,

1839. 596 p. 24 cm. Trial on a writ of quo warranto in the Supreme court for the Eastern district of Pennsylvania, at nisi prius, March, 1839, and motion for a new trial. "The simple question ... in deciding upon this case, is, whether certain persons, the relators in the suit, have been duly elected to fill the office of truetees of the General assembly ... The determination of the formal issue depends, altogether, upon the decision of another question ... viz; which of twobocies that met in 1838, each claiming the title, was, in fact, the true General assembly of the Presbyterian church."--p. 226-227. 32-34168
1. Presbyterian church in the U. S. A. General assembly, 1838. I. Todd, James, relator. II. Miller, Samuel, 1816-1883, reporter. III. Pennsylvania. Supreme court. IV. Title. V. Title: Presbyterian church case.

A handbook for Presbyterians, prepared by the officers of the Lexington Presbyterian Church, Lexington, Va., Edwin G. Adair [and others. 7th ed., rev.] Richmond, John Knox Press [1957] 111p. illus. 20cm.
1. Presbyterian Church in the U. S. 2. Prebyterianism. I. Lexington, Va. Lexington Presbyterian Church.

A handbook for Presbyterians, preapred by the officers of the Lexington Presbyterian Church, Lexington, Va., Edwin G. Adair [and others. 8th ed., rev.] Richmond, Va., John Knox Press [1958] 111p. illus. 21cm.
1. Presbyterian Church in the U. S. 2. Presbyterianism. I. Lexington, Va. Lexington Presbyterian Church.

HANZSCHE, William Thomson, 1891- 285.173
Know your church! The Presbyterian church; its history, organization, and program--revised, by William Thomson Hanzsche. Thirteen studies for young people and adults... Philadelphia, Board of Christian education of the Presbyterian church in the United States of America [1946] 94 p. 19 1/2 cm. "Originally prepared in co-operation with the General council [under title: Our Presbyterian church, published in 1935]"--p. [5] [BX8955.H3 1946] 46-20757
1. Presbyterian church in the U.S.A. I. Presbyterian church in the U.S.A. Board of Christian education. II. Title.

[HANZSCHE, William Thomson] 1891- 285.173
Our Presbyterian church; its history, organization, and program, a study unit of thirteen lessons. Philadelphia, Pa., Pub. for the General council by the Board of Christian education of the Presbyterian church in the U.S.A. [c1933] cover-title, 72 p. 19 cm. William Thomson Hanzsche, and outlined for use in the young people's Westminster departmental graded materials." [BX8955.H3] 34-2520
1. Presbyterian church in the U.S.A. I. Title.

HARLOW, Henry Addison, 1830-1913. 266.
A history of the Presbytery of Hudson. 1681-1888. By Rev. Henry A. Harlow ... Middletown, N. Y., Stivers, Slauson & Boyd, 1888. 251, [1] p. 19 cm. [BX8958.H8H3] 3-31802
1. Presbyterian church in the U. S. A. Presbytery of Hudson. I. Title.

HARRAH, Charles Clark. 225
The road: the ever-existent, universal and only religion of God: its presence in all the religious and civilizations of the world, and the present crisis in Christianity, by Charles Clarke Harrah ... Des Moines, Ia., Scott Heights book company [1902] 144 p. front. (port.) 18 x 14 cm. Cover-title: The road of Jesus. [BR121.H37] 2-30124
I. Title.

HIGGINBOTTOM, Sam, 1874- 285.173
What does Jesus expect of his church? Report of a lay missionary moderator and his wife, who visited the church, by Sam Higginbottom ... New York [etc.] Fleming H. Revell company [c1941] 128 p. 20 cm. "The woman's viewpoint', chapter six, was written by Mrs. Higginbottom."--Foreword. [BX8955.H5] 41-4589
1. Presbyterian church in the U. S. A. I. Higginbottom, Ethel (Cody) Mrs. 1880- II. Title.

HUTCHISON, John Russell, 1807-1878. 922.573
Reminiscences, sketches and addresses, selected from my papers during a ministry of forty-five years in Mississippi, Louisiana and Texas. By I. R. Hutchison, D. D. Houston, Tex., E. H. Cushing, 1874. 1 p. l.; [v]-vi, [7]-218 p. 20 cm. [BX9225.H85A8 1874 a] 36-11174
1. Presbyterian church in the U. S. 2. Southern states—Church history. I. Title.

JOHNSON, Thomas Cary, 1859-
... A history of the Southern Presbyterian church, with appendix, by Thomas C. Johnson ... New York, The Christian literature co., 1894. 1 p. l., p. 311-487. 21 cm. At head of title: American church history. "The peculiar pagination is due to the work first appearing as the concluding portion of vol. xi, American church history series."--Contents. Bibliography: p. 313-314. [BX8962.J7] 29-30632
1. Presbyterian church in the U. S. 2. Presbyterianism. I. Title.

JOSEPH, Oscar L. 220
Ringing realitites; a restatement of some abiding truths, by Oscar L. Joseph, LITT. D. New York and London, Harper & brothers, 1928. viii p., 2 l., 254 p., 1 l., 20 cm. "For further reading" at end of each chapter. [BR125.J73] 28-11116
I. Title.

LESLIE, John Douglass, 1860- 285.1
Presbyterian law and procedure in the Presbyterian church in the United States, by Rev. J. D. Leslie... Richmond, Va., Presbyterian committee of publication, 1930. 411 p. front. (port.) 1 illus., fold. diagr. 18 1/2 cm. [BX8966.L4] 33-3478
1. Presbyterian church in the U.S. I. Title.

LETTERS of William Hamilton, 1811-1891. Introduction by Charles A. Anderson. [Lancaster, Pa., 1957] 157-170p. 23cm. Excerpt from the Journal of the Presbyterian Historical Society, Vol. 35, no. 3, September, 1957.
1. Presbyterian Church in the U. S. A.—Presbyteries— Highland, Kan. 2. Presbyterian Church in the U. S. A. Board of Foreign Missions. 3. Indians of North America—Missions. I. Hamilton, William, 1811-1891.

LEXINGTON, Va. Lexington Presbyterian Church. 285.173
A handbook for Presbyterians, prepared by the officers of the Lexington Presbyterian Church, Lexington, Va., Edwin G. Adair [and others] Richmond, John Knox Press [1951] 100 p. illus. 21 cm. [BX8962.L4] 51-7680
1. Presbyterian Church in the U. S. 2. Presbyterianism. I. Title.

LEXINGTON, Va. Lexington Presbyterian Church. 285.173
A handbook for Presbyterians, Prepared by the officers of the Lexington Presbyterian Church, Lexington, Virginia. Ed in G. Adair and other. 11th print. rev. Richmond, Va., John Knox Press [1963, c1951] 109 p. illus., maps. 21 cm. [BX8965.L4] 63-22504
1. Presbyterian Church in the U.S. 2. Presbyterianism. I. Title.

LILLY, David Clay, 1870- 285.175
Faith of our fathers, by D. Clay Lilly, D. D. Richmond, Va., Texarkana, Ark.-Tex., Presbyterian committee of publication, 1935. 143 p. 19 cm. [BX8965.L5] 36-7426
1. Presbyterian church in the U. S. I. Title.

LONG, Roswell Curtis, 1893- 285.173
The story of our church, by Roswell C. Long ... Richmond, Va., Presbyterian committee of publication, 1932. 188, [5] p. 20 cm. "Books for further reading" at end of each chapter. [BX8965.L6] 33-3734
1. Presbyterian church in the U. S. I. Title.

MCINTOSH, William Alexander, 1884- 200
The story, a book for those who care to think. Springfield, Vt. [1950] 79 p. 18 cm. [BR126.M3554] 50-29217
I. Title.

MEMORANDA concerning Sheldon Jackson and the moderatorship of the 109th General assembly of the Presbyterian church in the United States of America. 922.573 Winona assembly grounds, Eagle lake, Indiana, May 20-28, 1897. For private circulation. Philadelphia, MacCalla & company, incorporated [1897?] 126 p. front. (port.) 21 cm. [BX9225.J25M4] 36-24279
1. Jackson, Sheldon, 1834-1909. 2. Presbyterian church in the U. S. A. General assembly. 1897.

MOORE, Ambrose Yoemans. 266.
History of the presbyterian of Indianapolis. By A. Y. Moore, Pub. by the presbytery. Indianapolis, J. G. Doughty, printer, 1876. vii, 132 p. 22 cm. [BX8958.I 4M6] 20-16420
1. Presbyterian church in the U. S. A. Presbytery of Indianapolis. I. Title.

MURRAY, Andrew E. 285.0973
Presbyterians and the Negro; a history, by Andrew E. Murray. Philadelphia, Presbyterian Hist. Soc. 1966. xiv, 270p. 24cm. (Presbyterian Hist. Soc. pubns., 7) Bibl. [BX8946. N4M8] 67-20 6.00
1. Prsbyterians. Negro. 2. Church and race problems—U. S. I. Title. II. Series: Presbyterian Historical Scoiety. Publications, 7
Publisher's address: 520 Withrspoon Bldg., Phila., Pa., 19107.

NEVIN, Alfred, 1816-1890, ed.
Encyclopaedia of the Presbyterian church in the United States of America: including the northern and southern assemblies. Alfred Nevin ... editor, assisted by B. M. Smith ... W. E. Schenck ... and other eminent ministers of the church. D. R. B. Nevin ... managing editor ... Philadelphia, Presbyterian encyclopaedia publishing co., 1884. viii, 9-1248 p. illus. (incl. facsim.) ports. 28 cm. [BX8909.N4] 10-31801
1. Presbyterian church in the U. S. A.—Dictionaries. 2. Presbyterian church in the U. S. A. 3. Presbyterian church in the U. S. I. Nevin, David Robert Bruce, 1828- joint ed. II. Title.

NEVIN, John Williamson, 1803-1886. 220.98
A summary of Biblical antiquities; for the use of schools, Bible-classes and families. By John W. Nevin, D. D. Philadelphia, American Sunday-school union [c1849] 447 p. incl. front., illus. plates. 20 cm. "List of principal writers": p. 439-443. [BS620.N4 1849] 40-23167
1. Bible—Antiq. I. American Sunday-school union. II. Title. III. Title: Biblical antiquities.

OSMOND, Jonathan, 1820-1903. 266.
History of the presbytery of Luzerne, state of Pennsylvania, By Rev. J. Osmond ... with introduction by Rev. N. G. Parke, D. D. [Philadelphia] The Presbyterian historical society [1897] xvii, 344 p. 21 cm. [BX8958.L9O8] 42-26728
1. Presbyterian church in the U. S. A. (Old school) Presbyterian of Luzerne. I. Presbyterian historical society. II. Title.

AN overview of Presbyterianism in the city of Philadelphia, Pennsylvania, by Charles Thorne, for the Presbytery of Philadelphia and the Department of City and Industrial Work, Board of National Missions, Presbyterian Church in the U. S. A. [n. p.] 1959. 179p.
I. Presbyterian Church in the U. S. A. Presbyteries. Philadelphia.

AN overview of Presbyterianism in the city of Philadelphia, Pennsylvania, by Charles Thorne, for the Presbytery of Philadelphia and the Department of City and Industrial Work, Board of National Missions, Presbyterian Church in the U. S. A. [n. p.] 1959. 179p.
I. Presbyterian Church in the U. S. A. Presbyteries. Philadelphia.

[PARSONS, Levi] 1828or29-1901, comp. 285.
History of Rochester presbytery from the earliest settlement of the country, embracing original records of Ontario assocaition, and the presbyteries of Ontario, Rochester (former) Genesee River, and Rochester city, to which are appended biographical sketches of deceased ministers and brief histories of individual churches. Rochester, N. Y., Democratchronicle press, 1889. 319 p. front. (port.) plates. 24 cm. "Published by Presbytery." Caption title: History of Rochester presbytery, compiled by Rev. Levi Parsons. D. D. [BX8958.R6P3] 1-26559
1. Presbyterian church in the U. S. A. Presbytery of Rochester. I. Title. II. Title: Rochester presbytery, History of.

PATTON, Francis Landey, 1843-1932. 285.
Before the Synod of Illinois, North. In the matter of the appeal of Francis L. Patton against the decision of the presbytery of Chicago, in the case of David Swing. Appellant's argument. Chicago, Ills., Beach, Barnard & co.'s printing house, 1872. 68 p. 23 cm. Errata slip inserted. [BX9193.S9P3] 39-7838
1. Swing, David, 1830-1894. 2. Presbyterian church in the U. S. A. Presbyterian of Chicago. I. Presbyterian church in the U. S. A. Synod of Illinois. II. Title.

THE plan of union of the Presbyterian Church in the United States of America and the United Presbyterian Church of North American to form the United Presbyterian Church in the United States of America [Approved by a Joint Conference of the Permanent Committee on Interchurch Relations and the Permanent Commission on Interchurch Relations, held in New York City on March 8-9, 1956. [n. p.] 1956. 308p. 17cm.
1. Presbyterian Church in the U. s.—Relations—United Presbyterian Church of North America 2. United Presbyterian Church of North America—Relations—Presbyterian Church in the U.S. I. Joint Conference of the Permanent Committee on Interchurch Relations and the Permanent Commission on Interchurch Relations.

PRESBYTERIAN brotherhood of America.
The brotherhood and the church; report of the third convention of the Presbyterian brotherhood of America, at Pittsburg, February twenty-third to twenty-fifth, nineteen-nine. Philadelphia, Pa., The Presbyterian board of publication, 1909. 328 p. front. (port.) 20 cm. 9-19816
I. Title.

PRESBYTERIAN church in the U. S. Executive committee of publication.
The church at work: organization and duties of the agencies of the Southern Presbyterian church; Executive committee of foreign missions, Executive committee of home missions. Executive committee of Christian education and ministerial relief. Executive committee on publication and Sabbath school work. The Woman's auxiliary. The assembly's stewardship committee. Richmond, Va., Presbyterian committee of publication [c1922] 118 p. illus. 19 cm. [BX8941.A5 1922] 22-16526
1. Presbyterian church in the U. S. I. Title.

PRESBYTERIAN church in the U. S. Presbytery of East Hanover. 285.175546
Manual of East Hanover presbytery. Revised 1932. Richmond, Va., Richmond press, inc., printers, 1932. 63 p. 16 cm. [BX8968.E3A5 1932] 32-28877
I. Title.

PRESBYTERIAN church in the U. S. Presbytery of Fayetteville.
Minutes of the Presbytery of Fayetteville. Fayetteville, N. C., v. tables. 22-23 cm. 15-22008
I. Title.

PRESBYTERIAN church in the U. S. A. 285.
The constitution of the Presbyterian church, in the United States of America: containing the confession of faith, the catechims [!] and the directory for the worship of God together with the plan of government and discipline, as ratified by the General assembly, at their sessions in May, 1821; and amended in 1833. Philadelphia, Barrington & Haswell [1850] 1 p. l., 466 p. 16 cm. [BX8955.A3 1850] 42-30174
1. Presbyterian church in the U. S. A.—Doctrianl and controversial works. 2. Presbyterian church in the U. S. A.—

Discipline. 3. Presbyterian church in the U. S. A.—Catechisms and creeds. I. Title.

PRESBYTERIAN church in the U. S. A. Board of foreign missions. 266.
Five hundred thousand of a hundred million; a sketch of the Evangelistic work of the Presbyterian church in non-Christian lands, the third of a series of booklets, pub. by the Presbyterian board of foreign missions ... New York, The Board of foreign missions of the Presbyterian church in the U. S. A. [1915] 87, [1] p. illus. 24 cm. [BV2570.A2A7 1915] 21-11313
I. Title.

PRESBYTERIAN church in the U. S. A. Board of foreign missions. 266.
Five hundred thousand of a hundred million; a sketch of the Evangelistic work of the Presbyterian church in non-Christian lands, the third of a series of booklets, pub. by the Presbyterian board of foreign missions ... New York, The Board of foreign missions of the Presbyterian church in the U. S. A. [1915] 87, [1] p. illus. 24 cm. [BV2570.A2A7 1915] 21-11313
I. Title.

PRESBYTERIAN church in the U. S. A. 285.
The government, discipline, and worship of the Presbyterian church in theUnited States of America, being the administrative standards subordinateto the word of God, viz.: the form of government, the book of discipline,and the directory for the worship of God as ratified and adopted by theSynod of New York and Philadelphia in the year of Our Lord 1788, andas amended in the years 1805-1924, together with the constitutional rulesadopted in 1893-1912, and general rules for judicatories. Philadelphia, Pa., Issued for the office of the General assembly by thepublication department of the Board of Christian education, 1924. 166 p. 18 cm. [BX8955.A3 1924] 25-10268
I. Title.

PRESBYTERIAN church in the U. S. A. (Old school) Board of publication. 285.173
A series of tracts on the doctrines, order, and polity of the Presbyterian church in the United States of America. Embracing several on practical subjects ... Philadelphia, Presbyterian board of publication, 1842. 2 v. 19 cm. Each tract has special t.p. and separate paging. [BX8953.A6 1842] 33-35172
1. Presbyterian church in the U. S. A. I. Title.

PRESBYTERIAN church in the U. S. A. Board of Christian education. 230.51
A teacher's guide for use with A manual of faith and life; prepared at the request of the committee appointed by the General assembly to co-operate with the Board of Christian education "in the preparation of a communicant's manual." Philadelphia, Presbyterian board of Christian education, 1938. xi, 83 p. 18 cm. "This teacher's guide has been prepared by Winfred P. Moody."--Introd. [BX9175.P72] 38-24548
1. Presbyterian church in the U. S. A. Board of Christian education. A manual of faith and life. 2. Presbyterian church—Membership. I. Moody, Winfred Pettit. II. Title.

PRESBYTERIAN church in the U. S. A. Board of Christian education. 285.
Ten minute lesson on the Presbyterian church in the United States of America. Philadelphia, Board of Christian education of the Presbyterian church in the U. S. A., 1924. 80 p. 19 cm. "Opening chapters ... revised by Dr. Lewis S. Mudge."--Pref. On cover: Revised edition. [BX8955.A5 1924] 24-18525
1. Presbyterian church in the U. S. A. I. Title.

PRESBYTERIAN church in the U.S. Presbyteries. East Hanover. 285.175546
Manual of East Hanover presbytery. Rev. 1932. Richmond, Va., Richmond press, inc., printers, 1932. 63 p. 15 1/2 cm. [BX8968.E3A5 1932] 32-28877
I. Title.

PRESBYTERIAN Church in the U.S. Presbyteries. Mobile. 285.1761
Minutes. [Mobile?] v. 22 cm. [BX8968.M6A3] 52-16066
I. Title.

PRESBYTERIAN Church in the U.S. Synods. Florida. 285.1759
Minutes of the annual meeting. [Orlando, etc.] v. 21-23 cm. [BX8967.F5A3] 52-36171
I. Title.

PRESBYTERIAN historical society. Library. 016.
Catalogue of books in the library of the Presbyterian historical society ... Philadelphia, J. B. Rodgers, 1865. 107 p. 25 cm. [Z7755.P92] 7-20051
1. Persbyterian church in the U. S. A.—Bibl. 2. Presbyterian—Bibl. I. Title.

PRESBYTERIAN historical society. 267.
Report. Philadelphia, 18 v. illus., pl., port. 18-25 cm. Report year ends in May, 18-93 (in January, 1894- Full title of 5th report: Annual report of the Executive committee of the Presbyterian historical society ... [BX8905.P7A3] ca 6
I. Title.

ST. Paul, Central Presbyterian Church
...Semicentennial of the Central Presbyterian Church, St. Paul, Minnesota, 1902 St. Paul, Press of Webb publishing co. [1902] 68 p. incl. front., illus. (ports.) 2 pl. 19 1/2 cm. At head of title: 1852-1902. Preface signed: T. D. Simonton. 15-1445
I. Simonton, T. D. II. Title.

SHERWOOD, James Manning, 1814-1890.
Plea for the old foundations. A sermon, doctrinal and historical, delivered at the re-dedication of the Presbyterian church of Bloomfield, N.J. ... Dec. 18, 1853. By Rev. James Manning Sherwood ... with an appendix of historical memoranda, by the Rev. Stephen Dodd ... New York, M. W. Dodd, 1854. 108 p. 18 1/2 cm. Published by request. 10-24988
I. Dodd, Stephen. II. Title.

A short history of American 285.
Presbyterianism from its foundations to the reunion of 1869. Philadelphia, Presbyterian board of publication and Sabbath-school work, 1903. 207 p. 17 1/2 cm. Contents.--The period from the founding of the Presbyterian church in the United States of America to the commencement of the war of the revolution, by the Rev. A. T. McGill.--The period from the war of the revolution to the adoption of the "Presbyterian form of government" (1786) by the Rev. S. M. Hopkins--The period from the adoption of the Presbyterian form of government to the reunion of 1869, by the Rev. S. J. Wilson. [BX8935.S5] 4-1855
1. Presbyterian church in the U.S.A. I. McGill, Alexander Taggart, 1807-1889. II. Hopkins, Samuel Miles, 1813-1901. III. Wilson, Samuel Jennings, 1828-1883.

THOMPSON, Ernest Trice, 1894- 285.175
The changing South and the Presbyterian Church in the United States. Richmond, John Knox Press [1950] 221 p. map. 21 cm. Bibliographical references included in "Notes and acknowledgements" (p. [215]-221) [BX8962.T5] 50-8262
1. Presbyterian Church in the U.S. 2. Southern States. I. Title.

THOMPSON, Ernest Trice, 1894- 285.173
Tomorrow's church; tomorrow's world. Richmond, John Knox Press [1960] 128 p. 21 cm. Includes bibliography. [BX8965.T5] 60-15825
1. Presbyterian Church in the United States. I. Title.

THOMPSON, Ernest Trice, 1894- 285.173
Tomorrow's church; tomorrow's world. Richmond, Va. John Knox Press [c.1960] 128p. 21cm. Bibl.: p.[125]-128. 60-15825 1.50 pap.,
1. Presbyterian Church in the United States. I. Title.

TRULL, George Harvey, comp. 278
Latin American stories, comp. by George H. Trull ... New York city, Sunday school department, Board of foreign missions of the Presbyterian church in the U.S.A. [c1916] 95 p. 18 1/2 cm. $0.25 [BV2830.T75] 16-25153
I. Title.

TULSA, Okla. First Presbyterian Church. 285.176686
A history of the First Presbyterian Church of Tulsa, Oklahoma, 1885-1960. [Tulsa, 1960] 60 p. illus. 20 x 28 cm. [BX9211.T8A3] 63-2728
I. Title.

VANCE, James Isaac, 1862- 248
The rise of a soul; a stimulus to personal progress and development, by James I. Vance ... New York, Chicago [etc.] Fleming H. Revell company, 1902. 1 p. l., 5-241 p. 20 cm. [BV4501.V23] 2-13646
I. Title.

Presbyterian church in the U.S.A. Associate reformed synod.

[ANNAN, Robert] 1761-1819.
A concise and faithful narrative of the various steps which led to the unhappy division, which hath taken place among the members of the Associate body in the United States; with a brief confutation of the high pretensions, unjust claims and ill-founded principles of those who call themselves the Associate presbytery of Pennsylvania ... By a ruling elder in the communion of the Associate reformed synod. Philadelphia; Printed by Zachariah Poulson, jun. in Fourth-street, between Market-street, and Arch-street, M DCC LXXXIX. 88 p. 22 cm. A 33
1. Presbyterian church in the U.S.A. Associate reformed synod. I. Title.

Presbyterian Church in the United States Board of Christian Education.

PRESBYTERIAN church in the U. S. A. Board of Christian education. 268.
Manual of the Presbyterian program for young people, Building with Christ; prepared by Young people's work of the Board of Christian education, working cooperatively with the Young people's department, Board of foreign missions, and the Department of young people's work, Board of national missions. Philadelphia, Pa., Publication department, Presbyterian board of Christian education, 1925. 144 p. 19 cm. Loose-leaf. Bibliography: p. 131-133. [BX8917.A5 1925] 25-15964
I. Title.

PRESBYTERIAN church in the U. S. A. Board of Christian education. 268.
Manual of the Presbyterian program for young people. Building with Christ, prepared by Young people's work of the Board of Christian education, working cooperatively with the Young people's department, Board of foreign missions, and the Department of young people's work, Board of national missions. Philadelphia, Pa., Publication department, Presbyterian board of Christian education, 1927. 150 p. 18 cm. On cover: Revised edition. Bibliography: p. 133-135. [BX8917.A5 1927] 27-13586
I. Title.

PRESBYTERIAN church in the U. S. A. Board of Christian education. 268.
Year book of the Presbyterian program for young people; Building with Christ ... prepared by Young people's work of the Board of christian education, working cooperatively with the Young people's department, Board of foreign missions, and the Department of Young people's work, Board of national missions. Philadelphia, Pa., Publication department, Presbyterian board of Christian education, 1925- v. 19 cm. [BX8917.A32] 25-16683
I. Presbyterian church in the U. S. A. Board of foreign missions. II. Presbyterian church in the U. S. A. Board of national missions. Building with Christ. III. Title.

WIDMER, Frederick W
Christian family education in the local church. Manual. Richmond, Virginia, Board of Christian Education Presbyterian Church, U.S. [c1957] 62 p. 21 cm. 67-27799
1. Presbyterian Church in the U.S. Board of Christian Education. I. Title.

Presbyterian church in the U.S.A. Board of foreign missions.

BROWN, Arthur Judson, 1856-
Report of a visitation of the China missions of the Presbyterian board of foreign missions, by the Rev. Arthur J. Brown... New York, Board of foreign missions of the Presbyterian church in the U.S.A., 1901. cover-title, 125, [1] p. 23 cm. Printed for the use of the Board and the Missions. 16-4829
1. Presbyterian church in the U.S.A. Board of foreign missions. I. Title.

TRULL, George Harvey. 276.
The tribe of Zambe, by George H. Trull ... New York city, Sunday school department, Board of foreign missions of the Presbyterian church in the U.S.A. [c1917] 3 p. l., 5-107 p. illus. (incl. maps) 18 1/2 cm. Bibliography: p. [103]-107. [BV3540.T8] 17-23957
I. Title.

Presbyterian church in the U.S.A. Board of publication.

THE Child's cabinet of things
both rare and useful, collected and arranged by the editor. Philadelphia, Presbyterian board of publication [1854] 128 p. plates. 15 1/2 cm. 10-30186
1. Presbyterian church in the U.S.A. Board of publication.

Presbyterian Church in the United States Board of Women's Work.

MCGAUGHEY, Janie W 267.4451
On the crest of the present; a history of women's work, Presbyterian Church in the United States. Atlanta, Board of Women's Work, Presbyterian Church in the United States [1961] 204p. illus. 22cm. [BX8966.M3] 61-29014
1. Presbyterian Church in the U. S. Board of Women's Work. I. Title.

Presbyterian Church in the U.S.—Catechisms and creeds.

OSTERWALD, Jean Frederic, 1663-1747. 238.
A catechism for youth, containing a brief but comprehensive summary of the doctrines and duties of Christianity; translated chiefly from a work of the late reverend and learned Professor Osterwald. With some alterations and additions by SamuL Bayard. New-York, Published by Whiting and Watson, for the benefit of the New Jersey Bible society, 1812. 216 p. 17 cm. [BX9184.O7] A 32
1. Presbyterian church in the U. S. A.—Catechisms and creeds. I. Bayard, Samuel, 1767-1840, tr. II. Title.

PRESBYTERIAN church in the U. S.
The Constitution of the Presbyterian church in the United States, containing the Confession of faith, the larger and shorther catechisms, as ratified by the General assembly, at Augusta, Ga., Dec. 1861, together with The book of church order, adopted 1879, The directory for the worship of God, with optional forms, adopted 1894, rules of parlimentary order, adoted 1866. Richmond, Va., Presbyterian committee of publication [1900!] v. 9-404, 189, [1] p. 16 cm. "The book of church order ... With amendments embodied up to and including those adopted in 1899" has special t.-p. and separate pagination. 16-24027
I. Title.

PRESBYTERIAN Church in the U.S. 238'.5'133
A declaration of faith / The Presbyterian Church in the United States. Atlanta : The Church, c1977. 29 p. ; 26 cm. Cover title. [BX8965.P73 1977] 77-154197 0.65
1. Presbyterian Church in the U.S.—Catechisms and creeds. I. Title.

PRESBYTERIAN church in the U. S. A. 285.
The constitution of the Presbyterian church in the United States of America: being ... the confession of faith, the larger and shorter catechisms, the form of government, the book of discipline, and the

directory for the worship of God as ratified and adopted by the synod of New York and Philadelphia in ... 1788 and as amended in the years 1805-1902, together with the constitutional rules adopted in 1893-1901, and administrative acts of the assembly of a general nature. Philadelphia, Presbyterian board of publication and Sabbath-school work, 1903. 527 p. 18 cm. [BX8955.A3 1908] 3-3761
I. Title.

PRESBYTERIAN church in the U. S. A. 285.
The constitution of the Presbyterian church in the United States of America, being ... the confession of faith, the larger and shorter catechisms, the form of government, the book of discipline, and the directory for the worship of God, as ratified and adopted by the Synod of New York and Philadelphia in ... 1788 and as amended in the years 1805-1924, together with the brief statemrny of the reformed faith, the constitutional rules adopted in 1893-1912, and general rules for judicatories. Philadelphia, Board of Christian education of the Presbyterian church in the U. S. A., 1924. 504 p. 19 cm. Parts iv-vii published separately under title: The government, discipline, and worship of the Presbyterian church in the United States of America ... (Philadelphia, 1924) [BX8955.A3 1924] 25-21887
I. Title.

PRESBYTERIAN church in the U. S. A. 285.
The constitution of the Presbyterian church in the United States of America, being ... the confession of faith, the larger and shorter catechisms, the form of government, the book of discipline, and the directory for the worship of God, as ratified and adopted by the Synod of New York and Philadelphia in ...1788 and as mended in the years 1805-1927, together with the constitutional rules adopted in 1893-1912 and general rules for judicatories. Philadelphia, Pub. for the office of the General assembly by the publication department of the Presbyterian board of Christian education, 1927. 2 p. l., iii-v, 3-512 p. 19 cm. [BX8955.A3 1927] 27-13584
I. Title.

PRESBYTERIAN church in the U. S. A. 285.
The constitution of the Presbyterian church in the United States of America, being ... the confession of faith, the larger and shorter catechisms, the form of government, the book of discipline, and the directory for the worship of God, as ratified and adopted by the Synod of New York and Philadelphia in ... 1788 and as amended in the years 1805-1927, together with the constitutional rules adopted in 1893-1912 and general rules for judicatories. Philadelphia, Pub. for the office of the General assembly by the publication department of the Presbyterian board of Christian education, 1928. 2 p. l., iii-v, 3-512 p. 19 cm. [BX8955.A5 1928] 28-13570
I. Title.

PRESBYTERIAN church in the U. S. A. 285.173
The constitution of the Presbyterian church in the United States of America, being ... the confession of faith, the larger and shorter catechisms, the form of government, the book of discipline, and the directory for the worship of God, as ratified and adopted by the Synod of New York and Philadelphia in ... 1788 and as amended in the years 1805-1930, together with the constitutional rules adopted in 1893-1912 and general rules for judicatories. Philadelphia, Pub. for the office of the General assembly by the publication department of the Presbyterian board of Christian education, 1930. 2 p. l., iii-v, 3-512 p. 19 cm. [BX8955.A3 1930] 30-30891
I. Title.

Presbyterian church in the U.S.A.—Clergy.

BEECHER, Willis Judson, 1838-1912.
Index of Presbyterian ministers, containing the names of all the ministers of the Presbyterian church in the United States of America; with references to the pages on which those names are found in its records and minutes, from A.D. 1706 to A.D. 1881. Compiled by the Rev. Willis J. Beecher, D.D., assisted by Mary A. Beecher. Philadelphia, Presbyterian board of publication [c1883] 599 p. 23 1/2 cm. [BX922-.B45] 7-13527
1. Presbyterian church in the U.S.A.—Clergy. I. Beecher, Mary A. II. Title.

SMITH, Elwyn Allen, 1919- 262.14
The Presbyterian ministry in American culture, a study in changing concepts, 1700-1900. Philadelphia, Published for the Presbyterian Historical Society by Westminster Press [1962] 269 p. 21 cm. (Presbyterian Historical Society. Studies in Presbyterian history) [BX8936.S4] 62-16251
1. Presbyterian Church in the U.S. — Clergy. 2. Clergy — Office. I. Title.

Presbyterian church in the U.S.A. Confession of faith.

PRESBYTERIAN church in the U. S. A. Presbytery of Pennsylvania. 266.
A display of the religious principles of the Associate presbytery of Pennsylvania ... 2d ed. Philadelphia, Printed and sold by John M'Culloch, 1802. 184 p. 18 cm. Preface signed: William Marshall. [BX8958.P4A5 1802] 18-1773
I. Marshall, William. II. Title.
Contents omitted.

WEED, Henry Rowland, 1789-1870.
Questions on the Confession of faith and Form of government of the Presbyterian church in the United States of America, with a selection of Scripture proofs: designed for the instruction of classes in the doctrines of said church. By Henry R. Weed, D.D. Philadelphia, Presbyterian board of publication, 1842. 108 p. 16 cm. Pages [3]-[4] bound between p. 6-7. [BX8923.W4] 38-24310
1. Presbyterian church in the U.S.A. Confession of faith. 2. Presbyterian church in the U.S.A. Form of government. I. Presbyterian church in the U.S.A. (Old school) Board of publication. II. Title.

Presbyterian church in the United States—Discipline.

PRESBYTERIAN church in the U. S. A. General assembly. 285.173
Digest of the acts and deliverances of the General assembly of the Presbyterian church in the United States of America ... Issued from the office of the General assembly and by its authority. Philadelphia, Pa., 1930. 2 v. 24 cm. On cover: The Presbyterian digest, 1930. Introduction signed: Lewis Seymour Mudge, editor; William P. Finney, associate editor. "Part i, consisting exclusively of historical documents has been placed in a separate volume, volume ii, together with such portions of the other several parts as do not have direct relation to the interpretation of the constitution or to the work of the agencies. Therefore volume i opens with part ii, containing the text of the Confession of faith, together with accompanying acts and deliverances consonat with the Assembly direction."--Explanatory note. BX8956.A5 1930 a -- The Presbyterian digest. Supplement to volumes i and ii, 1930 edition, containing the Book of discipline, 1934, with the pertiment acts and deliverances of the General assembly, 1789-1934, and acts and deliverances of the General assembly, 1931-1934 inclusive, relating to the sections of the form of government and the directory for worship. Issued from the office of the General assembly and by its authority. Philadelphia, Pa., 1934. xvi, 310 p. 24 cm. Introduction signed: Lewis Seymour Mudge, editor; William Parker Finney, associate editor. [BX8956.A5 1930 a] 31-3924
1. Presbyterian church in the U. S. A.—Discipline. I. Mudge, Lewis Seymour, 1868- ed. II. Finney, William Parker, 1861- joint ed. III. Title. IV. Title: The Presbyterian digest, 1930.

PRESBYTERIAN church in the U. S. A. General assembly. 285.173
Digest of the acts and deliverances of the General assembly of the Presbyterian church in the United States of America ... Issued from the office of the General assembly and by its authority. Philadelphia, Pa., 1938. 2 v. 24 cm. On cover: The Presbyterian digest, 1938. Introduction signed: Lewis Seymour Mudge, editor; William Parker Finney, associate editor. "Part i, consisting exclusively of historical documents, has been placed in a separate volume, volume ii, together with such portions of the other several parts as do not have direct relation to the interpretation of the constitution, or to the work of the agencies. Therefore volume i opens with part ii, containing the text of the Confession of faith, together with accompanying acts and deliverances consonant with the Assembly's direction."--Explanatory note. [BX8956.A5 1938 a] 39-32367
1. Presbyterian church in the U. S. A.—Discipline. I. Mudge, Lewis Seymour, 1868- ed. II. Finney, William Parker, 1861- joint ed. III. Title. IV. Title: The Presbyterian digest, 1938.

PRESBYTERIAN Church in the U. S. A. General Assembly. 262.9851
A digest of the acts and proceedings of the General Assembly of the Presbyterian Church in the United States, 1861-1965. Atlanta, 1966. ix, 489 p. 24 cm. [BX8956.A5] 66-5073
1. Presbyterian Church in the U. S. A.—Discipline. I. Title.

PRESBYTERIAN church in the U.S. General assembly. 285.173
A digest of the acts and proceedings of the General assembly of the Presbyterian church in the United States, 1861-1944 ... Richmond, Va., Presbyterian committee of publication, 1945. xi, 543 p. 24 cm. [BX8966.A5] 45-20561
1. Presbyterian church in the U.S.—Discipline. I. Title.

Presbyterian church in the U.S.A.—Doctrinal and controversial works.

BEECHER, Lyman, 1775-1863. 285.
Views in theology. By Lyman Beecher ... Published by request of the synod of Cincinnati. Cincinnati, Truman and Smith New York, Leavitt, Lord and co., 1836. ix, [11]-240 p. 19 cm. Contents.Introduction.--Natural ability.--Moral ability.--Original sin.--Total depravity.--Regeneration. [BX9193.B4V5] 39-3730
1. Presbyterian church in the U.S.A.—Doctrinal and controversial works. 2. Man (Theology). I. Presbyterian church in the U.S.A. Synod of Cincinnati. II. Title.

BEECHER, Lyman, 1775-1863. 285.
... Views of theology; as developed in three sermons, and on his trials before the presbytery and synod of Cincinnati, June, 1835. With remarks on the Princeton review, By Lyman Beecher, D.D. Boston, J.P. Jewett & company; Cleveland, O., Jewett, Proctor & Washington, 1853. iv, [5]-456 p. front. (port.) 19 cm. (Beecher's works. vol. III.) [BX9193.B4V52] 39-3731
1. Presbyterian church in the U.S.A.—Doctrinal and controversial works. 2. Man (Theology). I. Presbyterian church in the U.S.A. Presbytery of Cincinnati. II. Presbyterian church in the U.S.A. Synod of Cincinnati. III. Title.

BRIGGS, Charles Augustus, . 1841-1913. 285.
The defence of Professor Briggs before the Presbytery of New York, December 13, 14, 15, and 19, 1892. New York, C. Scribner's sons, 1892. xx, 182 p. 23 cm. [BX9193.B7A6 1892] 5-1545
1. Presbyterian church in the U.S.A.—Doctrinal and controversial works. 2. Presbyterian church in the U.S.A. Presbytery of New York. I. Title.

BRIGGS, Charles Augustus, 1841-1913. 220.1
Inaugural address and defense, 1891/1893. New York, Arno Press, 1972. iii, xx, 193 p. 23 cm. (Religion in America, series II) Reprint of the author's The authority of Holy Scripture, first published 1891; and of his The defence of Professor Briggs before the Presbytery of New York, first published 1893. [BS480.B64 1972] 70-38442 ISBN 0-405-04062-8 16.00
1. Presbyterian Church in the U.S.A.—Doctrinal and controversial works. 2. Presbyterian Church in the U.S.A. Presbyteries. New York. 3. Bible—Evidences, authority, etc. I. Briggs, Charles Augustus, 1841-1913. The defence of Professor Briggs before the Presbytery of New York. 1972. II. Title.

[HAMILTON, Edward John] 1834-1918. 225
Rational orthodoxy; essays on mooted questions, by a member of the Presbytery of New York. New York and London, Funk & Wagnalls company, 1917. ix, 565 p. 21 1/2 cm. Lettered on cover: Rational orthodozy, by a New York presbyter. [BR121.H2] 17-5704 1.50
I. Title.

[MURRAY, John] 1742-1793.
Bath-kol. A voice from the wilderness. Being an humble attempt to support the sinking truths of God, against some of the principal errors, raging at this time. Or, a joint testimony to some of the grand articles of the Christian religion, judicially delivered to the churches under their care. By the first presbytery of the Eastward. Boston: Printed by N. Coverly, between the Sign of the Lamb and the White horse. M,DCCLXXXMI. 4, [v]-xxi, [22]-360, vii, [4] p. 15 1/2 cm. A projected second volume was apparently not published. [BX9174.M8] 43-34013
1. Presbyterian church in the U.S.A.—Doctrinal and controversial works. I. Title. II. Title: A voice from the wilderness.

PRESBYTERIAN Church in the U. S. A. 285.173
The Constitution of the Presbyterian Church in the United States of America, being its standards subordinate to the Word of God; viz., the Confession of faith, the Larger and Shorter catechisms, the Form of government, the Book of discipline, and the Directory for the worship of God, as ratified and adopted by the Synod of New York and philadelphia in the year of Our Lord 1788 and as amended, together with the general rules for judicatories. [Rev. ed.] Philadelphia, Published for the Office of the General Assembly by the Board of Christian Education of the Presbyterian Church in the U. S. A. [1956] ix, 457p. 26cm. [BX8955.A3 1956a] 56-10495
1. Presbyterian Church in the U. S. A.—Doctrinal and controversial works. 2. Presbyterian Church in the U. S. A.—Discipline. 3. Presbyterian Church in the U. S. A.—Catechisms and creeds. I. Title.

PRESBYTERIAN church in the U. S. A. 285.
The constitution of the Presbyterian church in the United States of America, containing the confession of faith, the catechisms, the government and discipline, and the directory for the worship of God, ratified and adopted by the Synod of New-York and Philadelphia, held at Philadelphia May the 16th, 1788, and continued by adjournments until the 28th of the same month. Philadelphia, Printed by Thomas Bradford, 1789. 3 p. l., 215 p. 17 cm. [BX8955] A 34
1. Presbyterian church in the U. S. A.—Doctrinal and controversial works. 2. Presbyterian church in the U. S. A.—Discipline. 3. Presbyterian church in the U. S. A.—Catechism and creeds. I. Title.

PRESBYTERIAN church in the U. S. A. 285.
The constitution of the Presbyterian church, in the United States of America. Containing, the confession of faith, the catechisms, the government and discipline, and the directory for the worship of God. Ratified and adopted by the Synod of New-York and Philadelphia, held at Philadelphia, May the 16th, 1788, and continued by Adjournments, until the 28th of the same month. Wilmington: Printed and sold by Bonsal and Niles. Also sold at their book-store, no. 173, Market-street, Baltimore, 1801. iv, 407 p. 16 cm. [BX8955.A3 1801] 42-26729
1. Presbyterian church in the U. S. A.—Doctrinal and controversial works. 2. Presbyterian church in the U. S. A.—Discipline. 3. Presbyterian church in the U. S. A.—Catechisms and creeds. I. Title.

PRESBYTERIAN church in the U. S. A. 285.
The constitution of the Presbyterian church in the United States of America: containing ... the Confession of faith, the Larger and Shorter catechisms, the Form of government, the Book of discipline, and the Directory for the worship of God, as ratified and adopted by the Synod of New York and Philadelphia in ... 1788, and as amended in the years 1805-1894; together with the constitutional rule adopted in 1893, and administrative acts of the assembly of a general nature. Philadelphia, Presbyterian board of publication and Sabbath-school work, 1896. 525 p. 18 cm. [BX8955.A3 1896] 41-40831
1. Presbyterian church in the U. S. A.—Doctrinal and controversial works. 2. Presbyterian church in the U. S. A.—Discipline. 3. Presbyterian church in the U. S. A.—Catechisms and creeds. I. Presbyterian church in the U. S. A. Board of publication. II. Title.

PRESBYTERIAN church in the U. S. A. 285.173
The constitution of the Presbyterian church in the United States of America, being ... the confession of faith, the larger and shorter catechisms, the form of government, the book of discipline, and the directory for the worship of God, as ratified and adopted by the Synod of New York Philadelphia in ... 1788 and as amended in the years 1805-1934, together with the Constitutional rule adopted in 1912 and general rules for judicatories. iPhiladelphia, Pub. for the office of the General assembly by the publication department of the Presbyterian board of Christian education, 1934. 2 p. l., iii-v, 3-532 p. 19 cm. [BX8955.A3 1934] 34-22376
1. Presbyterian church in the U. S. A.—Doctrinal and controversial works. 2. Presbyterian church in the U. S. A.—Discipline. 3. Presbyterian church in the U. S. A.—Catechisms and creeds. I. Title.

PRESBYTERIAN church in the U. S. A. 285.173
The constitution of the Presbyterian church in the United States of America, being ... the Confession of faith, the Larger and Shorter catechisms, the Form of governement, the Book of discipline, and the Directory for the worship of God, as ratified and adopted by the Synod of New York and Philadelphia in ... 1788 and as amended in the years 1805-1938, together with the constitutional rule adopted in 1912 and general rules for judicatories. Philadelphia, Pub. for the office of the General assembly by the Publication department of the Presbyterian board of Christian education, 1938. 2 p. l., iii-v, 3-532 p. 19 cm. [BX8955.A3 1938] 39-11960
1. Presbyterian church in the U. S. A.—Doctrinal and controversial works. 2. Presbyterian church in the U. S. A.—Discipline. 3. Presbyterian church in the U. S. A.—Cathechisms and creeds. I. Presbyterian church in the U. S. A. General assembly. II. Presbyterian church in the U. S. A. Board of Christian education. III. Title.

PRESBYTERIAN church in the U. S. A. (Old school) 285.173
The constitution of the Presbyterian church in the United States of America, containing the confession of faith, the catechisms, and the directory for the worship of God: together with the plan of government and discipline, as ratified by the General assembly, at their sessions in May, 1821; and amended in 1833. Philadelphia, Presbyterian board of publication [1839] 549 p. 16 cm. [BX8955.A3 1839] 38-14617
1. Presbyterian church in the U. S. A.—Doctrinal and controversial works. 2. Presbyterian church in the U. S. A.—Discipline. 3. Presbyterian church in the U. S. A.—Cathechims and creeds. I. Title.

SHEDD, William Greenough Thayer, 1820-1894. 230'.5
Dogmatic theology / by William G. T. Shedd. 2d ed. Nashville : T. Nelson, c1980. 3 v. : port. ; 21 cm. [BT75.S63 1980] 19 80-19709 ISBN 0-8407-5223-7 (v. 1) ISBN 0-8407-5743-3 (pbk. : v. 1) set : 37.50
1. Presbyterian Church in the U.S.A.—Doctrinal and controversial works. 2. Theology, Doctrinal. I. Title.

[WHELPLEY, Samuel] 1766-1817. 230.
The triangle. A series of numbers upon three theological points, enforced from various pulpits in the city of New-York. By Investigator. New-York, J. Wiley, 1832. ix, [11]-396 p. 23 cm. On cover: Whelpley's Triangle. "The first of the ... numbers was published in the New-York courier."--Dedication. Attributed by Cushing to Samuel Wheeler. [BX9175.W5 1832 a] 38-33872
1. Presbyterian church in the U.S.A.—Doctrinal and controversial works. 2. Calvinism. I. Title.

Presbyterian church in the United States—Education.

BROWN, Benjamin Warren, 1885-
Report of the survey of the educational work and responsibility of the Presbyterian church in the United States [by] B. Warren Brown. Louisville, Ky., 1928. cover-title, 87, [1] p. incl. tables. 23 1/2 cm. Errata slip. "This survey was authorized at the meeting of the Presbyterian educational association of the South, July 6th, 1927."-p. 3. "Third edition, August, 1928." [LC580B7] E37
1. Presbyterian church in the U.S.—Education. 2. Educational survey—[Southern states] I. Presbyterian education association of the south. II. Title.

GEIGER, C. Harve, 1893- 377.85173
The program of higher education of the Presbyterian church in the United States of America; an historical analysis of its growth in the United States, by C. Harve Geiger. Cedar Rapids, Ia., Laurance press, 1940. viii p., 1 l., 237 p. incl. tables, diagrs. 23 cm. Issued also as thesis (PH. D.) Columbia university. Bibliography: p. 229-237. [LC580. G4 1940 a] 42-15120
1. Presbyterian church in the U. S. A.—Education 2. Universities and colleges—U. S. I. Title. II. Title: Higher education of the Presbyterian church in the United States of America.

LISTON, R T L 377.851
The neglected educational heritage of Southern Presbyterians. Bristol, Tenn. [1956] 78p. 22cm. (The Smyth lectures, 1952) [LC580.L5] 59-38493
1. Presbyterian Church in the U. S.—Education. I. Title.

MILLER, Howard, 1941- 377'.8'5
The revolutionary college : American Presbyterian higher education, 1707-1837 / Howard Miller. New York : New York University Press, 1976. xxiii, 381 p. : ill. ; 24 cm. (New York University series in education and socialization in American history) Includes bibliographical references and indexes. [LC580.M48] 75-27053 15.00
1. Presbyterian Church in the U.S.A.—Education. I. Title. II. Series.

PRESBYTERIAN church in the U. S. 377.
A North American study in the field of religious education. Richmond, Va., Published for the Madras conference by the Presbyterian committee on publication, Presbyterian church in the United States [1938?] 59 p. 23 cm. Compiled by Robert M. Hopkins, cf. Introductory statement. Bibliography: p. 58-59. [LC580.P913] E 40
1. Presbyterian church in the U. S.—Education. 2. Religious education. I. Hopkins, Robert Milton, 1878- comp. II. Title.

PRESBYTERIAN church in the U. S. A. College board.
Annual report. 1st- 1883/84 Chicago, 1884- v. in 23 cm. Title varies: 1883/84-1903/04, Annual report of the Board of aid for colleges and academies ... 1904/05-Annual report [of] the College board ... [LC579.P9] E 15
1. Presbyterian church in the U. S. A.—Education. I. Title.

PRESBYTERIAN Church in the U. S. A. Board of Christian Education. 285.132
Report. Philadelphia. v. 24cm. annual. [BX8950.A28] 57-52819
1. Presbyterian Church in the U. S. A.—Education. I. Title.

PRESBYTERIAN Church in the U.S.A. Board of Christian Education. 377.85173
The Presbyterian college handbook, 1955-1956. Philadelphia [1955] 95 p. illus. 26 cm. [LC580.P7] 55-12680
1. Presbyterian Church in the U.S.A.—Education. 2. Universities and colleges—United States. I. Title.

PRESBYTERIAN church in the U.S.A. College board. 377.85173
Annual report. 1st- 1883/84- [New York, etc.] 1884- v. in. 22 1/2 cm. Reports for 1883/84-1903/04 issued under the board's earlier name: Board of aid for colleges and academies. [BX8950.A3] E 15
1. Presbyterian church in the U.S.A.—Education. I. Title.

PRESBYTERIAN church in the U. S. Executive committee of Christian education and ministerial relief.
Annual report. First. Louisville, Ky., The Franklin company, 1911- v. pl. 24 cm. The first report comprises the seventh report of the Executive committee of ministerial education and relief, the fiftieth report of the Executive committee of education for the ministry, the tenth report of the Executive committee of ministerial relief, the eighteenth report of the Assembly's home and school, the fifth report of the Executive committee of schools and colleges, all these committees being conslidated to form the present executive committee. E 13
1. Presbyterian church in the U. S.—Education. I. Title.

PRESBYTERIAN church in the U. S. Executive committee of Christian education and ministerial relief. 377.
Our Presbyterian educational institutions; the Executive committee of Christian education and ministerial relief of the Presbyterian church in the United States, Henry H. Sweets, secretary ... [Louisville, Ky.] 1914. 206 p. illus. (incl. ports.) fold. map. 23 cm. On cover: 1913-1914. [LC580.P7] 14-10269
1. Presbyterian church in the U. S.—Education. I. Sweets, Henry Hayes, 1872- II. Title.

PRESBYTERIAN church in the U. S. Exevutive committee of Christian education and ministerial relief. 377.85173
The blue book, and A friendly guide ... Louisville, Ky., [19 v. illus. (port.) 23 cm. [LC580.A15] 37-35894
1. Presbyterian church in the U. S.—Education. 2. Presbyterian church in the U. S.—Clergy—salaries, pensions, etc. I. Title. II. Title: A friendly guide.

PRESBYTERIAN church in the U.S. General assembly. 377.851
Report of a survey of the colleges and theological seminaries of the Presbyterian church in the United States; George A. Works, director. 1941-1942. Louisville, Ky. [1942] 2 p. l., iii-xiv, 145, [6] p. incl. tables. 23 cm. "A survey ... order by the General assembly."--Introductory, message, signed: Assembly's Committee on the Christian education movement. [LC580.A45 1942] 43-4920
1. Presbyterian church in the U.S.—Education. 2. Universities and colleges—U.S. 3. Theological seminaries, Presbyterian. I. Works, George Alan, 1877- II. Title.

SHERRILL, Lewis Joseph, 1892- 268.851
Lift up your eyes, a report to the churches on the religious education re-study. Richmond, John Knox Press [1949] xi, 175 p. diagrs. 21 cm. [BX8917.S5] 49-9588
1. Presbyterian Church in the U. S.—Education. I. Presbyterian Church in the U. S. Committee on Religious Education Re-study. II. Title.

SHERRILL, Lewis Joseph, 1892- 377.8510973
Presbyterian parochial schools, 1846-1870, by Lewis Joseph Sherrill ... New Haven, Yale university press; London, H. Milford, Oxford university press, 1932. xv p., 1 l., 261 p. 23 1/2 cm. (On Cover: Yale studies in religious education, [IV]) "The present volume is the fourth work published by the Yale university press on the Samuel B. Sneath memorial publication fund."--p. [v] "In its original form this study was presented to the faculty of the Graduate school of Yale university in candidacy for the degree of doctor of philosophy [1929] That manuscript of more than eight hundred pages, giving more detail than is necessary in publication, has been reduced to the present form."--Acknowledgments. [LC580.S5 1932] 32-8679
1. Presbyterian church in the U.S.A.—Education. 2. Church schools. I. Yale university. Samuel B. Sneath memorial publication fund. II. Title.

Presbyterian church in the United States (General)

PRINCETON theological seminary. 207.
The centennial celebration of the Theological seminary of the Presbyterian church in the United States of America, at Princeton, New Jersey, May fifth--May sixth--May seventh, nineteen hundred and twelve. Princeton, At the Theological seminary, 1912. xvi p., 1 l., 565, [1] p. 2 fold. facsim. (incl. front.) 27 cm. "This volume has been printed under the supervision of Benjamin B. Warfield, William P. Armstrong, Harold McA. Robinson, committee." [BV4070.P765 1912] 13-3730
I. Title.

THOMPSON, Charles Lemuel, 1839-1924. 285.
... *The Presbyterians,* by Charles Lemuel Thompson ... New York, The Baker & Taylor co. [1903] 5 p. l., 9-312 p. front. 18 1/2 cm. (The story of the churches) [BX8935.T5] 3-6153
1. Presbyterian church in the U.S. (General) I. Title.

VANDER VELDE, Lewis George. 285.173
The Presbyterian churches and the federal Union, 1861-1869, by Lewis G. Vander Velde... Cambridge, Harvard university press; London, H. Milford, Oxford university press, 1932. XV, 575 p. 23 cm. (Half-title: Harvard historical studies...vol. XXXIII) Bibliography: p. [523]-542. [BX8937.V3] 32-30007
1. Presbyterian church in the U.S. (General) 2. Slavery and the church—Presbyterian church. I. Title.

ZENOS, Andrew Constantinides, 1855- 285.173
Presbyterianism in America; past--present and prospective, by Andrew C. Zenos. New York, T. Nelson and sons, 1937. 9 p. l., 13-216 p. 19 1/2 cm. [BX8935.Z4] 37-35141
1. Presbyterian church in the U.S. (General) 2. Presbyterian church—Doctrinal and controversial works. I. Title.

Presbyterian Church in the United States (General)—Bibliography.

TRINTERUD, Leonard J., 1904- 016.285'133
A bibliography of American Presbyterianism during the colonial period, compiled by Leonard J. Trinterud. Philadelphia, Presbyterian Historical Society, 1968. 1 v. (unpaged) 24 cm. (Presbyterian Historical Society. Publications, 8) Cover title: Bibliography of colonial American Presbyterianism. [Z7845.P9T7] 70-128
1. Presbyterian Church in the United States (General)—Bibliography. I. Title. II. Title: Bibliography of colonial American Presbyterianism. III. Series.

Presbyterian Church in the United States (General)—Bibliography—Catalogs.

HISTORICAL Foundation of the Presbyterian and Reformed Churches. 016.23
Historical Foundation holdings of eighteenth-century American publications / compiled by Ruth D. See ; prepared in the office of Mary G. Lane, research librarian, the Historical Foundation of the Presbyterian and Reformed Churches. Montreat, N.C. : The Foundation, 1976. 100 p. ; 27 cm. (Historical Foundation

working bibliographies) Includes index. [Z7751.H65 1976] [BR118] 77-351275
1. Presbyterian Church in the United States (General)—Bibliography—Catalogs. 2. Reformed Church in the United States—Bibliography—Catalogs. 3. Historical Foundation of the Presbyterian and Reformed Churches. 4. Theology—Bibliography—Catalogs. I. See, Ruth Douglas, 1910- II. Title. III. Series: Historical Foundation of the Presbyterian and Reformed Churches. Historical Foundation working bibliographies.

Presbyterian Church in the United States (General) — Clergy — Correspondence, reminiscences, etc.

RANKIN, Alexander Taylor, 1803-1885. 978.1'02'0924
Alexander Taylor Rankin, 1803-1885, his diary and letters; a pioneer minister who fought lawlessness with religion on the prairies of eastern Kansas and the frontier settlements of Denver, where life was harsh and brutal. [Edited] by Nolie Mumey. Boulder, Colo., Johnson Pub. Co., 1966. 188 p. illus.. ports. 29 cm. The diary and letters date from 1859 to 1861. "A limited edition of four hundred signed and numbered copies." No. 44. [BX9225.R33A3] 66-9515
1. Presbyterian Church in the U.S. (General)—Clergy—Correspondence, reminiscences, etc. 2. Frontier and pioneer life—Kansas. 3. Frontier and pioneer life—Colorado. I. Mumey, Nolie, 1891- ed.

Presbyterian church in the United States (General)—History

ARMSTRONG, Maurice Whitman, 1905- ed. 285.173
The Presbyterian enterprise; sources of American Presbyterian history, edited by Maurice W. Armstrong, Lefferts A. Loetscher [and] Charles A. Anderson. Philadelphia, Westminster Press [1956] 336p. 24cm. Bibliography: p. 323-328. [BX8935.A7] 56-7368
1. Presbyterian Church in the U. S. (General)—Hist. I. Title.

ARMSTRONG, Maurice Whitman, 1905- ed. 285.173
The Presbyterian enterprise; sources of American Presbyterian history, edited by Maurice W. Armstrong, Lefferts A. Loetscher [and] Charles A. Anderson. Philadelphia, Westminster Press [1956] 336p. 24cm. Bibliography: p. 323-328. [BX8935.A7] 56-7368
1. Presbyterian Church in the U. S. (General)—Hist. I. Title.

PATTON, Jacob Harris, 1812-1903. 285.
A popular history of the Presbyterian church in the United States of America, by Jacob Harris Patton ... New York, R. S. Mighill and company, 1900. xxiii, 560 p. front., ports. 24 cm. "The following authorities have been consulted": p. [vii] [BX8935.P3 1900] 0-3070
1. Presbyterian church in the U. S. (General)—Hist. 2. Presbyterian church in the U. S. A.—Hist. I. Title.

SLOSSER, Galus Jackson, 1887- ed. 285
They seek a country; the American Presbyterians, some aspects. Contributors: Frank H. Caldwell [and others] New York, Macmillan, 1955. xvi, 330 p. illus., ports. 22 cm. Bibliography: p. 322-324. [BX8935.S55] 55-14554
1. Presbyterian Church in the U.S. (General)—History. I. Title.

SPENCE, Irving, 1799-1836. 285.
Letters on the early history of the Presbyterian Church in America, addressed to the late Robert M. Laird; with a sketch of the life of the author and a selection from his religious writings. Philadelphia, H. Perkins, 1838. 199 p. 20 cm. Cover title: Early history of the Presbyterian Church. [BX8935.S7] 51-48837
1. Presbyterian Church in the U. S. (General)—Hist. I. Laird, Robert M. II. Title.

THOMPSON, Robert Ellis, 1844-1924. 284
... A history of the Presbyterian churches in the United States, by Robert Ellis Thompson, D.D. New York, The Christian literature co., 1895. xxxi, 424 p. 21 cm. (Half-title: The American church history series, vol. vi) Series title also at head of t.-p. Bibliography: p. xi-xxxi. [BR515.A5 vol. 6] 4-4660
1. Presbyterian church in the U.S. (General)—Hist. 2. Presbyterianism—Hist. I. Title.

TRINTERUD, Leonard J., 1904- 285'.173
The forming of an American tradition; a re-examination of colonial Presbyterianism [by] Leonard J. Trinterud. Freeport, N.Y., Books for Libraries Press [1970, c1949] 352 p. 24 cm. Bibliography: p. [309]-320. [BX8936.T7 1970] 78-124262
1. Presbyterian Church in the U.S. (General)—History. I. Title.

Presbyterian Church in the United States (General) — History — Sources.

SWEET, Willia, Warren, 1881-1959, ed. 285.173
The Presbyterians, a collection of source materials. New York, Cooper Square Publishers, 1964 [c1936] xii, 939 p. maps. 22 cm. (His Religions on the American frontier, 1783-1840, v. 2) Bibliography: p. 888-917. [BX8935.S75 1964] 65-1622
1. Presbyterian Church in the U.S. (General) — Hist. — Sources. 2. Presbyterian Church in the U.S. (General) — Hist. 3. Frontier and pioneer life — U.S. I. Title.

SWEET, William Warren, 1881- ed. 285.173
... The Presbyterians, 1783-1840, a collection of source materials, by William Warren Sweet. New York and London, Harper and brothers, 1936. xii, 939 p. 1 illus., maps. 22 cm. (His Religion on the American frontier, vol. II) "First edition." Bibliography: p. 888-917. [BX8935.S75] 36-15032
1. Presbyterian church in the U.S. (General)—Hist.—Sources. 2. Presbyterian church in the U.S. (General)—Hist. 3. Frontier and pioneer life—U.S. I. Title.

Presbyterian Church in the United States—Government.

GARRISON, Pinkney J 1906- 285.1
Presyterian policy and procedures: the Presbyterian Church, U. S. Richmond, John Knox Press [1953] 190p. 25cm. [BX8966.G37] 53-11602
1. Presbyterian Church in the U.S.—Government. I. Title.

JUMPER, Andrew A. 262.15
Chosen to serve: the deacon; a practical manual for the operation of the board of deacons in the Presbyterian Church in the United States. Richmond, Va., John Knox [c.1961] 128p. 61-18257 1.25 pap.,
1. Presbyterian Church in the United States—Government. 2. Deacons. I. Title.

JUMPER, Andrew A 262.14
The noble task: the elder; a practical manual for the operation of the church session in the Presbyterian Church in the United States, by Andrew A. Jumper. [Rev. ed.] Richmond, John Knox Press [1965] 158 p. 21 cm. Bibliographical footnotes. [BX8966.J8] 65-14420
1. Presbyterian Church in the U.S. — Government. I. Title.

JUMPER, Andrew A. 262.14
The noble task: the elder; a practical manual for the operation of the church session in the Presbyterian Church in the United States, [Rev. ed.] Richmond, Knox [c.1965] 158p. 21cm. Bibl. [BX8966.J8] 65-14420 1.50 pap.,
1. Presbyterian Church in the U.S.—Government. I. Title.

JUMPER, Andrew A. 262
The noble task: the elder; a practical manual for the operation of the church session in the Presbyterian Church in the United States. Richmond, Va., John Knox [c.1961] 143p. 61-18256 1.50 pap.,
1. Presbyterian Church in the U.S.—Government. I. Title.

LA ROE, Wilbur, 1888- 285.173
Lawyer, moderator. New York National Council of Presbyterian Men [1949] 192 p. 20 cm. [BX9225.L36A3] 49-1563
1. Presbyterian Church in the U. S. A.—Government. I. Title.

PRESBYTERIAN church in the U.S.A. 285.
Manual for church officers and members, of the govenment, discipline, and worship of the Presbyterian church in the United States of America. [Philadelphia] Pub. for the office of the General assembly by the publication department of the Board of Christian education, 1926. 387 p. 18 1/2 cm. Introduction signed: Lewis Seymour Mudge, William P. Finney. Bibliography: p. 11-12. [BX8956.A5 1926] 26-6679
1. Presbyterian church in the U.S.A.—Government. I. Mudge, Lewis Seymour, 1868- ed. II. Finney, William Parker, 1861-joint ed. III. Title.

PRESBYTERIAN church in the U.S.A. 285.173
Manual for church officers and members, of the government, discipline, and worship of the Presbyterian church in the United States of America. 13th ed. [Philadelphia] Pub. for the office of the General assembly by the Publication division of the Board of Christian education of the Presbyterian church in the United States of America, 1945. 412 p. 19 cm. On spine: Manual of Presbyterian law for church officers and members. Introduction signed: Lewis Seymour Mudge. William Parker Finney. "Amendments to the Manual ... enacted by the 1945 General assembly": [3] p. inserted. Bibliography: p. 11-12. [BX8956.A5 1945] 45-11399
1. Presbyterian church in the U.S.A.—Government. I. Mudge, Lewis Seymour, 1868- ed. II. Finney, William Parker, 1861-joint ed. III. Presbyterian church in the U.S.A. General assembly. IV. Presbyterian church in the U.S.A. Board of Christian education. V. Title.

PRESBYTERIAN Church in the U.S.A. 262.05'132
Presbyterian law for the local church; a handbook for church officers and members, edited by Eugene Carson Blake. 1967 revision by William P. Thompson. Philadelphia, Office of the General Assembly, United Presbyterian Church in the United States of America, 1967 [c1963] 145 p. 23 cm. [BX8956.A6 1967] 68-2613
1. Presbyterian Church in the U.S.A.—Government. I. Blake, Eugene Carson, 1906- ed. II. Thompson, William P., 1918- III. Title.

PRESBYTERIAN Church in the U.S.A. 262.05'132
Presbyterian law for the presbytery; a manual for ministers and ruling elders by Eugene Carson Blake [and] Edward Burns Shaw. 1967 revision by William P. Thompson. Philadelphia, Office of the General Assembly, United Presbyterian Church in the United States of America, 1967 [c1966] 187 p. 23 cm. [BX8956.A5 1967] 63-11693
1. Presbyterian Church in the U.S.A.—Government. I. Blake, Eugene Carson, 1906- II. Shaw, Edward Burns. III. Thompson, William P., 1918- IV. Title.

PRESBYTERIAN church in the U. S. A. 285.173
Manual for church officers and members of the govenment, discipline, and worship of the Presbyterian church in the United States of America. 5th ed. [Philadelphia] Pub. for the office of the General assembly by the publication dept. of the Board of Christian education, 1934. 405 p. 19 cm. Introduction signed: Lewis Seymour Mudge, William Parker Finney. Bibliography: p. 11-12. [BX8956.A5 1934] 34-1914
1. Presbyterian church in the U. S. A.—Government. I. Mudge, Lewis Seymour, 1868- ed. II. Finney, William Parker, 1861-joint ed. III. Title.

PRESBYTERIAN church in the U. S. A. 285.
Manual for church officers and members, of the government, discipline, and worship of the Presbyterian church in the United States of America. [Philadelphia] Pub. for the office of the General assembly by the publication department of the Board of Christian education, 1926. 387 p. 19 cm. Introduction signed: Lewis Seymour Mudge, William P. Finney. Bibliography: p. 11-12. [BX8956.A5 1926] 26-6679
I. Mudge, Lewis Seymour, 1868- ed. II. Finney, William Parker, 1861- joint ed. III. Title.

PRESBYTERIAN church in the U. S. A. 285.173
Manual for church officers and members, of the government, discipline, and worship of the Presbyterian church in the United States of America, 4th ed. [Philadelphia] Pub. for the office of the General assembly by the publication department of the Board of Christian education, 1930. 393 p. 19 cm. Introduction signed: Lewis Seymour Mudge, William P. Finney. Bibliography: p. 11-12. [BX8956.A5 1930] 30-30890
I. Mudge, Lewis Seymour, 1868- ed. II. Finney, William Parker, 1861- joint ed. III. Title.

PRESBYTERIAN church in the U. S. A. 285.173
Manual for church officers and members of the government, discipline, and worship of the Presbyterian church in the United States of America. 8th ed. [Philadelphia] Pub. for the office of the General assembly by the Publication department of the Board of Christian education, 1938. 405 p. 19 cm. Introduction signed: Lewis Seymour Mudge. William Parker Finney. Bibliography: p. 11-12. [BX8956.A5 1938] 39-11959
1. Presbyterian church in the U. S. A.—Government. I. Mudge, Lewis Seymour, 1868- ed. II. Finney, William Parker, 1861-joint ed. III. Presbyterian church in the U. S. A. General assembly. IV. Presbyterian church in the U. S. A. Board of Christian education. V. Title.

PRESBYTERIAN church in the U. S. A. General assembly. 285.173
The Presbyterian digest: a compend of the acts and deliverances of the General assembly of the Presbyterian church in the United States of America. Compiled by the order and authority of the General assembly. By William E. Moore, D. D., 1873. Philadelphia, Presbyterian board of publication [1874] 718 p. 23 cm. First published 1820 under title: A digest. [BX8956.A5 1874] 31-11219
I. Moore, William Eves, 1823-1899, ed. II. Title.

PRESBYTERIAN church in the U. S. A. General assembly. 285.173
The Presbyterian digest of 1886. A compend of the acts and deliverances of the General assembly of the Presbyterian church in the United States of America. Compiled by the order and authority of the General assembly. By the Rev. William E. Moore, D. D., embracing, with the contents of the edition of 1873, the acts of the Assembly from 1874 to 1885, inclusive and an addendum of the acts of the Assembly of 1886. Philadelphia, Presbyterian board of publication [1886] 876 p. 23 cm. [BX8956.A5] 31-11220
I. Moore, William Eves, 1828-1899, ed. II. Title.

PRESBYTERIAN church in the U. S. A. General assembly. 285.173
The Presbyterian digest of 1898. A compend of the acts, decisions, and deliverances of the General presbytery, General synod, and General assembly of the Presbyterian church in the United States of America, 1706-1897. Compiled by authority, and with the co-operation of a committee, of the General assembly. By the Rev. William E. Moore ... Philadelphia, Presbyterian board of publications and Sabbath-school work, 1898. xiviii, 909 p. 24 cm. [BX8956.A5 1898] 31-11221
I. Moore, William Eves, 1823-1899, ed. II. Title.

PRESBYTERIAN church in the U. S. A. General assembly. 285.173
The Presbyterian digest of 1907. A compend of the acts, decisions, and deliverances of the General presbytery, General synod, and General assembly of the Presbyterian church in the United States of America, 1706-1906. Compiled

for the years 1706-1897, by the Rev. William E. Moore ... with the cooperation of a committee of General assembly. Supplement for the years 1898-1906, edited by the Rev. William H. Roberts ... Philadelphia, Presbyterian board of publication and Sabbath-school work, 1907. ixi, 1127 p. 24 cm. [BX8956.A5 1907] 33-14917
I. Moore, William Eves, 1823-1899, ed. II. Roberts, William Henry, 1844-1920, ed. III. Presbyterian church in the U. S. A. Board of publication. IV. Title.

PRESBYTERIAN Church in 285.173
the U. S. A.
Presbyterian law for the local church; a handbook for church officers and members. Edited by Eugene Carson Blake. 3d ed., rev. [Philadelphia] Published for the Office of the General Assembly by the Division of Publication of the Board of Christian Education of the Presbyterian Church in the United States of America, 1956. 129p. 20cm. [BX8956.A6 1956] 56-10494
1. Presbyterian Church in the U. S. A.—Government. I. Blake, Eugene Carson, 1906- ed. II. Title.

PRESBYTERIAN Church in 285.173
the U. S. A.
Presbyterian law for the local church; a handbook for church officers and members, edited by Eugene Carson Blake. 4th ed. rev. [Philadelphia] Published for the Office of the General Assembly by the Division of Publication of the Board of Christian Education of the Presbyterian Church in the United States of America, 1957. 129p. 20cm. [BX8956.A6 1957] 57-11181
1. Presbyterian Church in the U. S. A.—Government. I. Blake, Eugene Carson, 1906- ed. II. Title.

PRESBYTERIAN Church in the 262.4
U. S. A.
Presbyterian law for the presbytery; a manual for ministers and ruling elders [by] Eugene Carson Blake [and] Edward Burns Shaw. Philadelphia, Published for the Office of the General Assembly by the General Division of Publication of the Board of Christian Education of the Presbyterian Church in the United States of America [1958] 157p. 23cm. 60-24677
1. Presbyterian Church in the U. S. A.—Government. I. Blake, Eugene Carson, 1906- II. Shaw, Edward Burns. III. Title.

PRESBYTERIAN Church in the U. 262
S. General Assembly.
The book of church order of the Presbyterian Church in the United States. Rev. ed. [n. p.] Printed by the Board of Christian Education for the General Assembly of the Presbyterian Church in the United States, 1961. 174p. 21cm. [BX8966.A45 1961] 61-42474
1. Presbyterian Church in the U. S.—Government. I. Title.

PRESBYTERIAN Church in the 262.4
U.S. General Assembly.
The book of church order of the Presbyterian Church in the United States. Rev. ed. Richmond, Printed for the General Assembly of the Presbyterian Church in the United States by the Board of Christian Education, 1963. 181 p. 21 cm. [BX8966.A45] 63-25949
1. Presbyterian Church in the U.S.—Government. I. Title.

. . . Presbyterian law for the local church; a handbook for church officers and members. 6th ed. Edited by Eugene Carson Blake. A treatment of Presbyterian law . . . based upon the Constitution of the United Presbyterian church in the United States of America and the Acts and deliverances of the General assembly. Revised 1960. [Philadelphia] Published for the Office of the General assembly by the General division of publication of the Board of Christian education of the Board of Christian education of the United Presbyterian church in the United States of America [c1960] 144p. 20cm.
I. Presbyterian Church in the U. S. A. II. Blake, Eugene Carson, 1906-

RAMSAY, Franklin Pierce, 1856-
An exposition of the form of government and the rules of discipline of the Presbyterian church in the United States. Richmond, Va., The Presbyterian committee of publication [1899] 298 p. 12 degree. 0-523
I. Title.

RAMSAY, Franklin Pierce, 1856-
An exposition of the form of government and the rules of discipline of the Presbyterian church in the United States. Richmond, Va., The Presbyterian committee of publication [1899] 298 p. 12 degree. 0-523
I. Title.

UNITED Presbyterian Church in
the U.S.A.
Presbyterian law for the Presbytery; a manual for ministers and ruling elders [by] Eugene Carson Blake [and] Edward Burns Shaw. Rev. 1963. Philadelphia, Office of the General Assembly, United Presbyterian Church in the U.S.A. [c1963] 156 p. 23 cm. On cover: 1962-63. 65-25778
I. Blake, Eugene Carson, 1906- II. Title.

WORKMAN, William Hay, comp.
Presbyterian rule, embracing the form of government, rules of discipline, and directory for worship, in the Presbyterian church in the United States ... Richmond, Va., The Presbyterian committee on publication [1898] 256 p. 16°. 98-204
I. Title.

WORKMAN, William Hay, 1858- 285.
1934, comp.
Presbyterian rule, embracing the form of government, rules of discipline, and directory for worship, in the Presbyterian church in the United States, re-arranged and annotated with the decisions of the General assembly of said church ... with remarks by the compiler, Rev. W. H. Workman. Richmond, Va., The Presbyterian committee on publication [1898] 256 p. 16 cm. [BX8966.W7 1898] 98-204
1. Presbyterian church in the U.S.—Government. I. Title.

WORKMAN, William Hay, 1858- 285.
1934, comp.
Presbyterian rule, embracing the form of government, rules of discipline and directory of worship in the Presbyterian church in the United States; rearranged and annotated with the decisions of the General assembly of said church ... and with remarks by the compiler, Rev. W. H. Workman. [n.p.] c1895 204, 21 p. 15 1/2 cm. [BX8966.W7 1895] 47-38443
1. Presbyterian church in the U.S.—Government. I. Title.

Presbyterian church in the U.S.A.—History

BAIRD, Samuel John, 1817- 285.
1893.
A history of the new school, and of the questions involved in the disruption of the Presbyterian church in 1838. By Sameul J. Baird ... Philadelphia, Claxton, Remsen & Haffelfinger, 1868. xii, 564 p. 20 cm. [BX8937.B3] 22-14656
1. Presbyterian church in the U. S. A.—Hist. I. Title.

CROSS CREEK, Ohio. Presbyterian
Church.
Sessional records of Cross Creek Presbyterian Church, Cross Creek Township, Jefferson Co., Ohio, from April 11, 1839 to Sept. 1, 1880. Copied from the original records by Helen Brodine, May, 1963. [n.p., 1963] i v. carbon copy in binder. Original volume is on file at the Wooster College, Wooster, Ohio. 64-38994
I. Brodine, Helen. II. Title.

HILL, William, 1769-1852. 285.
History of the rise, progress, genius, and character of American Presbyterianism; together with a review of "The constitutional history of the Presbyterian church in the United States of America, by Chas. Hodge ..." By William Hill ... Washington city, J. Gideon, jr., 1839. xv, 224 p. 24 cm. [BX8935.H5] 22-23423
1. Presbyterian church in the U.S.A.—Hist. I. Hodge, Charles, 1797-1878. The constitutional history of the Presbyterian church in the United States. II. Title.

HODGE, Charles, 1797-1878.
The constitutional history of the Presbyterian church in the United States of America. By Charles Hodge ... Philadelphia, W. S. Martien, 1839-40. 2 v. 23 1/2 cm. Contents.Pt. I, 1705 to 1741.--Pt. II. 1741 to 1788. [BX8936.H6 1839] 42-27085
1. Presbyterian church in the U.S.A.—Hist. I. Title.

HODGE, Charles, 1797-1878.
The constitutional history of the Presbyterian church in the United States of America. By Charles Hodge ... Philadelphia, Presbyterian Board of publication [1851] 2 pt. in 1 v. 23 1/2 cm. Contents.Pt. I. 1705 to 1741.--pt. II. 1741 to 1788. [BX8936.H6 1851] 42-27086
1. Presbyterian church in the U.S.A.—Hist. I. Presbyterian church in the U.S.A. (Old school) Board of publication. II. Title.

LAKE, Benjamin J 285.173
The story of the Presbyterian Church in the U.S.A. Philadelphia, Westminster Press [1956] 126p. 19cm. Presbyterian Church in the U.S.A.--Hist. [BX8952.L3] 56-7367
I. Title.

LAKE, Benjamin J 285.173
The story of the Presbyterian Church in the U. S. A. Philadelphia, Westminster Press [1956] 126p. 19cm. [BX8952.L3] 56-7367
1. Presbyterian Church in the U. S. A.—Hist. I. Title.

LOETSCHER, Lefferts 285.173
Augustine, 1904-
The broadening Church; a study of theological issues in the Presbyterian Church since 1869. Philadelphia, University of Pennsylvania Press, 1954. 195p. 24cm. Includes bibliographical references. [BX8952.L6] 54-7110
1. Presbyterian Church in the U. S. A.—Hist. I. Title. II. Title: Theological issues in the Presbyterian Church since 1869.

MARTIN, Isaac, 1758-1828. 922.
A journal of the life, travels, labours, and religious exercises of Isaac Martin. Philadelphia, Printed by W. P. Gibbons, 1834. 160 p. 19 cm. [BX7795.M333A3] 48-34206
I. Title.

PRESBYTERIAN Church in 285'.132
the U.S.A.
Records of the Presbyterian Church in the United States of America, 1706-1788. New York, Arno Press, 1969. 582 p. 24 cm. (Religion in America) Reprint of the 1904 ed. [BX8952.P73 1969] 75-83434
1. Presbyterian Church in the U.S.A.—History.

PRESBYTERIAN Church in 285.173
the U. S. Board of Church Extension.
Building the church. Edited by Patrick D. Miller, executive secretary. Atlanta, Dickson [1958] 93p. illus. 21cm. Includes bibliography. [BX8962.A4] 58-44411
1. Presbyterian Church in the U. S.—Hist. I. Title.

PRESBYTERIAN reunion: a 285
memorial volume. 1837-1871 ... New York, De W. C. Lent & company, 1870. 3 p. l., iii-viii, 568 p. front. (facsim.) plates, ports. 24 cm. Added t.-p., engraved. [BX8397.P8] 28-4990
1. Presbyterian church in the U. S. A.—Hist.

PRESBYTERIANS pioneer at Matawan; published as its history. Matawan, N. J. [author] 1959. 79p. illus.
I. Matawan, N. J. First Presbyterian Church.

STREET, T Watson. 285.10973
The story of southern Presbyterians. Richmond, John Knox Press [1960] 134 p. illus. 21 cm. Includes bibliography. [BX8962.S75] 60-11623
1. Presbyterian Church in the U.S. — Hist. I. Title.

THOMPSON, Ernest Trice, 285.175
1894-
Presbyterians in the South; v.1. Richmond, Va., Knox [c.1963] 629p. map (on lining papers) 24cm. Contents.v.1. 1607-1861. Bibl. 63-19121 9.75
1. Presbyterian Church in the U. S.—Hist. 2. Presbyterian Church in the Southern States. I. Title.

THOMPSON, Ernest Trice, 285.175
1894-.
Presbyterians in the South. Richmond, John Knox Press [c1963-] v. map (on lining papers) 24 cm. Contents.CONTENTS. -- v. 1. 1607-1861. Bibliography: v. 1, p. [597]-608. [BX8941.T5] 63-19121
1. Presbyterian Church in the U.S. — Hist. 2. Presbyterian Church in the Southern States. I. Title.

WOODS, Henry, 285.173
Presbyterian Minister.
The history of the Presbyterian controversey, with early sketches of Presbyterianism. By H. Woods ... Louisville [Ky.] Printed by N. H. White, 1843. viii, [9]-204 p. 19 cm. [BX8935.W7] 36-6886
1. Presbyterian church in the U.S.A.—Hist. 2. Presbyterian church—Hist. 3. Presbyterian church—Doctrinal and controversial works. I. Title. II. Title: The Presbyterian controversey.

Presbyterian church in the U.S.A.—History—Schism, 1837-1870.

BROWN, Isaac Van Arsdale, 285.173
1784-1861.
A historical vindication of the abrogation of the plan of union by the Presbyterian church in the United States of America. By the Rev. Isaac V. Brown... Philadelphia, W.S. & A. Martien, 1855. vi, [7]-325 p. 23 1/2 cm. On cover: Old school Presbyterianism vindicated. [BX8937.B8] 39-5063
1. Presbyterian church in the U.S.A.—Hist.—Schism, 1837-1870. 2. Presbyterian church in the U.S.A. (Old school) I. Title. II. Title: Old school Presbyterianism vindicated.

CROCKER, Zebulon. 285.173
The catastrophe of the Presbyterian church, in 1837, including a full view of the recent theological controversies in New England. By Zebulon Crocker ... New Haven, B. & W. Noyes, 1838. xii, 300 p. 19 cm. "List of publications on the Unitarian controversy": p. [298]: "List of publications on the New Haven controversy": p. 299-300. [BX8937.C8] 39-5791
1. Presbyterian church in the U. S. A.—Hist.—Schism, 1837-1870. 2. New England—Church history. I. Title.

PRESBYTERIAN church in 285.173
the U. S. A. General assembly.
Addresses delivered at the quarter-century anniversary of the reunion of the Old and New school Presbyterian churches, held in the Third Presbyterian church, Pittsburgh, Pa., May 23, 1895 ... Published by order of the General assembly. Philadelphia, Presbyterian board of publication and Sabbath-school work, 1895. 94 p. 19 cm. [BX8937.A5 1895] 39-5807
1. Presbyterian church in the U. S. A.—Hist.—Schism, 1837-1870. I. Presbyterian church in the U. S. A. Board of publication. II. Title.
Contents omitted.

PRESBYTERIAN church in the U. 280
S. A. (New school) Synod of New York
and New Jersey.
A history of the division of the Presbyterian church in the United States of America. By a committee of the Synod of New York and New Jersey. New York, M. W. Dodd, 1852. vii, [9]-278 p. 20 cm. [BX8937.A5 1852] 39-5808
1. Presbyterian church in the U. S. A.—Hist.—Schism, 1837-1870. I. Title.

Presbyterian church in the U.S.A.—Hymns.

COVERT, William Chalmers, 783.9
1864- ed.
Handbook to the Hymnal. William Chalmer Covert ... editor, Calvin Weiss Laufer ... associate editor ... Philadelphia. Presbyterian board of Christian education, 1935. ixi, 566 p. col. front. (music) 22 cm. "Principal sources consulted": p. ix. "Chronological table ... of the antecedents of 'The hymnal' (1933)": p. xx-xxi. [ML3176.C6H3] 35-9483
1. Presbyterian church in the U. S. A. Hymnal. 2. Presbyterian church—Hymns—

Hist. & crit. 3. Hymns. English—Hist & crit. I. Laufer, Calvin Weiss, 1874-1938. joint ed. II. Presbyterian church in the U. S. A. Board of Christian education. III. Title.

PRESBYTERIAN church in the U.S.A.
The hymnal. Edited by the Rev. Joseph T. Duryea, D.D. Philadelphia, J. A. Black [c1874] 2 p. l., 7-510 p. 19 x 14 1/2 cm. Also published under title: The Presbyterian hymnal. With music. [M2130.P7H9 1874a] 45-42166
1. Presbyterian church in the U.S.A—Hymns. 2. Hymns. 3. Hymns, English. I. Duryea, Joseph Tuthill, 1832-1898, ed. II. Title.

PRESBYTERIAN church in the U.S.A.
The Presbyterian hymnal. Philadelphia, Presbyterian board of publication [c1874] 510 p. 23 cm. Also published under title: The hymnal. "Compiled and edited by the Rev. Joseph T. Duryea." [M2130.P7H9 1874] 45-42029
1. Presbyterian church in the U.S.A.—Hymns. 2. Hymms, English. I. Duryea, Joseph Tuthill, 1832-1898, ed. II. Title.

Presbyterian Church in the United States—Missions.

AROUND the world: 266.
studies and stories of Presbyterian foreign missions: by a carefully selected company of students who personally visited and critically investigated most of the foreign mission stations of the Presbyterian church, U.S.A.: Charles Edwin Bradt ... William Robert King ... Herbert Ware Reherd ... assisted by Mrs. C. E. Bradt, Mrs. W. R. King. Miss Margaret Bradt. Wichita, Kan., The Missionary press co. (inc.) [c1912] 488 p. front., illus. (incl. maps) plates, ports. 20 1/2 cm. [BV2570.A8] 13-750
1. Presbyterian church in the U.S.A.—Missions. 2. Presbyterian church—Missions. I. Bradt, Charles Edwin, 1863?-1922 II. King, William Robert, 1868- III. Reherd, Herbert Ware, 1869- IV. Presbyterian church in the U.S.A. Board of foreign missions.

BROWN, Arthur Judson, 1856- 266.51
One hundred years; a history of the foreign missionary work of the Presbyterian church in the U.S.A., with some account of countries, peoples and the policies and problems of modern missions, by Arthur Judson Brown... with introduction by Charles R. Erdman... New York [etc] Fleming H. Revell company [c1936] 1140 p. maps, fold. tables. 23 1/2 cm. Map on front lining-paper. [BV2570.B7] 37-42
1. Presbyterian church in the U.S.A.—Missions. 2. Missions, Foreign. 3. Presbyterian church in the U.S.A. Board of foreign missions. I. Title.

CHESTER, Samuel Hall, 1851- 266.
Behind the scenes; an administrative history of the foreign work of the Presbyterian church in the United States, by Samuel H. Chester ... Austin, Tex., Press of Von Boeckmann-Jones co. [c1928] 145 p. 19 1/2 cm. "The chapters of this volume, with the exception of the last four, were given in substance in a series of missionary lectures to the faculty and students of Austin theological seminary in April of this year, 1928."--Introd. [BV2570.C4] 29-3919
1. Presbyterian church in the U.S.—Missions. 2. Missions, Foreign. I. Title.

CLARKE, James Everitt, 1868- 266.
See for yourself; an invitation and a challenge to Presbyterians, by James E. Clarke ... Philadelphia, Board of Christian education of the Presbyterian church in the U.S.A. [1927] v, 195 p. front., plates. 18 1/2 cm. [BV2570.C6] 27-10626
1. Presbyterian church in the U.S.A.—Missions. I. Title.

DOYLE, Sherman Hoadley, 1865- 277.
Presbyterian home missions: an account of the home missions of the Presbyterian church in the U.S.A., by Sherman H. Doyle ... Philadelphia. Presbyterian board of publication and Sabbath-school work, 1902. xiv, 318 p. front., plates, maps. 20 cm. [BV2766.P6D7] 2-16222
1. Presbyterian church in the U.S.A.—Missions. 2. Missions. Home. I. Title.

EASTMAN, Fred, 1886- 277.
Unfinished business of the Presbyterian church in America, by Fred Eastman; prepared under the direction of the Board of home missions of the Presbyterian church in the U.S.A., the Woman's board of home missions, the Board of publication and Sabbath school work, the Board of missions for freedmen. Philadelphia, The Westminster press, 1921. 176 p. front., plates. 19 1/2 cm. [BV2766.P6E2] 21-21580
1. Presbyterian church in the U.S.A.—Missions. 2. Missions. I. Title.

EDWARDS, Charles Eugene. 266'.5'132
The coming of the Slav. Philadelphia, Westminster Press, 1921. [San Francisco, R and E Research Associates, 1972] 148 p. map. 22 cm. Bibliography: p. 117. [BV2788.S68E4 1972] 71-165782 ISBN 0-88247-158-9 8.00
1. Presbyterian Church in the U.S.A.—Missions. 2. Slavs in the United States. I. Title.

EDWARDS, Charles Eugene. 922
The coming of the Slav, by Charles Eugene Edwards ... Philadelphia, The Westminster press, 1921. 148 p. ports., map. 18 1/2 cm. [BV2788.S68E4] 22-1225
1. Presbyterian church in the U.S.A.—Missions. 2. Slavs in the U.S. I. Title.

FULTON, Charles Darby, 1892- 266.51
Now is the time, by C. Darby Fulton ... Richmond, Va., Pub. for the executive committee of foreign missions, Presbyterian church, U.S., by John Knox press [1946] 188 p. 20 cm. [BV2570.F8] 47-18682
1. Presbyterian church in the U.S.—Missions. 2. Missions, Foreign. I. Presbyterian church in the U.S. Executive committee of foreign missions. II. Title.

GREEN, Ashbel, 1762-1848. 266.
Presbyterian missions, by Ashbel Green ... With supplemental notes by John C. Lowrie. New York, A. D. F. Randolph & company (incorporated) [c1893] 3 p. l., v-xiii, 249 p. 25 cm. Written at the request of the Board of foreign missions of the Presbyterian church. "This book is here reprinted as it left the author's pen, with a few omissions specified where they occur, and with some changes not affecting its meaning." cf. p. vii. "Of this large-paper edition three hundred copies have been printed. no. 150." "Presbyterian foreign missionaries": p. 243-245. "Books of reference": p. [246]-247. [BV2570.G74] 3-12157
1. Presbyterian church in the U. S. A.—Missions. I. Lowrie, John Cameron, 1808-1900, ed. II. Title.

JACKSON, Sheldon, 1834-1909. 266'.5'1798
Alaska, and missions on the north Pacific coast. With a new series introd. by Sidney Forman. Boston, Gregg Press, 1973 [c1880] p. (History of minority education) [E78.A3J32 1973] 73-1703 ISBN 0-8398-0964-6
1. Presbyterian Church in the United States of America—Missions. 2. Indians of North America—Alaska—Missions. 3. Alaska—Description and travel—1867-1896. I. Title. II. Series.

LOWRIE, John Cameron, 1808-1900. 266.51
A manual of missions; or, Sketches of the foreign missions of the Presbyterian church: with maps, showing the stations, and statistics of Protestant missions among unevangelized nations. By John C. Lowrie ... New York, A. D. F. Randolph, 1854. 74 p. double front., 1 illus., maps. 20 x 24 cm. [BV2570.L8 1854] 30-14938
1. Presbyterian church in the U. S. A.—Misssions. 2. Missions, Foreign. I. Title.

MCMILLAN, Homer, 1873- 277.3
Other men labored [by] Homer McMillan... Richmond, Va., Presbyterian committee of publication [c1937] vii, 151 p. 19 1/2 cm. "Prepared at the request of the Educational department of the Assembly's Executive committee of home missions...of the Presbyterian church in the United States."--Foreword. [BV2766.P6M27] [266.51] 37-11645
1. Presbyterian church in the U.S.—Missions. 2. Missions, Home. I. Presbyterian church in the U.S. Executive committee of home missions. II. Title.

MORRIS, Samuel Leslie, 1854- 922.573
Samuel Leslie Morris; an autobiography ... Richmond, Va., The Presbyterian committee of publication [c1932] 140 p. incl. front. (mounted port.) 21 cm. [BX9225.M63A3] 33-2539
1. Presbyterian church in the U.S.—Missions. 2. Missions, Home. I. Title.

MORSE, Hermann Nelson, 1887- 285.173
These moving times; the home mission of the church in the light of social trends and population shifts, by Hermann N. Morse ... Richmond, Va., John Knox press [1945] iv, 154 p. 17 1/2 cm. "For supplementary reading": p. 150-154. [BV2766.P6M72] [266.51] 45-7790
1. Presbyterian church in the U.S.A.—Missions. 2. Missions, Home. I. Title.

PRESBYTERIAN church in the U. S. Executive committee of foreign missions. 266.51
Foundations of world order: the foreign service of the Presbyterian church, U. S., by a missionary from each field, with an introduction. Richmond, Va., Published for the Executive committee of foreign mission, Presbyterian church, U. S., by John Knox press [c1941] 175 p. illus. (map) 19 cm. Maps on p. [2] and [3] of cover. Introduction signed: H. Kerr Taylor, educational secretary, Executive committee on foreign missions. [BV2570.P67] 42-1022
1. Presbyterian church in the U. S.—Missions. 2. Presbyterian church—Missions. I. Taylor, Hugh Kerr, 1891- II. Title.
Contents omitted.

PRESBYTERIAN church in the U. S. A. Board of missions for freedmen. 283
... Annual report of the Board of missions for freedmen of the Presbyterian church in the United States of America. Pittsburgh, 186. v. illus. 24 cm. Title varies: -5th (-1869/70) Annual report of the General assembly's Committee on freedmen of the Presbyterian church and the United States of America ... [6th- (1870/71-) Annual report of the Presbyterian committee of missions for freedmen of the Presbyterian church in the United States of America ... Annual report of the Board of missions for freedmen of the Presbyterian church, in the United States of America ... Library has Abstracts of Annual reports for 1872/73-1874/75, 1883/84-1887/88 in Presbyterian church in the U. S. A. (Old school) General assembly. Minutes. New series, v. 3, 8-11. [BV2783.P6] ca 30
1. Presbyterian church in the U. S. A.—Missions. 2. Negroes—Religion. 3. Negroes—Moral and social conditions. 4. Freedmen. I. Title.

PRESBYTERIAN Church in the U.S.A. Board of Foreign Missions. 266.51
New frontiers for old. New York, c1946. 181 p. illus., ports. 22 cm. Articles by various authors. [BV2570.A2A63] 47-7766
1. Presbyterian Church in the U.S.A.—Missions. 2. Presbyterian Church—Missions. I. Title.

PRESBYTERIAN Church in the U.S. Board of World Missions.
Consultation on World Missions, October 13-19, 1962, Montreat, N.C. Recommendations. [n.p., 1962] 63 p. 20 cm. 65-75594
1. Presbyterian Church in the U.S.—Missions. I. Title.

SHALOFF, Stanley, 1939- 266.5'133'09675
Reform in Leopold's Congo. Richmond, Va., John Knox Press [1970] 195 p. illus., map. 21 cm. Bibliography: p. [184]-189. [BV3625.C6S45] 77-103464 5.95
1. Presbyterian Church in the U.S.—Missions. 2. Missions—Kasai, Congo (Province) 3. Kasai, Congo (Province)—History. I. Title.

SMITH, Egbert Watson, 1862-1944. 266.51
From one generation to another, by Egbert W. Smith. Richmond, Va., Pub. for the Executive committee of foreign missions, Educational department, Presbyterian church, U.S., by John Knox press [c1945] xv p., 1 l., 136 p. incl. front. (port.) 20 cm. [BV2570.S68] 46-20690
1. Presbyterian church in the U.S.—Missions. I. Presbyterian church in the U.S. Executive committee of foreign missions. II. Title.

SPEER, Robert Elliott, 1867- 266.
Presbyterian foreign missions; an account of the foreign missions of the Presbyterian church in the U.S.A. By Robert E. Speer ... Philadelphia, Presbyterian board of publication and Sabbath-school work, 1901. 296 p. 18 1/2 x 10 1/2 cm. [BV2570.S7] 1-15244
1. Presbyterian church in the U.S.A.—Missions. 2. Missions, Foreign. I. Title.

THOMPSON, Charles Lemuel, 1839- 277.
The soul of America; the contribution of Presbyterian home missions, by Charles Lemuel Thompson ... New York, Chicago [etc.] Fleming H. Revell company [c1919] 251 p. front., plates, ports. 19 cm. [BV2766.P6T5] 19-19866
1. Presbyterian church in the U.S.A.—Missions. 2. Presbyterian church in the U.S.A. Board of home missions. 3. Presbyterian church in the U.S.A. Woman's board of home missions. 4. Missions, Home—Hist. I. Title.

THOMPSON, Ernest Trice, 1894- 277.5
Presbyterian missions in the southern United States, by Ernest Trice Thompson ... Richmond, Va., Texarkana, Ark., Tex., Presbyterian committee of publication, 1934. 6 p. l., 15-281 p. maps. 19 cm. [BV2793.T47] [266.5] 39-31300
1. Presbyterian church in the U.S.—Missions. 2. Missions—Southern states. 3. Missions, Home—Hist. I. Title.

WILLIAMS, Henry Francis, 1848-
In four continents; a sketch of the foreign missions of the Presbyterian church, U.S., by Rev. Henry F. Williams ... Richmond, Va., Presbyterian committee of publication, 1910. 230 p. incl. front. plates. 20 cm. $0.50. 10-22540
I. Title.

WILLIAMS, Henry Francis, 1848-
In four continents; a sketch of the foreign missions of the Presbyterian church, U.S., by Rev. Henry F. Williams ... Richmond, Va., Presbyterian committee of publication, 1910. 243 p. incl. front. plates, maps. 19 1/2 cm. $0.50. "Books suggested for missionary libraries": p. 241-243. 11-1766
I. Title.

WRIGHT, Julia (MacNair) 1840-1903. 266'.5'1798
Among the Alaskans. With a new series introd. by Sidney Forman. Boston, Gregg Press, 1973 [c1883] p. (History of minority education) [E78.A3W74 1973] 73-1701 ISBN 0-8398-2181-6
1. Presbyterian Church in the United States of America—Missions. 2. Indians of North America—Alaska—Missions. 3. Alaska—Description and travel—1867-1896. I. Title. II. Series.

Presbyterian Church in the U.S.A. (New school)

MARSDEN, George M., 1939- 285'.173
The evangelical mind and the new school Presbyterian experience; a case study of thought and theology in nineteenth-century America [by] George M. Marsden. New Haven, Yale University Press, 1970. xiii, 278 p. 23 cm. (Yale publications in American studies, 20) Bibliography: p. [256]-264. [BX8937.M37] 75-118731 ISBN 0-300-01343-4 10.00

1. Presbyterian Church in the U.S.A. (New school) 2. Evangelicalism—United States. I. Title. II. Series.

Presbyterian Church in the U.S.A. (Old School)—Government.

PRESBYTERIAN Church in the U.S.A. (Old School) 285.
The form of government, the discipline, and the directory for worship of the Presbyterian Church in the United States of America. [As amended and ratified by the General Assembly, in May, 1821] Philadelphia, Presbyterian Board of Publication; W. S. Martien, publishing agent, 1840. 401-528 p. 16 cm. [BX8955.A35 1840] 50-46170
1. Presbyterian Church in the U.S.A. (Old School)—Government. 2. Presbyterian Church in the U.S.A. (Old School)—Discipline. I. Title.

Presbyterian Church in the U.S.A. (Old School). Synods. Wheeling.

MITCHELL, Osborne. 285'.1771'6
The Synod of Zoheeling : an old Scotch-Irish synod. [Wheeling? W. Va., 1971] 16 p. 23 cm. [BX8957.W45M57] 74-153607
1. Presbyterian Church in the U.S.A. (Old School). Synods. Wheeling. I. Title.

Presbyterian Church in the U.S.A. Presbyteries. Chicago.

LYONS, John Frederick, 1878- 285.1773
Centennial sketch of the history of the Presbytery of Chicago. Chicago, 1947. 53 p. 24 cm. Bibliography: p. 48-51. [BX8958.C47L9] 47-29967
1. Presbyterian Church in the U.S.A. Presbyteries. Chicago. I. Title.

Presbyterian Church in the United States Presbyteries. Hanover.

COLE, Lucy (Cole) 285.175546
History of woman's work in East Hanover Presbytery, by Mrs. Charles F. Cole; introd. by Edward Mack. Richmond, Richmond Press, 1938. 151 p. ports. 19 cm. [BX8968.H3C6] 38-18517
1. Presbyterian Church in the U.S. Presbyteries. Hanover. 2. Presbyterian Church in the U.S. Woman's Auxiliary. 3. Women in church work — Virginia. I. Title.

PRESBYTERIAN Church in the U. S. Presbyteries. Honover. 285.1755
Minutes. [n. p.] v. 23cm. Issued [BX8968.H3A3] 52-16064
I. Title.

Presbyterian Church in the United States Presbyteries. Lexington.

WILSON, Howard McKnight. 285'.1755
The Lexington Presbytery heritage; the Presbytery of Lexington and its churches in the Synod of Virginia, Presbyterian Church in the United States. [Verona, Va.] McClure Press [1971] xiii, 510 p. illus., facsim., maps, ports. 24 cm. Bibliography: p. 399-412. [BX8947.V8W53] 72-156142 8.50
1. Presbyterian Church in the U.S. Presbyteries. Lexington. I. Title.

Presbyterian Church in the United States Presbyteries. Mecklenburg.

BROCKMANN, Charles Raven, 1888- 285.10975676
Mecklenburg Presbytery, a history Photos. by Bruce Roberts. Mecklenburg Presbytery [dist. Charlotte, N.C., McNally, & Loftin, c.]1962. 148p. 32cm. Bibl. 63-900 5.00
1. Presbyterian Church in the U.S. Presbyteries. Mecklenburg. I. Title.

BROCKMANN, Charles Raven, 1888- 285.10975676
Mecklenburg Presbytery, a history. Photos. by Bruce Roberts. Charlotte, N.C., Office of the Executive Secretary. Mecklenburg Presbytery, 1962. 148 p. illus. 32 cm. [BX8968.M4B7] 63-990
1. Presbyterian Church in the U.S. Presbyteries. Mecklenburg. I. Title.

Presbyterian Church in the United States Presbyteries. Orange.

STONE, Robert Hamlin, 1896- 262'.4
A history of Orange Presbytery, 1770-1970. Greensboro, N.C. [Orange Presbytery] 1970. xxviii, 430 p. illus., facsims. (part col.), maps (part col.), ports. 25 cm. Bibliography: p. 403-405. [BX8968.O7S75] 78-19371 10.00
1. Presbyterian Church in the U.S. Presbyteries. Orange. I. Title.

Presbyterian Church in the United States Presbyteries. Winchester.

WOODWORTH, Robert Bell, 1868- 285.1754
A history of the Presbytery of Winchester (Synod of Virginia); its rise and growth, ecclesiastical relations, institutions and agencies, churches and ministers, 1719-1945. Based on official documents. Staunton, Va., McClure Print. Co., 1947. x, 521 p. illus., ports., maps. 24 cm. [BX8968.W5W6] 48-522
1. Presbyterian Church in the U. S. Presbyteries. Winchester. 2. Churches—Virginia. I. Title.

Presbyterian church in the U.S.A. Presbytery of Blairsville.

HAYS, Calvin Cornwell, 1861- 285.174889
History of the Presbytery of Blairsville and its churches, by Calvin C. Hays ... Published by the Presbytery in celebration of the completion of one hundred years of activity, 1830-1930. [Pittsburgh, Pittsburgh printing company, 1931?] 193 p. incl. front., plates, ports., fold. map. 23 1/2 cm. [BX8958.B6H3] 32-35372
1. Presbyterian church in the U.S.A. Presbytery of Blairsville. I. Title.

Presbyterian Church in the U.S.A. presbytery of Chicago.

CHICAGO. Third Presbyterian church. Library association. 016.
... Catalogue. Constitution and by-laws. March 1, 1889. Chicago, Printed by Woman's temperance publication association [1889] 188 p. 15 cm. At head of title: Library association of the Third Presbyterian church, Chicago. [Z881.C536] 15-17228
I. Title.

Presbyterian church in the U.S.A. Presbytery of Cincinnati.

SKINNER, Thomas Harvey, 1820-1892. 266.
The complaint of the Rev. Thomas H. Skinner, against the action of the presbytery of Cincinnati, at its fall meeting, 1876, with the argument. Cincinnati, Gazette company print, 1876. 51 p. 23 cm. [BX8958.C53S5] 39-7031
1. Presbyterian church in the U.S.A. Presbytery of Cincinnati. I. Title.

Presbyterian church in the United States Presbytery of East Hanover.

COLE, Lucy (Cole) Charles F. Cole." "Mrs. 285.175546
History of woman's work in East Hanover Presbytery, by Mrs. Charles F. Cole; introduction by Rev. Edward Mack ... Richmond, Richmond press, inc., 1938. 151 p. ports. 19 cm. [BX8968.E3C6] 38-18517
1. Presbyterian church in the U.S. Presbytery of East Hanover. 2. Presbyterian church in the U.S. Woman's auxiliary. 3. Women in church work. I. Title.

Presbyterian church in the United States Presbytery of Greenbrier.

COURTNEY, Lloyd McFarland, 1889- 285.1754
The church on the western waters; an history of Greenbrier presbytery and its churches, by Lloyd McF. Courtney ... Richmond, Va., Whittet & Shepperson, 1940. 5 p. l., 13-123 p. 21 cm. [BX8968.G7C6] 41-11390
1. Presbyterian church in the U. S. Presbytery of Greenbrier. I. Title.

Presbyterian church in the U.S.A. Presbytery of Huntington.

WHITE, John White, 1828-1901, defendant. 285.
A full report of the trial of Rev. John W. White for heresy by the Huntington (Pa.) presbytery, September 4, 5, and 6, 1883. Philadelphia, E. Claxton and company [1883?] cover-title, 95 p. 21 1/2 cm. [BX9193.W65A3] 42-35126
1. Presbyterian church in the U.S.A. Presbytary of Huntington. I. Title.

Presbyterian church in the U.S.A. Presbytery of Huron.

MOORE, Robert Braden, 1835-1906. 266.
History of Huron presbytery, showing the working of the plan of union from its inception in 1801 till after the reunion in 1870; also the spirit of the presbytery regarding religious, general, and national interests; with biographical notice of some ministers, and sketches of the churches. Compiled and written by Rev. R. Braden Moore, D.D. Philadelphia, Press of W. F. Fell & co., 1892. ix, 486 p. 22 1/2 cm. [BX8958.H85.M6] 22-22544
1. Presbyterian church in the U.S.A. Presbytery of Huron. I. Title.

Presbyterian Church in the United States Presbytery of Kanawha.

PRESBYTERIAN Church in the U.S.A. Presbytery of Kanawha.
History of the Presbytery of Kanawha, 1895-1956. [Charleston, W. Va., Jarrett Printing Co. 1956?] vi, 804 p. illus. 24 cm. 68-98558
1. Presbyterian Church in the U. S. Presbytery of Kanawha. I. Title.

Presbyterian church in the U.S.A. Presbytery of Kansas City.

HILL, John Boynton, 1860- comp. 266.
The Presbytery of Kansas City and its predecessors 1821-1901; historical sketches and statistical matter by John B. Hill ... Kansas City, The Burd & Fletcher printing co., 1901. 336 p. front. (fold. map) ports. 23 cm. Published by the Presbytery of Kansas City, Presbyterian church in the United States of America. [BX8958.K3H5] 1-28234
1. Presbyterian church in the U.S.A. Presbytery of Kansas City. I. Title.

Presbyterian church in the U.S.A. Presbytery of Redstone.

SMITH, Joseph, 1796-1858. 285.1748
Old Redstone; or, Historical sketches of western Presbyterianism, its early ministers, its perilous times, and its first records. By Joseph Smith ... Philadelphia, Lippincott, Grambo & co., 1854. x, 11-459 p. front., plates, ports. 28 cm. [BX8958.R4S6] 35-36297
1. Presbyterian church in the U.S.A. Presbytery of Redstone. 2. Presbyterian church in Pennsylvania. 3. Presbyterian church in Virginia. 4. Presbyterian church in the U.S.A.—Biog. I. Title.

Presbyterian church in the U.S.A. Presbytery of San Francisco.

EDWARDS, Vina Howland, Mrs. 266.51
The story of the San Francisco presbyterial society, 1883-1933, by Vina Howland Edwards. With thumb-nail histories of societies. Oakland, Calif., A. Newman, 1933. 3 p. l. 9-80 p. incl. front., ports. 20 cm. "Thumb-nail histories of societies from reports edited by Mrs. Donald U. Ross": p. 61-80. On cover: Golden jubilee, 1883-1933. [BX8958.S3E3] 33-35343
1. Presbyterian church in the U.S.A. Presbyterial of San Francisco. I. Ross, Jessie Harriette (Slocombe) "Mrs. Donald U. Ross", 1876- II. Title.

Presbyterian church in the U.S.A. Presbytery of Westminster.

CLARK Robert Lorenzo, 1849- 285.1748
A history of the Presbytery of Westminser and its antecedents, 1732- 1924, compiled by Rev. Robert L. Clark...Published for the Presbytery by the Historical committee, Robert L. Clark, George H. Shea, Alex M. Grove. [Chicago, The Regan printing and publishing co., 1924. 9 p. l., 545 p. front., plates, ports. 24 cm. [BN958.W45C6] 31-35711
1. Presbyterian church in the U.S.A. Presbytery of Westminster. I. Shea, George Hopkins. II. Grove, Alex M. III. Title.

Presbyterian Church in the U.S.—Relations—Addresses, essays, lectures.

PRESBYTERIAN Church in the U.S. Ecumenical Consultation. 262'.001
Report of the Ecumenical Consultation, Kanuga Conference Center, Hendersonville, North Carolina, October 27-31, 1975. [Atlanta] : Office of the Stated Clerk, Presbyterian Church in the United States : available from Materials Distribution Service, c1976. 55 p. ; 25 cm. [BX9171.A1P73 1976] 77-150902 0.50
1. Presbyterian Church in the U.S.—Relations—Addresses, essays, lectures. 2. Christian union—Presbyterian Church—Addresses, essays, lectures.

Presbyterian church in the U.S.A.—Relations—Protestant Episcopal church in the U.S.A.

RICHARDSON, Cyril Charles, 1909- 285.173
The sacrament of reunion; a study in ecumenical Christianity with particular reference to the proposed concordat between the Presbyterian and Protestant Episcopal churches, by Cyril C. Richardson... New York, C. Scribner's sons; London, C. Scribner's sons, ltd., 1940. x p., 1 l., 120 p. 19 1/2 cm. "Important books": p. 113-115. [BX9171.P7R5] 40-6021
1. Presbyterian church in the U.S.A.—Relations—Protestant Episcopal church in the U.S.A. 2. Protestant Episcopal church in the U.S.A.—Relations—Presbyterian church in the U.S.A. 3. Christian union. I. Title.

Presbyterian Church in the U.S.—Relations—United Presbyterian Church in the U.S.A.

JOINT committee on organic union. 285.173
The plan of union providing for the organic union of the presbyterian church in the United States of American and the United Presbyterian church of North America, prepared, by the Joint committee on organic union. [Philadelphia?] 1934. 176 p. 22 x 13 cm. [BX8951.A75 1934] 36-104
1. Presbyterian church in the U. S. A.—Relations—United Presbyterian church of North America. 2. United Presbyterian church of North America—Relations—Presbyterian church in the U. S. A. I. Title.

PRESBYTERIAN Church in the U.S. 262'.001
Study draft of a plan for union of the Presbyterian Church in the United States and the United Presbyterian Church in the United States of America. Submitted to the 111th General Assembly (1971) of the Presbyterian Church in the United States and the 183d General Assembly (1971) of the United Presbyterian Church in the United States of America. [Philadelphia, 1971] 160 p. 23 cm. [BX9171.A1P73] 79-159762 0.50
1. Presbyterian Church in the U.S.—Relations—United Presbyterian Church in the U.S.A. 2. United Presbyterian Church in the U.S.A.—Relations—Presbyterian Church in the U.S. 3. Christian union—Presbyterian Church. I. United

Presbyterian Church in the U.S.A. II. Title. III. Title: A plan for union.

Presbyterian church in the U.S.A.—Sermons.

BROWN, William Adams, 1865- 243
Finding God in a new world, and other sermons preached at home and abroad, by William Adams Brown... New York and London, Harper & brothers, 1935. vii p., 21., 105 p. 19 cm. "First edition." [BX9178.B743F5] 252 35-38289
1. Presbyterian church—Sermon. 2. Sermons, American. I. Title.

BUTZER, Albert George, 252.051
1893-
You and yourself, by Albert George Butzer; with an introduction by Harry Emerson Foedick. New York and London, Harper & brothers, 1933. viii, 117 p. 20 cm. "First edition." [BX9178.B87Y6] 33-6200
1. Presbytrian church—Sermons. 2. Sermons, American. I. Title.

MCLEOD, Malcolm James, 252.051
1867-
Heavenly harmonies, by Malcolm James McLeod. With preface by Hon. John V. Farwell. Chicago, The Bible institute colportage association [c1901] 2 p. l., 9-124 p. 18 cm. (On cover: The colportage library, v. 7, no. 108) [BX9178.M27H4] 1-25587
1. Presbyterian church in the U.S.A.—Sermons. 2. Sermons, American. I. Title.

NEVINS, William, 1797-1855. 252
Sermons, by the late Rev. William Nevins, D. D. New York, J. S. Taylor, 1837. 3 p. l., [v]-viii, [13]-428 p. front. (port.) 20 cm. [BX9178.N4S4] 18-15921
1. Presbyterian church—Sermon. 2. Sermons, American. I. Title.

VAN DYKE, Henry, 1852-1933.
...The open door, by Henry Van Dyke... Philadelphia, Presbyterian board of publication and Sabbath-school work, 1903. v. 160 p. front. (port.) 19 1/2 cm. (The Presbyterian pulpit. [no. 5]) [PX9178.V307] 3-12773
1. Presbyterian cnurch—Sermons. 2. Sermons, American. I. Title.
Contents omitted.

Presbyterian church in the U.S.A.—Statistics

WEBER, Herman Carl, 1873-
Presbyterian statistics through one hundred years, 1826-1926, tabulated, visualized, and interpreted [by] Rev. Herman C. Weber ... [Philadelphia] The General council, Presbyterian church in the U.S.A., 1927. 206 p. incl. tables, diagrs. 24 cm. [BX8952.W4] 27-11306
1. Presbyterian church in the U.S.A.—Stat. 2. Presbyterian church—Stat. 3. Church statistics—U.S. I. Title.

Presbyterian Church in the United States — Synod of Appalachia.

CRAIG, Edward Marshall, 277.5
1867-1918, ed.
Highways and byways of Appalachia; a study of the work of the Synod of Appalachia of the Presbyterian church in the United States ... compiled and edited by Rev. Edward Marshall Craig ... [Kingsport, Tenn., Kingsport press] 1927. 3 p. l., ix-x, 183 p. illus. (incl. ports.) fold. mounted map. 20 cm. [BX8967.A6C7] 266.51 31-20218
1. Presbyterian church in the U. S. Synod of Appalachia. I. Title.

MONTREAT, N.C. College.
Montreat-Anderson College; fifty years of service in nineteen hundred and sixty-six, affiliated with Asheville Presbytery and the Synod of Appalachia. [Montreat, 1963] 1 v. 23 cm. Called Montreat Normal School, 1916-1937; Montreat College, 1938-1961. 64-11892
1. Presbyterian Church in the U.S. — Synod of Appalachia. I. Title.

Presbyterian church in the United States Synod of Missouri.

PRESBYTERIAN church in 285.1778
the U. S. Synod of Missouri. Home mission committee.
"Show me"; Presbyterian study book, synod Missouri, Presbyterian church, U. S. ... Compiled and edited by I. F. Swallow ... Kansas City, Mo., Simpson printing company [1927] 184 p. illus. (ports.) plates, fold. map. 20 cm. The folded map is attached to back cover. [BX8947.M8S85] 34-22105
1. Presbyterian church in the U. S. Synod of Missouri. 2. Missions—Missouri. I. Swallow, Isaac Francis, 1873- ed. II. Title.

Presbyterian church in the United States Synod Oklahoma.

PRESBYTERIAN church in the U. S.
Synodical of Oklahoma.
Oklahoma trails; a history of the work of the Synod of Oklahoma of the Presbyterian church in the United States. Prepared under the direction of the Synodical of Oklahoma, Mrs. Luther Fountain, president ... compiled and edited by Mrs. G. T. Ralls. [Atoka, Okla., Atoka press] 1927. 200 p. illus. (incl. ports.) 21 cm. [BN8967.O5A4] 28-5266
1. Presbyterian church in the U. S. Synod Oklahoma. I. Ralls, Elle Mae (Battenberg) "Mrs. G. T. Ralls," 1875- ed. II. Title.

Presbyterian Church in the U.S.A. Synods. New York.

NEW York tribune.
... The two Presbyterian assemblies of 1889 ... New York, The Tribune association [1889] cover-title, 96 p. 26 cm. (Library of Tribune extras. vol. 1., June, 1889, no. 6) "The two General assemblies. New-York and Chattanooga: May, 1889." 9-31578
I. Title.

NICHOLS, Robert 285.1747
Hastings, 1873-1955.
Presbyterianism in New York State; a history of the Synod and its predecessors. Edited and completed by James Hastings Nichols. Philadelphia, Published for the Presbyterian Historical Society by Westminister Press [1963] 288 p. 21 cm. (Presbyterian Historical Society. Studies in Presbyterian history) Includes bibliography. [BX8957.N7N5] 63-8820
1. Presbyterian Church in the U.S.A. Synods. New York. 2. United Presbyterian Church in the U.S.A. Synods. New York. 3. Presbyterian Church in New York. I. Nichols, James Hastings, 1915- II. Title.

PRESBYTERIAN church in 285.173
the U. S. A. General assembly.
A digest, compiled from the records of the General assembly of the Presbyterian church in the United States of America, and from the records of the late synod of New York and Philadelphia, of their acts and proceedings, that appear to be of permanent authority and interest; together with a short account of the missions conducted by the Presbyterian church. By order of the General assembly. Philadelphia: Printed for the trustees of the Assembly by R. P. M'Culloh, 1820. xii, [13]-391 p. illus. 19 cm. On cover: The assembly's digest. Edited by J. J. Janeway, William Neill. and E. S. Fly. cf. p. [iii] aJaneway, Jacob Jones, [BX8956.A5 1820] 31-11218
I. Neill, William, 1778-1860, joint ed. II. Ely, Ezra Stiles, 1786-1861, joint ed. III. Title. IV. Title: The assembly's digest.

Presbyterian Church in the United States — Synods — North Carolina.

DUDLEY, Harold James.
History of Synod of N.C., Presbyterian Church in the U.S. Cover title. Additions and corrections in MS. 65-44347
1. Presbyterian Church in the U.S. — Synods — North Carolina. I. Title.

DUDLEY, Harold James.
History of Synod of N.C., Presbyterian Church in the U.S. [Raleigh? N.C., 1963] 106 p. 28 cm. Cover title. Additions and corrections in MS. 65-44347
1. Presbyterian Church in the U.S. — Synods — North Carolina. I. Title.

GARTH, John Goodall, 1871- 277.56
Sixty years of home missions in the Presbyterian Synod of North Carolina. [Charlotte? 1948?] 86 p. illus., ports. 23 cm. [BX8957.N8G3] 49-54672 ISBN] 266.51:.
1. Presbyterian Church in the U. S. Synods. North Carolina. 2. Missions—North Carolina. I. Title.

PRESBYTERIAN Church in the U.S.
Synods. North Carolina.
Minutes of the sessions. Fayetteville. v. 22 cm. annual. [BX8967.N8A3] 50-45675
I. Title.

Presbyterian Church in the U.S.A. Synods. Virginia.

BRIMM, Henry M., comp. 285'.1755
Yesterday and tomorrow in the Synod of Virginia. Henry M. Brimm [and] William M. E. Rachal, editors. Richmond, Synod of Virginia, Presbyterian Church in the United States, 1962. 131 p. 21 cm. "The six addresses which make up this book were presented as the major feature of the Synod of Virginia's observance of the centennial of the Presbyterian Church in the United States." [BX8957.V57B74] 74-172641
1. Presbyterian Church in the U.S.A. Synods. Virginia. I. Rachal, William M. E., joint comp. II. Presbyterian Church in the U.S.A. Synods. Virginia. III. Title.

PRESBYTERIAN Church in the U. S.
Synods. Virginia.
Minutes. Richmond [etc.] v. 23cm. annual. [BX8967.V5A3] 58-52545
I. Title.

Presbyterian church in the United States—United States—Missions—Congress.

PRESBYTERIAN church in the 266.51
U. S. Laymen's missionary movement. General convention. 4th Charlotte, N. C., 1915.
Facing the situation; addresses delivered at the fourth General convention of the Laymen's missionary movement, Presbyterian church in the U. S., held in Charlotte, N. C., Feb. 16-18, 1915, Dallas, Texas, Feb. 23-25, 1915. Athens, Ga., Laymen's missionary movement, Presbyterian church in the United States [1915?] 5 p. l., 13-376 p. tables, diagr. 23 cm. [BV2570.A75L3 1915] 33-35970
1. Presbyterian church in the U. S.—U. S.—Missions—Congress. 2. Missions—Congress. I. Presbyterian church in the U. S. Laymen's missionary movement. General vonvention. 4th Dallas, Tex., 1915. II. Title.

Presbyterian church in the U.S.A. West Africa mission.

HALSEY, Abram Woodruff, 276.6
1853-1921.
A visit to the West Africa mission of the Presbyterian church in the U.S.A. ... by the Rev. A. W. Halsey. New York city, Board of foreign missions of the Presbyterian church in the U.S.A. [19-] 71, [1] p. illus. 24 cm. [BV3540.H3] [266.51] 45-52211
1. Presbyterian church in the U.S.A. West Africa mission. 2. Missions—Africa, West. I. Presbyterian church in the U.S.A. Board of foreign missions. II. Title.

Presbyterian church in the U.S.A. Western Indian mission. Miraj station.

WANLESS, William, Sir, 275.4
1865-
An American doctor at work in India, by Sir William Wanless ... introduction by Robert E. Speer. New York [etc.] Fleming H. Revell company [c1932] 2 p. l., 3-200 p. front. (port.) illus. (plans) 19 1/2 cm. "A brief history of the Miraj medical mission, together with a paper on medicine in India, read by invitation before the New York academy of medicine, November 13, 1929."--Prefatory note. [R722.W3] (266.51) 32-24846
1. Presbyterian church in the U.S.A. Western Indian mission. Miraj station. 2. Missions, Medical. 3. Missions—Miraj, India. 4. Medicine—India. I. Title.

Presbyterian church in the United States Woman's auxiliary.

SPRINKLE, Patricia 285'.132
Houck.
The birthday book; first fifty years. Atlanta, Board of Women's Work, Presbyterian Church in the United States, 1972. xii, 296 p. illus. 23 cm. Includes bibliographical references. [BX8960.S67] 72-191652
1. Presbyterian Church in the U.S. Woman's Auxiliary. 2. Presbyterian Church in the U.S. Board of Women's Work. I. Title.

WINSBOROUGH, Hallie 267.4451
(Paxson) Mrs., 1865-
Yesteryears, by Hallie Paxson Winsborough ... as told to Rosa Gibbins. [Atlanta] Assembly's cOmmittee on woman's work, 1937. 7 p. l., 17-224 p. incl. front., illus., ports. 19 cm. "The story of ... the Woman's auxiliary of the Presbyterian church, U.S."--Foreword. [BX8905.P68W5] 37-24102
1. Presbyterian church in the U.S. Woman's auxiliary. I. Gibbins, Rosa. II. Presbyterian church in the U.S. Committee on woman's work. III. Title.

Presbyterian church in Virginia.

BRIERY Presbyterian 285.175563
church, Hampden district, Prince Edward co., Va.
A manual for the members An exact from an old copy now owned by Mrs. George W. Harlan ... Cape Girardeau, Mo., Mrs. R. B. Oliver, 1907. 2 p. l., [3]-60 p. incl. tables. 18 cm. With reproduction of the original t.-p.: A manual for the members of the Briery Presbyterian church. Virginia. Compiled by James W. Douglas. Published by order of the session. Richmond, Printed by J. Macfarian, 1828. [BX9211.B77A5 1907] 15-10760
I. Douglas, James Walter, comp. II. Title.

GRAHAM, James Robert, 1825?- 285.
1914.
The planting of the Presbyterian church in northern Virginia, prior to the organization of Winchester presbytery, December 4, 1794. By James R. Graham ... Winchester, Va., The Geo F. Norton publishing co., 1904. 3 p. l., 168 p. 24 cm. [BX8947.V8G7] 26-22114
1. Presbyterian church in Virginia. I. Title.

JOHNSON, Thomas Cary, 1859- 285.
Virginia Presbyterianism and religious liberty in colonial and revolutionary times, by Thos. Cary Johnson ... Richmond, Presbyterian committee of publication, 1907. 128 p. illus. (incl. ports.) 20 cm. [BX8947.V8J6] 21-20405
I. Title.

RICE, John Holt, 1777-1831. 285.
Ann [!] illustration of the character & conduct of the Presbyterian church in Virginia. By John H. Rice ... Richmond: Printed by Du-Val & Burke, 1816. 56 p. 23 cm. [BX8947.V8R5] 22-13805
1. Presbyterian church in Virginia. I. Title.

Presbyterian church in Washington (State)

PRESBYTERIAN church in 285.1797
the U. S. A. Synod of Washington.
History of the Synod of Washington of the Presbyterian church in the United States of America, 1835-1909 ... Historian: Rev. Robert Boyd ... Assistants: Rev. W. Chalmers Gunn [and] Rev. Hazen T. Murray ... [Seattle] The Synod [1910?] 1 p. l., x p., 1 l., 287, [1] p. inncl. illus., plates, ports. front. 24 cm. [BX8957.W3A52] 41-17062
1. Presbyterian church in Washington (State) I. Boyd, Robert, 1849-1917. II. Title.

Presbyterian church in Wisconsin.

[BROWN, William Fiske] 1845- 285.
Past made prsent; the first fifty years of the First Presbyterian church and congregation of Beloit, Wisconsin...together with a history of Presbyterianism in our state up to the year 1900... [Chicago, The Marsh & Grant co., 1900] 276, xxxvi, 14 p., 1 l., incl. front., illus., plates, ports., facsims. plates. 23 1/2 cm. No more published. [BX8947.W6B8] 0-5913
1. Presbyterian church in Wisconsin. 2. Beloit, Wis. 1st Presbyterian church. I. Title.

PRESBYTERIAN Church in the U.S.A. Synods. Wisconsin. 285.1775
Early Presbyterianism in Wisconsin. Centennial ed. [Waukesha? Wis., 1951] 116 p. illus. 22 cm. [BX8947.W6A3] 51-33042
1. Presbyterian Church in Wisconsin. I. Title.

WICKLEIN, Edward C. 285'.1775 s
A Wisconsin history of the Associate Presbyterian Church of North America, Associate Reformed Presbyterian Church of the West (later of America) Reformed Presbyterian Church of North America, Reformed Presbyterian Church, General Synod, United Presbyterian Church of North America, with historical sketches of each congregation, 1840-1958, by Edward C. Wicklein. [Waukesha, 1974] 29 l. illus. 28 cm. (His Badger kirk, v. 1) Bibliography: leaves 28-29. [BX8947.W6W53 vol. 1] 285'.1775 74-166460
1. Presbyterian Church in Wisconsin. I. Title.

Presbyterian Church in Wisconsin—Collected works.

WICKLEIN, Edward C. 285'.1775
Badger kirk; an historical study in the bounds of the former Synod of Wisconsin United Presbyterian Church in the U.S.A., by Edward C. Wicklein. [Waukesha, 1974- v. illus. 28 cm. Contents.Contents.—v. 1. A Wisconsin history of the Associate Presbyterian Church of North America, Associate Reformed Presbyterian Church of the West (later of America) Reformed Presbyterian Church of North America, Reformed Presbyterian Church, General Synod, United Presbyterian Church of North America. Bibliography: v. 1, leaves 28-29. [BX8947.W6W53] 74-166461
1. Presbyterian Church in Wisconsin—Collected works. I. Title.

Presbyterian Church. Liturgy and ritual.

BARKLEY, John Monteith. 264.05'2
The worship of the Reformed Church; an exposition and critical analysis of the eucharistic, baptismal, and confirmation rites in the Scottish, English-Welsh, and Irish liturgies, by John M. Barkley. Richmond, John Knox Press [1967] 132 p. 22 cm. (Ecumenical studies in worship, no. 15) Bibliography: p. 130. [BX9185.B3 1967] 67-10330
1. Presbyterian Church. Liturgy and ritual. I. Title. II. Series.

JOINT Committee on Worship 264.0513
The book of common worship; provisional services and lectionary for the Christian year. Philadelphia, Westminster, 1966. 157p. 22cm. [BX9185.J63] 66-6880 price unreported
1. Presbyterian Church. Liturgy and ritual. I. Title.

SHAFER, Floyd Doud. 264.05131
Liturgy; worship and work. Philadelphia, Board of Christian Education, United Presbyterian Church U.S.A. [1966] xii, [1], 109 p. 19 cm. Bibliography: p. [xiii] [BV10.2.S48] 66-31857
1. Presbyterian Church. Liturgy and ritual. 2. Worship. I. Title.

Presbyterian Church. Liturgy and ritual.—History

BAIRD, Charles Washington, 1828-1887. 264.051
The Presbyterian liturgies: historical sketches. Grand Rapids, Baker Book House, 1957. 266p. 19cm. First ed. published in 1855 under title: Eutaxiao or, The Presbyterian liturgies: historical sketches. [BX9185.B2 1957] 57-8257
I. Presbyterian Church. Liturgy and ritual. II. Title.

MELTON, Julius. 264.05'1
Presbyterian worship in America: changing patterns since 1787. Richmond, John Knox Press [1967] 173 p. 21 cm. Bibliographical references included in "Notes" (p. 149-163) [BX9185.M4] 67-22003
1. Presbyterian Church. Liturgy and ritual.—Hist. 2. Presbyterian Church in the U.S. (General)—Hist. I. Title.

MELTON, Julius. 264.05'1
Presbyterian worship in America: changing patterns since 1787. Richmond, John Knox Press [1967] 173 p. 21 cm. Bibliographical references included in "Notes" (p. 149-163) [BX9185.M4] 67-22003
1. Presbyterian Church. Liturgy and ritual.—History. 2. Presbyterian Church in the U.S. (General)—History. I. Title.

Presbyterian Church-Membership.

GETTYS, Joseph Miller, 1907- 265.2
Meet your church; how Presbyterians think and live. Richmond, John Knox Press [1955] Richmond, John Knox Press [1955] 62p. illus. 22cm. 35p. 22cm. Includes bibliography. [BX9190.G4] 55-6999
1. Presbyterian church—Membership. I. Title. II. Title: —Leader's guide.

PRESBYTERIAN Church in the U. S. A. Board of Christian Education. 230.51
The pastor's guide for the training of church members. Philadelphia [c1957] 205p. illus. 27cm. Includes bibliography. [BX9177.A35] 57-5028
1. Presbyterian Church—Membership. 2. Presbyterian Church— Doctrinal and controversial works. 3. Church membership—Study and teaching. I. Title.

SHERRILL, Lewis Joseph, 1892- 265.2
Becoming a Christain, a manual for communicant classes, by Lewis Joseph Sherrill and Helen Hardwicke Sherrill. Richmond, John Knox press, 1943. 5 p. l., 13-174 p. 16 cm. [BX9175.S45] 43-6240
1. Presbyterian church—Membership. I. Sherrill, Helen (Hardwicke) joint author. II. Title.

UNITED Presbyterian Church in the U.S.A. Board of Christian Education.
The pastor's guide for the training of church members. Phildelphia [1959] 205 p. illus. 27 cm. Earlier ed. (1957) published by the board under the eariler name of the church: Presbyterian Church in the U.S.A. Includes bibliography. 63-59692
1. Presbyterian Church-Membership. 2. Presbyterian Church-Doctrinal and controversial works. 3. Church membership-Study and teaching. I. Title.

Presbyterian church-Missions.

HANZSCHE, William Thomson, 1891- 266.51
And they went forth, by William Thomson Hanzsche. With illustrations by Cyrus Leroy Baldridge ... New York, N.Y., The Board of foreign missions of the Presbyterian church in the U.S.A. [1937] 6 v. in 1. illus. 24 cm. "The object of this series is to provide for the celebration of the centennial of the presbyterian board of foreign missions an analysis of the ... century." Contents.v. 1. Pioneering--v. 2. Preaching.--v. 3. Teaching.--v. 4. Healing.--v. 5. Reaping.--v. 6. Tomorrow. [BV2570.H3] 42-9216
1. Presbyterian church—Missions. 2. Presbyterian church in the U.S.A.—Missions. I. Presbyterian church in the U.S.A. Board of foreign missions. II. Title.

THE Isle of Palms, 266'.515127
sketches of Hainan : the American Presbyterian Mission. New York : Garland Pub., c1980. 153 p., [13] leaves of plates : ill. ; 19 cm. (The Modern Chinese economy) Reprint of the 1919 ed. printed at the Commercial Press, Shanghai. Includes index. Bibliography: p. [vi] [BV3420.H3I84 1980] 78-74354 ISBN 0-8240-4269-7 lib. bdg. : 15.00
1. Presbyterian Church—Missions. 2. Missions—China—Hainan. 3. Hainan—History. I. Presbyterian Church in the U.S.A. South China Mission. II. Series: Modern Chinese economy.

UNITED Presbyterian Church in the U.S.A.
An Advisory study. New York, U.P.C., 1962. 94 p. 63-59687
1. Presbyterian church-Missions. I. Title.

Presbyterian Church—Missions—History

BENNETT, Charles, 1932- 266'.00972'6
Tinder in Tabasco; a study of church growth in tropical Mexico. Grand Rapids, Erdmans [1968] 213p. illus., maps. 20cm. (Church growth ser.) Bibl. [BV2837.T3B] 67-28370 2.95 pap.,
1. Presbyterian Church—Missions—Hist. 2. Missions—Tabasco, Mexico. I. Title.

DRURY, Clifford. 1897- [266.51]
Presbyterian panorama; one hundred and fifty years of National Missions history. Philadelphia, Board of Christian Education, Presbyterian Church in the United States of America, 1952. xvi, 458 p. illus., ports., maps. 24 cm. Bibliography: p. [424]-429. [BV2570.D7] 277.3 52-9984
1. Presbyterian Church—Missions—Hist. 2. Presbyterian Church in the U. S. A. Board of National Missions. I. Title.

Presbyterian church of Chosen.

CLARK, Charles Allen, 1878- 275.19
The Korean church and the Nevius methods, by Charles Allen Clark... New York, Chicago [etc.] Fleming H. Revell company [c1930] 278 p. front., plates, map, diagr. 21 cm. "A disseriation for the author's dictorate of philosophy at the University of Chicago, June, 1929"--Author's pref. "Authorities referred to in this discussion": p. 273-276. [BX9151.K8C6] [266.5] 30-25510
1. Presbyterian church of Chosen. 2. Missions—Korea. 3. Nevins, John Livingston, 1829-1893. 4. Presbyterian church in the U.S.A.—Missions. I. Title.

Presbyterian Church of Dover.

EHINGER, Aline Noren. 284'.1751'5
Bridge across the years : a history of the Presbyterian Church of Dover, including chapters on the life of the community and denomination / by Aline Noren Ehinger. [Dover? Del. : s.n.], 1975. xi, 419 p., [4] leaves of plates : ill. ; 24 cm. Includes index. Bibliography: p. 406-415. [BX9211.D64P73] 76-359392
1. Presbyterian Church of Dover. I. Title.

Presbyterian Church—Prayer-books and devotions—English.

FERGUSON, James, 1873- ed. 264.05
Prayers for public worship; a service book of morning and evening prayers following the course of the Christian year. Compiled and edited by James Ferguson. American editor: Charles L. Wallis. New York, Harper [1958] 370 p. 22 cm. "A revision of [the author's] Prayers for common worship." Includes bibliography. [BX9185.F4 1958] 58-10369
1. Presbyterian Church—Prayer-books and devotions—English. I. Presbyterian Church. Liturgy and ritual. II. Title.

Presbyterian Church — Relations — Lutheran Church.

EMPIE, Paul E., ed. 230.57
Marburg revisited; a reexamination of Lutheran and Reformed traditions, Editors: Paul C. Empie & James I. McCord. Minneapolis, Augsburg [1966] 193p. 22cm. Papers and summaries prepd. in connection with a ser. of annual meetings held from Feb. 1962 through Feb. 1966. sponsored by the North Amer. Area of the World Alliance of Reformed Churches Holding the Presbvterian Order and the U.S.A. Natl. Comm. of the Lutheran World Fed. Bibl. [BX9171.L8E4] 67-11715 1.75 pap.,
1. elations — Presbyterian Church. 2. Presbyterian Church — Relations — Lutheran Church. I. McCord. James I., joint ed. II. Alliance of Reformed Churches throughout the World Holding the Presbyterian System. North American Area. III. National Lutheran Council. IV. Title.

Presbyterian Church—Sermons.

ADAMS, Charles Francis, 1869- 285.
The life and sermons of Rev. T. DeWitt Talmage, by Charles Francis Adams... Chicago, M. A. Donohue & co. [c1902] xvi, 13-50, 29-252, 23-192 p. front. (port) plates 20 cm. [BX9225.T3A6] 3-17066
1. Talmage, Thomas De Witt, 1832-1902 2. Presbyterian church—Sermons. I. Title.

ALEXANDER, Archibald, 1772-1851. 252.651
Practical sermons: to be read in families and social meetings. By Archibald Alexander... Philadelphia, Presbyterian board of publication [1850?] 571 p. front. (port.) 24 cm. [BX9178.A4P7] 33-15996
1. Presbyterian church—Sermons. 2. Sermons, American. I. Presbyterian church in the U. S. A. [Old school] Board of publication. II. Title.

ALEXANDER, Maitland, 1867-1940. 252.05
The burning heart, sermons by Maitland Alexander ... introduction by Clarence Edward Macartney. New York [etc.] Fleming H. Revell company [1942] 175 p. front. (port.) 19 1/2 cm. [BX9178.A464B8] 42-25448
1. Presbyterian church—Sermons. 2. Sermons, American. I. Mccartney, Clarence Edward Noble, 1879- ed. II. Title.

ALSTON, Wallace McPherson, 1906- 252.051
Break up the night Richmond, J. Knox Press [1947] 155 p. 32 cm. [BX9178.A483B7] 48-1553
1. Presbyterian Church—Sermons. 2. Sermons, American. I. Title.

ALSTON, Wallace McPherson, 1906- 252.051
The throne among the shadows, by Wallace McPherson Alston. Richmond, Va., John Knox press, 1945. 4 p. l. [11]-157 p. 19 1/2 cm. Bibliographical references included in "Acknowledgements." [BX9178.A83T5] 45-7959
1. Presbyterian church—Sermons. 2. Sermons, American. I. Title.

ANDERSON, Harrison Ray. 252.051
God's way; messages for our time. [Westwood, N. J., Revell [1955] 160p. 21cm. [BX9178.A497G6] 55-6627
1. Presbyterian Church—Sermons. 2. Sermons. American I. Title.

ANDERSON, Neal Larkin, 1865-1931. 243
God's world and word; addresses for to-day, by Neal L. Anderson ... New York, Chicago [etc.] Fleming H. Revell company [c1926] 160 p. 20 cm. [BX9178.A5G6 1926] 27-5153
1. Presbyterian church—Sermons. 2. Sermons, American. I. Title.

ARMSTRONG, James Francis, 1750-1816. 252'.05'2
Light to my path : sermons / by James F. Armstrong ; edited by Marian B. McLeod. Trenton : First Presbyterian Church, c1976. 68 p. : ill. ; 22 cm. [BX9178.A67L53] 77-366763
1. Presbyterian Church—Sermons. 2. Sermons, American. I. Title.

BABCOCK, Maltbie Davenport, 1858-1901. 244
Fragments that remain from the ministry of Maltbie Davenport Babcock, pastor Brick church, New York city, 1899-1901,

reported and arranged by Jessie B. Goetschius ... New York, Chicago [etc.] Fleming H. Revell company [c1907] 3 p. l., 5-316 p. front. (port.) 20 cm. [BX8915.B25] 7-32160
1. Presbyterian church—Sermons. 2. Sermons, American. I. Gestschius, Jessie B. II. Title.

BAIN, John Wallace, 1833-1910. 252
The golden pot, by the Rev. John W. Bain ... Philadelphia, J. M. White & co. [1898] 293 p. incl. front. (port.) 19 1/2 cm. [BX9178.B329G6] 98-1182
1. Presbyterian church—Sermons. 2. Sermons, American. I. Title.

BARNES, Albert, 1798-1870. 252.051
Practical sermons; designed for vacant congregations and families. By Albert Barnes. Philadelphia, H. Perkins, 1841. 356 p. 19 cm. [BX978.B35P7 1841] 33-4905
1. Presbyterian church—Sermons. 2. Sermons, American. I. Title.

BARNES, Albert, 1798-1870. 252.051
Practical sermons, designed for vacant congregations and families. By Albert Barnes. Philadelphia, Perkins & Purves, 1845. 356 p. 20 cm. [BX9178.B35P7 1845] 33-4906
1. Presbyterian church—Sermons. 2. Sermons, American. I. Title.

BARNHOUSE, Donald Grey, 1895- 252.051
Guaranteed deposits. Philadelphia, Revelation Publications [1949] 160 p. 20 cm. [BX9178.B37G8] 49-2670
1. Presbyterian Church—Sermons. 2. Sermons, American. I. Title.

BARNHOUSE, Donald Grey, 1895-1960. 226'.6'07
Acts, an expositional commentary / Donald Grey Barnhouse, with Herbert Henry Ehrenstein. Grand Rapids : Zondervan Pub. House, c1979. 233 p. ; 23 cm. [BS2625.4.B32 1979] 79-16213 ISBN 0-310-20510-7 : 9.95
1. Presbyterian Church—Sermons. 2. Bible. N.T. Acts—Sermons. 3. Sermons, American. I. Ehrenstein, Herbert Henry, joint author. II. Title.

BARNHOUSE, Donald Grey, 1895-1960. 227'.81'07
Thessalonians—an expositional commentary / Donald Grey Barnhouse. Grand Rapids : Zondervan Pub. House, c1977. 111 p. ; 21 cm. [BS2725.B37 1977] 77-1507 5.95
1. Presbyterian Church—Sermons. 2. Bible. N.T. Thessalonians—Sermons. 3. Sermons, American. I. Title.

BARRON, Vance, 1916- 252'.6
Sermons for the celebration of the Christian year / Vance Barron. Nashville : Abingdon, c1977. 95 p. ; 19 cm. [BX9178.B375S47] 76-51402 ISBN 0-687-37775-7 pbk. : 3.95
1. Presbyterian Church—Sermons. 2. Church year sermons. 3. Sermons, American. I. Title.

BELK, John Blanton, 1893- 252.051
Our fighting faith, by J. Blanton Belk. Richmond, Va., The John Knox press, 1944. 89 p. 20 1/2 cm. [BX9178.B392O8] 44-3764
1. Presbyterian church—Sermons. 2. Sermons, American. 3. Moral rearmament. I. Title.

BEVERIDGE, Thomas Hanna, 1830-1860. 922.573
Life and diary of the late Rev. Thomas B. Hanna, A. M., pastor of the Associate congregation of Clinton, Pa. By Thos. Hanna Beveridge. With selections from his sermons, and a portrait ... ... Philadelphia, W. S. Young, 1852. ix, 1 l., [13]-261 p. front. (port.) 21 cm. [BX9225.H335B4] 36-24873
1. Hanna, Thomas Beveridge, 1828-1852 2. Presbyterian church—Sermons. 3. Sermons, American. I. Title.

BIEDERWOLF, Wiliam Edward, 1867- 252.051
Awake, O America! By Wm. Edward Biederwolf ... Grand Rapids, Mich., W. B. Eerdmans publishing co., 1937. 192 p. 20 cm. "First edition." [BX9178.B48A85] 38-5980
1. Presbyterian church—Sermons. 2. Sermons, American. I. Title.

BIEDERWOLF, William Edward, 1867- 252.051
The kiss of Judas, by Wm. Edward Biederwolf ... Grand Rapids, Mich., Wm. B. Eerdmans publishing co., 1939. 142 p. 20 cm. [BX9178.B48K5] 39-9140
1. Presbyterian church—Sermons. 2. Sermons, American. I. Title.

BIEDERWOLF, William Edward, 1867- 252.051
The new paganism, and other sermons, by William Edward Biederwolf ... Grand Rapids, Mich., Wm. B. Eederman publishing company [c1934] 159 p. 20 cm. [BX9178.B463N4] 35-4608
1. Presbyterian church—Sermons. 2. Sermons, American. I. Title.

BIEDERWOLF, William Edward, 1867- 252.051
The wonderful Christ, by Wm. Edward Biederwolf, D. D. Grand Rapids, Mich., Wm. B. Eerdmans publishing co. [c1937] 177 p. 20 cm. "First edition." [BX9178.B48W6] 38-10319
1. Presbyterian church—Sermons. 2. Sermons, American. I. Title.

BIEDERWOLF, William Edward, 1867- 252.051
The world's Saturday night, and other sermons, by William Edward Biederwolf ... Grand Rapids, Mich., Zondervan publishing house [c1939] 167 p. 20 cm. [BX9178.B48W63] 39-31943
1. Presbyterian church—Sermons. 2. Sermons, American. I. Title.

BIEDERWOLF, William Edward, 1867-1939. 252.051
... The cup of demons, and other sermons, by Wm. Edward Biederwolf. D.D. Grand Rapids, Mich., Wm. B. Eerdmans publishing co., 1945. 85, [1] p., 1 l. 20 cm. (Eerdmans devotional library) [BX9178.B48C8] 45-9479
1. Presbyterian church—Sermons. 2. Sermons, American. I. Title.

BILLINGSLEY, Amos Stevens, 1818-1897. 922.542
The life of the great preacher, Reverend Gerorge Whitfield, "prince of orators", with the secret of his success, and specimens of his sermons. By Rev. A. S. Billingsley ... Philadelphia, Pa., Chicago, Ill. [etc.] P. W. Ziegler & co. [c1878] vii, xx, 17-437 p. plates, 2 port. (incl. front.) 23 cm. "List of authors consulted": p. v-vii. [BX9225.W4B5] 36-31912
1. Whitefield, George, 1714-1770. 2. Presbyterian church—Sermons. 3. Sermons, English. I. Title.

BLACK, Hugh, 1868- 243
... The gift of influence, by Hugh Black ... New York, Chicago [etc.] Fleming H. Revell company [c1908] 2 p. l., 307 p. 20 1/2 cm. At head of title: University sermons. [BX9178.B62G5] 8-31998
1. Presbyterian church—Sermons. 2. Sermons, American. I. Title. II. Title: University sermons.

BLACKWOOD, Andrew Watterson, 1915- 252.05
The Holy Spirit in your life. Grand Rapids, Baker Book House, 1957. 169p. 21cm. [BX9178.B662H6] 57-14662
1. Presbyterian Church—Sermons. 2. Sermons, American. I. Title.

BLACKWOOD, Andrew Watterson, 1915- 232.922
When God came down. Grand Rapids, Baker Book House, 1955. 71p. 20cm. [BX9178.B662W5] 55-10435
1. Presbyterian Church—Sermons. 2. Sermons, American. 3. Incarnation. I. Title.

BLAIR, Hugh, 1718-1800. 252
Sermons, by Hugh Blair ... 2d complete American ed. ... Philadelphia, Hickman & Hazzard, 1822. 2 v. front. (port.) 22 1/2 cm. [BX9178.B465S4 1822] 4-24598
1. Presbyterian church—Sermons. 2. Sermons, English—Scotland. I. Title.

BLAKELY, Hunter Bryson, 1894- 252.051
Facing life's questions, byHunter B. Blakely, jr. ... New York [etc.] Fleming H. Revell company [c1938] 192 p. 19 1/2 cm. [BX9178.B668F3] 38-16773
1. Presbyterian church—Sermons. 2. Sermons, American. I. Title.

BODDY, William Henry, 1866-1940. 252.051
The defeat of death, and other sermons, by William Henry Boddy, D.D. Published by a group of Dr. Boddy's friends as a tribute to his victorious spirit. [Minneapolis, Printed by the Lund press, inc, c1941] 75 p. front. (port.) 21 cm. [BX9178.B66635D4] 41-7854
1. Presbyterian church—Sermons. 2. Sermons, American. I. Title.

BONNELL, John Sutherland, 1893- 252.05
Fifth avenue sermons, by J. Sutherland Bonnell. New York, London, Harper & brothers, 1936. x p., 1 l., 229 p. 19 1/2 cm. "First edition." [BX9178.B66653F5] 36-36574
1. Presbyterian church—Sermons. 2. Sermons, American. I. Title.

BONNELL, John Sutherland, 1893- 252.051
What are you living for? [Sermons] New York, Abingdon-Cokesbury Press [1950] 188 p. 20 cm. [BX9178.B66653W5] 50-5254
1. Presbyterian Church—Sermons. 2. Sermons, American. I. Title.

BOOTH, Henry Matthias, 1843-1899. 243
The heavenly vision and other sermons, by Henry M. Booth, d. d. Memorial ed. New York, R. R. Beam, 1902. 348 p. 19 1/2 cm. [BX9178.B47H4] 2-9160
I. Title.

[BOYD, Andrew Kennedy Hutchinson] 1825-1899. 243
Counsel and comfort spoken from a city pulpit. By the author of "The recreations of a country parson." Boston, Ticknor and Fields, 1864. 311 p. 19 cm. [BX9178.B7C6 1864] 24-19715
1. Presbyterian church—Sermons. 2. Sermons, English—Scotland. I. Title.

BOYD, Andrew Kennedy Hutchinson, 1825-1899. 243
Occasional and immemorial days, by the Very Reverend A. K. H. Boyd ... London and New York, Longmans, Green and co., 1895. 5 p. l., [3]-318 p. 20 cm. Sermons. [BX9178.B7O3] 1-5250
1. Presbyterian church—Sermons. 2. Sermons, English—Scotland. I. Title.

[BOYD, Andrew Kennedy Hutchison] 1825-1899. 248
The graver thoughts of a country parson. By the author of "The recreations of a country parson." 2d series. [Author's ed.] Boston, J. R. Osgood and company, 1873. 2 p. l., 332 p. 18 1/2 cm. [BX9178.B7G7 1873] 7-41480
1. Presbyterian church—Sermons. 2. Sermons, English—Scotland. I. Title.

[BOYD, Andrew Kennedy Hutchison] 1825-1899. 252
The graver thoughts of a country parson. [1st series] By the author of "The recreations of a country parson," ... [Author's ed.] Boston, J. R. Osgood and company, 1874. 307 p. 18 1/2 cm. [BX9178.B7G7 1874] 7-41481
1. Presbyterian church—Sermons. 2. Sermons, English—Scotland. I. Title.

BRANCH, Harold Francis, 1894- 252.051
Religious picture sermons; the Gospel messages of fifteen world-famous religious masterpieces, by Rev. Harold Francis Branch ... Philadelphia, Pa., H. M. Shelley [c1934] 283 p. 20 cm. [BX9178.B725R4] 34-34758
1. Presbyterian church—Sermons. 2. Sermons, American. 3. Bible—Pictorial illustrations. 4. Jesus Christ—Art. 5. Art and religion. I. Title.

BRUCE, Robert, 1778-1846. 252
Discourses on various points of Christian doctrine and practice. By Robert Bruce ... Pittsburgh, Printed by D. and M. Maclean, 1829. v p., 1 l., [9]-346 p. 18 1/2 cm. [BX9178.B744D5] 45-42927
1. Presbyterian church—Sermons. 2. Sermons, American. I. Title.

BUIST, George, 1770-1808. 252.051
Sermons by the Reverend George Buist, D. D., minister of the Presbyterian church and president of the college of Charleston. South-Carolina ... New-York: Printed for E. Sargeant, opposite Trinity church, by D. & G. Bruce. 1809. 2 v. 22 cm. [BX9178.B765S4] 5-21281
1. Presbyterian church—Sermons. 2. Sermons. American. I. Title.

BURNETT, Andrew Ian. 252.05
Lord of all life. New York, Rinehart [1952] 205p. 22cm. [BX9178.B78L6] 52-11251
1. Presbyterian Church— Sermons. 2. Sermons, English—Canada. I. Title.

BURRELL, David James, 1844-1926. 252
God and the people, and other sermons, by David James Burrell ... New York, W. B. Ketcham [1899] 350 p. 19 1/2 cm. [BX9178.B8G57] 99-4629
1. Presbyterian church—Sermons. 2. Sermons, American. I. Title.

CALDWELL, Charles Turner, 1865- ed. 252.051
In the swelling of Jordan; sermons by Texas Presbyterian preachers, edited by C. T. Caldwell ... Grand Rapids, Mich., Zondervan publishing house [c1940] 148 p. 20 cm. [BX9178.A1C3] 40-13354
1. Presbyterian church—Sermons. 2. Sermons, American. I. Title.

CAMPBELL, Ernest T. 261.8
Locked in a room with open doors [by] Ernest T. Campbell. Waco, Tex., Word Books [1974] 180 p. 23 cm. Includes bibliographical references. [BX9178.C26L6] 73-91554 5.95
1. Presbyterian Church—Sermons. 2. Sermons, American. I. Title.

CLOW, William Maccallum, 1853-1930. 252.054
The evangel of the strait, gate, by the Rev. W. M. Clow... London, New York [etc.] Hodder and Stoughton, 1916. xv, 306 p. 20 1/2 cm. [BX9178.C55E8] 37-14657
1. Presbyterian church—Sermons. 2. Sermons, English—Scotland. I. Title.

COFFIN, Henry Sloane, 1877- 252.051
God's turn, by Henry Sloane Coffin. New York and London, Harper & brothers, 1934. v p., 1 l., 100 p. 20 cm. "First edition." [BX9178.C56G6] 34-4559
1. Presbyterian church—Sermons. 2. Sermons, American. I. Title.

CONNING, Gordon. 252.05
The new shape of life. Wilmington, Del., Mercantile Press [1968] 157 p. illus. 24 cm. [BV4501.C71338] 68-59443
1. Presbyterian Church—Sermons. 2. Christian life—Presbyterian authors. 3. Sermons, American. I. Title.

CROSBY, Howard, 1826-1891. 252
Sermons by Howard Crosby. New York, A. D. F. Randolph & co. [1891] 247 p. 19 1/2 cm. [BX9178.C7S4] 45-33463
1. Presbyterian church—Sermons. 2. Sermons, American. I. Title.

CROSBY, Howard, 1826-1891. 252.051
Social hints for young Christians, in three sefmons. By Howard Crosby ... New-York, Broughton & Wyman, 1866. 56 p. 18 cm. [BV4310.C8] 37-38016
1. Presbyterian church—Sermons. 2. Sermons, American. I. Title.

CUSTIS, W. Keith. 252'.05'1
Into a new age and other sermons / W. Keith Custis. [Upper Marlboro? Md.] : Custis, c1975. 200 p. ; 24 cm. Includes bibliographical references. [BX9178.C85157] 75-29693
1. Presbyterian Church—Sermons. 2. Sermons, American. I. Title.

DAVIES, Samuel, 1724-1761. 252
Sermons on important subjects, by the late reverend and pious Samuel Davies ... The 6th ed. To which are now added, three occasional sermons, not included in the

English editions; memoirs and character of the author; and two sermons on occasion of his death, by the Rev. Drs. Gibbons and Finley ... 2d American ed. Philadelphia; Printed for Robert Campbell, bookseller, M.DCC.XCIV. 2 v. 22 cm. Edited by Thomas Gibbons. The sermons by Gibbons and Finley have special title-pages. L. C. copy imperfect: p. 169-176 of v. 2 wanting, replaced by p. 159-166 of v. 1. Pages 153-160 duplicated. [BX9178.D35S4 1794] 45-50075
1. Presbyterian church—Sermons. 2. Sermons, American. I. Gibbons, Thomas, 1720-1785, ed. II. Finley, Samuel, 1715-1766. III. Title.

DICKSON, Andrew Flinn, 1825-1879. 252.
Plantation sermons; or, Plain and familiar discourses for the instruction of the unlearned. By the Rev. A. F. Dickson ... Philadelphia, Presbyterian board of publication [c1856] xii, [13]-170 p. 18 cm. "The discourses ... first appeared as a monthly series in the Southern Presbyterian."--p. ix. [BV4316.S6D5] 39-808
1. Presbyterian church—Sermons. 2. Sermons, American. I. Presbyterian church in the U. S. A. (Old school) Board of publication. II. Title. III. Title: Plain and familiar discourses for the instruction of the unlearned.

DODD, Ira Seymour, 1842-1922. 248
The brother and the brotherhood, by Ira Seymour Dodd ... New York, Dodd, Mead, and company, 1908. x, 366, [1] p. 20 cm. [BX9178.D6B7] 8-19121
1. Presbyterian church—Sermons. 2. Sermons. American. I. Title.

EDMONDS, Henry Morris, 1878- 252.051
The way, the truth, and the life [by] Henry M. Edmonds. Nashville, Cokesbury press [c1936] 216 p. 19 1/2 cm. [BX9178.E35W3] 36-5077
1. Presbyterian church—Sermons. 2. Sermons, American. I. Title.
Contents omitted.

ELLIOTT, William Marion, 1903- 252.051
Coming to terms with life [by] William M. Elliott, jr. ... Richmond, John Knox press [1944] 142 p. 21 cm. Sermons. Bibliographical foot-notes. [BX9178.E48C6] 44-6846
1. Presbyterian church—Sermons. 2. Sermons, American. I. Title.

ELLIOTT, William Marion, 1903- 252.05
Lift high that banner! Richmond, John Knox Press, 1950. 153 p. 21 cm. "References and acknowledgments": p. [145]-153. [BX9178.E48L5] 50-5990
1. Presbyterian Church—Sermons. 2. Sermons, American. I. Title.

ELSON, Edward Lee Roy, 1906- 252.05
The inevitable encounter. Grand Rapids, Mich., Eerdmans [c.1962] 68p. 21cm. (Preaching for today) 62-21372 2.25
1. Presbyterian Church—Sermons. 2. Sermons, American. I. Title.

ESTEY, Stephen Sewall, 1861-1932. 252.061
"Laugh, and love, and lift", by Stephen Sewall Estey ... with an introduction by Charles M. Sheldon ... New York [etc.] Fleming H. Revell company [c1934] 127 p. front. (port.) 19 1/2 cm. [BX9178.E75L3] 34-40710
1. Presbyterian church—Sermons. 2. Sermons, American. I. Title.

EVANS, Llewelyn John, 1833-1892. 252
Preaching Christ. Sermons by the Rev. Llewelyn Ioan Evans ... With a sketch of his life by Henry Preserved Smith ... New York, The Christian literature co., 1893. 4 p. l., 388 p. 21 cm. [BX9178.E83P7] 45-34673
1. Presbyterian church—Sermons. 2. Sermons, American. I. Smith, Henry Preserved, 1847-1927. II. Title.

EVANS, Louis Hadley, 1897- 252.05
This is America's hour. [Westwood, N.J.] Revell [1957] 128p. 21cm. [BX9178.E84T5] 57-11323
1. Presbyterian Church—Sermons. 2. Sermons, American. 3. Lincoln, Abraham, Pres.U.S., 1809-1865. I. Title.

FERRIS, Frank Halliday. 252.05
Standing up to life. [1st ed.] Indianapolis, Bobbs-Merrill [1953] 190p. illus. 20cm. [BX9178.F43S8] 53-5231
1. Presbyterian Church—Sermons. 2. Sermons, American. I. Title.

FISHER, Samuel W[are] 1814-1874.
Presbytery. A sermon, preached at the opening of the synod of Cincinnati, in the Second Presbyterian church, Oxford, Ohio, October 18, 1850, by Samuel W. Fisher ... Cincinnati, Wright, Ferris & co., printers, 1850. 60 p. 22 1/2 cm. 6-15820
I. Title.

FLAVEL, John, 1630?-1691. 232
The fountain of life; or, A display of Christ in His essential and mediatorial glory. By Rev. John Flavel ... New-York, The American tract society [183-?] 559 p. 19 1/2 cm. Sermons. First published in 1671. "This edition has been carefully revised, and slightly abridged." [BX9178.F6F6] 37-10872
1. Presbyterian church—Sermons. 2. Sermons, English. I. American tract society. II. Title.

FLAVEL, John, 1630?-1691. 232
The fountain of life opened; or, A display of Christ, in his essential and mediatorial glory. Containing forty-two sermons, on various texts of Scripture. By the Revd. John Flavel ... 1st American ed. ... Richmond, J. Martin, 1824. xii, 676 p. front (port.) 22 cm. First published in 1671. [BX9178.F6F6] 37-14644
1. Presbyterian church—Sermons. 2. Sermons, English. I. Title.

FRANK, Robert Worth, 1890- 252.351
The Christian's duty and kindred sermons, by Robert Worth Frank ... New York [etc.] Fleming H. Revell company [1942] 2 p. l., 7-194 p. 20 cm. [BX9173.F75C4] 42-14675
1. Presbyterian church—Sermons. 2. Sermons, American. I. Title.

FREEMAN, Robert, 1878- 252.051
Castles in the air, by Robert Freeman ... Pasadena, Calif., A. C. Vroman, inc. [c1935] iii, 208 p. 20 cm. [BX9178.F77C3] 38-5766
1. Presbyterian church—Sermons. 2. Sermons, American. I. Title.

GEHMAN, John Luke. 252.05
The ceaseless circle; a series of sermon-lectures concerning a certain cyclic tendency strikingly evident in the course of human events and throughout the universe in general, by John Luke Gehman ... New York. Chicago [etc.] Fleming H. Revell company [c1931] 157 p. 20 cm. [BX9178.G4C4] 32-1555
1. Presbyterian church—Sermons. 2. Sermons, American. I. Title.

GIRARDEAU, John Lafayette, 1825-1898. 252.051
Sermons, by John L. Girardeau ... edited by Rev. George A. Blackburn under the auspices of the synods of South Carolina, Georgia, Alabama and Florida. Columbia, S. C., The State company, 1907. 412 p. front. (port.) 20 cm. [BX9178.G52S4] 41-38424
1. Presbyterian church—Sermons. 2. Sermons. American. I. Blackburn, George Andrew, 1861-1918. ed. II. Title.

GORDON, Ernest. 252.051
A living faith for today. New York, Coward-McCann [1956] 255p. 22cm. [BX9178.G55L5] 56-10622
1. Presbyterian Church—Sermons. 2. Sermons, American. I. Title.

GOSS, Charles Frederic, 1852-1930. 243
Hits and misses, by Charles Frederic Goss ... Chicago, New York [etc.] Fleming H. Revell company, 1899. 211, [1] p. 19 cm. A collection of nine sermons preached at the Avondale Presbyterian church. [BX9178.G57H5] 99-3064
1. Presbyterian church—Sermons. 2. Sermons, American. I. Title.

GOSSIP, Arthur John, 1873- 252.052
Experience worketh hope, being some thoughts for a troubled day, by Arthur John Gossip ... New York, C. Scribner's sons, 1945. 4 p. l., 200 p. 21 cm. [BX9178.G584E9] 45-9299
1. Presbyterian church—Sermons. 2. Sermons, English—Scotland. I. Title.

GOUWENS, Teunis Earl, 1886- 252.051
Keep your faith, by Teunis E. Gouwens ... New York, London [etc.] Fleming H. Revell company [1943] 142 p. 19 1/2 cm. [BN9178.G6K4] 43-9112
1. Presbyterian church—Sermons. 2. Sermons, American. I. Title.

GOUWENS, Teunis Earl, 1886- 252.051
The stirred nest, by Teunis E. Gouwens ... Nashville, Cokesbury press [c1933] 174 p. 19 cm. [BX9178.G6S8] 33-4608
1. Presbyterian church—Sermons. 2. Sermons, American. I. Title.

GOWAN, Donald E. 251
Reclaiming the Old Testament for the Christian pulpit / Donald E. Gowan. Atlanta : John Knox Press, c1980. vi, 163 p. ; 24 cm. Includes bibliographical references and index. [BS1191.5.G68] 79-87743 ISBN 0-8042-0166-8 : 12.50
1. Presbyterian Church—Sermons. 2. Bible. O.T.—Homiletical use. 3. Bible. O.T.—Sermons. 4. Sermons, American. I. Title.

GRAHAM, John, b.1794. 922.573
Autobiography and reminisences of Rev. John Graham, late pastor of the Associat, now the United Presbyterian congregation of Bovina, Delaware co., N. Y. With an appendix containing some interesting and important letters to the author from Rev. Dr. McCrie ... and other eminent ministers of Scotland of a former day. To which are added a few of his sermons. Philadelphia, W. S. Rentoul, 1870. vi, 206 p. 20 cm. "A brief sketch of Rev. Andrew Arnot": p. 124-129. [BX9225.G812A3] 36-24857
1. Arnot, Andrew, 1722-1808. 2. Presbyterian church—Sermons. 3. Sermons, American. I. Title.

GREGG, David, 1846-1919. 243
Facts that call for faith. A series of discourses. By Rev. David Gregg ... New York, E. B. Treat & co., 1898. 311 p. 19 cm. [BX9178.G7F3] 44-24518
1. Presbyterian church—Sermons. 2. Sermons, American. I. Title.

GUINN, B F 1897-
Sparks from the anvil of truth, by Rev. B. F. Guinn. Columbus, Miss., Fairview Cumberland Presbyterian Church, 1962. 72 p. 22 cm. 63-57101
1. Presbyterian church — Sermons. 2. Sermons, American. I. Title.

GULICK, Joseph Isaac, 1890- 252.051
The evangel of religion, by Rev. Joseph I. Gulick ... [Idaho Falls, 1942] [175] p. 20 1/2 cm. Various pagings. Plate mounted on fly-leaf. "Mimeographed." [BX9178.G78E8] 44-20356
1. Presbyterian church—Sermons. 2. Sermons, American. I. Title.

GURLEY, Ralph Randolph, 1797-1872. 922.573
Life and eloquence of the Rev. Sylvester Larned, first pastor of the First Presbyterian church in New-Orleans. By R. R. Gurley. New York, Wiley & Putnam, 1844. xii, [13]-412 p. front. (port.) 19 cm. "Sermons": p. [123]-412. [BX9225.L35G8] 36-29119
1. Larned, Sylvester, 1796-1820. 2. Presbyterian church—Sermons. 3. Sermons, American. I. Title.

GUTHRIE, Thomas, 1803-1873. 243
Speaking to the heart; or, Sermons for the people. By Thomas Guthrie, D. D. New ed. with much additional matter. New York, E. B. Treat & company [1891] 2 p. l., 492 p. 20 cm. nglish--Scotland. [BX9178.G8S6] 3-986
1. Presbyterian church—Sermons. I. Title.

GUTHRIE, Thomas, 1803-1873. 243
The way to life. Sermons by Thomas Guthrie, D. D. New York, E. B. Treat & company [1891] 1 p. l., 7-336 p. 20 cm. [BX9178.G8W3] 3-979
1. Presbyterian church—Sermons. 2. Sermons, English—Scotland. I. Title.

GWYNNE, John Harold, 1899- 252.051
One thing needful, by J. Harold Gwynne... Grand Rapids, Mich., Wm. B. Eerdmans publishing co., 1941. 120 p. 20 cm. [BX9178.G905] 41-23457
1. Presbyterian church—Sermons. 2. Sermons, American. I. Title.

HALVERSON, Richard C 252.051
Christian maturity. Los Angeles, Cowman Publications [1956] 137p. 21cm. [BX9178.H32C5] 57-32400
1. Presbyterian Church—Sermons. 2. Sermons, American. I. Title.

HASKELL, Thomas Nelson, 1826-1906. 922.573
The life and death of a Christian are our teachers. The funeral sermon of Elder David M. Wilson, the useful layman and unassuming benefactor of Washington city; delivered in the Western Presbyterian church, March 9, 1856, by the pastor, Rev. T. N. Haskell; to which is prefixed the funeral address, by Rev. B. Sunderland, D. D., delivered on the burial day, March 1, 1856. Washington, D. C., T. McGill, printer, 1856. 52 p. 22 cm. [BX9225.W46H3] 36-31917
1. Wilson, David Morris, 1798-1856. 2. Presbyterian church—Sermons. 3. Funeral sermons. I. Sunderland, Byron, 1819-1901. II. Title.

HELTZEL, Massey Mott. 252.051
The invincible Christ. Nashville, Abingdon Press [1957] 142p. 20cm. [BX9178.H39 I 5] 57-5278
1. Presbyterian Church—Sermons. 2. Sermons, American. I. Title.

HEZMALL, Everett F. 210
God speaks through nature / by Everett F. Hezmall. Lincoln, Neb. : Venture Pub., 1975. 102 p. ; 18 cm. [BT695.5.H49] 75-29556 1.25
1. Presbyterian Church—Sermons. 2. Nature (Theology)—Sermons. 3. Sermons, American. I. Title.

HILLS, Oscar Armstrong, 1837-1919. 252.051
New shafts in the old mine; an exposition on some classic passages of Holy Scripture, by O. A. Hills... Philadelphia, The Westminster press, 1906. xii, 185 p. 19 1/2 cm. [BX9178.H47N4] 6-37969
1. Presbyterian church—Sermons. 2. Sermons, American. I. Title.

HOWARD, Henry, 1859-1933. 252.051
Something ere the end; the last message of Henry Howard ... New York [etc.] Fleming H. Revell company [c1933] 157 p. front. (port.) 19 1/2 cm. [BX9178.H6S6] 33-35467
1. Presbyterian church—Sermons. 2. Sermons, American. I. Title.

HUDNUT, Robert K. 252'.05'1
An active man and the Christ, by Robert K. Hudnut. Philadelphia, Fortress Press [1972] xiv, 114 p. 18 cm. Includes bibliographical references. [BX9178.H7A25] 72-75650 ISBN 0-8006-0119-X 2.50
1. Presbyterian Church—Sermons. 2. Sermons, American. I. Title.

HUGHES, Daniel Lawrence, 1820-1902. 922.573
A sketch of the life, character, and writings of the Rev. James Y. M'Ginnes, of Shade Gap, Pa,, by the Rev. D. L. Hughes ... Philadelphia, J. M. Wilson, 1854. x p., 1 l., [13]-352 p. incl. front. (port.) 18 1/2 cm, "Sermons by the Rev. James Y. M'Ginnes": p. [175]-317. "An address delivered before the Philo and Franklin literary societies, of Jefferson college, at the annual commencement, August 5, 1851": p. [319]-352. [BX9225.M22H8] 36-24276
1. McGinnes, James Y., 1815-1851. 2. Presbyterian church—Sermons. 3. Sermons, American. I. Title.

HUTTON, John Alexander, 1868-1947. 252.051
The best of John A. Hutton, edited with an introd. by Edgar De Witt Jones. [1st

ed.] New York, Harper [1950] xiv, 176 p. 21 cm. [BX9178.H75B4] 50-5295
1. Presbyterian Church—Sermons. 2. Sermons. American. I. Title.

IMES, William Lloyd, 1889- 252.051
The black pastures, an American pilgrimage in two centuries; essays and sermons. [1st ed.] Nashville, Hemphill Press, 1957. 146p. illus. 24cm. [BX9178.I5B5] 57-11472
1. Presbyterian Church—Sermons. 2. Sermons, American. 3. U. S.—Race question. I. Title.

INGLIS, James, 1777-1820. 243
Sermons of the late Dr. James Inglis, pastor of the First Presbyterian church in Baltimore; with some of his forms of prayer. Vol. i. Baltimore: Published by N. G. Maxwell, no. 140, Baltimore-street, For the benefit of the orphan children of the author. Benjamin Edes, printer ... 1820. vii, [9]-389 p. front. (port.) 23 cm. No more published.? [BX9178.I6S4] 22-7801
1. Presbyterian church—Sermons. 2. Sermons, American. I. Title.

JENNEY, Ray Freeman, 1891- 253.051
Speaking boldly; essay-sermons, by Ray Freeman Jenney ... with a foreword by John McDowell ... New York [etc.] Fleming H. Revell company [c1935] 128 p. 20 cm. [BX9178.J4S6] 35-1424
1. Presbyterian church—Sermons. 2. Sermons, American. I. Title.

JOHNSON, Herrick, 1832-1913. 243
... From love to praise, by Herrick Johnson ... Philadelphia, Presbyterian board of publication and Sabbath-school work, 1903. v, 182 p. front. (port.) 20 cm. (The Presbyterian pulpit. [no. 4]) [BX9178.J5F7] 3-6551
I. Title.

JONES, Ilion Tingnal, 1889- 252.05'1
God's everlasting "yes", and other sermons [by] Ilion T. Jones. Waco, Tex., Word Books [1969] 138 p. 23 cm. [BX9178.J59G6] 69-12816 3.95
1. Presbyterian Church—Sermons. 2. Sermons, American. I. Title.

JONES, John Sparhawk, 1841-1910. 252
The invisible things, and other sermons, by J. Sparhawk Jones ... New York [etc.] Longmans, Green, and co., 1907. 3 p. l., 232 p. 19 1/2 cm. [BX9178.J616] 7-9535
1. Presbyterian church—Sermons. 2. Sermons, American. I. Title.

JONES, John Sparhawk, 1841-1910. 243
... Seeing darkly, by the Rev. J. Sparhawk Jones, D. D. Philadelphia, Presbyterian board of publication and Sabbath-school work, 1904. v, 188 p. front. (port.) 20 cm. (The Presbyterian pulpit) [BX9178.J6S4] 4-14388
1. Presbyterian church—Sermons. 2. Sermons, American. I. Title.

JOWETT, John Henry, 1864-1923. 252.05
Brooks by the traveller's way; twenty-six weeknight addresses, by J. H. Jowett ... [London] Hodder & Stoughton; New York, George H. Doran company [191-!] 280 p. 19 cm. (On cover: Library of standard religious authors) "The addresses in this volume were all originally published in the Examiner newspaper."--Foreword. [BX9178.J66B7] 41-30978
1. Presbyterian church—Sermons. 2. Sermons, English. I. Title.

KEARNS, Ralph D 252.051
Handling life; sermons of inspiration and coruage for living. [1st ed.] New York, Exposition Press [1957] 77p. 21cm. [BX9178.K25H3] 57-7658
1. Presbyterian Church—Sermons. 2. Sermons, American. I. Title.

KERR, Hugh Thomson, 1871-1950. 252.051
Design for Christian living sermons edited by Donald Craig Kerr Philadelphia, Westminster Press [1953] 157p. 21cm. [BX9178.K4D4] 52-11757
1. Presbyterian Church—Sermons. 2. Sermons, American. I. Title.

KIK, Jacob Marcellus, 1903- 252.05
The narrow and the broad way, and other sermons of salvation, by J. Marcellus Kik... Grand Rapids, Mich. Sondervan publishing house, 1934. 4 p. l., iii, [13]-106 p. 20 1/2 cm. [BX9178.K45N3] 36-17787
1. Presbyterian church—Sermons. 2. Sermons, English—Canada. I. Title.

KIRK, Harris Elliott, 1872- 221.92
A man of property; or, The Jacob saga, by Harris Elliott Kirk ... New York and London, Harper & brothers, 1935. 5 p. l., 109 p. 19 cm. "First edition." [BS580.J3K5] 35-3905
1. Jacob, the patriarch. 2. Presbyterian church—Sermons. 3. Sermons, American. I. Title.

LANSING, Dirck Cornelius, 1785-1857. 243
Sermons, on important subjects of doctrine and duty; by the Rev. D. C. Lansing. Auburn, Printed by R. Oliphant, 1825. xv, [17]-355 p. 22 cm. [BX9178.L3S4] 20-16817
1. Presbyterian church—Sermons. 2. Sermons, American. I. Title.

LARSON, Bruce. 252'.051
Believe and belong / Bruce Larson. Old Tappan, N.J. : Power Books, c1982. 155 p. ; 21 cm. [BX9178.L36B44] 19 81-23508 ISBN 0-8007-1288-9 : 6.95
1. Presbyterian Church—Sermons. 2. Sermons, American. I. Title.

LEE, John Lloyd, 1859-1906. 243
The message of to-morrow; or, The gospel of hope, by Rev. John Lloyd Lee... New York, Chicago [etc.] Fleming H. Revell co., 1901. 4 p. l., 5-311 p. 20 cm. [BX9178.L4M4] 1-27344
1. Presbyterian church—Sermons. 2. Sermons, American. I. Title.

LITTLE, Archibald Alexander, 1860- 252.051
The highway to happiness; sermons ... by Archibald Alexander Little ... Grand Rapids, Mich., Zondervan publishing house, 1935. 204 p. incl. port. 20 cm. [BX9178.L55H5] 35-34020
1. Presbyterian church—Sermons. 2. Sermons, American. I. Title.

LIVING in depth...
Edinburgh, Saint Andrew Press [1959] xii, 187p. 22cm. 'These articles have all appeared in the British weekly during the last few years.'
1. Presbyterian Church—Sermons. I. Reid, James, 1877-

LOVE, Larry. 252.051
Called to be saints. Grand Rapids, Zondervan Pub. House [1955] 137p. 20cm. [BX9178.L72C3] 55-24614
1. Presbyterian Church—Sermons. 2. Sermons. 3. Sermons, American. I. Title.

LOWE, Arnold Hilmar, 1888- 252.05
Beliefs have consequences. New York, Crowell [1959] 178p. 21cm. [BX9178.L73B4] 59-14573
1. Presbyterian Church—Sermons. 2. Sermons, American. I. Title.

LOWE, Arnold Hilmar, 1888- 252.051
The importance of being ourselves. [1st ed.] New York, Harper [1948] v, 179 p. 20 cm. [BX9178.L73 I 4] 48-11880
1. Presbyterian Church—Sermons. 2. Sermons, American. I. Title.

LOWE, Arnold Hilmar, 1888- 252.05
Start where you are. [1st ed.] New York, Harper [1950] vii, 179 p. 20 cm. [BX9178.L73S7] 50-10793
1. Presbyterian Church—Sermons. 2. Sermons, American. I. Title.

LOWE, Arnold Hilmar, 1888- 252.051
When God moves in. [1st ed.] New York, Harper, [1952] 191 p. 21 cm. [BX9178.L73W45] 52-8482
1. Presbyterian Church—Sermons. 2. Sermons, American. I. Title.

MACARTNEY, Clarence Edward Noble, b.1879. 252.051
The greatest question of the bible and of life / by Clarence Edward Macartney. Grand Rapids, MI : Baker Book House, 1977. 223p. ; 20 cm. [BX9178.M172G685] ISBN 0-8010-6018-4 pbk. : 2.95
1. Presbyterian Church — Sermons. 2. Sermons, American. I. Title.
L.C. card no. for 1948 Abingdon-Cokesbury Press ed. : 48-7240

MACARTNEY, Clarence Edward Noble, 1879- 252.051
Facing life and getting the best of it, by Clarence Edward Macartney ... Nashville, Cokesbury press c1940] 184 p. 19 1/2 cm. [BX9178.M172F3] 40-11529
1. Presbyterian church—Sermons. 2. Sermons, American. I. Title.

MACARTNEY, Clarence Edward Noble, 1879- 252.051
The faith once delivered. New York, Abingdon-Cokesbury Press [1952] 175 p. 20 cm. [BX9178.M172F32] 52-5384
1. Presbyterian Church—Sermons. 2. Sermons, American. I. Title.

MACARTNEY, Clarence Edward Noble, 1879- 252.051
Great interviews of Jesus, by Clarence Edward Macartney ... New York, Nashville, Abingdon-Cokesbury press [1944] 190 p. 19 1/2 cm. [BX9178.M172G68] 44-39794
1. Presbyterian church—Sermons. 2. Sermons, American. I. Title.

MACARTNEY, Clarence Edward Noble, 1879- 252.051
Great nights of the Bible. Nashville, Abingdon [1964, c.1943] 224p. 18cm. (Apex bk. Q4-125) 1.25 pap.,
1. Presbyterian church—Sermons. 2. Sermons, American. I. Title.

MACARTNEY, Clarence Edward Noble, 1879- 252.051
Great nights of the Bible, by Clarence Edward Macartney ... New York, Nashville, Abingdon-Cokesbury press [1943] 224 p. 19 1/2 cm. [BX9178.M172G67] 43-14422
1. Presbyterian church—Sermons. 2. Sermons, American. I. Title.

MACARTNEY, Clarence Edward Noble, 1879- 252.051
The greatest questions of the Bible and of life. New York, Abingdon-Cokesbury Press [1948] 223 p. 20 cm. [BX9178.M172G685] 48-7240
1. Presbyterian Church—Sermons. 2. Sermons, American. I. Title.

MACARTNEY, Clarence Edward Noble, 1879- 252.051
The greatest texts of the Bible. Nashville, Abingdon-Cokesbury Press [1947] 219 p. 20 cm. [BX9178.M172G69] 47-6813
1. Presbyterian Church—Sermons. 2. Sermons, American. I. Title.

MACARTNEY, Clarence Edward Noble, 1879- 252.051
The greatest words in the Bible and in Human speech, by Clarence Edward Macartney. Nashville, Abingdon [1963, c.1938] 193p. 18cm. (Apex Bks., M5) .95 pap.,
1. Presbyterian church—Sermons. 2. Sermons, American. I. Title.

MACARTNEY, Clarence Edward Noble, 1879- 252.051
The greatest words in the Bible and in human speech, by Clarence Edward Macartney ... Nashville, Cokesbury press [c1938] 193 p. 19 1/2 cm. [BX9178.M172G7] 38-38644
1. Presbyterian church—Sermons. 2. Sermons, American. I. Title.

MACARTNEY, Clarence Edward Noble, 1879- 252.051
More sermons from life, by Clarence Edward Macartney ... Nashville, Cokesbury press [c1939] 204 p. 19 1/2 cm. [BX9178.M172S42] 39-21185
1. Presbyterian church—Sermons. 2. Sermons, American. I. Title.

MACARTNEY, Clarence Edward Noble, 1879- 225.92
Peter and his Lord; sermons on the life of Peter, by Clarence Edward Macartney ... Nashville, Cokesbury press [c1937] 247 p. 19 1/2 cm. [BS2515.M25] [922.1] 37-16013
1. Peter, Saint, apostle. 2. Presbyterian church—Sermons. 3. Sermons, American. I. Title.

MACARTNEY, Clarence Edward Noble, 1879- 252.051
Strange texts, but grand truths. Nashville, Abingdon-Cokesbury Press [1953] 192p. 20cm. [BX9178.M174S8] 52-13756
1. Presbyterian Church—Sermons. 2. Sermons, American. I. Title.

MACARTNEY, Clarence Edward Noble, 1879- 252.051
Trials of great men of the Bible, by Clarence Edward Macartney. New York, Nashville, Abingdon [1967, c.1946] 189p. 18cm. (Apex bks., AA5-125) [BX9178.M172T7] 46-3923 1.25 pap.,
1. Presbyterian church—Sermons. 2. Sermons, American. I. Title.

MACARTNEY, Clarence Edward Noble, 1879- 252.051
Trials of great men of the Bible, by Clarence Edward Macartney ... New York, Nashville, Abingdon-Cokesbury press [1946] 189 p. 19 1/2 cm. [BX9178.M172T7] 46-3923
1. Presbyterian church—Sermons. 2. Sermons, American. I. Title.

MACARTNEY, Clarence Edward Noble, 1879- 232.
Twelve great questions about Christ, by Clarence E. Macartney ... with foreword by J. Gresham Machen ... New York, Chicago [etc.] Fleming H. Revell company [c1923] 221 p. 19 1/2 cm. [BT201.M18] 24-3492
1. Jesus Christ—Person and offices. 2. Presbyterian church—Sermons. 3. Sermons, American. I. Title.

MACARTNEY, Clarence Edward Noble, 1879- 252.051
You can conquer. Nashville, Abingdon Press [1954] 158p. 20cm. [BX9178.M172Y6] 54-5507
1. Presbyterian Church—Sermons. 2. Sermons, American. I. Title.

MACARTNEY, Clarence Edward Noble, 1879-1957. 252.05
Along life's highway. Compiled and edited by Harry E. Farra. Grand Rapids, Mich., Baker Book House [1969] 103 p. 21 cm. ([The New minister's handbook series]) [BX9178.M172A63] 75-97726 2.95
1. Presbyterian Church—Sermons. 2. Sermons, American. I. Title.

MACARTNEY, Clarence Edward Noble, 1879-1957. 252.051
Salute thy soul. New York, Abingdon Press [1957] 144p. 20cm. [BX9178.M172S3] 57-9787
1. Presbyterian Church—Sermons. 2. Sermons, American. I. Title.

MCCARTNEY, Albert Joseph. 252.085
The empire of silence and selected sermons. Boston, Christopher Pub. House [1957] 191p. 21cm. [BX9178.M1746E5] 57-9839
1. Presbyterian Church—Sermons. 2. Sermons, American. I. Title.

MACCOLL, Alexander, 1866-
The sheer folly of preaching, by Alexander MacColl ... New York, George H. Doran company [c1923] 217 p. 19 1/2 cm. Sermons. [BX178.M18S5] 23-13409
1. Presbyterian church—Sermons. 2. Sermons, American. I. Title.

MCCOMB, John Hess, 1898- 252.051
The faith once delivered. New York, F.H. Revel Co. [1949] 126 p. 20 cm. [BX9178.M192F25] 49-8156
1. Presbyterian Church—Sermons. 2. Sermons, American. I. Title.

MCCOMB, John Hess, 1898- 252.051
Sermons on Bible themes. Wheaton, Ill., Van Kampen Press [1955] 99p. 20cm. [BX9178.M192S4] 55-33683
1. Presbyterian Church—Sermons. 2. Sermons, American. I. Title.

MCCONAUGHY, David, 1775-1852. 220.92
Discourses,chiefly biographical, of persons eminent in sacred history. bY David McConaughy... Pittsburgh, Printed by G. Parkin & co., 1850. 3 p. l., [9]-494 p. front. (port.) 23 cm. [BX9178.M195D5] 35-36266

1. Presbyterian church—Sermons. 2. Sermons, American. 3. Bible—Biog. I. Title.

MCCONKEY, F Paul. 252.051
The ebony jewel box, and other sermons. Grand Rapids, W.B. Eerdmans Pub. Co., 1956. 150p. 23cm. [BX9178.M197E2] 56-14353
1. Presbyterian Church—Sermons. 2. Sermons, American. I. Title.

MCCOSH, James, 1811-1894. 248
Gospel sermons. By James McCosh ... New York, R. Carter and brothers, 1888. 336 p. 20 1/2 cm. [BX9178.M2G6] 45-34672
1. Presbyterian church—Sermons. 2. Sermons, American. I. Title.

MACHEN, John Gresham, 1881-1937. 252.051
God transcendent, and other selected sermons; ed. by Ned Bernard Stonehouse. Grand Rapids, W. B. Eerdmans Pub. Co., 1949. 189 p. 21 cm. [BX9178.M227G6] 49-9633
1. Presbyterian Church—Sermons. 2. Sermons, American. I. Title.

MACKENZIE, Lachlan, 1754-1819. 252'.05'2
The happy man : the abiding witness of Lachlan Mackenzie. Edinburgh ; Carlisle, Pa. : The Banner of Truth Trust, 1979. 249 p., [2] leaves of plates : ill. ; 23 cm. [BX9178.M245H36 1979] 79-320576 ISBN 0-85151-282-8 : 7.95
1. Presbyterian Church—Sermons. 2. Presbyterian Church—Doctrinal and controversial works—Presbyterian authors—Miscellanea. 3. Sermons, English. I. Title.

MACLEAN, Alistair, 1885-1936. 252.052
High country; studies of the inner life with some interpretative aids from modern literature. With a foreword by Henry Sloane Coffin. New York Scribner, 1952. 255 p. 20 cm. [BX9178.M262H5] 52-13544
1. Presbyterian Church—Sermons. 2. Sermons, English—Scotland. I. Title.

MACLEAN, John Allan, 1891- 252.051
The most unforgettable character I've ever met, by John Allan MacLean. Richmond, Va., John Knox press [c1945] 223 p. 21 cm. [BX9178.M263M6] 46-3125
1. Presbyterian church—Sermons. 2. Sermons, American. I. Title.

MACLENNAN, David Alexander, 1903- 252.05'1
Sermons from Thanksgiving to Easter [by] David A. MacLennan. Valley Forge [Pa.] Judson Press [1968] 156 p. 23 cm. [BX9178.M1786S4] 68-13607 3.95
1. Presbyterian Church—Sermons. 2. Sermons, American. I. Title.

MACLENNAN, David Alexander, 1903- 252.6
Sermons of faith and hope [by] David A. MacLennan. Valley Forge [Pa.] Judson Press [1971] 144 p. 23 cm. Includes bibliographical references. [BX9178.M265S4] 73-144083 ISBN 0-8170-0509-9 4.95
1. Presbyterian Church—Sermons. 2. Sermons, American. I. Title.

MACMILLAN, Ebenzer, 1881-1944. 252.052
"Happy seeker, happy finder," a memoir of Dr. Ebenezer Macmillan ... with some sermons and addresses ... Pretoria, J. L. van Schaik, limited, 1945. 174 p. front., plates, ports. 19 1/2 cm. Compiled by J. Lang. cf. Foreword. [BX9178.M293H3] A 47
1. Presbyterian church—Sermons. 2. Sermons, English—Africa, South. I. Lang, J., comp. II. Title.

MACWHORTER, Alexander, 1734-1807. 252.051
A series of sermons, upon the most important principles of our holy religion... by Alexander Macwhorter... Newark: Printed by Pennington & Gould, for the author. 1803. 2 v. 21 cm. Vol. II: Newark--Printed by John Wallis. 1803. [BX9178.M343S4] 33-16681

1. Presbyterian church—Sermons. 2. Sermons, American. I. Title.

MARSHALL, Peter, 1902-1949. 252
The exile heart. [1st ed.] [Washington] Peter Marshall Scottish Memorial Committee, 1949. 157 p. ports. 24 cm. "A compilation of the [author's] Scottish sermons and addresses." [BX9178.M363E9] 051 ISBN 50-5747
1. Presbyterian Church—Sermons. 2. Sermons, American. I. Title.

MARSHALL, Peter, 1902-1949. 252.05
John Doe, disciple; sermons for the young in spirit. Edited and with introd. by Catherine Marshall. Pref. by Peter John Marshall. New York, McGraw-Hill [1963] 222 p. 22 cm. [BX9178.M363J6 1963] 63-20813
1. Presbyterian Church—Sermons. 2. Sermons, American. I. Title.

MARSHALL, Peter, 1902-1949. 252.05
Keepers of the springs, and other messages from Mr. Jones, meet the Master. [Westwood, N. J.] Revell [1962] 60p. 17cm. [BX9178.M363M52] 61-13622
1. Presbyterian Church—Sermons. 2. Sermons, American. I. Title.

MARSHALL, Peter, 1902-1949 252.051
Mr. Jones, meet the Master; sermons and prayers. [New York] Dell [1961, c.1949, 1950] 253p. (F127) Bibl. .50 pap.,
1. Presbyterian Church—Sermons. 2. Sermons, American. 3. Prayers. I. Title.

MARSHALL, Peter, 1902-1949. 252.051
Mr. Jones, meet the Master; sermons and prayers. [Rev.] New York, Revell [1950] 192 p. port. 22 cm. [BX9178.M363M5 1950] 50-13247
1. Presbyterian Church—Sermons. 2. Sermons, American. 3. Prayers. I. Title.

MARSHALL, Peter, 1902-1949. 252.051
Mr. Jones, meet the Master; sermons and prayers. New York, F. H. Revell [1949] 192 p. port. 22 cm. [BX9178.M363M5] 49-50155
1. Presbyterian Church—Sermons. 2. Sermons, American. 3. Prayers. I. Title.

MARSHALL, Peter, 1902-1949. 252'.05'1
Mr. Jones, meet the Master; sermons and prayers of Peter Marshall. Boston, G. K. Hall, 1973 [c1950] 330 p. 25 cm. Large print ed. Includes bibliographical references. [BX9178.M363M5 1973] 73-9911 ISBN 0-8161-6132-1 9.95 (lib. bdg.)
1. Presbyterian Church—Sermons. 2. Sermons, American. 3. Prayers. I. Title.

MARTIN, William T 1921-1956. 252.051
The power of an upward look, and other sermons. Tallahassee, Peninsular Pub. Co. [1957] 176p. illus. 24cm. [BX9178.3653P6] 57-29433
1. Presbyterian Church—Sermons. 2. Sermons, American. I. Title.

MAULDIN, Kenneth, 1918- 252'.05'1
Table talk with Jesus / Kenneth Mauldin. Nashville : Abingdon Press, [1979] p. cm. [BS2595.4.M38] 78-13750 ISBN 0-687-40820-2 : 3.75
1. Presbyterian Church—Sermons. 2. Bible. N.T. Luke—Sermons. 3. Sermons, American. I. Title.

MECKLIN, R. W. 226.8
The twin parables, or; The mysteries of the kingdom of God: a series of expository sermons on some of the leading parables of Our Lord; to which is appended, a classification of these and other developed and undeveloped parables of Our Saviour. By Rev. R. W. Mecklin ... Richmond, Va., Whitet & Shepperson, 1892. 3 p. l., [5]-9, [9]-135, [6] p. 21 cm. [BT375.M4] 35-32582
1. Jesus Christ—Parables—Sermons. 2. Presbyterian church—Sermons. 3. Sermons, American. I. Title.

MEMORIALS of Rev. Elias R. Beadle, D. D., LL. D. 922.573 Philadelphia [The Chandler printing house] 1881. 2 p. l., 101, [1] p., 1 l. front. (port.) 23 cm. "Memorial sermon preached in the Second Presbyterian church, January 25, 1880, by Rev. Herrick Johnson": p. [1]-36. [BX9225.B45M4] 36-23721
1. Beadle, Elias Root, 1812-1879. 2. Presbyterian church—Sermons. I. Johnson, Herrick, 1832-1913.

MEMORIALS of Richard H. Richardson, D. D. 922.573 New York, A. D. F. Randolph and company [1893] 133 p. front. (mounted phot.) 23 cm. Contents.--Biographical sketch.--The Chicago pastorate.--The Newburyport pastorate.--The Trenton pastorate.--Funeral services and public tributes.-- Letters of sympathy.--Sermons by Dr. Richard H. Richardson. [BX9225.R52M4] 36-31461
1. Richardson, Richard Higgins, 1823-1892. 2. Presbyterian church—Sermons. 3. Sermons, American.

MERRILL, William Pierson, 1867- 252.051
We see Jesus, by William Pierson Merrill. New York and London, Harper & brothers, 1934. 4 p. l., 3-129 p. 20 cm. "First edition." [BX9178.M45W5 1934] 34-24840
1. Presbyterian church—Sermons. 2. Sermons, American. I. Title.

MILLER, James Russell, 1840-1912. 243
... Our new Edens, by J. R. Miller ... Philadelphia, Presbyterian board of publication and Sabbath-school work, 1903. v. 155 p. front. (port.) 19 cm. (The Presbyterian pulpit. [no. VIII]) [BX9178.M508] 3-26947
1. Presbyterian church—Sermons. 2. Sermons, American. I. Title.

MITCHELL, Samuel S., 1839-1919 243
...The staff method, by the Rev. S. S. Mitchell... Philadelphia, Presbyterian board of publication and Sabbath school work, 1904. v. 178 p. front. (port.) 19 1/2 cm. (The Presbyterian pulpit. [no. ix]) [BX9178.M5934S8] 4-16200
1. Presbyterian church—Sermons. 2. Sermons, American. I. Title.

MOFFATT, James, 1870- 252.05
His gifts & promises, being twenty-five reflections and directions on phases of our Christian discipline, from the inside, by James Moffatt ... New York, C. Scribner's sons [1934] vi, 245, [1] p. 21 cm. Half-title: "The scholar as preacher" (Fifth series)) "Printed in Great Britain." [BX9178.M5955H5] 35-772
1. Presbyterian church—Sermons. 2. Sermons, English. I. Title.

MUNGER, Robert Boyd. 252.05
What Jesus says; the master teacher and life's problems. [Westwood, N. J.] F. H. Revell Co. [1955] 185p. 22cm. [BX9178.M664W5] 55-8764
1. Presbyterian Church —Sermons. 2. Sermons, American. I. Title.

MURPHY, Wilkins Harper, 1891- 252.051
Flowers from Gethsemane and other sermons, by W. H. Murphy, jr. ... Grand Rapids, Mich., Wm. B. Eerdmans publishing company, 1939. 144 p. 20 cm. [BX9178.M667F5] 39-11395
1. Presbyterian church—Sermons. 2. Sermons, American. I. Title.

MURRAY, George, 1896- 252.054
The music of the golden bells, by George Murray. Grand Rapids, Mich., Wm. B. Eerdmans publishing company, 1942. 120 p. 20 cm. [BX9178.M669M8] 42-18321
1. Presbyterian church—Sermons. 2. Sermons, American. I. Title.

MURRAY, George Lewis, 1896- 252.054
The music of the golden bells. Grand Rapids, Mich., W.B. Eerdmans Pub. Co., 1942. 120 p. 20 cm. [BX9178.M669M8] 42-18321
1. Presbyterian Church—Sermons. 2. Sermons, American. I. Title.

MURRAY, Nicholas, 1802-1861. 243
Dying legacy to the people of his beloved charge. By Nicholas Murray, D. D. February fourth, 1861. Things unseen and eternal. New York, Harper & brothers, 1861. vi, [7]-78 p. 1 l. 24 cm. Sermons. [BX9178.M67D8] 39-8941
1. Presbyterian church—Sermons. 2. Sermons, American. I. Title.

NEILL, William, 1778?-1860. 922.573
Autobiography of William Neill, D. D., with a selection from his sermons. By the Rev. J. H. Jones ... Philadelphia. Presbyterian board of publication, 1861. 2 p. l., 272 p. front. (port.) 20 cm. [BX9225.N4A4] 36-22129
1. Presbyterian church—Sermons. 2. Sermons, American. I. Jones Joseph Huntington, 1797-1868, ed. II. Presbyterian church in the U. S. A. Board of publication. III. Title.

NICELY, Harold Elliott, 1900- 252.051
What religion does to men, by Harold Elliott Nicely. New York and London, Harper & brothers, 1936. 5 p. l., 97 p. 19 1/2 cm. "First edition." [BX9178.N48W5] 36-11252
1. Presbyterian church—Sermons. 2. Sermons, American. I. Title.

NOBLE, David A. 252.051
Words of truth, a series of radio messages by David A. Noble ... [St. Paul, Bruce publishing company, 1944] 111 p. 20 cm. [BX9178.N6W6] 45-17397
1. Presbyterian church—Sermons. 2. Sermons, American. I. Title.

OGILVIE, Lloyd John. 252'.051
The bush is still burning : the Christ who makes things happen in our deepest needs / Lloyd John Ogilvie. Waco, Tex. : Word Books, c1980. 257 p. ; 23 cm. [BX9178.O43B87] 19 79-55924 ISBN 0-8499-0128-6 : 8.95
1. Presbyterian Church—Sermons. 2. Sermons, American. I. Title.

OGILVIE, Lloyd John. 252'.05'1
Drumbeat of love : the unlimited power of the Spirit as revealed in the Book of Acts / Lloyd John Ogilvie. Waco, Tex. : Word Books, c1976. 291 p. ; 23 cm. Includes bibliographical references. [BS2625.4.O36] 76-19535 ISBN 0-87680-483-0 : 7.95
1. Presbyterian Church—Sermons. 2. Bible. N.T. Acts—Sermons. 3. Sermons, American. I. Title.

OGILVIE, Lloyd John. 227'.8106
Life as it was meant to be / Lloyd John Ogilvie. Ventura, Calif. : Regal Books, c1980. 157 p. ; 24 cm. [BS2725.4.O34] 19 80-50541 ISBN 0-8307-0740-9 : 8.95
1. Presbyterian Church—Sermons. 2. Bible. N.T. Thessalonians—Sermons. 3. Sermons, American. I. Title.
Publisher's address: 2300 Knoll Dr., Ventura, CA 93003

OGILVIE, Lloyd John. 248'.2
You've got charisma! / Lloyd John Ogilvie. Nashville : Abingdon Press, [1975] 175 p. ; 21 cm. [BT767.3.O28] 75-14414 ISBN 0-687-47269-5 : 6.95
1. Presbyterian Church—Sermons. 2. Gifts, Spiritual—Sermons. 3. Sermons, American. I. Title.

OGLESBY, Stuart Roscoe, 1888- 252.051
A practising faith; the relation of religious thinking to religious living. New York, F. H. Revell Co. [1948] 157 p. 21 cm. [BX9178.O44P7] 49-224
1. Presbyterian Church—Sermons. 2. Sermons, American. I. Title.

OGLESBY, Stuart Roscoe, 1888- 252.051
Think on these things, by Stuart R. Oglesby. Richmond, Va., John Knox press [1946] 103 p. 21 cm. [BX9178.O44T5] 46-3124
1. Presbyterian church—Sermons. 2. Sermons, American. I. Title.

OMAN, John Wood, 1860-1939. 243
The paradox of the world; sermons by John Oman, D. D. Cambridge [Eng.] The University press, 1921. viii, 292 p. 20 cm. [BX9178.O5P3] 21-18000
1. Presbyterian church—Sermons. 2. Sermons, English. I. Title.

PALMER, Robert E. 222'.16
Directions for living, by Robert E. Palmer. New York, Carlton Press [1967] 100 p. 22

cm. (A Hearthstone book) [BV4655.P33] 74-263269 2.50
1. Presbyterian Church—Sermons. 2. Commandments, Ten—Sermons. 3. Sermons, American. I. Title.

PARKHURST, Charles Henry, 1842-1933. 252
The blind man's creed, and other sermons by Charles H. Parkhurst ... New York, A. D. F. Randolph & company [1883] 2 p. l., 246 p. 20 cm. [BX9178.P3B6] 46-28941
1. Presbyterian church—Sermons. 2. Sermons, American. I. Title.

PARKHURST, Charles Henry, 1842-1933. 252
A little lower than the angels, by Charles H. Parkhurst ... New York, Chicago [etc.] F. H. Revell company [c1908] 287 p. 21 cm. [(BX9178.P3L)] 8-34617
1. Presbyterian church—Sermons. 2. Sermons, American. I. Title.

PARKHURST, Charles Henry, 1842-1933. 252
The pattern in the Mount, and other sermons by Charles H. Parkhurst ... New York, A. D. F. Randolph & company [1885] 2 p. l., 254 p. 19 1/2 cm. [BX9178.P3P3] 46-28332
1. Presbyterian church—Sermons. 2. Sermons, American. I. Title.

PARKHURST, Charles Henry, 1842-1933. 252
Three gates on a side, and other sermons by Charles H. Parkhurst ... New York, Chicago, Fleming H. Revell company [1891] 271 p. 19 cm. [BX9178.P3T4] 46-28952
1. Presbyterian church—Sermons. 2. Sermons, American. I. Title.

PHIFER, William Everette, 1909- 252.051
The cross and great living, by William E. Phifer, jr. New York, Nashville, Abingdon-Cokesbury press [1943] 192 p. 19 1/2 cm. [BX9178.P52C7] 43-3146
1. Presbyterian church—Sermons. 2. Sermons, American. I. Title.

PLEUNE, Peter Henry, 1883- 252.051
The whereabouts of God [by] Peter H. Pleune. NewYork, Nashville, Abingdon-Cokesbury press [1946] 185 p. 19 1/2 cm. [BX9178.P57W5] 46-7912
1. Presbyterian church—Sermons. 2. Sermons, American. I. Title.

PURVES, George Tybout, 1852-1901. 252
... The sinless Christ, by George Tybout Purves ... Philadelphia, Presbyterian board of publication and Sabbath-school work, 1902. ix, 186 p. front. (port.) 20 cm. (The Presbyterian pulpit. [no. 1]) [BX9178.P885] 2-28396
1. Presbyterian church—Sermons. 2. Sermons, American. I. Title.

READ, David Haxton Carswell. 252'.05'242
Curious Christians [by] David H. C. Read. Nashville, Abingdon Press [1973] 144 p. 19 cm. [BX9178.R367C87 1973] 72-5201 ISBN 0-687-10101-8 pap. 1.95
1. Presbyterian Church—Sermons. 2. Sermons, American. I. Title.

READ, David Haxton Carswell. 252'.05
An expanding faith, by David H. C. Read. Grand Rapids, Eerdmans [1973] 116 p. 18 cm. (An Eerdmans evangelical paperback) [BX9178.R367E96] 73-7620 ISBN 0-8028-1539-1 1.95 (pbk.)
1. Presbyterian Church—Sermons. 2. Sermons, American. I. Title.

READ, David Haxton Carswell 252.05
I am persuaded. New York, Scribners [1962, c.1961] 182p. 62-9641 3.00
1. Presbyterian Church—Sermons. 2. Sermons, American. I. Title.

READ, David Haxton Carswell. 252.05'131
The presence of Christ; sermons [by] David H. C. Read. [Denville, N.J.] Pannonia Press, 1968. 91 p. 21 cm. [BX9178.R367P7] 68-31878
1. Presbyterian Church—Sermons. 2. Sermons, American. I. Title.

READ, David Haxton Carswell. 252.05
Religion without wrappings, by David H. C. Read. Grand Rapids, Mich., Eerdmans [1970] 216 p. 21 cm. [BX9178.R367R4] 79-127626 4.95
1. Presbyterian Church—Sermons. 2. Sermons, American. I. Title.

READ, David Haxton Carswell. 253'.2
Unfinished Easter: sermons on the ministry / David H. C. Read. 1st ed. San Francisco : Harper & Row, c1978. 132 p. ; 20 cm. (Harper's ministers paperback library ; RD 263) [BX9178.R367U53 1978] 77-20454 ISBN 0-06-066812-1 pbk. : 4.95
1. Presbyterian Church—Sermons. 2. Sermons, American. I. Title.

READ, David Haxton Carswell. 252.05'131
Virginia Woolf meets Charlie Brown, by David H. C. Read. Grand Rapids, Eerdmans [1968] 225 p. 23 cm. A collection of sermons. [BX9178.R367V5] 68-28854 4.95
1. Presbyterian Church—Sermons. 2. Sermons, American. I. Title.

REDHEAD, John A. 252.05
Getting to know God, and other sermons. Nashville, Abingdon [1964, c.1954] 126p. 18cm. (Apex bks., Q6) .95 pap.,
1. Presbyterian Church—Sermons. 2. Sermons, American. I. Title.

REDHEAD, John A 252.05
Getting to know God, and other sermons. Nashville, Abingdon Press [c1954] 126p. 20cm. [BX9178.R368G4] 54-5230
1. Presbyterian Church—Sermons. 2. Sermons, American. I. Title.

REID, James, 1877- 252.05
Making friends with life, by Rev. James Reid ... Nashville, Tenn., Cokesbury press [1936] 288 p. 19 1/2 cm. "Printed in Great Britain." "These reflections first appeared in the columns of the British weekly."--Pref. Sermons. [BX9178.R37M3] 36-36976
1. Presbyterian church—Sermons. 2. Sermons, English. I. Title.

REID, James, 1877- 252.05
The temple in the heart [by] Rev. James Reid, D.D. Nashville, Tenn., Cokesbury press [c1938] 331 p. 19 1/2 cm. [BX9178.R37T4] 38-3040
1. Presbyterian church—Sermons. 2. Sermons, English (Selections: Extracts, etc.) I. Title.

REID, John Calvin, 1901- 252.05
On toward the goal; sermons of hope and encouragement. Richmond, John Knox Press, 1949. 159 p. 21 cm. Bibliographical references included in "Notes" (p. [155]-159) [BX9178.R38O5] 49-10904
1. Presbyterian Church—Sermons. 2. Sermons, American. I. Title.

REID, John Calvin, 1901- 252.051
Reserves of the soul, and other sermons by J. Calvin Reid ... Richmond, Va., John Knox press [c1942] vi, p., 1 l., 156 p. 19 1/2 cm. [BX9178.R38R4] 43-2795
1. Presbyterian church—Sermons. 2. Sermons, American. I. Title.

RIMMER, Harry, 1890- 232.95
From Cana to Calvary, by Harry Rimmer ... Grand Rapids, Mich., Wm. B. Eerdmans publishing company, 1940. 136 p. 20 cm. [BT340.R5] 40-8559
1. Jesus Christ—Biog.—Sermons. 2. Presbyterian church—Sermons. 3. Sermons, American. I. Title.

ROBERTS, David Everett, 1911-1955. 252.051
The grandeur and misery of man; [sermons] New York, Oxford University Press, 1955. 186p. 20cm. [BX9178.R56G7] 55-10931
1. Presbyterian Church—Sermons. 2. Sermons, American. I. Title.

ROBINSON, Charles Seymour, 1829-1899. 252
... Bethel and Penuel: twenty-six sermons preached in the Presbyterian memorial church, Madison avenue and Fifty-third street, N.Y., by Chas. S. Robinson ... New York, A. S. Barnes & company [1874] viii, 317 p. 19 1/2 cm. (His The Memorial pulpit, vol. II) [BX9178.R58B4] 46-28942
1. Presbyterian church—Sermons. 2. Sermons, American. I. Title.

ROBINSON, Charles Seymour, 1829-1899. 248
Sabbath evening sermons, by Chas. S. Robinson ... New-York, The Century co., 1887. vii, 306 p. 19 1/2 cm. [BX9178.R58S3] 45-34676
1. Presbyterian church—Sermons. 2. Sermons, American. I. Title.

ROBINSON, Charles Seymour, 1829-1899. 252
Studies of neglected texts. By Chas. S. Robinson ... New York, American tract society [1883] vii, 329 p. 19 1/2 cm. [BX9178.R58S8] 45-23091
1. Presbyterian church—Sermons. 2. Sermons, American. I. American tract society. II. Title.

ROBSHAW, Charles P 252.05
The wisdom that does not change. New York, Abingdon Press [1962] 125p. 20cm. [BX9178.R63W5] 62-8106
1. Presbyterian Church—Sermons. 2. Sermons, American. I. Title.

ROLSTON, Holmes, 1900- 227'.92'07
The Apostle Peter speaks to us today / Holmes Rolston. Atlanta : John Knox Press, c1977. 99 p.; 21 cm. [BS2795.4.R64] 76-44974 ISBN 0-8042-0201-X pbk. : 2.95
1. Presbyterian Church—Sermons. 2. Bible. N.T. 1 Peter—Sermons. 3. Sermons, American. I. Title.

ROSE, Stephen C. 252'.05'1
Sermons not preached in the White House, by Stephen C. Rose. Introductory essay by Reinhold Niebuhr. New York, R. W. Baron Pub. Co., 1970. 155 p. 21 cm. "A Cambria Press book." [BX9178.R67S47] 70-108974 4.95
1. Presbyterian Church—Sermons. 2. Sermons, American. I. Title.

RUSSELL, Daniel, 1873- 252.051
O stedfast face! Studies of the Christ of purpose, by Daniel Russell ... New York [etc.] Fleming H. Revell company [c1936] 159 p. 20 cm. [BX9178.R8O2] 36-21334
1. Presbyterian church—Sermons. 2. Sermons, American. I. Title.

SANDERS, James A., 1927- 252'.05'1
God has a story too : sermons in context / James A. Sanders. Philadelphia : Fortress Press, c1979. xi, 145 p. ; 22 cm. Includes bibliographical references and index. [BX9178.S28G62] 77-15244 ISBN 0-8006-1353-8 pbk. : 5.75
1. Presbyterian Church—Sermons. 2. Bible—Hermenenties. 3. Sermons, American. 4. Preaching.

SANTA, George Frederick, 1914- 252.051
Musings at twilight, by George F. Santa. Grand Rapids, Mich., Wm. B. Eerdmans publishing co., 1938. 133 p. 20 cm. [BX9178.S3M8] 39-2144
1. Presbyterian church—Sermons. 2. Sermons, American. I. Title.

SAWIN, Theophilus Parsons, 1841-1906. 232.96
The transfiguring of the cross; or, The trial and triumph of the Son of man. By Theophilus P. Sawin ... Troy, N.Y., Brewster and Packard, 1896. viii p., 2 l., [13]-239 p. 20 cm. [BT430.S2] 36-1511
1. Jesus Christ—Passion—Sermons. 2. Presbyterian church—Sermons. 3. Sermons, American. I. Title. II. Title: The trial and triumph of the Son of man.

SCOTT, William Anderson, 1813-1885. 222'.2'0924
Wedge of gold : [the folly and fall of Achan] : a careful look at the sin of covetousness / W. A. Scott. Swengel, Pa. : Reiner Publications, [1974?] 162 p. ; 19 cm. Discourses delivered in the Calvary Church, San Francisco. Reprint of the 1855 ed. [BX9178.S4W4 1974] 74-187954 2.95
1. Presbyterian Church—Sermons. 2. Sermons, American. 3. Achan (Biblical character) I. Title.

SCOTT, William Anderson, 1813-1885. 252
The wedge of gold: or, Achan in El Dorado ... By Rev. W. A. Scott, D. D. San Francisco, Whitton, Towne & co., 1855. xi, [13]-182 p. 18 cm. Discourses delivered in Calvary church, San Francisco. cf. Pref. [BX9178.S4W4] 20-23357
1. Presbyterian church—Sermons. 2. Sermons, American. 3. Achan (Biblical character) I. Title.

SEYMOUR, Otto Cleveland, 1891- 252.051
Precious things of the Bible, by Otto C. Seymour... New York [etc.] Fleming H. Revell company [c1935] 147 p. 19 1/2 cm. [BX9178.S443P7] 36-726
1. Presbyterian church—Sermons. 2. Sermons, American. I. Title.

SHEDD, William Greenough Thayer, 1820-1894. 252
Sermons to the natural man. By William G. T. Shedd ... New York, C. Scribner & co., 1871. x p., 1 l., 422 p. 21 1/2 cm. [BX9178.S45S4 1871] 42-43207
1. Presbyterian church—Sermons. 2. Sermons, American. I. Title.

SHEDD, William Greenough Thayer, 1820-1894. 252
Sermons to the natural man. By William G. T. Shedd ... New York, Scribner, Armstrong & co., 1873. x p., 1 l., 422 p. 21 cm. [BX9178.S45S4 1873] 42-43206
1. Presbyterian church—Sermons. 2. Sermons, American. I. Title.

SHEDD, William Greenough Thayer, 1820-1894. 252'.05'1
Sermons to the natural man / William G. T. Shedd. Edinburgh ; Carlisle, Pa. : Banner of Truth Trust, 1978. [2], xi, 422 p. ; 23 cm. Reprint of the 1st ed. published in 1871 by Scribner, New York. Includes bibliographical references. [BX9178.S45S4 1977] 78-312986 ISBN 0-85151-260-7 : 8.95
1. Presbyterian Church—Sermons. 2. Sermons, American. I. Title.

SHEDD, William Greenough Thayer, 1820-1894. 252
Sermons to the spiritual man. By William G. T. Shedd ... New York, C. Scribner's sons, 1884. v. p., 1 l., 421 p. 21 1/2 cm. [BX9178.S45S42] 42-43208
1. Presbyterian church—Sermons. 2. Sermons, American. I. Title.

SIBLEY, Josiah, 1877- 243
Pathfinders of the soul-country, and other sermons for today, by Josiah Sibley... New York, Chicago, [etc.] Fleming H. Revell company [c1918] 4 p. l., 11-209 p. 19 1/2 cm. [BX9178.S5P3] 18-18137
1. Presbyterian church—Sermons. 2. Sermons, American. I. Title.

SIZOO, Joseph Richard, 1884- 252.05
The way of faith, by Joseph R. Sizoo. New York and London, Harper & brothers, 1935. 6 p. l., 107 p. 19 cm. "First edition." [BX9178.S522 W3] 35-5132
1. Presbyterian church—Sermons. 2. Sermons, American. I. Title.

SMART, James D 252.05
The recovery of humanity. Philadelphia, Westminster Press [1953] 157p. 21cm. [BX9178.S526R4] 53-8528
1. Presbyterian Church—Sermons. 2. Sermons, American. I. Title.

SMITH, Asa Dodge, 1804-1877. 922.573
Memoir of Mrs. Louisa Adams Leavitt; comprised in a sermon occasioned by her death, and a supplementary sketch. By Rev. Asa D. Smith. New-York, J. F. Trow, 1843. 156 p. 16 cm. "Shed not a tear" (with music): p. 154-155. [BR1725.L33S6] 38-3079
1. Leavitt, Mrs. Louisa Adams, 1803-1842. 2. Presbyterian church—Sermons. I. Title.

SMITH, George Adam, Sir 1856- 243
The forgiveness of sins, and other sermons, by George Adam Smith ... New York, A. C. Armstrong & son, 1905. xii, 266 p. 20 cm. [BX9178.S53F7] 4-37000
1. Presbyterian church—Sermons. 2. Sermons, English. I. Title.

SPEAKMAN, Frederick B. 252.051
Love is something you do. [Westwood, N.J.] Revell [1959] 154 p. 22 cm. [BX9178.S68L6] 59-8724

1. Presbyterian Church — Sermons. 2. Sermons, American. I. Title.

SPEAKMAN, Frederick B 252.051
The salty tang; messages for today. [Westwood, N. J.] F. H. Revell Co. [1954] 160p. 21cm. [BX9178.S68S3] 54-5435
1. Presbyterian Church— sermons. 2. Sermons, American. I. Title.

SPEERS, Theodore Cuyler, 1899- 252.051
The power of the commonplace, by Theodore Cuyler Speers; with an introduction by Henry Sloane Coffin. New York and London, Harper & brothers, 1933. lx p., 1 l., 107 p. 19 1/2 cm. "First edition." [BX9178.S692P6] 33-22797
1. Presbyterian church—Sermons. 2. Sermons, American. I. Title.

SPENCER, Ichabod Smith, 1798-1854. 243
Sermons of Rev. Ichabod S. Spencer ... With a sketch of his life, By Rev. J. M. Sherwood ... New York, M. W. Dodd, 1855. 2 v. front. (port.) 20 cm. Contents.--I. Life, Practical and experimental sermons.--II. Doctrinal sermons. [BX9178.S694S4] 38-19174
1. Presbyterian church—Sermons. 2. Sermons, American. I. Sherwood, James Manning, 1814-1890. II. Title.

SPRUNT, James.
Windows on the word; a series of sermons based on the literature of the Bible symbolized by the chancel windows in the First Presbyterian Church of Raleigh, North Carolina. Preached by the minister, James Sprunt, D.D., June 24th-October 21st, 1956, including "Symbolism of the sanctuary," a prefactory sermon delivered on June 17, 1956 . . . and, in the appendix, a brief historical sketch of the church, 1816-1958. [Raleigh 1958] 88 p. illus. 28 cm. 66-52015
I. Title.

SPRUNT, James.
Windows on the word; a series of sermons based on the literature of the Bible symbolized by the chancel windows in the First Presbyterian Church of Raleigh, North Carolina. Preached by the minister, James Sprunt, D.D., June 24th-October 21st, 1956, including "Symbolism of the sanctuary," a prefactory sermon delivered on June 17, 1956 . . . and, in the appendix, a brief historical sketch of the church, 1816-1958. [Raleigh 1958] 88 p. illus. 28 cm. 66-52015
I. Title.

STEEN, Robert Service, 1880-1908. 252
The strength of quietness, and other sermons, by Robert Service Steen. New York, Dodd, Mead and company, 1908. xviii p., 2 l., 3-293 p. front. (port.) 18 cm. "Life of Robert Service Steen, by Henry Sloane Coffin": p. vii-xviii. [BX9178.S78S8] 8-30530
1. Presbyterian church—Sermons. 2. Sermons, American. I. Coffin, Henry Sloane, 1877- II. Title.

STEWART, George, 1892- 252.051
Jesus said "I am", by George Stewart. New York and London, Harper & brothers, 1934. 5 p. l., 89 p. 19 cm. "First edition." [BX9178.S7915J4] 34-1903
1. Presbyterian church—Sermons. 2. Sermons, American. I. Title.

STEWART, James Stuart, 1896- 252.052
The gates of new life, by James S. Stewart. Popular ed. New York, C Scribner's sons, 1940. x p., 1 l., 251 p. 21 cm. "Popular edition." [BX9178.S7917G3] 40-0444
1. Presbyterian church—Sermons. 2. Sermons, English—Scotland. I. Title.

STEWART, James Stuart, 1896- 252'.05'1
King for ever / James S. Stewart. Nashville, Tenn. : Abingdon Press, [1975] 160 p. ; 23 cm. [BX9178.S7917K5] 75-313215 ISBN 0-687-20883-1 : 5.95
1. Presbyterian Church—Sermons. 2. Sermons, English—Scotland. I. Title.

STEWART, James Stuart, 1896- 252'.05'2
River of life, by James S. Stewart. Nashville, Abingdon Press [1972] 160 p. 23 cm. [BX9178.S7917R58] 72-2031 ISBN 0-687-36480-9 3.50
1. Presbyterian Church—Sermons. 2. Sermons, English—Scotland. I. Title.

STEWART, James Stuart, 1896- 252.052
The strong name, by James S. Stewart ... New York, C. Scribner's sons, 1941. viii, 260 p. 21 1/2 cm. [BX9178.S7917S75] 41-6084
1. Presbyterian church—Sermons. 2. Sermons, English—Scotland. I. Title.

STEWART, James Stuart, 1896- 252.05'2
The wind of the spirit [by] James S. Stewart. Nashville, Abingdon Press [1969, c1968] 191 p. 23 cm. [BX9178.S7917W5 1969] 69-18447 3.95
1. Presbyterian Church—Sermons. 2. Sermons, English—Scotland. I. Title.

STOFFEL, Ernest Lee. 252.051
The strong comfort of God. Richmond, John Knox Press [1958] 159 p. 21 cm. [BX9178.S7932S7] 58-7774
1. Presbyterian Church — Sermons. 2. Sermons, American. I. Title.

STRYKER, Melancthon Woolsey, 1851-1929. 243
... The well by the gate, by the Rev. M. Woolsey Stryker ... Philadelphia, Presbyterian board of publication and Sabbath school work, 1903. v, 116 p. front. (port.) 19 1/2 cm. (The Presbyterian pulpit. no. 3]) [BX9178.S92W4] 3-7195
1. Presbyterian church—Sermons. 2. Sermons, American. I. Title.

SWEAZEY, George Edgar. 252.6
The keeper of the door, by George E. Sweazey ... St. Louis, Mo., The Bethany press [1946] 190 p. 19 1/2 cm. [BX9178.S97K4] 46-1744
1. Presbyterian church—Sermons. 2. Sermons, American. I. Title.

*TALMAGE, T. DeWitt. 252'.051
T. DeWitt Talmage. Introduction by Daniel A. Poling. Grand Rapids, Mich., Baker Book House [1973, c1950] 254 p. 19 cm. (Great pulpit masters series) [BX9178] ISBN 0-8010-8812-7. 2.95 (pbk.)
1. Presbyterian Church—Sermons. 2. Sermons, American. I. Title.

TALMAGE, Thomas De Witt, 1832-1902. 252.051
500 selected sermons. Grand Rapids, Baker Book House, 1956- v. illus. 22 cm. "A reprint of the printing originally made by the Christian herald in 1900." [[BN9178]] 56-10681
1. Presbyterian Church — Sermons. 2. Sermons, American. I. Title.

TALMAGE, Thomas DeWitt, 1832-1902. 252.05
The masque torn off. By T. DeWitt Talmage ... Chicago, J. Fairbanks & co. London, Eng., R. D. Dickenson; [etc., etc.] 1879. xviii, 21-526 p. incl. front. (port.) plates. 22 1/2 cm. "Discourses on the temptations and vices of city life."--Pref. [BX9178.T3M35 1879] 36-29977
1. Presbyterian church—Sermons. 2. New York (City)—Soc. condit. 3. Sermons, American. I. Title.

TALMAGE, Thomas DeWitt, 1832-1902. 252.05
The masque torn off. By T. DeWitt Talmage ... Chicago, J. Fairbanks & co. London, Eng., R. D. Dickenson; [etc., etc.] 1880. xviii, 21-526 p. incl. front., (port.) plates. 22 1/2 cm. [BX9178.T3M35 1880] 35-29978
1. Presbyterian church—Sermons. 2. New York (City)—Soc. condit. 3. Sermons, American. I. Title.

TALMAGE, Thomas DeWitt, 1832-1902. 301.41'2
Woman, her power and privileges : a series of sermons on the duties of the maiden, wife and mother, and of their influence in the home and society / by T. DeWitt Talmage. Washington : Zenger Pub. Co., 1975, c1888. p. cm. Reprint of the ed. published by J. S. Ogilvie, Chicago. [BT704.T34 1975] 75-41390 ISBN 0-89201-027-4
1. Presbyterian Church—Sermons. 2. Woman (Theology)—Sermons. 3. Sermons, American. I. Title.

TAYLOR, William Mackergo, 1829-1895. 252
Contrary winds, and other sermons by Wm. M. Taylor ... New York, A. C. Armstrong & son, 1883. 372 p. 21 1/2 cm. [BX9178.T33C6 1883] 45-23094
1. Presbyterian church—Sermons. 2. Sermons, American. I. Title.

TAYLOR, William Mackergo, 1829-1895. 252
The limitations of life, and other sermons by Wm. M. Taylor, D.D. ... With portrait on steel by Ritchie. New York, A. C. Armstrong & son, 1880 [i.e. 1879] v, 391 p. front. (port.) 21 1/2 cm. [BX9178.T33L5 1879] 46-33040
1. Presbyterian church—Sermons. 2. Sermons, American. I. Title.

TEMPLETON, Charles Bradley, 1915- 252.051
Life looks up. [1st ed.] New York, Harper [c1955] 192p. 22cm. [BX9178.T345L5] 54-12812
1. Presbyterian Church—Sermons. 2. Sermons, American. I. Title.

THOMAS, D Reginald. 252.05
Love so amazing. [Westwood, N.J.] Revell [1961] 127 p. 21 cm. [BX9178.T37L6] 61-5926
1. Presbyterian Church — Sermons. 2. Sermons, American. I. Title.

THOMAS, D. Reginald. 252.05131
To know God's way [by] D. Reginald Thomas. Westwood, N.J., Revell [1966] 154 p. 21 cm. [BX9178.T37T6] 66-21895
1. Presbyterian Church—Sermons. 2. Sermons, American. 3. Christian life—Presbyterian authors. I. Title.

TINKER, Reuben, 1799-1854. 252
Sermons by Rev. Reuben Tinker ... with a biographical sketch by M. L. P. Thomspon ... New York, Derby & Jackson, 1856. viii, 421 p. front. (port.) 19 cm. [BX9178.T5S4] 45-23092
1. Presbyterian church—Sermons. 2. Sermons, American. I. Thompson, Matthew La Rue Perrine, b. 1809. II. Title.

TURNBULL, Ralph G. 252.05
Triumph in Christ; the blessing of life in Him [by] Ralph G. Turnbull. Philadelphia, Pa., The Bethlehem book room [1945] 99 p. 19 cm. [BX9178.T8T7] 45-9649
1. Presbyterian church—Sermons. 2. Sermons, American. I. Title.

[VAN Dyke, Henry] 1852-1933. 922.573
Henry Jackson Van Dyke... New York, A. D. F. Randolph & company [1892] 1 p. l., iv, 168 p. front., (port.) 19 1/2 cm. "Life and character" signed: Henry Van Dyke. Paul Van Dyke. [BX9225.V3V3] 36-22123
1. Van Dyke, Henry Jackson, 1822-1891. 2. Presbyterian church—Sermons. 3. Sermons, American. I. Van Dyke, Paul, 1859-1933, joint author. II. Title. Contents omitted.

VANCE, James Isaac, 1862-1939. 289
Church portals. By James I. Vance ... Richmond, Va., The Presbyterian committee of publications, 1895. 145 p. 19 cm. [BX9178.V2C5] 45-23093
1. Presbyterian church—Sermons. 2. Sermons, American. I. Title.

WADSWORTH, Charles, 1814-1882. 252
Sermons. By Rev. Charles Wadsworth ... Philadelphia, Presbyterian publishing company, 18 v. 19 cm. [BX9178.W2S4] 46-34911
1. Presbyterian church—Sermons. 2. Sermons, American. I. Title.

WALKER, Harold Blake. 252.051
Upper room on Main Street. [1st ed.] New York, Harper [1954] 191p. 22cm. [BX9178.W29U6] 53-10981
1. Presbyterian Church—Sermons. 2. Sermons, American. I. Title.

WARD, John William George, 1879- 252.051
The refiner's fire, and other sermons, by J. W. G. Ward... New York and London, Harper & brothers, 1934. 4 p. l., 124 p. 19 1/2 cm. "First edition." [BX9178.W325R4] 34-40131
1. Presbyterian church—Sermons. 2. Sermons, American. I. Title.

WARFIELD, Benjamin Breckinridge, 1851-1921. 252'.05
Faith and life / Benjamin B. Warfield. Edinburgh ; Carlisle, Pa. : Banner of Truth Trust, 1974. viii, 458 p. ; 19 cm. First published 1916. [BX9178.W33F3 1974] 75-320416 ISBN 0-85151-188-0 : £0.90
1. Presbyterian Church—Sermons. 2. Sermons, American. I. Title.

WASSON, Samuel Carson, 1908- 252.05
Eleven o'clock Sunday morning; book of sermons. [Rye? N.Y., 1960] 245 p. illus. 20 cm. Includes bibliography. [BX9178.W347E4] 61-21272
1. Presbyterian Church — Sermons. 2. Sermons, American. I. Title.

WATSON, John, 1850-1907. 252
The inspiration of our faith; sermons by John Watson, D.D. "Ian Maclaren"... New York, A. C. Armstrong and son, 1905. 3 p. l., 9-359 p. 20 cm. [BX9178.W35I5] 5-41620
1. Presbyterian church—Sermons. 2. Sermons, English. I. Title.

WETTSTONE, Karl Frederick, 1894- 252.05
Christ at every turn, twelve popular Sunday evening sermons, by Karl Frederick Wettstone ... Grand Rapids, Mich., Wm. B. Eerdmans publishing company, 1938. 168 p. front. (port.) 20 cm. [Full name: Karl Frederick Humbert Wettstone] [BX9178.W464C5] 38-39350
1. Presbyterian church—Sermons. 2. Sermons, American. I. Title.

WHARTON, Lawrence Hay, 1892-1937. 252.051
Guideposts for youth; searching for right living, by Lawrence H. Wharton, edited by De Witt Reddick. Richmond, Va., John Knox press [1943] vii, 102 p. 20 1/2 cm. [BX9178.W47G8] 43-7828
1. Presbyterian church—Sermons. 2. Sermons, American. I. Reddick, De Witt Carter, ed. II. Title.

WHITEFIELD, George, 1714-1770. 252.05
Eighteen sermons preached by the late Rev. George Whitefield ... Taken verbatim in short hand, and faithfully transcribed by Joseph Gurney. Revised by Andrew Gifford, D.D. Printed at Springfield [Mass.] By Thomas Dickman. 1808. 4 p. l., 361 p. 18 cm. Originally published, London, 1771. [BX9178.W5E5 1808] 34-29194
1. Presbyterian church—Sermons. 2. Sermons, English. I. Gurney. Joseph, 1744-1815, reporter. II. Gifford, Andrew, 1700-1784, ed. III. Title.

WHYTE, Alexander, 1837-1921 252.052
The treasury of Alexander Whyte; ed. by Ralph G. Turnbull. Foreword by Clarence E. Macartney. Grand Rapids, Mich., Baker Bk. [1968, c. 1953] 256p. 19cm. (Treasury ser.) [BX9178.W55T7] 1.95 pap.,
1. Presbyterian Church—Sermons. 2. Sermons. 3. Sermons, English—Scotland. I. Title.

WILLIAMS, Richard John, 1881- 252.051
The creed of a slave, by Rev. R. J. Williams, M.A. Boston, The Christopher publishing house [c1939] x, 13-79 p. front. (port.) 20 1/2 cm. [BX9178.W565C7] 39-9781
1. Presbyterian church—Sermons. 2. Sermons, American. I. Title.

WILLISTON, Seth, 1770-1851. 252.051
Sermons of doctrinal and experimental subjects. By Seth Williston... Hudson [N.Y.]: Printed by A. Stoddard, no. 137, Warren-Street, 1812. 2 p. l., 236 p. 18 cm. [BX9198.W5835S4] 33-31540
1. Presbyterian church—Sermons. 2. Sermons, American. I. Title.

WILLS, Theodore O. M., 1905- 252.051
God with us, by Theodore O. M. Wills ... Pupit book club ed. New York, Colfax press, 1945. 5 p. l., 122 p. 20 cm. [BX9178.W584G6] 45-20011

1. Presbyterian church—Sermons. 2. Sermons, American. I. Title.

WILSON, Elijah, ed. 252
The living pulpit, or Eighteen sermons by eminent living divines of the Presbyterian church, with a biographical sketch of the editor, by Geo. W Bethune, D.D. Edited and published by Rev. Elijah Wilson 7th ed. Philadelphia, For sale by W. S. Martien [etc.] 1857. xvi, 414 p. front. (port.) 23 1/2 cm. [BX9178.A1W5 1857] 22-5359
1. Presbyterian church—Sermons. 2. Sermons, American. I. Bethune, George Washington, 1805-1862. II. Title.

WOOD, Francis Lloyd 252.05
Ferguson, 1909- ed.
Living echoes; sermons by twelve Georgia Presbyterian ministers, edited by Ferguson Wood ... Richmond, Va., John Knox press [1943] 112 p. 20 1/2 cm. [BX9178.A1W6] 43-8735
1. Presbyterian church—Sermons. 2. Sermons, American. I. Title.

YOUNG, Samuel Edward, 252.051
1906-
A zest for life [by] S. Edward Young ... Buffalo, N.Y., Foster & Stewart publishing corp., 1946. vii, 169 p. 19 cm. [BX9178.Y67Z4] 46-21902
1. Presbyterian church—Sermons. 2. Sermons, American. I. Title.

Presbyterian college, Clinton, States C.

PRESBYTERIAN college of South Carolina, Clinton, S. C. Surrey commission.
Report of the Survey commission of the Presbyterian college of South Carolina. Clinton, S. C. [1927] 146 p. incl. tables. diagrs. 22 cm. (On cover: Presbyterian college of South Carolina. Quarterly bulletin, vol. xxv, no. 2) Shelton Phelps, director of the survey. [LD456.P679] E 27
1. Presbyterian college, Clinton, S. C. 2. Educational surveys. I. Phelps, Shelton Joseph, 1884- II. Title.

Presbyterianism.

BRIGGS, Charles Augustus, 285
1841-1913.
Whither? A theological question for the times, by Charles Augustus Briggs ... New York, C. Scribner's sons, 1889. xv, 303 p. 21 cm. [BX8937.B7] 33-22267
1. Presbyterianism. I. Title.

BROWNLOW, William Gannaway, 1805-1877.
Helps to the study of Presbyterianism; or, An unsophisticated exposition of Calvinism, with Hopkinsian modifications and policy, with a view to a more easy interpretation of the same. To which is added a brief account of the life and travels of the author; interspersed with anecdotes. By William G. Brownlow ... Knoxville, T., F. S. Heiskell, printer, 1834. xiii, [15]-299 p. 20 cm. [BX9180.B7] 42-46859
1. Presbyterianism. I. Title.

BRYANT, Alfred, 1807- 230.5
The doctrine of decress, foresordination, predestination, and election, as held by Presbyterians, and taught in their Confesion of faith, explained and illustrated, by Rev. Alfred Bryant ... Lansing [Mich.] W. S. George & co., printers, 1870. 141 p. 21 cm. [BX9177.B75] 38-19146
1. Presbyterianism. I. Title.

CHURCH of Scotland.
The Confession of faith, the Larger and Shorter catechisms, with the Scripture proofs at large. Together with The sum of saving knowledge (contain'd in the Holy Scriptures, and held forth in the said Confession and catechisms) and practical use thereof; Covenants national and Solemn league, Acknowledgment of sins and engagement to duties, directions, Form of church-government, &c. Of publick-authority in the Church of Scotland. With acts of Assembly and Parliament, relative to, and approbative of the same ... Philadelphia, Printed and sold by B. Franklin, M.DCC.XLV. 567, [28] p. 17 1/2 cm. Signatures: A-Z8, Aa-Oo8. Imperfect: 2 l. (sig. Oo4-5) in table of contents wanting. Each part has special t.-p. Imprint varies slightly. Paged continuously with other parts. 2-668
1. Presbyterianism. 2. Church of Scotland—Catechisms and creeds. I. Westminster assembly of divines. II. Title.

[DICKINSON, Jonathan] 262.18
1688-1747.
The Scripture-bishop; or, The divine right of Presbyterian ordination & government considered in a dialogue between Preslaticus and Eleutherius. Boston: N. E. Printed for D. Henchman, in Corn-hill, 1732. 1 p. l., ii, 58 p. 16 cm. [BX9174.D48] 3-4368
1. Presbyterianism. I. Title.

DUNCAN, James, d.1829? 285
Polemic disquisitions on four general subjects: viz. I. On the unity of the church in a lecture from Matt, XXXVI. II. Strictures on the independent scheme of church government. III. A lecture on the subject of convenanting, from Psalm 105. 6-10. IV. An essay on creeds and confessions of faith. By James Duncan. Indianapolis, Printed by J. Douglass, 1828. 215 p. 19 cm. [BX9175.D8] 46-39537
1. Presbyterianism. 2. Church—Unity. 3. Creeds. I. Title.

HENDERSON, George David, 285.2
1888-
Why we are Presbyterians. [Edinburgh?] Church of Scotland Publications [1953?] 86p. 19cm. [BX9175.H4] 53-40457
1. Presbyterianism. I. Title.

HODGE, Charles, 1797-1878. 230.
What is Presbyterianism? An address delivered before the Presbyterian historical society at their anniversary meeting in Philadelphia, on Tuesday evening, May 1, 1855. By the Rev. Charles Hodge, D.D. Philadelphia, Presbyterian board of publication [c1855] 80 p. 15 cm. [BX9177.H63] 39-7827
1. Presbyterianism. I. Presbyterian church in the U.S.A. (Old school) Board of publication. II. Title.

KERR, Robert Pollok, 1850- 285
1923.
Presbyterianism for the people. By the Rev. Robert P. Kerr. Philadelphia, Presbyterian board of publication [1884] 80 p. 17 1/2 cm. [BX9177.K4] 45-26718
1. Presbyterianism. I. Presbyterian church in the U.S.A. Board of publication and Sabbath school work. II. Title.

LINGLE, Walter Lee, 1868- 285
Presbyterians, their history and beliefs, by Walter L. Lingle ... Richmond, Va. [etc.] Presbyterian committee of publication [c1928] 199 p. diagr. 20 cm. "Question and topics for study" at end of each chapter [BX8931.L5] 30-8494
1. Presbyterianism. 2. Presbyterianism—Hist. I. Title.

LINGLE, Walter Lee, 1868- 285
Presbyterians, their history and beliefs. [Rev. ed.] Rev. by T. Watson Street. Richmond, John Knox Press [c1960] 128p. 21cm. [BX8931.L5 1960] 60-16432
1. Presbyterianism. 2. Presbyterianism—Hist. I. Title.

LINGLE, Walter Lee, 1868- 285
Presbyterians, their history and beliefs, by Walter L. Lingle ... Richmond, Va., John Knox press [1944] 4 p. l., 11-127 p. 20 cm. [BX8931.L5 1944] 45-5368
1. Presbyterianism. 2. Presbyterianism—Hist. I. Title.

LINGLE, Walter Lee, 1868- 285
1956.
Presbyterians, their history and beliefs / by Walter L. Lingle and John W. Kuykendall. [4th rev. ed.]. Atlanta : John Knox Press, c1978. 110 p. : port. ; 21 cm. Includes index. [BX8931.2.L56 1978] 77-15750 ISBN 0-8042-0985-5 pbk. : 3.50
1. Presbyterian Church—History. 2. Presbyterianism. I. Kuykendall, John W., joint author. II. Title.

MACKAY, John Alexander, 1889- 285
The Presbyterian way of life. Englewood Cliffs, N. J., Prentice-Hall [1960] 238p. 21cm. [BX9175.2.M3] 60-14198
1. Presbyterianism. I. Title.

MILLER, James Russell, 1840-
Practical religion: a help for the common days. By J. R. Miller ... Philadelphia, Presbyterian board of publication [c1888] 320 p. 18 cm. 12-36791
I. Title.

MORRIS, Samuel Leslie, 1854- 285
Presbyterianism; its principles and practice, by S. L. Morris ... Richmond [etc.] Presbyterian committee of publication, 1922. vii, 177, viii-xiii p. 20 cm. [BX9175.M6] 22-15523
I. Title.

PECK, Thomas E. 1822-1893. 201
Miscellanies of Rev. Thomas E. Peck ... Selected and arranged by Rev. T. C. Johnson, D. D. Richmond, Va., The Presbyterian committee of publication, 1895-97. 3 v. 22 cm. Contents.--v. 1. Containing his more popular writings and lectures.--v. 2. Containing theological and evangelical, historical and expository, and ecclesiological writings.--v. 3. Containing the notes on the Acts of the apostles, and briefs and sermons ... with biographical sketch of Dr. Peck by Rev. C. R. Vaughan, D. D. [BR83.P4] 98-271
I. Johnson, Thomas Cary, 1859- ed. II. Vaughan, Clement Read, 1827- III. Title.

PHILADELPHIA. 285.174811
Overbrook Presbyterian Church.
The place where Thy glory dwells; the story of Overbrook Presbyterian Church, 1890-1958. [Philadelphia, 1958] 139p. illus. 24cm. [BX9211.P5O8] 59-33739
I. Title.

ROBINSON, Stuart, 1814-1881. 285
The church of God as an essential element of the Gospel, and the idea, structure, and functions thereof. A discourse in four parts. By Rev. Stuart Robinson ... With an Appendix, containing the more important symbols of Presbyterian church government ... Philadelphia, J. M. Wilson; Louisville, Ky., A. Davidson, 1858. 1 p. l., 9-130, xcvi p. 19 1/2 cm. [BX9175.R63] 15-16171
1. Presbyterianism. I. Title.

STAPLES, M. W. 285
Presbyterianism in her polity and practice. Defended in three discourses. By Rev. M. W. Staples ... delivered in Marshall, Texas, February, 1854. St. Louis, Mo., Published by the urgent request of the church and congregation, 1855. 142 p. 20 1/2 cm. [BX9175.S8] 27-9572
1. Presbyterianism. I. Title.

STOCKER Rhamanthus Menville, 1848-
History of the First Presbyterian society of Honesdale, by R. M. Stocker. Honesdale, Pa., Herald press association, 1906. vii, 336 p. 7 pl., 21 port. and group of ports. 24 cm. Library of Congress. 8-409
I. Title.

SWING, David, 1830-1894. 285.173
The world's edition of the great Presbyterian conflict: Patton vs. Swing. Both sides of the question. With portraits of Profs. Patton and Swing, and containing a full outline of the circumstances which preceded the trial... Pulpit sketches of Profs. Swing and Patton, by the Rev. Chas. L. Thompson...Also, the fourteen famous sermons preached by Prof. Swing, "for utterances in which" the prosecution has based its charges of heterodoxy. The celebrated "Charges and specifications": Prof. Swing's Declaration; Prof. Patton's famous argument; the answer to the same by Prof. Swing and his counsel; the closing argument by Prof. Patton, and the verdict of the Presbytery. Chicago, G. Macdonald & co., 1874. 168 p. ports. 24 cm. [BX9193.S9W6] 33-22266
1. Presbyterianism. I. Patton, Francis Landey, 1843-1932. II. Thompson, Charles Lemuel, 1839-1924. III. Title. IV. Title: The great Presbyterian conflict.

WARFIELD, Benjamin 233
Breckinridge, 1851-1921.
... The power of God unto salvation, by Benjamin B. Warfield ... Philadelphia, Presbyterian board of publication and Sabbath-school work, 1903. vi, 254 p. front. (port.) 19 1/2 cm. (The Presbyterian pulpit. [no. 5]) "The sermons included in this volume have all been preached in the Chapel of the Theological seminary at Princeton." [BT751.W25] 3-11305
I. Title.

Presbyterianism—History

KERR, Robert Pollok, 1850- 285
The people's history of Presbyterianism in all ages. By Robert P. Kerr... 5th ed. Richmond, Va., The Presbyterian committee of publication [c1899] 3 p. l., 5-10, [9]-284 p. plates, 2 port. (incl. front.) 20 cm. [BX8931.K4] 99-3960
1. Presbyterianism—Hist. I. Title.

PRESBYTERIAN church in the 285.
U. S. A. General assembly.
Twentieth century addresses, General assembly of the Presbyterian church in the U. S. A., Academy of music, Philadelphia, Pa., May 17, 1901. Philadelphia, Pa., Presbyterian board of publication and Sabbath-school work, 1902. 275 p. 20 cm. [BX8951.A7 1901] 2-13625
1. Presbyterian—Hist. I. Craig, Willis Green, 1834-1911. II. McCook, Henry Christopher, 1837-1911. III. Minton, Henry Collin, 1855-1924. IV. Purves, George Tybout, 1852-1901. V. Speer, Robert Elliott, 1867- VI. Brownson, Marcus Acheson, 1859- VII. Nicholis, Samuel Jack, 1838-1915. VIII. Dickey, Charles Andrews, 1838-1910. IX. Title.
Contents omitted.

SHRIVER, William Payne, 266.51
1872-
Adventure in missions; the story of Presbyterian work with Italians, by William Payne Shriver. New York, N.Y., Unit of city and industrial work, Board of national missions of the Presbyterian church in the United States of America, 1946. 3 p. l., ix-x p., 1 l., 93 (i.e. 81), [1] p. diagr. 23 cm. "First edition." [BX8946.I8S5] 47-1495
1. Presbyterian, Italian. 2. Presbyterian church in the U.S.A.—Missions. I. Title.

Presbyterians—Canada—Biography.

HOPE Evangeline. 266'.0092'4 B
Daisy : the fascinating story of Daisy Smith, wife of Dr. Oswald J. Smith, missionary, statesman, and founder of the Peoples Church, Toronto / Hope Evangeline. Grand Rapids : Baker Book House, c1978. xiii, 247 p., [8] leaves of plates : ill. ; 21 cm. [BX9225.S477H66] 78-103025 ISBN 0-8010-3328-4 : 6.95
1. Smith, Daisy, 1891-1972. 2. Toronto. Peoples Church. 3. Smith, Oswald J. 4. Presbyterians—Canada—Biography. I. Title.

Presbyterians in North Carolina—Drama.

BLYTHE, Le Gette 1900-
Voice in the wilderness; a play with music, song, dance and pantomime. Charlotte, W. Loftin, 1955. 87p. plates. 20cm. 'Staged in commemoration of the 200th anniversary of the establishment of Presbyterianism in the region of Old Mecklenburg.' A56
1. Presbyterians in North Carolina—Drama. 2. Presbyterian Church in Mecklenburg County, N. C.—Drama. I. Title.

Presbyterians in Pennsylvania.

KLETT, Guy Soulliard. 285.09748
Presbyterians in colonial Pennsylvania, by Guy Soulliard Klett. Philadelphia, University of Pennsylvania press; London, H. Milford, Oxford university press, 1937. xi p., 2 l., 297 p. illus. (maps) 24 cm. "Bibliographical notes": p. 267-286. [BX8947.P4K5] 37-24524
1. Presbyterians in Pennsylvania. 2. Presbyterian church in Pennsylvania. 3. Presbyterian church in the U. S. A. Presbytery of Philadelphia. 4. Scotch-Irish in Pennsylvania. 5. Pennsylvania—Hist.—Colonial period. I. Title.

PRESBYTERIAN Church in the 266.
U.S.A. Presbyteries. Carlisle.
The centennial memorial of the Presbytery of Carlisle; a series of papers, historical and biographical, relating to the origin and growth of Presbyterianism in the central and eastern part of southern Pennsylvania.

Harrisburg, Meyers Print. and Pub. House, 1889. 2 v. illus., ports. 24 cm. [BX8958.C3A5 1889] 51-51114
1. Presbyterians in Pennsylvania. 2. Presbyterians Church in Pennsylvania. I. Title.

Presbyterians in the Appalachian region—Statistics.

NELSEN, Hart M. 285'.175
The Appalachian Presbyterian: some rural-urban differences; a preliminary report, by Hart M. Nelsen. Bowling Green, Western Kentucky University, Office of Research and Services, 1968. iv, 59 l. 29 cm. ([Western Kentucky University. Office of Research and Services] Research bulletin no. 5) "[A report of a] two-year research project ... being carried out by Western Kentucky University for the Boards of Christian Education of the United Presbyterian Church in the United States of America and the Presbyterian Church in the United States." [BX8941.N44] 78-253230
1. Presbyterians in the Appalachian region—Statistics. I. Presbyterian Church in the U.S. Board of Christian Education. II. United Presbyterian Church in the U.S.A. Board of Christian Education. III. Title. IV. Series: Western Kentucky University. College of Commerce. Office of Research and Services. Research bulletin no. 5.

Presbyterians in the United States.

BUXBAUM, Melvin H. 277.3
Benjamin Franklin and the zealous Presbyterians [by] Melvin H. Buxbaum. University Park, Pennsylvania State University Press [1975] 265 p. ports. 24 cm. Includes bibliographical references. [E302.6.F8B94] 74-14932 ISBN 0-271-01176-9
1. Franklin, Benjamin, 1706-1790. 2. Presbyterians in the United States. I. Title.

WILLIAMSON, Lamar, 262.050207
1887-
. . . and a time to laugh; notes from the pen of anuntamed iconoclast. Comp., ed. by Jerry R. Tompkins. Camden, Ark., Hurley Co., 1966. xiv, 49p. 23cm. Excerpts from sessional records of the First Presbyterian Church of Monticello, Ark., written by Lamar Williamson. [BX9211.M78 F58] 66-23532 1.50 pap.,
I. Tompkins, Jerry R., ed. II. Monticello, Ark. First Presbyterian Church. III. Title.

Presbyterians in Virginia — Highland Co.

SHEPPERSON, Archibald Bolling, 1897-
A Presbyterian church on the Virginia frontier: 1784 -- 1872. [n.p.] 1961. [67] -- 79 p. 25 cm. Reprinted from the Virginia magazine of history and biography, vol. 69, no. 1 (January, 1961) Cover title.
1. Presbyterians in Virginia — Highland Co. 2. Blue Spring Meeting House. I. Title.

Presbyterians—Middle States—History.

HOOD, Fred J. 285.7'75
Reformed America : the Middle and Southern States, 1783-1837 / Fred J. Hood. University, Ala. : University of Alabama Press, c1980. p. cm. Includes index. Bibliography: p. [BX9496.M53H66] 79-28834 21.50 ISBN 0-8173-0036-8 (pbk.)
1. Reformed (Reformed Church) in the Middle States—History. 2. Reformed (Reformed Church) in the Southern States. 3. Presbyterians—Middle States—History. 4. Presbyterians—Southern States—History. 5. Middle States—Church history. 6. Southern States—Church history. I. Title.

Presbyterians—United States—Biography.

ALEXANDER, Archibald, 1772- 377.
1851.
Biographical sketches of the founder, and principal alumni of the Log college. Together with an account of the revivals of religion, under their ministry. Collected and ed. by A. Alexander, D.D. Princeton, N.J. Printed by J. T. Robinson, 1845. 369 p. 19 cm. "Log college" was the name commonly given to Rev. William Tennent's school at Neshaminy, Pa. [LC580.A5] 7-84849
1. Presbyterian church in the U.S.A.—Blog. 2. Nershaminy, Pa. Log college. I. Title.

GILLESPIE, Janet. 974'.04'0924 B
With a merry heart / Janet Gillespie. 1st ed. New York : Harper & Row, c1976. 231 p. ; 22 cm. [BX9225.G49A34 1976] 76-5125 ISBN 0-06-011537-8 : 8.95
1. Gillespie, Janet. 2. Wicks, Robert Russell, 1882- 3. Wickes family. 4. Presbyterians—United States—Biography. I. Title.

GILLESPIE, Janet. 974'.04'0924 B
With a merry heart / Janet Gillespie. Boston : G. K. Hall, 1977, c1976. 467 p. ; 24 cm. Large print ed. [BX9225.G49A34 1977] 77-5585 lib.bdg. : 12.95
1. Gillespie, Janet. 2. Wicks, Robert Russell, 1882- 3. Wickes family. 4. Presbyterians—United States—Biography. 5. Large type books. I. Title.

SANFORD, Charlotte, 285'.1'0924 B
1936-
Second sight : a miraculous story of vision regained / Charlotte Sanford and Lester David. New York : M. Evans, c1979. 203 p. ; 22 cm. [BX9225.S278A36] 79-10282 ISBN 0-87131-287-5 : 7.95 7.95
1. Sanford, Charlotte, 1936- 2. Presbyterians—United States—Biography. 3. Blind—Biography. I. David, Lester, joint author. II. Title.

SCOVEL, Myra. 285'.1'0922 B
In clover / Myra Scovel. 1st ed. Philadelphia : Westminster Press, c1980. 120 p. ; 21 cm. [BX9225.S355A34] 79-24882 ISBN 0-664-21366-9 : 8.95
1. Scovel, Myra. 2. Scovel, Frederick Gilman. 3. Presbyterians—United States—Biography. 4. Missionaries—Asia—Biography. 5. Retirement—United States—Biography. I. Title.

SHOWALTER, Carol. 248'.2 B
3D / Carol Showalter. Orleans, Mass. : Rock Harbor Press, 1978, c1977. 144 p. ; 22 cm. [BX9225.S43A35] 77-90947 5.95
1. Showalter, Carol. 2. Diet, Discipline, and Discipleship, inc. 3. Presbyterians—United States—Biography. 4. Reducing—Moral and religious aspects. I. Title.

WELLS, John Miller, 1870- 922.573
Southern Presbyterian worthies, by John Miller Wells ... Richmond, Va., Presbyterian committee of publication [c1936] 240 p. ports. 20 cm. [James Sprunt lectures, 1936] [BX9220.W4] 36-11946
1. Presbyterian church in the U.S.—Bioq. 2. Presbyterian church—Biog. I. Title.
Contents omitted.

Presbyterians—United States—South Dakota.

PARKER, Donald Dean, 1899-
Founding Presbyterianism in South Dakota. [Brookings, S.D., pref. 1963] 83 p. illus. 28 cm. 65-111081
1. Presbyterians—U.S.—South Dakota. I. Title.

Presence of God.

HARRISON, Norman B. 231
His indwelling presence, by Norman B. Harrison ... Chicago, The Bible institute colportage association [c1928] 96 p. 20 cm. [BT124.H3] 28-30463
I. Title.

LEFEBVRE, Georges, 1908- 231.7
God present / by Georges Lefebvre ; translated by John Otto, in collaboration with Marie Philip Haley, Mary Virginia Micka. Minneapolis, MN : Winston Press, c1979. 109 p. ; 22 cm. Translation of Dieu present. Includes bibliographical references. [BT180.P6L4313] 79-64653 ISBN 0-03-053436-4 pbk. : 3.95
1. Presence of God. 2. Spiritual life—Catholic authors. I. [Dieu present. English] II. Title.

MANN, Thomas Wingate. 296.3'11
Divine presence and guidance in Israelite traditions : the typology of exaltation / Thomas W. Mann. Baltimore : Johns Hopkins University Press, c1977. x, 310 p. ; 26 cm. (The Johns Hopkins Near Eastern studies) Includes indexes. Bibliography: p. 272-285. [BS1192.6.M36] 76-49846 ISBN 0-8018-1919-9 : 14.00
1. Bible. O.T. Pentateuch—Criticism, interpretation, etc. 2. Presence of God. 3. Assyro-Babylonian religion—Relations—Judaism. 4. Judaism—Relations—Assyro-Babylonian. I. Title. II. Series: Johns Hopkins University. Near Eastern studies.

Presentation of the Blessed Virgin Mary, Feast of the.

KISHPAUGH, Mary Jerome, 232.931
sister, 1900-
... The feast of the presentation of the Virgin Mary in the temple: an historical and literary study ... by Sister Mary Jerome Kishpaugh, O. R. Washington, D. C., The Catholic university of America press, 1941. xii, 159 p. 23 cm. Thesis (PH. D.)--Catholic university of America, 1941. Bibliography: p. 137-154. [BV50.P7K5] A 41
1. Presentation of the Blessed Virgin Mary, Feast of the. 2. Catholic church. Liturgy and ritual. I. Title.

SOLEMN dedication [of the] Church of the Presentation of the Blessed Virgin Mary, Saturday, November 11, 1961. [Midland, Pa., 1961] 57p. illus., ports. 28cm.
I. Midland, Pa. Church of the Presentation of the Blessed Virgin Mary.

Presentation Sisters in Victoria.

KANE, Kathleen 271'.977'094
Dunlop.
Adventure in faith : the Presentation sisters / [by] Kathleen Dunlop Kane. [Melbourne] : Congregation of the Presentation of the Blessed Virgin Mary, 1974. xi, 303, xxix p. : ill., diagrs., facsims., ports. ; 25 cm. Includes index. [BX4511.Z5 A84] 75-327894 ISBN 0-909246-05-X
1. Presentation Sisters in Victoria. 2. Victoria, Australia—Religion. I. Title.

Presidents—United States—Election.

DULCE, Berton 324.0973
Religion and the presidency, a recurring American problem, by Berton Dulce, Edward J. Richter. New York, Macmillan [c.]1962. 245p. 22cm. Bibl. 62-11354 6.00
1. Presidents—U. S.—Election. 2. Christianity and politics. I. Richter, Edward J., joint author. II. Title.

Presidents—United States—Election—1928.

MOORE, Edmund Arthur, 329.01
1903-
A Catholic runs for President; the campaign of 1928. New York, Ronald Press Co. [1956] 220p. illus. 21cm. Includes bibliography. [E796.M6] 56-10167
1. Smith, Alfred Emanuel, 1873-1944. 2. Presidents—U. S.—Election—1928. 3. Catholic Church in the U.S. 4. Church and state in the U.S I. Title.

MOORE, Edmund Arthur, 329.3'023
1903-
A Catholic runs for President; the campaign of 1928, by Edmund A. Moore. Gloucester, Mass., P. Smith, 1968 [c1956] xv, 220 p. illus., facsims., ports. 21 cm. Includes bibliographies. [E796.M6 1968] 68-5894
1. Smith, Alfred Emanuel, 1873-1944. 2. Presidents—United States—Election—1928. 3. Catholic Church in the United States. 4. Church and state in the United States. I. Title.

Presidents — United States — Religion.

ALLEY, Robert S., 1932- 261.7
So help me God: religion and the Presidency, Wilson to Nixon, by Robert S. Alley. Richmond, John Knox Press [1972] 160 p. illus. 20 cm. [BR516.A7] 70-37418 ISBN 0-8042-1045-4
1. Presidents—United States—Religion. 2. Nationalism and religion—United States. 3. Messianism, American. I. Title.

BONNELL, John 973'.099
Sutherland, 1893-
Presidential profiles; religion in the life of American presidents. Philadelphia, Westminster Press [1971] 253 p. ports. 21 cm. Bibliography: p. 249-253. [BR516.B65] 74-133250 ISBN 0-664-20897-5 4.95
1. Presidents—U.S.—Religion. I. Title.

MCCOLLISTER, John. 973'.09'92
"—so help me, God" : the faith of America's presidents / by John C. McCollister. Bloomington, Minn. : Landmark Books, c1982. 207 p. : ill. ; 24 cm. Includes index. Describes the religious backgrounds of the presidents of the United States and reveals their religious preferences while in office. [E176.1.M4 1982] 19 80-81279 ISBN 0-934086-08-7 : 10.95
1. Presidents—United States—Religion. 2. [Presidents—Religion.] I. Title.
Publisher's address: 7847 12th Ave., S., Bloomington, MN 55420

STORER, James Wilson. 242
These historic Scriptures; meditations upon the Bible texts used by our Presidents, from Lincoln to Truman, at their inaugurations. Portrait drawings of the Presideents by T. Victor Hall. Nashville, Broadman Press [1952] 136 p. illus. 21 cm. [BR516.S86] 52-7244
1. Presidents — U.S. — Religion. I. Title.

Press.

MORLEY, Hugh M. 262'.13'0924
The Pope and the press [by] Hugh Morley. With an introd. by James Doyle. Notre Dame [Ind.] University of Notre Dame Press [1968] xi, 143 p. 21 cm. Bibliographical references included in "Notes" (p. 137-143) [BX1378.3.M6] 68-25116 2.45
1. Paulus VI, Pope, 1897- 2. Press. I. Title.

PALMER, Edwin Reuben, 1869-
The printing press and the Gospel, by Edwin R. Palmer. Takoma Park, Washington, D.C., Review and herald publishing association, 1912. 224 p. 19 cm. $0.75 12-21177
I. Title.

Press, Baptist—Texas—History.

BERGER, Tom. 286'.1'764
Baptist journalism in nineteenth-century Texas. [Austin] Dept. of Journalism Development Program, University of Texas at Austin [1969?] iv, 73 p. illus. 24 cm. Bibliography: p. 71-72. [PN4897.T44B4] 75-633594 4.00
1. Press, Baptist—Texas—History. 2. Baptists—Texas. I. Title.

Press, Catholic—Congresses.

CANADIAN Catholic Press 070.4'82
Convention, 2d, Sudbury, Ont., 1959.
Second Canadian Catholic Press Convention [discussions] Kingston, Ont., Canadian register [1959] 80 p. 28 cm. Cover title. [PN4784.C3C3 1959] 76-270161
1. Press, Catholic—Congresses.

Press—Italy—Venice.

GRENDLER, Paul F. 274.5'31
The Roman Inquisition and the Venetian press, 1540-1605/ Paul F. Grendler Princeton, N.J. : Princeton University Press, c1977. xxiii, 374 p. : ill. ; 25 cm. Includes index. Bibliography: p. 325-348. [BX1723.G73] 76-45900 ISBN 0-691-05245-X : 21.50
1. Inquisition. Venice. 2. Press—Italy—Venice. 3. Counter-Reformation. I. Title.

Preston, Jennet, d. 1612.

POTTS, Thomas 133.4'09427'2
fl.1612-1618.
The trial of the Lancaster witches, A.D.

MDCXII; [recorded by Thomas Potts]. [1st ed. reprinted]; edited with an introduction by G. B. Harrison. London, Muller, 1971. xlvii, 188 p.; 1 illus. 23 cm. Facsimile of ed. published London, P. Davies, 1929. Originally published as The wonderfull discoverie of witches in the Countie of Lancaster, London, Barnes, 1613. Includes The arraignement and trial of Iennet Preston, of Gisborne in Craven, in the Countie of Yorke. [BF1581.P65 1971] 72-193427 ISBN 0-584-10921-0
1. Preston, Jennet, d. 1612. 2. Witchcraft—Lancashire, England. I. Harrison, George Bagshawe, 1894- ed. II. Title.
Available from Barnes and Noble, 6.50.

POTTS, Thomas, fl.1612-1618. 133.4'09427'2
The trial of the Lancaster witches, 1612. [Edited with an introd. by G.B. Harrison New York, Barnes & Noble [1971] xlvi, 188 p. 23 cm. Facsim. reprint of the 1929 ed. Includes original t.p. which reads: The wonderfvll discoverie of witches in the covntie of Lancaster ... Together with the Arraignement and triall of Iennet Preston ... by Thomas Potts, Esquier. London, Printed by W. Stansby for Iohn Barnes, dwelling neare Holborne Conduit, 1613. The Arraignement and triall of Iennet Preston has special t.p. with imprint: London, 1612. [BF1581.P65 1929a] 75-27610 ISBN 0-389-04140-8 6.50
1. Preston, Jennet, d. 1612. 2. Witchcraft—Lancashire, Eng. I. Harrison, George Bagshawe, 1894- ed. II. Title.

Presumptions (Canon law)

MANNING, John Joseph, 1900- 348
... Presumptions of law in marriage cases ... by John Joseph Manning ... Washington, D.C., The Catholic university of America, 1935. xi, 111 p. 23 cm. (The Catholic university of America. Canon law studies, no. 94) Thesis (J. C. D.)--Catholic university of America, 1965. Biography. Bibliography: p. 95-97. [BX1969.P55M3 1935] 35-10122
1. Presumptions (Canon law) 2. Marriage (Canon law) 3. Catholic church. Codex juris canonici. O. 1012-1143: De matrimonio. I. Title.

Pretheological education.

BRIDSTON, Keith R. 207.11
Pre-seminary education; report of the Lilly Endowment study, by Keith R. Bridston and Dwight W. Culver. Minneapolis, Augsburg Pub. House [1965] xi, 257 p. 23 cm. Includes bibliographical references. [BV4163.B7] 65-12141
1. Pretheological education. I. Culver, Dwight W., joint author. II. Lilly Endowment, Inc., Indianapolis.

Preus, Jacob Aall Ottesen, 1920-

ADAMS, James Edward, 1941- 284'.1'0924 B
Preus of Missouri and the great Lutheran civil war / James E. Adams. 1st ed. New York : Harper & Row, c1977. x, 242 p. ; 21 cm. Includes index. [BX8080.P73A65 1977] 76-62931 ISBN 0-06-060071-3 : 10.00
1. Preus, Jacob Aall Ottesen, 1920- 2. Lutheran Church—Clergy—Biography. 3. Lutheran Church—Missouri Synod—Doctrinal and controversial works. 4. Clergy—United States—Biography. I. Title.

Prewitt, Cheryl.

PREWITT, Cheryl. 280 B
A bright-shining place : the story of a miracle / by Cheryl Prewitt with Kathryn Slattery. 1st ed. Garden City, N.Y. : Doubleday, 1981. 257 p., [8] p. of plates : ill. ; 22 cm. "A Doubleday-Galilee original." [BR1725.P687A33] 19 80-2896 ISBN 0-385-17021-1 : 11.95
1. Prewitt, Cheryl. 2. Christian biography—United States. 3. Beauty contestants—United States—Biography. 4. Spiritual healing. I. Slattery, Kathryn. II. Title.

Price, Eugenia.

PRICE, Eugenia. 248'.2 B
The burden is light! The autobiography of a transformed pagan who took God at His word. Boston, G. K. Hall, 1973 [c1955] 326 p. 25 cm. Large print ed. [BV4935.P75A32 1973] 73-9986 ISBN 0-8161-6137-2 9.95 (lib. bdg.)
1. Price, Eugenia. 2. Converts. I. Title.

PRICE, Eugenia. 248.2'46'0924 B
The burden is light : the autobiography of a transformed pagan who took God at his word / Eugenia Price. Rev. and updated. New York : Dial Press, [1982], c1975. xiii, 174 p. : 22 cm. [BV4935.P75A32 1982] 19 81-17238 ISBN 0-385-27618-4 : 8.95
1. Price, Eugenia. 2. Converts—United States—Biography. I. Title.

Price, George McCready, 1870-

CLARK, Harold Willard, 1891- 213'.0924
Crusader for creation; the life and writings of George McCready Price, by Harold W. Clark. Incorporating biog. materials prepd. by R. Lyle James. Mountain View, Calif., Ppacific Pr. Pub. [c.1966] 102p. 22cm. (Destiny bk., D-110) Bibl. [BX6193.P7C5] 66-28531 1.50 pap.,
1. Price, George McCready, 1870- I. Title. II. Title: The life and writings of George McGready Price.

PRICE, George McCready.
Back to the Bible; or, The new Protestantism, by George McCready Price ... Washington, D. C., New York city [etc.] Review and Herald publishing association [c1916] viii, 9-215 p. 19 cm. 16-18306 0.50
I. Title. II. Title: The new Protestantism.

Price, John Milburn, 1884-

MAGUIRE, Clyde (Merrill) 922.673
J. M. Price; portrait of a pioneer. Nashville, Broadman Press. [1960] 138p. illus. 22cm. [BV1470.3.P7M3] 60-14145
1. Price, John Milburn, 1884- I. Title.

Price, Joseph Charles, 1854-1893.

YATES, Walter L ed.
He spoke, now they speak; a collection of speeches and writings of and on the life and works of J. C. Price. [Salisbury, N. C., Hood Theological Seminary] 1952. 165p. illus. 22cm. [BX8459.P7Y3] 54-43328
1. Price, Joseph Charles, 1854-1893. I. Title.

Price, Richard,

CUA, Antonio S. 171.1
Reason and virtue; a study in the ethics of Richard Price. Foreword by Stephen C. Pepper. [Athens] Ohio Univ. Pr. [c.1966] xv, 196p. 22cm. Bibl. [BJ1241.P82] 66-10868 5.00
1. Price, Richard, I. Title.

Price, Richard, 1728-1791.

THOMAS, Roland, 1885- 922.
Richard Price, philosopher and apostle of liberty, by Roland Thomas ... London, Oxford university press, H. Milford, 1924. vii [1], 194 p. front. (port.) pl., facsim. 19 1/2 cm. Bibliography: p. [171]-186. [BX9869.P75T5] 25-9805
1. Price, Richard, 1728-1791. I. Title.

Price, Thomas Frederick, 1860-1919.

[BYRNE, Patrick James] 1888- ed. 922.
Father Price of Maryknoll, a short sketch of the life of Reverend Thomas Frederick Price, missioner in North Carolina, co-founder of Maryknoll, missioner in China, compiled from the letters of his friends by a priest of Maryknoll. Maryknoll, N. Y., Catholic foreign mission society of America [c1923] xv, 93 p. front., plates, ports. 18 cm. Advertising matter: p. 93. [BX4705.P7B8] 23-12465
1. Price, Thomas Frederick, 1860-1919. I. Title.

MURRETT, John C 922.273
The story of Father Price: Thomas Frederick Price, cofounder of Maryknoll. New York, McMullen Books [1953] 116p. 20cm. 'An abridgment of the author's ... Tar Heel apostle.' [BX4705.P7M83] 53-12277
1. Price, Thomas Frederick, 1860-1919. I. Title.

MURRETT, John C. 922.273
... Tar heel apostle, Thomas Frederick Price, cofounder of Maryknoll. New York, Longmans, Green [1944] 6 p., l., 3-260 p. front. (port.) illus. 23 1/2 cm. At head of title: By John C. Merrett, M.M. Map on lining-papers. [BX4705.P7M8] 44-7789
1. Price, Thomas Frederick, 1860-1919. I. Title.

Prichard, John Lamb, 1811-1862.

HUFHAM, James Dunn, 1834-1921. 922.673
Memoir of Rev. John L. Prichard, late pastor of the First Baptist church, Wilmington, N.C., by Rev. J. D. Hufham. Raleigh, N.C., Hufman & Hughes, 1867. 2 p. l., [vii]-viii, [9]-182 p. 20 1/2 cm. [BX6495.P75H8] 34-28825
1. Prichard, John Lamb, 1811-1862. I. Title.

Priest, Arlis.

PRIEST, Arlis. 269'.2'0924
Love, Arlis / by Arlis Priest and Al Janssen. San Diego, CA : Beta Book Co., [1979] p. cm. [BR1725.P693A36] 78-31392 ISBN 0-89293-069-1 pbk. : 3.95
1. Priest, Arlis. 2. Christian biography—United States. I. Janssen, Al, joint author. II. Title.

Priest—worker movement.

THE worker-priests;
a collective documentation. Translated form the French by John Petrie [pseud.] New York, Macmillan [1956] xiv, 204p. Translation of Les pretres ouvriers.
1. Priest—worker movement. I. Hewison, Robert John Petrie, 1909- tr.

Priesthood.

BRUNEAU, Joseph.
Our priesthood, by the Rev. Joseph Bruneau ... St. Louis, Mo. [etc.] B. Herder, 1911. ix, 173 p. front. 19 1/2 cm. 11-2930 0.50.
I. Title.

FEUILLET, Andre. 232
The priesthood of Christ and his ministers. Translated by Matthew J. O'Connell. [1st ed.] Garden City, N.Y., Doubleday, 1975. 310 p. 22 cm. Translation of Le sacerdoce du Christ et de ses ministres. Bibliography: p. [286]-294. [BT260.F4813] 74-9446 ISBN 0-385-06009-2 7.95
1. Jesus Christ—Priesthood. 2. Priesthood. I. Title.

FRESENBORG, Bernard, 1847-
"Thirty years in hell"; or, "From darkness to light." By ex-priest, Bernard Fresenborg, who for thirty long years tread the slippery and deceitful path of abhorrent Catholicism ... St. Louis, Mo., North-American book house [1904] 328 p., 1 l. incl. front. (port.) illus., plates. 22 cm. 4-21076
I. Title.

GREELEY, Andrew M 1928-
Priests for tomorrow. Notre Dame, Indiana, Ave Maria Press [1964] 63 p. 19 cm. 64-69925
1. Priesthood. I. Title.

HALDEMAN, Isaac Massey, 1845- 296
The Tabernacle, priesthood and offerings, by I. M. Haldeman... New York, Chicago [etc.] Fleming H. Revell company [c1925] 5 p. l., 9-408 p. col. front., plates. 19 1/2 cm. [BM654.H28] 26-3291
I. Title.

HUCAL, Theodore P. 282
A shattered dream; the story of a priest who discovered the futility and utter emptiness of his calling, by Father Theodore P. Hucal. Kansas City, Mo., Mid-states publishing co. [c1924] 2 p. l., 7-162 p. 19 1/2 cm. [BX1765.H82] 24-16918
I. Title.

LELEN, Joseph Mary, 1873-
Towards the altar; papers on vocations to the priesthood, by Rev. J.M. Lelen. St. Louis, Mo., and Freiburg (Baden) B. Herder, 1910. 125 p. 14 1/2 cm. $0.15 10-14683
I. Title.

LELEN, Joseph Mary, 1873-
Towards the eternal priesthood; a treatise on the divine call, comp. from approved sources by Rev. J.M. Lelen. St. Louis, Mo., and Freiburg (Baden) B. Herder, 1910. 115 [1] p. 14 1/2 cm. $0.15 "List of books for seminarians' spiritual reading": 1 p. at end. 10-14683
I. Title.

PARKER, Percy G. 250
An acceptable minister of Christ, by Percy G. Parker; a present-day message for the man of God either in or out of the pulpit. Philadelphia, The Sunday school times company [c1924] 1 p. l., 5-98 p. 19 cm. [BV4010.P25] 25-1407
I. Title.

... Priesthood in English church; a study of the "Vindication of the bull Apostolicae curae." Pub. under the direction of the Tract committee. London [etc.] Society for promoting Christian knowledge; New York, E. & J. B. Young & co., 1898. 70 p. front. (fold. tab.) 22 cm. (The Church historical society. [Publications] xli) [BX5178.P7] 20-23074 262.

SCHEETZ, Leo A., 1896- 282'.0924 B
Going her way; the joy of fifty years in the priesthood [by] Leo A. Scheetz. [1st ed.] New York, Exposition Press [1971] 220 p. 22 cm. (An Exposition-testament book) [BX4705.S487A3] 70-171715 ISBN 0-682-47347-2 4.00
I. Title.

SCHEETZ, Leo A., 1896- 282'.0924 B
Going her way; the joy of fifty years in the priesthood [by] Leo A. Scheetz. [1st ed.] New York, Exposition Press [1971] 220 p. 22 cm. (An Exposition-testament book) [BX4705.S487A3] 70-171715 ISBN 0-682-47347-2 4.00
I. Title.

SCHMIDT, George Thomas, 1885- 262.
The American priest, by Rev. George T. Schmidt ... New York, Cincinnati [etc.] Benziger brothers, 1919. 147 p. 19 cm. [BX1912.S3] 19-16725
I. Title.

Priesthood—Biblical teaching.

BROWN, Raymond Edward. 253
Priest and bishop; Biblical reflections, by Raymond E. Brown. Paramus, Paulist Press [1970] v, 86 p. 21 cm. Includes bibliographical references. [BX1912.B77] 78-139594 1.50
1. Priesthood—Biblical teaching. 2. Bishops—Biblical teaching. I. Title.

SCHELKLE, Karl Hermann. 225.825
Discipleship and priesthood. [Rev. ed. translated by Joseph Disselhorst. New York] Herder and Herder [1965] 142 p. 21 cm. Translation of Jungerschaft und Apostelamt. Bibliographical footnotes. [BX1912.S2883] 65-13483
1. Priesthood—Biblical teaching. I. Title.

Priesthood — History

PALMER, Lee A 262
Aaronic priesthood through the centuries [by] Lee A. Palmer. Salt Lake City, Deseret Book Co., 1964. xi, 430 p. illus. 24 cm. Bibliography: p. [411]-414. [BX8657.P3] 64-66455
1. Priesthood — Hist. 2. Mormons and Mormonism — Clergy. I. Title.

Priesthood—History of doctrines.

WUERL, Donald W. 253'.2
The priesthood : the Catholic concept

today / by Donald W. Wuerl. Chicago : Franciscan Herald Press, c1976. 192 p. ; 21 cm. Bibliography: p. 167-192. [BX1912.W83] 75-33171 ISBN 0-8199-0591-7 : 6.95
1. Catholic Church—Clergy. 2. Priesthood—History of doctrines. I. Title.

Priesthood—Papal documents.

CATHOLIC Church. Pope. 253.082
The Catholic priesthood, according to the teaching of the Church; bk. 2 [Ed. by] Pierre Veuillot. Pref. by His Excellency Monsignor Montini. Westminster, Md., Newman [1965, c.1964] xxxix, 302p. 22cm. Bibl. [BX1912.A323] 58-1447 7.50
1. Priesthood—Papal documents. 2. Pastoral theology—Catholic Church—Addresses, essays, lectures. I. Veuillot, Pierre, ed. II. Title.
Contents omitted.

Priesthood, Universal.

BRUNGS, Robert A., 1931- 262'.1
A priestly people [by] Robert A. Brungs. New York, Sheed and Ward [1968] xii, 179 p. 21 cm. [BX1920.B76] 68-13849
1. Priesthood, Universal. 2. Laity—Catholic Church. I. Title.

BUSZIN, Walter Edwin, 1899- 262.4
The doctrine of the universal priesthood and its influence upon the liturgies and music of the Lutheran Church. Saint Louis, Concordia Pub. House [194-?] [32] p. 22 cm. Cover title. Bibliographical footnotes. [BT769.B8] 51-28818
1. Priesthood, Universal. 2. Lutheran Church. Liturgy and ritual. 3. Church music—Lutheran Church. I. Title.

EASTWOOD, Charles Cyril, 1916- 230
The priesthood of all believers; an examination of the doctrine from the Reformation to the present day. Minneapolis, Augsburg Pub. House [1962, 1960] 268 p. 22 cm. Includes bibliography. [BT767.5.E3 1962] 62-3573
1. Priesthood. Universal. I. Title.

EASTWOOD, Charles Cyril, 1916- 234.1
The royal priesthood of the faithful; an investigation of the doctrine from Biblical times to the Reformation. Minneapolis, Augsburg Pub. House [1963] 264 p. 23 cm. Bibliography: p. 251-255. [BT767.5.E32 1963] 63-16595
1. Priesthood, Universal. I. Title.

EASTWOOD, Cyril 230
The priesthood of all believers; an examination of the doctrine from the Reformation to the present day. Minneapolis, Augsburg [1962, c.1960] 268p. 22cm. Bibl. 62-3573 4.50
1. Priesthood. Universal. I. Title.

EDWARDS, Rex. 262'.15
A new frontier : every believer a minister / by Rex Edwards. Mountain View, Calif. : Pacific Press Pub. Association, c1979. 126 p. ; 22 cm. Includes bibliographical references. [BT767.5.E35] 78-59308 pbk. : 4.50
1. Priesthood, Universal. 2. Laity. I. Title. II. Title: Every believer a minister.

HERTZ, Karl H. 248.4
Everyman a priest. Philadelphia, Muhlenberg Press [1961, c.1960] 56p. (Fortress book) 61-6754 1.00 bds.,
1. Priesthood, Universal. I. Title.

KETCHERSIDE, W. Carl. 262.4
The royal priesthood; a plea for the restoration of the priesthood of all believers in the churches of God. St. Louis, Mission Messenger [1956] v, 193 p. 21 cm. [BT769.K44] 57-15264
1. Priesthood, Universal. I. Title.

LYONS, Bob E. 253
Kingdom of priests / Bob E. Lyons. Cleveland, Tenn. : Pathway Press, c1977. 160 p. ; 21 cm. "A publication of the Department of General Education." Bibliography: p. 160. [BT767.5.L96] 77-92990 ISBN 0-87148-478-1
1. Priesthood, Universal. 2. Laity—Church of God (Cleveland, Tenn.) I. Title.

MCCARTHY, Timothy. 262'.15
The postconciliar Christian; the meaning of the priesthood of the laity. Foreword by Dorothy Day. New York, P. J. Kenedy [1967] x, 142 p. 22 cm. Bibliography: p. 139-142. [BX1920.M3] 67-18427
1. Priesthood, Universal. 2. Laity—Catholic Church. I. Title.

PERSICH, Nicholas C
The priesthood in the mystical body. St. Louis [Society of the Congregationof the Missions] 1951. ix, 131p. 23cm. Diss.--Pontificio Istituto angelico, Rome. Bibliography: p.130-131. A53
1. Priesthood, Universal. 2. Jesus Christ—Priesthood. 3. Jesus Christ—Mystical body. I. Title.

ROBINSON, William, 1888- 234.1
Completing the reformation; the doctrine of the priesthood of all believers. Lexington, Ky., College of the Bible, 1955. 70p. 23cm. (The College of the Bible. Spring lectures, 1955) [BT769.R6] 56-783
1. Priesthood, Universal. I. Title. II. Series: Lexington, Ky. College of the Bible. Spring lectures, 1955

Priestley, Joseph, 1733-1804.

BELSHAM, Thomas, 1750-1829. 925.4
A vindication of certain passages in a discourse, on occasion of the death of Dr. Priestley, &c. By Thomas Belsham. To which is annexed the Discourse on the death of Dr. Priestley. By the same author. Boston: Printed and published by T. B. Wait & co. Sold by W. Wells ... Court-street. 1809. 3 p. l., [iii]-vi. [2], 83 p., 1 l., [85]-118 p. 19 cm. The "Vindication ... in reply to the animadversions of the Rev. John Pye Smith" and the "Discourse" have each a special t.-p. [BX9869.P8B4 1809] 37-8033
1. Priestley, Joseph, 1733-1804. 2. Smith, John Pye, 1774-1851. 3. Letters. 4. Unitarian churches—Sermons. I. Title.

HOLT, Anne, 1899- 540'.924 B
A life of Joseph Priestley. With an introd. by Francis W. Hirst. Westport, Conn., Greenwood Press [1970] xviii, 221 p. port. 23 cm. Reprint of the 1931 ed. Bibliography: p. [xv]-xviii. [BX9869.P8H6 1970] 75-109750 ISBN 0-8371-4240-7
1. Priestley, Joseph, 1733-1804. I. Title.

HOLT, Anne, 1899- 925.4
A life of Joseph Priestley, by Anne Holt. With an introduction by Francis W. Hirst. London, Oxford university press, H. Milford, 1931. xviii, 221, [1] p. front. (port.) 20 cm. "Bibliography and manuscript sources": p. [xv]-xviii. [BX9869.P8H6] 31-16860
1. Priestley, Joseph, 1733-1804. I. Title.

PURVES, James, 1734-1795. 289
Observations on Doctor Priestley's doctrines of philosophical necessity and materialism. By James Purves. Philadelphia, Printed by W. Pritchard, 1797. 244 p. 19 cm. [BX9178.P89S5] 10-20984
1. Priestley, Joseph, 1733-1804. 2. Liberty of the will. I. Title.

Priestley, Joseph, 1733-1804. An appeal to the serious and candid professors of Christianity.

AN answer to Dr. Priestley's appeal to the serious and candid professors of Christianity. Philadelphia, Printed for the author, by William W. Woodward, no. 36, Franklin's Head, (green sign,) south side of Chestnut street, 1795. 49 p. 20 1/2 cm. A 34
1. Priestley, Joseph, 1733-1804. An appeal to the serious and candid professors of Christianity.

Priests.

BARRETT, Edward John Boyd, 1883- 262.14
Shepherds in the mist. New York, D. X. McMullen [1949] x, 102 p. 20 cm. [BX1765.B24] 49-49718
1. Priests. I. Title.

BASTIAN, Ralph J. 253
Priesthood and ministry, by Ralph J. Bastian. Glen Rock, N.J., Paulist Press [1969] ix, 99 p. 21 cm. (Guide to the Fathers of the church, 5) Bibliography: p. 95. [BR63.B3] 69-18372 2.95
1. Priests. 2. Christian literature, Early. I. Title.

BELL, Stephen, 1864- 922.273
Rebel, priest and prophet; a biography of Dr. Edward McGlynn, by Stephen Bell. New York, The Devin-Adair company, 1937. xi p. 2 l 303p. front, pl.,ports. 21cm [BX4705.M2B4] 37-38552
I. McGlynn, Edward, 1837-1900 II. Title.

CATHOLIC Church. Pope. 262.14
The Catholic priesthood, according to the teaching of the Church papal documents from Pius x to Pius XII [by] Pierre Veuillot. Pref. by His Excellency Monsignor Montini. Translated by John A. O'Flynn, in collaboration with P. Birch and G. Canon Mitchell. Westminster, Md., Newman Press, 1958. 264, 374p. 22cm. Translation of Notre sacerdoce. [BX1912.A323] 58-1447
1. Priests. 2. Pastoral theology—Catholic Church—Addresses, essays, lectures. I. Veuillot, Pierre, ed. II. Title.

CHRYSOSTOMUS, Jeannes, Saint, patriarch of Constantinople, d.407. 250
Saint Chrysostom On the priesthood; translated from the original Greek: with notes and a life of the father, by the Rev. Henry M. Mason ... Philadelphia, E. Littell, 1826. 1 p. l., [v]-viii, [9]-194 p. 20 1/2 cm. [BV4009.C53] T-28735
1. Priests. I. Mason, Henry M., tr. II. Title.

FROST, Bede, father, 1877-
Priesthood and prayer, by the Rev. Father Bede Frost, O. S. B. London and Oxford, A. R. Mowbray & co. ltd.; Milwaukee, Morehouse publishing co. [1933] xi, 220 p. 22 cm. "List of books recommended": p. 212-216. [Secular name: Albert Ernest Frost] A 34
1. Priests. 2. Mysticism. I. Title.

GIVENS, Nick K.
"Echoes from hell," or, "Light after darkness" ... the Protestant world stands amazed at the awful deeds of the Filipino priestcraft. Undisputable truths from an eye witness, told in no uncertain manner ... By Captain Nick K. Givens ... St. Louis, Mo., Columbia book concern [1904] 330 p. incl. front. (port.) illus., plates. 22 cm. 4-26230
I. Title.

HOWITT, William, 1792-1879. 291.614
History of priestcraft in all ages and nations. By William Howitt. Edited by a clergyman of New York ... London, E. Wilson; New York, Reprinted for the booksellers, 1833. xii, [13]-260 p. 20 cm. London edition of the same year has title: Popular history of priestcraft. [BL635.H8 1833] 31-23882
1. Priests. 2. Catholic church—Clergy. 3. Church of England—Clergy. I. A clergyman of New York, ed. II. Title.

JAMES, Edwin Oliver, 1886- 291.61
The nature and function of priesthood; a comparative and anthropological study. [New York, Barnes & Noble, 1961, c.1955] 336p. Bibl. 61-45011 6.00
1. Priests. I. Title.

KELEHER, C Woods.
Romish priests' recent outrages. By C. Woods Keleher ... Chicago, Craig & Barlow, 1886. 1 p. l., iv, [3]-304 p. 21 cm. 6-25431
I. Title.

KELLY, Paul A. 250
The romance of a priest, by Rev. Paul A. Kelly ... New York, P. J. Kenedy & sons, 1927. viii, 120 p. 21 cm. [BX1912.K3] 27-19235
1. Priests. I. Title.

KLEIN, Walter Conrad, Bp., 1904- 253
A priest forever. New York, Morehouse [1965, c.1964] viii, 132p. 21cm. Bibl. [BX5965.K55] 65-14454 4.50
1. Priests. 2. Pastoral theology—Anglican Communion. I. Title.

LAUDER, Robert E. 262'.142
The priest as person : a philosophy of priestly existence / Robert E. Lauder. 1st ed. Whitinsville, Mass. : Affirmation Books, c1980. p. cm. [BX1912.L338] 19 81-3665 ISBN 0-89571-013-7 pbk. : 5.00
1. Catholic Church—Clergy. 2. Priests. I. Title.

[LOWELL, Robert Traill Spence] 1816-1891.
The new priest in Conception bay ... Boston, Phillips, Sampson and company, 1858. 2 v. 19 cm. [PS2349.L4N4 1858] 7-14748
I. Title.

MADDEN, William Joseph, d.1905. 250
Discourses on priesthood, with panegyric of St. Patrick by Rev. W. J. Madden: edited with additions by Rev. Ferreol Girardey, C.S.S.R. St. Louis, Mo., B. Herder, 1903. 115 p. 20 1/2 cm. "The discourse on Vocation to the priesthood and Thoughts on the celibacy of the clergy have been added by the editor."--Pref. [BX1912.M2] 3-14427
1. Priests. 2. Catholic church—Clergy. I. Girardey Ferreol, 1839-1930, ed. II. Title.

MEYER, Charles Robert, 1920- 253
Man of God; a study of the priesthood [by] Charles R. Meyer. [1st ed.] Garden City, N.Y., Doubleday, 1974. 168 p. 22 cm. Bibliography: p. [160]-168. [BX1912.M517] 73-10813 ISBN 0-385-01024-9 5.95
1. Priests. 2. Priesthood—History of doctrines. I. Title.

MURRAY, John, 1741-1815. 922.8173
The life of Rev. John Murray, preacher of universal salvation. Written by himself. With a continuation, by Mrs. Judith Sargent Murray. New ed., with an introduction and notes, by Rev. G. L. Demarest. Boston, Universalist publishing house, 1869. iv, 5-408 p. front. (port.) plates. 20 cm. [BX9969.M8A3 1869] 37-8743
I. Murray, Judith (Sargent) Mrs. 1751-1820. II. Demarest, George L., ed. III. Title.

POHLSCHNEIDER, Johannes, Bp., 1899- 253
Adsum a bishop speaks to his priests. Tr. [from German], adapted by Henry J. Grimmelsman. St. Louis, B. Herder [c.1962] 172p. 22cm. 62-15405 3.25
1. Priests. 2. Pastoral theology—Catholic church. I. Title.

POTAPENKO, Ignatii Nikolaevich, 1856-
A Russian priest, by J. N. Potapenko; with an introduction by James Adderley. New York, Dodd, Mead & company, 1916. 320 p. 20 cm. Printed in Great Britain. A 17
I. Title.

REINHOLD, Hans Ansgar, 1897- 282'.0924 B
H.A.R.; the autobiography of Father Reinhold. [New York] Herder and Herder [1968] x, 150 p. 21 cm. [BX4705.R433A3] 67-29678
I. Title.

RENISON, William Thomas, 1876- 922.373
Afterglow; memories of a happy ministry, by William T. Renison and Clara Shepherd Reid-Renison. [1st ed.] New York, Exposition Press [1953] 121p. 21cm. [BX5995.R44A3] 53-8514
I. Renison, Clara Shepherd Reid, joint author. II. Title.

SHEEN, Fulton John, Bp., 1895- 271.069
The priest is not his own. [1st ed.] New York, McGraw-Hill [1963] 276 p. 21 cm. [BX1912.5.S4] 63-15896
1. Priests. 2. Meditations. 3. Catholic Church—Clergy. I. Title.

SHEEN, Fulton John, Bp., 1895- 253'.2
Those mysterious priests [by] Fulton J. Sheen. [1st ed.] Garden City, N.Y., Doubleday, 1974. 333 p. 22 cm. Includes bibliographical references. [BX1912.S493] 74-1508 ISBN 0-385-08102-2 7.95
1. Priests. I. Title.

SHELDON, Henry Clay, 1845-1928. 270.
Sacerdotalism in the nineteenth century; a critical history, by Henry C. Sheldon ... New York, Eaton & Mains; Cincinnati, Jennings & Graham [c1909] 1 p. l., v-ix, 461 p. 22 cm. Bibliographical foot-notes. [BR477.S5] 9-4570
1. Priests. 2. Sacraments. 3. Ritualism. 4. Church history—19th cent. I. Title.

SMEDT, Emile Joseph de, Bp. 262.14
The priesthood of the faithful. Translated by Joseph F. M. Marique. New York, Paulist Press [1962] 126 p. 18 cm. (Paulist Press paperbacks. Deus books) [BX1913.S613] 62-11628
1. Priests. I. Title.

SNELLING, Joseph. 922.773
Life of Rev. Joseph Snelling, being a sketch of his Christian experience and labors in the ministry. Written by himself ... Boston, J. M'Leish, 1847. iv, [9]-163 p. front. (port.) 17 cm. [BX8495.S63A3] 36-37409
I. Title.

WALSH, James Joseph, 1865- 250
Priests and long life, by James J. Walsh ... New York, J. F. Wagner, inc.; London, B. Herder [c1927] iv p., 1 l., 171 p. 19 1/2 cm. [BX1912.W3] 28-3555
1. Priests. 2. Longevity. 3. Hygiene. I. Title.

WALSH, James Joseph, 1865-1942, comp. 282'.0922
These splendid priests. Freeport, N.Y., Books for Libraries Press [1968] 248 p. 22 cm. (Essay index reprint series) Reprint of the 1926 ed. Contents.Contents.—St. Benedict, founder of the Rule of St. Benedict, by C. F. de Tryon, Comte de Montalembert.—Friar William de Rubruquis, explorer and traveler in the Orient; his journal, translated by J. Mandeville.—Friar Odoric, missionary traveler in the East; his journal, translated by J. Mandeville.—St. Ignatius Loyola, founder of the Society of Jesus; from the Life by Father Bouhours, translated by J. Dryden. Life work of Ignatius Loyola.—St. Francis Xavier, apostle to the Indies; from the Life by Father Bouhours, translated by J. Dryden. Missionary labors of St. Francis Xavier, by J. Schurhammer.—Father James Marquette, explorer of the Mississippi and missionary to the Indians of North America, by J. G. Shea.—St. Vincent de Paul, founder of charitable orders, by F. Goldie.—Father Isaac Jogues, missionary to the Iroquois, by C. J. Devine.—Father Jerome Lobo, missionary to Abyssinia; account of his voyages, translated by S. Johnson.—Friar Junipero Serra, founder of the missions of California, by H. H. Bancroft. The work of Friar Junipero Serra, by Z. Engelhardt.—Father John MacEnery, pioneer palaeontologist, by J. J. Walsh. Other priest anthropologists, by H. G. Osborn. [BX4651.W3 1968] 68-29252
1. Catholic Church—Clergy—Biography. 2. Priests. I. Title.

Priests—Addresses, essays, lectures.

FULTON, Justin Dewey, 1828-1901.
Why priests should wed, by Justin D. Fulton, D. D. New ed. Toledo, O., L. J. King, 1911. xii, 393 p. illus. 20 cm. 12-274
I. Title.

TO be a priest : 262'.14
perspectives on vocation and ordination / edited by Robert E. Terwilliger, Urban T. Holmes, III ; with a foreword by John M. Allin. New York : Seabury Press, c1975. p. cm. "A Crossroad book." Bibliography: p. [BV662.T6] 75-28248 ISBN 0-8164-2592-2 : 4.95
1. Priests—Addresses, essays, lectures. 2. Priesthood—Addresses, essays, lectures. I. Terwilliger, Robert E. II. Holmes, Urban Tigner, 1930-

Priests, Buddhist—China—Biography.

HSU, Sung-peng. 294.3'6'10924
A Buddhist leader in Ming China : the life and thought of Han-shan Te-ch'ing / Sung-peng Hsu. University Park : Pennsylvania State University Press, 1978. p. cm. A revision of the author's thesis, University of Pennsylvania, 1970. Includes index. Bibliography: p. [BQ962.A557H78 1978] 78-50068 ISBN 0-271-00542-4: 16.95
1. Han-shan, 1546-1623. 2. Priests, Buddhist—China—Biography. I. Title.

YU, Chun-fang. 294.3'657'0924
The renewal of Buddhism in China : Chu-hung and the late Ming synthesis / Chung-fang Yu. New York : Columbia University Press, 1981. xvi, 353 p. : ill. ; 24 cm. (IASWR series) (Buddhist studies and translations) Includes index. Bibliography: p. [327]-343. [BQ946.U2Y8] 79-28073 ISBN 0-231-04972-2 : 20.00
1. Chu-hung, 1535-1615. 2. Priests, Buddhist—China—Biography. 3. Buddhism—China—History. I. Title. II. Series. III. Series: Institute for Advanced Studies of World Religions. IASWR series.

Priests, Buddhist—Thailand—Biography.

VAJIRANANA Varoros, Prince, Supreme Patriarch, 1859-1921. 294.3'657'0924 B
Autobiography, the life of Prince-Patriarch Vajirana of Siam, 1860-1921 / Prince Vajiranana-varorasa ; translated, edited, and introduced by Craig J. Reynolds. Athens : Ohio University Press, 1979. p. cm. (Southeast Asia translation series ; 3) [BQ994.A447A3513] 79-9725 ISBN 0-8214-0376-1 : 12.00
1. Vajiranana Varoros, Prince, Supreme Patriarch, 1859-1921. 2. Priests, Buddhist—Thailand—Biography. 3. Thailand—Princes and princesses—Biography. I. Reynolds, Craig J. II. Title. III. Series.

VAJIRANANA Varoros, Prince, Supreme Patriarch, 1859-1921. 294.3'657'0924 B
Autobiography, the life of Prince-Patriarch Vajiranana of Siam, 1860-1921 / Prince Vajiranana-varorasa ; translated, edited, and introduced by Craig J. Reynolds. Athens : Ohio University Press, 1979. p. cm. (Southeast Asia translation series ; 3) [BQ994.A447A3513] 79-9725 ISBN 0-8214-0376-1 : 12.00 12.00 ISBN 0-8214-0408-3 (pbk.)
1. Vajiranana Varoros, Prince, Supreme Patriarch, 1859-1921. 2. Priests, Buddhist—Thailand—Biography. 3. Thailand—Princes and princesses—Biography. I. Reynolds, Craig J. II. Title. III. Series.

Priests, Egyptian.

SAUNERON, Serge 299.31
The priests of ancient Egypt. Translated [from the French] by Ann Morrissett. New York, Grove Press [1960] 191p. illus. (Evergreen profile book P12) 59-10792 1.35 pap.,
1. Priests, Egyptian. I. Title.

SAUNERON, Serge. 299'.3'1
The priests of ancient Egypt / Serge Sauneron ; translated by Ann Morrissett. 1st Black cat ed. New York : Grove Press : distributed by Random House, 1979, c1960. p. cm. Translation of Les pretres de l'ancienne Egypte. [BL2443.S283 1979] 79-17050 ISBN 0-394-17410-0 : 3.50
1. Priests, Egyptian. I. Title.

Priests, Hindu.

SUBRAMANIAM, K. 294.5'6'1
Brahmin priest of Tamil Nadu [by]K. Subramaniam. New York, Wiley [1974] 183 p. illus. 22 cm. "A Halsted Press book." Based on the author's thesis, University of Saugar, 1969. Bibliography: p. [161]-167. [BL1215.P75S9] 74-13072 ISBN 0-470-83535-4
1. Priests, Hindu. I. Title.

VIDYARTHI, Lalita Prasad 294.53
The sacred complex in Hindu Gaya. New York, Asia Pub. House [dist. Taplinger, c.1961] xxiv 232p. illus. map. Bibl. 61-4851 4.50
1. Priests, Hindu. 2. Hinduism—Rituals. 3. Gaya-Ksetra. I. Title.

VIDYARTHI, Lalita Prasad. 294.53
The sacred complex in Hindu Gays. New York, Asia Pub. House [1961] xxiv. 232 p. illus. port., map. tables. 23 cm. Errata slip inserted. Bibliography: p. [219]-224. [BL1215.P75V5] 61-4851
1. Priests, Hindu. 2. Hinduism-Rituals. 3. Gaya-Ksetra. I. Title.

Priests-Meditations.

ESCRIBANO, Eugenio.
The priest at prayer. Translated from the Spanish ... Westminster, Md., Newman, 1962. 584 p. 17 cm. 68-42086
1. Priests-Meditations. I. Title.

SKWIRCZYNSKI, Wladyslaw.
My life in Christ, meditations for the reverend priests. New York, Arlington Print, Co., 1957. xviii, 217 p. 24 cm. Print. 68-103260
1. Priests—Meditations. I. Title.

Priests, Nichiren—Japan—Biography.

RODD, Laurel Rasplica. 294.3'64 B
Nichiren, a biography / Laurel Rasplica Rodd. [Tempe] : Arizona State University, 1978. 86 p. ; 23 cm. (Occasional paper - Arizona State University ; no. 11) Contents.Contents.—Nichiren.—Letter from Sado.—Letter to the wife of Lord Shijo Kingo.—Letter from Mt. Minobu. Bibliography: p. 77-86. [BQ8349.N577R6] 78-624123 pbk. : 2.50
1. Nichiren, 1222-1282. 2. Priests, Nichiren—Japan—Biography. I. Title. II. Series: Arizona. State University, Tempe. Center for Asian Studies. Occasional paper ; no. 11.

Priests of the Most Precious Blood. American Province.

BRUNNER, Francis de Sales, 1795-1859. 271.79
Four historical booklets regarding the American province of the most precious blood : a translation from the original German. Carthagena, Ohio, Messenger Press, 1957. 304p. 23cm. [BX3960.P7B72] 57-33578
1. Priests of the Most Precious Blood. American Province. I. Title.

KNAPKE, Paul Justin, 1910- 271.79
History of the American Province of the Society of the Precious Blood. Carthagena, Ohio, Messenger Press, 1958- v. illus., port., fold. map. 22cm. Bibliography: v. 1, p. 8-13. [BX3958.Z5A5] 60-22716
1. Priests of the Most Precious Blood. American Province. I. Title.

Priests—Prayer-books.

PRIESTLY prayers.
Springfield, Ill., Templegate [1961] 299p. 17cm.
1. Priests—Prayer-books. I. McEvoy, Hubert, ed.

Priests, Roman.

BOUCHE-LECLERCQ, Auguste, 1842-1923. 292'.6'1
Les pontifes de l'ancienne Rome / Auguste Bouche-Leclercq. New York : Arno Press, 1975. vii, 439 p. ; 23 cm. (Ancient religion and mythology) Reprint of the 1871 ed. published by Librairie A. Franck, Paris. Originally presented as the author's thesis, Paris, 1871. Bibliography: p. [viii]. [BL815.P7B68 1975] 75-10630 ISBN 0-405-07006-3
1. Priests, Roman. I. Title. II. Series.

Priests, Zen—Japan—Biography.

COVELL, Jon Etta Hastings Carter, 1910- 294.3'61'0924 B
Unraveling Zen's red thread : Ikkyu's controversial way / by Jon Carter Covell, in collaboration with Sobin Yamada. Elizabeth, N.J. : Hollym International Corp., 1980. 341 p., [12] leaves of plates : ill. ; 23 cm. Includes bibliographical references and index. [BQ9399.I567C68 1980] 19 80-123937 ISBN 0-930878-19-1 : 18.50
1. Ikkyu, 1394-1481. 2. Priests, Zen—Japan—Biography. I. Yamada, Sobin, joint author. II. Title.

KODERA, Takashi James, 1945- 294.3'64 B
Dogen's formative years in China : historical study and annotated translation of the Hokyo-ki / Takashi James Kodera. Boulder, Colo. : Prajna Press, 1979. p. cm. Based on the author's thesis, Columbia University, 1975. Includes Dogen's Hokyo-ki in the original and English translation. Bibliography: p. [BQ9449.D657K6] 79-12848 ISBN 0-87773-710-X : 25.00
1. Dogen, 1200-1253. 2. Priests, Zen—Japan—Biography. I. Dogen, 1200-1253. Hokyoki. 1979. II. Title.

Primers—1500-1800.

HARRIS, Benjamin, fl.1673-1716. 230'.2
The Protestant tutor / Benjamin Harris. The New England primer enlarged / with a pref. for the Garland ed. by Daniel Cohen. New York : Garland Pub., 1977. xxvii, 146, [77] p. : ill. ; 15 cm. (Classics of children's literature, 1621-1932) Reprint of 2 works, the first originally printed in 1679 for B. Harris, London; the 2d printed in 1737 by T. Fleet, Boston. The first of these works was intended to teach spelling and reading while pointing out the "evils" of Catholicism; the second was a combination religious instructor and reader used by children of early New England. [BX1763.H34 1977] 75-32135 ISBN 0-8240-2252-1 lib.bdg. : 27.00
1. Catholic Church—Doctrinal and controversial works—Protestant authors—Juvenile literature. 2. Catholic Church in England—Juvenile literature. 3. [Catholic Church—Doctrinal and controversial works—Protestant authors.] 4. [Catholic Church in England.] 5. Primers—1500-1800. 6. Catechisms, English. 7. [Primers.] 8. [Readers.] 9. [Christian life.] I. The New England primer enlarged. 1977. II. Title. III. Series.

Primers-1800-1870.

[CALKINS, Frances Manwaring] 1795-1869. 372.4
The Tract primer. New York, The American Tract Society [1848?] 108 p. illus. 19 cm. On cover: The pictorial Tract primer. [BV4510.C27] 34-36882
1. Primers-1800-1870. I. American Tract Society. II. Title. III. Title: The pictorial Tract primer.

Primers—1870—

FOX, Ethel. 221.95
Bible primer for the tiny tots, by Ethel Fox. New York, Block publishing company, 1930. vii p., 1 l., 102 p. illus. 19 cm. For Jewish children. [PE1125.F6] 30-14305
1. Primers—1870- 2. Readers and speakers—Bible. I. Title.

RUANE, Minnie (Halberstadt) Mrs. 1883- 244
My father's house, an alphabet of the church; verse by M. H. Ruane, drawings by Janet Robson. Paterson, N. J., Saint Anthony guild press, 1938. [28] p. col. illus. 29 cm. [Full name: Mrs. Wihlelmina Terresa Minnie (Halberstadt) Ruane] [PE123.R8] 39-13653
1. Primers—1870- I. Robson, Janet, 1902- II. Title. III. Title: An alphabet of the church.

Primers, Hebrew.

GOLDIN, Hyman Elias, 1881- 27-23571
(transliterated): Keriah. [New York, Hebrew publishing company, c1927] 96 p. illus. 20 cm. Author's name at head of title.
1. Primers, Hebrew. I. Title.

MARGALIT, Avi. 492.41'1
The Hebrew alphabet book, Me-alef 'ad tav. (romanized form) illustrated by Avi Margalit. New York, Funk and Wagnalls [1968] [25] p. (chiefly col. illus.) 22 x 30 cm. (A Sabra book) An introduction to the Hebraic alphabet through using each of its

letters in a Hebraic word, showing the word's pronunciation and giving its English translation. [PJ4569.M36] 68-55546 2.95
1. Primers, Hebrew. 2. [Alphabet books, Hebrew.] I. Title.

Primers (Prayer-books)

BUTTERWORTH, Charles C 1894- 264.03
The English primers, 1529-1545; their publication and connection with the English Bible and the Reformation in England Philadelphia, University of Pennsylvania Press, 1953. xiii, 340p. facsims. 24cm. Bibliography: p. 305-325. [BV4818.B85] 53-7051
1. Primers (Prayer-books) 2. Bible. English—Hist. 3. Reformation—England. I. Title.

BUTTERWORTH, Charles C., 1894-1957. 264.03
The English primers (1529-1545): their publication and connection with the English Bible and the Reformation in England. New York, Octagon Books, 1971 [c1953] xiii, 340 p. facsims. 24 cm. Bibliography: p. 305-325. [BV4818.B85 1971] 72-120240
1. Bible. English—History. 2. Primers (Prayer-books) 3. Reformation—England. I. Title.

CUSHMAN, Ralph Spaulding, 1879- 254
Dealing squarely with God; a stewardship primer, by Ralph S. Cushman. New York, Cincinnati, The Abingdon press [c1927] 69 p. 17 cm. [BV772.C78] 27-24622
I. Title.

THE Primer set furth by the Kinges Maiestie & his clergie (1545) 264'.02 A facsimile reproduction with an introd. by David Siegenthaler. Delmar, N.Y., Scholars' Facsimiles & Reprints, 1974. vii, [170] p. 23 cm. Original t.p. has imprint: Imprinted at London within the precinct of the late dissolued house of the Graye Friers by Richard Grafton Printer to the Princes grace, the xvii. day of August, the yeare of our Lorde M,D.XLVI. S.T.C. 16044. [BV4831.P7 1545a] 74-5335 ISBN 0-8201-1129-5 10.00
1. Primers (Prayer-books)

Primitive Baptists—Directories

THE Primitive Baptist church meeting directory. 286.4058 Elon College, N. C., Primitive Baptist Pub. House [1958] 96p. 16cm. [BX6380.P67] 58-28869
1. Primitive Baptists—Direct.

THE primitive Baptist church meeting directory. 284.405873 2d ed., rev. Elon College, N. C., Primitive Baptist Pub. House, 1959. 96p. 16cm. [BX6380.P67 1959] 59-39193
1. Primitive Baptists—Direct.

Primitive Baptists—Doctrinal and controversial works.

BANNER of love. 230.64
Primitive Baptist doctrine, a selected group of articles, reprinted from the Banner of love ... Aspermont, Tex., [1946] 109 p. illus. 25 cm. "Articles ... in the Banner of love between the period of January 1, 1933, and September 15, 1946."--p. [1] [BX6387.B3] 47-21350
1. Primitive Baptists—Doctrinal and controversial works. I. Title.

HOLDER, J D 230.64
Principles and practices of the church. Elon College, N. C., Primitive Baptist Pub. House [1961] 222p. 22cm. [BX6387.H6] 61-36014
1. Primitive Baptists—Doctrinal and controversial works. I. Title.

SAMMONS, Wiley W., 1907- 286'.4
Identity of the true Baptist Church; doctrine, precept & practice from 1701-1971 in west Tennessee, North Carolina and Alabama, by Wiley W. Sammons. [Collierville, Tenn., 1971] xx, 299 p. illus. 23 cm. [BX6387.S24] 77-31641
1. Primitive Baptists—Doctrinal and controversial works. I. Title.

Primitive Baptists—History

ASHBURN, Jesse Anderson 1861-
History of the Fisher's River primitive Baptist association from its organization, in 1832, to 1904, by Jesse A. Ashburn ... Laurel Fork, Va., F. P. Branscome, printer, 1905. 205 p. front., ports. 18 1/2 cm. 6-1534
I. Title.

BOOTON, John Kaylor, 1823- comp. 266.4
Footsteps of the flock; a compilation of the history of God's people from the creation of the world to the present day, as found in sacred and profane history, church records, documents, & c. by J. K. Booton. Luray, Va. [Printed by Hurst and company] 1902. vi, 407 p. 20cm. [BX6383.B6] 2-21129
1. Primitive Baptists—Hist. I. Title.

GRIFFIN, Benjamin. 286.
A history of the Primitive Baptists of Mississippi, from the first settlement by the Americans up to the middle of the xixth century; including a brief allusion to the course, doctrines, and practice of the Christian church from Jerusalem to America; also the doctrine and practice of modern missionaries, from the days of Andrew Fuller, and a brief notice of D. Benedict's late History of the Baptists; concluded with an address to the general reader. By Benjamin Griffin ... Jackson, Miss., Pub. for the author by Barksdale and Jones, 1853. 262 p., 1 l. 21 cm. [BX6384.M7G8] 1-26943
1. Primitive Baptists—Hist. I. Title.

KIRKLAND, John Vinus.
A condensed history of the Church of God from the days of John the Baptist under the present time, with a chapter on the interpretation of the Scriptures, and a treatise on the general government of the churches, and a plan suggested for the federal government of the churches, to correct the friction which produces factions. By Elder J. V. Kirkland ... [Fulton, Ky., 1904] 120 p. port. 15 1/2 cm. [BX6383.K5] 45-28484
1. Primitive Baptists—Hist. I. Title.

LAMBERT, Byron Cecil, 1923- 286'.4
The rise of the anti-mission Baptists : sources and leaders, 1800-1840 / Byron Cecil Lambert. New York : Arno Press, 1980. xv, 428 p. ; 24 cm. (The Baptist tradition) Originally presented as the author's thesis, University of Chicago, 1957. Bibliography: p. 414-428. [BX6383.L35 1980] 79-52573 ISBN 0-405-12441-4 : 34.00
1. Primitive Baptists—History. 2. Missions. I. Title. II. Title: Anti-mission Baptists. III. Series: Baptist tradition.

ROBINSON, John Thomas, 1859- comp.
A history of the church, beginning with the tree of life, up to the twentieth century ... together with the ... pastors and membership of the Primitive Baptist churches of Mississippi ... comp. by John T. Robinson ... Martin, Tenn., Cayces & Turner, 1912. 324 p. incl. front. (port.) illus. (ports.) 22 cm. $1.25 12-8677
I. Title. II. Title: Primitive Baptist churches of Mississippi.

Primitive Baptists. North Carolina. Fisher's River Primitive Baptist Association.

ASBHURN, Jesse Anderson, 1861- 286.4756
History of the Fisher s River Primitive Baptist Association from its organization in 1832, to 1904, by Jesse A. Ashburn; reprinted with a second volume, from 1905 to 1953, by Francis Preston Stone. [Elon College, N. C., Primitive Baptist Pub. House, [1953] 350p. illus. 23cm. [BX6384.N62F5 1953] 54-22114
1. Primitive Baptists. North Carolina. Fisher's River Primitive Baptist Association. I. Stone, Francis Pieston, 1872- II. Title.

Primitive Baptists. North Carolina. Kehukee Primitive Baptist association.

BIGGS, Joseph, 1776-1844. 286.
A concise history of the Kehukee Baptist association, from its original rise to the present time ... By Elder Joseph Biggs ... Part I. Contains the history of the Kehukee association, from its first organization until 1803, as compiled by Elders Burkitt and Read ... (omitting the history of the churches.) Part II. Embraces a continuation of the history of the association until the present time, (together with a history of the churches now in the association) by Joseph Biggs ... [Tarboro? N.C.] G. Howard, 1834. xxi, [27]-300 p. 18 cm. [BX6384.N62K415] 43-32265
1. Primitive Baptists. North Carolina. Kehukee Primitive Baptist association. I. Burkitt, Lemuel, 1750-1806. A concise history of the Kehukee Baptist association. II. Read, Jesse. A concise history of the Kehukee Baptist association. III. Title.

BURKITT, Lemuel, 1750-1806. 286.4
A concise history of the Kehukee Baptist association, from its original rise down to 1803 ... By Elders Lemuel Burkitt and Jesse Read ... Revised and improved by Henry L. Burkitt. Philadelphia, Lippincott, Grambo and co., 1850. xxiv, [31]-351 p. 17 cm. [BX6384.N62K42 1850] 33-10346
1. Primitive Baptists. North Carolina. Kehukee Baptist association. I. Read, Jesse, joint author. II. Burkitt, Henry Lemuel, 1818- ed. III. Title.

BURKITT, Lemuel, 1750-1806. 286.4
A concise history of the Kehukee Baptist association, from its original rise down to 1803 ... By Elders Lemuel Burkitt and Jesse Pead ... Revised and improved by Henry L. Burkitt. Philadelphia, Lippincott, Grambo and co., 1850. xxix, [31]-351 p. 17 cm. [BX6384.N62K42 1850] 33-103460
1. Primitive Baptists. North Carolina. Kekukee Primitive Baptist association. I. Read, Jesse, joint author. II. Burkitt, Henry Lemuel, b. 1818, ed. III. Title.

BURKITT, Lemuel, 1750-1806. 286'.4
A concise history of the Kehukee Baptist Association, from its original rise down to 1803 / Lemuel Burkitt and Jesse Read. Rev. and improved / by Henry L. Burkitt. New York : Arno Press, 1980. 351 p. ; 21 cm. (The Baptist tradition) Reprint of the 1850 ed. published by Lippincott, Grambo, Philadelphia. [BX6384.N84B87 1980] 19 79-52591 ISBN 0-405-12458-9 lib. bdg. : 25.00
1. Primitive Baptists. North Carolina. Kehukee Primitive Baptist Association. I. Read, Jesse, joint author. II. Burkitt, Henry Lemuel, b. 1818. III. Title. IV. Series: Baptist tradition.

Prince, Deborah, 1723-1744.

PRINCE, Thomas, 1687-1758. 922
Dying exercises of Mrs. Deborah Prince: and devout meditations of Mrs. Sarah Gill, daughters of the late Rev. Thomas Prince, minister of the South church, Boston. Edinburgh printed: Newbury-port [Mass.] re-printed and sold by John Mycall. m,dcc,lxxxix. 59 p. 19 x 10 cm. [BR1725.P7P7] 38-7494
1. Prince, Deborah, 1723-1744. I. Gill, Sarah (Prince) Mrs. 1728?-1771. II. Title.

The Princeton review.

FINNEY, Charles Grandison, 1792-1875. 230
The reviewer reviewed: or, Finney's Theology, and the Princeton review. By Professor C. G. Finney ... Oberlin [O.] J. M. Fitch, 1847. 1 p. l., 59 p. 22 cm. [BT75.F52] 46-42428
1. Finney, Charles Grandison, 1792-1875. Lectures on systematic theology. 2. The Princeton review. I. Title.

Princeton theological seminary—Biography

KERR, Hugh Thomson, 1909- ed. 922.5
Sons of the prophets; leaders in Protestantism from Princeton Seminary. Princeton, N. J., Princeton University Press, 1963. xix, 227 p. ports. 23 cm. "Essays in celebration of the sesquicentennial, Princeton Theological Seminary, Princeton, New Jersey, 1812-1962." Bibliographical footnotes. [BV4070.P759A2 1963] 63-12665
1. Princeton Theological Seminary — Biog. I. Title.

PRINCETON theological seminary. 207.74967
Biographical catalogue of the Princeton theological seminary, 1815-1932, compiled by Rev. Edward Howell Roberts ... Princeton, N. J., The trustees of the Theological seminary of the Presbyterian church, 1933. xxxii, 812 p. 24 cm. [BV4070.P74 1932] 33-21165
1. Princeton theological seminary—Biog. I. Roberts, Edward Howell, 1895- comp. II. Title.

PRINCETON theological seminary. 207.
... Bulletin ... Fall conference number. [Princeton, N. J., The Seminary, v. 25 cm. Cover-title. At head of title: The Princeton seminary. [BV4070.P712] ca 11
I. Title.

PRINCETON theological seminary. Alumni association.
Addresses before the Alumni association of Princeton theological seminary, at its annual meeting in Princeton, April 25th, 1876. Pub. at the request of the association. Philadelphia, Grant, Faires & Rodgers, printers, 1876. 82 p. 22 cm. E 15
I. Title.

PRINCETON theological seminary. Alumni association. 207.
Necrological reports and annual proceedings of the Alumni association of Princeton theological seminary. v. 1-1875 89-19 Princeton, N. J., 1891-19 v. 22 cm. On cover, 1907-The Princeton theological seminary bulletin ... Issued annually, with general t.-p. for ten-year periods (v. 1 covers 15 years) The issues for 1875-84 have imprint Philadelphia. 1875-99 prepared by a committee of the association; 1900-by the secretary (later, editor) J. H. Dulles. Contents.v. 1. 1875-1889.--v. 2. 1890-1899.--v. 3. 1900-1909.--v. 4. 1910-1919. [BV4070.P743] ca 9
1. Princeton theological seminary—Biog. I. Dulles, Joseph Heatly, 1853- ed. II. Title.

Princeton theological seminary—Registers.

PRINCETON theological seminary. 207.749
... General catalogue. 1872. Philadelphia, J. B. Rodgers co., printers, 1872. 109, [1] p., 1 l., xiv p. 24 cm. [BV4070.P74] 33-29235
1. Princeton theological seminary—Registers. I. Title.

PRINCETON theological seminary. 207.74967
... General catalogue. 1881. Trenton, N. J. W. S. Sharp, printer, 1881. 330 p. 25 cm. [BV4070.P74 1881] 8-34563
1. Princeton theological seminary—Registers. I. Title.

Princeton university. Chapel.

DUFFIELD, John Thomas, 1823-1901, ed.
The Princeton pulpit. Ed. by John T. Duffield ... New York, C. Scribner, 1852. viii, [9]-326 p. 24 cm. E 13
I. Title.

PRINCETON university. 726.
Service in dedication of the Milbank memorial choir, Princeton university chapel, in memory of Eliabeth Milbank Anderson. Princeton, New Jersey, October the twenty-fifth, MCMXXVIII [New York, Pub. for the University by the Milbank memorial fund, in consultation with the printing house of William Edwin Rudge, 1928] [52] p. incl. front. (port.) illus., col. pl. 28 1/2 cm. Cover-title: The Milbank memorial choir, Princeton university chapel. "Two hundred copies ... printed ... Number 128." [NA5235.P75P7] 44-31596
1. Princeton university. Chapel. I. Milbank memorial fund. II. Title.

STILLWELL, Richard, 1899- 917.49'67'034
The Chapel of Princeton University. Princeton, N.J., Princeton Univerisity Press, 1971. xiv, 137 p. illus. (part col.) 29 cm. [NA5235.P75S8] 76-90961 ISBN 0-691-03864-3 15.00
1. Princeton University. Chapel. I. Title.

Princeton university. Department of art and archaeology. Index of Christian art.

WOODRUFF, Helen. 704
The Index of Christian art at Princeton university; a handbook by Helen Woodruff, with a foreword by Charles Rufus Morey. Princeton, Princeton university press, 1942. ix, 83 p. front. (facsim.) illus. 23 cm. [N7832.W65] 42-21166
1. Princeton university. Dept. of art and archaeology. Index of Christian art. I. Title.

Printers—Pennsylvania—Biography.

LONGENECKER, Steve, 1951- 974.8'02'0922 B
The Christopher Sauers : courageous printers who defended religious freedom in early America / Steve Longenecker. Elgin, Ill. : Brethren Press, 1981. p. cm. Includes index. Bibliography: p. [BX7841.L63] 19 81-10075 ISBN 0-87178-141-7 pbk. : 7.95
1. Sower, Christopher, 1693?-1758. 2. Sower, Christopher, 1721-1784. 3. Church of the Brethren—Pennsylvania—Biography. 4. Sowers family. 5. Printers—Pennsylvania—Biography. 6. Pennsylvania—Biography. I. Title.

Priscilla, Saint, wife of Saint Aquila.

HOPPIN, Ruth. 227'.87'014
Priscilla, author of the Epistle to the Hebrews, and other essays. [1st ed.] New York, Exposition Press [1969] 158 p. 21 cm. Contents.Contents.—Priscilla, author of the Epistle to the Hebrews.—The sovereignty of God and the spiritual status of women.—Four devotions.—More than a day's journey. Includes bibliographies. [BS2775.2.H6] 72-8428 6.00
1. Priscilla, Saint, wife of Saint Aquila. 2. Bible. N.T. Hebrews—Criticism, interpretation, etc. 3. Woman (Theology)—Biblical teaching. 4. Devotional exercises. I. Title.

Priscillianus, Bp. of Avila, d. 385.

CHADWICK, Henry, 1920- 272'.1'0924 B
Priscillian of Avila : the occult and the charismatic in the early church / Henry Chadwick. Oxford : Clarendon Press, 1976. viii, 250 p. ; 23 cm. Includes index. Bibliography: 11th prelim. page. [BT1465.C44] 76-370521 ISBN 0-19-826643-X : 22.00
1. Priscillianus, Bp. of Avila, d. 385. 2. Christian martyrs—Biography.
Dist. by Oxford University Press NY NY

Prisoners—Czechoslovak Republic.

HATHAWAY, David. 266'.3'0924 B
Czech mate / David Hathaway. Old Tappan, N.J. : F. H. Revell Co., c1974. 187 p. ; 18 cm. Autobiographical. [BR1725.H245A33 1974] 75-6552 ISBN 0-8007-0742-7 pbk. : 1.95
1. Hathaway, David. 2. Bible—Publication and distribution—Europe, Eastern. 3. Prisoners—Czechoslovak Republic. I. Title.

Prisoners—France.

FESCH, Jacques. 248'.2'0924
Light upon the scaffold : prison letters of Jacques Fesch, executed October 1, 1957, age twenty-seven / edited by Augustin-Michel Lemonnier ; translated by Matthew J. O'Connell ; with a foreword by Michel Quoist. St. Meinrad, IN. : Abbey Press, 1975. ix, 153 p. ; 18 cm. (A Priority edition) Translation of Lumiere sur l'echafaud. [HV9667.F4813] 75-208 ISBN 0-87029-046-0 pbk. : 2.95
1. Prisoners—France. 2. Prisons—Religious life. I. Title.

Prisoners, Russian.

CISZEK, Walter J., 1904- 922.273
With God in Russia, by Walter J. Ciszek, with Daniel L. Flaherty. Garden City, N.Y., Doubleday [1966, c.1964] 357p. 18cm. (Image bks., D200) [DK268.3.C58] 1.25 pap.,
1. Prisoners, Russian. I. Title.

CISZEK, Walter J., 1904- 922.273
With God in Russia, by Walter J. Ciszek, with Daniel L. Flaherty. New York, Amer. Bk. [dist.] McGraw [c.1964] xv,302p. map. 22cm. 64-25167 5.95 bds.,
1. Prisoners, Russian. I. Title.

CISZEK, Walter J 1904- 922.273
With God in Russia, by Walter J. Ciszek, with Daniel L. Flaherty. [1st ed.] New York, McGraw=Hill [1964] xv, 302 p. map. 22 cm. Autobiographical. [DK268.3.C58] 64-25167
1. Prisoners, Russian. I. Title.

POPOFF, Haralan, 1907- 289.9
I was a Communist prisoner. Grand Rapids, Mich., Zondervan [c.1966] 287p. illus.,maps, ports. 23cm. [BX8764.Z8P6] 66-13695 4.95 bds.,
I. Title.

Prisons—Missions and charities.

ALLEE, George Franklin, 1897- 922
Beyond prison walls; the story of Frank Novak, once a desperate criminal and convict, now national prison chaplain no. 1 by the grace of God. Kansas City, Mo., Beacon Hill Press [1960] 96p. 20cm. [BV4465.A4] 60-12063
1. Novak, Frank, 1884- 2. Prisons—Missions and charities. I. Title.

BEASLEY, A Roy. 258
In prison ... and visited me, by Prison Parson A. Roy Beasley; as told to Ewart A. Autry. Grand Rapids, Mich., Eerdman, 1952. 188 p. 21 cm. [BV4465.B36] 52-10795
1. Prisons—Missions and charities. I. Autry. Ewart A. II. Title.

BONN, John Louis, 1906- 922.273
Gates of Dannemora. [1st ed.] Garden City, N. Y., Doubleday, 1951. 276 p. 21 cm. [BV4465.B57] 51-14075
1. Hyland, Ambrose R. 2. Prisons—Missions and charities. 3. Clinton Prison, Dannemora, N. Y. I. Title.

CHURCH of England. National Assembly. Prisons Commission. 365'.66
The church and the prisoner; the report of the Prisons Commission of the Church Assembly. Westminster, Church Information Office, 1960. 56p. 22cm. [BV4465.C45] 61-39382
1. Prisons—Missions and charities. I. Title.

KANDLE, George C. 253.7'5
Ministering to prisoners and their families [by] George C. Kandle and Henry H. Cassler. Englewood Cliffs, N.J., Prentice-Hall [1968] 140 p. illus. 21 cm. (Successful pastoral counseling series) Bibliography: p. 133-136. [BV4465.K3] 68-11944
1. Prisons—Missions and charities. 2. Pastoral counseling. I. Cassler, Henry H., joint author. II. Title. III. Series.

TUCKER, Park. 258
Prison is my parish; the story of Park Tucker as told to George Burnham. [Westwood, N. J.] Revell [1957] 191p. illus. 22cm. [BV4340.T8] 57-9963
1. Prisons—Missions and charities. I. Burnham, George. II. Title.

Prisons—Religious life.

AMERICAN society for visiting Catholic prisoners.
Annual report. Philadelphia, v. 24 cm. ca 5
I. Title.

AUSTIN, Robert A 248
Eternal energy; God and convicts, triangle of life, by a 23-year loser. Houston, Tex., Austin Pub. Co., 1948. 361 p. 23 cm. [BR126.A85] 49-16188
I. Title.

AUSTIN, Robert A 248
Eternal energy; God and convicts, triangle of life, by a 23-year loser. Houston, Tex., Austin Pub. Co., 1948. 361 p. 23 cm. [BR126.A85] 49-16188
I. Title.

CAMPBELL, Ora Mae, 1916- 258
Them that sit in darkness. Cleveland, Tenn., White Wing Pub. House & Press [1953] 174p. 20cm. [BV4595.C3] 54-17874
1. Prisons—Religious life. I. Title.

STOCKWELL, Francis Olin. 266.7
With God in Red China; the story of two years in Chinese Communist prisons. [1st ed.] New York, Harper [1953] 256p. 22cm. [BV3427.S825A3] [BV3427.S825A3] 275.1 53-6973 53-6973
I. Title.

WILLING, Ora Mae (Campbell) 1916- 258
Them that sit in darkness. Cleveland, Tenn., White Wing Pub. House & Press [1953] 174 p. 20 cm. [BV4595.W5] 54-17874
1. Prisons — Religious life. I. Title.

Prisons—Sermons.

BARTH, Karl, 1886- 252
Deliverance to the captives. [Sermons translated by Marguerite Wieser. 1st ed.] New York, Harper [1961] 160p. 22cm. [BV4316.P7B33] 61-7333
1. Prisons—Sermons. I. Title.

BARTH, Karl, 1886-1968. 252
Deliverance to the captives / Karl Barth. Westport, Conn. : Greenwood Press, 1979, c1961. 160 p. ; 23 cm. Translation of Den Gefangenen Befreiung. Reprint of the ed. published by Harper, New York. [BV4316.P7B33 1979] 78-12767 ISBN 0-313-21179-5 lib.bdg. : 14.50
1. Prisons—Sermons. I. Title.

Pritchett, Reuel B., 1884-

PRITCHETT, Reuel B., 1884- 286'.5 B
On the ground floor of heaven / by Reuel B. Pritchett, with Dale Aukerman. Elgin, IL : Brethren Press, 1980 c1980. 116 p. ; 18 cm. [BX7843.P73A34] 79-543 ISBN 0-87178-666-4 pbk. : 2.25
1. Pritchett, Reuel B., 1884- 2. Church of the Brethren—Clergy—Biography. 3. Clergy—Tennessee—Biography. 4. Tennessee—Biography. I. Aukerman, Dale, joint author. II. Title.

Private revelations.

†INMAN, W. Richard. 232.9'54
A message from heaven and things to think about / by W. Richard Inman. [Sunnyvale, CA] : Inman, c1976. iv, 134 p. ; 18 cm. Imprint from label mounted on p. [2] of cover. [BS2415.A2I55] 76-18436 2.95
1. Jesus Christ—Teaching. 2. Private revelations. I. Title.

SPRINGER, Rebecca Ruter, 1832-1904. 236'.24
My dream of heaven = originally published under the title Intra muros / Rebecca Ruter Springer. Old Tappan, N.J. : F. H. Revell Co., c1979. 160 p. ; 22 cm. [BV5091.R4S67 1979] 78-67820 ISBN 0-8007-0989-6 : 6.95
1. Private revelations. 2. Heaven. I. Title.

VOLKEN, Laurent, 1914- 231.74
Visions, revelations and the church. Tr. [from French] by Edward Gallagher. New York, Kenedy [1963] ix, 292p. 22cm. Bibl. 63-18883 5.50
1. Private revelations. I. Title.

Private schools—Hawaii.

HAWAII. University, Honolulu. College of Education. 371'.02'09969
A study of non-public schools in Hawaii : prepared for the 1972 session of the Legislature of the State of Hawaii / by John A. Thompson ... [et al.]. [Honolulu] : College of Education, University of Hawaii, 1971. xiii, 153 p. ; 28 cm. Includes bibliographical references. [LC50.H3H38 1971] 75-622200
1. Private schools—Hawaii. I. Thompson, John A., 1928- II. Hawaii. 6th Legislature, 1971-1972. III. Title.

Private schools—New York (State)

GARY, Louis R. 371'.02'09747
The collapse of nonpublic education: rumor or reality? By Louis R. Gary. In association with: Ernest J. Bartell [and others. New York, Implications Research, 1971] 2 v. 28 cm. "The report on nonpublic education in the State of New York for the New York State Commission on the Quality, Cost and Financing of Elementary and Secondary Education." Includes bibliographical references. [LC50.N4G37] 73-621061
1. Private schools—New York (State) I. New York (State). State Commission on the Quality, Cost, and Financing of Elementary and Secondary Education. II. Title.

Private schools—Religion.

COUNCIL for Religion in Independent Schools. 377.1
The Christian faith and youth today; [proceedings of the conference on religion in education held at Atlantic City, October 1956] Edited by Malcolm Strachan and Alvord M. Beardslee. Greenwich, Conn., Seabury Press, 1957. vii, 88p. 22cm. Bibliography: p. 87-88. [BV1609.C6] 57-4810
1. Private schools—Religion. 2. Religion education—U.S. 3. High schools—U. S. I. Strachan, Malcolm, ed. II. Beardslee, Alvord M., ed. III. Title. IV. Title: Conference on religion in education.

MILDRAM, Robert Cecil. 377.1
A study of religion in the independent schools. New York, Association Press, 1950. 78 p. tables. 22 cm. Much of the material has been drawn from a doctoral dissertation presented at Yale University, 1949. Bibliographical footnotes. [BV1609.M5] 51-3526
1. Private schools — Religion. 2. Religious-education — U.S. I. Title.

NATIONAL Conference on Religion in Education. 6th, Atlantic City, 1959. 377.1
Commitment and the school community; [proceedings] Edited by A. Graham Baldwin, Frank E. Gaebelein, and Earl G. Harrison, Jr. Greenwich, Conn., Seabury Press, 1960. vii, 118p. 22cm. [BV1609.N3 1959] 60-10070
1. Private schools—Religion. I. Baldwin, Alfred Graham, 1902- ed. II. Title.

NATIONAL Conference on Religion in Independent Education. 5th, Atlantic City, 1956. 377.1
The Christian faith and youth today; [proceedings of the Conference on Religion in Education, under the auspices of the Council for Religion in Independent Schools, held at Atlantic City, October 1956] Edited by Malcolm Strachan and Alvord M. Beardslee. Greenwich, Conn., Seabury Press, 1957. vii, 88 p. 22 cm. Bibliography: p. 87-88. [BV1609.N3] 57-4810
1. Private schools — Religion. 2. Religious education — U.S. 3. High schools — U.S. I. Strachan, Malcolm, ed. II. Beardslee, Alvord M., ed. III. Council for Religion in Independent Schools. IV. Title.

NATIONAL Conference on Religion in Independent Education. 6th, Atlantic City, 1959. 377.1
Commitment and the school community; [proceedings of the Conference on Religion in Education, held under the auspices of the Council for Religion in Independent Schools at Atlantic City, October 1959] Edited by A. Graham Baldwin, Frank E. Gaebelein, and Earl G. Harrison, Jr. Greenwich, Conn., Seabury Press, 1960. vii, 118 p. 22 cm. [BV1609.N3] 60-10070
1. Private schools — Religion. I. Baldwin, Alfred Graham, 1902- ed. II. Council for Religion in Independent Schools. III. Title.

NATIONAL Conference on Religion in Independent Education. 7th, Colorado Springs, 1962. 377.1
Education for decision; [addresses by] James H. Robinson [and others] Editors: Frank E. Gaebelein, Earl G. Harrison, Jr.

[and] William L. Swing. New York, Seabury Press, 1963. 125 p. 21 cm. "Held under the auspices of the Council for Religion in Independent Schools." Bibliography: p. 123-125. [BV1609.N3] 63-16289
1. Private schools — Religion. 2. Religious education — U.S. I. Robinson, James Herman. II. Gaebelein, Frank Ely, 1899- ed. III. Council for Religion in Independent Schools. IV. Title.

NATIONAL Conference on 377.1
Religion in Secondary Education, Atlantic City, 1946.
The preparatory schools & religion in our time, a symposium; addresses and papers. Editorial committee: L. Gertrude Angell [and others] New York, Association Press, 1947. vii, 124 p. 23 cm. [BV1609.N33 1946] 48-305
1. Private schools—Religion. I. Angell, Lisbeth Gertrude, ed. II. Title.

Private schools—Religious life.

NATIONAL conference of 377.1
preparatory school masters.
Religion in the preparatory schools; the proceedings of the National conference of preparatory school masters, held at Atlantic City, N. J., October 7-9, 1932. Edited by Boyd Edwards ... and Harold B. Ingalls ... New York, The National council of student Christian associations [1932?] 149 p. 24 cm. "Partial bibliography for further reading": p. 144-149. [BV1609.N3 1932] 34-13006
1. Private schools—Religious life. 2. Religious education—U. S. I. Edwards, Boyd, 1876- ed. II. Ingalls, Harold B., joint ed. III. National council of student Christian associations. IV. Title.

Private schools—United States

CHAMBERLAIN, Ernest 373.73
Barrett.
Our independent schools; the private school in American education, by Ernest Barrett Chamberlain ... New York, Cincinnati [etc.] American book company [1944] xii, 212 p. 20 1/2 cm. "Sponsored by the Carteret school scholarship and endowment fund, West Orange, New Jersey." Bibliographical foot-notes. [LC49.C45] 44-5852
1. Private schools—U.S. I. Title.

Private schools—United States—Directories.

B'NAI B'rith. 377.9602573
Vocational Service.
Prep school guide for Jewish youth; a comprehensive guide to selecting a prep school, for counselors, teachers, parents, and students. Edited and prepared under the supervision of S. Norman Feingold. Prepared by Sol Swerdloff and William Mead. 1966 ed. Washington [1966] 223 p. illus., forms. 23 cm. Bibliography: p. 217-218. [L901.B62 1966] 66-29565
1. Private schools—United States—Directories. 2. Jews in the United States—Education. I. Feingold, S. Norman, 1914- ed. II. Title.

Privilege (Canon law)

MATULENAS, Raymond Anthony, 262.9
1915-
... Communication, a source of privileges; an historical synopsis and commentary ... by Rev. Raymond Anthony Matulenas ... Washington, D.C., The Catholic university of America press, 1943. ix, p. 225 (i.e. 229) p. 23 cm. (The Catholic university of America. Canon law studies, no. 183) Thesis (J.C.D.)--Catholic university of America, 1943. "Biographical note": p. 215. Bibliography: p. 199-204. [BX1939.P6M3] A 44
1. Privilege (Canon law) I. Title.

Privileges and immunities, Ecclesiastical.

ANTON, Hans Hubert. 128'.3
Studien zu den Klosterprivilegien der Papste im fruhen Mittelalter : unter bes. Berucks. d. Privilegierung von St. Maurice d'Agaune / von Hans Hubert Anton. Berlin ; New York : de Gruyter, 1975. x, 172 p. ; 25 cm. (Beitrage zur Geschichte und Quellenkunde des Mittelalters ; Bd. 4) Errata slip inserted. Originally presented as the author's Habilitationsschrift, Bonn, 1970. Includes index. Bibliography: p. [150]-161. [LAW] 75-516225 ISBN 3-11-004686-5 : DM80.00
1. Saint Maurice, Switzerland (Augustinian abbey) 2. Privileges and immunities, Ecclesiastical. I. Title. II. Series.

FAIRCHILD, Joy Hamlet 1790-1859.
The new doctrine of clerical privilege. An address delivered in Fremont temple, on the 26th and 27th of January, 1852. By J. H. Fairchild ... Boston, Redding & co., 1852. 60 p. 20 cm. 6-26334
I. Title.

Pro Juarez, Miguel Agustin, 1891-1927.

[BLOUNT, Melesina Mary] 922.272
Mrs.
God's jester; the story of the life and martyrdom of Father Michael Pro, s.j., by Mrs. George Norman [pseud.] New York, Cincinnati [etc.] Benziger brothers, 1930. viii, 226 p. front. (port.) 19 1/2 cm. Bibliography: p. 226. [BX4705.PT2B6] 31-101
1. Pro Jares Miguel Augustin, 1898-1927. 2. Catholics in Mexico. 3. Mexico—Hist.—Revolution, 1910- I. Title.

DAUGHTERS of St. Paul 92
God s secret agent; the life of Michael Augustine Pro, S. J., written, illus. by the Daughters of St. Paul. [Boston] St. Paul Eds. [1967] 101p. illus. 22cm. (Their Encounter bks.) [BX4705.P75D34] 67-4290 1.50
1. Pro Juarez, Miguel Agustin, 1891-1927. I. Title.
Distributed by the Daughters of St. Paul.

DAUGHTERS of St. Paul. 92
God's secret agent; the life of Michael Augustine Pro, S.J., written and illustrated by the Daughters of St. Paul. [Boston] St. Paul Editions [1967] 101 p. illus. 22 cm. (Their Encounter books) A biography of a Jesuit priest and martyr for the Catholic faith in the early twentieth-century struggle between Church and State in Mexico. [BX4705.P72D34] AC 67
1. Pro Juarez, Miguel Agustin, 1891-1927. I. Title.

FORREST, Michael D. 922.272
The life of Father Pro, by Rev. M. D. Forrest, M.S.C., with foreword by His Grace Archbishop Mannix ... St. Paul, Minn., Fathers Rumble and Carty, Radio replies press, c1945. viii, 118 p. ports., facsim. 20 1/2 cm. [BX4605.P72F6] 46-5949
1. Pro Juarez, Miguel Agustin, 1891-1927. I. Title.

MULLER, Gerald 271'.5'0924 B
Francis, 1927-
With life and laughter; the life of Father Miguel Agustin Pro, by Gerald F. Muller. Notre Dame [Ind.] Dujarie Press [1969] 128 p. illus., ports. 22 cm. First ed. published in 1954 under title: The martyr laughed. [BX4705.P72M8 1969] 70-76774
1. Pro Juarez, Miguel Agustin, 1891-1927. I. Title.

ROBERTO, Brother, 1927- 922.272
Dawn brings glory; a story of Father Pro, S. J. Notre Dame, Ind., Dujarie Press [1956] 139p. illus. 22cm. High school ed. of the author's The martyr laughed. [BX4705.P72R57 1956] 56-59252
1. Pro Juarez, Miguel Augustin, 1891-1927. I. Title.

ROBERTO, Brother, 1927- 922.272
The martyr laughed; a story of Father Miguel Pro, S. J. Illus. by Anthony Joyce. Notre Dame, Ind., Dujarie Press [1954] 92p. illus. 24cm. [BX4705.P72R57] 54-41985
1. Pro Juar2s, Miguel Agustin, 1891-1927. I. Title.

ROYER, Fanchon, 1902- 922.272
Padre Pro. New York, P. J. Kenedy [1954] 248p. illus. 21cm. [BX4705.P72R6] 54-5016
1. Pro Juares, Miguel Augustin, 1891-1927. I. Title.

Pro Juarez, Miguel Agustin, 1891-1927—Juvenile literature.

ROYER, Fanchon, 1902- 920
Padre Pro, Mexican hero. Illus. by James J. Fox. New York, Kenedy [c.1963] 189p. illus. 22cm. (Amer. background bks. [23]) 63-11352 2.50
1. Pro Juarez, Miguel Agustin, 1891-1927—Juvenile literature. I. Title.

Probation after death.

EMERSON, George Homer, 237.3
1822-1898.
The doctrine of probation examined with reference to current discussions. By George H. Emerson ... Boston, Universalist publishing house, 1883. 175 p. 18cm. [BT927.E5] 37-39272
1. Probation after death. I. Title.

JACKSON, Green P 1840- 237.
Man an eternal probationer, by Rev. Green P. Jackson ... Nashville, Tenn., Printed for the author, 1902. 160 p. front. (port.) 22 cm. [BT927.J2] 2-21495
1. Probation after death. I. Title.

LOVE, William DeLoss, 1819- 237.3
1898.
Future probation examined. By William DeLoss Love ... New York, London, Funk & Wagnalls, 1888. x, 322 p., 1 l. 20 cm. [BT927.L8] 37-39271
1. Probation after death. I. Title.

MORRIS, Edward Dafydd. 1825- 237.
1915.
Is there salvation after death? A treatise on the gospel in the intermediate state. By E. D. Morris ... New York, A. C. Armstrong & son [c1887] 2 p. l., 252 p. 21 1/2 cm. [BT927.M6] 41-40821
1. Probation after death. I. Title.

PEMENT, Philemon. 237.3
Probation after death; or, Is the hope of salvation limited to this life? No. By Philemon Pement ... Moberly, Mo., P. Pement [1897] 203, [1] p. 20 cm. [BT927.P3] 37-39270
1. Probation after death. I. Title.

POND, Enoch, 1791-1882. 237.3
Probation. By Enoch Pond ... Bangor [Me.] Duren & Thatcher, 1837. xi, [13]-137 p. 17 cm. [BT927.P6] 37-39267
1. Probation after death. I. Title.

WRIGHT, George Frederick, 237.3
1838-1921.
An inquiry concerning the relation of death to probation. By G. Frederick Wright ... Boston, Congregational publishing society [1882] viii, [9]-114 p. 17 1/2 cm. [BT927.W7] 37-39276
1. Probation after death. I. Congregational Sunday-school and publishing society. II. Title.

Problem children.

WOODY, Robert Henley. 371.93
Behavioral problem children in the schools; recognition, diagnosis, and behavioral modification [by] Robert H. Woody. New York, Appleton-Century-Crofts [1969] xi, 264 p. 25 cm. Includes bibliographies. [LC4801.W65] 69-11951
1. Problem children. I. Title.

Problem children—Education.

SWIFT, Marshall S. 371.9'3
Alternative teaching strategies : helping behaviorally troubled children achieve : a guide for teachers and psychologists / Marshall S. Swift and George Spivack. Champaign, Il. : Research Press, [1975] xx, 217 p. ; 21 cm. Bibliography: p. 209-217. [LC4661.S94] 75-309120 ISBN 0-87822-117-4 pbk. : 4.50
1. Problem children—Education. I. Spivack, George, joint author. II. Title.

Problem children—Education—Illinois—Chicago.

WAGNER, Jon. 371.9'3'0977311
Misfits and missionaries : a school for Black dropouts / by Jon Wagner. Beverly Hills : Sage Publications, c1977. p. cm. (The City and society ; 2) [LC4801.W3] 77-22316 ISBN 0-8039-0722-2 : 15.00 ISBN 0-8039-0723-0 pbk. : 6.95
1. Mission Academy. 2. Problem children—Education—Illinois—Chicago. 3. Afro-American dropouts—Illinois—Chicago. 4. Juvenile delinquency—Illinois—Chicago. I. Title. II. Series.

Problem children—Education—New York (City)

GROSSMAN, Herbert, 371.9'3'097471
1934-
Nine rotten, lousy kids. [1st ed.] New York, Holt, Rinehart, and Winston [1972] viii, 407 p. 22 cm. [LC4801.G76 1972] 71-183535 ISBN 0-03-091386-1 ISBN 0-03-085189-0 (college) 8.95
1. Problem children—Education—New York (City) I. Title.

Probverbs—Bibliography

CHICAGO. Public library.
... Books on proverbs, quotations and toasts. Chicago, 1905. 23 p. 14 1/2 cm. [Z7191.C56] 13-10495
1. Probverbs—Bibl. 2. Quotations—Bibl. 3. Toasts—Bibl. I. Title.

Process theology.

BALTAZAR, Eulalio R. 230
God within process [by] Eulalio R. Baltazar. Paramus, N.J., Newman Press [1970] 186 p. 24 cm. Includes bibliographical references. [BT83.6.B3 1970] 73-118701 5.95
1. Process theology. I. Title.

BEARDSLEE, William A. 230
A house for hope; a study in process and Biblical thought, by William A. Beardslee. Philadelphia, Westminster Press [1972] 192 p. 21 cm. Includes bibliographical references. [BT83.6.B4] 75-181724 ISBN 0-664-20931-9 5.95
1. Process theology. 2. Hope. I. Title.

COBB, John B. 230
Process theology : an introductory exposition / John B. Cobb, Jr., and David Ray Griffin. Philadelphia : Westminister Press, c1976. p. cm. Includes index. Bibliography: p. [BT83.6.C6] 76-10352 ISBN 0-664-24743-1 pbk. : 6.95
1. Process theology. I. Griffin, David, 1939- joint author. II. Title.

COBB, John B. 261.8
Process theology as political theology / by John B. Cobb, Jr. 1st ed. Manchester : Manchester University Press ; Philadelphia : Westminister Press, c1982. xvi, 158 p. ; 22 cm. "Based on the Ferguson lectures delivered in the University of Manchester 1980"—T.p. verso. Includes bibliographical references. [BT83.6.C625 1982] 19 82-1845 ISBN 0-664-24417-3 (Westminster Press) pbk. : 7.95
1. Process theology. 2. Christianity and politics. I. Title.

FORD, Lewis S. 230
The lure of God : a Biblical background for process theism / Lewis S. Ford. Philadelphia : Fortress Press, c1978. xiii, 144 p. ; 24 cm. Includes bibliographical references annd indexes. [BT83.6.F67] 77-15230 ISBN 0-8006-0516-0 : 10.95
1. Bible—Theology. 2. Process theology. I. Title.

GRIFFIN, David, 1939- 232
A process Christology, by David R. Griffin. Philadelphia, Westminister Press [1973] 273 p. 21 cm. Includes bibliographical references. [BT205.G67] 73-10252 ISBN 0-664-20978-5 10.00
1. Jesus Christ. 2. Process theology. I. Title.

JAMES, Ralph E 230'.0924
The concrete God; a new beginning for theology; the thought of Charles Hartshorne, by Ralph E. James.

Indianapolis, Bobbs-Merrill [1967] xxviii, 236 p. 22 cm. Bibliography: p. 195-223. [B945.H354J3] 67-25172
1. Hartshorne, Charles, 1897- 2. Process theology. I. Title.

JAMES, Ralph E. 230'.0924
The concrete God; a new beginning for theology; the thought of Charles Hartshorne, by Ralph E. James. Indianapolis, Bobbs-Merrill [1967] xxviii, 236 p. 22 cm. Bibliography: p. 195-223. [B945.H354J3] 67-25172
1. Hartshorne, Charles, 1897- 2. Process theology. I. Title.

LEE, Bernard. 201'.1
The becoming of the Church; a process theology of the structures of Christian experience. New York, Paulist Press [1974] vii, 304 p. 23 cm. Bibliography: p. 299-304. [BT83.6.L43] 73-90718 ISBN 0-8091-1816-5 5.95 (pbk.)
1. Process theology. 2. Church. 3. Sacraments. I. Title.

MELLERT, Robert B. 230
What is process theology? / By Robert B. Mellert. New York : Paulist Press, [1975] 141 p. ; 18 cm. (Deus books) Includes bibliographical references. [BT83.6.M44] 74-28933 ISBN 0-8091-1867-X pbk. : 1.95
1. Whitehead, Alfred North, 1861-1947. 2. Process theology. I. Title.

NEVILLE, Robert C. 231
Creativity and God : a challenge to process theology / Robert C. Neville. New York : Seabury Press, 1980. xi, 163 p. ; 24 cm. "A Crossroad book." Includes bibliographical references and index. [BT83.6.N48] 79-25655 ISBN 0-8164-0120-9 : 9.95
1. Process theology. 2. God. I. Title.

RUST, Eric Charles. 200.1
Evolutionary philosophies and contemporary theology, by Eric C. Rust. Philadelphia, Westminster Press [1969] 256 p. 21 cm. Bibliographical references included in "Notes" (p. [231]-248) [BT83.6.R8] 69-10419 6.50
1. Process theology. 2. Philosophy, Modern. I. Title.

SMITH, Gregory Michael, 1941- 230'.2
Pilgrims in process : a pastoral theology / by Gregory Michael Smith. New York : Alba House, c1978. 145 p. : ill. ; 21 cm. Bibliography: p. [141]-145. [BX1751.2.S485] 78-4094 ISBN 0-8189-0366-X : 3.95
1. Catholic Church—Doctrinal and controversial works—Catholic authors. 2. Process theology. I. Title.

SPONHEIM, Paul R. 230
Faith and process : the significance of process thought for Christian faith / Paul R. Sponheim. Minneapolis : Augsburg Pub. House, c1979. 351 p. : ill. ; 23 cm. Includes bibliographical references and indexes. [BT83.6.S66] 78-66955 ISBN 0-8066-1680-6 : 12.50
1. Process theology. I. Title.

SUCHOCKI, Marjorie. 230'.044
God, Christ, Church : a practical guide to process theology / Marjorie Hewitt Suchocki. New York : Crossroad, 1982. xii, 227 p. : ill. ; 23 cm. [BT83.6.S93 1982] 19 81-22189 ISBN 0-8245-0464-X : 9.95
1. Process theology. 2. Theology, Doctrinal. I. Title.

Process theology—Addresses, essays, lectures.

COUSINS, Ewert H., comp. 230
Process theology: basic writings. Edited by Ewert H. Cousins. New York, Newman Press [1971] vii, 376 p. 23 cm. Contents.Contents.—Preface, by E. H. Cousins.—Introduction: process models in culture, philosophy, and theology, by E. H. Cousins.—Process thought: a contemporary trend in theology, by W. N. Pittenger.—Faith and the formative imagery of our time, by B. E. Meland.—The development of process philosophy, by C. Hartshorne.—Whitehead's method of empirical analysis, by B. M. Loomer.—God and the world, by A. N. Whitehead.—Philosophical and religious uses of "God," by C. Hartshorne.—The reality of God, by S. M. Ogden.—A Whiteheadian reflection on God's relation to the world, by W. E. Stokes.—The world and God, by J. B. Cobb.—God and man, by D. D. Williams.—The new creation, by B. E. Meland.—Bernard E. Meland, process thought, and the significance of Christ, by W. N. Pittenger.—The human predicament, by H. N. Wieman.—Teilhard de Chardin and the orientation of evolution: a critical essay, by T. Dobzhansky.—My universe, by P. Teilhard de Chardin.—The cosmic Christ, by H. de Lubac.—Cosmology and Christology, by N. M. Wildiers.—The problem of evil in Teilhard's thought, by G. Crespy.—Teilhard de Chardin and Christian spirituality, by C. F. Mooney.—Teilhard's process metaphysics, by I. G. Barbour.—Bibliography on process theology (p. 351-369) Includes bibliographies. [BT83.6.C68] 78-171961 4.95
1. Teilhard de Chardin, Pierre—Addresses, essays, lectures. 2. Process theology—Addresses, essays, lectures. I. Title.

PITTENGER, William Norman, 1905- 230
The lure of divine love : human experience and Christian faith in a process perspective / Norman Pittenger. New York : Pilgrim Press, c1979. viii, 193 p. ; 21 cm. [BT83.6.P57] 19 79-15611 ISBN 0-8298-0370-X pbk. 6.95
1. Process theology—Addresses, essays, lectures. I. Title.

RELIGIOUS experience and process theology : the pastoral implications of a major modern movement / edited by Harry James Cargas and Bernard Lee. New York : Paulist Press, c1976. xvi, 438 p. ; 23 cm. Includes bibliographies. [BT83.6.R4] 75-46065 ISBN 0-8091-1934-X : 9.95 230
1. Process theology—Addresses, essays, lectures. I. Cargas, Harry J. II. Lee, Bernard.

Process theology—Collections.

BROWN, Delwin, 1935- comp. 201
Process philosophy and Christian thought. Edited by Delwin Brown, Ralph E. James, Jr. [and] Gene Reeves. Indianapolis, Bobbs-Merrill [1971] xiv, 495 p. 23 cm. Bibliography: p. 475-489. [BT83.6.B76] 74-127586 6.95
1. Process theology—Collections. I. James, Ralph E., joint comp. II. Reeves, Gene, joint comp. III. Title.

Process theology—History—20th century.

MUELLER, J. J. (John J. 230'.044
Faith and appreciative awareness : the cultural theology of Bernard E. Meland / J.J. Mueller. Lanham, MD : University Press of America, 1981. p. cm. Bibliography: p. [BT83.6.M83] 19 81-3390 ISBN 0-8191-1560-6 : 17.75 ISBN 0-8191-1561-4 (pbk.) : 8.75
1. Meland, Bernard Eugene, 1899- 2. Process theology—History—20th century. 3. Christianity and culture—History—20th century. I. Title.

Processing (Libraries)

APPLEBAUM, Edmond L., comp. 025'.02
Reader in technical services, edited by Edmond L. Applebaum. [Washington, NCR Microcard Editions, 1973. xi, 266 p. 27 cm. (Reader series in library and information science) Includes bibliographies. [Z688.5.A66] 72-87717 ISBN 0-910972-21-4 10.95
1. Processing (Libraries) I. Title.

Procia, reputed with of Pontius Pilate.

VAN DYKE, Catherine. 232.
A letter from Pontius Pilate's wife, rewritten by Catherine Van Dyke. Indianapolis, The Bobbs-Merrill company [c1929] 53 p. 18 cm. [BT309.V3] 29-24205
1. Procia, reputed with of Pontius Pilate. I. Title.

Proclus Lycius, surnamed Diadochus. Commentarii.

PROCLUS, Diadochus.
Proclus' Metaphysical elements ... tr. from the original Greek by Thos. M. Johnson ... Osceola, Mo., Press of the Republican, 1909. 2 p. l., xvi, 201 p. diagrs. 22 1/2 cm. A 10
I. Johnson, Thomas Moore, 1851-1919, tr. II. Title.

WHITTAKER, Thomas, 1856-
The Neo-Platonists; a study in the history of Hellenism, by Thomas Whittaker. 2d ed., with a supplement on the Commentaries of Proclus. Cambridge [Eng.] The University press, 1928. xv, [1], 318 p., 1 l. 23 cm. "First edition 1901; second edition (enlarged) 1918, reprinted 1928." [B517.W5 1928] 29-948
1. Proclus Lycius, surnamed Diadochus. Commentarii. 2. Neoplatonism. I. Title.

Procopius of Sazava, Saint, d. 1053.

KADLEC, Jaroslav, doctor of theology. 922.22
Saint Procopius, guardian of the Cyrilo-Methodian legacy. Translated by Vitus Buresh. [Cleveland, Micro Photo Division, Bell & Howell Co., 1964. 331 p. illus. 23 cm. Photocopy of typescript reproduced by duopage process. Bibliograpical references included in "Footnotes" (p. 203-310) [BX4700.P8K313] 64-4477
1. Procopius of Sazava, Saint, d. 1053. I. Title.

Prodigal son.

BRENDLE, Daniel F 1824-1906 2268
The prodigal son. In four parts. Being a practical exposition of Luke XV. 11-32. Carefully revised and enlarged by Rev. D. F. Brendle, A.M. Translated from the German. Philadelphia, Lindsay & Blakiston, 1862. xii, 13-220 p. front., plates. 18 cm. "A translation from the German which the author published a year ago."--Pref. [BT378.P8B72] 35-29021
1. Prodigal son. I. Title.

BURRELL, David James. 1844- 252.
The Golden parable; studies in the story of the prodigal son, by Davie James Burrell ... New York, Chicago [etc.] Flemin H. Revell company [1926] 159 p. 19 1/2 cm. [BT378.P8B8] 26-8942
1. Prodigal son. I. Title.

GREENE, Joseph Nelson, 1868- 226.
The portrait of the prodigal; life studies in the experiences of the prodigal son, by Joseph Nelson Greene. New York, Cincinnati, The Methodist book concern [c1921] 215 p. 19 1/2 cm. [BT378.P8G7] 21-7270
I. Title.

HEISLER, Daniel Yost, 1820-1888. 226.8
Life-pictures of "The prodigal son." A gift-book for the million; genial, searching, and kind. By Rev. D. Y. Heisler... Author's ed. Philadelphia [Printed by Grant, Faires & Rodgers] 1877. vii, [9]-225 p. 19 cm. [BT378.P8H4] 35-30430
1. Prodigal son. I. Title.

LEYBURN, John, 1814-1894. 226.8
Hints to young men from the parable of the prodigal son. By the Rev. John Leyburn ... Philadelphia, Presbyterian board of publication and Sabbath-school work [1888] 183 p. 18 cm. [BT378.P8L4] 34-34401
1. Prodigal son. I. Presbyterian church in the U.S.A. Board of publication. II. Title.

MOTT, George Scudder, 1829-1901. 226.8
The prodigal son, by the Rev. George S. Mott ... Philadelphia, Presbyterian board of publication [1863] 143 p. 18 1/2 cm. [BT378.P8M6] 35-22767
1. Prodigal son. I. Presbyterian church in the U.S.A. Board of publication. II. Title.

THE prodigal; 226.8
chapters by Moorhouse, Moody, Spurgeon, Aitken, Talmage and others ... Chicago, New York [etc.] The Bible institute colportage association [1897] 126 p. 19 cm. (On cover: The Colportage library, v. 2, no. 48) [BT378.P8A15 1897] 35-34403
1. Prodigal son. I. Moorhouse, Henry. II. Moody, Dwight Lyman, 1837-1899. III. Spurgeon, Charles Haddon, 1834-1892.

ROSCAMP, Robert G. 226.
Lost and found; being a series of lectures on the prodigal son, by Rev. R. G. Roscamp, D. D. New York, London [etc.] The Abbey press [1902] 216 p. front. (port.) 21 cm. [BT378.P8R65] 2-24736
1. Prodigal son. I. Title.

TAPMAN, Lillian Smith. 226.8
The unprodigal son, by a wayfarer (Lillian Smith-Tapman) Richmond Hill, N.Y., L. S. Tapman [c1935] [BT378.P8T3] 36-4048
1. Prodigal son. I. Title.

WILLCOX, Giles Buckingham, 1826-1922. 226.8
The prodigal son, A monograph. With an excursus on Chirst as a public teacher, by G. B. Willcox... New York, American tract society, [1890] viii, [9]-112 p. 19 1/2 cm. [BT378.P8W5] 33-32579
1. Jesus Christ—Teaching methods. 2. Prodigal son. I. American tract society. II. Title.

ZABRISKIE, Francis Nicoll, 1832-1891. 226.8
The story of a soul; or, Thoughts on the parable of the prodigal son. By F. N. Zabriskie, D.D. New York, A. D. F. Randolph & company [1872] 14 p. 17 cm. [BT378.P8Z3] 35-29026
1. Prodigal son. I. Title.

Prodigal son (Parable)

BLACK, Harold Garnet. 226.8
The prodigal returns, by Harold Garnet Black...with an introduction by Roy L. Smith by Roy L. Smith... New York [etc.] Fleming H. Revel company [c1941] 1 p. l., 7-168 p. 20 cm. [BT378.P8B4] (813.5) 41-20857
1. Prodigal son—Fiction. I. Title.

BROWN, Robert Raymond, Bp., 1910- 248.42
Alive again. New York, Morehouse-Barlow [1964] 151 p. 21 cm. [BT378.P8B74] 64-15260
1. Prodigal son (Parable) 2. Christian life — Anglican authors. I. Title.

ELLIOTT, William Marion, 1903- 226.8
Two sons. Richmond, John Knox Press [1955] 62p. 21cm. [BT378.P8E47] 55-6742
1. Prodigal son (Parable) I. Title.

FREEMAN, Winfield, 1848- 252.
The prodigal son, by Winfield Freeman. Topeka, Kan., Capper printing company, 1921. 60 p. 20 cm. Ornamental borders. [BT378.P8F7] 22-543
I. Title.

MCCONNELL, Franz Marshall, 1861- 226.8
After the feast, by F. M. McConnell... Dallas, Tex., The Marshall company, 1932. 55 p. 20 1/2 cm. "The parable of the prodigal son...[8] supplementary story of his efforts."--Pref. [BV4515.M28] 33-3330
1. Prodigal son—Ficiton. I. Title.

MELTON, William Walter, 1879- 252.
The waste of sin; a study of the parable of the prodigal son, by W. W. Melton ... New York, Chicago [etc.] Fleming H. Revell company [c1922] 170 p. 20 cm. [BT378.P8M4] 23-5379
I. Title.

MOON, Robert D. 226.8
Love's conquest. Mountain View, Calif., Pacific Press Pub. Association [c.1960] xvii, 116p. 21cm. 60-8300 3.00
1. Prodigal son (Parable) I. Title.

MORGAN, George Campbell, 1863-1945. 226.8
The parable of the father's heart. New York, F. H. Revell Co. [1949] 96 p. 18 cm. [BT378.P8M57] 49-8772
1. Prodigal son (Parable) I. Title.

WARD, C. M. 248'.4
The playboy comes homes / C. M. Ward. Springfield, Mo. : Gospel Pub. House,

c1976. 107 p. ; 18 cm. (Radiant books) [BT378.P8W27] 75-32603 ISBN 0-88243-572-8 pbk. : 1.25
1. Prodigal son (Parable) I. Title.

WHITE, John Wesley. 226'.8
The runaway / John Wesley White. [Dallas : Crescendo Publications], c1976. 198 p. ; 18 cm. [BT378.P8W46] 77-371317 ISBN 0-89038-028-7 pbk. : 1.95
1. Prodigal son (Parable) I. Title.

Prodigal son (Parable)—Caricatures and cartoons—Juvenile literature.

WALSH, Bill. 226'.8
The prodigal son / Bill Walsh ; edited with an introduction by Charlie Shedd. Kansas City, Kan. : Sheed Andrews and McMeel, c1977. p. cm. (A Cartoon Bible story) A cartoon version of the parable of the prodigal son who, after squandering his inheritance, returns home to his forgiving father. [BT378.P8W24] 77-1146 ISBN 0-8362-0693-2 pbk. : 1.95
1. Prodigal son (Parable)—Caricatures and cartoons—Juvenile literature. 2. [Prodigal son (Parable)] 3. [Parables.] 4. [Bible stories—N.T.] 5. [Cartoons and comics.] I. Title.

Prodigal son (Parable)—Juvenile literature.

DUNCAN, Cleo. 226'.8
Woofy is forgiven, and The prodigal son. Illustrated by Beryl Bailey Jones. Boston, United Church Press, 1964. 1 v. (unpaged) col. illus. 21 cm. "Part of the United Church curriculum, prepared and published by the Division of Christian Education and the Division of Publication of the United Church Board for Homeland Ministries." [BT378.P8D75] 64-19469
1. Prodigal son (Parable) — Juvenile literature. I. i. United Church Board for Homeland Ministries. Division of Christian Education. II. ii. United Church Board for Homeland Ministries. Division of Publication. The prodigal son. III. Title.

ELMER, Irene 226
The boy who ran away: Luke 15:1-2 for children. Illus. by Sally Mathews. St. Louis, Concordia [c.1964] [32]p. col. illus. 21cm. (Arch bks.) 63-23143 .35 pap.,
1. Prodigal son (Parable)—Juvenile literature. I. Title.

ELMER, Irene 226
The boy who ran away; Luke 15: 1-2 for children. Illustrated by Sally Mathews. St. Louis, Concordia Pub. House [1964] [32] p. col. illus. 21 cm. (Arch books) Quality religious books for children. [BT378.P8E48] 63-23143
1. Prodigal son (Parable) — Juvenile literature. I. Title.

GRAHAM, Lorenz B. 226'.8
Hongry catch the foolish boy, by Lorenz Graham. Pictures by James Brown, Jr. New York, Crowell [1973] [40] p. illus. (part col.) 21 x 22 cm. Story first appeared in the author's How God fix Jonah, published in 1946. Retells the parable of the prodigal son in the speech patterns and images of African people newly acquainted with the English language. [BT378.P8G68 1973] 77-184981 ISBN 0-690-40111-6 3.95
1. Prodigal son (Parable)—Juvenile literature. 2. [Prodigal son (Parable)] 3. [Bible stories—N.T.] I. Brown, James, illus. II. Title.

NIXON, Joan Lowery. 226'.4'09505
The son who came home again : the prodigal son for beginning readers : Luke 15:11-32 for children / by Joan Lowery Nixon ; illustrated by Aline Cunningham. St. Louis : Concordia Pub. House, c1977. [48] p. : col. ill. ; 23 cm. (I can read a Bible story) Retells the parable of the son, who, after squandering his inheritance, returns home to a forgiving father. [BT378.P8N57] 77-6651 3.95
1. Prodigal son (Parable)—Juvenile literature. 2. [Prodigal son (Parable)] 3. [Parables.] 4. [Bible stories.] I. Cunningham, Aline. II. Title.

WIEMER, Rudolf Otto, 1905- 226
The prodigal son. Illus. and design by Reinhard Herrmann. Tr. by Paul T. Martinsen. Minneapolis, Augsburg [c.1967] 1v. (unpaged) col. illus. 27cm. Tr. of Der verlorene Sohn. [BT378.P8 W483] 67-8420 1.75 bds.,
1. Prodigal son (Parable)—Juvenile literature. I. Title.

Prodigal son (Parable)—Meditations.

SCHROEDER, Frederick W 226.8
Far from home. Philadelphia, Christian Education Press [1961] 123p. 20cm. [BT378.P8S314] 61-10557
1. Prodigal son (Parable)—Meditations. I. Title.

Prodigal son (Parable)—Sermons.

COX, Norman Wade, 1888- 226.8
God and ourselves. Nashville, Broadman Press [c.1960] x, 139p. 21cm. 60-5191 2.75 bds.,
1. Prodigal son (Parable)—Sermons. 2. Baptists—Sermons. 3. Sermons, American. I. Title.

SOMMER, Frederick, 1873- 226.8
The world's greatest short story, a study of present-day significance of the family pattern of life. [Oswego, Kan., Pub. by the Carpenter Press, 1948] xv, 166 p. 23 cm. [BT378.P8S6] 48-4861
1. Prodigal son (Parable)—Sermons. 2. Occasional sermons. I. Title.

WHITING, Thomas A. 226.8
Sermons on the prodigal son. Abingdon Press [c.1959] 111p. Bibl. footnotes: p2.00 bds., 60-5237
1. Prodigal son (Parable)—Sermons. 2. Methodist Church—Sermons. 3. Sermons, American. I. Title.

Prodigal son—Sermons.

BLACKWELL, George Lincoln, 1861- 226.8
The model homestead. Three pointed, practical and picturesque sermons on the parable of the prodigal son. By Rev. George L. Blackwell ... Introduction by Bishop Alexander Walters, D.D. Boston, Mass., H. Marshall & co., printers, 1893. 76 p. incl. front. (Ort.) 18 1/2 cm. [BT378.P8B5] 35-33917
1. Prodigal son—Sermons. 2. Sermons, American. I. Title.

DUTCHER, Jacob Conkling, 1820-1888. 226.8
The prodigal son. By the Rev. J. C. Dutcher. New York, E. B. Tripp & co., printers, 1870. 4 p. l., [5]-125 p. 16 cm. [BT378.P8D8] 35-22768
1. Prodigal son—Sermons. 2. Sermons, American. I. Title.

ELSEY, Charles William, 1880- 226.8
The prodigal's father, by Charles William Elsey. Nashville, Tenn., Broadman press [c1937] 159 p. 19 1/2cm. [BT378.P8E5] 37-29372
1. Prodigal son—Sermons. 2. God—Fatherhood. 3. Baptists—Sermons. 4. Sermons, American. I. Title.

ROWLAND, James, 1789?-1873. 226.8
Ruin and restoration; illustrated from the parable of the prodigal son. By Rev. James Rowland, late pastor of the First Presbyterian church, Circleville, Ohio. Albany, N. Y., Weed, Parsons and company, printers, 1862. 3 p. l., [5]-147 p. 23 cm. [BT378.P8R67] 35-30432
1. Prodigal son—Sermons. 2. Presbyterian church—Sermons. I. Title.

VINCENT, Marvin Richardson, 1834-1922. 226.8
The two prodigals. By Rev. Marvin R. Vincent ... New York, A. D. F. Randolph & company [1876] 59 p. 15 cm. [BT378.P8V5] 35-29035
1. Prodigal son—Sermons. 2. Presbyterian church—Sermons. I. Title.

WHITAKER, Walter Claiborne, 1867- 226.8
... The prodigal son; Christ's parable of mercy, by Rev. Walter C. Whitaker ... Jacksonville, Fla., The church yea pub. co., printers, 1890. cover-title, 52 p. 17 1/2 cm. (The church year series. no. 4) [BT378.P8W45] 35-33543
1. Prodigal son—Sermons. 2. Protestant Episcopal church in the U.S.A.—Sermons. 3. Sermons, American. I. Title.

Proefschrift — Amsterdam.

SNYDER, Dale Norman. 230'.4'20924
Karl Barth's struggle with anthropocentric theology. Gravenhage, Boekhandel Wattez. 1966. 224 p. 22 cm. unpriced (Ne66-40) Bibliography: p. [221]-[(223]) [BX4827.B3S6] 67-95170
1. Barth, Karl, 1886- 2. Proefschrift — Amsterdam. I. Title.

Profession, Choice of—Bibliography

JEWISH occupational council, New York. 016.371425
A bibliography for Jewish vocational agencies ... New York city, Jewish occupational council, 1940. 23, [1] p. 26 cm. (Its Report no. 3) [Z7164.C81J48] 41-10861
1. Profession, Choice of—Bibl. 2. Occupations—Bibl. 3. Jews—Political and social conditions—Bibl. I. Title.

Profession (in religious orders, congregations, etc.)

FRANCISCANS. Custody of St. Mary of the Angels. 265.9
Making a monk. [New Cannaan, Conn., Byzantine Franciscans, 1965] 65 p. 18 cm. "Translation from the Postrizenije monachov, published in 1952." [BX2049.F7P73] 65-26169
1. Profession (in religious orders, congregations, etc.) I. Title.

Professions—Social aspects—Addresses, essays, lectures.

PERILS of professionalism : essays on Christian faith and professionalism / Donald B. Kraybill and Phyllis Pellman Good, editors. Scottdale, Pa. : Herald Press, 1982. 240 p. ; 21 cm. Bibliography: p. [231]-237. [HT687.P47 1982] 19 82-3052 ISBN 0-8361-1997-5 (pbk.) : 9.95 261.8'34553
1. Professions—Social aspects—Addresses, essays, lectures. 2. Professions—Religious aspects—Christianity—Addresses, essays, lectures. 3. Professions—Religious aspects—Mennonites—Addresses, essays, lectures. I. Kraybill, Donald B. II. Good, Phyllis Pellman.

Progress.

CARTER, Paul Allen, 1926- 261
The idea of progress in American Protestant thought, 1930-1960, by Paul A. Carter. Philadelphia, Fortress Press [1969] xi, 27 p. 20 cm. (Facet books. Historical series, 11) First published in Church history, [v.] XXXII, no. 1 (March, 1963), [p.] 75-94, under title: The idea of progress in most recent American Protestant thought, 1930-1960. Includes bibliographical references. [BR479.C33] 69-14621 0.85
1. Progress. 2. Religious thought—20th century. I. Title.

CUNNINGHAM, William, 1849-1919. 225
The secret of progress, by W. Cunningham ... Cambridge, University press, 1918. xii, 179 p. 20 cm. [BR121.C915] 20-189
I. Title.

DAVIES, Thomas Frederick, bp., 1872- 248
Personal progress in religion, by Thomas Frederick Davies ... Milwaukee, Morehouse publishing co.; [etc., etc., c1925] 4 p. l., 90, [2] p. 20 cm. "References": [BV4501.D3] 25-4219
I. Title.

DAWSON, Christopher Henry, 1889- 200
Progress and religion; an historical enquiry [by] Christopher Dawson. Westport, Conn., Greenwood Press [1970] xvii, 254 p. 23 cm. Reprint of the 1929 ed. Bibliography: p. 251-254. [BL55.D3 1970] 79-104266
1. Progress. 2. Religion. 3. Civilization, Christian. 4. History—Philosophy. I. Title.

Prohibited books (Canon law)

PERNICONE, Joseph Maria, 1903- 098.11
... The ecclesiastical prohibition of books ... [by] Reverend Joseph M. Pernicone ... Washington, D. C., Catholic university of America, 1932. 3 p. l., [ix]-xii, 267 p. 23 cm. (Catholic university of America. Studies in canon law. no. 72) Thesis (J. C. D.)--Catholic university of America. "Biographical note". Bibliography: p. [249]-257. [BX1939.P67P4 1932] 32-21787
1. Prohibited books (Canon law) 2. Index liborum prohibitorum, 3. Catholic church. Codex juris canonici. C. 1384-1405: De Praevia cencura libroum eorumque prohibitione. I. Title.

Prohibition.

MANEVAL, Solomon H. 178.
Prohibition of intoxicating liquors the enemy of church and state; or, The precepts of men setting up the "man of sin." By Solomon H. Maneval... [Canton, O., Roller printing and paper company, printers, c1901] 409 p. 21 x 16 1/2 cm. [HV5183.M3] 3-5790
1. Prohibition. 2. Temperance—Biblical arguments. I. Title.

PENCE, Gilbert Eugene, 1883- 178.50973
Prohibition is wrong, by Gilbert E. Pence ... New Market, Va., The Henkel press, inc. [c1932] 167 p. 23 cm. [HV5088.P4] 32-13328
1. Prohibition. 2. Temperance—Biblical arguments. I. Title.

SMITH, Brooke. 178.50973
Prohibition and the Bible, the evils, the remedy, by Brooke Smith... [Brownwood, Tex., c1932] 207 p. 18 1/2 cm. [HV5089.S615] 32-8554
1. Prohibition. 2. Temperance—Biblical arguments. I. Title.

Prohibition—United States

RUSSELL, Jay Vance, 1879- 178.
Outlawing the Almighty; or, Prohibition carried to the high court of nature and nature's God, by J. Vance Russell. Springfield, Mass., J. J. McCathy, 1923. 4 p. l., 13-120 p. illus. 19 cm. [HV5089.R85] 23-14213
1. Prohibition—U. S. I. Title.

SCOTT, William Rufus, 1886- 178.5
Revolt on mount Sinai; the Puritan retreat from prohibition, by William Rufus Scott. Bookreviewers ed. ... [Pasadena, Calif., Login printing company, 1944] 187 p. 23 1/2 cm. [HV5089.S37] 44-35913
1. Prohibition—U.S. I. Title.

Project method in teaching.

SHAVER, Edwin Leander, 1890- 268.
The project principle in religious education; a manual of theory and practice for church-school leaders, by Erwin L. Shaver ... Chicago, Ill., The University of Chicago press [c1924] xix, 375 p. 18 cm. (Half-title: The University of Chicago publications in religious education ... Principles and methods of religious education) "Suggestions for further study" at end of part of the chapters. "Reference list of additional descriptions": p. 353-354. [BV1534.S45] 24-28982
1. Project method in teaching. 2. Sunday-schools. 3. Religious education. I. Title.

TOWNER, Milton Carsley. 268.
One hundred projects for the church school, by Milton Carsley Towner ... New York, George H. Doran company [c1925] xiii p., 2 l., 17-198 p. plates, fold. tab., diagrs. 19 1/2 cm. Contains bibliographies. [BV1534.T6] 25-7208
1. Project method in teaching. 2. Sunday-schools. I. Title.

Project Test Pattern.

DESPORTES, Elisa L. 254'.6
Congregations in change; a Project Test Pattern book in parish development [by] Elisa L. DesPortes. Foreword by Cynthia C. Wedel. Pref. by Loren B. Mead. New York, Seabury Press [1973] xvi, 201 p. illus. 21 cm. "A Crossroad book." [BV600.2.D49] 73-77768 ISBN 0-8164-2085-8 3.95
1. Project Test Pattern. 2. Church renewal—Case studies. I. Title.

MEAD, Loren B. 262'.001
New hope for congregations; a Project Test Pattern book in parish development [by] Loren B. Mead, with research assistance of Elisa L. DesPortes. Foreword by Reuel L. Howe. New York, Seabury Press [1972] 128 p. 21 cm. (An Original Seabury paperback, SP 78) [BV600.2.M4] 72-80715 ISBN 0-8164-2077-7 2.95
1. Project Test Pattern. 2. Church renewal. I. DesPortes, Elisa L. II. Project Test Pattern. III. Title.

Prometheus.

KERENYI, Karoly, 1897- 292.211
Prometheus: archetypal image of human existence. Tr. from German by Ralph Manheim. Bollingen Found. [dist. New York, Pantheon, c.1963] xxvi, 152p. 16 plates. 27cm. (Bollingen ser., 65. Archetypal images in Greek religion, v.1) Bibl. 63-1080 5.00
1. Prometheus. I. Title. II. Series: Bollingen series, 65 III. Series: Archetypal images in Greek religion, v.1)

KERENYI, Karoly, 1897- 292.211
Prometheus: archetypal image of human existence. Translated from the German by Ralph Manheim. [New York, Bollingen Foundation; distributed by] Pantheon Books [1963] xxvi, 152 p. 16 plates. 27 cm. (Bollingen series, 65. Archetypal images in Greek religion, v. 1) "Translated from Prometheus: die menschliche Existenz in griechischer Deutung ... 1959 ... Earlier version: Prometheus: das griechische Mythologem von der menschlichen Existenz, copyright 1946." Bibliography: p. 135-143. [BL820.P68K43] 63-1080
1. Prometheus. Bollingen series, 65. Archetypal images in Greek religion, v. 1) I. Title. II. Series.

Promise (Christian theology)—History of doctrines.

MORSE, Christopher, 1935- 230
The logic of promise in Moltmann's theology / Christopher Morse. Philadelphia : Fortress Press, c1979. xi, 179 p. ; 24 cm. Based on the author's thesis. Includes bibliographical references and indexes. [BX4827.M6M67] 78-54556 ISBN 0-8006-0523-3 : 11.95
1. Moltmann, Jurgen. 2. Promise (Christian theology)—History of doctrines. I. Title.

Prompt Succor, Our Lady of.

ROBERTO, Brother, 1927- 232.9317
The forgotten Madonna; a story of Our Lady of Prompt Succor. Notre Dame, Ind., Dujarie Press [1959] 143p. illus. 22cm. [BT660.P8R6] 59-2781
1. Prompt Succor, Our Lady of. I. Title.

ROBERTO, Brother, 1927- 232.9317
Our Lady comes to New Orleans. Illus. by Thekla Ofria. Notre Dame, Ind., Dujarie Press [1957] 95p. illus. 24cm. [BT660.P8R62] 59-2745
1. Prompt Succor, Our Lady of. I. Title.

Propers (Liturgy)

CHURCH of England. Book of common prayer. 264.036
The Christian year; the prayer book Collects, with Epistles and Gospels; tr. by J. B. Phillips; notes by H. W. Dobson. New York, Macmillan [1963, c.1961] 311p. diagr. 21cm. 63-953 1.45 pap.,
1. Propers (Liturgy) 2. Bible. N. T. Epistles and Gospels, Liturgical—Commentaries. I. Phillips, John Bertram, 1906- tr. II. Title.

Property—Biblical teaching.

†JOHNSON, Luke Timothy. 226'.4'06
The literary function of possessions in Luke-Acts / by Luke Timothy Johnson. Missoula, Mont. : Published by Scholars Press for the Society of Biblical Literature, c1977. viii, 241 p. ; 22 cm. (Society of Biblical Literature dissertation series ; no. 39 ISSN [0145-2770])oOriginally presented as the author's thesis, Yale, 1976. Bibliography: p. 223-241. [BS2545.P696J63 1977] 77-21055 ISBN 0-89130-200-X pbk. : 6.00
1. Bible. N.T. Luke and Acts—Criticism, interpretation, etc. 2. Property—Biblical teaching. I. Title. II. Series: Society of Biblical Literature. Dissertation series ; no. 39.

Property—Moral and religious aspects—History.

HENGEL, Martin. 261.8'5
Property and riches in the early church : aspects of a social history of early Christianity / Martin Hengel ; translated by John Bowden from the German. 1st American ed. Philadelphia : Fortress Press, 1974. viii, 96 p. ; 22 cm. Translation of Eigentum und Reichtum in der fruhen Kirche. Includes bibliographical references. [BR166.H4513 1974] 75-305658 ISBN 0-8006-1201-9 pbk. : 2.95
1. Property—Moral and religious aspects—History. 2. Wealth, Ethics of—History. 3. Sociology, Christian—Early church, ca. 30-600. I. Title.

Prophecies.

ANDERSON, Wing. 133.3
Seven years that change the world, 1941-1948, by Wing Anderson ... Los Angeles, Calif. [etc.] Kosmon press [1940] xviii, 269 p. illus., diagrs. 22 cm. Bibliography: p. 268-269 [BF1791.A5] 159.9613 41-489
1. Prophecies. I. Title.

ANDERSON, Wing, 1890- 133.3
Prophetic years, 1947-1953, by Wing Anderson ... Los Angeles, Kosmon press [1946] xvii, 234 p. illus. (incl. facsim.) 22 cm. [Full name: Earl Wing Anderson] Bibliography: p. 233-234. [BF1815.A5A3] 47-18417
1. Prophecies. I. Title.

AUCHINCLOSS, William Stuart
The only key to Daniel's prophecies, by W. S. Auchincloss. Philadelphia, 1902. 173 p. front. (tab.) 16 cm. Explanation of prophecies in red. 2-10815
1. Prophecies. 2. Bible. O. T. Daniel.—Criticism, interpretation, etc. I. Title.

BJORNSTAD, James. 133.3'0922
Twentieth century prophecy : Jeanne Dixon, Edgcor Cayce. Minneapolis, Minn., Bethany Fellowship [1969] 151 p. ports. 22 cm. On spine: Jeane Dixon, Edgar Cayce. Includes bibliographical references. [BF1812.U6B59] 73-7529 2.95
1. Dixon, Jeane. 2. Cayce, Edgar, 1877-1945. 3. Prophecies. 4. Twentieth century—Forecasts. I. Title.

BOSWELL, Rolfe. 133.3
Nostradamus speaks, [by] Rolfe Boswell. New York, Thomas Y. Crowell company, 1941. 5 p. l., 381 p. front. 22 1/2 cm. [BF1815.N8B55] [159.9613] 41-24921
1. Prophecies. I. Notredame, Michel de, 1508-1566. Les Propheties. II. Title.

BOSWELL, Rolfe. 133.3
Nostradamus speaks [by] Rolfe Boswell. New York, Thomas Y. Crowell company, 1943. 5 p. l., 381 p. front. 21 1/2 cm. "Third printing, 1943." Bibliography: p. 365. [BF1815.N8B55 1943] 43-9457
1. Prophecies. I. Notredame, Michel de, 1503-1566. Lee prophecies. II. Title.

BOSWELL, Rolfe. 133.3
Prophets and portents; seven seers foretell Hitler's doom [by] Rolfe Boswell. New York, Thomas Y. Crowell company [1942] 3 p. l., 154 p. 19 1/2 cm. [BF1785.B6] 159.9613 42-24209
1. Hitler, Adolf, 1889- 2. Prophecies. I. Title.

BRIEFS on prophetic themes. 224.
By a member of the Boston bar ... Boston, E.P. Dutton & company; New York, Hurd & Houghton, 1864. 112 p. 19 cm. [BS1198.B8 1864] 18-5836
I. A member of the Boston bar.
Contents omitted.

BRIEFS on prophetic themes; 224.
with an introductory chapter on the parable of the leaven, not before published. By a member of the Boston bar. 2d ed.-- rev. and enl. Boston, E.P. Dutton & company; New York, Hurd & Houghton, 1866. 168 p. 20 cm. [BS1198.B8 1866] 18-5837
I. A member of the Boston bar.
Contents omitted.

CARTER, Mary Ellen. 133.3'2
Edgar Cayce on prophecy; under the editorship of Hugh Lynn Cayce. [1st ed.] New York, Hawthorn Books [1968] 207 p. 22 cm. [BF1815.C28C3 1968b] 68-28124 4.95
1. Prophecies. I. Cayce, Edgar, 1877-1945.

COLLIER, Robert Gordon. 133.3
Something to hope for, by Robert Gordon Collier; including What old Nostradamus predicted that came true, and what he said will happen, by the Grand Duchess Marie of Russia, and The date of Hitler's fall, by Pierre van Passen ... New York, N.Y., The Book of gold [1942] xvi, 229 p. incl. front., illus. 21 cm. [BF1785.C56] [159.9613] 42-23300
1. Prophecies. I. Title.

CONNOR, Edward. 220.15
Prophecy for today. Fresno, Calif., Academy Library Guild, 1956. 110p. 21cm. [BX961] 57-524
1. Prophecies. I. Title.

COURNOS, John, 1881- ed. 133.3
A book of prophecy, from the Egyptians to Hitler, edited with an introduction by John Cournos. Decorations by John C. Wonsetler. New York, C. Scribner's sons, 1942. xi p., 1 l., 274 p. illus. 21 cm. [BF1785.C6] 159.9613 42-9210
1. Prophecies. I. Title.

CRISWELL, Jeron. 133.3'2
Your next ten years; Criswell predicts, by Criswell. Illustrated by Lewis N. Schilling, Jr. [1st ed.] Anderson, S.C., Droke House [1969] 128 p. illus. 24 cm. [CB161.C7] 72-79399 3.95
1. Prophecies. I. Title.

DIXON, Jeane. 232
The call to glory; Jeane Dixon speaks of Jesus. New York, Morrow, 1972 [c1971] 192 p. 22 cm. [BF1283.D48A53] 78-187805 4.95
1. Jesus Christ—Person and offices. 2. Prophecies. I. Title.

[FINDLING, Joseph] 1892- 133.3
When? Thy kingdom come. A book of revelation, when the impossible of today, will become a reality of tomorrow. By The Unknown [pseud.] New York, N.Y., Master age publishing company, 1933. 105 p., 2 l. 21 1/2 cm. Illustrated t.-p. [BF1815.F5A4] (159.9613) 33-28778
1. Prophecies. 2. Second advent. I. Title.

FORMAN, Henry James, 1879- 133.3
The story of prophecy, ir. the life of mankind from early times to the present day, by Henry James Forman. New York, Toronto, Farrar & Rinehart, incorporated, [c1936] viii p. 3 l., 3-347 p. front., plates., ports., facsim, diagr., 22 cm. Bibliography: p. 335-338. [BF1791.F6] [[159.9613]] 36-18269
1. Prophecies. I. Title.

GREENHOUSE, Herbert B. 133.3
Premonitions: a leap into the future. New York, Warner Paperback Lib. [1973, c.1971] 302 p. 18 cm. [BF1791.G69] ISBN 0-446-76016-1 pap., 1.25
1. Prophecies. I. Title.

GRIMMER, C A.
The coming catastrophe, being a prediction by Prof. C. A. Grimmer, (astrologer) of the terrible misfortunes, woes and miseries threatened to mankind by the malific conjunction now ruling the heavens; also, opinions from Doctor Cummings, Magus Biskerstaff, Sidney Brooks and others. Cambridge, Mass., Tribune publishing company, 1881. 96 p. 18 cm. First published in the Cambridge tribune, Sept. 24, 1880, and reprinted in the issue of Nov. 5, 1880. [BF1812.U6G8] 11-14515
1. Prophecies. 2. Astrology. I. Title.

HALPERN, Herman. 133.322
I predict, by Herman Halpern ... Newark, N.J., The Buckingham press [c1935] 255, [1] p. front. (port.) facsims. (1 fold.) diagrs. 23 1/2 cm. "A series of strange visitations ... have caused ... [the author] to predict many unusual occurrences which have come true during the past two years."--p. 9. [BF1815.H28A4] (159.961322) 36-721
1. Prophecies. 2. Spiritualism. I. Title.

JOYCE, Gilbert Cunningham.
The inspiration of prophecy: an essay in the psychology of revelation. By G. C. Joyce ... London, New York [etc.] H. Frowde, 1910. 4 p. l., 195 p. 21 cm. (Half-title: The S. Deinol's series. i) "This little book contains the substance of lectures delivered to the memoirs of the Society of sacred study in the dioceses of S. Asaph and Bangor."--Pref. A 11
1. Prophecies. 2. Psychology and religion. I. Title.

KING, Bruce. 133.3
Everything you want to know about nature's mysteries, the prophets, Nostradamus, tea leaf readings, herbs, candle burning, by Zolar. New York, Arco Pub. Co. [1973, c1972] 203 p. 18 cm. On spine: Nature's mysteries, the prophets, Nostradamus. [BF1791.K56] 72-3137 ISBN 0-668-02661-8 0.95 (pbk.)
1. Notredame, Michel de, 1503-1566. 2. Prophecies. 3. Fortune-telling by tea leaves. 4. Herbs (in religion, folk-lore, etc.) 5. Candles (in religion, folk-lore, etc.) I. Title. II. Title: Nature's mysteries, the prophets, Nostradamus.

KIRBAN, Salem. 133.3'2
20 reasons why this present earth may not last another 20 years. Huntingdon Valley, Pa., 1973. 191 p. illus. 22 cm. [BF1791.K57] 72-78026 ISBN 0-912582-07-3 2.95 (pbk.)
1. Prophecies. I. Title.

LEWINSOHN, Richard, 1894- 133.3
Science, prophecy, and prediction; man's efforts to foretell the future, from Babylon to Wall Street. Translated by Arnold J. Pomerans. New York, Harper [1961] 318 p. illus. 22 cm. Translation of Die Enthullung der Zukunft. [BF1793.L473] 61-6435
1. Prophecies. I. Title.

LUCAS, DeWitt Bannister, 1876- ed. 133.93
Thy kingdom come, edited by DeWitt B. Lucas ... [Atascadero, Calif., Beacon light publishers, 1940] 2 p l., 108 p., 1 l. 1 illus. 23 cm. "These letters were received through the medium of automatic writing.--Pref. "First printing September, 1940: second printing October, 1940." [BF1311.P75L8] 159.96173 41-10077
1. Prophecies. 2. Spiritualism. I. Title.

LUSSON, M., 1938- 133.3'2
The beginning or the end, where are we

going? / By the Lusson twins. Virginia Beach : Donning, c1975. 119 p. : ill. ; 22 cm. [BF1815.L8L87] 75-22487 ISBN 0-915442-02-7 : 5.95
1. Prophecies. I. Lusson, D., 1938- joint author. II. The Lusson twins. III. Title.

MACKENZIE, Chloris. 236.9
The popes of Saint Malachy's prophecy, by Chloris Mackenzie. New York, Fortuny's [c1941] 80 p. 19 cm. "First edition." Bibliography: p. 75. [BT875.M38] 41-20571
1. Malachy O'Morgair, Saint, 1094?-1148, supposed author. Prophetia de futuris pontificibus romanis. 2. Prophecies. 3. Popes. I. Title.

MORRIS, Alvin Marion, 1861-
The prophecies unveiled; or, Prophecy a divine system, by A. M. Morris ... Winfield, Kans., The Courier press, 1914. xvi, 496 p. incl. front. (port.) 3 diagr. 20 cm. $1.50 15-3978
I. Title.

NOTREDAME, Michel de, 1503- 1566. 133.3
The complete prophecies of Nostradamus, tr., ed. and interpreted by Henry C. Roberts. [2d ed.] N[ew] Y[ork] C[ity] Nostradamus, inc. [1949] vi, 350 p. port. 22 cm. Each French stanza in accompanied by English translation and comment by the editor. [BF1815.N8A3 1949] 49-9029
1. Prophecies. I. Roberts, Henry C., 1889- ed. and tr. II. Title.

NOTREDAME, Michel de, 1503- 1566. 133.3
The complete prophecies of Nostradamus, translated, edited and interpreted by Henry C. Roberts. New York, Crown publishers [1947] vi, 350 p. 22 cm. Each French stanza is accompanied by English translation and comment by the editor. [BF1815.N8A3 1947] 47-1275
1. Prophecies. I. Roberts, Henry C., ed. and tr. II. Title.

NOTREDAME, Michel de, 1503- 1566. 133.3
Nostradamus: life and literature. Including all the Prophecies in French and English, with complete notes and indexes. A critical biography of Nostradamus, his will, and personal letters. Bibl. of Nostradamus and his commentators. A review of theories about him, his method and other supplementary material. By Edgar Leoni. New York, Exposition [c.1961] 823p. illus. (Exposition-Univ. bk.) 61-15635 10.00
1. Prophecies. 2. Astrology. I. Leoni, Edgar. II. Title.

NOTREDAME, Michel de, 1503- 1566. 133.3
Nostradamus: life and literature. Including all the Prophecies in French and English, with complete notes and indexes. A critical biography of Nostradamus, his will, and personal letters. Bibliography of Nostradamus and his commentators. A review of theories about him, his method and other supplementary material. By Edgar Leoni. [1st ed.] New York. Exposition Press [1961] 823p. illus. 24cm. (An Exposition-University book) [BF1815.N8A213] 61-15635
1. Prophecies. 2. Astrology. I. Leoni, Edgar. II. Title.

NOTREDAME, Michel de, 1503- 1566. 133.3
Nostradamus sees all; detailed predictions regarding America, Hitler, Mussolini, Franco, Petain, Stalin, Churchill, the Jews, etc., with actual dates of forth coming events of importance as Europe's greatest prophet gives them [by] Andre Lamont. From 1555 to 1999 ... Philadelphia, W. Foulsham co. [c1942] vi p., 2 l., 3-341 p. front., plates, ports. 19 1/2 cm. [BF1815.N8A3 1942] [(159.9613)] 42-1939
1. Prophecies. I. Lamont, Andre, ed. and tr. II. Title. III. Title: Translation of Les prophetes.

NOTREDAME, Michel de, 1503- 1566. 133.3
Nostradamus sees all; detailed predictions regarding America, Hitler, Mussolini, Franco, Petain, Stalin, Churchill, the Jews, etc., with actual dates of forthcoming events of importance as Europe's greatest prophet gives them [by] Andre Lamont. From 1555 to 3797 ... 3d ed., rev. and enl. Philadelphia, W. Foulsham co. [1944] xiii, 363 p. front., plates, ports. 19 1/2 cm. "A practical bibliography on Nostradamus": p. 363. [BF1815.N8A3 1944] 44-10009
1. Prophecies. I. Lamont, Andre, ed. and tr. II. Title.

NOTREDAME, Michel de, 1503- 1566. 133.3
Nostradamus sees all; detailed predictions regarding America, Hitler, Mussolini, Franco, Petain, Stalin, Churchill, the Jews, etc., with actual dates of forthcoming events of importance as Europe's greatest prophet gives them [by] Andre Lamont. From 1555 to 1999 ... Philadelphia, W. Foulsham co. [c1942] vi p., 2 l., 3-341 p. front., plates, ports. 20 cm. [BF1815.N8A3 1942] 159.9613 42-1939
1. Prophecies. I. Lamont, Andre, ed. and tr. II. Title. III. Title: Translation of Les propheties.

*NOTRE DAME, Michel de, 1503-1566. 133.3
Prophecies on world events by Nostradamus translated and interpreted by Stewart Robb. New York, Ace Books, [1975 c1961] 158 p., 18 cm. [BF1815] 1.25 (pbk.)
1. Prophecies. I. Title.

O'KEARNEY, Nicholas. 133.3
The prophecies of SS. Columbkille, Maeltamlacht, Ultan, Seadhna, Coireall, Bearcan, Malachy, &c., together with the prophetic collectanea, or gleanings of several writers who have preserved portions of the now lost prophecies of our saints, with literal translation and notes. By Nicholas O'Kearney ... Reprinted 1939 from the original plates coast in the year 1858 [i.e. 1857. New York, 1939] 2 p. l., vii-xxxviii, [21]-144 p. 18 1/2 cm. [BF1785.O35 1939] 44-28666
1. Prophecies. I. Title.

O'KEARNEY, Nicholas. 133.3
The prophecies of SS, Columbkille, Macltamalacht, Ultan, Seadhna, Coireall, Bearean, Malachy, &c., together with the prophetic collectanea, or gleanings of several writers who have preserved portions of the now lost prophecies of our saints, with literal translation and notes. By Nicholas O'Kearney ... Reprinted 1939 from the original plates cast in the year 1858. [New York, 1939] 2 p. l., vii-xxxviii, [21]-144 p. 18 1/2 cm. [BF1785.O35 1939] 44-28666
1. Prophecies. I. Title.

PARACELSUS, 1493-1541. 133'.092'4
The prophecies of Paracelsus; occult symbols and magic figures with esoteric explanations, by Theophrastus Paracelsus of Hohenheim, and The life and teachings of Paracelsus, by Franz Hartmann. Introd. by Paul M. Allen. Blauvelt, N.Y., Rudolf Steiner Publications [1973] 86, xiii, 220 p. illus. 18 cm. (Steinerbooks, 1733) The prophecies of Paracelsus is a translation of Prognosticatio eximii doctoris Theophrasti Paracelsi. The life and teachings of Paracelsus is a reprint of the 1887 ed. published by G. Redway, London, under title: The life of Philippus Theophrastus, Bombast of Hohenheim known by the name Paracelsus. [BF1598.P19P7613] 72-81591 2.45 (pbk.)
1. Paracelsus, 1493-1541. 2. Prophecies. 3. Occult sciences. I. Hartmann, Franz, d. 1912. The life of Philippus Theophrastus, Bombast of Hohenheim. 1973. II. Title.

PETTINGILL, William Leroy, 1866- 230
God's prophecies for plain people [by] William L. Pettingill. Philadelphia, Pa., The Philadelphia school of the Bible [c1923] 240 p. 19 cm. "This book consists of a series of articles written for the Sunday school times and appearing in that periodical during 1919." [BT875.P4] 23-16787
I. Title.

PETTINGILL, William Leroy, 1866- 230
God's prophecies for plain people [by] William L. Pettingill. Philadelphia, Pa., The Philadelphia school of the Bible [c1923] 240 p. 19 cm. "This book consists of a series of articles written for the Sunday school times and appearing in that periodical during 1919." [BT875.P4] 23-16787
I. Title.

PRIEDITIS, Arthur, 1909- 133.3'2
The fate of the nations [by] Arthur Prieditis. [1st ed.] Saint Paul, Llewellyn Publications, 1974 [i.e. 1975] xiii, 428 p. 24 cm. Bibliography: p. 425-428. [BF1815.N8P7] 73-20450 ISBN 0-87542-624-7
1. Notredame, Michel de, 1503-1566. 2. Prophecies. I. Title.

PRIEDITIS, Arthur A., 1909- 133.3'2
The fate of the nations [by] Arthur A. Prieditis. [1st ed.] Saint Paul, Minn., Llewellyn Publications, 1973. p. [BF1815.N8P7] 73-20450 ISBN 0-87542-624-7 12.95
1. Notredame, Michel de, 1503-1566. 2. Prophecies. I. Title.

ROBB, Stewart. 133.3
Letters on Nostradamus and miscellaneous writings. [New York, Maranatha Publishers, 1945?] 128 p. 19 cm. [AC8.R532] 50-36977
1. Notredame, Michel de, 1506-1566. 2. Prophecies. I. Title.

ROBB, Stewart 133.5
Prophecies on world events by Nostradamus Tr. and interpreted by Stewart Robb [Kew Gardens] New York, Box 142, Oracle Pr., [c.1961] 144p. illus. p1.00 pap., 61-2912
1. Notredame, Michel de, 1503-1566. 2. Prophecies. I. Title.

ROBB, Stewart 133.5
Prophecies on world events by Nostradamus. Tr., interpreted by Stewart Robb. New York, Liveright [1964, c.1961] 144p. illus. 21cm. 1.95 pap.,
1. Notredame, Michel de, 1503-1566. 2. Prophecies. I. Title.

*ROBB, Stewart. 133.32
Prophecies on world events by Nostradamus, tr., interpreted by Stewart Robb. New York, Ace [1968, c. 1961] 158p. 18cm. (Ace star, H99) .60 pap.,
1. Prophecies. I. Nostradamus, 1503-1566. II. Title. III. Title: Prophecies.

SEAT, W H.
The Confederate States of America in prophecy. By the Rev. W. H. Seat ... Nashville, Tenn., Printed for the author, at the Southern Methodist publishing house, 1861. vi, 7-144 p. 16 cm. An attempt to apply the prophecies in the Book of Daniel to the confederacy. [E650.S44] 8-1152
1. Prophecies. I. Title.

SMITH, Robert William, 1884- comp. 236
The "last days"; a compilation [!] of prophecies pertinent to the present, gathered from secular and religious sources embracing George Washington's vision and others of a prophetic nature. With excerpts from prophetic writings of Joseph Smith, jr., Floyd Gibbons, Gus McKey, Christabel Pankhurst, and others ... Compiled by Robert W. Smith and Elisabeth A. Smith. [Salt Lake City, Pyramid press, 1931] 4 p. l., [3]-82 p. 20 cm. On cover: Scriptural and secular prophecy. Later editions published under title: Scriptural and secular prophecies pertaining to the last days. [BT875.S58 1931] 44-33893
1. Prophecies. 2. Bible—Prophecies. 3. Mormons and Mormonism—Doctrinal and controversial works. I. Smith, Elisabeth Augusta (Sauer) 1878- joint comp. II. Title. III. Title: The last days.

SMITH, Robert William, 1884- comp. 236
Scriptural and secular prophecies pertaining to the last days, comp. from prophetic utterances and writings of noted church leaders, statesmen, scientists, world famous writers, philosophers, commentators, etc. ... Comp. by Robert W. Smith and Elisabeth A. Smith. 10th ed., rev. and enl. [Salt Lake City? 1948] 296 p. 18 cm. "First issued in October, 1931 [under title: The 'last days]'" Cover title: The last days. [BT875.S58 1948] 48-4692
1. Prophecies. 2. Bible—Prophecies. 3. Mormons and Mormonism—Doctrinal and controversial works. I. Smith, Elisabeth Augusta (Sauer) 1878- joint comp. II. Title. III. Title: The last days.

SMITH, Robert William, 1884- comp. 236
...Scriptural and secular prophecies pertaining to the "last days," compiled from prophetic utterances and writings ascribed to famous men of former days...and, prominent men and women of today...compiled by Robert W. Smith and Elisabeth A. Smith. [Salt Lake City, Pyramid press, c1932] 5 p. l., [3]-128, [1] p. 20 cm. "Second edition, containing part II." [BT875.S58 1932] 32-18847
1. Prophecies. 2. Bible—Prophecies. 3. Mormons and Mormonism—Doctrinal and controversial works. I. Smith, Mrs. Elisabeth Augusta (Sauer) 1878- joint comp. II. Title.

SMITH, Robert William, 1884- comp. 236
...Scriptural and secular prophecies pertaining to the last days, compiled from prophetic utterances and writings ascribed to famous men of former days...and prominent men and women of today... compiled by Robert W. Smith and Elisabeth A. Smith. [Salt Lake City, Pyramid press, c1933] 204, [5] p. illus. 16 1/2 cm. "Third edition." [BT875.S58 1933] 33-33084
1. Prophecies. 2. Bible—Prophecies. 3. Mormons and Mormonism—Doctrinal and controversial works. I. Smith, Mrs. Elisabeth Augusta (Sauer) 1878- joint comp. II. Title.

SMITH, Robert William, 1884- comp. 236
...Scriptural and secular prophecies pertaining to the last days, compiled from prophetic utterances and writings of: George Washington, Joseph Smith, Brigham Young...and many others, compiled by Robert W. Smith and Elisabeth A. Smith. [Salt Lake City, Pyramid press, c1940] 3-223 p. 17 cm. "Fourth edition, October, 1940, revised and condensed." [BT875.S58 1940] 41-624
1. Prophecies. 2. Bible—Prophecies. 3. Mormons and Mormonism—Doctrinal and controversial works. I. Smith, Mrs. Elisabeth Augusta (Sauer) 1878- joint comp. II. Title.

SMITH, Robert William, 1884- comp. 236
... Scriptural and secular prophecies pertaining to the last days, compiled from prophetic utterances and writings of: George Washington, Joseph Smith, Brigham Young ... and many others, compiled by Robert W. Smith and Elisabeth A. Smith. [5th ed., December, 1942, rev. and enl.] [Salt Lake City, Pyramid press, 1943] 286 p. 17 1/2 cm. At head of title: ... First issued in October, 1931. Cover-title: The last days. [BT875.S58 1943] 43-2919
1. Prophecies. 2. Bible—Prophecies. 3. Mormons and Mormonism—Doctrinal and controversial works. I. Smith, Elisabeth Augusta (Sauer) 1878- joint comp. II. Title. III. Title: The last days.

SMITH, Robert William, 1884- comp. 236
... Scriptural and secular prophecies pertaining to the last days, compiled from prophetic utterances and writings of: George Washington, Joseph Smith, Brigham Young ... and many others, compiled by Robert W. Smith and Elisabeth A. Smith. [6th ed., July, 1943, rev. and enl.] [Salt Lake City, Pyramid press, 1943] 301 p. 20 cm. At head of title: ... First issued in October, 1931. Cover-title: The last days. [BT875.S58 1943 a] 43-17200
1. Prophecies. 2. Bible—Prophecies. 3. Mormons and Mormonism—Doctrinal and controversial works. I. Smith, Elisabeth Augusta (Sauer) 1878- joint comp. II. Title. III. Title: The last days.

SMITH, Robert William, 1884- comp. 236
... Scriptural and secular prophecies pertaining to the last days, compiled from prophetic utterances and writings of noted church leaders, statesmen, scientists, world famous writers, philosophers, commentators, etc. ... Compiled by Robert W. Smith and Elisabeth A. Smith. [8th ed., rev. and enl.] [Salt Lake City, Pyramid press, 1945] 288 p. 16 1/2 cm. At head of title: ... First issued in October, 1931

[under title: The "last days"] Cover-title: The last days. [BT875.S58 1945] 45-21592
1. Prophecies. 2. Bible—Prophecies. 3. Mormons and Mormonism—Doctrinal and controversial works. I. Smith, Elisabeth Augusta (Sauer) 1878- joint comp. II. Title. III. Title: The last days.

SMITH, Robert William, 1884- comp. 236
... Scriptural and secular prophecies pertaining to the last days, compiled from prophetic utterances and writings of noted church leaders, statesmen, scientists, world famous writers, philosophers, commentators, etc. ... Compiled by Robert W. Smith and Elisabeth A. Smith. [9th ed., rev. and enl.] [Salt Lake City, Printed by Pyramid press, 1947] 288 p. 16 1/2 cm. At head of title: ... First issued in October, 1931 [under title: The "last days"] Cover-title: The last days. [BT875.S58 1947] 47-18684
1. Prophecies. 2. Bible—Prophecies. 3. Mormons and Mormonism—Doctrinal and controversial works. I. Smith, Elisabeth Augusta (Sauer) 1878- joint comp. II. Title. III. Title: The last days.

SOLARYK, Sam 133.3
Fourth dimensional man; in search of prophecy. New York, Pageant Press [c.1959] 103p. 21cm. 60-295 2.50
I. Title.

SOLARYK, Sam, 1928- 133.3
Fourth dimensional man; in search of prophecy. [1st ed.] New York, Pageant Press [1960, c1959] 103 p. 21 cm. [BF1999.S57] 60-295
I. Title.

STEBBINS, Charles Maurice, 1871- 204
Past and future; an interpretation and a prophecy, by Charles M. Stebbins. Brooklyn, N. Y., Stebbins and company [c1928] vi p. 1 l., 9-154 p. 20 cm. "The book ... aims to give an interpretation of certain significant prophecies of the Bible."--Pref. [BR126.S78] 28-22161
I. Title.

STEPHENS, Kenneth D., 1919- comp. 289.3'3
So great a cause! A surprising new look at the Latter Day Saints, selected from sacred scriptures, including those of the Latter-day Saints, by Kenneth D. Stephens. [Healdsburg, Calif., Naturegraph Publishers, 1973] 215 p. illus. (part col.) 22 cm. Bibliography: p. [212]-215. [BX8635.2.S67 1973] 72-13406 ISBN 0-87961-007-7 6.50
1. Church of Jesus Christ of Latter-Day Saints—Doctrinal and controversial works. 2. Prophecies. I. Title.
pap. 3.50; ISBN 0-87961-006-9.

STRAUB, Jacob. 133.
Prophecy and prophets; or, The laws of inspiration and their phenomena. By Jacob Straub ... Chicago, S.W. Straub & co., 1888. viii,9-188 p. 20 cm. [BF1791.S8] 21-11305
I. Title.

TAYLOR, Barnard Cook, 1850- 221.
Prophecy and the prophets, by Barnard C. Taylor ... Philadelphia, Boston [etc.] The Judson press [c1923] 6 p. l., 3-143 p. 20 cm. [BS1505.T3] 23-17835
I. Title.

VAUGHAN, Alan. 133.3'2
Patterns of prophecy. New York, Hawthorn Books [1973] xii, 244 p. 22 cm. Includes bibliographical references. [BF1791.V38 1973] 72-11219 7.95
1. Prophecies. I. Title.

VOLDBEN, A. 133.32
After Nostradamus [by] A. Voldben. Translated from the Italian by Gavin Gibbons Secaucus, N.J., Citadel Press, 1974 xiii., 183 p. 22 cm. Bibliography: 184-186 [BF1815.N8V64] 74-80821 ISBN 0-8065-0431-5 6.95
1. Notredame, Michel de, 1503-1566. 2. Prophecies. I. Title.

WILKERSON, David R. 236'.9
The vision / David Wilkerson. New York : Pillar Books, 1975, c1974. 143 p. ; 18 cm. [BV5091.R4W54] 73-21088 ISBN 0-89129-088-5 pbk. : 1.50
1. Bible—Prophecies. 2. Prophecies. 3. Visions. I. Title.

*YOGANANDA, Paramahansa. 133.3
The road ahead. World prophecies by the great master, Paramahansa Yogananda. Edited with commentary by his disciple Swami Kriyananda. Nevada City, Calif., Ananda Publications [1973] 72 p., 14 cm. [BF1783] 1.25 (pbk.)
1. Prophecies. I. Title.

Prophecies (Occult sciences.)

AYLSWORTH, William Prince, 1844-
The growing miracle; a practical study of Hebrew prophecy, by William Prince Aylsworth ... Bethany, Neb., Reporter publishing company, 1911. 2 p. l., vii-xi, 222 p. 20 cm. 11-23066 1.00
I. Title.

BRIAN, Denis. 133.3'092'4
Jeane Dixon : the witnesses / Denis Brian. 1st ed. Garden City, N.Y. : Doubleday, 1976. 216 p. ; 22 cm. Bibliography: p. [213]-216. [BF1815.D57B74] 75-21212 ISBN 0-385-11243-2 : 6.95
1. Dixon, Jeane. 2. Prophecies (Occult sciences)

BRIAN, Dennis. 133.3'092'4
Jeane Dixon : the witness / [by]Denis Brian New York : Warner Books, 1977c1976 223p. ; 18 cm. Bibliography;p.220-223. [BF1815.D57B74] ISBN 0-446-89145-2 pbk. : 1.95
1. Dixon, Jeane. 2. Prophecies (Occult sciences) I. Title.
L.C. card no. for 1976 Doubleday ed.:75-21212

CARTER, Mary Ellen. 133.3'2
Edgar Cayce on prophecy. Under the editorship of Hugh Lynn Cayce. New York, Paperback Library [1968] 207 p. 18 cm. [BF1815.C28C3] 68-5982 0.75
1. Prophecies (Occult sciences) I. Cayce, Edgar, 1877-1945. II. Title.

CORRALL, Alice Enid, 1916- 133.3'09
They foresaw the future; the story of fulfilled prophecy [by] Justine Glass. [1st American ed.] New York, Putnam [1969] 256 p. 22 cm. [BF1791.C63 1969] 74-85286 5.95
1. Prophecies (Occult sciences) 2. Prophets. I. Title.

CRISWELL, Jeron. 133.3
Criswell's forbidden predictions; based on Nostradamus and the Tarot, by Criswell. [1st ed.] Atlanta, Droke House/Hallux [1972] 128 p. illus. 22 cm. [BF1815.N8C75] 72-83125 ISBN 0-8375-6769-6 4.95
1. Notredame, Michel de, 1503-1566. 2. Prophecies (Occult sciences) 3. Tarot. I. Title. II. Title: Forbidden reflections.

DELOUISE, Joseph. 133.3'2'0924 B
Psychic mission [by] Joseph DeLouise [with] Tom Valentine. Chicago, H. Regnery Co. [1971] ix, 224 p. 22 cm. [BF1791.D4] 75-143842 5.95
1. Prophecies (Occult sciences) 2. Clairvoyance. I. Valentine, Tom. II. Title.

DIXON, Jeane. 133.3'0924 B
Jeane Dixon: my life and prophecies; her own story as told to Rene Noorbergen. Boston, G. K. Hall, 1971 [c1969] 373 p. 25 cm. Large print ed. [BF1283.D48A3 1971] 70-38008 ISBN 0-8161-6004-X 7.95
1. Prophecies (Occult sciences) I. Noorbergen, Rene. II. Title.

DIXON, Jeane. 133.3'0924
Jeane Dixon: my life and prophecies; her own story as told to Rene Noorbergen. New York, W. Morrow, 1969. 219 p. 22 cm. [BF1283.D48A3] 70-94472 5.95
1. Prophecies (Occult sciences) I. Noorbergen, Rene. II. Title.

EBON, Martin. 133.8'4
Prophecy in our time. [New York] New American Library [1968] 238 p. 22 cm. Bibliography: p. 229-232. [BF1791.E2] 68-17055
1. Prophecies (Occult sciences) 2. Visions. I. Title.

EDELSON, Edward, 1932- 133.3
The book of prophecy. [1st ed.] Garden City, N.Y., Doubleday, 1974. 133 p. illus. 25 cm. [BF1791.E3] 73-22050 ISBN 0-385-01077-X 4.95
1. Prophecies (Occult sciences) I. Title.

FESTINGER, Leon, 1919- 133.3
When prophecy fails, by Leon Festinger, Henry W. Riecken and Stanley Schacter. Minneapolis, University of Minnesota Press [1956] vii, 256 p. 23 cm. Bibliographical references included in "Notes to chapter 1" (p. 253-254) [BF1809.F4] 56-11611
1. Prophecies (Occult sciences) I. Title.

FISHER, Joe. 133.3
Predictions / by Joe Fisher ; with ill. compiled by Peter Commins. New York : Van Nostrand Reinhold, c1980. 224 p. : ill. ; 24 cm. "A Jonathan-James book." Bibliography: p. 219-222. [BF1791.F5] 80-11167 ISBN 0-442-23375-2 : 12.95
1. Prophecies (Occult sciences) 2. Prophets. 3. Forecasting. I. Title.

GARDNER, Jeanne, 1930- 133.3'2'0924 B
A grain of mustard, by Jeanne Gardner, as told to Beatrice Moore. New York, Trident Press [1969] 189 p. 21 cm. [BF1815.G32A3] 72-92362 ISBN 0-671-27042-7 4.95
1. Prophecies (Occult sciences) I. Moore, Beatrice. II. Title.

GILLEN, Jack. 133.5
Jack Gillen predicts. 1st ed. Hollywood, Fla. : Grand Trine Publications, 1975- v. : diagrs. ; 22 cm. Contents.Contents.—v. 1. Thru 1980. [BF1791.G54] 75-2887 ISBN 0-915532-00-X : 9.95 (v. 1)
1. Prophecies (Occult sciences) 2. Astrology. I. Title.

GREENHOUSE, Herbert B. 133.3
Premonitions: a leap into the future, by Herbert B. Greenhouse. [New York] B. Geis Associates [1972, c1971] xiii, 327 p. 22 cm. [BF1791.G69] 74-134215 6.95
1. Prophecies (Occult sciences) I. Title.

HALL, Angus. 133.3
Signs of things to come / Angus Hall. Garden City, N.Y. : Doubleday, [1975] p. cm. [BF1791.H3 1975] 75-16747 7.95
1. Prophecies (Occult sciences) I. Title.

HATCH, Arthur Elmer, 1862-
A handbook of prophecy, by A. E. Hatch... Mendota, Ill., The Western advent Christian publication association, 1913. 289 p. front. (port.) 20 cm. 13-12603 1.00.
I. Title.

HOLZER, Hans W., 1920- 133.3'2
Predictions: fact or fallacy? By Hans Holzer. [1st ed.] New York, Hawthorn Books [1968] 191 p. 22 cm. [BF1791.H6] 68-14393
1. Prophecies (Occult sciences) I. Title.

JAMES, Paul, 1922- 133.3'2
California superquake, 1975-77? : Scientists, Cayce, psychics speak / Paul James ; foreword by Gina Cerminara. 1st ed. Hicksville, N.Y. : Exposition Press, [1974] xxxviii, 294 p., [4] leaves of plates : ill. ; 21 cm. Includes index. Bibliography: p. 277-286. [BF1812.U6J35] 75-301373 ISBN 0-682-48041-X : 10.00
1. Prophecies (Occult sciences) 2. Earthquakes—California—Miscellanea. I. Title.

LOGAN, Daniel, 1936- 133.3'2
The anatomy of prophecy / by Daniel Logan. Englewood Cliffs, N.J. : Prentice-Hall, [1975] viii, 172 p. ; 22 cm. Includes index. Bibliography: p. 165-166. [BF1791.L63] 74-23151 ISBN 0-13-035188-1 : 6.95
1. Prophecies (Occult sciences) I. Title.

MASSON, Francois, 1920- 133.3
The end of our era / by Francois Masson ; translated by David Michael Steinberg. Norfolk, Va. : Donning, c1982. p. cm. Translation of: Notre fin de siecle. [BF1791.M37 1982] 19 82-9725 ISBN 0-89865-202-2 (pbk.) : 6.95
1. Prophecies (Occult sciences) I. [Notre fin de siecle.] English II. Title.

NOTREDAME, Michel de, 1503-1566. 133.3
The prophesies of Nostradamus : including the "Preface to my son" and the "Epistle to Henry II" / illustrated by Shari de Miskey. Avenel 1980 ed. New York : Avenel Books ; distributed by Crown Publishers, [1980], c1975. 90 p. : ill. ; 19 cm. [BF1815.N8A3 1980] 79-24358 ISBN 0-517-30984-X : 2.49
1. Prophecies (Occult sciences) I. Title.

NOTREDAME, Michel de, 1503-1566. 133.3
The complete prophecies of Nostradamus. Translated, edited and interpreted by Henry C. Roberts. New York, Nostradamus, inc. [1962] vi, 350 p. port. 22 cm. Each French stanza is accompanied by English translation and comment by the editor. [BF1815.N8A3 1962] 62-5700
1. Prophecies (Occult sciences) I. Roberts, Henry C., 1889- ed. and tr.

ROBB, Stewart. 133.3
Strange prophecies that came true. New York, Ace Books [1967] 189 p. 18 cm. (Ace star book, K-228) [BF1791.R6] 67-66344
1. Prophecies (Occult sciences) I. Title.

SALTMARSH, Herbert Francis, 1881- 133.8'6
Foreknowledge / H. F. Saltmarsh. New York : Arno Press, 1975. p. cm. (Perspectives in psychical research) Reprint of the 1938 ed. published by G. Bell, London, in series: Psychical experiences. [BF1791.S24 1975] 75-7401 ISBN 0-405-06990-1 : 8.00
1. Prophecies (Occult sciences) I. Title. II. Series. III. Series: Psychical experiences.

SAXON, Kurt. 133.3'2
Keeping score on modern prophets. [1st ed. Eureka, Calif., Atlan Formularies, 1974] vi, 136 p. illus. 21 cm. [BF1791.S29] 74-176316
1. Prophecies (Occult sciences) I. Title.

SPICER, William Ambrose, 1866-
The hand of God in history; notes on important eras of fulfilling prophecy, by William A. Spicer ... Washington, D.C., South Bend, Ind. [etc.] Review and herald publishing assn. [c1913] 2 p. l., 7-246 p. illus. (incl. ports.) 19 cm. $0.50. 13-12602
I. Title.

THURSTON, Mark A. 133.8
Visions and prophecies for a new age : guidelines for the future from Edgar Cayce and other psychics and visionaries / by Mark A. Thurston. Virginia Beach, Va. : A.R.E. Press, c1981. ix, 228 p. : ill. ; 22 cm. Includes index. [BF1809.T47 1981] 19 82-146184 ISBN 0-87604-135-7 pbk. : 6.95 9.95 5.95
1. Cayce, Edgar, 1877-1945. 2. Prophecies (Occult sciences) 3. Visions. I. Title.

TIMBS, John, 1801-1875. 133.3'2
Predictions realized in modern times. Now first collected by John Timbs. New ed., rev. and corr. London, C. Lockwood, 1880. Ann Arbor, Mich., Gryphon Books, 1971. xii, 276 p. front. 22 cm. (His Things not generally known) Includes bibliographical references. [BF1809.T54 1971] 73-159861
1. Prophecies (Occult sciences) I. Title.

TIMMS, Moira, 1938- 133.3
Prophecies & predictions : everyone's guide to the coming changes / by Moira Timms. Santa Cruz : Unity Press, c1980. p. cm. Edition of 1979 published under title: The six o'clock bus. Bibliography: p. [BF1809.T55 1980] 19 80-25137 ISBN 0-913300-55-1 pbk. : 7.95
1. Prophecies (Occult sciences) I. Title.

TOMAS, Andrew. 133
Beyond the time barrier. [New York, Berkley Publishing Corp. [1976 c1974] 160 p. 18 cm. (A Berkley Medallion Book) [BF1791.T65] ISBN 0-425-03061-X 1.25 (pbk.)
1. Prophecies (Occult sciences.) I. Title.
L.C. card no. of 1974 Salisbury, Compton Russell edition: 74-183216.

VAUGHAN, Alan. 133.3
The edge of tomorrow / Alan Vaughan. New York, N.Y. : Coward, McCann & Geoghegan, 1981. p. cm. [BF1815.V35V35] 19 81-17264 ISBN 0-698-11090-0 : 11.95
1. Prophecies (Occult sciences) 2. Success. I. Title.

WARD, Charles A. 133.3'2
Oracles of Nostradamus / by Chas. A. Ward. New York : Gordon Press, 1975. xxix, 375 p. ; 24 cm. Originally published in 1891 by Leadenhall Press, London. Includes index. [BF1815.N8W2 1975] 75-16676 ISBN 0-87968-232-9
1. Notredame, Michel de, 1503-1566. 2. Prophecies (Occult sciences) I. Title.

Prophecies (Occult sciences)—Dictionaries.

GARRISON, Omar V. 133.3'2'03
The encyclopedia of prophecy / by Omar V. Garrison. 1st ed. Secaucus, N.J. : Citadel Press, c1978. 225 p., [5] leaves of plates : ill. ; 24 cm. [BF1786.G37 1978] 78-102241 ISBN 0-8065-0559-1 : 10.00
1. Prophecies (Occult sciences)—Dictionaries. I. Title.

Prophecies (Occult sciences)—History.

EDMONDS, I. G. 133.3
Second sight : people who read the future / I. G. Edmonds. 1st ed. Nashville : T. Nelson, c1977. p. cm. Includes index. Bibliography: p. [BF1791.E35 1977] 77-9881 ISBN 0-8407-6566-5 : 6.95
1. Prophecies (Occult sciences)—History. I. Title.

Prophecy.

BROTHERS, Richard, 1757-1824. 133.
A revealed knowledge of the prophecies and times... Wrote under the direction of the Lord God, and published by His sacred command; it being the first sign of warning for the benefit of all nations. Containing, with other great and remarkable things ... the restoration of the Hebrews to Jerusalem, by the year 1798; under their revealed prince and prophet Richard Brothers. Philadelphia; Printed for Robert Campbell, n". 40, South Second street. 1795. 2 v. in 1. 17 cm. Published also under title: God's awful warnings to a giddy, careless, sinful world. With this is bound: Helbed, N.B., Testimony of the authenticity of the prophecies of Richard Brothers ... and A calculation on the commencement of the millennium, Philadelphia, 1795. [BF1815.B8A3 1795a] 25-23574
I. Title.

CHADWICK, Nora Kershaw, 1891- 291.6'3
Poetry & prophecy / by N. Kershaw Chadwick. Folcroft, Pa. : Folcroft Library Editions, 1975. xvi, 110 p., [7] leaves of plates : ill. ; 23 cm. Reprint of the 1942 ed. published by the University Press, Cambridge, Eng. Includes bibliographical references and index. [BL633.C45 1975] 75-44139 ISBN 0-8414-3381-X lib.bdg. : 22.50
1. Prophecy. 2. Inspiration. 3. Religion and poetry. I. Title.

CHADWICK, Nora Kershaw, 1891- 291.6'3
Poetry & prophecy / by N. Kershaw Chadwick. Norwood, Pa. : Norwood Editions, 1976. xvi, 110 p., [8] leaves of plates : ill. ; 23 cm. Reprint of the 1942 ed. published by the University Press, Cambridge, Eng. Includes bibliographical references and index. [BL633.C45 1976] 76-8245 ISBN 0-8482-0350-X lib bdg. : 15.00
1. Prophecy. 2. Inspiration. 3. Religion and poetry. I. Title.

*EBON, Martin, ed. 133.8
True experiences in prophecy [New York] New Amer. Lib. [1967, c.1961] 128p. 18cm. (Signet bk., P3280) .60 pap.,
I. Title.

[HAYES, B. M. 228
A descriptive exhibition of four prophetical horses, and of what they are emblematic: and also of their riders and their riders' mission ... [Washington, D.C.] c1919. 68 p. 20 cm. [BS2826.H3] 20-2136
I. Title.

HOLBROOK, Edwin A.
The light of prophecy, or The religion of the future. By Edwin A. Holbrook. Boston, Colby & Rich, 1882. 156 p. 19 1/2 cm. In verse. Published also under title: The light of the future. "Miscellaneous poems": p. [127]-156. [PS1939.H34] 27-27
I. Title. II. Title: Religion of the future. III. Title: Light of the future.

KAPLAN, Jacob Hyman, 1874-
Psychology of prophecy; a study of the prophetic mind as manifested by the ancient Hebrew prophets, by Jacob H. Kaplan, PH. D. Philadelphia, J. H. Greenstone, 1908. xii, 148 p. 24 cm. "This book was originally presented as a thesis ... to the faculty of the University of Donver in partial fulfilment of the PH. D. degree." Bibliography: p. 145-148. 8-34134
I. Title.

MORRISON, Henry Clay, 1857-
Lectures on prophecy. By H. C. Morrison ... Louisville, Ky., Pentecostal publishing company, c1915. 101 p. 19 1/2 cm. $0.50 15-15809
I. Title.

SCHAEFFER, Henry, 1881- 250
The call to prophetic service, from Abraham to Paul, by Henry Schaeffer ... foreword by Cleland B. McAfee ... New York, Chicago [etc.] Fleming H. Revell company [c1926] 2 p. l., 459 p. 21 cm. [BV660.S3] 26-10265
I. Title.

*STEIGER, Brad 133.32
Strange powers of prophecy. New York, Popular Lib. [1967] 128p. 18cm. (60-2172) .60 pap.,
1. Prophecy. I. Title.

TAYLOR, Mary Abigail, Mrs.
The historic meaning of prophecy, by Mrs. Mary Abigail Taylor ... Cincinnati, Press of Jennings and Graham [c1910] xii, 371 p. front. (port.) fold. diagr. 20 1/2 cm. $1.50 10-29719
I. Title.

TAYLOR, Mary Abigail, Mrs.
The historic meaning of prophecy, by Mrs. Mary Abigail Taylor ... Cincinnati, Press of Jennings and Graham [c1910] xii, 371 p. front. (port.) fold. diagr. 20 1/2 cm. $1.50 10-29719
I. Title.

Prophecy (Christianity)

BORING, M. Eugene. 226'.015
Sayings of the risen Jesus : Christian prophecy in the synoptic tradition / M. Eugene Boring. Cambridge [Cambridgeshire] ; New York : Cambridge University Press, 1982. p. cm. (Monograph series / Society for New Testament Studies ; 46) Includes index. Bibliography: p. [BS2555.2.B63] 19 81-18022 ISBN 0-521-24117-0 : 39.50
1. Jesus Christ—Words. 2. Bible. N.T. Gospels—Criticism, interpretation, etc. 3. Prophecy (Christianity) I. Title.

HALL, Robert Benjamin. 248'.2
Anyone can prophesy / Robert Benjamin Hall. New York : Seabury Press, 1977. p. cm. "A Crossroad book." [BR115.P8H36] 77-8267 ISBN 0-8164-2158-7 pbk. : 3.95
1. Prophecy (Christianity) I. Title.

SANDFORD, John Loren. 231'.74
The Elijah task / John and Paula Sandford. Plainfield, N.J. : Logos International, c1977. ix, 240 p. ; 21 cm. [BR115.P8S26] 77-82331 ISBN 0-88270-191-6 pbk. : 4.95
1. Prophecy (Christianity) 2. Pentecostalism—United States. I. Sandford, Paula, joint author. II. Title.

SPRUNGER, J[ohn] A.
Outline on prophecy; Israel in the past and in the future. The kingdom of Antichrist. The coming of the Lord. The millennium. The new heaven and new earth. By Rev. J. A. Sprunger. Cleveland, O., Light and hope publishing company [1903] 4 p. l., 287 p. front., pl. 19 1/2 cm. 3-8669
I. Title.

TAYLOR, Mary Abigail (Mellott) Mrs., 1847- 224.
The doctrinal meaning of prophecy, by Mrs. Mary Abigail Taylor ... Cincinnati, O., Caxton press [c1926] 268 p. front. (port.) double diagr. 20 1/2 cm. [BS647.T25] 26-11642
I. Title.

TURNER, Samuel Hulbeart.
Thoughts on the origin, character, and interpretation of scriptual prophecy in seven discourses ... With notes ... New York, Harper & bros., 1852. 1 p., l., vi p., 1 l., 219 p. 12 cm. New York, T. N. Stanford, 1856. 1 p. 1., vi p., 1 l., 219 p. 12° 1-11912
I. Title.

Prophecy (Christianity)—Addresses, essays, lectures.

BAKER, John Austin. 231'.74
Prophecy in the Church / [by] John Austin Baker. London : Church Literature Association, 1976. [2], 9 p. ; 21 cm. "This essay was first given as a talk to the Westminster Deanery Chapter on 3 February 1976." [BR115.P8B34] 77-372457 ISBN 0-85191-086-6 : £0.25
1. Prophecy (Christianity)—Addresses, essays, lectures. 2. Prophets—Addresses, essays, lectures. I. Title.

MIDDLETON, Edmond
... The doomed Turk, the end of the "Eastern question;" a series of ten essays reviewing the historical evidences in parallel with the prophecies, foretelling the fortunes of Esau (the Turk) and Jacob (the British) showing that the "birthright" and the "Eastern question" are identical. New York [etc.] The Abbey press [1900] 152 p. port. 8°. Mar
I. Title.

STACY, James, 1830-
Hand-book of prophecy, containing a brief outline of the prophecies of Daniel and John, together with a critical essay on the second advent. By James Stacy ... Richmond, Presbyterian board of publication [c1906] 149 p. incl. front. 20 1/2 cm. 6-36467
I. Title.

Prophecy (Christianity)—Biblical teaching.

GRUDEM, Wayne A. 227'.2015
The gift of prophecy in 1 Corinthians / Wayne A. Grudem. Washington, D.C. : University Press of America, c1982. xxiv, 333 p. ; 22 cm. Includes indexes. Bibliography: p. 289-309. [BS2655.P87G78] 19 81-40583 ISBN 0-8191-2083-9 : 23.50 ISBN 0-8191-2084-7 (pbk.) : 13.25
1. Bible. N.T. Corinthians, 1st—Criticism, interpretation, etc. 2. Prophecy (Christianity)—Biblical teaching. I. Title.

Prophecy (Christianity)—Biblical teaching—Addresses, essays, lectures.

MINEAR, Paul Sevier, 1906- 226'.4'015
To heal and to reveal : the prophetic vocation according to Luke / Paul S. Minear. New York : Seabury Press, c1976. ix, 179 p. ; 21 cm. "A Crossroad book." Includes index. [BS2545.P72M56] 75-42213 ISBN 0-8164-0295-7 : 8.95
1. Bible. N.T. Luke—Criticism, interpretation, etc.—Addresses, essays, lectures. 2. Prophecy (Christianity)—Biblical teaching—Addresses, essays, lectures. 3. Gifts, Spiritual—Biblical teaching—Addresses, essays, lectures. I. Title.

Prophets.

ABRAVANEL, Isaac, 1437-1508. 200
Maimonides and Abrabanel on prophecy, by Alvin Jay Reines. Cincinnati, Hebrew Union College Press, 1970. lxxxi, 239 p. 24 cm. Translation of selections from Perush 'al Sefer Moreh nevukhim (romanized form) Includes bibliographical references. [BS1198.A2713] 73-119106
1. Moses ben Maimon, 1135-1204. Dalalat al-ha'irin. 2. Prophets. I. Reines, Alvin Jay, 1926- ed. II. Title.

ALTMAN, Addie (Richman) Mrs. 221.
God's agents--the prophets, and other Biblical tales, simplified for young people by Addie R. Altman. New York, Bloch publishing company, inc., 1926. xi, 86 p. front., plates 19 cm. [BM107.A46] 26-24170
1. Prophets. I. Title.

ASSAD'U'LLAH, mirza.
The school of the prophets, by Mirza Assad'u'llah; tr. from the original Persian by Ameen'u'llah Fareed, M.D. (Mirza Ameen); with an introduction by Edwin Hartley Pratt ... v. 1- Chicago, Ill., Bahai publishing society, 1907- v. 20 1/2 cm. 7-42319
I. Ameen'u'llah Fareed, mirza, tr. II. Title.

BEAUCAMP, Evode. 221.92'2
Prophetic intervention in the history of man. Staten Island, N.Y., Alba House [1971, c1970] xvii, 230 p. 22 cm. Translation of Le prophetisme et l'election d'Israel. [BS1198.B3613] 76-129176 ISBN 0-8189-0191-8 4.95
1. Prophets. I. Title.

BEECHER, Willis Judson, 1838-1912 224.06
The prophets and the promise. Grand Rapids, Mich., Baker Bk., 1963. xiv, 427p. 23cm. 63-19837 3.95
1. Prophets. 2. Messiah. I. Title.

BEECHER, Willis Judson, 1838-1912. 221.
The prophets and the promise; being for substance the lectures for 1902-1903 on the L.P. Stone foundation in the Princeton theological seminary, by the Rev. Willis Judson Beecher ... New York, T.Y. Crowell & company, [1905] xiv, 427 p. 21 1/2 cm. [BS1505.B4] 5-33904
1. Prophets. 2. Messiah. I. Title.

BLACKWOOD, Andrew W. 224.
The prophets, Elijah to Christ, by Andrew W. Blackwood, illustrated by original charts. New York, Chicago [etc.] Fleming H. Revell company [c1917] 232 p. charts. 19 1/2 cm. $1.25. [BS1198.B5] 17-19166
1. Prophets. I. Title.

BLACKWOOD, Andrew Waltterson, 1882-
The prophets, Elijah to Christ, by Andrew W. Blackwood, illustrated by original charts. New York, Chicago [etc.] Fleming H. Revell company [c1917] 282 p. charts. 19 1/2 cm. [BS1198.B5] 17-19166
1. Prophets. I. Title.

BLANK, Sheldon H. 221.92'2
Understanding the prophets, by Sheldon H. Blank. New York, Union of American Hebrew Congregations [1969] 138 p. 20 cm. (Issues of faith) [BS1198.B52] 74-92159 2.50
1. Prophets. I. Title. II. Series.

BRIGHT, John, 1908- 224'.06
Covenant and promise : the prophetic understanding of the future in pre-exilic Israel / John Bright. Philadelphia : Westminster Press, c1976. p. cm. Includes bibliographical references and indexes. [BS1505.2.B74] 76-13546 ISBN 0-664-20752-9 : 10.95
1. Jews—History—953-586 B.C. 2. Bible. O.T. Prophets—Theology. 3. Prophets. I. Title.

BRUEGGEMANN, Walter. 221.1'5
The prophetic imagination / by Walter Brueggemann. Philadelphia : Fortress Press, 1978. p. cm. Includes bibliographical references. [BS1198.B84] 78-54546 ISBN 0-8006-1337-6 pbk. : 4.95
1. Prophets. 2. Pastoral theology. I. Title.

BUTTENWIESER, Moses. 221.
The prophets of Israel, from the eighth to the fifth century; their faith and their message, by Moses Buttenwieser ... New York, The Macmillan company, 1914. xxii, 350 p. 20 cm. [BS1505.B8] 14-2222 2.00
1. Prophets. I. Title.

CADMAN, Samuel Parkes, 1864-1936. 224
The prophets of Israel, by S. Parkes Cadman ... illustrated by Frank O. Salisbury. New York, The Macmillan company, 1933. 6 p. l., 197 p. col. front., plates (1 col.) 24 cm. Frontispiece accompanied by guard sheet and each plate, by leaf, with descriptive letterpress. "Literature": p. 196-197. [BS1505.C3] 33-33100

1. Prophets. I. Salisbury, Frank O., 1874- illus. II. Title.

CHAPPELL, Clovis Gillham, 1882- 224.06
And the prophets . . . [by] Clovis G. Chappell. Nashville, Abingdon [1962, c.1946] 208p. 18cm. (Apex bk. J1) .95 pap.,
1. Prophets. I. Title.

CHAPPELL, Clovis Gillham, 1882- 224
And the prophets ... [by] Clovis G. Chappell. New York, Nashville, Abingdon-Cokesbury press [1946] 208 p. 20 cm. [BS1505.C53] 46-7357
1. Prophets. I. Title.

CHURCH, Brooke (Peters) 1885- 224
The private lives of the prophets and the times in which they lived. New York, Rinehart [1953] 246 p. 21 cm. [BS1505.C56] 52-14190
1. Prophets. I. Title.

CLAUSEN, Bernard Chancellor, 1892- 221.
Pen-portraits of the prophets, by Bernard C. Clausen ... New York, Chicago [etc.] Fleming H. Revell company [c1926] 175 p. 19 1/2 cm. [BS1505.C57] 26-10133
1. Prophets. I. Title.

CLEMENTS, Ronald Ernest, 1929- 224
The conscience of the nation: a study of early Israelite prophecy, by R. E. Clements. London, Oxford U. P., 1967. 119 p. maps, diagrs. 18 1/2 cm. (Approaching the Bible) (B 67-12744) Bibliography: p. 111-113. [BS1198.C55] 68-106116
1. Prophets. 2. Bible. O. T. Prophets—Study—Outlines, syllabi, etc. I. Title.

CLEMENTS, Ronald Ernest, 1929- 221.1'5
Prophecy and tradition [by] R. E. Clements. Atlanta, John Knox Press [1975, c1974] 104 p. 22 cm. (Growing points in theology) Bibliography: p. 93-99. [BS1198.C57 1975] 74-3713 ISBN 0-8042-0110-2 4.95 (pbk.)
1. Prophets. I. Title.

COHON, Beryl D. 224.06
God's angry men; a student's introduction to the Hebrew prophets. New York, Bloch [c.1961] 109p. front. 2.75
I. Title.

CORBETT, Jack Elliott, 1920- 224
The Prophets on Main Street / J. Elliott Corbett. Rev. and exp. Atlanta : John Knox Press, c1977. p. cm. Bibliography: p. [BS1505.7.C67 1977] 77-79597 ISBN 0-8042-0841-7 pbk. : 5.95
1. Bible. O.T. Prophets—Paraphrases, English. 2. Prophets. I. Title.

CORNILL, Carl Heinrich, 1854-1920. 221.
The prophets of Israel; popular sketches from Old Testament history by Carl Heinrich Cornill ... tr. by Sutton F. Corkran. Chicago. The Open court publishing company, 1895. xiv p., 1 l., 194 p. front. 21 cm. [BS1505.C6] 3-4371
1. Prophets. I. Corkran, Sutton Fraser, tr. II. Title.

CUTLER, Ethel, 1880- 224
One prophet--and another, a sequence of line drawings [by] Ethel Cutler. New York, N. Y., The Womans press [c1941] x, 126 p. 22 cm. Includes bibliographies. [BS1505.C8] 41-23376
1. Prophets. 2. Bible, O. T. Prophets—Critism interpretation, etc. 3. Bible—Criticism, interpretation, etc.—O. T. Prophets. I. Title.

DE VRIES, Simon John. 222'.53'06
Prophet against prophet : the role of the Micaiah narrative (I Kings 22) in the development of early prophetic tradition / by Simon J. De Vries. Grand Rapids : Eerdmans, c1978. xix, 162 p. ; 23 cm. Includes indexes. [BS1198.D43] 78-2590 7.95
1. Bible. O.T. 1 Kings XX—Criticism, interpretation, etc. 2. Bible. O.T. Former prophets—Criticism, interpretation, etc. 3. Prophets. I. Title.

THE doctrine of the prophets.
Grand Rapids, Zondervan, 1958. xix, 537p.
I. Kirkpatrick, Alexander Francis, 1849-1940.

EFIRD, James M. 224'.06
The Old Testament prophets then and now / James M. Efird. Valley Forge, PA : Judson Press, c1982. 125 p. : map ; 22 cm. Bibliography: p. 123-125. [BS1198.E33] 19 81-20850 ISBN 0-8170-0960-4 : 6.95
1. Prophets. I. Title.

FARRAR, Frederic William, 1831-1903. 224
... The Minor prophets, by Rev. F. W. Farrar ... New York, Chicago [etc.] Fleming H. Revell company [189-?] vi, [2], 245 p. 20 cm. (Men of the Bible) "Books on the prophets": p. [vii] [BS1560.F3] 37-10890
1. Prophets. I. Title.

FAUS, William Arthur. 224
The genius of the prophets, by W. Arthur Faus. New York, Nashville, Abingdon-Cokesbury press [1946] 190 p. 19 1/2 cm. "References": p. 177-180. "Suggestions for further reading": p. 181-182. [BS1505.F35] 46-20665
1. Prophets. 2. Bible. O. T. Prophets—Criticism, interpretation, etc. I. Title.

FLEG, Edmond, 1874- 221.
The boy prophet [by] Edmond Fleg; a translation made by D. L. Orns. New York, E. P. Dutton & co., inc. [c1929] 4 p. l., 7-153 p. 20 cm. [BM107.F6] 29-16324
I. Orna, Mrs. Doris Libetta, 1889- tr. II. Title.

GOLDBERG, David, 1886- 224
Meet the prophets. In collaboration with Samuel Halevi Baron and Leonard R. Sussman. Illustrated by F. Dzubas. New York, Bookman Associates [1956] 211p. illus. 23cm. [BS1505.G57] 56-2168
1. Prophets. I. Title.

GOODMAN, Hannah Grad. 224.095
The story of prophecy. Ed. by Eugene B. Borowitz. Illus. by Eli Levin, Robert Cenedella; maps by Stephen Kraft. New York, Behrman [c.1965] 248p. illus., maps. 24cm. [BS1198.G6] 65-24925 3.95
1. Prophets. I. Title.

GOODMAN, Hannah Grad. 224.095
The story of Prophecy. Edited by Eugene B. Borowitz. Iilustrated by Eli Levin and Robert Cenedella; maps by Stephen Kraft. New York,Behram House [1963] 248 p. illus., maps. 24 cm. [BS1198G6] 65-24925
1. Prophets. I. Title.

GRISINGER, George F., M.D. 248
A modern prophet speaks. New York, Carlton [c.1963] 58p. 21cm. 2.00
I. Title.

GRISINGER, George F., M.D. 248
A modern prophet speaks. New York, Carlton [c.1963] 58p. 21cm. 2.00
I. Title.

HAWLEY, Charles Arthur, 1889- 221.
The teaching of the prophets [by] Charles Arthur Hawley... New York, Association press, 1924. xv, 242 p. 16 1/2 cm. [BS1505.H3] 24-28014
I. Title.

HEATN, Eric William. 224.06
The Old Testament Prophets. 53Harmondsworth, Middlesex] Penguin Books [1958] 186p. 18cm. *A Pellcan book, A414) 'Completely revised and largely rewritten edition of [the author's] His servants the Prophets, published ... in 1949.' [BS1198.H4 1958] 59-4547
1. Prophets. 2. Bible. O. T. Prophets—Theology. I. Title.

HEATON, Eric William. 224'.06
The Old Testament prophets / E. W. Heaton. Atlanta : John Knox Press, c1977. p. cm. Includes indexes. Bibliography: p. [BS1198.H4 1977] 77-79589 ISBN 0-8042-0140-4 pbk. : 3.95
1. Bible. O.T. Prophets—Theology. 2. Prophets. I. Title.

HESCHEL, Abraham Joshua, 1907- 224.06
The Prophets. [1st ed.] New York, Harper & Row [1962] 518 p. 25 cm. [BS1505.2.H4] 62-7290
1. Bible. O.T. Prophets—Criticism, interpretation, etc. 2. Prophets. I. Title.

HESCHEL, Abraham Joshua, 1907- 224'.06
The Prophets, by Abraham J. Heschel. New York, Harper & Row [1969, c1962] xv, 235 p. 21 cm. (Harper torchbooks, TB 1421) "This edition comprises the first 220 pages of the Prophets, originally published in 1962." Bibliographical footnotes. [BS1505.2] 78-2376 1.75
1. Bible. O.T. Prophets—Criticism, interpretation, etc. 2. Prophets.

HOLT, Ivan Lee, Bp., 1886- 224
Yesterday speaks to today. New York, Abingdon Press [1956] 96p. 20cm. [BS1505.H63] 56-10147
1. Prophets. I. Title.

HUEY, F. B., 1925- 224'.06
Yesterday's prophets for today's world / F. B. Huey, Jr. Nashville, Tenn. : Broadman Press, c1980. 177 p. ; 21 cm. Bibliography: p. [176]-177. [BS1505.2.H8] 19 79-54922 ISBN 0-8054-1216-6 : 6.95
1. Bible. O.T. Prophets—Criticism, interpretation, etc. 2. Prophets. I. Title.

HYATT, James Philip, 1909- 223'.7'06
The prophetic criticism of Israelite worship [by] J. Philip Hyatt. Cincinnati, Hebrew Union College Press [1963] 24 p. 23 cm. (The Goldenson lecture of 1963) Bibliographical references included in "Notes" (p. 23-24) [BS1505.2.G6 1963] 68-6987
1. Prophets. 2. Worship (Judaism) I. Title. II. Series: The Goldenson lecture, 1963

INTERPRETING the prophetic tradition. 224 Introd. by Harry M. Orlinsky. Cinn. [i.e. Cincinnati] Hebrew Union College Press, 1969. xii, 343 p. 23 cm. (The Goldenson lectures, 1955-1966) Contents.Contents.—"Of a truth the Lord hath sent me": an inquiry into the source of the prophet's authority, by S. H. Blank.—The prophets: our concurrence and our dissent, by A. Cronbach.—The prophet in modern Hebrew literature, by J. B. Agus.—Prophets and philosophers: the scandal of prophecy, by L. H. Silberman.—The voice of prophecy in this satellite age, by E. F. Magnin.—The stone which the modern builders rejected, by L. A. Olan.—Samuel and the beginnings of the prophetic movement, by W. F. Albright.—Prophetic religion in an age of revolution, by L. I. Feuer.—The prophetic criticism of Israelite worship, by J. P. Hyatt.—The so-called "suffering servant" in Isaiah 53, by H. M. Orlinsky.—Jerusalem and the prophets, by R. De Vaux.—The changing image of the prophet in Jewish thought, by B. J. Bamberger. Includes bibliographical references. [BS1505.2.I5] 68-58444
1. Bible. O.T. Prophets—Addresses, essays, lectures. 2. Prophets. I. Orlinsky, Harry Meyer, 1908- ed. II. Title. III. Series. IV. Library of Biblical studies.

ISSERMAN, Ferdinand Myron, 1898- 224
Rebels and saints; the social message of the prophets of Israel, by Ferdinand M. Isserman ... introduction by William Scarlett ... St. Louis, The Bethany press [c1933] 162 p. 20 cm. [BS1505.18] 33-34449
1. Prophets. 2. Sociology, Biblical. 3. Religion and sociology. I. Title.

JOHNSON, Aubrey Rodway. 223'.2'06
The cultic prophet and Israel's psalmody / by Aubrey R. Johnson. Cardiff : University of Wales Press, 1979. xii, 467 p. ; 23 cm. Continues The cultic prophet in ancient Israel. Includes bibliographical references and indexes. [BS1430.2.J57] 79-311257 ISBN 0-7083-0707-8 : 60.00
1. Bible. O.T. Psalms—Criticism, interpretation, etc. 2. Prophets. I. Title.
Dist. by Verry, PO Box 98, Mystic CT 06355

JOHNSON, Aubrey Rodway 224.066
The cultic prophet in ancient Israel [2d ed.] Cardiff, Univ. of Wales Pr. Mystic, Conn., Verry, 1965] viii, 91p. 22cm. First pub. in 1960. Bibl. [BS1198.J6] 65-8444 3.50
1. Prophets. I. Title.

JURGENSEN, Barbara. 224'.06
The prophets speak again : a brief introduction to Old Testament prophecy / Barbara Jurgensen. Minneapolis : Augsburg Pub. House, c1977. 128 p. ; 20 cm. [BS1505.2.J87] 76-27084 ISBN 0-8066-1566-4 : 2.95
1. Bible. O.T. Prophets—Criticism, interpretation, etc. 2. Prophets. I. Title.

KLAGSBRUN, Francine. 222'.1'0924 B
The story of Moses. New York, F. Watts [1968] vxii, 171 p. map. 22 cm. (Immortals of philosophy and religion) Presents the life and teachings of the prophet and lawgiver who, after a revelation from God, devoted his life to leading his people out of slavery to the promised land. [BS580.M6K55] 68-27403 3.95
1. Moses—Juvenile literature. 2. [Moses.] 3. [Prophets.] I. Title.

KOCH, Klaus, 1926- 224'.06
The prophets / Klaus Koch. 1st Fortress Press ed. Philadelphia : Fortress Press, 1982- p. cm. Translation of: Die Profeten. Contents.Contents. v. 1. The Assyrian age Bibliography: v. 1, p. [BS1198.K6313 1982] 19 79-8894 ISBN 0-8006-1648-0 pbk. : 10.95
1. Prophets. I. [Profeten.] English II. Title.

KRAELING, Emil Gottlieb Heinrich, 1892- 221'.922
The prophets, by Emil G. Kraeling. [Chicago] Rand McNally [1969] 304 p. 22 cm. Bibliographical references included in "Notes and references" (p. 293-297) [BS1198.K7] 75-90839 6.95
1. Prophets.

KUHL, Curt 224
The prophets of Israel. Translated [from the German] by Rudolf J. Ehrlich and J. P. Smith. Richmond, John Knox Press, 1960[ ] vii, 199p. Bibl.: p.192-196. 23cm. 60-11624 3.50 bds.,
1. Prophets. I. Title.

LANDMAN, Isaac, 1880- 221.
Stories of the prophets (before the exile) by Isaac Landman. Cincinnati, O., Department of synagog and school extension of the Union of American Hebrew congregations [c1912] 7 p. l., 5-73 p., 1 l., 75-280 p. 20 cm. (Half-title: The union graded series, intermediate department) "First edition, September, 1911. Second edition, September, 1912." [BM107.L3] 12-25098
1. Prophets. I. Title.

LEISHMAN, Thomas Linton, 1900- 222'.1'095
The continuity of the Bible. Boston, Christian Science Pub. Society [1968- v. maps. 24 cm. Articles originally published in the Christian science journal, 1963- Contents.Contents.—[1] The patriarchs.—[2] Joshua to Elisha.—[3] Prophetic writings.—[4] The Gospels. [BS1225.2.L4] 68-31635 3.50 (v. 3)
1. Jews—History—To 1200 B.C. 2. Bible. O.T. Pentateuch—History of Biblical events. 3. Prophets. I. Title.

LIMBURG, James, 1935- 220.1'5
The prophets and the powerless / James Limburg. Atlanta : John Knox Press, c1977. vi, 104 p. ; 20 cm. Bibliography: p. [103]-104. [BS1198.L5] 76-12397 ISBN 0-8042-0156-0 pbk. : 3.45
1. Prophets. 2. Prophecy. I. Title.

LINEBERGER, Lawrence Otto, 1897- 224
Towering figures among the prophets, by L. O. Lineberger ... Philadelphia, Chicago [etc.] The John C. Winston company [c1928] ix, 181 p. front., pl. 19 cm. [BS1505.L5] 29-9351
1. Prophets. I. Title.

MCCONNELL, Francis John, bp., 1871- 224
The prophetic ministry, [by] Francis J. McConnell... New York, Cincinnati [etc.] The Abingdon press [c1930] 308 p. 20 1/2 cm. "The present course of lectures, being the fifty-sixth upon the Lyman Beecher foundation, was delivered in Battell Chapel. Yale university, April 28-May 2, 1930."--P. [6] [BS1505.M27] 30-29295
1. Prophets. 2. Bible. O.T. Prophets—Criticism, interpretation, etc. 3. Bible—

Criticism, interpretation,e tc.—O.T. Prophets. I. Title.

MCELENEY, Neil J. 220.1'5
The oracle of the Lord; introduction to the prophets, by Neil J. McEleney. New York, Paulist Press [1973] 55 p. illus. 23 cm. (Pamphlet Bible series, v. 24) [BS491.2.P3 vol. 24] [BS1198] 74-155418 1.00
1. Prophets. I. Title. II. Series.

MALY, Eugene H. 224'.06
Prophets of salvation [by] Eugene H. Maly. [New York] Herder & Herder [1967] 191p. 21cm. Orig. appeared in Hi-time magazine. [BS1198.M27] 67-14146 4.50
1. Prophets. 2. Bible. O.T. Prophets—Criticism, interpretation, etc. I. Title.

MARVIN, Dwight Edwards.
The church and her prophets, by Dwight Edwards Marvin. New York, Broadway publishing company [c1909] 4 p. l., 7-94 p. 18 cm. 9-16788
I. Title.

MERRILL, William Pierson, 221.
1867-
Prophets of the dawn; Amos, Hosea, Isaiah, Micah, the beginnings of the religion of the spirit, by William Pierson Merrill ... New York, Chicago [etc.] Fleming H. Revell company [c1927] 173 p. 20 cm. [BS1505.M4] 27-20135
1. Amos, the prophet. 2. Hosea, the prophet. 3. Isaiah, the prophet. 4. Micah, the prophet. 5. Prophets. I. Title.

MILLEY, C Ross. 224.06
The prophets of Israel. New York, Philosophical Library [1959] 143p. 22cm. Includes bibliography. [BS1505.5.M5] 59-16478
1. Prophets. 2. Bible. O. T. Prophets—Theology. I. Title.

MORTON, William Albert, 1866-
From plowboy to prophet; being a short history of Joseph Smith, for children, by William A. Morton (illustrations by L. A. Ramsey) Salt Lake City, Utah, W. A. Morton, 1912. 2 p. l., 130 p., 1 l. plates, 2 port. (incl. front.) 19 cm. $0.50. 12-18335
I. Title.

MOWVLEY, Harry. 224'.06
Reading the Old Testament prophets today / Harry Mowvley. Atlanta : John Knox Press, 1979. p. cm. Includes bibliographical references and indexes. [BS1198.M68] 79-87744 ISBN 0-8042-0167-6 : 4.95
1. Bible. O.T. Prophets—Criticism, interpretation, etc. 2. Prophets. I. Title.

MUZZEY, David Saville, 1870- 922
Spiritual heroes: a study of some of the world's prophets, by David Saville Muzzey ... New York, Doubleday, Page & company, 1902. xi, 305 p. 20 cm. [BL72.M8] 2-13784
1. Socrates. 2. Jesus Christ. 3. Aurelius Antoninus. Marcus, emperor of Rome, 121-180. 4. Paul, Saint, Apostle. 5. Augustinus Aurelius, Saint. bp. of Hippo. 6. Muhammad, the prophet. 7. Luther, Martin, 1483-1546. 8. Prophets. 9. Jeremiah, the prophet. 0. Buddha and Buddhism. I. Title.
Contents omitted.

PEARLMAN, Moshe, 1911- 221.9'22 B
In the footsteps of the prophets / Moshe Pearlman. New York : Crowell, 1975. 230 p. : ill. (some col.) ; 29 cm. Includes index. [BS1505.2.P4 1975] 75-11965 ISBN 0-690-00962-3 : 19.95
1. Prophets. I. Title.

PETRIE, George Laurens, 1840- 224
Israel's prophets, by George L. Petrie, D. D. New York, The Neale publishing company, 1912. 243 p. 19 cm. [BS1505.P4] 12-6533
1. Prophets. 2. Bible. O. T. Prophets—Biog. 3. Bible—Bible.—O. T. Prophets. I. Title.

RAD, Gerhard von, 1901-1971. 224
The message of the prophets. [1st U.S. ed.] New York, Harper & Row [1972, c1965] 289 p. 22 cm. Translation of Die Botschaft der Propheten, a revised version of material from the author's Theologie des Alten Testaments. Includes bibliographical references. [BS1505.2.R313 1972] 72-183633 3.95
1. Bible. O.T. Prophets—Theology. 2. Prophets. I. Title.

REID, David P. 224
What are they saying about the prophets? / By David P. Reid. New York : Paulist Press, 1980. 103 p. ; 19 cm. (A Deus book) Bibliography: p. 99-103. [BS1198.R43] 19 80-80869 ISBN 0-8091-2304-5 (pbk.) : 2.95
1. Prophets. I. Title.

REID, John Calvin, 1901- 224'.06
We spoke for God. Grand Rapids, Eerdmans [1967] 122 p. 23 cm. [BS1505.2.R4] 67-28376
1. Bible. O.T. Prophets—Introductions. 2. Prophets. I. Title.

ROBINSON, Henry Wheeler, 221.6
1872-1945.
Inspiration and revelation in the Old Testament / by H. Wheeler Robinson. Westport, Conn. : Greenwood Press, 1979, c1946. 298 p. ; 23 cm. Reprint of the ed. published by Clarendon Press, Oxford. Lectures delivered before the University of Oxford, 1942-1945. Includes bibliographical references and indexes. [BS1192.5.R62 1979] 78-9891 ISBN 0-313-21068-3 : 22.50
1. Bible. O.T.—Theology. 2. Prophets. 3. Revelation—Biblical teaching. I. Title.

ROWLEY, Harold Henry, 1890- 290
Prophecy and religion in ancient China and Israel. New York, Harper [1956] 154p. 22cm. 'Lectures ... originally delivered at the School of Oriental and African Studies of the University of London as the Louis H. Jordan lectures in comparative religion for 1954.' [BL633.R6 1956a] 56-12074
1. Prophets. 2. China—Religion—Relations—Judaism. 3. Judaism—Relations— Chinese. I. Title.

RUST, Eric Charles. 224
Covenant and hope; a study in the theology of the prophets [by] Eric C. Rust. Waco, Tex., Word Books [1972] 192 p. 23 cm. [BS1198.R87] 72-84170 5.95
1. Prophets. I. Title.

SCHULTZ, Samuel J. 224
The prophets speak; law of love, the essence of Israel's religion, by Samuel J. Schultz. [1st ed.] New York, Harper & Row [1968] 159 p. 21 cm. [BS1198.S35] 69-10478 5.00
1. Bible O.T. Prophets—Theology. 2. Prophets. I. Title.

SCOTT, Robert Balgarnie 224
Young, 1899-
The relevance of the prophets [by] R. B. Y. Scott. Rev. ed. New York, Macmillan [1968] viii, 248 p. 20 cm. Includes bibliographical references. [BS1505.S36 1968] 68-17519
1. Bible. O.T. Prophets—Criticism, interpretation, etc. 2. Prophets. I. Title.

SEILHAMER, Frank H. 224'.06
Prophets and prophecy : seven key messengers / Frank H. Seilhamer. Philadelphia : Fortress Press, c1977. x, 85 p. ; 22 cm. Bibliography: p. 84-85. [BS1198.S42] 76-62603 ISBN 0-8006-1254-X pbk. : 2.95
1. Bible. O.T. Prophets—Criticism, interpretation, etc. 2. Prophets. I. Title.

SILVERMAN, Althea Osber. 224
Behold my messengers! The lives and teachings of the prophets. Illus. by Reuben Leaf. New York, Bloch Pub. Co., 1955. 239p. illus. 21cm. [BS1505.S416] 55-11056
1. Prophets. I. Title.

SKELTON, Eugene. 224
Meet the prophets! Nashville, Tenn., Broadman Press [1972] 160 p. illus. 22 cm. [BS1198.S5] 72-79176 ISBN 0-8054-1510-6
1. Prophets. I. Title.

SMART, James D. 221.15
Servants of the Word; the prophets of Israel. Philadelphia, Westminster Press [1961, c.1960] 95p. (Westminster guides to the Bible) 60-11066 1.50
1. Prophets. I. Title.

SMITH, John Merlin Powis, 221.
1866-1932.
The prophets and their times, by J. M. Powis Smith ... Chicago, Ill., The University of Chicago press [c1925] ix, 277 p. 20 cm. (Half-title: The University of Chicago publications in religious education. Handbooks of ethics and religion) Bibliography: p. 265-266. [BS1505.S53] 25-6864
1. Prophets. I. Title.

SMITH, W. Robertson 224'.0922
1846-1894. (William Robertson),
The prophets of Israel and their place in history. New York : AMS Press, [1982] lviii, 446 p. ; 18 cm. Reprint. Originally published: New ed. London : A. & C. Black, 1895. With new introd. Includes index. [BS1198.S57 1982] 19 77-87666 ISBN 0-404-16403-X : 47.50
1. Prophets. I. Title.

STAACK, Hagen. 224
Prophetic voices of the Bible. Cleveland, World Pub. Co. [1968] 121 p. illus. 21 cm. [BS1198.S65 1968] 68-26840 3.50
1. Prophets. I. Title.

STORR, Vernon Faithfull, 221.
1869-
The prophets of the Old Testament and their message; lessons for school and Bible classes, by Vernon F. Storr ... London, Society for promoting Christian knowledge; New York, The Macmillan co., 1921. x, 86 p. 19 cm. [BS1505.S7] 22-17169
1. Prophets. 2. Bible. O.T.—Criticism, interpretation, etc. I. Title.

VAN DOLSON, Bobbie 224'.09'22
Jane.
Prophets are people, believe it or not / Bobbie Jane Van Dolson. Washington : Review and Herald Pub. Association, [1974] 92 p. : ill. ; 21 cm. [BS1560.V36] 74-78394 ISBN pbk. : 2.50
1. Prophets. I. Title.

WALKER, Rollin Hough.
Studies in the prophets of Israel; a normal course for Bible class teachers, by Rollin H. Walker, Ph. D. and Russell B. Miller... New York, Eaton & Mains; Cincinnati, Jennings & Graham [1909] 112 p. plates. 19 1/2 cm. $0.25. 9-28190
I. Miller, Russell Benjamin, joint author. II. Title.

WALKER, Rollin Hough, 1865- 221.
Men unafraid, four pioneers of prophecy; a study of Amos, Hosea Isaiah, and the herald of the restoration... by Rollin H. Walker. New York, Cincinnati, The Methodist book concern [1923] 164 p. illus. (incl. map.) 19 cm. "Literature": p. 12. [BS1505.W28] 23-11526
1. Prophets. I. Title.

WARD, James Merrill, 224'.06
1928-
The Prophets / James M. Ward ; Lloyd R. Bailey, Sr. and Victor P. Furnish, editors. Nashville : Abingdon, c1982. 159 p. ; 21 cm. (Interpreting Biblical texts) Bibliography: p. 157-159. [BS1505.2.W37 1982] 19 81-20575 ISBN 0-687-34370-4 pbk. : 6.95
1. Bible. O.T. Prophets—Criticism, interpretation, etc. 2. Prophets. I. Title. II. Series.

WARD, John William George, 224
1879-
Portraits of the prophets; character studies of men who blazed the trail, by J. W. G. Ward... New York, R. R. Smith, Inc., 1930. vii, 328 p. 20 1/2 cm. [BS1505.W35] 30-9987
1. Prophets. I. Title.

WEE, Mons Olson, 1871- 224
Men who knew God: Samuel, Amos, Haggai; prophets and their times, prophetism, and "the schools of prophets" in the Old Testament, by M. O. Wee. Minneapolis, Minn., Augsburg publishing house [c1932] xiii, 122 p. 20 1/2 cm. "Works for reference": p. 122. [BS1505.W4] 32-20843
1. Samuel, judge of Israel. 2. Amos, the prohpet. 3. Haggai, the prophet. 4. Prophets. I. Title.

WIFALL, Walter. 224'.06
Israel's prophets : envoys of the King / by Walter Wifall. Chicago : Franciscan Herald Press, [1975] p. cm. (Herald Biblical booklets) Bibliography: p. [BS1198.W5] 74-31167 ISBN 0-8199-0521-6 pbk. : 0.95
1. Prophets. I. Title.

WILLIAMS, Walter George, 224
1900-
The prophets: pioneers to Christianity. New York, Abingdon Press [1956] 23p. 23cm. [BS1505.W57] 56-6358
1. Prophets I. Title.

WILLIAMS, Walter George, 224
1903-
The prophets, pioneers to Christianity. New York, Abingdon Press [1956] 223 p. 23 cm. [BS1505.W57] 56-6358
1. Prophets. I. Title.

WILSON, Robert R., 1942- 224'.06
Prophecy and society in ancient Israel / Robert R. Wilson. Philadelphia : Fortress Press, c1979. p. cm. Includes indexes. Bibliography: p. [BS1198.W55] 78-14677 ISBN 0-8006-0537-3 : 15.95
1. Bible. O.T. Prophets—Criticism, interpretation, etc. 2. Prophets. 3. Sociology, Biblical. I. Title.

WOLFE, Rolland Emerson, 1902- 224
Men of prophetic fire; with illus. by Phillips E. Osgood. Boston, Beacon Press [1951] 316 p. illus. 22 cm. [BS1505.W67] 51-14955
1. Prophets I. Title.

WOOD, Leon James. 221.9'22
The prophets of Israel / Leon J. Wood. Grand Rapids : Baker Book House, c1979. 405 p. ; 24 cm. Includes indexes. Bibliography: p. 379-384. [BS1198.W66] 79-50172 ISBN 0-8010-9607-3 : 11.95
1. Bible. O.T. Prophets—Criticism, interpretation, etc. 2. Prophets. I. Title.

YOUNG, Edward Joseph. 224
My servants, the prophets. Grand Rapids, W. B. Eerdmans Pub. Co., 1952. 231 p. 23 cm. [BS1505.Y6] 52-14505
1. Prophets. 2. Bible. O. T. Prophets — Criticism, interpretation, etc. I. Title.

Prophets—Addresses, essays, lectures.

DI CESARE, Mario A. 224
Poetry and prophecy : reflections on the word / Mario A. Di Cesare. Amherst, Mass : Published for the Friends of the Amherst College Library, c1977. 42 p. ; 22 cm. (The Robert Frost lecture : 1976) [BS1198.D53] 77-150847
1. Prophets—Addresses, essays, lectures. 2. Poetry—Addresses, essays, lectures. I. Amherst College. Library. Friends. II. Title. III. Series.

ISRAEL'S prophetic 224'.06
tradition : essays in honour of Peter R. Ackroyd / edited by Richard Coggins, Anthony Phillips, and Michael Knibb. Cambridge [Cambridgeshire] ; New York : Cambridge University Press, 1982. xxi, 272 p., [1] leaf of plates : port. ; 22 cm. Includes bibliographies and index. [BS1505.2.I8 1982] 19 81-17065 ISBN 0-521-24223-1 : 39.50
1. Ackroyd, Peter R.—Addresses, essays, lectures. 2. Bible. O.T. Prophets—Criticism, interpretation, etc.—Addresses, essays, lectures. 3. Prophets—Addresses, essays, lectures. I. Ackroyd, Peter R. II. Coggins, R. J., 1929- III. Phillips, Anthony. IV. Knibb, Michael A. 1938- (Michael Anthony),

PROPHECY : 221 s
essays presented to Georg Fohrer on his sixty-fifth birthday, 6 September 1980 / edited by J. A. Emerton. Berlin ; New York : W. de Gruyter, 1980. p. cm. (Beiheft zur Zeitschrift fur die alttestamentliche Wissenschaft ; 150) Bibliography: p. [BS410.Z5 vol. 150] [BS1505.2] 221.6 19 80-21779 ISBN 3-11-007761-2 : 61.50
1. Fohrer, Georg. 2. Bible. O.T. Prophets—Criticism, interpretation, etc.—Addresses, essays, lectures. 3. Prophets—Addresses, essays, lectures. I. Fohrer, Georg. II. Emerton, John Adney. III. Series: Zeitschrift fur die alttestamentliche Wissenschaft. Beihefte ; 150.

Prophets—Biography—Juvenile literature.

BRAGG, Juliana. 224'.9209505
The story of Jonah / retold by Juliana Bragg ; illustrated by Charles E. Martin. New York : Golden Press ; Racine, Wis. : Western Pub. Co., c1981. [24] p. : col. ill. ; 21 cm. (A Golden look-look book) Jonah, trying to run away from the work God wants him to do, is swallowed by a whale, then put out on dry land to have another chance. [BS580.J55B67 1981] 19 80-84787 ISBN 0-307-11863-0 (pbk.) : 1.25
1. Jonah (Biblical prophet)—Juvenile literature. 2. [Jonah (Biblical prophet)] 3. Bible. O.T.—Biography—Juvenile literature. 4. Prophets—Biography—Juvenile literature. 5. Bible stories, English—O.T. Jonah. 6. [Bible stories—O.T.] I. Martin, Charles E., ill. II. Title.

HEIFNER, Fred. 224'.1'0924 B
Isaiah, messenger for God / Fred Heifner ; illustrated by Cliff Johnston. Nashville : Broadman Press, c1978. 48 p. : col. ill. ; 24 cm. (Biblearn series) Tells how Isaiah began prophesying for God. [BS580.I7H43] 78-105150 ISBN 0-8054-4243-X pbk. : 3.95
1. Isaiah, the Prophet—Juvenile literature. 2. [Isaish, the Prophet.] 3. Bible. O.T.—Biography. 4. Prophets—Biography—Juvenile literature. 5. [Bible stories—O.T.] I. Johnston, Cliff. II. Title.

MCMINN, Tom. 224'.092'2 B
Prophets, preachers for God / Tom McMinn ; illustrated by H. Don Fields. Nashville : Broadman Press, c1979. 48 p. : ill. ; 24 cm. (Biblearn series) Presents accounts of the lives of five Old Testament prophets: Elisha, Amos, Jeremiah, Jonah, and Micah. Discussion questions accompany each selection. [BS1198.M19] 79-111901 ISBN 0-8054-4250-2 : 3.95
1. Bible. O.T.—Biography—Juvenile literature. 2. Prophets—Biography—Juvenile literature. 3. [Prophets.] 4. [Bible stories—O.T.] I. Fields, H. Don. II. Title.

Prophets—England—Yorkshire—Biography.

HARRISON, William Henry, Spiritualist. 133.3'2'0924
Mother Shipton investigated : the result of critical examination in the British Museum Library of the literature relating to the Yorkshire sibyl / by William H. Harrison. Folcroft, Pa. : Folcroft Library Editions, 1977. p. cm. Reprint of the 1881 ed. published by W. H. Harrison, London. [BF1815.S5H37 1977] 77-3412 ISBN 0-8414-4911-2 lib. bdg. : 10.00
1. Shipton, Ursula. 2. Prophets—England—Yorkshire—Biography. 3. Yorkshire, Eng.—Biography. I. Title.

Prophets in the New Testament—Addresses, essays, lectures.

ELLIS, Edward Earle. 225.6'3
Prophecy and hermeneutic in early Christianity : New Testament essays / by E. Earle Ellis. Grand Rapids, Mich. : W. B. Eerdmans Pub. Co., [1978] p. cm. Reprint of the 1978 ed. published by J. C. B. Mohr, Tubingen, which was issued as no. 18 of Wissenschaftliche Untersuchungen zum Neuen Testament. Includes bibliographical references and indexes. [BS2370.E44 1978] 78-17382 ISBN 0-8028-1689-4 : 15.00
1. Bible. N.T.—Criticism, interpretation, etc.—Addresses, essays, lectures. 2. Bible. N.T.—Hermeneutics—Addresses, essays, lectures. 3. Prophets in the New Testament—Addresses, essays, lectures. I. Title. II. Series: Wissenschaftliche Untersuchungen zum Neuen Testament ; 18.

Prophets—Iraq—Babylon—Biography.

CAMPBELL, Donald K. 224'.5'077
Daniel, decoder of dreams / Donald K. Campbell. Wheaton, Ill. : Victor Books, c1977. 143 p. ; 21 cm. [BS1555.3.C35] 77-154330 ISBN 0-88207-747-3 pbk. : 1.95
1. Daniel, the prophet. 2. Bible. O.T. Daniel—Commentaries. 3. Bible. O.T.—Biography. 4. Bible. O.T. Daniel—Prophecies. 5. Prophets—Iraq—Babylon—Biography. 6. Babylon—Biography. I. Title.

Prophets (Mormon Church)

CROWTHER, Duane S. 231.7'4
Thus saith the Lord— : the role of prophets and revelation in the kingdom of God / Duane S. Crowther. Bountiful, Utah : Horizon Publishers, c1980. 340 p. ; 24 cm. Includes bibliographical references and index. [BX8643.P7C76] 19 80-83862 ISBN 0-88290-168-0 : 10.95
1. Prophets (Mormon Church) I. Title.

Prophets (Mormonism)—Juvenile literature.

BARNES, Kathleen H. 230'.9'3
Today I saw a prophet / Kathleen H. Barnes & Virginia H. Pearce. Salt Lake City : Deseret Book Co., c1977. 30 p. : col. ill. ; 26 cm. Identifies Biblical prophets from Moses to Peter, explains the role of prophet and lists the men who have served in this capacity for the Church of Jesus Christ of Latter-Day Saints. [BX8643.P7B37] 77-4986 ISBN 0-87747-646-2 : 4.95
1. [Church of Jesus Christ of Latter-Day Saints.] 2. Prophets (Mormonism)—Juvenile literature. 3. Prophets—Juvenile literature. 4. [Prophets (Mormonism)] 5. [Prophets.] I. Pearce, Virginia H., joint author. II. Title.

Prophets—Palestine—Biography—Juvenile literature.

BARTON, Peggy, 1931- 225.9'2'4 B
John the Baptist / Peggy Barton. Salt Lake City : Deseret Book Co., 1978. 24 p. : ill. ; 24 cm. Presents the life and work of John the Baptist who predicted the coming of the Messiah and baptized Jesus. Explains how the Priesthood of Aaron was conferred upon Joseph Smith and Oliver Cowdery. [BS2456.B29] 78-23616 ISBN 0-87747-727-2 : 3.95
1. John the Baptist—Juvenile literature. 2. [John the Baptist.] 3. [Church of Jesus Christ of Latter-Day Saints.] 4. Prophets—Palestine—Biography—Juvenile literature. 5. [Prophets.] I. Title.

Prophets—Study and teaching.

AMERICAN society for prophetic study. 224.
Papers read before the American society for prophetic study ... [Philadelphia, The Elite press, c19 v. 26 cm. [BS647.A1A6] ca 26
I. Title.

WILLIS, John T., 1933- 224
My servants, the prophets, by John T. Willis. Abilene, Tex., Biblical Research Press [1971- v. 22 cm. (The Way of life series, no. 116) [BS1198.W53] 76-180789
1. Prophets—Study and teaching. I. Title.

Prose poems, American.

DICKEY, James. 242
God's images : the Bible, a new vision / James Dickey & Marvin Hayes. 1st ed. Birmingham, Ala. : Oxmoor House, c1977. ca. 100 p. : ill. ; 29 x 32 cm. [BS491.5.D52] 76-40862 ISBN 0-8487-0479-7 : 19.95
1. Bible—Meditations. 2. Bible—Pictures, illustrations, etc. 3. Prose poems, American. I. Hayes, Marvin, joint author. II. Title.

DICKEY, James. 811'.5'4
God's images : the Bible, a new vision / James Dickey & Marvin Hayes. New York : Seabury Press, 1978. [122] p. : ill. ; 24 x 25 cm. "A Crossroad book." [BS491.5.D52 1978] 78-17465 ISBN 0-8164-2194-3 pbk. : 7.95
1. Bible—Meditations. 2. Bible—Illustrations. 3. Prose poems, American. I. Hayes, Marvin. II. Title.

HAWTHORNE, Nathaniel, 1804-1864.
The complete writings of Nathaniel Hawthorne. Autograph ed., with portraits, illustrations, and facsimiles... [Boston and New York, Houghton, Mifflin and company, 1900] 22 v. fronts., plates, ports., facsims. (1 double) 23 cm. Added t.-p., illustrated: "The writings of Nathaniel Hawthorne." Each volume has also special t.-p. "This edition of the writings of Nathaniel Hawthorne is limited to five hundred signed and numbered copies." This set not numbered. Contents.v. 1-2. Twice-told tales.--v. 3. The snow-image and other twice-told tales.--v. 4-5. Mosses from an old manse.--v. 6. The scarlet letter.--v. 7. The house of the seven gables.--v. 8. The Blithedale romance.--v. 9-10. The marble faun.--v. 11. Our old home.--v. 12. The whole history of grandfather's chair, and Biographical stories.--v. 13. A wonder book for girls and boys, and Tanglewood tales.--v. 14. The Dolliver romance, and kindred tales.--v. 15. Doctor Grimshawe's secret. 1900--v. 16. Tales and sketches.--v. 17. Miscellanies.--v. 18. Passages from the American notebooks.--v. 19-22. Notes of travel. [PS1850.F00] 13-21420
I. Lathrop, Mrs. Rose (Hawthorne) 1851-1928. II. Scudder, Horace Elisha, 1838-1903, ed. III. Title.

Proselytes and proselyting, Jewish.

BAMBERGER, Bernard Jacob, 1904- 296
Proselytism in the Talmudic period, by Bernard J. Bamberger. With a foreword by Julian Morgenstern and a new introd. by the author. New York, KTAV Pub. House [1968, 1939] xxxiii, 310 p. 24 cm. Bibliography: p. 304-310. [BM729.P7B3 1968] 68-25720
1. Proselytes and proselyting, Jewish. I. Title.

CASSIN, Elena. 296.83
San Nicandro; the story of a religious phenomenon. Tr. by Douglas West. Chester Springs, Pa., Dufour, 1962 [c.1959] 200p. illus. 22cm. Bibl. 62-8537 4.50
1. Proselytes and proselyting, Jewish. 2. Jews in Sannicandro, Italy. I. Title.

CRESSON, Warder, 1798-1860. 922.
The key of David. David the true Messiah; or, The wisdom, to represent the true and false churches and the living and dead child or Messiah. Also, reasons for becoming a Jew, with a revision of the late lawsuit for lunacy on that account, together with an appendix. Philadelphia, 5612 [1852] iv, 344 p. 20 cm. Cover title: King Solomon's two women and the living and dead child or Messiah. [BM755.C7A3] 50-46163
1. Proselytes and proselyting, Jewish. 2. Messiah. I. Title.

EICHHORN, David Max, ed. 296.71
Conversion to Judaism: a history and analysis. Contributing authors: Bernard J. Bamberger [others. New York] Ktav [1966, c.1965] xii, 288p. 24cm. Bibl. [BM729.P7E5] 65-21742 5.95
1. Proselytes and proselyting, Jewish. I. Bamberger, Bernard Jacob, 1904- II. Title.

LAPIDE, Phinn E 1922- 296
The prophet of San Nicandro. New York, Beechhurst Press [1953] 240p. illus. 25cm. [BM729.P7L32] 53-8027
1. Prosetytes and proselyting, Jewish. I. Title.

ROSENBLOOM, Joseph R. 296.7'1
Conversion to Judaism : from the Biblical period to the present / Joseph R. Rosenbloom. Cincinnati : Hebrew Union College Press, 1979. xiii, 178 p. ; 24 cm. Includes index. Bibliography: p. 161-167. [BM729.P7R67] 78-9409 ISBN 0-87820-113-0 : 10.00
1. Proselytes and proselyting, Jewish. I. Title.

Proselytes and proselyting, Jewish—Converts from Christianity.

CARMEL, Abraham, 1911- 296
So strange my path; a spiritual pilgrimage [2d ed.] New York, Bloch [1964] 234p. 22cm. 64-17487 4.95
1. Proselytes and proselyting, Jewish—Converts from Christianity. I. Title.

WIGDOER, Devorah. 296.71
Hope is my house. Englewood Cliffs, N. J., Prentice [1966] 282p. 22cm. [BM755.W43A3] 66-22101 4.95 bds.,
1. Proselytes and proselyting, Jewish—Converts from christianity. 2. Proselytes and proselyting, Jewish—Converts from Christianity I. Title.

WIGODER, Devorah. 296.71 B
Hope is my house. Englewood Cliffs, N. J., Prentice-Hall [1966] 282 p. 22 cm. [BM755.W43A3] 66-22101
1. Proselytes and proselyting, Jewish—Converts from Christianity. I. Title.

Proselytes and proselyting, Jewish—Converts from Christianity—Juvenile literature.

YOWA. 296.7'1
The becoming of Ruth; an autobiography. Written and illustrated by Yowa. New York, Crown Publishers [1972] 64 p. col. illus. 21 cm. A young girl's search for spiritual fulfillment leads her to convert from Christianity to Judaism. [BM729.P7Y69] 79-185069 4.95
1. Proselytes and proselyting, Jewish—Converts from Christianity—Juvenile literature. 2. [Judaism.] I. Title.

Proselytes and proselyting, Jewish—Converts from Shinto.

KOTSUJI, Abraham Setsujau, 1899- 296.7
From Tokyo to Jerusalem [New York] Geis; dist. Random [1965, c.1964] 215p. 22cm. [BM755.P75K6] 64-84810 4.95 bds.,
1. Proselytes and proselyting, Jewish—Converts from Shinto. I. Title.

Proserpine—Juvenile literature.

HODGES, Margaret. JUV
Persephone and the springtime; a Greek myth retold by Margaret Hodges. Illustrated by Arvis Stewart. [1st ed.] Boston, Little, Brown [1973] 32 p. illus. 24 cm. ([Her Myths of the world]) Retells the Greek legend that explains why Persephone brings springtime to the earth each year. [PZ8.1.H69Pe] 292'.2'11 72-7492 ISBN 0-316-36786-9 5.75
1. Proserpine—Juvenile literature. 2. [Proserpine.] 3. [Mythology, Greek.] I. Stewart, Arvis L., illus. II. Title.

"Protcols of the wise men of Zion."

BERNSTEIN, Herman, 1876- 296
The truth about "The protocols of Zion"; a complete exposure, by Herman Bernstein. New York, Covici, Friede [c1935] xiv, 15-397 p. facsims. 21 cm. Contains a long historical introduction on the origins of the "Protocols" and on the numerous versions in which they have continued to appear, and reprints of all the documents relating to the case, including "Dialogues in hell between Machiavelli and Montesquieu" (p. [75]-258) and "Protocols of the wise men of Zion" (295-359) [DS145.P7B45] 85-8225
1. "Protcols of the wise men of Zion." 2. Jewish question. I. Joly, Maurice, 1831-1878. Dialogue aux enfers entre Machiavel et Montesquieu. II. Title.

Protestant churches.

BELLAMY, Joseph, 1719-1790. 252.
The law, our school-master; a sermon preached at Litchfield June 8, 1756, before the Association of Litchfield County. By Joseph Bellamy ... Published with great enlargements ... New-Haven, Printed by J. Parker, and company [1762] 1 p. l., 77, [1] p. 19 cm. Head-piece. [BX7233.B58L3] 21-18449

I. Title.

CHURCH directory, 277.
Olean, New York; a complete directory of All Protestant churches, 1905. [Olean, N.Y.] The Olean directory company, c1905- v. 17 cm. Cover-title. [BR560.O5C5] Ca 5

MEAGHER, James Luke, 1848-
The Protestant churches. Their founders, histories and developments. How the reformation spread. The beliefs, practices, customs and forms of worship of the different demoninations. Their ministers, congregations, membership and cost of buildings. Information condensed from authentic sources in various languages, by Rev. James Luke Meagher... New York, Christian press association [c1914] 653 p. 19 1/2 cm. 14-10037 1.50
I. Title.

NEW York. Missionary Research 284
Library.
Protestant churches of Asia, the Middle East, Africa, Latin America, and the Pacific area. New York, 1959. 75p. 28cm. 'Revision of The younger churches--Some facts and observations.' [BX4805.2.N45 1959] 59-44072
1. Protestant churches. 2. Sects. 3. Missions. I. Title.

PROTESTANT churches of Asia,
the Middle East, Africa, Latin America, and the Pacific area. New York, Missionary research library, 1959. iii, 75p. 28cm. 'Revision of The younger churches-some facts and observations.'
I. Price, Francis Wilson, 1895-

A study of church membership for adults in certain selected Protestant churches. Denver, Colorado, Iliff School of Theology, 1956. 170p. Diss.--Iliff School of Theology.
I. Rose, Edwin Joseph.

Protestant churches—Armenia.

ARPEE, Leon. 275.66
A century of American Protestantism, 1846-1946, by Leon Arpee ... New York, N. Y., The Armenian missionary association of America, inc., 1946. 4 p. l., 96 p. 23 cm. Bibliographical foot-notes. [BR1100.A67] 266 266 46-21905
1. Protestant churches—Armenia. 2. Armenia—Church history. 3. Armenian church—Hist. 4. Armenian missionary association of America. I. Title.

Protestant churches—Australia—Clergy.

BLAIKIE, Norman W. H., 301.5'8
1933-
The plight of the Australian clergy : to convert, care or challenge? / Norman W. H. Blaikie. St. Lucia : University of Queensland Press ; Hemel Hempstead Eng., : distributed by Prentice-Hall International, c1979. xii, 253 p. ; 22 cm. Includes index. Bibliography: p. [233]-244. [BR1480.B52] 79-320956 ISBN 0-7022-1397-7 : 24.25
1. Protestant churches—Australia—Clergy. 2. Clergy—Australia. 3. Role conflict. I. Title.
Distributed by Technical Impex Corp., 5 South Union Street, Lawrence, MA 01843

Protestant churches — Biography

HARPER, Howard V. 280'.4'0922
Profiles of Protestant saints, by Howard V. Harper. Foreword by Richard Cardinal Cushing. New York, Fleet Press Corp. [1968] 231 p. 21 cm. [BX4825.H3] 67-24071
1. Protestant churches—Biography. I. Title.

SMART, William James, 1895-
Six mighty men. New York, Macmillan [1957] 151 p. 19 cm.
1. Protestant churches — Biog. I. Title.

Protestant churches—Brazil.

GATES, Charles W. 278.1
Industrialization: Brazil's catalyst for church growth; a study of the Rio area, by C. W. Gates. South Pasadena, Calif., William Carey Library [1972] xi, 78 p. illus. 22 cm. Bibliography: p. 68-72. [BX4836.B8G38] 72-81342 ISBN 0-87808-413-4 1.95
1. Protestant churches—Brazil. 2. Church growth. I. Title.

INTERNATIONAL missionary 284
council. Dept. of social and economic research and counsel.
How the church grows in Brazil, a study of the economic and social basis of the Evangelical church in Brazil; J. Merle Davis, director. New York, London, Dept. of social and economic research and counsel, International missionary council, 1943. 167 p. illus. (map) 21 1/2 cm. [BX4836.B8I5] 43-10905
1. Protestant churches—Brazil. I. Davis, John Merle, 1875- II. Title.

MIZUKI, John, 1922- 280'.4'0981
The growth of Japanese churches in Brazil / John Mizuki. South Pasadena, Calif. : William Carey Library, c1978. xxii, 212 p. : ill. ; 22 cm. Includes index. Bibliography: p. 193-207. [BX4836.B8M59] 78-5415 ISBN 0-87808-323-5 pbk. : 8.95
1. Protestant churches—Brazil. 2. Japanese in Brazil—Religion. 3. Church growth—Brazil. I. Title.

WILLEMS, Emilio. 280/.4/098
Followers of the new faith; culture change and the rise of Protestantism in Brazil and Chile. [Nashville] Vanderbilt Univ. Pr., 1967. x, 290p. 24cm. Bibl. [BX4836.B8W5] 67-27517 7.50
1. Protestant churches—Brazil. 2. Protestant churches—Chile. 3. Brazil—Soc. condit. 4. Chile—Soc. condit. I. Title.

Protestant churches—Brazil—Statistics.

MISSIONS Advanced 280'.4'0981
Research and Communication Center.
Continuing evangelism in Brazil; a MARC/MIB study project. Monrovia, Calif. [1971] xi, 107 p. illus. 28 cm. (Its Interpretive bulletin 1) Bibliography: p. 100-106. [BX4836.B8M57 1971] 73-180295
1. Protestant churches—Brazil—Statistics. 2. Evangelistic work—Brazil. I. Missionary Information Bureau. II. Title. III. Series.

READ, William R., 280'.4'0981
1923-
Brazil 1980: the Protestant handbook; the dynamics of church growth in the 1950's and 60's, and the tremendous potential for the 70's [by] William R. Read and Frank A. Ineson. Monrovia, Calif., MARC [1973] xxx, 405 p. illus. 23 cm. Bibliography: p. [368]-396. [BX4836.B8R4] 73-84887 ISBN 0-912552-04-2
1. Protestant churches—Brazil—Statistics. 2. Church growth. 3. Religious and ecclesiastical institutions—Brazil—Directories. I. Ineson, Frank Avery, 1902- joint author. II. Title.
Publisher's address: 919 W. Huntington Drive, Monrovia, Calif. 91016.

READ, William R., 280'.4'0981
1923-
Brazil 1980: the Protestant handbook; the dynamics of church growth in the 1950's and 60's, and the tremendous potential for the 70's [by] William R. Read & Frank A. Ineson. Monrovia, Calif., MARC [1973] xxx, 405 p. illus. 23 cm. Bibliography: p. [368]-396. [BX4836.B8R4] 73-84887 ISBN 0-912552-04-2
1. Protestant churches—Brazil—Statistics. 2. Church growth. 3. Religious and ecclesiastical institutions—Brazil—Directories. I. Ineson, Frank Avery, 1902- joint author. II. Title.

Protestant churches—China (People's Republic of China, 1949-)

JONES, Francis Price. 275.1
The church in Communist China; a Protestant appraisal. New York, Friendship Press [1962] 180p. 19cm. Includes bibliography. [BR1285.J6] 62-7859
1. Protestant churches—China (People's Republic of China, 1949-) 2. Communism and religion—1946- I. Title.

Protestant churches—Clergy.

WAYWARD shepherds: 253'.2
prejudice and the Protestant clergy [by] Rodney Stark [and others. 1st ed.] New York, Harper & Row [1971] x, 138 p. 24 cm. (Patterns of American prejudice series, v. 6) Includes bibliographical references. [BX5965.W38] 76-144187 ISBN 0-06-013973-0 6.95
1. Protestant churches—Clergy. 2. Antisemitism—United States. I. Stark, Rodney. II. Title. III. Series.

WHITAKER, N[icholas]
T[illinghast]
The pastor's helper; a complete ritual for the various services connected with his office, arranged for the Baptist, Congregational, Methodist Episcopal, Unitarian, and Universalist denominations. Boston, Lee & Shepard, 1900. v, 115 p. 16°. May
I. Title.

Protestant churches—Cuba.

DAVIS, John Merle, 1875- 277.291
The Cuban church in a sugar economy; a study of the economic and social basis of the Evangelical church in Cuba. J. Merle Davis, director. New York, London, Dept. of social and economic research & counsel, International missionary council, 1942. 144 p. 22 1/2 cm. [BX4835.C8D3] 42-9991
1. Protestant churches—Cuba. I. International missionary council. Dept. of social and economic research. II. Title.

INTERNATIONAL missionary 277.291
council. Dept of social and economic research and counsel.
The Cuban church in a sugar economy; a study of the economic and social basis of the evangelical church in Cuba. J. Merle Davis, director. New York, London, Dept. of social and economic research & counsel, International missionary council, 1942. 144 p. 22 1/2 cm. [BX4835.C8I5] 42-9991
1. Protestant churches—Cuba. 2. Cuba—Soc. condit. I. Davis, John Merle, 1875- II. Title.

Protestant churches—Czechoslovak Republic.

LOCHMAN, Jan Milic. 209'.437
Church in a Marxist society; a Czechoslovak view. [1st ed.] New York, Harper & Row [1970] 198 p. 22 cm. [BX4854.C9L6 1970b] 77-85067 5.95
1. Protestant churches—Czechoslovak Republic. 2. Communism and Christianity—Czechoslovak Republic. I. Title.

Protestant churches—Delaware Valley—History.

BUTLER, Jon. 280'.4'09749
Power, authority, and the origins of American denominational order : the English churches in the Delaware Valley, 1680-1730 / Jon Butler. Philadelphia : American Philosophical Society, 1978. 85 p. ; 29 cm. (Transactions of the American Philosophical Society ; v. 68, part 2 ISSN 0065-9746s) Includes index.IBibliography: p. 78-81.I[BR520.B96] 77-91661 ISBN 0-87169-682-7 pbk. : 8.00
1. Protestant churches—Delaware Valley—History. 2. Delaware Valley—Church history. 3. Delaware Valley—History—Colonial period, ca. 1600-1775. I. Title. II. Series: American Philosophical Society, Philadelphia. Transactions ; v. 68, part 2.

Protestant churches—Doctrinal and controversial works.

FORELL, George Wolfgang. 230
The Protestant faith / by George Wolfgang Forell. With revisions. Philadelphia : Fortress Press, 1975, c1960. xii, 308 p. ; 22 cm. Originally published by Prentice-Hall, Englewood Cliffs, N.J. Includes bibliographical references and index. [BX4811.F65 1975] 74-26341 ISBN 0-8006-1095-4 : 5.95
1. Protestant churches—Doctrinal and controversial works. 2. Theology, Doctrinal. 3. Creeds. I. Title.

GARVER, Stuart P. 230'.2
Watch your teaching! A comparative study of Roman Catholic and Protestant teaching since Vatican Council II, by Stuart P. Garver. Hackensack, N.J., Christ's Mission [1973] xvi, 167 p. illus. 22 cm. (Christian heritage series) Bibliography: p. 166-167. [BX1751.2.G36] 73-90020 2.95
1. Catholic Church—Doctrinal and controversial works. 2. Protestant churches—Doctrinal and controversial works. I. Title. II. Series.
Publisher's address: 275 State Street, Hackensack, N.J. 07601

GARVER, Stuart P. 230'.2
Watch your teaching! A comparative study of Roman Catholic and Protestant teaching since Vatican Council II, by Stuart P. Garver. Hackensack, N.J., Christ's Mission [1973] xvi, 167 p. illus. 22 cm. (Christian heritage series) Bibliography: p. 166-167. [BX1751.2.G36] 73-90020 2.95
1. Catholic Church—Doctrinal and controversial works. 2. Protestant churches—Doctrinal and controversial works. I. Title. II. Series.

A layman's guide to Protestant theology. New York, Macmillan, 1956. viii, 222p. 21cm. 'Suggestions for further reading': p.216-218.
1. Protestant churches—Doctrinal and controversial works. I. Hordern, William.

[MILLER, Robert Johnson] 1853-
The fundamentals of Protestantism, including a comparative study of the creed of Romanism, adapted to Bible class work. Pittsburgh, Pa., United Presbyterian board of publication [c1915] 192 p. illus. 22 cm. $0.75 Lettered on cover: By R. J. Miller, D.D. 15-8127
I. Title.

NESBITT, Ralph Beryl. 230
A Protestant believes. New York, 1962. 126p. 23cm. [BX4811.N4] 62-21475
1. Protestant churches— Doctrinal and controversial works. I. Title.

Protestant churches—Education.

AVERILL, Lloyd James, 378.01
1923-
A strategy for the Protestant college. Philadelphia, Westminister [c. 1966] 128p. 21cm. Bibl. [LC427.A95] 66-11807 2.25 pap.,
1. Protestant churches—Education. 2. Universities and colleges—U.S. I. Title.

AVERILL, Lloyd James, 1923- 378.01

A strategy for the Protestant college, by Lloyd J. Averill. Philadelphia, Westminster Press [1966] 128 p. 21 cm. Bibliographical references included in "Notes" (p. [120]-128) [LC427.A95] 66-11807
1. Protestant churches — Education. 2. Universities and colleges — U.S. I. Title.

CHAPIN, Edwin Hubbell, 1814- 016.
1880.
Catalogue of the library of the late Rev. E. H. Chapin, D. D., of New York ... To be sold at auction ... April 18, 1881, and five following days, by Bangs & co. ... [New York, Press of D. Taylor, 1881] 1 p. l., ii, 268 p. 25 cm. 4157 numbers prited in manuscript. [Z997.C463] 4-10272
I. Title.

GROTON, Mass. First Baptist 016.
church. Sunday school library.
Catalogue of books in the Sunday school library of the First Baptist church, Groton, Mass. Ayer, Printed at the office of the Public spirit, 1884. 1 p. l., 12 p. 16 cm. [Z881.G8785] 8-24190
I. Title.

LOWELL, Mass. First 016.
Unitarian society.
Catalogue of books of the Parish library. Lowell, S. J. Varney, printer, 1854. cover-title, [3]-40 p. 17 cm. [Z881.L9116] 5-12491
I. Title.

MILLS, W. Plumer. 378'.0025
Protestant colleges in Asia, the Near East, Africa, and Latin America; with notes on higher education in those areas. New York, Missionary Research Library, 1955. 31 l.

28 cm. Cover title. Includes bibliographical references. [LC531.M5] 74-188622 0.50
1. Protestant Churches—Education. 2. Church colleges. I. Title.

WYNN, Daniel Webster, 1919- 377'.8'4
The Protestant church-related college : a handbook for presidents and trustees / by Daniel W. Wynn. New York : Philosophical Library, [1975] 108 p. ; 22 cm. Includes index. Bibliography: p. 97-102. [LC531.W96] 74-84861 ISBN 0-8022-2157-2 : 6.00
1. Protestant churches—Education. 2. Church and college. 3. College presidents. I. Title.

Protestant churches—Europe.

LATOURETTE, Kenneth Scott, 1884-1968. 270.8 s
The nineteenth century in Europe: the Protestant and Eastern churches. Westport, Conn., Greenwood Press [1973, c1959] viii, 532 p. 23 cm. (His Christianity in a revolutionary age, v. 2) Bibliography: p. 495-512. [BR475.L33 vol. 2] [BX4837] 280'.4'094 72-11977 ISBN 0-8371-5702-1 95.00, 5 vol. set
1. Orthodox Eastern Church—Europe. 2. Protestant churches—Europe. I. Title. II. Series.

MCLEISH, Alexander. 284
... *Europe in transition* ... by Alexander McLeish ... London, New York [etc.] World dominion press [1942?- v. incl. tables. fold. front., fold. map. 19 1/2 cm. (War-time survey series, no. 5 "Questions for group study": p. [3] of cover. Contents.pt. I. The churches face the future.--pt. II. Churches under trial. [BX4837.M3] 43-1942
1. Protestant churches—Europe. I. Title.

Protestant churches— France.

HOUGHTON, Louise (Seymour) Mrs., 1838-1920.
Handbook of French and Belgin Protestantism, prepared by Louise Seymour Houghton. New York, Pub. for the Federal council of the churches of Christ in America, by the Missionary education movement [c1919] viii p., 2 l., 3-245 p. front., plates. 19 1/2 cm. [BX4843.H6] 19-9257
I. Federal council of the churches of Christ in America. II. Title.

POLAND, Burdette C 284
French Protestantism and the French Revolution; a study in church and state, thought and religion, 1685-1815. Princeton, Princeton University Press, 1957. ix, 315p. maps. 25cm. Bibliography: p. 301-309. [BX4843.P6] 57-5846
1. Protestant churches— France. 2. France—Hist.—Revolution—Religious history. I. Title.

POLAND, Burdette C 284
French Protestantism and the French Revolution; a study in church and state, thought and religion, 1685-1815. Princeton, Princeton University Press, 1957. ix, 315p. maps. 25cm. Bibliography: p. 301-309. [BX4843.P6] 57-5846
1. Protestant churches—France. 2. France—Hist.—Revolution—Religious history. I. Title.

Protestant churches—Germany.

DORNER, Isaak August, 1809-1884 260
Geschichte der protestantischen theologie, besonders in Deutschland, nach ihrer principiellen bewegung und im zusammenhang mit dem religiosen, sittlichen und intellectuellen leben betrachtet, von dr. I. A. Dorner. Munchen, J. G. Cotta, 1867; New York, Johnson Reprint, 1966. 2 p. 1., 924 p. 23 cm. 2 cm. (Geschichte der wissenschaften in Deutschland. Neuere zeit. 5. bd.) 28.00
I. Title.

SCHODDE, George Henry, 1854-1917.
The Protestant church in Germany. A general survey. By Professor GeorgeH. Schodde ... Philadelphia, Pa., Lutheran publication society [c1901] 112 p. 16 cm. (On cover: Lutheran hand-book series) [BX8020.S3] 2-1223
1. Protestant churches—Germany. I. Title.

Protestant churches—Hungary.

UJSZASZY, Kalman. 280'.4'094391
Hungarian Protestantism yesterday and today. [Denville, N.J., Pannonia Press, 196-] 48 p. 23 cm. [BX4854.H8U38] 67-30022
1. Protestant churches—Hungary. 2. Protestants in Hungary. I. Title.

Protestant churches—India—Madras.

NELSON, Amirtharaj, 1934- 280'.4'095482
A new day in Madras : a study of Protestant churches in Madras / Amirtharaj Nelson. Pasadena, Calif. : William Carey Library, [1974, i.e.1975] xxvi, 340 p. : ill. ; 23 cm. Bibliography: p. [311]-340. [BR1175.M3N44] 74-23951 ISBN 0-87808-420-7 pbk. : 7.95
1. Protestant churches—India—Madras. I. Title.

Protestant churches—Japan.

IGLEHART, Charles W. 284.0952
A century of Protestant Christianity in Japan. [Published in cooperation with the Japan Committee. Division of Foreign Missions, National Council of the Churches of Christ in the U.S.A.] Rutland, Vt., C. E. Tuttle Co. [1959] 384p. 22cm. 59-11758 3.00
1. Protestant churches—Japan. 2. Japan—Church history. I. Title.

THOMAS, Winburn T 284.0952
Protestant beginnings in Japan, the first three decades, 1859-1889 [1st ed.] Tokyo, Rutland, Vt., C. E. Tuttle Co. [1959] 258 p. group port. 22 cm. "Originally presented as a dissertation to the faculty of the Graduate School of Yale University ... for the degree of doctor of philosophy." Bibliographical references included in "Notes" (p. 213-233) "A bibliography concerning the post-restoration development of Christianity in Japan" (p. 241-247) [BR1305.T5 1959] 59-6489
1. Protestant churches — Japan. 2. Missions — Japan. I. Title.

YAMAMORI, Tetsunao, 1937- 281'.4'0952
Church growth in Japan; a study in the development of eight denominations, 1859-1939. South Pasadena, Calif., William Carey Library [1974] xi, 185 p. illus. 23 cm. Revised version of the author's thesis, Duke University. Bibliography: p. [175]-185. [BR1305.Y35] 74-4009 ISBN 0-87808-412-6 4.95
1. Protestant churches—Japan. 2. Church growth—Case studies. I. Title.

Protestant churches—Korea.

SHEARER, Roy E. 275.19
Wildfire: church growth in Korea. Grand Rapids, Mich., Eerdmans [c.1966] 242p. illus., maps. 21cm. (Church growth ser.) Bibl. [BR1320.S45] 65-18085 2.95 pap.,
1. Protestant churches—Korea. 2. Missions—Korea. I. Title.

Protestant churches—Latin America.

COSTAS, Orlando E. 266'.023'098
Theology of the crossroads in contemporary Latin America : missiology in mainline Protestantism, 1969-1974 / door O. E. Costas. Amsterdam, [Keizersgracht 302-304] : Rodopi, 1976. xiv, 413 p. ; 23 cm. Includes index. Bibliography: p. [359]-408. [BR600.C66] 76-361930 ISBN 9-06-203259-1 pbk. : 19.25
1. Protestant churches—Latin America. 2. Missions—Theory. I. Title.
Distributed by Humanities

Protestant churches—Latin America—Bibliography.

SINCLAIR, John H., 1924- 016.280'4'098
Protestantism in Latin America: a bibliographical guide; an annotated bibliography of selected references mainly in English, Spanish, and Portuguese and useful bibliographical aids to assist the student and researcher in the general field of Latin American studies. Edited by John H. Sinclair. South Pasadena, Calif., William Carey Library [1973] p. [Z7778.L3S57] 73-12837 ISBN 0-87808-126-7 6.95 (pbk.)
1. Protestant churches—Latin America—Bibliography. I. Title.

Protestant churches—Mexico.

INTERNATIONAL missionary council. Dept. of social and economic research. 284.0972
The economic basis of the Evangelical church in Mexico; a study made by the Department of social and economic research of the International missionary council, J. Merle Davis, director of the department. London, New York, International missionary council, 1940. 133 p. 21 1/2 cm. [BX4833.M4I5 1940] 41-3757
1. Protestant churches—Mexico. I. Davis, John Merle, 1875- II. Title.

INTERNATIONAL missionary council. Dept. of social and economic research and counsel. 284.0972
The economic basis of the evangelical church in Mexico; a study made by the Department of social and economic research of the International missionary council; J. Merle Davis, director of the department. London, New York, International missionary council, 1940. 133 p. 21 1/2 cm. [BX4833.M4I5 1940] 41-3757
1. Protestant churches—Mexico. I. Davis, John Merle, 1875- II. Title.

MCGAVRAN, Donald Anderson, 1897- 284.0972
Church growth in Mexico, by Donald McGavran, John Huegel, Jack Taylor. Grand Rapids, Mich., Eerdmans [c.1963] 136p. map, diagrs. 21cm. Bibl. 63-17788 1.95 pap.,
1. Protestant churches—Mexico. I. Title.

Protestant churches—Missions.

BEAVER, Robert Pierce, 1906- 266.4
From mission to mission; Protestant world mission today and tomorrow. New York, Association [c.1964] 126p. 16cm. (Reflection bk.) 64-11420 .50 pap.,
1. Protestant churches—Missions. I. Title.

BEAVER, Robert Pierce, 1906- 266.4
From missions to mission; Protestant world mission today and tomorrow. New York, Association Press [c1964] 126 p. 16 cm. (A Reflection book) [BV2061.B4] 64-11420
1. Protestant churches — Missions. I. Title.

LEBER, Charles Tudor, 1898- ed. 266
World faith in action; the unified missionary enterprise of Protestant Christianity. [1st ed.] Indianapolis, Bobbs-Merrill [1951] 345 p. ports. 22 cm. [BV2060.L44] 51-10349
1. Protestant churches—Missions. I. Title.
Contents Omitted.

MALASKA, Hilkka. 266'.4
The challenge for evangelical missions to Europe; a Scandinavian case study. South Pasadena, Calif., William Carey Library [1970] 178 p. illus. 22 cm. Bibliography: p. 161-176. [BV3060.M33] 71-132011 ISBN 0-87808-308-1 2.95
1. Protestant churches—Missions. 2. Missions—Scandinavia. I. Title.

NEW York. Missionary Research Library.
North American Protestant foreign mission agencies, 5th ed. New York, Missionary Research Library. 1962. xvii, 119 p. 65-38730
I. Title.

Protestant churches—Missouri—St. Louis—Directories

THE Blue book; 277.
a manual and directory of the Protestant evangelical churches and related organizations of the metropolitan area of St. Louis, Missouri, including the city and county of St. Louis, Missouri, Madison and St. Clair counties, Illinois. Compiled and published by the Metropolitan church federation ... v. 1- St. Louis, Mo., 1926- v. illus. 19 1/2 cm. [BR560.S2B5] 26-4507
1. Protestant churches—Missouri—St. Louis—Direct. 2. Protestant churches—Illinois—Direct. I. Metropolitan church federation, St. Louis.

Protestant churches—New South Wales.

BOLLEN, John David. 261
Protestantism and social reform in New South Wales 1890-1910 [by] J. D. Bollen. Clayton, Vic., Melbourne University Press, 1972. xiii, 199 p. illus., 4 plates, ports., tables. 23 cm. Bibliography: p. 187-193. [BR1483.N5B64] 73-163210 ISBN 0-522-84023-X
1. Protestant churches—New South Wales. 2. Church and social problems—New South Wales. I. Title.
Distributed by International Scholarly Book Service, 11.70.

Protestant churches—Prussia.

BIGLER, Robert M. 261.7
The politics of German Protestantism; the rise of the Protestant Church elite in Prussia, 1815-1848 [by] Robert M. Bigler. Berkeley, University of California Press [1972] xiv, 300 p. 24 cm. A revision of the author's thesis, University of California at Berkeley. Bibliography: p. 268-290. [BX4844.B53 1972] 77-142055 ISBN 0-520-01881-8
1. Protestant churches—Prussia. 2. Clergy—Prussia. 3. Christianity and politics. I. Title.

Protestant churches—Puerto Rico.

INTERNATIONAL missionary council. Dept. of social and economic research and counsel. 277.295
The church in Puerto Rico's dilemma; a study of the economic and social basis of the evangelical church in Puerto Rico; J. Merle Davis, director. New York, London, Dept. of social and economic research & counsel, International missionary council, 1942. viii, 80 p. 21 1/2 cm. [BX4835.P815] 43-3517
1. Protestant churches—Puerto Rico. 2. Puerto Rico—Soc. condit. I. Davis, John Merle, 1875- II. Title.

Protestant churches—Relations.

CONSULTATION on Church Union.
Consultation on church union 1967; principles of church union, guidelines for structure, and a study guide. [Cincinnati, Ohio, Foreward Movement Publications, 1967] 142 p. 17 cm. (Foreword Movement miniature books) 68-71142
1. Protestant churches—Relations. I. Title. II. Series.

Protestant churches—Relations—Catholic Church.

ADAM, Karl, 1876- 284
One and holy. Translated by Cecily Hastings. New York, Greenwood Press [1969, c1951] vii, 130 p. 23 cm. Translation of Una Sancta in katholischer Sicht. [BX4818.3.A313 1969] 79-95111
1. Catholic Church—Relations—Protestant churches. 2. Luther, Martin, 1483-1546. 3. Protestant churches—Relations—Catholic Church. 4. Reformation—Germany. I. Title.

BIANCHI, Eugene C. 282
John XXIII and American Protestants, by Eugene C. Bianchi. With a foreword by Albert C. Outler. Washington, Corpus Books [1968] 287 p. 21 cm. Bibliography: p. 269-277. [BX4818.3.B5] 67-17520
1. Catholic Church—Relations—Protestant

churches. 2. Joannes XXIII, Pope, 1881-1963. 3. Protestant churches—Relations—Catholic Church. I. Title.

BROWN, Robert McAfee, 1920- 282
An American dialogue: a Protestant looks at Catholicism and a Catholic looks at Protestantism, by Robert McAfee Brown and Gustave Weigel. With a foreword by Will Herberg. [1st ed.] Garden City, N. Y., Doubleday, 1960. 216 p. 22 cm. Includes bibliography. [BX4818.3.B7] 60-13750
1. Protestant churches—Relations—Catholic Church. 2. Catholic Church—Relations—Protestant churches. I. Weigel, Gustave, 1906- joint author. II. Title.

CALLAHAN, Daniel J., ed. 230
Christianity divided, Protestant and Roman Catholic theological issues; edited by Daniel J. Callahan, Heiko A. Oberman [and] Daniel J. O'Hanlon. New York, Sheed and Ward [1961] xiv, 335 p. 22 cm. Includes bibliographies. [BX4818.3.C3] 61-11789
1. Protestant churches—Relations—Catholic Church. 2. Catholic Church—Relations—Protestant churches. 3. Creeds—Comparative studies. I. Title.

CULLMANN, Oscar 280.1
Message to Catholics and Protestants. Translated [from the German] by Joseph A. Burgess. Grand Rapids, Eerdmans [1959] 57p. 20cm. 59-14590 1.50
1. Protestant churches—Relations—Catholic Church. 2. Catholic Church—Relations—Protestant churches. I. Title.

CURRY, Lerond. 262'.001
Protestant-Catholic relations in America, World War I through Vatican II. [Lexington] University Press of Kentucky [1972] xi, 124 p. 23 cm. Includes bibliographical references. [BX4818.3.C87] 79-183352 ISBN 0-8131-1265-6 7.25
1. Catholic Church—Relations—Protestant churches. 2. Protestant churches—Relations—Catholic Church. 3. United States—Religion. I. Title.

LETIS, Theodore P., 1951- 280'.042
Martin Luther and charismatic ecumenism / by Theodore P. Letis. Springfield, Mo. : Reformation Research Press, c1979. p. cm. Includes statements made at the 1977 Conference on the Charismatic Renewal in the Christian Churches. Bibliography: p. [BX4818.3.L48] 79-27854 pbk : 2.95
1. Catholic Church—Relations—Protestant churches. 2. Luther, Martin, 1483-1546—Theology. 3. Protestant churches—Relations—Catholic Church. 4. Theology, Catholic. 5. Pentecostalism and Christian union. I. Conference on the Charismatic Renewal in the Christian Churches, Kansas City, Mo., 1977. II. Title.

LOEWENICH, Walther von 282
Modern Catholicism. Translated by Reginald H. Fuller. New York, St. Martin's Press. 1959 [ ] viii, 378p. 23cm. (4p. bibl.) 59-65290 9.00
1. Protestant churches—Relations—Catholic Church. 2. Catholic Church—Relations—Protestant churches. 3. Catholic Church—Doctrinal and controversial works—Protestant authors. 4. Catholic Church—Hist.—Modern period. I. Title.

SKYDSGAARD, K E 280.1
One in Christ; translated by Axel C. Kildegaard. Philadelphia, Muhlenberg Press [1957] 220p. 20cm. [BX4817.S5] 57-9596
1. Protestant churches— Relations—Catholic Church. 2. Catholic Church—Relations— Protestant churches. I. Title.

WITTE, Paul W. 262'.001
On common ground : Protestant and Catholic evangelicals / Paul W. Witte. Waco, Tex. : Word Books, c1975. 135 p. ; 23 cm. Includes bibliographical references. [BX4818.3.W54] 74-82662 ISBN 0-87680-385-0 : 4.95
1. Catholic Church—Relations—Protestant churches. 2. Protestant churches—Relations—Catholic Church. 3. Evangelicalism. I. Title.

Protestant churches—Relations—Orthodox.

NATIONAL Council of the Churches of Christ in the United States of America. 280'.4'0973
American churchmen visit the Soviet Union; who went and what was achieved. [New York, 1956?] 24 p. illus., ports. 31 cm. [BX4817.N37] 73-253261
1. Orthodox Eastern Church, Russian—Relations—Protestant churches. 2. Protestant churches—Relations—Orthodox. I. Title.

Protestant churches—Relations—Orthodox Eastern Church.

MAKRAKES, Apostolos, 1831-1905. 281.9
An Orthodox-Protestant dialogue. Translated from the Greek by Denver Cummings. [2d ed.] Chicago, Orthodox Christian Educational Society [1966] 127 p. 23 cm. [BX324.5.M313 1966] 67-9736
1. Orthodox Eastern Church—Relations—Protestant churches. 2. Protestant churches—Relations—Orthodox Eastern Church. I. Title.

Protestant churches—Russia.

DURASOFF, Steve. 280'.4'0947
The Russian Protestants; evangelicals in the Soviet Union, 1944-1964. Rutherford, Fairleigh Dickinson University Press [1969] 312 p. 22 cm. Bibliography: p. 293-306. [BX4849.D87] 72-76843 ISBN 8-386-74658- 10.00
1. Protestant churches—Russia. I. Title.

HEBLY, J. A. 280'.4'0947
Protestants in Russia / by J. A. Hebly ; translated by John Pott. 1st American ed. Grand Rapids : Eerdmans, c1976. 192 p. ; 18 cm. Translation of Protestanten in Rusland. Includes bibliographical references. [BX4849.H413 1976b] 76-149 ISBN 0-8028-1614-2 : 2.45
1. Protestant churches—Russia. I. Title.

HEBLY, J A. 280'.4'0947
Protestants in Russia / by J. A. Hebly ; translated [from the Dutch] by John Pott. Belfast : Christian Journals Limited, 1976. 192 p. ; 18 cm. Translation of Protestanten in Rusland. [BX4849.H413 1976] 76-369830 ISBN 0-904302-14-8 : £1.50
1. Protestant churches—Russia. I. Title.

Protestant churches—South America.

FIELD, Jay C. 278
... Outlook in the western republics, by Jay C. Field. New York, Friendship press [1942] 64 p. illus. (maps) diagrs. 18 1/2 cm. (Outlook pamphlets on Latin America) "A brief reading list": p. 63-64. [BX4836.A2F5] [266] 43-5072
1. Protestant churches—South America. I. Title.

Protestant churches—Southern States.

CALDWELL, Erskine, 1903- 280'.4'0975
Deep South : memory and observation / Erskine Caldwell. Athens, GA : University of Georgia Press, [1980] p. cm. Part 1 published in 1966 under title: In the shadow of the steeple. [BR535.C29 1980] 80-16013 ISBN 0-8203-0525-1 pbk. : 5.95
1. Caldwell, Erskine, 1903- 2. Protestant churches—Southern states. 3. Southern States—Religion. I. Title.

HILL, Samuel S. 280'.4'0975
Southern churches in crisis [by] Samuel S. Hill. [1st ed.] New York, Holt, Rinehart and Winston [1967] xvii, 234 p. 22 cm. Bibliographical references included in "Notes" (p. 121-229) [BR535.H5] 66-10211
1. Protestant churches—Southern States. 2. Southern States—Church history. I. Title.

Protestant churches — Spain.

PATTEE, Richard, 1906- 284
The regilious question in Spain. Washington, National Council of Catholic Men [1950] 56 p. map. 22 cm. [BX4851.P3] 50-4304
1. Protestant churches — Spain. 2. Religious liberty — Spain. I. Title.

Protestant churches—Spanish America.

BARBIERI, Sante Uberto, Bp. 284.098
Land of Eldorado. New York, Friendship Press [1961] 161p. illus. 20cm. Includes bibliography. [BR600.B26] 61-6628
1. Protestant churches— Spanish America. 2. Spanish America—Religion. 3. Spanish America—Civilization. I. Title.

CARR, Wesley Moore. 278
Discussion and program suggestions for adults on Latin America, based primarily on On this foundation (by W. Stanley Rycroft) Suggestions for discussion groups by Wesley M. Carr; suggestions for program meetings and worship by Margaret W. Taylor ... New York, Friendship press [1942] 63 p. 18 1/2 cm. "Hymn: Consagracao" (words and music): p. 63. Bibliography: p. 8-11. [BR600.C3] [266] 43-3558
1. Protestant churches—Spanish America. 2. Missions—Study and teaching. I. Rycroft, William Stanley. On this foundation. II. Taylor, Margaret W. III. Title.

HOWARD, George Parkinson, 1882- 278
A spiritual adventure in South America. New York, Committee on Cooperation in Latin America, 1943. 68 p. 20 cm. [BR600.H7] [[266]] 50-50283
1. Protestant churches—Spanish America. I. Title.

HOWARD, George Parkinson, 1882- 278
We Americans: North and South. New York, Friendship Press [1951] x, 148 p. fold. col. map (inserted) 20 cm. Bibliography: p. 144-148. [BR600.H72] 51-3605
1. Protestant churches—Spanish America. I. Title.

RYCROFT, William Stanley. 284
Latin America's open doors as seen by W. Stanley Rycroft, executive secretary of the Committee on Co-operation in Latin America, on visits to eight of these republics during 1940. New York, Committee on Co-operation in Latin America [1940] 55 p. 22 cm. [BR600.R78] 47-43968
1. Protestant churches—Spanish America. I. Committee on Co-operation in Latin America. II. Title.

Protestant churches—Taiwan.

RABER, Dorothy A., 1930- 280'.4'0951249
Protestantism in changing Taiwan : a call to creative response / Dorothy A. Raber. South Pasadena, Calif. : William Carey Library, 1978. x, 353 p. : ill. ; 21 cm. Bibliography: p. 346-353. [BR1298.R32] 78-61042 ISBN 0-87808-329-4 pbk. : 3.95
1. Protestant churches—Taiwan. 2. Taiwan—Church history. I. Title.

Protestant Churches—United States

BRAUER, Jerald C. 277.3
Protestantism in America; a narrative history, by Jerald C. Brauer. Rev. ed. Philadelphia, Westminister Press [1965] 320 p. 21 cm. "Sources": p. [305]-308. "Suggestions for further reading": p. [309]-314. [BR515.B7] 66-12686
1. Protestant churches — U.S. 2. U.S. — Church history. I. Title.

BRAUER, Jerald C. 277.3
Protestantism in America; a narrative history. Philadelphia, Westminster Press [1953] 307 p. 21 cm. [BR515.B7] 53-6778
1. Protestant churches—U.S. 2. U.S.—Church history. I. Title.

BRILL, Earl H 261.8
The creative edge of American Protestantism [by] Earl H. Brill. New York, Seabury Press [1966] vii. 248 p. 22 cm. Bibliography: p. 239-243. [BR526.B7] 66-10834
1. Protestant churches — U.S. 2. Church and social problems — U.S. I. Title.

BUNDY, Edgar C 280.1
Collectivism in the churches; a documented account of the political activities of the Federal, National, and World Councils of Churches. Wheaton, Ill., Church League of America, 1958. 354p. 22cm. Includes bibliography. [BR516.B82] [BR516.B82] 280.6273 57- 57-13355
1. Protestant churches—U. S. 2. Federal Council of the Churches of Christ in America. 3. National Council of the Churches of Christ in the United States of America. 4. World Council of Churches. 5. Socialism in the U. S. I. Title.

DOUGLASS, Harlan Paul, 1871- 280
Church comity; a study of cooperative church extension in American cities, by H. Paul Douglass ... Garden City, N.Y., Doubleday, Doran & company, inc., 1929. vii p., 4 l., 181 p. diagrs. 22 1/2 cm. "The Institute of social and religious research ... is responsible for this publication." [BX8.D65] 29-19710
1. Protestant churches—U.S. I. Institute of social and religious research. II. Title.

DOUGLASS, Harlan Paul, 1871- 260
The Protestant church as a social institution, by H. Paul Douglass and Edmund de S. Brunner. New York and London, Pub. for the Institute of social and religious research by Harper and brothers [c1935] xv, 368 p. diagrs. 23 1/2 cm. "The Institute of social and religious research ... is responsible for this publication."--p. [ii] "First edition." Bibliography: p. 356-362. [BR516.D66] 35-2275
1. Protestant churches—U.S. 2. Sociology, Christian. I. Brunner, Edmund de Schweinitz, 1889- joint author. II. Institute of social and religious research. III. Title.

DOUGLASS, Harlan Paul, 1871- 234
Protestant cooperation in American cities, by H. Paul Douglass ... New York, Institute of social and religious research [c1930] xviii, 514 p. diagrs., fold. form. 22 1/2 cm. "The report of the investigation is in two volumes. The first entitled 'Church comity: a study of cooperative church extension in American cities'."--Pref. Bibliography: p. 494. [BX8.D67] 31-1893
1. Protestant churches—U.S. I. Institute of social and religious research. II. Title.

DOUGLASS, Harlan Paul, 1871-1953. 261.1
The Protestant church as a social institution, by H. Paul Douglass and Edmund deS. Brunner. New York, Russell & Russell [1972] xv, 368 p. illus. 24 cm. (Institute of Social and Religious Research studies) (Institute of Social and Religious Research Studies) Reprint of the 1935 ed. Bibliography: p. 356-362. [BR517.D6 1972] 72-173517
1. Protestant churches—United States. 2. Sociology, Christian. I. Brunner, Edmund de Schweinitz, 1889- joint author. II. Title. III. Series. IV. Series: Institute of Social and Religious Research. Studies.

DRUMMOND, Andrew Landale. 284
Story of American Protestantism. 2d ed. Boston, Beacon Press, 1951. xii, 418 p. 23 cm. Bibliography: p. 407-413. [BR515.D] A52
1. Protestant churches—U. S. 2. U. S.—Church history. I. Title.

HALL, Clarence Wilbur, 1902- 284
Protestant panorama; a story of the faith that made America free, by Clarence W. Hall and Desider Holisher. With an introd. by Charles P. Taft. New York, Farrar, Straus and Young [1951] 180 p. illus. 26 cm. Bibliography: p. 179-180. [BR525.H26] 51-13261
1. Protestant churches—U.S. 2. U.S.—Religion. I. Holisher, Desider, 1901- joint author. II. Title.

HUDSON, Winthrop Still, 1911- 277.3
American Protestantism. [Chicago] University of Chicago Press [1961] 198 p. 21 cm. (The Chicago history of American civilization) Includes bibliography. [BR515.H78] 61-15936
1. Protestant churches—United States. 2. United States—Church history. I. Title.

MARTY, Martin E., 1928- 280'.4'0973
Righteous empire; the Protestant experience in America [by] Martin E.

Marty. New York, Dial Press [1970] 295 p. 24 cm. (Two centuries of American life: a bicentennial series) Includes bibliographical references. [BR515.M33] 72-120468 8.95
1. Protestant churches—U.S. 2. U.S.—Church history. I. Title.

MARTY, Martin E., 1928- 280'.4'0973
Rightous empire : the protestant experience in America / Martin E. Marty. New York : Harper & Row, 1977,c1970. 95p. ; 21 cm. (Harper Torchbooks) Includes bibliographical references and index. [BR515.M33] ISBN 0-06-131931-7 pbk. : 4.95
1. Protestant churches-United States. 2. United States-Church history. I. Title.
L.C. card no. for c1970 Dial Press ed.:72-120468.

MEAD, Frank Spencer, 1898- 284.0973
See these banners go; the story of the Protestant churches in America, by Frank S. Mead ... Indianapolis, New York, The Bobbs-Merrill company [c1936] 3 p. l., ix-x p., 1 l., 13-273 p. 21 cm. "Published in Christian herald under the title 'Like a mighty army'." "First edition." [BR515.M4] [277.3] 36-5967
1. Protestant churches—U.S. 2. Sects—U.S. 3. U.S.—Church history. I. Title.

MILTON, Jennie Lou. 268.62
Let's go out-of-doors [by] Jennie Lou Milton. Prepared from a descriptive outline developed by Protestant Christian forces of the United States and Canada through the International council of religious education, and released to the constituent denominations. Leaders' manual. Co-operative vacation church school manual for kindergarten vacation church school groups. Nashville, Tenn., Printed for the International committee on co-operative publication of vacation church school curriculum, Cokesbury press [c1935] 151 p. 22 cm. [The co-operative series of vacation church school texts] Includes music. "Books for children": p. 19-20; "Bibliography for workers": p. 150-151. [BV1585.M5] 35-14066
I. Title.

MORRISON, Charles Clayton, 1874- 284
Can Protestantism win American? New York, Harper [1948] viii, 225 p. 21 cm. Based on a series of articles by the author pub. in the Christian century. Based on a series of articles by the author pub. in the Christian century. [BR515.M62] 48-9739
1. Protestant churches—U.S. 2. U.S.—Religion. I. Title.

MURCH, James DeForest, 1892- 280'.4'09B
The Protestant revolt; road to freedom for American churches. Foreword by Edmund A. Opitz. Arlington, Va., Crestwood Books, 1967. 326 p. ports. 21 cm. [BR516.M82] 67-21695
1. National Council of the Churches of Christ in the United States of America. 2. Protestant churches—United States. I. Title.

NIXON, Justin Wroe, 1886- 284.0973
Protestantism's hour of decision [by] Justin Wroe Nixon. Philadelphia, Chicago [etc.] The Judson press [1940] 154 p. 24 cm. "First printing, September, 1940." "References" at end of each chapter. [BR525.N63] 40-32975
1. Protestant churches—U. S. 2. Church and state in the U. S. 3. Sociology, Christian. I. Title.

PARKER, Thomas Valentine, 1878- 284.0973
American Protestantism, an appraisal. New York, Philosophical Library [1956] 219p. 22cm. [BR525.P27] 56-13948
1. Protestant churches—U. S. I. Title.

SCHOFIELD, Charles Edwin, 1894- ed. 208.2
The church looks ahead; American Protestant Christianity, an analysis and a forecast, edited by Charles E. Schofield. New York, The Macmillan company, 1933. xiv p., 1 l., 400 p. 23 cm. Bibliography: p. 391-400. [BR525.S35] 33-37689
1. Protestant churches—U. S. 2. U. S.—Religion. I. Title.

SEEBACH, Julius Frederick, 1869- 277.3
The path of Protestantism, by Julius F. Seebach. New York, Round table press, 1934. ix p., 2 l., 3-243 p. diagrs. 19 1/2 cm. Bibliography: p. 227-230. 34-40311
1. Protestant churches—U.S. 2. U.S.—Religion. I. Title.

SMITH, Timothy Lawrence, 1924- 269'.24'0973
Revivalism and social reform : American Protestantism on the eve of the Civil War / Timothy L. Smith ; with a new afterword by the author. Baltimore : Johns Hopkins University Press, 1980. 269 p. ; 20 cm. Originally published in 1957 by Abingdon Press, New York, under title: Revivalism and social reform in mid-nineteenth-century America. Includes index. Bibliography: p. 263-264. [BV3773.S6 1980] 19 80-8114 ISBN 0-8018-2477-X pbk. : 5.95
1. Protestant churches—United States. 2. Revivals—United States—History. 3. United States—Church history—19th century. 4. Church and social problems—United States. I. Title.

TEACHERS' manual for The Protestant Churches of America. Westminster, Md., Newman Press, 1957 57p. 20cm. 'Selected readings' at end of each chapter.
1. Protestant Churches—U. S. I. Hardon, John A

WAMBLE, G Hugh, 1923- 209'.73
The shape of faith. Nashville, Broadman Press [1962] 88 p. 20 cm. (A Broadman starbook) [BR526.W27] 62-9201
1. Protestant churches — U.S. I. Title.

WARD, Harry Frederick, 1873- 277.3
Which way religion? by Harry F. Ward... New York, The Macmillan company, 1931. 221 p. 19 1/2 cm. [BR515.W3] 31-5778
1. Protestant churches—U.S. 2. Sociology, Christian. 3. Christian ethics. I. Title.

Protestant churches—United States—Addresses, essays, lectures.

INGWALSON, Kenneth W. 260
Your church, their target; what's going on in the Protestant churches, a symposium by Harry R. Butman [others] Comp. by Kenneth W. Ingwalson. Arlington, Va., Better Bks. [1966] 275p. ports. 21cm. Bibl. [BR515.I46] 66-17578 4.50; 3.00 bds., pap.,
1. Protestant churches—U. S.—Addresses, essays, lectures. I. Butman, Harry R. II. Title.

Protestant churches—United States—Case studies.

OWENS, Owen D. 253'.0973
Growing churches for a new age / by Owen D. Owens. Valley Forge, PA : Judson Press, 1981. p. cm. Includes bibliographical references. [BR526.O95] 81-2919 ISBN 0-8170-0932-9 : 7.95
1. Protestant churches—United States—Case studies. 2. Church renewal—Case studies. I. Title.

Protestant churches—United States—Clergy.

QUINLEY, Harold E. 253'.2
The prophetic clergy: social activism among Protestant ministers [by] Harold E. Quinley. New York, Wiley [1974] ix, 369 p. illus. 24 cm. "A Wiley-Interscience publication." Includes bibliographical references. [BR517.Q56] 74-5175 ISBN 0-471-70265-X
1. Protestant churches—United States—Clergy. 2. Church and social problems—United States. I. Title.

Protestant churches—United States—Directories

PROTESTANT Council of the City of New York.
Protestant and Orthodox Church directory, giving the official status of the Protestant and Orthodox Churches of Metropolitan New York, including Nassau and Westchester Counties, as of October 1961. New York, 1962. 274 p. 23 cm. 66-2132
1. Protestant churches—U.S.—Direct. 2. Orthodox Eastern Churches—Direct. I. Title.

Protestant churches—United States—Education.

KENNEDY, William Bean 377
The shaping of Protestant education; an interpretation of the Sunday school and the development of Protestant educational strategy in the United States. 1789-1860. New York, Association [1966] 93p. 22cm. (Monographs in Christian educ., no. 4) Bibl. [BV1516.A1K4] 66-15749 2.50 pap.,
1. Protestant churches—U.S.—Education. 2. Sunday-schools—Hist. I. Title.

Protestant churches—United States—History.

PRIMER, Ben, 1949- 280'.4'0973
Protestants and American business methods / by Ben Primer. [Ann Arbor, Mich.] : UMI Research Press, c1979. v, 223 p. : ill. ; 24 cm. (Studies in American history and culture ; no. 7) Includes index. Bibliography: p. [195]-218. [BR517.P74 1978] 78-20879 ISBN 0-8357-0982-5 : 24.95. ISBN 0-8357-0983-3 pbk. : 21.95
1. Protestant churches—United States—History. 2. United States—Church history. 3. Church management. 4. Bureaucracy. I. Title. II. Series.

PROTESTANT Church in the U.S.A. Western New York (Diocese)
The story of 125 years. [Buffalo, N.Y., 1963] 35 p. illus. 65-83710
I. Title.

Protestant churches—United States—Relations—Eastern churches.

SHAW, Plato Ernest, 1883- 274.95
American contacts with the Eastern churches, 1820-1870, by P. E. Shaw ... Chicago, Ill., The American society of church history [c1937] 2 p. l., iii, 5-206 p. 22 cm. (Half-title: Monographs in church history, edited by Matthew Spinks, R. H. Nichols. vol. II) [Full name: Plato Ernest Oliver Shaw] Bibliography: p. 197-200. [BV3147.S45] [266.3] 38-959
1. Protestant churches—U.S.—Relations—Eastern churches. 2. Eastern churches—Relations—Protestant churches. I. Title.

Protestant Episcopal church in the Confederate States of America—History

CHESHIRE, Joseph Blount, bp., 1850-1932.
The church in the Confederate States; a history of the Protestant Episcopal church in the Conferate States, by Joseph Blount Cheshire ... New York, London [etc.] Longmans, Green and co., 1912. ix, 291 p. 19 1/2 cm. [BX5895.C5] 12-280
1. Protestant Episcopal church in the Confederate States of America—Hist. I. Title.

PROTESTANT Episcopal church in the Confederate States of America.
Journal of the proceedings of the General council of the Protestant Episcopal church in the Confederate States of America, held in St. Paul's church, Augusta, Ga. From Nov. 12th to Nov. 22d, inclusive, in the year of Our Lord, 1862. With an appendix, containing the constitution, a digest of the canons, a list of the clergy, and of the officers of the General council, etc. Augusta, Ga., Press of Chronicle & Sentinel, 1863. 216, 15 p., 2 l., [vii]-xii (i. e. xiii) p., 1 l., 59, viii p., 2 l. 22 cm. Page xiii incorrectly numbered xii. g"Pastoral letter fro m the bishops of the Protestant Episcopal church to the clergy and laity of the church in the Confederate States of America. Delivered before the General council, in St. Paul's church, Augusta, Saturday, Nov. 22d. 1862, Augusta, Ga., 1862": 15 p. [BX5823.A3 1863] 2-3344
I. Title.

Protestant Episcopal Church in the U.S.A.

ALLAN, Ethan, 1796-1879. 922.373
Clergy in Maryland of the Protestant Episcopal church since the independence of 1783. by Rev. Ethan Allen ... Baltimore, J. S. Waters, 1860. 106 p. 24 cm. [BX5917.M3A6] 283.752 34-24951
1. Protestant Epicopal church in the U. S. A.—Clergy. 2. Clergy—Maryland. I. Title.

ATWATER, George Parkin, 1874-1932. 283.73
The Episcopal Church: its message for men of today. Rev. ed. New York, Morehouse-Gorham Co., 1953. 190p. 21cm. [BX5930.A8 1953] 54-483
1. Protestant Episcopal Church in the U. S. A. I. Title.

AVERILL, Edward Wilson, 1870- 283.73
Talks on the Episcopal church. by the Rev. Edward W. Averill ... Fond du Lac, Wis., Parish press, 1936. 1 p. l., 62 p. 17 cm. [BX5935.A8] 36-7574
1. Protestant Episcopal church in the U. S. A. I. Title.

BERNARDIN, Joseph Buchanan, 1899- 283.73
An introduction to the Episcopal Church. [3d ed.] New York, Morehouse-Gorham Co. [1957] 116p. 19cm. [BX5930.B4 1957] 57-20940
1. Protestant Episcopal Church in the U. ,s. A. I. Title.

BERNARDIN, Joseph Buchanan, 1899- 286.73
An introduction to the Episcopal church, by Joseph Buchanan Bernardin. New York, E. S. Gorham, inc., 1935. 5 p. l., 116 p. 19 cm. "Books for further reading" at end of each chapter. "A partial list of Christian religious classics": p. ii6. [BX5990.B4] 36-1885
1. Protestant Episcopal church in the U. S. A. I. Title.

BERNARDIN, Joseph Buchanan, 1899- 283.73
An introduction to the Episcopal church, by Joseph Buchanan Bernardin. 2d ed. New York, Morehouse-Gorham company, 1949. 5 p. l., 116 p. 19 cm. "Books for further reading" at end of each chapter. "A partial list of Christian religious classics": p. 116. [BX5930.B4 1940] 40-14564
1. Protestant Episcopal church in the U. S. A. I. Title.

BESSLEY, Claude A 283.764
The Episcopal Church in northern Texas, until 1895. Wichita Falls, 1952. 65p. 23cm. [BX5918.D25B4] 54-27708
1. Protestant Episcopal Church in the U. S. A. Dallas (Diocese) 2. Protestant Episcopal Church in the U. S. A. Northern Texas (Missionary district) I. Title.

BROWN, William Montgomery, Bp., 1855-1937. 283.
The church for Americans. New York, T. Whittaker, 1896 [c1895] xiii. 440 p. illus., col. map. 21 cm. [BX5930.B8 1896] 50-46486
1. Protestant Episcopal Church in the U. S. A. I. Title.

BROWN, William Montgomery, Bp., 1855-1937. 283.
The church for Americans. 4th ed., rev. and enl. New York, T. Whittaker, 1896. xiv. 501 p. illus., col. map. 21 cm. [BX5930.B8 1896c] 50-46561
1. Protestant Episcopal Church in the U. S. A. I. Title.

BRYDON, George MacLaren, 1875- 262.9'8'373
Shall we accept the ancient canons as canon law? : A reply to the pamphlet "The ancient canons and an interpretation of the word discipline in the Book of common prayer" which was published by the Joint Commission on Discipline of the American Church Union and the Clerical Union / G. MacLaren Brydon. Richmond : Virginia

Diocesan Library, [1955] 58 p. ; 23 cm. Includes bibliographical references. [LAW] 75-322201
1. Protestant Episcopal Church in the U.S.A. 2. Canon law, Protestant Episcopal. I. Joint Committee on Discipline of the American Church Union and the Clerical Union. The ancient canons and an interpretation of the word discipline in the Book of common prayer. II. Title.

BURGESS, George, bp., 1809-1866. 286.
List of persons admitted to the order of deacons in the Protestant Episcopal church, in the United States of America, from A.D. 1785, to A.D. 1857, both inclusive. Prepared by the late Right Rev. George Burgess... Boston, A. Williams & co., 1874. 48, xvi p. 19 cm. "Index to Bishop Burgess's List of persons ordained deacons in the Protestant Episcopal church. Boston, A. Williams & co., 1874: xvi p. at end. Manuscript letter from the author to Rev. W. S. Perry attached to first leaf of advertisement at end. [BX5990.B8] 7-13528
1. Protestant Episcopal church in the U.S.A. I. Title.

CAMERON, Kenneth Walter, 1908- comp.
The Catholic revival in Episcopal Connecticut (1850-1925) Enl. ed. with an index. Hartford, Transcendental Books, 1965. 379 l. illus., facsims., ports. 29 cm. Chiefly facsimile reproductions of ms. and printed items. Bibliography: leaves 357-361. 66-83912
1. Portestant Episcopal Church in the U.S.A.—History—Sources. 2. Protestant Episcopal Church in the U.S.A.—Parties and movements. 3. Protestant Episcopal Church in the U.S.A.—Connecticut. I. Title.

CARTER, Hodding. 283.763
So great a good; a history of the Episcopal Church in Louisiana and of Christ Church Cathedral, 1805-1955, by Hodding Carter and Betty Werlein Carter. Sewanee, Tenn., University Press, 1955. 447p. illus. 24cm. [BX5918.L8C3] 56-28135
1. Protestant Episcopal Church in the U. S. A. Louisiana (Diocese)—Hist. 2. New Orleans. Christ Church Episcopal Cathedral. I. Carter, Betty Werlein, joint author. II. Title.

CHURCH Congress in the United States. 283.06373
Episcopalians united; ed. by Theodore P. Ferris, with a foreword by Walter H. Gray. New York. Morehouse-Gorham Co., 1948. viii, 149 p. 19 cm. Papers delivered at the Church Congress held in Toledo, April 22-24, 1947. [BX5820.A55] 48-5388
1. Protestant Episcopal Church in the U. S. A.—Addresses, essays, lectures. I. Ferris, Theodore Parker, 1908- ed. II. Title.

THE Church militant, Boston.
The Church militant. General convention number. v. 7, no. 5; Oct. 1904. Boston, 1904. cover-title, 152 p. illus. (incl. ports.) 27 cm. Pub. by the Board of missions of the diocese of Massachusetts. Presents the principal churches of the diocese with accounts of the parishes, history, description and statistics. 8-23411
I. Protestant Episcopal church in the U.S. Massachusetts, Diocese of. Diocesan board of missions. II. Title.

COCKE, Charles Francis 283.7557
Parish lines, Diocese of Southwestern Virginia. Richmond, Virginia State Library, 1960. 196p. col. maps, diagrs. (Virginia. State Library [Richmond] Publications, no. 14) Bibl.: p.179-180. 60-14622 4.00 pap.,
1. Protestant Episcopal Church in the U. S. A. Southwestern Virginia (Diocese) 2. Parishes—Virginia. I. Title. II. Series.

[CURTISS, Alonzo Parker] 1862- 283.
History of the diocese of Fond du Lac and its several congregations, compiled under the direction of the bishop, in commemoration on its fiftieth anniversary, a. d. 1857-1925. [Fond du Lac, Wis., P. B. Haber printing co., c1925] 96 p. front., plates, ports. 23 cm. Caption title: A history of the diocese of Fond du Lac, by Rev. A. Parker Curtiss. [BX5918.F6C8] 26-5010
1. Protestant Episcopal church in the U. S. A. Fond du Lac (Diocese) I. Title.

DE MILLE, George Edmed, 1898- 283.747
A history of the Diocese of Albany, 1704-1923. With foreword by the Bishop of Albany. Philadelphia, Church Historical Society [1946] 151 p. plates, ports., map. 24 cm. ([Church Historical Society, Philadelphia] Publication no. 16 [i. e. 17]) Bibliography: p. [137]-142. [BX5918.A3D4] 46-4488
1. Protestant Episcopal Church in the U. S. A. Albany (Diocese) I. Title. II. Series.

DOANE, George Washington, bp., 1799-1859, defendant.
The record of the proceedings of the Court of bishops, assembled for the trial of the Rt. Rev. George Washington Doane ... bishop of New Jersey, upon a presentment made by the Rt. Rev. William Meade ... the Rt. Rev. Charles Pettit McIlvaine ... and the Rt. Rev. George Burgess ... New York, Stanford and Swords, 1852. 1 p. l., 136 p. 23 cm. Court assembled Oct. 7, 1852. [BX5960.D7A2] 45-27725
I. Protestant Episcopal church in the U.S.A. Court of bishops for the trial of Bishop Doane. II. Title.

DU BOSE, William Porcher, 1836-1918. 230.3
Unity in the faith. Edited by W. Norman Pittenger. Greenwich, Conn., Seabury Press, 1957. 244p. 22cm. [BX5845.D78] 57-9536
1. Protestant Episcopal Church in the U. S. A.—Addresses, essays, lectures. 2. Theology—Addresses, essays, lectures. I. Title.

ELGIN, Kathleen, 1923- 283'.73
The Episcopalians; the Protestant Episcopal Church. Written and illustrated by Kathleen Elgin. With a foreword by Charles L. R. Pedersen. New York, D. McKay Co. [1970] 112 p. illus. 26 cm. (The Freedom to worship series) Bibliography: p. [110] [BX5930.2.E4 1970] 75-97805 4.95
1. Protestant Episcopal Church in the U.S.A. 2. Polk, Leonidas, Bp., 1806-1864. I. Title.

EMERY, Julia C. 266.
A century of endeavor, 1821-1921, a record of the first hundred years of the Domestic and foreign missionary society of the Protestant Episcopal church in the United States of America, by Julia C. Emery ... New York, The Department of missions, 1921. 2 p. l., vii-viii, 466 p. 19 cm. [BV2575.A5E6] 23-2671
1. Portestant Episcopal church in the U.S.A. Domestic and foreign missionary society. I. Title.

FENNER, Goodrich Robert, 1891- 250
The Episcopal church in town and country, by Goodrich R. Fenner. New York, N.Y., The National council, Division for rural work of the Department of Christian social service, 1935. 160 p. 19 cm. Bibliographies at end of each chapter. [BX5938.F4] 35-17220
1. Protestant Episcopal church in the U.S.A. 2. Rural churches—U.S. 3. Theology,Pastoral—Anglican communion. I. Protestant Episcopal church in the U.S.A. National council. Dept. of Christian social service. II. Title.

THE first 100 years;
being an historical review of the Diocese of Kansas of the Protestant Episcopal Church from its formation in 1859 to its centennial in 1959. The Right Reverend Goodrich Robert Fenner, S. T. D., Bishop; the Right Reverend Edward Clark Turner, D. D., Bishop Coadjutor. [Lawrence, Kansas, The Allen Press, 1959] 124p. illus., ports. 23cm.
1. Protestant Episcopal Church in the U. S. A.- Kansas—History. I. Protestant Episcopal Church in the U. S. A. Kansas (Diocese)

FRAZIER, Elizabeth P. 283.73
A treasure hunt; a work book about the Episcopal church, prepared by Elizabeth P. Frazier. New York, Morehouse-Gorham co [c1941] 56 p. 27 x 21 cm. "First printing, June, 1935 ... seventh printing, May, 1941." [BX5875.F7 1941] 41-12744
1. Protestant Episcopal church in the U. S. A. I. Title.

GALLAGHER, Mason.
A chapter of unwritten history. The Protestant Episcopacy of the revolutionary patriots. Lost and restored. A centennial offering, by Rev. Mason Gallagher ... Philadelphia, Reformed Episcopal rooms, 1882. iv, 102 p. 23 cm. [BX5881.G3] 23-5054
1. Protestant Episcopal church in the U. S. A. I. Title.

GOD is great, God is good.
[Greenwich, Conn., Seabury Press [c1959] 60p. 28cm. (Seabury series) Vacation church school primary book I. 'For use with the basic guide Weeks of growth.'
I. Protestant Episcopal Church in the U. S. A. National Council. Dept. of Christian Education.

GRAFTON, Charles Chapman, bp., 1830-1912. 252.
... The works of the Rt. Rev. Charles C. Grafton ... edited by B. Talbot Rogers ... [The Cathedral ed.] [New York, etc., Longmans, Green, and co.] 1914. 8 v. fronts. (v. 8, col.) plates, ports., map. 21 cm. At head of title: The Cathedral edition; on t.-p., v. 1-6: new edition. Each volume has also special t.-p. Vol. 2 contains references. Contents.--v. 1. Christian and Catholic.--v. 2. The lineage of the American Catholic church. Pusey and the church revival.--v. 3. A Catholic atlas; or, Idgest of Catholic theology.--v. 4. journey Godward Andler, (a servant of Jesus Christ) --v. 4. A journey Godward or, The call of the Divine Master of a sister's life, and other writtings on the religious life--v. 6. Plain suggestions for a reverent celebration of the holy communion. Fond du Lac tracts.--v. 7. Letters and addrumes--v. 8. Addresses and sermons. [BX5845.G7A3] 14-22600
1. Protestant Episcopal church in the U. S. A.—Collected works. 2. Theology—Collected works—20th cent. I. Title.

GRAY, William, 1927- 283'.73
The Episcopal Church welcomes you: an introduction to its history, worship, and mission [by] William and Betty Gray. Introd. by John Maury Allin. New York, Seabury Press [1974] xiv, 110 p. illus. 21 cm. "A Crossroad book." Bibliography: p. [109]-110. [BX5930.2.G7] 73-17898 ISBN 0-8164-0253-1 ISBN 0-8164-2087-4 (pbk.) 5.95
1. Protestant Episcopal Church in the U.S.A. I. Gray, Betty, joint author. II. Title.

HANCOCK, Henry Nicholas. 283.746
Transatlantic exchange; a look at the church in New England. London, A. R. Mowbray; New York, Morehouse-Gorham Co. [1951] 75 p. 19 cm. [BX5885.H3] 52-7472
1. Protestant Episcopal Church in the U. S. A.—New England. I. Title.

HATCHETT, Marion J. 264'.03
Commentary on the American prayer book / Marion J. Hatchett. New York : Seabury Press, 1980. p. cm. Includes index. Bibliography: p. [BX5945.H37] 19 80-20719 ISBN 0-8164-0206-X : 29.50
1. Protestant Episcopal Church in the U.S.A. Book of common prayer. I. Title.

HAUGHWOUT, Lefferd Merle Alexander, 1873- 230
The ways and teachings of the church; a course of instruction for confirmation candidates and for inquirers, by the Rev. Lefferd M. A. Haughwout...with foreword by the Rt. Rev. Cortiandt Whitehead... 6th ed., rev. Milwaukee, Morehouse publishing company [c1930] xii, 130 p. incl. front., illus., diagrs. 19 cm. [BX5930.H28 1930] [283] 30-9215
1. Protestant Episcopal Church in the U. S. A. 2. Confirmation. I. Title.

HAUGHWOUT, Lefferd Merle Alexander, 1873- 280
The ways and teachings of the church, a course of instruction by the Rev. Lefferd M. A. Haughwout, M.A. 7th ed., rev. New York, Morehouse-Gorham co., 1944. xiv, 128 p. incl. front., illus., diagrs. 20 cm. [BX5930.H28 1944] [283] 44-26254
1. Protestant Episcopal church in the U.S.A. 2. Confirmation—Instruction and study. I. Title.

THE Holy Cross magazine. 283.082
All for the love of God, a Holy Cross omnibus. [1st ed.] New York, Holy Cross Press [1957] 250p. 24cm. [BX5840.H6] 57-7735
1. Protestant Episcopal Church in the U. S. A.—Addresses, essays, lectures. I. Milligan, Ralph T., ed. II. Title.

HUTCHINS, Charles Lewis, 1838-1920, ed.
The chant and service book, containing the choral service for morning and evening prayer; chants for the canticles, with the pointing set forth by the General Convention, music for the communion service, chants and anthems for the burial office, etc., etc. Boston, Parish Choir [c1894] 253 p. 20 cm. [M2016.2.H] 49-37094
1. Protestant Episcopal Church in the U.S.A. I. Title.

INGRAM, Tolbert Robert, 1913- 230.3
Lambeth, unity and truth. A reply to the pastoral letter issued by the House of Bishops meetings in General Convention, Miami Beach, Florida, October 1958. Bellaire, Tex., St. Thomas Press [1959] 52p. 24cm. [BX5835 1958] 59-14078
1. Protestant Episcopal Church in the U. S. A.—Pastoral letters and charges. I. Title.

JACKSON, William, 1793-1844. 252.
Remains of the Rev. William Jackson, late rector of St. Paul's church, Louisville, Ky.; with a brief sketch of his life and character. By Rev. Wm. M. Jackson. New York, Stanford and Swords, 1847. 397 p. front. (port.) 20 cm. [BX5845.J3] 42-27030
1. Protestant Episcopal church in the U. S. A.—Collected works 2. Theology—Collected works—19th cent. I. Jackson, William M., 1809-1855, ed. II. Title.

JATHO, Charles Conrad, 1888- 283.73
The church visible; lessons on the outward and visible objects of the church's architecture, customs and organization. By Rev. Charles. C. Jatho. Royal Oak, Mich., Herald-review publishing company [c1935] 74 p. illus. (incl. plans) diagrs. 23 cm. [BX5935.J3] 36-7021
1. Protestant Episcopal church in the U. S. A. I. Title.

JOHNSON, Frederick A., 1909- 264.03
Brief topical index of the Book of common prayer [by Frederick A. Johnson. Morristown, N.J., 1968] 41 p. 22 cm. [BX5945.J565] 71-257080
1. Protestant Episcopal Church in the U.S.A. Book of common prayer—Indexes. I. Title.

JOHNSON, Howard Albert, 1915- ed. 283.73
This church of ours; the Episcopal Church: what it is and what it teaches about living, by Stephen F. Bayne, Jr. [and others] Foreword by the Bishop of New York. Greenwich, Conn., Seabury Press, 1958. 129p. 20cm. [BX5930.J6] 58-10841
1. Protestant Episcopal Church in the U. S. A. I. Bayne, Stephen Fielding, Bp., 1908- II. Title.

KRUMM, John McGill, 1913- 283.73
Why I am an Episcopalian. New York, Nelson [1957] 192 p. 21 cm. [BX5930.K8] 57-11897
1. Protestant Episcopal Church in the U.S.A. I. Title.

LEWIS, Henry Wilkins, 1916- 283.756
Northampton parishes. Jackson, N. C., 1951. ix, 120 p. illus., ports., map. 27 cm. Bibliographical footnotes. [BX5917.N8L4] 52-20939
1. Protestant Episcopal Church in the U. S. A.—Northampton Co.,N. C. 2. Churches—Northampton Co., N. C. I. Title.

LITTLE, Arthur Wilde, 1856-1910. 283
Reasons for being a churchman; addressed to English speaking Christians of every name, by Arthur W. Little ... Rev. ed. 25th thousand. Milwaukee, Wis., The Young

churchman co., 1905. xvi, 309 p. front. 20 cm. [BX5930.L5] 5-2766
1. Protestant Episcopal church in the U. S. A. 2. Church of England. I. Title.

MCCRADY, Edward, 1868-
Where the Protestant Episcopal church stands; a review of official definitions versus non-official theories concerning the nature and extent of the church catholic, by the Rev. Edward McCrady... New York, E. P. Dutton and company, 1916. 4 p. l., 336 p. 19 1/2 cm. $1.75 16-28332
I. Title.

MCKIM, Randolph Harrison, 1842-1920. 283.
The proposal to change the name of the Protestant Episcopal church, considered in the light of true catholic principles, by Rev. Randolph H. McKim... New York, E. P. Dutton & company [1913] xii p., 1 l., 252 p. 19 1/2 cm. Half-title: Catholic principles and the change of name. Essays and addresses delivered on different occasions. cf. Introd. [BX5925.M3] 14-24
1. Protestant Episcopal church in the U.S.A. 2. Protestantism. 3. Anglo-Catholicism. I. Title. II. Title: Catholic principles and the change of name.

MCMASTER, Vernon Cochrane. 283
That's our church, by the Rev. Vernon McMaster ... with a foreword by the Rev. D. A. McGregor ... Illustrated by Jessie Gillespie. New York, F. Fell, inc., 1944. 8 p., 2 l., 15-123 p. incl. front., plates. 21 cm. [BX5935.M35] 44-51114
1. Protestant Episcopal church in the U.S.A. I. Gillespie, Jessie, illus. II. Title.

MODERN Canterbury pilgrims, and why they chose the Episcopal Church. John H. Hallowell and others. Abridged 2nd ed. New York, More-house-Gorham [1959] 232p. 19cm. 'First printing.'
1. Protestant Episcopal Church in the U. S. A. 2. Converts, Anglican. I. Pike, James Albert, Bp., 1913- II. Hallowell, John Hamilton, 1913-

MOORE, Joseph Graessle, 1904-
A study of the Missionary District of Liberia, by Joseph G. Moore. Field staff: Lazarus O'KeeKee [and others. Evanston, Ill.] Unit of Research and Field Study of the National Council of the Protestant Episcopal Church [1955] 3 v. (xii, 907 l.) illus., maps (part fold. col. in pocket) plans. 30 cm. [BX6030.M6] 64-6348
1. Portestant Episcopal Church in the U.S.A. Liberia (Missionary district) I. Title.

MURPHY, Du Bose, 1893- 283.73
Life in the church. With a foreword by Henry W. Hobson. [Rev. ed.] Chicago, Wilcox & Follett [1950] 122 p. 20 cm. "A Cloister Press book." [BX5935.M8] 50-12071
1. Protestant Episcopal Church in the U.S.A. I. Title.

NATIONAL Council. Dept. of Christian Education. ... In God we trust ... Greenwich, Conn., The Seabury Press [c1961] 64p. (Vacation Church School. Younger Jr. Bk. 2) For use with Weeks of Growth.
I. Protestant Episcopal Church in the U. S. A.

NEWTON, William Wilberforce, 1843-1914. 283.
Yesterday with the fathers, by Wm. Wilberforce Newton, D.D. New York, Cochrane publishing company, 1910. 210 p. 20 cm. [BX5882.N5] 11-1376
1. Protestant Episcopal church in the U.S.A. I. Title.

PARET, William, bp., 1826-1911. 922
Reminiscences, by the Rt. Rev. William Paret ... Philadelphia, G. W. Jacobs & co. [1911] xv p., 1 l., 209 p. front. (port.) 20 cm. [BX5995.P3A3] 11-12706
1. Protestant Episcopal church in the U. S. A. Maryland (Diocese) I. Title.

PARSONS, Edward Lambe, Bp., 1868- 283.794
The diocese of California; a quarter century, 1915-1940. Austin, Tex., Church Historical Society [1958] 165p. illus. 24cm. (Church Historical Society. Publication no. 46) [BX5918.C2P3] 58-4045
1. Protestant Episcopal Church in the U. S. A. California (Diocese)—Hist. I. Title.

PIKE, James Albert, 1913- ed. 283.73
Modern Canterbury pilgrims and why they chose the Episcopal Church John H. Hallowell [and others] New York, Morehouse-Gorham, 1956. 317p. 21cm. [BX5990.P5] 56-6116
1. Protestant Episcopal Church in the U. S. A. 2. Converts, Anglican. I. Hallowell, John Hamilton, 1913- II. Title.

PIKE, James Albert, Bp., 1913- 283.73
Modern Canterbury pilgrims, and why they chose the Episcopal Church. John Hallowell and others. Abridged 2nd ed. New York, Morehouse-Gorham, 1956. 317p. 21cm. [BX5990.P5] 56-6116
1. Protestant Episcopal Church in the U. S. A. 2. Converts, Anglican. I. Hallowell, John Hamilton, 1913- II. Title.

PITTENGER, William Norman, 1905- 283.73
The Episcopalian way of life. Englewood Cliffs, N. J., Prentice-Hall [1957] 188 p. illus. 22 cm. [BX5930.P34] 57-5230
1. Protestant Episcopal church in the U.S.A. I. Title.

PRICE, Charles P., 1920- 264'.03
Introducing the proposed Book of common prayer / Charles P. Price. New York : Seabury Press, 1977, c1976. 121 p. ; 21 cm. "A Crossroad book." "Prepared at the request of the Standing Liturgical Commission." [BX5945.P74 1977] 77-6125 ISBN 0-8164-2171-4 pbk. : 1.75
1. Protestant Episcopal Church in the U.S.A. Book of common prayer. I. Protestant Episcopal Church in the U.S.A. Liturgical Commission. II. Title.

PROSTESTANT Episcopal church in the U. S. A. Western Michigan (Diocese) 283.774
Journal of the proceedings of the ... annual convention of the Protestant Episcopal church in the diocese of Western Michigan ... 1st-; 1875- Hastings, Mich. [etc.] 1875- v. in tables. 23 cm. With the Journal of the proceedings of the 1st-[6th] annual convention, 1875-80, are bound: Protestant Episcopal church in the U. S. A. Western Michigan (Diocese) Constitution and canons. [Hastings, Mich.] 1883 (issued also with the Journal of the proceedings of the 9th annual convention, 1883); and, Protestant Episcopal church in the U. S. A. Western Michigan (Diocese) Journal of the proceedings of the primary convention. Grand Rapids, 1875. [BX5918.W46A3] 40-699
I. Title.

PROSTESTANT Episcopal church in the U. S. A. Church congress. 283
The church and its American opportunity; papers by various writers read at the Church congress in 1919. New York, The Macmillan company, 1919. x, 235 p. 20 cm. [BX5820.A6 1919] 19-12689
1. Protestant Episcopal church in the U. S. A.—Addresses, essays, lectures. I. Title. Contents omitted.

PROTESTANT Episcopal church in the Confederate States of America.
Journal of the proceedings of the General council of the Protestant Episcopal church in the Confederate States of America, held in St. Paul's church, Augusta, Ga. From Nov. 12th to Nov. 22d, inclusive, in the year of Our Lord, 1862. With an appendix, containing the constitution, a digest of the canons, a list of the clergy, and of the officers of the General council, etc. Augusta, Ga., Press of Chronicle & Sentinel, 1863. 216, 15 p., 2 l., [vii]-xii (i. e. xiii) p., 1 l., 59, viii p., 2 l. 22 cm. Page xiii incorrectly numbered xii. g"Pastoral letter fro m the bishops of the Protestant Episcopal church to the clergy and laity of the church in the Confederate States of America. Delivered before the General council, in St. Paul's church, Augusta, Saturday, Nov. 22d. 1862, Augusta, Ga., 1862": 15 p. [BX5823.A3 1863] 2-3344
I. Title.

PROTESTANT Episcopal church in the U. S.
Constitutions and canons for the government of the Protestant Episcopal church in the United States of America, adopted in general conventions, 1789-1913. [New York] Printed for the Convention [Sherwood press] 1913. 187 p. 23 cm. 14-1488 0.40
I. Title.

PROTESTANT Episcopal church in the U. S. Lexington, Diocese of.
Journal of proceedings of the ... annual council of the diocese of Lexington ... Cincinnati [etc.] v. 23 cm. 6-967
I. Title.

PROTESTANT Episcopal church in the U. S. Joint commission on social service.
Social service at the General convention of 1913, the joint commission on social service of the Protestant Episcopal church New York city, The Church missions house [1913?] 3 p. l., 5-181 p., 1 l. fold. map, fold. form. 23 cm. 14-6680
I. Title.

PROTESTANT Episcopal church in the U. S. General convention, 1901.
The journal of the bishops, clergy and laity, assembled in general convention in the city of San Francisco, on the first Wednesday in October A. D. 1901; with appendices. [Boston, A. Mudge & son] Printed for the convention, 1902. xlii, 592 p. 24 cm. 2-12014
I. Title.

PROTESTANT Episcopal church in the U. S. General convention, 1910.
Who's who in the general convention of 1910 held at Cincinnati. Milwaukee, The Young churchman co., 1910. 122 p. illus. (ports.) fold. plan. 16 x 8 cm. 10-21358 0.50
I. Title.

PROTESTANT Episcopal church in the U. S. A. Virginia (Diocese) Diocesan missionary society.
Addresses delivered at the centennial celebration of the diocesan missionary society of the Protestant Episcopal church in the Diocese of Virginia, Held in St. John's, The Monumental and St. Paul's churches, Richmond, Virginia, May 14th and 15th, 1929. [Richmond! 1929] 122 p. 22 cm. [BS5918.V8A6 1929] 29-18013
I. Title.

PROTESTANT Episcopal church in the U. S. A. Liturgy and ritual. 264.03
... A book of offices; services for occasions not provided for in the Book of common prayer, comp. by a committee of the House of bishops. Presented to the House of bishops at Cincinnati, October 1910, and after further consideration, with suggestions from other bishops, revised and reported, October 1913. Referred back to the committee, and re-issued, 1914, with corrections, preliminary to presentation to the House of bishop at the General convention of 1916. Milwaukee, The Young churchman co., 1914. viii, 179 p. 18 cm. At head of title: Official. At the General convention at St. Louis, in 1916, a number of Changes were made, and the book was authorized for use in the church.--cf. Pref. to edition of 1917. [BX5947.B8A3 1914] 14-22599
1. Protestant Episcopal church in the U. S. A. House of bishops. Committee on a book of offices. I. Protestant Episcopal church in the U. S. A. Book of common prayer. II. Protestant Episcopal church in the U.S.A. House of bishops. Committee on a book of offices. III. Title.

PROTESTANT Episcopal church in the U. S. A. New York (Diocese) Committee on historical publications. 283.747
The centennial history of the Protestant Episcopal church in the diocese of New York, 1785-1885. Edited by James Grant Wilson. New York, D. Appleton and company, 1886. 5 p. l., [3]-454 p. front., illus. (facsims.) plates, ports. 24 cm. "Prepared for the press by a member of the Committee, under its direction."--Pref. [BX5918.N7A45] 38-10380
1. Protestant Episcopal church in the U. S. A. New York (Diocese) I. Wilson, James Grant, 1832-1914, ed. II. Title.

PROTESTANT Episcopal church in the U. S. A. 283.
A compilation for the use of the members of the Protestant Episcopal church, in Maryland: consisting of the constitution and canons of the church in the United States: the constitution and canons of the Maryland; with a connected statement of all testimonials required of candidates for holy orders, and the laws of the state of Maryland respecting the duties of clergy and vestries. Published by order of the convention of said church. Baltimore, Printed by Joseph Robinson, 1822. viii, [9]-69 p. 21 cm. Bound in a collection of pamphlets of the diocese lettered Maryland diocesan journals, 2, 1815-1827. [BX5918.M3A3] 23-2734
I. Protestant Episcopal church in the U. S. A. Maryland (Diocese) II. Maryland. Laws, statutes, etc. III. Title.

PROTESTANT Episcopal church in the U. S. A. Utah and Idaho (Missionary district) 283.
Journal of the ... annual convocation of the missionary district of Utah and Idaho ... 1st-; 1883- Salt Lake City, 1883- v. 21-23 cm. [BX5918.U8A3] 39-32792
I. Title.

PROTESTANT Episcopal church in the U. S. A. Quincy (Diocese) 283.
Journal of the ... annual synod of the diocese of Quincy ... 1st- [Galesburg, Ill., etc.] 1878-19 v. tables. 22-24 cm. Title varies slightly. The journal of the first annual convention was issued in combination with the journal of the primary convention and the special convention of 1878 under title: Journals of the first three conventions of the diocese of Quincy ... Primary convention, Dec. 11, 1877. Special convention. Feb. 26, 1878. First annual convention, May 28, 1878. Journal of the 15th annual convention was issued in combination with the journal of the 16th annual convention under cover-title: Diocese of Quincy. Journals of conventions, 1892 and 1808. Place of publication varies. [BX5918.Q5A3] 38-22088
I. Title.

PROTESTANT Episcopal church in the U. S. A. Ohio (Diocese) 283.771
Journals of the annual conventions of the Protestant Episcopal church, in the diocese of Ohio. Diocese organized, A. D. 1818. Columbus, Reprinted by Scott & Bascom, 1853. 2 p. l., [3]-167 p. 23 cm. Half-title: The first ten years of the Protestant Episcopal church in the diocese of Ohio. 1818-1827. [BX5918.O3A32 1827] 38-20518
I. Title.

PROTESTANT Episcopal church in the U. S. A. New York (Diocese) 283.
Journals of the conventions of the Protestant Episcopal church in the diocese of New York. Republished, under the supervision of the bishop of the diocese, and the secretary of the convention. from the several journals as originally printed. New-York, H. M. Onderdonk, 1844. v. 22 cm. [BX5918.N7A32] ca 7
I. Title.

PROTESTANT Episcopal church in the U. S. A. General convention. 283.
Journals of the general conventions of the Protestant Episcopal church, in the United States of America; from the year 1784, to the year 1814, inclusive. Also, first appendix, containing the constitution and canons. And second appendix, containing three pastoral letters. Philadelphia: Printed and published by John Bioren, no. 88, Chesnut street, 1817. 3 p. l., [3]-381 p., 1 l. 22 cm. [BX5820.A15 1814] 40-20213
I. Title.

PROTESTANT Episcopal church in the U. S. A. Commission on a nation-wide preaching mission.
The manual; a nation-wide preaching mission issued by the Commission on a nation-wide preaching mission. Milwaukee, Wis., Pub. for the Commission by the Young churchman company [c1915] 4 p. l., 139 p. 20 cm. 15-25244 0.50
I. Title. II. Title: A nation-wide preaching mission.

PROTESTANT Episcopal church in the U. S. A. New York (Diocese) Sunday school commission.
Teacher's notes on Hero stories of the Old Testament, prepared by the Sunday school

commission, diocese of New York. First[-second] year. Milwaukee, Wis., For the New York Sunday school commission by the Young churchman co., 1910-12. 4 v. fronts. (v. 1-3) illus., maps. 19 cm. 15-18963
I. Title.

PROTESTANT Episcopal church in the U. S. A. General convention, 1865. 283.73
Protestant Episcopal church. The debates and proceedings of the General triennial convention. Held in Philadelphia, Pa., from October 4 to 24, 1865 ... Philadelphia, Protestant Episcopal book society; New York, American news company; [etc., etc., 1865?] 2 p. l., 387 p. 28 cm. (The Reporter, vol. i) [BX5820.A3 1865] 33-31218
I. Title.

PROTESTANT Episcopal church in the U. S. A. Church congress, San Francisco, 1927. 283.
Christ in the world of to-day; a record of the Church congress in the United States on its fifty-third anniversary, A. D. mcmxxvii, with an introduction by the general chairman, Charles Lewis Slattery. New York, C. Scribner's sons, 1927. xi, 305 p. 20 cm. [BX5820.A6 1927] 27-27581
I. Title.
Contents omitted.

PROTESTANT Episcopal church in the U. S. A. Church congress, Ann Arbor, Mich., 1929. 283.063
The church and the future; a record of the Church congress in the United States on its fifty-fifth anniversary, A. D. mcmxxix, with an introduction by the general chairman, Charles Lewis Slattery. New York, E. S. Gorham, inc. [c1929] ix, 317 p. 20 cm. [BX5820.A6 1929] 31-6613
I. Title.
Contents omitted.

PROTESTANT Episcopal church in the U. S. A. Church congress, Hartford, 1932. 283.73
Hartford papers; a record of the Church congress in the United States on its fifty-eighth anniversary, A. D. mcmxxxii; with an introduction by the general secretary, Harold Adye Prichard. Spencer, Mass., The Heffernan press, 1932. x p., 1 l., 273 p. 20 cm. [BX5820.A6 1932] 33-820
I. Prichard, Harold Adye, 1882- II. Title.
Contents omitted.

PROTESTANT Episcopal church in the U. S. A. Church congress, Chicago, 1933. 283.06373
Chicago papers; a record of the Church congress in the United States on its fifty-ninth anniversary, A. D. mcmxxxiii; with an introduction by the general chairman, Harold Adye Prichard. Spencer, Mass., The Heffernan press, 1933. 6 p. l., 260 p. 20 cm. [BX5820.A6 1933] 34-3066
1. Protestant Episcopal church in the U. S. A.—Addresses, essays, lectures. I. Prichard, Harold Adye, 1882- II. Title.
Contents omitted.

PROTESTANT Episcopal church in the U. S. A. Church congress. 283.
... The church congress journal; papers and addresses of the ... Church congress in the United States ... New York, v. 23-24 cm. Title varies: Authorized report of the proceedings of the Church congress. -1909, Papers, addresses, and discussions ... 1910- The Church congress journal ... [BX5820.A3] 17-12443
I. Title.

PROTESTANT Episcopal Church in the U. S. A. Washington (Diocese) 283'.746
Opportunity for tomorrow; a survey of the Diocese of Washington. Washington, 1954. 111 l. illus. 28cm. [BX5918.W3A53] 55-23529
I. Title.

PROTESTANT Episcopal Church in the U. S. A. Western North Carolina (Diocese) 283.756
Journal of the annual convention. [Hendersonville, Flanagan Print. Co.] v. 23cm. First convention held 1923. [BX5918.W53A3] 54-27703
I. Title.

PROTESTANT Episcopal Church in the U.S.A. Joint Commission on Cooperation with the Eastern and Old Catholic Churches.
Parishes and clergy of the Orthodox, and other Eastern Churches in North and South America, together with the parishes and clergy of the Polish National Catholic Church, 1962-1963. [Buffalo, N.Y., 1962] 165 p. illus. (ports.) 63-63766
I. Title.

PROTESTANT Episcopal Church in the U.S.A. National Council. Dept. of Christian Education.
It's your choice; the church's teaching in the eleventh grade. Teacher's manual. Illus. by Randolph Chitwood. Greenwich, Conn., Seabury Press [1962] vi, 105 p. illus. 28 cm. (The Seabury series, T-11) Includes bibliographies. 63-36638
I. Title.

PROTESTANT Episcopal Church in the U.S.A. National Council. Dept. of Christian Education.
...Many messengers... Greenwich, Conn., Seabury Press [c1961] 124 p. 22 cm. (Seabury series, T-3B) "The Church's teaching in the third grade. Rev. Teacher's manual." 65-66507
I. Title.

PROTESTANT Episcopal church missionary society for seamen in the city and port of New York.
Annual report. New York, v. illus. 23 cm. Report year ends: April December. Second report has title: Second annual report of the Board of managers of the Protestant episcopal church missionary society for seamen in the city and port of New York. Read at the annual meeting, April, 1846. Title varies slightly. [BV2665.P7] ca 6
I. Title.

REPORT of the delegation sent to the Church of South India by General Convention. New York, Joint Commission on Ecumenical Relations, 1957. 84p.
I. Protestant Episcopal Church in the U. S. A. Joint Commission on Ecumenical Relations.

ROBERTS, Walter Coe, 1855-1930. 252.
Wings of the morning; by Walter C. Roberts ... New York and London, G. P. Putnam's sons, 1901. v. 144 p. 18 1/2 cm. [BX5937.R59W5] 1-80815
1. Protestant Episcopal church in the U.S.A—Addresses, essays, lectures. 2. Lent. I. Title.

RUDD, John C[hurchill] 1779-1848.
Questions upon the evidences of Christianity, the constitution and ministry of the Christian church, and upon the festivals, fasts, and usages, observed by the Protestant Episcopal church in the United States Intended to assist in the study of the "Companion for the festivals and fasts of the church." By the Rev. John C. Rudd [2d ed.] Elizabeth-Toun, (N. J.) Printed at the office of the Journal and gazette, 1823. 111 p. 17 cm. 6-30326
I. Title.

SANFORD, Louis Childs, Bp., 1867-1948. 283.79
The Province of the Pacific. Philadelphia, Church Historical Society [1949] xiii, 187 p. map. 24 cm. (Church Historical Society. Publication 28) [BX5917.5.P3S3] 49-10701
1. Protestant Episcopal Church in the U. S. A. Provinces. Pacific. 2. Protestant Episcopal Church in the U. S. A.—Government. I. Title. II. Series: Church Historical Society, Philadelphia. Publication 28

SIMCOX, Carroll Eugene, 1912- 283.73
An approach to the Episcopal Church. New York, 17, 14 E. 41 St., Morehouse-Barlow co.]1961. 184p. 61-5469 3.00
1. Protestant Episcopal Church in the U. S. A. I. Title.

SIMCOX, Carroll Eugene, 1912- 283.73
An approach to the Episcopal Church. New York, Morehouse-Barlow, 1961 181 p. 21 cm. [BX5930.2.S54] 61-5469
1. Protestant Episcopal Church in the U.S.A. I. Title.

SMITH, Harry Robert, 1894- 283
The church for you; an introduction to the Episcopal Church. Foreword by Norman B. Nash. Greenwich, Conn., Seabury Press, 1956. 93 p. 19 cm. Includes bibliography. [BX5935.S676] 56-1893
1. Protestant Episcopal Church in the U.S.A. I. Title.

SMITH, William Walter, 1868- comp. 268.
A complete handbook of religious pictures; a practical manual for pastors, Sunday school teachers, and Bible students ... comp. for the New York Sunday school commission, by the Rev. Wm. Walter Smith ... [New York!] c1905. 113 p. 21 cm. [BV1535.S6] 6-2534
I. Protestant Episcopal church in the U. S. A. New York (Diocese) Sunday school commission. II. Title.

SMYTHE, George Franklin, 1852- 283.771
A history of the diocese of Ohio until the year 1918, by George Franklin Smythe. Cleveland, Pub. by the Diocese, 1931. xii, 627 p. front., plates. ports. 25 cm. Map on back lining-papers. "Of this large paper edition, one hundred numbered copies have been printed by Horace Carr at Cleveland, Ohio, 1931." This copy not numbered. Bibliography: p. 565-576. [BX5918.O3S6] 31-19979
1. Protestant Episcopal church in the U. S. A. Ohio (Diocese) 2. Ohio—Church history. I. Title.

TANNER, George Clinton, 1834-
Fifty years of church work in the diocese of Minnesota, 1857-1907. With an account of the visitation of the Right Reverend Jackson Kemper, D.D., and the labors of the Reverend Ezekiel Gilbert Gear, D.D., the first Protestant clergyman to minister to the white settlers within the "Precinct of St. Peter's" which then included the present city of St. Paul, by the Rev. George Clinton Tanner, D.D., registrar of the diocese. St. Paul, Minn., Pub. by the committee, 1909. 3 p. l., x, 516 p. front., plates, ports. 24 cm. 11-25971
I. Protestant Episcopal church in the U.S. Minnesota, Diocese of. II. Title.

... Telling people about God ... Greenwich, Conn., Seabury Press [c1960] 58p. (Vacation Church School. Younger Junior, Bk. I)
I. Protestant Episcopal Church in the U. S. A. National Council. Dept. of Christian Education.

[TOMLINSON, David Gibson] b.1799. 283
The good way; or, Why Christians, of whatever name, may become churchmen ... New York, D. Dana, jr., The Gen. Prot. Epis. S. S. union and church book society, 1860. 79 p. 19 1/2 cm. [BX5930.T6] 43-20273
1. Portestant Episcopal church in the U.S.—Doctrinal and controversial works. I. General Protestant Episcopal Sunday school union and church work society. II. Title.

THE variorum constitution of the Diocese of Easton. [Baltimore?] Shrewsbury Press [1956] 1 v. (various pagings) 29cm. Revised by Rev. William Wylie, Jr., cf. Foreword.
I. Protestant Episcopal Church in the U. S. A. Easton (Diocese) II. Wyllie, William.

WALSH, Thomas Tracy. 283.
Church facts and principles, by the Rev. T. Tracy Walsh ... with an introduction by the Rt. Rev. Wm. Cabell Brown ... Milwaukee, Wis., Morehouse publishing co. [c1927] vi p., 2 l., 223 p., 1 l. 19 1/2 cm. "Facts and principles pertaining to the Episcopal church."--Pref. [BX5930.W3] 28-19267
1. Protestant Episcopal church in the U.S.A. 2. Church of England. I. Title.

WESTCOTT, Frank Nash, 1858-1915. 283.
Catholic principles as illustrated in the doctrine, history, and organization of the American Catholic church in the United States, commonly called the Protestant Episcopal church, by the Rev. Frank N. Westcott. Milwaukee, The Young churchman co. [1902] 410 p.19 cm. "Books quoted in the text": p. [400]-410. [BX5930.W4 1902] 2-20793
1. Protestant Episcopal church in the U.S.A. I. Title.

WHITTAKER'S churchman's almanac. The Protestant Episcopal almanac and parochial list... New York, T. Whittaker [etc.] 18 v. ports. 17-19 cm. Title varies: 18 The Protestant Episcopal almanac. 18 The Protestant Episcopal almanac and directory. 1875- Whittaker's churchman's almanac. The Protestant Episcopal almanac and church directory. 18 Whittaker's churchman's almanac. The Protestant Episcopal almanac and parochial list. Pub. by the Protestant Episcopal society for the promotion of evangelical knowledge, 18 United with the Living church annual which continued as the Living church annual and Whittaker's churchman's almanac, 1909- 6-7424
I. Protestant Episcopal society for the promotion of evangelical knowledge, New York.

WHITTEMORE, Lewis Bliss, Bp. 262.3
The care of all the churches; the background, work, and opportunity of the American episcopate. Greenwich, Conn., Seabury Press, 1955. 146p. 20cm. [BX5966.W5] 55-5456
1. Protestant Episcopal Church in the U. S. A.—Bishops. I. Title.

WILLIAMSON, Wayne B., 1918- 283'.73
Growth & decline in the Episcopal Church / Wayne B. Williamson. Pasadena, Calif. : William Carey Library, 1979. xii, 179 p. : ill. ; 28 cm. Bibliography: p. 174-176. [BX5933.W55] 79-12303 ISBN 0-87808-328-6 pbk. : 4.95
1. Protestant Episcopal Church in the U.S.A. 2. Church growth—United States. I. Title.

WILLIAMSON, William B. 283.73
A handbook for Episcopalians. New York, Morehouse-Barlow Co. [1961] 223 p. 21 cm. (Handbooks for churchmen series) Includes bibliography. [BX5930.2.W5] 61-14387
1. Protestant Episcopal Church in the U.S.A. I. Title.

Protestant Episcopal church in the U.S.A.—Addresses, essays, lectures.

BRENT, Charles Henry, bp., 1862-1929. 252.
Adventure for God, by The Rt. Rev. Charles H. Brent ... New York [etc.] Longmans, Green, and co., 1905. x p., 1 l., 158 p. 19 1/2 cm. (Half-title: The Bishop Paddock lectures, 1904) [BX5937.B75A3] 5-42042
1. Protestant Episcopal church in the U.S.A.—Addresses, essays, lectures. I. Title.

KINSMAN, Frederick Joseph, 1868- 225
Catholic and Protestant, by Frederick Joseph Kinsman ... New York, London [etc.] Longmans, Green, and co., 1913. 6 p. l., [3]-123 p. 19 1/2 cm. "The papers contained in this book were read before a conference for church workers in the cathedral of St. John the Divine, New York, July 1-4, 1913."--Pref. [BR121.K5] 13-20316
1. Protestant Episcopal church in the U.S.A.—Addresses, essays, lectures. I. Title.

RAINSFORD, William Stephen, 1850-1933. 252.
The reasonableness of faith, and other addresses, by W. S. Rainsford, D.D. New York, Doubleday, Page & co., 1902. 3 p. l., 300 p. 21 cm. [BX5937.R3R4] 2-14032
1. Protestant Episcopal church in the U.S.A.—Addresses, essays, lectures. 2. Brooks, Phillips, 1835-1893. I. Title.
Contents omitted.

STRENGTH to grow.
Illus. by Stanley Wyatt. Revised teacher's manual: grade 8. Greenwich, Conn., Seabury Press [c1959] x, 111p. illus. 28cm. (The Seabury series, T-8B)
I. Protestant Episcopal Church in the U. S. A. National Council. Dept. of Christian Education.

THOMPSON, Hugh Miller, 1830-1902. 230.
"Copy." Essays from an editor's drawer, on religion, literature, and life. By Hugh Miller Thompson ... Hartford, Conn., The Church press: M. H. Mallory and co., 1872. ix, [11]-360 p. 20 1/2 cm. [BX5845.T5 1872] 45-53775
1. Protestant Episcopal church in the U.S.A.—Addresses, essays, lectures. I. Title.

THOMPSON, Hugh Miller, 1830-1902. 204
"Copy"; essays from an editor's drawer on religion, literature and life, by Hugh Miller Thompson ... 3d ed. New York, T. Whittaker, 1885. 2 p. l., [iii]-ix, [11]-360 p. 19 1/2 cm. [BX5845.T5 1885] 12-39594
1. Protestant Episcopal church in the U.S.A.—Addresses, essays, lectures. I. Title.

Protestant Episcopal church in the U.S.A.—Alabama.

WHITAKER, Walter Claiborne, 1867- 283.
History of the Protestant Episcopal church in Alabama, 1763-1891, by Walter C. Whitaker ... Birmingham, Ala., Roberts & son, 1898. 317 p. ports. 20 cm. [BX5917.A2W5] 44-30272
1. Protestant Episcopal church in the U.S.A.—Alabama. 2. Protestant Episcopal church in the U.S.A. Alabama (Diocese) I. Title.

Protestant Episcopal church in the U.S.A. Albany (Diocese)

DE MILLE, George Edmed, 1898- 283.747
A history of the diocese of Albany, 1704-1923, by George E. De Mille ... with foreword by the Bishop of Albany ... Philadelphia, The Church historical society [1946] 6 p. l., 151 p. front., plates, ports., map. 23 1/2 cm. ([Church historical society, Philadelphia] Publication no. 16) Bibliography: p. [137]-142. [BX5918.A3D4] 46-4488
1. Protestant Episcopal church in the U.S.A. Albany (Diocese) I. Title.

Protestant Episcopal Church in the U.S.A. Bethlehem (Diocese)

RADDIN, George Gates, 1906- 262'.03'74822
Centennial survey of the Episcopal Diocese of Bethlehem, 1871-1971. Compiled by George Gates Raddin, Jr. Wilkes-Barre, Pa., King's College Press, 1972. 47 l. 28 cm. [BX5918.B5R3] 73-172399
1. Protestant Episcopal Church in the U.S.A. Bethlehem (Diocese) I. Title.

Protestant Episcopal Church in the U.S.A. — Biography

SMITH, Charles Ernest. 922.
Under the northern cross; or, Parochial memories, by C. Ernest Smith... Milwaukee, Wis., Morehouse publishing company [c1925] 3 p. l., 270 p. front. (port.) 19 cm. [BX5995.S47A3] 25-24295
I. Title.

TURNER, Samuel Hulbeart, 1790-1861. 922.373
Autobiography of the Rev. Samuel H. Turner, D. D., late professor of Biblical learning and the interpretation of Scripture in the General theological seminary of the Protestant Episcopal church in the United States of America. New York, A. D. F. Randolph. 1863. x, [9]-292 p. front. (port.) 19 1/2 cm. [BX5995.T77A3 1863] 35-23990
I. Title.

TURNER, Samuel Hulbeart, 1790-1861. 922.373
Autobiography of the Rev. Samuel H. Turner, D.D. late professor of Biblical learning and the interpretation of Scripture in the General theological seminary of the Protestant Episcopal church in the United States of America. New-York, A. D. F. Randolph, 1864. x, [9]-292 p. front. (port.) 19 cm. [BX5995.T77A3 1864] 35-23989
I. Title.

WILLIAMS, George Walton, 1922-
Early ministers at St. Michael's, Charleston. Charleston [S.C.] The Dalcho Historical Society, 1961. 78 p. ports. (1 col.) 22 cm. (Dalcho Historical Society of the Diocese of South Carolina. Publications, 14) 63-38808
1. Protestant Episcopal Church in the U.S.A. — Biog. 2. Clergy — South Carolina — Charleston. I. Title. II. Series.

Protestant Episcopal Church in the U.S.A. Book of common prayer.

-AVERILL, Edward Wilson 1870- 264.
Talks on the prayer book, by Edward W. Averill ... Fort Wayne, Ind., The Parish press, c1929. cover-title, 63 p. 17 cm. [BX5945.A85] 29-8123
1. Protestant Episcopal church in the U. S. A. Book of common prayer. I. Title.

BECKWITH, Charles Minnigerode, bp., 1851- 264.
The church school in the Book of common prayer ... [by] the Bishop of Alabama. [Montgomery, Ala., The Paragon press, c1928- v. 23 cm. Acknowledgment signed: C. M. Beckwith. Contents.grade III. The book of common prayer. [BX5945.B4] 28-11121
1. Protestant Episcopal church in the U.S.A. Book of common prayer. I. Title.

BIBLE. English. Lessons, Liturgical. 1850. 220.52
Proper lessons for the Sundays and holydays throughout the year. New-York, Stanford and Swords, 1850. 491 p. 13 cm. [With Protestant Episcopal church in the U. S. A. Book of common prayer. The Book of common prayer ... New York, 1850] [BX5943.A1 1850 b] 33-16672
I. Title.

BOGGIS, Robert James Edmund.
Praying for the dead, an historical review of the practice. By the Reverend R. J. Edmund Boggie ... London, New York [etc.] Longmans, Green and co., 1913. xiv, 272 p. 20 1/2 cm. "List of principal authorities": p. ix-xiv. A15
I. Title.

BOSS, Nelson Riley, d.1914. 264.03
The prayer book reason why; a text book of instruction on the history, doctrines, usages, and ritual of the church, by the Reverend Nelson R. Boss, M.A. New ed., rev. and enl. by the Rev. Marshall M. Day...with introduction by the Rt. Rev. Ernest Milmore Stires... Milwaukee, Wis., Morehouse publishing co. [c1930] viii p., 1 l., 210 p. 17 cm. "Second edition." "Books on the doctrines and usages of the church": p. [205]-206. [BX5145.B65 1930] 30-33763
1. Protestant Episcopal church in the U.S.A. Book of common prayer. 2. Protestant Episcopal church in the U.S.A.—Catechisms and creeds. I. Day, Marshall Mallory, 1884- ed. II. Title.

BURGESS, Francis Guild, 1856- 264.039
The romance of the Book of common prayer, by Franic G. Burgess. Milwaukee, Wis., Morehouse publishing co. [c1930] 5 p. l., 133, [1] p. 19 cm. First edition. [BX5945.B75] 30-33684
1. Protestant Episcopal church in the U.S.A. Book of common prayer. 2. Church of England. Book of common prayer. I. Title.

COX, William Edward, 1870- 264.03
The heart of the prayer book, by Rev. William E. Cox, D.D. Richmond, Va., The Dietz press, incorporated, 1944. xii p., 1 l., 163 p. 20 cm. [BX5945.C57] 45-60855
1. Protestant Episcopal church in the U.S.A. Book of common prayer. I. Title.

COXE, Arthur Cleveland, bp. 1818-1896. 264.03
Thoughts on the services; designed as an introduction to the liturgy, and an aid to its devout use. By Rt. Rev. A. Cleveland Coxe ... 12th American ed. Philadelphia, J. B. Lippncott & co., 1871. 370 p. 16 cm. [BX5940.C6 1871] 38-351
1. Protestant Episcopal church in the U. S. A. Book of common prayer. 2. Church year. I. Title.

DEARMER, Percy, 1867-1936. 264.
Everyman's history of the prayer book, by the Reverend Percy Dearmer ... New American edition, revised and edited for American use by Frederic Cook Morehouse ... with 103 illustrations. Milwaukee, Wis., Morehouse publishing co., 1931. xix, 268 p. illus. (incl. ports., chart., facsims.) 19 cm. A revision is published in 1933 under title: The story of the prayer book in the old and new world. "Second American edition." "Some books on the subject": p. viii. [BX5945.D35 1931] A 32
1. Protestant Episcopal church in the U. S. A. Book of common prayer. I. Morehouse, Frederic Cook, 1868- ed. II. Title.

DENNEN, Ernest Joseph, 1866- 264.
Introduction to the Prayer book, by Ernest J. Dennen ... New York, E. S. Gorham, 1906. 7 p. l., 19-117 p. front., 6 pl. 22 cm. Title within ornamental border. [BX5945.D4] 6-23683
1. Protestant Episcopal church in the U. S. A Book of common prayer. I. Title.

DOWDEN, John, bp. of Edinburgh, 1840-1910.
The Scottish communion office, 1764, with introduction, history of the office, notes and appendices, by John Dowden ... New ed., seen through the press by H. A. Wilson. Oxford, The Clarendon press, 1922. xii, 273, [1] p. 23 cm. First edition, 1884, published under title: The annotated Scottish communion office. "The American communion office": p. [135]-142. "Bibliography of the Scottish communion office": p. 195-203. [BX5337.C7D6 1922] 22-18548
I. Episcopal church in Scotland. Book of common prayer. Communion service. II. Protestant Episcopal church in the U.S.A. Book of common prayer. Communion service. III. Wilson, Henry Austin, 1854- ed. IV. Title.

EPISCOPAL evangelical fellowship. 264.03
A prayer book manual, prepared by the Boston clergy group of the Episcopal evangelical fellowship. Louisville, The Cloister press, 1943. 5 p. l., 123 p. 19 cm. "For further reading and study": p. [119] [BX5945.E65] 43-13885
1. Protestant Episcopal church in the U.S.A. Book of common prayer. I. Title.

EVANGELICAL Educational Society.
A prayer book manual, prepared by the Boston Clergy Group of the Evangelical Educational Society. [4th ed.] Philadelphia [1962?] 132 p. 19 cm. First published in 1943 under the society's former name: Episcopal Evangelical Fellowship. 68-42812
1. Protestant Episcopal Church in the U.S.A. Book of common prayer. I. Episcopal Evangelical Fellowship. II. Title.

*FILLMORE, Lowell 248.42
The prayer way to health, wealth and happiness. Lee's Summit, Mo., Unity Sch. of Christianity [1964] 252p. 24cm. 2.95 bds.,
I. Title.

GIRARDEY, Ferrol 1839-
Prayer, its necessity, its power, its conditions, by Rev. Ferrol Girardey, C. SS. R., with preface of Very Rev. Thos. P. Brown ... St. Louis, Mo. [etc.] B. Herder, 1916. xvi, 210 p. 20 cm. 16-17678 1.00
I. Title.

GRISWOLD, Latta, 1876- 264.
The teaching of the prayer book, by the Reverend Latta Griswold ... Milwaukee, Wis., Morehouse publishing co. [c1929] xi, 101, [1] p. 19 cm. "The text of the revised American prayer book is that to which ordinarily appeal is made."--Introd. [BX5945.G7] 29-30690
1. Protestant Episcopal church in the U. S. A. Book of common prayer. I. Title.

HALL, Arthur Crawshay Alliston, bp., 1847-1930. 264.
A companion to the Prayer book; a liturgical and spiritual exposition of the services for the holy communion, morning and evening prayer and the litany, by the Right Rev. A. C. A. Hall... New York, E. & J. B. Young & co. [c1902] 78 p. 15 1/2 cm. [BX5945.H82] 2-6069
1. Protestant Episcopal church in the U.S.A. Book of common prayer. I. Title.

HARNEY, William J.
Praying clear through; a book on a subject essential to all who would get into a state of grace and grow therein; also for those who study to shew themselves approved unto God, workmen that need not to be ashamed. By William J. Harney ... Cincinnati, O., God's revivalist press, 1915. 5 p. l., 7-253 p. 2 port. (incl. front.) 20 cm. 15-11660 1.00
I. Title.

HART, Samuel, 1845-1917. 264.
... The Book of common prayer, by Samuel Hart ... Sewanee, Tenn., The University press at the University of the South [c1910] x p., 1 l., 290 p. 20 cm. (Sewanee theological library) Bibliography at end of most of the chapters. [BX5945.H35] 10-12154
1. Protestant Episcopal church in the U. S. A. Book of common prayer. I. Title.

JONES, Bayard Hale, 1887-1957. 264.032
Dynamic redemption; reflections of the Book of common prayer. Greenwich, Conn., Seabury Press, 1961. 147p. 20cm. [BX5945.J58] 61-9107
1. Protestant Episcopal Church In the U.S.A. Book of common prayer. 2. Lords Supper—Anglican Communion. I. Title.

LARNED, Albert Cecil, 1883- 264.03
A spiritual treasury; short meditations on the Book of common prayer, by the Rev. Albert C. Larned ... Milwaukee, Wis., Morehouse publishing co. [c1932] 5 p. l., 78 p. 19 cm. [BX5945.L3] 32-23851
1. Protestant Episcopal church in the U. S. A. Book of common prayer. 2. Protestant Episcopal church in the U. S. A.—Prayer-books and devotions. 3. Meditations. I. Title.

MCCORMICK, John Newton, bp., 1863- 264.
The litany and the life; a series of studies in the litany designed more especially for use during the season of Lent, by the Rev. John Newton McCormick... Milwaukee, The Young churchman co., 1904. 3 p. l., [9]-304 p. 19 cm. [BX5944.L5M2] 4-3355
1. Protestant Episcopal church in the U.S.A. Book of common prayer. 2. Lent 3. Lent I. Title.

MULLER, James Arthur, 1884-1945. 264.039
... Who wrote the new prayers in the Prayer book? By James Arthur Muller. Philadelphia, The Church historical society [1946] 49 p. 23 cm. (Church historical society. Publication, no. 20) "Bibliography of the writings of James Arthur Muller": p. 9-10. [BX5945.M77] 47-5954
1. Protestant Episcopal church in the U.S.A. Book of common prayer. I. Title.

ODENHEIMER, William Henry, bp., 1817-1879. 264.
An offering to churchmen: or, A few historical hints connected with the origin and compilation of the prayer book, with notes and an appendix, containing various documents connected with our liturgy, by W. H. Odenheimer ... Philadelphia, R. S. H. George, 1841. 166 p., 1 l. 12 cm. [BX5945.O4] 28-3281
1. Protestant Episcopal church in the U. S. A. Book of common prayer. I. Title.

PRAYER--ITS deeper dimensions; a Christian Life symposium. Grand Rapids, Mich., Zondervan [1963] 88p. 21cm. 1.95 bds., 248.32

**PRAYER of love and silence (The),* by a Carthusian. Tr. from French by a Monk of Parkminster. Wilkes-Barre, Pa., Dimension [1968,c.1962] 18cm. 1.25 pap., 248.8'942

PROTESTANT Episcopal church in the U. S. A. Joint commission on the Book of common prayer. 264.
Fourth report of the Joint commission on the Book of common prayer, appointed by the General convention of 1913. New York, The Macmillan company, 1925. 1 p. l., 5-116 p. 20 cm. [BX5945.A6 4th rept.] 25-3858

1. Protestant Episcopal church in the U. S. A. Book of common prayer. I. Title.

PROTESTANT Episcopal church in the U. S. A. Joint commission on the Book of common prayer.
Report of the Joint commission on the Book of common prayer, appointed by the General convention of 1913. Boston, D. B. Updike, The Merrymount press, 1916. xi, 177, [1] p. 18 cm. A25
1. Protestant Episcopal church in the U. S. A. Book of common prayer. I. Title.

PROTESTANT Episcopal church 264. in the U. S. A. Joint commission on the Book of common prayer.
Second report of the Joint commission on the Book of common prayer appointed by the General convention of 1913. New York, The Macmillan company, 1919. xx, 301 p. 20 cm. [BX5945.A5 1919] 19-12582 1.50
1. Protestant Episcopal church in the U. S. A. Book of common prayer. I. Title.

PROTESTANT Episcopal church 264. in the U. S. A. Joint commission on the Book of common prayer.
Third report of the Joint commission, on the Book of common prayer, appointed by the General convention of 1913. New York, The Macmillan company, 1922. xviii, 231 p. 20 cm. [BX5945.A6] 22-8735
1. Protestant Episcopal church in the U. S. A. Book of common prayer. I. Title.

PROTESTANT Episcopal church 264. in the U. S. A. General convention, 1922.
Prayer book amendments, adopted by the General convention of 1922, and to be finally voted upon by the General convention of 1925, containing the substance of the official notification communicated by the secretary of the House of deputies to each diocese, edited by the Rev. Carroll M. Davis ... Milwaukee, Wis., Morehouse publishing co. [c1923] 2 p. l., 79, [1] p. 14 cm. [BX5945.A3 1922] 23-13760
1. Protestant Episcopal church in the U. S. A. Book of common prayer. I. Davis, Carroll Melvin, 1857- ed. II. Title.

PROTESTANT Episcopal church 264. in the U. S. A. General convention, 1925.
Prayer book alterations, finally adopted or ratified by the General convention of 1925, edited by the Rev. Charles L. Pardee ... and the Rev. Carroll M. Davis ... Pub. by authority of General convention. Milwaukee, Wis., Morehouse publishing co. [c1925] 3 p. l., 67, [1] p. 14 cm. [BX5945.A3 1925] 26-3610
1. Protestant Episcopal church in the U. S. A. Book of common prayer. I. Pardee, Charles Laban, 1864- ed. II. Davis, Carroll Melvin, 1857- joint ed. III. Title.

PROTESTANT Episcopal 264.03 Church in the U. S. A. Book of common prayer.
Our prayers and praise; the order for daily morning prayer and the order for the administration of the Lord's Supper or Holy Communion, with simplified rubrics and explanatory notes, together with notes on the church year and the collects to be used throughout the year. Illustrated by a Sister of the Community of the Holy Spirit. The notes on morning prayer and Holy Communion were prepared by Massey H. Shepherd, Jr., and Robert N. Rodenmayer. Greenwich, Conn., Seabury Press [1957] 108p. illus. 26cm. (The Seabury series, R-3) [BX5943.A1 1957] 57-8341
I. Shepherd, Massey Hamilton, 1913- ed. II. Title.

PROTESTANT Episcopal 264.03 Church in the U. S. A. Book of common prayer.
The prayer book office, Anglican divine service; morning prayer and evening prayer according to the American book of common prayer. With additional invitatories, antiphons for seasons and feasts, the hymns and other enrichments. [Revision of 1963] New York, Morehouse-Barlow, 1963. ixxxvii, 658 p. 17 cm. [BX5943.A4P7] 63-14273
I. Title.

PROTESTANT Episcopal church 264. in the U. S. A. Book of common prayer.
The proposed revision of the Book of common prayer, issued under authority and by resolution of General convention. Milwaukee, Morehouse publishing co., 1923. 3 p. l., 154 p. 20 cm. "Part i ... alterations in the Book of common prayer, finally adopted at the conventions of 1919 and 1922; part ii ... alterations proposed at the conventionof 1922, and to be finally acted upon at the convention of 1925." [BX5943.A1 1923] 23-9622
I. Title. II. Title: Book of common prayer, Proposed revision of.

PROTESTANT Episcopal 264.03 Church in the U.S.A. Book of common prayer.
The Oxford American prayer book commentary, by Massey Hamilton Shepherd, Jr. New York, Oxford University Press, 1950. 1 v. (various pagings) 21 cm. Facsimile reproduction of the Book of common prayer [New York, Oxford University Press, 1944) with commentary on opposite pages. Includes bibliography. [BX5945.S5] 50-10192
1. Protestant Episcopal Church in the U.S.A. Book of common prayer. I. Shepherd, Massey Hamilton, 1913- II. Title.

PROTESTANT Episcopal church in the U. S. Book of common prayer.
The prayer book of the Protestant Episcopal church simplified and arranged. Chicago, Ritzmann, Brookes & co. [c1910] 2 p. l., 3-25 p., p. 329-508. 16 cm. Preface signed: Frederic E. J. Lloyd. 10-27318 0.30
I. Lloyd, Frederic E. J., comp. II. Title.

PROTESTANT Episcopal 264.03 church in the U.S.A. Book of common prayer.
The Prayer book office, morning prayer and evening prayer, according to the American book of common prayer, with invitatories and hymns, antiphons to the gospel canticles and other enrichments. New York, Morehouse-Gorham co., 1944. ixv, 801, [1] p. 17 cm. [BX5943.A4P7] 44-8927
I. Title.

PROTESTANT Episcopal 264'.03 Church in the U.S.A. Book of common prayer.
The Prayer book office / compiled and edited by Howard Galley. New York : Seabury Press, 1980. xli, 771 p. ; 20 cm. [BX5943.A4P7 1980] 79-92533 ISBN 0-8164-0370-8 : 24.50
I. Galley, Howard. II. Title.

PROTESTANT Episcopal 264'.03 Church in the U.S.A. Liturgical Commission.
The draft proposed Book of Common Prayer and administration of the sacraments and other rites and ceremonies of the Church : according to the use of the Protestant Episcopal Church in the United States of America, otherwise known as the Episcopal Church, together with the Psalter or Psalms of David : presented to the General Convention of 1976 / by the Standing Liturgical Commission in compliance with the directions of the General Convention of 1973. New York : Church Hymnal Corp., 1976. 1001 p. ; 22 cm. [BX5945.A3 1976] 76-360414
1. Protestant Episcopal Church in the U.S.A. Book of Common Prayer. 2. Protestant Episcopal Church in the U.S.A. Liturgy and ritual. I. Protestant Episcopal Church in the U.S.A. Book of Common Prayer. II. Title: The draft proposed Book of Common Prayer.

PROTESTANT EPISCOPAL 264.03 CHURCH IN THE U.S.A. BOOK OF COMMON PRAYER
The prayer book office, Anglican divine service; morning prayer and evening prayer according to the American book of common prayer. With additional invitatories, antiphons for seasons and feasts, the hymns and other enrichments [Revision of 1963] New York, Morehouse, 1963 [c.1944, 1963] 1xxxvii, 658p. 17cm. 63-14273 10.95
I. Title.

ROACH, Corwin Carlyle, 264.03 1904-
For all sorts and conditions. Greenwich, Conn., Seabury Press, 1955. 215p. 21cm. [BX5945.R6] 55-6352
1. Protestant Episcopal Church in the U. S. A. Book of common prayer. I. Title.

SANFORD, Edgar Lewis, 264.03 1864-
The Christian life in the Book of common prayer; a year's lessons for church children, by Rev. Edgar L. Sanford ... Trenton, The Diocesan board of religious education of the Diocese of New Jersey [c1931] 2 p. l., 3-87 p. illus. 15 cm. [BX5945.S3] 31-19638
1. Protestant Episcopal church in the U.S.A. Book of common prayer. I. Protestant Episcopal church in the U.S.A. New Jersey (Diocese) Diocesan board of religious education. II. Title.

SANFORD, Edgar Lewis, 264.03 1864-
Lessons on the offices of instruction as contained in the Book of common prayer, by the Rev. Edgar L. Sanford ... Rev. ed. Trenton, N.J., The Diocesan board of religious education of the Diocese of New Jersey, 1933. 2 p. l., 3-93 p. 15 1/2 cm. [BX5944.O4S3 1933] 34-2440
1. Protestant Episcopal church in the U.S.A. Book of common prayer. I. Title. II. Title: Offices of instruction.

SANFORD, Edgar Lewis, 264.03 1864-
Life in the kingdom of God; sequel to The Christian life in the Book of common prayer, by Rev. Edgar L. Sanford, D.D. Trenton, The Diocesan board of religious education of the Diocese of New Jersey [c1932] 2 p. l., 3-90 p. 15 1/2 cm. [BX5945.S33] 32-23594
1. Protestant Episcopal church in the U.S.A. Book of common prayer. I. Protestant Episcopal church in the U.S.A. New Jersey (Diocese) Diocesan board of religious education. II. Title.

SHEPHERD, Massey Hamilton, 264.03 1913-
The worship of the church [by] Massey H. Shepherd Jr., with the assistance of the Authors' Committee of the Dept. of Christian Education of the Protestant Episcopal Church. Greenwich, Conn., Seabury Press, 1952. ix, 240 p. 22 cm. (The Church's teaching, v. 4) Bibliography: p. 213-236. [BX5945.S52] 52-13444
1. Protestant Episcopal Church in the U.S.A. Book of common prayer. 2. Public worship. I. Title. II. Series.

SIMCOX, Carroll Eugene, 264.03 1912-
The words of our worship; a study in prayer book meanings. Foreword by Horace W. B. Donegan. New York, Morehouse-Gorham, 1955. 239p. 21cm. (Bishop of New York books, 1955) [BX5945.S54] 55-7436
1. Protestant Episcopal Church in the U. S. A. Book of common prayer. 2. Theology—Terminology. I. Title.

STEVENSON, William Fleming, 1832-1886.
Praying and working; being some account of what men can do when in earnest. By the late Rev. William Fleming Stevenson. New York, T. Whittaker [1892!] xiv, 411 p. 18 cm. Introduction dated July 1892. 7-24508
I. Title.

SUTER, John Wallace, 1859- 264.
The people's book of worship; a study of the Book of common prayer, by John Wallace Suter and Charles Morris Addison. New York, The Macmillan company, 1919. 5 p. l., 76 p. 18 cm. (Half-title: Church principles for lay people) [BX5945.S8] 19-9156
1. Protestant Episcopal church in the U.S.A. Book of common prayer. I. Addison, Charles Morris, 1856- joint author. II. Title.

SYDNOR, William 264.032
How and what the church teaches. New York, Longmans, Green [c.]1960. xii, 177p. 22cm. 60-10536 4.00 pap.,
1. Protestant Episcopal Church in the U. S. A. Book of common prayer I. Title.

SYDNOR, William. 264.032
How and what the church teaches. [1st ed.] New York, Longmans, Green, 1960. 177 p. 22 cm. [BX5947.L4S9] 60-40536
1. Protestant Episcopal Church in the U.S.A. Book of common prayer. I. Title.

TIFFANY, Charles Comfort, 264. 1829-1907.
The prayer book and the Christian life; or, The Conception of the Christian life implied in the Book of common prayer, by Charles C. Tiffany ... New York, C. Scribner's sons, 1898. viii, 174 p. 19 1/2 cm. [BX5945.T5] 98-957
1. Protestant Episcopal church in the U.S.A. Book of common prayer. 2. Christian life. I. Title.

TYLER, William Seymour, 264. 1810-1897.
Prayer for colleges, a premium essay, written for "the Society for the promotion of collegiate and theological education at the West." By W. S. Tyler ... New York, The Society, 1859. viii, [7]-214 p. 19 cm. [BV283.C7T8 1859] 15-17307
I. Title.

Protestant Episcopal Church in the U.S.A. Book of common prayer. Collects.

MAY, Caroline, b.ca.1820.
Hymns on the collects for every Sunday in the year, by Caroline May ... New York, A. D. F. Randolph & company [1872] iv, 156 p. 18 1/2 cm. [PS2376.M15] 31-25888
1. Protestant Episcopal church in the U.S.A. Book of common prayer. Collects. 2. Hymns, American. I. Title.

PROTESTANT Episcopal church 264. in the U. S. A. Book of common prayer.
Revised service book. Revision of 1925. The order for morning and for evening prayer, together with prayers and thanksgivings, the new and altered collects, Epistles, and Gospels, and the order for the holy communion, solemnization of matrimony, burial of the dead, as modified by the action of General convention in the years 1919, 1922, and 1925; authorized for use in churches. Pub. by authority of General convention. Milwaukee, Morehouse publishing co. [c1925] xi, 115, [1] p. 15 cm. Lettered on cover: Edition A. [BX5943.A1 1925 a] 26-3609
I. Title.

TATE, Edward Engram, 1911-
The armour of light: an interpretation of the Prayer book Collects, by Edward E. Tate and Marjorie Shearer. Atlanta Lullwater Press, 1963] 92 p. 23 cm. 64-575
1. Protestant Episcopal Church in the U.S.A. Book of common prayer. Collects. I. Shearer, Marjorie, 1915-1963, joint author. II. Title.

Protestant Episcopal Church in the U.S.A. Book of common prayer. Communion service.

BABIN, David E. 264.03
Introduction to the liturgy of the Lord's Supper, by David E. Babin. New York, Morehouse-Barlow Co. [1968] 96 p. 19 cm. [BX5949.C5B25] 68-19700
1. Protestant Episcopal Church in the U.S.A. Book of common prayer. Communion service. 2. Lord's Supper (Liturgy) I. Title.

YOUNG, William Tate, 264.035 1900-
A commentary on the holy communion [by] the Reverend W. Tate Young. New York, Morehouse-Gorham [1944] 5 p. l., 101 p. 19 cm. [BK5944.C75Y6] 44-1014
1. Protestant Episcopal church in the U.S.A. Book of common prayer. Communion service. 2. Lord's supper (Liturgy) I. Title.

Protestant Episcopal Church in the U.S.A. Book of common prayer—Congresses.

PRAYER book renewal : 264'.03 worship and the new book of common prayer / edited by H. Barry Evans ; with a foreword by Charles M. Guilbert ; and an introd. by William S. Pregnall. New York : Seabury Press, 1978. 115 p. ; 21 cm. "A Crossroad book." Bibliography: p. 113-115.

[BX5945.P68] 77-16256 ISBN 0-8164-2157-9 pbk. : 4.95
1. Protestant Episcopal Church in the U.S.A. Book of common prayer—Congresses. 2. Liturgics—Congresses. I. Evans, Hayden Barry, 1936-

Protestant Episcopal church in the U.S.A. Book of common prayer. Offices of instruction.

WOODCOCK, Irene G 264.03
A first work book study on the Offices of instruction, by Irene Woodcock, in association with Helen Beckett, edited by Dr. Maurice Clarke. Pupil's work book. Louisville [1944] 79 p. illus. 27 cm. -- Teacher's guide. Louisville [1944] 59 p. 20 cm. [BX5875.W6] 44-10003
1. Protestant Episcopal church in the U.S.A. Book of common prayer. Offices of instruction. I. Beckett, Helen, joint author. II. Clarke, Maurice, 1882- ed. III. Title.

Protestant Episcopal church in the U.S.A. Book of common prayer. Psalter.

HUTCHINS, Charles Lewis, 1838-1920, ed. and arr.
The church psalter, containing the psalter, proper psalms, and twenty selections, with the pointing set forth and authorized for use by the General convention, together with special settings of certain psalms; arranged with appropriate chants by the Rev. Charles L. Hutchins... Boston, Parish choir, 1897. vi, 332, ii p. 20 x 15 cm. Principally close score. [M2169.H9C4] 45-46816
1. Protestant Episcopal church in the U.S.A. Book of common prayer. Psalter. 2. Bible. O.T. Psalms. English. 1897. Coverdale. I. Title.

PROTESTANT Episcopal 264'.038
Church in the U.S.A. Book of common prayer. Psalter.
The Psalter : a new version for public worship and private devotion / introduced by Charles Mortimer Guilbert. New York : Seabury Press, 1978, c1977. xxviii, 228 p. ; 19 cm. A revision of the traditional text. "A Crossroad book." [BX5946.A1 1978] 78-50084 ISBN 0-8164-0311-2 : 3.50
I. Bible. O.T. Psalms. English. II. Title.

PROTESTANT Episcopal 264.038
church in the U. S. A. Book of common prayer. Psalter.
The morning and evening canticles and occasional anthems, together with the Psalter or Psalms of David, pointed for chanting in accordance with the action of the General convetions of 1892 and 1895. [Concord? Mass.] Printed for the commission, 1896. 202 p. 20 x 16 cm. "Twelve copies only printed. No. 10." [BX5946.A1 1896] 223.5 35-22142
I. Protestant Episcopal church in the U. S. A. Joint commission on a uniform pointing of the canticles and Psalter. II. Bible. O. T. Psalms. English. 1896. III. Bible. English. O. T. Psalms. 1896. IV. Title.

PROTESTANT Episcopal church 783.9
in the U. S. A. Book of common prayer. Psalter.
The Psalter; pointed for singing and set to music, according to the use of Trinity parish, New York. New ed. The pointing revised, and the music, chiefly double chants, selected and arranged by A. H. Messiter ... New York, E. & J. B. Young & co., 1889. vi p., 1 l., 344 p. 21 cm. On cover: Double chant edition. [M2169.P96P38] 40-15421
I. Messiter, Arthur Henry, 1834-1916. II. Bible. O. T. Psalms. English. 1889. III. Bible. English. O. T. Psalms. 1889. IV. New York. Trinity parish. V. Title.

PROTESTANT Episcopal church in
the U.S.A. Book of common prayer. Psalter.
The Psalter, Canticles and selections of Psalms, pointed for singing according to the use of Trinity parish, New York, the pointing revised by A. H. Messiter ... New York, E. & J. B. Young & co. [1892] 2 p. l., 326 p. 15 1/2 cm. [BX5946.A1 1892] 45-44803
I. Messiter, Arthur Henry, 1834-1916. II. Bible. O.T. Psalms. English. 1889. III. New York. Trinity church. IV. Title.

PROTESTANT Episcopal church in
the U.S.A. Book of common prayer. Psalter.
The psalter, or, Psalms of David; together with the canticles of the morning and evening prayer, and occasional offices of the church. Figured for chanting. To which are prefixed an explanatory preface and a selection of chants. New York, D. Appleton & company; Philadelphia, G. S. Appleton, 1847. 36, 224 p. illus. (music) 20 cm. Preface signed: W.A.M. [i.e. W. A. Muhlenberg] [BX5946.A1 1847] 46-28064
I. Muhlenberg, William Augustus, 1796-1877, ed. II. Bible. O.T. Psalms. English. 1847. III. Title.

PROTESTANT Episcopal church in
the U.S.A. Book of common prayer. Psalter.
The Psalter, or, Psalms of David, ec., ec. Printed for chanting Compiled from the arrangements of Robert Janes and James Stimpson. 3d ed. New York, Stanford and Swords, 1848. 224 p., 1 l. 15 cm. With this is bound, as issued: Protestant Episcopal church in the U.S.A. Book of common prayer. Canticles of the church. New-York, 1848. [BX5946.J3 1848] 45-42156
I. Janes, Robert, 1806-1866. II. Stimpson, James, 1820-1886. III. Bible. O.T. Psalms. English. 1848. Coverdale. IV. Title.

Protestant Episcopal church in the U.S.A. Catechism.

GARDNER, Vera C. ed. 238.3
The child of God; ten-minute instructions for the upper school, based on the catechism to be used at the worship service, edited by Vera C. Gardner, illustrations by Lucia Patton. New York, Morehouse-Gorham co., 1941. 160 p. incl. front., illus., diagrs. 19 1/2 cm. "Prepared ... by the Curriculum committee of the Department of Christian education of the province of the Mid-west."--Foreword. [BX5939.A3G3] 41-21163
1. Protestant Episcopal church in the U.S.A. Catechism. I. Protestant Episcopal church in the U.S.A. Provinces. Mid-west. Dept. of Christian education. II. Title.

GRAY, Andrew, D. D.
What every Christian ought to know and believe; or, The church catechism with notes expository and practical (for Sunday schools and Bible classes) A book for the times, by Rev. Andrew Gray ... New York, J. Pott and company, 1892. 1 p. l., [v]-xv, 71 p. 23 cm. [BX5969.G7] 46-40258
1. Protestant Episcopal church in the U.S.A. Catechism. I. Title.

KEAN, Charles Duell, 1910- 238.3
The meaning of the quadrilateral. New York, Seabury Press [c1963] 56 p. 21 cm. Bibliography: p. 54-56. [BX5939.K4] 63-25956
1. Protestant Episcopal Church in the U.S.A. — Catechisms and creeds. I. Title.

LITTELL, John Stockton, 238.3
1870-
500 questions & answers in religion, by the Reverend John S. Littell ... Milwaukee, Wis., Morehouse publishing co.; London, A. R. Mowbray & co., ltd. [c1931] 84 p. 23 cm. "Books which have helped": p. 77; "Materials in religious education by the Rev. John S. Littell, D. D.": p. 82-84. [BX5939.L55] 32-9568
1. Protestant Episcopal church in the U. S. A.—Catechisms and creeds. I. Title.

NELSON, Richard Henry, bp., 238.
1859-1931.
The Christian faith and the Christian life; a catechism on the doctrine of the church, by the Rev. R. H. Nelson. New York, J. Pott & co., 1888. 127 p. 17 cm. [BX5939.N4] 39-24042
1. Protestant Episcopal church in the U. S. A.—Catechisms and creeds—English. I. Title.

OLDHAM, George Ashton, 238.3
Bp., 1887-
The catechism today; primary principles of the faith. Greenwich, Conn., Seabury Press, 1961 [c1956] 143 p. 19 cm. [BX5139.O55] 61-9109
1. Protestant Episcopal Church in the U.S.A. Catechism. I. Title.

RANDALL, Edwin Jarvis, Bp. 238.3
The church catechism and the living Word. [New York] Parthenon Press [1954] 88p. 16cm. [BX5939.R3] 55-18972
1. Protestant Episcopal Church in the U. S. A. Catechism. I. Title.

SANFORD, D. P., Mrs. 238.3
Lessons on the church catechism, with Scripture references, by Mrs. D. P. Sanford ... New York, E. P. Dutton and company, 1894. 111 p. 16 cm. [BX5939.S3] 31-8962
1. Protestant Episcopal church in the U.S.A.—Catechisms and creeds. I. Title.

TUCKER, Beverly D
Questions on the way; a catechism for Episcopalians. [Alexandria, Va., Seminary Book Service, 1965?] 131 p. 17 cm. 68-98677
1. Protestant Episcopal Church in the U.S.A.—Catechisms and creeds. I. Title.

WHITE, William, bp., 1748-1836.
Lectures on the catechism of the Protestant Episcopal church. With supplementary lectures; one on the ministry, the other on the public service. And dissertations on select subjects in the lectures. By William White ... Philadelphia: Published by Bradford and Inskeep; also, by Inskeep and Bradford, New York; and Edward J. Coale, Baltimore. Printed at the office of the United States' gazette, 1813. x p., 1 l., 506 p. front. (port.) 23 1/2 cm. [BX5139.W6] 45-30099
1. Protestant Episcopal church in the U.S.A. Catechism. 2. Protestant Episcopal church in the U.S.A.—Doctrinal and controversial works. I. Title.

Protestant Episcopal church in the U.S.A.—Ceremonies and practices.

MCMASTER, Vernon Cochrane. 264.03
The church's way, by the Rev. Vernon McMaster ... With a foreword by the Right Reverend Henry St. George Tucker ... New York, F. Fell, inc., 1946. 94 p. incl. front. 21 cm. [BX5940.M3] 46-2851
1. Protestant Episcopal church in the U.S.A.—Ceremonies and practices. I. Title.

Protestant Episcopal church in the U.S.A. Chicago (Diocese)

HOPKINS, John Henry, 283.7731
1861-
The great forty years in the diocese of Chicago, A.D. 1893 to 1934, by the Reverend John Henry Hopkins... Chicago, The Centenary fund of the diocese of Chicago, inc., 1936. xii, 242, [1] p. front., plates, ports. 23 1/2 cm. [BX5918.C5H6] 37-4620
1. Protestant Episcopal church in the U.S.A. Chicago (Diocese) 2. Episcopalians in Chicago. I. Title.

PROTESTANT Episcopal Church 283.
in the U. S. A. Chicago (Diocese)
Journal of the primary convention of the clergy and laity of the Protestant Episcopal Church in the Diocese of Illinois, held in Peoria ... March 9, 1835. Peoria, Printed at the Champion Off., 1835. 16 p. 21 cm. [BX5918.C5A32] 49-57665
I. Title.

Protestant Episcopal church in the U.S.A.—Clergy.

BUTLER, John V 262.14
What is the priesthood? A book on vocation, by John V. Butler and W. Norman Pittenger. New York, Morehouse-Gorham Co., 1954. 221p. 20cm. [BX5965.B8] 54-7264
1. Protestant Episcopal Church in the U. S. A.—Clergy. 2. Clergy—Office. I. Pittenger, William Norman, 1905- II. Title.

CAMERON, Kenneth Walter, 262'.14
1908- comp.
American Episcopal clergy; registers of ordinations in the Episcopal Church in the United States from 1785 through 1904, with indexes. Hartford, Transcendental Books [1970] 31, 43, 35, 36 l. illus., port. 28 cm. [BX5965.C35] 74-15966
1. Protestant Episcopal Church in the U.S.A.—Clergy. I. Title.

CASE histories of 253'.2
tentmakers / edited by James L. Lowery, Jr. Wilton, Conn. : Morehouse-Barlow Co., c1976. xvii, 83 p. ; 22 cm. Includes bibliographical references. [BV676.5.C37] 76-374762 ISBN 0-8192-1216-4 pbk. : 3.50
1. Protestant Episcopal Church in the U.S.A.—Clergy. 2. Clergy, Part-time—Case studies. I. Lowery, James L.

LOWRIE, Randolph W., 1839- 254
1913.
How to behave in the parish, by the Rev. R. W. Lowrie. New York, J. Pott, 1882. 2 p. l., 3-98 p. 17 cm. [BX5965.L6] 46-28145
1. Protestant Episcopal church in the U.S.A.—Clergy. 2. Church work. I. Title.

MELISH, John Howard, 922.373
1874-
Autumn days; a recollection. Brooklyn, Bromwell Press, 1954. 80p. illus. 24cm. [BX5995.M47A3] 55-22775
1. Protestant Episcopal Church in the U. S. A.—Clergy—Correspondence, reminiscences, etc. I. Title.

MOORE, Paul, 1919- 253'.2
Take a Bishop like me / Paul Moore, Jr. 1st ed. New York : Harper & Row, c1979. viii, 200 p. ; 22 cm. Includes index. [BX5695.M66 1979] 78-2148 ISBN 0-06-013018-0 : 8.95
1. Protestant Episcopal Church in the U.S.A.—Clergy. 2. Moore, Paul, 1919- 3. Ordination of women—Protestant Episcopal Church in the U.S.A. 4. Homosexuality and Christianity. I. Title.

PRATT, Sarah (Smith) 283.772
Mrs. 1853-
Episcopal bishops in Indiana; a churchwoman's restrospect, by Sarah S. Pratt. Indianapolis, The Pratt poster co., 1934. 4 p. l., 3-83 p. front., ports. 19 cm. [Full name: Mrs. Sarah Greene (Smith) Pratt] [BX5917.I6P7] 35-20282
1. Protestant Episcopal church in the U. S. A.—Clergy. 2. Clergy—Indiana. 3. Bishops—Indiana. I. Title.

RAY, Randolph, 1886- 283.747
My Little Church Around the Corner. In collaboration with Villa Stiles. New York, Simon and Schuster, 1957. 365p. illus. 22cm. [BX5995.R37A3] 57-12396
1. Protestant Episcopal Church in the U. S. A.—Clergy—Correspondence, reminiscences, etc. 2. New York. Church of the Transfiguration. I. Title.

SEAGLE, Nathan A 1868- 922.373
The memoirs of a metropolitan minister; sixty years of service in the Diocese of New York. Foreword by the Rt. Rev. Horace W. B. Donegan. [1st ed.] New York, Exposition Press [1955] 99p. illus. 21cm. [BX5995.S314A3] 55-11831
1. Protestant Episcopal Church in the U. S. A.—Clergy—Correspondence, reminiscences, etc. I. Title.

WHITE, William, bp., 1748-1836.
A charge to the clergy of the Protestant Episcopal church in the commonwealth of Pennsylvania, delivered in Christ church, in the city of Philadelphia, on Wednesday, May 27, 1807. By William White... Philadelphia: Printed at the office of the United States gazette. 1807. 56 p. 23 1/2 cm. [BX5837.W5 1807] 27-9553
1. Protestant Episcopal church in the U.S.A.—Clergy. 2. Protestant Episcopal church in the U.S.A. Pennsylvania (Diocese) I. Title.

Protestant Episcopal Church in the U.S.A.—Clergy—Biography.

SLOSSER, Bob. 283'.092'4 B
Miracle in Darien / Bob Slosser. Plainfield, N.J. : Logos International, c1979. 268 p. ; 22 cm. [BX5995.F78S58] 79-83791 ISBN 0-88270-355-2 : 6.95
1. Fullman, Terry. 2. St. Paul's Episcopal Church, Darien, Conn. 3. Protestant Episcopal Church in the U.S.A.—Clergy—Biography. 4. Clergy—United States—Biography. I. Title.

Protestant Episcopal Church in the U.S.A. Colorado (Diocese)

BRECK, Allen duPont. 283.788
The Episcopal Church in Colorado, 1860-1963. [1st ed.] Denver, Big Mountain Press [c1963] ix, 450 p. plates (part col.) ports. (part col.) 27 cm. (The West in American history, no. 2) Bibliography: p. 419-431. [BX5918.C6B7] 63-23029
1. Protestant Episcopal Church in the U.S.A. Colorado (Diocese) I. Title. II. Series.

BRECK, Allen duPont 283.788
The Episcopal Church in Colorado, 1860-1963. Denver, Big Mountain Pr. [dist. Swallow, c.1963] ix, 450p. plates (pt. col.) ports. (pt. col.) 27cm. (West in Amer. hist., no. 2) Bibl. 63-23029 10.00
1. Protestant Episcopal Church in the U.S.A. Colorado (Diocese) I. Title.

Protestant Episcopal Church in the U.S.A.—Colorado Springs.

PERKINS, Mary Louise. 283'.788'56
An house not made with hands; a century of the Episcopal faith in Colorado Springs, Colorado, 1872-1972. [Colorado Springs] Episcopal Centennial Committee of Colorado Springs [1972] xii, 84 p. illus. 28 cm. Includes the history of Grace Church and St. Stephen's, Church of the Holy Spirit, Church of St. Michael the Archangel, and Chapel of Our Saviour. [BX5919.C6P47] 74-152285
1. Protestant Episcopal Church in the U.S.A.—Colorado Springs. I. Title.

Protestant Episcopal church in the U.S.A. Communion service.

HURLBUT, Stephen Augustus, ed. 264.035
The liturgy of the Church of England before and after the reformation, together with the service of the holy communion of the Episcopal church in the United States, edited with an introduction and notes by Stephen A. Hurlbut, M.A. Mount St. Alban, Washington, D.C., The St. Albans press, 1941. 2 p. l., iv p., 1 l., 34, 60 p. 2 facsim. (incl. front.) 24 cm. A complete mass for a particular day (the Ascesion) has been exhibited in a four-column arrangement, in which the first two columns (on the left-hand page) contain the Latin text and a translation of the Roman mass (as used at Sarum) in England; the third column, the reformed service of the first English prayer book (1549): the fourth column, the Communion service of the Episcopal church. cf. Pref. "375 copies have been printed on Worthy Aurelian paper...This is copy number 35." "A short list of books on liturgy": p. [59]-60. [BX5944.C75H8] 41-8659
1. Protestant Episcopal church in the U.S.A. Communion service. 2. Lord's supper (Liturgy) 3. Lord's supper—Hist. I. Title.

Protestant Episcopal church in the U.S.A.—Congresses.

CHURCH congress in the United States. 283.06373
A record of the Church congress in the United States, -59th; -1933. Spencer, Mass., The Heffernan press [etc., etc.] 18 - 1933. v. 19 1/2-24 cm. At head of title, 18 -19 :The Protestant Episcopal church. Publication began with report of the 1st congress, 1874; no reports published for the 6th, 25th and 36th congresses. cf. Union list of serials. Volume numbers irregular: 39th-49th omitted. Issued under variant names of the congress: 18 -75, Church congress in the Protestant Episcopal church in the United States; 18 Congress of the Protestant Episcopal church in the United States. Title varies: 18 Authorized report (varies slightly) 18 - 1909, Papers, addresses and discussions. 1910- The Church congress journal; papers and addresses. 19 -22, Papers by various writers read at the Church congress. 1924-33, A record of the Church congress in the United States. Several volumes have also distinctive title: 1919, The church and its American opportunity: 1922, The influence of the church on modern problems; 1924, Honest liberty in the church; 1925, Problems of faith and worhsip; 1926, The church and truth: 1927, Christ in the world of to-day; 1928, Forthright opinions within the church; 1929, The church and the future; 1930, Charleston papers; 1931, Cincinnati papers; 1932, Hartford papers; 1933, Chicago papers. Imprint varies: 18 - 19 New York, T. Whittaker, inc.--19 -26, New York, the Macmillan company.--1927-28, New York, C. Scribner's sons.--1929, New York, E. S. Gorham, inc.--1930, New York, R. R. Smith, inc. Superseded by its Papers read at the ... triennial Church congress, 1939- [BX5820.A5] 17-12443
1. Protestant Episcopal church in the U.S.A.—Congresses. I. Title. II. Title: The church and its American opportunity. III. Title: Problems of faith and worhsip. IV. Title: The church and truth. V. Title: Christ in the world of to-day. VI. Title: Forthright opinions within the church. VII. Title: The church and the future. VIII. Title: Honest liberty in the church. IX. Title: The influence of the church on modern problems.

CHURCH historical society, Philadelphia. 261
Proceedings. pt. 1- Philadelphia, 1915- v. 24 cm. Cover-title. [BX5810.C8] 16-7474
I. Title.

THE Convention militant : 57th General Convention, Protestant Episcopal Church, Boston, 1952. [Boston : The Church militant, 1952] 48 p. : ill. ; 28 cm. Cover title. [BX5820.C6 1952] 75-317099 283'.73
1. Protestant Episcopal Church in the U.S.A.—Congresses. I. Protestant Episcopal Church in the U.S.A. General Convention, Boston, 1952. II. The Church militant.

PROTESTANT Episcopal church in the U. S. A. Church congress, Cincinnati, 1931. 283.063
Cincinnati papers; a record of the Church congress in the United States on its fifty-seventh anniversary, A. D. mcmxxxi; with an introduction by the general secretary, Harold Adye Prichard. Spencer, Mass., The Heffernan press, 1931. x p., 1 l., 271 p. 20 cm. [BX5820.A6 1931] 31-29496
I. Prichard, Harold. II. Title.
Contents omitted.

PROTESTANT Episcopal church in the U. S. A. Church congress. 283.
Honest liberty in the church; a record of the Church congress in the United States on its fiftieth anniversary, A. D. mcmxxiv, with an introduction by the general chairman, Charles Lewis Slattery. New York, The Macmillan company, 1924. xvii, 408 p. 20 cm. [BX5820.A6 1924] 24-28805
I. Title.
Contents omitted.

PROTESTANT Episcopal church in the U. S. A. Church congress. 37th, Baltimore, 1922. 283.
The influence of the church on modern problems; papers by various writers read at the Church congress in 1922. New York, The Macmillan company, 1922. ix, 223 p. 20 cm. [BX5820.A6 1922] 22-23139
I. Title.
Contents omitted.

PROTESTANT Episcopal church in the U. S. A. Church congress. 37th, Baltimore, 1922. 283.
The influence of the church on modern problems; papers by various writers read at the Church congress in 1922. New York, The Macmillan company, 1922. ix, 223 p. 20 cm. [BX5820.A6 1922] 22-23139
I. Title.
Contents omitted.

PROTESTANT Episcopal church in the U. S. A. Church congress. St. Louis, 1925. 283.
Problems of faith and worship; a record of the Church congress in the United States on its fifty-first anniversary, A. D. mcmxxv, with an introduction by the general chairman, Charles Lewis Slattery. New York, The Macmillan company, 1926. ix p., 1 l., 13-313 p. 20 cm. [BX5820.A6 1925] 26-7065
I. Title.
Contents omitted.

Protestant Episcopal church in the U.S.A.—Connecticut.

CAMERON, Kenneth Walter, 1908- comp. 283'.746
The Anglican Episcopate in Connecticut (1784-1899); a sheaf of biographical and institutional studies for churchmen and historians with early ecclesiastical documents. Hartford, Transcendental Books [1970] 252 l. illus., ports. 29 cm. Bibliography: leaves 250-251. [BX5917.C8C28] 71-13537
1. Protestant Episcopal Church in the U.S.A.—Connecticut. I. Title.

COIT, Richard M. 779'.4'0924
Churches in Episcopal Connecticut : photographs / by Richard M. Coit ; edited by Kenneth Walter Cameron. Hartford : Transcendental Books, [1974] 186 leaves : chiefly ill. ; 29 cm. [BX5917.C8C64] 74-193173
1. Protestant Episcopal Church in the U.S.A.—Connecticut. 2. Churches—Connecticut—Pictorial works. I. Title.

SHEPARD, James, 1838-1926.
The Episcopal church and early ecclesiastical laws of Connecticut; preceded by a chapter on the church in America, by James Shepard; reprinted from his History of St. Mark's church, New Britain, Conn., and of its predecessor, Christ church, Wethersfield and Berlin. New Britain, Conn., 1908. 3 p. l., [iii]-xi p., 1 l., [15]-129 p. 5 port., facsim. 24 cm. A 41
1. Protestant Episcopal church in the U.S.A.—Connecticut. 2. Protestant Episcopal church in the U.S.A.—Hist. 3. Clery—Connecticut. 4. Ecclesiastical law—Connecticut. I. Title.

Protestant Episcopal Church in the U.S.A. Connecticut Diocese.

BURR, Nelson Rollin, 1904- 283'.746
First American diocese: Connecticut, its origin, its growth, its work, by Nelson R. Burr. Hartford, Church Missions Pub. Co. [1970] 48 p. map. 21 cm. [BX5918.C7B79] 72-169342
1. Protestant Episcopal Church in the U.S.A. Connecticut Diocese. I. Title.

BURR, Nelson Rollin, 1904- 283.746
The story of the diocese of Connecticut, a new branch of the vine. [Hartford, Church Missions Pub. Co., c1962] 568 p. illus 24 cm. [BX5918.C7B8] 63-35497
1. Protestant Episcopal Church in the U.S.A. Connecticut Diocese. I. Title.

CAMERON, Kenneth Walter, 1908- comp. 283'.746
Historical resources of the Episcopal Diocese of Connecticut. Index by Carolyn Hutchens. Hartford, Transcendental Books [1966] iv, 315 l. illus., maps (part col.), ports. 29 cm. Based on the Inventory of the church archives of Connecticut. Protestant Episcopal, by the Historical Records survey. Connecticut. [BX5918.C7C3] 76-218714
1. Protestant Episcopal Church in the U.S.A. Connecticut (Diocese) 2. Churches—Connecticut. 3. Archives—Connecticut. I. Historical Records Survey. Connecticut. Inventory of the church archives of Connecticut. Protestant Episcopal. II. Title.

YOUNG, Howard Palmer. 248
The youth of to-day in the life of to-morrow by Howard Palmer Young... New York, Chicago [etc.] Fleming H. Revell company [c1923] 224 p. 19 1/2 cm. [BV639.Y7Y8] 23-18244
I. Title.

Protestant Episcopal Church in the U.S.A.—Connecticut—History—Sources.

CAMERON, Kenneth Walter, 1908- comp. 283'.746
Anglican climate in Connecticut; historical perspectives from imprints of the late colonial and early national years. Hartford, Transcendental Books [1974] 237 l. illus. 29 cm. [BX5917.C8C27] 74-173630
1. Protestant Episcopal Church in the U.S.A.—Connecticut—History—Sources. 2. Protestant Episcopal Church in the U.S.A.—Doctrinal and controversial works. I. Title.

CAMERON, Kenneth Walter, 1908- comp. 283'.746
Connecticut churchmanship; records and historical papers concerning the Anglican Church in Connecticut in the eighteenth and early nineteenth centuries. Hartford, Transcendental Books [1969] 1 v. (various pagings) illus., facsims., ports. 29 cm. [BX5917.C8C34] 70-10390
1. Protestant Episcopal Church in the U.S.A.—Connecticut—History—Sources. I. Title.

Protestant Episcopal Church in the U.S.A.—Dictionaries.

BENTON, Angelo Ames, 1837-1912, ed. 283'.03
The church cyclopaedia : a dictionary of church doctrine, history, organization, and ritual ... designed especially for the use of the laity of the Protestant Episcopal Church in the United States of America / edited by A. A. Benton. Detroit : Gale Research Co., 1975, c1883. 810 p. ; 23 cm. Reprint of the ed. published by M. H. Mallory, New York. [BR95.B5 1975] 74-31499 ISBN 0-8103-4204-9 : 28.00
1. Protestant Episcopal Church in the U.S.A.—Dictionaries. 2. Theology—Dictionaries. I. Title.

BENTON, Angelo Ames, 1937- ed. 220.
The church cyclopaedia. A dictionary of church doctrine, history, organization and ritual, and containing original articles on special topics, written expressly for this work by bishops, presbyters, and laymen. Designed especially for the use of the laity of the Protestant Episcopal church in the United States of America. Edited by Rev. A. A. Benton ... Philadelphia, L. R. Hamersly & co., 1884. 810 p. 26 cm. [BR95.B5] 10-27520
1. Protestant Episcopal church in the U. S. A.—Dictionaries. 2. Theology—Dictionaries. 3. Religious—Dictionaries. I. Title.

CRUM, Rolfe Pomeroy, 1889- 283.03
A dictionary of the Episcopal Church, compiled from various authentic sources; with a foreword by Henry St. George Tucker. 11th ed., with pronunciations according to Webster's and Thorndike-Barnhart's dictionaries. Baltimore, Trefoil Pub. Society, c1954. 98p. illus. 20cm. [BX5007.C7 1954] 55-15394
1. Protestant Episcopal Church in the U. S. A.—Dictionaries. I. Title.

CRUM, Rolfe Pomeroy, 1889- 283.03
A dictionary of the Episcopal Church, compiled from&various authentic sources; with a foreword by Frederick Deane Goodwin. 8th ed., rev. and enl., including an addendum (page 94) Baltimore, Trefoil Pub. Society, c1951. 96 p. illus. 19 cm. [BX5007.C7 1951] 52-17002
1. Protestant Episcopal Church in the U. S. A.—Dictionaries. I. Title.

CRUM, Rolfe Pomeroy, 1889- 283.03
A dictionary of the Episcopal Church, compiled from various authentic sources; with a foreword by Henry St. George Tucker. 10th ed., rev. and enl. Baltimore, Trefoil Pub. Society, c1953. 96p. illus. 19cm. [BX5007.C7 1953] 53-38199
1. Protestant Episcopal Church in the U. S. A.—Dictionaries. I. Title.

CRUM, Rolfe Pomeroy, 1889- 283.03
A dictionary of the Episcopal Church, compiled from various authentic sources; with a foreword by Frederick Deane Goodwin. 8th ed., rev. and enl., including an addendum (page 94) Baltimore, Trefoil Pub. Society, '1951. 96 p. illus. 19 cm. [BX5007.C7 1951] 52-17002
1. Protestant Episcopal Church in the U. S. A.—Dictionaries. I. Title.

ECKEL, Frederick L., Jr. 283.03
A concise dictionary of ecclesiastical terms. Drawings by William Duncan. Boston 8, 16 Ashburton Place Whittemore Associates, [c.1960] 64p. illus. 19cm. 60-50385 .60 pap.,
1. Protestant Episcopal Church in the U. S.

A.—Dictionaries. 2. Liturgics—Dictionaries. I. Title.

HARPER, Howard V. 230'.3'03
The Episcopalian's dictionary: church beliefs, terms, customs, and traditions explained in layman's language [by] Howard Harper. New York, Seabury Press [1975, c1974] viii, 183 p. 21 cm. "A Crossroad book." [BX5007.H37 1975] 74-12105 ISBN 0-8164-1166-2 ISBN 0-8164-1166-2 5.95
1. Protestant Episcopal Church in the U.S.A.—Dictionaries. I. Title.
Pbk. 3.95, ISBN 0-8164-2100-5.

MILLER, William James, 1850- 283.
The American church dictionary and cyclopedia, by the Rev. William James Miller ... New York, T. Whittaker [c1901] 296 p. 21 cm. [BX5007.M6] 2-3105
1. Protestant Episcopal church in the U.S.A.—Dictionaries. 2. Theology—Dictionaries. I. Title.

PROTESTANT Episcopal Church 203
in the U. S. A. National Council. Dept. of Christian Education.
More than words; a resource book for church school teachers and for students in junior high school classes. Rev. ed. Greenwich, Conn., Seabury Press [1958] 216p. 22cm. (The Seabury series, R-7B) [BX5007.P7 1958] 58-9264
1. Protestant Episcopal Church in the U. S. A.—Dictionaries. I. Title.

Protestant Episcopal church in the U.S.A.—Directories

MOREHOUSE, Clifford 283.73
Phelps, 1904- comp.
Who's who in the General convention of the Episcopal church, 1934, compiled and edited by Clifford P. Morehouse and the Publishers' editorial staff. Milwaukee, Wis., Morehouse publishing co. [c1934] viii, 91, [1] p. incl. front. (map) 21 1/2 cm. [BX5830.M6 1934] 34-34002
1. Protestant Episcopal church in the U.S.A.—Direct. I. Protestant Episcopal church in the U.S.A. General convention, 1934. II. Morehouse publishing company, Milwaukee. III. Title.

STOWE'S clerical directory 922.
of the American church ... Minneapolis, Minn., A. D. Stowe, v. front., port. 24 1/2 - 26 cm. Title varies: Lloyd's clerical directory. 1917 - Stowe's clerical directory of the American church. Editors: F. E. J. Lloyd.--1917. A.D. Stowe. [BX5830.S8] 10-4250
1. Protestant Episcopal church in the U. S. A.—Directories. I. Stowe, Andrew David, 1851-1925, ed. II. Lloyd's clerical directory. III. Lloyd, Frederick Ebenezer John, 1850—ed. IV. Lloyd, Frederick Ebenezer John, 1850—ed.

STOWE'S clerical 922.373
directory of the Protestant Episcopal Church in the United States of America New York [etc.] Pub. by the Church Hymnal Corporation for the Church Pension Fund. v. plates, ports. 26 cm. No issue pub. for 1944. Title varies: Lloyd'sclerical directory.--1917-1938 Editors: F. R. J. Lloyd.--1917-24, A. D. Stowe.--1926 Began publication with issue for 1898. [BX5830.S8] 10-4250
1. Protestant Episcopal Church in the U. S. A.—Direct. I. Lloyd, Frederic Ebenezer John, 1859-1933, ed. II. Stowe, Andrew David, 1851-1925, ed. III. Fish, Grace (Stowe) ed.

Protestant Episcopal church in the U.S.A.—Doctrinal and controversial works.

ALLEN, Alexander Viets 283.
Griswold, 1841-1908.
Freedom in the church; or, The doctrine of Christ as the Lord hath' commanded, and as this church hath received the same according to the commandments of God. By Alexander V. G. Allen ... New York, The Macmillan company; London, Macmillan & co., ltd., 1907... xiv p., 1 l., 228 p. 19 1/2 cm. [BX5930.A5] 7-7180
1. Protestant Episcopal church in the U.S.A.—Doctrinal and controversial works. I. Title.

BUTLER, Clement Moore, 1810- 283.
1890.
Protestant Episcopal doctrine and church unity. By the Rev. C. M. Butler ... New York, T. Whittaker, 1887. 174 p. 17 1/2 cm. [BX5930.B9] 16-3268
I. Title.

CHAPMAN, George Thomas, 283.
1786-1872.
Sermons, upon the ministry, worship, and doctrines of the Protestant Episcopal church, and other subjects; by G. T. Chapman ... Lexington, K., Printed by Smith and Palmer, 1828. viii, 399 p. 22 cm. [BX5930.C4 1828] 6-4149
1. Protestant Episcopal church in the U. S. A.—Doctrinal and controversial works. 2. Protestant Episcopal church in the U. S. A.—Sermons. 3. Sermons, American. I. Title.

CLARK, Howard Gordon. 230.3
Friends, Romans, countrymen; a friendly answer to questions Roman Catholics ask concerning the relationship of the Anglican churches to the one, holy, catholic, and apostolic church of Jesus Christ. New York, Morehouse- Gorham [1956] 58p. 19cm. [BX5132.C57] 56-11862
1. Protestant Episcopal Church in the U.S. A.—Doctrinal and controversial works. 2. Catholic Church—Doctrinal and controversial works—Protestant authors. I. Title.

CLARK, John Alonzo, 1801- 283
1843.
A walk about Zion, revised and enlarged. By Rev. John A. Clark... 2d ed. Philadelphia, W. Marshall and co., Providence, Marshall, Brown & co., 1836. 244 p. 19 1/2 cm. [BX5930.C5 1836] 37-39640
1. Protestant Episcopal church in the U.S.A.—Doctrinal and con- troversial works. I. Title.

CLARK, John Alonzo, 1801- 283.
1843.
A walk about Zion, rev. and enl. By Rev. John A. Clark... 5th ed. New York, R. Carter, 1842. 2 p. l., [3]-244 p. front. 20 cm. Added to.-p. engraved. [BX5930.C5 1842] 9-25710
1. Protestant Episcopal church in the U.S.A.—Doctrinal and controversial works. I. Title.

CLARK, John Alonzo, 1801- 283.
1843.
A walk about Zion, revised and enlarged. By Rev. John A. Clark... 6th ed. New York, R. Carter; Pittsburg, T. Carter, 1843. 2 p. l., [3]-244 p. front. 20 cm. Half-title, engraved. [BX5930.C5 1848] 40-25724
1. Protestant Episcopal church in the U.S.A.—Doctrinal and controversial works. I. Title.

COUBURN, John B ed. 283.73
Viewpoints; some aspects of Anglican thinking, edited by John B. Coburn and W. Norman Pittenger. Foreword by Robert F. Gibson. Greenwich, Conn., Seabury Press, 1959. 267p. 22cm. Includes bibliography. [BX5930.2.C6] 59-9804
1. Protestant Episcopal Church in the U. S. A.—Doctrinal and controversial works. 2. Theology—Addresses, essays, lectures. I. Pittenger, William Norman, 1905- joint ed. II. Title.

DAMROSCH, Frank, 1888- 283
The faith of the Episcopal church [by] Frank Damrosch, jr. New York, Morehouse-Gorham co., 1946. 4 p. l., 146 p. 19 cm. [BX5131.D3] 46-22619
1. Protestant Episcopal church in the U.S.A.—Doctrinal and controversial works. I. Title.

DUBOIS, Albert Julius, 230.3
1906- ed.
The truth and the life; essays on doctrine by priests of the American Church Union [by] Robert F. Capon [others] Foreword by Henry I. Louttit. New York, Published for the American Church Union by Morehouse-Barlow Co. [c.1961] 207p. 61-7805 4.25 lea. cl.,
1. Protestant Episcopal Church in the U. S. A.—Doctrinal and controversial works. I. Title.

THE faith of the church,
by James A. Pike and W. Norman Pittenger, with the editoriol collaboralion of Arthur C. Lichter berger, and with the assistance f the Authors Committee of the Dept. of Christian Education. Greenwich, Conn., Seabury Press [1957] 214p. 22cm. (The Church's teaching, v. 3) Bibliography: p.193-207.
1. Protestant Episcopal Church in the U. S. A. —Doctrinal and controversial works. I. Pike, James Albert, Bp., 1913- II. Pittenger, William Norman, 1905- joint author. III. Series.

FERGUSON, Franklin C. 230'.3
A pilgrimage in faith / by Franklin C. Ferguson. New York : Morehouse-Barlow Co., [1975] 170 p. ; 22 cm. Bibliography: p. 165-170. [BX5930.2.F47 1975] 75-5220 ISBN 0-8192-1200-8 pbk. : 3.95
1. Protestant Episcopal Church in the U.S.A.—Doctrinal and controversial works. I. Title.

FITZROY, Anne, Lady, 1787- 244
1871.
Little Mary's first going to church. Intended as a familiar exposition, for young children, of the service and chief holy days of the church. By Lady Charles Fitzroy...Rev. and cor., and adapted to use in this country. New York, General Protestant Episcopal Sunday school union and church book society, 1859. viii, [9]-216 p. front. 17 cm. [BX5875.F5 1859] 31-71
1. Protestant Episcopal church in the U.S.A.—Doctrinal and controversial works. I. Title.

FRIENDS, Romans, 230.3
countrymen a friendly answer to questions Roman Catholics ask concerning the relationship of the Anglican churches to the one, holy catholic, and apostolic church of Jesus Christ. New York, Morehouse-Gorham [1956] 58p. 19cm. [BX5132.C57] 56-11862
1. Protestant Episcopal Church in the U. S. A.—Doctrinal and constroversial works. 2. Catholic Church—Doctrinal and controversial works—Protestant authors.

GRAFTON, Charles Chapman, 283.
bp., 1830-1912.
Christian and Catholic, by the Right Reverend Charles C. Grafton ... New York, London [etc.] Longmans, Green, and co., 1905. xvii, 367 p. 21 cm. [BX5930.G82] 5-6477
1. Protestant Episcopal church in the U. S. A.—Doctrinal and controversial works. 2. Catholic church—Doctrinal and controversial works—Protestant authors. I. Title.

HAVERSTICK, Alexander 283.
Campbell.
The churchman's ready reference, by the Rev. Alexander C. Haverstick. With introduction by the Rt. Rev. Leighton Coleman ... Milwaukee, The Young churchman co., 1900. 329 p. 19 1/2 cm. [BX5930.H3] 0-6915
1. Protestant Episcopal church in the U.S.—Doctrinal and controversial works. 2. Church history. I. Title.

HIGGINS, John Seville, 264.033
Bp., 1904-
The hope of glory. Foreword by Horace W. B. Donegan. New York, Morehouse-Gorham Co., 1953. 146p. 19cm. (Bishop of New York books, 1953) [BX5933.H5] 53-544
1. Protestant Episcopal Church in the U. S. A.—Doctrinal and controversial works. 2. Protestant Episcopal Church in the U. S. A. Book of common prayer. A general thanksgiving. I. Title.

HODGES, George, 1856-1919. 283.
The Episcopal church; its faith and order, by George Hodges ... New York, The Macmillan company, 1915. vii p., 2 l., 3-204 p. 19 1/2 cm. Half-title: Church principles for lay people. The Episcopal church. [BX5930.H63] 15-2866
1. Protestant Episcopal church in the U.S.A.—Doctrinal and controversial works. I. Title.

HODGES, George, 1856-1919. 230.3
The Episcopal church, its faith and order, by George Hodges ... revised to accord with the new prayer book, by James Arthur Muller ... New York, The Macmillan company, 1932. ix, 204 p. 18 cm. (Half-title: Church principles for lay people) [BX5930.H63] 32-8943
1. Protestant Episcopal church in the U.S.A.—Doctrinal and controversial works. I. Muller, James Arthur, 1884- ed. II. Title.

HOW, Thomas Yardley. 283.
A vindication of the Protestant Episcopal church, in a series of letters addressed to the Rev. Samuel Miller, D.D., in reply to his late writings on the Christina ministry, and to the charges contained in his life of the Rev. Dr. Rodgers; with preliminary remarks. By Thomas Y. How ... New York; Published by Eastburn, Kirk, & co., T. & J. Swords, and P. A. Mesier. T. & J. Swords, printers, no. 160 Pearl street, 1816. xxxvi, [5]-492 p. 21 cm. [BX5930.H7] 23-16542
1. Miller, Samuel, 1769-1850. Memoirs of the Rev. J. Rodgers. 2. Protestant Episcopal church in the U.S.A.—Doctrinal and controversial works. I. Title.

KEAN, Charles Duell, 1910- 261
The Christian gospel and the parish church; an introduction to parish dynamics. Greenwich, Conn., Seabury Press, 1953. 142p. 22cm. [BX5930.K35] 53-12395
1. Protestant Episcopal Church in the U. S. A.—Doctrinal and controversial works. I. Title.

KENNEDY, James William, 230.03
1905-
The man who wanted to know, by James W. Kennedy. New York, Morehouse-Gorham, 1944. x p., 1 l., 160 p. 21 cm. [BX5930.K4] 44-44876
1. Protestant Episcopal church in the U.S.A.—Doctrinal and controversial works. I. Title.

LITTLE, Arthur Wilde, 1856- 283
1910.
Reasons for being a churchman. Addressed to English speaking Christians of every name. By the Rev. Arthur Wilde Little ... 8th thousand. Milwaukee, Wis., The Young churchman company [188-?] xvi, 269 p. front. 20 cm. [BX5930.L5] 38-20527
1. Protestant Episcopal church in the U. S. A.—Doctrinal and controversial works. I. Title.

MORTIMER, Alfred Garnett, 283.
1848-1924.
Catholic faith and practice ... by the Rev. Alfred G. Mortimer ... New York, London [etc.] Longmans, Green, and co., 1897-98. 2 v. 20cm. "List of works referred to": [pt. I] p. xii-xiv; pt. II, p. lxv-lxix. Contents.[I] A manual of theological instruction for confirmation and first communion.--II. A manual of theology. [BX5930.M65 1897] 1-17061
1. Protestant Episcopal church in the U.S.A.—Doctrinal and controversial works. 2. Anglo-Catholicism. I. Title.

MORTIMER, Alfred Garnett, 283.
1848-1924.
Catholic faith and practice ... by the Rev. Alfred G. Mortimer ... 2d ed., rev. London, New York [etc.] Longmans, Green, and co., 1901. v. 20cm. Vol. I wanting. [BX5930.M65 1901] 1-15287
1. Protestant Episcopal church in the U.S.A.—Doctrinal and controversial works. 2. Anglo-Catholicism. I. Title.

MOSS, Claude Beaufort, D. 230.3
D. 1888-
A summary of the faith. New York, Morehouse-Barlow [c.]1961. 47p. 61-13583 1.25 bds.,
1. Protestant Episcopal Church in the U. S. A.—Doctrinal and controversial works. I. Title.

PELL, Walden, 1902- 264.03
The religion of the prayer book; a course of study designed to review the faith and practice of the Book of common prayer, by Walden Pell, II, and P. M. Dawley. [2d ed.] New York, Morehouse-Gorham Co., 1950. vi, 232 p. 19 cm. Bibliography: p. 232. [BX5930.P4 1950] 50-12570
1. Protestant Episcopal Church in the U.S.A. — Doctrinal and controversial works. 2. Protestant Episcopal Church in the U.S.A. Book of common prayer. I. Dawley, Powel Mills, 1907- joint author. II. Title.

PELL, Walden, 1902- 264.03
The religion of the prayer book, a course of study designed to review the faith and practice of the Book of common prayer, by the Rev. Walden Pell, ii ... and the Very Rev. P. M. Dawley ... New York, Morehouse-Gorham co., 1943. vi p., 1 l. 219 p. 19 cm. "Books recommended for reference": p. 219. [BX5930.P4] 43-47167
1. Protestant Episcopal church in the U.S.A.—Doctrinal and controversial works. 2. Protestant Episcopal church in the U.S.A. Book of common prayer. I. Dawley, Powel Mills, joint author. II. Title.

PELL, Walden, 1902- 283
The religion of the prayer book, a course of study designed to review the faith and practice of the Book of common prayer, by the Rev. Walden Pell, ii ... and the Very Rev. P. M. Dawley ... New York, Morehouse-Gorham co., 1943. vi p. 1 l. 232 p. 18 1/2 cm. On cover: Textbook ed. "Books recommended for reference": p. 232. [BX5930.P4 1943a] 264 43-18216
1. Protestant Episcopal church in the U.S.A.—Doctrinal and controversial works. 2. Protestant Episcopal church in the U.S.A. Book of common prayer. I. Dawley, Powel Mills, joint author. II. Title.

PIKE, James Albert, 1913- 230.3
The faith of the church, by James A. Pike and W. Norman Pittenger, with the editorial collaboration of Arthur C. Lichtenberger, and with the assistance of the Authors' Committee of the Dept. of Christian Education. New York, The National Council, Protestant Episcopal Church, 1951. 214 p. 22 cm. (The Church's teaching, v. 3) Bibliography: p. 193-207. [BX5930.P5] 51-13489
1. Protestant Episcopal Church in the U.S.A. — Doctrinal and controversial works. I. Pittenger, William Norman, 1905- joint author. II. Title. III. Series.

PROTESTANT Episcopal Church in the U. S. A. Homilies. 252.
Sermons; or, Homilies appointed to be read in churches in the time of Queen Elizabeth of famous memory. 1st American from the last Oxford ed. New-York, T. and J. Swords, 1815. xii, 516 p. 23 cm. On spine: Homilies. [BX5937.A1A3 1815] 49-55973
1. Protestant Episcopal Church in the U. S. A.—Doctrinal and controversial works. I. Title.

PROTESTANT Episcopal church in the U.S.A. Homilies. 264.
Selections from the Homilies of the Protestant Episcopal church; with a preface, by the Rt. Rev. William Meade, D.D. Philadelphia, Pub. by the Executive committee of the "Protestant Episcopal society for the promotion of evangelical knowledge" [185-?] xvii, 19-251 p. 19 1/2 cm. [BX5947.H6A5] 43-40040
1. Protestant Episcopal church in the U.S.A.—Doctrinal and controversial works. I. Meade, William, bp., 1789-1862, ed. II. Protestant Episcopal society for the promotion of evangelical knowledge, New York. III. Title.

USHER, Edward Preston, 1851-1923. 283.73
The church's attitude towards truth, by Edward P. Usher ... Grafton, Mass., The author, 1907. xviii, 173 p. 19 1/2 cm. [BX5933.U8] 7-10031
1. Protestant Episcopal church in the U.S.A.—Doctrinal and controversial works. I. Title.

WESTCOTT, Frank Nash, 1858-1915. 283.
The heart of Catholicity ... by the Rev. Frank N. Westcott ... Milwaukee, The Young churchman co., 1905. ix, 215, [1] p. 19 cm. Bibliography: [1] p. at end. [BX5930.W43] 5-27429
1. Protestant Episcopal church in the U.S.A.—Doctrinal and controversial works. I. Title.

WILL, Theodore St. Clair, 1886- 283
The Episcopal church: heritage of American Christians, by Theodore St. Clair Will...with foreword by the Rt. Rev. Arthur C. Thomson... Milwaukee, Wis., Morehouse publishing co., 1934. xv, 135, [1] p. front. 19 cm. [BX5930.W44] 34-37260
1. Protestant Episcopal church in the U.S.A.—Doctrinal and controv- ersial works. I. Title.

Protestant Episcopal Church in the U.S.A.—Doctrinal and controversial works—Addresses, essays, lectures.

REALITIES and visions : 260
the church's mission today / edited by Furman C. Stough and Urban T. Holmes III. New York : Seabury Press, c1976. p. cm. "A Crossroad book." Bibliography: p. [BX5935.R4] 76-21086 pbk. : 4.95
1. Protestant Episcopal Church in the U.S.A.—Doctrinal and controversial works—Addresses, essays, lectures. 2. Mission of the church—Addresses, essays, lectures. I. Stough, Furman C., 1928- II. Holmes, Urban Tigner, 1930-

SHARING the vision : 230'.3
the Church's teaching series reader / edited by Ruth Cheney ; contributions by Robert A. Bennett ... [et al.]. New York : Seabury Press, 1980. viii, 123 p. ; 21 cm. "Contains excerpts from the seven volumes of the Church's teaching series." Includes index. [BX5935.S43] 79-27021 ISBN 0-8164-2044-0 pbk. : 2.95
1. Protestant Episcopal Church in the U.S.A.—Doctrinal and controversial works—Addresses, essays, lectures. I. Bennett, Robert A., 1933- II. Cheney, Ruth.

Protestant Episcopal church in the U.S.A. Domestic and foreign missionary society.

EMERY, Julia C. 266.
A century of endeavor, 1821-1921, a record of the first hundred years of the Domestic and foreign missionary society of the Protestant Episcopal church in the United States of America, by Julia C. Emery ... New York, The Department of missions, 1921. 2 p. l., vii-viii, 466 p. 19 cm. [BV2575.A5E6] 23-2671
1. Portestant Episcopal church in the U.S.A. Domestic and foreign missionary society. I. Title.

Protestant Episcopal Church in the U.S.A.—Education.

BREWER, Clifton Hartwell, 1876- 268.83
Early Episcopal Sunday schools (1814-1865) by Clifton Hartwell Brewer ... Milwaukee, Morehouse publishing co., London, A. R. Mowbray & co. [c1933] xviii p., 2 l., [3]-179, [1] p. front., plates. 19 cm. Bibliography: p. [164]-171. [BX5850.B78] 33-22273
1. Protestant Episcopal church in the U.S.A.—Education. 2. Sunday-schools—Hist. I. Title.

BREWER, Clifton Hartwell, 1876- 268.
A history of religious education in the Episcopal church to 1835, by Clifton Hartwell Brewer ... New Haven, Yale university press; [etc., etc.] 1924. xi p., 2 l., [3]-362 p. plates, facsims. 23 1/2 cm. (Half-title: Yale studies in the history and theory of religious education ... II) Bibliography: p. [331]-343. [BX5850.B8] 24-28681
1. Protestant Episcopal church in the U.S.A.—Education. 2. Religious education—U.S. I. Title.

BREWER, Clifton Hartwell, 1876- 268.23
Later Episcopal Sunday schools. by Clifton Hartwell Brewer ... New York, Morehouse-Gorham co., 1939. xx, 197 p. front. 19 cm. Bibliography: p. 177-184. [BX5850.B782] 40-2585
1. Protestant Episcopal church in the U.S.A.—Education. 2. Sunday-schools—Hist. I. Title.

BREWER, Clifton Hartwell, 1876- 207
Nurturing young churchmen; the development of the idea of spiritual growth, by Clifton Hartwell Brewer ... Milwaukee, Wis., Morehouse publishing co. [c1930] xii, 153, [1] p. 19 cm. Bibliography at end of each chapter. [BX5859.B35] 31-3803
1. Protestant Episcopal church in the U.S. A.—Education. 2. Religious education. I. Title.

BREWER, Clifton Hartwell, 1876-1947. 268'.8'373
The history of religious education in the Episcopal Church to 1835. New York, Arno Press, 1969. xi, 362 p. facsims. 23 cm. (American education: its men, ideas, and institutions) On spine: Religious education in the Episcopal Church. Reprint of the 1924 ed., first published as Yale studies in the history and theory of religious education, 2. Bibliography: p. [331]-348. [BX5850.B8 1969] 73-89152
1. Protestant Episcopal Church in the U.S.A.—Education. 2. Christian education—United States. I. Title. II. Title: Religious education in the Episcopal Church. III. Series.

CAMBRIDGE, Mass. Episcopal theological school.
Catalogue. Cambridge, [Mass.] v. plans. 18 1/2 cm. On cover: 1913 CA15
I. Title.

[CRUSE, Mary Anne]
The little Episcopalian; or, The child taught by the prayer-book. By M. A. C. ... New York, E. P. Dutton and company, 1885. vi, [7]-271 p. 16 1/2 cm. First edition published 1854. [BX5140.C7 1885] 44-19674
I. Title.

CULLY, Kendig Brubaker, ed. 377.83
The Episcopal Church and education. New York, Morehouse-Barlow Co. [1966] 256 p. 22 cm. Bibliographical references included in "Notes" (p. 241-251) [LC582.C8] 66-23709
1. Protestant Episcopal Church in the U.S.A — Education — Collections. I. Title.

EVANGELICAL education society of the Protestant Episcopal church. 283.73
Annual report of the Evangelical education society of the Protestant Episcopal church. Philadelphia, Pa., v. 18 cm. [BX5850.A1E8] 37-36743
I. Title.

HINES, John Elbridge, Bp., 1910- 378.73
Episcopal colleges; a case for church relationship in education [by] John E. Hines. New York, Newcomen Society in North America, 1968. 24 p. illus. 23 cm. (Newcomen address, 1968) Delivered at a national dinner of the Newcomen Society held in New York City on Jan. 25, 1968, honoring the Association of Episcopal Colleges. [LC583.H5] 68-26784
1. Protestant Episcopal Church in the U.S.A.—Education. 2. Church colleges—U.S. I. Association of Episcopal Colleges. II. Title. III. Series.

INSTITUTE for Christian Learning, Evanston, Ill.
A program of education and research through the establishment of a Christian center for higher learning at the college and post-graduate levels in affiliation with the University of Chicago, proposed by the Institute for Christian Learning, a community of scholars, teachers, clergy and laity of the Episcopal Church, sponsored by Christ the King Foundation,m Inc., Evaston, Illinois. [n.p., 1960?] 1 v. (various pagings) 63-30581
1. Protestant Episcopal Church in the U.S. — Education I. Title.

MISSION renewed:
a study guide on the mission of the Church with special emphasis on the mission of the Episcopal Church to Japan. Prepared under the auspices of the Youth Division, Department of Christian Education, Protestant Episcopal Church. Greenwich, Conn., Seabury Press [c1957] 60p.
I. Protestant Episcopal Church in the U. S. A. National Council. Dept. of Christian Education.

1. Protestant Episcopal church in the U. S. A.—Education. I. Title.

PROTESTANT Episcopal church in the U. S. A. National council. Dept. of Christian education.
Church ideals in education; a preconvention statement, 1916. A description of the work and aims of the General board of religious education of the Protestant Episcopal church. Presented to the church preparatory to the General convention. [New York, 1916] 258 p., 1 l. 24 cm. E 16
1. Protestant Episcopal church in the U. S. A.—Education. I. Title.

*PROTESTANT Episcopal Church in the U. S. A. National Council. Dept. of Christian Education. 248.83
Mission: the Christian's calling; leader's guide for Called to be, Bigger than all of us, These rebellious powers. For use with young people. Prepared by the Dept. of Christian Educ. of the Protestant Episcopal Church at the direction of General Convention. New York, Seabury [c.1965] 63p. 21cm. .95 pap.,
I. Title.

PROTESTANT Episcopal Church in the U.S.A. National Council. Dept. of Chrisian Education. 268.433
It's your choice. Illus. by Randolph Chitwood. Greenwich, Conn., Seabury [c.1962] 105p. illus. (The church's teaching inthe 11th grade, teacher's manual) 2.10 pap.,
I. Title.

PROTESTANT Episcopal Church in the U.S.A. National Council. Dept. of Christian Education.
God, His world, and me; the church's teaching in the second grade. Revised teacher's manual. New York, Seabury Press [c1964] v, 98 p. 65-96854
I. Title.

PROTESTANT Episcopal Church in the U.S.A. National Council. Dept. of Christian Education.
Living in the church; the church's teaching in the fifth grade. Revised teacher's manual. Illus. by Frank Giusto. New York, Seabury Press [1964] 216 p. 65-98328
I. Title.

PROTESTANT Episcopal Church in the U.S.A. National Council. Dept. of Christian Education.
Unit book A for the primary course: God in our widening world. To be used with the manual for primary teachers. Greenwich, Conn., Seabury Press [1962] 96 p. illus. 28 cm. (The Seabury series, P-A) At head of title: The Church's teaching for small church schools. 63-36639
I. Title.

PROTESTANT Episcopal church in the U.S.A. National council. Dept. of religious education.
Church ideals in education; a preconvention statement, 1916. A description of the work and aims of the General board of religious education of the Protestant Episcopal church. Presented to the church preparatory to the General convention. [New York, 1916] 258 p., 1 l. 23 1/2 cm. [LC582.P95] E 16
1. Protestant Episcopal church in the U.S.A.—Education. I. Title.

SANDT, Eleanor E., ed.
Small church schools bulletin. New York, Seabury Press [1964] 128 p. 24 cm. 68-350
1. Protestant Episcopal Church in the U.S.A.—Education. 2. Religious education—Teacher training. I. Title. II. Title: Education in the small church,

...THINE own child...
Greenwich, Conn., Seabury Press [c1960] 60p. (Vacation Church School. Older Junior Book I)
I. Protestant Episcopal Church in the U. S. A. National Council. Dept. of Christian Education.

Protestant Episcopal Church in the U.S.A.—Education—Collections.

BEHOLD the church.
Prepared under the Auspices of the Youth

Division, Department of Christian Education, Protestant Episcopal Church. Greenwich, Connecticut, Seabury Press [1958] 58p. 22cm.
I. Myers, Chauncie Kilmer, 1916-

CULLY, Kendig Brubaker, ed. 377.83
The Episcopal Church and education. New York, Morehouse [1966] 256p. 22cm. Bibl. [LC582.C8] 66-23709 7.95 bds.,
1. Protestant Episcopal Church in the U.S.A.—Education—Collections. I. Title.

Protestant Episcopal Church in the U.S.A.—Florida.

CUSHMAN, Joseph D 283.759
A goodly heritage; the Episcopal Church in Florida, 1821-1892 [by] Joseph D. Cushman, Jr. Gainesville, University of Florida Press, 1965. xiii, 219 p. illus., ports. 24 cm. Bibliography: p. [207]-212. [BX5917.F55C8] 65-28693
1. Protestant Episcopal Church in the U.S.A. — Florida. 2. Protestant Episcopal Church in the U.S.A. South. Florida (Diocese). I. Title.

Protestant Episcopal Church in the U.S.A. General Convention.

CHURCH'S teaching for small church schools (The) 268.432 Unit Bks. B, C [Drawings by Maurice Rawson, others] Prep. by the Dept. of Christian Educ. of the Protestant Episcopal Church at the direction of Gen. Convention. New York, Seabury, c.1964. 2v. (95; 96p.) illus. 28cm. (Church's teaching ser.) 2.00 pap.,
Contents omitted.

CHURCH'S teaching in the [closely graded church schools (The) 268.432 2d grade. Photos by Ken Heyman; drawings by Randolph Chirwood] Materials for Christian educ. prep. [by the Dept. of Christian Educ. of the Protestant Episcopal Church] at the direction of Gen. Convention. New York, Seabury [c.1955-1964] 98p. illus. 28cm. (Church's teaching ser.) 2.10 pap.,
Contents omitted.

CHURCH'S teaching in the [closely graded church schools (The) 268.433 7th grade. Photos by Edward Wallowitch, Wayne Miller] Materials for Christian educ. prep. [by the Dept. of Christian Educ. of the Protestant Episcopal Church] at the direction of Gen. Convention. New York, Seabury [c.1955-1964] 96p. illus. 28cm. (Church's teaching ser.) 2.10 pap.,
Contents omitted.

PROTESTANT Episcopal church in the U. S. General convention. Joint commission on Sunday school instruction.
Report. Philadelphia [etc.] 1907- v. 23 cm. A 10
I. Title.

PROTESTANT Episcopal church in the U. S. A. General convention. 283.
Journal of the General convention of the Protestant Episcopal chruch in the United States of America. [n. p.] Printed for the convention, 1790- v. 23 cm. Title varies: General form, 1790-1904: Journal of the proceedings of the bishops, clergy and laity of the Protestant church in the United States of America. Published 1790, 1792, 1795, 1799, 1801, 1804, 1808 and triennially thereafter. Extra volumes for special conventions, 1821. Early volumes have slight minor variations. Imprint varies: 1790-1868. Beginning with 1832 Constitution and canons have separate t.-p. and paging and are also published separately. Title from General Theol. sem. [BX5820.A15] A 21
I. Title.

WALLACE, Bob N., 1932- 262'.03
The General Convention of the Episcopal Church / Bob N. Wallace ; foreword by Scott Field Bailey. New York : Seabury Press, c1976. xiii, 105 p. ; 21 cm. "A Crossroad book." [BX5820.W34] 76-10156 ISBN 0-8164-1212-X : 2.95
1. Protestant Episcopal Church in the U.S.A. General Convention. I. Title.

Protestant Episcopal Church in the U.S.A.—Georgia.

MALONE, Henry Thompson 283.758
The Episcopal Church in Georgia, 1733-1957. Atlanta, Protestant Episcopal Church in the Diocese of Atlanta [c.1960] 334p. illus. end paper map 25cm. 60-53599 2.95
1. Protestant Episcopal Church in the U.S.A.—Georgia. I. Title.

MALONE, Henry Thompson. 283.758
The Episcopal Church in Georgia, 1733-1957. Atlanta, Protestant Episcopal Church in the Diocese of Atlanta [1960] 334p. illus. 25cm. [BX5917.G4M3] 60-53599
1. Protestant Episcopal Church in the U. S. A.—Georgia. I. Title.

PROTESTANT Episcopal church in the U. S. Georgia, Diocese of.
The Protestant Episcopal church of the diocese of Georgia, vs. Rev. J. G. Armstrong, D. D. ... Report of the above state case, authorized and authenticated by J. W. Beckwith, bishop of Georgia. Atlanta, Ga., J. P. Harrison & co., 1886. 308 p. 23 cm. 10-21404
I. Armstrong, James G. II. Title.

PROTESTANT Episcopal church in the U.S.A. Georgia (Diocese)
The Protestant Episcopal church of the diocese of Georgia vs. Rev. J. G. Armstrong, D.D. ... Report of the above stated case, authorized and authenticated by J. W. Beckwith, bishop of Georgia. Atlanta, Ga., J. P. Harrison & co., 1886. 308 p. 22 1/2 cm. [BX5960.A6A5] 10-21404
I. Armstrong, James G. II. Title.

Protestant Episcopal Church in the United States—Government.

ANDERSON, Charles Palmerston, bp. 1864?-1930. 262
Letters to laymen, by the Most Reverend Charles P. Anderson ... New York, Milwaukee, Morehouse publishing co., 1935. 64 p. incl. front. (port.) 16 cm. "Abridged edition." [BX5968.A63] 35-17211
1. Protestant Episcopal church in the U. S. A.—Government. 2. Church officers. 3. Laity. I. Title.

BOLLES, James Aaron, 1810-1894. 283.73
The Episcopal church defended; with an examination into the claims of Methodist episcopacy; in a series of letters addressed to the Rev. Allen Steele, with his replies. By James A. Bolles ... Batavia, N. Y., Printed by F. Follett [1843] 100 p. 19 cm. Errata slip inserted at end. Cover dated: 1843. [BX5132.B7] 33-32119
1. Protestant Episcopal church in the U.S.A.—Government. 2. Methodist Episcopal church—Government. 3. Episcopacy. I. Steele, Allen. II. Title.

BOWEN, V. S. 254'.03'73
A vestryman's guide / by Van S. Bowen. Rev. ed. New York : Seabury Press, 1976. 70 p. ; 21 cm. "Sponsored by the Episcopal Church Foundation." "A Crossroad book." includes index. Bibliography: p. 67. [BX5967.5.B68 1976] 76-44386 ISBN 0-8164-2136-6 : 2.50
1. Protestant Episcopal Church in the U.S.A.—Government. 2. Church officers. I. Title.

BOWEN, V. S. 254'.03
A vestryman's guide, by V. S. Bowen. New York, Seabury Press [1972] 64 p. illus. 21 cm. [BX5967.5.B68] 72-82210 ISBN 0-8164-2078-5 1.25
1. Protestant Episcopal Church in the U.S.A.—Government. 2. Church officers. I. Title.

ERVIN, Spencer, 1886- 348.83
Some deficiencies in the canon law of the American Episcopal Church, and related matters. New York 17, [347 Madison Ave., Amer. Church Pubns. 1961] 73p. 61-19225 1.25 pap.,
1. Protestant Episcopal Church in the U.S.—Government. I. Title.

HOFFMAN, Murray, 1791-1878. 283.
A treatise on the law of the Protestant Episcopal church in the United States. By Murray Hoffman, esq. New-York, Stanford and Swords, 1850. 480 p. 24 cm. [Full name: David Murray Hoffman] [BX5955.H6] 45-53781
1. Protestant Episcopal church in the U.S.A.—Government. I. Title.

JEWEL, Alice. 265.
Scriptural psychology of eternal youth; a discussion of the harmony between the teaching of the Scriptures and modern applied psychology, by Alice Jewel ... Washington, D. C., Alice Jewel [c1926] xvii, 179 p. front. (port.) 19 cm. [Her Eternal youth series] [BR115.H4J4] 26-16607
I. Title.

PROTESTANT Episcopal Church in the U.S.A. 262.9'83'73
Constitution and canons for the government of the Protestant Episcopal Church in the United States of America, otherwise known as the Episcopal Church, adopted in general conventions, 1789-1967. [New York?] Printed for the convention, 1967. xx, 210 p. 23 cm. [BX5955.A5 1967] 74-799
1. Protestant Episcopal Church in the U.S.A.—Government. I. Title.

PROTESTANT Episcopal church in the U. S.
Constitution and canons for the government of the Protestant Episcopal church in the United States of America, adopted in general conventions. 1789-1910. [New York] Printed for the Convention, 1910. 163 p. 24 cm. 11-1073 0.75
I. Title.

PROTESTANT Episcopal church in the U.S.A. 283.
Constitution and canons of the Protestant Episcopal church in the United States. New York, Swords, Stanford & co., 1841. 1 p. l., 4-76 p. 10 1/2 cm. [BX5955.A5 1841] 44-23220
I. Title.

PROTESTANT Episcopal Church in the U.S.A.
Digest of the canons for the government of the Protestant Episcopal Church in the United States of America, passed and adopted in the General Conventions of 1859, 1862, and 1865, together with the Constitution. Boston, Hall, 1865. [Cleveland, Micro Photo Division, Bell & Howell, 1965?] 122, 465-478 p. 23 cm. Reproduced by Duopage process. 67-1058
1. Protestant Episcopal Church in the United States—Government. 2. Canon law, Protestant Episcopal I. Title.

PROTESTANT Episcopal Church in the U. S. A. 283.73
Annotated constitution and canons for the government of the Protestant Episcopal Church in the United States of America, adopted in general conventions, 1789-1952. By Edwin Augustine White. 2d ed., rev., 1954, by Jackson A. Dykman. Published after review by a joint committee of General Convention. Greenwich, Conn., Seabury Press [1954] 2v. 24cm. [BX5955.A5 1954] 54-1136
I. White, Edwin Augustine, 1856-1925. II. Dykman, Jackson Annan, 1887- III. Title. IV. Title: Constitution and canons.

PROTESTANT Episcopal church in the U. S. A. 283.
Constitution and canons for the government of the Protestant Episcopal church in the United States of America, adopted in general convention, 1789-1904. [New York?] Printed for the Convention, 1905. 150 p. 24 cm. [BX5955.A5 1905] 5-3718
I. Title.

PROTESTANT Episcopal church in the U. S. A. 283.
Constitution and canons for the government of the Protestant Episcopal church in the United States of America, adopted in general conventions, 1789-1907. [New York] Printed for the convention [The Winthrop press] 1907. 154 p. 23 cm. [BX5955.A7 1907] 8-1484
I. Title.

PROTESTANT Episcopal church in the U. S. A. 283.73
Constitution and canons for the government of the Protestant Episcopal church in the United States of America adopted in general conventions, 1789-1922, annotated, with an exposition of the same, and reports of such cases as have arisen and been decided thereunder. By the Reverend Edwin Augustine White ... Published by order of the House of deputies. New York, E. S. Gorham, 1924. vii, 1061 p. 25 cm. [BX5955.A5 1924] 40-2829
I. White, Edwin Augustine, 1856- II. Title.

PROTESTANT Episcopal church in the U. S. A.
Constitution and canons for the government of the Protestant Episcopal church in the United States of America, adopted in general conventions, 1789-1916. [New York] Printed for the Convention [Sherwood press, inc.] 1916. 192 p. 23 cm. 17-3742 0.40
I. Title.

PROTESTANT Episcopal church in the U. S. A. General convention. 283.73
Digest of the canons for the government of the Protestant Episcopal church in the United States of America, passed and adopted in general conventions. Together with the constitution. [n. p.] Printed for the convention, 1896. 167 p. 24 cm. [BX5955.A5 1896] 262 35-28529
1. Protestant Episcopal church in the U. S. A.—Government. I. Title.

PROTESTANT Episcopal church in the U. S. A. General convention, 1859. 283.73
Digest of the canons for the government of the Protestant Episcopal church in the United States of America, passed and adopted in general convention, in Richmond, Virginia, October, 1859; together with the constitution. New-York, Pudney & Russell, 1860. xxix, 97 p. 23 cm. Prefatory note signed: Francis L. Hawks, Murray Hoffman, committee. [BX5955.A5 1860] 33-11039
1. Protestant Episcopal church in the U. S. A.—Government. I. Hawks, Francis Lister, 1798-1866. II. Title.

PROTESTANT Episcopal Church in the U. S. A. Washington (Diocese)
The constitution and canons of the Diocese of Washington of the Protestant Episcopal Church, together with the Maryland vestry act of 1798, as amended, rules of order and order of business, by-laws of the Executive Council, corporate charter of the Diocese of Washington, corporate charter of the Cathedral Foundation of the District of Columbia and forms. Compiled by the Committee on Canons and Other Business. Washington, The Convention, 1962. 99p. 23cm. [BX5957.W3A5 1962] 62-52148
I. Protestant Episcopal Church in the U. S. A. Washington (Diocese) Committee on Canons and Other Business. II. Title.

WOODS, Leonard, 1774-1854. 262
Lectures on church government, containing objections to the Episcopal scheme. Delivered in the Theological seminary, Andover, August, MDCCCXLIII. By Leonard Woods ... New York, Turner & Hayden, 1844. viii, 198 p. 17 1/2 cm. [BX5936.W8] 34-7190
1. Protestant Episcopal church in the U.S.A.—Government. 2. Episcopacy. I. Title.

Protestant Episcopal Church in the U.S.A. Harrisburg (Diocese)—History

WOLFGANG, Ralph T 283.748
History of the Diocese of Harrisburg Protestant Episcopal Church, 1904-1954. With foreword by John Thomas Hiestand, Bishop of Harrisburg. [Harrisburg, Pa.] Diocese of Harrisburg, 1954. 135p. illus. 23cm. [BX5918.H3W6] 55-15390
1. Protestant Episcopal Church in the U.S.A. Harrisburg (Diocese)—Hist. I. Title.

Protestant Episcopal church in the U.S.A.—History

ADDISON, James Thayer, 1887- 283'.73
The Episcopal Church in the United States, 1789-1931. [Hamden, Conn.] Archon Books, 1969 [c1951] xii, 400 p. 23

cm. Bibliography: p. 382-385. [BX5880.A33 1969] 69-15786
1. Protestant Episcopal Church in the U.S.A.—History. I. Title.

ADDISON, James Thayer, 1887- 283.73
The Episcopal Church in the United States, 1789-1931 New York, Scribner, 1951. xii, 400 p. 24 cm. Bibliography: p. 382-385. [BX5880.A33] 51-10050
1. Protestant Episcopal Church in the U. S. A.—Hist. I. Title.

ALBRIGHT, Raymond Wold, 1901- 283.73
A history of the Protestant Episcopal Church [by] Raymond W. Albright. New York, Macmillan [c1964] x. 406 p. 24 cm. Bibliography: p. 382-397. [BX5880.A4] 64-21168
1. Protestant Episcopal Church in the U.S.A.—Hist. I. Title.

BURR, Nelson Rollin 1904- 283.73
The story of the Episcopal church in the United States, by Nelson R. Burr ... Hartford, Conn., Church missions publishing company, 1935. 2 v. in 1. 21 1&2 cm. (Story and pageant series) Contents.pt. 1. From the colonial beginnings to the organization of the church in the U.S.--pt. 2. From the General convention of 1789 to the present day. [BX5880.B83] 37-4834
1. Protestant Episcopal church in the U.S.A.—Hist. 2. Church of England in America. I. Title.

CASWALL, Henry, 1810-1870. 283'.73
America and the American church. New York, Arno Press, 1969. xviii, 368 p. illus., map. 22 cm. (Religion in America) Reprint of the 1839 ed. [BX5880.C3 1969] 77-83413
1. Protestant Episcopal Church in the U.S.A.—History. 2. Kenyon College, Gambier, Ohio. 3. U.S.—Description and travel—1848-1865. I. Title.

DE MILLE, George Edmed, 1898- 283.73
The Episcopal Church since 1900; a brief history New York, Morehouse-Gorham, 1955. 223p. 22cm. [BX5882.D45] 55-7433
1. Protestant Episcopal Church in the U. S. A.—Hist. I. Title.

GRAFTON, Charles Chapman, bp., 1830-1912.
The lineage from apostolic times of the American Catholic church, commonly called the Episcopal church, by the Right Rev. C. C. Grafton ... Milwaukee, The Young churchman company [c1911] xxi, 296 p. front., illus. (map) plates. 20 cm. On cover: The lineage of the American Catholic church. "Books referred to" at end of each chapter. [BX5883.G8] 11-12514
1. Protestant Episcopal church in the U. S. A.—Hist. I. Title. II. Title: The lineage of the American Catholic church.

THE Historiographer. 283.73
v. 1- Whitsuntide 1938- [Philadelphia, Church historical society] 1938- v. 23-26 cm. annual. No issues for 1940-42. Includes reports of the president, librarian, etc., of the society. [BX5810.C53] 47-17737
1. Protestant Episcopal church in the U.S.A.—Hist. I. Church historical society, Philadelphia.

HODGES, George, 1856-1919. 283.
Three hundred years of the Episcopal church in America, by George Hodges ... Philadelphia, For the Missionary thank offering committee by G. W. Jacobs & co. [1906] 153 p. front., 11 port. 17 cm. "Suggested readings": p. 151-152. [BX5880.H7] 6-41777
1. Protestant Episcopal church in the U.S.A.—Hist. I. Title.

KANSAS City, Mo. St. Andrew's Episcopal Church. 283.778411
The spirit of St. Andrew's, 1913-1963. Kansas City [1963?] 112 p. illus., ports. 29 cm. [BX5980.K3S3] 64-56060
I. Title.

LOVELAND, Clara O 283.73
The critical years; the reconstitution of the Anglican Church in the United States of America: 1780-1789. Greenwich, Conn., Seabury Press, 1956. vi, 311p. 22cm. 'Catalogue of correspondence': p. (289)-293. Bibliography: p. [294]-306. [BX5881.L6] 56-10567
1. Protestant Episcopal Church in the U.S.A.—Hist. I. Title.

MCCONNELL, Samuel David, 1845- 283.
History of the American Episcopal church, by S. D. McConnell... 10th ed., rev. and enl. and continued to the year 1915. Milwaukee, The Young churchman co.; London, A. R. Mowbray & co., 1916. xx p., 1 l., [5]-468 p. plates. ports. 21 cm. [BX5880.M3 1916] 16-14820
1. Protestant Episcopal Church, in the U.S.A.—Hist. I. Title.

MCCONNELL, Samuel David, 1845-1939. 283.
History of the American Episcopal church, by S. D. McConnell ... 7th ed., rev. and enl. New York, T. Whittaker, 1897. xviii p., 1 l., [5]-452 p. 22 cm. [BX5880.M3 1897] 45-53086
1. Protestant Episcopal church in the U.S.A.—Hist. I. Title.

MCCONNELL, Samuel David, 1845-1939. 283.
History of the American Episcopal church from the planting of the colonies to the end of the civil war, by S. D. McConnell ... New York, T. Whittaker, 1890. xiv p., 1 l., [5]-392 p. 21 cm. [BX5880.M3 1890] 45-25703
1. Protestant Episcopal church in the U.S.A.—Hist. I. Title.

MANROSS, William Wilson, 1905- 283.73
The Episcopal church in the United States, 1800-1840, a study in church life, by William Wilson Manross ... New York [Columbia university press] 1938. 1 p. l., 5-270 p., 1 l. 22 1/2 cm. Thesis (PH.D.)--Columbia university, 1938. Vita. Published also as Studies in history, economics and public law, ed. by the Faculty of political science of Columbia university, no. 441. Bibliography: p. 240-257. [BX5882.M35 1938] 38-38021
1. Protestant Episcopal church in the U.S.A.—Hist. I. Title.

MANROSS, William Wilson, 1905- 283.73
The Episcopal church in the United States, 1800-1840, a study in church life, by William Wilson Manross ... New York, Columbia university press. London, P. S. King & son, ltd., 1938. 270 p. 23 cm. (Half-title: Studies in history, economics and public law, ed. by the Faculty of political science of Columbia university, no. 441) Issued also as thesis (PH. D.) Columbia university. Bibliography: p. 240-257. [H31.C7 no. 441] [BX5882.M35 1938a] (308.2) 38-38020
1. Protestant Episcopal church in the U.S.A.—Hist. I. Title.

MANROSS, William Wilson, 1905- 283.73
A history of the American Episcopal Church. [3d ed., rev.] New York, Morehouse-Gorham, 1959. 420p. 21cm. Includes bibliography. [BX5880.M35 1959] 59-1356
1. Protestant Episcopal Church in the U. S. A.—Hist. I. Title. II. Title: American Episcopal Church.

MANROSS, William Wilson, 1905- 283.73
A history of the American Episcopal Church. [2d ed., rev. and enl.] New York, Morehouse-Gorham, 1950. xiv. 415 p. 24 cm. Bibliography: p. 373-386. [BX5880.M35 1950] 50-8326
1. Protestant Episcopal Church in the U. S. A.—Hist. I. Title.

MANROSS, William Wilson, 1905- 283.73
A history of the American Episcopal church, by the Reverend William Wilson Manross ... New York, Milwaukee, Morehouse publishing co., 1935. xvi p., 1 l., 404 p. front., plates (1 fold.) ports. 21 cm. Maps on lining-papers. Bibliography: p. 361-375. [BX5880.M35] 35-33564
1. Protestant Episcopal church in the U.S.A.—Hist. I. Title.

MILLER, William James, 1850-
The American church; being a brief historical sketch of the body known as the Protestant Episcopal church in the United States of America, by the Rev. William James Miller ... New York, T. Whittaker [1904] 87 p. 18 1/2 cm. "Books recommended": p. 87. 4-6890
I. Title.

PROTESTANT Episcopal church in the U. S. A. General convention. 283.73
Journals of general conventions of the Protestant Episcopal church, in the United States, 1785-1835. Published by authority of General convention. Edited by William Stevens Perry ... Claremont, N. H., The Claremont manufacturing company, 1874. 3 v. 24 cm. Binder's title: A half century of the legislation of the American church. Vol. iii has also special t.-p. Contents.--i. 1785-1821.--ii. 1823-1835.--iii. Historical notes and documents. [BX5820.A15 1835] 33-25814
1. Protestant Episcopal church in the U. S. A.—Hist. I. Perry, William Stevens, bp., 1832-1898, ed. II. Title. III. Title: A half century of the legislation of the American church.

PROTESTANT Episcopal church in the U. S. A. General convention. 283.73
Journals of the general conventions of the Protestant Episcopal church, in the United States of America, from A. D. 1785 to A. D. 1853, inclusive. Published by order of the General convention. With illustrative historical notes and appendices, by the Rev. Francis L. Hawks ... and the Rev. William Stevens Perry, M. A. Vol. i. Philadelphia, J. W. Raynor, 1861. 4, vii, 653 p. 24 cm. No more published. [BX5820.A15 1853] 33-25815
1. Protestant Episcopal church in the U. S. A.—Hist. I. Hawks, Francis Lister, 1798-1866, ed. II. Perry, William Stevens, bp., 1832-1898, joint ed. III. Title.
Contents omitted.

PROTESTANT Episcopal church in the U. S. A. Maine(Diocese) 283.
One hundreth anniversary of the diocese of Maine, 1820-1920, Christ church, Gardiner, Maine, May thirtieth to June third. Gardiner, Me., 1920. xi, [1], 159, [1] p. 1 l. incl. illus., plates, ports. 29 cm. Bibliography: 1 page at end. [BX5918.M25A5 1920] 21-2532
I. Title.

PROTESTANT Episcopal church in the U. S. A. Church congress, Richmond, 1926. 283.
The church and truth; a record of the Church congress in the United States on its fifty-second anniversary A. D. mcmxxvi with an introduction by the general chairman, Charles Lewis Slattery. New York, The Macmillan company, 1926. 317 p. 20 cm. [BX5820.A6 1926] 26-18481
I. Title.
Contents omitted.

STOWE, Walter Herbert, 1895- 283.73
The Episcopal Church; a miniature history. [2d ed., rev. and enl.] Philadelphia, Church Historical Society [1952, c1944] 64p. 19cm. (Church Historical Society publications, no. 15) [BX5880.S8 1952] 53-6879
1. Protestant Episcopal Church in the U. S. A.—Hist. I. Title.

TIFFANY, Charles Comfort, 1829-1907. 283
... A history of the Protestant Episcopal church in the United States of America, by Charles C. Tiffany ... New York, The Christian literature co., 1895. xxiv, 593 p. 21 cm. (Half-title: The American church history series, vol. XII) Series title also at head of t.-p. Bibliography: p. xvi-xxiv. [BR515.A5] 4-4661
1. Protestant Episcopal church in the U.S.A.—Hist. I. Title.

WHITE, William, bp., 1748-1836. 283.73
Memoirs of the Protestant Episcopal church in the United States of America, from its organization up to the present day: containing, I. A narrative of the early measures of the church; II. Additional statements and remarks; III. An appendix of original papers. By William White ... 2d ed. New York, Swords, Stanford, and co., 1836. xiii p., 1 l., 17-393 p. 24 1/2 cm. [BX5880.W5 1836] 37-13877
1. Protestant Episcopal church in the U.S.A.—Hist. I. Title.

WILSON, Frank Elmer, bp., 1885- 283.73
An outline history of the Episcopal church, by the Rt. Rev. Frank E. Wilson ... Milwaukee, Wis., Morehouse publishing co.; London, A. R. Mowbray & co. [1932] 3 p. l., 65, [1] p. illus. (incl. ports.) 15 1/2 cm. "Table of presiding bishops in the American church": p. [2-3] of cover. [BX5880.W65] 32-14315
1. Protestant Episcopal church in the U.S.A.—Hist. I. Title.

WILSON, Frank Elmer, Bp., 1885-1944. 283.73
An outline history of the Episcopal Church. Rev. by Edward R.. Hardy, Jr. [5th ed.] New York, Morehouse-Gorham Co., 1949. 78 p. illus., ports. 16 cm. [BX5880.W651949] 49-3695
1. Protestant Episcopal Church in the U. S. A.—Hist. I. Hardy, Edward Rochie, 1908- II. Title.

Protestant Episcopal Church in the U.S.A.—History—Sources.

CAMERON, Kenneth Walter, 1908- comp.
Early Anglicanism in Connecticut; materials on the missionary career of Roger Viets, Samuel Seabury's Communion office, and aids for scholarly research. Hartford, Transcendental Books, 1962. 1 v. (various pagings, chiefly facsims.) 29 cm. Facsimile reproductions of ms. and printed items. [BX5833.C3] 63-37040
1. Protestant Episcopal Church in the U.S.A.—Hist.—Sources. 2. Viets, Roger, 1738-1811. 3. Seabury, Samuel, Bp., 1729-1796. I. Title.
Contents omitted.

FACSIMILES of early Episcopal Church documents (1759-1789) 283'.73
Edited by Kenneth Walter Cameron. Hartford, Transcendental Books [1970] 68 l. port. 29 cm. Cover title: Early Episcopal Church documents, 1759-1789. Facsim. reproduction of the New York? 1880? ed. Documents 29-33 omitted. Original t.p. reads: Fac-similes of church documents; papers issued by the Historical Club of the American Church, 1874-79. Privately printed. [BX5881.F3 1970] 74-268868
1. Protestant Episcopal Church in the U.S.A.—History—Sources. I. Cameron, Kenneth Walter, 1908- ed. II. Historical Club of the American Church. III. Title: Early Episcopal Church documents, 1759-1789.

Protestant Episcopal Church in the U.S.A. Hymnal.

PROTESTANT Episcopal Church in the U.S.A. 783.9
The hymnal 1940 companion; prepared by the Joint Commission on the Revision of the Hymnal of the Protestant Episcopal Church in the United States of America. 2d ed., rev. New York, Church Pension Fund [1951] xxviii, 740 p. illus., port., music. 22 cm. Bibliography: p. viii. [ML3166.P77 1951] 51-32683
1. Protestant Episcopal Church in the U.S.A. Hymnal. 2. Protestant Episcopal Church in the U.S.A.—Hymns—Hist. & crit. 3. Hymns—Hist. & crit. 4. Hymns-Dictionaries. I. Title.
Contents omitted

PROTESTANT Episcopal Church in the U.S.A.
The hymnal of the Protestant Episcopal church in the United States of America, 1940. With supplemental liturgical Index and collection of service music, 1961. New York, Church pension Fund [c1961] vi, 857 p. music. 22 cm. 66-24429
1. Protestant Episcopal Church in the U.S.A. Hymnal. 2. Protestant Episcopal Church in the U.S.A.—Hymns—Hist. & crit. 3. Hymns—Hist. & crit. 4. Hymns—Dictionaries. I. Title.

PROTESTANT Episcopal Church 783.9
in the U. S. A.
The hymnal 1940 companion, prepared by the Joint Commission on the Revision of the Hymnal. New York, Church Pension Fund [1949] xxviii, 732 p. illus., port. 22 cm. Contents.Historica essays on texts and tunes.--Biographies of authors, composers, translators, and arrangers. Bibliography: p. viii. [ML3166.P77] 49-5947
1. Protestant Episcopal Church in the U. S. A. Hymnal. 2. Protestant Episcopal Church in the U. S. A.—Hymns—Hist. & crit. 3. Hymns—Dictionaries, indexes, etc. I. Title.

Protestant Episcopal church in the U.S.A.—Hymns.

ANKETELL, John. 245.
Gospel and epistle hymns for the Christian year. By the Reverend John Anketell ... [New York] The Church rcord company [1890] iv, [2], [7]-71, [1] p. 19 cm. Without music. [BV372.A6 1890] 45-44801
1. Protestant Episcopal church in the U. S. A.—Hymns. 2. Hymns, English. I. Title.

BIBLE. O. T. Psalms. 223.
English. Paraphrases. 1791.
The whole book of Psalms, in metre; with hymns, suited to the feasts and fasts of the church, and other occasions of public worship. Philadelphia: Printed by Hall & Sellers. mdccxci 221, [3] p. 15 cm. [With Protestant Episcopal church in the U. S. A. Book of common prayer. The Book of common prayer ... Philadelphia, mdccxci] Title within line borders. [BX5943.A1 1791] 6-26907
1. Protestant Episcopal church in the U. S. A.—Hymns. 2. Hymns, English. I. Bible. English. Paraphrases. O. T. Psalms. 1791. II. Title.

BIBLE. O. T. Psalms. 223.
English. Paraphrases. 1801.
The whole book of Psalms, in metre; with hymns, suited to the feasts and fasts of the church, and other occasions of public worship. Whitehall: Printed by William Young, bookseller & stationer, n. 52 S. 2d-street, Philadelphia, 1801. 2 p. l., [3], 171, [4] p. 15 cm. [With Protestant Episcopal church in the U. S. A. Book of common prayer. The Book of common prayer ... Philadelphia, 1795. Copy 1] [BX5943.A1 1795 copy 1] 5-31224
1. Protestant Episcopal church in the U. S. A.—Hymns. 2. Hymns, English. I. Bible. English. Paraphrases. O. T. Psalms. 1801. II. Title.

BIBLE. O.T. Psalms. English.
Paraphrases. 1819.
The whole book of Psalms, in metre; with hymns, suited to the feasts and fasts of the church, and other occasions of public worship. New-York, W. B. Gilley, 1819. 224 p. 22 1/2 cm. [With Protestant Episcopal church in the U.S.A. Book of common prayer. The Book of common prayer, and administration of the sacraments ... New-York, 1819] Without music. [BS5943.A1 1819] 42-48023
1. Protestant Episcopal church in the U.S.A.—Hymns. 2. Hymns, English. I. Bible. English, Paraphrases. O.T. Psalms. 1819. II. Title.

BIBLE. O. T. Psalms. 223.5
English. Paraphrases. 1840.
Psalms, in metre, selected from the Psalms of David. New-York, New York Bible and Common prayer book society, 1840. 51, 48 p. 15 cm. [With Protestant Episcopal church in the U. S. A. Book of common prayer. The Book of common prayer ... New York, 1841] "Hymns of the Protestant Episcopal church, in the United States of America, set forth in the years ... 1782, 1808 and 1826": 48 p. at end. Without music. [BX5943.A1 1841 a] 33-36475
1. Protestant Episcopal church, in the U. S. A.—Hymns. 2. Hymns, English. I. Bible. Paraphrases. O. T. Psalms. 1840. II. Title.

BIBLE. O. T. Psalms. 223.5
English. Paraphrases. 1844.
Psalms, in metre, selected from the Psalms of David; suited to the feasts and fasts of the church. and other occasions of public worship. Philadelphia, King & Baird [1844] 105 p. 16 cm. [With Protestant Episcopal church in the U. S. A. Book of common prayer. The Book of common prayer, and administration of the sacraments ... Hartford, Ct., 1844] "Hymns of the Protestant Episcopal church" (p. [45]-92) has special t.-p. [BX5943.A1 1844 b] 34-38082
1. Protestant Episcopal church in the U. S. A.—Hymns. 2. Hymns, English. I. Bible. English Paraphrases. O. T. Psalms. 1844. II. Title.

BIBLE. O. T. Psalms, 264.
English. Paraphrases. 1845.
Psalms, in metre, selected from the Psalms of David; with Hymns, suited to the feasts and fasts of the church, and other occasions of public worship. Buffalo, W. B. & C. E. Peck, 1845. 105, [1] p. 16 cm. [With Protestant Episcopal church in the U. S. A. Book of common prayer. The Book of common prayer, and administration of the sacraments ... Buffalo, 1845] "Hymns suited to the feasts and fasts of the church" has special t.-p. Without music. [BX5943.A1 1845 a] 39-30701
1. Protestant Episcopal church in the U. S. A.—Hymns. 2. Hymns, English. I. Bible. English. Paraphrases. O. T. Psalms. 1845. II. Title.

BIBLE. O. T. Psalms. 223.
English. Paraphrases. 1869.
Selections from the Psalms of David in metre, with hymns suited to the feasts and fasts of the church, and other occasions of public worship. Oxford, Printed at the University press; New York, Sold by T. Nelson & sons, 1869. 334 p. 11 cm. [With Protestant Episcopal church in the U. S. A. Book of common prayer. Oxford, 1869] Without music. "Additional hymns ... Oxford, 1869" (p. [285]-334) has special t.-p. [BX5943.A1 1869] 31-15750
1. Protestant Episcopal church in the U. S. A.—Hymns. I. Protestant Episcopal church in the U. S. A. Hymnal. II. Bible. English. Paraphrases. O. T. Psalms. 1869. III. Title.

DAVIES, George C. 264.
hymnologist, comp.
Songs of the church: or, Psalms and hymns of the Protestant Episcopal church, arranged to appropriate melodies. With a full set of chants for each season of the Christian year. By George C. Davies. The whole carefully harmonized in four parts and forming a complete choral service for the church; with special reference to the use of congregations, with or without choirs ... Cincinnati, Applegate and company, 1858. x, 11-456 p. 20 cm. [M2125.D27S5 1858] 45-44980
1. Protestant Episcopal church in the U.S.A.—Hymns. 2. Hymns, English. I. Bible. O.T. Psalms. English. Paraphrases 1858. II. Title.

GREATOREX, Henry Wellington, 783.
1813-1858, comp.
A collection of psalm and hymn tunes, chants, anthems, and sentences, original and selected from the best standard composers: adapted for the use of the Protestant Episcopal church in America, and for congregations of other denominations, as well as for societies and schools. By H. W. Greatorex ... Hartford, A. C. Goodman & co.; New York, Stanford & Swords; [etc., etc., c1851] xvi, 223, [1] p. 17 x 25 cm. Organ accompaniment. [M2125.G77] 43-21121
1. Protestant Episcopal church in the U.S.A.—Hymns. 2. Hymns, English. I. Title.

HUTCHINS, Charles Lewis, 783.
1838-1920, comp.
A church hymnal, compiled from the Prayer book hymnal, and from "The additional hymns", "Hymns ancient and modern", and "Hymns for church and home", with music: by Rev. C. L. Hutchins ... Buffalo, Breed, Lent & co., 1870. iv p., 1 l., 240 p. 19 cm. [M2125.H97C42B] 24-24654
1. Protestant Episcopal church in the U. S. A.—Hymns. 2. Hymns, English. I. Title.

HUTCHINS, Charles Lewis, 783.
1838-1920. comp.
A church hymnal, compiled from the Prayer book hymnal, and from "The additional hymns", "Hymns ancient and modern", and "Hymns for church and home", with music: by the Rev. C. L. Hutchins ... 6th ed. Buffalo, Breed, Lent & co., 1871. iv p., 1 l., 240 p. 18 cm. [M2125.H97C42E] 30-5302
1. Protestant Episcopal church in the U. S. A.—Hymns. 2. Hymns, English. I. Title.

HUTCHINS, Charles Lewis, 245.
1838-1920, comp.
A church hymnal, compiled from "Additional hymns," "Hymns ancient and modern," and Hymns for church and home," as authorized by the House of bishops: by the Rev. C. L. Hutchins... Buffalo, Breed, Lent & co., 1870. 1 p. 1., v -vi, f -263, 1 p. 17cm. 6 cm. Without music. [BV372.H8] 45-42814
1. Protestant Episcopal church in the U.S.A.—Hymns. 2. Hymns, English. I. Title.

HUTCHINS, Charles Lewis, 783.
1838-1920, ed.
The church hymnal, revised; containing hymns approved and set forth by the general conventions of 1892 and 1916; together with hymns for the use of guilds and brotherhoods, and for special occasions. Ed. and arranged with music by the Rev. Charles L. Hutchins. D. D. Boston, The Parish choir, 1920. xxxii, 736 p. 20 cm. [M2125.H97C48] 20-6291
1. Protestant Episcopal church in the U. S. A.—Hymns. 2. Hymns, English. I. Title.

HUTCHINS, Charles Lewis, 264.
1838-1920, ed.
The first 108 hymns from the revised and enlarged hymnal, with music, edited by the Rev. Charles L. Hutchins... Boston, Parish choir [1893] 2 p. l., 131 p. 19 1/2 cm, [M2125.H97C45 1893] 45-45717
1. Protestant Episcopal church in the U.S.A.—Hymns. 2. Hymns, English. I. Title.

MUHLENBERG, William 245.
Augustus, 1796-1877.
Church poetry: being portions of the Psalms in verse, and hymns suited to the festivals and fasts, and various occasions of the church. Selected and altered from various authors. By Wm. Augustus Muhlenberg ... Philadelphia, S. Potter & co., 1823. vi, 267 p. 16 1/2 cm. Errata slip inserted. [BV372.M8] 45-47064
1. Protestant Episcopal church in the U.S.A.—Hymns. 2. Hymns, English. I. Bible. O.T. Psalms. English. Paraphrases. 1823. II. Title.

PROTESTANT Episcopal church 264.
in the U.S.A.
Episcopal common praise: consisting of the chants in the morning and evening service of the Book of common prayer. And the Psalms of David in metre. With hymns suited to the feasts and fasts of the church; together with the additional hymns licensed for use in the congregations of the Protestant Episcopal church, by the General convention of 1865. All set to appropriate music. New York, A. S. Barnes & company, 1867. 600 p. 21 1/2 cm. Music revised by John P. Morgan. cf. p. 3. [M2125.P9E6 1867] 45-46646
1. Protestant Episcopal church in the U.S.A.—Hymns. 2. Hymns, English. I. Bible. O.T. Psalms. English. Paraphrases. 1867. II. Morgan, John Paul, 1841-1879, arr. III. Title.

PROTESTANT Episcopal 245.203
church in the U. S. A. Joint commission on the revision of the hymnal.
Report of the Joint commission on the revision of the Hymnal to the General convention of the Protestant Episcopal church in the United States of America. [New York] 1940. 1 p. l., v-xv, [472], xix-ixx p. 19 cm. H. J. Mikell chairman. "Printed not published, solely for consideration by members of General convention of 1940." [BV372.A3 1940] 40-32126
1. Protestant Episcopal church in the U. S. A.—Hymns. 2. Hymns, English. I. Protestant Episcopal church in the U. S. A. II. Mikell, Henry Judah, bp., 1873- III. Title.

PROTESTANT Episcopal Church 223.
in the U. S. A. Book of common prayer.
The Book of common prayer and administration of the sacraments and other rites and ceremonies of the church according to the use of the Protestant Episcopal Church in the United States of America together with the Psalter; or, Psalms of David. New York, Auxiliary New York Bible and Common Prayer Book Society, 1831. xxi, 38-395, 4-56 p. 15 cm. "The whole book of Psalms in metre; with hymns" (p. [319]-395, 4-56 p.) has special t.-p. [BX5943.A1 1831] 48-42282
1. Protestant Episcopal Church in the U. S. A.—Hymns. 2. Hymns, English. 3. Bible. O. T. Psalms. English. Paraphrases, 1831. I. Title.

[PROTESTANT Episcopal church 245.
in the U. S. A. New York (Diocese)]
The mission hymnal; words only. New York, Chicago, Biglow & Main [1885] cover-title, [68] p. 14 cm. "The committee appointed by the Assistant Bishop of New York has authorized the publication of this hymnal."--Pref. Published also under title: Hymns for special services. [BV372.A32 1885] 45-47062
1. Protestant Episcopal church in the U.S.A.—Hymns. 2. Hymns, English. I. Title.

PROTESTANT Episcopal church 783.9
in the U.S.A. Hymnal.
The hymnal of the Protestant Episcopal church in the United States of America, 1940. New York, The Church pension fund [1943] vii, 828, [3] p. 21 1/2 cm. With music. Three pages at end lined for music. "Service music": p. 697-794. [M2125.P94 1940] 43-48116
1. Protestant Episcopal church in the U.S.A.—Hymns. 2. Hymns, English. I. Title.

[PROTESTANT Episcopal church 245.
in the U.S.A. New York (Diocese))
Hymns for special services. New York, Chicago, Biglow & Main [1885] [68] p. 14 x 11 cm. Title from p. [2] of cover. Without music. Published also under title: The mission hymnal. [BV372.A32 1885 a] 45-47063
1. Protestant Episcopal church in the U.S.A.—Hymns. 2. Hymns, English. I. Title.

PROTESTANT Episcopal church 264.
in the U.S.A. New York (Diocese) Mission committee, 1885.
The mission hymnal; a hymnal issued by the Mission committee appointed by the assistant bishop of New York. New York, Chicago, Biglow & Main, c1885. viii, 168 p. 20 cm. With music. [M2125.P94N4 1885] 45-42031
1. Protestant Episcopal church in the U.S.A.—Hymns. 2. Hymns, English. I. Title.

SISTERHOOD of St Mary 783.9
The Saint Dunstan hymnal; plainsong hymns with accompaniments, from the manuscripts of the late Winfred Douglas. Foreword by Leo Sowerby. Ed. by Sisters of Saint Mary. New York, H. W. Gray, 1968. 1v. (unpaged) 24cm. [M2125.S59S3] 68-12664 3.50
1. Protestant Episcopal Church in the U.S.A.—Hymns. 2. Hymns, English. I. Douglas, Charles Winfred, 1867-1944. II. Title.
Publisher's address, 159 E. 48th St., New York, N.Y. 10017.

THE Sunday school chant and 783
tune book; a collection of canticles, hymns and carols, for the Sunday schools of the Episcopal church. Boston, E. P. Dutton & company; New York, Hurd & Houghton, 1866. 191 p. 17 cm. With music. Prepared by a committee: Treadwell Walden, C. A. L. Richards, George A. Strong, Phillipe Brooks and D. Otis Kellogg, jr., appointed by Alonso Potter, bishop of the diocese of Pennsylvania. [M2193.S] [BX3873.W3 1866] 26-22279
1. Protestant Episcopal church in the U.S.A.—Hymns. 2. Sunday schools—Hymn-books.

Protestant Episcopal church in the U.S.A.—Hymns—History and criticism

HUTCHINS, Charles Lewis, 245.
1838-1920.
Annotations of the Hymnal: consisting of notes, biographical sketches of authors, originals and references. By the Rev. Charles L. Hutchins, M.A. Hartford, Conn., The Church press: M. H. Mallory

and co., 1872. xix, [20]-206 p. 21 x 17 cm. [BV372.A1H8] 45-47236
1. Protestant Episcopal church in the U.S.A.—Hymns—Hist. & crit. 2. Hymns, English—Hist. & crit. I. Protestant Episcopal church in the U.S.A. Hymnal. II. Title.

Protestant Episcopal Church in the U.S.A. — Illinois — Fulton Co.

SWARTZBAUGH, Constance 283.77348 H
The Episcopal Church in Fulton County, Illinois, 1835-1959; with some early history of the Episcopal Church in Illinois and the English settlement at Albion. [Canton? Ill., 1959] 187 p. illus. 24 cm. Includes bibliography. [BX5917.I3S9] 61-22285
1. Protestant Episcopal Church in the U.S.A. — Illinois — Fulton Co. I. Title.

Protestant Episcopal church in the U.S.A.—Law.

VINTON, Francis, 1809- 1872. 283.73
A manual commentary on the general canon law and the constitution of the Protestant Episcopal church in the United States. By Francis Vinton ... New York, E. P. Dutton and company, 1870. viii p., 1 l., 223 p. 21 1/2 cm. "Index of authorities": p. [218]-223. [BX5955.V5] 37-31948
1. Protestant Episcopal church in the U.S.A.—Law. I. Title.

Protestant Episcopal Church in the U.S.A. Lexington (Diocese)

SWINFORD, Frances Keller. 283'.769
The great elm tree; heritage of the Episcopal Diocese of Lexington, by Frances Keller Swinford & Rebecca Smith Lee. With an epilogue by William R. Moody. Lexington, Ky., Faith House Press, 1969. xii, 456 p. illus., ports. 24 cm. Bibliographical footnotes. [BX5918.L5S9] 78-8747 9.50
1. Protestant Episcopal Church in the U.S.A. Lexington (Diocese) I. Lee, Rebecca Washington (Smith) 1894- joint author. II. Title.

Protestant Episcopal Church in the U.S.A. Liturgical Commission.

PARSONS, Donald J., 1922- 264'.035
The Holy Eucharist, rite two : a devotional commentary / Donald J. Parsons. New York : Seabury Press, 1976. 114 p. ; 21 cm. "A Crossroad book." [BX5944.C75P37] 76-15636 ISBN 0-8164-2129-3 pbk. : 3.95
1. Protestant Episcopal Church in the U.S.A. Liturgical Commission. The draft proposed Book of Common Prayer. The Holy Eucharist, rite two. 2. Lord's Supper (Liturgy) I. Title.

Protestant Episcopal Church in the U.S.A. Liturgy and ritual.

BIBLE. O. T. Psalms. English. Paraphrases. 1858. 783.
The Psalter, or Psalms of David; together with appropriate chants, adapted to each portion as set forth by the church for the morning and evening prayer. To which are added the morning and evening canticles, arranged to be sung to the Gregorian tones ... Boston, Ide & Dutton; New York, D. Dana, jr.; [etc., etc.] 1858. viii, [9]-320 p. 18 cm. Editors' preface signed: H. S., F. E. O. [M2125.P97] 10-18548
I. Protestant Episcopal church in the U. S. Liturgy and ritual. Psalter. II. Southgate, Horatio, 1812-1894. III. Oliver, Fitch Edward, 1819-1892. IV. Title.

BURGESS, Thomas, 1880- 264.035
The Celebrant's manual, by the Reverend Thomas Burgess, D.D. Milwaukee, Wis., Morehouse publishing co., 1934. viii, 75, [1] p. illus. 17 cm. Bibliography: p. [73]-75. [BX5947.R5B8] 34-17346
1. Protestant Episcopal church in the U.S.A. Liturgy and ritual. I. Title.

COXE, Arthur Cleveland, bp. 1818-1896. 264.03
Thoughts on the services; designed as an introduction to the liturgy, and an aid to its devout use, by the late Rt. Rev. A. Cleveland Coxe ... Rev. and enl. by Rt. Rev. Cortlandt White-head ... Philadelphia, J. B. Lippincott company, 1900. 361 p. front. (port.) 17 cm. [BX5940.C6 1900] 0-1414
1. Protestant Episcopal church in the U. S. A. Liturgy and ritual. 2. Protestant Episcopal church in the U. S. A. Book of common prayer. I. Whitehead, Cortlandt, bp., 1842-1922, ed. II. Title.

GAVITT, Loren N 264.03
Our offering; some notes on the liturgy. West Park, N. Y., Holy Cross Press, 1949. viii, 50 p. 19 cm. [BX5949.C5G3] 49-4664
1. Protestant Episcopal Church in the U. S. A. Liturgy and ritual. 2. Lord's Supper (Liturgy) I. Title.

GRISWOLD, Latta, 1876- 264.
The middle way; suggestions for a practicable ceremonial, by the Reverend Latta Griswold ... Milwaukee, Wis., Morehouse publishing co.; London, A. R. Mowbray & co. [c1928] 3 p. l., 115, [1] p. illus. 19 cm. [BX5940.G7] 28-31135
1. Protestant, Episcopal church in the U. S. A. Liturgy and ritual. I. Title.

GUTHRIE, William Norman, 1868- comp. 264.08
Evangelical offices of worship and meditation derived chiefly from the New Testament, compiled and edited by William Norman Guthrie. New York, Issued for the Petrus Stuyvesant book guild ... by the Schulte press [c1930] 2 p. l., iii-xi, 289 p. 20 cm. [BX5947.B8G7] 31-502
1. Protestant Episcopal church in the U. S. A. Liturgy and ritual. I. Title.

HINES, John M. 234'.16
By water and the Holy Spirit; new concepts of baptism, confirmation, and communion [by] John M. Hines. Foreword by Alfred R. Shands. New York, Seabury Press [1973] 95 p. 21 cm. "A Crossroad book." [BX5940.H5] 74-155336 ISBN 0-8164-5703-4 2.95 (pbk.).
1. Protestant Episcopal Church in the U.S.A. Liturgy and ritual. 2. Baptism—Anglican Communion. 3. Confirmation—Anglican Communion. 4. Lord's Supper—Anglican Communion. 5. Children—Religious life. I. Title.

JONES, Hosea Williams. 264.
A half-year in the prayer book. For Sunday-schools. By H. W. Jones ... Philadelphia, G. W. Jacobs & co., 1899. 156 p. 17 cm. [BX5945.J6] 99-5271
1. Protestant Episcopal church in the U. S. A. Liturgy and ritual. I. Title. II. Title: Prayer book.

THE kingdom, the power and the glory; services of praise and prayer for occasional use in churches. An American ed. of the Grey book. New York, Oxford university press [c1933] v, 87 p. 17 cm. "The third volume of the Grey book, one of the several proposed revisions of the English Book of common prayer, none of which was adopted by Parliament."--Pref. to the American ed. [BX5943.A4K5] 33-21161 264.03
I. Protestant Episcopal church in the U.S.A. Liturgy and ritual.

LADD, William Palmer, 1870-1941. 264.03
Prayer book interleaves; some reflections on how the Book of common prayer might by made more influential in our English-speaking world. Foreword by Massey H. Shepherd. Jr. Greenwich, Conn., Seabury Press [c1957] 193p. 19cm. [BX5910.L27 1957] 58-386
1. Protestant Episcopal Church in the U. S. A. Liturgy and ritual. I. Title.

LADD, William Palmer, 1870-1941. 264.08
Prayer book interleaves; some reflections on how the Book of common prayer might be made more influential in our English-speaking world, by William Palmer Ladd ... New York, London [etc.] Oxford university press [c1942] ix, [1], 188 p. front. 20 cm. Foot-note to preface signed: A. T. Ladd. [BX5940.L27] 42-3560
1. Protestant Episcopal church in the U. S. A. Liturgy and ritual. I. Ladd, Allsie (Taylor) Mrs. ed. II. Title.

LADD, William Palmer, 1870-1941. 264.
Prayer book interleaves; some reflections on how the Book of common prayer might be made more influential in our English-speaking world, by William Palmer Ladd ... New York, London [etc.] Oxford university press [1943] ix, [1], 193 p. front., pl. 19 1/2 cm. Foot-note to preface signed: A. T. Ladd. "Second edition, November 1943." [BX5940.L27 1943] 44-1887
1. Protestant Episcopal church in the U.S.A. Liturgy and ritual. I. Ladd, Ailsie (Taylor) ed. II. Title.

PRICE, Charles P., 1920- 264'.03'009
Liturgy for living / Charles P. Price and Louis Weil, with assistance of a group of editorial advisors under the direction of the Church's Teaching Series Committee. New York : Seabury Press, c1979. xv, 345 p. ; 22 cm. (The Church's teaching series ; v. 5) Includes index. Bibliography: p. 332-337. [BX5940.P74] 78-26605 ISBN 0-8164-0422-4 : 9.50
1. Protestant Episcopal Church in the U.S.A. Liturgy and ritual. 2. Protestant Episcopal Church in the U.S.A. Book of common prayer. 3. Liturgics. I. Weil, Louis, 1935- joint author. II. Title. III. Series.

THE propers for the minor holy days. New York, Church Pension Fund, 1958. 185p.
I. Protestant Episcopal Church in the U. S. A. Liturgy and ritual.

PROTESTANT Episcopal church in the U. S. A. House of bishops. Commission on memorial of Rev. Dr. Muhlenberg and others.
Memorial papers. The memorial: with circular and questions of the episcopal Commission; report of the Commission; contributions of the commissioners; and communications from Episcopal and non-Episcopal divines. With an introduction, by Rt. Rev. Alonzo Potter, D. D., one of the Commission. Philadelphia, E. H. Butler & co., 1857. xii p., 1 l., 27-444 p. 19 cm. "Memorial" (signed: W. A. Muhlenberg [and others]): 1 l., 27-31 p. [BX5840.A5] 4-6860
1. Protestant Episcopal church in the U. S. A. Liturgy and ritual. 2. Protestant Episcopal church in the U. S. A.—Government. I. Potter, Alonzo, bp., 1800-1865, ed. II. Muhlenberg, William Augustus, 1796-1877. III. Title.

PROTESTANT Episcopal Church in the U. S. A. Liturgy and ritual. 264.03
The Book of offices; services for certain occasions not provided for in the Book of common prayer, compiled by the Liturgical Commission and commended for use by General Convention. 2d ed. New York, Church Pension Fund, 1949. ix, 81 p. 18 cm. [BX5947.B8A3 1949] 51-3351
1. Protestant Episcopal Church in the U. S. A. Liturgical Commission. I. Title.

PROTESTANT Episcopal Church in the U. S. A. Liturgy and ritual. 264.03
The Book of offices; services for certain occasions not provided in the Book of common prayer. Compiled by the Standing Liturgical Commission, commended for use by General Convention. 3d ed. New York, Church Pension Fund, 1960. x, 106p. 18cm. [BX5947.B8A3 1960] 60-34864
1. Protestant Episcopal Church in the U. S. A. Liturgical Commission. I. Title.

PROTESTANT Episcopal Church in the U.S.A. Liturgical Commission.
The collects, epistles, and gospels for the lesser feasts and fasts. A supplement to Prayer Book studies, XII. New York, Church Pension Fund, 1960. vii, 160 p. 19 cm. (Its Prayer Book studies, no. xii, supplement) Printed for the information of the Church by direction of the General Convention. 65-66572
1. Protestant Episcopal Church in the U.S.A. Liturgy and ritual. 2. Prayers. I. Title.

PROTESTANT Episcopal Church in the U.S.A. Liturgical Commission.
Morning and evening prayer [and] The Penitential Office. New York, Church Pension Fund, 1957. vii, 63 p. 19 cm. (Its Prayer Book studies, no. 6-7) 65-66569
1. Protestant Episcopal Church in the U.S.A. Liturgy and ritual. 2. Prayers. I. Title.

PROTESTANT Episcopal Church in the U.S.A. Liturgical Commission.
The order for the burial of the dead [and] An office of institution of rectors into parishes. New York, Church Pension Fund, 1959. vii, 52 p. 19 cm. (Prayer Book studies, no. 13-14) 65-66570
1. Protestant Episcopal Church in the U.S.A. Liturgy and ritual. I. Title.

PROTESTANT Episcopal Church in the U.S.A. Liturgical Commission.
The ordinal. New York, Church Pension Fund, 1957. vii, 57 p. 19 cm. (Its Prayer Book studies, no.8) 65-66571
1. Protestant Episcopal Church in the U.S.A. Liturgy and ritual. 2. Ordination—Anglican Church. 3. Consecration of bishops. I. Title.

ST. George's school, Middletown, R.I. 264.03
The form of consecration of St. George's chapel, April XXIII, anno Domini, MDCCCCXXVIII. Middletown, R.I., St. George's school [1928] 2 p. l., 57, [2] p. 17 cm. "Six hundred copies printed at the Merrymount press, Boston, April, 1928." [BX5947.C55S3] 41-24299
1. Protestant Episcopal church in the U.S.A. Liturgy and ritual. I. Title.

[ST. George's school, Jerusalem] 264.03
Service book for schools. New York, The Macmillan company, 1932. xiv p., 1 l., 194 p. 17 cm. An American adaptation of "Saint George's service book for schools" (London, St. Christopher press) edited by J. W. Suter, jr., using the ritual of the Protestant Episcopal church in the U.S.A. cf. Pref. to the American ed. "Compiled and arranged by E. W. Hamond [and others]--Introd., p. xi. "Sources and acknowledgments": p. 191-194. [BX5147.S3S3 1932] 32-2485
I. Protestant Episcopal church in the U.S.A. Liturgy and ritual. II. Hamond, E. W., comp. III. Suter, John Wallace, 1890- ed. IV. Title.

SHEPHERD, Massey Hamilton Jr. 1913- 264
Liturgy and education. New York, Seabury [c.1965] 112p. 20cm. Bibl. [BX5940.S49] 65-10354 3.50
1. Protestant Episcopal Church in the U.S.A. Liturgy and ritual. I. Title.

SHEPHERD, Massey Hamilton, 1913- 264.03
The living liturgy, by Massey Hamilton Shepherd, jr. New York, Oxford university press, 1946. x, 139 p. 19 1/2 cm. [BX5940.S5] 47-427
1. Protestant Episcopal church in the U.S.A. Liturgy and ritual. I. Title.

SHEPHERD, Massey Hamilton, 1918- ed. 264.021
Holy Week offices, editred for the Associated Parishes, incorporated. Greenwich, Conn, Seabury Press, 1958. 6 pts. (viii, 106 p.) in 1 v. illus. 19 cm. "Published under the auspices of the Adult Division of the Department of Christian Education, Protestant Episcopal Church." [BX5147.H6S5] 58-5054
I. Associated Parishes. II. Protestant Episcopal Church in the U.S.A. Liturgy and ritual. III. Title.

SOCIETY of Saint John the Evangelist. 264.03
An American Holy week manual, the liturgy from Palm Sunday through Easter day together with tenebrae. Cambridge, Mass., Society of Saint John the Evangelist, 1946. 3 p. l., v-viii, 363 p. 16 cm. Cover-title: Holy week. Edited by E. H. Maddux. cf. Pref. [BX5947.H5S6] 47-18888
I. Protestant Episcopal church in the U.S.A. Liturgy and ritual. II. Maddux, Earle Hewitt, 1906- ed. III. Title. IV. Title: Holy week manual.

SOCIETY of St. John the Evangelist. 264.03
A manual for priests of the American church, complementary to the occasional offices of the Book of common prayer. Cambridge, Mass., Society of Saint John the Evnagelist, 1944. xi, 276 p. 16 cm. Edited by E. H. Maddux, cf. Pref. [BX5947.R5S6] 45-724
1. Protestant Episcopal church in the U.S.A. Liturgy and ritual. II. Maddux, Earle Hewitt, 1906- ed. III. Title.

VAUGHAN, Charles John, 1816-1897. 264.03
Ten discourses on subjects connected with public worship and the liturgy. By C. J. Vaughan ... Revised and adapted to the liturgy and worship of the Protestant Episcopal church in the United States of America, with an introduction by Henry C. Potter, D.D. New York, E. P. Dutton & company, 1872. 2 p. l., 3-283 p. 18 cm. [BX5133.V3T4] 40-22681
1. Protestant Episcopal church in the U.S.A. Liturgy and ritual. 2. Church of England—Doctrinal and controversial works. I. Title.

WATERBURY, William Penfield, ed.
Offices for the burial of the dead, ed. by the Reverend William Penfield Waterbury, B.D. Milwaukee, The Young churchman company, 1911. v p., 1 l., 93 p. 14 cm. $0.75. 11-22852
I. Protestant Episcopal church in the U.S. Liturgy and ritual. II. Title.

Protestant Episcopal Church in the U.S.A. Liturgy and ritual — Sermons.

GOODRICH, William Lloyd. 283.73
Black rubric 1965; sermons on the Anglican view of the new liturgy, [1st ed. Washinton, St. James' Parish, [1965] xi, 64 p. 23 cm. 200 copies printed. Bibliography: p. 63-64. [BX5940.G6] 67-7336
1. Protestant Episcopal Church in the U.S.A. Liturgy and ritual — Sermons. 2. Sermons, American. 3. Protestant Episcopal Church in the U.S.A. — Sermons. I. Title. II. Title: Sermons on the Anglican view of the new liturgy.

Protestant Episcopal Church in the U.S.A. Louisiana (Diocese)

DUNCAN, Herman Cope. 283.
The Diocese of Louisiana, some of its history, 1838-1888; also some of the history of its parishes and missions, 1805-1888. New Orleans, A. W. Hyatt, printer, 1888. 268, viii p., plates, ports. 24 cm. On spine: History of the Diocese of Louisiana, 1806-1888. [BX5918.L8D8] 50-40811
1. Protestant Episcopal Church in the U.S.A. Louisiana (Diocese) I. Title.

Protestant Episcopal Church in the U.S.A.—Membership.

BROCK, Horace, Mrs. 287.6
The green book; church membership--what it is, what are its privileges and obligations, and what is its end, by Mrs. Horace Brock ... Philadelphia, St. Mark's league of intercession [1919?] 4 p. l., 5-245 p. 19 cm. [BX5950.B7] 34-13689
1. Protestant Episcopal church in the U.S.A.—Membership. 2. Church membership. I. Title.

WITSELL, William Postell, 1874- 265.2
Come. Boston, Christopher Pub. House [1955] 127p. 21cm. [BX5950.W55] 55-14258
1. Protestant Episcopal Church in the U.S.A.—Membership. I. Title.

Protestant Episcopal church in the U.S.A.—Minnesota.

WHIPPLE, Henry Benjamin, bp., 1822-1901. 283
Lights and shadows of a long episcopate; being reminiscences and recollections of the Right Reverend Herry Benjamin Whipple ... bishop of Minnesota ... New York, The Macmillan company [etc.] 1899. vi p., 1 l., 576 p. front., illus., 5 pl., 5 port., 4 facsim. 23 cm. [E78.M7W5] 0-209
1. Indians of North America—Missions. 2. Protestant Episcopal church in the U.S.A.—Minnesota. I. Title.

WHIPPLE, Henry Benjamin, bp., 1822-1901. 922.373
Lights and shadows of a long episcopate; being reminiscences and recollections of the Right Reverend Henry Benjamin Whipple, D.D., LL.D., bishop of Minnesota. New York, The Macmillan company; London, Macmillan & co., ltd., 1902. vi p., 1 l., 576 p. front., plates, ports., facsims. 23 cm. "Set up and electrotyped November, 1899, reprinted January, 1900, July 1902." [E78.M7W52] 4-16977
1. Indians of North America—Missions. 2. Protestant Episcopal church in the U.S.A.—Minnesota. I. Title.

Protestant Episcopal church in the U.S.A. Minnesota (Diocese)—History

TANNER, George Clinton, 1834-1923. 283.776
Fifty years of church work in the diocese of Minnesota, 1857-1907. With an account of the visitation of Right Reverend Jackson Kemper, D.D., and the labors of the Reverend Ezekiel Gilbert Gear, D.D., the first Protestant clergyman to minister to the white settlers within the "Precinct of St. Peter's" which then included the present city of St. Paul, by the Rev. George Clinton Tanner, D.D., registrar of the diocese. St. Paul, Minn., The Committee, 1909. 3 p. l., x, 516 p. front., plates, ports. 24 cm. Index to the history of the diocese of Minnesota, by the Rev. George Clinton Tanner, D.D., "Fifty years of church work in the diocese of Minnesota, 1857-1907" ... Compiled in 1937 by Rev. Dr. Francis L. Palmer ... [St. Paul] 1937. 12 p. 24 cm. [BX5918.M6T3] 11-25971
1. Kemper, Jackson, bp., 1789-1870. 2. Gear, Ezekiel Gilbert, 1793-1873. 3. Protestant Episcopal church in the U.S.A. Minnesota (Diocese)—Hist. I. Palmer, Francis Leseure, 1863- comp. II. Title.

Protestant Episcopal church in the U.S.A.—Missions.

ADDISON, James Thayer, 1887- 266.3
Our expanding church; foreword by the presiding bishop. New York, National Council [1951] 132 p. 21 cm. Bibliography: p. 125-132. [BV2575.A8 1951] 51-5327
1. Protestant Episcopal Church in the U. S. A.—Missions. I. Title.

ADDISON, James Thayer, 1887- 266.3
Our expanding church. A new and completely rev. ed. By James Thayer Addison, with a foreword by the presiding bishop. New York, The National council of the Protestant Episcopal church, 1944. 4 p. l., 3-130 p. 20 1/2 cm. "First published in 1930."--Foreword. "Books for further reading": p. 123-130. [BV2575.A8 1944] 45-18694
1. Protestant Episcopal church in the U.S.A.—Missions. I. Protestant Episcopal church in the U.S.A. National council. II. Title.

BURGESS, Thomas, 1880- 277.
Foreign-born Americans and their children; our duty and opportunity for God and country from the standpoint of the Episcopal church, by Thomas Burgess... New York, Department of missions and church extension of the Episcopal church [1921?] 3 p. l., 80 p. incl. front., illus. 24 1/2 cm. "Best books to read": p. 80. [BV2785.B75] 22-10533
1. Protestant Episcopal church in the U.S.A.—Missions. 2. U.S.—Foreign population. 3. Americanization. I. Protestant Episcopal church in the U.S.A. Dept. of missions and church extension. II. Title.

BURGESS, Thomas, 1880- 277.
Foreigners or friends, a handbook; the churchman's approach to the foreigh-born and their children, by Thomas Burgess...Charles Kendall Gilbert...Charles Thorley Bridgeman... New York, N.Y., Department of missions and church extension, 1921. 9 p. l., 263 p. incl. charts. 19 cm. "The work has been done by the Foreign-born American division of the Department of missions and church extension of the Presiding bishop and council assisted by the secretary of the New York Social service commissions."--Pref. Reading lists at ends of chapters. "Literature in foreign language to guide the foreign-born:" p. 249-253. [BV2785.B8] 22-10469
1. Protestant Episcopal church in the U.S.A.—Missions. 2. U.S.—Foreign population. 3. Americanization. I. Gilbert, Charles Kendall, 1878- joint author. II. Bridgeman, Charles Thorley, 1893- joint author. III. Protestant Episcopal church in the U.S.A. Dept. of missions and church extension. IV. Title.

BURLESON, Hugh Latimer, bp., 1865- 277.
The conquest of the continent, by Hugh Latimer Burleson ... New York, Domestic and foreign missionary society [c1911] 3 p. l., 5-207 p. incl. port. plates, ports., 2 fold. maps (incl. front.) 19 1/2 cm. Bibliography: p. 187-188. [BV2775.B9] 11-28831
1. Protestant Episcopal church in the U.S.A.—Missions. 2. Missions, Home. 3. Missions—U.S. I. Title.

EMHARDT, William Chauncey, 1874-
The eastern church in the western world, by Wm. Chauncey Emhardt, PH.D., Thomas Burgess, D.D., Robert Frederick Lau, D.D., officers of the Foreign-born Americans division, Department of missions, National council, Episcopal church. Milwaukee, Wis., Morehouse publishing co.; London, A. R. Mowbray & co. [c1928] x, 149, [1] p. front., plates, ports. 19 cm. "These chapters were delivered as a series of lectures in St. Pau' chapel. Trinity parish. New York city, daily at noon in the Advent season of 1926."--Pref. [BX733.E5] 28-21078
I. Burgess, Thomas, 1880- joint author. II. Lau, Robert Frederick, 1885- joint author. III. Protestant Episcopal church in the U.S.A. National council. Dept. of missions and church extension. IV. Title.

GARDNER, Mary Tracy. 277.
Conquerors of the continent for Christ and His church, by Mary Tracy Gardner. New York, Domestic and foreign missionary society [c1911] 1 p. l., 5-71 p. illus. (incl. ports., map) 20 cm. "Six conquerors of the continent": John Henry Hobart, Jackson Kemper, William Hobart Hare, Olla E. Ostenson, Dr. Marcus Whitman, Peter Trimble Rowe. [BV2766.P9G3] 21-9098
1. Hobart, John Henry, 1775-1830. 2. Kemper, Jackson, 1789-1870. 3. Hare, William Hobart, bp., 1838-1909. 4. Ostenson, Olla, 1849-1905. 5. Whitman, Marcus, 1802-1847. 6. Rowe, Peter Trimble, bp., 1856- 7. Protestant Episcopal church in the U.S.A.—Missions. I. Title.

HENING, E. F. 266.3'73
History of the African mission of the Protestant Episcopal Church. Freeport, N.Y., Books for Libraries Press, 1971 [c1849] 300 p. map. 23 cm. (The Black heritage library collection) Reprint of the 1850 ed., published under title: History of the African mission of the Protestant Episcopal Church in the United States, with memoirs of deceased missionaries, and notices of native customs. [BV3540.H4 1971] 77-173608 ISBN 0-8369-8900-7
1. Protestant Episcopal Church in the U.S.A.—Missions. 2. Missions—Africa, West. I. Title. II. Series.

AN Historical sketch of the China mission of the Protestant Episcopal church in the U.S.A., from the first appointments in 1834 to include the year ending August 31st, 1884. New York, Foreign committee, 1885. 74 p. front., plates, ports. 23 1/2 cm. [BV3415.H53] [266.3] 37-9275 275.1
1. Protestant Episcopal church in the U.S.A.—Missions. 2. Missions—China.

HOBART, Margaret Jefferys. 266
Institutions connected with the Japan mission of the American church, Comp. by Margaret Jeffreys Hobart. B.A. New York, The Domestic and foreign missionary society [1912] 87 p. front., plates. 18 cm. [BV3445.H6] 19-9806
1. Protestant Episcopal church in the U.S.A.—Missions. 2. Missions—Japan. I. Title.

PROTESTANT Episcopal church in the U. S. Domestic and foreign missionary society. 266.
Proceedings ... Together with the Report of the Board of directors ... Philadelphia, v. illus. 22-23 cm. Report year ends: May; October. 1827/28 has title: Proceedings of the Board of directors of the Domestic and foreign missionary society of the Protestant Episcopal church in the United States of America, at a stated meeting, May 13th, 1828. Together with the report of the Executive committee, from May 17th, 1827, to May 13th, 1828. Title varies: 1831/32 Proceedings of the Domestic and foreign missionary society ... Together with the report of the Board of directors ... [BV2575.A5A3] ca 6
I. Title.

PROTESTANT Episcopal Church in the U. S. A. Niobrara (Missionary District) 283.
Annual report of the missionary bishop of Niobara. [n. p.] v. plates. 26 cm. [BX5918.N76A3] 48-43533
I. Title.

[PROTESTANT Episcopal church in the U.S.A. National council] 266.3
A calendar of prayer for missions. [New York, 1944] cover-title, 80 p. 21 1/2 cm. "Descriptive list of active missionaries of the Episcopal church ... arranged in the form of a calendar with specific suggestions for each day." [BV2575.A5A43] 45-16717
1. Protestant Episcopal church in the U.S.A.—Missions. 2. Prayers. I. Title.

PROTESTANT Episcopal church in the U.S.A. National council.
The Christian fellowship in action ... New York: The National council, Protestant Episcopal church [1945?] 128 p. incl. illus., 25 pl. 22 1/2 cm. A 45
1. Protestant Episcopal church in the U.S.A.—Missions. I. Title.

PROTESTANT Episcopal Church in the U.S.A. National Council.
Our overseas missions: Brazil; a memorandum prepared in the office of the Director of the Overseas Department. [New York] 1964. 101 p. maps. 65-85088
I. Protestant Episcopal Church in the U.S.A. Overseas Dept. II. Title.

RICHMOND, Annette B. 275.
The American Episcopal church in China, by Annette B. Richmond ... New York, The Domestic and foreign missionary society of the Protestant Episcopal church in the United States of America, 1907. xi p., 1 l., 170 p. front., plates, ports. 18 1/2 cm. "References to the Spirit of missions" at end of chapters. "List of books prepared by members of the American church mission": p. 137-138. [BV3415.R5] 8-9517
1. Protestant Episcopal church in the U.S.A.—Missions. 2. Missions—China. I. Title.

SCOTT, Anna M. (Steele) 266.3'66'6
Day dawn in Africa; or, Progress of the Prot. Epis. Mission at Cape Palmas, West Africa, by Anna M. Scott. New York, Negro Universities Press [1969] 314 p. illus., map. 18 cm. Reprint of the 1858 ed. [BV3625.L5S3 1969] 69-18659
1. Protestant Episcopal Church in the U.S.A.—Missions. 2. Missions—Africa, West. I. Title.

TWING, Mary A. E. 266.
Twice around the world. Hartford, Junior Auxiliary Pub. Co. [pref. 1898] 244 p. illus., ports. 23 cm. [BV2575.T85] 50-44059
1. Protestant Episcopal Church in the U.S.A.—Missions. I. Title.

Protestant Episcopal Church in the U.S.A.—Montana.

DEHNERT, Amy Hales, comp.
A history of Episcopal churchwomen in Montana, 1892-1958. [Billings] Epsicopal Churchwomen of Montana [1959?] 112 p. 68-34289
1. Protestant Episcopal Church in the

U.S.A.—Montana. 2. Women in church work. I. Title.

Protestant Episcopal Church in the U.S.A. — Name.

SHOEMAKER, Robert W., 1924- 283.73
The origin and meaning of the name "Protestant Episcopal." [New York, American Church Publications, 1959] 338 p. 24 cm. Includes bibliography. [BX5935.S62] 59-16467
1. Protestant Episcopal Church in the U.S.A. — Name. I. Title.

Protestant Episcopal Church in the U.S.A.—New Jersey.

BURR, Nelson Rollin, 283.749
1904-
The Anglican Church in New Jersey. Philadelphia, Church Historical Society [1954] xvi, 768p. maps, tables. 24cm. (Church Historical Society [Philadelphia] Publication no. 40) [BX5917.N55B8] 54-12793
1. Protestant Episcopal Church in the U. S. A.—New Jersey. I. Title. II. Series.

STOWE, Walter Herbert 267.183
The Christian Knowledge Society and the revival of the Episcopal Church in New Jersey. [Austin 5, Tex., 606 Rathervue Place, Church Historical Society, 1960] 40p. port., facsims. 22cm. (Church Historical Society. Publication no. 49) Cover title. Bibliographical footnotes. 60-3399 .50 pap.,
1. Protestant Episcopal Church in the U.S.A.—New Jersey. 2. Episcopal Society of New Jersey for the Promotion of Christian Knowledge and Piety. 3. Christian Knowledge Society of New Jersey. I. Title. II. Series.

Protestant Episcopal church in the U.S.A. New York (Diocese)—Finance.

PROTESTANT Episcopal church 283.
in the U.S.A. New York (Diocese) Survey of the beneficiaries of the program of the church and the assessment.
General report of the Survey of the beneficiaries of the program of the church and / or the assessment in the diocese of New York. [New York?] 1940. 3 p. l., 60 p., 1 l. incl. fold. tables. 22 1/2 cm. Folded map laid in. [BX5918.N7A48] 258 ISBN 42-34395
1. Protestant Episcopal church in the U.S.A. New York (Diocese)—Finance. I. Title.

Protestant Episcopal church in the U.S.A. New York (Diocese) Sunday school commission.

PALMER, Margaretta.
Teachers' notes on the church catechism, illustrated and explained; part of the combined course on catechism, church year, and prayer book, or to be used separately as a distinct course, prepared for the New York Sunday school commission, inc., by Margaretta Palmer... Milwaukee, Wis., Pub. for the New York Sunday school commission, inc., by the Morehouse publishing co., 1918. xix, 175 p. illus. (incl. charts) 18 1/2 cm. $0.40 "Suggested books and supplies for teachers": p. xi-xv. Advertising matter: p. 167-173. [BX5049.P3] 19-2203
1. Protestant Episcopal church in the U.S.A. New York (Diocese) Sunday school commission. I. Title.

Protestant Episcopal Church in the U.S.A. — North Carolina.

DUNCAN, Norvin C
Pictorial history of the Episcopal Church in North Carolina, 1701-1964, by xxviii, 154 p. illus., facsim., ports. 29 cm.
1. Protestant Episcopal Church in the U.S.A. — North Carolina. I. Title. II. Title: History of the Episcopal Church in North Carolina, 1701-1964.

DUNCAN, Norvin C 283.756
Pictorial history of the Episcopal Church in North Carolina, 1701-1964, by Norvin C. Duncan. Asheville, N.C. [1965] xxviii, 154 p. illus., facsim., ports. 29 cm. [BX5917.N8D8] 65-3103
1. Protestant Episcopal Church in the U.S.A. — North Carolina. I. Title. II. Title: History of the Episcopal Church in North Carolina, 1701-1964.

PRESBYTERIAN church in the 266.
U. S. Presbytery of Mecklenburg.
Minutes of Mecklenburg presbytery. [Charlotte, N. C., Press of Presbyterian standard publishing company, v. 23 cm. [BX8958.M4A3] 29-4159
I. Title.

RALEIGH, N. C. Christ 283.756
church.
Centennial ceremonies held in Christ church parish, Raleigh, North Carolina, A. D. 1921, including historical addresses. Published by order of the vestry. Raleigh, Bynum printing company, 1922. 55 p. front., plates., ports. 23 cm. [BX5980.R3C5] 37-14660
1. Protestant Episcopal church in the U. S. A.—North Carolina. I. Cheshire, Joseph Blount, bp., 1850-1932. II. Haywood, Marshall De Lancey, 1871-1933. III. Ashe, Samuel A'Court, 1840- IV. Title.
Contents omitted

Protestant Episcopal church in the U.S.A. North Carolina (Diocese)

[MASON, Richard Sharp] 1795- 283.
1875.
A letter to the Bishop of North Carolina on the subject of his late pastoral on the Salisbury convention; by the chairman of the Committee on the state of the church. New-York, Stanford and Swords, 1850. 71 p. 19 1/2 cm. Signed: R. S. Mason. Addressed to Levi Silliman Ives, bishop of North Carolina. [BX5917.N8M3] 24-19628
1. Ives, Levi Silliman, 1797-1867. A pastoral letter to the clergy and laity of his diocese. 2. Protestant Episcopal church in the U.S.A. North Carolina (Diocese) I. Title.

ROOF, Wade Clark. 301.5'8
Communsity & commitment : religious plausibility in a liberal Protestant church / Wade Clark Roof. New York : Elsevier, c1978. x, 277 p. ; 24 cm. Includes bibliographical references and index. [BR526.R66] 77-16329 ISBN 0-444-99038-0 : 16.95
1. Protestant Episcopal Church in the U.S.A. North Carolina (Diocese) 2. Liberalism (Religion)—United States. 3. Commitment to the church. 4. Faith—Psychology. I. Title.

Protestant Episcopal Church in the U.S.A. — North Dakota.

WILKINS, Robert p. 283.784
God giveth the increase; the history of the Episcopal Church in North Dakota by Robert P. Wilkins and Wynona H. Wilkins. Fargo, North Dakota Institute for Regional Studies, 1959. xiv, 206 p. illus., ports., map (on lining paper) 24 cm. Biliography: p. 194-199. [BX5917;N9W5] 59-62934
1. Protestant Episcopal Church in the U.S.A. — North Dakota. I. Wilkins, Wynona H., joint author. II. Title.

Protestant Episcopal Church in the U.S.A.—Oklahoma.

THE Episcopal Church in Oklahoma. Oklahoma City, American Bond Print. Co., 1958. 158p. illus. 24cm. Issued also as thesis, University of Oklahoma.
1. Protestant Episcopal Church in the U.S.A.—Oklahoma. I. Botkin, Samuel Lee, 1921-

PROTESTANT Episcopal 283.766
Church in the U.S.A. Oklahoma (Diocese)
Journal of the annual meeting of the convention together with reports. [n.p.] v. 22 cm. [BX5918.O4A3] 52-29974
I. Title.

Protestant Episcopal Church in the United States Olympia (Diocese)—History

JESSETT, Thomas Edwin 283.79
1902 1902-
Pioneering God's country; the history of the Diocese of Olympia, 1853- 1953. Tacoma, Wash., Church Lantern Press, 1953. 54p. illus. 23cm. [BX5918.O5J3] 54-30473
1. Protestant Episcopal Church in the U.S. Olympia (Diocese)—Hist. I. Title.

Protestant Episcopal Church in the U.S.A.—Parties and movements.

CHORLEY, Edward Clowes, 283.73
1865-
... Men and movements in the American Episcopal church, by E. Clowes Chorley ... New York, C. Scribner's sons, 1946. ix, 501 p. 21 cm. (The Hale lectures) Bibliography: p. 445-474. [BX5925.C5] 46-3383
1. Protestant Episcopal church in the U.S.A.—Parties and movements. 2. Protestant Episcopal church in the U.S.A.—Hist. I. Title.

CHORLEY, Edward Clowes, 283.73
1865-1949
Men and movements in the American Episcopal Church. Hamden, Conn., Archon Books, 1961 [c.1946] ix, 501p. (Hale lectures) Bibl. 61-4971 10.00
1. Protestant Episcopal Church in the U.S.A.—Parties and movements. 2. Protestant Episcopal Church in the U. S. A.—Hist. I. Title. II. Series: Seabury-Western Theological Seminary, Evanston, Ill. The Hale lectures

Protestant Episcopal church in the U.S.A.—Pastoral letters and charges.

MEADE, William, bp., 1789- 252.
1862.
The law of proportion in the church of God: considered in a pastoral address of the Right Rev. William Meade, D.D., bishop of the Protestant Episcopal church in the diocese of Virginia, to the ministers and members thereof, in compliance with the 27th canon of the General convention. Alexandria, Printed at the Sou: churchman office, 1843. 56 p. 21 1/2 cm. [BX5937.M42L3] 24-16964
1. Protestant Episcopal church in the U.S.A.—Pastoral letters and charges. 2. Protestant Episcopal church in the U.S.A. Virginia (Diocese) I. Title.

Protestant Episcopal Church in the U.S.A. Pennsylvania (Diocese)

PROTESTANT Episcopal Church in
the U.S.A. Pennsylvania (Diocese)
Constitution and canons for the government of the Protestant Episcopal Church in the Diocese of Pennsylvania. Ordered printed by the Convention of the Diocese, held in May, A.D. 1959, together with the charter and by-laws of The church Foundation and the recommended form of articles of incorporation for parishes and the proposed by-laws for a church. Philadelphia, 1959. 167 p. 63-69472
I. Title.

TWELVES, J. Wesley, 283'.748
1890-
A history of the Diocese of Pennsylvania of the Protestant Episcopal Church in the U.S.A., 1784-1968, by J. Wesley Twelves. [Philadelphia, Diocese of Pennsylvania, 1969] vii, 270 p. illus., ports. 24 cm. Bibliography: p. 265. [BX5918.P4T9] 79-78366
1. Protestant Episcopal Church in the U.S.A. Pennsylvania (Diocese) I. Title.

Protestant Episcopal church in the U.S.A.—Periodicals

WASHINGTON diocese of the 283.753
Protestant Episcopal church. v. 1- Jan. 1933- [Washington, D.C., Department of publicity of the diocese of Washington, 1933- v. illus. (incl. ports.) 25 1/2 cm. 10 no. a year. "Published ... as the official organ of the diocese of Washington of the Protestant Episcopal church in the United States and under the auspices of the diocesan Department of publicity." [BX5918.W3A33] 36-22883
1. Protestant Episcopal church in the U.S.A.—Period. I. Protestant Episcopal church in the U.S.A. Washington (Diocese)

Protestant Episcopal Church in the U.S.A.—Prayer books and devotions.

[ADDISON, Charles Morris] 264.03
1856- comp.
A book of offices and prayers for priest and people; compiled by two presbyters of the church. New York, E.S. Gorham, 1899. 2 p. l., [iii]-iv. [2], 220 p. 16 1/2 cm. Compiled by Charles M. Addison and John W. Suter. "Third edition." [BX5947.B8A5 1899] 3-228
1. Protestant Episcopal church in the U.S.A.—Prayer-books and devotions. 2. Prayers. I. Protestant Episcopal church in the U.S.A. Liturgy and ritual. II. Suter, John Wallace 1859- joint author. III. Title.

DYER, Henry Page, 1853- 264.03
1917.
The divine service; being devotions and suggestions for those present at the blessed sacrament, whether receiving or not...17th thousand. Baltimore, Md., H.P. Dyer, 1899. 5 p. l., 2-121 p. illus. 12 1/2 cm. [BX5949.C5D91899] 90-3520
1. Protestant Episcopal church in the U.S.A.—Prayer-books and devotions. I. Title.

GAVITT, Loren N ed. 264.03
Saint Augustine's prayer book; a book of devotion for members of the Episcopal Church. Compiled and edited by Loren Gavitt and Archie Drake, [2d ed.] West Park, N. Y., Holy Cross Press [1949] xii, 367 p. front. 15 cm. [BV260.G3 1949] 50-4486
1. Protestant Episcopal Church in the U. S. A.—Prayer-books and devotions—English. I. Drake, Archie, joint ed. II. Title.

GIFFORD, Frank Dean, 1891- 264.03
The Christian way; a book of instructions and devotions for members of the Episcopal Church. New York, Morehouse-Barlow [c.1961] 136p. 61-12880 2.50; 1.50 pap.,
1. Protestant Episcopal Church in the U.S.A.—Prayer books and devotions. I. Title.

HAINES, Elwood Lindsay, 264.03
1893- comp.
A children's service book for the Sundays of the church year and special occasions, compiled by the Reverend Elwood L. Haines. New York, The Century co. [c1931] xiii, 294 p. 19 1/2 cm. "Services based on the Book of common prayer."--Foreword. [BX5873.H3] [(268.7)] 31-12714 1.25
1. Protestant Episcopal church in the U.S.A.—Prayer-books and devotions. 2. Sunday-schools—Exercises, recitations, etc. I. Title.

IVINS, Benjamin Franklin 264.03
Price, bp., 1884- comp.
A book of devotions for men and boys, by the Right Reverend Benjamin F. P. Ivins ... Milwaukee, Morehouse publishing co. [c1931] 3 p. l., 82 p. 14 cm. [BV4855.I 8] 31-8777
1. Protestant Episcopal church in the U. S. A.—Prayer-books and devotions. I. Title.

KNOWLES, Archibald 264.03
Campbell, 1865-
The practice of religion; a short manual of instructions and devotions ... by the Reverend Archibald Campbell Knowles ... Milwaukee, Wis., Morehouse publishing co., 1935. xiii p., 1 l., 256 p. front., plates. 14 cm. [BX5930.K63 1935] 35-4613
1. Protestant Episcopal church in the U. S. A.—Prayer-books and devotions—English. I. Title.

LOARING-CLARK, Ada, Mrs. 248
comp.
A book of devotions for women and girls, compiled by Ada Loaring Clark with a foreword by the Rt. Rev. Thomas Campbell Darst ... Milwaukee, Morehouse

publishing co. [c1931] xiv, 98 p. 14 cm. [BV4860L6] 31-9709
1. Protestant Episcopal church in the U. S. A.—Prayer-books and devotions. I. Title.

ODENHEIMER, William Henry, bp., 1817-1879, comp. 264.
The private prayer book; being a collection of devotions for daily and hourly use; compiled from Holy Scriptures and godly writings, by W. H. Odenheimer ... Philadelphia, H. Hooker; New York, Stanford and Swords, 1851. 9, [1], [13]-257 p. 16 1/2 cm. [BV245.O3] 45-34924
1. Protestant Episcopal church in the U.S.A—Prayer-books and devotions—English. I. Title.

PROTESTANT Episcopal church in the U. S. A. Book of common prayer. 264.
The daily service. Edition of 1923. The order for morning and for evening prayer, together with prayers and thanksgivings and the order for the use of thePsalter, as modified by the action of General convention in the years 1916, 1919, and 1922; authorized for use in churches, with footnotes showing the further changes proposed in morning and evening prayer by the General convention of 1922 but not finally adopted. Milwaukee, Morehouse printing co. [c1923] 2 p. l., 57 p., 1 l. 15 cm. [BX5944.D2 1923] 23-13759
I. Title.

ROBBINS, Howard Chandler, 1876- comp. 249
... Family devotions, compiled by Howard Chandler Robbins. New York, London, The Century co. [c1927] 5 p. l., 3-183 p. 18 cm. (The Century devotional library) [BV255.R6] 27-18914
1. Protestant Episcopal church in the U. S. A.—Prayer-books and devotions—England. I. Title.

STEVENS, William Bacon, Bp. 1815-1887. 264.
Home service: a manual intended for those who are occasionally hindered from attending the house of God. With sermons and a selection of hymns. Philadelphia, E. H. Butler, 1856. 347 p. 19 cm. [BX5940.S8] 48-42262
1. Protestant Episcopal Church in the U. S. A.—Prayer-books and devotions—English. I. Title.

Protestant Episcopal Church in the U.S.A.—Prayer books and devotions—English.

A manual of Catholic worship, based on the Book of common prayer. Milwaukee, Wis., Morehouse publishing co., 1934. viii p., 1 l., 120 p., 1 l. 13 1/2 cm. [BX5947.M3M3] 34-42134 264.03
1. Protestant Episcopal church in the U.S.A.—Prayer-books and devotions—English.

PREGNALL, William S., 1931- 264'.03
Laity and liturgy : a handbook for parish worship / William S. Pregnall. New York : Seabury Press, [1975] p. cm. "A Crossroad book." Includes bibliographical references. [BX5948.P73] 75-22482 ISBN 0-8164-2593-0 pbk. : 3.95
1. Protestant Episcopal Church in the U.S.A.—Prayer books and devotions—English. I. Title.

PROSTESTANT Episcopal church in the Confederate States of America. Virginia. Diocesan missionary society.
Prayer book for the camp. Diocesan missionary society Protestant Episcopal church in Va. Richmond, Macfarlane & Fergusson, 1863. 64 p. 14 cm. Mainly from the "Book of common prayer." "A prayer for the president of the Confederate States and all in civil authority": p. 12-13. p. [53]-64: Hymns. 17-8248
I. Title.

PROTESTANT Episcopal Church in the U.S.A. Committee on the Observance of the Bicentennial. 264'.03
This Nation under God : a book of aids to worship in the bicentennial year 1976 / prepared by the Committee on the Observance of the Bicentennial, in cooperation with the Standing Liturgical Commission ; and recommended for use by the presiding Bishop and the President of the House of Deputies of the General Convention of the Episcopal Church in the United States of America. New York : Seabury Press, c1976. 64 p. ; 21 cm. [BV135.A45P76 1976] 76-378 ISBN 0-8164-7809-0 : 1.00
1. Protestant Episcopal Church in the U.S.A.—Prayer-books and devotions—English. 2. American Revolution Bicentennial, 1776-1976—Prayer-books and devotions—English. 3. Worship programs. I. Protestant Episcopal Church in the U.S.A. Liturgical Commission. II. Title.

SUTER, John Wallace, 1890- 264.1
Prayers of the spirit, by John Wallace Suter ... New York and London, Harper & brothers, 1943. xii, 50 p., 1 l. 18 cm. "First edition." [BV245.S86] 44-35
1. Protestant Episcopal church in the U.S.A.—Prayer-books and devotions—English. 2. Prayers. I. Title.

Protestant Episcopal Church in the U.S.A.—Pueblo, Colo.

DANEY, Isabel Stevenson 283.78855
Pueblo's first cross: Episcopal church history. Denver, Big Mountain dist. Swallow c.1966 246p. illus., group ports. 23cm. Bibl. [BX5919.P8D3] 66-4044 4.50
1. Protestant Episcopal Church in the U.S.A.—Pueblo, Colo. 2. Pueblo, Colo.—Church history. I. Title.

Protestant Episcopal Church in the U.S.A.—Relations—Addresses, essays, lectures.

A Communion of communions : one Eucharistic fellowship : the Detroit report and papers of the triennial ecumenical study of the Episcopal Church, 1976-1979 / edited by J. RobertWright. New York : Seabury Press, 1979. xvii, 302 p. ; 23 cm. "A Crossroad book." Includes index. [BX5926.C65] 79-65999 ISBN 0-8164-2008-4 pbk. : 8.95 283'.73
1. Protestant Episcopal Church in the U.S.A.—Relations—Addresses, essays, lectures. I. Wright, John Robert, 1936-

KEAN. CHARLES DUELL, 1910- 280.1
The road to reunion. Greenwich, Conn., Seabury Press, 1958. 145p. 20cm. [BX5926.K4] 58-5507
1. Protestant Episcopal Church in the U. S. A.—Relations. 2. Ecumenical movement. I. Title.

[SEABURY, Samuel] bp., 1729-1796.
An address to the ministers and congregations of the Presbyterian and independent persuasions in the United States of America. By a member of the Episcopal church ... [New Haven, T. and S. Green] Printed in the year m,dcc,xc. 53 p. 17 cm. [BX5926.5.P65S4] 42-26732
1. Protestant Episcopal church in the U. S. A.—Relations—Presbyterian church in the U. S. A. 2. Presbyterian church in the U. S. A.—Relations—Protestant Episcopal church in the U. S. A. 3. Protestant Episcopal church in the U. S. A.—Relations—Congregational churches in the U. S. 4. Congregational churches in the U. S.—Relations—Protestant Episcopal church in the U. S. A. I. Title.

Protestant Episcopal Church in the U.S.A.—Relations—Church of England.

HERKLOTS, Hugh Gerard Gibson, 1903- 283
The Church of England and the American Episcopal Church, from the first voyages of discovery to the first Lambeth Conference. London. Mowbray; New York, Morehouse [c.] 1966. xiii, 183p. illus. 22cm. Bibl. [BX5927.8.H4] 66-70108 6.00 bds.,
1. Protestant Episcopal Church in the U.S.A.—Relations—Church of England. 2. Church of England—Relations—Protestant Episcopal Church in the U.S.A. I. Title.

HERKLOTS, Hugh Gerard Gibson, 1903- 283
The Church of England and the American Episcopal Church, from the first voyages of discovery to the first Lambeth Conferencey [by] H. G. G. Herklots. London, Mowbray; New York, Morehouse-Barlow, 1966. xiii, 183 p. illus. 22 cm. (B66-5892) Bibliographical footnotes. [BX5927.8.H4] 66-70108
1. Protestant Episcopal Church in the U.S.A. — Relations — Church of England. 2. Church of England — Relations — protestant Episcopal Church in the U.S.A. I. Title.

Protestant Episcopal church in the U.S.A.—Rhode Island.

UPDIKE, Wilkins, 1784-1867. 726.
A history of the Episcopal church in Narragansett, Rhode Island, including a history of other Episcopla churches in the state, by Wilkins Updike. With a transcript of the Narragansett parish register, from 1718 to 1774; an appendix containing a reprint of a work entitled: America dissected by the Rev. James MacSparran, D.D., and copies of other old papers; together with notes containing genealogical and biographical accounts of distinguished men, families, &c. 2d ed., newly edited, enlarged, and corrected by the Reverend Daniel Goodwin...Illustrated by fifty portraits after old paintings; together with six views of historic localities, and several facsimiles. Boston, D. B. Updike, 1907. 3 v. plates, ports., facsims. (part fold.; incl. plans) 23 cm. [BX5980.N2P3] 8-266
1. Protestant Episcopal church in the U.S.A.—Rhode Island. 2. Narragansett, R.I.—Hist. 3. Rhode Island—Hist. I. MacSparran, James, d. 1757. II. Goodwin, Daniel, 1835-1922, ed. III. Title.

Protestant Episcopal Church in the U.S.A.—Sermons.

BEDELL, Gregory Townsend, 1793-1834. 252.03
Sermons, by Rev. Gregory T. Bedell ... With a biographical sketch of the author, by Stephen H. Tyng ... Philadelphia, W. Stavely--J.C. Pechin, 1835. 2 v, front. (port.) 24 1/2 cm. Vol. II contains sermons on the epistles to the seven churches of Asia. [BX5937.B43S4] 34-23416
1. Protestant Episcopal church in the U.S.A.—Sermons. 2. Sermons, American. 3. Bible, N.T. Revelation II-III—Sermons. I. Tyng, Stephen Higginson, 1800-1885. II. Title.

BOWIE, Walter Russell, 1882- 232.9
Remembering Christ [by] Walter Russell Bowie. New York, Cincinnati [etc.] The Abingdon press [c1940] 183 p. 20 cm. [BX5937.B6R4] 40-5929
1. Protestant Episcopal church in the U. S. A.—Sermons. 2. Sermons, American. I. Title.

BREWER, Darius Richmond, 1802-1881. 25203
The rector's offering. Selections from sermons, by the Rev. D.R. Brewer. New York A. D. F. Randolph 1860 79 p. 17 cm. [BX5937.B77R4] 35-34767
1. Protestant Episcopal church in the U.S.A.—Sermons 2. Sermons, American (Selections: Extracts, etc.) I. Title.

BROOKLYN. St. Ann's church (Protestant Episcopal) 283.74723
Inaugural sermons, preached at the opening services of St. Ann's on the heights. Brooklyn, N.Y. Published by the vestry. Brooklyn, Printed by H. M. Gardner, jr., 1869. 87 p. 23 1/2cm. [BX5980.B8S3 1869a] 39-30713
1. Protestant Episcopal church in the U.S.A.—Sermons. 2. Sermons, American. I. McIlvaine, Charles Pettit, bp., 1799-1878. II. Littlejohn, Abram Newkirk, bp., 1824-1901. III. Schenck, Noah Hunt, 1825-1885. IV. Title.

BROOKS, Phillips, bp., 1835-1893. 252.
Addresses, [by] Phillips Brooks; illustrated by Moore Smith. New York, Frederick A. Stokes company [c1899] 3 p. l., 180 p. front., 2 pl., port. 11 x 6 1/2 cm. [BX5845.B7A4 1899] 99-4790
1. Lincoln, Abraham, pres. U.S.—Addresses, sermons, etc. 2. Protestant Episcopal church in the U.S.A.—Sermons. 3. Sermons, American. I. Title.
Contents omitted

BROOKS, Phillips bp., 1835-1893. 252.03
Addresses by the Right Reverend Phillips Brooks ... Boston, J. Knight company, 1894. 165 p. front., pl., ports. 18 cm. [BX5845.B7A4 1894] 37-16306
1. Lincoln, Abraham,pres. U.S.—Addresses, sermons, etc. 2. Protestant Episcopal church in the U.S.A.—Sermons. 3. Sermons, American. I. Title.
Contents omitted

BROOKS, Phillips, bp. 1835-1893. 252.03
The candle of the Lord, and other sermons, by the Rev. Phillips Brooks ... Second series. New York E. P. Dutton and company, 1903. vii 370 p. 19 1/2 cm. [BX5845.B7S42 1903] 4-10407
1. Protestant Episcopal church in the U.S.A.—Sermons. 2. Sermons, American. I. Title.

BROOKS, Phillips, bp., 1835-1893. 252.03
The law of growth and other sermons, by the Rt. Rev. Phillips Brooks ... 9th series. New York, E. P. Dutton and company, 1902. v, 381 p. 20 cm. [BX5845.B7S49] 4-10408
1. Protestant Episcopal church in the U.S.A.—Sermons. 2. Sermons, American. I. Title.

BROOKS, Phillips, Bp., 1835-1893.tAddresses. With introd. by Julius H. Ward 252.
Prefect freedom. Boston, C. E. Brown [c1893] 204 p. ports. 16 cm. On cover: Prefect freedom. [BX5845.B7A4 1893a] 52-52837
1. Protestant Episcopal Church in the U. S. A—Sermons. 2. Sermons, American. 3. Lincoln, Abraham, Press. U. S.—Addresses, sermons, etc. I. Title.

BROOKS, Phillips, Bp., 1835-1893. 252.03'73
Selected sermons, edited and with an introd. by William Scarlett. Freeport, N.Y., Books for Libraries Press [1971, c1949] 377 p. port. 23 cm. (Essay index reprint series) [BX5937.B83S39 1971] 79-142610 ISBN 0-8369-2146-1
1. Protestant Episcopal Church in the U.S.A.—Sermons. 2. Sermons, American.

CHAPMAN, George Thomas, 1786-1872. 283.
Sermons, upon the ministry, worship, and doctrines of the Protestant Episcopal church. By G. T. Chapman ... 2d ed. Burlington [Vt.] C. Goodrich, 1832. 324 p. 20 cm. [BX5930.C4 1832] 6-4148
I. Title.

COBURN, John B. 248'.48'3
The hope of glory : exploring the mystery of Christ in you / John B. Coburn. New York : Seabury Press, c1976. p. cm. "A Crossroad book." [BX5937.C63H66] 75-37751 ISBN 0-8164-1208-1 : 7.95. ISBN 0-8164-2117-X pbk. : 3.95
1. Protestant Episcopal Church in the U.S.A.—Sermons. 2. Sermons, American. I. Title.

CRAVNER, William Charles.
The faith magnificent. [1st ed.] New York, Vantage Press [c1961] 93 p. 21 cm. 68-84386
1. Protestant Episcopal Church in the U.S.A.—Sermons. 2. Sermons, American. I. Title.

DIX, Morgan, 1827-1908. 232.958
Blessing and ban from the cross of Christ; meditations on the seven words on the cross given in Trinity church, New York, on Good Friday, A. D. 1894, by Morgan Dix ... New York, J. Pott & company, 1898. [84] p. 20 cm. [BT455.D6] 37-7787
1. Jesus Christ—Seven last words. 2. Protestant Episcopal church in the U. S. A.—Sermons. 3. Sermons, American. I. Title.

DOUGLAS, George William, 1850-1926. 252.
Christ's challenge to man's spirit in this world crisis; advent addresses at the Cathedral of St. John the Divine, New York, by George William Douglas ... published by request of the dean and others. New York [etc.] Longmans, Green and co., 1918. x p., 1 l., 54, [4] p. 19 1/2 cm. [BX5937.D7C5] 18-6812

1. Protestant Episcopal church in the U.S.A.—Sermons. 2. Sermons, American. I. Title.

DOUGLASS, William, of Philadelphia.
Sermons preached in the African Protestant Episcopal church of St. Thomas, Philadelphia. By William Douglass, rector. Philadelphia, King & Baird, 1854- 251 p. 19 1/2 cm. 2-16348
I. Title.

EDWARDS, Otis Carl, 1928- 251'.08
The living and active word : one way to preach from the Bible today / by O. C. Edwards, Jr. New York : Seabury Press, [1975] 178 p. ; 22 cm. "A Crossroad book." Bibliography: p. [173]-178. [BS534.5.E38] 74-30038 ISBN 0-8164-0265-5 : 6.95
1. Protestant Episcopal Church in the U.S.A.—Sermons. 2. Bible—Homiletical use. 3. Preaching. 4. Sermons, American. I. Title.

FERRIS, Theodore Parker, 1908- 252'.0373
This is the day : selected sermons / Theodore Parker Ferris. 2d ed. Dublin, N.H. : Yankee, c1980. 368 p. : port. ; 23 cm. [BX5937.F42T5 1980] 19 76-39640 ISBN 0-911658-16-5 (pbk.) : 10.00
1. Protestant Episcopal Church in the U.S.A.—Sermons. 2. Sermons, American. I. Title.

FISKE, Charles, bp., 1868- 252.03
From skepticism to faith, by Charles Fiske ... New York and London, Harper & brothers, 1934. ix, 124 p. 20 cm. "First edition." [BX5937.F54F7] 34-17344
1. Protestant Episcopal church in the U.S.A.—Sermons. 2. Sermons, American. I. Title.

FRANKS, Vincent Chesley, 1891- 252.03
Top of the mount; sermons for the Christian year, by Vincent C. Franks ... New York, Morehouse-Gorham co., 1946. ix, 182 p. 22 1/2 cm. [BX5937.F65T6] 47-51
1. Protestant Episcopal church in the U.S.A.—Sermons. 2. Sermons, American. I. Title.

GIFFORD, Frank Dean, 1891- 252.03
Traveling the King's highway, a book of sermons especially suitable for lay readers, by Frank Dean Gifford ... Foreword by the Right Reverend Oliver James Hart ... bishop of Pennsylvania. New York, Morehouse-Gorham co., 1944. xii p., 2 l., 190 p. 20 1/2 cm. Bibliographical foot-notes. [BX5937.G5T7] 44-14954
1. Protestant Episcopal church in the U.S.A.—Sermons. 2. Sermons, American. I. Title.

GREEN, Rachel W. (Cope) Mrs. d.1859. 922
Grace filling an earthen vessel with glory; or, Letters of Rachel W. Green ... Edited by W. R. Carroll ... Philadelphia, Protestant Episcopal book society [1860] xii p., 1 l., 15-190 p., 1 l. 16 cm. [BR1725.G85A4] 37-31953
I. Carroll, William R., ed. II. Protestant Episcopal book society. III. Title.

GRISWOLD, Asa. 252.
Sermons, by Asa Griswold ... Chicago, C. Scott, printer, 1856. vi p., 1 l., [7]-365 p. 19 cm. [BX5937.G865S4] 45-29869
1. Protestant Episcopal church in the U.S.A.—Sermons. 2. Sermons. American. I. Title.

HINES, John Elbridge, Bp., 1910- 231'.7
Thy kingdom come, by John E. Hines. [1st ed.] New York, Morehouse-Barlow, 1967. 123 p. 21 cm. [BX5937.H5T5] 67-12971
1. Protestant Episcopal Church in the U.S.A.—Sermons. 2. Sermons, American. 3. Kingdom of God—Sermons. I. Title.

HODGES, George, 1856-1919. 252.
The battles of peace, by George Hodges ... New York, T. Whittaker [c1899] ix, 273 p. 19 cm. Second edition. "All of these sermons have been preached in St. John's memorial chapel of the Episcopal theological school."--Pref. [BX5937.H6B3 1899] 7-8272
1. Protestant Episcopal church in the U.S.A.—Sermons. 2. Sermons, American. I. Title.

JENKINS, Holt M. 252'.53
A haunted house and other sermons for the family service, by Holt M. Jenkins. New York, Morehouse-Barlow Co. [1967] 128 p. 21 cm. [BV4315.J47] 67-12970
1. Protestant Episcopal Church in the U.S.A.—Sermons. 2. Children's sermons. 3. Sermons, American. I. Title.

JESUS, dollars and sense 248'.6
: a practical and effective stewardship guide for clergy and lay leaders / edited by Oscar C. Carr, Jr. ; foreword by Furman C. Stough. New York : Seabury Press, c1976. p. cm. "A Crossroad book." [BV772.J45] 76-14362 ISBN 0-8164-2132-3 pbk. : 3.95
1. Protestant Episcopal Church in the U.S.A.—Sermons. 2. Stewardship, Christian—Addresses, essays, lectures. 3. Stewardship, Christian—Sermons. 4. Sermons, American.

JOHNSON, John Howard, 1897- 252.03
Harlem, The war, and other addresses, by John Howard Johnson ... New York, W. Malliet and company, 1942. 6 p. l., 163 p. front. (port.) 22 cm. "First edition." [BX5937.J4H3] 42-22629
1. Protestant Episcopal church in the U.S.A.—Sermons. 2. Sermons, American. I. Title.

LONSDALE, Herman Lilienthal, 1858- 232.96
Some actors in Our Lord's passion, by Rev. Hermann Lilienthal ... with an introduction by the Rt. Rev. Thomas March Clark ... New York, T. Whittaker, 1903. xii, 157 p. 19 cm. "A course of sermons preached in Lent, 1902, in Christ church, Hartford, Conn."--Pref. [Name originally: Herman Lilienthal] [BT430.L6] 3-6444
1. Jesus Christ—Passion—Sermons. 2. Protestant Episcopal church in the U. S. A.—Sermons. 3. Sermons, American. I. Title.

LYONS, James Gilborne, d.1868. 208.
Selections from the sermons and poems of the late Rev. James Gilbourne Lyons, LL.D. With a commemorative discourse by the Rt. Rev. the Bishop of New Jersey. Philadelphia, J.B. Lippincott co., 1868. lviii, 227 p. front. (port.) 2 pl. 22 cm. Introduction signed: L. H. L. [i.e. Mrs. L. H. Lyons] [BX5037.L98S4] 8-870
1. Protestant Episcopal church in the U.S.A.—Sermons. 2. Sermons, American. I. Odenhelmer, William Henry, bp., 1817-1879. II. Lyons, Mrs. L. H., comp. III. Title.

MCCONNELL, Samuel David, 1845-1939. 252.
Sons of God; sermons by the Rev. S. D. McConnell... New York, T. Whittaker, 1891. v, 259 p. 19 cm. [BX5937.M25S6] 14-2113
1. Protestant Episcopal church in the U.S.A.—Sermons. 2. Sermons, American. I. Title.

MACDONALD, David Ferguson, 1835-1894. 222.
The moral law: a series of practical sermons on the Decalogue; or, The ten commandments; preached in Emmanuel church, Coloma, California, by the Rev. David F. Macdonald, A.M., of the Protestant Episcopal church. Sacramento, J. Anthony & co., printers, 1858. 2 p. l., 152 p. 23 1/2 cm. [BV4655.M35] 22-11424
I. Title.

MANNING, William Thomas, bp., 1866- 252.03
Be strong in the Lord; sermons and addresses on various occasions, by Willliam T. Manning ... New York, Morehouse-Gorham co., 1947. x p., 1 l., 196 p. 19 cm. [BX5937.M289B4] 47-20026
1. Protestant Episcopal church in the U.S.A.—Sermons. 2. Sermons, American. I. Title.

MILLER, Robert Bryce, 1877-1918. 243
"He yet speaketh"; a selection of sermons preached by the Rev. Robert Bryce Miller, D.D., ed. by the Rev. John S. Duncan, D.D.; foreword by the Rev. John McNaugher ... New York, Chicago [etc.] Fleming H. Revell company [c1920] 163 p. front. (port.) 19 1/2 cm. [BX9178.M56H4] 21-3692
I. Duncan, John S., ed. II. Title.

MITCHELL, Charles Baird, 1875-1938. 252.03
The things that cannot die, and other addresses and writings by Charles Baird Mitchell...with foreword by the Hon. John W. Davis. Baltimore, Md., The Remington, Putnam book co., 1939. x p., 2 l., [3]-643, [1] p. front. (port.) 24 1/2 cm. [BX5937.M56T5] 39-21768
1. Protestant Episcopal church in the U.S.A.—Sermon. 2. Sermons, American. I. Davis, John William, 1873- ed. II. Title.

MORRIS, Frederick M. 252.03
God in action, by Frederick M. Morris. Grand Rapids, W. B. Eerdmans Pub. Co. [1968] 77 p. 21 cm. [BX5937.M65G59] 68-12789
1. Protestant Episcopal Church in the U.S.A.—Sermons. 2. Sermons, American. I. Title.

MORRIS, Frederick M 252.03
God's way and ours. [1st ed.] New York, Exposition Press [1952] 124 p. 21 cm. [BX5937.M65G6] 52-12344
1. Protestant Episcopal Church in the U.S.A. — Sermons. 2. Sermons, American. I. Title.

NEVILLE, Edmund. 252.
Gleanings among the wheat sheaves; or, Sermons preached at Trinity church. Newark, N. J., by the Rev. Edmund Neville ... Newark, N.J., S. C. Atkinson, printer, 1860. [254] p. 21 1/2 cm. Each sermon separately paged. [BX5937.N36G6] 46-35349
1. Protestant Episcopal church in the U.S.A.—Sermons. 2. Sermons, American. I. Title.

NORWOOD, Robert Winkworth, 1874-1932. 252.03
Increasing Christhood by Robert Norwood ... with a tribute of the author by Walter Russell Bowie ... Memorial ed. New York, London, C. Scribner's sons, 1932. ixxlv, 232 p. front. (port.) 22 cm. "An extension of The steep ascent, and of his glorious body ... noontide meditations at St. Bartholomews--Foreword. [BX5937.N6S72] 33-4367
1. Protestant Episcopal church in the U.S.A.—Sermons. 2. Sermons, American. I. Title.

PACKARD, A. Appleton 252.03
An open door; sermons by A. Appleton Packard. Boston, Christopher Pub. House [1966] 328p. 20cm. Bibl. [BX5937.P26O6] 66-19216 4.00; 2.50 pap.,
1. Protestant Episcopal Church in the U.S.A.—Sermons. 2. Sermons, American. I. Title.

PAUL, James Albert, 1905-1957. 252.03
Faith is the victory; a selection of sermons. Edited by Horace W.B. Donegan. New York, Morehouse-Barlow Co., 1959. 143p. 16cm. [BX5937.P36F3] 59-14477
1. Protestant Episcopal Church in the U.S.A.—Sermons. 2. Sermons, American. I. Title.

SAYRE, Francis B. 252'.62
To stand in the cross : a book of meditations / Francis B. Sayre, Jr. ; with prayers by Jeffrey Cave ; ill. by Babs Gaillard. New York : Seabury Press, 1978. 80 p. : ill. ; 21 cm. "A Crossroad book." [BV95.S29] 77-13259 ISBN 0-8164-0380-5 : 5.95
1. Protestant Episcopal Church in the U.S.A.—Sermons. 2. Good Friday sermons. 3. Sermons, American. I. Cave, Jeffrey, joint author. II. Title.

SERMONS preached before the 252.
Bishop Seabury association of Brown university, Providence, R.I.; with a preface by the Rev. Henry Waterman ... New York, The Association, 1868. 68 p. 28 1/2 cm. [BX5937.A1S42] 45-41233
1. Protestant Episcopal church in the U.S.A.—Sermons. 2. Sermons, American. I. Dix, Morgan, 1827-1908. II. Ewer, Ferdinand Cartwright, 1826-1883. III. Brown university. Bishop. Seabury association.
Contents omitted.

SHOEMAKER, Samuel Moor, 1893- 252.03
Christ and this crisis, by Samuel M. Shoemaker ... New York, London [etc.] Fleming H. Revell company [1943] 151 p. 19 cm. [BX5937.S45C45] 43-14429
1. Protestant Episcopal church in the U.S.A.—Sermons. 2. Sermons, American. I. Title.

SHOEMAKER, Samuel Moor, 1893- 252.03
The gospel according to you, and other sermons, by Samuel M. Shoemaker ... New York [etc.] Fleming H. Revell company [c1934] 192 p. 19 1/2 cm. "These sermons were preached in Calvary church, New York, most of them during the winter of 1933-34."--Pref. [BX5937.S45G6] 35-1384
1. Protestant Episcopal church in the U.S.A.—Sermons. 2. Sermons, American 3. Oxford group. I. New York. Calvary church (Protestant Episcopal) II. Title.

SHOEMAKER, Samuel Moor, 1893- 232.08
National awakening, by Samuel M. Shoemaker. New York and London, Harper & brothers, 1936. 5 p. l., 108 p. 19 cm. "First edition." [BX5937.S45N3] 36-35590
1. Protestant Episcopal church in the U.S.A.—Sermons. 2. Sermons, American. 3. Oxford group. I. Title.

SPALDING, John Franklin, bp., 1818-1902. 232
Jesus Christ the proof of Christianity ... by John F. Spalding ... Milwaukee, Wis., The Young churchman co., 1891. 220 p. 20 cm. [BT201.S75] 37-13892
1. Jesus Christ—Person and offices. 2. Protestant Episcopal church in the U.S.A.—Sermons. 3. Sermons, American. I. Title. II. Title: The proof of Christianity.

STEWART, Alexander Doig. 252.03
The shock of revelation [by] Alexander Stewart. New York, Seabury Press [1967] vii, 152 p. 22 cm. Based on a series of television appearances.—Cf. dust jacket. Bibliographical references included in "Notes" (p. 149-152) [BX5937.S842S5] 67-11469
1. Protestant Episcopal Church in the U.S.A.—Sermons. 2. Sermons, American. I. Title.

STURGES, Philemon Fowler, 1875- 252.03
Our common loyalty, by Philemon F. Sturges. New York and London, Harper & brothers, 1936. 5 p. l., 100 p. 19 cm. "First edition." Good Friday meditations on the seven last words of Jesus: p. 68-100. [BX5967.S89O8] 36-7422
1. Jesus Christ—Seven last words. 2. Protestant Episcopal church in the U.S.A.—Sermons. 3. Sermons, American. I. Title.

SUTTON, Joseph Wilson, 1881- 232.958
The cross, our hope; addresses on the seven words from the cross by the Reverend J. Wilson Sutton ... New York, Morehouse-Gorham co., 1940. 89 p., 1 l. 21 cm. [BT455.S82] 40-4921
1. Jesus Christ—Seven last words. 2. Protestant Episcopal church in the U.S.A.—Sermons. 3. Sermons, American. I. Title.

TYNG, Stephen Higginson, 1800-1885. 283
The Israel of God By Stephen H. Tyng ... 4th thousand. Enl. New York, R. Carter & brothers, 1849. vi p., 1 l., 9-387 p. front. (port.) 23 1/2 cm. [BX5937.T85 I 75] 42-49722
1. Protestant Episcopal church in the U.S.A.—Sermons. 2. Sermons, American. I. Title.

URBANO, Paul. 232.9'63
The marks of the nails. St. Paul, Minn., Yellow Bird Division, Economic Information, inc. [1973] vii, 111 p. 22 cm. Includes bibliographical references. [BX5937.U7M37] 73-90039 ISBN 0-913514-04-7 3.50
1. Protestant Episcopal Church in the U.S.A.—Sermons. 2. Jesus Christ—Seven

last words—Sermons. 3. Sermons, American. I. Title.

WELLES, Edward Randolph, bp., 1830-1888. 252.
Sermons and addresses by the late Rt. Rev. Edward Randolph Welles ... With portraits and memoirs. Edited by his son, the Rev. Edward Sprague Welles ... Milwaukee, Wis., The Young churchman co., 1889. lxxxiv, 237 p. front. (port.) 20 cm. [BX5937.W4S4] 5-28791
1. Protestant Episcopal church in the U.S.A.—Sermons. 2. Sermons, American. I. Welles, Edward Sprague, ed. II. Title.

WHITTINGHAM, William Rollinson, bp., 1805-1879. 252.
Fifteen sermons by William Rollinson Whittingham, fourth bishop of Maryland ... New York, D. Appleton and company, 1880. 312 p. 19 1/2 cm. [BX5937.W46F5] 45-53085
1. Protestant Episcopal church in the U.S.A.—Sermons. 2. Sermons, American. I. Title.

WHITTLE, Arthur Ernest, 1887- 252.03
The Christ of the dawn, by Rev. Arthur Ernest Whittle. Boston, The Christopher publishing house [c1935] xi, 13-134 p. 19 1/2 cm. [BX5937.W463C5] 35-21556
1. Protestant Episcopal church in the U.S.A.—Sermons. 2. Sermons, American. I. Title.

WILLIAMS, Granville Mercer, 1889- 252'.03'3
Joy in the Lord [by] Granville M. Williams. Wakefield, Mass., Parameter Press [1972] 123 p. 24 cm. "Retreat addresses given at various times to the Sisters of the Society of St. Margaret." [BX5937.W475J69] 71-189764 ISBN 0-88203-001-9 2.00
1. Protestant Episcopal Church in the U.S.A.—Sermons. 2. Sermons, American. I. Title.

WILSON, Frank Elmer, bp., 1885- 252.03
The promises of Christ, and other sermons, by the Rt. Rev. Frank E. Wilson ... New York, Morehouse-Gorham co., 1944. xii p., 1 l., 174 p. 20 cm. [BX5937.W529P7] 44-1013
1. Protestant Episcopal church in the U.S.A.—Sermons. 2. Sermons, American. I. Title.

WORCESTER, Elwood, 1862-1940. 252.
The allies of religion, by Elwood Worcester. Boston, Mass., Marshall Jones company [1929] xix, 322 p. front. (port.) pl. 21 cm. Sermons. "First edition." [BX5937.W56A5] 29-20665
1. Protestant Episcopal church in the U.S.A.—Sermons. 2. Sermons, American. I. Title.

Protestant Episcopal Church in the U.S.A.—South Carolina.

DALCHO, Frederick, 1770?-1836. 283'.757
An historical account of the Protestant Episcopal Church in South-Carolina. New York, Arno Press, 1972. vii, 613 p. 23 cm. (Religion in America, series II) Reprint of the 1820 ed. [BX5917.S6D2 1972] 71-38445 ISBN 0-405-04064-4
1. Protestant Episcopal Church in the U.S.A.—South Carolina. 2. South Carolina—History—Colonial period, ca. 1600-1775. I. Title.

DALCHO, Frederick, 1770?-1836. 283.
An historical account of the Protestant Episcopal church in South Carolina, from the first settlement of the province, to the war of the revolution; with notices of the present state of the church in each parish; and some account of the early civil history of Carolina, never before published. To which are added: the laws relating to religious worship; the journals and rules of the convention of South-Carolina; the constitution and canons of the Protestant Episcopal church, and the course of ecclesiastical studies ... By Frederick Dalcho ... Charleston, Published by E. Thayer, at his theological book-store, Broad Stree. Arch'd. E. Miller, Printer, 120 Broad-street 1820. vii, [1], 613, [3] p. 22 cm. [BX5917.S6D2] 8-26486
1. Protestant Episcopal church in the U. S. A.—South Carolina. 2. South Carolina—Hist.—Colonial period. I. Title.

PROTESTANT Episcopal church in the U. S. A. Church congress, Charleston, S. C., 1930. 283
Charleston papers; a record of the Church congress in the United States on its fifty-sixth anniversary, A. D. mcmxxx; with and introduction by the general secretary, Harold Adye Prichard. New York, R. R. Smith, inc., 1930. x p., 1 l., 220 p. 20 cm. [BX5820.A6 1930] 30-31386
I. Title.
Contents omitted.

Protestant Episcopal Church in the U.S.A. — South Carolina — History

THOMAS, Albert Sidney, 1873-
A historical account of the Protestant Episcopal Church in South Carolina, 1820-1957; being a continuation of Dalcho's account, 1670-1820. [Columbia, c1957] x, 879 p. plates, map (on lining papers) 24 cm. A58
1. Protestant Episcopal Church in the U.S.A. — South Carolina — Hist. I. Title.

Protestant Episcopal Church in the U.S.A.—South Carolina—History—Chronology.

†CLARKE, Philip G. 283'.757
Anglicanism in South Carolina, 1660-1976 : a chronological history of dates and events in the Church of England and the Episcopal Church in South Carolina / compiled by Philip G. Clarke, Jr. Easley, S.C. : Southern Historical Press, c1976. 156 p. ; 24 cm. Bibliography: p. 154-155. [BX5917.5.S6C56] 76-23346 ISBN 0-89308-042-X : 10.00
1. Protestant Episcopal Church in the U.S.A.—South Carolina—History—Chronology. 2. Church of England in South Carolina—History—Chronology. I. Title.

Protestant Episcopal Church in the U.S.A.—South Dakota.

SNEVE, Virginia Driving Hawk. 283'.783
That they may have life : the Episcopal Church in South Dakota, 1859-1976 / Virginia Driving Hawk Sneve. New York : Seabury Press, c1977. xiv, 224 p. : ill. ; 23 cm. Includes index. Bibliography: p. 218-220. [BX5917.5.S8S65] 76-55342 ISBN 0-8164-2141-2 : 5.95
1. Protestant Episcopal Church in the U.S.A.—South Dakota. 2. South Dakota—Church history. I. Title.

Protestant Episcopal Church in the U.S.A. South Florida (Diocese)

CUSHMAN, Joseph D. 283'.759'3
The sound of bells : the Episcopal Church in South Florida, 1892-1969 / Joseph D. Cushman, Jr. Gainesville : University Presses of Florida, 1976. xiv, 378 p., [10] leaves of plates : ill. ; 24 cm. Continues A goodly heritage: The Episcopal Church in Florida, 1821-1892. "A University of Florida book." Includes index. Bibliography: p. 359-367. [BX5918.S65C87] 75-30946 ISBN 0-8130-0518-3 : 15.00
1. Protestant Episcopal Church in the U.S.A. South Florida (Diocese) 2. Protestant Episcopal Church in the U.S.A.—Florida. 3. Florida—Church history. I. Title.

Protestant Episcopal church in the U.S.A. Southern Ohio (Diocese)

VINCENT, Boyd, bp., 1845- 283.771
Recollections of the diocese of Southern Ohio, by Boyd Vincent ... Milwaukee, Wis., Morehouse publishing co. London, A. R. Mowbray & co., 1934. viii p., 1 l., 189, [1] p. 19 cm. [BX5918.S9V5] 34-14510
1. Protestant Episcopal church in the U.S.A. Southern Ohio (Diocese) I. Title.

Protestant Episcopal Church in the U.S.A. Southern Virginia (Diocese)

COCKE, Charles Francis 283.755
Parish lines, Diocese of Southern Virginia. Richmond, Va. State Lib., 1964. 287p. col. maps. 24cm. Bibl. A64 5.00 pap.,
1. Protestant Episcopal Church in the U.S.A. Southern Virginia (Diocese) 2. Parishes—Virginia. I. Title.

PROTESTANT Episcopal Church in the U. S. A. Southwestern Virginia (Diocese) 283.755
Journal of the annual council. [Roanoke?] v. 23cm. [BX5918.S922A3] 53-16396
I. Title.

Protestant Episcopal Church in the U.S.A. Springfield (Diocese)

FORBES, John Van Gelder. 283'.773
The Springfield mitre; a history of the politics and consequences of an Episcopal election in Illinois, 1962-1967 [by] John Forbes. Pelham, N.Y., American Church Publications [1971] xii, 263 p. 22 cm. Bibliography: p. 249-263. [BX5918.S93F67] 72-27489 2.50
1. Protestant Episcopal Church in the U.S.A. Springfield (Diocese) I. Title.

Protestant Episcopal Church in the U.S.A.—Tennessee.

DAVIES-RODGERS, Ellen 283.768
The romance of the Episcopal Church in west Tennessee, 1832-1964. Photos., reproductions by Nadia Price. Brunswick, Tenn., Plantation Pr. [1964] 232p. illus., facsims., ports. 24cm. Bibl. 64-20656 8.00
1. Protestant Episcopal Church in the U. S. A.—Tennessee. 2. Protestant Episcopal Church in the U. S. A.—Tennessee (Diocese) I. Title.

NASHVILLE. Christ church. 283
Christ church, Nashville, 1829-1929 ... Nashville, Tenn., Marshall & Bruce co. [c1929] 297 p. front., plates, ports., map, facsim. 24 cm. "History publication committee: Mrs. Anne Rankin. editor-in-chief." [BX5960.N25C5] 29-11490
1. Protestant Episcopal church in the U. S. A.—Tennessee. 2. Tennessee—Church history. I. Rankin, Anne, Mrs. ed. II. Title.

RODGERS, Ellen (Davies) 283.768
The romance of the Episcopal Church in west Tennessee, 1832-1964 by Ellen Davies-Rodgers. With illus., photos. and reproductions by Nadia Price. Brunswick, Tenn., Plantation Press [1964] 232 p. illus., facsims., ports. 24 cm. Bibliographical footnotes. [BX5918.T2R6] 64-20656
1. Protestant Episcopal Church in the U. S. A.—Tennessee. 2. Protestant Episcopal Church in the U. S. A. Tennessee (Diocese) I. Title.

RODGERS, Ellen (Davies) 283.768
The romance of the Episcopal Church in west Tennessee, 1832-1964. Photos, and reproductions by Nadia Price. Brunswick, Tenn., Plantation Press [1964] 232 p. illus., facsims., ports. 24 cm. Bibliographical footnotes. [BX5917.T2D3] 64-20656
1. Protestant Episcopal Church in the U.S.A.—Tennessee. 2. Protestant Episcopal Church in the U.S.A.—Tennessee (Diocese) I. Title.

Protestant Episcopal Church in the U.S.A. — Texas.

BROWN, Lawrence L 283.764
The Episcopal Church in Texas, 1838-1874; from its foundation to the division of the diocese Austin, Tex., Church Historical Society, 1963. 271 p. illus., ports., maps, facsim, 24 cm. [BX5917.T4B7] 63-19457
1. Protestant Episcopal Church in the U.S.A. — Texas. I. Title.

MURPHY, Du Bose, 1893- 283.764
A short history of the Protestant Episcopal church in Texas, by the Reverend Du Bose Murphy ... Dallas, Tex., Turner company [c1935] ix, 173 p. front., illus. (maps) ports. 24 cm. Bibliography: p. 157-160. [BX5917.T4M8] 36-36
1. Protestant Episcopal church in the U. S. A.—Texas. I. Title.

Protestant Episcopal Church in the U.S.A. Vermont (Diocese)

PROTESTANT Episcopal church in the U. S. Vermont (Diocese) 283.743
The documentary history of the Protestant Episcopal church in the diocese of Vermont, including the journals of the conventions from the year 1790 to 1832, inclusive. New York, Pott & Armery [etc.]; Claremont, N. H., The Claremont manufacturing company, 1870. 418 p. 23 cm. [BX5918.V5A2] 38-33858
I. Title.

ROTHWELL, Kenneth S. 283'.743
A goodly heritage; the Episcopal Church in Vermont. Edited by Kenneth S. Rothwell. Photography by Edward P. Lyman, Jr., with Samuel J. Hatfield and William W. Stone. Burlington, Vt., Document Committee, Cathedral Church of Saint Paul [1973] 56 p. illus. 28 cm. Includes bibliographical references. [BX5917.V5R67] 73-88188
1. Protestant Episcopal Church in the U.S.A. Vermont (Diocese) 2. Protestant Episcopal Church in the U.S.A.—Vermont. I. Title.

Protestant Episcopal Church in the U.S.A.—Virginia—Addresses, essays, lectures.

UP from independence : 283'.755
the Episcopal Church in Virginia : articles / by George J. Cleaveland ... [et al.]. [s.l.] : Interdiocesan Bicentennial Committee of the Virginias, 1976. iii, 125 p. : ill. ; 23 cm. Includes bibliographical references. [BX5917.V8U6] 76-380758
1. Protestant Episcopal Church in the U.S.A.—Virginia—Addresses, essays, lectures. 2. Virginia—Church history—Addresses, essays, lectures. I. Cleaveland, George Julius.

Protestant Episcopal Church in the U.S.A. Virginia (Diocese)

BRYDON, George MacLaren, 1875- 283.755
Highlights along the road of the Anglican Church; the Church of England in England and her oldest daughter, the Protestant Episcopal Church of Virginia. Richmond, Virginia Diocesan Library, 1957. 58p. illus. 23cm. [BX5917.V8B725] 58-2675
1. Protestant Episcopal Church in the U. S. A.—Virginia. 2. Church of England in Virginia. I. Title.

COCKE, Charles Francis. 283'.746
Parish lines, Diocese of Virginia. Richmond, Virginia State Library, 1967. xv, 321 p. col. maps. 23 cm. (Virginia State Library publications, no. 28) "Parish changes of 1967": p. 275-276. Bibliography: p. 271-274. [BX5918.V8C6] A 67
1. Protestant Episcopal Church in the U.S.A. Virginia (Diocese) 2. Parishes—Virginia. I. Title. II. Series: Virginia. State Library, Richmond. Publications, no. 28

DASHIELL, Thomas Grayson, 1830-1893. 283.
A digest of the proceedings of the conventions and councils in the diocese of Virginia, by T. Grayson Dashiell ... Richmond, W. E. Jones, 1883. vii, 431 p. 23 cm. "A list of the clergy": p. [7]-17, [349]-364 [BX5918.V8A4] 39-24022
I. Protestant Episcopal church in the U. S. A. Virginia (Diocese) II. Title.

Protestant Episcopal church in the U.S.A.—West Virginia.

PETERKIN, George William, bp., 1841-1916. 283.
A history and record of the Protestant Episcopal church in the diocese of West Virginia, and, before the formation of the diocese in 1878, in the territory now known as state of west Virginia. Comp., arranged and contributed by Geo. W. Peterkin ... [Charleston, W. Va., The Tribune company, printers] 1902. 3 p. l., xv, 856, xx p. front., plates, ports., maps. 24 cm. [BX5917.W4P4] 2-12935
1. Protestant Episcopal church in the U. S. A.—West Virginia. I. Title.

STRIDER, Robert Edward Lee, bp., 1887- 922.
The life and work of George William Peterkin, by Robert Edward Lee Strider ... Philadelphia, G. W. Jacobs & company [c1929] xiii p., 1 l., 331 p. front., ports. 21 1/2 cm. [BX5995.P45S8] 29-20805
1. Peterkin, George William, bp., 1841-1916. 2. Protestant Episcopal church in the U.S.A.—West Virginia. I. Title.

Protestant Episcopal Church in the U.S.A.—West Virginia—History.

HAMILTON, Eleanor Meyer. 283'.754
The flair & the fire : the story of the Episcopal Church in West Virginia, 1877-1977 / by Eleanor Meyer Hamilton. Charleston : Diocese of West Virginia, Protestant Episcopal Church, 1977. 395 p., [24] leaves of plates : ill., maps (on lining papers) ; 24 cm. Includes index. [BX5917.W4H35] 77-151356
1. Protestant Episcopal Church in the U.S.A.—West Virginia—History. I. Title.

Protestant Episcopal church in the U.S.A. Western New York (Diocese)

BURROWS,George Sherman, 1865- 283.747
The diocese of Western New York, 1897-1931, by G. Sherman Burrows, [Buffalo] The Diocese of Western New York, 1935. xix, 565 p., 1 l. front., plates. ports. map. diagr. 24 cm. "The book is intended to be supplementary to the very excellent "Diocese of Western New York" published by the Rev. Charles Welles Hayes [1904]"--Pref. [BX5918.W5H32] 35-34894
1. Protestant Episcopal church in the U.S.A. Western New York (Diocese) 2. Protestant Episcopal church in the U.S.A.—New York (State) I. Title.

HAYES, Charles Wells, 1828-1908. 283.
The diocese of Western New York; history and recollections, by Charles Wells Hayes. Rochester, N.Y., Scrantom, Wetmore & co., 1904. viii, 406, [2] p. front., plates, ports., facsims. 24 cm. History of the Protestant Episcopal church in the western half of the state of New York. "Publications by the Rev. Charles Wells Hayes": [2] p. at end. Contents.--pt. I. Colonial: 1615-1785.--pt. II. Diocese of New York: 1785-1838--pt. III. Diocese of Western New York: 1838-68.--pt. IV. The present diocese. [BX5918.W5H3] 3-32546
1. Protestant Episcopal church in the U.S.A. Western New York (Diocese) 2. Protestant Episcopal church in the U.S.A.—New York (State) I. Title.

PROTESTANT Episcopal church in the U. S. A. Western New York (Diocese) 283.
Journal of the ... annual council of the Protestant Episcopal church, in the diocese of Western New-York ... [1st]-1838- Utica [etc.] 1838- v. in tables. 22-24 cm. Title varies: 1838, Journal of the proceedings of the primary convention of the Protestant Episcopal church in the diocese of Western New York. 1839-65, Journal of the proceedings of the 2d[-28th] annual convention of the Protestant Episcopal church in the diocese of Western New York. 1866-77, Journal of the 29th[-40th] annual convention of the Protestant Episcopal church in the diocese of Western New York. 1878 Journal of the 41st annual council of the Protestant Episcopal church in the diocese of Western New York. With Journal of the proceedings of the 2d annual convention, 1839, is bound: Protestant Episcopal church in the U. S. A. Western New York (Diocese) Journal of the proceedings of a special convention ... 1839. Utica, 1839. [BX5918.W5A3] 40-15247
I. Title.

Protestant Episcopal Church in the U.S.A. Western Texas (Missionary district)

A brief history of the Church in West Texas ... Austin, Texas, Seminary of the Southwest [1959] vi, 74p. 19cm.
1. Protestant Episcopal Church in the U.S.A. Western Texas (Missionary district) I. Brown, Lawrence L

Protestant Episcopal church in the U.S.A.—Wyoming.

PROTESTANT Episcopal church in the U.S.A. Wyoming (Missionary district) 283.787
The Episcopal church in Wyoming. [Laramie, 19 v. illus. (incl. ports.) 23 cm. Compiled by the Committee on the state of the church, Missionary district of Wyoming. [BX5918.W85A25] 44-44065
1. Protestant Episcopal church in the U.S.A.—Wyoming. 2. Protestant Episcopal church in the U.S.A.—Missions. I. Title.

WEST, Samuel Earnest, 1889- 922.373
Cross on the range; missionary in Wyoming. Philadelphia, Church Historical Society [1947] 105 p. illus., ports., map. 23 cm. (Church Historical Society [Philadelphia] Publication no. 21) "Published serially in the St. James tower." [BX5995.W475A3] 48-11582
1. Protestant Episcopal Church in the U. S. A.—Wyoming. I. Title. II. Series.

Protestant Episcopal Church in the U.S.A.—Yearbooks.

... The American church almanac and year book ... 922. New York, 18-19 v. illus. 17-20 cm. Title varies: 18-1889. The Church almanac. 1889-1882. The Church almanac and year book. 1803-19 The American church almanac and year book. 18-81 published by the Protestant Episcopal tract society: 1882-89, by the Protestant Episcopal tract society, J. Pott; 1890-1902, by J. Pott & co.: 1903-21, by E. S. Gorham. 1874-81, 1883 and 1889 include the Parish list, paged continuously with the Almanac, but with special t.-p. Merged into the Living church annual in 1922. [BX5830.A5] 0-1074
1. Protestant Episcopal church in the U.S.A.—Year-books. I. The Church almanac.

... The American church almanac and year book ... 922. New York, 18-19 v. illus. 17-20 cm. Title varies: 18-1889. The Church almanac. 1889-1882. The Church almanac and year book. 1803-19 The American church almanac and year book. 18-81 published by the Protestant Episcopal tract society: 1882-89, by the Protestant Episcopal tract society, J. Pott; 1890-1902, by J. Pott & co.: 1903-21, by E. S. Gorham. 1874-81, 1883 and 1889 include the Parish list, paged continuously with the Almanac, but with special t.-p. Merged into the Living church annual in 1922. [BX5830.A5] 0-1074
1. Protestant Episcopal church in the U.S.A.—Year-books. I. The Church almanac.

THE Churchman's year book and American church almanac. 283. v. [1]-1830- New York, Churchman co. [etc., 1829]-19 v. illus., plates, ports., tables. 17-20 cm. Vols. for 1897-1901 issued a Pott's library. Title varies: 1830-40, The Churchman's almanac ... 1841-89, The Church almanac. 1890-92, The Church almanac and year book. 1893-1917, The American church almanac and year book. 1918-21, The Churchman's year book and American church almanac. Publisher varies: 1830-40, Portestant Episcopal press, by J. R. M'Gown [etc.]--1841-81, Protestant Episcopal tract society.--1882-89, Protestant Episcopal tract society, J. Pott & co. [etc.]--1890-1902, J. Pott & co.--1903-17, E. S. Gorham. Vols. for 18 include the Parish list, paged continuously with the almanac, but with special t.-p. Absorbed in 1922 by the Living church annual. [BX5830.C53] 0-1074
1. Protestant Episcopal church in the U.S.A.—Year-books. I. The Parish list. II. Title: The Churchman's almanac. III. Title: The Church almanac. IV. Title: The American church almanac and year book.

EPISCOPAL Church annual (The) 283.058 1964. [Ed.: Clifford P. Morehouse. Asst. ed. William V. Albert] New York, Morehouse [1965, c.1964] 1v. (various p.) illus. 22cm Title varies. 46-33254 6.25
1. Protestant Episcopal Church in the U.S.A.—Year-books. I. Morehouse, Clifford P., ed. II. Albert, William V., assistant ed.

EPISCOPAL Church annual (The) 283.058 1964 [Ed.: Clifford P. Morehouse. Assist. ed.: Rev. Rodney F. Cobb] New York, Morehouse [1964, c.1963] various p. illus. 22cm. title varies. 46-33254 6.25
1. Protestant Episcopal Church in the U.S.A.—Yearbooks. I. Morehouse, Clifford P., ed. II. Cobb, Rodney F., ed.

EPISCOPAL Church annual (The) 283.058 1967. New York, Morehouse [1967] illus. 22cm. Ed.: 1964- C. P. Morehouse. Title varies. 46-33254 7.50
1. Protestant Episcopal Church in the U.S.A.—Yearbooks. I. Morehouse, Clifford P., ed.

EPISCOPAL Church annual (The) 283.058 1961. [ed. Clifford P. Morehouse] New York, Morehouse-Barlow Co. [c.1961] 567, a-115 p. illus., ports. Title varies 46-33254 5.75
1. Protestant Episcopal Church in the U.S.A.—Yearbooks.

EPISCOPAL Church annual (The) 1963. 283.058 New York, Morehouse [c.1962] 573p. illus. 22cm. Ed: C. P. Morehouse; asst. ed.: R. F. Cobb. Title varies. 46-33254 6.25
1. Protestant Episcopal Church in the U.S.A.—Yearbooks. I. Morehouse, Clifford P., ed. II. Cobb, Rodney F., ed.

EPISCOPAL Church annual (The) 1968. 283.058 New York, Morehouse Barlow [1968] v. illus., ports., maps (pt. fold.) 22cm. The 5th-21st years, 1886-1902 (called v. 1-17) issued quarterly, one number each year retaining the features of the annual, the other numbers being clergy lists. Title varies: 1882-85, 1903-08, 1922-52, The Living church annual; the yearbook of the Episcopal Church (subtitle varies)--1886-89, Living church and clergy list quarterly, containing an almanac and calendar.--1890-1902, The Living Church quarterly, containing an almanac and calendar (varies slightly)--1909-14, The Living church annual and Whittaker's churchman's almanac.--1915-21, The Living church annual and churchman's almanac. Vols. for 1882-85 edited by C. W. Leffingwell and A. Seymour. Imprint varies: 1882-85. Chicago, S. A. Maxwell [etc.]--1886-1938, Milwaukee, Morehouse Pub. Co. [etc.] Absorbed Whittaker's churchman's almanacin 1909, and the Churchman's year book and American church almanac in 1922. [BX5830.L5] 46-33254 7.50
1. Protestant Episcopal Church in the U.S.A.—Yearbooks. I. Leffingwell, Charles Wesley, 1840-1928, ed. II. Seymour, Arthur. ed.

WHITTAKER'S churchman's almanac; 283. the Protestant Episcopal almanac and parochial list. New York, T. Whittaker [etc.] 18 -19 v. illus., ports., tables. 16 1/2-19 1/2 cm. Issued for the years 1854-1907? Vols. for 1894-1901 issued as Whittaker's library. Title varies: -1874. The Protestant Episcopal almanac and directory (varies slightly) 1875-19 Whittaker's churchman's almanac; the Protestant Episcopal almanac and parochial list (subtitle varies slightly) On cover, 1874-91: Whittaker's American churchman's almanac. Vols. for 18 -73 published by the Protestant Episcopal society for the promotion of evangelical knowledge. [BX5830.W6] 6-7424
1. Protestant Episcopal church in the U.S.A.—Year-books. I. Protestant Episcopal society for the promotion of evangelical knowledge, New York. II. Title: The Protestant Episcopal almanac and directory. III. Title: Whittaker's American churchman's almanac.

Protestant Reformed Churches of America.

GOD'S covenant faithfulness : 285'.7 the 50th anniversary of the Protestant Reformed Churches in America / Gertrude Hoeksema, editor. Grand Rapids : Reformed Free Pub. Association ; distributed by Kregel Publications, [1975] 117, 64 p. : ill. ; 23 cm. [BX9250.G6] 75-990 ISBN 0-8254-2824-6 : 5.95
1. Protestant Reformed Churches of America. I. Hoeksema, Gertrude.

Protestant Reformed Churches of America—Doctrinal and controversial works.

ENGELSMA, David. 234
Hyper-Calvinism and the call of the Gospel / by David Engelsma. Grand Rapids, Mich. : Reformed Free Pub. Association : Distributed by Kregel Publications, c1980. ix, 150 p. ; 22 cm. Includes index. Bibliography: p. 147-150. [BT761.2.E5] 19 80-52562 ISBN 0-916206-23-8 (pbk.) : 4.95
1. Protestant Reformed Churches of America—Doctrinal and controversial works. 2. Grace (Theology) 3. Predestination. I. Title. II. Title: Call of the Gospel.

Protestant Reformed Churches of America—Sermons.

HOEKSEMA, Herman. 227'.106
God's eternal good pleasure / Herman Hoeksema ; edited and partially rev. by Homer C. Hoeksema. Grand Rapids, Mich. : Reformed Free Pub. Association : distributed by Kregel Publications, [c1979] 371 p. ; 23 cm. [BS2665.4.H63] 79-65565 ISBN 0-916206-19-X : 9.95
1. Protestant Reformed Churches of America—Sermons. 2. Bible. N.T. Romans IX-XI—Sermons. 3. Sermons, American. I. Hoeksema, Homer C. II. Title.

Protestant theology—United States.

FOSTER, Frank Hugh, 1851-1935. 230'.0973
The modern movement in American theology; sketches in the history of American protestant thought from the Civil War to the World War. Freeport, N.Y., Books for Libraries Press [1969] 219 p. 23 cm. (Essay index reprint series) Reprint of the 1939 ed. Includes bibliographical references. [BT30.U6F6 1969] 76-86751 ISBN 0-8369-1131-8
1. Protestant theology—United States. 2. New England theology. I. Title.

Protestantism.

ANDERSON, William Ketcham, 1888- ed. 284
Protestantism, a symposium, edited by William K. Anderson. Nashville, Tenn., Commission on courses of study, The Methodist church [1944] vi, 282 p. 24 cm. Contents.--Introduction, by S. M. Cavert.--pt. i: History: Was the reformation needed? By J. T. McNeill. Protestantism and the primitive church, by Martin Rist. Protestantism before Luther, by E. P. Booth. Luther and his tradition, by A. R. Wentz. Zwingli and the reformed tradition, by G. W. Richards. Calvin and his tradition, by Georgia Harkness. The Anglican tradition, by A. C. Zabriskie. The independent tradition, by J. M. Batten. Protestantism in American history, by W. W. Sweet. Sectarianism run wild, by C. S. Braden-pt. ii. Interpretations: Cardinal principles of Protestantism, by A. C. Knudson. Protestantism and the Bible,by W. G. Chanter. Christian theology, by H. F. Rall. Worship and the sacraments, by O. T. Olson. Protestantismsis on preaching, by H. E. Luccock. The mystical spirit, by W. E. Hocking. Ethics, by F. J. McConnell. The open mind, by R. W. Sockman.--pt. iii. Opportunities: in the Far East, by K. S. Kathourette. In Europe, by H. S. Leiper. In Latin America, by Gonzalo Baez-Camargo. In world, by P. B. Kern. A growing ecumenicity. by H. P. Van Dusen.--Biographical notes (p. 278-282) Bibliographical foot-notes. [BX4810.A53] 44-5603
1. Protestantism. 2. Protestant churches. I. Methodist church (United States) Commission on courses of study. II. Title.

ANDERSON, William Ketcham, 1888-1947. 284
Protestantism, a symposium. Edited by William K. Anderson. Freeport, N.Y., Books for Libraries Press [1969, c1944] vi, 282 p. 24 cm. (Essay index reprint series) Contents.Contents.—Introduction, by S. M.

Cavert.—Was the Reformation needed? By J. T. McNeill.—Protestantism and the primitive church, by M. Rist.—Protestantism before Luther, by E. P. Booth.—Luther and his tradition, by A. R. Wentz.—Zwingli and the reformed tradition, by G. W. Richards.—Calvin and his tradition, by G. Harkness.—The Anglican tradition, by A. C. Zabriskie.—The independent tradition, by J. M. Batten.—Protestantism in American history, by W. W. Sweet.—Sectarianism run wild, by C. S. Braden.—Cardinal principles of Protestantism, by A. C. Knudson.—Protestantism and the Bible, by W. G. Chanter.—Christian theology, by H. F. Rall.—Worship and the sacraments, by O. T. Olson.—Protestantism and music, by C. and H. A. Dickinson.—The Protestant emphasis on preaching, by H. E. Luccock.—The mystical spirit, by W. E. Hocking.—Ethics, by F. J. McConnell.—The open mind, by R. W. Sockman.—In the Far East, by K. S. Latourette.—In Europe, by H. S. Leiper.—In Latin America, by G. Baez-Camargo.—In American education, by E. C. Colwell.—Our responsibility for a new world, by P. B. Kern.—A growing ecumenicity, by H. P. Van Dusen. Bibliographical footnotes. [BX4810.A53 1969] 69-18918
1. Protestantism. 2. Protestant churches.

BAILEY, Edwin Dunton.
Protestants and Catholics; a candid book for candid readers, by Rev. Edwin Dunton Bailey ... Washington, D. C., The Protestant league, c1924. 1 p. l., 93 p. 20 cm. [BN810.B3] 24-31608
1. Protestantism. 2. Catholic church. I. Title.

BASS, Archer Bryan. 270
Protestantism in the United States, by Archer B. Bass ... New York, Thomas Y. Crowell company [c1929] xii, 364 p. 22 cm. Bibliography: p. 323-326. [BR515.345]
1. Protestantism. 2. Protestant churches—U. S. 3. Christian union. I. Title.

*BOUYER, Louis 284
The spirit and forms of Protestantism. Tr. by A. V. Littledale. Cleveland, World [1964] 234p. 21cm. (Meridian bks., M180) 1.95 pap.,
I. Title.

BOYER, Merle William, 1910- 270.6
Luther in Protestantism today. New York, Association Press [1958] 188p. 20cm. [BX4817.B68] 58-6468
1. Protestantism. 2. Luther, Martin—Influence. I. Title.

BROWN, Robert McAfee, 1920- 280.4
The spirit of Protestantism. New York, Oxford University Press, 1965 [i.e. 1966] xxx, 270 p. 21 cm. (A Galaxy book, GB 151) Bibliographical references included in "Notes" (p. 227-254) "Supplementary bibliography": p. 255-259. [BX4811.B74 1966] 67-732
1. Protestantism. I. Title.

BROWN, Robert McAfee, 1920- 284
The spirit of Protestantism. New York, Oxford University Press, 1961. 264 p. 21 cm. Includes bibliographies. [BX4811.B74] 61-8367
1. Protestantism. I. Title.

CAVANAGH, William Henry, 1858- 284.
The word protestant in literature, history, and legislation, and its introduction into the American church, by the Rev. William Henry Cavanagh. Philadelphia, G. W. Jacobs & co., 1899. 1 p. l., v p., 1 l., v, [2], 188 p. double diagr. 19 cm. [BX4805.C4] 99-2644
1. Protestantism. 2. Protestant Episcopal church in the U. S. A.—Name. I. Title. II. Title: Protestant. The word in literature, history and legislation.

CHILLINGWORTH, William, 1602-1644.
The works of W. Chillingworth, M.A., containing his book, entitled The religion of Protestants a safe way to salvation, together with his sermons, letters, discourses, controversies, &c., &c. 1st American, from the 12th English ed., complete in one volume. With life by Birch ... Philadelphia, Pub. by an association of gentlemen, R. Davis, agent, 1848. xv, 17-764 p. 23 1/2 cm. [BX4809.C45 1848] 24-10098
1. Protestantism. 2. Theology—Collected works—17th cent. I. Birch, Thomas, 1705-1766. II. Title.

CHILLINGWORTH, William, 1602-1644.
The works of William Chillingworth ... Oxford, University press, 1838. 8 v. 22 1/2 cm. [BX4809.C45 1838] 4-17826
1. Protestantism. 2. Theology—Collected works—17th cent. I. Title.

COBB, John B 230
Living options in Protestant theology: a survey of methods. Philadelphia, Westminster Press [1962] 336p. 24cm. [BX4811.C6] 62-10568
1. Protestanitism. 2. Theology, Doctrinal. I. Title. II. Title: Protestant theology.

COBB, John B. 284
Varieties of Protestantism. Philadelphia, Westminister Press [1960] 271 p. 21 cm. Includes bibliography. [BX4810.C54] 60-5082
1. Protestantism. 2. Sects. I. Title.

DAVIES, Alfred Thomas, Sir 1861- 284
John Calvin, many-sided genius. New York, American Tract Society [1947] 92 p. illus., port. 20 c. "Published originally in England [under title: John Calvin and the influence of Protestantism on national life and character] ... now issued in a revised and enlarged form in this first American edition." "References": p. 87-92. [BX9418.D3 1947] 48-5390
1. Calvin, Jean,1509-1564 2. Protestantism. I. Title.

DITTERICH, Richard, 1865- 284
Protestantism; its principles and reasons, by Rev. R. Ditterich ... Chicago, The Bible institute colportage ass'n [c1924] 62 p. 20 cm. [BX4817.D5] 24-5610
1. Protestantism. I. Title.

DOWDING, Henry Wallace. 280
Will Protestantism be overthrown? By Henry Wallace Dowding ... Norfolk, Va., International Christian union league [c1923] 6 p. l., 3-266 p. port. 19 1/2 cm. [BX4810.D7] 23-6725
1. Protestantism. I. Title.

DUNNING, Annie Ketchum. Mrs.
Little Annie's first thoughts about God. By Nellie Grahame [pseud.] Philadelphia, Presbyterian board of publication [1860] 87 pp. front. 16 cm. (Presbyterian board of publication. Series for youth) 1-161
I. Title.

DUNSTAN, John Leslie, 1901- ed. 284
Protestantism. New York, Washington Sq. [1962, c.1961] 257p. 17cm. (Great religions of modern man) Bibl. .60 pap.,
1. Protestantism. I. Title.

DUNSTAN, John Leslie, 1901- ed.
Protestantism. New York, Washington Square Press, c1961. 255 p. (Great religions of modern man) Includes bibliography. 64-34219
I. Title.

DUNSTAN, John Leslie, 1901- ed.
Protestantism. New York, Washington Square Press [1962] xi, 257 p. 17 cm. (Great religions of modern man) "New edition." 64-34220
1. Protestantism. I. Title.

DUNSTAN, John Leslie, 1901- ed.
Protestantism. New York, Washington Square Press, c1961. 255 p. (Great religions of modern man) Paperback. Includes bibliography. 64-34219
1. Protestantism. I. Title.

DURNBAUGH, Donald F. 280'.4
The believers' church; the history and character of radical Protestantism [by] Donald F. Durnbaugh. New York, Macmillan [1968] xi, 315 p. 21 cm. Bibliographical footnotes. [BX4817.D8] 68-23631
1. Protestantism. 2. Dissenters, Religious. I. Title.

EDDY, Howard Ranney.
The Protestant ethic and the spirit of Labour. [n.p.] 1962. 1 v. Honors thesis-Harvard. 64-33984
1. Protestantism. I. Title.

EDDY, Howard Ranney.
The Protestant ethic and the spirit of Labour. [n.p.] 1962. 1 v. Honors thesis-Harvard. 64-33984
1. Protestantism. 2. Labour Party (Gt. Brit.) I. Title.

THE Evangelistic message of Protestantism; a series of messages by eight of the bishops of the Methodist Church. Nashville, Tidings [1948] 80 p. 19 cm. "The first seven messages ... were delivered ... at 'The hour of evangelism' during the session of the General Conference in Boston." Contents.The Protestant spirit, by F. P. Corson.--The authority of the Scriptures, by J. C. Broomfield.--The priesthood of believers, by R. S. Cushman.-- Justification by faith, by W. T. Watkins.--The right of private judgment, by C. W. Brashares.--Separation of church and state, by W. A. Smith.--The church and the sacraments, by W. J. King.--The sanctity of the common life, by C. C. Selecman. [BX4810.E85] 49-13305 284
1. Protestantism.

FIELDHOUSE, Marvin L. 284
The modern menace of Protestantism. New York, Vantage [c.1964] 62p. 21cm. 64-56576 2.00 bds.,
1. Protestantism. I. Title.

FIELDHOUSE, Marvin L 284
The modern menace of Protestantism, by Marvin L. Fieldhouse. [1st hard cover ed.] New York, Vantage Press [1964] 62 p. 21 cm. [BX4815.F5] 64-56576
1. Protestantism. I. Title.

FLEW, Robert Newton, 1886- ed. 284
The catholicity of Protestantism; being a report presented to His Grace the Archbishop of Canterbury by a group of Free Churchmen. Edited by R. Newton Flew and Rupert E. Davies. With a foreword by the Archbishop of Canterbury. Philadelphia, Muhlenberg Press [1954] 159p. 21cm. Bibliographical footnotes. [BX4817] 54-3942
1. Protestantism. 2. Catholicity. I. Fisher, Geoffrey Francis, Abp. of Canterbury, 1887- II. Davies, Rupert Eric, 1909- joint ed. III. Title.

FLEW, Robert Newton, 1886-1962, ed. 280'.4
The catholicity of Protestantism : being a report presented to His Grace the Archbishop of Canterbury by a group of Free Churchmen / edited by R. Newton Flew and Rupert E. Davies ; with a foreword by the Archbishop of Canterbury. Westport, Conn. : Greenwood Press, [1981] p. cm. Reprint of the 1950 ed. published by Lutterworth Press, London. Includes bibliographical references. [BX4817.F55 1981] 19 80-29108 ISBN 0-313-22825-6 lib. bdg. : 17.50
1. Protestantism. 2. Catholicity. I. Fisher, Geoffrey Francis, Abp. of Canterbury, 1887- II. Davies, Rupert Eric, 1909- III. Title.

FORELL, George Wolfgang 230.4
The Protestant faith. Englewood Cliffs, N.J., Prentice [1967,c.1960] 321p. 22cm. Bibl. [BX4811.F65] 60-10133 2.95 pap.,
1. Protestantism. 2. Theology, Doctrinal. 3. Creeds. I. Title.

GARRISON, Winfred Ernest, 1874- 284
A Protestant manifesto. New York, Abingdon-Cokesbury Press [1952] 207 p. 24 cm. [BX4810.G28] 52-5377
1. Protestantism. I. Title.

GLEN, John Stanley, 1907- 208
Erich Fromm; a Protestant critique, by J. Stanley Glen. Philadelphia, Westminster Press [1966] 224 p. 21 cm. Bibliography: p. [213]-224. [BX4817.G5] 66-21807
1. Fromm, Erich, 1900- 2. Protestantism.

HAMILTON, Kenneth. 284
The Protestant way. Fair Lawn, N. J., Essential Books, 1956. 264p. 22cm. [BX4810.H23] 56-4967
1. Protestantism. I. Title.

HAMILTON, Kenneth Gardiner, 1893- 284
The Protestant way. Fair Lawn, N. J., Essential Books, 1956. 264p. 22cm. [BX4810.H23] 56-4967
1. Protestantism. I. Title.

HAMMOND, William E. 280
The dilemma of Protestantism, by William E. Hammond ... New York and London, Harper & brothers, 1929. xi p., 1 l., 150 p., 1 l., 19 1/2 cm. [BX4810.H25] 29-11362
1. Protestantism. I. Title.

HARDON, John A 284
Christianity in conflict; a Catholic view of Protestantism. Westminster, Md., Newman Press, 1959. 300p. 23cm. Sequel to The Protestant churches of America. [BX4811.H3] 59-14802
1. Protestantism. 2. Catholic Church—Doctrinal and controversial works—Catholic authors. I. Title.

HARTSHORNE, Marion Holmes 284
The faith to doubt; a Protestant response to criticisms of religion. Englewood Cliffs, N.J., Prentice [c.1963] 111p. 21cm. (Spectrum bk.) 63-9947 3.95; 1.75 pap.,
1. Protestantism. 2. Faith. I. Title.

HAWKS, Edward, 1878- 284
A pedigree of Protestanism, by Edward Hawks... Philadelphia, The Peter Reilly company; London, B. Herder, 1936. x p., 1 l., 95 p. 19 1/2 cm. "A brief description of the Protestant sects."--p. 1. Reprinted from the Missionary. [BX4807.H34] 37-1389
1. Protestantism. 2. Sects. 3. Catholic church—Doctrinal and controversial works—Catholic authors. I. Title.

HEIM, Karl, 1874- 284
The nature of Protestantism. Translated and with a foreword by John Schmidt. Philadelphia, Fortress Press [1963] 164 p. 18 cm. "Transalation from the fourth and fifth revised and expanded edition of Das Wesen des evangelischen Christentums." Includes bibliography. [BX4810.H42] 63-12534
1. Protestantism. I. Title.

HOBSON, Alphonzo Augustus. 280
Positive Protestantism; a concise statement of the historical origins, the positive affirmations, and the present position of Protestantism, by A. Augustus Hobson ...Complete ed. Phildelphia, Boston [etc.] The Griffith and Rowland press [c1917] xii, 313 p. 18 1/2 cm. "Booklist for reference and study": p. [302]-303. [BX4810.H7 1917a] 17-29477
I. Title.

HOBSON, Alphonzo Augustus. 280
Positive Protestantism; a concise statement of the historical origins, the positive affirmations, and the present position of Protestantism, by A. Augustus Hobson ...Text-book ed. Phildelphia, Boston [etc.] The Griffith and Rowland press [c1917] viii, p., 1 l., 224 p. 18 1/2 cm. "Book-list for reference and study": p. 223-224. [BX4810.H7] 17-18716
I. Title.

JENKINS, Burris Atkins, 1869- 284
The world's debt to Protestantism, by Burris Jenkins. Boston, Mass., The Stratford company [c1930] 3 p. l., 270 p. 20 cm. [BX4810.J4] 30-10962
1. Protestantism. I. Title.

JENNEY, Ray Freeman, 1891- 284
I am a Protestant. [1st ed.] Indianapolis, Bobbs-Merrill [1951] 239 p. 21 cm. [BX4810.J43] 51-12229
1. Protestantism. I. Title.

KELLER, Adolf, 1872- 284
Protestant Europe; its crisis and outlook, by Adolf Keller ... and George Stewart ... New York, George H. Doran company [c1927] 2 p. l., vii-xv p., 1 l., 19-385 p. front., plates, maps (1 fold.) diagr. 23 cm. Bibliography: p. 362-369. [BX4837.K4] 27-5881
1. Protestantism. 2. Protestant churches—Europe. I. Stewart, George, 1892- joint author. II. Title.

KERR, Hugh Thomson, 1909- 284
Positive Protestantism; an interpretation of the gospel. Philadelphia, Westminster Press [1950] 147 p. 21 cm. [BX4810.K4] 50-10304

1. Protestantism. 2. Christianity—Essence, genius, nature. I. Title.

KIRK, Harris Elliott, 1872- 284
The spirit of Protestantism, by Harris Elliott Kirk ... Nashville, Tenn., Cokesbury press, 1930. 233 p. 19 1/2 cm. (Half-title: The Cole lectures for 1930 delivered before Vanderbilt university) [BX4810.K5] 30-17544
1. Protestantism. I. Title.

LAWRENCE, Emeric Anthony, 1908- 230'.2
Understanding our neighbor's faith / by Emeric A. Lawrence. Collegeville, Minn. : Liturgical Press, c1975. xii, 281 p. ; 20 cm. Includes bibliographical references. [BX1751.2.L38] 76-353618 ISBN 0-8146-0868-X
1. Catholic Church—Doctrinal and controversial works—Catholic authors. 2. Protestantism. I. Title.

LEARY, Lewis Gaston, 1877- 284
Problems of Protestantism, by Lewis Gaston Leary. New York, R. M. McBride & company, 1933. 310 p. 22 cm. "Notes": p. 298-310. [BR515.L4] 33-5321
1. Protestantism. 2. Protestant churches—U. S. 3. U. S.—Religion. 4. Christian union. I. Title.

LE PAPPE DE TREVERN, Jean Francois Marie, 1754-1842. 282
An amicable discussion on the Church of England and on the reformation in general, dedicated to the clergy of every Protestant communion, and reduced into the form of letters, by the Right Rev. J. F. M. Trevern... Translated by the Rev. William Richmond... Baltimore, F. Lucas, jun. [n. d.] 2 v. 18 1/2 cm. [BX4820.L4 1800] 1-11915
1. Protestantism. 2. Church of England—Doctrinal and controversial works—Debates, etc. 3. Reformation. 4. Catholic church—Doctrinal and controversial works—Debates, etc. I. Richmond, William, tr. II. Title.

LITTELL, Franklin Hamlin. 284
The free church. Boston, Starr King Press [1957] 171p. 22cm. [BX4817.L55] 57-10927
1. Protestantism. 2. Dissenters. 3. Anabaptists. I. Title.

MCELROY, Paul Simpson, 1902- 230.4
Protestant beliefs, [by] Paul Simpson McElroy. New York, Cincinnati [etc.] The Abingdon press [c1940] 110 p. 17 cm. Includes bibliographies. [BX4810.M32] 40-31578
1. Protestantism. 2. Theology, Doctrinal—Popular works. I. Title.

MACGREGOR, Geddes. 284
The coming reformation. Philadelphia, Westminster Press [1960] 160p. 22cm. [BX4811.M25] 60-11071
1. Protestantism. 2. Lord's Supper (Liturgy) I. Title.

MACGREGOR, Geddes [John Geddes MacGregor] 284
The coming reformation. Philadelphia, Westminister Press [c.1960] 160p. 22cm. 60-11071 3.50
1. Protestantism. 2. Lord's Supper (Liturgy) I. Title.

MACMANUS, Theodore Francis, 1873- 280
"An enemy sowed cockle", by Theodore F. MacManus and George Barry O'Toole. New York, The Devin-Adair company [c1926] xii p., 2 l., 194 p. 19 1/2 cm. [BX4820.M35] 27-1931
1. Protestantism. I. O'Toole, George Barry, joint author. II. Title.

MANSCHRECK, Clyde Leonard, 1917- 284
The Reformation and Protestantism today. New York, Association Press [1960] 128p. 16cm. (An Association Press reflection book) Includes bibliography. [BX4811.M3] 60-6570
1. Protestantism. 2. Reformation. I. Title.

MARTY, Martin E., 1928- 280'.4
Protestantism. Garden City, N.Y., Doubleday [1974, c1972] 440 p. 18 cm. (Image books, D334) Includes bibliographical references. [BX4811.M347] ISBN 0-385-07610-X 2.45 (pbk.)
1. Protestantism. I. Title.
L.C. card no. for the hardbound edition: 76-182759.

MARTY, Martin E., 1928- 280'.4
Protestantism [by] Martin E. Marty. [1st ed.] New York, Holt, Rinehart and Winston [1972] xii, 368 p. 25 cm. (History of religion series) Includes bibliographical references. [BX4811.M347] 76-182759 ISBN 0-03-091353-5 8.95
1. Protestantism.

*MECKLENBURG, George, D. D. 253.081
Never a dull moment; reflections on sixty years in the Protestant ministry. New York, Exposition [c.1964] 128p. 22cm. (EP42114) 3.00
I. Title.

MIELKE, Arthur W 284
This is Protestantism. [Westwood, N. J.] F. H. Revell Co. [1961] 127p. 24cm. [BX4811.M5] 61-9243
1. Protestantism. I. Title.

MOEHLMAN, Conrad Henry, 1879- 284
Protestantism's challenge; an historical study of the survival value of Progestantism, by Conrad Henry Moehlman. New York and London, Harper & brothers [c1939] 5 p. l., 286 p. 21 1/2 cm. "First edition." [BX4810.M6] 40-2583
1. Protestantism. 2. Theology, Doctrinal—Hist. 3. Christianity—20th cent. I. Title.

MUNRO, Harry Clyde, 1890- 284
Be glad you're a Protestant! St. Louis, Bethany Press [1948] 188 p. 21 cm. [BX4810.M8] 48-11078
1. Protestantism. I. Title.

NICHOLS, James Hastings, 1915- 280'.4
Primer for Protestants. Westport, Conn., Greenwood Press [1971, c1947] 151 p. 23 cm. Includes bibliographical references. [BX4810.N5 1971] 78-152620 ISBN 0-8371-6019-7
1. Protestantism. I. Title.

NICHOLS, James Hastings, 1915- 280
Primer for Protestants. New York, Association Press, 1947. 151 p. 21 cm. (A Haddam House book) [BX4810.N5] 47-30372
1. Protestantism. I. Title. II. Series.

NICHOLS, James Hastings, 1915- 280
A short primer for Protestants; an abridgement of his full length Haddam House book. New York, Association Press [c1957] 127p. 16cm. (An Association Press reflection book) [BX4810.N52] 57-5492
1. Protestantism. I. Title.

THE nineteenth century in Europe: the Protestant and Eastern churches. New York, Harper [c1959] 532p. (His Christianity in a revolutionary age; a history of Christianity in the nineteenth and twentieth centuries, 2)
1. Protestantism. 2. Eastern Churches—Hist. I. Latourette, Kenneth Scott, 1884-

OCKENGA, Harold John, 1905- 284
Our Protestant heritage, a series of sermons, by Harold John Ockenga... Grand Rapids, Mich., Zondervan publishing house [c1938] 6 p. l., 11-140 p. 19 12 cm. Contents.Martin Luther and Germany.--Ulrich Zwingli and Switzerland.--John Calvin and Geneva.--William of Orange and the Netherlands.--John Knox and Scotland.--Oliver Cromwell and England.--Roger Williams and America.--Whither Protestantism? [BX4810.O3] 38-29187
1. Protestantism. 2. Reformation—Biog. 3. Congregational churches—Sermons. 4. Sermons, American. I. Title.

OLMSTEAD, Dwight Hinckley, 1827?-1901.
A lecture on the Protestant faith. By Dwight H. Olmstead. New-York, 1874. 3 p. l., [13]-71 p. 19 cm. "Lecture ... delivered before the Young Men's Christian union of New York in 1856." [BX4815.O5 1874 a] 39-10474
1. Protestantism. I. Title.

OLMSTEAD, Dwight Hinckley, 1827?-1901.
A lecture on the Protestant faith. By Dwight H. Olmstead. New-York, 1874. 8 p. l., [13]-70 p. 19 cm. "Lecture ... delivered before the Young Men's Christian union of New York in 1856." [BX4815.O5 1874] 39-10475
1. Protestantism. I. Title.

OLMSTEAD, Dwight Hinckley, 1827?-1901.
The Protestant faith; or, Salvation by belief, by Dwight Hinckley Olmstead. 3d ed., with an introduction on the limitations of thought. New York and London, G. P. Putnam's sons, 1897. v, 97, [1] p. 20 cm. "The following essay ... was read ... before the Young Men's Christian union of New York in 1856."--Pref. to 2d ed. [BX4815.O52 1897] 38-35223
1. Protestantism. I. Title. II. Title: Salvation by belief.

OLMSTEAD, Dwight Hinckley, 1827?-1901.
The Protestant faith; or, Salvation by belief. An essay upon the errors of the Protestant church, by Dwight Hinckley Olmstead. New York & London, G. P. Putnam's sons, 1885. 77 p. 20 cm. "The following essay ... was read ... before the Young Men's Christian union of New York in 1856."--Introd. [BX4815.O52 1885] 38-35221
1. Protestantism. I. Title. II. Title: Salvation by belief.

PAUCK, Wilhelm, 1901- 280'.4
The heritage of the Reformation. Rev., enl. ed. London New York, Oxford Univ. Pr. [1968] x, 399p. 21cm. (Galaxy bk. GB251) Bibl. refs. [BX4810.P3 1968] 68-115753 2.75 pap.,
1. Protestantism. I. Title.

PAUCK, Wilhelm, 1901- 284
The heritage of the Reformation. Rev. and enl. ed. Glencoe [Ill.] Free Press [1961] 399p. 22cm. Includes bibliography. [BX4810.P3 1961] 60-7096
1. Protestantism. I. Title.

PAUCK, Wilhelm, 1901- 284
The heritage of the Reformation. Boston, Beacon Press, 1950. 312 p. 23 cm. (The Phoenix series, 2) Bibliographical references included in "Notes" (p. 295-306) [BX4810.P3] 50-7345
1. Protestantism. I. Title.

POL, Willem Hendrik van de, 1897- 284
World Protestantism. Rev. ed., translated by T. Zuydwijk. New York] Herder and Herder [1964] xii, 316 p. 22 cm. [BX4811.P613] 64-19733
1. Protestantism. I. Title.

SCHAFF, David Schley, 1852-1941 280
Our fathers faith and ours; a comparison between Protestantism and Romanism, by David S. Schaff ... New York, London, G. P. Putnam's sons, 1928. iv, 680 p. 24 1/2 cm. "Literature and notes": p. 629-661. [BX4810.S25] 28-11223
1. Protestantism. 2. Catholic church—Doctrinal and controversial works—Protestant authors. I. Title.

SCHAFF, Philip, 1819-1893 284
The principle of Protestantism. Tr. from German by John W. Nevin, 1845. Philadelphia, United Church [c.1964] 268p. facsim. 23cm. (Lancaster ser. on the Mercersburg theology, v.1) Bibl. 64-14141 4.50 pap.,
1. Protestantism. 2. Mercersburg theology. I. Title. II. Series.

SIMMS, Paris Marion, 1874-
What must the church do to be saved? The necessity and possiblity of the unity of Protestantism, by P. Marion Simms... New York, Chicago [etc.] Fleming H. Revell company [c1913] 3 p. l., 11-324 p. 21 1/2 cm. $1.50. 13-17693
I. Title.

SOPER, David Wesley, 1910- ed. 284
Room for improvement; next steps for Protestants. with chapters by Chad Walsh [and others] Chicago, Wilcox and Follett Co. [1951] 126 p. 22 cm. [BX4817.S6] 51-14846
1. Protestantism. 2. U.S. — Religion. 3. Theology — 20th cent. I. Title.

THE spirit and forms of protestantism. Translated by A. V. Littledale. Westmister, Md., Newman Press, 1956. 234p.
I. Boyer, Louis, 1913-

TAVARD, Georges Henri 270.6
Protestantism. Translated from the French by Rachel Attwater. New York, Hawthorn Books [c.1959] 139p. 21cm. (The Twentieth century encyclopedia of Catholicism, v.137. Section 13: Outside the church) (2p. bibl.) 59-12170 2.95 bds.,
1. Protestantism. I. Title.

TAVARD, Georges Henri, 1922- 270.6
Protestantism. Translated from the French by Rachel Attwater. [1st ed.] New York, Hawthorn Books [1959] 139 p. 21 cm. (The Twentieth century encyclopedia of Catholicism, v. 137. Section 13: Outside the church) Includes bibliography. [BX4817.T313] 59-12170
1. Protestantism. I. Title.

TILLICH, Paul, 1886- 284
The Protestant era. Translated by James Luther Adams. Abridged ed. [Chicago] University of Chicago Press [1957] 242p. 21cm. (Phoenix books, P19) [BX4817] 57-14060
1. Protestantism. 2. Theology. Doctrinal—Addresses, essays, lectures. 3. Christianity—Philosophy. I. Title.

TILLICH, Paul, 1886- 284
The Protestant era; tr., and with a concluding essay, by James Luther Adams. Chicago, Univ. of Chicago Press [1948] xxxi, 323 p. 24 cm. Essays an addrsses. Full name: Paul Johannes Oskar Tillich. [BX4817.T53] 48-6650
1. Protestantism 2. Theology, Doctrinal—Addresses, essays, lectures. 3. Christianity—Philosophy. I. Adams, James Luther, 1901- tr. II. Title.

TORREY, David Clarence, 1859-
Protestant modernism; or, Religious thinking for thinking men, by David C. Torrey... Author's ed. [Boston, Press of C. W. Calkins & co.] 1910. 172 p. 20 cm. $1.00. 10-389
I. Title.

TORREY, David Clarence, 1859-
Protestant modernism; or, Religious thinking for thinking men, by David C. Torrey... [Rev. and enl. ed.] New York and London, G. P. Putnam's sons, 1910. xi, 172 p. 19 cm. (On cover: Crown theological library) $1.50. 10-25795
I. Title.

VON ROHR, John Robert. 280'.4
Profile of Protestantism; an introduction to its faith and life [by] John Von Rohr. Belmont, Calif., Dickenson Pub. Co. [1969] 240 p. 22 cm. Bibliography: p. 226-230. [BX4811.V6] 70-76139
1. Protestantism. I. Title.

WEIGEL, Gustave, 1906- 230
A survey of Protestant theology in our day. Westminster, Md., Newman Press, 1954. 56p. 22cm. [BX 4820.W37] 54-12085
1. Protestantism. 2. Catholic Church—Doctrinal and controverstal works—Catholic authors. 3. Theology, Doctrinal—Hist. I. Title.

WHALE, John Seldon, 1896-
The Protestant tradition; an essay in interpretation. [1st paperback edition] Cambridge [Eng.] University Press, 1960. xiv, 359 p. Bibliography: p. 345-347.
1. Protestantism. I. Title.

WHALE, John Seldon, 1896- 284
The Protestant tradition; an essay in interpretation. Cambridge [Eng.] University Press, 1955. 359 p. 20 cm. [BX4810.W5] 55-4857
1. Protestantism. 2. Theology, Doctrinal—History—Modern period. I. Title.

WILBURN, Ralph Glenn, 1909- 284
The prophetic voice in Protestant Christianity. St. Louis, Bethany Press [1956] 298p. 23cm. [Bethany history series] [BX4817.W5] 56-10171

1. Protestantism. 2. Revelation. 3. Ecumenical movement. I. Title.

Protestantism—20th century.

DENBEAUX, Fred J. 280'.4
The premature death of protestantism; an invitation to a future [by] Fred J. Denbeaux. [1st ed.] Philadelphia, Lippincott [1967] 155 p. 19 cm. Bibliographical footnotes. [BX4811.D4] 67-25897
1. Protestantism—20th century. I. Title.

DODGE, Ralph Edward. 280'.4'0973
The pagan church; the Protestant failure in America [by] Ralph E. Dodge. [1st ed.] Philadelphia, Lippincott [1968] 144 p. 21 cm. Bibliographical footnotes. [BR526.D6] 68-54413 2.25
1. Protestantism—20th century. 2. United States—Religion—1945- I. Title.

GARRISON, R. Benjamin 284
Portrait of the church: warts and all. Nashville, Abingdon [c.1964] 160p. 20cm. Bibl. 64-20771 3.00 bds.,
1. Protestantism—20th cent. 2. Church—Addresses, essays, lectures. I. Title.

KEGERREIS, Robert B 280.4
[Catalogue of the Poe collection of Robert B. Kegerreis. Richland, Pa., 1965] New York, Harper & Row [1965] 1 v. (various pagings) 36 cm. v. 282 p. 22 cm. Bibliographical footnotes. [BX4811.K35] 66-81401 65-20453
1. Poe, Edgar Allan, 1809-1849 — Bibl. 2. Protestantism — 20th cent. I. Kegley, Charles W II. Title. III. Title: Protestantism in transition

KEGLEY, Charles W. 280.4
Protestantism in transition. New York, Harper [c.1965] v, 282p. 22cm. Bibl. [BX4811.K35] 65-20453 5.75
1. Protestantism—20th cent. I. Title.

KERR, Hugh Thomson, 1909- 284
Positive Protestantism, a return to first principles. Englewood Cliffs, N.J., Prentice [c.1950, 1963] 108p. 21cm. (Spectrum bk.) 63-7989 1.75 pap.,
1. Protestantism—20th cent. I. Title.

KERR, Hugh Thomson, 1909- 284
Positive Protestantism, a return to first principles. Englewood Cliffs, N. J., Prentice-Hall [1963] 108 p. 21 cm. (A Spectrum book) [BX4811.K4] 63-7989
1. Protestantism — 20th cent. I. Title.

MARTY, Martin E. 284.0973
Second chance for American Protestants. New York, Harper [c.1963] 175p. 22cm. 63-10962 3.50 bds.,
1. Protestantism—20th cent. I. Title.

OURSLER, William Charles, 1913- 260
Protestant power and the coming revolution [by] Will Oursler. [1st ed.] Garden City, N.Y., Doubleday, 1971. xi, 203 p. 22 cm. [BX4805.2.O9] 78-131099 5.95
1. Protestantism—20th century. I. Title.

STRINGFELLOW, William 284.0973
A private and public faith. Grand Rapids, Mich., Eerdmans [c.1962] 93p. 22cm. 62-21368 3.00
1. Protestantism—20th cent. 2. U. S.—Religion. I. Title.

Protestantism—Addresses, essays, lectures.

FERM, Vergilius Ture Anselm, 1896- ed. 284
The Protestant credo. New York, Philosophical Library [1953] 241p. 22cm. [BX4815.F4] 53-7907
1. Protestantism—Addresses, essays, lectures. I. Title.

MACMILLAN, Kerr Duncan, 1871- 274.
Protestantism in Germany, by Kerr D. Macmillan... Princeton, Princeton university press; [etc., etc.] 1917. viii, 282 p. 21 1/2 cm. The chapters of this volume were delivered in 1916-17 as lectures on the L. P. Stone foundation at Princeton theological seminary. cf. Pref. [BR305.M2] 18-31
I. Title.

PROTESTANTISM / 280'.4
Hugh T. Kerr, editor. Woodbury, N.Y. : Barron's Educational Series, [1976] p. cm. Includes bibliographies. [BX4815.P74] 76-16065 ISBN 0-8120-0665-8 pbk. : 2.95
1. Protestantism—Addresses, essays, lectures. I. Kerr, Hugh Thomson, 1909-

WATERS, F W
Protestantism - a Baptist interpretation; a treatise from the pens and discussion of a number of Ministers of the Baptist Convention of Ontario and Quebec, recast and re-written by Doctor F. W. Waters. [n.p.] Published by ... The Baptist Federation of Canada, 1958. 67 p.
I. Title.

Protestantism and capitalism.

KITCH, M. J., comp. 261.8'5
Capitalism and the Reformation. New York, Barnes & Noble [1968, c1967] xx, 217 p. 22 cm. (Problems and perspectives in history) Bibliography: p. 209-212. [BR115.E3K52 1968] 68-2564
1. Protestantism and capitalism. I. Title.

Protestantism—Collections.

BOWIE, Walter Russell, 1882- ed. 280.408
What is Protestantism? ed. by Walter Russell Bowie Kenneth Seeman Giniger. New York, Watts [c.1965] xiii, 190p. 25cm. [BX4801.B6] 65-11755 5.95; 4.46 lib. ed.,
1. Protestantism—Collections. I. Giniger, Kenneth Seeman, 1919- joint ed. II. Title.

FERM, Robert L., comp. 280'.4'0973
Issues in American Protestantism; a documentary history from the Puritans to the present. Edited with an introd. and notes by Robert L. Ferm. Garden City, N.Y., Anchor Books [1969] xxii, 418 p. 18 cm. Includes bibliographical references. [BX4801.F43] 69-11012 1.95
1. Protestantism—Collections. 2. Protestant churches—U.S. 3. U.S.—Church history—Sources. I. Title.

Protestantism—Controversial literature.

ECK, Johann, 1486-1543. 230'.2
Enchiridion of commonplaces against Luther and other enemies of the church / John Eck ; translated by Ford Lewis Battles. Grand Rapids, Mich. : Baker Book House, c1979. 2, 2, 10, 312 p. ; 23 cm. (Twin brooks series) Translation of Enchiridion locorum communium adversus Lutteranos. Includes bibliographical references and index. [BX1780.E2313 1979] 79-127360 ISBN 0-8010-3352-7 : 9.95
1. Catholic Church—Doctrinal and controversial works—Catholic authors. 2. Protestantism—Controversial literature. I. Title.

PATERSON, F. William. 230'.2 s
The Protestants theologie / [by] William Paterson. Ilkley [etc.] : Scolar Press, 1976. [29], 309, [3] p. ; 21 cm. (English recusant literature, 1558-1640 ; v. 316) (Series: Rogers, David Morrison, comp. English recusant literature, 1558-1640 ; v. 316.) Reprint of the 1620 ed. STC 19461; Allison and Rogers 597. [BX1750.A1E5 vol. 316] [BX1752] 230'.2 77-362661 ISBN 0-85967-330-8
1. Catholic Church—Apologetic works. 2. Protestantism—Controversial literature. I. Title. II. Series.

TEAGUE, Hosea Holcombe. 248
The phenomenal mirror ... by Hosea H. Teague ... Mansfield, O., 1933. 2 p. l., 195 p. illus. 24 cm. "The phenomenal mirror is a religious book, written with a view to prove the corruption of Protestantism, and its fulfillment of the period of deception spoken of in the Bible. The writer's spiritual biography, Christian experience and prophecy, dealing with the many intricate angles of Christianity, embody the import." Erratum noted on 1st prelim. leaf (type-written) [BR125.T4] 33-32390
I. Title.

WALSINGHAM, Francis. 230'.2 s
A search made into matters of religion / [by] Francis Walsingham. Ilkley : Scolar Press, 1976. [29], 520 p. ; 21 cm. (English recusant literature, 1558-1640 ; v. 286) (Series: Rogers, David Morrison, comp. English recusant literature, 1588-1640 ; v. 286.) Reprint of the 1609 ed. "Reproduced ... from a copy in the library of Stonyhurst College." STC 25002 Includes index. [BX1750.A1E5 vol. 286] [BX1752] 230'.2 76-380512 ISBN 0-85967-287-5 : £10.00
1. Catholic Church—Apologetic works. 2. Walsingham, Francis. 3. Protestantism—Controversial literature. I. Title. II. Series.

Protestantism—History

BATTEN, Joseph Minton. 1893- 270
Protestant backgrounds in history. New York, Abingdon-CokesburyPress [1951] 160 p. 19 cm. [BX4805.B3] 51-10322
1. Protestantism—Hist. I. Title.

DANIEL-ROPS, Henry, 19011965 270.8
Our brothers in Christ. 1870-1959, by H. Daniel-Rops; tr. from French by J. M. Orpen. John Warrington, ed. by A. Cox J. Hetherington. London, Dent; New York, Dutton. 1967. x. 496p. tables, diagrs. 23cm. (His History of the church of Christ, 10) Orig. pub. as L'Eglise des revolutions: ces chretiens nos freres. Paris, Fayard, 1965. [BX4805.2.D313] 68-86851 10.00
1. Protestantism—Hist. 2. Eastern churches—Hist. 3. Christian union—Catholic Church I. Title.

DILLENBERGER, John 284
Protestant Christianity interpreted through its development [by] John Dillenberger [and] Claude Welch. New York, Scribner [c.1958] xii, 340p. 21cm. (Scribner library SL17) 1.45 pap.,
1. Protestantism—Hist. I. Welch, Claude, joint author. II. Title.

FERM, Vergilius Ture Anselm, 1896- 284.09
Pictorial history of Protestantism; a panoramic view of western Europe and the United States. New York, Philosophical Library [1957] xi, 368 p. illus., ports., maps, facsims., music. 29 cm. [BX4805.F4] 57-14163
1. Protestantism—History. 2. Protestantism—History—Pictures, illustrations, etc. I. Title.

INGE, William Ralph, 1860- 284
... Protestantism, by the Very Rev. W. R. Inge ... Garden City, New York, Doubleday, Doran & company, inc., 1928. 1 p. l., 77 p. 18 cm. (The little books of modern knowledge) "First edition." [BX4807.I] A 35
1. Protestantism—History. I. Title.

KINGTON-OLIPHANT, Thomas Laurence, 1831-1902. 274
Rome and reform. Port Washington, N.Y., Kennikat Press [1971] 2 v. 22 cm. Reprint of the 1902 ed. Includes bibliographical references. [BX1304.K5 1971] 76-118541
1. Catholic Church—History. 2. Protestantism—History. 3. Europe—Church history. I. Title.

LAGRANGE, Marie Joseph, 1855-1938.
The meaning of Christianity according to Luther and his followers in Germany, by the Very Rev. M. J. Lagrange ... translated by the Rev. W. S. Reilly, S. S. New York, London [etc.] Longmans, Green and co., 1920. 381 p. 19 cm. Lectures delivered in the Catholic institute of Paris, 1917 and 1918. Bibliographical foot-notes. [BX4844.L3] 20-22092
1. Protestantism—Hist. 2. Theology, Doctrinal—Hist.—Germany. 3. Bible. N. T.—Criticism, interpretation, etc.—Hist.—N. T. 4. Catholic church—Doctrinal and controversial works—Catholic authors. I. Reilly, Wendell Stephen, 1875- tr. II. Title. III. Title: Christianity, The meaning of.

LEONARD, Emile G., 1891- 280'.4'09
A history of Protestantism [by] Emile G. Leonard. Edited by H. H. Rowley. Translated by Joyce M. H. Reid. Indianapolis, Bobbs-Merrill [1968- v. maps. 24 cm. Translation of Histoire generale du protestantisme. Contents.Contents.—v. 1. The Reformation. Includes bibliographical references. [BX4805.2.L4133] 68-12987
1. Protestantism—History. I. Title.

PIETTE, Maximin. 922.742
John Wesley in the evolution of Protestantism, by Maximin Piette ... translated by the J. B. Howard, with forewords by Bishop F. C. Kelley [and] Dr. H. B. Workman. New York, Sheed & Ward, 1937. xlviii, 569 p. front., plates, ports., facsim. 22 cm. "Printed in Great Britain." Bibliography: p. xxxi-xlviii. [BX8495.W5P48] 38-2954
1. Wesley, John, 1703-1791. 2. Protestantism—Hist. 3. Reformation. I. Howard, Joseph Bernard, 1892- tr. II. Title.

RICHMOND Union Theological Seminary 284.09
Our Protestant heritage, by members of the faculty of Union Theological Seminary in Virginia. Richmond, John Knox Press [1948] 224 p. 21 cm. A series of lectures given in 1946. [BX4805.R5] 48-10711
1. Protestantism—Hist. I. Title.
Contents omitted.

Protestantism—History—Pictures, illustrations, etc.

HAVERSTICK, John. 280'.4'09
The progress of the Protestant; a pictorial history from the early reformers to present-day ecumenism. Design by Al Corchia, Jr. [1st ed.] New York, Holt, Rinehart and Winston [1968] 273 p. illus., ports. 31 cm. [BX4805.2.H3] 66-22065
1. Protestantism—History—Pictures, illustrations, etc. I. Title.

Protestantism—History—Sources.

FOSDICK, Harry Emerson, 1878- ed. 270.6
Great voices of the Reformation; an anthology. Edited, with an introd. and commentaries. New York, Modern Library [1954, c1952] 546p. 21cm. (The Modern library of the world's best books.[A Modern library giant, G-9]) [BX4801] 54-9973
1. Protestantism—Hist.—Sources. 2. Reformation— Sources. 3. Theology—Collections. I. Title.

FOSDICK, Harry Emerson, 1878-1969. ed. 270.6
Great voices of the Reformation, an anthology. New York, Random House [1952] xxx, 548 p. 22 cm. [BX4801.F6] 52-5550
1. Protestantism—History—Sources. 2. Reformation—Sources. 3. Theology—Collected works. I. Title.

Protestantism—Relations—Catholic church.

THE Inquiry, New York. 282
The Fairfield experiment; the story of one episode in an effort towards a better understanding of Catholics by Protestants. With suggestions for group discussion of religious differences. New York city, The Inquiry [c1927] 3 p. l., 5-74 p. 20 cm. [BX4817.I6] 31-31511
1. Protestantism—Relations—Catholic church. 2. Catholic church—Relations—Protestantism. I. Title.

Protestantism—United States.

GREVEN, Philip J. 301.5'8
The protestant temperament : patterns of child-rearing, religious experience, and the self in early America / Philip Greven. 1st ed. New York : Knopf, 1977. xiv, 431 p. ; 25 cm. Includes index. Bibliography: p. [404]-410. [BR515.G75 1977] 77-74989 ISBN 0-394-40423-8 : 15.00
1. Protestantism—United States. 2. Child development. 3. Temperament. 4. Experience (Religion) 5. Religious thought—United States. I. Title.

Protestants — 20th century

GARRISON, R. Benjamin. 284
Portrait of the church: warts and all [by]

R. Benjamin Garrison. New York, Abingdon Press [1964] 160 p. 20 cm. Bibliographical footnotes. [BX4811.G3] 64-20771
1. Protestants — 20th cent. 2. Church — Addresses, essays, lectures. I. Title.

WINCHESTER, Charles Wesley, 1843-
What Protestants believe, by C. W. Winchester ... Chicago, Ill., The Christian witness company [c1915] 240 p. 20 cm. $1.00. 15-14675
I. Title.

Protestants and Other Americans United for Separation of Church and State.

CREEDON, Lawrence P. 261.7
United for separation; an analysis of POAU assaults on Catholicism, by Lawrence P. Creedon and William D. Falcon. Milwaukee, Bruce Pub. Co. [c.1959] 259p. 23cm. (bibl. footnotes) 59-13646 3.95
1. Protestants and Other Americans United for Separation of Church and State. 2. Church and state in the U. S. 3. Catholic Church—Doctrinal and controversial works—Catholic authors. I. Falcon, William D., joint author. II. Title.

FEY, Harold Edward, 1898- 261.7'06'273
With sovereign reverence; the first twenty-five years of Americans United, by Harold E. Fey. Rockville, Md., R. Williams Press [1974] 87 p. illus. 21 cm. [BR516.F48] 73-94001 4.95
1. Protestants and Other Americans United for Separation of Church and State. 2. Church and state in the United States. I. Title.

WHO'S who in the P. O. A. U.? 261.7
Huntington, Ind., Our Sunday Visitor Press, 1951. 128p. 20cm. [BR516.W45] 53-26243
1. Protestants and Other Americans United for Separation of Church and State. 2. Church and state in the U S. 3. Catholic Church— Doctrinal and controversial works—Catholic authors.

Protestants in France.

CLAUDE, Jean, 1619-1687. 272.
Cruel persecutions of the Protestants in the kingdom of France. First American reprint of the English translation, pub. in London in 1707, with a biographical sketch of the author Jean Claude, by Narcisse Cyr, publisher. Boston, 1893. xiv, 212 p. front. (port.) 15 cm. Contains reproduction of t.-p. of original London edition: A short account of the complaints. and cruel persecutions of the Protestants in the kingdom of France. London Printed by W. Redmayne, 1707. French original published in 1686. [DC111.C5] 17-15255
1. Protestants in France. 2. Huguenots in France. I. Cyr, Narcisse, 1823?-1894. II. Title.

LE BRAS, Gabriel. 301.5'8'0944
Etudes de sociologie religieuse / Gabriel Le Bras. New York : Arno Press, 1975, c1955-1956. p. cm. (European sociology) Reprint of the ed. published by Presses universitaires de France, Paris, in series: Bibliotheque de sociologie contemporaine. Contents.Contents.—t. 1. Sociologie de la pratique religieuse dans les campagnes francaises.—t. 2. De la morphologie a la typologie. "Bibliographie des travaux de Gabriel Le Bras sur la sociologie religieuse": v. 1, p. [BX1528.L3972] 74-25763 ISBN 0-405-06517-5
1. Catholic Church in France. 2. Protestants in France. 3. Rural churches—France. I. Title. II. Series.

WILL, Joseph Stanley.
Protestantism in France. Volume two, 1598-1629. By Joseph Stanley Will... [Toronto] University of Toronto press, 1921. 4 p. l., 7-265, [5] p. 21 cm. Thesis (PH.D.)--Columbia university, 1921. Vita. The complete work, which is to consist of 3 vols., has not yet been published. cf. Pref. Bibliography: 4 p. at end. [BX4843.W8] 22-4192
1. Protestants in France. 2. France—Church history. I. Title.

Protestants in Ireland.

WHITE, Jack, 1920- 280'.4'09417
Minority report : the Protestant community in the Irish Republic / Jack White. Dublin : Gill and Macmillan, 1975. 208 p. ; 23 cm. Includes bibliographical references and index. [BX4839.W45] 75-332310 ISBN 0-7171-0766-3 : £6.50
1. Protestants in Ireland. I. Title.

Protestants in Latin America.

LEE, Elizabeth Meredith. 278
He wears orchids, & other Latin American stories. With an epilogue by W. Stanley Rycroft. Drawings by Rafael Palacios. Freeport, N.Y., Books for Libraries Press [1970, c1951] x, 178 p. illus. 23 cm. (Biography index reprint series) Includes bibliographical references. [BR600.L4 1970] 76-117327 ISBN 8-369-80190-
1. Protestants in Latin America. 2. Latin America—Religion. I. Title.

Protestants in Nicaragua.

MOODY Bible Institute of Chicago.
Evangelism-in-depth; experimenting with a new type of evangelism; as told by team members of the Latin America Mission. Chicago, Moody press [c1961] 126 p. 20 cm. 65-34434
1. Protestants in Nicaragua. 2. Nicaragua — Religion. I. Title.

Protestants in Northern Ireland.

WILSON, Ron, 1932- 209'.416
A flower grows in Ireland / Ron Wilson. Elgin, Ill. : D. C. Cook Pub. Co., c1976. xiv, 144 p., [2] leaves of plates : ill. ; 22 cm. Bibliography: p. 144. [BX4839.W54] 75-18646 ISBN 0-912692-78-2 : 3.95
1. Protestants in Northern Ireland. 2. Catholics in Northern Ireland. 3. Northern Ireland—History—1969- I. Title.

Protestants in Russia.

BLUMIT, Oswald A. 922
Sentenced to Siberia the story of the ministry, persecution, imprisonment and God's wonderful deliverance of Pastor Basil malof, Apostl of Russia. With 50 illustrations By Rev. Oswald A. Blumit. Berne, Ind. Mayflower press, 1940. 4 p. l., [7]-204 p. incl. illus. plates, ports., plan, facsims. front. 19 cm. "First edition--3000 copies." "Russia, dark Russia" (words and music): p. [110] [BX4849.B5] 41-3607
1. Malof, Basil A., 1883- 2. Protestants in Russia. 3. Missions—Russia. I. Title.

BLUMIT, Oswald A. 922
Sentenced to Siberia; the story of the ministry, persecution, imprisonment and God's wonderful deliverance of Pastor Basil A. Malof, Russian missionary. With 43 illustrations. By Rev. Oswald A. Blumit and Dr. Oswald J. Smith. 5th rev. ed. Wheaton, Ill., Mayflower publishers, 1943. 192 p. incl. illus., plates, ports., double plan, facsims. front., 2 port. on 1 l. 19 cm. "First edition ... 1940." "Russia, dark Russia" (words and music): p. [110] Bibliography: p. [9]-[10] [BX4849.B5 1943] 44-6784
1. Malof, Basil A., 1883- 2. Protestants in Russia. 3. Missions—Russia. I. Smith, Oswald J., joint author. II. Title.

POLLOCK, John Charles 274.7
The faith of the Russian Evangelicals. New York, McGraw [c.1964] 190p. 21cm. London ed. (Hodder and Stoughton) has title: The Christians from Siberia. Bibl. 64-25603 3.95 bds.,
1. Protestants in Russia. 2. Baptists—Russia. 3. Persecution—Russia. I. Title.

POLLOCK, John Charles. 284'.0947
The faith of the Russian Evangelicals, by J. C. Pollock. Grand Rapids, Zondervan Pub. House [1969, c1964] 190 p. 21 cm. Bibliography: p. 187-190. [BX4849.P6 1969] 71-81037
1. Protestants in Russia. 2. Baptists—Russia. 3. Persecution—Russia. I. Title.

Protestants in Spain.

ARANJO, Garcia Carlos. 274.6
Religion in the republic of Spain, by C. Araujo Garcia and Kenneth G. Grubb. London, New York city [etc.] World dominion press, 1933. 4 p. l., 109 p. front., plates, fold. maps, diagrs. 25 cm. [World dominion survey series] [BX4851.A7] 23-31231
1. Protestants in Spain. 2. Spain—Church history. 3. Spain—Religion. I. Grubb, Kenneth George. II. Title.

DELPECH, Jacques, 1887- 261.73
The oppression of Protestants in Spain. Translation from the French by Tom and Dolores Johnson. Pref. by Howard Schomer; introd. by John A. Mackay. Boston, Beacon Press [1955] 114p. 22cm. [BX4851.D415] 55-7802
1. Protestants in Spain. 2. Religious liberty—Spain. I. Title.

IRIZARRY, Carmen. 280.40946
The thirty thousand; modern Spain and Protestantism. [1st ed.] New York, Harcourt, Brace & World [1966] x, 399 p. illus., facsims. 22 cm. Bibliography: p. 383-385. [BX4851.I7] 66-22276
1. Protestants in Spain. 2. Religious liberty—Spain. I. Title.

VOUGHT, Dale G., 1937- 280'.4'0946
Protestants in modern Spain; the struggle for religious pluralism [by] Dale G. Vought. South Pasadena, Calif., William Carey Library [1973] xiv, 153 p. illus. 23 cm. Originally presented as the author's thesis (M.A. in Missions), Fuller Theological Seminary. Bibliography: p. 141-153. [BX4851.V68 1973] 73-9744 ISBN 0-87808-311-1 3.45
1. Protestants in Spain. 2. Protestant churches—Spain. I. Title.

Protestants in Spanish America.

LEE, Elizabeth Meredith. 278
He wears orchids, & other Latin American stories; with an epilogue by W. Stanley Rycroft. Drawings by Rafael Palacios. New York, Friendship Press [1951] x, 181 p. illus. 22 cm. Bibliography: p. 179-180. [BR600.L4] 51-5044
1. Protestants in Spanish America. 2. Spanish America—Religion. I. Title.

RYCROFT, William Stanley. 278
On this foundation; the evangelical witness in Latin America, by W. Stanley Rycroft. New York, Friendship press [1942] xiii, 210 p. incl. tab. fold. map. 19 1/2 cm. "Reading list": p. [194]-199. [BR600.R8] [266] 42-14672
1. Protestants in Spanish America. 2. Spanish America—Religion. I. Title.

Protestants in the Tyrol.

KIDDER, Daniel Parish, 1815-1891, ed.
The exiles; or, Scenes in the Tyrol. Edited by Daniel P. Kidder. New York, Carlton & Phillips, 1852. 159 p. incl. front. 15 cm. [BX4841.K5] 39-3716
1. Protestants in the Tyrol. 2. Persecution. 3. Hillerthal, Tyrol. I. Title.

Protestants in the United States

ANDERSON, Charles H., 1938- 301.45'28
White Protestant Americans; from national origins to religious group [by] Charles H. Anderson. Englewood Cliffs, N.J., Prentice-Hall [1970] xx, 188 p. 24 cm. (Ethnic groups in American life series) Includes bibliographical references. [BR517.A55] 73-108810 ISBN 0-13-957423-9 6.95
1. Protestants in the United States. I. Title.

DEMERATH, Nicholas Jay 301.4460973
Social class in American Protestantism. Chicago, RandMcNally [1965] xxvi, 228p. 22cm. (Rand McNally sociol. ser.) Pub. from the Res. Program in the Sociol. of Religion. Survey Res. Ctr., Univ. of Calif., Berkeley. Bibl. [BR517.D4] 65-14103 5.00; 3.50 pap.,
1. Protestants in the U.S. 2. Religion and social status—U.S. I. California. University. Survey Research Center. II. Title.

RILEY, Elihu Samuel, 1845-
... The national debt that American Protestants owe to their brethren of the Roman Catholic church, by Elihu S. Riley ... Annapolis, Md. [The author] 1914. 51 p. 23 cm. (Riley's historic series, no. 1) 14-18287 0.25
I. Title.

SOPER, David Wesley, 1910- ed. 920
Highways to faith; autobiographies of Protestant Christians. Philadelphia, Westminster Press [1954] 168p. 22cm. [BR569.S63] 54-5289
1. Protestants in the U. S. 2. Christian biography. I. Title.

Protestants—United States—Attitudes—Addresses, essays, lectures.

THE Holy Land in American Protestant life, 1800-1948 : a 280'.4'0973
documentary history / edited with commentary by Robert T. Handy. New York : Arno Press, 1980. p. cm. Includes bibliographical references and index. [BR525.H64] 19 80-1052 ISBN 0-405-13466-5 lib. bdg. : 20.00
1. Protestants—United States—Attitudes—Addresses, essays, lectures. 2. Palestine—Addresses, essays, lectures. 3. United States—Church history—19th century—Addresses, essays, lectures. 4. United States—Church history—20th century—Addresses, essays, lectures. I. Handy, Robert T.

Proudfit, Alexander Moncrief, 1770-1843.

FORSYTH, John, 1810-1886. 922.573
Memoir of the late Rev. Alexander Proudfit, D.D., with selections from his diary and correspondence, and recollections of his life, &c., by his son. By John Forsyth ... New York, Harper & Brothers, 1846. viii, [9]-384 p. incl. front. (port.) 17 1/2 cm. [BX9225.P77F6] 36-31799
1. Proudfit, Alexander Moncrief, 1770-1843. I. Proudfit, John Williams, 1803-1870. II. Title.

Prout, Ebenezer, 1835-1909, ed.

HANDEL, Georg Friedrich, 1685-1759. 783.
The Messiah; a sacred oratorio composed in the year 1741 by G. F. Handel. Edited, and the additonal accompaniments largely re-written by Ebenezer Prout. Full score. London, Novello and company, limited; New York, Novello, Ewer and co., c1902. xvii p., 1 l., 351 p. 33 1/2 x 26 cm. Preface by the editor contains a critical comparison of his own edition, editions. [M3000.H22M4] 2-30462
1. Prout, Ebenezer, 1835-1909, ed. I. Title.

Proverbs.

BEAMER, Jacob 1830-
Book of proverbs, containing seven thousand gems. It is an epitome of the most brilliant sparklets of thought, from the galaxy of the world's genius, since the days of Solomon to the present time, forming the cream of the world's literature, as embodied in small compass by its greatest thinkers. Art, science, mirth, social culture and literature. Prof. J. Beamer, author... Greensburg, Pa., Review publishing co. [c1904] 264 p. front., ports. 20 cm. "Selecting the best from all nations...adding thousands of his own composition, eradicating crude and "ncouth expressions" [sic]-p. 3-4. 5-34381
I. Title.

DOWNEY, William Scott. 398.9
Proverbs. By Rev. William Scott Downey ... 5th ed. Boston, J. M. Hewes & co., printers, 1854. 104 p. 17 1/2 cm. "Opinions of the press": p. [100]-104. [BV4515.D6 1854] 13-21641
1. Proverbs. I. Title.

DOWNEY, William Scott. 244
Proverbs. By Rev. William Scott Downey ... 6th ed. Boston, J. M. Hewes, printer, 1854. 110 p. 18 cm. [BV4515.D6 1854a] 35-34431
1. Proverbs. I. Title.

DOWNEY, William Scott. 398.9
Proverbs. By Rev. William Scott Downey ... 10th ed. New York, Pub. for the author by E. Walker, 1856. 128 p. 19 cm. "Opinions of the Boston press": p. [115]-128. [BV4501.D63 1856] 32-7869
I. Title.

DOWNEY, William Scott. 248
Proverbs. By Rev. William Scott Downey ... 11th ed. New York, Pub. for the author, by E. Walker, 1858. 128 p. 19 cm. [BV4501.D63 1858] 13-21640
1. Proverbs. I. Title.

LE COMPTE, Irville Charles, 1872-
The sources of the Anglo-French commentary on the Proverbs of Solomon contained in manuscript 24862 (Fonds. francais) of the Bibliotheque nationale of Paris Collegeville, Pa., Thompson brothers, 1906. 3 p. l., xx p., 1 l., 63 p., 2 l. (1 fold.) 23 cm. Inaug.-diss.--Strassburg. Vita. 7-34253
I. Title.

A new book of proverbs; or, The economy of human life. tr. from an Indian mansucript, written by an Indian Bramin. Top which is prefixed, An account of the manner in which the said manuscript was discovered, in a letter from an English gentleman residing in China to the Earl of ... Robinson'a ed. ... Louisville, Ky., Pickett publishing co. [1902] 112, [2] p. front. (port.) 20 cm. 2-26072
I. Robinson, Luther R., tr.

SCHOLZ, G[ustave]
Choice proverbs for grammatical analysis; or, Grammar through proverbs, by G. Scholz ... Chicago, New York, A. Flanagan company [1903] 92 p. 19 cm. 3-18276
I. Title.

SOSSO, Lorenzo.
Wisdom for the wise; a book of proverbs, by Lorenzo Sosso ... New York, Dodge publishing company [c1907] [86] p. illus. 16 cm. 7-28934
I. Title.

SPURGEON, Charles Haddon, 1834-1892.
The salt-cellars. Being a collection of proverbs, together with homely notes thereon, by C. H. Spurgeon ... New York, A. C. Armstrong and son, 1889. viii, 334 p. 19 1/2 cm. A 13
I. Title.

Proverbs, Hebrew.

TALMUD, Selections. 296
Light from the Talmud by Charles L. Russell ... New York, Bloch publishing company, 1942. iv, 220 p. incl. tab. 20 cm. Hebrew and English on opposite pages. [PN6519.H5T35] 42-11653
1. Proverbs, Hebrew. I. Talmud, Selections. English. II. Russell, Charles L., ed. and tr. III. Title.

Providence and government of God.

ALLEN, Nancy (Armistead) Mrs. 231.7
...The will of God and prayer, by Nancy Armistead Allen. New York [etc.] Fleming H. Revell company [c1937]. 3 p. l., 5-125 p. 17 1/2 cm. (Her Little studies on great themes, v. 2). Bibliography: p. 125. [BT96.A4] 38-1427
1. Providence and government of God. 2. Prayer. I. Title.

AUGUSTINUS, Aurelius, Saint, bp. of Hippo. 231.5
Divine providence and the problem of evil, a translation of St. Augustine's De ordine, with annotations by Robert P. Russell ... New York, N.Y., Cosmopolitan science & art service co., inc. [1942] 4 p. l., iv, 191 p. 21 1/2 cm. Latin and English on opposite pages. [BR65.A69 1942] 42-22220
1. Providence and government of God. 2. Good and evil. I. Russell, Robert P., ed. and tr. II. Title.

BARKER, William Pierson. 220.9'2 B
When God says no [by] William P. Barker. Old Tappan, N.J., F. H. Revell Co. [1974] 160 p. 20 cm. [BS571.B344] 73-18148 ISBN 0-8007-0643-9 4.95
1. Bible—Biography. 2. Providence and government of God. I. Title.

BAXTER, James Sidlow. 231'.5
Does God still guide? Or, more fully, what are the essentials of guidance and growth in the Christian life? [By] J. Sidlow Baxter. Grand Rapids, Mich., Zondervan Pub. House [1971] 191 p. 23 cm. Reprint of the 1968 ed. [BT135.B35 1971] 71-120047 4.95
1. Providence and government of God. I. Title.

BELEW, Pascal P 231.5
The philosophy of providence. Butler, Ind. Higley Press [c1955] 176p. 22cm. [BT135.B38] 56-29678
1. Providence and government of God. I. Title.

BIERBAUM, Athanasius, father, 1874- 231.5
Why are you fearful? Adapted from the German of Father Athanase ... by Marion A. Habig ... Paterson, N. J., St. Anthony guild press, Franciscan monastery, 1937. 3 p. l., 96 p. incl. front. 17 cm. [Secular name: Frederick Bierbaum] [BT135.B47] 38-2114
1. Providence and government of God. 2. God—Love. I. Habig, Marion Alphonse, father, 1901- tr. II. Title. III. Title: Translation of Keine angst vor Gott!

BLAMIRES, Harry 231.5
The will and the way; a study of divine providence and vocation. Greenwich, Conn., Seabury, 1962. 128p. 19cm. 1.50 pap.,
1. Providence and government of God. 2. Vocation. I. Title.

BLAMIRES, Harry. 231.5
The will and the way; a study of divine providence and vocation. New York, Macmillan, 1957. 128 p. 22 cm. [BT135.B57] 57-10290
1. Providence and government of God. 2. Vocation. I. Title.

BRIDGMAN, Raymond Landon, 1848-1925. 231
The master idea, by Raymond L. Bridgman. Boston, Chicago, The Pilgrim press [c1899] 357 p. 19 1/2 cm. [BT101.B8] 99-4879
1. Providence and government of God. I. Title.

BRUCE, Alexander Balmain, 1831-1899. 214
The providential order of the world, by Alexander Balmain Bruce ... New York, C. Scribner's sons, 1897. viii p., 1 l., 346 p. 20 1/2 cm. (Half-title: The Gifford lectures, 1897) Lectures delivered before the University of Glasgow in 1897. [BT135.B7] 4-4019
1. Providence and government of God. I. Title.

BURR, Enoch Fitch, 1818-1907. 210
Ecce terra; or, The hand of God in the earth. By the Rev. E. F. Burr ... Philadlephia, Presbyterian board of publication [1883]. 320 p. 19 cm. [BL225.B8] 30-28790
1. Providence and government of God. 2. Creation. I. Title.

CHACE, George Ide, 1808-1885. 214
The relation of divine providence to physical laws. A discourse delivered before the Porter rhetorical society, of Andover theological seminary, August 1, 1854. By George I. Chace ... Boston, Ticknor and Fields, 1854. 66 p. 24 cm. [BT135.C4] 40-37281
1. Providence and government of God. 2. Religion and science—1800-359. I. Title.

CLOUD, Fred. 231.5
God's hand in our lives; a study of providence. Nashville, Tidings [c1964] 71 p. 19 cm. Bibliographical footnotes. [BT96.2.C5] 64-7793
1. Providence and government of God. I. Title.

DAVIES, David Richard. 231.8
Divine judgment in human history, by D. R. Davies ... London, The Sheldon press; New York, The Macmillan company [1943] vii, [1], 64 p. 18 1/2 cm. (Half-title: The Christian news-letter books, no. 18) "First published 1943." [BT96.D3] 44-4302
1. Providence and government of God. 2. World war, 1939-1945—Religious aspects. 3. Reconstruction (1939-)—Religious aspects. I. Title.

DAVIS, Andrew Jackson, 1826-1910. 133.9
The philosophy of special providence. A vision. By Andrew Jackson Davis ... Third. Revised, restereotyped, and enlarged [ed.] Boston, Banner of light publishing company [c1872?] 69 p. 20 cm. [BF1291.D32 1872] 32-21761
1. Providence and government of God. I. Title.

DAVIS, Andrew Jackson, 1826-1910. 133.
The philosophy of special providences. A vision. By Andrew Jackson Davis ... Rev., restereotyped, and enl. Boston, W. White and company; New York, Banner of light branch office, 1872. 69 p. 20 cm. [BF1291.D32 1872] 11-3608
1. Providence and government of God. I. Title.

DAVIS, Andrew Jackson, 1826-1910. 133.
The philosophy of special providences: a vision. By Andrew Jackson Davis ... Boston, B. Marsh, 1850. 55 p. 24 cm. [BF1291.D32 1850] 11-3607
1. Providence and government of God. I. Title.

DEWEY, Orville, 1794-1882. 124
... The problem of human destiny, or, The end of Providence in the world and man. By Rev. Orville Dewey, D. D. New York, J. Miller, 1864. viii, 278 p. 24 cm. (Lowell lectures) [BD541.D5] 11-23105
1. Providence and government of God. I. Lowell institute lectures, 1851-52. II. Title.

DEWEY, Orville, 1794-1882. 124
... The problem of human destiny; or, The end of Providence in the world and man. By Rev. Orville Dewey, D. D. 3d ed. New York, J. Miller, 1866. viii, 280 p. 24 cm. (Lowell lectures) [BD541.D52] 11-23106
1. Providence and government of God. I. Lowell institute lectures. II. Title.

THE divine purpose; 214
displayed in the works of providence and grace; in a series of twenty letters. Addressed to an inquiring friend. 2d ed. ... Richmond, Va., Pollard and Converse, 1827. 138 p. 19 cm. [BT135.D6 1827] 41-30181
1. Providence and government of God.

DOWNEY, Richard, abp., 1881- 214
Divine providence, by the Most Reverend Richard Downey ... introduction by Rt. Rev. Monsignor Joseph H. McMahon ... New York, The Macmillan company, 1928. xi, [1], 84 p. 17 1/2 cm. (Half-title: The treasury of the faith series: 7) [BT135.D7 1928a] 28-20847
1. Providence and government of God. I. Title.

DUNCAN, James Foulis, 1812-1895. 231.5
God in disease, or. The manifestations of design in morbid phenomena. By James F. Duncan ... Philadelphia, Lindsay & Blakiston, 1852. viii, [9]-232 p. 18 cm. [BT135.D8] 33-24563
1. Providence and government of God. I. Title.

DUNCAN, John Mason, 1790-1851. 231.7
Lectures on the general principles of moral government, as they are exhibited in the first three chapters of Genesis. By John M. Duncan ... Baltimore, Cushing & sons, 1832. 1 p. l., [vii]-xii, [13]-376 p. 19 cm. [BT96.D8 1832] 40-25482
1. Providence and government of God. 2. Bible. OT. Genesis I-III Criticism, interpretation, etc. I. Title.

DUNCAN, John Mason, 1790-1851. 231.7
Lectures on the general principles of moral government, as they are exhibited in the first three chapters of Genesis. By John M. Duncan ... 2d ed., rev. and enl. Baltimore, Cushing & sons, 1836. 2 v. 18 cm. [BT96.D8 1836] 40-25483
1. Providence and government of God. 2. Bible, OT, Genesis I-III—Criticism, interpretation, etc. I. Title.

DYE, Harold Eldon, 1907- 231.7
Through God's eyes, by Harold E. Dye ... Nashville, Tenn., Broadman press [1947] vii, 116 p. 20 1/2 cm. [BT135.D9] 47-23426
1. Providence and government of God. I. Title.

EDDY, George Sherwood, 1871- 231.5
I have seen God do it, by Sherwood Eddy. [New York] Harper & brothers [c1940] viii p., 1 l., 231 p. 20 cm. "First edition." [BT135.E3] 40-27319
1. Providence and government of God. I. Title.

EDWARDS, Francis Henry, 1897- 231
God our help, by F. Henry Edwards. Independence, Mo., Herald publishing house, 1943. 230 p. 20 1/2 cm. Bibliographical foot-notes. [BT101.E35] 43-17195
1. God. 2. Providence and government of God. 3. Faith. I. Title.

ELLIOTT-BINNS, Leonard Elliott, 1885-
Divine providence and human destiny, by L. E. Elliott-Binns ... London, Society for promoting Christian knowledge; New York, The Macmillan co. [1943] vii, 86 p. 1 l. 19 cm. "First published 1943." Bibliographical foot-notes. A 43
1. Providence and government of God. I. Title.

FARIS, John Thomson, 1871-
The book of God's providence, by John T. Faris ... New York, Hodder & Stoughton, George H. Doran company [c1913] 5 p. l., 278 21 cm. 13-25394 1.00
I. Title.

FARRER, Austin Marsden 231.8
Love almighty and ills unlimited; an essay on providence and evil, containing the Nathaniel Taylor lectures for 1961. Garden City, N.Y., Doubleday [c.1961] 168p. (Christian faith series) 61-8883 3.50 bds.,
1. Providence and government of God. 2. Theodicy. 3. Good and evil. I. Title.

FAUNCE, Daniel Worcester, 1829-1911. 214
Shall we believe in a divine providence? By D. W. Faunce ... New York and London, Funk & Wagnalls company, 1900. 202 p. 19 cm. [BT135.F2] 1-29300
1. Provedence and government of God. I. Title.

FERNALD, Woodbury M. 214
God in his Providence; a comprehensive view of the principles and particulars of an active Divine Providence over man,--his fortunes, changes, trails, entire discipline as a spiritual being, from birth to eternity. By Woodbury M. Fernald ... 2d ed. Boston, O. Clapp [etc.]; New York, D. Appleton & co., 1859. xv, 437 p. 20 cm. [BT135.F4] 24-13103
1. Providence and government of God. I. Title.

GARRIGOU-LAGRANGE, Reginald, pere, 1877- 231.5
Providence, by the Rev. Reginald Garrigou-Lagrange; translated by Dom Bede Rose ... St. Louis, Mo. and London, B. Herder book co., 1937. xi, 360 p. 21 cm. "God and ... providence ... in their relation to the spiritual life--Catholic authors. [Secular name: Gontrau Garrigou-Lagrange] [BT135.G32] 37-3379
I. Rose, Bede, father, 1880- tr. II. Title.

GILKEY, James Gordon, 1889- 281.7
God will help you, by James Gordon Gilkey ... New York, The Macmillan company, 1943. viii p., 2 l., 114 p. 19 cm. "First printing." [BT135.G5] 43-15041
1. Providence and government of God. I. Title.

GOODWIN, Abb L. 231'.5
God's eternal purpose revealed, by Abb L. Goodwin. Rev. ed. Dallas, Crescendo Book Publications [1973] 261 p. illus. 23 cm. [BT96.2.G64 1973] 73-83082 5.95
1. Providence and government of God. I. Title.
Publisher's address: 2580 Gus Thomasson, Dallas, Texas 75228.

GOODWIN, Abb L 231
God's eternal purpose revealed. Jacksonville, Fla. Direct Mail Advertising Co. 1948. 241 p. illus., port. 22 cm. [BT96.G6] 48-17664
1. Providence and government of God. I. Title.

GORDON, William Robert, 1811-1897. 221.92
Particular providence, in distinction from general, necessary to the fulfillment of the purposes and promises of God: illustrated by a course of lectures on the history of Joseph. By William R. Gordon ... New York, R. & R. Brinkerhoff, 1855. cxii, [13]-492 p. plates. 20 cm. [BS580.J6G6] 31-25329
1. Joseph, the patriarch. 2. Providence and government of God. I. Title.

GRIFFITH-JONES, Ebenezer, 1860- 214
Providence--divine and human, a study of the world-order in the light of modern thought, by E. Griffith-Jones ... New York, George H. Doran company [1925]- v. 21 cm. Contents.i. Some problems of divine providence. [BT135.G7] 27-1380
1. Providence and government of God. I. Title.

GWALTNEY, Leslie Lee, 1876- 248
A message for today on the chariots of fire; or, The Triumph of the spiritual. With notes on the times, [by] L. L. Gwaltney... [Birmingham, Ala., Birmingham printing company, 1941] 57 p. 18 cm. [BT96.G85] 42-2525
1. Providence and government of God. 2. Sprituality. 3. World War, 1939—Religious aspects. I. Title.

HALL, Charles Henry, 1763-1827. 231.5
Sermons preached before the University of Oxford, at St. Mary's church, in the year mdccxcviii, at the lecture founded by the Rev. John Bampton, M.A. By the Rev. Charles Henry Hall... Oxford, The University press for the author: [etc., etc.] 1799. 3 pc l., [v]-viii, 277, [1] p. 22 cm. Binder's title: Bampton lectures. 1798. [BR45.B3 1798] [(280.082)] 88-16044
1. Providence and government of God. 2. Church of England—Sermons. 3. Sermons, English. I. Title.

HARKNESS, Georgia Elma 231.5
The providence of God. Nashville, Abingdon Press [c.1960] 192p. 23cm. (bibl. footnotes) 60-6932 3.50
1. Providence and government of God. I. Title.

HARKNESS, Georgia Elma, 1891- 231.5
The providence of God. New York, Abingdon Press [1960] 192p. 23cm. Includes bibliography. [BT135.H27] 60-6932
1. Providence and government of God. I. Title.

HASTINGS, Horace Lorenzo, 1833- 231.7
The great controversy between God and man. Its origin, progress, and end... By H. L. Hastings... Providence, R. I., H. L. Hastings; New York, G. W. Young; [etc., etc.,] 1861. v p., 1 l., [11]-167 p. 17 1/2 cm. "Third thousand." [BT96.H3] 41-41797
1. Providence and government of God. I. Title.

HASTINGS, Horace Lorenzo, 1833- 214
The guiding hand; or, Providential direction illustrated by authentic instances; recorded and collected by H. L. Hastings... Boston, Scriptual tract repository, 1881. 382 p. 19 cm. (On cover: Faith series) [BT135.H3] 41-30182
1. Providence and government of God. I. Title.

HASTINGS, Horace Lorenzo, 1833?-1899. 231.
The great controversy between God and man, its origin, progress, and end... By H. L. Hastings. Rochester, N.Y., H. L. Hastings; New York, G. Young; [etc., etc., 1858] v p., 1 l., [11]-167 p. 18 cm. [BT96.H3 1858] 47-35879
1. Providence and government of God. I. Title.

HAYNES, Carlyle Boynton, 1882- 231.5
On the throne of the world; an analysis of the Bible teaching of the sovereignty of God and His providential supervision of the affairs of men and nations, particularly as it is manifested in the lives of His disciples. Nashville, Southern Pub. Association ['1951] 124 p. 21 cm. [BT135.H33] 52-24898
1. Providence and government of God. 2. Seventh-Day Adventists—Doctrinal and controversial works. I. Title.

HAZELTON, Roger, 1909- 231.5
God's way with man; variations on the theme of providence. New York, Abingdon Press [1956] 204p. 21cm. [BT135.H34] 56-101463
1. Providence and government of God. I. Title.

HEISLEY, Charles Wesley, 1826-
Providence and calamity, by Charles W. Heisley. Boston, Sherman, French & company, 1909. 6 p. l., 182 p. 20 cm. 9-15766
I. Title.

HIGGINS, Solomon, 1792-1867, comp. 214
Illustrations of the divine government in remarkable providences. Collected and arranged by S. Higgins and W. H. Brisbane. With an introductory essay on providence. By Rev. Joseph Castle, D. D. Philadelphia, Perkinpine & Higgins, 1859. xiii, 15-425 p. 19 cm. On cover: Divine government in remarkable providence. [BT135.H6] 40-38460
1. Providence and government of God. I. Brisbane, William H., 1824-1862, joint comp. II. Castle, Joseph, 1801-1881. III. Title. IV. Title: Divine government in remarkable providences.

HOWE, Lee Arthur, 1905- 231.5
--Yet we can hope, by Lee A. Howe, jr. Philadelphia, Chicago [etc.] The Judson press [1938] 7 p. l., 3-164 p. 20 cm. "Published September, 1938." [BT135.H67] 39-16212
1. Providence and government of God. I. Title.

HUNTER, John Edward, 1909- 231'.5
World in rebellion / by John E. Hunter. San Diego, Calif. : Beta Books, [1978] p. cm. Reprint of the 1972 ed. published by Moody Press, Chicago. [BT96.2.H86 1978] 78-2528 ISBN 0-89293-055-1 pbk. : 2.95
1. Providence and government of God. 2. Revolution (Theology). 3. Man (Christian theology). I. Title.

JACOCKS, Abel B. 231.7
The general features of the moral government of God. By A. B. Jacocks, M. A. Boston, W. Crosby and H. P. Nichols, 1848. iv, 90 p. 18 cm. [BT96.J2] 40-25484
1. Providence and government of God. I. Title.

JOHNSON, Paul Gordon, 1931- 231'.5
Caution—God at work / Paul G. Johnson. Maryknoll, N.Y. : Orbis Books, c1976. xiv, 137 p. ; 21 cm. Includes bibliographical references. [BT96.2.J63] 75-7781 ISBN 0-88344-052-0 : 3.95
1. Providence and government of God. 2. Theology. I. Title.

JOHNSON, Paul Gordon, 1931- 231'.5
Caution—God at work / by Paul G. Johnson. Maryknoll, N.Y. : Orbis Books, [1976] p. cm. Includes bibliographical references. [BT96.2.J63] 75-7781 ISBN 0-88344-052-0
1. Providence and government of God. 2. Theology. I. Title.

KEARNS, Mary Kenneth, comp. 231.5
Divine providence; [anthology. Scranton, Pa., Manus Langan Press, 1959] 112p. illus. 23cm. Includes bibliography. [BT135.K37] 59-14066
1. Providence and government of God. I. Title.

LITTLETON, Mary Brabson. 264.1
Whence victory? By Mary Brabson Littleton. Sea Isle City, N.J., New York [etc.] Scapular press [1943] 11 p. l., 19-181 p. front., plates, ports. 21 cm. A new and enlarged edition of the author's Whence cometh victory? [BT135.L5 1943] 43-13442
1. Providence and government of God. 2. World war, 1939—Religious aspects. I. Title.

LLOYD, Marjorie Lewis. 231'.8
Why the cookie crumbles / Marjorie Lewis Lloyd. Mountain View, Calif. : Pacific Press Pub. Association, c1981. p. cm. [BT96.2.L58] 19 80-22481 ISBN 0-8163-0400-9 pbk. : .95
1. Providence and government of God. 2. Theodicy. 3. Christian life—Seventh-Day Adventist authors. I. Title.
Distributed by the Greater New York Bookstore, 12 W. 40th St., New York, NY

LOCKERBIE, Jeanette W. 231'.5
Just take it from the Lord, brother [by] Jeanette Lockerbie. Old Tappan, N.J., F. H. Revell Co. [1975] 124 p. 21 cm. [BT135.L6] 74-18021 ISBN 0-8007-0698-6 3.95
1. Providence and government of God. 2. Christian life—1960- I. Title.

LUIS DE GRANADA, 1504-1588. 231.5
God cares for you, translated from the Spanish of the Venerable Father Louis of Granada ... By Father E. C. McEniry, O.P. ... Columbus, O., College book company, 1944. ix, 163, [2], 164-335 p. illus., plates. 23 1/2 cm. "First edition." Translation of Introduccion al simbolo de la fe. [BT135.L8] 44-1457
1. Providence and government of God. 2. Philosophy of nature. I. McEniry, Edmond Ceslas, father, 1891- tr. II. Title.

MCCOSH, James, 1811-1894. 231.
The method of the divine government, physical and moral. By James McCosh ... New York, R. Carter and brothers, 1880. vi p., 2 l., [ix]-xiii, 549 p 23 1/2 cm. [BT96.M2 1880] 45-44239
1. Providence and government of God. I. Title.

MCCOSH, James, 1811-1894. 231
The method of the divine government, physical and moral, by Rev. James McCosh. New York, R. Carter & brothers, 1852. viii, [9]-515 p. 23 1/2 cm. [BT96.M2 1852] 15-9184
1. Providence and government of God. I. Title.

MCCOSH,James, 1811-1894. 231.7
The method of the divine government, physical and moral. By Rev. James McCosh. New York, R. Carter & brothers, 1853. viii, [9]-515 p. 22 1/2 cm. [BT96.M2 1853] 38-20506
1. Providence and government of God. I. Title.

MCCOSH, James, 1811-1894. 231.7
The method of the divine government, physical and moral. By James McCosh... 4th ed. New York, R. Carter & brothers, 1858. 1 p. l., [b]-xiii, 546, [1] p. 24 cm. [BT96.M2 1858] 35-22781
1. Providence and government of God. I. Title.

MATHER, Increase, 1639-1723. 231'.5
Remarkable providences / Increase Mather. New York : Arno Press, 1977. p. cm. (International folklore) Reprint of the 1856 ed. published by J. R. Smith, London. [BT135.M34 1977] 77-70610 ISBN 0-405-10107-4 : 18.00
1. Providence and government of God. 2. Legends—New England. I. Title. II. Series.

MEYER, Carl Stamm, 1907- 231'.5
The caring God; perspectives on providence. Edited by Carl S. Meyer and Herbert T. Mayer. St. Louis, Concordia Pub. House [1973] 240 p. 24 cm. Includes bibliographical references. [BT135.M4 1973] 72-91151 ISBN 0-570-03228-8 8.95
1. Providence and government of God. I. Mayer, Herbert T., joint author. II. Title.

MORICE, Henri. 231.5
The gospel of divine providence, translated from the French of Henri Morice, by Rev. J. M. Lelen. Milwaukee, The Bruce publishing company [c1930] 4 p. l., 191 p. 18 1/2 cm. [BT135.M57] 31-102
1. Providence and government of God. I. Leien, Joseph Mary, 1873- tr. II. Title.

MUMFORD, Bob. 248.4
Take another look at guidance; a study of divine guidance. Edited by Jorunn Oftedal Ricketts. Plainfield, N.J., Logos International [1971] xi, 156 p. 21 cm. [BT96.2.M84] 77-166498 ISBN 0-912106-17-4 4.95
1. Providence and government of God. 2. Christian life—1960- I. Title.

OUTLER, Albert Cook, 1908- 231'.5
Who trusts in God; musings on the meaning of providence [by] Albert C. Outler. New York, Oxford University Press, 1968. xvi, 141 p. 21 cm. Bibliographical footnotes. [BT96.2.O8] 68-17616
1. Providence and government of God. I. Title.

PEARSON, Abel. 231.
An analysis of the principles of the divine government, in a series of conversations, and also conversations on some other interesting subjects, particularly relating to the same principles between A. P. and N. P. and a dissertation on the prophecies, in reference to the rise and fall of the beast ... together with a calculation shewing the exact time of the death of Christ, and, also, calculations shewing the precise time of the rise and fall of the beast, and the beginning of the millenium, &c. By Abel Pearson. Athens, Tenn., T. A. Anderson, 1832-33. xii, 419 p. 22 cm. [BT96.P3] 44-52873
1. Providence and government of God. I. Title.

PINK, Arthur Walkington, 1886-1952. 231
The sovereignty of God. [6th ed.] Swengel, Pa., Bible Truth Depot, 1959[c.1930] 320p. 60-52356 3.75 bds.,
1. Providence and government of God. I. Title.

PINK, Arthur Walkington, 1886-1952. 231.7
The sovereignty of God. Grand Rapids, Baker Book House, 1965 [c1930] 320 p. 21 cm. [BT135.P5. 1965] 63-18713
1. Providence and government of God. I. Title.

PITTENGER, William Norman, 1905- 230
God's way with men; a study of the relationship between God and man in providence, "miracle," and prayer, by Norman Pittenger. Valley Forge [Pa.] Judson Press [1969] 184 p. 22 cm. [BT135.P54 1969] 71-86853 4.95
1. Providence and government of God. 2. Miracles. 3. Prayer. I. Title.

PLUMER, William Swan, 1802-1880. 231.
Jehovah-jireh: a treatise on providence. By William S. Plumer ... Richmond, Presbyterian committee of publication, 1867. 233 p. 19 cm. [BT135.P55] 43-48412
1. Providence and government of God. I. Presbyterian church in the U.S. Executive committee of publication. II. Title.

POLLARD, William Grosvenor, 1911- 231.5
Chance and providence; God's action in a world governed by scientific law. New York, Scribner [1958] 190 p. 21 cm. [BT135.P6] 58-5722
1. Providence and government of God. 2. Religion and science—1900- I. Title.

THE providence of God 231.
displayed in a series of interesting facts. Philadelphia, Presbyterian board of publication [1848] iv, 5-215 p. front. 16 cm. [BT135.P8] 41-31255
1. Providence and government of God. I. Presbyterian church in the U. S. A. (Old school) Board of publication.

READ, Hollis, 1802-1887. 270
The hand of God in history; or, Divine providence historically illustrated in the extension and establishment of

Christianity. By Hollis Read ... Hartford, H. Huntington, 1849. x, [11]-402 p., 1 l. 21 cm. "Some of the authors consulted": leaf at end. [BR148.R4 1849] 36-29111
1. Providence and government of God. I. Title.

READ, Hollis, 1802-1887. 270
The hand of God in history; or, Divine providence historically illustrated in the extension and establishment of Christianity. By Hollis Read ... Hartford, H. E. Robins and co., 1851. x, [11]-402 p. plates. 20 cm. "Some of the authors consulted": p. [vi] [BR148.R4 1851] 36-24597
1. Providence and government of God. I. Title.

READ, Hollis, 1802-1887. 270
The hand of God in history; or, Divine providence historically illustrated in the extension and establishment of Christianity. By Hollis Read ... Part second. Hartford, H. E. Robins and co., 1856. x, [11]-408 p. plates. ports. 21 cm. On cover: God in history ... vol. 2. Supplements the author's work (with same title) published in 1849. The two were combined in one volume, Philadelphia, 1870. [BR148.R42] 37-17426
1. Providence and government of God. I. Title.

READ, Hollis, 1802-1887. 270
The hand of God in history; or, Divine providence illustrated in the extension and establishment of Christianity throughout the world. By Rev. Hollis Read ... Philadelphia, J. E. Potter and company; New York [etc.] J. W. Goodspeed & co. [1870] 860 p. incl. illus., 24 pl., 5 port. fornt., plates, ports. 23 cm. [BR148.R4 1870] 36-25165
1. Providence and government of God. I. Title.

A review of Doct. Emmons's 231.7
theory of God's agency on mankind; addressed to the Congregational clergy of New England. Also, a refutation of the views entertained by advocates of that theory, respecting the necessity of the moral evil existing in the universe to a display of the divine glory. New-York, J. Sayre, 1821. viii, [13]-388 p. 19 1/2 cm. [BT96.R4] 40-37130
1. Emmons, Nathanael, 1745-1840. 2. Providence and government of God. 3. Free will and determination.

SALVIANUS, 5thcent. 231.7
On the government of God; a treatise wherein are shown by argument and by examples drawn from the abandoned society of the times the ways of God toward His creatures, indited by Salvian...as a warning and counsel. This fifth century polemic done into English by Eva M. Sanford. New York, Columbia university press, 1930. viii, 241 p. front. 23 1/2 cm. (Added t.-p.: Records of civilization: sources and studies, ed. under the auspices of the Department of history, Columbia university) Bibliography: p. 233-234. [BR65.S25] (967.09) 31-3925
1. Providence and government of God. 2. Christianity. 3. Rome—Soc. condit. I. Sanford, Eva Matthews, tr. II. Title.

SEWARD, Theodore 214
Frelinghuysen, 1835-1902.
The school of life; divine providence in the light of modern science, the law of development applied to Christian thinking and Christian living, by Theodore F. Seward ... New York, J. Pott & co., 1894. xi, 267 p. 21 cm. [BT135.S4 1894] 40-37137
1. Providence and government of God. 2. Religion and science—1860-1899. I. Title.

SEWARD, Theodore 231.5
Frelinghuysen, 1835-1902.
The school of life; divine providence in the light of modern science, the law of development applied to Christian thinking and Christian living by Theodore F. Seward ... New York, J. Pott & co.; London, S. Bagster & sons limited, 1895. xi, 267 p. 21 cm. [BT135.S4 1895] 40-37282
1. Providence and government of God. 2. Religion and science—1860-1899. I. Title.

SHEBBEARE, Charles John, 214
1865-
Problems of providence, by Rev. Charles J. Shebbeare ... London, New York [etc.] Longmans, Green and co., 1929. vi p., 1 l., 119, [1] p. 19 1/2 cm. (Half-title: Anglican library of faith and thought) $1.35. [BT135.S47] 29-21163
1. Providence and government of God. I. Title.

SHERLOCK, William, 1641?- 231.5
1707.
A discourse concerning the divine providence. By William Sherlock, D.D. From the 2d London edition. Cincinnati, Pub. by M. Ruter, for the Methodist Episcopal church, 1823. iv, [5]-362, [5] p. 17 1/2 cm. [BT135.S5 1823] 32-35382
1. Providence and government of God. I. Title.

SHERLOCK, William, 1641?- 231.5
1707.
A discourse concerning the divine providence, by William Sherlock, D.D. 3d American ed. Nashville, Tenn., E. Stevenson & F. A. Owen, agents, for the Methodist Episcopal church, South, 1856. 336 p. 20 cm. [BT135.S5 1856] 35-23133
1. Providence and government of God. I. Title.

SHUMAKER, Elmer Ellsworth, 218
1862-
God and man; philosophy of the higher life, by E. Ellsworth Shumaker... New York and London, G. P. Putnam's sons, 1909. xi, 408 p. 21 cm. [BD431.S55] 9-30420
1. Providence and government of God. 2. Man. 3. Religion. I. Title.

SMITH, C Billings. 231.7
The philosophy of reform in which are exhibited the design, principle and plan of God, for the full development of man, as a social, civil, intellectual and moral being; thereby elevating him in the scale of being to the position he was created to occupy. By Rev. C. Billings Smith... New York, Gates and Stedman, 1846. 4 p. l., [v]-xiv, [17]-352 p. 19 1/2 cm. [BT96.S6] 40-37131
1. Providence and government of God. I. Title.

SPICER, William Ambrose, 214
1866-
The hand that intervenes, by W. A. Spicer ... Washington, D.C., South Bend, Ind. [etc.] Review and herald publishing association [c1918] 3 p. l., 11-334 p. front., illus. (incl. ports) 21 cm. $1.50. [BT135.S7] 18-18482
I. Title.

SPICER, William Ambrose, 231.7
1866- comp.
Stories of providential deliverance ... compiled by W. A. Spicer ... Takoma Park, Washington, D.C., South Bend, Ind. [etc.] Review and herald publishing association [c1936] 2 p. l., 3-121 p. 19 1/2 cm. [BV4515.S615] 36-11481
1. Providence and government of God. I. Title. II. Title: Providential deliverance, Stories of.

SQUIER, Miles Powell, 1792- 231.
1866.
The being of God; moral government and theses in theology. By Miles P. Squier ... Edited by Rev. James R. Boyd. Rochester, N.Y., E. Darrow & Kempshall, 1868. xvi p., 1 l., [19]-247 p. front. (port.) 20 cm. [BT96.S72] 43-48459
1. Providence and government of God. I. Boyd, James Robert, 1804-1890, ed. II. Title.

SUMMERS, Thomas Osmond, 1812- 214
1882.
Remarkable escapes from peril. Revised by Thos. O. Summers, D.D. Nashville, Tenn., Pub. by E. Stevenson & F. A. Owen, agents, for the Methodist Episcopal church, South, 1856. v, 7-158 p. 15 1/2 cm. [BT135.S85] 39-3014
1. Providence and government of God. I. Title.

SWEDENBORG, Emanuel, 1688- 228
1772.
Angelic wisdom concerning the divine love and the divine wisdom. Translated from the Latin of Emanuel Swedenborg. Originally published at Amsterdam MDCCLXIII. From the last London ed. New York, American Swedenborg printing and publishing society, 1851. xii, 180 p. 23 1/2 cm. One of the reprints of the London edition of 1843, which was revised by Dr. J. J. G. Wilkinson. cf. Hyde, J. A bibliography of the works of Emanuel Swedenborg ... 1906. no. 2047. [BX8712.D4 1851] 36-3257
1. Providence and government of God. I. Wilkinson, James John Garth, 1812-1899. II. Title.

SWEDENBORG, Emanuel, 1688- 230.9
1772.
Angelic wisdom concerning the divine love and the divine wisdom. Translated from the Latin of Emanuel Swedenborg ... Originally pub. at Amsterdam, MDCCLXIII. From the last London edition. New York, American Swedenborg printing and publishing society, 1864. xii, 180 p. 23 cm. One of the reprints of the London edition of 1843, which was revised by Dr. J. J. G. Wilkinson. cf. J. Hyde, A bibliography of the works of Emanuel Swedenborg, 1906, p. 427 (no. 2044) [BX8712.D4 1864] 17-4645
1. Providence and government of God. I. Wilkinson, James John Garth, 1812-1899. II. Title.

SWEDENBORG, Emanuel, 1688- 230.94
1772.
Angelic wisdom concerning the divine love and the divine wisdom [by] Emanuel Swedenborg; originally published in Latin at Amsterdam, 1763. New York, American Swedenborg printing and publishing society, 1885. viii, 246, [2] p. 23 cm. "Translated by the Rev. J. C. Ager, and an edition of 3491 printed."-- J. Hyde, A bibliography of the works of Emanuel Swedenborg, 1906, p. 432 (no. 2070) Copy 2. To this is appended the author's The nature of the intercourse between the soul and the body ... Neu York, 1882. On cover: Divine love and wisdom. The soul and body. [BX8712.D4 1885] 17-4647
1. Providence and government of God. I. Ager, John Curtis, 1835-1913, tr. II. Title.

SWEDENBORG, Emanuel, 1688- 230.94
1772.
Angelic wisdom concerning the divine love and the divine wisdom. By Emanuel Swedenborg. New York, The American Swedenborg printing and publishing society, 1923. xx, 617 p. 15 cm. Translator's note signed: John C. Ager. "Theological works of Emanuel Swedenborg": p. 605-617. [BX8712.D4 1923] 36-30571
1. Providence and government of God. I. Ager, John Curtis, 1835-1913, tr. II. Title.

SWEDENBORG, Emanuel, 1688- 230.94
1772.
Angelic wisdom concerning the divine love and the divine wisdom. Translated from the Latin of Emanuel Swedenborg ... Originally published at Amsterdam, MDCCLXIII. From the last London edition. New York, American Swedenborg printing and publishing society, 1872. xii, 199 p. 23 cm. One of the reprints or the London edition of 1843, which was revised by Dr. J. J. G. Wilkinson. cf. J, Hyde, A bibliography of the works of Emanuel Swedenborg, 1906, p. 427 (no. 2044) [BX8712.D4 1872] 17-4646
1. Providence and government of God. I. Wilkinson, James John Garth, 1812-1899. II. Title.

SWEDENBORG, Emanuel, 1688- 230.94
1772.
Angelic wisdom concerning the divine providence. Translated from the Latin of Emanuel Swedenborg ... Originally published at Amsterdam, MDCCLXIV. From the last London edition. New York, American Swedenborg printing and publishing society, 1857. xiii, 274 p. 23 1/2 cm. On cover: The divine providence. Reprinted from the London edition of 1833, which was revised by A. Maxwell. cf. J. Hyde. A bibliography of the works of Emanuel Swedenborg (no. 2117) [BX8712.D6 1857] 36-30568
1. Providence and government of God. I. Maxwell, Alexander, 1776-1849, ed. II. Title.

SWEDENBORG, Emanuel, 1688- 228
1772.
Angelic wisdom concerning the divine Providence. Translated from the Latin of Emanuel Swedenborg ... Originally published at Amsterdam, MDCCLXIV. From the last London ed. New York, American Swedenborg printing and publishing society, 1865. xiii, 308 p. 23 cm. One of the reprints of the London edition of 1833, which was revised by A. Maxwell. cf. J. Hyde, A bibliography of the works of Emanuel Swedenborg, 1906, p. 439 (no. 2105) [BX8712.D6 1865] 17-4665
1. Providence and government of God. I. Maxwell, Alexander, ed. II. Title.

SWEDENBORG, Emanuel, 1688- 230.94
1772.
Angelic wisdom concerning the divine providence. By Emanuel Swedenborg. From the original Latin as edited by Dr. J. F. I. Tafel. Translated by R. Norman Foster. Philadelphia, J. B. Lippincott & co., 1868. 2 p. l., 340 p. 21 cm. [BX8712.D6 1868] 33-39246
1. Providence and government of God. I. Tafel, Johann Friedrich Immanuel, 1796-1863, ed. II. Foster, R. Norman, tr. III. Title.

SWEDENBORG, Emanuel, 1688- 230.94
1772.
Angelic wisdom concerning the divine providence. From the Latin of Emanuel Swedenborg. Rotch ed. New York, The New church board of publication; Boston, Massachusetts New church union, 1877. 1 p. l., [v]-xxi, 422 p. 19 1/2 cm. On cover: The divine providence. Reprinted from the 3d American edition of 1856, revised by Rev. S. H. Worcester. cf. J. Hyde. A bibliography of the works of Emanuel Swedenborg (no. 2132) [BX8712.D6 1877] 36-30569
1. Providence and government of God. I. Worcester, Samuel Howard, 1824-1891, ed. II. Title.

SWEDENBORG, Emanuel, 1688- 230.94
1772.
Angelic wisdom concerning the divine providence, by Emanuel Swedenborg; first published in Latin at Amsterdam, 1764. New York, The American Swedenborg printing and publishing society, 1920. xxiv, 605 p. 16 cm. Translated by J. C. Ager; index by George W. Colton. cf. Translator's note. [BX8712.D6 1920] 36-30570
1. Providence and government of God. I. Ager, John Curtis, 1835-1913, tr. II. Colton, George Woolworth, 1827-1901. III. Title.

SWEDENBORG, Emanuel, 1688- 228
1772.
Angelic wisdon concerning the divine providence, by Emanuel Swedenborg; originally published in Latin at Amsterdam, 1764. Library ed. New York, The American Swedenborg printing and publishing society, 1908. xxii, 446 p. 21 1/2 cm. Translated by J. C. Ager; index by George W. Colton. [BX8712.D6 1908] 10-6154
1. Providence and government of God. I. Ager, John Curtis, 1835-1913, tr. II. Colton, George Woolworth, 1827-1901. III. Title.

SWEDENBORG, Emanuel, 1688- 230.94
1772.
The wisdom of angels, concerning divine love and divine wisdom. In five parts. Translated from the original Latin of the Hon. Emanuel Swedenborg. Printed at Boston, by Isaish Thomas and Ebenezer T. Andrews. Faust's statue, no. 45, Newbury street, 1794. 1 p. l., [v]-xxiii, 358 p. 21 cm. Translated also under title: Angelic wisdom concerning divine love and divine wisdom. [BX8712.D4 1794] 36-29969
1. Providence and government of God. I. Title.

SWEDENBORG, Emanuel, 1688- 228
1772.
The wisdom of angels concerning the divine providence. Translated from the Latin of the Hon. Emanuel Swedenborg. Originally published at Amsterdam, anno 1764. Printed at Boston, By Isaish Thomas and Ebenezer T. Andrews, 1796. xxxvi, [37]-543 p. 24 cm. [BX8712.D] A 35

1. Providence and government of God. I. Title.

TAYLOR, Jack R. 231'.5
God's miraculous plan of economy / Jack R. Taylor. Nashville : Broadman Press, c1975. 168 p. ; 23 cm. [BT135.T39] 75-27411 ISBN 0-8054-5565-5 : 5.95
1. Providence and government of God. 2. Stewardship, Christian. I. Title.

TAYLOR, Nathaniel William, 1786-1858. 231
Lectures on the moral government of God, by Nathaniel W. Taylor ... New York, Clark, Austin & Smith, 1859. 2 v. front. (port.) 23 cm. [BT96.T2] 15-25931
1. Providence and government of God. 2. Christian ethics. I. Title.

WAGNER, Ernst.
Means. New York [etc.] F. T. Neely co. [1900] 2 p. l., 75 p. 12 cm. Imperfect: wants p. 37-52, a duplicate sig. (p. 21-36) inserted instead. "How God operates through means."--Pref. 1-29978
I. Title.
Contents omitted.

WATKIN, Edward Ingram, 1888- 201
The bow in the clouds; an essay towards the integration of experience, by E. I. Watkin ... New York, The Macmillan company, 1932. xi p., 1 l., 174 p. 19 1/2 cm. (Half-title: Essays in order: 4) [BX1395.E72 no. 4] (204) 32-13158
1. Providence and government of God. 2. Experience. 3. Experience (Religion) 4. Philosophy and religion. 5. Religion and science—1900- I. Title.

WATSON, William Henry, 1864- 133
Providence, by William Henry Watson... Chicago, Art school publishing co. [c1923] 92 p., 1 l. incl. front., illus. 23 1/2 cm. [BF1999.W32] 23-8426
I. Title.

WEEKS, William Raymond, 1783-1848. 231
The doctrine of the universal decrees and agency of God, asserted and vindicated: nine sermons, from Ephesians 1. 11. Who worketh all things after the counsel of his own will. By William R. Weeks ... Second edition. Providence, R.I., Miller and Hutchens, 1819. 203 p. 14 1/2 cm. [BX9178.W4D6] A 32
1. Providence and government of God. I. Title.

WELCH, Mary Artie Barrington. 248'.4
More than sparrows : how God supplies our human needs / by Mary Welch ; foreword by Eugenia Price. Grand Rapids : Zondervan Pub. House, 1976. 123 p. ; 18 cm. [BT135.W38 1976] 75-45487 pbk. : 1.75
1. Providence and government of God. 2. Christian life—1960- I. Title.

WICKER, John Jordan. 231.7
The march of God in the age-long struggle, by John J. Wicker ... Nashville, Tenn., Broadman press [1943] 234 p. front. (port.) 20 1/2 cm. [BT96.W5] 43-7258
1. Providence and goverment of God. 2. Kingdom of God. I. Title.

Providence and government of God—Addresses, essays, lectures.

VINER, Jacob, 1892-1970. 081 s
The role of providence in the social order; an essay in intellectual history. Philadelphia, American Philosophical Society, 1972. viii, 113 p. 25 cm. (Memoirs of the American Philosophical Society, v. 90) (Jayne lectures for 1966) [Q11.P612 vol. 90] [BT135] 330 72-184168 ISBN 0-87169-090-X 2.00
1. Providence and government of God—Addresses, essays, lectures. 2. Christianity and economics—Addresses, essays, lectures. I. Title. II. Series: American Philosophical Society, Philadelphia. Memoirs, v. 90. III. Series: Jayne lectures, 1966.

Providence and government of God—Biblical teaching.

CARSON, D. A. 231.7
Divine sovereignty and human responsibility : some aspects of Johannine theology against a Jewish background / D. A. Carson. Atlanta : J. Knox Press, 1980. p. cm. (New foundations theological library) Includes bibliographical references. [BS2615.5.C37] 79-27589 ISBN 0-8042-3707-7 : 18.50 ISBN 0 ISBN 0-8042-3727-1 pbk. : 9.95
1. Bible. N.T. John—Theology. 2. Providence and government of God—Biblical teaching. 3. Man (christian theology)—Biblical teaching. 4. Providence and government of God (Judaism)—History of doctrines. 5. Man (Jewish theology)—History of doctrines. I. Title. II. Series.

HOWARD, David M. 223'.1'066
How come, God? Reflections from Job about God and puzzled man. [1st ed.] Philadelphia, A. J. Holman Co. [1972] 117 p. 21 cm. [BS1415.2.H67] 72-3477 ISBN 0-87981-010-6 3.95
1. Bible, O.T. Job—Criticism, interpretation, etc. 2. Providence and government of God—Biblical teaching. I. Title.

MCCALLUM, Martha. 231'.5
God's incredible plan / Martha McCallum and Jane Hamblin. Old Tappan, N.J. : Revell, c1978. p. cm. [BS544.M33] 78-621 ISBN 0-8007-0905-5 : 5.95
1. Providence and government of God—Biblical teaching. I. Hamblin, Jane, joint author. II. Title.

Providence and government of God—Devotional literature.

AUSTIN, Elva M. 242
The potter's shop, by Alice Glen [pseud.] Decorations by Iris Johnson. Washington, Review and Herald [1952] 94 p. illus. 18 cm. [BV4832.A8] 52-41518
1. Providence and government of God—Devotional literature. I. Title.

Providence and government of God—Early works to 1800.

SALVIANUS, 5thcent. 231.7
On the government of God; a treatise wherin are shown by argument and by examples drawn from the abandoned society of the times the ways of God toward His creatures. Indited by Salvian as a warning and counsel. This 5th century polemic done into English by Eva M. Sanford. New York, Octagon Books, 1966. viii, 241 p. front. 24 cm. (Records of civilization; sources and studies no. 12) Reprint of the 1931 ed. Bibliography: p. 233-234. [BR65.S25 1966] 66-28329
1. Providence and government of God—Early works to 1800. 2. Christian life—Early church, ca. 30-600. 3. Rome—Social conditions. I. Sanford, Eva Matthews, tr. II. Title.

SWEDENBORG, Emanuel, 1688-1772 231.5
Angelic wisdom about divine providence. Newly tr. [from Latin] by William Frederic Wunsch. Introd. by Walter M. Horton. New York, Citadel [1964, c.1963] xvii, 419p. 19cm. (C-155) 63-21204 1.95 pap.,
1. Providence and government of God—Early works to 1800. I. Title.

SWEDENBORG, Emanuel, 1688-1772 231
Angelic wisdom concerning divine love and wisdom. Tr. by John C. Ager. Introd. by Helen Keller. New York Citadel [1965, c.1963] xxiii, 306p. 19cm. (C-189) [BX8712.D6] 65-2713 1.50 pap.,
1. Providence and government of God—Early works to 1800. I. Title.

SWEDENBORG, Emanuel, 1688-1772. 230.94
Angelic wisdom concerning the divine love and the divine wisdom. Translation by John C. Ager. New York, Swedenborg Foundation, 1962. xvi, 313 p. 18 cm. On cover: Divine love and wisdom. [BX8712.D4 1962] 63-1052
1. Providence and government of God — Early works to 1800. I. Title. II. Title: Divine love and wisdom.

Providence and government of God (Judaism)

NEHER, Andre. 296.3
The exile of the Word, from the silence of the Bible to the silence of Auschwitz / Andre Neher ; translated from the French by David Naisel. Philadelphia : Jewish Publication Society of America, 1980. p. cm. Translation of L'Exil de la Parole, du silence biblique au silence d'Auschwitz. Includes bibliographical references. [BM645.P7N413] 80-12612 ISBN 0-8276-0176-X : 16.95
1. Bible. O.T.—Theology. 2. Providence and government of God (Judaism) 3. Silence. 4. Holocaust (Jewish theology) 5. God—Biblical teaching. I. Title.

Providence and government of God (Judaism)—Addresses, essays, lectures.

THE Divine helmsman : 296.3'11
studies on God's control of human events, presented to Lou H. Silberman / edited by James L. Crenshaw and Samuel Sandmel. New York : KTAV Pub. House, c1980. xviii, 273 p. : port. ; 24 cm. Contents.Contents.—A Bibliography of Lou Silberman's writings.—Crenshaw, J. L. The birth of skepticism in ancient Israel.—Harrelson, W. Ezra among the wicked in 2 Esdras 10.—Keck, L. E. The law and "the law of sin and death" (Rom 8:1-4).—Meyer, P. W. Romans10:4 and the end of the law.—Sandmel S. Some comments on providence in Philo.—Knight, D. A. Jeremiah and the dimensions of the moral life.—Berg, S. B. After the exile.—Talbert, C. H. Prophecies of future greatness.—Greenberg, M. The vision of Jerusalem in Ezekiel 8-11.—Patte, D. Charting the way of the helmsman on the high seas.—Fackenheim, E. L. New hearts and the old covenant.Hauer, C., Jr. When history stops.—Samuelson, N. Causation and choice in the philosophy of Ibn Daud.—Mills, L. O. The self as helmsman. Includes bibliographical references and index. [BM645.P7D58] 19 79-29644 ISBN 0-87068-700-X : 20.00
1. Silberman, Lou H.—Addresses, essays, lectures. 2. Bible—Criticism and interpretation, etc.—Addresses, essays, lectures. 3. Providence and government of God (Judaism)—Addresses, essays, lectures. I. Silberman, Lou H. II. Crenshaw, James L. III. Sandmel, Samuel.

Providence and government of God — Juvenile literature.

AVEN, Del. 231'.5
God has special places / Del Aven ; illustrated by Debra Aven. Nashville : Broadman Press, c1978. 32 p. : col. ill. ; 24 cm. A little girl discovers that God has a special place on Earth for all creatures. [BT135.A9] 78-113120 ISBN 0-8054-4253-7 pbk. : 2.95
1. Providence and government of God—Juvenile literature. 2. [God.] 3. [Christian life.] I. Aven, Debra. II. Title.

BEERS, Victor Gilbert, 1928- 231'.5
Cats and bats and things like that, and other wonderful things about God's world, by V. Gilbert Beers. Illustrated by Juel Krisvoy. Chicago, Moody Press [1972] [30] p. col. illus. 20 x 26 cm. Describes some of God's gifts in nature, such as the bats' sonar, the changing colors of leaves, and the life contained in a seed. [BT96.2.B43] 72-88038 ISBN 0-8024-1211-4
1. Providence and government of God—Juvenile literature. 2. [Nature.] I. Krisvoy, Juel, illus. II. Title.

HEIDE, Florence Parry. 231'.5
By the time you count to 10 / written by Florence Parry Heide ; illustrated by Pam Erickson. St. Louis : Concordia Pub. House, c1979. [28] p. : col. ill. ; 26 cm. Discusses the omnipotence of God and His continued creation and sustaining love in the world around us. [BT96.2.H43] 79-110408 ISBN 0-570-07797-4 pbk. : 2.95
1. Providence and government of God—Juvenile literature. 2. [God.] I. Erickson, Pamela. II. Title.

HEIDE, Florence Parry. 231'.5
Who taught me? / Florence Parry Heide. St. Louis : Concordia Pub. House, 1978,c1977. p. cm. Explains the concept of God's control over all aspects of our lives. [BT96.2.H44] 77-17383 ISBN 0-570-07786-9 pbk. : 2.95
1. Providence and government of God—Juvenile literature. 2. [Christian life.] I. Title.

MONCURE, Jane Belk. 231'.5
God's care is everywhere / by Bruce Wannamaker ; illustrated by Helen Endres. Elgin, IL : Dandelion House, c1982. p. cm. Affirms the evidences of God's love and care in nature and in human relationships. [BT135.M56] 19 82-7244 ISBN 0-89693-202-8 pbk. : 4.95
1. Providence and government of God—Juvenile literature. 2. [God.] 3. [Christian life.] I. Endres, Helen, ill. II. Title.

WOLCOTT, Carolyn Muller. 231
God planned it that way, by Carolyn Edna Muller. Pictures by Lloyd Dotterer. New York, Abingdon-Cokesbury Press, c1952. unpaged. illus. 19 x 23 cm. [BT135.W6] 52-11653
1. Providence and government of God — Juvenile literature. I. Title.

Providence and government of God—Popular works.

ANDERSON, Margaret J. 296.3
It couldn't happen, but it did / Margaret J. Anderson. Irvine, Calif. : Harvest House Publishers, c1980. 127 p. ; 18 cm. [BT135.A5] 79-56817 ISBN 0-89081-213-6 (pbk.) : 1.95
1. Providence and government of God—Popular works. 2. Prayer—Popular works. I. Title.

ROHDE, J. Martin.
Wonders of Providence; remarkable and authentic providential stories; original and comp. by Rev. J. Martin Rohde... Chicago, The Evangelical publishing co. [c1911] 344 p. 19 1/2 cm. 11-25442
I. Title.

Providence and government of God—Sermons.

CARROLL, Benajah Harvey, 1843-1914. 231.7
The providence of God; comprising heart-searching sermons on vital themes concerning God and his overruling providence among men, by B. H. Carroll ... compiled by J. W. Crowder ... edited by J. B. Cranfill ... Dallas, Tex., Helms printing company [c1940] 217 p. incl. front. (port.) 20 cm. [BT135.C3] 41-1351
1. Providence and government of God—Sermons. 2. Baptists—Sermons. 3. Sermons, American. I. Crowder, Joseph Wade, 1873- comp. II. Cranfill, James Britton, 1858- ed. III. Title.

Providence Baptist Church, Monrovia, Liberia.

PROVIDENCE Baptist Church, Monrovia, Liberia. 286'.1666'2
Providence Baptist Church official souvenir program dedicatorial ceremonies. Monrovia, Liberia : The Church, [1976] 43 p., [5] leaves of plates : ill. ; 28 cm. Cover title. [BX6490.M6P766] 77-372079
1. Providence Baptist Church, Monrovia, Liberia.

Providence. Bell street chapel.

SPENCER, Anna (Garlin) Mrs., 1851- 288.
The history of the Bell street chapel movement, May, 1888, to July, 1902, by Anna Garlin Spencer ... [Providence, R.I. Printed by R. Grieve, 1903] xiv, 208 p. 20 1/2 cm. [BX9861.P9B4] 24-10100
1. Providence. Bell street chapel. I. Title.

Providence. Beneficent Congregational church.

VOSE, James Gardiner, 1830-1908. 285.87452
Commemorative discourses preached in the Beneficent Congregational church, Providence, R.I., October 18, 1868, by

James G. Vose, pastor. To which are appended some historical notes and reminiscences, and a list of the members of the church. Providence, Beneficent Congregational church, 1869. 135, [1] p. front., ports. 19 cm. [BX7255.P9B48] 38-14616
1. Wilson, James, 1760-1830. 2. Providence. Beneficent Congregational church. I. Title.

VOSE, James Gardiner, 1830-1908. 285.87452
Sketches of Congregationalism in Rhode Island, with special reference to the history of the Beneficent church. By James Gardiner Vose. New York, Boston (etc.] Silver, Burdette & company [1894] 236 p. front. 20 cm. [BX7255.P9B5] 38-12921
1. Providence. Beneficent Congregational church. 2. Congregational churches in Rhode Island. I. Title.

Providence—Biography.

WALSH, Richard A. 282'.745'2
The centennial history of Saint Edward Church, Providence, Rhode Island, 1874-1974, by Richard A. Walsh. With an introd. by Louis E. Gelineau. [Providence? R.I., 1974] 242 p. illus. 24 cm. Bibliography: p. [240]-242. [BX4603.P7S258] 74-163508
1. Saint Edward Church, Providence. 2. Providence—Biography. I. Title.

Providence. First Baptist church.

KING, Henry Melville, 1838-1919. 286.17452
The mother church; a brief account of the origin and early history of the First Baptist church in Providence, by Henry Melville King, D.D. Philadelphia, American Baptist publication society [1896] 85 p. front. 17 1/2 cm. [BX6480.P9F5] 40-11356
1. Providence. First Baptist church. I. American Baptist publication society. II. Title.

Providence Presbyterian Church, Mecklenburg Co., N.C.

MATTHEWS, Louise Barber. 285'.1756'76
A history of Providence Presbyterian Church, Mecklenburg County, North Carolina. Illus. by Al Fincher. [Charlotte, N.C., Brooks Litho] 1967. xvi, 338 p. illus., ports. 24 cm. Bibliography: p. 311-320. [BX9211.M38P75] 67-9139
1. Providence Presbyterian Church, Mecklenburg Co., N.C. I. Title.

Providence. St. John's church.

CLARK, Thomas March, bp. 1812-1903. 283.7452
An historical discourse, delivered in St. John's church, Providence, R.I., on St. Barnabas's day, June 11, 1872, in commemoration of the one hundred and fiftieth anniversary of the parish. By the Rt. Rev. Thomas M. Clark...Published, with an appendix, at the request of the vestry, with a photograph of the old parsonage. Hartford, Conn, M. H. Mallory & co., 1872. 52 p. 22 1/2 cm. "Photograph of the old parsonage" not included in L. C. copy. [BX5980.P983 1872] 35-25958
1. Providence. St. John's church. I. Title.

Providence. Saint Stephen's Church.

CATIR, Norman Joseph. 283.7452
Saint Stephen's Church in Providence; the history of a New England Tractarian parish, 1839-1964. Providence, St. Stephen's Church, 1964. xvi, 222 p. illus., ports. 22 cm. Bibliography: p. [211]-214. [BX5980.P9S3] 64-20900
1. Providence. Saint Stephen's Church. I. Title.

Province of Papua New Guinea—History.

WETHERELL, David Fielding. 266'.3'953
Reluctant mission : the Anglican Church in Papua New Guinea, 1891-1942 / by David Wetherell. St. Lucia, Australia : University of Queensland Press, c1977. xiv, 430 p. : ill. ; 22 cm. Includes index. Bibliography: p. [390]-405. [BX5720.8.A4W47] 78-310118 ISBN 0-7022-1411-6 : 18.00
1. Province of Papua New Guinea—History. I. Title.
Available from Technical impex Corp. Lawrence, MA.

Provoost, Samuel, bp., 1742-1815.

NORTON, John Nicholas, 1820-1881. 922
Life of Bishop Provoost, of New York. By John N. Norton ... New York, General Protestant Episcopal S. school union, and Church book society, 1859. 183 p. incl. front. (port.) 18 cm. [BX5995.P7N6] 1-10265
1. Provoost, Samuel, bp., 1742-1815. I. Title.

Pruden, Edward Hughes.

PRUDEN, Edward Hughes. 286'.1'0924 B
A window on Washington / Edward Hughes Pruden. 1st ed. New York : Vantage Press, c1976. 136 p. ; 21 cm. Includes bibliographical references. [BX6495.P78A38] 77-353145 ISBN 0-533-02086-7 : 5.95
1. Pruden, Edward Hughes. 2. Baptists—Clergy—Biography. 3. Clergy—Washington, D.C.—Biography. 4. Washington, D.C.—Biography. 5. Statesmen—United States—Biography. I. Title.

Prudentius Clement, Aurelius.

DEFERRARI, Roy Joseph, 1890- comp. 245.7
A concordance of Prudentius [by] Joseph Deferrari [and] James Marshall Campbell ... Cambridge, Mass., The Mediaeval academy of America, 1932. ix, 833 p. 25 cm. (Half-title: The Mediaeval academy of America. Publication no. 9) [BR65.P67D4] 871 32-5968
1. Prudentius Clements, Aurelisu—Concordances. I. Campbell, James Marshall, 1895- joint comp. II. Title.

MAHONEY, Albertus, brother. 871
... Vergil in the works of Prudentius ... by Brother Albertus Mahoney ... Washington, D.C., The Catholic university of America, 1934. xv, 214 p. 23 1/2 cm. (The Catholic university of America. Patristic studies. vol. xxxix) Thesis (PH.D.)--Catholic university of America, 1934. "Select bibliography": p. vii-x. [BR65.P67M3 1934] 34-22778
1. Prudentius Clement, Aurelius. 2. Vergilius Maro, Publius—Influence. 3. Literature, Comparative—Latin, Classical and postclassical. I. Title.

SMITH, Macklin, 1944- 233'.7
Prudentius' Psychomachia : a reexamination / Macklin Smith. Princeton, N.J. : Princeton University Press, c1976. xii, 310 p. ; 23 cm. Includes bibliographical references and index. [BR65.P783S6] 75-29436 ISBN 0-691-06299-4 : 17.50
1. Prudentius Clemens, Aurelius. Psychomachia. I. Title.

Prynne, William, 1600-1669.

BAKER, Richard, Sir, 1568-1645. 792'.013
Theatrum redivivum; or, The theatre vindicated. Introductory note by Peter Davison. New York, Johnson Reprint Corp., 1972. 141 p. 16 cm. (Theatrum redivivum) Running title: The theatre vindicated. "Written in response to Prynne's Histrio-mastix." Reprint of the 1662 ed. printed by T. R. for F. Eglesfield, London (Wing B513) [PN2047.B3 1972] 76-175650 13.50
1. Prynne, William, 1600-1669. Histrio-mastix. 2. Theater—Moral and religious aspects. I. Prynne, William 1600-1669. Histrio-mastix. II. Title. III. Title: The theatre vindicated.

MR. William Prynn, his 792'.013
defence of stage-plays, anonymous. The vindication of William Prynne by William Prynne. Theatrum redivivum; or, The theatre vindicated by Sir Richard Baker. With a pref. for the Garland ed. by Arthur Freeman. New York, Garland Pub., 1973. 7, 8, 141 p. 21 cm. (The English stage: attack and defense, 1577-1730) Reprint of the 1649 ed. of Mr. William Prynn, his defence of stage-plays, printed in London; of the 1649 broadside of The vindication of William Prynne; and of the 1662 ed. of Theatrum redivivum, printed by T. R. for F. Eglesfield, London. [PN2047.M5 1973] 79-170427 ISBN 0-8240-0598-8
1. Prynne, William, 1600-1669. Histrio-mastix. 2. Theater—Moral and religious aspects. I. Prynne, William, 1600-1669. The vindication of William Prynne. 1973. II. Baker, Richard, Sir, 1568-1645. Theatrum redivivum. 1973. III. Title. IV. Series.

MR. William Prynn, his 792'.013
defence of stage-plays, anonymous. The vindication of William Prynne [by] William Prynne. Theatrum redivivum; or, The theatre vindicated [by] Sir Richard Baker. With a pref. for the Garland ed. by Arthur Freeman. New York, Garland Pub., 1973. 7, 8, 141 p. 21 cm. (The English stage: attack and defense, 1577-1730) Reprint of the 1649 ed. of Mr. William Prynn, his defence of stage-plays, printed in London; of the 1649 broadside of The vindication of William Prynne; and of the 1662 ed. of Theatrum redivivum, printed by T. R. for F. Eglesfield, London. [PN2047.M5 1973] 76-170429 ISBN 0-8240-0598-8 22.00
1. Prynne, William, 1600-1669. Histrio-mastix. 2. Theater—Moral and religious aspects. I. Prynne, William, 1600-1669. The vindication of William Prynne. 1973. II. Baker, Richard, Sir, 1568-1645. Theatrum redivivum. 1973. III. Title. IV. Series.

Psalmody.

ANDERSON, John. 264.2
Vindiciae cantus dominici. In two parts: i. A discourse on the duty of singing the book of Psalms in solemn worship. ii. A vindication of the doctrine taught in the preceding discourse. With an appendix containing essays and observations on vatious subjects. By John Anderson ... Philadelphia: Printed and sold by David Hogan, n. 51, South third-street, opposite the Bank of the United States, 1800. xii, [13]-403, viii p. 18 cm. "Subscribers' names": p. at end. [BV290.A55] 19-17672
1. Psalmody. I. Title.

BAIRD, Thomas Dickson 1773-1839.
Science of praise, or An illustration of the nature and design of sacred psalmody, as used in the worship of God; and a consideration of the precepts and examples of Scripture, and the practice of the Christian church, relating to its exercise, in a series of letters. By T. D. Baird ... Zanesville, O., Putnam & Clark 1816. ix, 10-108 p. 18 cm. 6-26896
I. Title.

BIBLE. O. T. Psalms. English. Paraphrases. 1771. 223.
The Psalms of David imitated in the language of the New Testament, and applied to the Christian state and worship. With the preface, or, an enquiry into the right way of fitting the book of Psalms for Christian worship, and notes. By I. Watts, D. D. The 27th ed. ... Boston: Printed by Thomas and John Fleet, at the Heart & Crown in Cornhill, 1771. xxiv, 298, [20] p. 16 cm. Signatures: a-o12, p4 (is blank) With this copy are bound Watts' "Hymns and spiritual songs", Boston, 1772 and "The Essex harmony", by Daniel Bailey, Newbury Port, 1770. [BS1440.W3 1771] 6-14393
1. Psalmody. I. Bible. English. Paraphrases. O. T. Psalms. 1771. II. Watts, Isaac, 1674-1748. III. Title.

BLACK, John, 1750-1802.
An examination of the Reverend John Anderson's Discourse, on the divine ordinance of singing psalms; wherein the inconclusive reasoning, and many inconsistencies of that writer, are detected: and the truth vindicated; agreeably to the principles exhibited in a sermon on the subject of psalmody, published by the author hereof, in the year 1790. By John Black, pastor of the upper Presbyterian congregation of Marsh-creek, Pennsylvania. York [Pa.] Printed by John and James Edie, 1792. 114 p., 1 l. 16 1/2 cm. "Errata": 1 leaf at end. A 35
1. Anderson, John, 1767-1835. A discourse on the divine ordinance of singing psalms. 2. Psalmody. I. Title.

BONNER, David Findley.
The psalmody question. an examination of the alleged divine appointment of the book of Psalms as the exclusive manual of praise, by the Rev. David Findley Bonner ... Middletown, N.Y., Hanford and Horton, 1908. viii, 98 p. 19 cm. "In a way this work is an expansion of a series of articles published in August-September, 1904 in the Westminster."--Pref. 8-10301
I. Title.

GELINEAU, Joseph. 783.9
Psalmody in the vernacular, the theory and application of the Gelineau method of psalmody. Translated by Louis Cyr. Toledo, Gregorian Institute of America [1965] 95 p. music. 23 cm. [ML3086.G44] 65-4879 MN
1. Psalmody. I. Title.

[JOCELIN, Simeon] 1746-1823. 783.
The chorister's companion; or, Church music revised. Containing, besides the necessary rules of psalmody, a variety of plain and fuging psalm tunes. Together with a collection of approved hymns and anthems, many of which never before printed. New Haven, Printed for and sold by Simeon Jocelin and Amos Doolittle [1783] 1 p. l., 18, [2] p.: (music) illus. (music) 12 x 18 1/2 cm. "Amos Doolittle sculp. 178 [2?]" (last figure obliterated) Preface dated December 16, 1782. Brinley cat. (5932), describing this copy, says, "It was advertised, as just published, in the Conn. gazette, Feb. 21, 1783." The chorister's companion. Part third. Containing a collection of approved hymns and anthems. In three and four parts. Some of which never before printed. New Haven; Printed by T. and S. Green, for Simeon Jocelin and Amos Doolittle[1783]. 15, [1] p.; 32 p. (music) 12 x 18 1/2 cm [With [Jocelin, Simeon] The chorister's companion, New Haven. [1783]) [M2116.J65C5 1783] 41-26610
1. Psalmody. 2. Hymns, English I. Title.

[JOCELYN, Simeon] 1746-1823. 783.
The chorister's companion; or, Church music revised. Containing, besides the necessary rules of psalmody, a variety of plain and fuging Psalm tunes. Together with a collection of approved hymns and anthems, many of which never before printed. New Haven, Printed for and sold by Simeon Jocelin and Amos Doolittle [1783] 1 p. l., 18, [2] p.; 64 p. (music) illus. (music) 12 x 19 cm. "Amos Doolittle sculp. 178[2!]" (Last figure obilterated) Preface dated December 16, 1782. Brinley cat. (5932), describing this copy, says: "It was advertised, as just published,in the Conn. gazette, Feb. 21, 1783." --The chorister's companion. Part third. Containing a collection of approved hymns and anthems. In three and four part. Some of which never before printed. New-Haven; Printed by T. and S. Green, for Simeon Jocelin and Amos Doolittle [1783] 15, [1] p.; 32 p. (music) 12 x 19 cm. [With [Jocelyn Simeon] The chorister's companion. New Haven. [1783]] [M2116.J65C5] 41-26610
1. Psalmody. 2. Hymns, English. 3. Anthems. I. Title.

JOHNSTON, J. B.
Psalmody. An examination of authority for making uninspired songs, and for using them in the formal worship of God. By J. B. Johnston ... St. Clairsville, O., J. Stuart, 1871. 172 p. 19 cm. [BV290.J6] 43-48093
1. Psalmody. 2. Hymns—Hist. & crit. I. Title.

LATTA, James, 1732-1801. 264.2
A discourse on psalmody: in which it is clearly shewn, that it is the duty of Christians to take the principal subjects and occasions of their Psalms, hymns, and spiritual songs from the gospel of Christ. By James Latta ... Philadelphia: Printed for the author, by William W. Woodward, at Franklin's head, no. 41, Chesnut-street, 1794. xv, [17]-146 p. 22 cm. [BV310.L3] 19-16946

1. Psalmody. I. Title.

LATTA, James, 1732-1801. 245
A discourse on psalmody; in which it is clearly shewn that it is the duty of Christians to take the principal subjects and occasions of their psalms, hymns, and spiritual songs, from the gospel of Christ. 4th ed., with corrections and additions. By James Latta ... Philadelphia: Printed by William W. Woodward, no. 17 Chesnut near Front street ... 1801. xvi, [17]-107 p. 22 cm. [BV310.L3 1801] 20-10826
1. Psalmody. I. Title. II. Title: Psalmody, A discourse on.

MATSON, Albert.
Psalmodic science vs. psalmodic sciolism, by Albert Matson. San Diego, Cal., Press of Frye & Smith, 1907. 176 p. incl. port. 18 1/2 cm. 8-14527
I. Title.

PIERIK, Marie, 1884- 783.9
The Psalter in the temple and the church. Washington, Catholic University of America Press, 1957. xi, 101p. diagrs., music. 21cm. [ML3086.P54] A57
1. Psalmody. 2. Chants (Plain, Gregorian, etc.)—Instruction and study. 3. Bible. O. T. Psalms—Criticism, interpretation, etc. I. Title.

PIERIK, Marie, 1884- 783.9
The Psatter in the temple and the church. Washington, Catholic University of America Press, 1957. xi, 101p. diagrs., music. 21cm. [ML3086.P54] A57
1. Psalmody. 2. Chants (Plain, Gregorian, etc.)—Instruction and study. 3. Bible. O. T. Psalms—Criticism, interpretation, etc. I. Title.

PRATT, Waldo Selden, 1857- 783.9
The music of the French Psalter of 1562; a historical survey and analysis, with the music in modern notation, by Waldo Selden Pratt. New York, Columbia university press, 1939. x p., 1 l., 213 p. front. (facsim.: music) 24 cm. (Half-title: Columbia university studies in musicology, no. 3) "The reproduction of the ... tunes in modern notation is based primarily upon one of the first editions of the completed Psalter, the title page of which reads as follows: Pseavines de David mis en rime francaise par Clement Marot & Theodore de Beze ... A Paris Par Adrian le Roy & Robert Ballard ... m.d.lxii."--p. 79. "Douen's contention seems plausible that for all the official editions from late in 1542 till 1557 Louis Bourgeois was the chief. If not the only musical supervisor"--p. 59. [ML3102.P92M9] 40-4909
1. Psalmody. 2. Church music—Reformed church. 3. Church music—France. I. Bible. O. T. Psalms. French. Paraphrases. 1562. Marot. II. Bible. French. Paraphrases. O. T. Psalms. 1562. Marot. III. Bourgeois, Louis, 16th cent. IV. Marot, Clement, 1495?-1544. V. Beze, Theodore de, 1519-1605. VI. Title.

[Psalms.]

BIBLE. O. T. Psalms. English. 1947.
My daily Psalm book; the book of Psalms arranged for each day of the week. New English translation from the new Latin version. [Arr. by] Rev. Joseph B. Frey. Brooklyn, N. Y., Confraternity of the Precious Blood [c1947] xii. 368 p. illus. 13 cm. On cover: The perfect prayer book. A 48
I. Frey, Joseph B. II. Title.

BIBLE. O.T. Psalms. 223'.2
English. Authorized. Selections. 1968.
The Psalms; a selection, by Elvajean Hall. Illustrated by Charles Mozley. New York, F. Watts [1968] xv, 78 p. illus. 22 cm. Presents thirty-six well-known psalms arranged in verse form. [BS1423.H3] 68-24125 2.95
1. [Psalms.] I. Hall, Elvajean, comp. II. Mozley, Charles, illus. III. Title.

BOSTON. Brattle Square church.
A selection from Tate and Brady's version of the Psalms; with hymns by various authors; for the use of the church in Brattle-Square. Compiled by a committee of that church. Boston, Richardson and Lord, 1825. (205) p. 18 1/2 cm. Hymns. Part I. 2-9870
I. Title.

BROWN, Elijah P. 1842-
Lifting the latch; an hour with the twenty-third psalm; new thoughts on an old theme, by Elijah P. Brown... Cincinnati, Jennings and Graham; New York, Eaton and Mains [c1907] 90 p. 19 cm. 7-26994
I. Title.

CARTER, John Pim, 1880- 223.5
Psalms in the spirit of Jesus; interpretations of the spirit of Jesus in the manner of the ancient Psalms ... gathered and transmitted by John Pim Carter. Boston, Mass., Bellman publishing company, inc, [1941-42] 3 v. 23 1/2 cm. Reproduced from type-written copy. "They are neither a new translation, a paraphrase, nor a metrical version of the Hebrew Psalms. They are now, yet of the old."--v. 1, p. 7. "Acknowledgements": v. 1, 119-120. [PS3505.A7923P7] 41-18941
I. Title.

DEAN, Susie Kelly.
Psalms for today, and other poems. [West Palm Beach, Fla., Boykin Press, c1959] 53 p. 22 cm. 68-53871
I. Title.

DRIVER, Samuel Rolles, 1846-1914.
Studies in the Psalms, by the S. R. Driver ... Ed., with a preface, by C. F. Burney ... London, New York [etc.] Hodder and Stoughton, 1915. xi, 305 p. 20 cm. 16-12759
I. Burney, Charles Fox, 1868- ed. II. Title.

ENELOW, Hyman Gerson, 1876- 223.
The varied beauty of the Psalms, by H. G. Enelow ... New York, Bloch publishing company, 1917. 102 p. 18 cm. $0.35. [BS1430.E6] 17-29751
I. Title.

FREEMAN,John Dolliver 1864-
Life on the uplands; an interpretation of the twenty-third psalm, by J. D. Freeman. New York, A. C. Armstrong & son, 1907. 139 p. 20 cm. 7-8267
I. Title.

HAFER, W Keith.
Psalm of life. Los Angeles, Calif., De Vorss [c1962] 56 p. 22 cm. 64-43622
I. Title.

HALL, Arthur Crawshay Alliston, bp., 1847-
Notes on the proper Psalms for holy days, by A. C. A. Hall... New York, London [etc.] Longmans, Green, and co., 1914. xxviii, 141 p. 17 1/2 cm. $0.75 14-22565
I. Title.

HUGHSON, Shirley Carter, 223.5
1867-
The Gloria psalter, arranged by S. C. Hughson ... West Park, N.Y., Holy cross press, 1946. 93 p. 17 cm. [BS1436.H8] 46-16313
I. Bible. O.T. Psalms. English. Selections. 1946. II. Gloria in excelsis. III. Title.

LIKUTE batar likute:
Tehilim. [New York: P. Feldheim, 1957- v. 24cm. Added t. p.: L'kuteibosar l'kutei, a commentary on the Psalms. In Hebrew characters.
I. Alter, Samuel.

MCKILLOP, Sybil L. 223.206
Twenty psalms for schools, from the Prayer Book, the Scottish Psalter and a fresh tr., selected and arranged for singing at morning worship. Foreword by M. E. Popham [dist. Westminster, Md., Canterbury, c.1962] 63p. 22cm. 1.00 pap.,
I. Title.

MCNAUGHER, John, 1857- ed.
The Psalms in worship; a series of convention papers bearing upon the place of the Psalms in the worship of the church; ed. by John McNaugher... Pittsburgh, The United Presbyterian board of publication, 1907. 572 p. 24 cm. 7-18116
I. Title.

MACNICOL, Nicol, tr.
Psalms of Maratha saints; one hundred and eight hymns translated from the Marathi by Nicol Macnicol...Calcutta, Associaton press; London, New York [etc.] Oxford university press [1920] 4 p.l., [5]-94 p., 1 l. front. 19 cm. (The heritage of India) Bibliography: p. [91] [PK2405.E3M3] 21-14964
I. Title.

MILLER, L David.
Psalms for today; meditations for speech choirs. Philadelphia, Muhlenberg Pr. [1962] 54 p. 23 cm. 63-51631
I. Title.

THE Psalms around 223'.2'00222
us. Philadelphia, Countryside Press; [distributed to the book trade by] Doubleday, Garden City, N.Y. [1970] 95 p. illus. (part col.) 29 cm. "Quotations from the Psalms are taken from the Revised standard version of the Bible." [BS1423.C68] 72-114340
I. Bible. O.T. Psalms. English. Revised standard. Selections. 1970.

SELECT psalms and hymns,
designed chiefly for the use of public worship... Shrewsbury, J. and W. Eddowes, 1807. 1 p. l., [5]-318, [11] p. 14 1/2 cm. 16-18860

Psalters.

ARNOLD-FORSTER, Frances Egerton, 1857-
The hymn-book of the church; or, The growth of the Psalter, by Frances Arnold-Forster, S. TH. London, Society for promoting Christian knowledge; New York, The Macmillan company, 1920. x, 198 p. 20 cm. [BX5146.A7] 21-10197
I. Title.

BIBLE. O. T. Psalms. 223.2
English. 1808.
The Psalter; or, Psalms of David: with the Proverbs of Solomon, and Christ's Sermon on the mount. Being an introduction for the training up of children to the reading of the Holy Scriptures. Boston: Published by Hastings, Etheridge & Bliss, no. 8 State street. And by said Etheridge, Charlestown ... Charlestown, Mass. S. Etheridge, printer, 1808 ... 157, [1] p. 17 cm. [BS1422 1808a] 31-15770
I. Bible. O. T. Proverbs. English. 1808. II. Bible, N. T. Matthew. v-vii, English. 1808. III. Bible. English. O. T. Psalms. 1808. IV. Bible. English. O. T. Proverbs. 1808. V. Title.

BIBLE. O. T. Psalms. English. 1902.
The Psalter or Psalms of David, from the Bible of Archbishop Cranmer. [London, E. Arnold; New York, S. Buckley & co., 1902] 1 p. l., 87, [1] p. 30 cm. Colophon: Here ends the Psalter; edited from the Cranmer Bible of mdxl,by Janet E. Ashbee, and reprinted in honour of David the great singer, at the Essex house press, Mile End, E. in the year mdcccii, under the care of C. R. Ashbee, who has also designed and drawn the woodcuts. Printed in red and black; title vignette; initials and tail-pieces. "250 copies; 10 on vellum. no. 224." Bound in blue vellum. The version of Miles Coverdale. 15-22804
I. Coverdale, Miles, bp. of Exeter, 1488-1568, tr. II. Ashbee, Charles Robert. III. Ashbee, Janet E. IV. Title.

BIBLE. O.T. Psalms. English. 1902. Coverdale.
The Psalter or Psalms of David, from the Bible of Archbishop Cranmer. [London, E. Arnold; New York, S. Buckley & co., 1902] 1 p. l., 87, [1] p. 30 cm. Colophan: Here ends the Psalter: edited from the Crammer Bible of MDXL by Janet E. Ashbee, and reprinted in honour of David the great singer, at the Essex house press, Mile End. E in the year MDCCCII, under the care of C. R. Ashbee, who has also designed and drawn the woodcuts. Title vignette; initials and tall-pieces. "250 paper copies; 10 on vellum. No. 224." From the version of Miles Coverdale, in which Cranmer's prologue first appeared in 1540. cf. British and foreign Bible society. Historical catalogue of the printed editions of Holy Scripture. v. 1. p. 21-22. [BS1422.1540a] 15-22804
I. Coverdale, Miles, bp. of Exeter, 1488-1568, tr. II. Ashbee, Charles Robert, 1863-1942. III. Ashbee, Janet Elizabeth (Forbes) IV. Bible. English. O.T. Psalms. 1902. Coverdale. V. Title.

BIBLE. O. T. Psalms. 783.
English. Paraphrases. 1900.
The Psalter in metre and Scripture paraphrases with tunes, authorized for use in public worship by the Church of Scotland, the Free church of Scotland, the United Presbyterian church, the Presbyterian church in Ireland. [Standard ed. for the organ] Edinburgh, New York [etc.] H. Frowde, 1900. xvi, 247, [1] p. 25 cm. With this is bound The church hymnary ... London, New York [etc.] 1914. [M2136.P7] 17-22443
I. Title.

BIBLE. O. T. Psalms. 783.9
English. Paraphrases. 1938. Pilgrim psalter.
... The Ainsworth psalter ... New York, The New York public library, 1938- v. 28 x 22 cm. (Early psalmody in America, series i) Preface signed: Carleton Sprague Smith. Contents.--[v. 1] Psalm 65, with settings by Claude Goudimel. [M2.A3N4] 40-34369
I. Bible. English. Paraphrases. O. T. Psalms. 1938. Pilgrim psalter. II. Ainsworth, Henry, 1571-1622? III. Goudimel, Claude, d. 1572. IV. Smith, Carleton Sprague, 1905- V. Title.

BIBLE. O. T. Psalms. 223.
English. Selections. 1894.
The Psalter; a selection of Psalms arranged for responsive readings in the house of God, with selections for chanting, and tables of lessons, by T. Ralston Smith ... New York, Maynard, Merrill & co. [c1894] 157 p. 17 cm. (Lettered on cover: Maynard's English classic series. no. 135-136) [BS1436.S6] 14-6764
I. Bible. English. Selections. O. T. Psalms. 1894. II. Smith, Thomas Ralston, ed. III. Title.

BIBLE. O. T. Psalms. 223.2
Hebrew. Selections. 1899.
The classified Psalter arranged by subjects. The Hebrew text with a new English translation on opposite pages ... By J. D. Eisenstein. Reader for Hebrew schools. New York [A. Ginsberg & bro.] 1899. 8 p. l., 123 p., 2 l. 20 cm. Added t.-p. in Hebrew. [BS1420.E5] 99-1283
I. Bible. Hebrew. Selections. O. T. Psalms. 1899. II. Bible. O. T. Psalms. English. Selections. 1899. III. Bible. English. Selections. O. T. Psalms. 1899. IV. Eisenstein, Judah David, 1855- V. Title.

BIBLE. O. T. Psalms. Latin. 1884.
The Psalter, or Psalms of David and certain canticles, with a translation and exposition in English by Richard Rolle of Hampole; ed. from manuscripts by the Rev. H. R. Bramley ... With an introduction and glossary. Oxford, Clarendon press, 1884. xxiv, 556 p. 23 cm. [BS1425.L3R7] A11
I. Bible. O. T. Psalms. English (Middle English) 1884. II. Rolle, Richard, of Hampole, 1290-1349 tr. III. Bramley, Henry Ramsden, 1833-1917, ed. IV. Bible, English (Middle English) O. T. Psalms. 1884. V. Bible, Latin O. T. Psalms. 1884. VI. Title.

CHURCH of England. Book of common prayer. Psalter.
The cathedral paragraph Psalter, containing the canticles, proper psalms and the twenty selections of psalms arranged in paragraphs and pointed for chanting with brief notes on the Psalter. Edited by the Rev. J. Troutbeck, D.D. New York and Chicago, Novello, Ewer and co. [1900?] xix, 184 p. 20 1/2 cm. Without music. [BX5146.A1 1900] 45-51993
I. Troutbeck, John, 1832-1899, ed. II. Title.

CHURCH of England. Book of 265
common prayer. Psalter.
The simple Psalter & canticles, pointed for ancient tones by Rev. H. Kynaston Hudson ... the tones harmonized by B. Vme Westbrook ... 2d ed., rev. London, New York etc., Pub. for the St. Alban's plainsong society by H. Milford, 1916. 282 p. 15 cm. [BX5148.A1 1916] 17-24382
I. Bible. O.T. Psalms. English. II. Hudson, Herbert Kynaston. III. Westbrook, B. Vine. IV. Title.

GLASS, Henry Alexander. 223'.2'05209
The story of the Psalters; a history of the metrical versions of Great Britain and America from 1549 to 1885. London, K. Paul, Trench, 1888. [New York, AMS Press, 1972] vii, 208 p. 19 cm. [BS1440.A1G58 1972] 72-1635 ISBN 0-404-08308-0
1. Bible. O.T. Psalms—Paraphrases, English—History and criticism. 2. Psalters. I. Title.

ORTHODOX Eastern Church. Liturgy and ritual. Psalter. English. 264'.01'9
The Psalter, according to the Seventy, of St. David, the prophet and King : together with the nine odes and an interpretation of how the Psalter should be recited throughout the whole year / translated from the Septuagint version of the Old Testament by the Holy Transfiguration Monastery. Boston : The Monastery, 1974. 296 p. : ill. ; 24 cm. [BX370.A5H64 1974] 74-76941 ISBN 0-913026-09-3
1. Psalters. I. Holy Transfiguration Monastery. II. Title.

PROSTESTANT Episcopal church in the U. S. A. Book of common prayer. Psalter. 264.038
The American Psalter; the Psalms and canticles according to the use of the Protestant Episcopal church, pointed and set to Anglican chants. together with the choral service, prepared by the Joint commission on church music, under authority of General convention. New York, The H. W. Gray company, 1930. xiii, 256 p. 21 cm. "the revised Psalms and canticles of the prayer book of 1929."--Pref. [M2125.P94 1930] 783.9 30-23572
I. Bible. O. T. Psalms. English. II. Protestant Episcopal church in the U. S. A. Joint Commission on church music. III. Title.

THE Psalter; 223.
or, Psalms of David, with the Proverbs of Solomon, and Christ's Sermon on the mount. Being an introduction for children to the reading of the Holy Scriptures. Carefully copied from the Holy Bible. Worcester, Massachusetts, Printed by Isaiah Thomas, for Ebenezer Battelle, in Boston, 1784. 160 p. 17 cm. [BS1422 1784a] 24-13121
I. Sermon on the mount. II. Bible. O. T. Proverbs. English. III. Bible. O. T. Psalms. English. 1784. IV. Bible. O. T. Psalms. English. 1724.

VAUGHAN, John, 1855-
A mirror of the soul; short studies in the Psalter by the Rev. John Vaughan ... New York, C. Scribner's sons, 1913. vii, 141, [1] p. 18 1/2 cm. (Half-title: The short course series; ed. by Rev. John Adams. Series title also at head of t.p. A 14
I. Title.

Psalters—Texts.

BIBLE. 264'.028
The abbey psalter : the book of Psalms used by the Trappist monks of Genesee Abbey. Ramsey, N.J. : Paulist Press, c1981. [350] p. : ill. ; 29 cm. [BX2049.T73P74 1981] 19 81-80871 ISBN 0-8091-0316-8 : 24.95
1. Catholic Church—Liturgy—Texts. 2. Psalters—Texts. I. Genesee Abbey. II. Title.

BIBLE. O.T. Psalms. English. 1911. 223'.2'52
The Hexaplar Psalter. Edited by William Aldis Wright. Hildesheim, New York, G. Olms, 1969. vi, 389 p. 22 cm. (Anglistica & Americana, 55) Reprint of the ed. published in Cambridge by University Press in 1911. Coverdale (1535) Great Bible (1539) Geneva (1560) Bishops (1568) Authorised (1611) Revised (1885) in parallel columns. [BS1421.W7 1969] 72-483998
I. Wright, William Aldis, 1831-1914, ed. II. Title. III. Series.

BIBLE. O. T. Psalms. English. 1911.
The hexaplar Psalter; being the book of Psalms in six English versions, ed. by William Aldis Wright ... Cambridge, The University press, 1911. vi, 389, [1] p. 26 cm. Coverdale (1535) Great Bible (1539) Geneva (1560) Bishops (1568) Authorised (1611) Revised (1885) in parallel columns. 11-18103
I. Wright, William Aldis, ed. II. Title.

BIBLE. O.T. Pslams. English. 1911.
The hexaplar Psalter; being the book of Psalms in six English versions ed. by William Aldis Wright ... Cambridge, The University press, 1911. vi, 389, [1] p. 20 cm. Coverdale (1535) Great Bible (1539) Geneva (1560) Bishops (1568) Authorized (1611) Revised (1885) in parallel columns. [BS1421.W7] 11-18103
I. Wright, William Aldis, 1831-1914, ed. II. Bible. English. O.T. Psalms. 1911. III. Title.

Psellus, Michael.

ZERVOS, Christian. 189 B
Un philosophe neoplatonicien du XIe siecle: Michel Psellos, sa vie, son ouvre, ses luttes philosophiques, son influence. Pref. de Francois picavet. New York, B. Franklin [1974] xix, 269 p. 23 cm. (Burt Franklin research and source works series. Byzantine series, 41) Reprint of the 1920 ed. published by E. Laroux, Paris. Bibliography: p. 1-42. [B765.P84Z4 1974] 74-2050 ISBN 0-8337-3921-2
1. Psellus, Michael. I. Title.

Pseudo-Messiahs—Biography.

MANDEL, Arthur. 296.6'1'0924 B
The militant messiah : or, The flight from the ghetto : the story of Jacob Frank and the Frankist movement / by Arthur Mandel. Atlantic Highlands, N.J. : Humanities Press, c1979. 185 p., [3] leaves of plates : ill. ; 22 cm. "A Peter Bergman book." Includes bibliographical references and index. [BM755.F68M36] 79-443 ISBN 0-391-00973-7 : 10.00
1. Frank, Jacob, 1726 (ca.)-1791. 2. Pseudo-Messiahs—Biography. 3. Jews in Poland—Biography. I. Title.

Psychiana movement.

ROBINSON, Frank Bruce. 211
Blood on the tail of a pig, by Dr. Frank B. Robinson. Moscow, Id., "Psychiana", inc., 1941. 2 p. l., 76 p. 19 cm. Illustrated t.-p. [BL2790.R6A27] 41-3892
1. Psychiana movement. I. Title.

ROBINSON, Frank Bruce. 211
Ye men of Athens, by Frank B. Robinson... Moscow, Id., "Psychiana" inc. [c1940] 130 p. 20 1/2 cm. [BL2775.R64] 40-32363
1. Psychiana movement. I. Title.

ROBINSON, Frank Bruce, 1886- 211
For rent, a cross, by Dr. Frank B. Robinson ... Moscow, Id., "Psychiana" inc., 1941. 2 p. l., 7-64 p. 21 1/2 cm. [BL2775.R632] 43-49381
1. Psychiana movement. I. Title.

ROBINSON, Frank Bruce, 1886- 211
The pathway to God, by Frank B. Robinson. Moscow, Id., Psychiana, inc. [1943] 10 p. l., 19-185 p. front. (port.) 20 1/2 cm. [BL2775.R637] 43-9598
1. Psychiana movement. I. Title.

ROBINSON, Frank Bruce, 1886- 210
... A prophet speaks; the cause and cure of war. Moscow, Id., "Psychiana," inc. [1943] 143 p. incl. front. (port.) 20 1/2 cm. At head of title: By Dr. Frank B. Robinson. [BL2775.R638] 43-10544
1. Psychiana movement. I. Title.

ROBINSON, Frank Bruce, 1886- 922.91
The strange autobiography of Frank B. Robinson, founder of "Psychiana," Moscow, Idaho. Moscow, Id., "Psychiana," inc., 1941. 284 p. front., plates, ports. 22 1/2 cm. [BL2790.R6A35] 41-16258
1. Psychiana movement. I. Title.

ROBINSON, Frank Bruce, 1886- 211
Your God-power, with twenty lessons showing how to find and use it, by Frank B. Robinson ... Moscow, Id., "Psychiana," inc. [c1943] 2 p. l., 348 p. front. (port.) 23 1/2 cm. [BL2775.R643] 44-468
1. Psychiana movement. I. Title.

Psychiatry and religion.

CHRISTIAN essays in psychiatry. New York, Philosophical Library, 1956. 187p.
I. Mairet, Philippe, 1886- ed.

PSYCHIATRY and religion; some steps toward mutual understanding and usefulness, formulated by the Committee on psychiatry and religion. New York, 1960. 317-373p. 23cm. (Its Report no. 48)
1. Psychiatry and religion. I. Group for the Advancement of Psychiatry. Committee on Psychiatry and Religion. II. Series.

ROSENBERG, Stuart E. 291.12
More loves than one; the Bible confronts psychiatry. New York, Ungar [1965, c.1963] 190p. 22cm. Bibl. [BM652.5.R6] 1.45 pap.,
1. Psychiatry and religion. 2. Love (Judaism) I. Title.

ROSENBERG, Stuart E. 291.12
More loves than one; the Bible confronts psychiatry. New York, T. Nelson [1963] 190 p. 22 cm. [BM652.5.R6] 63-10927
1. Psychiatry and religion. 2. Love (Judaism) I. Title.

SIEGMUND, Georg, 1903- 200.19
Belief in God and mental health. Tr. by Isabel and Florence McHugh. Pref. by James H. Van der Veldt. New York, Desclee, 1965[c.1962] 210p. 22cm. [RC455.S5313] 65-20315 4.50
1. Psychiatry and religion. I. Title.

Psychiatry and religion—Congresses.

JOHN G. Finch Symposium on Psychology and Religion, 2d, Pasadena, Calif., 1973. 261.8'32'2
After therapy, what? Lay therapeutic resources in religious perspective. Finch lectures by Thomas C. Oden, with responses by Neil C. Warren [and others] Edited by Neil C. Warren. Springfield, Ill., Thomas [1974] 205 p. 24 cm. Includes bibliographical references. [RC480.5.J63 1973] 73-21983 ISBN 0-398-03105-3
1. Psychiatry and religion—Congresses. 2. Psychotherapy—Congresses. 3. Pastoral counseling—Congresses. I. Oden, Thomas C. II. Warren, Neil Clark, ed. III. Title.

Psychiatry—Congresses.

PSYCHIATRY and mysticism / Stanley R. Dean, editor. Chicago : Nelson-Hall Co., [1975] p. cm. Includes bibliographies and index. [RC454.4.P785] 75-8771 ISBN 0-88229-189-0 : 12.95 133.8'01'9
1. Psychiatry—Congresses. 2. Psychical research—Congresses. I. Dean, Stanley R.

Psychical research.

ALLISON, Lydia W., Mrs. 133.
Leonard and Soule experiments in psychical research, also experiments with Sanders, Brittain, Peters and Dowden, by Lydia W. Allison; supplementary material by the research officer of the Boston society for psychic research. Boston, Mass., Boston society for psychic research 1929. 399 p. 23 1/2 cm. Mrs. Allison gives records of sittings in which communications are purported to have come from her husband, Dr. Edward W. Allison. Research officer of the Boston society for psychic research: Walter F. Prince. [BF1301.A35] 29-6365
1. Psychical research. I. Leonard, Mrs. Gladys. II. Soule, Mrs. Minnie Meserve. III. Allison, Edward Wood, 1857-1920. IV. Prince, Walter Franklin 1863- V. Title.

ANSPACHER, Louis Kaufman, 1878- 133.072
Challenge of the unknown; exploring the psychic world; with an introd. by Waldemar Kaempffert. New York, Current Books, 1947. 327 p. 22 cm. [BF1031.A5] 47-4286
1. Psychical research. I. Title.

ARNOLD, James Oliver. 130
Advanced thought on electrical and spiritual voltage; two invisible forces of nature: spirit supreme, and the induction of spirit into man, by James Oliver Arnold ... Dayton, O., Advanced thought co., c1902. 68 p. 17 cm. [BD701.A7] 3-23386
I. Title.

ASHBY, Robert H. 016.1339'072
The guidebook for the study of psychical research [by] Robert H. Ashby. New York, S. Weiser, 1972. 190 p. 21 cm. Bibliography: p. 33-101. [BF1031.A8 1972b] 72-78575 ISBN 0-87728-188-2 2.95
1. Psychical research. 2. Psychical research—Bibliography. I. Title.

BAILEY, Wilson Gill, 1865- 133.072
We live outside our bodies; a challenge to your pet opinions about the future of life, by Wilson Gill Bailey, M.D. Philadelphia, Dorrance and company [c1937] 248 p. front. (port.) plates. 20 cm. [BF1031.B22] 159.961 37-8559
1. Psychical research. 2. Immortality. I. Title.

BANISTER, Corrilla.
A modern miracle, psychic power made plain, by Corrilla Banister ... New York, The Grafton press [1905] vii, l., 9-113 p. 19 cm. Published in 1901 under title: I'm a brick, a congress of religions. 5-2775
I. Title.

BANNISTER, Paul. 133.8
Strange happenings / by Paul Bannister. New York : Grosset & Dunlap, c1978. ix, 148 p. : ill. ; 28 cm. [BF1031.B23] 77-87112 ISBN 0-448-14390-9 : 12.95 ISBN 0-448-14391-7 pbk. : 6.95
1. Psychical research. 2. Occult sciences. I. Title.

BARTLETT, Laile E. 133.8
Psi trek : a world-wide investigation into the lives of psychic people and the researchers who test such phenomena as healing, prophecy, dowsing, ghosts, and life after death / Laile E. Bartlett. New York : McGraw-Hill, c1981. xi, 337 p. ; 24 cm. Includes index. Bibliography: p. 325-332. [BF1031.B312] 19 80-22178 ISBN 0-07-003915-1 : 12.95
1. Psychical research. I. Title.

BATES, Emily Katharine. 133.
Psychical science and Christianity, a problem of the xxth century, by E. Katharine Bates ... New York, Dodge publishing company [c1909] 5 p. l., vii-x. 233 p. 20 cm. [BF1275.C5B33] 9-29570 1.50
1. Psychical research. I. Title.

BATES, Emily Katharine. 133.8'092'4 B
Seen and unseen / by E. Katharine Bates. Popular ed. Folcroft, Pa. : Folcroft Library Editions, 1975. xvi, 323 p. ; 24 cm. Reprint of the 1908 ed. published by Greening & Co., London. [BF1261.B35 1975] 75-32535 ISBN 0-8414-3234-1 lib. bdg. : 20.00
1. Psychical research. 2. Spiritualism. I. Title.

BENDIT, Phoebe Daphne (Payne) 1891- 133.07
The psychic sense [by] Phoebe D. Payne, L. J. Bendit. New York, Citadel [1961, c.1958] 227p. Bibl. 61-4647 3.95
1. Psychical research. 2. Spiritualism. I. Bendit, LaurenceJohn, 1898- joint author. II. Title.

BENDIT, Phoebe Daphne (Payne) 1891- 133
The psychic sense [by] Phoebe D. Payne and L. J. Bendit. Wheaton, Ill., Theosophical Pub. House [1967, c1958] 227 p. 18 cm. (A Quest book) Bibliography: p. 225-226. [BF1031.B33] 67-7911
1. Psychical research. 2. Spiritualism. I. Bendit, Laurence John, 1898- joint author. II. Title.

BENDIT, Phoebe Daphne (Payne) 1891- 133
The psychic sense, by Phoebe D. Payne and Laurence J. Bendit. With a foreword by L. A. G. Strong. [1st American ed.] New York, E. P. Dutton, 1949. 224 p.

diagrs. 20 cm. "Books recommended": p. 223-224. [BF1031.B33 1949] 49-8694
1. Psychical research. 2. Spiritualism. I. Bendit, Lawrence John, 1898- joint author. II. Title.

BENDIT, Phoebe Daphne (Payne) 1891- 133
This world and that; an analytical study of psychic communication, by Phoebe D. Payne (Mrs. L. J. Bendit) and Laurence J. Bendit. Wheaton, Ill., Theosophical Pub. House [1969, c1950] 194 p. 20 cm. (A Quest book) Bibliographical footnotes. [BF1031] 73-1927 1.75
1. Psychical research. I. Bendit, Laurence John, 1898- joint author. II. Title.

BENNETT, Edward T. 133.
Psychic phenomena; a brief account of the physical manifestations observed in psychical research, with facsimile illustrations of thought-transference drawings and automatic writing by Edward T. Bennett ... with a foreword by Sir Oliver Lodge. New York, Brentano's, 1909. 3 p. l., 9-140 p. illus. 18 cm. "Extracts from the Proceedings of the Society [for psychical research], from the privately printed Journal, and from 'Phantasms of the living.'" [BF1371.B4] 10-8550
1. Psychical research. I. Title.

BENNETT, Ernest Nathaniel, Sir 1868- 133.
Apollonius; or, The present and future of psychical research, by E. N. Bennett ... New York, E. P. Dutton & company [c1927] 3 p. l., 3-79 p. 16 cm. [BF1031.B4] 27-18814
1. Psychical research. I. Title.

BOIRAC, Emile, 1851-1917. 133.
Our hidden forces("La psychologie inconnue") An experimental study of the psychic sciences, by Emile Boirac ... tr. and ed., with an introduction, by W. De Kerlor ... New York, Frederick A. Stokes company [c1917] xxiii p., 2 l., 302 p. front. (port.) plates. 21 cm. "The report presented to the Academie des sciences de Paris by the Commission board of the prize endowment 'Fanny Emden.'"--Pref. to the 2d edition. "Compiled during the period extendi-g from 1893 to 1906. Certain parts... which already had appeared in various periodicals ... have been credited and completed."--Introd. [BF1031.B65] 17-13485
1. Psychical research. I. Kerlor, Willie Wendt de, 1883- tr. II. Title.

BOIRAC, Emile, 1851-1917. 133.
The psychology of the future ("L'avenir des sciences psychiques") by Emile Boirac ... tr. and ed. with an introduction by W. de Kerlor ... New York, Frederick A. Stokes company [c1918] ix p., 2 l., 822 p. front., plates. 21 cm. [BF1061.B62] 18-5754
1. Psychical research. I. Kerlor, Willie Wendt de, 1868- tr. II. Title.

BONNAR, William. 133.
The mathematical laws of psychic phenomena discovered, formulated and elucidated with practical diagrams, by William Bonnar. Chicago, 1912. 2 p. l., xx, [7] 4-193, [2] p. incl. plates. front. (port.) 26 cm. [BF1031.B7] 13-11261
1. Psychical research. I. Title.

BREITFELD, Rose. 133
Your psychic self; a treatise on the various forms of psychic powers and how to develop them. New York, N.Y., Rose Breitfeld. [c1932] 63 p. 21 cm. [BF1040.B65] 32-13436
1. Psychical research. I. Title.

BRUCE, Henry Addington Bayley, 1874- 133.
Adventurings in the psychical, by H. Addington Bruce. Boston, Little, Brown, and company, 1914. vi. p., 1 l., 318 p. 19 1/2 cm. "The present volume is somewhat in the nature of a sequel to "The riddle of personality."--Pref. [BF1031.B8] 14-6675 1.35
1. Psychical research. I. Title.

BUCKLAND, Raymond. 133.9
Amazing secrets of the psychic world / Raymond Buckland and Hereward Carrington. West Nyack, N.Y. : Parker Pub. Co., [1975] 201 p. ; 24 cm. Includes bibliographies. [BF1261.B883] 74-22327 ISBN 0-13-024042-7 : 7.95
1. Psychical research. 2. Occult sciences. I. Carrington, Hereward, 1880- joint author.

CARRINGTON, Hereward, 1880- 133.
The coming science, by Hereward Carrington ... with an introduction by James H. Hyslop ... Boston, Small, Maynard & company, 1908. xii p., 1 l., 393 p. 20 cm. Partly reprinted from the Journal of the American society for psychical research, the Metaphysical magazine, and elsewhere. cf. Pref. [BF1031.C3] 8-37615
1. Psychical research. I. Title.

CARRINGTON, Hereward, 1880- 133.072
The invisible world, by Hereward Carrington ... New York, The Beechhurst press, B. Ackerman, inc. [1946] 190 p. 21 1/2 cm. [BF1031.C32] 46-5442
1. Psychical research. I. Title.

CARRINGTON, Hereward, 1880- 133.
Modern psychical phenomena; recent researches and speculations, by Hereward Carrington ... New York, Dodd, Mead and company, 1919. xi p., 3 l., 3-331 p. front., illus., plates. 21 cm. "Several chapters in this book have already appeared in various psychical and other journals."--Pref. [BF1031.C35] 19-14535
1. Psychical research. I. Title.

CARRINGTON, Hereward, 1880- 133.07
... Modern psychical phenomena, recent researches and speculations, by Hereward Carrington ... New York, American universities publishing company, 1920. xi, [2] p., 1 l., 3-331 p. front., illus. (incl. diagr.) plates. 21 cm. (The occult and psychical sciences) "Several chapters in this book have already appeared in various psychical and other journals."--Pref. [BF1031.C35 1920] 32-6505
1. Psychical research. I. Title.

CARRINGTON, Hereward, 1880- 133.07
A primer of psychical research, by Hereward Carrington ... New York, I. Washburn, 1932. 3 p. l., 3-117 p. 20 cm. [BF1031.C36] 32-26229
1. Psychical research. I. Title.

CARRINGTON, Hereward, 1880- 133.
The problems of psychical research; experiments and theories in the realm of the supernormal, by Hereward Carrington ... New York, Dodd, Mead and company, 1921. vii p., 3 l., 288 p. front., illus., plates. 21 cm. [BF1031.C37] 21-2456 3.00
1. Psychical research. I. Title.

CARRINGTON, Hereward, 1880- 133.072
Psychic science and survival; an essay in psychical research, by Hereward Carrington ... New York, The American psychical institute [1939] 90 p. 19 cm. ([American psychical institute] Bulletin v) "Printed and made in Great Britain." [BF1031.C3715] 159.961 40-33482
1. Psychical research. 2. Spiritualism. I. Title.

CARRINGTON, Hereward, 1880- 133.072
Psychic science and survival. New York, Beechhurst Press [1947] 142 p. 21 cm. [BF1031.C3715 1947] 47-5071
1. Psychical research. 2. Spiritualism. I. Title.

CARRINGTON, Hereward, 1880- 133.072
The psychic world, by Hereward Carrington ... New York, G. P. Putnam's sons, 1937 xvi, 311 p. diagr. 23 cm. [BF1031.C345] 159.961 37-21814
1. Psychical research. 2. Supernatural. I. Title.

CARRINGTON, Hereward, 1880- 133.072
Psychology in the light of psychic phenomena, by Hereward Carrington ... Philadelphia, David McKay company [c1940] 4 p. l., 3-214 p. diagrs. 20 cm. [BF1031.C373] 159.961 40-12220
1. Psychical research. I. Title.

CARRINGTON, Hereward, 1880- 133.072
Your psychic powers and how to develop them. Brooklyn, Astrol Co., 1949. xvii, 358 p. 19 cm. [BF1031.C4 1949] 49-49435
1. Psychical research. 2. Spiritualism. I. Title.

CARRINGTON, Hereward, 1880- 133.07
... Your psychic powers and how to develop them, by Hereward Carrington ... New York, American universities publishing company, 1920. xvii p., 1 l., 358 p. front. 21 cm. (The occult and psychical sciences) [BF1031.C4 1920a] 32-6504
1. Psychical research. 2. Spiritualism. I. Title.

CARRINGTON, Hereward, 1880- 133.
Your psychic powers and how to develop them, by Hereward Carrington ... New York, Dodd, Mead and company, 1920. xvii p., 1 l., 358 p. 21 cm. [BF1031.C4] 20-5132
1. Psychical research. 2. Spiritualism. I. Title.

CARRINGTON, Hereward, 1880- 133.072
Your psychic powers and how to develop them, by Hereward Carrington ... Brooklyn, N.Y., Astrol company, 1939. 5 p. l., ix-xvii, 358 p. 19 cm. [BF1031.C4 1939] 159.961 40-7178
1. Psychical research. 2. Spiritualism. I. Title.

CAYCE, Edgar, 1877-1945. 133.8'08 S
Healing, prayer, and the revelation. Virginia Beach, Va., Association for Research and Enlightenment [1974] viii, 306 p. 24 cm. (His Meditation, pt. 1) (The Edgar Cayce readings, v. 2) [BF1023.C37 vol. 2, pt. 1] [BF1031] 133.8 74-176204 ISBN 0-87604-072-5
1. Psychical research. I. Title.

CHEVEREUIL, L . 133.
Proofs of the spirit world (On ne meurt pas) by L. Chevreuil; tr. by Agnes Kendrick Gray. New York, E. P. Dutton & company [c1920] v p., 1 l., 297 p. illus. 21 cm. [BF1031.C5] 20-6884
1. Psychical research. 2. Spiritualism. I. Gray, Agnes Kendrick, tr. II. Title.

CHRISTOPHER, Milbourne. 133.8
Mediums, mystics, & the occult / Milbourne Christopher. New York : Crowell, [1975] x, 275 p. : ill. ; 24 cm. Includes index. Bibliography: p. [259]-264. [BF1031.C53 1975] 74-26812 ISBN 0-690-00476-1 : 6.95
1. Psychical research. 2. Occult sciences. 3. Mysticism—East (Far East) I. Title.

COBLENTZ, Stanton Arthur, 1896- 133.8
Light beyond : the wonderworld of parapsychology / Stanton A. Coblentz. New York : Cornwall Books, c1981. p. cm. Includes bibliographical references and index. [BF1031.C5684] 19 80-69585 ISBN 0-8453-4712-8 : 15.00
1. Psychical research. I. Title.

COHEN, Daniel. 133
The far side of consciousness / Daniel Cohen. New York : Dodd, Mead, [1975] c1974. x, 214 p., [8] leaves of plates : ill. ; 22 cm. Includes index. Bibliography: p. 207-209. [BF1031.C58 1975] 74-11797 ISBN 0-396-07002-7 : 6.95
1. Psychical research. 2. Faith-cure. 3. Experience (Religion) I. Title.

COOPER, Irving Steiger, 1882- 133.
... Methods of psychic development, by Irving S. Cooper, with a foreword by C. W. Leadbeater. Rev. American ed. Chicago, Theosophical book concern; [etc., etc.] 1912. ix, [2], 113, [2] p. 16 cm. (Manuals of occultism: no. 1) [BF1325.C6] 12-23098 0.50
1. Psychical research. 2. Clairvoyance. I. Title.

CRAWFORD, William Jackson, 1880-1920. 133.
Experiments in psychical science, levitation, contact, and the direct voice, by W. J. Crawford ... New York, E. P. Dutton & company [c1919] ix, p. 1 l., 201 p. illus., plates, diagrs. 20 cm. "Although complete in itself, the present volume is partly a continuation of my previous book. 'The reality of psychic phenomena'." [BF1261.C87] 19-11580
1. Psychical research. 2. Spiritualism. I. Title.

CRAWFORD, William Jackson, 1880-1920. 133.
The psychic structures at the Goligher circle, by W. J. Crawford ... New York, E. P. Dutton & company [c1921] viii p., 1 l., 176 p. illus., plates, diagrs. 21 cm. Part of the plates are printed on both sides. [BF1261.C89] 21-22160
1. Psychical research. 2. Spiritualism. I. Title.

CRAWFORD, William Jackson, 1880-1920. 133.07
The reality of psychic phenomena, raps, levitations, etc. By W. J. Crawford ... New York, E. P. Dutton & company [1919] vii, 246 p. front. (port.) illus., plates. 20 cm. "First printing May, 1918; second printing Feb. 1919." [BF1031.C83 1919] 32-21760
1. Psychical research. 2. Spiritualism. I. Title.

CROOKALL, Robert, 1890- 133
The interpretation of cosmic and mystical experiences; foreword by J. D. Pearce-Higgins. Cambridge, James Clarke, 1969. xii, 175, [1] p. (1 fold.) 23 cm. Includes bibliographical references. [BF1031.C855] 72-579453 ISBN 0-227-67729-3 £1.25
1. Psychical research. 2. Mysticism. I. Title.

CROWE, Catherine (Stevens) Mrs. d.1876. 133.
The night-side of nature; or, Ghosts and ghost-seers. By Catherine Crowe ... New York, J. S. Redfield; Boston, B. B. Mussey & co., 1850. 451 p. 19 cm. First edition published in 1848. [BF1031.C86 1850] 10-29913
1. Psychical research. 2. Ghosts. I. Title.

CROWE, Catherine (Stevens) Mrs. d.1876. 133.
The night side of nature; or, Ghosts and ghosts seers, by Catherine Crowe ... London, New York, G. Routledge and sons [1866] 1 p. l., 502 17 cm. First edition published in 1848. [BF1031.C86 1866] 10-29914
1. Psychical research. 2. Ghosts. I. Title.

CROWE, Catherine (Stevens) Mrs. d.1876. 133.07
The night side of nature; or, Ghosts and ghost seers, by Catherine Crowe ... London, New York [etc.] G. Routledge and sons [1882?] iv, [5]-155 p. 23 cm. [BF1031.C86 1800] 32-21765
1. Psychical research. 2. Ghosts. I. Title.

CROWE, Catherine (Stevens) Mrs. d.1876. 133.
The night-side of nature; or, Ghosts and ghost seers, by Catherine Crowe. New ed., with an introduction by Thomson Jay Hudson ... Philadelphia, H. T. Coates & company, 1901. xiv, [7]-451 p. 20 cm. [BF1031.C86 1901] 1-25495
1. Psychical research. 2. Ghosts. I. Title.

DALLAS, Helen A. 133.
Death, the gate of life? (Mors janua vitae?) A discussion of certain communications purporting to come from Frederic W. H. Myers, by H. A. Dallas; with an introduction by Professor W. F. Barrett ... New York, E. P. Dutton & company [1919] xix, 147, [1] p. illus. 19 cm. Previously published (London, 1910) under title: Mors janua vitae? [BF1301.M9] 19-13017
1. Myers, Frederic William Henry, 1843-1901. 2. Psychical research. I. Title.

DAVIS, Andrew Jackson, 1826-1910. 133.9
The great harmonia; being a philosophical revelation of the natural, spiritual, and celestial universe. By Andrew Jackson Davis ... Boston, B. Marsh, 1852-66. 5 v. front. (v. 5) illus., plates. 20 cm. Title varies slightly. Imprint of vol. iii: Boston, B. B. Mussey & co.; New York, J. S. Redfield, 1852; vol. v: New York, C. M. Plumb & co., 1865. Vol. i: 5th edition; vol. v: 6th edition. Contents.i. The physician.--ii. The teacher.--iii. The seer.--iv. The reformer.--v. The thinker. [BF1291.D27 1852] 32-11975

1. Psychical research. 2. Spiritualism. I. Title.

DAVIS, Andrew Jackson, 1826-1910. 133.9
The great harmonia: being a philosophical revelation of the natural, spiritual, and celestial universe. By Andrew Jackson Davis ... New York, A. J. Davis & co., 1864-80. 5 v. front. (v. 5) illus., plates. 20 cm. Title varies slightly. Imprint of vol. ii: Boston, Colby & Rich, 1880; vol. iii: Boston, B. Marsh, 1864. Contents.i. The physician.--ii. The teacher.--iii. The seer.--iv. The reformer.--v. The thinker. [BF1291.D27 1864] 32-11976
1. Psychical research. 2. Spiritualism. I. Title.

DEARDEN, Harold, 1882- 133
Devilish but true; the doctor looks at spiritualism. [New York] EP Pub. Ltd., 1975. p. cm. Reprint of the 1936 ed. published by Hutchinson, London. [BF1031.D33 1975] 74-19281 ISBN 0-8277-3274-0
1. Psychical research. 2. Spiritualism. I. Title.

DE MONCO, Almo, 1857- 133.
Experimental psychology; a treatise on the anatomy and physiology of the human soul, by Almo De Monco ... Los Angeles, Calif., J. F. Rowny press, 1922. 2 p. l., vii-xi, [1], 13-188 p. 20 cm. [BF1031.D488] 22-15677
1. Psychical research. I. Title.

DENDY, Walter Cooper, 1794-1871. 133.
The philosophy of mystery. By Walter Cooper Dendy ... New-York, Harper & brothers, 1845. vi, [7]-442 p. 19 cm. An English edition was published in 1841. [BF1031.D5 1845] 11-6861
1. Psychical research. I. Title.

DENDY, Walter Cooper, 1794-1871. 133.
The philosophy of mystery. By Walter Cooper Dendy ... New-York, Harper & brothers, 1847. vi, [7]-442 p. 17 cm. [BF1031.D5 1847] 18-8661
1. Psychical research. I. Title.

DENIS, Leon, 1846-1927. 133.
Life and destiny, by Leon Denis ... tr. into English by Ella Wheeler Wilcox. New York, G. H. Doran company [1919] xii p., 1 l., 15-315 p. 21 cm. [BF1032.D42] 19-16917
1. Psychical research. I. Wilcox, Ella (Wheeler) Mrs. 1855-1919. II. Title.

DONNELLY, John J. 133.
Subjective concepts of humans; source of spiritistic manifestations, by John J. Donnelly. New York, The International press, 1922. xiii p., 1 l., 555 p. 21 cm. [BF1042.D68] 22-21267
1. Psychical research. I. Title.

DONNELLY, Joseph W., 1899- 133.9
Diary of a psychic; the anecdotes and personal experiences in the development of extra sensory perception (E.S.P.), by Joseph W. Donnelly. [Hollywood, Fla., Graphic Press] c1966. 60 p. 28 cm. Caption title. [BF1027.D65A3] 75-17817 2.50
I. Title.

DRESSER, Horatio Willis, 1866- 133.
The open vision; a study of psychic phenomena, by Horatio W. Dresser... New York, Thomas Y. Crowell Company [1920] x p., 1 l., 352 p. 19 1/2 cm. [BF1031.D7] 20-6883
1. Psychical research. I. Title.

EDDY, George Sherwood, 1871- 133.9
You will survive after death. New York, Rinehart [1950] xi, 210 p. 20 cm. [BF1031.E33] 50-12070
1. Psychical research. I. Title.

[EDGERLY, Webster] 133.
The great psychic, the master mind of the universe, a study of all phenomena including other world life and its control over human existence, by Edmund Shaftesbury [pseud.] Hopewell, N.J., Ralston company [c1925] 416 p. 25 cm. [BF1031.E4] 25-15862
1. Psychical research. I. Title.

[EDGERLY, Webster] 1852-1926. 133.
The great psychic, the master power of the universe; a study of the origin, meaning and purpose of those controlling influences that precede, attend and follow human existence on earth. An all-inclusive educational system based on new sources of knowledge. By Edmund Shaftesbury [pseud.] Meriden, Conn., Ralston unversity press, 1928. 416 p. 25 cm. [BF1031.E4 1928] 28-16323
1. Psychical research. I. Title.

FLAMMARION, Camille, 1842-1925. 133.07
L'inconnu. The unknown, by Camille Flammarion. London and New York, Harper & brothers, 1900. xiii, 488 p. front. 23 cm. [Full name: Nicolas Camille Flammarion] [BF1032.F5 1900a] 32-21752
1. Psychical research. I. Title. II. Title: The unknown.

FLAMMARION, Camille, 1842-1925. 133.
L'inconnu, The unknown. By Camille Flammarion. New York and London, Harper & brothers, 1900. xiii, 488 p. pl., diagrs. 20 1/2 cm. [Full name: Nicolas Camille Flammarion] [BF1032.F5] 0-2009
1. Psychical research. I. Title. II. Title: The unknown.

FLAMMARION, Camille, 1842-1925. 133.
Mysterious psychic forces; an account of the author's investigations in psychical research, together with those of other European savants, by Camille Flammarion... Boston, Small, Maynard and company, 1907. 3 p. l., v-xxiv p., 1 l., 466 p. illus., xiii pl. 21 1/2 cm. [Full name: Nicolas Camille Flammarion] [BF1032.F55] 7-30610
1. Psychical research. 2. Spiritualism. I. Title.

FLOURNOY, Theodore, 1854-1920. 133.
Spiritism and psychology, by Theodore Flournoy...tr, abridged, and with an introduction by Hereward Carrington... New York and London, Harper & brothers, 1911. ix, [1] p., 1 l., 353, [1] p. front., plates, ports., facsims. 21 1/2 cm. [BF1032.F6] 11-25954
1. Psychical research. 2. Spiritualism. I. Carrington, Hereward, 1880- ed. and tr. II. Title.

FRANCIS, John Reynolds, d.1909, comp. 133.
Gems of thought from leading intellectual lights ... Designed to illustrate certain grand truths which are connected with the spiritual philosophy. Comp. by John R. Francis. Chicago, Ill., The Progressive thinker publishing house, 1906. 3 p. l., 356 p. 20 cm. [BF1023.F68] 6-16204
1. Psychical research. 2. Spiritualism. 3. Religion—Addresses, essays, lectures. I. Title.

FRANK, Henry, 1854- 133.07
Psychic phenomena, science and immortality; being a further excursion into unseen realms beyond the point previously explored in "Modern light on immortality", and a sequel to that previous record, by Henry Frank ... 2d ed. Boston, Sherman, French & company, 1916. 23 p. l., [13]-556 p. 21 cm. [BT921.F782 1916] 128 32-15892
1. Psychical research. 2. Immortality. I. Title.

FRANK, Henry, 1854-1933. 237.
Psychic phenomena, science and immortality; being a further excursion into unseen realms beyond the point previously explored in "Modern light on immortality," and a sequel to that previous record, by Henry Frank ... Boston, Sherman, French & company, 1911. 8 p. l., [12]-556 p. 21 cm. [BT921.F782 1911] 11-11680
1. Psychical research. 2. Immortality. I. Title.

**FRONTIERS of healing :* 133.8
new dimensions in parapsychology / edited by Nicholas M. Regush. New York : Avon, 1977. xxi, 309p. [BF1031] 77-72357 ISBN 0-380-00707-X pbk. : 2.25 Bibliography:p.307-309. ; 18 cm.
1. Psychical research. I. Regush, Nicholas m., ed.

GANDEE, Lee R. 133
Strange experience; the autobiography of a hexenmeister [by] Lee R. Gandee. Englewood Cliffs, N.J., Prentice-Hall [1971] 355 p. illus. 24 cm. [BF1027.G25A3] 76-157053 ISBN 0-13-850966-2 6.95
1. Psychical research. 2. Occult sciences. 3. Reincarnation. I. Title.

GARFIELD, Rorke. 133.8
Superforce : the ancient laws of magic at work / by Rorke Garfield. Wellingborough [Eng.] : Thorsons Publishers, 1976. 127 p. ; 22 cm. [BF1031.G17 1976] 76-373268 ISBN 0-87728-353-2 pbk. : 4.50
1. Psychical research. 2. Witchcraft. I. Title.
Distributed by S. Weiser, N.Y.

GARLAND, Hamlin, 1860- 133.072
Forty years of psychic research; a plain narrative of fact, by Hamlin Garland... New York, The Macmillan company, 1936. viii p., 1 l., 394 p. front. (port.) 22 1/2 cm. [BF1031.G19] [[159.961]] 36-27232
1. Psychical research. I. Title.

GARLAND, Hamlin, 1860- 133.072
The mystery of the buried crosses: a narrative of psychic-exploration, by Hamlin Garland...Illustrated with photographs and endpapers. New York, E. P. Dutton and company, 1939. 351, [1] p. front., illus. (incl. ports., map, plan) "First edition." [BF1031.G195] 39-15054 159
1. Psychical research. I. Title. II. Title: The buried crosses, The mystery of.

GARRETT, Eileen Jeanette (Lyttle) 1893- 133.07
Awareness, by Eileen J. Garrett. New York, Creative age press, inc., 1943. xvi p., 1 l., 308 p. diagrs. 21 cm. [BF1031.G3] 43-15460
1. Psychical research. 2. Consciousness. 3. Spiritualism. I. Title.

GIBIER, Paul, 1851-1900. 133.
Psychism; analysis of things existing; essays by Paul Gibier ... 3d ed. New York, Bulletin publishing co. [c1899] 287 p. 20 cm. [BF1261.G4] 99-2099
1. Psychical research. 2. Spiritualism. I. Title.

GLASS, Kate Elizabeth (Perkins) "Mrs. C. W. Glass," 1874- 133.
Her invisible spirit mate; a scientific novel, and psychological lessons on how to make the world more beautiful, by Reverend Mrs. Charles Wilder Glass. [Los Angeles, Printed by McElheney, c1917] 2 p. l., [2]-115, [2] p. illus. (incl. ports.) 18 cm. [BF1301.G5] 17-11675 0.50
1. Psychical research. I. Title.

GOOCH, Stan. 133.8
The paranormal / Stan Gooch. New York : Harper Colophon Books, 1980, c1978. 313 p. ; 18 cm. Includes bibliographical references ad index. [BF1031.G54] ISBN 0-06-090749-5 pbk. : 4.95
1. Psychical research. 2. Occult sciences. I. Title.
L.C. card no. for 1978 Wildwood House ed.: 78-318971

GORDON, William, 1893- 133.072
A course in psychic unfoldment, by William Gordon ... Hollywood, Calif. [Printed by the Oxford press, c1932] 171 p. mounted port. 20 cm. [Full name: William Reeves Gordon] [BF1040.G6] 159.961 33-1184
1. Psychical research. I. Title. II. Title: Psychic unfoldment, A course in.

HALEY, Philip S. 133
A guide to the psychic life, by Philip S. Haley ... Los Angeles, Calif, The Austin publishing co., 1928. 3 p. 1., [9]-94 p. 19 cm. [BF1040.H3] 28-16246
1. Psychical research. I. Title.

HALEY, Philip S. 133.072
Modern loaves and fishes, and other studies in psychic phenomena, by Philip S. Haley ... San Francisco, Calif., P. S. Haley [c1935] 1 p. 1., l, 118 p. illus., 2 diagr. 23 x 17 1/2 cm. "Lithographed." [BF1040.H33] [[159.961]] 36-23284
1. Psychical research. I. Title. II. Title: Psychic phenomena.

HALEY, Philip Sheridan, 1884- 130
A guide to the psychic life, by Philip S. Haley ... Los Angeles, Calif., The Austin publishing co., 1928. 3 p. l., [9]-94 p. 19 cm. [BF1040.H3] 28-16246
1. Psychical research. I. Title.

HALEY, Philip Sheridan, 1884- 133.072
Modern loaves and fishes, and other studies in psychic phenomena, by Philip S. Haley... San Francisco, Calif., P. S. Haley [1935] 1 p. l., 1, 118 p., illus, 2 diagr. 23 x 17 1/2 cm. "Lithographed." [BF1040.H33] [159.961] 36-23284
1. Psychical research. I. Title. II. Title: Psychic phenomena.

HALPHIDE, A[lvan] C[avala]
The Psychic and Psychism ... 1st ed. Chicago, Authors' pub. co., 1901. xi, 19-228 p. 8 cm. 1-8194
I. Title.

*HAMMOND, Sally. 133.9
We are all healers. New York, Ballantine Books [1974, c1973] 296 p. 18 cm. [BF1027] ISBN 0-345-24152-5. 1.95 (pbk.)
1. Psychical research. I. Title.
L.C. card number for original ed.: 73-6331.

HAPGOOD, Charles H. 133.93
Voices of spirit : through the psychic experience of Elwood Babbitt / Charles H. Hapgood New York : Leisure Books [1976 c1975] xiii, 336 p. : ill. ; 18 cm. Includes index Bibliography: pp. 329-332 [BF1283.B25H37] pbk. : 1.75
1. Babbitt, Elwood, 1922- 2. Psychical research. I. Title.
L.C. card no. for 1975 Delacorte Press / S. Lawrence edition: 74-22238.

HAPGOOD, Charles H. 133.9'3
Voices of spirit : through the psychic experience of Elwood Babbitt / by Charles H. Hapgood. New York : Delacorte Press/S. Lawrence, [1975] p. cm. [BF1283.B25H37] 74-22238 ISBN 0-440-05983-6
1. Babbitt, Elwood, 1922- 2. Psychical research. I. Title.

HAPGOOD, Charles H. 133.9'3
Voices of spirit : through the psychic experience of Elwood Babbitt / by Charles H. Hapgood. New York : Delacorte Press/S. Lawrence, [1975] p. cm. [BF1283.B25H37] 74-22238 ISBN 0-440-05983-6
1. Babbitt, Elwood, 1922- 2. Psychical research. I. Title.

*HARLOW, Samuel Ralph. 133'.01
A life after death. [New York] Macfadden [1968, c.1961] 176p. 18cm. (75-212) .75 pap.,
1. Psychical research. 2. Future life. I. Title.

HARLOW, Samuel Ralph, 1885- 133.07
A life after death. [1st ed.] Garden City, N. Y., Doubleday, 1961. 264 p. 22 cm. [BF1031.H26] 61-6508
1. Psychical research. 2. Future life. I. Title.

HART, William E. 133.93
Psychic instructions, by William E. Hart. Boston, The Christopher publishing house [c1937] 62 p. 21 cm. [BF1040.H37] 159.96173 38-2317
1. Psychical research. I. Title.

HENKEL, Fred, 1867-
Creative psychics, the art of regeneration; the science and art of the religion of the future; a positive science of metapsychics and the art expression of regenerative mysticism; an interpretation of the emancipation of the age, by Fred Henkel. Los Angeles, Cal., Printed for the author by the Golden press, 1917. 81, [1] p. 19 1/2 cm. Back cover paged in. 18-2470
I. Title.

HILL, John Arthur, 1872- 133.
Man is a spirit; a collection of spontaneous cases of dream, vision, and ecstasy, by J. Arthur Hill ... London, New York [etc.] Cassell and company, ltd., 1918. 2 p. l., vii-x, [2], 13-199, [1] p. 21 cm. [BF1031.H38] 18-6179
1. Psychical research. I. Title.

HILL, John Arthur, 1872- 133.
Man is a spirit; a collection of spontaneous cases of dream, vision and ecstasy, by J. Arthur Hill ... New York, George H. Doran company [c1918] ix, [2], 13-199 p. 21 1/2 cm. $1.50. [BF1031.H38 1918a] 18-8146
1. Psychical research. I. Title.

HILL, John Arthur, 1872- 133.
Psychical investigations; some personally-observed proofs of survival, by J. Arthur Hill ... London, New York [etc.] Cassell and company, ltd., 1917. viii, 288 p. 21 1/2 cm. "Chapters I., II., and X. have appeared as articles in the Quest, Nineteenth century and after, and Occult review respectively."-- Pref. [BF1301.H5] 17-12729
1. Psychical research. I. Title.

HILL, John Arthur, 1872- 133.
Psychical investigations; some personally-observed proofs of survival, by J. Arthur Hill ... New York, George H. Doran company [c1917] viii p., 1 l., 11-308 p. 21 cm. Reprinted in part from various periodicals. [BF1031.H42] 17-13827
1. Psychical research. I. Title.

HILL, John Arthur, 1872- 133.
Psychical miscellanea, being papers on psychical research, telepathy, hypnotism, Christian science, etc., by J. Arthur Hill ... New York, Harcourt, Brace & Howe, 1920. 3 p. l., 118 p. 19 1/2 cm. "Printed in England." Reprinted in part from various periodicals. [BF1031.H5] 20-26542
1. Psychical research. I. Title.

*HILL, Raymond Putnam 133.8
My family of souls; The story of a journey through time; 1st. ed. Jericho, N.Y. Exposition Press [1974] 145 p. 22 cm. [BF1038] ISBN 0-682-47900-4 6.00
1. Psychical research. 2. Reincarnation. I. Title.

HOLT, Henry, 1840-1926. 133.
The cosmic relations and immortality, by Henry Holt, being a second edition of the author's treatise "On the cosmic relations"... Boston and New York, Houghton Mifflin company, 1919. 2 v. 23 cm. Paged continuously. [BF1031.H65 1919] 20-26562
1. Psychical research. 2. Thought-transference. 3. Spiritualism. I. Title.

HOLT, Henry, 1840-1926. 133.
On the cosmic relations, by Henry Holt... Boston and New York, Houghton Mifflin company, 1914. 2 v. 22 cm. Paged continuously. [BF1031.H65] 14-20555
1. Psychical research. 2. Through-transference. 3. Spiritualism. I. Title.

HOLZER, Hans W., 1920- 133.9'0924
The psychic world of Bishop Pike [by] Hans Holzer. New York, Crown Publishers [1970] 224 p. 22 cm. [BX5995.P54H6 1970] 70-119164 5.95
1. Pike, James Albert, Bp., 1913-1969. 2. Psychical research. I. Title.

HUBBARD, Henry Seward, 1854- 133.
Beyond, by Henry Seward Hubbard. Boston, Arena publishing company, 1896. 2 p. l., [7]-179 p. 17 cm. [BF1031.H75] 20-13242
1. Psychical research. I. Title.

HUDSON, Thomson Jay, 1834-1903. 133.
The evolution of the soul, and other essays, by Thomson Jay Hudson ... with portrait and biographical sketch. Chicago, A. C. McClurg & co., 1904. xi p. 1 l., 344 p. front (port.) 19 1/2 cm. Preface signed: C. B. H. [BF1031.H84] 4--7869
1. Psychical research. I. Title.
Contents omitted.

HUDSON, Thomson Jay, 1834-1903. 133.
The law of psychic phenomena; a working hypothesis for the systematic study of hypnotism, spiritism, mental therapeutics, etc., by Thomson Jay Hudson. Chicago, A. C. McClurg and company, 1894. 3 p. 1., [v]-xvii, [19]-409 p. 20 cm. [BF1031.H86 1804] 10-29910
1. Psychical research. I. Title.

HUDSON, Thomson Jay, 1834-1903. 133.
The law of psychic phenomena; a working hypothesis for the systematic study of hypnotism, spiritism, mental theapeutics, etc., by Thomson Jay Hudson. 9th ed. Chicago, A. C. McClurg and company, 1896. 1 p. l., xvii, [19]-409 p. 19 1/2 cm. [BF1061] 3-26449
1. Psychical research. I. Title.

HUDSON, Thomson Jay, 1834-1903. 133.072
The law of psychic phenomena; a working hypothesis for the systematic study of hypnotism, spiritism, mental therapeutics, etc., by Thomson Jay Hudson ... 17th ed. Chicago, A. C. McClurg and company, 1899. 3 p. l., [v]-xvii, [19]-409 p. 19 1/2 cm. [BF1031.H86 1899] 40-21008
1. Psychical research. I. Title.

HUDSON, Thomson Jay, 1834-1903. 133.
The law of psychic phenomena; a working hypothesis for the systematic study of hypnotism, spiritism, mental therapeutics, etc. by Thomson Jay Hudson ... 18th ed. Chicago, A. C. McClurg and company, 1899. 3 p. l., [v]-xvii, [19]-409 p. 19 cm. [BF1031.H86 1899] 10-29911
1. Psychical research. I. Title.

HUDSON, Thomson Jay, 1834-1903. 133.
The law of psychic phenomena; a working hypothesis for the systematic study of hypnotism, spiritism, mental therapeutics, etc., by Thomson Jay Hudson ... 20th ed. Chicago, A. C. McClurg & co. 1900. 3 p. l., [v]-xvii, [19]-409 p. 19 cm. [BF1031.H86 1900] 10-29912
1. Psychical research. I. Title.

HUDSON, Thomson Jay, 1834-1903. 133.072
The law of psychic phenomena, a working hypothesis for the systematic study of hypnotism, spiritism, mental therapeutics, etc., by Thomson Jay Hudson ... 51st thousand. Chicago, A. C. McClurg & co., 1902. 3 p. 1., [v]-xvii, [19]-409 p. 19 1/2 cm. [BF1031.H86 1902] (159.961) 36-5007
1. Psychical research. I. Title.

HUDSON, Thomson Jay, 1834-1903. 133.072
The law of psychic phenomena, a working hypothesis for the systematic study of hypnotism, spiritism, mental therapeutics, etc., by Thomson Jay Hudson ... 30th ed. Chicago, A. C. McClurg & co., 1905. 3 p. l., [v]-xvii, [19]-409 p. 19 1/2 cm. [BF1031.H86 1905] (159.961) 32-32116
1. Psychical research. I. Title.

HUDSON, Thomson Jay, 1834-1903. 133.
The law of psychic phenomena; a working hypothesis for the systematic study of hypnotism, spiritism, mental therapeutics, etc., by Thomson Jay Hudson ... 47th ed. Chicago, A. C. McClurg & co., 1925. 3 p. l., [v]-xviii, [19]-409 p. 19 cm. [BF1031.H86 1925] 25-25440
1. Psychical research. I. Title.

HUDSON, Thomson Jay, 1834-1903. 133.072
The law of the psychic phenomena; a working hypothesis for the systematic study of hypnotism, spiritism, mental therapeutics, etc., by Thomson Jay Hudson ... 32d ed. Chicago, A. C. McClurg & co., 1909. 3 p. l., [v]-xvii, [19]-409 p. 19 cm. [BF1031.H86 1909] [(159.961)] 37-8483
1. Pyschical research. I. Title.

HUTCHINGS, Emily Grant. Mrs. 133.9072
Where do we go from here? The journey of life, by Emily Grant Hutchings. New York, London, G. P. Putnam's sons, 1933. xiii p., 1 l., 17-306 p. 21 cm. [BF1031.H87] 159.9617072 33-29359
1. Psychical research. 2. Spiritualism. 3. Future life. I. Title.

HYSLOP, James Harvey, 1854-1920. 133.
Contact with the other world; the latest evidence as to communication with the dead, by James H. Hyslop ... New York, The Centry co., 1919. 5 p. l., 3-493 p. plates. 23 cm. [BF1031.H9] 19-12304
1. Psychical research. I. Title.

HYSLOP, James Hervey, 1854-1920. 133.
Borderland of psychical research, by James H. Hyslop ... Boston, H. B. Turner & co., 1906. viii p., 1 l., 425 p. 20 cm. [BF1031.H88] 6-33631
1. Psychical research. I. Title.
Contents omitted.

HYSLOP, James Hervey, 1854-1920. 133.07
Contact with the other world, the latest evidence as to communication with the dead, by James H. Hyslop ... New York, The Century co., 1920. 5 p. l., 3-493 p. plates. 23 cm. "Published, June, 1919." [BF1031.H9 1920] 32-21751
1. Psychical research. I. Title.

HYSLOP, James Hervey, 1854-1920. 133.
Engigmas of psychical research, by James H. Hyslop ... Boston, H. B. Turner & co., 1906. x p., 1 l., 427 p. illus. 20 cm. "The present volume may be considered as a supplement to the one on Science and a future life, which has been published."-- Pref. [BF1031.H92] 6-6896
1. Psychical research. I. Title.
Contents omitted.

HYSLOP, James Hervey, 1854-1920. 133.
Psychical research and the resurrection, by James H. Hyslop ... Boston, Small, Maynard and company, 1908. 3 p. l., ix-xiv p., 1 l., 409 p. 20 cm. Partly reprinted from various sources. [BF1031.H94] 8-18413
1. Psychical research. 2. Ressurection. I. Title.

HYSLOP, James Hervey, 1854-1920. 133.
Science and a future life, by James H. Hyslop ... Boston, H. B. Turner & co., 1905. xi, 372 p. 20 cm. [BF1031.H97] 5-17300
1. Psychical research. 2. Spiritualism. 3. Future life. I. Title.
Contents omitted.

JACOBSON, Nils-Olof, 1937- 133.9'013
Life without death? On parapsychology, mysticism, and the question of survival [by] Nils O. Jacobson. Translated from the Swedish by Sheila La Farge. [New York] Delacorte Press [1974] viii, 339 p. illus. 24 cm. Translation of Liv efter doden? Includes bibliographical references. [BF1038.S7J313] 73-12714 10.00
1. Psychical research. 2. Future life. I. Title.

JACOBSON, Nils-Olof, 1937- 133.9013
Life without death? On parapsychology, mysticism, and the question of survival [by] Nils O. Jacobsen. Translated from the Swedish by Sheila La Forge. [New York, Dell, 1974] 334 p. 18 cm. "Translation of Liv efter d oden?" [BF1038.S7J313] 1.75 (pbk.)
1. Psychical research. 2. Future life. I. Title.
L.C. card number for original edition: 73-12714.

JARVIS, Stinson, 1854- 133
The ascent of life; or, The psychic laws and forces in nature. By Stinson Jarvis ... Boston, Arena publishing company, 1894. 3 p. l., iii, 120 p. front. (port.) 23 x 18 cm. [Full name: Thomas Stinson Jarvis] [BF1999.J3] 3-1601
1. Psychical research. 2. Hypnotism. I. Title.

JASTROW, Joseph, 1863- 130
Fact and fable in psychology, by Joseph Jastrow ... Boston and New York, Houghton, Mifflin and company, 1900. xviii, 375, [1] p. illus. 21 cm. [BF1081.J25] 1-29066
1. Psychical research. 2. Psychology. I. Title.
Contents omitted.

JOIRE, Paul Martial Joseph, 1856- 133.07
Psychical and supernormal phenomena, their observation and experimentation, the secrets of life unveiled, by Dr. Paul Joire ... translated by Dudley Wright, with 22 illustrations. Chicago, The Marlowe press [1917] 490 p. illus. 20 cm. [BF1031.J7 1917] 32-35398
1. Psychical research. I. Wright, Dudley, 1868- tr. II. Title.

KENILWORTH, Walter Winston. 133.
Practical occultism, by Walter Winston Kenilworth. Boston, R. G. Badger [c1921] 308 p. 21 cm. [BF1031.K25] 21-7200
1. Psychical research. 2. Occult sciences. 3. New thought. I. Title.

KENILWORTH, Walter Winston. 131
Thoughts on things psychic, by Walter Winston Kenilworth ... New York, R. F. Fenno & company [1911] 3 p. l., 230 p. 20 cm. [BF639.K48] 11-6021
1. Psychical research. I. Title.

KINGSFORD, S. M., Miss. 133.
Psychical research for the plain man, by S. M. Kingsford. London, K. Paul, Trench, Trubner & co., ltd.; New York, E. P. Dutton & co., 1920. vi p., 1 l., 271 p. 19 1/2 cm. [BF1031.K5] 22-5233
1. Psychical research. I. Title.

KITTLER, Glenn D. 133.8
Edgar Cayce on the Dead Sea scrolls, by Glenn D. Kittler, under the editorship of Hugh Lynn Cayce. New York, Paperback Library [1970] 205 p. 18 cm. [BF1311.E75K5] 73-20586 0.95
1. Dead Sea scrolls. 2. Psychical research. 3. Essenes. I. Cayce, Edgar, 1877-1945. II. Title.

KRESKIN, 1935- 133.8'092'4 B
The amazing world of Kreskin. [New York] Avon [1974, c1973] 252 p. 18 cm. Bibliography: p. 243-252. [BF1027.K75A3] ISBN 0-380-00121-7 1.50 (pbk.)
1. Kreskin, 1935- 2. Psychical research. 3. Occult sciences. I. Title.
L.C. card number for original ed.: 72-11411.

KRESKIN, 1935- 133.8'092'4 B
The amazing world of Kreskin. [1st ed.] New York, Random House [1973] xi, 209 p. 22 cm. Bibliography: 203-209. [BF1027.K75A3] 72-11411 ISBN 0-394-48440-1 5.95
1. Kreskin, 1935- 2. Psychical research. 3. Occult sciences. I. Title.

LAMBERT, Helen Churchill (Smith) Mrs. 133.
A general survey of psychical phenomena, by Helen C. Lambert; foreword by Stanley De Brath. New York, The Knickerbocker press, 1928. xxiii, 165 p. front., plates, ports., facsims. 23 cm. [BF1031.L25] 28-10983
1. Psychical research. 2. Spiritualism. I. Title. II. Title: Psychical phenomena A general survey of.

LANG, Andrew, 1844-1912. 133.
Cock Lane and common-sense, by Andrew Lang. London and New York, Longmans, Green, and co., 1894. xvi, 357 p. 20 cm. [BF1031.L27] 10-29933
1. Psychical research. 2. Ghosts. I. Title.
Contents omitted.

LANG, Andrew, 1844-1912. 133.04
Cock lane and common-sense by Andrew Lang. New ed. London and New York, Longmans, Green and co., 1894. xvi, 357 p. 20 cm. [BF1031.L27 1894 a] 159.96104 32-35018
1. Psychical research. 2. Ghosts. I. Title.
Contents omitted.

*LESHAN, Lawrence, 1920- 133.8'012
Alternate realities : the search for the full human being / Lawrence LeShan. New York : Ballantine Books, 1977,c1977. xiv, 193p. ; 18 cm. Includes bibliograhical references. [BF1031.L42] ISBN 0-345-25370-1 pbk. : 1.95
1. Psychial research. 2. Reality. I. Title.
L.C. card no. for 1976 M. Evans ed.: 76-14488.

LESHAN, Lawrence L., 1920- 133.8
The medium, the mystic, and the physicist; toward a general theory of the paranormal, by Lawrence LeShan. New York, Viking Press [1974] xix, 299 p. 22 cm. (An Esalen book) Includes bibliographical references. [BF1031.L43 1974] 73-8147 ISBN 0-670-46566-6 8.95
1. Psychical research. I. Title.

LISEMER, Louis. 133
Fate or destiny? a new optimism (the story of the soul) by Louis Lisemer ... Boston, The Christopher publishing house [c1923] 4 p. l., [vii]-viii, 9-210 p. 2 port. (incl. front.) 22 cm. [BF1031.L5] 23-11849
1. Psychical research. I. Title.

LODGE, Oliver Joseph, Sir 133.
1851-
Phantom walls, by Sir Oliver Lodge ... New York, London, G. P. Putnam's sons, 1930. xiv, 255 p. front. (port.) 21 cm. "First American edition." [BF1031.L65 1930] 30-8611
1. Psychical research. 2. Immortality. 3. Science—Philosophy. I. Title.

LODGE, Oliver Joseph, Sir. 133.
1851-
The survival of man; a study in unrecognized human faculty, by Sir Oliver Lodge, F. R. S. New and enl. ed. New York, George H. Doran company [c1920] 3 p. l., v-viii p., 3 l., 379 p. 23 cm. [BF1031.L7 1920] 20-5130
1. Psychical research. I. Title.

LODGE, Oliver Joseph, Sir 133.
1851-
Why I believe in personal immortality, by Sir Oliver Lodge. Garden City, N. Y., Doubleday, Doran & company, inc., 1929. viii p., 1 l., 206 p. 20 cm. [BF1031.L75 1929] 29-786
1. Psychical research. 2. Immortality. I. Title.

LODGE, Oliver Joseph, Sir 133.
1851-1940.
Th survival of man; a study in unrecongnized human faculty, by Sir Oliver Lodge, F. R. S. New York, Moffat, Yard and company, 1909. 6 p. l., 361 p. 21 cm. [BF1031.L7 1909 a] 9-30857
1. Psychical research. I. Title.

LOEHR, Franklin. 264.1
The power of prayer on plants. [1st ed.] Garden City, N. Y., Doubleday, 1959. 144p. illus. 22cm. [BF1031.L77] 58-11320
1. Psychical research. 2. Prayer. 3. Plants, Effect of prayer on. I. Title.

LOGAN, Daniel, 1936- 133.8
Vibrations : improving your psychic environment / by Daniel Logan. Englewood Cliffs, N.J. : Prentice-Hall, c1976. 193 p. ; 22 cm. Includes index. [BF1031.L774] 75-45412 ISBN 0-13-941666-8 : 7.95
1. Psychical research. 2. Occult sciences. I. Title.

LYTTELTON, Edith Sophy 130
(Balfour) Hon. Mrs., 1865-
Our superconscious mind, by Edith Lyttelton, D.D.E. New York, D. Appleton and company, 1931. 4 p. l., 3-264 p. 21 cm. [BF1031.L8 1931a] 31-32016
1. Psychical research. 2. Subconsciousness. I. Title. II. Title: Superconscious mind.

MCADAMS, Elizabeth E., 133.9'01'3
1945-
The case for life after death : parapsychologists look at survival evidence / Elizabeth E. McAdams and Raymond Bayless. Chicago : Nelson-Hall, c1981. viii, 157 p. ; 23 cm. Includes index. Bibliography: p. 151-153. [BF1040.M3] 19 80-29289 ISBN 0-88229-592-6 : 14.95
1. Psychical research. 2. Future life. I. Bayless, Raymond, joint author. II. Title.

*MCCREERY, Charles, 1942- 133
Psychical phenomena and the physical world. With a foreword by Sir George Joy. [1st Amer. ed. New York, Ballantine Books [1973] ix, 139 p. 18 cm. Includes bibliographical references. [BF1021] ISBN 0-345-23602-5 1.25 (pbk.)
1. Psychical research. 2. Occult sciences. I. Title.

MAETERLINCK, Maurice, 1862- 133.
The unknown guest, by Maurice Maeterlinck; tr. by Alexander Teixeira de Mattos. New York, Dodd, Mead and company, 1914. 410 p. 20 cm. Reprinted in part from various periodicals. [BF1032.M24] 14-13577
1. Psychical research. I. Teixeira de Mattos, Alexander Louis, 1865-1921, tr. II. Title.
Contents omitted.

MASON, Eveleen Laura, Mrs. 1838-
The discovery of discoveries, climaxingly collated in the month of Una-and-her-lion (1908) inclusive of August: and fulfilling "the message of Ishtar" ... By Mrs. Eveleen Laura Mason ... [Brookline? Mass.] c1909. 2 p. l., 119 p. illus. 18 1/2 x 16 cm. Cover-title: My book of the discovery and rescue from wreckage of the discoveries which have been made by me and others in the weird-realm of spiritual facts. Illus. t.-p. 9-11696
I. Title.

MASON, Eveleen Laura, Mrs. 1838-
The discovery of discoveries, climaxingly collated in the month of Una-and-her-lion (1908) inclusive of August: and fulfilling "the message of Ishtar" ... By Mrs. Eveleen Laura Mason ... [Brookline? Mass.] c1909. 2 p. l., 119 p. illus. 18 1/2 x 16 cm. Cover-title: My book of the discovery and rescue from wreckage of the discoveries which have been made by me and others in the weird-realm of spiritual facts. Illus. t.-p. 9-11696
I. Title.

MASON, Rufus Osgood, 1830- 133.
1903.
Telepathy and the subliminal self; an account of recent investigations regarding hypnotism, automatism, dreams, phantasms, and related phenomena, by R. Osgood Mason ... New York, H. Holt and company, 1897. viii, 343 p. front., illus. 19 1/2 cm. [BF1031.M38] 3-10771
1. Psychical research. 2. Thought transference. I. Title.

MASON, Rufus Osgood, 1830- 133.
1903.
Telepathy and the subliminal self; an account of recent investigations regarding hypnotism, automatism, dreams, phantasms, and related phenomena, by R. Osgood Mason ... 4th impression. New York, H. Holt and company, 1899. viii, 343 p. front., illus. 19 cm. [BF1031.M38 1899] 22-14680
1. Psychical research. 2. Thought-transference. I. Title.

MEYER, Ann Porter. 248'.22
Being a Christ! : The basic course of the teaching of the inner Christ / by Ann Porter Meyer and Peter Victor Meyer. San Diego, Calif. : Dawning Publications, 1975- v. in ; 28 cm. [BF1031.M54] 74-32528
1. Psychical research. 2. Spiritual life. I. Meyer, Peter Victor, joint author. II. Title.

MISHLOVE, Jeffrey, 1946- 133
The roots of consciousness : psychic liberation through history, science, and experience / Jeffrey Mishlove. New York : Random House, c1975. p. cm. "A Random House/Bookworks book." Includes bibliographical references and index. [BF1031.M56] 75-10311 9.95 ISBN 0-394-73115-8 pbk. : 8.95
1. Psychical research. 2. Occult sciences. I. Title.

MONTGOMERY, John Lawrence, 133.
1890-
The mastery of mysteries, the result of research, observation and personal experience, by Dr. John L. Montgomery ... Los Angeles, Cal., Gem publishing company [c1927] 156 p. incl. front. (port.) illus. 20 cm. [BF1031.M65] 27-11084
1. Psychical research. 2. Hypnotism. I. Title.

MOORE, Evelyn Garth. 133.8
Try the spirits / by E. Garth Moore. New York : Oxford University Press, [1977] p. cm. Includes index. Bibliography: p. [BF1031.M673] 77-24734 8.95 ISBN 0-19-519973-1 pbk. : 2.95
1. Psychical research. 2. Christianity and psychical research. I. Title.

MULDOON, Sylvan Joseph. 133.923
The case for astral projection, by Sylvan Muldoon ... Chicago, The Aries press, G. Engelke, 1936. 173 p., 1 l. 21 cm. [BF1389.A7M75] 159.961723 37-1815
1. Psychical research. I. Title. II. Title: Astral projection, The case for.

MURCHISON, Carl Allanmore, 133.
1887- ed.
The case for and against psychical belief, by Sir Oliver Lodge, Sir Arthur Conan Doyle, Frederick Bligh Bond, L. R. G. Crandon, Mary Austin, Margaret Deland, William McDougall, Hans Driesch, Walker Franklin Prince, F. C. S. Schiller, John E. Coover, Gardner Murphy, Joseph Jastrow, Harry Houdini, edited by Carl Murchison. Worcester, Mass., Clark university, 1927. 6 p. l., [3]-365 p. illus., plates, ports. 24 cm. [BF1023.M8] 27-6665
1. Psychical research. I. Title.

MYERS, Frederic William 133.9'013
Henry, 1843-1901.
Human personality and its survival of bodily death / Frederic William Henry Myers ; with an introd. by Gardner Murphy. New York : Arno Press, 1975, c1954. 2 v. : ill. ; 24 cm. (Perspectives in psychical research) Reprint of the ed. published by Longmans, Green, New York. Includes bibliographical references and index. [BF1031.M85 1975] 75-7391 ISBN 0-405-07038-1
1. Psychical research. 2. Personality. 3. Immortality. I. Title. II. Series.

NEHER, Andrew. 133.8'01'9
The psychology of transcendence / Andrew Neher. Englewood Cliffs, N.J. : Prentice-Hall, c1980. p. cm. (A Spectrum book) Includes index. Bibliography: p. [BF1031.N43] 19 80-19797 ISBN 0-13-736652-3 : 12.95 pbk. : 6.95
1. Psychical research. 2. Occult sciences. 3. Mysticism—Psychology. I. Title.

NELSON, Robert A. 133.072
The encyclopedia of mentalism and allied arts, by Robert A. Nelson; humorous illustrations by Nelson Hahne. Columbus, O., Nelson enterprises [1944] 118 p. incl. front. (port.) illus. 23 1/2 cm. "Recommended books for further study": p. 118. [BF1042.N4] 793.8 44-35814
1. Psychical research. I. Title.

NICHOLS, Beverley, 1899- 133
Powers that be. New York, Popular Lib. [1967] 192p. 18cm. (60-2195) Bibl. [BF1031.N5] .60 pap.,
1. Psychical research. 2. Occult sciences. I. Title.

NICHOLS, Beverley, 1899- 133
Powers that be. New York, St. Martin's Press [1966] 240 p. illus. 22 cm. Bibliographical footnotes. [BF1031.N5] 65-23600
1. Psychical research. 2. Occult sciences. I. Title.

OSBORN, Arthur Walter, 133.9
1891-
The expansion of awareness; one man's search for meaning in living [by] Arthur W. Osborn. Foreword by Raynor C. Johnson. [2d ed.] Adyar [India] Wheaton, Ill., Theosophical Pub. House [1967] 272p. 22cm. (Quest bk.) Bibl. [BF1031.O74 1961] 67-4806 pap., price unreported
1. Psychical research. I. Title.

OSBORN, Arthur Walter, 133.9'013
1891-
The superphysical : a review of the evidence for continued existence, reincarnation, and mystical states of consciousness / Arthur W. Osborn. Rev. ed. New York : Barnes & Noble, 1974. xviii, 350 p. ; 23 cm. Includes bibliographical references and index. [BF1031.O75 1974] 74-2674 ISBN 0-06-495304-1 : 13.00
1. Psychical research. 2. Reincarnation. I. Title.

OSTRANDER, Sheila. 133.8
Handbook of psi discoveries / by Sheila Ostrander and Lynn Schroeder. New York : Berkley Pub. Corp. : distributed by Putnam, [1974] 342 p., [8] leaves of plates : ill. ; 22 cm. Includes index. Bibliography: p. 315-335. [BF1031.O78 1974] 73-88532 ISBN 0-399-11288-X : 8.95
1. Psychical research. I. Schroeder, Lynn, joint author. II. Title.

PAGE, Howard L. 133.
The dual mind, by H. L. Page ... Chicago, Green leaf publishing co. [1909] 2 p. l., 7-194 p. 20 cm. [BF1031.P15] 9-24681
1. Psychic research. 2. Hypnotism. I. Title.

PAINE, Albert Ware, 1812- 133.
1907.
The new philosphy. By Albert W. Paine... Bangor, Me., O. F. Knowles & co., printers, 1884. 168 p. 20 1/2 cm. [BF1031.P2] 10-29934
1. Psychical research. I. Title.
Contents omitted.

PARAPSYCHOLOGICAL 133.8
Association.
Research in parapsychology 1973, [edited by] W. G. Roll, R. L. Morris and J. D. Morris. Metuchen, N.J., Scarecrow Press, 1974. vi, 249 p. 23 cm. Abstracts and papers taken from the sixteenth annual convention of the Parapsychological Association, 1973. [BF1021.P28] ISBN 0-8108-0708-4 8.00
1. Psychial research—Congresses. I. Roll, William George, 1926- II. Title.
L.C. card number for original ed.: 66-28580.

PENDRAGON, John. 133.8'4'0924
Pendragon: a clairvoyant's power of prophecy, written in collaboration with Brad Steiger. New York, Award Books [1968] 222 p. 18 cm. [BF1283.P43A3] 68-4494
1. Psychical research. I. Steiger, Brad. II. Title.

PHARNES, Henry. 133
Spiritual truth; my research into the subconscious and how I received my spiritual vibration through, by Henry Pharnes. [Minneapolis, c1926] 183 p. incl. front. (port.) 21 cm. [BF1999.P54] 26-11577
I. Title.

PLAYFAIR, Guy Lyon. 133.8
The indefinite boundary : an investigation into the relationship between matter and spirit / Guy Lyon Playfair ; with an appendix by Hernani Guimaraes Andrade. New York : St. Martin's Press, c1976. 320 p., [4] leaves of plates : ill. ; 22 cm. Includes bibliographical references and index. [BF1031.P6] 76-28051 ISBN 0-312-41195-2 : 8.95
1. Psychical research. 2. Occult sciences. 3. Spirit writings. I. Title.

PODMORE, Frank, 1856-1910. 133
The naturalisation of the supernatural, by Frank Podmore ... New York and London, G. P. Putnam's sons, 1908. viii p., 1 l., 374 p. illus., pl. 23 cm. "The illustrative narratives quoted in the following pages are selected partly from the Proceedings, but mainly from the unpublished Journal of the Society for psychical research."--Pref. note. [BF1031.P72] 8-22271
1. Psychical research. I. Title.

PODMORE, Frank, 1856-1910. 133
Studies in psychical research, by Frank Podmore ... New York [etc.] G. P. Putnam's sons, 1897. ix, 458 p. illus. 23 cm. [BF1031.P74] 10-29908
1. Psychical research. I. Title.

PRATT, Joseph Gaither, 133.8072
1910-
Extra-sensory perception after sixty years; a critical appraisal of the research in extra-sensory perception [by] J. G. Pratt ... J. B. Rhine ... Burke M. Smith ... Charles E. Stuart ... and Joseph A. Greenwook ... New York, H. Holt and company [c1940] xiv, 463 p. illus. (incl. plates) plates, diagrs. 23 cm. "References": p. 425-451. [BF1171.P77] 159.9616072 40-11662
1. Psychical research. I. Rhine, Joseph Banks, 1895- joint author. II. Smith, Burke M., joint author. III. Stuart, Charles Edward, 1907- joint author. IV. Greenwood, Joseph Albert, joint author. V. Title.

PRICE, Harry, 1881- 133.072
Fifty years of psychical research, a critical survey, by Harry Price ... London, New York [etc.] Longmans, Green and co. [1939] xii, 383 p. front., illus., 14 pl. (incl. facsims., diagr.) on 7 l. 23 cm. "First published 1939." "Psychic practitioners (regulation) bill": p. 326-344. "The best books to read": p. 345-359. [BF1031.P758] 159.961 40-9461
1. Psychical research. 2. Spritualism. I. Title.

PRICE, Harry, 1881-1948. 133.9
Fifty years of psychical research : a critical survey / Harry Price. New York : Arno Press, 1975. xii, 383 p., 14 leaves of plates : ill. ; 23 cm. (Perspectives in psychical research) Reprint of the 1939 ed. published

by Longmans, Green, London, New York. Includes index. Bibliography: p. 345-359. [BF1031.P758 1975] 75-7394 ISBN 0-405-07043-8
1. Psychical research. 2. Spiritualism—Case studies. I. Title. II. Series.

PRICHARD, Harold Adye, 1882- 130
God's communicating door; some suggestions from the philosophy of psychic research, by the Rev. H. Adye Prichard ... Boston, R. G. Badger [c1929] 99 p. 20 cm. [BF1040.P7] 30-33232
1. Psychical research. 2. Death. 3. Future life. I. Title.

PRINCE, Walter Franklin, 1863- 133.07
The enchanted boundary; being a survey of negative reactions to claims of psychic phenomena, 1820-1930, by Walter Franklin Prince ... Boston, Mass., Boston society for psychic research, 1930. x p., 1 l., 348 p. 24 cm. [BF1031.P77] 31-3884
1. Psychical research. I. Title.

[PRINCE, Walter Franklin] 1863- comp. 133.
Noted witnesses for psychic occurrences; incidents and biographical data, with occasional comments, compiled by the research officer of the Boston society for psychic research. Boston, Mass., Boston society for psychic research, 1928. 336 p. 23 cm. Lettered on cover: Prince. [BF1023.P7] 28-12887
1. Psychical research. I. Boston society for psychic research. II. Title.

PRINCE, Walter Franklin, 1863- 133
The psychic in the house, by Walter Franklin Prince ... Boston, Boston society for psychic research, 1926. vi, 284 p . 23 cm. "The psychic is Theodosia, my foster-daughter ... the same person who, under the pseudonym Doris, is known as having been formerly one of the most extraordinary cases in the records of abnormal psychology ... This volume is equivalent to a 'Proceedings, volume 1', of the Boston society for psychic research."--Introd. [BF1283.T5P7] 26-4726
1. Psychical research. I. Boston society for psychic research. II. Title.

PRINCE, Walter Franklin, 1863-1934. 133.9
The case of Patience Worth. New Hyde Park, N. Y., University Books [1964] 509 p. port. 24 cm. (Library of the mystic arts: a library of ancient and modern classics) Includes messages sent by P. Worth, alleged seventeenth century spirit, through P. L. Curran, a medium. [BF1301.W865P7] 63-23268
1. Psychical research. I. Worth, Patience. II. Worth, Patience. III. Curran, Pearl Lenore (Pollard) 1883-1937. IV. Title.

PRINCE, Walter Franklin, 1863-1934. 133.8
The enchanted boundary / Walter Franklin Prince. New York : Arno Press, 1975 [c1930] p. cm. (Perspectives in psychical research) Reprint of the ed. published by Boston Society for Psychic Research, Boston. [BF1031.P77 1975] 75-7396 ISBN 0-405-07045-4 : 20.00
1. Psychical research. I. Title. II. Series.

PURYEAR, Herbert B. 248'.3
Reflections on the path : based on the Edgar Cayce readings / by Herbert B. Puryear. Virginia Beach, Va. : A.R.E. Press, c1979. vii, 183 p. : ill. ; 22 cm. [BF1999.P87] 79-112092 ISBN 0-87604-113-6 pbk. : 3.95
1. Cayce, Edgar, 1877-1945. Edgar Cayce readings. 2. Psychical research. I. Cayce, Edgar, 1877-1945. Edgar Cayce readings. II. Title.

RANDALL, John Herman, 1871- 130
The new light on immortality; or, The significance of psychic research, by John Herman Randall. New York, The Macmillan company, 1921. vii p., 1 l., 174 p. 20 cm. [BF1031.R22] 21-1446
1. Psychical research. I. Title.
Contents omitted.

RANDALL, John L. 133.8'01'57
Parapsychology and the nature of life / John L. Randall. 1st U.S. ed. New York : Harper & Row, c1975. x, 256 p., [4] leaves of plates : ill. ; 22 cm. Includes index. Bibliography: p. [244]-252. [BF1045.S35R36 1975] 75-30341 ISBN 0-06-013509-3 : 8.95
1. Psychical research. 2. Biology. I. Title.

RAO, Koneru Ramakrishna. 133
Experimental parapsychology; a review and interpretation, By K. Ramakrishna Rao. Springfield, Ill., Thomas [1966] x, 255 p. 24 cm. Bibliography: p. 192-243. [BF1031.R23] 65-27587
1. Phychical research. I. Title.

RAUE, Charles Godlove, 1820-1896. 133
Psychology as a natural science applied to the solution of occult psychic phenomena, by C. G. Raue, M. D. Philadelphia, Porter & Coates, 1889. 541 p. 23 cm. [BF1031.R24] 10-29935
1. Psychical research. 2. Psychology. I. Title.

RAUSCHER, William V. 133
The spiritual frontier / William V. Rauscher with Allen Spraggett. 1st ed. Garden City, N.Y. : Doubleday, 1975. x, 204 p. ; 22 cm. Bibliography: p. [186]-201. [BF1031.R27] 73-15361 ISBN 0-385-07189-2 : 7.95
1. Psychical research. 2. Occult sciences. I. Spraggett, Allen, joint author. II. Title.

REYNER, John Hereward. 291.2'3
No easy immortality / J. H. Reyner. London ; Boston : G. Allen & Unwin, 1979. 90 p. ; 22 cm. Includes index. Bibliography: p. 87-88. [BF1031.R352] 78-41235 ISBN 0-04-200032-7 : 13.50
1. Psychical research. 2. Future life. 3. Spiritualism. I. Title.

RHINE, Joseph Banks. 133.072
Extra-sensory perception [by] J. B. Rhine ... with a foreword by Professor William McDougall ... and an introduction by Walter Franklin Prince ... Boston, Mass., Boston society for psychic research, 1934. 2 p. l., iii-xiv, 169 p. front. (5 port.) 2 pl., diagrs. 23 cm. [BF1031.R37] [159.961072] 34-34415
1. Psychical research. I. Title.

RHINE, Joseph Banks, 1895- 133.8
The reach of the mind. New York, W. Sloane Associates [1947] [5] l., 3-234 p. illus. 22 cm. "Additional reading": p. [225]-[226] [BF1031.R38] 47-30743
1. Psychical research. I. Title.

[RICHARDSON, John Emmett] 1853- 133.
The spirit of the work, by the author of "The great psychological crime"... 1st ed. Chicago, Ills., Indo-American book co., 1915. 7 p. l., 11-331 p. front. 18 cm. (The spirit of the work series. vol. I) "Foreword" signed: TK. [BF1031.S75 vol. I] 16-2875
1. Psychical research. I. Title.

RICHARDSON, Mark Wyman, 1867- 133.
Margery, Harvard, veritas; a study in psychics [by] Mark W. Richardson...Charles S. Hill [and others]... Boston, Blanchard printing co., 1925. 82 p. incl. illus. (facsim.) pl. 24 cm. [BF1283.C85R5] 26-1333
1. Crandon, Mrs. Mina (Stinson) 2. Psychical research. I. Hill, Charles Stanton, 1870- joint author. II. Title.

RICHET, Charles Robert, 1850-1935. 133.8
Thirty years of psychical research / Charles Richet. New York : Arno Press, 1975. p. cm. (Perspectives in psychical research) Translation of Traite de metapsychique. Reprint of the 1923 ed. published by Macmillan, New York. [BF1031.R513 1975] 75-7397 ISBN 0-405-07046-2 : 37.00
1. Psychical research. 2. Spiritualism I. Title. II. Series.

ROGERS, Edward Coit. 133.9
Philosophy of mysterious agents, human and mundane; or, The dynamic laws and relations of man. Embracing the natural philosophy of phenomena styled "spiritual manifestations." By E. C. Rogers... Boston, J. P. Jewett and company; Cleveland, O., Jewett, Proctor & Worthington, 1853. 1 p. l., [v]-xii, [13]-336 p. 21 cm. [BF1251.R7 1853] 159.9617 33-24157
1. Psychical research. 2. Spiritualism. I. Title.

ROGERS, Edward Coit. 133.
Philosophy of mysterious agents, human and mundane; or The dynamic laws and relations of man. Embracing the natural philosophy of phenomena styled "spiritual manifestations." By E.C. Rogers... Boston, J. P. Jewett and company; Cleveland, O., Jewett, Proctor, & Worthington, 1856. 1 p. l., [v]-xiv, [15]-336 p. 21 cm. [BF1251.R7] 11-2430
1. Psychical research. 2. Spiritualism. I. Title.

SAMADHI, Delta. 133
The master key to psychic unfoldment, a physiological, psychical and philosophical analysis, by Delta Samadhi, edited by Felicie O. Crossley... Los Angeles, Calif., The Crossley publishing company, c1931. 2 p. l., 152 p. 19 1/2 cm. [BF1999.S313] 31-19767
I. Crossley, Fellcie O., ed. II. Title.

SCHEUING, Herman Aloysius, 1872- 133.
Is Jesus of Nazareth the son of God? By H. Scheuing... Boston, The Christopher publishing house [1926] 175 p. 20 1/2 cm. The result of the author's psychic researches. ef. Dedication. [BF1311.J5S35] 26-18648
1. Jesus Christ—Divinity. 2. Psychical research I. Title.

SCIENS, pseud. 133.9
How to speak with the dead, a practical handbook, by Sciens ... London, K. Paul, Trench, Trubner & co., ltd.; New York, E. P. Dutton & co. [1918?] xiii, 183 p. 19 cm. [BF1031.S42] 159.9617 33-24147
1. Psychical research. 2. Spiritualism. I. Title.

SCIENS, pseud. 133
How to speak with the dead; a practical handbook, by Sciens ... New York, E. P. Dutton & co. [1918] xv, 136 p. 20 cm. [BF1031.S4] 19-26087
1. Psychical research. 2. Spiritualism. I. Title.

*SHAVER, Ruth, ed. 133.8
She follows the psychic path; psychic experiences of Jessie Shaver Jones. New York, Vantage [c.1964] 48p. 21cm. 2.00 bds.,
I. Title.

SOPHOMORE, A., pseud. 133.
Bridging the great divide between the physical and the spiritual worlds, by A. Sophomore ... 1st ed. Chicago, M. A. Donohue and co., 1914. 4 p. l., 11-262 p. 18 cm. (Great divide series, vol. I) $1.00. [BF1261.S6] 15-2776
1. Psychical research. I. Title.

SOWERBY, Joseph Henry, 1859- 133.
Psychic phenomena in the light of the Bible; a treatise on the philosophy of non-medicinal healing and other psychic phenomena, in accordance with the ordinary theological science of evangelical Christianity. By Rev. J. H. Sowerby, PH. B. Cedar Rapids, Ia., Laurance press company, [c1905] 2 p. l., 205, [1] p., 1 l. front. (port.) 28 cm. [BF1031.S7] 10-29907
1. Psychical research. 2. Mental healing. I. Title.

SPRAGGETT, Allen. 133
Probing the unexplained. New York, World Pub. [1971] 256 p. 22 cm. [BF1031.S757] 79-160481 6.95
1. Psychical research. 2. Occult sciences. I. Title.

STANTON, Horace Coffin. 133
Telepathy of the celestial world, psychic phenomena here but foreshadowings of our transcendent faculties hereafter. Evidences from psychology and Scripture that the celestials can instantaneously and freely communicate across distance indefinitely great. By Horace C. Stanton ... New York, Chicago [etc.] Fleming H. Revell company [c1913] xxix, 473 p. 21 cm. $2.00. p. 472-473, advertising matter. [BF1171.S65] 13-26187
1. Psychical research. 2. Thought-transference. I. Title.

STEIGER, Brad. 133.9
Words from the source / Brad Steiger. Englewood Cliffs, N.J. : Prentice-Hall, [1975] 168 p. : ill. ; 22 cm. Includes index. [BF1031.S7684] 74-25571 ISBN 0-13-963348-0 : 6.95
1. Psychical research. 2. Occult sciences. I. Title.

STEINER, Rudolf, 1861- 133
The threshold of the spiritual world, by Rudolph Steiner. London and New York, G. P. Putnam's sons, 1918. xi, 140 p. 19 cm. "Authorized English translation edited by H. Colleson." [BF1033.S82] 20-4791
1. Psychical research. I. Colleson, H., ed. II. Title.

SWANN, Ingo, 1933- 133.8
To kiss earth good-bye / Ingo Swann ; foreword by Gertrude Schmeidler. New York : Hawthorn Books, [1975] xix, 217 p., [9] leaves of plates : ill. ; 24 cm. Includes index. Bibliography: p. 199-207. [BF1031.S96 1975] 73-21321 ISBN 0-8015-7774-8 : 10.00
1. Psychical research. 2. Prophecies (Occult sciences) I. Title.

SWANN, Ingo, 1933- 133.8
To kiss earth good-bye / Ingo Swann. New York : Dell Pub. Co., 1977,c1975. 254[16] p. : ill. ; 18 cm. Includes index. Bibliography p.:[238]-246. [BF1031.S96 1975] ISBN 0-440-38914-3 pbk. : 1.95
1. Psychical research. 2. Prophecies (Occult sciences) I. Title.
L.C. card no. for 1975 Hawthorn ed.:73-21321.

TALAMONTI, Leo. 133.8
Forbidden universe : mysteries of the psychic world / Leo Talamonti ; pref. by William MacKenzie ; translated by Paul Stevenson. New York : Stein and Day, 1975, c1974. 230 p., [8] leaves of plates : ill. ; 24 cm. Translation of Universo proibito. Includes bibliographical references. [BF1034.T313 1975] 74-23121 ISBN 0-8128-1767-2 : 8.95
1. Psychical research. 2. Occult sciences. I. Title.

TANNER, Amy Eliza. 133.
Studies in spiritism, by Amy E. Tanner, PH.D. with an introduction by G. Stanley Hall ... New York and London, D. Appleton and company, 1910. xxxviii p., 1 l., 406 p. 21 1/2 cm. Bibliography: p. 406-408. [BF1042.T3] 10-22113
1. Psychical research. 2. Spiritualism. I. Title.

TENHAEFF, Wilhelm Heinrich Carl. 133.8
Telepathy and clairvoyance; views of some little investigated capabilities of man, by W. H. C. Tenhaeff. With a foreword by Berthold Eric Schwarz. Springfield, Ill., Thomas [1972, i.e. 1973] xii, 161 p. illus. 24 cm. Translation of Telepathie en helderzienheid. Bibliography: p. 149. [BF1038.D8T4513] 77-187679 ISBN 0-398-02455-3 12.50
1. Psychical research. 2. Reincarnation. I. Title.

THOMAS, John Frederick, 1874-1940. 133.9'3
Beyond normal cognition / John F. Thomas. New York : Arno Press, 1975 [c1973] p. cm. (Perspectives in psychical research) Reprint of the ed. published by the Boston Society for Psychic Research, Boston. Originally presented as the author's thesis, Duke. [BF1031.T54 1975] 75-7405 ISBN 0-405-06992-8 : 19.00
1. Psychical research. 2. Spiritualism. I. Title. II. Series.

THURSTON, Mark A. 289.9
Experiments in a search for God : the Edgar Cayce path of application / Mark A. Thurston. Virginia Beach, Va. : A.R.E. Press, c1976. vi, 139 p. : ill. ; 22 cm. Bibliography: p. 139. [BX9999.V5T48] 76-373076 ISBN 0-87604-090-3 pbk. : 2.95
1. Association for Research and Enlightenment, Virginia Beach, Va. A search for God. 2. Cayce, Edgar, 1877-1945. 3. Psychical research. I. Title.

TUBBY, Gertrude Ogden. 133.072
Psychics and mediums; a manual and bibliography for students, by Gertrude Ogden Tubby ... Boston, Marshall Jones company [c1935] viii, 168 p. 22 cm. "How to conduct a scientific seance": folded leaf laid in. Bibliography: p. 152-165. [BF1031.T73] [159.961 35-7300

1. Psychical research. 2. Spiritualism. 3. Psychical research—Bibl, I. Title.

TUTTLE, Hudson, 1836- 133.
Studies in the out-lying fields of psychic science, by Hudson Tuttle ... New York, M. L. Holbrook & co. [c1889] 250 p. diagr. 19 cm. [BF1261.T8] 11-3403
1. Psychical research. I. Title.

TWINING, Harry La Verne, 1863- 133.
The physical theory of the soul; a presentation of psychic phenomena from the phyisical and scientific [!] standpoint in order to form a real basis upon which to build a logical and probable theory of the constitution of the soul, and a real scientific explanation of its phenomena, by H. La V. Twining ... Westgate, Cal., The author [c1915] 4, xv, [5]-182 p. illus. 20 1/2 cm. $1.50. [BF1031.T8] 15-18895
1. Psychical research. I. Title.

UPHOFF, Walter Henry, 1913- 133.8
New psychic frontiers : your key to new worlds / Walter and Mary Jo Uphoff ; foreword by Harold Sherman. 2d ed. Gerrards Cross, Eng. : C. Smythe ; New York : distributor, S. Weiser, 1977. xvii, 271 p. : ill. ; 22 cm. Includes index. Bibliography: p. [245]-271. [BF1031.U63 1977] 77-81683 ISBN 0-901072-74-5 : 9.50 (U.S.)
1. Psychical research. 2. Occult sciences. I. Uphoff, Mary Jo, joint author. II. Title.

VANDEMAN, George E. 133
Psychic roulette [by] George E. Vandeman. [1st ed.] Nashville, T. Nelson [1973] 176 p. 21 cm. [BF1031.V33] 73-9628 5.95
1. Psychical research. 2. Future life. 3. Devil. I. Title.

WAHLETKA, Cherokee princess, 1888- 133.
Lifting the veil; how you yourself may acquire mystic power and develop mind, body and spirit, by Princess Wahletka ... New York, Ashfield & Royal [1923] 183 p. incl. front. plates, ports. 19 1/2 cm. [BF1286.W3] 24-3095
1. Psychical research. I. Title.

WALKER, Dick, 1917- 133.9'092'4
Do not test us : one man's ventures into the psychic world / by Dick Walker. 1st ed. Portland, Or. : Binford & Mort, 1978. viii, 191 p. ; 22 cm. Bibliography: p. 189-190. [BF1031.W32] 78-57020 ISBN 0-8323-0307-0 pbk. : 4.95
1. Walker, Dick, 1917- 2. Psychical research. 3. Psychical research—Biography. I. Title.

WARCOLLIER, Rene. 133.82
Experimental telepathy, by Rene Warcollier; edited and abridged by Gardner Murphy from La telepathie, articles in the Revue metapsychique, and recent unpublished studies. Translated by Josephine B. Gridley, with the collaboration of Maud King Murphy. Boston, Mass., Boston society for psychic research, inc., 1938. viii, 296 p. illus., diagrs. 22 cm. [BF1171.W22 1938a] [159.96162] 41-27553
1. Psychical research. 2. Thought-transference. I. Murphy, Gardner, 1895- ed. II. Gridley, Josephine B., tr. III. Murphy, Maud King, joint tr. IV. Title.

WARCOLLIER, Rene. 133.82
Experiments in telepathy, by Rene Warcollier; edited and abridged by Gardner Murphy from La telepathic, articles in the Revue metapsychique, and recent unpublished studies; translated by Josephine B. Girdley. New York and London, Harper & brothers, 1938. viii, 250 p. illus. 22 cm. [BF1171.W22] [159.96162] 38-28764
1. Psychical research. 2. Thought-transference. I. Murphy, Gardner, 1895- ed. II. Girdley, Josephine B., tr. III. Title.

WARRICK, F. W. 133.072
Experiments in psychics; practical studies in direct writing, supernormal photography and other phenomena, mainly with Mrs. Ada Emma Deane, by F. W. Warrick. With six hundred and fifty illustrations. New York, E. P. Dutton & co., inc., 1939. xxxi, 399 p. incl. front., illus. (incl. ports., facsims.) 25 1/2 x 19 1/2 cm. "Printed in Great Britain." Bibliography: p. 380-382. "Some books on psychic photography": p. 11. [BF1031.W37] [159.961] 40-6896
1. Deane, Mrs. Ada Emma. 2. Psychical research. 3. Spiritualism. I. Title. II. Title: Psychics, Experiments in.

WILLIAMS, John West, 1867- 133.
Divine inspiration, psychic research of the great beyond, by J. W. Williams... St. Louis, Mo., The Assembly press [1916] 4 p. l., [13]-91 p. 23 cm. $1.50. [BF1031.W6] 16-17081
1. Psychical research. I. Title.

WILLSON, Beckles, 1869- 133.072
Occultism and common-sense, by Beckles Willson; with an introduction by Prof. W. F. Barrett ... New York, R. F. Fenno & company [1908?] xv, 291 [1] p. 19 cm. "Originally appeared in the ... Westminster gazette." [Full name: Henry Beckles Willson] [BF1031.W72] [159.961] 34-13043
1. Psychical research. I. Barrett, Sir William Fletcher, 1844-1925. II. Title.

WOELFL, Genevieve. 133.8
Psychic experience : an introduction to spiritualism / Genevieve Woelfl. Menlo Park, Calif. : Redwood Publishers, c1976. xv, 188 p. : ill. ; 22 cm. Bibliography: p. 181-182. [BF1031.W75] 76-151432 ISBN 0-917928-00-8 : 6.95 ISBN 0-917928-01-6 pbk. : 4.95
1. Psychical research. I. Title.

WOODREW, Greta. 133.8
On a slide of light / Greta Woodrew. New York : Macmillan, c1981. xii, 176 p. ; 25 cm. [BF1999.W696] 19 80-24577 12.95
1. Psychical research. 2. Occult sciences. I. Title.

WORRALL, Ambrose A. 1899- 133.8
Explore your psychic world / by Ambrose A. Worall and Olga N. Worrall, with Will Oursler. New York : Harper & row, 1976c1970. xi, 144p. ; 21 cm. Based on a series of seminars conducted by the authors at Wainwright House, Rye, N.Y. 1967-68. Sponsored by the Commission for the Study of Healing of the Laymen's Movement. [BF1041.W64] ISBN 0-06-069686-9 pbk. : 3.95
1. Laymen's Movement. Commission for the Study of healing. 2. Psychical research. 3. Mental healing. I. Worrall, Olga Nathalie (Ripich) 1906- joint author II. Oursler, William Charles, 1913- joint author. III. Title.
L.C. card no. for original ed. 79-85062.

WRIGHT, George E. 133
Practical views on psychic phenomena, by George E. Wright. New York, Harcourt, Brace & Howe, 1920. viii, 136 p. 19 cm. Printed in Great Britain. [BF1031.W8] 20-27481
1. Psychical research. 2. Spiritualism. I. Psychic phenomena, Practical views on. II. Title.

YOUNG, Frank Rudolph. 133.4
Cyclomancy, the secret of psychic power control. West Nyack, N.Y., Parker Pub. Co. [1966] xiv, 209 p. 24 cm. [BF1031.Y66] 66-26238
1. Psychical research. I. Title.

Psychical research—Addresses, essays, lectures.

BROAD, Charlie Dunbar, 1887- 133.072
Religion, philosophy, and psychical research; selected essays. New York, Harcourt, Brace, 1953. 308 p. 22 cm. (International library of psychology, philosophy, and scientific method) [BF1031.B74] 53-5653
1. Psychical research—Addresses, essays, lectures. 2. Theology—Addresses, essays, lectures. I. Title.

DUCASSE, Curt John, 1881- 133.9
Paranormal phenomena, science, and life after death, [by] C. J. Ducasse. New York, Parapsychology Foundation [1969] 63 p. 22 cm. (Parapsychological monographs, no. 8) Bibliographical footnotes. [BF1031.D9] 79-76282
1. Psychical research—Addresses, essays, lectures. I. Title. II. Series.

THE Edgar Cayce reader, 133'.08
under the editorship of Hugh Lynn Cayce. New York, Paperback Library [1969] 187 p. 18 cm. A selection of articles by Edgar Cayce and others, previously published in the A.R.E. journal of the Association for Research and Enlightenment, including verbatim extracts from Edgar Cayce's telepathic-clairvoyant readings. Bibliography: p. 181-182. [BF1031.E34 1969] 79-2344 0.75
1. Psychical research—Addresses, essays, lectures. I. Cayce Edgar, 1877-1945. II. Cayce, Hugh Lynn, ed. III. Association for Research and Enlightenment, Virginia Beach, Va. The A.R.E. journal.

FRONTIERS of the spirit : 133.8
studies in the mystical and psychical areas in observance of the twentieth anniversary of the founding of Spiritual Frontiers Fellowship / edited by Paul Lambourne Higgins. Minneapolis : T. S. Denison, c1976. 133 p. ; 24 cm. [BF1031.F76] 76-358476 6.95
1. Psychical research—Addresses, essays, lectures. 2. Mysticism—Addresses, essays, lectures. 3. Prayer—Addresses, essays, lectures. 4. Meditation—Addresses, essays, lectures. 5. Faith-cure—Addresses, essays, lectures. I. Higgins, Paul Lambourne. II. Spiritual Frontiers Fellowship.

HARVEST of light : 133.8
approaches to the paranormal / edited by Neville Armstrong. London : Spearman, 1976. 260 p. ; 23 cm. Contains articles originally published in the journal Light. [BF1031.H29 1976] 77-369744 ISBN 0-85435-452-2 : £3.25
1. Psychical research—Addresses, essays, lectures. 2. Occult sciences—Addresses essays, lectures. I. Armstrong, Neville. II. Light.

MURCHISON, Carl Allanmore, 1887- ed. 133.8
The case for and against psychical belief / edited by Carl Murchison. New York : Arno Press, 1975. p. cm. (Perspectives in psychical research) Reprint of the 1927 ed. published by Clark University, Worcester, Mass. [BF1023.M8 1975] 75-7389 ISBN 0-405-07037-3 : 22.00
1. Psychical research—Addresses, essays, lectures. I. Title. II. Series.

PSYCHOENERGETIC systems : 133.8
the interaction of consciousness, energy, and matter / edited by Stanley Krippner ; Mary Lou Carlson, managing editor. New York : Gordon and Breach Science Publishers, c1979. xxvi, 264 p. : ill. ; 28 cm. Includes bibliographies. [BF1031.P797] 79-5167 ISBN 0-677-14870-4 : 29.50
1. Psychical research—Addresses, essays, lectures. 2. Mental healing—Addresses, essays, lectures. 3. Acupuncture—Addresses, essays, lectures. 4. Kirlian photography—Addresses, essays, lectures. 5. Occult sciences—Addresses, essays, lectures. I. Krippner, Stanley. II. Carlson, Mary Calley.

SCIENCE and the 133.8'01'5
paranormal / edited by George O. Abell and Barry Singer. New York : Scribner, 1981. p. cm. Includes index. Bibliography: p. [BF1045.S33S38] 19 80-26839 ISBN 0-684-16655-0 : 12.95
1. Psychical research—Addresses, essays, lectures. 2. Occult sciences—Addresses, essays, lectures. 3. Science—Addresses, essays, lectures. I. Abell, George Ogden, 1927- II. Singer, Barry.

Psychical research—Bibliography.

MORGAN, Samuel Rowland, 1877- 016.133
Index to psychic science; an introduction to systematized knowledge of psychical experience. Swarthmore, pa., 1950. v, 117 p. illus., ports. 24 cm. Errata slip inserted. [Z6878.P8M6] 50-58006
1. Psychical research—Bibliography. I. Title: Psychic science.

WHITE, Rhea A. 016.1338
Parapsychology: sources of information. Compiled under the auspices of the American Society for Psychical Research by Rhea A. White and Laura A. Dale. Metuchen, N.J., Scarecrow Press, 1973. 302 p. 22 cm. [Z6878.P8W47] 73-4853 ISBN 0-8108-0617-7 7.50
1. Psychical research—Bibliography. I. Dale, Laura A., joint author. II. American Society for Psychical Research (Founded 1906) III. Title.

ZORAB, George. 016.133072
Bibliography of parapsychology. New York, Parapsychology Foundation [1957] 127 p. 20 cm. [Z6878.P8Z6] 57-8446
1. Psychical research—Bibl. I. Title.

ZORAB, George. 016.133072
Bibliography of parapsychology. New York, Parapsychology Foundation [1957] 127 p. 20 cm. [Z6878.P8Z6] 57-8446
1. Psychical research—Bibliography. I. Title.

Psychical research—Bibliography—Catalogs.

LONDON. University. Council for Psychical Investigation. Research Library. 016.133
Short-title catalogue of works on psychical research, spiritualism, magic, psychology, legerdemain and other methods of deception, charlatanism, witchcraft, and technical works for the scientific investigation of alleged abnormal phenomena, from circa 1450 A.D. to 1929 A.D.; with a supplement of additional items acquired between 1929 and 1935. Compiled by Harry Price. Detroit, Gale Research Co., 1975. p. cm. Reprint in 1 v., with a new foreword, of the 1929 ed. issued by the National Laboratory of Psychical Research (later the University of London Council for Psychical Investigation) as its Proceedings, v. 1., no. 2, and the Supplement issued in 1935 by the Council as its Bulletin 1. [Z6880.L84 1975] 74-19203 ISBN 0-8103-4102-6 26.00
1. London. University. Council for Psychical Investigation. Research Library. 2. Psychical research—Bibliography—Catalogs. 3. Occult sciences—Bibliography—Catalogs. I. Price, Harry, 1881-1948. II. Title. III. Series: London. University. Council for Psychical Investigation. Proceedings of the National Laboratory of Psychical Research, v. 1, pt. 2. IV. Series: London. University. Council for Psychical Investigation. Bulletin, 1935- no. 1.

SOCIETY for Psychical Research, London. Library. 016.1338
Catalogue of the Library of the Society for Psychical Research, London, England. Boston : G. K. Hall, 1976. v, 341 p. ; 37 cm. [Z6878.P8S6 1976] [BF1031] 76-358758 ISBN 0-8161-0008-X lib.bdg. : 49.00
1. Society for Psychical Research, London. Library. 2. Psychical research—Bibliography—Catalogs. 3. Occult sciences—Bibliography—Catalogs. I. Title.

Psychical research—Biography.

KINGSTON, Kenny. 133.8
Sweet spirits / Kenny Kingston and Brenda Marshall. Chicago : Contemporary Books, c1978. p. cm. Includes index. [BF1027.K53A35 1978] 78-57439 ISBN 0-8092-7625-9 : 9.95
1. Kingston, Kenny. 2. Psychical research—Biography. 3. Psychical research. I. Marshall, Brenda, joint author. II. Title.

PLEASANTS, Helene, ed. 921
Biographical dictionary of parapsychology. 1964-66- New York, Garrett Publications Heix Press. v. 25 cm. Editors: 1964-66- Helene Pleasants. [BF1026.B5] 64-4288
1. Psychical research—Biog. I. Title.

WILSON, Colin, 1931- 133.9
Strange powers. [1st American ed.] New York, Random House [1975, c1973] 146 p. illus. 22 cm. [BF1026.W53 1975] 74-17353 ISBN 0-394-49585-3 6.95
1. Leftwich, Robert. 2. Beattie, Eunice. 3. Guirdham, Arthur. 4. Psychical research—Biography. 5. Occult sciences—Biography. I. Title.

WILSON, Colin, 1931- 133.9'0922
Strange powers / Colin Wilson. New York : Vintage Books, 1976, c1973. 163 p. ; 18 cm. [BF1026.W53 1976] 75-28138 ISBN 0-394-72045-8 pbk. : 1.95
1. Leftwich, Robert. 2. Beattle, Eunice. 3. Guirdham, Arthur. 4. Psychical research—Biography. 5. Occult sciences—Biography. I. Title.

Psychical research—Biography—Juvenile literature.

NEIMARK, Anne E. 133.8'092'4
With this gift : the story of Edgar Cayce / by Anne E. Neimark. 1st ed. New York : Morrow, 1978. 192 p. ; 22 cm. Includes index. Bibliography: p. 188. A biography of the psychic whose powers included long-distance diagnoses of illnesses and prescriptions for their cure. [BF1027.C3N44] 92 B 78-4159 ISBN 0-688-22147-5 : 6.95 ISBN 0-688-32147-X lib.bdg. : 6.43
1. Cayce, Edgar, 1877-1945—Juvenile literature. 2. [Cayce, Edgar, 1877-1945.] 3. Psychical research—Biography—Juvenile literature. 4. [Psychical research—Biography.] I. Title.

Psychical research—Case studies.

BELL, Clark, 1832- ed.
Spiritism, hypnotism and telepathy as involved in the case of Mrs. Leonora E. Piper and the Society of psychical research, by Clark Bell ... and the discussion before the New York medico-legal society and its psychological section by Thomson Jay Hudson, LL. D., John Duncan Quackenbos ... and others. New York, Medico-legal journal, 1902. 3 p. l., 171 p. port. 25 cm. 2-19746
I. Title.

GREELEY, Andrew M., 1928- 133.8'092'6
The sociology of the paranormal : a reconnaissance / Andrew M. Greeley. Beverly Hills, Calif. : Sage Publications, c1975. 88 p. : diagrs. ; 22 cm. (Sage research papers in the social sciences ; 90-023) (Studies in religion and ethnicity) Bibliography: p. 87-88. [BF1029.G73] 75-9046 ISBN 0-8039-0543-2 pbk. : 3.00
1. Psychical research—Case studies. 2. Mysticism—Case studies. I. Title. II. Series.

KING, Clyde S. 016.1338
Psychic and religious phenomena limited : a bibliographical index / compiled by Clyde S. King. Westport, Conn. : Greenwood Press, 1978. xvii, 245 p. ; 25 cm. [BF1029.K55] 78-13535 ISBN 0-313-20616-3 lib.bdg. : 22.50
1. Psychical research—Case studies. 2. Psychical research—Bibliography. I. Title.

ROBERTS, Jane, 1929- 133.9'3
The God of Jane : a psychic manifesto / Jane Roberts. Englewood Cliffs, N.J. : Prentice-Hall, c1981. x, 262 p. ; 24 cm. Includes index. [BF1029.R6] 19 81-321 ISBN 0-13-357517-9 : 10.95
1. Roberts, Jane, 1929- 2. Psychical research—Case studies. I. Title.

Psychical research—Collected works.

CAYCE, Edgar, 1877-1945. 133.8'08
The Edgar Cayce readings. Virginia Beach, Va., Association for Research and Enlightenment [1973- v. 24 cm. Contents.Contents.—v. 1. On life and death.—v. 2. Meditation: pt. 1. Healing, prayer, and the revelation. [BF1023.C37] 74-176203
1. Psychical research—Collected works. I. Association for Research and Enlightenment, Virginia Beach, Va. II. Title.

CAYCE, Edgar, 1877-1945. 133.8'08 S
Meditation. Virginia Beach, Va., Association for Research and Enlightenment [1974- v. 24 cm. (The Edgar Cayce readings, v. 2) Contents.Contents.—pt. 1. Healing, prayer, and the revelation. [BF1023.C37 vol. 2 etc.] [BF1031] 133.8 74-176205
1. Psychical research—Collected works. I. Title.

Psychical research—Congresses.

THE Philosophy of parapsychology : proceedings of an international conference held in Copenhagen, Denmark, August 25-27, 1976 / edited by Betty Shapin and Lisette Coly. New York : Parapsychology Foundation, c1977. 295 p. ; 24 cm. Includes bibliographical references. [BF1021.P48] 77-75663 13.50 133.8'01
1. Psychical research—Congresses. I. Shapin, Betty. II. Coly, Lisette. III. Parapsychology Foundation, New York.

PSI and states of awareness 133.8
: proceedings of an international conference held in Paris, France, August 24-26, 1977 / edited by Betty Shapin and Lisette Coly. New York : Parapsychology Foundation, c1978. 278 p. : ill. ; 24 cm. Includes bibliographies. [BF1021.P17] 78-50167 ISBN 0-912328-30-4 : 13.50
1. Psychical research—Congresses. I. Shapin, Betty. II. Coly, Lisette. III. Parapsychology Foundation, New York.

Psychical research—Controversial literature.

BIRDSONG, Robert E. 133.8
Sensory awareness and psychic manifestation / by Robert E. Birdsong. 1st ed. Eureka, Calif. : Sirius Books, c1978. ii, 114 p., [1] leaf of plates : ill. ; 21 cm. Includes bibliographical references. [BF1042.B5] 78-65000 ISBN 0-917108-24-8 : 4.75
1. Psychical research—Controversial literature. 2. Senses and sensation. I. Title.

KOREM, Danny. 133.8
The fakers / Danny Korem and Paul Meier. Old Tappan, N.J. : F. H. Revell Co., c1980. p. cm. Includes bibliographical references. [BF1042.K67] 19 80-23180 ISBN 0-8007-1130-0 : 8.95
1. Psychical research—Controversial literature. 2. Occult sciences—Controversial literature. 3. Christianity and psychical research. 4. Christianity and occult sciences. I. Meier, Paul D., joint author. II. Title.

MARKS, David. 133.8'01'9
The psychology of the psychic / by David Marks and Richard Kammann ; foreword by Martin Gardner. Buffalo, N.Y. : Prometheus Books, 1980. 232 p. [7] leaves of plates : ill. ; 24 cm. Bibliography: p. 227-232. [BF1042.M33] 19 80-7458 ISBN 0-87975-121-5 : 16.95 ISBN 0-87975-122-3 pbk. : 7.95
1. Psychical research—Controversial literature. I. Kammann, Richard, joint author. II. Title.

SMITH, Susy. 133.9'0924 B
Confessions of a psychic. New York, Macmillan [1971] 315 p. illus., ports. 21 cm. Autobiographical. [BF1283.S62A3] 78-156993 6.95
I. Title.

Psychical research—Dictionaries.

FODOR, Nandor 133.903
Encyclopaedia of psychic science [New Hyde Park, N.Y.] University Bks. [c.1966] xxxix, 415p. 26cm.Bibl. [BF1025.F6] 66-16316 17.50, bxd.
1. Psychical research — Dictionaries. 2. Spiritualism — Dictionaries. I. Title.

FODOR, Nandor. 133.903
An encyclopaedia of psychic science. Secaucus, N.J., Citadel Press [1974, c1966] [416 p.] 25 cm. [BF1025.F6 1974] 66-16316 5.95 (pbk.)
1. Psychical research—Dictionaries. 2. Spiritualism—Dictionaries. I. Title.

THE Steinerbooks 133'.03
dictionary of the psychic, mystic, occult. Blauvelt, N.Y., Rudolf Steiner Publications [1973] 235 p. illus. 18 cm. (Steinerbooks, 1767) [BF1025.S8] 72-86344 1.95 (pbk.)
1. Psychical research—Dictionaries. 2. Occult sciences—Dictionaries. 3. Religion—Dictionaries. I. Rudolf Steiner Publications.

Psychical research—Early works to 1900.

DU PREL, Karl Ludwig August Friedrich Maximilian Alfred, Freiherr, 1839-1899 149'.3
The philosophy of mysticism / Carl Du Prel. New York : Arno Press, 1976. p. cm. (The Occult) Translation of Die Philosophie der Mystik. Reprint of the 1889 ed. published by G. Redway, London. [BF1033.D9 1976] 75-36838 ISBN 0-405-07951-6 : 38.00
1. Psychical research—Early works to 1900. 2. Mysticism. 3. Somnambulism. 4. Soul. I. Title. II. Series: The Occult (New York, 1976-)

GURNEY, Edmund, 1847-1888. 133.8
Phantasms of the living, by Edmund Gurney, Frederic W. H. Myers and Frank Podmore. A fascim. reproduction with an introd., by Leonard R. N. Ashley. Gainesville, Fla., Scholars' Facsims. & Reprints, 1970. 2 v. illus. 24 cm. (History of psychology series) Facsim. reprint of the 1886 ed. [BF1031.G8 1886a] 71-119868 ISBN 0-8201-1075-2
1. Psychical research—Early works to 1900. I. Myers, Frederic William Henry, 1843-1901. II. Podmore, Frank, 1856-1910. III. Title.

Psychical research—Indexes.

CHICOREL, Marietta. 016.133
Chicorel index to parapsychology and occult books / edited by Marietta Chicorel. 1st ed. New York : Chicorel Library Pub. Corp., c1978. 354 p. ; 26 cm. (Her Chicorel index series ; v. 24) [Z6878.P8C45] [BF1031] 77-17989 60.00
1. Psychical research—Indexes. 2. Occult sciences—Indexes. I. Title. II. Title: Index to parapsychology and occult books.

Psychical research—Juvenile literature.

BERGER, Melvin. 133
The supernatural : from ESP to UFO's / Melvin Berger. New York : John Day Co., [1977] p. cm. Includes index. Bibliography: p. Discusses ESP, parapsychology, astrology, psychokinesis, spiritualism, faith healing, witchcraft, and UFO's. [BF1031.B43] 77-2829 ISBN 0-381-90054-1 : 6.95
1. Psychical research—Juvenile literature. 2. Occult sciences—Juvenile literature. 3. [Occult sciences.] 4. [Psychical research.] I. Title.

Psychical research—Societies.

AMERICAN society for psychical research. (Founded 1884) 133.
Proceedings. Boston. pl. 23 cm. No more published after 1889; in 1890 the society became the American branch of the Society for psychical research. [BF1010.A36] 20-7836
1. Psychical research—Societies. I. Title.

AMERICAN society for psychical research. (Founded 1884) 133.
Proceedings. v. 1, no. 1-4; July 1885-Mar. 1889. Boston, Damrell and Upham [etc.] 1885-[89] iv, 584 p. incl. illus., tables, diagrs. fold. pl. 23 cm. No more published. L. C. set incomplete: no. 2 wanting. [BF1010.A36] 20-7836
1. Psychical research—Societies. I. Title.

AMERICAN society for psychical research. (Founded 1906) 133.072
Proceedings of the American society for psychical research. v. 1- New York [etc.] American society for psychical research, 1907- v. illus. (incl. plans) plates, ports., facsims., diagrs. 24 cm. Vols. 1-13, 1907-19, edited by J. H. Hysolp; subsequent volumes by various editors. Vols. 1 published in Boston by H. B. Turner & co. In 1926 the society decided to discountinue the regular publication of its Journal. The Proceedings are continued therefore, only for material unsuited to the Journal, the volumes appearing at irregular intervals. Vols. 20-21 form a combined volume issued in two parts with continuous paging, published 1928 and 1933, respectively. [BF1010.A5] 159.96106273 8-14134
1. Psychical research—Societies. I. Hyslop, James Hervey, 1854-1920, ed. II. Title.

Psychical research—Tibet.

DAVID-NEEL, Alexandra, 1868-1969. 299.54
Magic and mystery in Tibet. Introd. by Aaron Sussman. [New ed.] New Hyde Park, N.Y., University Books [1965] xv, 320 p. 24 cm. Translation of Mystiques et magiciens du Thibet. [DS785.D272 1965] 65-23524
1. Psychical research—Tibet. 2. Occult sciences—Tibet. 3. Tibet—Description and travel. 4. Lamaism. 5. Tibet—Religion. I. Title.

Psychical research—United States—Biography.

ROBBINS, Shawn. 133.3'092'4 B
Ahead of myself : confessions of a professional psychic / Shawn Robbins, as told to Milton Pierce. Englewood Cliffs, N.J. : Prentice-Hall, c1980. p. cm. Includes index. [BF1027.R56A32] 19 80-20486 ISBN 0-13-004002-9 : 9.95
1. Robbins, Shawn. 2. Psychical research—United States—Biography. I. Pierce, Milton, joint author. II. Title.

Psychoanalysis.

HUDSON, Cyril Edward, 1888- 201
Recent psychology and the Christian religion; some points of contact and divergence, by Cyril E. Hudson ... New York, George H. Doran company [c1923] [BL53.H7] 23-9625
1. Paychoanalysis. I. Title.

*REIK, Theodor, 1888- 222.11
The creation of woman. New York, McGraw [1973, c.1960] 159 p. front. 21 cm. (McGraw-Hill paperbacks) Includes bibliography. [BS580] ISBN 0-07-051813-0 pap., 1.95
1. Eve (Biblical character) 2. Psychoanalysis. 3. Initiations (in religion, folk-lore, etc.) I. Title.
L.C. card no. for Knopf edition: 60-5613.

REIK, Theodor, 1888-1970. 222.11
The creation of woman. New York, G. Braziller, 1960. 159 p. illus. 22 cm. Includes bibliography. [BS580.E85R4] 60-5613
1. Eve (Biblical character) 2. Psychoanalysis. 3. Initiations (in religion, folk-lore, etc.) I. Title.

VON DER HEYDT, Vera. 128'.1
Prospects for the soul : soundings in Jungian psychology and religion / [by] Vera von der Heydt. London : Barton, Longman and Todd, 1976. xvi, 110 p. ; 22 cm. Bibliography: p. 109-[110] [BF173.J85V26 1976] 76-376737 ISBN 0-232-51338-4 : £2.00
1. Jung, Carl Gustav, 1875-1961. 2. Psychoanalysis. 3. Psychology, Religious. I. Title.

Psychoanalysis and religion.

BROWN, Clifford A. (Clifford Alan) 230'.01'9
Jung's hermeneutic of doctrine : its theological significance / Clifford A. Brown. Chico, CA : Scholars Press, c1981. vii, 226 p. ; 22 cm. (American Academy of Religion dissertation series ; no.32) Includes indexes. Bibliography: p. 203-211. [BF175.B69] 19 80-20795 ISBN 0-89130-437-1 pbk. : 12.50
1. Jung, Carl Gustav, 1875-1961. 2. Psychoanalysis and religion. 3. Theology, Doctrinal—History—20th century. I. Title. II. Series.
Publisher's address: 101 Salem St., Chico, CA 95926.

CUTTEN, George Barton, 1874.
The psychological phenomena of Christianity, by George Barton Cutten ... New York, C. Scribner's sons, 1908. xviii, 497 p. 21 cm. 8-31997
I. Title.

DE LUCA, Anthony J. 200'.1'9
Freud and future religious experience / Anthony J. De Luca. Totowa, N.J. : Littlefield, Adams, 1977, c1976. 263 p. ; 21 cm. (Littlefield, Adams quality paperback ; 330) Includes index. Bibliography: p. 251-261. [BF173.F85D4 1977] 77-6798 ISBN 0-8226-0330-6 : 4.95
1. Freud, Sigmund, 1856-1939. 2. Psychoanalysis and religion. I. Title.

DE LUCA, Anthony J. 200'.1'9
Freud and future religious experience / Anthony J. De Luca. New York : Philosophical Library, c1976. 263 p. ; 22

cm. Includes index. Bibliography: p. 251-261. [BF173.F85D4] 75-3782 ISBN 0-8022-2173-4 : 12.50
1. Freud, Sigmund, 1856-1939. 2. Psychoanalysis and religion. I. Title.

DE LUCA, Anthony J. 200'.1'9
Freud and future religious experience / Anthony J. De Luca. Totowa, N.J. : Littlefield, Adams, 1977, c1976. 263 p. ; 21 cm. (Littlefield, Adams quality paperback ; 330) Includes index. Bibliography: p. 251-261. [BF173.F85D4 1977] 77-6798 ISBN 0-8226-0330-6 : 4.95
1. Freud, Sigmund, 1856-1939. 2. Psychoanalysis and religion. I. Title.

FABER, Heije, 1907- 200'.1'9
Psychology of religion / by Heije Faber ; [translated by Margaret Kohl]. Philadelphia : Westminster Press, c1975. p. cm. Translation of Cirkelen om een geheim. Includes index. Bibliography: p. [BF175.F1513] 75-43721 ISBN 0-664-20748-0 : 12.50
1. Psychoanalysis and religion. I. Title.

FABER, Heije, 1907- 200'.1'9
Psychology of religion / Heije Faber ; [translated from the Dutch by Margaret Kohl]. London : S.C.M. Press, 1976. ix, 338 p. ; 23 cm. Translation of Cirkelen om een geheim. Includes indexes. Bibliography: p. 326-331. [BF175.F1513 1976] 77-366213 ISBN 0-334-01354-2 : £6.50
1. Psychoanalysis and religion. I. Title.

GILL, Richard Hooker Keller, 1880-
The psychological aspects of Christian experience, by Richard H. K. Gill ... Boston, Sherman, French & company, 1915. 3 p. l., 104 p. 20 cm. 15-5303 1.00
I. Title.

HEISEY, Paul Harold.
Psychological studies in Lutheranism, by Paul Harold Heisey, M.A., introduction by the Rev. Professor J. A. Clutz... Burlington, Ia., The German literary board, 1916. 5 p. l., [9]-143 p. 20 cm. Reprinted in part from the Lutheran quarterly and the Lutheran church review. 16-14103
I. Title.

HOMANS, Peter. 230
Theology after Freud; an interpretive inquiry. Indianapolis, Bobbs-Merrill [1970] xvii, 254 p. 21 cm. Bibliography: p. 233-245. [BF175.H64] 76-84162 4.25
1. Freud, Sigmund, 1856-1939. 2. Psychoanalysis and religion. I. Title.

PSYCHOANALYSIS and Christianity. [White Pigeon, Michigan, Harvey E. Swihart, 1958] 99p. 22cm.
I. Oehlschlegel, Lydia.

RIZZUTO, Ana-Maria. 291.2'11'019
The birth of the living God : a psychoanalytic study / Ana-Maria Rizzuto. Chicago : University of Chicago Press, 1979. x, 246 p. : ill. ; 24 cm. Includes index. Bibliography: p. 231-239. [BF175.R59] 78-10475 ISBN 0-226-72100-0 : 15.00
1. Psychoanalysis and religion. 2. Developmental psychology. 3. God. I. Title.

RIZZUTO, Ana-Maria. 291.2'11'019
The birth of the living God : a psychoanalytic study / Ana-Maria Rizzuto. Chicago : University of Chicago Press, 1981, c1979. 246 p : ill. ; 23 cm. Includes index. Bibliography: p. 231-239. [BF175.R59] 78-10475 ISBN 0-226-72100-0 pbk. : 6.50
1. Psychoanalysis and religion. 2. Developmental psychology. 3. God. I. Title.

Psychological research.

CANADIAN Opinicon Conference, Lake Opinion, Ont., 1960. 150
Training for research in psychology. Edited by Karl S. Bernhardt. [Toronto] University of Toronto Press [c1961] x, 130p. 24cm. Bibliography: p. [129]-130. [BR76.5.C28 1960] 62-1792
1. Psychological research. I. Bernhardt, Karl Schofield, 1901- ed. II. Title.

Psychologists—United States—Correspondence, reminiscences, etc.

SPOERL, Howard Davis, 1903- 289.4'092'4
There was a man; the letters, papers and poems of Howard Davis Spoerl. Edited by Paul B. Zacharias. North Quincy, Mass., Christopher Pub. House [1972] 193 p. port. 21 cm. [BF109.S69A25 1972] 72-78904 4.95
1. Psychologists—United States—Correspondence, reminiscences, etc. I. Zacharias, Paul B., ed. II. Title.

Psychology.

ANDERSON, Louis Francis, 1859- 201
Psychology and the cosmic order, by Louis F. Anderson ... [New York, The Society for the elucidation of religious principles, 1939?] 5 p. l., 185 p. 24 cm. [BL53.A58] A39
1. Psychology. 2. Religion—Philosophy. I. Title. II. Title: Cosmic order, Psychology of the.

BAILEY, Alice A. Mrs. 1881- 133
The soul and its mechanism (the problem of psychology) by Alice A. Bailey ... New York city, Lucis publishing co. [c1930] xii p., 1 l., 17-136 p. 24 cm. Bibliography: p. 135-136. [BF1999.B36] 31-995
I. Title.

BAILEY, Alice Anne (LaTrobe-Bateman) 1880- 133
The soul and its mechanism (the problem of psychology) by Alice A. Bailey ... New York city, Lucis publishing co. [c1930] xiii p., 1 l., 17-136 p. 23 1/2 cm. Bibliography: p. 135-136. [BF1999.B36] 133 ISBN 31-995 Revised
I. Title.

BROWN, George, of Dallas. 133.
Occult Psychology, by George Brown. Dallas, Tex., The Psychological society [c1919] 3 p. l., 67, [1] p. port. 23 1/2 cm. [BF1031.B75] 20-453
1. Psychology. 2. Occult sciences. 3. Psychical research. I. Title.

CHRISTIAN perspectives on psychology / edited by Richard Ruble. New York : MSS Information Corp., [1975] p. cm. [BF121.C49] 75-15956 ISBN 0-8422-0456-3 pbk. : 3.75 261.8
1. Psychology. 2. Psychology, Religious. I. Ruble, Richard.

*ENSLEY, Francis Gerald 248
Persons can change. Nashville, Abingdon [1964, c.1963] 127p. 20cm. 1.00
I. Title.

MCGRATH, Joseph Edward, 1927-
Value-orientations, personal adjustment and social behavior of members of three American religious groups in Fiedler, Fred Edward. Age, sex and religious background as determinants of interpersonal perception among Dutch children. Urbana, Group Effectiveness Research Laboratory, Dept. of Psychology, University of Illinois, 1962.
I. Title.

MATTHEWS, Walter Robert, 1881- 201
Psychology and the church, by W. R. Matthews, L. W. Grensted, J. A. Hadfield, H. M. Relton, L. F. Browne and O. Hardman (editor) New York, The Macmillan company, 1925. 203 p. 20 cm. [BL53.M42] 25-20426
1. Psychology. 2. Psychology, Religious. 3. Mental healing. I. Grensted, Laurence William, 1884- II. Hadfield, James Arthur 1882- III. Relton, Herbert Maurice, 1882- IV. Brown, Leonard Foster. V. Hardman, Oscar, 1880- ed. VI. Title.
Contents omitted.

NEW York Academy of Medicine. 253
Ministry and medicine in human relations. Iago Galdston, editor. Freeport, N.Y., Books for Libraries Press [1971, c1955] xviii, 165 p. 23 cm. (Essay index reprint series) Papers presented at conferences held by the academy, May 11, 1950 and April 18-19, 1952. Includes bibliographical references. [BF47.N48 1971] 77-142682 ISBN 0-8369-2120-8
1. Psychology. 2. Ethics. 3. Pastoral psychology. I. Galdston, Iago, 1895- ed. II. Title.

SANFORD, John A. 222'.110922
The man who wrestled with God : light from the Old Testament on the psychology of individuation / John A. Sanford. New York : Paulist Press, c1981. vi, 119 p. ; 23 cm. Includes bibliographical references. [BS571.S26 1981] 19 80-84829 ISBN 0-8091-2367-3 (pbk.) : 6.95
1. Jacob (Biblical patriarch) 2. Joseph (Son of Jacob) 3. Moses (Biblical leader) 4. Adam (Biblical figure) 5. Eve (Biblical figure) 6. Psychology. I. Title.

STOLZ, Karl Ruf, 1884- 253
Pastoral psychology, by Karl R. Stolz ... Nashville, Tenn., Cokesbury press [c1932] 259 p. 22 1/2 cm. "A selected bibliography": p. 249-258. [BV4012.S7] [150.13] 32-25301
1. Psychology. 2. Theology, Pastoral. I. Title.

STOLZ, Karl Ruf, 1884- 253
Pastoral psychology, by Karl R. Stolz ... Rev. ed. New York, Nashville, Abingdon-Cokesbury press [c1940] 284 p. 22 1/2 cm. "A selected bibliography": p. 273-277. [BV4012.S7 1940] 41-11139
1. Psychology. 2. Theology, Pastoral. I. Title.

STONE, Margaret Manson (Barbour) Mrs., 1841- 133.
A practical study of the soul, by Margaret M. Barbour Stone ... New York, Dodd, Mead & company, 1901. xiv, 350 p. 19 1/2 cm. [BF1031.S85] 1-25596
1. Psychology. 2. Soul. 3. Psychical research. I. Title.

Psychology—Addresses, essays, lectures.

PEASTON, Monroe. 248'.092'4 B
Personal living; an introduction to Paul Tournier. [1st ed.] New York, Harper & Row [1972] xvii, 107 p. 22 cm. Bibliography: p. [101]-104. [BF149.P35 1972] 70-184418 4.95
1. Tournier, Paul. 2. Psychology—Addresses, essays, lectures. I. Title.

Psychology, Applied.

BIETZ, Arthur Leo. 248
Conquering personal problems [by] Arthur L. Bietz ... Mountain View, Calif., Brookfield, Ill. [etc.] Pacific press publishing association [1944] 159 p. 20 cm. [BF636.B48] 44-47929
1. Psychology, Applied. I. Title.

EVANS, Melvin James, 1890- 170
It works, by Melvin J. Evans. [Chicago, Democracy in action, inc, 1946] iii-xx, 223 p. illus. 20 1/2 cm. "First edition." Bibliography: p. 222-223. [BF636.E78] 47-16518
1. Psychology, Applied. 2. Christian life. I. Title.

HAND, Henry, 1860- 213
The art and wisdom of living; the story and principles of practical psychology and esoteric philosophy, by Henry Hand... San Diego, Calif., Indo-American press [c1930] xi, 13-241 p. incl. illus., pl., diagrs. 23 1/2 cm. "Books to study" at end of each part. [Full name: Henry William Hand] [BF1999.H345] 30-11525
I. Title.

HOUSE, Elwin Lincoln, 1861- 220
The drama of the face, and other studies in applied psychology, by Elwin Lincoln House... New York, Chicago [etc.] Fleming H. Revell company [c1919] 4 p. l., 11-258 p. 21 cm. [BR125.H72] 19-19946
I. Title.

LEWIS, Harve Spencer, 1883- 299
Rosicrucian principles for the home and business, by Dr. H. Spencer Lewis. San Jose, Calif., AMORC [c1929] 2 p. l., 7-170 p. 17 cm. [BF1623.R7L4] 29-18992
1. Rosicrucians. 2. Psychology, Applied. I. Ancient and mystical order rosae crucis. II. Title.

PEALE, Norman Vincent, 1898- 248
The power of positive thinking. by Robert Todd, Greenwich, Conn., Fawcett [1963, c.1952] 223p. 18cm. (Crest bk., R608) .60 pap.,
1. Psychology, Applied. I. Title.

PEALE, Norman Vincent, 1898- 248
The power of positive thinking. New York, Prentice-Hall [1952] 276 p. 21 cm. [BF636.P37] 52-10833
1. Psychology, Applied. I. Title.

PEALE, Norman Vincent, 1898- 248
The power of positive thinking for young people. Illus. by Robert Todd. New York, Prentice-Hall [1954] 214 p. illus. 21 cm. Abridged ed. of the author's The power of positive thinking. [BF636.P38] 54-11547
1. Psychology, Applied. I. Title.

PEALE, Norman Vincent, 1898- 248
Stay alive all your life. Greenwich, Conn., Fawcett [1964, c.1957] 256p. 18cm. (Crest R712) .60 pap.,
1. Psychology, Applied. I. Title.

PEALE, Norman Vincent, 1898- 248
Stay alive all your life. Greenwich, Conn., Fawcett [1968,c.1957] 256p. 18cm. (Crest bk., T1143) [BF636.P39] .75 pap.,
1. Psychology, Applied. I. Title.

PEALE, Norman Vincent, 1898- 248
Stay alive all your life. Englewood Cliffs, N. J., Prentice-Hall [1957] 300p. 21cm. [BF636.P39] 57-6179
1. Psychology, Applied. I. Title.

ROBERSON, Harriette Gunn. Mrs. 270
Christ on the American road; or, The psychology of power, by Harriette Gunn Roberson; photographs by John W. Gummo. [Portland, Or., Arcady press, c1928] 229 p. illus. 19 cm. [BR125.R6295] 29-1031
I. Title. II. Title: The psychology of power.

Psychology of religion.

ANDERSON, James Burns, 1889- 201
Applied religious psychology, by James B. Anderson ... Boston, R. G. Badger [c1919] 83 p. 19 cm. (On cover: Library religious thought) [BR110.A6] 19-13050
I. Title.

[BEGBIE, Harold] 1871-1929.
Painted windows; studies in religious personality by a gentleman with a duster ... with an introduction by Kirsopp Lake ... with illustrations by Emile Verpilleux. New York and London, G. Putnam's sons, 1922. xxi, 229 p. front., illus. (ports.) 23 1/2 cm. Contents.Bishop Gore.--Dean Inge.--Father Knox.--Dr. L. P. Jacks.--Bishop Hensley Henson.--Miss Maude Royden.--Canon E. W. Barnes.--General Bramwell Booth.--Dr. W. E. Orchard.--Bishop Temple.--Principal W. B. Selbie.--Archbishop Randall Davidson.--Conclusion. [BR767.B4 1922 a] 22-6538
I. Title.

CLARK, Walter Houston, 1902- 201.6*
The psychology of religion; an introduction to religious experience and behavior. New York, Macmillan [1958] 485 p. illus. 22 cm. Includes bibliography. [BL53.C57] 58-5210
I. Title.

FREUD and religious belief.
New York, Pitman [1956] xi, 140p. 23cm. Includes bibliographical references.
1. Freud, Sigmund, 1856-1939. 2. Psychology of religion. 3. Psychoanalysis. I. Philp, Howard Littleton.

FREUD and religious belief.
New York, Pitman [1956] xi, 140p. 23cm. Includes bibliographical references.
1. Freud, Sigmund, 1856-1939. 2. Psychology of religion. 3. Psychoanalysis. I. Philp, Howard Littleton.

PRUYSER, Paul W. 200.'19
A dynamic psychology of religion / Paul W. Pruyser. New York : Harper & Row, 1976c1968. x, 367 ; 24 cm. Includes bibliographical references and index. [BL53.P82] pbk. : 5.95
I. Title.
L.C. card no. for 1968 ed. 68-17589.

STEVENS, Charles Mcclellan 1861-
The analysis of moral man: an outline of

the conditions of human righteousness, by C. M. Stevens [!] ... Chicago, The Popular publishing company [1900] 160 p. 18 x 13 cm. Aug
I. Title.

Psychology, Pastoral.

ANDERSON, Stanley E 253
Every pastor a counselor. Wheaton, Ill., Van Kampen Press [1949] 111 p. 20 cm. Bibliography: p. 107-111. [BV4012.A6] 49-8239
1. Psychology, Pastoral. I. Title.

BELGUM, David Rudolph, 1922- 258
Clinical training for pastoral care. Philadelphia, West-minister Press [1956] 136p. illus. 21cm. [BV4012.B38] 56-5102
1. Psychology, Pastoral. I. Title.

BERGSTEN, Gote 258
Pastoral psychology; a study in the care of souls. London, Allen & Unwin [dist. Mystic, Conn., Verry, 1964] 227p. 23cm. 4.50
1. Psychology, Pastoral. I. Title.

BERGSTEN, Gote. 258
Pastoral psychology; a study in the care of souls. London. Allen and Unwin; New York, Macmillan [1951] 227 p. 22 cm. [BV4012.B4] 51-10759
1. Psychology. Pastoral. I. Title.

BLANTON, Smiley, 1882- 201
Faith is the answer; a pastor and a psychiatrist discuss your problems. By Norman Vincent Peale and Smiley Blanton. [New and rev. ed.] New York, Prentice-Hall, 1950. vi, 243 p. 21 cm. In the earlier edition Blanton's name appeared on the title page. [BV4012.B53 1950] 50-8115
1. Psychology, Pastoral. I. Peale, Norman Vincent, 1898- II. Title.

BONNELL, John Sutherland, 1893- 258
Psychology for pastor and people, a book on spiritual counseling. [1st ed.] New York, Harper [1948] xii. 225 p. 21 cm. (The James Sprunt lectures, 1948) Series: James Sprunt lectures delivered at Union Theological Seminary in Virginia 1943. Bibliographical references in "Notes" (p. 203-210) "Selected bibliography": p. 211 217. [BV4012.B585] 48-5426
1. Psychology, Pastoral. I. Title. II. Series.

DEWAR, Lindsay, 1891- 250
Psychology and the parish priest. London, A. R. Mowbray. New York, Morehouse-Gorham Co. [1949] 122 p. 19 cm. [BV4012.D39] 49-9412
1. Psychology, Pastoral. I. Title.

FAITH is the answer; 253.5
a pastor and a psychiatrist discuss your problems [by] Norman Vincent Peale [and] Smiley Blanton. [Enl. and rev. ed.] Carmel, N. Y., Guideposts Associates [1955] 280 p. 22 cm. In the 1940 ed. Blanton's name appeared first on the title page. [BV4012.B53 1955] [BV4012.B53 1955] 258 55-4168 55-4168
1. Psychology, Pastoral. I. Blanton, Smiley, 1882- II. Peale, Norman Vincent, 1898-

FAITH is the answer; 253.5
a pastor and a psychiatrist discuss your problems [by] Norman Vincent Peale [and] Smiley Blanton. [Enl. and rev. ed.] Englewood Cliffs, N. J., Prentice-Hall [1955] 280 p. 21 cm. In the 1940 ed. Blanton's name appeared first on the title page. [BV4012.B53 1955a] [BV4012.B53 1955a] 258 56-5645 56-5645
1. Psychology, Pastoral. I. Blanton, Smiley, 1882- II. Peale, Norman Vincent, 1898-

GOULOOZE, William, 1903- 250
Pastoral psychology; applied psychology in pastoral theology in America. Grand Rapids, Baker Book House, 1950. 266 p. 24 cm. Bibliography: p. [211]-236. [BV4012.G58] 50-4210
1. Psychology, Pastoral. I. Title.

HILTNER, Seward, 1909- 258
The counselor in counseling; case notes in pastoral counseling. New York, Abingdon-Cokesbury Press [1952] 188 p. 22 cm. [BV4012.H48] 52-375
1. Psychology, Pastoral. 2. Counseling. I. Title.

HULME, William Edward, 1920- 253.5
Counseling and theology. Philadelphia, Muhlenberg Press [1956] 249p. 22cm. [BV4012.H827] 258 56-5643
1. Psychology, Pastoral. 2. Counseling. I. Title.

INSTITUTE on Religion and Psychiatry, Temple Israel, Boston, 1947. 258
Psychiatry and religion, ed. by Joshua Loth Liebman. Introd. by Albert A. Goldman. Boston, Beacon Press, 1948. xix. 202 p. 22 cm. Addresses, with discussion, given at the Temple Israel Institute of Religion and Psychiatry held in Boston, Oct. 1947. [BV4012.I6 1947a] 48-10344
1. Psychology, Pastoral. 2. Psychotherapy. I. Liebman, Joshua Loth, 1907-1948 ed. II. Title.

JOHNSON, Paul Emanuel, 1898- 250
Psychology of pastoral care. Nashville, Abingdon [1964, c.1963] 362p. 23cm. (Apex bks., R2) 1.95 pap.,
1. Psychology, Pastoral. 2. Theology, Pastoral. I. Title.

JOHNSON, Paul Emanuel, 1898- 250
Psychology of pastoral care. Nashville, Abingdon-Cokesbury [1953] 362p. 24cm. [BV4012.J64] 53-8134
1. Psychology, Pastoral. 2. Theology, Pastoral. I. Title.

MCKENZIE, John Grant, 1882- 258
Nervous disorders and character; a study in pastoral psychology and psychotherapy ... New York [etc.] Harper [1947] 126 p. 20 cm. Pub. also in London as the 1944 Tate lectures. [BV4012.M29 1947a] Med
1. Psychology, Pastoral. 2. [Psychotherapy] I. Title.

MCKENZIE, John Grant, 1882- 258
Nervous disorders and religion; a study of souls in the making. New York, Collier [1962] 160p. 18cm. (Tate lects., 1947) (AS407V) Bibl. .95 pap.,
1. Psychology, Pastoral. 2. Psychotherapy. I. Title.

MAVES, Paul B ed. 253.5
The church and mental health. New York, Scribner, 1953. 303p. 24cm. Includes bibliography. [BV4012.M36] [BV4012.M36] 258 53-12856 53-12856
1. Psychology, Pastoral. 2. Mental hygiene. I. Title.

MUEDEKING, George H 248
Emotional problems and the Bible.. Philadelphia, Muhlenberg Press [c1956] 188p. 20cm. [BV4012.M76] 55-11317
1. Psychology, Pastoral. I. Title.

OATES, Wayne Edward, 1917- 253.5
Religious factors in mental illness. New York, Association Press [1955] 239p. 20cm. [BV4012.O24] [BV4012.O24] 258 55-7416 55-7416
1. Psychology, Pastoral. 2. Psychology, Religious. 3. Mental illness. I. Title.

OUTLER, Albert Cook, 1908- 258
Psychotherapy and the Christian message. New York, Harper [1966, c.1954] 286p. 21cm. (Chapel bks., CB26K) [BV4012.O72] 53-10975 1.75 pap.,
1. Psychology, Pastoral. 2. Psychotherapy. I. Title.

OUTLER, Albert Cook, 1908- 253.5
Psychotherapy and the Christian message. [1st ed.] New York, Harper [1954] 286p. 22cm. [BV4012.O72] [BV4012.O72] 258 53-10975 53-10975
1. Psychology, Pastoral. 2. Psychotherapy. I. Title.

PASTORAL psychology. 253.5
The minister's consultation clinic; pastoral psychology in action, a selection of questions submitted by ministers to the magazine Pastoral psychology, and answered by a board of psychiatrists, psychologists, social scientists, and clergymen. Edited by Simon Doniger. Great Neck, N. Y., Channel Press [1955] 316p. illus. 21cm. [BV4012.P34] [BV4012.P34] 258 55-4568 55-4568
1. Psychology, Pastoral. I. Doniger, Simon, ed. II. Title.

PASTORAL psychology in practice; 253.5
contributions to a psychology for priests and educators. Translated from the German by Joachim Werner Conway. New York, P. J. Kenedy [1955] 249p. 23cm. [BX1912] [BX1912] 258 55-8364 55-8364
1. Psychology, Pastoral. 2. Theology, Pastoral—Catholic Church. I. Demal, Willibald, 1908-

PEALE, Norman Vincent, 1898- 253.5
The art of real happiness, by Norman Vincent Peale and Smiley Blanton. 2d ed. Englewood Cliffs, N. J., Prentice-Hall [1956] 280p. 21cm. [BV4012.P35 1956] [BV4012.P35 1956] 258 56-9773 56-9773
1. Psychology, Pastoral. I. Blanton, Smiley, 1882- joint author. II. Title.

PEALE, Norman Vincent, 1898- 258
The art of real happiness / Norman Vincent Peale and Smiley Blanton revised edition Greenwich, Coon. : Fawcett Crest [1976 c1950] 204 p. ; 18 cm. [BV4012.P35] ISBN 0-449-23039-2 pbk. : 1.75
1. Psychology, Pastoral. I. Blanton, Smiley, 1882- , joint author. II. Title.
L.C. card no. for 1950 Prentice-Hall edition: 50-5426.

PEALE, Norman Vincent, 1898- 258
The art of real happiness, by Norman Vincent Peale and Smiley Blanton. [1st ed.] New York, Prentice-Hall [1950] vi, 247 p. 21 cm. [BV4012.P35] 50-5426
1. Psychology, Pastoral. I. Blanton, Smiley, 1882- joint author. II. Title.

PEALE, Norman Vincent, 1898- 258
A guide to confident living. [1st ed.] New York, Prentice-Hall [1948] 248 p. 22 cm. [BV4012.P37] 48-5754
1. Psychology, Pastoral. 2. Psychology, Applied. I. Title.

PEUGNET, Claire Adele. 258
The missing value in medical social case work, by Claire A. Peugnet ... [St. Louis, Pub. by Hilton printing co., inc., 1943] 145, [1] p. 21 cm. (School of social service, Saint Louis university. Studies no. 1) Bibliography: p. 101-109. [BV4012.P48] 44-8926
1. Psychology, Pastoral. 2. Medical social work. I. Title.

PIKE, James Albert, 1913- 248
Beyond anxiety; the Christian answer to fear, frustration. guilt, indecision, inhibition, loneliness, despair. New York, Scribners [1962, c.1953] 149p. 21cm. (SL74) 1.25 pap.,
1. Psychology, Pastoral. 2. Christian ethics. I. Title.

PIKE, James Albert, Bp., 1913-1969. 248
Beyond anxiety; the Christian answer to fear, frustration, guilt, indecision, inhibition, loneliness, despair. New York, Scribner, 1953. 149 p. 22 cm. [BV4012.P53] 53-12237
1. Psychology, Pastoral. 2. Christian ethics. I. Title.

PSYCHOLOGY for pastor and people; a book on spiritual counseling. Rev. ed. New York, Harper [1960] 2 40p. 21cm.
I. Bonnell, John Sutherland, 1893-

RINGEL, Erwin. 253.5
The priest and the unconscious, by Erwin Ringel and Wenzel van Lun. Edigted and translated from the German by Meyrick Booth. Westminster, Md., Newman Press, 1954. 118p. 19cm. Translation of Die Tiefenpsychologie hilft dem Seelsorger. [BV4012.R543] 55-14201
1. Psychology. Pastoral. 2. Psychotherapy. I. Lun, Wenzel van, joint author. II. Title.

ROBERTS, David Everett 201
Psychotherapy and a christian view of man. New York, Scriber [1960, c.1950] xiv, 161 p. (Bibl.: p. 155-156) 21 cm. (Scriber Library, SL 29) pap., 1.25
1. Psychology Pastoral. 2. Christianity—Psychology. 3. Psychotherapy. I. Title.

ROBERTS, David Everett, 1911- 201
Psychotherapy and a Christian view of man. New York, Scribner, 1950. xiv, 161 p. 21 cm. Bibliography: p. 155-156. [BV4012.R59] 50-6770
1. Psychology, Pastoral. 2. Christianity — Psychology. 3. Psychotherapy. I. Title.

STOLZ, Karl Ruf, 1884-1943. 258
The church and psychotherapy, by Karl R. Stolz ... with an introduction by Elmer G. Homrighausen. New York, Nashville, Abindgon-Cokesbury press [1943] 312 p. 22 1/2 cm. "Selected bibliography": p. 303-306. [BV4012.S68] 44-3491
1. Psychology, Pastoral. I. Title.

THOMAS, George Ernest, 1907- 248
Faith can master fear. New York, Revell [1950] 160 p. 21 cm. Bibliographical references: p. 159-560. [BV4012.T5] 50-10876
1. Psychology, Pastoral. 2. Fear. I. Title.

VAN DER VELDT, James Herman, 1893- 616.89
Psychiary and Catholicism [by] James H. Van der Veldt [and] Robert P. Odenwald. 1st ed. New York, McGraw-Hill, 1952. ix, 433 p. 24 cm. Includes bibliographies. [BX1759.V3] 51-12652
1. Psychology, Pastoral. 2. Psychiatry. 3. Christian ethics — Catholic authors. I. Odenwald, Robert P., 1809- joint author. II. Title.

WERNER, Hazen Graff, 1895- 258
And we are whole again, by Hazen G. Werner ... New York, Nashville, Abingdon-Cokesbury press [1945] 195 p. 19 1/2 cm. "References": p. 187-195. [BV4012.W4] 45-924
1. Psychology, Pastoral. I. Title.

WISE, Carroll Alonzo, 1903- 253.5
Psychiatry and the Bible. New York, Harper [1966, c.1956] 169p. 21cm. (Harper Chapel bk., CB23H) [BV4012.W53] 56-7025 1.45 pap.,
1. Psychology, Pastoral. 2. Bible—Psychology. 3. Medicine and religion. I. Title.

WISE, Carroll Alonzo, 1903- 253.5
Psychiatry and the Bible. [1st ed.] New York, Harper [1956] 169p. 22cm. [BV4012.W53] 258 56-7025
1. Psychology, Pastoral. 2. Bible—Psychology. 3. Medicine and religion. I. Title.

Psychology, Pastoral—Dictionaries.

A dictionary of pastoral psychology. 253
New York, Philosophical Library [c1955] xi, 336p. 22cm. [BV4012.F44] [BV4012.F44] 258 54-13510 54-13510
1. Psychology, Pastoral—Dictionaries. 2. Psychology—Dictionaries. I. Ferm, Vergilius Ture Anselm, 1896-

Psychology, Pathological.

BOISEN, Anton Theophilus, 1876- 132.14
The exploration of the inner world: a study of mental disorder and religious experience, by Anton T. Boisen ... Chicago, New York, wIllett, Clark & company, 1936. xi, p., 1 l., 322 p. diagrs. 23 1/2 cm. [BL53.B6] [258 [159.9724 38-10801
1. Psychology, Pathological. 2. Psychology, Religious. 3. Medicine and religion. 4. Church work with the insane. I. Title.

JUNG, Carl Gustav, 1875-1961. 133.4
Psychology and alchemy / C. G. Jung ; translated by R. F. C. Hull. 1st Princeton / Bollingen paperback printing. Princeton, NJ : Princeton University Press, 1980, c1968. xxxiv, 571p. : ill. ; 22 cm. (The collected works of C. G. Jung; v.12) (Bollingen series; 20) (Princeton/Bollingen paperbacks) "From second edition, completely revised, 1968. Bibliography: p. 487-523. [BF23.J763 vol. 12] 75-156 ISBN 0-691-01831-6 pbk. : 8.95
1. Psychology, Pathological. 2. Psychology, Religious. 3. Alchemy. I. Title. II. Series: Bollingen series; 20
LC card no. for 1968 ed.: 76-167

Psychology—Philosophy.

ARIETI, Silvano. 222'.11'0924
Abraham and the contemporary mind / Silvano Arieti. New York : Basic Books, c1981. viii, 181 p. : ill. ; 22 cm. Includes bibliographical references and index.

[BS580.A3A74] 19 80-68187 ISBN 0-465-00005-3 : 11.95
1. Abraham, the patriarch. 2. Psychology—Philosophy. 3. Civilization, Modern—20th century. I. Title.

Psychology, Religious.

AGUDO, Philomena, 1925- 248'.4
Affirming the human and the holy / Philomena Agudo. 1st ed. Whitinsville, Mass. : Affirmation Books, c1979. 101 p. : ill. ; 21 cm. Includes bibliographical references. [BR110.A37] 79-1499 ISBN 0-89571-006-4 pbk. : 4.95
1. Psychology, Religious. 2. Personality. 3. Holy, The. I. Title.

ALLPORT, Gordon Willard 201
The individual and his religion, a psychological interpretation. New York, Macmillan, 1960 [c.1950] xi, 147p. (Bibl. footnotes) 21cm. (Macmillan paperback 1) 1.25 pap.,
1. Psychology, Religious. I. Title.

ALLPORT, Gordon Willard, 201
1897-1967.
The individual and his religion, a psychological interpretation. New York, Macmillan, 1950. xi, 147 p. 21 cm. Bibliographical footnotes. [BL53.A428] 50-5982
1. Psychology, Religious. I. Title.

AMES, Edward Scribner, 1870- 201
The psychology of religious experience, by Edward Scribner Ames ... Boston and New York, Houghton Mifflin company, 1910. xi, [1]. 427, [1] p., 1 l. 23 cm. [BL58.A5] 10-22984
1. Psychology, Religious. 2. Religion. 3. Experience (Religion) I. Title.

ANDERSON, George Christian. 201.6
Man's right to be human; to have emotions without fear. New York, Morrow, 1959. 191 p. 21 cm. [BL53.A57] 59-8188
1. Psychology, Religious. I. Title.

ANDERSON, George Christian. 201.6
Man's right to be human to have emotions withour fear. New York, Morrow, 1959. 191p. 21cm. [BL53.A57] 59-8188
1. Psychology, Religious. I. Title.

ANDERSON, George 200'.19
Christian.
Your religion: neurotic or healthy? [1st ed.] Garden City, N.Y., Doubleday, 1970. 191 p. 22 cm. [BL53.A573] 74-123682 5.95
1. Psychology, Religious. I. Title.

ARGYLE, Michael. 201.6
Religious behavior. Glencoe, Ill., Free Press [1959] 196p. illus. 23cm. Includes bibliography. [BL53.A7 1959] 59-16264
1. Psychology, Religious. I. Title.

ARGYLE, Michael. 301.5'8
The social psychology of religion / Michael Argyle and Benjamin Beit-Hallahmi. London ; Boston : Routledge & K. Paul, 1975. x, 246, 14 p. : ill. ; 22 cm. (International library of sociology) Previous editions published under title: Religious behavior. Includes bibliographical references and index. [BL53.A7 1975] 75-324056 ISBN 0-7100-7997-4 : 18.50 ISBN 0-7100-8043-3 pbk. : 8.75
1. Psychology, Religious. I. Beit-Hallahmi, Benjamin, joint author. II. Title.

AUBREY, Edwin Ewart. 201
Religion and the next generation, by Edwin Ewart Aubrey. New York and London, Harper & brothers, 1931. xi, 188 p. diagr. 20 cm. "First edition." [BR110.A8] 31-6900
1. Psychology, Religious. I. Title.

BAKAN, David. 200.19
The duality of human existence; an essay on psychology and religion. Chicago, Rand McNally [1966] 242 p. 23 cm. Bibliographical footnotes. [BL53.B29] 66-13438
1. Psychology, Religious. I. Title.

BAKER, Oren Huling, 1894- 201.6
Human nature under God; or, Adventure of personality. New York. Association Press [1958] 316p. 20cm. [BL53.B3] 58-11524
1. Psychology, Religious. 2. Bible—Psychology. 3. Personality. I. Title.

BARKER, Charles Edward, 201.6
1908-
Psychology's impact on the Christian faith. London, Allen & Unwin [dist. Hollywood-by-the-Sea, Fla., Transatlantic, c.1964] 220p. 23cm. Bibl. 64-56250 7.50 bds.,
1. Psychology, Religious. I. Title.

BARKMAN, Paul Friesen. 157
Man in conflict, by Paul F. Barkman. Grand Rapids, Zondervan Pub. House [1965] 189 p. 23 cm. Bibliographical footnotes. [BR110.B34] 65-19510
1. Psychology, Religious. I. Title.

BENNETT, John Godolphin, 248
1897-
A spiritual psychology [London] Hodder & Stoughton [dist. Mystic Conn., Verry [1965, c.1964] 256p. 22cm. Bibl. [BP605.B376] 65-3270 6.00
1. Psychology, Religious. I. Title.

BENNETT, John Godolphin, 212'.5
1897-
A spiritual psychology / J. G. Bennett. 1st American ed., rev. Lakemont, Ga. : CSA Press, 1974. 268 p. : ill. ; 22 cm. Includes bibliographical references and index. [BP605.S7B4 1974] 73-81620 ISBN 0-87707-128-4 : 6.95
1. Psychology, Religious. 2. Subud. I. Title.

BIDDLE, William Earl, 1906- 201.6
Integration of religion and psychiatry. New York, Macmillan, 1955. 171p. 22cm. [BL53.B45] 55-14123
1. Psychology, Religious. I. Title.

BIDDLE, William Earl, 1966-
Integration of religion and psychiatry. New York, Collier [1962] 188 p. 18 cm. Bibilography: 173-176. 66-83392
1. Psychology, Religious. I. Title.

BLANTON, Smiley, 1882- 201
Faith is the answer; a psychiatrist and a pastor discuss your problems [by,) Smiley Blanton, M.D. and Norman Vincent Peale, D.D. New York, Nashville, Abingdon-Cokesbury press [c1940] 223 p. 20 1/2 cm. [BL53.B5] 41-619
1. Psychology, Religious. 2. Faith—cure. I. Peale, Norman Vincent, 1898- joint author. II. Title.

BOISEN, Anton Theophilus, 201.6
1876-
Religion in crisis and custom; a sociological and psychological study. [1st ed.] New York, Harper [1955] 271p. 22cm. [BL53.B62] 55-8519
1. Psychology, Religious. 2. Religion and sociology. 3. U. S.—Religion. I. Title.

BOISEN, Anton Theophilus, 261.8'3
1876-
Religion in crisis and custom; a sociological and psychological study, by Anton T. Boisen. Westport, Conn., Greenwood Press [1973, c1955] xv, 271 p. 22 cm. Includes bibliographical references. [BL53.B62 1973] 72-10977 ISBN 0-8371-6642-X 14.25
1. Psychology, Religious. 2. Religion and sociology. 3. United States—Religion. I. Title.

BONTHIUS, Robert Harold, 201
1918-
Christian paths to self-acceptance. New York; King's Crown Press, 1948. xi, 254 p. 21 cm. Biblioaphy p. 238-247. [BL53.B63] 48-8777
1. Psychology, Religious. 2. Psychology, Pastoral. 3. Psychotherapy. I. Title.

BOOTH, Howard J. 200'.1'9
Edwin Diller Starbuck, pioneer in the psychology of religion / Howard J. Booth. Washington, D.C. : University Press of America, c1981. p. cm. Bibliography: p. [BL43.S85B66] 19 80-5731 ISBN 0-8191-1703-X (pbk.) : 13.00 ISBN 0-8191-1702-1 : 24.50
1. Starbuck, Edwin Diller, 1866-1947. 2. Psychology, Religious. I. Title.

BOURGUIGNON, Erika, 1924- 200'.19
Religion, altered states of consciousness, and social change. Edited by Erika Bourguignon. Columbus, Ohio State University Press, 1973. x, 389 p. illus. 22 cm. Includes bibliographies. [BL53.B643] 72-8448 ISBN 0-8142-0167-9 12.50
1. Psychology, Religious. 2. Trance. 3. Sects. 4. Religion and sociology. I. Title.

BOVET, Pierre, 1878- 270
The child's religion; a study of the development of the religious sentiment, by Pierre Bovet ... authorized translation of "Le sentiment religieux", by George H. Green ... New York, E. P. Dutton & co., inc., 1928. xiii, 202 p. 19 1/2 cm. [BR110.B6]
1. Psychology, Religious. 2. Child study. 3. Religious education—Psychology. I. Green, George Henry, 1881- II. Title.

*BROWN, L. B., ed. 200.19
Psychology and religion; selected readings, edited by L. B. Brown. [Harmondsworth, Eng., Penguin, 1973] 400 p. 20 cm. (Penguin Modern Psychology Readings) Includes bibliographical references. [BL53] ISBN 0-14-080538-9
1. Psychology, Religious. I. Title.
Available from Penguin, Baltimore for 4.95 (pbk)

BROWN, William Adams, 1865- 201
Imperialistic religion and the religion of democracy; a study in social psychology, by William Adams Brown... New York, C. Scribner's sons, 1923. xiv, 223 p. 20 1/2 cm. Printed in Great Britain. "The substance of the following pages was delivered as the Martha Upton lectures in religion for 1922, at Manchester college, Oxford, under the title 'Three great religions'. Parts of chapters I, III., IV., and V. were delivered at King's college of the University of London, in the fall of the same year, under the title 'The religion of demoncracy'. The main thesis to which the work is devoted was presented to the Aristotelian society of London in January 1923, in a paper entitled 'The problem of classification in religion'."--Pref. [BR110.B75] 24-11459
1. Psychology, Religious. 2. Religion. 3. Social psychology. I. Title. II. Title: The religion of democracy.

BURR, Anna Robeson (Brown) 922
Mrs. 1873-
Religious confessions and confessants; with a chapter on the history of introspection, by Anna Robeson Burr. Boston and New York, Houghton Mifflin company, 1914. viii p., 2 l., [3]-562 p. 21 cm. $2.50 "Bibliography of cases": p. [525]-548. [BR1690.B8] 14-10467
1. Psychology, Religious. 2. Mysticism. 3. Autobiography. I. Title.

BURR, Anna Robeson 200'.1'9
Brown, 1873-1941.
Religious confessions and confessants. With a chapter on the history of introspection. [Folcroft, Pa.] Folcroft Library Editions, 1974 [c1914] p. cm. Reprint of the ed. published by Houghton Mifflin, Boston. Bibliography: p. [BR1690.B8 1974] 74-18010 45.00
1. Psychology, Religious. 2. Mysticism. 3. Autobiography. I. Title.

CARRIER, Blanche, 1895- 258
Free to grow. [1st ed.] New York, Harper [1951] vii, 241 p. 22 cm. Bibliography:p. 235-238. [BL53.C28] 51-11275
1. Psychology, Religious. 2. Psychology, Pastoral. I. Title.

CATES, Wayne Edward, 1917- 201.6
The religious dimensions of personality. New York, Association Press [1957] 320p. 21cm. [BL53.O3] 57-11600
1. Psychology, Religious. 2. Personality. I. Title.

CATTELL, Raymond Bernard, 201
1905-
Psychology and the religious quest; an account of the psychology of religion and a defence of individualism, by Raymond B. Cattell ... London and New York [etc.] T. Nelson and sons, ltd. [1938] viii, 9-195, [1] p. 19 cm. (Half-title: Discussion books. General editors: Richard Wilson and A. J. J. Ratcliff. no. 23) "First published, autumn 1938." "Further related reading" at end of each chapter. [BL53.C3] 39-19890
1. Psychology, Religious. I. Title.

CHESEN, Eli S. 218
Religion may be hazardous to your health. New York, Collier Books [1973, c.1972] ix, 145 p. 18 cm. Bibliography: p. 137-139. [BL53.C45] 1.50 (pbk.)
1. Psychology, Religious. 2. Religious education of children. I. Title.
L.C. card no. for the hardbound edition: 76-189524.

CHRISTIAN paths to self-acceptance. 210
New York, King's Crown Press, 1948. xi, 254 p. 21 cm. Thesis--Columbia Univ. Pub. also without thesis statement. Bibliography: p. [238]-247. [BL53.B63 1948a] A 49 1918-
1. Psychology, Religious. 2. Psychology, Pastoral. 3. Psychotherapy.

/CHURCHILL, Winston, 1871- 201
The uncharted way; the psychology of the gospel doctrine, by Winston Churchill. Philadelphia, Dorrance and company [c1940] 266 p. 19 1/2cm. [BL53.C5] 201 ISBN 40-9468
1. Psychology, Religious. I. Title.

CLARK, Elmer Talmage, 1886- 201
The psychology of religious awakening, by Elmer T. Clark... New York, The Macmillan company, 1929. 170 p. fold. tables, diagrs. 24 1/2 cm. Bibliography: p. 161-166. [BR110.C6] 29-3621
1. Psychology, Religious. 2. Conversion. 3. Religion. I. Title. II. Title: Religious awakening, The psychology of.

COE, George Albert, 1862- 201
The psychology of religion, by George Albert Coe ... Chicago, Ill., The University of Chicago press [1916] xvii, 365 p. 20 cm. (Half-title: The University of Chicago publications in religious education, ed. by E. D. Burton, Shailer Mathews, T. G. Soares. Handbooks of ethics and religion) Alphabetical bibliography: p. 327-345; Topical bibliography: p. 346-355. [BL53.C6] 17-212
1. Psychology, Religious. I. Title.

COE,George Albert 1862- 201
The spiritual life; studies in the science of religion, by George A. Coe ... New York, Eaton & Mains; Cincinnati, Curts & Jennings, 1900. 279 p. diagrs. 19 cm. [BL53.C63] 0-2003
1. Psychology, Religious. 2. Religion. 3. Mental healing. I. Title.

COLLINS, Gary R. 248'.092'4 B
The Christian psychology of Paul Tournier [by] Gary R. Collins. Grand Rapids, Mich., Baker Book House [1973] 222 p. port. 23 cm. Bibliography: p. 211-213. [BF109.T63C64] 72-93076 4.95
1. Tournier, Paul. 2. Psychology, Religious. I. Title.

CONFERENCE on Christianity 250
and mental hygiene, Greenwich, Conn., 1938.
Christianity and mental hygiene; report of the Conference held at Rosemary hall, Greenwich, Conn., August 24-30, 1938. Issued by Committee on religion and health, Federal council of the churches of Christ in America, Editorial committee, Seward Hiltner, Otis R. Rice, Webb H. York. [New York, 1939] v. 2 p., 1 l., 53 p. 28 cm. "References made during the conference": p. 52-53. [BR110.C63] 40-620
1. Psychology, Religious. 2. Mental physiology and hygiene. I. Federal council of the churches of Christ in America. II. Hiltner, Seward, 1909- ed. III. Title.

CONKLIN, Edmund Smith, 1884- 201
The psychology of religious adjustment; by Edmund S. Conklin ... New York, The Macmillan company, 1929. xiv p., 1 l., 340 p. 19 1/2 cm. [BR110.C65] 29-28337
1. Psychology, Religious. I. Title.

COOPER, W. Norman. 248
Finding your self, by W. Norman Cooper. Santa Monica, Calif., DeVorss [1974] 88 p. 21 cm. [BL53.C655] 74-78511 ISBN 0-87516-183-9 3.00 (pbk.)
1. Psychology, Religious. I. Title.

COX, Richard H. 200'.19
Religious systems and psychotherapy, edited by Richard H. Cox. With a foreword by E. Mansell Pattison. Springfield, Ill., Thomas [1973] xxiv, 519 p. 26 cm. Includes bibliographies. [BL53.C66] 72-93207 ISBN 0-398-02753-6
1. Psychology, Religious. 2. Psychotherapy. I. Title.

CRABB, Cecil Van Meter. 201
Psychology's challenge to Christianity, by Rev. Cecil V. Crabb ... Richmond, Va., Presbyterian committee of publication [c1923] 210 p. 19 cm. [BL53.C7] 24-19342
1. Psychology, Religious. I. Title.

CRABB, Cecil Van Meter, 1889- 248
The individual in our present-day world, making the grade today, by Cecil V. Crabb ... New York [etc.] Fleming H. Revell company [c1938] 93 p. 20 cm. [BL53.C67] 39-2409
1. Psychology, Relligious. 2. Personality. I. Title.

CURRAN, Charles Arthur. 201'.9
Psychological dynamics in religious living [by] Charles A. Curran. [New York] Herder and Herder [1971] 228 p. 22 cm. [BL53.C78] 72-170968 6.95
1. Psychology, Religious. I. Title.

CUTTEN, George Barton, 1874- 201
Instincts and religion, by George Barton Cutten ... New York and London, Harper & brothers [c1940] 6 p. l., 154 p. 20 cm. "First edition." [BL53.C8] 40-7906
1. Psychology, Religious. 2. Instinct. I. Title.

DEWAR, Lindsay. 201
Psychology for religious works, by Lindsay Dewar ... and Cyril E. Hudson ... New York, R. Long & R. R. Smith, inc., 1932. 2 p. 1 l., 13 288 p. 23 cm. [BR110.D4] 32-22690
1. Psychology, Religious. 2. Psychoanlysis. 3. Theology, Pastoral. I. Hudson, Cyril Edward, joint author. II. Title.

THE Dialogue between 200'.19
theology and psychology, by LeRoy Aden [and others] Edited by Peter Homans. Chicago, University of Chicago Press [1968] x, 295 p. 24 cm. (Essays in divinity, v. 3) Many of the papers were first presented at the Alumni Conference of the Religion and Personality Field, Jan. 27-29, 1969, celebrating the 75th anniversary of the University of Chicago and the 100th anniversary of its Divinity School. Bibliographical footnotes. [BL53.D47] 68-16698
1. Psychology, Religious. I. Homans, Peter, ed. II. Aden, LeRoy. III. Chicago. University. Divinity School. IV. Title. V. Series.

DOOLEY, Anne Mary. 253.5
A quest for religious maturity : the obsessive-compulsive personality : implications for pastoral counseling / Anne Mary Dooley. Lanham, MD : University Press of America, c1981. xii, 111 p. ; 22 cm. Includes indexes. Bibliography: p. 93-104. [BL53.D64] 19 80-67255 ISBN 0-8191-1442-1 lib. bdg. : 16.00 ISBN 0-8191-1443-X (pbk.) : 7.50
1. Psychology, Religious. 2. Obsessive-compulsive neurosis. 3. Pastoral counseling. I. Title.

DRAKEFORD, John W. 201.6
Psychology in search of a soul. Nashville, Broadman *c.1964] 301p illus. 22cm. Bibl. 64-15096 5.75
1. Psychology, Religious. 2. Soul. I. Title.

DRESSER, Horatio Willis, 1866-
Outlines of the psychology of religion, by Horatio W. Dresser... New York, Thomas Y. Crowell company, [c1929] xiii, 451 p. 21 cm. Bibliography at end of each chapter. [BL.53.D7] 29-8011
1. Psychology, Religious. I. Title. II. Title: Psychology of religion.

DUGUID, Julian, 1902- 201
I am persuaded, by Julian Duguid; introduction by John Haynes Holmes. New York, London, D. Appleton-Century company, incorporated, 1941. ix p., 2 l., 3-367, [1] p. 21 cm. [Full name: Julian Thomas Duguid] [BL53 D8] 41-23467
1. Psychology, Religious, I. Title.

[EDGERLY, Webster]
Book of the Psychic society; a study of the fourteen unseen powers that control human life, and containing immortality, a scientific demonstration of life after death, by Edmund Shaftesbury [pseud.] Washington, D.C., Ralston university publishing company, 1908. 320 p. 22 1/2 cm. 8-32496
I. Title.

[EDGERLY, Webster] ed.
Book of the Psychic society; a study of the unseen powers that surround human life, based on fixed natural laws. Ed. by Edmund Shaftesbury [pseud.] and the committee of the Society. Washington, D. C., Ralston company, 1907. 303 p. 22 1/2 cm. 7-42322
I. Title.

EDWARDS, Ethel.
Instinct in religion. Cincinnati, Psyche book Service [1964] 199 p. 64-66781
1. Psychology, Religious. 2. Instinct. I. Title.

EDWARDS, Ethel.
Instinct in religion. Cincinnati, Psyche book Service [1964] 199 p. 64-66781
1. Psychology, Religious. 2. Instinct. I. Title.

ELLIOTT, Harrison Sacket, 201
1882-
The bearing of psychology upon religion [by] Harrison Sacket Elliott... New York, Association press, 1927. 77 p. 19 1/2 cm. [BL53.E56] 28-6317
1. Psychology, Religious. I. Title.

EVERETT, Charles Carroll, 201
1829-1900.
The psychological elements of religious faith; lectures by Charles Carroll Everett ... edited by Edward Hale ... New York, The Macmillan company; London, Macmillan & co., ltd., 1902. xiii, 215 p. 19 cm. [BL53.E8] 2-20332
1. Psychology, Religious. 2. Religion. I. Hale, Edward, 1858-1918, ed. II. Title.

FEINSILVER, Alexander, 201.6
In search of religious maturity. [Yellow Springs, Ohio] Antioch Press [c.]1960. 124p. 22cm. 60-15084 3.50
1. Psychology, Religious. I. Title.

FERM, Vergilius Ture 200'.19
Anselm, 1896- ed.
Religion in transition [by] S. Radhakrishnan [and others] Edited by Vergilius Ferm. Freeport, N.Y., Books for Libraries Press [1969] 266 p. facsims. 21 cm. (Essay index reprint series) Reprint of the 1937 ed. Contents.Contents.—My search for truth, by S. Radhakrishnan.—A pilgrim's progress, by C. F. Andrews.—My own little theatre, by G. A. Coe.—From credence to faith, by A. Loisy.—The making of a psychologist of religion, by J. H. Leuba.—Religion's use of me, by E. D. Starbuck. Includes bibliographies. [BL53.F4 1969] 68-29204
1. Psychology, Religious. I. Radhakrishnan, Sarvepalli, Pres. India, 1888- II. Title.

FLOWER, John Cyril, 1886- 201
An approach to the psychology of religion, by J. Cyril Flower... New York, Harcourt, Brace & company, inc.; London, K. Paul, Trench, Trubner & co., ltd., 1927. xi, 248 p. 22 1/2 cm. "The substance of a Cambridge PH. D. dissertations submitted... in 1925, entitled The bearing of recent developments of psychological study upon religion."--Introd. Printed in Great Britain. Contents.What is religion?--The mechanism of the religious response.--A study of the religion of the Winnebago Indians.--The peyote cult among the Winnebago. --George Fox.--Psychopathology and religion.--Conversion.--Religion and prehistory.--Rudolph Otto's The idea of the holy.--Note on responses to a questionnaire.--Index to authors quoted and referred to (p. 243-245) [BL53.F47] 28-13400
1. Fox, George, 1624-1691. 2. Psychology,Religious. 3. Winnebago Indians. 4. Indians of North America—Religion and mythology. 5. Mescal. I. Title.

FREUD, Sigmund, 1856-1939. 201
The future of an illusion. Translated by W. D. Robson-Scott. Garden City, N. Y., Doubleday, 1957. 102p. 18cm. (Doubleday anchor books, A99) [BL53] 57-1077
1. Psychology, Religious. 2. Religion. 3. Psychoanalysis. I. Title.

FREUD, Sigmund, 1856- 200'.1'9
1939.
The future of an illusion / Sigmund Freud ; newly translated from the German and edited by James Strachey. New York : Norton, [1975] c1961. 63 p. ; 20 cm. Translation of Die Zukunft einer Illusion. Includes indexes. Bibliography: p. 57-59. [BL53.F67 1975] 75-15645 ISBN 0-393-01120-8 : 5.95
1. Psychology, Religious. 2. Religion. 3. Psychoanalysis. I. Strachey, James. II. Title.

FREUD, Sigmund, 1856-1939. 201
The future of an illusion. Translated by W. D. Robson-Scott. New York, Liveright Pub. Corp., 1949. 98 p. 23 cm. (The International psycho-analytical library no. 15) [BL5.F67 1949] 49-9624
1. Psychology. Religious. 2. Religion. 3. Psychoanalysis. I. Title. II. Series.

GILL, Mabel K., R. N. 130.1
Mind, body and religion. Nashville, Southern Pub. Assn. [c.1965] 143p. 21cm. Bibl. [BX6111.W9G5] 65-16371 3.75 bds.,
1. White, Ellen Gould (Harmon) 1827-1915. 2. Psychology, Religious. I. Title.

GLEASON, John J., 1934- 200'.19
Growing up to God; eight steps in religious development [by] John J. Gleason, Jr. Nashville, Abingdon Press [1975] 141 p. 19 cm. Includes bibliographical references. [BL53.G58] 74-17093 ISBN 0-687-15972-5 3.50 (pbk.)
1. Erikson, Erik Homburger, 1902- 2. Psychology, Religious. I. Title.

GOODENOUGH, Erwin Ramsdell, 201.6
1893-
The psychology of religous experiences. New York, Basic Books [1965] xii, 192 p. 22 cm. Bibliographical footnotes. [BR110.G63] 65-15280
1. Psychology, Religious. I. Title.

GRENSTED, Laurence William, 201
1884-
Psychology and God; a study of the implications of recent psychology for religious belief and practice ... by the Rev. L. W. Grensted ... London, New York [etc.] Longmans, Green and co., 1930. xi, 257 p. 23 cm. (On cover: Bampton lectures 1930) [BR45.B3 1930] 230 30-20852
1. Psychology, Religious. I. Title.

GRENSTED, Laurence William, 201.6
1884-
The psychology of religion. London, New York, Oxford University Press, 1952. 181 p. 18 cm. (The Home university library of modern knowledge, 221) [BL53.G75 1952a] 52-4100
1. Psychology, Religious. I. Title.

GRENSTED, Laurence William, 201.6
1884-
The psychology of religion. New York, Oxford University Press, 1952. 181 p. 19 cm. [BL53.G75] 52-12536
1. Psychology, Religious. I. Title.

GROSS, Leonard. 201
God and Freud. New York, D. McKay Co. [1959] 215 p. 21 cm. [BL53.G78] 59-6696
1. Freud, Sigmund, 1856-1939. 2. Psychology, Religious. 3. Pastoral psychology. I. Title.

HARDY, Thomas John, 1868- 201
The religious instinct. by the Rev. Thomas J. Hardy ... London, New York [etc.] Longmans, Green, and co., 1913. 4 p. l., 300 p. 20 cm. [BL53.H3] A 15
1. Psychology, Religious. 2. Religion. I. Title.

HAUGHTON, Rosemary. 200'.19
The liberated heart; transactional analysis in religious experience. New York, Seabury Press [1974] xxi, 192 p. 21 cm. "A Crossroad book." Bibliography: p. 191-192. [BL53.H35] 74-18271 ISBN 0-8164-1167-0 7.95
1. Psychology, Religious. 2. Transactional analysis. I. Title.

HAVENS, Joseph, 1919- 200.19
Psychology and religion; a contemporary dialogue [by] Joseph Havens, with the collaboration of David Bakan [and others] Princeton, N.J., Van Nostrand [1968] vii, 151 p. 19 cm. (An Insight book, 42) Bibliography: p. 140-147. [BL53.H36] 68-4750
1. Psychology, Religious. I. Bakan, David. II. Title.

HERR, Vincent V 201.6
Religious psychology [by] Vincent V. Herr. Staten Island, N. Y., Alba House [c1965] 277 p. 22 cm. (Mental health series, 5) Bibliography: p. [265]-267. [BR110.H4] 64-20109
1. Psychology, Religious. I. Title.

HERRING, Daniel Boone, 1876- 130
Mind surgery, by Daniel Boone Herring. Holyoke, Mass., The Elizabeth Towne co., inc.; London, L. N. Fowler & company [c1931] 112 p. 119 cm. [BR126.H387] 201 31-31507
1. Psychology, Religious. I. Title.

HICKMAN, Franklin Simpson, 201
1886-
... Introduction to the psychology of religion, by Frank S. Hickman. New York, Cincinnati, The Abingdon press [c1926] 558 p. 20 cm. (The Abingdon religious education texts, D. G. Downey, general editor. College series. G. H. Betts, editor) Bibliography: p. 540-542. [BL53.H45] 27-1507
1. Psychology, Religious. I. Title.

HILL, Owen Aloysius, 1863- 201
Psychology and natural theology, by Owen A. Hill ... New York, The Macmillan company, 1921. xiii, 351 p. 22 cm. [BL53.H5] 21-3788
1. Psychology, Religious. 2. Natural theology. I. Title.

HOFFMAN, William Henry, 131.
1853-
Questions and answers on material and spiritual psychology and symposium of subjects on the psychology of morals and religious truths for the betterment of mankind, by W. H. Hoffman. Los Angeles, The Austin publishing company, 1926. 144 p. incl. front. (port.) 20 1/2 cm. Poems and essays: p. 44-144. [BF636.H65] 26-15083
I. Title.

HOLLINGTON, Richard Deming, 201
1870-
Psychology serving religion; a practical guide to life adjustments, by Richard D. Hollington. New York, Cincinnati [etc] The Abingdon press [c1938] 248 p.21 cm. Includes bibliographies. [BL53.H56] 38-38256
1. Psychology, Religious. 2. Psychology, Applied. 3. Personality. 4. Theology, Pastoral I. Title.

HOLMAN, Charles Thomas, 1882- 248
Psychology and religion for everyday living. New York, Macmillan Co., 1949. x, 178 p. 20 cm. [BL53.H564] 49-10280
1. Psychology, Religious. I. Title.

HOLMAN, Charles Thomas, 1882- 201
The religion of a healthy mind, by Charles T. Holman. New York, Round table press, inc., 1939. xi, 210 p. 20 cm. [BL53.H565] 39-19881
1. Psychology, Religious. 2. Mental physiology and hygiene. I. Title.

HOLMES, Walter Herbert Greame.
Memories of the supernatural in east and west London and Oxford, A.R. Mowbray & co. limited; New York, Morehouse Gorham co. [1941] 160 p. 19cm. "First published in 1941." A42
1. Psychology, Religious. 2. India—Religion. I. Title.

HOPKINS, Pryns, 1885- 201
From gods to dictators; psychology of religions and their totalitarian substitutes, by Pryns Hopkins ... Girard, Kan., Haldeman-Julius publications [c1944] 168 p. illus. 23 cm. [BL53.H568] 45-1792
1. Psychology, Religious. 2. Religious. 3. Totalitarianism. I. Title.

HOPKINS, Pryns, 1885- 201.6
The social psychology of religious experience. New York, Paine-Whitman, 1962. 135 p. illus. 24 cm. [BL53.H569] 62-18494
1. Psychology, Religious. I. Title.

HORTON, Walter Marshall, 201
1895-
A psychological approach to theology [by] Walter Marshall Horton ... New York and London, Harper & brothers, 1931. xii p., 1 l., 279 p. 20 cm. (Half-title: Living issues in religion, ed. by M. H. Krumbine) "First edition." [BL53.H57] 31-19632

1. Psychology, Religious. 2. Theology, Doctrinal. I. Title.

HOSTIE, Raymond, 1920- 201.6
Religion and the psychology of Jung. Translated by G. R. Lamb. New York, Sheed & Ward [1957] 249p. 21cm. Translation of Analytische psychologie en godsdienst. Includes bibliography. [BL53.H583] 57-6049
1. Jung, Carl Gustav, 1875- 2. Psychology, Religious. I. Title.

HOWLAND, Elihu S. 200'.1'9
Speak through the earthquake: religious faith and emotional crisis [by] Elihu S. Howland. Philadelphia, Pilgrim Press [1972] 125 p. 22 cm. Includes bibliographical references. [BL53.H65] 79-185180 ISBN 0-8298-0229-0 4.95
1. Psychology, Religious. I. Title.

HOWLEY, John F. Whittington, 1866- 201
Psychology and mystical experience, by John Howley ... London, K. Paul, Trench, Trubner & co., ltd.; St. Louis, Mo., B. Herder book company, 1920. 6 p. l, 275, [1] p. 23 cm. Bibliographical foot-notes. [BR110.H6] SG 21
1. Psychology, Religious. I. Title.

HUGHES, Thomas Hywel, 1875- 201
Psychology and religious origins, by Thomas Hywel Hughes... New York, C. Scribner's sons, 1937. 242 p. 19 cm. [Studies in theology series, ed. by A. W. Harrison] Bibliography: p. 236-240. [BL53.H73] 38-15269
1. Psychology, Religious. 2. Religion, Primitive. I. Title.

THE idea of the holy,
an inquiry into the non-rational factor in the idea of the divine and its relation to the rational; translated by John W. Harvey. 2d ed. London, New York, Oxford University Press [1957] xix, 232p. 22cm.
1. Psychology, Religious. I. Otto, Rudolf, 1869-1937.

THE idea of the holy,
an inquiry into the non-rational factor in the idea of the divine and ts relation to the rational; translated by John W. Harvey. 2d ed. London, New York, Oxford University Press [1957] xix, 232p. 22cm.
1. Psychology, Religious. I. Otto, Rudolf, 1869-1937.

JACKS, Lawrence Pearsall, 1860- 201
Religious perplexities, by L. P. Jacks ... New York, George H. Doran company [1923] 5 p. l., 9-92 20 cm. "The substance of this little book was delivered in the forms of two lectures given at the invitation of the Hibbert trustees in Manchester, Liverpool, Leeds and Birmingham during March and April, 1922."-- Foreword. [BR110.J2 1923 a] 23-9473
1. Psychology. Religious. 2. Christianity—Apologetic works—20th cent. I. Title. II. Title: Perplexities, Religious.

JOHNSON, Paul Emanuel, 1898- 201.6
Psychology of religion. Rev. and enl. New York, Abingdon Press [1959] 304p. 24cm. Includes bibliography. [BL53.J56 1959] 59-8198
1. Psychology, Religious. I. Title.

JOHNSON, Paul Emanuel, 1898- 201
Psychology of religion [by] Paul E. Johnson ... New York, Nashville, Abingdon-Cokesbury press [1945] 288 p. 20 cm. Bibliography: p. 273-280. [BL53.J56] 45-8728
1. Psychology, Religious. I. Title.

JONES, Rufus Matthew, 1863- 201
Social law in the spiritual world; studies in human and divine inter-relationship, by Rufus M. Jones ... Philadelphia, Chicago [etc.] The John C. Winston co. [1904] 272 p. diagrs. 21 cm. Contents.--Introduction.--The quest.--The meaning of personality.--The realization of persons.--Self-sacrifice.--The subconscious life.--The testimony of mysticism.--The inner light.--The test of spiritual guidance.--Faith as a pathway to reality.--The self and the over-self.--The divine-human life. [BL53.J6 1904] 4-31294
1. Psychology, Religious. 2. Religion. I. Title.

JOSEY, Charles Conant, 1893- 201
The psychology of religion, by Charles Conant Josey New York, The Macmillan company, 1927. xi p., 1 l., 362 p. 20 cm. "References for further reading" at end of most of the chapters. [BL53.J65] 27-10944
1. Psychology, Religious. I. Title.

JUNG, Carl Gustav 201
Psychology and religion. New Haven, [Conn.,] Yale University Press [1960, c.1938] 131 p. Bibl. notes: p.[115]-131. 21 cm. (Yale paperbound Y-14) pap., .90
1. Psychology, Religious. 2. Symbolism. I. Title.

JUNG, Carl Gustav, 1875- 201
Psychology and religion, by Carl Gustav Jung ... New Haven, Yale university press; London, H. Milford, Oxford university press, 1938. 3 p. l., 131 p. 21 cm. (Half-title: The Terry lectures) "Notes": p. [115]-131. Contents.--The autonomy of the unconscious mind.--Dogma and natural symbols.--The history and psychology of a natural symbol. [BL53.J8] 38-27254
1. Psychology, Religious. 2. Symbolism. I. Title.

JUNG, Carl Gustav, 1875-1961. 133.4
Psychology and alchemy. Translated by R. F. C. Hull. 2d ed. completely rev. [Princeton, N.J.] Princeton University Press [1968] xxxiv, 581 p. 270 illus. 24 cm. (His Collected works, v. 12) (Bollingen series, 20.) Bibliography: p. 487-523. Bibliographical footnotes. [BF23.J763 1953 vol. 12] 76-167 7.50
1. Psychology, Religious. 2. Alchemy. 3. Dreams. 4. Symbolism (Psychology) I. Title. II. Series: Bollingen series, 20

JUNG, Carl Gustav, 1875-1961. 201.6
Psychology and religion. New Haven, Yale University Press [1962, c1938] 131 p. 21 cm. "Based on the Terry lectures delivered [in 1937] at Yale University." Bibliographical references included in "Notes" (p. [115]-131) [[BL53]] A 63
1. Psychology, Religious. 2. Symbolism. I. Title.

JUNG, Carl Gustav, 1875-1961. 200'.19
Psychology and religion: West and East. Translated by R. F. C. Hull. 2d ed. [Princeton, N.J.] Princeton University Press [1969] xiii, 699 p. illus. 24 cm. (His Collected works, v. 11) (Bollingen series, 20.) Translation of Zur Psychologie westlicher und ostlicher Religion. Bibliography: p. [609]-640. [BL53.J8413 1969] 74-13858 12.50
1. Psychology, Religious. I. Title. II. Series.

KAO, Charles C. L., 1932- 200'.1'9
Psychological and religious development : maturity and maturation / Charles C.L. Kao. Washington, D.C. : University Press of America, c1981. p. cm. Includes index. Bibliography: p. [BL53.K28] 19 80-5852 ISBN 0-8191-1759-5 : 22.25 ISBN 0-8191-1760-9 (pbk.) : 12.75
1. Psychology, Religious. 2. Developmental psychology. 3. Maturation (Psychology). I. Title.

KEYSER, Leander Sylvester, 1856- 201
A handbook of Christian psychology, by Leander S. Keyser ... Burlington, Ia., The Lutheran literary board, 1928. 169 p. 20 cm. "First published as a brochure and only in outline form."--Pref. to "second edition". Bibliography: p. 157-163. [BL53.K4] 28-20335
1. Psychology, Religion. I. Title. II. Title: Christian psychology.

KING, Irving.
The development of religion; a study in anthropology and social psychology, by Irving King ... New York, The Macmillan company, 1910. xxiii, 371 p. 21 cm. Bibliography: p. 355-361. 10-5028 1.75.
I. Title.

KUPKY, Oskar. 201
The religious development of adolescents, based upon their literary productions, by Oskar Kupky ... authorized translation with a preface by Wm. Clark Trow. New York, The Macmillan company, 1928. vii p., 1 l., 138 p. 20 cm. Bibliography: p. 132-138. [BL53.K8] 28-6821
1. Psychology, Religious. 2. Adolescence. I. Trow, William Clark, 1894- tr. II. Title.

LEE, Roy Stuart. 201
Freud and Christianity. New York, A. A. Wyn, 1949. 204 p. 20 cm. "For further reading": p. [11]-12. [BL53.L3] 49-4504
1. Psychology, Religious. 2. Psychoanalysis. I. Freud, Sigmund, 1856-1939. II. Title.

LEE, Roy Stuart.
Psychology and worship. New York, Philosophical Library, 1956. 110p. (Burroughs Memorial Lectures, 1953)
1. Psychology, Religious. 2. Worship. I. Title. II. Series: Burroughs memorial lectures, Leeds University, 1953

LEUBA, James Henry, 1868- 201
God or man? A study of the value of God to man, by James H. Leuba ... New York, H. Holt and company [c1933] xii, 338 p. 21 cm. [BL53.L38] 33-34982
1. Psychology, Religious. 2. God. I. Title.

†LEUBA, James Henry, 1868-1946. 200'.1'9
The psychological origin and the nature of religion / by James H. Leuba. Folcroft, Pa. : Folcroft Library Editions, 1978. 94 p. ; 23 cm. Reprint of the 1909 ed. published by A. Constable, London, which was issued in the series: Religions, ancient and modern. Includes bibliographical references. [BL85.L48 1978] 78-1577 ISBN 0-8414-5837-5 lib. bdg. : 12.50
1. Psychology, Religions. 2. Magic. I. Title.

LEUBA, James Henry, 1868-1946. 200'.19
A psychological study of religion, its origin, function, and future. New York, AMS Press [1969] xiv, 371 p. 23 cm. Reprint of the 1912 ed. "The author's publications on the psychology of religion": p. 361-362. [BL53.L4 1969] 75-98628
1. Psychology, Religious. 2. Religion—Philosophy. I. Title.

LEYS, Wayne Albert Risser. 201
The religious control of emotion, by Wayne Leys, PH. D. New York, R. Long & R. R. Smith, inc., 1932. x, 229 p. diagrs. 19 1/2 cm. "Selected bibliography": p. 219-222 [BL53.L44] 32-4877
1. Psychology, Religious. 2. Emotions. 3. Control (Psychology) I. Title.

LINK, Henry Charles, 1889- 201
The return to religion, by Henry C. Link ... New York, The Macmillan company, 1936. 5 p. l., 3-181 p. 21 cm. [BL53.L5] 36-8628
1. Psychology, Religious. 2. Personality. 3. Psychology, Applied. 4. Christianity—Apologetic works—20th cent. I. Title.

LINK, Henry Charles, 1889- 201
The return to religion, by Henry C. Link, PH. D. New York, The Macmillan company, 1937. 5 p. l., 3-181 p. 21 cm. "Published March, 1936 ... eighteenth printing, February, 1937." [BL53.L5 1937 a] 37-3813
1. Psychology, Religious. 2. Personality. 3. Psychology, Applied. 4. Apologetics. I. Title.

LINK, Henry Charles, 1889-1952. 239'.09'04
The return to religion / by Henry C. Link. Folcroft, Pa. : Folcroft Library Editions, 1977 [c1936] 181 p. ; 23 cm. Reprint of the ed. published by Macmillan, New York. [BL53.L5 1977] 77-17291 ISBN 0-8414-5846-4 lib. bdg. : 12.50
1. Psychology, Religious. 2. Personality. 3. Psychology, Applied. 4. Apologetics—20th century. I. Title.

LODER, James Edwin 201.9
Religious pathology and Christian faith. Philadelphia, Westminster [c.1966] 255p. 21cm. Bibl. [BR110.L62] 66-11918 5.00
1. Psychology, Religious. I. Title.

LODER, James Edwin.
Religious pathology and Christian faith, by James E. Loder. Philadelphia, Westminster Press [1966] 255 p. 21 cm. Bibliographical references included in "Notes" (p. 231-247)
1. Psychology, Religious. I. Title.

LOFLAND, John. 299.57
Doomsday Cult; a study of conversion, proselytization, and maintenance of faith. Englewood Cliffs, N.J., Prentice-Hall [1966] x, 276 p. 22 cm. Bibliographical footnotes. [BL53.L6] 66-19893
1. Psychology, Religious. 2. Religion and sociology. I. Title.

LOFLAND, John. 299
Doomsday Cult : a study of conversion, proselytization, and maintenance of faith / John Lofland. Enl. ed. New York : Irvington Publishers : distributed by Halsted Press, c1977. p. cm. Includes index. Bibliography: p. [BL53.L6 1977] 77-23028 ISBN 0-470-99249-2 : 15.95
1. Psychology, Religious. 2. Religion and sociology. I. Title.

LOFLAND, John. 299
Doomsday cult : a study of conversion, proselytization, and maintenance of faith / John Lofland. Enl. ed. New York : Irvington Publishers, [1980] c1977. p. cm. Includes index. Bibliography: p. [BL53.L6 1980] 80-16426 ISBN 0-8290-0095-X pbk. : 8.95
1. Psychology, Religious. 2. Religion and sociology. I. Title.

MCCOMAS, Henry Clay, 1875 200'.19
The psychology of religious sects; a comparison of types, by Henry C. McComas. New York, F. H. Revell Co. [New York, AMS Press, 1973] 235 p. 23 cm. Reprint of the 1912 ed. [BL53.M3 1973] 70-172763 ISBN 0-404-04107-8 10.00
1. Psychology, Religious. 2. Sects. I. Title.

MCCOMAS, Henry Clay, 1875- 201
The psychology of religious sects; a compromise of types, by Henry C. McComas ... New York, Chicago [etc.] Fleming H. Revell company [1912] 235 p. 21 cm. [BL53.M3] 13-1166
1. Psychology, Religious. 2. Sects. Religious sects, Psychology of. I. Title. II. Title: Religious sects, Psychology of III. Title: Religious sects, Psychology of

MACGREGOR, Geddes 201.9
God beyond doubt; an essay in the philosophy of religion. Philadelphia, Lippincott [c.1966] 240p. 21cm. Bibl. [BR110.M2] 66-16660 3.95
1. Psychology, Religious. I. Title.

MCKERROW, James Clark, 1888- 201
An introduction to pneumatology, by James Clark McKerrow, M.B. London, New York [etc.] Longmans, Green and co., 1932. 3 p. l., 178, [1] p. 20 1/2 cm. [BL53.M35] 32-22678
1. Psychology, Religious. 2. Experience (Religion) 3. Spiritual life. I. Title. II. Title: Pneumatology, An introduction to.

MCLAUGHLIN, Barry 271.069
Nature, grace, and religious development. Westminster, Md., Newman [c.]1964. ix, 164p. 22cm. 63-12253 3.95
1. Psychology, Religious. 2. Spiritual life—Catholic authors. I. Title.

MCLAUGHLIN, Barry. 271.069
Nature, grace, and religious development. Glen Rock, N. J., Paulist [1968,c.1964] ix, 164p. 18cm. (Deus bks.) [BR110M33] 1.45 pap.,
1. Psychology, Religious. 2. Spiritual life—Catholic authors. I. Title.

MAHONEY, Carl K. 201
The religious mind; a psychological study of religious experience, by C. K. Mahoney ... New York, The Macmillan company, 1927. xxii p., 1 l., 214 p. 19 1/2 cm. Bibliography: p. 207-210. [BR110.M28] 27-18637
1. Psychology, Religious. I. Title.

MARTIN, Everett Dean, 1880- 201
The mystery of religion, a study in social psychology, by Everett Dean Martin ... New York and London, Harper & brothers, 1924. xii p., 1 l., 391 p. 22 cm. [BL53.M37] 24-13283
1. Psychology, Religious. 2. Social psychology. I. Title.

MASLOW, Abraham Harold. 201.6
Religions, values, and peak-experiences, by Abraham H. Maslow. Columbus, Ohio State University Press [1964] xx, 123 p. 21 cm. ([The Kappa Delta Pi lecture series])

Bibliography: p. 117-123. [BL53.M38] 64-23886
1. Psychology, Religious. 2. Experience (Religion) I. Title. II. Series.

MATTHEWS, Walter Robert, 1881- 201
The psychological approach to religion, by the Rev. W. R. Matthews ... London, New York [etc.] Longmans, Green and co., 1925. 3 p. l., 73, [1] p. 18 cm. (Half-title: The Liverpool diocesan board of divinity publications, 1924) $1.00 [BL53.M4] 25-5221
1. Psychology. Religious. I. Title.

MAY, Rollo. 201
The springs of creative living; a study of human nature and God, by Rollo May ... New York, Nashville, Abingdon-cookesbury press [c1940] 271 p. 20 1/2 cm. Includes bibliographies. [BL58.M43] 41-934
1. Psychology, Religious. I. Title.

MEISSNER, William W. 234.1
Foundations for a psychology of grace, by William W. Meissner. Glen Rock, N.J., Paulist [1966] vii, 246p. 21cm. Includes selections from the works of William James, others. Bibl. [BT761.2.M4] 66-24896 2.95 pap.,
1. Psychology, Religious. 2. Grace (Theology) I. Title.

MONROE, Harriet (Earhart) Mrs. 1842-
Twice-born men in America; or, The psychology of conversion as seen by a Christian psychologist in rescue mission work, by Harriet Earhart Monroe ... Philadelphia, Pa., The Lutheran publication society [c1914] vi, 7-118 p. front., plates. 20 cm. 14-20374 0.75
I. Title.

MORENO, Antonio, 1918- 200'.19
Jung, gods, & modern man. Notre Dame [Ind.] University of Notre Dame Press [1970] xiii, 274 p. 24 cm. Bibliography: p. 265-269. [BL53.M64] 73-122047 7.95
1. Jung, Carl Gustav, 1875-1961. 2. Nietzsche, Friedrich Wilhelm, 1844-1900. 3. Psychology, Religious. I. Title.

MUDGE, Evlyn Leigh, 1879- 201
The God-experience; a study in the psychology of religion, by E. Leigh Mudge ... Cincinnati, Printed for the author by the Caxton press [c1923] 88 p. 23 cm. [BL53.M77] 24-744
1. Psychology, Religious. I. Title.

MURPHY, Edward Francis, 1892- 201
New psychology and old religion, by Edward F. Murphy ... foreword by Rev. Fulton J. Sheen ... New York, Cincinnati [etc.] Benziger brothers, 1933. xiii, 265 p. 23 cm. [BL53.M9] 34-2165
1. Psychology, Religious. I. Title.

NAGLE, Urban, brother, 1905- 201
... An empirical study of the development of religious thinking in boys from twelve to sixteen years old [by] Urban Nagle ... Washington, D. C., The Catholic university of America, c1934. 126 p. diagrs. 23 cm. At head of title: The Catholic university of America. Thesis (PH. D.)--The Catholic university of America, 1934. [Secular name: Edward John Nagle] Bibliography: p. 115-124. [BL53.N3 1934] 34-40700
1. Psychology, Religious. 2. Boys. 3. Adolescence. 4. Youth—Religious life. I. Title. II. Title: Religious thinking in boys.

NORTHRIDGE, William Lovell, 1886- 258
Health for mind and spirit [by] W. L. Northridge. New York, Cincinnati [etc.] The Abingdon press [c1938] 200 p. 20 cm. London edition (The Epworth press) has title: Psychology and pastoral practice. Bibliography at end of some of the chapters. [BV4012.N6 1938a] 39-9779
1. Psychology, Religious. 2. Theology, Pastoral. 3. Psychology, Pathological. I. Title.

OATES, Wayne Edward, 1917- 200'.1
The psychology of religion, by Wayne E. Oates. Waco, Tex., Word Books [1973] 291 p. 24 cm. Includes bibliographical references. [BL53.O29] 73-77951 7.95
1. Psychology, Religious. I. Title.

OATES, Wayne Edward, 1917- 201.6
What psychology says about religion. New York, Association Press [1958] 128p. 16cm. (An Association Press reflection book) Includes bibliography. [BL53.O33] 58-11533
1. Psychology, Religious. I. Title.

OATES, Wayne Edward, 1917- 253.5
When religion gets sick, by Wayne E. Oates. Philadelphia, Westminster Press [1970] 199 p. 19 cm. [BL53.O334] 76-114727 2.95
1. Psychology, Religious. I. Title.

ODEN, Thomas C. 200'.19
The structure of awareness [by] Thomas C. Oden. Nashville, Abingdon Press [1969] 283 p. 24 cm. Bibliographical footnotes. [BL53.O35] 75-84711 6.50
1. Psychology, Religious. 2. Phenomenology. 3. Philosophical anthropology. I. Title.

O'DOHERTY, Eamonn Feichin. 137
Religion and personality problems by E. F. O'Doherty. Staten Island, N.Y., Alba House [1964] 240 p. 22 cm. (Mental health series, 2) Title on three pages. [BV4012.O32] 64-15373
1. Psychology, Religious. I. Title.

OLT, Russell, 1895- 201.6
An approach to the psychology of religion. Boston, Christopher Pub. House [c1956] 183p. 21cm. [BL53.O44] 56-13760
1. Psychology, Religious. I. Title.

OSTOW, Mortimer. 201.6
The need to believe; the psychology of religion, by Mortimer Ostow and Ben-Ami Scharfstein. New York, International Universities Press [1954] 162p. 23cm. [BL53.O8] 54-8070
1. Psychology, Religious. I. Scharfstein, Ben-Ami, 1919- joint author. II. Title.

OWENS, Claire Myers. 920.7
Awakening to the good--psychological or religious? An autobiographical inquiry. Boston, Christopher Pub. House [1958] 273p. illus: 21cm. Includes bibliography. [CT275.O87A3] 58-6719
I. Title.

PANZARELLA, Andrew. 200'.1'9
Religion and human experience / by Andrew Panzarella. Winona, Minn. : St. Mary's College Press, [1974] 109, [1] p. : ill. ; 21 cm. Bibliography: p. 109-[110] [BL53.P2] 73-87024 ISBN 0-88489-058-9 : 3.00
1. Psychology, Religious. I. Title.

*PARKER, William R. 248
Prayer can change your life, by William R. Parker and Elaine St. Johns. New York, Pocket Books [1974, c1957] 253 p. 18 cm. [BV220.P24] 57-6777 ISBN 0-671-78372-6 1.25 (pbk.)
1. Psychology, Religious. I. St. Johns, Elaine, joint author. II. Title.

PEAR, Tom Hatherley, 1886- 201
... Religion and contemporary psychology, delivered before the University of Durham at Armstrong college, Newcastle-upon-Tyne, in November 1936, by T. H. Pear ... London, Oxford university press, H. Milford, 1937. 51, [1] p. 23 cm. (Riddell memorial lectures, 9th ser.) References: p. [50]-51. [BL53.P3] 37-33937
1. Psychology, Religious. 2. Reality. I. Title.
Contents omitted.

PRATT, James Bissett, 1875- 201
The psychology of religious belief, by James Bissett Pratt ... New York, The Macmillan company; London, Macmillan & co., ltd., 1907. xii, 327 p. 20 cm. "A selected bibliography of the psychology of religion": p. 310-319. [BL53.P7] 7-4164
1. Psychology, Religious. 2. Faith. 3. Mysticism—Psychology. I. Title.

PRATT, James Bissett, 1875- 201
The religious consciousness; a psychological study, by James Bissett Pratt ... New York, The Macmillan company, 1920. viii p., 1 l., 488 p. 22 cm. Reprinted in part from various periodicals. Bibliographical foot-notes. [BL53.P8] 20-10634
1. Psychology, Religious. 2. Religion. I. Title.

PRATT, James Bissett, 1875-1944. 200.1'9
The religious consciousness; a psychological study. New York, Hafner Pub. Co., 1971 [c1920] viii, 488 p. 22 cm. "Facsimile of the 1920 edition." Includes bibliographical references. [BL53.P8 1920a] 72-153585
1. Psychology, Religious. 2. Religion. I. Title.

PRUYSER, Paul W. 200'.19
A dynamic psychology of religion [by] Paul W. Pruyser. [1st ed.] New York, Harper & Row [1968] x, 367 p. 25 cm. Bibliographic references included in "Notes" (p. 341-355) [BL53.P82] 68-17589
1. Psychology, Religious. I. Title.

PSYCHOLOGY and religion: West and East. Translated by R. F. C. Hull. [New York] Pantheon Books [c1958] xiii, 699p. front. (His Collected works, v. 11) Bollingen series, 20. Pages 691-699, advertising matter. A collection of Jung's shorter works on religion and psychology.
1. Psychology, Religious. I. Jung, Carl Gustav, 1875- II. Series.

PSYCHOLOGY and worship.
New York, Philosophical Library, 1956. 110p. (Burroughs MemoiralLectures, 1953)
1. Psychology, Religious. 2. Worship. I. Lee, Roy Stuart. II. Series: Burroughs memorial lectures, Leeds University, 1953

PYM, Thomas Wentworth, 1885- 201
Psychology and the Christian life, by T. W. Pym ... New York, George H. Doran company [c1922] xii p., 1 l., 15-175 p. 20 cm. "For further reading": p. 172. [BL53.P85] 23-7115
1. Psychology, Religious. 2. Christian life. I. Title.

RAHN, Carl Leo, 1881- 201
Science and the religious life; a psycho-physiological approach, by Carl Rahn. New Haven, Yale university press; London, H. Milford, Oxford university press, 1928. vii p., 1 l. 221 p. 25 cm. [BL53.R25] 28-10719
1. Phychology, Religious. 2. Religion and science—1900. I. Title.

RAUPERT, John Godfrey Ferdinand, 1858-1929. 236
Human destiny and the new psychology, by J. Godfrey Raupert ... Philadelphia, Peter Reilly, 1921. 5 p. l., 138 p. 19 cm. [BT821.R3] 21-18680
I. Title.

RAYMOND, George Lansing, 1839- 201
The psychology of inspiration; an attempt to distinguish religious from scientific truth and to harmonize Christianity with modern thought, by George Lansing Raymond ... New York and London, Funk and Wagnalls company, 1923. 7 p. l., [xi]-xix, 340 p. 20 cm. "Revised edition." [BL53.R3 1923] 23-16275
1. Psychology, Religious. 2. Inspiration. I. Title.

RAYMOND, George Lansing, 1839-1929. 201
The psychology of inspiration; an attempt to distinguish religious from scientific truth and to harmonize Christianity with modern thought, by George Lansing Raymond. New York and London, Funk and Wagnalls company, 1908. xix, 340 p. 21 cm. [BL53.R3] 8-794
1. Psychology, Religious. 2. Inspiration. I. Title.

REDDING, David A. 200'.19
The couch and the altar [by] David A. Redding. [1st ed.] Philadelphia, Lippincott [1968] 125 p. 21 cm. Bibliographical references included in "Notes" (p. [123]-125) [BL53.R35] 68-29729 3.95
1. Psychology, Religious. I. Title.

REIK, Theodor, 1888- 201
Dogma and compulsion psychoanalytic studies of religion and myths. [Translated by Bernard Miall] New York, International Universities Press [1951] 332 p. 23 cm. Bibliographical footnotes. [BL53.R37] 51-10993
1. Psychology, Religious. 2. Dogma. 3. Authority (Religion) 4. Bible — Psychology. I. Title.

REIK, Theodor, 1888- 291
The psychological problems of religion ... By Theodor Reik ... New York, Farrar, Straus and company, inc., 1946- v. 22 1/2 cm. Bibliographical foot-notes. [BL53.R4] 46-8632
1. Psychology, Religious. I. Bryan, Douglas, tr. II. Title.
Contents omitted.

REIK, Theodor, 1888-1969. 201'.1
Dogma and compulsion; psychoanalytic studies of religion and myths. Westport, Conn., Greenwood Press [1973, c1951] 332 p. 22 cm. Includes bibliographical references. [BL53.R37 1973] 72-9369 ISBN 0-8371-6577-6
1. Bible—Psychology. 2. Psychology, Religious. 3. Dogma. 4. Sphinxes. I. Title.

THE return to religion.
New York, Macmillan, 1956. 181p. 20cm.
1. Psychology, Religious. 2. Personality. 3. Psychology, Applied. 4. Apologetics. I. Link, Henry Charles, 1889-

RICE, William Francis, 1871- 201
The psychology of the Christian life [by] William Francis Rice ... Chicago, Ill., Blessing book stores, inc. [c1937] 2 p. l., [iii]-vi p., 1 l., 220 p. diagrs. 22 cm. Bibliography: p. [169]-177. [BR110.R5] 37-20459
1. Psychology, Religious. 2. Christian life. 3. Character. 4. Conduct of life. I. Title.

RITUAL; psycho-analytic studies. With a preface by Sigm. Freud. Translated from the 2d German edition by Douglas Bryan. New York, International Universities Press [1958] 367p. Bibliographical footnotes.
1. Psychology, Religious. 2. Rites and ceremonies. I. Reik, Theodor, 1888-

RONALDSON, Agnes Sutherland. 155.2
The spiritual dimension of personality. Philadelphia, Westminster Press [1965] 156 p. 21 cm. Bibliography: p. [143]-148. [BR110.R6] 65-20339
1. Psychology, Religious. I. Title.

RUDIN, Josef. 200'.19
Psychotherapy and religion. Translated by Elisabeth Reinecke and Paul C. Bailey. Notre Dame [Ind.] University of Notre Dame Press [1968] xiii, 244 p. 22 cm. Bibliographical footnotes. [BL53.R813] 68-12291 5.95
1. Psychology, Religious. 2. Psychotherapy. I. Title.

SANDWEISS, Samuel H. 294.5'6'2
Sai Baba, the holy man ... and the psychiatrist / Samuel H. Sandweiss. San Diego, Calif. : Birth Day Pub. Co., c1975. 240 p. : ill. ; 23 cm. Includes bibliographical references. [BL1175.S385S26] 75-28784 4.25
1. Sathya Sai Baba, 1926- 2. Psychology, Religious. I. Title.

SARGANT, William Walters. 291.4'2
The mind possessed; a physiology of possession, mysticism, and faith healing [by] William Sargant. Philadelphia, Lippincott, 1974 [c1973] xii, 212 p. illus. 22 cm. Bibliography: p. [200]-203. [BL53.S27 1974] 73-15627 ISBN 0-397-01011-7 7.95
1. Psychology, Religious. 2. Spirit possession. 3. Demoniac possession. I. Title.

SARGANT, William Walters. 291.4'2
The mind possessed; a physiology of possession, mysticism and faith healing. Baltimore, Penguin Books [1975, c1974] xii, 212 p. illus. 20 cm. Bibliography: p. [200]-203. [BL53.S27 1975] ISBN 0-14-004034-X 2.50 (pbk.)
1. Psychology, Religious. 2. Spirit possession. 3. Demoniac possession. I. Title.
L.C. card number for original ed.: 73-15627

SAUNDERS, Kenneth James, 1883-
Adventures of the Christian soul; being chapters in the psychology of religion, by K. J. Saunders ... with a preface by the Very Rev. W. R. Inge ... Cambridge, University press, 1916. xii p., 1 l., 145, [1] p. 20 cm. A 17
1. Psychology, Religious. I. Title.

SCHNEIDERMAN, Lee, 1925- 291'.01'9
The psychology of myth, folklore, and religion / Lee Schneiderman. Chicago : Nelson-Hall, 1981. p. cm. Includes index. [BL53.S34] 19 81-9471 ISBN 0-88229-363-X : 18.95 ISBN 0-88229-783-X : 8.95
1. Psychology, Religious. 2. Mythology—Psychological aspects. 3. Folk-lore—Psychological apsects. I. Title.

SCOBIE, Geoffrey E. W. 200'.1'9
Psychology of religion / Geoffrey E. W. Scobie. New York : Wiley, 1975. 189 p. ; 23 cm. "A Halsted Press book." Includes index. Bibliography: p. [170]-179. [BL53.S35] 74-21832 ISBN 0-470-76712-X : 8.95
1. Psychology, Religious. I. Title.

SEABURY, David, 1885- 248
How Jesus heals our minds today, by David Seabury. Boston, Little, Brown and company, 1940. xxx, 317 p. 21 cm. "First edition." [BR115.H4S4 1940] 40-32056
1. Jesus Christ—Teachings. 2. Psychology, Religious. 3. Mental physiology and hygiene. I. Title.

SEARS, Annie Lyman. 201
The drama of the spiritual life; a study of religious experience and ideals, by Annie Lyman Sears ... New York, The Macmillan company, 1915. xxiv p., 1 l., 495 p. 23 cm. [BL53.S4] 15-16210
1. Psychology, Religious. 2. Spiritual life. 3. Experience (Religion) I. Title.

SELBIE, William Boothby, 1862- 201
The psychology of religion, by W. B. Selbie... Oxford, The Clarendon press, 1924. xii, 310 p. 23 cm. [Oxford handbooks of theology. I] "The substance of two courses of lectures delivered under the Wilde foundation at Oxford."--p. [vii] [BL53.S45] 25-2167
1. Psychology, Religious. I. Wilde lectures in natural and comparative religion, 1922, 1923. II. Title.

SHELDON, William Herbert, 1899- 201
Psychology and the Promethean will; a constructive study of the acute common problem of education, medicine and religion, by William H. Sheldon ... New York and London, Harper & brothers, 1936. x, 265 p. 21 cm. "First edition." [BL53.S5] 36-8629
1. Psychology, Religious. 2. Will. 3. Happiness. 4. Psychology. I. Title. II. Title: The Promethean will.

SHIPP, Nelson McLester, 1892- 201
Where psychology breaks down (spiritual biology) by Nelson M. Shipp. A "shirt-sleeve" newspaper man in protest against some of the ideas being expressed upon this planet. Critical preface by Dr. Frederick S. Porter ... Columbus, Ga., Gilbert printing co., 1935. 84 p. incl. front. 20 cm. [BR110.S5] 35-8535
1. Psychology, Religious. 2. Psychology, Applied. 3. Faith-cure. I. Title.

SNOWDEN, James Henry, 1852- 201
The psychology of religion, and its application in preaching and teaching, by James H. Snowden ... New York, Chicago [etc.] Fleming H. Revell company [1916] 390 p. 21 cm. "Bibliographical note": p. 379-381. [BL53.S6] 17-1025
1. Psychology, Religious. 2. Preaching. 3. Christian life. I. Title.

SPINKS, George Stephens 200.19
Psychology and religion; an introduction to contemporary voews. by G. Stephens Spinks. Boston. Beacon [1967. c.1963] xv, 221p. 21cm. (BP273) [BL53.S63 1965] 65-23471 2.45 pap.,
1. Psychology, Religious. I. Title.

SPURR, Frederic Chambers, 1862- 201
The new psychology and the Christian faith, by Frederic C. Spurr ... New York, Chicago [etc.] Fleming H. Revell company [c1925] 190 p. 19 1/2 cm. [BR110.S7] 25-20514
1. Psychology, Religious. I. Title.

STARBUCK, Edwin Diller, 1866- 201
The psychology of religion: an empirical study of the growth of religious consciousness , by Edwin Diller Starbuck ... With a preface by William James ... London, W. Scott; New York, C. Scribner's sons, 1901. xx, 423 p. incl. tables, diagrs. 19 cm. (Half-title: The Contemporary science series. Ed. by H. Ellis) [BL53.S65 1901] 2-5200
1. Psychology, Religious. 2. Conversion. 3. Adolescence. 4. Experience (Religion) I. Title.

STARBUCK, Edwin Diller, 1866- 201
The psychology of religion: an empirical study of the growth of religious consciousness, by Edwin Diller Starbuck ... Preface by William James ... 3d ed. London, The Walter Scott publishing co., ltd.; New York, C. Scribner's sons, 1911. xx, 423 p. diagrs. 19 cm. (Half-title: The contemporary science series) [BL53.S65 1911] 12-16917
1. Psychology, Religious. I. Title.

STEVENS, Samuel Nowell. 201
... Religion in life adjustments [by] Samuel Nowell Stevens ... New York, Cincinnati [etc.] The Abingdon press [c1930] 147 p. 21 cm. (The Abingdon religious education monographs) Bibliography: p. 146-147. [BL53.S68] 30-29288
1. Psychology, Religious. I. Title.

STOLZ, Karl Ruf, 1884- 201
The psychology of religious living, by Karl R. Stolz--- Nashville, Cokesbury press [c1937] 375 p. 22 cm. Bibliography: p. 357-368. [BL53.S686] 37-22093
1. Psychology, Religious. 2. Personality. I. Title.

STRICKLAND, Francis Lorette, 1871- 201
Psychology of religious experience; studies in the psychological interpretation of religious faith, by Francis L. Strickland ... New York, Cincinnati, The Abingdon press [c1924] 320 p. 21 1/2 cm. [BL53.S75] 24-19433
1. Psychology, Religious. 2. Faith. 3. Experience (Religion) I. Title.

STRUNK, Orlo. 201.6
Mature religion; a psychological study [by] Orlo Strunk, Jr. New York, Abingdon Press [1965] 160 p. 20 cm. Includes bibliographical references. [BR110.S77] 65-15235
1. Psychology, Religious. I. Title.

STRUNK, Orlo, comp. 200'.19
The psychology of religion; historical and interpretative readings. Nashville, Abingdon Press [1971] 152 p. 23 cm. (Apex books) "A revision and enlargement of part I of [the editor's] Readings in the psychology of religion." Bibliography: p. 135-144. [BL53.S763] 77-158672 ISBN 0-687-34862-5
1. Psychology, Religious. I. Title.

STRUNK, Orlo, ed. 201.6
Readings in the psychology of religion. Nashville, Abingdon Press [1959] 288 p. 24 cm. Includes bibliography. [BL53.S76] 59-12787
1. Psychology, Religious. I. Title. II. Title: Psychology of religion.

STRUNK, Orlo. 201.6
Religion, a psychological interpretation. New York, Abingdon Press [1962] 128 p. 20 cm Includes bibliography. [BL53.S77] 62-9386
1. Psychology, Religious. I. Title.

STRUNK, Orlo 201.6
Religion, a psychological interpretation. Nashville, Abingdon [c.1962] 128p. 20cm. Bibl. 62-9386 2.50
1. Psychology, Religious. I. Title.

SYMINGTON, Thomas Alexander, 1883- 218
Religious liberals and conservatives; a comparison of those who are liberal in their religious thinking and those who are conservative, by Thomas A. Symington. New York, Bureau of Publications, Teachers College, Columbia University, 1935. [New York, AMS Press, 1972, ie 1973] v, 104 p. 22 cm. Reprint of the 1935 ed., issued in series: Teachers College, Columbia University. Contributions to education, no. 640. Originally presented as the author's thesis, Columbia. Bibliography: p. 76-77. [BR1615.S9 1972] 70-177727 ISBN 0-404-55640-X 10.00
1. Psychology, Religious. 2. Attitude (Psychology) 3. Liberalism (Religion) 4. Religious education. I. Title. II. Series: Columbia University. Teachers College. Contributions to education, no. 640.

SYMINGTON, Thomas Alexander, 1883- 201
Religious liberals and conservatives; a comparison of those who are liberal in their religious thinking and those who are conservative, by Thomas A. Symington... New York city, Teachers college, Columbia university, 1935. v, 104 p. 23 1/2 cm. (Teachers college. Columbia university. Contributions to education. no. 640) Issued also as thesis (PH.D.) Columbia university. Bibliography: p. 76-77. [BR1615.S9 1935a] [LB5. C8 no. 640] 35-14700
1. Psychology, Religious. 2. Attitude (Psychology) 3. Liberalism (Religion) 4. Religious education. I. Title. II. Title: Conservatives.

TENNEY, Edward Vernon.
An outline for the study of the meaning, and the origin and development of the religious experience. [Fresno? Calif,] 1956. 105 l. 30 cm. Mimeographed. Bibliography: l. 98-105. 65-62302
1. Psychology, Religious. 2. Mysticism. I. Title. II. Title: The religious experience.

THOULESS, Robert Henry, 1894- 201
Authority and freedom; some psychological problems of religious belief. Greenwich, Conn., Seabury Press [1954] 124p. 19cm. (The Hulsean lectures delivered at the University of Cambridge, 1952) [BL53] 55-14293
1. Psychology, Religious. 2. Authority (Religion) 3. Religious though—Gt. Brit. I. Title.

THOULESS, Robert Henry, 1894- 201.6
An introduction to the psychology of religion. [New York] Cambridge [c.]1961. 286p. 61-16140 1.75 pap.,
1. Psychology, Religious. I. Title.

THOULESS, Robert Henry, 1894-
An introduction to the psychology of religion. Second edition. Cambridge, At the University Press, 1956. vii, 286 p. 19 cm.
I. Title.

THOULESS, Robert Henry, 1894- 201.6
An introduction to the psychology of religion. [1st paperback ed.] Cambridge [Eng.] University Press, 1961. 286 p. 19 cm. [BL53.T5 1961] 61-16140
1. Psychology, Religious. I. Title.

THOULESS, Robert Henry, 1894- 200'.19
An introduction to the psychology of religion [by] Robert H. Thouless. 3rd ed. London, Cambridge University Press, 1971. viii, 152 p. 23 cm. Includes bibliographical references. [BL53.T5 1971] 76-184142 ISBN 0-521-08149-1 ISBN 0-521-09665-0 (pbk) £2.40 ($7.50 U.S.)
1. Psychology, Religious. I. Title.

THOULESS, Robert Henry, 1894- 201
An introduction to the psychology of religion, by Robert H. Thouless... New York, The Macmillan company, 1923. 5 p. l., 286 p. 20 1/2 cm. "Lectures delivered to ordination candidates during the long vacation at Cambridge."--Pref. [BL53.T5 1923] 28-3846
1. Psychology. Religious. I. Title.

TOURNIER, P. 233
To resist or to surrender? Tr. by John S. Gilmour. Richmond, Va., Knox [1967, c.1964] 63p. 19cm. (Chime paperbacks) The German orig. ed. was pub. under title: Sich Durchsetzen order [i.e. oder] Nachgeben [BL53.T663] 1.00 pap.,
1. Psychology, Religious. 2. Christian ethics. 3. Social interaction. I. Title.

TOURNIER, Paul. 201'.9
A place for you; psychology and religion. [1st U.S. ed.] New York, Harper & Row [1968] 224 p. 22 cm. Translation of L'homme et son lieu. Bibliographical footnotes. [BL53.T6563] 68-29559
1. Psychology, Religious. 2. Self. I. Title.

TOURNIER, Paul. 201.6
The seasons of life Translated by John S. Gilmour. Richmond, John Knox Press [1963] 63 p. 21 cm. [BR110.T613] 63-8709
1. Psychology, Religious. 2. Christian life. I. Title.

TOURNIER, Paul. 201
The strong and the weak. Translated by Edwin Hudson. Philadelphia, Westminster Press [1963] 254 p. 23 cm. [BL53.T653] 63-8898
1. Psychology, Religious. I. Title.

TOURNIER, Paul. 233.7
To resist or to surrender? Translated by John S. Gilmour. Richmond, John Knox Press [1964] 63 p. 21 cm. Translation of Tenir tete ou ceder. [BL53.T663] 64-16284
1. Psychology, Religious. 2. Christian ethics. 3. Social interaction. I. Title.

TOURNIER, Paul. 233
The whole person in a broken world. Translated by John and Helen Doberstein. [1st ed.] New York, Harper & Row [1964] 180 p. illus. 22 cm. Translation of Desharmonie de la vie moderne. Bibliography: p. 171-175. [BL53.T643] 64-14377
1. Psychology, Religious. I. Title.

TOURNIER, Paul. 233
The whole person in a broken world / Paul Tournier ; translated by John and Helen Doberstein. San Francisco : Harper & Row, [1981] c1964. p. cm. Translation of Desharmonie de la vie moderne. Includes index. Bibliography: p. [BL53.T643 1981] 19 81-6885 ISBN 0-06-068312-0 pbk. : 6.10
1. Psychology, Religious. I. [Desharmonie de la vie moderne.] English II. Title.

TRANSPERSONAL 200'.1'9
psychologies / edited by Charles T. Tart. 1st ed. New York : Harper & Row, [1975] 502 p. : ill. ; 24 cm. Includes indexes. Bibliography: p. [473]-485. [BL53.T67 1975] 73-18672 ISBN 0-06-067823-2 : 12.50
1. Psychology, Religious. I. Tart, Charles T., 1937-

TRANSPERSONAL 291.4'2
psychologies / edited by Charles T. Tart. London : Routledge and Kegan Paul, 1975. [7], 502 p. : ill. ; 24 cm. Includes indexes. Bibliography: p. [475]-485. [BL53.T67 1975b] 76-373802 ISBN 0-7100-8298-3 : 23.50
1. Psychology, Religious. I. Tart, Charles T., 1937-
Distributed by Routledge and Kegan Paul,Boston.

TRANSPERSONAL 200'.1'9
psychologies / edited by Charles T. Tart. New York : Harper & Row, 1977c1975. 504p. : ill. ; 21 cm. (Harper Colophon Books) Includes index. Bibliography: p. [480]-490. [BL53R67] ISBN 0-06-090486-0 pbk. : 6.95
1. Psychology, Religious. I. Tart, Charles T., 1937-
L.C. card no. for original ed.: 73-18672.

TROUT, David McCamel. 201
Religious behavior; an introduction to the psychological study of religion, by David M. Trout ... New York, The Macmillan company, 1931. xiv, 528 p. 22 1/2 cm. "Selected bibliography": p. 493-509. [BL53.T7] 31-30540
1. Psychology, Religious. 2. Religion. I. Title.

ULANOV, Ann Belford. 200'.19
Religion and the unconscious / by Ann and Barry Ulanov. Philadelphia : Westminster Press, [1975] 287 p. ; 24 cm. Includes bibliographical references and index. [BL53.U45] 75-16302 ISBN 0-664-20799-5 : 10.00
1. Psychology, Religious. 2. Subconsciousness. 3. Ethics. I. Ulanov, Barry, joint author. II. Title.

UMPHREY, Marjorie. 253.5
Why don't I feel ok? / By Marjorie Umphrey & Richard Laird. Irvine, Calif. : Harvest House Publishers, c1977. 160 p. ; 21 cm. Bibliography: p. 160. [BR110.U45] 77-24826 ISBN 0-89081-041-9 : pbk. : 2.95
1. Psychology, Religious. 2. Transactional analysis. I. Laird, Richard, joint author. II. Title.

VALENTINE, Cyril Henry. 201
Modern psychology and the validity of Christian experience, by Cyril H. Valentine ... With a preface by the Rev. Alfred E. Garvie ... London, Society for promoting Christian knowledge; New York and Toronto, The Macmillan co., 1926. xix, 236 p. 23 cm. "Thesis approved for the degree of doctor of philosophy in the University of London." [BR110.V3] 27-6833
1. Psychology, Religious. 2. Christianity. I. Title.

VAN KAAM, Adrian L., 1920- 248
Religion and personality [by] Adrian van Kaam. Englewood Cliffs, N.J., Prentice-Hall [1964] viii, 170 p. 21 cm. Bibliography: p. 161-163. [BX2350.V15] 64-15831
1. Psychology, Religious. 2. Personality. 3. Spiritual life—Catholic authors. I. Title.

VERGOTE, Antoine. 200'.19
The religious man; a psychological study of religious attitudes. Translated by Marie-Bernard Said. Dayton, Ohio, Pflaum Press, 1969. vii, 306 p. 21 cm. Translation of Psychologie religieuse. Bibliographical footnotes. Bibliography: p. 305-306. [BL53.V3813] 70-93006 6.95
1. Psychology, Religious. I. Title.

VETTER, George B. 201
Magic and religion, their psychological nature, origin, and function. New York, Philosophical Library [1958] 555 p. illus. 22 cm. [BL53.V4] 58-59410
1. Psychology, Religious. 2. Magic.

WARNER, Horace Emory. 201
The psychology of the Christian life; a contribution to the scientific study of Christian experience and character, by Horace Emory Warner ... with introduction by John R. Mott, LL.D. New York, Chicago [etc.] Fleming H. Revell company [c1910] 401 p. incl. fold. chart. charts (part fold.) 21 cm. [BR110.W3] 11-717
1. Psychology, Religious. 2. Christian life. I. Title.

WATERHOUSE, Eric Strickland, 201
1879-
Psychology and religion: a series of broadcast talks, by the Rev. E. S. Waterhouse ... New York, R. R. Smith, inc., 1931. 3 p. l., ix-xxii, 232 p. 19 1/2 cm. [BL53.W3] 31-32817
1. Psychology, Religious. I. Title.

WELLS, George Ross, 1884- 201.6
Sense and nonsense in religion [1st ed.] New York, Vantage Press [1962, c1961] 182 p. 21 cm. [BL53.W4] 62-16028
1. Psychology, Religious. 2. Christianity — Essence, genius, nature. I. Title.

WHEELER, Robert Fulton, 1883- 201
A study in the psychology of the spirit, by Robert F. Wheeler ... Boston, R. G. Badger [c1929] 2 p. l., 7-250 p. 21 cm. [BL53.W5] 30-3331
1. Psychology, Religious. 2. Soul. I. Title.

WHITE, Victor 201.6
Soul and psyche; and enquiry into the relationship of psychotherapy and religion. New York, Harper [1960] 312p. Bibl. notes: p.262-308. 22cm. (Edward Cadbury lectures, 1958-1959) 60-11790 5.00
1. Psychology, Religious. 2. Soul. 3. Psychotherapy. 4. Psychoanalysis. I. Title.

WHITE, Victor, 1902-1960 201.6
God and the unconscious. Foreword by C. G. Jung. Cleveland, World Pub. Co. [1961, c.1952] 287p. (Meridian bks., M120) Bibl. 61-15741 1.35 pap.,
1. Jung, Carl Gustav, 1875-1961. 2. Psychology, Religious. I. Title.

WHITE, Victor, 1902-1960. *201.6
God and the unconscious. With a foreword by C. G. Jung, and an appendix by Gebhard Frei. Chicago, H. Regnery Co., 1953. xxv, 277 p. 22 cm. Bibliography: p. 269-273. [[BL53]] 53-5779
1. Jung, Carl Gustav, 1875-1961. 2. Psychology, Religious. I. Title.

WHITE, Victor, 1902- 200'.1'9
1960.
God and the unconscious / by Victor White ; with a foreword by C.G. Jung and an introduction by William Everson. Dallas, Tex. : Spring Publications, 1982, c1952. p. cm. (The Jungian classics series ;) Originally published: London : Harvill Press, 1952. Includes index. [BL53.W52 1982] 19 82-19153 ISBN 0-88214-503-7 pbk. : 13.50
1. Jung, C. G. (Carl Gustav), 1875-1961. 2. Psychology, Religious. I. Title. II. Series.

WIEMAN, Henry Nelson, 201'.9
1884-
Normative psychology of religion, by Henry Nelson Wieman and Regina Westcott-Wieman. Westport, Conn., Greenwood Press [1971] x, 564 p. 23 cm. Reprint of the 1935 ed. Includes bibliographies. [BL53.W55 1971] 70-109876 ISBN 0-8371-4367-5
1. Psychology, Religious. I. Westcott, Regina (Hanson) 1886- joint author. II. Title.

WIEMAN, Henry Nelson, 1884- 201
Normative psychology of religion, by Henry Nelson Wieman and Regina Westcott-Wieman. New York, Thomas Y. Crowell company [c1935] x, 564 p. 22 1/2 cm. "Collateral readings" at end of each chapter. [BL53.W55] 35-16175
1. Psychology, Religious. I. Wieman, Mrs. Regina (Hanson) Westcott, 1886- joint author. II. Title.

WITHERINGTON, Henry Carl. 201.6
Psychology of religion; a Christian interpretation. Grand Rapids, W. B. Eerdmans Pub. Co., 1955. 344p. 22cm. [BL53.W58] 55-13911
1. Psychology, Religious. 2. Christianity—Psychology. I. Title.

WOODBURNE, Angus Stewart. 201
The religious attitude: a psychological study of its differentiation, by Angus Stewart Woodburne: introduction by Shailer Mathews. New York, The Macmillan company, 1927. vi p., 2 l., 353 p. 19 1/2 cm. [BL53.W6] 27-21248
1. Psychology. Religious. 2. Religion. I. Title.

WOODWARD, Luther Ellis, 1897- 218
Relations of religious training and life patterns to the adult religious life; a study of the relative significance of religious training and influence and of certain emotional and behavior patterns for the adult religious life. New York, Bureau of Publications, Teachers College, Columbia University, 1932. [New York, AMS Press, 1973, c1972] v, 75 p. 22 cm. Reprint of the 1932 ed., issued in series: Teachers College, Columbia University. Contributions to education, no. 527. Originally presented as the author's thesis, Columbia. Includes bibliographical references. [BL53.W65 1972] 71-177627 ISBN 0-404-55527-6 10.00
1. Psychology, Religious. 2. Religious education. I. Title. II. Series: Columbia University. Teachers College. Contributions to education, no. 527.

WOODWARD, Luther Ellis, 1897- 201
Relations of religious training and life patterns to the adult religious life: a study of the relative significance of religious training and influence and of certain emotional and behavior patterns for the adult religious life, by Luther Ellis Woodward ... New York city, Teachers college, Columbia university, 1932. v, 75 p. tables (1 fold.) 23 1/2 cm. (Teachers college, Columbia university. Contributions to education, no. 527) Issued also as thesis (PH.D.)--Columbia university. [BL53.W65 1932a] [LB5.C8 no. 527] 32-28925
1. Psychology, Religious. 2. Man—Influence of environment. 3. Religious education. I. Title.

YEAXLEE, Basil Alfred, 1883- 201
Religion and the growing mind. [3d ed.] Greenwich, Conn., seabury Press, 1952. 220 p. 23 cm. [BL53.Y4 1952] 52-12151
1. Psychology, Religious. 2. Child study. 3. Religious education. I. Title.

YELLOWLEES, David. 201
Psychology's defence of the faith, by David Yellowlees ... New York, R. R. Smith, inc. [1930] 190 p. 19 1/2 cm. Printed in Great Britain. "The lectures on which this book is based were delivered at the summer conference of the Student Christian movement at Swanwick, July, 1929."--Pref. [BR110.Y4] 31-30903
1. Psychology, Religious. I. Title.

ZIELINSKI, Stanislaw A. 200'.1'9
Psychology & silence / by Stanislaw Zielinski ; edited by Daniel Bassuk. Wallingford, Pa. : Pendle Hill Publications, 1975. 32 p. : port. ; 19 cm. (Pendle Hill pamphlet ; 201) Contents.Contents.—The role of psychology in religious mysticism.—Silent meeting. [BL53.Z48] 75-7413 ISBN 0-87574-201-7 : 0.95
1. Friends, Society of—Doctrinal and controversial works. 2. Psychology, Religious. 3. Silence. I. Title.

Psychology, Religious—Addresses, essays, lectures.

BEIT-HALLAHMI, Benjamin, 200'.19
comp.
Research in religious behavior: selected readings. Edited by Benjamin Beit-Hallahmi. Monterey, Calif., Brooks/Cole Pub. Co. [1973] x, 404 p. 23 cm. (Core books in psychology series) Includes bibliographies. [BL53.B38] 72-95822 ISBN 0-8185-0091-3 4.50
1. Psychology, Religious—Addresses, essays, lectures. I. Title.
Contents Omitted. Contents Omitted.

BEIT-HALLAHMI, Benjamin, 200'.19
comp.
Research in religious behavior: selected readings. Edited by Benjamin Beit-Hallahmi. Monterey, Calif., Brooks/Cole Pub. Co. [1973] x, 404 p. 23 cm. (Core books in psychology series) Contents.Contents.—Elkind, D. Piaget's semi-clinical interview and the study of spontaneous religion.—Nunn, C. Z. Child-control through a "coalition with God."—Crandall, V. C. and Gozali, J. The social desirability responses of children of four religious-cultural groups.—Ezer, M. The effect of religion upon children's responses to questions involving physical causality.—Allport, G. W. The religious context of prejudice.—Allport, G. W. and Ross, J. M. Personal religious orientation and prejudice.—Rokeach, M. Religion, values, and social compassion.—Stark, R. Age and faith: a changing outlook or an old process.—Shaw, B. W. Religion and conceptual models of behavior.—Nunn, C. Z., Kosa, J., and Alpert, J. J. Causal locus of illness and adaptation to family disruptions.—Lindenthal, J. J., Myers, J. K., Pepper, M. P., and Stern, M. S. Mental status and religious behavior.—Alland, A., Jr. "Possession" in a revivalistic Negro church.—Hine, V. H. Pentecostal glossolalia—toward a functional interpretation.—Allison, J. Adaptive regression and intense religious experiences.—Anderson, C. H. Religious communality and party preference.—Johnson, B. Ascetic Protestantism and political preference.—Marx, G. T. Religion: opiate or inspiration of civil rights militancy among Negroes. Includes bibliographies. [BL53.B38] 72-95822 ISBN 0-8185-0091-3
1. Psychology, Religious—Addresses, essays, lectures. I. Title.

CURRENT perspectives in 200'.1'9
the psychology of religion / edited by H. Newton Malony. Grand Rapids : Eerdmans, c1976. p. cm. Includes indexes. Bibliography: p. [BL53.C79] 76-44493 ISBN 0-8028-1660-6 pbk. : 4.95
1. Psychology, Religious—Addresses, essays, lectures. I. Malony, H. Newton.

DU PREEZ, J. P. 200'.1'9
Psychology and religion : an inaugural lecture given in the University of Fort Hare on the 18th March 1976 / by J. P. du Preez. [Fort Hare, South Africa] : Fort Hare University Press, 1976. 24 p. ; 22 cm. (Fort Hare inaugural lectures ; C. 33) Bibliography: p. 24. [BL53.D86] 77-371609 ISBN 0-949974-32-3
1. Psychology, Religious—Addresses, essays, lectures. I. Title. II. Series.

GODIN, Andre, ed. 200.19
Child and adult before God. Chicago, Loyola [c.]1965. 160p. illus. 24cm. (Loyola pastoral ser.: Lumen vitae studies) Bibl. [BL53.G6] 65-16549 3.50
1. Psychology, Religious—Addresses, essays, lectures. I. Title.

GODIN, Andre, ed. 200.19
Child and adult before God, edited by A. Godin. Chicago, Loyola University Press, 1965. 160 p. illus. 24 cm. (Loyola pastoral series: Lumen vitae studies) Includes bibiolographies. [BL53.G6] 65-16549
1. Psychology, Religious — Addresses, essays, lectures. I. Title.

GROWING edges in the 200'.1'9
psychology of religion / [edited by] John R. Tisdale. Chicago : Nelson-Hall, [1980] p. cm. Includes index. Bibliography: p. [BL53.G784] 79-20116 ISBN 0-88229-338-9 : 22.95 ISBN 0-88229-748-1 pbk. : 11.95
1. Psychology, Religious—Addresses, essays, lectures. I. Tisdale, John R.

HEANEY, John J., comp. 200'.19
Psyche and spirit; readings in psychology and religion, edited by John J. Heaney. New York, Paulist Press [1973] ix, 310 p. 23 cm. Bibliography: p. 305-310. [BL53.H37] 73-83810 ISBN 0-8091-1786-X 5.95 (pbk.)
1. Psychology, Religious—Addresses, essays, lectures. I. Title.

SADLER, William Alan, 200'.19
comp.
Personality and religion; the role of religion in personality development. Edited by William A. Sadler, Jr. [1st U.S. ed.] New York, Harper & Row [1970] 245 p. 21 cm. (Harper forum books, RD 12) Contents.Contents.—Introduction. The scientific study of religion and personality, by W. A. Sadler, Jr.—Religion and the formation of a personal world: The religious dimension of human experience, by D. Lee. Obsessive actions and religious practices, by S. Freud. Thought organization in religion, by P. Pruyser. The religious context of prejudice, by G. W. Allport. The prophet, by M. Weber. Formation of the need to achieve, by D. C. McClelland. Individual and social narcissism, by E. Fromm. Christ, a symbol of the self, by C. G. Jung. Father and son in Christianity and Confucianism, by R. N. Bellah. Religious aspects of peak-experiences, by A. H. Maslow.—The role of religion in existential crises: Religion in times of social distress, by T. F. O'Dea. Crises in personality development, by A. Boisen. Coming to terms with death, by D. Bakan.—Re-evaluating religion in relation to personality development and the personality sciences: Paradoxes of religious belief, by M. Rokeach. The common enemy, by K. Menninger. Includes bibliographical references. [BL53.S23 1970] 74-109076 3.95
1. Psychology, Religious—Addresses, essays, lectures. I. Title.

YUNGBLUT, John R. 200'.1'9
Seeking light in the darkness of the unconscious / John Yungblut. [Wallingford, Pa. : Pendle Hill Publications], 1977. 24 p. ; 19 cm. (Pendle Hill pamphlet ; 211 ISSN 0031-4250s) "Presented March 19, 1976, at Ben Lomond, California, at the first Conference on Psychology and Religion held by Friends on the West Coast." Includes bibliographical references. [BL53.Y86] 77-71933 ISBN 0-87574-211-4 : 0.95
1. Psychology, Religious—Addresses, essays, lectures. I. Title.

Psychology, Religious — Bibliography

CAPPS, Donald. 016.200'1'9
Psychology of religion : a guide to information sources / Donald Capps, Lewis Rambo, and Paul Ransohoff. Detroit : Gale Research Co., [1975] p. cm. (Philosophy and religion information guide series ; v. 1) (Gale information guide library) Includes index. [Z7204.R4C36] 73-17530 ISBN 0-8103-1356-1 : 18.00
1. Psychology, Religious—Bibliography. 2. Religion—Bibliography. 3. Mythology—Bibliography. I. Rambo, Lewis, joint author. II. Ransohoff, Paul, joint author. III. Title.

ELLIS, Charles Calvert, 016.
1874-
The religion of religious psychology, by Charles Calvert Ellis... Los Angeles, Calif., The Biola book room, Bible institute of Los Angeles [c1928] 60 p. 19 1/2 cm. "Revised and enlarged edition." Bibliography: p. 58-60. [Z7204.R4E4] 29-12146
1. Psychology, Religious—Bibl. I. Title.

MEISSNER, William W
Annotated bibliography in religion and psychology. New York, Academy of Religion and Mental Health, 1961. xi, 235 p. 27 cm. 63-680
1. Psychology, Religious — Bibl. 2. Pastoral psychology — Bibl. I. Title.

MEISSNER, William W. 016.612'022
Annotated bibliography in religion and psychology [by] W. W. Meissner. New York, Academy of Religion and Mental Health, 1961. xi, 235 p. 27 cm. [Z7204.R4M4] A 63
1. Psychology, Religious—Bibliography. 2. Pastoral psychology—Bibliography. I. Title.

Psychology, Religious—Case studies.

ROWLAND, Stanley J. 248
Hurt and healing; modern writers speak [by] Stanley J. Rowland, Jr. New York, Friendship Press [1969] 96 p. 19 cm. Includes bibliographies. [BL53.R65] 68-57231 1.50
1. Psychology, Religious—Case studies. I. Title.

Psychology, Religious—Collected works.

BROWN, Laurence Binet, 200'.19
1927- comp.
Psychology and religion: selected readings, edited by L. B. Brown. Harmondsworth, Penguin Education, 1973. 400 p. 20 cm. (Penguin modern psychology readings) (Penguin education) Includes index. Bibliography: p. 383-389. [BL53.B68] 74-158980 ISBN 0-14-080538-9
1. Psychology, Religious—Collected works. I. Title.
Distributed by Penguin, Baltimore, Md., 4.95 (pbk.).

CAPPS, Donald, comp. 200'.19
The religious personality, edited by Donald Capps and Walter H. Capps. Belmont, Calif., Wadsworth Pub. Co. [1970]. 381 p. 23 cm. Includes bibliographies. [BL53.C27] 76-125185
1. Psychology, Religious—Collections. I. Capps, Walter H., joint comp. II. Title.

Psychology, Religious—Congresses.

CATHOLIC University of 271.069
America, Institute of Pastoral Counseling.
Psychological aspects of spiritual development; proceedings of the Insts. of Catholic Pastoral Counseling and of the Confs. for Religious Superiors of Men under the auspices of the director of summer session and workshops, the Catholic Univ. of Amer. Ed. by Michael J. O'Brien, Raymond J. Steimel. Washington, D.C., Catholic Univ. of Amer. Pr. [c.1965] vii, 234p. 22cm. Bibl. [BV4012.C34] 65-12987 3.75 pap.,
1. Psychology, Religious—Congresses. 2. Pastoral psychology—Congresses. 3. Monastic and religious life. I. O'Brien, Michael J., ed. II. Steimel, Raymond J., ed. III. Catholic University of America. Conference for Superiors on the Psychological Aspects of the Religious Life. IV. Title.

HICK, John, ed. 201
Faith and the philosophers. New York, St. Martin's press, 1964. viii, 255 p. 23 cm. "Product of a two day conference...held at the Princeton Theological Seminary, Princeton, New Jersey, in December 1962." Bibliographical footnotes. [BR110.H5] 64-16778
1. Psychology, Religious — Congress. 2. Faith — Psychology. I. Princeton Theological Seminary. II. Title.

Psychology, Religious—History.

HEISIG, James W., 1944- 200'.1'9
Imago Dei : a study of C. G. Jung's psychology of religion / James W. Heisig. Lewisburg [Pa.] : Bucknell University Press, c1978. p. cm. (Studies in Jungian thought) Includes index. Bibliography: p. [BL53.H378] 77-74405 ISBN 0-8387-2076-5 : 16.00
1. Jung, Carl Gustav, 1875-1961. 2. Psychology, Religious—History. I. Title. II. Series.

ROSENBERG, Ann Elizabeth, 201'.9
1942-
Freudian theory and American religious journals, 1900-1965 / by Ann Elizabeth Rosenberg. Ann Arbor, Mich. : UMI Research Press, c1980. p. cm. (Studies in American history and culture ; no. 17) Includes index. Bibliography: p. [BL53.R59 1980] 80-17544 ISBN 0-8357-1099-8 : 26.95
1. Freud, Sigmund, 1856-1939. 2. Psychology, Religious—History. 3. Religious newspapers and periodicals—United States. I. Title. II. Series.

Psychology, Religious—Miscellanea.

TOURNIER, Paul. 200'.8
A Tournier companion. London : S.C.M. Press, 1976. xii, 177, [1] p. ; 23 cm. Contains extracts from the author's works. [BL53.T666] 77-359978 ISBN 0-334-01664-9 : £2.80
1. Psychology, Religious—Miscellanea. 2. Conduct of life—Miscellanea. I. Title.

Psychometry (Occult sciences)

BUCHANAN, Joseph Rodes, 133.
1814-1899.
Manual of psychometry: the dawn of a new civilzation, By Joseph Rodes Buchanan ... Published by the author Boston ... Boston, Holman brothers, press of the Roxbury advocate, 1885. 8 p. l., 212, 194, 94 p. front. (port.) illus. 20 cm. [BF1261.B86] 11-3136
1. Psychometry (Occult sciences) I. Title.

DENTON, William, 1823-1883. 133.
The soul of things: or, Psychometric researches and discoveries. By William and Elizabeth M. F. Denton ... 3d ed., rev. Boston, Walker, Wise and company, 1866. viii, [9]-370 p. 20 cm. Pt. i: Psychometric researches and discoveries. By William Denton. Pt. ii: Questions, considerations and suggestions. By Elizabeth M. F Denton. [BF1325.D4] 10-33699
1. Psychometry (Occult science) I. Denton, Mrs. Elizabeth M. Foote, joint author. II. Title.

DENTON, William, 1823-1883. 133
Soul of things: or, Psychometric researches and discoveries. By William Denton ... Wellesley, Mass., Mrs. E. M. F. Denton [1873] 3 v. front., illus. 20 cm. [BF1325.D4 1873] 32-16701
1. Psychometry (Occult sciences) I. Title.

DENTON, William, 1823-1883. 133.
The soul of things; or, Psychometric researches and discoveries. By William and Elizabeth M. F. Denton ... Wellesley, Mass., Denton publishing company, 1881-84. 3 v. fronts. (v. 2-3) illus. 20 cm. Vol. 1, 7th edition, revised, 1884: v. 2-3 (by William Denton) have imprint: Boston, Pub. by W. Denton, 1881. [BF1325.D4 1884] 20-19108
1. Psychometry (Occult sciences) I. Denton, Elizabeth M. Foote, Mrs. joint author. II. Title.

DENTON, William, 1823-1883. 133
The soul of things; or, Psychometric researches and discoveries. By William and Elizabeth M. F. Denton ... Boston, Walker, Wise and company, 1863. viii, [2], 11-370 p. 20 cm. [BF1325.D4 1863] 44-30397
1. Psychometry (Occult sciences) I. Denton, Elizabeth M. Foote. II. Title.
Contents omitted.

HOLZER, Hans W., 1920- 133.8
Window to the past; exploring history through ESP [by] Hans Holzer. Illustrated by Catherine Buxhoeveden. [1st ed.] Garden City, N.Y., Doubleday, 1969. 254 p. illus. 22 cm. [BF1286.H6] 69-10957 5.95
1. Psychometry (Occult sciences) I. Title.

MCDERMOTT, Charles Henry. 133.
Outline of psychometry, psychic life and phantasm of the dying; a study of telepathy, telesthenia, hypnotism, thought suggestion, spiritism, transliminality, mental therapeutics, the spiritual science, by Charles Henry McDermott. Chicago, Occult publishing company, 1926. 2 p. l., 9-259 p. 23 1/2 cm. "One thousand copies have been printed of this work numbered from 1 to 1000. This is copy no. 9." Signed: C. H. McDermott. [BF1031.M3] 26-14358
1. Psychometry (Occult sciences) 2. Psychical research. I. Title.

Puberty rites—India.

BHATTACHARYYA, 392'.14'0954
Narendra Nath, 1934-
Indian puberty rites / by Narendra Nath Bhattacharyya. 2d ed., rev. and enl. New Delhi : Munshiram Manoharlal, 1980, c1979. viii, 124 p. ; 23 cm. Includes index. Bibliography: p. [111]-115. [GT2487.I4B47 1980] 19 80-903984 11.00
1. Puberty rites—India. 2. India—Social life and customs. I. Title.
Distributed by South Asia Books, P.O. Box 502, Columbia, MO 65205

Puberty rites—Papua New Guinea—Addresses, essays, lectures.

RITUALS of manhood : 392'.14
male initiation in Papua New Guinea / edited by Gilbert H. Herdt ; with an introduction by Roger M. Keesing. Berkeley : University of California Press, c1982. xxvi, 365 p. : ill. ; 24 cm. Includes bibliographies and index. [GN671.N5R55 1982] 19 81-1807 ISBN 0-520-04448-7 : 22.50
1. Puberty rites—Papua New Guinea—Addresses, essays, lectures. 2. Papua New Guinea—Social life and customs—Addresses, essays, lectures. I. Herdt, Gilbert H., 1949-

Public opinion polls—Religion.

GALLUP, George Horace, 1901-
comp.
Gallup opinion index; special report on religion. [Trenton, N.J., American Institute of Public Opinion, 1967] [64] p. 28 cm. 68-86457
1. Public opinion polls—Religion. I. American Institute of Public Opinion. II. Title.

Public relations—Churches.

BARROWS, William J. 254.4
How to publicize church activities. [Westwood, N.J.] Revell [c.1962] 62p. illus. 21cm. (Revell's better church ser.) 62-17112 1.00 pap.,
1. Public relations—Churches. I. Title.

BARROWS, William J 254.4
How to publicize church activities. [Westwood, N.J.] Revell [1962] 62 p. illus. 21 cm. (Revell's better church series) [BV653.B3] 62-17112
1. Public relations — Churches. I. Title.

COMMUNICATIONS Seminar 254.4
Manhattan College, 1959
The church and communications arts; [proceedings. 2d ed.] Washington, D.C., 1312 Massachusetts Ave. Bur. of Info., Natl. Catholic Welfare Conference, [1962] 183p. 26cm. 62-16968 3.00 pap.,
1. Public relations—Churches. 2. Communication. I. Title.

CRAIG, Floyd A. 254.4
Christian communicator's handbook; a practical guide for church public relations [by] Floyd A. Craig. Nashville, Broadman Press [1969] 96 p. illus. 28 cm. Includes bibliographical references. [BV653.C7] 69-17893
1. Public relations—Churches. I. Title.

GREIF, Edward L. 254.4
The silent pulpit; a guide to church public relations. New York, Holt [1964] x, 213p. 22cm. 64-11277 4.95
1. Public relations—Churches. I. Title. II. Title: A guide to church public relations.

JOHNSON, Philip A 254.8
Telling the good news; a public relations handbook for churches, edited by Philip A. Johnson, Norman Temme [and] Charles C. Hushaw. Saint Louis, Concordia Pub. House [1962] 202p. illus. 21cm. [BV653.J6] 62-14145
1. Public relations—Churches. I. Title.

LEIDT, William E. 254.4
Publicity goes to church. Greenwich, Conn., Seabury Press, 1959. 122 p. 20 cm. Includes bibliography. [BV653.L45] 58-9227
1. Public relations—Churches. 2. Advertising—Churches. I. Title.

LESCH, Gomer R 254.4
Church public relations at work. Nashville, Convention Press [1962] 142p. 19cm. Includes bibliography. [BV653.L47] 62-9621
1. Public relations—Churches. I. Title.

SOUTHERN Baptist 254.4
Convention. Sunday School Board.
The church public relations committee. [Nashville, 1972] 23 p. 21 cm. (Its Program help series) Cover title. Bibliography: p. 22-23. [BV653.S74] 73-150730
1. Public relations—Churches. I. Title.

WOLSELEY, Roland Edgar, 1904- 259
Interpreting the church through press and radio. Philadelphia, Muhlenberg Press [1951] xv, 352 p. illus. 22 cm. "A booklist for the church journalist": p. 337-341. [BV653.W6] 51-11395
1. Public relations — Churches. I. Title.

Public relations—Churches—Addresses, essays, lectures.

INSTITUTE on Modern 659.2'9'28
Religious Communication Dilemmas, Syracuse University, 1971.
The challenge of modern church-public relations. Edited by Michael V. Reagen and Doris S. Chertow. [Syracuse, N.Y.] Publications in Continuing Education, Syracuse University, 1972 [c1973] iii, 67 p. 23 cm. ([Syracuse University. Publications in Continuing Education] Occasional papers, no. 33) Sponsored by the Religious Public Relations Council and others. Includes bibliographical references. [BV653.I58 1971] 72-5637 3.00
1. Public relations—Churches—Addresses, essays, lectures. 2. Communication (Theology)—Addresses, essays, lectures. 3. Christianity—20th century—Addresses, essays, lectures. I. Reagen, Michael V., ed. II. Chertow, Doris S., ed. III. Religious Public Relations Council. IV. Title. V. Series.

Public relations—Clergy.

MEAD, Frank Spencer, 1898- 254.4
ed.
Reaching beyond your pulpit. [Westwood, N.J.] Revell [1962] 190p. 21cm. 62-10730 3.50 bds.,
1. Public relations—Clergy. I. Title.

Public speaking.

LITFIN, A. Duane. 808.5'1
Public speaking : a handbook for Christians / A. Duane Litfin. Grand Rapids, Mich. : Baker Book House, c1981. 352 p. : ill. ; 23 cm. Includes bibliographies and index. [PN4121.L56] 19 81-65993 ISBN 0-8010-5605-5 (pbk.) : 9.95
1. Public speaking. 2. Public speaking—Religious aspects—Christianity. I. Title.

WEST, Emerson Roy. 251
How to speak in church / Emerson Roy West. Salt Lake City : Deseret Book Co., 1976. viii, 168 p. : ill. ; 24 cm. Includes index. Bibliography: p. 162-163. [BX8638.W47] 76-3818 5.95
1. Church of Jesus Christ of Latter-Day Saints. 2. Public speaking. 3. Preaching. I. Title.

Public worship.

ABBA, Raymond. 264
Principles of Christian worship. New York, Oxford University Press, 1957. 196 p. 21cm. Includes bibliography. [BV15.A15] 57-14051
1. Public worship. I. Title. II. Title: Christian worship.

ALLEN, Ronald Barclay. 248.2
Worship, rediscovering the missing jewel /

by Ronald Allen and Gordon Borror. Portland, OR : Multnomah Press, c1982. 200 p. ; 23 cm. Includes indexes. Bibliography: p. 199-200. [BV15.A39 1982] 19 82-2198 ISBN 0-930014-86-3 : 9.95
1. Public worship. 2. God—Worship and love. I. Borror, Gordon, 1936- II. Title.
Publisher's address: 10209 S.E. Division St., Portland, OR 97266

ANDERSON, Robert Grant, 1896- 264
The unified Sunday morning church service; a movement now under way among Protestant churches to unite the study and worship program of the Sunday school with the Sunday morning worship service of the church [by] Robert Grant Anderson. New York, Cincinnati [etc.] The Abingdon press [1936] c55 p. 20 cm. [BV10.A6] 39-1559
1. Public worship. 2. Sunday-schools. I. Title. II. Title: Sunday morning church service.

BAILEY, Robert W. 264
New ways in Christian worship / Robert W. Bailey. Nashville, Tenn. : Broadman Press, c1981. 164 p. ; 21 cm. Bibliography: p. 163-164. [BV15.B32] 19 81-65390 ISBN 0-8054-2311-7 pbk. : 5.95
1. Public worship. 2. Worship services. 3. Baptists—Liturgy—Texts. I. Title.

BAILEY, Wilfred M. 248'.4
Awakened worship; involving laymen in creative worship [by] Wilfred M. Bailey. Nashville, Abingdon Press [1972] 157 p. 20 cm. Bibliography: p. 157. [BV15.B34] 73-185543 ISBN 0-687-02338-6 2.95
1. Public worship. I. Title.

BEACHY, Alvin J. 264.09'7
Worship as celebration of covenant and incarnation [by] Alvin J. Beachy. Newton, Kan., Faith and Life Press [1968] 73 p. 20 cm. Bibliography: p. 73. [BV10.2.B4] 68-57497
1. Public worship. 2. Liturgics—Mennonites. I. Title.

BENSON, Dennis C. 264
Electric liturgy [by] Dennis C. Benson. Richmond, John Knox Press, 1972. 96 p. 22 cm. Accompanied by 2 phonodiscs (4 s. 8 in. 33 1/3 rpm.) [BV15.B44] 72-175179 ISBN 0-8042-1593-6 4.95
1. Public worship. I. Title.

BEVERIDGE, William, bp. of St. Asaph 1637-1708. 264
The great necessity and advantage of public prayer, and frequent communion, designed to revive primitive piety. By William Beveridge ... New York, J. A. Sparks, 1845. xiv, [2], [17]-331, [1] p. 15 cm. Preface signed: H. E. M. [BV20.B4] 34-8094
1. Public worship. I. Title.

BLACKWOOD, Andrew Watterson, 1882- 264
The fine art of public worship, [by] Andrew W. Blackwood ... Nashville, Cokesbury press [c1939] 247 p. 20 1/2 cm. "The literature of the subject": p. 230-241. [BV10.B45] 39-21402
1. Public worship. I. Title.

BLACKWOOD, Andrew Watterson, 1882- 264.1
Leading in public prayer. New York, Abingdon Press [1958] 207p. 21cm. Includes bibliography. [BV226.B6] 58-7429
1. Public worship. 2. Pastoral prayers. I. Title.

BRENNER, Scott Francis, 1903- 264
The art of worship; a guide in corporate worship techniques. New York, Macmillan [c.]1961. 95p (Oikoumene) Bibl. 61-16541 2.75
1. Public worship. I. Title.

BRENNER, Scott Francis, 1903- 264
Ways of worship for new forms of mission. With action suggestions by Miriam Brattain. New York, Friendship Press [1968] 96 p. 19 cm. Bibliography: p. 95-96. [BV15.B73] 68-24792
1. Public worship. I. Title.

COFFIN, Henry Sloane, 1877- 264
The public worship of God, a source book [by] Henry Sloane Coffin. Philadelphia, The Westminster press [1946] 208 p. 21 cm. (The Westminster source books) "A selected bibliography": p. [199]-205. [BV10.C65] 46-5948
1. Public worship. I. Title.

COFFIN, Henry Sloane, 1877-1954. 264
The public worship of God; a source book. Freeport, N.Y., Books for Libraries Press [1972, c1946] 208 p. 22 cm. (Essay index reprint series) Original ed. issued in series: The Westminster source books. Bibliography: p. [199]-205. [BV10.C65 1972] 75-167327 ISBN 0-8369-7272-4
1. Public worship.

DEARMER, Percy, 1867-1936. 264
The art of public worship, by Percy Dearmer ... London [etc.] A. R. Mowbray & co. ltd.; Milwaukee, The Morehouse publishing co. [1919] vii, 213, [1] p. 19 cm. "The following chapters were originally delivered as the Bohien lectures at Philadelphia in January, 1919. Part of their substance was afterwards repeated at S. Martin-in-the-Fields, London, during Leut."--Pref. [BV10.D4] 20-5397
1. Public worship. 2. Church of England. Book of common prayer. 3. Protestant Episcopal church in the U. S. A. Book of common prayer. I. Title.

DOBBINS, Gaines Stanley, 1886- 264.1
The church at worship. Nashville, Broadman [1963, c.1962] 147p. 22cm. Bibl. 63-7334 3.25 bds.,
1. Public worship. I. Title.

DOLLOFF, Eugene Dinsmore. 264
Sunday night services can be successful, by Eugene Dinsmore Dolloff, S.T.D. Philadelphia, The Blackiston company, distributed by Fleming H. Revell company, New York and London [c1943] 144 p. 19 cm. [BV27.D6] 44-2452
1. Public worship. I. Title.

FAUTH, Robert T. 264
When we worship. Philadelphia [2][1505 Race St., Christian Education Press c.1961] 88p. Bibl. 61-7446 1.50 bds.,
1. Public worship. I. Title.

FISCHER, Helmut, 1929- 248'.4
Thematischer Dialog-Gottesdienst / Helmut Fischer. Hamburg : Furche-Verlag, 1975. 119 p. ; 20 cm. Includes bibliographical references. [BV15.F57] 76-456278 ISBN 3-7730-0254-8 : DM19.80
1. Public worship. 2. Dialogue sermons. I. Title.

FISKE, George Walter, 1872- 264
The recovery of worship; a study of the crucial problem of the Protestant churches, by George Walter Fiske ... New York, The Macmillan company, 1931. xi p., 1 l., 269 p. 19 1/2 cm. "Selected bibliography": p. 265-266. [BV10.F5] 31-12843
1. Public worship. I. Title.

FORD, Murray J. S. 264
Planning, preparing, praising / by Murray J. S. Ford. Valley Forge, PA : Judson Press, [1978] p. cm. Bibliography: p. [BV25.F56] 78-3475 ISBN 0-8170-0798-9 : pbk. : 3.50
1. Public worship. 2. Worship programs. I. Title.

GOLDSWORTHY, Edwin Arthur, 1906- 264
Plain thoughts on worship, by Edwin A. Goldsworthy. Chicago, New York, Willett, Clark & company, 1936. xii p., 1 l., 134 p. 21 cm. [The minister's professional library] [BV10.G63] 38-11149
1. Public worship. 2. Theology, Pastoral. I. Title.

HARDIN, H. Grady. 264
The leadership of worship / Grady Hardin ; with ill. by Bruce A. Sayre. Nashville, Tenn. : Abingdon, c1980. 110 p. : ill. ; 23 cm. Includes bibliographical references. [BV15.H37] 19 79-26863 ISBN 0-687-21160-3 : 6.95
1. Public worship. I. Title.

HARRIS, Thomas Leonard, 1901- 264
Christian public worship, its history, development and ritual for to-day, by Thomas L. Harris. Garden City, N. Y., Doubleday, Doran & company, inc., 1928. xvi p., 1 l., 259 p. 20 cm. "Books on public worship": p. 255-259. [BV10.H3] 28-28969
1. Public worship. I. Title.

HEDLEY, George Percy, 1899- 264
When Protestants worship. Nashville, Pub. for the Cooperative Pubn. Assn. by Abingdon [c.1961] 96p. (Faith for life ser.) 62-16016 1.00 pap.,
1. Public worship. I. Title.

HEIMSATH, Charles Herman, 1894- 264
The genius of public worship, by Charles H. Heimsath. New York, C. Scribner's sons, 1944. xiv p., 1 l., 204 p. 19 1/2 cm. [BV10.H43] 44-47471
1. Public worship. I. Title.

HOVDA, Robert W. 264'.02
Dry bones; living worship guides to good liturgy, by Robert Hovda. Washington, Liturgical Conference, 1973. vi, 152 p. 23 cm. Includes bibliographical references. [BV15.H69] 73-76658 4.95
1. Public worship. I. Title.

HOYT, Arthur Stephen, 1851-1924. 264
Public worship for non-liturgical churches, by Arthur S. Hoyt ... New York, Hodder & Stoughton, G. H. Doran company [1911] 6 p. l, 3-164 p. 19 1/2 cm. "Books on worship": p. 164. [BV10.H85] 11-19553
1. Public worship. I. Title.

HUTTON, Samuel Ward, 1886- comp. 264
Worship highways; guideposts for spiritual engineers, by Samuel Ward Hutton and Noel Leonard Keith. St. Louis, The Bethany press [1943] 264 p. incl. front., illus. 20 cm. Bibliography: p. 259-260. [BV25.H8] 43-4201
1. Public worship. 2. Liturgies. I. Keith, Noel Leonard, joint comp. II. Title.

JONES, Ilion Tingnal, 1889- 264
A historical approach to evangelical worship. Nashville, Abingdon Press [1954] 319p. 24cm. [BV10.J6] 53-11339
1. Public worship. I. Title.

KEIR, Thomas H. 264
The word in worship; preaching and its setting in common worship. New York, Oxford [c.]1962. 150p. 19cm. 62-51116 3.50
1. Public worship. 2. Preaching. I. Title.

KILLINGER, John. 264
Leave it to the Spirit; commitment and freedom in the new liturgy. [1st ed.] New York, Harper & Row [1971] xviii, 235 p. 22 cm. Includes bibliographical references. [BV15.K47 1971] 78-149749 6.95
1. Public worship. I. Title.

KING, William, abp. of Dublin, 1650-1729. 264
A discourse, concerning the inventions of men in the worship of God. By the Right Rev. William King... Philadelphia, Printed by J. Harding, 1828. ix, [5]-112 p. 18 1/2 cm. [BV9.K5 1828] 39-3975
1. Public worship. 2. Church of England. Liturgy and ritual. I. Title.

KING, William, abp. of Dublin, 1650-1729. 264
A discourse concerning the inventions of men in the worship of God. By the Right Rev. William King... Philadelphia, J. Harding. 1828. 94 p., 1 l., 18 cm. [Waterman pamphlets, v. 134, no. 5] [AC901.W3 vol. 134, no. 5] 39-10923
1. Public worship. 2. Church of England. Liturgy and ritual. I. Title.

KNIGHT, Cecil B. 264
Pentecostal worship / edited by Cecil B. Knight. Cleveland, Tenn. : Pathway Press, [1974] 140 p. ; 20 cm. Includes bibliographies. [BV15.K56] 74-83548 ISBN 0-87148-684-9
1. Public worship. 2. Pentecostalism. I. Title.

KOENKER, Ernest Benjamin. 264
Worship in word and sacrament. Saint Louis, Concordia Pub. House [1959] 109p. illus. 19cm. [BV10.2.K6] 59-10270
1. Public worship. 2. Lutheran Church. Liturgy and ritual. I. Title.

MCDORMAND, Thomas Bruce. 264
The art of building worship services. Rev. ed. Nashville, Broadman Press, 1958. 123p. 21cm. Includes bibliography. [BV10.M24 1958] 58-11547
1. Public worship. 2. Worship (Religious education) I. Title.

MCDORMAND, Thomas Bruce. 264
The art of building worship services, by Thomas Bruce McDormand ... Nashville, Tenn., Broadman press [1942] 131 p. 20 1/2 cm. Includes bibliographies. [BV10.M24] 42-21737
1. Public worship. 2. Worship (Religious education) I. Title.

MCGAVRAN, Grace Winifred. 264
We gather together, by Grace W. McGavran; drawings by Margaret Ayer. New York, Friendship press [c1941] 3 p. l., 121 p. illus., plates. 19 1/2 cm. Includes songs with music. "Plans and procedures for using We gather together will be found in A junior teacher's guide on 'Worship around the world,' by Lola Hanzelwood." [BV10.M27] 41-5995
1. Public worship. I. Title.

MACGREGOR, Geddes. 264
The rhythm of God; a philosophy of worship. New York, Seabury Press [1974] 120 p. 22 cm. "A Crossroad book." [BV15.M28] 74-13598 ISBN 0-8164-1174-3 6.95
1. Public worship. I. Title.

MCILWAIN, Orene, 1891- 264
Worship God, a guide toward genuineness in worship, by Orene McIlwain. Richmond, Va., John Knox press [1947] 4 p. l., [1]-157 p. illus. 20 cm. Includes bibliographies. [BV15.M3] 47-26355
1. Public worship. 2. Worship (Religious education) 3. Worship programs. I. Title.

MACLEOD, Donald, 1914- 264.05
Presbyterian worship; its meaning and method. Richmond, Va., Knox [c.1965] 152p. illus. 21cm. Bibl. [BX9185.M23] 65-11499 3.25
1. Public worship. I. Title.

MCNUTT, William Roy, 1879- 264
Worship on the churches, by William Roy McNutt. Philadelphia, Chicago [etc.] The Judson press [1941] 275 p. plates. plans, diagr. 20 cm. "A selected bibliography": p. 267-272. [BV10.M28] 41-20127
1. Public worship. I. Title.

MARTIN, Ralph P. 264
The worship of God : some theological, pastoral, and practical reflections / by Ralph P. Martin. Grand Rapids, Mich. : W.B. Eerdmans Pub. Co., c1982. ix, 237 p. ; 21cm. Includes bibliographical references and indexes. [BV15.M34 1982] 19 82-7397 ISBN 0-8028-1934-6 pbk. : 7.95
1. Public worship. 2. Liturgics. I. Title.

MASSEY, James Earl. 264
The worshiping church; a guide to the experience of worship. Anderson, Ind., Warner Press [1961] 106p. 19cm. [BV15.M35] 61-15360
1. Public worship. I. Title.

MILLIGAN, Oswald Bell, 1879-1940. 264
The ministry of worship; being the Warrack lectures for 1940, by the Rev. Oswald B. Milligan ... London, New York [etc.] Oxford university press, 1941. vii p., 1 l., 115, [1] p. 19 cm. Edited by George Shaw Stewart. [BV10.M56] 42-4102
1. Public worship. 2. Sacraments. I. Stewart, George Shaw, ed. II. Title.

MOORE, Ralph. 264
Toward celebration, with suggestions for using the celebration packet. Philadelphia, Published for Joint Educational Development [by] United Church Press [1973] 126 p. illus. 22 cm. (A Shalom resource book) Part of the Celebration packet which also includes Celebration sharings and sounds, and Liturgical simulation exercise. Bibliography: p. [101]-113. [BV15.M66] 73-6754
1. Public worship. I. Joint Educational Development. II. Title.

NEUFER Emswiler, Thomas, 1941- 264

Wholeness in worship / Thomas Neufer Emswiler, Sharon Neufer Emswiler. 1st ed. San Francisco : Harper & Row, c1980. xi, 171 p. : ill. ; 23 cm. Filmography: p. 161-164. [BV15.N49 1980] 79-2982 ISBN 0-06-062247-4 : 6.95

1. Public worship. I. Neufer Emswiler, Sharon, joint author. II. Title.

O'DAY, Rey, 1947- 264'.05834
Theatre of the spirit : a worship handbook / Rey O'Day, Edward A. Powers. New York : Pilgrim Press, c1980. viii, 200 p. : ill. ; 23 cm. Bibliography: p. 193-200. [BV15.O3] 80-14165 ISBN 0-8298-0381-5 pbk. : 7.95
1. Public worship. I. Powers, Edward A., joint author. II. Title.

ODGERS, J Hastie, 1863- 264
The technique of public worship, by J. Hastie Odgers and Edward G. Schutz. New York, Cincinnati, The Methodist book concern [c1928] 300 p. front., illus., plates. 20 cm. [BV10.O4] 28-14558
1. Public worship. I. Schutz, Edward G., 1876- joint author. II. Title.

OSBORN, George Edwin, 1897- 264.1
The Glory of Christian worship. Indianapolis, Christian Theological Seminary Press, 1960. 84p. 27cm. 'First appeared in Encounter, vol. xx (1959) 172-243.' Includes bibliography. [BV15.O8] 60-23461
1. Public worship. 2. Worship. I. Title.

PALMER, Albert Wentworth, 1879-
The art of conducting public worship. New York, Macmillan, 1961. 207 p. 65-49080
1. Public worship. I. Title.

PALMER, Albert Wentworth, 1879- 264
The art of conducting public worship [by] Albert W. Palmer... New York, The Macmillan company, 1939. 6 p. l., 211 p. front., pl. 21 cm. "Published March, 1939. First printing." "Annotated book-list": p. 203-207. [BV10.P23 1939] 39-7283
1. Public worship. I. Title.

PALMER, Albert Wentworth, 1879- 264
Come, let us worship, by Albert W. Palmer. New York, TheMacmillan company, 1941. xx p., 1 l., 136 p. 19 1/2 cm. "First printing." "Annotated book-list": p. 125-131. [BV10.P235 1941] 41-5996
1. Public worship. I. Title.

PATTISON, Thomas Harwood, 1838-1904. 264
Public worship, by T. Harwood Pattison ... Philadelphia, American Baptist publication society, 1900. vi p., 1 l., 271 p. 20 cm. [BV10.P3] 0-5802
1. Public worship. 2. Theology, Pastoral. 3. Worship. I. Title.

PERKINS, Ruth. 264
Planning services of worship, by Ruth Perkins ... New York, The Womans press [c1929] 4 p. l., 5-60 p. 19 cm. "Annotated bibliography": p. 46-60. [BV10.P4] 30-10065
1. Public worship. I. Title.

RANDOLPH, David James, 1934- 264
God's party: a guide to new forms of worship. Nashville, Abingdon Press [1975] 144 p. illus. 22 cm. Bibliography: p. 135-138. [BV15.R36] 74-18293 ISBN 0-687-15445-6 3.50 (pbk.)
1. Public worship. I. Title.

RAYBURN, Robert Gibson, 1915- 264
O come, let us worship : corporate worship in the evangelical church / Robert G. Rayburn. Grand Rapids, Mich. : Baker Book House, c1980. 319 p. ; 22 cm. [BV15.R39] 79-55192 ISBN 0-8010-7690-0 : 8.95
1. Public worship. I. Title.

REID, Clyde H. 264
Let it happen: creative worship for the emerging church [by] Clyde Reid and Jerry Kerns. [1st ed.] New York, Harper & Row [1973] 86 p. 21 cm. and phonodisc (2 s. 7 in. 33 1/3 rpm.) in pocket. Bibliography: p. 82-86. [BV15.R44 1973] 72-78063 ISBN 0-06-066821-0 4.95
1. Public worship. I. Kerns, Jerry, joint author. II. Title.

RIVERS, Clarence Joseph. 264
Soulfull worship. [Washington, National Office for Black Catholics, 1974] 160 p. illus. 28 cm. [BX1970.R57] 73-93702
1. Public worship. 2. Liturgies. I. Title.

ROCHELLE, Jay C. 264
Create and celebrate! [by] Jay C. Rochelle. Philadelphia, Fortress Press [1971] iv, 124 p. 22 cm. Includes hymns, with music, and liturgical melodies by the author. Bibliography: p. 114-124. [BV15.R6] 79-139345 2.95
1. Public worship. 2. Worship programs. I. Title.

SEIDENSPINNER, Clarence. 264
Form and freedom in worship, by Clarence Seidenspinner. Chicago, New York, Willett, Clark & company, 1941. xii p., 1 l., 186 p. 20 1/2 cm. [The minister's professional library] Bibliography at end of each chapter. [BV10.S425] 41-2886
1. Public worship. 2. Liturgies. I. Title.

SELLERS, Ernest Orlando, 1869- 264
Worship, why and how; principles of worship in non-liturgical churches, by Ernest O. Sellers...Introduction by Dr. W. W. Hamilton... Grand Rapids, Mich., Zondervan publishing house [c1941] 7 p. l., 13-148 p. 19 1/2 cm. Bibliography: p. 147-148. [BV10.S428] 41-9700
1. Public worship. I. Title.

SNYDER, Ross. 264
Contemporary celebration. Nashville, Abingdon Press [1971] 202 p. 24 cm. [BV15.S56] 74-162458 4.75
1. Public worship. I. Title.

SPERRY, Willard Learoyd, 1882- 264
Reality in worship; a study of public worship and private religion, by Willard L. Sperry ... New York, The Macmillan company, 1925. 346 p. 19 1/2 cm. [BV10.S6] 25-17833
1. Public worship. I. Title.

STEVICK, Daniel B. 264.001'4
Language in worship; reflections on a crisis [by] Daniel B. Stevick. New York, Seabury Press [1970] viii, 184 p. 22 cm. Bibliography: p. [177]-184. [BV15.S7] 76-106518 5.95
1. Public worship. 2. Prayer. 3. Religion and language. I. Title.

SUSOTT, Albert A. 264
A practical handbook of worship, by Albert A. Susott. New York [etc.] Fleming H. Revell company [c1941] 173 p. 19 cm. [BV15.S8] 41-19008
1. Public worship. I. Title.

TURKEL, Roma Rudd 264
Who's zoo in church? [people are likened to animals in their behavior in church]. New York, Paulist Press [c.1959] unpaged illus. (col.) 16cm. .10 pap.,
I. Title.

UNITED Presbyterian Church of North America. General Assembly. 264.051
The manual of worship, approved by the General Assembly; prepared by a committee and rev. by a commission of the General Assembly. [Pittsburgh,] Board of Christian Education of the United Presbyterian Church of North America, [1947] xv, 212 p. 17 cm. [BX9185.A42 1947] 48-14506
1. Public worship. I. United Presbyterian Church of North America. Liturgy and ritual. II. Title.

WEBBER, Robert. 264
Worship, old and new / Robert E. Webber ; [edited by Maureen LeLacheur and Gerard Terpstia]. Grand Rapids, Mich. : Zondervan Pub. House, c1982. 256 p. ; 23 cm. Includes indexes. Bibliography: p. 236-242. [BV15.W4 1982] 19 82-1969 ISBN 0-310-36650-X : 11.95
1. Public worship. I. Title.

WHITE, James F. 264
Christian worship in transition / James F. White. Nashville : Abingdon, c1976. 160 p. ; 21 cm. Includes index. [BV15.W46] 76-16848 ISBN 0-687-07659-5 : 6.75
1. Public worship. I. Title.

WHITE, James F. 264
New forms of worship [by] James F. White. Nashville, Abingdon Press [1971] 222 p. 23 cm. Includes bibliographical references. [BV15.W48] 72-160797 ISBN 0-687-27751-5 5.75
1. Public worship. I. Title.

WILLIMON, William H. 264'.34
The Bible, a sustaining presence in worship / William H. Willimon. Valley Forge, PA : Judson Press, c1981. 109 p. ; 22 cm. Includes bibliographical references. [BV15.W53] 19 81-8301 ISBN 0-8170-0918-3 : 5.95
1. Bible. N.T.—Theology. 2. Public worship. 3. Worship—History—Early church, ca. 30-600. I. Title.

WILLIMON, William H. 264
Worship as pastoral care / William H. Willimon. Nashville : Abingdon, c1979. 237 p. ; 23 cm. Includes bibliographical references and indexes. [BV15.W54] 79-894 ISBN 0-687-46389-0 : 9.95
1. Public worship. 2. Liturgies. 3. Pastoral theology. I. Title.

WINTER, Miriam Therese. 264'.02
Preparing the way of the Lord / Miriam Therese Winter. Nashville : Abingdon, c1978. 256 p. : music ; 22 cm. Includes bibliographical references. [BV25.W54] 78-7571 pbk.: 6.5
1. Public worship. I. Title.

WOLFE, Paul Austin, 1898- 264
The choir loft and the pulpit; fifty-two complete services of worship with sermon text, Psalter, Scripture readings, hymns, anthems, and organ numbers related to the theme of each service. By Rev. Paul Austin Wolfe ... Helen A. Dickinson ... [and] Clarence Dickinson ... New York, N.Y., The H. W. Gray company, inc. [1943] 127 p. 22 1/2 cm. "Fifty-two morning services of the Brick church, New York city."--p. 3. [BV25.W6] 44-19672
1. Public worship. 2. Liturgies. I. Dickinson, Helena Adell (Snyder) 1875- joint author. II. Dickinson, Clarence, 1873- joint author. III. New York. Brick Presbyterian church. IV. Title.

ZDENEK, Marilee. 264
Catch the new wind [by] Marilee Zdenek and Marge Champion. Waco, Tex., Word Books [1972] 191 p. illus. 19 x 23 cm. Bibliography: p. 182-187. [BV15.Z39] 77-188073 8.95
1. Public worship. 2. Worship programs. I. Champion, Marge (Belcher) joint author. II. Title.

Public worship—Case studies.

ABERNETHY, William Beaven, 1939- 264'.05'8
A new look for Sunday morning / William Beaven Abernethy. Nashville : Abingdon, [1975] 176 p. ; 20 cm. Includes bibliographical references. [BX7255.M63S682] 74-34387 ISBN 0-687-27805-8 pbk. : 4.50
1. South Congregational Church, Middletown, Conn. 2. Public worship—Case studies. 3. Religious education—Case studies. I. Title.

Public worship—Congresses.

CONFERENCE on the Layman as a Leader of Worship, Charleston, S.C., 1968. 264
The layman as a leader of worship. The study papers presented at, and a report on the considerations and recommendations of, the Conference on the Layman as a Leader of Worship. [Washington? 1969] v, 82 p. 26 cm. "NAVPERS 15155." "Jointly sponsored by Commander, Submarine Force, U.S. Atlantic Fleet [and] Chief of Chaplains, U.S. Navy." Includes bibliographical references. [BV10.2.C65] 75-605351
1. Public worship—Congresses. 2. Laity—Congresses. I. U.S. Navy. Chaplain Corps. II. U.S. Navy. Atlantic Fleet. Submarine Force. III. Title.

INTER-LUTHERAN Conference on Worship, Minneapolis, 1973. 264'.04'1
Worship: good news in action. Edited by Mandus A. Egge. Minneapolis, Augsburg Pub. House [1973] 144 p. 20 cm. Lectures presented at the conference. [BV15.I57 1973] 73-88598 ISBN 0-8066-1402-1 3.50
1. Public worship—Congresses. I. Egge, Mandus A., ed. II. Title.

Public worship—Handbooks, manuals, etc.

CLARK, Linda, 1937- 264
Image-breaking/image-building : a handbook for creative worship with women of Christian tradition / Linda Clark, Marian Ronan, Eleanor Walker. New York : Pilgrim Press, c1981. 144 p. ; 21 cm. Bibliography: p. 142-144. [BV25.C58] 19 80-28896 ISBN 0-8298-0407-2 (pbk) : 7.95
1. Public worship—Handbooks, manuals, etc. 2. Women (Christian theology)—Handbooks, manuals, etc. I. Ronan, Marian, 1947- joint author. II. Walker, Eleanor Myrtle, 1922- joint author. III. Title.

ROBERTSON, James Douglas. 264'.002'02
Minister's worship handbook, by James D. Robertson. Grand Rapids, Baker Book House [1974] 136 p. 20 cm. Includes bibliographical references. [BV25.R6] 74-172781 ISBN 0-8010-7619-6 3.95
1. Public worship—Handbooks, manuals, etc. I. Title.

Public worship — History.

BISHOP, John, 1908- 264'.07
Methodist worship in relation to free church worship / by John Bishop. New York : Scholars Studies Press, [1975] p. cm. A revision of the author's thesis (M.A.), Bristol University, England published under title: The forms and psychology of workship in the free church with special reference to Methodism. Includes indexes. Bibliography: p. [BX8337.B55 1975] 75-20379 ISBN 0-89177-001-1 : 6.95
1. Methodist Church. Liturgy and ritual. 2. Public workship—History. I. Title.

BRENNER, Scott Francis, 1903- 264.009
The way of worship, a study in ecumenical recovery [by] Scott Francis Brenner, TH.D. Introduction by John R. Mott. New York, The Macmillan company, 1944. xxv, 200 p. 21 cm. "First printing." "Bibliography: p. 176-179. [BV5.B7] 44-7057
1. Public worship—Hist. 2. Liturgies. I. Title.

MICKLEM, Nathaniel 1888- 3d.
Christian worship, studies in its history and meaning, by members of Mansfield College. [London, New York] Oxford University Press [1959] xi, 259 p. 23 cm. 66-37517
1. Public worship — History. I. Title.

MICKLEM, Nathaniel, 1888- ed. 264.009
Christian worship, studies in its history and meaning, by members of Mansfield college; edited by Nathaniel Micklem. Oxford, The Clarendon press, 1936. xi, 259, [1] p. 22 1/2 cm. [BV10.M53] 37-5730
1. Public worship—Hist. I. Title.
Contents omitted.

Public worship in hospitals.

†BASSETT, S. Denton. 264
Public religious services in the hospital / by S. Denton Bassett ; with a foreword by Myron C. Madden. Springfield, Ill. : Thomas, c1976. xiv, 65 p. ; 24 cm. Includes index. Bibliography: p. 47. [BV4335.B33] 76-2356 ISBN 0-398-03563-6 : 7.50
1. Public worship in hospitals. 2. Church work with the sick. I. Title.

Public worship—Methodist authors.

*RANDOLPH, David James. 264
Ventures in worship 3. Nashville, Abindgon Press [1973] 223 p. illus. 28 cm. [BV15] ISBN 0-687-43689-3 3.95 (pbk.)
1. Public worship—Methodist authors. I. Title.

Publicity.

KNESEL, Dave. 659.2
Free publicity : a step by step guide / Dave Knesel. New York : Sterling Pub. Co., c1982. 160 p. : ill. ; 24 cm. Includes

index. [HM263.K57 1982] 19 81-85027 ISBN 0-8069-0240-X : 12.95 ISBN 0-8069-0241-8 : 11.69 ISBN 0-8069-7588-1 pbk. : 6.95
1. Publicity. I. Title.

WINSTON, Martin Bradley, 1948- 659.2
Getting publicity / Martin Bradley Winston. New York : Wiley, c1982. x, 193 p. : ill. ; 23 cm. Includes index. [HM263.W593 1982] 19 81-16217 ISBN 0-471-08225-2 : 7.95
1. Publicity. I. Title.

Pudaite, Rochunga.

HEFLEY, James C. 266'.022'0924 B
God's tribesman; the Rochunga Pudaite story [by] James and Marti Hefley. [1st ed.] Philadelphia, A. J. Holman Co. [1974] 144 p. illus. 21 cm. [BV3269.P8H43] 74-3346 ISBN 0-87981-031-9 5.95
1. Pudaite, Rochunga. I. Hefley, Marti, joint author. II. Title.

Pueblo Indians—Juvenile literature.

CLARK, Ann (Nolan) 1898- 299'.7
Circle of seasons. Illustrated by W. T. Mars. New York, Farrar, Straus & Giroux [1970] 113 p. illus. 22 cm. (A Bell book) Describes the ceremonies and festival rituals of the Pueblo Indians to recognize and celebrate the changing of the seasons. [E99.P9C57] 73-113772 3.95
1. Pueblo Indians—Juvenile literature. 2. [Pueblo Indians—Rites and ceremonies.] I. Mars, Witold T., illus. II. Title.

[Pueblo Indians—Legends.]

MCDERMOTT, Gerald. JUV
Arrow to the sun; a Pueblo Indian tale. Adapted and illustrated by Gerald McDermott. 1st ed. New York, Viking Press [1974] [42] p. col. illus. 25 x 29 cm. An adaptation of the Pueblo Indian myth which explains how the spirit of the Lord of the Sun was brought to the world of men. [PZ8.1.M159Ar] 291.2'12 398.2 E 73-16172 6.95
1. [Pueblo Indians—Legends.] I. Title.

Pueblo Indians—Religion and mythology.

PARSONS, Elsie Worthington (Clews) Mrs. 1875- 970.62
Pueblo Indian religion ... by Elsie Clews Parsons. Chicago, Ill., The University of Chicago press [c1939] 2 v. fronts. (maps) illus., plates (1 col.) port., fold. tables. 21 cm. (Half-title: The University of Chicago publications in anthropology Ethnalogical series) Paged continuously. Bibliography: v. 2. p. 1195-1200. [E99.P9P3] [299.7] 39-19032
1. Pueblo Indians—Religion and mythology. 2. Indians of North America—Religion and mythology. I. Title.

SWITZER, Ronald R. 299'.7
The origin and significance of snake-lightning cults in the Pueblo Southwest, by Ronald R. Switzer. [El Paso, Tex., El Paso Archaeological Society, 1972?] iii, 48 p. illus. 29 cm. (El Paso Archaeological Society. Special report no. 11) Bibliography: p. 44-48. [E99.P9S9] 72-171715
1. Pueblo Indians—Religion and mythology. I. Title. II. Series.

TYLER, Hamilton A. 299'.7
Pueblo animals and myths / by Hamilton A. Tyler. 1st ed. Norman : University of Oklahoma Press, [1975] xiii, 274 p. : ill. ; 21 cm. (The Civilization of the American indian series ; v. 134) Includes index. Bibliography: p. 246-255. [E99.P9T89] 74-15902 ISBN 0-8061-1245-X : 8.95
1. Pueblo Indians—Religion and mythology. 2. Animal lore. I. Title. II. Series.

TYLER, Hamilton A. 299'.7
Pueblo birds and myths / Hamilton A. Tyler ; illustrated by Donald Phillips. Norman : University of Oklahoma Press, c1979. xix, 308 p. : ill. ; 21 cm. (The Civilization of the American Indian series ; [147]) Includes index. Bibliography: p. 293-301 [E99.P9T893] 78-58069 ISBN 0-8061-1483-5 : 12.50
1. Pueblo Indians—Religion and mythology. 2. Indians of North America—Southwest, New—Religion and mythology. 3. Folk-lore of birds. 4. Birds—Southwest, New. I. Title. II. Series.

TYLER, Hamilton A. 299.7
Pueblo gods and myths. [1st ed.] Norman, University of Oklahoma Press [1964] xxii, 313 p. illus., map. 23 cm. (The Civilization of the American Indian series, 71) Bibliography: p. 293-300. [E99.P9T9] 64-11317
1. Pueblo Indians—Religion and mythology. I. Title. II. Series.

Pulkingham, Betty.

PULKINGHAM, Betty. 283'.092'4 B
Little things in the hands of a big God / Betty Pulkingham. Waco, Tex. : Word Books, 1978,c1977. 142 p. : ill. ; 21 cm. [BR1725.P84A34] 79-63930 ISBN 0-8499-2855-9 : 4.95
1. Pulkingham, Betty. 2. Christian biography—United States. 3. Christian life—1960- I. Title.

Pulkingham, W. Graham.

A Charismatic reader. 234'.1
New York, Religious Book Club [1974] 281, 160, 162, 138 p. illus. 22 cm. Includes bibliographies. [BR110.C43] 74-81757 8.95
1. Pulkingham, W. Graham. 2. Church of the Redeemer, Houston, Tex. 3. Experience (Religion) 4. Theology, Doctrinal—History. 5. Pentecostalism 6. Glossolalia—Addresses, essays, lectures. I. Religious Book Club.
Contents omitted.

PULKINGHAM, W. Graham. 283'.092'4 B
Gathered for power, by Graham Pulkingham. Illus. by Cathleen. New York, Morehouse-Barlow Co. [1972] 138, [5] p. illus. 22 cm. Bibliography: p. [141]-143] [BX5995.P767A33] 72-80885 ISBN 0-8192-1130-3 2.50
1. Pulkingham, W. Graham. 2. Church of the Redeemer, Houston, Tex. I. Title.

Pumphrey, Stanley, 1837-1881.

NEWMAN, Henry Stanley. 922.
Memories of Stanley Pumphrey, by Henry Stanley Newman ... New York, Friends' book and tract committee, 1883. iv, 292 p. front. (port.) 19 cm. First published, 1882, under title: The young man of God. Memories of Stanley Pumphrey. [BX7795.P8N4 1883] 39-19568
1. Pumphrey, Stanley, 1837-1881. I. Title.

Puppet-plays.

RACE, Martha.
Missionary marionette plays [by] Martha Race. Boston, Chicago, The Pilgrim press [c1927] 2 p. l., 65 p. illus. (incl. music) 24 cm. [BV2086.R3] [791] 27-9194
1. Puppet-plays. I. Title.

Puppets and puppet-plays in Christian education.

CHAPMAN, Marie M. 791.5'3
Puppet animals tell Bible stories / Marie M. Chapman ; cover and ill. by Caroline A. Cleaveland. Denver : Accent Books, c1977. 96 p. : ill. ; 26 cm. Includes bibliographical references. [BV1535.9.P8C48] 77-75134 ISBN 0-916406-74-1 pbk. : 2.95
1. Puppets and puppet-plays in Christian education. 2. Puppet making. I. Title.

FAUST, David. 791.5'3
Puppet plays with a point / by David and Candy Faust. Rev. Cincinnati : Standard Pub., c1979. 157 p. : ill. ; 28 cm. "Songs for puppets to sing": p. [127]-157. [BV1535.9.P8F38 1979] 79-63769 ISBN 0-87239-248-1 pbk. : 6.95
1. Puppets and puppet-plays in Christian education. I. Faust, Candy, joint author. II. Title.

GILBERTSON, Irvy. 812'.5'4
Practical puppet plays / Irvy Gilbertson. Springfield, Mo. : Gospel Pub. House, c1977. 61 p. ; 22 cm. [BV1535.9.P8G54] 77-75600 ISBN 0-88243-746-1 pbk. : 2.50
1. Puppets and puppet-plays in Christian education. I. Title.

MARSH, Fredda. 268'.432
Putting it all together in a puppet ministry / Fredda Marsh, with Dow Mooney. Springfield, MO : Gospel Pub. House, c1978. p. cm. [BV1535.9.P8M37] 77-91674 ISBN 0-88243-578-7 : 6.95
1. Puppets and puppet-plays in Christian education. I. Mooney, Dow, joint author. II. Title.

MILLER, Sarah Walton. 268'.67
A variety book of puppet scripts / Sarah Walton Miller. Nashville : Broadman Press, c1978. 79 p. ; 22 cm. [BV1535.9.P8M54] 78-57276 ISBN 0-8054-7515-X pbk. : 2.50
1. Puppets and puppet-plays in Christian education. I. Title.

Puppets and puppet-plays in Christian education—Juvenile literature.

FERGUSON, Helen. 791.5'3
Bring on the puppets! / By Helen Ferguson. New York : Morehouse-Barlow, c1975. 31 p. : ill. ; 28 cm. Gives instructions for making puppets representing Biblical figures and includes scripts of Bible stories for putting on shows. [BV1535.9.P8F47] 75-5217 ISBN 0-8192-1195-8 pbk. : 3.25
1. Puppets and puppet-plays in Christian education—Juvenile literature. 2. [Puppets and puppet-plays.] 3. [Bible stories.] I. Title.

Puppets and puppet-plays in religious education.

MYERS, Galene J. 268.67
Puppets can teach too; using puppetry in religious education. Illus. adapted by Betty Ellingboe. Minneapolis. Augsburg [c.1966] 64p. illus., ports. 26cm. Bibl. [BV1535.9.P8.M9] 66-13058 3.50, pap., plastic bdg.
1. Puppets and puppet-plays in religious education. I. Title.

REYNOLDS, Joyce. 268'.67
Puppet shows that reach & teach children. Springfield, Mo., Gospel Pub. House [1972] 62 p. illus. 29 cm. [BV1535.9.P8R48] 73-185586 2.95
1. Puppets and puppet-plays in religious education. I. Title.

Puranas. Bhagavatapurana.

BHAKTIVEDANTA, A.C., Swami 1896- 294.5'925
Krsna : the supreme personality of Godhead : a summary study of Srila Vyasadeva's Srimad-Bhagavatam, tenth canto / A. C. Bhaktivedanta Swami. New York ; Bombay: Bhaktivedanta Book Trust, c1970, 1974 printing. 3 v. : col. ill. ; 28 cm. [BL1220.B44 1974] 75-304945 ISBN 0-912776-60-9
1. Krishna. 2. Puranas. Bhagavatapurana. I. Title.

PURANAS. Bhagavatapurana. English. 294.5
Srimad Bhagavatam; The wisdom of God, translated by Swami Prabhavananda; frontispiece by Suzanne Miller. New York, G. P. Putnam's sons [1943] xii, 340 p. front. 17 1/2 cm. Frontispiece accompanied by guard sheet with descriptive letterpress. [BL1135.P7A25] 43-11610
I. Prabhavananda, swami, 1893- II. Title. III. Title: The wisdom of God.

PURANAS. Devibhagavatapurana. English 294.5'925
The Sri Mad Devi Bhagavatam. Translated by Swami Vijnanananda, alias Hari Prasanna Chatterji. Allahabad, Panini Office, 1921-23. [New York, AMS Press, 1974] p. cm. Original ed. issued as v. 26, pts. 1-4, of The Sacred books of the Hindus. Parts 2 and 4 have title: The Srimad Devi Bhagavatam; pt. 3 has title: The Devi Bhagavatam. [BL1135.P72A36 1974] 73-3819 ISBN 0-404-57826-8
I. Vijnanananda, Swami, 1868-1938, ed. II. Title. III. Title: The Srimad Devi Bhagavatam. IV. Title: The Devi Bhagavatam. V. Series: The Sacred books of the Hindus, v. 26, pts. 1-4.

Puranas. Bhagavatapurana—Paraphrases, English—Juvenile literature.

YOGESVARA Dasa. 294.5'211
Gopal the Invincible / retold by Yogesvara dasa and Jyotirmayi-devi dasi ; illustrations by Sunita-devi dasi. Long Island, N.Y. : Bala Productions, c1982. p. cm. (The Childhood pastimes of Krishna) "Based on the Bhagavatapurana ... translated from the original Sanskrit by ... A.C. Bhaktivedanta Swami Prabhupada"—Verso t.p. Krishna, known as Gopal the cowherd boy, proves himself a worthy match for the nefarious creatures who come to disturb the life of his peaceful forest village. [BL1140.4.B435Y63 1982] 19 82-16396 ISBN 0-89647-017-2 : 6.95
1. Puranas. Bhagavatapurana—Paraphrases, English—Juvenile literature. 2. [Krishna (Hindu deity)] 3. [Mythology, Hindu.] I. Jyotirmayi-devi. II. Sunita-devi, ill. III. Puranas. Bhagavatapurana. IV. Title. V. Series.

Puranas. Brahmavaivartapurana.

*BROWN, Cheever Mackenzie. 294.5'925
God as mother: a feminine theology in India; an historical and theological study of the Brahmavaivarta Purana. Hartford, Vt. Claude Stark [1974] xiii, 264 p. 23 cm. Bibliography: p. 245-254. [BL1135] 74-76006 ISBN 0-89007-004-0 15.00
1. Puranas. Brahmavaivartapurana. I. Title.

Puratana janama sakhi.

MCLEOD, W. H. 294.6'8'2
Early Sikh tradition : a study of the janam-sakhis / by W. H. McLeod. Oxford : Clarendon Press ; New York : Oxford University Press, 1980. xiv, 317 p. ; 23 cm. Includes indexes. Bibliography: p. [292]-294. [BL2017.48.M32] 79-40397 ISBN 0-19-826532-8 : 43.00
1. Puratana janama sakhi. I. Title.

Purdie, Samuel Alexander, 1843-1897.

KNOWLES, James Purdie. 922.
Samuel A. Purdie, his life and letters, his work as a missionary and Spanish writer and publisher in Mexico and Central America, by James Purdie Knowles, with an introduction by Allen Jay ... Plainfield, Ind., Publishing association of Friends [1908] xvi, [17]-251 p. 23 cm. [BX7795.P85K55] 43-44590
1. Purdie, Samuel Alexander, 1843-1897. 2. Friends, Society of—Missions. I. Title.

Purdy, Alexander Converse, 1890-

MCARTHUR, Harvey K., ed. 220.04
New Testament sidelight. essays in honor of Alexander Converse Purdy. . . Hartford 5, Conn., 55 Elizabeth St. Hartford Seminary Foundation, [c.]1960 vii, 135p. bibl. p.129-35 and bibl. notes. port. 21cm. 60-2687 4.25
1. Purdy, Alexander Converse, 1890- 2. Bible. N. T.—Addresses, essays, lectures. I. Title.

MCARTHUR, Harvey K ed. 220.04
New Testament sidelights; essays in honor of Alexander Converse Purdy ... Hartford, Hartford Seminary Foundation Press, 1960. vii, 135p. port. 21cm. Includes bibliographies. [BS2280.M3] 60-2687
1. Purdy, Alexander Converse, 1890- 2. Bible. N. T.—Addresses, essays, lectures. I. Title.
Contents omitted.

Pure Land Buddhism in art.

FUKUYAMA, Toshio, 726'.1'43920952 1905-
Heian temples : Byodo-in and Chuson-ji / by Toshio Fukuyama ; translated by Ronald K. Jones. 1st English ed. New York : Weatherhill, 1976. 168 p., [2] fold. leaves of plates : ill. (some col.) ; 24 cm. (The Heibonsha survey of Japanese art ; v. 9) Translation of Byodoin to Chusonji. [N8193.3.P8F8413] 75-41337 ISBN 0-8348-1023-9 : 12.50
1. Pure Land Buddhism in art. 2. Art, Japanese—Heian period, 794-1185. I. Title. II. Series.

Purgative way to perfection.

SHAMON, Albert J. 234
First steps to sanctity. Westminster, Md., Newman Press, 1958. 128 p. 23 cm. [BX2350.52.S5] 58-11028
1. Purgative way to perfection. I. Title.

Purgatory.

ARENDZEN, John Peter 236.5
Purgatory and heaven. New York, Sheed and Ward [1960] 96p. 18cm. (Canterbury books) 'From What becomes of the dead?' 60-7317 .75 pap.,
1. Purgatory. 2. Heaven. I. Title.

BARROWS, William, 1815- 236.5 1891.
Purgatory; doctrinally, practically, and historically opened. By William Barrows ... with an introduction, by Alexander McKenzie, d. d. New York, American tract society [1882] ix, 228 p. 20 cm. [BT841.B2] 40-37167
1. Purgatory. I. Title.

DOOLEY, Lester M., 1898- 236.5
God's guests of tomorrow, a mystical visit to purgatory and a consideration of the sabbatine privilege, by Rev. L. M. Dooley, S.V.D. Sea Isle City, N.J., New York [etc.] Scapular press, 1943. 111 p. 21 cm. [BT841.D6] 44-2628
1. Purgatory. I. Title.

HUBERT, Father, O.F.M. 236'.5 Cap.
The mystery of purgatory / Father Hubert. Chicago : Franciscan Herald Press, [1975] p. cm. Includes bibliographical references. [BT842.H8] 74-28028 ISBN 0-8199-0559-3
1. Purgatory. I. Title.

LASANCE, Francis Xavier, 264. 1860- ed.
Holy souls book reflections on purgatory; a complete prayer-book including special prayers and devotions in behalf of the poor souls in purgatory, ed. by Rev. F. X. Lasance ... New York, Cincinnati [etc.] Benziger brothers, 1922. 443 p. front., pl. 15 cm. [BX2170.D5L3] 22-16904
1. Purgatory. 2. Catholic church—Prayer-books and devotions. I. Title.

MCLAUGHLIN, James Bede 236. Benedict, 1866-
Purgatory; or, The church suffering, by the Reverend J. B. McLaughlin, O. S. B.; introduction by Rt. Rev. Patrick J. McCormick ... New York, The Macmillan company, 1929. vii p., 1 l., 87 p. 17 cm. (Half-title: The treasury of the faith series: 32) [BT841.M3 1929a] 29-22403
1. Purgatory. I. Title.

MARY of St. Austin, mother. 236.5
The divine crucible of purgatory, by Mother Mary of St. Austin ... Revised and edited by Nicholas Ryan, S.J. New York, P. J. Kenedy & sons, 1940. viii p., 1 l., 185 p. 22 1/2 cm. Bibliographical references included in "Notes" at end of each chapter. [BT841.M35 1940a] 43-39521
1. Purgatory. I. Ryan, Nicholas, ed. II. Title.

NAGELEISEN, John August, 236.5 1861-
Charity for the suffering souls. An explanation of the Catholic doctrine of purgatory. With a treatise on the Arch-confraternity of the most precious blood of Our Lord Jesus Christ, and on the spiritual benevolent fraternity for the relief and ransom of the suffering souls. By Rev. John A. Nageleisen ... Cincinnati, O., Press of S. Rosenthal & co., 1895. xvi, 578 p. front., pl. 20 cm. [Full name: John August Albert Nageleisen] [BT841.N2] 41-30216
1. Purgatory. 2. Confraternity of the precious blood. I. Title.

SADLIER, Mary Anne (Madden) 236.5 "Mrs. James Sadlier," 1820-1903.
Purgatory: doctrinal, historical and poetical. By Mrs. J. Sadlier ... New York, D. & J. Sadlier & company [1886] 500 p. 21 cm. [BT841.S2] 40-37168
1. Purgatory. I. Title.
Contents omitted.

SIMMA, Maria, 1915- 248'.2
My personal experiences with the poor souls / Maria Simma. Chicago : Franciscan Herald Press, [1978] p. cm. Translation of Meine Erlebnisse mit Armen Seelen. [BX4705.S6355A313] 78-16270 ISBN 0-8199-0744-8 : 7.95
1. Simma, Maria, 1915- 2. Purgatory. 3. Spiritualism. I. Title.

Purgatory—Early works to 1800.

CATERINA da Genova, Saint, 236'.5 1447-1510.
Purgation and purgatory ; The spiritual dialogue / Catherine of Genoa ; translation and notes by Serge Hughes ; introd. by Benedict J. Groeschel ; pref. by Catherine De Hueck Doherty. New York : Paulist Press, c1979. xvi, 163 p. ; 24 cm. (The Classics of Western spirituality) Translation of Libro de la vita mirabile ... de la beata Caterinetta. Includes indexes. Bibliography: p. 153-154. [BT840.C33 1979] 19 79-88123 ISBN 0-8091-2207-3 pbk. : 7.95 ISBN 0-8091-0285-4 : 11.95
1. Purgatory—Early works to 1800. 2. Mysticism—Middle Ages, 600-1500. I. Title. II. Series: Classics of Western spirituality.

Purim (Feast of Esther)

CONE, Molly. 296.4
Purim. Illustrated by Helen Borten. New York, Crowell [1967] [40] p. illus. (part col.) 22 cm. (A Crowell holiday book) The story and customs of the gayest of Jewish holidays which celebrate how Queen Esther saved her people from the wicked Haman. [GT4995.P8C65] AC 67
1. Purim (Feast of Esther) 2. Fasts and feasts—Judaism. I. Borten, Helen, illus. II. Title.

DONIACH, Nakdimon 296 Shabbethary.
Purim; or, The feast of Esther; an historical study, by N. S. Doniach ... Philadelphia, The Jewish publication society of America, 1933. 5 p. l., 277 p. 20 cm. "Bibliography of the works in European languages and most frequently consulted": p. 267-268. [BM695.P8D6] 33-9255
1. Purim (Feast of Esther) 2. Jews—Rites and ceremonies. I. Title.

GARVEY, Robert. 296.4
When it's Purim. Pictures by Laszlo Matulay. [New York] Ktav Pub. House [1954] unpaged. illus. 22cm. (A Two-in-one holiday book) Bound with the author's When it's Passover. [New York, 1954] [BM695.P3G33] 54-1853
1. Purim (Feast of Esther) I. Title.

GASTER, Theodor Herzl, 1906- 296
Purim and Hanukkah, in custom and tradition; Feast of Lots, Feast of Lights. New York, Schuman [1950] xvi, 134 p. illus., map. 22 cm. (Great religious festivals series) Bibliography: p. [119]-126. [BM695.P8G3] 50-10632
1. Purim (Feast of Esther) I. Title.

GOLDIN, Hyman Elias, 1881- 296
Purim, a day of joy and laughter, by Hyman E. Goldin, illustrated by Howard Simon. New York, Hebrew publishing company [c1941] 96 p. incl. front., illus. 20 cm. [BM695.P8G6] 41-4340
1. Purim (Feast of Esther) I. Title.

GOODMAN, Philip, 1911- ed.
The Purim anthology. Philadelphia, Jewish Publications Society of America, 1960 [c1949] xxxi, 525 p. illus. 22 cm. "Music supplement, compiled by A. W. Binder": p. [441]-489. Bibliography: p. 495-512. 67-94893
1. Purim (Feast of Esther) I. Title.

GOODMAN, Philip, 1911- ed. 296
The Purim anthology. Philadelphia, Jewish Publication Society of America, 1949. xxxi, 525 p. illus. 22 cm. "Music supplement, compiled by A. W. Bindex": p. [441]-489. Bibliography: p. 495-512. [BM695.P8G63] 49-8892
1. Purim (Feast of Esther) I. Title.

Purim (Feast of Esther)—Addresses, essays, lectures.

PURIM : 296.4'36
the face and the mask : essays and catalogue of an exhibition at the Yeshiva University Museum, February-June 1979, New York City. New York : The Museum, [1979] p. cm. Bibliography: p. [BM695.P8P87] 79-23953 pbk. : 10.00
1. Purim (Feast of Esther)—Addresses, essays, lectures. 2. Purim (Feast of Esther)—Exhibitions. I. Yeshiva University, New York. Museum.

Purim (Feast of Esther)—Juvenile literature.

SIMON, Norma 296.436
Happy Purim night. Illus. by Ayala Gordon. [New York 27] 3080 Bway.] United Synagogue Commission on Jewish Education, c.1959 unpaged. illus. (col.) 25x15cm. 59-12531 .95 bds.,
1. Purim (Feast of Esther)—Juvenile literature. I. Title.

SIMON, Norma. 296.436
The Purim party. Illus. by Ayala Gordon. [New York 27] 3080 Bway., United Synagogue Commission on Jesish Education, c.1959. unpaged. illus. (col.) 25 x 15cm. 59-12532 .95 bds.,
1. Purim (Feast of Esther)—Juvenile literature. I. Title.

Purisima Concepcion mission.

ENGELHARDT, 271.30979491 Zephyrin, father, 1851-
Mission La Concepcion Purisima de Maria Santisima, by Fr. Zephyrin Engelhardt... Santa Barbara, Calif., Mission Santa Barbara, 1932. ix, [1] 131 p. incl. front., illus., maps, plans, diagr. 22 cm. (Missions and missionaries of California. New series. Local history) With the author's Mission Santa Ines. Santa Barbara, Calif., 1932. Running title: Mission Putisima Concepcion. [Secular name: Charles Anthony Engelhardt] [F864.E569] [F370.M6E45] 979.40082 33-29506
1. Purisima Concepcion mission. I. Title.

Puritans.

[ALDEN, Joseph] 1807-1885.
Anecdotes of the Puritans ... New York, M. W. Dodd, 1849. vii, [9]-144 p. 15 1/2 cm. [BX9327.A6] 42-45368
1. Puritans. I. Title.

BANKS, Charles Edward, 1854- 1931.
The Winthrop fleet of 1630; an account of the vessels, the voyage, the passengers and their English homes from original authorities. Baltimore, Genealogical Pub. Co., 1961. 118p. maps. 23cm.
1. Winthorop, John, 1588-1649. 2. Puritans. 3. Arbella (Ship) I. Title.

BEECHER, Henry Ward, 1813- 081 1887.
Lectures and orations. Edited by Newell Dwight Hillis. New York, AMS Press [1970] 330 p. 19 cm. Reprint of the 1913 ed. Contents.Contents.—Puritanism.—The wastes and burdens of society.—The reign of the common people.—Eloquence and oratory.—William Ellery Channing.—Charles Sumner.—Wendell Phillips.—Eulogy on Grant.—Abraham Lincoln. [BX7260.B3A54 1970] 72-126662 ISBN 0-404-00699-X
I. Hillis, Newell Dwight, 1858-1929. II. Title.

BROWN, John, 1830-1922. 250.
Puritan preaching in England; a study of past and present, by John Brown... New York, C. Scribner's sons, 1900. 5 p. l., [3]-290 p. 19 1/2 cm. (On verso of half-title: The Lyman Beecher lectures on preaching at Yale university. 1899) [BV4208.G7B7] 0-1399
1. Puritans. 2. Preaching. I. Title.

BYINGTON, Ezra Hoyt, 1825- 285'.9 1901.
The Puritan in England and New England. 4th ed., with a chapter on witchcraft in New England. New York, B. Franklin [1972] xlii, 457 p. illus. 22 cm. (Burt Franklin research & source works series. American classics in history and social science, 233) Reprint of the 1900 ed. Bibliography: p. [xxvii]-xxxi. [BX9321.B8 1972] 70-183241 ISBN 0-8337-4017-2
1. Puritans. 2. Witchcraft—New England. I. Title.

BYINGTON, Ezra Hoyt, 1828- 973. 1901.
The Puritan in England and New England. By Ezra Hoyt Byington ... With an introduction by Alexander McKenzie ... Boston, Roberts bros., 1896. xi, 406 p. front. (port.) 22 cm. "Authorities": p. [xxv]-xxix. [BX9321.B8 1896] [F7.B96] 1-151
1. Pynchon, William, 1590?-1662. 2. Breck, Robert, 1713-1784 3. Breck, Robert, 1713-1784 4. Puritans. 5. Witchcraft. I. Title.
Contents omitted

BYINGTON, Ezra Hoyt, 1828-1901.
The Puritan in England and New England, by Ezra Hoyt Byington ... 4th ed., with a chapter on witchcraft in New England. Boston, Little, Brown, and company, 1900. xiii, 457 p. pl., 2 port. (incl. front.) 22 cm. "List of authorities": p. [xxvii]-xxxi. [F7.B97] [BX9321.B8 1900] 0-6595
1. Puritans, 2. Witchcraft—New England. I. Title.

COIT, Thomas Winthrop, 1803- 289 1885.
Puritanism; or, A churchman's defense against its aspersions, by an appeal to its own history... By Thomas W. Coit... New York, D. Appleton & co.; Philadelphia, G. S. Appleton, 1845. [BX9329.C7] 10-13334
1. Puritans. 2. New England—Hist.—Colonial period. I. Title.

COOLIDGE, John S. 285'.9'0942
The Pauline Renaissance in England: Puritanism and the Bible, by John S. Coolidge. Oxford, Clarendon, 1970. xiv, 162 p. 23 cm. Bibliography: p. [152]-158. [BX9322.C6 1970] 73-17854 42/-
1. Puritans. I. Title.

CRAGG, Gerald 285'.9'0942 Robertson.
Puritanism in the period of the great persecution, 1660-1688, by Gerald R. Cragg. New York, Russell & Russell [1971] 325 p. 23 cm. Reprint of the 1957 ed. with new pref. Bibliography: p. 303-320. [BX9334.C7 1971] 76-143557
1. Puritans. 2. Gt. Brit.—Church history—17th century. I. Title.

FLYNN, John Stephen. 285.
The influence of Puritanism on the political & religious thought of the English, by John Stephen Flynn... New York, E.P. Dutton and company, 1920. 2 p. l., vii-xii, 257 p. 22 1/2 cm. [BX9334.F5] 20-22021
1. Puritans. 2. Gt. Brit.—Church history. I. Title.

FRERE, Walter Howard, bp. of Truro, 1863- ed.
... Puritan manifestoes. A study of the origin of the Puritan revolt. With a reprint of the Admonition to the Parliament and kindred documents, 1572. Ed. by the Rev. W. H. Frere, M. A., and the Rev. C. E. Douglas. London [etc.] Society for promoting Christian knowledge; New York, E. S. Gorham, 1907. xxxi, 155, [1] p. incl. front., facsims. 22 cm. (The Church historical society ... [Publications] lxxiii) "Published under the direction of the Tract committee."--p. [iv] Richard Bancroft in his "A survey of the pretended holy Discipline", London, 1598, attributes "An admonition to the Parliament" to Anthony Gilby, Thomas Sampson, Thomas Lever or Leaver, Thomas Wilcox, and John Feilde or Field. [BX9631.F7] 8-19127
1. Puritans. I. Douglas, Charles Edward, joint ed. II. Feilde, John, d. 1588. III. Wilcox, Thomas, 1549?-1608. IV. Cartwright, Thomas, 1535-1603. V. An admonition to the Parliament. VI. A

second admonition to the Parliament. VII. Title. VIII. Title: A second admonition to the Parliament.
Contents omitted.

GARRETT, Christina Hallowell 285.942
The Marian exiles, a study in the origins of Elizabethan Puritanism, by Christina Hallowell Garrett, M.A. Cambridge [Eng.] Univ. Pr., 1938. ix, 388p. front. 22cm. Bibl. [BX9338.G3] 38-25099 8.50
1. Puritans. 2. Gt. Brit.—Pol. & govt.—1553-1558. 3. Gt. Brit.—Biog. 4. Gt. Brit.—Church history—16th cent. I. Title.
Available from Cambridge in New York.

GARRETT, Christina Hallowell. 285.942
The Marian exiles, a study in the origins of Elizabethan Puritanism. by Christina Hallowell Garrett, M. A. Cambridge [Eng.] The University press, 1938. ix, 388 p. front. 22 1/2 cm. "The lives of exiles": p. [61]-349. Bibliographies: p. [65]-66, [373]-378. [BX9338.G3] 38-25099
1. Puritans. 2. Gt. Brit.—Pol. & govt.—1553-1558. 3. Gt. Brit.—Biog. 4. Gt. Brit.—Church history—16th cent. I. Title.

GT. Brit. Army. 285.942
Puritanism and liberty, being the Army debates (1647-9) from the Clarke manuscripts with supplementary documents selected, ed., introd. by A. S. P. Woodhouse. Foreword by A. D. Lindsay. [2d ed. Chicago] Univ. of Chic. Pr. [1965] 100, 506p. 22cm. [BX9331.A55] A51 price unreported
1. Puritans. 2. Gt. Brit.—Pol. & govt.—1642-1649. 3. Religious liberty—Gt. Brit. I. Woodhouse, Arthur Sutherland Pigott, ed. II. Clarke, Sir William, 1623-1666. III. Title.

GT. Brit. Army Council. 285.942
Puritanism and liberty, being the Army debates (1647-9) from the Clarke manuscripts with supplementary documents selected and edited with an introd. by A. S. P. Woodhouse. Foreword by A. D. Lindsay. [2d ed. Chicago] University of Chicago Press [1951] 100, 506 p 22 cm. Includes the debates in the General Council of the Army at Putney, Oct. 28-29 and Nov. 1. 1647, and in the Council of Officers at Whitehall, Jan. 13 and Dec. 14, 1648 and Jan. 8-11, 1649. [BX9331.A55] A51
1. Puritans. 2. Gt. Brit.—Pol. & govt.—1642-1649. 3. Religious liberty—Gt. Brit. I. Gt. Brit. Army. Council of Officers. II. Woodhouse. Arthur Sutherland Pigott. ed. III. Clarke, William, Sir 1623-1666. IV. Title.

HALLER, William, 1885- 274.2
Liberty and reformation in the Puritan Revolution [Gloucester, Mass., P. Smith, 1964, c.1955] xv, 410p. 21cm. (Columbia Univ. Pr. bk. rebound) Bibl. 4.50
1. Puritans. 2. Gt. Brit.—Church history—17th cent. 3. Church and state in Great Britain. 4. Gt. Brit.—Pol. & govt.—1625-1649. I. Title.

HALLER, William, 1885- 274.2
Liberty and reformation in the Puritan Revolution. New York, Columbia [1963, c.1955] 410p. 21cm. (47) Bibl. 2.45 pap.,
1. Puritans. 2. Gt. Brit.—Church history—17th cent. 3. Church and state in Great Britain. 4. Gt. Brit.—Pol. & govt.—1625-1649. I. Title.

HALLER, William, 1885- 285.942
The rise of Puritanism; or, The way to the New Jerusalem as set forth in pulpit and press from Thomas Cartwright to John Lilburne and John Milton, 1570-1643. [Gloucester, Mass., P. Smith, 1965, c.1938] 464p. illus. 21cm. (Harper torchbks., TB22 rebound) Bibl. [BX9334.H3] 4.25
1. Puritans. 2. Religious literature, English. 3. English literature—Early modern (to 1700)—Hist. & crit. I. Title.

HALLER, William, 1885- 285.942
The rise of Puritanism; or, The way to the New Jerusalem as set forth in pulpit and press from Thomas Cartwright to John Lilburne and John Milton, 1570-1643, by William Haller ... New York, Columbia university press, 1938. xiii p., 2 l. [3]-464 p. front. 23 1/2 cm. "Notes": p. [379]-404. "Bibliographical notes": p. [406]-440. [BX9334.H3] 38-36498
1. Puritans. 2. Religious literature, English. 3. English literature—Early modern (to 1700)—Hist. & crit. I. Title.

HOPKINS, Samuel, 1807-1887. 274.
The Puritans; or, The church, court, and Parliament of England, during the reigns of Edward VI. and Queen Elizabeth. By Samuel Hopkins ... Boston, Gould and Lincoln; New York, Sheldon and company; [etc., etc.] 1860-61. 3 v. 23 1/2 cm. Half-title: The Puritans and Queen Elizabeth. Bibliography: v. 1, p. [v]-viii. [BX9334.H7 1860] 46-28138
1. Puritans. 2. Gt. Brit.—Church history—16th cent. I. Title.

HOPKINS, Samuel, 1807-1887. 274.
The Puritans and Queen Elizabeth: or, The church, court, and Parliament of England, from the reign of Edward VI. to the death of the queen. By Samuel Hopkins. With an introductory note by Mark Hopkins ... New York, A. D. F. Randolph & co. [c1875] 3 v. 21 cm. First published under title: The Puritans. Bibliography: v. 1, p. [v]-viii. [BX9334.H7 1875] 45-22336
1. Puritans. 2. Gt. Brit.—Church history—16th cent. I. Title.

HOWE, Daniel Wait, 1839-1920. 922
The Puritan republic of the Massachusetts bay in New England. By Daniel Wait Howe ... Indianapolis, The Bowen-Merrill company [1899] xxxviii, 422 p. 23 1/2 cm. "Table of citations": p. xxxiii-xxxviii. [F67.H85] 99-5081
1. Puritans. 2. Massachusetts—Hist.—Colonial period. 3. Massachusetts—Pol. & govt.—Colonial period. I. Title.

KNAPPEN, Marshall Mason, 1901- 285.942
Tudor puritanism, a chapter in the history of idealism [New preface by the author] Chicago, Univ. of Chic. [1965, c.1939] xvi, 555p. 21cm. (Phoenix bk. P194) [BX9334.K5] 39-10082 3.45 pap.,
1. Puritans. 2. Idealism. I. Title.

KNAPPEN, Marshall Mason, 1901- 285.942
Tudor puritanism, a chapter in the history of idealism, by M. M. Knappen. Gloucester, Mass., P. Smith [1964, c.1938] xii, 555p. 21cm. Bibl. 7.50
1. Puritans. 2. Idealism. I. Title.

KNAPPEN, Marshall Mason, 1901- 285.942
Tudor puritanism, a chapter in the history of idealism, by M. M. Knappen ... Chicago, The University of Chicago press [1939] xii, 555 p. 25 cm. "Select bibliography": p. [521]-531. [BX9834.K5] 39-10082
1. Puritans. 2. Idealism. I. Title.

KNAPPEN, Marshall Mason, 1901- ed. 285.9
Two Elizabethan Puritan diaries, by Richard Rogers and Samuel Ward, edited, with and introduction, by M. M. Knappen ... Chicago, The American society of church history [c1933] xiii, 148 p. illus. (map) 2 port. (incl. front.) facsims. 25 cm. (Half-title: Studies in church history. vol. ii) [BX9339.R6K6] 34-853
1. Puritans. I. Rogers, Richard, 1550?-1618. II. Ward, Samuel, d. 1643. III. Title.
Contents omitted.

MCGINN, Donald Joseph. 285.942
The Admonition controversy. New Brunswick, Rutgers University Press, 1949. xii. 580 p. 24 cm. (Rutgers studies in English, no. 5.) Includes "selections from the Admonition (1572). Whitgift's Answers (1572), Cartwright's Replye (1573), Whitgift's Defense (1574), and finally Cartwright's Second replie (1575) and The rest of the second replie (1577)." Bibliographical references included in "Notes" (p. 541-566). [BX9331.M3] 49-11605
1. Puritans. 2. An admonition to the Parliament. I. Cartwright, Thomas, 1535-1603. II. Whitgift, John, Abp. of Canterbury, 1530-1604. III. Title. IV. Series: Rutgers University, New Brunswick, N.J. Rutgers studies in English.

MARCHANT, Ronald Albert 285.9
The Puritans and the church courts in the Diocese of York, 1560-1642 [London] Longmans [Mystic, Conn., Verry, 1965, c.1960] xii, 330p. maps. 23cm. Bibl. [BX9335.Y6M3] 61-237 12.50
1. Puritans. 2. York, Eng. (Diocese) I. Title.

MERRIMAN, Titus Mooney, 1822-1912. 922
The Pilgrims, Puritans, and Roger Williams, vindicated: and his sentence of banishment, ought to be revoked. By Rev. T. M. Merriman ... Boston, Bradley & Woodruff, 1892. xii, 312 p. 20 x 15 cm. [F67.M57] 1-12041
1. Williams, Roger, 1604?-1683. 2. Puritans. 3. Pilgrim fathers. 4. Massachusetts—Hist.—Colonial period. I. Title.

MERRIMAN, Titus Mooney, 1822-1912. 922
"Welcome, Englishmen"; or, Pilgrims, Puritans and Roger Williams vindicated and his sentence of banishment ought to be revoked. By Rev. T. M. Merriman ... 2d ed. Boston, Arena publishing company, 1896. xii, 320 p. 20 x 16 cm. [F67.M58] 1-12042
1. Williams, Roger, 1604?-1683. 2. Puritans. 3. Pilgrim fathers. 4. Massachusetts—Hist.—Colonial period. I. Title.

MILLER, Perry, 1905-
The New England mind: the seventeenth century. Cambridge, Harvard University Press, 1963 [c1954] xi, 528 p. 24 cm. Bibliographical references included in Appendix A-B and "Notes" (p. 493-523) 68-58444
1. Puritans. 2. Religious literature, American. 3. American literature—Colonial period—Hist. & crit. 4. American literature—New England. I. Title.

MONK, Robert C. 287.0924
John Wesley; his puritan heritage; a study of the Christian life [by] Robert C. Monk. Nashville, Abingdon [1966] 286p. 24cm. Based on thesis. Priceton Univ. Bibl. [BX8495.W5M6] 66-15494 5.50
1. Wesley, John, 1703-1791. 2. Puritans. I. Title.

MORGAN, Edmund Scars.
Visible saints; the history of a Puritan idea. Ithaca, N. Y., Cornell University Press [1965, c1963] ix, 159 p.19 cm. (Cornell paperbacks) 67-30682
1. Puritans. 2. Church — History of doctrines. I. Title.

MORGAN, Edmund Sears 285.9
Visible saints; the history of a Puritan idea. [New York] N. Y. Univ. Pr. [c.]1963. 159p. 22cm. Bibl. 63-9999 4.50
1. Puritans. 2. Church—History of doctrines. I. Title.

NEAL, Daniel, 1678-1743. 274.
The history of the Paritans, of Protestant Nonconforaists; form the reformation in 1517, to the revolution in 1688; comprising an account of their principles; their attempts for a farther reformation in the church; their sufferings; and the lives and characters of their most considerable divines. By Daniel Neal, M. A. Reprinted from the text of Dr. Toulmin's edition: with his life of the author and account of his writings. Rev. cor., and enl., with additional notes, by John O. Choules, M. A. With nine protraits on steel ... New York, Harper & brothers, 1856. 2 v. & port. (incl. fronts.) 24 cm. [BX9333.N4 1856] 7-30197
1. Puritans. I. Toulmin, Hoshus, 1740-1814, ed. II. Choules, John Overton, 1801-1858, ed. III. Title.

NEAL, Daniel, 1678-1743 274.2
The history of the Puritans, or Protestant non-conformists ... with an account of their principles; their attempts for a further reformation in the church; their sufferings: and the lives and characters of their most considerable divines ... By Daniel Neal, M. A. A new ed. rev., cor., and enl., by Joshna Toulmin, D. D. To which are prefixed, some memoirs of the life and writings of the author ... Published by Charles Ewer, Portsmouth, N. H. and Wm. B. Allen 3 co. Newburyport, Mns. Wm. B. Allen & co. printers, 1816-17. 5 v. 22 cm. Vols. ii-iii have imprint-Published by Charles Ewer, Boston; and William B. Allen & co. Newburport, Ms. 1817. Wm. B. Allen & co. printers: vol. iv-v: Published by Charles Ewer, Boston: and E. W. Allen, Newburyport. Mass. 1817. E. W. Allen, printer (vol. v. omits "Mass") Contents.--i. From the reformation to the death of Queen Elizabeth.--ii. From the death of Queen Elizabeth to the beginning of the civil war in the year 1642,--iii. From the battle of Edgehill, to the death of King Charles i., with a supplement.--iv. From the death of King Charles i. to the King's Declaration of indulgence, in the year 1672.--v. From the death of King Charles ii. to the Act of toleration in the reign of King William and Queen Mary, in the year 1688. With an index to the five volumes. [BX9333.N4 1816] 36-25378
1. Puritans. 2. Gt. Brit.—Pol. & govt.—1485-1603. 3. Gt. Brit.—Ind. & govt.—1664-1714. I. Toulmia, Joshua, 1740-1815, ed. II. Title.

NEAL, Daniel, 1678-1743. 274.
The history of the Puritans, or Protestant nonconformists; from the reformation in 1517, to the revolution in 1688; comprising an account of their principles; their attempts for a farther reformation in the church; their sufferings; and the lives and characters of their most considerable divines. By Daniel Neal, M, A. Reprinted from the text of Dr. Toulmin's ed. with his life of the author...rev., cor., and enl., with additional notes, by John O. Choules, M. A. with nine portraits of steel New York, Harper & brothers, 1844. 2 v. 9 port. (incl. fronts.) 24 cm. "Supplement, containing a sketch of the history of the Baptists and Quakers": v. 2, p. [353]-435. [BX9333.N4 1844] 16-9643
1. Puritans. 2. Gt. Brit.—Pol. & govt.—1485-1603. 3. Gt. Brit.—Pol. & govt.—1603-1714. I. Toulmin, Joshus, 1740-1815. ed. II. Choules, John Overton, 1801-1856, ed. III. Title.

PEARSON, Andrew Forrest Scott, 1886- 922.
Thomas Cartwright and Elizabethan Puritanism, 1535-1603, by The Rev. A. F. Scott Pearson. Cambridge [Eng.] The University press, 1925. xvi, 511 p. incl. front. 23 cm. "References and abbreviations": p. [xiii]-xvi. [BX9339.C35P4] 25-16113
1. Cartwright, Thomas, 1535-1603 2. Puritans. I. Title.

PEARSON, Andrew Forret Scot, 1886- 285.
Church & state; political aspects of sixteenth century Puritanism, by the Rev. A. F. Scott Pearson ... Cambridge [Eng.] The University press, 1928. ix p., 1 l., 153, [1] p. 23 cm. [BX9334.P4] 29-69
1. Puritans. 2. Church and state. 3. Church and state in Great Britain. I. Title.

PEARSON, Andrew Forret Scott, 1886- 285.90924(B)
Tomas Cartwright and Elizabethan Puritanism, 1535-1603, by A. F. Scott Pearson. Gloucester, Mass., P. Smith, 1966. xvi. 511p. port. 21cm. First pub. in 1925. Bibl. [BX9339.C35P4 1966] 67-869 8.50
1. Cartwright, Thomas, 135-1603. 2. Puritans. I. Title.

*PERRY, Ralph Barton, 1876- 285.9
Puritanism and democracy. New York, Harper [1964, c.1944] xvi, 688p. 21cm. (Acad. Lib.; Torchbk. TB-1138) 3.95 pap.,
I. Title.

PLUM, Harry Grant, 1868- 274.2
Restoration puritanism, a study of the growth of English liberty, by Harry Grant Plum. Chapel Hill, The University of North Carolina press, 1943. ix, 129 p. 22 1/2 cm. "Selected bibliography": p. [108]-128. [BX9334.P55] 43-18437
1. Puritans. 2. Gt. Brit.—Church history—17th cent. 3. Gt. Brit.—Pol. & govt.—1660-1714. I. Title.

... *The Puritans in Old England.* 274.
Boston, Old South meeting house, 1895. cover-title, [161] p. 18 cm. (Old South leaflets. xiii. [no. 57-64] 895) Various pagings. The t.-p. reads: The Old South leaflets. Thirteenth series, 1895. Contents.--57. The English Bible; extracts from the important English versions of the Bible from Wiclif's to the King James version.--58. Letters of Hooper to Bullinger.--59. Sir John Eliot's "Apologie for Socrates."--60. Ship-money papers.--61. Pym's speech against Strafford ... 1641.--62. Cromwell's second speech ... 1654.--63.

A free commonwealth, by John Milton.--64. Sir Henry Vane's defence, 1662. [BX9334.P8] 4-8879
1. Puritans. 2. Gt. Brit.—Hist.—Puritan revolution, 1642-1660.

SAUNDERSON, Henry Hallam, 1871- 270
Modern religion from Puritan origins, by Henry Hallam Saunderson ... Boston, Mass., The Beacon press, inc., 1930. xiv p., 1 l., 288 p. 19 1/2 cm. Bibliography included in appendix. [BX9321.S3] 30-13733
1. Puritans. 2. Church history. I. Title.

SCHNEIDER, Herbert Wallace, 1892- 285.9
The Puritan mind. [Ann Arbor] University of Michigan Press [1958] 267 p. 21 cm. (Ann Arbor paperbacks, AA21) Bibliographical footnotes. [BX9321.S4 1958] 58-14941
1. Puritans. 2. New England—Church history. I. Title.

SCHNEIDER, Herbert Wallace, 1892- 285.9
The Puritan mind, by Herbert Wallace Schneider. New York, H. Holt and company, [c1930] 6 p. l., 3-301 p. 23 cm. (Half-title: Studies in religion and culture American religion series. i) Bibliography: p. 265-297. [BX9321.S4] 30-31233
1. Puritans. 2. New England—Church history. I. Title.

SHEPARD, Thomas, 1605-1649. 285'.9'0924 B
God's plot; the paradoxes of Puritan piety; being The autobiography & journal of Thomas Shepard. Edited with an introd. by Michael McGiffert. [Amherst] University of Massachusetts Press, 1972. vii, 252 p. 24 cm. (The Commonwealth series [v. 1]) Bibliography: p. [239]-241. [BX7260.S53A32] 71-181364 ISBN 0-87023-100-6 12.00
I. Shepard, Thomas, 1605-1649. The autobiography. 1972. II. Shepard, Thomas, 1605-1649. The journal. 1972. III. Title. IV. Series: The Commonwealth series (Amherst, Mass.) v. 1.

SHEPARD, Thomas, 1605-1649. 285'.9'0924 B
God's plot; the paradoxes of Puritan piety; being The autobiography & journal of Thomas Shepard. Edited with an introd. by Michael McGiffert. [Amherst] University of Massachusetts Press, 1972. vii, 252 p. 24 cm. (The Commonwealth series [v. 1]) Bibliography: p. [239]-241. [BX7260.S53A32] 71-181364 ISBN 0-87023-100-6 12.00
I. Shepard, Thomas, 1605-1649. The autobiography. 1972. II. Shepard, Thomas, 1605-1649. The journal. 1972. III. Title. IV. Series: The Commonwealth series (Amherst, Mass.) v. 1.

SIMPSON, Alan 285.9
Puritanism in old and New England. [Chicago] Univ. of Chic. Pr. [1961, c.1955] 125p. (Charles R. Walgreen Found. lectures; Phoenix bk. P66) Bibl. 1.35 pap.,
1. Puritans. I. Title.

SIMPSON, Alan.
Puritanism in old and New England. [1st Phoenix ed. Chicago] University of Chicago Press [1961] vii, 125 p. 20 cm. (Phoenix books, P66] Charles R. Walgreen Foundation lectures. 63-74093
1. Puritans. I. Title.

STECK, James S. 285'.9
The intellectual pleasures of the Puritans [by] James S. Steck. [Shippensburg, Pa.] Shippensburg Collegiate Press, 1967. 16 p. 23 cm. (Shippensburg State College, Shippensburg, Pa. Faculty monograph series, v. 2, no. 1) Bibliography: p. 16. [BX9327.S68] 67-65700
1. Puritans. I. Title. II. Series: Pennsylvania. State College, Shippensburg. Faculty monograph series, v. 2, no. 1.

STOUGHTON, John, 1807-1897. 285'.9
Spiritual heroes; or, Sketches of the Puritans, their character and times. With and introductory letter, by Joel Hawes. Freeport, N.Y., Books for Libraries Press [1973] p. (Essay index reprint series) "First published 1848." [BX9334.S7 1973] 73-1194 ISBN 0-518-10066-9
1. Puritans. I. Title.

TOON, Peter, 1939- 285'.9
Puritans and Calvinism. Swengel, Pa., Reiner Publications, 1973. 110 p. 23 cm. "First five chapters ... originally appeared as nine separate articles in the monthly magazine, The Gospel magazine." Includes bibliographical references. [BX9322.T66] 73-166984 3.25
1. Puritans. 2. Calvinism. I. Title.

WALLER, George Macgregor, 1919- ed.
Puritanism in early America. Boston, Heath [1965] 115 p. (Problems in American civilization) Bibliography: p. [113]-115. 68-24165
I. Title.

WATKINS, Owen C. 285'.9
The Puritan experience; studies in spiritual autobiography [by] Owen C. Watkins. New York, Schocken Books [1972, c1971] x, 270 p. 23 cm. Bibliography: p. 241-260. [BX9322.W36 1972b] 70-150987 ISBN 0-8052-3425-X
1. Friends, Society of. 2. Puritans. 3. Witness bearing (Christianity) I. Title.

Puritans—Addresses, essays, lectures.

INTRODUCTION to Puritan theology : a reader / Edward Hindson, editor ; foreword by James I. Packer. Grand Rapids : Baker Book House, c1976. 282 p. : ill. ; 23 cm. "A Canon Press book." Includes index. Contents.Contents.—Preston, J. Natural theology.—Jewel, J. Scripture.—Charnock, S. God.—Manton, T. Man and sin.—Ussher, J. Christ.—Perkins, W. Salvation: introduction.—Owen, J. The atonement.—Hopkins, S. Regeneration and conversion.—Downame, G. Justification.—Bunyan, J. Sanctification.—Baxter, R. The church.—Edwards, J. Eschatology. Bibliography: p. 267-275. [BX9327.I58] 75-38235 ISBN 0-8010-4143-0 : 8.95 230'.5'9
1. Puritans—Addresses, essays, lectures. 2. Theology, Doctrinal—Addresses, essays, lectures. I. Hindson, Edward E.

[LEE, Samuel] 1625-1691.
The triumph of mercy in the chariot of praise. A treatise of preventing secret & unexpected mercies, with some mixt reflexions ... Boston, Reprinted by B. Green, for Benj. Eliot, and sold at his shop, 1718. 4 p. l., 194 p. 15 cm. Title vignette. "Epistle dedicatory" signed: Samuel Lee. First published in London, 1677. [BX9318.L4] 24-28194
I. Title. II. Title: The triumph of mercy. III. Title: Eleothriambos.

THE New Puritanism. 285'.9
Papers by Lyman Abbott [and others] during the semi-centennial celebration of Plymouth Church, Brooklyn, N.Y., 1847-1897. With introd. by Rossiter W. Raymond. Freeport, N.Y., Books for Libraries Press [1972] 275 p. 23 cm. (Essay index reprint series) "First published in 1897." [BX9327.N46 1972] 70-39672 ISBN 0-8369-2732-X
1. Puritans—Addresses, essays, lectures. 2. Theology—Addresses, essays, lectures. I. Abbott, Lyman, 1835-1922. II. Brooklyn. Plymouth Church.

THE Old Puritanism and the new age; addresses before the Woburn conference of Congregational churches at Malden, Massachusetts, April, 1903. Boston, Chicago, The Pilgrim press [1903] 106 p. 19 1/2 cm. (On cover: Beacon hill series) [BX9327.O4] 43-39390
1. Puritans—Addresses, essays, lectures.

Puritans—Collected works.

HOWE, John, 1630-1705.
The works of the Rev. John Howe ... with memoirs of his life by Edmund Calamy ... New-York, J. P. Haven, 1838. 2 v. 26 1/2 cm. Paged continuously. [BX9315.H6 1838] 46-37769
1. Puritans—Collected works. 2. Theology—Collected works—17th cent. I. Calamy, Edmund, 1671-1732. II. Title.

Puritans—Collections.

REINITZ, Richard, comp. 285'.9'0973
Tensions in American Puritanism. New York, Wiley [1970] xiii, 192 p. 22 cm. (Problems in American history) Bibliography: p. 188-192. [BX9313.R4] 70-100325
1. Puritans—Collections. I. Title.

Puritans—Controversial literature.

BANCROFT, Richard Abp. of Canterbury. 1544-1610, supposed author. 285.9
Tracts ascribed to Richard Bancroft, edited from a manuscript in the Library of St. John's College, Cambridge, by Albert Peel. Cambridge, University Press, 1953. xxix, 168p. 21cm. Bibliographical footnotes. [BX9320.B3] 53-7565
1. Puritans—Controversial literature. 2. Brownists. 3. Presbyterians in England. I. Peel, Albert, 1887-1949, ed. II. Title. Contents omitted.

DARK, Sidney, 1874- 285.9
The passing of the Puritan, by Sidney Dark. London, New York [etc.] Skeffington & son limited [1946] 100 p. 19 cm. [Full name: Sidney Ernest Dark] [BX9329.D3] A 46
1. Puritans—Controversial literature. I. Title.

EDWARDS, Jonathan, 1703-1758. 208.1
Puritan sage; collected writings of Jonathan Edwards, edited by Vergilius Ferm. New York, Library Publishers [1953] xxvii, 640p. illus., facsims. 23cm. [BX7117.E3 1953] 53-3143
I. Title.

Puritans—England.

BERRY, Boyd M. 821'.4
Process of speech : Puritan religious writing & Paradise lost / Boyd M. Berry. Baltimore : Johns Hopkins University Press, c1976. xi, 305 p. ; 24 cm. Includes bibliographical references and index. [PR3562.B4] 75-36933 ISBN 0-8018-1779-X : 13.50
1. Milton, John, 1608-1674. Paradise lost. 2. Puritans—England. 3. Preaching—History—England. I. Title.

BROWN, John, 1830-1922. 285'.9'0942
The English Puritans. [Folcroft, Pa.] Folcroft Library Editions, 1973. p. Reprint of the 1910 ed. published at the University Press, Cambridge, in series: The Cambridge manuals of science and literature. Bibliography: p. [BX9334.B7 1973] 73-12821 15.00
1. Puritans—England. I. Title.

BROWN, John, 1830-1922. 285.
The English Puritans, by John Brown, D.D. Cambridge [Eng.] The University press, 1910. vi p., 1 l., 160 p. 17 cm. (Half-title: The Cambridge manuals of science and literature) "Authorities": p. [156]-157. [BX9334.B7] A 11
I. Title.

FLYNN, John Stephen. 942.06
The influence of Puritanism on the political & religious thought of the English. Port Washington, N.Y., Kennikat Press [1970] xii, 257 p. 21 cm. "First published in 1920." Bibliographical footnotes. [BX9334.F5 1970] 72-102569 ISBN 0-8046-0729-X
1. Puritans—England. 2. Great Britain—Church history—Modern period, 1485- I. Title.

HALLER, William, 1885- 285.9
Elizabeth I and the Puritans Ithaca, N. Y., Pub. for the Folger Shakespeare Lib. [by] Cornell [1965, c.1964] 40p. facsims., ports. 22cm. (Folger bklets. on Tudor and Stuart civilization) Bibl. [BX9334.2.H3] 64-7542 1.00 pap.,
1. Elizabeth, Queen of England, 1533-1603. 2. Puritans—England. I. Title. II. Series.

HENSON, Herbert Hensley, Bp. of Durham, 1863-1947. 285'.9'0942
Puritanism in England. New York, B. Franklin [1972] viii, 294 p. 22 cm. (Burt Franklin research and source works series. Selected studies in history, economics, and social science, n.s. 19. (c) Modern European studies) Reprint of the 1912 ed. [BX9334.H37 1972] 70-185944 ISBN 0-8337-4177-2 15.00
1. Puritans—England. I. Title.

KNOTT, John Ray, 1937- 230
The sword of the spirit : Puritan responses to the Bible / John R. Knott, Jr. Chicago : University of Chicago Press, 1980. p. cm. Includes index. [BS500.K6] 79-23424 ISBN 0-226-44848-7 : 18.00
1. Bible—Criticism, interpretation, etc.—History—17th century. 2. Puritans—England. I. Title.

PLUM, Harry Grant, 1868-1956. 274.2
Restoration puritanism; a study of the growth of English liberty. Port Washington, N.Y., Kennikat Press [1972, c1943] ix, 129 p. 22 cm. Bibliography: p. [103]-123. [BX9334.P55 1972] 72-159101 ISBN 0-8046-1644-2
1. Puritans—England. 2. Great Britain—Church history—17th century. 3. Great Britain—Politics and government—1660-1714. I. Title.

PORTER, Harry Culverwell, comp. 285'.9'0942
Puritanism in Tudor England. [Edited by] H. C. Porter. Columbia, University of South Carolina Press [1970] xv, 311 p. 23 cm. (History in depth) Bibliography: p. 301-304. [BX9334.2.P67 1970b] 75-145532 ISBN 0-87249-222-2 9.95
1. Puritans—England. I. Title.

SCHUCKING, Levin Ludwig, 1878-1964. 301.42'0942
The Puritan family; a social study from the literary sources. Translated from the German by Brian Battershaw. New York, Schocken Books [1970, c1969] xv, 196 p. 23 cm. Translation of Die Familie im Puritanismus. Bibliography: p. 185-191. [BX9334.S313 1970] 79-86315 6.00
1. Puritans—England. 2. Family—History. 3. Great Britain—Social conditions. 4. English literature—History and criticism. I. Title.

TRINTERUD, Leonard J., 1904- comp. 285'.9'08
Elizabethan Puritanism, edited by Leonard J. Trinterud. New York, Oxford University Press, 1971. xv, 454 p. 24 cm. (A Library of Protestant thought) Bibliography: p. 441-444. [BX9334.2.T75] 74-141652 11.50
1. Puritans—England. 2. Gt. Brit.—Church history—16th century—Sources. I. Title. II. Series.

WILSON, John Frederick. 251'.00942
Pulpit in Parliament; Puritanism during the English civil wars, 1640-1648, by John F. Wilson. Princeton, N.J., Princeton University Press, 1969. x, 289 p. 23 cm. Bibliographical footnotes. [BX9333.W5] 69-18074 ISBN 0-691-07157-8 10.00
1. Puritans—England. 2. Preaching—History—England. I. Title.

Puritans—England—Addresses, essays, lectures.

THE English Puritan tradition / Barrington R. White, editor. Limited ed. Nashville, Tenn. : Broadman Press, c1980. 415 p. ; 24 cm. (Christian classics) Includes bibliographical references. [BX9333.E53] 19 78-75163 ISBN 0-8054-6543-X : 24.95 285'.9
1. Puritans—England—Addresses, essays, lectures. 2. Dissenters, Religious—England—Addresses, essays, lectures. I. White, B. R. (Barrington Raymond) II. Title. III. Series.

Puritans—England—History.

FOSTER, Stephen, 1942- 285'.9'0922
Notes from the Caroline underground : Alexander Leighton, the Puritan Triumvirate, and the Laudian reaction to nonconformity / by Stephen Foster. Hamden, Conn. : Published for the Conference on British Studies and Wittenberg University by Archon Books, c1978. p. cm. (Studies in British history

and culture ; v. 6) Includes index. Bibliography: p. [BX9339.L4F67] 78-9595 ISBN 0-208-01758-5 : 12.50
1. Leighton, Alexander, 1568-1649. 2. Land, William, Abp. of Canterbury, 1573-1645. 3. Puritans—England—History. 4. England—Church history—17th century. 5. Persecution—England. I. Title. II. Series.

Puritans—England—History—16th century.

LAKE, Peter. 285'.9'0922
Moderate Puritans and the Elizabethan church / Peter Lake. Cambridge ; New York : Cambridge University Press, 1982. viii, 357 p. ; 23 cm. Revision of thesis (Ph.D.)—Cambridge. Includes index. Bibliography: p. 343-347. [BX9334.2.L34 1982] 19 81-17052 ISBN 0-521-24010-7 : 49.50
1. Church of England—History—16th century. 2. Puritans—England—History—16th century. 3. England—Church history—16th century. I. Title.

Puritans—Frankfurt am Main.

[WHITTINGHAM, William] 283
d.1579.
A brieff discours off the troubles begonne at Franckford in Germany, Anno Domini 1554. Abowte the Booke off off [sic] common prayer and ceremonies and contienued by the Englishe men theyre to thende off Q. Maries raigne ... [Amsterdam, Theatrum Orbis Terrarum; Da Capo Press, 1972] ccxv p. 21 cm. (The English experience, its record in early printed books published in facsimile, no. 492) "S.T.C. no. 25442." Reprint of the 1574 ed. Cover title: Troubles abowte the Booke of common prayer. Title on spine: Booke of Common prayer, 1574. [BX5653.F8W6 1574a] 71-38228 ISBN 9-02-210492-3 9.00
1. Frankfurt am Main. English Church. 2. Church of England—Doctrinal and controversial works. 3. Puritans—Frankfurt am Main. 4. British in Frankfurt am Main. I. Title. II. Title: Troubles abowte the Booke of common prayer. III. Title: Booke of common prayer, 1574. IV. Series.

Puritans—Great Britain

FRERE, Walter Howard, 285'.9'0942
Bp. of Truro, 1863-1938, ed.
Puritan manifestoes; a study of the origin of the Puritan revolt with a reprint of the Admonition to the Parliament and kindred documents, 1572. Edited by W. H. Frere and C. E. Douglas. New York, B. Franklin [1972] xxxi, 155 p. 22 cm. (Burt Franklin research and source works series. Philosophy & religious history monographs, 107) Reprint of the 1907 ed. published as no. 72 of the Church Historical Society's publications. Contents.Contents.—Puritan manifestoes.—An admonition to the Parliament.—The letters of Gualter and Beza.—An exhortation to the byshops to deale brotherly with theyr brethren.—An exhortation to the bishops and their clergie to aunswer a little booke, etc.—A second admonition. Includes bibliographical references. [BX9331.F7 1972] 79-183703 ISBN 0-8337-4119-5 15.00
1. Puritans—Great Britain. I. Douglas, Charles Edward, joint author. II. Title. III. Series: Church Historical Society (Gt. Brit.) Publications, 52.

HALLER, William, 1885- 285.942
The rise of Puritanism; or, The way to the New Jerusalem as set forth in pulpit and press from Thomas Cartwright to John Lilburne and John Milton, 1570-1643. New York, Harper [1957, c1938] 464 p. illus. 21 cm. (Harper torchbooks, TB22) [BX9334.H3 1957] 57-10117
1. Puritans—Great Britain. 2. Christian literature, English. 3. English literature—Early modern, 1500-1700—History and criticism. I. Title.

KNAPPEN, Marshall Mason, 1901-
Tudor Puritanism; a chapter in the history of idealism. Chicago, University of Chicago Press [1965] xvi,555 p. (Phoenix books, P194) NUC66
1. Puritans—Gt. Brit. 2. Gt. Brit.—Church hist.—1528-1603. I. Title.

SEAVER, Paul S. 251
The Puritan lectureships; the politics of religious dissent, 1560-1662 [by] Paul S. Seaver. Stanford, Stanford University Press, 1970. ix, 402 p. 24 cm. Bibliography: p. [311]-373. [BX9334.2.S4] 71-93497 12.50
1. Puritans—Gt. Brit. 2. Preaching—History—Gt. Brit. 3. Church and state in Great Britain. I. Title.

Puritans-Massachusetts.

ERIKSON, Kai T. 301.15
Wayward Puritans; a study in the sociology of deviance [by] Kai T. Erikson. New York, Wiley, [1966] xv, 228 p. illus. 22 cm. Bibliography: p. 217-223. [BX9355.E7] 66-16140
1. Puritans—Massachusetts. I. Title.

MIDDLEKAUFF, Robert. 285'.9'0922
The Mathers : three generations of Puritan intellectuals, 1596-1728 / [by] Robert Middlekauff. New York : Oxford University Press, 1976,c1971. 440p. ; 21 cm. Includes index. Includes bibliographical notes. [F67.M4865] 79-140912 ISBN 0-19-502115-0 pbk. : 4.50
1. Mather, Richard, 1596-1669. 2. Mather, Increase, 1639-1723. 3. Mather, Cotton, 1663-1728. 4. Puritans-Massachusetts. I. Title.
The 1971hardcover ed.is available for 13.95

Puritans—Massachusetts—Biography.

WENDELL, Barrett, 285.8'32'0924 B
1855-1921.
Cotton Mather / Barrett Wendell ; introd. by David Levin. New York : Chelsea House, 1980. xix, 321 p. ; 21 cm. (American and women of letters) Reprint of the 1891 ed. published by Dodd, Mead, New York, in series: Makers of America. Includes index. [F67.M43W46 1980] 19 80-23335 ISBN 0-87754-166-3 pbk. : 5.95
1. Mather, Cotton, 1663-1728. 2. Puritans—Massachusetts—Biography. I. Title. II. Series. III. Series: Makers of America.

Puritans—Massachusetts—History—Sources.

PURITAN personal 974.4'02
writings : autobiographies and other writings. New York : AMS Press, 1982. p. cm. (A Library of American Puritan writings ; v. 8) Contents.Contents. Governour Bradford's letter book / by William Bradford — The Autobiographical memoranda of John Brock, 1636-1659 / edited by Clifford K. Shipton — The Journal of Esther Burr / edited by Josephine Fisher — Memoirs of Captain Roger Clap — John Dane's Narrative — The complete book of Joseph Green (1675-1715) — Edward Taylor's "Spiritual relation" / edited by Donald E. Stanford — John Winthrop's Christian experience. [F67.P97] 19 78-270 ISBN 0-404-60808-6 : 57.50
1. Puritans—Massachusetts—History—Sources. 2. Massachusetts—History—Colonial period, ca. 1600-1775—Sources. I. Title. II. Series.

PURITAN personal 974.4'02'0924
writings : diaries. New York : AMS Press, 1982. p. cm. (A Library of American Puritan writings ; v. 7) Reprint (1st work). Originally published: Biographical sketch and diary of Rev. Joseph Green, of Salem Village / by Samuel P. Fowler. (Historical collections of the Essex Institute ; v. 8, 10, 36 (June 1866-Oct. 1900)) Reprint (2nd work). Originally published: The diaries of John Hull, mint-master and treasurer of the colony of Massachusetts Bay, with a memoir of the author. Boston : Printed by J. Wilson and Son, 1857. Reprint (3rd work). Originally published: The diary of a Colonial clergyman, Peter Thacher of Milton / Edward Pierce Hamilton. (Proceedings of the Massachusetts Historical Society ; v. 71 (Oct. 1953-May 1957) [F67.P98 1982] 19 78-269 ISBN 0-404-60807-8 : 57.50
1. Green, Joseph, 1675-1715. 2. Thacher, Peter, 1651-1727. 3. Puritans—Massachusetts—History—Sources. 4. Massachusetts—History—Colonial period, ca. 1600-1775—Sources. I. Fowler, Samuel Page, 1800-1888. Biographical sketch and diary of Rev. Joseph Green, of Salem Village. 1982. II. Hull, John, 1624-1683. The diaries of John Hull, mint-master and treasurer of the colony of Massachusetts Bay, with a memoir of the author. 1982. III. Hamilton, Edward Pierce. The diary of a Colonial clergyman, Peter Thacher of Milton. 1982. IV. Series.

Puritans—New England.

BACON, Leonard, 1802- 285'.9'0974
1881.
The genesis of the New England churches. New York, Arno Press, 1972. 485 p. illus. 23 cm. (Religion in America, series II) Reprint of the 1874 ed. [F68.B12 1972] 74-38435 ISBN 0-405-04056-3
1. Puritans—New England. 2. Pilgrim Fathers. 3. New England—Church history. 4. Massachusetts—History—Colonial period, ca. 1600-1775. 5. Massachusetts—History—New Plymouth, 1620-1691. I. Title.

MILLER, Perry, 1905-1963. 974'.02
Sources for The New England mind : the seventeenth century / by Perry Miller ; edited by James Hoopes. Williamsburg, Va. : Institute of Early American History and Culture, c1981. xxiv, 120 p. ; 24 cm. Bibliography: p. xxii. [F7.M56 1954 Suppl.] 19 81-81411 ISBN 0-910776-01-6 (pbk.) : 5.95
1. Miller, Perry, 1905-1963. New England mind. 2. Puritans—New England. 3. Christian literature, American. 4. American literature—Colonial period, ca. 1600-1775—History and criticism. 5. American literature—New England. I. Hoopes, James, 1944- II. Miller, Perry, 1905-1963. New England mind. III. Title.
Publisher's address: P. O. Box 220, Williamsburg, VA 23185.

RUTMAN, Darrett 285'.9'0974
Bruce.
American Puritanism / by Darrett B. Rutman. New York : Norton, c1977. p. cm. Reprint of the 1970 ed. published by Lippincott, Philadelphia, in series: Pilotbooks and The Lippincott history series. Includes bibliographical references and index. [F7.R8 1977] 76-49541 ISBN 0-393-00842-8 pbk. : 2.95
1. Puritans—New England. 2. New England—Religious life and customs. I. Title.

RUTMAN, Darrett 285'.9'0974
Bruce.
American Puritanism; faith and practice, by Darrett B. Rutman. Philadelphia, Lippincott [1970] xii, 139 p. 21 cm. (Pilotbooks) (The Lippincott history series.) Includes bibliographical references. [F7.R8] 79-100370
1. Puritans—New England. I. Title.

Puritans—New England—Addresses, essays, lectures.

JAMES, Sydney V., 285'.9'0974
comp.
The New England Puritans, edited by Sydney V. James. New York, Harper & Row [1968] vi, 169 p. 21 cm. (Interpretations of American history) Includes bibliographical references. [BX9354.2.J3] 69-11114
1. Puritans—New England—Addresses, essays, lectures. I. Title.

PURITAN New England 285'.9'0974
: essays on religion, society, and culture / Alden T. Vaughan and Francis J. Bremer, editors. New York : St. Martin's Press, c1977. vii, 395 p. ; 24 cm. Includes bibliographical references. [BX9355.N35P87] 76-52589 ISBN 0-312-65695-5 : 5.95
1. Puritans—New England—Addresses, essays, lectures. 2. New England—Civilization—Addresses, essays, lectures. I. Vaughan, Alden T., 1929- II. Bremer, Francis J.

Puritans—New England—History—Sources.

GREGORY, J.
Puritanism in the Old world and in the New, from its inception in the reign of Elizabeth to the establishment of the Puritan theocracy in New England: a historical handbook, by Rev. J. Gregory, Edinburgh: introduction by Rev. Amory 41. Bradford ... New York, Chicago [etc.] Fleming H. Revell company, 1896. 4 p. l., v-x. 406 p. 22 cm. 12-32648
I. Title.

VAUGHAN, Alden T., 285'.9'0974
1929- comp.
The Puritan tradition in America, 1620-1730. Edited by Alden T. Vaughan. New York, Harper & Row [1972] xxviii, 348 p. 21 cm. (Documentary history of the United States) Includes bibliographical references. [F7.V32 1972] 78-174703 ISBN 0-06-139641-9
1. Puritans—New England—History—Sources. I. Title.

Puritans—United States.

EMERSON, Everett H., 285'.9'0973
1925-
Puritanism in America, 1620-1750 / by Everett Emerson. Boston : Twayne Publishers, c1977. p. cm. (Twayne's world leaders series ; TWLS 71) Includes index. Bibliography: p. [BX9354.2.E47] 77-4354 ISBN 0-8057-7692-3 lib.bdg. : 8.50
1. Puritans—United States. I. Title.

KNAPPEN, Marshall Mason, 285'.9
1901-
Two Elizabethan Puritan diaries : by Richard Rogers and Samuel Ward. Edited, with an introd., by M.M. Knappen. Gloucester, Mass., P. Smith, 1966 [c1933] xiii, 148 p. facsims., map. ports. 21 cm. (Studies in church history, v. 21. Reprint of the 1933 edition. Contents.Contents.--The diary of Richard Rogers.--The diary of Samuel Ward.--Historical notes from Ward's ms. "Adversarian."--Selected Bibliography: (p. 137-140) [BX9339.R6K6 1966] 67-3219
1. Puritans. Rogers, Richard, 1550?-1618. Diary. Ward, Samuel, d. 1643. Diary. 2. Studies in church history (Hartford) v. 2) I. Title.

KOFOID, Carrie Prudence.
Puritan influences in the formative years of Illinois history, by Carrie Prudence Kofoid. Springfield, Illinois state journal company, 1906. cover-title, 79 p. 23 cm. "Paper ... accepted by the University of Illinois as a thesis for the degree of master of arts in history." Bibliographical foot-notes. 7-145730
I. Title.

Puritans—U.S.—Addresses, essays, lectures.

MCGIFFERT, Michael, 285'.9'0973
comp.
Puritanism and the American experience. Edited by Michael McGiffert. Reading, Mass., Addison-Wesley [1969] viii, 280 p. 22 cm. (Themes and forces in American history series) Essays. Bibliography: p. 275-280. Bibliographical footnotes. [BX9354.2.M3] 69-18403
1. Puritans—U.S.—Addresses, essays, lectures. 2. U.S.—Civilization—Addresses, essays, lectures. I. Title.

Purnell, Benjamin Franklin.

STERLING, Anthony 922.89
King of the harem heaven; the amazing true story of a daring charlatan who ran a virgin love cult in America. Derby, Conn., Monarch Books [c.1960] 159p. 19cm. (Monarch Americana bk. MA300) .35 pap.,
1. Purnell, Benjamin Franklin. I. Title.

Purviance, David, 1766-1847.

ROGERS, James Richard, 1840- 286.
The Cane Ridge meeting-house, by James R. Rogers; to which is appended the autobiography of B. W. Stone, and a sketch of David Purviance by William Rogers. Cincinnati, The Standard publishing company [c1910] 237 p. incl. front. plates, ports. 20 cm. [BX7331.C3R6] 10-20166
1. Purviance, David, 1766-1847. I. Stone,

Barton Warren, 1772-1844. II. Rogers, William 1784-1862. III. Title.

Pusey, Edward Bouverie, 1800-1882.

GRAFTON, Charles Chapman, bp., 1830-1912. 922.
Pusey and the church revival, by the Rt. Rev. Chas. Chapman Grafton ... Milwaukee, The Young churchman co., 1902. 76 p. front. (port.) 20 cm. [BX5199.P9G7] 2-10811
1. Pusey, Edward Bouverie, 1800-1882. I. Title.

JACKSON, Thomas, 1783-1873. 230.7
A letter to Rev. Edward B. Pusey ... being a vindication of the tenets and character of Wesleyan Methodists, against his misrepresentations and censures. By Thomas Jackson ... New York, Pub. by G. Lane & P. P. Sandford, for the Methodist Episcopal church, 1843. 208 p. 16 cm. [BX8331.J25] 34-6003
1. Pusey, Edward Bouverie, 1800-1882. 2. Methodism. I. Title.

LIDDON, Henry Parry, 1829-1890. 922.
Life of Edward Bouverie Pusey, doctor of divinity, canon of Christ church; regius professor of Hebrew in the University of Oxford, by Henry Parry Liddon...Edited and prepared for publication by the Rev. J. O. Johnston...and the Rev. Robert J. Wilson... London and New York, Longmans, Green, and co., 18 v. fronts. (ports.) illus. 23 cm. Vol. 4 edited and prepared for publication by J. O. Johnston, Robert J. Wilson and W. C. E. Newbolt. Vol. 2: 3d ed.; v. 4: 3d impression. "A bibliographical list of the printed works of Dr. Pusey": v. 4, p. [393]-446. "Dr. Pusey's sermons arranged in order of the texts": v. 4, p. [447]-453. [BX5199.P9L52] 46-43851
1. Pusey, Edward Bouverie, 1800-1882. I. Johnston, John Octavius, 1852-1923, ed. II. Title.

LIDDON, Henry Parry, 1829-1890. 922.
Life of Edward Bouverie Pusey, doctor of divinity, canon of Christ church; regius professor of Hebrew in the University of Oxford, by Henry Parry Liddon...Edited and prepared for publication by the Rev. J. O. Johnston...and the Rev. Robert J. Wilson... London and New York, Longmans, Green, and co., 1893-97. 4 v. fronts, illus., ports., facsim. 22 1/2 cm. Vol. 4, edited and prepared for publication by J. O. Johnston, R. J. Wilson and W. C. E. Newbolt. Vols. 1, 3-4, 2d ed. "A bibliographical list of the printed works of Dr. Pusey": v. 4, p. [395]-446. "Dr. Pusey's sermons arranged in order of the texts": v. 4. p. [447]-453. [BX5199.P9L5] 46-43585
1. Pusey, Edward Bouverie, 1800-1882. I. Johnston, John Octavius, 1852-1923, ed. II. Title.

[TRENCH, Maria Marcia Fanny] 922.342
The story of Dr. Pusey's life, by the author of 'Charles Lowder' ... London, New York [etc.] Longmans, Green, and co., 1900. xix, 570 p. front. (port.) 21 cm. [BX5199.P9T7] 1-28075
1. Pusey, Edward Bouverie, 1800-1862. I. Title.

Pusey, Edward Bouverie, 1800-1882. A letter to ... the Archbishop of Canterbury.

GOODE, William, 1801-1868. 283
The case as it is: or, A reply to the letter of Dr. Pusey to His Grace the Archbishop of Canterbury; including a compendious statement of the doctrines and views of the tractors as expressed by themselves. By William Goode ... 1st American, from the 2d London ed. ... Philadelphia, H. Hooker, 1842. 1 p. l., [5]-57 p. 24 cm. [BX5099.P83G6 1842] 36-33989
1. Pusey, Edward Bouverie, 1800-1882. A letter to ... the Archbishop of Canterbury. 2. Oxford movement. I. Title.

Putman, Jimmy, 1946-

PUTMAN, Jimmy, 1946- 248'.246 B
A new life to live : Jimmy Putman's story / [edited] by William Bradford Huie. Nashville : T. Nelson, c1977. 157 p., [4] leaves of plates : ill. ; 21 cm. [BV4935.P87A36] 77-24956 ISBN 0-8407-5124-9 : 5.95
1. Putman, Jimmy, 1946- 2. Converts—Alabama—Biography. 3. Church work with juvenile delinquents—Alabama—Oneonta. I. Huie, William Bradford, 1910- II. Title.

Putnam, Hilary.

SALMON, Nathan U., 1951- 110
Reference and essence / Nathan U. Salmon. Princeton, N.J. : Princeton University Press, c1981. xvi, 293 p. ; 24 cm. Based on the author's thesis (Ph.D.)—University of California at Los Angeles, 1979. Includes indexes. Bibliography: p. 265-278. [B105.R25S24] 19 81-8687 ISBN 0-691-07264-7 : 45.00
1. Putnam, Hilary. 2. Reference (Philosophy) 3. Essence (Philosophy) 4. Object (Philosophy) I. Title.

Puzzles.

CASTO, Earle Ray, 1884- 220.088
Building Bible names, by E. Ray Casto. Boston, W. A. Wilde company [c1939] [123] p. diagrs. 20 cm. [BS613.C3] 793.73 39-31941
1. Puzzles. 2. Bible—Study—Text-books. I. Title.

ROOTS, Anne Frances. 290.3
Mythological aids for cross-word puzzle solvers; also includs Arbic-Greek-Hebrew alphabets and Hebrew-Roman months, by Anne Frances Roots. Old Greenwich, Conn. [c1938] 59 p. 15 cm. [BL315.R6] 39-3770
1. Puzzles. 2. Mythology—Dictionaries, indexes, etc. I. Title. II. Title: Cross-words puzzle solvers, Mythological aids for.

Pygmalion—Juvenile literature.

ESPELAND, Pamela, 1951- 292'.13 E
The story of Pygmalion / Pamela Espeland ; pictures by Catherine Cleary. Minneapolis : Carolrhoda Books, c1981. [30] p. : col. ill. ; 24 cm. Pygmalion, a sculptor, falls in love with one of his statues and prays to Venus for help. [PZ8.1.E83Sw 1981] 80-15792 ISBN 0-87614-127-0 (lib. bdg.) : 6.95
1. Pygmalion—Juvenile literature. 2. Galatea—Juvenile literature. 3. [Pygmalion.] 4. [Galatea.] 5. [Mythology, Roman.] I. Cleary, Catherine. II. Title.

Pyinmana agricultural school.

CASE, Brayton Clarke, 1887-1944. 922.6591
Lazy-man-rest-not: the Burma letters of Brayton C. Case, selected by Randolph L Howard Philadelphia, Chicago [etc.] The Judson press [1946] 128 p. plates. 20 1/2 cm. [BV3271.C33A32] 47-21353
1. Pyinmana agricultural school. I. Howard, Randolph Levi, 1883- ed. II. Title.

Pyke, James Howell.

PYKE, Frederick Merrill. 266'.7'10924 B
The first of three generations of White Wolves in China; James Howell Pyke's secret. [Timonium, Md., c1973] 109 p. illus. 18 cm. [BV3427.P9P94] 74-157956 1.95
1. Pyke, James Howell. I. Title.

Pynchon, William, 1590?-1662.

BYINGTON, Ezra Hoyt, 1828-1901. 973.
The Puritan in England and New England. By Ezra Hoyt Byington ... With an introduction by Alexander McKenzie ... Boston, Roberts bros., 1896. xi, 406 p. front. (port.) 22 cm. "Authorities": p. [xxv]-xxix. [BX9321.B8 1896] [F7.B96] 1-151
1. Pynchon, William, 1590?-1662. 2. Breck, Robert, 1713-1784 3. Breck, Robert, 1713-1784 4. Puritans. 5. Witchcraft. I. Title.
Contents omitted

Pyramids—Curiosa and miscellany.

DARTER, Francis M. 913.32
Our Bible in stone, its divine purpose and present day message, the mystery of the ages unveiled [by] Francis M. Darter ... Salt Lake City, Utah, Deseret news publishing co. [c1931] 179 p. pl., fold. plan, diagrs, 20 cm. [DT63.5.D28] 133.32 31-14613
1. Pyramids—Curisa and miscellany. 2. Mormons and Mormonism. 3. Prophecies. I. Title.

LEWIS, Harve Spencer, 1883- 913.32
The symbolic prophecy of the Great pyramid, by Dr. H. Spencer Lewis ... San Jose, Calif., Supreme grand lodge of AMORC [c1936] 208 p. incl. illus., plates, plans. 20 cm. (Rosicrucian library, vol. xiv) "First edition." Pages 193-208, advertising matter. [BF1623.R7R65 vol. 14bis] (133.082) [(159.961082)] 37-3808
1. Rosicrucians. 2. Pyramids—Curiosa and miscellany. I. Title.

THE symbolic prophecy of the great pyramid. San Jose, Calif., Supreme Grand Lodge of AMORC [1961] 207p. illus. 20cm. (Rosicrucian Library, XIV)
I. Lewis, Harve Spencer, 1883-1939.

WAKE, Charles Staniland, 1835-1910. 932
The origin and significance of the great pyramid / by C. Staniland Wake. Minneapolis : Wizards Bookshelf, 1975. viii, 131 p. : ill. ; 23 cm. (Secret doctrine reference series) Reprint of the 1882 ed. published by Reeves & Turner, London. "The substance of this little work was read as a paper before the Hull Literary Club on the 13th March, 1882." [DT63.W14 1975] 73-84047 ISBN 0-913510-10-6 : 6.50
1. Cheops, King of Egypt. 2. Pyramids—Miscellania. I. Title.

Pyrros (Greek mythology)

FONTENROSE, Joseph Eddy, 1903- 292.213
The cult and myth of Pyrros at Delphi. Berkeley, University of California Press, 1960. iv, 191-266p. illus., map. 26cm. (University of California publications in classical archaeology, v. 4, no. 3) Bibl. 61-62773 2.50 pap.,
1. Pyrros (Greek mythology) I. Title. II. Series: California. University. University of California publications in classical archaeology, v. 4, no. 3

Q document.

MANSON, Thomas Walter, 1893-1958. 226'.2'06
The sayings of Jesus : as recorded in the Gospels according to St. Matthew and St. Luke / arranged with introd. and commentary by T. W. Manson. Grand Rapids : Eerdmans, 1979. p. cm. Originally published as pt. 2 of The mission and message of Jesus by H. D. A. Major. Includes index. Bibliography: p. [BS2575.M34 1979] 79-16611 ISBN 0-8028-1812-9 pbk. : 7.95
1. Jesus Christ—Words. 2. Bible. N.T. Matthew—Commentaries. 3. Bible. N.T. Luke—Commentaries. 4. Q document. I. Major, Henry Dewsbury Alves, 1872- The mission and message of Jesus. II. Title.

Q document (Biblical criticism)

EDWARDS, Richard Alan. 226'.06
A theology of Q : eschatology, prophecy, and wisdom / Richard A. Edwards. Philadelphia : Fortress Press, c1976. xiii, 173 p. ; 24 cm. Includes indexes. Bibliography: p. 159-164. [BS2555.2.E34] 75-13042 ISBN 0-8006-0432-6 : 11.95
1. Q document (Biblical criticism) I. Title.

Q document (Biblical criticism)—Concordances.

EDWARDS, Richard Alan. 226
A concordance to Q / Richard A. Edwards. Missoula, Mont. : Society of Biblical Literature : distributed by Scholars Press, [1975] p. cm. (Sources for Biblical study ; 7) [BS2555.5.E38] 75-6768 ISBN 0-88414-052-0 (Society of Biblical Literature) : 7.00
1. Q document (Biblical criticism)—Concordances. I. Title. II. Series.

Quakers—Fiction.

NEWMAN, Daisy. FIC
Indian summer of the heart / Daisy Newman. Boston : Houghton Mifflin, 1982. 376 p. ; •22 cm. [PS3527.E87715 1982] 813'.52 19 82-6226 ISBN 0-395-32517-X : 14.95
1. Quakers—Fiction. I. Title.

Quakers—Sermons.

THE beginnings of Quakerism.
By the late William C. Braithwaite. Second edition revised by Henry J. Cadbury. Cambridge [Eng.] at the University Press, 1961. xxviii, 585p. fold. map. 23cm.
I. Brathwaite, William Charles, 1862-1922.

BRAITHWAITE, William Charles.
The message and mission of Quakerism, by William C. Braithwaite and Henry T. Hodgkin ... Pub. by direction of the Five years meeting. Philadelphia, The John C. Winston company, 1912. 115 p. 20 cm. "The two addresses which compose this book were delivered at the Five years meeting of the Society of Friends held in Indianspolis, Indians, from October 15th to 22nd, 1912"--Foreword. Bibliography: p. 115. 13-1313 0.60
I. Hodgkin, Henry T. II. Title.

FOX, George, 1624-1691.
Selections from the epistles of George Fox. By Samuel Tuke. Abeidged. Philadelphia, Association of Friends, for the diffusion of religious and useful knowledge, 1858. xx, 114 p. 16 cm. 16-8269
I. Tuke, Samuel, 1784-1857, ed. II. Title.

LETCHWORTH, Thomas, 1739-1784.
Twelve discourses, delivered chiefly at the meeting-house of the people called Quakers, in the park, Southwark. By the late Thomas Letchworth. Salem, Reprinted by T. C. Cushing, 1794. xiii, [15]-248 p. 21 cm. 9-23105
I. Title.

MOTT, Lucretia, 1793-1880. 252'.0963
Lucretia Mott, her complete speeches and sermons / edited [with an introduction] by Dana Greene. New York : E. Mellen Press, c1980. ix, 401 p., [1] p. of plates : port. ; 23 cm. Includes bibliographical references. [BX7733.M59L82 1980] 19 80-81885 ISBN 0-88946-968-7 pbk. : 24.95
1. Quakers—Sermons. 2. Sermons, American. 3. Church and social problems—Addresses, essays, lectures. I. Greene, Dana. II. [Speeches] III. Title.

SHARING our Quaker faith.
Edwin B. Bronner, editor. Birmingham, Eng., Philadelphia, Pa., Friends World Committee for Consultation, 1959. iv, 140p. 20cm.
I. Bronner, Edwin B 1920- ed.

Quality assurance.

BROH, Robert A. 658.5'62
Managing quality for higher profits / Robert A. Broh. New York : McGraw-Hill, c1982. p. cm. Includes index. [TS156.6.B76] 19 81-19292 ISBN 0-07-007975-7 : 15.95
1. Quality assurance. I. Title.

QUALITY assurance : 658.5'62
methods, management, and motivation / Hans J. Bajaria, editor. 1st ed. Dearborn, Mich. : Society of Manufacturing Engineers, Marketing Services Dept. ; Milwaukee, Wis. : American Society for Quality Control, c1981. v, 248 p. : ill. ; 29 cm. Includes bibliographies and index. [TS156.6.Q343] 19 81-50392 ISBN 0-87263-067-6 : 29.00
1. Quality assurance. I. Bajaria, Hans J.
Publisher's address : P. O. Box 930, Dearborn, MI 48128.

Quality circles.

DEWAR, Donald L. 658.4'036
The quality circle guide to participation management / Donald L. Dewar. Englewood Cliffs, N.J. : Prentice-Hall, [1982] c1980. 414 p. : ill. ; 24 cm. [HD66.D48 1982] 19 81-15724 ISBN 0-13-744987-9 : 19.95
1. Quality circles. I. Title. II. Title: Participation management.

INGLE, Sud. 658.4'036
Quality circles master guide : increasing productivity with people power / Sud Ingle. Englewood Cliffs, N.J. : Prentice-Hall, c1982. ix, 246 p. : ill. ; 29 cm. (A Spectrum book) Bibliography: p. 244-246. [HD66.I47] 19 81-13874 ISBN 0-13-745018-4 : 25.95 ISBN 0-13-745000-1 pbk. : 14.95
1. Quality circles. I. Title.

Quality of work life—Case studies.

PERKINS, Dennis N. T., 658.1'1 1942-
Managing creation : the challenge of building a new organization / Dennis N.T. Perkins, Veronica F. Nieva, Edward E. Lawler III. Chichester [West Sussex] ; New York : Wiley, c1983. p. cm. (Wiley series on organizational assessment and change,) "A Wiley-Interscience publication." Includes bibliographical references and indexes. [HD4905.P47 1983] 19 82-17548 ISBN 0-471-05204-3 (U.S.) : 21.95
1. Quality of work life—Case studies. 2. Organizational change—Case studies. 3. Employees' representation in management—Case studies. 4. Machinery in industry—Case studies. I. Nieva, Veronica F. II. Lawler, Edward E. III. Title. IV. Series.

Quaracchi, Italy. Collegium States Bonaventura.

ARCHIVUM franciscanum historicum. 271.3
Periodica publicatio trimestris cura pp. Collegii D. Bonaventura, annus 1-3 1908-1910 Ad Claras Aquas prope Florentiam, 1908-; New York, Johnson Reprint, 1967. v. plates. 25cm. [BX3601.A7] 10-2408 set; pap.; 75.00; ea., pap., 27.50
1. Quaracchi, Italy. Collegium S. Bonaventura.

Quarreling.

DE MOSS, Lucy King. 241
Learning how to settle disputes; a weekday church school unit in Christian citizenship series for grades three and four [by] Lucy King De Moss. St. Louis, Mo., Printed for the International committee on cooperative publication of weekday church school curriculum, by the Bethany press [c1941] 122 p. 22 cm. Songs with music: p. 77-82. Bibliography: p. [119]-122. [BV4627.Q8D4] 43-38934
1. Quarreling. I. International council of religious education. Interdenominational committee on co-operative publication of vacation and church school curriculum. II. Title.

Quayle, William Alfred, bp., 1860-1925.

QUAYLE, William Alfred, bp., 1860-1925. 252.
The dynamite of God, by William A. Quayle. New York, Cincinnati, The Methodist book concern [c1918] 2 p. l., 7-330 p. 21 cm. [BX8333.Q3D9] 18-19133
I. Title.

RICE, Merton Stacher, 1872- 922.
William Alfred Quayle, the skylark of Methodism, by M. S. Rice ... New York, Cincinnati, The Abingdon press [c1928] 249 p. front., plates, ports., facsims. 20 1/2 cm. [BX8495.Q75R5] 28-14479
1. Quayle, William Alfred, bp., 1860-1925. I. Title.

Queen Anne's Bounty.

BEST, Geoffrey Francis Andrew 283.42
Temporal pillars: Queen Anne's Bounty, the Ecclesiastical Commissioners, and the Church of England. [New York] Cambridge [c.]1964. xiv, 582p. fold. maps. 24cm. Bibl. 64-2873 12.50
1. Queen Anne's Bounty. 2. Gt. Brit. Ecclesiastical Commissioners for England. I. Title.

BEST, Geoffrey Francis Andrew. 283.42
Temporal pillars: Queen Anne's Bounty, the Ecclesiastical Commissioners, and the Church of England. Cambridge [Eng.] University Press, 1964. xiv, 582 p. fold. maps. 24 cm. Bibliography: p. 558-569. [BX5165.B39] 64-2873
1. Queen Anne's Bounty 2. Gt. Brit. Ecclesiastical Commissioners for England I. Title.

Queen of All Saints, Chicago.

CHICAGO. Queen of All Saints.
Celebration of the Consecration, October, 29, 1960. [Chicago, The New World, 1960] 1 v. (unpaged) illus. ports., 30 cm. 68-35468
1. Queen of All Saints, Chicago. I. Title.

Queen of the Most Holy Rosary Church, Elysburg, Pa.

25TH anniversary of the Queen of the Most Holy Rosary Church, October, 1975, Elysburg, Pennsylvania. 282'.748'31
New York : Park Pub. Co., c1975. [32] p. : ill. ; 26 cm. [BX4603.E47O437] 75-41695
1. Queen of the Most Holy Rosary Church, Elysburg, Pa.

The querists.

BLAIR, Samuel, 1712-1751. 285.
A particular consideration of a piece, entitled, The quersists: wherein sundry passages extracted from the printed sermons, letters and journals of the Rev. Mr. Whitefield are vindicated from the false glosses and erroneous senses put upon them in said Querists;... Mr. Whitefield's soundness in the true scheme of Christian doctrine maintained; and the author's disingenuous dealing with him exposed. By Samuel Blair ... Philadelphia: Printed and sold by B. Franklin, 1741. iii, 4-63 p. 16 1/2 cm. Signatures: A-D. [BX9225.W4B6] 2-11333
1. Whitefield, George, 1714-1770. 2. The querists. I. Title.

[Questions and answers.]

BEERS, Victor Gilbert, 1928- 220*.07
The ABQ book, by V. Gilbert Beers. Illustrated by Alla Skuba. Chicago, Moody Press [1972] [44] p. col. illus. 20 x 26 cm. An alphabetically arranged Bible quiz with more than one hundred questions about such topics as Abraham, bulrushes, Calvary, and vineyards. Answers are at the back. [BS539.B44] 72-88039 ISBN 0-8024-0134-1
1. Bible—Juvenile literature. 2. [Bible.] 3. [Questions and answers.] I. Skuba, Alla, illus. II. Title.

CAMPBELL, James Mann, 1840-
Bible questions; a series of studies arranged for every week in the year. New York and London, Funk & Wagnalls co., 1900. xv, 267 p. 12 cm. 0-728
I. Title.

DAUGHTERS of St. Paul. 238'.2
Basic catechism : with Scripture quotations / by the Daughters of St. Paul. Boston, Ma. : St. Paul Editions, c1980. 207 p. ; 19 cm. Presents the basic tenets of the Catholic Church in question and answer format with related scriptural quotations. [BX1961.D27 1980] 80-10149 ISBN 0-8198-0622-6 : 3.00 ISBN 0-8198-0623-4 pbk. : 1.50
1. Catholic Church—Catechisms and creeds—English. 2. [Catholic Church—Catechisms and creeds.] 3. [Questions and answers.] I. Title.

MARTI, Retta. Mrs. 220
Bible questions for the study of church, ladies', and young people's organizations, by Mrs. Retta Marti ... [Weatherford, Tex., 1925] cover-title, 1 p. l., 171 p. 22 cm. [BS612.M3] 25-5275
I. Title.

PUTNAM, Charles Elsworth, 1859- 230
Where now is Jesus! and nine kindred questions, with the Word's clear answers, by C. E. Putnam ... Chicago, The Bible institute colportage association [c1924] 58 p. 17 cm. [BT885.P95] 24-5491
I. Title.

RAY, Charles Wayne.
Bible questions answered, by Rev. Charles Wayne Ray ... Cincinnati, O., Press of Jennings & Pye [1903] 59 p. incl. front. (port.) 19 cm. 3-28946
I. Title.

[WILKINSON, Horace] 220.
A Bible question book; outlines, questions and answers on the persons and events of the Bible, arranged into periods. Bedford, Va., Bedford printing company [1919] 95 p. 23 cm. On cover: By Horace Wilkinson. [BS615.W7] 19-5067
I. Title.

Questions and answers—Christian life.

BIBLE. English. Selections. 1973. 248'.4
Answers, compiled by David Shibley. Wheaton, Ill., Tyndale House [1973] 80 p. 20 cm. [BS391.2.S54 1973] 72-97652 ISBN 0-8423-0080-5 1.00 (pbk.)
1. Questions and answers—Christian life. I. Shibley, David, comp. II. Title.

FAGAL, William A 253.5
Pastor, this is my problem. Mountain View, Calif., Pacific Press Pub. Association [1963] 144 p. 23 cm. [BV4612.F3] 63-10645
1. Questions and answers — Christian life. 2. Casuistry. I. Title.

FAGAL, William A. 253.5
Pastor. this is my problem. Mountain View, Calif., Pac. Pr. Pub. [c.1963] 144p. 23cm. 63-10645 3.75 bds.,
1. Questions and answers—Christian life. 2. Casuistry. I. Title.

MURRAY, Walter Brown, 1864-
Who is Jesus? ... Is he God? or God in man? or man only? [by] Walter B. Murray. Minneapolis, Minn., The Nunc licet press [c1915] 203 p. 19 cm. 15-25526
I. Title.

Questions and answers—Jews.

APPLEBAUM, Morton M 296.076
What everyone should know about Judaism; answers to the questions most frequently asked about Judaism. Foreword by John Haynes Holmes. New York, Philosophical Library [1959] 87p. 22cm. [BM51.A65] 59-4504
1. Questions and answers—Jews. I. Title.

BARISH, Louis. 296.076
Basic Jewish beliefs, by Louis and Rebecca Barish. New York, J. David [1961] 221p. 22cm. [BM51.B3] 61-8453
1. Questions and answers—Jews. I. Barish, Rebecca, joint author. II. Title.

KAPLAN, Mordecai Menahem, 1881- 296
Questions Jews ask: reconstructionist answers. New York, Reconstructionist Press [1956] 532p. 23cm. [BM197.7.K3] 56-8577
1. Questions and answers—Jews. 2. Reconstructionist Judaism. I. Title.

KAPLAN, Mordecai Menahem, 1881- 296
Questions Jews ask: reconstructionist answers. New York, Reconstructionist Press [1956] 532p. 23cm. [BM197.7.K3] 56-8577
1. Questions and answers—Jews. 2. Reconstructionist Judaism. I. Title.

WEINBERG, Albert Katz, comp. 296
Ask the rabbi; two thousand questions and answers about the Jew, compiled by Albert K. Weinberg, M.A., in collaboration with Rabbi Morris S. Lazaron, M.A. New York, Bloch publishing company, 1927. 192 p. 21 1/2 cm. [DS118.5.W4] 27-18978
1. Questions and answers—Jews. I. Lazaron, Morris Samuel, 1888- joint comp. II. Title.

Questions and answers—Marriage.

CONWAY, James D 1906- 265.5
What they ask about marriage. Chicago, Fides [1955] 322p. 21cm. [BX2250.C62] 55-7774
1. Questions and answers—Marriage. 2. Marriage—Catholic Church. I. Title.

Questions and answers—Theology.

ASKING them question; 230
a selection from the three series. Edited by Ronald Selby Wright. London, New York, Oxford University Press, 1953. 254p. 19cm. [BR96.A815] 54-22119
1. Questions and answers—Theology. I. Wright, Ronald Selby, 1908- ed.

ASKING them questions. 230
3d ser. Edited by Ronald Selby Wright. London, New York, Oxford University Press, 1950. xviii, 194 p. 19 cm. [BR96.A83] 50-8143
1. Questions and answers—Theology. I. Wright, Ronald Selby, 1908- ed.

BROWN, Charles Ewing, 1883- 230.076
Questions and answers. Anderson, Ind., Gospel Trumpet Co. [1949] 188 p. 22 cm. [BR96.B68] 49-5039
1. Questions and answers—Theology. I. Title.

BRUCE, Frederick Fyvie, 1910- 220.6'6
Answers to questions [by] F. F. Bruce. Grand Rapids, Mich., Zondervan [1973, c1972] 264 p. 25 cm. Questions and answers previously printed in the Harvester. [BS612.B78] 72-95520 ISBN 0-85364-101-3 6.95
1. Bible—Examinations, questions, etc. 2. Questions and answers—Theology. I. Title.

BURTON, Charles J. 220
Biblical exegesis; or, The Bible explained in the light of two thousand exegetical questions, by Chas. J. Burton... [Minneapolis] Standard press, 1920. 126 p. 1 l., 19 1/2 cm. [BS605.B8] 21-900
I. Title.

CHAPLIN, Dora P 230.076
We want to know; originally intended for young people but frequently borrowed by the other generation especially parents, godparents, clergy, and other leaders. Foreword by Lawrence Rose. New York, Morehouse-Gorham, 1957. 216p. 21cm. Includes bibliography. [BR96.C5] 57-6775
1. Questions and answers— Theology. I. Title.

CLARKE, William R. 230'.076
Pew ask pulpit answers. by W. R. Clarke. Boston, Christopher Pub. House [c.1967] 161p. 21cm. [BR96.C55] 67-13543 3.95
1. Questions and answers—Theology. I. Title.

CLARKE, William R. 230'.076
Pew asks; pulpit answers, by W. R. Clarke. Boston, Christopher Pub. House [c1967] 161 p. 21 cm. [BR96.C55] 67-13543
1. Questions and answers — Theology. I. Title.

CONNELL, Francis Jeremiah 230.2
Father Connell answers moral questions. Edited by Eugene J. Weitzel. Washington, Catholic University of America Press, [c.] 1959. xiii, 210p. 23cm. 59-16744 3.95
1. Questions and answers—Theology. 2. Christian ethics—Catholic authors. 3. Catholic Church—Doctrinal and controversial works. I. Title.

CONNELL, Francis Jermiah, 1888- 241.076
More answers to today's moral problems. Ed. by Eugene J. Weitzel. Washington, D.C., Catholic Univ. [c.1965] xiii, 249p.

23cm. Bibl. [BX1758.2.C647] 65-16255 4.95
1. Questions and answers—Theology. 2. Christian ethics—Catholic authors. 3. Casuistry. I. Title.

DAVIS, Denver Jackson, 1915- 248
Across the pastor's desk; problems and questions faced by ourpeople in these troubled times. With an introd. by Norman Vincent Peale. Philadelphia, Dorrance [1954] 187p. 20cm. [BR96.D3] 54-8892
1. Questions and answers-Theology. I. Title.

DAVISON, Frank Elon, 1887- 250.76
Let's talk it over; questions on church work and church problems asked by ministers and lay people, answered with brevity, candor, humor, and understanding. St. Louis, Bethany Press [1953] 159p. 21cm. [BR96.D35] 53-32883
1. Questions and answers—Theology. 2. Church work. I. Title.

EMCH, William N 230.41
The question box. Columbus, Ohio, Wartburg Press [1956] 188 p. 20 cm. Compiled from 'The question box, conducted by ... [the author, as] a regular feature of the Lutheran standard. [BR96.E5] 57-16411
1. Questions and answers—Tehology. 2. Lutheran Church—Doctrinal and controversal works. I. Title.

FINEGAN, Jack, 1908- 230.076
Youth asks about religion. New York, Association Press, 1949. 192 p. 20 cm. (A Haddam House book) Includes bibliographies. [BR96.F7] 49-8332
1. Questions and answers—Theology. 2. Theology, Doctrinal—Popular works. I. Title.

FITZGERALD, Lawrence P. 230'.076
Questions that bother me [by] Lawrence P. Fitzgerald. Valley Forge [Pa.] Judson [1967] 94p. 20cm. [BR96.F75] 67-14359 1.95 pap.,
1. Question sQuestion and answers Theology. 2. Questions and answers—Christian life. I. Title.

GIESEN, Heinrich, ed. 230.03
When you are asked about faith and life. Tr. [from German] by Elmer Foelber. Philadelphia, Fortress [c.1963] 190p. 18cm. 63-7903 3.75
1. Questions and answers—Theology. I. Title.

GRAHAM, William Franklin, 1918- 207.6
My answer. New York, Pocket Bks. [1967. c.1960] 243p. 18cm. (50550) [BR96.G7] .50 pap.,
1. Questions and answers—Theology. I. Title.

GRAHAM, William Franklin, 1918- 207.6
My answer. [1st ed.] Garden City, N.Y., Doubleday, 1960. 259 p. 22 cm. [BR96.G7] 60-15942
1. Questions and answers—Theology. I. Title

HALL, Frederick Fairchild, 1873- 207
Your faith and your neighbors; a quiz book of world religions ... By Frederick Hall. Boston, W. A. Wilde company [c1946] 142 p. 20 cm. [BR96.H3] 46-5361
1. Questions and answers—Theology. I. Title.

HARING, Bernhard, 1912- 230'.2'076
Bernard Haring replies; answers to 50 moral and religious questions [by] Bernard Haring. Staten Island, N.Y., Alba [1967] 205p. 19cm. Tr. of Padre Bernard Haring risponde. [BX1754.3.H313] 67-15201 3.95
1. Questions and answers—Theology. 2. Catholic Church—Doctrine and controversial works—Catholic authors. I. Title.

HARING, Bernhard, 1912- 230'.2'076
Bernard Haring replies; answers to 50 moral and religious questions [by] Bernard Haring. Staten Island, N.Y., Alba House [1967] 205 p. 19 cm. Translation of Padre Bernard Haring risponde. [BX1754.3.H313] 67-15201
1. Questions and answers — Theology. 2. Catholic Church — Doctrinal and controversal works — Catholic authors. I. Title.

HASKIN, Dorothy (Clark), 1905- 248
Your questions answered. Chicago, Moody Press [1952] 128 p. 17 cm. (Colportage library, 223) [BR96.H34] 52-4343
1. Questions and answers—Theology. I. Title.

HAYWARD, Percy Roy, 1884- 248
This business of living; the questions young people ask, with answers. New York, Association Press, 1949. 159 p. 21 cm. Bibliography: p. 157-159. [BR96.H38] 49-9943
1. Questions and answers—Theology. I. Title.

HOWARD, Philip Eugene, 1898- 207
Answers for inquiring Christians; notes on open letters to the Sunday school times. [Westwood, N. J.] F. H. Revell Co. [1954] 172p. 22cm. [BR96.H6] 54-8001
1. Questions and answers—Theology. I. Title.

IRONSIDE, Henry Allan, 1876- 220.076
What's the answer? 362 answers to Bible questions, by Harry A. Ironside... Grand Rapids, Mich., Zondervan publishing house [1944] 164 p. 20 cm. [BR96.I7] 45-15770
1. Questions and answers—Theology. I. Title.

KERR, Clarence Ware, 1893- 252.051
Questions that must be answered. Los Angeles, Cowman Publications [1956] 190p. 20cm. [BR96.K4] 56-2694
1. Questions and answers—Theology. 2. Presbyterian Church— Sermons. 3. Sermons, American. I. Title.

KNIGHT, Marcus. 230.076
There's an answer somewhere, by Marcus Knight and L. S. Hawkes. With a foreword by the Bishop of Portsmouth. London, New York, Longmans, Green [1953] 134p. 19cm. [BR96.K5] 53-13316
1. Questions and answers—Theology. I. Hawkes, Leonard Stephen, joint author. II. Title.

KUNG, Hans, 1928- 230.2
That the world may believe. Tr. by Cecily Hastings. New York, Sheed [c.1963] 149p. 20cm. 63-10676 3.00 bds.,
1. Questions and answers—Theology. 2. Catholic Church—Apologetic works. I. Title.

KUNG, Hans, 1928- 230.2
That the world may believe. Translated by Cecily Hastings. New York, Sheed and Ward [1963] 149 p. 20 cm. [BX1754.K78] 63-10676
1. Questions and answers — Theology. 2. Catholic Church — Apologetic works. I. Title.

MCCARTHY, John, 1909- 230.2
Problems in theology. vol. II. Westminster, Md., Newman Press, 1960. 22cm. Contents.v. 2, The commandments. 57-8610 7.50
1. Questions and answers—Theology. 2. Catholic Church—Doctrinal and controversial works. I. Title.

MCCARTHY, John, 1909- 230.2
Problems in theology. Westminister, Md., Newman Press [1956- v. 22cm. Contents.v.1. The sacraments. [BX1751.M14] 57-8610
1. Questions and answers—Theology. 2. Catholic Churc; –Doctrinal and controversial works. I. Title.

MOSS, Claude Beaufort, 1888- 283.076
Answer me this. [1st ed.] New York, Longmans, Green, 1959. 212p. 21cm: [BX5930.2.M66] 59-13546
1. Questions and answers—Theology. 2. Protestant Episcopal Church in the U. S. A.—Doctrinal and controversial works. I. Title.

O'REILLY, Philip 230.2
1000 questions and answers on Catholicism. [Rev. ed.] New York, Guild Press; distributed by Golden Press [c.1956, 1960] 384p. 17cm. (An Angelus book) 60-4878 1.25 bds.,
1. Questions and answers—Theology. 2. Catholic Church—Doctrinal and controversial works—Catholic authors. I. Title.

O'REILLY, Philip. 230.2
1000 questions and answers on Catholicism. [Rev. ed.]iNew York, Guild Press; distributed by Golden Press [1960] 384p. 17cm. (An Angelus book) [BX1754.3.O7 1960] 60-4878
1. Questions and answers—Theology. 2. Catholic Church—Doctrinal and controversial works— Catholic authors. I. Title.

POLING, Daniel Alfred, 1884- 230.076
Your questions answered with comforting counsel. Great Neck, N.Y., Channel Press [1956] 312p. 21cm. [BR96.P57] 56-12006
1. Questions and answers—Theology. I. Title.

POOVEY, William Arthur, 1913- 230
Qeustions that trouble Christians. Columbus, Ohio, Wartburg Press [1946] 187 p. 21 cm. [BR96.P6] 47-7011
1. Questions and answers—Theology. I. Title.

PRICE, Eugenia. 241
Never a dull moment; honest questions by teen agers, with honest answers by Eugenia Price. Grand Rapids, Zondervan Pub. House [1955] 121p. 20cm. [BR96.P7] 55-13639
1. Questions and answers—Theology. I. Title.

REDHEAD, John A 248.4076
Putting your faith to work. New York, Abingdon Press [1959] 128p. 20cm. [BR96.R4] 59-12784
1. Questions and answers—Theology. I. Title.

RICE, John R., 1895- 220.076
Dr. Rice, here is my question: Bible answers to 294 important questions in forty years' ministry. Wheaton, Ill., Sword of the Lord Publishers [c1962] 367 p. 21 cm. [BR96.R47] 63-23940
1. Questions and answers — Theology. I. Title.

RIMMER, Harry, 1890- 207
'That's a good question!' Grand Rapids, W. B. Eerdmans Pub. Co., 1954. 137p. 20cm. [BR96.R5] 54-6233
1. Questions and answers—Theology. I. Title.

SAINT'S herald. 289.3
Question time. Independence, Mo., Herald House, 1955-67. 2 v. 21 cm. A collection of questions and answers from the Saints' herald, official organ of the Reorganized Church of Jesus Christ of Latter Day Saints. [BX8671.Q4] 55-12245
1. Questions and answers—Theology. 2. Reorganized Church of Jesus Christ of Latter Day Saints—Doctrinal and controversial works. I. Title.

SAINT'S herald Question time 289.3 [answers to 457 often-asked questions from the Saint's herald, well indexed for ready use; questions about the church, the scriptures, and problems of life, Reorganized Church of Jesus Christ of Latter-Day Saints. Independence, Mo.] Herald House [1967] v. 21cm. has as subtitle: A collection of often-asked questions and answers from the Saint's herald. Well indexed for ready use [BX6871.S23] 55-12245 5.95
1. Questions and answers—Theology. 2. Reorganized Church of Jesus Christ of Latter-Day Saints

SANGSTER, William Edwin, 1900- 207
Questions people ask about religion. New York, Abingdon Press [1959] 142p. 21cm. London ed. (Epworth) has title: Give God a chance. [BR96.S22 1959] 60-5235
1. Questions and answers—Theology. I. Title.

SANGSTER, William Edwin Robert, 1900- 207
Questions people ask about religion. Nashville, Abingdon [1965, c.1959] 142p. 21cm. (Apex bk. T6) London ed. (Epworth) has title: Give God a chance. [BR96.S22] 1.00 pap.,
1. Questions and answers—Theology. I. Title.

SHERIDAN, John V. 230.2
Questions and answers on the Catholic faith. Foreword by James Francis Cardinal McIntyre. New York, Hawthorn [c.1963] 319p. 21cm. Bibl. 63-11862 4.95
1. Questions and answers—Theology. 2. Catholic Church—Doctrinal and controversial works—Catholic authors. I. Title.

SIEMENS, David F., Jr. 230
Exploring Christianity, a guided tour. Chicago, Moody [1963, c.1962] 156p. 18cm. (Moody pocket bks., 78) Bibl. 62-21957 .59 pap.,
1. Questions and answers—Theology. I. Title.

SOHN, Otto E 230.41
What's the answer? Saint Louis, Concordia Pub. House [1960] 210 p. 20 cm. Selections from the author's column with the same title, which has appeared regularly in the Lutheran witness since Jan. 1954. [BR96.S6] 60-44457
1. Questions and answers — Theology. 2. Lutheran Church — Doctrinal and controversial works. I. Title.

STONE, Nathan J 230.076
Answering your questions. Chicago, Moody Press [1956] 509 p. 22 cm. [BR96.S86] 57-23348
1. Questions and answers — Theology. I. Title.

THOMAS, John Lawrence. 249
The family clinic; a book of questions and answers. Westminster, Md., Newman Press, 1958. 336 p. 23 cm. [BX2351.T5] 58-13641
1. Questions and answers — Theology. 2. Family — Religious life. 3. Church and social problems — Catholic Church. I. Title.

THORNTON, Francis Beauchesne, 1898- 282.076
What is your Catholic I. Q., by Francis Beauchesne Thornton and Timothy Murphy Rowe. New York, P. J. Kenedy [1951] 216 p. 20 cm. [BX1754.T5] 51-14705
1. Questions and answers — Theology. 2. Catholic Church — Doctrinal and controversial works, Popular. I. Title.

UTT, Charles D 230.076
Answers to 343 bible questions Mountain View, Calif., Pacific Press Pub. Association [1957] 383p. 18cm. (Christian home library) [BR96.U8] 57-7780
1. Questions and answers—Theology. I. Title.

WOODBRIDGE, Charles Jahleel, 1902- 230.076
Tell us, please; answers to Life's great questions. [Westwood, N.J.] Revell [1958] 127 p. 21 cm. [BR96.W63] 58-8601
1. Questions and answers — Theology. I. Title.

Quiches—Religion and mythology.

GIRARD, Rafael. 299'.7
Esotericism of the Popol Vuh / Raphael Girard ; translated from the Spanish with a foreword by Blair A. Moffett. 1st English ed. Pasadena, Calif. : Theosophical University Press, 1979. xiv, 359 p. : ill. ; 22 cm. Translation of Esoterismo del Popol-vuh. Includes index. [F1465.P84513] 78-74712 ISBN 0-911500-13-8 : 12.50 ISBN 0-911500-14-6 pbk. : 7.50
1. Popul-vuh. 2. Quiches—Religion and mythology. 3. Indians of Central America—Guatemala—Religion and mythology. I. Title.

JACKSON, Donald, 1895- 299'.7
Religious concepts in ancient America and in the Holy Land : as illustrated by the Sacred book of the Quiche Mayans and by the Bible : quotes, notes, and notions / Donald Jackson. 1st ed. Hicksville, N.Y. : Exposition Press, c1976. viii, 142 p. ; 22 cm. (An Exposition-university book) Bibliography: p. 141-142. [F1465.P8466] 76-363012 ISBN 0-682-48503-9 : 8.00
1. Popol vuh. 2. Bible—Criticism,

interpretation, etc. 3. Quiches—Religion and mythology. I. Title.

POPOL vuh. & Quiche 299'.7
The book of counsel: the Popol vuh of the Quiche Maya of Guatamala. [By] Munro S. Edmonson. New Orleans, Middle American Research Institute, Tulane University, 1971. xvii, 273 p. 27 cm. (Tulane University. Middle American Research Institute. Publication 35) Bibliography: p. 257-259. [PM4231.6.A1 1971] 72-197628
1. Quiches—Religion and mythology. I. Edmonson, Munro S., tr. II. Title. III. Series: Tulane University of Louisiana. Middle American Research Institute. Publication 35.

POPOL vuh. English. 299'.7
Popol vuh : the great mythological book of the ancient Maya / newly translated, with an introd., by Ralph Nelson ; with drawings from the Codices mayas. Boston : Houghton Mifflin, 1976. 86 p. : ill. ; 24 cm. [F1465.P813 1976] 75-42451 ISBN 0-395-24302-5 : 5.95
1. Quiches—Religion and mythology. I. Nelson, Ralph, 1940-

SPENCE, Lewis, 1874-1955. 299'.7
The Popol vuh; the mythic and heroic sagas of the Kiches of Central America. New York, AMS Press [1972] 63 p. 19 cm. Reprint of the 1908 ed., which was issued as no. 16 of Popular studies in mythology, romance and folklore. Bibliography: p. [57]-59. [F1465.P875 1972] 75-139178 ISBN 0-404-53516-X 5.50
1. Popol vuh. 2. Quiches—Religion and mythology. I. Title. II. Series: Popular studies in mythology, romance and folklore, no. 16.

Quick, Robert Hebert, 1831-1891.

QUICK, Robert Hebert, 1831-1891. 922
Life and remains of the Rev. R. H. Quick, ed. by F. Storr. Cambridge, University press, 1899. vi p., 1 l., 544 p. front. (port.) 20 cm. [LB775.Q38] E 10
1. Quick, Robert Hebert, 1831-1891. I. Storr, Francis, 1839- ed. II. Title.

Quietism.

FENELON, Francois de Salignac de la Mothe-, 1651-1715. 242
A guide to true peace; or, A method of attainment to inward and spiritual prayer. Compiled chiefly from the writings of Fenelon, archbishop of Cambray, Lady Guion, and Michael de Molinos. First American edition. New-York, Printed and sold by Samuel Wood & sons, 1816. iv, [5] -108 p. 14 1/2 cm. [BX2183.F4] A 32
1. Quietism. I. Guyon, Jeanne Marie (Bouvier de La Motte) 1648-1717. II. Molinos, Miguel de, 1628-1696. III. Title.

FENELON, Francois de Salignac de La Mothe-, abp., 1651-1715. 242
A guide to true peace; or, The excellency of inward and spiritual prayer. Compiled chiefly from the writings of Fenelon, Guyon, and Molinos. New York and London, Pub. in association with Pendle Hill by Harper & brothers [1946] xvi p., 1 l., 118 p., 1 l. 14 cm. Compiled by William Backhouse and James Janson. cf. Introd. "The present printing ... is taken from the 1839 edition published in Philadelphia."--p. XII. [BV5099.F45] 47-16904
1. Quietism. I. Guyon, Jeanne Marie (Bouvier de La Motte) 1648-1717. II. Molinos, Miguel de, 1628-1696. III. Backhouse, William 1779- or 80-1844, comp. IV. Janson, James, joint comp. V. Title.

GUYON, Jeanne Marie (Bouvier de La Motte) 1648-1717. 242
Spiritual torrents, by Madame J. M. B. de la Mothe Guyon. Translated by A. E. Ford. With parallel passages from the writings of Emanuel Swedenborg. Boston, O. Clapp, 1853. viii, [11]-308 p. 17 1/2 cm. [BV5099.G8] 43-45939
1. Quietism. 2. Mysticism. I. Ford, A. K., tr. II. Swedenborg, Emanuel, 1688-1772. III. Title.

Quietude.

ROGERS, Harold, 1907- 248'.3
A handful of quietness / Harold Rogers. Waco, Tex. : Word Books, c1977. 140 p. ; 23 cm. [BJ1533.Q5R63] 77-75463 ISBN 0-8499-0010-7 : 5.95
1. Rogers, Harold, 1907- 2. Quietude. 3. Spiritual life—Methodist authors. I. Title.

ROGERS, Harold, 1907- 248'.3
A handful of quietness / Harold Rogers. Boston : G. K. Hall, 1979, c1977. xi, 218 p. ; 24 cm. Large print ed. [BJ1533.Q5R63 1979] 79-11192 ISBN 0-8161-6696-X : 9.95
1. Rogers, Harold, 1907- 2. Quietude. 3. Spiritual life—Methodist authors. 4. Large type books. I. Title.

Quimby, Paul Elmore.

†QUIMBY, Paul Elmore. 266'.6'73 B
Yankee on the Yangtze : one missionary's saga in revolutionary China / Paul Quimby with Norma Youngberg. Nashville, Tenn. : Southern Pub. Association, c1976. 176 p. ; 21 cm. [BV3427.Q55A36] 76-49387 ISBN 0-8127-0131-3 pbk. : 4.95
1. Quimby, Paul Elmore. 2. Missionaries—China—Biography. 3. Missionaries—United States—Biography. I. Youngberg, Norma R., joint author. II. Title.

Quimby, Phineas Parkhurst, 1802-1866.

HAWKINS, Ann Ballew, 1892- 922.8573
Phineas Parkhurst Quimby, revealer of spiritual healing to this age; his life and what he taught. [1st ed.] Jackson, Tenn. [1951] 56 p. 18 cm. "Based on the Quimby manuscripts and original letters in the Library of Congress." [RZ401.Q63] 51-5939
1. Quimby, Phineas Parkhurst, 1802-1866. I. Title.

Quincy, Mass. First Congregational society (Unitarian)

FROTHINGHAM, Nathaniel Langdon, 1793-1870. 288.
The manifestation of Christ. A sermon, preached at the installation of Rev. William Parsons Lunt, as colleague pastor with Rev. Peter Whitney, over the Congregational church in Quincy, June 3, 1835. By N. L. Frothingham ... Boston, L. C. Bowles, 1835. 63 p. 24 cm. Contains also "Charge, by Rev. Dr. Parkman, of Boston. Right hand of fellowship, by Rev. F. Cunningham, of Dorchester. Address to the society, by Rev. E. S. Gannett, of Boston ... With a sermon preached on the first Sunday after his installation, by William P. Lunt. [BX9861.Q8F7] 22-13829
1. Quincy, Mass. First Congregational society (Unitarian) 2. Lunt, William Parsons, 1805-1857. 3. installation sermons. I. Title.

Quinlan, Karen Ann.

COLEN, B. D. 174'.2
Karen Ann Quinlan : dying in the age of eternal life / B. D. Colen. New York : Nash Pub., c1976. 204 p. ; 22 cm. Includes index. [R726.C64] 76-7144 ISBN 0-8402-1368-9 : 7.95
1. Quinlan, Karen Ann. 2. Terminal care—Moral and religious aspects. 3. Death. 4. Coma—Biography.

Quinn, Clinton Simon, Bp.

CHIDSEY, Alan Lake. 283.09
The bishop; a portrait of the Right Reverend Clinton S. Quin. Houston, Tex., Gulf Pub. Co. [1966] 239 p. 22 cm. [BX5995.15C5] 65-29026
1. 1. Quinn, Clinton Simon, Bp. I. Title.

Quinn, Edel Mary, 1907-1944.

BROWN, Evelyn M. 92
Edel Quinn, beneath the Southern Cross, by Evelyn M. Brown. Illustrated by Harold Lang. New York, Vision Books [1967] xv, 175 p. illus. 22 cm. A biography of an Irish girl who dedicated her life to missionary service in East Africa. [BV3557.Q8B7] AC 67
1. Quinn, Edel Mary, 1907-1944. 2. Missions—Africa, South.

MCAULIFFE, Marius 266'.2'0924 B
Envoy to Africa : the interior life of Edel Quinn / Marius McAuliffe. Chicago : Franciscan Herald Press, [1975] p. cm. [BV3557.Q8M32] 74-31153 ISBN 0-8199-0560-7 pbk. : 1.95
1. Quinn, Edel Mary, 1907-1944. I. Title.

Quinn, James, 1775-1847.

WRIGHT, John F. 922.773
Sketches of the life and labors of James Quinn, who was nearly half a century a minister of the gospel in the Methodist Episcopal church. By John F. Wright ... Cincinnati, Printed at the Methodist book concern, 1851. 324 p. front. (port.) 19 1/2 cm. [BX8495.Q8W7] 32-31783
1. Quinn, James, 1775-1847. I. Title.

Quiroga, Gaspar, Cardinal, d. 1594.

BOYD, Maurice, 1921- 922.246
Cardinal Quiroga, inquisitor general of Spain. Dubuque,Iowa, W. C. Brown Co. [c1954] 163p. illus. 24cm. [BX4705.Q65B6] 55-14535
1. Quiroga, Gaspar, Cardinal, d. 1594. I. Title.

Qumran.

MANUAL of discipline 221.4
The Rule of Qumran and its meaning: introduction, translation, and commentary. R. C. Leaney. Philadelphia, Westminster [c.1966] 310p. 23cm. (New Testament lib.) Bibl. [BM488.M3A3] 66-16966 7.50
I. Leaney, Alfred Robert Clare, ed. and tr. II. Title.

TREVER, John C., 1915- 221.4
The Dead Sea scrolls : a personal account / by John C. Trever. Rev. ed. Grand Rapids : Eerdmans, 1977. p. cm. Published in 1965 and 1966 under title: The untold story of Qumran. Includes bibliographical references and index. [BM487.T7 1977] 77-10808 ISBN 0-8028-1695-9 pbk. : 3.95
1. Trever, John C., 1915- 2. Dead Sea scrolls. 3. Qumran. I. Title.

VAUX, Roland de, 1903- 221.4
L'archeologie et les manuscrits de la mer Morte. [New York] Pub. forthe British Acad. by Oxford [c.]1961[ ] xv, 107p. illus., fold. map, 25cm. (Schweich lectures of the British Acad., 1959) Bibl. 62-245 6.90
1. Qumran. 2. Dead Sea scrolls. I. Title. II. Series: The Schweich lectures, 1959

VAUX, Roland de, 1903-1971. 221'.44
Archaeology and the Dead Sea scrolls. London, published for the British Academy by the Oxford University Press, 1973. xv, 142 p. illus., fold maps. 26 cm. (The Schweich lectures of the British Academy, 1959) Revised ed. in an English translation of L'archeologie et les manuscrits de la mer Morte. Includes bibliographical references. [DS110.Q8V313 1973] 73-174845 ISBN 0-19-725931-6
1. Qumran. 2. Dead Sea scrolls. I. British Academy, London (Founded 1901). II. Title. III. Series: The Schweich lectures, 1959.
Distributed by Oxford University Press, New York, 12.00.

Qumran community.

ALLEGRO, John Marco, 1923- 221.44
The people of the Dead Sea scrolls in text and pictures by John Marco Allegro. [1st ed.] Garden City, N. Y., Doubleday, 1958. 192 p. illus. 27 cm. [BM175.Q6A4] 58-13267
1. Dead Sea scrolls. 2. Qumran community. I. Title.

BADIA, Leonard F. 296.4
The Qumran baptism and John the Baptist's baptism / Leonard F. Badia. Lanham, Md. : University Press of America, [1980] p. cm. Includes index. Bibliography: p. [BM175.Q6B32] 19 80-5438 ISBN 0-8191-1095-7 : 14.50 ISBN 0-8191-1096-5 (pbk.) : 6.75
1. John the Baptist. 2. Qumran community. 3. Baptism—Judaism. I. Title.

BLACK, Matthew. 296.81
The scrolls and Christian origins; studies in the Jewish background of the New Testament. New York, Scribner [1961] 206p. illus. 22cm. Includes bibliography. [BM175.Q6B5] 61-7223
1. Qumran community. 2. Dead Sea scrolls. 3. Christianity—Origin. I. Title.

BLACK, Matthew 296.81
The scrolls and Christian origins; studies in the Jewish background of the New Testament. New York, Scribners [c.1961] 206p. illus. Bibl. 61-7223 3.95
1. Qumran community. 2. Dead Sea scrolls. 3. Christianity—Origin. I. Title.

CROSS, Frank Moore, Jr. 296
The ancient library of Qumran and modern biblical studies. Garden City, N.Y., Doubleday, 1961[c.1958, 1961] 260.p. illus. (Anchor bk., A272) 1.25 pap.,
1. Qumran community. 2. Dead Sea scrolls. I. Title.

CROSS, Frank Moore. 296.8'1
The ancient library of Qumran and modern Biblical studies / by Frank Moore Cross, Jr. Westport, Conn. : Greenwood Press, 1976. p. cm. Reprint of the 1958 ed. published by Doubleday, Garden City, N.Y., which was issued as the 1956-1957 Haskell lectures at Oberlin College. Bibliography: p. [BM175.Q6C7 1976] 76-29736 ISBN 0-8371-9281-1 lib.bdg. : 15.25
1. Dead Sea scrolls. 2. Dead Sea scrolls—Relation to the New Testament. 3. Qumran community. I. Title. II. Series: The Haskell lectures, Oberlin College ; 1956-1957.

CROSS, Frank Moore. 296
The ancient library of Qumran and modern Biblical studies. [1st ed.] Garden City, N.Y., Doubleday, 1958. 196 p. illus. 22 cm. (The Haskell lectures, 1956-1957) Includes bibliography. [BM175.Q6C7] 58-5933
1. Dead Sea scrolls. 2. Qumran community. I. Title.

FRITSCH, Charles Theodore, 1912- 221.6'7
The Qumran community: its history and scrolls, by Charles T. Fritsch. With a new introd. by the author. New York, Biblo and Tannen, [1973 c1956] viii, 147 p. illus. 22 cm. Bibliography: p. 131-141. [BM487.F7 1972] 72-7327 ISBN 0-8196-0279-5 7.50
1. Dead Sea scrolls. 2. Qumran community.

GARTNER, Bertil. 296.81
The temple and the community in Qumram and the New Testament; a comparative study in the temple symbolism of the Qamran texts and the New Testament. Cambridge, Univerity Press, 1965. xii, 164 p. 23 cm. (Society for New Testament Studies. Monograph series, 1) Bibliography: p. 143-151. [BM175.Q6G3] 64-21545
1. Qumran community. 2. Bible. N.T. — Symbolism. 3. Christianity, and other religions — Judaism. 4. Judaism — Relations — Christianity. I. Title. II. Title: Temple symbolism of the Qumran texts and the New Testament. III. Series. IV. Series: Studiorum Novi Testamenti Societas. Monograph series, 1

GARTNER, Bertil 296.81
The temple and the community in Qumran and the New Testament; a comparative study in the temple symbolism of the Qumran texts and the New Testament [New York] Cambridge [c.]1965. xii, 164p. 23cm. (Soc. for N.T. Studies. Monograph ser., 1) Bibl. [BM175.Q6G3] 64-21545 4.75
1. Qumran community. 2. Bible. N.T.—Symbolism. 3. Christianity and other religions—Judaism. 4. Judaism—Relations—Christianity. I. Title. II. Title: Temple symbolism of the Qumran texts and the New Testament. III. Series: Studiorum Novi Testamenti Societas. Monograph series, 1

GARTNER, Bertil. New Testament 296.81
Temple symbolism of the Qumran texts and the New Testament. Cambridge, Univerity Press, 1965. xii, 164 p. 23 cm. (Society for New Testament Studies. Monograph series, 1) Bibliography: p. 143-151. [BM175.Q6G3] 64-21545
1. Qumran community. 2. Bible. N.T. — Symbolism. 3. Christianity, and other religions — Judaism. 4. Judaism — Relations — Christianity. I. Title. II. Series. III. Series: Studiorum Novi Testamenti Societas. Monograph series, 1

GILLIAM, Olive Kuntz. 296.8'1
Qumran and history : the place of the teacher in religion / Olive Gilliam. 1st ed. New York : Vantage Press, c1974. ix, 67 p. : map ; 21 cm. [BM175.Q6G54] 75-306758 ISBN 0-533-01167-1 : 3.95
1. Qumran community. I. Title.

MANUAL of discipline, English. 296
The manual of discipline, translated and annotated with an introd. by P. Wernberg-Moller. Grand Rapids, Eerdmans, 1957. 180p. 24cm. (Studies on the texts of the desert of Judah, v. 1) Bibliography: p. [167]-178. [BM488.M3A3 1957] 58-14626
1. Qumran community. I. Wernberg-Moller, Preben, ed. and tr. II. Title. III. Series.

NEW directions in Biblical archaeology. 220.93 Edited by David Noel Freedman and Jonas C. Greenfield. [1st ed.] Garden City, N.Y., Doubleday, 1969. xix, 191 p. illus. 22 cm. Based on papers originally presented at a symposium on Biblical archaeology, held in the San Francisco Bay area, Mar. 14-16, 1966. Includes bibliographies. [BS621.N46] 69-15185 6.95
1. Bible—Antiquities. 2. Dead Sea scrolls. 3. Qumran community. I. Freedman, David Noel, 1922- ed. II. Greenfield, Jonas C., 1926- ed.

PIKE, Diane Kennedy. 232
The wilderness revolt; a new view of the life and death of Jesus based on ideas and notes of the late Bishop James A. Pike [by] Diane Kennedy Pike and R. Scott Kennedy. [1st ed.] Garden City, N.Y., Doubleday, 1972. xxxiii, 385 p. 22 cm. "Quotations from Bishop James A. Pike ... are excerpted and edited from transcripts of a seminar on Christian Origins given in May of 1969 for the Esalen Institute in San Francisco." Bibliography: p. [365]-375. [BT202.P53] 72-171311 7.95
1. Jesus Christ—Person and offices. 2. Qumran community. I. Kennedy, R. Scott, joint author. II. Pike, James Albert, Bp., 1913-1969. III. Title.

PLOEG, J. P. M. van der, 1909- 296.81
The excavations at Qumran; a survey of the Judaean brotherhood and its ideas. Tr. [from Dutch] by Kevin Smyth. London, Longmans [dist. Mystic, Conn., Verry, 1965, c.1958] 233p. illus. 21cm. Bibl. [BM175.Q6P513] 4.00 bds.,
1. Qumran community. 2. Dead Sea scrolls. I. Title.

PLOEG, J. P. M. van der, 1909- 296
The excavations at Qumran; a survey of the Judaean brotherhood and its ideas. Translated by Kevin Smyth. London, New York, Longmans, Green 1958 233 p. illus. 21 cm. Translation of Vondsten in de weestijn van Juda. Includes bibliography. [BM175.Q6P513] 58-4029
1. Dead Sea scrolls. 2. Qumran community. I. Title.

RABIN, Chaim. 296
Qumran studies. [London] Oxford University Press, 1957. 135p. 22cm. (Scripta Judalca, 2) Bibliographical footnotes. [BM175.Q6R3] 57-59398
1. Qumran community. 2. Judaism—Relations—Mohammedanism. 3. Mohammedanism—Relations—Judaism. I. Title.

RABIN, Chaim. 296.8'1
Qumran studies / Chaim Rabin. New York : Schocken Books, 1975, c1957. xv, 135 p. : 21 cm. Reprint of the ed. published by Oxford University Press, London, which was issued as no. 2 of Scripta Judaica. Includes bibliographical references and indexes. [BM175.Q6R3 1975] 74-26735 ISBN 0-8052-0482-2 pbk. : 3.95
1. Qumran community. 2. Judaism—Relations—Islam. 3. Islam—Relations—Judaism. I. Title. II. Series: Scripta Judaica ; 2.

RABIN, Chaim. 296.8'1
Qumran studies / by Chaim Rabin. Westport, Conn. : Greenwood Press, 1976, c1957. p. cm. Reprint of the ed. published by Oxford University Press, London, which was published as no. 2 of Scripta Judaica. Includes indexes. [BM175.Q6R3 1976] 76-40116 ISBN 0-8371-9060-6 lib.bdg. : 11.25
1. Qumran community. 2. Judaism—Relations—Islam. 3. Islam—Relations—Judaism. I. Title. II. Series: Scripta Judaica ; 2.

ROTH, Cecil, 1899- 296.81
The Dead Sea scrolls; a new historical approach. New York, Norton [c.1958, 1965] xx, 99p. 22cm. First pub. in London in 1958 under title: The historical background of the Dead Sea scrolls. Bibl. [BM175.Q6R6] 65-13329 4.50
1. Qumran community. 2. Zealots (Jewish party) 3. Dead Sea scrolls. I. Title.

ROTH, Cecil, 1899- 296.81
The Dead Sea scrolls: a new historical approach. New York, Norton [1966. c.1958. 1965] xx, 99p. 20cm. First pub. in London under the title: The historical background of the Dead Sea scrolls (Norton Lib. N303) Bibl. [BM175.Q6R6 1965] 65-13329 1.25 pap.,
1. Qumran community. 2. Zealots (Jewish party) 3. Dead Sea scrolls. I. Title.

ROTH, Cecil, 1899- 221.4
The historical background of the Dead Sea scrolls. New York, Philosophical Library, 1959 [c1958] 87p. 23cm. Includes bibliography. [BM175.Q6R6 1959] 59-16249
1. Qumran community. 2. Zealots (Jewish party) 3. Dead Sea scrolls. I. Title.

SCHARLEMANN, Martin Henry, 1910- 296.81
Qumran and Corinth. New York, Bkman [c.1962] 78p. Bibl. 62-10887 1.95 pap.,
1. Qumran community. 2. Bible. N. T. 1 Corinthians—Criticism, interpretation, etc. 3. Corinth, Greece—Religion. I. Title.

SCHUBERT, Kurt, 1923- 296.81
The Dead Sea community; its origin and teachings. [Eng. tr. from German by John W. Doberstein] London, A. & C. Black [New York, Humanities, 1966, c.1958, 1959] 178p. 21cm. Bibl. [BM175.Q6S363] 2.50 bds.,
1. Qumran community. 2. Dead Sea scrolls. I. Title.

SCHUBERT, Kurt, 1923- 296.81
The Dead Sea community: its origin and teachings. Translated by John W. Doberstein. New York, Harper [1959] 178 p. 22 cm. Includes bibliography. [BM175.Q6S363 1959a] 59-7162
1. Dead Sea scrolls. 2. Qumran community. I. Title.

SCHUBERT, Kurt, 1923- 296.8'1
The Dead Sea community: its origin and teachings. Translated by John W. Doberstein. Westport, Conn., Greenwood Press [1973] xi, 178 p. 22 cm. Reprint of the 1959 ed. published by Harper, New York, which was a translation of Die Gemeinde vom Totem Meer. Bibliography: p. 165-168. [BM175.Q6S363 1973] 73-15245 ISBN 0-8371-7169-5 9.95
1. Dead Sea scrolls. 2. Qumran community. I. Title.

SUTCLIFFE, Edmund Felix 296.81
The monks of Qumran as depicted in the Dead Sea scrolls, with translations in English. Westminster, Md., Newman Press, 1960[ ] xvi, 272p. illus., diagrs., map, 23cm. Bibl. and bibl. notes: p.241-259 60-14813 5.50
1. Qumran community. I. Dead Sea scrolls. English. II. Title.

VERMES, Geza, 1924- 296.8'1
The Dead Sea scrolls : Qumran in perspective / Geza Vermes, with the collaboration of Pamela Vermes. Cleveland : Collins World, 1978, c1977. 238 p. ; 22 cm. Includes index. Bibliography: p. [231]-232. [BM175.Q6V47 1978] 78-55467 ISBN 0-529-05491-4 : 9.95
1. Dead Sea scrolls—Criticism, interpretation, etc. 2. Qumran community. I. Vermes, Pamela, joint author. II. Title.

VERMES, Geza, 1924- 296.8'15
The Dead Sea scrolls : Qumran in perspective / Geza Vermes, with the collaboration of Pamela Vermes. Rev. ed., 1st Fortress Press ed. Philadelphia : Fortress Press, 1981, c1977. 238 p. ; 21 cm. Includes index. Bibliography: p. [231]-232. [BM175.Q6V47 1981] 19 80-2382 ISBN 0-8006-1435-6 pbk. : 8.50
1. Dead Sea scrolls—Criticism, interpretation, etc. 2. Qumran community. I. Vermes, Pamela, joint author. II. Title.

WAR of the Sons of Light against the Sons of Darkness. English. 296
The rules for the War of the Sons of Light with the Sons of Darkness. [Translated by Robert G. Jones from the Dea Sea scrolls in the Hebrew University. New Haven? 1956] [49] p. 21 cm. [BM488.W3A3 1956] 58-29041
1. Qumran community. I. Jones, Robert G., tr. II. Title.

Quotations.

GAER, Joseph, 1897- 290.82
The wisdom of the living religions. New York, Apollo Eds. [1961, c.1956] Bibl. 1.95 pap.,
1. Quotations. 2. Religious literature (Selections: Extracts, etc.) I. Title.

GAER, Joseph, 1897- 290.82
The wisdom of the living religions. New York, Dodd, Mead, 1956. 338 p. 21 cm. [BL29.G27] 56-8362
1. Quotations. 2. Religious literature (Selections: Extracts, etc.) I. Title.

LAWSON, James Gilchrist, 1874- comp. 808.8
The world's best religious quotations, compiled by James Gilchrist Lawson ... New York, Chicago [etc.] Fleming H. Revell company [c1930] 192 p. 21 cm. [BR53.L3] 30-27098
1. Quotations. I. Title. II. Title: Religious quotations, The world's best.

MEAD, Frank Spencer, 1898- ed. 808.882
The encyclopedia of religious quotations. Ed., comp. by Frank S. Mead. Westwood, N. J., Revell [1965] 534p. 26cm. [PN6084.R3M4] 65-236232 11.95
1. Quotations. 2. Religious literature (Selections: extracts, etc.) I. Title.

PROCHNOW, Herbert Victor, 1897- ed. 808.8
A family treasury of inspiration and faith. Boston, W. A. Wilde Co. [1958] 121p. 21cm. [PN6084.R3P7] 58-12417
1. Quotations. 2. Aphorisms and apothegms. I. Title.

[WELLFORD, Clarence] comp. 242
Answers of the ages [by] I. K. L. [and] L. C. W. Chicago and New York, H. S. Stone and company, 1900. 5 p. l., 3-135 p., 1 l. 15 cm. "These answers have been gathered from the note-books of two friends"--Pref. note. [BL29.W4] 0-1206
1. Quotations. I. L. I. K. II. I. K. L. III. W. L. C. IV. L. C. W. V. Title.

Quotations, English.

BACHELDER, Louise, comp. 242'.08
Golden words of faith, hope & love. Illus. by Chrystal Corcos. Mount Vernon, N.Y., Peter Pauper Press [1969] 62 p. col. illus. 20 cm. [PN6081.B15] 75-5771 1.25
1. Quotations, English. I. Title.

BACHELDER, Louise, comp. 290.82
Time for reflection. With illus. by Pat Stewart. Mount Vernon, N.Y., Peter Pauper Press [1968] 62 p. col. illus. 19 cm. [PN6081.B17] 68-3278
1. Quotations, English. I. Title.

HUOT, Patricia W., comp. 242'.4
The Lord is my shepherd. Compiled by Patricia W. Huot. New York, World Pub. Co. [1970] 45 p. 21 cm. Verse and prose. [PN6084.C57H8 1970] 71-131160
1. Quotations, English. 2. Consolation. I. Title.

WIRT, Sherwood Eliot, comp. 808'.88'2
Living quotations for Christians, compiled and edited by Sherwood Eliot Wirt and Kersten Beckstrom. [1st ed.] New York, Harper & Row [1974] xv, 290 p. 24 cm. [PN6084.R3W5] 73-6330 ISBN 0-06-069598-6 7.95
1. Quotations, English. I. Beckstrom, Kersten, joint comp. II. Title.

Quotations, Jewish.

BARON, Joseph Louis, 1894- ed. 808.882
A treasury of Jewish quotations. New rev. ed. New York, Yoseloff [c.1956, 1965] xiv, 623p. 24cm. Bibl. [PN6095.J4B3] 65-24576 6.95
1. Quotations, Jewish. I. Title. II. Title: Jewish quotations.

BARON, Joseph Louis, 1894- ed. 808.8
A treasury of Jewish quotations. New York, Crown Publishers [1956] 623p. 23cm. [PN6095.J4B3] 56-7194
1. Quotations, Jewish. I. Title. II. Title: Jewish quotations.

ROSTEN, Leo Calvin, 1908- 808.88'2
Leo Rosten's Jewish treasury. New York, McGraw-Hill [1972] xi, 716 p. 25 cm. Bibliography: p. 699-710. [PN6095.J4R6] 72-298 ISBN 0-07-053978-2 10.95
1. Quotations, Jewish. I. Title. II. Title: Treasury of Jewish quotations.

SILVER, Samuel M., comp. 808.88'2
The quotable American rabbis, comp., ed. by Samuel M. Silver and the staff of Quote. [1st ed.] Anderson. S.C., Droke House; Dist. by Grosset, New York [1967] xii, 244p. 20cm. [PN6095.J4S5] 67-13274 4.95
1. Quotations, Jewish. 2. Rabbis—U.S. I. Quote: The weekly digest. II. Title.

WOODS, Ralph Louis, 1904- comp. 808.88'2
The joy of Jewish humor. Compiled by Ralph L. Woods. New York [Essandess Special Editions, 1969] [56] p. illus. 16 cm. [PN6095.J4W6] 76-229941 ISBN 6-7110-3555- 2.00
1. Quotations, Jewish. I. Title.

Ra (Egyptian deity)

LITANY of the sun 299.31
The Litany of Re. Texts tr., commentary by Alexandre Pinakoff [New York, Bollingen Found.; dist.] Pantheon [c.1964] xv, 182p. illus., facsims. (pt. fold.) 31cm. (Bollingen ser., 40:4. Egyptian religious texts and representations, v.4) Bibl. 64-24858 7.50
1. Ra (Egyptian deity) I. Piankoff, Alexandre, ed. and tr. II. Title. III. Series: Bollingen series, 40:4 IV. Series: Egyptian religious texts and representations, v.4)

PLANKOFF, Alexandre, ed. and tr. 299.31
The Litany of Re. Texts translated with commentary by Alexandre Piankoff. [New York, Bollingen Foundation; distributed by]Pantheon Books [1964] xv, 182 p. illus., facsims. 31 cm. (Bollingen series, 40: 4. Egyptian religious texts and representations, v. 4) Bibliographical footnotes. [PJ1551.E4 vol. 4] 64-24858
1. Ra (Egyptian deity) I. Title. II. Series: Bollingen series, 40: 4 III. Series: Egyptian religious texts and representations, v. 4)

ZABKAR, Louis Vico, 1914- 299'.3'1
A study of the ba concept in ancient Egyptian texts, by Louis V. Zabkar. Chicago, University of Chicago Press [1968] xiv, 163 p. 6 plates. 24 cm. (The Oriental Institute of the University of Chicago. Studies in ancient oriental civilization, no. 34) Bibliographical footnotes. [BL2450.B2Z3] 68-55393
1. Ba (Egyptian religion) 2. Eschatology, Egyptian. I. Title. II. Title: The ba concept in ancient Egyptian texts. III. Series: Chicago. University. Oriental Institute.

Studies in ancient oriental civilization, no. 34

Rabbinical literature—Addresses, essays, lectures.

LIEBERMAN, Saul, 1898- 296.1'08
Texts and studies. New York Ktav Pub. House [1974] viii, 318 p. 24 cm. Includes bibliographical references. [BM496.5.L5] 72-12046 ISBN 0-87068-210-5 20.00
1. Rabbinical literature—Addresses, essays, lectures. 2. Jews in Palestine—Addresses, essays, lectures. 3. Hellenism—Addresses, essays, lectures.

Rabbinical literature—History and criticism.

DALMAN, Gustaf 296.1'206'6
Hermann, 1855-1941, comp.
Jesus Christ in the Talmud, Midrash, Zohar, and the liturgy of the synagogue. New York, Arno Press, 1973. vi, 47, 108 p. 23 cm. (The Jewish people: history, religion, literature) Translation of Jesus Christus im Thalmud. English and Hebrew. Reprint of the 1893 ed. published by Deighton, Bell, Cambridge. "Jesus Christ in the Talmud, by Heinrich Laible. Translated by Rev. A. W. Streane": p. 1-108 (3d group) [BM620.D313 1973] 73-2190 ISBN 0-405-05256-1
1. Jesus Christ—Jewish interpretations. 2. Rabbinical literature—History and criticism. I. Title. II. Series.

GOLDIN, Hyman Elias, 1881- 296
comp. and tr.
Legends of our fathers; a collection of legends from ancient rabbinical writings from the creation to Joseph, comp. and tr. by Hyman E. Goldin. New York, Sinai publishing co., 1921. 164 p. 27 cm. [BM530.G57] 21-8040
I. Title.

HANDELMAN, Susan A. 121'.68
The slayers of Moses : the re-emergence of rabbinic interpretation in modern literary theory / by Susan A. Handelman. Albany : State University of New York Press, c1982. p. cm. (SUNY series on modern Jewish literature and culture) Bibliography: p. [BM496.5.H34] 19 81-16522 39.00 ISBN 0-87395-577-3 pbk. : 12.95
1. Rabbinical literature—History and criticism. 2. Talmud—Influence—Civilization, Occidental. 3. Criticism. I. Title. II. Series.

KADUSHIN, Max, 1895- 296.1'4
The rabbinic mind. With an appendix by Simon Greenberg. 3d ed. New York, Bloch Pub. Co. [1972] xxix, 414 p. 22 cm. Includes bibliographical references. [BM496.5.K3 1972] 75-189016 ISBN 0-8197-0007-X 9.95
1. Rabbinical literature—History and criticism. I. Title.
Pap. 4.95.

LEIMAN, Sid Z. 081 s
The canonization of Hebrew scripture : the Talmudic and Midrashic evidence / by Sid Z. Leiman. Hamden, Conn. : Published for the Academy by Archon Books, 1976. 234 p. ; 24 cm. (Transactions - The Connecticut Academy of Arts and Sciences ; v. 47, p. 1-234) Includes indexes. Bibliography: p. 205-218. [Q11.C9 vol. 47, p. 1-234] [BS1135] 221.1'2 76-359773 ISBN 0-208-01561-2 : 17.50
1. Bible. O.T.—Canon. 2. Rabbinical literature—History and criticism. I. Title. II. Series: Connecticut Academy of Arts and Sciences, New Haven. Transactions ; v. 47, p. 1-234.

MARMONSTEIN, Arthur.
The doctrine of merits in old Rabbinical literature by A. Marmorstein, PH. D. London [Oxford university press] 1920. 199 p. 22 cm. (Jews' college, London. Publication no. 7) Bibliographical footnotes. [BM645.M4M3] 20-20347
I. Title. II. Title: Rabbinical literature.

MONTEFIORE, Claude Joseph 220.6'6
Goldsmid, 1858-1938.
The Old Testament and after. Freeport, N.Y., Books for Libraries Press [1972] xi, 601 p. 22 cm. Reprint of the 1923 ed. [BM565.M62 1972] 72-2566 ISBN 0-8369-6862-X 18.75
1. Bible. O.T.—Criticism, interpretation, etc. 2. Bible. N.T.—Criticism, interpretation, etc. 3. Rabbinical literature—History and criticism. 4. Hellenism. 5. Reform Judaism. I. Title.

OESTERLEY, William Oscar 296.1
Emil, 1866-1950.
A short survey of the literature of Rabbinical and mediaeval Judaism, by W. O. E. Oesterley and G. H. Box. New York, B. Franklin [1973] xi, 334 p. 22 cm. (Burt Franklin bibliography & reference series 490) Reprint of the 1920 ed. published by Macmillan, New York. Includes bibliographical references. [BM495.5.O35 1973] 72-82352 ISBN 0-8337-2602-1 18.50
1. Jews. Liturgy and ritual—History. 2. Rabbinical literature—History and criticism. 3. Hebrew literature, Medieval—History and criticism. I. Box, George Herbert, 1869-1933, joint author. II. Title.

Rabbinical literature—History and criticism—Addresses, essays, lectures.

UNDERSTANDING the 296.1'206'6
Talmud / selected with introductions by Alan Corre. New York : Ktav Pub. House, 1975. xii, 468 p. ; 23 cm. Includes bibliographical references. [BM496.5.U52] 78-138459 ISBN 0-87068-140-0 : 15.00 pbk. : 5.95
1. Talmud—Theology—Addresses, essays, lectures. 2. Rabbinical literature—History and criticism—Addresses, essays, lectures. I. Corre, Alan D.

Rabbinical literature—History and criticism, Christian.

FLETCHER, Harris Francis, 821'.4
1892-
Milton's rabbinical readings. [Hamden, Conn.] Archon Books, 1967. 334 p. facsims. 23 cm. Reprint of the 1930 ed. Bibliography: p. [316]-333. [PR3592.R2F6 1967] 67-22303
1. Milton, John, 1608-1674—Knowledge—Judaism. 2. Rabbinical literature—History and criticism, Christian. I. Title.

Rabbinical literature—Outlines, syllabi, etc.

WHITNEY, John Raymond, 291.8'2
1920-
Comparative religious literature : Tanach, Apocrypha, Pirke Avot, Midrash, New Testament, Koran / John R. Whitney and Susan W. Howe ; edited and rev. for Jewish studies by Jay Stern. New York : Ktav Pub. House, 1977. 326 p. : ill. ; 23 cm. Published in 1971 under title: Religious literature of the West. Includes index. Bibliography: p. 318-320. [BS592.W48 1977] 77-155915 5.95
1. Bible—Study—Outlines, syllabi, etc. 2. Koran—Study—Outlines, syllabi, etc. 3. Rabbinical literature—Outlines, syllabi, etc. I. Howe, Susan W., joint author. II. Stern, Jay B. III. Title.

Rabbinical literature—Relation to the New Testament.

DAUBE, David. 225.6'6
The New Testament and rabbinic Judaism. New York, Arno Press, 1973 [c1956] xviii, 460 p. 23 cm. (The Jewish people: history, religion, literature) Reprint of the ed. published by University of London, Athlone Press, London, which was issued as no. 2 of Jordan lectures in comparative religion. Includes bibliographical references. [BM535.D34 1973] 73-2191 ISBN 0-405-05257-X 25.00
1. Bible. N.T.—Criticism, interpretation, etc. 2. Rabbinical literature—Relation to the New Testament. I. Title. II. Series. III. Series: Jordan lectures in comparative religion, 2.

MONTEFIORE, Claude Joseph 296.3
Goldsmid, 1858-1938.
Judaism and St. Paul: two essays. New York, Arno Press, 1973. 240 p. 21 cm. (The Jewish people: history, religion, literature) Reprint of the 1914 ed. published by M. Goschen, London. Includes bibliographical references. [BS2652.M6 1973] 73-2222 ISBN 0-405-05284-7 15.00
1. Paul, Saint, apostle. 2. Bible. N.T. Epistles of Paul—Theology. 3. Rabbinical literature—Relation to the New Testament. 4. Reform Judaism. I. Title. II. Series.

MONTEFIORE, Claude Joseph 226
Goldsmid, 1858-1938.
Rabbinic literature and Gospel teachings. New York, Ktav Pub. House, 1970. xlii, 442 p. 24 cm. (The Library of Biblical studies) Reprint of the 1930 ed. with Prolegomenon by Eugene Mihaly. Bibliography: p. xxxiii-xxxiv. [BS2555.M632 1970] 68-19731 ISBN 0-87068-088-9
1. Bible. N.T. Gospels—Criticism, interpretation, etc. 2. Rabbinical literature—Relation to the New Testament. I. Title. II. Series.

Rabbinical literature—Translations into English.

THE Day God laughed 296.1'205'21
: sayings, fables, and entertainments of the Jewish sages / chosen and translated by Hyam Maccoby ; with conversations between Wolf Mankowitz and Hyam Maccoby. New York : St. Martin's Press, [1978] p. cm. [BM495.D38] 78-53502 ISBN 0-312-18403-4 : 10.00
1. Rabbinical literature—Translations into English. 2. Tales, Jewish. I. Maccoby, Hyam, 1924- II. Mankowitz, Wolf.

PORTON, Gary G. 296.1'7
The traditions of Rabbi Ishamel / by G. Porton. Leiden : Brill, 1976- v. ; 25 cm. (Studies in Judaism in late antiquity ; v. 19) Contents.Contents.—The non-exegetical materials. Bibliography: v. 1, p. [226]-229. [BM502.3.I8P67] 76-381618 ISBN 9-00-404526-0 (v. 1) : fl 64.00 (v. 1)
1. Ishmael, tanna, fl. 2d cent. 2. Rabbinical literature—Translations into English. 3. Rabbinical literature—History and criticism. I. Title. II. Series.

SPERKA, Joshua Sidney, 223'.8'066
1904- comp.
Ecclesiastes: stories to live by. A modern translation with a story illustrating each verse translated, edited, and compiled by Joshua S. Sperka. New York, Bloch Pub. Co. [1972] 232 p. 23 cm. Bibliography: p. 215-222. [BS1475.4.S64] 73-150613 5.95
1. Bible. O.T. Ecclesiastes—Homiletical use. 2. Rabbinical literature—Translations into English. 3. Tales, Jewish. I. Bible. O.T. Ecclesiastes. English. Sperka. 1972. II. Title.

Rabbinical seminaries—United States.

BRAV, Stanley 378.77178
Rosenbaum, 1908- ed.
Telling tales out of school; seminary memories of the Hebrew Union College-Jewish Institute of Religion. Cincinnati, Alumni Assn. of the H.U.C.-J.I.R., 1965 x, 184p. 25cm. [BM90.H465] 65-11568 price unreported
1. Rabbinical seminaries—U.S. I. Title.

HELMREICH, William 296'.07'1173
B.
The yeshiva in America / William B. Helmreich. New York : Free Press, c1982. p. cm. Includes index. Bibliography: p. [BM75.H44] 19 81-67440 ISBN 0-02-914640-2 : 19.95
1. Rabbinical seminaries—United States. 2. Orthodox Judaism—United States. I. Title.

Rabbis.

THE activities of the 296
rabbi. A course of lectures delivered under the auspices of the Jewish theological seminary, February-May, 5652 New York, Jewish theological seminary association, 5652-1892. 114 p. 18 1/2 cm. Preface signed: Max Cohen, chairman Seminary committee. [BM652.A2] 24-17619
I. Cohen, Max, ed. II. Jewish theological seminary of America

DUCKAT, Walter B. 296
Opportunities in Jewish religious vocations. New York, Vocational Guidance Manuals [1952] 128 p. 20 cm. (Vocational guidance manuals) [BM652.D8] 52-12236
1. Rabbis. I. Title.

FELDMAN, Abraham Jehiel, 296
1893-
The rabbi and his early ministry, by Abraham J. Feldman. The alumni lectures of the Hebrew union college, Cincinnati, Ohio, delivered in March, 1940, with a foreword by President Julian Morgenstern. New York, Bloch publishing co., 1941. ix, 146 p. 20 cm. Bibliographical references included in "Notes" (p. [141]-146) [BM652.F4 1940] 41-11136
1. Rabbis. I. Title.

FRIEDMAN, Bear Leib, 1845-1920.
Rabbis of ancient times. Biographical sketches of the Talmudic period. (300 B.C.E. to 500 C.E.) Supplemented with maxims and proverbs of the Talmud. By D. A. (B. L.) Friedman. Rochester, N.Y. [c1896] xv, [1], 135 p. 22 cm. [BM750.F7] 44-52686
1. Rabbis. 2. Jews—Biog. I. Title.

GRADE, Chaim, 1910- FIC
Rabbis and wives / Chaim Grade ; translated by Harold Rabinowitz and Inna Hecker Grade. 1st ed. New York : A.A. Knopf : Distributed by Random House, 1982. p. cm. Contents.Contents. Rebbetzin — The courtyard — The oath. [PJ5129.G68A2 1982] 839'.0933 19 82-14 ISBN 0-394-50979-X : 15.95
I. [Selections.] English. 1982 II. Title.

[JULIE DU ST. ESPRIT, 242
Sister] 1868-
Rabboni; heart to heart before the tabernacle, by J. S. E. [Cincinnati, c1920] 58 p. front. 16 cm. [BX2182.J5] 24-1104
I. E. J. S. II. J. S. E. III. Title.

MAYERBERG, Samuel Spier, 922.96
1892-
Chronicle of an American crusader; alumni lectures delivered at the Hebrew union collge, Cincinnati, Ohio, December 7-10, 1942, by Samuel S. Mayerberg ... Foreword by Julian Morgenstern ... New York, Bloch publishing company, 1944. xiii p., 1 l., 148 p. 20 1/2 cm. [BM755.M34A3] 44-7756
1. Rabbis. 2. Kansas City, Mo.—Pol & govt. I. Title.

MIDRASH. Pirke de Rabbi 296.14
Eliezer. English
Pirke de Rabbi Eliezer (The chapters of Rabbi Eliezer the Great) according to the text of the manuscript belonging to Abraham Epstein of Vienna, tr. annotated,introd. indices by Gerald Friedlander. [2d ed.] New York, Hermon Pr. 10 E. 40th St., 1965. 1x, 490p. 24cm. [BM517.P7E5] 65-15088 9.75
I. Friedlander, Gerald, 1871- ed. and tr. II. Title.

NEWMAN, Louis Israel, 922.96
1893-
A "chief rabbi" of Rome becomes a Catholic; a study in fright and spite, by Louis I. Newman ... New York, The Renascence press, 1945. xii, 233 p. 21 cm. Bibliographical foot-notes. [BM755.Z6N4] 46-1245
I. Zolli, Israele, 1881- II. Title.

PIRKE, de-Rabbi Eliezer, 296.14
Pirke de Rabbi Eliezer (The chapters of Rabbi Eliezer the Great) according to the text of the manuscript belonging to Abraham Epstein of Vienna, translated and annotated, with intro. and indices, by Gerald Friedlander. [2d. American ed.] New York, Hermon Press, 1965. ix, 490 p. 24 cm. This translation was first published in London in 1916. [BM517.P7E5] 65-15088
I. Friedlander, Gerald, 1871- ed. and tr. II. Title. III. Title: The chapters of Rabbi Eliezer.

PIRKE de rabbi Eliezer, 296
Pirke de rabbi Eliezer (The chapters of Rabbi Eliezer the Great) according to the text of the manuscript belonging to Abraham Epstein of Vienna, tr. and annotated with introduction and indices by Gerald Friedlander. London, K. Paul, Trench, Trubner & co., ltd.; New York, The Bloch publishing company, 1916. ix, 490 p. 22 cm. [BM520.P5A3 1916] 22-2665
I. Friedlander, Gerald, 1871- ed. and tr. II. Title.

PIRKE de-Rabbi Eliezer. 296.1'4
English.
Pirke de Rabbi Eliezer (The chapters of Rabbi Eliezer the Great) according to the text of the manuscript belonging to Abraham Epstein of Vienna. Translated and annotated with introd. and indices by Gerald Friedlander. New York, B. Blom, 1971. lx, 490 p. 21 cm. "First published London, 1916." [BM517.P7E5 1971] 70-174366
1. Friedlander, Gerald, 1871-1923, ed. II. Title: The chapters of Rabbi Eliezer the Great.

. . . The role of the rabbi in human relations. Experimental ed. Cincinnati, H. U. C.-J. I. R., Department of Human Relations, 1957. 287 l. 28cm. Alternate pages blank. At head of title: Selected readings.
I. Katz, Robert Langdon, ed.

SIEGEL, Martin. 296.6'1 B
Amen: the diary of Rabbi Martin Siegel. Edited by Mel Ziegler. New York [Maddick Manuscripts; distributed by] World Pub. Co. [1971] xi, 276 p. 22 cm. [BM755.S528A3] 73-142133 6.95
I. Title.

Rabbis—Anecdotes, facetiae, satire, etc.

BENGIS, Esther (Rosenberg) 296
Mrs.
I am a rabbi's wife, by Esther Bengis. Moodus, Conn., Esther Bengis, 1934. vii, 136 p. 20 cm. "A brief record of experiences, facts and observations, covering a period of over a dozen years."--Introd. [BM755.B43 I 2] 35-5751
I. Title. II. Title: A rabbi's wife.

GOLDBURG, Norman M., 296.6'1'0207
1902-
Patrick J. McGillicuddy and the rabbi, by Norman M. Goldburg. Drawings by Stephen Osborn. Los Altos, Calif., Geron-X [1969] viii, 247 p. illus. 22 cm. [PN6268.J4G6] 77-90818 5.95
1. Rabbis—Anecdotes, facetiae, satire, etc. I. Title.

Rabbis—Biography

FEUCHTWANGER, O. 296.61
Righteous lives. New York, Bloch [1966] 169p. facsims., plates. 23cm. Rev. versions of sketches which, except one, have appeared in the London Jewish review. [BM750.F4] 66-1637 3.00
1. Rabbis—Biog. I. Title.

MELCHIOR, Marcus. 296.6'1'0924
A rabbi remembers. [Tr. from Danish by Werner Melchior] New York, Lyle Stuart [1968] 256p. 21cm. Tr. of Levet og oplevet; erindringer. [BM755.M445A313] 67-15887 4.95
I. Title.

Rabbis—Czechoslovakia—Biography.

SHERWIN, Byron L. 296.8'33 B
Mystical theology and social dissent : the life and works of Judah Loew of Prague / Byron L. Sherwin. Rutherford [N.J.] : Fairleigh Dickinson University Press ; London ; East Brunswick, N.J. : Associated University Presses, c1981. p. cm. Includes index. Bibliography: p. [BM755.J8S45] 19 80-67968 ISBN 0-8386-3028-6 : 25.00 25.00
1. Judah Loew ben Bezalel, ca. 1525-1609. 2. Rabbis—Czechoslovakia—Biography. I. Title.

Rabbis—Egypt—Biography.

HESCHEL, Abraham 296.8'2'0924 B
Joshua, 1907-1972.
Maimonides : a biography / Abraham Joshua Heschel ; translated from the German by Joachim Neugroschel. New York : Farrer, Straus, Giroux, c1982. x, 273 p. ; 22 cm. Translation of: Maimonides. Includes bibliographical references and index. [BM755.M6H413 1982] 19 81-15308 ISBN 0-374-19874-8 : 15.00
1. Maimonides, Moses, 1135-1204. 2. Rabbis—Egypt—Biography. 3. Philosophers, Jewish—Egypt—Biography. I. [Maimonides.] English II. Title.

Rabbis—France—Biography.

TWERSKY, Isadore. 296.1'7
Rabad of Posquieres : a twelfth-century Talmudist / Isadore Twersky. Rev. ed. Philadelphia, Pa. : Jewish Publication Society of America, 1980. xxv, 368 p. ; 22 cm. Includes index. Bibliography: p. 307-343. [BM755.A226T8 1980] 19 79-88696 ISBN 0-8276-0123-9 (pbk.) : 6.95
1. Abraham ben David, of Posquieres, 1125 (ca.)-1198. 2. Moses ben Maimon, 1135-1204. Mishneh Torah. 3. Rabbis—France—Biography. 4. Scholars, Jewish—France—Biography. I. Title.

Rabbis—Germany—Biography.

BAKER, Leonard. 296.6'1'0924 B
Days of sorrow and pain : Leo Baeck and the Berlin Jews / by Leonard Baker. New York : Macmillan, c1978. xiii, 396 p., [16] leaves of plates : ill. ; 25 cm. Includes index. Bibliography: p. 339-350. [BM755.B32B34 1978] 77-28872 ISBN 0-02-506340-5 : 12.95
1. Baeck, Leo, 1873-1956. 2. Rabbis—Germany—Biography. 3. Jews in Germany—History—1933-1945. 4. Germany—History—1933-1945. I. Title.

Rabbis—Handbooks, manuals, etc.

CENTRAL Conference of 296.4
American Rabbis.
Rabbi's manual. Rev. ed. New York, 1961. 156p. 18cm. [BM676.C4 1961] 61-10418
1. Rabbis—Handbooks, manuals, etc. I. Title.

Rabbis—Jerusalem—Biography.

RAZ, Simhah. 296.6'1'0924 B
A tzaddik in our time : the life of Rabbi Aryeh Levin / Simcha Raz ; translated from the Hebrew, rev., and expanded by Charles Wengrov ; foreword by Isser Judah Unterman ; introd. by Chaim Herzog ; [edited by Isaiah Dvorkas]. 1st ed. Jerusalem ; New York : Feldheim Publishers, c1976. 468 p. : ill. ; 25 cm. Translation of Ish tsadik hayah. [BM755.L446R3813] 77-371079 ISBN 0-87306-130-6 : 12.50
1. Levin, Arieh, 1885-1969. 2. Rabbis—Jerusalem—Biography. 3. Chaplains, Prison—Jerusalem—Biography. 4. Jews in Jerusalem—Social life and customs. I. Title.

Rabbis—New York (N.Y.)—Biography.

BIRSTEIN, Ann. 296.8'32'0924 B
The rabbi on Forty-seventh Street : the story of her father / by Ann Birstein. New York : Dial Press, c1982. xv, 202 p. ; 22 cm. [BM755.B573B57] 19 81-17456 ISBN 0-385-27429-7 : 13.95
1. Birstein, Bernard, 1892-1959. 2. Rabbis—New York (N.Y.)—Biography. 3. New York (N.Y.)—Biography. I. Title.

REICHEL, Aaron. 296.8'32'0924 B
The Jewish Billy Sunday / by Aaron Reichel. Norfolk, Va. : Donning, c1982. p. cm. [BM755.G624R44 1982] 19 82-9664 ISBN 0-89865-174-3 : 12.95
1. Goldstein, Herbert Samuel, 1890- 2. Rabbis—New York (N.Y.)—Biography. 3. Jews—New York (N.Y.)—Biography. 4. New York, N.Y.—Biography. I. Title.

Rabbis—Office.

GOTTSCHALK, Alfred. 296.6'1
Your future as a rabbi; a calling that counts. [1st ed.] New York, R. Rosen Press [1967] 127 p. 22 cm. (Careers in depth, 72) Cover title: A definitive study of your future as a rabbi. [BM652.G63] 67-12679
1. Rabbis—Office. I. Title. II. Title: A definitive study of your future as a rabbi.

LENN, Theodore I., 296.8'346
1914-
Rabbi and synagogue in Reform Judaism [by] Theodore I. Lenn and associates. Commissioned by the Central Conference of American Rabbis. New York, 1972. xvii, 412 p. illus. 24 cm. Includes bibliographical references. [BM652.L37] 72-189571
1. Rabbis—Office. 2. Rabbis—United States. 3. Pastoral theology (Judaism) 4. Reform Judaism—United States. I. Central Conference of American Rabbis. II. Title.

Rabbis—Poland—Biography.

GREEN, Arthur, 296.6'1'0924 B
1941-
Tormented master : a life of Rabbi Nahman of Bratslav. University : University of Alabama Press, 1979. p. cm. (Judaic studies series ; 9) Bibliography: p. [BM755.N25G73] 78-16674 ISBN 0-8173-6907-4 : 19.50
1. Nahman ben Simhah, of Bratzlav, 1770?-1810? 2. Rabbis—Poland—Biography. 3. Hasidim—Poland—Biography. I. Title. II. Series: Judaic studies ; 9.

GREEN, Arthur, 296.6'1'0924 B
1941-
Tormented master : a life of Rabbi Nahman of Bratslav / Arthur Green. New York : Schocken Books, 1981, c1979. viii, 395 p. : ill. ; 23 cm. Reprint of the 1979 ed. published by University of Alabama Press, University, which was issued as no. 9 of Judaic studies series. Includes indexes. Bibliography: p. 381-388. [BM755.N25G73 1981] 80-14668 ISBN 0-8052-0663-9 pbk. : 11.95
1. Nahman ben Simhah, of Bratzlav, 1770?-1810? 2. Rabbis—Poland—Biography. 3. Hasidim—Poland—Biography. I. Title. II. Series: Judaic studies ; 9.

SCHOCHET, Elijah 296'.092'4
Judah.
"TaZ", Rabbi David Halevi / by Elijah J. Schochet. New York : Ktav Pub. House, 1979. 79 p. ; 24 cm. Includes bibliographical references. [BM755.D33S36] 78-31657 7.50
1. David ben Samuel, ha-Levi, 1536 (ca.)-1667. 2. Rabbis—Poland—Biography. 3. Scholars, Jewish—Poland—Biography. I. Title.

Rabbis—Spain—Toledo—Biography.

SEPTIMUS, Bernard, 296.3'092'4 B
1943-
Hispano-Jewish culture in transition : the career and controversies of Ramah / Bernard Septimus. Cambridge, Mass. : Harvard University Press, 1982. ix, 180 p. ; 24 cm. (Harvard Judaic monographs ; 4) Includes bibliographical references and index. [BM755.A29S46 1982] 19 81-13275 ISBN 0-674-39230-2 : 20.00
1. Abulafia, Meir, 1180 (ca.)-1244. 2. Maimonides, Moses, 1135-1204—Theology. 3. Rabbis—Spain—Toledo—Biography. 4. Resurrection (Jewish theology)—History of doctrines. 5. Toledo (Spain)—Biography. I. Title. II. Series.

Rabbis—United States

GELBER, Sholome Michael 296.61
The failure of the American rabbi; a program for the revitalization of the rabbinate in Amerca. Foreword by Salo W. Baron. New York, Twayne Pubs. [1962, c.1961] 79p. 61-18506 2.75
1. Rabbis—U.S. 2. Judaism—U. S. I. Title.

JEWISH Statistical Bureau, 296
New York.
Necrology of rabbis. New York, Jewish Statistical Bureau. no. in v. 28 cm. annual. Title varies slightly. no. 1-8, 1952/53-1959/60, in no. 9. [BM750.N4] 68-7052
1. Rabbis—U. S. 2. Rabbis—Canada. I. Title.

POLNER, Murray. 296.6'1'0973
The American rabbi / by Murray Polner. 1st ed. New York : Holt, Rinehart and Winston, c1977. p. cm. Includes index. Bibliography: p. [BM652.P6] 8.95
1. Rabbis—United States. 2. Rabbis—Office. 3. Judaism—United States. 4. Jews in the United States—Politics and government. I. Title.

ZEITLIN, Joseph, 1906- 296
Disciples of the wise; the religious and social opinions of American rabbis, by Joseph Zeitlin ... New York, Teachers college, Columbia university, 1945. 4 p. l., xi-xiii p., 1 l., 233 p. incl. tables. 23 1/2 cm. (Teachers college, Columbia university. Contributions to education, no. 908) Issued also as thesis (PH.D.) Columbia university. Bibliography: p. 199-202. [BM652.Z4] [LB5.C8 no. 908] A 45
1. Rabbis—U.S. 2. Jews—Religion. 3. Attitude (Psychology) I. Title.

Rabbis—United States—Addresses, essays, lectures.

THE American rabbi : 296.6'1
a tribute on the occasion of the bicentennial of the United States, and the ninety-fifth birthday of the New York Board of Rabbis / edited by Gilbert S. Rosenthal. New York : Ktav Pub. House, 1977. x, 200 p. : port. ; 24 cm. "This volume is in honor of Rabbi Harold H. Gordon." Includes bibliographical references and index. [BM652.A4] 77-1047 10.00
1. Gordon, Harold H. 2. New York Board of Rabbis. 3. Rabbis—United States—Addresses, essays, lectures. 4. Rabbis—Office—Addresses, essays, lectures. I. Gordon, Harold H. II. Rosenthal, Gilbert S. III. New York Board of Rabbis.
Contents omitted

Rabbis—United States—Biography.

FEIBELMAN, Julian 296.6'1'0924 B
Beck, 1897-
The making of a rabbi / by Julian B. Feibelman. 1st ed. New York : Vantage Press, c1980. 508 p. ; 24 cm. [BM755.F37A34] 19 79-65053 ISBN 0-533-04325-5 : 11.95
1. Feibelman, Julian Beck, 1897- 2. Rabbis—United States—Biography. I. Title.

GOLDMAN, Alex J. 922.96
Giants of faith; great American rabbis, by Rabbi Alex J. Goldman. New York, Citadel [1965, c.1964] 349p. ports. 24cm. [BM750.G57] 64-8163 6.95
1. Rabbis—U. S.—Biog. I. Title.

KERTZER, Morris 296'.092'4 B
Norman, 1910-
Tell me, rabbi / Morris N. Kertzer. New York : Bloch Pub. Co., 1977,c1976 xii, 196 p. ; 22 cm. [BM755.K37A35] 76-8324 ISBN 0-8197-0395-8 : 7.95
1. Kertzer, Morris Norman, 1910- 2. Rabbis—United States—Biography. 3. Jews in the United States—Anecdotes, facetiae, satire, etc. I. Title.

KERTZER, Morris 296'.092'4 B
Norman, 1910-
Tell me, rabbi / Morris N. Kertzer. New York : Collier Books, 1978, c1976. xii, 196 p. ; 18 cm. [BM755.K37A35 1978] 77-20929 ISBN 0-02-086340-3 pbk. : 2.95
1. Kertzer, Morris Norman, 1910- 2. Rabbis—United States—Biography. 3. Jews in the United States—Anecdotes, facetiae, satire, etc. I. Title.

NOVECK, Simon. 296.6'1'0924 B
Milton Steinberg : portrait of a rabbi / by Simon Noveck. New York : Ktav Pub. House, c1978. xii, 353 p., [8] leaves of plates : ill. ; 24 cm. Includes index. Bibliography: p. 330-337. [BM755.S67N68] 77-25943 ISBN 0-87068-444-2 : 12.50
1. Steinberg, Milton, 1903-1950. 2. Rabbis—United States—Biography.

ROSENBLATT, Samuel, 296.6'1 B
1902-
The days of my years : an autobiography / by Samuel Rosenblatt. New York : Ktav Pub. House, 1976. 207 p., [7] leaves of plates : ill. ; 22 cm. [BM755.R565A33] 76-47616 ISBN 0-87068-494-9 : 10.00
1. Rosenblatt, Samuel, 1902- 2. Rabbis—United States—Biography. I. Title.

UROFSKY, Melvin 296.8'346'0924 B
I.
A voice that spoke for justice : the life and times of Stephen S. Wise / Melvin I. Urofsky. Albany : State University of New York Press, 1981. p. cm. (SUNY series in modern Jewish history) Includes index. Bibliography: p. [BM755.W53U76] 19 81-

5676 ISBN 0-87395-538-2 : 49.00 ISBN 0-87395-539-0 pbk. : 16.95
1. Wise, Stephen Samuel, 1874-1949. 2. Rabbis—United States—Biography. 3. Zionists—United States—Biography. I. Title. II. Series.

VOSS, Carl Hermann. 288'.33'0924 B
Rabbi and minister : the friendship of Stephen S. Wise and John Haynes Holmes / Carl Hermann Voss. 2d ed. Buffalo, N.Y. : Prometheus Books, c1980. 383 p. ; 22 cm. (Library of liberal religion) Bibliography: p. 377-379. [BM755.W53V6 1980] 80-7453 ISBN 0-87975-130-4 pbk. : 6.95
1. Wise, Stephen Samuel, 1874-1949. 2. Holmes, John Haynes, 1879-1964. 3. Rabbis—United States—Biography. 4. Unitarian churches—Clergy—Biography. 5. Clergy—United States—Biography. I. Title. II. Series.

WEINSTEIN, Jacob Joseph, 1902- 296.6'1'0924 B
Rabbi Jacob J. Weinstein, advocate of the people / edited by Janice J. Feldstein. New York : KTAV Pub. House, c1980. xii, 226 p., [8] leaves of plates : ill. ; 24 cm. Includes bibliographical references and index. [BM755.W359A37] 79-25654 ISBN 0-87068-699-2 : 15.00
1. Weinstein, Jacob Joseph, 1902- 2. Rabbis—United States—Biography. I. Feldstein, Janice J. II. Title.

Rabelais, Francois, 1490 (ca.)-1553?—Religion and ethics.

FEBVRE, Lucien Paul Victor, 1878-1956. 843'.3
The problem of unbelief in the sixteenth century, the religion of Rabelais / by Lucien Febvre ; translated by Beatrice Gottlieb. Cambridge, Mass. : Harvard University Press, 1982. p. cm. Translation of: Le probleme de l'incroyance au XVIe siecle, la religion de Rabelais. Includes index. Bibliography: p. [PQ1697.R4E3 1982] 19 82-1009 ISBN 0-674-70825-3 : 35.00
1. Rabelais, Francois, 1490 (ca.)-1553?—Religion and ethics. I. [Probleme de l'incroyance au XVIe siecle, la religion de Rabelais.] English II. Title.

Rabi'ah, al-'Adawiyah, d. 801?

SMITH, Margaret. 922.
Rabi'a the mystic & her fellow-saints in Islam; being the life and teachings of Rabi'a al-'Adwiyya al-Qaysiyya of Basra together with some account of the place of the women saints in Islam, by Margaret Smith... Cambridge, Eng., The University press, 1928. xxv, 219, [1] p. 22 1/2 cm. "Survey of sources": p. [xiii]-xxv; "List of authors quoted": p. [205]-209. [BP80.R3S6] 29-10771
1. Rabi'ah, al-'Adawiyah, d. 801? 2. Saints, Mohammedan. 3. Sufism. 4. Saints, Women. I. Title.

Rabten, Geshe.

RABTEN, Geshe. 294.3'61'0924 B
The life and teaching of Geshe Rabten : a Tibetan Lama's search for truth / translated [and edited] by B. Alan Wallace. London ; Boston : G. Allen & Unwin, 1979. p. cm. [BQ982.A27A3413 1979] 79-42715 ISBN 0-04-922030-6 : 13.50
1. Rabten, Geshe. 2. Lamas—Tibet—Biography. 3. Buddhist doctrines. I. Wallace, B. Alan. II. Title.

Race.

BUSWELL, James Oliver. 301.451
Slavery, segregation, and Scripture. Grand Rapids, Eerdmans [1964] 101 p. 21 cm. Bibliography: p. 93-97. [BT734.B8] 63-20683
1. Race. I. Title.

CONSIDINE, John Joseph, 1897- 261.83
Fundamental Catholic teaching on the human race. Maryknoll, N. Y., Maryknoll Publications [c.1961] 92p. 25cm. (World horizon reports. Report no. 27) Bibl. 61-9083 1.00 pap.,
1. Race. I. Title.

FOWLER, Grady. 261.8
Three races under God. [1st ed.] New York, Vantage Press [1956] 172p. illus. 21cm. [BR115.R3F6] 55-11657
1. Race. I. Title.

MCLAIN, C. E. 261.83
Place of race. New York, Vantage [c.1965] 56p. 21cm. Bibl. [BT734.M22] 65-4154 2.50 bds.,
1. Race. I. Title.

OLIVER, C Herbert, 1925- 261.83
No flesh shall glory. [Nutley, N. J.] Presbyterian and Reformed Pub. Co., 1959. 96p. 21cm. [BT734.O4] 59-14513
1. Race. 2. Segregation—Religious aspects. 3. Sociology, Biblical. I. Title.

Race—Addresses, essays, lectures.

DAANE, James. 261.8308
The anatomy of anti-semitism, and other essays on religion and race. Grand Rapids, Eerdmans [1965] 84 p. 21 cm. [BT734.D3] 65-18090
1. Race — Addresses, essays, lectures. I. Title.

Race—Biblical teaching.

*FIGART, Thomas O. 261.8'345196073
A Biblical perspective on the race problem. Grand Rapids, Mich., Baker Book House [1973] 185 p. 20 cm. Bibliography: p. 171-176. [BR563] ISBN 0-8010-3457-4 3.95 (pbk.)
1. Race—Biblical teaching. 2. Church and social problems. I. Title.

Race problems.

BOER, Hans Alfred de. 261.8
The bridge is love; jottings from a traveller's notebook. Foreword by Martin Niemoller. [1st English ed.] Grand Rapids, Eerdmans, 1958. 255p. illus. 23cm. Translation of Unterwegs notiert: Bericht einer Weitreise. [BT734.2.B613 1958] 58-3886
1. Race problems. 2. Voyages around the world. I. Title.

CAMPBELL, Will D. 261.83
Race and the renewal of the church. Philadelphia, Westminster [c.1962] 90p. 19cm. (Christian perspectives on soc. problems) 62-12146 1.25 pap.,
1. Race problems. 2. Segregation—Religious aspects. I. Title.

FARRAHER, Joseph J
Catholic doctrine on race relations. Los Gatos, Alma College, 1964. 1 v. 66-60707
I. Alma College, Alma, Calif. II. Title.

FELTON, James Andrew, 1919-
Fruits of enduring faith; a story of racial unity. New York, Exposition Press [c1965] 96 p. 21 cm. 67-90408
I. Title.

LAFARGE, John. 261.83
The Catholic viewpoint on race relations. Introd. by John J. Delaney. Rev. ed. Garden City, N. Y., Hanover House, 1960 [c.1956, 1960] 192 p. 22 cm. (Catholic viewpoint series) (Bibl. footnotes) 60-9760 3.50
1. Race problems. 2. Church and social problems—Catholic Church. 3. U. S.—Race question. I. Title.

LA FARGE, John, 1880- *261.8
The Catholic viewpoint on race relations. [1st ed.] Garden City, N. Y., Hanover House [1956] 190p. 22cm. (The Catholic viewpoint series) [HT1521.L18] 56-10767
1. Race problems. 2. Church and social problems—Catholic Church. 3. U. S.—Race question. I. Title.

MACDONALD, Allan John Macdonald, 1887- 261.8
Trade politics and Christianity in Africa and the East, by A. J. Macdonald. With an introd. by Sir Harry Johnston. New York, Negro Universities Press [1969] xxi, 295 p. 23 cm. "Originally published in 1916." Includes bibliographical references. [BV2105.M3 1969] 77-89007
1. Race problems. 2. Native races. 3. Missions. I. Title. II. Title: Christianity in Africa and the East.

MACDONALD, Allan John Macdonald, 1887-
Trade politics and Christianity in Africa and the East, by A. J. Macdonald ... with an introduction by Sir Harry Johnston ... London, New York [etc.] Longmans, Green and co., 1916. xxi, 295, [1] p. 22 1/2 cm. "Awarded the Maitland prize at Cambridge in 1915."--Pref. [BV2105.M3] 16-22960
1. Race problems. 2. Native races. 3. Missions. I. Johnston, Sir Harry Hamilton, 1858-1927. II. Maitland prize essay, 1915. III. Title. IV. Title: Christianity in Africa and the East.

MCMANUS, Eugene P 261.83
Studies in race relations. Baltimore, Josephite Press, 1961. 163p. 23cm. Includes bibliography. [HT1521.M23] 61-18523
1. Race problems. 2. U. S.—Race question. 3. Church and social problems—Catholic Church. I. Title.

'MASON, Philip. 261.8
Christianity and race. New York, St. Martin's Press, 1957. 174p. 19cm. (The Burroughs memorial lectures, 1956) [BR115.R3M27 1957] 57-816
1. Race problems. 2. Church and social problems. I. Title.

MAYS, Benjamin Elijah, 1895- 261.8
Seeking to be Christian in race relations. New York, Friendship Press, 1957. 84p. 20cm. [BR115.R3M3 1957] 57-6580
1. Race problems. 2. Church and social problems. I. Title.

OLDHAM, Joseph Houldsworth, 1874- 265.
Christianity and the race problem, by J. H. Oldham ... New York, George H. Doran company [1924] xx p., 1 l., 280 p. 21 cm. "Index of authors quoted": p. 276-280. [BR115.R3O4] 24-25550
1. Race problem. I. Title.

OLDHAM, Joseph Houldsworth, 1874-1969. 261.8'3
Christianity and the race problem. New York, Negro Universities Press [1969] xx, 280 p. 23 cm. Reprint of the 1924 ed. Bibliographical footnotes. [BT734.2.04 1969] 73-75534
1. Race problems. I. Title.

TARPLEE, Cornelius C. 268.433
Racial prejudice. Preface by Gordon Allport. Greenwich, Conn., Seabury [c.1962] 67p. illus. 21cm. (Senior-high-sch. unit) .75 pap.,
I. Title.

WEST, Robert Frederick 261.83
Preaching on race. St. Louis, Bethany Press [1962] 160 p. 23 cm. [BT734.2.W45] 62-8760
1. Race problems. 2. Sermons, American. 3. Disciples of Christ — Sermons. I. Title.

Race (Theology)

BALTAZAR, Eulalio R. 261.8'34'5196
The dark center; a process theology of Blackness [by] Eulalio R. Baltazar. New York, Paulist Press [1973] 181 p. 23 cm. Includes bibliographical references. [BT734.B3] 73-83811 ISBN 0-8091-1788-6 4.95
1. Race (Theology) 2. Black (in religion, folk-lore, etc.) 3. Symbolism. I. Title.

CLEVELAND, Earl E. 261.8'3
The middle wall [by] E. E. Cleveland. Washington, Review and Herald Pub. Association [1969] 96 p. 18 cm. [BT734.C56] 77-81305
1. Race (Theology) I. Title.

JACKSON, Warner. 261.8'34'5196073
Theology: White, Black, or Christian? Scottdale, Pa., Herald Press, 1974. 47 p. 18 cm. (Focal pamphlet no. 25) [BT734.J3] 74-6543 ISBN 0-8361-1743-3 0.75 (pbk.)
1. Race (Theology) I. Title.

JONES, William Ronald. 231
Is God a white racist? A preamble to Black theology, by William R. Jones. [1st ed.] Garden City, N.Y., Anchor Press, 1973. xxii, 239 p. 22 cm. (C. Eric Lincoln series on Black religion) Includes bibliographical references. [BT734.J66] 72-96245 ISBN 0-385-00909-7 7.95
1. Race (Theology) 2. Negroes—Religion. I. Title. II. Series.

REIST, Benjamin A. 261.8'34'51
Theology in red, white, and black / by Benjamin A. Reist. Philadelphia : Westminster Press, [1975] 203 p. ; 22 cm. Includes bibliographical references. [BT734.R44] 74-27936 ISBN 0-664-20723-5 : 7.50
1. Race (Theology) I. Title.

ROBERTS, James Deotis. 261.8'34'51042
Liberation and reconciliation: a Black theology, by J. Deotis Roberts. Philadelphia, Westminster Press [1971] 205 p. 19 cm. Includes bibliographical references. [BT734.2.R6] 73-140601 ISBN 0-664-24911-6 3.50
1. Race (Theology) 2. Negroes—Religion. I. Title. II. Title: Black theology.

SALLEY, Columbus. 261.8'34'51042
Your God is too white [by] Columbus Salley & Ronald Behm. Downers Grove, Ill., Inter-Varsity Press [1970] 114 p. 21 cm. Includes bibliographical references. [BT734.2.S25] 76-132957 ISBN 0-87784-478-X
1. Race (Theology) I. Behm, Ronald, joint author. II. Title.

Race (Theology)—Biblical teaching.

HUMAN relations 261.8'34'51042
and the South African scene in the light of scripture : official translation of the report Ras, volk en nasie en volkereverhoudinge in die lig van die Skrif : approved and accepted by the General Synod of the Dutch Reformed Church, October 1974. Cape Town : Dutch Reformed Church Publishers, 1976. 100 p. ; 22 cm. [BS680.R2R3713] 77-463450 ISBN 0-86991-158-9
1. Reformed Church in South Africa. 2. Race (Theology)—Biblical teaching. 3. Church and social problems—South Africa. 4. Church and race problems—South Africa. I. Nederduits Gereformeerde Kerk (South Africa). Algemene Sinode.

Rad, Gerhard von, 1901-1971.

CRENSHAW, James L. 221'.092'4
Gerhard von Rad / by James L. Crenshaw. Waco, Tex. : Word Books, c1978. 193 p. ; 23 cm. (Makers of the modern theological mind) Bibliography: p. 190-193. [BS1161.R3C73] 78-59463 ISBN 0-8499-0112-X : 7.95
1. Rad, Gerhard von, 1901-1971.

Rader, Paul, 1879-

TUCKER, Walter Leon, 1871- 922
The redemption of Paul Rader, by W. Leon Tucker ... New York city, The Book stall [c1918] 201 p. 1 l. incl. plates ports. front. 20 cm. [BV3785.R2T8] 18-12196
1. Rader, Paul, 1879- I. Title.

Radhakrishnan, Sarvepalli, Pres. India, 1888-

ARAPURA, John Geeverghese, 1920- 181.4
Radhakrishnan and integral experience; the philosophy and world vision of Sarvepalli Radhakrishnan [by] J. G. Arapura. New York, Asia Pub. House [1966] xiv, 211 p. 23 cm. Bibliography: p. 205-208. [B5134.R34A7 1966] 66-29814
1. Radhakrishnan, Sarvepalli, Pres. India, 1888- I. Title. II. Title: Integral experience.

*RADHAKRISHAN, Sarvepalli, Pres. india, 1888- 201
An idealist view of life; being the Hibbert lectures for 1929. New York, Barnes & Noble [1963, c.1932] 352p. 22cm. 4.00
I. Title.

SAMARTHA, S J 1920- 181.4
Introduction to Radhakrishnan; the man and his thought. New York, Association

Press [1964] 127 p. 21 cm. [B133.R16S3] 64-11596
1. Radhakrishnan, Sarvepalli, Pres. India, 1888- I. Title.

SCHILPP, Paul Arthur, 1897- ed. 181.4
The philosophy of Sarvepalli Radhakrishnan. [1st ed.] New York, Tudor Pub. Co. [1952] xiv, 883 p. port., facsim. 25 cm. (The Library of living philosophers) "Bibliography of the writings of Sarvepalli Radhakrishnan to March 1952, compiled by T. R. V. Murti": p. [843]-862. [B133.R16S4] 52-10747
1. Radhakrishnan, Sarvepalli, Sir, 1888- I. Title. II. Series.

SINGH, Surjit 232.9
Christology and personality. Foreword by Nels F. S. Ferre. Philadelphia, Westminster Pr. [c.1961] 206p. Bibl. 61-6102 4.50
1. Radhakrishnan, Sarvepalli, Sir 1888- 2. Jesus Christ—Person and offices. 3. Man (Theology) I. Title.

SINGH, Surjit. 232.9
Christology and personality. Foreword by Nels F. S. Ferre. Philadelphia, Westminster Press [1961] 206 p. 21 cm. "Revision of a monograph originally published in India under the title: Preface to personality ... 1952." Includes bibliography. [BT212.S5 1961] 61-6102
1. Radhakrishnan, Sir Sarvepalli, 1888- 2. Jesus Christ — Person and offices. 3. Man (Theology) I. Title.

Radini Tedeschi, Giacomo Maria, 1857-1914.

JOANNES XXIII, Pope, 1881-1963. 282'.0924 B
My bishop; a portrait of Mgr. Giacomo Maria Radini Tedeschi. With a foreword by H. E. Cardinale, and an introd. by Loris Capovilla. Translated by Dorothy White. New York, McGraw-Hill [1969] 143 p. illus., ports. 25 cm. Translation of Mons. Giacomo Maria Radini Tedeschi. [BX4705.R286J63] 69-13212 6.95
1. Radini Tedeschi, Giacomo Maria, 1857-1914. I. Title.

Radio broadcasting.

KREMER, Nicholas J. 170
Electrons of inspiration; radio talks delivered over WGES, Chicago, by Rev. Nicholas J. Kremer (Father Nick) Techny, Ill., Mission press, S. V. D., 1928. 5 p. l., [7]-192 p. front. (port.) 19 cm. [BJ1661.K7] 28-18550
I. Title.

LOVELESS, Wendell Phillips, 1892- 259
Manual of gospel broadcasting, by Wendell P. Loveless ... Chicago, Ill., Moody press [1946] 352 p. front., plates. 19 1/2 cm. Bibliography: p. 346-348. [BV656.L57] 46-5770
1. Radio broadcasting. 2. Radio in religion. I. Title. II. Title: Gospel broadcasting.

SCHROEDER, Mary Agnes (Tynan) 791.4
Catholics, meet the "mike," a radio workbook giving professional guidance to the amateur, by Mary Agnes Schroeder, with an introduction by Daniel A. Lord, S.J. St. Louis, Mo., The Queen's workshop of the air, the Queen's work [1944] 127, [1] p. illus. 20 1/2 cm. "First printing, March 1944." Bibliography: p. 125-[128]. [BV656.S35] 44-38715
1. Radio broadcasting. I. Queen's workshop of the air. II. Title.

Radio Church of God.

KIRBAN, Salem. 291'.08 s
Armstrong's Church of God. Huntingdon Valley, Pa., S. Kirban Inc. [1970] 53 p. illus. (part col.), ports. 22 cm. (His Doctrines of devils, no. 1) [BL85.K56 no. 1] 70-21613 1.50
1. Radio Church of God. 2. Armstrong, Herbert W. I. Title.

Radio in missionary work.

CUNNINGHAM, Milton E. 254.3
New drums over Africa [by Milton E. Cunningham, Jr.] Nashville, Convention Press [1971] 115 p. illus., map, ports. 20 cm. (Foreign mission graded series) "Text for course number 5136-17 of the New church study course." [BV2082.R3C85] 78-139665
1. Radio in missionary work. 2. Missions—Africa, East. 3. Baptists—Missions. I. Title.

FREED, Paul E. 266'.023'73
Let the Earth hear : the thrilling story of how radio goes over barriers to bring the gospel of Christ to unreached millions / Paul E. Freed. Nashville : T. Nelson, c1980. 207 p., [8] leaves of plates : ill. ; 21 cm. Includes bibliographical references. [BV2082.R3F68] 80-169 ISBN 0-8407-5199-0 : 7.95
1. Trans World Radio. 2. Freed, Paul E. 3. Radio in missionary work. I. Title.

FREED, Paul E. 253.7'8
Towers to eternity, by Paul E. Freed. Waco, Tex., Word Books [1968] 154 p. 22 cm. [BV2082.R3F7] 68-54118 3.95
1. Trans World Radio. 2. Radio in missionary work. I. Title.

LEDYARD, Gleason H. 266'.023'095
Sky waves; the incredible Far East Broadcasting Company story, by Gleason H. Ledyard. Chicago, Moody Press [1968] 227 p. illus., ports. 17 cm. (Moody giants, no. 55) [BV2082.R3L4 1968] 68-3590
1. Far East Broadcasting Company. 2. Radio in missionary work. I. Title.

REED, Jane. 266.6'0966'6
Voice under every palm; the story of radio station ELWA, by Jane Reed and Jim Grant. Grand Rapids, Zondervan Pub. House [1968] 150 p. illus., ports. 23 cm. [BV2082.R3R4] 68-56089 3.95
1. ELWA (Radio station) Monrovia, Liberia. 2. Radio in missionary work. 3. Missions—Africa. I. Grant, Jim, joint author. II. Title.

Radio in religion.

ARMSTRONG, Ben. 253.7'8
The electric church / by Ben Armstrong. Nashville : T. Nelson, c1979. 191 p., [8] leaves of plates : ill. ; 21 cm. Includes bibliographical references. [BV656.A75] 78-27699 ISBN 0-8407-5157-5 : 7.95
1. Radio in religion. 2. Television in religion. I. Title.

BACHMAN, John W 259
The church in the world of radio-television. New York, Association Press [1960] 191p. 22cm. Includes bibliography. [BV656.B3] 60-6554
1. Radio in religion. 2. Television in religion. I. Title.

BENSON, Dennis C. 269'.2
Electric evangelism [by] Dennis C. Benson. Nashville, Abingdon Press [1973] 144 p. illus. 23 cm. [BV656.B45] 72-7425 ISBN 0-687-11633-3 3.95
1. Radio in religion. 2. Television in religion. I. Title.

CLEVELAND, Denton E. 252.
Radio heart throbs, by Denton E. Cleveland, radio pastor of WNAX. Yankton, S. D., The Gurney seed and nursery co. [1929] 133 p., 1 l., port. 23 1/2 cm. "Printed on cornstalk paper." Contains music. Lettered on cover: wnax. House of Gurney. Sermons. [BV4301.C6] 29-12415
I. Title.

ELLENS, J. Harold, 1932- 253.7'8
Models of religious broadcasting, by J. Harold Ellens. [Grand Rapids] Eerdmans [1974] 168 p. 21 cm. Bibliography: p. 153-163. [BV656.E43] 74-8382 ISBN 0-8028-3437-X ISBN 0-8028-3437-X 3.45 (pbk.)
1. Radio in religion. 2. Television in religion. I. Title.

EPP, Theodore H
Twenty -- five years of adventuring by faith. Lincoln, Neb., Back to the Bible Broadcast [c1964] 78 p. 65-53432
1. Radio in religion. I. Title.

FREEMAN, Wendell K, 1928- 254.3
Why not broadcast the gospel? Radio broadcasting methods, sermons, questions. [Huntington? W. Va.] 1952. 179 p. illus. 20 cm. [BV656.F7] 259 52-32351
1. Radio in religion. 2. Churches of Christ—Sermons. 3. Sermons, American. I. Title.

GRANT, Clara Odessa (Winkler) Mrs. John Grant." 1901- 244
Radio stories that live, by Mrs. John Grant. Evansville, Ind., 1934. 64 p. illus. (ports.) 23 cm. "These stories were first told over WG.BF Evansville, Ind. at the children's hour of our radio program."--Introd. [BV4315.G73] unr
I. Title.

GRISWOLD, Clayton T comp. 254.3
Broadcasting religion, compiled by Clayton T. Griswold and Charles H. Schmitz. [Rev., enl. ed.] New York, National Council of the Churches of Christ, Broadcasting and Film Commission [c1954] 103p. illus. 23cm. Bibliography: p. 102. [BV656.G7 1954] 259 55-4080
1. Radio in religion. 2. Radio broadcasting. 3. Television broadcasting. I. Schmitz, Charles Henry, joint comp. II. Title.

GRISWOLD, Clayton T comp. *254.3
How you can broadcast religion, compiled by Clayton T. Griswold and Charles H. Schmitz; edited by Lois J. Anderson. New York, National Council of the Churches of Christ in the United States of America, Broadcasting and Film Commission [1957] 128p. illus. 23cm. [BV656.G72] 259 57-4638
1. Radio in religion. 2. Radio broadcasting. 3. Television broadcasting. I. Schmitz, Charles Henry., joint comp. II. Title.

HOW to conduct religious radio programs. St. Louis, Bethany Press [1958] 63p. 22cm. 'Originally part of the author's thesis written in the School of Religion in Butler University ... for the bachelor of divinity degree.' Includes bibliography. [BV656.K5] 259 58-12745 254.3
1. Radio in religion. 2. Radio broadcasting. I. Kimsey, James E

IVERSEN, John Orville. 254.3
So you're going on the air, written and compiled by J. Orville Iversen. [Washington, Review and Herald Pub. Association, 1969] 320 p. illus., ports. 24 cm. Bibliography: p. 315-320. [BV656.I9] 68-57039
1. Radio in religion. I. Title.

*JESS, John D. 253.78
Escape from emptiness, [by] John D. Jess. Grand Rapids, Baker Book House, [1975 c1968] 87 p. 18 cm. (Direction books) [BV4301] ISBN 0-8010-5071-5 1.25 (pbk.)
1. Radio in religion. I. Title.

JONES, Clarence W. 259
Radio, the new missionary, by Clarence W. Jones ... Chicago, Ill., Moody press [1946] 147 p. plates, ports. 20 cm. The story of HCJB, a missionary radio station in Quito, Ecuador. [BV656.J6] 46-4039
1. Radio in religion. 2. Missions—Ecuador. 3. Quito. Radio difusoras HCJB. 4. Radio broadcasting—Ecuador. 5. Christian and missionary alliance. I. Title.

LOWE, Samuel Franklin, 1890- 259
Successful religious broadcasting, by S. F. Lowe ... with an introduction by the Honorable Walter F. George ... Atlanta, Ga., The Radio press [1945] 154 p. 19 1/2 cm. [BV656.L6] 46-12157
1. Radio in religion. 2. Oratory. I. Title.

NORTH American radio commission. 269
Broadcasting the advent message; the technique of radio ministry, prepared under the joint auspices of the North American radio commission and the Ministerial association of Seventh-day Adventists ... Takoma Park, Washington, D.C., Review and herald publishing association [1944] 317 p. incl. front., illus., forms, diagr. 20 cm. (Ministerial reading course selection for 1944. Ministerial association of Seventh-day Adventists) Bibliography: p. 303-317. [BV656.N6] 44-2166
1. Radio in religion. 2. Seventh-day Adventists—Sermons. I. Seventh-day Adventists. Ministerial association. II. Title.

PATTERSON, Sherwood Hofele, 1893- 261
Radio sermons ... by Pastor S. H. Patterson. Denver, Colo. [Hayes printing co., c1926] 3 p. l., [9]-92, [1] p. ports. 19 cm. [BV4301.P3] 28-6314
I. Title.

THE Petition against God : the full story behind the filing of "The Lansman-Milam petition" : including an unauthorized biography of the petitioners, filings by Christian groups, and the full texts of the original petition, the response petition, and the final Federal Communications Commission decision / compiled by A. W. Allworthy. Dallas, Tex. : Christ the Light, 1976, c1975. 149 p. : ill. ; 21 cm. [BV656.P48] 75-43375 pbk. : 7.95 384.54'53
1. Radio in religion. 2. Television in religion—United States. 3. Radio in education—United States. 4. Television in education—United States. 5. Broadcasting—Law and legislation—United States. I. Allworthy, A. W., 1933-

POLING, Daniel Alfred, 1884- 248
Dr. Poling's radio talks with questions and answers, by Rev. Daniel A. Poling ... with an introduction by Rev. William B. Millar ... index by Leonard M. Miller ... New York, George H. Doran company [c1927] xii, 15-321 p. 20 cm. Addresses and answers to questions of the second season of the Young people's conference, under the auspices of the General radio committee of the Greater New York federation of churches. cf. Introd. [BV4531.P6 1927] 27-19500
I. Title.

POLING, Daniel Alfred, 1884- 248
Radio talks to young people with the questions and answers, by Rev. Daniel A. Poling ... with an introduction by Rev. William B. Millar ... New York, George H. Doran company [c1926] xvii p., 2 l., 23-268 p. 20 cm. [BV4531.P6] 26-17843
I. Millar, William Bell, 1866- II. Title.

ROBERTS, Philip I. ed. 252
Radio preaching; far-flung sermons by pioneers in broadcasting, introduction by Bernard C. Clausen, D. D., edited by Philip I. Roberts. New York, Chicago [etc.] Fleming H. Revell company [c1924] 217 p. 20 cm. [BV4241.R6] 25-1566
I. Title.

SMITH, Everett St. Clair. 252.066
Bits of evergreen; fifty select broadcasts, by Everett St. Clair Smith ... Cincinnati, O., The Standard publishing company [c1931] 240 p. 20 cm. "The ... essays ... appeared first on the editorial page of the Miami herald."--p. 10. [BX7327.S55B5] 31-7424
I. Title.

Radio in religion—Directories.

INTERNATIONAL Christian Broadcasters. 791.45'5
World directory of religious radio and television broadcasting. South Pasadena, Calif., William Carey Library [1973] 808 p. maps. 24 cm. Bibliography: p. 805. [BV656.I53] 73-8853 ISBN 0-87808-133-X 19.95
1. Radio in religion—Directories. 2. Television in religion—Directories. I. Title.

INTERNATIONAL Christian Broadcasters. 791.45'5
World directory of religious radio and television broadcasting. South Pasadena, Calif., William Carey Library [1973] 808 p. maps. 24 cm. Bibliography: p. 805. [BV656.I53] 73-8853 ISBN 0-87808-133-X
1. Radio in religion—Directories. 2. Television in religion—Directories. I. Title.

Rahner, Karl, 1904-

BACIK, James J., 1936- 230
Apologetics and the eclipse of mystery : mystagogy according to Karl Rahner / James J. Bacik. Notre Dame, Ind. : University of Notre Dame Press, c1980. xvi, 166 p. ; 24 cm. Includes indexes. Bibliography: p. 143-159. [BT1102.B2] 80-123 ISBN 0-268-00592-3 : 15.00
1. Rahner, Karl, 1904- 2. Apologetics—20th century. 3. Mystery. I. Title.

CARR, Anne. 230'.2'0924
The theological method of Karl Rahner / by Anne Carr. Missoula, Mont. : Published by Scholars Press for the American Academy of Religion, c1977. vii, 281 p. ; 22 cm. (Dissertation series - American Academy of Religion ; no. 19) Originally presented as the author's thesis, University of Chicago, 1971. Bibliography: p. 271-281. [BX4705.R287C37 1977] 76-51639 ISBN 0-89130-129-1 : 4.50
1. Rahner, Karl, 1904- I. Title. II. Series: American Academy of Religion. Dissertation series — American Academy of Religion ; no. 19.

GELPI, Donald L., 1934- 230.0924
Life and light; a guide to the theology of Karl Rahner, by Donald L. Gelpi. New York, Sheed [c.1966] xiv,301p. 22cm. Bibl. [BX4705.R287G4] 66-12274 6.00
1. Rahner, Karl, 1904- I. Title.

KING, J. Norman. 231.7
The God of forgiveness and healing in the theology of Karl Rahner / by J. Norman King. Washington, D.C. : University Press of America, c1982. p. cm. Includes bibliographical references. [BT102.R272K56] 19 81-40932 ISBN 0-8191-2237-8 : 17.50 ISBN 0-8191-2238-6 (pbk.) : 6.75
1. Rahner, Karl, 1904- 2. God—History of doctrines—20th century. I. Title.

OCHS, Robert, 1930- 236'.1
The death in every now. New York, Sheed and Ward [1969] 159 p. 21 cm. Bibliography: p. 158-159. [BT825.O25] 69-19253 4.25
1. Rahner, Karl, 1904- Schriften zur Theologie. 2. Death. I. Title.

ROBERTS, Louis. 201
The achievement of Karl Rahner. [New York] Herder and Herder [1967] viii, 312 p. 22 cm. Includes bibliographical references. [BX4705.R287R6] 67-25883
1. Rahner, Karl, 1904- I. Title.

SICA, Joseph F. 231.7'4
God so loved the world / Joseph F. Sica. Washington, D.C. : University Press of America, c1981. p. cm. Includes index. [BT127.2.S53] 19 81-40441 ISBN 0-8191-1677-7 : 16.50 ISBN 0-8191-1678-5 (pbk.) : 7.50
1. Rahner, Karl, 1904- 2. Niebuhr, Helmut Richard, 1894-1962. 3. Revelation—History of doctrines—20th century. I. Title.

VORGRIMLER, Herbert. 230.20924
Karl Rahner; his life, thought and works. Translated by Edward Quinn. Glen Rock, N.J., Paulist Press [1966, c1965] 96 p. 19 cm. (Deus books) Translation of Karl Rahner; Denkers over God en Wereld. "Notes and bibliography": p. 89-95. "Books by Karl Rahner available in English": p. 96. [BX4705.R287V63 1966a] 66-4765
1. Rahner, Karl, 1904- I. Title. II. Series.

WEGER, Karl-Heinz. 230'.2'0924
Karl Rahner, an introduction to his theology / Karl-Heinz Weger ; [translated from the German by David Smith]. New York : Seabury Press, 1980. viii, 200 p. ; 22 cm. Translation of Karl Rahner, Eine Einfuhrung in sein theologisches Denken. "A Crossroad book." Includes bibliographical references. [BX4705.R287W4313] 19 79-27424 ISBN 0-8164-0127-6 : 8.95
1. Rahner, Karl, 1904- I. Title.

Rahner, Karl, 1904- —Addresses, essays, lectures.

THEOLOGY and discovery : 230'.2
essays in honor of Karl Rahner, S.J. / edited by William J. Kelly. Milwaukee, Wis. : Marquette University Press, c1980. 365 p. : port. ; 24 cm. Includes bibliographical references and indexes. [BR50.T4296] 19 80-82361 ISBN 0-87462-521-1 : 24.95
1. Rahner, Karl, 1904- —Addresses, essays, lectures. 2. Theology—Addresses, essays, lectures. I. Rahner, Karl, 1904- II. Kelly, William J., 1924-

A World of grace : 230'.2'0924
an introduction to the themes and foundations of Karl Rahner's theology / edited by Leo J. O'Donovan. New York : Seabury Press, 1980. xiii, 198 p. ; 23 cm. "A Crossroad book." Bibliography: p. 185-186. [BX4705.R287W67] 79-25588 ISBN 0-8164-0212-4 : 14.95 ISBN 0-8164-2006-8 (pbk.) : 7.95
1. Rahner, Karl, 1904- —Addresses, essays, lectures. I. O'Donovan, Leo J.

A World of grace : 230'.2'0924
an introduction to the themes and foundations of Karl Rahner's theology / edited by Leo J. O'Donovan. New York : Crossroad, 1981, c1980. p. cm. Bibliography: p. [BX4705.R287W67 1981] 19 81-5441 ISBN 0-8245-0406-2 pbk. : 9.95
1. Rahner, Karl, 1904- —Addresses, essays, lectures. 2. Theology, Doctrinal—History—20th century—Addresses, essays, lectures. I. O'Donovan, Leo J.

Rahway, N. J. First Presbyterian church.

[DAVIS, William 285.174938
Franklin] 1880-
200 years of Christian ministry of the First Presbyterian church, Rahway, N. J., 1741-1941. [Rahway? N.J., 1941?] [3]-80 p. illus. (incl. ports.) 24 cm. "Foreword" signed: William F. Davis, historian. [BX9211.R3F15] 42-456670
1. Rahway, N.J. First Presbyterian church. I. Title.

PAYSON, George Hubbard, 285.
1852-1934.
... Jubilee souvenir of the First Presbyterian church of Rahway, N. J., by the pastor, Rev. Geo. Hubbard Payson ... Rahway, N. J., The Mershon company press, 1891. 92 p. front., pl. ports. 19 cm. At head of title: 1741, 1891. "Biographical": p. 58-60. [BX9211.R3F3] 42-5722
1. Rahway, N. J. First Presbyterian church. I. Title.

POMEROY, John Jay, 1834- 285.
1889.
... Historical sketch of the First Presbyterian church of Rahway, N. J., by Rev. J. Jay Pomeroy, the pastor. Published by the Ladies association of the church. New York, Printing house of W. C. Martin, 1377. 3 p. l., 15-88 p. 23 cm. At head of title: 1741-1877. [BX9211.R3F2] 24-6558
1. Rahway, N. J. First Presbyterian church. I. Title.

Raibolini, Francesco, called ii Francia, 1450-1518.

CARMICHAEL, Montgomery, 1857-
Francia's masterpiece; an essay on the beginnings of the Immaculate conception in art, by Montgomery Carmichael ... New York, E. P. Dutton and co., 1909. xxxiv, 167 p. front., plates. 20 cm. [ND628.R55C] A11
1. Raibolini, Francesco, called ii Francia, 1450-1518. 2. Mary, Virgin—Art. 3. Lucca. San Frediano (Church) I. Title. II. Title: Immaculate conception in art.

Raikes, Robert, 1736-1811.

HARRIS, J. Henry. 200
The story of Robert Raikes for the young, by J. Henry Harris ... With a prefatory note to the authorized American edition, by Edwin W. Rice ... Philadelphia, The Union press [c1900] 112 p. front., pl. port. 20 cm. [BV1518.R3H3] 0-1599
1. Raikes, Robert, 1736-1811. I. Title.

ROBERT Raikes: his Sunday 268.09
schools and his friends; including historical sketches of the Sunday school cause in Europe and America. Philadelphia, American Baptist publication society [1859] 311 p. front. (port.) plates. 16 cm. [BV1518.R3R6] 33-397
1. Raikes, Robert, 1735-1811. 2. Sunday-schools—Hist. I. American Baptist publication society.

Raines, Robert Arnold.

RAINES, Robert 287'632'0924 B
Arnold.
Going home / Robert A. Raines. 1st ed. San Francisco : Harper & Row, c1979. x, 145 p. ; 21 cm. [BR1725.R25A33 1979] 78-15834 ISBN 0-06-066768-0 : 6.95
1. Raines, Robert Arnold. 2. Christian biography—United States. I. Title.

Rains, Francis Marion, 1854-1919.

RAINS, Paul Boyd. 922.
Francis Marion Rains, by Paul Boyd Rains. St. Louis, Christian board of publication, 1922. 168 p. front., ports. 19 cm. [BX7343.R3R3] 22-21275 1.00
1. Rains, Francis Marion, 1854-1919. I. Title.

Rajaneesh, Acharya, 1931-

BELFRAGE, Sally, 1936- 291.4
Flowers of emptiness : reflections on an ashram / Sally Belfrage. 1st ed. New York : Dial Press, c1981. 240 p. ; 22 cm. [B5134.R3464B44] 19 80-25283 ISBN 0-8037-2523-X : 9.95
1. Rajaneesh, Acharya, 1931- 2. Belfrage, Sally, 1936- 3. Philosophers—India—Biography. 4. Life. I. Title.

GUNTHER, Bernard. 294.5'43
Dying for enlightenment : living with Bhagwan Shree Raineesh / by Bernard Gunther ; photographed by Swami Krishna Bharti. 1st ed. San Francisco : Harper & Row, c1979. 151 p. : ill. ; 28 cm. "Books by Bhagwan Rajneesh": p. 151. [BL1175.R2513G86 1979] 78-15841 ISBN 0-06-063527-4 : 6.95
1. Rajaneesh, Acharya, 1931- 2. Meditation. I. Krishna Bharti, Swami. II. Title.

JOSHI, Vasant S., 1941- 299'.93 B
The awakened one : the life and work of Bhagwan Shree Rajneesh / by Vasant Joshi (Swami Satya Vedant). 1st ed. San Francisco : Harper & Row, c1982 p. cm. Bibliography: p. [BP605.S553R344 1982] 19 81-48209 ISBN 0-06-064205-X pbk. : 6.95
1. Rajaneesh, Acharya, 1931- 2. Gurus—United States—Biography. I. Title.

RAJANEESH, Acharya, 1931- 299'.93
Zorba tha Buddha : a darshan diary / Bhagwan Shree Rajneesh; editing and commentary, Ma Prem Maneesha. 1st ed. Antelope, Or. : Rajneesh Foundation International, 1982. 326 p. : ill. ; 22 x 28 cm. [BP605.S553R342 1982] 19 82-50463 ISBN 0-88050-694-6 (pbk.) : 21.95
1. Rajaneesh, Acharya, 1931- 2. Gurus—United States—Biography. I. Prem Maneesha, Ma. II. Title.

SATYA Bharti, Ma. 291.4
Drunk on the divine : life in a Rajneesh Ashram / Ma Satya Bharti. 1st Evergreen ed. New York : Grove Press, 1980. p. cm. [BP605.S553S27 1980] 79-6168 ISBN 0-394-17656-1 (pbk.) : 4.95
1. Rajaneesh, Acharya, 1931- I. Shree Rajneesh Ashram, Pune, India. II. Title.

Raleigh, N. C.-Edenton Street Methodists Church.

RALEIGH, N. C. Edenton Street Methodist Church. Sesquicentennial Committee.
Edenton Street in Methodism: 1811-1961. Sesquicentennial, Edenton Street Methodist Church, a memorial book. [Raleigh, N. C., Capital Printing Co., 1961] 95p. illus. 28cm.
1. Raliegh, N. C. Edenton Street Methodist Church—Anniversaries. I. Title.

Raleigh, N. C. First Baptist Church. Anniversaries, etc.

RALEIGH, N. C. First Baptist Church.
The struggles and fruits of faith. Sesquicentennial celebration, March 4-11, 1962. [Raleigh, 1962] 64 p. illus., ports. 25 cm. 63-52945
1. Raleigh, N. C. First Baptist Church. Anniversaries, etc. I. Title.

Raleigh, Walter, Sir, 1552?-1618.

STRATHMANN, Ernest 211.7'092'4
Albert, 1906-
Sir Walter Ralegh; a study in Elizabethan skepticism, by Ernest A. Strathmann. New York, Octagon Books, 1973 [c1951] ix, 292 p. 23 cm. Reprint of the ed. published by Columbia University Press, New York. Includes bibliographical references. [DA86.22.R2S86 1973] 73-8897 ISBN 0-374-97640-6 11.50
1. Raleigh, Walter, Sir, 1552?-1618. 2. Skepticism.

Rall, Harris Franklin, 1870-1964.

MCCUTCHEON, 230'.7'6320924 B
William John, 1928-
Essays in American theology: the life and thought of Harris Franklin Rall, by W. J. McCutcheon. New York, Philosophical Library [1973] xii, 345 p. 22 cm. Includes bibliographical references. [BX8495.R24M33] 72-190198 ISBN 0-8022-2085-1 12.50
1. Rall, Harris Franklin, 1870-1964. I. Title.

THEOLOGY and modern life; 204
essays in honor of Harris Franklin Rall, edited by Paul Arthur Schilpp. Chicago, New York, Willett, Clark & company, 1940. x p., 1 l., 297 p. front. (port.) 20 1/2 cm. Contents.Harris Franklin Rall, by I. G. Whitchurch.--Our immortality, by S. S. Cohon.--The significance of critical study of the Gospels for religious thought today, by F. C. Grant.--The Christian doctrine of man, by A. C. Knudson.--Facing the problem of evil, by F. J. McConnell.--The realistic movement in religious philosophy, by E. W. Lyman.--The meaning of rational faith, by P. A. Schilpp.--Interpreting the religious situation, by I. G. Whitchurch.--The kingdom of God and the life of today, by C. C. McCown.--The church, the truth, and society, by E. S. Brightman.--Let the church be the church! By E. F. Tittle.--Bibliography of the writings of Harris Franklin Rall (p. 285-297) Bibliographical references in "Notes" at end of most of the chapters. [BT10.T53] 40-8892
1. Rall, Harris Franklin, 1870- 2. Theology—Addresses, essays, lectures. I. Schilpp, Paul Arthur, 1897- ed.

Ram Dass.

RAM Dass. 294
Grist for the mill / by Ram Dass, in collaboration with Stephen Levine. Santa Cruz, Calif. : Unity Press, 1977. 173 p. : ill. ; 22 cm. (The Mindfulness series) [BP610.R3514] 76-40447 ISBN 0-913300-17-9 : 7.95. ISBN 0-913300-16-0 pbk. : 3.95
1. Ram Dass. 2. Spiritual life. I. Levine, Stephen, joint author. II. Title.

Rama (Hindu deity)

BHOOTHALINGAM, Mathuram 294.5211
The story of Rama. New York, Asia Pub. [dist. Taplinger, c.1964] 94p. plates. 26cm. 64-56070 6.50 bds.,
I. Valmiki. Ramayana. II. Title.

SCHURE. EDOUARD, 1841- 291.6
1929.
The ancient mysteries of the East: Rama/Krishna. Introd. by Paul M. Allen. Blauvelt, N.Y., Rudolf Steiner Publications [1971] 11-134 p. 18 cm. (Steinerbooks) Published also in 1961 as the 1st and 2d chapters of the author's The great initiates which was G. Rasberry's translation of Les grands inities. Includes bibliographical references. [BL1225.R3S3813] 70-125797 1.45
1. Krishna. 2. Rama (Hindu deity) I. Schure, Edouard, 1841-1929. Les grands inities. Krishna. English. 1971. II. Title. III. Title: Rama/Krishna.

Rama, Swami, 1925-

BOYD, Doug. 181'.4
Swami / Douglas Boyd. 1st ed. New York : Random House, c1976. xx, 330 p. ; 22 cm. [BL2003.B6] 75-40566 ISBN 0-394-49603-5 : 10.00

1. Rama, Swami, 1925- 2. Boyd, Doug. 3. Sadhus—India. 4. India—Religion. I. Title.

RAMA, Swami, 1925- 294.5'42
Living with the Himalayan masters : spiritual experiences of Swami Rama / edited by Swami Ajaya. Honesdale, Pa. : Himalayan International Institute of Yoga Sciences & Philosophy, c1978. xix, 490 p., [2] leaves of plates : ill. ; 24 cm. [BL1228.R317] 78-103055 ISBN 0-89389-034-0 : 13.95
1. Rama, Swami, 1925- 2. Spiritual life (Hinduism) 3. Himalaya Mountains—Description and travel. I. Ajaya, Swami, 1940- II. Title.

RAMA, Swami, 1925- 294.5'42
Living with the Himalayan masters : spiritual experiences of Swami Rama / edited by Swami Ajaya. Honesdale, Pa. : Himalayan International Institute of Yoga Science & Philosophy, c1980. xv, 490 p., [4] leaves of plates : ill. ; 23 cm. [BL1228.R317 1980] 19 80-82974 ISBN 0-89389-070-7 (pbk.) : 7.50
1. Rama, Swami, 1925- 2. Spiritual life (Hinduism) I. Ajaya, Swami, 1940- II. Title.

Rama, Swami, 1925- —Quotations.

RAMA, Swami, 1925- 294.5'6'1 B
Swami Rama of the Himalayas : photographs & quotations / edited by L. K. Misra. Glenview, Ill. : Himalayan Institute, c1976. [80] p. : ill. ; 23 cm. [BL1175.R253A55] 77-150898
1. Rama, Swami, 1925- —Quotations. 2. Rama, Swami, 1925- —Portraits, etc. 3. Gurus—India—Portraits. I. Title.

Ramabai Sarasvati, Pandita, 1858-1922.

BUTLER, Clementina. 922
Pandita Ramabai Saravati: pioneer in the movement for the education of the child-widow of India, by Clementina Butler ... New York, Chicago [etc.] Fleming H. Revell company [c1922] 96 p. front., plates, ports. 19 1/2 cm. [DS479.1.B3B8] 23-5211
1. Ramabai Sarasvati, pundita, 1858-1922. I. Title.

DYER, Helen S. 922
Pandita Ramabai; the story of her life, by Helen S. Dyer. New York, Chicago [etc.] Fleming H. Revell company [1900] 170 p. 20 cm. [DS479.1.R8D8] 0-6773
1. Ramabai Sarasvati, pandita, 1858- 2. Women in India. I. Title.

FULLER, Mary Lucia Bierce. 922
The triumph of an Indian widow; the life of Pandita Ramabai, by Mary Lucia Bierce Fuller. New York, N. Y., The Christian alliance publishing company [c1928] 72 p. front. (port.) plates. 19 cm. [DS479.1.R3F8] 28-1711
1. Ramabai Sarasvati, pandita, 1858-1922. I. Title.

MILLER, Basil William, 1897- 922
Pandita Ramabai, India's Christian pilgrim. Grand Rapids, Zondervan [1949] 121 p. 20 cm. [DS479.1.R3M5] 49-10439
1. Ramabai Sarasvati, Pandita, 1858-1922. I. Title.

Ramakrishna, 1836-1886.

DEVAMATA, Sister. 921.
Sri Ramakrishna and his disciples, by Sister Devamata ... La CrescNta, Calif., Ana-Ashrama [c1928] xiv p., 1 l., 201 p. 20 cm. "Advertisements": p. 197-201. [B133.R2D4] 28-12838
1. Ramakrishna, 1836-1886. I. Title.

FRENCH, Harold W. 294.5'55
The swan's wide waters : Ramakrishna and Western culture / Harold W. French. Port Washington, N.Y. : Kennikat Press, 1974. viii, 220 p. ; 24 cm. (National university publications) Includes bibliographical references and index. [BL1270.R3F73] 74-77657 ISBN 0-8046-9055-3 : 11.95
1. Ramakrishna, 1836-1886. 2. Vivekananda, Swami, 1863-1902. I. Title.

[GUPTA, Mahendra Nath] 181.4
1855-1932.
The gospel of Sri Ramakrishan, translated into English with an introduction by Swami Nikhilananda. New York, Ramakrishna-Vivekananda center, 1942. xxiii p., 2 l., 3-1063 p. front., plates, ports. 24 cm. "Translation [from the Bengali] of the Sri Sri Ramakrishna Kathamrita, the conversations of Sri Ramakrishna with his disciples, devotees, and visitors, recorded by Mahendranath Gupta, who wrote the book under the pseudonym of 'M'."--Pref. [B133.R3G72] 42-22750
1. Ramakrishna, 1836-1886. I. Nikhilananda, swami, ed. and tr. II. Ramakrishna-Vivekananda center, New York. III. Title.

ISHERWOOD, Christopher, 921.9
1904-
Ramakrishna and his disciples. New York, Simon and Schuster [1965] 348 p. illus., map, ports. 24 cm. Bibliography: p. 335-337. [BL1270.R3I8] 65-17100
1. Ramakrishna, 1836-1886. I. Title.

LEMAITRE, 294.5'55'0924 B
Solange.
Ramakrishna and the vitality of Hinduism. Translated by Charles Lam Markmann. New York, Funk & Wagnalls [1969] xviii, 244 p. illus. 21 cm. Bibliography: p. 232-234. [BL1270.R3L43] 68-54059 4.95
1. Ramakrishna, 1836-1886. 2. Hinduism. I. Title.

MUKERJI, Dhan Gopal, 1890- 921.
1936.
The face of silence, by Dhan Gopal Mukerji ... New York, E. P. Dutton & company, [c1926] vii p., 1 l., 255 p. 22 cm. [B133.R3M85] 26-16160
1. Ramakrishna, 1836-1886. I. Title.

MULLER, Friedrich Max, 1823- 921.
1900.
Ramakrishna; his life and saying, by the Right Hon. F. Max Muller ... New York, C. Scribner's sons, 1899. x p., 1 l., 290 p. 20 cm. Printed in Great Britain. [B133.R2M8] 22-10346
1. Ramakrishna, 1836-1886. I. Ramakrishna 1833-1886. II. Title.

MULLER, 294.5'55'0924 B
Friedrich Max, 1823-1900.
Ramakrishna, his life and sayings / by F. Max Muller. New York : AMS Press, [1975] p. cm. Reprint of the 1899 ed. published by Scribner, New York. [B5134.R38M83 1975] 73-18812 ISBN 0-404-11452-0 : 14.50
1. Ramakrishna, 1836-1886. I. Ramakrishna, 1836-1886. Ramakrishna, his life and sayings. 1975. II. Title.

ROLLAND, Romain, 1866- 181.4
...Prophets of the new India. New York, A. & C. Boni, 1930. xxxiv p., 2 l., 3-683 p. 22 1/2 cm. "Translated from the French by E. F. Malcolm-Smith." Translation of Essal sur la mystique et l'action de l'Indevivante. Bibliography on Ramakrishna: p. 270-275. [B131.R62] 30-25250
1. Ramakrishna, 1836-1886. 2. Vivekananda, swami, 1863-1902. 3. Philosophy, Hindu. I. Malcolm-Smith, Elizabeth Frances, 1891- tr. II. Title.

SATPRAKASHANANDA, 294.5'55'0924 B
Swami.
The significance of Sri Ramakrishna's life and message in the present age : with the author's reminiscences of Holy Mother and some direct disciples / by Swami Satprakashananda. St. Louis : Vedanta Society of St. Louis, 1976. 208 p. ; 20 cm. On spine: Sri Ramakrishna's life and message in the present age. Includes bibliographical references and index. [BL1175.R26S26] 75-46386 ISBN 0-916356-54-X : 6.00
1. Ramakrishna, 1836-1886. 2. Hinduism—Biography. I. Title. II. Title: Sri Ramakrishna's life and message in the present age.

STARK, Claude 294.5'55'0924 B
Alan.
God of all: Sri Ramakrishna's approach to religious plurality. Cape Cod, Mass. [1974] xvii, 236 p. port. 23 cm. Bibliography: p. 216-233. [BL1175.R26S8] 74-76001 ISBN 0-89007-000-8 12.00
1. Ramakrishna, 1836-1886. I. Title.

THORNE, Sabina. 181.48
Precepts for perfection; teachings of the disciples of Sri Ramakrishna. Hollywood, Calif., Nedanta Press [1961] 235 p. 22 cm. Includes bibliography. [B132.V3T5] 61-65951
1. Ramakrishna, 1836-1886. 2. Vedanta. I. Title.

VIDYATMANANDA, Swami. 294.555
Ramakrishna's teachings illustrated. Hollywood, Calif., Vedanta [c.1965] 63p. illus. 18cm. [BL1270.R3V5] 65-1620 1.00 pap.,
1. Ramakrishna, 1836-1886. I. Title.

VIVEKANANDA, swami, 1863- 921.
1902.
My master; by the Swami Vivekananda; with an appended extract from the Theistic quarterly review. New York, The Baker & Taylor co., 1901. viii, 9-89 p. front. 19 1/2 cm. "Param haman Scrimat Ramakrishna, bg. Portab Chunder Masoomdar from the Theistic quarterly review. October 1879 [B133.R3V5] 1-31799
1. Ramakrishna, 1836-1886. I. Pratapachandra Majundar. II. Title.

Ramakrishna, 1836-1886—Addresses, essays, lectures.

SRI Ramakrishna, in 294.5'55'0924
the eyes of Brahma and Christian admirers / edited by Nanda Mookerjee. 1st ed. Calcutta : Firma KLM, 1976. xiv, 141, [9] p., [2] leaves of plates : ill. ; 22 cm. Includes bibliographical references and index. [BL1175.R26S693] 76-904430 Rs22.00 ($4.00 U.S.)
1. Ramakrishna, 1836-1886—Addresses, essays, lectures. I. Mookerjee, Nanda.

Ramakrishna, 1836-1886- Friends and associates.

GAMBHIRANANDA, 294.5'55'0922
Swami
The apostles of Shri Ramakrishna, comp., ed. by Swami Gambhirananda. [1st. ed.] Calcutta, Advaita Ashrama [1967] 401p. ports. 19cm. Partially replaces The disciples of Ramakrishna . . . [BL1270.R3G3] SA67 3.50 bds.,
1. Ramakrishna, 1836-1886- Friends and associates. I. Title.
American distributor: Vedanta Pr., Hollywood, Calif.

Ramamohana Raya, raja, 1774-1833.

RAMACHANDSRA Vasu. 294.552
Brahmoism; or, History of reformed Hinduism from its origin in 1830, under Rajah Mohun Roy, to the present time. With a particular account of Babu Keshub Chunder Sen's connection with the movement. By Ram Chandra Bose ... New York, London, Funk & Wagnalls, 1884. 222 p. 20 cm. "These papers embody the substance of lectures delivered in various places in India, both in Urdu and in English ... The second, the third, and the fifth have appeared as articles in the Indian evangelical review."--Pref. [BL1263.B6] 32-12698
1. Ramamohana Raya, raja, 1774-1833. 2. Brahmasamaj. 3. India—Religion. 4. Kesavachandra Sena I. Title.

Ramana, Maharshi.

MAHADEVAN, 294.5'6'1 B
Telliyavaram Mahadevan Ponnambalam, 1911-
Ramana Maharshi : the sage of Arunacala / T. M. P. Mahadevan. London : Allen & Unwin, 1977. 186 p. ; 21 cm. Includes bibliographical references and index. [BL1175.R342M33] 77-354800 ISBN 0-04-149040-1 : 9.95 ISBN 0-04-149041-X pbk. : 4.50
1. Ramana, Maharshi. 2. Hindus—Biography.

MAHADEVAN, Telliyavaram 181'.48
Mahadevan Ponnambalam, 1911-
Ramana Maharshi and his philosophy of existence / by T. M. P. Mahadevan. 3d ed. Tiruvannamalai : Sri Ramanasramam, 1976. vii, 190 p., [1] leaf of plates : ill. ; 20 cm. Appendices (in Tamil (romanized)) (p. [158]-172): 1. Ulladu narpadu.—2. Ulladu narpadu, anubandham. Includes bibliographical references and index. [BL1175.R342M32 1976] 76-904993 Rs6.00
1. Ramana, Maharshi. I. Title.

OSBORNE, Arthur, 294.5'6'10924 B
1906-
Ramana Maharshi and the path of self-knowledge. Foreword by S. Radhakrishnan. New York, S. Weiser [1970] 207 p. port. 21 cm. Reprint of the 1954 ed. [BL1146.R352O8 1970b] 76-18194 3.00 (pbk)
1. Ramana, Maharsi.

RAMANA, Maharshi. 294.5'4
The collected works of Ramana Maharshi. Edited and annotated by Arthur Osborne. New York, S. Weiser [1970, c1959] 192 p. 21 cm. [BL1146.R35A1 1970] 75-18518 2.75
I. Osborne, Arthur, 1906-

Ramanuja, founder of sect.

CARMAN, John B. 294.5'2'110924
The theology of Ramanuja; an essay in interreligious understanding [by] John Braisted Carman. New Haven, Yale University Press, 1974. xii, 333 p. illus. 24 cm. (Yale publications in religion, 18) Revision of the author's thesis, Yale University, 1962, issued under title: The ideas of divine supremacy and accessibility in the theology of Ramanuja. Bibliography: p. 317-323. [BL1245.V33C37 1974] 73-77146 ISBN 0-300-01521-6 17.50
1. Ramanuja, founder of sect. I. Title. II. Series.

VIDYARTHI, Pandeya 294
Brahmeshwar.
Early Indian religious thought : a study in the sources of Indian theism with special reference to Ramanuja / P. B. Vidyarthi. 1st ed. New Delhi : Oriental Publishers & Distributors, 1976. xv, 239 p. ; 22 cm. (World's wisdom series ; no. 1) Includes indexes. Bibliography: p. [228]-233. [BL2001.2.V5] 76-904388 Rs55.00
1. Ramanuja, founder of sect. 2. India—Religion. 3. Religious thought—India. 4. Theism. I. Title. II. Series.

Rameses VI, King of Egypt.

THE tomb of Ramesses VI. 299.31
[New York] Pantheon Books [1954] 2 v. illus. (part col.) 32cm. (Bollingen series, 40: 1. Egyptian religious texts and representations, v. 1) 'This study is based on the work of an expedition sponsored by the Bollingen Foundation ... October. 1949. to June, 1951.' Contents.pt. I. Texts, translated with introductions by A. Plankoff; edited by N. Rambova.--pt. 2. Plates, recorded by N. Rambova; photographed by L. F. Husson. [PJ1551.E3 vol.1] 54-5646
1. Rameses VI, King of Egypt. 2. Egypt—Religion. 3. Egyptian literature. I. Piankoff, Alexandre, tr. II. Series: Bollingen series, 40: 1 III. Series: Egyptian religious texts and representations, v. 1)

Rammohun Roy, Raja, 1772?-1833.

CARPENTER, Mary, 294.5'562'0924 B
1807-1877.
The last days in England of the Rajah Rammohun Roy / by Mary Carpenter. Riddhi ed. / edited by Swapan Majumdar. Calcutta : Riddhi, 1976. xii, 159 p., [1] leaf of plates : ill. ; 22 cm. Running title: Rammohun Roy. First published in 1866 by Trubner, London. Includes bibliographical references. [BL1265.R3C3 1976] 76-903877 Rs25.00
1. Rammohun Roy, Raja, 1772?-1833. 2. Brahma-samaj—Biography. 3. Hindus—Biography. I. Majumdar, Swapan, 1946- II. Title.

RAY, Ajit Kumar. 294.5'2
The religious ideas of Rammohun Roy : a survey of his writings on religion particularly in Persian, Sanskrit, and Bengali / Ajit Kumar Ray ; with pref. by A. L. Basham. 1st ed. New Delhi : Kanak Publications (Books India Project), 1976. xii, 112 p. ; 22 cm. "Appendix A: Jawab

tuhfatu'l muwahhidin; an anonymous defence of Rammohun Roy's "Tuhfatu'l muwahhidin' against the attacks of the Zoroastrians; translated with text, introduction, and notes": p. [66]-91. Bibliography: p. [99]-112. [BL1265.R3R39] 77-900843 Rs30.00 ($6.00 U.S.)
1. Rammohun Roy, Raja, 1772?-1833. I. Rammohun Roy, Raja, 1772?-1833. Tuhfatu'l muwahhidin. 1976. II. Title.

Ramos, Alex M.

RAMOS, Alex M. 287'.6'0924 B
Stranded no longer / Alex M. Ramos ; [foreword by D. Elton Trueblood]. Nashville, Tenn. : Broadman Press, c1980. 191 p. : ill. ; 20 cm. [BX8495.R25A37] 19 80-66229 ISBN 0-8054-5281-8 pbk. : 4.95
1. Ramos, Alex M. 2. Methodist Church—Clergy—Biography. 3. Clergy—United States—Biography. I. Title.

Ramquist, Grace Bess (Chapman) 1907-comp.

CHAPMAN, James Blaine, 1884-1947. 208.1
The wit and wisdom of J. B. Chapman, unsual stories Dr. Chapman told, comp. by Grace Chapman Ramquist. Grand Rapids, Zondevan Pub. House [1948] 72 p. 20 cm. [BX8699.N3C36] 48-8084
1. Ramquist, Grace Bess (Chapman) 1907-comp. I. Title.

Ramsay, Sir William Mitchell, 1851-1939.

GASQUE, W. Ward 225.6
Sir William M. Ramsay, archaeologist and New Testament scholar; a survey of his contribution to the study of the New Testament, by W. Ward Gasque. Foreword by F. F. Bruce. Grand Rapids, Baker Bk. [1966] 95p. 22cm. (Baker studies in Biblical archaeology) Issued also as thesis (Master of Theol.) Fuller Theol. Seminary. Bibl. [BS2351.R3G3 1966] 66-18312 1.50 pap.,
1. Ramsay, Sir William Mitchell, 1851-1939. I. Title.

Ramsey, Arthur Michael, Abp. of Canterbury, 1904-

SIMPSON, James Beasley 922.342
The hundredth Archbishop of Canterbury. New York, Harper [c.1962] 262p. illus. 22cm. 62-14581 6.00
1. Ramsey, Arthur Michael, Abp. of Canterbury, 1904- I. Title.

SIMPSON, James Beasley. 922.342
The hundredth Archbishop of Canterbury. [1st ed.] New York, Harper & Row [1962] 262 p. illus. 22 cm. [BX5199.R2S5] 62-14581
1. Ramsey, Arthur Michael, Abp. of Canterbury, 1904- I. Title.

Ramsey, Ian T.

EDWARDS, David Lawrence. 283'.092'4 B
Ian Ramsey, Bishop of Durham; a memoir [by] David L. Edwards. London, New York, Oxford University Press, 1973. 101 p. illus., port. 23 cm. [BX5199.R22E38] 73-179441 ISBN 0-19-213111-7 £2.00
1. Ramsey, Ian T. I. Title.

GILL, Jerry H. 201
Ian Ramsey : to speak responsibly of God / by Jerry H. Gill. London : Allen and Unwin, 1976. 13-166 p. ; 22 cm. (Contemporary religious thinkers series) Includes index. Bibliography: p. 159-164. [BR100.G478] 76-363853 ISBN 0-04-230014-2 : 12.25
1. Ramsey, Ian T. 2. Experience (Religion) 3. Religion and language. 4. Knowledge, Theory of (Religion)
Distributed by Allen and Unwin Inc. 198 Ash St. Reading, Mass. 01867

Ramsey, Paul.

CURRAN, Charles E. 241'.6'2
Politics, medicine, and Christian ethics; a dialogue with Paul Ramsey [by] Charles E. Curran. Philadelphia, Fortress Press [1973] viii, 228 p. 24 cm. Includes bibliographical references. [BR115.P7C83] 72-91521 ISBN 0-8006-0500-4 6.95
1. Ramsey, Paul. 2. Christianity and politics. 3. War and religion. 4. Medical ethics. 5. Human genetics. I. Title.

LOVE and society : 241
essays and epics and Paul Ramsey / [edited by] James T. Johnson, David Smith. Missoula, Mont. : Scholars Press, [1975] p. cm. (AAR studies in religious ethics) Contents.Contents.—Smith, D. H. Paul Ramsey, love and killing.—Evans, D. Paul Ramsey on exceptionless moral rules.—Curran, C. E. Paul Ramsey and traditional Roman Catholic natural law theory.—Camenisch, P. F. Paul Ramsey's task, some methodological clarifications and questions.—Johnson, J. T. Morality and force in statecraft.—Walters, L. Historical applications of the just war theory.—Little, D. The structure of justification in the political ethics of Paul Ramsey.—O'Brien, W. V. Morality and war, the contribution of Paul Ramsey.—Outka, G. Social justice and equal access to health care.—McCormick, R. A. Proxy consent in the experimentation situation.—May, W. F. Attitudes toward the newly dead.—Bibliography of Paul Ramsey's works (p.) Includes bibliographies. [BJ1251.L68] 74-19665 ISBN 0-88420-123-6
1. Ramsey, Paul. 2. Ramsey, Paul—Bibliography. 3. Christian ethics—Addresses, essays, lectures. 4. Social ethics—Addresses, essays, lectures. I. Johnson, James Turner, ed. II. Smith, David H., 1939- ed. III. Series: American Academy of Religion. AAR studies in religious ethics.

Ramsey, William.

BEATTY, Charles, d.1772. 252.7
Double honour due to the laborious gospel minister. Represented in a sermon, preached at Fairfield, in New Jersey, the 1st of December, 1756. At the ordination of the Reverend Mr. William Ramsey. Published at the desire of the hearers, by Charles Beatty, minister of the gospel at Nishaminy ... Philadelphia, Printed by William Bradford, at the corner of Front- and Market-streets [1757] 1 p. l., 56 p. 16 1/2 cm. Signatures: A-C. Fly-leaf, containing half-title is missing. Margins trimmed when re-bound. [BX7233.B37D6] 2-10520
1. Ramsey, William. I. Title.

Ramseyer, Joseph Eicher, 1868 or 9-1944.

RAMSEYER, Macy (Garth) 922.89
Joseph E. Ramseyer--"yet speaking," by Macy Garth Ramseyer (Mrs. J. E. Ramseyer) ... Fort Wayne, Ind., The Fort Wayne Bible institute [1945] 298 p. front., plates, ports., map. 20 cm. [BX8530.M5R3] 45-19786
1. Ramseyer, Joseph Eicher, 1868 or 9-1944. 2. Missionary church association—Hist. I. Fort Wayne, Ind. Bible institute. II. Title.

Ranade, Mahadev Govind, 1842-1900.

RANADE, Ramabai. 920.7
Himself: the autobiography of a Hindu lady, translated and adapted by Katherine Van Akin Gates from a book written in the Marathi language by Mrs. Ramabai Ranade; with illustrations by Louise Spalding Carter. New York, Toronto, Longmans, Green and co., 1938. xiv, [2], 253 p. illus. 20 cm. "First edition." [HQ1742.R28] 38-27884
1. Ranade, Mahadev Govind, 1842-1900. I. Gates, Katharine (Van Akin) Mrs. 1882-ed and tr. II. Title.

Rance, Armand Jean Le Bouthillier de, 1626-1700.

KRAILSHEIMER, A. J. 271'.125'024 B
Armand-Jean de Rance, Abbot of La Trappe : his influence in the cloister and the world / by A. J. Krailsheimer. Oxford : Clarendon Press, 1974. xvi, 376 p., [5] leaves of plates : ill. ; 23 cm. Includes index. Bibliography: p. [345]-362. [BX4705.R3K7] 74-186609 ISBN 0-19-815744-4 : 25.00
1. Rance, Armand Jean Le Bouthillier de, 1626-1700.
Distributed by Oxford University Press, New York.

LUDDY, Ailbe J. 922.244
The real de Rance, illustrious penitent and reformer of Notre Dame de la Trappe. By Ailbe J. Luddy ... London, New York [etc.] Longmans, Green and co., 1931. xxi, 314 p. front.)port.) 20 1/2 cm. Bibliography: p. 312-313. [BX4705.R3L8] 31-12717
1. Rance, Armand Jean le Bouthiller de, 1626?-1700. 2. Trappists. I. Title.

LUDDY, Ailbe John, 1883- 922.24
The real de Rance, illustrious penitent and reformer of Notre Dame de la Trappe. By Ailbe J. Luddy ... London, New York [etc.] Longmans, Green and co., 1931. xxi, 314 p. front. (port.) 20 1/2 cm. Bibliography: p. 312-313. [BX4705.R3L8] 31-12717
1. Rance, Armand Jean le Bouthiller de, 1626?=1700. 2. Trappists. I. Title.

Randall, Benjamin, 1749-1808.

BUZZELL, John, 1798-1863.
The life of Elder Benjamin Randal. Principally taken from documents written by himself. By John Buzzell ... Limerick [Me.] Hobbs, Woodman & co., 1827. 306 p. 18 cm. [BX6379.B3B8] 22-20231
1. Randal, Benjamin, 1749-1808. I. Title.

WILEY, Frederick Levi, 1836-
Life and influence of the Rev. Benjamin Randall, founder of the Free Baptist denomination... By Rev. Frederick L. Wiley. Philadelphia, Boston [etc.] American Baptist publication society [c1915] 9 p. l., 3-310 p. front., 1 illus., pl., ports. 20 cm. $1.00. 15-14120
1. Randall, Benjamin, 1749-1808. I. Title.

Randall, Richard William, 1824-1906.

BRISCOE, John Fetherstonhaugh, 1877- 922.342
A tractarian at work; a memoir of Dean Randall, by J.F. Briscoe... and H.F.B. Mackay...with a foreword by Viscount Halifax. London and Oxford, A.R. Mowbray & co., ltd.; Milwaukee, Morehouse publishing co. [1932] xi, 211, [1] p. front., plates, ports. 22 cm. "First published, September, 1932; second impression, December, 1932." [BX5199.R23B7 1932a] 33-9562
1. Randall, Richard William, 1824-1906. 2. Oxford movement. I. Mackay, Henry Falconer Barclay, joint author. II. Title.

Randolph, Paschal Beverly, b. 1825.

CLYMER, Reuben Swinburne, 1878- ed. 299
The Rose cross order; a short sketch of the history of the Rose cross order in America, together with a sketch of the life of Dr. P. B. Randolph, the founder of the order... Introduction and notes by Dr. R. Swinburne Clymer... Allentown, Pa., The Philosophical publishing co., 1916. 208 p. illus. 20 1/2 cm. [BF1623.R7C67] 17-3898 1.00
1. Randolph, Paschal Beverly, b. 1825. 2. Rosicrucians. I. Title.

Rankin, Milledge Theron, 1804-1953.

WEATHERSPOON, Jesse Burton, 1886- 922.651
M. Theron Rankin, Apostle of Advance. Nashville, Broadman Press [1958] 137 p. illus. 21 cm. [BV3427.R2W4] 58-11550
1. Rankin, Milledge Theron, 1804-1953. I. Title.

Rankin, Molly K.

RANKIN, Molly K. 266'.673 B
No chance to panic / Molly K. Rankin ; [cover ill. by Don Muth]. Mountain View, Calif. : Pacific Press Pub. Association, 1980. 128 p. ; 22 cm. (A Destiny book ; D186) [BV3680.N52R367] 79-87734 pbk. : 4.95
1. Rankin, Molly K. 2. Missionaries—Papua New Guinea—Biography. 3. Missionaries—New Zealand—Biography. I. Title.

Rapture (Christian eschatology)

BEECHICK, Allen. 236
The pretribulation rapture / Allen Beechick. Denver, Colo. : Accent Books, c1980. 288 p. : ill. ; 21 cm. Includes bibliographical references. [BT887.B43] 19 79-53291 ISBN 0-89636-040-7 (pbk.) : 4.95
1. Rapture (Christian eschatology) I. Title.

BETZER, Dan. 236
Countdown, a newsman looks at the rapture / Dan Betzer. Springfield, Mo. : Radiant Books, c1979. 112 p. ; 18 cm. [BT887.B47] 79-53943 ISBN 0-88243-481-0 pbk. : 1.50
1. Rapture (Christian eschatology) 2. Eschatology. I. Title.

†CRIBB, C. C. 236
Armageddon, dead ahead / C. C. Cribb. Raleigh, N.C. : Manhattan, c1977. 160 p. ; 19 cm. Selections from the author's From now till eternity. [BS647.2.C72 1977] 77-70212 1.75
1. Bible—Prophecies. 2. Rapture (Christian eschatology) 3. Tribulation (Christian eschatology) I. Title.
Publisher's address: P. O. Box 18601 Raleigh, NC 27609

MACPHERSON, Dave. 236
The incredible cover-up : the true story on the pre-trib rapture / by Dave MacPherson. Rev. and combined ed. Plainfield, N.J. : Logos International, c1975. xiii, 162 p., [2] leaves of plates : ill. ; 21 cm. Combines The unbelievable pre-trib origin and The late great pre-trib rapture, both written by the author and originally published in 1973 and 1974 respectively. Bibliography: p. [158]-162. [BT887.M3 1975] 75-25171 ISBN 0-88270-143-6 : 5.95. pbk. : 2.95
1. Rapture (Christian eschatology) 2. Tribulation (Christian eschatology) I. Title.

RYRIE, Charles Caldwell, 1925- 236
What you should know about the Rapture / by Charles C. Ryrie. Chicago : Moody Press, c1981. 118 p. ; 21 cm. (Current Christian issues) [BT887.R95] 19 81-4019 ISBN 0-8024-9416-1 pbk.: 2.95
1. Rapture (Christian eschatology) 2. Tribulation (Christian eschatology) 3. Eschatology. I. Title. II. Series.

SMITH, Chuck, 1927- 236'.9
Snatched away! / Chuck Smith. Costa Mesa, Calif. : Maranatha Evangelical Association of Calvary Chapel, c1976. 70 p. ; 18 cm. [BT887.S6] 76-26645 ISBN 0-89337-004-5 pbk. : 1.25
1. Bible—Prophecies. 2. Rapture (Christian eschatology) 3. Tribulation (Christian eschatology) 4. Second Advent. I. Title.

TOMBLER, John W. 236
The raptured : a Catholic view of the latter days and the Second Coming / John W.

Tombler and Hubert J. Funk. East Orange, N.J. : Trumpet Press, c1977. viii, 179 p. ; 23 cm. [BT887.T65] 77-80110 ISBN 0-918952-01-8 : 4.95
1. Rapture (Christian eschatology) I. Funk, Hubert J., joint author. II. Title.

WALVOORD, John F. 236
The rapture question / John F. Walvoord. Rev. and enl. ed. Grand Rapids : Zondervan Pub. House, c1979. 304 p. ; 21 cm. Includes indexes. Bibliography: p. 287-293. [BT887.W34 1979] 79-11907 ISBN 0-310-34111-6 pbk. : 2.95
1. Rapture (Christian eschatology) 2. Millennialism. I. Title.

WOOLSEY, Raymond H. 236'.8
The secret of the rapture / Raymond H. Woolsey. Washington : Review and Herald Pub. Association, [1975] 64 p. ; 19 cm. Bibliography: p. 64. [BT887.W66] 75-9364
1. Rapture (Christian eschatology) I. Title.

Ras Shamra.

KAPELRUD, Arvid Schou, 1912- 299.269
The Ras Shamra discoveries and the Old Testament. Translated by G. W. Anderson. [1st U.S. ed.] Norman, University of Oklahoma Press [1963] 91 p. 21 cm. Bibliographical footnotes. [BL1670.K33 1963] 63-17164
1. Bible. O. T.—Criticism, interpretation, etc. 2. Ras Shamra. 3. Palestine—Religion. I. Title.

PFEIFFER, Charles F. 220.93
Ras Shamra and the Bible. Grand Rapids, Mich., Baker Bk. [c.]1962. 73p. illus. 22cm. (Baker studies in Biblical archaeology) Bibl. 62-15162 1.50 pap.,
1. Ras Shamra. 2. Bible. O.T.—Antiq. I. Title.

Ras Tafari movement.

BARRETT, Leonard E. 299'.6
The Rastafarians : sounds of cultural dissonance / Leonard E. Barrett. Boston : Beacon Press, [1977] p. cm. Includes index. Bibliography: p. [BL2530.J3B37] 76-48491 ISBN 0-8070-1114-2 : 10.95 ISBN 0-8070-1115-0 pbk. : 3.95
1. Ras Tafari movement. 2. Jamaica—Religion. 3. Jamaica—History. I. Title.

NICHOLAS, Tracy. 299'.6
Rastafari : a way of life / text by Tracy Nicholas ; photos. by Bill Sparrow. 1st ed. Garden City, N.Y. : Anchor Books, 1979. viii, 92 p., [36] leaves of plates : ill. ; 20 x 27 cm. Includes bibliographical references. [BL2530.J3N5] 77-76285 ISBN 0-385-11575-X pbk. : 6.95
1. Ras Tafari movement. 2. Jamaica—Religion. I. Sparrow, Bill. II. Title.

Ras Tafari movement—England.

CASHMORE, Ernest. 299'.67
Rastaman : the Rastafarian movement in England / Ernest Cashmore. London : Boston : G. Allen & Unwin, 1979. xi, 263 p. ; 23 cm. Includes index. Bibliography: p. [249]-257. [BL980.G7C37] 79-40684 ISBN 0-04-301108-X : 27.50
1. Ras Tafari movement—England. I. Title.

Ras Tafari movement—Jamaica—Miscellanea.

FARISTZADDI, Millard. 299'.67
Iations of Jamaica and I Rastafari / by Millard Faristzaddi. 1st Evergreen ed. New York : Grove Press, 1982. p. cm. [BL2352.R37F37 1982] 19 82-82460 ISBN 0-394-62435-1 : 9.95
1. Ras Tafari movement—Jamaica—Miscellanea. 2. Jamaica—Miscellanea. I. Title.

Rashdall Hastings 1858-1924

MATHESON, Percy Ewing, 1859-
The life of Hastings Rashdall, D.D., dean of Carlisle, fellow of the British academy, honorary fellow of New College, by P. E. Matheson... London, Oxford university press, H. Milford, 1928. xi, 287, [1] p. front., plates, ports. 28 cm. "Writings by Dr. Hastings Rashdall": p. 237. [BX5199.R24M3] 28-28974
1. Rashdall Hastings 1858-1924 I. Title.

Raskin, Saul, 1878- illus.

JEWS. Liturgy and ritual. Hagadah. 1941. 296
Hagadah for Passover. [New York, Printed by the Academy photo offset, inc., 1941] 82 p. illus. (part col.) 35 cm. Hebrew and English. [BM675.P4A3 1941] 46-39184
1. Raskin, Saul, 1878- illus. I. Title.

Raskolniks.

AVVAKUM, Protopope, 1621?-1682 922.147
The life of the Archpriest Avvakum, by himself. Tr. from seventeenth century Russian by Jane Harrison, Hope Mirrlees. Pref. by Prince D. S. Mirsky. Hamden, Conn., Archon [dist. Shoe String, 1963] 155p. 18cm. 63-18279 5.00
1. Raskolniks. I. Title.

CRUMMEY, Robert O. 281.9'47'2
The Old Believers & the world of Antichrist; the Vyg community & the Russian State, 1694-1855 [by] Robert O. Crummey. Madison, University of Wisconsin Press, 1970. xix, 258 p. illus., maps. 25 cm. Bibliography: p. 227-247. [BX601.C78 1970] 79-98121 ISBN 0-299-05560-4 10.00
1. Raskolniks. I. Title.

HEARD, Albert F. 281.9'47
The Russian church and Russian dissent, comprising orthodoxy, dissent, and erratic sects, by Albert F. Heard. New York, Harper, 1887. [New York, AMS Press, 1971] ix, 310 p. 23 cm. Bibliography: p. [vii]-ix. [BX510.H4 1971] 70-127909 ISBN 0-404-03198-6
1. Orthodox Eastern Church, Russian. 2. Raskolniks. 3. Sects—Russia. I. Title.

Rasmussen, Bertha, 1885-1901.

RASMUSSEN, Hannah, Mrs.
A young missionary; or, The life of Bertha Rasmussen, written by her mother, Mrs. Hannah Rasmussen ... Chicago, S. B. Shaw [c1904] 143 p. incl. pl., ports. front. (port.) pl. 21 cm. 5-32508
1. Rasmussen, Bertha, 1885-1901. I. Title.

Rasputin, Grigorii Efimovich, 1871-1916.

JUDAS, Elizabeth, 1897- 281.90924
Rasputin, neither devil nor saint, [2d ed.] Miami, Fla., Allied Publishers [1965] 216 p. illus. ports. 21 cm. [DK254.R3J8] 65-8566
1. Rasputin, Grigoril Efimovich, 1871-1916. I. Title.

JUDAS, Elizabeth, Mrs. 1897- 922.147
Rasputin, neither devil nor saint, by Dr. Elizabeth Judas. Los Angeles, Calif., Wetzel publishing co., inc. [1942] 283 p. incl. front., plates, ports., facsims. 21 cm. [DK254.R3J8] 42-12961
1. Rasputin, Grigoril Efimovich, 1871-1916. I. Title.

JUDAS, Elizabeth, 1897- 281.90924
Rasputin, neither devil nor saint. [2d ed.] Miami, Fla. 33127, Allied Pubs. 220 N.W. 47 St. [c.1942-1965] 216p. illus. ports. 21cm. [DK254.R3J8] 65-8566 3.95
1. Rasputin, Grigorii Efimovich, 1871-1916. I. Title.

TRUFANOV, Sergiei Mikhailovich, 1880- 922
The life of Rasputin, by Sergius Michailow Trufanoff (Illiodor) ... New York, The Metropolitan magazine co., 1916. 67 p. 18 1/2 cm. $0.25 [DK254.R3T8] 16-22130
1. Rasputin, Grigoril Efimovich. I. Title.

WILSON, Colin, 1931- 922.147
Rasputin and the fall of the Romanovs. New York, Farrar, Straus [1964] 240 p. ports. 22 cm. Bibliography: p. 218-220. [DK254.R3W5] 64-23120
1. Rasputin, Grigorii Efimovich, 1871-1916. I. Title.

Ratana, Tahupotiki Wiremu, 1873-1939.

HENDERSON, J. McLeod 299.94
Ratana; the origins and the story of the movement. Wellington, N.Z., Polynesian Soc. [dist. Detroit, Cellar Bk. Shop, 1963] vii, 128p. illus., ports., map. geneal. table. 25cm. (Polynesian Soc. memoir, v. 36) Bibl. 64-854 4.25 bds.,
1. Ratana, Tahupotiki Wiremu, 1873-1939. 2. Maoris. I. Title. II. Series: Polynesian Society, Wellington. Memoirs, v. 36

Rationalism.

ADAMS, Robert Chamblet, 1839- 211
Good without God, by Robert Chamblet Adams... New York P. Eckler [1902] 118 p. 19 1/2 cm. [BL2775.A38] 2-20064
1. Rationalism. I. Title.

ADAMS, Robert Chamblet, 1839- 211
Travels in faith from tradition to reason, by Robert C. Adams... New York, London, G. P. Putnam's sons, 1884. 2 p. l., 238 p. 20 cm. [BL2775.A4] 38-33863
1. Rationalism. I. Title.

ALLEN, Ethan, 1737-1789. 211
Reason, the only oracle of man; or, A compendious system of natural religion. Boston, J. P. Mendum, 1854. 171 p. 19 cm. [BL2773.A5 1854] 48-42285
1. Rationalism. I. Title.

ALLEN, Ethan, 1737-1789. 211
Reason the only oracle of man, or A compenduous system of natural religion. Alternately adorned with confutations of a variety of doctrines incompatible to it; deduced from the most exalted ideas which we are able to form of the divine and human characters, and from the universe in general. By Ethan Allen, esq. Bennington: state of Vermont: Printed by Haswell & Russell, M[DOC]-LXXXIV. xxi, [28]-477 p. 21 cm. The scarcest of his works; the greater part of the edition was destroyed by fire in the printing office, and was not reprinted entire. An abridged edition was published in New York, by G. W. & A. I. Matseil, 1836. This is the first publication in the United States openly directed against the Christian religion. [BL2773.A5] 2-8989
1. Rationalism. I. Title. II. Title: Natural religion, A compenduous system of.

ALLEN, Ethan, 1737-1789. 211
Reason the only oracle of man, by Ethan Allen; with an introduction by John Pell. New York, N.Y., Scholars' facsimiles & reprints, 1940. xii p. 2 l, facsim (xxi, [23]-477 p.), 1 l. 70 p. 21 cm. [Scholars' facsmiles & reprints]. "Facsmile reproduction of a copy [of the 1794 edition] in Fort Ticonderoga museum." Title of facsmile: Reason the only oracle of man, or A compenduous system of natural religion ... "The appendix to Reason" (reprinted from the Historical magazine, Boston, April, May, June and July, 1878): 1 l. 70 p. at end. "Bibliographical note": p. xi-xii. [BL2773.A5 1784a] 40-36196
1. Rationalism. I. Pell, John. II. Title. III. Title: Natural religion, A compenduous system of.

ANDERSON, Robert, Sir 1841-
Christianized rationalism and the higher criticism; a reply to Professor Harnack's "What is Christianity," by Sir Robert Anderson ... Chicago, Ill., Winona Lake, Ind., The Winona publishing company, 1903. 2 p. l., 89 p. 17 cm. 4-44
I. Title.

BARTLEY, William Warren, 1934- 149.7
The retreat to commitment. [1st ed.] New York, Knopf, 1962. 223 p. 22 cm. [BL2775.2.B3] 62-8674
1. Rationalism. I. Title.

BENNETT, George H.
Challenge of the church, rationalism refuted; a reply to the Oregon rationalist society, containing expositions of cosmogony, inspiration, prayer, etc., which offer practical solutions of certain great issues between science and the Bible. By George H. Bennett ... Cincinnati, Press of the Methodist book concern [c1914] 164 p. 19 cm. 15-6546 1.00
I. Title.

CAMPBELL, Douglas. 211
The rational and true gospel of the world's divine order, By Douglas Campbell. New ed., rev. ... London, Trubner & co.; [etc., etc., 1878] viii, 363 p. 22 cm. [BL2775.C27 1878a1] 36-8470
1. Rationalism. I. Title.

CHUBB, Thomas, 1679-1747. 211'.4
The comparative excellence and obligation of moral and positive duties, 1730, and A discourse concerning reason, 1731 / Thomas Chubb. New York : Garland Pub., 1979 85, 83 p. ; 23 cm. (British philosophers and theologians of the 17th & 18th centuries) Reprint of the works printed in London, respectively, for J. Roberts and T. Cox. [BL2773.C52 1978] 75-11205 ISBN 0-8240-1760-9 : 29.50
1. Rationalism. 2. Natural theology. I. Chubb, Thomas, 1679-1747. A discourse concerning reason. 1978. II. Title. III. Title: The comparative excellence and obligation of moral and positive duties ... IV. Series.

COBBE, Frances Power, 1822-1904. 211
Broken lights: an inquiry into the present condition and future prospects of religious faith. By Frances Power Cobbe. Boston, Lee and Shepard; New York, C. T. Dillingham [189-?] 2 p. l., 7-243 p. 18 cm. (On cover: Good company) [BL2775.C59] 43-37122
1. Rationalism. I. Title.

COLLINS, James Daniel 190
The continental rationalists: Descartes, Spinoza, Leibniz, by James Collins. Milwaukee, Bruce [1967] viii, 177p. 22cm. First pub. as chapters 5-7 of the author's History of modern European philosophy. Bibl. [B1875.C63] 67-26507 2.50 pap.,
1. Descartes, Rene, 1596-1650. 2. Spinoza, Benedictus de, 1632-1677. 3. Leibniz, Gottfried Wilhelm, Freiherr von, 1646-1716. 4. Rationalism. I. Title.

COLLINS, James Daniel. 190
The continental rationalists: Descartes, Spinoza, Leibniz, by James Collins. Milwaukee, Bruce Pub. Co. [1967] viii. 177 p. 22 cm. First published as chapters 5-7 of the author's History of modern European philosophy. Includes bibliographical references. [B1875.C63] 67-26507
1. Descartes, Rene, 1596-1650. 2. Spinoza, Benedictus de, 1632-1677. 3. Leibniz, Gottfried Wilhelm, Freiherr von. 1646-1716. 4. Rationalism. I. Title.

EISENSTEIN-BARZILAY, Isaac, 1915- 149'.7
Between reason and faith. Anti-rationalism in Italian Jewish thought 1250-1650, by Isaac E. Barzilay. The Hague, Paris, Mouton & Co. 1967 [1968] 248p. 24cm. (Pubns. in Near & Middle East studies, Columbia Univ. Series A, 10) Bibl. [B833.E57] 67-24376 11.75
1. Rationalism. 2. Philosophy, Jewish. I. Title. II. Series: Columbia University. Publications in Near and Middle East studies. Ser. A., 10
Distributed by Humanities, New York.

[ENGLISH, George Bethune] 1787-1826. 211
A letter to the Reverend Mr. Cary, containing remarks upon his Review of The grounds of Christianity examined, by comparing the New Testament with the Old. By the author of that work... Boston: Printed for the author..... 1813. 133 p. 18 1/2 cm. With this is bound the author's A letter respectfully addressed to the Reverend Mr. Channing. Boston, 1813. [BL2775.E64] 36-19298
1. Cary, Samuel, 1785-1815. Review of a book entitled The grounds of Christianity examined. 2. Rationalism. I. Title.

ENGLISH, George Bethune, 1787-1828. 211
The grounds of Christianity examined, by comparing the New Testament with the Old. By George Bethune English... Boston; Printed for the author... 1813. xxi, 182 p., 1 l., 18 cm. [BL2775.E63] 38-19300
1. Rationalism. I. Title.

ENGLISH, George Bethune, 1787-1828. 211
The grounds of Christianity examined by comparing the New Testament with the Old. To which is added a review of the

Sermon on the Mount, &c. by the Rev. Dr. Zipser. [Boston?] 1852 [cover 1868] xii, 128 p. 23 cm. "Re-printed from the Boston edition, 1813." [BL2775.E63 1868] 50-47701
1. Rationalism. I. Title.

FISKE, Asa Severance, 1833- 289
Reason and faith, by Rev. A. S. Fiske, D.D. Washington, D.C., The Neale company, 1900. vii, 9-167 p. front. (port.) 18 cm. [BT1210.F52] 0-6903
1. Rationalism. 2. Christianity—Evidences. I. Title.
Contents omitted.

GAUVIN, Marshall J. 211
The Gauvin-Olson debates on God and the Bible, at the Auditorium building, Minneapolis, Minn., on Sunday afternoons, May 1 and May 8, 1921; speeches revised by both disputants. New York, Peter Eckler publishing co., 1921. 127 p. 20 cm. $0.75 [BL2778.G3] 21-11259
I. Olson, David Eugene, joint author. II. Title.

GERHARD, Frederick. 211
The coming creed of the world. Is there not a faith more sublime and blissful than Christianity? A voice crying in the wilderness. By Frederick Gerhard ... Philadelphia, W. H. Thompson, 1884. 526 p. incl. front. (port.) 20 cm. [B12775.G4]
1. Rationalism. 2. Free thought. I. Title.

HALDEMAN-JULIUS, Emmanuel, 1889- 211
This tyranny of bunk. Girard, Kan., Haldeman-Julius Publications, [c1927]. 128 p. 22 cm. (Big blue book no. B-40) [BL2775.H133] ISBN 48-33714
1. Rationalism. I. Haldeman-Julius, Emmanuel, II. Title. III. Series.

HANVILLE, Merrill F. 211
The heavenly alibi, by Merrill F. Hanville. [Gary, Ind.] The author, 1940. 5 p. l., 92 p. 20 1/2 cm. [BL2775.H14] 40-5555
I. Title.

HASTINGS, George T. 211
Love, evolution and religion, by George T. Hastings. White Plains, N.Y., George T. Hastings publishing co., 1924. xii p., 1 l., 15-308 p. 20 1/2 cm. "References and bibliography : p. 305-308. [BL2775.H28] 24-11892
I. Title.

HURST, John Fletcher, bp., 1834-1903. 211
History of rationalism; embracing a survey of the present state of Protestant theology, by John Fletcher Hurst ... with appendix of literature. Rev., 1901. New York, Eaton & Mains; Cincinnati, Jennings & pye [1901] 3 p. l., [ix]-xix, 633 p. 23 cm. Literature of rationalism: p. 591-621. [BL2750.H8 1901] 2-744
1. Rationalism. 2. Protestantism. I. Title.

LECKY, William Edward Hartpole, 1838-1903. 211
History of the rise and influence of the spirit of rationalism in Europe. By W. E. H. Lecky, M. A. Rev. ed. New York, D. Appleton and company, 1870. 2 v. 21 cm. [BL2750.L4 1870] 17-8230
1. Rationalism. I. Title.

LECKY, William Edward Hartpole, 1838-1903. 211
History of the rise and influence of the spirit of rationalism in Europe. By W. E. H. Lecky, M. A. Rev. ed. ... New York, D. Appleton and company, 1872. 2 v. 21 cm. [BL2750.L4 1872] 17-8231
1. Rationalism. I. Title.

LECKY, William Edward Hartpole, 1838-1903. 211
History of the rise and influence of the spirit of rationalism in Europe. By W. E. H. Lecky, M. A. Rev. ed. New York and London, D. Appleton and company, 1925. 2 v. 21 cm. [BL2750.L4 1925] 31-34280
1. Rationalism. I. Title.

LEWIS, Joseph. 211
The tyranny of God, by Joseph Lewis. New York city, The Truth publishing company [c1921] 122 p. 19 1/2 cm. [BL2775.L4] 21-11124
I. Title.

LOVE, Alonzo Robert. 211
Under the ban, by Alonzo Robert Love. Boston, Mass., The Stratford company, 1927. 5 p. l., x, 326 p. front. (port.) 21 cm. [BL2775.L5] 27-6159
I. Title.

MACY, Christopher. 149'.7
Science, reason, and religion, edited by Christopher Macy. [Buffalo, N.Y.] Prometheus Books [1974] 111 p. 19 cm. First published in 1973 under title: Rationalism in the 1970s. Includes bibliography. [B833.M3 1974] 74-174354 ISBN 0-87975-028-6 ISBN 0-87975-027-8 (pbk.) 6.95
1. Rationalism. 2. Science—Philosophy. 3. Religion and science—1946- I. Title.

MANGASARIAN, Mangasar Mugwiditch, 1859- 211
The truth about Jesus. Is he a myth? Illustrated. [By] M. M. Mangasarian Chicago, Independent religious society [c1909] 295 p. illus. 21 cm. Illustrated t.-p. [BL2775.M35] 9-3546
1. Jesus Christ—Historicity. 2. Rationalism. I. Title.

MUNDAY, William. 211
An examination of the Bible; or, An impartial investigation of supernatural & natural theology: wherein the foundations of true religion are illustrated and established. To which are added, A rational system of faith, and Remarks on the union of church and state. By William Munday ... Baltimore: Printed for the author, 1908. xv, [17]-280 p. 17 cm. [BL2775.M8] 39-3980
1. Rationalism. I. Title. II. Title: An impartial investigation of supernatural & natural theology.

PAINE, Thomas, 1737-1809. 211
The age of reason: being an investigation of true & fabulous theology. By Thomas Paine... Life by Richard Carlile. Philadelphia, Pa., Manchester, Eng., G. Walton [18-] 207 p. 16 1/2 cm. Printed in Manchester, Eng. With this is bound the author's Common Sense... Manchester [18-] [BL2740.A1 1820] 4-1970
1. Rationalism. I. Title.
Contents omitted.

PAINE, Thomas, 1737-1809. 211
Age of reason, being an investigation of true and fabulous theology. By Thomas Paine... New York, P. Eckler [1891] 2 v. in 1. 21 cm. (Library of liberal classics) Paged continuously. Portrait on cover. [BL2740.A1 1891] 34-10935
1. Rationalism. I. Title.

PAINE, Thomas, 1737-1809. 211
The age of reason; being an investigation of true and fabulous theology. By Thomas Paine, M.A., a pioneer of Biblical criticism. New York, The Truth seeker co. [1898] 1 p. l., xxii p., 1 l., 194 p. front., pl., port., facsim. 22 1/2 cm. With facsimile of original t.-p. [BL2740.A1 1898] 4-1972
1. Rationalism. I. Title.

PAINE, Thomas, 1737-1809. 211
The age of reason. Being an investigation of true and of fabulous theology. By Thomas Paine... [Part 1] New York: Printed by T. and J. Swords, for J. Fellows, no. 131, Water-Street, 1794. vi, [7]-192, 191-202 p. 17 1/2 cm. Signatures: A-Q, A. Advertising matter: p. 195-102. "Epitome of Lequinio's Prejudices destroyed": p. [153]-188. "Twenty-five precepts of reason", by J. Grasset de Saint-Sauveur: p. [189]-192. "France. National convention... (8 May 1793) [Decree concerning the institution of national festivals]": p. 192 [a] -194. [BL2740.A2 pt. 1 1794n] 12-12056
1. Rationalism. I. Lequinio, Joseph Marie, b. 1755. II. Grasset de Saint-Sauveur, Jacques, 1757-1810. III. France. Convention nationale, 1792-1795. IV. Title.

PAINE, Thomas, 1737-1809. 211
The age of reason. Being an investigation of true and of fabulous theology. By Thomas Paine [Part I] 7th American ed. New-York: Printed and sold by George Forman, no. 156, Front-Street.-- 1795. 96 p. incl. front. (port.) 15 1/2 cm. [BL2740.A2 pt. 1 1795] 5-28256
1. Rationalism. I. Title.

PAINE, Thomas, 1737-1809. 211
The age of reason; being an investigation of true and of fabulous theology. Part the second. By Thomas Paine ... London, printed, New-York, Re-printed by Mott & Lyon, for Fellows & Adam and J. Reid, 1796. xiii, [15]-199, [1] p. front. 15 cm. [BL2740.A2 pt. 2 1796] 5-28257
1. Rationalism. I. Title.

PAINE, Thomas, 1737-1809. 211
The age of reason; being an investigation of true and fabulous theology, by Thomas Paine ... New York, The Truth seeker company [189-?] 180 p. 20 cm. [BL2740.A1] 45-49526
1. Rationalism. I. Title.

PAINE, Thomas, 1737-1809. 211
Age of reason, being an investigation of true and fabulous theology. By Thomas Paine ... New York, P. Eckler, 1915. 186 (i.e. 184) p. 20 cm. [BL2740.A1 1915] 42-35996
1. Rationalism. I. Title.

PAINE, Thomas, 1737-1809. 211
Inspiration and wisdom from the writings of Thomas Paine. With three addresses on Thomas Paine by Joseph Lewis. New York, Freethought Press Association, 1954. 303p. illus. 20cm. [BL2735.A1 1954] 54-429
1. Rationalism. I. Lewis, Joseph, 1889- comp. II. Title.

PAINE, Thomas, 1737-1809.
The theological works of Thomas Paine. To which are added the Profession of faith of a Savoyard vicar, by J. J. Rousseau; and other miscellaneous pieces. New-York, W. Carver, 1830. xiv p., 2 l., [1]-424 p. front. (port.) 23 cm. [BL2735.A1 1930] 4-1951
1. Rationalism. I. Rousseau, Jean Jacques, 1712-1778. II. Title.
Contents omitted.

PAINE, Thomas, 1787-1809. 211
Age of reason; being an investigation of true and fabulous theology. Baltimore, Ottenheimer [1956] 2pts. in 1. 22cm. [BL2740] 57-2505
1. Rationalism. I. Title.

POWELL, Benjamin F. 211
Bible of reason ... Collected and rendered by B. F. Powell ... New-York, Wright & Owen, 1831, '28. 2 v. 20 cm. Title of v. 2 varies slightly; imprint: New York, G. H. Evans. Contents.--i. Scriptures of ancient morilists.--[ii] Scriptures of modern autors. [BL2775.P7 1828] 39-10937
1. Rationalism. 2. Free thought. I. Title.

PRIESTLEY, Joseph, 1733-1804. 192
A continuation of the Letters to the philosophers and politicians of France on the subject of religion, and of the Letters to a philosophical unbeliever in answer to Mr. Paine's Age of reason / by Joseph Priestley. Millwood, N.Y. : Kraus Reprint Co., 1977. vii, 96 p. ; 24 cm. Reprint of the 1794 ed. printed by A. Kennedy, Northumberland-Town. [BL2740.P7 1977] 77-2935 ISBN 0-527-72705-9 lib.bdg. : 30.00
1. Paine, Thomas, 1737-1809. The age of reason. 2. Rationalism. I. Priestley, Joseph, 1733-1804. Letters to a philosophical unbeliever. Pt. 3. 1977. II. Title: A continuation of the Letters to the philosophers and politicians of France on the subject of religion ...

PRIESTLEY, Joseph, 1733-1804.
Observations on the increase of infidelity. By Joseph Priestley ... The 3d ed. To which are added, animadversions on the writings of several modern unbelievers, and especially The ruins of Mr. Volney ... Philadelphia, Printed for Thomas Dobson, no. 41, South Second street. 1797. xxvi, 179 p. 21 cm. "Originally prefixed to the American edition of ... [the author's] Letters to the philosophers and politicians of France ... here much enlarged, and printed separately."--p. [111] [BL2747.P7 1797a] 43-20437
1. Rationalism. 2. Volney, Constantin Francois Chasseboeuf, comte de, 1757-1820. Les ruines. I. Title.

QUINN, Henry. 211
Temple of reason, and dignity of self-government. Dedicated to the American republic, as a compendium of political, philosophical, and moral elements, applicable to our republican form of government. By Henry Quinn ... Riegelsville [Pa.] The author, 1856. xv, [17]-404 p. front. 19 cm. [BL2775.Q5] 38-38918
1. Rationalism. I. Title.

REMSBURG, John Eleazer, 1848-1919. 232.9
The Christ; a critical review and analysis of the evidences of His existence, by John E. Remsburg ... New York, The Truth seeker company [1909] 599 p. 20 1/2 cm. [BL2775.R476] 37-19959
1. Jesus Christ—Historicity. 2. Rationalism. I. Title.

RYLANCE, Joseph Hine, 1826-1907. 211
Christian rationalism; essays on matters in debate between faith and unbelief. By J. H. Rylance, D.D. New York, T. Whittaker, 1898. 220 p. 19 1/2 cm. [BL2775.R9] 41-37865
1. Rationalism. I. Title.

SLACK, David B. 211
The celestial magnet. By David B. Slack ... no. [1]-5; 1820-[21?] Providence, R.I., Printed by Miller & Hutchens, 1820-[21?] 1 v. 24 cm. Nos. [1]-3 have title-pages; each number has separate paging. No. [1] was published in 1820; nos. 2-3 in 1821; nos. 4-5 are undated. No more published? [BL2775.S63] 20-20341
1. Rationalism. I. Title.

STEARNS, George. 211
The mistake of Christendom; or, Jesus and His gospel before Paul and Christianity. By George Stearns ... Boston, B. Marsh, 1857. xii, [13]-312 p. 20 cm. [BL2775.S687] 39-10310
1. Jesus Christ—Rationalistic interpretations. 2. Rationalism. I. Title. II. Title: Jesus and His gospel before Paul and Christianity.

STEWART, Charles D. 211
Five points in faith. Self-evident statement of truth that the church avoids ... By Charles D. Stewart. Milwaukee, Wis., University publishing co. [1896] 93 p. 20 cm. [BL2775.S73] 39-10811
1. Rationalism. I. Title.
Contents omitted.

STRAUSS, David Friedrich, 1808-1874. 211
The old faith and the new, a confession by David Friedrich Strauss; authorized translation from the 6th edition by Mathilde Blind. American ed. ... The translation revised and partly rewritten, and preceded by an American version of the author's "Prefatory postscript"... New York, H. Holt and company, 1873. 2 v. in 1. 19 1/2 cm. Vol. II has caption title only. [BL2775.S76 1873] 38-29418
1. Rationalism. 2. Philosophy and religion. I. Blind, Mathilde, 1841-1896, tr. II. Title.

TAYLOR, Robert, 1784-1844. 211
The astronomico-theological lectures of the Rev. Robert Taylor ... New York, C. Blanchard, 1857. vii, [7]-406 p. 19 cm. Published also as V. 2 of the author's The Devil's pulpit. [London?] 1831-32. [BL2775.T32] 39-13392
1. Rationalism. I. Title.

TAYLOR, Robert, 1784-1844. 211
The devil's pulpit; or, Astro-theological sermons, by the Rev. Robert Taylor ... with a sketch of his life, and an astronomical introduction. New York, C. Blanchard, 1856. 2 p. l., [x]-xii, [iii]-viii, 341 p. 1 illus. 19 1/2 cm. Published also as v. 1 of the author's collected sermons and lectures. [London?] 1831-32. "Sketch of the life of the Rev. Robert Taylor" (p. [x]-xii) signed: G. V. [BL2775.T33 1856] 40-2843
1. Rationalism. I. V., G. II. G. V. III. Title. IV. Title: Astro-theological sermons.

TAYLOR, Robert, 1784-1844. 211
The devil's pulpit; or, Astro-theological sermons by the Rev. Robert Taylor ... with a sketch of his life, and an astronomical introduction. New York, C. Blanchard, 1857. 2 p. l., [iii]-viii, [x]-xii, 341 p. 1 illus. 19 cm. Published also as v. 1 of the author's collected sermons and lectures, also with title, The devil's pulpit. [London?] 1831-32. [BL2775.T33 1857] 39-13394
1. Rationalism. I. Title. II. Title: Astro-theological sermons.

TAYLOR, Robert, 1784-1844. 211
The diegesis; being a discovery of the origin, evidences, and early history of Christianity, never yet before or elsewhere so fully and faithfully set forth. by The Rev. Robert Taylor ... Boston, J. Gilbert, 1832. viii, 440 p. 23 cm. First edition, London, 1829. [BL2775.T35 1832] 15-17275
1. Rationalism I. Title.

TAYLOR, Robert, 1784-1844. 211
The diegesis; being a discovery of the origin, evidences, and early history of Christianity, never yet before or elsewhere so fully and faithfully set forth. By the Rev. Robert Taylor ... Boston, J. P. Mendum, 1883. viii, 440 p. front. (port.) 23 1/2 cm. First edition, London, 1829. [BL2775.T35 1883] 32-31785
1. Rationalism. I. Title.

THE three imposters. 211
Translated (with notes and illustrations.) from the French edition of the work, published at Amsterdam, 1776 New York, Republished by G. Vale, 1846. 84 p. 19 cm. A translation of Traite des trois imposteurs, from the revision by Vroes, J. Aymon and J. Rousset de Missy of the 2d pt. of "La vie et lesprit de m. Benoft Spinoss", a work attributed by some authorities to J. M. Lucas. cf. Barbier, Dictionnaire des ouvrages anonymes, and Brit. mus. Catalogue. "Disquisition on the book entitled "The three imposters" (by B. de La Monnoye): p. [7]-22. "Answer to the dissertation of M. de La Monnoye on the work entitled "The three impostors'" (p. 23-30) signed: J. L. R. L. [i.e. P. F. Arpe] "Copy of part 2d, vol. I. article IX. of 'Literary memoirs', published at the Hague...1716": p. 31-32. [BL2773.V523 1846] 34-23425
1. Rationalism. 2. Spinoza, Benedictus de 1632-1677. 3. De tribues impostoribus. I. Lucas, Jean Maximillen, d. 1697, supposed author. II. Vroes. III. Aymon, Jean, 1661-ca. 1720 IV. Rousset de Missy, Jean, 1686-1762. V. La Monnoye, Bernard de, 1641-1728. VI. Arpe, Peter Friedrich, 1682-1740.

TINDAL, Matthew, 1653?-1733. 211'.5
Christianity as old as the creation, 1730 / Matthew Tindal. New York : Garland Pub., 979 viii, 432 p. ; 24 cm. (British philosophers and theologians of the 17th & 18th centuries) Reprint of the 1730 ed. printed in London. [BL2773.T4 1978] 75-11256 ISBN 0-8240-1806-0 : 29.50
1. Rationalism. 2. Natural theology. I. Title. II. Series.

TOLAND, John, 1670-1722. 211'.4
Christianity not mysterious / John Toland. New York : Garland Pub., 1979 xxxii, 176 p. ; 19 cm. (British philosophers and theologians of the 17th & 18th centuries) Reprint of the 1st ed. published in 1696, London. [BL2773.T6 1978] 75-11257 ISBN 0-8240-1807-9 : 29.50
1. Rationalism. I. Title. II. Series.

VAIDEN, Thomas J. 211
Rational religion and morals: presenting analysis of the functions of mind, under the operations and directions of reason; the first, eliciting the necessary, rational, and only religion, monotheism ... the second, the obvious duties and precautions of society. By Thomas J. Vaiden ... New York, The author, 1852. viii, 1021 p. 24 cm. Lettered on cover: The bible of rational mind and religion. [BL2775.V35] 31-6638
1. Rationalism. I. Title. II. Title: The bible of rational mind and religion.

VOLTAIRE, Francois Marie Arouet de, 1694-1778. 211
Toleration and other essays, by Voltaire; translated, with an introduction, by Joseph McCabe. New York and London, G. P. Putnam's sons, 1912. xix, 263 p. 20 1/2 cm. [BL2773.V65] 13-7808
1. Rationalism. I. MacCabe, Joseph, 1867- tr. II. Title.

[WHITE, Albert C.] 239
Authordoxy, being a discursive examination of Mr. G. K. Chesterton's "Orthodoxy." By Alan Handsacre [pseud.] London, John Lane; New York, John Lane company, 1921. 3 p. l., 9-120, [1] p. 19 cm. [BR121.C56W5] 21-18111
1. Chesterton, Gilbert Keith, 1874- Orthodoxy. 2. Rationalism. I. Title.

YOUNG, John, 1805-1881. 201
The province of reason: a criticism of the Bampton lecture on "The limits of religious thought." By John Young... New York, R. Carter & brothers, 1860. xiv p., 1 l., [17]-305 p. 19 1/2 cm. [BL51.M33Y7 1860 a] 15-22010
1. Mansel, Henry Longueville, 1820-1871. The limits of religious thought. 2. Rationalism. 3. Religion—Philosophy. I. Title.

YOURS truly, Pseud. 211
The trinity of civilization; or, Love, divorce and religion, by Yours truly. [New York, J. J. Little & Ives company, c1924] 165 p. double front. 21 cm. [BL2775.Y6] 25-11180
I. Title.

Rationalism—Biography

[BRADLAUGH, Charles,] 1833-1891. 922.91
Biographies of ancient and modern celebrated freethinkers. Reprinted from an English work, entitled "Half-hours with the freethinkers." By "Iconoclast." Collins [pseud.], & Watts. Boston, J. P. Mendum, 1877. 2 p. l., 344 p. 18 cm. On cover: Half hours with freethinkers. [BL2785.B7 1877] 38-33086
1. Rationalism—Biog. I. Collins, Anthony, pseud., joint author. II. Watts, John, joint author. III. Title. IV. Title: Half-hours with freethinkers.
Contents omitted.

Rationalism—Collected works.

PAINE, Thomas, 1737-1809.
The theological works of Thomas Paine. To which are added the Profession of faith of a Savoyard vicar, by J. J. Rousseau; and other miscellaneous pieces. Boston, Printed for the advocates of common sense, 1834. 384 p. front. (port.) 20 1/2 cm. Title vignette. [BL2735.A1 1834] 5-28255
1. Rationalism—Collected works. I. Rousseau, Jean jacques, 1712-1778. II. Title.
Contents omitted.

THRASHER, Marion. 211
The harlot and the Virgin, by Dr. Marion Thrasher. San Francisco, Calif. [1918?] 2 p. l., v, 58 p. 17 cm. Or why the world is not Christianized: in ms. on t.-p. [BL2775.T45] 19-17331
I. Title.

Rationalism—Controversial literature.

BENNETT, George Henry, 1864- 289
Challenge of the church, rationalism refuted; a reply to the Oregon rationalist society, containing expositions of cosmogony, inspiration, prayer, etc., which offer practical solutions of certain great issues between science and the Bible. By George H. Bennett ... Cincinnati, Press of the Methodist book concern [c1914] 164 p. 19 cm. [BT1210.B45] 15-6546
1. Rationalism—Controversial literature. 2. Bible and science. I. Title.

BREMOND, Andre. 211
Religions of unbelief [by] Andre Bremond... Milwaukee, The Bruce publishing company [c1939] xv, 163 p. 22 1/2 cm. (Half-title: Science and culture series, Joseph Husslein ... general editor) [BL2750.B7] 39-14236
1. Rationalism—Controversial literature. 2. Apologetics—20th cent. I. Title.

ENGELDER, Theodore Edward William, 1865- 239.7
Reason or revelation? By Th. Engelder. St. Louis, Mo., Concordia publishing house, 1941. iii, 176 p. 19 1/2 cm. [BT1210.E75] 41-23096
1. Rationalism—Controversial literature. I. Title.

KIRK, Kenneth Escott, 1886- 211
The crisis of Christian rationalism, three lectures by K. E. Kirk ... London, New York [etc.] Longmans, Green and co., [1936] 4 p. l., 119 p. 20 cm. "First published, 1936." "These addresses were delivered, in the autumn of 1935, in Sir Giles Gilbert Scott's new chapel at Lady Margaret hall."--Introd. [BT78.K53] 37-5739
1. Rationalism—Controversial literature. 2. Revelation. 3. Christian ethics. I. Title.
Contents omitted.

MANGASARIAN, Mangasar M. 1859-
The Bible unveiled, by M. M. Mangasarian... Chicago, Independent religious society (Rationalist) [c1911] 269 p. 20 1/2 cm. $1.50 11-26215
I. Title.

Rationalism—Dictionaries.

MCCABE, Joseph, 1867-1955. 103
A rationalist encyclopaedia; a book of reference on religion, philosophy, ethics, and science. London, Watts. Ann Arbor, Mich., Gryphon Books, 1971. vi, 633 p. 22 cm. Reprint of the 1948 ed. [BL2705.M2 1971] 79-164054
1. Rationalism—Dictionaries. I. Title.

Rationalism—History

BUDD, Susan. 211
Varieties of unbelief : atheists and agnostics in English society, 1850-1960 / Susan Budd. London : Heinemann Educational Books, 1977. vii, 307 p. ; 22 cm. Imprint covered by label which reads: Holmes & Meier Publishers, New York. Bibliogrpahy: p. [282]-299. Includes index. [BL2765.G7B83] 77-363322 ISBN 0-435-82100-8 : £9.50 ($20.00 U.S.)
1. Rationalism—History. 2. Religious thought—England. I. Title.

CAIRNS, John, 1818-1892. 211
Unbelief in the eighteenth century as contrasted with its earlier and later history, being the Cunningham lectures for 1880, by John Cairns ... New York, Harper & brothers, 1881. 2 p. l., [vi]-ix, [11]-216 p. 19 1/2 cm. [BL2750.C3] 43-49236
1. Rationalism—Hist. I. Cunningham lectures. II. Title.

HALLEY, Ebenezer. 211
The pantheism of Germany; a sermon, delivered before the synod of Albany, at Saratoga Springs, October 9, 1850, by Ebenezer Halley ... Albany, Gray & Sprague, 1850. 64 p. 23 cm. "Published by request of the synod." [BL2765.G3H3] 40-2727
1. Rationalism—Hist. 2. Religious thought—Germany. I. Title.

HURST, John Fletcher, bp., 1834-1903. 211
History of rationalism; embracing a survey of the present state of Protestant theology. By the Rev. John F. Hurst, A. M. With appendix of literature. New York, C. Scribner & co., 1865. xv, 623 p. 23 cm. Bibliography: p. [590]-610. [BL2750.H8 1865] 37-13879
1. Rationalism—Hist. 2. Protestantism. I. Title.

HURST, John Fletcher, bp., 1834-1903. 211
History of rationalism, embracing a survey of the present state of Protestant theology, by John Fletcher Hurst ... With appendix of literature. New York, Junt & Eaton; Cincinnati, Cranston & Curts [1893?] 2 p. l., [ix]-xix, 623 p. 23 cm. Bibliography: p. [590]-610. [BL2750.H8] 37-15490
1. Rationalism—Hist. 2. Protestantism. I. Title.

HURST, John Fletcher, bp., 1834-1903. 211
History of rationalism, embracing a survey of the present state of Protestant theology, by John Fletcher Hurst ... With appendix of literature. New York, Eaton & Mains; Cincinnati, Curts & JNnings [1898?] 2 p. l., [ix]-xix, 623 p. 23 cm. Bibliography: p. [590]-610. [BL2750.H8] 37-15959
1. Rationalism—Hist. 2. Protestantism. I. Title.

LECKY, William Edward Hartpole, 1838-1903. 211
History of the rise and influence of the spirit of rationalism in Europe. Introd. by C. Wright Mills. New York, G. Braziller, 1955. 405, 386p. 21cm. Bibliographical footnotes. [BL2750.L4 1955] 55-37386
1. Rationalism—Hist. I. Title.

LECKY, William Edward Hartpole, 1838-1903. 211
History of the rise and influence of the spirit of rationalism in Europe. By W. E. H. Lecky ... Rev. ed. New York, D. Appleton and company, 1903. 2 v. 21 cm. [BL2750.L4 1903] 4-10384
1. Rationalism—Hist. I. Title.

LECKY, William Edward Hartpole, 1838-1903. 211
History of the rise and influence of the spirit of rationalism in Europe. By W. E. H. Lecky, M. A. Rev. ed. ... New York and London, D. Appleton and company, 1914. 2 v. 21 cm. [BL2750.L4 1914] 15-5668
1. Rationalism—Hist. I. Title.

OGILVIE, John, 1733-1813. 211'.4
An inquiry into the causes of the infidelity and scepticism of the times, 1783 by John Ogilvie. New York : Garland Pub., 1975. xvi, 462, 2 p. ; 19 cm. (The Life & times of seven major British writers) (Gibboniana ; 12) Reprint of the ed. printed for Richardson and Urquhart, London, and W. Gordon, W. Creech, and J. Dickson, Edinburgh. [DG206.G5G52 vol. 12] [BL2758] 75-31549 ISBN 0-8240-1348-4 lib.bdg. : 28.00
1. Rationalism—History. 2. Deism—History. 3. Skepticism—History. I. Title. II. Series.

Rationalism—History—Sources.

THE Infidel tradition from Paine to Bradlaugh / edited by Edward Royle. London : Macmillan, 1976. xvii, 228 p. ; 23 cm. (History in depth) Includes index. Bibliography: p. [221]-224. [BL2751.I53] 77-353219 ISBN 0-333-17434-8 : £10.00 211'.4
1. Rationalism—History—Sources. 2. Radicalism—History—Sources. I. Royle, Edward.

Rationalism—Periodicals

UNITED Secularists of America.
Progressive world. [Portland, Ore., etc.] v. illus. 21 cm. monthly. Began publication in 1947. Cf. Ulrich's periodicals directory, 1963. Published by United Secularists of America (called Progressive World Associates) [BL2700.P85] 65-56521
1. Rationalism—Period. I. Title.

Rationalists.

[FROTHINGHAM, Washington] b.1822. 922.
Atheos; or, The tragedies of unbelief ... New York, Sheldon & company, 1862. 331 p. 20 cm. [BL2785.F7] 42-44681
1. Rationalists. I. Title.
Contents omitted.

MCCABE, Joseph, 1867- 922.91
A biographical dictionary of ancient, medieval and modern freethinkers [by] Joseph McCabe. Girard, Kans., Haldeman-Julius publications [1945] 96 p. 21 1/2 cm. [BL2785.M23] 46-686
1. Rationalists. I. Title.

Rationalists—Germany—Biography.

GROSSMANN, Walter, 1918- 211'.4'0924 B
Johann Christian Edelmann : from orthodoxy to enlightenment / by Walter Grossman. The Hague : Mouton, [1976] ix, 209 p. ; 24 cm. (Religion and society ; 3) Includes index. Bibliography: p. [199]-203. [BL2790.E33G76] 76-377412 ISBN 9-02-797691-0 : 14.00
1. Edelmann, Johann Christian, 1698-1767. 2. Rationalists—Germany—Biography. I. Title. II. Series: Religion and society (The Hague) ; 3.
Distributed by Humanities

Ratisbon, Colloquy of, 1941.

MATHESON, Peter. 270.6'092'4 B
Cardinal Contarini at Regensburg. Oxford, Clarendon Press, 1972. x, 193 p. 23 cm. Bibliography: p. [183]-190.

[BX4705.C774M38] 72-180270 ISBN 0-19-826431-3 £3.25
1. Contarini, Gasparo, Cardinal, 1484-1542. 2. Ratisbon, Colloquy of, 1941. I. Title.

Ratisbonne, Marie Alphonse, 1812?-1894.

BUSSIERRE, Marie Theodore 928.
Renouard, vicomte de, 1802-1865.
The conversion of Marie-Alphonse Ratisbonne: original narrative of Baron Theodore de Bussieres [!] followed by a letter from Mr. Ratisbonne to Rev. Mr. Dufriche-Deegenettes ... Edited by the Rev. W. Lockhart ... New York, T. W. Strong [1876?] 147 p. 15 1/2 cm. [BX4668.B82] 41-28173
1. Ratisbonne, Marie Alphonse, 1812?-1894. I. Lockhart, William, 1820-1892, ed. II. Title.

Ratiu, Alexander.

RATIU, Alexander. 272'.9
Stolen church, martyrdom in Communist Romania / Alexander Ratiu & William Virtue. Huntington, Ind. : Our Sunday Visitor, c1979. 192 p. ; 21 cm. [BX4711.495.R37A37] 79-87926 ISBN 0-87973-730-1 pbk. : 4.95
1. Ratiu, Alexander. 2. Catholic Church—Clergy—Biography. 3. Catholic Church in Romania—Clergy. 4. Clergy—Romania—Biography. 5. Prisoners—Romania—Biography. 6. Persecution—Romania. I. Virtue, William, joint author. II. Title.

Rato Khyongla Nawang Losang.

RATO Khyongla 294.3'61'0924 B
Nawang Losang.
My life and lives : the story of a Tibetan incarnation / Rato Khyongla Nawang Losang ; edited with an introd. by Joseph Campbell. 1st ed. New York : Dutton, c1977. p. cm. [BQ982.A767A35] 77-8399 ISBN 0-525-47480-3 pbk. : 3.50
1. Rato Khyongla Nawang Losang. 2. Lamas—Tibet—Biography. I. Campbell, Joseph, 1904- II. Title.

Ratramnus, monk of Corble, d. ca. 868.

FAHEY, John F 265.3
The eucharistic teaching of Ratramn of Corbie. Mundelein, Ill., Saint Mary of the Lake Seminary, 1951. 176p. 23cm. (Pontificia Facultas Theologica Seminarii Sanctae Mariae ad Lacum. Dissertationes ad lauream, 22) Bibliography: p. 166-176. [BV823.F22] 52-11867
1. Ratramnus, monk of Corble, d. ca. 868. 2. Lord's Supper—Hist. I. Title. II. Series: St. Mary of the Lake Seminary, Mundelein, Ill. Dissertationes ad laurcam, 22

Rauschenbusch, Walter, 1861-1918.

BODEIN, Vernon Parker. 922.673
The development of the social thought of Walter Rauschenbusch, by Vernon Parker Bodein ... [New York, 1937] 1 p. l., p. 420-431. 24 cm. "Part of a dissertation entitled 'The relation of the social gospel of Walter Rauschenbusch to religious education' presented to Yale university for the degree of doctor of philosophy [1936]" "Reprinted...from Religion in life, summer issue, 1937." [BX6495.R3B6 1937] 38-8544
1. Rausechenbusch, Walter, 1861-1918. 2. Sociology, Christian. I. Title.

BODEIN, Vernon Parker.
The social gospel of Walter Rauschenbusch and its relation to religious education, by Vernon Parker Bodein. New Haven, Yale university press; London, H.Milford, Oxford university press, 1944. ix p., 1 l., 168, [2] p. 23 1/2 cm. (Half-title: Yale studies in religious education. XVI) Originally the author's thesis (PH.D.) Yale university, 1936; rewritten for this publication. cf. Pref. "The publication of this volume has been aided by the Samuel B. Sneath memorial publication fund." Bibliography: p. [158]-168. A 44
1. Rauschenbusch, Walter, 1861-1918. 2. Sociology, Christian. 3. Religious education. I. Yale university. Samuel B. Sneath memorial publication fund. II. Title.

FISHBURN, Janet 261'.0973
Forsythe, 1937-
The fatherhood of God and the Victorian family : the Social Gospel in America / Janet Forsythe Fishburn. Philadelphia : Fortress Press, [1982] c1981. p. cm. Includes index. Bibliography: p. [BX6495.R3F57 1982] 19 81-43090 ISBN 0-8006-0671-X : 19.95
1. Rauschenbusch, Walter, 1861-1918. 2. Social gospel—History. 3. United States—Church history—19th century. 4. United States—Church history—20th century. I. Title.

JAEHN, Klaus 230'.6'10924 B
Juergen.
Rauschenbusch, the formative years / [Klaus Juergen Jaehn]. Valley Forge, PA : Judson Press, c1976. 58 p. ; 22 cm. A revision of the author's thesis (Master of Divinity) which was first published in two parts in Foundations, Oct.-Dec., 1973, v. 16, no. 4 and Jan.-Mar., 1974, v. 17, no. 1. Bibliography: p. 49-52. [BX6495.R3J3 1976] 75-38191 ISBN 0-8170-0707-5 pbk. : 1.50
1. Rauschenbusch, Walter, 1861-1918. I. Title.

SHARPE, Dores Robinson, 922.673
1886-
Walter Rauschenbusch, by Dores Robinson Sharpe. New York, The Macmillan company, 1942. xiii p., 1 l., 463 p. front. (port.) 21 cm. "First printing." [BX6495.R3S48] 42-12945
1. Rauschenbusch, Walter, 1861-1918. I. Title.

SINGER, Anna M. 922.673
Walter Rauschenbusch and his contribution to social Christianity, by Anna M. Singer, A.M. Boston, R. G. Badger [c1926] xi, 13-136 p. 21 1/2 cm. "Sources": p. 133. Bibliography of Walter Bauschenbusch's publications: p. 135-136. [BX6495.R3S5] 26-9623
1. Rauschenbusch, Walter, 1861-1918. 2. Socialogy, Christian. I. Title.

Raven, Charles Earle, 1885-1964.

DILLISTONE, 230'.3'0924 B
Frederick William, 1903-
Charles Raven : naturalist, historian, theologian / by F. W. Dillistone. 1st ed. Grand Rapids, Mich. : Eerdmans, [1975] 448 p., [4] leaves of plates : ill. ; 24 cm. Includes index. "Bibliography of Charles Raven": p. 439-440. [BX5199.R26D54 1975] 74-20580 ISBN 0-8028-3455-8 : 12.95
1. Raven, Charles Earle, 1885-1964.

RAVEN, Charles Earle, 1885- 922.
A wanderer's way, by Charles E. Raven ... New York, H. Holt and company [c1929] x p., 2 l., 3-220 p. 20 cm. A spiritual autobiography. [BX5199.R26A3 1929] 29-5192
I. Title.

Ravenna. San Giovanni in Fonte (Baptistery)

KOSTOF, Spiro K 726.69
The Orthodox Baptistery of Ravenna [by] Spiro K. Kostof. New Haven, Yale University Press, 1965. xviii, 171 p. illus. (part col.) plans. 29 cm. (Yale publications in the history of art, 18) Revision of thesis, Yale University. "Bibliographical note": p. 157-165. [NA5621.R3K6] 65-22328
1. Ravenna. San Giovanni in Fonte (Baptistery) I. Title.

Ravenscroft, John Stark, bp., 1772-1830.

NORTON, John Nicholas, 922.373
1820-1881.
The life of Bishop Ravenscroft. By John N. Norton ... New York, General Protestant Episcopal Sunday school union, and church book society, 1859. xii, [13]-152 p. incl. front. (port.) 16 cm. [BX5995.R35N6] 35-29987
1. Ravenscroft, John Stark, bp., 1772-1830. I. General Protestant Episcopal Sunday school union and church book society. II. Title.

Ravetch, Isadore Shalom, 1899-

JEWS. Liturgy and ritual. 296
Sabbath prayers.
Menuchat Shalom; late service for Sabbath eve, arranged by I. Shalom Ravetch ... Long Beach (Calif.) 1943. xx, 90, 2-59 p., 3 l. 23 cm. Text paged in duplicate. Hebrew and English (with transliteration of text) on opposite pages. Title transliterated: Menuhath Shalom. [BM675.S3R3] 45-13457
1. Ravetch, Isadore Shalom, 1899- I. Title.

Rawlings, Maurice.

RAWLINGS, Maurice. 236'.11
Before death comes / by Maurice S. Rawlings. Nashville : T. Nelson Publishers, c1980. 180 p. ; 21 cm. Includes bibliographical references. [BT825.R34] 80-13250 ISBN 0-8407-5191-5 : 8.95
1. Rawlings, Maurice. 2. Death. 3. Future life. 4. Religion and science—1946- I. Title.

Ray, Jefferson Davis, 1860-1951.

RAY, Georgia Miller, 922.673
1887-
The Jeff Ray I knew; a pioneer preacher in Texas. With introd. by W. R. White. San Antonio, Naylor Co. [1952] 192 p. illus. 22 cm. [BX6495.R35R3] 52-9348
1. Ray, Jefferson Davis, 1860-1951. I. Title.

Rayburn, James C.

CAILLIET, Emile, 1894- 267.61
Young life. New York, Harper [1964, c.1963] viii, 120p. 22cm. 64-10614 2.95
1. Rayburn, James C. 2. Young Life Campaign. I. Title.

Raymond, Father, 1903-

RAYMOND, Father, 271'.125'024 B
1903-
Forty years behind the wall / M. Raymond. Huntington, Ind. : Our Sunday Visitor, c1979. 336 p. ; 21 cm. [BX4705.R3744A29] 79-83875 ISBN 0-87973-644-5 : 5.95
1. Raymond, Father, 1903- 2. Trappists in the United States—Biography. I. Title.

Raymond, Henry Jarvis, 1820-1869.

BROWN, Ernest Francis, 920.5
1903-
Raymond of the Times. [1st ed.] New York, Norton [1951] viii, 345 p. illus., ports. 25 cm. "Some notes on bibliography": p. [335]-340. [PN4874.R3B7] 51-5183
1. Raymond, Henry Jarvis, 1820-1869. I. Title.

Raymundus de Pennaforte, Saint, 1175?-1275.

ERNEST, Brother, 1897- 922.246
When all ships failed; a story of St. Raymond of Pennafort. Illus. by Brother Bernard Howard. Notre Dame, Ind., Dujarie Press [1953] 93p. illus. 24cm. [BX4700.R35E7] 53-3998
1. Raymundus de Pennaforte, Saint, 1175?-1275. I. Title.

SCHWERTNER, Thomas Maria, 922.246
1883-1933.
Saint Raymond of Pennafort of the Order of friars, by Thomas M. Schwertner ... revised and edited by C. M. Antony [pseud.]; introduction by the Most Reverend Amleto Giovanni Cicognani ... Milwaukee, The Bruce publishing company [c1935] xxiii p., 1 l., 158 p. 21 cm. (Half-title: Dominican library of spiritual works) "Writings": p. 135-137: "References": p. 138-152. [BX4700.R35S35] 35-12051
1. Raymundus de Pennaforte, Saint, 1175?-1275. I. Woodcock, Catherine Mary Antony, ed. II. Title.

Raymundus de Vineis, 1330-1399.

CORMIER, Hyacinthe Marie, 922.245
1832-1916.
Blessed Raymund of Capua, twenty-third master general of the Order of preachers, by Father Hyacinth M. Cormier ... Translated with the author's sanction by J. Dillon Trant. Boston, Marlier, Callanan & co.; London and Leamington, Art & book company; [etc., etc.] 1900. xi, 163 p. front., plates, ports. 19 cm. [BX4705.R38C6] 0-1254
1. Raymundus de Vineis, 1330-1399. I. Trant, J. Dillon, tr. II. Title.

Rayyis, Rufqah, 1832-1914.

ZAYEK, Francis M. 271'.9 B
Rafka, the blind mystic of Lebanon / Francis M. Zayek. Still River, Mass. : St. Bede's Publications, c1980. viii, 83 p. : ill. ; 21 cm. [BX4713.595.R39Z39] 19 80-21176 ISBN 0-932506-02-X : 3.95
1. Rayyis, Rufqah, 1832-1914. 2. Nuns—Lebanon—Biography. I. Title.
Publisher's address P. O. Box 61, Still River, MA 01467.

Read, Maureen Hay, 1937-

READ, Maureen Hay, 248'.2'0924 B
1937-
Like a watered garden / Maureen Hay Read ; introduction by Sherwood E. Wirt. Scottdale, Pa. : Herald Press, 1977. 156 p. : ill. ; 21 cm. [BR1725.R37A34] 77-5858 ISBN 0-8361-1818-9 : 5.95
1. Read, Maureen Hay, 1937- 2. Christian biography—United States. I. Title.

Readers and speakers.

ABARBANEL, Henry. 221.
English school and family reader, for the use of Israelites, containing selections in prose and verse, historical accounts, biographies, narratives, notices, and characteristics on Judaism, past, present and future. By H. Abarbanel... New York, Rogers & Sherwood, 1883. 3 p. l., viii, 7-441, [1] p. 22 1/2 cm. [PE1125.A2] 17-16393
1. Readers and speakers. 2. Jews—Hist. 3. Jews—Biog. I. Title. II. Title: Reader for Israelites.

BROTHERS of the Christian
schools.
First[-seventh] reader. (Rev. ed., 1915) By the Brothers of the Christian schools ... [St. Louis, Woodward & Tiernan printing co., 1915] 7 v. illus., ports. 19 1/2 cm. (De la Salle series) Ports. on title-pages. E15
1. Readers and speakers. I. Title.

BROTHERS of the Christian
schools.
Reader[s]. By the Brothers of the Christian schools ... [St. Louis, Woodward & Tiernan printing co., c1913] 7 v. illus., ports. 19 1/2 cm. (De la Salle series) Ports. on title-pages. Contents.Primer. New series--First reader--Second reader--Third reader.--Fourth reader.--Fifth reader.--Selections from classic authors. E13
1. Readers and speakers. I. Title.

MARY, Irmina Sister, 1893- 226
An evaluation of the vocabulary content of twelve series of primary readers. Washington, Catholic Education Press [1929] 52 p. 23 cm. (The Catholic University of America. Educational research bulletins, v. 4, no. 7) "The series of readers used in the study: P. 17. Bibliograph: p. 51-52. [LB1525.M42] 30-2207
1. Readers and speakers. 2. Vocabulary. I. Title. II. Series: Catholic University of America. Educational research monographs, v. 4, no. 7

Readers and speakers—1800-1870.

[BULLARD, Asa] 1804-1888. 171.
The youth's museum ... Boston, Massachusetts Sabbath school society [1852] 216 p. incl. front., illus. 16 cm. [BV4531.B8] 19-14059
1. Readers and speakers—1800-1870. I. Massachusetts Sabbath school society. II. Title.

CLARK, Mary Latham, Mrs. 244
Dialogues and recitations, for Sabbath school concerts. By Mrs. Mary Latham Clark. Dover, [N.H.] The Freewill Baptist printing establishment, 1861. 60 p. 19 cm. [PN4231.C58] 13-20086
1. Readers and speakers—1800-1870. 2. Sunday-schools—Recitations, exercises, etc. I. Title.

[ETHERIDGE, Samuel] 244
The Christian orator; or, A collection of speeches, delivered on public occasions before religious benevolent societies. To which is prefixed an abridgment of Walker's Elements of elocution. Designed for the use of colleges, academies, and schools. By a gentleman of Massachusetts. Charlestown [Mass.] Printed by Samuel Etheridge, 1818. v, [1], 264 (i.e. 258) p. 19 1/2 cm. Nos. 223-228 omitted in paging. [PN4231.E8 1818] 13-20084
1. Readers and speakers—1800-1870. 2. Elocution. I. Walker, John, 1732-1807. Elements of elocution. II. Title.

[ETHERIDGE, Samuel] comp. 244
The Christian orator, or A collection of speeches, delivered on public occasions, before religious benevolent societies. To which is prefixed an abridgment of Walker's Elements of elocution. Designed for the use of colleges, academies and schools. By a gentleman of Massachusetts. 3d ed. Charlestown [Mass.] Printed by S. Etheridge, for Cushing & Jewett, and F. Lucas, Baltimore, 1819. 1 p. l., iv, [2], ix-x, [11]-298 (i. e. 300) p. incl. diagr. 14 cm. No. 11-12 repeated in paging. [PN4231.E8 1819] 13-19893
1. Readers and speakers—1800-1870. 2. Elocution. I. Walker, John, 1732-1807. Elements of elocution. II. Title.

HESTON, Newton. 244
The anniversary speaker, or, Young folks on the Sunday school platform. Designed as an assistant in Sunday school celebrations and anniversaries; being a collection of addresses, dialogues, recitations, infant class exercises, hymns, etc. By Rev. Newton Heston ... Philadelphia, Higgins & Perkinpine, 1858. vii, &98 1 l., 11-204 p. 16 cm. [PN4231.H5] 12-34015
1. Readers and speakers—1800-1870. 2. Sunday schools—Recitation, exercises, etc. I. Title.

HESTON, Newton. 268
The anniversary speaker, or Young folks on the Sunday school platform. Designed as an assistant in Sunday school celebrations and anniversaries; being a collection of addresses, dialogues, recitations, infant class exercises, hymns, etc. By Rev. Newton Heston ... 2d series. Philadelphia, Perkinpine & Higgins, 1865. 215 p. 15 cm. [PN4231.H62] 12-34177
1. Readers and speakers—1800-1870. 2. Sunday-schools—Exercises, recitations, etc. I. Title.

HESTON, Newton. 244
The universary speaker, or Young folks n the Sunday school platform. Designed as an assistant in Sunday school celebrations and anniversaries; being a collection of addresses, dialogues, recitations, infant class exercises, hymns, etc. By Rev. Newton Heston ... 2d series. Philadelphioa, Perkinpine & Higgins [c1865] 215 p. 15 cm. [PN4231.H6] 12-14246
1. Readers and speakers—1800-1870. 2. Sunday-schools-Recitations, exercises, etc. I. Title.

MCCURDY, Convers L., comp. 244
Sunday school and band of hope speaker. A collection of dialogues and addresses adapted to "Band of hope" anniversaries and Sunday school exhibitions. Comp. by the Rev. C. L. McCurdy. Boston, J. P. Magee, 1860. iv, [5]-200 p. 16 cm. [PN4231.M2] 17-6841
1. Readers and speakers—1800-1870. 2. Schools—Exercises and recreations. I. Title.

MURRAY, Grace, comp. 244
The Sunday school celebration book. A collection of dialogues, speeches, hymns, etc., for anniversaries and other occasions. By Grace and Ida Murray. 3d ed. Philadelphia, Perkinpine & Higgins [c1860] 262 p. 15 cm. [PN4231.M8] 13-19886
1. Readers and speakers—1800-1870. 2. Sunday-schools—Recitation, exercises, etc. I. Murray, Ida, joint author. II. Title.

MURRAY, Grace, comp. 244
The Sunday school celebration book. A collection of dialogues, speeches, hymns, etc., for anniversaries and other occasions. By Grace and Ida Murray. 2d ed. Philadelphia, Perkinpine & Higgins, 1861. 202 p. 16 cm. [PN4231.M82] 13-19887
1. Readers and speakers—1800-1870. 2. Sunday-schools—Exercises, recitations, etc. I. Murray, Ida, joint comp. II. Title.

SPENCER, Albert J., ed. 244
Spencer's book of comic speeches and humorous recitations ... Ed. by Albert J. Spencer. New York, Dick & Fitzgerald [c1867] lv, [5]-192 p. 17 cm. [PN4231.S6] [PN4251.B3 1871] 815. CA 17
1. Readers and speakers—1800-1870. I. Title. II. Title: Comic speeches.

Readers and speakers—1870—

BECHTEL, John Hendricks, 1841- ed. 244
Sunday school selections, comprising a wide range of reading and recitations adapted to church and Sunday school entertainments and to all gatherings of a moral or religious character; ed. by John H. Bechtel ... Philadelphia, The Penn publishing company, 1892. vi, 7-200 p. 18 1/2 cm. [PN4231.B35] 20-16377
1. Readers and speakers—1870- 2. Sunday-school literature. I. Title.

FILLMORE, James Henry, 1849- comp. 244
Religious recitations for Sunday school and church use, compiled by J. H. Fillmore... Cincinnati, O., Fillmore music house, c1923. 63 p. 23 cm. [PN4231.F5] 23-15290
1. Readers and speakers—1870- 2. Sunday-schools—Exercises, recitations, etc. I. Title.

GENTRY, Curtis Gavin, 1891- 377.
A character book for the grade, by Curtis Gentry ... Boston, New York [etc.] D. C. Heath and company [c1929]- v. 26 cm. [LC268.G4] 29-9497
1. Readers and speakers—1870- 2. Moral education. I. Title.

GILMORE, Joseph Henry, 1834- comp. 244
Declamations and dialogues. 118 choice pieces for the Sunday-school. By Prof. J. H. Gilmore ... Philadelphia, J. E. Potter and company [c1889] viii p., 1 l., [1]-251 p. 19 cm. [PN4231.G5] 13-19891
1. Readers and speakers—1870- 2. Sunday-school—Recitations, exercises, etc. I. Title.

GILMORE, Joseph Henry, 1834-1918, comp. 244
Declamations and dialogues for the Sunday-school. By Prof. J. H. Gilmore ... Boston, H. A. Young & co. [c1871] viii p., 1 l., [11]-251 p. 16 cm. [PN4231.G4] 13-19892
1. Readers and speakers—1870- 2. Sunday-schools—Exercises, recitations, etc. I. Title.

GRACEY, Samuel Levis, 1835-1911, comp. 244
Anniversary gems; consisting of addresses, recitations, conversations, and Scripture illustrations, for the Sunday-school concert, or anniversary. By Rev. Samuel L. Gracey ... Philadelphia, Perkinpine & Higgins [c1870] vi p., 1 l., 9-215 p. 15 cm. [PN4231.G7] 13-19890
1. Readers and speakers—1870- 2. Sunday-schools—Exercises, recitations, etc. I. Title.

KENNEDY, M. G. Mrs. 244
Anniversary leaves. By Mrs. M. G. Kennedy ... Philadelphia, American Baptist publication society [1879] 1 p. l., 5-224 p. 17 cm. [PN4231.K4] 20-17786
1. Readers and speakers—1870- 2. Sunday-schools—Exercises, recitations, etc. I. Title. Contents omitted

KINSEY, J. F., Mrs., comp. 244
Juvenile speaker and songster. For use in Sunday-school entertainments. Appropriate selections for all special occasions. Ed. and comp. by Mrs. J. F. Kinsey ... Lafayette, Ind., The Echo music company, c1893. 157, [1] p. illus. 18 1/2 cm. [PN4231.K5] 13-19889
1. Readers and speakers—1870- 2. Sunday-schools—Hymn-books. 3. Song, English. I. Title.

KOHAUS, Hannah More. 244
Recitation poems, especially adapted for Sabbath schools, mission bands, concerts, Easter, children's day, harvest homes, Christmas festivals, &c. By Hannah More Kohaus ... Chicago, New York, F. H. Revell [c1889] 144 p. 19 cm. [PN4231.K7] 13-19888
1. Readers and speakers—1870- 2. Sunday-schools—Recitations, exercises, etc. I. Title.

LOEHR, E L ed. 244
Paramount Sunday school recitations comprising three hundred choice selections for Sunday school anniversaries, Easter, children's day, patriotic, flag day, rally day, harvest home, Thanksgiving, Christmas, little folks, temperance, missionary and miscellaneous. Ed. by E. L. Loehr ... Chicago, Ill., Meyer & brother, 1902. 114 p. 20 cm. [PN4231.L6] 12-36293
1. Readers and speakers—1870- I. Title.

LYSNES, Olaf, comp. 248
Better readings, collected by Olaf Lysnes. Minneapolis, Minn., Augsburg publishing house, 1927. 1 p. l., iv, [3]-298 p. 20 cm. [BV4495.L9] 28-2248
1. Readers and speakers—1870- I. Title.

LYSNES, Olaf, comp. 244
Readings for live programs, collected by Olaf Lysnes. Minneapolis, Augsburg publishing house [c1937] xiv, 224 p. 20 1/2 cm. [PN4231.L95] 37-10305
1. Readers and speakers—1870- I. Title.

[METHODIST Episcopal church, South. Woman's missionary council. Educational department. 266
Missionary entertainments for the Junior missionary society and the Sunday school. Nashville, Tenn., The Sunday school supply department, Smith & Lamar [c1922] 164 p. 20 cm. "Written, compiled, and edited in the Educational department of the Woman's missionary council."--Pref. [BV2087.M4] 22-23591
1. Readers and speakers—1870- 2. Church entertainments. I. Title.

SLADE, Mary Bridges (Canedy) Mrs., comp. 244
The holiday concert, a collection of dialogues, recitations, and concert exercises, for the use of Sunday-school anniversaries and holiday exhibitions; by Mrs. M. B. C. Slade. Chicago, J. E. Miller & co., 1873. 56 p. 17 1/2 cm. [PN4231.S5] 13-19884
1. Readers and speakers—1870- 2. Sunday-schools—Exercises, recitations, etc. I. Title.

SUNDAY school entertainments, together with ninety-nine other choice readings and recitations ... Chicago, The Henneberry company [c1901] 134 p. 1 illus. 16 1/2 cm. [PN4231.S8] CA 17 244
1. Readers and speakers—1870- 2. Sunday-schools—Exercises, recitations, etc.

WHITE, James Edson. 220.
Best stories from the best book; an illustrated Bible companion for the home, by James Edson White; with an introductory department of easy lessons for children, by Ella King Sanders. New York City [etc.] Pacific press publishing co.; Chicago [etc.] Review and Herald pub. co., c1900. 194 p. incl. front., illus. (part col.) 21 1/2 cm. [BS551.W55] 1-29854
1. Readers and speakers—1870- 2. Bible—History of Biblical events. I. Title.

WOOD, R. H., Mrs. 244
The Sunday-school olio; containing original dialogues and single pieces for Sunday-school exhibitions and Sabbath evening concerts. By Mr. R. H. Wood. New York, Carlton & Lanahan; San Francisco, E. Thomas; [etc., etc., c1871] 84 p. 17 cm. [PN4231.W6] 13-19885
1. Readers and speakers—1870- 2. Sunday-schools—Exercises, recitations, etc. I. Murray, Ida, joint comp. II. Title.

Readers and speakers—Bible.

EGERMEIER, Elsie Emilie, 1890- 220.95
Bible picture A B C book, by Elsie E. Egermeier ... Anderson, Ind., The Warner press, 1939. [63] p. col. illus. 23 cm. [PE1127.B5E4] 39-32160
1. Readers and speakers—Bible. 2. Primers—1870- I. Title.

HOGARTH, Grace Allen. 220.95
A Bible A B C [by] Grace Allen Hogarth. New York, Frederick A. Stokes co., 1941. [55] p. col. illus. 16 cm. Illustrated lining-papers. [PE1127.B5H6] 41-16358
1. Readers and speakers—Bible. 2. Primers—1870- I. Title.

MARY Bartholomeu, Sister. 244
The book of the Holy Child [by] Sister Mary Bartholomew ... edited by Dr. Edward A. Fitzpatrick ... Milwaukee, New York [etc.] The Bruce publishing company [c1931] 3 p. l., 89 p. col. illus. 20 1/2 cm. [BX930.M35] [372.4] 31-21207
1. Readers and speakers—Bible. 2. Primers—1870- I. Fitzpatrick, Edward Augustus, 1884- ed. II. Title. III. Title: The Holy Child, The book of.

MARY Bartholomeu, sister. 244
The book of the Holy Child [by] Sister Mary Bartholomew ... Milwaukee, New York [etc.] The Bruce publishing company [c1935] 4 p. l., 88 p. col. illus. 20 1/2 cm. (Half-title: Highway to heaven series. [book 1]) [Secular name: Elizabeth Eva Frederick] [BX980.M37 1935] [372.4] 35-29158
1. Readers and speakers—Bible. 2. Primers—1870- I. Title. II. Title: The Holy Child, The book of.

SANDERS, Ella King. 220.95
The Bible story primer, by Ella King Sanders. Nashville, Tenn., Atlanta, Ga. [etc.] Southern publishing association [c1929] 136 p. incl. col. front., col. illus. 21 cm. [PE1127.B5S3] (372.4) 30-17551
1. Readers and speakers—Bible. 2. Primers—1870- I. Title.

Readers and speakers — Black Muslims.

JOHNSON, Christine (Claybourne) 1909-
Muhammad's children; a first grade reader. [Chicago? 1963] 130 p. illus. 23 cm. On spine: University of Islam No. 2. [PE1125.5.B5J6] 63-25928
1. Readers and speakers — Black Muslims. I. Title. II. Title: University of Islam No. 2

Readers and speakers—Missions.

HOLLOWAY, Pearl.
The paramount missionary book; exercises, dialogs, plays, pantomimes, songs and recitations, by Pearl Holloway... Chicago, Ill., Meyer & brother, c1926. 1 p. l., 5-62, [5] p.19 1/2 cm. At head of title: A paramount line publication. Music: [5] p. at end. [BV2085.H6] 26-13437
1. Readers and speakers—Missions. I. Title. II. Title: Missionary book, The paramount.

Reading—Addresses, essays, lectures.

LEARNING to read in different languages / edited by Sarah Hudelson. Washington, D.C. : Center for Applied Linguistics, 1981, c1980. p. cm. (Linguistics and literacy series ; 1) "July 1980." Includes bibliographies. [BL1050.L385] 80-36878 ISBN 0-87281-118-2 pbk. : 7.95 428.4
1. Reading—Addresses, essays, lectures. 2. Miscue analysis—Addresses, essays, lectures. 3. Education, Bilingual—Addresses, essays, lectures. 4. Reading, Psychology of—Addresses, essays, lectures. I. Hudelson, Sarah. II. Series.

Reading (Adult Education)

HEDING, Howard William, 1917- 428.6'2
The Missouri adult vocational-literacy materials development project [by] Howard W. Heding, Wilbur S. Ames [and] A. Sterl

Artley, with the assistance of William G. Grimsley and Larry Andrews. Columbia, University of Missouri, 1967. vi, 320 l. 27 cm. "Final report, project no. 034-65, contract no. OE-5-85-027 [prepared under contract with the U.S. Office of Education] " Includes bibliographies. [LC5225.R4H4] 68-63982
1. Reading (Adult education) I. Ames, Wilbur S., joint author. II. Artley, A. Sterl, joint author. III. Missouri. University. IV. Title.

LANGUAGE and faith. 418'.02
[Edited by Cornell Capa and Dale Kietzman, in association with Yvonne Kalmus, and assisted by Peter Anderson, Carey Moore, and Hugh Steven] Santa Ana, Calif., Wycliffe Bible Translators, in cooperation with Summer Institute of Linguistics [1972] 159 p. illus. 28 cm. [BS450.L35] 73-153883
1. Bible—Versions. 2. Reading (Adult Education) 3. Ethnology. I. Capa, Cornell, ed. II. Kietzman, Dale, ed. III. Wycliffe Bible Translators. IV. Summer Institute of Linguistics.

Reading (Elementary)

GORDON, Emma K. 226
A manual for teachers of primary reading, by Emma K. Gordon ... Boston, D. C. Heath & co., 1910. vii, 203 p. illus. 19 cm. (On cover: Gordon readers) [LB1525] 13-16841
1. Reading (Elementary) I. Title.

Reading, Pa. First Reformed Church.

WETZEL, Daniel Jacob, 1888- 284.2748
Two hundredth anniversary history of First Reformed Church, Reed and Washington Streets, Reading, Pennsylvania. [Reading] The Consistory, 1953. 119p. illus. 24cm. [BX7481.R4F5] 54-30219
1. Reading, Pa. First Reformed Church. I. Title.

Reading, Pa. Trinity Lutheran church.

FRY, Jacob, 1834-1920. 284.174816
The history of Trinity Lutheran church, Reading, Pa., 1751-1894. By Jacob Fry ... Reading, Pa. [Press Eagle job office] 1894. 300 p. incl. front. 20 cm. Published by the congregation. [BX8076.R3T8] 31-7329
1. Reading, Pa. Trinity Lutheran church. I. Title.

Realino, Bernardino, Saint, 1530-1616.

SWEENEY, Francis W 1916- 922.245
Bernardine Realino, Renaissance man. New York, Macmillan, 1951. 173 p. 21 cm. Bibliography: p. 165-167. [BX4700;R36S8] 51-14334
1. Realino, Bernardino, Saint, 1533-1616. I. Title.

†SWEENEY, Francis W., 1916- 282'.092'4 B
Every man my brother / Francis Sweeney. [Boston] : St. Paul Editions, c1976. 172 p. ; 22 cm. Includes index. Bibliography: p. 165-167. [BX4700.R36S83] 77-370075 4.00
1. Realino, Bernardino, Saint, 1530-1616. 2. Christian saints—Italy—Biography. I. Title.

Realism.

ASHCROFT, Edgar A. 211
The world's desires: or, The results of monism, an elementary treatise on a realistic religion and philosophy of human life, by Edgar A. Ashcroft. London, K. Paul, Trench, Trubner & co., ltd.; Chicago, The Open court publishing co. ltd., 1905. xii, 440 p. 22 1/2 cm. [B835.A7] 31-7916
1. Realism. 2. Monism. 3. Philosophy and religion. I. Title.

GOODSELL, Willystine.
The conflict of naturalism, by Willystine Goodsell ... New York city, Teachers college, Columbia university, 1910. vii, 183 p. 24 cm. (Teachers college, Columbia university. Contributions to education, no. 33) Bibliography: p. 179-183. A 10 1.50.
1. Realism. 2. Humanism. I. Title.

Reality.

BRENNER, Harry Lyon.
"Christian efficiency," by Harry Lyon Brenner, an exposition of Christianity in its relation to life. Not based upon traditions and beliefs, but upon reason and logic. Written for Christian and non-Christian thinkers ... Kansas City, Mo., Tiernan-Dart printing company, 1915. 99 p. incl. front. (port) 19 1/2 cm. 15-12654 1.00
I. Title.

CULLITON, Joseph T. 201
A processive world view for pragmatic Christians / by Joseph T. Culliton. New York : Philosophical Library, c1975. 302 p. ; 22 cm. Includes bibliographical references. [BD331.C84] 75-3781 ISBN 0-8022-2170-X : 12.50
1. Teilhard de Chardin, Pierre. 2. Dewey, John, 1859-1952. 3. Reality. 4. Evolution. 5. Christianity—Philosophy. 6. Pragmatism. I. Title.

FAIRBAIRN, Robert Edis, 1880- 220
The appeal to reality, by R. Edis. Fairbairn. New York, Cincinnati, The Abingdon press [c1927] 192 p. 19 cm. [BR125.F2] 28-4248
I. Title.

JOHNSON, Raynor Carey. 133.072
The imprisoned splendour; an approach to reality, based upon the significance of data drawn from the fields of natural science, psychical research and mystical experience. London, Hodder and Stoughton [1953] 424p. illus. 23cm. [BD331.J59] 53-2874
1. Reality. 2. Science—Philosophy. 3. Psychical research. 4. Mysticism. I. Title.

OSBORN, Merton b., comp. 248.2'4
Quest for reality Chicago, Moody [1967] [BV4930.D8] 67-14386 2.95
1. eality. 2. Converts. I. Title.
Contents omitted

THOMAS, Evan Edward, 1884-
Lotze's theory of reality, by the Rev. E. E. Thomas ... London, New York [etc.] Longmans, Green, and co., 1921. 1, 217 p. 22 cm. $5.00 [B3298.O2T4] 21-17999
1. Lotze, Hermann i.e. Rudolf Hermann, 1817-1881. 2. Reality. I. Title.

WHEELER, Charles Kirkland.
Hundredth century philosophy, by Charles Kirkland Wheeler. Boston, Press of J. H. West company, 1906. 3 p.l., [5]-171 p. front. (diagr.) 18 cm. [BD553.W5] 6-38883
1. Reality. 2. Materialism. I. Title.

WODEHOUSE, Helen.
Presentation of reality, by Helen Wodehouse ... Cambridge, University press, 1910. x, 163 p. 19 cm. Index of authors referred to: p. 161-163. A 11
1. Reality. I. Title.

Reason.

BRAY, Henry Truro, 1846-1922. 922
The evolution of a life; or, From the bondage of superstition to the freedom of reason. By Rev. Henry Truro Bray ... Chicago, Holt publishing company, 1890. xii, 436 p. front. (port.) 21 cm. Autobiography. [Full name: Thomas Henry Truro Bray] [BL2775.B68] 32-28857
I. Title.

BRAY, Henry Truro, 1846-1922. 922
The evolution of a life; or, From the bondage of superstition to the freedom of reason. By Rev. Henry Truro Bray ... Chicago, Holt publishing company, 1890. xii, 436 p. front. (port.) 21 cm. Autobiography. [Full name: Thomas Henry Truro Bray] [BL2775.B68] 32-28857
I. Title.

[GINZBERG, Asher] 1856-1927.
... The supremacy of reason, by Achad Ha-Am [pseud.] Translated from the Hebrew by Leon Simon ... New York city, Maimonides octocentennial committee, 1935. 52 p. 23 cm. (Maimonides octocentennial series, no. i) Title vignette: autograph of Maimonides reproduced from a manuscript in the museum of the Jewish theological seminary. A38
1. Moses ben Maimon, 1135-1204. 2. Reason. I. Simon, Leon, 1881- tr. II. Title.

GOLDBERG, Henry.
The voice of reason and truthful echoes ... Boston, Investigator co., 1901. 2 p. l., 193 p. port. 12 degrees. Contents.--What is God?--The Holy Bible and book of nature.--Moses and the Bible miracles.--Is a universal brotherhood of man possible without a universal religion?--Immortality; or, Continued existence. 1-15246
I. Title.

[JOHNSON, Francis] 1562-1618.
Certayne reasons and arguments proving that it is not lawfull to heare or have any spiritual communion with the present ministerie of the Church of England ... [Amsterdam] 1608. 4 p. l., 112 p. 19 cm. Preface signed: Francis Johnson. ca 17
I. Title.

KEARY, Charles Francis, 1848-1917.
The pursuit of reason. By Charles Francis Keary, M. A. Cambridge, University press, 1910. vi p., 1 l., 456 p. 22 cm. A 11
1. Reason. I. Title.

MYERS, Edward De Los, ed. 230.04
Christianity and reasons, seven essays. New York, Oxford University Press, 1951. xiii, 172 p. 21 cm. Includes bibliographical references. [BT10.M9] 51-9721
I. Title.
Contents omitted.

NIXON, Leroy 230.42
John Calvin's teachings on human reason; a synthesis from Calvin's writings according to established categories, and a study of their implications for theory of Reformed Protestant Christian education. Foreword by Lee A. Belford. New York, Exposition [c1963] xi, 276p. 22cm. (Exposition-testament bks.) Bibl. 63-11689 6.00
1. Calvin, Jean, 1509-1564. 2. Reason. 3. Religious education. I. Title.

NIXON, Leroy. 230.42
John Calvin's teachings on human reason; a synthesis from Calvin's writings according to established categories, and a study of their implications for the theory of Reformed Protestant Christian education. Foreword by Lee A. Belford. [1st ed.] New York, Exposition Press [1963] xi, 276 p. 22 cm. (An Exposition-testament book) Revision of thesis -- New York University. Bibliography: p. [267]-276. [BX9418.N58] 63-11689
1. Calvinm Jean, 1509-1564. 2. Reason. 3. Religious education. I. Title.

NUESCH, John, 1846-
Christianity in the light of reason; a contribution for the uplifting of the true religion and the overthrow of Babylon, by John Nuesch, sr. ... [Malvern? Ark., 1906] 2 p. l., [7]-118 p. 23 cm. 8-28273
I. Title.

NUESCH, John, 1846-
Christianity in the light of reason; a contribution for the uplifting of the true religion and the overthrow of Babylon, by John Nuesch, sr. ... [Malvern? Ark., c1906] 2 p. l., [7]-118 p. 23 cm. 8-28273
I. Title.

WICKIZER, George Edward. 286.7
The aquarian age of man, by G. E. W. ... Denver, Colo., G. E. Wickizer [c1931] 5 p. l., 226 p., 1 l. 20 1/2 cm. [BR126.W6] 31-23312
I. Title.

Reasoning.

HAWLEY, Thomas De Riemer.
How to reason infallibly; a practical and exact system of logical reasoning by means of the reasoning frame. By Thomas D. Hawley... Chicago, T. D. Hawley, 1900. 3 p. l., 222, [4] p. 20 cm. [BC138.H3] Feb
1. Reasoning. 2. Logic. I. Title.

Reba Place Fellowship (Evanston, Ill.)

JACKSON, Dave. 261.8'33
Dial 911 : peaceful Christians and urban violence / Dave Jackson. Scottdale, Pa. : Herald Press, 1981. p. cm. [BV4407.8.J3] 19 81-2541 ISBN 0-8361-1952-5 (pbk.) : 5.95 ($6.90 Can)
1. Reba Place Fellowship (Evanston, Ill.) 2. Violence—Moral and religious aspects. 3. Crime and criminals—Illinois—Evanston. I. Title. II. Title: Peaceful Christians and urban violence.

Rebekah.

KURTZ, Edward Cuyler. 221.92
... "And behold, the camels were coming" (Genesis 24: 63) by Edward Cuyler Kurtz ... Grand Rapids, Mich., Zondervan publishing house [c1941] 2 p. l., 3-332 p. 20 cm. [BS580.R4K8] 41-19354
1. Rebekah. 2. Bible—Prophecies. I. Title.

STEBBINS, John Wesley.
The half-century history of Rebekah odd fellowship of the I. O. O. F. from its organization in 1851 to 1901 ... [Rochester? N. Y., 1901] 100 p. front., port. 8 degrees. 1-9375
I. Title.

Rebirth (Game)

TATZ, Mark. 294.3'4'23
Rebirth : the Tibetan game of liberation / by Mark Tatz and Jody Kent. 1st ed. Garden City, N.Y. : Anchor Press, 1977. 231 p. : ill. ; 26 cm. Includes bibliographical references. [BQ7566.5.T37] 76-2845 ISBN 0-385-11421-4 : 6.95
1. Rebirth (Game) 2. Eschatology, Buddist. 3. Spiritual life (Lamaism) 4. Cosmology, Buddhist. I. Kent, Jody, joint author. II. Title.

Recife, Brazil, Kahal Kadosh Sur Israel.

WIZNITZER, Arnold. 296
The records of the earliest Jewish community in th New World; with a foreword by Salo W. Baron. New York, American Jewish Historical Society, 1954. xiii, 108p. illus., port., maps, facsims 24cm.*Translation of the Minute book of the Congregations Zur Israel of Recife and Magen Abraham of Mauricia, Brazil, 1648-1653;: p. 58-91. Bibliographical footnotes. [F2659.J5W5] 54-2217
1. Recife, Brazil, Kahal Kadosh Sur Israel. 2. Mauritia. Kahal Kadosh Maguen Abraham. 3. Jews in Brazil. I. Recife, Brazil Kahal Kadosh Sur Israel. Minute book. II. Mauritia. Kathal Kadosh Maguen Abraham. Minute book. III. Title.

Recitations.

BARNES, Annie Maria, b.1857 comp.
Helps and entertainments for juvenile and your people's missionary societies Compiled and arr. by Miss A. M. Barnes. Nashville, Tenn., Barbee & Smith, 1901. 206 p. front. 19 cm. [BV2085.B3] 2-3566
1. Recitations. I. Title.

FERNIE, Benjamin J.
Select readings and recitations, by Benjamin J. Fernie, PH.D. New York, The Christian herald [c1905] 3 p. l., 11-321 p. 15 1/2 cm. 5-19225
I. Title.

GABRIEL, Charles H. ed.
Rodeheaver recitations; Children's day, for Sunday schools, young peoples' societies, etc., ed. by Chas. H. Gabriel ... Chicago, Philadelphia, The Rodeheaver company, c1916. cover-title, 64 p. 23 cm. 16-11199 0.15
I. Title. II. Title: Children's day.

HOYLE, Frances P.
The world's peaker, reciter and entertainer for home, school, church and platform; recitations, readings, plays, drills, tableaux, etc. ... By Frances P. Hoyle ... Philadelphia, Pa., World Bible house [c1905] 7 p. l. 27-484 p. incl. illus., plates. col. front., plates (partly col.) 25 cm. 5-34642
I. Title.

Recollection (Theology)

GOLLAND TRINDADE, Henrique 248
Heitor, Bp., 1897-
Recollection the soul of action. Translated by Conall O'Leary from the Portuguese. [1st ed.] Paterson, N. J., St. Anthony Guild Press [1957] 166p. illus: 20cm. [BX2350.6.G6] 57-39769
1. Recollection (Theology) I. Title.

Reconciliation.

COMPTON-RICKETT, Joseph, Sir 225
1847-1919
Origins and faith; an essay of reconciliation, by Joseph Compton-Rickett ... New York, Chicago [etc.] Fleming H. Revell company [c1909] 11 p., 1 l., 13-276 p. 22 cm. [BR121.C64] 10-13178
I. Title.

*GERSTNER, John H. 231
A reconciliation primer. Grand Rapids, Mich., Baker Bk. [c.]1965. 51p. 22cm. .85 pap.,
I. Title.

[HALES, Jacob Cecil] 1864-
"That they all may be one;" a plea for the reunion of Christians ... by a layman. Petersburg, Va., The Franklin press company, c1908. 183, [6] p. 19 1/2 cm. 8-20483
I. Title.

HARKNESS, Georgia Elma, 1891- 261
The ministry of reconciliation [by] Georgia Harkness. Nashville, Abingdon Press [1971] 160 p. 20 cm. [BV4509.5.H3] 79-134243 2.45
1. Reconciliation. I. Title.

HUNTER, Gordon C. 261
When the walls come tumblin' down, by Gordon C. Hunter. Foreword by Bruce Larson. Waco, Tex., Word Books [1970] 139 p. 23 cm. Includes bibliographical references. [BV4509.5.H85] 79-135354 3.95
1. Reconciliation. I. Title.

MORRISON, Mary Chase. 234'.5
Re-conciliation : the hidden hyphen / by Mary Morrison. Wallingford, Pa. : Pendle Hill Publications, 1974. 24 p. ; 19 cm. (Pendle Hill pamphlet ; 198 ISSN 0031-4250) [BV4509.5.M67] 74-24007 ISBN 0-87574-198-3 : 0.95
1. Reconciliation. I. Title.

POTE, Lawrence. 234'.1
Acceptance : balancing our differences in grace / by Lawrence Pote. Kalamazoo : Master's Press, c1977. ix, 54 p., [1] leaf of plates : ill. ; 18 cm. (Master's moments) [BV4509.5.P67] 77-70117 ISBN 0-89251-030-7 pbk. : 1.50
1. Reconciliation. 2. Church controversies. 3. Acceptance in the Bible. I. Title.

UNDERWOOD, Joseph B. 234'.5
New persons in an old world : adventures in reconciliation in many lands / Joseph B. Underwood. Nashville : Broadman Press, c1976. 127 p. ; 21 cm. [BV4509.5.U5] 75-39447 ISBN 0-8054-8510-4 pbk. : 2.50
1. Reconciliation. I. Title.

Reconciliation—Addresses, essays, lectures.

HOWE, John, 1630-1705.
The Redeemer's tears wept over lost souls: union among Protestants: carnality of religious contention: man's enmity to God; and reconcilation between God and man. By John Howe, A.M. With life of the author, by the Rev. W. Urwick ... New York, Wiley & Putnam, 1846. 2 p. l., liii, 286 p. 17 1/2 cm. [BX9318.H65 1846] 22-22547
I. Urwick, William, 1826-1905. II. Title.

RECONCILIATION in today's 260
world; six study papers [by Donald G. Miller and others] introducing the theme of the uniting general council of the World Alliance of Reformed and Presbyterian Churches and the International Congregational Council, Nairobi, Kenya, August 1970. Grand Rapids, Eerdmans [1969] 122 p. 20 cm. "Prepared ... for the North American Area Theological Committee of the World Alliance of Reformed and Presbyterian Churches, Allen O. Miller, chairman and editor." [BT265.2.R4] 70-95464 1.95
1. Reconciliation—Addresses, essays, lectures. I. Miller, Allen O., ed. II. Miller, Donald G. III. Alliance of Reformed Churches throughout the World Holding the Presbyterian System. North American Area. Theological Committee.

SACRAMENTAL 234'.5
reconciliation. Edited by Edward Schillebeeckx. [New York] Herder and Herder [1971] 156 p. 23 cm. (Concilium: religion in the seventies, v. 61. Dogma) Includes bibliographical references. [BV4509.5.S24] 76-129760 2.95
1. Reconciliation—Addresses, essays, lectures. 2. Penance—Addresses, essays, lectures. I. Schillebeeckx, Edward Cornelis Florentius Alfons, 1914- ed. II. Series: Concilium (New York) v. 61

Reconciliation—Biblical teaching.

ELLIOTT, Ralph H. 261
Reconciliation and the new age [by] Ralph H. Elliott. Valley Forge [Pa.] Judson Press [1973] 125 p. 22 cm. (Lakeview books) Includes bibliographical references. [BS680.R28E45] 72-9568 ISBN 0-8170-0586-2 2.95
1. Reconciliation—Biblical teaching. I. Title.

MARTIN, Ralph P. 230'.12
Reconciliation : a study of Paul's theology / Ralph P. Martin. Atlanta : John Knox Press, c1980. p. cm. (New foundations theological library) [BS2655.R29M37 1980] 80-16340 ISBN 0-8042-3709-3 : 18.50 pbk. : 11.95 ISBN 0-8042-3729-8 :
1. Bible. N.T. Epistles of Paul—Theology. 2. Reconciliation—Biblical teaching. I. Title. II. Series.

STUHLMUELLER, Carroll. 234'.5
Reconciliation : a Biblical call / by Carroll Stuhlmueller. Chicago : Franciscan Herald Press, [1975] p. cm. (Herald Biblical booklets) Bibliography: p. [BS680.R28S8] 74-34059 ISBN 0-8199-0522-4 pbk. : 0.95
1. Reconciliation—Biblical teaching. I. Title.

WORKMAN, George Coulson.
At onement; or, Reconciliation with God, by George Coulson Workman ... New York, Chicago [etc.] Fleming H. Revell company [c1911] 2 p. l., 3-237 p. 19 1/2 cm. $1.25 11-26968
I. Title.

Reconstruction (1914-1939)—Europe.

JONES, Mary Hoxie. 267'.18'9673
Swords into ploughshares; an account of the American Friends Service Committee, 1917-1937. Westport, Conn., Greenwood Press [1971] xix, 374 p. illus., ports. 23 cm. Reprint of the 1937 ed. [BX7635.A1F65 1971] 70-109757 ISBN 0-8371-4247-4
1. Friends, Society of. American Friends Service Committee. 2. Friends, Society of—Charities. 3. Reconstruction (1914-1939)—Europe. I. Title.

Reconstruction (1939-1951)—Religious aspects.

RUSSELL, Ralph, father. 261
Essays in reconstruction. Port Washington, N.Y., Kennikat Press [1968] xi, 176 p. 22 cm. (Essay and general literature index reprint series) Reprint of the 1946 ed. Contents.Contents.—Reconstruction and the natural man, by R. Russell.—The leaven, by R. Russell.—The Catholic action, by I. Trethowan.—Christian education, by C. Butler.—Catholicism and science, by F. S. Taylor.—Catholicism and English literature, by H. Steuert and S. Moore.—The reconstruction of philosophic thought, by I. Trethowan.—Catholics and economic reconstruction, by M. Fogarty.—The aims of youth in peace and war, by A. Lytton-Milbanke.—Youth and the young Christian workers, by J. Fitzsimons. Bibliographical footnotes. [D825.R88 1968] 68-15835
1. Reconstruction (1939-1951)—Religious aspects. 2. Church and social problems—Catholic Church. I. Title.

Reconstruction (1939-)—Jews.

GOTTSCHALK, Max, 1889- 296
Jews in the post-war world, by Max Gottschalk ... and Abraham G. Duker ... New York, The Dryden press, 1945. xiv, 224 p. 21 1/2 cm. [D829.J4G65] 45-45
1. Reconstruction (1939-)—Jews. 2. Jewish question. I. Duker, Abraham Gordon, 1907- joint author. II. Title.

Reconstructionist Judaism.

DININ, Samuel, 1902- 917.3'06'924
Judaism in a changing civilization. New York, Bureau of Publications, Teachers College, Columbia University, 1933. [New York, AMS Press, 1972, ie. 1973] x, 213 p. 22 cm. Reprint of the 1933 ed., issued in series: Teachers College, Columbia University. Contributions to education, no. 563. Originally presented as the author's thesis, Columbia. Includes bibliographies. [BM197.7.D55 1972] 70-176722 ISBN 0-404-55563-2 10.00
1. Reconstructionist Judaism. I. Title. II. Series: Columbia University. Teachers College. Contributions to education, no. 563.

EISENSTEIN, Ira, 1906- 296
Judaism under freedom. With a foreword by Mordecai M. Kaplan. New York, Reconstructionist Press, 1956. 262p. 22cm. [BM197.7.E5] 56-12814
1. Reconstructionist Judaism. I. Title.

KAPLAN, Mordecai Menahem, 296
1881-
Basic values in Jewish religion. [New York] Reconstructionist Press [1957] 111p. 25cm. 'Reprinted from The future of the American Jew, chapters 14 & 15.' [BM197.7.K24] 57-12333
1. Reconstructionist Judaism. I. Title.

KAPLAN, Mordecai Menahem, 296
1881-
Judaism as a civilization: toward a reconstruction of American-Jewish life. [Enl. ed.] New York, Reconstructionist Press, 1957. xvi, 601p. 24cm. Bibliographical references included in 'Notes' (p. 525- 554) [BM197.7.K26 1957] 57-8533
1. Reconstructionist Judaism. 2. Jews in the U. S. I. Title.

KAPLAN, Mordecai Menahem, 296
1881-
Judaism as a civilization; toward a reconstruction of American-Jewish life. [Enl. ed.] New York, T. Yoseloff [1957] xvi, 601p. diagr. 25cm. Bibliographical references included in 'Notes' (p. 525-554) [BM197.7.K26 1957a] 57-2633
1. Reconstructionist Judaism. 2. Jews in the U. S. I. Title.

KAPLAN, Mordecai Menahem, 296
1881-
Judaism as a civilization ; toward a reconstruction of American-Jewish life. [Enl. ed.] New York, Reconstructionist Press, 1957. xvi, 601p. 24cm. Bibliographical references included in 'Notes' (p.525-554) [BM197.7.K26 1957] 57-8533
1. Reconstructionlist Judaism. 2. News in the U. S. I. Title.

KAPLAN, Mordecai 910.03'176'6
Menahem, 1881-
Judaism as a civilization; toward a reconstruction of American-Jewish life, by Mordecai M. Kaplan. New York, Schocken Books [1967] xvi, 601 p. 21 cm. Reprint of the 1957 ed. Bibliographical references included in "Notes" (p. 525-554) [BM197.7.K26 1967] 67-26990
1. Reconstructionist Judaism. 2. Jews in the United States. I. Title.

KAPLAN, Mordecai 296.8'344
Menahem, 1881-
Judaism as a civilization : toward a reconstruction of American Jewish life / Mordecai M. Kaplan ; introduction by Arthur Hertzberg. Philadelphia : Jewish Publication Society of America and the Reconstructionist Press, 1981. p. cm. Reprint. Originally published: New York : Reconstructionist Press, 1957. Includes bibliographical references and index. [BM197.7.K26 1981] 19 81-6057 ISBN 0-8276-0193-X : 25.00 ISBN 0-8276-0194-8 (pbk.) : 10.95
1. Reconstructionist Judaism. 2. Judaism—United States. 3. Jews—United States—Politics and government. I. Title.

KAPLAN, Mordecai Menahem, 296
1881-
Judaism without supernaturalism; the only alternative to orthodoxy and secularism. [1st ed.] New York, Reconstructionist Press, 1958. 254p. 21cm. [BM197.7.K28] 58-10056
1. Reconstructionist Judaism. 2. Supernatural. I. Title.

KAPLAN, Mordecai 296.8'344
Menahem, 1881-
A new approach to Jewish life / by Mordecai M. Kaplan ; with a new introd. by Jacob Neusner. Bridgeport, Conn. : Published for the Jewish Reconstructionist Foundation by Hartmore House, c1973. 88 p. ; 21 cm. Reprint of the 1924 ed. published by the Society for the Advancement of Judaism, New York, under title: A new approach to the problem of Judaism. [BM197.7.K29 1973] 75-322744 ISBN 0-87677-142-8 : 4.95
1. Reconstructionist Judaism. I. Title.

KAPLAN, Mordecal Menahem, 296
1881-
Judaism as a civilization; toward a Reconstructionist Press [1957] 111p. 25cm. 'Reprinted from The future of the American Jew, chapters 14 & 15.' [BM197.7.K26 1957] 57-8533
1. Reconstructionist Judaism. I. Title.

KOHN, Eugene, 1887-
Religious humanism: a Jewish interpretation. New York, Reconstructionist Press [1963] x, 154 p. 21 cm. 65-18340
1. Reconstructionist Judaism. I. Title.

Reconstructionist Judaism—Addresses, essays, lectures.

BEN-HORIN, Meir, 296.8'344'08
1918-
Common faith, uncommon people; essays in Reconstructionist Judaism. With a foreword by Ira Eisenstein. New York, Reconstructionist Press [1970] 245 p. 23 cm. Includes bibliographies. [BM197.7.B46] 71-80691 ISBN 0-910808-00-7
1. Jews—Education—Addresses, essays, lectures. 2. Reconstructionist Judaism—Addresses, essays, lectures. I. Title.

Recreation.

CLEMENS, Frances, ed. 259
Recreation and the local church, edited by Frances Clemens, Robert Tully [and] Edward Crill. Illustrated by Frances Clemens. Elgin, Ill., Brethren Pub. House [1956] 191p. illus. 24cm. Includes bibliographies. [BV1640.C56] 57-18412
1. Recreation. 2. Church work. I. Title.

PYLANT, Agnes (Durant) 259
Church recreation. Nashville, Convention Press [c1959] 150p. illus. 19cm. Includes bibliography. [BV1620.P9] 60-507
1. Recreation. 2. Church entertainments. I. Title.

PYLANT, Agnes Durant. 259
Fun plans for church recreation. Illustrated by Murray McKeehan. Nashville, Broadman Press [1958] 125p. illus. 22cm. Includes bibliography. [BV1640.P9] 58-8924
1. Recreation. 2. Church entertainments. I. Title.

Recreation in church work.

BOYD, Bob M. 259
Recreation for churches, compiled by Bob M. Boyd. Nashville, Convention Press [1967] x. 146 p. 19 cm. "Church study course [of the Sundy School Board of Southern Baptist Convention] This book is number 1109 in category 11, section for adults and young people." Bibliography: p. 142-146. [BV1640.B6] 67-21665
1. Recreation in church work. I. Southern Baptist Convention. Sunday School Board. II. Title.

Recreation—United States

YOUNG men's Christian associations. International committee. Bureau of records, studies and trends. 267.3973
The Y.M.C.A. and public recreation, informal education, and leisure-time programs; a study of relationships by Helen E. Davis, with a final chapter contributed by a review committee charged with preparing specific implications for Y.M.C.A. policy and practice. Published under the auspices of the Bureau of records, studies and trends, National board of Y.M.C.A.'s, New York, N.Y. New York, Association press, 1946 [i.e. 1947] ix, 196 p. 20 1/2 cm. "Copyright, 1946." [BV1140.Y6] 47-21695
1. Recreation—U.S. I. Davis, Helen Edna, 1898- II. Title.

YOUNG Men's Christian Associations. National Board. Bureau of Records, Studies and Trends. 267.3973
The Y. M. C. A. and public recreation, informal education and leisure-time programs, a study of relationships by Helen E. Davis with a final chapter contributed by a review committee charged with preparing specific implications for Y. M. C. A. policy and practice. Pub. under the auspices of the Bureau of Records, Studies and Trends, National Board of Y. M. C. A.'s, New York, N. Y. New York, Association Press, 1946 [i. e. 1947] ix, 196 p. 21 cm. [BV1140.Y6] 47-21695
1. Recreation—U. S. I. Davis, Helen Edna, 1898- II. Title.

Red cross (Symbol)

[JOHNSON & Johnson] 291.37
Brief on historical use of the symbol and words "red cross." [New Brunswick, N.J., 1943] 92 p. illus. (part col., incl. facsims.) 28 1/2 cm. On spine: Historical use of the symbol and words "red cross." Bibliography: p. 87-92. [BL604.C7J6] 43-6419
1. Red cross (Symbol) 2. Cross and crosses. 3. Signs and symbols. I. Title. II. Title: Historical use of the symbol and words "red cross."

Red Mass sermons.

WRIGHT, John Joseph, Bp., 1909- 252.02
The Christian and the law, selected Red Mass sermons. Notre Dame, Ind., Fides Publishers [1962] 98 p. 21 cm. [BX1756.W7C5] 62-20572
1. Red Mass sermons. 2. Catholic Church — Sermons. 3. Sermons, American. I. Title.

Red Wing, Minn.—Churches.

NELSON, Lowry, 1893-
... Red Wing churches during the war, by Lowry Nelson ... Minneapolis, The University of Minnesota press [1946] iii, 21 p. tables. 23 cm. (The Community basis for postwar planning, no. 7) A 46
1. Red Wing, Minn.—Churches. 2. World war, 1939-1945—Religious aspects. I. Title.

Reddington, Joanna Woodberry, 1817-1829.

MALLERY, Samuel S. 922
Memoir of Joanna Woodberry Reddington, by Samuel S. Mallery. Written for the New England Sabbath school union, and revised by the Committee of publication. Boston, New England Sabbath school union, 1837. viii, [9]-92 p. front. 15 cm. [BR1715.R4M3] 922 ISBN 37-19927
1. Reddington, Joanna Woodberry, 1817-1829. I. New England Sabbath school union. II. Title.

Redemption.

BALDWIN, P. C. 234.
The redemption of sinners by the free grace of God. Or, The doctrines of unconditional election, perseverance of the saints, assurance of hope, sanctification and glorification, freely discussed. By the Rev. P. C. Baldwin. Philadelphia, H. Perkins, 1849. 298 p. 19 cm. [BT775.B2] 45-44701
1. Redemption. I. Title.

BRADLEY, Joseph Henry, 1838-
The love of God revealed to the entire universe by man's redemption. New York, Chicago [etc.] F. H. Revell co. [1899] 59 p. nar. 16 cm. 0-566
I. Title.

BRYANT, John Delavan, 1811-1877.
Redemption, a poem, by John D. Bryant, M. D. Philadelphia, J. Penington & son, 1859. 366 p. 19 cm. [PS1149.B5R4 1859] 21-13043
I. Title.

CAREY, Walter Julius, bp., 1875- 234.
Evolution & redemption, by the Right Rev. Walter J. Carey, D. D., bishop of Bloemfontein. Milwaukee, Morehouse publishing co.; London, A. R. Mowbray & co. ltd. [1930] vii, 56 p. diagr. 18 cm. "Printed in England." [BT775.C3] A 40
1. Redemption. I. Title.

CARTLEDGE, Samuel Jackson, 1864-1940. 230
The drama of redemption, by Samuel Jackson Cartledge ... Grand Rapids, Mich., Zondervan publishing house [c1940] 7 p. l., 11-142 p. 20 cm. "Brief biographical sketch, by Samuel A. Cartledge": 5th prelim. leaf. [BT775.C35] 40-12216
1. Redemption. I. Cartledge, Samuel Antoine, 1903- II. Title.

CASTER, Marcel van. 234.3
The redemption; a personalist view. Translated by Eileen O'Gorman and Olga Guedatarian. Glen Rock, N. J., Paulist Press [1965] 155 p. 18 cm. (Deus books, T895H) Translation of La redemption situee dans une perspective personnaliste. Bibliographical footnotes. [BT775.C373] 65-26793
1. Redemption. I. Title.

DAWSON, John Leard.
A race's redemption. by John Leard Dawson. Boston, Sherman, French & company, 1912. 5 p. l., 428 p. 21 cm. 12-17651 1.50
I. Title.

DOUTY, Norman Franklin, 1899- 234'.3
The death of Christ; a treatise which answers the question: "Did Christ die only for the elect?" [By] Norman F. Douty. Swengel, Pa., Reiner Publications, 1972. 120 p. 23 cm. Includes bibliographical references. [BT775.D68] 73-153887 3.95
1. Redemption. 2. Election (Theology) I. Title.

DURRWELL, F. X. 232.97
The resurrection, a Biblical study. Translated [from the French] by Rosemary Sheed, and with an introd. by Charles Davis. New York, Sheed and Ward [c.1960] 371p. 60-15679 6.00
1. Redemption. 2. Jesus Christ—Resurrection I. Title.

EDWARDS, Jonathan, 1703-1758. 234.3
A history of the work of redemption: comprising an outline of church history. By President Edwards. New York, American tract society [1839?] 3 p. l., [5]-444 p. 15 cm. (Added t.-p.: The Evangelical family library, vol. ix) Added t.-p. engraved, with vignette. Originally a series of sermons preached in Northampton in 1739, edited after the author's death, from his manuscripts, by John Erskine and published in Edinburgh, 1774. [BT775.E2 1839] 38-33142
1. Redemption. I. Erskine, John, 1721-1803, ed. II. American tract society. III. Title.

EDWARDS, Jonathan, 1703-1758. 234.
A history of the work of redemption; comprising an outline of church history. By President Edwards. Rev. and slightly abridged. New-York, American tract society [184-?] 3 p. l., [5]-446 p. 16 cm. (Added t.-p.: The Evangelical family library, vol. ix) Added t.-p. engraved, with vignette. Originally a series of sermons preached in Northampton in 1739, edited after the author's death, from his manuscripts, by John Erskine and published in Edinburgh, 1774. [BT775.E2] 39-22839
1. Redemption. I. Erskine, John, 1721-1808, ed. II. American tract society. III. Title.

FISHER, Fred L. 234.3
The purpose of God and the Christian life. Philadelphia, Westminster [1963, c.1962] 189p. 21cm. Bibl. 62-14174 3.75
1. Redemption. 2. Salvation. 3. Election (Theology) I. Title.

FLOOD, Edmund 264.02
In memory of me; God's plan for men: present in history, made active in the Eucharist. New York, Sheed [1963, c.1962] 117p. 22cm. First pub. in London in 1962 under title: No small plan. Bibl. 63-17149 3.00
1. Redemption. 2. Mass. I. Title.

GALLOWAY, Allan Douglas, 1920- 234.3
The cosmic Christ. New York, Harper [1951] 274 p. 22 cm. [BT775.G3 1951a] 52-4212
1. Redemption. I. Title.

GARDNER, Charles. 225
The redemption of religion, by Charles Gardner ... London, New York [etc.] Longmans, Green, and co., 1919. xi, 191 p. 22 1/2 cm. "This book is my attempt to extract what I suppose to be ... [the] value of the higher criticism"--Pref. [BR121.G25] 20-7673
I. Title.

GOODE, Francis, 1797?-1842. 234.
The better covenant. By the late Rev. Francis Goode ... 5th thousand. From the 5th London ed. With a preface by the late Rev. James H. Fowles ... Philadelphia, Smith, English & co., 1868. 312 p. 23 cm. [BT775.G57] 42-40135
1. Redemption. 2. Covenants (Theology) I. Title.

GRAHAM, James R. jr. 234.3
The divine unfolding [by] James R. Graham, jr. Grand Rapids, Mich., Zondervan publishing house [c1938] vii p., 1 l., 11-128 p. 20 cm. [BT775.G67] 38-33186
1. Redemption. I. Title.

GRIFFITH, George W. 234.
The divine program; an interpretation of the divine method of redemption and of the nature and nurture of the Christian life, by Rev. G. W. Griffith ...introduction by Bishop William Pearce. Chicago, Ill., W. B. Rose, 1923. 256 p. 19 cm. [BT775.G75] 23-9126
I. Title.

GRIFFITH, George W. 234.
The divine program; an interpretation of the divine method of redemption and of the nature and nurture of the Christian life, by Rev. G. W. Griffith ...introduction by Bishop William Pearce. Chicago, Ill., W. B. Rose, 1923. 256 p. 19 cm. [BT775.G75] 23-9126
I. Title.

GRIFFITH-JONES, Ebenezer, 1860- 234.
The ascent through Christ; a study of the doctrine of redemption in the light of the theory of evolution, by E. Griffith-Jones, B. A., with special preface for the American ed. by the author. New York, E. S. Gorham [c1901] xxxvi, 469 p. 20 cm. [BT775.G8] 3-19200
1. Redemption. 2. Evolution. I. Title.

HENNESSY, Augustine Paul. 232'.3
The paschal mystery : core grace in the life of the Christian / Augustine Paul Hennessy. Chicago : Franciscan Herald Press, [1976] p. cm. (Synthesis series) [BT775.H37] 76-43245 ISBN 0-8199-0707-3 pbk. : 0.65
1. Redemption. 2. Atonement. 3. Paschal mystery. I. Title.

HICKOK, Laurens Perseus, 1798-1888. 234.3
Humanity immortal; or, Man tried. fallen, and redeemed. By Laurens P. Hickok ... Boston, Lee and Shepard; New York, Lee, Shepard and Dilingham, 1872. 362 p. 23 cm. [BT775.H6] 35-31056
1. Redemption. 2. Man (Theology) I. Title.

HOOKER, Thomas, 1586-1647. 234'.3
The application of redemption by the effectual work of the word and spirit of Christ, for the bringing home of lost sinners to God / Thomas Hooker New York : Arno Press, 1972. 451 [i.e. 431] p. ; 23 cm. (Research library of colonial Americana) Reprint of the 1657 ed. printed by P. Cole, London. [BT775.H75] 70-141111
1. Redemption. I. Title. II. Series.

HUFFMAN, Jasper Abraham. 234.
Redemption completed; a treatise on the work of complete redemption, by Rev. Jasper Abraham Huffman ... with an introduction by Rev. A. B. Yoder. Cincinnati, O., For the author by Western Methodist book concern [1903] 196 p. front. (port.) 19 cm. [BT775.H8] 4-45
1. Redemption. I. Title.

KAGAWA, Toyohiko, 1888- 234.3
The challenge of redemptive love [by] Toyohiko Kagawa, translated by Marion R. Draper. New York, Cincinnati [etc.] The Abingdon press [c1940] 160 p. 20 cm. [BT775.K25] 40-6515
1. Redemption. 2. God—Love. I. Draper, Marion Romer, 1891- tr. II. Title.

KENYON, Essek William, 1867-1948. 234.3
New creation realities; a revelation of redemption. [Seattle, c1945] 180 p. port. 22 cm. [BT775.K4] 48-18809
1. Redemption. I. Title.

KENYON, Essek William, 1867-1948. 234.3
What happened from the cross to the throne. Should have been written 400 years ago. [Seattle, 1946, c 1945] 205 p. port. 22 cm. [BT775.K42] 48-19437
1. Redemption. I. Title.

LEFEBVRE, Gaspar, 1880- 234.3
Redemption through the blood of Jesus. Translated by Edward A. Maziarz. Westminster, Md., Newman Press, 1960. 233p. 23cm. [BT775.L513] 59-14811
1. Redemption. I. Title.

MCDOWELL, Alexander. 234.
Transformation the way into the kingdom of God, by Alexander McDowell. Ansonia, Conn., c1905. 85 p. 17 x 13 1/2 cm. [BT775.M2] 45-53468
1. Redemption. I. Title.

MCKINSTRY, Levi C., 1834- 234.3
The redemption. by Eld. L. C. McKinstry. Published by request... Portland [Me.] Printed by B. Thurston & company, 1884. cover-title, 108 p. 18 1/2 cm. [BT775.M24 1884] 36-5743
1. Redemption. I. Title.

MCKINSTRY, Levi C., 1834- 234.3
Redemption by the blood of Christ; or, Why the blood in the scheme of redemption? By L. C. McKinstry... Haverhill, Mass., 1887. 1 p. l., 108 p. 20 cm. [BT775.M24 1887] 36-5742
1. Redemption. I. Title.

MARTIN, Thomas Theodore, 1862-
Redemption and the new birth, by T. T. Martin ... New York, Chicago [etc.] Fleming H. Revell company [c1913] 220 p. 19 1/2 cm. $1.00 13-12604
I. Title.

MURRAY, John, 1898- 232.3
Redemption, accomplished and applied. Grand Rapids, W. B. Eerdmans Pub. Co., 1955. 236p. 23cm. [BT775.M8] 55-13972
1. Redemption. I. Title.

MURRAY, John, 1898-
Redemption, accomplished and applied. Grand Rapids, Eerdmans, 1965. 192 p. 19 cm. 68-38997
1. Redemption. I. Title.

NASH, Charles Ellwood, 1855-1932. 234.
... The Saviour of the world. By Charles Ellwood Nash ... Boston, Universalist publishing house, 1895. 3 p. l., [5]-105 p. 17 cm. (Added t.-p.: Manuals of faith and duty, ed. by J. S. Cantwell. no. vii) Series in part at head of t.-p. [BT775.N3] 38-33139
1. Redemption. I. Title.

OWEN, John, 1616-1683. 234.3
The death of death in the death of Christ. A treatise of the redemption and reconciliation that is in the blood of Christ, with the merit thereof, and the satisfaction wrought thereby: wherein the proper end of the death of Christ is asserted; the immediate effects and fruits thereof assigned, with their extent in respect of its object; and the whole controversy about universal redemption fully discussed. By John Owen, D. D. Philadelphia, Green and M'Laughlin, 1827. xvii, [1], [19]-392 p., 1 l. 18 cm. [BT775.O9 1827] 33-1381
1. Redemption. 2. Atonement. I. Title.

PACE, Charles Nelson. 232.
Bring him to me; or, The sufficient remedy being a short study of modern methods in the redemption of man, by Charles Nelson Pace. New York, Cincinnati, The Methodist book concern [c1917] 72 p. 17 1/2 cm. [BT265.P3] 17-23443
I. Title.

PETERSON, Ephraim.
Redemption, by E. Peterson. Independence, Mo., The author [c1909] cover-title, 140 p. 19 cm. 9-27579 0.25
I. Title.

PHILIPPE DE LA TRINITE, 234.3
Father.
What is redemption? Translated from the French by Anthony Armstrong. [1st ed.] New York, Hawthorn Books [1961] 151p. 21cm. (Twentieth century encyclopedia of Cathllcism, v. 25. Section 2: The basic truths) Translation of La redemption par le sang. Includes bibliographies. [BT775.P533] 61-17220
1. Redemption. I. Title.

POHLE, Joseph, 1852-1922. 234.
Soteriology; a dogmatic treatise on the redemption, by the Reverend Joseph Pohle ... Authorized English version, based on the 5th German ed., with some abridgement and added references, by Arthur Preuss. St. Louis, Mo. [etc.] B. Herder, 1914. 3 p. l., 160 p. 21 cm. Published 1913. Half-title: Dogmatic theology v. "Readings": p. 108-100, 163-164. [BT775.P7] 13-22501
1. Redemption. 2. Atonement. I. Preuss, Arthur, 1871- tr. II. Title.

PRESSENSE, Edmond Dehault 234.
de, 1824-1891.
The Redeemer: a sketch of the history of redemption. By Edmond de Pressense. Translated from the second edition, by Rev. J. H. Myers ... Boston, American tract society [1867] x, 11-412 p. 19 cm. Errata slip inserted. [BT775.P8] 45-47163
1. Redemption. I. Myers, J. H., tr. II. American tract society. III. Title.

RHYNARD, Peter. 234.
"Redemption;" old paths made plain, by Rev. Peter Rhynard. Chicago, Ill., Herald publishing company [1920] 4 p. l., [17]-123 p. illus. (incl. plates, port.) 23 1/2 cm. [BT775.R45] 20-14130
I. Title.

RICHARD, Louis, 1880-1956 234.3
The mystery of the redemption. Foreword by Frank B. Norris. [Tr. from French by Joseph Horn] Helicon [dist. New York, Taplinger, c.1966] 358p. 21cm. Bibl. [BT775.R4713] 65-24129 5.95 bds.,
1. Redemption. I. Title.

RICHARD, Louis, 1880-1956. 234.3
The mystery of the redemption. With a foreword by Frank B. Norris. [Translated from the French by Joseph Horn] Baltimore, Helicon [1966] 358 p. 21 cm. Translation of Le mystere de la redemption, which was first published under the title, Le dogme de la redemption. Bibliography: p. 353-356. [BT775.R4713] 65-24129
1. Redemption. I. Title.

ROBINSON, Henry Wheeler, 1872-
Redemption and revelation in the actuality of history, by H. Wheeler Robinson ... New York and London, Harper & brothers [1942] xlviii, 320 p. 22 1/2 cm. (Half-title: The Library of constructive theology. Editors: W. R. Matthews ... H. W. Robinson) Bibliographical foot-notes. 42-23294
1. Redemption. 2. Revelation. I. Title.

SHEETS, John R., comp. 234'.3
The theology of the atonement; readings in soteriology. Edited by John R. Sheets. Englewood Cliffs, N.J., Prentice-Hall [1967] vi, 233 p. 22 cm. Bibliography: p. 230-233. Bibliographical footnotes. [BT775.S45] 67-15180
1. Redemption. 2. Atonement. 3. Salvation. I. Title.

SHERRILL, Lewis Joseph, 234.3
1892-
Guilt and redemption [reissue of] rev. ed. Richmond, Knox [1963, c.1945, 1957] 255p. illus. 21cm. 2.00 pap.,
1. Redemption. 2. Guilt. I. Title.

SHERRILL, Lewis Joseph, 234.3
1892-
Guilt and redemption. Rev. ed. Richmond, John Knox Press [c1957] 255 p. illus. 21 cm. [BT775.S47 1957] 56-13378
1. Redemption. 2. Guilt. I. Title.

SHERRILL, Lewis Joseph, 234.3
1892-
Guilt and redemption, by Lewis Joseph Sherrill ... Richmond, Va., John Knox press, 1945. 254 p. 21 cm. [James Sprunt lectures delivered at Union theological seminary in Virginia, 1945] Biographical references included in "Notes" (p. [245]-254) [BT775.S47] 46-3269
1. Redemption. 2. Guilt. I. Title.

SIMPSON, William John 232.3
Sparrow, 1859-
The Redeemer, by the Rev. W. J. Sparrow Simpson ... London, New York [etc.] Longmans, Green and co. [1937] xx, 226 p. 19 cm. "The substance of the following pages was delivered in the form of lectures to the Men's lecture society at St. Paul's cathedral, to a group of clergy in the diocese of Chelmsford, and to a summer school for priests at Exeter."--Pref. "First published 1937." [BT265.S53] 38-17080
1. Jesus Christ—Person and offices. 2. Redemption. I. Title.

SWAIN, Joseph, 1761-1796.
Redemption. A poem, in eight books. By Joseph Swain ... 1st American from 2d London ed. To which is prefixed memoirs of the author's life. Boston, Printed by Nathaniel Willis, 1812. xxxvi, [37]-209, 6 p. 24 1/2 cm. A different work from the author's "Redemption, a poem in five books." "A selection from 'Walworth hymns' by Joseph Swain": 6 p. at end. [PR3719.S7 1812] 14-14005
I. Title. II. Title: Redemption, a poem in eight books.

SWAIN, Joseph, 1761-1796.
Redemption, a poem in five books. By Joseph Swain ... Charleston, S.C., Printed for Robert Missildine, by J. Hoff, 1819. x, [11]-114 p., 1 l., [4] p. 18 1/2 cm. A different work from the author's "Redemption, a poem in eight books." "A sketch of the life of the author": p. [iii]-v. "List of subscribers": [4] p. at end. [PR3719.S7 1819] 14-14003
I. Title.

THOLUCK, August, 1799-1877. 234.
Guido and Julius; or, Sin and the propitiator exhibited in the true consecration of the sceptic. By Frederick Aug. D. Tholuck ... Translated from the German by Jonathan Edwards Ryland, with an introductory preface by John Pye Smith, D.D. Boston, Gould and Lincoln, 1854. 238 p. 18 1/2 cm. Translation of Die lehre von der sunde und vom versohner; oder, Die weihe der sweifiers. [Full name: Friedrich August Gotttreu Tholuck] [BT775.T45] 40-37308
1. Redemption. 2. Skepticism—Controversial literature. 3. Apologetics—19th cent. I. Ryland, Jonathan Edwards, 1798-1866, tr. II. Title. III. Title: Sin and the propitiator.

WARD, Wayne E 234.3
The drama of redemption [by] Wayne E. Ward. Nashville, Broadman Press [1966] 128 p. 20 cm. Bible -- History of Biblical events. [BS635.2.W3] 1559932 66-26221
I. Title.

WHALE, John Seldon, 1896- 234.3
Victor and victim; the Christian doctrine of redemption. [New York] Cambridge University Press, 1960[ ] 172p. Bibl. notes. 60-16320 3.75
1. Redemption. I. Title.

WILKIN, Vincent 234.3
From limbo to heaven; an essay on the economy of the redemption. Pref. by Maurice Bevenot. New York, Sheed & Ward [c.1961] 145p. 61-11799 3.00 bds.,
1. Redemption. I. Title.

WILKIN, Vincent. 234.3
From limbo to heaven; an essay on the economy of the redemption. With a pref. by Maurice Bevenot. New York, Sheed and Ward [1961] Brooklyn [1958] 145 p. 20 cm. 154 p. illus. 22 cm. [BT775.W68] [PE1128.W725] 428.24 61-11709 58-7703
1. Redemption. 2. English language — Text-books for foreigners. I. Wilkins, C D II. Title. III. Title: Let us speak English;

WILLEMS, Boniface A., 234'.3
1926-
The reality of redemption [by] Boniface A. Willems. [New York] Herder and Herder [1970] 128 p. 23 cm. Translation of Verlossing in kerk en wereld. Includes bibliographical references. [BT775.W6913] 78-105366 4.95
1. Redemption. I. Title.

WINCHESTER, Elhanan, 1751- 252.
1797.
The seed of the woman bruising the serpent's head. A discourse delivered at the Baptist meeting house, in Philadelphia, Sunday April 22, 1781. By Elhanan Winchester. Published by request. Philadelphia: Printed [by Benjamin Towne] in the year 1781. 58 p. 20 cm. "Silas Winchester, his book A 1780", in manuscript on fly-leaf. An attempt to collect the Scripture in favor of the doctrine of universal redemption and final restitution of all things: p. 19-35. The objections usually brought from the Scriptures, against the doctrine of the restitution of all things, answered, for the satisfaction of all serious inquirers: p. 36-58. Imperfect: corner of t.-p. torn off, and p. 57-58 missing. [BX6333.W62S4] 25-18764
I. Title.

WRIGHTON, William Hazer. 234.3
The human quest and the divine plan, by William Hazer Wrighton ... Grand Rapids, Mich., Zondervan publishing house [c1938] 165 p. 19 1/2 cm. [BT775.W85] 38-30212
1. Redemption. I. Title.

Redemption—Biblical teaching.

ACHTEMEIER, Paul J 234'.3
To save all people; a study of the record of God's redemptive acts in Deuteronomy and Matthew [by] Paul J. and Elizabeth Achtemeier. Boston, United Church Press [1967] 154 p. 21 cm. [BT775.A23] 67-19499
1. Redemption—Biblical teaching. 2. Bible. O. T. Deuteronomy—Study—Outlines, syllabi, etc. 3. Bible. N.T. Matthew—Study—Outlines, syllabi, etc. I. Achtemeier, Elizabeth Rice, 1926-joint author. II. Title.

AN exposition and defense of the scheme of redemption, as it is revealed and taught in the Holy Scriptures.... St. Louis, Bethany press, 1960. 582p. 21cm. First printed in 1868.
1. Redemption—Biblical teaching. I. Milligan, Robert. II. Title: The scheme of redemption.

MCGEE, J. Vernon 1904- 222'.3506
(John Vernon),
Ruth, the romance of Redemption / by J. Vernon McGee. Nashville : T. Nelson, c1982. 200 p. ; 21 cm. Includes bibliographical references. [BS1315.2.M35 1982] 19 81-18892 ISBN 0-8407-5795-6 pbk. : 4.95
1. Bible. O.T. Ruth—Criticism, interpretation, etc. 2. Redemption—Biblical teaching. I. Title.

MCGEE, John Vernon, 221.92'4
1904-
In a barley field, by J. Vernon McGee. Glendale, Calif., G/L Regal Books [1968] 192 p. 18 cm. On cover: Ruth's romance of redemption. 1943 and 1954 editions published under title: Ruth: the romance of redemption. Bibliography: p. 192. [BS580.R8M3 1968] 68-22387
1. Ruth (Biblical character) 2. Redemption—Biblical teaching. I. Title.

SCROGGIE, William Graham, 220.9'5
1877-1958.
The unfolding drama of redemption; the Bible as a whole. Old Tappan, N.J., F. H. Revell Co. [1970] 3 v. illus. 22 cm. (His The unfolding drama of redemption; the Bible as a whole) At head of title: Know your Bible. Vol. 1 first published in 1953; v. 2 in 1957. Contents.Contents.—v. 1. The prologue and act I of the drama, embracing the Old Testament.—v. 2. The interlude and act II of the drama embracing the inter-Testament period, the gospels and acts.—v. 3. Act II and the epilogue of the drama embracing the Epistles and the Book of Revelation. [BS635.2.S362] 72-152551 ISBN 0-7208-0192-3 (v. 1) 34.95
1. Bible—History of Biblical events. 2. Bible—Study—Outlines, syllabi, etc. 3. Redemption—Biblical teaching. I. Title. II. Title: Know your Bible. III. Series.

SCROGGIE, William Graham, 220.9'5
1877-1958.
The unfolding drama of redemption; the Bible as a whole. Grand Rapids, Zondervan Pub. House [1972, c1953-70] 505, 493, 443 p. maps. 23 cm. [BS635.2.S362 1972] 74-163555 16.95
1. Bible—History and Biblical events. 2. Bible—Study—Outlines, syllabi, etc. 3. Redemption—Biblical teaching. I. Title.

WAHLSTROM, Eric Herbert. 234.3
God who redeems; perspectives in Biblical theology. Philadelphia. Muhlenberg Press [1962] 198 p. 22 cm. [BT775.W17] 62-15701
1. Redemption — Biblical teaching. I. Title.

Redemption—Early works to 1800.

EDWARDS, Jonathan, 1703- 234.
1758.
A history of the work of redemption. Containing the outlines of a body of divinity, in a method entirely new. By the late Reverend Mr. Jonathan Edwards ... New York; Printed by Shepard Kollock, for Robert Hodge, no. 38, Maiden-lane. M,DCC,LXXVI. xxiv p., 1 l., [25]-402 p. 20 1/2 cm. Originally a series of sermons preached in Northampton in 1739, edited after the author's death, from his manuscripts, by John Erskine and published in Edinburgh, 1774. [BT775.E2 1786] 44-36298
1. Redemption—Early works to 1800. I. Erskine, John, 1721-1803, ed. II. Title.

EDWARDS, Jonathan, 1703- 234.
1758.
A history of the work of redemption. Containing the outlines of a body of divinity, in a method entirely new. By the late Reverend Jonathan Edwards ... Printed at Worcester, for Isaiah Thomas, jun. Sold by him, in Worcester; by Thomas & Whipple, Newburyport, and by Thomas & Tappan, Portsmouth ... March, 1808. Isaac Sturtevant, printer. viii, [9]-392 p. 21 cm. Originally a series of sermons preached in Northampton in 1739, edited after the author's death, from his manuscripts, by John Erskine and Published in Edinburgh, 1774. [BT775.E2 1808] 43-31955
1. Redemption—Early works to 1800. I. Erskine, John, 1721-1803, ed. II. Title.

HOOKER, Thomas, 1586-1647. 234.3
Redemption : facsimile reproductions With an introd. by Everett H. Emerson Gainesville, Fla., Scholars' Facsimiles & Reprints, 1956. xvi, 139p. facsims. 23cm. [BT775.H77 1938a] 56-9145
1. Redemption —Early works to 1800. I. Title.
Contents omitted.

OWEN, John, 1616-1683. 234.
The death of death in the death of Christ. Being a treatise of the redemption and reconciliation that is in the blood of Christ; wherein the whole controversy about universal redemption, is fully discussed ... By John Owen, D. D. 1st American ed., carefully rev. and cor. Carlisle, (Pennsylvania) Printed by George Kline. M,DCC,XCII. xv, [17]-320 p. 21 cm. [BT775.O9 1792] 42-26088

1. Redemption—Early works to 1800. 2. Atonement—Early works to 1800. I. Title.

Redemption—History of doctrines.

THE doctrine of our redemption. With an introduction by William Temple, late Archbishop of Canterbury. 2d ed. London, Oxford University Press, 1960. xii, 115p. 19cm.
I. Micklem, Nathaniel, 1888-

HENNESSY, Augustine Paul. 234.3
...The victory of Christ over Satan in John Driedo's "De captivitate et redemptione generis humani." His sources and his influence. By Rev. Augustine P. Hennessy ...Washington, D.C., The Catholic University of America press, 1945 [i.e. 1946] xvii, 133 p. 23 cm. (The Catholic university of America. Studies in sacred theology, no. 99 [i.e. 99A]) Thesis (P.H. D.)--Catholic university of America, 1945. Bibliography: p. 124-130. [BT775.H38] A 48
1. Redemption-History of doctrines. I. Title.

HOGAN, William F., 1920- 234.3
Christ's redemptive sacrifice. Englewood Cliffs, N.J., Prentice [c.1963] 118p. illus. 23cm. (Found. of Catholic theology ser.) Bibl. 63-17628 3.95; 1.50 pap.,
1. Redemption—History of doctrines. 2. Atonement—Hist. I. Title.

MICKLEM, Nathaniel, 1888- 234.3
The doctrine of our redemption. Nashville, Abingdon-Cokesbury Press [1948] 155 p. 20 m. [BT775.M55 1948a] 48-2766
1. Redemption—History of doctrines. I. Title.

Redemption (Jewish theology)—History of doctrines—Sources.

REVELATION and redemption 296.3'2 : Jewish documents of deliverance from the fall of Jerusalem to the death of Nahmanides / introd., translation, conclusions, and notes by George Wesley Buchanan. 1st ed. Dillsboro, N.C. : Western North Carolina Press, c1978. vi, 632 p. ; 24 cm. Includes bibliographical references and indexes. [BM645.R4R48] 78-65146 ISBN 0-915948-04-4 : 29.50
1. Redemption (Jewish theology)—History of doctrines—Sources. 2. Messianic era (Judaism)—History of doctrines—Sources. I. Buchanan, George Wesley.

Redemption-Study and teaching—Text-books.

BJORNARD, Reidar B.
Toward man's redemption. Illus. by John Gretzer; cover by David Monyer. Valley Forge, Judson Press [1964] 128 p. illus. 21 cm. (The redemptive purpose of God. Year 11, part 1: The place of Israel in the redemptive purpose of God) "An official publication of the American Baptist Board of Education and Publication." NUC65
1. Redemption-Study and teaching—Text-books. 2. Israel—Hist.—Study and teaching—Text-books. 3. Religious education—Text-books—Baptist. I. American Baptist Convention. Board of Education. II. Title.

Redemptorists.

MAURON, Nicholas, 1818-1893. 271.6
Circular letters (selected) of Redemptorist generals, the Most Reverend Nicholas Mauron ... [and] the Most Reverend Methias Ruas ... with introductory study of the spirit of St. Alphonsus and his institute. Milwaukee, The Bruce publishing company [c1933] xiii, 297 p. 22 cm. Edited by Rev. D. F. Miller. [BX4020.M34] 33-11131
1. Liguori, Alfonso Maria de', Saint, 1696-1787. 2. Redemptorists. I. Raus, Mathias, 1829-1917. II. Miller, Donald Ferdinand, 1903- ed. III. Title.

WERGUET, Stanislaus, 1879- 271.6
The model Redemptorist brother; a manual of spiritual direction and prayer, by Rev. Stanislaus Werguet...Translated and adpated by Rev. Joseph W. Printon... St. Louis, Mo., Redemptorist fathers [c1932] xvii, 448 p. incl. front. 17 cm. Portions of "The lay-brother's prayer book" (p. 245-448) in Latin and English. [BX4020.W4] 33-3614
1. Redemptorists. I. Printon, Joseph W., 1882- ed. and tr. II. Catholic church. Liturgy and ritual. Redemptorist. III. Title.

Redemptorists in the United States

BYRNE, John F.
The Redemptorist centenaries: 1732, founding of the Congregation of the Most Holy Redeemer; 1832, establishment in United States, by John F. Byrne ... Philadelphia, Pa., The Dolphin press, 1932. xvi, 628 p. front. 24 cm. "Foreword" (2 p.) inserted between p. [vi] and vii. Bibliography: p. 589-595. A 41
1. Redemptorists in the U. S. 2. Redemptorists. I. Title.

SKINNER, Thomas Lawrence, 1886- 271.6
The Redemptorists in the West, by T. L. Skinner, C.SS.R. St. Louis, Mo., Redemptorists fathers [c1933] xiii, 514 p. front. (port.) 23 1/2 cm. Bibliography: p. 497-499. [BX4020.S5] 33-9783
1. Redemptorists in the U.S. I. Title.

WISSEL, Joseph, 1830-1912. 252'.02
The Redemptorist on the American missions / Joseph Wissel. New York : Arno Press, 1978. 3 v. in 2 ; 21 cm. (The American Catholic tradition) Reprint of the 1920 ed. privately printed and issued in 3 v. [BX4020.Z5U548 1978] 77-11322 ISBN 0-405-10867-2 : 86.00
1. Redemptorists in the United States. 2. Spiritual exercises. 3. Sermons—Outlines. I. Title. II. Series.

Redfield, John Wesley, 1810-1863.

TERRILLE, Joseph Goodwin. 922
The life of Rev. John Wesley Redfield, M.D. By Rev. Joseph Goodwin Terrill ... Chicago, Ill., The author, 1889. xx, 464, [1] p. front. (port.) 20 cm. [BX8495.R35T4] 37-7026 37-7026
1. Redfield, John Wesley, 1810-1863. I. Title.

Redmond, Sidney Dillion. 1871-1948.

WILSON, Charles H 1905- 920
God! Make me a man! A biographical sketch of Dr. Sidney Dillion Redmond. Boston, Meador Pub. Co. [1950] 61 p. port. 21 cm. [E185.97.R4W5] 50-7852
1. Redmond, Sidney Dillion. 1871-1948. I. Title.

Redner, Lewis H., 1831-1908.

BANCROFT, Charles W. H. 783.6'5'54
O little town of Bethlehem; the story of the carol, 1868-1968, by Charles Bancroft. Philadelphia, Church of the Holy Trinity [1968] v, 19 p. facsims., music, photos. 22 cm. Facsim. of holograph: p. 19. Words by Phillips Brooks, music by Lewis H. Redner. [ML410.R242B4] 76-2023
1. Redner, Lewis H., 1831-1908. O little town of Bethlehem. 2. Brooks, Phillips, Bp., 1835-1893. O little town of Bethlehem. I. Title.

Reducing—Moral and religious aspects.

KREML, Patricia Banta. 248'.86
Slim for Him : Biblical devotions on diet / by Patricia Banta Kreml. Plainfield, N.J. : Logos International, c1978. 163 p. ; 21 cm. [RM222.2.K73] 78-53422 ISBN 0-88270-300-5 pbk. : 2.95
1. Reducing—Moral and religious aspects. 2. Christian life—1960- I. Title.

Redwood Chapel Community Church, Castro Valley, Calif.

PALMER, Bernard Alvin, 1914- 254
Pattern for a total church : Sherman Williams and his staff share ways any church can grow / Bernard Palmer. Wheaton, Ill. : Victor Books, c1975. 135 p. : ill. ; 21 cm. Includes index. [BX9999.C3P34] 75-8026 ISBN 0-88207-717-1 : 2.50
1. Redwood Chapel Community Church, Castro Valley, Calif. I. Williams, Sherman. II. Title.

Reeb, James Joseph, 1927-1965.

HOWLETT, Duncan 288.330924
No greater love: the James Reeb Story. New York, Harper [c.1966] xii, 242p. illus., ports. 22cm. [BX9869.R4H6] 66-11489 4.95
1. Reeb, James Joseph, 1927-1965. I. Title.

Reed, Fred M., 1894-

BUROKER, Leonard Peres, 1902- 922
A man made whole; the life story of Fred M. Reed, by L. Peres Buroker. Des Moines, Ia., F. M. Reed [c1935] 99 p. front., pl. ports. 19 cm. [BV3785.R4B8] 43-21220
1. Reed, Fred M., 1894- I. Title.

Reed, John, 1751-1831. A sermon preached before the Plymouth association of ministers.

NILES, Samuel, 1743-1814. 233.2
Remarks on a sermon preached before the Plymouth association of ministers in the third Congregational society in Milldeborough, Sept. 26, 1810, by John Reed, D. D., pastor of the 1st church and congregation in Bridgewater. By Samuel Niles A. M., pastor of the 1st church and congregation in Abington ... Boston; Printed and sold by Lincoln & Edmands, no. 53 Cornhill, 1813. 62 p. 24 cm. [BX7233.R397S43] 35-32286
1. Reed, John, 1751-1831. A sermon preached before the Plymouth association of ministers. 2. Sin. 3. Free will and determinism. 4. Congregational churches—Sermons. I. Title.

Reed, Mary, 1854-

JACKSON, John, 1853-1917. 266
Mary Reed, missionary to the lepers, by John Jackson ... with introductory note by Rev. F. B. Meyer ... New York, Chicago [etc.] Fleming H. Revell company [1900?] 127, [1] p. ports. (incl. front.) 19 cm. An account of the work of the Mission to lepers. [BV2637.J2] 12-18629
1. Reed, Mary, 1854- 2. Leprosy—India. 3. Mission to lepers. 4. Missions—Lepers. I. Title.

Reed, Rebecca Theresa, b. ca. 1813.

†REED, Rebecca Theresa. 271'.974'024 B
Six months in a convent, and supplement / Rebecca Theresa Reed. New York : Arno Press, 1977. 192, 264 p. ; 21 cm. (Anti-movements in America) Reprint of the 1835 ed. published by Russell, Odiorne & Metcalf, Boston. Includes bibliographical references. [BX4668.3.R38A37 1977] 76-46097 ISBN 0-405-09970-3 : 26.00
1. Reed, Rebecca Theresa, b. ca. 1813. 2. Charlestown, Mass. Ursuline Convent. 3. Ex-nuns—Massachusetts—Biography. I. Title. II. Series.

Reed, Rebecca Theresa, b. ca. 1813. Six months in a convent.

[MOFFATT, Mary Anne Ursula] 264 in religion Mary Edmont Saint George.
An answer to Six months in a convent, exposing its falsehoods and manifold absurdities. By the lady superior. With some preliminary remarks. Boston, J. H. Eastburn [etc.] 1835. xxxvii, [1], 66 p. 24 cm. [F74.C4R35] [AC901.M2 vol. 21] 974. 13-7172
1. Reed, Rebecca Theresa, b. ca. 1813. Six months in a convent. 2. Charlestown, Mass. Ursuline convent. I. Title.

Rees, Emory J., 1870-1947.

EMERSON, Elizabeth Holaday. 266'.96'0924 B
Emory J. Rees language pioneer; a biographical sketch, by Elizabeth H. Emerson. [Gowanda, N.Y., Niagara Frontier Pub. Co., 1958] 25 p. 23 cm. Includes bibliographical references. [BV3625.K42R433] 74-156675
1. Rees, Emory J., 1870-1947. 2. Logooli language. I. Title.

Rees, Seth Cook, 1854-1933.

REES, Paul Stromberg. 922.89
Seth Cook Rees, the warrior-saint, by Paul S. Rees. Indianapolis, Ind., The Pilgrim book room, 1934. ix, p., 2 l., 194 p. front., pl., ports. 19 1/2 cm. [BX7990.H62R47] 44-22353
1. Rees, Seth Cook, 1854-1933. I. Title.

REES, Paul Stromberg. 922.89
Seth Cook Rees, the warrior-saint, by Paul S. Rees ... Indianapolis, Ind., The Pilgrim book room, 1934. ix p., 2 l., 194 p. front. pl., ports. 19 1/2 cm. [BX7990.H62R47] 44-22353
1. Rees, Seth Cook, 1854-1933. I. Title.

REES, Seth Cook.
Fire from heaven. Cincinnati, O., M. W. Knapp, 1899. 329 p. port. 12° A collection of sermons. 31,
I. Title.

Reeve, Becky.

REEVE, Becky. 289.3'3 B
The spirit knows no handicap / Becky Reeve. [Salt Lake City? Utah] : Bookcraft, c1980. 94 p., [4] leaves of plates : ports. ; 24 cm. [BX8695.R42A34] 19 80-65245 ISBN 0-88494-397-6 : 4.95
1. Reeve, Becky. 2. Mormons and Mormonism in Utah—Biography. 3. Quadriplegics—Utah—Biography. 4. Utah—Biography. I. Title.

Reeves, Mrs. Hannah (Pearce) 1800-1868.

BROWN, George, b.1792. 922.773
The lady preacher; or, The life and labors of Mrs. Hannah Reeves, late the wife of the Rev. Wm. Reeves, D.D., of the Methodist church. By the Rev. George Brown, D.D. Philadelphia, Daughaday & Becker; Springfield, O., Methodist publishing house, 1870. 343 p. front. (port.) 19 cm. [BX8495.R42B7] 37-7027
1. Reeves, Mrs. Hannah (Pearce) 1800-1868. I. Title.

Reeves, William, 1779-1852.

CORDEROY, Edward. 922.742
Father Reeves, the Methodist class-leader; a brief account of Mr. William Reeves, thirty-four years a class-leader in the Westelyan Methodist society, Lambeth. By Edward Corderoy. New-York, Carlton & Phillips, 1853. 160 p. 16 cm. [BX8495.R44C6] 37-7036
1. Reeves, William, 1779-1852. I. Title.

Reference books—Catholic Church.

ATCHLEY, Edward Godfrey Cuthbert Frederic. 220.
The churchman's glossary of ecclesiastical terms, by E. G. Cuthbert F. Atchley ... and E. G. P. Wyatt. London [etc.] A. R. Mowbray & co. ltd. Milwaukee, The Morehouse publishing co. [1923] viii, 206 p., 1 l. 22 cm. [BR95.A37] 24-4543
I. Wyatt, Edward Gerald Penfold, 1869- joint author. II. Title.

MCCABE, James Patrick. 011'.02
Critical guide to Catholic reference books / by James Patrick McCabe ; with an introd. by Russell E. Bidlack. 2d ed. Littleton, Co : Libraries Unlimited, 1980. 282 p. ; 24 cm. (Research studies in library science ; no. 2) Includes index. [Z674.R4 no. 2, 1980] [Z7837] [BX1751.2] 80-16209 ISBN 0-87287-203-3 : 22.50
1. Catholic Church—Bibliography. 2. Reference books—Catholic Church. I. Title. II. Series.

Reference books—Catholic literature.

MCCABE, James Patrick. 011'.02
Critical guide to Catholic reference books. With an introd. by Russell E. Bidlack. Littleton, Colo., Libraries Unlimited, 1971. 287 p. 24 cm. (Research studies in library science, no. 2) Based on the author's thesis, University of Michigan. Bibliography: p. 246-248. [Z674.R4 no. 2] 78-144202 ISBN 0-87287-019-7
1. Reference books—Catholic literature. 2. Catholic literature—Bibliography. I. Title. II. Series.

Reference books—Theology.

KEPPLE, Robert J. 016.2
Reference works for theological research : an annotated selective bibliographical guide / Robert J. Kepple. 2nd ed. Washington, D.C. : University Press of America, c1981. xiv, 283 p. ; 23 cm. Includes index. [Z7751.K46 1981] [BR118] 19 81-40350 ISBN 0-8191-1679-3 : 21.50 ISBN 0-8191-1680-7 (pbk.) : 11.75
1. Reference books—Theology. 2. Reference books—Religion. 3. Theology—Bibliography. 4. Religion—Bibliography. I. Title.

Reference (Philosophy)

SALMON, Nathan U., 1951- 110
Reference and essence / Nathan U. Salmon. Princeton, N.J. : Princeton University Press, c1981. xvi, 293 p. ; 24 cm. Based on the author's thesis (Ph.D.)—University of California at Los Angeles, 1979. Includes indexes. Bibliography: p. 265-278. [B105.R25S24] 19 81-8687 ISBN 0-691-07264-7 : 45.00
1. Putnam, Hilary. 2. Reference (Philosophy) 3. Essence (Philosophy) 4. Object (Philosophy) I. Title.

Reference services (Libraries)—Moral and ethical aspects.

ETHICS and reference 174'.9092
services / Bill Katz and Ruth Fraley, editors. New York : Harworth Press, c1982. p. cm. (The Reference librarian ; no. 4) Includes bibliographical references. [Z711.E85 1982] 19 82-11862 ISBN 0-86656-112-9 (pbk.) : 15.00
1. Reference services (Libraries)—Moral and ethical aspects. I. Katz, William A., 1924- II. Fraley, Ruth. III. Series.

Reform church in America—Hymns.

REFORMED church in 264.057
America.
The Psalms of David, with hymns and spirtual songs, having the proper metre prefixed to each. Also, the Catechism, Compendium, Confession of faith and Liturgy, of the Reformed church in the Netherlands. For the use of the Reformed Dutch church in North-America. Albany: Printed and sold, by Charles R. and George Webster, at their printing-office and bookstore, in the white house, corner of State & Pearl streets M, D.CC,XCVI 530, [10] p. 14 1/2 cm. Signatures: A-Z 13-4 (incl. w): As-Ee 8-13. Certification signed: John H. Livingston. Without music. [Ten] pages at end, advertising matter. [BV434.A3 1796] 32-18634
1. Reform church in America—Hymns. 2. Hymns. English. I. Bible. O.T. Psalms. English. Paraphrases. 1796. II. Bible. English. Paraphrases O.T. Psalms. 1796. III. Heidelberg catechism. IV. Nationale synode te Dordrecht, 1618-1619. V. Livingston, John Henry. 1746-1825. VI. Title.

Reform Judaism.

FREEHOF, Solomon Bennett, 292
1892-
Reform Jewish practice and its rabbinic background. [v. 1 & 2. combined ed.] New York, Union of Amer. Hebrew Congregations [1963, c.1944] 196; 138p. 20cm. Bibl. 5.95
1. Reform Judaism. I. Title.

HERTZ, Richard C 296
The American Jew in search of himself; a preface to Jewish commitment. New York, Bloch Pub. Co. [1962] 209p. 21cm. Includes bibliography. [BM197.H4] 62-14460
1. Reform Judaism. I. Title.

LENN, Theodore I.
Rabbi and synagogue in Reform Judaism [by] Theodore I. Lenn and Associates. New York, KTAV Pub. House [1972] Commissioned by the Central Conference of American Rabbis. pap. 8.50.

SCHWARTZMAN, Sylvan David. 296
Reform Judaism in the making. New York, Union of AmericanHebrew Congregations [1955] 194p. illus. 24cm. (Commission on Jewish Education of the Union of American Hebrew Congregations and Central Conference of American Rabbis. Union graded serie Includes bibliography. [BM197.S33] 56-204
1. Reform Judaism. I. Title.

SCHWARTZMAN, Sylvan David. 296
The story of Reform Judaism. New York, Union of American Hebrew Congregations [1953] 191p. illus. 24cm. (Commission on Jewish Education of the Union of American Hebrew Congregations and Central Conference of American Rabbis. Union graded series) [BM197.S34] 54-1803
1. Reform Judaism. I. Title.

SILVERMAN, William B. 296.8'346
Basic reform Judaism, by William B. Silverman. New York, Philosophical Library [1970] xiii, 292 p. 22 cm. Bibliography: p. 277-285. [BM197.S48] 69-15531 8.50
1. Reform Judaism. I. Title.

Reform Judaism—Addresses, essays, lectures.

BLAU, Joseph Leon, 296.8'346
1909- comp.
Reform Judciism : essays from the Yearbook of the Central Conference of American Rabbis. Selected, edited, and with an introd. by Joseph L. Blau. New York, Ktav Pub. House, 1973. viii, 529 p. 24 cm. Includes bibliographical references. [BM197.B55] 72-428 ISBN 0-87068-191-5 15.00
1. Reform Judaism—Addresses, essays, lectures. 2. Judaism—United States—Addresses, essays, lectures. I. Central Conference of American Rabbis. Yearbook. II. Title.

CONTEMPORARY Reform 296.8'346
Jewish thought. Edited by Bernard Martin. Chicago, Published in cooperation with the Central Conference of American Rabbis by Quadrangle Books [1968] 216 p. 22 cm. Includes bibliographical references. [BM197.C62] 67-13461 5.95
1. Reform Judaism—Addresses, essays, lectures. I. Martin, Bernard, 1928- ed. II. Central Conference of American Rabbis.

FELDMAN, Abraham Jehiel, 296.61
1893-
The American Reform rabbi; a profile of a profession, by Abraham J. Feldman. With an introd. by Nelson Glueck. New York, Published for Hebrew Union College Press by Bloch Pub. Co. [c1965] xiii, 242 p. 22 cm. [BM197.F44] 63-22502
1. Reform Judaism—Addresses, essays, lectures. I. Title.

GEIGER, Abraham, 1810- 296.8'346
1874.
Abraham Geiger and liberal Judaism : the challenge of the nineteenth century / compiled with a biographical introduction by Max Wiener ; translation from the German by Ernst J. Schlochauer. Cincinnati : Hebrew Union College Press ; New York, N.Y. : Distributed by KTAV Pub. House, 1981, c1962. p. cm. Reprint. Originally published: Philadelphia : Jewish Publication Society of America, 1962. [BM197.G38213 1981] 19 81-4524 ISBN 0-87820-800-3 (pbk.) ; 9.95
1. Geiger, Abraham, 1810-1874—Addresses, essays, lectures. 2. Reform Judaism—Addresses, essays, lectures. 3. Judaism—History—Addresses, essays, lectures. 4. Rabbis—Germany—Biography—Addresses, essays, lectures. I. Wiener, Max, 1882-1950. II. [Selections.] English III. Title.

Reform Judaism—Canada.

ROSE, Albert, 1917- ed. 296.834
A people and its faith; essays on Jews and reform Judaism in a changing Canada. [Toronto] University of Toronto Press, 1959. 204p. 22cm. [BM197.R6] 60-4797
1. Reform Judaism—Canada. 2. Jews in Canada—Hist. I. Title.

Reform Judaism—Ceremonies and practices.

BIAL, Morrison David, 296.8'346
1917-
Liberal Judaism at home; the practices of modern reform Judaism. [Rev. ed. New York] Union of American Hebrew Congregations [1971] xiii, 208 p. illus. 22 cm. Bibliography: p. 207-208. [BM197.B5 1971] 76-32236
1. Reform Judaism—Ceremonies and practices. I. Title.

DOPPELT, Frederic Aubrey. 296.4
A guide for Reform Jews, by Frederic A. Doppelt and David Polish. Rev. ed., by David Polish. New York, Ktav Pub. House [1974, c1973] 124 p. 22 cm. Bibliography: p. 124. [BM700.D6 1974] 73-20243 ISBN 0-87068-237-7 2.50 (pbk.).
1. Reform Judaism—Ceremonies and practices. I. Polish, David, joint author. II. Title.

Reform Judaism—Charleston, S.C.

SILBERMAN, Lou 296.8'346'09757915
H.
American impact: Judaism in the United States in the early nineteenth century [by] Lou H. Silberman. [Syracuse, N.Y., Syracuse University, 1964] [30] p. 23 cm. (B. G. Rudolph lectures in Judaic studies) Lecture delivered on April 29, 1964, at Syracuse University. Includes bibliographical references. [BM225.C4S5] 73-171337
1. Reformed Society of Israelites, Charleston, S.C. 2. Reform Judaism—Charleston, S.C. I. Title. II. Series.

Reform Judaism—Collected works.

GEIGER, Abraham, 1810- 296.834
1874
Abraham Geiger and liberal Judaism; the challenge of the nineteenth century. Comp., biographical introd. by Max Wiener. Tr. from German by Ernst J. Schlochauer. [Philadelphia, Jewish Pubn. [c.]1962. 305p. 22cm. 61-11705 4.50
1. Reform Judaism—Collected works. I. Wiener, Max, 1882-1950, comp. II. Title.

PLAUT, W. Gunther, 1912- 296.834
ed.
The rise of Reform Judaism. [v.2] [Foreword by Jacob K. Shankman] New York, World Union for Progressive Judaism [1966, c.1965] 383p. 25cm. Contents.[v.2] The growth of Reform Judaism, American and European sources until 1948. Bibl. [BM197.P6] 63-13568 1.50
1. Reform Judaism—Collections. I. Title.

PLAUT, W. Gunther, 1912- 296.834
ed.
The rise of Reform Judaism. Pref. by Solomon B. Freehof. New York, World Union for Progressive Judaism [dist. Union of Amer. Hebrew Cong. [c.1963] 288p. 25cm. Contents.[1] A sourcebook of its European origins. Bibl. 63-13568 6.00
1. Reform Judaism—Collections. I. Title.
Contents omitted.

PLAUT, W Gunther, 1912- 296,834
ed.
The rise of Reform Judaism. Pref. by Solomon B. Freehof. New York, World Union for Progressive Judaism [1963-65] 2 v. 25 cm. Vol. 2, with foreword by Jacob K. Shankman, has title: The growth of Reform Judaism. Contents.--A sourcebook of its European origins.--American and European sources until 1948. Includes bibliographies. [BM197.P6] 65-18555
1. Reform Judaism—Collections. I. Title. II. Title: The growth of Reform Judaism.

Reform Judaism—Controversial literature.

ANTELMAN, Marvin S., 296.8'346
1933-
To eliminate the opiate, by Marvin S. Antelman. [New York, Zahavia, 1974- v. illus. 18 cm. [BM197.A7] 74-180467 2.97 (pbk. vol. 1)
1. Bund der Kommunisten. 2. Reform Judaism—Controversial literature. 3. Illuminati. I. Title.
Publisher's address: 249 South Lafayette Park Place, Los Angeles, Ca 90057.

Reform Judaism—Controversial literature—History and criticism.

GUTTMANN, Alexander. 296.8'346
The struggle over reform in Rabbinic literature of the last century and a half / Alexander Guttmann. New York : Union of American Hebrew Congregations, [1976] p. cm. Includes index. "Hebrew sources": p. [BM197.G86] 75-45046 ISBN 0-8074-0005-X
1. Reform Judaism—Controversial literature—History and criticism. 2. Responsa—1800- —History and criticism. I. Title.

Reform Judaism—History.

PHILIPSON, David, 296.8'346'09
1862-1949.
The reform movement in Judaism. A reissue of the new and rev. ed., with an introd. by Solomon B. Freehof. [New York] Ktav Pub. House [1967] xxi, 503 p. 23 cm. Bibliographical references included in "Notes" (p. 437-491) [BM197.P55 1967] 67-11906
1. Reform Judaism—History. I. Freehof, Solomon Bennett, 1892- II. Title.

SCHWARTZMAN, Sylvan 296.8'346
David.
Reform Judaism then and now [by] Sylvan D. Schwartzman. New York, Union of American Hebrew Congregations [1971] xi, 339 p. illus. 27 cm. Bibliography: p. 329-332. [BM197.S334] 76-31681
1. Reform Judaism—History. I. Title.

Reform Judaism—Juvenile literature.

FREEMAN, Grace R. 296
Inside the synagogue, by Grace R. Freeman, Joan G. Sugarman. Photography by Justin E. Kerr, others. Illus. by Judith Oren. New York, Union of Amer. Hebrew Congregations [c.1963] unpaged. illus. 62-19996 2.50; 2.63 bds., lib. ed.,
1. Reform Judaism—Juvenile literature. I. Sugarman, Joan G., joint author. II. Title.

FREEMAN, Grace R
Inside the synagogue, by Grace R. Freeman and Joan G. Sugarman. Photography by Justin E. Kerr and others. Illus. by Judith Oren. [2d ed.] New York, Union of American Hebrew Congregations [1965] [57] p. illus. 32 cm. 68-45987
1. Reform Judaism—Juvenile literature. I. Sugarman, Joan G., joint author. II. Union of American Hebrew Congregations. III. Title.

Reform Judaism—United States.

BOROWITZ, Eugene B. 296.8'346
Reform Judaism today / by Eugene B. Borowitz. New York : Behrman House, c1977. p. cm. Contents.Contents.—Book 1. Reform in the process of change.—Book 2. What we believe.—Book 3. How we live. [BM197.B67] 77-24676 ISBN 0-87441-271-4 pbk. : 2.45
1. Central Conference of American Rabbis. Reform Judaism, a centenary perspective. 2. Reform Judaism—United States. I. Title.

POLISH, David. 296.8'34
Renew our days : the Zionist issue in Reform Judaism / by David Polish ; with a foreword by Richard G. Hirsch. [Jerusalem] : World Zionist Organization, 1976. 276 p. ; 20 cm. Includes index. Bibliography: p. 269. [BM197.P68] 77-356707 pbk. : 2.95
1. Reform Judaism—United States. 2. Zionism. I. Title.

SOFFIN, Joel. 296.8'346
A leader's guide / prepared by Joel Soffin. New York : Behrman House, c1979. xii, 178 p. ; 19 cm. On spine: IV, Reform Judaism today: leader's guide. Prepared for Reform Judaism today, by E. B. Borowitz. [BM197.B673S64] 79-120372 ISBN 0-87441-277-3 pbk. : 3.50
1. Borowitz, Eugene B. Reform Judaism today. 2. Central Conference of American Rabbis. Reform Judaism, a centenary perspective. 3. Reform Judaism—United States. I. Borowitz, Eugene B. Reform Judaism today. II. Title: Reform Judaism today.

Reform Judaism — United States — Directories

UNION of American Hebrew Congregations.
Handbook; basic information about the Union of American Hebrew Congregations. [New York] 1961. ix, 334 p. ports., tables. 16 cm. [BM60.U5] 63-32871
1. Reform Judaism — U.S. — Direct. I. Title.

Reform Judaism—United States—History—20th century.

GREENSTEIN, Howard R. 296.3'877
Turning point, Zionism and reformed Judaism / by Howard R. Greenstein. Chico, CA : Scholars Press, c1981. p. cm. (Brown Judaic studies ; no. 12) Bibliography: p. [BM197.G72] 19 81-8996 ISBN 0-89130-511-4 ISBN 0-89130-512-2 pbk. : 12.00
1. Reform Judaism—United States—History—20th century. 2. Zionism and Judaism. I. Title. II. Series.
Publisher's address: 101 Salem St., Chico, CA 95926.

Reformation.

AGATE, Leonard D.
Luther and the reformation, by Leonard D. Agate. London [etc.] T. C. & E. C. Jack. New York, Dodge publishing co. [1914] 93, [1] p. incl. front. (port.) 16 cm. (half-title: The people's books) Bibliography: p. 92-93. A 15
1. Luther, Martin, 1483-1546. 2. Reformation. I. Title.

AGATE, Leonard Dendy, 1886-
Luther and the reformation, by Leonard D. Agate ... London [etc.] T. C. & E. C. Jack; New York, Dodge publishing co. [1914] 93, [1] p. incl. front. (port.) 16 cm. (Half-title: The people's books) Bibliography: p. 92-93. A 15
1. Luther, Martin, 1483-1546. 2. Reformation. I. Title.

ALLEN, Fred Hovey, 1845-1926. 270.6
Popular history of the reformation, by Fred A. (1) Allen ... Boston, Estes and Lauriat, [1894]. 570 p. incl. front., illus., plates, ports, 18 cm. (On cover: The popular historical series.) "The principal part of this work appeared in serial form in the Golden Rule."--Pref. Published in 1887 under title: Young folks' history of the reformation. [BR305.A5 1894] 34-14832
1. Reformation. I. Title.

ALLEN, Fred Hovey, 1845-1926. 270.6
Young folk's history of the reformation, by Fred H. Allen ... Boxton, Estes and Lauriat, [c1887] 570 p. incl. front., illus., plates, ports. 18 1/2 cm. "The principal part of this work appeared in serial form in the Golden rule"--Pref. Published in 1894 under title: Popular history of the reformation. [BR305.A5 1887] 34-17926
1. Reformation. I. Title.

ANDERSON, Charles S. 270.6
The Reformation ... then and now [by] Charles S. Anderson. Minneapolis, Augsburg Pub. House [1966] 119, [1] p. 20 cm. (A Tower book) Bibliography: p. [120] [BR305.2.A5] 66-9710
1. Reformation. 2. Christianity—20th century. I. Title.

ATKINSON, James, 1914- 270.6
The great light; Luther and Reformation. Grand Rapids, W. B. Eerdmans Pub. Co. [1968] 287 p. 23 cm. (The Advance of Christianity through the centuries, v. 4) Bibliography: p. 266-276. [BR305.2.A73] 68-20590
1. Reformation. I. Title. II. Series.

AULEN Gustaf Emanuel Hildebrand Bp., 1879- 270.6
Reformation and catholicity. Tr. [from Swedish] by Eric H. Wahlstrom. Philadelphia, Muhlenberg [c.1961] 203p. Bibl. 61-10281 3.75
1. Reformation. 2. Justification—History of doctrines. 3. Authority (Religion) 4. Catholicity. I. Title.

AULEN, Gustaf Emanuel Hildebrand, Bp., 1879- 270.6
Reformation and Catholicity / by Gustaf Aulen ; translated by Eric H. Wahlstrom. Westport, Conn. : Greenwood Press, 1979, c1961. viii, 203 p. ; 23 cm. Translation of Reformation och katolicitet. Reprint of the ed. published by Muhlenberg Press, Philadelphia. Includes bibliographical references and index. [BR305.2.A813 1979] 78-25981 ISBN 0-313-20809-3 lib. bdg. : 17.50
1. Jesus Christ—History of doctrines. 2. Reformation. 3. Theology, Doctrinal—History—16th century. 4. Tradition (Theology) 5. Catholicity. I. Title.

BABINGTON, John Albert, 1843- 270.6
The Reformation; a religious and historical sketch. Port Washington, N.Y., Kennikat Press [1971] x, 362 p. 22 cm. Reprint of the 1901 ed. [BR305.B3 1971] 71-118513
1. Reformation.

BAINTON, Roland Herbert, 1894- 270.6
The age of the Reformation. Princeton, N.J., Van Nostrand [1956] 192 p. 18 cm. (An Anvil original, no. 13) [BR305.B33] 56-6880
1. Reformation. I. Title.

BAINTON, Roland Herbert, 1894- 270.6
The Reformation of the sixteenth century [Gloucester, Mass. Peter Smith 1962, c.1952] 278p. illus. 21cm. (Beacon Pr. bk. rebound) Bibl. 3.75
1. Reformation. I. Title.

BAINTON, Roland Herbert, 1894- 270.6
The Reformation of the sixteenth century. Boston, Beacon Press [1952] xi, 276 p. illus. 22 cm. Bibliography: p. 262-268. [BR305.B35] 52-5244
1. Reformation. I. Title.

BAINTON, Roland Herbert, 1894- 270.6
Studies on the Reformation. Boston, Beacon Press [1963] 289 p. illus. 21 cm. (His Collected papers in church history, ser. 2) Includes bibliographies. [BR305.2.B3] 63-17527
1. Reformation. I. Title.

BAUSLIN, David Henry, 1854-1922. 274.
The Lutheran movement of the sixteenth century; an interpretation, by David H. Bauslin ... Philadelphia, Pa., The Lutheran publication society [c1919] 368 p. 23 1/2 cm. [BR305.B4] 19-6062
1. Reformation. 2. Luther, Martin, 1483-1546. I. Title.

BEARD, Charles, 1827-1888. 270.6
The Reformation of the 16th century in its relations to modern thought and knowledge / by Charles Beard ; foreword by Joseph Dorfman ; introd. by Ernest Barker. Westport, Conn. : Greenwood Press, 1980. xxviii, 450 p. ; 23 cm. Reprint of the 1962 ed. published by University of Michigan Press, which was issued as no. AA61 of Ann Arbor paperbacks. Includes bibliographical references and index. [BR305.B45 1980] 80-12915 ISBN 0-313-22410-2 lib. bdg. : 33.50
1. Reformation. I. Title.

BEARD, Charles, 1827-1888. 270.6
The Reformation of the 16th century in its relation to modern thought and knowledge. Foreword by Joseph Dorfman. Introd. by Ernest Barker. [Ann Arbor] University of Michigan Press [1962] 450 p. 20 cm. (Ann Arbor paperbacks, AA61) [BR305.B45 1962] 62-53003
1. Reformation.

BELLOC, Hilaire, 1870- 274.
How the reformation happened by Hilaire Belloc ... New York, R. M. McBride & company, 1928. 3 p. l., 9-290 p. 23 cm. Illustrated lining-papers. [Full name: Joseph Hilaire Pierre Belloc] [BR305.B47] 28-13799
1. Reformation. I. Title.

BELLOC, Hilaire [Joseph Hilaire Pierre Belloc] 1870-1953. 270.6
How the Reformation happened [New York 16, Apollo Eds. Inc. 425 Park Ave., S. 1961, c.1928] 290p. (A-10) 1.95 pap.,
1. Reformation. I. Title.

CARTER, Thomas. 270.6
History of the great reformation in England, Ireland, Scotland, Germany, France, and Italy. By Rev. Thomas Carter. New York, Carlton & Porter; Boston, J. P. Magee, 1860. 1 p. l., 372 p. 20 cm. [BR305.C3] 34-16228
1. Reformation. I. Title.

CHADWICK, Owen 270.6
The Reformation. Grand Rapids, Mich., Eerdmans [1965, c,1964] 463p. maps. 22cm. Bibl. [BR305.2.C5] 5.95
1. Reformation. I. Title.

CHADWICK, Owen 270.6
The Reformation [Gloucester, Mass., P. Smith, c.1964] 463p. 19cm. (Pelican bk. A504. Pelican hist. of the Church v. 3) Bibl. 4.00
1. Reformation. I. Title.

CHADWICK, Owen 270.6
The Reformation. Baltimore, Penguin [1964] 463p. maps. 19cm. (Pelican hist. of the church, v. 3, A504) Bibl. 64-3925 1.95 pap.,
1. Reformation. I. Title.

CHADWICK, Owen. 270.6
The Reformation. [1st ed.], reprinted with revisions. Harmondsworth, Penguin, 1972. 463 p. 18 cm. (The Pelican history of the church, v. 3) (Pelican books) Bibliography: p. [446]-449. [BR305.2.C5 1972] 73-331082 ISBN 0-14-020504-7 £0.50
1. Reformation.

CHADWICK, Owen. 270.6
The Reformation. Grand Rapids, Eerdmans [1965, c1964] 463 p. 22 cm. (The Pelican history of the church, v. 3) "Suggestions for further reading": p. [446]-449. [BR305.2.C5 1965] 65-5283
1. Reformation.

COURVOISIER, Jaques. 270.6
Reformation and politics. Translated from the French by Grace A. Gibson. [Newcastle upon Tyne, University of Newcastle upon Tyne, 1971] 20 p. 21 cm. (Earl Grey memorial lecture, 50) [BR309.C6313] 73-157357 ISBN 0-900565-37-3 £0.25
1. Reformation. 2. Christianity and politics—History. I. Title. II. Series.

COWIE, Leonard W. 270.6
The Reformation [by] Leonard W. Cowie. Drawings by Elizabeth Hammond. [1st American ed.] New York, John Day Co. [1968] 112 p. illus., maps, ports. 23 cm. (Young historian books) [BR308.C6 1968] 68-11309
1. Reformation.

COWIE, Leonard W. 270.6
The Reformation [by] Leonard W. Cowie. Drawings by Elizabeth Hammond. [1st American ed.] New York, John Day Co. [1968] 112 p. illus., maps, ports. 23 cm. (Young historian books) Traces the events leading to the Reformation, the movements of Luther and Calvin, the reforms within the Catholic Church itself, the unique course of the reform movement in England, and the influence of the Reformation on New World settlements. [BR308.C6 1968] AC 68
1. Reformation. I. Hammond, Elizabeth, illus. II. Title.

COWIE, Leonard W. 270.6
The Reformation of the sixteenth century, by Leonard W. Cowie. New York, Putnam [1970] 128 p. illus., ports. 24 cm. (The Putnam documentary history series) Includes bibliographical references. [BR305.2.C65 1970b] 75-116150 4.95
1. Reformation. I. Title.

[CRAMP, John Mockett] 1796-1881. 270.6
The reformation in Europe. By the author of "The council of Trent." With a chronology of the reformation. New-York, The American tract society [184-?] 432 p. 16 cm. [BR305.C8] 34-17173
1. Reformation. I. American tract society. II. Title.

CRISTIANI, Leon [Augustin Louis Leon Pierre Cristiani] 270.6
The revolt against the church. Tr.from French by R. F. Trevett. New York, Hawthorn [c.1962] 142p. 21cm. (Twentieth century ency. of Catholicism, v.78. Sect. 7: The hist. of the church) Bibl. 62-12933 3.50 bds.,
1. Reformation. 2. Counter-Reformation. I. Title.

CROSBY, Ernest S. 270.6
Reformation and the reformers; a layman's story for laymen [Hartford 3, Conn., South Congregational Church, 1964] vii, 622p. illus., ports. 21cm. Bibl. 64-633 4.95
1. Reformation. I. Title.

DANIEL-ROPS, Henry, 1901-
The Protestant Reformation. Translated from the French by Audrey Butler. Garden City, N.Y., Image Books [1963] 2 v. in 1. 18 cm. Translation of Une revolution religieuse: la Reforms protestante. 66-5252
I. Title.

*D'AUBIGNE, J. H. Merle 270.'6
History of the reformation of the sixteenth century / by J. H. Merle D'Aubigne ; translated by H. White. Grand Rapids : Baker Book House, 1976. xxi, 867 p. ; 23 cm. (Religious heritage library) Contents.Vol. 1-5. [BR305.2] ISBN 0-8010-2859-0 : 14.95
1. Reformation. 2. Church history—Modern period, 1500- I. White, H. tr. II. Title.

DESMOND, Humphrey Joseph, 1858--1932. 904
Mooted questions of history By Humprey J. Desmond ... Re. ed. Boston, Marlier & co., 1901. viii, 328 p. 19 cm. [BX946.D4 1901] 1-30667
1. Reformation. 2. History—Addresses, essays, lectures. I. Title.

DICKENS, Arthur Geoffrey. 270.6
Reformation and society in sixteenth-century Europe [by] A. G. Dickens. [1st American ed. New York] Harcourt, Brace & World [1966] 216 p. illus. (part col.) facsims., maps (1 fold.) ports. (part col.) 21 cm. (History of European civilization library) Bibliography: p. 203-206. [BR305.2.D5 1966a] 66-19863
1. Reformation. I. Title.

DOLAN, John Patrick 270.6
History of the Reformation; a conciliatory assessment of opposite views. New York, Desclee [1965] xvii, 417p. 22cm. [BR305.2.D6] 65-22364 6.75
1. Reformation. I. Title.

DOLAN, John Patrick 270.6
History of the Reformation; a concilliatory assessment of opposite views. Introd. by Jaroslav Pelikan. New York, New Amer. Lib. [1967, c.1965] xv, 366p. 18cm. (Mentor-Omega MQ712) [BR305.2D6] .95 pap.,
1. Reformation. I. Title.

DONNELLY, John Patrick, 1934- 270.6
Reform and renewal / John Patrick Donnelly. [Wilmington, N.C.] : Consortium, c1977. 177 p. ; 23 cm. (Faith of our fathers ; v. 2) Bibliography: p. 176-177. [BR305.2.D64] 77-9994 9.50
1. Reformation. I. Title. II. Series.

ERASMUS, Desiderius, d.1536. 879.7
Inquisitio de fide; a colloquy, 1524. Edited with introd. and commentary by Craig R. Thompson. New Haven, Yale University Press, 1950. vi, 131 p. 25 cm. (Yale studies in religion, no. 15) Latin text accompanied by revision of English translation made by Nathan Bailey in 1725. Includes bibliographical references. [PA8509.I 6 1950] 50-14222
1. Reformation. I. Bailey, Nathan, d. 1742,

tr. II. Thompson, Craig Ringwalt, 1911- ed. III. Title. IV. Series.

ERASMUS, Desiderius, d.1536. 878'.04'07
Inquisitio de fide : a colloquy, 1524 / by Desiderius Erasmus Roterodamus ; edited with introd. and commentary by Craig R. Thompson. 2d ed. / introd. by Roland H. Bainton ; bibliography by Craig R. Thompson. Hamden, Conn. : Archon Books, 1975, c1950. p. cm. Latin text accompanied by revision of English translation made by Nathan Bailey in 1725. This "2d ed." is a reprint of the ed. published by Yale University Press, New Haven, which was issued as no. 15 of Yale studies in religion. Includes index. [PA8509.I6 1975] 74-31476
1. Reformation. I. Title. II. Series: Yale studies in religion ; no. 15.

FISHER, George Park, 1827-1909. 270.6
The reformation. By George P. Fisher... New York, Scribner, Armstrong and co., 1873. xxxiv, 620 p. 22 1/2 cm. "A list of works on the reformation": p. [567]-591. [BR305.F5 1873] 34-17925
1. Reformation. I. Title.

FISHER, George Park, 1827-1909. 274.
The reformation; by George P. Fisher... [New ed.] New York, Charles Scribner's sons, 1903. xxxiv, 620 p. 21 cm. "This work has grown out of a course of lectures...given at the Lowell institute in Boston...in the spring of 1871."--Pref. First published in 1873. "A list of works on the reformation": p. [537]-591. [BR305.F5 1908] 4-5621
1. Reformation. I. Title.

FISHER, George Park, 1827-1909. 274.
The reformation, by George Park Fisher... New and rev., ed. New York, C. Scribner's sons, 1906. xxx, 525 p. 22 cm. "A list of works on the reformation": p. 475-502. [BR305.F5 1906] 6-11660
1. Reformation. I. Title.

GAILLARD, Thomas. 270.6
The history of the reformation in the church of Christ; continued form the close of the fifteenth century. By Thomas Gaillard ... New York, M. W. Dodd, 1847. xv, 557 p. 23 cm. [BR305.G2] 34-19429
1. Reformation. I. Title.

GELDER, Herman Arend Enno van, 1889- 270.6
The two reformations in the 16th century: a study of the religious aspects and consequences of Renaissance and humanism. [Tr. from Dutch by Jan F. Finlay, Alison Hanham] The Hague, M. Nijhoff [dist. New York, Heinman, 1962, c.]1961. x, 406p. 25cm. Bibl. 63-228 12.50
1. Reformation. 2. Humanism. I. Title.

GOOD, James Isaac, 1850-
The Reformed reformation, by Rev. Prof. James I. Good ... [Philadelphia] The Heidelberg press, 1916. 4 p. l., 143, [1] p. 23 cm. [BR307.G6] 17-3325
1. Reformation. I. Title.

GOOD, James Isaac, 1850-1924.
Famous reformers of the Reformed and Presbyterian churches; a mission study manual on the reformation, by Rev. Prof. James. I. Good ... Published by the home and foreign mission boards of the Reformed church in the United States. Philadelphia, Pa., The Heidelberg press, 1916. xiii, 160 p. front., plates, port. 18 cm. [BR306.G6] 16-16154
1. Reformation. 2. Reformation—Biog. 3. Reformed church—Biog. I. Reformed church in the United States. Board of home missions. II. Reformed church in the United States. Board of foreign missions. III. Title.

GREEN, Vivian Hubert Howard 922.443
Luther and the Reformation. London, B. T. Batsford. New York, Putnam [c.1964] 208p. illus., ports., facsims. 23cm. Bibl. 64-13032 5.95
1. Luther, Martin, 1483-1546. 2. Reformation. I. Title.

GREEN, Vivian Hubert Howard. 922.443
Luther and the Reformation. London, B. T. Batsford; New York, Putnam [1964] 208 p. illus., ports., facsims. 23 cm. "Books for further reading": p. 200-201. [BR325.G68] 64-13032
1. Luther, Martin, 1483-1546. 2. Reformation. I. Title.

GREEN, Vivian Hubert Howard.
Luther and the Reformation. New York, Capricorn Books [c1964] 192 p. illus. Bibliography: p. 184-185. 65-109476
1. Luther, Martin, 1483-1546. 2. Reformations. I. Title.

GREENWALD, Emanuel, 1811-1885. 274.
Discourses on Romanism and the reformation, by Rev. E. Greenwood ... Lancaster, Pa., J. Baer's sons, printers, 1880. 185 p. 18 cm. [BR305.G7] 24-24525
1. Reformation. 2. Catholic church—Doctrinal and controversial works—Protestant authors. I. Title.

GRIMM, Harold John, 1901- 270.6
The Reformation [by] Harold J. Grimm. Washington, American Historical Association [1972] 34 p. 23 cm. (AHA pamphlets, 403) First published in 1964 under title: The Reformation in recent historical thought. Bibliography: p. 32-34. [BR309.G74 1972] 72-76717
1. Reformation. I. Series: American Historical Association. AHA pamphlets, 403.

GRIMM, Harold John, 1901- 270.6
The Reformation era, 1500-1650 [by] Harold J. Grimm. 2d ed. New York, Macmillan [1973] xiii, 594 p. illus. 24 cm. Bibliography: p. 509-580. [BR305.2.G74 1973] 72-91167 10.95
1. Reformation. I. Title.

GRIMM, Harold John, 1901- 270.6
The Reformation era, 1500-1650; with a revised and expanded bibliography [by] Harold J. Grimm New York, Macmillan [1965] xiii, 703 p. maps. 22 cm. Bibliography: p. 617-684. [BR305.2.G74 1965] 65-25864
1. Reformation. I. Title.

GRIMM, Harold John, 1901- 270.6
The Reformation era, 1500-1650 New York, Macmillan [1954] 675 p. illus. 22 cm. [BR305.G74] 54-12610
1. Reformation. I. Title.

HARBISON, Elmore Harris, 1907-1964. 940.22
The Age of Reformation. Ithaca, N.Y., Cornell University Press [1955] 145 p. illus. 22 cm. (The Development of Western civilization) [BR305.H28] 55-14204
1. Reformation. I. Title.

HARRY, Carolus Powel, 1884-
Protest and progress in the sixteenth century, by Carolus P. Harry. Philadelphia, Joint Lutheran committee on celebration of the quadricentennial of the reformation, 1917. xv, 162 p. front., plates, ports. 18 1/2 cm. [BR306.H3] 17-25089
1. Reformaton. I. Title.

HILLERBRAND, Hans J. 270.6
The world of the Reformation / Hans J. Hillerbrand. Grand Rapids, Michigan : Baker Book House, 1981, c1973. viii, 229 p. : map. ; 21 cm. Includes index. Bibliography :p.215-220. [BR305.2.H53 1973] ISBN 0-8010-4248-8 pbk.: 6.95
1. Reformation. I. Title.
L.C. card no. for the 1973 Scribner edition: 73-5175

HILLERBRAND, Hans Joachim. 270.6
Christendom divided; the Protestant Reformation [by] Hans J. Hillerbrand. New York, Corpus [1971] xiii, 344 p. 24 cm. (Theological resources) Bibliography: p. 321-336. [BR305.2.H49 1971] 70-93573 ISBN 0-664-20912-2 9.95
1. Reformation. I. Title.

HILLERBRAND, Hans Joachim, ed. 270.6082
The Reformation; a narrative history related by contemporary observers and participants [edited by] Hans J. Hillerbrand. [1st ed.] New York, Harper & Row [1964] 495 p. illus., facsims., ports. 25 cm. London ed. (Student Christian Movement Press) has title: The Reformation in its own words. Includes bibliographies. [BR305.2.H5 1964] 64-15480
1. Reformation.

HILLERBRAND, Hans Joachim. 270.6
The world of the Reformation [by] Hans J. Hillerbrand. New York, Scribner [1973] x, 229 p. map. 24 cm. Bibliography: p. 215-220. [BR305.2.H53 1973] 73-5175 ISBN 0-684-13534-5 10.00
1. Reformation. I. Title.

HOLL, Karl, 1866-1926. 270.6
The cultural significance of the Reformation. Introd. by Wilhelm Pauck. Translated by Karl and Barbara Hertz and John H. Lichtblau. New York, Meridian Books [1959] 191 p. 19 cm. (Living age books [LA25]) [BR307.H643] 59-7188
1. Reformation. I. Title.

HOLMIO, Armas Kustaa Ensio, 1897- 270.6
The Lutheran Reformation and the Jews; the birth of the Protestant Jewish missions. Hancock, Mich., Print. by Finnish Lutheran Book Concern [1949] 218 p. 22 cm. Thesis--Boston Univ. Bibliography: p. [191]-207. [BR355.J4H6] 49-6401
1. Reformation. 2. Jewish question. 3. Missions—Jews. I. Title.

HOUGH, Lynn Harold, 1877-
the significance of the Protestant reformation; a series of lectures delivered in connection with the observance of the four hundredth anniversary of the posting of the theses by Luther, by Lynn Harold Hough... New York, Cincinnati, The Abingdon press [c1918] 106 p. 17 1/2 cm. [BR397.H7] 18-9757
1. Reformation. I. Title.

HOW the reformation happened. [New York] Dodd, Mead, 1959. 290p. 21cm.
1. Reformation. I. Belloc, Hilaire, 1870-1953.

HUGHES, Philip, 1895-
A popular history of the Reformation. [New, rev. ed.] Garden City, N. Y., Image Books [1960] 313 p. (Doubleday Image book D92) 68-56313
1. Reformation. I. Title.

HUGHES, Philip, 1895- 270.6
A popular history of the Reformation. [1st ed.] Garden City, N. Y., Hanover House [1957] 343 p. 22 cm. [BR305.H68] 57-5788
1. Reformation. I. Title.

HURST, John Fletcher, bp., 1834-1903. 270.6
Short history of the reformation, by John F. Hurst ... New York, Harper & brothers, 1884. 3 p. l., 125 p. front., illus. (incl. port.) map. 16 cm. [BR305.H7] 31-10007
1. Reformation. I. Title.

ILLUSTRATED history of the Reformation. 270.6 Edited by Oskar Thulin. Translators: Jalo E. Nopola [and others] St. Louis, Concordia Pub. House [1967] 327 p. illus., facsims., maps, ports. 23 cm. Translation of Reformation in Europa. Bibliography: p. 319-321. [BR305.2.R413] 67-20941
1. Reformation. I. Thulin, Oskar, ed.

JONES, Alonzo T. 270.6
Lessons from the Reformation. Boston, Forum [1961] 404p. 3.00
I. Title.

JONES, Alonzo Trevier, 1850-
The reformation 14th-16th century; what it meant then, what it means now [by] Alonzo Trevier Jones. [Battle Creek, Mich., Printed at the Ellis publishing company] 1913. viii, 481 p. front. (port.) 21 cm. 13-13748 2.00
I. Title.

KIDD, Berenford James, 1863- ed. 270.
Documents illustrative of the continental reformation, edited by Rev. B. J. Kidd ... Oxford, The Clarendon press, 1911. xix, 742, [2] p. 20 cm. [BR301.K4] 11-23789
1. Reformation. I. Title.
Contents omitted.

KINGDON, Robert McCune, 1927- 914'.03'23
Transition and revolution; problems and issues of European Renaissance and Reformation history, edited by Robert M. Kingdon. Minneapolis, Burgess Pub. Co. [1974] viii, 274 p. 23 cm. Includes bibliographies. [BR309.K5] 74-75575 ISBN 0-8087-1118-0 3.95 (pbk.).
1. Reformation. 2. State, The—History. 3. Humanism. 4. Witchcraft—History. 5. Printing—History. I. Title.

KLASSEN, Peter James. 274
Europe in the Reformation / Peter J. Klassen. Englewood Cliffs, N.J. : Prentice Hall, c1979. vi, 297 p. : ill. ; 23 cm. Includes bibliographies and index. [BR305.2.K57] 78-11023 ISBN 0-13-292136-7 pbk. : 8.95
1. Reformation. 2. Europe—History—1492-1648. I. Title.

KRAUTH, Charles Porterfield, 1823-1883. 230.41
The Conservative Reformation and its theology. Minneapolis, Augsburg Pub. House [1963, c1899] xvii, 840 p. 24 cm. Bibliographical references included in footnotes. [BX8065.K7] 63-16600
1. Reformation. 2. Lutheran Church — Doctrinal and controversial works. I. Title.

KRAUTH, Charles Porterfield, 1823-1883. 230.41
The Conservative Reformation and its theology. Minneapolis, Augsburg Pub. House [1963, c1899] xvii, 840 p. 24 cm. Bibliographical references included in footnotes. [BX8065.K7 1963] 63-16600
1. Reformation. 2. Lutheran Church—Doctrinal and controversial works. I. Title.

LILJE, Hanns, 1899- 270.6
Luther now; translated by Carl J. Schindler. Philadelphia, Muhlenberg Press [1952] 190 p. 20 cm. Translation of Luther; Anbruch und Krise der Neuzeit. [BR325.L473] 52-9119
1. Luther, Martin, 1483-1546. 2. Reformation. I. Title.

LINDSAY, Thomas Martin, 1843-1914. 270.
... A history of the reformation, by Thomas M. Lindsay ... New York, C. Scribner's sons, 1906-07. 2 v. 21 cm. (Half-title: The International theological library. Ed. by C. A. Briggs ... and ... S. D. F. Salmond) Series title also at head of t.-p. Map in pocket (v. 2) Bibliographical foot-notes. Contents.--1. The reformation in Germany from its beginning to the religious peace of Augsburg.--ii. The reformation in Switzerland, France, the Netherlands, Scotland and England, the Anabaptists and Socinian movements, the counter-reformation. [BR305.L7 vol.1] 6-23686
1. Reformation. 2. Counter-reformation. 3. Socinianism. 4. Anabaptists. I. Title.

LORTZ, Joseph, 1887- 270.6
The Reformation: a problem for today. Translated by John C. Dwyer. Westminster, Md., Newman Press, 1964. 261 p. 23 cm. Translation of Die Reformation als religioses Anliegen heute. Bibliographical footnotes. [BR305.2.L613] 63-12239
1. Reformation. I. Title.

LUTHER, Martin, 1483-1546. 208.1
Reformation writings. Translated with introd. and notes from the definitive Weimar ed. by Bertram Lee Woolf. New York, Philosophical Library [1953- v. port. 23 cm. "A chronological table of Luther's writings...and of contemporary events": v. 1, p. [381]-387. Contents.Contents.—v. 1. The basis of the Protestant Reformation.—[BR331.E5W6] 53-8176
1. Reformation. I. Title.

MCCABE, James Dabney, 1842-1883. 270.
Cross and crown; or, The sufferings and triumphs of the heroic men and women who were persecuted for the religion of Jesus Christ. By James D. McCabe ... With illustrations on steel by Sartain and Illman ... Cincinnati, O., National publishing company; Philadelphia, Pa., Jones brothers & co., 1875. 619 p. front., plates. 23 1/2 cm. [BR315.M3] 18-5844
1. Reformation. 2. Persecution. 3. Waldenses. 4. Huguenots in France. 5.

Reformation—Gt. Brit. I. Sartain, John, 1808-1897, illus. II. Title.

MACKINNON, James, 1860- 922.
Luther and the reformation, by James Mackinnon... London, New York [etc.] Longmans, Green, and co., 1925-30. 4 v. 22 1/2 cm. L. C. copy incomplete: vol. II wanting. Contents.I. Early life and religious development to 1517.--II. The breach with Rome (1517-21)--III. Progress of the movement (1521-29)--IV. Vindication of the movement (1530-46) [BR325.M27] 25-20520
1. Luther, Martin, 1483-1546. 2. Reformation. I. Title.

MACKINNON, James, 1860- 922.443
1945.
Luther and the Reformation. New York, Russell & Russell, 1962. 4v. 22cm. Contents.v.1. Early life and religious development to 1517.--v.2. The breach with Rome (1517-21)--v.3. Progress of the movement (1521-29)--v.4. Vindication of the movement (1531-46) Bibliographical footnotes. [BR325.M27 1962] 62-10691
1. Luther, Martin, 1483-1546. 2. Reformation. I. Title.

MCLELLAND, Joseph C. 270.6
The Reformation and its significance today. Philadelphia, Westminster Press [1962] 238 p. 21 cm. Includes bibliography. [BR305.2.M3] 62-9810
1. Reformation. I. Title.

MEAD, Edwin Doak, 1849- 922.
Martin Luther; a study of reformation, by Edwin D. Mead. Boston, G. H. Ellis, 1884. 194 p. 18 cm. [BR325.M4] 12-36693
1. Luther, Martin, 1483-1546. 2. Reformation. I. Title.

MEE, Charles L. 270.6'092'4 B
White robe, black robe [by] Charles L. Mee, Jr. New York, Putnam [1972] 316 p. 22 cm. Bibliography: p. 301-303. [BR325.M4125 1972] 76-183547 7.95
1. Luther, Martin, 1483-1546. 2. Leo X, Pope, 1475-1521. 3. Reformation. I. Title.

MERLE d'Aubigne, Jean 922.443
Henri, 1794-1872.
The life and times of Martin Luther. Selections from D'Aubigne's famed History of the Reformation of the sixteenth century. Translated from the French by H. White and rev. by the author. Chicago, Moody Press, 1950. 559 p. 21 cm. (The Tyndale series of great biographies) [BR305.M52] 51-5666
1. Luther, Martin, 1483-1546. 2. Reformation. I. Series.

MERLE D'AUBIGNE, Jean Henri, 270.
1794-1872.
History of the great reformation of the sixteenth century in Germany, Switzerland, etc., by J. H. Merle d'Aubigne ... Philadelphia, Sorin & Ball, 1847. vi, 644 p. 24 cm. [BR305.M35 1847a] 43-36205
1. Reformation. I. Title.

MERLE D'AUBIGNE, Jean Henri, 274.
1794-1872.
History of the reformation in Europe in the time of Calvin. By J. H. Merle d'Aubigne ... New York, R. Carter & brothers, 1870. 5 v. 19 cm. Contents.--v. 1-2. Geneva and France--v. 3. France, Switzerland, Geneva.--v. 4. England, Geneva, France, German, and italy.--v. 5. England, Geneva, Ferrara. [BR305.M7 1870] 15-617
1. Reformation. I. Title.

MERLE D'AUBIGNE, Jean 270.6
Henri, 1794-1872.
History of the reformation in the sixteenth century. By J. H. Merle d'Augigne, D. D.; with twelve engravings on steel, after P. A. Labouchere, and two hundred illustrations on wood, including portraits of the most eminent reformers. New York, G. P. Putnam & sons, 1872. xxvi, 724 p. front., illus. (incl. ports.) plates. 28 cm. In double columns. [BR305.M5 1872a] 940.22 30-12930
1. Reformation. I. Title.

MERLE D'AUBIGNE, Jean Henri, 274.
1794-1872.
History of the reformation of the sixteenth century. By J. H. Merle d'Aubigne ... Tr. by H. White ... The translation carefully rev. by Dr. d'aubigne, who has also made various additions not hitherto published ... New York, American tract society, 1849-53. 5 v. fronts. (v. 1-2: ports.) facsim. 19 cm. Vol. 5. with subtitle "The reformation is England", published by R. Carter & brothers. "Messrs. Oliver & Boyd ... having stereotyped a new edition of this work under the immediate supervision of the author, a duplicate set of theirr stereotype plates ... procured from them and imported, from which, as revised by the author for the American tract society, the present edition is printed."--Note, verso of t.-p. of v. 1. [BR305.M5 1849] 12-30423
1. Reformation. I. White, Henry, 1812-1880, tr. II. Title.

MERLE D'AUBIGNE, Jean Henri, 274.
1794-1872.
History of the reformation of the sixteenth century. By J. H. Merle d'Aubigne ... Translated by H. White ... The translation carefully revised by Dr. d'Aubigne, who has also made various additions not hitherto published ... New York, R. Carter & brothers, 1872. 5 v. 20 cm. [BR305.M5 1872] 16-9635
1. Reformation. I. White, Henry, 1812-1880, tr. II. Title.

MOSSE, George Lachmann 270.6
The Reformation. 3d ed. [Gloucester, Mass., P. Smith, 1964, c.1953, 1963] 136p. 18cm. (Berkshire studies in European hist. rebound) Bibl. 2.50
1. Reformation. I. Title.

MOSSE, George Lachmann. 270.6
The Reformation. 3d ed. New York, Holt, Rinehart and Winston [1963] 136 p. 19 cm. (Berkshire studies in European history) [BR305.M96 1963] 63-11339
1. Reformation.

THE 'New Light Christians'; initiators of the nineteenth-century reformation. [Fort Worth, Texas, Copyright Colby D. Hall] 1959. 152p. 23cm.
I. Hall, Colby Dixon, 1875-

NICKERSON, Hoffman, 1888- 270.6
The loss of unity. Garden City, N. Y., Doubleday [1961] 360p. 61-12562 4.95
1. Reformation. I. Title.

PAINTER, Franklin Verzelius
Newton, 1852-
The reformation dawn... Philadelphia, Lutheran pub. society [1901] vi, 7-245 p. 16° (Lutheran hand-book series) 1-9367
I. Title.

PAINTER, Franklin Verzelius
Newton, 1852-1931.
The reformation dawn. By F. V. N. Painter ... Philadelphia, Lutheran pub. society [1901] vi, 7-245 p. 15 1/2 cm. (Lutheran hand-book series) [BR307.P3] 1-9367
1. Reformation. I. Lutheran publication society, Philadelphia. II. Title.

PELIKAN, Jaroslav Jan, 270.6
1923-
Obedient rebels; Catholic substance and Protestant principle in Luther's Reformation. [1st ed.] New York, Harper & Row [1964] 212 p. 24 cm. Bibliographical footnotes. [BR307.P4] 64-20200
1. Reformation. 2. Catholic Church—Relations—Protestant churches. 3. Protestant church—Relations—Catholic Church. I. Title.

PELIKAN, Jaroslav Jan, 270.6'0924
1923-
Spirit versus structure; Luther and the institutions of the church [by] Jaroslav Pelikan. [1st ed.] New York, Harper & Row [1968] x, 149 p. 21 cm. Bibliographical references included in "Notes" (p. 140-149) [BR325.P45] 68-29557
1. Luther, Martin, 1483-1546. 2. Reformation. I. Title.

PELIKAN, Jaroslaw, 1923- 270.6
Obedient rebels; Catholic substance and Protestant principle in Luther's Reformation. New York, Harper [c.1964] 212p. 24cm. Bibl. 64-20200 5.00
1. Reformation. 2. Catholic Church—Relations—Protestant churches. 3. Protestant church—Relations—Catholic Church. I. Title.

PHILLIPS, Margaret Mann. 922.2492
Erasmus and the northern Renaissance. New York, Macmillan, 1950. xxv, 236 p. map (on lining paper) 19 cm. (Teach yourself history) Bibliography: p. 228. [BR350.E7P5] 928.79 50-7057
1. Erasmus, Desiderius, d. 1536. 2. Reformation. I. Series: Teach yourself history library (New York)

PLUMMER, Alfred, 1841-1926.
The continental reformation in Germany, France and Switzerland from the birth of Luther to the death of Calvin, by the Rev. Alfred Plummer ... New York, C. Scribner's sons; London, R. Scott, 1912. xiii, 217 p. 21cm. "This volume reproduces the substance and for the most part the exact words of four lectures, delivered at Oxford, July, 1911, and which have appeared in a somewhat abbreviated form in the Churchman, October, 1911-May, 1912."--Pref. Chronological table: p. 192-197. Appendices: i, Extracts from the Epistolae obscurorum virorum, illustrating their treatment of Erasmus.--ii. Dollinger on Luther and the reformation in Germany-- iii. Specimens of Luther's teaching. Bibliography: p. ix-xiii. W17
1. Reformation. I. Title.

A popular history of the Reformation. Garden City, N. Y., Image Books [1960, c1957] 313p. 18cm.
1. Reformation. I. Hughes, Philip, 1895-

PORTEOUS, David. 270.6
Calendar of the Reformation. Pref. by Joseph Zacchello. New York, Loizeaux Bros. [1960] 96p. 21cm. Includes bibliography. [BR307.P65] 60-51665
1. Reformation. 2. Calendars. I. Title.

THE Reformation;
a history of European civilization from Wyclif to Calvin, 1300-1564. New York, Simon and Schuster, 1957. xviii, 1025p. illus., ports. (His The story of civilization. part 6)
1. Reformation. 2. Renaissance. I. Durant, William James, 1885-

THE Reformation.
New York, Holt [1960] vi, 103p. 19cm. (Berkshire studies in European history) 'Expanded edition.' Includes bibliography.
1. Reformation. I. Mosse, George Lachmann.

THE Reformation of the sixteenth century. Boston, Beacon Press [1956, c1952] xi, 276p. illus. 21cm. (Bacon paperbooks, BP22)
1. Reformation. I. Bainton, Roland Herbert, 1894-

THE Reformation of the sixteenth century. Boston, Beacon Press [1959, c1952] xi, 276p. illus. 21cm. (Beacon paperbacks, BP 22)
1. Reformation. I. Bainton, Roland Herbert, 1894-

THE Reformation of the sixteenth century. Boston, Beacon Press [1959, c1952] 278p. illus. 21cm. Bibliography: p. 262-269.
1. Reformation. I. Bainton, Roland Herbert, 1894-

ROBINSON, William Childs, 270.6
1897-
The Reformation; a rediscovery of grace. Grand Rapids, Eerdmans [1962] 189 p. 23 cm. [BT27.R6] 62-21373
1. Reformation. 2. Theology, Doctrinal—History—16th cen.

RUPP, Ernest Gordon. 270
The old Reformation and the new [by] Gordon Rupp. Philadelphia, Fortress Press [1967] 68 p. 18 cm. (The Cato lecture, 1966) [BR305.2.R8 1967b] 67-21530
1. Reformation. 2. Christianity—20th cent. 3. Church renewal. I. Title. II. Series.

SAMPLE, Robert Fleming, 270.6
1829-1905.
Beacon-lights of the reformation; or, Romanism and the reformers. By the Rev. Robert F. Sample, D.D. With introduction by the Rev. John Hall... Philadelphia, Presbyterian board of publication and Sabbath-school work [c1889] 1 p.l., viii, 452 p. 19 1/2 cm. [BR305.S3] 34-19437
1. Reformation. I. Hall, John, 1800-1894. II. Presbyterian church in the U.S.A. Board of publication. III. Title. IV. Title: Romanism and the reformers.
Contents omitted.

SANFORD, Elias Benjamin, 1843-
1932.
A history of the reformation, by Elias B. Sanford ... Hartford, Conn., The S. S. Scranton company [c1917] xiii p., 1 l., 287 p. 19 1/2 cm. Bibliography: p. xiii. [BR306.S3] 17-21496
1. Reformation. I. Title.

SCHMUCKER, Samuel Simon, 270.6
1799-1873.
Discourse in commemoration of the glorious reformation of the sixteenth century. Delivered before the Evangelical Lutheran synod of West Pennsylvania, by S. S. Schmucker ... Published by synod. New-York, Gould & Newman, 1838. 131 p. 16 cm. [BR309.S4 1838] 39-7368
1. Reformation. 2. Catholic church—Doctrinal and controversial works—Protestant authors. I. Evangelical Lutheran synod of West Pennsylvania. II. Title.

SCHMUCKER, Samuel Simon, 270.6
1799-1873.
Discourse in commemoration of the glorious reformation of the sixteenth century. Delivered before the Evangelical Lutheran synod of West Pennsylvania, by S. S. Schmucker ... Published by synod. 2d ed., improved. New York, Gould & Newman; Philadelphia, H. Perkins, 1838. vi, [7]-137 p. 15 cm. [BR309.S4 1838 a] 39-7367
1. Reformation. 2. Catholic church—Doctrinal and controversial works—Protestant authors. I. Evangelical Lutheran synod of West Pennsylvania. II. Title.

SCHMUCKER, Samuel Simon, 270.6
1799-1873.
Discourse in commemoration of the glorious reformation of the sixteenth century. Delivered before the Evangelical Lutheran synod of West Pennsylvania, by S. S. Schmucker ... Published by synod. 3d ed., with additions. New York, Gould & Newman; Philadelphia, H. Perkins, 1838. vi, 7-142 p. 15 cm. [BR309.S4 1838 b] 39-7369
1. Reformation. 2. Catholic church—Doctrinal and controversial works—Protestant authors. I. Evangelical Lutheran synod of West Pennsylvania. II. Title.

SCHWARTZ, Werner, 1905- 220.52
Principles and problems of Biblical translation; some Reformation controversies and their background. Cambridge [Eng.] University Press, 1955. xiv, 224 p. 23 cm. Bibliography: p. 213-214. Bibliographical footnotes. [BS450.S3] 55-3878
1. Bible—Versions. 2. Bible—Hermeneutics. 3. Bible—History. 4. Reformation. I. Title.

SCHWIEBERT, Ernest 922.443
George.
Luther and his times; the Reformation from a new perspective. St. Louis, Concordia Pub. House [1950] xxii, 892 p. illus., ports., maps. 26 cm. Bibliographical references included in "Notes" (p. 765-878) [BR325.S335] 50-11670
1. Luther, Martin, 1483-1546. 2. Reformation. I. Title.

SCHWIEBERT, Ernest 922.443
George, 1895-
Luther and his times; the Reformation from a new perspective. St. Louis, Concordia Pub. House [1950] xxii, 892p. illus., ports., maps. 26cm. Bibliographical references included in 'Notes' (p. 765-878) [BR325.S335] 50-11670
1. Luther, Martin, 1483-1546. 2. Reformation. I. Title.

SCRIBNER, Robert W. 274.3'06
For the sake of simple folk : popular propaganda for the German Reformation / R.W. Scribner. Cambridge [England] ; New York, NY : Cambridge University Press, 1981. xi, 299 p. : ill. ; 24 cm. (Cambridge studies in oral and literate culture ; no. 2) Includes index. Bibliography: p. 281-293. [BR307.S464] 19 81-7710 ISBN 0-521-24192-8 : 44.50
1. Reformation. 2. Propaganda, German. 3. Illustrated books—Germany. 4. Illustrated books—15th and 16th centuries. I. Title. II. Series.

SEEBACH, Margaret Rebecca (Himes) Mrs., 1875- 284
Missionary milestones, a study of the reformation in its influence on civil and religious liberty and home mission activities in America, by Margaret R. Seebach. New York city, Council of women for home missions [c1917] ix, 198 p. front., pl., ports. 19 cm. (Interndenominational home mission study course) Bibliography: p. 197-198. [BX4807.S4] 17-13208
1. Reformation. 2. U.S.—Church history. 3. Missions, Home. I. Council of women for home missions. II. Title.

SEEBOHM, Frederic, 1833-1912. 270.6
The era of the Protestant revolution. 2d ed. New York, AMS Press [1971] xv, 250 p. maps. 19 cm. Reprint of the 1903 ed. Bibliography: p. 239-246. [D228.S4 1971] 77-147114 ISBN 0-404-05695-4
1. Reformation. I. Title.

SEEBOHM, Frederic, 1833-1912. 274.2
The Oxford reformers, by Frederic Seebohm... London & Toronto, J. M. Dent & sons, Ltd.; New York, E. P. Dutton & co. [1929] xi, 331 p. 17 1/2 cm. (Half-title: Everyman's library, ed. by Ernest Rhys. Biography. [no. 665]) "First published in this edition, 1914; reprinted, 1929." Caption title: The Oxford reformers: Colet, Erasmus, and More. Bibliography: p. viii. [AC1.E8 no. 665] 37-9300
1. Colet, John, 1467?-1519. 2. Erasmus, Desiderius, d. 1536. 3. More, Sir Thomas, Saint, 1478-1535. 4. Reformation. 5. Education—England—Hist. I. Title.

SEEBOHM, Frederic, 1833-1912.
The Oxford reformers, by Frederic Seebohm. London, J. M. Dent & sons, ltd.; New York, E. P. Dutton & co. [1914] xi, 331 p. 17 cm. (Half-title: Everyman's library ed. by Ernest Rhys. Bibliography [no. 665]) Bibliography: p. viii. [BR378.S] A 14
1. Colet, John, 1467?-1519. 2. Erasmus, Desiderius, d. 1536. 3. More, Sir Thomas Saint, 1478-1535. 4. Reformation. 5. Education—England—History. I. Title.

SEEBOHM, Frederic, 1833-1912. 270.5'0922 B
The Oxford reformers: John Colet, Erasmus, and Thomas More. Being a history of their fellow-work. London, New York, Longmans, Green, 1913. [New York, AMS Press, 1971] xvi, 551 p. 23 cm. [BR378.S4 1971] 70-147115 ISBN 0-404-05696-2
1. Colet, John, 1467?-1519. 2. Erasmus, Desiderius, d. 1536. 3. More, Thomas, Sir, Saint, 1478-1535. 4. Reformation. 5. Education—England—History. I. Title.

[SHOBER, Gottlieb] 1756-1838. 274.
A comprehensive account of the rise and progress of the blessed reformation of the Christian church. By Doctor Martin Luther: began on the thirty-first of October, A.D. 1517. Interspersed with views of his character and doctrine, extracted from his books; and how the church, established by him, arrived and progressed in North America--as also, the constitution and rules of that church, in North Carolina and adjoining states, as existing in October, 1817. Printed for the German and English Lutheran synod of North Carolin and adjoining states, by Schaeffer & Maund, printers, booksellers and stationers. Baltimore, 1818. xii, 218 p. 17 cm. By resolution of the synod of the Evangelical Lutheran German and English church in North Carolina, 1816, the secretary, G. Shober, "was charged to compile an abbreviated history of the rise, progress and present situation of the said church". cf. Pref. Fifteen hundred copies directed to be printed. cf. Pref. [BR305.S5] A 34
1. Luther, Martin, 1483-1546. 2. Reformation. 3. Lutheran church in the U.S. I. Evangelical Lutheran synod of North Carolina. II. Title.

SIMON, Edith. 270.6
Luther alive; Martin Luther and the making of the Reformation. [1st ed.] Garden City, N.Y., Doubleday, 1968. xi, 371 p. col. map (on lining papers) 24 cm. (The Crossroads of world history series) Bibliography: p. [361]-364. [BR325.S49] 68-14194
1. Luther, Martin, 1483-1546. 2. Reformation. I. Title.

SIMON, Edith, 1917- 270.6
The Reformation, by Edith Simon and the editors of Time-Life books. New York, Time, inc. [1966] 191 p. illus. (part col.) facsims., col. maps, ports. (part col.) 28 cm. (Great ages of man) Bibliography: p. 186. [BR305.2.S5] 66-22782
1. Reformation.

SMELLIE, Alexander.
The reformation in its literature, by Alexander Smellie... London & New York, A. Melrose ltd. [1925] v. 320 p. 23 cm. [BR307.S5] 26-13699
1. Reformation. I. Title.

SMITH, Frederick George, 1880- 230
The last reformation, by F. G. Smith. Anderson, Ind., Gospel trumpet company [c1919] vii, 9-256 p. 20 cm. $1.00 [BV600.S57] 19-16102
I. Title.

SMYTH, Hugh Patrick, 1855-
The reformation, by the Rev. Hugh P. Smyth. 2d ed. Chicago, Extension press, 1920. 243 p. 20 cm. "Seven of these discourses were delivered at St. Mary's church, Evanston, during the Lent of 1918."--Pref. [BR306.S6 1930] 20-20658
1. Reformation. I. Title.

SPALDING, Martin John, abp., 1810-1872. 270.6
D'Aubigne's "History of the great reformation in Germany and Switzerland," reviewed; or, The reformation in Germany examined in its instruments, causes and manner, and in its influence on religion, government, literature, and general civilization. By M. J. Spalding... Baltimore, J. Murphy; Pittsburgh, G. Quigley, 1844. 4 p. l., [xv]-xxii p., 1 l., [25]-379 p. front. 19 1/2 cm. [BR305.M8S7] 34-5249
1. Marie d'Aubigne, Jean Henri, 1794-1872. Histoire de in reformation. 2. Reformation. I. Title.

SPALDING, Martin John, abp., 1810-1872. 270.6
The history of the Protestant reformation... In a series of essays; reviewing D'Aubigne, Menzel, Hallan...and others... By M. J. Spalding... 7th ed., rev. and enl. Baltimore, J. Murphy & co., 1876. 2 v. in 1. 23 cm. Contents.1. Reformation in Germany and Switzerland.--II. Reformation in England, Ireland, Scotland, the Netherlands, France, and northern Europe. [BR305.S7] 34-16729
1. Reformation. I. Title.

STEVENSON, William, 1901- 270.6
The story of the Reformation. Richmond, John Knox Press [1959] 206 p. 21 cm. Includes bibliography. [BR305.2.S8] 59-10517
1. Reformation.

SWANSON, Guy E. 270.6
Religion and regime; a sociological account of the reformation, by Guy E. Swanson. Ann Arbor, University of Michigan Press [1967] x, 295 p. 21 cm. Bibliographical references included in "Notes" (p. 263-291) [BR307.S9] 67-11979
1. Reformation. 2. Protestantism. 3. Religion and sociology. I. Title.

SYKES, Norman, 1897-1961. 270.6
The crisis of the Reformation. New York, W. W. Norton [1967, c1946] 122 p. 21 cm. [BR305.S8 1967] 67-3850
1. Reformation. I. Title.

TILLMANNS, Walter G 270.6
The world and men around Luther. Illus. by Edmund Kopietz. Minneapolis, Augsburg Pub. House [1959] 384 p. illus. 23 cm. Includes bibliography. [BR305.2.T54] 59-11714
1. Luther, Martin, 1483-1546. 2. Reformation. 3. Reformation—Biog. I. Title.

TODD, John Murray. 270.6
Reformation [by] John M. Todd. Garden City, N.Y., Doubleday, 1971. 377 p. 22 cm. Bibliography: p. [360]-371. [BR305.2.T58] 75-157629 7.95
1. Reformation.

TULLOCH, John, 1823-1886. 270.
Leaders of the reformation: Luther, Calvin, Latimer, Knox, the representative men of Germany, France, England and Scotland. By John Tulloch ... Boston, Gould and Lincoln; New York, Sheldon and company; [etc., etc.] 1860. 309 p.20 cm. [BR315.T9 1860] 6-26894
1. Luther, Martin 1483-1546. 2. Calvin, Jean, 1509-1561. 3. Latimer, Hugh, bp., Worcester. 1485?-1555. 4. Knox, John, 1506-1572. 5. Reformation. I. Title.

VERDUIN, Leonard. 270.6
The reformers and their stepchildren. Grand Rapids, Mich., Eerdmans [1964] 292 p. 24 cm. "Bibliographical footnotes": p. 282-288. [BR307.V4] 64-16595
1. Reformation. 2. Church — History of doctrines — 16th cent. 3. Church and state — Hist. I. Title.

VILLERS, Charles Francois Dominique de, 1765-1815. 274.
An essay on the spirit and influence of the reformation by Luther. The work which obtained the prize on this question, (proposed by the National institute of France, in the public sitting of the 15th Germinal, in the year x.) "What has been the influence of the reformation by Luther on the political situation of the different states of Europe, and on the progress of knowledge?" By C. Villers. Faithfully translated from the last Paris edition by B. Lambert. Dover, N.H., Printed by Samuel Bragg, jun., 1807. ix, [11]-328 p. 21 1/2 cm. "Appendix. Sketch of the history of the church": p. [209]-328 [BR305.V74e 1807] A 32
1. Luther, Martin, 1483-1546. 2. Reformation. 3. Sixteenth century. 4. Church history. I. Lambert, B., tr. II. Title.

WALKER, Williston, 1860-1922. 270.6
...The reformation, by Williston Walker. New York, C. Scribner's sons, 1909. ix, 478 p. 19 1/2 cm. (Half-title: Ten epochs of church history, ed. by J. Fulton...vol. IX.) Series title also at head of t.-p. [BR141.T4 vol. 9] 1-30202
1. Reformation. I. Title.

WHITNEY, James Pounder.
The reformation; being an outline of the history of the church from A.D. 1503 to A.D, 1648, by the Rev. James Pounder Whitney... New York, The Macmillan company, 1907. viii, 501 p. 19 cm. (On back of cover: The church universal [vol. VI]) Bibliography: p. 457-463. 7-37538
I. Title.

WHITNEY, James Pounder, 1857-1939. 270.6
The history of the reformation, by James Pounder Whitney...Published for the Church historical society. London, Society for promoting Christian knowledge; New York, The Macmillan company [1940] xv, 526, [2] p. 22 cm. Prepared for publication by Miss M. T. Stead. cf. Prefatory note. "New edition 1940." First published 1907 under title: The reformation: being an outline of the history of the church from A.D. 1503 to A.D. 1648. "Memoir of Dr. Whitney" (p. vii-xii) and "Bibliography of Dr. Whitney's works" (p. xiii-xiv) by R. E. Balfour. [BR305.W45 1940] 41-18462
1. Reformation. I. Stead, M. T., ed. II. Balfour, Ronald Edmond. III. Church historical society. IV. Title.

WILLIAMS, George Huntston, 1914- 270.5
The Radical Reformation. Philadelphia, Westminster Press [1962] xxxi, 924 p. map (on lining paper) 24 cm. Bibliographical footnotes. [BR307.W5] 62-7066
1. Reformation. 2. Anabaptists. I. Title.

WILSON, John Churchwood, 1862-1903.
The struggle for religious liberty in the fifteenth and sixteenth centuries; being a series of six lectures delivered on Sunday evenings in the South Congregational church, Brooklyn, in the winter of 1903, by John Churchwood Wilson ... New York [Press of J. J. Little & co.] 1905. xii p., 1 l., 231 p. incl. front. (port.) 20 cm. Prefatory note by Albert J. Lyman. [BR290.W5] 5-28195
1. Reformation. 2. Religious liberty. I. Lyman, Albert Josiah, 1845-1915. II. Title.

ZWIERLEIN, Frederick James, 1881- 270.6
Reformation studies, by Frederick J. Zwierlein ... Rochester, N.Y., The Art print shop, 1938. 4 p. l., 166 p. 23 1/2 cm. "All of these ... studies, except the last ... have been printed repeatedly in pamphlet form."--Pref. [BR301.Z3] 40-4658
1. Reformation. I. Title.
Contents omitted.

Reformation — Addresses, essays, lectures.

GASQUET, Francis Aidan, 1846-
Breaking with the past; or, Catholic principles abandoned at the reformation; four sermons delivered at St. Patrick's cathedral, New York, on the Sundays of Advent, 1913, by Francis Aidan Gasquet ... with a preface by His Eminence Cardinal Farley. New York, P.J. Kenedy & sons, 1914. viii p., 2 l., [3]-84 p. 1 l., 17 1/2 cm. $0.60. "Books suggested for reading": 11 at end. 14-7895
I. Title.

GERRISH, B. A. 1931- (Brian Albert), 230'.044'0903
The old Protestantism and the new : essays on the Reformation heritage / B.A. Gerrish. Chicago : University of Chicago Press, 1982. p. cm. Includes index. Bibliography: p. [BR309.G39] 19 82-2730 ISBN 0-226-28869-2 : 35.00
1. Reformation—Addresses, essays, lectures. 2. Theology, Doctrinal—History—Addresses, essays, lectures. I. Title.

GREENALL, Raphael. 200
The second fall. Liverpool, Keys Pub. Co. [1963] 112 p. 22 cm. Bibliographical footnotes. [BR307.G7] 64-1769
1. Reformation—Addresses, essays, lectures. 2. Civilization, Modern—Addresses, essays, lectures. I. Title.

HURSTFIELD, Joel, ed. 270.608
The Reformation crisis. New York, Barnes & Noble [1966, c1965] ix, 126 p. 21 cm. Consists chiefly of talks broadcast by the B. B. C. in 1962, here revised with two new chapters added. Bibliography: p. [119]-120. [BR309.H77 1966] 66-3534
1. Reformation — Addresses, essays, lectures. Title. I. Title.

HURSTFIELD, Joel, ed. 270.608
The Reformation crisis. New York, Barnes & Noble [1966, c1965] ix, 126 p. 21 cm. Consists chiefly of talks broadcast by the B. B. C. in 1962, here revised with two new chapters added. Bibliography: p. [119]-120. [BR309.H77 1966] 66-3534
1. Reformation — Addresses, essays, lectures. Title. I. Title.

HURSTFIELD, Joel, ed.
The Reformation crisis. New York, Harper & Row [1966, c1965] vii, 126 p. 21 cm. (Harper torchbooks. The Academy library TB1267G) Bibliography: p. [119]-120.
1. Reformation — Addresses, essays, lectures. I. Title.

LITTELL, Franklin Hamlin, ed. 270.6
Reformation studies; essays in honor of Roland H. Bainton. Richmond, Va., Knox [c.1962] 285p. front. 25cm. Bibl. 62-16259 5.50
1. Bainton, Roland Herbert, 1894- 2. Reformation-Addresses, essays, lectures. I. Title.

LITTELL, Franklin Hamlin, ed. 270.6
Reformation studies : essays in honor of Roland H. Bainton. Richmond, John Knox Press [1962] 285p. port. 25cm. Bibliographical references included in 'Notes and acknowledgments' (p. [254]-285) [BR309.L5] 62-16259
1. Bainton, Roland Herbert, 1894- 2. Reformation—Ad- dresses, essays, lectures. I. Title.
Contents omitted.

LUTHER, Erasmus, and the Reformation; 270.6 a Catholic-Protestant reappraisal. Edited by John C. Olin, James D. Smart [and] Robert E. McNally. New York, Fordham University Press, 1969. x, 150 p. ports. (on lining papers) 22 cm. Essays presented at a conference held Oct. 20-21, 1967, and sponsored by Union

Theological Seminary and Fordham University. Includes bibliographical references. [BR309.L84] 68-8749 6.00
1. Luther, Martin, 1483-1546. 2. Erasmus, Desiderius, d. 1536. 3. Reformation—Addresses, essays, lectures. I. Olin, John C., ed. II. Smart, James D., ed. III. McNally, Robert E., ed. IV. New York. Union Theological Seminary. V. Fordham University, New York.

OZMENT, Steven E., comp. 270.6
The Reformation in medieval perspective. Edited with an introd. by Steven E. Ozment. Chicago, Quadrangle Books, 1971. xiv, 267 p. 22 cm. (Modern scholarship on European history) Contents.Contents.—Romantic and revolutionary elements in German theology on the eve of the Reformation, by G. Ritter.—Piety in Germany around 1500, by B. Moeller.—The crisis of the Middle Ages and the Hussites, by F. Graus.—On Luther and Ockham, by P. Vignaux.—Facientibus quod in se est Deus non denegat gratiam: Robert Holcot O. P. and the beginnings of Luther's theology, by H. A. Oberman.—Home viator: Luther and late medieval theology, by S. E. Ozment.—The Windesheimers after c. 1485: confrontation with the reformation and humanism, by R. R. Post.—Paracelsus, by A. Koyre.—Simul gemitus et raptus: Luther and mysticism, by H. A. Oberman.—Bibliography (p. 253-256) [BR309.O93] 72-152100 ISBN 0-8129-0194-0 ISBN 0-8129-6166-8 (pbk.) 12.50
1. Reformation—Addresses, essays, lectures. I. Title.

REFORMATIO perennis : 270.6
essays on Calvin and the Reformation in honor of Ford Lewis Battles / edited by B.A. Gerrish, in collaboration with Robert Benedetto. Pittsburgh, Pa. : Pickwick Press, 1981. p. cm. (Pittsburh theological monograph series : 32) Includes bibliographical references. [BX9418.R36] 19 81-1007 ISBN 0-915138-41-7 : 12.95
1. Calvin, Jean, 1509-1564—Addresses, essays, lectures. 2. Battles, Ford Lewis Addresses, essays, lectures. 3. Reformation—Addresses, essays, lectures. 4. Church and state—Addresses, essays, lectures. I. Battles, Ford Lewis. II. Gerrish, B. A. 1931- (Brian Albert), III. Benedetto, Robert. IV. Series.
Contents omitted.

THE Reformation : 270.6
change and stability / edited with an introd. by Peter J. Klassen. St. Louis, Mo. : Forum Press, c1980. 74 p., [1] leaf of plates : ill. ; 24 cm. (Problems in civilization) Bibliography: p. 73-74. [BR309.R37] 79-54030 ISBN 0-88273-408-3 pbk. : 3.95
1. Reformation—Addresses, essays, lectures. I. Klassen, Peter James. II. Series.

REID, William Stanford, 270.6
1913- comp.
The Reformation: revival or revolution? Edited by W. Stanford Reid. New York, Holt, Rinehart and Winston [1968] 122 p. illus. 24 cm. (European problem studies) Bibliography: p. 119-122. [BR309.R4] 68-28181
1. Reformation—Addresses, essays, lectures. I. Title.

THE Social history of the 270.6
Reformation. Edited by Lawrence P. Buck and Jonathan W. Zophy. Columbus, Ohio State University Press [1972] xxiv, 397 p. 24 cm. "In honor of Harold J. Grimm." [BR307.S6] 72-5952 ISBN 0-8142-0174-1 12.50
1. Grimm, Harold John, 1901- 2. Reformation—Addresses, essays, lectures. I. Grimm, Harold John, 1901- II. Buck, Lawrence P., 1944- ed. III. Zophy, Jonathan W., 1945- ed.

SPITZ, Lewis William, 1922- 270.6
ed.
The Reformation; basic interpretations. Edited and with an introd. by Lewis W. Spitz. 2d ed. Lexington, Mass., Heath [1972] xxi, 221 p. 21 cm. (Problems in European civilization) Contents.Contents.—Bainton, R. H. Interpretations of the Reformation.—Dilthey, W. The interpretation and analysis of man in the 15th and 16th centuries.—Troeltsch, E. Renaissance and Reformation.—Spitz, L. W. The third generation of German Renaissance humanists.—Walker, P. C. G. Capitalism and the Reformation.—Holborn, H. The social basis of the German Reformation.—Grimm, H. J. Social forces in the German Reformation.—Lea, H. C. The eve of the Reformation.—Lortz, J. Why did the Reformation happen?—Ritter, G. Why the Reformation occured in Germany.—Barth, K. Reformation as decision.—Luther, M. Luther's road to the Reformation.—Erikson, E. H. Young man Luther.—Bainton, R. H. Luther's struggle for faith.—Bibliography (p. 213-221) [CB359.S64 1972] 72-2273 ISBN 0-669-81620-5
1. Reformation—Addresses, essays, lectures. I. Title. II. Series.

Reformation—Biography

ALAND, Kurt. 280'.4 B
Four reformers : Luther, Melanchthon, Calvin, Zwingli / Kurt Aland ; translated by James L. Schaff. Minneapolis : Augsburg Pub. House, c1979. 174 p. ; 20 cm. Translation of Die Reformatoren. Bibliography: p. 159-174. [BR315.A4513] 79-50091 ISBN 0-8066-1709-8 pbk. : 4.95
1. Luther, Martin, 1483-1546. 2. Melanchthon, Philipp, 1497-1560. 3. Calvin, Jean, 1509-1564. 4. Zwingli, Ulrich, 1484-1531. 5. Reformation—Biography. 6. Reformation. I. Title.

BAINTON, Roland 199'.492 B
Herbert, 1894-
Erasmus of Christendom / Roland H. Bainton. New York : Crossroad, 1982, c1969. xii, 308 p. : ill. ; 23 cm. Includes index. Bibliography: p. 285-299. [BR350.E7B25 1982] 19 81-70875 ISBN 0-8245-0415-1 (pbk.) : 12.95
1. Erasmus, Desiderius, d. 1536. 2. Reformation—Biography. I. Title.

BAINTON, Roland 277.6'0922 B
Herbert, 1894-
Women of the Reformation, from Spain to Scandinavia / Roland H. Bainton. Minneapolis : Augsburg Pub. House, c1977. 240 p. : ill. ; 22 cm. Includes bibliographies and index. [BR317.B28] 76-27089 ISBN 0-8066-1568-0 : 9.95
1. Reformation—Biography. 2. Women—Biography. I. Title.

BAINTON, Roland 270.6'092'2 B
Herbert, 1894-
Women of the Reformation in France and England [by] Roland H. Bainton. Minneapolis, Augsburg Pub. House [1973] 287 p. illus. 23 cm. Bibliography: p. 277. [BR317.B29] 73-78269 ISBN 0-8066-1333-5 8.95
1. Reformation—Biography. 2. Woman—Biography. I. Title.

BAINTON, Roland 270.6'092'2 B
Herbert, 1894-
Women of the Reformation in France and England / Roland H. Bainton. Boston : Beacon Press, 1975, c1973. 287 p. : ill. ; 20 cm. Reprint of the ed. published by Augsburg Pub. House, Minneapolis, Includes index. Bibliography: p. 277. [BR317.B29 1975] 75-19393 ISBN 0-8070-5649-9 pbk. : 4.45
1. Reformation—Biography. 2. Women—Biography. I. Title.

BAINTON, Roland 270.6'092'2 B
Herbert, 1894-
Women of the Reformation in Germany and Italy, by Roland H. Bainton. Boston, Beacon Press [1974, c1971] 279 p. illus. 21 cm. (Beacon paperback, 485) Reprint of the ed. published by Augsburg Pub. House, Minneapolis. Includes bibliographies. [BR317.B3 1974] 74-6085 ISBN 0-8070-5651-0 3.95
1. Reformation—Biography. 2. Woman—Biography. I. Title.

BAINTON, Roland 270.6'0922 B
Herbert, 1894-
Women of the Reformation in Germany and Italy, by Roland H. Bainton. Minneapolis, Augsburg Pub. House [1971] 279 p. illus., facsims., geneal. table, maps, ports. 23 cm. Includes bibliographies. [BR317.B3 1971] 70-135235 7.95
1. Reformation—Biography. 2. Woman—Biography. I. Title.

BELLOC, Hilaire, 1870- 270.6
Characters of the reformation, by Hilaire Belloc. Twenty-three portraits by Jean Charlot. New York, Sheed & Ward, 1936. v, 342 p. col. front., col. ports. 21 cm. Printed in Great Britain [Full name: Joseph Hilaire Pierre Belloc] [BR315.B35] 37-1317
1. Reformation-Biog. I. Charlot, Jean, 1896- illus. II. Title.
Contents omitted.

BELLOC, Hilaire, 1870- 270.6
Characters of the reformation, by Hilaire Belloc. New York, Sheed & Ward, 1940. v. 342 p. 19 cm.]Catholic masterpieces. no.7: "First published, July 1936." [Full name: Joseph Hilarie Pierre Belloc] [BR315.B35 1940] 40-30902
1. Reformation—Biog. I. Title.
Contents omitted.

BELLOC, Hilaire, 940.2'3'0922 B
1870-1953.
Characters of the Reformation. Portraits by Jean Charlot. Freeport, N.Y., Books for Libraries Press [1970] 342 p. ports. 23 cm. (Essay index reprint series) Reprint of the 1936 ed. [BR315.B35 1970] 72-121449
1. Reformation—Biography. I. Title.

BELLOC, Hilaire, 1870-1953. 270.6
Characters of the Reformation. New York, Image Books [1958] 200 p. 19 cm. (Image books, D71) [BR315.B35 1958] 58-9384
1. Reformation—Biography. I. Title.

DUBBS, Joseph Henry, 1838- 270.6
1910.
Leaders of the reformation, by Joseph Henry Dubbs ... Philadelphia, Pa., The Heidelberg press [1898] vi, [7]-212 p. front., ports. 19 1/2 cm. (The world's benefactors series) [BR315.D8] 922 99-1675
1. Hus, Jan, 1369-1415. 2. Luther, Martin, 1483-1546. 3. Zwingli, Ulrich, 1484-1531. 4. Calvin, Jean, 1509-1564. 5. Cranmer, Thomas, abp. of Canterbury, 1489-1556. 6. Knox, John, 1505-1572. 7. Friedrich III, Elector Palatine, 1515-1576. 8. Olevianus, Kaspar, 1536-1587. 9. Ursinus, Zacharias, 1534-1583. 0. Reformation—Biog. I. Title.

GARVER, Isobel M. 270.6'092'2 B
Our Christian heritage. Artist: Isobel M. Garver. Author: Stuart P. Garver. Hackensack, N.J., Christ's Mission [1973] 103 p. illus. (part col.) 29 cm. [BR315.G3] 73-77907
1. Reformation—Biography. I. Garver, Stuart P. II. Title.
Publisher's address: 275 State, Hackensack, N.J. 07304.

GERRISH, Brian Albert, 270.6'0922
1931-
Reformers in profile. Ed. by B. A. Gerrish. Philadelphia, Fortress [1967] vii, 264p. 23cm. Bibl. [BR315.G4] 67-27134 5.95
1. Reformation—Biog. I. Title.
Contents Omitted.

HAILE, Harry Gerald, 284.1'092'4
1931-
Luther, an experiment in biography / H. G. Haile. 1st ed. Garden City, N.Y. : Doubleday, 1980. x, 422 p. : map (on lining papers) ; 22 cm. Includes bibliographical references and index. [BR325.H23] 79-6282 ISBN 0-385-15960-9 : 14.95
1. Luther, Martin, 1483-1546. 2. Reformation—Biography. I. Title.

HENDRIX, Scott H. 284.1'092'4 B
Luther and the papacy : stages in a reformation conflict / Scott H. Hendrix. Philadelphia : Fortress Press, c1981. p. cm. Includes index. Bibliography: p. [BR333.5.P3H46] 19 80-2393 ISBN 0-8006-0658-2 : 14.95
1. Luther, Martin, 1483-1546. 2. Reformation—Biography. I. Title.

NESTINGEN, James 284.1'092'4 B
Arne.
Martin Luther, his life and teachings / James Arne Nestingen. Philadelphia : Fortress Press, c1982. p. cm. [BR325.N47 1982] 19 82-71829 ISBN 0-8006-1642-1 : 3.95
1. Luther, Martin, 1483-1546. 2. Reformation—Biography. I. Title.

RITTER, Gerhard, 230'.4'10924 B
1888-1967.
Luther, his life and work / by Gerhard Ritter ; translated from the German by John Riches. Westport, Conn. : Greenwood Press, 1978, c1963. 256 p. ; 23 cm. Translation of Luther, Gestalt und Tat. Reprint of the ed. published by Harper & Row, New York. [BR325.R633 1978] 78-2717 ISBN 0-313-20347-4 lib. bdg. : 18.50
1. Luther, Martin, 1483-1546. 2. Reformation—Biography. I. Title.

STEINMETZ, David 270.6'0922 B
Curtis.
Reformers in the wings [by] David C. Steinmetz. Philadelphia, Fortress Press [1971] viii, 240 p. 23 cm. Includes bibliographies. [BR315.S83] 75-135266 ISBN 0-8006-0051-7 8.50
1. Reformation—Biography. I. Title.

[STOKES, George] 1789-1847.
The lives of the British reformers. Embellished with twelve portraits. Philadelphia, Presbyterian board of publication, 1844. [496] p. front., ports. 19 cm. Various pagings. Appeared originally as two works, under titles: The Lollards and The days of Queen Mary; amalgamated under title: A brief history of the British reformation [1932?] cf. Brit. mus. Catalogue. [BR378.S8 1844] 44-14516
1. Reformation—Biog. 2. Reformation—England. 3. Gt. Brit.—Biog. I. Presbyterian church in the U.S.A. Board of publication. II. Title. III. Title: British reformers.

TODD, John Murray. 284.1'092'4 B
Luther, a life / John M. Todd. New York : Crossroad, 1982. xix, 396 p., [4] p. of plates : ill. map ; 24 cm. Includes bibliographical references and index. [BR325.T59 1982] 19 82-5009 ISBN 0-8245-0479-8 : 17.50
1. Luther Martin, 1483-1546. 2. Reformation—Biography. I. Title.

YELVERTON, Eric Esskildsen.
An archbishop of the Reformation, Laurentius Petri Nericius, Archbishop of Uppsala, 1531-73; a study of his liturgical projects. Minneapolis, Augsburg pub. house [1959] xxi, 153 p. facsim. 20 cm. "Printed in Great Britain." With reproduction of original t.-p. of Laurentius Petri's Church order (Then swenska kyrkeordningen), 1571. Bibliography: p. [xv]-xx.
I. Title.

Reformation—Biography—Juvenile literature.

BENSON, Kathleen. 284.1'092'4 B
A man called Martin Luther / Kathleen Benson. St. Louis : Concordia, c1980. 128 p. : ill. ; 24 cm. A biography of the German monk who led the Prostestant Reformation in Europe from its beginning in 1517 until his death in 1546. [BR325.B43] 92 80-100 ISBN 0-570-03625-9 : 6.95
1. Luther, Martin, 1483-1546—Juvenile literature. 2. [Luther, Martin, 1483-1546.] 3. Reformation—Biography—Juvenile literature. 4. [Reformers.] I. Title.

Reformation—Bohemia.

MEARS, John William, 1825-1881.
Heroes of Bohemia; Huss, Jerome and Zisea. by The Rev. John W. Mears... Philadelphia, Presbyterian board of publication [c1879] 350 p. front. (fold. map) 18 cm. [BX4916.M4] 12-36692
1. Huss, Jan 1369-1415. 2. Herinymus von Prag, ca. 1365-1416. 3. Zisea, Jan, ca. 1360-1424. 4. Reformation—Bohemia. I. Title.

Reformation — Causes.

LORTZ, Joseph, 1887- 200
How the Reformation came. [Translated by Otto M. Knab. New York] Herder and Herder [1964] 115 p. 21 cm. [BR307.L613] 63-18152
1. Reformation — Causes. I. Title.

LORTZ, Joseph, 1887- 270.6
How the Reformation came. [Tr. from German by Ott M. Knab. New York]

Herder [c.1964] 115 p. 21 cm. 63-18152 2.95
1. Reformation—Causes. I. Title.

WACE, Henry, 1836-
Principles of the Reformation practical and historical, by the Very Rev. Henry Wace ... New York, American tract society [1911] vii, 252 p. 21 1/2 cm. A 12
I. Title.

Reformation—Congresses.

LUTHER, Erasmus, and the 270.6
Reformation : a Catholic-Protestant reappraisal / edited by John C. Olin, James D. Smart, Robert E. McNally. Westport, Conn. : Greenwood Press, 1982, c1969. p. cm. Reprint. Originally published: New York : Fordham University Press, 1969. Includes index. Bibliography: p. [BR300.L87 1982] 19 82-15500 ISBN 0-313-23652-6 lib. bdg. : 22.50
1. Luther, Martin, 1483-1546—Congresses. 2. Erasmus, Desiderius, d. 1536—Congresses. 3. Reformation—Congresses. I. Olin, John C. II. Smart, James D. III. McNally, Robert E.

Reformation—Czechoslavakia—Biography.

SPINKA, Matthew, 1890- 284'.3 B
1972.
John Hus, a biography / Matthew Spinka. Westport, Conn. : Greenwood Press, 1979, c1968. v, 344 p. ; 22 cm. Reprint of the ed. published by Princeton University Press, Princeton, N.J. Includes index. Bibliography: p. 323-330. [BX4917.S69 1979] 78-14366 ISBN 0-313-21050-0 lib. bdg. : 21.00
1. Hus, Jan, 1369-1415. 2. Reformation—Czechoslavakia—Biography.

Reformation—Czechoslovakia—Bohemia—Biography.

GILLETT, Ezra Hall, 284'.3 B
1823-1875.
The life and times of John Huss : or, The Bohemian reformation of the fifteenth century / by E. H. Gillett. New York : AMS Press, [1978] p. cm. Reprint of the 1863 ed. published by Gould and Lincoln, Boston. [BX4917.G5 1978] 77-85271 ISBN 0-404-16150-2 : 28.50
1. Hus, Jan, 1369-1415. 2. Reformation—Czechoslovakia—Bohemia—Biography. 3. Bohemia—Church history. I. Title.

LUTZOW, Franz Heinrich 284'.3 B
Hieronymus Valentin, Graf von, 1849-1916.
The life & times of Master John Hus / by the Count Lutzow. 1st AMS ed. New York : AMS Press, 1978. xi, 398 p., [7] leaves of plates : ill. ; 23 cm. Reprint of the 1909 ed. published by J. M. Dent, London. Includes index. Bibliography: p. 383-386. [BX4917.L83 1978] 77-84728 ISBN 0-404-16128-6 : 28.50
1. Hus, Jan, 1369-1415. 2. Reformation—Czechoslovakia—Bohemia—Biography. 3. Bohemia—Church history. I. Title.

Reformation—Early movements.

CHARACTERS, scenes, and 270.
incidents, of the reformation; from the rise of the Culdees to the times of Luther. Revised by D. P. Kidder. New York, Carlton & Phillips, 1853. 176 p. incl. front. 15 cm. [BR295.C5] 41-31832
1. Reformation—Early movements. I. Kidder, Daniel Parish, 1815-1891, ed.

ERASMUS, Desiderius, d.1536.
Selections from Erasmus, principally from his Epistles, by P. S. Allen. Oxford, The Clarendon press, 1908. 159, [1] p. 4 port. (incl. front.) facsim. 17 1/2 cm. Latin text. Vocabulary: p. [158]-159. List of place-names: p. [160] W9-131
I. Allen, Percy Stafford, 1869-1963, ed. II. Title.

MCFARLANE, Kenneth 270.5'0924
Bruce.
John Wycliffe and the beginnings of English noncomformity [by] K. B. McFarlane [London] English Universities Pr. [1972, c.1952] xiii, 188 p. maps. 23 cm. ([Men & their times]) Bibliography: p. [174]-175 [BX4905.M3] A53 ISBN 0-340-16648-7
1. Wycliffe, John, d. 1384. 2. Reformation—Early movements. 3. Reformation—England. I. Title. II. Title: English nonconformity. III. Series.
Available from Verry, Mystic, Conn., for 5.00.

MACKINNON, James, 1860- 270.5
The origins of the reformation, by James Mackinnon... London, New York [etc.] Longmans, Green, and co. [1939] xi, 448 p. 22 1/2 cm. "First published, 1939." [BR295.M3] 39-22339
1. Reformation—Early movements. 2. Religious thought—Middle ages. 3. Church history—Middle ages. I. Title.

MCNALLY, Robert E. 270.4
Reform of the church; crisis and criticism in historical perspective. [NewYork] Herder & Herder [c.1963] 140p. 21cm. Bibl. 63-18153 3.50
1. Reformation—Early movements. 2. Papacy—Hist.—1309-1378. I. Title.

WORKMAN, Herbert Brook, 270.6
1862-
The dawn of the Reformation / by Herbert B. Workman. 1st AMS ed. New York : AMS Press, 1978. 2v. ; 19 cm. Reprint of the 1901-1902 ed. published by C. H. Kelly, London, in series: Books for Bible students. Contents.Contents.— v. 1. The age of Wyclif.—v. 2. The age of Hus. Includes bibliographical references and index. [BR295.W67 1978] 77-85273 ISBN 0-404-16170-7 : 52.50
1. Reformation—Early movements. I. Title. II. Series: Books for Bible students.

Reformation—England.

ALLEN, Benjamin, 1789-1829. 274.2
History of the reformation. Being an abridgment of Burnet's History of the reformation of the Church of England. Together with sketches of the lives of Luther, Calvin and Zuingle, the three celebrated reformers of the continent. By the Rev. Benjamin Allen... Washington city, Printed for the author, by Jacob Gideon, junior, 1820. 297 p. 18 1/2 cm. [BR305.A4 1820] 34-14828
1. Luther, Martin, 1483-1546. 2. Calvin, Jean, 1509-1564. 3. Zwingll, Ulrich, 1484-1531. 4. Reformation—England. I. Burnet, Gilbert, bp. of Salisbury, 1643-1715. History of the reformation of the Church of England. II. Title.

ALLEN, Benjamin, 1789-1829. 274.2
History of the reformation. Being an abridgment of Burnet; together with sketches of the lives of Luther, Calvin and Zuingle, the three celebrated reformers of the continent. By the Rev. Benjamin Allen... 2d ed. Philadelphia, E. Littell, 1823. xii, [13]-297 p. 18 1/2 cm. [BR305.A4 1923] 34-14829
1. Luther, Martin, 1483-1546. 2. Calvin, Jean, 1500-1564. 3. Zwingli, Ulrich, 1484-1531. 4. Reformation—England. I. Burnet, Gilbert, bp. of Salisbury, 1643-1715. History of the reformation of the Church of England. II. Title.

BAILEY, Derrick Sherwin, 922.342
1910-
Thomas Becon and the reformation of the church in England. Edinburgh, Oliver and Boyd [1952] xiv, 155p. ports., facsims. 22cm. 'In its original form this study was submitted as a thesis for the doctorate of philosophy (in theology) at Edinburgh University.' [BX5199.B346B2] 53-1160
1. Becon, Thomas, 1512-1567. 2. Reformation—England. I. Title.

BURNET, Gilbert, bp. of 274.
Salisbury, 1643-1715.
The history of the reformation of the Church of England, by Gilbert Burnet ... A new ed., carefully rev., and the records collated with the originals, by Nichols Pocock ... Oxford, Clarendon press, 1865. 7 v. 23 1/2 cm. Contents.v. 1. The first part: Of the progress made in the reformation during the reign of King Henry VIII.--v. 2. The second part: Of the progress made in the reformation till the settlement of it in the beginning of Queen Elizabeth's reign.--v. 3. The third part: Being a supplement to the two formerly published. --v. 4-5. A collection of records, letters, and original papers, with other instruments referred to in the first [and second] part[s] ... [Appendices] concerning some of the errors and falsehoods in Sanders' book of the English schism.--v. 6. A collection of records ... [etc.] referred to in the third part ...--v. 7. Editor's preface. Corrigenda et addenda. Chronological index of records. General index. [BR375.B9 1865] 1-3744
1. Reformation—England. 2. Sanders, Nicholas, 1530?-1581. De origine ac progressu schismatis anglicanl. I. Pocock, Nicholas, 1814-1897, ed. II. Title.

CAMPBELL, William Edward, 274.2
1875-
Erasmus, Tyndale, and More. Milwaukee, Bruce Pub. Co. [1950] 288 p. plate, ports. 22 cm. Bibliography: p. 280-281. [B R378. C3 1950] 49-539
1. Erasmus, Desiderius, d. 1536. 2. Tyndale, William, d. 1536. 3. More, Sir Thomas, Saint, 1478-1535. 4. Reformation—England. I. Title.

CARTER, Charles Sydney.
The English church and the reformation, by the Rev. C. Sydney Carter ... London & New York, Longmans, Green and co., 1915. x, 150 p. 20 cm. First published October, 1912. Bibliographical foot-noites. A 21
1. Reformation—England. 2. Church of England—History—[Reformation] I. Title.

CLAYTON, Joseph, 1868- 274.2
The Protestant reformation in Great Britain, by Joseph Clayton ... Milwaukee [etc.] The Bruce publishing company [c1934] xviii p., 1 l., 252 p. 22 cm. (Half-title: Science and culture series) "A note on authorities": p. 243-245. [BR375.C55] 34-32385
1. Reformation—England. I. Title.

CLEAVELAND, George Julius. 283
Reformation and reunion; Protestant-Catholic tensions and suggested solutions. New York, Carlton Press [1963] 126 p. 21 cm. (A Reflection book) Bibliography: p. 125-126. [BR375.C57] 63-2665
1. Reformation — England. 2. Church of England — Relations — Catholic Church. 3. Catholic Church — Relations — Anglican Communion. 4. Anglican orders. 5. Christian union. I. Title.

CLEBSCH, William A 274.2
England's earliest Protestants, 1520-1535, by William A. Clebsch. New Haven, Yale University Press, 1964. xvi, 358 p. illus. 25 cm. (Yale publications in religion, 11) Bibliography: p. 319-345. [BR375.C58] 64-20912
1. Reformation — England. I. Title. II. Series.

CLEBSCH, William A. 280'.4'0942
England's earliest Protestants, 1520-1535 / by William A. Clebsch. Westport, Conn. : Greenwood Press, 1980, c1864. xvi, 358 p. ; 24 cm. Reprint of the ed. published by Yale University Press, New Haven, which was issued as v. 11 of Yale publications in religion. Includes index. Bibliography: p. 319-345. [BR375.C58 1980] 80-15226 ISBN 0-313-22420-X : 29.25
1. Reformation—England. I. Title. II. Series: Yale publications in religion ; 11.

CLEVELAND, George Julius 283
Reformation and reunion; Protestant-Catholic tensions and suggested solutions. New York, Carlton [c.1963] 126p. 21cm. (Reflection bk.) Bibl. 63-2665 2.50
1. Reformation—England. 2. Church of England—Relations—Catholic Church. 3. Catholic Church—Relations—Anglican Communion. 4. Anglican orders. 5. Christian union. I. Title.

COBBETT, William, 1763-1835. 274.
A history of the Protestant reformation in England & Ireland, written in 1824-1827, by William Cobbett. A new edition revised with notes and a preface, by Francis Aidan Gasquet ... Authorized American ed. New York, Cincinnati [etc.] Benziger brothers [1905] xix, [1], 406 p. 19 cm. [BR375.C6 1905] 8-20205
1. Reformation—England. 2. Reformation—Ireland. I. Gasquet, Francis Aidan, cardinal, 1846-1929, ed. II. Title.

COBBETT, William, 1763- 274.2
1835.
A history of the Protestant reformation in England and Ireland, by William Cobbett, revised by Francis Aidan cardinal Gasquet ... New York, Cincinnati [etc.] Benziger brothers [193-?] xix, [1], 406 p. 20 cm. [BR375.C3] 41-37872
1. Reformation—England. 2. Reformation—Ireland. I. Gasquet, Francis Aidan, cardinal, 1846-1929, ed. II. Title.

COLLINS, William Edward, 274.
bp. of Gibraltar, 1867-1911.
...The English reformation and its consequences, Four lectures, with notes and an appendix. By William Edward Collins ... 2d ed., rev. London [etc.] Society for promoting Christian knowledge; New York, E. & J. B. Young & co., 1901. vi, 314 p. 17 cm. (The Church historical society) [BR375.C7] 4-13620
1. Reformation—England. I. Title.

CONSTANT, Gustave Leon 274.2
Marie Joseph, 1869-
The reformation in England ... by G. Constant ... translated by the Rev. R. E. Scantlebury; with a preface by Hilaire Belloc. New York, Sheed & Ward inc., 1934- v. 22 cm. Bibliography: v. 1, p. 439-468. [BR375.C76] 35-768
1. Reformation—England. 2. Gt. Brit.—Pol. & govt.—1485-1603. I. Scantlebury, Robert E., tr. II. Title.

CONSTANT, Gustave Leon 274.2
Marie Joseph, 1869-
The reformation in England... by G. Constant...translated by the Rev. R. E. Scantlebury; with a preface by Hilaire Belloc. New York, Sheed & Ward inc., 1934- v. 22 cm. Contents.I. The English schism. Henry VIII (1509-1547) Bibliography: v. 1, p. 439-468. [BR375.C76 1934] 35-768
1. Reformation—England. 2. Gt. Brit.—Pol. & govt.—1485-1608. I. Scantlebury, Robert Elliott, tr. II. Title.

CONSTANT, Gustave Leon 274.2
Marie Joseph, 1869-1940
The Reformation in England; [v.1. Tr. from French] New York, Harper [1966] 531p. 21cm. (Torchbk. TB314S. Cathedral lib.) Reprint of the Eng. ed. pub. in 1934. First French ed. pub in 1929. [BR375.C76] 66-4630 3.45 pap.,
1. Reformation—England. 2. Gt. Brit—Pol &govt.—1485-1603. I. Scantlebury, Robert Elliott, tr. II. Title.
Contents omitted.

DICKENS, Arthur Geoffrey. 274.2
The English Reformation [by] A. G. Dickens. New York, Schocken [1968,c.1964] x, 374p. 20cm. (SB177) Bibl. [BR375.D5] 64-22987 2.45 pap.,
1. Reformation—England. I. Title.

EDWARDS, Maxwell D 274.2
The Tudors and the church, 1509-1553. [n. p.] 1957. 58 p. 24 cm. (Utah State Agricultural College. Monograph series, 5, no.2p [BR375.E3] 57-62995
1. Reformation—England. 2. Church and state in Great Britain. 3. Gt. Brit.—Hist.—Tudors, 1485-1603. I. Title.

ELLIOTT-BINNS, Leonard 274.2
Elliott, 1885-
The Reformation in England by L. Elliot Binns. Hamden, Conn., Archon Books, 1966. 244 p. 19 cm. First published in 1937. Bibliography: p. 235-238. [BR375.E5 1966] 66-18644
1. Reformation — England. I. Title.

FLETCHER, Joseph Smith, 274.2
1863-1935.
The Reformation in northern England, six lectures. Port Washington, N.Y., Kennikat Press [1971] 191 p. 22 cm. Reprint of the 1921 ed. Bibliography: p. 181-188. [BR375.F5 1971] 71-118469
1. Reformation—England. I. Title.

FORSYTH, Peter Taylor, 1848-
1921.
Faith, freedom, and the future, by Peter Taylor Forsyth ... New York and London, Hodder and Stoughton [n.d.] xvi, 348 p. 20 cm. A 13
1. Reformation—England. 2. Congregationalism. 3. Calvinism. 4. Anabaptists. I. Title.

GEIKIE, John Cunningham, 1824-1906. 274.
The English reformation: how it came about, and why we should uphold it. By Cunningham Geikie ... New York, D. Appleton and company, 1879. xviii, 512 p. 20 cm. [BR375.G4] 11-13440
1. Reformation—England. I. Title.

GEORGE, Charles H. 274.2
The Protestant mind of the English Reformation, 1570-1640, by Charles H. George, Katherine George. Princeton, N.J., Princeton Univ. Press [c.]1961. x, 452p. front. port. 25cm. Bibl. 61-7399 8.50
1. Reformation—England. 2. Gt. Brit.—Church history—16th cent 3. Gt. Brit.—Church history—17th cent. 4. Church and social problems—Gt. Brit. I. George, Katherine, joint author. II. Title.

HORNE, Thomas, 1772?-1847. 274.2
The religious necessity of the reformation asserted, and the extent to which it was carried in the Church of England vindicated, in eight sermons preached before the University of Oxford, in the year mdcccxxviii., at the lecture founded by the late Rev. John Bampton ... By Thomas Horne ... Oxford, The University press for the author; [etc., etc.] 1828. 1 p. l., [v]-xv, 310 p. 22cm. Binder's title: Bampton lectures. 1828. [BR45.B3 1828] (230.082) 38-16176
1. Reformation—England. 2. Catholic church—Doctrinal and controversial works—Protestant authors. I. Title.

HUGHES, Philip, 1895- 274.2
The Reformation in England. Rev. [i. e. 5th] ed. New York, Macmillan [1963] 3 v. in 1 illus., ports., maps, facsims. 24 cm. Contents.Contents.—"The King's proceedings."—Religio depopulata.—"True religion now established." "Bibliographical note to the revised edition": p. [vi] Includes bibliographies. [BR375.H752] 63-16363
1. Reformation—England. 2. Catholic Church in England—History. 3. Gt. brit.—Church history—16th century.

HUTCHINSON, Francis Ernest, 1871- 274.2
Cranmer and the English Reformation. New York, Collier [1962] 128p. 18cm. (Men & hist., AS266V) .95 pap.,
1. Cranmer, Thomas, Abp. of Canterbury, 1489-1556. 2. Reformation—England. I. Title.

LACEY, Thomas Alexander, 1853- 274.
The reformation and the people, by T. A. Lacey ... London, New York [etc.] Longmans, Green and co., 1929. vi, [2], 120 p. 20 cm. (Half-title: Anglican library of faith and thought, edited by Leonard Prestige) [BR375.L3] 29-19219 1.35
1. Reformation—England. 2. Reformation. I. Title.

MCCONICA, James Kelsey 942.052
English humanists and Reformation politics under Henry VIII and Edward VI. Oxford, Clarendon Pr. [New York, Oxford, 1966, c.]1965. xii,340p. 22cm. Bibl. [BR375.M27] 66-1503 7.20
1. Reformation—England. I. Title.

MAITLAND, Samuel Roffey, 1792-1866. 274.
Essays on subjects connected with the reformation in England, by the late Samuel Roffey Maitland ... With an introduction by Arthur Wollaston Hutton ... London & New York, J. Lane, 1899. xix, [1] 467 p. 19 1/2 cm. [BR375.M3 1899]
1. Reformation—England. I. Title.

MAITLAND, Samuel Roffey, 1792-1866. 274.
The reformation in England, by S. R. Maitland ... London, J. Lane; New York, John Lane company, 1906. 4 p. l., 467 p. 1 illus., 16 port. (incl. front.) 20 cm. First published in 1849, under the title Essays on subjects connected with the reformation in England. [BR375.M3 1906] 7-25559
1. Reformation—England. I. Title.

MARTI, Oscar Albert.
Economic causes of the reformation in England, by Oscar Albert Marti ... New York, The Macmillan company, 1929. xxi p., 1 l., 254 p. 21 cm. Bibliography: p. 243-254. [BR377.M35] 30-1113
1. Reformation—England. 2. Tithes—Gt. Brit. 3. Catholic church in England—Clergy. I. Title.

NICHOLS, John Gough, 1806-1873, ed.
Narrative of the days of the reformation, chiefly from the manuscripts of John Foxe the martyrologist; with two contemporary biographies of Archbishop Cranmer ... Ed. by John Gough Nichols ... [Westminster] Printed for the Camden society, 1859. xxviii, 366, 3, [1] p. illus. 22 1/2 c 17 cm. [Camden society. Publications, LXXVII] [DA20.R91 vol. 77 R.R.] A 17
1. Reformation—England. 2. Cranmer, Thomas, abp. of Canterbury, 1489-1556. I. Foxe, John, 1516-1587. II. Title.

PARKER society, London. 289
The Parker society ... for the publication of the works of the fathers and early writers of the reformed English church. [Publications] [Cambridge, Eng., Printed at the University press, 1841-55] 55 v. plates, facisms., tables. 16-27 cm. Title vignette (coat of arms) [[BX5035.P2]] A C33
1. Reformation—England. 2. Church of England—Collections. 3. Theology—Collection. I. Title.
Contents omitted.

PARKER, Thomas Maynard, 1906-
The English Reformation to 1558. London, New York, Oxford University Press [1963] viii, 200 p. 18 cm. (The Home university library of modern knowledge, 217) "First edition 1950. Reprinted...with revisions 1963." Bibliography: p. 189-195. 65-80380
1. Reformation—England. I. Title.

PARKER, Thomas Maynard, 1906- 274.2
The English Reformation to 1558 [by] T. M. Parker. 2d ed. London iNew York, Oxford Univ. Pr. 1966. vi, 168p. 20cm. (Oxford paperbacks univ. ser., opus 2) Bibl. [BR375.P3 1966] 66-8422 1.85 pap.,
1. Reformation—England. I. Title.

PARKER, Thomas Maynard, 1906- 274.2
The English Reformation to 1558 London, New York, Oxford University Press, 1950. viii, 200 p. 18 cm. (The Home university library of modern knowledge, 217) Bibliography: p. 189-195. [BR375.P3] 50-9769
1. Reformation — England. I. Title.

PERRY, George Gresley, 1820-1897. 274.
History of the reformation in England, by George G. Perry ... 6th ed. London, New York and Bombay, Longmans, Green, and co., 1898. xv, 222 p. 18 cm. (Half-title: Epochs of church history) [BR375.P5] 3-823
1. Reformation—England. I. Title.

PILL, David H. 274.2
The English Reformation, 1529-58 [by] David H. Pill. Totowa, N.J., Rowman and Littlefield [1973] 224 p. 22 cm. Includes bibliographies. [BR375.P54 1973] 72-11733 ISBN 0-87471-159-2 ISBN 0-87471-163-0 (pbk.) 7.00
1. Reformation—England. I. Title.

POCOCK, Nicholas, 1814-1897, ed.
Records of the reformation; the divorce 1527-1533. Mostly now for the first time printed from mss. in the British museum, the Public record office, the Venetian archives and other libraries. collected and arranged by Nicholas Pocock ... Oxford, Clarendon press, 1870. 2 v. 24 cm. [DA338.P6] 1-13096
1. Henry viii, king of England, 1491-1547—Divorce from Catharine. 2. Reformation—England. I. Title.

POLE, Reginald Cardinal 1500-1558 262
Defense of the unity of the church. Tr. [from Latin] introd. by Joseph G. Dwyer. Wesminster, Md., Newman [c.]1965. xli, 349p. port. 24cm. Bibl. [BR377.P713] 65-25980 6.50
1. Henry VIII, King of England, 1491-1547. 2. Reformation—England. 3. Church—Unity. I. Dwyer, Joseph G., ed. and tr. II. Title.

POWICKE, Frederick Maurice, Sir 1819- 274.2
The Reformation in England. [New York] Oxford Univ. Press [1961] 153p. (Oxford paperbacks, no. 24) Bibl. 1.25 pap.,
1. Reformation—England. I. Title.

POWICKE, Frederick Maurice, 1879-
The Reformation in England. London, Oxford University Press, 1965. 153 p. 20 cm. (Oxford Paperbacks, no. 24) 68-65901
1. Reformation—England. I. Title.

POWICKE, Frederick Maurice, Sir, 1879- 274.2
The reformation in England, by F. M. Powicke. London, New York [etc.] Oxford university press, 1941. vi, 137, (l) p. 22 cm. The essay here re-issued was written for the fourth volume of European civilisation; its origin and development, edited by E. Eyre ... 1936."--Pref. Bibliographical foot-notes. "Some recent books and articles": p. 137. [BR375.P58] A 41
1. Reformation—England. I. Title.

POWICKE, Frederick Maurice, 1879-
The reformation in England, by F. M. Powicke. London, New York [etc.] Oxford university press, 1941. vi, 137, [1] p. 22 cm. "The essay here re-issued was written for the fourth volume of European civilization: its origin and development, edited by E. Eyre ... 1936."--Pref. Bibliographical foot-notes. "Some recent books and articles": p. 137. A 41
1. Reformation—England. I. Title.

READ, Conyers, 1881- 274.2
Social and political forces in the English reformation. Houston [Tex.] Elsevier Press, 1953. 87p. 22cm. (The Rockwell lectures) [BR375.R4] 53-5960
1. Reformation—England. 2. Gt. Brit.—Pol. & govt.—1485-1606. I. Title.

THE reformation in England.
[4th ed.] New York, Macmillan, 19 v. illus., maps, facsims. Includes bibliographies.
1. Reformation—England. 2. Gt. Brit.—Pol. & govt.— 1485-1603. I. Hughes, Philip, 1895-

ROSS Williamson, Hugh 1901- 274.2
The beginning of the English Reformation. New York, Sheed and Ward [1957] 113p. 20cm. [BR375.R7] 57-10179
1. Reformation—England. I. Title.

RUPP, Ernest Gordon 274.2
Studies in the making of the English Protestant tradition, mainlv in the reign of Henrv VIII. Cambridge [eng.] Univ. Pr. 1966. xvi. 220p. 19cm. Bibl. [BR375.R8] 48-15338 1.75 pap.,
1. Reformation—England. I. Title.

SHORT, Ruth Gordon. 274.2
Stories of the reformation in England and Scotland, by Ruth Gordon Short, illustrated by Russell M. Harlan. Washington, D.C., Review and herald publishing association [1944] 249 p. illus. 20 cm. Bibliography: p. 246-249. [BR375.S45] 44-3713
1. Reformation—England. 2. Reformation—Scotland. I. Title.

SMYTH, Charles Hugh Egerton, 1903- 274.2
Cranmer & the Reformation under Edward VI, by C. H. Smyth Westport, Conn., Greenwood Press [1970] x, 315 p. 23 cm. Reprint of the 1926 ed. Bibliography: p. [303]-306. [BR375.S6 1970] 75-100842 ISBN 0-8371-4025-0
1. Cranmer, Thomas, Abp. of Canterbury, 1489-1556. 2. Reformation—England. I. Title.

SPENCER, Jesse Ames, 1816-1898. 274.
History of the reformation in England. By Rev. J. A. Spencer ... New York, Stanford and Swords, 1846. 2 p. l., [iii]-x, [9]-205 p. 16 1/2 cm. Bibliography: p. 205. [BR375.S8] 15-24186
1. Reformation—England. I. Title.

WILSON, Derek A. 274.2
A Tudor tapestry; men, women and society in Reformation England [by] Derek Wilson. [Pittsburgh] University of Pittsburgh Press [1972] viii, 287 p. illus. 23 cm. Bibliography: p. [273]-278. [BR375.W74 1972] 71-158187 ISBN 0-8229-3242-3 9.95
1. Reformation—England. I. Title.

Reformation—England—Collections.

PARKER, Thomas Henry Louis, ed. 274.2
English reformers, edited by T. H. L. Parker. Philadelphia, Westminster Press [1966] xxiv, 360 p. 24 cm. (The Library of Christian classics, v. 26) Includes bibliographies. [BR375.P26 1966] 66-10354
1. Reformation—England—Collections. I. Title.

Reformation—England—Essex.

OXLEY, James Edwin 274.267
The Reformation in Essex to the death of Mary [Manchester. Eng.] Manchester Univ. Pr. [New York, Barnes & Noble, 1966, c.1965] xii, 320p. fold. map. 23cm. Bibl. [BR377.5.E8O9] 66-879 8.00
1. Reformation—England—Essex. I. Title.

Reformation—England—Lancashire.

HAIGH, Christopher. 274.27'6
Reformation and resistance in Tudor Lancashire / Christopher Haigh. London ; New York : Cambridge University Press, 1975. xiii, 377 p. ; 22 cm. Includes index. Bibliography: p. 336-348. [BR377.5.L36H34] 73-88308 ISBN 0-521-20367-8 : 23.50
1. Reformation—England—Lancashire. 2. Lancashire, Eng.—Church history. I. Title.

Reformation—England—Sources.

DICKENS, Arthur Geoffrey. 270.6'0942
The Reformation in England, to the accession of Elizabeth I. edited by A. G. Dickens and Dorothy Carr. New York, St. Martin's Press, 1968 [c1967] vii, 167, [1] p. 20 cm. (Documents of modern history) Bibliography: p. [168] [BR375.D52 1968] 67-29568
1. Reformation—England—Sources. I. Carr, Dorothy, joint author. II. Title.

Reformation—England—Wales.

WILLIAMS, Glanmor. comp. 274.29
Welsh Reformation essays. Cardiff. Univ. of Wales Pr., 1967. 232p. 23cm. Bibl. [BR775.W5] 68-82089 5.00 bds.,
1. Reformation—England—Wales. 2. Wales—Church history. I. Title.
Distributed by Verry, Mystic. Conn.

Reformation—Europe.

*FISCHER, Robert H. 922.443
Luther. Frank W. Klos, ed. Gustav Rehberger, illustrator. Philadelphia. Lutheran Church Pr. [1966] 192p. illus. 21cm. (LCA sch. of religion ser.) Bibl. 1.25 pap. 1.50
1. Luther, Martin, 1483-1546. 2. Reformation—Europe. I. Title. II. Series.

Reformation—France.

FARMER, James Eugene, 1867-1915.
Essays on French history; The rise of the reformation in France, The club of the Jacobins, by James Eugene Farmer ... New York [etc.] G. P. Putnam's sons, c1897. 1 p. l., 120 p. 22 cm. "Authorities consulted": p. 2, 56. [DC5.F23] 5-35808
1. Reformation—France. 2. Jacobins. I. Title.

Reformation—France—Strasbourg.

STAFFORD, William S. 274.4'3835
Domesticating the clergy : the inception of the Reformation in Strasbourg, 1522-1524 / by William S. Stafford. Missoula, Mont. : Published by Scholars Press for the American Academy of Religion, c1976. vii, 296 p. ; 21 cm. (Dissertation series - American Academy of Religion ; no. 17) Originally presented as the author's thesis, Yale, 1974. Bibliography: p. 289-296.

[BR372.S8S8 1976] 76-15567 ISBN 0-89130-109-7 : 3.00
1. Reformation—France—Strasbourg. 2. Clergy—France—Strasbourg. 3. Strasbourg—Church history. I. Title. II. Series: American Academy of Religion. Dissertation series — American Academy of Religion ; no. 17.

STAFFORD, William S. 274.4'3835
Domesticating the clergy : the inception of the Reformation in Strasbourg, 1522-1524 / by William S. Stafford. Missoula, Mont. : Published by Scholars Press for the American Academy of Religion, c1976. p. cm. (Dissertation series - American Academy of Religion ; no. 17) Originally presented as the author's thesis, Yale, 1974. Includes bibliographical references. [BR372.S8S8 1976] 76-15567 ISBN 0-89130-109-7 : 3.00
1. Reformation—France—Strasbourg. 2. Clergy—France—Strasbourg. 3. Strasbourg—Church history. I. Title. II. Series: American Academy of Religion. Dissertation series — American Academy of Religion ; no. 17.

Reformation—Germany.

EELLS, Hastings, 284'.1'0924 B 1895-
Martin Bucer. New York, Russell & Russell [1971] 539 p. port. 23 cm. "First published in 1931." Bibliography: p. [424]-432. [BR350.B93E4 1971] 79-151547
1. Butzer, Martin, 1491-1551. 2. Reformation—Germany.

EELLS, Hastings, 1895- 922.443
Martin Bucer, by Hastings Eells ... New Haven, Yale university press. London, H. Milford, Oxford university press, 1931. xii, 539 p. front. (port.) 24 1/2 cm. "Published on the Louis Stern memorial fund." Bibliography: p. [424]-432. [BR350.B93E4] 31-24504
1. Butzer, Martin, 1491-1551. 2. Reformation—Germany. I. Yale university. Louis Stern memorial fund. II. Title.

[GELZER, Heinrich] 1813- 922.443 1889.
The life of Martin Luther, and the reformation in Germany. With an introduction by the Rev. Theophilus Stork ... Phrladelphia, Lindsay & Blakiston, 1854. viii, 360 p. front., plates. 29 cm. "The present work is a translation from the German work entitled 'Dr. Martin Luther, der deutache reformator. In bildlichen darstellungen, von Gustav Konig. In geschichtilchen umrissen, von Heinrich Gelzer. Hamburg, 1851'."--Introd., p. 13. [Full name: Johann Heinrich Gelzer] [BR325.G4 1854] 31-3532
1. Luther, Martin, 1483-1546. 2. Reformation—Germany. I. Stork, Theophilus, 1814-1874, ed. II. Konig, Gustav Ferdinand Leopold, 1808-1869, illus. III. Title.

[GELZER, Heinrich, 1813- 922.443 1889.
The life of Martin Luther, and the reformation in Germany. With an introduction by the Rev. Theophilus Stork ... Philadelphia. Lindsay & Blakiston, 1858. viii, 360 p. front., plates. 24 cm. "The present work is a translation from the German work entitled Dr. Martin Luther, der deutsce refrmator. In bildllchen darstellungen, von Gustav Konig. In geschichtllchen umrissen, von Heinrich Gelzer. Hamburg, 1851."--Introd., p. 13. [Full name: Johann Heinrich Gelzer] [BR325.G4 1858] 31-3531
1. Luther, Martin, 1483-1546. 2. Reformation—Germany. I. Stork, Theophilus, 1814-1874, ed. II. Konig, Gustav Ferdinand Leopold, 1808-1869, illus. III. Title.

GRISAR, Hartmann, 1845- 922.443 1932.
Martin Luther, his life and work, by Hartman Grisar ... adapted from the second German edition by Frank J. Eble M. A., edited by Arthur Preuss. St. Louis, Mo and London, B. Herber book co., 1930. x, 609 p. 24 cm. Bibliography: p. 586-600. [BR325.G75] 30-28687
1. Luther, Martin, 1483-1546. 2. Reformation—Germany. I. Eble, Frank J., tr. II. Preuss, Arthur, 1871-1934, ed. III. Title.

GRISAR, Hartmann, 1845- 922.443 1932.
Martin Luther, his life and work; adapted from the 2d German ed. by Frank J. Eble, edited by Arthur Preuss. Westminster, Md., Newman Press, 1950. x, 609 p. 23 cm. Bibliography: p. 586-600. [BR325.G75 1950] 50-10519
1. Luther, Martin, 1483-1546. 2. Reformation—Germany. I. Title.

GRISAR, Hartmann, 230'.4'10924 B 1845-1932.
Martin Luther: his life and work. Adapted from the 2d German ed. by Frank J. Eble. New York, AMS Press [1971] x, 609 p. 23 cm. Reprint of the 1930 ed. Bibliography: p. 586-600. [BR325.G75 1971] 71-137235 ISBN 0-404-02935-3
1. Luther, Martin, 1483-1546. 2. Reformation—Germany.

HOLBORN, Hajo, 1902- 922.443
Ulrich von Hutten and the German Reformation. Tr. [from German] by Roland H. Bainton [Gloucester, Mass., P. Smith, 1966, c.1937, 1965] viii, 214p. (Harper torchbk., TB1238, Acad. lib. rebound) First. pub. in 1937 by Yale in the Yaie Hist. pubns. studies, 11. Bibl. [PA8535.H62] 3.75
1. Hutten Ulrich von, 1488-1523. 2. Reformation—Germany. I. Bainton, Roland Herbert, 1894- tr. II. Title.

HOLBORN, Hajo, 1902- 922.443
Ulrich von Hutten and the German reformation. Tr. [from German] by Roland H. Bainton. New York, Harper [c.1937, 1965] viii, 214p. front. 21cm. (Torchbk., TB1238 Acad. lib.) Bibl. [PA8535.1162] 1.60 pap.,
1. Hutten, Ulrich von, 1488-1523. 2. Reformation—Germany. I. Bainton, Roland Herbert, 1894- tr. II. Title.

KONIG, Gustav Ferdinand 922.443 Leopold, 1808-1869.
The life of Martin Luther, the German reformer, in fifty pictures, from designs by Gustav Konig. To which is added, A sketch of the rise and progress of the reformation in Germany. London, N. Cooke; Philadelphia, J. W. Moore, 1855. xii, [13]-207 p. front., plates. 26 cm. The explanatory text and the "Sketch" are by Heinrich geizer. [BR325.K6 1855 a] 37-23871
1. Luther, Martin, 1483-1546. 2. Reformation—Germany. I. Gelzer, Heinrieh, 1813-1889 II. Title.

LINDSAY, Thomas 270.6'0924 B Martin, 1843-1914.
Luther and the German Reformation. Freeport, N.Y., Books for Libraries Press [1970] xii, 300 p. 23 cm. Reprint of the 1900 ed. "Chronological summary of the history of the Reformation": p. 267-291. Bibliography: p. 293-296. [BR325.L48 1970] 71-133524
1. Luther, Martin, 1483-1546. 2. Reformation—Germany. I. Title.

MOELLER, Bernd, 1931- 274.3
Imperial cities and the Reformation; three essays. Edited and translated by H. C. Erik Midelfort and Mark U. Edwards, Jr. Philadelphia, Fortress Press [1972] xi, 115 p. illus. 22 cm. "Translated from the expanded French version of 1966 [of Reichsstadt und Reformation]" Includes Problems of Reformation research (translation of Probleme der Reformationsgeschichtsforschung) and The German humanists and the beginnings of the Reformation (translation of Die deutschen Humanisten und die Anfange der Reformation). Includes bibliographical references. [BR307.M613] 72-75660 ISBN 0-8006-0121-1 3.25
1. Reformation—Germany. 2. Imperial cities (Holy Roman Empire) I. Moeller, Bernd, 1931- Probleme der Reformationsgeschichtsforschung. English. 1972. II. Moeller, Bernd, 1931- Die deutschen Humanisten und die Anfange der Reformation. English. 1972. III. Title.

OZMENT, Steven E. 280'.4'0943
The Reformation in the cities : the appeal of Protestantism to sixteenth-century Germany and Switzerland / Steven E. Ozment. New Haven : Yale University Press, 1975. xi, 237 p. ; 22 cm. Includes bibliographical references and index. [BR305.2.O9] 75-8444 ISBN 0-300-01898-3 : 12.50
1. Reformation—Germany. 2. Reformation—Switzerland. 3. Protestantism. I. Title.

PASCAL, Roy, 1904- 309.1'43'03
The social basis of the German Reformation; Martin Luther and his times. New York, A. M. Kelley, 1971. ix, 246 p. illus., port. 22 cm. (Reprints of economic classics) Reprint of the 1933 ed. Includes bibliographical references. [BR325.P3 1971] 68-30539 ISBN 0-678-00549-4
1. Luther, Martin, 1483-1546. 2. Reformation—Germany. 3. Germany—Social conditions. I. Title.

RANKE, Leopold von, 1795- 274.3 1886.
History of the Reformation in Germany. [Translated by Sarah Austin. Edited by Robert A. Johnson] New York, F. Unger Pub. Co. [1966] 2 v. (xx, 792 p.) 27 cm. "Reprinted from the edition of 1905." Bibliographical footnotes. [BR305.R4 1966] 66-26513
1. Reformation—Germany. I. Austin, Sarah (Taylor) 1793-1867, tr. II. Johnson, Robert A., ed.

RANKE, Leopold von, 1795- 270. 1886.
History of the reformation in Germany. By Leopold Ranke ... Tr. from the last edition of the German, by Sarah Austin ... Philadelphia, Lea and Blanchard, 1844. vi, [2], [25]-453 p. 24 cm. [BR305.R4 1844] 22-22539
1. Reformation—Germany. I. Austin, Sarah (Taylor) Mrs. 1793-1867, tr. II. Title.

RANKE, Leopold von, 1795- 270. 1886.
History of the reformation in Germany, by Leopold von Ranke, translated by Sarah Austin, edited by Robert A. Johnson, M. A. (Oxon) London, G. Routledge and sons, limited; New York, E. P. Dutton & co., 1905. xxiv, 792 p. 23 cm. First German edition, 6 vols, 1839-47; Sarah Austin's translation, 3 vols, published London, 1845-47, cf. Eng. cat. Bibliography: p. xv-xvii. [BR305.R4 1905] 6-15
1. Reformation—Germany. I. Austin, Sarah (Taylor) Mrs. 1793-1867, tr. II. Johnson, Robert A., ed. III. Title.

SEHLBREDE, G. E.
Wittenberg and its association with the reformation of Germany, by Rev. G. E. Sehlbrede...Introduction by Rev. W. L. McEwan... Philadelphia, The J. C. Winston co. [c1906] 1 p. l., vii-x p., 4 l., 3-128 p. front. (port.) 4 pl. 17 1/2 cm. 7-2152
I. Title.

STRAUSS, Gerald, 1922- 371.3'0943
Luther's house of learning : introduction of the young in the German reformation / Gerald Strauss. Baltimore : Johns Hopkins University Press, 1979, c1978 xii, 390 p. ; 24 cm. Includes bibliographical references and index. [BR307.S76] 77-18705 ISBN 0-8018-2051-0. : 20.00
1. Lutheran Church—Education—History. 2. Reformation—Germany. 3. Education—Germany—History. I. Title.

VEDDER, Henry Clay, 1853- 274. 1935.
The reformation in Germany, by Henry C. Vedder ... New York, The Macmillan company, 1914. xiix p., 2 l., 3-406 p. 22 1/2 cm. Bibliography: p. xi-xii. [BR305.V4] 14-1922
1. Reformation—Germany. I. Title.

Reformation—Germany—Addresses, esseys, lectures.

SHAPERS of traditions in 274.3'06 *Germany, Switzerland, and Poland, 1560-1600* / edited with an introd. by Jill Raitt ; pref. by Robert M. Kingdon. New Haven : Yale University Press, c1981. p. cm. Includes bibliographical references and index. [BR855.S53] 19 80-23287 ISBN 0-300-02457-6 : 22.50
1. Reformation—Germany—Addresses, esseys, lectures. 2. Counter-Reformation—Germany—Addresses, essays, lectures. 3. Reformation—Switzerland—Address, essays, lectures. 4. Counter-Reformation—Switzerland—Addresses, essays, lectures. 5. Reformation—Poland—Addresses,esssays, lectures. 6. Counter-Reformation—Poland—Addresses, essays, lectures. 7. Creeds—History and crticism—Addresses, essays, lectures. 8. Switzerland—Church history—Addresses, essays, lectures. 9. Poland—Church history—Addresses, essays, lectures. I. Raitt, Jill.

Reformation—Germany—Bibliography

KIEFFER, George Linn, 1883-1937, comp.
... List of references on the history of the reformation in Germany, comp. by George Linn Kieffer ... ed. and annotated by William Walker Rockwell ... and Otto Hermann Pannkoke ... White Plains, N.Y., and New York city, The H. W. Wilson company, 1917. 60 p. 19 cm. "This bibliography is gotten out by the Reformation quadricestenary committee of New York city."--Introd. (Practical bibliographies) [Z7830.K65] 17-17197
1. Reformation—Germany—Bibl. I. Rockwell, William Walker, 1874-ed. II. Paunkoke, Otto Hermann, joint ed. III. Title.

Reformation—Germany—Biography.

HOLBORN, Hajo, 270.6'092'4 B 1902-1969.
Ulrich von Hutten and the German Reformation / by Hajo Holborn ; translated by Roland H. Bainton. Westport, Conn. : Greenwood Press, 1978, c1937. viii, 214 p., [3] leaves of plates : ill. ; 23 cm. A rev. and expanded translation of Ulrich von Hutten. Reprint of the ed. published by Yale University Press, New Haven, which was issued as no. 11 of Yale historical publications studies. Includes index. Bibliography: p. [203]-209. [BR350.H8H6413 1978] 77-25067 ISBN 0-313-20125-0 lib.bdg. : 16.50
1. Hutten, Ulrich von, 1488-1523. 2. Reformation—Germany—Biography. I. Title. II. Series: Yale historical publications : Studies ; 11.

O'NEILL, Judith, 230'.4'10924 B 1930-
Martin Luther / Judith O'Neill. Minneapolis : Lerner Publications Co., 1978, c1975. p. cm. (A Cambridge topic book) (The Cambridge history library) Includes index. [BR325.O64 1978] 78-56804 ISBN 0-8225-1215-7 lib bdg. : 4.95
1. Luther, Martin, 1483-1546. 2. Reformation—Germany—Biography. I. Title. II. Series.

Reformation—Germany—Biography—Juvenile literature.

FEHLAUER, Adolph. 284.1'092'4 B
The life and faith of Martin Luther / Adolph Fehlauer ; illustrations by Steven D. MacLeod. Milwaukee, Wis. : Northwestern Pub. House, 1981. 129 p., [2] p. of plates : ill. ; 23 cm. [BR325.F46] 19 80-84134 ISBN 0-8100-0125-X pbk. : 5.95
1. Luther, Martin, 1483-1546—Juvenile literature. 2. Reformation—Germany—Biography—Juvenile literature. I. Title.

Reformation — Germany — fiction.

CHARLES, Elizabeth (Rundle) 1828-1896.
Our neighbour, Martin Luther: chronicles of the Schonberg-Cotta family. Chicago, Moody Press [1964] 384 p. 18 cm. (Moody diamonds, no. 9) Published in 1864 under title: Chronicles of the Schonberg-Cotta family. [PQ3.C38Ou] 64-3889
1. Luther, Martin — Fiction. 2. Reformation — Germany — fiction. I. Title. II. Title: Chronicles of the Schonberg-Cotta family. III. Title: Schonberg-Cotta family.

Reformation—Germany—History

LINDSAY, Thomas Martin, 922. 1843-1914.
... Luther and the German reformation, by Thomas M. Lindsay ... New York, C. Scribner's sons, 1900. xii, 300 p. 29 cm.

(The world's epoch-makers. [xv]) "Chronological summary of the history of the reformation": p. 367-291. "A list of some of the books read or consulted for this volume": p. 293-296. [BR325.L48] 2-12314
1. Luther, Martin, 1483-1546. 2. Reformation—Germany—Hist. I. Title.

LINDSAY, Thomas Martin, 1843-1914. 922.
... Luther and the German reformation, by Thomas M. Lindsay ... New York, C. Scribner's sons, 1900. xii, 300 p. 29 cm. (The world's epoch-makers. [xv]) "Chronological summary of the history of the reformation": p. 267-291. "A list of some of the books read or consulted for this volume": p. 293-296. [BR325.L48] 2-12314
1. Luther, Martin, 1483-1546. 2. Reformation—Germany—Hist. I. Title.

Reformation—Germany, Southern.

HANNEMANN, Manfred, 1938- 910 s
The diffusion of the Reformation in southwestern Germany, 1518-1534 / Manfred Hannemann. [Chicago] : University of Chicago, Dept. of Geography, 1975. p. cm. (Research paper - University of Chicago, Department of Geography ; no. 167) Bibliography: p. [H31.C514 no. 167] [BR305.2] 270.6'0943'4 75-14120 ISBN 0-89065-074-8 : 20.00
1. Reformation—Germany, Southern. I. Title. II. Series: Chicago. University. Dept. of Geography. Research paper ; no. 167.

Reformation—Germany—Strassburg.

CHRISMAN, Miriam Usher. 274.4'3835
Strasbourg and the Reform; a study in the process of change. New Haven, Yale University Press, 1967. xii, 351 p. illus., map. 22 cm. (Yale historical publications. Miscellany, 87) "Bibliographical note": p. 319-322. Bibliography: p. 323-333. [BR848.S7C45] 67-13431
1. Reformation — Germany — Strassburg. 2. Strassburg — Church history. I. Title. II. Series.

Reformation—Germany, West—Nuremberg—Biography.

GRIMM, Harold John, 1901- 270.6'092'4 B
Lazarus Spengler : a lay leader of the Reformation / by Harold J. Grimm. Columbus : Ohio State University Press, [1978] p. cm. Includes index. Bibliography: p. [BR350.S67G74] 78-13508 ISBN 0-8142-0290-X : 15.00
1. Spengler, Lazarus, 1479-1534. 2. Reformation—Germany, West—Nuremberg—Biography. 3. Nuremberg—Biography.

Reformation—Germany—Wittenberg.

PREUS, James Samuel. 274.3'18
Carlstadt's ordinaciones and Luther's liberty : a study of the Wittenberg Movement, 1521-22 / James S. Preus. Cambridge, Mass. : Harvard University Press, 1974. 88 p. ; 24 cm. (Harvard theological studies ; 26 [i.e. 27]) Includes bibliographical references. [BR359.W57P73] 74-190635 4.50
1. Karlstadt, Andreas Rudolf, 1480 (ca.)-1541. 2. Luther, Martin, 1483-1546. 3. Reformation—Germany—Wittenberg. I. Title. II. Series: Harvard theological studies ; 27.

Reformation—Great Britain

BLUNT, John Henry, 1823-1884. 274.
The reformation of the Church of England; its history, principles, and results, by the Rev. John Henry Blunt. ... London and New York, Longmans, Green, and co., 1892-96. 2 v. double tab. 23 cm. Contents.v. l. A.D. 1514-1547. 7th ed. 1892.--v. 2 A.D. 1547-1662. New ed. 1896. [BR375.B6] 1-18458
1. Reformation—Gt. Brit. 2. Church of England—Hist. I. Title.

CARTER, Charles Sydney, 1876- 274.
The English church and the reformation, by the Rev. C. Sydney Carter ... 2d ed. London, New York [etc.] Longmans. Green and co., 1925. xii, 273 p. front., plates. ports., facsims. 19 cm. [BR375.C3 1925] 28-28085
1. Reformation—Gt. Brit. 2. Church of England—Hist. I. Title.

CLARK, William Robinson, 1829-1912.
...The Anglican reformation, by William Clark... New York, The Christian literature co., 1897. vii, 482 p. 20 cm. (Ten epochs of church history. [vol. x]) 28-28081
1. Reformation—Gt. Brit. 2. Church of England—Hist. I. Title.

CLARKE, Henry Lowther, abp., 1850-
Studies in the English reformation, by Henry Lowther Clarke ... London, Society for promoting Christian knowledge; New York, E. S. Gorham [etc.] 1912. xi, [1], 13-250 p. front. ports. 19 cm. (The Moorhouse lectures, 1912). A13
1. Reformation—Gt. Brit. I. Title.

POYNTER, James William, 1885- 274.2
The reformation, Catholicism and freedom; a study of Roman Catholic and other martyrs, and of the struggles for liberty of conscience, by J. W. Poynter. With a preface by the Rt. Rev. A. C. Headlam ... London, Society for promoting Christian knowledge; New York [etc.] The Macmillan co. [1930] xiv, 209, [1] p. 20 cm. "A short bibliography": p. 203-205. [BR375.P6] 31-14215
1. Reformation—Gt. Brit. 2. Catholic church in Great Britain. 3. Martyrs—England. I. Title.

Reformation—Great Britain—Bibliography.

INTERNATIONAL Committee of Historical Sciences. Commission internationale d'histoire ecclesiastique comparee. British Sub-Commission. 016.2741
The bibliography of the Reform, 1450-1648, relating to the United Kingdom and Ireland for the years 1955-70 / edited by Derek Baker ; compiled by D. M. Loades, J. K. Cameron, Derek Baker for the British Sub-Commission, Commission Internationale d'Histoire Ecclesiastique Comparee. Oxford : Blackwell, 1975. x, 242 p. ; 23 cm. [Z7830.I522 1975] [BR375] 76-360869 ISBN 0-631-15960-6 : 20.00
1. Reformation—Great Britain—Bibliography. 2. Reformation—Ireland—Bibliography. 3. Great Britain—Civilization—Bibliography. 4. Ireland—Civilization—Bibliography. I. Baker, Derek. II. Loades, D. M. III. Cameron, James Kerr. IV. Title.
Distributed by International Schol. Bk. Service.

Reformation—History

CARPENTER, Sanford Ner.
The reformation in principle and action; a bird's eye view of the reformation, by Sanford N. Carpenter. Philadelphia, The Lutheran publication society [c1917] xii, 294 p. 20 cm. "Sermon-lectures." "References": p. xi-xxi. [BR306.C3] 17-17637
1. Reformation—Hist. I. Title.

HARRY, Carolus P.
Protest and progress in the sixteenth century, by Carolus P. Harry. Philadelphia, Joint Lutheran committee on celebration of the Quadricentennial of the reformation, 1917. xv, 162 p. front., plates, ports. 19 cm. [BR306.H3] 17-25089 0.50
1. Reformation—Hist. I. Title.

SMYTH, Hugh P.
The reformation, by the Rev. Hugh P. Smyth. Chicago, Extension press, 1919. 241p. 20 cm. [BR306.S6] 19-15031
1. Reformation—Hist. I. Title.

TORBET, Robert George, 1912- 270.6
The Protestant Reformation, a cooperative text. Philadelphia, Published for the Cooperative Publication Association, by the Judson Press [1961] 96 p. 19 cm. (Faith for life series) [BR306.T65] 61-19282
1. Reformation — Hist. I. Title.

Reformation in literature.

CHRISTOPHER, Georgia B., 1932- 821'.4
Milton and the science of the saints / Georgia B. Christopher. Princeton, N.J. : Princeton University Press, c1982. xii, 264 p. ; 22 cm. Includes bibliographical references and index. [PR3592.R4C56 1982] 19 81-47911 ISBN 0-691-06508-X : 20.00
1. Milton, John, 1608-1674—Religion and ethics. 2. Reformation in literature. 3. Theology, Puritan, in literature. 4. Calvinism in literature. I. Title.

Reformation—Ireland.

HOLLOWAY, Henry, 1876-
The reformation in Ireland; a study of ecclesiastical ligislation, by Henry Holloway... London, Society ofr pormoting Christian knowledge; New York, The Macmillan company, 1919. 3 p. l., 5-240 p. 20 cm. (Studies in church history) "List of authorities used":p. [234]-235. [BR380.H6] 20-9572
1. Reformation—Ireland. 2. Ecclesiastical law—Gt. Brit. I. Title.

LAWLOR, Hugh Jackson, 1860-
... The reformation and the Irish episcopate. By Hugh Jackson Lawlor ... London [etc.] Society for promoting Christian knowledge; New York, E. S. Gorham, 1906. 57, [3] p. 17 cm. (The Church historical society. [Publications] xciii) "The substance of a paper read on January 8, 1906, before the Dublin clerical association."--Prefatory note. [BR380.L3] 20-16440
1. Reformation—Ireland. 2. Church of Ireland. 3. Bishops—Ireland. I. Title.

MOONEY, Canice, 1911-1963. 282.415 s
The first impact of the Reformation [by] Canice Mooney. The counter-reformation [by] Frederick M. Jones. Dublin, Gill [1967] [4], 40, 53 p. 21 cm. (A History of Irish Catholicism, v. 3, 2/3) Bibliography: 3d-4th prelim. pages. [BX1503.H55 vol. 3, no. 2/3] 78-17594 7/6
1. Reformation—Ireland. 2. Counter-Reformation—Ireland. I. Jones, Frederick M. The counter-reformation. 1967. II. Title. III. Series.

RONAN, Myles Vincent, 1877-
The reformation in Dublin, 1536-1558 (from original sources) by Myles V. Roman, C. C. London, New York [etc.] Longmans, Green and co., ltd., 1926. xxxii, 543 p. 23 cm. Bibliography: p. xxix-xxxii. [BR380.R6] 26-18030
1. Reformation—Ireland. 2. Ireland—Church history. 3. Dublin—Hist. I. Title.

RONAN, Myles Vincent, 1877-
The reformation in Ireland under Elizabeth, 1558-1580 (from original sources) by Myles V. Bonan, C. C. ... London, New York [etc.] Longmans, Green and co., 1930. xxxii, 678 p. fold. map. 23 cm. Bibliography: p. xxix-xxxii. [BR380.B65] 30-8693 7.00
1. Reformation—Ireland. 2. Ireland—Church history. 3. Ireland—Hist.—1558-1608. I. Title.

Reformation—Italy.

BROWN, George Kenneth. 274.5
Italy and the Reformation to 1550, by G. K. Brown. New York, Russell & Russell [1971] vii, 324 p. 23 cm. A reprint of the 1933 modification of the author's thesis, University of Edinburgh. Bibliography: p. 299-309. [BR390.B7 1971] 70-139908
1. Reformation—Italy. 2. Italy—Church history. I. Title.

CHURCH, Frederic Corss. 274.5
The Italian reformers, 1534-1564, by Frederic C. Church. New York, Columbia university press, 1932. xii p., 1 l., 428 p., 1 l. 22 1/2 cm. Bibliography: p. [387]-399. [BR300.C5] 32-11232
1. Reformation—Italy. 2. Counter-reformation. I. Title.

CHURCH, Frederic Corss. 274.5
The Italian reformers, 1534-1564, by Frederic C. Church. New York, Octagon Books, 1974 [c1932] xii, 428 p. 23 cm. Reprint of the ed. published by Columbia University Press, New York. Bibliography: p. [387]-399. [BR390.C5 1974] 73-19934 ISBN 0-374-91595-4 14.50
1. Reformation—Italy. 2. Counter-Reformation. I. Title.

MCCRIE, Thomas, 1772-1835. 274.5
History of the progress and suppression of the Reformation in Italy in the sixteenth century; including a sketch of the history of the Reformation in the Grisons. A new ed. edited by his son. Edinburgh, W. Blackwood, 1856. [New York, AMS Press, 1974] xiv, 266 p. port. 23 cm. Includes bibliographical references. [BR390.M29 1974] 72-1006 ISBN 0-404-04118-3 13.00
1. Reformation—Italy. 2. Reformation—Switzerland—Grisons. I. Title.

Reformation—Italy—Addresses, essays, lectures.

REFORM thought in sixteenth-century Italy / 230'.0945 [edited and translated by] Elisabeth G. Gleason. Chico, Calif. : Scholars Press, 1981. 223 p. ; 23 cm. (Texts and translations series / American Academy of Religion ; no. 4) Bibliography: p. 219-223. [BR390.R43] 19 81-5648 ISBN 0-89130-497-5 : 13.50
1. Reformation—Italy—Addresses, essays, lectures. 2. Counter-Reformation—Italy—Addresses, essays, lectures. 3. Theology—16th century—Addresses, essays, lectures. I. Gleason, Elisabeth G.
Contents omitted. Publisher's address: 101 Salem St., Chico, CA 95926.

Reformation—Netherlands.

SHORT, Ruth Gordon. 274.92
Stories of the Reformation in the Netherlands; illus. by Russell M. Harlan. Washington, Review and Herald Pub. Assn., 1948 271 p. illus. 21 cm. [BR395.S5] 49-770
1. Reformation—Netherlands. I. Title.

Reformation—Norway.

QUAM, John Elliott. 284'.1'0924
Jorgen Eriksson; a study in the Norwegian reformation, 1571-1604. [New Haven, Conn.] 1968. xii, 272 l. port. 28 cm. Thesis—Yale University. Bibliography: leaves 259-272. [BR403.Q3] 77-2688
1. Jorgen Eriksson, 1535-1604. 2. Reformation—Norway.

Reformation—Poland.

FOX, Paul, 1874- 943.8'02
The reformation in Poland; some social and economic aspects. Westport, Conn., Greenwood Press [1971] viii, 153 p. 23 cm. (Johns Hopkins University. Studies in historical and political science, ser. 42) Reprint of the 1924 ed. Bibliography: p. 149-150. [BR420.P7F6 1971] 71-104272 ISBN 0-8371-3924-4
1. Reformation—Poland. 2. Poland—Social conditions. 3. Poland—Economic conditions. I. Title. II. Series.

FOX, Paul, 1874- 274.38
The Reformation in Poland: some social and economic aspects. Baltimore, Johns Hopkins Press, 1924. [New York, AMS Press, 1971] viii, 153 p. 23 cm. (Johns Hopkins University. Studies in historical and political science, ser. 42, no. 4) Originally presented as the author's thesis, Johns Hopkins University. Includes bibliographical references. [BR420.P7F6 1971b] 72-136395 ISBN 0-404-02544-7
1. Reformation—Poland. 2. Poland—Social conditions. 3. Poland—Economic conditions. I. Title. II. Series.

FOX, Paul, 1874- 943
... The reformation in Poland, some social and economic aspects, by Paul Fox, PH. D. Baltimore, The Johns Hopkins press, 1924. viii, 9-153 p. 25 cm. (Johns Hopkins university studies in historical and political

science ... ser. xlii, no. 4) Published also as thesis (PH. D.) Johns Hopkins university, 1922. Bibliography: p. 149-150. [H31.J6 ser. xlii. no. 4] [BR420.P7F6 1924] 25-1605
1. Reformation—Poland. 2. Poland—Soc. condit. 3. Poland—Econ. condit. I. Title.

KRASINSKI, Walerjan 274.38
Skorobohaty, d.1855.
Historical sketch of the rise, progress, and decline of the Reformation in Poland, and of the influence which the scriptural doctrines have exercised on that country in literary, moral, and political respects, by Count Valerian Krasinski. New York, B. Franklin [1974] p. cm. Reprint of the 1838-40 ed. [BR420.P7K8 1974] 72-82255 ISBN 0-8337-1957-2 42.50
1. Reformation—Poland. 2. Poland—Church history. I. Title.

Reformation—Scotland.

COWAN, Ian Borthwick. 274.11'06
The Scottish Reformation : church and society in sixteenth century Scotland / Ian B. Cowan. New York : St. Martin's Press, 1982. x, 244 p. : map ; 23 cm. Includes index. Bibliography: p. 224-230. [BR385.C76 1982] 19 82-5834 ISBN 0-312-70519-0 : 25.00
1. Reformation—Scotland. 2. Scotland—Church history—16th century. I. Title.

DONALDSON, Gordon 274.1
The Scottish Reformation. [New York] Cambridge University Press, 1960[ ] 242p. illus. 'Based on the Birkbeck lectures delivered in the University of Cambridge in 1957-8. bIncludes bibl. 60-16183 5.50
1. Reformation—Scotland. 2. Scotland—Church history—16th cent. 3. Church of Scotland—Hist. 4. Scotland—Soc. life & cust. I. Title.

FREE Presbyterian Church of 274.1
Scotland. Synod.
Quater-centenary of the Scottish Reformation, as commemorated by the Synod of the Free Presbyterian Church of Scotland, at Edinburgh, May, 1960, by the reading of papers on the Reformation of 1560 [Inverness, Free Presbyterian Church of Scotland (Synod) 1967]. 3-68 p. front. (port.). 22 cm. Includes bibliographical references. [BR385.F7] 68-119620 6/-
1. Reformation—Scotland. I. Title.

INNES review (The) 274.1
Essays on the Scottish Reformation, 1513-1625. Ed. by David McRoberts. Glasgow, Burns [dist. Chester Springs, Dufour, 1964] xxix, 496p. illus., ports., maps, facsims. 25cm. Essays which appeared in the Innes review. Bibl. 63-24324 15.00
1. Reformation—Scotland. I. McRoberts, David, ed. II. Title.

KNOX, John, 1505-1572. 274.1
History of the Reformation in Scotland. Edited by William Croft Dickinson. London, New York, Nelson [1949] 2 v. 25 cm. Bibliography: v. 2, p. 343-350. [BR385.K6 1949] 50-12368
1. Reformation—Scotland. I. Title.

RENWICK, A. M. 274.1
The story of the Scottish Reformation. Grand Rapids, Mich., Eerdmans [1960] 176p. 18cm. (Eerdmans pocket editions) Includes bibliography. 60-2957 1.25
1. Reformation—Scotland. I. Title. II. Title: Scottish Reformation.

Reformation—Sources.

CALVIN, Jean, 1509-1564 270.6
A Reformation debate; Sadoleto's letter to the Genevans and Calvin's reply [by] John Calvin, Jacopo Sadoleto. With an appendix on the justification of controversy. Ed., introd. by John C. Olin [Gloucester, Mass., P. Smith, c.1966] 136p. 21cm. (Harper torchbk., TB1239G, Acad. lib. rebound) Bibl. [BR301.C3 1966] 3.25
1. Reformation—Sources. 2. Church—Authority. 3. Justification. I. Sadoleto, Jacopo, Cardinal, 1477-1547. II. Olin, John C., ed. III. Title.

CALVIN, Jean, 1509-1564 270.6
A Reformation debate; Sadoleto's letter to the Genevans and Calvin's reply. [By] John Calvin, Jacopo Sadoleto. With an appendix on the justification controversy Ed., introd., by John C. Olin. New York, Harper [c.1966] 136p. 21cm. (Torchbk. TB1239G. Acad. lib.) Bibl. [BR301.C3] 66-10529 1.25 pap.,
1. Reformation—Sources. 2. Church—Authority. 3. Justification. I. Sadoleto, Jacopo, Cardinal, 1477-1547. II. Olin, John C., ed. III. Title.

CHRISTIANITY and revolution 270.6
: radical Christian testimonies, 1520-1650 / edited by Lowell H. Zuck. Philadelphia : Temple University Press, 1975. xiv, 310 p. ; 23 cm. (Documents in free church history) Includes indexes. Bibliography: p. 287-297. [BR301.C45] 74-25355 ISBN 0-87722-040-9 : 20.00 ISBN 0-87722-044-1 pbk. : 5.00
1. Reformation—Sources. 2. Anabaptists—History—Sources. I. Zuck, Lowell H. II. Title. III. Series.

CROZER theological seminary, 270.
Chester, Pa.
Historical leaflets. no. 1-9. [Chester, Printed by J. Spencer] c1901-12. 9 v. 20 cm. Issued under the supervision of the Department of church history of the seminary. Edited by Prof. Henry Clay Vedder. Contents.--no. 1. Protest of Spiers, 1529. The protest at Speler. [c1901]--no. 2. Tetzel's teses on indulgences. c1901.--no. 3. The decree of Worms. c1901.--no. 4. Brief reformation documents.--no. 5. The Peace of Augsburg. c1901.--no. 6. Luther, Martin. Two Luther documents. c1902.--no. 7. Pithou, P. Liberties of the Gallican church. c1911.--no. 8-9. Trent, Council of, 1545-1563. ... Decrees of Trent on reformation. c1912. [BR301.C8] 19-3069
1. Reformation—Sources. 2. Reformation—Germany. I. Vedder, Henry Clay, 1853- ed. II. Title.

HILLERBRAND, Hans 270.6'08
Joachim, comp.
The Protestant Reformation, edited by Hans J. Hillerbrand. New York, Walker [1968] xxvii, 290 p. 24 cm. (Documentary history of Western civilization) Includes bibliographical references. [BR301.H64 1968b] 68-3924
1. Reformation—Sources. I. Title.

HILLERBRAND, Hans 270.6'08
Joachim, comp.
The Protestant Reformation, edited by Hans J. Hillerbrand. [1st ed.] New York, Harper & Row [1968] xxvii, 290 p. 21 cm. (Documentary history of Western civilization) (Harper torchbooks, TB1342.) Includes bibliographical references. [BR301.H64 1968] 68-13328
1. Reformation—Sources. I. Title.

KIDD, Beresford James, 270.6'08
1863-1948.
Documents illustrative of the Continental Reformation; edited by B. J. Kidd. 1st ed. reprinted. Oxford, Clarendon P., 1967. xix, 743 p. 20 cm. Contributions in English, Latin and French. [BR301.K4 1967] 68-75422 50/-
1. Reformation—Sources. I. Title.

THE Reformation—Luther, the 270.6
Anabaptists / W. R. Estep, editor. [Nashville] : Broadman Press, c1979. 416 p. : ill. ; 24 cm. (Christian classics) Contents.Contents.—Desiderius Erasmus.—Martin Luther.—Ulrich Zwingli.—The Anabaptists. Bibliography: p. 413-415. [BR301.R43] 78-59979 ISBN 0-8054-6537-5 : 4.95
1. Reformation—Sources. 2. Anabaptists—History—Sources. I. Estep, William Roscoe, 1920- II. Title. III. Series.

SPINKA, Matthew, 1890- ed. 270.5
Advocates of reform, from Wyclif to Erasmus. Philadelphia, Westminster Press [1953] 399 p. 24 cm. (The Library of Christian classics, v. 14) Bibliography: p. 380-382. [BR301.S65] 53-13092
1. Reformation—Sources. 2. Reformation—Early movements. I. Title. II. Series: The Library of Christian classics (Philadelphia) v. 14

SPIRITUAL and Anabaptist 270.6
writers. Documents illustrative of the Radical Reformation, edited by George Huntston Williams, and Evangelical Catholicism as represented by Juan de Valdes, edited by Angel M. Mergal. Philadelphia, West-minster Press [1957] 421 p. 24 cm. (The Library of Christian classics, v. 25) [BR301.S67] 57-5003
1. Reformation—Sources. 2. Anabaptists. I. Williams, George Hunston, 1914- ed. II. Valdes, Juan de, d. 1541.

SPITZ, Lewis William, 1922- 270.6
ed.
The Protestant Reformation. Edited by Lewis W. Spitz. Englewood Cliffs, N.J., Prentice-Hall [1966] viii, 178 p. 21 cm. (A Spectrum book, S-140.) (Sources of civilization in the West) Bibliography: p. 177-178. [BR301.S68] 66-16344
1. Reformation—Sources. I. Title. II. Series.

ZIEGLER, Donald 230'.09'031
Jenks, comp.
Great debates of the Reformation, edited, with commentaries, by Donald J. Ziegler. New York, Random House [1969] vii, 358 p. map. 21 cm. [BR301.Z5] 69-11973
1. Reformation—Sources. I. Title.

Reformation—Spain.

MCCRIE, Thomas, 1772-1835. 274'.6
History of the progress and suppression of the Reformation in Spain in the sixteenth century, by Thomas M'Crie. New York, AMS Press [1971] viii, 424 p. 23 cm. Reprint of the 1829 ed. Includes bibliographical references. [BR405.M3 1971] 75-120206 ISBN 0-404-04117-5
1. Reformation—Spain. I. Title.

MCCRIE, Thomas, 1772-1835.
History of the progress and suppression of the reformation in Spain in the sixteenth century. By Thomas McCrie, D.D. Philadelphia, Presbyterian board of publication, 1842. 314 p. 20 cm. [BR405.M3 1842] 20-16824
1. Reformation—Spain. I. Title.

Reformation—Sweden.

ANJOU, Lars Anton, bp. of
Wisby, 1803-1884.
The history of the reformation in Sweden. By L. A. Anjou ... Translated from the Swedish by Henry M. Mason, D.D. New York, General Protestant Episcopal Sunday school union and church book society, 1859. x. 668 p. 19 1/2 cm. [BR404.A6] 7-30191
1. Reformation—Sweden. 2. Sweden—Church history. I. Mason, Henry M., tr. II. Title.

BERGENDOFF, Conrad John 274.85
Immanuel, 1895-
Olavus Petri and the ecclesiastical transformation in Sweden, 1521-1552; a study in the Swedish Reformation [New introd. by the author] Philadelphia, Fortress [c.1965] xvi, 267p. 20cm. Orig. pub. in 1928. Bibl. [BR350.P4B4] 3.75
1. Petri, Olavus, 1493-1552. 2. Reformation—Sweden. 3. Sweden—Church history. 4. Church and state in Sweden. I. Title.

BERGENDOFF, Conrad John 922.
Immanuel, 1895-
Olavus Petri and the ecclesiastical transformation in Sweden [1521-1552]; a study in the Swedish reformation, by Conrad Bergendoff. New York, The Macmillan company, 1928. 6 p. l., 264 p. 20 cm. Bibliography: p. 252-257. [BR350.P4B4] 28-14024
1. Petrl. Olavus, 1493-1552. 2. Reformation-Sweden 3. Sweden—Church history. 4. Church and state in Sweden. I. Title.

Reformation—Switzerland.

JACKSON, Samuel Macauley, 1851-
1912.
Huldreich Zwingli, the reformer of German Switzerland, by Samuel Macauley Jackson ... together with an historical survey of Switzerland before the reformation, by Prof. John Martin Vincent ... and a chapter on Zwingli's theology, by Prof. Frank Hgh Foster ... New York and London, G. P. Putnam's sons, 1901. 3 p. l., v-xxvi, 519 p. 27 pl. (1 double) 2 port. (incl. front.) fold. map, plan, 2 fold. facsim. 20 cm. (Half-title: Heroes of the reformation. [v. 5]) Bibliography: p. xxi-xxvi. [BR345.J3] 1-30597
1. Zwingli, Ulric, 1484-1531. 2. Reformation—Switzerland. I. Vincent, John Martin, 1857- II. Foster, Frank Hugh, 1851-1935. III. Title.

JACKSON, Samuel 270.6'0924 B
Macauley, 1851-1912.
Huldreich Zwingli, 1484-1531, the reformer of German Switzerland. Together with an historical survey of Switzerland before the Reformation, by Prof. John Martin Vincent ... and a chapter on Zwingli's theology, by Prof. Frank Hugh Foster. New York, Putnam, 1901. St. Clair Shores, Mich., Scholarly Press [1969] xxvi, 519 p. illus., facsims., plan, ports. 22 cm. (Heroes of the Reformation [v. 5]) Bibliography: p. xxi-xxvi. [BR345.J3 1969] 70-8883
1. Zwingli, Ulrich, 1484-1531. 2. Reformation—Switzerland. I. Vincent, John Martin, 1857-1939. II. Foster, Frank Hugh, 1851-1935.

JACKSON, Samuel 270.6'092'4 B
Macauley, 1851-1912.
Huldreich Zwingli, the reformer of German Switzerland, 1484-1531. Together with an historical survey of Switzerland before the Reformation, by John Martin Vincent; and a chapter on Zwingli's theology by Frank Hugh Foster. 2d ed. rev. New York, Putnam. [New York, AMS Press, 1972] xxvi, 519 p. illus. 19 cm. Reprint of the 1901 ed., which was issued as v. 5 of Heroes of the Reformation. Bibliography: p. xxi-xxvi. [BR345.J3 1972] 75-170836 ISBN 0-404-03543-4
1. Zwingli, Ulrich, 1484-1531. 2. Reformation—Switzerland. I. Vincent, John Martin, 1857-1939. II. Foster, Frank Hugh, 1851-1935. III. Title.

ZWINGLI, Ulrich, 270.6'092'4
1484-1531.
Selected works. Edited by Samuel Macauley Jackson. Introd. by Edward Peters [Translations from the German by Lawrence A. McLouth; translations from the Latin by Henry Preble and George W. Gilmore] Philadelphia, University of Pennsylvania Press [1972, c1901] xxx, 258 p. 21 cm. Original ed. issued as v. 1 of Translations and reprints from the original sources of European history, ser. 2. Bibliography: p. xxx. [BR410.Z87 1972b] 73-151482 ISBN 0-8122-7670-1 12.50
1. Reformation—Switzerland. I. Series: Pennsylvania. University. Dept. of History. Translations and reprints from the original sources of history, ser. 2, v. 1.

ZWINGLI, Ulrich, 1484-1531.
Selected works of Huldreich Zwingli, (1484-1531) the reformer of German Switzerland. Translated for the first time from the originals. The German works by Lawrence A. McLouth ... and the Latin by Henry Preble ... and George W. Gilmore ... Edited with general and special introductions and occasional notes by Samuel Macauley Jackson ... Philadelphia, University of Pennsylvania, 1901. 8 p. l., 9-258 p. front. (port.) 19 cm. [BR346.A25 1901] 1-14418
1. Reformation—Switzerland. I. Jackson, Samuel Macauley, 1851-1912, ed. II. McLouth, Lawrence Amos, 1863- tr. III. Preble, Henry, 1853-1929, tr. IV. Gilmore, George, W., tr. V. Title.

Reformation—Switzerland—Geneva—Sources.

COMPAGNIE des pasteurs et 270.6
professeurs de Geneve.
The register of the Company of Pastors of Geneva in the time of Calvin, Ed., tr. [from French & Latin] by Philip Edgcumbe Hughes. Grand Rapids, Mich., Eerdmans [c.1966] xvi, 380p. 24cm. Bibl. [BR410.C6] 65-18095 12.50
1. Reformation—Switzerland—Geneva—Sources. I. Hughes, Philip Edgcumbe ed. and tr. II. Title.

Reformation—Switzerland—History—Sources.

ZWINGLI, Ulrich, 1484- 282'.494
1531.
Selected works. Edited by Samuel Macauley Jackson. Introd. by Edward

Peters. [Translations from the German by Lawrence A. McLouth; translations from the Latin by Henry Preble and George W. Gilmore] Philadelphia, University of Pennsylvania Press [1972, c1901] xxx, 258 p. 21 cm. (Pennsylvania paperback, 49) Original ed. issued as v. 1 of Translations and reprints from the original sources of European history, new ser. Includes bibliographical references. [BR410.Z87 1972] 72-80383 ISBN 0-8122-7670-1 3.95
1. Reformation—Switzerland—History—Sources. I. Series: Pennsylvania. University. Dept. of History. Translations and reprints from the original sources of history, ser. 2, v. 1.

Reformation—Switzerland—Zurich.

ORIGINAL letters relative to the English reformation, 220. written during the reigns of King Henry viii., King Edward vi., and Queen Mary: chiefly from the archivesz of Zurich. Translated from authenticated copies of the authographs, and edited for the Parker society, by the Rev. Hastings Robinson ... 1st [-2d] portion Cambridge [Eng.] Printed at the University press, 1846-47. 2 v. 23 cm. (Half-title: The Parker society. [Publications. v. 37-38]) Paged continuously. General t.-p. bound at back of v. 2. This volume forms the third series of the Zurich letters, and includes letters from 1531 to 1558. [BX5035.P2 vol. 37-38] A C
1. Reformation—Switzerland—Zurich. 2. Reformation—England. I. Zurich letters. II. Robinson, Hastings, 1792?-1866, ed. and tr.

ORIGINAL letters relative to the English reformation, 289 written during the reigns of King Henry VIII., King Edward VI., and Queen Mary: chiefly from the archives of Zurich. Translated from authenticated copies of the autographs, and edited for the Parker society, by the Rev. Hastings Robinson ... Cambridge [Eng.] Printed at the University press, 1847. 2 v. in 1. 23 cm. (Half-title: The Parker society. [Publications. v. 53]) Paged continuously. General t.-p. bound at back of v. 2. Each vol. has also special t.-p., v. 1 dated 1846; v. 2, 1847. This volume forms the third series of the Zurich letters, and includes letters from 1531 to 1558. [BX5035.P2] A C
1. Reformation—Switzerland—Zurich. 2. Reformation—England. I. Zurich letters. II. Robinson, Hastings, 1792?-1866, ed. and tr.

WALTON, Robert Clifford. 321.5
Zwingli's theocracy [by] Robert C. Walton. [Toronto] University of Toronto Press [1967] 258 p. 24 cm. (C***) Bibliography: p. [227]-232. [Zwingli, Ulrich, 1484-1531.] [BR345.W3] 68-80869
1. Reformation—Switzerland—Zurich. I. Title.

THE Zurich letters: 289
or, The correspondence of several English bishops and others, with some of the Helvetian reformers, during the reign of Queen Elizabeth. Chiefly from the archives of Zurich. Translated from the authenticated copies of the autographs, and edited for the Parker society, by the Rev. Hastings Robinson ... Second edition, chronologically arranged in one series. Cambridge [Engl.] Printed at the University press, 1846. xv, [1], 576 p. 23 cm. [The Parker society. Publications. v. 52] A rearrangement, with many additions, of the English translations in the collections of the Zurich letters published by the Parker society in 1842 and 1845. [BX5035.P2] AC 33
1. Reformation—Switzerland—Zurich. 2. Reformation—England. I. Robinson, Hastings, 1792-1866, ed. and tr.

THE Zurich letters, 270.6
comprising the correspondence of several English bishops and others, with some of the Helvetian reformers, during the early part of the reign of Queen Elizabeth. Translated from authenticated copies of the autographs preserved in the archives of Zurich, and edited for the Parker society, by the Rev. Hastings Robinson ... Cambridge [Eng.] Printed at the University press, 1842. 2 p. l., vii -xvi, 378, vi, 189 p. facsims. 23 cm. (Half-title: The Parker society. [Publications. v. 50]) Edited from the original collection made by Mr. John Hunter for his own use. cf. Introd. English translations, with Latin originals at end. Half-title: The Zurich letters. A.D. 1558-1579. [BX5035.P2] [(283.082)] AC
1. Reformation—Switzerland—Zurich. 2. Reformation—England. I. Hunter, John, of Bath. II. Robinson, Hastings, 1792?-1866, ed. and tr.

THE Zurich letters (second series) 270.6 comprising the correspondence of several English bishops and others with some of the Helvetian reformers, during the reign of Queen Elizabeth Translated from authenticated copies of the autographs, and edited for the Parker society, by the Rev. Hastings Robinson ... Cambridge [Eng.] Printed at the University press, 1845. xxiii, 377, vi, 207 p. facsims. 23 cm. (Half-title: The Parker society. [Publications. v. 51]) Edited from the original collection made by Mr. Steuart A. Pears. English translations, with Latin originals at end. Half-title: The Zurich letters. (Second series) A.D. 1558-1602. [BX5035.P2] [(283.082)] AC 33
1. Reformation—Switzerland—Zurich. 2. Reformation—England. I. Pears, Steuart Adolphus, 1815-1875. II. Robinson, Hastings, 1792?-1866, ed. and tr.

Reformed Church.

BOSMA, Menno John, 1874-
Exposition of Reformed doctrine; a popular explanation of the most essential teachings of the Reformed churches, by Rev. M. J. Bosma. Grand Rapids, Mich. [1907] 4 p. l., 307, [4] p. 20 cm. 7-25554
I. Title.

BOSMA, Menno John, 1874-
Exposition of Reformed doctrine; a popular explanation of the most essential teachings of the Reformed churches, by Rev. M. J. Bosma. Grand Rapids, Mich. [1907] 4 p. l., 307, [4] p. 20 cm. 7-25554
I. Title.

HAUSER, Conrad Augustine, ed.
...Outline studies on the church; ,part I. Reformed church doctrine [by] Rev. Conrad A. Hauser. Part II. The Reformed church at work. Part III. The Reformed church and missions, by various authors in the Reformed church. Part IV. Church history (general and denominational) [by] Rev. Theodore P. Bolliger, ed. by Rev. Conrad A. Hauser... Philadelphia, Pa., The Heidelberg press [c1915] [365] p. 19 1/2 cm. (Advanced Heidelberg teacher training course, Vol. III) $0.75 Each part has separate pagination. "Additional reading references" at end of some of the chapters. 15-14579
I. Bolliger, Theodore P. II. Title.

HOUTZ, Alfred, 1844-
Triple life of the aged, by Rev. A. Houtz... Philadelphia, Reformed church publication board, 1911. 2 p. l, [9]-212 p. front. (port.) 19 1/2 cm. $0.75 11-20526
I. Title.

MACLEOD, Donald, 1914- 264.057
Word and sacrament; a preface to preaching and worship. Englewood Cliffs, N. J., Prentice-Hall, 1960. 176p. 22cm. Includes bibliography. [BX9422.2.M3] 60-14662
1. Reformed Church. 2. Preaching. 3. Public worship. 4. Reformed Church. Liturgy and ritual. I. Title.

REFORMED church in America. General synod.
The acts and proceedings of the General synod of the Reformed Dutch church, in North America, at Albany, June, 1817. Albany, Webster & Skinner, 1817. 53 pp. 8 degrees. 1-20008
I. Title.

REFORMED church in America. General synod.
The acts and proceedings of the General synod of the Reformed Protestant Dutch church in North America. New York, Board of publication of the Reformed Protestant Dutchchurch, 1859. v. 8 degrees. Contents.--v. 1. Embracing the period from 1771 to 1812, preceded by the minutesof the coetus (1738-1754) and the proceedings of the conferentie (1733-1767)and followed by the minutes of the original particular synod (1794-1799) 1-20239
I. Title.

SCHICK, John M.
Catechumen's counselor for the edification of baptized members of the Reformed church. Cleveland, O., Central pub. house of the Ref. church in the U.S. 1900. 170 [2] p. incl. form. 24 cm. Mar
I. Title.

Reformed Church—Addresses, essays, lectures.

BARTH, Karl, 1886-1968. 261.704
Community, state, and church; three essays. With an introd. by Will Herberg. [1st ed.] Garden City, N.Y., Doubleday, 1960. 193 p. 18 cm. (Anchor books, A221) Translated from the German. Contents.Contents.—Gospel and law.—Church and state.—The Christian community and the civil community.—Bibliography (p. 191-193) [BX9410.B323] 60-13233
1. Reformed Church—Addresses, essays, lectures. 2. Theology—20th century—Addresses, essays, lectures. I. Title.

CHRISTIAN perspectives. 208.2
1960- [Toronto, Association for Reformed Scientific Studies] v. ports. 28cm. annual. Includes bibliography. [BX9409.C5] 60-9912
1. Reformed Church—Addresses, essays, lectures. I. Association for Reformed Scientific Studies.

DE BOER, Cecil. 261.8
Responsible society. Grand Rapids, Eerdmans [1957] 247p. 23cm. [BX9410.D4] 57-6670
1. Reformed Church—Addresses, essays, lectures. 2. Church and social problems—Reformed Church. I. Title.

Reformed Church—Catechisms and creeds—Collections.

COCHRANE, Arthur C ed 238.42
Reformed confessions of the 16th century, edited, with historical introductions, by Arthur C. Cochrane Philadelphia, Westminster Press [1966] 336 p. 23 cm. [BX9428.A1C6] 66-13084
1. Reformed Church — Catechisms and creeds — Collections. I. Title.

TORRANCE, Thomas Forsyth, 238.42
1913- ed. and tr.
The school of faith; the catechisms of the Reformed Church. Translated and edited with an introd. by Thomas F. Torrance. New York, Harper [1959] cxxvi, 208 p. 20 cm. Contents.The larger catechisms: Calvin's Geneva catechism, 1541. The Heidelberg catechism, 1563. Craig's catechism, 1581. The new catechism, 1644. The larger catechism, 1648. -- The shorter catechisms: The little catechism, 1556. -- Craig's short catechism, 1592. A catechism for young children 1641. The shorter catechism, 1648. The Latin catechism, 1595. [BX9428.A1T613] 59-10932
1. Reformed Church — Catechisms and creeds — Collections. 2. Church of Scotland — Catechisms and creeds — Collections. I. Title.

Reformed church—Catechisms and creeds—English.

GOOD, James Isaac, 1850- 238.
1924.
Aid to the Heidelberg catechism, by Rev. James I. Good ... Cleveland, O., Central publishing house, 1904. 287 p. 15 cm. [BX9428.G6] 4-21585
1. Reformed church—Catechisms and creeds—English. 2. Reformed church in the United States—Hist. I. Heidelberg catechism. English II. Van Horne, David. III. Title.
Contents omitted.

HEIDELBERG catechism. 238.
English.
The Heidelberg catachism, with proof--texts and explanations as used in the Palatinate. Translated from the German by Rev. H. Harbaugh, D.D. With forms of devotion. Reading, Pa., D. Miller [c1892] 279 [1] p. 16 cm. [BX9428.A3 1892] 22-25629
1. Reformed church—Catachisms and creeds—English. I. Harbaugh, Henry, 1817-1867 tr. II. Title.

HEIDELBERG catechism. 238.85
English.
The Heidelberg catechism with commentary. 400th anniversary ed., 1563-1963. Philadelphia, United Church [c.1962, 1963] 224p. 23cm. This ed. of the Heidelberg catechism is a tr. from orig. German and Latin texts by Allen O. Miller and M. Eugene Osterhaven. 63-10981 3.00 pap.,
1. Reformed Church—Catechisms and creeds—English. I. Pery, Andre. Le cathechisme de Heidelberg. II. Title.

HEIDELBERG catechism. 238.85
English.
The Heidelberg catechism with commentary. 400th anniversary ed., 1563-1963. Philadelphia, United Church Press [1963] 224 p. 23 cm. "This ... edition of the Heidelberg catechism is a translation from original German and Latin texts by Allen O. Miller and M. Eugene Osterhaven. The commentary is a translation by Allen O. Miller ... from Le cathechisme de Heidelberg, by And[r]e Pery." [BX9428.A3] 63-1098
1. Reformed Chruch — Catechisms and creeds — English. I. Pery, Andre. Le cathechisme de Heidelberg. II. Title.

HEIDELBERG catechism. 238.
English.
The Heidelberg catechism, with proof-texts and explanations as used in the Palatinate. Tr. from the German by Rev. H. Harbaugh, D.D. With forms of devotion. Reading, Pa., D. Miller [1891] 287, [1] p. 16 cm. [BX9428.A3 1891] 3-22853
1. Reformed church—Catechisms and creeds—English. I. Harbaugh, Henry, 1817-1867, tr. II. Title.

HEIDELBERG catechism. 238.41
English.
The Heidelbergh catechism, or, Method of instruction in the Christian religion, as the same is taught in the Reformed churches & schools of the United States of America, and Europe. Translated from the German. Hagers-Town, Printed by J. Gruber and D. May, 1818. 70 p. 13 cm. [BX9428.A3 1818] 35-32350
1. Reformed church—Catechisms and creeds—English. I. Title.

HEIDELBERG CATECHISM. 238.5
ENGLISH
The Heidelberg catechism. 400th anniversary ed., 1563-1963. [Tr. from orig. German and Latin texts by Allen O. Miller, M. Eugene Osterhaven] Philadelphia, United Church [c.1962] 127p. 17cm. 62-20891 1.00 pap.,
1. Reformed Church—Catechisms and creeds—English. I. Title.

PETERSEN, Henry, 262.9'8'5731
1915-
The Canons of Dort; a study guide. Grand Rapids, Baker Book House [1968] 115 p. 22 cm. First published as articles in the Banner, official weekly periodical of the Christian Reformed Church. "The Canons of Dort": p. 93-115. [BX9478.P4] 68-5351
1. Dort, Synod of, 1618-1619. 2. Reformed Church—Catechisms and creeds—English. I. Canons of Dort.

Reformed Church—Clergy—Biography.

SCHMIDT, Elisabeth, 284'.23 B
1908-
When God calls a woman : the struggle of a woman pastor in France and Algeria / by Elisabeth Schmidt ; translated, with notes, by Allen Hackett. New York : Pilgrim Press, c1981. p. cm. Translation of: Quand Dieu appelle des femmes. Includes bibliographical references. [BX9459.S35A3613] 19 81-12009 ISBN 0-8298-0430-7 pbk. : 7.95
1. Schmidt, Elisabeth, 1908- 2. Reformed Church—Clergy—Biography. 3. Clergy—France—Biography. 4. Clergy—Algeria—Biography. I. [Quand Dieu appelle des femmes.] English II. Title.

Reformed Church—Collected works.

CALVIN, Jean, 1509-1564. 230.42
By John Calvin, a reflection book introduction to the writings of John Calvin. Selected and edited by Hugh T. Kerr. New York, Association Press [c.1960] 124p. (An Association Press reflection book) Bibl.: p. [123]-124. 16p. 60-12725 .50 pap.,
1. Reformed Church—Collected works. 2. Theology—Collected works—16th cent. I. Title.

CALVIN, Jean, 1509-1564. 230.42
By John Calvin, a reflection book introduction to the writings of John Calvin. Selected and edited by Hugh T. Kerr. New York, Association Press [1960] 124p. 16cm. (An Association Press reflection book) Bibliography: p. [123]-124 [BX9420.A32K4] 60-12725
1. Reformed Church—Colleced works. 2. Theology—Collected works—16th cent. I. Title.

CALVIN, Jean, 1509-1564. 201'.1
John Calvin: selections from his writings. Edited and with an introd. by John Dillenberger. Garden City, N.Y., Anchor Books, 1971. viii, 590 p. 18 cm. Bibliography: p. [574]-575. [BX9420.A32D54] 72-123715 2.45
1. Reformed Church—Collected works. 2. Theology—Collected works—16th century. I. Dillenberger, John, ed.

CALVIN, Jean, 1509-1564. 248
The piety of John Calvin; an anthology illustrative of the spirituality of the reformer of Geneva. Selected, translated, and edited by Ford Lewis Battles. Pittsburgh, Pittsburgh Theological Seminary, 1969. vii, 190 p. 23 cm. [BX9420.A32B3] 71-2831
1. Reformed Church—Collected works. 2. Theology—Collected works—16th century. I. Battles, Ford Lewis, ed. II. Title.

CALVIN, Jean, 1509-1564. 248
The piety of John Calvin : an anthology illustrative of the spirituality of the reformer / translated and edited by Ford Lewis Battles ; music edited by Stanley Tagg. Grand Rapids : Baker Book House, c1978. 180 p. : music ; 23 x 27 cm. "Metrical psalms translated by Calvin," for unison chorus with keyboard acc.: p. 137-165. Includes bibliographical references and index. [BX9420.A32B3 1978] 77-88698 ISBN 0-8010-0701-1 : 9.95
1. Reformed Church—Collected works. 2. Theology—Collected works. I. Battles, Ford Lewis. II. Title.

CALVIN, Jean, 1509-1564. 284.2
Theological threatises. Translated with introductions and notes by J. K. S. Reid. Philadelphia, Westminster Press [1954] 355p. 24cm. (The Library of Christian classics, v. 22) Bibliography: p. 344-346. [BX9420.T68] 54-9956
1. Reformed Church— Collected works. 2. Theology—Collected works—16th cent. I. Title. II. Series: The Library of Christian classics (Philadelphia) v. 22

CALVIN, Jean, 1509-1564. 284.2
Tracts and treatises. With a short life of Calvin by Theodore Bezu. Translation from the original Latin by Henry Beveridge. Historical notes and intord. added to the present ed. by Thomas F. Torrance. [Grand Rapids, Eerdmans [c1958] 3v. 23cm. Vols. 2-3 translated from the original Latin and French. Contents.v. 1. On the Reformation of the church.--v. 2, On the doctrine and worship of the church.--v.3. In defense of the Reformed faith. [BX9420.A3 1958] 58-9546
1. Reformed Church—Collected works. 2. Theology—Collected works—16th cent. I. Title.

ZWINGLI, Ulrich, 1484-1531. 230'.4
Huldrych Zwingli / [edited by] G. R. Potter. New York : St. Martin's Press, [1978] p. cm. (Documents of modern history) Bibliography: p. [BR346.A2513 1978] 78-5311 ISBN 0-312-39633-3 : 19.95
1. Reformed Church—Collected works. 2. Theology—Collected works—16th century. I. Potter, George Richard, 1900-

ZWINGLI. ULRICH, 1484-1531. 270.6
Zwingli and Bullinger: selected translations with introductions and notes by G. W. Bromiley. Philadelphia, Westminster Press [1953] 364p. 24cm. (The Library of Christian classics, v. 24) Bibliography: p. 353-357. [BR346.A24] 53-1533
1. Reformed Church—Collected works. 2. Theology—Collected works—16th cent. I. Bullinger, Heinrich, 1504-1575. II. Bromiley, G. W., ed. and tr. III. Title. IV. Series.

Reformed church—Doctrinal and controversial works.

BERKOUWER, Gerrit Cornelis, 1903- 230.42
Modern uncertainty and Christian faith. Grand Rapids, W. B. Eerdmans Pub. Co., 1953. 86p. 23cm. (The Calvin Foundation lectures, 1952) [BX9422.B4] 53-13122
1. Reformed Church—Doctrinal and controversial works. 2. Apologetics—20th cet. I. Title. II. Series.

BRINCKERHOFF, Theodore. 280.42
The Christian faith and life; an introduction to the Christian religion [by] Theodore Brinckerhoff. New York, The Half moon press [c1941] 72 p. 18 1/2 cm. [BX9422.5.B75] 41-12745
1. Reformed church—Doctrinal and controversial works. 2. Church membership. I. Title.

BROWN, Willard Dayton, 1874- 230.42
My confession of faith, a manual for catechetical and communicants' classes [by] Willard Dayton Brown. New York The Half moon press [c1941] 71 p. 19 cm. [BX9422.5.B76] 41-12746
1. Reformed church—Doctrinal and controversial works. 2. Church membership. I. Title.

CALVIN, Jean, 1509-1564. 230.42
A compend of the Institutes of the Christian religion. Edited by Hugh T. Kerr. Philadelphia, Westminister Press [1964] viii, 228 p. 23 cm. [BX9420.I652] 65-3389
1. Reformed Church—Doctrinal and controversial works. 2. Theology, Doctrinal. I. Kerr, Hugh Thomson, 1900- ed. II. Title.

CALVIN, Jean, 1509-1564. 230.42
A compend of the Institutes of the Christian religion, by John Calvin. Edited by Hugh Thomson Kerr ... Philadelphia, Presbyterian Board of Christian education, 1939. v. 228 p. 23 1/2 cm. [BX9420.I 652 1939] 40-2885
1. Reformed church—Doctrinal and controversial works. 2. Theology, Doctrinal. I. Kerr, Hugh Thomson, 1871- ed. II. Presbyterian church in the U.S.A. Board of Christian education. III. Title.

CALVIN, Jean, 1509-1564. 248'.48'42
Concerning scandals / by John Calvin ; translated by John W. Fraser. Grand Rapids : Eerdmans, c1978. p. cm. Translation of De scandalis. [BX9420.D4213] 78-8675 ISBN 0-8028-3511-2 : 6.95
1. Reformed Church—Doctrinal and controversial works. 2. Christian life—Reformed authors. I. Title.

CALVIN, Jean, 1509-1564. 230.42
Institutes of the Christian religion. Translated by Haenry Beveridge. Grand Rapids, Eerdmans, 1957. 2v. 22cm. [BX9420.I 65 1957] 59-2119
1. Reformed Church— Doctrinal and controversial works. 2. Theology, Doctrinal. I. Title.

CALVIN, Jean, 1509-1564 230.42
Institutes of the Christian religion. Ed. by John T. McNeill. Tr. by Ford Lewis Battles, in collaboration with the ed. and a committee of advisers. Philadelphia, Westminster Press [c.1960] 2 v. (lxxi, 1734 p.) (Library of Christian classics, v.20-21) bibl. 60-5379 12.50, set.
1. Reformed Church—Doctrinal and controversial works. 2. Theology, Doctrinal. I. Title. II. Series.

CALVIN, Jean, 1509-1564. 230.
Institutes of the Christian religion. By John Calvin. Translated from the original Latin, and collated with the author's last edition in French, by John Allen ... 6th American ed., rev. and cor. ... Philadelphia, Presbyterian board of Christian education, 1928. 2 v. 24 cm. The first edition was published in 1813. [BX9420.I65 1928] 29-17180
1. Reformed church—Doctrinal and controversial works. 2. Theology, Doctrinal. I. Allen, John, 1771-1839 tr. II. Title.

CALVIN, Jean, 1509-1564. 230.42
Institutes of the Christian religion, by John Calvin. Translated from the Latin and collated with the author's last edition in French by John Allen. 7th American ed., rev. and cor., with an introduction on the literary history of the Institutes by Benjamin B. Warfield ... and on account of the American editions by Thomas C. Pears ... Philadelphia, Presbyterian board of Christian education, 1936. 2 v. port., facsims. 23 1/2 cm. [BX9420.I65 1936] 38-15978
1. Reformed church Doctrinal and controversial works. 2. Theology, Doctrinal. I. Allen, John, 1771-1839 tr. II. Warfield, Benjamin Breckinridge, 1851-1921. III. Jears, Thomas Clinton, 1884- IV. Presbyterian church in the U.S.A. Board of Christian education. V. Title.

CALVIN, Jean, 1509-1564. 230'.4'2
Institution of the Christian religion : embracing almost the whole sum of piety & whatever is necessary to know the doctrine of salvation : a work most worthy to be read by all persons zealous for piety, and recently published ; Preface to the most Christian King of France, wherein this book is offered to him as a confession of faith / John Calvin of Noyon, author ; translated and annotated by Ford Lewis Battles. Atlanta : John Knox Press, 1975. p. cm. Translation of Christianae religionis institutio ... published in 1536. Includes indexes. [BX9420.I65 1975] 74-3718 ISBN 0-8042-0489-6 : 9.95
1. Reformed Church—Doctrinal and controversial works. 2. Theology, Doctrinal. I. Battles, Ford Lewis. II. Title.

CALVIN, Jean, 1509-1564. 230.42
... John Calvin's "Instruction in Christianity," an abbreviated edition of "The institutes of the Christian religion," translated from the Latin into simple modern English by Joseph Pitt Wiles ... edited and abridged by David Otis Fuller ... Grand Rapids, Mich., Wm. B. Eerdmans publishing company, 1947. 246 p. 20 cm. (Gems from giants of yesterday) [BX9420.I 65 1947] 47-23428
1. Reformed church—Doctrinal and controversial works. 2. Theology, Doctrinal. I. Wiles, Joseph Pitts, 1849- tr. II. Fuller, David Otis, 1903- ed. III. Title.

FULL declaration of 230'.424343
the faith and ceremonies professed in the dominions of the most illustrious noble Prince Fredericke 5, Prince Elector Palatine.
A Declaration of the faith professed in the Palatinate. Amsterdam : Theatrum Orbis Terrarum ; Norwood, N.J. : W. J. Johnson, 1979. 188 p. ; 22 cm. (The English experience, its record in early printed books published in facsimile ; no. 947) Photoreprint ed. Includes original t.p.: A full declaration of the faith and ceremonies professed in the dominions of the most illustrious and noble Prince Fredericke 5, Prince Elector Palatine ... according to the originall printed in the High Dutch tongue, translated into English by John Rolte. London, Imprinted for William Welby ... 1614. STC 19130. [BX9466.P34F84 1979] 19 79-84129 ISBN 90-221-0947-X : 20.00
1. Reformed Church—Doctrinal and controversial works. 2. Reformed Church—Germany, West—Palatinate—Early works to 1800. I. Rolte, John. II. Series: English experience, its record in early printed books published in facsimile ; no. 947.

O'MALLEY, John Steven. 284'.2
Pilgrimage of faith: the legacy of the Otterbeins, by J. Steven O'Malley. Metuchen, N.J., Scarecrow Press, 1973. xiii, 212 p. 22 cm. (ATLA monograph series, no. 4) Thesis—Drew University, 1970. Bibliography: p. 197-207. [BX9422.2.O4 1973] 73-5684 ISBN 0-8108-0626-6 6.50
1. Reformed Church—Doctrinal and controversial works. 2. Otterbein, Georg Gottfried, 1731-1800. 3. Otterbein, Johann Daniel, 1736-1804. 4. Otterbein, Philip William, Bp., 1726-1813. 5. Pietism—History. I. Title. II. Series: American Theological Library Association. ATLA monograph series, no. 4.

Reformed Church—Doctrinal and controversial works—Reformed authors.

BARTH, Karl, 1886-1968. 238'.5'2
The knowledge of God and the service of God according to the teaching of the Reformation, recalling the Scottish confession of 1560 / by Karl Barth ; translated by J. L. M. Haire and Ian Henderson. 1st AMS ed. New York : AMS Press, 1979. xxix, 255 p. ; 23 cm. Reprint of the 1939 ed. published by Scribner, New York, which was issued as Gifford lectures, 1937-1938. Includes index. [BX9183.B37 1979] 77-27187 ISBN 0-404-60495-1 : 24.00
1. Reformed Church—Doctrinal and controversial works—Reformed authors. 2. Scottish confession of faith, 1560. 3. Theology, Doctrinal. I. Title. II. Series: Gifford lectures ; 1937-1938.

Reformed church—Hymns.

REFORMED church in the United States.
The hymnal of the Reformed church in the United States, Prepared by a committee appointed by the General synod. Cleveland, O., Publishing house of the Reformed church [1892] 2 p. l., 638 p. 14 cm. Without music. [BV435.A5 1892] 99-4457
1. Reformed church—Hymns. 2. Hymns, English. I. Title.

REFORMED church in the United States.
The hymnal of the Reformed church in the United States. Prepared by a committee appointed by the General synod. Cleveland, O., Publishing house of the Reformed church [1892] 2 p. l., 490 p. 12 1/2 cm. Without music. [BV435.A5 1892a] 99-4458
1. Reformed church—Hymns. 2. Hymns, English. I. Title.

Reformed Church in America.

ASSOCIATE Reformed church in North America. 285.6
The constitution and standards of the Associate-Reformed church in North-America. New-York: Printed by T. & J. Swords, no. 99 Pearl-street, 1799. 612, [2] p. 21 1/2 cm. Signatures: [A]-Z4, 2A-2Z4, 2A-1Z4, 4A-4H4. Signature [A1] (half-title?) wanting. In five parts, each with special t.-p. Contents.[v. 1] The confession of faith.--[v. 2] The larger catechism--[v. 3] The shorter catechism.--[v. 4] The government, discipline, and worship ... Appendix I. Forms of ecclesiastical papers. II. Rules of procedure in judicatories. III. Solemnization of marriage. IV. Burial of the dead.--[v. 5] The sum of saving knowledge ... together with the practical use thereof. [BX8999.A7A2 1799] 32-25198
I. Title.

CORWIN, Edward Tanjore, 1834-1914. 285.
A manual of the Reformed church in America (formely Ref. Prot. Dutch church). 1628-1902. By Edward Tanjore Corwin ... 4th ed., rev. and enl. New York, Board of publication of the Reformed church in America, 1902. viii p., 2 l., 1082 p. front., illus., plates, ports., facsim. 24 cm. [BX9515.C8 1902] 2-22180
1. Reformed church in America. I. Title.

LILY among the thorns.
New York, Board of Education, Reformed Church in America Distr. by Half Moon Press, Teaneck, N. J., 1961. 154p. 18cm.
1. Reformed Church in America. 2. Reformation—Netherlands. I. Hageman, Howard G

MANUAL of the Sacred Heart.
Comp. and tr. from approved sources. New ed. Philadelphia, H. L. Kilner & co. [1891] 355 p. 24° 1-14608

NEW York. Collegiate church.
Historical sketch of the origin and organization of the Reformed church in America and of the Collegiate church of the city of New York... 3d ed. [New York] The Consistory [of the Collegiate reformed church] 1904. 54, [6] p. illus. (incl. ports.) 19 1/2 cm. 4-24603
I. Title.

NEW York. Collegiate church.
Historical sketch of the origin and organization of the Reformed church in America and of the Collegiate church of the city of New York... 3d ed. [New York] The Consistory [of the Collegiate reformed church] 1904. 54, [6] p. illus. (incl. ports.) 19 1/2 cm. 4-24603
I. Title.

READINGTON, N.J. Reformed church. 289
... Historical discourse and addresses delivered at the 175th anniversary of the Reformed church Readington, N. J. October 17th, 1894. [Somerville, N.J., Press of the Unionist-gazette association. 1894?] 82 p. front., plates, ports. 20 cm. At head of title: 1719-1894. [BX9531.R4A4] 44-30300
I. Title.

READINGTON, N.J. Reformed church. 289
... Historical discourse and addresses delivered at the 175th anniversary of the Reformed church Readington, N. J. October 17th, 1894. [Somerville, N.J., Press of the Unionist-gazette association. 1894?] 82 p. front., plates, ports. 20 cm. At head of title: 1719-1894. [BX9531.R4A4] 44-30300
I. Title.

REFORMED church in America. General synod.
The acts and proceedings ... of the General synod of the Reformed church in America ... New York, The Board of publication and Bible-school work, 1812-19. v. illus. (incl. port.) maps (part fold.) diagrs. 21-23 1/2 cm. Title varies: v. 1, The acts and proceedings of the General synod of the Reformed Protestant Dutch church in North America ... [v. 1a]-4. The acts and proceedings of the General synod of the Reformed Dutch church in North America ... v. 5-10, The acts and proceedings of the General Synod of the Reformed Protestant Dutch church in North America ... v. 11- Acts and proceedings of the General synod of the Reformed church in America ... Published in New York with the exception of v. 1a, no. 1-7, which were printed in Albany by Ferrand and Green [etc.] Vol. 1, a translation includes "the period from 1771 to 1812, preceded by the Minutes of the Coetus (1738-1754) and the Proceedings of the Conferentle (1755-1767) and followed by the Minutes of the original particular synod (1794-1799)" [BX9518.A3] 1-20238
I. Title.

REFORMED church in America. General synod.
The constitution of the Reformed Dutch church of North America, with an appendix, containing formularies for the use of the churches; together with the rules and orders for the government of the general synod. The catechism, articles of faith, canons of synod of Dordrecht, and liturgy. Philadelphia, G. W. Mentz & son, 1840. 131 p. 13 1/2 cm. 4-34273
I. Title.

REFORMED church in the U.S. Classis of North Carolina
Historic sketch of the Reformed church in North Carolina, by a board of editors under the Classis of North Carolina. With an introduction by the late Geo. Wm. Welker, D.D. Philadelphia, Pa., Publication board of the Reformed church in the United States [c1908] 327 p. front, plates, ports. 20 cm. Edited by J. C. Clapp, J. C. Leonard and others. 8-10428
I. Clapp, Jacob Crawford, 1832- ed. II. Leonard, Jacob C., joint ed. III. Title.

REFORMED church in the U.S. Classis of North Carolina
Historic sketch of the Reformed church in North Carolina, by a board of editors under the Classis of North Carolina. With an introduction by the late Geo. Wm. Welker, D.D. Philadelphia, Pa., Publication board of the Reformed church in the United States [c1908] 327 p. front, plates, ports. 20 cm. Edited by J. C. Clapp, J. C. Leonard and others. 8-10428
I. Clapp, Jacob Crawford, 1832- ed. II. Leonard, Jacob C., joint ed. III. Title.

REFORMED church in the United States. General convention, Jan. 17-23, 1863. 238.41
Tercentenary monument. In commemoration of the three hundredth anniversary of the Hiedelberg catechism. of the Heidelberg catechism. New York, A. D. F. Randolph; [etc., etc.] 1863. ixxii, 573, [1] P. 23 cm. "The essays contained in this volume ... were read before a general convention of the church, held in Philadelphia, January 17-28, 1863. In honor of the three hundredth anniversary of the Heidelberg catechism."--Pref. [BX9428.A5 1863] 40-1669
I. Title.

ROMIG, Edgar Franklin, 1890-
The tercentenary year; a record of the celebration of the three hundredth anniversary of the founding of the first church in New Netherland. now New York, and the beginning of organized religious life under the Reformed (Dutch) church in America, held under the auspices of the General synod, R. C. A., A. D. 1928; prepared by Edgar Franklin Romig ... 1628-1928. [New York,] The Church, 1929. xv, 542 p. front., illus. (incl. music, map) plates (2 double) ports., facsims. 26 cm. [BX9515.R6] 29-18347
1. Reformed church in America. I. Title.

Reformed church in America — Church government and discipline.

REFORMED Church in America. Constitution.
The constitution of the Reformed church in America. Teaneck, N.J., Board of education, Dept. of publications, Reformed church in America, 1962. 56 p. 19 cm. 63-47521
1. Reformed church in America — Church government and discipline. I. Reformed Church in America. Board of Education. II. Title.

Reformed church in America. Classis Montgomery.

DAILEY, William Nelson Potter, 1863-
... The history of Montgomery classis, R. C. A. To which is added sketches of Mohawk valley men and events of early days, the Iroquois, Palatines, Indian isons, Tyron county committee of safety, Sir Wm. Johnson, Joseph Brant, Arendt Van Curler, Gen. Herkimer, Reformed church in America, doctrine and progress, revolutionary residences, etc. By W. N. P. Dailey. Amsterdam, N. Y., Recorder press [116] 197, [1] p. illus. (incl. ports.) 24 cm. Biblorgaphy: p. 197. [BX9519.M7D3] 16-19315
1. Reformed church in America. Classes. Montgomery. I. Title.

Reformed church in America. Classis of Bergen.

TAYLOR, Benjamin Cook, 1801-1881.
Annals of the classis of Bergen, of the Reformed Dutch church, and of the churches under its care: including, the civil history of the ancient township of Bergen, in New Jersey; by Benjamin C. Taylor ... 3d ed. New York, Board of publication of the Reformed Protestant Dutch church [1857] xii, [13]-479 p. 17 pl. (incl. front.) 4 port. 20 cm. [BX9519.B5T3] 17-14850
1. Reformed church in America. Classis of Bergen. 2. Bergen co., N.J.—Hist. I. Title.

Reformed Church in America. Classis of Schenectady.

BIRCH, John Joseph, 1894-
As the fields ripened; being a history of the Schenectady Classis of the Reformed Church in America. [Schenectady, N.Y.] Schenectady Classis, 1960. 126 p. 23 cm. NUC64
1. Reformed Church in America. Classis of Schenectady. I. Title.

Reformed church in America. Constitution.

DEMAREST, David D. 1819-1898. 285.7
Notes on the constitution of the Reformed (Dutch) church in America. Printed for the use of the students of the Theological seminary of the Reformed (Dutch) church in America. At New Brunswick, N. J. By Rev. David D. Demarest ... New Brunswick, N. J., J. Heidingsfield's press, 1896. 186 p. 1 l. 21 cm. (New Brunswick N. J. Theological ceminary of the Reformed Church in America. Publications) [BX9522.D4] 36-16646
1. Reformed church in America. Constitution. 2. Reformed church in America—Government. I. Title.

REFORMED church in America. General synod. 285.7
A digest of constitutional and synodical legislation of the Reformed church in America (formerly the Ref. Prot. Dutch church) by Edward Tanjore Corwin, D.D. Prepared by order of General synod. New York, The Board of publication of the Reformed church in America, 1906. ixxxvii, 851 p. 24 cm. Constitutions: p. vii-ixxxvii. [BX9522.A52] 38-12468
1. Reformed church in America. Constitution. 2. Reformed church in America—Government. I. Corwin, Edward Tanjore, 1834-1914, ed. II. Reformed church in America. Board of publication. III. Title.

Reformed Church in America—Directories.

REFORMED Church in America. Commission on History. 285.73205
Historical directory of the Reformed Church in America, 1628-1965. Peter N. VandenBerge, ed. New Brunswick, N.J. [1966] xix, 348p. 23cm. Successor to C. E. Corwin's A manual of the Reformed Church in America (formerly Reformed Protesant Dutch Church) 1628-1922, 5th ed., 1922 [BX9507.A55] 66-21948 5.00
1. Reformed Church in America—Direct. I. VandenBerge. Peter N., ed. II. Corwin, Charles Edward, 1868-1958. A manual of the Reformed Church in America. III. Title.

REFORMED Church in America. Commission on History. 285'.732'02573
Historical directory of the Reformed Church in America, 1628-1978 / [edited] by Peter N. VandenBerge. 2d ed. Grand Rapids : Eerdmans, c1978. xvii, 385 p. ; 23 cm. (The Historical series of the Reformed Church in America ; no. 6) [BX9507.A55 1978] 78-6736 ISBN 0-8028-1746-7. : 15.00
1. Reformed Church in America—Directories. I. VandenBerge, Peter N. II. Title. III. Series: Reformed Church in America. Historical series ; no. 6.

Reformed church in America—Doctrinal and controversial works.

REMARKS on liberty of conscience, human creeds, and theological schools, suggested by the facts in a recent case. By a layman of the Reformed Dutch church ... New York, Printed by J. & J. Harper, 1828. 102 p. 22 1/2 cm. [BX9543.V3R4] 36-22152 922.573
1. Van Dyck, Leonard B., 1802?-1877. 2. Reformed church in America—Doctrinal and controversial works. 3. New Brunswick, N.Y. Theological seminary of the Reformed church in America. 4. Liberty of conscience. I. A layman of the Reformed Dutch church.

Reformed Church in America. General Synod—Indexes.

SCHUPPERT, Mildred W. 262'.5'5732
A digest and index of the minutes of the General Synod of the Reformed Church in America, 1958-1977 / by Mildred W Schuppert. Grand Rapids : Eerdmans, c1979. xix, 120 p. ; 23 cm. (The Historical series of the Reformed Church in America ; no. 7) [BX9518.A2] 79-10043 ISBN 0-8028-1774-2. : 8.95
1. Reformed Church in America. General Synod—Indexes. I. Reformed Church in America. General Synod. II. Title. III. Series. IV. Series: Reformed Church in America. Historical series ; no. 7

Reformed church in America—Government.

REFORMED church in America. 289
The constitution of the Reformed church in America, (known for a time as the "Reformed Dutch church," and also designated in the Act of incorporation passed by the Legislature of New York, April 7, 1819, as "The Reformed Protestant Dutch church") Embracing the catacism, the compendium, the Confession of faith, the canons of the Synod of Dordrecht, and the liturgy ... New York, Board of publication of the Reformed church in America, 1905. 96 p. incl. forms. 18 cm. Cover-title: The constituion of the R.C.A. "This volume contains only the title page, the prefatory note and the organic law of the constitution; with an appendix comprising: I. Formularies II. Rules of order. III. Order of busines. IV. Permanent resolutions." [BX9522.A5] 45-49718
1. Reformed church in America—Government. I. Title.

REFORMED church in America. 285.773
The constitution of the Reformed Dutch church of North America: with an appendix, containing formularies for the use of the churches; together with the rules and orders for the government of the General synod. New-York, Printed by L. Nichols, 1834. 72 p. incl. forms. 14 1/2 cm. [BX9522.A5 1834] 38-11346
1. Reformed church in America—Government. I. Title.

Reformed church in America—History

†BROUWER, Arie R. 285'.732'09
Reformed Church roots : thirty-five formative events / by Arie R. Brouwer. 1st ed. New York : Reformed Church Press, c1977. 195 p. : ill. ; 22 x 25 cm. Includes index. [BX9515.B68] 77-155910 write for information
1. Reformed Church in America—History. I. Title.

BROWN, Willard Dayton, 1874-
A history of the Reformed church in America [by] Willard Dayton Brown ... New York city, Board of publication and Bible school work [c1928] 3 p. l., 5-140 p. front., illus., plates, ports. 19 1/2 cm. Bibliography: p. 123. [BN9515.B7] 28-13395
1. Reformed church in America—Hist. I. Title.

CORWIN, Charles Edward, 1868-
A manual of the Reformed church in America (formerly Reformed Protestant Dutch church) 1628-1922. By Charles E. Corwin. 5th ed., rev. New York, Board of publication and Bible-school work of the Reformed church in America, 1922. 2 p. l., [iii]-xxix, 782 p. front. (port.) 24 cm. 60 p. 14 cm. Earlier editions by Edward Tanjore Corwin. Supplement to Corwin's manual (5th edition, 1922) of the Reformed church in America, compiled by Rev. Charles E. Corwin; edited by Rev. James Boyd Hunter, D.D., and Rev. W. N. P. Dailey, D.D. New York, The Board of publication and Bible-school work, 1933. Bibliography: p. xxviii-xxix. [BX9515.C8 1922] 22-14218
1. Reformed church in America—Hist. 2. Reformed church in America—Clergy. I. Corwin, Edward Tanjore, 1834-1914. II. Hunter, James Boyd, 1863- ed. III. Dailey, William Nelson Potter, 1863- ed. IV. Title.

CORWIN, Edward Tanjore, 1834-1914. 285.
A manual of the Reformed church in America (formerly Ref. Prot. Dutch church) 1628-1878. By Edward Tanjore Corwin ... 3d ed., rev. and enl. New York, Board of publication of the Reformed church in America, 1879. xiv p., 1 l., 675,

[1] p. fold. front., illus., plates, ports. 24 cm. "First edition, 1859, 1,000 copies. Second edition, 1869. 1,000 copies. Third edition, 1879, electrotyped: first issued, 1,000 copies." [BX9515.C8 1879] 9-23108
1. Reformed church in America—Hist. 2. Reformed church in America—Clergy. I. Title.

DE JONG, Gerald Francis, 1921- 285'.73
The Dutch Reformed Church in the American colonies / by Gerald F. De Jong. Grand Rapids : Eerdmans, c1978. 279 p. : ill. ; 21 cm. (The Historical series of the Reformed Church in America ; no. 5) Includes index. Bibliography: p. 266-272. [BX9515.D39] 78-17216 ISBN 0-8028-1741-6 : 6.95
1. Reformed Church in America—History. I. Title. II. Series: Reformed Church in America. The historical series ; no. 5.

DEMAREST, David D. 1819-1898. 285.7
History and characteristics of the Reformed Protestant Dutch church. By David D. Demarest ... New York, Board of publication of the Reformed Protestant Dutch church, 1856. xxviii, [13]-221 p. front., plates. 19 cm. [New Brunswick N. J. Theological seminary of the Reformed church in America. Publications] Based on a course of lectures delivered in the Reformed Dutch church, Hudson N. Y., in the winter of 1853-4. cf. Pref. Published later under title: The Reformed church in America. [BX9515.D4 1856] 36-16664
1. Reformed church in America—Hist. I. Reformed church in America. Board of publication. II. Title.

DEMAREST, David D. 1819-1898. 285.7
The Reformed church in America. Its origin, development and characteristics. By David D. Demarest ... 4th ed. Rev. and enl. New York, Board of publication of the Reformed church in America, 1889. xiii, [3], 215 p. col. front. (coat of arms) illus., ports. 23 cm. [New Brunswick, N. J. Theological seminary of the Reformed church in America. Publications] Based on a course of lectures delivered in the Reformed Dutch church, Hudson, N. Y., in the winter of 1853-4. cf. Pref. Published earlier under title: History and characteristics of the Reformed Protestant Dutch church. "Works ... consulted": p. iv-v. "The history of the coat-of-arms. By John S. Bussing": p. [ix]-xiii. [BX9515.D4 1889] 36-25401
1. Reformed church in America—Hist. I. Reformed church in America. Board of publication. II. Bussing, John Stuyvesant, 1838-1916. III. Title.

HARMELINK, Herman. 285'.732'09
Ecumenism and the Reformed Church. Grand Rapids, Eerdmans [1968] 112 p. 21 cm. (The Historical series of the Reformed Church in America, no. 1) Bibliography: p. 95-98. Bibliographical references included in "Notes" (p. 99-106) [BX9515.H3] 68-57154 2.45
1. Reformed Church in America—History. 2. Christian union—Reformed Church in America—History. I. Title. II. Series: Reformed Church in America. The historical series, no. 1

KINDERHOOK, N. Y. Reformed Dutch Church.
The two hundred fiftieth anniversary of the Kindernook Reformed Church ... 1712-1962. Incorporated on December 25th, 1788 by the name of "Minister, Elders and Deacons of the Reformed Protestant Dutch Church of Kinderhook in the County of Columbia." A congregation of the Reformed Church in America, the classis of Columbia -- Greene, the particular Synod of Albany. [Kinderhook] 1962. 67 p. illus., port. facsims. 23 cm. 65-3791
I. Title.

REFORMED church in America. Tercentenary committee on research and publication. 285.
Tercentenary studies, 1928, Reformed church in America; a record of beginnings, compiled by the Tercentenary committee on research and publication. [New York] The Church, 1928. vi, 515 p. 24 cm. W. H. S. Demarest, chairman. Contains bibliographies. [BX9515.A4 1928] 29-9894
1. Reformed church in America—Hist. I. Demarest, William Henry Steele, 1863- II. Title.

STOUDT, John Baer, 1878-
A history of Grace reformed church, Northampton, Pennsylvania, arranged and prepared by Rev. John Bear Stoudt, Preston D. Borger, James W. Smith, Herbert T. Werner; together with an account of the Dry Run and Stemton Union Sunday schools, a complete record of baptisms, confirmations, marriages, deaths, the officers and members of the congregation and Sunday school; in commemoration of the fifteenth anniversary of the laying of the cornerstone, October 18, 1897-October 20, 1912. Northampton, Pa. [Clement news print] 1912. 65, [1] p. front., pl., ports., facsim. 23 1/2 cm. "Edition limited to one hundred and twenty-five copies of which this is no. 43." 13-19453
I. Borger, Preston D., joint author. II. Smith, James W., joint author. III. Werner, Herbert T., joint author. IV. Title.

STOUDT, John Baer, 1878-
A history of Grace reformed church, Northampton, Pennsylvania, arranged and prepared by Rev. John Bear Stoudt, Preston D. Borger, James W. Smith, Herbert T. Werner; together with an account of the Dry Run and Stemton Union Sunday schools, a complete record of baptisms, confirmations, marriages, deaths, the officers and members of the congregation and Sunday school; in commemoration of the fifteenth anniversary of the laying of the cornerstone, October 18, 1897-October 20, 1912. Northampton, Pa. [Clement news print] 1912. 65, [1] p. front., pl., ports., facsim. 23 1/2 cm. "Edition limited to one hundred and twenty-five copies of which this is no. 43." 13-19453
I. Borger, Preston D., joint author. II. Smith, James W., joint author. III. Werner, Herbert T., joint author. IV. Title.

VAN EYCK, William O.
Landmarks of the Reformed-fathers; or, What Dr. Van Raalte's people believed, by William O. van Eyck... Grand Rapids, Mic., The Reforemd press [c1922] 319 p. incl. front., ports. 22 cm. [BX9515.V3] 22-20449
1. Reformed church in America—Hist. I. Title.

WARWICK, N.Y. Reformed church.
1804-1904; the record of a century of church life of the Reformed church, Warwick N.Y. [Warwick, N.Y., Press of the Warwick Valley dispatch, 1904] 5 p. l., [7]-129, [2] p. front., illus., plates, ports., plan. 25 cm. Taber Knox, chairman of Publication committee. 7-11200
I. Knox, Taber, 1863- II. Title.

Reformed Church in America—History—Addresses, essays, lectures.

PIETY and patriotism : 285'.709
Bicentennial studies of the Reformed Church in America, 1776-1976 / edited by James W. Van Hoeven. Grand Rapids : Eerdmans, c1976. 191 p. ; 21 cm. (The Historical series of the Reformed Church in America ; no. 4) Includes bibliographical references. [BX9515.P5] 76-369401 ISBN 0-8028-1663-0 : 3.95
1. Reformed Church in America—History—Addresses, essays, lectures. 2. Reformed Church in America—Doctrinal and controversial works—Addresses, essays, lectures. I. Van Hoeven, James w. II. Series: Reformed Church in America. The historical series ; no. 4.

Reformed church in America—Hymns.

REFORMED church in America. 245.2057
Additional hymns. Adopted by the General synod of the Reformed Protestant Dutch church in North America, at their session, June, 1846, and authorized to be used in the churches under their care. Philadelphia, Mentz & Rovoudt, 1848. 238 p. 18 1/2 cm. Without music. [BV434.A3 1848 a] 32-18630
1. Reformed church in America—Hymns. 2. Hymns, English. I. Title.

REFORMED church in America.
... *Hymns of prayer and praise.* New York, A. S. Barnes & company, 1871. 188 p. 17 1/2 cm. Preface signed: Ashbel G. Vermilye, William J. R. Taylor, Alex R. Thompson. "Compiled mainly from 'Hymns of the church'."--Pref. With music. [M2124.D7R28 1871] 45-31672
1. Reformed church in America—Hymns. 2. Hymns, English. I. Vermilye, Ashbel Green, 1822-1905, ed. II. Taylor, William James Romeyn, 1823-1891, joint ed. III. Thompson, Alexander Ramsay, 1822-1895, joint ed. IV. Title.

REFORMED church in America.
Hymns of prayer and praise. New York, A. S. Barnes & company, 1874. 192 p. 17 1/2 cm. Preface signed: Ashbel G. Vermilye, William J. R. Taylor, Alex R. Thompson. Compiled mainly from "Hymns of the church." With music. [M2124.D7R28 1874] 45-31556
1. Reformed church in America—Hymns. 2. Hymns, English. I. Vermilye, Ashbel Green, 1822-1895, ed. II. Taylor, William James, Romeyn, 1823-1891, joint ed. III. Thompson, Alexander Ramsay, 1822-1895, joint ed. IV. Title.

REFORMED church in America.
Hymns of the church. With tunes. New York, A. S. Barnes & company, 1869. iv, [4], 495, [1] p. 21 1/2 cm. Preface signed: John R. Thompson, Ashbel G. Vermilye, Alex R. Thompson. "The musical part of the book, except a portion of the chants, has been arranged and edited by Mr. U. C. Burnap."--Pref. [M2124.D7R3 1869] 45-31548
1. Reformed church in America—Hymns. 2. Hymns, English. I. Thompson, John Bodine, 1830-1907, ed. II. Vermilye, Ashbel Green, 1822-1905, joint ed. III. Thompson, Alexander Ramsay, 1822-1895, joint ed. IV. Burnap, Uzzlah Cicero, ed. and arr. V. Title.

REFORMED Church in America. 238'.5'732
Our song of hope : a provisional confession of faith of the Reformed Church in America ; with commentary and appendixes by Eugene P. Heideman. Grand Rapids : Eerdmans, [1975] c1974. vi, 90 p. ; 21 cm. [M2124.R26O8] 74-28219 ISBN 0-8028-1604-5 pbk. : 2.95
1. Reformed Church in America—Hymns. 2. Reformed Church in America—Catechisms and creeds—English. 3. Hymns, English. I. Heideman, Eugene P., ed. II. Title.

REFORMED church in America. 264.057
The Psalms and hymns, with the Catechism, Confession of faith and Liturgy of the Reformed Dutch church in North America. Selected at the request of the General synod. By John H. Livingston ... New York: Printed and sold by George Forman, corner of Partition and Greenwich streets. 1814. xx, 601 p. 15 cm. [BV434.A3 1814] 19-19193
1. Reformed church in America—Hymns. 2. Hymns, English. I. Bible. O.T. Psalms. English. Paraphrases. 1814. II. Bible. English. Paraphrases. O.T. Psalms. 1814. Heidelberg catechism. III. Nationale synode te Dordrecht, 1618-1619. IV. Livingston, John Henry, 1746-1825, comp. V. Title.

REFORMED church in America. 264.057
The Psalms & hymns, with the Catechism, Confession of faith, and Liturgy of the Reformed Dutch church in North America. Selected at the request of the General synod. By John H. Livingston ... New-York, D. D. Smith and J. Montgomery [1827] xvi, [17]-493 p. 12 1/2 cm. Without music. [BV434.A3 1827] 32-18626
1. Reformed church in America—Hymns. 2. Hymns. English. I. Bible. O.T. Psalms. English. Paraphrases. 1827. II. Bible, English Paraphrases. O.T. Psalms. 1827. III. Heidelberg catechism. IV. Nationale synode te Dordrecht, 1618-1619. V. Livingston, John Henry, 1746-1825, comp. VI. Title.

REFORMED church in America. 264.057
The Psalms and hymns, with the Catechism, Confession of faith, and Liturgy, of the Reformed Dutch church in North America. Selected at the request of the General synod. By John H. Livingston ... New York; Published by John Montgomery, no. 472 Greenwich-street, 1820. 20, [25]-536 p. 11 1/2 cm. Without music. [BV434.A3 1820] 32-18627
1. Reformed church in America—Hymns. 2. Hymns, English. I. Bible. O.T. Psalms. English. Paraphrases. 1820. II. Bible. English. Paraphrases. O.T. Psalms. 1820. III. Heidelberg catechism. IV. Nationale synode te Dordrecht, 1618-1619. V. Livingston, John Henry, 1746-1825, comp. VI. Title.

REFORMED church in America. 264.057
... *The Psalms and hymns, with the Catechism,* Confession of faith, and Liturgy, of the Reformed Dutch church in North America, selected at the request of the General synod. By John H. Livingston ... To which are added the Additional hymns, and the Canons of the Synod of Dordrecht, with a new and copious index. New York, W. A. Mercein, 1832. iv, [5]-316, 89, [9], [323]-330, 77 p. 19 1/2 cm. At head of title: Mercein's stereotyped edition. "Additional hymns ... 3d ed." has special t.p. Without music. [BV434.A3 1832] 32-18624
1. Reformed church in America—Hymns. 2. Hymns, English. I. Bible. English. Paraprases. O. T. Psalms. 1832. II. Heidelberg catechism. III. Nationale synode te Dordrecht, 1618-1619. v. Livingston, John Henry, 1746-1825, comp. IV. Title.

REFORMED church in America. 264.057
The Psalms and hymns, with the Catechism, Confession of faith, and Liturgy, of the Reformed Dutch church in North America. Selected at the request of the General synod. By John H. Livingston ... To which are added, the Additional hymns, and the Canons of the Synod of Dordrecht, with a new and copious index. Philadelphia, Mentz & Rovoudt, 1842. iv, 5-592, 81 p. 19 cm. Without music. [BV434.A3 1842] 32-18625
1. Reformed church in America—Hymns. 2. Hymns, English. I. Bible. O.T. Psalms. English. Paraphrases. 1842. II. Bible. English. Paraphrases. O. T. Psalms. 1842. III. Heidelberg catechism. IV. Nationale synode te Dordrecht, 1618-1619. V. Livingston, John Henry, 1746-1825, comp. VI. Title.

REFORMED church in the United States.
The hymnal of the Reformed church in the United States. Prepared by a committee appointed by the General synod. Cleveland, Publishing house of the Reformed church [1892] Oct
I. Title.

REFORMED church in the United States.
The hymnal of the Reformed church in the United States. Prepared by a committee appointed by the General synod. Cleveland, O., Publishing house of the Reformed Church [1892] 2 p. 1., 490 p. 24°. Text only. Oct
I. Title.

Reformed church in America—Missions.

APPLEGARTH, Margaret Tyson, 1886- 266
Junior missionary stories; fifty-two junior missionary stories, by Margaret T. Applegarth. New York city, Board of publication and Bible school work, [c1917] 406 p. illus. 19 1/2 cm. Prepared and published under the auspices of the Reformed church in America. [BV2087.A65] 18-3822
1. Reformed church in America—Missions. I. Title.

APPLEGARTH, Margaret Tyson, 1886- 266
Missionary stories for little folks. First series: Primary, by Margaret T. Applegarth ... with 52 drawings and verses. New York, George H. Doran company, [1921] 2 p. l., 3-6. [2]. 7-343 p. illus. 19 1/2 cm. Prepared and published under the auspices of the Reformed church in America. First

published in 1917 under title "Fifty-two primary missionary stories." [BV2087.A5] 21-16739
1. Reformed church in America—Missions. I. Title.

APPLEGARTH, Margaret Tyson, 1886-
Missionary stories for little folks. Second series: Junior, by Margaret T. Applegarth ... with 52 drawings and verses. New York, George H. Doran company, [c1921] ix, 11-406 p. illus. 19 1/2 cm. Prepared and published under the auspices of the Reformed church in America. First published in 1917 under title "Junior missionary stories; fifty-two junior missionary stories." [BC2087.A52] 21-16738
1. Reformed church in America—Missions. I. Title.

MENNENGA, George H 266.57
All the families of the earth, a study of Christian missions. Grand Rapids, Baker Book House, 1950. 109 p. 21 cm. [BV2580.M4] 51-31453
1. Reformed Church in America — Missions. 2. Missions, Foreign. 3. Missions — Study and teaching. I. Title.

REFORMED Church in America. Board of Domestic Missions. Women's Executive Committee. 266.57
Report 1st-1884- New York [etc.] v. 17-24 cm. annual. Report year for 1884-86 ends Apr. 1; for 1887-19 Apr. 30. Vols. for 1884-93 issued by the committee under a variant name: Women's Executive Committee of Domestic Missions. [BV2580.A2244] 51-38653
1. Reformed Church in America — Missions. I. Title.

RYDER, Stephen Willis, 1880- 275.2
A historical sourcebook of the Japan mission of the Reformed church in America (1859-1930) by Stephen Willis Ryder, Ph. D. York, Penna., The York printing co., 1935. 156 p. 23 1/2 cm. Chapters I-III (p. 15-128) published also as chapters I to III of the author's thesis (PH.D.) Columbia university, "A historical-educational study of the Japan mission of the Reformed church in America". Bibliography: p. 147-156. [BV3445.R92] [266.57] 35-11736
1. Reformed church in America—Missions. 2. Missions—Japan. I. Title.

STRING, Margaret Lancaster. 922
Miss Wistaria at home; a tale of modern Japan, by Margaret Lancaster String. Philadelphia, Pa., Board of foreign missions, Reformed church in the United States [c1918] 6 p. 1., 80 p. illus. 20 1/2 cm. [BV3445.S7] 18-12849
I. Title.

WEDDELL, Suzanne E., 1885- 277.3
Marching thousands; a story of the domestic mission program, carried on within the United States and Mexico, by the Reformed church in America [by] Sue Weddell... New York city, Boards of domestic missions and Dept. of missionary education, Reformed church in America [c1933] xiv p., 1 l., 159 p. 19 1/2 cm. Bibliography: p. [vi] [BV2766.R5W4] [266.57] 33-24469
1. Reformed church in America—Missions. 2. Missions, Home. I. Title.

Reformed church in America—New Jersey—History

HARMELINK, Herman. 285'.7749
The Reformed Church in New Jersey [1660-1969] by Herman Harmelink, III, William W. Coventry [and] Sharon Thoms Scholten. [n.p.] Synod of New Jersey, 1969. 110 p. illus. 23 cm. Bibliography: p. 108-110. [BX9516.N5H37] 78-91396
1. Reformed Church in America—New Jersey—History. I. Coventry, William W., 1930- joint author. II. Scholten, Sharon Thoms, 1933- joint author. III. Title.

LEIBY, Adrian Coulter. 285'.7749
The United Churches of Hackensack and Schraalenburgh, New Jersey, 1686-1822 / Adrian C. Leiby ; drawings by Richard G. Belcher. River Edge, N.J. : Bergen County Historical Society, 1976. 336 p. : ill. ; 24 cm. Includes index. Bibliography: p. 315-322. [BX9516.N5L44] 76-12114
1. Reformed Church in America—New Jersey—History. 2. Dutch in New Jersey. I. Title: The United Churches of Hackensack ...

REFORMED church in America. Classis of Paramus.
... A history of the classis of Paramus of the Reformed church in America; containing the proceedings of the centennial meeting of the classis, the historical discourse, and the addresses, statistical history and the histories of the individual churches [1800-1900] New York, The Board of publications R.C.A., 1902. 599 p. illus. 24 cm. [BX9519.P3A5] 2-14697
1. Reformed church in America—New Jersey—Hist. I. Title.

REFORMED church in America. Classes. Paramus.
History of the classis of Paramus of the Reformed church in America; containing the proceedings of the centennial meeting of the classis, the historical discourse, and the addresses, statistical history and histories of the indiviual churches [1800-1902] New York, The Board of publication R. C. A., 1902. 59 p. llus. 24 cm. [BX9519.P3A5] 2-14697
1. Reformed church in America—New Jersey—Hist. 2. Churches—New Jersey 3. Clergy—New Jersey. I. Title.

Reformed Church in America — Sermons.

GOSSELINK, Marion Gerard. 252.05'732
The things eternal; sermons of a Dutch dominie. Grand Rapids, Baker Book House, 1967. 85 p. 22 cm. [BX9527.G57T49] 67-28326
1. Reformed Church in America—Sermons. 2. Sermons, American. I. Title.

VANDENBERG, William Ernest 1916- 242
Devotions for church groups, by William E. Vanden Berg. Grand Rapids, Baker Book House [1966] 126 p. 20 cm. [BX9527.V3] 67-2210
1. Reformed Church in America—Sermons. 2. Sermons, American. I. Title.

Reformed church in America—Somerset co., N. J.

MESSLER, Abraham, 1800-1882.
Forty years at Raritan. Eight memorial sermons, with notes for a history of the Reformed Dutch churches in Somerset county, N. J., by Abraham Messler ... New-York, A. Lloyd, 1873. viii, [5]-327 p. 24 cm. [BX9516.N5M5] 41-28025
1. Reformed church in America—Somerset co., N. J. I. Title.

Reformed church in America. Woman's board of foreign missions.

CHAMBERLAIN, Mary Eleanor (Anable) "Mrs. W. I. Chamberlain."
Fifty years in foreign fields, China, Japan, India, Arabia; a history of five decades of the Woman's board of foreign missions, Reformed church in America, by Mrs. W. I. Chamberlain, 1875-1925, issued in its jubilee year by the Woman's board of foreign missions, Reformed church in America ... New York [c1925] xv, 292 p. front., plates, ports., fold. maps. 25 cm. "List of women missionaries, Reformed church in America": p. 287-292. [BV2580.C5] 26-6526
1. Reformed church in America. Woman's board of foreign missions. 2. Reformed church in America—Missions. 3. Missions—Asia. I. Title.

Reformed Church in America—Yearbooks.

REFORMED Church in America.
Almanac and year-book. New York, Board of Publ. of the Reformed Church in America. v. illus., ports. 20 cm. Began publication with issue for 1902. "Published by authority of the General Synod." [BX9507.A3] 48-32953
1. Reformed Church in America—Yearbooks. I. Title.

Reformed church in Germany—History

BYRUM, Isabel (Coston) Mrs. 1870-1938. 922.89
The tread of years, by Isabel C. Byrum. Anderson, Ind., Gospel trumpet company [c1938] vi, 7-136 p. 19 cm. [BX7990.G7B87] 38-35277
I. Title.

GOOD, James Isaac, 1850-1924.
History of the Reformed church of Germany. 1620-1890. By Rev. James I. Good ... Reading, Pa., D. Miller, 1894. 646 p., 1 l. plates, ports., double ma. 20 cm. [BX9464.G6] 2-670
1. Reformed church in Germany—Hist. I. Title.

GOOD, James Isaac, 1850-1924.
The origin of the Reformed church in Germany. By Rev. James I. Good, D.D. Reading, Pa., D. Miller, 1887. viii, [9]-507 p. 2 front. (incl. double map) plates, ports. 20 cm. [BX9464.G65] 45-40600
1. Reformed church in Germany—Hist. I. Title.

Reformed Church in South Africa.

HUMAN relations 261.8'34'51042
and the South African scene in the light of scripture : official translation of the report Ras, volk en nasie en volkereverhoudinge in die lig van die Skrif : approved and accepted by the General Synod of the Dutch Reformed Church, October 1974. Cape Town : Dutch Reformed Church Publishers, 1976. 100 p. ; 22 cm. [BS680.R2R3713] 77-463450 ISBN 0-86991-158-9
1. Reformed Church in South Africa. 2. Race (Theology)—Biblical teaching. 3. Church and social problems—South Africa. 4. Church and race problems—South Africa. I. Nederduits Gereformeerde Kerk (South Africa). Algemene Sinode.

Reformed church in Switzerland—History

GOOD, James Isaac, 1850-1924.
History of the Swiss reformed church since the reformation, by Rev. Prof. James I. Good ... Philadelphia, Publication and Sunday school board of the Reformed church in the United States, 1913. xii p., 2 l., 3-504 p. front., pl., ports. 22 1/2 cm. [BX9434.G6] 13-10996
1. Reformed church in Switzerland—Hist. I. Reformed church in the United States. Publication and Sunday school board. II. Title.

Reformed church in the United States.

HARTLEY, Issac S[mithson] 1830-
Historical discourse delivered on the occasion of the semi-centennial year of the Reformed church, Utica, N. Y. By the pastor Isaac S. Hartley, D. D. January, 1880... Utica, N. Y., Curtiss & Childs, printers, 1880. 68 p. front., pl. 24 cm. 6-37731
I. Title.

HARTLEY, Issac S[mithson] 1830-
Historical discourse delivered on the occasion of the semi-centennial year of the Reformed church, Utica, N. Y. By the pastor Isaac S. Hartley, D. D. January, 1880... Utica, N. Y., Curtiss & Childs, printers, 1880. 68 p. front., pl. 24 cm. 6-37731
I. Title.

KURTZ, H.
"Praise the Lord!" A collection of anthems, motettos, antiphons, etc., for the use of church choirs. Arranged and in part composed by H. Kurtz; edited and translated by M. Vitz ... Cleveland, O., Publishing house of the Reformed church in the U. S. [1897] 242 p., 1 l. 4 degrees. With music. German and English title-page and text. Oct
I. Title.

REFORMED church in America.
Public services at the inauguration of the Rev. John H. Gillespie,D. D. as Thomas De Witt professor of Hellenistic Greek and NewTestament exegesis in the Theological seminary of the Reformed (Dutch)church in Amerida, at New Brunswick, N. J. ... New York, Board of publication of the Reformed church in America, 1899. 58 pp. 8 degrees. 1-23304
I. Title.

REFORMED Church in America. Synods. Particular Synod of Albany.
Minuties. Albany. v. 23 cm. annual. Vols. for ... issued by the synod under the church's earlier name: Reformed Portestant Dutch Church in North America. [BX9518.A8A3] 51-36183
I. Title.

REFORMED church in the United States.
Prayers for the family and for special occasions ... Philadelphia, Pa., The Publication board of the Reformed church in the United States, 1903. 268 p. 19 cm. 4-5002
I. Title.

REFORMED church in the United States. Laymen's missionary movement.
A survey of the Reformed church in the United States, under the auspices of the Laymen's missionary movement, by four commissions. [Philadelphia] The Laymen's missionary movement, Reformed church in the U.S., c1914] 3 p. i., 9-212 p. illus., maps (2 fold.) diagrs. 23 cm. $0.25. 14-9874
I. Title.

REFORMED church in the United States. Liturgy and ritual. 264.
An order of service with the heidelberg Catehism for use in the family, the Sunday-school, the catechetical class and church work societies. New and enl. ed. Compiled and arranged by Nathaniel Z. Snyder, D.D. South Bethlehem, Pa., 1904. 233 p. 14 1/2 cm. [BX9573.A5 1904] 4-14344
I. Snyder, Nathaniel Z., comp. II. Heidelberg catechism. III. Title.

REFORMED church in the United States. Liturgy and ritual. 264.
An order of worship for the Reformed church. Philadelphia, S. R. Fisher & co., 1867. 388 p. 19 1/2 cm. [BX9573.A2 1867] 42-26730
I. Title.

REFORMED church in the United States. Synod of the Northwest
Students' manual of the Reformed church in the United States. Part one, The history of the church, by Rev. D. W. Vriesen, D.D. Part two, The activities of the church, by Rev. Alvin Grether. Cleveland, O., Central publishing house [1923]. vii, 168 p. 19 cm. [BX9571.A6] 28-3289
1. Reformed church in the United States. 2. Church history. I. Vriesen, D. W., ed. II. Grether, Alvin, ed. III. Title.

Reformed Church in the United States—Biography

REFORMED Church in the United States. Classes. Somerset, Pa. 284.274879
Pastors and people of Somerset Classis; the Reformed Church in the United States. [De luxe ed.] Berlin, Pa., Berlin Pub. Co., 1940. 432 p. front., illus., ports. 21 cm. An account of events prior to the union of the Reformed Church in the United States with the Evangelical Synod of North America to form the Evangelical and Reformed Church. "Committee on publication: Rev. D. Snider Stephhn ... chairman ... Rev. L. Nevin Wilson, editor." "Pastors of Somerset Classis": p. [346]-412. [BX9569.S6A5 1940] 41-2059
1. Reformed Church in the United States—Biog. 2. Churches—Pennsylvania. I. Stephan, David Snider, 1870- II. Wilson, Levi Nevin, 1879- ed. III. Title.

Reformed church in the United States—Catechisms and creeds.

HEIDELBERG catechism. 238.
The Heidelberg catechism, with questions for the catechsical class and the Sunday--school, by Rev. Aaron Spangler, A.M. Cleveland, O., Central publishing house

[c1899] 94 p. 15 cm. [BX9428.A3 1899] 99-3655
1. Reformed church in the United States—Catechisms and creeds. I. Spangler, Aaron, ed. II. Title.

Reformed church in the United States—Chester co., Pa.

FLUCK, Jonathan Lewis, 1864- ed.
A history of the Reformed churches in Chester county, compiled and edited by J. Lewis Fluck... Norristown, Pa., Herald printing and binding rooms, 1892. vii p., 2 l., [13]-139 p., 1 l. plates. 2 port. (incl. front.) 19 1/2 cm. [BX9566.P4F6] 3-18337
1. Reformed church in the United States—Chester co., Pa. I. Title.

Reformed church in the United States. Classis of Gettysburg.

SANDO, Edwin Milton, 1876- 285.7484
History of Gettysburg classis of the synod of the Potomac, Reformed church in the United States, by Rev. Edwin M. Sando, D.D., stated clerk. Sketches of the congregations by their pastors. [Hanover, Pa., Anthony printing company, 1941] 2 p. l., 7-135 p. illus. 23 1/2 cm. [BX9569.G4S3] 42-1019
1. Reformed church in the United States. Classis of Gettysburg. I. Title.

Reformed church in the United States. Classis of Lancaster, Pa.

GLASS, Daniel Grant, 1870- ed. 287.5748
History of the classis of Lancaster of the Eastern synod of the Reformed church in the United States, 1852-1940. Editors Rev. Daniel G. Glass ... Rev. C. George Bachman, Rev. Harry E. Shepardson [and others] ... [New Holland, Pa., The New Holland clarion, 1942] xiv, 431 p. incl. illus., ports. col. pl. (coat of arms) ports., fold. map. 23 1/2 cm. Bibliography: p. 420. [BX9569.L2G55] 42-25209
1. Reformed church in the United States. Classis of Lancaster, Pa. 2. Churches—Pennsylvania. I. Bachman, Calvin George, 1892- joint ed. II. Title.

Reformed church in the United States. Classis of Maryland.

BREADY, Guy Pearre, 1882- 285.7752
History of Maryland classis of the Reformed church in the United States; or,The History of the Reformed church in Maryland since 1820. By Rev. Guy P. Bready. [Taney-town, Md., The Carroll record print. c1938] 320 p. incl. front., illus., ports. 24 cm. "Ministers and licentiates of Maryland classis": p. 274-296. [BX9569.M3B7] 38-24550
1. Reformed church in the United States. Classis of Maryland. 2. Reformed church in the United States—Clergy. I. Title. II. Title: Maryland classis of the Reformed church in the United States.

Reformed church in the United States. Classis of Somerset, Pa.

MEYERSDALE, Pa. St. Paul's church. Historical committee. 284.
A history of the Wilhelms and the Wilhelm charge, by the Historical committee ... Meyersdale, Pa., The Wilhelm press, 1919. 3 p. l., [9]-205 p. incl. front., plates, ports. 24 cm. [BX9569.S6M4] 20-632
1. Wilhelm family. 2. Reformed church in the United States. Classis of Somerset, Pa. I. Title.

Reformed Church in the United States—Doctrinal and controversial works—Collected works.

NEVIN, John Williamson, 1803-1886. 230'.5'733
Catholic and Reformed : selected theological writings of John Williamson Nevin / edited by Charles Yrigoyen, Jr. and George H. Bricker. Pittsburgh : Pickwick Press, 1978. ix, 411 p. : port. ; 22 cm. (Pittsburgh original texts & translations series ; 3) Includes bibliographical references. [BX9559.N48 1978] 78-2567 ISBN 0-915138-37-9 : 9.50
1. Reformed Church in the United States—Doctrinal and controversial works—Collected works. 2. Theology—Collected works—19th century. 3. Mercersburg theology—Collected works. I. Yrigoyen, Charles, 1937- II. Bricker, George H. III. Title.

Reformed Church in the United States. Eastern Synod.

HARNER, Nevin Cowger, 1901-1951. 268'.8'5733
Factors related to Sunday school growth and decline in the Eastern Synod of the Reformed Church in the United States. New York, Bureau of Publications, Teachers College, Columbia University, 1931. [New York, AMS Press, 1973, c1972] vi, 101 p. illus. 22 cm. Reprint of the 1931 ed., issued in series: Teachers College, Columbia University. Contributions to education, no. 479. Originally presented as the author's thesis, Columbia. Bibliography: p. 101. [BX9563.H3 1972] 71-176839 ISBN 0-404-55479-2 10.00
1. Reformed Church in the United States. Eastern Synod. 2. Sunday schools—Pennsylvania. 3. Churches—Pennsylvania. I. Title. II. Series: Columbia University. Teachers College. Contributions to education, no. 479.

KLEIN, Harry Martin John, 1873- 285.7748
The history of the Eastern synod of the Reformed church in the United States, prepared by H. M. J. Klein ... [Lancaster, Pa.] The Eastern synod, 1943. 6 p. l., 414 p. col. front., plates, ports. (part fold.) 23 1/2 cm. On spine: 1747-1940. [BX9568.E2K55] 43-4832
1. Reformed church in the United States. Eastern synod. I. Title.

Reformed church in the United States—Education.

LIVINGOOD, Frederick George. 377.84109748
Eighteenth century Reformed church schools. Part xxv of a narrative and critical history prepared at the request of the Pennsylvania German society. [By] Frederick George Livingood ... Norristown, Pa., 1930. xix, [2], 313 p. front., illus., plates, ports., facsims. 26 cm. "Reprinted from Proceedings of the Pennsylvania German society, vol. xxxviii." Forms pt. 35 of the series "Pennsylvania: the German influence in its settlement and development", published in the Proceedings and adrresses of the Society. Bibliography: p. [299]-313. [LC586.R35L5] 30-28276
1. Reformed church in the United States—Education. 2. Church schools—Pennsylvania. 3. Education—Pennsylvania—Hist. 4. Schools, German—Pennsylvania. I. Pennsylvania-German society. II. Title.

Reformed church in the United States—Goshenhoppen, Pa.

HINKE, William John, 1871-
A history of the Goshenhoppen Reformed charge, Montgomery County, Pennsylvania (1727-1819) Part xxix of a narrative and critical history prepared at the request of the Pennsylvania German society. By Rev. William John Hinke... Lancaster [Press of the New era printing company] 1920. xvii, 5-490 p. incl. front., illus., plates, ports., facsims. 25 1/2 cm. "Autograph edition, 230 copies; no. 107." [BX9566.P4H5] 22-16905
1. Reformed church in the U.S.—Goshenhoppen, Pa. I. Pennsylvania-German society. II. Title. III. Title: Goshenhoppen Reformed charge.

Reformed church in the United States—History

APPEL, Theodore, 1823-
The beginnings of the Theological seminary of the Reformed church in the United States, from 1817 to 1832. By Rev. Theodore Appel... Philadelphia, Reformed church publication board, 1886. viii p., 1 l., 11-116 p. 22 1/2 cm. 3-4678
I. Title.

GOOD, James Isaac, 1850-1924.
History of the Reformed church in the United States. 1725-1792. By Rev. Prof. James I. Good ... Reading, Pa., D. Miller, 1899. vii, 701 p. plates. 20 cm. [BX9565.G7] 0-137
1. Reformed church in the United States—Hist. I. Title.

NEW York. Collegiate church. 289
1628-1928. Collegiate Reformed Protestant Dutch Church of the City of New York; her organization and development, a record of the proclamation of the truth over three centuries... Collated and edited by William Leverich Brower...and Henry P. Miller....Published by the Consistory of the Collegiate Reformed Dutch Church to commemorate the tercentory of her organization of Manhattan Island. New York, 1928. 133 p. 23 1/2 cm. [BX9531.N5C72] 29-208
I. Brower, William Leverich. II. Miller, Henry P. III. Title.

Reformed church in the United States—Hymns.

REFORMED church in the United States.
The hymnal of the Reformed church in the United States. Prepared by a committee appointed by the General synod ... Cleveland, O., Publishing house of the Reformed church [c1890] iv p., 1 l., 342 p. 19 1/2 cm. Without music. Preface signed: H. M. Kieffer, J. A. Hoffheins, John M. Schick, H. H. W. Hibshman. [BV435.A5 1890] 17-31590
1. Reformed church in the United States—Hymns. 2. Hymns, English. I. Kieffer, Henry Martyn, 1845- II. Title.

REFORMED church in the United States. Liturgy and ritual. 264.057
A liturgy: or, Order of Christian worship. Prepared and published by the direction and for the use of the German Reformed church in the United States of America. Philadelphia, Lindsay & Blakiston, 1858. v. 7-840, 68 p. 20 cm. "A selection of hymns for public and private worship": 68 p. at end. [BX9573.A2 1858] 38-331233
1. Reformed church in the U.S.—Hymns. 2. Hymns, English. I. Title.

Reformed church in the United States. Liturgy and ritual—History

KUHNS, Benjamin, comp.
The liturgical conflict and the peace movement of the Reformed church in the United States as exhibited by the official records of the General synod. Published by Elders Benjamin Kuhns ... [and] Rudolph F. Kelker ... Dayton, O., Press of U. B. publishing house, 1896. vi p., 1 l., 9-96 p. front. (ports.) 20 cm. [BX9565.K8] 39-7356
1. Reformed church in the United States. Liturgy and ritual—Hist. 2. Reformed church in the United States—Doctrinal and controversial works. 3. Reformed church in the United States—Government. 4. Reformed church in the United States. General synod. Peace commission. I. Kelker, Rudolph Frederick, 1820-1906 joint comp. II. Reformed church in the United States. General synod. III. Title.

Reformed church in the United States—Missions.

CASSELMAN, Arthur Vale, 1874- 266.42
The end of the beginning; a narrative of the missionary enterprise of the Reformed church, by Arthur V. Casselman ... Philadelphia, Heidelberg press, 1936. x p., 3 l., [3]-209 p. incl. front. (port.) maps. plates, ports. 20 cm. [BV2585.C3] 36-17242
1. Reformed church in the United States—Missions. 2. Missions, Foreign. I. Title.

MILLER,, Henry K. ed. 266
History of the Japan mission of the Reformed church in the United States, 1879-1904. Edited by Rev. Henry K. Miller. Philadelphia, Board of foreign missions, Reformed church in the United States, 1904. vii, [1], 127 p. incl. front., illus. 24 cm. [BV3445.M5] 5-26547
1. Reformed church in the United States—Missions. 2. Missions—Japan. I. Reformed church in the United States. Board of foreign missions. II. Title.

Reformed Church in the United States—Missions—History.

CALLENDER, S N
Historical sketch of the work of foreign missions of the Reformed Church in the United States. Revised ed. [Lebanon, Pa.] By direction of the Board (n.d.] l., 50 p. illus. 20 cm. 66-53944
1. Reformed Church in the United States—Missions—History. I. Reformed Church in the United States. Board of Foreign Missions. II. Title.

Reformed Church in the United States—North Carolina.

REFORMED Church in the United States. Classes. North Carolina.
Historic sketch of the Reformed Church in North Carolina, by a board of editors under the Classis of North Carolina. With an introd. by Geo. Wm. Welker. Philadelphia, Pub. Board of the Reformed Church in the United States [1908] 327 p. plates, ports. 20 cm. Edited by J. C. Clapp, J. C. Leonard and others. [BX9566.N8A4] 8-10428
1. Reformed Church in the United States—North Carolina. I. Clapp, Jacob Crawford, 1832- ed. II. Title.

Reformed church in the United States—Pennsylvania.

BOEHM, John Philip, 1653-1749. 922.
Life and letters of the Rev. John Philip Boehm, founder of the Reformed church in Pennsylvania, 1683-1749, edited by the Rev. William J. Hinke. Philadelphia, Publications and Sunday school board of the Reformed church in the United States, 1916. xxiv, [2], 501 p. front., plates, ports., double map, facsims. 24 cm. "This volume is made uniform with 'The minutes of the Coetus,', its companion."--Pref. Contents.pt. i. Life--pt. ii. Correspondence, containing the letters and reports of Mr. Boehm sent to Holland and the letters from Holland addressed to him, 1728-1748, tr. and ed. by W. J. Hinke (p.[153]-468) --Appendix x. i. Documents relating to Boehm's death and property; ii. List of reformed churches founded before 1750.--Index. [BX9593.B6A3] 19-17589
1. Reformed church in the United States—Pennsylvania. I. Hinke, William John, 1871- ed. II. Title.

BOEHM, John Philip, 1683-1749. 285'.7'0924 B
Life and letters of the Rev. John Philip Boehm, founder of the Reformed Church in Pennsylvania, 1683-1749. Edited by the Rev. William J. Hinke. New York, Arno Press, 1972 [c1916] xxiv, 501 p. illus., map (1 fold.) 24 cm. (Religion in America, series II) [BX9593.B6A3 1972] 71-38784 ISBN 0-405-04069-5
1. Reformed Church in the United States—Pennsylvania. I. Hinke, William John, 1871-1947, ed.

HISTORICAL notes relating to the Pennsylvania Reformed church. Edited by Harry S. Dotterer. v. 1 [May 10, 1899-Apr. 10, 1900] Philadelphia, Perkiomen publishing company, 1900. 1 p. l., 201 p. 26 cm. Publication discontinued. Includes records of "Marriages by Rev. George Wack". "List of Huguenot galley-slaves. Released by the king of France in ... seventeen hundred and thirteen and seventeen hundred and fourteen": p. 43-47, 63-64, 77-80. [BX9496.P4H5] 1-1136
1. Reformed church in the United States—Pennsylvania. 2. Registers of births, etc.—Pennsylvania. 3. Huguenots in France. I. Dotterer, Henry Sassaman, 1841-1908, ed.

MILLER, David, 1843-
Early history of the Reformed church in Pennsylvania. By Daniel Miller. With

introduction by Prof. W. J. Hinke, D.D. Reading, Pa., D. Miller, 1906. viii, [9]-280 p. illus. (incl. ports.) 20 1/2 cm. [BX9566.P4M5] 6-36204
1. Reformed church in the U.S.—Pennsylvania. I. Title.

REFORMED church in the United States. 289
Minutes and letters of the Coetus of the German reformed congregations in Pennsylvania, 1747-1792. Together with three preliminary reports of Rev. John Philip Boehm, 1734-1744. Published by authority of the eastern synod of the Reformed church in the United States. Philadelphia, Reformed church publishing board, 1903. xxii, 463 p. front. (facsim.) 24 cm. Edited by the Rev. J. I. Good, and the Rev. Mm. J. Hinke. [BX9568.P4A5 1792] 3-26946
I. Good, James Isaac, 1850-1924, ed. II. Hinke, William John, 1871- ed. III. Boehm, John Philip, 1683-1749. IV. Title.

REFORMED church in the United States. Classes. Westmoreland, Pa. 289
A history of the Reformed church within the bounds of the Westmoreland classis Edited by a committee of classis. Philadelphia, Reformed church publication board, 1877. 4 v-vi, 232 p. 20 cm. [BX9569.W6A5] 44-24283
1. Reformed church in the United States—Pennsylvania. I. Title.

Reformed church in the United States—Reading, Pa.

MILLER, Daniel, 1843-
History of the Reformed church in Reading, Pa., by Daniel Miller...Introduction by Rev. B. Bausman, D.D. Reading, Pa., D. Miller, 1905. viii, [9]-468 p. front., illus., ports., facsim. 20 1/2 cm. [BX9567.R4R5] 5-36157
1. Reformed church in the U.S.—Reading, Pa. I. Title.

Reformed church in the United States—Sermons.

PETERS, Madison Clinton, 1859-1918. 252.
The panacea for poverty, by Madison C. Peters ... New York, W. B. Ketcham [1898] 207 p. front. (port.) 1 illus. 19 cm. [BX9577.P4P3] 44-50995
1. Reformed church in the United States—Sermons. 2. Sermons, American. I. Title.

STAMM, Frederick Keller, 1883- comp. 252.
The Reformed church pulpit, by Frederick K. Stamm; introduction by the Rev. Joseph Fort Newton ... New York, The Macmillan company, 1928. xiii, 329 p. 19 1/2 cm. [BX9577.A1S7] 28-2250
1. Reformed church in the United States—Sermons. 2. Sermons, American. I. Title.

Reformed Church. Liturgy and ritual.

HAGEMAN, Howard G. 264.057
Pulpit and table; some chapters in the history of worship in the Reformed churches. Richmond, Va., Knox [c.1962] 139p. 21cm. Bibl. 62-12080 3.00
1. Reformed Church. Liturgy and ritual. I. Title.

REFORMED church in America. Liturgy and ritual.
A liturgy, or, Order of worship for the Reformed church. Cincinnati, T. P. Bucher, 1869. xii, 11-276 p. 19 cm. 16-24039
I. Title.

REFORMED church in the United States. Liturgy and ritual. 264.
A liturgy, or, Order of worship for the Reformed church. Cincinnati, T. P. Bucher, 1869. xii, 11-276 p. 19 cm. [BX9573.A2 1869] 16-24089
I. Title.

Reformed Church. Liturgy and ritual—History.

NICHOLS, James Hastings, 1915- 264.04'2
Corporate worship in the reformed tradition. Philadelphia, Westminster Press [1968] 190 p. 21 cm. Bibliographical references included in "Notes" (p. 177-182) [BX9427.N5] 68-13957
1. Reformed Church. Liturgy and ritual—History. 2. Worship—History. I. Title.

Reformed church of the United States.

RUETENIK, Herman Julius, 1826-1914.
The pioneers of the Reformed church in the United States of America. By H. J. Ruetenik ... Cleveland, O., Central publishing house, 1901. 123 p. front. (port.) plates. 19 cm. Published simultaneously in German and English. [BX9565.R8] 2-1228
1. Reformed church of the United States. I. Title.
Contents omitted.

Reformed church—Prayer-books and devotions—English.

STOUDT, John Joseph, 1911- ed. and tr. 264.042
Private devotions for home and church. Translated and compiled by John Joseph Stoudt. Philadelphia, Christian Education Press [c1956] 173p. 23cm. [BV260.S85] 56-13071
1. Reformed Church—Prayer-books and devotions—English. I. Title.

ZOLLIKOFER, Johannes, 1633-1692.
A newly opened treasury of heavenly incense; or, Christian's companion, containing instructions, hymns, and prayers, applicable to all persons, situations, and circumstances in life. Translated and compiled chiefly from the celebrated work on these subjects of the Rev. John Zollikoffer ... To which is prefixed a justly celebrated sermon, In vindication of the religious spirit of the present age. By Alexander McClelland ... By John S. Ebaugh ... Carlisle [Pa.] Printed by G. Fleming, 1833. iv, [5]-608 p. front. (port.) 22 cm. Translation of Himmlischer weihrauschatz [BV247.Z63 1833] 46-35350
1. Reformed church—Prayer-books and devotions—English. I. McClelland, Alexander, 1796?-1864. II. Ebaugh, John S., 1795-1874, ed. and tr. III. Title.

ZOLLIKOFER, Johannes, 1633-1692.
A newly opened treasury of heavenly incense; or, Christian's companion, containing instructions and devotional exercises, applicable to all persons and circumstances in life. Translated and compiled chiefly from the celebrated work on these subjects of the Rev. John Zollikoffer ... To which are prefixed three celebrated sermons, by the late Rev. John M. Mason, D.D. and Rev. Alexander M'Clelland D.D. ... By John S. Ebaugh, V.D.M. ... 6th ed. New York Printed by Martin, Lambert & co., 1839. 612 p. front. (port.) 25 1/2 cm. Translation of Himmlischer weihrauchschatz. [BV247.Z63 1869] 46-42585
1. Reformed church—Prayer-books and devotions—English. I. Mason, John Mitchell, 1770-1829. II. McClelland, Alexander, 1796?-1864. III. Ebaugh, John S., 1795-1874, ed. and tr. IV. Title.

Reformed church—Sermons.

BARTH, Karl, 1886- 252.04'2
Call for God. [Translated by A. T. Mackay. 1st U.S. ed.] New York. Harper & Row [1967] 125 p. 22 cm. Translation of Rufe mich an. Collection of 12 sermons delivered to convicts in a prison at Basel. [BX9435.B2613] 67-21543
1. Reformed Church — Sermons. 2. Sermons, English — Translations from German. 3. Sermons. German — Translations into English. 4. Prisons — Sermons. I. Title.

BARTH, Karl, 1886- 252.04'2
Call for God: new sermons from Basel Prison; translated [from the German] by A. T. Mackay. London, S. C. M. Press, 1967. 125 p. 19 1/2 cm. 12/6 (B67-14128) Originally published as 'Rufe mich an.' Zurich, Evangelischer Veriag, 1965. [BX9426.B3R13] 67-100978
1. Reformed Church — Sermons. 2. Sermons, German — Translations into English. 3. Sermons, English — Translations from German. I. Title.

BARTH, Karl, 1886- 252.042
Come, Holy Spirit; sermons, by Karl Barth ... and Eduard Thurneysen ... English translation by Professor George W. Richards ... Reverend Elmer G. Homrighausen ... [and] Professor Karl J. Ernst ... Translation read and approved by Karl Barth. New York, Round table press, inc., 1933. xvi, 267 p. 20 cm. [BX9426.A1B3] 34-563
1. Reformed church—Sermans. 2. Sermons, English—Translations from German. 3. Sermons, German—Translations into English. I. Thurneysen, Eduard, 1888- II. Richards, George Warren, 1869- tr. III. Homrighausen, Elmer George, 1900- joint tr. IV. Ernst, Karl Julius, 1884- joint tr. V. Title.

BARTH, Karl, 1886- 252.042
God's search for man; sermons, by Karl Barth ... and Eduard Thurneysen ... English translation by Profesor George W. Richards ... Reverend Elmer C. Homrighausen ... [and] Professor Karl J. Ernst ... translation read and approved by Karl Barth. New York, Round table press, inc., 1935. viii p., 1 l., 235 p. 20 cm. [BX9426.A1B34] 35-5808
1. Reformed church—Sermons, 2. Sermons, English—Translations from German. 3. Sermons, German—Translations into English. I. Thurneysen, Eduard, 1888- II. Richards, George Warren, 1869- tr. III. Homrighausen, Elmer George, 1900- joint tr. IV. Ernst, Karl Jullus, 1884- joint tr. V. Title.

BEETS, Nicolaas, 1814-1903. 922-4492
Life and character of J. H. van der Palm ... Sketched by Nicolaas Beets, D.D. Translated from the Dutch by J. P. Westervelt. New York, Hurd and Houghton. Boston, F. P. Dutton and company, 1865. xii, 401 p. 19 1/2 cm. "Sermons of J. H. van der Palm ...": p. [175]-401. "Articles relating to van der Palm ...": p. 172-173. [BX9479.P3B42] 36-22145
1. Palm, Johannes Heuricus van der, 1763-1840. 2. Reformed church—Sermons. I. Westervelt, John P., 1816-1879, tr. II. Title.

BERSIER, Eugene Arthur Francois, 1831-1889.
Saint Paul's vision, and other sermons by Rev. Eugene Bersier ... translated by Marie Stewart. New York, A. D. F. Randolph and company [1881] 2 p. l., [iii]-viii p., 1 l., 283 p. 19 cm. [BX9455.B4] 46-28069
1. Reformed church—Sermons. 2. Sermons, French—Translations into English. 3. Sermons, English—Translations from French. I. Stewart, Marie, tr. II. Title.

BRUNNER, Heinrich Emil, 1889- 252
The great invitation, and other sermons. Translated by Harold nninght. Philadelphia, Westminster Press [1955] 188p. 22cm. Translation of Fraumunster-Predigten. [BX9435.B675 1955] 55-8594
1. Reformed Church—Sermons. 2. Sermons, German —Translations into English. 3. Sermons, English—Translations from German. I. Title.

BULLINGER, Heinrich, 1504-1575. 252.042
The decades of Henry Bullinger ... Translated by H. I. ... Edited for the Parker society, by the Rev. Thomas Harding ... Cambridge [Eng.] Printed at the University press, 1849-52. 4 v. 23 cm. (Half-title: The Parker society. [Publications. Vol. 7-10]) Contains reprints of original title-pages. "Biographical notice of Henry Bullinger": v. 4, p. [vii]-xxxi. [BX5035.P2] 283.082 A C
1. Reformed church—Sermons. 2. Sermons, Latin—Translations into English. 3. Sermons, English—Translations from Latin. I. Harding, Thomas, ed. II. I., H., student of divinitie, tr. III. H. I., student of divinitie, tr. IV. Title.

CALVIN, John. 252.042
Sermons on the saving work of christ / John Calvin ; selected and translated by Leroy Nixon. Grand Rapids, Michigan : Baker Book House, 1980,c1950 302 p. ; 22 cm. esus Christ-Divinity-sermons. Reprint of c 1950 by Wm. B. Eerdmans Publishing Company Formmerly published under the title The deity of Christ. [BX420.A32] ISBN 0-8010-2463-3 pbk. : 7.95
1. Reformed church-sermons. 2. ermons English-translations from French 3. ermons, English-Translations from Latin 4. ermons french -translations into English. 5. ermons, Latin-translation into english. I. Title. II. Series.

COFFIN, William Sloane. 252'.051
The courage to love / William Sloane Coffin. 1st ed. San Francisco : Harper & Row, c1982. 100 p. ; 22 cm. Contents.Contents. Introduction — The courage to love — The limits of life — Thorns in the flesh — Being called — Homosexuality — Abortion — The promised time — The arms race — The soviets — Beating burn-out. Includes bibliographical references and index. [BX9426.C63C68 1982] 19 81-48386 ISBN 0-06-061508-7 : 9.95
1. Reformed Church—Sermons. 2. Sermons, American. I. Title.

THE deity of Christ, and other sermons; translated from the French and Latin by Leroy Nixon. Grand Rapids, Eerdmans, 1950. 302 p. 23 cm. [BX A32 Nd] 50-8898 252.042
1. Reformed Church—Sermons. 2. Sermons, English—Translations from French. 3. Sermons, English—Translations from Latin. 4. Sermons, French—Translations into English. Sermons, Latin—Translations into English. 5. Jesus Christ—Divialty—Sermons.

GOULOOZE, William, 1903- 252.057
Consider Christ Jesus. Grand Rapids, Mich., Baker Bk., 1964[c.1947] 121p. 22cm. 1.00 pap.,
1. Reformed Church—Sermons. 2. Sermons, American. I. Temple time (Radio program) II. Title.

GOULOOZE, William, 1903- 252.057
Consider Christ Jesus; Temple time radio sermons. Grand Rapids, Pub. in cooperation with the Reformed Church Book Stores, 1947. 121 p. port. 21 cm. [BX9527.G6C6] 48-18149
1. Reformed Church—Sermons. 2. Sermons, American. I. Temple time (Radio program) II. Title.

MACKAY, Donald Sage, 1863-1908. 252.
The religion of the threshold, and other sermons, by Donald Sage Mackay...with introduction by Professor Hugh Black, D.D. New York, A. C. Armstrong & son, 1908. xxiii, [25]-354 p. front. (port.) 21 1/2 cm. [BX9527.M3] 8-37755
1. Reformed church—Sermons. 2. Sermons, American. I. Black, Hugh, 1868- II. Title.

MCKEEHAN, Hobart Deitrich, 1897- 252.057
...What men need most. New York, Fortuny's [c1940] 90 p. 20 cm. At head of title: Hobart D. McKeehan. "First edition." [BX9577.M3W5 1940] 40-9538
1. Reformed church—Sermons. 2. Sermons, American. I. Title.

MILLER, Charles Ervine, 1867-1939. 252.05'7
Sermons and addresses. Edited by Herman Albert Klahr. Fostoria, Ohio, Gray Print. Co., 1967. xi, 328 p. port. 24 cm. [BX9426.M5S4] 67-28570
1. Reformed Church—Sermons. 2. Sermons, American. I. Klahr, Herman Albert, ed. II. Title.

SCHAAP, Theodore. 252.057
What of tomorrow? By Theodore Schaap ... Grand Rapids, Mich., Zondervan publishing house [1945] 144 p. 20 cm. [BX9527.S35] 45-16396
1. Reformed church—Sermons. 2. Sermons, American. I. Title.

VAN SANTVOORD, Cornelius, 1816-1901. 922.573
Memorials of the Rev. John Cantine Farrell Hoss, D.D. Edited by the Rev. C. Van Santvoord, D.D. [New York, C. Scribner's sons] Printed, not published, 1883. 124 p. front. (port.) 26 1/2 cm. [BX9543.H6V3] 36-30778
1. Hoss, John Cantine Farrell, 1811-1883. 2. Reformed church—Sermons. I. Title.
Contents omitted.

Reformed Episcopal Church.

FOUNDATIONS of our faith,
[Prepared by the Committee on Christian Education of the Reformed Episcopal Church. n. p., 1959] 56p. illus. 23cm. 'A confirmation manual designed especially for junior age boys and girls.'
1. Reformed Episcopal Church. I. Mueller, Walter. II. Reformed Episcopal Church. Committee on Christian Education.

OSBORNE, Richard B.
Poems of living truth. Philadelphia, Reformed, Episcopal pub. society, 1899. 148 p. port. 12 degrees. Apr
I. Title.

Reformed[Episcopal church—Clergy.

CUMMINS, George David, bp., 1822-1876. 262.12
Primitive episcopacy; a retiern to the "old paths" of Scripture and the early church. A sermon, preached in Chicago, Dec. 14, 1873. At this consecration of the Rev. Charles Edward Cheney, D. D., as a bishop in the Reformed Episcopal church. By the Rt. Rev. George[David Cummins, D. D. New York, Printed by E. O. Jenkins, 1874. 57 p. 25 cm. [BX6076.C8] 35-34768
1. Reformed[Episcopal church—Clergy. 2. Episcopacy. I. Title.

Reformed Episcopal[church—History—Sources.

CUMMINS, George David, bp., 1822-1876. 922.373
Memoir of George David Cummins, D D., first bishop of the Reformed Episcopal church. By his wife ... New York, Dodd, Mead & company [1879] 8 p. l., vii, [13]-544 p. front., plates, ports. 21 cm. [BX6093.C78A3] 36-25149
1. Reformed Episcopal[church—History—Sources. I. Cummins, Alexandrine Macomb (Balch) Mrs. ed. II. Title.

PRICE, Annie Darling. Mrs.
A history of the formation and growth of the Reformed Episcopal church, 1873-1902. By Mrs. Annie Darling Price ... Philadelphia, J. M. Armstrong, 1902. viii, 308, [4] p. front., pl., port. 20 cm. "Books and pamphlets consulted in the writing of this volume": 2 p. at end. 2-26081
I. Title.

Reformed Episcopal church—Hymns.

REFORMED Episcopal church. 264.
Hymnal of the Reformed Episcopal church, being a selection of spiritual songs, with music. Authorized by the General council, May, 1883. New York, The Century co. [1884] x, 288 p. 20 1/2 cm. [M2125.R4H9 1884] 45-44307
1. Reformed Episcopal church—Hymns. 2. Hymns, English. I. Title.

REFORMED Episcopal church.
Hymnal of the Reformed Episcopal church, adopted in General council, Chicago, May, 1879. Philadelphia, Covenant publishing co., 1880. 336 p. 19 cm. Without music. [BV373.A3 1880] 45-47065
1. Reformed Episcopal church—Hymns. 2. Hymns, English. I. Title.

Reformed Mennonite Church—Doctrinal and controversial works.

BEAR, Robert L. 261.8'34'2
Delivered unto Satan / by Robert L. Bear. Carlisle, Pa. : Bear, c1974. 331 p. ; 23 cm. [BX8129.R4B4] 75-303200 6.95
1. Reformed Mennonite Church—Doctrinal and controversial works. 2. Bear, Robert L. 3. Excommunication. I. Title.
Distributed by Stackpole Books

MUSSER, Daniel.
The Reformed Mennonite church, its rise and progress, with its principles and doctrines. By Daniel Musser. 2d ed. Lancaster, Pa., Inquirer printing & publishing co., 1878. iv, 5-608 p. 22 cm. 5-41199
I. Title.

Reformed Presbyterian church in North America.

PRITCHARD, John W 1851-
Soldiers of the church; the story of what the Reformed Presbyterians (Covenanters) of North America, Canada, and the British Isles, did to win the world war of 1914-1918, by John W. Pritchard ... New York, Christian nation publishing company, 1919. 190 p. col. front., pl., ports. 20 cm. [BX8992.P7] 20-2497
1. Reformed Presbyterian church in North America. 2. European war, 1914- I. Title.

REFORMED church in America. Litury and ritual.
The liturgy of the Reformed Protestant Dutch church in North America. Printed according to the order of the General synod, June, 1857. New York, Board of publication of the Reformed Protestant Dutch church [1857?] vi, [7]-96 p. 19 cm. [BX9523.A2] 36-29093
I. Title.

REFORMED Presbyterian congregation of Pittsburgh, Pa.
Wuarter-centennial of thePittsburgh congregation of the Covenater church, 1866 to 18919 1866 to 1891. Allegheny, Pa., The Covenanter publishing co. [1891] 1 p. 1., [7]-198 p. pl., 2 port. (incl. front.) 18 1/2 cm. 5-9399
I. Title.

Reformed Presbyterian church in North America—History

GLASGOW, William Melancthon, 1856-1909.
History of the Reformed Presbyterian church in America: with sketches of all her ministry, congregations, missions, institutions, publications, etc., and embellished with over fifty portraits and engravings. By W. Melancthon Glasgow ... Baltimore, Hill & Harvey, 1888. xix, [20]-788 p. front., plates, ports. 21 cm. [BX8992.G6] 28-22541
1. Reformed Presbyterian church in North America—Hist. 2. Reformed Presbyterian church in North America—Clergy. 3. Reformed Presbyterian church in North America—Missions. I. Title.

REFORMED Presbyterian church in North America. General synod.
Minutes of Reformed Presbytery of America, from 1798 to 1809, and digest of the acts of the Synod of the Reformed Presbyterian church in North America, from 1809 to 1898. With appendix. Philadelphia, J. B. Rodgers printing co., 1888. 2 p. l., 219 p. 24 1/2 cm. 4-9168
I. Title.

Reformed (Reformed Church) in the Middle States—History.

HOOD, Fred J. 285.7'75
Reformed America : the Middle and Southern States, 1783-1837 / Fred J. Hood. University, Ala. : University of Alabama Press, c1980. p. cm. Includes index. Bibliography: p. [BX9496.M53H66] 79-28834 21.50 ISBN 0-8173-0036-8 (pbk.)
1. Reformed (Reformed Church) in the Middle States—History. 2. Reformed (Reformed Church) in the Southern States. 3. Presbyterians—Middle States—History. 4. Presbyterians—Southern States—History. 5. Middle States—Church history. 6. Southern States—Church history. I. Title.

Reformed Society of Israelites, Charleston, S.C.

ELZAS, Barnett Abraham, 1867-
The Reformed society of Israelites of Charleston, S.C., by Dr. Barnett A. Elzas, with an appendix: The constitution of the society. New York, Bloch publishing company, 1916. 2 p. l., 7-54 p. 19cm. "The story of the Reformed society of Israelites ... is virtually reproduced here from the author's The Jews of South Carolina, (Philadelphia, 1905)."--Pref. The appendix has special t.-p.: The constitution of the Reformed society of Israelites for promoting true principles of Judaism according to its purity and spirit, founded in Charleston, South-Carolina, 16th of January, 1825. Charleston, Printed by B. Levy, 1825. 17-10183
I. Reformed society of Israelites, Charleston, S.C. II. Title.

REFORMED society of Israelites, Charleston, S.C. New York, Bloch publishing company, 1916. 4 p. 1., [3]-69 p. 19 1/2 cm. With reproduction of original t.-p., Charleston, 1830. Comp. by Isaac Harby, Abraham Moise and D. N. Carvalho. 16-10704
I. Jews. Liturgy and ritual. II. Harby, Isaac, 1788-1828, comp. III. Moise, Abraham, 1799-1869, comp. IV. Carvalho, David Nunez, 1774-1860, comp. V. Elzas, Barneet Abraham, 1867- ed. VI. Title: The Sabbath service and miscellaneous prayers,

SILBERMAN, Lou H. 296.8'346'09757915
American impact: Judaism in the United States in the early nineteenth century [by] Lou H. Silberman. [Syracuse, N.Y., Syracuse University, 1964] [30] p. 23 cm. (B. G. Rudolph lectures in Judaic studies) Lecture delivered on April 29, 1964, at Syracuse University. Includes bibliographical references. [BM225.C4S5] 73-171337
1. Reformed Society of Israelites, Charleston, S.C. 2. Reform Judaism—Charleston, S.C. I. Title. II. Series.

Reformers.

AUSUBEL, Herman. 309.142
In hard times; reformers among the late Victorians. New York, Columbia University Press, 1960. 403 p. 24 cm. Includes bibliography. [HN385.A84] 60-14400
1. Reformers. 2. Gt. Brit.—Social policy. I. Title.

[CARTER, John Franklin, 1897- 920.073
American messiahs, by the Unofficial observer. New York, Simon and Schuster, 1935. x p., 1 l., 238 p. 24 cm. Portraits on lining-papers. By John Franklin Carter and others. [E806.C3843] 35-27206
1. Reformers. 2. U.S.—Pol. & govt.—1933-3. U.S.—Soc. condit. I. Title.

HAGSTOTZ, Gideon David, 1896- 270.6
Heroes of the Reformation [by] Gideon David Hagstotz and Hilda Boettcher Hagstotz. Mountain View, Calif., Pacific Press Pub. Association [1951] 307 p. 23 cm. [BR315.H3] 51-7544
1. Reformers. 2. Reformation. I. Title.

SCHENK, Wilhelm. 309.142
The concern for social justice in the Puritan Revolution. London, New York, Longmans, Green [1948] xi, 180 p. illus., ports. 23 cm. Bibliographical references included in "Notes." [HN388.S3] 49-980
1. Reformers. 2. Gt. Brit.—Soc. condit. 3. Gt. Brit.—Hist.—Puritan Revolution, 1642-1660. I. Title.

WALTON, John, 1895- 923.642
... Six reformers: William Wilberforce, Sir Robert Peel, Elizabeth Fry, Lord Shaftesbury, Florence Nightingale, Dr. Barnardo, by John Walton. [London, New York, etc.] Oxford university press, 1941. 2 p. l., 84 p. 18 1/2 cm. (Living names) [HN385.W3] 42-50303
1. Reformers. 2. Gt. Brit.—Soc. condit. I. Title.

Refugees, Jewish.

DEKEL, Ephraim, 1903- 325'.247'095694
B'riha: flight to the homeland. Translated from the Hebrew by Dina Ettinger. Edited by Gertrude Hirschler. New York, Herzl Press [1973] 352 p. illus. 23 cm. Translation of Bi-netive ha-"Berihah." [JV8749.P3D4513] 72-94056 6.95
1. Berihah (Organization) 2. Refugees, Jewish. 3. Palestine—Emigration and immigration. I. Title.

Refugio, Tex. Our Lady of refuge church.

OBERSTE, William H. 976.4
Our Lady comes to Refugio, by William H. Oberste ... Centennial ed. Corpus Christi, Jones publishing company, 1944. xiii, 150 p. front., plates, ports. 24 cm. [BX4603.R4208] 44-39308
1. Refugio, Tex. Our Lady of refuge church. 2. Neustra Sefiore del Refugio mission. I. Title.

Regeneration.

BACKUS, Charles, 1749-1803. 234.4
The Scripture doctrine of regeneration, considered in six discourses. By Rev. Charles Backus ... Published in the year 1800, revised and somewhat abridged. New York, American tract society [18-] 184 p. 16 cm. [BT790.B2 1800 a] 31-10009
I. Title.

CAREY, George Washington, 1845- 133
The tree of life; an expose of physical regenesis on the three-fold plane of bodily, chemical and spiritual operation. By Dr. George W. Carey ... Los Angeles, Cal., G. W. Carey, 1917. 2 p. l., 7-60 p. 23 cm. [X3.C2] 17-23676 1.00
I. Title.

DODDRIDGE, Philip, 1702-1751.
Practical discourses on regeneration in ten sermons ... Preached at Northampton, and published at the earnest request of many that heard them. By P. Doddridge, d. d. The first American ed. Providence, R. I., Printed by Carter and Wilkinson, 1794. xxii, 207 p. 17 cm. Contents.--1. The character of the unregenerate.--ii-iii. The nature of regeneration.--vi-vi. The necessity and importance of it.--vii. The divine influences necessary to produce it.--viii. The various methods in which those influences operate.--ix. Directions to the awakened sinner.--x. An address to the regenerate. 15-4353
I. Title.

DOWD, F[reeman] B[enjamin]
Regeneration; being pt. II of The temple of the rosy cross. New York, The Temple pub. co., 1900. 158 p. 12°. Aug
I. Title.

GUTHRIE, Kenneth Sylvan, 1871- 133
Regeneration applied; being the sequel and practical application of regeneration, the gate of heaven. By Rev. Kenneth Sylvan Guthrie ... Medford, Mass., The Prophet publishing house, c1900. 3 p. l., 165-318 p. 21 cm. [BF1611.G9] 0-2239
I. Title.

JOHN, S B. 234.
Regeneration and reconstruction, by S. B. John. With a foreword by the Rev. John Clifford ... New York, George H. Doran company, 1923. 93 p. 19 cm. Printed in Great Britain. [BT790.J6] 23-4632
I. Title.

LEE, Charles Follen. 234.4
The birth from above. By Rev. Charles Follen Lee ... Boston, Universalist publishing house, 1889. 3 p. l., [5]-104 p. 17 1/2 cm. (Added t.-p: Manuals of faith and duty,Ed. By J. S. Contwell no. vi) Series title in part at head of t.-p. [BT790.L4] 38-11181
1. Regeneration. I. Title.

ROMMEL, Jon. 133
Regeneration, by Rev. Jon Rommel ... founder of the Regenerate church. [Niagara Falls, N. Y., c1932] 243 p. 21 cm. [BF1999.R64] 32-16086
I. Title. II. Title: Regenerate church.

WORMAN, Alwin Emmanuel. 248
The regeneration of David Bancroft, by the Rev. Alwin E. Worman. Boston, Mass., William B. Rand co., inc. [c1922] 4 p. l., 11-62 p. 15 cm. [BV4515.W65] 22-14289
I. Title.

Regeneration (Theology)

BACKUS, Charles, 1749-1803. 234.
Discourses of Rev. Charles Backus, D. D.

of Somers, Conn. on the Scripture doctrine of regeneration; abridged, and put into the form of an essay. Boston, American doctrinal tract society, 1846. 108 p. 16 cm. [BT790.B2 1846] 39-3016
1. Regeneration (Theology) I. Doctrinal tract and book society. II. Title.

BAILLIE, John, 1886-1960. 234.4
Baptism and conversion; [lectures] New York, Scribner [1963] 121 p. 20 cm. Bibliographical footnotes. [BT790.B3 1963] 63-17936
1. Regeneration (Theology) 2. Conversion—History of doctrines. 3. Conversion—Psychology. I. Title.

*BEST, W. E. 248.24
Regeneration and conversion [By] W. E. Best. Grand Rapids, Baker Book House, [1975] 126 p. 20 cm. [BV4916] ISBN 0-8010-0643-0 2.95 (pbk.)
1. Regeneration (Theology). 2. Conversion. I. Title.

CITRON, Bernhard, 1905- 234
New birth; a study of the evangelical doctrine of conversion in the Protestant Fathers. With a pref. by Hugh Watt. Edinburgh, University Press, 1951. xvi, 214p. 23cm. (Edinburgh University publications; theology. no. 1) Bibliography: p. 203-207. [BT790.C5] 54-19256
1. Regeneration (Theology) I. Title. II. Series: Edinburgh. University. Edinurgh University publications: theology, no. 1

CRICHLOW, Cyril A 1889- 234.4
The new birth; a handbook of Scriptu[r]al documentation. [1st ed.] New York, Pageant Press [1956] 143 p. 21 cm. [BT790.C7] 56-11348
1. Regeneration (Theology) I. Title.

DODDRIDGE, Philip, 1702-1751. 234.
Practical discourses on regeneration, in ten sermons ... Preached at Northampton, and published at the earnest request of many that heard them. By P. Doddridge, D.D. The first American ed. Providence, R.I., Printed by Carter and Wilkinson, 1794. xxii, 207 p. 17 cm. Contents.--I. The character of the unregenerate.--II-III. The nature of regeneration.--IV-VI. The necessity and importance of it.--VII. The divine influences necessary to produce it.--VIII. The various methods in which those influences operate.--IX. Directions to the awakened sinner.-- X. An address to the regenerate. [BT790.D6 1794] 15-4353
1. Regeneration (Theology) I. Title.

ELVY, Cora. 234.4
The light of God, lost and found; a message of the second birth. New York, Exposition Press [1952] 71 p. 21 cm. [BT790.E4] 52-6086
1. Regeneration (Theology) I. Title.

GODWIN, Johnnie C. 234'.4
What it means to be born again / Johnnie C. Godwin. Nashville : Broadman Press, 1977, c1976. 138 p. ; 19 cm. Includes bibliographical references. [BT790.G57] 76-44039 ISBN 0-8054-1944-6 pbk. : 2.50
1. Regeneration (Theology) I. Title.

GRAHAM, Balus Joseph Winzer, 1862- 234.4
The gist of Christian doctrine, by B. J. W. Graham ... Palmetto, Ga., B. J. W. Graham [c1941] 120 p. port. 20 cm. [BT790.G65] 42-6478
1. Regeneration (Theology) I. Title.

HOYT, Herman Arthur, 1909- 234.4
The new birth. Findlay, Ohio, Dunham Pub. Co. [c1961] 122p. 20cm. [BT790.H85] 62-4946
1. Regeneration (Theology) I. Title.

MCILVAINE, Charles Pettit, bp., 1799-1873. 234.
Spiritual regeneration with reference to present times: a charge delivered to the clergy of the diocese of Ohio, at the thirty-fourth annual convention of the same, in St. Paul's church, Cleveland, October 11th, 1851. By Charles Pettit M'Ilvaine ... New York, Harper & brothers, 1851. 53 p. 24 1/2 cm. [BT790.M25] 45-50104
1. Regeneration (Theology) 2. Protestant Episcopal church in the U.S.A.—Pastoral letters and charges. I. Title.

MASTRICHT, Peter von, 1630-1706. 234.
A treatise on regeneration. By Peter Van Mastricht...Extracted from his system of divinity, called Theologia theoretico-practica; and faithfully tr. into English with an appendix containing extracts from many celebrated divines of the reformed church, upon the same subject. New Haven, Printed and sold by Thomas and Samuel Green, in the old- council-chamber [1769] viii, 9-94 p. 20 1/2 cm. [BT790.M3] 21-18453
1. Regeneration (Theology) I. Title.

RIMMER, Harry, 1890- 234.4
Flying worms, by Harry Rimmer ... Grand Rapids, Mich., Wm. B. Eerdmans publishing co., 1943. 71 p. 20 cm. [BT790.R55] 43-6421
1. Regeneration (Theology) I. Title.

SEARS, Edmund Hamilton, 1810-1876. 234.4
Regeneration. By Edmund H. Sears ... Printed for The American Unitarian association. 3d thousand. Boston, Crosby, Nichols, and company, 1854. 248 p. 20 cm. [BT790.S4 1854] 42-12090
1. Regeneration (Theology) I. American Unitarian association. II. Title.

SEARS, Edmund Hamilton, 1810-1876. 234.4
Regeneration. By Edmund H. Sears ... 6th ed. Boston, Walker, Wise, and company, 1859. 248 p. 20 cm. Published by the American Unitarian association. [BT790.S4 1859] 35-22150
1. Regeneration (Theology) I. American Unitarian association. II. Title.

SEARS, Edmund Hamilton, 1810-1876. 234.4
Regeneration. By Edmund H. Sears ... 7th ed. Boston, American Unitarian association; New York, J. Miller, 1866. 248 p. 20 cm. [BT790.S4 1866] 35-32552
1. Regeneration (Theology) I. American Unitarian association. II. Title.

SEARS, Edmund Hamilton, 1810-1876. 234.4
Regeneration. By Edmund H. Sears ... 9th ed., rev. and enl. Philadelphia, Claxton, Remsen & Haffelfinger; Boston, Noyes, Holmes & co., 1873. 264 p. 20 cm. [BT790.S4 1873] 35-32553
1. Regeneration (Theology) I. Title.

STURGES, Thomas H. 234.4
Evidences of the new birth, by T. H. Sturges ... Weatherford, Tex., The author, 1899. 104 p. 17 cm. [BT790.S8] 99-4473
1. Regeneration (Theology) I. Title.

WOODS, Thomas Edward Peck, 1875- 234.4
Born of the spirit; two true stories: 1. Nicodemus of the first century. 2. Nicodemus of the twentieth century. By T. E. P. Woods ... Grand Rapids, Mich., Wm. E. Eerdmans publishing co., 1941. 56 p. 15 cm. [BT790.W8] 41-10404
1. Regeneration (Theology) I. Title.

WRIGHT, Samuel, 1683-1746. 234.
A treatise on being born again, without which no man can be saved. By Samuel Wright, D.D. to which is added, The communicant's spiritual companion; or, An evangelical preparation for the Lord's supper ... by the Rev. Thomas Haweis ... Philadelphia: Published by George W. Mentz, no. 71 Race-street ... 1812. xxiv, [25]-286 p. 17 1/2 cm. Each article has special t.-p. [BT790.W9 1812] 4-30764
1. Regeneration (Theology) I. Haweis, Thomas, 1734-1820. II. Title.

WRIGHT, Samuel, 1683-1746. 234.
A treatise on that being born again, without which no man can be saved. By Samuel Wright, D.D. To which is added, The communicant's spiritual companion; or, An evangelical preparation for the Lord's supper ... by the Rev. Thomas Haweis ... Whitehall, Printed by William Young, for William Barlas, New-York, 1802. [224] p. 17 1/2 cm. Various pagings. Each article has special t.-p. [BT790.W9] [BT790.W] 234. A 34
1. Regeneration (Theology) I. Haweis, Thomas, 1734-1820. II. Title.

WRIGHT, Samuel, 1683-1746. 234.
A treatise on that being born again, without which no man can be saved. By Samuel Wright, D.D. To which is added, The communicant's spiritual companion: or, An evangelical preparation for the Lord's supper ... by the Rev. Thomas Haweis ... New York, W. Barlas, 1813. xxxi, [33]-141 p., 1 l., [cixv]-cixvii, [149]-270, [ccixxi]-ccixxvi p. 18 cm. Each article has special t.-p. [BT790.W9 1813] 43-42766
1. Regeneration (Theology) I. Haweis, Thomas, 1734-1820. II. Title.

Regeneration (Theology)—Popular works.

GRAHAM, William Franklin, 1918- 234'.4
How to be born again / by Billy Graham. Waco, Tex. : Word Books, c1977. 187 p. ; 23 cm. Includes bibliographical references. [BT790.G66] 77-76057 ISBN 0-8499-0017-4 : 6.95
1. Regeneration (Theology)—Popular works. 2. Salvation—Popular works. I. Title.

GRAHAM, William Franklin, 1918- 234'.4
How to be born again / by Billy Graham. New York : Warner Books, 1979, c1977. 222p. ; 18 cm. Includes bibliographical references. [BT790.G66] ISBN 0-446-92037-1 pbk. : 2.25
1. Regeneration (Theology) — Popular works. 2. Salvation — Popular works. I. Title.
L.C. card no. for 1977 Word Books ed.: 77-76057.

Reginald de Saint Gilles, 1183-1220.

[BAYONNE, Emmanuel Ceslas], 1832-1885. 922.244
Life of Blessed Reginald of St. Giles, O.P. Translated by a Dominican nun. With an introduction by Very Rev. J.A. Rotchford ... Westchester, N.Y., Printed at the Boy's protectory, 1877. xxxix, 142 p. 17 1/2 cm. [BX4705.R42B3] 37-18511
1. Reginald de Saint Gilles, 1183-1220. I. Dominin nun, tr. II. Title.

Regis, Jean Francois, Saint, 1597-1640.

FOLEY, Albert Sidney, 1912- 922.244
St. Regis, a social crusader [by] Albert S. Foley, S. J. Milwaukee, The Bruce publishing company [c1941] xi, 268 p. front. (port.) illus. (maps, facsim.) plates. 22 cm. (Half-title: Religion and culture series; Joseph Husslein...general editor) Bibliography: p. 266-268. [BX4700.R4F6] 41-24147
1. Title. II. Series.

HOLLAND, Robert E. 922.
Life of Saint John Francis Regis of the Society of Jesus, by Robert E. Holland, s.j. Chicago, Ill., Loyola university press, 1922. x p., 1 l., 145 p. incl. front. (port.) plates. 20 cm. [BX4700.R4H6] 22-8146
1. Regis, Jean Francois, Saint, 1597-1640. I. Title.

Register, Susanne Haines, 1947-

REGISTER, Susanne Haines, 1947- 248'.246 B
Take it all off / Susanne Haines Register. San Diego : Beta Books ; [New York] : distributed by Two Continents Pub. Group, c1977. p. cm. Autobiography. [BV4935.R36A37] 77-17285 ISBN 0-89293-074-8 pbk. : 2.95
1. Register, Susanne Haines, 1947- 2. Converts—United States—Biography. 3. Entertainers—United States—Biography. I. Title.

Registers of births, etc.

FRANKLIN, Conn. Congregational church and society.
Records of the Congregational church, Franklin, Connecticut, 1718-1860, and a record of deaths in Norwich eighth society, 1763, 1778, 1782, 1784-1802. Published jointly by the Society of Mayflower descendants in the state of Connecticut, and the Society of the founders of Norwich, Connecticut. Hartford, Conn., 1938. 128 p. front. (fold. map) pl. 24 cm. A 42
1. Registers of births, etc. I. Franklin, Conn. II. Society of Mayflower descendants. Connecticut. III. Society of the founders of Norwich, Conn. IV. Title. V. Title: Franklin, Conn. Pautipaug hill Congregational church.

O'ROURKE, James John, 1905- 348
... Parish registers, an historical synopsis and commentary ... by Rev. James J. O'Rourke ... Washington, D. C., The Catholic university of America, 1934. vii p., 1 l., 109 p. 23 cm. (The Catholic university of America. Canon law studies, no. 88) Thesis (J. C. D.)--Catholic university of America, 1934. Biographical note. Bibliography: p. 98-95. [BX1939.P25O7 1934] 34-19833
1. Registers of births, etc. 2. Registers of births, etc. (Canon law) 3. Catholic church. Codex juris canonici. I. Title.

Registers of births, etc.—Bethel, Vt.

MILLER, J. Wesley, 1869-1934. 287'.632'0924 B
"All my days for Jesus"; the diary of the Rev. J. Wesley Miller of Bethel, Vermont. Edited by J. W. Miller, III. Springfield, Mass., 1959. [50] l. 28 cm. [BX8495.M525A3] 75-304150
1. Miller, J. Wesley, 1869-1934. 2. Registers of births, etc.—Bethel, Vt. 3. Bethel, Vt.—History. I. Title.

Registers of births, etc.—Bocking, Eng.

BOCKING, Eng. Saint Mary's church. 254
The first register of Saint Mary's church, Bocking, Essex, England. Baptisms, 1561-1605; marriages, 1593-1639; burials, 1558-1628. Transcribed from the original for, and privately printed by James Junius Goodwin. [Hartford, Conn.] 1903. xii, 276 p. front. 1 pl. 25 1/2 cm. "An edition of fifty copies of which this is number 15." [CS436.B68] 3-18666
1. Registers of births, etc.—Bocking, Eng. I. Title.

Registers of births, etc.—Charleston, S.C.

BULL, Elias B. 288'.757'915
Founders and pew renters of the Unitarian Church in Charleston, S.C., 1817-1874, by Elias B. Bull. [Charleston] Unitarian Church in Charleston, S.C., Press [1970] iii, 47 p. 22 cm. [F279.C445B8] 76-268863
1. Charleston, S.C. Unitarian Church. 2. Registers of births, etc.—Charleston, S.C. I. Title.

Registers of births, etc.—Gloucester Co., N.J.

MORAVIAN Church at Oldman's Creek. 929.3
The records of the Moravian Church at Oldman's Creek, Gloucester County, New Jersey. Transcribed, compiled, and edited by Paul Minotty for the Gloucester County Historical Society, Woodbury, New Jersey. [Woodbury?] Published for the society by E. G. Van Name [1968] xvi, 134 p. 2 illus., map. 23 cm. "Transcribed from a microfilm of the original church books and related materials ... in the possession of the archives of the Moravian Church at Bethlehem, Pennsylvania." [BX8581.O4M6] 68-31120
1. Registers of births, etc.—Gloucester Co., N.J. I. Minotty, Paul, ed. II. Gloucester County Historical Society, Woodbury, N.J. III. Title.

Registers of births, etc.—New York (City)

NEW York. French church du Saint Esprit. 929.3097471
Registers of the births, marriages, and deaths, of the "Eglise francoise a la Nouvelle York," from 1688 to 1804, edited by the Rev. Alfred V. Wittmeyer...and historical documents relating to the French Protestants in New York during the same

period. New York, 1886. lxxviii, 431, xii p. 3 pl. fold. facsim. 25 1/2 cm. (Added t.-p.: Collections of the Hugenot society of America. vol. i) The "eglise francoise" was incorporated in 1804 as an Episcopal church, under the names "French church du Saint-Esprit." The "Historical documents...1696-1804" (p. [327]-431) are edited by Edward F. de Lancey. "500 copies printed." [E184.H9H63 vol. 1] (284.573) 4-7493

1. Registers of births, etc.—New York (City) 2. Huguenots in New York (State) I. Wittmeyer, Alfred Victor, 1847-1926, ed. II. De Lancey Edward Floyd, 1821-1905. III. Title.

Registers of births, etc.—Oconee County, Ga.

REID, Frances W. 286
Mars Hill Baptist Church (constituted 1799) Clarke-Oconee Co., Georgia [by] Frances W. Reid and Mary B. Warren. Athens, Ga., Heritage Papers, 1966. 71 p. 28 cm. Cover title. [F292.O3R4] 70-15343
1. Mars Hill Baptist Church. 2. Registers of births, etc.—Oconee County, Ga. I. Warren, Mary Bondurant, joint author.

Registers of births, etc.—Poole, Ky.

WILLIAMS, Irene Aldridge, 1904- 286'.6769'883
A record of Poole Church of Christ, Poole, Webster County, Kentucky. Evansville, Ind., 1969. v, 97 l. 28 cm. Cover title: Poole Church of Christ. Typescript. [F459.P65W5] 74-275312
1. Poole Church of Christ. 2. Registers of births, etc.—Poole, Ky. I. Title.

Registers of births, etc.—Prestwich, Eng.

PRESTWICH, Eng. Church of St. Mary. 254
The registers of the parish church of Prestwich; baptisms, burials and weddings, 1603-1688, transcribed by Henry Brierley ... Printed and pub. with the permission of the Rev. F. W. Cooper, M. A., rector of Prestwich ... Cambridge, Printed for the Lancashire parish register society by J. Clay, at the University press, 1909. vi, [2], 276 p. front. 23 cm. (Half-title: Lancashire parish register society [Publications] 34) [CS435.L3 vol. 34] 10-27053
1. Registers of births, etc.—Prestwich, Eng. I. Brierley, Henry. II. Title.

Regular Baptists—Doctrinal and controversial works.

JACKSON, Paul Rainey, 1903- 230.86'1
The doctrine and administration of the church, by Paul R. Jackson. Des Plaines, Ill., Regular Baptist Press [1968] 210 p. 22 cm. Rev. and enl. ed. of the author's Doctrine of the local church. Bibliography: p. 209-210. [BX6389.37.J3 1968] 68-28699 3.95

1. Regular Baptists—Doctrinal and controversial works. I. Title.

Rehmeyer, Nelson D., 1868-1928.

LEWIS, Arthur H., 1906- 133.4
Hex, by Arthur H. Lewis. New York, Trident Press [1969] 255 p. 22 cm. [BF1577.P4L4] 69-14545 4.95

1. Rehmeyer, Nelson D., 1868-1928. 2. Blymyer, John H. 3. Curry, John, 1915-1962. 4. Hess, Wilbert G. 5. Witchcraft—Pennsylvania. I. Title.

Rehrersburg, Pa. Altalaha Evangelical Lutheran Church.

DIEFFENBACH, Ray J. 284'.1748'16
An historical account of the building of Altalaha Lutheran Church, Rehrersburg, Pa. in 1808 and the bell tower of 1849. Compiled by Ray J. Dieffenbach and Schuyler C. Brossman. Edited by Larry R. Hassler. Rehrersburg, Pa., Church Council of Altalaha Lutheran Church, 1973. 27 p. 22 cm. [BX8076.R34A63] 73-299016
1. Rehrersburg, Pa. Altalaha Evangelical Lutheran Church. 2. Rehrersburg, Pa.—Biography. I. Brossman, Schuyler C. II. Title.

Rehrersburg, Pa.—Biography.

DIEFFENBACH, Ray J. 284'.1748'16
An historical account of the building of Altalaha Lutheran Church, Rehrersburg, Pa. in 1808 and the bell tower of 1849. Compiled by Ray J. Dieffenbach and Schuyler C. Brossman. Edited by Larry R. Hassler. Rehrersburg, Pa., Church Council of Altalaha Lutheran Church, 1973. 27 p. 22 cm. [BX8076.R34A63] 73-299016
1. Rehrersburg, Pa. Altalaha Evangelical Lutheran Church. 2. Rehrersburg, Pa.—Biography. I. Brossman, Schuyler C. II. Title.

Reichel, Willy.

REICHEL, Willy. 133.9'092'4 B
An occultist's travels / by Willy Reichel. Philadelphia : Running Press, [1975] 244 p. ; 22 cm. Originally published in 1908. [BF1241.R3 1975] 74-31539 ISBN 0-914294-10-5 pbk. : 3.95
1. Reichel, Willy. 2. Spiritualism. I. Title.

Reichert, George, 1837-1855.

[GIRARDEY, Ferrol] 1839-1930. 922.273
George Reichert, C. SS. R., a model for youth. By one of his companions ... Kansas City, Mo., J. A. Heilmann, 1891. 93 p 12 cm. [BX4705.R43G5] 37-16736
1. Reichert, George, 1837-1855. I. Title.

Reid, Jim.

REID, Jim. 286'.132'0924 B
Praising God on the Las Vegas Strip / Jim Reid ; foreword by Creath Davis. Grand Rapids : Zondervan Pub. House, [1975] 183 p. ; 21 cm. [BV3775.L3R44] 74-25335 5.95
1. Reid, Jim. 2. Evangelistic work—Las Vegas, Nev. I. Title.

Reid, Thomas F.

REID, Thomas F. 289.9
The exploding church / by Thomas F. Reid, with Doug Brendel. Plainfield, N.J. : Logos International, c1979. 156 p. ; 21 cm. [BR1725.R39A34] 78-73575 ISBN 0-88270-299-8 pbk. : 3.50
1. Reid, Thomas F. 2. Full Gospel Tabernacle, Orchard Park, N.Y. 3. Clergy—United States—Biography. I. Brendel, Doug, joint author. II. Title.

Reims. Notre-Dame (Cathedral)

HOLBROOK, Sabra. 914.4'32
Joy in stone; the Cathedral of Reims. Illustrated by Herbert Danska. New York, Farrar, Straus and Giroux [1973] xii, 163 p. illus. 24 cm. Bibliography: p. 155-158. [BX4629.R42N674 1973] 73-82696 ISBN 0-374-33941-4 5.95
1. Reims. Notre-Dame (Cathedral) I. Title.

Reincarnation.

ABHEDANANDA, swami. 129.4
Vedanta philosophy; five lectures on reincarnation, by Swami Abhedananda... 3d ed. West Cornwall, Conn., The Vendanta society [c1907] 2 p. l., 99 p. front. (port.) 18 1/2 cm. Contents.Reincarnation.--Heredity and reincarnation.--Evolution and reincarnation.--Which is scientific, resurrection or reincarnation?--... Theory of transmigration. [B133.A2R372] 294.1 32-5674
1. Reincarnation I. Title.

ABHEDANANDA, swami, 1866- 129.4
vedanta philosophy; five lectures on reincarnation, by Swami Abhedananda ... 4th ed. San Francisco, Cal., The Vedanta ashrama [191-?] 2 p. l., 99 p. front. (port.) 18 1/2 cm. Contents.Reincarnation.--Heredity and reincarnation.--Evolution and reincarnation.--Which is scientific, resurrection or reincarnation?--Theory of transmigration. [B133.A2R373] 294.1 39-15998
1. Reincarnation. I. Title.

ABHENDANANDA, swami. 181
Vedanta philosophy; three lectures by Swami Abhedananda on reincarnation, delivered under the auspices of the Vedanta society, in Assembly hall, New York, 1898-1899. New York, Vedanta society [c1899] 61 p. front. (port.) 18 1/2 cm. Advertising matter: p. [50]-61. Contents.Reincarnation.--Evolution and reincarnation.--Which is scientific, resurrection or reincarnation? [B133.A2R35] 4-80
1. Reincarnation. I. Title.

APPLEBY, Hazel F, 1899- 129.4
The reward of reincarnation, by Vyrne Montanique [pseud.] Boston, Meador Pub. Co. [1951] 88 p. 19 cm. [BL515.A6] 52-18169
1. Reincarnation. I. Title.

ATKINSON, William Walker, 1862-
Reincarnation and the law of karma; a study of the old-new world-doctrine of rebirth and spiritual cause and effect, by William Walker Atkinson. Chicago, Ill., Advanced thought publishing company; [etc., etc., c1908] 249 p. 19 cm. 8-28414
I. Title.

BANERJEE, H. N. 133
Lives unlimited; reincarnation East and West [by] H. N. Banerjee and Will Oursler. [1st ed.] Garden City, N.Y., Doubleday, 1974. 187 p. 22 cm. Includes bibliographical references. [BL515.B26] 73-9171 ISBN 0-385-03912-3 5.95
1. Reincarnation. I. Oursler, William Charles, 1913- joint author. II. Title.

BAUGHMAN, Harold A. 133.9
The ladder, by H. A. Baughman. [Sacramento, Celestial Press, c1971- v. 19 cm. (A Wisdom book) [BL515.B36] 73-143776
1. Reincarnation. I. Title.

BESANT, Annie (Wood) Mrs. 1847- 212
... *Reincarnation,* by Annie Besant. 3d and rev. ed. London, New York [etc.] Theosophical publishing society, 1898. 2 p. l., 66 p. 16 x 12 cm. (Theosophical manuals, no. 2 [BP563.R4 1898] 5-37172
1. Reincarnation. I. Title.

BRADFORD, Columbus.
Birth a new chance, by Columbus Bradford, A. M. Chicago, A. C. McClurg & co., 1901. 363 p. 20 cm. A theory of reincarnation. [BD426.B7] 1-31411
1. Reincarnation. I. Title.

BROWNE, Merry. 128
The ladder of life. New Albany, Ind. [1971] c1968-69. 44 l. 28 cm. Original imprint covered by label: New Albany, Ind., Merry Browne Institute of Ontology, c1971. [BL515.B76 1971] 73-30024
1. Reincarnation. 2. Conduct of life. I. Title.

BUCHANAN, Frances (Grant) Mrs. 1872- 133
The ladder of initiation, by Frances Buchanan, M. D. [Los Angeles, Printed by Wetzel publishing co., inc., c1934] vii p., 1 l., 11-78 p. pl. 20 cm. [BF1999.B73] 159.961 34-17948
1. Reincarnation. I. Title.

BURR, Henry, 1889- 129.4
Christianity crucified, by Henry Burr ... and Marguerite Geighton Pless ... The Bert Rose company c1932 86 p. 19 1/2 cm. "Reincarnation" ...used ... as meaning part of the true Christianity of Christ."--Foreword. [BR148.B8] 32-31850
1. Reincarnation. I. Pless, Marguerite Beighton, joint author. II. Title.

CAYCE, Edgar, 1877-1945 291.2'3
Edgar Cayce on reincarnation, by Noel Langley; under editorship of Hugh Lynn Cayce. [1st hardbound ed.] New York, Hawthorn [1968,c.1967] 286p. 22cm. Presents data from 2500 readings given by Edgar Cayce from 1925 through 1944. Bibl. [BL515.C3 1968] 68-14394 4.95
1. Reincarnation. I. Langley, Noel, 1911- comp. II. Title.

CERMINARA, Gina. 291.23
Many lives, many loves. [New York] New American Library [1974, c1963] 170 p. 18 cm. (A Signet book) [BL515.C38] 1.50 (pbk.)
1. Reincarnation. I. Title.
L.C. card no. for original: 63-13710.

CERMINARA, Gina. 291.23
Many lives, many loves. New York, W. Sloane Associates, 1963. 246 p. illus. 21 cm. [BL515.C38] 63-13710
1. Reincarnation. I. Title.

CERMINARA, Gina. 129.4
Many mansions. [New York] New Amer. Lib. [1967,c.1950] 240p. 18cm. (Signet mystic bk., Q3307) [BL515.C4] .95 pap.,
1. Reincarnation. I. Title.

CERMINARA, Gina. 129'.4
Many mansions. New York, Morrow [1968, c1950] 310 p. illus. 22 cm. [BL515.C4 1968] 70-5404 5.00
1. Reincarnation. I. Title.

CERMINARA, Gina. 129.4
Many mansions. New York, Sloane [1950] 304 p. 22 cm. [BL515.C4] 50-11101
1. Reincarnation. I. Title.

CERMINARA, Gina. 129.4
The world within. New York, W. Sloane Associates, 1957. 215p. illus. 21cm. [BL515.C45] 57-5941
1. Reincarnation. I. Title.

CERMINARA, Gina. 129.4
The world within. [New York] New American Library [1974, c1958] 153 p. 18 cm. [BL515.C45] 57-5941 1.25 (pbk.)
1. Reincarnation. I. Title.

CHRISTIE-MURRAY, David. 291.2'37
Reincarnation : ancient beliefs and modern evidence / David Christie-Murray. Newton Abbot : David and Charles, c1981. 287 p. ; 23 cm. Includes index. Bibliography: p. 267-274. [BL515.C49] 19 81-149385 ISBN 0-7153-7861-9 : 26.50
1. Reincarnation. I. Title.

COHEN, Daniel. 129'.4
The mysteries of reincarnation / Daniel Cohen ; illustrated with photos. and reproductions. New York : Dodd, Mead, [1975] 172 p. : ill. ; 24 cm. Includes index. Bibliography: p. 163-167. [BL515.C58] 74-25517 ISBN 0-396-07077-9 : 5.50
1. Reincarnation. I. Title.

COLTON, Ann Ree. 291.2'3
Draughts of remembrance. [1st ed.] Glendale, Calif., Arc Pub. Co. [1959] iv, 177 p. 20 cm. [BL515.C6] 67-9622
1. Reincarnation. I. Title.

COOPER, Irving Steiger, Bp., 1882-1935. 129.4
Reincarnation, the hope of the world. 4th ed. Wheaton, Ill., Theosophical Press, 1951. 121 p. 20 cm. [BP573.R5C6 1951] 52-3162
1. Reincarnation. I. Title.

COOPER, Irving Steiger, bp., 1882- 212
Reincarnation, the hope of the world, by the Rt. Rev. Irving S. Cooper ... 2d ed. Chicago, The Theosophical press [c1927] xiii, 121, [5] p. 20 cm. "Suggested courses of reading in theosophy": 5 p. at end. [BP573.R5C6 1927] 27-7278
1. Reincarnation. I. Title.

COOPER, Irving Steiger, Bp 1882-1935. 212
Reincarnation, the hope of the world. 3d ed. Wheaton, Iii., Theosophical Press, 1947. xiii. 121 p. 20 cm. [BP573.R5C] A 50

1. Reincarnation. I. Title.

COOPER, Irving Steiger, Bp., 1882-1935. 129'.4
Reincarnation, a hope of the world / Irving S. Cooper. 1st Quest ed. Wheaton, Ill. : Theosophical Pub. House, 1979. ix, 106 p. ; 18 cm. (A Quest book) Previously published under title: Reincarnation, the hope of the world. [BP573.R5C6 1979] 79-11475 ISBN 0-8356-0528-0 pbk. : 2.95
1. Reincarnation. I. Title.

COOPER, Irving Steiger, Bp., 1882-1935. 129.4
Reincarnation, the hope of the world, by Irving S. Cooper. 6th ed. Wheaton, Ill., Theosophical Press, 1959. xiii, 121 p. 20 cm. [BP573.R5C6 1959] 65-8145
1. Reincarnation.

CRAWFORD, Merwin Richard. 129.4
Aztirc, by Merwin Richard Crawford, recording a successful experience with a philosophy of life adaptable to the evolutionary status of any man or woman desirous of karmic improvement. Philadelphia, Dorrance & company [1945] xi p., 1 l., 15-130 p. front. (group port.) plates. 19 1/2 cm. [BP573.R5C7] 45-7385
1. Reincarnation. I. Title.

DAS, Ranendra Kumar. 129.4
Reincarnation, by Ranendra Kumar Das. Los Angeles, Cal. De Vores & co. [1943] 127 p. 18 cm. "First edition." [BL515.D3] 43-4540
1. Reincarnation. I. Title.

DETHLEFSEN, Thorwald. 133.9'013
Voices from other lives : reincarnation as a source of healing / by Thorwald Dethlefsen ; translated by Gerhard Hundt. New York : M. Evans, [1977] p. cm. Translation of Das Erlebnis der Wiedergeburt. Includes bibliographical references. [BL515.D4513] 76-30454 ISBN 0-87131-233-6 : 7.95
1. Reincarnation. 2. Mental healing. I. Title.

DIXON, Jeane. 200
Reincarnation and prayers to live by. New York, W. Morrow, 1970 [c1969] 62 p. 18 cm. [BL515.D57 1970] 77-115439
1. Reincarnation. 2. Prayers. I. Title.

DOUMETTE, Hanna Jacob, 1884- 129.4
Life after death, by Hanna Jacob Doumette. Kansas City; Mo., Christian institute of spiritual science, 1938. 3 p. l., 120 p. 21 1/2 cm. "First edition." [BF1999.D63] 40-487
1. Reincarnation. I. Title.

ELLIS, Edith, 1876- 133.93
Incarnation; a plea from the masters, by Wilfred Brandon, transcribed by Edith Ellis. New York, London, A. A. Knof, 1936. xxi, [1], 171, [1] p., 1 l. 21 cm. "First edition." [BF1311.R35E6] 159.96173 36-20413
1. Reincarnation. 2. Automatism. I. Title.

ELLIS, Edith, 1876- 133.93
Incarnation; a plea from the masters, by Wilfred Brandon, transcribed by Edith Ellis. New York, London, A. A. Knof, 1936. xxi, [1], 171, [1] p., 1 l. 21 cm. "First edition." [BF1311.R35E6] 159.96173 36-20413
1. Reincarnation. 2. Automatism. I. Title.

FULK, Augustus Marion. 129.4
Reincarnation (time--space--matter) by Augustus Marion Fulk, LL. B. Boston, The Christopher publishing house [c1940] 3 p. l., 5-462 p. front., plates, diagrs. 24 cm. [BL515.F8] 40-5094
1. Reincarnation. 2. Religion and science—1900- 3. Space and time. 4. Matter. I. Title.

GESTEFELD, Ursula Newell, 1845-1921.
Reincarnation or immortality? By Ursula N. Gestefeld ... New York, The Alliance publishing co., 1899. 165 p. 22 cm. [BD426.G4] 2-12095
1. Reincarnation. I. Title.

GIBSON, Axel Emil, 1863- 129.4
Immortality in the light of reason, by Dr. Axel Emil Gibson. Los Angeles, Calif., Catterlin publishing company, printers [c1933] 2 p. l., 7-82 p. 18 cm. [BL515.G5] 34-8169
1. Reincarnation. 2. Immortality. I. Title.

GLASKIN, Gerald M., 1924- 236'.2
Windows of the mind: discovering your past and future lives through massage and mental exercise [by] G. M. Glaskin. New York, Delacorte Press [1974] 268 p. 22 cm. [BL515.G55] 73-19760 6.95
1. Reincarnation. I. Title.

GOUDEY, Ray Freeman. 129'.4
Reincarnation: a universal truth. Rev. and republished by Balwant Singh Grewal. [2d ed.] Detroit, B. S. Grewal [1967] 160 p. 24 cm. Bibliography: p. 139-160. [BL515.G6 1967] 67-8686
1. Reincarnation. I. Grewal, Balwant Singh.

GOUDEY, Ray Freeman. 129.
Reincarnation, a universal truth [by] R. F. Goudey. Los Angeles, The Aloha press [c1928] 160 p. 24 cm. [BL515.G6] 28-14566
1. Reincarnation. I. Title.

GRAHAM, David, 1927- 129'.4
The practical side of reincarnation / David Graham ; introd. by Brad Steiger. Englewood Cliffs, N.J. : Prentice-Hall, c1976. xv, 210 p. ; 22 cm. Includes index. [BL515.G67 1976] 76-2603 ISBN 0-13-693903-1 : 7.95
1. Reincarnation. I. Title.

GREEN, Harry L. 133.901'3
Echoes of thunder : a unique experience in reincarnation / by Harry L. Green. Santa Rosa, CA : Emerald House, c1980. 167 p. ; 24 cm. [BL518.G73] 19 80-66322 ISBN 0-936958-00-6 : 10.95 ISBN 0-936958-01-4 pbk. : 5.95
1. Reincarnation. I. Title.
Publisher's address: P. O. Box 388, Santa Rosa, CA 95402

HACKETT, Ann. 129.4
Tilak of Tibet reveals life's purpose, by Ann Hackett. San Francisco, Sentinel press, 1944. 5 p. l., 144 p. 18 cm. [BL515.H2] 44=19247
1. Reincarnation. I. Title.

HALL, Manly Palmer. 129.4
Reincarnation; the cycle of necessity, by Manly P. Hall. 1st ed. Los Angeles, Calif., The Philosophers press, 1939. 3 p. l., 9-198 p. 2 pl. (1 fold.) 24 cm. Bibliography: p. 191-196. [BL515.H3] 40-3328
1. Reincarnation. I. Title.

HALL, Manly Palmer, 1901- 129'.4
Past lives and present problems : how to prepare for a fortunate rebirth / by Manly P. Hall. 3d ed. Los Angeles : Philosophical Research Society, c1977. p. cm. [BL515.H28 1977] 77-6164 ISBN 0-89314-381-2 : 1.50
1. Reincarnation. I. Title.

HALL, Manly Palmer, 1901-
Reincarnation; the cycle of necessity. 5th ed. rev. and enl. Los Angeles, The Philosophical Research Society, 1967. 224 p. 2 plates (1 fold.) Bibliography: p. 203-210. 68-50336
1. Reincarnation. I. Title.

HALL, Manly Palmer, 1901-
Reincarnation, the cycle of necessity. 4th ed., rev. and enl. Los Angeles, Philosophical Research Society, 1956. 217 p. illus. 24 cm. Bibliography: p. 203-210. 65-108681
1. Reincarnation. I. Title.

HAMMER, Frank L. 129.4
Life and its mysteries, by Frank L. Hammer. Philadelphia, Dorrance & company [1945] vii, [1], 9-124 p. 20 cm. "First appeared in serial form in the New age magazine-"--Pref. [BF1999.H342] 46-520
1. Reincarnation. I. Title.

HEAD, Joseph, comp. 291.2'3
Reincarnation; an East-West anthology including quotations from the world's religions & from over 400 Western thinkers. Compiled and edited by Joseph Head and S. L. Cranston. Wheaton, Ill., Theosophical Pub. House [1968, c1961] x, 341 p. 21 cm. (A Quest book) [BL515.H38 1968] 68-146
1. Reincarnation. I. Cranston, S. L., joint comp.

HEAD, Joseph, ed. 291.23
Reincarnation; an East-West anthology including quotations from the world's religions & from over 400 Western thinkers. Compiled and edited by Joseph Head and S. L. Cranston. New York, Julian Press, 1961. 341 p. 25 cm. [BL515.H38] 61-14420
1. Reincarnation. I. Cranston, S. L., joint ed. II. Title.

HEAD, Joseph, comp. 291.2'3
Reincarnation in world thought; a living study of reincarnation in all ages; including selections from the world's religions, philosophies, and sciences, and great thinkers of the past and present, compiled and edited by Joseph Head [and] S. L. Cranston. New York, Causeway Books; published by arrangement with The Julian Press, New York, c1967. 461 p. illus. Based on the compiler's Reincarnation, an East-West anthology. [BL515.H39] 67-17571
1. Reincarnation. I. Cranston, S. L., joint comp. II. Title.

HOLZER, Hans. 133.9'013
The reincarnation primer: patterns of destiny. New York, Harper & Row [1975, c1974] xi, 163 p., 18 cm. [BL515.H63] ISBN 0-06-465042-1 1.75 (pbk.)
1. Reincarnation. I. Title.
L.C. card no. for original ed.: 73-12714

HOLZER, Hans W., 1920- 129.'4
Born again; the truth about reincarnation. New York, Pocket Books [1973, c.1970] xii, 227 p. 18 cm. [BL515.H6] ISBN 0-671-77461-1 pap., 0.95
1. Reincarnation. I. Title.
L.C. card no. for the hardbound ed.: 71-119920.

HOLZER, Hans W., 1920- 129'.4
Born again [by] Hans Holzer. [1st ed.] Garden City, N.Y., Doubleday, 1970. xvi, 267 p. 22 cm. [BL515.H6] 71-119920 5.95
1. Reincarnation. I. Title.

HOLZER, Hans W., 1920- 133.9'013
Patterns of destiny, by Hans Holzer. Los Angeles, Nash Pub. [1974] xi, 163 p. 23 cm. [BL515.H63] 73-83535 ISBN 0-8402-1323-9 6.95
1. Reincarnation. I. Title.

HOWE, Quincy, 1934- 236'.2
Reincarnation for the Christian. Philadelphia, Westminster Press [1974] 112 p. 21 cm. Bibliography: p. [109]-112. [BL515.H65] 73-19758 ISBN 0-664-20996-3 4.95
1. Reincarnation. I. Title.

HUDSON, Charles Frederic. 236
Debt and grace, as related to the doctrine of a future life. By C. F. Hudson ... 4th thousand. New York, Rudd and Carleton, 1861. vii, [1], 489 p. 19 1/2 cm. [BT901.H88 1861] 8-17106
I. Title.

INGRAHAM, E V. 204
Incarnation and re-incarnation [by] E. V. Ingraham. Los Angeles, De. Vorss & co., 1930. 3 p. l., 5-106 p. 18 cm. [BR123.I55] 30-17550
I. Title.
Contents omitted.

*IVERSON, Jeffrey. 129'.4
More lives than one? : the evidence of the remarkable Bloxham Tapes / Jeffrey Iverson ; foreword by Magnus Magnusson. New York : Warner Books, 1977,c1976. 270p. : ill.,ports. ; 18 cm. Orginally published by Souvenir Press. Bibliography:p.269-270. [BL515] ISBN 0-446-89372-2 pbk. : 1.95
1. Reincarnation. I. Title.

JAST, Louis Stanley, 1868- 129.4
Reincarnation and karma, a spiritual philosophy applied to the world today, by L. Stanley Jast ... New York, B. Ackerman incorporated [1944] 190 p. 21 cm. [BL515.J28] 44-3065
1. Reincarnation. 2. Karma. I. Title.

JONES, Gladys V. 291.23
The flowering tree. New York, W. Sloane Associates, 1965. 316 p. 22 cm. Bibliography: p. 315-316. [BL518.J6] 65-20504
1. Reincarnation. 2. Karma. I. Title.

JUDGE, William Quan, 1851-1896. 212.5
The scope of reincarnation. Alhambra, Calif., Cunningham Press [1960] 98p. 21cm. 'Passages taken from [the author's] . . . Ocean of theosophy, which first appeared in 1893.' [BP573.R5J8] 60-52058
1. Reicearnation. 2. Theosophy. I. Title.

LANGLEY, Noel, 1911- 133.8'0924
Edgar Cayce on reincarnation. Under the editorship of Hugh Lynn Cayce. [1st hardbound ed.] New York, Hawthorn Books [1968, c1967] 286 p. 22 cm. "Presents data from 2500 readings given by Edgar Cayce from 1925 through 1944." Bibliography: p. 279. [BL515.L35 1968] 68-14394
1. Reincarnation. I. Cayce, Edgar, 1877-1945. II. Title.

LANGLEY, Noel, 1911- ed.
The hidden history of reincarnation; the historical 61 p. 23 cm. Bibliography: p. 61. 67-99035
1. Cayce, Edgar, 1877-1945. 2. Reincarnation. I. Title.

LANGLEY, Noel, 1911- ed.
The hidden history of reincarnation; the historical evidence in support of the Edgar Cayce readings. Virginia Beach, Va., A.R.E. Press, 1965. 61 p. 23 cm. Bibliography: p. 61. 67-99035
1. Reincarnation. 2. Cayce, Edgar, 1877-1945. I. Title.

LEEK, Sybil. 291.2'3
Reincarnation: the second chance. New York, Stein and Day [1974] 262 p. 24 cm. Bibliography: p. 249-256. [BL515.L43] 73-93034 ISBN 0-8128-1693-5 7.95
1. Reincarnation.

LEEK, Sybil. 291.2'3
Reincarnation: the second chance. New York, Bantam Books [1975, c1974] 212 p. 18 cm. Bibliography: p. 199-205. [BL515.L43] 1.50 (pbk.)
1. Reincarnation. I. Title.
L.C. card number for original ed.: 73-93034.

LEWIS, Harve Spencer, 1883- 129.4
Mansions of the soul; the cosmic conception, by H. Spencer Lewis ... San Jose, Calif., Rosicrucian press, AMORC college [1930] 339 p. illus. 20 cm. (Rosicrucian library, v. no. 11) Advertisements: p. 335-339. "First edition, November 1930." [BF1623.R7R65 vol. 11] (133) 30-34218
1. Reincarnation. I. Title.

LEWIS, Harve Spencer, 1883-
A thousand years of yesterdays, by H. Spencer Lewis ... a strange story of mystic revelations, with an introduction by Reverend George R. Chambers. San Francisco, Calif., The College press, 1920. 80 p. 21 cm. [BD426.L4] 20-9068
1. Reincarnation. I. Title.

LEWIS, Harve Spencer, 1883-1939.
Mansions of the soul; the cosmic conception. [10th ed.] San Jose, Calif., Supreme Grand Lodge of AMORC [1961] 352 p. illus. 20 cm. (Rosicrucian library, v. 11) 65-28495
1. Reincarnation. I. Title. II. Series.

LEWIS, Harve Spencer, 1883-1939. 129.4
Mansions of the soul; the cosmic conception. [7th ed.] San Jose, Calif., Supreme Grand Lodge of AMORC [1954] 352 p. illus. 20 cm. (Rosicrucian library, v. 11) [BF1623.R7R65 vol. 11, 1954] 54-30272
1. Reincarnation. I. Title.

LEWIS, Harve Spencer, 1883-1939.
A thousand years of yesterdays; a strange story of mystic revelations, with an introd. by George R. Chambers. [12th ed.] San Jose, Calif., Supreme Grand Lodge of AMORC [1961] 77 p. 20 cm. 64-47905
1. Reincarnation. I. Title.

LEWIS, Harve Spencer, 1883-1939. 129.4
A thousand years of yesterdays, by H. Spencer Lewis ... a strange story of mystic revelations, with an introduction by Reverend George R. Chambers ... San Jose, Calif., Supreme Grand lodge of AMORC [1935] 80 p. 20 cm. (Rosicrucian

library. vol. vi) "Fifth edition, November, 1935." [BF1623.R7R65 vol. 6] (133.082) [(159.961082)] 38-33864
1. Reincarnation. I. Title.

LUNTZ, Charles E 129.4
The challenge of reincarnation. With foreword by Morey Bernstein. St. Louis, C. E. Luntz Publications [1957] 154p. 22cm. [BL515.L8] 57-29430
1. Reincarnation. I. Title.

MANAS, John H. 133
Life's riddle solved through the law of metempsychosis, by John H. Manas ... New York, N.Y., Pythagorean society [1944] xxvi, 262 p. incl. front. (port.) illus., diagrs. 21 cm. "Second edition revised and enlarged ... 1944." First published, 1941, under title: Metempsychosis. [BL535.M3 1944] 44-24516
1. Reincarnation. 2. Soul. 3. U.S.—Commercial policy. I. Pythagorean society. II. Title.

MANAS, John Helen, 1890- 133
Life's riddle solved through the law of metempsychosis, by John H. Manas ... New York, N.Y., Pythagorean society [1944] xxvi, 262 p. incl. front. (port.) illus., diagrs. 21 cm. "Second edition revised and enlarged ... 1944." First published, 1941, under title: Metempsychosis. [BL535.M3 1944] 44-24516
1. Reincarnation. 2. Soul. I. Pythagorean society. II. Title.

MANAS, John Helen, 1890- 133
Metempsychosis, reincarnation; pilgrimage of the soul through matter; "solution of the riddle of life," by John H. Manas. New York city, Pythagorean society [1941] xxii (i.e. xxiv), 23-206 (i.e. 208) p., 1 l. incl. illus., plates, ports., diagrs. 20 1/2 cm. [BL535.M3 1941] [[159.961]] 42-4530
1. Reincarnation. 2. Soul. I. Pythagorean society. II. Title.

MARTIN, Asa Roy, 1887- 129.4
Researches in reincarnation and beyond ... by A. R. Martin. Sharon, Pa., Author [1942- v. 24 1/2 cm. [BL515.M3] 42-22749
1. Reincarnation. I. Title.

MILLER, Richard De Witt, 1910- 129.4
Reincarnation, the whole startling story. New York, Bantam Books [1956] 118p. 18cm. (Bantam books, 1507) [BL515.M54] 56-10493
1. Reincarnation. I. Title.

MILLS, Janet Melanie Ailsa, 1894- 133.9'013
The wheel of rebirth : an autobiography of many lifetimes / by H. K. Challoner [i.e. J. M. A. Mills] Wheaton, Ill. : Theosophical Pub. House, 1976, c1969. 285 p. ; 21 cm. (A Quest book) [BP573.R5M5 1976] 75-26759 ISBN 0-8356-0468-3 pbk. : 3.50
1. Reincarnation. I. Title.

MILLS, Janet Melanie Ailsa, 1894- 139.'4
The wheel of rebirth, by H. K. Challoner. 2nd ed. London, Wheaton, Ill., Theosophical Publishing House, 1969. 287 p. 20 cm. Bibliography: p. [287] [BP573.R5M5 1969] 75-413821 ISBN 7-229-01100- 25/-
1. Reincarnation. I. Title.

MONTGOMERY, Ruth (Shick) 1912- 129'.4
Here and hereafter; by Ruth Montgomery. New York, Coward-McCann [1968] 224 p. 22 cm. [BL515.M6] 68-23375
1. Reincarnation. I. Title.

MOORE, Marcia. 133.9
Hypersentience : exploring your past lifetime as a guide to your character and destiny / Marcia Moore. New York : Crown Publishers, c1976. xiii, 210 p. ; 24 cm. [BL515.M62 1976] 76-8199 ISBN 0-517-52536-4 : 7.95
1. Reincarnation. I. Title.

MOORE, Marcia. 291.2'3
Reincarnation, key to immortality [by] Marcia Moore [and] Mark Douglas. [1st ed.] York Cliffs, Me., Arcane Publications [1968] xv, 394 p. 23 cm. Bibliography: p. 349-352. [BL515.M63] 67-19603 5.95
1. Reincarnation. I. Douglas, Mark, joint author. II. Title.

MULIER, pseud. 129.
Signor: a segment from the eternal cycle, by Mulier ... San Diego, Cal., The Gnostic press [c1917] 2 p. l., iii-ix, 11-219 p. front. 20 cm. [BL515.M7] 18-4365
1. Reincarnation. I. Title.
Contents omitted.

MULIER, pseud. 129.
Sojourners by the wayside; travelers on the long road, by Mulier ... San Diego, Cal., The Gnostic press [c1917] 2 p. l., vii-xiii, 15-203 p. 20 cm. [BL515.M8] 17-30235
1. Reincarnation. I. Title.
Contents omitted.

MURPHY, Joseph, 1898- 129.4
The meaning of reincarnation. San Gabriel, Calif., Willing Pub. Co. [1954] 86p. 20cm. [BL515.M85] 54-43974
1. Reincarnation. I. Title.

PARAMANANDAS, swami, 1883- 237.2
Reincarnation and immortality, by Swami Paramananda ... Boston, Mass., The Vedanta centre [c1923] 102 p. 19 cm. "Reprinted from the Vedanta monthly 'The message of the East'." [B132.V3P36] 34-5864
1. Reincarnation. 2. Immortality. I. Title.

PEEBLES, James Martin, 1822-1922. 129.4
Reincarnation; or, The doctrine of the "soul's" successive embodiments, examined and discussed pro and con by Dr J. M. Peebles versus Dr. Helen Densmore and W. J. Colville. Battle Creek, Mich., The Peebles medical institute [c1904] 105 p. 23 cm. "Catalogue of Dr. Peebles' most important books and pamphlets": p. [101]-105. [BL515.P4] 33-20370
1. Reincarnation. I. Densmore, Helen. II. Colville, William Wilberforce Juvenal, 1862-1917. III. Title.

PERKINS, James Scudday. 236
Experiencing reincarnation / James S. Perkins ; pen drawings by author. Wheaton, Ill. : Theosophical Pub. House, c1977. ix, 192 p. : ill. ; 21 cm. (A Quest book) Includes index. Bibliography: p. 187-189. [BL515.P465] 77-5249 ISBN 0-8356-0500-0 pbk. : 3.95
1. Reincarnation. I. Title.

PETTYJOHN, Marie Louise. 236'.2
One immortal being / by Marie Louise Pettyjohn. New York : Philosophical Library, c1975. 117 p., [1] leaf of plates : ill. ; 22 cm. [BL515.P47] 75-7966 ISBN 0-8022-2168-8 : 8.75
1. Reincarnation. I. Title.

PRYSE, James M.
Reincarnation in the New Testament. New York, E. B. Page & co., 1900 [1899] 1 p. l., 92 p. 12 degree. Feb
I. Title.

PRYSE, James Morgan, 1859- 212
Reincarnation in the New Testament, by James M. Pryse. New York, Theosophical society, 1904. 1 p. l., 92 p. 18 cm. First published 1900. [BP573.R5P8] 4-22959
1. Reincarnation. I. Title.

ROGERS, Louis William, 1859- 236
Reincarnation, and other lectures by L. W. Rogers. Chicago, Theo book concern [c1925] 138 p. 18 1/2 cm. [BT901.R6] 25-16745
1. Reincarnation. 2. Future life. I. Title.
Contents omitted.

RUSSELL, Lao, 1904- 129'.4
Why you cannot die! The continuity of life; reincarnation explained. [1st ed.] Swannanoa, Va., University of Science and Philosophy [1972] xiv, 252 p. illus. 25 cm. [BL515.R85] 72-172725
1. Reincarnation. I. Title.

RYALL, Edward W., 1902- 133.9'013 B
Born twice : total recall of a seventeenth-century life / by Edward W. Ryall ; with an introd. and appendix by Ian Stevenson. 1st U.S. ed. New York : Harper & Row, [1975] c1974. 214 p., [4] leaves of plates : ill. ; 22 cm. Includes index. [BL515.R9 1975] 74-20412 ISBN 0-06-013713-4 : 8.95
1. Ryall, Edward W., 1902- 2. Reincarnation. 3. [Parapsychology—Personal narratives.] I. Title.

ST. Cyr, Emil, 1865- 129.4
The essay Let us think it over, by Dr. Emil St. Cyr ... 12th ed. augm. Chicago, Ill., The Publisher's book review [1936] 4 p. l., iv, 141 p. illus., mounted port. 20 1/2 cm. Four unnumbered pages between pages [54] and [55] On cover: The cycle of life. "Let us think it over." "Linotyped April 1935. Revised and rearranged March 1936." [Full name: Emil De Haye St. Cyr] [BL515.S3 1936] 36-10367
1. Reincarnation. I. Let us think it over. II. Title. III. Title: The cycle of life.

SALMON, Ruth (Barcafer) Mrs. 1885- 129.4
Radiant horizons; a book on reincarnation, by Dr. R. B. Salmon. Los Angeles, DeVorss & co., 1938. 3 p. l., 180 p., 1 l. 22 1/2 cm. "First edition." [Full name: Mrs. Ruth Emmaline (Barcafer) Salmon] [BR126.S24] 38-35765
1. Reincarnation. I. Title.

SHARMA, I. C. 1921- (Ishwar Chandra), 291.2'37
Cayce, Karma, & reincarnation / I.C. Sharma ; introduction by Hugh Lynn Cayce. 1st Quest ed. Wheaton, Ill. : Theosophical Pub. House, 1982, c1975. xiii, 172 p. ; 21 cm. Includes bibliographical references. [BL515.S45 1982] 19 81-23214 ISBN 0-8356-0563-9 pbk. : 5.50
1. Cayce, Edgar, 1877-1945. 2. Reincarnation. 3. Karma. 4. Religion. I. Title. II. Title: Cayce, Karma and reincarnation.

SHARMA, Ishwar Chandra. 291.2'3
Cayce, Karma, and reincarnation / I. C. Sharma ; introd. by Hugh Lynn Cayce. 1st ed. New York : Harper & Row, [1975] xiii, 172 p. ; 20 cm. Includes bibliographical references. [BL515.S45 1975] 74-25707 ISBN 0-06-067328-1 pbk. : 3.95
1. Cayce, Edgar, 1877-1945. 2. Reincarnation. 3. Karma. 4. Religion. I. Title.

SHEDD, Arthur B.
Soul life; or, Art and nature, by Arthur B. Shedd ... South Braintree, Mass., 1904. 1 p. l., 61, [1] p. 21 cm. [BD426.S5] CA 11
1. Reincarnation. I. Title.

SIWEK, Paul. 129.4
The enigma of the hereafter; the re-incarnation of souls. New York, Philosophical Library [1952] 140p. 23cm. [BL515.S49] 53-5812
1. Reincarnation. I. Title.

SMITH, Orlando Jay, 1842-1908.
Eternalism; a theory of infinite justice by Orlando J. Smith. Boston and New York, Houghton, Mifflin and company, 1902. viii, 321, [1] p. 20 1/2 cm. [BD573.S65] 2-14880
1. Reincarnation. 2. Fate and fatalism. I. Title.
Contents omitted.

SMITH, Orlando Jay, 1842-1908.
A short view of great questions, by Orlando J. Smith. New York, The Brandur company [1899] 1 p. l., 75 p. 18 cm. Treatise touching questions of reincarnation, immortality, pre-existence, etc. [BD426.S6] 99-2603
1. Reincarnation. I. Title.

*SMITH, Susy. 133.8
Do we live after death? New York, Manor Books, [1974] 191 p. 18 cm. Bibliography: p. 187-191 [BF1321] 1.50 (pbk.)
1. Reincarnation. 2. Occult sciences. 3. Extrasensory perception. I. Title.

SMITH, Susy. 291.2'3
Reincarnation for the millions, by Suzy [i. e. Susy] Smith. Los Angeles, Sherbourne Press [c1967] 160 p. 21 cm. (For the millions series, FM-13) [BL515.S6] 67-21875 1.95
1. Reincarnation. I. Title.

SPIRITUAL light; 133
new scripture, by many authors and translations from ancient manuscripts previously unpublished. Los Angeles, J. M. Pryse, 1940. 1 p. l., iv, 192 p. 20 cm. [BF1999.S63] 159.961 41-1661
1. Reincarnation.

STEARN, Jess. 291.2'3
The search for the girl with the blue eyes. [1st ed.] Garden City, N.Y., Doubleday, 1968. 304 p. 22 cm. [BL518.S7] 67-20920
1. MacIver, Joanne. 2. Reincarnation. 3. Hypnotism. I. Title.

STEIGER, Brad. 133.9
Other lives, by Brad Steiger and Loring G. Williams. New York, Hawthorn Books [1969] 189 p. 22 cm. [BL515.S73] 77-86056 4.95
1. Reincarnation. 2. Hypnotism. I. Williams, Loring G., joint author. II. Title.

STEVENSON, Ian.
Twenty cases suggestive of reincarnation. New York, American Society for Psychical Research, 1966. x, 362 p. 24 cm. (American society for psychical research, inc. Proceedings. New York. v. 26, Sept. 1966) Bibliographical footnotes. 67-66415
1. Reincarnation. I. Title. II. Series.

STREET, Noel. 129.4
The man who can look backward. New York, S. Weiser [1969] 90 p. 21 cm. [BL515.S77 1969] 73-16550
1. Reincarnation. I. Title.

TICHENOR, Henry Mulford, 1858-
... *Theory of reincarnation* [by] Henry M. Tichenor. Girard, Kan., Haldeman-Julius company [c1922] 59 p. 13 cm. (Ten cent pocket series, no. 124, ed. by E. Haldeman-Julius) Advertising matter: p. 54-59. [BD426.T5] CA 22
1. Reincarnation. I. Title.

TOYNE, Clarice Joy, 1906- 133.9'013
Heirs to eternity : a study of reincarnation with illustrations / [by] Clarice Toyne. London : Spearman, 1976. 204 p., [10] p. of plates, leaf of plate : ports. ; 23 cm. Includes bibliographical references. [BL515.T65 1976] 77-357519 ISBN 0-85435-113-2 : £3.50
1. Reincarnation. I. Title.

WALKER, Edward Dwight, 1859-1890 291.23
Reincarnation; a study of forgotten truth. Introd. by S. Digby Smith. New Hyde Park, N. Y. Univ. Bks. [c.1965] xix, 383p. 22cm. Bibl. [BP573.R5W3] 65-13657 5.00
1. Reincarnation. 2. Theosophy. I. Title.

WALKER, Edward Dwight, 1859-1890. 212
Reincarnation; a study of forgotten truth, by E. D. Walker ... New York, John W. Lovell company [c1888] xiii, [1], 350 p. 19 cm. "Bibliography of reincarnation": p. [329]-343. [BP573.R5W3 1888a] 39-19576
1. Reincarnation. 2. Theosophy. I. Title.

WALKER, Edward Dwight, 1859-1890. 212
Reincarnation; a study of forgotten truth, by E. D. Walker ... New York, Theosophical society, 1904. ix, [1] p., 1 l., [xi]-xiii, [3], [3]-350 p. 19 cm. Appendix: Bibliographhy of reincarnation: p. [327]-342. [BP573.R5W3 1904] 4-22849
1. Reincarnation. 2. Theosophy. I. Title.

WALKER, Edward Dwight, 1859-1890.
Reincarnation; a study of forgotten truth, by E. D. Walker ... Boston and New York, Houghton, Mifflin and company, 1888. xiii, [1], 4, 350 p. 19 1/2 cm. "Bibliography of reincarnation": p. [329]-343. [DB426.W4] 18-27485
1. Reincarnation. I. Title.

WALKER, Edward Dwight, 1859-1890.
Reincarnation; a study of forgotten truth, by E. D. Walker ... Point Loma ed. Point Loma, Calif., The Aryan theosophical press, 1923. xv, [8], 4-375 p. 19 1/2 cm. Bibliography: p. [345]-361. [BD426.W4 1923] 23-16090
1. Reincarnation. I. Title.

WEBB, Richard, 1915- 133.9'013
These came back / by Richard Webb. New York : Hawthorn Books, c1974. xix, 188 p. ; 22 cm. Includes index. Bibliography: p. 181. [BL515.W38 1974] 73-21324 ISBN 0-8015-7580-X : 8.95
1. Reincarnation. I. Title.

WILLIS, Frederick Milton, 1868- 212
Recurring earth-lives, how and why; reincarnation described and explained, by

F. Milton Willis ... New York, E. P. Dutton & company [c1921] xiii, 92 p. 19 cm. (His Sacred occultism series) [BP573.R5W5] 21-4422
1. Reincarnation. I. Title.

WILSON, Ernest C. 129.
Have we lived before? By Ernest C. Wilson. Kansas City, Mo., Unity school of Christianity, 1936. 130 p., 1 l. 20 cm. [BL515.W5] 42-43352
1. Reincarnation. I. Unity school of Christianity, Kansas City, Mo. II. Title.

WILSON, Ernest C. 129.4
Have we lived before? By Ernest C. Wilson. Kansas City, Mo., Unity school of Christianity, 1946. 130 p., 1 l. 17 1/2 cm. "First appeared in 1936." [BL515.W5 1946] 47-21449
1. Reincarnation. I. Unity school of Christianity, Kansas City, Mo. II. Title.

WILSON, Ernest Charles, 1896- 129.4
Have you lived other lives? Englewood Cliffs, N. J., Prentice-Hall [c1956] 163p. 22cm. [BL515.W48] 57-5232
1. Reincarnation. 2. Unity School of Christianity—Doctrinal and controversial works. I. Title.

WRIGHT, Leoline L. 129'.4
Reincarnation; a lost chord in modern thought, by Leoline L. Wright, with additional chapters by Helen Todd and Steele O'Hara. Wheaton, Ill., Published for Point Loma Publications by the Theosophical Pub. House [1975] viii, 113 p. 18 cm. (Theosophical manual, no. 2) [BP573.R5W72] 74-18350 ISBN 0-8356-0453-5 2.25 (pbk.)
1. Reincarnation. I. Title. II. Series.

WRIGHT, Leoline L 129.4
... *Reincarnation:* a lost chord in modern thought, by Leoline L. Wright. Covina, Calif., Theosophical university press, 1943. 3 p. l., 112, [3] p. 15 cm. (Theosophical manual no. II) "Third edition, revised, 1938. Second printing, 1943." [BP573.R5W7 1943] 44-9141
1. Reincarnation. I. Title.

YOUNG, Robert, 1943- 129'.4
Reincarnation, your denied birthright / by Robert and Loy Young ; [compiled by Violet Buettner, Louisa Antares, Simon Lind ; photos. by Simon Lind, Robert Young, Robert Baxter]. Santa Monica, Calif. : Awareness Pub. Co., c1978. v, 295 p. ; 22 cm. [BL515.Y68] 78-65006 ISBN 0-932872-01-8 pbk. : 7.95
1. Reincarnation. I. Young, Loy, joint author. II. Title.

Reincarnation—Addresses, essays, lectures.

REINCARNATION : 133.9'013
the phoenix fire mystery : an East-West dialogue on death and rebirth from the worlds of religion, science, psychology, philosophy, art, and literature, and from great thinkers of the past and present / compiled and edited by Joseph Head and S. L. Cranston. New York : Julian Press, c1977. xix, 620 p. ; 24 cm. Includes index. Bibliography: p. 607-610. [BL515.R43 1977] 76-30439 ISBN 0-517-52893-2 : 10.00
1. Reincarnation—Addresses, essays, lectures. I. Head, Joseph. II. Cranston, S. L.

REINCARNATION, the 133.9'013
phoenix fire mystery : an East-West dialogue on death and rebirth from the worlds of religion, science, psychology, philosophy, art, and literature, and from great thinkers of the past and present / compiled and edited by Joseph Head and S. L. Cranston ; foreword by Elisabeth Kubler-Ross. New York : Warner Books, [1979] c1977. xix, 620 p. ; 23 cm. Reprint of the ed. published by Julian Press, New York. Includes index. Bibliography: p. 607-610. [BL515.R43 1979] 79-10714 ISBN 0-446-97140-5 pbk. : 5.95
1. Reincarnation—Addresses, essays, lectures. I. Head, Joseph. II. Cranston, S. L.

Reincarnation—Case studies.

BANERJEE, Hemendra Nath. 133.9'01'3
Americans who have been reincarnated / H. N. Banerjee. New York : Macmillan ; London : Collier Macmillan, c1980. xiii, 196 p. ; 22 cm. Includes bibliographical references. [BL515.B47] 80-12702 ISBN 0-02-506740-0 : 10.95
1. Reincarnation—Case studies. I. Title.

EBON, Martin, comp. 133
Reincarnation in the twentieth century. New York, World Pub. Co. [1969] 157 p. 22 cm. Contents.Contents.—But can you prove it? By M. Ebon.—Lullaby from a previous life, by F. Portland.—The two Alexandrinas, by E. Brenner.—A Canadian soldier who "took the walls," by A. Mackenzie.—Reincarnation in Burma, by L. Markham.—The return of a woman who died in childbirth, by J. S. Singer.—Rebirth of a salesman: an Edgar Cayce reading, by V. M. Shelly.—Thirty centuries later, by H. Curtis.—I will come back and be your son, by D. Harding.—Bridey Murphy revisited, by C. J. Ducasse.—From the files of Dr. Ian Stevenson, by H. McCarthy.—Judge Fraser's son was reborn, and so perhaps was I, by C. K. Shaw.—Now I am convinced, by I. Ammann.—Was he a surgeon in a previous life? By J. Krause.—The case of Joanne MacIver, by A. Spraggett.—Her favorite incarnation, by A. Vaughan. [BL518.E2 1969] 71-79065 4.95
1. Reincarnation—Case studies. I. Title.

FURST, Jeffrey. 129'.4
The return of Frances Willard; her case for reincarnation. New York, Coward, McCann & Geoghegan [1971] xix, 171 p. 22 cm. [BL515.F86] 73-154778 5.95
1. Willard, Frances Elizabeth, 1839-1898. 2. Hale, Stephanie Elizabeth, 1939- 3. Reincarnation—Case studies. I. Title.

FURST, Jeffrey. 129'.4
The return of Frances Willard: her case for reincarnation. New York, Pyramid Books [1973, c.1971] 173 p. 18 cm. [BL515.F86] ISBN 0-515-03044-9 1.25 (pbk.)
1. Willard, Frances Elizabeth, 1839-1898. 2. Hale, Stephanie Elizabeth, 1939- 3. Reincarnation—Case studies. I. Title.
L.C. card no. for the hardbound edition: 73-154778.

GUIRDHAM, Arthur. 133.9
The Cathars and reincarnation / Arthur Guirdham. Wheaton, Ill. : Theosophical Pub. House, 1978, c1970. 207 p. : ill. ; 21 cm. (A Quest book) Includes index. Bibliography: p. 199-204. [BL515.G8 1978] 77-17012 ISBN 0-8356-0506-X pbk. : 3.75
1. Reincarnation—Case studies. I. Title.

LENZ, Frederick, 1950- 133.9'013
Lifetimes : true accounts of reincarnation / Frederick Lenz. Indianapolis : Bobbs-Merrill, c1979. p. cm. Bibliography: p. [BL515.L46] 78-11209 ISBN 0-672-52490-2 : 10.00
1. Reincarnation—Case studies. I. Title.

LEONARDI, Dell. 133.9'3
The reincarnation of John Wilkes Booth : a study in hypnotic regression / by Dell Leonardi. Old Greenwich, Conn. : Devin-Adair Co., c1975. 180 p. ; 22 cm. Bibliography: p. 180. [BF1311.R35L46] 74-27952 ISBN 0-8159-6716-0 : 6.95
1. Booth, John Wilkes, 1838-1865. 2. Reincarnation—Case studies. 3. Spirit writings. I. Title.

MOSS, Peter. 133.9'01'3
Encounters with the past : how man can experience and relive history / Peter Moss, with Joe Keeton. 1st ed. Garden City, N.Y. : Doubleday, 1980. ix, 227 p., [16] leaves of plates : ill. ; 22 cm. Includes index. [BF1311.R35M67] 79-8010 ISBN 0-385-15307-4 : 14.00
1. Reincarnation—Case studies. 2. Hypnotism—Case studies. I. Keeton, Joe, joint author. II. Title.

*STEIGER, Brad. 129.4
The enigma of reincarnation. New York, Ace [1973, c.1967] 189 p. 18 cm. [BL515] pap., .95
1. Reincarnation—Case studies. I. Title.

STEVENSON, Ian. 133.9'013
Cases of the reincarnation type / Ian Stevenson. Charlottesville : University Press of Virginia, 1975- v. ; 26 cm. Includes indexes. Contents.Contents.—v. 1. Ten cases in India. [BL515.S746] 74-28263 ISBN 0-8139-0602-4(v.1) : 20.00
1. Reincarnation—Case studies. I. Title.

STEVENSON, Ian. 133.9'013
Twenty cases suggestive of reincarnation. 2d ed., rev. and enl. Charlottesville, University Press of Virginia [1974] xvi, 396 p. 27 cm. "Originally published in 1966 as volume 26 of the Proceedings of the American Society for Psychical Research." [BL515.S75 1974] 73-93627 ISBN 0-8139-0546-X 15.00
1. Reincarnation—Case studies. I. Title.

WAMBACH, Helen. 133.9'013
Reliving past lives : the evidence under hypnosis / by Helen Wambach. 1st ed. New York : Harper & Row, c1978. 200 p. : graphs ; 21 cm. [BL515.W34 1978] 77-11805 ISBN 0-06-014513-7 : 8.95
1. Reincarnation—Case studies. 2. Hypnotism—Case studies. I. Title.

Reincarnation—Case studies—Juvenile literature.

ATKINSON, Linda. 129
Have we lived before? / by Linda Atkinson ; illustrations by Michele Chessare. New York : Dodd, Mead, [1981] p. cm. Considers the theory that a person may live more than once, and recounts the experiences of several persons who have remembered incidents and details from past lives. [BL515.A85] 19 81-43234 ISBN 0-396-07999-7 lib. bdg. : 6.95
1. Reincarnation—Case studies—Juvenile literature. 2. [Reincarnation.] I. Chessare, Michele, ill. II. Title.

Reincarnation—Collections.

MARTIN, Eva M., ed. 291.23
Reincarnation: the ring of return. Comp., introd. by Eva Martin. New Hyde Park, N.Y., University Bks. [1963] xi, 306p. 22cm. 63-18492 5.00
1. Reincarnation—Collections. I. Title.

Reincarnation—Juvenile literature.

EDMONDS, I. G. 291.2'3
Our other lives : the story of reincarnation / by I. G. Edmonds. New York : McGraw-Hill, [1979] p. cm. Includes index. Bibliography: p. Discusses reincarnation, its occurrence in the folklore of primitive people around the world, and some of the famous people who have believed in it. [BL515.E35] 79-14689 ISBN 0-07-018987-0 : 7.95
1. Reincarnation—Juvenile literature. 2. [Reincarnation.] I. Title.

†RISEDORF, Gwen, 1923- 236
Born today, born yesterday : Contemporary Perspectives ; New York : Contemporary Perspectives ; Milwaukee, Wis. : distributor, Raintree Publishers, c1977. 48 p. : ill. (some col.) ; 24 cm. "A CPI book from Raintree Childrens Books." Briefly investigates the possibility of reincarnation by presenting accounts of people who claim remembrances from past lives. [BL515.R57] 77-21406 ISBN 0-8172-1045-8 lib. bdg. : 7.32
1. Reincarnation—Juvenile literature. 2. [Reincarnation.] I. Title. II. Title: Milwaukee, Wis. :

Reines, Isaac Jacob, 1839-1915.

WANEFSKY, Joseph. 296.6'1'0924
Rabbi Isaac Jacob Reines; his life and thought. New York, Philosophical Library [1970] 171 p. 23 cm. Bibliography: p. 171. [BM755.R348W35] 79-118314 ISBN 0-8022-2349-4 5.95
1. Reines, Isaac Jacob, 1839-1915.

Reiss, Marguerite.

REISS, Marguerite. 248'.4
Holy nudges / Marguerite Reiss. Plainfield, N.J. : Logos International, c1976. xiii, 141 p. ; 20 cm. [BV4501.2.R45] 76-23362 ISBN 0-88270-185-1 : 5.95 ISBN 0-88270-186-X pbk. : 3.50
1. Reiss, Marguerite. 2. Christian life—1960- I. Title.

Relativity—Addresses, essays, lectures.

RELATIVISM, cognitive and 121
moral / edited with introductions by Jack W. Meiland and Michael Krausz. Notre Dame : University of Notre Dame Press, c1982. x, 260 p. ; 23 cm. Includes index. Bibliography: p. 245-253. [BD221.R44 1982] 19 81-19834 ISBN 0-268-01611-9 : 20.00 ISBN 0-268-01612-7 (pbk.) : 8.95
1. Relativity—Addresses, essays, lectures. 2. Ethical relativism—Addresses, essays, lectures. I. Meiland, Jack W. II. Krausz, Michael.
Contents omitted.

Relics and reliquaries—Thefts.

GEARY, Patrick J., 1948- 364.1'62
Furta sacra : thefts of relics in the central Middle Ages / Patrick J. Geary. Princeton, N.J. : Princeton University Press, c1978. xiv, 227 p. ; 23 cm. Includes index. Bibliography: p. 191-217. [BX2333.G42] 77-85538 ISBN 0-691-05261-1 : 14.50
1. Relics and reliquaries—Thefts. 2. Relics and reliquaries—Europe. 3. Social history—Medical, 500-1500. I. Title.

Religion.

ACADEMY of Religion and Mental Health. Academy Symposium.
Religion in the developing personality. Proceedings of the second Academy Symposium [on Inter-discipline Responsibility for Mental Health, 1958. Academy of Religion and Mental Health, with the aid of the Josiah Macy, Jr. Foundation. [New York] New York University Press, 1960. xiii, 110p. 22cm.
I. Title.

ADAM, John Douglas.
Religion and the growing mind, by John Douglas Adam, D.D. New York, Chicago [etc.] Fleming H. Revell company [c1912] 142 p. 19 112 cm. $0.75 13-953
I. Title.

ADAMS, Hannah, 1755-1831.
A view of religious, in two parts. Pt. I. containing an alphabetical compendium of the various religious denominations, which have appeared in the world, from the beginning of the Christian era to the present day. Pt. II. containing a brief account of the different schemes of religion now embraced among mankind. The whole collected from the best authors, ancient and modern. By Hannah Adams ... The 3d ed., with large additions ... Published according to act of Congress. Boston, Printed by and for Manning & Loring, proprietors, No. 2, Cornhill, Boston. October, 1801. xxxv, [36]-504 p. 22 cm. A 31
1. Religion. I. Title.

AGEE, James, 1909- 211
Religion and the intellectuals; a symposium with James Agee [and others. New York, 1950] 139 p. 23 cm. (PR series, no. 3) First published in Partisan review, v. 17, no. 2-5, Feb.-May/June, 1950. [BL237.R4] 51-620
1. Religion. 2. Intellectuals. I. Partisan review. II. Title.

ALLEN, Douglas, 1941- 291'.01
Structure and creativity in religion : hermeneutics in Mircea Eliade's phenomenology and new directions ; foreword by Mircea Eliade / Douglas Allen. The Hague : Mouton, 1978. xviii. 265 p. ; 24 cm. (Religion and reason ; 14) Includes index. Bibliography: p. [247]-256. [BL43.E4A68] 78-320515 ISBN 9-02-797594-9 : 29.00
1. Eliade, Mircea, 1907- 2. Religion. 3. Hermeneutics. I. Title. II. Series.
Available from Mouton, New York.

AMES, Edward Scribner, 1870- 201
Religion, by Edward Scribner Ames ... New York, H. Holt and company [c1929] vi p., 2 l., 3-824 p. 23 cm. The chapters on "Religion and philosophy" and on "Religion and art" appearedin the Journal of religion: the substance of the chapter on "Religion and morality" appeared in the International journal of ethics. cf. Pref. [BL48.A5] 29-6025
1. Religion. 2. God. I. Title.

ANDREWS, George Arthur, 1870-
What is essential? By George Arthur Andrews. New York, T. Y. Crowell & co. c1910. x, 153 p. 20 cm. "Concerning the essentials of our religion."--Pref. 10-14957
I. Title.

AUSTIN, C Grey. 377.1
A century of religion at the University of Michigan; a case study in religion and the state university, commemorating the centennial of student religious activity at the University of Michigan. [Ann Arbor [BR561.M5A8] 57-63107
I. Title.

BADLEY, John Haden, 1865- 290
Form and spirit; a study in religion. Boston, Beacon Press [1952] 247 p. 22 cm. [BL48.B17 1952] 52-6215
1. Religion. I. Title.

BADLEY, John Haden, 1865- 1967. 291
Form and spirit; a study in religion. Port Washington, N.Y., Kennikat Press [1971] 247 p. 22 cm. (Essay and general literature index reprint series) Reprint of the 1951 ed. [BL48.B17 1971] 77-113347
1. Religion. I. Title.

BAGGS, Ralph L 204
Religion could be wonderful, if! [1st ed.] New York, Greenwich Book Publishers, 1955. 87p. 22cm. [BL50.B25] 55-11467
1. Religion. I. Title.

BAILLIE, John, 1886- 201
The interpretation of religion; an introductory study of theological principles. Nashville, Abingdon [1965, c.1928] xv, 477p. 21cm. (Apex bk., V1) [BL48B2] 2.45 pap.,
1. Religion. 2. Religion—Philosophy. 3. Theology, Doctrinal. I. Title.

BAILLIE, John, 1886- 201
The interpretation of religion; an introductory study of theological principles, by John Baillie ... New York, C. Scribner's sons, 1928. xv, 477 p. 24 cm. [BL48.D2] 23-30166
1. Religion. 2. Religion—Philosophy. I. Title.

BAILLIE, John, 1886-1960. 200'.1
The interpretation of religion : an introductory study of the theological principles / by John Baillie. Westport, Conn. : Greenwood Press, [1977] c1928. xv, 477 p. ; 23 cm. Reprint of the ed. published by Scribner, New York. Includes bibliographical references and index. [BL48.B2 1977] 76-49990 ISBN 0-8371-9038-X lib. bdg. : 25.00
1. Religion. 2. Religion—Philosophy. 3. Theology, Doctrinal. I. Title.

BAKER, Arthur Mulford, 1880- 201
The river of God, the source-stream for morals and religion, by Arthur Mulford Baker ... Nashville, Tenn., Cokesbury press, 1930. 172 p. 19 cm. [BL48.B35] 30-20848
1. Religion. 2. Ethics. 3. Christianity. 4. Spiritual life. I. Title.

BALLOU, Robert Oleson, 1892- 200
The nature of religion [by] Robert O. Ballou. New York, Basic Books [1968] vi, 246 p. 22 cm. (Culture & discovery) Bibliography: p. 229-236. [BL48.B36] 68-22858
1. Religion. I. Title.

BARNHART, Joe E., 1931- 200'.1
The study of religion and its meaning : new explorations in the light of Karl Popper and Emile Durkheim / J. E. Barnhart. The Hague : Mouton, 1977. xiii, 216 p. ; 23 cm. (Religion and reason ; nr. 12) Includes indexes. Bibliography: p. [197]-207. [BL48.B364] 78-307820 ISBN 90-279-7762-3 : 27.00
1. Durkheim, Emile, 1858-1917. 2. Popper, Karl Raimund, Sir, 1902- 3. Religion. I. Title.
Distributed by Walter de Gruyter, Hawthorne, NY 10523

BARREAU, Jean Claude. 200'.1
The religious impulse / by Jean-Claude Barreau ; translated by John George Lynch. New York : Paulist Press, c1979. ix, 70 p. ; 18 cm. (A Deus book) Translation of Du bon usage de la religion. [BL48.B36513] 78-71436 ISBN 0-8091-2186-7 pbk. : 1.95
1. Religion. I. Title.

BARRY, Joseph Gayle Hurd, 1858- 283.
The religion of the prayer book, by the Rev. J. G. H. Barry, D. D., and the Rev. Selden Peabody Delany, D. D. New York, E. S. Gorham, 1919. 3 p. l., 275 p. 19 cm. [BX5930.B3] 19-7936
I. Delany, Selden Peabody, 1874- joint author. II. Title.

BARTLETT, Frederic Charles, Sir, 1887- 200
Religion as experience, belief, action, by Sir Frederic Bartlett. London, New York, G. Cumberlege, 1950. 38 p. 24 cm. (Riddell memorial lectures, 22d ser.) Includes bibliographical references. [BL50.B346] 73-172237
1. Religion. 2. Experience (Religion) I. Title. II. Series.

BELANGER, Merlyn. 201
On religious maturity. New York, Philosophical Library [1962] 82p. 23cm. [BL2775.2.B4] 61-15238
1. Religion. I. Title.

BELL, Hermon Fiske, 1880- 204
Talks on religion. New York, Philosophical Library [1958] 73p. 21cm. [BL50.B38] 58-59400
1. Religion. I. Title.

BELL, Ralcy Husted, 1869-
The religion of beauty and the impersonal estate, by Ralcy Husted Bell ... New York city, Hinds, Noble & Eldredge [c1911] 5 p. l., 3-262 p. 20 cm. 11-1350 1.25
I. Title.
Contents omitted.

BELLAH, Robert Neelly, 1927- 306'.6
Varieties of civil religion / Robert N. Bellah, Phillip E. Hammond. 1st ed. San Francisco : Harper & Row, c1980. xv, 208 p. ; 22 cm. Includes index. [BL48.B38 1980] 19 80-7742 ISBN 0-06-060776-9 : 14.95
1. Religion. 2. United States—Religion. I. Hammond, Phillip E., joint author. II. Title.

BENNETT, Charles Andrew Armstrong, 1855-1930. 201
The dilemma of religious knowledge, by Charles A. Bennett ... edited, with a preface, by William Ernest Hocking ... New Haven, Yale university press; London, H. Milford, Oxford university press, 1931. xv p., 1 l., 126 p. 24 cm. "Published on the foundation established in memory of James Wesley Cooper of the class of 1865, Yale college."--p. [iii] "The chapters of this volume had been given as a series of Lowell lectures in King's chapel, Boston, during the spring of 1960." "Philosophical articles and reviews [by C. A. Bennett] ... a partial list": p. xiv. "Notes": p. [121]-123. [BL48.B4] 31-24040
1. Religion. 2. Religion—Philosophy. 3. Supernatural. I. Hocking, William Ernest, 1873- ed. II. Yale university. James Wesley Cooper memorial publication fund. III. Lowell institute lectures, 1960. IV. Title. V. Title: Religious knowledge, The dilemma of.

BENNETT, Charles Andrew Armstrong, 1885-1930. 200'.1
The dilemma of religious knowledge. Edited, with a pref., by William Ernest Hocking. Port Washington, N.Y., Kennikat Press [1969] xv, 126 p. 22 cm. (Lowell lectures, 1930) (Essay and general literature index reprint series.) Reprint of the 1931 ed. Bibliographical references included in "Notes" (p. [121]-123) [BL48.B4 1969] 71-85986
1. Religion. 2. Religion—Philosophy. 3. Supernatural. I. Title. II. Series: Lowell Institute lectures, 1930

BENNION, Lowell Lindsay, 1908-
The religion of the Latter-day Saints, by Lowell L. Bennion. [2d ed.] Provo, Utah, L.D.S. Dept. of Education, 1964 [1965, c1940] 319 p. 20 cm. On cover: "Revised edition." Bibliography: p. 315-319. NUC68
I. Title.

BENSON, Purnell Handy, 1913- 208.1
Religion in contemporary culture; a study of religion through social science. New York, Harper, 1960. 839 p. 25 cm. (Harper's social science series) Includes bibliography. [BL48.B43] 60-7021
1. Religion. I. Title.

BINDER, Rudolph Michael, 1865- 201
Religion as man's completion; a socio-religious study, by Rudolph M. Binder ... New York and London, Harper & brothers, 1927. 7 p. l., 417 p. 19 cm. "Questions problems and references": p. 399-411. [BL48.B5] 27-12959
1. Religion. I. Title.

BLAKE, Clinton Hamlin, 1920- 201
An elementary introduction to religion and Christianity. Boston, Christopher Pub. House [1954] 63p. 21cm. [BL50.B26] 54-12019
1. Religion. 2. Christianity—Essence, genius, nature. I. Title.

BLISS, Kathleen. 200
The future of religion [Baltimore] Penguin [1972, c.1969] x, 193 p. 18 cm. (Pelican book) Bibl.: p. 182-186 [BL48.B56] ISBN 0-14-021366-X pap., 2.25
1. Religion. 2. Religions. I. Title.

BLUMHORST, Roy.
Faithful rebels; does the old-style religion fit the new style of life? Saint Louis, Concordia Pub. House [1967] 100 p. illus. 23 cm. 68-61826
I. Title.

BONES, Ben Roland, 1885- 290
Ben Roland gospels. [1st ed.] New York,

Pageant Press [1956] 116p. 21cm. [BL50.B65] 56-12554
1. Religion. I. Title.

BOWER, William Clayton, 1878- 248
... *Religion and the good life* [by] William Clayton Bower ... New York, Cincinnati [etc.] The Abingdon press [c1933] 231 p. 20 cm. (The Abingdon religious education monographs, J. W. Langdale, general editor) [BJ47.B65] (170) 33-5421
1. Religion. 2. Conduct of life. 3. Religion and sociology. I. Title. II. Title: The good life, Religion and.

BOWKER, John. 211
The sense of God; sociological, anthropological and psychological approaches to the origin of the sense of God. Oxford, Clarendon P., 1973. xiii, 237 p. 23 cm. "Based on the Wilde Lectures, given in Oxford in 1972." Includes index. Bibliography: p. 219-229. [BL48.B63] 73-180543 ISBN 0-19-826632-4 16.00
1. Religion. 2. God. I. Title.
Distributed by Oxford University Press, New York; Library edition 12.64

BOWKER, John Westerdale. 291.2'11
The religious imagination and the sense of God / by John Bowker. Oxford ; New York : Clarendon Press, 1978. p. cm. Continues the author's Wilde lectures of which the first part was published as The sense of God. Includes index. Bibliography: p. [BL48.B635] 77-30459 ISBN 0-19-826646-4 : 28.50
1. Religion. 2. God. I. Title.

BOWKER, Richard Rogers, 1848-
... *Of religion,* by Richard Rogers Bowker. Boston and New York, Houghton, Mifflin and company, 1903. 73, [1] p. 18 cm. Reprinted from the author's "The arts of life." 3-10363
I. Title.

BOWNE, Borden Parker, 1847- 261
1910.
The essence of religion, by Borden Parker Bowne. Boston and New York, Houghton Mifflin company, 1910. vi p., 2 l., [3]-298 p., 1 l. 21 cm. Sermons. [BR85.B8] 10-30039
I. Title.

BOYNTON, Richard Wilson, 201
1870-
Beyond mythology; a challenge to dogmatism in religion. [1st ed.] Garden City, N. Y., Doubleday, 1951. xiv, 257 p. 21 cm. [BL48.B644] 51-9244
1. Religion. 2. Humanism, Religious. 3. Religions (Proposed, universal, etc.) I. Title.

BRADLEY, Dwight, 1889- 201
The recovery of religion, by Dwight Bradley ... Garden City, N. Y., Doubleday, Doran & company, inc., 1929. 4 p. l., 235 p. 20 cm. [BL48.B68] 29-19209
1. Religion. 2. Religion and science. I. Title.

BREWSTER, Edwin Tenney, 1866- 201
The understanding of religion, by Edwin Tenney Brewster... Boston and New York, Houghton Mifflin company, 1923. xiii, [1] p. 1 l., 182 p. front., illus. 19 cm. [BL48.B7] 23-5138
1. Religion. 2. Religion and science—1900- I. Title.

BREWSTER, Edwin Tenney, 1866- 258
What laymen want, by Edwin Tenney Brewster... Boston, The Four seas company [c1925] 98 p. 19 1/2 cm. [BV4012.B8] 26-10484
1. Religion. I. Title.

BROAD, FitzGerald. 218
The problem of life; a solution, a solution, by FitzGerald Broad. New York, For the author, Brentano's, 1918. 3 p. l., 162 p. 19 cm. [BD431.B8] 18-14388
1. Religion. 2. Life. 3. Future life. I. Title.

BROOKE, Stopford Augustus, 220
1832-1916.
Religion in literature and religion in life. Being two papers written by Stopford A. Brooke ... New York, T. Y. Crowell & company, 1901. 3 p. l., 58, [1] p. 19 1/2 cm. [BR125.B735] 1-30873
1. Religion. 2. Religion in literature. I. Title.

BROUGHTON, Leonard Gaston, 1864-
Christianity and the commonplace, by Rev. Len G. Broughton ... New York and London, Hodder and Stoughton [1914] vi, 201 p. 29 cm. A15
1. Religion. I. Title.

BROUGHTON, Leonard Gaston, 133
1864-
Religion and health, by Len G. Broughton ... New York, Chicago [etc.] F. H. Revell company [c1909] 62 p. 1 l., 19 cm. On cover: A review of the Immanuel movement, with suggestions to the Christian church. [RZ400.B75] 9-9046
I. Title.

BROWN, Charles Reynolds, 225
1862-
The modern man's religion, by Charles Reynolds Brown... New York city, Teachers college, Columbia university, 1911. viii, 166 p., 1 l. 20 cm. (Half-title: Teachers college lectures on the religious life. ser. 1) [BR121.B658] 11-14771
I. Title.

BROWN, Charles Reynolds, 226.
1862-
The religion of a layman, by Charles R. Brown... New York, The Macmillan company, 1920. vii p., 1 l., 84 p. 19 1/2 cm. [BT380.B7] 20-20982
I. Title.

BROWNE, Thomas Sir 1605-1682 755
Religio medici. A letter to a friend, Christian morals, Urn-burial, and other papers. 2d ed. Boston, Ticknor and Fields, 1862. xviii, 440 p. port. 18 cm. Half-title: The writings of Sir Thomas Browne. [PR3327.A73 1862a] 48-40275
1. Religion. 2. Christian life. 3. Christian ethics. 4. Urn burial. I. Title.

BROWNE, Thomas, Sir, 1605- 755
1682.
The Religio medici & other writings of Sir Thomas Browne. London, J. M. Dent & co.; New York, E. P. Dutton & co. [1906] xvi p., 1 l., 296 p. 17 1/2 cm. (Half-title: Everyman's library, ed. by Ernest Rhys. Theoloby & philosophy. [no. 92]) Introduction by Prof. C. H. Herford. Bibliography: p. xv-xvi. [[PR3327.A]] A10
1. Religion. 2. Christian life. I. Title.

BROWNE, Thomas, Sir, 1605- 755
1682.
Religio medici. Its sequel, Christian morals. By Sir Thomas Browne ... Wtih resemblant passages from Cowper's Task, and a verbal index. Philadelphia, Lea and Blanchard, 1844. xxii p., 1 l., [25]-226 p. 20 cm. Editor's preface signed: John Peace. "Religio medici" is a careful reprint from the edition of 1643; that of Christian morals," from the edition of 1716. [PR3327.A73 1844] 18-23612
1. Religion. 2. Christian life. 3. Christian ethics. I. Peace, John, 1785-1861, ed. II. Cowper, William, 1731-1800. III. Title. IV. Title: The task.

BUCK, Oscar MacMillan, 1885-
... *Out of their own mouths;* an elective course for young people on the religions of the world, by Oscar MacMillan Buck ... New York, Cincinnati, The Methodist book concern [c1926] 136 p. 19 cm. (World friendship series) "Approved by the Committee on curriculum of the Board of education of the Methodist Episcopal church." An account of a voyage around the world made to observe different religions. [BL95.B8] 26-6655
1. Religion. I. Title.

BUCKHAM, John Wright, 1864- 220
Religion as experience, by John Wright Buckham ... New York, Cincinnati, The Abingdon press [c1922] 128 p. 20 cm. [BR125.B92] 22-5384
I. Title.

BURR, Enoch Fitch, 1818-1907. 290
Universal beliefs; or, The great consensus. By Rev. E. F. Burr ... New York, American tract society, [1887] 312 p. 19 cm. [BL85.B9] 30-17984
1. Religion. I. Title. II. Title: Beliefs, Universal.

CAILLOIS, Roger, 1913- 306'.6
Man and the sacred / by Roger Caillois ; translated by Meyer Barash. Westport, Conn. : Greenwood Press, 1980, c1959. 190 p. ; 23 cm. Translation of L'homme et le sacre. Reprint of the ed. published by Free Press of Glencoe, Ill. Includes bibliographical references and index. [BL48.C2813 1980] 79-8709 ISBN 0-313-22196-0 lib. bdg. : 17.25
1. Religion. 2. Religion and sociology. 3. Rites and ceremonies. I. Title.

CALVIN, Jean, 1509-1564.
Commentary on a harmony of the Evangelists, Matthew, Mark, and Luke. Translated from the original Latin and collated with the author's French version by William Pringle. Grand Rapids, W.B. Eerdmans Pub. Co. [c1949, 1965- v. ports., facsims. 23 cm. 68-34999
1. On spine: Harmony of Matthew, Mark, Luke. 2. Bible. N. T. Gospels—Commentaries. 3. Bible. N. T. Gospels—Harmonies. I. Title.

CANALE, Andrew. 200'.1
Masters of the heart : a modern spiritual seeker dialogues with the great sages of history / by Andrew Canale. New York : Paulist Press, c1978. v, 151 p. : ill. ; 24 cm. Bibliography: p. 148-151. [BL48.C33] 78-58953 ISBN 0-8091-0271-4 : 9.95
1. Religion. I. Title.

CARREL, Alexis, 1873-1944. 264.1
Prayer; tr. by Dulcie de Ste. Croix Wright. New York, Morehouse-Gorham Co., 1948. 54 p. 20 cm. [BV210.C335] 48-5941
1. Prayer. I. Wright, Dulcie de Ste. Croix tr. II. Title.

CASSILLY, Francis Bernard, 230.2
1860-
Religion, doctrine and practice, for use in Catholic high schools, by Francis B Cassilly ... 9th and rev. ed. ... Chicago, Ill., Loyola university press, 1931. xv, 480 p. incl. front., plates, ports, 21 cm. [BX930.C3 1931] 31-34622
I. Title.

CHEATHAM, Katharine Smiley. 289.
America triumphant under God and His Christ, by Kitty Cheatham. New York and London, G. P. Putnam's sons, 1920. v, 84 p. incl. col. front. 17 cm. [BX6947.C45] 20-21078
I. Title.

CHESTERTON, Gilbert Keith, 290
1874-1936.
The everlasting man. Garden City, N. Y., Image Books [1955, c1925] 274p. 19cm. (A Doubleday image book, D18) [BL48.C5 1955] 55-14903
1. Religion. 2. Christianity and other religions. 3. Catholic Church—Apologetic works. I. Title.

CHESTERTON, Gilbert Keith, 261.2
1874-1936.
The everlasting man. Westport, Conn., Greenwood Press [1974, c1925] xxv, 344 p. 22 cm. Reprint of the ed. published by Dodd, Mead, New York. [BL48.C5 1974] 72-11233 ISBN 0-8371-6636-5 14.50
1. Catholic Church—Apologetic works. 2. Religion. 3. Christianity and other religions. I. Title.

CHESTERTON, Gilbert Keith, 230
1874-1936.
The everlasting man. Garden City, N.Y., Image Books [1974, c1925] 280 p. 18 cm. [BL48.C5 1974b] 74-2114 ISBN 0-385-07198-1 1.95 (pbk.)
1. Catholic Church—Apologetic works. 2. Religion. 3. Christianity and other religions. I. Title.

CHESTERTON, Gilbert Keith, 201
1874-1936.
The everlasting man, by G. K. Chesterton ... New York, Dodd, Mead & company, 1925. xxv p., 1 l., 344 p. 21 cm. [BL48.C5 1925a] 25-23426
1. Religion. 2. Christianity. I. Title.

CLANCY, William 208.2
Religion and American society; a statement of principles, by William Clancy [others] Introd. by Henry P. Van Dusen. Santa Barbara, Calif., Center for the Study of Democratic Insts. [c.1961] 79p. gratis pap.,
I. Title.

COGLEY, John. 200'.9'04
Religion in a secular age; the search for final meaning. Pref. by Arnold Toynbee. New York, Praeger [1968] xxi, 147 p. 24 cm. (Britannica perspective) Bibliographical footnotes. [BL48.C556] 68-28156 5.95
I. Title.

COHEN, Jack Joseph. 296
The case for religious naturalism; a philosophy for the modern Jew. New York, Reconstructionist Press [1958] 296p. 21cm. Includes bibliography. [BL48.C558] 57-14412
1. Religion. 2. Judaism. I. Title.

COLE, Stewart Grant, 1892- 204
ed.
This is my faith the convictions of representative Americans today. [1st ed.] New York, Harper [1956] 291p. 22cm. [BL48.C56] 55-11403
1. Religion. I. Title.

COLLINS, John J., 1938- 291'.042
Primitive religion / John J. Collins. Totowa, N.J. : Rowman and Littlefield, 1978, c1977. Includes index. Bibliography: p. [BL48.C565 1978b] 78-7052 ISBN 0-8476-6076-1 10.00
1. Religion. 2. Religion, Primitive. I. Title.

COMFORT, Alexander, 1920- 200'.1
I and that / by Alex Comfort. New York : Crown Publishers, 1979. p. cm. Includes bibliographical references and index. [BL48.C57 1979] 79-421 ISBN 0-517-53749-4 : 6.95
1. Religion. 2. Experience (Religion) I. Title.

COMSTOCK, W. Richard. 200'.7
The study of religion and primitive religions [by] W. Richard Comstock. New York, Harper & Row [1972] 117 p. illus. 24 cm. (Religion and man) Bibliography: p. 107-112. [BL50.C67] 76-185899 ISBN 0-06-041338-7
1. Religion. 2. Religion, Primitive. I. Title. II. Series.

[CONFERENCE on religion as 291.17
a factor in shaping conduct and character, Northwestern university, 1929]
Religion and conduct; the report of a conference held at Northwestern university, November 15-16, 1929; editorial committee: George H. Betts, Frederick C. Eiselen, George A. Goe. New York, Cincinnati [etc.] The Abingdon press [c1929] 288 p. 20 cm. Contains References." [BR41.C65 1929] 30-12159
I. Betts, George Herbert, 1903-1934, ed. II. Title.

COOPER, Charles Champlin, 201
1874- ed.
Religion and the modern mind, edited by Charles C. Cooper ... New York and London, Harper & brothers, 1929. vi, 227, [1] p. 20 cm. [BL48.C6] 29-25337
1. Religion. I. Title.
Contents omitted.

COOPER, John Montgomery, 264.
1881-
The content of the advanced religion course, by John M. Cooper ... Washington, D. C., The Catholic education press, 1924. 61 p. 21 cm. [BX903.C6] 24-2095
I. Title.

COOPER, John Montgomery, 282.
1881-
Notebook for religion ... Catholic university of America [by] John M. Cooper, D. D. Washington, D. C., 19 v. 23 cm. [BX904.C6] ca 24
I. Catholic university of America. II. Title.

CORLETT, William. 200
The question of religion / William Corlett and John Moore. 1st American ed. Scarsdale, N.Y. : Bradbury Press, 1980. 100 p. ; 22 cm. (Their Questions) Examines the world's major religions' answers to the fundamental questions of life. [BL48.C64 1980] 79-15140 ISBN 0-87888-149-2 : 7.95
1. Religion. 2. [Religion.] I. Moore, John, 1932- joint author. II. Title. III. Series.

COVERT, William Chalmers, 243
1864-
Religion in the heart, and other addresses, by William Chalmers Covert ... New York, Chicago [etc.] Fleming H. Revell company [c1926] 192 p. 20 cm. [BX9178.C66R4] 26-10139
I. Title.

COX, Harvey Gallagher. 201'.1
The seduction of the spirit; the use and misuse of people's religion [by] Harvey Cox. New York, Simon and Schuster [1973] 350 p. 22 cm. Bibliography: p. 331-334. [BX4827.C68A37] 73-2314 ISBN 0-671-21525-6 8.95
1. Cox, Harvey Gallagher. 2. Religion. I. Title.
Pbk. 2.95.

CREEL, Richard E., 1940- 200'.1'9
Religion and doubt : toward a faith of your own / Richard E. Creel. Englewood Cliffs, N.J. : Prentice-Hall, 1976c1977 p. cm. Bibliography: p. [BL48.C725] 76-23102 ISBN 0-13-771949-3 : 8.95
1. Religion. I. Title.

CRITIQUE of religion and *philosophy.* Garden City, N. Y., Doubleday, 1961. xx, 453p. 19cm. (Anchor books. A252)
1. Religion. 2. Philosophy of religion. I. Kaufmann, Walter Arnold.

CUMONT, Franz Valery Marie, 1868-1947 292
Astrology and religion among the Greeks and Romans [Tr. from French. Gloucester, Mass., Peter Smith, 1962] 115p. 21cm. (Dover bk., rebound) 3.35
1. Religion. 2. Greece—Religion. 3. Rome—Religion. 4. Astrology. I. Title.

CUMONT, Franz Valery Marie, 1868-1947. 292
Astrology and religion among the Greeks and Romans. New York, Dover Publications [1960] 115p. (T581) Bibl. footnotes 60-50835 1.35 pap.,
1. Religion. 2. Greece—Religion. 3. Rome—Religion. 4. Astrology. I. Title.

CURRY, Albert Bruce, 1887- 248
Speaking of religion--, by Bruce Curry. New York, London, C. Scribner's sons, 1935. xiv, p., 2 l., 3-205 p. 20 cm. "Suggested readings": p. 205. [BL48.C8] 35-4713
1. Religion. 2. Christianity—20th cent. I. Title.

DAMERON, James Palatin, b.1828. 133.
Spiritism; the origin of all religions. By J. P. Dameron ... San Francisco, Cal., The author, 1885. cover-title, 108 p. port. 25 cm. Bound with this are three pamphlets: Autobiography and writings of J. P. Dameron; Who shall we elect U. S. senator? (Signed: A voice from the people): and Speech of J. P. Dameron, before the Printer's Hancock and English club, San Francisco. [BF1261.D2] 11-3138
I. Title.

DAS, Bhagavan, 1869-1958, comp. 290
The essential unity of all religions. Wheaton, Ill., Theosophical Press [1966] liv, 683 p. 20 cm. Reprint of the "Second edition, greatly enlarged, 1939." [BL48] 66-6517
1. Religion. 2. Religions. 3. Sacred books. I. Title.

DAVIS, Charles, 1923- 200
Temptations of religion. [1st U.S. ed.] New York, Harper & Row [1974, c1973] 89 p. 21 cm. Includes bibliographical references. [BL48.D3725 1974] 73-6341 ISBN 0-06-061701-2 4.95
1. Religion. I. Title.

DAWSON, Christopher Henry, 1889- 290
Religion and culture. New York, Sheed & Ward, 1948 [i. e. 1949] v. 225 p. 23 cm. (Gifford lectures, 1947) "Delivered in the University of Edinburgh." Bibliographical footnotes. [BL55.D32 1949] 49-7957
1. Religion. I. Title. II. Series.

DAY, Albert Edward, 1884- 287
Present perils in religion, by Albert Edward Day. New York, Cincinnati [etc.] The Abingdon press [c1928] 215 p. 20 cm. Sermons. [BX8333.D37P7] 28-20147
I. Title.

DECLARATION of the Lord's own religion--church--nation or, for short, Renation with His real peace ... Salem, Or., Renational publishing association, 1900. 152 p. 21 cm. "The following work, up to page 140,--excepting that the first four pages are now somewhat changed,--was published seven years ago."--Pref. Signed on p. 140; "Henry" (the Christian name of the author) 6-30325

DEMERSCHMAN, Lucille. 200
New light upon old tradition, with spiritual guidelines for the new age. Los Angeles, DeVorss [1969] 279 p. 24 cm. [BL48.D385] 79-101300
1. Jesus Christ—Biography. 2. Religion. 3. Christianity. I. Title.

DEWEY, John 201
A common faith. New Haven, [Conn.], Yale University Press [1960, c.1934] 87p. 21cm. (Yale paperbound Y-18) .95 pap.,
1. Religion. I. Title.

DEWEY, John, 1859- 201
A common faith [by] John Dewey ... New Haven, Yale university press; London, H. Milford, Oxford university press, 1934. 3 p. l., 87 p. 21 cm. (Half-title: The Terry lectures) [BL48.D4] 34-27264
1. Religion. I. Title.

DIAMOND, Herbert Maynard. 201
Religion and the commonweal; an analysis of the social economy of religion, by Herbert Maynard Diamond ... New York and London, Harper & brothers, 1928. xx, 305, [1] p. 22 cm. "Serial publications": p. 288; Bibliography: p. 289-301. [BL60.D5] 28-18011
1. Religion. 2. Religion. Primitive. 3. Sociology. I. Title.

DICKINSON, Goldsworthy Lowes, 1862-1932. 261
Religion; a criticism and a forecast, by G. Lowes Dickinson. New York, McClure, Phillips & co., 1905. x, 83, [1] p. 18 cm. These chapters originally appeared in the Independent review for October 1903, and May, June and November, 1904. cf. Introd. [BR123.D5] 5-10559
I. Title.

DOAN, Frank Carleton.
Religion and the modern mind, and other essays in modernism, by Frank Carleton Doan. Boston, Sherman, French & company, 1909. 3 p. l., iii-ix, 201 p. 20 cm. [A251164] 9-28386 1.00
I. Title.

DOBBS, John Francis.
The modern man and the church, by John Francis Dobbs. New York, Chicago [etc.] Fleming H. Revell company [c1911] 3 p. l., 5-268 p. 22 cm. 12-308 1.25
I. Title.

DOUGLAS, Mary (Tew) 301.5'8
Natural symbols; explorations in cosmology [by] Mary Douglas. [1st American ed.] New York, Pantheon Books [1970] xvii, 177 p. 22 cm. Bibliography: p. [169]-174. [BL48.D67 1970b] 77-110128 5.95
1. Religion. 2. Ritual. 3. Symbolism. I. Title.

DOUGLAS, Mary (Tew) 113
Natural symbols; explorations in cosmology [by] Mary Douglas. New York, Vintage Books [1973] 218 p. 19 cm. Bibliography: p. 202-208. [BL48.D67 1973] 73-5908 ISBN 0-394-71942-5 1.95 (pbk.)
1. Religion. 2. Ritual. 3. Symbolism. I. Title.

DRAKE, Durant, 1878-1933. 200
Problems of religion; an introductory survey. New York, Greenwood Press, 1968 [c1916] xiii, 425 p. 20 cm. Includes bibliographies. [BL48.D7 1968] 68-19268
1. Religion. 2. Christianity. 3. Religion—Philosophy. I. Title.

DRAKE, Durant, 1878-1933. 201
Problems of religion; an introductory survey, by Durant Drake... Boston, New York [etc.] Houghton Mifflin company [c1916] xiii, 425 p. 21 cm. Bibliography at end of each chapter. [BL48.D7] 16-18757
1. Religion. 2. Christianity. I. Title.

DUCASSE, Curt John, 1881- 200
A philosophical scrutiny of religion. New York, Ronald Press Co. [1953] x, 441 p. illus. 22 cm. Bliographical footnotes. [BL48.D78] 53-5700
1. Religion. I. Title.

DUNLAP, Knight, 1875- 291
Religion, its functions in human life, a study of religion from the point of view of psychology by Knight Dunlap ... 1st ed. New York, London, McGraw-Hill book company, inc., 1946. xi, 362 p. 23 cm. (McGraw-Hill publications in psychology, J. F. Dashiell, PH.D., consulting editor) "Important references on religion and religions": p. 345-358. [BL48.D8] 46-7061
1. Religion. I. Title.

DUNLAP, Knight, 1875-1949. 291
Religion: its functions in human life; a study of religion from the point of view of psychology. Westport, Conn., Greenwood Press [1970, c1946] xi, 362 p. 23 cm. (McGraw-Hill publications in psychology) Reprint of the 1946 ed. Includes bibliographical references. [BL48.D8 1970] 77-100158
1. Religion. I. Title.

DUPRE, Louis K., 1925- 248.2
The other dimension; a search for the meaning of religious attitudes [by] Louis Dupre. [1st ed.] Garden City, N.Y., Doubleday, 1972. 565 p. 22 cm. Includes bibliographical references. [BL48.D84] 78-144261 10.00
1. Religion. 2. Experience (Religion) I. Title.

DUPRE, Louis K., 1925- 291.4'2
The other dimension : a search for the meaning of religious attitudes / Louis Dupre. Seabury abridged paperback ed. New York : Seabury Press, 1979. 418 p. ; 23 cm. (The Seabury library of contemporary theology) "A Crossroad book." Includes bibliographical references. [BL48.D842] 79-88311 ISBN 0-8164-9108-9 pbk. : 9.95
1. Religion. 2. Experience (Religion) I. Title.

DUTCH, Andrew K. 200
The God within : brotherhood nyet / by Andrew K. Dutch. Boca Raton, Fla. : Dutch Treat Syndicate, [1975] xxix, 277 p. ; 23 cm. [BL48.D87] 74-24542
1. Religion. I. Title.

...DYNAMIC religion; 204
a personal experience, by Alfred Noyes, Zona Gale, Leo Tolstoi...[and others] New York city, Eddy and Page [193-] 67 p. 19 1/2 cm. (Personal problems series, no. 11) [BL25.D6] 38-4282
1. Jesus Christ—Biog.—Study. 2. Religion. 3. Christianity—20th cent.
Contents omitted.

EAKIN, Frank E., 1936- 209'.182'1
Religion in Western culture : selected issues / Frank E. Eakin, Jr. Washington : University Press of America, c1977. xviii, 328 p. : ill. ; 22 cm. Includes indexes. Bibliography: p. 286-292. [BL48.E15] 78-100453 ISBN 0-8191-0256-3 pbk. : 10.50
1. Bible—Criticism, interpretation, etc. 2. Religion. 3. Christianity. 4. Judaism. I. Title.

EDWARDS, David Lawrence. 301.5'8
Religion and change, by David L. Edwards. [1st ed.] New York, Harper & Row [1969] 383 p. 24 cm. Bibliographical footnotes. [BL48.E35] 69-19778 8.00
1. Religion. 2. Secularism. 3. Christianity—20th century. I. Title.

EDWARDS, Jonathan, 1703-1758. 285.
The treatise on religious affections. by the late Rev. Jonathan Edwards, A. M. Somewhat abridged. New-York, American tract society [185-?] iv, [5]-276 p. front. 15 cm. "This edition ... is that of W. Ellerby, slightly abridged."--p. [ii] [BX7230.E4 1850] 20-10840
I. Ellerby, W., ed. II. Title.

EDWARDS, Loren M. 1877- 248
The spectrum of religion [by] Loren M. Edwards. New York, Cincinnati, The Methodist book concern [c1919] 159 p. 19 cm. [BV4501.E3] 19-15941
I. Title.

EINIG, Peter, 1852-1908. 231
Religion--faith--the church; a series of apologetic discourses, by Canon P. Einig, D.D. New York, Joseph F. Wagner,...[etc., etc, c1919] 2 p., l., 158 p. 21 1/2 cm. [BT1101.E5] 20-3805
I. Title.

ELIADE, Mircea 290
The sacred and the profane; the nature of religion. Tr. from French by Wilard R. Trask. New York, Harper [1961, c.1957-1959] 256p. (Harper torchbks. Cloister lib., TB81) Bibl. 1.45 pap.,
1. Religion. I. Title.

ELIADE, Mircea, 1907- 200'.9
The quest; history and meaning in religion. Chicago, University of Chicago Press [1969] 180 p. 23 cm. Bibliographical footnotes. [BL50.E46] 69-19059
1. Religion. I. Title.

ELIADE, Mircea, 1907- 290
The sacred and the profane; the nature of religion. Translated from the French by Willard R. Trask. [1st American ed.] New York, Harcourt, Brace [1959] 256 p. 22 cm. Includes bibliography. [BL48.E413] 58-10904
1. Religion. I. Title.

ELLWOOD, Robert S., 1933- 200.1
Introducing religion : from inside and outside / Robert S. Ellwood, Jr. Englewood Cliffs, N.J. : Prentice-Hall, c1978. xi, 196 p. : ill. ; 23 cm. Includes index. Bibliography: p. 183-191. [BL48.E43] 77-13837 ISBN 0-13-477505-8 pbk. : 6.95
1. Religion. I. Title.

ELY, Richard Theodore, 1854- 377.
...The universities and the churches; an address delivered at the 31st university convocation, Senate chamber, Albany, N.Y., July 5, 1893, by Professor Richard T. Ely ... Albany, University of the state of New York, 1893. p. 349-367. 25cm. A reprint from the Regents' bulletin of the New York state university, no. 22, Sept., 1893, p. 350-367. [LC383.E5] 16-8576
I. Title.

EVANS, Morris Owen, 1857- 220
The healing of the nations, by Morris O. Evans ... Boston, R. G. Budger [c1922) 3 p. l., ix-x p., 1 l., 13-246 p. 21 1/2 cm. "In the interweaving of Lord Tennyson's poems with the treatment of my theme the object was ... to trace the organic development of Christian thought and ideals from medieval times to the present day along the lines of the laureate's own conception of the movements of history. [BR125.E8] 24-4638
1. Tennyson, Alfred Tennyson, 1st baron, 1809-1892. Idylls of the King. 2. Religion. I. Title.

EXPLORING religious meaning 200
[by] Robert Monk [and others] Englewood Cliffs, N.J., Prentice-Hall [1974, c1973] xviii, 395 p. illus. 24 cm. Includes bibliographical references. [BL48.E95] 73-4888 ISBN 0-13-297499-1 9.95
1. Religion. 2. Religious literature (Selections: Extracts, etc.) I. Monk, Robert C.
Pbk. 5.95; ISBN 0-13-297481-9.

EXPLORING religious meaning 200
/ Robert C. Monk ... [et al.]. 2d ed. Englewood Cliffs, N.J. : Prentice-Hall, c1980. xvii, 394 p. : ill. ; 24 cm. Includes bibliographical references and indexes. [BL48.E95 1980] 79-19608 ISBN 0-13-297515-7 : 11.95
1. Religion. 2. Relgious literature—Collected works. I. Monk, Robert C.

FALLDING, Harold. 301.5'8
The sociology of religion; an explanation of the unity and diversity in religion. Toronto, New York, McGraw-Hill Ryerson [1974] xii, 240 p. 23 cm. Includes bibliographical references. [BL48.F25] 73-10793 ISBN 0-07-077640-7
1. Religion. 2. Religion and sociology. I. Title.

FALLDING, Harold. 301.5'8
The sociology of religion : an explanation of the unity and diversity in religion / [by] Harold Fallding. London ; New York [etc.] : McGraw-Hill, 1974. xii, 240 p. : ill., map ; 23 cm. Includes bibliographical references and index. [BL48.F25 1974b] 74-189012 ISBN 0-07-084039-3 : £3.95
1. Religion. 2. Religion and sociology. I. Title.

FARMER, Herbert Henry, 1892- 290
Revelation and religion; studies in the theological interpretation of religious types.

New York, Harper [1954] 244p. 23cm. [The Gifford lectures, 1950] [BL48] 54-10941
1. Religion. I. Title.

FARNELL, Lewis Richard, 1856-1934. 290
The evolution of religion: an anthropological study, by L. R. Farnell ... London, Williams & Norgate; New York, G. P. Putnam's sons, 1905. ix, 234 p. 19 cm. (Half-title: Crown theological library, vol. xii) "Lectures for the Hibbert trust."--Pref. Bibliographical foot-notes. [BL85.F3] 6-25146
1. Religion. 2. Rites and ceremonies. 3. Prayer. I. Title.
Contents omitted.

FERGUSON, Charles.
The religion of democracy; a manual of devotion, by Charles Ferguson. San Francisco, D. P. Elder [etc.] 1900. iv p., 1 l., 7-160 p. 19 cm. 3-14779
I. Title.

FEUERBACH, Ludwig Andreas, 1804-1872.
The essence of religion. God the image of man. Man's dependence upon nature the last and only source of religion. By Ludwig Feuerbach...Tr. by Alexander Loos, A.M. New York, A. K. Butts & co., 1873. 1 p. l., iv, 75 p. 19 1/2 cm. "Forms the basis and substance of the author's larger work, published under the same title, as a complement to his previous: 'Essence of Christianity'."--p. [1] [B2971.W5E51873] 12-32488
I. Loos, Alexander, tr. II. Title.

FEUERBACH, Ludwig Andreas, 1804-1872. 200'.1
Lectures on the essence of religion. Translated by Ralph Manheim. [1st ed.] New York, Harper & Row [1967] xv, 359 p. 22 cm. Translation of Vorlesungen uber das Wesen der Religion. Bibliography: p. 357-359. [B2971.W62E5 1967] 67-21548
I. Title.

FISKE, Charles, bp., 1868- 283.
The faith by which we live; a plain, practical exposition of the religion of the incarnate Lord, by the Right Reverend Charles Fiske ... Milwaukee, Wis., Morehouse publishing co. [c1919] xii, 322 p. 19 cm. [BX5930.F5] 19-8311
I. Title.

FISKE, Charles, bp., 1868- 283.
The faith by which we live; a plain, practical exposition of the religion of the incarnate Lord, by the Right Reverend Charles Fiske ... Rev. ed.; with questions on the faith appended. Milwaukee, Wis., Morehouse publishing co. [1927] xii, 334 p. 19 cm. [BX5930.F5 1927] 28-18903
I. Title.

FLUEGEL, Maurice. 180
Philosophy, Qabbala and Vedanta. Comparative meta- physics and ethics, rationalism and mysticism, of the Jews, the Hindus and most of the historic nations, as links and developments of one chain of universal philosophy. By Maruice Fluegel ... Baltimore, H. Fluegel & co., 1902. v. 25 cm. [B723.F6] 2-3563
1. Religion. 2. Hinduism. 3. Cabala. 4. Vedanta. 5. Philosophy—Hist. I. Title.

FORMAN, Henry James, 1879- 290
Have you a religion? The supreme hygiene of life, by Henry James Forman. New York, Toronto, Farrar & Rinehart, inc. [c1941] viii, p., 2 l., 3-246 p. 21 cm. [BL48.F57] 41-13654
1. Religion. 2. Religious (Proposed, universal, etc.) I. Title.

FOSDICK, Harry Emerson, 1878- 201
As I see religion, by Harry Emerson Fosdick. New York and London, Harper & brothers, 1932. v. 201 p. 20 cm. "First edition." "Reference notes": p. 190-198. [BL48.F6] 32-26506
1. Religion. I. Title.

FOSDICK, Harry Emerson, 1878-1969. 200'.1
As I see religion / by Harry Emerson Fosdick. Westport, Conn. : Greenwood Press, 1975, c1932. v, 201 p. ; 20 cm. Reprint of the ed. published by Harper, New York. Includes bibliographical references and index. [BL48.F6 1975] 75-11835 ISBN 0-8371-8142-9
1. Religion. I. Title.

FOSTER, George Burman, 1858-1918. 201
The function of religion in man's struggle for existence, by George Burman Foster ... Chicago, The University of Chicago press; [etc., etc.] 1909. xi, [1], 293 p. 19 cm. Enlarged from an address first published in the University of California chronicle, vol. xl. no. 1. cf. Pref. [BL51.F6] 9-12412
1. Religion. I. Title.

FOSTER, John, 1770-1843. 204
An essay on the importance of considering the subject of religion. Addressed particularly to men of education. By John Foster ... Boston, S. H. Parker and Crocker & Brewster, 1827. 172 p. 21 cm. "The essay ... was written as an introduction to Doddridge's Rise and progress of religion in the soul."--Pref. [BL50.F6] 37-39278
1. Religion. I. Title.

FOX, James Joseph.
Religion and morality, their nature and matual relations, historically and doctrinally considered; dissertation for the doctorate in theology at the Catholic university of America. New York, W. H. Young & co., 1899. 8 p. l., 335 p. 8 degree. Bibliography: prelim. leaf 5-6 99-2533
I. Title.

FRANCIS, Genevieve Mae (Hilliard) Mrs. 1874- 131
Keeper of the temple, by Geneieve Mae Francis ... Essence of truth in laws of life, psychology--metaphysics--occultism; practical lessons in spiritual unfoldment. Los Angeles, Calif., The Austin publishing company, 1928. 221 p. incl. front. (port.) 20 cm. [BF640.F55] 29-2960
I. Title.

GAEBELEIN, Arno Clemens, 1861- 201
Christianity or religion? A study of the origin and growth of religion and the supernaturalism of Christianity, by Arno Clemens Gaebelein ... New York city, Publication office "Our hope" [c1927] 176 p. 19 cm. Bibliography: p. [4] [BL48.G25] 28-1334
1. Religion. 2. Christianity. I. Title.

GARRISON, Winfred Ernest, 1874- 220
Affirmative religion, by Winfred Ernest Garrison. New York and London. Harper & brothers, 1928. viii p., 1 l., 292 p., 1 l. 19 1/2 cm. [BR125.G32] 28-24262
I. Title.

GIFFORD, Miram Wentworth, 1851- 201
Laws of the soul; or, The science of religion and the future life. By M. W. Gifford ... Cincinnati, Cranston & Curts; New York, Hunt & Eaton, 1893. 204 p. 20 cm. [BL48.G5] 30-11340
1. Religion. I. Title.

GITTELSOHN, Roland Bertram, 1910- 215
Man's best hope. New York, Random House [1961] 200 p. 21 cm. [BL48.G57] 61-14892
1. Religion. I. Title.

GLEASON, John J., 1934- 200'.1'9
Consciousness & the ultimate / John J. Gleason, Jr. Nashville : Abingdon, c1981. 192 p. : ill. ; 22 cm. Includes bibliographical references. [BL48.G578] 19 80-21397 ISBN 0-687-09470-4 pbk. : 6.95
1. Jesus Christ—Person and offices. 2. Religion. 3. Religions. 4. Psychology, Religious. I. Title.

GOPI Krishna, 1903- 215'.7
The biological basis of religion and genius. With an introd. by Carl Friedrich Freiherr von Weizsacker. [1st ed.] New York, Harper & Row [1972] xvi, 118 p. 22 cm. (Religious perspectives, v. 22) [BL263.G63 1972] 71-178013 ISBN 0-06-064789-2 5.95
1. Religion. 2. Evolution. I. Title. II. Series.

GORDIS, Robert, 1908- 200
A faith for moderns. New York, Bloch Pub. Co., [c.]1960. xii, 316p. 24cm. 60-15012 5.00 bds.,
1. Religion. I. Title.

GORDIS, Robert, 1908- 200
A faith for moderns. Rev. and augm. ed. New York, Bloch Pub. Co. [1971] xviii, 340 p. 23 cm. [BL48.G64 1971] 76-136424 ISBN 0-8197-0001-0 3.95
1. Religion. I. Title.

GOWEN, Herbert Henry, 1864- 291.
The universal faith; comparative religion from the Christian standpoint, by the Rev. H. H. Gowen ... Milwaukee, Wis., Morehouse publishing co.; [etc., etc., c1926] x, 210 p., 1 l. 17 cm. (Half-title: Biblical and oriental series, S. A. B. Mercer, general editor) Bibliography: p. 210. [BR127.G6] 26-8104
1. Religion. I. Title.

GRAHAM, Aelred, 1907- 200
The end of religion; autobiographical explorations. New York, Harcourt [1973, c.1971] xii, 292 p. 21 cm. (Harvest Book, HB249) Includes bibliographical references. [BL48.G68] 77-139461 ISBN 0-15-628790-0 pap., 2.85
1. Religion. 2. Religions. I. Title.

GRANT, Percy Stickney, 1860-1927. 220
The religion of Main street, by Rev. Dr. Percy Stickney Grant. New York, American library service, 1923. 200 p. 20 cm. [BR125.G719] 23-7416
I. Title.

GRIMES, Hezekiah, 1861-
The thunderbolt; did man create the god's, or did the god's create man, flashes of thought, by H. Grimes. [Ottumwa, Ia., Ottumwa printing co.] c1915. 1 p. l., 85 p. 20 cm. 15-23086 0.75
I. Title.

GRONBECH, Vilhelm Peter, 1873-1948 201
Religious currents in the nineteenth century. Tr. from Danish by P. M. Mitchell, W. D. Paden. Lawrence, Univ. of Kan. Pr. [c.]1964. 201p. port. 24cm. Bibl. [BR477.G713] 64-20567 4.50
1. Religion. 2. Evolution. 3. Nineteenth century. I. Title.

GRONBECH, Vilhelm Peter, 1873-1948. 201
Religious currents in the nineteenth century, by Vilhelm Gronbech. Translated from the Danish by P. M. Mitchell and W. D. Paden. Lawrence, University of Kansas Press, 1964. 201 p. port. 24 cm. Bibliographical references included in "Notes" (p. 195-198) [BR477.G713] 64-20567
1. Religion. 2. Evolution. 3. Nineteenth century. I. Title.

GROSE, George Richmond, 1869-
The outlook for religion, by George Richmond Grose ... Cincinnati, Jennings and Graham; New York, Eaton and Mains [c1913] 137 p. 20 cm. 13-13400 0.75
I. Title.

GROSE, George Richmond, 1869-
Religion and the mind, by George Richmond Grose ... New York, Cincinnati, The Abingdon press [c1915] 112 p. 20 cm. First appeared as a series of articles in the Adult Bible class montly. 15-18634 0.75
I. Title.

GRoNBECH, Vilhelm Peter, 1873-1948. 201
Religious currents in the nineteenth century. Translated from the Danish by P. M. Mitchell and W. D. Paden. Carbondale, Southern Illinois University Press [1973, c1964] 201 p. port. 20 cm. (Arcturus books, AB110) Translation of Religiose stromninger i det nittende aarhundrede. Includes bibliographical references. [BR477.G713 1973] 72-11829 ISBN 0-8093-0629-8 2.45 (pbk.)
1. Religion. 2. Religion and evolution. 3. Nineteenth century. I. Title.

GRoNBECH, Vilhelm Peter, 1873-1948. 201
Religious currents in the nineteenth century. Translated from the Danish by P. M. Mitchell and W. D. Paden. Carbondale, Ill., Arcturus Books [1973, c1964] p. Translation of Religiose stromninger i det nittende aarhundrede. Includes bibliographical references. [BR477.G713 1973b] 72-11830 ISBN 0-8093-0630-1 (pbk)
1. Religion. 2. Religion and evolution. 3. Nineteenth century. I. Title.

EL Guindi, Fadwa. 301.5'8
Religion in culture / Fadwa El Guindi. Dubuque, Iowa : W. C. Brown Co., c1977. viii, 71 p. ; 24 cm. (Elements of anthropology) Includes bibliographies and index. [BL48.G85] 76-11977 ISBN 0-697-07549-4 pbk. : 2.50
1. Religion. 2. Myth. 3. Ritual. I. Title.

GUTHRIE, W. K. C. 292
The religion and mythology of the Greeks. v.2, chap. 40. [New York] Cambridge [c.] 1961[ ] 55p. Bibl. 1.25 pap.,
I. Title.

GUYAU, Jean Marie, 1854-1888. 211
The non-religion of the future, a sociological study; translated from the French of M. Guyau. New York, H. Holt and company, 1897. xi, 543 p. 22 cm. [BL2747.G83 1897] 1-928
1. Religion. 2. Social sciences. I. Title.

GUYAU, Jean Marie, 1854-1888. 211
The non-religion of the future, a sociological study; translated from the French of M. Guyau. New York, H. Holt and company, 1897. xi, 543 p. 22 cm. [BL2747.G83] 1-928
1. Religion. 2. Social sciences. I. Title.

GUYAU, Jean Marie, 1854-1888. 211
The non-religion of the future; a sociological study. Introd. by Nahum N. Glatzer New York, Schocken Books [1962] 538 p. 21 cm. (Schocken paperbacks, SB39) [BL2747.G83 1962] 62-19393
1. Religion. 2. Social sciences. I. Title.

HACKMAN, George Gottlob. 200
Religion in modern life [by] George G. Hackman, Charles W. Kegley [and] Viljo K. Nikander. New York, Macmillan [1957] 480 p. 22 cm. Includes bibliography. [BL48.H23] 57-5545
1. Religion. 2. Christianity—20th century.

HALL, Thomas Cuming, 1858- 201
Religion and life, by Thomas Cuming Hall ... New York, Eaton & Mains; Cincinnati, Jennings & Graham [c1913] xiv, 161 p. 19 1/2 cm. "The literature" at end of each chapter. [BL48.H3] 13-4784
1. Religion. I. Title.

HALSTEAD, William Riley, 1848-
A cosmic view of religion, by William Riley Halstead. Cincinnati, Jennings and Graham; New York, Eaton and Mains [c1913] 337 p. 21 cm. $1.50 13-3845
I. Title.

HAMMANN, Louis J., 1929- 200
The puzzle of religion : the parts and the whole / Louis J. Hammann. Washington : University Press of America, 1977. 175 p. ; 22 cm. Includes bibliographical references. [BL48.H354] 78-100511 ISBN 0-8191-0309-8 : 8.75
1. Religion. I. Title.

HANNAY, James Ballantyne, 1855- 291.3'7
Symbolism in relation to religion; or, Christianity: the sources of its teaching and symbolism. Port Washington, N.Y., Kennikat Press [1971] xv, 394 p. illus., port. 23 cm. "First published circa 1915." Includes bibliographical references. [BL48.H355 1971] 79-118523
1. Religion. 2. Christianity—Origin. I. Title.

HARRIS, Ben, 1884- 290
Human gods, by Ben Harris. Philadelphia, Dorance and company [c1939] 304 p. 20 cm. [BL2775.H24] 40-485
1. Religion. 2. Free thought. 3. Religion and science—1900- I. Title.
Contents omitted.

HAYDON, Albert Eustace, 1880- 201
The quest of the ages, by A. Eustace Haydon. New York and London, Harper & brothers, 1929. xiii p., 1 l., 243 p. 21 1/2 cm. [BL48.H37] 29-29726
1. Religion. I. Title.

HOBART, Alvah Sabin, 1847-
Religion for men, by Alvah Sabin Hobart... New York [etc.] Association press, 1912.

192 p. 19 cm. (On cover: Men and religion series) 12-19361
I. Title.

HOFFMAN, Frank Sargent, 1852- 1928. 290
The sphere of religion; a consideration of its nature and of its influence upon the progress of civilization, by Frank Sargent Hoffman... New York and London, G. P. Putnam's sons, 1908. viii p., 1 l., 394 p. 20 cm. "Two of the chapters, the first and the ninth, have already appeared in the North American review, and the others have been printed wholly or in part in the Proceedings of the associations before which they were read and discussed."--Pref. [BL85.H7] 8-5160
1. Religion. 2. Civilization—Hist. 3. Sacred books—Hist. & crit. I. Title.

HOLMER, Paul L. 200
Theology and the scientific study of religion. Minneapolis, T. S. Denison [1961] 233 p. 22 cm. (The Lutheran studies series, v. 2) [BL48.H53] 61-18613
1. Religion. 2. Faith. I. Title.

HOLMES, Edmond Gore Alexander, 1850- 290
Dying lights & dawning; the Martha Upton lectures given in Manchester college, Oxford, 1923, by Edmond Holmes. London & Toronto. J. M. Dent & sons ltd; New York, E. P. Dutton & co., 1924. ix, 222 p. 19 1/2 cm. [BL100.H7] 25-23601
1. Religion. 2. Christianity. 3. Supernatural. I. Martha Upton Lectures,1923. II. Title.

HOLZER, Hans W. 1920- 131'.32
The human dynamo / Hans Holzer. Millbrae, Calif. : Celestial Arts, [1975] p. cm. [BL48.H55] 75-9097 ISBN 0-89087-053-5 : 4.95
1. Religion. 2. Psychical research. 3. Success. I. Title.

HOLZER, Hans W., 1920- 131'.32
The human dynamo / Hans Holzer. Millbrae, Calif. : Celestial Arts, [1975] ix, 117 p. ; 22 cm. [BL48.H55] 75-9097 ISBN 0-89087-053-5 : 4.95
1. Religion. 2. Psychical research. 3. Success. I. Title.

HOUF, Horace Thomas, 1889- 201
What religion is and does; an introduction to the study of its problems and values, by Horace T. Houf... New York and London, Harper & brothers, 1935. viii, 411 p. diagrs. 22 1/2 cm. "First edition." Contents.--pt. 1. Generic religion.--pt. 2. Hebrew-Christian religion. Books for further reading (p. 371-888) [BL48.H6] 35-9009
1. Religion. 2. Christianity—20th cent. I. Title.

HOUF, Horace Thomas, 1889- 201
What religion is and does; an introduction to the study of its problems and values, by Horace T. Houf ... Rev. ed. New York and London, Harper & brothers [1945] viii, 413 p. 22 1/2 cm. Contents.pt. 1. Generic religion.--pt. 2. Hebrew-Christian religion.--Books for further reading (p. 369-390) [BL48.H6 1945] 45-3473
1. Religion. 2. Christianity—20th cent. I. Title.

HUBBARD, Sara Anderson, Mrs. 1832-
The religion of cheerfulness, by Sara A. Hubbard. Chicago, A. C. McClurg & co., 1906. 3 p. l., 11-62, [1] p. port. 20 x 12 cm. 6-39460
I. Title.

HUXLEY, Julian Sorell, Sir, 1887- 211
Religion without revelation. [New and rev. ed.] New York, Harper [1957] 252 p. 22 cm. Includes bibliography. [BL48.H8 1957] 57-8170
1. Religion. I. Title.

HUXLEY, Julian Sorell, 1887- 201
Religion without revelation [by] J. S. Huxley. New York and London, Harper & brothers [c1927] 392 p. 20 cm. [What I believe series] Bibliography: p. 383-384. [BL48.H8 1927 a] 27-24378
1. Religion. I. Title.

HUXLEY, Julian Sorell, Sir, 1887-1975. 210
Religion without revelation / by Julian Huxley. Westport, Conn. : Greenwood Press, 1979. vi, 203 p. ; 23 cm. Reprint of the 1967 ed. published by C. A. Watts, London, as no. 19 of the New thinker's library. Includes index. Bibliography: p. 196-198. [BL48.H8 1979] 78-12065 ISBN 0-313-21225-2 lib.bdg. : 16.50
1. Religion. I. Title.

HUXLEY, Sir Julian Sorell, 1887-
Religion without revelation. [New and rev. ed. New York] The New American Library [1961] 222 p. (A Mentor book, MD244) 64-20360
1. Religion. I. Title.

HYDE, William De Witt, 1858- 1917.
Abba Father; or, The religion of everyday life, by William De Witt Hyde. New York, Chicago [etc.] F. H. Revell company [c1908] 71 p. 19 cm. 8-28412
I. Title.

INGRAM, Kenneth, 1882- 201
Christianity, communism and society. London, New York, Rider [1951] 216p. 19cm. [BL48.I5] 53-20
1. Religion. 2. Christianity—Essence, genius, nature. 3. Sociology, Christian. I. Title.

INTELLECTUAL honesty and religious commitment [by] Henry D. Aiken [and others] Edited and with an introd. by Arthur J. Bellinzoni, Jr. and Thomas V. Litzenburg, Jr. Philadelphia, Fortress Press [1969] xii, 84 p. 20 cm. "This volume has grown out of a symposium ... sponsored by the Departments of Philosophy and Religion at Wells College, February 21-22, 1964." [BL237.I5] 71-83677 1.95 201
1. Religion. 2. Faith. I. Aiken, Henry David, 1912- II. Bellinzoni, Arthur J., ed. III. Litzenburg, Thomas V., ed.

ISHERWOOD, Margaret. 201
The root of the matter; a study in the connections between religion, psychology, and education. With a foreword by Gerald Heard. New York, Harper [1954] 238p. illus. 21cm. [BL48] 54-8957
1. Religion. I. Title.

ISHERWOOD, Margaret. 200'.1
The root of the matter; a study in the connections between religion, psychology, and education. With a foreword by Gerald Heard. Westport, Conn., Greenwood Press [1970, c1954] 236 p. 23 cm. Includes bibliographical references. [BL48.I8 1970] 72-90534 ISBN 0-8371-3962-7
1. Religion. I. Title.

JACKS, Lawrence Pearsall, 1860- 252
Elemental religion; the Lyman Beecher lectures for 1933, with three sermons on the main topic, by L. P. Jacks ... New York and London, Harper & brothers, 1934. 5 p. l., 143 p. 20 cm. "First edition." [BR85.J25] 34-7583
1. Religion. 2. Preaching. 3. Sermons, English. I. Title.

JACKS, Lawrence Pearsall, 1860- 201
The inner sentinel; a study of ourselves and of something more, by L. P. Jacks ... New York and London, Harper & brothers, 1930. v. p., 1 l., 183 p. 20 cm. "First edition." [BL43.J3] 30-25728
1. Religion. I. Title.

JACKSON, Alvin R., 1889- 201
Religious sanity, the philosophy of individual life; an abridgment by A. R. Jackson of the literature of the Great School of Natural Science, addressed to the progressive intelligenceof the age. With a foreword by J. W. Norwood. New York, Exposition Press [1951] 94 p. 22 cm. "A condensation of the Harmonic series of books (eight in all), andother literature of natural science and the philosophy of individual life." [BL50.J3] 51-10212
1. Religion. I. Great School of Natural Science, Hollywood, Calif. II. Title.

JAMES, William, 1842-1910. 201
The varieties of religious experience; a study in human nature. Foreword by Jacques Barzun. [New York] New American Library [1958] 406p. 19cm. (Gifford lectures, 1901-02) A Mentor book, MD221. 'Delivered at Edinburgh.' Bibliographical footnotes. [BR110.J3 1958] 58-1697
1. Religion. 2. Philosophy and religion. 3. Conversion. 4. Psychology. Religious. I. Title. II. Series.

JAMES, William, 1842-1910. 201.6
The varieties of religious experience; a study in human nature. With a new introd. by Reinhold Niebuhr. New York, Collier Books [1961] 416p. 18cm. (Collier books, AS39) Bibliographical footnotes. [BR110.J3 1961] 61-17497
1. Religion. 2. Philosophy and religion. 3. Conversion. 4. Psychology. Religious. I. Title.

JAMES, William, 1842-1910. 201
The varieties of religious experience; a study in human nature. Enl. ed., with appendices and introd. by Joseph Ratner. New Hyde Park, N. Y., University Books [1963] xiii, 626 p. 24 cm. (Gifford lectures on natural religion, 1901-02) Bibliographical footnotes. [BR110.J3 1963] 63-14505
1. Religion. 2. Philosophy and religion. 3. Conversion. 4. Psychology, Religious. I. Title. II. Series: Gifford lectures, 1901-02

JAMES, William, 1842-1910. 201
The varieties of religious experience; a study in human nature, being the Gifford lectures on natural religion delivered at Edinburgh in 1901-1902, by William James ... New York, London, [etc.] Longmans, Green, and co., 1902. xii, 534 p., 1 l. 23 cm. [BR110.J3 1902 a] 2-16221
1. Religion. 2. Philosophy and religion. 3. Conversation. 4. Psychology. Religious. I. Title.

JAMES, William, 1842-1910. 201
The varieties of religious experience; a study in human nature; being the Gifford lectures on natural religion delivered at Edinburgh in 1901-1902, by William James ... New York [etc.] Longmans, Green, and co., 1902. xii, 534 p., 1 l. 22 cm. "Bibliographical note: First edition, June, 1902.--Reprinted, with revisions, August, 1902." [BR110.J3 1902 a] 2-26239
1. Religion. 2. Philosophy and religion. 3. Conversion. 4. Psychology, Religious. I. Gifford lectures. II. Title.

JAMES, William, 1842-1910. 201
The varieties of religious experience; a study in human nature; being the Gifford lectures on natural religion delivered at Edinburgh in 1901-1902, by William James 28th impression. New York [etc.] Longmans, Green, and co., 1917. 3 p. l., [v]-xii, 534 p., 1 l. 23 cm. [BR110.J3 1917] 19-10944
1. Religion. 2. Philosophy and religion. 3. Conversion. 4. Psychology, Religious. I. Title.

JAMES, William, 1842-1910. 201
The varieties of religious experience; a study in human nature; being the Gifford lectures on natural religion delivered at Edinburgh in 1901-1902, by William James. 37th impression. London, New York [etc.] Longmans, Green and co., 1929. 3 p. l., [v]-xii, 534 p. 21 cm. [BR110.J3 1929] 31-13198
1. Religion. 2. Philosophy and religion. 3. Conversion. 4. Psychology, Religious. I. Title.

JAMES, William, 1842-1910. 201
The varieties of religious experience; a study in human nature; being the Gifford lectures on natural religion delivered at Edinburgh in 1901-1902, by William James, 38th impression. London, New York [etc.] Longmans, Green and co., 1935. 3 p. l., [v]-xii, 534 p. 21 cm. "Printed in the United States of America." [BR110.J3 1935] 38-31406
1. Religion. 2. Philosophy and religion. 3. Conversion. 4. Psychology, Religious. I. Title.

JAMES, William, 1842-1910. 201
The varieties of religious experience, a study in human nature; being the Gifford lectures on natural religion delivered at Edinburgh in 1901-1902 by William James. New York, The Modern library [1936] xviii, 526 p. 18 cm. (Half-title: The modern library of the world's best books) "First modern library edition, 1936." [BR110.J3 1936] 37-27013
1. Religion. 2. Philosophy and religion. 3. Conversion. 4. Psychology, Religious. I. Title.

JAMES, William, 1842-1910. 201
The varieties of religious experience / William James ; [introd. by Andrew M. Greeley]. Garden City, N.Y. : Image Books, 1978. 516 p. ; 18 cm. (Gifford lectures on natural religion ; 1901-1902) Includes bibliographical references and index. [BR110.J3 1978] 77-76278 ISBN 0-385-13267-0 : pbk. : 2.95
1. Religion. 2. Philosophy and religion. 3. Conversion. 4. Psychology, Religious. I. Title. II. Series: Gifford lectures ; 1901-1902.

JAMES, William, 1842-1910. 201
The varities of religious experience; a study in human nature; being the Gifford lectures on natural religion delivered at Edinburgh in 1901-1902 by William James. 35th impression. New York [etc.] Longmans, Green, and co., 1925. 3 p. l., [v]-xii, 534 p. 23 cm. [BR110.J3 1925] 27-3530
1. Religion. 2. Philosophy and religion. 3. Conversation. 4. Psychology. I. Title.

JARRATT, Devereux, 1733-1801. 283'.0924 B
The life of the Reverend Devereux Jarratt. New York, Arno Press, 1969. 223 p. 23 cm. (Religion in America) "A series of letters addressed to the Rev. John Coleman." Reprint of the 1806 ed. [BX5995.J27A3 1969] 79-83427
I. Coleman, John, 1758?-1816. II. Title.

JENKINS, Burris Atkins, 1869-
The man in the street and religion, by Burris A. Jenkins. New York, Chicago [etc.] Fleming H. Revell company [c1917] 248 p. 20 cm. 17-11447 1.25
I. Title.

JOHNSON, Claude M. 211
Human religion, by Claude M. Johnson. [New York] C. Mercer [c1917] 68 p. 19 cm. [BL2775.J6] 19-11002
I. Title.

JOLLY, David E 200
Knowledge beyond understanding; a topic essay book of enlightenment, by David E. Jolly. [Seattle, 1967] 153 p. 24 cm. [BL50.J55] 67-9692
1. Religion. I. Title.

*JONES, Irene 248.8
Needed: a righteous generation. Independence, Mo., Herald House [c.1964] . 64p. 22cm. .60 pap.,
I. Title.

JONES, Rufus Matthew, 1863- 922.
A boy's religion from memory, by Rufus M. Jones. Philadelphia, Ferris & Leach, 1902. 141 p. front., plates, port. 18 cm. [BX7795.J55A3] 3-36
I. Title.

JORDAN, David Starr, 1851- 1931. 220
The religion of a sensible American, by David Starr Jordan ... Boston, American Unitarian association, 1909. 84 p. 20 cm. Enlarged from an article first published in "The Hibbert journal." [BR125.J7] 9-23502 0.80
I. Title.

JURJI, Edward Jabra, 1907- 290
The Christian interpretation of religion; Christianity in its human and creative relationships with the world's cultures and faiths. New York, Macmillan, 1952. 318 p. 21 cm. [BL48.J8] 52-10200
1. Religion. 2. Religions. 3. Christianity and other religions. 4. Apologetics—20th cent. I. Title.

KALLEN, Horace Meyer, 1882- 201
Why religion [by] Horace M. Kallen ... New York, Boni & Liveright, 1927. 6 p. l., 11-316 p. 23 cm. [BL48.K3] 27-5437
1. Religion. I. Title.

KAUFMANN, Walter 201
Critique of religion and philosophy. Garden City, N.Y., Doubleday 453p. (Anchor bk. A252) Bibl. 1.45 pap.,
1. Religion. 2. Philosophy and religion. I. Title.

KAUFMANN, Walter Arnold. 201
Critique of religion and philosophy. [1st ed.] New York, Harper [1958] 325 p. 22

cm. Includes bibliography. [BL48.K38] 58-7097
1. Religion. 2. Philosophy and religion. I. Title.

KEESEY, Wilbur Ruth, 1869-
The problem of religion, by Rev. Wilbur R. Keesey ... Cincinnati, Jennings and Graham; New York, Eaton and Mains [c1911] 139 p. 18 cm. 11-20602 0.50
I. Title.

KEETON, Morris T. 290
Values men live by; an invitation to religious inquiry. Nashville, Abingdon Press [c.1960] 224 p. 23 cm. Bibl.: p. 213-218. 60-10909 3.50
1. Religion. I. Title.

KELLOGG, Samuel Henry, 1839-1899. 201
The genesis and growth of religion; the L. P. Stone lectures for 1892, at Princeton theological seminary ... by the Rev. S. H. Kellogg ... New York and London, Macmillan and co., 1892. xiii, 275 p. 20 cm. [BL48.K4] 30-11342
1. Religion. I. Title.

KELLOGG, Samuel Henry, 1839-1899. 290
A handbook of comparative religion, by Rev. S. H. Kellogg ... Philadelphia, The Westminister press, 1899. viii, 179 p. 19 cm. (On cover: Westminister handbooks) [BL85.K45] 99-1701
1. Religion. 2. Christianity and other religions. I. Title. II. Title: Comparative religion, A handbook of.

KERSHNER, Frederick Doyle, 1875- 225
The religion of Christ, an interpretation, by Frederick D. Kershner... Cincinnati, The Standard publishing company [c1917] 189 p. 19 1/2 cm. [BR121.K4 1917] 17-29480
I. Title.

KERSHNER, Frederick Doyle, 1875-
The religion of Christ; an interpretation, by Frederick D. Kershner... New York, Chicago [etc.] Fleming H. Revell company [c1911] 159 p. 19 1/2 cm. 12-6249
I. Title.

KIMPEL, Benjamin Franklin. 290
The symbols of religious faith; a preface to an understanding of the nature of religion. New York, Philosophical Library [1954] 198p. 22cm. [BL48.K47] 54-11306
1. Religion. I. Title.

KING, Winston Lee, 1907- 200
Introduction to religion. [1st ed.] New York, Harper [c1954] 563p. 24cm. Includes bibliography. [BL48.K48] 53-10970
1. Religion. I. Title.

KING, Winston Lee, 1907- 200
Introduction to religion; a phenomenological approach [by] Winston L. King. New York, Harper & Row [1968] vii, 391 p. illus. 24 cm. Includes bibliographies. [BL48.K48 1968] 68-11455
1. Religion. I. Title.

KINGDON, Frank, 1894- 220
Humane religion [by] Frank Kingdon. New York, Cincinnati [etc.] The Abingdon press [c1930] 351 p. 19 cm. [BR125.K57] 30-8386
I. Title.

KIRN, George John. 201
Religion a rational demand. By Rev. G. J. Kirn ... Cleveland, O., Press of Thomas & Mattill. 1900. 230 p. 20 cm. [BL48.K5] 0-6925
1. Religion. 2. Rationalism. I. Title.

KISCH, H J.
Religion of the civilized world and Judaism, by H. J. Kisch. London, G. Routledge and sons limited; New York, E. P. Dutton & co. [1910] iii, 68 p. 20 cm. Label of Bloch publishing company, New York, mounted over American imprint. Bibliographical foot-notes. 15-14919 0.35
I. Title.

KNOWLES, Archibald Campbell, 1865- 264.
The practice of religion, a short manual of instructions and devotions ... by the Reverend Archibald Campbell Knowles ... 12th ed. With a preface by the Right Reverend Charles Chapman Grafton ... New York, E. S. Gorham, 1918. xii p., 1 l., 200 p. front., plates. 14 cm. [BX5947.K6 1918] 18-15371
I. Title.

KNOWLES, Archibald Campbell, 1865-
The practice of religion, a short manual of instructions and devotions ... by the Reverend Archibald Campbell Knowles ... 19th ed., with a preface by the Right Reverend Charles Chapman Grafton ... New York, E. S. Gorham, 1922. xiv p., 1 l., 240 p. incl. front. plates. 14 cm. [BX5948.K6 1922] 22-15680
I. Title.

KNOWLES, Archibald Campbell, 1865-
The practice of religion, a short manual of instructions and devotions ... by the Reverend Archibald Campbell Knowles ... 28th ed. With a preface by the Right Reverend Charles Chapman Grafton ... New York, E. S. Gorham, 1926. xiv p., 1 l., 256 p. incl. front. plates. 14 cm. [BX5948.K6 1926] 26-7064
I. Title.

KNOWLES, Archibald Campbell, 1865-
The practice of religion; a short manual of instructions and devotions ... by the Reverend Archibald Campbell Knowles ... 38th ed. With a preface by the Right Reverend Charles Chapman Grafton ... New York, E. S. Gorham, inc., 1930. xiv p., 1 l., 256 p. incl. front. plates. 14 cm. [BX5948.K6 1930] 30-7734
I. Title.

KNOWLES, Archibald Campbell, 1865-
The pratice of religion, a short manual of instructions and devotions ... by the Reverend Archibald Campbell Knowles ... 3d ed. With a preface by the Right Reverend the Bishop of Fond du Lac. New York, E. S. Gorham, 1911. xiv, 181 p. front., plates. 14 cm. 11-1429
I. Title.

KNOX, Ronald Arbuthnott, 1888- 201
Caliban in Grub street, by Ronald A. Knox ... New York, E. P. Dutton and co., inc. [c1930] xii p., 1 l., 221, [1] p. 20 cm. [PR6021.N6C3 1930 a] 30-20191
1. Religion. 2. Religion in literature. I. Title.

KNUDSON, Albert Cornelius, 1873- 230
Present tendencies in religious thought, by Albert C. Knudson ... New York, Cincinnati, The Abingdon press [c1924] 328 p. 20 cm. (Half-title: The Mendenhall lectures, ninth series, delivered at De Pauw university) [BR479.K5] 24-14497
1. Religion. 2. Christianity. I. Title.

KRAEMER, Hendrik, 1888- 290
Religion and the Christian faith. Philadelphia, Westminster Press [1957] 461p. 24cm. [BL48.K67 1957] 57-5016
1. Religion. 2. Christianity and other religions. I. Title.

KRING, Walter Donald. 201
Religion is the search for meaning. Boston, Starr King Press [1955] 63p. 24cm. [BL50.K7] 55-4547
1. Religion. I. Title.

LA BARRE, Weston, 1911- 200
The ghost dance; origins of religion. [1st ed.] Garden City, N.Y., Doubleday, 1970. xvi, 677 p. 24 cm. Includes bibliographical references. [BL48.L25] 71-89094 12.50
1. Religion. 2. Psychology, Religious. I. Title.

LAMBERT, Bernard. 262'.001
Ecumenism: theology and history; translated [from the French] by Lancelot C. Sheppard. London, Burns & Oates; New York, Herder & Herder [1967] x, 533 p. 24 1/2 cm. 90/- (B 67-19374) Bibliographical footnotes. [BX8.2.L2713] 67-21091
1. Originally published as Le probleme oecumenique. Paris, Editions du Centurions, 1962. 2. Christian union. I. Title.

LANIER, John Jabez.
... Religion on the thinking man. Fredericksburg, Va., J. J. Lanier [c1915] xiv, 232 p. 19 cm. (His The larger church ... vol. ii) 15-19424 1.25
I. Title.

LAWSON, Albert Gallatin, 1842- 270
The religion of Jesus, by Albert G. Lawson. Philadelphia, Boston [etc.] The Judson press [c1920] 6 p. l., 3-86 p. 19 cm. [BR121.L35] 21-1296
I. Title.

LEE, Jung Young. 291.2
Cosmic religion. New York, Philosophical Library [1973] 109 p. 23 cm. [BL48.L33] 73-82163 ISBN 0-8022-2125-4 4.50
1. Religion. I. Title.

LEIGHTON, Joseph Alexander, 1870- 230
Religion and the mind of today, by Joseph Alexander Leighton ... New York, London, D. Appleton and company, 1924. x, 372 p. 21 1/2 cm. Bibliography: p. 363-372. [BR479.L4] 24-14894
1. Religion. I. Title.

LEVI, Carlo, 1902- 290
Of fear and freedom. Translated from the Italian by Adolphe Gourevitch. New York, Farrar, Straus, 1950. xix, 135 p. 21 cm. Translation of Paura della liberta. [BL50.L413] 50-5061
1. Religion. I. Title.

LEWIS, Norman, 1903- 204
Light from God; essays on the true religious principles. [1st ed.] New York, Exposition Press [1956] 65p. illus. 21cm. [BL50.L43] 56-9560
1. Religion. I. Title.

LIGHTFOOT, Joseph Barber, bp. of Durham, 1828-1889.
Essays on the work entitled Supernatural religion; reprinted from the Contemporary review. By J. B. Lightfoot ... London and New York, Macmillan and co., 1889. 3 p. l., [vii]-ix p., 2 l., 324 p. 23 cm. Contents.--Introduction.--The silence of Eusebius.--The Iguatian epistles.--Polycarp of Smyrna.--Papias of Hierapolis. i, ii.--The later school of St. John.--The churches of Gaul.--Tatian's Diatessaron.--Discoveries illustrating the Acts of the Apostles. 10-19823
I. Cassels, Walter Richard, 1826- Supernatural religion. II. Title.

LOWRIE, Walter, 1868- 201
Religion or faith, by Walter Lowrie. Boston, Mass., Marshall Jones company [c1930] xvii, 178 p. 20 cm. [BL48.L6] 30-12767
1. Religion. I. Title.

MACCARTHY, Joseph Patrick, 1862- 201
The philosophy of religion, by Joseph P. MacCarthy ... with an introduction by Albert C. Dieffenbach. Boston, The author, 1927. viii, 180 p. 20 cm. [BL51.M15] 27-14225
1. Religion. 2. Philosophy and religion. I. Title.

MCDOWELL, William Fraser, bp. 1858- 250
In the school of Christ, by William Fraser McDowell... New York, Cincinnati, The Abingdon press [c1923] 303 p. 17 1/2 cm. [BV4010.M32 1923] 23-10358
I. Title.

MACEACHEN, Roderick Aloysius. 239
Religion; course, by Roderick MacEachen... New York, The Macmillan company, 1922. v. front., illus. 19 cm. (Lettered on cover: MacEachen's course in religion) Companion texts to Religion manual. [BX930.M3] 22-24691
I. Title.

MACEACHEN, Roderick Aloysius. 239
...Religion; first[-] manual, by Roderick MacEachen... New York, The Macmillan company, 1921- v. 19 1/2 cm. (MacEachen's course in religion) Companion text to Religion; first- course. [BX930.M32] 21-901
I. Title.

MCGEE, James Ellington.
The religion of a person, by James Ellington McGee ... Cincinnati, Jennings and Graham; New York, Eaton and Mains [c1912] 355 p. 20 1/2 cm. $1.00 12-20215
I. Title.
Contents omitted.

MACHEN, John Gresham, 1881- 227
The origin of Paul's religion ... by J. Gresham Machen ... New York, The Macmillan company, 1921. 6 p. l., 3-329 p. 22 1/2 cm. (The James Sprunt lectures delivered at Union theological seminary in Virginia) [BS2651.M3] 21-17445
I. Title.

MACKINTOSH, Charles Henry, 1885- 220
Reasonable religion [by] Charles Henry Mackintosh. 1st ed. Chicago, Mackintosh service [c1925] 99 p. port. 15 1/2 cm. Lettered on cover: What is reasonable religion? [BR125.M326] 25-22002
1. Religion. 2. Religion and science. I. Title. II. Title: What is reasonable religion?

MCMURRAY, De Witt.
Religion of a newspaper man, by De Witt McMurray. New York, Chicago [etc.] Fleming H. Revell company [c1916] 316 p. front. (port.) 21 cm. $1.50. "The contents of this book consist of religio-philosophical editorials which appeared in Sunday issues of two of America's well-known newspapers--the Dallas morning news and the Galveston daily news, also in two semi-weekly agricultural publications published by the same company."--Pref. 17-729
I. Title.

MAGEE, John Benjamin, 1917- 200
Religion and modern man; a study of the religious meaning of being human [by] John B. Magee. New York, Harper [1967] xiv, 510.p. 24cm. Bibl. [BL41.M28] 67-15791 8.00
1. Religion. I. Title.

MALINOWSKI, Bronislaw, 1884- 291
... The foundations of faith and morals; an anthropological analysis of primitive beliefs and conduct with special reference to the fundamental problems of religion and ethics ... by Bronislaw Malinowski. London, Oxford university press, H. Milford, 1936. x p., 1 l., 62 p. 23 cm. (Riddell memorial lectures. 7th ser., 1934-5) At head of title: University of Durham. "Delivered before the University of Durham at Armstrong college, Newcastle-upon-Tyne, Febrauy 1935." [GN470.M2] 37-11258
1. Religion. 2. Ethics. 3. Religion, Primitive. I. Title.

MARTIN, Alfred Wilhelm, 1862-1933. 290
Comparative religion and the religion of the future, by Alfred W. Martin ... New York, London, D. Appleton and company, 1926. 5 p. l., 121, [1] p. 20 cm. Bibliography: p. 121-[122] [BL82.M45] 26-1282
1. Religion. 2. Religions. I. Title.

MARTINEAU, James, 1805-1900. 201
The seat of authority in religion, by James Martineau ... 2d ed., rev. London and New York, Longmans, Green, and co., 1890. xi, 664 p. 22 1/2 cm. [BR121.M38] 4-4011
1. Religion. 2. Christianity. I. Title. II. Title: Authority.
Contents omitted.

MARX, Karl, 1818-1883. 201
On religion [by] Karl Marx and Friedrich Engels. Introd. by Reinhold Niebuhr. New York, Schocken Books [1964] 382 p. 21 cm. (Schocken paperbacks) "SB67." Bibliographical references included in "Notes" (p. [348]-359) [BL2775.M3983 1964] 64-15219
1. Religion. I. Engels, Friedrich, 1820-1895. II. Title.

MATHESON, George, 1842-1906.
The Bible definition of religion. New York, Chicago [etc.] F. H. Revell co. [1899] 53 p. 16 degree. Jun
I. Title.
Contents omitted.

MEHTA, Phirozshah Dorabji. 291
The heart of religion / P. D. Mehta. Tisbury [Eng.] : Compton Russell, 1976. vi, 436 p. ; 24 cm. Includes index.

Bibliography: p. [391]-401. [BL48.M37 1976] 76-364994 ISBN 0-85955-029-X : £7.50
1. Religion. 2. Religions. I. Title.

MEISS, Millard.
Painting in Florence and Siena after the Black Death; the arts, religion and society in the mid-fourteenth century. New York, Harper & Row [1964] xii, 195 p. illus. (Harper torchbooks, TB 1148) 66-38852
I. Title.

MENCKEN, Henry Louis, 1880- 201
Treatise on the gods [by] H. L. Mencken. New York, London, A. A. Knopf, 1930. ix p., 2 l., 363, [1], xii p., 1 l. 22 cm. "Bibliographical note": p. 354-363, [1] [BL48.M4] 30-8107
1. Religion. 2. Gods. I. Title.

MENCKEN, Henry Louis, 1880- 290
Treatise on the gods [by] H. L. Mencken. 2d ed.: corr. and rewritten. New York, A. A. Knopf, 1946. ix, 302, xvii p., 1 l. 22 cm. "Bibliographical note": p. 294-302. [BL48.M4 1946] 46-6976
1. Religion. 2. Gods. I. Title.

MENCKEN, Henry Louis, 1880- 290
1956
Treatise on the gods. [Rev. ed.] New York, Random [1963, c.1930] 287p. 19cm. (Vintage Bk., V-232) Bibl. 1.95 pap.,
1. Religion. 2. Gods. I. Title.

MICKLEM, Nathaniel, 1888- 200
Religion. Westport, Conn., Greenwood Press [1973] 224 p. 17 cm. Reprint of the 1948 ed., which was issued as no. 201 of The Home university library of modern knowledge. Bibliography: p. 216-220. [BL48.M48 1973] 73-168964 ISBN 0-8371-6234-3 10.00
1. Religion. 2. Religions.

MICKLEM, Nathaniel, 1888- 290
Religion. London, New York, Oxford Univ. Press, 1948. 224 p. 17 cm. (The Home university library of modern knowledge, 201) Bibliography: p. 216-220. [BL48.M48] 49-7025
1. Religion. 2. Religions. I. Title. II. Series: Home university library of modern knowledge. London, 201

MILL, John Stuart, 1806-1873.
Three essays on religion, by John Stuart Mill. New York, H. Holt and company, 1874. xi, 302 p. 21 cm. "Introductory notice" signed: Helen Taylor. [B1601.T4T2] E 16
1. Berkeley, George, bp. of Cloyne, 1685-1753. 2. Religion. I. Taylor, Helen, ed. II. Title.
Contents omitted.

MILLER, James Russell, 1840- 248
1912.
Week-day religion. By the Rev. James Russell Miller. Philadelphia, Presbyterian board of publication [1880] 315 p. 18 cm. [BV4501.M5845] 27-10779
I. Title.

MOLINARI, Gustave de, 1819- 239
1912.
... Religion, by G. de Molinari ... translated from the 2d (enl.) ed. with the author's sanction, by Walter K. Firminger ... London, S. Sonnenschein & co.; New York, Macmillan & co., 1894. xii, 200 p. 19 1/2 cm. ("Philosophy at home" series) "Press opinions": p. 196-200. [BR100.M65 1894] 1-21029
I. Firminger, Walter Kelly, 1870- tr. II. Title.

MOORE, Edward Le Roy. 201
The Robinson from Mars papers; dialogues and lectures on truth and reality. [1st ed.] New York, Exposition Press [1956- v. 21cm. [BL50.M6] 56-12375
1. Religion. I. Title.

MOORE, Justin Hartley, 1884- 242
comp.
The world beyond, passages from oriental and primitive religions, comp. and arranged by Justin Hartley Moore. New York, Thomas Y. Crowell company [c1920] 143 p. 18 cm. Bibliographical notes at end of each chapter. [BL29.M6] 20-12826
I. Title.

MULLENDORE, William. 230
The urge of the unrational in religion, by William Mullendore. Boston, Mass., The Stratford company [c1930] 4 p. l., 255 p. 21 cm. [BR125.M774] 30-20995
I. Title.

MULLER, Friedrich Max, 1823- 291
1900.
Anthropological religion / by F. Max Muller. New York : AMS Press, [1975] xxvii, 464 p. ; 18 cm. Reprint of the 1892 ed. published by Longmans, Green, London, New York, which was issued as Gifford lectures, 1891. Includes bibliographical references and index. [BL48.M76 1975] 73-18822 ISBN 0-404-11428-8 24.00
1. Religion. 2. Religions. 3. Soul. I. Title. II. Series: Gifford lectures ; 1891.

MULLER, Friedrich Max, 1823- 290
1900.
Anthropological religion; the Gifford lectures delive. ed. before the University of Glasgow in 1891, by F. Max Miller ... London and New York, Longmans, Green, and co., 1892. xxvii, 464 p. 20 cm. [BL85.M85] 2-6303
1. Religion. 2. Natural theology. I. Title.

MUNSTER, Ernest Greve. 290
A new Bible. [1st ed.] Brooklyn, G. J. Rickard [1958] 91p. 17cm. [BL50.M85] 58-10103
1. Religion. I. Title.

MUNSTER, Ernest Greve.
A new Bible. Amherst, Wisc., Amherst Press [1964?] 89 p. 18 cm. 65-108244
1. Religion. I. Title.

MURRAY, Lindley, 1745-1826. 922
The power of religion on the mind, in retirement, afflication, and at the approach of death: exemplified in the testimonies and experience of persons distinguished by their greatness, learning, or virtue ... By Lindley Murray ... From the 18th ed., improved. New York, Printed by order of the trustees of the residuary estate of Lindley Murray, M. Day's press, 1838. xii, 378 p. 19 cm. [BR1703.M8] 17-28565
1. Religion. 2. Biography. I. Title.

MYERS, Cortland, 1864- 231
How do we know? By Cortland Myers ... Philadelphia. Boston [etc.] The Judson press [1927] 4 p. l., 118 p. 21 cm. [BT1101.M93] 27-5436
I. Title.

NAGARAJA Rao$, P., 1910- 181'.4
Essays in Indian philosophy and religion [by] P. Nagaraja Rao. Bombay, Lalvani Pub. House [1971] ix, 185 p. 22 cm. Includes bibliographical references. [BL48.N23] 72-902383
1. Religion. 2. Vedanta. I. Title.
Distributed by Verry 9.00.

THE natural & the supernatural, by John Oman ... Cambridge [Eng.] The University press, 1931. xiii, 506 p. 22 cm. [BL48.O6 1931] 31-30414 201
1. Religion. 2. Philosophy and religion. 3. Reality. 4. Supernatural. 5. Knowledge, Theory of. 6. Religious—Classification. I. Oman, John Wood, 1860-1939.

NEWBOLT, William Charles Edmund,
1844-
Religion, by the Rev. W. C. E. Newbolt ... London, New York [etc.] Longmans, Green & co., 1899. 4 p. l., 301 p. 19 1/2 cm. (Half-title: The Oxford library of practical theology ...) A 21
1. Religion. I. Title.

*NEWLAND, Mary (Reed) 268.434
Religion in the home; a parents' guide to the Our life with God series for use with In Christ Jesus, gr. 3. New York, Sadlier [1968] .80 pap.,
I. Title.

NORBECK, Edward, 1915- 200
Religion in human life: anthropological views. New York, Holt, Rinehart and Winston [1974] p. (Basic anthropology units) Bibliography: p. [BL48.N67] 73-7862 ISBN 0-03-091284-9
1. Religion. I. Title.

NOVAK, Michael. 200.1
Ascent of the mountain, flight of the dove; an invitation to religious studies. [1st ed.] New York, Harper & Row [1971] xvi, 240 p. front. 22 cm. Includes bibliographical references. [BL48.N68] 70-128050 ISBN 0-06-066320-0 5.95
1. Religion. 2. Religion and sociology. I. Title.

NOVAK, Michael. 200'.1
Ascent of the mountain, flight of the dove : an invitation to religious studies / by Michael Novak. Rev. ed. San Francisco : Harper & Row, c1978. xx, 258 p. ; 21 cm. Includes index. Bibliography: p. 251-256. [BL48.N68 1978] 78-106542 ISBN 0-06-066322-7 : pbk. : 4.95
1. Religion. 2. Religion—Study and teaching. 3. Religion and sociology. I. Title.

OAKESMITH, John.
The religion of Plutarch, a pagan creed of apostolic times; an essay by John Oakesmith ... London, New York and Bombay, Longmans, Green, and co., 1902. xxviii, 229 p. 20 cm. Practically a reprint of the author's "Religion of Plutarch as expounded in his 'Ethics.'" 1901. The difference consists mainly in the translation or removal of various quotations from Greek and Latin sources which were given in full in the first edition of the book. cf. Introd. note. 3-12790
I. Title.

OMAN, John Wood, 1860-1939. 200.1
The natural & the supernatural. Freeport, N.Y., Books for Libraries Press [1972] xiii, 506 p. 23 cm. Reprint of the 1931 ed. [BL48.O6 1972] 79-39696 ISBN 0-8369-9941-X
1. Religion. 2. Philosophy and religion. 3. Reality. 4. Supernatural. 5. Knowledge, Theory of. 6. Religions—Classification. I. Title.

OMAN, John Wood, 1860-1939. 201
The natural & the supernatural, by John Oman ... New York, The Macmillan company; Cambridge, Eng., The University press, 1931. xiii, 5o6 p. 23 cm. [BL48.O6 1931 a] 31-24864
1. Religion. 2. Philosophy and religion. 3. Reality. 4. Supernatural. 5. Knowledge, Theory of. 6. Religions—Classification. I. Title.

ORCHARD, William Edwin, 1877- 225
The outlook for religion, by W. E. Orchard ... New York and London, Funk & Wagnalls company, 1917. 5 p. l., 3-271, [1] p. 22 cm. Printed in Great Britain. [BR121.O6] 17-31685
I. Title.

ORCHARD, William Edwin, 1877- 230
The present crisis in religion, by the Rev. W. E. Orchard ... London, New York [etc. Cessell and company, ltd. [1929] v p., 1 l, p. 20 cm. [BR479.O7] 29-12417
I. Title.

ORCHARD, William Edwin, 1877- 230
The present crisis in religion [by] the Rev. W. E. Orchard ... New York and London, Harper & brothers, 1929. vii p., 1 l., 281, [1] p. 21 cm. [BR479.O7 1929 a] 29-14782
I. Title.

OTTO, Rudolf, 1869-1937. 201
The idea of the holy; an inquiry into the non-rational factor in the idea of the divine and its relation to the rational. Translated by John W. Harvey. New York, Oxford University Press, 1958. xix, 232p. 21cm. (A Galaxy book, GB14) Translation of Das Heilige. Bibliographical footnotes. [BL48.O82 1958] 58-776
1. Religion. I. Title.

OTTO, Rudolf, 1869-1937. 201
The idea of the holy; an inquiry into the non-rational factor in the idea of the divine and its relation to the rational, by Rudolf Otto ... translated by John W. Harvey ... London, New York [etc.] H. Milford, Oxford university press, 1923. xv, 228 p. 22 cm. "This translation of ... 'Das heilige' has been made from the ninth German edition ..."--p. [v] [Full name: Karl Ludwig Rudolf Otto] [BL48.O82] 24-11216
1. Religion. 2. Psychology, Religious. I. Harvey, John Wilfred, tr. II. Title.

OTTO, Rudolf, 1869-1937. 201
The idea of the holy; an inquiry into the non-rational factor in the idea of the divine and its relation to the rational, by Rudolf Otto ... translated by John W. Harvey ... Revised with additions. London, Oxford university press, H. Milford [1936] xix, [1], 239, [1] p. 22 cm. (On cover: The Oxford bookshelf) "First impression, November 1923 ... sixth impression, May 1931; reprinted in The Oxford bookshelf, May 1936." "This translation of ... Das heilige has been made from the ninth German edition."--p. ix. [Full name: Karl Ludwig Rudolf Otto] [BL48.O82 1936] 38-24342
1. Religion. I. Harvey, John Wilfred, 1889- tr. II. Title. III. Title: Holy, The.

OURSLER, William Charles, 200
1913-
The road to faith. New York, Rinehart [1960] 223p. 21cm. [BL48.O86] 60-5227
1. Religion. I. Title.

OWENS, Gene, 1930- 200'.1
Confessions of a religionless Christian / Gene Owens. Nashville : Abingdon Press, [1975] 112 p. ; 20 cm. Includes bibliographical references. [BR121.2.O94] 75-14317 ISBN 0-687-09386-4 : 4.95
1. Religion. 2. Christianity—Essence, genius, nature. I. Title.

PALMER, E H 230
This thing called religion. [1st ed.] New York, Exposition Press [1952] 132 p. 23 cm. Includes bibliography. [BL48.P26] 52-9241
1. Religion. I. Title.

PARKER, Theodore, 1810-1860. 204
Views of religion. By Theodore Parker. With an introduction, by James Freeman Clarke. 5th ed. Boston, American Unitarian association, 1900. x p., 1 l., 466 p. 21 1/2 cm. "Selections from the writings of Theodore Parker."--Introd. [BX9815.P39 1900] 4-10381
1. Religion. 2. Unitarianism. I. Clarke, James Freeman, 1810-1888, ed. II. American Unitarian association. III. Title.

PARRISH, Herbert. 248
What is there left to believe? By Herbert Parrish ... New York, Holston house, Sears publishing company, inc. [c1931] 277 p. 20 cm. [BL48.P3] 31-33133
1. Religion. 2. Christianity. I. Title.

PATTON, Carl Safford, 1866- 220
Religion in the thought of today, by Carl S. Patton. New York, The Macmillan company, 1924. vi p., 2 l., 159 p. 20 cm. "The following chapters contain the substance of a course of lectures given at Berkeley, California, in the winter of 1922, on the Earl Foundation."--Pref. [BR125.P25] 24-8575
I. Title.

PEABODY, Francis Greenwood, 252.
1847-
... Religion of an educated man, by Francis Greenwood Peabody ... New York, The Macmillan company; London, Macmillan & co., 1903. 5 p. l., [3]-89 p. 20 cm. (Haverford library lectures) [BV4310.P5] 3-27912
I. Title.
Contents omitted.

PEASE, Eugene Moody. 200
Religion can be amazing, how religion can and will evolve. [1st ed.] New York, Pageant Press [1957] 83p. 21cm. [BL50.P43] 57-8309
1. Religion. I. Title.

PELIKAN, Jaroslav, 1923- 230
Fools for Christ; essays on the true, the good, and the beautiful. Philadelphia, Muhlenberg Press [1955] 172p. 20cm. [BT45.P4] 55-7766
1. Religion. 2. Worth. 3. Holiness. 4. Truth. 5. Good and evil. 6. Aesthetics. I. Title.
Contents omitted.

PELIKAN, Jaroslav Jan, 1923- 230
Fools for Christ; essays on the true, the good, and the beautiful. Philadelphia, Muhlenberg Press [1955] 172 p. 20 cm. [BT45.P4] 55-7766
1. Religion. 2. Worth. 3. Holiness. 4. Truth 5. Good and evil. 6. Aesthetics. I. Title.
Contents Omitted

PELL, Edward Leigh, 1861- 220
Our troublesome religious questions, by Edward Leigh Pell. New York, Chicago [etc.] Fleming H. Revell company [c1916] 251 p. 21 cm. [BR125.P4] 16-21244 1.25
I. Title.

PENTER, John. 200'.1
Circumstantial evidence / John Penter. 1st ed. San Francisco : Faraday Press, 1981. 144 p. ; 23 cm. Bibliography: p. 137-144. [BL48.P36] 19 81-67265 ISBN 0-939762-00-5 : 11.95
1. Religion. I. Title.
487 Noe St., San Francisco, CA 94131

PHENIX, Philip Henry, 1915- 201
Intelligible religion. New York, Harper [1954?] 189p. 21cm. [BL48] 54-13475
1. Religion. I. Title.

PHILLIPS Brooks house 204
association, Harvard university.
Religion and modern life, lectures given for the Phillips Brooks house association, Harvard university. New York, C. Scribner's sons, 1927. x, 370 p. 20 cm. [BR50.P5] 27-9193
1. Religion. I. Title.

PHILLIPS, Dorothy Berkley, 208.2
1906- ed.
The choice is always ours; an anthology on the religious way, chosen from psychological, religious, philosophical, poetical, and biographical sources, edited by Dorothy Berkley Howes Phillips, co-edited by Elizabeth Boyden Howes [and] Lucille M. Nixon. Rev. and enl. ed. New York, Harper [1960] 430 p. 24 c,. [BL48.P5 1960] 59-5222
1. Religion. 2. Mysticism. I. Title.

PIKE, John Gregory. 248
Religion and eternal life; or, Irreligion and perpetual ruin, the only alternative for mankind. By J. G. Pike ... New-York, The American tract society [1834] viii, [5]-246 p. 15 1/2 cm. [BV4501.P5] 8-25604
I. Title.

PISE, Charles Constantine, 1802-
1866.
The pleasures of religion; and other poems ... By Charles Constantine Pise, D.D. Philadelphia, E. L. Carey & A. Hart, 1833. ix, [11]-251 p. 16 cm. [PS2593.P3] 25-3140
1. Religion. 2. Cozumel Island—Hist. 3. Tabasco, Mexico—Hist. I. Title.
Contents omitted.

POTTER, Bernard. 200
Mortals and gods. [1st ed.] New York, Vantage Press [1955] 200p. illus. 23cm. [BL50.P6] 54-13132
1. Religion. I. Title.

POWYS, John Cowper, 1872- 211
The religion of a sceptic, by John Cowper Powys. New York, Dodd, Mead and company, 1925. 4 p. l., 51 p. 19 cm. [BL2775.P73] 25-7959 1.00
I. Title.

PYNE, Mable Mandeville, 1903- 200
The story of religion, written and illustrated by Mable Mandeville Pyne. Boston, Houghton Mifflin, 1954. 54 p. illus. 29 cm. [BL50.P85] 54-12232
1. Religion.

RADHAKRISHNAN, Sarvepalli, 291'.1
Pres. India, 1888-
Recovery of faith. New York, Greenwood Press, 1968 [c1955] xvii, 205 p. 20 cm. (World perspectives, v. 4) Bibliographical footnotes. [BL48.R23 1968] 68-21329
1. Religion. 2. Belief and doubt. I. Title. II. Series.

RADHAKRISHNAN, Sarvepalli, 201
Sir 1888-
Recovery of faith. [1st ed.] New York, Harper [1955] 205 p. 20 cm. (World perspectives, v. 4) [BL48.R23] 55-7219
1. Religion. 2. Belief and doubt. I. Title.

RADHAKRISHNAN, Sarvepalli, 200
Pres. India, 1888-
Religion in a changing world [by] S. Radhakrishnan. London, Allen & Unwin; New York, Humanities, 1967. 3-187 p. 21cm. Bibl. [BL55.R33] 67-85914 5.00
1. Religion. 2. Civilization. I. Title.

RANDALL, John Herman, 1871- 230
... Religion and the modern world, by John Herman Randall and John Herman Randall, jr. New York, Frederick A. Stokes company, 1929. xii, 249 p. 20 cm. ("Religion and the modern age" series) [BR479.R3] 29-10523
I. Randall, John Herman, 1899- joint author. II. Title.

RANDALL, John Herman, 1899- 200
The meaning of religion for man. New York, Harper & Row [1968] 125 p. 21 cm. (Harper torchbooks, TB1379) "Originally published in 1946 ... as part IV of Preface to philosophy: textbook ... The author has made revisions [with a new introduction] for the Torchbook edition." [BL48.R27] 70-3431 1.60
1. Religion. I. Title.

RASCHKE, Carl A. 291
Religion and the human image / Carl A. Raschke, James A. Kirk, Mark C. Taylor. Englewood Cliffs, N.J. : Prentice-Hall, c1977. xi, 274 p. ; 23 cm. Includes bibliographies and index. [BL48.R29] 76-43047 ISBN 0-13-773424-7 pbk. : 6.95
1. Religion. 2. Religions. I. Kirk, James A., joint author. II. Taylor, Mark C., 1945- joint author. III. Title.

RAUGHLEY, Leonard C 1898- 290
Must we have religion? Philadelphia, Dorrance [1948] 135 p. 20 cm. [BL48.R33] 48-9538
1. Religion. I. Title.

RAUSCHENBERG, Lina 268.6
(Andrews) Mrs. 1890-
A-visiting we will go; a world friendship unit for primary children, by Lina A. Rauschenberg ... Nashville, Cokesbury press [c1938] 80 p. 23 cm. "Issued by General board of Christian education and General board of missions, Methodist Episcopal church, South, through the Joint committee on co-operation and counsel." Includes music. "List of materials": p. 17-18. [BV1545.R3] 39-2878
I. Title. II. Title: A world friendship unit for primary children.

RAVINDRANATHA, Thakura, Sir, 201
1861-
... The religion of man ... New York, The Macmillan company, 1931. 244 p. front. (port.) 21 cm. (The Hibbert lectures for 1930) At head of title: Rabindranath Tagore. "Delivered in Oxford, at Manchester college, during the month of May 1930."--Pref. [BL25.H5 1930] [BL48.R3] 204 31-6500
1. Religion. I. Title.

RELIGION and man; 291
an introduction [by] Robert D. Baird [and others]. W. Richard Comstock, general editor. New York, Harper & Row [1971] viii, 676 p. illus. 24 cm. Includes bibliographies. [BL48.R4] 79-141175 ISBN 0-06-041337-9
1. Religion. 2. Religions. I. Baird, Robert D., 1933- II. Comstock, W. Richard, ed.

RELIGION and the psychology of Jung. Translated by G. R. Lamb. London and New York, Sheed and Ward [1957] 249p. Bibliography: p. 224-244.
I. Hostie, Raymond, 1920-

RELIGION at Michigan. . .
1857-58. 100 years of student religious activity. [Ann Arbor, 1956] 1 v.
I. Michigan. University. Office of Religious Affairs.

RELIGION in the making;
Lowell lectures, 1926. New York, Macmillan, 1926 [i. e. 1956? c1954] 160p. 20cm.
1. Religion. I. Whitehead, Alfred North, 1861-1947. II. Lowell Institute lectures, 1926.

RELIGION in the making;
Lowell lectures, 1926. New York, Macmillan, 1926 [i. e. 1956? c1954] 160p. 20cm.
1. Religion. I. Whitehead, Alfred North, 1861-1947. II. Lowell Institute lectures, 1926.

RELIGION reconsidered...
Grand Rapids, Mich., Foundation Street Baptist Church, 1957. 1v. (various pagings) 20cm. Five sermons, each with its own pagination.
I. Littlefair, Duncan Elliot, 1912-

REMENSNYDER, Junius Benjamin,
1843-
The post-apostolic age and current religious problems. By Junius B. Remensnyder ... Philadelphia, Pa., Lutheran publication society [c1909] x, 11-333 p. 19 1/2 cm. $1.25. 9-32671
I. Title.

RICHARDSON, Edward Elliott, 201
1873-
First principles of religion, by Edward Elliott Richardson ... New York [etc.] Fleming H. Revell company [1942] 281 p. 21 1/2 cm. [BL48.R45] 42-7721
1. Religion. I. Title.

ROBINSON, Ethel Blackwell.
The religion of joy; God-consciousness, or the religion of joy with God, by Ethel Blackwell Robinson, S.B., M.D. Boston, Sherman, French & company, 1911. 4 p. l., 122 p. 20 cm. $1.00. 11-26486
I. Title.

ROHRBAUGH, Lewis Guy. 201
The science of religion; an introduction, by Lewis Guy Rohrbaugh... New York, H. Holt and company [c1927] xii, 291 p. 1 illus. 21 cm. Bibliography at end of most of the chapters. [BL48.R5] 27-25322
1. Religion. I. Title.

ROSZAK, Theodore, 1933- 200
Unfinished animal : the aquarian frontier and the evolution of consciousness / Theodore Roszak. 1st ed. New York : Harper & Row, [1975] ix, 271 p. : ill. ; 22 cm. Includes bibliographical references and index. [BL48.R56 1975] 75-9333 ISBN 0-06-067016-9 : 10.00
1. Religion. 2. Evolution. I. Title.

ROSZAK, Theodore, 1933- 200
Unfinished animal : the acquarian frontier and the evolution of consciousness / Theodore Roszak. New York : Harper & Row [1977]c1975. ix, 271p. : ill. ; 20 cm. (Harper Colophon Books) Includes bibliographical references and index. [BL48.R56] ISBN 0-06-090537-9 pbk. : 3.45
1. Religion. 2. Evolution. I. Title.
L.C. card no. for original ed.: 75-9333.

SANDERS, Charles Finley, 201
1869-
The taproot of religion and its fruitage, by Charles F. Sanders ... New York, The Macmillan company, 1931. viii p., 2 l., 266 p. 19 1/2 cm. [BL48.S27] 31-23311
1. Religion. 2. Spiritual life. 3. Psychology, Religious. 4. Religion and science—1900- I. Title.

SANDMEL, Samuel. 200'.1
A little book on religion (for people who are not religious) / Samuel Sandmel. Chambersburg, Pa. : Wilson Books, c1975. xi, 146 p. ; 21 cm. [BL48.S274] 75-1831 ISBN 0-89012-002-1 : 4.95
1. Religion. 2. God. I. Title.

SAVAGE, Minot Judson, 1841-
The religion of evolution. By M. J. Savage ... Boston, Lockwood, Brooks, & company, 1876. 253 p. 18 1/2 cm. 12-38428
I. Title.

SAVAGE, Minot Judson, 1841- 230.
1918.
The passing and the permanent in religion, a plain treatment of the great essentials of religion, being a sifting from these of such things as cannot outlive the results of scientific, historical and critical study,--so making more clearly seen "the things which cannot be shaken", by Minot Judson Savage ... New York & London, G. P. Putnam's sons, 1901. 2 p. l., iii-vii, 336 p. 21 1/2 cm. [BX9841.S25] 1-25474
1. Religion. 2. Unitarianism. I. Title.

SAVARD, Wilfred, Rev. 248.8
The A.B.C. institute of the holy faith. New York, Vantage [c.1965] 73p. 21cm. 2.50 bds.,
I. Title.

SCHLEIERMACHER, Friedrich 204
Ernst Daniel, 1768-1834.
On religion: speeches to its cultured despisers. Translated by John Oman. With an introd. by Rudolf Otto. New York, Harper [1958] 287p. 21cm. (The Library of religion and culture) Harper torchbooks, TB36. [BL48.S33 1958] 58-7108
1. Religion. I. Title.

SCHLEIERMACHER, Friedrich 200
Ernst Daniel, 1768-1834.
On religion: addresses in response to its cultured critics. Translated, with introd. and notes, by Terrence N. Tice. Richmond, John Knox Press [1969] 383 p. 21 cm. (Research in theology) Translation of Uber die Religion. Bibliographical references included in "Notes" (p. [348]-373) [BL48.S33 1969] 72-82936
1. Religion. I. Tice, Terrence N., ed. II. Title.

SCHMID, Georg. 200'.7
Principles of integral science of religion / by Georg Schmid ; [translated from the German by John Wilson. [2514GC] The Hague, [Noordeinde 41] : Mouton, [1979] viii, 211 p. ; 24 cm. (Religion and reason ; v. 17) Includes indexes. Bibliography: p. [199]-206. [BL48.S368] 79-308165 ISBN 90-279-7864-6 37.75
1. Religion. 2. Religion—Study and teaching. I. Title.
Available from Mouton, Hawthorne, NY 10532

SCHMIDT, Nathaniel, 1862- 201
1939.
The coming religion, by Nathaniel Schmidt ... New York, The Macmillan company, 1930. 262 p. 20 cm. [BL48.S37] 30-23582
1. Religion. I. Title.

SCHMIDT, Roger, 1931- 200
Exploring religion / Roger Schmidt. Belmont, Calif. : Wadsworth, c1980. xvi, 393 p. : ill. ; 24 cm. Includes index. Includes bibliographies and index. [BL48.S372] 80-10978 ISBN 0-87872-244-0 : 12.95
1. Religion. I. Title.

SCHNEIDER, Herbert 200'.1
Wallace, 1892-
Civilized religion; an historical and philosophical analysis. [1st ed.] New York, Exposition Press [1972] 112 p. 22 cm. (An Exposition-university book) [BL48.S373] 79-186484 ISBN 0-682-47426-6 5.00
1. Religion. I. Title.

SEIFERT, Harvey. 200'.9
Reality and ecstasy; a religion for the 21st century. Philadelphia, Westminster Press [1974] 173 p. 19 cm. Includes bibliographical references. [BL48.S43] 74-9713 ISBN 0-664-24990-6 3.25 (pbk.).
1. Religion. I. Title.

SELLARS, Roy Wood, 1880- 225
Religion coming of age, by Roy Wood Sellars... New York, The Macmillan company, 1928. xi p., 1 l., 293 p. 20 1/2 cm. (Half-title: Philosophy for the layman series) [BR121.S482] 28-23055
1. Religion. 2. Christianity. 3. Humanism—20th cent. I. Title.

SHAIRP, John Campbell, 1819- 265.
1885.
Culture and religion in some of their relations, By J. C. Shairp... [Reprinted form the Edinburgh ed.] New York, Hurd and Houghton, 1873. 2 p. l., 631, [vii]-ix, [11]-187 p. 18 cm. [BR115.C8S3 1873] 15-22018
1. Religion. 2. Culture. I. Title.

SHAW, Charles Gray, 1871- 201
The precinct of religion in the culture of humanity, by Charles Gray Shaw ... London, S. Sonnenschein & co., lim.; New York, The Macmillan co., 1908. xiii, 279, [1] p. 22 cm. "The following work contains the substance of the lectures delivered in the Graduate school of New York university in the course entitled, Philosophy of religion."--Pref. [BL48.S5] 9-9816
1. Religion. I. Title.

SHEPARD, Sheldon, ed. 212
The Awman translations, edited by Sheldon Shepard ... Los Angeles, Calif., Wetzel publishing co., inc. [1944] 124 p. 21 cm. [BP605.S5] 45-1052
I. Title.

SHEPARDSON, George Defrees, 220
1864-
The religion of an electrical engineer, by George D. Shepardson ... New York, Chicago [etc.] Fleming H. Revell company [c1926] 186 p. 19 1/2 cm. [BR125.S449] 26-20265
I. Title.

SHINN, Larry D., 1942- 200
Two sacred worlds : experience and structure in the world's religions / Larry D. Shinn. Nashville : Abingdon, [1977] p. cm. [BL48.S516] 76-45645 ISBN 0-687-42781-9 pbk. : 6.95
1. Religion. 2. Religions. I. Title.

SHRYOCK, John Knight, 1890- 291
Desire and the universe; a study of religions, by John K.Shryock... Philadelphia, The Centaur press, 1935. 352 p. 24 cm. "General bibliography": p. 331-333; "Chapter notes and bibliographies": p. 334-343. [BL48.S53] 36-3978
1. Religion. I. Title.

SILVER, Abba Hillel, 1893- 200
Religion in a changing world, by Abba Hillel Silver ... New York, R. R. Smith, inc., 1930. 5 p. l., 204 p. 19 1/2 cm. [BL48.S55] 31-97
1. Religion. 2. Religion and science—1900- 3. Religion and sociology. I. Title.

SILVERMAN, William B 200
God help me! From kindergarten religion to the radical faith. New York, Macmillan, 1961. 294 p. 22 cm. [BL50.S55] 61-8111
1. Religion. I. Title. II. Title: From kindergarten religion to the radical faith.

SIMMEL, Georg 201
Sociology of religion. Translated from the German by Curt Rosenthal. New York, Philosophical Library [c.1959] x, 76p. 20cm. 60-2684 3.75 bds.,
1. Religion. I. Title.

SIMMEL, Georg, 1858-1918. 201
Sociology of religion. Translated from the German by Curt Rosenthal. New York, Philosophical Library [c1959] 76 p. 20 cm. Translation of Die Religion. [BL48.S573] 60-2684
1. Religion. I. Title.

SMART, Ninian, 1927- 200'.1
The phenomenon of religion [by] Ninian Smart. [New York] Herder and Herder [1973] v, 157 p. 22 cm. (Philosophy of religion series) Bibliography: p. 153-156. [BL48.S592 1973b] 72-8067 ISBN 0-07-073792-3 6.95
1. Religion. I. Title.

SMART, Ninian, 1927- 200'.1
The science of religion & the sociology of knowledge: some methodological questions. [Princeton, N.J.] Princeton University Press [1973] vii, 164 p. 21 cm. (The Virginia and Richard Stewart memorial lectures, 1971) Bibliography: p. 161-164. [BL48.S5923] 72-12115 ISBN 0-691-07191-8 8.50
1. Religion. I. Title. II. Series.

SMITH, Ethel (Sabin) 1887- 200'.1
God and other gods; essays in perspective on persisting religious problems. [1st ed.] New York, Exposition Press [1973] xiii, 185 p. 22 cm. (An Exposition-university Book) [BL48.S594] 73-154811 ISBN 0-682-47619-6 7.50
1. Religion. 2. Religions. I. Title.

SMITH, Fred Burton, 1865-
A man's religion [by] Fred B. Smith ... New York [etc.] Association press, 1913. 267 p. 19 1/2 cm. $0.75 [BV4440.S6] 13-1163
I. Title.

SMITH, Gerrit, 1797-1874.
Religion of reason. Gerrit Smith. Peterboro, N.Y., C. A. Hammond, 1864. 203 p. front. (port.) 23 1/2 cm. 5-17707
I. Title.

SMITH, John Merlin Powis, 223.26
1866-1932.
The religion of the Psalms, by J. M. Powis Smith ... Chicago, Ill., The University of Chicago press [c1922] ix, 170 p. 19 cm. "Books for the general reader": p. 158-159. [BS1430.S55] 22-5471
I. Title.

SPALDING, John Lancaster, 261
abp., 1840-1916.
Religion, agnosticism and education, by J. L. Spalding... Chicago, A. C. McClurg & co., 1902. 285 p., 1 l. 18 cm. [BR85.S55 1902] 2-16947
1. Religion. 2. Agnosticism. 3. Education. I. Title.
Contents omitted.

SPALDING, John Lancaster, abp., 1840-1916.
Religion and art, and other essays, by Rt. Rev. J. L. Spalding, bishop of Peoria. Chicago, A. C. McClurg & co., 1905. 235 p. 18 cm. 5-8659
I. Title.
Contents omitted.

STACE, Walter Terence, 1886-
Religion and the modern mind. Philadelphia, J. B. Lippincott, 1960. 320 p. (Keystone books. KB-21)
I. Title.

STENSON, Sten H. 201
Sense and nonsense in religion; an essay on the language and phenomenology of religion [by] Sten H. Stenson. Nashville, Abingdon Press [1969] 255 p. 24 cm. Bibliography: p. 237-246. [BL51.S655] 69-19737 5.95
1. Religion. 2. Philosophy and religion. I. Title.

STEVENSON, John Gilchrist.
Religion and temperament; a popular study of their relations, actual and possible, by Rev. J. G. Stevenson ... London, New York [etc.] Cassell and company, ltd., 1913. 3 p. l., 323, [1] p. 21 cm. 14-3762
I. Title.

STEWARD, George, 1803-1866. 230
Religion, the weal of the church and the need of the times. By George Steward. New-York, Lane & Scott, 1851. 256 p. 19 cm. [BR121.S85] 31-9296
1. Religion. 2. Methodism. I. Title.

STRAND, Grace Browne, comp.
Faith, hope, love, comp. by Grace Browne Strand. Chicago, A. C. McGlurg & co., 1910 3 p. l., 72 p., 1 l. 19 1/2 cm. $0.50. Title within colored ornamental border. 10-23135
I. Title.

STRENG, Frederick J. 200
Understanding religious life / Frederick J. Streng. 2d ed. Encino, Calif. : Dickenson Pub. Co., c1976. 207 p. : ill. ; 23 cm. (The Religious life of man) First ed. published in 1969 under title: Understanding religious man. Includes bibliographies and index. [BL48.S77 1976] 75-26540 ISBN 0-8221-0168-8 pbk. : 4.95
1. Religion. I. Title.

STRENG, Frederick J. 291.4
Understanding religious man [by] Frederick J. Streng. Belmont, Calif., Dickenson Pub. Co. [1969] 132 p. 23 cm. (The Religious life of man) Includes bibliographies. [BL48.S77] 70-76372
1. Religion. I. Title.

STRICKLAND, Reba Carolyn, 1904-
Religion and the state in Georgia in the eighteenth century. New York, AMS Press, 1967. 211 p. Reprint of New York, Columbia University Press, 1939 ed. Originally published as Studies in history, economics and public law, no. 460. 68-27071
I. Title.

SUMMERBELL, Martyn, 1847-
Religion in college life; college sermons and addresses, by Martyn Summerbell ... New York, Chicago [etc.] Fleming H. Revell company [c1913] 215 p. 19 1/2 cm. $1.00. 13-24474
I. Title.

SWISHER, Walter Samuel, 1882- 201
Religion and the new psychology, a psycho-analytic study of religion, by Walter Samuel Swisher, D.D. Boston, Marshall Jones company, 1920. xv, 261 p. 20 1/2 cm. Bibliography: p. 267-256. [BL53.S8] 20-12542
1. Religion. 2. Psychoanalysis. I. Title.

SZUNYOGH, Bela, 1923- 291
Crisis in religion; an introduction to the science and philosophy of religion. [1st ed.] New York, Exposition Press [1955] 135p. illus. 21cm. [BL48.S965] 55-10306
1. Religion. 2. Religion—Philosophy. I. Title.

TAGORE, Rabindranath, Sir, 201
1861-1941.
... The religion of man, being the Hibbert lectures for 1930. New York, The Macmillan company, 1931. 244 p. front. (port.) 20 1/2 cm. (Half-title: The Hibbert lectures for 1930) Delivered in Oxford, at Manchester college, during the month of May 1930."--Pref. [BL48.T26] (204) 31-6500
1. Religion. I. Title.

THIS believing world;
a simple account of the great religions of mankind. With more than seventy illustrations and animated maps drawn by the author. New York, Macmillan, 1961. 347p. illus., maps. 21cm. (Macmillan Paperbacks, MP83)
I. Browne, Lewis, 1897-1949.

THOMAS, James Bishop, 1871- 225
Religion--its prophets and false prophets, by James Bishop Thomas ... New York, The Macmillan company, 1918. xxvii p., 1 l., 256 p. 20 cm. [BR121.T5] 18-12364
I. Title.

TIELE, Cornelis Petrus, 200'.1
1830-1902.
Elements of the science of religion / by C. P. Tiele. 1st AMS ed. New York : AMS Press, 1979. 2 v. ; 18 cm. Translation of Inleiding tot de godsdienst wetenschap. Reprint of the 1897-1899 ed. published by W. Blackwood, Edinburgh, in series: The Gifford lectures, 1896 and 1898. Contents.Contents.—pt. 1. Morphological.—pt. 2. Ontological. Includes bibliographical references and index. [BL48.T4513 1979] 79-9495 ISBN 0-404-60480-3 : 49.50 (set)
1. Religion. I. Title. II. Title: The science of religion. III. Series: Gifford lectures ; 1896 [etc.]

TOFFTEEN, Olof Alfred, 1863- 232
A forgotten religion, by Olof A. Toffteen... Chicago,Ill., The Academic press, 1926. 2 p. l., 128 p. 23 cm. (On cover: Researches in Biblical archaeology, vol. III, pt. I) [BT201.T55] 26-10873
I. Title.

TOLSTOI, Lev Nikolaevich, 270
graf, 1828-1910.
What is religion? and other new articles and letters, by Lyof N. Tolstoi, tr. by V. Tchertkoff and A. C. Fifield. New York, T. Y. Crowell & company [1902] vi, 177 p. front. (port.) 19 1/2 cm. [BR125.T72] 2-16340
I. Cherthev, Vladimer Grigor'evich, 1854- II. Title.
Contents omitted.

TOYNBEE, Arnold Joseph, 1889- 290
An historian's approach to religion; based on Gifford lectures delivered in the University of Edinburgh in the years 1952 and 1953. London, New York, Oxford University Press, 1956. 316p. 23cm. [BL48.T68 1956a] 56-14616
1. Religion. 2. Civilization—Hist. I. Title.

TOYNBEE, Arnold Joseph, 1889- 290
An historian's approach to religion; based on Gifford lectures delivered in the University of Edinburgh in the years 1952 and 1953. New York, Oxford University Press, 1956. 318 p. 22 cm. [BL48.T68] 56-10187
1. Religion. 2. Civilization—History. I. Title.

TREMMEL, William C. 200'.1
Religion : what is it? / William Calloley Tremmel. New York : Holt, Rinehart and Winston, c1976. x, 277 p. ; 21 cm. Includes index. Bibliography: p. 251-264. [BL48.T7] 75-38955 ISBN 0-03-015551-7 pbk. : 4.95
1. Religion. I. Title.

THE truth about religion;
a dissertation of comparative religion and kindered [!] philosophical subjects. [1st. ed.] New York, Pythagorean Society [1957] 132p. illus. 19cm.
I. Manas, John Helen, 1890-

TUCKWELL, James Henry. 200'.1
Religion and reality; a study in the philosophy of mysticism. Port Washington, N.Y., Kennikat Press [1971] ix, 318 p. 22 cm. Reprint of the 1915 ed. Includes bibliographical references. [BL53.T77 1971] 77-118552
1. Religion. 2. Experience (Religion) 3. Mysticism. I. Title.

VAUGHAN, John Gaines, 1858- 290
Religion; a comparative study, by John Gaines Vaughan ... Cincinnati, Printed for the author by the Abingdon press, c1919. 362 p. 20 1/2 cm. $1.50. "A brief comparison of the Christian and non-Christian religions, arranged by Martin J. Van der Linden." p. [343]-360. Bibliography: p. 361-362. [BL80.V3] 19-8831
I. Van der Linden, Martin J. II. Title.

VEIBY, John. 204
Jingo, by John Veiby. South Bend, Ind. [c1927] 157 p. 18 1/2 cm. "The object of this book is to create interest in a national religion."--Introd. [BL50.V4] 27-23929
I. Title.

VROOMAN, Hiram.
The federation of religions, by Rev. Hiram Vrooman ... Philadelphia and London, The Nunc licet press, 1903. 138 p. 19 1/2 cm. Library of Congress, no. 3-31498
I. Title.

VROOMAN, Hiram. 230.
Religion rationalized, intended as an introduction to the writings of Emanual Swedenborg, by Hiram Vrooman. Chicago, Saul brothers, 1918. 3 p. l., [9]-188 p. 19 1/2 cm. $1.00 [BX8721.V8] 18-15270
I. Title.

WALLACE, Anthony F. C., 1923- 201
Religion; an anthropological view, by Anthony F. C. Wallace. New York, Random House [1966] xv, 300 p. map. 22 cm. Bibliography: p. 271-290. [BL48.W185] 66-15811
1. Religion. I. Title.

WALSH, James Joseph, 1865- 265.
Religion and health, by James J. Walsh ... Boston, Little, Brown, and company, 1920. 4 p. l., 341 p. 21 cm. [BR115.H4W3] 20-21211
I. Title.

WALTER, William Wilfred, 289.
1869-
The allness of good, by William W. Walter. Aurora, Ill., W. W. Walter [c1924] 63 p. 15 cm. [BX6947.W25] 25-4995
I. Title.

WARD, Harry Frederick, 1873- 230
The opportunity for religion in the present world situation, by Harry F. Ward. New York, The Womans press, 1919. 66 p. 19 1/2 cm. [BR479.W3] 19-16098
I. Title.

WATERMAN, Leroy, 1875- 261
Religion faces the world crisis, a study of the religious aspects and motivations of civilization, by Leroy Waterman ... Ann Arbor, G. Wahr, 1943. x, [2], 206 p. 21 1/2 cm. [BL55.W3] 43-2081
1. Religion. 2. Civilization. 3. Ethics. I. Title.

WATERS, Nacy McGee, 1866-
A young man's religion and his father's faith, by N. McGee Waters. New York, T. Y. Crowell & co. [1905] 4 p. l., 289 p. 18 1/2 cm. 5-29084
I. Title.

WATES, George Frederick. 270
The religion of wise men, by George Frederick Wates ... New York, George H. Doran company, 1924. 127, [1] p. 19 cm. Printed in Great Britain. [BR125.W32] 24-17720
I. Title.

WELLS, Charles Arthur, 1897- 290
Journey into light; a study of the long search for truth in a world darkened by dogma, and an examination of first century Christianity as the only solution for the moral dilemmas of the nuclear age. With illus. by the author. New York, Between the Lines Press [1958] 142 p. illus. 23 cm. [BL50.W36] 58-36372
1. Religion. 2. Dogma. I. Title.

WHITEHEAD, Alfred North, 1861-
Religion in the making: Lowell, lectures, 1926, by Alfred North Whitehead ... New York, The Macmillan company, 1926. 100 p. 19 1/2 cm. 26-15643
1. Religion. I. Lowell institute lectures, 1926. II. Title.

WHITEHEAD, Alfred North, 1861-1947.
Religion in the making; Lowell lectures, 1926. New York, Macmillan, 1926 [i.e. 1956? c1954] 160 p. 20 cm.
1. Religion. I. Lowell Institute lectures, 1926. II. Title.

WHITEHEAD, Alfred North, 1861-1947. 201
Religion in the making. New York, Meridian Books [1960, c1954] 154 p. 19 cm. (Living age books, LA 28) "Four lectures ... delivered in King's Chapel, Boston ... February, 1926." [BL48.W35 1960] 60-6736
1. Religion. I. Title.

WHITTAKER, Thomas, 1856-1935. 291
Priests, philosophers and prophets; a dissertation on revealed religion. Port Washington, N.Y., Kennikat Press [1970] 251 p. 22 cm. Reprint of the 1911 ed. Bibliographical footnotes. [BL48.W4 1970] 77-102589
1. Religion. 2. Christianity and other religions. I. Title.

WHYTE, Alexander, 1837-
The four temperaments, by Alexander Whyte, D.D. London, Hodder and Stoughton; New York, Dodd, Mead and company, 1895. 5 p. l., 3-101, [1] p. 17 1/2 cm. (Half-title: Little books on religion; ed. by W. R. Nicoli) 8-17114
I. Title.

WIEMAN, Henry Nelson, 1884- 201
The wrestle of religion with truth, by Henry Nelson Wieman ... New York, The Macmillan company, 1927. vii p., 2 l., 256 p. 22 1/2 cm. [BL48.W48] 27-19143
1. Religion. I. Title.

WILSON, John, 1928- 200
Religion. London, Heinemann Educational, [1972, i.e 1973] viii, 119 p. 20 cm. (Concept books, 14) Imprint covered by label: Distributed in the USA by Humanities Press, New York. Bibliography: p. 117. [BL48.W49] 73-161650 ISBN 0-435-46194-X 2.00 (pbk.)
1. Religion.

WILSON, John Francis. 200
Religion : a preface / John Francis Wilson. Englewood Cliffs, N.J. : Prentice-Hall, c1982. xiii, 209 p. : ill. ; 23 cm. Includes bibliographical references and index. [BL48.W494] 19 81-15316 ISBN 0-13-773192-2 pbk. : 9.95
1. Religion. 2. Religions. I. Title.

WINANS, Ross, 1796-1877. 211
Extracts from One religion: many creeds. By Ross Winans. Baltimore, 1871. 1 p. l., 59 p. 22 cm. "Response to an Unitarian clergyman": p. [47]-59. [BL48.W52] 36-2827
1. Religion. I. Title. II. Title: One religion: many creeds. Extracts from.

WINANS, Ross, 1796-1877. 211
One religion: many creeds. By Ross Winans ... Baltimore, J. P. Des Forges, 1870. x, 343, 127 p. 23 1/2 cm. "List of books consulted": p. [121]-122 at end. [BL48.W5 1870] 30-12951
1. Religion. I. Title.

WINANS, Ross, 1796-1877. 211
One religion: many creeds. By Ross Winans ... 2d ed. Baltimore, J. P. Des Forges, 1870. x, 343, 127 p. 23 1/2 cm. "List of books consulted": p. [121]-122 at end. [BL48.W5 1870a] 30-12952
1. Religion. I. Title.

WINANS, Ross, 1796-1877.
One religion: many creeds, by Ross Winans ... 3d ed., with an introduction by Rev. Charles Voysey ... New York and London, G. P. Putnam's sons, 1903. xxiv p., 1 l., 452 p. front. (port.) 22 1/2 cm. "List of books consulted": p. 451-452. 3-25603
I. Title.

WISEMAN, Adam John. 236.
The first religion handed down by the wise men who were chosen of God to worship God and believed God when he said, "Behold, the man is become as one of us" ... by A. J. Wiseman. Detroit [Wolverine printing co.] 1920. 61 p. incl. front. (port.) 20 cm. [BR126.W77 1920] 20-13338
I. Title.

WISEMAN, Adam John. 236.
The first religion handed down by the wise men who were chosen of God to worship God and believed God when he said, "Behold, the man is become as one of us" ... by A. J. Wiseman. Detroit [Wolverine printing co.] 1920. 61 p. incl. front. (port.) 20 cm. [BR126.W77 1920] 20-13338
I. Title.

WISHART, Alfred Wesley.
Primary facts in religious thought; seven essays dealing in a simple and practical manner with the nature, expressions, and relations of religion, by Alfred Wesley Wishart ... Chicago, The University of Chicago press, 1905. vii, 122 p. 19 1/2 cm. 5-37166
I. Title.

WOELFKIN, Cornelius, 1859-1928. 252.
Religion, thirteen sermons by Cornelius Woelfkin; edited by Robert A. Ashworth, with an introduction by Harry Emerson Fosdick. Garden City, N.Y., Doubleday, Doran & company, inc., 1928. xiii p., 1 l., 221 p. 19 1/2 cm. [BX6333.W65R4] 28-28970
I. Ashworth, Robert Archibald, 1871- ed. II. Title.

WOMEN, Parley Paul
A valid religion for the times; a study of the central truths of spiritual religion. By Parley P. Womer ... with a foreword by Washington Gladden. New York, Broadway publishing company, 1910. 2 p. l., ii, iii p., 1 l., 180 p. 20 cm. 10-10987
I. Title.

WOOD, Eugene Halsey.
Three new concepts; religion and authority: the correct concepts, also, a hitherto unnamed mental faculty, by E. H. Wood ... Chicago, R. E. Wood, 1901. 2 p. l., x p., 1 l., 40 p. 17 1/2 cm. 1-25488
1. Religion. 2. Authority. I. Title. II. Title: Religion and authority.

WOODS, James Haughton, 1864- 201
The value of religious facts; a study of some aspects of the science of religion, by James Haughton Woods ... New York, E. P. Dutton & company, 1899. v, 165 p. 18 1/2 cm. [BL48.W7] 99-2185
1. Religion. I. Title.

WOOLSEY, Theodore Dwight, 1801-1889. 252.
The religion of the present, and of the future; sermons preached chiefly at Yale college, by Theodore D. Woolsey. New ed. New York, C. Scribner's sons, 1887. ix, 9-394 p. front. (port.) 21 cm. [BV4310.W6 1887] 23-16510
I. Title.

WORCESTER, Elwood, 1863- 225
Religion and life, by Elwood Worcester ... New York and London, Harper & brothers, 1914. 5 p. l., 3-263, [1] p. 21 cm. $1.25 [BR121.W66] 14-3984
I. Title.

YINGER, John Milton. 200
The scientific study of religion [by] J. Milton Yinger. [New York] Macmillan [1970] x, 593 p. illus. 24 cm. Bibliography: p. 536-576. [BL48.Y46 1970] 75-95188
1. Religion. I. Title.

YOGANANDA, swami. 211
The science of religion, [by] Swami Yogananda ... Swami Dhirananda, M.A., associate. 2d ed. Boston, Sat-Sanga [c1924] xv, 107 p. front. (port.) 18 1/2 cm. "First edition published in India." [BL48.Y5 1924] 24-29431
1. Religion. I. Dhirananda, swami, joint author. II. Title.

YOGANANDA, paramhansa. 211
The science of religion [by] Swami Yogananda ... [and] Swami Dhirananda ... 2d ed. Boston, Sat-sanga [1924] xv, 107 p. front. (port.) 18 1/2 cm. "First edition published in India." [BL48.Y5 1924] 24-29431
1. Religion. I. Dhirananda, swami, joint author. II. Self-realization fellowship. III. Title.

YOUNGHUSBAND, Francis Edward, Sir, 1863-
Mutual influence; a re-view of religion, by Sir Francis Younghusband. New York, Duffield & co., 1915. xiv, 144 p. 21 cm. A 16
1. Religion. I. Title.

ZUEBLIN, Charles, 1866-1924. 239
The religion of a democrat, by Charles Zueblin ... New York, B. W. Huebach, 1908. 192 p. 19 1/2 cm. Contents.Temperament and personality.--The coustraint of orthodoxy.--The decay of authority.--Religion and the church.--Religion and the state.-- Impersonal immortality. [BR121.Z9] 8-12540
I. Title.

ZWEMER, Samuel Marinus, 1867- 290
The origin of religion, based on the Smyth lectures delivered at Columbia theological seminary, Decatur, Georgia, 1935, by Samuel M. Zwemer ... Nashville, Tenn., Cokesbury press [c1935] 256 p. 19 1/2 cm. "Classified select bibliography": p. [239]-248. [BL430.Z75] 35-20701
1. Religion. 2. Religion, Primitive. 3. Revelation. I. Title.

Religion—20th century.

ANDREWS, George Arthur, 1870-
Efficient religion, by George Arthur Andrews ... New York, Hodder & Stoughton, George H. Doran company [c1912] 178 p. 20 1/2 cm. $0.75 12-27815
I. Title.

HARRIS, Theodore, 1828-
A banker's views on religious and other important subjects, by Theodore Harris ... [Cincinnati, O., Press of C. J. Krehbiel & co., c1908] xxiv, 329 p. front. (port.) 22 cm. 8-12826
I. Title.

RASCHKE, Carl A. 291
The interruption of eternity : modern gnosticism and the origins of the new religious consciousness / Carl A. Raschke. Chicago : Nelson-Hall, c1980. xi, 271 p. ; 23 cm. Includes bibliographical references and index. [BL98.R37] 79-16460 ISBN 0-88229-374-5 : 18.95
1. Religion—20th century. I. Title.

THE religion of Christ in the twentieth century ... New York and London, G. P. Putnam's sons, 1906. vii, 197 p. 19 cm. (On cover: Crown theological library) 6-2998

RESPOND. 268'.4
Valley Forge, PA : Judson Press.
Vol. 5, Resources for Senior Highs in the church, c1977 and edited by Robert Howard, is available for 5.95 (pbk.) ISBN 0-8170-0767-9. L.C. card no.: 77-159050.

Religion — 20th century — Addresses, essays, lectures.

MCCORMICK, Scott 200.9
Religion in a changing world [by] Scott McCormick, Jr. [and others] Washington, Pa., Washington and Jefferson College, 1965. 69 p. 23 cm. (Topic: a journal of the liberal arts, 10) Contents. -- Man and morality, by S. McCormick, Jr. -- Martin Ruber and the life of dialogue, by P. L. Urban, Jr. -- The Dead Sea Scrolls and the baptism of John, by J. R. Hookey. -- The religious interpretation of disaster, by R. R. Dynes and D. Yutzy. -- The faith of the faculty, by R. Rankin. -- A laymen's viewpoint; crisis in the church, by A. N. Farley. Bibliographical footnotes. [AS30.T6] 66-6940
1. Religion — 20th cent. — Addresses, essays, lectures. I. Title. II. Series. III. Series: Topic 10

ROWE, Gilbert Theodore, 1875- 211
Reality in religion, by Gilbert T. Rowe ... Nashville, Tenn., Cokesbury press, 1927. 320 p. 20 cm. (The Quillian lectures for 1927) [BL48.R6] 27-19789
I. Title.

SHANNON, Frederick Franklin, 1877- 252
Doors of God, and other addresses, by Frederick F. Shannon ... New York, Chicago [etc.] Fleming H. Revell company [c1929] 152 p. 19 1/2 cm. [BV4253.S515] 29-24206
I. Title.

SIMMONS, Henry Martyn, 1841-1905. 261
New tables of stone, and other essays, by Henry M. Simmons. Boston, James H. West company [c1904] 4 p. l., [3]-328 p. 20 1/2 cm. [BR85.S46] 4-28226
I. Title.

Religion—Addresses, essays, lectures.

ADLER, Felix, 1851-1933. 200
Creed and deed: a series of discourses. New York, Arno Press, 1972 [c1877] iv, 243 p. 22 cm. (Religion in America, series II) Contents.Contents.—Immortality.—Religion.—The new ideal.—The priest of the ideal.—The form of the new ideal.—The religious conservatism of women.—Our consolations.—Spinoza.—The founder of Christianity.—The anniversary discourse. Appendix: The evolution of Hebrew religion.—Reformed Judaism, I, II, III. [BL50.A33 1972] 76-38430 ISBN 0-405-04051-2
1. Religion—Addresses, essays, lectures. 2. Ethics—Addresses, essays, lectures. 3. Ethical culture movement—Addresses, essays, lectures. I. Title.

ANSTRUTHER, William, Sir, d.1711. 201
Essays, moral and divine. With a pref. for the Garland ed. by Arthur Freeman. New York, Garland Pub., 1973. 5, 238 p. 23 cm. (The English stage: attack and defense, 1577-1730) Reprint of the 1701 ed. printed by G. Mosman, Edinburgh. [BL50.A697 1973] 74-170474 ISBN 0-8240-0623-2 22.00 ea.
1. Religion—Addresses, essays, lectures. I. Title. II. Series.
Part of a 50 volume series selling for 1050.00 set.

ANTHONY, Alfred Williams, 1860- ed.
New wine skins, present-day problems; lectures delivered before the Maine ministers' institute at Cobb divinity school, Lewiston, Me., September 3-8, 1900. Boston, Mass., The Morning star publishing house, 1901. x, p., 2 1., [15]-302 p. 20 cm. Preface signed: Alfred Williams Anthony. 9-3367
I. Title.
Contents omitted.

BALDWIN-SLOCUM lectures.
Chicago, A. C. McClurg & co., [etc., etc.] 1887- v. 18-21 cm. Delivered under the auspieces of the Hobart Guild of the University of Michigan. The place of publication and publishers vary. 1886/87. Coxe, A. C. Institutes of Christian history. 1887. (Baldwin lecture) 1887/88. Clark, W. Witnesses to Christ. 1888 (Baldwin lecture) 1888/89. Gray G. Z. The church's certain faith. 1890. (Baldwin lecture) 1889/90. Thompson, H. M. The world and the man. 1890. (Baldwin lecture) 1890/91. Garrett, A. C. The philosophy of the incarnation. 1891. (Baldwin lecture) 1891/92. Fulton, J. The Chalcedonian decree. 1892. (Slocum lecture) 1892/93. 1893/94. Holland, R. A. The commonwealth of man. 1905. (Slocum lecture) 1894/95. Rulison, N.S. A study in conscience. [1901] (Baldwin lecture) 1896/97. Hall, A. C. A., Christ's temptation and ours. 1897. (Baldwin lecture) 1897/98. Doane, W. C. The manifestations of the risen Jesus ... 1898. (Slocum lecture) 1898/99. Prall, W. The state and the church. [1900] (Baldwin lecture) 1899. Clark. The Paraclete ... 1900. (Slocum lecture) 1900/1901. Brewster, C. B. Aspects of revelation. 1901. (Baldwin lecture) 1901/1902. Du Moulin, J. P. The eternal law. 1903. (Slocum lecture) 1902/1903. Baldwin lectures for 1902-1903. Delivered under the direction of the Harris memorial trust. [1903?] CA 6

BASILIUS, Harold A ed. 204
Contemporary problems in religion. Detroit, Wayne University Press, 1956. viii, 128p. port. 21cm. (The Leo M. Franklin lectures in human relations, 1953-54) 'References': p. 123-126. [BL25.B3] 56-7842
1. Religion—Addresses, essays, lectures. I. Title. II. Series.

BEECHER, Henry Ward, 1813-1887. 252.058
A summer in England with Henry Ward Beecher; giving the addresses, lectures, and sermons delivered by him in Great Britain during the summer of 1886. Together with an account of the tour, expressions of public opinion, etc., edited by James B. Pond ... New York, Fords, Howard, & Hulbert, 1887. 2 p. l., [iii]-vi, [3]-125, 100 p., 1 l., 118, 208 p. front. (port.) facsim. (7 pl. on 41.) 19 cm. Contents.Account of the trip, by J.B. Pond.--Addresses.--Lectures.--Sermons and prayers. [BX7200.R3A4 1886] 35-33496
1. Religion—Addresses, essays, lectures. 2. Congregational churches—Sermons. 3. Sermons, American. 4. Gt. Brit.—Descr. & trav. I. Pond, James Burton, 1838-1903, ed. II. Title.

BELL, Bernard Iddings, 1886- 204
Perface to religion [by] Bernard Iddings Bell ... New York, London, Harper & brothers, 1935. xii, 196 p. 20 cm. (The Lyman Coleman foundation lectures delivered at Lafayette college in 1935) "First edition." [BL27.B38] 35-4860
1. Religion—Addresses, essays, lectures. 2. Protestant Episcopal church in the U. S. A.—Addresses, essays, lectures. I. Title.

BELL, Bernard Iddings, 1886- 204
Unfashionable convictions, by Bernard Iddings Bell ... New York and London, Harper & brothers, 1931. xviii p., 1 l., 190 p. 20 cm. "First edition." [BL27.B4] 31-82250
1. Religion—Addresses, essays, lectures. I. Title.

BELL, Hermon Fiske, 1880- 208.2
Current problems in religion. New York, Philosophical Library [1956] viii, 648p. 22cm. Includes bibliographical references. [BL27.B44] 56-14029
1. Religion—Addresses, essays, lectures. 2. Religious literature (Selections: Extracts, etc.) I. Title.

BELONGING and alienation : 201
religious foundations for the human future / edited by Philip Hefner and W. Widick Schroeder. Chicago : Center for the Scientific Study of Religion, c1976. vii, 248 p. ; 23 cm. (Studies in religion and society) Includes bibliographical references. [BL50.B39] 75-30254 ISBN 0-913348-07-4 : 10.95 ISBN 0-913348-08-2 pbk. :
1. Religion—Addresses, essays, lectures. 2. Sociology, Christian—United States—Addresses, essays, lectures. I. Hefner, Philip J. II. Schroeder, W. Widick. III. Series.

BERRIGAN, Daniel. 200
The raft is not the shore : conversations toward a Buddhist/Christian awareness / Daniel Berrigan, Thich Nhat Hanh. Boston : Beacon Press, [1975] 139 p., [3] leaf of plates : ill. ; 21 cm. (Beacon paperback ; 523) [BL50.B46] 75-5287 ISBN 0-8070-1124-X : 7.95. ISBN 0-8070-1125-8 pbk. : 3.45
1. Religion—Addresses, essays, lectures. I. Nhat Hanh, Thich, joint author. II. Title.

BRANDON, Samuel George Frederick. 291
Religion in ancient history: studies in ideas, men, and events [by] S. G. F. Brandon. New York, Scribner [1969] xiv, 412 p. illus. 25 cm. Bibliography: p. 387-396. [BL27.B7] 73-82691 12.50
1. Religion—Addresses, essays, lectures. I. Title.

BRIDGMAN, Howard Allen, 1860-
Real religion; friendly talks to the average man on clean and useful living, by Howard Allen Bridgman ... Boston, New York [etc.] The Pilgrim press [c1910] ix, 184 p. 19 1/2 cm. $0.75. 10-23349
I. Title.

CHADWICK, John White, 1840-1904. 252.08
The faith of reason. A series of discourses on the leading topics of religion. By John W. Chadwick ... Boston, Roberts brothers, 1880. 2 p. l., [7]-254 p. 18 cm. "Discourses preached ... in the months of January and February, 1879."--Pref. Contents.-Introductory discourses: Agnostic religion. The nature of religion--The faith of reason: Concerning God. Concerning immortality. Concerning prayer. Concerning mortals. [BX9843.C35F3 1880] 32-28856
1. Religion—Addresses, essays, lectures. 2. Sermons, American. I. Title.

CHURCH, Richard William, 1815-1890.
Christianity and civilisation; five lectures delivered at St. Paul's cathedral, London, by the late R. W. Church ... New York, The Macmillan company, 1914. v. p., 1 l., 143 p. 19 cm. (On cover: The Macmillan standard library) A 15
1. Religion—Addresses, essays, lectures. 2. Christianity. I. Title.

COBBE, Frances Power, 1822-1904.
Darwinism in morals, and other essays. Reprinted from the Theological and Fortnightly reviews. Fraser's and Macmillan's magazines, and the Manchester friend. By Frances Power Cobbe. Boston, G. H. Ellis, 1883. 422 p. 20 cm. First published in London, 1872. A 14
1. Religion—Addresses, essays, lectures. I. Title.
Contents omitted.

CONTEMPORARY problems in religion. 208
Harold Albert Basilius, editor. Freeport, N.Y., Books for Libraries Press [1970, c1956] viii, 128 p. port. 23 cm. (Essay index reprint series) Includes bibliographical references. [BL25.C6 1970] 78-93315 ISBN 8-369-15453-
1. Religion—Addresses, essays, lectures. I. Basilius, Harold Albert, ed.

CRANE, Frank, 1861-
Lame and lovely; essays on religion for modern minds, by Frank Crane ... Chicago, Forbes & company, 1912. 2 p. l., 7-215 p. 20 cm. 12-18337 1.00
I. Title.

CUNNINGHAM, William, 1849- 261
The increase of true religion; addresses to the clergy and church workers of the archdeaconry of Ely, by W. Cunningham ... Cambridge, The University press, 1917. viii, 50 p. 18 cm. "Books and papers, chiefly on religious subjects, and sermons by Dr. Cunningham": p. [43]-50. [BR123.C8] 17-31091
I. Title.

DAWSON, Christopher Henry, 1889- 200
Enquiries into religion and culture, by Christopher Dawson. Freeport, N.Y., Books for Libraries Press [1968] xi, 347 p. 22 cm. (Essay index reprint series) Reprint of the 1933 ed. Bibliographical footnotes. [BL55.D27 1968] 68-29200
1. Religion—Addresses, essays, lectures. 2. Civilization—Addresses, essays, lectures. I. Title.

DAWSON, Christopher Henry, 1889- 204
Enquiries into religion and culture, by Christopher Dawson ... New York, Sheed & Ward, 1933. xi, 347 p. fold. tab. 23 cm. Essays, most of which are reprinted from various sources. cf. Introd. [BL55.D27] 33-22277
1. Religion—Addresses, essays, lectures. 2. Civilization—Addresses, essays, lectures. I. Title.
Contents omitted.

DIMOCK, Marshall Edward, 1903- 208.1
Creative religion, as seen by a social scientist. Boston, Beacon Press [1963] viii, 133 p. 21 cm. Bibliography: p. 125-133. [BL50.D47] 63-18731
1. Religion—Addresses, essays, lectures. I. Title.

DOLE, Charles Fletcher, 1845-1927. 225
The theology of civilization, by Charles F. Dole ... New York, Boston, T. Y. Crowell & company [c1899] 3 p. l., v-xxiv, 256 p. 18 cm. [BR121.D622] 99-5391
1. Religion—Addresses, essays, lectures. 2. Civilization, Christian. I. Title.

DUMONT, Henry.
The average man, by Henry Dumont ... Chicago, M. B. Haver [c1911] 2 p. l., [9]-52 p. 20 cm. "This little work is not presumed to be an exhaustive treatise upon any subject. It is simply intended to present a slightly different viewpoint from that of the average man upon the subject, mainly, of religion." 11-649 0.50
I. Title.

DURKEE, James Stanley, 1866- 252.058
The pull of the invisible, and other addresses, by J. Stanley Durkee ... New York, Chicago [etc.] Fleming H. Revell company [c1931] 197 p. 20 cm. "Messages given to radio audience during the summer of 1930."--Pref. [BX7233.D77P8] 31-8700
I. Title.

DURKHEIM, Emile, 1858-1917. 200
Durkheim on religion : a selection of readings with bibliographies / [compiled by] W. S. F. Pickering ; new translations by Jacqueline Redding and W. S. F. Pickering. London ; Boston : Routledge & K. Paul, 1975. x, 376 p. ; 23 cm. Includes bibliographies and indexes. [BL50.D85 1975] 75-325445 ISBN 0-7100-8108-1 : 21.75
1. Religion—Addresses, essays, lectures. I. Pickering, W. S. F. II. Title.

EGGLESTON, Margaret (White) Mrs., 1878- 252
Seventy-five stories for the worship hour, by Margaret White Eggleston ... Garden City, N. Y., Doubleday, Doran & company, inc., 1929. xviii p., 1 l., 155 p. 19 1/2 cm. [BV4315.E4] 29-21159
I. Title.

FAITH of the free, 204
by Van Meter Ames, William Clayton Bower, Margueritte Harmon Bro [and others] ... Edited by Winfred Ernest Garrison. Chicago, New York, Willett, Clark & company. 1940. 276 p. 21 cm. "The immediate occasion for the writing and publication of this book is the completion, in October 1940, of the forty-year ministry of Edward Scribner Ames with the University church of Disciples of Christ, Chicago."--Introd. [BR50.F36] 40-35158
1. Religion—Addresses, essays, lectures. 2. Ames, Edward Scribner, 1870- I. Garrison, Winfred Ernest, 1874- ed.
Contents omitted.

FREE religious association, Boston.
Freedom and fellowship in religion. A collection of essays and addresses, edited by a committee of the Free religious association. Boston, Roberts brothers, 1875. 2 p. l., 424 p. 18 cm. [BR21.F85] 38-20490
1. Religion—Addresses, essays, lectures. 2. Unitarianism—Addresses, essays, lectures. I. Title.
Contents omitted.

FRIEDER, Emma. 291
Essays in religion. [1st ed.] New York, Exposition Press [1968] 152 p. 22 cm. (An Exposition-testament book) Bibliography: p. [147]-152. [BL50.F73] 68-24888 5.00
1. Religion—Addresses, essays, lectures. I. Title.

FRIEDER, Emma. 291
Essays in religion. 2d rev. ed. New York, Hurst Pub. Co. [1971] 152 p. 22 cm. Bibliography: p. [147]-152. [BL50.F73 1971] 77-26292 5.00
1. Religion—Addresses, essays, lectures. I. Title.

FRIEDMAN, Maurice S. 200
Searching in the syntax of things; experiments in the study of religion. Essays by Maurice Friedman, T. Patrick Burke [and] Samuel Laeuchli. With an introd. by Franklin H. Littell. Philadelphia, Fortress Press [1972] xv, 144 p. 23 cm. [BL50.F75] 70-171494 ISBN 0-8006-0103-3 3.75
1. Religion—Addresses, essays, lectures. I. Burke, Thomas Patrick, 1934- II. Laeuchli, Samuel. III. Title.

GALLAHER, James, 1792-1853. 204
The western sketch-book. By James Gallaher. Boston, Crocker and Brewster; New York, M. W. Dodd; [etc., etc.] 1850. iv, [5]-408 p. 20 cm. "The articles ... are mostly on religious subjects."--Pref. [PS1729.G7W5 1850] [BR82.G3 1850] A 15
1. Religion—Addresses, essays, lectures. I. Title.

GALLAHER, James, 1792-1853. 204
The western sketch-book. By James Gallaher. 3d ed. Boston, Crocker and Brewster; New York, M. W. Dodd; [etc., etc.] 1852. iv, [5]-408 p. 20 cm. "The articles ... are mostly on religious subjects."--Pref. [BR85.G3 1852] 24-19063
1. Religion—Addresses, essays, lectures. I. Title.

GEACH, Peter Thomas. 208
God and the soul, by Peter Geach. New York, Schocken Books [1969] xxi, 138 p. 23 cm. (Studies in ethics and the philosophy of religion) [BL50.G36] 69-17835 4.50
1. Religion—Addresses, essays, lectures. I. Title.

GILKEY, Charles Whitney, 1882- 220
Present-day dilemmas in religion, by Charles W. Gilkey ... Nashville, Tenn., Cokesbury press, 1928. xi, 180 p. 19 cm. (Half-title: The Cole lectures for 1927 delivered before Vanderbilt university) [BR125.G494] 28-8828
I. Title.

GOUWENS, Teunis Earl, 1886- 243
The rock that is higher, and other addresses, by Teunis E. Gouwens ... New York, Chicago [etc.] Fleming H. Revell company [c1922] 160 p. 20 cm. [BX9178.G6R6] 22-5232
I. Title.

GRAMMER, Carl Eckhardt, 1858- 225
Things that remain ... by Carl E. Grammer ... New York, The Macmillan company, 1929. 219 p. 21 cm. (The Bohlen lectures, 1928) "The special task that I have taken upon myself here is to point out some of the truths of Christianity which show no signs of decomposition under modern analysis."--Introd. [BR121.G673] 29-21157
I. Title.

HAMLIN, Benjamin Baird.
The voice out of the cloud, and other discourses. Harrisburg, Pa., The Evangelical press [1899] 3 p. l., 499 p. port. 8°. 0-1812
I. Title.

HEBARD, John J. 204
The philosophy of an opinion, by John J. Hebard. Denver, Col., App & Stott, 1890. 99 p. front. (port.) 20 cm. [BL50.H4] 30-11317
1. Religion—Addresses, essays, lectures. I. Title.

HEILIG, Matthias R. 200
Discussions on the Styx [by] Matthias R. Heilig. New York, Philosophical Library [1969] 118 p. 23 cm. [BL50.H46] 69-20333 4.50
1. Religion—Addresses, essays, lectures. I. Title.

*HILLIS, Don W. 248.83
When God calls the signals: the will of God and how to find it. Foreword by Jack Wyrtzen. Chicago, Moody [c.1965] 63p. (Compack bk. no. 54) .29, pap.,
I. Title.

HUTTON, Richard Holt, 1826-1897. 261
Aspects of religious and scientific thought, by the late Richard Holt Hutton; selected from the Spectator and edited by his niece, Elizabeth M. Roscoe. London, Macmillan and co., limited; New York, The Macmillan company, 1899. xi, 415 p. front. (port.) 19 cm. [BR85.H8] 38-83873
1. Religion—Addresses, essays, lectures. I. Roscoe, Elizabeth Mary, tr. II. Title.

INGE, William Ralph, 1860- 261
The church in the world, collected essays by William Ralph Inge ... London, New York [etc.] Longmans, Green and co., ltd., 1927. xi, 275 p. 20 cm. [BR85.I6] 27-19722
1. Religion—Addresses, essays, lectures. I. Title.
Contents omitted.

INGE, William Ralph, 1860-
Types of Christian saintliness, by William Ralph Inge ... London, New York [etc.] Longmans, Green and co., 1915. 2 p. l., 3-93 p. 18 cm. A 16
1. Religion—Addresses, essays, lectures. I. Title.

INGE, William Ralph, 1860-1954. 201
The church in the world; collected essays. Freeport, N.Y., Books for Libraries Press [1969] xi, 275 p. 23 cm. (Essay index reprint series) Reprint of the 1927 ed. Contents.Contents.—The condition of the Church of England.—The crisis of Roman Catholicism.—The Quakers.—Hellenism in Christianity.—Science and theology.—Science and ultimate truth.—Faith and reason.—The training of the reason. Bibliographical footnotes. [BR85.I6 1969] 68-57324
1. Religion—Addresses, essays, lectures. I. Title.

INSTITUTE for Religious and Social Studies. Jewish Theological Seminary of America. 200'.1
Moments of personal discovery. Edited by R. M. MacIver. Port Washington, N.Y., Kennikat Press [1969, c1952] ix, 170 p. 23 cm. (Essay and general literature index reprint series.) (Religion and civilization series) "Based on lectures given at the Institute for Religious and Social Studies of the Jewish Theological Seminary of America during the winter of 1951-1952." Contents.Contents.—What a poem did to me, by D. Moore.—Ants, galaxies, and men, by H. Shapley.—The neurosis wears a mask, by L. S. Kubie.—Out of the things I read, by M. Mead.—Persons, places, and things, by P. Weiss.—The road to understanding, by L. Bryson.—The sum of it all, by J. M. Proskauer.—There really is a God, by H. E. Fosdick.—How to live creatively as a Jew, by M. M. Kaplan.—A philosopher meditates on discovery, by R. McKeon.—Thinkers who influenced me, by H. Taylor.—Arnold Toynbee kindles a light, by D. Auchincloss.—Sometimes a miracle happens, by W. G. Constable. [BL50.I5 1969] 68-26194
1. Religion—Addresses, essays, lectures. I. MacIver, Robert Morrison, 1882- ed. II. Title. III. Series.

INTRODUCTION to the study of religion / T. William Hall, general editor, with Ronald R. Cavanagh ; contributors, Alan L. Berger ... [et al.]. 1st ed. New York : Harper & Row, c1978. p. cm. Bibliography: p. [BL48.I56 1978] 78-4427 ISBN 0-06-063572-X pbk. : 7.95 pbk. : 7.95 200'7
1. Religion—Addresses, essays, lectures. I. Hall, Thomas William, 1921- II. Cavanagh, Ronald R. III. Berger, Alan L., 1939-

JAMES, William, 1842-1910. 200
Essays in religion and morality / William James ; [Frederick H. Burkhardt, general editor ; Fredson Bowers, textual editor ; Ignas K. Skrupskelis, associate editor ; introduction by John J. McDermott]. Cambridge, Mass. : Harvard University Press, 1982. xxviii, 345 p. : port. ; 24 cm. (The works of William James) (Series: James, William, 1842-1910. Works.) Includes index. [BL50.J35 1982] 19 81-7040 ISBN 0-674-26735-4 : 25.00
1. Religion—Addresses, essays, lectures. 2. Ethics—Addresses, essays, lectures. I. Burkhardt, Frederick Henry, 1912- II. Bowers, Fredson Thayer. III. Skrupskelis, Ignas K., 1938- IV. Title. V. Series. VI. (Series: 1975.)

KNOX, Thomas Malcolm, Sir, 1900- 208
A heretic's religion / by Sir Malcolm Knox. Dundee : University of Dundee, 1976. 93 p. ; 21 cm. [BL50.K56] 77-354224 ISBN 0-901396-11-7
1. Religion—Addresses, essays, lectures. I. Title.

LEAMING, Jeremiah, 1717-1804.
Dissertations upon various subjects, which may be well worth the attention of every Christian; and of real service to the sincere inquirer after true religion. By Jeremiah Leaming, A. M. rector of Christ's church, in Stratford ... Litchfield [Conn.] Reprinted by T. Collier, 1798. vi, [7]-68 p. 23 cm. [BX5929.L] A 33
I. Title.

LICHTENWALLNER, William A 270
Problems vital to our religion, by W. A. Lichtenwallner. Los Angeles, Calif., Times-Mirror printing and binding house, 1920. 5 p. l., [7]-183 p. 20 cm. [BR125.L72] 22-1389
I. Title.

MACALPINE, Robert J. 243
What is true religion? and other addresses, by Robert J. MacAlpine ... New York, Chicago [etc.] Fleming H. Revell company [c1923] 206 p. 19 1/2 cm. [BX9178.M16W5] 23-11003
I. Title.

*MCELVANY, Harold. 248
Are Americans a chosen people? New York, Vantage [1968] 80p. 20cm. 2.50 bds.,
I. Title.

MARTIN, David A. 209
The dilemmas of contemporary religion / David Martin. New York : St. Martin's Press, [1978] p. cm. Includes bibliographical references. [BL50.M323] 78-17704 ISBN 0-312-21055-8 : 14.50
1. Religion—Addresses, essays, lectures. I. Title.
Contents omitted

MASSEY, Gerald, 1828-1907. 208
Gerald Massey's Lectures / with foreword by John G. Jackson ; introd. by Sibyl Ferguson. New York : S. Weiser, 1974. vii, 287 p. ; 24 cm. "Originally published in a private edition c. 1900." [BL50.M327 1974] 73-92165 ISBN 0-87728-249-8 : 12.50
1. Religion—Addresses, essays, lectures.

MEAD, Margaret, 1901- 200'.9'04
Twentieth century faith: hope and survival. [1st ed.] New York, Harper & Row [1972] xviii, 172 p. 22 cm. (Religious perspectives, v. 25) [BL50.M35 1972] 72-78081 ISBN 0-06-065549-6 6.95
1. Religion—Addresses, essays, lectures. I. Title. II. Series.

MORIARTY, Theodore W. C. 128
The mystery of man / [by] Theodore W. C. Moriarty ; [editor, Eleanor E. Whittall]. Southall : Blackburn Business Services Ltd, 1976- v. : 2 ports. ; 30 cm. "Lectures given in England in 1921-23" Two errata sheets laid in. [BL50.M63] 77-363215 ISBN 0-9504728-0-8 (v. 1)
1. Religion—Addresses, essays, lectures. I. Title.

MULLER, Frederich Max, 1823-1900.
Last essays by the Right Hon. Professor F. Max Muller ... Second series. Essays on the science of religion. London, New York [etc.] Longmans, Green and co., 1901. vi p., 1 l., 375, [1] p. 20 cm. (Half-title: Collected works ... 18) [PJ27.M7 vol. 18] 2-2241
1. Religion—Addresses, essays, lectures. I. Title.
Contents omitted.

MULLER, Friedrich Max, 1823-1900. 291
Last essays, second series : essays on the science of religion / by F. Max Muller. New York : AMS Press, 1978. vi, 375 p. ; 18 cm. (Series: Muller, Friedrich Max, 1823-1900. Collected works of the Right Hon. F. Max Muller ; 18.) Reprint of the 1901 ed. published by Longmans, Green, London, which was issued as no. 18 of the author's Collected works. Includes index. Contents.Contents.—Forgotten Bibles.—Ancient prayers.—Indian fables and esoteric Buddhism.—The alleged sojourn of Christ in India.—The Kutho-daw.—Buddha's birthplace.—Mohammedanism and Christianity.—The religions of China.—The parliament of religions at Chicago.—Why I am not an agnostic.—Is man immortal? [BL50.M77 1978] 73-18815 ISBN 0-404-11439-3 : 24.50
1. Religion—Addresses, essays, lectures. 2. Religions—Addresses, essays, lectures. I. Title. II. Series.

MULLER, Friedrich Max, 1823-1900. 200
Life and religion : an aftermath from the writings of the Right Honourable Professor F. Max Muller / [edited] by his wife. New York : AMS Press, 1978. viii, 237 p. ; 19 cm. Reprint of the 1905 ed. published by Doubleday, New York. [BL50.M78 1978] 73-18821 ISBN 0-404-11448-2 : 17.50.
1. Religion—Addresses, essays, lectures. I. Muller, Georgina Adelaide Grenfell. II. Title.

MURPHY, Carol R. 200.8
Many religions, one God; toward a deeper dialogue, by Carol R. Murphy. [Wallingford, Pa., 1966] 31 p. 19 cm. (Pendle Hill pamphlet 150) Bibliography: p. 31. [BL50.M88] 66-30689
1. Religion—Addresses, essays, lectures. 2. Christianity and other religions—Addresses, essays, lectures. I. Title.

MURRAY, Gilbert, 1866- 204
Stoic, Christian, and humanist. Essays] Boston, Beacon Press, 1950. 180 p. 19 cm. Bibliography: p. 17-18. [BL87.M8] 51-4096
1. Religion — Addresses, essays, lectures. I. Title.

MURRAY, Gilbert, 1866-1957. 208
Stoic, Christian, and humanist. Freeport, N.Y., Books for Libraries Press [1969] 189 p. 23 cm. (Essay index reprint series) Reprint of the 1940 ed. Bibliography: 17-18. [BL87.M8 1969] 75-99712
1. Religion—Addresses, essays, lectures. I. Title.

NEEDLEMAN, Jacob, comp. 200'.8
Religion for a new generation / edited by Jacob Needleman, Arthur K. Bierman, James A. Gould. 2d ed. New York : Macmillan, c1977. xiii, 572 p. ; 24 cm. Includes bibliographical references. [BL50.N39 1977] 76-10540 ISBN 0-02-385990-3 : 7.95
1. Religion—Addresses, essays, lectures. I. Bierman, Arthur Kalmer, 1923- joint comp. II. Gould, James A., 1922- joint comp. III. Title.

NEEDLEMAN, Jacob, comp. 200'.8
The sword of gnosis : metaphysics, cosmology, tradition, symbolism. essays by Frithjof Schuon [and others] Baltimore, Penguin Books [1974] 464 p. illus. 18 cm. (The Penguin metaphysical library) Includes bibliographical references. [BL50.N4] 73-81717 ISBN 0-14-003768-3 4.95 (pbk.)
1. Religion—Addresses, essays, lectures. I. Schuon, Frithjof, 1907- II. Title.

NOCK, Arthur Darby, 1902-1963. 200'.8
Essays on religion and the ancient world. Selected and edited, with an introd., bibliography of Nock's writings, and indexes, by Zeph Stewart. Cambridge, Mass., Harvard University Press, 1972. 2 v. (xvii, 1029 p.) port. 25 cm. Includes bibliographical references. [BL50.N562] 74-135192 ISBN 0-674-26725-7 35.00 (set)
1. Religion—Addresses, essays, lectures. I. Stewart, Zeph, 1921- ed. II. Title.

OFFICIAL and popular religion : analysis of a theme for religious studies / ed. by Pieter Hendrik Vrijhof and Jacques Waardenburg. [2514 GC] The Hague, [Noordeinde 41] : Mouton, 1979. xiv, 739 p. ; 24 cm. (Religion and society ; 19) Includes bibliographies and indexes. [BL48.O4] 79-319323 ISBN 90-279-7998-7 : 59.50 291
1. Religion—Addresses, essays, lectures. 2. Religions—Addresses, essays, lectures. I. Vrijhof, P. H., 1919- II. Waardenburg, Jean Jacques. III. Title. IV. Series.
Dist. by Walter De Gruyter, Hawthorne, NY.

THE Other side of God : a polarity in world religions / edited by Peter L. Berger. 1st ed. Garden City, N.Y. : Anchor Books, 1981. p. cm. Includes index. [BL48.O78] 19 80-2844 ISBN 0-385-17423-3 pbk. : 7.95 291
1. Religion—Addresses, essays, lectures. 2. Religions—Addresses, essays, lectures. I. Berger, Peter L. II. Title: Polarity in world religions.

OTTO, Rudolf, 1869-1937. 204
Religious essays; a supplement to 'The idea of the holy', by Rudolf Otto ... Translated by Brian Lunn ... London, Oxford university press, H. Milford, 1931. vii p., 1 l., 160 p. 23 cm. "The second portion of this book contains certain supplementary chapters whichhave already appeared in earlier German editions of The idea of the holy." "The form of divine service": p. [53]-67. [Full name: Karl Ludwig Rudolf Otto] [BL48.O83] 32-8447
1. Religion—Addresses, essays, lectures. 2. Liturgies. I. Lunn, Brian, tr. II. Title. III. Title: Divine service, The form of.

THE Persistence of religion. Edited by Andrew Greeley and Gregory Baum. [New York] Herder and Herder [1973] 160 p. 23 cm. (Concilium, 81) Series statement also appears as: The New concilium. Includes bibliographical references. [BL50.P474] 72-3947 ISBN 0-8164-2537-X 3.95 200'.1
1. Religion—Addresses, essays, lectures. I. Greeley, Andrew M., 1928- ed. II. Baum, Gregory, 1923- ed. III. Series: Concilium (New York) 81.

PHILLIPS, Bernard, 1915-1974. 291.4'4
Religion and the life of man / by Bernard Phillips ; edited by O'Hyun Park. Lakemont, Ga. : CSA Press, c1977. 186 p. ; 21 cm. Includes bibliographical references. [BL50.P49 1977] 77-74731 ISBN 0-87707-181-0 pbk. 3.75
1. Religion—Addresses, essays, lectures. 2. Logical positivism—Addresses, essays, lectures. I. Title.

PHILLIPS Brooks House Association, Harvard University. 200
Religion and modern life; lectures given for the Phillips Brooks House Association, Harvard University. Freeport, N.Y., Books for Libraries Press [1972] x, 370 p. 23 cm. (Essay index reprint series) Reprint of the 1927 ed. [BL50.P5 1972] 75-39104 ISBN 0-8369-2713-3
1. Religion—Addresses, essays, lectures. I. Title.

PLOTKIN, Frederick. 200'.1
Faith and reason; essays in the religious and scientific imagination. New York, Philosophical Library [1970] 192 p. 23 cm. Includes bibliographical references. [BL50.P55] 72-97937 4.95
1. Religion—Addresses, essays, lectures. I. Title.

PORTER, John William, 1863-
Random remarks, by J. W. Porter ... Louisville, Ky., Baptist book concern [1917] 76 p. 16 cm. On apostasy, baptismal remission, and other religion subjects. 17-11106 0.25
I. Title.

PRINCE, Leon Cushing, 1875- 208.
Pharaoh's question, and other addresses, by Leon C. Prince ... New York, Cincinnati, The Abingdon press [c1927] 180 p. 20 cm. [BR85.P7] 27-24568
I. Title.

A Quest anthology / with an introd. by James Webb. New York : Arno Press, 1976. p. cm. (The Occult) Reprint of articles originally published in the Quest, London, 1909-1927. Includes bibliographical references. [BL50.Q47 1976] 75-36916 ISBN 0-405-07971-0 : 35.00 200'.4
1. Grail—History and criticism—Addresses, essays, lectures. 2. Religion—Addresses, essays, lectures. 3. Mysticism—Addresses, essays,lectures. I. Webb, James, 1946- II. The Quest (London, 1909-1930) III. Series: The Occult (New York, 1976-)

RAINSFORD, William Stephen, 1850-
The reasonableness of faith, and other addresses, by W. S. Rainsford, D. D. New York, Doubleday, Page & co., 1902. 3 p. l., 309 p. 21 cm. 2-14032
1. Brooks, Phillips, 1835-1893. 2. Religion—Addresses, essays, lectures. I. Title.
Contents omitted.

READINGS on religion : from inside and outside / edited by Robert S. Ellwood, Jr. Englewood Cliffs, N.J. : Prentice-Hall, c1978. xv, 336 p. ; 23 cm. Includes bibliographical references. [BL25.R23] 77-17973 ISBN 0-13-760942-6 : 7.95 208
1. Religion—Addresses, essays, lectures. I. Ellwood, Robert S., 1933-

REISS, Joseph 291.13
Language, myth, and man. New York, Philosophical [c.1963] 134p. 21cm. 63-15605 4.50 bds.,
1. Religion—Addresses, essays, lectures. I. Title.

RELIGION and social sciences: 1973; pre-printed papers for the Section on Religion and Social Sciences, American Academy of Religion, annual meeting, 1973. Compiled by Henry B. 301.5'8

Clark. [Tallahassee, American Academy of Religion; order from CSR Executive Office, Waterloo Lutheran University, Waterloo, Ont., 1973] iii, 94 p. 23 cm. Includes bibliographical references. [BL50.R45] 74-176328 ISBN 0-88420-108-2
1. Religion—Addresses, essays, lectures. I. Clark, Henry, 1930- ed. II. American Academy of Religion.

RELIGIOUS life, by E. Sapir, Shailer Mathews, Ernest F. Tittle [and others] ... New York, D. Van Nostrand company, inc. [c1929] 6 p. l., [3]-134 p., 1 l. illus. 18 cm. (Man and his world, v. 11, ed. by B. Brownell) Contents.Religions and religious phenomena, by Edward Sapir.--The religious life, by Shailer Mathews.--Religion and personality, by E. F. Tittle.--The spirit, by R. M. Jones.--Fact and faith, by F. J. McConnell. [BD493.M3 vol. 11] 29-21933
1. Religion—Addresses, essays, lectures. I. Sapir, Edward, 1884- II. Mathews, Shailer, 1863- III. Title. Ernest Fremont, 1885- IV. Jones, Rufus Matthew, 1803- V. McConnell, Francis John, bp., 1871-

RENAN, Ernest, 1823-1892. 204
Studies in religious history. New York, Scribner and Welford, 1887. vi, 481 p. 20 cm. Running title: New studies of religious history. Full name: Joseph Ernest Renan. [BL27.R47] 49-32072
1. Joachim, Abbot of Fiore, 1132 (ca.)-1202. 2. Francesco d'Assisi, Saint, 1182-1226. 3. Port Royal. 4. Spinoza, Benedictus de, 1632-1677. 5. Molinism. 6. Religious—Addresses, essays, lectures. 7. Christianity—Addresses, essays, lectures. 8. Buddha and buddhism. I. Title.

ROHEIM, Geza, 1891-1953. 200'.1
The panic of the gods and other essays. Edited with an introd. by Werner Muensterberger. [1st Harper torchbook ed.] New York, Harper & Row [1972] xxiii, 227 p. 21 cm. (Harper torchbooks, TB1674) Contents.Contents.—Primitive high gods.—Animism and religion.—Aphrodite, or the woman with a penis.—The panic of the gods. [BL50.R55 1972] 72-80870 ISBN 0-06-131674-1 3.95
1. Religion—Addresses, essays, lectures. 2. Mythology—Addresses, essays, lectures. I. Title.

RUSSELL, Bertrand Russell, 3d earl, 1872-
Why I am not a Christian, and other essays on religion and related subjects. Edited, with an appendix on the Bertrand Russell Case, by Paul Edwards. New York, Simon and Schuster [1966] xvii, 266 p. (Essandess paperback) 67-60800
I. Title.

RUSSELL, Bertrand Russell, 3d earl, 1872-
Why I am not a Christian, and other essays on religion and related subjects. Edited, with an appendix on the Bertrand Russell Case, by Paul Edwards. New York, Simon and Schuster [1966] xvii, 266 p. (Essandess paperback) 67-60800
I. Title.

SCHOPENHAUER, Arthur, 1788- 198.7 1860.
Religion: a dialogue, and other essays, by Arthur Schopenhauer ... selected and tr. by T. Bailey Saunders, M. A. London, S. Sonnenschein & co., limited; New York, The Macmillan co., 1899. 4 p. l., 140 p. 20 cm. [The philosophy at home series] Contents.--Religion: a dialogue.--A few words on pantheism.--On books and reading.--On physiognomy.--Psychological observations.--The Christian system.--The failure of philosophy.--The metaphysics of fine art. [B3118.E5S45 vol. 3] 4-17569
1. Religion—Addresses, essays, lectures. 2. Philosophy. I. Saunders, Thomas Bailey, 1860- tr. II. Title.

SELBIE, William Boothby, 204 1862-
Religion and life; being the William Belden Noble lectures delivered in Harvard university, 1930, by W. B. Selbie... London, Oxford university press, H. Milford, 1930. 2 p. l., [iv]-v, [2], 135, [1] p. 19 cm. Contents.Religion and history.--The psychological interpretation of religion--Belief in God.--Religion and ethics.--The Christian contribution.--Eternal life. [BR85.S34] 31-14213
1. Religion—Addresses, essays, lectures. I. Title.

SELLARS, Roy Wood, 1880- 225
The next step in religion; an essay toward the coming renaissance, by Roy Wood Sellars ... New York, The Macmillan company, 1918. 5 p. l., 228 p. 19 1/2 cm. $1.50 [BR121.S48] 18-18974
I. Title.

SELLECK, Willard Chamberlain, 1856-
Main questions in religion; a study of fundamentals. Crane theological school lectures and other essays, by Willard Chamberlain Selleck... Boston, R. G. Badger; [etc., etc., c1916] 140 p. 19 1/2 cm. (Lettered on cover: Library of religious thought) $1.25 16-19095
I. Title.

SIEGEL, Meyer D., 1883- 208.1
Religion is here to stay, whether you like it or not; a new concept of what religion is and what it is not. 'Christian Science' debuked [2d ed.] Scarsdale, N. Y., 30 E. 42nd St., New York 17, Author's Bk. Distributors [dist. Author, c.1963] vii, 184p. port. 22cm. Bibl. 63-25558 1.95 pap.,
1. Religion—Addresses, essays, lectures. 2. Christian Science—Legal aspects. I. Title.

SKOTTOWE, John Coulson. 220
Four religious essays, by John C. Skottowe. Boston, R. G. Badger [c1920] 64 p. 19 1/2 cm. (Lettered on cover: Library of religious thought) [BR125.S53] 20-9304
I. Title.

SMITH, Goldwin, 1823-1910. 220
In quest of light, by Goldwin Smith. New York, The Macmillan company; London, Macmillan & co., ltd., 1906. viii p., 1 l., 177 p. 19 1/2 cm. "The following papers...appeared in different forms, chiefly as letters, in the New York sun."--Pref. [BR125.S62] 6-14776
1. Religion—Addresses, essays, lectures. I. Title.

SMITH, Wilfred Cantwell, 200 1916-
Questions of religious truth. New York, Scribner [1967] 127 p. 21 cm. "The material ... was delivered first as the Taylor lectures for 1963 at Yale Divinity School, except the opening chapter." Contents.Contents.—The "Death of God"?—Is the Qur'an the word of God?—Can religions be true or false?—Christian—noun, or adjective? Bibliographical footnotes. [BL27.S45] 67-14494
1. Religion—Addresses, essays, lectures. 2. Truth—Addresses, essays, lectures. I. Title.

SMITH, Wilfred Cantwell, 200 1916-
Religious diversity : essays / by Wilfred Cantwell Smith ; edited by Willard B. Oxtoby. 1st ed. New York : Harper & Row, c1976. p. cm. (A Harper forum book) Includes index. Bibliography: p. [BL50.S58 1976] 76-9968 ISBN 0-06-067463-6 : 10.00. ISBN 0-06-067464-4 pbk. : 4.95
1. Religion—Addresses, essays, lectures. 2. Religions—Addresses, essays, lectures. I. Title.

SOME religious views; four papers read before the Chicago literary club, Monday evening, December, 5, 1904. 204 [Chicago] Chicago literary club, 1905. 80 p., 1 l. illus. 18 x 10 1/2 cm. (On cover: Club papers) "This edition consists of four hundred and thirty copies privately printed for the members of the Chicago literary club." [BL25.S56] 43-47827
1. Religion—Addresses, essays, lectures.
Contents omitted.

SORELY, William Ritchie, 250 1855-1935.
Reconstruction and the renewal of life; three lay sermons, by W. R. Sorley ... Cambridge, The University press, 1919. 4 p. l., 52 p. 18 1/2 cm. Contents.--Life.--Faith.--Vision. [BV4017.S6] A 20
1. Religion—Addresses, essays, lectures. 2. European war, 1914-1918—Addresses, sermons, etc. I. Title.

SPECULUM religionis, 208 being essays and studies in religion and literature from Plato to Von Hugel, with an introduction by F. C. Burkitt ... Presented by members of the staff of University college, Southampton, to their president, Claude G. Montefiore ... Oxford, The Clarendon press, 1929. viii, 216 p. front. (port.) 22 1/2 x 17 1/2 cm. Bibliographical foot-notes. [BL25.S6] 31-6502
1. Montefiore, Claude Joseph Goldsmid, 1858- 2. Religion—Addresses, essays, lectures. 3. Literature—Addresses, essays, lectures. I. Burkitt, Francis Crawford, 1864-
Contents omitted.

SPERRY, Willard Learoyd, 294. 1882-
The paradox of religion, by Willard L. Sperry ... New York, The Macmillan company, 1927. 2 p. l., ix-xi, 13-63 p. 19 cm. (Half-title: Hibbert lectures, 1927) Printed in Great Britain. [BL25.H5 1927] 28-9676
1. Religion—Addresses, essays, lectures. I. Title.

SPERRY, Willard Learoyd, 201 1882-1954.
The paradox of religion / by Willard L. Sperry. 1st AMS ed. New York : AMS Press, 1979. 63 p. ; 19 cm. Reprint of the 1927 ed. published by Macmillan, New York, which was issued as the 1927 Hibbert lectures. [BL50.S65 1979] 77-27146 ISBN 0-404-60424-2 : 11.00
1. Religion—Addresses, essays, lectures. I. Title. II. Series: Hibbert lectures (New York) ; 1927.

STUDIES in the history of 294. *religions,* presented to Crawford Howell Toy by pupils, colleagues and friends; ed. by David Gordon Lyon [and] George Foot Moore. New York, The Masmillan company, 1912. viii p., 1 l., 373 p. 2 pl. 24 1/2 cm. [BL25.S7] 12-25968
1. Toy, Crawford, Howell, 1836-1919. 2. Religion—Addresses, essays, lectures. I. Lyon, David Gordon, 1852-1965, ed. II. Moore, George Foot, 1851-1931, joint ed.
Contents omitted.

SUNDAR SINGH, 1889- 220
Reality and religion; meditations on God, man and nature, by Sadhu Sundar Singh, with an introduction by Canon Streeter. New York, The Macmillan company, 1924. xvi, 80 p. 18 cm. [BR125.S935 1924a] 24-9366
1. Religion—Addresses, essays, lectures. I. Title.

SWIFT, Arthur Lessner, 208.2 1891- ed.
Religion today, a challenging enigma, edited by Arthur L. Swift, jr. ... New York, and London, Whittlesey house, McGraw-Hill book. company, inc., 1933. xvi, 300 p. 22 1/2 cm. "First presented in 1932 as a series of lectures on religion at the New school for social research in New York city."--Pref. "First edition." Bibliography: p. 267-271. [BL25.S8] 33-4053
1. Religion—Addresses, essays, lectures. 2. Religion and sociology. I. Title.

TAGORE, Rabindranath, 200'.1 Sir, 1861-1941.
The religion of man / [Rabindranath Tagore]. New York : AMS Press, [1981] c1931. p. cm. Reprint. Originally published: New York : Macmillan, 1931. (The Hibbert lectures for 1930). Includes index. [BL50.T253 1981] 19 77-27145 ISBN 0-404-60426-9 : 27.50
1. Religion—Addresses, essays, lectures. I. Title.

TOYNBEE, Arnold Joseph, 1889- 200 1975.
An historian's approach to religion / Arnold Toynbee. New ed. Oxford ; New York : Oxford University Press, 1978. p. cm. Includes the author's essay Gropings in the dark. Includes index. [BL50.T69 1978] 78-40536 ISBN 0-19-215260-2 : 12.95
1. Religion—Addresses, essays, lectures. 2. Civilization, Occidental—History—Addresses, essays, lectures. I. Title.

UNITARIAN club of California.
Addresses at the thirtieth meeting of the Unitarian club of California, held at San Francisco, Cal., April 26, 1897. [San Francisco] C. A. Murdock & co. [1897] 52 p. 24 cm. Cover-title: Addresses on religion ... Title from Leland Stanford Jr. Univ. A 10
1. Religion—Addresses, essays, lectures. I. Title.
Contents omitted.

WACH, Joachim, 1898-1955. 291'.08
Understanding and believing : essays / by Joachim Wach ; edited with an introd. by Joseph M. Kitagawa. Westport, Conn. : Greenwood Press, 1975, c1968. p. cm. Reprint of the 1st ed. published by Harper & Row, New York, which was issued as no. TB1399 of the Harper torchbooks. "Bibliography of Joachim Wach (1922-55)": p. [BL27.W26 1975] 75-31987 ISBN 0-8371-8488-6 : 12.75
1. Wach, Joachim, 1898-1955—Bibliography. 2. Religion—Addresses, essays, lectures. I. Title.
Contents omitted.

WACH, Joachim, 1898-1955. 291'.08
Understanding and believing; essays. Edited with an introd. by Joseph M. Kitagawa. [1st ed.] New York, Harper & Row [1968] xviii, 204 p. 21 cm. (Harper torchbooks, TB1399) Contents.Contents.—The self-understanding of modern man.—Stefan George; poet and priest of modern paganism.—The problem of death in modern philosophy.—General revelation and the religions of the world.—The paradox of the gospel.—Redeemer of man.—Seeing and believing.—Belief and witness.—The meaning and task of the history of religions.—Religious commitment and tolerance.—The problem of truth in religion.—The Christian professor.—The crisis in the university.—Hugo of St. Victor on virtues and vices.—To a rabbi friend.—On felicity.—A prayer.—Bibliography of Joachim Wach, 1922-55 (p. 188-196) Bibliographical footnotes. [BL27.W26] 68-29897 2.95
1. Wach, Joachim, 1898-1955—Bibliography. 2. Religion—Addresses, essays, lectures. I. Title.

WALKER, Gerald Bromhead. 301.29'3
Diffusions : five studies in early history / by Gerald Bromhead Walker. London : The Research Pub. Co., [1976] 142 p. : ill. ; 23 cm. [BL50.W23] 76-363596 ISBN 0-7050-0030-3 : £3.00
1. Religion—Addresses, essays, lectures. 2. Religion, Primitive—Addresses, essays, lectures. 3. Mythology—Addresses, essays, lectures. I. Title.

WATKIN, Edward Ingram, 100'.8 1888-
Men and tendencies, by E. I. Watkin. Freeport, N.Y., Books for Libraries Press [1968] ix, 316 p. 23 cm. (Essay index reprint series) Reprint of 1937 ed. [BX890.W35 1968] 68-16986
1. Religion—Addresses, essays, lectures. 2. Philosophy—Addresses, essays, lectures. I. Title.

WATTS, Alan Wilson, 1915- 200'.1
Cloud-hidden, whereabouts unknown; a mountain journal [by] Alan Watts. [1st ed.] New York, Pantheon Books [1973] xi, 179 p. illus. 25 cm. [BL50.W32 1973] 72-12384 ISBN 0-394-48253-0 6.95
1. Religion—Addresses, essays, lectures. I. Title.

WATTS, Alan Wilson, 1915- 200'.1
Cloud-hidden, whereabouts unknown; a mountain journal [by] Alan Watts. New York, Vintage Books [1974, c1973] xi, 208 p. 18 cm. [BL50.W32 1974] 73-13747 ISBN 0-394-71999-9 1.95 (pbk.)
1. Religion—Addresses, essays, lectures. I. Title.

THE Weekly monitor; 248 a series of essays on moral and religious subjects. By a layman. Philadelphia, Published by Brannan & Morford; Charleston, South Carolina, E. Morford, Willington, & co., James Maxwell, Printers, 1810. xv, 310 p. 20 1/2 cm. Contains 41 papers, originally published in weekly numbers, in the Charleston courier. Revised and reprinted. [BV4501.W44] 9-22528
I. Charleston daily courier.

WERBLOWSKY, Raphael 301.5'8 Jehudah Zwi, 1924-
Beyond tradition and modernity : changing religions in a changing world / by R. J. Zwi Werblowsky. London : Athlone Press,

1976. ix, 146 p. ; 23 cm. (Jordan lectures in comparative religion ; 11) Distributed in the USA and Canada by Humanities Press, Atlantic Highlands, N.J. "Delivered ... in June 1974." Bibliography: p. [134]-146. [BL50.W397] 76-375007 ISBN 0-485-17411-1 : 9.00
1. Religion—Addresses, essays, lectures. 2. Religions—Addresses, essays, lectures. I. Title. II. Series.

WHAT is religion? : 200'.1
an inquiry for Christian theology / edited by Mircea Eliade and David Tracy ; English language editor Marcus Lefebure. Edinburgh : T. & T. Clarke ; New York : Seabury Press, 1980. ix, 88 p. ; 22 cm. (Concilium ; 136) Includes bibliographical references. [BL48.W34] 19 80-50583 ISBN 0-8164-2278-8 (Seabury Press) : 5.95
1. Religion—Addresses, essays, lectures. 2. Christianity and other religions—Addresses, essays, lectures. I. Eliade, Mircea, 1907- II. Tracy, David. III. Lefebure, Marcus.

WHAT religion means to me, 204
by Harry Emerson Fosdick, A. Bruce Curry, Ernest Fremont Tittle ... [and others] Garden City, N.Y., Doubleday, Doran & company, inc. [c1929] 3 p. l., 5-88 p. 19 1/2 cm. (Added t.-p.: Personal problems series, no. 7) [BR50.W5] 29-10767
1. Religion—Addresses, essays, lectures. I. Fosdick, Harry Emerson, 1878- II. Curry, Albert Bruce, 1887- III. Tittle, Ernest Fremont, 1885-

WHY [I am a Catholic; 204
[by] Clarence Darrow ... Rabbi Solomon Goldman ... Dr. John A. Lapp ... Dr. Charles W. Gilkey ... Chicago, M. M. Cole publishing co. [c1932] 2 p. l., 3-62 p. 23 cm. "Delivered at Orchestra hall, Chicago, Ill., Dr. A. Eustace Haydon, chairman; reporting by George F. FitzGerald."--2d prelim. leaf. [BL87.W5] 32-16083
1. Religion—Addresses, essays, lectures. I. Lapp, John Augustus, 1880- II. Gilkey, Charles Whitney, 1882- III. Goldman, Solomon, 1893- IV. Darrow, Clarence Seward, 1857- V. Fitzgerald, George Francis, 1886-

YOUARD, Henry George.
Showing ourselves men, addresses for men's services, by the Rev. H. G. Youard... London, Brighton, Society for promoting Christian knowledge; New York, E. S. Gorham, 1911. v, 7-79, [1] p. 19 cm. A 34
1. Religion—Addresses, essays, lectures. I. Title.
Contents omitted.

ZAEHNER, R. C. 1913-1974. 291
(Robert Charles)
The city within the heart / R.G. Zaehner. New York : Crossroad, 1981, c1980. p. cm. Includes bibliographical references and index. [BL50.Z328 1981] 19 81-9779 ISBN 0-8245-0109-8 pbk. : 7.95
1. Religion—Addresses, essays, lectures. I. Title.

Religion and astronautics.

ALLAN, John Robertson, 1906- 231
The gospel according to science fiction : God was an ancient astronaut, wasn't he? / John Allan. Libertyville, Ill. : Quill Publications, [1976] p. cm. Includes bibliographical references. [BL254.A44 1976] 76-6920 ISBN 0-916608-02-6
1. Bible—Miscellanea. 2. Religion and astronautics. I. Title.

CHEVILLE, Roy Arthur, 248.42
1897-
Spirituality in the space age. Prepared for the Dept. of Religious Education, Reorganized Church of Jesus Christ of latter Day Saints. [Independence, Mo., Herald Pub. house] 1962. 264p. 20cm. [BL254.C47] 62-12899
1. Religion and astronautics. 2. Reorganized Church of Jesus Christ of Latter-Day Saints—Sermons. I. Title.

CHEVILLE, Roy Arthur, 248.42
1897-
Spirituality in the space age. Prepared for the Dept. of Religious Education, Reorganized Church of Jesus Christ of Latter Day Saints. [Independence, Mo., Herald, c.]1962. 264p. 20cm. 62-12899 2.75
1. Religion and astronautics. 2. Reorganized Church of Jesus Christ of Latter-Day Saints—Sermons. I. Title.

DRAKE, Walter Raymond. 215'.25
Gods and spacemen in the ancient East, by W. Raymond Drake. [New York] New American Library [1973, c.1968] 247 p. 18 cm. (Signet Book, W5737) First published in 1930 in London under title: Spacemen in the ancient East. Bibliography: p. 230-242. [BL254.D7] 1.50 (pbk.)
1. Religion and astronautics. 2. Flying saucers. I. Title.
L.C. card no. for the hardbound (London) edition: 71-353952.

HEINECKEN, Martin J. 215
God in the space age. [1st ed.] Philadelphia, Winston [1959] 216 p. 22 cm. Includes bibliography. [BL254.H4] 59-5327
1. God. 2. Religion and astronautics. I. Title.

KLOTZ, John William 215
The challenge of the space age. St. Louis, Concordia [c.1961] 112p. (Concord bks.) 61-13456 1.00 pap.,
1. Religion and astronautics. 2. Atomic energy. I. Title.

OSTLIN, Melvin T 215
Thinking out loud about the space age. Is the Christian faith adequate for a space age? Philadelphia, Dorrance [1962] 144p. 20cm. Includes bibliographies. [BL254.O8] 62-11977
1. Religion and astronautics. I. Title.

PARROTT, Bob W. 215'.2
Earth, moon, and beyond [by] Bob W. Parrott. Waco, Tex., Word Books [1969] 176 p. illus. (part col.) 23 cm. [BL254.P37] 77-85828 4.95
1. Religion and astronautics. 2. Astronautics—U.S. I. Title.

RICHARDS, Harold Marshall 230.67
Sylvester, 1894-
Look to the stars, Washington, D. C, Review & Herald [c.1964] 156p. 21cm. [BL254.R5] 64-17663 3.00
1. Religion and astronautics. I. Title.

RICHARDS, Harold Marshall 230.67
Sylvester, 1894-
Look to the stars, by H. M. S. Richards. Washington, Review and Herald Pub. Association [1964] 156 p. 21 cm. [BL254.R5] 64-17663
1. Religion and astronautics. I. Title.

Religion and civilization.

FROST, William P. 170'.202
The future significance of civilization, nature, and religion [by] William P. Frost. [1st ed.] New York, Exposition Press [1974, c1973] 104 p. 22 cm. (An Exposition-university book) [BL55.F76 1974] 73-82086 ISBN 0-682-47769-9 4.00
1. Religion and civilization. I. Title.

LOPER, W. Harold. 215
The curious layman : science, belief, and the common man / W. Harold Loper. 1st ed. Hicksville, N.Y. : Exposition Press, [1975] xii, 96 p. ; 22 cm. (An Exposition-university book) Bibliography: p. 93-96. [BL55.L56] 74-21444 ISBN 0-682-48170-X : 5.50
1. Religion and civilization. 2. Cosmology. I. Title.

*SMART. NINIAN 290
World religions: a dialogue. Baltimore, Penguin [1966] 154p. 19cm. (Pelican bk., A 786) 1.25 pap.,
I. Title.

Religion and culture.

ACADEMY of Religion and Mental Health. Academy Symposium.
Religion, culture and mental health; with an introduction by Talcott Parsons. Proceedings of the third Academy Symposium, 1959, Academy of Religion and Mental Health, with the aid of the Josiah Macy, Jr. Foundation. [New York] New York University Press, 1961. xv, 157p. 22cm.
I. Title.

CONFERENCE on Religion and American Culture, Boston? 1965?
Proceedings of the Conference on Religion and American Culture, sponsored by Daedalus, journal of the American Academy of Arts and Sciences and the Church Society for College Work. Boston. House of the Academy, 1965. 161 p. 28 cm. Mimeographed. 66-58029
I. Daedalus. II. American Academy of Arts and Sciences, Boston. III. Title.

JESUS in literature and art.
Philadelphia, Published by Friends Central Bureau for Committee on Education. Religious and Secular, Friends General Conference [1957?] 64p. 20cm.
I. Hubben, William, 1895-

**RELIGION in human* 290.76
culture; a guide. Iowa City, Sernoll, inc., 410 E. Market St. [c.1965] 134 l. 28cm. Prep. by the teachers and assistants of the course Religion in human culture, State Univ., Iowa City, Iowa. 5.75 pap., plastic bdg.

SCOTT, Nathan A. 246
The wild prayer of longing; poetry and the sacred [by] Nathan A. Scott, Jr. New Haven, Yale University Press, 1971. xix, 124 p. 23 cm. Includes bibliographical references. [BL65.C8S36 1971] 72-140538 ISBN 0-300-01389-2 6.75
1. Roethke, Theodore, 1908-1963. 2. Religion and culture. 3. Holy, The. 4. Religion and poetry. I. Title.

Religion and culture—Addresses, essays, lectures.

THE Bent world : 261
essays on religion and culture / [edited by] John R. May. Chico, Calif. : Scholars Press, c1981. p. cm. (The Annual publication of the College Theology Society) "Most of the essays were presented as papers at the 1979 meeting of CTS, though some in quite different form"—Pref. Includes bibliographical references. [BL65.C8B46] 19 81-5801 ISBN 0-89130-503-3 : 18.00
1. Religion and culture—Addresses, essays, lectures. I. May, John R. II. College Theology Society. III. Title. IV. Series.
Contents omitted. Publisher's address: 101 Salem St., Chico, CA 95926.

GILKEY, Langdon Brown, 1919- 261
Society and the sacred : toward a theology of culture in decline / Langdon Gilkey. New York : Crossroad, c1981. p. cm. [BL65.C8G54] 19 81-9775 ISBN 0-8245-0089-X : 14.95
1. Religion and culture—Addresses, essays, lectures. I. Title.

LOOS, Amandus William, 261.8
1908- ed.
Religious faith and world culture. Freeport, N.Y., Books for Libraries Press [1970, c1951] viii, 294 p. 23 cm. (Essay index reprint series) Contents.Contents.—Introduction, by A. W. Loos.—What do we mean by religion? By H. E. Fosdick.—The situation we face: a sociological analysis, by K. G. Collier.—The situation we face: a psychological analysis, by G. W. Allport.—Religion and reality, by M. Buber, translated by N. Guterman.—Individualism reconsidered, by D. Riesman.—The individual and authority, D. J. Bradley.—Technology and personality, by J. E. Burchard.—Faith and freedom, by N. F. S. Ferre.—Prophetic religion and world culture, by A. H. Silver.—The world impact of the Russian Revolution, by P. E. Mosely.—The whole world in revolt, by M. S. Bates.—The unity of interdependence: a case study in international economics, by J. P. Condliffe.—Religious faith and human brotherhood, by A. Paton.—Ideal democracy and global anarchy, by M. B. Lucas.—World organization and world culture, by E. D. Canham.—Individual ethics and world culture, by W. R. Matthews.—World faith for world peace, by A. Chakravarty.—Is there a nascent world culture? By M. C. D'Arcy.—Cathedral lamp, translated by F. Mousseau. Bibliography (p. 285-287) [BL65.C8L6 1970] 71-128270 ISBN 0-8369-1976-9
1. Religion and culture—Addresses, essays, lectures. I. Title.

MAJOR, Henry Dewsbury Alves, 201
1872-
Civilisation and religious values / by H. D. A. Major. 1st AMS ed. New York : AMS Press, 1979. 140 p. ; 19 cm. Reprint of the 1948 ed. published by G. Allen & Unwin, London, which was issued as the 1946 Hibbert lectures. Includes bibliographical references. [BL65.C8M34 1979] 77-27137 ISBN 0-404-60431-5 : 15.00
1. Religion and culture—Addresses, essays, lectures. I. Title. II. Series: Hibbert lectures (London) ; 1946.

Religion and culture—Juvenile literature.

KING, Basil, 1859-1928. 220
Adventures in religion, by Basil King. Garden City, N.Y., Doubleday, Doran & company, inc., 1929. 3 p. l., 252 p. 21 1/2 cm. [Full name: William Benjamin Basil King] [BR125.K52] 29-23810
I. Title.

MOSKIN, Marietta D. 291
In the name of God : religion in everyday life / by Marietta Moskin. New York : Atheneum, 1980. p. cm. Examines the role played by the various religious systems and institutions of the world in the development of modern culture and civilization. [BL65.C8M67] 80-12319 ISBN 0-689-30783-7 : 10.95
1. Religion and culture—Juvenile literature. 2. Religions—Juvenile literature. 3. [Religion and culture.] 4. [Religions.] I. Title.

Religion and economics.

NATIONAL Study Conference on the Church and Economic Life. 4th, Pittsburgh,1962.
Rapid economic change - its impact on people and the churches; major addresses by churchmen - lay and clergy - on various aspects of "The ethical implications of rapid change in the U.S.A." [New York, Dept. of the Church and Economic Life in the U.S.A., 1963?] 1 v. (various pagings) 65-57953
I. Title.

OPITZ, Edmund A. 261.8'5
Religion and capitalism: allies, not enemies [by] Edmund A. Opitz. New Rochelle, N.Y., Arlington House [1970] 318 p. 24 cm. Bibliography: p. [303]-309. [BR115.E3O6] 72-101955 ISBN 0-87000-079-9 7.00
1. Religion and economics. 2. Capitalism. I. Title.

WATSON, Kenneth, 261.8'5'0973
1913-
Religion in the market place; or, Religious characteristics of business and labor leaders in America. Tujunga, Calif., 196- vi, 174 [5] l. 28 cm. Bibliography: leaves [175]-[180] [HB72.W34] 72-192080
1. Religion and economics. I. Title.

Religion and ethics.

BAELZ, Peter. 241
Ethics and belief / Peter Baelz. New York : Seabury Press, 1977. 117 p. ; 21 cm. (Issues in religious studies) "A Crossroad book." Includes index. Bibliography: p. 114-115. [BJ47.B33 1977] 76-15425 ISBN 0-8164-1229-4 pbk. : 3.95
1. Religion and ethics. I. Title.

BURTON, Ernest DeWitt, 1856- 232.
1925.
A source book for the study of the teaching of Jesus in its historical relationships, by Ernest DeWitt Burton... Chicago, Ill., The University of Chicago press [1923] x, 277 p. 20 cm. (Half-title: The University of Chicago publications in religious education, ed. by E. D. Burton, Shailer Mathews, T. G. Soares. Handbooks of ethics and religion) Bibliography: p. 275-277. [BS2415.B8] 23-8750
I. Title.

BURTON, Ernest DeWitt, 1856- 232.
1925.
A source book for the study of the

teaching of Jesus in its historical relationships, by Ernest DeWitt Burton... [2d ed.] Chicago, Ill., The University of Chicago press [1924] x, 277. 20 cm. (Half-title: The University of Chicago publications in religious education, ed. by E. D. Burton, Shailer Mathews, T. G. Soares. Handbooks of ethics and religion) Bibliography: p. 275-277. [BS2415.B8 1924] 24-4063
1. Title.

MACLAGAN, William Gauld 170
The theological frontier of ethics; an essay based on the Edward Cadbury lectures in the University of Birmingham, 1955-56. New York, Macmillan [c.1961] 202p. (Muirhead library of philosophy) Bibl. 61-3766 5.00
1. Religion and ethics. I. Title.

MACLAGAN, William Gauld 170
The theological frontier of ethics; an essay based on the Edward Cadbury lectures in the University of Birmingham, 1955-56. London, Allen & Unwin New York, Macmillan [1961] 202p. 23cm. (The Muirhead library of philosophy) Includes bibliography. [BJ47.M27 1961] 61-3766
1. Religion and ethics. I. Title.

PORTER, Burton Frederick. 200'.1
Deity and morality, with regard to the naturalistic fallacy [by] Burton F. Porter. New York, Humanities Press, 1968. 176 p. 23 cm. Includes bibliographical references. [BJ47.P62 1968] 68-16017
1. Religion and ethics. I. Title.

VAN TIL, Cornelius, 1895-
Christian theistic ethics. Philadelphia, Westminster Theological Seminary, 1958. 135 p. Syllabus.
1. Title.

Religion and ethics—Addresses, essays, lectures.

DIVINE commands and morality / edited by Paul Helm. Oxford ; New York : Oxford University Press, 1981. 186 p. ; 21 cm. (Oxford readings in philosophy) Includes bibliographical references and index. [BJ47.D58] 19 80-41066 ISBN 0-19-875049-8 (pbk.) : 6.95 291.5
1. Religion and ethics—Addresses, essays, lectures. I. Helm, Paul.

Religion and geography.

SOPHER, David Edward 200'.91
Geography of religion [by] David E. Sopher. Englewood Cliffs, N.J., Prentice [1967] x, 118p. illus., maps. 23cm. (Founds. of cultural geog. ser.) Bibl. [BL65.G4S6] 67-13357 4.50; 1.95 pap.,
1. Religion and geography. I. Title.

Religion and labor.

ANDERSON, Robert Phillips, 1866- 287.
The new junior workers' manual; a text-book on junior work, by Rev. Robert P. Anderson ... Boston, Chicago, United society of Christian endeavor [c1921] ix, 11-187 p. 17 cm. [BV1429.A6] 21-14935
I. Title.

CARTER, John A d.1911.
Christianity vs. railroading, by a Rock Island locomotive engineer, John A. Carter ... Kansas City, Mo., The Western Baptist publishing co., 1911. 94 p. front. (port.) 18 cm. 12-1324 0.75
I. Title.

CHARTIER, Myron Raymond. 261.8'3'0924
The social views of Dwight L. Moody and their relation to the workingman of 1860-1900. [Hays, Fort Hays Kansas State College] 1969. x, 79 p. port. 23 cm. (Fort Hays studies. New series. History series, no. 6) Bibliography: p. 74-79. [D6.F6 no. 6] 77-627350
1. Moody, Dwight Lyman, 1837-1899. 2. Religion and labor. I. Title. II. Series.

THE Christian laborer--the Christian hero. Memoirs of a useful man... New York, Carlton & Phillips, 1853. 200 p. 15 1/2 cm. The manuscript of the present volume has been purchased and presented as a donation to the Tract society of the Methodist Episcopal church under whose auspices it is now sent forth. cf. Introd. 7-32063
I. Miller, Roger Woods, 1808-1847. II. Methodist Episcopal church. Tract society.

MILLER, Herbert Sumner, 1867- 250
The Christian workers' manual, by H. S. Miller ... New York, George H. Doran company [c1922] xi p., 1 l., 13-254 p. 19 1/2 cm. $1.50 [BV4400.M45] 22-15591
I. Title.

Religion and language.

ACHTEMEIER, Paul J. 225.6'3
An introduction to the new hermeneutic, by Paul J. Achtemeier. Philadelphia, Westminster Press [1969] 190 p. 21 cm. Bibliographical references included in "Notes" (p. [166]-183) [BS2331.A23] 74-79666 6.50
1. Fuchs, Ernst, 1903- 2. Bible. N.T.—Hermeneutics. 3. Religion and language. I. Title.

ALTIZER, Thomas J. J. 201'.4
The self-embodiment of God / Thomas J. J. Altizer. 1st ed. New York : Harper & Row, c1977. 96 p. ; 21 cm. [BL65.L2A45 1977] 76-62952 ISBN 0-06-060160-4 : 6.95
1. Religion and language. I. Title.

BOCHENSKI, Innocentius M., 1902- 200.1
The logic of religion, by Joseph M. Bochenski [New York] N.Y.U. [c.1965] x, 179p. 22cm. A re-elaboration of a ser. of lects. delivered in March, 1963, at N.Y.U. and sponsored by the Deems Fund. [BL65.L2B6] 65-11762 5.00
1. Religion and language. 2. Semantics (Philosophy) I. Title.

BOLDUAN, Miriam F. 200'.1'4
Words to see by, by Miriam F. Bolduan. Philadelphia, Fortress Press [1970] vi, 122 p. 22 cm. [BL65.L2B63] 73-94816 2.95
1. Religion and language. 2. Meditations. I. Title.

BURKE, Kenneth, 1897- 201'.4
The rhetoric of religion; studies in logology. Berkeley, University of California Press, 1970. vi, 327 p. 21 cm. "Cal 188." Includes bibliographical references. [BL65.L2B8 1970] 70-89892 2.95
1. Augustinus, Aurelius, Saint, Bp. of Hippo. Confessiones. 2. Bible. O.T. Genesis—Language, style. 3. Religion and language. 4. Semantics (Philosophy) I. Title.

BURKE, Kenneth, [Kenneth Duva Burke] 1897- 201.4
The rhetoric of religion; studies in logology. Boston, Beacon [c.1961] vi, 327p. 61-7249 6.95
1. Augustinus, Aurelius, Saint, Bp: of Hippo. Confessiones. 2. Religion and language. 3. Semantics (Philosophy) 4. Bible. O. T. Genesis—Language, style. I. Title.

CAMPBELL, James Ian, 1935- 200'.1
The language of religion [by] James I. Campbell. New York, Bruce Pub. Co. [1971] 183 p. 22 cm. (Horizons in philosophy) Bibliography: p. 164-176. [BL65.L2C33] 76-121005
1. Religion and language. I. Title.

CHARLESWORTH, Maxwell John, comp. 200'.1
The problem of religious language [compiled by] M. J. Charlesworth. Englewood Cliffs, N.J., Prentice-Hall [1974] viii, 253 p. 21 cm. (Contemporary problems in philosophy) Contents.Contents.—Charlesworth, M. J. Introduction.—Marshall, G. D. Religious language must be descriptive.—Otto, R. Religious language describes religious experiences I.—Horsburgh, H. J. N. Religious language describes religious experiences II.—Joyce, G. H. Religious language is analogously descriptive.—Carnap, R. Religious language is meaningless.—Randall, J. H., Jr. Religious language is symbolic and "impressive."—Ramsey, I. T. Religious language is paradoxically evocative.—Le Roy E. Religious language is "practical."—Arnold, M. Religious language is moral-emotive.—Santayana, G. Religious language is poetic-ethnic.—Hare, R. M. Religious language expresses quasi-metaphysical "attitudes."—Hudson, W. D. Religious language has its own proper meaning. Includes bibliographical references. [BL65.L2C48] 73-17263 ISBN 0-13-720011-0 7.95
1. Religion and language. I. Title.
Contents omitted.

DEWART, Leslie. 200'.1'4
Religion, language, and truth. [New York] Herder and Herder [1970] 174 p. 21 cm. Includes bibliographical references. [BL65.L2D44] 70-127870 5.95
1. Religion and language. 2. Christianity—Philosophy. I. Title.

DONOVAN, Peter, 1940- 200'.1'4
Religious language / Peter Donovan. New York : Hawthorn Books, 1976. 113 p. ; 21 cm. Includes index. Bibliography: p. 111-112. [BL65.L2D66 1976] 75-31372 ISBN 0-8015-6278-3 : 3.50
1. Religion and language. I. Title.

DONOVAN, Peter, 1940- 200'.1'4
Religious language / [by] Peter Donovan. London : Sheldon Press, 1976. ix, 114 p. : 20 cm. (Issues in religious studies) Includes index. Bibliography: p. 111-112. [BL65.L2D66 1976b] 76-373614 ISBN 0-85969-054-7 : £1.60
1. Religion and language. I. Title.

DUDLEY, Guilford, 1932- 200
The recovery of Christian myth, by Guilford Dudley III. Philadelphia, Westminster Press [1967] 127 p. 21 cm. Bibliographical references included in "Notes" (p. 119-123) [BL65.L2D8] 67-15869
1. Religion and language. 2. Myth. 3. Bible. N.T. Revelation — Criticism, interpretation, etc. I. Title.

FAWCETT, Thomas. 200'.14
The symbolic language of religion. Minneapolis, Augsburg Pub. House [1971] 288 p. 23 cm. Includes bibliographical references. [BL65.L2F37 1971] 79-140423 ISBN 0-8066-1117-0
1. Religion and language. 2. Symbolism. I. Title.

GILKEY, Langdon Brown, 1919- 230'.09'04
Naming the whirlwind; the renewal of God-language, by Langdon Gilkey. Indianapolis, Bobbs-Merrill [1969] x, 483 p. 22 cm. Bibliographical footnotes. [BL65.L2G5] 68-11146 2.75
1. Religion and language. 2. Theology—20th century. I. Title.

HALLETT, Garth. 230'.2
Darkness and light : the analysis of doctrinal statements / by Garth L. Hallett. New York : Paulist Press, c1975. vi, 174 p. ; 23 cm. Includes bibliographical references. [BX1753.H23] 75-21734 ISBN 0-8091-1897-1 pbk. : 6.95
1. Wittgenstein, Ludwig, 1889-1951. 2. Religion and language. 3. Theology, Catholic. I. Title.

HAMILTON, Kenneth. 201
Words and the word. Grand Rapids, Mich., Eerdmans [1971] 120 p. 21 cm. "A slightly expanded version of the Payton lectures delivered at Fuller Theological Seminary during spring quarter of 1970." Bibliography: p. 111-115. [BL65.L2H3] 76-132031 2.95
1. Bible—Criticism, interpretation, etc. 2. Religion and language. 3. Myth. I. Title.

HEIMBECK, Raeburne Seeley. 200'.1'4
Theology and meaning: a critique of metatheological scepticism [by] Raeburne S. Heimbeck. Stanford, Stanford University Press, 1969. 276 p. 23 cm. Bibliography: p. [261]-269. [BL65.L2H4 1969b] 68-13146 7.50
1. Religion and language. 2. Semantics (Philosophy) I. Title.

HUTCHEON, Robert James, 1869- 230.
Frankness in religion, by Robert J. Hutcheon. New York, The Macmillan company, 1929. vii p., 1 l., 307 p. 20 cm. [BX9841.H8] 29-3915
I. Title.

JENSON, Robert W. 201'.4
The knowledge of things hoped for; the sense of theological discourse [by] Robert W. Jenson. New York, Oxford University Press, 1969. viii, 243 p. 21 cm. Bibliographical footnotes. [BR96.5.J4] 79-75601 5.75
1. Religion and language. 2. Theology—Terminology. I. Title.

LADRIERE, Jean. 234'.2
Language and belief. Translated by Garrett Barden. [American ed. Notre Dame, Ind.] University of Notre Dame Press [1972] 204 p. 22 cm. Translation of L'articulation du sens. Includes bibliographical references. [BL65.L2L3313 1972] 72-3506 ISBN 0-268-00479-X 10.95
1. Religion and language. 2. Science—Language. I. Title.

LUNDEEN, Lyman T. 200'.1
Risk and rhetoric in religion; Whitehead's theory of language and the discourse of faith [by] Lyman T. Lundeen. Philadelphia, Fortress Press [1972] xii, 276 p. 23 cm. Includes bibliographical references. [BL65.L2L85] 71-171501 9.50
1. Whitehead, Alfred North, 1861-1947. 2. Religion and language. I. Title.

MACCORMAC, Earl R. 200'.1'4
Metaphor and myth in science and religion / Earl R. MacCormac. Durham, N.C. : Duke University Press, 1976. xviii, 167 p. ; 23 cm. Includes bibliographical references and indexes. [BL65.L2M26] 75-23941 ISBN 0-8223-0347-7 : 7.95
1. Religion and language. 2. Science—Language. 3. Metaphor. 4. Religion and science—1946- I. Title.

MACQUARRIE, John. 291.2
God-talk; an examination of the language and logic of theology. [1st Amer. ed.] New York, Harper [1967] 255p. 22cm. Bibl. [BR115.L25M3 1967] 67-14993 6.00
1. Religion and language. 2. Communication (Theology) I. Title.

MEYNELL, Hugo Anthony. 291
Sense, nonsense, and Christianity; an essay on the logical analysis of religious statements [by] Hugo A. Meynell. London, New York, Sheed and Ward [1964] 281 p. 18 cm. (Stagbooks) Bibliography: p. [271]-278. [BL65.L2M43] 67-66331
1. Religion and language. 2. Semantics (Philosophy) I. Title.

PING, Charles J. 230.014
Meaningful nonsense, by Charles J. Ping. Philadelphia, Westminster [1966] 143p. 21cm. Bibl. [BL65.L2P5] 66-15545 2.25 pap.,
1. Religion and language. 2. Theology—Terminology. I. Title.

PRELLER, Victor. 201'.4
Divine science and the science of God; a reformulation of Thomas Aquinas. Princeton, N.J., Princeton University Press, 1967. ix, 281 p. 23 cm. "Original version ... was submitted as a doctoral dissertation to the Department of Religion at Princeton University." Bibliography: p. 273-278. [BX1749.T7P7] 66-21838
1. Thomas Aquinas, Saint, 1225?-1274—Theology. 2. Religion and language. I. Title.

PRELLER, Victor. 201'.4
Divine science and the science of God; a reformulation of Thomas Aquinas. Princeton, N.J., Princeton University Press, 1967. ix, 281 p. 23 cm. "Original version ... was submitted as a doctoral dissertation to the Department of Religion at Princeton University." Bibliography: p. 273-278. [BX1749.T7P7] 66-21838
1. Thomas Aquinas, Saint, 1225?-1274—Theology. 2. Religion and language. I. Title.

SANTONI, Ronald E., comp. 200'.1'4
Religious language and the problem of religious knowledge, edited with an introd. by Ronald E. Santoni. Bloomington, Indiana University Press [1968] 382 p. 22 cm. Includes bibliographies. [BL65.L2S2] 68-27352 8.50
1. Religion and language. 2. Knowledge, Theory of (Religion) I. Title.

STAHMER, Harold. 200'.1'4
"Speak that I may see Thee!" The religious

significance of language. New York, Macmillan [1968] xi, 304 p. 21 cm. Bibliography: p. 287-293. [BL65.L2S7] 68-21305
1. Religion and language. I. Title.

TESELLE, Sallie 808'.066'202
McFague.
Speaking in parables : a study in metaphor and theology / by Sallie McFague TeSelle. Philadelphia : Fortress Press, [1975] vi, 186 p. ; 22 cm. Includes bibliographical references and index. [BR115.L25T47] 74-26338 ISBN 0-8006-1097-0 pbk. : 4.25
1. Religion and language. 2. Parables. I. Title.

VAN BUREN, Paul Matthews, 200'.1
1924-
The edges of language; an essay in the logic of a religion [by] Paul M. van Buren. New York, Macmillan [1972] 178 p. 22 cm. Includes bibliographical references. [BL65.L2V35] 70-187077 7.95
1. Religion and language. I. Title.

WINQUIST, Charles E., 201'.1
1944-
The communion of possibility / Charles E. Winquist. Chico, Calif. : New Horizons Press, [1975] 155 p. ; 22 cm. (The religious quest ; v. 2) Includes bibliographical references and index. [BL65.L2W52] 75-2420 ISBN 0-914914-05-7 lib.bdg. : 8.95 ISBN 0-914914-04-9 pbk. : 4.95
1. Religion and language. 2. Hermeneutics. 3. Church. I. Title. II. Series.

Religion and language—Addresses, essays, lectures.

THE Autonomy of religious 200'.1
belief : a critical inquiry / edited with an introduction by Frederick J. Crosson. Notre Dame, Ind. : University of Notre Dame Press, c1981. p. cm. (Notre Dame studies in the philosophy of religion ; v. 2) [BL65.L2A95] 19 81-50461 ISBN 0-268-00596-6 : 14.95
1. Religion and language—Addresses, essays, lectures. 2. Religion —Philosophy—Addresses, essays, lectures. I. Crosson, Frederick James, 1926- II. Series.

GOULBURN, Edward Meyriok, 1818-
1897.
The idle word: short religious essays upon the gift of speech, and its employment in conversation. By Edward Meyrick Goulburn ... New York, D. Appleton and company, 1866. 2 p. l., [5]-208 p. 18 cm. 8-16867
I. Title.

HIGH, Dallas M., comp. 200'.1'4
New essays on religious language. Edited by Dallas M. High. New York, Oxford University Press, 1969. xv, 240 p. 21 cm. Contents.—Introduction, by D. M. High.—Ludwig Wittgenstein: unphilosophical notes, by E. Heller.—Wittgenstein and theology, by P. L. Holmer.—Religion and science: a philosopher's approach, by I. T. Ramsey.—Mapping the logic of models in science and theology, by F. Ferre.—Metaphysics and the limits of language, by C. B. Daly.—God and the "private I", by W. H. Poteat.—Paradox in religion, by I. T. Ramsey.—Birth, suicide, and the doctrine of creation, by W. H. Poteat.—The justification of religious belief, by B. Mitchell.—Assertion and analogy, by T. McPherson.—A neglected use of theological language, by R. C. Coburn. Bibliographical footnotes. [BL65.L2H53] 73-75116 5.00
1. Religion and language—Addresses, essays, lectures. I. Title.

LANGUAGE in religious 200'.1'4
practice / edited by William J. Samarin. Rowley, Mass. : Newbury House Publishers, c1976. xi, 177 p. ; 23 cm. (Series in sociolinguistics) Includes bibliographies and index. [BL65.L2L37] 76-17553 ISBN 0-88377-059-8 pbk. : 7.95
1. Religion and language—Addresses, essays, lectures. I. Samarin, William J.

RELIGIOUS language and 200'.1
knowledge. Edited by Robert H. Ayers and William T. Blackstone. Athens, University of Georgia Press [1972] x, 149 p. 22 cm. Essays originally presented in the 1965 Great Thinkers Forum sponsored by the Dept. of Philosophy and Religion at the University of Georgia, the 1st of a series of meetings; papers of the 2d are entered under the title: Education and ethics. Includes bibliographical references. [BL65.L2R43] 72-169950 ISBN 0-8203-0269-4 4.00
1. Religion and language—Addresses, essays, lectures. I. Ayers, Robert Hyman, ed. II. Blackstone, William T., ed.

Religion and language—History.

BOYLE, Marjorie O'Rourke, 201'.4
1943-
Erasmus on language and method in theology / Marjorie O'Rourke Boyle. Toronto ; Buffalo : University of Toronto Press, c1977. p. cm. (Erasmus studies ; 2) Includes index. Bibliography: p. [B785.E64B69] 77-2606 ISBN 0-8020-5363-7 : 17.50
1. Erasmus, Desiderius, d. 1536. 2. Religion and language—History. 3. Theology—Methodology—History. I. Title. II. Series.

TILLEY, Terrence W. 231'.01'4
Talking of God : an introduction to philosophical analysis of religious language / by Terrence W. Tilley. New York : Paulist Press, c1978. vii, 131 p. ; 21 cm. (An Exploration book) Includes bibliographical references and index. [BL65.L2T5] 78-51592 ISBN 0-8091-2110-7 pbk. : 4.95
1. Religion and language—History. 2. God—History of doctrines. I. Title.

Religion and law.

ABBOTT, Edwin Milton, 200.0134
1877-
The law and religion, by Edwin M. Abbott. Philadelphia, Dorance and company [c1938] 4 p. l., 7-92 p. 20 cm. [BL65.L33A3] 39-488
1. Religion and law. I. Title.

RELIGION and the law : 261.7
a handbook of suggestions for laymen and clergymen preparing Law Day addresses. [Chicago : American Bar Association, c1975] 64 p. ; 23 cm. Cover title. Bibliography: p. 59-62. [BL65.L33R44] 76-356405 pbk. : 0.75
1. Religion and law. I. American Bar Association.

ROSENIUS, Carl Olaf, 1816- 242
1868.
The believer free from the law, by C. O. Rosenius; translated, with an introduction, by Adolf Hult. Rock Island, Ill., Augustana book concern [c1923] 132 p. 20 cm. [BV4836.R6] 23-6591 0.75
I. Hult, Adolf, 1869- tr. II. Title.

Religion and literature.

BALL, Timothy Horton, 1826-
The home of the redeemed and other discourses. Crown Point, Ind., Register print, 1899 [1898] 200 p. port. 12. 99-233
I. Title.

BELCHER, Kate H. Mrs. 248
Home nurture for the little ones of the church, by Kate H. Belcher. Prepared at the request of a committee on home nurture and religion in the province of New York and New Jersey. Milwaukee, Wis., Morehouse publishing co.; [etc., etc., c1919] xiii, 142 p. 27 pl. (in pocket) 21 cm. Part of the pages are blank on which the plates are to be mounted. [BV1590.B4] 19-16091
I. Title.

FITCH, Robert Elliot, 822.3'3
1902-
Shakespeare: the perspective of value, by Robert E. Fitch. Philadelphia, Westminster Press [1969] 304 p. 21 cm. "Notes and references": p. [249]-290. [PR3011.F5] 73-78481 3.50
1. Shakespeare, William, 1564-1616—Religion and ethics. 2. Religion and literature. I. Title.

FRYE, Roland Mushat. 822.33
Shakespeare and Christian doctrine. Princeton, N.J., Princeton University Press, 1963. ix, 314 p. 23 cm. Bibliography: p. 295-303. [PR3011.F7] 63-9990
1. Shakespeare, William, 1564-1616—Religion and ethics. 2. Religion and literature. I. Title.

FUNK, Robert Walter, 809'.933'51
1926-
Jesus as precursor / by Robert W. Funk. Philadelphia : Fortress Press, c1975. vii, 165 p. ; 22 cm. (Semeia supplements ; no. 2) Bibliography: p. 161-165. [PN49.F8] 75-18949 ISBN 0-8006-1502-6 : 3.95
1. Religion and literature. I. Title. II. Series.

GLICKSBERG, Charles 809.9'33
Irving, 1901-
Modern literature and the death of God, by Charles I. Glicksberg. The Hague, Martinus Nijhoff, 1966. 162 p. 24 cm. fl 19.80 Bibliographical footnotes. [PN49.G55] 67-77029
1. Religion and literature. 2. Literature, Modern — Hist. & crit. I. Title.

JARRETT-KERR, Martin, 808.84'9'31
1912-
Studies in literature and belief. Freeport, N.Y., Books for Libraries Press [1970, c1954] xi, 203 p. 23 cm. (Essay index reprint series) Includes bibliographical references. [PN49.J37 1970] 74-134101 ISBN 0-8369-1978-5
1. Religion and literature. I. Title.

LYNCH, William F., 809'.933'1
1908-
Christ and Apollo : the dimensions of the literary imagination / William F. Lynch. Notre Dame : University of Notre Dame Press, 1975, c1960. p. cm. Reprint of the ed. published by Sheed and Ward, New York; with a new pref. and without the 4 supplements in the back. Bibliography: p. [PN49.L9 1975] 75-19873 ISBN 0-268-00711-X : 8.95. ISBN 0-268-00712-8 pbk. : 3.25
1. Religion and literature. 2. Creation (Literary, artistic, etc.) I. Title.

MCKAY, Llewelyn R 922.8373
Home memories of President David O. McKay. compiled. and written by Llewelyn R. McKay. Salt Lake City, Desert Book Co., 1956. 280p. illus. 24cm. [BX8695.M27M3] 56-26187
1. McKay, David Oman, 1873- II. Title.

MIMS, Edwin, 1872- 809'.933'1
1959.
Great writers as interpreters of religion. Freeport, N.Y., Books for Libraries Press [1970, c1945] 176 p. 23 cm. (Essay index reprint series) [PN49.M46 1970] 70-134116 ISBN 0-8369-1988-2
1. Religion and literature. I. Title.

MOLLENKOTT, Virginia R. 809.9'33
Adamant & stone chips; a Christian humanist approach to knowledge [by] Virginia R. Mollenkott. Waco, Tex., Word Books [1968, c1967] 113 p. 21 cm. Bibliography: p. 111-113. [PN49.M55] 67-30568
1. Religion and literature. 2. Literature and morals. 3. Humanism. I. Title.

PANICHAS, George 808.84'9'3
Andrew, comp.
Mansions of the spirit; essays in literature and religion. Edited by George A. Panichas. [1st ed.] New York, Hawthorn Books [1967] 414 p. 24 cm. Includes bibliographical references. [PN49.P28 1967] 67-14862
1. Religion and literature. 2. Literature, Modern—19th century—Addresses, essays, lectures. 3. Literature, Modern—20th century—Addresses, essays, lectures. I. Title.

RAVEN, Charles Earle, 1885- 270
The quest of religion, by Charles E. Raven ... Garden City, N. Y., Doubleday, Doran & company, inc., 1928. 141 p. 19 cm. [BR121.R29] 29-222
I. Title.
Contents omitted.

RELIGION as story / 809'.933'1
edited by James B. Wiggins. 1st ed. New York : Harper & Row, [1975] p. cm. (A Harper forum book ; RD 103) Includes bibliographical references. [PN49.R4 1975] 75-9339 ISBN 0-06-069353-3 pbk. : 4.50
1. Religion and literature. 2. Narration (Rhetoric) I. Wiggins, James B., 1935-

SCOTT, Nathan A. 809.933
The broken center; studies in the theological horizon of modern literature [by] Nathan A. Scott, Jr. New Haven, Yale University Press, 1966. xv, 237 p. 23 cm. "Chapter 5 was delivered as the first William Lyon Phelps lectures at Yale University in ... 1965." Bibliographical footnotes. [PN49.S325] 66-12511
1. Religion and literature. I. Title.

TATE, Allen, 1899- 809.9'33
Mere literature and the lost traveller. Nashville, George Peabody College for Teachers, 1969. [13] p. 2 ports. 28 cm. (Fourth annual C. C. Williamson memorial lecture) [PN49.T3] 70-259827
1. Religion and literature. I. Title. II. Series: C. C. Williamson memorial lecture, 4

THOMPSON, Lawrance Roger, 1906-
Melville's quarrel with God. Princeton, Princeton University Press, 1952 [i.e. 1966, c1952] 474 p. 25 cm. 68-15743
1. Melville, Herman, 1819-1891. 2. Religion and literature. I. Title.

WILDER, Amos Niven, 809.9'33
1895-
The new voice; religion, literature, hermeneutics [by] Amos N. Wilder. [New York] Herder and Herder [1969] 269 p. 22 cm. "Amplification of the material and themes presented as the first Paul Tillich Commemoration Lectures under the title 'Modern reality and the renewal of the word' ... delivered at New Harmony, Indiana, in May 1968." Bibliographical footnotes. [PN49.W48] 76-87775 6.50
1. Bible—Hermeneutics. 2. Religion and literature. 3. Religion and language. I. Title.

Religion and literature—Addresses, essays, lectures.

GARDNER, Helen Louise. 809'.933'1
Religion and literature [by] Helen Gardner. New York, Oxford University Press, 1971. 194 p. 22 cm. Includes bibliographical references. [PN49.G34 1971b] 72-27742 ISBN 0-19-501457-X 6.00
1. Religion and literature—Addresses, essays, lectures. I. Title.

GUNN, Giles B., comp. 809.9'33'1
Literature and religion. Edited by Giles B. Gunn. [1st U.S. ed.] New York, Harper & Row [1971] xi, 238 p. 21 cm. (Harper forum books, RD13) Contents.Contents.—Introduction: Literature and its relation to religion, by G. B. Gunn.—The uses of a theological criticism, by A. N. Wilder.—Specifying the sacred, by V. Buckley.—Voice as summons for belief: literature, faith, and the divided self, by W. J. Ong.—Hold on hard to the huckleberry bushes, by R. W. B. Lewis.—The idea of man in literature, by E. Auerbach.—Hamlet's moment of truth, by P. T. Roberts, Jr.—Meditative poetry, by L. L. Martz.—Religious poetry in the United States, by R. P. Blackmur.—The hazard of modern poetry, by E. Heller.—The poetry of reality, by J. H. Miller.—Poetry and prayer, by N. A. Scott, Jr.—The symbol gives rise to thought, by P. Ricoeur.—The poetry of meaning, by S. R. Hopper. Includes bibliographical references. [PN49.G76 1971b] 71-109078 3.95
1. Religion and literature—Addresses, essays, lectures. I. Title.

TENNYSON, G. B., comp. 809'.933'1
Religion and modern literature; essays in theory and criticism. Edited by G. B. Tennyson and Edward E. Ericson, Jr. Grand Rapids, Eerdmans [1975] 424 p. 24 cm. Includes bibliographical references. [PN49.T37] 74-13237 ISBN 0-8028-3459-0 8.95
1. Religion and literature—Addresses, essays, lectures. I. Ericson, Edward E., joint comp. II. Title.

Religion and music.

FOWLER, Alfred.
The ministry and melody of angels; a gift book for every day in the year ... by Alfred Fowler ... with introductions by Margaret E. Sangster and Chancellor Burwash, S. T. D. Chicago, Philadelphia, Monarch book company, [c1903] 542 p. incl., front.,

plates. 25 cm. Issued also under the title: Our angel friends in ministry and song. 4-21506
I. Title.

HANCOCK, Tyre. 783.
Church error; or, Instrumental music condemned. By Tyre Hancock... Dallas, The author, 1902. 72 p. 22 cm. [ML3001.H24] 2-19743
I. Title.

HANDEL, Georg Friedrich, 1685-1759. 783.3
The Messiah, a sacred oratorio composed in the year 1741, by G. F. Handel. Edited, and the pianoforte accompaniment largely re-written, by Ebenezer Prout... London, Novello and company, limited; New York, Novello, Ewer and co., c1902. vi p., 1 l., 209, [1] p. 29 cm. (Novello's original octavo edition) With preface by the editor. Vocal score with pianoforte accompaniment. [M2003.H] 3-7596
I. Title.

HERRINGTON, J Wells and Pitney, J H
The new century: a book containing music, well graded and adapted for the use of singing classes public and high schools, church choirs, choral societies, musical conventions, the home circle, etc. ... Eagle Bridge, N. Y., Herrington & Pitney, 1899. 158 pp., 1 l. front. (port.) 4 degrees. 1-268
I. Title.

LADD, Paul R comp.
Christian life in song, the Christian year; a community song book for church, school and home. illustrated by Eva Maria Ladd. Boston, McLaughlin & Reilly Co., c1963. xv, 206 p. illus. 27 cm. For various combinations of voices, mostly SATB; the voice parts may be used for optional piano aco. 65-64597
I. Title.

LADD, Paul R comp.
Christian life in song, the Christian year; a community song book for church, school and home. illustrated by Eva Maria Ladd. Boston, McLaughlin & Reilly Co., c1963. xv, 206 p. illus. 27 cm. For various combinations of voices, mostly SATB; the voice parts may be used for optional piano aco. 65-64597
I. Title.

LARSON, Bob. 780'.09
Rock & the church. [1st ed.] Carol Stream, Ill., Creation House [1971] 90 p. 22 cm. Includes bibliographical references. [ML3007.L37] 76-158992 1.95
1. Religion and music. I. Title.

MENDL, Robert William Sigismund, 1892- 780.1
The divine quest in music. New York, Philosophical Library [1957] 252p. 23cm. [ML2900.M4 1957a] 57-14057
1. Religion and music. I. Title.

MYRA, Harold Lawrence, 1939- 780'.09
Rock, Bach & superschlock [by] Harold Myra and Dean Merrill. [1st ed.] Philadelphia, Holman [1972] 123 p. illus. 27 cm. [ML3865.M97] 71-39852 ISBN 0-87981-007-6 4.95
1. Religion and music. I. Merrill, Dean, joint author. II. Title.

PATTON, John Danie] and others.
Christian life songs. Dalton, Ga.; Dallas, Tex. [etc.] The A. J. Showalter co., 1899. 224 p. 12 degrees. Words and music. Mar
I. Title.

PENN, W. E. Mrs. 783
New harvest bells, for Sunday schools, revivals, and all religious meetings. Containing selections from the most popular song writers of the day, together with the unpublished songs of the late W. E. Penn. By Mrs. W. E. Penn. Associate editors, W H. Morris and E. A. Hoffman. Eureka Springs Ark., Mrs. W. E. Penn., c1900. 1 p. l., 222 [4] p. front. (port.) 20 cm. [M2193.P4H3] 0-2737
I. Morris, W. H. joint comp. II. Hoffman, Elisha A., 1839- joint comp. III. Title.

SHIELDS, Elizabeth McEwen, 1879- 783
Music in the religious growth of children, by Elizabeth Mc.E. Shields. New York, Nashville, Abingdon-Cokesbury press [1943] 128 p. 22 1/2 cm. Includes children's hymns with music. "Song books": p. 38-39. [MT10.S5M8 1943] 43-16914
1. Religion and music. 2. Religious education of children. I. Title.

STONE, Alonzo.
The Resurrection; a sacred cantata for three solo voices (contralto, tenor, bass), chorus and organ; music by Alonzo Stone ... Words selected and arranged from the Holy Scriptures by Rev. Nathaniel Seymour Thomas. Boston, New York [etc.] White-Smith music publishing co., 1902. 1 p. l., 49 p. 28 cm. Vocal score. 2-16744
I. Title.

TOVEY, Herbert George, 1888- *264 268.73
Music levels in Christian education, a book on Sunday school music. Wheaton, Ill., Van Kampen Press [1952] 143 p. 20 cm. [MT10.T68] 52-1877
1. Religion and music. 2. Religious education of children. I. Title.

Religion and parapsychology.

BRO, Harmon Hartzell, 1919- 133.80924
Edgar Cayce on religion and psychic experience. Under the editorship of Hugh Lynn Cayce. New York, Paperback Library [1970] 265 p. 18 cm. [BF1027.C3B7] 72-9626 0.95
1. Cayce, Edgar, 1877-1945. 2. Religion and parapsychology. I. Title.

HERON, Laurence Tunstall. 220.8'1338
ESP in the Bible. [1st ed.] Garden City, N.Y., Doubleday, 1974. 212 p. 21 cm. Includes bibliographical references. [BS534.H45] 73-14050 ISBN 0-385-09603-8 5.95
1. Bible—Miscellanea. 2. Religion and parapsychology. I. Title.

NEFF, H. Richard, 1933- 133
Psychic phenomena and religion: ESP, prayer, healing, survival, by H. Richard Neff. Philadelphia, Westminster Press [1971] 176 p. 19 cm. Includes bibliographical references. [BL65.P3N44] 70-158122 ISBN 0-664-24931-0 3.50
1. Religion and parapsychology. I. Title.

Religion and politics.

THE Christian, the state and the New Testament. Altona, Manitoba, D. W. Frieson & Sons, 1959. 128p. Includes bibliography and bibliographical footnotes.
I. Penner, Archie.

LEVY, Bernard Henri. 296.3'877
Testament of God / Bernard-Henri Levy ; translated from the French by George Holoch. 1st ed. New York : Harper & Row, c1980. p. cm. Translation of Le testament de Dieu. Includes bibliographical references and index. [BL65.P7L4413 1980] 80-7589 ISBN 0-06-012616-7 : 15.00
1. Religion and politics. 2. World politics—20th century. 3. Covenants (Theology) I. Title.

PELLEY, Wiley Hall, 1869- 265.
Christian government, by W. H. Pelley. Boston, The Christopher publishing house [c1925] 263 p. plates, map. 21 cm. [BR115.P7P4] 25-10269
I. Title.

SCHONFIELD, Hugh Joseph, 1901- 261
The politics of God [by] Hugh J. Schonfield. Chicago, Regnery [1971, c1970] xx, 231 p. 22 cm. Includes bibliographical references. [BL65.P7S33 1971] 77-143848 5.95
1. Religion and politics. 2. Messianism. 3. Judaism—Relations—Christianity. 4. Christianity and other religions—Judaism. I. Title.

SCHONFIELD, Hugh Joseph, 1901- 261
The politics of God / Hugh J. Schonfield. Boulder Creek, Ca : University of the Trees Press, c1970, 1978 printing. xx, 243 p. : ill. ; 22 cm. Includes bibliographical references and index. [BL65.P7S33 1978] 78-9024 ISBN 0-916438-25-2 pbk. : 9.95
1. Religion and politics. 2. Messianism. 3. Judaism—Relations—Christianity. 4. Christianity and other religions—Judaism. I. Title.

SHEPHEARD, Harold B.
Jesus and politics; an essay towards an ideal, by Harold B. Shepheard, M.A., with introduction by Vida D. Scudder. New York, E. P. Dutton & company [c1915] 2 p. l., iii-xxxii, 145 p. 19 1/2 cm. $1.00. 15-5395
I. Title.

SMITH, Donald Eugene, 1927- 322'.1
Religion and political development, an analytic study. Boston, Little, Brown [1970] xvii, 298 p. illus. 21 cm. (The Little, Brown series in comparative politics) Includes bibliographical references. [BL65.P7S6] 76-112757
1. Religion and politics. I. Title.

SMITH, Donald Eugene, 1927- comp. 291'.17
Religion, politics, and social change in the Third World; a sourcebook. Edited with introductory notes by Donald Eugene Smith. New York, Free Press [1974, c1971] xv, 286 p. 21 cm. Bibliography: p. 267-271. [BL65.P7S635] 3.95 (pbk)
1. Religion and politics. 2. Religion and state. 3. Religion and sociology. 4. Socialism and religion. I. Title.
L.C. card number for original ed.: 73-143516.

TOWNSEND, Luther Tracy, 1838-
"Manifest destiny" from a religious point of view. An address delivered before the Boston music hall patriotic association, November 6, 1898. Baltimore, Md., Baltimore Methodist [1898] 61 p. 16°. Dec
I. Title.

WESTOCTT, Brooke Foss, bp. of Durham, 1825-1901.
Christian social union addresses, by the late Brooke Foss Westcott ... London, New York, Macmillan and co., limited, 1903. 4 p. l., 76 p. 19 cm. 3-31452
I. Title.
Contents omitted.

Religion and politics—Case studies.

LEWY, Guenter, 1923- 301.6'333
Religion and revolution. New York, Oxford University Press, 1974. xvii, 694 p. 25 cm. Includes bibliographical references. [BL65.P7L46] 73-87610 ISBN 0-19-501744-7 17.50
1. Religion and politics—Case studies. 2. Revolutions—Case studies. I. Title.

Religion and politics—United States.

MENENDEZ, Albert J. 261.7'0973
Religion at the polls / by Albert J. Menendez. Philadelphia : Westminster Press, c1977. 248 p. ; 21 cm. Bibliography: p. 237-248. [BL2530.U6M46] 76-30655 ISBN 0-664-24117-4 pbk. : 5.95
1. Religion and politics—United States. 2. Presidents—United States—Election—History. I. Title.

Religion and Psychiatry.

JUDAISM and psychiatry . . .
New York, Basic Books, c1956. xl, 197p. 22cm.
1. Religion and Psychiatry. 2. Psychology, Pastoral. 3. Psychology of the Jew. I. Noveck, Simon, ed.

Religion and race.

CAMPBELL, Charles Grimshaw, 1912-1953. 261.8'34'51
Race and religion. Westport, Conn., Greenwood Press [1970] viii, 238 p. 23 cm. Reprint of the 1953 ed. Includes bibliographical references. [BL65.R3C3 1970] 71-104256 ISBN 0-8371-3262-2
1. Religion and race. I. Title.

Religion and race—Congresses.

NATIONAL Conference on Religion and Race, Chicago, 1963. 261.8'34'5196073
Race : challenge to religion : original essays and An appeal to the conscience / edited by Mathew Ahmann. Westport, Conn. : Greenwood Press, 1979, c1963. xiv, 178 p. ; 22 cm. "Convened by agencies of the National Council of Churches, the Synagogue Council of America, and the National Catholic Welfare Conference." Reprint of the ed. published by H. Regnery Co., Chicago. Includes bibliographical references. [BL65.R3N37 1979] 78-24276 ISBN 0-313-20796-8 lib. bdg. : 16.00
1. Religion and race—Congresses. 2. Church and race relations—United States—Congresses. I. Ahmann, Mathew H. II. National Council of the Churches of Christ in the United States of America. Dept. of Racial and Cultural Relations. III. Title.

Religion and science.

ALLEN, John Harden, 1847-
The spirit man; or, The hidden man of the heart. A work on pneumatology and psychology showing the Biblical distinctions between the soul and the spirit of man, and the harmony of these with the objective and the subjective man of science ... by Rev. J. H. Allen ... [Los Angeles, Press of the Grafton publishing corporation, c1915] 232 p. incl. front. (port.) 19 1/2 cm. $1.00 16-1028
I. Title.

BALLARD, Frank. 215
The mystery of painlessness; an appeal to facts, by Frank Ballard ... with foreword by S. Parkes Cadman ... New York, Chicago [etc.] Fleming H. Revell company [c1926] 95 p. 19 1/2 cm. An appreciation of the benevolent marvels of our daily existence. cf. p. 94. [BL262.B3] 26-21513
1. Religion and science. 2. Pain. I. Title. II. Title: Painlessness, The mystery of.

BARRICKMAN, Van Ara, 1874- 215
Science and the Bible; excerpts from some inspiring addresses delivered before several Bible classes. by Van A. Barrickman ... general theme: evolution of our spiritual life and ideals. Pittsburgh, Pa., Pittsburgh printing company 1927. 152 p. incl. front. (mounted port.) 24 cm. [BL240.B27] 27-5673
1. Religion and science. 2. Bible and science. I. Title.

BEST, John Henry, 1856- 215
From the seen to the unseen, by John H. Best ... London, New York [etc.] Longmans, Green and co., 1929. xi, [1], 552 p. illus., pl., diagrs. 23 cm. "List of authors quoted or otherwise referred to": p. ix-xi. [BL340.B36] 29-7586 7.00
1. Religion and science. 2. Science. 3. Evolution. I. Title.

BROMAN, Oscar Francis. 215
Transcendent evolution, by Oscar Francis Broman. Boston, Mass., The Stratford company [c1928] xii, 162 p. 19 1/2 cm. [BL263.B73] 28-22162
1. Religion and science. 2. Evolution. I. Title.

DARROW, Floyd Lavern, 1880- 215
Through science to God, by Floyd L. Darrow ... Indianapolis, The Bobbs-Merrill co. [c1925] 309 p. front., plates. 21 cm. [BL240.D33] 25-21594
1. Religion and science. 2. Evolution. I. Title.

DRAPER, John William, 1811-1882. 215
History of the conflict between religion and science. By John William Draper ... 3d ed. New York, D. Appleton and company, 1875. xxii, 373 p. 19 1/2 cm. (The International scientific series [vol. xii)] [BL245.D7 1875] 6-46128
1. Religion and science. I. Title.

DRAPER, John William, 1811-1882. 215
History of the conflict between religion and science, by John William Draper original text edited and abridged by Charles T. Sprading. New York. Vanguard

press. 1926. vii. 116 p. 18 1/2 cm. [BL245.D7 1926] 26-19853
1. Religion and science. I. Sprading, Charles T., ed. II. Title.

FISHER, Hiram Thomas, 1839- 215
Cosmos and man, by H. T. Fisher. [Eustis, Fla., The author [c1926] viii, 170 p. front. (port.) 19 1/2 cm. [BL240.F5] 27-1207
1. Religion and science. 2. Evolution. I. Title.

GILBERT, George Holley, 1854- 232.
Jesus for the men of today, when science aids religion, by George Holley Gilbert ... New York, Hodder & Stoughton, George H. Doran company [c1917] xv p., 2 l., 21-176 p. 20 cm. [BT301.G5] 17-17183 1.00
I. Title.

GLENN, Jacob B 1905- 221.861
The Bible and modern medicine; an interpretation of the basic principles of the Bible in the light of present day medical thought. New York, Bloch Pub. Co. [1963] 222 p. 23 cm. [R135.5.G55] 63-6032
1. Pible — Medicine, hygiene, etc. 2. Jewish way of life. 3. Jews — Rites and ceremonies. I. Title.

GOD in the space age.
Philadelphia, Lippincott [c1959] 216p.
1. Religion and science. I. Heinecken, Martin J

GOODCHILD, Frank Marsden, 1860-1928. 252.
God in everything, a series of popular nature studies, by Frank M. Goodchild ... Philadelphia, Boston [etc.] The Judson press [c1928] 6 p. l., 3-271 p. 20 cm. [BX6333.G57G6] 28-13132
1. Religion and science. I. Title. II. Title: Nature studies.

HARDWICK, John Charlton.
Religion and science from Galileo to Bergson, by John Charlton Hardwick... London, Society for promoting Christian knowledge; New York, Macmillan, 1920. ix, 148 p. 20 cm. A 21
1. Religion and science. I. Title.

HARRIS, James Coffee, 1858- 215
Nature and God, by James Coffee Harris ... Cave Spring, Ga., c1928. [254] p. illus., plates, diagrs. 22 cm. Various pagings. Copyright date corrected in manuscript to 1929. [BL240.H3] 29-12997
1. Religion and science. 2. Cosmology. 3. Evolution. I. Title.

HITCHCOCK, Edward, 1793-1864. 215
The religion of geology and its connected sciences. By Edward Hitchcock ... Boston, Phillips, Sampson, and company, 1852. xvi, 511 p. col. front. 20 cm. [BS657.H53 1852] G S
1. Religion and science. I. Title.

HITCHCOCK, Edward, 1793-1864.
The religion of geology and its connected sciences. By Edward Hitchcock ... A new ed.: With an additional lecture, giving a summary of the author's present views of the whole subject ... Boston, Phillips, Sampson, and company, 1859. XX, 592 p. col. front., col. pl. 29 1/2 cm. G S
1. Religion and science. I. Title.

HOOD, Alice Watkins, 1877- 215
And the new earth, by Alice Watkins Hood... Baltimore, Waverly press, 1927. 214 p. 19 cm. [BL240.H72] 27-22170
1. Religion and science. I. Title.
Contents omitted.

HOYT, Wilbur Franklin, 1864- 215
Science and life; a philosophy of science, by Wilbur F. Hoyt ... [Peru, Neb.] c1927. 59 p. illus. (port.) 21 1/2 cm. Bibliography: p. [6] [BL241.H65] 27-13583
1. Religion and science. 2. Science—Philosophy. I. Title.

HUBBIRT, John c. 215
The great globe, a place of everlasting opportunity, by John C. Hubbirt. Des Moines, Ia., The Gold press [c1928] 3 p. l., 213 p. 20 1/2 cm. [BL240.H78] 28-30525
1. Religion and science. 2. Evolution. I. Title.

JACOBS, Thornwell, 1877- 215
The new science and the old religion, by Thornwell Jacobs ... Oglethorpe University, Ga., Oglethorpe university press [c1927] xv, [1], 463 p. incl. front., illus. diagrs. fold. tab. 24 cm. [BL240.J3] 27-3331
1. Religion and science. 2. Evolution. I. Title.

JOHNSON, Francis Howe, 1835-1920. 201
God in evolution; a pragmatic study of theology, by Francis Howe Johnson ... New York [etc.] Longmans, Green, and co., 1911. vii, 354 p. 21 cm. [BL51.J6] 11-31905 1.60
1. Religion and science. 2. Evolution. I. Title.

KAUFMANN, Peter. 133
The temple of truth, or The science of ever-progressive knowledge; containing the foundation and elements of a system for arriving at absolute certainty in all things; being a message of never ending joy, and the abiding herald of better times to all men of a good-will, or desirous of acquiring it ... by Peter Kaufmann ... Cincinnati, Truman & Spofford [etc.]; Canton, O., The author, 1858. vi, 9-290 p. 20 cm. Published also in German, same year. [X3.K3] 15-8283
I. Title.

LE CONTE, Joseph, 1823-1901.
Religion and science. A series of Sunday lectures on the relation of natural and revealed religion, or the truths revealed in nature and Scripture. By Joseph Le Conte ... New York, D. Appleton and company, 1880. 324 p. 18 1/2 cm. 15-3388
I. Title.

LE CONTE, Joseph, 1823-1901.
Religion and science. A series of Sunday lectures on the relation of natural and revealed religion, or the truths revealed in nature and Scripture. By Joseph Le Conte ... New York, D. Appleton and company, 1884. 324 p. 18 1/2 cm. 17-8254
I. Title.

LE CONTE, Joseph, 1823-1901.
Religion and science. A series of Sunday lectures on the relation of natural and revealed religion, or the truths revealed in nature and Scripture, by Joseph Le Conte ... New York, D. Appleton and company, 1898. 324 p. 18 1/2 cm. A 11
1. Religion and science. I. Title.

LEIGHTON, Gerald Rowley, 1868-
Scientific Christianity; a study in the biology of character, by Gerald Leighton ... New York, Moffat, Yard and company, 1910. xii, 289 p. illus. 20 cm. A 10
1. Religion and science. I. Title.

LODGE, Oliver Joseph, Sir 1851- 215
Man and the universe, by Sir Oliver Lodge ... New York, George H. Doran company [c1920] vi p., 3 l., 294 p. 23 cm. "This book appeared originally under the title 'Science and immortality,' but this represents only a portion of its theme and is inadequate. Its true title, by which it is known in England, is now restored to it--'Man and the universe.'"--Pref. note to American ed. [BL240.L6 1920] 20-5129 3.00
1. Religion and science. 2. Cosmology. I. Title.

LUCKEY, Leonard Wilson Arnold, 1857- 215
Whence comest thou? Whither goest thou? A very comprehensive treatise on creation and the endless progression of life as is clearly seen, through science and religion, by the Rev. Leonard W. A. Luckey ... Boston, Mass., The Stratford company, 1927. 209 p. 19 1/2 cm. [BL240.L8] 27-3427
1. Religion and science. I. Title.

MERCER, John Edward, bp. of Tasmania.
The science of life and the larger hope, by the Right Rev. John Edward Mercer ... New York, Bombay [etc.] Longmans, Green, and co., 1910. 3 p. l., 195, [1] p. 20 cm. A 11
1. Religion and science. I. Title.

MOLINARE, Nicholas.
DNA, RNA and the atom; what does God say about them. New York, Vantage Press [1963] 134 p. 21 cm. 65-105291
1. Religion and science. I. Title.

MOORE, Albert Weston, 1842- 225
The rational basis of orthodoxy, by Albert Weston Moore, D. D. Boston and New York, Houghton, Mifflin and company, 1901. vi p., 1 l., 378 p. 1 l. 21 cm. [BR121.M73] 1-23597
1. Religion and science. 2. Christianity—Evidences. I. Title.

NEEDHAM, Joseph, ed. 215
Science, religion and reality [by] Arthur James, earl of Balfour ... Bronislaw Malinowski [and others] ... edited by Joseph Needham. London, The Sheldon press; New York and Toronto, The Macmillan co., 1925. 6 p. l., [3]-396 p. 23 cm. [Full name: Noel Joseph Terence Montgomery Needham] [BL240.N4] 25-22892
1. Religion and science. I. Balfour, Arthur James Balfour, 1st earl of, 1848- II. Title.
Contents omitted.

NELSON, Harry Tracy. 215
The heavens and earth declare, by H. T. Nelson ... Dallas, Atlanta [etc.] B. Upshaw and company [c1934] 5 p. l., 60 p. 19 cm. [BL241.N4] 35-1030
1. Religion and sicence—1900- 2. Cosmogony. I. Title.

PIKE, Granville Ross. 215
Vital modifications of religious thought; contributions by science to religion, by Granville Ross Pike ... Boston, Mass., The Stratford company, 1926. 4 p. l., 126 p. 19 1/2 cm. [BL240.P55] 26-17491
1. Religion and science. I. Title.

POTEAT, William L.
Laboratory and pulpit; the relation of biology to the preacher and his message ... Philadelphia, The Griffith & Rowland press, 1901. 103 p. 12 degree. (The Gay lectures, 1900) May
I. Title.

POTEAT, William Louis, 1856-
The new peace; lectures on science and religion, by William Louis Poteat ... Boston, R. G. Badger; [etc., etc., c1915] 160 p. 20 cm. (Lettered on cover: Library of religious thought) "The lectures which are here published were given in May, 1905, on the Brooks foundation in Hamilton theological seminary of Colgate university. In October and November of the same year they were repeated in Crozer theological seminary, Newton theological institution, Rochester theological institution, and the Divinity school of the University of Chicago."--Prefatory note. 15-13344 1.00
I. Title.

QUESTIONS on natural science and the harmonic philosophy, consisting of interrogatories, the answers to which are disclosed in the three volumes of the Harmonic series, prepared and comp. by students of the work. 1st ed., 1913. Chicago, Ill., Indo-American book co. [1913] 355 p. 20 cm. 13-17989 2.00
I. Harmonic series.

RELIGION and science.
London, New York, Oxford University Press [1956] 255p. (Home university library of modern knowledge, 178)
1. Religion and science. 2. Religion and science—History of controversy. I. Russell, Bertrand Russell, 3d earl, 1872-

RELIGION& science.
New York, Oxford University Press, 1961. 255, [1]p. 21cm. (A Galaxy book [GB 50])
I. Russell, Bertrand Russell, 3d earl, 1872-

REUTERDAHL, Arvid, 1876- 215
The God of science, by Arvid Reuterdahl ... Minneapolis, Minn., The Arya company, 1928. xiv p., 1 l., 312 p. incl. front. 22 cm. [BL240.R35] 29-942
1. Religion and science. I. Title.

RICE, William North, 1845- 215
Science and religion; five so-called conflicts, by William North Rice. New York, Cincinnati. The Abingdon press [c1925] 53 p. 17 1/2 cm. [BL240.R53] 26-878
1. Religion and science. I. Title.

RIGDON, Jonathan, 1858- 215
Science and religion as they look to a layman, by Jonathan Rigdon ... Danville, Ind., The author, 1928. 136 p. 18 cm. [BL240.R56] 29-9893
1. Religion and science. I. Title.

ROBERTS, Joseph.
Perthynas crefydd a gwyddoreg. Utica, N. Y., T. J. Griffiths, 1897. 828p. illus., port, 19cm. [PB2342.R59] 54-50804
1. Religion and science. I. Title.

SHEEN, Fulton John Bp., 1895-
Science, psychiatry and religion. [New York, Dell Pub. Co., 1957, 1962] 190 p. illus. 17 cm. (A Chapel book) "First Dell printing - December, 1962." 66-65149
1. Religion and science. 2. Psychiatry. I. Title.

SHIELDS, Charles Woodruff, 1825-1904.
Religion and science in their relation to philosophy. An essay on the present state of the sciences. Read before the Philosophical society of Washington, By Charles W. Shields ... New York, Scribner, Armstrong, and company, 1875. 69 p. 19 cm. 12-38720
I. Title.

SIMPSON, Thomas Jefferson.
Simpson's Bible; a comparison of science and religion, the great moral way of facts, truths and reasons, by Thomas Jefferson Simpson ... [St. Louis, Nixon-Jones ptg. co.] 1912. 376 p. illus., pl., 3 port. (incl. front.) 20 1/2 cm. Bound with this: The Simpson-Paine combination of facts, truths and reasons, the great moral way, Thomas Paine's Age of reason, rev. ... by Thomas Jefferson Simpson ... St. Louis, Mo., 1912. "I wish I was a baby. Song by T. J. Simpson," inserted between p. 30-31. 8 ruled pages, preceding front., for marriages, births, deaths, memorandum. 12-12701
I. Title.

SINGER, Charles Joseph, 1876-
Religion & science, considered in their historical relations. New York, R. M. McBride & Co. [n.d.] 130 p. 18 cm. 66-83977
I. Title.

SPEARS, Samuel T. 215
Evolution; the Bible and science reconciled, by Samuel T. Spears. [Morgantown, W.Va., 1927] 5 p. l., 75 p. 19 1/2 cm. [BL263.S62] 27-2796
1. Religion and science. 2. Evolution. I. Title.

SPRADING, Charles T. 213
Science versus dogma, by Charles T. Sprading ... Los Angeles, Calif., The Libertarian publishing company, 1925. 212 p. 20 cm. [BL245.S7] 25-19631
1. Religion and science. 2. Evolution. 3. Modernist-fundamentalist controversy. I. Title.

STRAUS, Herbert Cerf, 1895- 215
Reason and religion; or, Religion and science co-ordinated on the basis of personal realism, by H. Cerf Straus, D.D. Boston, Mass., The Stratford company, 1928. 3 p. l., ii, 56 p. 19 1/2 cm. Bibliography: p. 56. [BL240.S757] 28-5570
1. Religion and science. I. Title.

*TINER, John Hudson. 215
When science fails. Grand Rapids, Baker Book House [1974] 136 p. 18 cm. (Direction books.) [BL245] ISBN 0-8010-8823-2 1.25 (pbk.)
1. Religion and science. I. Title.

TYNDALL, Charles Herbert, 1857- 215
Nature and religion; a handbook of religious education, by Charles H. Tyndall. New York, Chicago [etc.] Fleming H. Revell company [c1930] 275 p. diagr. 19 1/2 cm. [BL240.T83] 30-24065
1. Religion and science. 2. Religious education. I. Title.

TYNDALL, Charles Herbert, 1857- 215
Through science to God; nature a medium in the revelation of spiritual truth, by Charles H. Tyndall ... New York, Chicago [etc.] Fleming H. Revell company [c1926] 269 p. front. (port.) illus., plates, fold. tab. 19 1/2 cm. [BL240.T85] 26-22397
1. Religion and science. I. Title.

VAN DER KIEL, Aldert, 1910-
The natural sciences and the Christian message. Minneapolis. T. S. Denison [1960] 259 p. diagrs. 23 cm.
I. Title.

WAGGETT, Philip Napier, 1862-
Religion and science; some suggestions for the study of the relations between them, by P. N. Waggett ... London, New York [etc.] Longmans, Green & co., 1904. xii, 174 p. 18 cm. (Half-title: Handbooks for the clergy, ed. by Arthur W. Robinson) Bibliography: p. 165-174. A22
1. Religion and science. I. Title.

WARD, Duren James Henderson, 1851- 215
A receivership for civilization from Bibilical church with its primitive world and Jewish legends to Aryan science with its infinite universe and established facts, by Duren J. H. Ward. Boston, The Four seas company [c1922] 328 p. 1 illus. 20 cm. [BL240.W27] 22-16984
I. Title. II. Title: Civilization, A receivership for.

WHALING, Thornton, 1858- 215
Science and religion today, by Thornton Whaling ... Chapel Hill, The University of North Carolina press, 1929. 3 p. l., [ix]-xi p., 2 l., 74 p. 19 cm. (Half-title: The John Calvin McNair lectures) [BL240.W42] 29-9051
1. religion and science. I. Title.

WHELAN, Edward H. 215
Evolution, God and immortality; a new philosophy, by Edward H. Whelan ... Author's own edition. San Diego, Calif., c1923. 196, [2] p. 20 cm. [BL240.W43] 23-6608
1. Religion and science. 2. Evolution. I. Title.

WHITE, Andrew Dickson, 1832-1918. 213
New chapters in the warfare of science, by Andrew Dickson White. xix. From creation to evolution ... New York, D. Appleton and company, 1894. 67 p. 23 1/2 cm. Reprinted from the Popular science monthly for February, April, May and June, 1894. [BL263.W5] 21-3002
1. Religion and science. 2. Evolution. I. Title.

*WHITE, Joseph L. 212
The creation of a God. By Joseph L. White Madison, Tenn., White Publications [1975] 119 p. 22 cm. [BT98] 6.50
1. Religion and Science. 2. God-Proof. 3. Creation. I. Title.
Available from author 221 Neely's Bend Road Madison, Tenn. 37115

WILLIAMS, Esther. 215
A new pebble in science, by Esther Williams. St. Catherine, Mo., The author [c1926] 75 p. 19 1/2 cm. [BL240.W52] 26-17602
1. Religion and science. 2. Evolution. I. Title.

WILLISTON, Arthur Lyman, 1868- 215
Beyond the horizon of science, by Arthur L. Williston, S.B. Boston, W. A. Wilde company, 1944. xiv, [2], 56 p. illus. 21 cm. [BL241.W48] 44-7053
1. Religion and science. I. Title.

WOOD, William Hamilton, 1874- 215
The religion of science, by William Hamilton Wood ... New York, The Macmillan company, 1922. x p., 1 l., 176 p. 19 1/2 cm. "A selected bibliography": p. 175-176. [BL240.W65] 22-19726
1. Religion and science. I. Title.

WOODBURNE, Angus Stewart. 215
The relation between religion and science: a biological approach, by Angus Stewart Woodburne. Chicago, Ill., The University of Chicago press [1920] vii, 103 p. 24 cm. Published also as thesis (PH.D.) University of Chicago, 1918. Bibliography: p. 96-103. [BL240.W63] 20-2682
1. Religion and science. I. Title.

YEATER, Samuel Horatio, 1856- 270
Christianity; a biologic fact, by S. H. Yeater ... Upland, Ind., Yeater printing company [c1922] 72 p. 19 1/2 cm. [BR125.Y4] 22-18545
I. Title.

ZERBE, Alvin Sylvester, 1847-1935. 213
Christianity and false evolutionism, by Alvin Sylvester Zerbe... Cleveland, O., Central publishing house [c1925] xx, 321 p. 21 1/2 cm. [BL263.Z5] 25-16110
1. Religion and science. 2. Christianity. 3. Evolution. I. Title.

Religion and science—1860-1899.

ABBEY, Richard, 1805-1891. 215
Diuturnity; or, The comparative age of the world, showing that the human race is in the infancy of its being, and demonstrating a reasonable and rational world, and its immense future duration. By Rev. R. Abbey. Cincinnati, Applegate & company, 1766. xii, 13-300 p. 10 cm. [BL240.A2] 31-9286
1. Religion and science—1860-1899. 2. Millennium. I. Title.

[ALLEN, Stephen Merrill] 1819-1894. 215
Religion and science; the letters of "Alpha" on the influence of spirit upon imponderable actienic molecular substances, and the life-forces of mind and matter. Embracing a review of the address of Prof. John Tyndall...before the British association at Belfast, August 19, 1874, with additional evidence, through the law of "evolution", of the immortality of the soul, its relations to physical life, and accountability to the Deity, By The author of "Fibrilla and fibrous manufactures"... Boston, A. Mudge & son, Printers, 1874. 2 p. l., [iii]-vi, [7]-171 p. col. front., col. plates. 20 cm. "Mostly compiled from the letters of 'Alpha', written for the 'Boston daily Transcript', and quotations from distinguished writers upon the subjects therein treated."--Pref. [BL240.A6] 31-9285
1. Religion and science—1860-1899. 2. Tyndall, Joh, 1820-1893. Address delivered before the British association assembled at Belfast, 1874. I. Title.

[ALLEN, Stephen Merrill] 1819-1894. 215
Religion and science; the letters of "Alpha" on the influence of spirit upon imponderable actienic molecular substances, and the life-forces of mind and matter. Embracing a review of the address of Prof. John Tyndall...before the British association at Belfast, August 19, 1874, with additional evidence, through the law of "evolution", of the immorality of the soul, its relations to physical life, and accountability to the Deity. By the author of "Fibrilia and fibrous manufactures"... Boston, J. Campbell, 1875. 2 p. l., (lll)-vi, [7]-171 p. col. front col. plates. 20 cm. "Mostly compiled from the letters of 'Alpha' written for the 'Boston daily transcript', and quotations from distinguished writers upon the subjects therein treated."--Pref. [BL240.A6] 35-31552
1. Religion and science—1860-1899. 2. Tyndall, John, 1820-1893. Address delivered before the British association assembled at Belfast, 1874. I. Title.

ARGYLL, George Douglas Campbell, 8th duke of, 1823-1900. 215
The reign of law. By the Duke of Argyll. 4th American ed. New York, G. Routledge & sons, 1873. xxvii, 462 p. 4 pl. 18 cm. From the fifth London edition. [BL240.A7 1873] 11-23092
1. Religion and science—1860-1899. 2. Cosmology. I. Title.

ARGYLL, George Douglas Campbell, 8th duke of, 1823-1900. 215
The reign of law. By the Duke of Argyll. 5th American ed. New York, G. Routledge & sons, 1879. xxvii, 462 p. 4 pl. 18 cm. From the fifteenth London edition. [BL240.A7 1879] 18-4909
1. Religion and science—1860-1899. 2. Cosmology. I. Title.

ARGYLL, George Douglas Campbell, 8th duke of, 1823-1900. 215
The reign of law. By the Duke of Argyll ... New York, J. B. Alden, 1884. xv, [1], 265 p. 4 pl. 19 1/2 cm. [BL240.A7 1884] 33-16403
1. Religion and science—1860-1899. 2. Cosmology. I. Title.

ARGYLL, George Douglas Campbell, 8th duke of, 1823-1900. 215
The reign of law. By the Duke of Argyll ... New York, J. W. Lovell company [1888] xv, [1], 265 p. 4 pl. 19 cm. (On cover: Lovell's library, no. 1175) [BL240.A7 1888] 11-23098
1. Religion and science—1860-1899. 2. Cosmology. I. Title.

ARGYLL, George Douglas Campbell, 8th duke of, 1823-1900. 215
The unity of nature, by the Duke of Argyll ... New York, London, G. P. Putnam's sons, 1884. xv, 571 p. incl. front. 23 cm. A sequel to "The reign of law". cf. Pref. [BL240.A8] 11-21992
1. Religion and science—1860-1899. 2. Cosmology. 3. Philosophy and religion. I. Title.

BARR, Enoch Fitch, 1818-1907. 215
Pater mundi; or, Doctrine of evolution. Being in substances lectures delivered in various colleges and theological seminaries By Rev. E. F. Burr ... Second series. Boston, Noyes, Holmes and company, 1873. xi p., 1 l., [9]-308 p. 20 cm. [BL240.B82] 31-9994
1. Religion and science—1800-1899. 2. Evolution. I. Title.

BARRY, Alfred, 1826-1910. 215
Some lights of science on the faith. Eight lectures preached before the University of Oxford in the year 1892 on the foundation of the late Rev. John Bampton ... by Alfred Barry ... London and New York, Longmans, Green, and co., 1892. xvi, 348 p. 23 cm. (Half-title: The Bampton lectures for m dccc xcii) [BR45B3 1892] 230.082 38-16296
1. Religion and science—1860-1899. I. Title.

BETTEX, Frederic, 1837-1915. 215
Science and Christianity, by F. Bettex; translated from the German. Cincinnati, Jennings & Pye; New York, Eaton & Mains [c1901] 326 p. 21 cm. [BL240.B45] 1-25531
1. Religion and science, 1860-1899. I. Title.

BIXBY, James Thompson, 1843-1921. 215
Religion and science as allies: or, Similarities of physical and religious knowledge, by James Thompson Bixby. Chicago, C. H. Kerr & company, 1889. 226 p. 19 1/2 cm. Published previously under title: Similarities of physical and religious knowledge. [BL240.B5] 31-8984
1. Religion and science—1800-1899. I. Title.

BIXBY, James Thompson, 1843-1921. 215
Similarities of physical and religious knowledge. By James Thompson Bixby. New York, D. Appleton and company, 1876. 226 p. 19 cm. Lettered on cover: Physical and religious knowledge. Published also under title: Religion and science as allies. [BL240.B53] 31-8985
1. Religion and science—1860-1899. I. Title. II. Title: Physical and religious knowledge.

BRADEN, Clark. 211
The problem of problems, and its various solutions; or, Atheism, Darwinism and theism. By Clark Braden ... Cincinnati, Chase & Hall, 1877. xii, 13-480 p. 20 cm. [BL200.B75] 30-28760
1. Religion and science—1860-1899. 2. Theism. I. Title.

CALDERWOOD, Henry, 1830-1897. 215
The relations of science and religion. The Morse lecture, 1880, connected with the Union theological seminary, New York. By Henry Calderwood ... New York, R. Carter & brothers, 1881. xiii, [9]-323 p. front., plates. 20 cm. [BL240.C27] 31-9988
1. Religion and science—1860-1899. I. Title.

CARUS, Paul, 1852-1919. 215
Homilies of science by Dr. Paul Carus ... Chicago, The Open court publishing company, 1892. x p., 1 l., 317 p. 21 cm. First published as editorial articles in the Open court. cf. Pref. [BL240.C33] 27-12039
1. Religion and science—1860-1899. I. Title.

CARUS, Paul, 1852-1919. 215
The religion of science, by Dr. Paul Carus ... Chicago, The Open court publishing company, 1893. vi, p. 2 l., [3]-103 p. 20 cm. (On cover: The religion of science library v. 1 no. 1) [BL240.C35 1893] 3-3546
1. Religion and science—1860-1899. I. Title.

CARUS, Paul, 1852-1919. 215
The religion of science, by Dr. Paul Carus. 2d ed., rev. and enl. ... Chicago [etc.] The Open court publishing company, 1896. 2 p. l., [iii]-vi p., 2 l., [3]-125 p. 20 cm. [The religion of science library, no. 1] [BL240.C35 1806] 31-9985
1. Religion and science—1860-1899. I. Title.

CHALMERS, Thomas, 1780-1847. 215
A series of discourse on the Christian revelation, viewed in connexion with the modern astronomy ... By Thomas Chalmers ... New York: Published by Kirk & Mercein. No. 22 Wall-Street ..... 1817 12, [17]-218 p. 23 cm. With this is bound the author's A sermon preached in St. Andrew's Church, Edinburgh ... April 18, 1813. New-York, 1817. [BL253.C5 1817] 1-3229
1. Religion and science—1800-1859. 2. Astronomy. I. Title.

CHALMERS, Thomas, 1780-1847. 215
A series of discourses on the Christian revelation, viewed in connexion with the modern astronomy. By Thomas Chalmers ... New-York: Published by Kirk & Mercein, no. 22 Wall-street, 1818. 7, [11]-306 p. 24 cm. "An address to the inhabitants of the parish of Kilmany": p. [227-271]: "The influence of Bible societies, on the temporal necessities of the poor": p. [273]-306. With this is bound the author's A sermon, delivered in the Tron church Glasgow, on Wednesday, Nov. 19th, 1817, the day of the funeral of Her Royal Highness the Princess Charlotte of Wales. New-York, 1818. [BL253.C5 1818] 37-33202
1. Religion and science—1800-1859. 2. Astronomy. I. Title.

CHAPIN, James Henry, 1832-1892. 215
The creation and the early developments of society, by James H. Chapin... New York, G. P. Putnam's sons [c1880] 5 p. l., [3]-276 p. col. front. 21 cm. [BL240.C47] 31-9984
1. Religion and science—1860-1899. 2. Cosmology. 3. Civilization—Hist. I. Title.

CHILD, George Chaplin. 215
The great architect. Benedicite; illustrations of the power, wisdom, and goodness of God, as manifested in His works. By G. Chaplin Child ... New York, G. P. Putnam and son, 1867. 2 p. l., 376 p. 19 cm. "Reprinted from the London edition of John Murray, issued December, 1866." 2 vols. [BL240.C5 1867] 31-9987
1. Religion and science—1860-1899. 2. Natural history. 3. God—Attributes. I. Title. II. Title: Benedicite.

CHILD, George Chaplin. 215
The Great Architect. Benedicite: illustrations of the power, wisdom, and goodness of God, as manifested in His works. By G. Chaplin Child ... New York, G. P. Putnam and sons, 1871. 2 p. l., 376 p. 19 1/2 cm. "Reprinted from the London edition of John Murray, issued December, 1866." 2 v. [BL240.C5 1871] 31-35782
1. Religion and science—1860-1899. 2. Natural history. 3. God—Attributes. I. Title. II. Title: Benedicite.

CHRISTIAN truth and modern opinion. 215
Seven sermons preached in New York by clergymen of the Protestant Episcopal church. New York, T. Whittaker, [c1874] 229 p. 19 1/2 cm. Contents.The Christian doctrine of Providence, by C. S. Henry.--The Christian doctrine of prayer, py H. M. Thompson.--Moral responsibility and Physical law, by E. A. Washburn.--The relation of miracles to the Christian faith, by J. H. Rylance.--The oneness of Scripture, by W. R. Huntington.-- Immortality, by Rt. Rev. T. M. Clark.--Evolustion and a personal creator, by J. C. Smith [BL240.C55 1874] 31-9982
1. Religion and science—1860-1899. 2.

Sermons, American. I. Henry, Caleb Sprague, 1804-1884.

CHRISTIAN truth and modern opinion. Seven sermons preached in New York, by Clergymen of the Protestant Episcopal church. 4th ed.. with a preface by the Rt. Rev. Hugh Miller Thompson ... New York, T. Whittaker, 1885. 1 p., l., vi p., 3 l., [9]-229 p. 19 cm. First edition. 1874. Contents.The Christian doctrine of Providence, by C. S. Henry.--The Christian doctrine of prayer, by H. M. Thompson.--Moral responsibility and physical law, by E. A. Washburn.--The relation of miracle to the Christian faith, by J. H. Rylance.--The oneness of Scripture, by W. R. Huntington.-- Immortality, by the Rt. Rev. T. M. Clark.--Evolution and a personal creator, by J. C. Smith. [BL240.C55 1884] 31-9983 215
1. Religion and science—1860-1899. 2. Sermons, American. I. Henry, Caleb Sprague, 1804-1884.

COMBE, George, 1788-1858. 215
Science and religion. By George Combe ... London [etc.] Cassell and company, limited; New York. The Cassell publishing company, 1893. xi, 222 p. 18 cm. (Half-title: The select works of George Combe) Enlarged from a pamphlet published in 1847 under title: On the relation between science and religion. [BL240.C6] 31-9980
1. Religion and science—1800-1859. 2. Providence and government God. 3. Natural theology. I. Title.

COOKE, Josiah Parsons, 1827-1894. 215
The credentials of science the warrant of faith. By Josiah Parsons Cooke ... 2d ed. New York, D. Appleton and company, 1893. viii p., 1 l., 324 p. diagr. 23 cm. [Ely lectures] Amplified from lectures prepared at the invitation of the Union theological seminary, and delivered during the spring of 1887. cf. Pref. [BL240.C65 1893] 31-9071
1. Religion and science—1860-1899. I. Title.

COOKE, Josiah Parsons, 1827-1894. 215
Religion and chemistry; a re-statement of an old argument, by Josiah Parsons Cooke ... Newly rev. ed. ... New York, C. Scribner's sons, 1880. ix, 331 p. 20 cm. [Graham lectures] "Lectures ... first delivered before the Brooklyn institute ... January and February, 1861."--p. vii. [BL265.C4C7 1880] 31-1164
1. Religion and science—1800-1899. 2. Chemistry—Addresses, essays, lectures. 3. Atmosphere. I. Title.

CRAFTS, Wilbur Fisk, 1850-1922. 215
Before the lost arts and other lectures, by Rev. Wilbur Crafts ... Washington, D. C., The Reform bureau [c1896] 96 p. incl. illus. (incl. port.) plates, diagr. 20 cm. [BL240.C7] 15-22022
1. Religion and science—1860-1809. I. Title.
Contents omitted.

CUNNINGHAM, J A. 215
Light on the mysteries of nature and the Bible in the form of letters to our children, by J. A. Cunningham. vol i. Cincinnati, Standard publishing company, 1886. xiii, 15-198 p. 18 cm. No more published? [BL240.C8] 31-9973
1. Religion and science—1860-1899. I. Title.

DALE, Thomas Nelson, 1845- 215
The outskirts of physical science, essays, philosophical and religious, by T. Nelson Dale ... Boston, Lee and Shepard : New York, C. T. Dillingham, 1884. iv p., 2 l., [9]-187 p. 18 cm. [BL240.D3] 31-9977
1. Religion and science—1800-1899. I. Title.

DAWSON, John William Sir, 1820-1899. 215
Facts and fancies in modern science; studies of the relations of science to prevalent speculations and religious belief. Being the lectures on the Samuel A. Crozer foundation in connection with the Crozer theological seminary, for 1881. By J. W. Dawson ... Philadelphia, American Baptist publication society [1882] 238 p. illus. 19 cm. [BL240.D35] 31-9972
1. Religion and science—1860-1899. 2. Evolution. I. Title.

DAWSON, John William, Sir 1820-1899. 215
Points of contact between science and revelation, by Principal Dawson ... [New York, Princeton review, 1879] 1 p. l., [579]-606 p. 24 cm. "Articles no. seventeen from the Princeton review." [BL241.D3] 31-13533
1. Religion and science—1860-1899. I. Title.

DICK, Thomas, 1774-1857. 215
The Christian philosopher; or, The connection of science and philosophy with religion. Illustrated with engravings. By Thomas Dick ... 4th American ed. New York, G. & C. & H. Carvill, 1829. vi, [7]-399 illus., diagrs. 21 cm. "List of popular works on the different science treated of in this volume": p. 391-399. [BL240.D5 1829] 31-11676
1. Religion and science—1800-1859. I. Title.

DICK, Thomas, 1774-1857. 215
The Christian philosopher; or, The connection of science and philosophy with religion. Illustrated with engravings. By Thomas Dick ... New York, Robinson, Pratt, & co., 1835. 2 p. l., [ix]-x, [11]-350 p. front., illus., diagrs. 20 cm. [BL240.D5 1835] 7-6267
1. Religion and science—1800-1859. I. Title.

DICK, Thomas, 1774-1857. 236
... The Christian philosopher; or, The connexion of science and philosophy with religion. Illustrated with engravings. By Thomas Dick ... From the 8th London ed., rev., cor., and greatly enl. Philadelphia, E. C. & J. Biddle, 1847. xv, 17-422 p. front., illus., diagrs. 19 cm. (Label on cover: Dick's works, v. 1-2) At head of title: Uniform edition. Vol. ii of Dick's works. With this is bound, as issued, vol. i: The philosophy of a future state. Philadelphia, 1847. "List of popular works on the different sciences treated of in this volume": p. 405-412. [BT901.D5 1847] 33-35176
1. Religion and science—1800-1859. I. Title.

DRUMMOND, Henry, 1851-1897. 215
Natural law, in the spiritual world. By Henry Drummond... New York, J. Pott & co., 1884. xxiv, 414 p. 19 cm. [BL240.D8 1884] 31-11678
1. Religion and science—1860-1899. 2. Natural theology. I. Title.

DRUMMOND, Henry, 1851-1897 215
Natural law in the spiritual world, by Henry Drummond... New ed. New York, J. Pott & co., 1889. xxiv, 414 p. 19 cm. [BL240.D6 1889] 29-29154
1. Religion and science—1800-1899. 2. Natural theology. I. Title.

DRUMMOND, Henry, 1851-1897. 215
Natural law in the spiritual world, by Henry Drummond... New York, J. Pott & co., 1890. xxiv, 414 p. 19 cm. On cover: Author's edition. [BL240.D6 1890] 32-9303
1. Religion and science—1800-1899. 2. Natural theology. I. Title.

DRUMMOND, Henry, 1851-1897. 215
Natural law in the spiritual world, by Henry Drummond... New York, Home book company [1895?] 391 p. 15 cm. [BL340.D6 1895] 35-31640
1. Religion and science—1860-1899. 2. Natural theology. I. Title.

DRUMMOND, Henry, 1851-1897. 215
Natural law in the spiritual world, by Henry Drummond... New York, J. Pott & co. [190-?] xxiv, 414 p. 19 cm. First published in 1883. [BL240.D6 1904] 4-10883
1. Religion and science—1860-1899. 2. Natural theology. I. Title.

DRUMMOND, Henry, 1851-1897. 215
Natural law in the spiritual world, by Professor Henry Drummond. Philadelphia, H. Altemus [190-?] 4 p. l., [v]-xxii, 371 p. front., ports. 16 1/2 cm. [BL240.D8] 39-34100
1. Religion and science-1800-1899. 2. Natural theology. I. Title.

DRUMMOND, Henry, 1851-1897. 215
Natural law in the spiritual world, by Henry Drummond... Chicago, W.B. Conkey company [1900] 391 p. front. (port.) plates. 16 cm. [BL240.D8 1900] 0-4962
1. Religion and science-1800-1899. 2. Natural theology. I. Title.

DRUMMOND, Henry, 1851-1897. 215
Natural law in the spiritual world. By Henry Drummond ... New York, A. L. Burt company [190-] 388 p. 19 cm. (On cover: Cornell series) [BL240.D8] 46-44347
1. Religion and science—1860-1899. 2. Natural theology. I. Title.

ELDER, William, 1840-1903. 215
Ideas from nature; talks with students, by William Elder... Philadelphia. American Baptist publication society [c1898] 202 p. 19 cm. [BL240.E5] 12-31979
1. Religion and science—1860-1899. I. Title.

FARRAR, Adam Storey, 1826-1905. 215
Science in theology. Sermons preached in St. Mary's Oxford, before the university. By Adam S. Farrar ... Philadelphia, Smith, English & co.; New York, Sheldon & co.; [etc., etc.] 1860. xxiii, [25]-250 p. 20 cm. [BL240.F2] 36-25382
1. Religion and science—1800-1859. 2. Church of England—Sermons. 3. Sermons, English. I. Title.

FISHER, Arabella Burton (Buckley) Mrs., 1840- 170
Moral teachings of science, by Arabella B. Buckley [Mrs. Fisher]. New York, D. Appleton and company, 1892. vi p., 1 l.,122 p. 19 cm. [BJ57.B9] 10-4684
1. Religion and science—1860-1899. 2. Ethics. I. Title.

FROUDE, James Anthony, 1818-1894. 215
... Theological unrest; discussions in science and religion ... New York, A. S. Barnes & co., c1880. cover-title, [3]-62 p. 23 cm. (Atlas series, no. 11) From the International review. [BL240.F83] 31-14269
1. Religion and science—1860-1899. 2. Draper, John William, 1811-1882. History of the conflict between religion and science. I. Tait, Peter Guthrie. II. Washburn, Edward Abiel, 1819-1881. III. Title.
Contents omitted.

GIBBES, Emily Oliver. 225.92
Reflections on Paul according to the Acts in the New Testament; reflections on: Darwin's Origin of the species; Darwin's Descent of man; Cain--Chico, the chimpanzee; Bourget--The disciple; Moses--Egyptian religion; Electricity--the works of Jesus. By Emily Oliver Gibbes. New York, C. T. Dillingham & co., 1895. iii, 5-7, ix p., 1 l., 13-271 p. 19 cm. [BS2505.G45] 922.1 34-17154
1. Paul, Saint, apostle. 2. Religion and science—1860-1899. I. Title.

GMEINER, John, 1847-1913. 215
Modern scientific views and Christian doctrines compared, By Rev. John Gmeiner ... Milwaukee, Wis., J. H. Yewdal & sons, printers, 1884. viii, 212 p. 20 cm. Bibliographical foot-notes. [BL240.G6] 27-7861
1. Religion and science—1860-1899. 2. Christianity—Evidences. I. Title.

GOULD, George Milbry, 1848-1922. 215
The meaning and the method of life; a search for religion in biology, by George M. Gould ... New York, London, G. P. Putnam's sons, 1893. iii, 297 p. 21 cm. [BL262.G6] 31-1160
1. Religion and science—1860-1899. 2. Biology. I. Title. II. Title: Life, The meaning and the method of.

GRANT, Frederick W. 215
Spiritual law in the natural world: an attempt to develop, according to Scripture-truth, the interpretation of nature. By F. W. Grant ... New York, Loizeaux brothers [c1891] 205 p. illus. 19 cm. [BL240.G8] 31-11660
1. Religion and science—1860-1899. 2. Natural theology. I. Title.

GRAY, Asa, 1810-1888. 215
Natural science and religion; two lectures delivered to the Theological school of Yale college, by Asa Gray. New York, C. Scribner's sons, 1880. 111 p. 21 cm. Agr
1. Religion and science—[1860-1899] 2. [Natural history] I. Title.

GRUBER, Jacob W 213.5
A conscience in conflict: the life of St. George Jackson Mivart. New York, Published for Temple University Publications by Columbia University Press, 1960. 266p. illus. 24cm. [BL263.G68 1960] 60-10645
1. Mivart. St. George Jackson, 1827-1900. 2. Religion and science—1860-1899. 3. Evolution. I. Title.

HALL, J.A. 215
Glimpses of great fields, by Rev. J.A. Hall... Boston, D. Lothrop company [1888] 289, [1] p. 19 cm. [BL240.H23] 31-11659
1. Religion and science—1860-1899. I. Title.

HITCHCOCK, Edward, 1793-1864. 215
Religious truth, illustrated from science, in addresses and sermons on special occasions. By Edward Hitchcock ... Boston, Phillips, Sampson and company, 1857. 422 p. col. front. 20 cm. [BL240.H7] G S
1. Religion and science—1800-1859. I. Title.

HUDSON, Thomson Jay, 1834-1903. 215
The divine pedigree of man, or The testimony of evolution and psychology to the fatherhood of God, by Thomson Jay Hudson ... Chicago, A. C. McClurg & co., 1899. xxviii, [29]-379 p. 19 cm. [BL240.H8] 0-502
1. Religion and science—1800-1899. 2. Man. 3. God. 4. Evolution. I. Title.

HUDSON, Thomson Jay, 1834-1903. 215
The divine pedigree of man; or, The testimony of evolution and psychology to the fatherhood of God, by Thomas Jay Hudson ... 2d ed. Chicago, A. C. McClurg & co., 1900. xxviii p., 1 l., [31]-379 p. 19 1/2 cm. [BL240.H8 1900] 35-32282
1. Religion and science—1860-1899. 2. Man. 3. God. 4. Evolution. 5. Natural theology. I. Title.

HUXLEY, Thomas Henry, 1825-1895. 215
Science and Christian tradition; essays. New York, Greenwood Press [1968] xxxiv, 419 p. 23 cm. (His Collected essays, v. 5) "Originally published in 1897." Contents.Contents.—Prologue (controverted questions, 1892).—Scientific and pseudo-scientific realism (1887).—Science and pseudo-science (1887).—An Episcopal trilogy (1887).—The value of witness to the miraculous (1889).—Possibilities and impossibilities (1891).—Agnosticism (1889).—Agnosticism: a rejoinder (1889).—Agnosticism and Christianity (1889).—The keepers of the herd of swine (1890).—Illustrations of Mr. Gladstone's controversial methods (1891) [Q171.H902 vol. 5] [BL240] 79-29963
1. Religion and science—1860-1899. 2. Agnosticism. 3. Miracles—Controversial literature. I. Title.

HUXLEY, Thomas Henry, 1825-1895. 215
Science and Christian tradition; essays, by Thomas H. Huxley. New York, D. Appleton and company, 1894. 2 p. l., [v] ixxxiv, 419 p. 19 cm. (Half-title: Collected essays by T. H. Huxley, vol. v) "Authorized edition." [BL240.H85 1894] 41-30619
1. Religion and science—1860-1899. 2. Agnosticism. 3. Miracles—Controversial literature. I. Title.
Contents omitted.

HUXLEY, Thomas Henry, 1825-1895. 215
Science and Christian tradition; essays by Thomas H. Huxley. New York, D. Appleton and company, 1896. 1 p. l., [v]-xxxiv, 419 p. 19 cm. "Authorized edition." [BL240.H85 1896] 32-24205
1. Religion and science—1860-1899. 2. Agnosticism. 3. Miracles—Controversial literature. I. Title.
Contents omitted.

HUXLEY, Thomas Henry, 1825- 1895. 215
Science and Christian tradition. Essays by Thomas H. Huxley. New York, D. Appleton and company, 1902. xxxiv, 419 p. 19 cm. (Half-title: Collected essays by T. H. Huxley, vol. v) On verso of t.-p.: Authorized edition. [Q171.H9 vol. 5] 3-16507
1. Religion and science—1860-1899 2. Agnosticism. 3. Miracles—Controversial literature. I. Title.
Contents omitted.

IVERACH, James, 1839-1922. 215
Christianity and evolution. New York, T. Whittaker, 1894. viii, 232 p. 18 cm. (The Theological educator) Series: The Theological educator. New York) [BL263.I8] 48-35814
1. Religion and science—1860-1899. 2. Evolution. I. Title. II. Series.

KINSLEY, William Wirt, 1837- 1923. 215
Old faiths and new facts, by William W. Kinsley ... New York, D. Appleton and company, 1896. v, 345 p. 19 1/2 cm. [BL240.K5] 31-11658
1. Religion and science—1800-1809. I. Title.
Contents omitted.

[LAZELLE, Henry Martyn] 1832- 117
Matter, force, and spirit; or, Scientific evidence of a supreme intelligence ... New York [etc.] G. P. Putnam's sons, 1895. vii, 144 p. 20 cm. [BD701.L4] 11-24654
1. Religion and science—1860-1899. I. Title.

LE CONTE, Joseph, 1823-1901. 215
Religion and science. A series of Sunday lectures on the relation of natural and revealed religion, or the truths revealed in nature and Scripture. By Joseph Le Conte ... New York, D. Appleton and company, 1874. 324 diagrs. 18 1/2 cm. [BL240.L4 1874] 31-11657
1. Religion and science—1860-1899. I. Title.

LEWIS, Tayler, 1802-1877. 211
..."The light by which we see light": or, Nature and the Scriptures. A course of lectures delivered before the Theological seminary and Rutgers college... By Tayler Lewis... New York, Board of publications of the R.C.A., 1875. vi p., 2 l., 11-246 p. 19 1/2 cm. (The Vedder lectures, 1875) [BL240.L55] 31-11656
1. Religion and science—1860-1899. 2. Bible and science. I. Title.

MACKALL, Louis, 1801-1876. 219
Analogy of science, physical and metaphysical, to natural and revealed religion. By Louis Mackall, M.D. Washington, D.C. McGill & Witherow, printers, 1876. 106 p. 17 cm. Running title: American science. [BL240.M3] 31-11655
1. Religion and science—1860-1899. I. Title. II. Title: American science.

MADDEN, William Joseph. 239
The reaction from agnostic science, by Rev. W. J. Madden... 2d revised ed. St. Louis, Mo., B. Herder, 1899. viii, 9-206 p. 20 cm. First edition published 1898 under title: The reaction from science. [BT1220.M3 1899] 99-4823
1. Religion and science—1860-1899. 2. Agnosticism. I. Title.

MADDEN, William Joseph. 239
The reaction from agnostic science, by Rev. W. J. Madden... 2d revised ed. St. Louis, Mo., B. Herder, 1899. viii, 9-206 p. 20 cm. First edition published 1898 under title: The reaction from science. [BT1220.M3 1899] 99-4823
1. Religion and science—1860-1899. 2. Agnosticism. I. Title.

MARTINEAU, James, 1805-1900. 215
Religion as affected by modern materialism; an address delivered in Manchester New college, London, at the opening of its eighty-ninth session, on Tuesday, October 6, 1874. By James Martineau, LL.D., with an introduction by the Rev. Henry W. Bellows, D.D. New York, G. P. Putnam's sons, 1875. 68 p. 17 1/2 cm. [BL241.M27] 27-4874
1. Religion and science—1860-1899. 2. Materialism. 3. Religion—Philosophy. I. Title.

MARY Frederick, Sister 213
Religion and evolution since 1859; some effects of the theory of evolution on the philosophy of religion, by Sister Mary Frederick, C.S.C. Chicago, Loyola university press, 1935. ix p., 3 l., 3-189 p. 23 cm. Issued also as thesis (PH.D) University of Notre Dame. Bibliography: p. 187-189. [BL240.M345 1935] 36-7660
1. Religion and science—1860-1899. 2. Religion and science—1900- 3. Evolution. I. Title.

MEAGHER, James Luke, 1848- 1920. 215
Man, the mirror of the universe; or, The agreement of science and religion, explained for the people, by Rev. James L. Meagher... New York, Russell brothers, 1887. iv, 375 p. 19 1/2 cm. [BL240.M4] 31-13195
1. Religion and science—1860-1899. I. Title.

MITCHELL, Thomas, b.1818. 215
Cosmogony: the geological antiquity of the world, evolution, atheism, pantheism, deism and infidelity refuted, by science, philosophy and Scripture, by Prof. Thomas Mitchell. In two volumes [v. 1] ... New York, The American news company, 1881. xxviii, 29-450 p. 19 cm. No more published? [BL240.M6] 31-13181
1. Religion and science—1800-1899. 2. Cosmology. 3. Evolution. I. Title.

MONELL, Gilbert Chichester, d.1881. 215
The creation and the Scripture, the revelation of God, by Gilbert Chichester Monell, M. D. New York, G. P. Putnam's sons, 1882. 2 p. l., 233 p. 20 cm. [BL240.M7] 31-13180
1. Religion and science—1860-1899. I. Title.

NATURAL law in the spiritual world by Henry Drummond ... [New York] A. L. Burt company [n.d.] 388 p. front. (port.) 19 cm. (On cover: The home library) [BL240.D6 1926] 26-12888 215
1. Religion and science—1800-1899. 2. Religion and science—1800-1899. 3. Natural theology.

NEWTON, William, 1820?-1893. 215
Nature's testimony to nature's God. Four sermons, preached in the Church of the Nativity, Philadelphia. By Wm. Newton... Philadelphia, Claxton, Remsen & Haffelfinger, 1873. 1 p. l., v-ix, 11-97 p. 18 cm. [BL240.N5] 31-13189
1. Religion and science—1800-1890. 2. Sermons, American. I. Title.

ORTON, Azariah Giles, 1789- 1869. 215
An address on the internal evidence of divine authorship, in nature and revelation; delivered before the Erodelphian and Eecritean societies of Miami university, June 1854; by Rev. A. G. Orton ... Cincinnati, C. F. Bradley & co., printers, 1855. 55 p. 23 cm. Cover-title: Nature and revelation ... [BL241.O7] 41-30620
1. Religion and science—1800-1859. I. Title. II. Title: Nature and revelation.

PEDDER, Henry C. 215
Religion and progress: an essay. by Henry C. Pedder ... New York. E. P. Dutton & company, 1876. 82 p. 20 cm. [BL240.P35] 31-13188
1. Religion and science—1860-1899. I. Title.

PONTON, Mungo, 1802-1880. 215
The great architect; as manifested in the material universe. By Mungo Ponton ... 2d ed. London, Edinburgh and New York, T. Nelson and sons, 1866. 1 p. l., vi p., 2 l., [9]-276 p. col. front., col. plates. 19 cm. [BL240.P6 1866] 31-8494
1. Religion and science—1860-1899. 2. Astronomy. 3. Light. I. Title.
Contents omitted.

PORTER, Charles Talbot, 1826- 210
Mechanics and faith. By Charles T. Porter. New York, Evening post job printing office, 1885. 2 p. l., 5-230 numb. l. 24 cm. "Put in type and a few copies printed in this form, for the purpose of submitting it to criticism in advance of its publication." [BL240.P7 1885] 31-13177
1. Religion and science—1860-1899. 2. Natural theology. I. Title.

PORTER, Charles Talbot, 1826- 210
Mechanics and faith; a study of spiritual truth in nature, by Charles Talbot Porter. New York & London, G. P. Putnam's sons, 1886. viii p., 1 l., 295 p. 20 cm. [BL240.P7 1886] 31-13176
1. Religion and science—1860-1899. 2. Natural theology. I. Title.

REYNOLDS, Joseph William, 1821- 1899.
The supernatural in nature; a verification by free use of science, by Joseph William Reynolds ... New and cheaper ed. (rev.) London, New York [etc.] Longmans, Green, and co., 1897. xxviii, 479 p. 19 cm. [RD555.R4] 1-5908
1. Religion and science—1860-1899. I. Title.

RICHARDS, Harry Edward, d.1923. 215
The mystery of life: a study of revelation in the light of science, by Harry E. Richards ... New York, Dodd, Mead and company, 1898. 292 p. 19 cm. [BL240.R55] 31-13182
1. Religion and science—1800-1899. 2. Life. I. Title.

ROE, Edward Reynolds. 215
God reigns; lay sermons, by Edward Reynolds Roe, M.D. Chicago, Laird & Lee [c1888] 187 p. 17 1/2 cm. [BL240.R57] 31-13173
1. Religion and science—1860-1899. 2. Sermons, American. I. Title.

ROMANES, George John, 1848- 1894. 215
Thoughts on religion, by the late George John Romanes...Edited by Charles Gore... Chicago, The Open court publishing company, 1895. 1 p. l., 184 p. 18 1/2 cm. [BL240.R6 1895] 3-14725
1. Religion and science—1860-1899. I. Gore, Charles, 1853-1932, ed. II. Title.

ROMANES, George John, 1848- 1894. 215
Thoughts on religion, by the late George John Romanes...Edited by Charles Gore... 3d ed. Chicago, The Open court publishing company, 1897. 3 p. l., 5-196 p. 20 cm. (On cover: The religion of science library, no. 25) [BL240.R6 1897] 3-15828
1. Religion and science—1860-1899. I. Gore, Charles, 1853-1932, ed. II. Title.

SAVAGE, Minot Judson, 1841- 1918. 215
The irrepressible conflict between two world-theories. Five lectures dealing with Christianity and evolutionary thought, to which is added "The inevitable surrender of orthodoxy." By Rev. Minot J. Savage ... Boston, Arena publishing co., 1892. 198 p. 19 cm. [BL263.S355] 33-20361
1. Religion and science—1860-1899. 2. Evolution. I. Title.

SCIENCE and revelation: 215
a series of lectures in reply to the theories of Tyndall, Huxley, Darwin, Spencer, etc. BLfast, W. Mullan; New York, Scribner, Welford & Armstrong, 1875. [326] p. illus. 22 cm. Various pagings. Lectures delivered in the Presbyterian church, Rosemary street, Belfast, during the winter of 1874-75. cf. Pref. [BL240.S37] 31-13172
1. Religion and science—1860-1899. I. Porter, Josias Leslie, 1823-1889.
Contents omitted.

SHALER, Nathaniel Southgate, 1841-1906. 215'.7
The interpretation of nature. Freeport, N.Y., Books for Libraries Press [1973] p. (Essay index reprint series) "Lectures on the Winkley Foundation ... delivered before the students of Andover Theological Seminary in 1891." Reprint of the 1893 ed. [BL240.S435 1973] 72-14095 ISBN 0-518-10023-5
1. Religion and science—1860-1899. I. Title.

SHAW, Robert, M.A. 213
Four cosmical lectures; or, Cosmotheological essays, which were delivered in different places, on different occasions ... and are here intended to complete the work, "Creator and cosmos". By Robert Shaw ... Revised. St. Louis, Becktold & company, 1889. 122 p. fold. map. illus. (plan) 26 1/2 cm. [With his Creator and cosmos. St. Louis, 1889] [BL225.S55 1889] 30-31428
1. Religion and science—1860-1899. 2. Pyramids—Construction. 3. Natural theology. I. Title.
Contents omitted.

SPURLOCK, James Aquila, b.1825. 215
A philosophy of heaven, earth, and the millennium ... By James A. Spurlock ... St. Louis, Mo., W. J. Gilbert [c1869] vii, [9]-310 p. 17 1/2 cm. [BL240.S75] 31-13165
1. Religion and science—1800-1899. I. Title.

SWANDER, John I. 1833-1925. 215
The substantial philosophy. Eight hundred answers to as many questions concerning the most scientific revolution of the age. By J. I. Swander ... New York, Hudson & co. [c1886] 352 p. front. (port.) 20 1/2 cm. "Other authorities consulted and quoted": p. [8] [BL240.S8] 31-14257
1. Religion and science—1860-1899. I. Title.

TEMPLE, Frederick, abp. of Canterbury, 1821-1902. 230
The relations between religion and science; eight lectures preached before the University of Oxford, in the year 1884, on the foundation of the late Rev. John Bampton ... by the Right Rev. Frederick, lord bishop of Exeter. London, Macmillan and co., limited; New York, The Macmillan company, 1903. xi, 252 p. 19 1/2 cm. (Half-title: The Bampton lectures for M.DCCC.LXXXIV) "First edition, 8vo, 1884, reprinted January and February (twice), 1885, April 1885; reissue (crown 8vo) November, 1885, 1903." [BR45.B3 1884 a] 3-17687
1. Religion and science—1860-1899. I. Title.
Contents omitted.

THOMAS, Jesse Burgess, 1832- 1915. 215
The old Bible and the new science. An essay and four lectures delivered before the New York Baptist ministers' conference, by J. B. Thomas ... stenographically reported by C. C. Urquhart. New York, D. C. Potter [c1877] 2 p. l., 3-234 p. 19 1/2 cm. [BL240.T55] 31-13162
1. Religion and science—1860-1899. I. Title.

THOMPSON, Lewis Olson, 1839- 1887. 215
Nothing lost; or, The universe a recording machine. By Rev. Lewis O. Thompson ... New York, De W. C. Lent; Peoria, D. H. Tripp & co., 1877. 56 p. 23 cm. [BL241.T5] 31-14268
1. Religion and science—1860-1899. I. Title.

TUTTLE, Hudson, 1836-1910. 211
Religion of man and ethics of science. By Hudson Tuttle ... New York, M. L. Holbrook & co., 1890. xii, [9]-313 p. 10 cm. [BL240.T8] 31-13161
1. Religion and science—1860-1899. I. Title.

VAHEY, John W. 215
The visible and invisible worlds. By Rev. J. W. Vahey ... Milwaukee, Wis., Hoffmann bros., 1890. 276 p. 19 1/2 cm. [BL240.V3] 31-13547
1. Religion and science-1860-1899. 2. Catholic church—Doctrinal and controversial works—Catholic authors. I. Title.

WARD, James, 1843-1925. 215'.08
Naturalism and agnosticism. 4th ed. London, A. & C. Black, 1915. New York, Kraus Reprint Co., 1971. xvi, 623 p. 23 cm. (Gifford lectures, 1896-1898) Includes bibliographical references. [BD541.W3 1971] 78-149170
1. Religion and science—1860-1899. 2. Natural theology. 3. Agnosticism. 4. Monism. I. Title. II. Series.

WARD, James, 1843-1925. 124
Naturalism and agnosticism; the Gifford lectures delivered before the University of Aberdeen in the years 1896-1898, by James Ward... New York, The Macmillan company; London, Macmillan & co., ltd., 1899. 2 v. 21 cm. [BD541.W3] 99-3429
1. Religion and science—1860-1899. 2.

Natural theology. 3. Agnosticism. 4. Mosism. I. Title.

WELCH, Ransom Bethune, 1824- 1890. 215
Faith and modern thought, by Ransom B. Welch...with introduction by Tayler Lewis. New York, G. P. Putnam's sons, 1876. 3 p. l., [v]-xxx, [3]-272 p. 19 1/2 cm. [BL240.W4] 31-13545
1. Religion and science—1860-1899. 2. Positivism. I. Title.

WISEMAN, Nicholas Patrick Stephen, cardinal, 1802-1865. 215
Twelve lectures on the connexion between science and revealed religion. Delivered in Rome by Nicholas Wiseman... 1st American from the 1st London ed. Andover, New York, Gould and Newman, 1837. xii, [9]-404 p. front. (fold map) III fold. pl., diagrs. 23 1/2 cm. [BL240.W6 1837] 5-28244
1. Religion and science—1800-1859. I. Title.

WOODROW, James, 1828-1907. 215
An examination of certain recent assaults on physical science. By James Woodrow ... Columbia, S.C., Printed at the Presbyterian publishing house, 1873. 53 p. 21 cm. "Reprinted from the Southern Presbyterian review for July, 1873." [BL240.W648] 31-13539
1. Dabney, Robert Lewis, 1820-1898. 2. Religion and science—1860-1899. I. Title.

WRIGHT, George Frederick, 1838-1921. 215
Studies in science and religion. By G. Frederick Wright ... Andover, W. F. Draper, 1882. xvi, 390 p. illus. (incl. maps) 18 1/2 cm. [BL240.W7] 31-13538
1. Religion and science—1860-1899. I. Title.

WYTHE, Joseph Henry, 1822- 215
The agreement of science and revelation. By Rev. Jos. H. Wythe ... Philadelphia, J. B. Lippincott & co.; London, Trubner & co., 1872. 290 p. 20 cm. "Glossary": p. 267-284. [BL240.W8 1872] 31-13537
1. Religion and science—1860-1899. I. Title.

WYTHE, Joseph Henry, 1822- 215
The agreement of science and revelation, by Rev. Jos. H. Wythe ... 2d ed., rev. Philadelphia, J. B. Lippincott & co., 1877. 306 p. 19 1/2 cm. "Glossary": p. 283-300. [BL240.W8 1877] 31-13536
1. Religion and science—1860-1899. I. Title.

ZAHM, John Augustine, 1851- 1921. 213
Evolution and dogma, by the Reverend J. A. Zahm... Chicago, D. H. McBride & co., 1896. 11, [2], xiii-xxx, 13-461 p. 20 cm. "Authors and works cited": p. 439-449. [BL263.Z3] 4-4018
1. Religion and science—1800-1899. 2. Evolution. I. Title.

ZAHM, John Augustine, 1851- 1921. 215
Science and the church, by the Reverend J. A. Zahm... Chicago, D. H. McBride & co., 1896. 299 p. 20 cm. Articles reprinted from various periodicals. cf. Pref. [BL240.Z37] 31-13535
1. Religion and science—1800-1899. 2. Catholic church. I. Title.

ZAHM, John Augustine, 1851- 1921. 215
...Scientific theory and Catholic doctrine, by the Reverend J. A. Zahm... Chicago, D. H. McBridge & co., 1896. 307 p. 16 cm. (Catholic summer and winter school library) "References": p. 305-307. [BL240.Z45] 31-13534
1. Religion and science—1800-1899. 2. Evolution. 3. Teleology. I. Title.

Religion and science—1900—

AMERICAN Scientific Affiliation. 215
Modern science and Christian faith; a symposium on the relationship of the Bible to modern science, by members of the American Scientific Affiliation. 2d ed., enl. Wheaton, Ill., Van Kampen Press [1950] xii, 316 p. illus. 22 cm. Bibliographical footnotes. [BL240.A64 1950] 50-54737
1. Religion and science—1900- I. Title.

AMERICAN Scientific Affiliation. 215
Modern science and Christian faith, eleven essays on the relationship of the Bible to modern science by members of the American Scientific Affiliation. [F. Alton Everest, editor] Wheaton, Ill., Van Kampen Press [1948] 289 p. illus. 21 cm. On cover: The Christian student's science symposium. Bibliographical footnotes. [BL240.A64] 411755
1. Religion and Science—1900- I. Everest, Frederick Alton, 1900- ed. II. Title.

THE American weekly (New York) 215
The faith of great scientists; a collection of "My faith" articles from the American weekly. [New York, Hearst Pub. Co., 1950] 63 p. ports. 23 cm. Cover title. [BL240.A643] 50-3271
1. Religion and science—1900- I. Title.

ARNOLD, Frank Stutesman, 1863- 215
Through nature to nature's God, by Frank S. Arnold... New York, Chicago [etc.] Fleming H. Revell company [c1930] 191 p. 19 1/2 cm. [BL240.A86] 30-25518
1. Religion and science—1900- I. Title.

ATWOOD, Elijah Francis, 1871- 215
The Bible and science; especially devoted to proving that evolution as a whole is unscientific and impossible, and the Bible, when that book touches upon any fact of nature, is apt to speak scientifically. By Elijah Francis Atwood ... Sisseton, S. D., The Atwood publishing company, 1931. 6 p. l., 85 p. port. 21 cm. [BL263.A6] 31-21550
1. Religion and science—1900- 2. Bible and science. I. Title.

BARNES, Ernest William, bp. of Birmingham, 1874- 215
Scientific theory and religion; the world described by science and its spiritual interpretation, by Ernest William Barnes ... Cambridge [Eng.] The University press, 1933. xxiv, 685, [1] p. diagrs. 24 cm. [The Gifford lectures at Aberdeen. 1927-1929] [BL240.B26] 33-13154
1. Religion and science—1900- 2. Religion—Philosophy. 3. Science—Philosophy. 4. Religion—Addresses, essays, lectures. I. Title.

BARNES, Ernest William, bp. of Birmingham, 1874- 215
Scientific theory and religion; the world described by science and its spiritual interpretation, by Ernest William Barnes ... New York, The Macmillan company; Cambridge, Eng., The University press, 1933. xxiv, 685 p. diagrs. 24 1/2 cm. [The Gifford lectures of Aberdeen, 1927-1929] [BL240.B26 1933a] 33-17816
1. Religion and science—1900- 2. Religion—Philosophy. 3. Science—Philosophy. 4. Religion—Addresses, essays, lectures. I. Title.

BARRY, William Francis, 1849- 215
The triumph of life; or, Science and the soul, by William Barry ... London, New York [etc.] Longmans, Green and co. ltd., 1928. xi, 247, [1] p. 23 cm. [BL240.B28] 28-12636
1. Religion and science, 1900- I. Title. II. Title: Science and the soul.

BAVINK, Bernhard, 1879- 215
Science and God. by Bernhard Bavink, translated by H. Stafford Hatfield. New York, Reynal & Hitchcock, inc., 1934. ix, 174 p. 19 1/2 cm. [BS240.B32] 34-11194
1. Religion and science—1900- I. Hatfield, Henry Stafford, tr. II. Title.

BENSON, Clarence Herbert, 1879- 215
The greatness and grace of God, conclusive evidence that refutes evolution; arranged to be used as a textbook in Christian evidences. Chicago, Scripture Press [1953] 224p. illus. 21cm. [BL253.B38] 54-652
1. Religion and science—1900- 2. Astronomy. I. Title.

BENSON, Clarence Herbert, 1879- 215
Immensity; God's greatness seen in creation, by Clarence H. Benson. Chicago, The Scripture press [1937] 140 p. front., illus., plates. 20 cm. [BL253.B4] 40-622
1. Religion and science—1900- 2. Bible and science. 3. Astronomy. I. Title.

BIXBY, James Thompson, 1843- 1921. 215
The new world and the new thought, by James Thompson Bixby... New York, TWhittacker 1902. 219 p. 19 1/2 cm. [BL240.B49] 2-8358
1. Religion and science 1900- I. Title.
Contents omitted.

BOLE, Simeon James, 1873- 215
The battlefield of faith, by S. J. Bole...with an introduction by President Stephen W. Paine... University Park, Ia., The College press, 1940. 6 p. l., 15-320, [10] p. plates, ports., maps, tables, 21 cm. Bibliography at the end of each chapter. [BL240.B57] 41-9490
1. Religion and science—1900- 2. Sceince—Study and teaching. I. Title.

BROWN, Arthur Isaac, 1897- 215
Miracles of science, by Arthur I. Brown ... Findlay, O., Fundamental truth publishers [1945] 287 p. 20 cm. "Talks ... delivered by transcription over various radio stations--several along the entire Pacific coast, and also in Chicago where the two stations owned and operated by the Moody Bible institute have recently carried the program, Miracles of science."--Foreword. [BL240.B73] 46-12275
1. Religion and science—1900- I. Moody Bible institute of Chicago. II. Title.

BROWNE, Laurence Edward, 1887- 215
Where science and religion meet. Wallington, Surrey, Religious Education Press, 1950. 128 p. 20 cm. (Gateway handbooks of religious knowledge, 3) Bibliography: p. 126. [BL240.B74] 51-27683
1. Religion and science—1900- I. Title. II. Series.

BURROUGHS, John, 1837-1921.
The light of day; religious discussions and criticisms from the naturalist's point of view, by John Burroughs. Boston & New York, Houghton, Mifflin company, 1900. 4 p., l., [vii]-ix p. 1 l., 224 p. front. (port.) 19 1/2 cm. (Added t.-p. engraved: The writings of John Burroughs. Riverside edition. [vol. xi]) [PS1220.E95 vol. 11] 0-2941
1. Religion and science—1900- 2. Natural theology. I. Title.

BURTT, Edwin Arthur, 1892- 215
...Religion in an age of science, by Edwin A. Burtt... New York, Frederick A. Stokes company, 1929. xiii, 158 p. 19 1/2 cm. ("Religion and the modern age" series) "Most of the material in the following chapters was presented in lecture form before the Institute of world unity at Green Acre, Maine, during the week of August 13, 1928, and has been published as a serial in World unity."--foreword. [BL240.B83] 29-10527
1. Religion and science—1900- 2. Science—Philosophy. I. Title.

CATHOLIC Church. Pope (Pius XII), 1939- Le Prove della esistenza di D10(22 nov. 1951) 215
Modern science and God. [Edited and translated] by P. J. McLaughlin. New York, Philosophical Library [1954] 89p. 19cm. Address delivered to the members of the Pontificial Academy of Science. [BL240] 54-13051
1. Religion and science—1900- 2. God—Proof. I. McLaughlin, P. J., ed. and tr. II. Title.

CLAYTON, Charles Lincoln, 1860- 213
God, evolution, and mind healing, by Charles Lincoln Clayton ... [Wellington, Kan., The American school of science and religion] 1923. 220 p. 20 cm. [BL240.C57] 31-21963
1. Religion and science—1900- 2. Evolution. 3. Mental healing. I. Title.

COFFIN, William Carey, 1862- 215
Enduring faith [by] William Carey Coffin. Boston, Mass., The Christopher publishing house [1943] 69 p. 17 cm. "Revised edition." [BL241.C58 1943] 43-10906
1. Religion and science—1900- I. Title.

COLLIER, Frank Wilbur, 1870- 922.
John Wesley among the scientists, by Frank W. Collier ... New York, Cincinnati [etc.] The Abingdon press [c1928] 351 p. front. (port.) pl. 20 cm. Bibliography: p. 323-326. [BX8495.W5C75] 28-31129
1. Wesley, John, 1703-1791. 2. Religion and science—1900- I. Title.

COULSON, Charles Alfred.
Christianity in an age of science. London, New York, Oxford University Press, 1953. 53p. 23cm. (Riddell memorial lectures, 25th ser.) At head of title: University of Durham. A56
1. Religion and science—1900- I. Title. II. Series.

COULSON, Charles Alfred. 215
Science and Christian belief. Chapel Hill, University of North Carolina Press, 1955. 127p. 20cm. (The John Calvin McNair lectures) [BL240] 55-12908
1. Religion and science—1900- I. Title.

CRISWELL, Wallie A 215
Did man just happen? Grand Rapids, Zondervan Pub. House [1957] 121 p. 21 cm. [BL240.C73] 57-38983
1. Religion and science—1900- 2. Evolution. I. Title.

CROSS, Frank Leslie, 1900- 215
Religion and the reign of science, by F. Leslie Cross ... London, New York [etc.] Longmans, Green and co., 1930. ix p., 1 l., 110 p., 1 l. 20 cm. (Half-title: Anglican library of faith and thought) Bibliography: 1 p. at end. [BL240.C75] 30-30525
1. Religion and science—1900- I. Title.

CURTIS, Heber Doust, 1872- 1942. 215
One scientist's religion, from articles by Professor Heber Doust Curtis, synthesized and edited by his colleague, Will Carl Rufus. Ann Arbor, Mich., Wesley foundation [1944] 52 p. incl. front. (port.) illus. 23 cm. Bibliography: p. 51-52. [BL241.C8] 45-2162
1. Religion and science—1900- I. Rufus, Will Carl, 1876- ed. II. Wesley foundation, University of Michigan. III. Title.

D'ARCY, Charles Frederick, abp. of Armagh, 1859-1938. 215
Science and creation: the Christian interpretation, by Charles F. D.'Arcy ... London, New York [ect.] Longmans, Green and co., 1925. vi, 125, [1] p. 18 cm. (Half-title: The Liverpool diocesan board of divinity publications, 1924) [BL225.D3] 25-5220
1. Religion and science—1900- 2. Creation. I. Title.

DINSMORE, Charles Allen, 1860- 215
Religious certitude in an age of science; the McNair lectures, 1922, delivered at the University of North Carolina, by Charles Allen Dinsmore ... Chapel Hill, N. C., The University of North Carolina press; [etc., etc.] 1924. 4 p. l., vi p., 1 l., 102 p. 20 cm. [BL240.D6] 24-7739
1. Religion and science—1900- I. Title.

DINSMORE, Charles Allen, 1860-1941. 215
Religious certitude in an age of science; the McNair lectures, 1922, delivered at the University of North Carolina, by Charles Allen Dinsmore ... Chapel Hill, N.C., The University of North Carolina press; London, H. Milford, 1924. 4 p. l., vi p., 1 l., 102 p. 20 cm. [BL240.D6] 24-7739
1. Religion and science—1900- I. Title.

DONAT, Josef, 1868- 215
The freedom of science, by Joseph Donat ... New York, J. F. Wagner [c1914] ix, 419 p. 23 cm. [BL240.D7] 14-16951
1. Religion and science—1900- 2. Free thought. 3. Teaching, Freedom of. 4. Modernism—Catholic church. I. Title.
Contents omitted.

[DOWSON, Mary Emily] 1848- 215
Where science and religion meet, by William Scott Palmer [pseud] ... London, New York [etc.] Hodder and Stoughton [1919] 287. [1] p. 19 cm. Bibliography: p. 287-[288] [BL240.D75] 20-4475
1. Religion and science—1900- 2. Christianity. I. Title.

DRAWBRIDGE, Cyprian Leycester, 1868- ed. 215
The religion of scientists, being recent opinions expressed by two hundred fellows of the Royal society on the subject of religion and theology; edited by C. L. Drawbridge, M.A., on behalf of the Christian evidence society. New York, The Macmillan company, 1932. 160 p. 20 1/2 cm. "Names and descriptions of fellows of the Royal society mentioned": p. 150-158. [BL240.D77 1962a] 32-16948
1. Religion and science-1900- 2. Royal society of London. 3. Christian evidence society. I. Title.

DUNHAM, Chester Forrester, 1891- 215
Christianity in a world of science, by Chester Forrester Dunham. New York, The Macmillan company, 1930. 185 p. 21 cm. [BL240.D87] 30-24938
1. Religion and science—1900- I. Title.

DWIGHT, Thomas, 1843-1911. 215
Thoughts of a Catholic anatomist, by Thomas Dwight... New York, London [etc.] Longmans, Green, and co., 1911. vii p., 2 l., 3-243 p. 19 cm. [BL240.D9] 11-17630
1. Religion and science—1900- I. Title.

EDDINGTON, Arthur Stanley, Sir 1882- 215
Science and the unseen world, by Arthur Stanley Eddington ... New York, The Macmillan company, 1929. 91 p. 21 cm. (Swarthmore lecture, 1929) [BL241.E4 1929a] 29-19461
1. Religion and science—1900- 2. Friends, Society of. I. Title.

FENDRICH, Joseph Lowrey, 1897- 215
Science discovers God. New York, Dodd, Mead [1949] xii, 176 p. 20 cm. [BL240.F4] 49-8195
1. Religion and science—1900- I. Title.

FERBER, Adolph C 215
Where is heaven? [1st ed.] New York, Pageant Press [1955] 243p. 24cm. [BL240.F45] 55-7358
1. Swedenborg, Emanuel. 1688-1772. 2. Religion and science—1900- 3. Heaven. 4. Extrasensory perception. I. Title.

FOSTER, Allyn King, 1868- 215
The new dimensions of religion, by Allyn K. Foster ... New York, The Macmillan company, 1931. x p., 1 l., 291 p. 20 cm. [BL240.F6] 31-29500
1. Religion and science—1900- 2. Religion. I. Title.

FOSTER, George Sanford, 1882- 239
Why I believe in God and immortality, by George Sanford Foster, M. D. New York [etc.] Fleming H. Revell company [c1939] 128 p. 20 cm. [BT1101.F72] 39-10871
1. Religion and science—1900- 2. Apologetics—20th cent. I. Title.

GAGER, Charles Stuart, 1872- 215
The relation between science and theology; how to think about it, by C. Stuart Gager. Chicago, London, The Open court publishing co., 1925. 4 p. l., 87 p. 21 cm. [BL240.G25] 25-19202
1. Religion and science—1900- I. Title.

GARRISON, Webb B 599.8
Wonders of man; mysteries that point to God, by Gary Webster [pseud.] New York, Sheed & Ward [1957] 152p. 21cm. [BL243.G33] [BL243.G33] 599.9 57-6055 57-6055
1. Religion and science—1900- I. Title.

GARRISON, Webb B 215
Wonders of science; mysteries that point to God, by Gary Webster [pseud.] New York, Sheed & Ward [1956] 135p. 21cm. [BL243.G3] 56-6132
1. Religion and science—1900- I. Title.

GASPAR, Geza. 215
Science, conscience and God. Should the scientist believe New York, Helicon Books [1950] 64 p. 24 cm. [BL240.G29] 50-9312
1. Religion and science—1900- I. Title.

GREENWOOD, William Osborne, 1871- 215
Biology and Christian belief, by William Osborne Greenwood ... with a foreword by Theodore Savory ... New York, The Macmillan company, 1939. 191, [1] p. illus. 21 cm. [BL262.G74 1939] 39-3100
1. Religion and science—1900- 2. Biology. I. Title.

HAAS, John Augustus William, 1862-1937. 215
The unity of faith and knowledge, [by] John A. W. Haas... New York, The Macmillan company, 1926. 251 p. 19 1/2 cm. Bibliography: p. 239-251. [BL240.H2] 26-20267
1. Religion and science—1900- 2. Philosophy and religion. I. Title.

HAND, James Edward, 1862- ed. 215
Ideals of science & faith; essays by various authors, ed. by the Rev. J. E. Hand... New York, Longmans, Green, & co.; London, G. Allen, 1904. xix, 333 p. 19 1/2 cm. [BL240.H25 1904] 4-14996
1. Religion and science-1900- I. Title.
Contents omitted.

HANDRICH, Theodore Lewis, 1906- 215
The creation: facts, theories, and faith. Chicago, Moody Press [1953] 311p. 22cm. [BL240.H258] 53-3667
1. Religion and science—1900- I. Title.

HANDRICH, Theodore Lewis, 1906- 215
Everyday science for the Christian. [3d ed.] St. Louis, Concordia Pub. House, 1947. xx, 188 p. 20 cm. [BL240.H26 1947] 47-26327
1. Religion and science—1900- 2. Bible and science. I. Title.

HARMAN, Nathaniel Bishop, 1869- 215
Science and religion, by N. Bishop Harman ... New York, The Macmillan company, 1935. 174, [1] p. 20 cm. [BL240.H27 1935 a] 35-16176
1. Religion and science—1900- 2. Religion—Philosophy. I. Title.

HARRIS, Errol E 215
Revelation through reason; religion in the light of science and philosophy. New Haven, Yale University Press, 1958. 158p. 21cm. (The Terry lectures) [BL240.H29] 58-11253
1. Religion and science—1900- 2. Revelation. I. Title.

HARRISON, Norvell. 215
The chamber in the heart, by Norvell Harrison. New York, Lucis publishing company [c1931] 86 p. 20 cm. Contents.--The chamber in the heart.--The path. [BL241.H3] ca 31
1. Religion and science—1900- I. Title.

HARTSHORNE, Marion Holmes. 215
The promise of science and the power of faith. Philadelphia, Westminster Press [1958] 143p. 21cm. [BL240.H35] 58-8940
1. Religion and science—1900- I. Title.

HEIM, Karl, 1874- 215
Christian faith and natural science. [1st Harper torchbook ed.] New York, Harper [1957] 256p. 21cm. (Harper torchbooks, TB 16) Translation by N. Horton Smith of Der christliche Gottesglaube und die Naturwissenschaft, I, Grundiegung. [BT75] 57-7536
1. Religion and science—1900- I. Title.

HEIM, Karl, 1874- 215
Christian faith and natural science. [Translation by N. Horton Smith] New York, Harper [1953] 256p. 22cm. Translation of Der chfistliche Gottesglaube und die Naturwissenschaft, i, Grundlegung. [BT75.H536 1953a] 53-8371
1. Religion and science—1900- I. Title.

HEIM, Karl, 1874- 215
The transformation of the scientific world view. New York, Harper [c1953] 262p. 22cm. Translation of Der christliche Gottesglaube und die Naturwissenschaft, ii, Die Wandlung im naturwissenschaftlichen Weltbild. [BT75.H537 1953a] 53-109666
1. Religion and science—1900- I. Title.

HEYL, Paul Renno, 1872- 215
The philosophy of a scientific man, by Paul R. Heyl. New York, The Vanguard press, 1933. ix p., 2 l., 15-182 p. diagrs. 20 cm. "References notes". p. [177]-182. [BL240.H4] 215 ISBN 33-4056
1. Religion and science—1900- 2. Religion—Philosophy. 3. Science—Philosophy. I. Title.

HILL, Mabel, 1864- comp. 215.04
Wise men worship; a compilation of excerpts from scientists, philosophers and professional men concerning science and religion, compiled and edited by Mabel Hill; with a preface by Prof. William Lyon Phelps; introduction by the compiler. New York, E. P. Dutton & company, inc. [c1931] xvii p.. 1 l., 21-134 p. 19 1/2 cm. "First edition." [BL240.H52] 31-30536
1. Religion and science—1900- I. Title.

HOCKING, William Ernest, 1873- 215
Science and the idea of God, by William Ernest Hocking. Chapel Hill, The University of North Carolina press, 1944. ix p., 1 l., 124 p. 21 cm. (Half-title: The John Calvin McNair lectures) [BL240.H715] 44-8718
1. Religion and science—1900- I. Title.

HOUCK, Frederick Alfons, 1866- 215
Our palace wonderful; or, Man's place in visible creation, by the Rev. Frederick A. Houck... Chicago, Ill., D. B. Hansen & sons, 1915. 2 p. l., 7-173 p. front., plates (Art double, part col.) 19 1/2 cm. [BL240.H75] 15-1797
1. Religion and science—1900- I. Title.

INGE, William Ralph, 1860- 215
God and the astronomers; containing the Warburton lectures, 1931-1933, by William Ralph Inge... London, New York [etc.] Longmans, Green and co., 1933. xiii, 308 p. 22 1/2 cm. [BL240.I5] 33-36225
1. Religion and science—1900- 2. Religion—Philosophy. I. Title.
Contents omitted.

JACOBS, Thornwell. 213
The new science and the old religion, by Thornwell Jacobs ... Oglethorpe University, Ga., Oglethorpe university press [1935] xv, [1], 526 p. incl. front., illus., maps, diagrs. fold. tab. 24 cm. "Second edition, revised and enlarged." "Acknowledgments": p. xi-[xiii] [BL240.J3 1935] 35-11731
1. Religion and science—1900- 2. Evolution. I. Title.

KERR, Alva Martin. 213
Thinking through; facts and principles to clarify the controversial thinking in the church, by Alva Martin Kerr... New York, George H. Doran company [c1926] 125 p. 19 1/2 cm. [BL263.K46] 26-10869
1. Religion and science—1900- 2. Modernist-fundamentalist controversy. I. Title.

KIMBALL, John Calvin, 1832-1910. 213
The romance of evolution, and its relation to religion, by John C. Kimball. Boston, American Unitarian association, 1913. vii, 323 p. 19 cm. "Many of the essays in this book were prepared for delivery as lectures before the Brooklyn ethical society and were also delivered at the Meadville theological school and before various clubs and scientific societies in different parts of the country."--Pref. [BL263.K5] 13-22503
1. Religion and science—1900- 2. Evolution. I. Title.

KIRK, Harris Elliott, 1872- 215
Stars, atoms, and God, by Harris Elliott Kirk ... Chapel Hill, The University of North Carolina press, 1932. xv p., 2 l., 3-100 p. 19 1/2 cm. (Half-title: The John Calvin McNair lectures) Bibliography: p. 95-100. [BL240.K53] 32-11469
1. Religion and science 1900- 2. Science—Philosophy. 3. Astronomy. 4. Physics. I. Title.

KISKADDON, Jesse Fulton, 1890- 215
Scientific support for Christian doctrines [by] J. Fulton Kiskaddon, M. A. [Ripley, N. Y., c1933] 76 p. 22 cm. Bibliography: p. 76. [BL240.K533] 33-12629
1. Religion and science—1900- 2. Virgin birth. I. Title.

KRIMSKY, Joseph Hayyim. 215
A doctor's soliloquy. New York, Philosophical Library [1953] 116p. 20cm. [BL241.K7] 53-6244
1. Religion and science—1900- 2. Religion—Philosophy. I. Title.

LANGMACK, Holger Christian. 215
God and the universe; unity of science and religion. New York, Philosophical Library [1953] 173p. illus. 22cm. [BL240.L28] 53-13071
1. Religion and science—1900- I. Title.

LEE, James Wideman, 1849-1919. 215
The religion of science, the faith of coming man, by James W. Lee ... New York, Chicago [etc.] Fleming H. Revell company [c1912] 304 p. 21 1/2 cm. [BL240.L5] 12-17649
1. Religion and science—1900- 2. Science—Philosophy. I. Title.

LEETE, Frederick De Land, bp., 1866- 215
Christianity in science, by Frederick D. Leete. New York, Cincinnati, The Abingdon press [c1928] 387 p. 23 cm. Bibliographical foot-notes. [BL240.L53] 28-12030
1. Religion and science—1900- I. Title.

LEIMAN, Harold. 296
Science and Judaism, by Harold Leiman and Joseph Elias. New York, Jewish Pocket Books, 1947. 70 p. 17 cm. (Jewish pocket books, 7) [BM538.S3L4] 48-24540
1. Religion and science-1900- 2. Jews—Religion—Apologetic works. 3. Bible. O. T.—Evidences, authority, etc. I. Elias, Joseph, joint author. II. Title. III. Series.

LEVER, Jan. 213.5
Creation and evolution. Translated from the Dutch by Peter G. Berkhout. Grand Rapids, Grand Rapids International Publications; distributed by Kregel, 1958. 244p. illus. 23cm. Includes bibliography. [BL263.L443] 57-13247
1. Religion and science—1900- 2. Evolution. I. Title.

LIVELY, James Madison, 1852- 215
Science of mind; or, Individual and communal knowledge, by J. Madison Lively. [Portland, Or., Printed by Metropolitan press] 1933. 6 p. l., [3]-211, [3] p. front. (port.) diagrs. 21 cm. [BL240.L58] 33-33470
1. Religion and science—1900- I. Title.

LODGE, Oliver Joseph, Sir 1851- 215
The substance of faith allied with science; a catechism for parents and teachers, by Sir Oliver Lodge ... New York and London, Harper & brothers, 1907. viii, 144 p. 20 cm. [BL240.L65] 7-9613
1. Religion and science—1900- I. Title.

LODGE, Oliver Joseph, Sir 1851-1940. 215
Science and immortality, by Sir Oliver Lodge, F.R.S. New York, Moffat, Yard and company, 1910. 7 p. l., 294 p. 21 cm. "Published October, 1908 ... Fourth printing, March, 1910." [BL240.L6 1910] 48-42016
1. Religion and science—1900- 2. Christianity—20th cent. 3. Immortality. I. Title.

LODGE, Oliver Joseph Sir 1851-1940. 215
Science and immortality, by Sir Oliver Lodge, F. R. S. New York, Moffat, Yard and company, 1908. 7 p. l., 294 p. 22 cm. "This book is based upon articles by the author which have appeared in the Hibbert journal and in the Contemporary review, and incorporates the substance of many of those articles."--Prefatory note to American edition. The original edition was published under the title "Man and the universe." London, Methuen & co., 1908, and contains a "Glossary of technical terms," etc., and an index not found in the present edition. [BL240.L6 1908] 8-28409
1. Religion and science—1900- 2. Christianity. 3. Immortality. I. Title.

LONG, Edward Le Roy. 213
Religious beliefs of American scientists. Philadelphia, Westminster Press [1952] 108 p. 21 cm. Revision of thesis, Columbia University, published in microfilm form in 1951 under title: Religious philosophies of natural scientists. [BL240.L66 1952] 52-9193
1. Religion and science—1900- I. Title.

LONG, Edward Le Roy. 215
Science & Christian faith; a study in

partnership. New York, Association Press, 1950. 125 p. 20 cm. (A Haddam House book) [BL240.L67] 50-6377
1. Religion and science—1900- I. Title.

LUNN, Arnold Henry Moore, 1888- 215
The revolt against reason. London, Eyre & Spottiswoode [1950] 252p. 23cm. Bibl. [BL240.L825] 51-546 2.50 bds.,
1. Religion and science — 1900- 2. Science — Philosophy. I. Title.
Now available from Hillary House, New York.

LUNN, Arnold Henry Moore, 1888- 215
The revolt against reason. New York, Sheed & Ward, 1951. 273 p. 22 cm. [BL240.L825 1951] 51-12845
1. Religion and science—1900- 2. Science—Philosophy. I. Title.

LUNN, Arnold Henry Moore, 1888- 215
Science and the supernatural; a correspondence between Arnold Lunn and J. B. S. Haldane... New York, Sheed & Ward, inc., 1935. vi p., 1 l., 412 p. 22 1/2 cm. [BL240.L83] 36-1052
1. Religion and science—1900- I. Haldane, John Burdon Sanderson, 1892- II. Title.

MCCRADY, Edward, 1868- 213
Reason and revelation; argument for the truth of revealed religion based solely upon the evidences of science and philosophy, by Edward McCrady... Grand Rapids, Mich., Wm. B. Eerdmans publishing co. [c1936] 4 p. l., [11]-411 p. diagrs. 23 1/2 cm. Bibliography: p. 403-406. [BL240.M2] 36-9300
1. Religion and science—1900- 2. Christianity—Evidences—20th cent. 3. Evolution 4. Evolution I. Title.

MCCUTCHEN, Duval Talmadge, 1908- 215
The creation story and modern man. [1st ed.] Arlington, Va., 1954. 56p. 20cm. [BL941.M17] 55-32976
1. Religion and science—1900- 2. Creation. I. Title.

MACDONALD, Greville, 1856- 201
The religious sense in its scientific aspect, by Greville Macdonald ... New York, A. C. Armstrong and son; London, Hodder and Stoughton, 1903. xvi, 243 p. vi pl. 20 1/2 cm. "Three lectures given before students ... at King's college, London, June, 1902." [BL240.M25] 5-10562
1. Religion and science—1900- I. Title.
Contents omitted.

MCLAUGHLIN, P. J. 215
The church and modern science. New York, Philosophical Library [1957] 374p. 22cm. 'The second part . . . consists almost entirely of addresses delivered by H. H. Pope Plus xii to scientific and other professional bodies.' 'Acts of Pius xii relating to science and technology':p. 351-359. 'Acts of Pius xii relating to atomic energy':p. 360. Bibliography: p. 361-366. [BL240.M318] 57-59054
1. Religion and science—1900- I. Pius XII, Pope, 1876- II. Title.

MAINS, George Preston, 1844-1930. 215
Science, Christianity and youth, by George Preston Mains. New York, George H. Doran company [c1926] xvii p., 1 l., 19-146 p. 19 1/2 cm. [BL240.M33] 26-17844
1. Religion and science—1900- I. Title.

MARSH, Frank Lewis, 1899- 213
Evolution, creation and science. 2d ed., rev. Washington, Review and Herald Pub. Assn. [1947] 381 p. 18 cm. (Christian home library) [BL240.M3445 1947] 48-107
1. Religion and science—1900- 2. Evolution. I. Title.

MARSH, Frank Lewis, 1899- 215
Life, man, and time. Mountain View, Calif., Pacific Press Pub. Association [1957] 200p. 21cm. [BL240.M3447] 57-11332
1. Religion and science—1900- I. Title.

MASCALL, Eric Lionel, 1905- 215
Christian theology and natural science: some questions on their relations. London, New York, Longmans, Green [1956] 328p. 23cm. (The Bampton lectures, 1956) [BR45.B3 1956] 56-58533
1. Religion and science—1900- I. Title.

MATHER, Kirtley Fletcher, 1888- 215
Crusade for life. Chapel Hill, University of North Carolina Press, 1949. xi, 87 p. 21 cm. (The John Calvin McNair lectures) [BL240.M352] 49-11804
1. Religion and science—1900- 2. Communism and religion. I. Title. II. Series.

MATHER, Kirtley Fletcher, 1888-
Science in search of God, by Kirtley F. Mather... New York, H. Holt and company [c1928] vii p., 3 l., 3-159 p. 19 1/2 cm. A revision of six lectures delivered at the Institute of world unity during a session held at Green Acre, Maine, in 1927. cf. Pref. [BL240.M36] 28-19951
1. Religion and science—1900- I. Title.

MAY, James Lewis, 1873- ed. 215
God and the universe; the Christian position; a symposium, by Rev. S. C. Carpenter ... Rev. Father M. C. D'Arcy ... Rev. Bertram Lee Woolf ... edited by J. Lewis May ... New York, L. MacVeagh, The Dial press, 1931. 209 p. 21 1/2 cm. [BL240.M36] 31-22185
1. Religion and science—1900- 2. God. 3. Apologetics. I. Carpenter, Spencer Cecil, 1877- II. D'Arcy, Martin Cyril, 1868- III. Woolf, Bertram Lee, 1884- IV. Title.

MONSMA, John Clover, ed. 215.082
The evidence of God in an expanding universe; forty American scientists declare their affirmative views on religion. New York, Putnam [1958] 250 p. 21 cm. [BL240.M715] 58-8903
1. God—Proof. 2. Religion and science—1900- I. Title.

MORRIS, Daniel Luzon. 215
Possibilities unlimited; a scientist's approach to Christianity. With a foreword by Kirtley F. Mather. [1st ed.] New York, Harper [1952] 191 p. illus. 20 cm. [BL240.M736] 52-5465
1. Religion and science — 1900- I. Title.

MORRISON, Abraham Cressey, 1864- 215
Man does not stand alone, by A. Cressy Morrison. New York, London [etc.] Fleming H. Revell company [1944] 107 p. 19 cm. [BL240.M738] 44-6967
1. Religion and science—1900- 2. God—Proof. 3. Apologetics—20th cent. I. Title.

NEEDHAM, Joseph, 1900- ed. 215
Science, religion & reality. Introductory essay by George Sarton. New York, G. Braziller, 1955. 355p. 21cm. [BL240.N4 1955] 55-13670
1. Religion and science—1900- I. Title.

NEEDHAM, Joseph, 1900- ed. 215
Science, religion and reality [by] Arthur James, earl of Balfour ... Bronislaw Malinowski [and others] ... edited by Joseph Needham [2d impression, corrected] London, The Sheldon press; New York and Toronto, The Macmillan co., 1926. 6 p. l., [3]-396 p. 22 cm. "Second impression, corrected." [Full name: Noel Joseph Terence Montgomery Needham] [BL240.N4 1926] 26-1609
1. Religion and science—1900- I. Balfour, Arthur James Balfour, 1st earl of, 1848-1930. II. Title.
Contents omitted.

A new answer to Darwinism.
[Chicago(M. E. Baldwin, 1957] vi, 120p. illus. 21cm.
1. Religion and science—1900- 2. Creation. 3. Evolution. I. Baldwin, James Lauer, 1882-

NEWMAN, Barclay Moon. 215
Science rediscovers God [by] Barclay Moon Newman. New York, G. P. Putnam's sons, 1936. 234 p. 21 cm. [BL240.N45] 43-37440
1. Religion and science—1900- I. Title.

NEWMAN, Barclay Moon.
Science rediscovers God [by] Barclay Moon Newman. Princeton, N.J., Science index press, 1936. 234 p. 20 1/2 cm. A 37
1. Religion and science—1900- I. Title.

NISSENBAUM, Mordecai. 215
Scientific work ... Supplemented by a Critique on the State laws. New York, Moinester Pub. Co., 1948. 140 p. illus. 24 cm. Contents.--What is evolution? Critique on Darwin's theory; a logical treatment of the evolution question from the religious and scientific viewpoints.--Proof that the earth is immovable: critique on Newton's gravitation theory, critique on Einstein's theory of relativity, concrete proof that the earth stands on one place.--Critique on the State laws. [BL240.N55] 49-3088
1. Religion and science—1900- I. Title.

NYE, Ernest J 215
Secret power of life. New York, Vantage Press [1953] 115p. 22cm. [BL240.N9] 53-12147
1. Religion and science— 1900- I. Title.

OTEY, William Wesley, 1867- 213
Creation or evolution, by W. W. Otey. Austin, Tex., Firm foundation publishing house, 1930. 148 p., 1 l. 22 cm. [BL263.O8] 31-3882
1. Religion and science—1900- 2. Evolution. I. Title.

OTEY, William Wesley, 1867- 239.8
The origin and destiny of man, by W. W. Otey ... Grand Rapids, Mich., Wm. B. Eerdmans publishing co., 1938. 179 p. 20 cm. [BT1220.O8] 39-2408
1. Religion and science—1900- 2. Apologetics—20th cent. 3. Man—Origin. 4. Evolution. I. Title.

OTTO, Rudolf, 1869-1937. 215
Naturalism and religion, by Dr. Rudolf Otto ... Translated by J. ArthurThomson ... and Margaret R. Thomson. Edited with an introduction by Rev. W. D. Morrison, LL. D. New York, G. P. Putnam's sons; London, Williams and Norgate, 1907. xi, 374 p. 19 cm. (Half-title: Crown theological library. [vol. xvii]) Printed in Great Britain. [Full name: Karl Ludwig Rudolf Otto] [BL240.O8 1907 a] 7-32826
1. Religion and science—1900- I. Thomson, John Arthur, 1861-1933, tr. II. Thomson, Margaret R., joint tr. III. Morrison, William Douglas, 1853- ed. IV. Title.

OWEN, Derwyn Randolph Grier. 215
Scientism, man, and religion. Philadelphia, Westminster Press [1952] 208 p. 21 cm. [BL240.O85] 52-8226
1. Religion and science — 1900- I. Title.

PILKINGTON, Roger. 215
World without end. London, Macmillan; New York, St. Martin's Press, 1960. 165p. 21cm. [BL210.2.P52] 60-2762
1. Religion and science—1900- I. Title.

PIRONE, Frank John, 1912- 215
Science and the love of God. New York, Philosophical Library [1957] 233p. 22cm. [BL240.P57] 57-2753
1. Religion and science—1900- I. Title.

POTEAT, William Louis, 1856- 215
Can a man be a Christian to-day? By William Louis Poteat ... 2d ed. Chapel Hill, The University of North Carolina press; London, H. Milford, Oxford university press, 1926. x p., 2 l., 110 p. 19 cm. (Half-title: The John Calvin McNair lectures. [1925]) [BL240.P717 1926] 26-22869
1. Religion and science—1900- I. Title.

POTEAT, William Louis, 1856-1938. 215
Can a man be a Christian to-day? By William Louis Poteat ... Chapel Hill, The University of North Carolina press; London, H. Milford, Oxford university press, 1925. 6 p. l., 110 p. 20 cm. (Half-title: The John Calvin McNair lectures [1925]) [BL240.P717] 25-13856
1. Religion and science—1900- I. Title.

POTEAT, William Louis, 1856-1938. 215
Laboratory and pulpit; the relation of biology to the preacher and his message. By William L. Poteat ... Philadelphia, the Griffith & Rowland press, 1901. 103 p. 19 cm. (The Gay lectures, 1900) [BL262.P7] 1-31776
1. Religion and science—1900- 2. Biology. I. Title.

POWELL, Arthur Edward, 1882- 215
The nature of man; a synthesis of science and religion. [1st ed.] New York, Vantage Press [1957] 295p. 21cm. Includes bibliography. [BL240.P726] 56-12925
1. Religion and science—1900- I. Title.

PRICE, George McCready, 1870- 215
God's two books; or, Plain facts about evolution, geology, and the Bible, by George McCready Price ... Washington, D. C., New York city [etc.] Review and herald publishing association, 1911. 2 p. l., 9-183 p. front., illus. (incl. ports.) 19 cm. [BL240.P74] 11-3949
1. Religion and science—1900- 2. Evolution. I. Title.

PRICE, George McCready, 1870- 215
Outlines of modern Christianity and modern science, by Geo. E. McCready Price ... Oakland, Cal., New York [etc.] Pacific press publishing company [1902] xi, 13-271 p. front., pl. diagr. 20 cm. [BL240.P75] 2-21886
1. Religion and science—1900- 2. Evolution. I. Title.

PRICE, George McCready, 1870- 215
Some scientific stories and allegories, by George McCready Price ... Grand Rapids, Mich., Zondervan publishing house [c1936] 107 p. 20 cm. [BL240.P765] 36-15026
1. Religion and science—1900- 2. Evolution. 3. Bible and geology. I. Title. II. Title: Scientific stories and allegories.
Contents omitted.

PRICE, Henry Habberley, 1899-
Some aspects of the conflict between science & religion. Cambridge [Eng.] University Press, 1953. v, 53p. 19cm. (Arthur Stanley Eddington memorial lecture, 7) A55
1. Religion and science—1900- I. Title. II. Series.

RANSOM, John Crowe, 1888- 215
God without thunder, an unorthodox defense of orthodoxy, by John Crowe Ranson. New York, Harcourt, Brace and company [c1930] x, 334 p. 22 cm. "First edition." [BL240.R25] 30-29297
1. Religion and science—1900- I. Title.

RAVEN, Charles Earle, 1885- 215
Christianity and science. New York, Association Press [1955] 96p. 20cm. (World Christian books) [BL240.R314] 55-7566
1. Religion and science—1900- I. Title.

RAVEN, Charles Earle, 1885- 213
... Evolution and the Christian concept of God; delivered before the University of Durham at Armstrong college, New-castle-upon-Tyne, November, 1935, by Charles E. Raven ... London, Oxford university press, H. Milford, 1936. 56 p. 24 cm. (Riddell memorial lectures, 8th ser.) [BL241.R3] 36-18452
1. Religion and science—1900- 2. Evolution. 3. God. I. Title.
Contents omitted.

RAVEN, Charles Earle, 1885- 215
Science, religion, and the future, a course of eight lectures by Charles E. Raven ... Cambridge [Eng.] The University press, 1943. x, 125, [1] p. 20 cm. Bibliographical foot-notes. [BL240.R32 1943] 43-8868
1. Religion and science—1900- 2. Religion and science—History of controversy. I. Title.

RAVEN, Charles Earle, 1885- 215
Science, religion, and the future; a course of eight lectures by Charles E. Raven ... Cambridge [Eng.] The University press; New York, The Macmillan company, 1943. x, 125 p. 19 1/2 cm. Bibliographical foot-notes. [BL240.R32 1943a] 43-10231
1. Religion and science—1900- 2. Religion and science—History of controversy. I. Title.

REUTERDAHL, Arvid, 1876- 215
Scientific theism versus materialism; the space-time potential, by Arvid Reuterdahl ... New York, The Devin-Adair company, 1920. 298 p. diagrs. 23 cm. [BL240.R4] 20-19926
1. Religion and science—1900- I. Title.

RICE, William North, 1845-1928. 215
Christian faith in an age of science, by William North Rice ... New York, A. C. Armstrong and son, 1903. xi, 425 p. illus.,

diagrs. 21 cm. Contents.Introduction.--pt. I. History of scientific discoveries which have affected religious beliefs.--pt. II. Status of certain doctrines of Christianity in an age of science.--pt. III. General status of Christian evidences. [BL240.R5 1903] 3-32540
1. Religion and science—1900- I. Title.

RICH, James Walter, 1870- 215
The message of the stars. Nashville, Southern Pub. Association [c1950] 128p. illus. 20cm. [BL253.R5] 54-22105
1. Religion and science—1900- 2. Astronomy. 3. Seventh-Day Adventists—Doctrinal and controversial works. I. Title.

RIMMER, Harry, 1890- 215
Lot's wife and the science of physics, by Harry Rimmer, SC. D. Grand Rapids, Mich., Wm. B. Eerdmans publishing company, 1947. 160 p. illus. 20 cm. "First printing, January, 1947." [BL240.R562] 47-17991
1. Religion and science—1900- 2. Bible and science. I. Title.

ROBINSON, James E. 215
Evolution and modern thought, by J. E. Robinson. Bloomington, Ill. [Miller ptg. co., c1917] 208 p. 22 1/2 cm. Photograph of author mounted on inside of front cover. [BL240.R565] 36-29970
1. Religion and science—1900- 2. Religious thought—20th cent. 3. Evolution. I. Title.

RUFFINI, Ernesto, Cardinal. 213
The theory of evolution judged by reason and faith; translated by Francis O'Hanlon. Foreword by Thomas A. Boland; introd. by John E. Steinmueller. New York, J. F. Wagner [1959] 205p. 21cm. Includes bibliography. [BL263.R813] 59-16903
1. Religion and science—1900- 2. Evolution. I. Title.

RUSSELL, Bertrand Arthur Russell, 3rd earl 1872- 215
Religion & science. New York, Oxford, 1961 255p. (Galaxy bk. gb50) 1.25 pap.,
1. Religion and science—1900- 2. Religion and science—History of controversy. I. Title.

RUSSELL, Bertrand Russell, 3d earl, 1872- 215
Religion and science. New York, H. Holt [1935] 256 p. 17 cm. (Home university library of modern knowledge [New York] No. 150) Gull name: Bertrand Arthur William Russell, 3d earl Russell. [BL245.R8 1935a] 48-34372
1. Religion and science—1900- 2. Religion and science—History of controversy. I. Title. II. Series.

RUSSELL, Bertrand Russell, 3d earl, 1872- 215
Religion and science, by Bertrand Russell. New York, H. Holt and company [c1935] 4 p. l., 3-271 p. 23 cm. [Full name: Bertrand Arthur William Russell, 3d earl Russell] [BL245.R8] 36-373
1. Religion and science—1900- 2. Religion and science—History of controversy. I. Title.

SABINE, Paul Earls, 1879- 215
Atoms, men, and God. New York, Philosophical Library [1953] 226p. 23cm. [BL240.S2] 53-7918
1. Religion and science—1900- I. Title.

SAJOUS, Charles Euchariste de Medicis, 1852-1929. 213
Strength of religion as shown by science, facilitating also harmony within, and unity among, various faiths, by Charles E. de M. Sajous... Philadelphia, F. A. Davis company [c1926] 252 p. col. front. (port.) illus., plates. 20 cm. [BL240.S3] 215
1. Religion and science—1900- I. Title.

SANDEN, Oscar Emanuel, 1901- 215
The Bible in the age of science; or, The correlation of science and religion, by O. E. Sanden. Chicago, Ill., Moody press [1947] 141 p. 20 cm. "Copyright 1946." [BL240.S33] 47-1315
1. Religion and science—1900. 2. Bible and science. I. Title.

SCIENCE and your faith in God; 215.082
a selected compilation of writings and talks by prominent Latter-Day Saints scientists on the subjects of science and religion: Henry Eyring [and others] Salt Lake City, Bookcraft, 1958. 317p. 24cm. [BL240.2.S35] 59-902
1. Religion and science—1900- I. Eyring, Henry, 1901-

SCIENCE, history and faith.
London, New York, Oxford University Press [1956] vi, 210p. 19cm. 'First published 1950.'
1. Religion and science—1900- 2. Apologetics—20th cent 3. Theology, Doctrinal—Popular works. I. Richardson, Alan, 1905-

SECRIST, Jacob S 1861- 270
Creation, time and eternity, a book devoted to the unfolding of the great fundamental truths as found in science, nature and revelation ... By J. S. Secrist; with numerous diagrams and comparative charts for reference. Elgin, Ill., Brethren publishing house, 1911. 311 p. front. (port.) diagrs. 23 cm. [BR125.S36] 12-13933
1. Religion and science—1900- 2. Man (Theology) 3. Bible Prophecies. I. Title.

SECRIST, Jacob S 1861- 220.6
Creation, time and eternity; a book devoted to the unfolding of the great fundamental truths as found inscience, nature and revelation ... By J. S Secrist: with numerous diagrams and comparative charts for refernce. Elgin, Ill., Brethren publishing house, [1940] 311 p. front. (port.) illus., diagrs. 23 cm. "Fourt edition." [BR125.S36 1940] 41-1738
1. Religion and science 1900- 2. Man (Theology) 3. Bible—Prophecies. I. Title.

SHAFER, Robert, 1889-
Christianity and naturalism; essays in criticism, second series, by Robert Shafer. New Haven, Yale university press; [etc., etc.] 1926. viii p. 1 l., 307 p. 24 1/2 cm. [Full name: Samuel Robert Shafer] Contents.Religious thought in England in the XVIIth and XVIIIth centuries.--Coleridge.--Cardinal Newman.--Huxley.--Matthew Arnold.--Samuel Butler.--Thomas Hardy.--Naturalism and Christianity. [BL.240.S42] 26-10485
1. Coleridge, Samuel Taylor, 1772-1834. 2. Newman, John Henry, cardinal, 1801-1890. 3. Huxley, Thomas Henry, 1825-1895. 4. Arnold, Matthew, 1822-1888. 5. Butler, Samuel, 1835-1902. 6. Hardy, Thomas, 1840-1928. 7. Religion and science—1900- 8. Religious thought—Gt. Brit. I. Title.

SHUTTER, Marion Daniel, 1853- 215
Applied evolution, by Marion D. Shutter ... Boston, E. F. Endicott, 1900. vii p., 2 l., 3-290 p. 18 1/2 cm. [BL263.S5] 0-6838
1. Religion and science—1900- 2. Evolution. I. Title.

SIMMONS, John Walter, 1872- 215
Checking up on the Bible by facts of science. 2d ed. [Simpson? Kan., 1947] 131 p. illus. 21 cm. [BL240.S52 1947] 47-7767
1. Religion and science—1900- 2. Bible and science. I. Title.

SIMPSON, James Young, 1873-1934. 215
The spiritual interpretation of nature, by James Y. Simpson ... London, New York [etc.] Hodder and Stoughton [1912] xv, 383, [1] p. illus. 20 1/2 cm. [BL262.S5] 13-1885
1. Religion and science—1900- 2. Nature. 3. Evolution. I. Title.

SINNOTT, Edmund Ware, 1888- 215
Two roads to truth; a basis for unity under the great tradition. New York, Viking Press, 1953. 241 p. 22 cm. [BL240.S54] 52-12885
1. Religion and science—1900- I. Title.

SMETHURST, Arthur F 215
Modern science and Christian beliefs. Nashville, Abingdon Press [1957, c1955] 300p. 23cm. [BL240.S58 1957] 57-13655
1. Religion and science—1900- 2. Philosophy, Modern. I. Title.

SMITH, Orlando Jay, 1842-1908. -215
Balance, the fundamental verity, by Orlando J. Smith... Boston and New York, Houghton, Mifflin and company, 1904. ix, 146 p., 1 l. 20 1/2 cm. [BL240.S63 1904] 4-11542
1. Religion and science—1900- 2. Natural theology. I. Title.

SMYTH, Nathan Ayer, 1876- 215
Through science to God, by Nathan A. Smyth. New York, The Macmillan company, 1936. vi p., 2 l., 213 p. 21 cm. [BL240.S64] 36-12798
1. Religion and science—1900- 2. Religion—Philosophy. I. Title.

SMYTH, Newman, 1843-1925. 215
Through science to faith, by Newman Smyth ... New York, C. Scribner's sons, 1902. x p., 1 l., 282 p. 21 cm. "Lectures ... given before the Lowell institute in Boston during the winter ... of 1900-1901."--Pref. [Full name: Samuel Phillips Newman Smyth] [BL240.S65] 2-4986
1. Religion and science—1900- 2. Natural theology. I. Title.

SNOWDEN, James Henry, 1852-1936. 215
Old faith and new knowledge, by James H. Snowden. New York and London, Harper & brothers, 1928. xiii p., 1 l., 279 p. 23 cm. [BL240.S67] 28-18008
1. Religion and science—1900- 2. Modernism. I. Title.

SPILMAN, John M 215
My universe and my faith; a Catholic layman's views on science and his religion. [1st ed.] New York, Exposition Press [1959] 179 p. 21 cm. [BL240.2.S68] 59-4163
1. Religion and science — 1900- I. Title.

STREETER, Burnett Hillman, 1874-1937. 215
Adventure; the faith of science and the science of faith, by Burnett H. Streeter ... Catherine M. Chilcott ... John Macmurray ... Alexander S. Russell ... New York, The Macmillan company, 1928. ix, 247 p. 20 1/2 cm. [BL240.S76 1928] 28-2521
1. Religion and science—1900- 2. Philosophy and religion. 3. Ethics. I. Chilcott, Catherine Mary. II. Macmurray, John, 1891- III. Russell, Alexander Smith, 1869- IV. Title.

STROMBERG, Gustaf, 1882- 215
The searchers. Philadelphia, D. McKay Co. [1948] xiv, 242 p. 21 cm. Full name: Gustaf Benjamin Stromberg. [BL240.S764] 48-1906
1. Religion and science—1900- 2. Physics—Philosophy. I. Title.

TAYLOR, Robert Oswald Patrick, 1873- 215
The universe within us; a scientific view of God and man, by R. O. P. Taylor ... New York, R. R. Smith, inc., 1931. xi, 13-168 p. 22 cm. English edition, 1931, has title: The meeting of the roads. [BL240.T35 1931] 31-22633
1. Religion and science—1900- 2. God. 3. Man. I. Title.

THOMAS, Wendell Marshall, 1896- 215
On the resolution of science and faith [by] Wendell Thomas. New York, Island press [1947] xii, 300 p. 20 cm. "Copyright 1946." "References": p. 266-285. Bibliography: p. 286-294. [BL240.T56] 47-17199
1. Religion and science—1900. I. Title.

THOMSON, John Arthur, Sir, 1861-1933. 215
Science and religion; being the Morse lectures for 1924, by J. Arthur Thomson ... New York, C. Scribner's sons, 1925. viii, 280 p. 19 1/2 cm. Appendix, by David Landsborough Thomson: p. 243-274. Bibliography: p. 275-278. [BL240.T57 1925a] 25-8491
1. Religion and science—1900- I. Thomson, David Landsborough. II. Title.

TUTE, Richard Clifford, Sir 1874- 215
... After materialism--what? New York, E. P. Dutton & co. inc., 1945. 222 p. 21 cm. "First edition." [BL240.T78] 45-2340
1. Religion and science—1900- 2. Philosophy and religion. I. Title.

TYNDALL, Charles Herbert, 1857- 215
Electricity and its similitudes; the analogy of phenomena, natural and spiritual [by] Charles H. Tyndall ... New York, London [etc.] Fleming H. Revell company [1902] 215 p. front., plates, diagr. 20 cm. [BL265.E6T8] 2-23928
1. Religion and science—1900- 2. Electricity. I. Title.

WARD, Duren James Henderson, 1851-1942. 215
The modern God. With an introd. by Claude W. Blake. [Denver? 1956] 62p. illus. 23cm. [BL241.W25] 56-33038
1. Religion and science—1900- 2. God. I. Title.

WATSON, John M. 215
Science as revelation, by John M. Watson. New York, The Macmillan company, 1925. 303 p. plates. 19 1/2 cm. [BL240.W28] 25-21398
1. Religion and science—1900- 2. Natural theology. I. Title.

WELLS, Albert N. 261.75
The Christian message in a scientific age. Richmond, John Knox Press [1962] 160 p. 21 cm. Bibliographical footnotes. [BL240.2.W4] 62-19483
1. Religion and science — 1900- I. Title.

WILLET, Nathaniel Louis, 1831- 215
Nature in the witness-box; or, Suggestive parallels, by N. L. Willet. Philadelphia, Griffith and Rowland press, 1903. 4 p. l., vii-viii, 224 p. 19 cm. "This book is an attempt at the making plain of certain of nature's laws and phenomenn, and at the finding of their certain parallels in kingdoms that are higher."--Preface. [BL240.W5] 3-988
1. Religion and science—1900. 2. Natural theology. I. Title.

WINDLE, Bertram Coghill Alan, Sir 1858-1929. 215
The church and science, by Sir Bertram C. A. Windle ... [2d ed.] St. Louis, Mo., B. Herder book co.; London, Catholic truth society, 1917. xvi, 415 p. 22 cm. Printed in Great Britain. Bibliographical foot-notes. [BL240.W57 1917] 19-8091
1. Religion and science—1900- 2. Catholic church. I. Title.

WISHART, Alfred Wesley, 1865-1933. 215
Evolution and religion, by Alfred Wesley Wishart ... Grand Rapids, Mich., 1923. 63 p. 19 1/2 cm. [BL263.W59] 42-7271
1. Religion and science—1900- 2. Evolution. I. Title.

WYCHE, Charles David, 1861- 215
God, science, and the Bible, by Charles David Wyche, M.D. Boston, Mass., The Stratford company [c1931] 1 p. l., ix p. 2 l., 284 p. 19 cm. [BL240.W78] 31-35508
1. Religion and science—1900- 2. Bible and science. I. Title.

YARNOLD, Greville Dennis
The spiritual crisis of the scientific age. New York, Macmillan [1959] 207 p. 22 cm.
1. Religion and science — 1900- I. Title.

Religion and science — 1900-1925.

BOUTROUX, Emile, 1845-1921. 215
Science & religion in contemporary philosophy. Translated by Jonathan Nield. Port Washington, N.Y., Kennikat Press [1970] xi, 400 p. 22 cm. Reprint of the 1909 ed. Bibliographical footnotes. [B56.B72 1970] 70-102563
1. Religion and science—1900-1925. 2. Philosophy, Modern. I. Title.

GATEWOOD, Willard B 213
Preachers, pedagogues & politicians; the evolution controversy in North Carolina, 1920-1927, by Willard B. Gatewood, Jr. Chapel Hill, University of North Carolina Press [1966] viii, 268 p. illus. 24 cm. Errata slip inserted. Bibliography: p. [251]-259 [BL263.G34] 66-15504
1. Religion and science — 1900-1925. 2. Evolution. I. Title.

GATEWOOD, Willard B., Jr. 213
Preachers, pedagogues & politicians; the evolution controversy in North Carolina. 1920-1927. Chapel Hill, Univ. of N. C. Pr. [c.1965, 1966] viii, 268p. illus. 24cm. Bibl. [BL263.G34] 66-15504 5.95
1. Religion and science — 1900-1925. 2. Evolution. I. Title.

SHAFER, Robert, 1889-1956. 215
Christianity and naturalism; essays in criticism, second series. Port Washington, N.Y., Kennikat Press [1969] viii, 307 p. 22 cm. Reprint of the 1926 ed. Contents.Contents.—Religious thought in England in the XVIIth and XVIIIth centuries.—Coleridge.—Cardinal Newman.—Huxley.—Matthew Arnold.—Samuel Butler.—Thomas Hardy.—Naturalism and Christianity. Bibliographical footnotes. [BL240.S42 1969] 68-26206
1. Coleridge, Samuel Taylor, 1772-1834—Religion and ethics. 2. Newman, John Henry, Cardinal, 1801-1890. 3. Huxley, Thomas Henry, 1825-1895. 4. Arnold, Matthew, 1822-1888—Religion and ethics. 5. Butler, Samuel, 1835-1902. 6. Hardy, Thomas, 1840-1928. 7. Religion and science—1900-1925. 8. Religious thought—Great Britain. I. Title.

Religion and science—1909—

BILL, Annie C. Mrs. 215
Science and religion, by Annie C. Bill. New York, London, A. A. Beauchamp, 1931. 63 p. 19 cm. "The study presented in this booklet is the extension of a lecture given by me in the McAlpiu hotel, New York, on January. 4th."--Note. [BL241.B45] 31-8058
1. Religion and science—1909- I. Title.

KEYSER, Cassius Jackson, 1862- 215
Science and religion, the rational and the superrational; an address delivered May 4, 1914 before the Phi beta kappa alumni in New York, by Cassius J. Keyser ... New Haven, Yale university press. London, H. Milford, Oxford university press, 1914. 3 p. l., 75 p. 19 1/2 cm. "First printed September, 1914, 1000 copies." [BL240.K4] 14-17499
1. Religion and science—1909- I. Title.

Religion and science—1926-1945.

MORRISON, Abraham Cressy, 1864-1951. 215
Seven reasons why a scientist believes in God. [Westwood, N. J.,] Revell [1962] 61p. 17cm. (A Revell inspirational classic) [BL240.M7383] 62-17109
1. Religion and science—1926-1945. 2. God—Proof. I. Title.

RANSOM, John Crowe, 1888- 215
God without thunder; an unorthodox defense of orthodoxy [Reissue] Hamden, Conn., Archon [dist. Shoe String, 1965, c.1930] x, 334p. 21cm. [BL240.R25] 65-17410 9.00
1. Religion and science—1926-1945. I. Title.

SCIENCE & religion; 215
a symposium. With a foreword by Michael Pupin. Freeport, N.Y., Books for Libraries Press [1969] xi, 175 p. 23 cm. (Essay index reprint series) Reprint of the 1931 ed. Twelve talks, by Julian Huxley, J. Arthur Thomson, J. S. Haldane and others, broadcast between September and December 1930 by the British Broadcasting Corporation. [BL240.S367 1969] 75-84336
1. Religion and science—1926-1945. I. British Broadcasting Corporation.

TUTE, Richard Clifford, Sir, 1874- 215
After materialism—what? Freeport, N.Y., Books for Libraries Press [1973, c1945] 222 p. 23 cm. (Essay index reprint series) Reprint of the 1945 ed. [BL240.T78 1973] 72-13176 ISBN 0-8369-8175-8
1. Religion and science—1926-1945. 2. Philosophy and religion. I. Title.

Religion and science—1926-1945—Addresses, essays, lectures.

COTTON, Edward Howe, 1881-1942, ed. 215
Has science discovered God? A symposium of modern scientific opinion. Freeport, N.Y., Books for Libraries Press [1968] lviii, 308 p. ports. 23 cm. (Essay index reprint series) Reprint of the 1931 ed. [BL240.C68 1968] 68-8452
1. Religion and science—1926-1945—Addresses, essays, lectures. I. Title.

EDDINGTON, Arthur Stanley, Sir, 1882-1944. 215
Science and the unseen world / by Arthur Stanley Eddington. Folcroft, Pa. : Folcroft Library Editions, 1979. p. cm. Reprint of the 1929 ed. published by Allen & Unwin, London, which was issued as the 1929 Swarthmore lecture. Bibliography: p. [BL241.E4 1979] 79-15894 ISBN 0-8414-4004-2 (lib. bdg.) : 8.50
1. Friends, Society of—Addresses, essays, lectures. 2. Religion and science—1926-1945—Addresses, essays, lectures. I. Title. II. Series: Swarthmore lecture ; 1929.

LINDSAY, Alexander Dunlop, Baron Lindsay of Birker, 1879-1952. 261.7
Religion, science, and society in the modern world. Freeport, N.Y., Books for Libraries Press [1972, c1943] vi, 73 p. 23 cm. (Essay index reprint series) Original ed. issued in series: The Terry lectures. [BL241.L55 1972] 70-37847 ISBN 0-8369-2604-8
1. Religion and science—1926-1945—Addresses, essays, lectures. 2. Sociology, Christian—Addresses, essays, lectures. I. Title. II. Series: The Terry lectures, Yale University.

Religion and science—1930—

SCIENCE & religion; 215
a symposium, with a foreword by Michael Pupin. New York, C. Scribner's sons, 1931. xi, 175 p. 20 cm. Twelve talks, by Julian Huxley, J. Arthur Thomson, J. S. Haldane and others, broadcast between September and December 1930 by the British broadcasting corporation. [BL240.S367 1931 a] 31-16030
1. Religion and science—1930-

Religion and science—1945—

BURNABY, John. 215
Darwin and the human situation. Cambridge, W. Heffer [1959] iii, 30 p. 19 cm. Bibliographical footnotes. [BL263.B87] 68-32238
1. Religion and science—1945- 2. Evolution. I. Title.

MORRIS, Henry Madison, 1918- 261.5
Evolution and the modern Christian, by Henry M. Morris. Philadelphia, Presbyterian and Reformed Pub. Co. [1967] 72 p. 20 cm. Bibliography: p. 69-72. [BL263.M58] 68-2233
1. Religion and science—1945- 2. Evolution. I. Title.

Religion and science-1946-

APPLING, Phillip Holden, 1910- 215
Gospel in the twentieth century; essays on science and religion. Illustrated by Frances Elois Appling. [1st ed.] New York, Exposition Press [1973] 127 p. illus. 21 cm. Bibliography: p. 125-127. [BL240.2.A66] 72-90060 ISBN 0-682-47594-7 5.00
1. Religion and science—1946- I. Title.

AUBERT, Jean Marie. 215
A God for science? Translated by Paul Barrett. Westminster, Md., Newman Press [1967] vi, 154 p. 21 cm. Translation of Recherche scientifique et foi chretienne. Bibliographical footnotes. [BL240.2.A813] 67-23605
1. Religion and science—1946- I. Title.

AUSTIN, William H. 215
The relevance of natural science to theology / William H. Austin. New York : Barnes & Noble Books, 1976. 132 p. ; 23 cm. (Library of philosophy and religion) Includes bibliographical references and index. [BL240.2.A87 1976b] 75-43222 ISBN 0-06-490240-4 : 22.50
1. Religion and science—1946- I. Title.

AUSTIN, William H. 215
The relevance of natural science to theology / [by] William H. Austin. London : Macmillan, 1976. ix, 132 p. ; 23 cm. (Library of philosophy and religion) Includes bibliographical references and index. [BL240.2.A87 1976] 76-368460 ISBN 0-333-18660-5 : £7.95
1. Religion and science—1946- I. Title.

BARBOUR, Ian G 215
Christianity and the scientist. New York, Association Press [1960] 128p. 20cm. (The Haddam House series on the Christian in his vocation) A Haddam House book. Includes bibliography. [BL240.2.B35] 60-12715
1. Religion and science—1946- I. Title.

BARBOUR, Ian G. 200'.1
Myths, models, and paradigms; a comparative study in science and religion [by] Ian G. Barbour. [1st ed.] New York, Harper & Row [1974] vi, 198 p. 21 cm. Includes bibliographical references. [BL240.2.B36 1974] 73-18698 6.95
1. Religion and science—1946- I. Title.

BARBOUR, Ian G., comp. 215
Science and religion; new perspectives on the dialogue, edited by Ian G. Barbour. [1st ed.] New York, Harper & Row [1968] xi, 323 p. 21 cm. (Harper forum books) Bibliographical footnotes. [BL240.2.B37 1968] 68-11744
1. Religion and science—1946- I. Title.

BECK, Stanley D. 215
Modern science and Christian life [by] Stanley D. Beck. Minneapolis, Augsburg Pub. House [1970] 157 p. illus. 22 cm. Includes bibliographies. [Q125.B36] 73-121965 2.95
1. Religion and science—1946- I. Title.

BIANCHI, Joseph Salvatore, 1915- 200'.1
Philosophy of the unknown [by] Joseph S. Bianchi. Santa Monica, Calif., DeVorss [1973] 325 p. illus. 23 cm. On spine: The unknown. [BL240.2.B54] 73-77352
1. Religion and science—1946- I. Title. II. Title: The unknown.

BIRCH, L. Charles, 1918- 215
Nature and God. Philadelphia, Westminster [1966, c.1965] 128p. 19cm. (Adventures in faith) Bibl. [BL240.2.B58] 66-10066 1.45 pap.,
1. Religion and science — 1946- I. Title.

BIRCH, L. Charles, 1918- 215
Nature and God [by] L. Charles Birch. Philadelphia, Westminster Press [1965] 128 p. 29 cm. (Adventures in faith) Bibliography: p. [118]-125. [BL240.2.B58] 66-10066
1. Religion and science—1946- I. Title.

BRAIN, Walter Russell Brain, baron, 1895- 215
Science, philosophy, and religion. Cambridge [eng.] University Press, 1959. 30 p. 19 cm. (Arthur Stanley Eddington memorial lecture, 12) [BL240.2.B7] 59-1912
1. Religion and science — 1946- 2. Science — Philosophy. 3. Philosophy — Addresses, essays, lectures. I. Title. II. Series.

BROPHY, Donald, comp. 215
Science and faith in the 21st century. New York, Paulist Press [1968] ix, 118 p. 18 cm. (Deus books) Contents.Contents.—Breaking the genetic code, by V. G. Dethier.—Experiment: man, by K. Rahner.—Reflections on biological engineering, by G. M. Schurr.—Birth control: time for a second look, by R. Tobias.—Life in a test tube, by P. R. Gastonguay.—Terrestrial and cosmic polygenism, by R. J. Pendergast.—Teilhard de Chardin, by B. Towers.—Cybernetics and the knowledge of God, by S. Beer.—The God of contradiction, by R. B. McLaren. [BL240.2.B76] 67-31105
1. Religion and science—1946- I. Title.

BUBE, Richard H., 1927- 215
The encounter between Christianity and science, edited by Richard H. Bube. Grand Rapids, W. B. Eerdmans Pub. Co. [1968] 318 p. 21 cm. Includes bibliographical references. [BL240.2.B8] 67-13987
1. Religion and science—1946- I. Title.

BUBE, Richard H., 1927- 215
The human quest; a new look at science and the Christian faith [by] Richard H. Bube. Waco, Tex., Word Books [1971] 262 p. illus. 23 cm. Bibliography: p. 254-257. [BL240.2.B82] 70-160294 5.95
1. Religion and science—1946- I. Title.

CAUTHEN, Wilfred Kenneth. 215
Science, secularization & God; toward a theology of the future [by] Kenneth Cauthen. Nashville, Abingdon Press [1968, c1969] 237 p. 24 cm. Bibliographical footnotes. [BL240.2.C3] 69-12010 5.50
1. Religion and science—1946- 2. Church and the world. 3. Theology, Doctrinal. I. Title.

CHAUCHARD, Paul, 1912- 215
Science and religion. Translated from the French by S. J. Tester. [1st ed.] New York, Hawthorn Books [1962] 156p. 21cm. (The Twentieth century encyclopedia of Catholicism, v. 130. Section 13: Catholicism and science) Translation of La science detruit-elle la religion? Includes bibliographies. [BL240.2.C473] 62-16132
1. Religion and science—1946- I. Title.

CHAUCHARD, Paul Albert, 1912- 215
Science and religion. Tr. from French by S. J. Tester. New York, Hawthorn [c.1962] 156p. 21cm. (Twentieth cent. encyclopedia of Catholicism, v.130. Section 13: Catholicism and sci.) Bibl. 62-16132 3.50
1. Religion and science—1946- I. Title.

CHAUVIN, Remy 215
God of the scientists. God of the experiment. Translated by Salvator Attanasio. Baltimore. Helicon Press [c.] 1960. 152p. Bibl.:p.149-152. 60-15633 3.95
1. Religion and science—1946- 2. God—Proof. I. Title.

CHAUVIN, Remy. 215
God of the scientists, God of the experiment. Translated by Salvator Attanasio. Baltimore, Helicon Press, 1960. 152p. 23cm. Includes bibliography. [BL240.2.C513] 60-15633
1. Religion and science—1946- 2. God—Proof. I. Title.

CHEN, Philip Stanley, 1903- 261.75
A new look at God. South Lancaster, Mass., Chemical Elements [c.]1962. 238p. 23cm. 62-4924 3.95
1. Religion and science—1946- I. Title.

CHEN, Philip Stanley, 1903- 215
A new look at God / by Philip S. Chen. 2d ed. Camarillo, Calif. : Chemical Elements Pub. Co., [1975] 228 p. ; 23 cm. Includes bibliographical references. [BL240.2.C52 1975] 75-5419 5.95
1. Religion and science—1946- I. Title.

CLARK, John Ruskin, 1911- 215
The great living system : new answers from the sciences to old religious questions / by John Ruskin Clark. Pacific Grove, CA : Boxwood Press, [1977] p. cm. Includes index. Bibliography: p. [BL240.2.C548] 76-53812 pbk. : 4.95
1. Religion and science—1946- 2. Religion—Philosophy. I. Title.

CLARK, Robert Edward David 215
Christian belief and science; a reconciliation and a partnership. Philadelphia, Muhlenberg [1961, c.1960] 160p. Bibl. 61-19759 2.25 pap.,
1. Religion and science—1946- I. Title.

CLARK, Robert Edward David. 215
The Christian stake in science, by Robert E. D. Clark. Chicago, Moody Press [1967] 160 p. 22 cm. Bibliographical footnotes. [BL240.2] 68-1816
1. Religion and science—1946- I. Title.

CLARK, Robert Edward David. 215
Science and Christianity—a partnership, by Robert E. D. Clark. Mountain View, Calif., Pacific Press Pub. Association [1972] 192 p. 22 cm. (Dimension 114) Bibliography: p. 177-183. [BL240.2.C577] 72-80665
1. Religion and science—1946- I. Title.

CLARK, Robert Edward David 215-62-1412
The universe: plan or accident? The religious implications of modern science. Philadelphia, Muhlenberg [1962, c.1961] 240p. illus. 3.50
1. Religion and science—1946- I. Title.

CLARK, Robert Edward David. 215
The universe: plan or accident? The religious implications of modern science, by Robert E. D. Clark. Grand Rapids, Zondervan Pub. House [1972, c1961] 236 p. illus. 21 cm. (Contemporary evangelical

perspectives) "First published 1949. Third ed. (rev. and enl.) 1961." Includes bibliographical references. [BL240.C5673 1972] 78-171204 2.95
1. Religion and science—1946- I. Title.

COOK, Melvin Alonzo.
Science and Mormonism; correlations, conflicts and conciliations, by Melvin Alonzo Cook and Melvin Garfield Cook. [Salt Lake City, Deseret News Press, 1967] xii, 295 p. illus. 24 cm. 68-105032
1. Religion and science-1946- 2. Mormons and Mormonism—Doctrinal and controversial works. I. Cook, Melvin Garfield, joint author. II. Title.

COULSON, Charles Alfred 215
Science, technology, and the Christian. Nashville, Abingdon Press [1961, c.1960] 111p. 19cm. 61-826 2.50 bds.,
1. Religion and science—1946- 2. Technology. I. Title.

COULSON, Charles Alfred. 261.5
Science, technology, and the Christian / by C. A. Coulson. Westport, Conn. : Greenwood Press, [1978] c1960. p. cm. Reprint of the ed. published by Epworth Press, London, which was issued as the Beckly social service lecture, 1960. [BL265.T4C6 1978] 78-16421 ISBN 0-8371-9041-X lib.bdg. : 13.50
1. Religion and science—1946- 2. Technology. I. Title. II. Series: The Beckly social service lecture ; 1960.

CUPITT, Don. 215
The worlds of science & religion / Don Cupitt. New York : Hawthorn Books, 1976. 115 p. ; 21 cm. (Issues in religious studies) Includes index. Bibliography: p. 110-112. [BL240.2.C86 1976] 75-41795 ISBN 0-8015-8924-X pbk. : 3.50
1. Religion and science—1946- I. Title.

DANKENBRING, William F. 213
The first genesis : a new case for creation / William F. Dankenbring. Altadena, Calif. : Triumph Pub. Co., [1975] xxii, 359 p. : ill. ; 22 cm. Bibliography: p. [355]-359. [BL240.2.D27] 75-10841 8.95
1. Religion and science—1946- 2. Creation. 3. Evolution. I. Title.

DAY, John A 248.4
Science, change and the Christian [by] John A. Day. New York, Published for the Cooperative Publication Association by Abingdon Press [1965] 96 p. 20 cm. (Faith for life series) Bibliography: p. 95-96. [BL240.2.D3] 65-4238
1. Religion and science — 1946- I. Cooperative Publication Association. II. Title.

DYE, David L. 261.5
Faith and the physical world: a comprehensive view, by David L. Dye. Grand Rapids, W. B. Eerdmans Pub. Co. [1966] 214 p. illus. 21 cm. Bibliography: p. 183-199. [BL240.2.D9] 66-18729
1. Religion and science—1946- I. Title.

ESTERER, Arnulf K 215
Towards a unified faith. New York, Philosophical Library [1963] 102 p. illus. 22 cm. [BL240.2.E8] 62-20870
1. Religion and science — 1946- I. Title.

GILKEY, Langdon Brown, 1919- 215
Religion and the scientific future; reflections on myth, science, and theology, by Langdon Gilkey. [1st ed.] New York, Harper & Row [1970] x, 193 p. 22 cm. (The Deems lectures, 1967) Includes bibliographical references. [BL240.2.G54 1970] 72-109070 5.95
1. Religion and science—1946- I. Title. II. Series.

HABGOOD, John Stapylton. 215
Truths in tension; new perspectives on religion and science by John Habgood. Foreword by Sir Bryan Matthews. [1st ed.] New York, Holt, Rinehart and Winston [1965, c1964] 157 p. illus., maps. 22 cm. First published in London in 1964 under title: Religion and science. Bibliography: p. 152-153. [BL240.2.H3 1965] 65-13820
1. Religion and science—1946- I. Title.

HARDY, Alister Clavering, 215'.74
Sir.
The biology of God : a scientist's study of man, the religious animal / Alister Hardy. [Pittsburgh] : University of Pittsburgh Press, [1976] p. cm. Includes index. [BL262.H27] 75-30984
1. Religion and science—1946- 2. Evolution and religion. 3. Biology. I. Title.

HEIM, Karl, 1874- 213
The world: its creation and consummation; the end of the present age and the future of the world in the light of the Resurrection. Tr. [from German] by Robert Smith. Philadelphia, Muhlenberg [c.]1962. 159p. 23cm. illus. 62-9748 3.00
1. Religion and science—1946- 2. Cosmogony. 3. Creation. 4. Resurrection. I. Title.

HEIM, Karl, 1874- 213
The world: its creation and consummation; the end of the present age and the future of the world in the light of the Resurrection. Translated by Robert Smith. Philadelphia, Muhlenberg Press, 1962. 159p. 23cm. 'A translation of the second German edition of Weltschopfung und Weltende, published in 1958 ... as Bd. VI of Der evangellsche Glaube und das Denken der Gegenwart: Grundzilge einer christichen Lebensanschanung [sic]' [BL245.H413 1962] 62-9748
1. Religion and science—1946- 2. Cosmogony. 3. Creation 4. Resurrection. I. Title.

ISAACS, Alan, 1925- 215
The survival of God in the scientific age. Harmondsworth, Penguin, 1966. 224 p. diagrs. 18 cm. (Pelican book A843) Bibliography: p. 216-218. [BL240.2.I8] 67-70936
1. Religion and science—1946- I. Title.

JEEVES, Malcolm A. 215
The scientific enterprise & Christian faith [by] Malcolm A. Jeeves. Downers Grove, Ill., Inter-varsity Press [1969] 168 p. 22 cm. Based on papers and discussions prepared for the International Conference of Science and Faith, held at Oxford, 1965. Bibliographical footnotes. [BL240.2.J4 1969] 74-93034 4.50
1. Religion and science—1946- I. International Conference of Science and Faith, Oxford, 1965. II. Title.

JOHNSON, Roger A., 1930- 200'.1
Critical issues in modern religion [by] Roger A. Johnson and Ernest Wallwork, with Clifford Green, H. Paul Santmire [and] Harold Y. Vanderpool. Englewood Cliffs, N.J., Prentice-Hall [1973] viii, 472 p. 23 cm. Includes bibliographies. [BL240.2.J55] 72-10829 ISBN 0-13-193987-4 6.50
1. Religion and science—1946- 2. Religion—Addresses, essays, lectures. I. Wallwork, Ernest, joint author. II. Title.

JOHNSTONE, Parker Lochiel. 215
Quandary of life, science, and religion / by Parker Lochiel Johnstone and Frank Johnstone. Philadelphia, Pa. : Theoscience Foundation, c1980. p. cm. Includes index. [BL240.2.J56] 19 80-83297 ISBN 0-917802-04-7 : 7.95
1. Religion and science—1946- I. Johnstone, Frank, 1880- II. Title.
Publisher's address 193 Los Robles Dr., Burlingame, CA 94010.

JONES, James William, 1943- 215
The texture of knowledge : an essay on religion and science / James W. Jones. Lanham, MD : University Press of America, 1981. p. cm. Includes bibliographical references. [BL240.2.J58] 19 80-69036 ISBN 0-8191-1360-3 lib. bdg. : 15.75 ISBN 0-8191-1361-1 (pbk.) : 6.75
1. Religion and science—1946- I. Title.

KLOTZ, John William. 215
Modern science in the Christian life. Saint Louis, Concordia Pub. House [1961] 191p. 21cm. Includes bibliography. [BL210.2.K53] 60-15575
1. Religion and science—1946- I. Title.

LANGMACK, Holger 215.0151
Christian.
Science, faith and logic; scientific faith substantiated by a logical science. New York, Philosophical [c.1965] xviii, 146p. illus., port. 22cm. [BL240.2.L34] 64-13325 6.00
1. Religion and science—1946- I. Title.

LEVER, Jan. 215
Where are we headed? A biologist talks about origins, evolution, and the future. Translated by Walter Lagerwey. Grand Rapids, Mich., W. B. Eerdmans [1970] 59 p. 22 cm. Cover title: Where are we headed? A Christian perspective on evolution. Translation of Waar blijven we? Een bioloog over de wording van deze aardse werkelijkheid. [BL240.2.L4713] 78-127631 1.65
1. Religion and science—1946- 2. Philosophical anthropology. I. Title.

LONG, Edward Le Roy. 215
Religious beliefs of American scientists [by] Edward LeRoy Long, Jr. Westport, Conn., Greenwood Press [1971, c1952] 168 p. 23 cm. [BL240.2.L65 1971] 70-141415 ISBN 0-8371-4693-3
1. Religion and science—1946- I. Title.

LONSDALE, Kathleen (Yardley) 248
1903-
I believe . . . [New York] Cambridge [c.] 1964. 56p. 19 cm. (Arthur Stanley Eddington memorial lect. 18) Bibl. [BX7795.L65A3] 65-588 .95 pap.,
1. Religion and science—1946- I. Title. II. Series.

LONSDALE, Kathleen (Yardley) 248
1903-
I believe... by Kathleen Lonsdale. Cambridge [Eng.] University Press, 1964. 56 p. 19 cm. [Arthur Stanley Eddington memorial lecture, 18) Delivered 6 November 1964. Bibliography: p. 58. [BX7795.L65A3] 65-588
1. Religion and science — 1946- I. Title. II. Series.

LUNN, Arnold Henry Moore, 215
Sir, 1888-
The revolt against reason, by Arnold Lunn. Westport, Conn., Greenwood Press [1971, c1951] xiv, 273 p. 23 cm. Includes bibliographical references. [BL240.L825 1971] 72-108396 ISBN 0-8371-3819-1
1. Religion and science—1946- 2. Science—Philosophy. I. Title.

*MCGOWEN, C. H. 213
In six days / C. H. McGowen. Van Nuys, Calif. : Bible Voice, 1976. 108, [1]p. ; 21 cm. Bibliography: p. [109] [BS650] pbk. : 2.95
1. Religion and science-1946- 2. Creation. 3. Evolution. I. Title.
Pub. address P.O. Box 7491 91409.

MACKAY, Donald MacCrimmon, 261.5
1922-
The clock work image : a Christian perspective on science / Donald M. MacKay. Downers Grove, Ill. : InterVarsity Press, 1974. 112 p. ; 18 cm. Includes index. [BL240.2.M29] 74-83475 ISBN 0-87784-557-3 pbk. : 2.25
1. Religion and science—1946- I. Title.

MARSH, Frank Lewis, 1899- 261.5
Life, man, and time. Rev. ed. Escondido, Calif., Outdoor Pictures [1967] 238 p. illus. 23 cm. Bibliography: p. 226-229. [BL240.2.M39 1967] 66-21121
1. Religion and science—1946- I. Title.

*MOLINARE, Nicholas 220.85
DNA, RNA and the atom: what does God say about them? New York, Vantage [1964, c.1963] 134p. 21cm. 2.95 bds.,
I. Title.

MONSMA, John Clover, ed. 215.082
Science and religion; twenty-three prominent churchmen express their opinions. New York, Putnam [1962] 253 p. 21 cm. [BL240.2.M6] 62-7350
1. Religion and science—1946- I. Title.

MORRIS, Henry Madison, 261.5
1918-
Evolution and the modern Christian, by Henry M. Morris. Philadelphia, Presbyterian and Reformed Pub. Co. [1967] 72 p. 20 cm. Bibliography: p. 69-72. [BL263.M585] 68-2233
1. Religion and science—1946- 2. Evolution. I. Title.

NEEDHAM, Joseph, 1900- ed. 215
Science, religion, and reality [by] Arthur James, Earl of Balfour [and others] Edited by Joseph Needham. Port Washington, N.Y., Kennikat Press [1970] 396 p. 22 cm. (Essay and general literature index reprint series) Reprint of the 1925 ed. [BL240.N4 1970] 70-108706
1. Religion and science—1946- I. Balfour, Arthur James Balfour, 1st Earl of, 1848-1930. II. Title.

NELSON, J. Robert, 1920- 261.5'5
Science and our troubled-conscience / J. Robert Nelson. Philadelphia : Fortress Press, c1980. p. cm. [BL240.2.N44] 80-8045 ISBN 0-8006-1398-8 : 6.95
1. Religion and science—1946- I. Title.

ONG, Walter J., ed. 213.5
Darwin's vision and Christian perspectives; [papers] Foreword by JohnWright. New York, Macmillan, [c:]1960. 154p. Bibl. 22cm. 60-14486 4.00
1. Darwin, Charles Robert, 1809-1882. 2. Religion and science—1946- 3. Evolution. I. Title.

OSBORNE, Denis. 215
The Andromedans & other parables of science and faith / Denis Osborne. Downers Grove, Ill. : InterVarsity Press, 1978, c1977. 95 p. : ill. ; 18 cm. Includes bibliographical references. [BL241.O76 1977] 78-18550 ISBN 0-87784-600-6 : 2.50
1. Religion and science—1946- I. Title.

OVERMAN, Ralph T. 215
Who am I? The faith of [a] scientist [by] Ralph T. Overman. Waco, Tex., Word Books [1971] 94 p. 21 cm. [BL240.2.O88] 79-170908 1.95
1. Religion and science—1946- I. Title.

PEACOCKE, Arthur Robert. 215
Science and the Christian experiment, [by] A. R. Peacocke. London, New York, Oxford University Press, 1971. xiii, 214 p. 23 cm. Bibliography: p. 206-207. [BL240.2.P34 1971] 76-881338 ISBN 0-19-213953-3 ISBN 0-19-213956-8 (pbk.) £4.00
1. Religion and science—1946- I. Title.

PILKINGTON, Roger 215
Heavens alive; the impact of science on the image of God. London, Macmillan; New York, St. Martin's [c.]1964. x, 149p. 21cm. 64-4435 3.50 bds.,
1. Religion and science—1946- I. Title.

PLAUT, W Gunther, 1912- 296.38
Judaism and the scientific spirit. New York, Union of American Hebrew Congregations [1962] 82p. 20cm. (Issues of faith) Includes bibliography. [BM538.S3P5] 61-17139
1. Religion and science—1946- I. Title.

POLLARD, William Grosvenor, 215
1911-
Physicist and Christian, a dialogue between the communities. Greenwich, Conn., Seabury Pr. [c.]1961. 178p. Bibl. 61-14381 4.25 bds.,
1. Religion and science—1946- I. Title.

POLLARD, William Grosvenor, 215
1911-
Physicist and Christian, a dialogue between the communities. New York, Seabury [1964, c.1961] 178p. 21cm. Orig. given as the Bishop Paddock lects. (1959) at the General Theological Seminary, New York City. (SP11) Bibl. 1.65 pap.,
1. Religion and science—1946- I. Title.

POLLARD, William Grosvenor, 215
1911-
Science and faith: twin mysteries, by William G. Pollard. New York, T. Nelson [1970] xiv, 116 p. illus. 21 cm. (A Youth forum book, YF 11) Examines the relationship of religion and science and maintains that the two fields are not necessarily in opposition. [BL240.2.P58] 76-127076 1.95
1. Religion and science—1946- 2. [Religion and science.] I. Title. II. Series: Youth forum series, YF 11

QUEFFELEC, Henri, 1910- 215
Technology and religion. Tr. from French by S. J. Tester. New York, Hawthorn [c.1964] 110 [1]p. 21cm. (Twentieth cent. ency. of Catholicism, v.94. Section 9: The church and the modern world) Bibl. 64-13009 3.50 bds.,
1. Religion and science—1946- I. Title. II. Series. III. Series: The Twentieth century encyclopedia of Catholicism, v.94

RABUT, Olivier A. 215
God in an evolving universe [by] Olivier

A. Rabut. Translated by William Springer. [New York] Herder and Herder [1966] 154 p. 22 cm. "The French edition of this work contains four 'Notes justificatives' which have been omitted from this translation." Originally published in 1962 under title: "Le probleme de Dieu inscrit dans l'evolution." Bibliographical references included in footnotes. [BL240.2.R283] 66-13069
1. Religion and science—1946- 2. Natural theology. 3. Cosmology. I. Title.

REAM, Robert J. 261.5
A Christian approach to science and science teaching, by Robert J. Ream. [Nutley, N.J.] Presbyterian and Reformed Pub. Co., 1972. v, 130 p. 21 cm. Cover title: Science teaching: a Christian approach. [BL240.2.R37] 78-187332
1. Religion and science—1946- I. Title. II. Title: Science teaching: a Christian approach.

REID, William Stanford, 1913- 215
Christianity and scholarship [by] W. Stanford Reid. Nutley, N.J. Craig Press, 1966. viii, 110 p. 26 cm. (University series: philosophical studies) Bibliographical footnotes. [BL240.2.R4] 66-21725
1. Religion and science—1946- 2. Learning and scholarship. 3. Philosophy and religion. I. Title.

RITLAND, Richard M., 1925- 215
A search for meaning in nature; a new look at creation and evolution [by] Richard M. Ritland. Mountain View, Calif., Pacific Press Pub. Association [1970] 320 p. illus., map, ports. 22 cm. Includes bibliographies. [BL240.2.R55] 71-115432
1. Religion and science—1946- I. Title.

ROY, Rustum. 200 s
Experimenting with truth : the fusion of religion with technology needed for humanity's survival / Rustum Roy. 1st ed. Oxford ; New York : Pergamon Press, 1980. p. cm. (The Hibbert lectures ; 1979) (Pergamon international library of science, technology, engineerig, and social studies) [BL25.H5 1979] [BL240.2] 261.5'5 19 80-40658 ISBN 0-08-025820-4 : 27.00 ISBN 0-08-02519-0 pbk. : 13.50
1. Religion and science—1946- I. Title. II. Series: Hibbert lectures (London) ; 1979.

RUPERT, Frank F.
The scientist and the soul. Wilmington, Del., Kaumagraph, 1965. 232 p. 25 cm. 67-57712
1. Religion and science—1946- 2. Scientists—Correspondence, reminiscences, etc. 3. Scientists—Religion. I. Title.

RUSHDOONY, Rousas John. 215
The mythology of science. Nutley, N.J., Craig Press, 1967. 134 p. 20 cm. (University series: historical studies) Bibliographical footnotes. [BL240.2.R78] 67-28460
1. Religion and science—1946- I. Title.

RUST, Eric Charles 215
Science and faith; towards a theological understanding of nature, by Eric C. Rust. New York, Oxford Univ. Pr., 1967. xiii, 330p. 21cm. Bibl. [BL240.2.R8] 67-28130 6.50
1. Religion and science—1946- I. Title.

SALISBURY, Frank B. 215
Truth by reason and by revelation. Salt Lake City, Deseret, 1965. x, 362p. illus. 24cm. Bibl. [BL240.2.S25] 65-18576 price unreported
1. Religion and science—1946- I. Title.

SCHILLING, Harold Kistler, 1899- 215
The new consciousness in science and religion [by] Harold K. Schilling. Philadelphia, United Church Press [1973] 288 p. 21 cm. "A Pilgrim Press book." Bibliography: p. 287-288. [BL240.2.S28] 72-13792 ISBN 0-8298-0247-9 7.95
1. Religion and science—1946- I. Title.

SCHILLING, Harold Kistler, 1899- 215
Science and religion, an interpretation of two communities. New York, Scribner [1962] 272 p. illus. 22 cm. [BL240.2.S3] 62-17732
1. Religion and science—1946- I. Title.

SCHNABEL, A. O. 215
Has God spoken? By A. O. Schnabel. Rev. and enl. San Diego, Ca., Creation-Life Publishers [1974] iv, 118 p. illus. 19 cm. Includes bibliographical references. [BS480.S335] 74-81483 ISBN 0-89051-009-1 1.95 (pbk.)
1. Bible—Evidences, authority, etc. 2. Religion and science—1946- I. Title.
Publisher's address: Box 15666, San Diego, Calif. 92115.

SEMINAR on Science and the Spiritual Nature of Man. 2d, Rye, N. Y., 1958. 215
Second Seminar on Science and the Spiritual Nature of Man. [Rye? N. Y.] c1959. ii, 113p. 28cm. [BL240.2.S4 1958] 60-29872
1. Religion and science—1946- I. Title.

SEMINAR on Science and the Total Nature of Man. 2d, Rye, N. Y., 1958. 215
Second Seminar on Science and the Spiritual Nature of Man; [papers. Rye? N. Y.] c1959. ii, 113p. 28cm. 'Sponsored by the Laymen's Movement for a Christian World.' [BL240.2.S4 1958] 60-29872
1. Religion and science—1946- I. Laymen's Movement for a Christian World. II. Title.

SEMINAR on Science and the Total Nature of Man. 3d, Rye, N. Y., 1960. 215
Seminar on Science and the Total Nature of Man; [papers. Rye] c1962. 70p. diagrs. 30cm. 'Sponsored by the Laymen's Movement.' [BL240.2.S4 1960] 62-43477
1. Religion and science—1946- I. Laymen's Movement for a Christian World. II. Title.

SHAPLEY, Harlow, ed. 215
Science ponders religion. New York, Appleton-Century-Crofts [c.1960] x, 308p. Bibl. footnotes 22cm. 60-15840 5.00
1. Religion and science—1946- I. Title.

SHIDELER, Emerson W. 215
Believing and knowing: the meaning of truth in Biblical religion and in science [by] Emerson W. Shideler. [1st ed.] Ames, Iowa State University Press, 1966. xvii, 196 p. 24 cm. Bibliography: p. 185-188. [BL240.2.S56] 66-14588
1. Religion and science—1946- I. Title.

THE single reality. 215
Preston Harold, author of The shining stranger. Winifred Babcock, author of The Palestinian mystery play. Introduction and summary by Oliver L. Reiser. Preface for the Physical scientist by Robert M. L. Baker, Jr. [Winston-Salem, N.C., Harold Institute]; distributed by Dodd, Mead, New York [1971] 386 p. illus. 24 cm. Contents.Contents.—The Palestinian mystery play, by W. Babcock.—If thine eye be single, by W. Babcock.—On the nature of universal cross-action, by P. Harold.—Bibliography (p. 375-376) [BL240.2.S58] 78-121985 ISBN 0-396-06206-7 7.95
1. Jesus Christ—Miscellanea. 2. Religion and science—1946- 3. Occult sciences. I. Harold, Preston. On the nature of universal cross-action. 1971. II. Babcock, Winifred. The Palestinian mystery play. 1971.

STUERMANN, Walter Earl, 1919- 261.75
Logic and faith, a study of the relations between science and religion. Philadelphia, Westminster Press [1962] 192 p. illus. 21 cm. (Westminster studies in Christian communication) [BL240.2.S8] 62-12647
1. Religion and science—1946- I. Title.

TEILHARD de Chardin, Pierre. 128'.3
Activation of energy. Translated by Rene Hague. [1st American ed.] New York, Harcourt Brace Jovanovich [1971, c1970] 416 p. 21 cm. "A Helen and Kurt Wolff book." Includes bibliographical references. [B2430.T373A313 1971] 75-142104 ISBN 0-15-103276-9 7.50
1. Religion and science—1946- I. Title.

TEILHARD de Chardin, Pierre. 215
Science and Christ. Translated from the French by Rene Hague. [1st U.S. ed.] New York, Harper & Row [1968] 230 p. 22 cm. [B2430.T373S313] 69-10470 5.00
1. Religion and science—1946- I. Title.

TEMPLETON, John M. 210
The humble approach : scientists discover God / John M. Templeton. New York : Seabury Press, 1981. 248 p. : ill. ; 22 cm. Bibliography: p. [133]-248. [BL240.2.T45] 19 80-25106 ISBN 0-8164-0481-X : 10.95
1. Religion and science—1946- I. Title.

THORPE, William Homan, 1902- 215
Science, man, and morals. Ithaca, N. Y., Cornell Univ. Pr. [1966, c.1965] xii, 176p. illus. 23cm. Based upon the Fremantle lects. delivered in Balliol Coll., Oxford, Trinity term, 1963. Bibl. [BL240.2.T47] 66-17580 4.95
1. Religion and science — 1946- 2. Science and ethics. I. Title.

THORPE, William Homan, 1902- 215
Science, man, and morals : based upon the Fremantle lectures delivered in Balliol College, Oxford, Trinity term, 1963 / W. H. Thorpe. Westport, Conn. : Greenwood Press, 1976, c1965. p. cm. Reprint of the ed. published by Scientific Book Club, London. Includes bibliographical references and index. [BL240.2.T47 1976] 76-14962 ISBN 0-8371-8143-7 lib.bdg. : 13.25
1. Religion and science—1946- 2. Science and ethics. I. Title.

TRINKLEIN, Frederick E. 215
The God of science; personal interviews with 38 leading American and European scientists on the nature of truth, the existence of God, and the role of the church [by] Frederick E. Trinklein. Grand Rapids, Eerdmans [1971] xxii, 192 p. 22 cm. [BL241.T74] 72-162034 3.45
1. Religion and science—1946- I. Title.

VAN DER ZIEL, Aldert, 1910- 215
The natural sciences and the Christian message. Minneapolis, T. S. Denison [1960] 259 p. diagrs. 23 cm. (The Lutheran studies series, v. 1) "This book is the result of a series of lectures on the natural sciences given for Lutheran pastors in the Lutheran Student Hall of the St. Paul campus of the University of Minnesota." Includes bibliographies. [BL240.2.V3] 60-9802
1. Religion and science — 1946- I. Title. II. Title: The Christian message. III. Series.

WALTER, R. Kenneth. 215
Science, saints, & sense, by R. Kenneth Walter. Salt Lake City, Bookcraft [1973] ix, 140 p. 24 cm. Includes bibliographical references. [BL240.2.W29] 73-84592 3.50
1. Religion and science—1946- I. Title.

WARD, Rita Rhodes. 261.5
In the beginning; a study of creation versus evolution for young people. Illus. by Charles Valentine. Grand Rapids, Baker Book House [1967, c1965] 110 p. (p. 110 blank for "Notes") illus. 22 cm. Includes bibliographies. [BL263.W3] 67-18200
1. Religion and science—1946- 2. Evolution—Study and teaching. 3. Creation—Study and teaching. I. Title.

WATERS, F. William, 1889- 215
The way in and the way out; science and religion reconciled [by] F. W. Waters. Toronto, Oxford University Press, 1967. x, 269 p. 19 cm. Bibliography: p. [260]-266. [BL240.2.W32] 68-78081 4.75
1. Religion and science—1946- I. Title.

WHITEHOUSE, Walter Alexander 215
Order, goodness, glory. New York, Oxford University Press, 1960[ ] 83 p. (bibl. notes: p. 81-83) 19 cm. (The Riddell memorial lectures, 31st series) 60-1974 1.55
1. Religion and science—1946- I. Title.

WIER, Frank E., 1930- 215
The Christian views science [by] Frank E. Wier. Nashville, Published for the Cooperative Publication Association by Abingdon Press [1969] 192 p. illus. 22 cm. (The Cooperative through-the-week series) Bibliography: p. 189-192. [BL240.2.W52] 71-10212
1. Religion and science—1946- I. Title.

WILLIAMS, John Gordon. 215
Christian faith and the space age, by John G. Williams. [1st American ed.] Cleveland, World Pub. Co. [1968] 123 p. 20 cm. First published in 1964 under title: The faith and the space age. [BL240.2.W55] 67-24756
1. Religion and science—1946— 2. Chrisianity—20th cent. I. Title.

WOLTHUIS, Enno, 1911- 215
Science, God, and you. Grand Rapids, Mich., Baker Bk. [c.]1963. 121p. 20cm. 63-21464 2.50 bds.,
1. Religion and science—1946- I. Title.

Religion and science — 1946- — Addresses, essays, lectures.

BOOTH, Edwin Prince, 1898- ed. 215.082
Religion ponders science. New York, Appleton-Century [dist. Meredith, c.1964] xii, 302p. diagrs. 22cm. Bibl. 64-12457 5.95
1. Religion and science—1946- — Addresses, essays, lectures. I. Title.

BOOTH, Edwin Prince, 1898- ed. 215
Religion ponders science. [1st ed.] New York, Appleton-Century [1964] xii, 302 p. diagrs. 22 cm. Bibliographical footnotes. [BL240.2B66] 64-12457
1. Religion and science — 1946- — Addresses, essays, lectures. I. Title.

CUSTANCE, Arthur C. 230
Science and faith / Arthur C. Custance. Grand Rapids : Zondervan Pub. House, c1978. 249 p. ; 23 cm. (His The doorway papers ; v. 8) Includes bibliographical references. [BS543.A1C87 vol. 8] [BL241] 231'.7 77-28310 ISBN 0-310-23018-7 : 8.95
1. Religion and science—1946- — Addresses, essays, lectures. 2. Creation—Addresses, essays, lectures. 3. Man—Addresses, essays, lectures. I. Title.

EYRING, Henry, 1901- 215
The faith of a scientist. Salt Lake City, Bookcraft [1967] 196 p. illus., ports. 24 cm. Essays. Includes bibliographical references. [BL240.2.E9] 67-25432
1. Religion and science—1946- — Addresses, essays, lectures. I. Title.

FAITH, science, and the future / editorial committee, Charles Birch ... [et al.] ; Paul Abrecht, editor. 1st Fortress Press ed. Philadelphia : Fortress Press, 1979, c1978. 236 p. : ill. ; 22 cm. Originally published as preparatory readings for the Conference of Faith, Science, and the Future, to be held at Massachusetts Institute of Technology, July 12-24, 1979. Includes bibliographical references. [BL226.F34 1979] 79-7035 ISBN 0-8006-1365-1 pbk. : 3.95 261
1. Religion and science—1946- — Addresses, essays, lectures. 2. Nature (Theology)—Addresses, essays, lectures. 3. Human ecology—Moral and religious aspects—Addresses, essays, lectures. I. Abrecht, Paul. II. Conference of Faith, Science, and the Future, Massachusetts Institute of Technology, 1979.

HOLUM, John R 261.5
Of test tubes & testaments; thoughts for youth on science and the Christian faith, by John R. Holum. Minneapolis, Augsburg Pub. House [1965] ix, 69 p. illus. 20 cm. "Reprint of articles in One magazine, February, June, and October, 1963, and February and June, 1964." Bibliographical footnotes. [BL241.H625] 65-22832
1. Religion and science — 1946- — Addresses, essays, lectures. I. Title.

HORIZONS of science : 234
Christian scholars speak out / edited by Carl F. H. Henry. 1st ed. San Francisco : Harper & Row, c1978. xii, 281 p. ; 21 cm. (Contemporary evangelical thought series) "Partly an outgrowth of the International Conference on Human Engineering and the Future of Man held in Wheaton, Illinois, July 21-24, 1975." Bibliography: p. [277]-281. [BL240.2.H67 1978] 77-18038 ISBN 0-06-063866-4 pbk. : 5.95
1. Religion and science—1946- — Addresses, essays, lectures. I. Henry, Carl Ferdinand Howard, 1913- II. International Conference on Human Engineering and the Future of Man, Wheaton, Ill., 1975.

SCIENCE and human values in the 21st century. Edited by Ralph Wendell Burhoe Philadelphia, Westminster Press [1971] 203 p. 22 cm. Includes bibliographical references. [BL241.S317] 74-146667 ISBN 0-664-20907-6 6.95 215'.09'05
1. Religion and science—1946- —

Addresses, essays, lectures. 2. Technology and ethics—Addresses, essays, lectures. I. Burhoe, Ralph Wendell, 1911- ed.

TORRANCE, Thomas Forsyth, 1913- 231
The ground and grammar of theology / Thomas F. Torrance. Charlottesville : University Press of Virginia, 1980. xii, 180 p. ; 24 cm. (The Richard lectures for 1978-79, University of Virginia) Four of the lectures were given in an earlier form at Princeton Theological Seminary's Summer Institute in July 1977. [BL241.T68] 79-21429 ISBN 0-8139-0819-1 : 9.95
1. Religion and science—1946- — Addresses, essays, lectures. 2. Creation—Addresses, essays, lectures. 3. Natural theology—Addresses, essays, lectures. I. Title. II. Series: Richard lectures, University of Virginia ; 1978-79.

Religion and science—Early works to 1800.

CAMPANELLA, Tommaso, 1568-1639. 215'.2
The defense of Galileo / Thomas Campanella ; [translated and edited, with introd. and notes by Grant McColley]. New York : Arno Press, 1975. xliv, 93 p. ; 23 cm. (History, philosophy and sociology of science) Translation of Apologia pro Galileo. Reprint of the 1937 ed. published by the Dept. of History of Smith College, Northampton, Mass., which was issued as v. 22, no. 3-4 of Smith College studies in history. Includes bibliographical references and index. [QB36.G2C32 1975] 74-26254 ISBN 0-405-06582-5 : 8.00
1. Galilei, Galileo, 1564-1642. 2. Copernicus, Nicolaus, 1473-1543. 3. Religion and science—Early works to 1800. I. Title. II. Series. III. Series: Smith College studies in history ; v. 22, no. 3-4.

CAMPANELLA, Tommaso, 1568-1639. 215'.2
The defense to Galileo of Thomas Campanella : for the first time translated and edited, with introd. and notes / by Grant McColley. Merrick, N.Y. : Richwood Pub. Co., 1976. p. cm. Translation of Apologia pro Galileo. Reprint of the 1937 ed. published by the Dept. of History of Smith College, Northampton, Mass., which was issued as v. 22, no. 3-4 of Smith College studies in history. Includes bibliographical references and index. [QB36.G2C32 1976] 76-1114 ISBN 0-915172-20-8 : 12.50 lib.bdg. : 14.50
1. Galilei, Galileo, 1564-1642. 2. Copernicus, Nicolaus, 1473-1543. 3. Religion and science—Early works to 1800. I. McColley, Grant. II. Title. III. Series: Smith College studies in history ; v. 22, no. 3-4.

Religion and science—History

COTTON, Edward Howe, 1881- ed. 215.04
Has science discovered God? A symposium of modern scientific opinion, gathered and edited by Edward H. Cotton. New York, Thomas Y. Crowell company [c1931] iviii, 308 p. front., ports. 23 cm. [B1240.C68] 31-30634
1. Religion and science—Hist. I. Title.

Religion and science — History of controversy.

ABELE, Jean, 1886- 215
Christianity and science. Translated from the French by R. F. Trevett. [1st ed.] New York, Hawthorn Books [1961] 140p. 21cm. (The Twentieth century encyclopedia of Catholicism, v. 14. Section 1: Knowledge and faith) Translation of Le christianisme se desinteresse-t-ii de la science? Includes bibliography. [BL240.2.A213] 61-17755
1. Religion and science—History of controversy. I. Title.

AGAR, William Macdonough, 1894- 215
Catholicism and the progress of science, by William M. Agar, PD. D. New York, The Macmillan company, 1940. xi, 109 p. 19 1/2 cm. [The Christendom series] "First printing." "Bibliographical note": p. 101-104. [BX961.S4A33 1940] 40-31207
1. Religion and science—History and controversy 2. Religion and science—1900- I. Title. II. Series.

CLARK, Gordon Haddon 501
The philosophy of science and belief in God. Nutley, N.J., Craig Pr. [c.]1964. 95p. 20cm. (Univ. ser.; philosophical studies) Bibl. [BL1245.C55] 64-25833 1.50 pap.,
1. Religion and Science—History of controversy. I. Title.

CLARK, Gordon Haddon. 501
The philosophy of science and belief in God [by] Gordon H. Clark. Nutley, N.J., Craig Press, 1964. 95 p. 20 cm. (University series: philosophical studies) Bibliography: p. [3]-[4] [BL245.C55] 64-25833
1. Religion and science — History of controversy. I. Title.

CURTIS, Winterton Conway, 1875-- 215
Fundamentalism vs. evolution at Dayton, Tennessee; abstracts from the autobiographical notes of Winterton C. Curtis. [n. p.] c1956. 64p. illus. 23cm. 'Reprinted in part from the Falmouth enterprise, July 20 to August 31, 1956.' [BL245.C78] 57-1913
1. Religion and science—History of controversy. 2. Scopes, John Thomas, defendant. I. Title.

DILLENBERGER, John 215
Protestant thought and natural science; a historical interpretation. Nashville, Abingdon [1967, c.1960] 320p. 21cm. (Apex bks., Z-1p Bibl. [BL240.2.D5] 2.25 pap.,
1. Religion and science—History of controversy. 2. Religious thought—Modern period. I. Title.

DILLENBERGER, John.
Protestant thought and natural science; a historical interpretation. Nashville, Abingdon Press [c1960] 320 p. 21 cm. (Apex books) 67-87283
1. Religion and science — History of controversy. 2. Religious thought — Modern period. I. Title.

DILLENBERGER, John. 215
Protestant thought and natural science : a historical interpretation / by John Dillenberger. Westport, Conn. : Greenwood Press, 1977 [c1960] p. cm. Reprint of the 1st ed., published by Doubleday, Garden City, N.Y. Includes index. Bibliography: p. [BL240.2.D5 1977] 77-7200 ISBN 0-8371-9670-1 lib.bdg. : 18.50
1. Religion and science—History of controversy. 2. Religious thought—Modern period, 1500- I. Title.

DILLENBERGER, John. 215
Protestant thought and natural science; a historical interpretation. [1st ed.] Garden City, N.Y., Doubleday, 1960. 310 p. 22 cm. Includes bibliography. [BL240.2.D5] 60-13517
1. Religion and science—History of controversy. 2. Religious thought—Modern period. I. Title.

DRAPER, John William, 1811-1882. 215
History of the conflict between religion and science. By John William Draper ... New York, D. Appleton and company, 1875. xxii, 373 p. 19 cm. (Half-title: The International scientific series. [vol. xii]) Series title also at head of t.-p. [BL245.D7 1875] 14-
1. Religion and science—History of controversy. I. Title.

DRAPER, John William, 1811-1882. 215
History of the conflict between religion and science. By John William Draper ... 5th ed. New York, D. Appleton and company, 1875. xxii, 373 p. 19 cm. (Half-title: The international scientific series, [American ed.] vol xii) Series title also at head of t.-p. [BL245.D7 1875d] 8-881
1. Religion and science—History of controversy. I. Title.

DRAPER, John William, 1811-1882. 215
History of the conflict between religion and science. By John William Draper ... 8th ed. New York, D. Appleton and company, 1876. xxii, 373 p. 19 1/2 cm. (Half-title: The international scientific series. [American ed.] vol. xii) Series title also at head of t.-p. [BL245.D7 1876] 31-
1. Religion and science—History of controversy. I. Title.

DRAPER, John William, 1811-1882. 215
History of the conflict between religion and science, By John William Draper ... 8th ed. New York, D. Appleton and company, 1877. xxii. 373 p. 19 1/2 cm. (Half-title: The international scientific series [American ed.] vol. xii) Series title also at head of t.-p. [BL245.D7 1877] 30-
1. Religion and science—History of controversy. I. Title.

DRAPER, John William, 1811-1882. 215
History of the conflict between religion and science, by John William Draper ... New York, D. Appleton and company, 1897. 1p. 1., [v]-xxii, 373 p. 19 1/2 cm. [BL245.D7 1897] 33-33644
1. Religion and science—History of controversy. I. Title.

DRAPER, John William, 1811-1882. 215
History of the conflict between religion and science. By John William Draper ... New York, D. Appleton and company, 1903. xxiii, 373 p. 19 1/2 cm. (The International scientific series. [American ed. vol. xii]) [BL245.D7 1903] 3-32831
1. Religion and science—History of controversy. I. Title.

DRAPER, John William, 1811-1882. 215
... History of the conflict between religion and science. By John William Draper. 4th ed. New York, D. Appleton and company, 1875. xxii, 373 p. 19 1/2 cm. (Half-title: The International scientific series. [American ed.] Vol. XII) Series title also at head of t.-p. [BL245.D7 1875 c] 43-41622
1. Religion and science—History of controversy. I. Title.

GILLISPIE, Charles Coulston. 213
Genesis and geology, a study in the relations of scientific thought, natural theology, and social opinion in Great Britain, 1790-1850. Cambridge, Harvard University Press, 1951. xiii, 315 p. 22 cm. (Harvard historical studies, v. 58) "Bibliographical essay": p. [229]-258. Bibliographical referencesincluded in "Notes" (p. [259]-302) [BS657.G55] 51-10449
1. Religion and science—History of controversy. 2. Geology. I. Title. II. Series.

GILLISPIE, Charles Coulston. 213
Genesis and geology; a study in the relations of scientific thought, natural theology, and social opinion in Great Britain, 1790-1850. New York, Harper [1959, c1951] 306 p. 21 cm. (Harper torchbooks, TB51) Includes bibliography. [BS657.G55 1959] 59-6649
1. Religion and science—History of controversy. 2. Geology. I. Title.

GREENE, John C. 215
Darwin and the modern world view, the Rockwell lectures, Rice University. New York, New Amer. Lib. [c.1961, 1963] 126p. 18cm. (Mentor Bk. MP485) Bibl. .60 pap.,
1. Religion and science—History of controversy. 2. Natural theology. 3. Ethics, Evolutionary. I. Title.

GREENE, John C 215
Darwin and the modern world view. Baton Rouge, Louisiana State University Press [1961] 141p. 21cm. (Rockwell lectures, Rice University) Includes bibliography. [BL263.G66] 61-15489
1. Religion and science—History of controversy. 2. Natural theology. 3. Ethics, Evolutionary. I. Title.

HABER, Francis C 215
The age of the world: Moses to Darwin. Baltimore, Johns Hopkins Press, 1959. xi, 303p. 23cm. 'An extension of ... [the author's] dissertation, Revolution in the concept of historical time: a study in the relationship between Biblical chronology and the rise of modern science ... Johns Hopkins University, 1957. Bibliographical footnotes. Includes bibliography. [BL245.H3] 59-14893
1. Religion and science—History of controversy. 2. Earth—Age. I. Title.

HABER, Francis C. 215
The age of the world : Moses to Darwin / Francis C. Haber. Westport, Conn. : Greenwood Press, 1978 c1959. xi, 303 p. ; 23 cm. Based on the author's thesis, Johns Hopkins University, 1957, which was issued under title: Revolution in the concept of historical time. Reprint of the ed. published by Johns Hopkins Press, Baltimore. Includes bibliographical references and index. [BL245.H3 1978] 77-13854 ISBN 0-8371-9898-4 lib.bdg. : 19.50
1. Religion and science—History of controversy. 2. Earth—Age. I. Title.

HEDLEY, George Percy 1899- 215
Religion and the natural world. Seattle, Dist. by the Univ. of Wash.Pr. [1963] 49p. 22cm. Three lects. given in the med. student res. training program at the Univ. of Wash. Sch. of Med. 63-4038 1.50
1. Religion and science—History of controversy. 2. Washington (State) University. School of Medicine. I. Title.

HOOYKAAS, Reijer, 1906- 215'.09
Religion and the rise of modern science, by R. Hooykaas. [1st American ed.] Grand Rapids, Mich., Eerdmans Pub. Co. [1972] xiii, 162 p. 21 cm. Based on the Gunning lectures which were delivered under the auspices of the Faculty of Divinity in the University of Edinburgh, Feb. 1969. Includes bibliographical references. [BL245.H63 1972] 72-75568 ISBN 0-8028-1474-3 2.65
1. Religion and science—History of controversy. I. Title. II. Series: The Gunning lectures, 1969.

KLAAREN, Eugene M., 1940- 509
Religious origins of modern science / by Eugene M. Klaaren. Grand Rapids : Eerdmans, c1977. p. cm. Includes bibliographical references and index. [BL245.K52] 76-53838 ISBN 0-8028-1683-5 pbk. : 4.95
1. Religion and science—History of controversy. 2. Creation.

KOCHER, Paul Harold, 1907- 215
Science and religion in Elizabethan England. San Marino, Calif., Huntington Library, 1953. xii, 340p. 24cm. (Huntington Library publications) Bibliographical footnotes. [BL245.K6] 53-9115
1. Religion and science—History of controversy. I. Title. II. Series: Henry E. Huntington Library and Art Gallery, San Marino, Calif. Huntington Library publications

KOESTLER, Arthur, 1905- 215
The sleep walkers; a history of man's changing vision of the universe. Introd. by Herbert Butterfield. New York, Grosset [1963, c.1959] 624p. diagrs. 21cm. (Universal lib., 0159) Bibl. 2.65 pap.,
1. Religion and science—History of controversy. I. Title.

KOESTLER, Arthur, 1905- 215
The sleep walkers; a history of man's changing vision of the universe. With an introd. b Herbert Butterfield. New York, Macmillan, 1959. 624p. illus. 22cm. Includes bibliography. [BL245.K63 1959a] 59-7218
1. Religion and science—History of controversy. I. Title.

LANGFORD, Jerome J. 215
Galileo, science, and the church. Foreword by Stillman Drake. New York. Desclee. [c.1966] xv, 237p. 21cm. Bibl. [BL245.L27] 66-17861 5.95
1. Galilei Galileo, 1564-1642. 2. Religion and science — History of controversy. I. Title.

RAVEN, Charles Earle, 1885- 215
Natural religion and Christian theology. Cambridge [Eng.] University Press, 1953. 2v. 23cm. (Gifford lectures, 1951-52) Contents.1st ser. Science and religion.--2d ser. Experience and Interpretation. [BL245.R28] 53-8684

1. Religion and science—History of controversy. 2. Theology, Doctrinal—Addresses, essays, lectures. I. Title.

SHAPIRO, Barbara J. 283'.0924 B
John Wilkins, 1614-1672; an intellectual biography [by] Barbara J. Shapiro. Berkeley, University of California Press, 1969. 333 p. port. 24 cm. Bibliographical references included in "Notes" (p. 251-320) [LF724.W5S5] 73-84042 9.50
1. Wilkins, John, Bp. of Chester, 1614-1672. 2. Religion and science—History of controversy.

SIMPSON, James Young, 215'.09
1873-1934.
Landmarks in the struggle between science and religion. Port Washington, N.Y., Kennikat Press [1971] xiii, 288 p. 22 cm. "First published in 1925." Includes bibliographical references. [BL245.S5 1971] 75-118549 ISBN 8-04-611742-
1. Religion and science—History of controversy. I. Title.

SIMPSON, James Young, 1873- 215
1934.
Landmarks in the struggle between science and religion, by James Y. Simpson ... New York, George H. Doran company [1926] xiii p., 1 l., 288 p. 20 1/2 cm. [BL245.S5] 26-7593
1. Religion and science—History of controversy. I. Title.

WHEELER, Gerald W. 213
The two-taled dinosaur : why science and religion conflict over the origin of life / by Gerald W. Wheeler. Nashville : Southern Pub. Association, c1975. 224 p. ; 22 cm. Includes index. Bibliography: p. 211-217. [BL245.W47] 75-28530 ISBN 0-8127-0090-2
1. Religion and science—History of controversy. 2. Evolution. 3. Creation. I. Title.

WHITE, Andrew Dickson, 1832- 215
1918
A history of the warfare of science and theology in Christendom, Abridged. New York, Free Pr. [c.1965] 538p. 22cm. (93507) Bibl. [BL245.W5] 2.95 pap.,
1. Religion and science—History of controversy. 2. Science—Hist. I. Title.

WHITE, Andrew Dickson, 1832- 213
1918.
A history of the warfare of science uith theology in christendom, by Andrew Dickson White ... New York, D. Appleton & company, 1896. 2 v. 23 cm. [BL245.W5] 9-20218
1. Religion and science—History of controversy. I. Title.

WHITE, Andrew Dickson, 1832- 215
1918
A history of the warfare of science with theology in Christendom; 2 v. [Gloucester, Mass., P. Smith, 1965] 2 v. (various p.) 21cm. [Dover bk. rebound] Unabridged, unaltered repubn. of the first ed. of 1896. Bibl. [BL245.W5] 8.00 set.,
1. Religion and science—History of controversy. 2. Science—Hist. I. Title.

WHITE, Andrew Dickson, 1832- 215
1918.
A history of the warfare of science with theology in Christendom. New York, Dover Publications [1960] 2 v. 21 cm. "Unabridged and unaltered republication of the first edition that appeared in 1896." Includes bibliography. [BL245.W5 1960] 60-2524
1. Religion and science — History of controversy. 2. Science — Hist. I. Title.

WHITE, Andrew Dickson, 1832- 215
1918.
A history of the warfare of science with theology in Christendom. Abridged for the modern reader, with a pref. and epilogue by Bruce Mazlish. New York, Free Press [1965] 538 p. 21 cm. (A Free Press paperback) Bibliographical footnotes. [BL245.W5 1965] 63-7311
1. Religion and science — History of controversy. 2. Science — Hist. I. Mazlish, Bruce, 1923- ed. II. Title.

WHITE, Andrew Dickson, 1832- 215
1918.
A history of the warfare of science with theology in Christendom, by Andrew Dickson White ... New York and London, D. Appleton and company, 1910. 2 v. 22 1/2 cm. Published first in 1896. [BL245.W5 1910] 13-6463
1. Religion and science—History of controversy. 2. Science—Hist. I. Title.

WHITE, Andrew Dickson, 1832- 215
1918.
A history of the warfare of science with theology in Christendom, by Andrew Dickson White ... New York and London, D. Appleton and company, 1930. 2 v. 23 cm. Published first in 1896. Bibliographies interspersed. [BL245.W5 1930] 31-35762
1. Religion and science—History of controversy. 2. Science—Hist. I. Title.

WHITE, Andrew Dickson, 1832- 215
1918.
A history of the warfare of science with theology in Christendom, by Andrew Dickson White ... New York and London, D. Appleton and company, 1932. 2 v. 22 1/2 cm. First published in 1896. Bibliographies interspersed. [BL245.W5 1932] 33-1590
1. Religion and science—History of controversy. 2. Science—Hist. I. Title.

WHITE, Andrew Dickson, 1832- 215
1918.
The warfare of science. By Andrew Dickson White ... New York, D. Appleton and company, 1876. 151 p. 16 cm. [BL245.W6 1876] 31-14786
1. Religion and science—History of controversy. I. Title.

Religion and science—History of controversy—England.

JACOB, Margaret C., 215.0942
1943-
The Newtonians and the English Revolution, 1689-1720 / Margaret C. Jacob. Ithaca, N.Y. : Cornell University Press, 1976. p. cm. Includes bibliographical references and index. [BL245.J3 1976] 75-36995 ISBN 0-8014-0981-0 : 14.50
1. Religion and science—History of controversy—England. 2. Physics—History. 3. England—Intellectual life—17th century. 4. Great Britain—History—Revolution of 1688. I. Title.

KOCHER, Paul Harold, 1907- 215
Science and religion in Elizabethan England, by Paul H. Kocher. New York, Octagon Books, 1969 [c1953] xii, 340 p. 24 cm. Bibliographical footnotes. [BL245.K6 1969] 73-96198
1. Religion and science—History of controversy—England. I. Title.

TURNER, Frank Miller. 261.5
Between science and religion; the reaction to scientific naturalism in late Victorian England. New Haven, Yale University Press, 1974. x, 273 p. 25 cm. (Yale historical publications, miscellany, 100) Based on the author's thesis, Yale. Bibliography: p. 257-267. [BL245.T87] 73-86920 ISBN 0-300-01678-6 12.50
1. Religion and science—History of controversy—England. I. Title. II. Series: Yale historical publications. Miscellany 100.

WESTFALL, Richard S. 215'.0942
Science and religion in seventeenth-century England [by] Richard S. Westfall. [Hamden, Conn.] Archon Books, 1970 [c1958] vii, 235 p. 23 cm. Includes bibliographical references. [BL245.W4 1970] 72-103992 ISBN 2-08-008438-
1. Religion and science—History of controversy—England. 2. Gt. Brit.—Church history—17th century. I. Title.

Religion and science—History of controversy—France.

PAUL, Harry W. 215'.0944
The edge of contingency : French Catholic reaction to scientific change from Darwin to Duhem / Harry W. Paul. Gainesville : University Presses of Florida, 1979. 213 p. ; 24 cm. "A University of Florida book." Includes index. Bibliography: p. 195-203. [BL245.P38] 78-11168 ISBN 0-8130-0582-5 : 15.00
1. Religion and science—History of controversy—France. 2. Catholic Church in France. I. Title.

Religion and science—History of controversy—India.

GOSLING, David L., 1939- 215
Science and religion in India / by David L. Gosling. Madras : Published for Christian Institute for the Study of Religion and Society, Bangalore, by Christian Literature Society, 1976. 176 p. ; 23 cm. (Series on religion ; no. 21) A portion of the author's thesis, University of Lancaster. Includes bibliographical references. [BL245.G67] 76-904188 Rs12.50
1. Religion and science—History of controversy—India. I. Title.

Religion and science—History of controversy—United States.

BOZEMAN, Theodore Dwight, 261.5
1942-
Protestants in an age of science : the Baconian ideal and ante-bellum American religious thought / by Theodore Dwight Bozeman. Chapel Hill : University of North Carolina Press, c1977. xv, 243 p. ; 24 cm. Includes index. Bibliography: p. 211-239. [BL245.B7] 76-25962 ISBN 0-8078-1299-4 : 14.95
1. Bacon, Francis, Viscount St. Albans, 1561-1626. 2. Religion and science—History of controversy—United States. 3. Protestantism. I. Title.

HOVENKAMP, Herbert. 215
Science and religion in America, 1800-1860 / Herbert Hovenkamp. Philadelphia : University of Pennsylvania Press, 1978. p. cm. Includes index. Bibliography: p. [BL245.H66] 78-53332 ISBN 0-8122-7748-1 : 16.00
1. Religion and science—History of controversy—United States. I. Title.
Available from Technical Impex Corp. Lawrence, MA.

KENNEDY, Gail, 1900- ed. 215.082
Evolution and religion; the conflict between science and theology in modern America. Boston, Heath [1957] 114 p. 24 cm. (Problems in American civilization; readings selected by the Dept. of American Studies, Amherst College) [BL245.K4] 57-1698
1. Religion and science—History of controversy—United States. I. Title.

WHITE, Edward Arthur, 1907- 215
Science and religion in American thought; the impact of naturalism [by] Edward A. White. New York, AMS Press [1968] viii, 117 p. 22 cm. (Stanford University publications. University series. History, economics, and political science, v. 8) Reprint of the 1952 ed. Bibliographical footnotes. [BL245.W63 1968] 68-54307
1. Religion and science—History of controversy—United States. I. Title. II. Series: Stanford studies in history, economics, and political science, v. 8

Religion and science — History of doctrines.

WESTFALL, Richard S. 215
Science and religion in seventeenth-century England. New Haven, Yale University Press, 1958. ix, 235 p. 25 cm. (Yale historical publications. Miscellany 67) "Bibliographical essay": p. 221-228. Bibliographical footnotes. [BL245.W4] 58-6548
1. Religion and science — History of doctrines. 2. Gt. Brit. — Church history — 17th cent. I. Title. II. Series.

WESTFALL, Richard S. 215
Science and religion in seventeenth-century England. [Ann Arbor] Univ. of Michigan Pr. [1973, c.1958] x, 239 p. 21 cm. (Ann Arbor paperbacks, AA190) (Yale historical publications. Miscellany, 67) "Bibliographical essay": p. 221-228. [BL245.W4] ISBN 0-472-06190-9 2.95 (pbk.)
1. Religion and science—History of doctrines. 2. Gt. Brit.—Church history—17th cent. I. Title. II. Series.
L.C. card no. for the hardbound edition: 58-6548.

Religion and sociology.

ACQUAVIVA, Sabino S. 301.5'8
The decline of the sacred in industrial society / S. S. Acquaviva ; translated by Patricia Lipscomb. New York : Harper & Row, c1979. xiii, 289 p. ; 22 cm. Translation of L'eclissi del sacro nella civilta industriale. Includes index. Bibliography: p. [247]-282. [BL60.A2513 1979b] 78-59910 ISBN 0-06-136180-1 : 23.50
1. Religion and sociology. I. Title.

ASPECTS of the rise of economic individualsm; a criticism of Max Weber and his school. New York, Kelley & Millman, 1959. xvi, 223p. 22cm. 'First written in 1928-9 as a dissertation for the degree of doctor of philosophy in the University of Cambridge. 'Pref. 'First published in 1933.' Paper read to the University of Cape Town Senior Seminar, 18gh May, 1949, entitled European economic developments in the 16th century by H. M. Robertson, inserted between pages viii and [xi]
1. Weber, Max, 1864-1920. Die protestantische Ethik und der geist der Kapitalismus. 2. Religion and sociology. 3. Capitalism. I. Robertson Hector Menteith.

BECKFORD, James A. 289.9
The trumpet of prophecy : a sociological study of Jehovah's Witnesses / James A. Beckford. New York : Wiley, [1975] xii, 244 p. ; 25 cm. "A Halsted Press book." Includes indexes. Bibliography: p. 224-234. [BX8526.B4] 75-14432 ISBN 0-470-06138-3 : 17.95
1. Jehovah's Witnesses. 2. Religion and sociology. I. Title.

BERGER, Peter L. 261.8
The precarious vision : a sociologist looks at social fictions and Christian faith / Peter L. Berger. Westport, Conn. : Greenwood Press, 1976, c1961. 238 p. ; 23 cm. Reprint of the ed. published by Doubleday, Garden City, N.Y. Includes bibliographical references. [BL60.B4 1976] 76-1981 ISBN 0-8371-8657-9 lib.bdg. : 14.00
1. Religion and sociology. 2. Sociology, Christian. I. Title.

BERGER, Peter L. 261.8
The precarious vision; a sociologist looks at social fictions and Christian faith. [1st ed.] Garden City, N.Y., Doubleday, 1961. 238 p. 22 cm. Includes bibliography. [BL60.B4] 61-12493
1. Religion and sociology. 2. Sociology, Christian. I. Title.

BERGER, Peter L. 301.5'8
The sacred canopy; elements of a sociological theory of religion, by Peter L. Berger. [1st ed.] Garden City, N.Y., Doubleday, 1967. vii, 230 p. 22 cm. Bibliographical references included in "Notes" (p. [189]-211) [BL60.B42] 67-19805
1. Religion and sociology. I. Title.

BIANCHI, Eugene C. 200'.1
The religious experience of revolutionaries [by] Eugene C. Bianchi. [1st ed.] Garden City, N.Y., Doubleday, 1972. 223 p. 22 cm. Includes bibliographies. [BL60.B45] 72-76122 ISBN 0-385-05412-2 6.95
1. Religion and sociology. I. Title.

CAILLOIS, Roger 291
Man and the sacred; translated [from the French] by Meyer Barash. [Glencoe] Ill., Free Press of Glencoe [1960, c.1959] 190p. 22cm. Includes bibliography. 59-6826 4.50 bds.,
1. Religion and sociology. 2. Religion. 3. Rites and ceremonies. I. Title.

CARRIER, Herve, 1921-. 201.6
The sociology of religious belonging. [Translated by Arthur J. Arrieri. New York] Herder and Herder [1965] 335 p. 22 cm. Bibliography: p. 302-318. [BL60.C37] 64-13684
1. Religion and sociology. 2. Psychology, religious. I. Title.

CONFERENCE on New Approaches 291
in Social Anthropology, Jeses College, Cambridge, Eng., 1963.
Anthropological approaches to the study of religion, edited by Michael Banton. New York, F. A. Praeger [1966] xiii, 176 p. illus. 23 cm. (A. S. A. Monographs, 3)

Derived from material presented at a conference sponsored by the Association of Social Anthropologists of the Commonwealth. Includes bibliographies. [BL60.C58 1963c] 65-16223
1. Religion and Sociology. 2. Religion, Primitive. I. Banton, Michael P. ed. II. Association of Social Anthropologists of the Commonwealth. III. Cambridge. University. Jesus College. IV. Title. V. Series.

COOKE, George Willis, 1848-1923. 201
The social evolution of religion, by George Willis Cooke. Boston, The Stratford company, 1920. xxiv, 416 p. 20 cm. [BL60.C6] 20-4088
1. Religion and sociology. I. Title.

CORWIN, Charles. 261.1
East to Eden? Religion and the dynamics of social change. Grand Rapids, Eerdmans [1972] 190 p. 21 cm. Includes bibliographical references. [BL60.C67] 77-184693 ISBN 0-8028-1444-1 2.95
1. Religion and sociology. 2. Asia—Religion. I. Title.

CRAFTS, Wilbur Fisk, 1850-
The march of Christ down the centuries. [Rev. 4th ed. of Social progress] By Rev. Wilbur F. Crafts ... Washington, D. C., The International reform bureau, c1897. 3 p. l., [9]-128 p. 20 cm. 15-24962
I. Title.

DEMERATH, Nicholas Jay. 200
Religion in social context; tradition and transition [by] N. J. Demerath III and Phillip E. Hammond. New York, Random House [1968, c1969] ix, 246 p. 21 cm. Bibliography: p. [233]-238. [BL60.D45] 68-20032 5.95
1. Religion and sociology. I. Hammond, Phillip E., joint author. II. Title.

DEMERATH, Nicholas Jay. 301.5'8
A tottering transcendence; civil v. cultic aspects of the sacred [by] N. J. Demerath III. Indianapolis, Bobbs-Merrill [1973, i.e.1974] p. (The Bobbs-Merrill studies in sociology) Bibliography: p. [BL60.D454] 73-10476 1.25 (pbk.)
1. Religion and sociology. I. Title.

DESROCHE, Henri. 261.8'3
Jacob and the angel; an essay in sociologies of religion. Translated by John K. Savacool. Amherst, University of Massachusetts Press [1973] xiv, 187 p. 24 cm. Translation of Sociologies religieuses. Includes bibliographical references. [BL60.D4813] 72-77575 12.50
1. Religion and sociology. I. Title.

*EBBERT, George C. FIC
Satan will never die : a socio-religious novel, by George C. Ebbert. Hicksville, N.Y. Exposition Press [1974] 223 p. 22 cm. ISBN 0-682-48072-X 7.50
I. Title.

EDDY, George Sherwood, 1871- 220
Facing the crisis; a study in present day social and religious problems, by Sherwood Eddy. New York, George H. Doran company [c1922] xii, 15-241 p. 19 1/2 cm. (Half-title: The Fondren lectures for 1922, delivered before the School of theology of Southern Methodist university) "Appendix iii, Books on current social problems": p. 237-238. [BR125.E3] 22-19728
I. Title.

ELWANG, William Wilson. 201
...The social function of religious belief, by William Wilson Elwang, ph. d. [Columbia, Mo.] University of Missouri, 1908. ix, 103 p. 27 1/2cm. (The university of Missouri studies: ed. by W. G. Brown. Social science series vol. II. no. 1) "Written and accepted originally as a doctor's thesis in the University of Missouri, in 1905, but slightly expanded since ..."--Pref. "Works of reference": p. 101-103. [BL60.E6] 8-16560
1. Religion and sociology. 2. Religion—Philosophy. I. Title.

FINNEY, Ross L 1875-.
Personal religion and the social awakening, by Ross L. Finney ... Cincinnati, Jennings and Graham; New York, Eaton and Mains [c1913] 147 p. 20 1/2cm. $0.75 13-20315
I. Title.

GLOCK, Charles Y. 301.58
Religion and society in tension [by] Charles Y. Glock [and] Rodney Stark. Chicago, Rand McNally [1965] xii, 316 p. 23 cm. (Rand McNally sociology series) [BL60.G55] 65-25356
1. Religion and sociology. 2. United States—Religious life and customs. I. Stark, Rodney, joint author. II. Title.

GLOCK, Charles Y. 301.58
Religion and society in tension [by] Charles Y. Glock [and] Rodney Stark. Chicago, Rand McNally [1965] xii, 316 p. 23 cm. (Rand McNally sociology series) [BL60.G55] 65-25356
1. Religion and sociology. 2. United States—Religious life and customs. I. Stark, Rodney, joint author. II. Title.

GOODE, William J. 291
Religion among the primitives; with an introd. by Kingsley Davis. Glencoe, Ill., Free Press ['1951] 321 p. 25 cm. Bibliography: p. 259-269. [BL60.G6] 51-11596
1. Religion and sociology. 2. Religion, Primitive. I. Title.

GOODE, William Josiah 291
Religion among the primitives. Introd. by Kingsley Davis. New York, Free Pr. [1964, c.1951] 321p. 21cm. Bibl. 1.95 pap.,
1. Religion and sociology 2. Religion, Primitive. I. Title.

GOODE, William Josiah. 291
Religion among the primitives; with an introd. by Kingsley Davis. Glencoe, Ill., Free Press [1951] 321 p. 25 cm. Bibliography: p. 259-269. [BL60.G6] 51-11596
1. Religion and sociology. 2. Religion, Primitive. I. Title.

GOODE, William Josiah.
Religion among the primitives; with an introd. by Kingsley Davis. [New York] Free Press of Glencoe [1964, c1951] 321 p. 21 cm. (A Free Press paperback) Bibliography: p. 259-269. 64-70123
1. Religion and sociology. 2. Religion, Primitive I. Title.

GREELEY, Andrew M., 1928- 301.5'8
Unsecular man; the persistence of religion [by] Andrew M. Greeley. New York, Schocken Books [1972] 280 p. 21 cm. Includes bibliographical references. [BL60.G73] 72-79446 ISBN 0-8052-3463-2 7.95
1. Religion and sociology. I. Title.

GREELEY, Andrew M., 1928- 301.58
Unsecular man; the persistence of religion [by] Andrew M. Greeley. [New York, Dell, 1974, c1973] 280 p. 21 cm. (A Delta book) Includes bibliographical references. [BL60.G73] 2.95 (pbk.)
1. Religion and sociology. I. Title.
L.C. card no. for hardbound ed.: 72-79446.

HARGROVE, Barbara W. 301.5'8
Reformation of the holy; a sociology of religion [by] Barbara W. Hargrove. Philadelphia, F. A. Davis Co. [1971] x, 315 p. 23 cm. Bibliography: p. 293-305. [BL60.H288] 79-158651
1. Religion and sociology. I. Title.

HARGROVE, Barbara W. 306'.6
The sociology of religion : classical and contemporary approaches / Barbara Hargrove. Arlington Heights, Ill. : AHM Pub. Corp., c1979. viii, 342 p. ; 23 cm. A revision of the author's Reformation of the holy, published in 1971. Includes index. Bibliography: p. 317-331. [BL60.H289 1979] 79-50879 ISBN 0-88295-211-0 pbk. : 9.95
1. Religion and sociology. I. Title.
Publisher's Address: 3110 N. Arlington Hts. Rd., Arlington Heights, IL 60004

HILL, Michael, 1943- 301.5'8
A sociology of religion. New York, Basic Books [1974, c1973] x, 285 p. illus. 23 cm. Includes bibliographies. [BL60.H48 1974] 72-96918 ISBN 0-465-08039-1 10.00
1. Religion and sociology. I. Title.

HOULT, Thomas Ford. 201
The sociology of religion. New York, Dryden Press [1958] 436p. 22cm. (The Dryden Press sociology publications) Includes bibliography. [BL60.H64] 58-7384
1. Religion and sociology. I. Title.

IRELAND, John, abp., 1838-1918. 230.
The church and modern society; lectures and addresses by John Ireland ... New York [etc.] D. H. McBride & co. [etc] 1903-04. 2 v. front. (port., v.2) 20 cm. Vol. 2 published at St. Paul, Minn., by The Pioneer press mfg. depts. Contents.[v.1] The Catholic church and civil society. The mission of Catholics in America. The church and the age. Human progress. Patriotism. American citizenship. State schools and parish schools. The Catholic church and liberal education. Intemperance and law. The Catholic church and the saloon. Charity is the Catholic church. Social purity. America in France. The pontiff of the age.--v. 2. The friend of America: Gilbert Motier, marquis de La Fayette. Jeanne d'Arc, patron saint of patriotism. War and peace. Conscience: The mainstay of democracy. The American republic: The ideal embodiment of democracy. Abraham Lincoln: the savior of the union, the exemplar of democracy. Devotion to truth: The virtue of the teacher. Leo XIII. The pope's civil princedom. The church in America. Fifty years of Catholicity in the Northwest. A Catholic sisterhood in the Northwest. A Catholic sisterhood and education. Personal liberty and labor strikes. Labor and capital. Religion, deepest instinct of the human soul. Jesus Christ, yesterday, and today; and the same forever. [BX1753.I7 1903] 3-16805
I. Title.

IRELAND, John, abp., 1838-1918. 230.
The church and modern society; lectures and addresses by John Ireland ... St. Paul, Minn., The Pioneer press mfg. depts., 1904- v. 19 1/2 cm. [BX1753.I7 1904] 4-36949
I. Title.

JOHNSTONE, Ronald L. 301.5'8
Religion and society in interaction : the sociology of religion / Ronald L. Johnstone. Englewood Cliffs, N.J. : Prentice-Hall, [1975] x, 345 p. ; 24 cm. (Prentice-Hall sociology series) Includes bibliographical references and index. [BL60.J63] 74-30049 ISBN 0-13-773085-3 : 9.95
1. Religion and sociology. I. Title.

KIRKPATRICK, Clifford, 1898- 201
Religion in human affairs, by Clifford Kirkpatrick ... New York, J. Wiley & sons, ind.; London, Chapman & Hall, limited, 1929. xiii, 530 p. diagrs. 21 cm. (Half-title: Wiley social science series, ed. by H. P. Fairchild) Bibliography: p. 491-496. [BL60.K5] 29-14115
1. Religion and sociology. 2. Religion and science—1900- 3. Religion—Hist. 4. Sociology, Christian. I. Title.

KNUDTEN, Richard D., comp. 261
the sociology of religion, an anthology, edited by Richard D. Knudten. New York, Appleton--Century--Crofts [1967] xiii, 500 p. illus. 24 cm. (Sociology series) Bibliographical footnotes. [BL60.K55] 67-14572
1. Religion and sociology. I. Title.

KRESAGE, Elijah Everett, 1875- 265.
The church and the ever-coming kingdom of God (A discussion of the evolution of a righteous social order with special reference to the mission of the church in the process.) By Elijah Everett Kresge ... New York, The Macmillan company, 1922. xiv, 316 p. 21 cm. [BR115.Sk7] 22-19305
I. Title.

LUCKMANN, Thomas. 301.58
The invisible religion; the problem of religion in modern society. New York, Macmillan [c1967] 128 p. 21 cm. Translation of Das Problem der Religion in der modernen Gesellschaft. Includes bibliographical references. [BL60.L813] 67-11631
1. Religion and sociology. I. Title.

MCGUIRE, Meredith B. 306'.6
Religion, the social context / Meredith B. McGuire. Belmont, Calif. : Wadsworth Pub. Co., c1981. xii, 297 p. ; 24 cm. Includes indexes. Bibliography: p. 259-285. [BL60.M27] 19 80-21807 ISBN 0-534-00951-4 : 12.95
1. Religion and sociology. I. Title.

MATHEWS, Shailer, 1863- 261
Christianity and social process ... by Shailer Mathews. New York and London, Harper & brothers, 1934. viii p., 1 l., 221 p. 20 cm. (Barrows lectures for 1933-1934) Half-title: Living issues in religion, ed. by M. H. Krumbine. "First edition." [BR115.S6M44] 34-40132
1. Religion and sociology. 2. Christianity—Addresses, essays, lectures. 3. Sociology, Christian—Addresses, essays, lectures. I. Title.
Contents omitted.

MENNONITE Church. General Conference.
Church and society conference. YMCA Hotel, Chicago, Illinois October 31-November 3, 1961. 1 v. 29 cm. 65-43438
I. Title.

MOL, J. J. 260
The breaking of traditions: theological convictions in colonial America [by] J. J. Mol. Berkeley, Glendessary Press [1968] 94 p. 21 cm. Bibliography: p. 73-78. [BL60.M6] 68-25005
1. Religion and sociology. 2. Assimilation (Sociology) 3. United States—Church history—Colonial period, ca. 1600-1775. I. Title.

MOL, J. J. 301.5'8
Identity and the sacred : a sketch for a new social-scientific theory of religion / Hans Mol. 1st American ed. New York : Free Press, 1977, c1976. xvi, 326 p. : 22 cm. Includes indexes. Bibliography: p. [267]-301. [BL60.M62 1977] 76-27153 ISBN 0-02-921600-1 : 13.95
1. Religion and sociology. I. Title.

NEF, John Ulric, 1899- 261
Religion and study of man. Houston [Tex.] Univ. of St. Thomas [c.1961] 53p. illus. 16cm. (Smith hist. lecture, 1961) 61-65160 2.00 pap.,
1. Religion and sociology. I. Title.

NEF, John Ulric, 1899- 261
Religion and the study of man. Houston [Tex.] University of Saint Thomas, 1961. 53p. illus. 16cm. (The Smith history lecture, 1961) [BL60.N4] 61-65160
1. Religion and sociology. I. Title.

NOTTINGHAM, Elizabeth Kristine, 1900- 301.5'8
Religion: a sociological view [by] Elizabeth K. Nottingham. [1st ed.] New York, Random House [1971] xiii, 332 p. 22 cm. Bibliography: p. 315-324. [BL60.N597] 75-122976 ISBN 0-394-31021-7
1. Religion and sociology. I. Title.

NOTTINGHAM, Elizabeth Kristine, 1900- 291
Religion and society. Garden City, N.Y., Doubleday, 1954. 84 p. 24 cm. (Doubleday short studies in sociology, SSS5) [BL60.N6] 54-11418
1. Religion and sociology. I. Title.

O'DEA, Thomas F. 301.5
Sociology and the study of religion; theory, research, interpretation [by] Thomas F. O'Dea. New York, Basic Books [1970] x, 307 p. 25 cm. Includes bibliographical references. [BL60.O28 1970] 79-94307 8.50
1. Religion and sociology. I. Title.

O'DEA, Thomas F. 200.1
The sociology of religion. Englewood Cliffs. N.J., Prentice [c.1966] viii, 120p. 24cm. (Founds. of mod. soc. ser.) Bibl. [BL60.O3] 66-10807 3.95; 1.50 pap.,
1. Religion and sociology. I. Title.

PARSONS, Talcott, 1902- 201
Religious perspectives of college teaching in sociology and social psychology. New Haven, Edward W. Hazen Foundation [1951?] 47 p. 23 cm. [BL60.P3] 52-4258
1. Religion and sociology. I. Title.

RADHAKRISHNAN, Sarvepalli, Pres. India, 1888- 294.5
Religion and society. [2d ed.] London, Allen & Unwin. [dist. New York, Barnes & Noble, 1962] 248p. illus. 22cm. (Kamala lectures) Based on notes of lectures

delivered in the Univ. of Calcutta and Benares in the winter of 1942. 62-53406 3.75
1. Religion and sociology. 2. Sociology, Hindu. I. Title.

RAUSCHENBUSCH, Walter, 1861- 241 1918
Christianity and the social crisis. Ed. by Robert D. Cross [Gloucester, Mass., P. Smith, 1965, c.1964] xxv, 429p. (Harper torchbk., TB3059, Univ. lib. rebound) First pub. in 1907. 4.25
I. Title.

*RAUSCHENBUSCH, Walter, 1861- 241 1918
Christianity and the social crisis. New York, Harper [1964, c.1920] 1v. 21cm. (Universal Lib.; Torchbk TB-3059) 2.25 pap.,
I. Title.

ROBERTSON, Hector Menteith. 261
Aspects of the rise of economic individualism; a criticism of Max Weber and his school, by H. M. Robertson ... Cambridge [Eng.] The University press, 1933. xvi, 223 p. 22 cm. (Half-title: Cambridge studies in economic history) "First written in 1928-9 as a dissertation for the degree of doctor of philosophy in the University of Cambridge ... has now been revised and rewritten."--Pref. [BR115.E3R62] 34-12397
1. Weber, Max, 1864-1920. Die protestantische ethik und der geist der kapitalismus. 2. Religion and sociology. 3. Capitalism. I. Title. II. Title: Economic individualism. Aspects of the rise of.

ROBERTSON, Hector Menteith.
Aspects of the rise of economic individualism; a criticism of Max Weber and his school. New York, Kelley & Millman, 1959. 223 p. 22 cm. "First written in 1928-9 as a dissertation for the degree of doctor of philosophy in the University of Cambridge ... has now been revised and rewritten." Bibliographical footnotes. 64-57204
1. Weber, Max, 1864-1920. Dis protestantische Ethik und der Geist des Kapitalismus. 2. Religion and sociology. 3. Capitalism. I. Title.

ROBERTSON, Roland. 301.5
The sociological interpretation of religion. New York, Schocken Books [1970] 256 p. 21 cm. (Introductions to sociology) Includes bibliographical references. [BL60.R59] 77-79124 6.50
1. Religion and sociology. I. Title.

ROGERS, Edward H.
National life in the spirit world: a sociologic essay. By Edward H. Rogers... [Chelsea? Mass.] The author, 1891. iv, 66 p. port. 20 cm. 4-34271
I. Title.

SCHARF, Betty R. 301.5'8
The sociological study of religion [by] Betty R. Scharf. [1st Harper torchbook ed.] New York, Harper & Row [1971] 190 p. 21 cm. (Harper torchbooks, TB 1601) Reprint of the 1970 ed. Bibliography: p. 181-184. [BL60.S28 1971] 70-171975 ISBN 0-06-131601-6 1.95
1. Religion and sociology. I. Title.

SCHNEIDER, Louis, 1915- 261
Sociological approach to religion. New York, Wiley [1970] viii, 188 p. 23 cm. Includes bibliographical references. [BL60.S32] 78-94915
1. Religion and sociology. I. Title.

SIMMEL, Georg, 1858-1918. 301.5'8
Sociology of religion / Georg Simmel ; translated from the German by Curt Rosenthal. New York : Arno Press, 1979. x, 76 p. ; 21 cm. (Perennial works in sociology) Translation of Die Religion. Reprint of the 1959 ed. published by Philosophical Library, New York. [BL60.S5513 1979] 79-7021 ISBN 0-405-12120-2 : 13.00
1. Religion and sociology. I. Title. II. Series.

SMITH, Richard Bonham. 220
Christianity vs. selfishness, by Richard Bonham Smith, containing the Archaeological writings of the Sanhedrim and Talmuds of the Jews, together with a pertinent, direct, and comprehensive discussion and survey of our present social and economic system. Archaeological writings taken from manuscripts in Constantinople and the Records of the senatorial docket taken from the Vatican at Rome; archaeological writings translated by Drs. McIntosh and Twyman. Hendersonville, N.C., Skyland publishing co., 1927. xiii p., 1 l., 119 p. 19 1/2 cm. The "Archaeological writings of the Sanhedrin and Talnuds of the Jews" are from a book bearing this title, published in 1887, by W. D. Mahan and J. W. Damon. [BR125.S646] 27-22569
I. Mahan, W. D. II. Damon, J. W. III. Title.

SOCIOLOGY, theology, and 261 *conflict.* Edited by D. E. H. Whiteley and R. Martin. New York, Barnes & Noble, 1969. vii, 167 p. 23 cm. Papers from a conference organized by the Modern Churchmen's Union held at Oxford, Easter 1968. Bibliographical footnotes. [BL60.S63] 78-5351 5.50
1. Religion and sociology. I. Whiteley, Denys Edward Hugh, ed. II. Martin, Roderick, ed. III. Modern Churchmen's Union.

STAHMER, Harold, ed. 261.83
Religion & contemporary society. New York, Macmillan [1963] 282 p. 21 cm. [BL60.S67] 63-15052
1. Religion and sociology. 2. U.S.—Religion. I. Title.

STARK, Werner, 1909- 301.5'8
The sociology of religion; a study of Christendom. New York, Fordham University Press, 1966-67. 3 v. 23 cm. Contents.--v. 1. Established religion.--v. 2. Sectarian religion.--v. 3. The universal church. Bibliographical footnotes. [BL60.S732] 66-27652
1. Religion and sociology. I. Title.

STARK, Werner, 1909- 301.5'8
The sociology of religion; a study of Christendom. New York, Fordham University Press, 1966- v. 23 cm. Contents.Contents.—v. 1. Established religion.—v. 2. Sectarian religion.—v. 3. The universal church.—v. 4. Types of religious man. Bibliographical footnotes. [BL60.S732] 66-27652
1. Religion and sociology. I. Title.

TEAGUE, Wilbur A
Decline in American democracy. New York, Vantage Press [c1963] 98 p. 65-23669
1. Religion and sociology. 2. Negroes — Moral and social conditions. 3. Juvenile delinquency — U.S. I. Title.

TOWLER, Robert. 301.5'8
Homo religiosus : sociological problems in the study of religion / Robert Towler. New York : St. Martin's Press, 1974. ix, 206 p. : diagrs. ; 23 cm. Includes bibliographical references and index. [BL60.T68 1974] 74-78939 10.95
1. Religion and sociology. I. Title.

VERNON, Glenn M 201
Sociology of religion. New York, McGraw-Hill, 1962. 413 p. 24 cm. (McGraw-Hill series in sociology) Includes bibliography. [BL60.V4] 61-18136
1. Religion and sociology. I. Title.

WACH, Joachim, 1898- 201
Sociology of religion. [Chicago] University of Chicago Press [1958, c1944] xii, 418 p. 21 cm. (Phoenix books, P25) Bibliography: p. 391-395. [BL60.W3 1958] 58-14679
1. Religion and sociology. 2. Sociology. I. Title.

WACH, Joachim, 1898- 201
Sociology of religion, by Joachim Wach ... Chicago, Ill., The University of Chicago press [1944] xii, 412 p. 23 1/2 cm. Bibliographical foot-notes. [BL60.W3] A 44
1. Religion and sociology. 2. Sociology. I. Title.

WACH, Joachim, 1898-1955. 201
Sociology of religion. [Chicago] Univ. of Chic. Pr. [1962, c.1944] 418p. 21cm. (Phoenix bks., P92) Bibl. 1.95 pap.,
1. Religion and sociology. 2. Sociology. I. Title.

WALLIS, Louis.
Egoism: a study in the social premises of religion, by Louis Wallis. Chicago, The University of Chicago press, 1905. xiii, [1], 121 p. 18 cm. 5-41736
I. Title.

WATT, William Montgomery 290
Truth in the religions: a sociological and psychological approach. [dist. Chicago, Aldine, Edinburgh at the University Pr. 1963] 190p. 23cm. Bibl. 6.00
I. Title.

WATT, William Montgomery. 290
Truth in the religions, a sociological and psychological approach. Edinburgh, University Press;[U.S. & Canadian agent: Aldine Pub. Co., Chicago, 1963] viii, 190 p. 24 cm. Bibliographical references included in "Notes" (p. [176]-179) [BL60.W37] 63-22839
1. Religion and sociology. 2. Psychology, Religious. I. Title.

WEBER, Max 261.85
The Protestant ethic and the spirit of capitalism. Translated [from the German] by Talcott Parsons. With a foreword by R. H. Tawney. New York, Scribner [c.1958] xvii, 1(a)-1(e), 292p. 21cm. (Scribner library SL21) Bibliographical references included in Notes (p. 185-284) 1.45 pap.,
1. Religion and sociology. 2. Christian ethics. 3. Capitalism. 4. Christianity and economics. 5. Protestantism I. Title.

WEBER, Max, 1864-1920. 261.85*
The Protestant ethic and the spirit of capitalism. Translated by Talcott Parsons. With a foreword by R. H. Tawney. [Student's ed.] New York, Scribner [1958] xvii, 292 p. 21 cm. Bibliographical references included in "Notes" (p. 185-284) [BR115.E3W4 1958] 58-4170
1. Religion and sociology. 2. Christian ethics. 3. Protestantism and captialism. I. Title.

WEBER, Max, 1864-1920. 290
The sociology of religion. Translated by Ephraim Fischoff. Introd. by Talcott Parsons. Boston, Beacon Press [1963] lxvii, 304 p. 22 cm. "First published in Germany, in 1922 ... under the title 'Religionssoziologie,' from Wirtschaft und Gesellschaft." [BL60.W433] 62-16644
1. Religion and sociology. I. Title.

WHITLEY, Oliver Read. 201
Religious behavior; where sociology and religion meet [by] Oliver R. Whitley. Englewood Cliffs, N.J., Prentice-Hall [1964] xiii, 177 p. 22 cm. Bibliographical footnotes. [BL60.W5] 64-8062
1. Religion and sociology. I. Title.

WILCOX, Francis McLellan. 296
Facing the crisis; present world conditions in the light of the Scriptures, by Francis McLellan Wilcox... Washington, D.C., New York city [etc.] Review and herald publishing assn. [c1920] 128 p. incl. front., illus. 19 1/2 cm. [World's crisis series] [BT875.W5] 20-10779
I. Title.

WILSON, Bryan R. 301.5'8
Magic and the millennium; a sociological study of religious movements of protest among tribal and third-world peoples [by] Bryan R. Wilson. [1st U.S. ed.] New York, Harper & Row [1973] xi, 547 p. 25 cm. Bibliography: p. 505-531. [BL60.W54 1973b] 72-9762 ISBN 0-06-014671-0 15.00
1. Religion and sociology. 2. Sects. 3. Magic. I. Title.

WILSON, John, 1942- 301.5'8
Religion in American society : the effective presence / John Wilson. Englewood Cliffs, N.J. : Prentice-Hall, c1978. xv, 492 p. ; 24 cm. (Prentice-Hall series in sociology) Includes index. Bibliography: p. 454-486. [BL60.W55] 77-16808 ISBN 0-13-773259-7 : 13.95
1. Religion and sociology. 2. United States—Religion. I. Title.

WINTER, Jerry Alan. 301.5'8
Continuities in the sociology of religion : creed, congregation, and community / J. Alan Winter. New York : Harper & Row, c1977. x, 307 p. : ill. ; 25 cm. Includes bibliographies and indexes. [BL60.W56] 76-27674 ISBN 0-06-047158-1 : 11.95
1. Religion and sociology. I. Title.

YINGER, John Milton 261.8
Religion in the struggle for power; a study in the Sociology of religion. New York, Russell & Russell, 1961 [c.1946] 275p. (Duke Univ. Pr. soc. ser., 3) Bibl. 61-13820 6.50
1. Religion and sociology. 2. Church and social Problems. I. Title.

YINGER, John Milton. 201
Religion in the struggle for power; a study in the sociology of religion, by J. Milton Yinger. Durham, N.C., Duke university press, 1946. xix, 275 p. diagr. 23 1/2 cm. (Half-title: Duke university press. Sociological series. H. E. Jensen and C. A. Ellwood, consulting editors) Bibliography: p. [259]-268. [BL60.Y5] 46-3047
1. Religion and sociology. 2. Church and social problems. I. Title.

YINGER, John Milton. 306'.6
Religion in the struggle for power : a study in the sociology or religion / J. Milton Yinger. New York : Arno Press, 1980, c1946. xix, 275 p. ; 24 cm. (Dissertations on sociology) Reprint of the ed. published by Duke University Press, Durham, N.C., in series: Duke University Press sociological series. Includes index. Bibliography: p. [259]-268. [BL60.Y5 1980] 79-9040 ISBN 0-405-13007-4 lib. bdg. : 23.00
1. Religion and sociology. 2. Church and social problems. I. Title. II. Series.

YINGER, John Milton. 201
Religion, society, and the individual; an introduction to the sociology of religion. New York, Macmillan [1957] 655 p. 24 cm. Includes bibliography. [BL60.Y52] 57-8266
1. Religion and sociology. I. Title.

YINGER, John Milton. 261.83
Sociology looks at religion. New York, Macmillan [1963] 192 p. 18 cm. (Macmillan paperbacks, 139) [BL60.Y53] 63-15705
1. Religion and sociology. I. Title.

Religion and sociology—Addresses, essays, lectures.

BELLAH, Robert Neelly, 200.1 1927-
Beyond belief essays on religion in a post-traditional world /Robert N. Bellah New York Harper and Row [1976 c1970] xxii, 298 p.; 20 cm. Includes bibliographical references and index [BL60.B37] ISBN 0-06-060775-0 pbk.: 4.95
1. Religion and sociology—Addresses, essays, lectures. I. Title.
L.C. card no. for original edition: 77-109058.

BELLAH, Robert Neelly, 200'.1 1927-
Beyond belief; essays on religion in a post-traditional world [by] Robert N. Bellah. [1st ed.] New York, Harper & Row [1970] xxi, 298 p. 22 cm. Includes bibliographical references. [BL60.B37] 77-109058 7.95
1. Religion and sociology—Addresses, essays, lectures. I. Title.

CHRISTIANITY and the 261.8'345 *bourgeoisie* / edited by Johann Baptist Metz. New York : Seabury Press, 1979. viii, 126 p. ; 23 cm. (Concilium : Religion in the seventies ; 125) Includes bibliographical references. [BL60.C46 1979] 79-65696 ISBN 0-8164-2233-8 pbk. : 4.95
1. Religion and sociology—Addresses, essays, lectures. 2. Middle classes—Addresses, essays, lectures. I. Metz, Johann Baptist. II. Series: Concilium (New York) ; 125.

CHURCHES and states: 291'.17 the religious institution and modernization, by Victor D. Du Bois [and others] Edited by Kalman H. Silvert. With a foreword by Kenneth W. Thompson. New York, American Universities Field Staff [1967] xiv, 224 p. 24 cm. "This vol. grew out of a conference on 'the religious institution and modernism', sponsored by the American Universities Field Staff and held at Indiana University in October 1966." [BL60.C47] 67-22384
1. Religion and sociology—Addresses, essays, lectures. I. Du Bois, Victor D. II. Silvert, Kalman H., ed. III. American

Universities Field Staff. IV. Title: The religion institution and modernization.

GLOCK, Charles Y., comp. 200
Religion in sociological perspective; essays in the empirical study of religion. Edited by Charles Y. Glock. With contributions by Earl R. Babbie [and others] Belmont, Calif., Wadsworth Pub. Co. [1973] ix, 315 p. 23 cm. (The Wadsworth series in sociology) "From the Research Program in Religion and Society, Survey Research Center, University of California, Berkeley." Includes bibliographical references. [BL60.G553] 72-87021 ISBN 0-534-00216-1 4.95
1. Religion and sociology—Addressses, essays, lectures. I. Title.

HADDEN, Jeffrey K., comp. 301.5'8
Religion in radical transition. Edited by Jeffrey K. Hadden. New Brunswick, N.J., Transaction Books [1973, c1970] ix, 166 p. 20 cm. (Transaction/society book series) [BL60.H26] 74-133305 ISBN 0-87855-567-6. 2.95 (pbk.)
1. Religion and sociology—Addresses, essays, lectures. I. Title.

NEWMAN, William M. 301.5'8
The social meanings of religion : an integrated anthology / William M. Newman. Chicago : Rand McNally, [1974] 373 p. ; 23 cm. Includes bibliographical references and indexes. [BL60.N43] 74-6560 ISBN 0-528-68212-1 pbk. : 5.95
1. Religion and sociology—Addresses, essays, lectures. I. Title.

OTSUKA, Hisao, 1907- 261.8'5
Max Weber on the spirit of capitalism / Otsuka Hisao ; translated by Kondo Masaomi. Tokyo : Institute of Developing Economies, 1976. 95 p. ; 25 cm. (I.D.E. occasional papers series ; no. 13) Includes bibliographical references. [BR115.E3W43513] 76-376652
1. Weber, Max, 1864-1920. Die protestantische Ethik und der Geist des Kapitalismus. 2. Religion and sociology—Addresses, essays, lectures. 3. Christian ethics—Addresses, essays, lectures. 4. Protestantism and capitalism—Addresses, essays, lectures. I. Title. II. Series: Ajia Keizai Kenkyujo, Tokyo. I.D.E. occasional papers series ; no. 13.

THE Religious dimension 301.5'8
: new directions in quantitative research / edited by Robert Wuthnow. New York : Academic Press, c1979. xiv, 376 p. ; 24 cm. Includes bibliographies and index. [BL60.R44] 79-6948 ISBN 0-12-766050-X : 25.00
1. Religion and sociology—Addresses, essays, lectures. I. Wuthnow, Robert.

ROBERTSON, Roland, comp. 301.5'8
Sociology of religion; selected readings. Baltimore, Penguin Books [1969] 473 p. 18 cm. (Penguin modern sociology readings) Bibliography: p. 451-455. [BL60.R6 1969b] 70-11072 2.25
1. Religion and sociology—Addresses, essays, lectures. I. Title.

ROBERTSON, Roland, comp. 301.5'8
Sociology of religion: selected readings. Harmondsworth, Penguin, 1969. 473 p. 19 cm. (Penguin modern sociology readings) (Penguin education.) Includes bibliographies. [BL60.R6] 78-445564 10/-
1. Religion and sociology—Addresses, essays, lectures. I. Title.

Religion and sociology — Case studies.

LENSKI, Gerhard Emmanuel, 1924- 261.8
The religious factor; a sociological study of religion's impact on politics, economics, and family life. Garden City, N.Y., Doubleday, [c.]1961 xvi, 381p. illus., 61-9197 5.95
1. Religion and sociology—Case studies. I. Title.

LENSKI, Gerhard Emmanuel, 1924- 261.8
The religious factor; a sociological study of religion's impact on politics, econimics, and family life. Rev. ed. Garden City, N.Y., Doubleday [c.1961, 1963] xvi, 414p. 18cm. (Anchor bk., A337) Bibl. 1.45 pap.,
1. Religion and sociology—Case studies. I. Title.

LENSKI, Gerhard Emmanuel, 1924-
The religious factor; a sociological study of religion's impact on politics, economics, and family life. Rev. ed. Garden City, N.Y., Doubleday [1963] xvi, 414 p. (Doubleday Anchor books, A337) Bibliographical footnotes. 63-26383
1. Religion and sociology — Case studies. I. Title.

LENSKI, Gerhard Emmanuel, 1924- 261.8
The religious factor : a sociological study of religion's impact on politics, economics, and family life / by Gerhard Lenski. Westport, Conn. : Greenwood Press, [1977, c1961] p. cm. Reprint of the 1st ed. published by Doubleday, Garden City, N.Y. Includes bibliographical references and indexes. [BL60.L44 1977] 77-1275 ISBN 0-8371-9506-3 lib.bdg. : 21.75
1. Religion and sociology—Case studies. 2. Detroit—Religion—Case studies. I. Title.

Religion and sociology—Collections.

BIRNBAUM, Norman, comp. 201
Sociology and religion; a book of readings [by] Norman Birnbaum [and] Gertrud Lenzer. Englewood Cliffs, N.J., Prentice-Hall [1969] x, 452 p. 24 cm. Includes bibliographical references. [BL60.B48] 68-28878 7.95
1. Religion and sociology—Collections. I. Lenzer, Gertrud, joint comp. II. Title.

BROCKMAN, Norbert, comp. 261.8'3
Contemporary religion and social responsibility. Edited by Norbert Brockman [and] Nicholas Piediscalzi. New York, Alba House [1973] xvi, 366 p. 23 cm. Includes bibliographical references. [BL60.B68] 72-11982 ISBN 0-8189-0257-4 4.95 (pbk.)
1. Religion and sociology—Collections. 2. Social ethics—Collections. I. Piediscalzi, Nicholas, joint comp. II. Title.

BROTHERS, Joan, 1938- ed. 261'.08
Readings in the sociology of religion. [1st ed.] Oxford, New York, Pergamon Press [1967] x, 239 p. 20 cm. (The Commonwealth and international library. Readings in sociology) Includes bibliographical references. [BL60.B7 1967] 66-29582
1. Religion and sociology—Collections. I. Title.

FAULKNER, Joseph E., comp. 301.5'8
Religion's influence in contemporary society; readings in the sociology of religion. Edited by Joseph E. Faulkner. Columbus, Ohio, C. E. Merrill Pub. Co. [1972] xiv, 578 p. 24 cm. (Merrill sociology series) Includes bibliographical references. [BL60.F38] 72-76586 ISBN 0-675-09105-5
1. Religion and sociology—Collections. I. Title.

O'DEA, Thomas F., comp. 261
Readings on the sociology of religion [compiled by] Thomas F. O'Dea [and] Janet K. O'Dea. Englewood Cliffs, N.J., Prentice-Hall [1973] xi, 244 p. illus. 23 cm. (Readings in modern sociology series) Includes bibliographical references. [BL60.O27] 72-8593 ISBN 0-13-761940-5 5.95
1. Religion and sociology—Collections. I. O'Dea, Janet K., joint author. II. Title.

SCHNEIDER, Louis, 1915- ed. 201
Religion, culture, and society; a reader in the sociology of religion. New York, Wiley [1964] xvii, 663 p. fold. map. 25 cm. Includes bibliographical references. [BL60.S3] 64-23859
1. Religion and sociology—Collections. I. Title.

Religion and sociology—History.

BEIDELMAN, Thomas O. 200'.92'4 B
W. Robertson Smith and the sociological study of religion / T. O. Beidelman ; with a foreword by E. E. Evans-Pritchard. Chicago : University of Chicago Press, 1975. xiv, 92 p. ; 23 cm. Bibliography: p. 69-92. [BX9225.S55B46] 74-7568 ISBN 0-226-04158-1 : 8.95 pbk. : 1.95
1. Smith, William Robertson, 1846-1894. 2. Religion and sociology—History. I. Title.

STONE, Ronald H. 261.8'092'4
Paul Tillich's radical social thought / Ronald H. Stone. Atlanta : John Knox Press, c1980. 180 p. ; 20 cm. Includes bibliographical references and index. [BX4827.T53S76] 79-87740 ISBN 0-8042-0679-1 : 6.95
1. Tillich, Paul, 1886-1965. 2. Religion and sociology—History. I. Title.

Religion and sociology—History—Addresses, essays, lectures.

BROWN, Peter Robert Lamont. 270.2'08
Religion and society in the age of Saint Augustine [by] Peter Brown. [1st U.S. ed.] New York, Harper & Row [1972] 351 p. 23 cm. Includes bibliographical references. [BL60.B75 1972b] 70-181609 ISBN 0-06-010554-2 12.00
1. Augustinus, Aurelius, Saint, Bp. of Hippo—Sociology—Addresses, essays, lectures. 2. Religion and sociology—History—Addresses, essays, lectures. I. Title.

Religion and sociology—History—Congresses.

CENTER for Hermeneutical Studies in Hellenistic and Modern Culture. 261.83
A social context to the religious crisis of the third century A.D. : protocol of the fourteenth colloquy, 9 February 1975 / The Center for Hermeneutical Studies in Hellenistic and Modern Culture ; Peter R. L. Brown. Berkeley, CA : The Center, c1975. 52 p. ; 21 cm. (Protocol series of the colloquies of the Center for Hermeneutical Studies in Hellenistic and Modern Culture ; no. 14 ISSN 0098-0900s) Includes bibliographical references..[BL60.C43 1975] 75-38688IISBN 0-89242-013-8XV
1. Religion and sociology—History—Congresses. 2. Sociology, Christian—Early church, ca. 30-600—Congresses. I. Brown, Peter Robert Lamont. II. Title. III. Series: Center for Hermeneutical Studies in Hellenistic and Modern Culture. Protocol series of the colloquies ; no. 14.

Religion and state.

CARAYON, Jean. 261.7
Essai sur les rapports du pouvoir politique et du pouvoir religieux chez Montesquieu. New York, B. Franklin [1973] p. Reprint of the 1903 ed. Bibliography: p. [JC179.M8C25 1973] 75-168919 ISBN 0-8337-4024-5
1. Montesquieu, Charles Louis de Secondat, baron de La Brede et de, 1689-1755—Political science. 2. Religion and state. I. Title.

Religion and state—Africa.

PAYNE, Denis, ed. 209.6
African independence and Christian freedom; addresses delivered at Makerere University College, Uganda, in 1962. London, Oxford University Press, 1965. 89 p. 19 cm. (A Three crowns book) Includes bibliographical references. [BR1360.P3] 66-5878
1. Religion and state—Africa. 2. Christianity—Africa. I. Title.

Religion and state—India.

BLOOMFIELD, Maurice, 1855
... The religion of the Veda, the ancient religion of India (from Big-Veda to Upanishads) by Maurice Bloomfield ... New York and London, G. P. Putnam's sons, 1908. xv, 300 p. 21 cm. (American lectures on the history of religions. Seventh series--1906-1907) 8-5569
I. Title.

LUTHERA, Ved Prakash 342.5401
The concept of the secular state and India. [New York] Oxford [1965, c.1964] ix, 187p. 23cm. Bibl. [BL2003.L8] SA64 3.35
1. Religion and state—India. I. Title.

Religion and state—India—History

NIZAMI, Khaliq Ahmad 297
Some aspects of religion and politics in India during the thirteenth century. Foreword by C. Collin Davies. Introd. by Mohd Habib. Pub. for the Dept. of Hist., Aligarh Muslim Univ. New York, Asia House [dist. Taplinger, 1965, c.1961] xxii, iv, 421p. illus. 25cm. Bibl. [BL2003.N5] SA65 8.75
1. Religion and state—India—Hist. 2. I sIslam—India—Hist. I. Aligarh, India. Muslim University. Dept. of History. II. Title.

NIZAMI, Khaliq Ahmad. 297
Some aspects of religion and politics in India during the thirteenth century. With a foreword by C. Collin Davies, & an introd. by Mohd. Habib. Bombay, New York, Asia Pub. House [c1961] xxii, iv, 421 p. illus. 25 cm. Label mounted on t.p.: Published for the Dept. of History, Allgarh Muslim University. Bibliography: p. 381-402. [BL2003.N5] S A
1. Religion and state — India — Hist. 2. Islam and state — India — Hist. 3. Islam — India — Hist. I. Agigarh, India. Muslim University. Dept. of History. II. Title.

Religion and state—Israel.

ASCHAM, John Bayne, 1873- 296
... The religion of Israel, by John Bayne Ascham. New York, Cincinnati, The Abingdon press [c1918] 239 p. illus. (map) 19 cm. (Kingdom of God series, ed. by H. H. Meyer and D. G. Downey) Bibliography at end of each chapter. [BM155.A8] 18-9792
I. Title.

BARTON, George Aaron, 1859- 296
The religion of Israel, by George A. Barton ... New York, The Macmillan company, 1918. 8 p. l., 289 p. 21 cm. (Half-title: Religious science and literature series, ed. by E. H. Sneath) "Topics for further study" at end of each chapter. [BM165.B3] 18-18346
I. Title.

MARMORSTEIN, Emile. 322'.1'095694
Heaven at Bay; the Jewish Kulturkampf in the Holy Land. London, New York, Oxford University Press, 1969. xi, 215 p. 23 cm. (Middle Eastern monographs 10) Bibliography: p. 211-212. [BM390.M3] 76-444963 6.25
1. Religion and state—Israel. 2. Judaism—Israel. I. Title. II. Series.

Religion and state—Pakistan.

BINDER, Leonard 297.09547
Religion and politics in Pakistan. Berkeley, Univ. of California Press [c.]1961. cxviii, 440p. Bibl. 61-7537 7.50
1. Religion and state—Pakistan. 2. Pakistan—Constitutional history. I. Title.

Religion and state—South Asia.

SMITH, Donald Eugene, 1927- ed. 291.1770954
South Asian politics and religion. Princeton, N. J., Princeton, 1966. xii, 563p. 25cm. Articles contributed to a seminar held in Colombo, Ceylon, in July 1964, which was sponsored by the Council on Religion and Intl. Affairs. Bibl. [BL65.S8S6] 66-8738 15.00
1. Religion and state—South Asia. I. Council on Religion and International Affairs. II. Title.

Religion and state—United States

BOONE, Abbott 261.7
Our hypocritical new national motto: In God we trust; a study of the congressional substitution for E pluribus unum and its theological implications. New York, Expostion [c.1963] 114p. 21cm. 62-21054 3.00
1. Religion and state—U.S. 2. Religion—Controversial literature. 3. Mottoes. I. Title.

BOONE, Abbott. 261.7
Our hypocritical new national motto: In God we trust; a study of the congressional substitution for E pluribus unum and its theological implications. [1st ed.] New York, Exposition Press [1963] 114 p. 21 cm. [BL2775.2.B6] 62-21054
1. Religion and state — U.S. 2. Religion — Controversial literature. 3. Mottoes. I. Title.

HARRISON, George Leib, plaintiff, 1811-1885.
Report of Harrison et al. vs. St. Mark's church, Philadelphia. A bill to restrain the ringing of bells so as to cause a nuisance to the occupants of the dwellings in the immediate vicinity of the church. In the Court of common pleas, no.2. In Equity. Before Hare, P.J. and Mitchell, associate j., Philadelphia, February, 1877. [Philadelphia] Printed by Allen, Lane & Scott [187-?] x, 491 p. front. (fold. plan) 23 1/2 cm. On cover: Case St. Mark's church, Philadelphia, to regulate ringing of bells. "Contains all the pleadings and depositions used in the cause, also all documents submitted to the court for their decision together with reports of the arguments of counsel and the opinion and decree of the court, with the exception of summaries of the plaintiff's affidavits prepared by both sides." 44-29239
I. Philadelphia. St. Mark's church, defendant. II. Pennsylvania. Court of common pleas (Philadelphia co.) III. Title. IV. Title: Ringing of bells.

JONES, Cave, 1769-1829, plaintiff.
Report of the case between the Rev. Cave Jones, and The recor and inhabitants of the city of New-York in communion of the Protestant episcopal church in the state of New-York. As the same was argued before the five judges of the Supreme court of the state of New-York--arbitrators to whom the difference between the parties were referred a rule of the said court. By Matthew L. Davis. New-York: Printed by William A. Davis. 1813. vii, 587, [1] p. 24 cm. "Cave Jones ... commenced an action in the Supreme court ... to recover his salary and compensation as an assistant minister in the employ and service of the said Rector and inhabitants."--p. [561] 33-39044
I. New York. Trinity church, defendant. II. Davis, Matthew Livingston, 1773-1850, reporter. III. New York (State) Supreme court. IV. Title.

JORSTAD, Erling, 1930- 320.5'2
The politics of doomsday; fundamentalists of the Far Right. Nashville, Abingdon Press [1970] 190 p. 24 cm. Includes bibliographical references. [BR516.P7J73] 70-112332 ISBN 0-687-31730-4 4.95
1. Religion and state—United States. 2. Fundamentalism. 3. United States—Politics and government—1945- 4. Christianity and politics. I. Title.

*SWEET, William Warren. 261.7'0973
The story of religion in America. Grand Rapids, Mich., Baker Book House [1973, c1950] ix, 492 p, 22 cm. (Twin brooks series) [BL65.S8] ISBN 0-8010-8019-3 4.95 (pbk.)
1. Religion and state.—U.S. I. Title.

Religion and the humanities—Addresses, essays, lectures.

HUNTER, Howard. 200
Humanities, religion, and the arts tomorrow. Edited by Howard Hunter. New York, Holt, Rinehart and Winston [1972] vii, 247 p. illus. 24 cm. Includes bibliographical references. [BL65.H8H85] 77-186568 ISBN 0-03-085391-5
1. Religion and the humanities—Addresses, essays, lectures. I. Title.

Religion—Anecdotes, facetiae, satire, etc.

BARTON, William Eleazar, 1861-
The wit and wisdom of Safed the sage, by William E. Barton. Boston, Chicago, The Pilgrim press [c1919] x, 134 p. 19 cm. [PS1074.B38W55 1919] 19-18171
I. Title.

BARTON, William Eleazar, 1861-
The wit and wisdom of Safed the sage, by William E. Barton. Boston, Chicago, The Pilgrim press [c1919] x, 134 p. 19 cm. [PS1074.B38W55 1919] 19-18171
I. Title.

CANDLER, Warren Akin bp., 1857-1941. 287
Wit and wisdom of Warren Akin Candler, ed, by Elam Franklin Dempsey, with and introduction by Rev. Andrew J. Lamar ... Nashville, Tenn., Dallas, Tex. [etc.] Publishing house of the M.E. church, South, Smith & Lamar, agents, 1922. 285 p. front., plates, ports. 20 cm. [BX8217.C35] 22-6944
I. Dempsey, Elam Franklin, 1878-ed. II. Title.

CANDLER, Warren Akin bp., 1857-1941. 287
Wit and wisdom of Warren Akin Candler, ed, by Elam Franklin Dempsey, with and introduction by Rev. Andrew J. Lamar ... Nashville, Tenn., Dallas, Tex. [etc.] Publishing house of the M.E. church, South, Smith & Lamar, agents, 1922. 285 p. front., plates, ports. 20 cm. [BX8217.C35] 22-6944
I. Dempsey, Elam Franklin, 1878-ed. II. Title.

GRAHAM, William Franklin, 1918- 243
The wit and wisdom of Billy Graham. Edited and compiled by Bill Adler. New York, Random House [1967] 165 p. 22 cm. [BV3797.G675] 66-21481
I. Adler, Bill, ed. II. Title.

GRAHAM, William Franklin, 1918- 243
The wit and wisdom of Billy Graham. Edited and compiled by Bill Adler. New York, Random House [1967] 165 p. 22 cm. [BV3797.G675] 66-21481
I. Adler, Bill, ed. II. Title.

HOWARD, J. Freeman.
Wit and wisdom of Christianity, by J. Freeman Howard ... Chicago, T. H. Devereaux & co. [1904] 159 p. 16 cm. 4-24537
I. Title.

HOWARD, J. Freeman.
Wit and wisdom of Christianity, by J. Freeman Howard ... Chicago, T. H. Devereaux & co. [1904] 159 p. 16 cm. 4-24537
I. Title.

MARTY, Martin E., 1928- 208.8
Pen-ultimates: comment on the folk religions of America, by Martin E. Marty, Dean G. Peerman. New York, Holt [c.1960-1963] 110p. 20cm. 63-11876 2.95 bds.,
1. Religion—Anecdotes, facetiae, satire, etc. I. Peerman, Dean G., joint author. II. Title.

RICHTER, Johann Paul Friedrich, 1863-1825.
Wit, wisdom, and philosophy of Jean Paul Fred. Richter; ed. by Giles P. Hawley. New York, Funk & Wagnalls, 1884. xix, [21]-228 p. 19 1/2 cm. (On cover: standard library, no. 117) [PT2455.A15H3] 12-38038
I. Hawley, Giles P. II. Title.

RICHTER, Johann Paul Friedrich, 1863-1825.
Wit, wisdom, and philosophy of Jean Paul Fred. Richter; ed. by Giles P. Hawley. New York, Funk & Wagnalls, 1884. xix, [21]-228 p. 19 1/2 cm. (On cover: standard library, no. 117) [PT2455.A15H3] 12-38038
I. Hawley, Giles P. II. Title.

SCHWEITZER, Albert, 1875- 208.1
The wit and wisdom of Albert Schweitzer; edited, with an introd., by Charles R. Joy. Boston, Beacon Press, 1949. vii, 104 p. 25 cm. Bibliography: p. 101-104. [B3329.S52E5 1949] 49-11511
I. Joy, Charles Rhind, 1885- ed. II. Title.

SCHWEITZER, Albert, 1875- 208.1
The wit and wisdom of Albert Schweitzer; edited, with an introd., by Charles R. Joy. Boston, Beacon Press, 1949. vii, 104 p. 25 cm. Bibliography: p. 101-104. [B3329.S52E5 1949] 49-11511
I. Joy, Charles Rhind, 1885- ed. II. Title.

SHEEN, Fulton John, Bp., 1895- 081
The wit and wisdom of Bishop Fulton J. Sheen. Edited by Bill Adler. Englewood Cliffs, N.J., Prentice-Hall [1968] xviii, 172 p. 22 cm. [BX4705.S612A25] 68-27798 3.95
I. Adler, Bill, ed. II. Title.

SHEEN, Fulton John, Bp., 1895- 081
The wit and wisdom of Bishop Fulton J. Sheen. Edited by Bill Adler. Englewood Cliffs, N.J., Prentice-Hall [1968] xviii, 172 p. 22 cm. [BX4705.S612A25] 68-27798 3.95
I. Adler, Bill, ed. II. Title.

SHEEN, Fulton John, Bp., 1895- 081
The wit and wisdom of Bishop Fulton J. Sheen, edited by Bill Adler. Garden City, N.Y., Image Books [1969] 188 p. 18 cm. [BX4705.S612A25 1969] 78-82959 0.95
I. Adler, Bill, ed. II. Title.

SHEEN, Fulton John, Bp., 1895- 081
The wit and wisdom of Bishop Fulton J. Sheen, edited by Bill Adler. Garden City, N.Y., Image Books [1969] 188 p. 18 cm. [BX4705.S612A25 1969] 78-82959 0.95
I. Adler, Bill, ed. II. Title.

SMITH, Sydney, 1771-1845.
Wit and wisdom of the Rev. Sydney Smith. Being selections froms his writings and passages of his letters and table talk, with a biographical memoir and notes by Evert A. Duyckink. New York, Renfield, 1856. 458 p. front. (port.) fold. facism. 19 cm. "Biographical memoir." p. [9]-104. [PR5456.D6 1856] 29-2293
I. Duyckink, Evert Augustus, 1816-1878, ed. II. Title.

SMITH, Sydney, 1771-1845.
Wit and wisdom of the Rev. Sydney Smith. Being selections froms his writings and passages of his letters and table talk, with a biographical memoir and notes by Evert A. Duyckink. New York, Renfield, 1856. 458 p. front. (port.) fold. facism. 19 cm. "Biographical memoir." p. [9]-104. [PR5456.D6 1856] 29-2293
I. Duyckink, Evert Augustus, 1816-1878, ed. II. Title.

SMITH, Sydney, 1771-1845.
Wit and wisdon of the Rev. Sydney Smith, being selections from his writings and passages of his letters and table-talk, with a biographical memoir and notes by Everet A. Duyckink and a prefatory memior of E. A. Duyckinck by R. H. Stoddard. New York, A. C. Armstrong & son, 1880. 1 p. l., v, [2], 9-458 p. front. (port.) 21 cm. "Bibliographical memoir": p. [9]-164. [PR5456.D8 1880] 29-2294
I. Duyckinck, Evert Augustus, 1816-1878, ed. II. Stoddard, Richard Henry, 1825-1903 III. Title.

SMITH, Sydney, 1771-1845.
Wit and wisdon of the Rev. Sydney Smith, being selections from his writings and passages of his letters and table-talk, with a biographical memoir and notes by Everet A. Duyckink and a prefatory memior of E. A. Duyckinck by R. H. Stoddard. New York, A. C. Armstrong & son, 1880. 1 p. l., v, [2], 9-458 p. front. (port.) 21 cm. "Bibliographical memoir": p. [9]-164. [PR5456.D8 1880] 29-2294
I. Duyckinck, Evert Augustus, 1816-1878, ed. II. Stoddard, Richard Henry, 1825-1903 III. Title.

VAN DYKE, Dick. 202'.07
Altar egos. Westwood, N.J., Revell [1967] 1v. (in paged ports. 16x220 cm. [PN6231.R4V3] 67-28866 1.00 pap.,
1. Religion—Anecdotes, facetiae, satire, etc. I. Title.

WAGONER, Walter D., comp. 200'.2'07
Bittersweet grace; a treasury of twentieth-century religious satire, edited by Walter D. Wagoner. Cleveland, World Pub. Co. [1967] x, 181 p. 22 cm. Bibliography: p. 179-181. [BL50.W2] 67-11437
1. Religion—Anecdotes, facetiae, satire, etc. I. Title.

Religion, Assyro-Babylonian.

JASTROW, Morris, 1861-1921. 299.219
... The religion of Babylonia and Assyria, by Morris Jastrow ... Boston, Ginn & company, 1898. xii p., 1 l., 780 p. map. 22 cm. (Handbooks on the history of religions. [ii]) Bibliography: p. [703]-738. [BL1620.J3] 98-607
1. Religion, Assyro-Babylonian. 2. Omens. 3. Cultus—Assyro-Babylonian. I. Title.

Religion—Bibliography

*BARBER, Cyril J. 016.20
The minister's library / Cyril J. Barber. Grand Rapids : Baker Book House, 1976. 106p. ; 26 cm. (Periodic supplement ; 1) Includes index. [Z7751] ISBN 0-8010-0647-3 pbk. : 2.95.
1. Religion-Bibliography. I. Title.

BERKOWITZ, Morris I. 016.2
Social scientific studies of religion: a bibliography, by Morris I. Berkowitz and J. Edmund Johnson. [Pittsburgh] University of Pittsburgh Press [1967] xvii, 258 p. 29 cm. [Z7751.B47] 67-18692
1. Religion—Bibliography. I. Johnson, J. Edmund, joint author. II. Title.

BODINGTON, Charles, 1836-1918.
Books on devotion, by the Rev. Charles Bodington ... London, New York, and Bombay, Longmans, Green, and co., 1903. xviii p. 1l., 319 p. 19 1/2 cm. (Half-title: The Oxford library of practical theology ...) Title vignette. "Appendix iii: ...List of...devotional books...reprinted from the 'Bibliotheca sacerdotalis' of the Priest's prayer book, with the permission of the Rev. J. Edward Vauz": p. 311-316. [BV207.B6] 3-12785
I. Title.

DIEHL, Katharine Smith 016.2
Religions, mythologies, folklores: an annotated bibliography. 2d ed. New York, Scarecrow Pr. [c.]1962. 573p. 62-16003 12.50
1. Religion—Bibl. 2. Mythology—Bibl. 3. Folk-lore—Bibl. I. Title.

DIEHL, Katharine Smith. 016.2
Religions, mythologies, folklores: an annotated bibliography. New Brunswick, N. J., Scarecrow Press, 1956. 315p. 23cm. Classified by subject, with author index. [Z7751.D54] 56-1859
1. Religion—Bibl. 2. Mythology—Bibl. 3. Folk-lore—Bibl. I. Title.

FOUST, Roscoe T
Books for the church library, Compiled for the Church Library Dept. of Christian herald. [New York? 1964] 57 p. 22 cm. Cover title.
1. Religion — Bibl. 2. Libraries, Church. I. Title.

FOUST, Roscoe T 016.0162
Books for the church library, Compiled for the Church Library Dept. of Christian herald. [New York? 1964] 57 p. 22 cm. Cover title. [Z7751.F65] 64-4413
1. Religion — Bibl. 2. Libraries, Church. I. Christian herald (New York, 1878-) Church Library Dept. II. Title.

HALL, Manly Palmer, 1901- 016.2
Great books on religion and esoteric philosophy. With a bibl. of related material selected from the writings of Manly P. Hall. Los Angeles Angeles. Philosophical Res. [1966] 85p. illus. 23cm. [Z7751.H3] 66-2943 1.50 pap.,
1. Religion—Bibl. 2. Philosophy—Bibl. 3. Occult sciences—Bibl. I. Title.

JORDAN, Louis Henry, 1855- 016.
Comparative religion, its adjuncts and allies, by Louis Henry Jordan ... London, New York [etc.] H. Milford, Oxford university press, 1915. xxxii, 574 p., 1 l. 23 cm. [Z7751.J75] A 16
1. Religion—Bibliography. 2. Religions—Bibliography. I. Title.

KARPINSKI, Leszek M. 016.2
The religious life of man : guide to basic literature / compiled by Leszek M. Karpinski. Metuchen, N.J. : Scarecrow Press, 1978. xx, 399 p. ; 23 cm. Includes indexes. [Z7751.K36] [BL41] 77-19338 ISBN 0-8108-1110-3 : 16.00

1. Religion—Bibliography. I. Title.

NATIONAL Library Service 016.2
for the Blind and Physically Handicapped.
Religion : a selected list of books that have appeared in Talking book topics and Braille book review / [National Library Service for the Blind and Physically Handicapped, Library of Congress]. Washington : Library of Congress, 1980 68 p. ; 28 cm. Includes index. [Z7751.N35 1979] [BL48] 79-14952 ISBN 0-8444-0286-9 : 6.60
1. Religion—Bibliography. 2. Blind, Books For the—Bibliography. 3. Talking books—Bibliography. I. Talking book topics. II. Braille book review. III. Title.

RELIGIONS, mythologies, folklores: an annotated bibliography. New York, Scarecrow Press, 1956. 315p. 23cm. Classified by subject, with author index.
1. Religion—Bibl. 2. Mythology—Bibl. 3. Folk-lore—Bibl. I. Diehl, Katharine Smith.

RICHARDSON, Ernest Cushing, 016.
1860-1939.
An alphabetical subject index and index encyclopaedia to periodical articles on religion, 1890-1899; compiled and edited by Ernest Cushing Richardson with the co-operation of Charles S. Thayer, William C. Hawks, Paul Martin, and various members of the faculty of the Hartford theological seminary, and some help from A. D. Savage, Solon Librescot and many others. New York, For the Hartford seminary press by C. Scribner's sons; [etc., etc., c1907] xiii, 1168 p. 24 1/2 cm. [Z7753.R55] 8-2949
1. Religion—Bibl. 2. Theology—Bibl. 3. Indexes. I. Thayer, Charles Snow, 1865- joint comp. II. Hawks, William Cushman, 1862-1905, joint comp. III. Martin, Paul, 1862- joint comp. IV. Title.

RICHARDSON, Ernest Cushing, 016.
1860-1939.
Periodical articles on religion, 1890-1899, comp. and ed., by Ernest Cushing Richardson, with the co-operation of Charles S. Thayer, William C. Hawks, Paul Martin, and various members of the faculty of the Hartford theological seminary, and some help from A. D. Savage, Solon Librescot and many others. Author index. New York, For the Hartford seminary press by C. Scribner's sons; [etc., etc., c1911] 4 p. l., 876 p. 24 1/2 cm. [Z7753.R55A] 11-18734
1. Religion—Bibl. 2. Theology—Bibl. 3. Indexes. I. Thayer, Charles Snow, 1865- II. Hawks, William Cushman, 1862-1905. III. Martin, Paul, 1862- IV. Title.

SAYRE, John L., 1924- 016.2
An index of Festschriften in religion in the Graduate Seminary Library of Phillips University. Compiled by John L. Sayre and Roberta Hamburger. Enid, Okla., Haymaker Press, 1970. iv, 121 p. 28 cm. [Z7751.S38] 73-32108
1. Religion—Bibliography. 2. Festschriften—Bibliography. I. Hamburger, Roberta, joint author. II. Phillips University, Enid, Okla. Graduate Seminary. Library. III. Title.

SOUTHERN Baptist 016.0162
Convention. Historical Commission.
Index of graduate theses in Baptist theological seminaries, 1894-1962. Nashville, 1963. v l., 182 p. 28 cm. [Z7751.S67] 66-93695
1. Religion—Bibliography. 2. Dissertations, Academic—United States—Bibliography. I. Title.

TROSS, Joseph Samuel 248
Nathaniel.
This thing called religion, by J. S. Nathaniel Tross ... Charlotte, N.C., 1934. xviii, 21-132 p., 1 l. 19 cm. "A brief bibliography": p. 128-132. [BR125.T76] 34-33849
I. Title.

TURNER, Harold W. 016.2
Bibliography of new religious movements in primal societies / Harold W. Turner. Boston : G. K. Hall, c1977- v, ; 25 cm. (Bibliographies and guides in African studies) Includes index. Contents.Contents.—v. 1. Black Africa. [Z7833.T87] [BL80] 77-4732 ISBN 0-8161-7927-1 lib.bdg. : 25.00

1. Religion—Bibliography. 2. Religion, Primitive—Bibliography. I. Title. II. Series.

Religion-Bibliography-Catalogues.

*BILL, E.G.W. 013'.942
A catalogue of manuscripts in Lambeth Palace Library / E.G.W. Bill. Oxford : Clarendon Press, 1976. 379p. ; 22 cm. Includes index. [Z2029] ISBN 0-19-920079-3 : 55.00
1. Religion-Bibliography-Catalogues. I. Title.
Distributed by Oxford University Press, New York.

Religion—Biography.

AKENS, David. 291.6 B
World's greatest leaders : the Akens book of supernatural records / by David Akens. Huntsville, Ala. : Strode Publishers, c1980. 192 p. : ill. ; 23 cm. [BL72.A37] 19 80-52087 ISBN 0-87397-181-7 (pbk.) : 4.95
1. Religion—Biography. 2. Psychical research—Biography. I. Title.

ARCHIBALD, Warren 933.973
Seymour.
Horace Bushnell, by Warren Seymour Archibald. Hartford, Conn., E.V. Mitchell, 1930. 5 p. l., 156 p. 19 1/2 cm. [BX7360.B9A7] 31-11813
I. Bushnell, Horace, 1903-1976. II. Title.

BOYD, Robert, 1792-
Personal memoirs: together with a discussion upon the hardships and sufferings of itinerant life; and also a discourse upon the pastoral relation. By Rev. Robert Boyd ... Cincinnati, Printed at the Methodist book concern, 1867. 228 p. front. (port.) 16 cm. 6-17631
I. Title.

CHAUCER, Geoffrey, d. 1400.
ABC., called La priere de Nostre Dame, made, as some say, at the request of Blanche, Duchess of Lancaster, as a prayer for her private use, being a woman in her religion very devout. San Francisco, Grabhorn-Hoyem, 1967. 1 v. (unpaged) 18 cm. 68-89765
I. Title. II. Title: La priere de Nostre Dame.

CHRISTLIKE Christian 248.42
(The) by an unknown Christian. Grand Rapids, Mich., Zondervan [1962] 144p. 21cm. 1.95 bds.,

COOKE, Harriet B Mrs. 923.773
b.1786?
Memories of my life work. The autobiography of Mrs. Harriet B. Cooke ... New York, R. Carter & brothers, 1858. viii, [9]-356 p. front. (port.) 20 c. [BR1725.C67A3] 37-31950
I. Title.

DAUGHERTY, Edgar Fay. 922.673
A Hoosier parson; his boosts and bumps (an apologia promea vita) Boston, Meador [1951] 224 p. illus. 21 cm. [BX7343.D27A3] 51-7594
I. Title.

DE MONBRUN, Sarah Ann, 1861- 922
1912.
Honey out of the rock, by Sallie De Monbrun ... Elk City, Kan., God's messenger publishing co. [1912] 193 p. front., ports. 20 cm. Autobiography. Introduction signed: G. W. Hood. [BR1725.D4A3] 37-36765
I. Hood, George W., ed. II. Title.

DURAND, Silas Horton, 1833- 230.
1918.
Fragments; autobiography and later writings, by Silas H. Durand. Philadelphia, The Biddle press, 1920. 2 p. l., 353 p. front., plates, ports. 24 cm. [BX6387.D8] 20-18183
I. Title.

[FLANDERS, George Truesdell] 230
Life's problems, here and hereafter; an autobiography. Boston, Cupples and Hurd, 1887. vi, [4], [3]-317 p. 18 1/2 cm. [BT78.F5] 12-32200
I. Title.

GANSFORT, Johan Wessel, 204
1420?-1489.
Wessel Gansfort, life and writings by Edward Waite Miller ... Principal works tr. by Jared Waterbury Scudder ... New York and London, G. P. Putnam's sons, 1917. 2 v. fronts., plates, ports., plan, facsims. 23 1/2 cm. "This work is published as Special volume number one [and] two in the Papers of the American society of church history." "Bibliography by Hardenberg": v. 2, p. 317-344. [BX890.G3] 18-2731
I. Miller, Edward Waite. II. Scudder, Jared Waterbury, tr. III. Hardenberg, Albert Rizaeus, 1510-1574. IV. Title.

GOODPASTURE, John Ridley.
The hope of his calling; or, The anointed life. Nashville, The Cumberland press, 1899. ix, 174 p. 12 degree. Oct
I. Title.

GRANT, Perley Cummings 254
The prophet of Calvary church. New York, Vantage [c.1962] 142p. 21cm. 3.00 bds.,
I. Title.

HORATIUS Bonar, D. D.; 922.541
a memorial. New York, R. Carter & brothers, 1889. 116 p. front. (mounted port.) 19 1/2 cm. Printed in Great Britain. [BX9225.B58H6] 32-92
I. Bonar, Horatius, 1808-1889.
Contents omitted.

KIRKE, Sarah Maria, 1827-1913.
The life of one of God's saints; notes by the way, or glimpses of a busy life from mss. of Sister Sarah (Sarah Maria Kirke) comp. and ed. by a kinsman, with an introduction by the Reverend Harrisson B. Wright ... Milwaukee, The Young churchman co.; [etc., etc.] 1915. xiii, 174 p. illus., 2 port. (incl. front.) plates, facsims. 19 cm. 15-7206 1.25
I. Title.

LONG, Mason, b.1842. 248
The life of Mason Long, the converted gambler. Being a record of his experience as a white slave; a soldier in the Union army; a professional gambler; a patron of the turf; a variety theater and minstrel manager; and, finally, a convert to the Murphy cause, and to the gospel of Christ. Written by himself. With a portrait, and six illustrations. Chicago, Donnelley, Loyd & co., printers, 1878. 256 (i.e. 254) p. incl. front., plates. pl. 19 cm. [BV4935.L6A3 1878] 44-13748
I. Title.

LONG, Mason, 1842- 248'.2'0924
1903.
The life of Mason Long, the converted gambler. Being a record of his experience as a white slave; a soldier in the Union Army; a professional gambler; a patron of the turf; a variety theater and minstrel manager; and, finally, a convert to the Murphy cause and to the Gospel of Christ. 4th ed. Fort Wayne, Ind., 1883. 280p. illus., ports. 18cm. [BV4935.L6A3 1883] 59-58984
I. Title.

MEMORIES of Lottie. 922
By a pastor. New York, The American tract society [1863] 128 p. front. (port.) 16 cm. [BR1715.Z9M4] 37-21305
I. American tract society. II. A pastor.

MILLER, Esther.
A prophet of the real, by Esther Miller ... New York, J. F. Taylor & company, 1902. 2 p. l., 269 p. front., pl. 20 cm. 2-28597
I. Title.

MOLZAHN, Kurt Emil Bruno. 922.473
Prisoner of war. Philadelphia, Muhlenberg Press [1962] 251p. 20cm. Autobiographical. [BX8080.M 556A3] 62-8203
I. Title.

MOODY, Granville, 1812- 922.773
1887.
A life's retrospect. Autobiography of Rev. Granville Moody ... Edited by Rev. Sylvester Weeks ... Cincinnati, Cranston and Stowe; New York, Hunt and Eaton, 1890. 486 p. front. (port.) 20 cm. [BX8495.M55A3] 37-15234
I. Weeks, Sylvester, 1836-1921, ed. II. Title.

POTTER, Charles Francis, 922.8173
1885-1962.
The preacher and I, an autobiography. New York, Crown Publishers [1951] 429 p. 22 cm. [BX9869.P74A3] 51-12006
I. Title.

SCHNITTKIND, Henry Thomas, 922
1888-
Living biographies of religious leaders, by Henry Thomas [pseud.) and Dana Lee Thomas [pseud.) Garden City, N.Y., Perma Giants [1950, c1942] viii, 297 p. 22 cm. [BL72.S37 1950] 51-30711
1. Religious — Biog. I. Schnittkind, Dana Arnold, 1918- joint author. II. Title.

TROLLOPE, Anthony, 1815-1882.
Framley parsonage, by Anthony Trollope ... Philadelphia, Gebbie & company, 1900. 2 v. fronts., plates. 21 1/2 cm. (Half-title: Collector's edition. The writings of Anthony Trollope. v. 6-7) "Limited to two hundred and fifty copies." [PR5680.F00 vol. 6-7] 1-29599
I. Title.

TROLLOPE, Anthony, 1815-1882.
Framley parsonage, by Anthony Trollope. London, J. M. Dent & co. New York, E. P. Dutton & co. [1907] xi, 470 p. 17 1/2 cm. (Half-title: Everyman's library, ed. by Ernest Rhys. Fiction. [no. 181]) Title within ornamental border; illustrated lining-papers. Bibliography: p. viii. A 10
I. Title.

WARBURTON, John, 1776-1857 248.2
Mercies of a covenant God; being an account of some of the Lord's dealings in providence and grace with John Warburton, minister of the gospel, Trowbridge. Together with an account of the author's last days. Swengel, Pa., Reiner Pubns. 1964. xvi, 285p. illus., facsim., ports. 20cm. [BX6419.69.W3A3] 65-1231 3.95; 2.75 pap.,
I. Title.

Religion—Biography—Addresses, essays, lectures.

THE Biographical process 200'.92
: studies in the history and psychology of religion / edited by Frank E. Reynolds and Donald Capps. The Hague : Mouton, 1977 xi, 436 p. ; 23 cm. (Religion and reason ; 11) Based on seminars held at the Divinity School, University of Chicago, 1972 and 1973. Includes indexes. Bibliography: p. 413-426. [BL72.B56] 77-352279 ISBN 9-02-797522-1 : 31.25
1. Religion—Biography—Addresses, essays, lectures. 2. Biography (as a literary form)—Addresses, essays, lectures. I. Reynolds, Frank, 1930- II. Capps, Donald. III. Chicago. University. Divinity School.
Distributed by Humanities Press

Religion—Collected works.

BRADY, Donald, comp. 108
Philosophy in the flesh : a reader / edited by Donald Brady. New York : MSS Information Corp., [1975] p. cm. [BL29.B7] 74-32419 ISBN 0-8422-0492-X
1. Religion—Collected works. 2. Ethics—Collected works. I. Title.

CARD, Claudia F., comp. 200'.8
Religious commitment and salvation; readings in secular and theistic religion. Edited by Claudia F. Card [and] Robert R. Ammerman. Columbus, Ohio, Merrill [1974] xiv, 370 p. 23 cm. Bibliography: p. 357-370. [BL25.C33] 73-87527 ISBN 0-675-08871-2 6.95
1. Religion—Collected works. 2. Theology—Collected works. I. Ammerman, Robert R., joint author. II. Title.

FRAZIER, Allie M., comp. 200'.8
Issues in religion : a book of readings / Allie M. Frazier. 2d ed. New York : Van Nostrand, [1975] viii, 435 p. ; 24 cm. Includes bibliographies and index. [BL25.F65 1975] 74-21155 ISBN 0-442-21680-7 : 7.25
1. Religion—Collected works. 2. Religion—Philosophy—Collected works. I. Title.

OUTKA, Gene H. 200'.1
Religion and morality; a collection of essays. Edited by Gene Outka and John P. Reeder, Jr. [1st ed.] Garden City, N.Y.,

Anchor Press [1973] viii, 448 p. 21 cm. Bibliography: p. [389]-392. [BL25.O9] 72-84966 ISBN 0-385-03992-1 4.95 (pbk.)
1. Religion—Collected works. 2. Ethics—Collected works. I. Reeder, John P., ed. II. Title.

VOLTAIRE, Francois Marie Arouet de, 1694-1778. 208
Voltaire on religion: selected writings. Translated and introduced by Kenneth W. Appelgate. New York, F. Ungar Pub. Co. [1974] xiii, 222 p. 22 cm. Includes bibliographical references. [BL27.V64213 1974] 74-127204 ISBN 0-8044-5975-4 7.50
1. Religion—Collected works. I. Appelgate, Kenneth W., tr. II. Title.

Religion—Collections.

CAPPS, Walter H., comp. 200'.8
Ways of understanding religion [by] Walter H. Capps. New York, Macmillan [1971, c1972] xvi, 399 p. 24 cm. Includes bibliographies. [BL25.C3 1972] 77-151166 4.95
1. Religion—Collections. I. Title.

NEEDLEMAN, Jacob, comp. 200'.8
Religion for a new generation. [Edited by] Jacob Needleman, A. K. Bierman [and] James A. Gould. New York, Macmillan [1973] xiv, 592 p. 24 cm. Includes bibliographies. [BL25.N43] 72-77149 9.95
1. Religion—Collections. I. Bierman, Arthur Kalmer, 1923- joint comp. II. Gould, James A., 1922- joint comp. III. Title.

SIMONSON, Harold Peter, 1926- comp. 200'.8
Dimensions of man [compiled by] Harold P. Simonson [and] John B. Magee. New York, Harper & Row [1973] xxviii, 368 p. 24 cm. [BL25.S5] 73-1037 ISBN 0-06-046177-2 4.95 (pbk.)
1. Religion—Collections. I. Magee, John Benjamin, 1917- joint comp. II. Title.

STRENG, Frederick J., comp. 208
Ways of being religious; readings for a new approach to religion [compiled by] Frederick J. Streng, Charles L. Lloyd, Jr. [and] Jay T. Allen. Englewood Cliffs, N.J., Prentice-Hall [1973] xii, 627 p. illus. 24 cm. Includes bibliographical references. [BL25.S65] 72-7388 ISBN 0-13-946277-5 9.95
1. Religion—Collections. I. Lloyd, Charles L., 1935- joint comp. II. Allen, Jay T., 1934- joint comp. III. Title.

Religion—Congresses.

THE American Academy of Religion, annual meeting, San Francisco, California, December 28-December 31, 1977 : abstracts / compiled by John F. Priest. Missoula, Mont. : Scholars Press, [1977] p. cm. [BL21.A47] 77-13208 ISBN 0-89130-191-7 pbk. : 2.50 200
1. Religion—Congresses. I. Priest, John F. II. American Academy of Religion.

COLLOQUIUM on Religious Studies, Auckland, N.Z., 1975. 200
The religious dimension : a selection of essays presented at a Colloquium on Religious Studies held at the University of Auckland, New Zealand in August, 1975 / edited by John C. Hinchcliff. Auckland : Rep Prep, 1976. 103 p. ; 29 cm. Errata slip inserted. Includes bibliographies. [BL21.C64 1975] 77-351054
1. Religion—Congresses. I. Hinchcliff, John C. II. Title.

CONFERENCE Towards a Global Congress of World Religions, 1st, San Francisco, 1977. 291
Towards a global congress of world religions : conference proceedings at San Francisco, Barrytown, Bristol / sponsored by Unification Theological Seminary ; edited by Warren Lewis. 1st ed. Barrytown, N.Y. : Unification Theological Seminary ; New York : distributed by Rose of Sharon Press, c1978. viii, 297 p. : ill. ; 23 cm. (Conference series - Unification Theological Seminary ; no. 2) Includes proceedings of the 1st annual Conference Towards a Global Congress of World Religions held Nov. 27-28, 1977 and proceedings of the 1st and 2d Conferences on Contemporary African Religion held May 26-28, 1978 and Sept. 3-5, 1978. Includes bibliographical references. [BL21.C65 1977] 78-73771 ISBN 0-932894-01-1 pbk. : 8.95
1. Religion—Congresses. 2. Religions—Congresses. 3. Africa—Religion—Congresses. I. Lewis, Warren. II. Unification Theological Seminary. III. Conference on Contemporary African Religion, 1st, Barrytown, N.Y., 1978; IV. 2d, Bristol, Eng., 1978. V. Title. VI. Series: Unification Theological Seminary. Conference series — Unification Theological Seminary ; no. 2.

CONFERENCE Towards a Global Congress of World Religions, 2d, Boston, 1978. 291
Towards a global congress of world religions : conference proceedings at Boston / sponsored by Unification Theological Seminary ; edited by Warren Lewis. 1st ed. Barrytown, N.Y. : Unification Theological Seminary ; New York : distributed by Rose of Sharon Press, c1979. viii, 63 p. : ill. ; 23 cm. (Conference series - Unification Theological Seminary ; no. 4) Includes bibliographical references. [BL21.C65 1978] 79-56121 ISBN 0-932894-03-8 pbk. : 2.95
1. Religion—Congresses. 2. Religions—Congresses. I. Lewis, Warren. II. Unification Theological Seminary. III. Title. IV. Series: Unification Theological Seminary. Conference series — Unification Theological Seminary ; no. 4.

INTERNATIONAL Congress of Anthropological and Ethnological Sciences, 9th, Chicago, 1973. 291
The Realm of the extra-human : agents and audiences / ed. Agehananda Bharati The Hague : Mouton ; Chicago : distributed by Aldine, c1976. xii, 556 p., [6] leaves of plates : ill. ; 24 cm. (World anthropology) Includes bibliographies and index. [BL21.I64 1973a] 77-353256 ISBN 0-202-90026-6 : 27.50
1. Religion—Congresses. 2. Rites and ceremonies—Congresses. 3. Shamanism—Congresses. I. Agehananda Bharati, Swami, 1923- II. Title. III. Series.

INTERNATIONAL Congress of Anthropological and Ethnological Sciences, 9th, Chicago, 1973. 291
The realm of the extra-human : ideas and actions / editor Agehananda Bharati The Hague : Mouton ; Chicago : distributed by Aldine, c1976. xi, 521 p., [5] leaves of plates : ill. ; 24 cm. (World anthropology) Includes bibliographies and indexes. [BL21.I64 1973] 77-353259 ISBN 0-202-90027-4 : 24.50
1. Religion—Congresses. 2. Rites and ceremonies—Congresses. I. Agehananda Bharati, Swami, 1923- II. Title. III. Series.

RELIGIOUS syncretism in antiquity : essays in conversation with Geo Widengren / edited by Birger A. Pearson. Missoula, Mont. : Published by Scholars Press for the American Academy of Religion and the Institute of Religious Studies, University of California, Santa Barbara, 1975. p. cm. (Symposium series - American Academy of Religion and Institute of Religious Studies, University of California, Santa Barbara ; no. 1) Based on a symposium held in Santa Barbara, Calif., on April 21-22, 1972, sponsored by the Institute of Religious Studies of the University of California, Santa Barbara. Includes bibliographical references. [BL21.R45] 75-29421 ISBN 0-89130-037-6 : 4.90 291
1. Religion—Congresses. I. Widengren, Geo, 1907- II. Pearson, Birger Albert. III. California. University, Santa Barbara. Institute of Religious Studies. IV. Series: American Academy of Religion. Symposium series — American Academy of Religion and Institute of Religious Studies, University of California, Santa Barbara ; no. 1.

Religion—Controversial literature.

BARD, Andreas, 1878- 222.16
Shall we scrap the Ten commandments! By Andreas Bard ... Burlington, Ia., The Lutheran literary board, 1940. 67 p. 21cm. [BV4655.B88] 40-10259
I. Title.

DOW, Lorenzo, 1777-1834. 922.
History of Cosmopolite; or, The writings of Rev. Lorenzo Dow: containing his experience and travels in Europe and America, up to near his fiftieth year. Also, his polemic writings. To which is added, the "Journey of life," by Peggy Dow. Rev. and cor. with notes ... Philadelphia, J. B. & co., 1859. vii, [9]-720 p. 2 port. (incl. front.) 22 cm. [BX8495.D57A3 1859] 35-3443
I. Dow, Mrs. Peggy, 1780-1820. II. Title.

ELDER, Frederick Stanton, 1868- 211.4
Morals and religion. New York, Philosophical [c.1963] 179p. 22cm. 62-18534 3.75
1. Religion—Controversial literature. I. Title.

ELFENBEIN, Hiram. 230
Organized religion; the great game of make-believe. New York, Philosophical Library [1968] 239 p. 22 cm. Bibliographical footnotes. [BL2775.2.E43] 67-27264
1. Religion—Controversial literature. I. Title.

GARDAVSKY, Vitezslav. 200
God is not yet dead; translated from the German by Vivienne Menkes. Harmondsworth, Penguin, 1973. 224 p. 18 cm. (Pelican books) The German ed. Gott ist nicht ganz tot was translated from the original Czech entitled Buh neni zcela mrtev. Includes bibliographical references and index. [BL2775.2.G313] 73-168508 ISBN 0-14-021322-8
1. Religion—Controversial literature. 2. Atheism. I. Title.
Distributed by Penguin, Baltimore, Md. 2.25 (pbk.)

MESLIER, Jean, 1664-1729. 210
Le Testament / Jean Meslier. Hildesheim ; New York : G. Olms, 1974. 3 v. in 1 ; 20 cm. Reprint of the ed. published in 1864 in Amsterdam by R. C. Meijer. [BL2773.M45 1974] 74-194533 ISBN 3-487-05278-4
1. Religion—Controversial literature. 2. Christianity—Controversial literature. I. Title.

PRUDENT, Julia Ann, ed.
Seven nights: or, Several conversations, containing arguments from Scripture, reason, fact, and experience, between individuals of different demoniations ... edited by Julia Ann Prudent. Sobriety [N. J.] Published by Plain truth and honesty, Jazer Meanwell, printer, 1821. 191 p. 15 cm. A 31
I. Title.

TURKEL, Roma Rudd 241
Church is for the birds [about people who scoff at religion]. New York, Paulist Press [c.1959] unpaged illus. (col.) 16cm. .10 pap.,
I. Title.

Religion—Dictionaries.

ADAMS, Hannah, 1755-1831. 208
An alphalbetical compendium of the various acts which have appeared in the world from the beginning of the Christian era to the present day. With an appendix, containing a brief account of the different schemes of religion now embraced among mankind. The whole collected from the best authors, ancient and modern. By Hannah Adams ... Boston: Printed by B. Edes & sons, no. 42, Cornhill, M,DCC,LXXXIV. 1 p. l., ii p., 1 l., 204, ixxxiii, [23] p. 21 cm. Second and third editions (Boston. 1791 and 1801, respectively) published with title: View of religious; fourth edition (Boston, 1817) has title: A dictionary of all religious. of. Sabin, Bibliothere americana. [BL31.A3 1784] 30-11331
1. Religion—Dictionaries. I. Title.

ADAMS, Hannah, 1755-1831. 208
A dictionary of all religious and religious denominations. Jewish, heathen, Mahometan and Christian, ancient and modern. With an appendix, containing a sketch of the present state of the world, as to population, religion, toleration, missions, etc., and the articles in which all Christian denominations agree. By Hannah Adams ... Fourth ed., with corrections and large additions. N. York; and by Cummings and Hilliard, no. 1, Cornhill, published by James Eastburn and company, at the Litery rooms, corner of Broadway and Pine street Boston. 1817. 4 p. l., [5]-376 p. 22 cm. Frist published. Boston, 1784, with title: An alphabetical compendium of the various sects which have appeared in the world. "A brief sketch of the state of religious throughout the world, by Mr. T. Williams": p. [325]-365. [BL31.A3 1817] 30-11332
1. Religion—Dictionaries. I. Williams, Thomas. II. Title.

BROWN, John Newton, 1803-1868, ed. 208
Encyclopedia of religious knowledge; or, Dictionary of the Bible, theology, religious biography, all religions, ecclesiastical history, and missions... To which is added a missionary gazetteer, containing descriptions of the various missionary stations throughout the globe; by Rev. B.B. Edwards... Edited by Rev. J. Newton Brown. Revised and corrected to date by Rev. Geo. P. Tyler... Brattleboro', Vt., J. Steen & co.; Philadelphia, J.B. Lippincott & co., 1858. 2 p. l., [iii]-vi, [7]-1275 p. front., illus. (incl. ports.) plates, maps, plans. 27 1/2 cm. Added t.-p., with portrait vignette. [BL31.B8 1858] 30-11336
1. Religion—Dictionairies. 2. Theology—Dictionaries. 3. Missions—Dictionaries. I. Edwards, Bela Bates, 1802-1852. II. Tyler, George Palmer, 1800-1896, ed. III. Title.

BROWN, John Newton, 1803-1868, ed. 208
Fessenden & co's Encyclopedia of religious knowledge; or, Dictionary of the Bible, theology, religious biography, all religions, ecclesiastical history, and missions... To which is added a missionary gazetteer, containing descriptions of the various missionary stations throughout the globe; by Rev. B.B. Edwards... The whole brought down to the present time, and...edited by Rev. J. Newton Brown... Brattleboro', Fessenden and co.; Boston, Shattuck & co., 1835. 2 p. l., [iii]-vi, [7]-1275 p. front., illus. (incl. ports.) plates, maps, plans. 27 1/2 cm. Engraved half-title, with vignette. [BL31.B8 1835] 30-11334
1. Religion—Dictionaries. 2. Theology—Dictionaries. 3. Missions—Dictionaries. I. Edwards, Bela Bates, 1802-1852. II. Title. III. Title: Encyclopedia of religious knowledge.

BROWN, John Newton, 1803-1868, ed. 208
Fessenden & co's Encyclopedia of religious knowledge; or, Dictionary of the Bible, theology, religious biography, all religions, ecclesiastical history, and missions... To which is added a missionary gazetteer, containing descriptions of the various mission stations throughout the globe; by Rev. B.B. Edwards... The whole brought down to the present time and...edited by Rev. J. Newton Brown... Brattleboro', Fessenden and co., 1836. 2 p. l., [iii]-vi, [7]-1275 p. front., illus. (incl. ports.) plates, maps, plans. 27 1/2 cm. Added t.-p., engraved: The encyclopedia of religious knowledge...Brattleboro, Vt., Fessenden and co. [BL31.B8 1836] 30-11335
1. Religion—Dictionaries. 2. Theology—Dictionaries. 3. Missions—Dictionaries. I. Edwards, Bela Bates, 1802-1852. II. Title. III. Title: Encyclopedia of religious knowledge.

BROWN, John Newton, 1803-1868, ed. 208
Fessenden & co's Encylcopedia of religious knowledge; or, Dictionary of the Bible, theology, religious biography, all religions, ecclesiastical history, and missions... To which is added, a missionary gazetteer, containing descriptions of the various missionary stations throughout the globe; by Rev. B.B. Edwards... Edited by Rev. J. Newton Brown... Brattleboro', Vt., Brattleboro' typographic company, 1847. 2 p. l., [iii]-vi, [7]-1275 p. front., illus. (incl. ports.) plates, maps, plans. 27 1/2 cm. Added t.-p., engraved: The encyclopedia of religious knowledge... Brattleboro', Vt. Fessenden & co. [BL31.B8 1837] 11-14600
1. Religion—Dictionaries. 2. Theology—Dictionaries. 3. Missions—Dictionaries. I. Edwards, Bela Bates, 1802-1852. II. Title. III. Title: Encyclopedia of religious knowldege.

BUMPUS, John Skelton, 1861- 1913. 203
A dictionary of ecclesiastical terms; being a history and explanation of certain terms used in architecture, ecclesiology, music, ritual, cathedral constitution, etc. London, T. W. Laurie [1910] Detroit, Gale Research Co., 1969. 323 p. 23 cm. [BR95.B8 1969] 68-30653
1. Religion—Dictionaries. 2. Encyclopedias and dictionaries. I. Title.

CANNEY, Maurice Arthur, 1872- 208
An encyclopedia of religions, by Maurice A. Canney. London, G. Routledge & sons, ltd.; New York, E. P. Dutton & co., 1921. ix, 397 p. 25 1/2 x 20 1/2 cm. "Chief authorities": p. [vii]-ix. [BL31. C3]
1. Religion—Dictionaries. I. Title.

CANNEY, Maurice Arthur, 1872-1942. 200'.3
An encyclopadia of religions. Detroit, Gale Research Co., 1970. ix, 397 p. 28 cm. Reprint of the 1921 ed. Bibliography: p. [vii]-ix. [BL31.C3 1970] 75-123370
1. Religion—Dictionaries. I. Title.

CATTELL, Ann, 1893- 200.3
A dictionary of esoteric words. [1st ed.] New York, Citadel Press [1967] 128 p. 21 cm. [BL31.C35] 67-25648
1. Religion—Dictionaries. I. Title.

ENCYCLOPAEDIA of religion and ethics, edited by James Hastings, with the assistance of John A. Selbie, and other scholars. New York, Scribner, 1951. 13v. in 7. illus., plates, facsims., taples. 27cm. [BL31.E] A53 200'.4
1. Religion—Dictionaries 2. Ethics—Dictionaries. 3. Theology—Dictionaries. I. Hastings, James, 1852-1922, ed.

ENCYCLOPAEDIA of religion and ethics, by James Hastings...With the assistance of John A. Selbie...and other scholars... Edinburgh, T. & T. Clark; New York, C. Scribner's sons, 1908-26. 13 v. illus., plates, facsims. tables. 29 cm. Vols. 6-12, "edited by James Hastings, with the assistance of John A. Selble and Louis H. Gray". Contents.V. 1. A-art.--V. 2. Arthur-Bunyan.--v. 3. Burial-confession.--v. 4. Confirmation-Drama.--v. 5. Dravidians-Fichte.--v. 6. Fictions-hyksons.--v. 7 Hymns-Liberty.--v. 8 Life and death-Mulla.--v. 9. Mundas-Phrygians.--v. 10. Picts-Sacraments--v. 11. Sacrific-Sundra.--v. 12. Suffering- Zwingll.--v. 13. Indexes. [BL31.E4] 8-35833 208
1. Religion—Dictionaries. 2. Ethics—Dictionaries. 3. Theology—Dictionaries. I. Hastings, James, 1852-1922, ed. II. Selbie, John Alexander, 1856- joint ed. III. Gray, Louis Herbert, 1857- ed.

ENCYCLOPAEDIA of religion and ethics edited by James Hasting...with the assistance of John A. Selbie...and other scholars... Edinburgh, T. & T. Clark; New York, C. Scribner's sons [1910]-34. 13 v. illus. (incl. plans. music) plates, facims., tables., diagrs. 29 cm. Vols. 6-12 edited by James Hasints, with the assistance of John A. Selbie...and Louis H. Gray." Vol. 1, 2d impression, 1925: v. 2, 8-10, 2d impression, 1930; v. 3-7. 1910-14; v. 11-12, 2d impression, 1934; v. [13] 1926. Contents.--I. A-Art.--II. Arthur-Bunyan.--III. Burial-Confessions--IV. Confirmation-Drama.--V. Dravidians-Fichte.--VI. Fiction-Hyksos.--VII. Hymns-Liberty.--VIII. Life and death-Mulla.--IX. Mundas-Phrygians.--X. Picts-Sacraments.--XI. Sacrifice-Sudra.--XII. Suffering-Zwingli.--[XIII] Index volume. [BL31.E44] 39-7345 203
1. Religion—Dictionaries. 2. Ehtics—Dictionaries. 3. Theology—Dictionaries. I. Hastings. James, 1852-1922, ed. II. Selbie, John Alexander, 1856-1931. joint ed. III. Gray, Louis Herbert, 1875- joint ed.

ENCYCLOPAEDIA of religion and ethics, edited by James Hastings...with the assistance of John A. Selbie...and other scholars... New York, C. Scribner's sons; Edinburg, T. & T. Clark, 1920-[30] 13 v. illus., plates, plan, facsim., tables. 29 cm. Vols. 6-12, "edited by James Hastings, with the assistance of John A. Selbie...and Louis H. Gray". Vol. 10, Edinburgh, T. & T. Clark; New York, C. Scribner's sons. Vols. 1-2, 7-8, 1926; v. 3, 5-6, 9, 11-12, 1925; v. 4, 1920; v. 10, 2d impression, 1930; v. [13] 1927. Contents.--I. A-Art.--II. Arthur-Bunyan.--III. Burial-Confessions.--IV. Confirmation-Drama.--V. Dravidians-Fichte.--VI. Fiction-Hyksos.--VII. Hymns-Liberty.--VIII. Life and death-Mulla.--IX. Mundas-Phrygians.--X. Picts-Sacraments.--XI. Sacrifice-Sudra.--XII. Suffering-Zwingli.--[XIII] Index volume. [BL31.E42] 34-9086 203
1. Religion—Dictionaries. 2. Ethics—Dictionaries. 3. Theology—Dictionaries. I. Hastings, James, 1852-1922, ed. II. Selbie, John Alexander, 1856- joint ed. III. Gray, Louis Herbert, 1875- joint ed.

ENCYCLOPAEDIA of religion and ethics, edited by James Hastings...with the assistance of John A. Seible...and other scholars... New York, C. Scribner's sons; Edinburgh, T. & T. Clark, 1924-27. 13 v. illus., plates., palsn., facsims., tables. 20 cm. Vols. 5-12, "edited by James Hastings, with the assistance of John A. Selbie...and Louis H. Gray". Vols. 1-2, 1926; v. 3, 1924; v. 4-6, 1925; v. 7-8, 1926; v. 9-12, 1925; v. [13] 1927. Contents.--I. A-Art.--II. Arthur-Bunyan.--III. Burial-Confessions.--IV. Confirmation-Drama.--V. Dravidians-Fichte.--VI. Fiction-Hyksos.--VII. Hymns-Liberty.--VIII. Life and death-Mulla.--IX. Mundas-Phrygians.--X. Picts-Sacraments.--XI. Sacrifice-Sudra.--XII. Suffering-Zwingli.--[XIII] Index volume. [BL31.E4 1924] 30-20143 203
1. Religion—Dictionaries. 2. Ethics—Dictionaries. 3. Theology—Dictionaries. I. Hastings, James, 1852-1922, ed. II. Selbie, John Alexander, 1856- joint ed. III. Gray, Louis Herbert, 1875- joint ed.

ENCYCLOPAEDIA of religion and ethics, edited by James Hasting...with the assistance of John A. Seible...and other scholars... New York, C. Scribner's sons; Edinburgh, T. & T. Clark, 1925-[32] 13 v. illus., plates, plan, facsims., tables. 20 cm. Vols. 6-12 edited by James Hastings, with the assistance of John A. Seible...and Louis H. Gray". Vols. 3, 10, Edinburgh, T. & T. Clark; New York, C. Scribner's sons. Vols. 1-2, 7-8, 1926; v. 3, 2d ed., 1932; v. 4-6, 9, 11-12, 1925; v. 10, 2d impression, 1930; v. [13] 1927. Contents.--I. A-Art.--II. Arthur-Bunyan.--III. Burial-Confessions.--IV. Confirmation-Drama.--V. Dravidians-Fichte.--VI. Fiction-Hyksos.--VII. Hymns-Liberty.--VIII. Life and death-Mulla.--IX. Mundas-Phrygians.--X. Picts-Sacraments.--XI. Sacrifice-Sudra.--XII. Suffering-Zwingli.--[XIII] Index volume. [BL31.E43] 34-9087 203
1. Religion—Dictionaries. 2. Ethics—Dictionaries. 3. Theology—Dictionaries. I. Hastings, James, 1852-1922, ed. II. Selbie, John Alexander, 1856- joint ed. III. Gray, Louis Herbert, 1875- joint ed.

FERM, Vergilius Ture Anselm, 1896- ed.
An encyclopedia of religion [1959 ed.] Paterson, N.J., Littlefield, Adams, 1959. xix, 844 p. 23 cm. (New Students outline series) 63-15620
1. Religion—Dictionaries. I. Title.

FERM, Vergilius Ture Anselm, 1896- ed. 203
An encyclopedia of religion, edited by Vergilius Ferm ... New York, The Philosophical library [c1945] xix, 844 p. 23 1/2 cm. Includes bibliographies. [BL31.F4] 46-3249
1. Religion—Dictionaries. I. Title.

FERM, Vergilius Ture Anselm, 1896-1974, ed. 200'.3
An encyclopedia of religion / edited by Vergilius Ferm. Westport, Conn. : Greenwood Press, 1976, c1945. xix, 844 p. ; 24 cm. Reprint of the ed. published by Philosophical Library, New York. Includes bibliographies. [BL31.F4 1976] 75-36508 ISBN 0-8371-8638-2 lib.bdg. : 40.00
1. Religion—Dictionaries. I. Title.

FORLONG JAMES GEORGE ROCHE 1904 203
Faiths of man; encyclopedia of religions [3v.] Introd. by Margery Silver. New Hyde Park, N. Y., Univ. Bks. [c.1964] 3v. (569;582;527p.) port. 24cm. Repub. verbatim from the London 1906 ed. 64-19387 25.50 set,
1. Religion—Dictionaries. I. Title.

FUERBRINGER, Ludwig Ernst, 1864- ed. 220.
The Concordia cyclopedia; a handbook of religious information, with special reference to the history, doctrine, work, and usages of the Lutheran church; L. Fuerbringer ... Th. Engelder ... P. E. Kretzmann ... editor-in-chief. St. Louis, Mo., Concordia publishing house, 1927. iv p., 1 l., 848 p. 23 cm. [BR95.F8] 27-13940
1. Religion—Dictionaries. 2. Lutheran church—Dictionaries. I. Engelder, Theodore Edward William, 1865- joint ed. II. Kretzmann, Paul Edward, 1883- joint ed. III. Title.

GAYNOR, Frank, 1911- ed. 290.3
Dictionary of mysticism. New York, Philosophical Library [1953] 208p. 24cm. [BL31.G32] 53-13354
1. Religion—Dictionaries. 2. Occult sciences —Dictionaries. 3. Mysticism—Dictionaries. I. Title.

GODS, a dictionary of the deities of all lands : including supernatural beings, mythical heroes, and kings, sacred books of principal religions, etc. / compiled and edited by Bessie G. Redfield. New York : Gordon Press, 1981, c1931. p. cm. Reprint. Originally published: New York : Putnam, 1931. Bibliography: p. [BL31.G62 1981] 19 80-53929 ISBN 0-03-057673-3 ISBN 0-8490-1894-3 lib. bdg. : 69.95 291'.03'21
1. Religion—Dictionaries. 2. Mythology—Dictionaries. I. Redfield, Bessie Gordon, 1868-

THE illustrated hand-book to all religions: from the earliest ages to the present time. Including the rise, progress, doctrines and government of all Christian denominations. Compiled from their own publications, and viewed from their own standpoint. Together with an account of the Jewish and all other systems of religion ... Philadelphia, J. E. Potter and company [1877] xix, [17]-593 p. illus. (incl. ports.) 21 cm. [BL31.I 6] 30-11341 208
1. Religion—Dictionaries. 2. Sects. I. Title: Hand-book to all religions.

KAUFFMAN, Donald T. ed. 200'.3
Baker's pocket dictionary of religious terms, [edited by] Donald T. Kauffman. Grand Rapids, Baker Book House, [1975 c1967] 445 p. 18 cm. Formerly published under the title, the dictionary of religious terms. [BL31.K34] ISBN 0-8010-5361-7 2.95 (pbk.)
1. Religion—Dictionaries. I. Title.
L.C. card no. for original ed.: 67-22570.

KAUFFMAN, Donald T. 200'.3
The dictionary of religious terms, by Donald T. Kauffman. Westwood, N.J., Revell [1967] 445 p. 24 cm. [BL31.K34] 67-22570
1. Religion—Dictionaries. I. Title.

MATHEWS, Shailer, 1863- ed. 203
A dictionary of religion and ethics, ed. by Shailer Mathews...and Gerald Birney Smith.. New York, The Macmillan company, 1921. 2 p. l., iii-vii, 513 p. 26 1/2 cm. Bibliography: p. 485-513. [BL31.M3] 21-16239
1. Religion—Dictionaries. 2. Ethics—Dictionaries. I. Smith, Gerald Birney, 1868-1929, joint ed. II. Title.

MATHEWS, Shailer, 1863- ed. 208
A dictionary of religion and ethics, edited by Shailer Mathews... and Gerald Birney Smith... New York, The Macmillan company, 1923. 2 p. l., iii-vii, 513 p. 26 1/2 cm. Bibliography: p. 485-513. [BL31.M3 1923] 31-24963
1. Religion—Dictionaries. 2. Ethics—Dictionareis. I. Smith, Gerald Birney, 1868-1929, joint ed. II. Title.

MATHEWS, Shailer, 1863-1941, ed. 200'.3
A dictionary of religion and ethics. Edited by Shailer Mathews and Gerald Birney Smith. London, Waverly Book Co. Detroit, Gale Research Co., 1973 [c1921] vii, 513 p. 23 cm. Bibliography: p. 485-513. [BL31.M3 1973] 70-145713 17.50
1. Religion—Dictionaries. 2. Ethics—Dictionaries. I. Smith, Gerald Birney, 1868-1929, joint ed. II. Title.

PIKE, Edgar Royston, 1896- 203
Encyclopaedia of religion and religions. New York, Meridian Books [1958] 406p. 21cm. (Meridian library, ML9) [BL31.P5 1958] 58-8530
1. Religion—Dictionaries. 2. Religions—Dictionaries. I. Title.

REDFIELD, Bessie Gordon, 1869- comp. 290.3
Gods; a dictionary of the deities of all lands, including supernatural beings, mythical heroes and kings, sacred books of principal religions, etc. Compiled and edited by Bessie G. Redfield. New York, London, G. P. Putnam's sons, 1931. 347 p. 17 cm. "Chief authorities": p. 9-10. [BL31.R38] 31-19637
1. Religion—Dictionaries. 2. Mythology—Dictionaries, indexes, etc. I. Title.

SHARPE, Eric J., 1933- 200'.3
Fifty key words: comparative religion, by Eric J. Sharpe. Richmond, John Knox Press [1971] 85 p. 20 cm. [BL31.S47 1971] 70-161840 ISBN 0-8042-3897-9 1.95
1. Religion—Dictionaries. I. Title. II. Title: Comparative religion.

THEIN, John. 220.
Ecclesiastical dictionary; containing, in concise form, information upon ecclesiastical, Biblical, archaeological, and historical subjects, by Rev. John Thein ... New York, Cincinnati [etc.] Benziger brothers, 1900. 2 p. l., iii-v, 749 p. 26 1/2 cm. "Works used in compiling the Ecclesiastical dictionary": p. v. [BR95.T4] 0-2157
1. Religion—Dictionaries. I. Title.

WARSHAW, Thayer S., 1915- 203'.21
Abingdon glossary of religious terms / Thayer S. Warshaw. Nashville : Abingdon, 1980. p. cm. "A Festival book." [BS440.W35] 80-13121 ISBN 0-687-00472-1 pbk. : 1.50
1. Bible—Dictionaries. 2. Religion—Dictionaries. I. Title.

WYGAL, Winnifred, 1884- 203
Our religious vocabulary, a glossary of terms in current use, compiled by Winnifred Wygal. New York, N.Y., The Womans press [c1939] xiii, 50 p. 21 1/2 cm. [Full name: Winnifred Crane Wygal] [BL31.W9] 39-21393
1. Religion—Dictionaries. I. Title.

Religion education.

CASE, Adelaide Teague. 201
Liberal Christianity and religious education; a study of objectives in religious education, by Adelaide Teague Case ... New York, The Macmillan company, 1924. viii p., 2 l., 3-194 p. 20 cm. Bibliography: p. 189-194. [BR1615.C3] 24-24836
I. Title.

DAY, Albert Edward. 220
... Revitalizing religion, by Albert Edward Day. New York, Cincinnati [etc.] The Abingdon press [c1930] 132 p. 20 cm. (The Abingdon religious education memographs) [BR125.D44] 30-8389
I. Title.

DUREN, Stephen.
Cards--Bible--church--religion; or, Bible--church--religion explained by a deck of fifty-three playing cards, by Rev. Stephen Duren ... Chicago, J. S. Hyland & company, 1912. 430 p. front. (port.) illus. (part col.) 17 cm. 13-1393 0.40
I. Title.

FALLAW, Wesner. 268
The modern parent and the teaching church, by Wesner Fallaw. New York, The Macmillan company, 1946. xiv p., 1 l., 228 p. 21 cm. "First printing." "A selected bibliography": p. 215-219. [BV1471.F3] 47-1262
1. Religion education. 2. Family—Religious life. I. Title.

MCCONNELL, Francis John, bp., 1871- 231
The Christlike God; a survey of the divine attributes from the Christian point of view, by Francis John McConnell ... New York, Cincinnati, The Abingdon press [c1927] 275 p. 19 cm. [BT101.M315] 27-14223
I. Title.

THWING, Charles Franklin, 1853-
A liberal education and a liberal faith; a series of baccalaureate addresses, by Charles Franklin Thwing ... New York,

The Baker & Taylor co. [1903] v, 233 p. 17 1/2 cm. 3-23510
I. Title.

Religion — Exhibitions and museums.

HUNTER, Stanley Armstrong, 1888- 290.74
Temple of religion and tower of peace at the 1839 Golden gate international exposition, by Stanley Armstrong Hunter. San Francisco, Temple of religion and tower of peace, inc., 1940. xxx, 96 p. incl. front., 1 illus., plates, ports, facsims. double plan 24 cm. [BL46.S3H8] 40-10548
1. Religion—Exhibitions and museums. 2. San Francisco Golden gate international exposition, 1939. I. Title.

JEWISH Theological Seminary of America. Jewish Museum.
Thou shalt have no other gods before me. [Exhibition] New York, 1964. [55] p. illus. 25 cm. Contents.CONTENTS. -- Pref. by A. R. Soloman. -- Neolithic religion at Catal Huyuk, by J. Mellaart. -- Introd. by A. Farkas. -- Catalogue by A. Farkas with sections by R. Arnold. [BL46.J4A53] 64-20950
1. Religion — Exhibitions and museums. I. Farkas, Ann. II. Title.

PENNSYLVANIA. University. Dept. of archoeology. 290.
... Loan exhibition, objects used in religious ceremonies and charms and implements for divination; edited by Stewart Culin. Philadelphia, The University, 1892. 2 p. l., 3-174 p. 19 cm. At head of title: University of Pennsylvania. Department of archaeology and palaeontology. [BL46.P5A5 1892] 12-10527
1. Religion—Exhibitions and museums. 2. Charms. 3. Divination. 4. Rite and ceremonies. I. Culin, Stewart, 1858-1929, ed. II. Title.

Religion — Greece.

MURRAY, Gilbert, 1866-1957.
Five stages of Greek religion, by Gilbert Murray. Garden City, N.Y., Doubleday [196-] xvi, 221 p. 18 cm. (Doubleday anchor books) 3. ed. First ed. published with title: Four stages of Greek religion. 65-44163
1. Religion — Greece. I. Title.

Religion historians—United States—Biography.

ELIADE, Mircea, 1907- 291'.092'4 B
Autobiography / Mircea Eliade ; translated from the Romanian by Mac Linscott Ricketts. 1st ed. San Francisco : Harper & Row, 1981- p. cm. Includes index. Contents.Contents.—v. 1. Journey east, journey west [BL43.E4A315] 19 81-6308 ISBN 0-06-065227-6 : 10.95 (vol.1)
1. Eliade, Mircea. 2. Religion historians—United States—Biography. I. Title.

ELIADE, Mircea, 1907- 291'.092'4 B
No souvenirs : journal, 1957-1969 / Mircea Eliade ; translated from the French by Fred H. Johnson, Jr. 1st ed. New York : Harper & Row, c1977. xiv, 343 p. ; 22 cm. Includes index. [BL43.E4A34 1977] 76-9969 ISBN 0-06-062141-9 : 15.00
1. Eliade, Mircea, 1907- 2. Religion historians—United States—Biography. I. Title.

Religion—Historiography—Congresses.

METHODOLOGICAL issues in religious studies / edited by Robert D. Baird ; contributions from Wilfred Cantwell Smtih [sic], Jacob Neusner, Hans Penner. [Chico, Ca.] : New Horizons Press, c1975. vi, 129 p. ; 22 cm. Proceedings of a symposium held Apr. 15-17, 1974, at the School of Religion of the University of Iowa. Includes bibliographical references. [BL41.M43] 75-44170 ISBN 0-914914-08-1 : 8.50. ISBN 0-914914-07-3 pbk. : 4.50 200'.7'2
1. Religion—Historiography—Congresses. 2. Religions—Historiography—Congresses. I. Baird, Robert D., 1933- II. Smith, Wilfred Cantwell, 1916-

Religion—History

ALLEN, Grant, 1848-1899.
The evolution of the idea of God; an inquiry into the origins of religion, by Grant Allen ... New York, H. Holt and company, 1897. ix, 447 p. 22 cm. 12-30313
I. Title.

BASS, Reginald Howard 209
The story of natural religion. New York, Lyle Stuart [1964, c.1963] 192p. 21cm. Bibl. 62-7779 4.95 bds.,
1. Religion—Hist. I. Title.

BIBLE. N.T. Apocryphal books. Gospels. Syrian. 1899. 220.6'6 s
The history of the Blessed Virgin Mary and The history of the likeness of Christ which the Jews of Tiberias made to mock at : the Syriac texts / edited with English translations by E. A. Wallis Budge. New York : AMS Press, 1976. 2 v. ; 23 cm. "The history of the likeness of Christ" purports to be written by "Philotheus, the deacon of the country of the East." Reprint of the 1899 ed. published by Luzac, London, which was issued as v. 4-5 of Luzac's Semitic text and translation series. Contents.Contents.—v. 1. The Syriac texts.—v. 2. English translations. [BS2850.S8B8 1976] 229'.8 73-18848 ISBN 0-404-11341-9 : 32.50 (2 vols)
I. Budge, Ernest Alfred Thompson Wallis, 1857-1934. II. Philotheus, deacon of the country of the East, fl. 5th cent.? III. Title: The history of the Blessed Virgin Mary ... IV. Title: The history of the likeness of Christ. V. Series: Luzac's Semitic text and translation series.

BROW, Robert. 209
Religion: origins and ideas. [1st ed. Chicago, Inter-varsity Press [1966] 128 p. 21 cm. Includes bibliographical footnotes. [BL48.B73 1966a] 66-30594
1. Religion—History. I. Title.

CAMERON, Ruth Hazelle. 220.6
Supplanters of history and God's pattern of the ages of man. Boston, Chritstopher Pub. House [1947] 302 p. map. 21 cm. [BS534.C3] 47-26841
I. Title.

CAMERON, Ruth Hazelle. 220.6
Supplanters of history and God's pattern of the ages of man. Boston, Chritstopher Pub. House [1947] 302 p. map. 21 cm. [BS534.C3] 47-26841
I. Title.

CENTRE, Michael. 291
In search of God : the solar connection : the evolution of God and civilization : a concise study of history and anthropology / [Michael Centre]. 1st ed. San Francisco : Centre Enterprise, c1978. 190 p. : ill. ; 22 cm. Bibliography: p. 184. [BL48.C42] 78-73706 ISBN 0-932876-01-3 : 6.50
1. Religion—History. 2. Egypt—Religion. 3. God—History of doctrines. I. Title.

DIBBLE, Charles Lemuel, 1881- 290
When half-gods go; a sketch of the emergence of religions, by Charles Lemuel Dibble, D. C. L. New York, Milwaukee, Morehouse publishing co., 1937. 202 p. 20 cm. (Half-title: The layman's library) "A reading course": p. 199-202. [BL85.D5] 37-7824
1. Religion—Hist. 2. Religion, Primitive. 3. Religions. 4. Christianity and other religions. I. Title.

DUPUIS, Charles Francois, 1742-1809.
The origin of all religious worship. Translated from the French of Dupuis ... Containing also a description of the zodiac of Denderah. New Orleans, 1872. 3 p. l., 5-433 p. fold. pl. 22 cm. [BL75.D82] 30-13609
1. Religious—Early works to 1800. 2. Astronomy—Early works to 1800. 3. Sun-worship. 4. Zodiac. 5. Mysteries, Religious. 6. Mythology. 7. Denderah. I. Title.

EASTWOOD, Charles Cyril, 1916- 209
Life and thought in the ancient world. Philadelphia, Westminster [1965, c.1964] 187p. 22cm. Bibl. [BL96.E25] 65-21055 2.25 pap.,
1. Religion Hist— 2. Religions—Hist. I. Title.

ELIADE, Mircea, 1907- 291
A History of religious ideas / Mircea Eliade ; translated from the French by Willard R. Trask. Chicago : University of Chicago Press, c1978- v. ; 24 cm. Translation of Histoire des croyances et des idees religieuses. Includes index. Contents.Contents.—1. From the stone age to the Eleusinian mysteries. Bibliography: v. 1, p. [376]-479. [BL48.E3813] 77-16784 ISBN 0-226-20400-6 : 20.00
1. Religion—History. 2. Religions—History. I. Title.

FRADENBURGH, Jason Nelson, 1843-
History of Erie conference ... by Rev. J. N. Fradenburgh ... Published for the author. Oil City, Pa., Derrick publishing company, 1907. 2 v. fronts. (v. 1: port.) illus. 24 cm. "This work is published in a limited edition from type and will not re-published." 8-10302
I. Title.

GOODE, M. M.
The church in history. A study, By M. M. Goode. St. Joseph, Mo., Hardman, printer, 1892. 69 p. 14 cm. 4-3175
I. Title.

GOWEN, Herbert Henry, 1864- 290
A history of religion, by Herbert H. Gowen ... Milwaukee, Wis., The Morehouse publishing co., [1934] ix, 698 p. 23 cm. The present volume follows the general lines of the author's The universal faith. cf. Foreword. "First published, 1934." Bibliographies interspersed. [BL80.G64] 34-35486
1. Religion—Hist. 2. Religions—Hist. I. Title.

HARDWICK, Charles, 1821-1859. 238.8
A history of the Articles of religion; to which is added a series of documents, from A.D. 1536 to A.D. 1615; together with illustrations from contemporary sources. By Charles Hardwick... Philadelphia, H. Hooker, 1852. 366 p. 23 1/2 cm. [BX5137.H3 1852] 40-25717
1. Church of England. Articles of religion. II. Title.
Contents omitted.

HIGGINS, Godfrey, 1773-1833. 290
Anacalypsis. An attempt to draw aside the veil of the Saitic Isis; or, An inquiry into the origin of languages, nations, and religions. New Hyde Park, N.Y., University Books [1965] 2 v. illus., port. 31 cm. Bibliography: v. 2, p. [463]-464. [BL430.H46] 64-24126
1. Religion — Hist. I. Title.

HOLDER, Charles Frederick, 1851-
The Quakers in Great Britain and America; the religious and political history of the Society of Friends from the seventeenth to the twentieth century ... by Charles Frederick Holder ... New York, Los Angeles [etc.] The Neuner company, 1913. 3 p. l., [11]-669 p. front., plates, ports., facsims. 24 cm. Plates printed on both sides. Contents.--book i. The Quakers in Great Britain.--book ii. The Quakers in American and other colonies, 1656-1913. 14-1512
I. Title.

HUTCHISON, John Alexander, 1912- 200'.9
Paths of faith [by] John A. Hutchison. 2d ed. New York, McGraw-Hill [1975] xvii, 667 p. illus. 24 cm. Includes bibliographies. [BL80.2.H78 1975] 74-2432 ISBN 0-07-031531-0 10.95
1. Religion—History. 2. Religions. I. Title.

HUTCHISON, John Alexander, 1912- 200'.9
Paths of faith [by] John A. Hutchison. New York, McGraw-Hill [1969] xv, 656 p. illus., ports. 24 cm. Includes bibliographies. [BL80.2.H78] 68-11930
1. Religion—History. 2. Religions. I. Title.

INTERNATIONAL congress for the history of religious. 3d, Oxford. 1908. 206.
Transactions of the third International congress for the history of religions ... Oxford, The Clarendon press, 1908. 2 v. illus., plates. 26 cm. "Edited under the general direction of the Papers committee by Mr. P. S. Allen ... assisted by Mr. J. de M. Johnson." Contents.--v. i. List of officers. List of members. Rules of the Congress ... [etc.] President's address. Papers: Section i. Religions of the lower culture. Section ii. Religions of China and Japan. Section iii. Religions of the Wegyptians. Sections iv. Religions of the Semites.--v. 2. Sections v. Religions of India and Iran. Section vi. Religions. of the Greeks and Romans. Section vii. Religions of the Germans. Celts, and Slavs. Section viii. The Christian religion. Section ix Method and scope of the history of religions. [BL21.I6 1908] 9-8428
I. Allen, Percy Stafford, 1869-19336, ed. II. Johnson, John de Monins, joint ed. III. Title.

INTERNATIONAL congress of arts and science, St. Louis, 1904.
Congress of arts and science, Universal exposition, St. Louis, 1904, ed. by Howard J. Rogers ... Boston and New York, Houghton, Mifflin and company, 1905-07. 8 v. 24 cm. Contents.--v. 1. History of the congress, by the editor. Scientic plan of the congress, by Professor Hugo Minsterberg. Philosophy and mathematics.--v. 2. History of politics and economics; history of law: history of religion.--v. 3. History of language: history of literature; history of art.--v. 4. Physics; chemistry; astronomy; sciences of the earth--v. 5. Biology; anthropology; psychology; sociology.--v. 6. Medicine; technology.--v. 7. Economics: politics: jurisprudence; social science--v. 8. Education: religion. Contains bibliographies. [AS3 1904] 6-2103
I. Rogers, Howard Jason, 1861- ed. II. Munsterburg, Hugo, 1863-1916. III. Title.

JOHNSON, Ryder Channing, 1928-
The church in history. Geneva, N. Y., Hobart & William Smith Colleges, 1965. unpaged. frontis. (port.) (Hobart papers) 66-71777
I. Title.

JONES, Louis Thomas.
The Quakers of Iowa, by Louis Thomas Jones. Iowa City, Ia., The State historical society of Iowa, 1914. 360 p. 24 cm. Published also as thesis (PH. D.)--University of Iowa, 1913. "Notes and references": p. 293-336. 14-31105
I. Title.

KANE, John Francis, 1942- 200'.1
Pluralism and truth in religion : Karl Jaspers on existential truth / John F. Kane. Chico, CA : Scholars Press, c1981. viii, 193 p. ; 22 cm. (Dissertation series - American Academy of Religion ; no. 33) Originally presented as the author's thesis, McMaster University, 1978. Includes index. Bibliography: p. 179-189. [BL48.K36 1981] 19 80-20659 ISBN 0-89130-413-4 : 13.50 ISBN 0-89130-414-2 pbk. : 9.00
1. Jaspers, Karl, 1883-1969. 2. Religion—History. 3. Truth (Theology)—History of doctrines. I. Title. II. Series: American Academy of Religion. Dissertation series — American Academy of Religion ; no. 33.
Publisher's address: 101 Salem St., Chico, CA 95926.

LANG, Andrew, 1844-1912. 200'.1
The making of religion. New York, AMS Press [1968] 380 p. 23 cm. Reprint of the 1898 ed. Includes bibliographical references. [BL430.L3 1968] 68-59286
1. Religion—History. 2. Religion, Primitive. 3. Spiritualism. I. Title.

LANG, Andrew, 1844-1912. 291
The making of religion, by Andrew Lang ... 2d ed. London, New York [etc.] Longmans, Green, and co., 1900. xxii p., 2 l., 355 p. 20 cm. [BL430.L3 1900] 8-6812
1. Religion—Hist. 2. Religion, Primitive. 3. Spiritualism. I. Title.

LEWIS, John, 1889- 290
The religions of the world made simple. New York, Made Simple Books; distributed to the book trade by Garden City Books, Garden City, N. Y. [1958] 191p. 27cm. (The Made simple series) [BL82.L4] 58-14937
1. Religion—Hist. I. Title.

LEWIS, John, 1889- 200'.9
The religions of the world made simple. Rev. ed. Garden City, N.Y., Doubleday [1968] 191 p. 26 cm. (Made simple books) Includes bibliographies. [BL82.L4 1968] 68-14221

1. Religion—History. I. Title.

LOOMIS, William Farnsworth, 1914- 200
The God within; an up-to-date sketch of the genesis of man and of the personal God within him, by W. Farnsworth Loomis. Foreword by James A. Pike. [1st ed.] New York, October House [1968,c.1967] ix, 117p. illus. 27cm. [BL430.L6] 67-14086 5.95
1. Religion—Hist. I. Title.

MCCABE, Joseph, 1867- 211
The story of religious controversy, by Joseph McCabe, edited, with an introduction, by E. Haldeman-Julius. Boston, Mass., The Stratford company [c1929] 2 p. l., xviii p., 1 l., 628 p. 24 cm. [BL2775.M2] 29-14064
1. Religion—Hist. 2. Religions. I. Haldeman-Julius, Emanuel, 1889- ed. II. Title.

PARRISH, Fred Louis 200.9
History of religion: the destiny-determining factor in the world's cultures. New York, Pageant [c.1965] 279p. 21cm. [BL96.P3] 65-19181 5.00
1. Religion—Hist. I. Title.

PARRISH, Fred Louis. 200.9
History of religion; the destiny-determining factor in the world's cultures. [1st ed.] New York, Pageant Press [1965] 279 p. 21 cm. [BL96.P3] 65-19181
1. Religion—Hist. I. Title.

POTTER, Charles Francis, 1885- 290
The great religious leaders. New York, Washington Sq. Pr. [1962, c.1929, 1958] 496p. (W1077) Bibl. .90 pap.,
1. Religion—Hist. 2. Christian biography. 3. Religions—Hist. I. Title.

POTTER, Charles Francis, 1885- 290
... *The story of religion* as told in the lives of its leawders, with special reference to atavisms, common elements, and parallel customs in the religions of the world. New York, Simon and Schuster, inc., 1929. xx, 627 p. plates, ports. 25 cm. "Designed by Andor Braun. Portraits designed by Karl S. Woerner." Bibliography: p. [607]-611. [BL80.P6] 29-12634
1. Religion—Hist. 2. Christian biography. 3. Religions—Hist. I. Title.

POTTER, Charles Francis, 1885- 290
The story of religion as told in the lives of its leaders, by Charles Francis Potter. De luxe ed. Garden City, N. Y., Garden City publishing co., inc. [1937] viii p., 2 l., xv-xx, 627 p. plates, ports. 26 cm. Bibliography: p. [607]-611. [BL80.P6 1937] 37-1318
1. Religion—Hist. 2. Christian biography. 3. Religions—Hist. I. Title.

POTTER, Charles Francis, 1885-1962. 290
The great religious leaders. A revision and updating of "The story of religion" in the light of recent discovery and research including the Qumran scrolls. New York, Simon and Schuster, 1958. 493 p. 24 cm. [BL80.P6 1958] 58-13791
1. Religion—History. 2. Christian biography. 3. Religions—History. I. Title.

RAO, K. L. Seshagiri, 1929- 291
Mahatma Gandhi and comparative religion / K. L. Seshagiri Rao. 1st ed. Delhi : Motilal Bandarsidass, 1978. xvi, 154 p. ; 22 cm. Includes index. Bibliography: p. [149]-150. [BL98.R36] 79-901503 ISBN 0-89684-034-4 : 11.50
1. Gandhi, Mohandas Karamchand, 1869-1948. 2. Religion—History. 3. Religions—History. I. Title.
Dist. by Orient Book Distributors, P.O. Box 100, Livingston, N.J.

REDDING, William A. 270
... *The three churches,* showing many mysterious and wonderful things just now coming to the surface after traveling down the path of the ages 6000 years. By William A. Redding. [n. p.] 1897. 396 p. 20 cm. At head of title: No. 7. No. 7 of a series of books by the author on "Our near future." cf. Advertisement at end. [BR125.R4] 28-3278
I. Title.

ROWE, Henry Kalloch, 1869- 200
The history of religion in the United States, by Henry Kalloch Rowe ... New York, The Macmillan company, 1924. viii p., 2 l., 213 p. 20 cm. [BR515.R6] 24-23151
I. Title.

RUST, Eric Charles. 200'.9
Positive religion in a revolutionary time, by Eric C. Rust. Philadelphia, Westminster Press [1970] 233 p. 21 cm. Includes bibliographical references. [BL48.R84] 78-90782 3.65
1. Religion—History. 2. Secularism. 3. Christianity—20th century. I. Title.

SALIBA, John A. 291
"Homo religiosus" in Mircea Eliade : an anthropological evaluation / by John A. Saliba. Leiden : Brill, 1976. vi, 210 p. ; 25 cm. (Supplementa ad Numen : Altera series) (Dissertaiones ad historiam religionum pertinentes ; v. 5) Bibliography: p. [178]-209. [BL48.S26] 76-482577 ISBN 9-00-404550-3 : fl 48.00
1. Eliade, Mircea, 1907- 2. Religion—History. 3. Anthropology—History. I. Title. II. Series. III. Series: Numen : Supplementa : Altera series.

SCHOFFELEERS, Matthew. 301.5'8
Religion, nationalism and economic action : critical questions on Durkheim and Weber / Matthew Schoffeleers, Daniel Meijers. Assen : Van Gorcum, 1978. 94 p. ; 21 cm. Includes bibliographies. [BL48.S375] 79-301366 ISBN 9-02-321614-8 pbk. : 8.75
1. Durkheim, Emile, 1858-1917. 2. Weber, Max, 1864-1920. 3. Religion—History. 4. Religion and capitalism—History. I. Meijers, Daniel, joint author. II. Title.

SMITH, Homer William, 1895-
Man and his gods. Foreword by Albert Einstein. New York, Grosset & Dunlap [1956] x, 501p. 20cm. (Grosset's universal library, UL-5)
1. Religion—Hist. I. Title.

SMITH, Homer William, 1895-
Man and his gods. Foreword by Albert Einstein. New York, Grosset & Dunlap [1956] x, 501 p. 20 cm. (Grosset's universal library, UL-5)
1. Religion — Hist. I. Title.

SMITH, Homer William, 1895- 290
Man and his gods Foreword by Albert Einstein. [1st ed.] Boston, Little, Brown, 1952. 501 p. 22 cm. [BL80.S65] 52-5512
1. Religion—Hist. I. Title.

TUTTLE, Hudson, 1836-
Evolution of the God, and Christ ideas [by] Hudson Tuttle. Berlin Heights, O., The Tuttle publishing company; Chicago, Ill., J. B. Francis [c1906] 3 p. l., 5-279 p. 20 cm. 6-45731
I. Title.

ZIGLER, D. H.
A history of the Brethren in Virginia, by D. H. Zigler. Elgin, Ill., Brethren publishing house, 1908. xvi p., 1 l., 19-278 p. incl. illus., ports., facsims. double map. 20 1/2 cm. "The following pages were the outgrowth of a series of lectures on the Second district of Virginia delivered at Bridgewater college during the Bible term of 1904."--Pref. 8-17710
I. Title.

Religion—History—Juvenile literature.

APPLETON, Ernest Robert, 1891- 290
An outline of religion, by E. R. Appleton, with a foreword by the Reverend S. Parkes Cadman ... New York, Garden City publishing co., inc. [1939] xi, 712 p. illus. 24 cm. London edition (Hodder and Stoughton) has title: An outline of religion for children. Bibliography included in preface. [BL82.A6 1939] 39-18648
1. Religion—Hist.—Juvenile literature. 2. Church history—Juvenile literature. I. Title.

BAXTER, Edna M. 1895- 200
How our religion began, by Edna M. Baxter; drawings by Edward F. Dugmore. New York, London, Harper & brothers [c1939] xiv p 1 l., 225 p. illus. (incl. maps) 24 cm. Maps on lining-papers. On cover: Teachers' edition. "First edition." Includes bibliographies. [BL96.B38 1939] 39-23627
1. Religion—Hist.—Juvenile literature. 2. Religion, Primitive. I. Title.

Religion—History—[Teaching]

JORDAN, Louis Henry, 1855-1923.
The study of religion in the Italian universities, by Louis Henry Jordan ... in collaboration with Baldassare Labanca ... London, New York [etc.] H. Frowde, Oxford university press, 1909. xxviii, 324 p. front. (port.) 20 cm. E 10
1. Religion—History—[Teaching] 2. Religion—Study [and teaching] 3. Universities and colleges—Italy. I. Labanca, Baldassare, 1829-1913. II. Title.

Religion in literature.

ANDERSON, John.
A mirror, representing some religious characters of the present times. By Mr. John Anderson ... Philadelphia: Printed by Young, Stewart, and M'Culloch, the corner of Chesnut and Second-streets. MDCC. LXXX. V I 59 p. 19 cm. A 34
I. Title.

ANDREWS, Emerson, 1806- 269
Pearls of words or, Works and wonders. By Rev. Emerson Andrews ... 1st ed. ... Boston, J. H. Earle, 1881. 383 p. front. (port.) 19 1/2 cm. [BV3797.A45] 38-3742
I. Title.

BATTENHOUSE, Henry Martin, 1885- 808.81
Poets of Christian thought; evaluations from Dante to T. S. Eliot. New York, Ronald Press Co. [1947] vii, 175 p. 21 cm. Contents.Dante.--Shakespeare.--Milton.--Wordsworth.--Tennyson.--Browning.--Emerson.--T. S. Eliot. [PN1077.B3] 47-31329
1. Religion in literature. 2. Poetry—Addresses, essays, lectures. 3. English poetry—Addresses, essays, lectures. I. Title.

BOCKING, Hannah (Dakin), Mrs. 1762-1855. 922.
Light in the valley; or, The life and letters of Mrs. Hannah Bocking. By Miss M. Annesley. New York, Carlton & Porter [1860] 176 p. front. (port.) 15 1/2 cm. [BX8495.B6A2] 922 ISBN 36-34750
I. Annesley, M., ed. II. Title.

CARMICHAEL, Charles Theophilus, 1877- 220
Light and life, by Rev. C. T. Carmichael. Jackson, Miss., Tucker printing house [c1919] 133 p. 21 cm. [BR125.C258] 20-771
I. Title.

[CRABBE, J. K.]
The listener in the church, by a workingman. Chicago, Newford publishing co., 1914. 3 p. l., 9-88 p. 18 cm. 14-5136 0.65
I. Title.

CROSS, Joseph, 1813-1893. 922.373
Days of my years, by the Rev. Joseph Cross ... New York, T. Whittaker, 1891. viii, 319 p. front. (port.) 19 cm. [BX5995.C75A3] 34-11510
I. Title.

DANTE ALIGHIERI
Selections from Dante's Divine commedia; chosen, tr. and annotated by R. J. Cross ... New York, H. Holt and co., 1901. iv, 225 p. front. (port.) 16 degree. Original and translation on opposite pages. 1-31164
I. Title.

DANTE ALIGHIERI 1265-1321.
Selections from Dante's Divina commedia; chosen, translated and annotated by Richard James Cross. The original and translation on opposite pages. New York, H. Holt and co., 1901. iv, 225 p. front. (port.) 16 cm. [PQ4303.C8 1901] 1-31164
I. Cross, Richard James, 1845-1917, ed. and tr. II. Title.

DARLEY, George M.
The pastor [by] George M. Darley. Boston, The Gorham press; [etc., etc. c1916] 239 p. 20 cm. 17-57 1.25
I. Title.

DAVIES, Trevor H 1871- 230
To live is Christ, by Trevor H. Davies ... London, New York [etc.] Oxford university press, 1938. x, 250 p. 20 cm. "Lectures ... delivered ... on Sunday evenings at the Eaton memorial church. Toronto."--P. vii. [BR85.D33] 38-23019
1. Religion in literature. 2. Religious literature—Hist. & crit. I. Title.
Contents omitted.

DIXON, A[mzi] C[larence] 1854-
Lights and shadows of American life, by Rev. A. C. Dixon ... Boston, W. H. Smith, 1903. 197 p. incl. front. (port.) 19 cm. First published, 1898. 3-33070
I. Title.
Contents omitted.

FEELY, Raymond T. 248
... *The pale Galilean,* by Raymond T. Feely ... San Francisco, Cal., Ecclesiastical supply association, 1927. 88 p. 15 1/2 cm. (Path of gold series) [BX2350.F4] 2713938
I. Title.

FOSTER, Henry, 1821-1901.
Life's secrets; spiritual insights of a Christian physician, Henry Foster, M. D.; comp. and arranged by Theodora Crosby Bliss. New York, Chicago [etc.] F. H. Revell company, 1902. 2 p. l., viii p., 1 l., 7-241 p. front., port. 20 cm. 2-22182
I. Bliss, Theodora Crosby, comp. II. Title.
Contents omitted.

FRYE, Roland Mushat 821.4
God, man, and Satan; patterns of Christian thought and life in Paradise lost, Pilgrim's progress, and the great theologians. Princeton, N. J., Princeton University Press [c.]1960. x, 184p. Bibliography: p.175-177. 23cm. 60-5747 3.75
1. Milton, John, Paradise lost. 2. Bunyan, John. The pilgrim's progress. 3. Religion in literature. 4. Religion and literature. I. Title.

GAUTIER, Judith, Mme., 1846-1917.
The daughter of heaven, by Pierre Loti [pseud.] and Judith Gautier; tr. by Ruth Helen Davis. New York, Duffield & company, 1912. viii p., 1 l., [4], [3]-192 p. 19 1/2 cm. Drama. Translation of La fille du ciel: drame chinois, par Judith Gautier et Pierre Loti. [PQ2257.G9F55] 12-23151
I. Vlaud, Julien, 1850-1928, joint author. II. Davis, Ruth Helen, tr. III. Title.

GEBHARD, Anna Laura Munro, 1914- 253
Parsonage doorway; illustrated by Janet Smalley. New York, Abingdon-Cokesbury [1950] 144 p. illus. 20 cm. [BV4395.G4] 50-10109
I. Title.

HISPERICA famina. Verses 1-156.
Hisperica famina : the garden of God : the prologue and a part of the Book of days / translated by Winthrop Palmer Boswell. San Francisco : Distributed by the Brick Row Book Shop, 1974. xxiv, 56 p. : ill. ; 24 x 30 cm. The original Latin text, with interpretive English paraphrase. "Privately printed." "400 copies." Erratum slip inserted. Includes bibliographical references. [PA8330.H72E5 1974] 75-323420
I. Boswell, Winthrop Palmer.

HISPERICA famina. Verses 1-156.
Hisperica famina : the garden of God : the prologue and a part of the Book of days / translated by Winthrop Palmer Boswell. San Francisco : Distributed by the Brick Row Book Shop, 1974. xxiv, 56 p. : ill. ; 24 x 30 cm. The original Latin text, with interpretive English paraphrase. "Privately printed." "400 copies." Erratum slip inserted. Includes bibliographical references. [PA8330.H72E5 1974] 75-323420
I. Boswell, Winthrop Palmer.

HUMPHREY, Jerry Miles, 1872-
Dew drops from the rifted clouds, by J. M. Humphrey ... Lima, O., True gospel grain pub. co., 1917. 54 p. front. 16 1/2 cm. $0.40 17-9580
I. Title.

INSTITUTE for Religious and Social Studies, Jewish Theological Seminary of America. 809.9'33
Spiritual problems in contemporary

literature. Edited by Stanley Romaine Hopper. Gloucester, Mass., P. Smith, 1969 [c1957] xvi, 298 p. 21 cm. (The Library of religion and culture) Bibliographical footnotes. [PN49.I64 1969] 71-3236 5.00
1. Religion in literature. I. Hopper, Stanley Romaine, 1907- ed. II. Title.

IWAHASHI, Takeo. 922
Light from darkness, by Takeo Iwahashi ... introductory notes by Rufus M. Jones, Toyohiko Kagawa [and] Dr. C. J. K. Bates. Philadelphia, Chicago [etc.] Pub. for the Book committee of the Religious society of Friends, at the Press of the John C. Winston company [c1933] 103 p. front. (port.) 21 cm. The author, a blind Japanese youth tells the story of his life and his conversion to Christianity. [BR1725.I 85A3] 33-9991
I. Title.

KING, Thomas A. 289.
Pearls of great price, by Thomas A. King... Minneapolis, Minn., The Nunc licet press, 1918. 386 p. 17 1/2 cm. "The chapters...were written from week to week as explanations of the spiritual sense of the International Sunday school lessons...from October, 1917. to October, 1918."--Pref. [BX8723.K5] 18-20118
I. Title.

LARSON, Christian Daa, 1874- 248
The pathway of roses, by Christian D. Larson ... Los Angeles, The New literature publishing company; [etc., etc., c1912] 360 p. 20 cm. [BV4501.L3] 12-15489 1.25
I. Title.

LAWSON, William, 1851- 208.
Life on Patmos, and Voices of the silent, by Rev. William Lawson. Boston, The Christopher publishing house [c1930] 138 p. 21 cm. [BR85.L43] 30-6189
I. Title. II. Title: Voices of the silent.

LEWIS, William Henry, 1815- comp.
A little casket of precious jewels; a daily companion which, when rightly used, will bring the Christian into a life of abiding fellowship with God, by Rev. W. H. Lewis... Nashville, Tenn., Dallas, Tex., Publishing house of the M.E. Church, South, Bigham & Smith, agents, 1903. xiv, 100 p. front. (port.) 19 1/2 cm. 3-20465
I. Title.

THE Light of the world.
A household treasury of Christian knowledge. Philadelphia [etc.] J. D. Carson [c1880]-83. 2 v. illus., pl. 4 degrees. 1-21470

LUCE, Alice Eveline. 296
The little flock in the last days, by Alice Eveline Luce ... Springfield, Mo., Gospel publishing house [c1927] 1 l., v-xii p., 1 l., 15-250 p. 20 cm. [BT875.L85] 28-3451
I. Title.

MCLACHLAN, Herbert, 1876- 230'.0942
The religious opinions of Milton, Locke, and Newton, by H. McLachlan. New York, Russell & Russell [1972] 217 p. 20 cm. (Publications of the University of Manchester, no. 276. Theological series no. 6) Reprint of the 1941 ed. Includes bibliographical references. [PR145.M27 1972] 74-173539
1. Milton, John, 1608-1674—Religion and ethics. 2. Locke, John, 1632-1704. 3. Newton, Isaac, Sir, 1642-1727. 4. Religion in literature. I. Title. II. Series: Victoria University of Manchester. Publications, no. 276. III. Series: Victoria University of Manchester. Publications. Theological series, no. 6.

MCPHERSON, George Wilson, 1865- 922
A parson's adventures, by G. W. McPherson... Yonkers, N.Y., Yonkers book company [c1925] 3 p. l., 5-298 p. front. plates (incl.music) ports. 20 cm. [BV3785.M3A3] 25-25
I. Title.

MANNING, William Thomas, bp., 1866- 280
The call to unity; the Bedell lectures for 1919 delivered at Kenyon college, May 24th and 25th, 1920, by William T. Manning ... New York, The Macmillan company, 1920. xi, 162 p. 20 cm. [BX8.M3] 20-21308
I. Title.

MENDL, Robert William Sigismund, 1892- 822.33
Revelation in Shakespeare; a study of the supernatural, religious and spiritual elements in his art. London, J. Calder [dist. New York, Humanities, 1965, c.1964] 223p. 22cm. Bibl. [PR3011.M45] 65-5764 6.00
1. Shakespeare, William, 1564-1616—Religion and ethics. 2. Religion in literature. I. Title.

MONTGOMERY, Henry Hutchinson, 1847- 248
Life's journey, by Henry Hutchinson Montgomery ... with an introduction by the Bishop of London. 3d impression. London, New York [etc.] Longmans, Green and co., 1916. xi, 149, [1] p. front. 20 cm. [BV4501.M6] 19-13016
I. Title.

MORTON, Arthur Leslie, 1903-
The everlasting gospel; a study in the sources of William Blake. New York, Haskell House, 1966. 64 p. 20 cm. 68-63227
1. Blake, William, 1757-1827. 2. Religion in literature. I. Title.

MUNTSCH, Albert, 1873- 248
The higher life, by Albert Muntsch ... St. Louis, Mo., and London, B. Herder book co., 1925. xii, 291 p. 20 cm. [BX2350.M87] 25-10793
I. Title.

ORR, Charles Ebert, 1861-
The hidden life; or, Walks with God, by Chas. E. Orr ... Anderson, Ind., Gospel trumpet company [c1908] 3 p. l., 9-224 p. 19 cm. 8-12600
I. Title.

PACE, Charles Nelson. 242
A candle of comfort, by Charles Nelson Pace ... New York, Cincinnati, The Abingdon press [c1923] 80 p. 15 1/2 cm. [BV4905.P2] 23-12539
I. Title.

PALMER, Mary, 1775-1800.
Miscellaneous writings on religious subjects; together with some extracts from a diary. By Mary Palmer...The whole written during six years lingering sickness... Windsor, Vt., Printed by A. Spooner, 1807. viii, [9]-119. 17 cm. Preface by Azel A. Palmer. Poems: p. 89-119. 7-13072
I. Title.

RADER, William, 1862-
The elegy of faith; a study of Alfred Tennyson's In memoriam, by William Rader. New York, T. Y. Crowell and company, 1902. 2 p. l., 56, [1] p. 20 cm. [PR5562.R3] 1-19595
1. Tennyson, Alfred Tennyson, baron, In memoriam. 2. Religion in literature. I. Title.

RANDOLPH, Percilla Lawyer. 248
Light on the path; or, Emmanuel, by Percilla Lawyer Randolph. Los Angeles, "The Books of light", 1932. 4 p. l., [7]-118 p. 20 cm. [BR125.R265] 32-5885
I. Title.

REESE, Clarence Herbert, 1882- 922.373
Pastoral adventure. by Clarence Herbert Reese ... New York [etc.] Fleming H. Revell company [c1938] 2 p. l., 3-205 p. front. (port.) 19 1/2 cm. [BX5995.R4A3] 38-13295
I. Title.

REESE, Clarence Herbert, 1882- 922.373
Pastoral adventure. by Clarence Herbert Reese ... New York [etc.] Fleming H. Revell company [c1938] 2 p. l., 3-205 p. front. (port.) 19 1/2 cm. [BX5995.R4A3] 38-13295
I. Title.

RICHARDSON, Simon Peter, 1818-1899. 922.
The lights and shadows of itinerant life: an autobiography of Rev. Simon Peter Richardson ... with an introduction by Rev. John B. Robins, D.D. Nashville, Tenn., Dallas, Tex., Barbee & Smith, 1901. xix, 288 p. ports. 19 cm. [BX8495.R5A3] 1-16628
I. Title.

ROEDER, Adolph, 1857- 290.
Light in the clouds, being glimpses of the inner word, by Adolph Roeder. New York, The New-church press [c1925] xi p., 1 l., [5]-105 p., 1 l., 18 cm. [BS534.R6] 25-16399
I. Title.

ROHDE, John Martin, 1852-
Heroes and heroines of the cross; or, One hundred thrilling life stories of gospel service and sacrifice, by J. Martin Rohde...forewords by Secretary of state William Jennings Bryan and ex-Vice president Charles W. Fairbanks. Introduction by Rev. S. H. Wainright... Chicago, Ill., The Glad tidings publishing co. [c1914] 2 p. l., 7-386 p. front., plates, groups of ports. 19 cm. $1.00 14-12306
I. Title.

[SHARP, William] 1856-1905.
By sundown shores; studies in spiritual history by Fiona Macleod [pseud.] Portland, Me., T. B. Mosher, 1902. xi, [3], 15-93, [1] p., 1 l. 23 1/2 cm. [The brocade series, XXXVI] "Four hundred and twenty-five copies of this book have been printed on japan vellum, and type distributed, in the month of September, A.D. MDCCCII, at the press of George D. Loring, Portland, Maine." 2-25636
I. Title.
Contents omitted.

SIEKMANN, T. C., Rev. 242
Modern reflections. Derby, N.Y., St. Paul Pubns. [dist.] St. Paul Bk. Ctr., Queen of Apostles Seminary [1962] 147p. 19cm. 1.00 pap.,
I. Title.

SMITH, Almiron, 1841-1919. 922
Light among the shadows; or, How and when I became blind. With other fragments of the story of my life in the dark and in the light... By Rev. Almiron Smith... Syracuse, N.Y., Faith tract house, 1899. 217 p. incl. front., illus., ports. 20 1/2 cm. [BV3785.S55A3] 99-4317
I. Title.

SPIVEY, Ted Ray, 1927- 330.9'73 S
Religious themes in two modern novelists, by Ted R. Spivey. [Atlanta] 1965. vi, 31 l. 28 cm. (Georgia. State College, Atlanta. School of Arts and Sciences Research papers, no. 12) Bibliographical footnotes. [AS36.G378A3] 65-65509
1. Hemingway, Ernest, 1899-1961. 2. Gary, Romain. 3. Religion in literature. I. Title. II. Series: Georgia. State College, Atlanta. School of Arts and Sciences. Research papers, no. 12

STANLEY, E. S.
Life's perilous places. By Rev. E. S. Stanley ... Hartford, Press of Case, Lockwood and co. [1863] 30 p. 15 x 12 cm. In verse. [PS2904.S3] 30-28357
I. Title.

THOMPSON, Hugh Miller, 1830-
"Copy"; essays from an editor's drawer on religion, literature and life, by Hugh Miller Thompson ... 3d ed. New York. T. Whittaker, 1885. 2 p. l., [iii]-ix, [11]-360 p. 19 1/2 cm. 12-39594
I. Title.

THURSTON, John, 1880- 248
The mission of man, by John Thurston ... Boston. The Christopher publishing house [c1934] 109 p. 21 cm. Prose and verse. "The sequel to ... [this] is June Gordon; or, The missing link, by Gladys Thurston." [BR126.T45] 34-16161
I. Title.

TOLSTOI, Lev Nikolaevich, graf, 1828-1910.
Selections. Edited by N. Duddington and N. Gorodetzky. Oxford, Clarendon Press, 1959. xv, 207 p. (Oxford Russian readers) Text in Russian.
I. Duddington, Nataliia Aleksandrovna (Ertel') II. Title.

VEGA, Jose M. 133.
Miracular; or, The warning of the spirit mother, by Jose M. Vega. Tampa, Fla. [c1923] 154 p. front. (port.) 20 cm. [BF1301.V4] 25-7033
I. Title.

WHITING, Lilian.
Lilies of eternal peace, by Lilian Whiting ... New York, T. Y. Crowell & co. [1908] 3 p. l., 40 p., 1 l. 19 1/2 cm. 8-11731
I. Title.

WINSTON, Annie Steger. 270
The deeper voice, by Annie Steger Winston ... New York, George H. Doran company [c1923] viii p., 3 l., 15-134 p. 19 1/2 cm. [BR125.W76] 25-357
I. Title.

Religion in poetry.

CROW, Martha (Foote) Mrs. 1854-1924.
The ministry of a child; a book of verses, by Martha Foote Crow. Chicago, The Wind-tryst press, 1899. 94 p., 1 l. front. (port.) 16 cm. No. 5a of a small edition printed for friends only. of. Colophon. [PS1473.C7M5] 41-38274
I. Title.

KING, Lillian[Estelle Day]
Who and what and where is God? [Poems] By L. Estelle Day King... New London, O., The author 1901. 64 pp. front. [port.] 18 1/2 cm. 2-3430
I. Title.

KLOPSTOCK, Friedrich Gottlieb, 1724-1803. 264
The Messiah, a poem; attempted in English blank verse; from the German of the celebrated Mr. Klopstock. By Solmon Halling ... Georgetown, (S. C.) Printed by Francis M. Baxter, 1810. 2 p. l., 37 p. 23 cm. First canto. [PT2381.Z3H3] [AC901.M5] 24-2875
I. Halling, Solmon, d. 1813, tr. II. Title.

WAHR, Mary Huebner. 248
Rainbow dream; a preachment in prose and poetry, by Mary Huebner Wahr. [Ann Arbor, Mich., c1929] 47 p. 22 1/2 cm. [BV4510.W25] 29-29387
I. Title.

WEATHERBY, Harold L., 1934- 809'.933'1
The keen delight : the Christian poet in the modern world / Harold L. Weatherby. Athens : University of Georgia Press, c1975. 167 p. ; 23 cm. Includes index. Bibliography: p. [160]-164. [PN1077.W4] 74-80043 ISBN 0-8203-0367-4 : 7.50
1. Thomas Aquinas, Saint, 1225?-1274. 2. Newman, John Henry, Cardinal, 1801-1890. 3. Religion in poetry. I. Title.

WISEMAN, George W. 242
Life begins with faith; poems and meditations [by] George W. Wiseman ... [Newton Centre, Mass., Printed by Modern printing company, inc., c1941] 195 p. port. 19 1/2 cm. [PS3545.I 832L5 1941] 41-19857
I. Title.

Religion in the public schools.

AMERICAN Association of School Administrators. Commission on Religion in the Public Schools.
Religion in the public schools. Washington [c1964] 67 p. NUC66
1. Religion in the public schools. I. Title.

BEDSOLE, Adolph. 377.1
The Supreme Court decision on Bible reading and prayer; America's black letter day. Grand Rapids, Baker Book House, 1964. 55 p. 22 cm. [LC111.B43] 64-57928
1. Religion in the public schools. I. Title.

BOLES, Donald Edward, 1926-
The Bible, religion, and the public schools. New, rev. ed. New York, Collier Books [1963, c1962] 320 p. 64-8815
1. Religion in the public schools. 2. Bible in the schools. I. Title.

DELFINER, Henry.
Church state relations and religious instruction in the public elementary schools of Switzerland, West-Germany and US. [Lexington, Mass. 1965] 350 p. 29 cm. Mimeographed. 67-29994
1. Religion in the public schools. 2. Church and state. I. Title.

DIERENFIELD, Richard B. 377.1
Religion in American public schools. Foreword by James A. Pike. Washington, D.C., Public Affairs Pr. [c.1962] 115p. illus. 24cm. Bibl. 62-18457 3.25
1. Religion in the public schools. I. Title.

DOUGLAS, William Orville, 1898- 323.442
The Bible and the schools. Boston, Little [c.1966] 65p. 20cm. Bibl. [LC111.D78] 66-10975 3.75 bds.,
1. Religion in the public schools. 2. Church and state in the U.S. I. Title.

DOUGLAS, William Orville, 1898- 323.442
The Bible and the schools, by William O. Douglas. [1st ed.] Boston, Little, Brown [1966] 65 p. 20 cm. Includes bibliographical references. [LC111.D78] 66-10975
1. Religion in the public schools. 2. Church and state in the U.S. I. Title.

FROMMER, Arthur, ed. 377.1
The Bible and the public schools. [New York, Frommer/Pasmantier, dist. Pocket Bks.] 190p. 21cm. (Liberal Pr. bk., 10542) 63-20920 1.25 pap.,
1. Religion in the public schools. I. Title.

FROMMER, Arthur, ed. 377.1
The Bible and the public schools. [New York, Frommer,/Pasmantier Pub. Corp., 1963] 190 p. 21 cm. [LC111.F73] 63-20920
1. Religion in the public schools. I. Title.

GRIFFITHS, William Edward, 1924- 377.10973
Religion, the courts, and the public schools; a century of litigation, by William E. Griffiths. Cincinnati, W. H. Anderson Co. [1966] x, 244 p. 24 cm. (American school law series) Bibliography: p. 233-236. [LC111.G7] 66-4636
1. Religion in the public schools. 2. Church and state in the U.S. I. Title.

LODER, James Edwin. 377
Religion and the public schools, by James E. Loder. New York, Association Press [1965] 125 p. 15 cm. (A Reflection book) [LC111.L57] 65-11091
1. Religion in the public schools. I. Title.

MCLAUGHLIN, Raymond, Sister, 1897- 377
Religious education and the state: democracy finds a way, by Sister M. Raymond McLaughlin. Washington, Catholic Univ. of Amer. Pr. [1967] ix, 439p. 22cm. Bibl. [LC473.M24] 67-21368 4.95 pap.,
1. Religion in the public schools. I. Title.

MINOR, John D., et al., plaintiffs. 377'.0973
The Bible in the public schools. Arguments before the Superior Court of Cincinnati in the case of Minor v. Board of Education of Cincinnati, 1870 with the opinions of the court and the opinion on appeal of the Supreme Court of Ohio. New Introd. by Robert G. McCloskey. New York, Da Capo Press, 1967. xvii, 438 p. 24 cm. Reprint of the 1870 ed. [LC113.C5M6 1967] 67-27464
1. Religion in the public schools. I. Cincinnati, Board of Education, et al, defendants. II. Cincinnati, Superior Court. III. Title.

MINOR, John D., et al., plaintiffs. 377'.0973
The Bible in the public schools. Arguments before the Superior Court of Cincinnati in the case of Minor v. Board of Education of Cincinnati, 1870 with the opinions of the court and the opinion on appeal of the Supreme Court of Ohio. New introd. by Robert G. McCloskey. New York, Da Capo, 1967. xvii, 438p. 24cm. Reprint of the 1870 ed. [LC113.C5M6 1967] 67-27464 15.00
1. Religion in the public schools. I. Cincinnati. Superior Court. II. Title.

Religion in the public schools—Baltimore.

O'HAIR, Madalyn Murray. 377'.1
An atheist epic: Bill Murray, the Bible, and the Baltimore Board of Education. Austin, Tex., American Atheist Press, 1970. xi, 316 p. illus., group port. 22 cm. On spine: Bill Murray, the Bible, and the Baltimore Board of Education. [LC113.B3O35] 72-129002 ISBN 0-911826-01-7
1. Religion in the public schools—Baltimore. I. Title. II. Title: Bill Murray, the Bible, and the Baltimore Board of Education.

Religion in the public schools—Law and legislation—United States

RICE, Charles E. 377.102673
The Supreme Court and public prayer, the need for restraint. New York, Fordham Univ. Pr. [c.1964] xiii, 202p. 24cm. Bibl. 64-18392 5.00
1. Religion in the public schools—Law and legislation—U.S. I. Title.

Religion in the public schools—Pittsburgh.

NATIONAL Conference of Christians and Jews. Committee on Religion in the Social Studies Curriculum of the Pittsburgh Public Schools. 377.1'09748'86
Religion in the social studies; report. Lawrence C. Little, editor. New York, National Conference of Christians and Jews, Religious Freedom and Public Affairs Project, 1966. 122 p. 29 cm. Bibliography: p. 120-122. [LC113.P56N3] 67-4159
1. Religion in the public schools—Pittsburgh. I. Little, Lawrence Calvin, 1897- ed. II. Title.

Religion in the public schools—United States

ADAMS, Marjorie E. Cook, comp. 377'.1
God in the classroom, edited by Marjorie E. Cook Adams. Westchester, Ill., Good News Publishers; [distributed by National Educator's Fellowship, South Pasadena, Calif., 1970] 94 p. 19 cm. (A "One evening" book) [LC111.A63] 74-24379 1.00
1. Religion in the public schools—U.S. I. Title.

NIELSEN, Niels Christian, 1921- 377
God in education; a new opportunity for American schools, by Niels C. Nielsen, Jr. New York, Sheed and Ward [1966] viii, 245 p. 22 cm. Includes bibliographical references. [111.N5] 65-20860
1. Religion in the public schools—U.S. 2. Church and state in the U.S. I. Title.

RELIGION and the schools: from prayer to public aid. 377'.0973 [Washington] National School Public Relations Association [1970] 55 p. 28 cm. (Education U.S.A. special report) Cover title. "Produced by the staff of Education U.S.A." Bibliography: p. 52-54. [LC111.R44] 77-19352 4.00
1. Religion in the public schools—U.S. I. National School Public Relations Association. II. Education U.S.A. III. Title. IV. Series.

Religion in the public schools—United States—Addresses, essays, lectures.

RELIGION and public education. 377'.1'0973 Edited by Theodor R. Sizer. Contributors: Nicholas Wolterstorff [and others] Boston, Houghton Mifflin [1967] xix, 361 p. 24 cm. Includes bibliographical references. [LC111.R4] 68-8656
1. Religion in the public schools—United States—Addresses, essays, lectures. I. Sizer, Theodor R., ed. II. Wolterstoff, Nicholas.

Religion in the public schools—United States—Handbooks, manuals, etc.

PANOCH, James V. 377'.1'0973
Religion goes to school; a practical handbook for teachers [by] James V. Panoch [and] David L. Barr. [1st ed.] New York, Harper & Row [1968] vii, 183 p. 21 cm. Bibliography: p. 114-183. [LC405.P3] 68-17598 5.95
1. Religion in the public schools—United States—Handbooks, manuals, etc. 2. Religious education—Bibliography. I. Barr, David L., joint author. II. Title.

Religion—Indexes—Bibliography.

CORNISH, G. P. 016.0162
A brief guide to abstracting and indexing services relevant to the study of religion / prepared on the occasion of the 13th Congress of the International Association for the History of Religions, at Lancaster, 15-22 August, 1975 by G. P. Cornish. Harrogate : Theological Abstracting and Bibliographical Services, [1975] [3], 14 p. ; 21 cm. [Z7751.C665] [BL48] 76-359019 ISBN 0-905098-00-5 : £0.20
1. Religion—Indexes—Bibliography. 2. Religion—Abstracts—Bibliography. I. International Association for the History of Religions.

DRURY, Clifford Merrill, 1897- comp.
Index to references to churches, clergymen and religious subjects mainly on the Pacific Coast, in The Pacific, organ of the Northern California Congregational Conference, 1851-1868, made at the San Francisco Theological Seminary, San Anselmo, California, under the direction of the Reverend Clifford M. Drury. [n.p.] 1961. 64-69155
I. Title.

Religion—Information services.

MOBERG, David O. 200
International directory of religious information systems. David O. Moberg, editor. Milwaukee, Wis., Dept. of Sociology and Anthropology, Marquette University [1971] 88 p. 23 cm. [BL35.M62] 75-156952
1. Religion—Information services. I. Marquette University, Milwaukee. Dept. of Sociology and Anthropology. II. Title.

Religion—Juvenile literature.

CAIN, Arthur H. 291
Young people and religion [by] Arthur H. Cain. New York, John Day Co. [1970] 159 p. 21 cm. Bibliography: p. 156-159. Examines the philosophic principles of the world's major religions and discusses the nature of the religious experience and its importance to man. [BL48.C3] 73-124155 4.95
1. Religion—Juvenile literature. 2. Religions—Juvenile literature. 3. [Religions.] I. Title.

FARIS, John Thomson, 1871- comp. 248
Pleasant Sunday afternoons for the children; a book for parents, comp. by John T. Faris ... Philadelphia, The Sunday school times company [c1937] 3 p. l., 5-110 p. illus. 19 cm. "Books for Sunday afternoon use": p. 99-102. [BV1590.F3] 7-32352
I. Title.

Religion—Miscellanea.

COULT, Allan D. 200
Psychedelic anthropology : the study of man through the manifestation of the mind / Allan D. Coult. Philadelphia : Dorrance, c1977. xxix, 296 p. : ill. ; 22 cm. Bibliography: p. 287-296. [BL50.C68] 77-151025 ISBN 0-8059-2270-9 : 10.95
1. Religion—Miscellanea. 2. Anthropology—Miscellanea. I. Title.

THE Master library... 221.
Cleveland, O., Springfield, Mass., The Foundation press, inc. [c1923] v. col. front., illus., plates (part col.) 24 1/2 cm. General editor: W. S. Athearn. "My best book...arranged and edited by Walter Scott Athearn... Alberta Munkres...and Minetta Sammis Leonard." Contents.--v. 1. Leaders of olden days.--v. 2. The book of the kingdom.--v. 3. Heroes and heroines.--v. 4. The living wisdom.--v. 5. Songs of the seers.--v. 6. Everyday life in old Judea.--v. 7. The perfect life.-- v. 8. Pioneers of the faith. Supplement: My best book. [BS551.M37] 24-21484
I. Athearn, Walter Scott, 1872- ed.

SWIFT, Morrison Isaac, 1856- 211
The evil religion does, by Morrison I. Swift. Boston, The Liberty press, 1927. 2 p. l., 111 p. 20 1/2 cm. [BL2775.C85] 28-6648
I. Title.

SWIFT, Morrison Isaac, 1856- 211
The evil religion does, by Morrison I. Swift. Boston, The Liberty press, 1927. 2 p. l., 111 p. 20 1/2 cm. [BL2775.C85] 28-6648
I. Title.

Religion, Modern.

FEELY, Raymond T. 242
... Thoughts for today, by Raymond T. Feely, S. J. New York, Cincinnati [etc.] Benziger brothers, 1925. 110 p. 14 cm. (Morning-star series. I) [BX2182.F4] 25-23432
I. Title.

HENRY, Francis Augustus, 1847- 220
The knowledge of religious truth, and other papers, by Francis A. Henry. Boston, New York, The Cornhill publishing company [c1922] ix, 297 p. 25 cm. [BR125.H5] 22-19077
I. Title.
Contents omitted.

SKIDMORE, Sydney Tuthill, 1844- 244
The new pilgrim's progress; a modern aspect ... by Sydney T. Skidmore. Philadelphia, Dorrance and company, 1925. 290 p. 20 cm. [BV4515.S56] 25-20146
I. Title.

Religion—New York (City)—Statistics.

PROTESTANTS Council of the City of New York. Dept. of Church Planning and Research. Religious affiliations, New York, 1958-59. 2 v. in 1. tables.
1. Religion—New York (City)—Statistics. 2. New York (City)—Statistics. I. National Council of the Churches of Christ in the United States of America.

Religion—Periodicals—Bibliography.

WALSH, Michael J. 016.200'5
Religious bibliographies in serial literature : a guide / complied by Michael J. Walsh, with the help of John V. Howard, Graham P. Cornish, and Robert J. Duckett, on behalf of the Association of British Theological and Philosophical Libraries ; foreword by John V. Howard. Westport, Conn. : Greenwood Press, 1981. p. cm. Includes index. Bibliography: p. [Z7753.W34] [BL1] 19 81-312 ISBN 0-313-22987-2 lib. bdg. : 39.95
1. Religion—Periodicals—Bibliography. 2. Theology—Periodicals—Bibliography. I. Title.

Religion—Periodicals—Indexes.

AMERICAN Theological Library Association. 016.22592
Index to religious periodical literature; an author and subject index to periodical literature, including an author index to book reviews. 1949-52-- [Chicago] v. 24cm. [Z7753.A5] A54
1. Religion—Period.—Indexes. 2. Religious literature—Bibl. I. Title.

Religion, Personal.

ALLPORT, Gordon Willard, 1897-
The individual and his religion; a psychological interpretation. New York, Macmillan, 1960. xi, 147 p. 21 cm. (Macmillan paperbacks) Bibliographical footnotes. NUC65
1. Religion, Personal. I. Title.

ANTHONY, Alfred Williams, 1860-
The method of Jesus; an interpretation of personal religion. New York, Boston, [etc.] Silver, Burdett & co., 1899. 364 p. 12 cm. Jan
I. Title.

BEGBIE, Harold, 1871- 248
Life changers (More twice-born men) narratives of a recent movement in the spirit of personal religion, by Harold Begbie ... New ed. New York & London, G. O. Putnam's sons, 1927. xi, 142 p. 21 cm. "Published in 1923 under title: More twice-born men." [BV4915.B43 1927] 27-27946
I. Title.

CAREY, Walter Julius. 225
My ideals of religion, by Walter J. Carey ... London, New York [etc.] Longmans, Green and co., 1917. xv, 77, [1] p. 19 cm. [BR121.C35] 18-13345
I. Title.

... *Christianity and problems* 204
of to-day, lectures delivered before Lake Forest college on the foundation of the late William Bross. New York, C. Scribner's sons, 1922. 5 p. l., 3-159 p. 19 1/2 cm. (The Bross lectures, 1921) Half-title: The Bross library, vol. xi. Contents.From generation to generation, by J.H. Finley.--Jesus' social plan, by C.F. Kent.--Personal religion and public morals, by R.B. Taylor.--Religion and social discontent, by P.E. More.--The teachings of Jesus as factors in international politics, with especial reference to Far-Eastern problems, by J.W. Jenks. [BR50.C55] 22-18944
I. Finley, John Huston, 1863- II. Kent, Charles Foster, 1867-1925. III. Taylor, Robert Bruce. IV. More, Paul pelmer, 1864- V. Jenks, Jeremiah Whipple, 1856-1929.

CRAIG, Clarence Tucker. 248
... *The Christian's personal religion;* an elective course for young people, by Clarence Tucker Craig ... New York, Cincinnati, The Methodist book concern [c1925] 122 p. 19 cm. (Studies in Christian living) "Approved by the Committee on curriculum of the Board of education of the Methodist Episcopal church." [BV4501.C74] 26-881
I. Title.

CROWLEY, Dale. 286'.1'0924 B
My life, a miracle. Washington, National Bible Knowledge Association [1971] xi, 211 p. illus., facsims., ports. 23 cm. [BV3785.C86A3] 73-155933 5.00
I. Title.

GILLIES, Andrew, 1870- 261
The individualistic gospel, and other essays, by Andrew Gillies. New York, Cincinnati, The Methodist book concern [c1919] 208 p. 20 cm. [BR85.G45] 19-15947
I. Title.

GILLIES, Andrew, 1870- 261
The individualistic gospel, and other essays, by Andrew Gillies. New York, Cincinnati, The Methodist book concern [c1919] 208 p. 20 cm. [BR85.G45] 19-15947
I. Title.

GORDON, George Angier, 1853- 922.
1929.
My education and religion, an autobiography, by George A. Gordon ... Boston and New York, Houghton Mifflin company, 1925. 6 p. l., 352 p. plates, 2 port. (incl. front.) 23 cm. [BX7260.G65A3] 25-18281
I. Title.

HUIZINGA, A. v. C. P.
Belief in a personal God, by A. v. C. P. Huizinga. Boston, Sherman, French & company, 1910. 52 p. 19 1/2 cm. $0.50 10-6164
I. Title.

*JOHNSON, Mel. 248.4'2
Straight from the shoulder; answers to questions teens ask. Chicago, Moody [1967] 63p. 19cm. .95 pap.,
I. Title.

MANGASARIAN, Mangasar M., 1859-
The story of my mind; or, How I became a rationalist, by M. M. Mangasarian. Chicago, Independent religious society [c1909] 125 p. 16 1/2 cm. $0.50 10-1680
I. Title.

ORAISON, Marc. 282'.0924 B
Strange voyage; the autobiography of a non-conformist. Translated by J. F. Bernard. [1st ed.] Garden City, N.Y., Doubleday, 1970 [c1969] 236 p. 22 cm. Translation of Tete dure. [BX4705.O498A33] 77-116243 5.95
I. Title.

RUST, Charles Herbert, 1869-
Personal religion, by Charles Herbert Rust... Boston, The Gorham press; [etc., etc., c1915] 279 p. 19 1/2 cm. (Lettered on cover: Library of religious thought) $1.25 15-23095
I. Title.

WALKER, Alan.
My faith is enough. Nashville, Tidings [1963?] 94 p. 20 cm. Published in London, Epworth Press, 1963, as Christ is enough. NUC68
I. Title.

WILLIAMS, Laura, 1896- 922
My life and vision, the story of Bishop (Mother) Laura Williams; her own trials, in service to the Highest, and her revelations, told by herself to the glory of God. Detroit, Starlight Temple of Truth [1948] 86 p. illus., ports. 23 cm. [BX9998.W5A3] 48-2832
I. Title.

Religion—Philosophy.

ABBOT, Francis Ellingwood, 201
1836-1903.
The way out of agnosticism; or, The philosophy of free religion, by Francis Ellingwood Abbot... Boston, Little, Brown, and company, 1890. xi, 83 p. 20 cm. "Based on notes of forty-one lectures delivered in 1888, in the 'Advanced course, Philosophy 13', Harvard university. Originally published during...1889 as a series of contributions to a monthly periodical in Boston."--p [v] "Press notices of [the author's] Scientific theism": p. [77]-83. [BL51.A3] 30-11307
1. Religion—Philosophy. 2. Agnosticism. I. Title.

ABBOT, Francis Ellingwood, 210
1936-1903.
The way out of agnosticism : or, The philosophy of free religion / by Francis Ellingwood Abbot. New York : AMS Press, 1980. p. cm. Reprint of the 2d ed., 1890, published by Little, Brown, Boston. [BL51.A3 1980] 75-3014 ISBN 0-404-59008-X : 15.00
1. Religion—Philosophy. 2. Agnosticism. I. Title.

ABERNETHY, George L., ed. 201
Philosophy of religion, a book of readings, edited by George L. Abernethy and Thomas A. Langford. New York, Macmillan [1962] 542 p. 24 cm. Includes bibliography. [BL51.A32] 62-7056
1. Religion—Philosophy. I. Langford, Thomas A., joint ed. II. Title.

ABERNETHY, George L. 201
Philosophy of religion; a book of readings, edited by George L. Abernethy and Thomas A. Langford. 2d ed. New York, Macmillan [1968] xvii, 586 p. 24 cm. Includes bibliographies. [BL51.A32 1968] 68-10237
1. Religion—Philosophy. I. Langford, Thomas A., joint ed. II. Title.

ADAMS, Charles Coffin, 1810- 201
1888.
Anthroposophy, by the Rev. Charles C. Adams,... New York, W. B. Smith & co. [1881] 81 p. 19 1/2 cm. (Lettered on cover: Current thought series, no.1) [BL51.A4] 30-11308
1. Religion—Philosophy. I. Title.

ALEXANDER, Hartley Burr, 201
1873-
God and man's destiny; inquiries into the metaphysical foundations of faith, by Hartley Burr Alexander. New York, Oxford university press, 1936. viii p., 1 l., 235 p. 22 cm. "First edition." [BL51.A47] 36-
1. Religion—Philosophy. I. Title.

ALLIBACO, W. A. 201
The philosophic and scientific ultimatum, written in the constitution and laws of universe by the omnipotent hand of divine intelligence, and spread before all mankind in the universal language of organic mind and matter, cause and effect, for the guide of nations and the promotion of human happiness. Copied, as read from the divine original, by W. A. Allibaco ... New-York, The author, 1864. 3 p. l., [5]-420 p. 19 1/2 cm. [BL51.A5] 26-22124
1. Religion—Philosophy. I. Title.

ANDERSON, Paul Russell, 1907- 215
Science in defense of liberal religion; a study of Henry More's attempt to link seventeenth century religion with science, by Paul Russell Anderson, PH. D. New York and London, G. P. Putnam's sons, 1933. 232 p. 21 cm. Thesis (ph. d.)--Columbia university, 1963. Without thesis note. Bibliography: p. 215-221. [BL239.M6A6 1933] 33-33090
1. More, Henry, 1614-1687. 2. Religion—Philosophy. 3. Religion and science—History of controversy. I. Title.

ARNETT, Willard Eugene, 1921- 201
Religion and judgment; an essay on the method and meaning of religion. New York, Appleton-Century-Crofts [1966] xi, 835 p. 22 cm. (The Century philosophy series) Bibliography: p. 323-327. [BL51.A7] 66-11680
1. Religion — Philosophy. I. Title.

*ASHTON, John. 211'.7
Why were the gospels written? Notre Dame, Ind., Fides Publishers [1973] 91 p. 18 cm. (Theology today series, no. 15) Bibliography: p. 90-91. [BL51.] ISBN 0-85342-261-3 0.95 (pbk.)
1. Religion—Philosophy. I. Title.

AVEY, Albert Edwin, 1886- 201
Re-thinking religion, by Albert E. Avey ... New York, H. Holt and company [c1936] vii p. 1 l., 294 p. 21 cm. [BL51.A85] 36-35588
1. Religion—Philosophy. I. Title.

BAILLIE, John, 1886-1960.
The sense of the presence of God. London, Oxford UP, 1962. 269 p. (Gifford lectures, 1961-2) NUC63
1. Religion—Philosophy. I. Title. II. Series.

BARNHART, Joe E., 1931- 200'.19
Religion and the challenge of philosophy / by J. E. Barnhart. Totowa, N.J. : Littlefield, Adams, 1975. x, 312 p. ; 21 cm. (A Littlefield, Adams quality paperback ; no. 291) Includes bibliographical references and indexes. [BL51.B245] 75-16364 ISBN 0-8226-0291-1 pbk. : 4.95
1. Religion—Philosophy. I. Title.

BARROW, George Alexander. 201
The validity of the religious experience, a preliminary study in the philosophy of religion, by George A. Barrow ... Boston, Sherman, French & company, 1917. 3 p. l., xi, 247 p. 21 cm. The latter part of lecture ii appeared in the Journal of religious psychology under the title "The reality of the religious experience". cf. "Note." [BL51.B25] 17-13311
1. Religion—Philosophy. I. Title.

BASCOM, John, 1827-1911. 201
A philosophy of religion; or, The rational grounds of religious belief, by John Bascom ... New York, G. P. Putnam's sons, 1876. 1 p. l., [v]-xx, 566 p. 19 cm. [BL51.B3] 12-30361
1. Religion—Philosophy. I. Title.

BEECHER, Catherine Esther, 201
1800-1878.
Common sense applied to religion, or, The Bible and the people. By Catharine E. Beecher ... New York, Harper & brothers; Montreal, B. Dawson, 1857. 2 p. l., [vii]-xxxv, [9]-358 p. 20 cm. Running title: The Bible and the people. [BL51.B5] 30-11309
1. Religion—Philosophy. I. Title. II. Title: The Bible and the people.

BERDIAEV, Nikolai 201
Aleksandrovich, 1874-1948.
Freedom and the spirit. [by] Nicolas Berdyaev. Translated by Oliver Fielding Clarke. Freeport, N.Y., Books for Libraries Press [1972] xix, 361 p. 22 cm. Translation of Filosofiia svobodnago dukha. [BL51.B5244 1972] 72-2567 ISBN 0-8369-6848-4
1. Religion—Philosophy. 2. Apologetics—20th century. I. Title.

BERTOCCI, Peter Anthony. 201
Introduction to the philosophy of religion. New York, Prentice-Hall, 1951. 565 p. 22 cm. (Prentice-Hall philosophy series) [BL51.B54] 51-14584
1. Religion—Philosophy. I. Title.

BERTOCCI, Peter Anthony. 201
Religion as creative insecurity [by] Peter A. Bertocci. Westport, Conn., Greenwood Press [1973, c1958] 128 p. 22 cm. Reprint of the ed. published by Association Press, New York. Bibliography: p. 127-128. [BL51.B543 1973] 73-1836 ISBN 0-8371-6803-1 8.00
1. Religion—Philosophy. 2. Security (Psychology) I. Title.

BERTOCCI, Peter Anthony. 201
Religion as creative insecurity. New York, Association Press [1958] 128 p. 20 cm. Includes bibliography. [BL51.B543] 58-6471
1. Religion—Philosophy. 2. Security (Psychology) I. Title.

BETTIS, Joseph Dabney, 200'.1
comp.
Phenomenology of religion; eight modern descriptions of the essence of religion. [1st U.S. ed.] New York, Harper & Row [1969] viii, 245 p. 21 cm. (Harper forum books) Contents.Contents.—Introduction, by J. D. Bettis.—An introduction to phenomenology: What is phenomenology? by M. Merleau-Ponty.—The phenomenology of religion: The meaning of religion, by W. B. Kristensen.—A naturalistic description: Religion in essence and manifestation, by G. van der Leeuw.—A supernaturalistic description: Approaches to God, by J. Maritain.—A projective description: The essence of Christianity, by L. Feuerbach.—Religion as a faculty: On religion, by F. Schleiermacher. The Christian faith, by F. Schleiermacher.—Religion as a dimension: Religion as a dimension in man's spiritual life, by P. Tillich.—Religion as a social function: Magic, science, and religion, by B. Malinowski.—Religion as structure and archetype: The sacred and the profane, by M. Eliade.—Religion as encounter: I and thou, by M. Buber. Bibliographical footnotes. [BL51.B547 1969] 69-17005 3.50
1. Religion—Philosophy. 2. Phenomenology. I. Title.

BLOOD, Benjamin Paul, 1832- 201
1919.
The philosophy of justice between God and man; being an attempt to show, from a candid examination of the Scripture and the powers of entities, that the existing philosophy of religion, both Calvinist and Arminian, is opposed to the Bible and to reason. By Benjamin Blood ... New York, J.S. Taylor, 1851. viii, 209 p. 19 1/2 cm. [BL51.B6] 30-11310
1. Religion—Philosophy. I. Title.

BODKIN, Maud. 201
Studies of type-images in poetry, religion, and philosophy. London, New York, Oxford University Press, 1951. xii, 184 p. 21 cm. [BL51.B62] 51-14429
1. Religion—Philosophy. I. Title.

BODKIN, Maud. 201
Studies of type-images in poetry, religion, and philosophy. [Folcroft, Pa.] Folcroft Library Editions, 1974. p. cm. Reprint of the 1951 ed. published by the Oxford University Press, London. [BL51.B62 1974] 74-14665 15.00 (lib. bdg.).
1. Religion—Philosophy. I. Title.

BOSTROM, Christopher Jacob, 201
1797-1866.
Philosophy of religion. Translation with introd. [by] Victor E. Beck [and] Robert N. Beck. New Haven, Yale University Press, 1962. lvi, 187p. 23cm. 'The original research and translation ... were done by [Victor E. Beck] ... and submitted to Boston University ... as a dissertation, 'A translation of C. J. Bostrom's Philosophy of religion with a critical commentary,' 1947.' 'The translation is the third part of Bostrom's lectures on religion ... recorded from class notes and edited by Sigurd Ribbing ... in the volume Chr. Jac. Bostrom's forelisningar I religionsfilosofi.' Bibliography: p.177-181. [BL51.B642] 62-8236
1. Religion— Philosophy. I. Beck, Victor Emanuel, 1894- ed. and tr. II. Title.

BRADSHAW, Marion John, 1886- 201
Philosophical foundations of faith, a contribution toward a philosophy of religion. New York, AMS Press [1969, c1941] x, 254 p. 23 cm. Includes bibliographical references. [BL51.B6485 1969] 78-99248
1. Religion—Philosophy. 2. Philosophy and religion. I. Title.

BRADSHAW, Marion John, 1886- 201
Philosophical foundations of faith, a contribution towards a philosophy of religion by Marion John Bradshaw. New York, Columbia university press, 1941. x p., 1 l., 254 p. 21 cm. Bibliography: p.233-242. [BL51.B6435] 41-9269
1. Religion—Philosophy. 2. Philosophy and religion. I. Title.

BRANN, Henry Athanasius, 1837-1921.
Curious questions. By Rev. Henry A. Brann, D.D. Newark, N. J., J. J. O'Connor & co., 1866. vii, [9]-292 p 20 cm. [BD573.B7] 11-24753
1. Religion—Philosophy. I. Title.

BRIGHTMAN, Edgar Sheffield, 1884- 201
A philosophy of religion. London, New York, Sheffington [1947] 291 p. 22 cm. "Historical bibliography": p. 268-270. "General bibliography": p. 271-284. [BL51.B689 1947] 48-1258
1. Religion—Philosophy. I. Title.

BRIGHTMAN, Edgar Sheffield, 1884- 201
A philosophy of religion, by Edgar Sheffield Brightman... New York, Prentice-Hall, inc., 1940. xvii, 539 p. 21 cm. [Prentice-Hall philosophy series: A. E. Murphy, PH.D., editor] "Historical bibliography": p. 490-494; "General bibliography": p. 495-522. [BL51.B689] 40-9467
1. Religion—Philosophy. I. Title.

BRIGHTMAN, Edgar, Sheffield, 1884- 201
Religious values, by Edgar Sheffield Brightman... New York, Cincinnati, The Abingdon press [c1925] 285 p. 21 1/2 cm. [BL51.B7] 25-19441
1. Religion—Philosophy. I. Title.

BRIGHTMAN, Edgar Sheffield, 1884-1953. 200'.1
Personality and religion / Edgar Sheffield Brightman. 1st AMS ed. New York : AMS Press, 1979, c1934. 160 p. ; 23 cm. (Philosophy in America) Reprint of the ed. published by Abingdon Press, New York, and issued as the Lowell Institute lectures, 1934. Includes bibliographical references and index. [BL51.B688 1979] 75-3084 ISBN 0-404-59083-7 : 14.50
1. Religion—Philosophy. 2. Personalism. 3. Theism. I. Title. II. Series: Lowell Institute lectures ; 1934.

BRIGHTMAN, Edgar Sheffield, 1884-1953. 200'.1
A philosophy of religion. New York, Greenwood Press [1969, c1940] xvii, 539 p. 23 cm. Bibliography: p. 490-522. [BL51.B689 1969] 72-95112
1. Religion—Philosophy. I. Title.

BRINTON, Daniel Garrison, 1837-1899. 201
The religious sentiment, its source and aim; a contribution to the science and philosophy of religion. By Daniel G. Brinton ... New York, H. Holt and company, 1876. iv p., 1 l., 234 p. 20 cm. [BL51.B75]
1. Religion—Philosophy. I. Title.

BROD, Max, 1884-1968. 200'.1
Paganism, Christianity, Judaism; a confession of faith. Translated from the German by William Wolf. University, University of Alabama Press [1970] x, 276 p. 24 cm. Translation of Heidentum, Christentum, Judentum. [BL51.B75713] 78-104937 10.00
1. Religion—Philosophy. I. Title.

BRONSTEIN, Daniel J 1908- ed. 201
Approaches to the philosophy of religion; a book of readings, edited by Daniel J. Bronstein and Harold M. Schulweis. New York, Prentice- Hall, 1954. 532p. 22cm. Includes bibliography. [BL51.B76] 54-11638
1. Religion—Philosophy. I. Schulweis, Harold M., joint ed. II. Title.

BRONSTEIN, Daniel J., 1908- ed. 200'.1
Approaches to the philosophy of religion; a book of readings, edited by Daniel Jay Bronstein and Harold M. Schulweis. Freeport, N.Y., Books for Libraries Press [1969, c1954] ix, 532 p. 22 cm. (Essay index reprint series) Bibliography: p. 519-522. [BL51.B76 1969] 77-93320
1. Religion—Philosophy. I. Schulweis, Harold M. II. Title.

BROWN, Stuart C. 200'.1
Do religious claims make sense? [By] Stuart C. Brown. New York, Macmillan [1969] xx, 188 p. 23 cm. Includes bibliographical references. [BL51.B777 1969b] 71-93568 5.95
1. Religion—Philosophy. I. Title.

BROWN, William Adams, 1865- 201
Pathways to certainty, by William Adams Brown... New York, London, C. Scribner's sons, 1930. xiv, p., 2 l., 3-296 p. 20 1/2 cm. Bibliography: p. [277]-284. [BR100.B67] 30-32177
1. Religion—Philosophy. 2. Christianity. I. Title.

BROWNELL, Baker, 1887- 201
Earth is enough; an essay in religious realism, by Baker Brownell ... New York and London, Harper & brothers, 1933. viii p., 2 l., 3-347, [1] p. illus. 22 1/2 cm. "First edition." "References": p. 313-317. [BL51.B78] 33-3042
1. Religion—Philosophy. I. Title.

BRUNNER, Heinrich Emil, 1889- 201
The philosophy of religion from the standpoint of Protestant theology, by Emil Brunner; translated by A. J. D. Farrer and Bertram Lee Woolf. New York, C. Scribner's sons, 1937. 2 p. l., vii-x, 11-194 p. 21 cm. (Half-title: The international library of "hristian knowledge, ed. by W. A. Brown and B. L. Woolf) "Printed in Great Britain." [BL51.B786] 37-13664
1. Religion—Philosophy. 2. Theology, Doctrinal. 3. Protestantism. I. Farrar, Augustine John Daniel, 1872- tr. II. Title.

BRUNNER, Heinrich Emil, 1889-1966. 201
The philsosphy of religion from the standpoint of Protestant theology / by Emil Brunner ; translated by A. J. D. Farrer and Bertram Lee Woolf. Westport, Conn. : Hyperion Press, [1979] p. cm. Translation of Religionsphilosophie evangelischer theologie. Reprint of the 1937 ed. published by Scribner, New York, in series: The International library of Christian knowledge. Includes index. [BL51.B78613 1979] 78-14106 ISBN 0-88355-779-7 : 17.00
1. Religion—Philosophy. 2. Theology, Doctrinal. 3. Protestantism. I. Title. II. Series: The International library of Christian knowledge.

BRYANT, William McKendree, 1843- 201
Life, death and immortality; with kindred essays, by William M. Bryant ... New York, The Baker and Taylor co., 1898. vi, [2], 442 p. 21 cm. Four of the essays have previously appeared in periodicals; the last one has been printed separately. cf. Pref. [BL51.B8] 11-24745
1. Religion—Philosophy. 2. Immortality. 3. Christianity and other religions. I. Title.
Contents omitted.

BUBER, Martin, 1878- 201
Eclipse of God; studies in the relation between religion and philosophy. New York, Harper [1957, c1952] 152p. 21cm. (Harper torchbooks, TB12) Includes bibliography. [BL51.B82 1957] 61-678
1. Religion—Philosophy. 2. Philosophy and religion. I. Title.

BUBER, Martin, 1878- 201
Eclipse of God; studies in the relation between religion and philosophy. [1st ed.] New York, Harper [1952] 192 p. 20 cm. [BL51.B82] 52-8464
1. Religion—Philosophy. 2. Religion and philosophy. I. Title.

BUBER, Martin, 1878-1965. 201
Eclipse of God : studies in the relation between religion and philosophy / Martin Buber. Westport, Conn. : Greenwood Press, 1977. p. cm. Translation of Gottesfinsternis. Reprint of the 1952 ed. published by Harper, New York, which was issued as TB12 of Harper torchbooks. Includes index. Bibliography: p. [BL51.B8213 1977] 77-10030 ISBN 0-8371-9718-X lib.bdg. : 14.00
1. Religion—Philosophy. 2. Philosophy and religion. I. Title.

BUBER, Martin, 1878-1965. 201
Eclipse of God; studies in the relation between religion and philosophy. New York, Harper [1957, c1952] 152 p. 21 cm. (Harper torchbooks, TB12) Includes bibliography. [BL51.B82 1957] 61-678
1. Religion—Philosophy. 2. Philosophy and religion. I. Title.

BURCH, George Bosworth, 1902- 200'.1
Alternative goals in religion; love, freedom, truth. With a foreword by W. Norris Clarke. Montreal, McGill-Queen's University Press, [1973 c1972] 118 p. 22 cm. Includes bibliographical references. [BL51.B84] 72-82248 ISBN 0-7735-0122-3 6.50
1. Religion—Philosophy. 2. Absolute, The. 3. Christianity. 4. Buddha and Buddhism. 5. Vedanta. I. Title.
Publisher's Address: 136 South Broadway N.Y. 10533. pap 2.50; ISBN 0-7735-0163-0.

BURKE, Thomas Patrick, 1934- 200'.1
The fragile universe : an essay in the philosophy of religions / Patrick Burke. New York : Barnes & Noble Books, 1979. viii, 129 p. ; 22 cm. (Library of philosophy and religion series) Includes bibliographical references and index. [BL51.LB853 1979] 78-17885 ISBN 0-06-490776-7 : 22.50
1. Religion—Philosophy. I. Title.

BURKE, Thomas Patrick, 1934- 200'.1
The reluctant vision; an essay in the philosophy of religion [by] T. Patrick Burke. Philadelphia, Fortress Press [1974] 136 p. 19 cm. Includes bibliographic references. [BL51.B854] 73-88354 ISBN 0-8006-1068-7 3.00
1. Religion—Philosophy. I. Title.

BURRELL, David B. 200'.1
Exercises in religious understanding [by] David B. Burrell. Notre Dame, University of Notre Dame Press [1974] x, 243 p. 22 cm. Includes bibliographical references. [BL51.B858] 74-12566 ISBN 0-268-00548-6 ISBN 0-268-00549-4 (pbk.) 9.95
1. Religion—Philosophy. I. Title.

BURROUGHS, James H 201
In praise of zero; thoughts on revealed religion and nature, by James H. Burroughs. Philadelphia, Dorrance [1964] 84 p. illus 20 cm. [BL51.B86] 63-22254
1. Religion — Philosophy. I. Title.

BURTT, Edwin Arthur, 1892- 201
Types of religious philosophy. Rev. ed. New York, Harper [1951] xi, 468 p. 22 cm. Includes bibliographies. [BL51.B87 1951] 51-11521
1. Religion—Philosophy. 2. Religion—Philosophy—History. I. Title.

BURTT, Edwin Arthur, 1892- 201
Types of religious philosophy, by Edwin A. Burtt... New York and London, Harper & brothers [c1939] ix p., 1 l., 512 p. 22 cm. "First edition." "Selected bibliography" at end of most of the chapters. [BL51.B87] 38-29086
1. Religion—Philosophy. 2. Religion—Philosophy—Hist. I. Title.
Contents omitted.

BUTLER, Frederick William James. 239
Christian thought, a grammar of reinterpretation; or, Christianity and nature, by F. W. Butler ... London, Society for promoting Christian knowledge. New York and Toronto, The Macmillan co. [1929] xii, 147, [1] p. 20 cm. [BR100.B8] 30-8849
1. Religion—Philosophy. 2. Christianity. I. Title. II. Title: Christianity and nature.

CAIRD, John, 1820-1898. 200'.1
An introduction to the philosophy of religion. New ed. New York, AMS Press [1970] xi, 343 p. 23 cm. Reprint of the 1901 ed. [BL51.C25 1970] 75-113569
1. Religion—Philosophy. I. Title.

CALHOUN, Robert Lowry, 1896- 201
God and the common life. Hamden, Conn., Shoe String Press [1954, c1935] 303p. 23cm. Includes bibliography. [BL51.C32 1954] 59-40376
1. Religion—Philosophy. 2. God. 3. Vocation. I. Title.

CALHOUN, Robert Lowry, 1896- 201
God and the common life, by Robert Lowry, Calhoun ... New York, London, C. Scribner's sons, 1935. xxiv, 303 p. 21 cm. "Notes": p. [251]-286. [BL51.C32] 35-10870
1. Religion—Philosophy. 2. God. 3. Profession, Choice of. I. Title.

CAPITAN, William H. 200'.1
Philosophy of religion; an introduction [by] William H. Capitan. Indianapolis, Pegasus [1972] viii, 214 p. 21 cm. (Traditions in philosophy) Bibliography: p. 207-209. [BL51.C324] 70-128669
1. Religion—Philosophy. I. Title.

CARPENTER, William Boyd, bp. of Ripon, 1841-1918. 201
The permanent elements of religion. Eight lectures preached before the University of Oxford in the year 1887 on the foundation of the late Rev. John Bampton ... by W. Boyd Carpenter ... London and New York, Macmillan and co., 1889. 3 p. l., [ix]-ixiv, 423, [1] p. 23 cm. (Half-title: The Bampton lectures for mdccclxxxvii) [BR45.B3 1887] 230.082 38-16291
1. Religion—Philosophy. I. Title.

*CASSELS, Louis. 201'.1
Forbid them not. New York, Family library, 1973 94 p., illus, 18 cm. [BT77] ISBN 0-515-03207-7. 0.95 (pbk.)
1. Religion—Philosophy. I. Title.

CERMINARA, Gina. 200'.1
Insights for the age of aquarius. Englewood Cliffs, N.J., Prentice-Hall [1973] 314 p. 24 cm. Includes bibliographical references. [BL51.C44 1973] 72-8449 ISBN 0-13-467589-4 7.95
1. Religion—Philosophy. 2. General semantics. I. Title.

CERMINARA, Gina. 200'.1
Insights for the age of aquarius : a guide to religious realism / by Gina Cerminara. Wheaton, Ill. : Theosophical Pub. House, 1976, c1973. p. cm. (A Quest book) Includes bibliographical references and index. [BL51.C44 1976] 76-6173 ISBN 0-8356-0483-7
1. Religion—Philosophy. 2. General semantics. I. Title.

CHARLESWORTH, Maxwell John. 200'.1
Philosophy of religion: the historic approaches [by] M. J. Charlesworth. [New York] Herder and Herder [1972] xiv, 216 p. 22 cm. (Philosophy of religion series) Includes bibliographical references. [BL51.C49 1972b] 75-176367 8.95
1. Religion—Philosophy. I. Title.

CHARTIER, Emile, 1868-1951. 200'.1
The gods [by] Alain. Translated by Richard Pevear. [New York, New Directions Pub. Corp., 1974] 186 p. 21 cm. (A New Directions book) Translation of Les dieux. Contents.Contents.—Aladdin.—Pan.—Jupiter.—Christophorous.—Selected bibliography (p. 185-186.) [BL51.C513 1974] 74-8291 ISBN 0-8112-0547-9 ISBN 0-8112-0547-9 8.95
1. Religion—Philosophy. 2. Truth. 3. Gods. I. Title.
Pbk. 3.95, ISBN 0-8112-0548-7

CLARK, Gordon Haddon. 370.1
A Christian philosophy of education, by Gordon H. Clark. Grand Rapids, Mich.; Wm. B. Eerdmans publishing company [1946] 217 p. 20 cm. [BL51.C54] 46-8097
1. Religion—Philosophy. I. Title.

CLARK, Gordon Haddon. 201
Religion, reason, and revelation. Philadelphia, Presbyterian and Reformed Pub. Co., 1961. 241 p. 22 cm. (International library of philosophy and theology. Philosophical and historical studies series) [BL51.C544] 61-11012

1. Religion—Philosophy. 2. Ethics. 3. Free will and determinism. I. Title.

*COKER, Marie. 218
So tomorrow. New York, Vantage Press [1974] 57 p. 21 cm. [BL53] ISBN 0-533-01123-X 3.95
1. Religion—Philosophy. 2. Conduct of life. I. Title.

COLLINGWOOD, Robin George, 1889-1943. 200'.1
Faith & reason; essays in the philosophy of religion. Edited with an introd. by Lionel Rubinoff. Chicago, Quadrangle Books, 1968. 317 p. 22 cm. Bibliography: p. [305]-311. [BL51.C595] 67-21641
1. Religion—Philosophy. I. Rubinoff, Lionel, ed. II. Title.

CONGER, George Perrigo, 1884- 201
The ideologics of religion, by George Perrigo Conger ... New York, Round table press, inc., 1940. viii, 271 p. 22 1/2 cm. "References: at end of each chapter. [BL51.C636] 40-33408
1. Religion—Philosophy. I. Title.

CONGER, George Perrigo, 1884- 200'.1
The ideologies of religion. Freeport, N.Y., Books for Libraries Press [1969] viii, 271 p. 23 cm. (Essay index reprint series) Reprint of the 1940 ed. Includes bibliographical reference. [BL51.C636 1969] 70-93329
1. Religion—Philosophy. I. Title.

COOK, Stanley Arthur, 1873- 201
The foundations of religion. By Stanley A. Cook ... London and Edinburgh, T. C. & E. C. Jack; New York, Dodge publishing co. [1914] 1 p. l., v-vii, 9-96 p. 1/2 cm. (Lettered on cover: The People's books. [119]) Bibliography: p. 93-94. [BL51.C65] A 15
1. Religion—Philosophy. I. Title.

CRANE, Wendell K. 248.84
Life is a Journey. New York, Vantage [c.1962] 101p. 21cm. 2.75 bds.
I. Title.

CULVERWEL, Nathanael, d.1651? 211'.6
An elegant and learned discource of the light of nature : with other treatises, including Spiritual opticks, 1652 / Nathanael Culverwel. New York : Garland Pub., 1978. 215, 212 p. ; 23 cm. (British philosophers and theologians of the 17th & 18th centuries) Spine title: Discourse of the light of nature. Reprint of the ed. printed by T. R. and E. M. for J. Rothwell, London. [BL51.C8 1978] 75-11215 ISBN 0-8240-1769-2 : lib.bdg. : 29.50
1. Religion—Philosophy. I. Title. II. Series.

DAKIN, Arthur Hazard, jr. 201
Von Hugel and the supernatural, by A. Hazard Dakin, jr. ... London, Society for promoting Christian knowledge; New York, The Macmillan company [1934] xii, 273, [1] p. front., ports., facsim. 22 cm. "Erratum" slip mounted on p. 257. Bibliography: p. [263]-270. [BX4705.H77D6] 35-1684
1. Hugel, Friedrich, frelherr von, 1852-1925. 2. Religion—Philosophy. 3. Supernatural. I. Title.

[D'ARCY, Charles Frederick] abp. of Armagh, 1859-1938. 201
God and the struggle for existence; by the Archbishop of Dublin Lily Dougall and Canon B. H. Streeter (editor) New York, Association press, 1919. 206 p. 19 cm. [BL51.D35] 20-636
1. Religion—Philosophy. 2. God. I. Streeter, Burnett Hillman, 1874- II. Dougall, Lily, 1858-1923. III. Title.
Contents omitted

DAVIS, William Hatcher. 200'.1
Philosophy of religion, by William H. Davis. Abilene, Tex., Biblical Research Press [1969] 78 p. 22 cm. (The Way of life series, no. 114. Adult class series) [BL51.D365] 75-92048
1. Religion—Philosophy. I. Title.

DEWART, Leslie. 201
The foundations of belief. [New York] Herder and Herder [1969] 526 p. 21 cm. Bibliographical footnotes. [BL51.D417] 69-17777 9.50
1. Religion—Philosophy. I. Title.

DE WOLF, Lotan Harold, 1905- 201
The religious revolt against reason, by L. Harold DeWolf. [1st ed.] New York, Greenwood Press, 1968 [c1949] 217 p. 22 cm. Bibliographical footnotes. [BL51.D42 1968] 68-23282
1. Religion—Philosophy. 2. Reason. I. Title.

DE WOLF, Lotan Harold, 1905- 201
The religious revolt against reason. [1st ed.] New York, Harper [1949] 217 p. 21 cm. [BL51.D42] 49-10389
1. Religion—Philosophy. 2. Reason. I. Title.

DIAMOND, Malcolm Luria. 200'.1
Contemporary philosophy and religious thought: an introduction to the philosophy of religion [by] Malcolm L. Diamond. New York, McGraw-Hill [1974] xiii, 450 p. 23 cm. Includes bibliographical references. [BL51.D48] 73-17084 ISBN 0-07-016721-4
1. Religion—Philosophy. 2. God. I. Title.

DIAMOND, Malcolm Luria, comp. 200'.1
The logic of God; theology and verification, edited by Malcolm L. Diamond and Thomas V. Litzenburg, Jr. Introd., The challenge of contemporary empiricism, by Malcolm L. Diamond. [1st ed.] Indianapolis, Bobbs-Merrill [1975] x, 552 p. 24 cm. Bibliography: p. [525]-552. [BL51.D49] 74-32235 ISBN 0-672-60792-1 9.95
1. Religion—Philosophy. I. Litzenburg, Thomas V., joint comp. II. Title.

DONNELLY, Dorothy (Boillotat) 1903- 201
The bone and the star, two perspectives on the scene of time, by Dorothy Donnelly. New York, Sheed & Ward, 1944. x, 205 p. 19 1/2 cm. Bibliographical references included in "Notes" (p. 195-205) [BL51.D56] 44-7908
1. Religion—Philosophy. 2. Psychology, Religious. 3. Religion and science—1900-4. Teleology. I. Title.

DRESSER, Horatio Willis, 1866-
Man and the divine order; essays in the philosophy or religion and in constructive idealism, by Horatio W. Dresser... New York and London, G. P. Putnam's sons, 1903. v, 448 p. 20 cm. [BL.51.D65] 3-24955
1. Religion-Philosophy. I. Title.

DRISCOLL, John Thomas, 1866- 201
Christian philosophy, God; being a contribution to a philosophy of theism. New York, Cincinnati [etc.] Benziger bros., 1900. xvi, 342 p. 19 1/2 cm. [BL51.D7] 0-2398
1. Religion—Philosophy. 2. God. 3. Theism. 4. Catholic church—Doctrinal and controversial-works—Catholic authors. 5. Apologetics—20th cent. I. Title.

*DRURY, John. 200.1
Angels and dirt; an inquiry into theology and prayer. New York, Macmillan. [1974, c1972]. 104 p. 18 cm. [BL51] 1.95 (pbk.)
1. Religion—Philosophy. I. Title.
L.C. card number for original ed.: 73-14427.

DUMERY, Henry. 201
Faith and reflection. Edited and with an introd. by Louis Dupre. Translated by Stephen McNierney and Mother M. Benedict Murphy. [New York] Herder and Herder [1968] xxxiii, 220 p. 22 cm. Includes bibliographical references. [BL51.D83] 68-54078 7.50
1. Religion—Philosophy. I. Dupre, Louis K., 1925- ed. II. Title.

EATON, Gai. 200'.1
King of the castle : choice and responsibility in the modern world / [by] Gai Eaton. London : Bodley Head [for] the Imperial Iranian Academy of Philosophy, 1979. 219 p. ; 23 cm. Bibliography: p. 217-[219] [BL51.E29] 78-314992 ISBN 0-370-30062-9 : 10.95
1. Religion—Philosophy. 2. Civilization—Philosophy. 3. Philosophy and religion. I. Title.
Distributed by Merrimack, 99 Main St., Salem, NH 03079

EDWARDS, David Miall, 1873- 201
The philosophy of religion, by D. Miall Edwards ... New York, George H. Doran company [1924] 1 p. l., 5-318 p. 19 1/2 cm. (On cover: Library of philosophy & religion) Bibliography: p. 310-313. [BL51.E4] 25-3332
1. Religion—Philosophy. I. Title.

EDWARDS, Rem B. 200'.1
Reason and religion; an introduction to the philosophy of religion [by] Rem B. Edwards. New York, Harcourt Brace Jovanovich [1972] xiv, 386 p. 21 cm. Includes bibliographies. [BL51.E42] 72-80882 ISBN 0-15-576002-5
1. Religion—Philosophy. I. Title.

EHLMAN, Dobbs Frederick 201
The religious aim and human perplexity [by] Dobbs Frederick Ehlman ... Boston, Mass., The Stratofrd company [c1937] 3 p. l., iv, 115 p. 19 cm. "Suggested readings": p. 114-115. [BR100.E5] 37-10282
1. Religion—Philosophy. 2. Religion and sociology. I. Title.

EUCKEN, Rudolf Christof, 1846-1926. 201
Christianity and the new idealism, a study in the religious philosophy of to-day, by Rudolf Eucken ... Translated by Lucy Judge Gibson ... and W. R. Boyce Gibson ... London and New York, Harper & brothers, 1912. xiv, 162, [2] p. 17 1/2 cm. (Half-title: Harper's library of living thought) Added title-page, illustrated. "First edition, October 1909; second edition, January 1912." "This book is the outcome of lectures given at Jena on October 23 and 24, 1906, in connection with the Theological vacation course."--p. vii. Translated from the third German edition. Translation of Hauptprobleme der religionsphilosophie der gegenwart. [BL51.E7] 12-20382
1. Religion—Philosophy. I. Gibson, Mrs. Lucy Judge (Peacock) tr. II. Gibson, William Ralph Boyce, 1869- joint tr. III. Title.

EUCKEN, Rudolf Christof, 1846-1926. 201
The truth of religion, by Rudolf Eucken ... tr. by W. Tudor Jones ... London, Williams and Norgate; New York, G. P. Putnam's sons, 1911. xiv, 622 p. 22 cm. (Half-title: Theological translation library, vol. xxx) [[BL51.E8]] A 12
1. Religion—Philosophy. 2. Christianity. I. Jones, William Tudor, 1865- tr. II. Title.

EUCKEN, Rudolf Christof, 1846-1926. 201
The truth of religion, by Rudolf Eucken ... tr. by W. Tudor Jones ... New York, G. P. Putnam's sons; [etc., etc.] 1911. xiv, 622 p. 22 1/2 cm. (Half-title: Theological translation library. vol. xxx) "Now first translated into English from the second and revised edition, with a special preface for this edition by the author." [BL51.E82] 12-9635
1. Religion—Philosophy. 2. Christianity. I. Jones, William Tudor, 1865- tr. II. Title.

FAIRBAIRN, Andrew Martin, 1838-1912. 201
Studies in the philosophy of religion and history. By A. M. Fairbairn ... New York, Lovell, Adam, Wesson & company [pref. 1876] 348 p. 20 cm. "The first and third essays, and part third of the fourth, originally appeared in the Contemporary review. The other parts of the latter formed the substance of two lectures delivered, in ... 1874, to the Philosophical institution, Edinburgh."--Pref. [BL51.F3] 13-10006
1. Religion—Philosophy. 2. History—Philosophy. I. Title.

FARRER, Austin Marsden 200.1
Finite and infinite; a philosophical essay. Westminster [London] Dacre pr. [New York, Humanities, c.1966] xii, 300p. 24cm. First pub. March 1943. 6.50
1. Religion — Philosophy. 2. Substance (Philosophy) 3. God. I. Title.

FAUSSET, Hugh L'Anson, 1895- 290
Fruits of silence; studies in the art of being. London, New York, Abelard-Schuman [1963] 224 p. 23 cm. [BL51.F37] 63-10584
1. Religion — Philosophy. 2. Yoga. I. Title.

FEE, Zephyrus Roy, 1890- 201
The Christian's philosophy of religion. Part I. Fundamental considerations. Part II. Christian experience and revelation in the light of philosophy. [Dallas? 1951] 128 p. 20 cm. [BL51.F42] 52-17001
1. Religion—Philosophy. I. Title.

FERM, Vergilius Ture Anselm, 1896- 201
First chapters in religious philosophy, by Vergilius Ferm ... New York, Round table press, inc., 1937. xii, 319 p. 21 1/2 cm. "A selected list of readings": p. 296-305. [BL51.F45] 37-8532
1. Religion—Philosophy. I. Title.

FERM, Vergilius Ture Anselm, 1896- 201
What can we believe? New York, Philosophical Library [1948] xi, 211 p. 23 cm. [BL51.F46] 48-8463
1. Religion—Philosophy. I. Title.

FERRE, Frederick. 200'.1
Basic modern philosophy of religion. New York, Scribner [1967] viii, 465 p. 24 cm. Includes bibliographies. [BL51.F48] 67-15490
1. Religion—Philosophy. I. Title.

FERRE, Nels Fredrick Solomon, 1908- 200'.1
The universal word; a theology for a universal faith, by Nels F. S. Ferre. Philadelphia, Westminster Press [1969] 282 p. 24 cm. [BL51.F494] 69-12907 9.00
1. Religion—Philosophy. I. Title.

FEUERBACH, Ludwig Andreas, 1804-1872. 230
The essence of Christianity. Translated from the German by George Eliot. Introductory essay by Karl Barth. Foreword by H. Richard Niebuhr. New York, Harper [1957] xiiv, 339p. 21cm. (The Library of religion and culture) Harper torchbooks, TB 11. [B2971.W4E5 1957] 57-13606
1. Religion—Philosophy. 2. Christianity—Controversial literature. I. Title.

FEUERBACH, Ludwig Andreas, 1804-1872. 201
The essence of Christianity; edited and abridged by E. Graham Waring and F. W. Strothmann. New York, F. Ungar Pub. Co. [1957] 65 p. 21 cm. (Milestones of thought in the history of ideas) [B2971.W4E52] 57-8650
1. Religion—Philosophy. 2. Christianity—Controversial literature. I. Title.

FRANTZ, Ezra, 1895- 201
Preface to a religious philosophy of living. [1st ed.] New York, Pageant Press [1952] 246p. 24cm. [BL51.F6812] 53-856
1. Religion—Philosophy. I. Title.

FREEMAN, David Hugh. 201
A philosophical study of religion [by] David Hugh Freeman in collaboration with David Freeman. Nutley, N.J., Craig Press, 1964. vii, 270 p. 23 cm. Includes bibliographical references. [BL51.F6813] 63-21699
1. Religion — Philosophy. I. Title.

FRIEDMAN, Maurice S. 200'.1
The human way : a dialogical approach to religion and human experience / Maurice Friedman. [Chambersburg, Pa.] : Anima Books, 1981. p. cm. Bibliography: p. [BL51.F6818] 19 81-8011 ISBN 0-89012-025-0 : 13.95
1. Religion—Philosophy. 2. Philosophical anthropology. I. Title.

FROTHINGHAM, Ephraim Langdon. 201
Christian philosophy. [By] Ephraim L. Frothingham and Arthur L. Frothingham. Baltimore, A. L. Frothingham, 1888-90. 2 v. 25 cm. Paged continuously. [BL51.F75] 40-17128
1. Religion—Philosophy. 2. Theism. I. Frothingham, Arthur Lincoln, joint author. II. Title.

A functional philosophy of religion ... Denver, The Criterion Press, 1958. iii, 167 numb. l. 28cm. Bibliographical references included in footnotes.
1. Religion— Philosophy. I. Bernhardt, William H

GALLOWAY, George.
... *The philosophy of religion,* by George Galloway ... New York, C. Scribner's sons,

1914. xii p., 1 l., 602 p. 21 cm. (Half-title: The International theological library, ed. by C. A. Brigg and S. D. F. Salmond) Series title also at head of t.-p. Bibliography: p. 591 593. a 14
I. Title.

*GANDHI, Ramchandra. 200.1
The availability of religious ideas / Ramchandra Gandhi. New York : Barnes & Noble, c1976. 109p. ; 23 cm. (Library of philosophy and religion) Includes index. [BL51] 75-46318 ISBN 0-06-492324-X : 22.50
1. Religion-Philosophy. I. Title.

GARNETT, Arthur Campbell, 1894- 201
A realistic philosophy of religion, by A. Campbell Garnett ... Chicago, New York, Willett, Clark & company, 1942. xii p., 1 l., 331 p. 20 1/2 cm. Bibliography: p. 323-326. [BL51.G33] 42-23106
1. Religion—Philosophy. I. Title.

GARNETT, Arthur Campbell, 1894- 170
Religion and the moral life. New York, Ronald Press Co. [c1955] 223p. 22cm. [BJ47.G3] 55-6085
1. Religion—Philosophy. 2. Ethics. I. Title.

GEHRING, Albert, 1870- 201
The religion of thirty great thinkers: together with miscellaneous essays on religious subjects, by Albert Gehring. Boston, Mass., Marshall Jones company [c1925] xiii, 268 p. 20 cm. "Partial list of writings in which the religious views of the men considered in this book are laid down": p. 123-124. [BL51.G37] 25-8871
1. Religion—Philosophy. I. Title.

GIBSON, Alexander Boyce, 1900- 211'.3
Theism and empiricism, by A. Boyce Gibson. New York, Schocken Books [1970] vii, 280 p. 23 cm. Includes bibliographical references. [BL51.G57 1970b] 70-111210 8.00
1. Religion—Philosophy. 2. Empiricism. 3. God—Proof. 4. Faith. I. Title.

GLANVILL, Joseph, 1636-1680. 200'.1
Collected works of Joseph Glanvill; facsimile editions prepared by Bernhard Fabian. Hildesheim, New York, G. Olms, 1970- v. 23 cm. Contents.Contents.——v. 5. Philosophia pia. Logou threskeia. (romanized form) [BL51.G665] 77-560142
1. Religion—Philosophy. 2. Faith and reason. I. Fabian, Bernhard, ed.

GOODALL, J. L. 201
An introduction to the philosophy of religion [by] J. L. Goodall. London, Longmans, 1966. viii, 182p. 21cm. (Educ. today) Bibl. [BL51.G712] 66-78165 2.25 pap.,
1. Religion—Philosophy. I. Title.
American distributor: Humanities, New York.

GOODSPEED, Edgar Johnson, 1871- 201
The four pillars of democracy, by Edgar J. Goodspeed. New York, London, Harper & brothers [c1940] 5 p. l., 148 p. 20 cm. "First edition." [BL51.G714 1940] 40-36195
1. Religion—Philosophy. 2. Civilization. 3. Faith. I. Title.
Contents omitted.

GRANT, Vernon W. 248
The roots of religious doubt and the search for security [by] Vernon W. Grant. New York, Seabury Press [1974] 243 p. 22 cm. "A Crossroad book." Includes bibliographical references. [BL51.G724] 74-9779 ISBN 0-8164-1165-4
1. Religion—Philosophy. 2. Belief and doubt. I. Title.

GREEN, Ronald Michael. 200'.1
Religious reason : the rational and moral basis of religious belief / by Ronald M. Green. New York : Oxford University Press, 1978. p. cm. Includes index. Bibliography: p. [BL51.G727] 77-26156 ISBN 0-19-502388-9 : 14.95. ISBN 0-19-502389-7 pbk. : 4.00
1. Kant, Immanuel, 1724-1804. 2. Religion—Philosophy. 3. Reason. 4. Ethics. 5. Religions. I. Title.

GRISEZ, Germain Gabriel, 1929- 201'.1
Beyond the new theism : a philosophy of religion / Germain Grisez. Notre Dame [Ind.] : University of Notre Dame Press, [1975] xiii, 418 p. ; 24 cm. Includes bibliographical references and index. [BL51.G743] 74-27885 ISBN 0-268-00567-2 : 16.95 ISBN 0-268-00568-0 pbk. : 6.95
1. Religion—Philosophy. 2. God—Proof. 3. Religion and language. 4. Apologetics—20th century. I. Title.

GROSS, Mark, 1918- 200'.1
Quattlebaum's truth. [1st ed.] New York, Harper & Row [1970] 145 p. 22 cm. Includes bibliographical references. [BL51.G76] 70-124706 4.95
1. Religion—Philosophy. I. Title.

HALL, James, 1933- 200'.1
Knowledge, belief, and transcendence : philosophical problems in religion / James Hall. Boston : Houghton Mifflin, [1975] xiii, 237 p. ; 24 cm. Includes bibliographical references and index. [BL51.H255] 74-11952 ISBN 0-395-19502-0 pbk. : 5.95
1. Religion—Philosophy. 2. Knowledge, Theory of (Religion) 3. Theism. 4. Religion and language. I. Title.

HALL, Robert William, comp. 201
Studies in religious philosophy [compiled by] Robert W. Hall. [New York] American Book Co. [1968, c1969] viii, 408 p. 23 cm. Includes bibliographies. [BL51.H26] 78-1746
1. Religion—Philosophy. I. Title.

HANSEN, Matthew, 1873- 201
Mr. Jones and his Maker. San Anselmo, Calif., 1951. 108 p. 24 cm. [BL51.H34] 52-29136
1. Religion—Philosophy. I. Title.

HARKNESS, Georgia Elma, 1891- 201
Conflict in religious thought, by Georgia Harkness ... New York, H. Holt and company [c1929] xv, 326 p. 21 cm. [BL51.H32] 29-18346
1. Religion—Philosophy. I. Title.

HARKNESS, Georgia Elma, 1891- 201
Conflicts in religious thought. [Rev. ed.] New York, Harper [1949] xix, 326 p. 21 cm. [BL51.H32 1949] 49-5703
1. Religion—Philosophy. I. Title.

HARKNESS, Georgia Elma, 1891- 201
The recovery of ideals, by Georgia Harkness ... New York, C. Scribner's sons; London, C. Scribner's sons, ltd., 1937. xiii p., 1 l., 237 p. 21 cm. "Books suggested for further reading": p. 227-229. [BL51.H323] 37-6570
1. Religion—Philosophy. 2. Idealism. I. Title.

HARMAN, John William, 1869- 290
Man and religion, by John William Harman ... a philosophic view of life and religion. Parsons, W. Va., Advance publishing company [c1934] 2 p. l., vii-x p., 1 l., 215 p., 2 l. 20 cm. [BL51.H325] 35-164
1. Religion—Philosophy. 2. Religions. I. Title.

HARNED, David Baily. 200'.1
The ambiguity of religion. Philadelphia, Westminster Press [1968] 158 p. 21 cm. Bibliographical references included in "Notes" (p.[153]-158) [BL51.H326] 68-11584
1. Religion—Philosophy. 2. Secularization (Theology) 3. Church and the world. I. Title.

HARRINGTON, John B. 200'.1
Issues in Christian thought [by] John B. Harrington. New York, McGraw-Hill [1968] x, 452 p. 23 cm. Bibliography: p. 439-452. [BL51.H328] 68-13515
1. Religion—Philosophy. 2. Religious thought—20th century. I. Title.

HART, Hornell Norris, 1888- 211
Skeptic's quest, by Hornell Hart ... New York, The Macmillan company [1938] 5 p. l., 3-173 p. 21 cm. "First printing." "An annotated list of books related to the skeptic's quest": p. 167-169. [BL2778.H35] 38-8542
1. Religion—Philosophy. 2. Youth—Religious life. 3. Skepticism. I. Title.

HATCH, Benjamin Franklin. 201
The constitution of man, physically, morally, and spiritually considered: or, The Christian philosopher. By B. F. Hatch, M.D. ... New York, The author, 1866. 654 p. illus. 23 1/2 cm. [BL51.H35] 30-11316
1. Religion—Philosophy. I. Title.

HAUGHT, John F. 200'.1
Religion and self-acceptance / by John F. Haught. New York : Paulist Press, c1976. vii, 189 p. ; 21 cm. (An exploration book) Includes bibliographical references. [BL51.H36] 75-44805 ISBN 0-8091-1940-4 pbk. : 4.95
1. Religion—Philosophy. 2. Self-acceptance. I. Title.

HAUGHT, John F. 200'.1
Religion and self-acceptance : a study of the relationship between belief in God and the desire to know / by John F. Haught. Washington, D.C. : University Press of America, c1980. p. cm. Includes bibliographical references. [BL51.H36 1980] 19 80-5872 ISBN 0-8191-1296-8 lib. bdg. : 17.00 ISBN 0-8191-1297-6 (pbk.) : 8.75
1. Religion—Philosophy. 2. Self-acceptance. I. Title.

HEARD, Gerald, 1889- 201
The eternal gospel, by Gerald Heard. New York and London, Harper & brothers [1946] 234 p. 19 1/2 cm. [The Ayer lectures] [Full name: Henry Fitzgerald Heard] [BL51.H38] 46-7575
1. Religion—Philosophy. I. Title.

HEARD, Gerald, 1889- 201
The human venture. [1st ed.] New York, Harper [1955] 310p. 22cm. [BL51.H3816] 55-8532
1. Religion— Philosophy. 2. Civilization—Hist. I. Title.

HEARD, Gerald, 1889- 210
Is God in history? An inquiry into human and prehuman history, in terms of the doctrine of creation, fall and redemption. [1st ed.] New York, Harper [1950] xii, 269 p. 22 cm. Bibliographical references included in "Notes" (p. 245-262) [BL51.H382] 50-8535
1. Religion—Philosophy. 2. History—Philosophy. 3. Creation. 4. Fall of man. 5. Redemption. I. Title.

HEARD, Gerald, 1889- 201
Social substance of religion; an essay on the evolution of religion, by Gerald Heard. New York, Harcourt, Brace & company, 1931. 3 p. l., [11]-318 p. 2 tab. 22 1/2 cm. Printed in Great Britain. [Full anme: Henry FitzGerald Heard] [BL60.H4] 31-33603
1. Religion—Philosophy. 2. Religion—Hist. 3. Psychology, Religions. 4. Religion, Primitve. 5. Religion and sociology. I. Title.

HERBERG, Will, ed. 201
Four existentialist theologians; a reader from the works of Jacques Maritain, Nicolas Berdyaev, Martin Buber, and Paul Tillich. Selected, and with an introd. and biographical notes, by Will Herberg. [1st ed.] Garden City, N. Y., Doubleday, 1958. 346p. 22cm. (Doubleday anchor books) [BL51.H469 1958a] 58-7578
1. Religion—Philosophy. 2. Existentialism. I. Title.

HERBERG, Will, ed. 200'.1
Four existentialist theologians : a reader from the works of Jacques Maritain, Nicolas Berdyaev, Martin Buber, and Paul Tillich / selected and with an introd. and biographical notes by Will Herberg. Westport, Conn. : Greenwood Press, 1975, c1958. p. cm. Reprint of the ed. published by Doubleday, Garden City, N.Y. [BL51.H469 1975] 75-17472 ISBN 0-8371-8303-0 lib.bdg. : 17.25
1. Religion—Philosophy. 2. Existentialism. I. Title.

HESCHEL, Abraham Joshua, 1907- 201
Man is not alone; a philosophy of religion. New York, Harper [1966, c.1951] 303p. 21cm. (Torchbk., TB838. Temple lib.) [BL51.H476] 2.95 pap.,
1. Religion — Philosophy. 2. Judaism. I. Title.

HESCHEL, Abraham Joshua, 1907-
Man is not alone; a philosophy of religion. New York, Harper & Row [1966, c1951] 303 p. (Harper Torchbooks. The Temple Library/TB 838 Q) 68-48566
1. Religion—Philosophy. 2. Judaism. I. Title.

HESCHEL, Abraham Joshua, 1907- 201
Man is not alone; a philosophy of religion. New York, Farrar, Straus & Young, 1951. 305 p. 22 cm. [BL51.H476] 51-9992
1. Religion—Philosophy. 2. Judaism. I. Title.

HESCHEL, Abraham Joshua, 1907- 200'.1
Man is not alone; a philosophy of religion. New York, Octagon Books, 1972 [c1951] 305 p. 23 cm. [BL51.H476 1972] 74-169258 ISBN 0-374-93879-2
1. Religion—Philosophy. 2. Judaism. I. Title.

HICK, John. 200'.1
Philosophy of religion. 2d ed. Englewood Cliffs, N.J., Prentice-Hall [1973] ix, 133 p. 23 cm. (Foundations of philosophy series) Bibliography: p. 130. [BL51.H494 1973] 72-5429 ISBN 0-13-663948-8 2.95
1. Religion—Philosophy. I. Title.

HICK, John. 201
Philosophy of religion. Englewood Cliffs, N.J., Prentice-Hall [1963] 111 p. 23 cm. (Prentice-Hall foundations of philosophy series) [BL51.H494] 63-10528
1. Religion—Philosophy. I. Title.

HICKOK, Laurens Perseus, 1798-1888. 201
Creator and creation; or, The knowledge in the reason of God and His work. By Laurens P. Hickok ... Boston, Lee and Shepard; New York, Lee, Shepard and Dillingham, 1872. 360 p. 23 cm. [BL51.H5] 30-11318
1. Religion—Philosophy. I. Title.

HOCKING, William Ernest, 1873- 201
The meaning of God in human experience; a philosophic study of religion. New Haven, Conn., Yale [1963, c.1912] 586p. 21cm. (Y-98) 2.95 pap.,
1. Religion—Philosophy. 2. God. I. Title.

HOCKING, William Ernest, 1878- 201
The meaning of God in human experience; a philosophic study of religion, by William Ernest Hocking ... New Haven, Yale university press; [etc., etc.] 1912. xxxix, 586 p., 1 l. 23 1/2 cm. [BL51.H6] 12-14946
1. Religion—Philosophy. 2. God. I. Title.

HOFFDING, Harald, 1843-1931. 201
The philosophy of religion, by Dr. Harald Hoffding ... tr. from the German ed. by B. E. Meyer. London, Macmillan and co., limited: New York, The Macmillan company, 1906. viii, 410 p. 23 cm. [BL51.H67] 6-18580
1. Religion—Philosophy. I. Meyer, B. Ethel, tr. II. Title.
Contents omitted.

HOUSER, James Alfred.
Life here and hereafter, by J. A. Houser... Indianapolis, Phalenx printing company, c1913. 70 p. 17 cm. $1.00 13-5081
I. Title.

HoFFDING, Harald, 1843-1931. 200'.1
The philosophy of religion. Translated from the German ed. by B. E. Meyer. Freeport, N.Y., Books for Libraries Press [1971] viii, 410 p. 22 cm. Translation of Religionsfilosofi. Reprint of the 1906 ed. Includes bibliographical references. [BL51.H67 1971] 71-152987 ISBN 0-8369-5739-3
1. Religion—Philosophy. I. Title.

HUGEL, Friedrich, Freiherr von, 1852-1925. 201'.1
Essays & addresses on the philosophy of religion. Westport, Conn., Greenwood Press [1974] xix, 308 p. 22 cm. Reprint of the 1921 ed. published by J. M. Dent, London. Contents.Contents.—Responsibility in religious belief.—Religion and illusion; and religion and reality.—Progress in religion.—Preliminaries to

religious belief.—The apocalyptic element in the teaching of Jesus.—The specific genius of Christianity.—What do we mean by heaven? and what do we mean by hell?—The essentials of Catholicism.—The convictions common to Catholicism and Protestantism.—Institutional Christianity.—Christianity and the supernatural. Includes bibliographical references. [BL51.H9 1974] 72-9828 ISBN 0-8371-6219-X
1. Jesus Christ—Messiahship. 2. Troeltsch, Ernst, 1865-1923. 3. Catholic Church—Doctrinal and controversial works—Catholic authors. 4. Religion—Philosophy. 5. Theism. 6. Heaven. 7. Hell. I. Title.

HUGEL, Friedrich, freiherr von, 1852-1925. 201
Essays & addresses on the philosophy of religion, by Baron Friedrich von Hugel. London & Toronto, J.M. Dent & sons limited; New York, E.P. Dutton & co., 1921. xix, 308 p. 23 1/2 cm. Contents.Responsibility to religious belief.--Religion and illusion: and religion and reality.--Progress in religion.--Preliminaries to religious belief.--The apocalyptic element in the teaching of Jesus.--The specific genius of Christianity.--What do we mean by heaven? And what do we mean by hell?--The essentials of Catholicism.--The convictions common to Catholicism and Protestantism.--Institutional Christianity.--Christianity and the supernatural. [BL51.H9] A21
1. Religion—Philosophy. 2. Theism. 3. Jesus Christ—Messiahship. 4. Troeltach, Ernst, 1865-1923. 5. Heaven. 6. Hell. 7. Catholic church—Doctrinal and controversial works—Catholic authors. I. Title.

HUGEL, Friedrich, freiherr von, 1852-1925. 201
Essays & addresses on the philosophy of religion, by Baron Friedrich von Hugel ... London & Toronto, J. M. Dent & sons, limited; New York, E. P. Dutton & co., 1921. xix, 309 p. 23 1/2 cm. [BL51.H9] A21
1. Jesus Christ—Messiahship. 2. Troeltsch, Ernst, 1865-1923. 3. Religion—Philosophy. 4. Theism. 5. Heaven. 6. Hell. 7. Catholic church—Doctrinal and controversial works—Catholic authors. I. Title.

HUGEL, Friedrich, freiherr von, 1852-1925. 201
Essays & addresses on the philosophy of religion. First series. By Baron Friedrich von Hugel ... London & Toronto, J. M. Dent & sons, ltd.; New York, E. P. Dutton & co., inc. [1931] xix, 308 p. 20 1/2 cm. "First published 1921, reprinted ... 1931." [BL51.H9 1st ser. 1931] 33-1399
1. Jesus Christ—Messiahship. 2. Troeltsch, Ernst, 1865-1923. 3. Religion—Philosophy. 4. Theism. 5. Heaven. 6. Hell. 7. Catholic church—Doctrinal and controversial works—Catholic authors. I. Title.

HUGEL, Friedrich, freiherr von, 1852-1925. 201
Essays & addresses on the philosophy of religion. Second series. By Baron Friedrich von Hugel ... London and Toronto, J. M. Dent & sons, limited; New York, E. P. Dutton & co., 1926. ix, 287, [1] p. 23 cm. [BL51.H9 2d ser.] 27-12780
1. Religion—Philosophy. I. Title.

HUGEL, Friedrich, freiherr von, 1852-1925. 201
Essays & addresses on the philosophy of religion. Second series. By Baron Friedrich von Hugel ... London and Toronto, J. M. Dent & sons, limited; New York, E. P. Dutton & co., inc. [1930] ix, 287, [1] p. 20 1/2 cm. "First edition 1926 ... reissued ... 1930." [BL51.H9 2d ser. 1930] 33-1398
1. Religion—Philosophy. 2. God. I. Title.

HUGEL, Friedrich, freiherr von, 1852-1925. 201
Readings from Friedrich von Hugel, selected by Algar Thorold, with an introductory essay on his philosophy of religion. London and Toronto, J. M. Dent & sons ltd.; New York, E. P. Dutton & co. inc., 1928. xxvi, 359, [1] p. front. (port.) 20 cm. [BL51.H95] 29-8140
1. Caterina da Genova, Saint, 1447-1510. 2. Religion—Philosophy. I. Thorold, Algar Labouchere, 1866- ed. II. Title.

HUGEL, Friedrich, freiherr von, 1852-1925. 231
The reality of God, and Religion & agnosticism; being the literary remains of Baron Friedrich von Hugel ... Edited by Edmund G. Gardner ... London & Toronto, J. M. Dent & sons, ltd.; New York, E. P. Dutton & co., inc. [1931] xi, 264 p. 23 1/2 cm. The present volume contains portions of one, and all that remains of another, of two books left unfinished by the author: The reality of God, and Religion and agnosticism; Sir Alfred Comyn Lyall and his attitude towards religion. cf. Pref. [BT101.H83] 31-21024
1. God. 2. Lyall, Sir Alfred Comyn, 1835-1911. 3. Religion—Philosophy. 4. Agnosticism. 5. Euhemerism. I. Gardner, Edmund Garratt, 1869- ed. II. Title.

HUGHES, John A. 230.96
...The Light of the world. Delivered at Arch street meeting house, Philadelphia, by John A. Hughes... Philadelphia, Published by the Book committee of the Religious society of Friends of Philadelphia and vicinity [c1933] viii, 56 p. 18 1/2 cm. (William Penn lecture, 1933) [BR100.H8] 34-20012
1. Religion—Philosophy. 2. Logos. I. Friends, Society of. Philadelphia Yearly meeting. Book committee. II. Title.

HUMBLE, Emil. 201
The gods in plain garb; a study in psychology, by Emil Humble. New York, London, G. P. Putnam's sons, 1935. ix, [1] p., 1 l., 13-314 p. 21 cm. Bibliography: p. 303-306. [BL51.H96] 35-15608
1. Religion—Philosophy. 2. Psychology, Religious. I. Title.

HUME, David, 1711-1776. 201
The natural history of religion. Edited with an introd. by H. E. Root. Stanford, Calif., Stanford University Press [1957] 76p. 23cm. (A Library of modern religious thought) 'The text followed ... is that established by T. H. Green and T. H. Grose and printed in their critical edition of Hume's Essays, moral, political, and literary (London: Longmans, 1875)' [BL51] 57-9373
1. Religion—Philosophy. I. Title. II. Series.

HUME, David, 1711-1776. 210
The natural history of religion / by David Hume; edited by A. Wayne Colver, and Dialogues concerning natural religion / by David Hume ; edited by John Valdimir Price. Oxford [Eng.] : Clarendon Press, 1976. 299 p. ; 22 cm. The natural history of religion is from the text of the 1st ed. of 1757; Dialogues concerning natural religion is edited from the author's original manuscript. Includes index. Bibliography: p. [287]-295. [BL51.H963 1976] 77-354407 ISBN 0-19-824379-0 : 21.00
1. Religion—Philosophy. 2. Natural theology—Early works to 1900. I. Colver, Anthony Wayne. II. Price, John Valdimir. III. Hume, David, 1711-1776. Dialogues concerning natural religion. 1976. IV. Title: The natural history of religion.
Dist. by Oxford University Press NY NY

HUTCHISON, John Alexander, 1912- 201
Faith, reason, and existence; an introduction to contemporary philosophy of religion. New York, Oxford University Press, 1956. 306 p. 21 cm. [BL51.H974] 56-5670
1. Religion—Philosophy. 2. Faith and reason. I. Title.

HUXLEY, Aldous Leonard, 1894- 201
The perennial philosophy. Cleveland, World [1962, c.1944, 1945] 311p. 19cm. (Meridian bks., M144) 62-18675 1.55 pap.,
1. Religion—Philosophy. 2. Philosophy and religion. I. Title.

HUXLEY, Aldous Leonard, 1894- 201
The perennial philosophy, by Aldous Huxley. New York and London, Harper & brothers, 1945. xi p., 1 l., 312 p., 1 l. 21 cm. "Third edition." "A list of recommended books": p. 303-306. [BL51.H98 1945b] 45-10379
1. Religion—Philosophy. 2. Philosophy and religion. I. Title.

HUXLEY, Aldous Leonard, 1894-1963.
The perennial philosophy. New York, Harper & Row [1964] xi, 312 p. 65-110989
1. Religion — Philosophy. I. Title.

HUXLEY, Aldous Leonard, 1894-1963. 201
The perennial philosophy. Freeport, N.Y., Books for Libraries Press [1972, c1945] xi, 312 p. 23 cm. (Essay index reprint series) Bibliography: p. 303-306. [BL51.H98 1972] 76-167362 ISBN 0-8369-2773-7
1. Religion—Philosophy. 2. Philosophy and religion. I. Title.

INTRODUCTION to religious philosophy. London, New York, Macmillan, 1960. xvi, 375p. Bibliographical footnotes.
1. Religion—Philosophy. I. MacGregor, Geddes.

INTRODUCTION to the philosophy of religion. Englewood Cliffs, N. J., Prentice-Hall [1956] xv, 565p. 22cm. (Prentice-Hall philosophy series) 'Suggestions for further reading': at end of each chapter.
I. Bertocci, Peter Anthony.

JOHNSON, Francis Howe, 1835-1920. 201
What is reality? An inquiry as to the reasonableness of natural religion, and the naturalness of revealed religion, by Francis Howe Johnson. Boston and New York, Houghton, Mifflin and company, 1891. xxvii, 510 p. 21 cm. [BL51.J7] 30-11319
1. Religion—Philosophy. 2. Reality. I. Title.

JONES, Henry, Sir 1852-1922. 201
A faith that enquires; the Gifford lectures delivered in the University of Glasgow in the years 1920 and 1921, by Sir Henry Jones. New York, The Macmillan company, 1922. x p., 1 l., 278 p. 21 cm. [BL51.J8] 22-4842
1. Religion—Philosophy. I. Title.

JORDAN, Rudolf, 1905- 201
Bridges to the unknown, an essay on religion. New York, Fell [1966, c.1957] 109p. 21cm. (Concept bk. 101) [BL51.J82] 57-7883 1.95 pap.,
1. Religion — Philosophy. I. Title.

JORDAN, Rudolf, 1905- 201
Bridges to the unknown, an essay on religion. New York, F. Fell [1957] 109p. 23cm. [BL51.J82 1957] 57-7883
1. Religion—Philosophy. I. Title.

JUNG, Carl Gustav, 1875- 201
Answer to Job. Translated by R. F. C. Hull. New York, Meridian Books [1960, c1954] 223p. 19cm. (Meridian books, M86) Includes bibliography. [BL51.J853 1960] 60-6738
1. Religion—Philosophy. 2. Bible. O. T. Job—Criticism, interpretation, etc. I. Title.

JUNG, Carl Gustav, 1875-1961.
Answer to job. Translated by R.F.C. Hull. Cleveland, World Pub. Co. [1963] 223 p. (Meridian books, M86) First Meridan books edition published 1960. Reprinted. Includes bibliography. 64-52411
1. Religion — Philosophy. 2. Bible. O.T. Job-Criticism, interpretation, etc. I. Title.

JUNG, Carl Gustav, 1875-1961. 201
Answer to Job [by] C. G. Jung [2d ed.] [Princeton] Princeton Univ. Pr. [1973, c.1969] xv, 121 p. 22 cm. (Bollingen paperbacks; Bollingen series, XX) Includes bibliography. [BL51.J853 1969] ISBN 0-691-01785-9 pap., 2.95
1. Bible. O.T. Job—Criticism, interpretation, etc. 2. Religion—Philosophy. I. Title.
L.C. card no. for the 1960 ed.: 60-6738.

JUNG, Carl Gustav, 1875-1961. 223'.1'06
Answer to Job. Translated by R. F. C. Hull. [1st Princeton/Bollingen paperback ed. Princeton, N.J.] Princeton University Press [1972, c1969] xv, 121 p. 21 cm. (Princeton/Bollingen paperbacks, 283) Translation of Antwort auf Hiob. Extracted from v. 11 of the author's Collected works, issued as no. 20 in the Bollingen series. Bibliography: p. 109. [BL51.J853 1972] 72-6097 ISBN 0-691-01785-9 2.95
1. Bible. O.T. Job—Criticism, interpretation, etc. 2. Religion—Philosophy. I. Title.

KEAN, Charles Duell, 1910- 201
The meaning of existence, by Charles Duell Kean. New York and London, Harper & brothers [1947] xiv, 222 p. 21 1/2 cm. "First edition." [BL51.K37] 47-4199
1. Religion—Philosophy. 2. Civilization, Modern. 3. Reconstruction (1939)—Religious aspects. I. Title.

KENDALL, Guy, 1876- 201
Religion in war and peace. London, New York, Hutchinson, [1947] 126 p. 22 cm. [BL51.K42] 48-10656
1. Religion—Philosophy. I. Title.

KEYSER, Leander Sylvester, 1856- 239
The philosophy of Christianity, by Leander S. Keyser ... Burlington, Ia., The Lutheran literary board, 1928. 266 p. 21 cm. [BR100.K4] 28-23126
1. Religion—Philosophy. 2. Christianity. I. Title.

KIERKEGAARD, Soren Aabye, 1813-1855. 248
For self-examination and Judge for yourselves! And three discourses, 1851, by Soren Kierkegaard: tr. by Walter Lowrie. Princeton, Princeton [1968] vii p., 5 l., [9]-243p. 21 cm. (115) First pub. in Great Britain, 1941. Reprinted by offset in the U.S.A., 1944. [BR100.K] A44 2.45 pap.,
1. Religion—Philosophy. 2. Lutheran church—Sermons. 3. Sermons, Danish—Translations into English. 4. Sermons, English—Translations from Danish. I. Lowrie, Walter, 1868- tr. II. Title. III. Title: Judge for yourselves!

KIERKEGAARD, Soren Aabye, 1813-1855. 248
For self-examination and Judge for yourselves! And three discourses, 1851, by Soren Kierkegaard; translated by Walter Lowrie, D.D. Princeton, Princeton university press; London, H. Milford, Oxford university press, 1944. vii p., 5 l., [9]-243 p. 20 1/2 cm. "First published in Great Britain, 1941. Reprinted by offset in the United States of America, 1944." [[BR100.K]] A 44
1. Religion—Philosophy. 2. Lutheran church—Sermons. 3. Sermons, Danish—Translations into English. 4. Sermons, English—Translations from Danish. I. Lowrie, Walter, 1868- tr. II. Title. III. Title: Judge for yourselves!

KIERKEGAARD, Soren Aabye, 1813-1855. 248
For self-examination and Judge for yourselves! And three discourses, 1851, by Soren Kierkegaard; translated by Walter Lowrie, D. D. London, New York [etc.] Oxford university press, 1941. vii p., 5 l., [9]-243, [1] p. 24 cm. [BR100.K54] 41-21842
1. Religion—Philosophy. 2. Lutheran church—Sermons. 3. Sermons, Danish—Translations into English. 4. Sermons, English—Translations from Danish. I. Lowrie, Walter, 1863- tr. II. Title. III. Title: Judge for yourselves!

KIERKEGAARD, Soren Aabye, 1813-1855 201
Philosophical fragments; or. A fragment of philosophy, by Johannes Climacus [pseud.] . . . . Responsible for publication: S. Kierkegaard. Orig. tr. introd. by David F. Swenson. New introd. and commentary by Niels Thulstrup. Tr. rev. and commentary tr. by Howard V. Hong. [2d ed.] Princeton, N. J., Princeton [1967,c.1962] xcvii, 260p. 21cm. [BL51.K487 1962] 62-7408 2.95 pap.,
1. Religion—Philosophy. I. Title.

KIERKEGAARD, Soren Aabye, 1813-1855. 201
Philosophical fragments; or, A fragment of philosophy, by Johannes Climacus [pseud.] ... responsible for publication. S. Kierkegaard; translated from the Danish with introduction and notes by David F. Swenson ... Princeton, Princeton university press. New York, American-scandinavian foundation, 1936. xxx p., 1 l., 105 p. 22 1/2 cm. [BL51.K487] 37-712
1. Religion—Philosophy. I. Swenson, David Ferdinand, 1876- tr. II. Title.

KIMPEL, Benjamin Franklin. 201
Language and religion; a semantic preface to a philosophy of religion. New York, Philosophical Library [1957] 153p. 22cm. [BL51.K497] 57-2538
1. Religion—Philosophy. 2. Semantics (Philosophy) I. Title.

KING-FARLOW, John. 200'.1
Faith and the life of reason. By John King-Farlow and William Niels Christensen. Dordrecht, Reidel, [1973] xiii, 253 p. 23 cm. Bibliography: p. [244]-248. [BL51.K498] 72-83376 ISBN 9-02-770275-6
1. Religion—Philosophy. I. Christensen, William Niels, joint author. II. Title.
Distributed by Reidel, Boston; 22.00 (lib. bdg.).

KING, Henry Churchill, 1858- 218
1934.
Seeing life whole, a Christian philosophy of life; the Deems lectures for 1922, New York university, by Henry Churchill King ... New York, The Macmillan company, 1923. ix p., 1 l., 163 p. 19 1/2 cm. [BD431.K45] 23-13302
I. Title.

KINGDON, Frank. 201
When half-gods go [by] Frank Kingdon. New York, Cincinnati [etc.] The Abingdon press [c1933] 206 p. 19 1/2 cm. [BL51.K5] 33-4923
1. Religion—Philosophy. I. Title.

KINSOLVING, Wythe Leigh, 220
1878-
"Thoughts on religion" [by] Wythe Leigh Kinsolving ... [New York city, On sale with Gorham book sellers] c1923. 63 p. 22 cm. [BR125.K595] CA 24
I. Title.

KOLENDA, Konstantin. 200'.1
Religion without God / by Konstantin Kolenda. Buffalo : Prometheus Books, 1976. 125 p. ; 23 cm. Includes bibliographical references. [BL51.K65] 76-19349 ISBN 0-87975-073-1 : 8.95
1. Religion—Philosophy. I. Title.

KRONER, Richard, 1884- 201
... *The religious function of imagination,* by Richard Kroner ... New Haven, Pub. for Keyon college by Yale university press. London, H. Milford, Oxford university press, 1941. 5 p. l., 70 p. 19 cm. (Bedell lectures delivered at Keyon college) [BL51.K7] 41-23466
1. Religion—Philosophy. 2. Imagination. I. Title.

LADD, George Trumbull, 1842- 201
1921.
The philosophy of religion; a critical and speculative treatise of man's religious experience and development in the light of modern science and reflective thinking, by George Trumbull Ladd ... New York, C. Scribner's sons, 1905. 2 v. 23 cm. [BL51.L3] 5-35578
1. Religion—Philosophy. I. Title.

LARSEN, Bernhard, 1888- 201
Religion and relations, by Bernhard Larsen ... Boston, Mass., The Stratford company [c1934] 4 p. l., 131 p. 20 cm. "The greater part of the material in this little book first belonged to a series of lectures which were delivered in the fall of 1932 before the Pastors' summer school of the Lutheran free church."--Pref. "Books for consultation" at end of each chapter. [Full name: Christian Bernhard Larsen] [BL51.L38] 35-3975
1. Religion—Philosophy. I. Title.

LAW, Edmund, Bp. of 211
Carlisle, 1703-1787.
An enquiry into the ideas of space, time, immensity, and eternity : 1734 / Edmund Law. New York : Garland Pub., 1976. 196 p. ; 23 cm. (British philosophers and theologians of the 17th & 18th centuries) Original t.p. has subtitle: In answer to a book lately publish'd by Mr. Jackson, entitled, The existence and unity of God proved from His nature and attributes. Reprint of the 1734 ed. printed by W. Fenner and R. Beresford, for W. Thurlbourn, Cambridge, Eng. "A dissertation upon the argument a priori," by D. Waterland: p. 98 [BL51.L45 1976] 75-11230 ISBN 0-8240-1783-8 lib.bdg. : 25.00
1. Jackson, John, 1686-1763. The existence and unity of God proved from His nature and attributes. 2. Religion—Philosophy. I. Waterland, Daniel, 1683-1740. II. Title. III. Series.

LEEUW, Gerardus van der, 201
1890-
Religion in essense and manifestation, 2. v. Tr. [from German] by J. E. Turner. With appendices to the Torch-bk. ed. incorporating the additions of the 2d German ed. by Hans H. Penner. New York, Harper [c.1963] 2v. 714p. 21cm. (Harper torchbks., Cloister lib., TB100-101) Bibl. 1.95 pap., ea.,
1. Religion—Philosophy. 2. Phenomenology. I. Turner, John Evans, tr. II. Title.

LEEUW, Gerardus van der, 201
1890-1950.
Religion in essence and manifestation. Translated by J. E. Turner, with appendices to the Torchbook ed. incorporating the additions of the 2d German ed. by Hans H. Penner. New York, Harper & Row [1963] 2 v. 21 cm. (Harper torchbks. The Cloister library) Translation of Phanomenologie der Religion. [BL51.L456] 63-1870
1. Religion — Philosophy. 2. Phenomenology. I. Title.

LESTER-GARLAND, Lester 201
Vallis, 1860-
The religious philosophy of Baron F. von Hugel, by L. V. Lester-Garland ... New York, E. P. Dutton & co., inc. [1933] vii, 115, [1] p. 19 cm. "The substance, and for the most part the actual text, of four public lectures" delivered at the University of Bristol in February and March, 1932. cf. Pref. Printed in Great Britain. "First published 1933." [BL51.H955L4] 33-11725
1. Hugel, Friedrica, freiberr von, 1852-1925. 2. Religion—Philosophy. I. Title.

LEUBA, James Henry, 1868- 201
A psychological study of religion, its origin, function, and future, by James H. Leuba ... New York, The Macmillan company, 1912. xiv, 371 p. 21 cm. "The author's publications on the psychology of religion": p. 361-362. [BL53.L4] 12-21976
1. Religion—Philosophy. 2. Psychology, Religious. I. Title.

LEVINSON, Henry S. 201
The religious investigations of William James / Henry Samuel Levinson. Chapel Hill : University of North Carolina Press, c1981. xii, 311 p. ; 24 cm. (Studies in religion) Includes index. Bibliography: p. 291-299. [B945.J24L437] 19 80-26109 ISBN 0-8078-1468-7 : 24.00
1. James, William, 1842-1910—Religion. 2. Religion—Philosophy. 3. Experience (Religion) I. Title. II. Series: Studies in religion (Chapel Hill, N.C.

LEWIS, Hywel David 201
Philosophy of religion, by H. D. Lewis. London, English Univ. Pr. Imprint covered by label: New York, Barnes ; Noble [1965] x, 338p. 19cm. (Teach yourself bks.) Bibl. [BL51.L468] 66-8804 2.50 bds.,
1. Religion — Philosophy. I. Title.
Available from Barnes & Noble, New York.

LING, Trevor Oswald. 200.1
Buddha, Marx, and God: some aspects of religion in the modern world, by Trevor Ling. London, Melbourne [etc.] Macmillan New York, St. Martin's P., 1966. xii, 228 p. 22 1/2 cm. (B 66-21487) Bibliography: p. 218-222. [BL51.L52] 67-10332
1. Religion — Philosophy. 2. Buddha and Buddhism — 20th cent. I. Title.

LION, Aline. 201
The idealistic conception of religion; Vico, Hegel, Gentile, by Aline Lion ... with a preface by Clement C. J. Webb. Oxford, The Clarendon press, 1932. xvi, 208 p. 23 cm. [BL51.L55] 32-22685
1. Vico, Giovanni Battista, 1668-1743. 2. Hegel, Georg Wilhelm Friedrich, 1770-1831. 3. Gentile, Giovanni, 1875- 4. Religion—Philosophy. I. Title.

LOFTON, George Augustus, 1839-
1914.
The masterwheel; or, The power of love; being a discussion of that passion by which God transmits moving force of His being to the universe, through whose highest development man becomes like unto Deity, and without which he would cease to be in his Maker's image, by George A. Lofton ... with illustrations by the author. Nashville, Tenn., Macon, Ga. [etc.] The Southwestern company [c1906] 477 p. incl. front. (port.) plates. 26 cm. [BJ4521.L746] 7-21433
I. Title.

LOTZE, Hermann, 1817-1881. 201
Outlines of a philosophy of religion. By Hermann Lotze. Ed. by F. C. Conybeare, M. A. London, G. Allen & Unwin ltd.; New York, C. Scribner's sons, 1916. xx, 176 p. 20 cm. [Full name: Rudolf Hermann Lotze] [BL51.L] A 17
1. Religion—Philosophy. I. Conybeare, Frederic Cornwallis, 1856-1924, ed. II. Title.

LOTZE, Hermann, 1817-1881. 201
Outlines of the philosophy of religion; dictated portions of the lectures of Hermann Lotze. Translation ed. by George T. Ladd ... Boston, Ginn, Heath, & co., 1885. viii p., 1 l., 162 p. 20 cm. (Half-title: Lotze's Outlines of philosophy. ii) [Full name: Rudolf Hermann Lotze] [BL51.L6] 11-24754
1. Religion—Philosophy. I. Ladd, George Trumbull, 1842-1921, ed. and tr. II. Brastow, Lewis Orsmond, 1834-1912, tr. III. Title.

LUIJPEN, Wilhelmus 200'.1
Antonius Maria, 1922-
Myth and metaphysics / William A. Luijpen ; translated by Henry J. Koren. The Hague : Nijhoff, 1976. viii, 186 p. ; 24 cm. Translation of Theologie is anthropologie. Includes bibliographical references. [BL51.L7213] 76-369438 ISBN 9-02-471750-7 : 18.00
1. Religion—Philosophy. I. Title.

LUIJPEN, Wilhelmus 200'.1
Antonius Maria, 1922-
Theology as anthropology; philosophical reflections on religion, by William A. Luijpen. Pittsburgh, Duquesne University Press; distributed by Humanities Press, New York [1973] 148 p. 21 cm. (Duquesne studies. Theological series, 12) Translation of De erwtensoep is klaar! Includes bibliographical references. [BL51.L713] 72-90638 ISBN 0-391-00324-0 6.50 (pbk.)
1. Religion—Philosophy. I. Title. II. Series.

LYMAN, Eugene William, 1872- 201
The meaning and truth of religion, by Eugene William Lyman ... New York, London, C. Scribner's sons, 1933. xvi, 468 p. 23 cm. Bibliography: p. 457-463. [BL51.L77] 33-8768
1. Religion—Philosophy. I. Title.

LYMAN, Eugene William, 1872- 201
Theology and human problems, a comparative study of absolute idealism and pragmatism as interpreters of religion. The Nathaniel William Taylor lectures for 1909-10, given before the Divinity school of Yale university, by Eugene William Lyman ... New York, C. Scribner's sons, 1910. ix p., 1 l., 232 p. 19 1/2 cm. [BL51.L8] 10-21646
1. Religion—Philosophy. I. Title.

MCCLENDON, James William. 200'.1
Understanding religious convictions / James Wm. McClendon, Jr., and James M. Smith. Notre Dame [Ind.] : University of Notre Dame Press, [1975] viii, 230 p. ; 24 cm. Includes bibliographical references and index. [BL51.M17] 74-34519 ISBN 0-268-01903-7 : 14.95
1. Religion—Philosophy. 2. Religion and language. I. Smith, James Marvin, 1933- joint author. II. Title.

MCCOSH, James, 1811-1894. 201
Christianity and positivism; a series of lectures to the times on natural theology and apologetics, delivered in New York, Jan. 16 to March 20, 1871, on the "Ely foundation" of the Union theological seminary. By James McCosh... New York, R. Carter and brothers, 1871. vii, 369 p. 19 1/2 cm. (Ely lectures) [BL51.M2] 30-11323
1. Religion—Philosophy. 2. Natural theology. 3. Apologetics. I. Title.

MACGREGOR, Geddes. 201
Introduction to religious philosophy. Boston, Houghton Mifflin [1959] 366p. 22cm. Includes bibliography. [BL51.M214] 59-3231
1. Religion—Philosophy. I. Title.

MACGREGOR, Geddes. 200'.1
Introduction to religious philosophy / Geddes MacGregor. [Washington, D.C.] : University Press of America, [c1981] p. cm. Reprint. Originally published: Boston : Houghton, Mifflin, 1959. Includes index. Bibliography: p. [BL51.M214 1981] 19 81-40257 ISBN 0-8191-1669-6 : 21.75 ISBN 0-8191-1670-X (pbk.) : 12.50
1. Religion—Philosophy. I. Title.

MACGREGOR, Geddes. 200'.1
Philosophical issues in religious thought. Boston, Houghton Mifflin [1972, c1973] xii, 500 p. 25 cm. Includes bibliographical references. [BL51.M2148] 72-5247 ISBN 0-395-14045-5
1. Religion—Philosophy. I. Title.

MACINTOSH, Douglas Clyde, 201
1877- ed.
Religious realism, by A. K. Rogers, J. B. Pratt, J. S. Bixler ... [and others] edited by D. C. Macintosh. New York, The Macmillan company, 1931. viii, 502 p. diagr. 22 1/2 cm. Bibliography at end of chap. iii (p. 97-98). [BL51.M22] 31-22639
1. Religion—Philosophy. 2. Realism. 3. Philosophy and religion. 4. God. I. Rogers, Arthur Kenyon, 1868- II. Title.

MACKEY, James Patrick. 200'.1
The problems of religious faith, by James P. Mackey. Chicago, Franciscan Herald Press [1973] p. Includes bibliographical references. [BL51.M225] 73-6670 ISBN 0-8199-0454-6 12.95
1. Religion—Philosophy. 2. Faith. I. Title.

MCPHERSON, Thomas 201
The philosophy of religion. Princeton, N. J., Van Nostrand [c.1965] ix, 207p. 20cm. Bibl. [BL51.M246] 65-20160 5.95; 2.95 pap.,
1. Religion — Philosophy. I. Title.

MALLOCK, William Hurrell, 201
1849-1923.
The reconstruction of religious belief, by W. H. Mallock ... New York and London, Harper & brothers, 1905. ix, [1], 302, [1] p. 21 1/2 cm. [BL51.M25] 5-34664
1. Religion—Philosophy. I. Title.

MALLOCK, William Hurrell, 201
1849-1923.
Religion as credible doctrine; a study of the fundamental difficulty, by W. H. Mallock ... New York, The Macmillan company, 1903. xiv, 287 p. 23 cm. Side notes. [BL51.M27] 3-867
1. Religion—Philosophy. 2. Religion and science—1900- 3. Theism. I. Title.

MANSEL, Henry Longueville, 201
1820-1871.
The limits of religious thought examined in eight lectures delivered before the University of Oxford, in the year mdccclviii, on the Bampton foundation. By Henry Longueville Mansel ... 1st American, from the 3d London, edition. With notes translated. Boston, Gould and Lincoln; New York, Sheldon and company: [etc., etc.] 1859. viii, [9]-364 p. 19 1/2 cm. [BL51.M3 1859] 30-11326
1. Religion—Philosophy. 2. Rationalism. I. Title.

MANSEL, Henry Longueville, 201'.1
1820-1871.
The limits of religious thought examined in eight lectures delivered before the University of Oxford, in the year MDCCCLVIII, on the Bampton Foundation. 1st American, from the 3d London ed., with the notes translated. Boston, Gould and Lincoln, 1859. [New York, AMS Press, 1973] 364 p. 19 cm. Includes bibliographical references. [BL51.M3 1973] 72-172840 ISBN 0-404-04182-5 15.00
1. Religion—Philosophy. 2. Rationalism. I. Title.

MARSHALL, Richard Maynard, 201
1880-
"What is truth!" The approach by infinition, by R. Maynard Marshall. [Charleston, S. C., Walker, Evans, & Cogswell co., c1934] 4 p. l., [11]-189 p., 1

l. 21 cm. "First edition." [BL51.M35] 34-42136
1. Religion—Philosophy. I. Title. II. Title: Infinition.

MARTI, Fritz, 1894- 200'.1
Religion, reason, and man / by Fritz Marti. St. Louis : W. H. Green, c1974. xi, 127 p. : port. ; 24 cm. Includes index. [BL51.M352] 74-9353 ISBN 0-87527-141-3 : 7.75
1. Religion—Philosophy. I. Title.

MARTIN, Charles Burton. 201
Religious belief. Ithaca, N. Y., Cornell University Press [1959] 168p. 23cm. (Contemporary philosophy) Includes bibliography. [BL51.M353] 59-4815
1. Religion—Philosophy. I. Title.

MARTIN, James Alfred, 1917- 200'.1
Empirical philosophies of religion, with special reference to Boodin, Brightman, Hocking, Macintosh and Wieman. Freeport, N.Y., Books for Libraries Press [1970, c1945] xii, 146 p. 23 cm. (Essay index reprint series) Bibliography: p. [138]-146. [BL51.M355 1970] 78-111850 ISBN 8-369-16182-
1. Religion—Philosophy. I. Title.

MARTIN, James Alfred, 1917-
Empirical philosophies of religion, with special reference to Boodin, Brightman, Hocking, Macintosh and Wieman, by James Alfred Martin, jr. New York, King's crown press, 1945. 2 p. l., [vii]-xii, 146 p. 23 cm. Bibliography: p. [138]-146. A 45
1. Religion—Philosophy. I. Title.

MARTINEAU, James, 1805-1900. 201
Modern materialism in its relations to religion and theology, comprising an address delivered in Manchester new college, October 6th, 1874, and two papers reprinted from "The Contemporary review," by James Martineau, LL.D., with an introduction by Henry W. Bellows, D.D. New York, G. P. Putnam's sons, 1877. 211 p. 16 1/2 cm. Cover-title: Materialism, theology and religion. [BL51.M37] 24-9309
1. Religion—Philsophy. 2. Religion and science—1860-1899. I. Title. II. Title: Materialism, theology and religion.

MARTINEAU, James, 1805-1900. 201
A study of religion, its sources and contents, by James Martineau ... American ed., rev. by the author ... Oxford, Clarendon press; New York, Macmillan and co., 1888. 2 v. 20 1/2 cm. [BL51.M4] 4-10380
1. Religion—Philosophy. 2. Theism. I. Title.

MARTINEAU, James, 1805-1900. 201
A study of religion, its sources and contents [by] James Martineau ... 2d ed., rev. ... Oxford, The Clarendon press, 1900. 2 v. 20 cm. [BL51.M4 1900] 38-19173
1. Religion—Philosophy. 2. Theism. I. Title.

MAURER, Herrymon, 1914- 201
What can I know? The prophetic answer. [1st ed.] New York, Harper [1953] 253p. 22cm. [BL51.M475] 53-5442
1. Religion—Philosophy. I. Title.

MAURICE, Frederick Denison, 1805-1872. 230
What is revelation? : A series of sermons on the Epiphany, to which are added letters to a student of theology on the Bampton lectures of Mr. Mansel / by Frederick Denison Maurice. New York : AMS Press, [1975] p. cm. Reprint of the 1859 ed. published by Macmillan, Cambridge. [BL51.M33M3 1975] 76-173061 ISBN 0-404-04276-7 : 37.50
1. Mansel, Henry Longueville, 1820-1871. The limits of religious thought. 2. Religion—Philosophy. 3. Rationalism. 4. Revelation. I. Title.

MILL, John Stuart, 1806-1873. 200'.1
Three essays on religion. New York, Greenwood Press [1969] xi, 302 p. 23 cm. Reprint of the 1874 ed. Contents.Contents.—Nature.—Utility of religion.—Theism.—Berkeley's life and writings. [BL51.M62 1969] 69-13997
1. Berkeley, George, Bp. of Cloyne, 1685-1753. 2. Religion—Philosophy. 3. Nature. 4. Theism. I. Title.

MILL, John Stuart, 1806-1873. 200'.1
Three essays on religion. [1st AMS ed.] New York, AMS Press [1970] xi, 302 p. 23 cm. Reprint of the New York 1874 ed. Contents.Contents.—Nature.—Utility of religion.—Theism.—Berkeley's life and writings. [BL51.M62 1970] 76-130995 ISBN 0-404-04325-9
1. Berkeley, George, Bp. of Cloyne, 1685-1753. 2. Religion—Philosophy. 3. Nature. 4. Theism. I. Title.

MILLER, Eddie L., 1937- 201'.1
God and reason; a historical approach to philosophical theology [by] Ed. L. Miller. New York, Macmillan [1972] xi, 244 p. 21 cm. Includes bibliographical references. [BL51.M624] 70-176059
1. Religion—Philosophy. I. Title.

MITCHELL, Basil. 200'.1
The justification of religious belief. New York, Seabury Press [1974] v, 180 p. 22 cm. (Philosophy of religion series) "A Crossroad book." Bibliography: p. 170-176. [BL51.M654 1974] 73-17904 ISBN 0-8164-1152-2 8.95
1. Religion—Philosophy. I. Title.

MITCHELL, Basil. 200'.1
The justification of religious belief. [London, New York] Macmillan [1973] 180 p. 23 cm. (Philosophy of religion series) Bibliography: p. 170-176. [BL51.M654 1973] 74-154832 ISBN 0-333-09942-7 £3.95
1. Religion—Philosophy. I. Title.

A modern in search of truth, by S. T. New York, Frederick A. Stokes company, 1931. xiii, 322 p. 19 1/2 cm. "Suggestions for further reading": p. 319-322. [BL51.M66] 31-12984 201
1. Religion—Philosophy. 2. Science—Philosophy. 3. Philosophy, Modern. 4. Ontology. I. T., S. II. S. T.

MONTAGUE, William Pepperell, 1873- 201
Belief unbound; a Promethean religion for the modern world, by Wm. Pepperell Montague ... New Haven, Yale university press; London, H. Milford, Oxford university press [1930] 4 p. l., 98 p. 21 cm. (Half-title: The Terry lectures) "First published, October, 1930. Second printing, October, 1930." [BL51.M67 1930 a] 30-32176
1. Religion—Philosophy. I. Title.

MONTAGUE, William Pepperell, 1873-1953. 200'.1
Belief unbound; a Promethean religion for the modern world. Freeport, N.Y., Books for Libraries PRess [1970] 98 p. 23 cm. Reprint of the 1930 ed. [BL51.M67 1970] 72-109630
1. Religion—Philosophy. I. Title.

MOORE, Edward Caldwell, 1857- 201
The nature of religion, by Edward Caldwell Moore ... New York, The Macmillan company, 1936. ix, 368 p. 21 cm. [BL51.M678] 36-10850
1. Religion—Philosophy. I. Title.

MORE, Paul Elmer, 1864-1937. 200.1
The sceptical approach to religion. Princeton, Princeton University Press, 1934 [i.e. 1958] 201p. 17cm. 'Fifth printing. 1958.' [BL51.M] A 59
1. Religion—Philosophy. 2. Skepticism. 3. Incarnation. I. Title.
Contents omitted.

MORELL, John Daniel, 1816-1891. 201
The philosophy of religion. By J. D. Morell... New York, D. Appleton & company; Philadelphia, G. S. Appleton, 1849. 2 p. l., [7]-359 p. 19 cm. [BL51.M7] 30-11328
1. Religion—Philosophy. I. Title.

MORGAN, Barbara (Spofford) 1887- 201
Skeptic's search for God, by Barbara Spofford Morgan. New york and London, Harper & brothers [1947] xiv, 248 p. 20 cm. "First edition." [BL51.M72] 47-4099
1. Religion—Philosophy. I. Title.

MORGAN, William Sacheus, 1865- 201
The philosphy of religion; a consideration of the more profound aspects of religious thought. New York, Philosophical Library [1950] xv, 413 p. 23 cm. Bibliographical references included in "Notes" (p. 399-408) [BL51.M74] 50-9827
1. Religion — Philosophy. I. Title.

MOURANT, John Arthur, 1903- ed. 201
Readings in the philosophy of religion. New York, Crowell, 1954. 500p. 22cm. [BL51.M75] 54-7581
1. Religion—Philosophy. I. Title.

MOURANT, John Arthur, 1903- ed.
Readings in the philosophy of religion. New York, Crowell [1965, c 1954] 500 p. 22 cm. 67-104020
1. Religion — Philosophy. I. Title.

MUELLER, Gustav Emil, 1898- 211
Discourse on religion. New York, Bookman Associates [c1951] 203 p. 23 cm. [BL51.M78] 52-6474
1. Religion — Philosophy. I. Title.

MUNSON, Thomas N. 200'.1
Reflective theology : philosophical orientations in religion / by Thomas N. Munson. Westport, Conn. : Greenwood Press, 1976, c1968. xi, 211 p. ; 23 cm. Reprint of the ed. published by Yale University Press, New Haven. Includes index. Bibliography: p. [189]-202. [BL51.M87 1976] 75-36099 ISBN 0-8371-8624-2 lib.bdg. : 13.00
1. Religion—Philosophy. I. Title.

MUNSON, Thomas N. 200'.1
Reflective theology; philosophical orientations in religion, by Thomas N. Munson. New Haven, Yale University Press, 1968. xi, 211 p. 22 cm. Bibliography: p. [189]-202. [BL51.M87] 68-27763 6.00
1. Religion—Philosophy. I. Title.

MUYSKENS, James L., 1942- 200'.1
The sufficiency of hope : conceptual foundations of religion / James L. Muyskens. Philadelphia : Temple University Press, [1979] p. cm. (Philosophical monographs) Includes index. Bibliography: p. [BL51.M93] 79-18714 ISBN 0-87722-162-6 lib. bdg. : 15.00
1. Religion—Philosophy. 2. Hope. 3. Faith. I. Title. II. Series: Philosophical monographs (Philadelphia, 1978-)

NASS, Raoul B.
Two popular philosophic-scientific essays in the spirit of faith and religion: I. The idea of God and of the notion of reality. II. The world--all of our Creator (an astronomic-Biblical universal outlook of God's kingdom.) By: Dr. Raoul B. Nass. Brooklyn, N.Y. [Printed by Twersky bros., 1943] 4 p. l., 70 p. 22 cm. A 44
1. Religion—Philosophy. 2. Religion and science. I. Title. II. Title: The idea of God and of the notion of reality. III. Title: The world—all of our Creator.

NEGRI, Vitali, 1887- 201
The Creator and the created; the philosophy of "existence" and the knowledge of the "first cause", by Vitali Negri. Los Angeles, DeVorss & co. [c1933] 2 p. l., xi-xxi, 289 p. diagrs. 22 cm. [BL51.N4] 33-35342
1. Religion—Philosophy. 2. Religion and science—1900- I. Title.

NEVISON, R. L. B. 200
The last problem / [by] R. L. B. Nevison. [Harrogate] : [The author], 1976. [3], ii, 97 p. ; 21 cm. Includes bibliographical references. [BL51.N447] 76-380959 ISBN 0-9505166-0-0 : £1.00
1. Religion—Philosophy. I. Title.

NEVIUS, Warren Nelson, 1877- 201
Religion as experience and truth; an introduction to the philosophy of religion, by Warren Nelson Nevius ... Philadelphia, The Westminister press, 1941. 438 p. 21 cm. "Notes and readings": p. 397-429. [BL51.N45] 41-25066
1. Religion—Philosophy. I. Title.

NICHOLSON, John Angus. 201
Philosophy of religion. New York, Ronald Press Co. [1950] viii, 419 p. 22 cm. Bibliography: p. 411-413. [BL51.N8] 50-7613
1. Religion — Philosophy. I. Title.

NIELSEN, Kai. 200'.1
Contemporary critiques of religion. [New York] Herder and Herder [1971] vii, 163 p. 22 cm. Bibliography: p. 150-160. [BL51.N496 1971b] 72-170200 6.95
1. Religion—Philosophy. I. Title.

NYGREN, Anders, Bp., 1890- 200'.1
Meaning and method; prolegomena to a scientific philosophy of religion and a scientific theology. Authorized translation by Philip S. Watson. [1st American ed.] Philadelphia, Fortress Press [1972] xv, 412 p. 26 cm. Bibliography: p. 387-401. [BL51.N88 1972] 72-157541 ISBN 0-8006-0038-X 12.95
1. Religion—Philosophy. 2. Meaning (Philosophy) I. Title.

OMAN, John Wood, 1860-1939. 230
Honest religion, by John Oman ... With an introduction by Frank H. Ballard, M. A., and a memoir of the author by George Alexander, M. A., and H. H. Farmer, D. D. Cambridge [Eng.] The University press, 1941. xi, 198 p. 19 cm. [BL48.O] A 41
1. Religion—Philosophy. 2. Authority (Religion) I. Alexander, George. II. Farmer, Herber Henry, 1892- III. Title.

OMAN, John Wood, 1860-1939. 230
Honest religion, by John Oman ... with an introduction by Frank H. Ballard, M. A., and a memoir of the author by George Alexander, M. A. and H. H. Farmer, D. D. New York, The Macmillan company. Cambridge, Eng., The University press, 1941. xi, 198 p. 19 cm. Printed in Great Britain. [BL48.O58] 41-12704
1. Religion—Philosophy. 2. Authority (Religion) I. Alexander, George. II. Farmer, Herbert Henry, 1892- III. Title.

ORMOND, Alexander Thomas, 1847-1915. 201
The philosophy of religion; lectures written for the Elliott lectureship at the Western theological seminary, Pittsburgh, Penna., U. S. A., 1916, by Alexander Thomas Ormond ... Princeton, Princeton university press; [etc., etc.] 1922. xiv p., 1 l., 195 p. front. (port.) 21 cm. [BL51.O7] 22-12184
1. Religion—Philosophy. I. Title.

OXFORD. University. Socratic Club.
Contemporary philosophy and Christian faith. Oxford, Blackwell, 1952. 63p. 22cm. (The Socratic, no. 5) Cover title. A53
1. Religion—Philosophy. I. Title.
Contents omitted.

PARKES, James William, 1896- 231
God at work in science, politics and human life. New York, Philosophical Library [1952] 180 p. 19 cm. [BL51.P27] 52-12431
1. Religion — Philosophy. 2. Revelation. I. Title.

PATERSON, W. P. 1860-1939. (William Paterson) 200'.1
The nature of religion / by W.P. Paterson. New York, N.Y. : AMS Press, 1981. p. cm. (Gifford lectures ; 1924-1925) Reprint. Originally published: London : Hodder and Stoughton, 1925. (Gifford lectures ; 1924-1925) Includes index. [BL51.P3 1981] 19 77-27202 ISBN 0-404-60476-5 : 20.00
1. Religion—Philosophy. I. Title. II. Series.

PATON, Herbert James, 1887- 201
The modern predicament; a study in the philosophy of religion. New York, Collier [1962, c.1955] 414p. 18cm. (BS146V) 1.50 pap.,
1. Religion—Philosophy. I. Title.

PATON, Herbert James, 1887- 201
The modern predicament; a study in the philosophy of religion. Based on Gifford lectures delivered in the University of St. Andrews. London, Allen & Unwin; New York, Macmillan [1955] 405p. 23cm. (The Muirhead library of philosophy) [BL51.P316 1955] 55-4627
1. Religion—Philosophy. I. Title.

PATTERSON, Robert Leet. 201
An introduction to the philosophy of religion. New York, Holt [1958] 342p. 22cm. Includes bibliography. [BL51.P319] 58-6325

1. Religion—Philosophy. I. Title.

PATTERSON, Robert Leet. 201
Irrationalism and rationalism in religion. Westport, Conn., Greenwood Press [1973, c1954] 155 p. 22 cm. Reprint of the ed. published by Duke University Press, Durham, N.C. [BL51.P32 1973] 73-436 ISBN 0-8371-6769-8 8.75
1. Religion—Philosophy. I. Title.

PATTERSON, Robert Leet. 200'.1
A philosophy of religion. Durham, N.C., Duke University Press, 1970. 571 p. 25 cm. Includes bibliographical references. [BL51.P324] 74-101130
1. Religion—Philosophy. I. Title.

PENELHUM, Terence, 1929- 200'.1
Religion and rationality; an introduction to the philosophy of religion. [1st ed.] New York, Random House [1971] xvi, 392 p. 22 cm. Includes bibliographical references. [BL51.P345] 75-135893 ISBN 0-394-31022-5
1. Religion—Philosophy. I. Title.

PERRIN, Raymond St. James, 201
1849-1915.
The religion of philosophy; or, The unification of knowledge: a comparison of the chief philosophical and religious systems of the world made with a view to reducing the categories of thought, or the most general terms of existence, to a single principle, thereby establishing a true conception of God. By Raymond S. Perrin. New York, G. P. Putnam's sons; London, Williams & Norgate, 1885. xix, 566 p. 24 cm. [BL51.P4] 2-14081
1. Religion—Philosophy. I. Title.
Contents omitted.

PFLEIDERER, Otto, 1839- 200'.1
1908.
The philosophy of religion on the basis of its history / by Otto Pfleiderer ; translated from the German of the 2d and greatly enl. ed., by Alexander Stewart and Allan Menzies. Millwood, N.Y. : Kraus Reprint Co., 1975. 4 v. in 2 ; 24 cm. Translation of Religionsphilosophie auf geschichtlicher Grundlage. Vols. 2-4: translated by A. Menzies. Reprint of the 1886-88 ed. published by Williams and Norgate, London. Includes index. Contents.Contents.—1. History of the philosophy of religion from Spinoza to the present day. 2 v.—2. Genetic-speculative philosophy of religion. 2 v. [BL51.P4713 1975] 75-23050 ISBN 0-527-03238-7 (v. 1/2) : 42.00
1. Religion—Philosophy. 2. Religion—History. 3. Religions. 4. Cultus. I. Title.

POTEAT, Edwin McNeill, 1892- 201
Coming to terms with the universe; a study in the philosophy of religion for the semi-sophisticated [by] Edwin McNeill Poteat, jr. New York, Association press, 1931. x, 85 p. 20 cm. [BL51.P6] 31-17634
1. Religion—Philosophy. 2. Philosophy and religion. 3. Religion and science—1900- I. Title.

POTEAT, Edwin McNeill, 1892- 201
God makes the difference; studies in the faith of nature and the nature of faith. [1st ed.] New York, Harper [1951] ix, 242 p. 21 cm. [BL51.P62] 51-10343
1. Religion — Philosophy. 2. God. I. Title.

†PROUDFOOT, Wayne, 1939- 200'.1
God and the self : three types of philosophy of religion / Wayne Proudfoot. Lewisburg [Pa.] : Bucknell University Press, c1976. 241 p. ; 22 cm. Includes index. Bibliography: p. 233-237. [BL51.P74] 75-28983 ISBN 0-8387-1769-1 : 13.00
1. Religion—Philosophy. I. Title.

PRZYWARA, Erich, 1889- 201
Polarity; a German Catholic's interpretation of religion, by P. Erich Przywara, S. J., translated by A. C. Bouquet ... London, Oxford university press, H. Milford, 1935. xii, 150 p., 1 l. 23 cm. Translated from an article in "Handbook on philosophy". cf. p. [v], foot-note. [BL51.P752] 35-38562
1. Religion—Philosophy. 2. Knowledge, Theory of (Religion) 3. Philosophy and religion. 4. Catholic church—Doctrinal and controversial works—Catholic authors. I. Bouquet, Alan Coates, 1884- tr. II. Title.

PURTILL, Richard L., 1931- 210
Reason to believe [by] Richard L. Purtill. Grand Rapids, Eerdmans [1974] 166 p. 21 cm. Bibliography: p. 163-164. [BL51.P87] 73-21905 ISBN 0-8028-1567-7 2.95 (pbk.)
1. Religion—Philosophy. I. Title.

PURTILL, Richard L., 1931- 200'.1
Thinking about religion : a philosophical introduction to religion / Richard L. Purtill. Englewood Cliffs, N.J. : Prentice-Hall, c1978. xiii, 175 p. ; 23 cm. Includes bibliographies and indexes. [BL51.P88] 77-13616 ISBN 0-13-917724-8 pbk. : 5.95
1. Religion—Philosophy. I. Title.

QUICK, Oliver Chase, 1885- 204
The gospel of divine action, by Olivr Chase Quick ... New York, E. P. Dutton & company, inc. [c1933] 2 p. l., vii-ix, 11-143 p. 20 cm. "First edition." [BR100.Q5] 33-25963
1. Religion—Philosophy. I. Title.

RAHNER, Karl, 1904- 201
Hearers of the word. Translated by Michael Richards. [New York] Herder and Herder [1969] x, 180 p. 22 cm. Translation of Horer des Wortes. Bibliographical footnotes. [BL51.R2413] 69-14389 6.50
1. Religion—Philosophy. 2. Knowledge, Theory of (Religion) I. Title.

REISCHAUER, August Karl, 200.1
1879-
The nature and truth of the great religions; toward a philosophy of religion. Rutland, Vt., Tuttle [c.1966] xvii, 340p. 22cm. Bibl. [BL51.R34] 65-20612 7.50
1. Religion — Philosophy. I. Title.

REISCHAUER, August Karl, 200.1
1879-
The nature and truth of the great religions; toward a philosphy of religion. Tokyo, Rutland, Vt., C.E. Tuttle Co. [1966] xvii, 340 p. 22 cm. Bibliography: p. [333]-354. [BL51.R34] 65-20612
1. Religion — Philosophy. I. Title.

RELIGIOUS perspectives and problems : 200'.1 an introduction to the philosophy of religion / edited by Allen V. Eikner. Lanham, MD : University Press of America, [1980] p. cm. Includes bibliographical references. [BL51.R355] 19 80-67265 ISBN 0-8191-1215-1 lib. bdg. : 21.00 ISBN 0-8191-1216-X (pbk.) : 12.50
1. Religion—Philosophy. I. Eikner, Allen V.

REYNOLDS, Ferris E 201
Thinking about religion; an introduction to the problems of interpreting religion, by Ferris E. Reynolds. [1st ed.] New York, American Press [c1965] 233 p. 23 cm. Includes bibliographies. [BL51.R39] 65-26017
1. Religion — Philosophy. I. Title.

RICHARDSON, Edward Elliott, 201
1873-
The philosophy of religion; the principles of Christianity and other religions, by Edward E. Richardson... Philadelphia, Boston [etc.] The Judson press [c1928] 6 p. l., 3-148 p. 20 cm. [BL51.R45] 28-31145
1. Religion—Philosophy. 2. Christianity and other religions. I. Title.

RICHMOND, James, 1931- 200.1
Faith and philosophy. Philadelphia, Lippincott [1966] 224 p. 21 cm. (Knowing Christianity) Bibliographical footnotes. [BL51.R47 1966a] 66-25411
1. Religion—Philosophy. I. Title.

ROGERS, Arthur Kenyon, 1868- 201
The religious conception of the world; an essay in constructiive philosophy, by Arthur Kenyon Rogers... New York, The Macmillan company; London, Macmillan & co., ltd., 1907. v, 285 p. 20 cm. [BL51.R58] 7-5078
1. Religion—Philosophy. 2. Theism. I. Title.

ROSS, James F., 1931- 201
Introduction to the philosophy of religion, by James F. Ross. [New York] Macmillan [1969] 185 p. 20 cm. Bibliography: p. [177]-178. [BL51.R597] 74-80298
1. Religion—Philosophy. I. Title.

ROTH, Robert J. 200'.1
American religious philosophy [by] Robert J. Roth. New York, Harcourt, Brace & World [1967] vi, 211 p. 21 cm. Bibliography: p. 191-199. [BL51.R598] 67-18540
1. Religion—Philosophy. 2. Philosophy, American. 3. Religious thought—United States. I. Title.

ROWE, William L., 1931- 200'.1
Philosophy of religion : an introduction / William L. Rowe. Encino, Calif. : Dickenson Pub. Co., c1978. xi, 207 p. ; 23 cm. Includes index. Bibliography: p. 200-202. [BL51.R5988] 77-16021 ISBN 0-8221-0208-0 pbk. : 6.95
1. Religion—Philosophy. I. Title.

ROYCE, Josiah, 1855-1916 201
The sources of religious insight. New York, Scribners [1963, c.1912, 1940] 297p. 21cm. (Scribner lib., SL88) 1.65 pap.,
1. Religion—Philosophy. I. Title. II. Title: Religious insight, the sources of.

ROYCE, Josiah, 1855-1916. 201
... The sources of religious insights; lectures delivered before Lake Forest college on the foundation of the late William Bross, by Josiah Royce ... New York, C. Scribner's sons, 1912. xvi, 297 p. 20 cm. (Half-title: The Bross library, vol. vi) At head of title: The Bross lectures ... 1911. [BL51.R6] 12-9515
1. Religion—Philosophy. I. Title. II. Title: Religious insight, The sources of.

RUPP, George. 200'.1
Beyond existentialism and Zen : religion in a pluralistic world / George Rupp. New York : Oxford University Press, 1979. xiv, 113 p. ; 22 cm. Includes bibliographical references and index. [BL51.R68] 78-15681 9.95
1. Religion—Philosophy. 2. Apologetics—20th century. 3. Christianity and existentialism. 4. Zen Buddhism—Philosophy. I. Title.

RUSSELL, Henry Norris, 1877- 201
Fate and freedom, by Henry Norris Russell ... New Haven, Yale university press; London, H. Milford, Oxford university press, 1927. viii, 176 p. 21 cm. (Half-title: The Terry lectures) [BL51.R7] 27-19147
1. Religion—Philosophy. 2. Religion and science—1900- 3. Free will and determinism. 4. God. 5. Immortality. I. Title.
Contents omitted.

SABATIER, Auguste, 1839-1901. 201
Outlines of a philosophy of religion based on psychology and history. New York, Harper [1957] 337p. 21cm. (Harper torchbooks, TB 28) The Library of religion and culture. [BL51.S3 1957] 57-10121
1. Religion—Philosophy. 2. Christianity—Philosophy. 3. Dogma. I. Title.

SABATIER, Auguste, 1839-1901. 201
Outlines of a philosophy of religion based on psychology and history, by Auguste Sabatier London, Hodder & Stoughton; New York, J. Pott & company, 1902. xv, 348 p. 20 1/2 cm. [Full name: Louis Auguste Sabatier] Contents.book I. Religion.--book II. Christianity.--book III. Dogma.--Appendix: Reply to criticisms. [BL51.S3] 2-28400
1. Religion—Philosophy. 2. Christianity—Philosophy. 3. Dogma. I. Title.

SAVAGE, Minot Judson, 1841- 237.2
1918.
Life beyond death; being a review of the world's beliefs on the subject, a consideration of present conditions of thought and feeling, leading to the question as to whether it can be demonstrated as a fact ... by Minot Judson Savage ... New York and London, G. P. Putnam's sons, 1899. 2 p. l., iii-xv, 336 p. 20 cm. [BF1031.S3] [159.9617] [133.9] 99-5542
I. Title.

SCHILPP, Paul Arthur, 1897- 201
Do we need a new religion? By Paul Arthur Schilpp ... New York, H. Holt and company [c1929] xvii, 325 p. 19 1/2 cm. [BL51.S43] 29-18534
1. Religion—Philosophy. I. Title.

SCHLETTE, Heinz Robert 261.2
Towards a theology of religions. [Tr. from German by W. J. O'Hara. New York] Herder & Herder [c.1966] 151p. 22cm. (Questiones disputatae, 14) Bibl. [BR127.S2413] 66-10760 2.50 pap.,
1. Religion—Philosophy. 2. Christianity and other religions. I. Title.

SCHMIDT, Karl, 1874- 201
From science to God: prolegomena to a future theology, by Karl Schmidt... New York, London, Harper & brothers [1944] x p., 1 l. 169 p. 20 cm. "First edition." [BL51.S457] 44-3300
1. Religion—Philosophy. 2. Theism. 3. Apologetics—20th cent. I. Title.

SCHOEN, Max, 1888- 201
Thinking about religion [by] Max Schoen. New York, Philosophical library [1946] 156 p. 1 l. 20 1/2 cm. [BL51.S458] 46-5933
1. Religion—Philosophy. I. Title.

SCHUON, Frithjof, 1907- 189.1
Gnosis: divine wisdom. Translated from the French by G. E. H. Palmer. London, J. Murray label: Hollywood-by-the-Sea, Fla., Transatlantic Arts [c1959]; 151p. 23cm. Translation of Sentlers de gnose. [BL51.S46573] 60-50745
1. Religion— Philosophy. I. Title.

SCHUON, Frithjof, 1907- 201
Stations of wisdom. Tr. from French by G. E. H. Palmer [Hollywood-by-the-Sea, Fla., Transatlantic 1962, c.1961] 157p. Bibl. 62-2622 5.25
1. Religion—Philosophy. I. Title.

SCHUON, Frithjof, 1907- 201
The transcendent unity of religions; translated by Peter Townsend. [New York] Pantheon [1953] 199p. 22cm. [BL51.S4643] 53-9950
1. Religion—Philosophy. 2. Christianity and other religions. 3. Religions. I. Title.

SCHUON, Frithjof, 1907- 200'.1
The transcendent unity of religions / Frithjof Schuon ; translated by Peter Townsend ; introd. by Huston Smith. Rev. ed. New York : Harper & Row, 1975. xxxii, 156 p. ; 21 cm. (Harper torchbooks ; TB 1818) Translation of De l'unite transcendante des religions. Includes bibliographical references and index. [BL51.S4643 1975] 74-9137 ISBN 0-06-139415-7 : 3.95
1. Religion—Philosophy. 2. Christianity and other religions. 3. Religions. I. Title.

SCHWEITZER, Albert, 1875- 201
1965.
The essence of faith; philosophy of religion. Translated and edited, with a foreword, by Kurt F. Leidecker. New York, Philosophical Library; [distributed to the trade by Book Sales, inc., 1966] 124 p. 20 cm. [B2799.R4S313] 66-23987
1. "Study...based on Kantian metaphysics, from The critique of pure reason to Religion within the limits of reason alone." 2. Kant, Immanuel, 1724-1804. 3. Religion—Philosophy. I. Leidecker, Kurt Friedrich, 1902- ed. and tr. II. Title.

SEGNO, A. Victor, 1870-
Life in the great beyond; or, The law of life and death, by A. Victor Segno. Los Angeles, Cal., The Segnogram press, 1911. 64 p. 18 1/2 cm. $1.00 11-4457
I. Title.

SETH PRINGLE PATTISON, 209
Andrew, 1856-1931.
Studies in the philosophy of religion, partly based on the Gifford lectures delivered in the University of Edinburgh in the year 1923, by A. Seth Pringle-Pattison ... Oxford, The Clarendon press, 1930. vi p., 1 l., 256 p. 22 1/2 cm. "The chapters which were originally given as lectures ... have been subjected to frequent revision, and eleven new chapters have been added."--Pref. [BL51.S47] 30-30523
1. Religion—Philosophy. I. Title.

SHEEN, Fulton John, 1895- 201
Philosophy of religion, the impact of modern knowledge on religion. New York, Appleton-Century-Crofts [1948] xvii. 409 p. 22 cm. Includes bibliographies. [BL51.S515] 48-8752
1. Religion—Philosophy. I. Title.

SHEEN, Fulton John, Bp., 201
1895-
Religion without God. 368p. 22cm. arden City, N. Y., [BL51] 54-4711
1. Religion—Philosophy. sPhilosophy and religion. 2. God. I. Title.

SHEEN, Fulton John, 1895- 201
Religion without God, by Fulton J. Sheen ... New York [etc.] Longmans, Green and co., 1928. xiv, 368 p. 21 cm. [BL51.S52] 28-25556
1. Religion—Philosophy. 2. Philosophy and religion. 3. God. I. Title.

SHERRY, Patrick. 200'.1
Religion, truth, and language-games / Patrick Sherry. New York : Barnes & Noble Books, 1977. p. cm. (Library of philosophy and religion) Includes index. Bibliography: p. [BL51.S5226 1977] 75-41579 ISBN 0-06-496236-9 : 18.50
1. Wittgenstein, Ludwig, 1889-1951. 2. Religion—Philosophy. 3. Religion and language. I. Title.

SHESTOV, Lev, 1866-1938 200.1
Athens and Jerusalem [by] Lev Shestov. Tr., introd. by Bernard Martin. New York, S. & S. [1968,c.1966] 447p. 21cm. (CL 017) Bibl. [BL51.S52273] 2.45 pap.,
1. Religion—Philosophy. 2. Philosophy and religion. I. Title.

SHESTOV, Lev, 1866-1938. 200.1
Athens and Jerusalem [by] Lev Shestov. Translated, with an introd., by Bernard Martin. Athens, Ohio University Press [1966] 447 p. 22 cm. Bibliographical footnotes. [BL51.S52273] 66-18480
1. Religion—Philosophy. 2. Philosophy and religion. I. Title.

SHIMER, William Allison, 201
1894-
Conscious clay; from science via philosophy to religion. New York, C. Scribner's Sons, 1948. xii, 199 p. 21 cm. [BL51.S5425] 48-11079
1. Religion—Philosophy. I. Title.

SLATER, Peter, 1934- 200'.1
The dynamics of religion : meaning and change in religious traditions / Peter Slater. 1st ed. San Francisco : Harper & Row, c1978. xiv, 204 p. : 20 cm. Includes bibliographical references and index. [BL51.S558 1978] 78-4426 ISBN 0-06-067389-3 pbk : 6.95
1. Religion—Philosophy. 2. Religions. I. Title.

SLATER, Robert Henry Lawson. 201
God of the living; or, Human destiny, by R. H. L. Slater... New York, C. Scribner's sons, 1939. xi, 13-325 p. diagr. 20 1/2 cm. (Half-title: The international library of Christian knowledge, ed. by B. L. Woolf and W. A. Brown) Printed in Great Britain. Bibliography: p. 309-311. [BL51.S56] 40-2877
1. Religion—Philosophy. 2. Philosophy and religion. I. Title.

SMART Ninian, 1927-
Reasons and faiths; an investigation of religious discourse, Christian and non-Christian. New York, Humanities Press [1959, c1958] 211 p. 23 cm. (International library of psychology, philosophy and scientific method) Bibliography: p. 204-205.
1. Religion — Philosophy. I. Title.

SMART, Ninian, 1927- ed. 201
Historical selections in the philosophy of religion. New York, Harper [c.1962] 510p. 22cm. Bibl. 62-14582 7.00
1. Religion—Philosophy. I. Title.

SMITH, Huston. 200'.1
Forgotten truth : the primordial tradition / Huston Smith. 1st ed. New York : Harper & Row, c1976. x, 182 p. : ill. ; 22 cm. Includes bibliographical references and index. [BL51.S572 1976] 74-15850 ISBN 0-06-013902-1 : 7.95
1. Religion—Philosophy. I. Title.

SMITH, John Edwin. 200'.1
Experience and God / John Edwin Smith. London ; New York : Oxford University Press, 1974. ix, 209 p. ; 21 cm. (A Galaxy book) Includes bibliographical references and index. [BL51.S573 1974] 75-323360 ISBN 0-19-501847-8 pbk. : 2.95
1. Religion—Philosophy. I. Title.

SMITH, John Edwin. 200'.1
Experience and God [by] John E. Smith. New York, Oxford University Press, 1968. viii, 209 p. 21 cm. Bibliographical footnotes. [BL51.S573] 68-18566
1. Religion—Philosophy. I. Title.

SMITH, John Edwin. 200'.1
Religion and empiricism, by John E. Smith. Milwaukee, Marquette University Press, 1967. 68 p. 19 cm. (The Aquinas lecture 1967) "Under the auspices of the Wisconsin-Alpha Chapter of Phi Sigma Tau." Bibliographical references included in "Notes" (p. [67]-68) [BL51.S579] 67-20684
1. Religion—Philosophy. 2. Empiricism. I. Title. II. Series.

SMITH, Wilfred Cantwell 201
The meaning and end of religion; a new approach to the religious traditions of mankind [New York] New Amer. Lib. [1964, c.1962, 1963] 352p. 18cm. (Mentor bk., MT575) Bibl. .75 pap.,
1. Religion—Philosophy. 2. Religions. I. Title.

SMITH, Wilfred Cantwell, 201
1916-
The meaning and end of religion; a new approach to the religious traditions of mankind. New York, Macmillan [c.1962, 1963] 340p. illus. 22cm. 62-21207 7.00
1. Religion—Philosophy. 2. Religions. I. Title.

SMITH, Wilfred Cantwell, 201
1916-
The meaning and end of religion; a new approach to the religious traditions of mankind. New York, Macmillan [1963] 340 p. illus. 22 cm. [BL51.S587] 62-21207
1. Religion — Philosophy. 2. Religions. I. Title.

SMITH, Wilfred Cantwell, 1916-
The meaning and end of religion; a new approach to the religious traditions of mankind. [New York] New American Library [1964] 352 p. (Mentor books, MT575) Bibliographical references included in "Notes" (p. 182-344) 65-76103
1. Religion — Philoslphy. 2. Religions. I. Title.

SMITH, Wilfred Cantwell, 291
Towards a world theology : faith and the comparative history of religion / by Wilfred Cantwell Smith. Philadelphia, Pa. : Westminster Press, 1981. vi, 206 p. ; 23 cm. "A revision of the Cadbury lectures given at the University of Birmingham"—p. vi. Includes bibliographical references and index. [BL51.S588] 19 80-50826 ISBN 0-664-21380-4 : 8.95
1. Religion—Philosophy. 2. Religions. 3. Christianity and other religions. 4. Faith. I. Title.

SNAITH, John. 201
The philosophy of spirit, by John Snaith. London, New York [etc.] Hodder and Stoughton, 1914. vii, 405, [1] p. 24 cm. [BL51.S59] 34-36375
1. Religion—Philosophy. 2. Ontology. 3. Christianity—Evidences. I. Title.

SOLOV'EV, Vladimir 201
Sergeevich, 1853-1900.
Godmanhood as the main idea of the philosophy of Vladimir Solovyev, by Peter P. Zouboff ... [Poughkeepsie, N.Y., Harmon printing house, 1944] 233 p., 1 l. 22 cm. Thesis (PH.D.)--Columbia university, 1942. Published also without thesis note, under title: Vladimir Solovyev's Lectures on Godmanhood. Vita. Chtenie o Bogochelovechestve) Bibliography: p. 227-233. [BL51.S617 1944 a] A 47
1. Religion—Philosophy. I. Zouboff, Peter Petrovich, 1893- ed. II. Title.

SOLOV'EV, Vladimir 201
Sergeevich, 1853-1900.
Vladimir Solovyev's Lectures on Godmanhood, with an introduction by Peter Peter Zouboff. [New York] International university press, distributor [1944] 233 p. 20 1/2 cm. Cover-title: Solovyev on Godmanhood. Title from t.-p. mounted on original t.-p. which reads: Godmanhood as the main idea of the philosophy of Vladimir Solovyev, by Peter P. Zouboff. Corrected pages mounted on p. 48-49. [BL51.S617] 46-14007
1. Religion—Philosophy. I. Zouboff, Peter Peter. II. Title. III. Title: Godmanhood as the main idea of the philosophy of Vladimir Solovyev.

SONTAG, Frederick. 200'.1
How philosophy shapes theology; problems in the philosophy of religion. New York, Harper & Row [1971] xv, 495 p. 21 cm. Includes bibliographical references. [BL51.S622 1971] 71-170618 ISBN 0-06-046349-X
1. Religion—Philosophy. I. Title.

STACE, Walter Terence 201
Time and eternity: an essay in the philosophy of religion. Princeton, N. J., Princeton University Press [1959, c.1952] vii, 169p. 22cm. 1.45 pap.,
1. Religion—Philosophy. I. Title.

STACE, Walter Terence, 1886- 201
Religion and the modern mind / W. T. Stace. Westport, Conn. : Greenwood Press, 1980, c1952. 285 p. ; 23 cm. Reprint of the 1st ed. published by Lippincott, Philadelphia. Includes index. [BL51.S6256 1980] 19 80-24093 ISBN 0-313-22662-8 lib. bdg. : 22.50
1. Religion—Philosophy. 2. Skepticism—Controversial literature. I. Title.

STACE, Walter Terence, 1886- 201
Time and eternity: an essay in the philosophy of religion. Princeton, Princeton University Press, 1952. vii, 169 p. 23 cm. [BL51.S6257] 52-5835
1. Religion — Philosophy. I. Title.

STACE, Walter Terence, 200'.1
1886-
Time and eternity; an essay in the philosophy of religion, by W. T. Stace. Princeton, N.J., Princeton University Press, 1952. New York, Greenwood Press [1969] vii, 169 p. 23 cm. Bibliographical footnotes. [BL51.S6257 1969] 69-14094
1. Religion—Philosophy. I. Title.

STACE, Wlater Terence, 1886- 201
Religion and the modern mind. [1st ed.] Philadelphia, Lippincott [1952] 285 p. 22 cm. [BL51.S6256] 52-7471
1. Religion—Philosophy. 2. Skepticism—Controversial literature. I. Title.

STARRATT, Alfred B. 210
Your self, my self & the self of the universe / Alfred B. Starratt. 1st ed. Owings Mills, Md. : Stemmer House Publishers, 1979. 183 p. ; 24 cm. "A Barbara Holdridge book." [BL51.S6259 1979] 79-9971 ISBN 0-916144-38-0 : 12.95. ISBN 0-916144-39-9 pbk. : 7.95
1. Religion—Philosophy. I. Title.

STERRETT, James Macbride, 1847-
1923.
Studies in Hegel's Philosophy of religion, with a chapter on Christian unity in America, by J. Macbride Sterrett ... New York, D. Appleton and company, 1890. xiii, 348 p. 21 cm. [B2940.S6] 15-22824
1. Hegel, Georg Wilhelm Friedrich, 1770-1831. Vorlesungen tiber die philosophie der religion. 2. Religion—Philosophy. I. Title.

STEVENS, Edward, 1928- 200'.973
The religion game, American style / by Edward Stevens. New York : Paulist Press, c1976. 152 p. ; 23 cm. Includes bibliographical references. [BL51.S657] 76-9367 ISBN 0-8091-1951-X pbk. : 5.95
1. Religion—Philosophy. 2. Religion and sociology. 3. Religious thought—United States. I. Title.

STIRLING, James Hutchison, 200'.1
1820-1909.
Philosophy and theology : being the first Edinburgh University Gifford lectures / by James Hutchison Stirling. 1st AMS ed. New York : AMS Press, 1979. xvi, 407 p. ; 19 cm. Reprint of the 1890 ed. published by T. & T. Clark, Edinburgh. Includes index. [BL51.S67 1979] 77-27233 ISBN 0-404-60451-X : 31.50
1. Religion—Philosophy. 2. Natural theolgy—Early, works to 1900. 3. Evolution and religion. I. Title. II. Series: Gifford lectures ; 1889-90.

STRAW, Walter E. 201
Philosophy of religion [by] W. E. Straw. Berrien Springs, Mich., Emmanuel missionary college, 1944. 3 p. l., 143 numb. l. 27 1/2 x 21 1/2 cm. Reproduced from type-written copy. Bibliography: leaves 141-143. [BL51.S678] 44-25474
1. Religion—Philosophy. I. Emmanuel missionary college, Berrien Springs, Mich. II. Title.

STREETER, Burnett Hillman, 201
1874-1937.
Reality; a new correlation of science and religion, by Burnett Hillman Streeter ... New York, The Macmillan company, 1926. xiii, 350 p. 20 1/2 cm. [BL51.S68] 26-20636
1. Religion—Philosophy. I. Title.

STRICKLAND, Francis Lorette, 239
1871-
Foundations of Christian belief; studies in the philosophy of religion, by Francis L. Strickland ... New York, Cincinnati, The Abingdon press c1915] 319 p. 21 1/2 cm. Contains bibliographies. [BR100.S8] 15-26891
1. Religion—Philosophy. I. Title.

TENNANT, Frederick Robert, 201
1866-
Philosophical theology, by F. R. Tennant ... Cambridge [Eng.] The University press, 1928- v. 24 cm. [BL51.T4] 29-3316
1. Religion—Philosophy. I. Title.

TENNANT, Frederick Robert, 201
1866-
Philosophical theology, by F. R. Tennant ... Cambridge [Eng.] The University press, 1928-30. 2 v. 24 cm. Contents.I. The soul and its faculties.--II. The world, the soul, and God. [BL51.T4] 29-3316
1. Religion—Philosophy. I. Title.

THOMAS, George Finger, 200'.1
1899-
Philosophy and religious belief [by] George F. Thomas. New York, Scribner [1970] xii, 372 p. 24 cm. Includes bibliographical references. [BL51.T438] 76-106534 10.00
1. Religion—Philosophy. I. Title.

[THOMPSON, George Western] 201
1806-1888.
Deus-semper. The norm plus the germ by the conditions minus the fruit. By the author of "Semper-Deus". Philadelphia, Claxton, Remsen & Haffelfinger, 1869. 435 p. 19 1/2 cm. Title vignette. [BL51.T5] 30-12957
1. Religion—Philosophy. I. Title.

THOMPSON, George Western, 201
1806-1888.
Deus-semper. The norm plus the germ by the conditions minus the fruit. By George W. Thompson ... Philadelphia, Claxton, Remsen & Haffelfinger, 1869. 435 p. 19 1/2 cm. Title vignette. [BL51.T5 1869a] 30-12958
1. Religion—Philosophy. I. Title.

THOMPSON, Samuel Martin. 201
A modern philosophy of religion. Chicago, H. Regnery Co., 1955. 601 p. 22 cm. [BL51.T53] 55-1237
1. Religion—Philosophy. I. Title.

TILLICH, Paul, 1886-1965. 200.1
What is religion? Edited and with an introduction by James Luther Adams. New York, Harper [1973, c.1969] 191 p. 20 cm. (Harper torchbooks, TB1732) [BL51.T58] 67-17014 ISBN 0-06-131732-2 2.25 (pbk.)
1. Religion—Philosophy. I. Title.

TRETHOWAN, Illtyd, 1907- 201
The basis of belief. New York, Hawthorn Books [c.1961] 142p. (Twentieth century encyclopedia of Catholicism, v.13. Section 1: Knowledge and faith) Bibl. 61-9457 3.50 bds.,
1. Religion—Philosophy. I. Title.

TRETHOWAN, Illtyd, 1907- 201
The basis of belief. [1st ed.] New York, Hawthorn Books [1961] 142 p. 21 cm. (Twentieth century encyclopedia of Catholicism, v. 13. Section 1: Knowledge and faith) Includes bibliography. [BL51.T64] 61-9457
1. Religion — Philosophy. I. Title.

TRUEBLOOD, David Elton. 201
The essence of spiritual religion, by D. Elton Trueblood ... with a foreword by Willard L. Sperry ... [New York] Harper and brothers, 1936. xiv, 156 p. 19 1/2 cm. [BR100.T75] 36-9449
1. Religion—Philosophy. 2. Mysticism. 3. Spiritual life. I. Title.

TRUEBLOOD, David Elton, 200'.1
1900-
The essence of spiritual religion / D. Elton Trueblood. New York : Harper & Row,

1975, c1936. xii, 156 p. ; 21 cm. Includes index. [BR100.T75 1975] 74-7684 pbk. : 1.95
1. Religion—Philosophy. 2. Mysticism. 3. Spiritual life. I. Title.

TRUEBLOOD, David Elton, 1900- 201
The logic of belief, an introduction to the philosophy of religion [by] David Elton Trueblood ... New York and London, Harper & brothers [1942] ix p., 2 l., 3-327 p. 22 1/2 cm. "First edition." [BL51.T68] 42-13750
1. Religion—Philosophy. I. Title.

TRUEBLOOD, David Elton, 1900- 201
Philosophy of religion. [1st ed.] New York, Harper [1957] 324 p. 22 cm. Includes bibliography. [BL51.T683] 57-7342
1. Religion — Philosophy. I. Title.

TRUEBLOOD, David Elton, 1900- 201
Philosophy of religion. Grand Rapids, Mich., Baker Book, [1973, c1957] xv, 324, 22 cm. [BL51.T683] 3.95 (pbk.)
1. Religion—Philosophy. I. Title.
L.C. card no. for hardbound ed.: 57-7342

TRUEBLOOD, David Elton, 1900- 200'.1
Philosophy of religion / David Elton Trueblood. Westport, Conn. : Greenwood Press, 1975 [i.e.1976] c1957 xv, 324 p. ; 22 cm. Reprint of the ed. published by Harper, New York. Includes bibliographical references and indexes. [BL51.T683 1975] 75-31446 ISBN 0-8371-8514-9 : 16.00
1. Religion—Philosophy.

TRUEBLOOD, David Elton, 1900- 201
Philosophy of religion. [1st ed.] New York, Harper [1957] 324 p. 22 cm. Includes bibliography. [BL51.T683] 57-7342
1. Religion—Philosophy.

TSANOFF, Radoslav Andrea, 1887- 201
Religious crossroads, by Radoslav A. Tsanoff ..., New York, E. P. Dutton & co., inc., 1942. xiv, 384 p. 22 cm. "First edition." "Notes (bibliographical)", p. 365-375. [BL51.T7] 42-12946
1. Religion—Philosophy. I. Title.

TYLER, Charles Mellen, 1832-1918. 201
Bases of religious belief, historic and ideal; an outline of religious study, By Charles Mellen Tyler ... New York, London, G. P. Putnam's sons, 1897. x, 273 p. 20 1/2 cm. [BL51.T8] 30-12959
1. Religion—Philsophy. 2. Faith. I. Title.

VANDEN Burgt, Robert J., 1936- 210

The religious philosophy of William James / Robert J. Vanden Burgt. Chicago : Nelson-Hall, c1981. vii, 167 p. ; 22 cm. Includes index. Bibliography: p. 161-163. [B945.J24V36] 19 80-22936 ISBN 0-88229-594-2 pbk. : 8.95
1. James, William, 1842-1910—Religion. 2. Religion—Philosophy. I. Title.

VAN DUSEN, Henry Pitney, 1897- 231
The plain man seeks for God, by Henry P. Van Dusen... New York, London, C. Scribner's sons, 1933. xiv p., 2 l., 3-213 p. 21 cm. Bibliography: p. 205-209. [BT101.V34] 33-16574
1. God. 2. Religion—Philosophy. I. Title.

VON HILDEBRAND, Alice M. (Jourdain) 200'.1
Introduction to a philosophy of religion, by Alice von Hildebrand. Chicago, Franciscan Herald Press [1970] ix, 178 p. 22 cm. Includes bibliographical references. [BL51.V58] 79-139972 6.95
1. Religion—Philosophy. I. Title.

WALHOUT, Donald 208.2
Interpreting religion. Englewood Cliffs, N.J., Prentice [c.]1963. 481p. 24cm. Bibl. 63-9965 9.00
1. Religion—Philosophy. 2. Theology—Collections. I. Title.

WALPOLE, George Henry Somerset, bp. of Edinburgh, 1854-1929.
Life in the world to come. By the Right Rev. G. H. S. Walpole ... London, R. Scott; Milwaukee, Wis., Young churchman co., 1917. 3 p. l., 142 p. 19 cm. A 18
I. Title.

WATTS, Alan Wilson 201
Nature, man, and woman. [New York] New American Library [1960, c.1958] 176p. (bibl. p. [174]-176) illus. 18cm. (Mentor bk. MD282) .50 pap.,
1. Religion—Philosophy. 2. Philosophy, Chinese. 3. Sex and religion. I. Title.

WATTS, Alan Wilson, 1915-
Nature, man, and woman. [New York] New American Library [1960, c1958] x, [11]-176 p. 18 cm. (A Mentor book, MD 282) "First Printing." "Reprint of the original ... edition published by Pantheon Books [in 1958]" Bibliography: p. [174]-176.
1. Religion — Philosophy. 2. Philosophy, Chinese. 3. Sex and religion. 4. Nature. I. Title.

WATTS, Alan Wilson, 1915- 201
Nature, man, and woman. [New York] Pantheon [1958] 209 p. illus. 22 cm. Includes bibliography. [BL51.W3713] 58-8266
1. Religion—Philosophy. 2. Philosophy, Chinese. 3. Sex and religion. I. Title.

WATTS, J. C. 133.
The orb of day. A treatise on spiritual philosophy and intellectual astronomy. Spiritual science against the world. A celestial Bible. By Prof. J. C. Watts, LL.D. Chicago, M. B. Kenny, printer, 1883. 200 p. front. (port.) illus. 19 1/2 cm. [BF1301.W3] CA 11
I. Title.

WEBB, Clement Charles Julian, 1865- 201
Group theories of religion and the individual. By Clement C. J. Webb ... London, G. Allen & Unwin ltd.; New York, The Macmillan company [1916] 207, [1] p. 20 1/2 cm. "The substance of a course of lectures delivered ... 1914 as Wilde lecturer on natural and comparative religion in the University of Oxford."--Pref . [BL51.W375] A 16
1. Religion—Philosophy. 2. Religion and sociology. I. Wilde lectures in natural and comparative religion, 1914. II. Title.

WEBB, Clement Charles Julian, 1865-
Religious experience; a public lecturedelivered in the hall of Oriel Collegeon Friday 19 May 1944. With a forwardby L. W. Grensted. Printed, togetherwith a bibliography of his published writings and presented to him by some of his friends and pupils on the occasion of his eightieth birthday, 25 June 1945. London, Oxford Univ. Press [1945] 70 p. port. 23 cm. A 48
1. Webb, Clement Charles Julian, 1865- 2. Webb, Clement Charles Julian, 1865-Bibl. 3. Religion—Philosophy. I. Title.

WEISS, Paul, 1901-
A draft of a book in religion tentatively entitled For the love of God. [New Haven, 1963?] 2 v. (viii, 572 l.) 28 cm. Cover title. 63-72938
1. Religion — Philosophy. 2. God. 3. God-Worship and love. I. Title. II. Title: For the love of God.

WEISS, Paul, 1901- 200'.1
The God we seek. Carbondale, Southern Illinois University Press [1973, c1964] 258 p. 20 cm. (Arcturus paperbacks, AB106) [B945.W396G6 1973] 72-11838 ISBN 0-8093-0628-X 2.95
1. Religion—Philosophy. 2. Experience (Religion) I. Title.

WEISS, Paul, 1901- 211
The God we seek. Carbondale, Southern Illinois University Press [1964] 258 p. 22 cm. [B945.W396G6] 64-13476
1. Religion—Philosophy. 2. Experience (Religion) I. Title.

WELLS, Donald A. 201
God, man, and the thinker: philosophies ofreligion. [New York, Dell, 1967, c. 1962] 507p. 21cm. (Delta bk., 9697) [BL51.W379] 2.45 pap.,
1. Religion—Philosophy. 2. Theology. I. Title.

WELLS, Donald A. 201
God, man, and the thinker: philosophies of religion. New York, Random House [1962] 507 p. 24 cm. [BL51.W379] 62-10778
1. Religion—Philosophy. 2. Theology. I. Title.

WIEMAN, Henry Nelson, 1884- 201
American philosophies of religion, by Henry Nelson Wieman ... [and] Bernard Eugene Meland ... Chicago, New York, Willett, Clark & company, 1936. xiii, 370 p. diagrs. 23 1/2 cm. Bibliography: p. 353-359. [BL51.W55] 36-15871
1. Religion—Philosophy. 2. Religious thought—U.S. I. Meland, Bernard Eugene, 1899- joint author. II. Title.

WIEMAN, Henry Nelson, 1884- 201
The growth of religion, by Henry Nelson Wieman ... [and] Walter Marshall Horton ... Chicago, New York, Willett, Clark & company, 1938. xviii p., 1 l., 505 p. 23 1/2 cm. Contents.pt. I. The historical growth of religion, by W. M. Horton.--pt. II. Contemporary growth of religion, by H. N. Wieman. Bibliography at end of each chapter. [BL51.W56] 39-31167
1. Religion—Philosophy. 2. Religion—Hist. I. Horton, Walter Marshall, 1895- II. Title.

WIEMAN, Henry Nelson, 1884- 201
Intellectual foundation of faith. New York, Philosophical Library [1961] 212 p. 22 cm. Includes bibliography. [BL51.W565] 60-13665
1. Religion — Philosophy. I. Title.

WIEMAN, Henry Nelson, 1884- 201
Man's ultimate commitment. Carbondale, Southern Ill. Univ. Pr. [1963, c.1958] 318p. 21cm. (ARCTURUS bk., ABI) Bibl. 6.00; 1.95 pap.,
1. Religion—Philosophy. 2. Creative ability. I. Title.

WIEMAN, Henry Nelson, 1884- 201
Man's ultimate commitment. Carbondale, Southern Illinois University Press, 1958. 318 p. 24 cm. Includes bibliography. [BL51.W376] 58-5488
1. Religion — Philosophy. 2. Creative ability. I. Title.

WIEMAN, Henry Nelson, 1884- 201
Religious experience and scientific method. Westport, Conn., Greenwood Press [1970] 387 p. 23 cm. Reprint of the 1926 ed. [BL51.W58 1970] 73-109877 ISBN 0-8371-4368-3
1. Religion—Philosophy. 2. Religion and science—1926-1945. I. Title.

WIEMAN, Henry Nelson, 1884- 201
Religious experience and scientific method, by Henry Nelson Wieman ... New York, The Macmillan company, 1926. 3 p. l., 5-387 p. 19 1/2 cm. [BL51.W58] 26-3507
1. Religion—Philosophy. 2. Relgiion and science—1900- I. Title.

WILM, Emil Carl, 1877-1932. 201
The problem of religion, by Emil Carl Wilm ... Boston, New York, [etc.,] The Pilgrim press [c1912] xii, 240 p. 21 1/2 cm. "Literature" at end of each chapter. [BL51.W6] 12-25969
1. Religion—Philosophy. 2. Theism. 3. Idealism. I. Title.

WINBURN, Oscar Edgar.
Unhand me! A comment on religion, by Oscar Edgar Winburn; illustrated with reproductions from original drawings by the author. New York, O. E. Winburn, 1905. 96 p. illus. 17 1/2 cm. 5-6471
I. Title.

WOBBERMIN, Georg, 1869- 234
Christian belief in God. A German criticism of German materialistic philosophy, by Georg Wobbermin ... Tr. from the 3d German ed. by Daniel Sommer Robinson ... New Haven, Yale university press, 1918. xix, 175 p. 19 1/2 cm. "Published on the foundation established in memory of James Wesley Cooper of the class of 1865, Yale college." "Notes and references": p. 153-175. [BT51.W7] 19-1878
1. Religion—Philosophy. 2. Belief and doubt. 3. G. I. Robinson, Daniel Sommer, 1888- tr. II. Yale university. James Wesley Cooper memorial publication fund. III. Title.

WOBBERMIN, Georg, 1869- 201
The nature of religion, by Georg Wobbermin ... translated by Theophil Menzel ... and Daniel Sommer Robinson ... with an introduction by Douglas Clyde Macintosh ... New York, Thomas Y. Crowell company [c1933] xvi, 379 p. front. (port.) 22 1/2 cm. An interpretation of religion based upon Schleiermacher's conception. Translation of "Systematische theologie nach religionspsychologischer methode". pt. 2, "Das wesen der religion". [BL51.W73] 33-39320
1. Schlieiermacher, Frederick Ernst Daniel, 1768-1834. 2. Religion—Philosophy I. Menzel, Theophil, tr. II. Robinson, Daniel Sommer, 1888- joint tr. III. Title.

WODEHOUSE, Helen, 1880- 201
One kind of religion, by Helen Wodehouse ... Cambridge [Eng.] The University press, 1944. 4 p. l., 208 p. 19 cm. [Full name: Helen Marion Wodehouse.] [BL51.W755] 45-4820
1. Religion—Philosophy. I. Title.

WOOD, Allen W. 200'.1
Kant's moral religion [by] Allen W. Wood. Ithaca, Cornell University Press [1970] xii, 283 p. 22 cm. Bibliography: p. [273]-279. [B2799.E8W6] 71-99100 ISBN 8-01-405483- 9.00
1. Kant, Immanuel, 1724-1804—Ethics. 2. Religion—Philosophy. I. Title.

WRIGHT, Henry Wilkes, 1878- 201
The religious response; an introduction to the philosophy of religion, by Henry Wilkes Wright ... New York and London, Harper & brothers, 1929. 4 p. l., 256 p. 19 1/2 cm. [BL51.W77] 29-24204
1. Religion—Philosophy. I. Title.

WRIGHT, Theodore Francis, 1845-1907. 201
The human and its relation to the divine ... By Theodore F. Wright, PH.D. Philadelphia, J. B. Lippincott company, 1892. 271 p. 19 cm. [BL51.W79] 30-12960
1. Religion—Philosophy. 2. Self. I. Title.

WRIGHT, William Kelley, 1877- 201
A student's philosophy of religion, by William Kelley Wright ... New York The Macmillan company, 1922. 3 p. l., v-xii p., 1 l., 472 p. 22 1/2 cm. "The book is an outgrowth of lecture courses given at Cornell university from 1913 to 1916."--Pref. "References" at end of chapters. [BL51.W8] 22-4841
1. Religion—Philosophy. 2. Religions. 3. Psychology, Religious. I. Title. II. Title: Philosophy of religion.

WRIGHT, William Kelley, 1877- 201
A student's philosophy of religion, by William Kelley Wright ... Rev. ed. New York, The Macmillan company, 1935. xvi p., 1 l., 566 p. 21 cm. "This book is an outgrowth of lecture courses given at Cornell university from 1913 to 1916."--Pref. "Notes": p. 526-555, and "References" at end of most of the chapters. [BL51.W8 1935] 35-1154
1. Religion—Philosophy. 2. Religions. 3. Psychology, Religious. I. Title. II. Title: Philosophy of religion.

YANDELL, Keith E., 1938- 200'.1
Basic issues in the philosophy of religion [by] Keith E. Yandell. Boston, Allyn and Bacon [1971] ix, 238 p. 24 cm. Includes bibliographical references. [BL51.Y27] 72-107427
1. Religion—Philosophy. I. Title.

ZEIGLER, Earle F
A brief introduction to the philosophy of religion. Champaign, Ill., Stipes Pub. Co., 1965. iii, 27 l. 28 cm. Errata slip inserted. Bibliography: leaves 26-27. 65-102874
1. Religion — Philosophy. I. Title.

ZUURDEEG, Willem Frederik. 201
An analytical philosophy of religion. New York, Abingdon Press [1958] 320 p. illus. 24 cm. [BL51.Z8] 58-9527
1. Religion—Philosophy. I. Title.

ZUVER, Dudley. 200.01157224
Salvation by laughter; a study of religion and the sense of humor, by Dudley Zuver. New York and London, Harper & brothers, 1933. 5 p. l., 270 p. 21 cm. "First edition." [Full name: Dudley De Forest Zuver] [BL65.L3Z8] [200.01159942324] 33-25036
1. Religion—Philosophy. 2. Comic, The. 3. Wit and humor. I. Title.

Religion—Philosophy—Addresses, essays, lectures.

BAMBROUGH, Renford. 201
Reason, truth and God. London, Methuen [1973, c.1969] 164 p. 21 cm. (University paperbacks, UP490) Bibliography: p. [159] -160. [BL51.B23] 73-390962 ISBN 0-416-70240-6 3.50 (pbk.)
1. Religion—Philosophy—Addresses, essays, lectures. I. Title.
Available from Barnes & Noble, New York, for 5.35.

BLOCH, Ernst, 1885- 200'.1
Man on his own; essays in the philosophy of religion. Translated by E. B. Ashton. [New York] Herder and Herder [1970] 240 p. 22 cm. Translation of Religion im Erbe. Contents.Contents.—Foreword, by H. Cox.—Introduction, by J. Moltmann.—Karl Marx; death and apocalypse.—Incipit vita nova.—Biblical resurrection and apocalypse.—Christ, or The uncovered countenance.—Religious truth.—Christian social utopias.—The nationalized God and the right to community.—Man's increasing entry into religious mystery. [BL51.B584513] 79-87749 5.50
1. Religion—Philosophy—Addresses, essays, lectures. I. Title.

*BUEHNE, Willis G. 201
Why is religion? New York, Exposition Pr. [1973] 42 p. 21 cm. [BR121.2] ISBN 0-682-47674-9 3.00
1. Religion—Philosophy—Addresses, essays, lectures. 2. Christianity—20th century. I. Title.

THE Challenge of religion 200'.1
today : essays on the philosophy of religion / John King-Farlow, editor. New York : Science History Publications, 1976. p. cm. (Canadian contemporary philosophy series) Bibliography: p. [BL51.C48] 76-13492 ISBN 0-88202-157-5 pbk. : 3.95
1. Religion—Philosophy—Addresses, essays, lectures. I. King-Farlow, John.

DUPRE, Louis K., 1925- 200'.1
A dubious heritage : studies in the philosophy of religion after Kant / by Louis Dupre. New York : Paulist Press, 1978,c1977 v, 177 p. ; 23 cm. "Collection of essays written over the past ten years." "A Newman book." Includes bibliographical references. [BL51.D85] 77-83577 ISBN 0-8091-2068-2 pbk. : 4.95
1. Religion—Philosophy—Addresses essays, lectures. I. Title.

EXPLORING the philosophy 200'.1
of religion / [edited by] David Stewart. Englewood Cliffs, N.J. : Prentice-Hall, c1980. x, 404 p. ; 23 cm. Includes bibliographical references and index. [BL51.E96] 79-18903 ISBN 0-13-297366-9 pbk. : 10.95
1. Religion—Philosophy—Addresses, essays, lectures. I. Stewart, David, 1938-

FEAVER, J. Clayton. 200.1
Religion in philosophical and cultural perspective; a new approach to the philosophy of religion through cross-disciplinary studies, edited by J. Clayton Feavor and William Horosz. Princeton, N.J., Van Nostrand [1967] xiv, 504 p. 24 cm. Includes bibliographies. [BL51.F39] 67-3112
1. Religion-Philosophy—Addresses, essays, lectures. I. Horosz, William, joint author. II. Title.

GANDHI, Ramchandra, 1937- 200'.1
The availability of religious ideas / Ramchandra Gandhi. London : Macmillan, 1976. 109 p. ; 23 cm. (Library of philosophy and religion) Includes index. [BL51.G325 1976b] 76-378093 ISBN 0-333-13757-4 : £7.95
1. Religion—Philosophy—Addresses, essays, lectures. I. Title.

HICK, John. 200'.1
God and the universe of faiths; essays in the philosophy of religion. New York, St. Martin's Press [1974, c1973] xii, 201 p. 23 cm. Includes bibliographical references. [BL51.H493 1974] 73-88027 12.95
1. Religion—Philosophy—Addresses, essays, lectures. I. Title.

HISTORY, religion, and 191
spiritual democracy : essays in honor of Joseph L. Blau / Maurice Wohlgelernter, editor, James A. Martin, Jr. [et al.] co-editors. New York : Columbia University Press, 1980. lxxiv, 375 p. : port. ; 24 cm. Includes index. "Joseph L. Blau: a bibliography [by] Sam Dekay": p. [341]-364. [BL51.H58] 79-23234 ISBN 0-231-04624-3 : 27.50
1. Blau, Joseph Leon, 1909- —Addresses, essays, lectures. 2. Religion—Philosophy—Addresses, essays, lectures. 3. Philosophy, American—History—Addresses, essays, lectures. 4. Political science—Addresses, essays, lectures. 5. Judaism—Addresses, essays, lectures. 6. Philosophy, Jewish—History—Addresses, essays, lectures. I. Blau, Joseph Leon, 1909- II. Wohlgelernter, Maurice.

INGE, William Ralph, 1860-1954. 215
Science and ultimate truth. [Folcroft, Pa.] Folcroft Library Editions, 1973. 32 p. 24 cm. "Delivered at Guy's Hospital Medical School, March 25, 1926." Reprint of the 1926 ed. published by Longmans, Green, New York and issued as the Fison memorial lecture, 1926. [BL51.I6 1973] 73-7513 ISBN 0-8414-2109-9 (lib. bdg.)
1. Religion—Philosophy—Addresses, essays, lectures, 2. Religion and science—1926-1945—Addresses, essays, lectures. I. Title. II. Series: The Fison memorial lecture, 1926.

INGE, William Ralph, 1860-1954. 215
Science and ultimate truth / by W. R. Inge. Norwood, Pa. : Norwood Editions, 1976. 32 p. ; 23 cm. "Delivered at Guy's Hospital Medical School, March 25, 1926." Reprint of the 1926 ed. published by Longmans, Green, New York, which was issued as the Fison memorial lecture, 1926. [BL51.I6 1976] 76-8218 ISBN 0-8482-1154-5 lib. bdg. : 6.50
1. Religion—Philosophy—Addresses, essays, lectures. 2. Religion and science—1926-1945—Addresses, essays, lectures. I. Title. II. Series: The Fison memorial lecture, 1926.

KUNG, Hans, 1928- 200'.1
Freud and the problem of God / Hans Kung ; translated by Edward Quinn. New Haven : Yale University Press, 1979. ix, 126 p. ; 22 cm. (The Terry lectures ; 41) Translation of a portion of Existiert Gott? Includes bibliographical references and index. [BL50.K83213] 78-25581 ISBN 0-300-02350-2 : 8.95
1. Freud, Sigmund, 1856-1939—Addresses, essays, lectures. 2. Religion—Philosophy—Addresses, essays, lectures. 3. God—History of doctrines—Addresses, essays, lectures. I. Title. II. Series: Terry lectures, Yale University ; 41.

MCLEAN, George F. 200'.1
Religion in contemporary thought. [by] George F. McLean. Staten Island, N.Y., Alba House [1973] xiv, 326 p. 21 cm. Includes bibliographical references. [BL51.M236] 72-6837 ISBN 0-8189-0256-6 4.95
1. Religion—Philosophy—Addresses, essays, lectures. 2. Death of God theology—Addresses, essays, lectures. I. Title.

MILLER, Oscar W 201
Thunder on the left: some religio-philosophical essays. New York, Philosophical Library [1959] 95p. 23cm. Includes bibliography. [BL51.M63] 59-16366
1. Religion—Philosophy—Addresses, essays, lectures. I. Title.

PATTERSON, Robert Leet. 200'.1
Adventures in the philosophy of religion / Robert Leet Patterson. 1st ed. Hicksville, N.Y. : Exposition Press, c1977. 87 p. ; 21 cm. (An Exposition-university book) Includes bibliographical references. [BL51.P318] 77-74567 ISBN 0-682-48827-5 : 5.50
1. Religion—Philosophy—Addresses, essays, lectures. I. Title.

PFLEIDERER, Otto, 1839-1908. 200'.1
Philosophy and development of religion / by Otto Pfleiderer. 1st AMS ed. New York : AMS Press, 1979. 2 v. ; 19 cm. "Delivered before the University of Edinburgh, 1894." Reprint of the 1894 ed. published by W. Blackwood, Edinburgh, in series: Gifford lectures, 1894. Contents.Contents.—v. 1. Philosophy of religion.—v. 2. Origin and development of Christianity. [BL51.P46 1979] 77-27229 ISBN 0-404-60470-6 : 57.50
1. Religion—Philosophy—Addresses, essays, lectures. 2. Christianity—Addresses, essays, lectures. 3. Theology, Doctrinal—History—Addresses, essays, lectures. I. Title. II. Series: Gifford lectures ; 1894.

PHILLIPS, Dewi Zephaniah, comp. 200'.1
Religion and understanding, edited by D. Z. Phillips. New York, Macmillan [1967] vii, 216 p. 23 cm. Bibliographical footnotes. [BL51.P52 1967] 67-22156
1. Religion—Philosophy—Addresses, essays, lectures. I. Title.

PHILLIPS, Dewi Zephaniah. 200'.1
Religion without explanation / D. Z. Phillips. Oxford : Blackwell, c1976. xi, 200 p. ; 23 cm. Includes indexes. Bibliography: p. [192]-195. [BL51.P523] 77-356891 ISBN 0-631-17100-2 : £7.00
1. Religion—Philosophy—Addresses, essays, lectures. I. Title.

PHILOSOPHY of religion and 200'.1
theology: 1971. Edited by David Griffin. Chambersburg, Pa., American Academy of Religion, 1971. 240 p. 23 cm. Proceedings of the Philosophy of Religion and Theology Section of the 1971 American Academy of Religion annual meeting. Includes bibliographical references. [BL51.P53] 72-192659
1. Religion—Philosophy—Addresses, essays, lectures. 2. Nature (Theology)—Addresses, essays, lectures. I. Griffin, David, 1939- ed. II. American Academy of Religion.

PRICE, Henry Habberley, 1899- 200'.1
Essays in the philosophy of religion: based on the Sarum lectures, 1971 [by] H. H. Price. Oxford, Clarendon Press, 1972. [7], 125 p. 21 cm. (The Sarum lectures, 1971) Includes bibliographical references. [BL51.P73] 72-195626 ISBN 0-19-824376-6
1. Religion—Philosophy—Addresses, essays, lectures. 2. Psychical research—Addresses, essays, lectures. 3. Experience (Religion)—Addresses, essays, lectures. I. Title. II. Series.
Available from Oxford Univ. Pr., 7.25.

RATIONALITY and religious 200'.1
belief / C. F. Delaney, editor. Notre Dame, Ind. : University of Notre Dame Press, c1979. p. cm. (Notre Dame studies in the philosophy of religion ; no. 1) Includes bibliographical references. [BL51.R29] 79-63359 ISBN 0-268-01602-X : 10.95. ISBN 0-268-01603-8 pbk. : 3.95
1. Religion—Philosophy—Addresses, essays, lectures. I. Delaney, Cornelius F. II. Title. III. Series.

THE Role of reason in 200'.1
belief / edited by George F. McLean. Lancaster, Pa. : Concorde Pub. Co., c1974. vi, 148 p. ; 23 cm. Includes bibliographical references. [BL51.R596] 74-84465
1. Religion—Philosophy—Addresses, essays, lectures. I. McLean, George F.

ROYCE, Josiah, 1855-1916. 200'.9
The religious philosophy of Josiah Royce / edited, with an introductory essay, by Stuart Gerry Brown. Westport, Conn. : Greenwood Press, 1976, c1952. 239 p. ; 23 cm. Reprint of the ed. published by Syracuse University Press, Syracuse, N.Y. Contents.Contents.—The possibility of error.—Individuality and freedom.—The temporal and the eternal.—The conception of immortality.—Loyalty and religion.—The idea of the universal community.—The moral burden of the individual.—The realm of grace.—Time and guilt.—Atonement. [B945.R61B7 1976] 76-4496 ISBN 0-8371-8810-5 lib.bdg. : 14.00
1. Religion—Philosophy—Addresses, essays, lectures. I. Title.
Contents omitted.

ROYCE, Josiah, 1855-1916. 201
The sources of religious insight : lectures delivered before Lake Forest College on the foundation of the late William Bross / by Josiah Royce. New York : Octagon Books, 1977, c1912. xv, 297 p. ; 19 cm. Reprint of the ed. published by Scribner, New York, as v. 6 in series: The Bross library. [BL51.R6 1977] 76-56454 ISBN 0-374-96989-2 lib.bdg. : 14.50
1. Religion—Philosophy—Addresses, essays, lectures. I. Title. II. Series: The Bross library ; v. 6.

TALAFOUS, Camillus D., ed. 210.8
Readings in science and spirit Englewood Cliffs, N.J. Prentice c.1966 xi, 271p. 22cm. Bibl. xi, 271p. 22cm. Bibl. [BL51.T34] 66-10611
1. Religion — sReligion— Philosophy — Addresses, essays, lectures. 2. Science — Philosophy — Addresses, essays, lectures. 3. Philosophical anthropology — Addresses, essays, lectures. I. Title.

WIEMAN, Henry Nelson, 1884- 200'.1
Seeking a faith for a new age ; essays on the interdependence of religion, science, and philosophy / by Henry Nelson Wieman ; edited and introduced by Cedric L. Hepler. Metuchen, N.J. : Scarecrow Press, 1975. ix, 313 p. ; 22 cm. Includes index. Bibliography: p. 295-304. [BL51.W585] 74-34052 ISBN 0-8108-0795-5 : 12.50
1. Religion—Philosophy—Addresses, essays, lectures. 2. Worth—Addresses, essays, lectures. 3. Religion and science—1946- —Addresses, essays, lectures. I. Title.

WILLIAMSON, William Bedford, 1918- 200'.1
Decisions in philosophy of religion / William B. Williamson. Columbus, Ohio : Merrill, c1976. viii, 407 p. ; 26 cm. Includes bibliographical references and indexes. [BL51.W59] 75-32716 ISBN 0-675-08629-9 : 11.95
1. Religion—Philosophy—Addresses, essays, lectures. I. Title.

Religion—Philosophy and theories.

PAGANISM in Christianity,
a new testament for rational believers. New York, Exposition Press [1961] 258p. 21cm. (Exposition--Banner bk.)
1. Religion—Philosophy and theories. 2. Christianity—Origin. 3. Paganism. I. Pratt, Charles Edgar, 1877-

PRATT, Charles Edgar 201
Paganism in Christianity; a new testament for rational believers. New York, Exposition Press [c.1961] 258p. (Exposition-Banner bk.) 5.00
1. Religion—Philosophy and theories. I. Title.

Religion—Philosophy—Bibliography.

WAINWRIGHT, William J. 016.2'001
Philosophy of religion : an annotated bibliography of twentieth-century writings in English / William J. Wainwright. New York : Garland Pub., 1978. p. cm. (Garland reference library of the humanities ; v. 111) Includes index. [Z7821.W34] [BL51] 77-83374 ISBN 0-8240-9849-8 : lib.bdg. : 40.00
1. Religion—Philosophy—Bibliography. I. Title.

Religion—Philosophy—Collected works.

BRODY, Boruch A., comp. 200'.1
Readings in the philosophy of religion; an analytic approach. Edited by Baruch A. Brody. Englewood Cliffs, N.J., Prentice-Hall [1974] xii, 667 p. 24 cm. Bibliography: p. 664-667. [BL51.B758] 73-20485 ISBN 0-13-759340-6 11.95
1. Religion—Philosophy—Collected works. I. Title.

HUME, David, 1711-1776. 201
Hume on religion. Ed., introd. by Richard Wollheim. Cleveland, World [1964, c.1963] 287p. 18cm. (Meridian bks., M172) 64-10002 1.95 pap.,
1. Religion—Philosophy—Collected works. I. Title. II. Title: On religion.

SCHEDLER, Norbert O., comp. 200'.1
Philosophy of religion: contemporary perspectives [by] Norbert O. Schedler. New York, Macmillan [1974] xix, 564 p.

24 cm. Includes bibliographies. [BL51.S419] 73-1959 ISBN 0-02-406720-2 8.95
1. Religion—Philosophy—Collected works. I. Title.

Religion—Philosophy— Collections.

ARNETT, Willard Eugene, 1921- ed. 200.1
A modern reader in the philosophy of religion [edited by] Willard E. Arnett. New York, Appleton-Century-Crofts [1966] x, 563 p. 22 cm. (The Century philosophy series) Includes bibliographical references. [BL51.A68] 66-20470
1. Religion—Philosophy—Collections. I. Title.

CAHN, Steven M., comp. 200'.1
Philosophy of religion, edited by Steven M. Cahn. New York, Harper & Row [1970] vi, 397 p. 21 cm. (Sources in contemporary philosophy) Bibliography: p. [395]-397. [BL51.C23] 75-108414
1. Religion—Philosophy—Collections. I. Title.

FRAZIER, Allie M., comp. 200'.8
Issues in religion; a book of readings [by] Allie M. Frazier. [New York] American Book Co. [1969] viii, 373 p. illus. 24 cm. Includes bibliographical references. [BL51.F68127] 70-2733
1. Religion—Philosophy—Collections. I. Title.

HICK, John, ed. 200'.1
Classical and contemporary readings in the philosophy of religion. 2d ed. Englewood Cliffs, N.J., Prentice-Hall [1970] xviii, 558 p. 24 cm. Includes bibliographical references. [BL51.H487 1970] 75-98092 11.95
1. Religion—Philosophy—Collections. 2. Theology—Collections. I. Title. II. Title: Philosophy of religion.

HICK, John, ed. 201
Classical and contemporary readings in the philosophy of religion. Englewood Cliffs, N. J., Prentice-Hall [1964] xv, 494 p. 24 cm. "Introductory notes and bibliographies": p. 465-485. [BL51.H487] 64-16056
1. Religion—Philosophy—Collections. 2. Theology—Collections. I. Title.

MAVRODES, George I., comp. 200'1
Problems and perspectives in the philosophy of religion, ed. by George I. Mavrodes. Stuart C. Hackett. Boston, Allyn [1967] viii, 492p. illus. 22cm. Bibl. [BL51.M476] 67-17758 7.95
1. Religion—Philosophy— Collections. I. Hackett, Stuart Cornelius, joint comp. II. Title.

MILLER, Eddie L., 1937- comp. 200'.1
Philosophical and religious issues: classical and contemporary statements [by] Ed L. Miller. Encino, Calif., Dickenson Pub. Co. [1971] xii, 448 p. 24 cm. Includes bibliographical references. [BL51.M626] 75-162678
1. Religion—Philosophy—Collections. I. Title.

ROGERS, Lewis M., 1918- comp. 201
And more about God. Lewis M. Rogers [and] Charles H. Monson, Jr., editors. Salt Lake City, University of Utah Press [1969] 363 p. 21 cm. Includes bibliographical references. [BL51.R592] 72-80722
1. Religion—Philosophy—Collections. I. Monson, Charles H., joint comp. II. Title.

ROWE, William L., comp. 200'.1
Philosophy of religion; selected readings. Edited by William L. Rowe [and] William J. Wainwright. Under the general editorship of Robert Ferm. New York, Harcourt Brace Jovanovich [1972, c1973] xv, 489 p. 24 cm. Includes bibliographical references. [BL51.R599] 72-93725 ISBN 0-15-570580-6 pap. 6.95
1. Religion—Philosophy—Collections. I. Wainwright, William J., joint comp. II. Title.

SAHAKIAN, William S ed. 210.8
Philosophies of religion [by] William S. Sahakian. Cambridge, Mass., Schenkman Pub. Co. [1965] xi, 476 p. 24 cm. Bibliographical footnotes. [BL51.S347] 65-20304
1. Religion—Philosophy—Collections. I. Title.

SMITH, John Edwin, ed. 201
Philosophy of religion [by] John E. Smith. New York, Macmillan [1965] 124 p. 23 cm. (Sources in philosophy) Bibliography: p. 123-124. [BL51.S575] 65-11875
1. Religion — Philosophy — Collections. I. Title. II. Series.

YANDELL, Keith E., 1938- 200'.1
God, man, and religion; readings in the philosophy of religion [by] Keith E. Yandell. New York, McGraw-Hill [1973] xii, 541 p. 23 cm. Includes bibliographical references. [BL51.Y272] 72-1978 ISBN 0-07-072247-1 6.95
1. Religion—Philosophy—Collections. 2. Experience (Religion)—Collections. 3. Ethics—Collections. I. Title.

Religion—Philosophy—Congresses.

CONFERENCE on the Philosophy of Religion, University of Birmingham, 1970. 291
Truth and dialogue in world religions: conflicting truth-claims. Edited by John Hick. Philadelphia, The Westminster Press [1974] 164 p. 21 cm. Selected papers of the conference held in April, 1970. British ed. published under title: Truth and dialogue, the relationship between world religions. [BL51.C635 1970] 74-7244 ISBN 0-664-20713-8 5.95
1. Religion—Philosophy—Congresses. 2. Religions—Congresses. I. Hick, John, ed. II. Title.

PHILOSOPHY of religion and theology : 1976 proceedings / compiled by Peter Slater. Missoula, Mont. : Published by Scholars Press for the American Academy of Religion, c1976. p. cm. Papers prepared for the 1976 annual meeting of the American Academy of Religion. Includes bibliographies. [BL51.P54] 76-29664 ISBN 0-89130-089-9 pbk. : 3.50 200'.1
1. Religion—Philosophy—Congresses. 2. Theology—Congresses. I. Slater, Peter, 1934- II. American Academy of Religion.

REASON and religion / edited by Stuart C. Brown. Ithaca, N.Y. : Cornell University Press, c1977. 315 p. ; 21 cm. (Cornell paperbacks) Papers originated at a conference sponsored by the Royal Institute of Philosophy and held at the University of Lancaster in 1975. Includes bibliographical references and index. [BL51.R325] 77-3115 ISBN 0-8014-1025-8 : 15.00 ISBN 0-8014-9166-5 pbk. : 6.95 200'.1
1. Religion—Philosophy—Congresses. 2. Good and evil—Congresses. 3. Immortality—Congresses. I. Brown, Stuart C. II. Royal Institute of Philosophy.

Religion—Philosophy—History

COLLINS, James Daniel. 200.1
The emergence of philosophy of religion, by James Collins. New Haven, Yale University Press, 1967. xv. 517 p. 25 cm. (St. Thomas More lectures, 1963) Bibliography: p. [492]-506. [BL51.C62] 67-13432
1. Religion — Philosophy — Hist. I. Title. II. Series. III. Series: The St. Thomas More lectures, 1963

COLLINS, James Daniel 200.1
The emergence of philosophy of religion, by James Collins. New Haven, Yale, 1967. xv, 517p. 25cm. (St. Thomas More lects., 1963) Bibl. [BL51.C62] 67-13432 12.50
1. Religion—Philosophy—Hist. I. Title. II. Series: The St. Thomas More lectures, 1963

MCKENZIE, David, 1943- 230'.044
Wolfhart Pannenberg and religious philosophy / David McKenzie. Washington, D.C. : University Press of America, 1980. p. cm. A revision of the author's thesis, University of Texas, 1977. Includes index. Bibliography: p. [BX4827.P3M32 1980] 19 80-8171 ISBN 0-8191-1314-X lib. bdg. : 17.50 ISBN 0-8191-1315-8 (pbk.) : 9.00
1. Pannenberg, Wolfhart, 1928- 2. Religion—Philosophy—History. I. Title.

ROTH, John K. 200.1
Problems of the philosophy of religion [by] John K. Roth. Scranton, Chandler Pub. Co. [1971] x, 203 p. 21 cm. (Chandler publications in philosophy.) (Problems of philosophy: a Chandler series) Bibliography: p. 195-196. [BL51.R5976] 74-126546 ISBN 0-8102-0396-0 2.95
1. Religion—Philosophy—History. I. Title.

THOMAS, George Finger, 1899- . 201
Religious philosophies of the West [by] George F. Thomas. New York, Scribner [1965] xviii, 454 p. 24 cm. Bibliography: p. 439-444. [BL51.T44] 65-13662
1. Religion — Philosophy — Hist. 2. Religious thought — Hist. I. Title.

WOLFSON, Harry Austryn, 1887-1974. 200'.1
From Philo to Spinoza : two studies in religious philosophy / by Harry Austryn Wolfson ; introd. by Isadore Twersky. New York : Behrman House, c1977. p. cm. Contents.Contents.—What is new in Philo?—Spinoza and the religion of the past. Includes bibliographical references. [B689.Z7W685 1977] 77-1909 ISBN 0-87441-262-5 pbk. : 3.95
1. Philo Judaus. 2. Spinoza, Benedictus de, 1632-1677. 3. Religion—Philosophy—History. I. Wolfson, Harry Austryn, 1887-1974. Spinoza and the religion of the past. 1977. II. Title.

Religion, Primitive.

BACHOFEN, Johann Jakob, 1815-1887. 291.3'7
Myth, religion, and mother right; selected writings of J. J. Bachofen. Translated from German by Ralph Manheim. With a preface by George Boas and an introd. by Joseph Campbell. [Princeton, N.J.] Princeton University Press [1973, c.1967] lvii, 309 p. 22 cm. (Princeton/Bollingen paperbacks) (Bollingen series, 84) Translated and adapted from Johann Jakob Bachofen: Mutterrecht und Urreligion. Bibliography: p. 257-270. [D7.B2713] 67-22343 ISBN 0-691-01797-2 3.45 (pbk.)
1. Religion, Primitive. 2. Symbolism. 3. Mythology, Classical. 4. Matriarchy. I. Title. II. Series.

BACHOFEN, Johann Jakob, 1815-1887. 291.3'7
Myth, religion, and mother right; selected writings of J. J. Bachofen. Translated from the German by Ralph Manheim. With a pref. by George Boas and an introd. by Joseph Campbell. New Jersey, Princeton University Press , [1967] lvii, 309 p. illus. 24 cm. (Bollingen series, 84) Translation of Mutterrecht und Urreligion. Includes bibliographies. [D7.B2713] 67-22343
1. Religion, Primitive. 2. Symbolism. 3. Mythology, Classical. 4. Matriarchy. I. Title. II. Series.

BERGOUNIOUX, Frederic Marie 291
Primitive and prehistoric religions, by F.-M. Bergounioux, Joseph Goetz. Tr. from French by C. R. Busby. New York, Hawthorn [c.1966] 160p. 21cm. (20th century encyclopedia of Catholicism, v.140. Sect. 15: Non-Christian beliefs) Title. (Series: The Twentieth century encyclopedia of Catholicism, v.140) Bibl. [GN470.B3413] 64-14166 3.50 bds.,
1. Religion, Primitive. I. Goetz, Joseph. II. Title. III. Series.
Contents omitted.

BERGOUNIOUX, Frederic Marie. 291
Primitive and prehistoric religions, by F.-M. Bergounioux and Joseph Goetz. Translated from the French by C. R. Busby. [1st ed.] New York, Hawthorn Books [1966] 160 p. 21 cm. (The Twentieth century encyclopedia of Catholicism, v. 140. Section 15: Non-Christian beliefs) Translation of Les religions des prehistoriques et des primitifs. Contents.Contents.—Prehistoric religion, by F.-M. Bergounioux.—Primitive religion, by J. Goetz. Bibliography: p. 159-160. [GN470.B3413] 64-14166
1. Religion, Primitive. I. Goetz, Joseph. II. Title. III. Series: The Twentieth century encyclopedia of Catholicism, v. 140

BROWN, Hiram Chellis. 290
The historical bases of religions, primitive, Babylonian and Jewish, by Hiram Chellis Brown. Boston, H.B. Turner & co., 1906. 3 p. l., [v]-vii p., 2 l., 3-319 p. 20 cm. [BL85.B8] 6-33632
1. Religion. Primitive. 2. Assyro-Bbaylonian religion. 3. Jews—Religion. I. Title.

CAMPBELL, Joseph, 1904- 291.1'3
Primitive mythology / Joseph Campbell. New York : Penguin Books, [1976] p. cm. (His The masks of God ; v. 1) Includes bibliographical references and index. [GN470.C33 1976] 76-25192 ISBN 0-670-00298-4 pbk. : 3.75
1. Religion, Primitive. 2. Mythology. I. Title. II. Series.

CARMODY, Denise Lardner, 1935- 291
The oldest god : archaic religion yesterday & today / Denise Lardner Carmody. Nashville : Abingdon, 1981. 190 p. ; 21 cm. Includes bibliographies and index. [BL430.C37] 19 80-25499 ISBN 0-687-28813-4 pbk. : 6.95
1. Religion, Primitive. 2. Religions. I. Title.

CLES-REDEN, Sibylle Emilie (von Reden) Baronin von Cles, 1910- 291.213
The realm of the great goddess; the story of the megalith builders. [Tr. from German by Eric Mosbacher] Englewood Cliffs, N.J., Prentice, 1962 [c.1960, 1961] 328p. illus. 26cm. Bibl. 62-5936 10.00
1. Religion, Primitive. 2. Salvation—Comparative studies. I. Title.

†DE RIOS, Marlene Dobkin. 291'.042
The wilderness of mind : sacred plants in crosscultural perspective / Marlene Dobkin De Rios. Beverly Hills : Sage Publications, c1976. 79 p. ; 22 cm. (Sage research papers in the social sciences ; ser. no. 90.039 : Cross-cultural studies series) Sponsored by the East-West Center. Bibliography: p. 73-78. [GN472.4.D47] 76-55088 ISBN 0-8039-0752-4 pbk. : 3.00
1. Religion, Primitive. 2. Hallucinogenic plants. 3. Hallucinogenic drugs and religious experience. I. East-West Center. II. Title. III. Series: Sage research papers in the social sciences : Cross-cultural studies series.

DESHMUKH, Panjabrao Shamran, 1898- 294.1
The origin and development of religion in Vedic literature, by P. S. Deshmukh ... with a foreword by A. Berriedale Keith ... London, New York [etc.] Oxford university press, 1933. xxi, 378 p. 23 cm. "What is published here was a thesis presented and approved for the degree of doctor of philosophy ... by the University of Oxford."--Pref. "Literature" interspersed. [BL1115.D4 1938] 34-83266
1. Religion, Primitive. 2. Vedas—Criticism, intwrpretation, etc. 3. Aryans. 4. Brahmanism. I. Title. II. Title: Religion in Vedic literature.
Contents omitted.

DE WAAL MALEFIJT, Annemarie, 1914- 290
Religion and culture; an introduction to anthropology of religion. New York, Macmillan [1968] vii, 407 p. illus., map. 21 cm. Bibliography: p. 360-389. [GN470.D4] 68-12717
1. Religion. Primitive. I. Title.

DUNLAP, Samuel Fales, 1825-1905. 290
Vestiges of the spirit-history of man. By S. F. Dunlap ... New York, D. Appleton and company, 1853. vi p., 1 l., 404 p. 24 cm. Bibliographical foot-notes. [BL80.D85] 23-32
1. Religion, Primitive. 2. Religions. I. Title.

DURKHEIM, Emile, 1858-1917.
The elementary forms of the religious life. Translated from the French by Joseph Ward Swain. New York, Collier Books [1961] 507 p. 19 cm. (Collier Books, AS 26) 63-9851
1. Religion, Primitive. 2. Totemism. 3. Religion—Philosophy. I. Title.

DURKHEIM, Emile, 1858-1917. 291
The elementary forms of the religious life, a study in religious sociology. Translated

from the French by Joseph Ward Swain. Glencoe, Ill., Free Press [1947] xi, 456 p. 22 cm. Bibliographical footnotes. [[GN470.D]] A 50
1. Religion, Primitive. 2. Cultus. 3. Totemism. 4. Religion—Philosophy. I. Title.

DURKHEIM, Emile, 1858-1917. 291
The elementary forms of the religious life, a study in religious sociology, by Emile Durkheim ... Translated from the French, by Joseph Ward Swain, M. A. London, G. Allen & Unwin, ltd.; New York, The Macmillan company [1915] xi, 456 p. 23 cm. [Full name: David Emile Durkheim] [GN470.D8 1915] 15-24224
1. Religion, Primitive. 2. Cultus. 3. Totemism. 4. Religion—Philosophy. I. Swain, Joseph Ward, 1891- tr. II. Title.

DURKHEIM, Emile, 1858-1917. 291
The elementary forms of the religious life, a study in religious sociology, by Emile Durkheim ... Translated form the French by Joseph Ward Swain, M. A. London, G. Allen & Unwin, ltd.,; New York, The Macmillan company [1926] xi, 456 p. 22 cm. [Full name: David Emile Durkheim] [GN470.D8] 33-25177
1. Religion, Primitive. 2. Cultus. 3. Totemism. 4. Religion-Philosophy. I. Swain, Joseph Ward, 1891- tr. II. Title.

THE elementary forms of the religious life. Translated from the French by Joseph Ward Swain. New York, Collier Books [1961] 507 p. 19 cm. (Collier Books, AS 26) 63-9851
1. Religion, Primitive. 2. Totemism. 3. Religion—Philosophy.

EVANS-PRITCHARD, Edward Eban 291
1902-
Theories of primitive religion. Oxford, Clarendon Pr. [New York, Oxford, c.] 1965. 132p. 23cm. (Sir D. Owen Evans lects., 1962) Bibl. [GN470.E9] 65-29790 4.00
1. Religion, Primitive. I. Title. II. Series.

EVANS-PRITCHARD, Edward Evan, 291
1902-
Theories of primitive religion. Oxford, Clarendon Pr., [1967, c.1965] 132p. 22cm. (Sir Owen Evans. lects., 1962) Bibl. [GN470.E9] 65-29790 2.00 pap.,
1. Religion, Primitive. I. Title. II. Series.
Available from Oxford Univ. Pr., New York.

GELFAND, Michael 299.6
An African's religion: the spirit of Nyajena; case history of a Karanga people. Cape Town, Juta, 1966. x, 135p. illus., fold. map. ports. 23cm. Bibl. [GN470.G4] 67-851 8.50 bds.,
1. Religion, Primitive. 2. Mashona—Religion. I. Title.
American distributor: Verry, Mystic, Conn.

THE gods of prehistoric man. Translated from the German by Mary Ilford. London, Weidenfeld and Nicolson; [New York, Knopf, c1960] xviii, 219p. illus. 25cm. 'First published in Switzerland under the title: Vorgeschichtliche Religion.'
1. Religion, Primitive. 2. Stone age—Europe. I. Maringer, Johannes, 1902-

HALBWACHS, Maurice, 1877- 291.211
1945.
Sources of religious sentiment. Tr. [from French] by John A. Spaulding. [New York] Free Pr. of Glencoe [c.1962] 109p. Bibl. 62-10589 4.00
1. Durkheim, Emile, 1858-1917. 2. Religion, Primitive. I. Title.

HAYS, Hoffman Reynolds. 291
In the beginnings; early man and his gods. New York, Putnam [1963] 575 p. illus., maps. 24 cm. Bibliography: p. 539-558. [BL430.H39] 63-16173
1. Religion, Primitive. I. Title.

HOPKINS, Edward Washburn, 291
1857-1932.
Origin and evolution of religion. New York, Cooper Square Publishers, 1969. 370 p. 23 cm. Reprint of the 1923 ed. Bibliographical footnotes. [BL430.H6 1969] 76-79199 10.00
1. Religion, Primitive. 2. Folk-lore. 3. Religions. 4. Nature worship. 5. Trinities. I. Title.

HOPKINS, Edward Washburn, 291
1857-1932.
Origin and evolution of religion, by E. Washburn Hopkins... New Haven, Yale university press; London, H. Milford, Oxford university press, 1923. 3 p. l., 370 p., 1 l. 24 cm. Bibliographical foot-notes. [BL430.H6] 23-7668
1. Religion, Primitive. 2. Folk-lore. 3. Religions. 4. Nature-worship. 5. Trinities. I. Title.

HOWELLS, William White, 1908- 290
The heathens, primitive man and his religions. Pub. in co-operation with the Amer. Mus. of Natural Hist. Garden City, N.Y., Doubleday [c.1948, 1962] 306p. illus., map. (Natural hist, lib.; Anchor bks., N19) Bibl. 1.45 pap.,
1. Religion, Primitive. I. Title.

HOWELLS, William White, 1908- 290
The heathens, primitive man and his religions 1st ed. Garden City, N.Y., Doubleday, 1948. 306 p. illus., map (on lining-papers) 22 cm. Bibliographical footnotes. [GN470.H6] 48-5578
1. Religion, Primitive. I. Title.

HUGHS, Milton A.
The crucified Lamb, or, The origin of the Christian religion and how it came down to us. By Milton A. Hughs... Wellsville, Kan., M. A. Hughs [c1922] 2 p. l., 94 p. illus. 20 cm. [BS2391.H8] 22-20923
I. Title.

JAMES, Edwin Oliver, 1886-
The beginnings of religion; an introductory and scientific study. London, New York, Hutchinson's University Library [1950?] 159 p. 19 cm. (Hutchinsou's university library: World religions, n Bibliography at end of each chapter. A52
1. Religion, Primitive. I. Title.

JAMES, Edwin Oliver, 291'.042
1886-
The beginnings of religion; an introductory and scientific study, by E. O. James. Westport, Conn., Greenwood Press [1973] 159 p. 22 cm. Reprint of the 1950 ed., which was issued as no. 8 of Hutchinson's university library: World religions. Includes bibliographies. [BL430.J29 1973] 72-11737 ISBN 0-8371-6706-X 8.50
1. Religion, Primitive. I. Title.

JAMES, Edwin Oliver, 291'.042
1886-
The beginnings of religion; an introductory and scientific study, by E. O. James. Westport, Conn., Greenwood Press [1973] 159 p. 22 cm. Reprint of the 1950 ed., which was issued as no. 8 of Hutchinson's university library: World religions. Includes bibliographies. [BL430.J29 1973] 72-11737 ISBN 0-8371-6706-X
1. Religion, Primitive. I. Title.

JAMES, Edwin Oliver, 1886- 291
The beginnings of religion; an introductory and scientific study. London, New York, Hutchinson's University Library [1950?] 159 p. 19 cm. (Hutchinson's university library: World religions, no. 8) Bibliography at end of each chapter. [BL430.J29] A 52
1. Religion, Primitive. I. Title.

JAMES, Edwin Oliver, 1886- 290
Prehistoric religion a study in prehistoric archaeology. New York, Praeger [1957] 300p. illus. 23cm. (Books that matter) [BL480.J32] 57-11090
1. Religion, Primitive. 2. Religions—Hist. I. Title.

JAMES, Edwin Oliver, 1886- 290
Prehistoric religion; a study in prehistoric archaeology. New York, Barnes & Noble [1961, c.1957] 300 p. illus. Bibl. 61-3103 6.50
1. Religion, Primitive. 2. Religions—Hist. I. Title.

JENSEN, Adolf Ellegard, 1899- 291
Myth and cult among primitive peoples. Translated by Marianna Tax Choldin and Wolfgang Weissledger. Chicago, University of Chicago Press [c1963] x, 349 p. 22 cm. [GN470.J413] 63-20909
1. Religion, Primitive. I. Title.

JEVONS, Frank Byron, 291.214
1858-
The idea of God in early religions. By F. B. Jevons ... Cambridge, University press, 1910. x, 170 p. 17 cm. (Half-title: The Cambridge manuals of science and literature. [4]) Title within ornamental border. Bibliography: p. [ix]-x. [BL41.J38] A 11
1. Religion, Primitive. 2. God. I. Title.

JEVONS, Frank Byron, 1858- 291.13
... An introduction to the study of comparative religion, by Frank Byron Jevons ... New York, The Macmillan company, 1908. xxv, 283 p. 20 cm. (The Hartford-Lamson lectures on the religions of the world. v.1) Bibliography: p. 271-273. [BL41.J4] 8-30157
1. Religion, Primitive. 2. Religion. I. Title.
Contents omitted.

KEARY, Charles Francis, 1848- 291
1917.
Outlines of primitive belief among the Indo-European races by Charles Francis Keary ... New York, C. Scribner's sons, 1882. xxi, 534 p. 22 cm. [BL430.K3] 12-34922
1. Religion, Primitive. 2. Mythology, Aryan. I. Title.

KING, Irving, 1874- 291.1
The development of religion; a study in anthropology and social psychology, by Irving King ... New York, The Macmillan company, 1910. xxiii, 371 p. 21 cm. Bibliography: p. 355-361. [BL430.K5] 10-5028
1. Religion, Primitive. 2. Social psychology. I. Title.

KUHN, Alvin Boyd, 1880- 290
The lost light; an interpretation of ancient scriptures, by Alvin Boyd Kuhn ... [Rahway, N. J., Printed by Quinn & Boden company, inc., c1940] 5 p. l., 602 p. diagr. 22 cm. Bibliographical references included in "Notes" (p. 595-602) [BL96.K8] 40-33409
1. Religion, Primitive. I. Title.

LANG, Andrew, 1844-1912. 291
The making of religion, by Andrew Lang ... London, New York [etc.] Longmans, Green, and co., 1898. 5 p. l., 380 p. 23 cm. [BL430.L3 1898] 31-6640
1. Religion, Primitive. 2. Spiritualism. 3. Religion—Hist. I. Title.

LAWRENCE, Peter, ed. 299.9
Gods, ghosts, and men in Melanesia; some religions of Australian New Guinea and the New Hebrides, ed. by P. Lawrence. M. J. Meggitt. New York, Oxford, 1965. 298p. 23cm. Bibl. [GN475.9.L3] 66-1121 9.75; 3.25 pap.,
1. Religion, Primitive. 2. Ethnology—Melanesia. I. Meggitt, M. J., joint ed. II. Title.

LE ROY, Alexandre, Abp., 299'.6
1854-1938.
The religion of the primitives, by Alexander Le Roy. Translated by Newton Thompson. New York, Negro Universities Press [1969] x, 334 p. 23 cm. Reprint of the 1922 ed. Bibliographical footnotes. [GN470.L43 1969] 72-78769
1. Religion, Primitive. I. Title.

LE ROY, Alexandre, bp., 1854- 291
1938.
The religion of the primitives, by Most Rev. Alexander Le Roy... tr. by Rev. Newton Thompson. New York, The Macmillan company, 1922. x p., 2 l., 334 p. 22 1/2 cm. Bibliographical foot-notes. [GN470.L43] 22-23345
1. Religion, Primitive. I. Thompson, Newton W., tr. II. Title.

LEVY, Gertrude Rachel, 1883-
The gate of horn; a study of the religious conceptions of the stone age, and their influence upon European thought. New York, Book Collectors Society [1965?] xxxi, 349 p. illus., maps. 23 cm. Bibliographical footnotes. 65-27708
1. Religion, Primitive. I. Title.

LEVY, Gertrude Rachel, 1883- 290
Religious conceptions of the stone age, and their influence upon European thought [Gloucester, Mass., P. Smith, 1966] xxxii, 349p. illus., maps. 21cm. First pub. in England in 1948 by Faber & Faber under title: The gate of horn; a study of the religious conceptions of the stone age and their influence upon European thought (Harper torchbk., Cloister lib. rebound) Bibl. [GN470.L47] 4.00
1. Religion, Primitive. I. Title.

LEVY, Gertrude Rachel, 1883- 290
Religious conceptions of the stone age, and their influence upon European thought. New York, Harper [1963] 349p. illus. 21cm. First pub. in England under title: The gate of horn. (Harper torchbk., cloister lib., TB106) Bibl. 1.95 pap.,
1. Religion, Primitive. I. Title.

LOWIE, Robert Harry, 1883- 291
Primitive religion. New York, Liveright Pub. Corp. [1948] xxiii, 382 p. illus. 23 cm. (Black and gold library) [GN470.L6 1948] 48-10086
1. Religion, Primitive. I. Title.
Contents omitted.

LOWIE, Robert Harry, 1883- 291
Primitive religion, by Robert H. Lowie ... New York, Boni and Liveright, 1924. xix, 346 p. 23 cm. Bibliography: p. 331-341. [GN470.L6] 24-24282
1. Religion, Primitive. I. Title.
Contents omitted.

LOWIE, Robert Harry, 1883-1957.
Primitive religion. New York, Grosset [1958, c1952] "Black and gold edition reprint." Bibliography: p. 364-378. 63-33175
1. Religion, Primitive. I. Title.

LOWIE, Robert Harry, 1883-1957.
Primitive religion. New York, Grosset [1958, c1952] 378 p. 21 cm. (Universal library, UL-35) "Black and gold edition reprint." Bibliography: p. 364-378. 63-33175
1. Religion, Primitive. I. Title.

LOWIE, Robert Harry, 1883- 291
1957.
Primitive religion. New York, Liveright [1970, c1948] xxii, 388 p. 21 cm. (Black and gold library) Bibliography: p. 367-381. [GN470.L6 1970] 75-114373 2.95
1. Religion, Primitive.

MACDONALD, Elizabeth Stone. 290
Primitive faiths, by Elizabeth Stone Macdonald. Leader's manual. Introductory unit in a series of brief reviews of what our neighbors believe. Boston, The Beacon press, inc., 1937. 54 p. 24 1/2 cm. Bibliography: p. 53-54. [BV1561.M2] 40-16563
1. Religion, Primitive. 2. Religious education—Text-books for children. I. Title.

MALINOWSKI, Bronislaw, 291'.042
1884-1942.
The foundation of faith and morals : an anthropological analysis of primitive beliefs and conduct with special reference to the fundamental problems of religion and ethics : delivered before the University of Durham at Armstrong College, Newcastle-upon-Tyne, February 1935 / by Bronislaw Malinowski. [Folcroft, Pa.] : Folcroft Library Editions, 1974. p. cm. Reprint of the 1936 ed. published by Oxford University Press, H. Milford, London, which was issued as Riddell memorial lectures, 7th ser., 1934-35. [GN470.M2 1974] 74-20949 ISBN 0-8414-5965-7 lib. bdg. : 6.50
1. Religion, Primitive. 2. Trobriand Islands—Religion. 3. Religion. I. Title. II. Series: Riddell memorial lectures ; 7th ser., 1934-35.

MALINOWSKI, Bronislaw, 291'.042
1884-1942.
The foundations of faith and morals : an anthropological analysis of primitive beliefs and conduct with special reference to the fundamental problems of religion and ethics : delivered before the University of Durham at Armstrong College, Newcastle-upon-Tyne, February 1935 / by Bronislaw Malinowski. Folcroft, Pa. : Folcroft Library Editions, 1974. x, 62 p. ; 26 cm. Reprint of the 1936 ed. published by Oxford University Press, H. Milford, London, which was issued as Riddell memorial lectures, 7th ser., 1934-35. Includes bibliographical references. [GN470.M2 1974] 74-20949 ISBN 0-8414-5965-7 lib. bdg.
1. Religion, Primitive. 2. Trobriand Islands—Religion. 3. Religion. I. Title. II.

Series: Riddell memorial lectures ; 7th ser., 1934-35.

MARETT, Robert Ranulph, 1866- 291.12
Faith, hope, and charity in primitive religion, by R. R. Marett ... New York, The Macmillan company, 1932. 6 p. l., 239 p. 22 cm. "These lectures were originally given in Boston in the fall of 1930 under the auspices of the Lowell institution. They were then amplified and, as gifford lectures, were delivered before the University of St. Andrews during the academic year 1931-2."--Pref. [GN470.M23] 32-9123
1. Religion, Primitive. I. Lowell institute lectures, 1930. II. Title.

MARETT, Robert Ranulph, 1866- 291.12
Faith, hope and charity in primitive religion, by R. R. Marett ... Oxford, The Clarendon press, 1932. 4 p. l., 181, [1] p. 23 cm. "These lectures were originally given in Boston in the fall of 1930 under the auspices of the Lowell institution. They were then amplified and, as Gifford lectures, were delivered before the University of St. Andrews during the academic year 1931-2."--Pref. [GN470.M23 1932a] 32-11244
1. Religion, Primitive. I. Lowell institute lectures, 1930. II. Title.

MARETT, Robert Ranulph, 1866- 291
Sacraments of simple folk, by R. R. Marett ... Oxford, The Clarendon press, 1933. 4 p. l., 230 p., 1 l. 23 cm. [Gillford lectures, 1932-33] "This second course of lectures was delivered on Lord Gifford's foundation before the University of St. Andrews during the academic year 1932-3."--Pref. The first course of lectures was entitled: Faith, hope, and charity in primitive religion. [GN473.M3] 572 33-31136
1. Religion, Primitive. 2. Rites and ceremonies. I. Title.

MASSEY, Gerald, 1828-1907. 299'.31
Ancient Egypt, the light of the world; a work of reclamation and restitution in twelve books. New York, S. Weiser, 1970. 2 v. (944 p.) illus. 26 cm. "Edition limited to five hundred copies." Reprint of the 1907 ed. [BL313.M35 1970] 79-138084 ISBN 0-87728-029-0
1. Religion, Primitive. 2. Mythology. 3. Egypt—Religion. I. Title.

MILLS, Philo Laos. 200
Prehistoric religion; a study in pre-Christian antiquity: an examination of the religious beliefs of the Oceanic, Central African, and Amazonian primitives, their development among the later Indo-Asiatic and Totemic peoples, their interpretation by the western-Asiatic and Caucasian races of Neolithic culture, and their possible connexion with the earliest religion of mankind. By Philo Laos Mills, S.T.L. Washington, Capital publishers, inc., 1918. 4 p. l., 18, lxxii, 2, 600, 16, [3] p. front., illus., plates (part col.) maps, facsims. 27 1/2 cm. Contains bibliographical foot-notes. [BL96.M7] 18-22525
1. Religion, Primitive. 2. God. 3. Creation. 4. Paradise. 5. Sacrifice. 6. Immortality. I. Title.

MULLER, Friedrich Max, 1823-1900. 291'.042
Physical religion / by F. Max Muller. New York : AMS Press, 1975. xii, 410 p. ; 19 cm. Reprint of the 1891 ed. published by Longmans, Green, London and New York, which was issued as Gifford lectures, 1890. Includes bibliographical references and index. [BL430.M83 1975] 73-18811 ISBN 0-404-11451-2 : 31.00
1. Vedas. 2. Religion, Primitive. 3. Natural theology. I. Title. II. Series: Gifford lectures ; 1890.

MULLER, Friedrich Max, 1823-1900.
Physical religion; the Gifford lectures delivered before the University of Glasgow in 1890, by F. Max Muller ... London & New York, Longmans, Green & co., 1891. xii, 410 p. 20 cm. A 22
1. Religion, Primitive. 2. Natural theology. 3. Vedas. I. Gifford lectures, 1890. II. Title.

NEWBERRY, John Strong, 1883- 291
The rainbow bridge; a study of paganism, by John Strong Newberry. Boston and New York, Houghton Mifflin company, 1934. xiv, [1], 345, [1] p. 22 1/2 cm. "Notes": p. 265-[314] [BL96.N45] 34-12860
1. Religion, Primitive. 2. Paganism. 3. Mythology. 4. Jews—Religion—Hist. 5. Civilization, Pagan. I. Title.

OWEN, David Cymmer. 291
The infancy of religion, by D. C. Owen ... London, New York [etc.] H. Milford, 1914. vi p., 1 l., 143 p. 21 cm. (Half-title: The S[aint] Deiniol's series. iv) Bibliographical foot-notes. [GN470.O8] 15-13479
1. Religion, Primitive. I. Title.

PERRY, William James. 291
Gods and men, the attainment of immortality, by W. J. Perry. New York, W. Morrow & company, 1929. 3 p. l., 85 p., 1 l. 19 cm. (On cover: The beginning of things) "Bibliographical note": leaf at end. [BL430.P38 1929] 29-15058
1. Religion, Primitive. 2. Creation. 3. Immortality. I. Title.

PERRY, William James. 291'.042
The origin of magic and religion, by W. J. Perry. Port Washington, N.Y., Kennikat Press [1971] ix, 212 p. front. 21 cm. Reprint of the 1923 ed. Includes bibliographical references. [BL430.P4 1971] 73-118543
1. Religion, Primitive. 2. Magic. I. Title.

RADIN, Paul, 1883- 291
Primitive religion: its nature and origin [Gloucester, Mass., P. Smith, 1964, c.1937, 1957] 322p. 21cm. (Dover bk. rebound) Bibl. 3.85
1. Religion, Primitive. I. Title.

RADIN, Paul, 1883- 291
Primitive religion: its nature and origin. New York, Dover Publications, 1957. 322p. 21cm. 'An unabridged republication of the first edition [published in 1937] with a new perface by the author.' [GN470.R3 1957] 57-4452
1. Religion, Primitive. I. Title.

RADIN, Paul, 1883- 291
... Primitive religion; its nature and origin. New York, The Viking press, 1937. x, 322 p. 22 cm. Bibliography: p. 307-314. [GN470.R3] 37-21906
1. Religion, Primitive. I. Title.

RADIN, Paul, 1883-1959. 291
Primitive religion: its nature and origin. New York, Dover Publications, 1957. 322 p. 21 cm. "An unabridged republication of the first edition [published in 1937] with a new preface by the author." [GN470.R3 1957] 57-4452
1. Religion, Primitive. I. Title.

RENNER, George Thomas, 1900- 291
Primitive religion in the tropical forests; a study in social geography, by George Thomas Renner, jr. ... [New York?] 1927. 109 p. map. 23 1/2 cm. Issued also as thesis (PH.D.) Columbia university. Bibliography: p. 107-109. [GN470.R4 1927 a] 36-24738
1. Religion. Primitive. 2. Tropics. 3. Man—Influence of environment. I. Title.

SCHLEITER, Frederick, 1884- 291
Religion and culture: a critical survey of methods of approach to religious phenomena, by Frederick Schleiter, PH. D. New York, Columbia university press, 1919. x, 206 p. 20 cm. Bibliography: p. 194-206. [BL430.S3] 19-9320
1. Religion, Primitive. 2. Religion—Philosophy. 3. Magic 4. Culture, Religion and. I. Title.

SCHMIDT, Wilhelm, 1868-1954. 200'.9
The origin and growth of religion; facts and theories. Translated from the original German by H. J. Rose. New York, Cooper Square Publishers, 1972. xvi, 302 p. 24 cm. Translation of Ursprung und Werden der Religion; Theorien und Tatsachen. Reprint of the 1931 ed. Includes bibliographical references. [BL430.S43 1972] 78-184909 ISBN 0-8154-0408-5 9.00
1. Religion, Primitive. 2. Religion—History. 3. Religion—Historiography. I. Title.

SHROPSHIRE, Denys William Tinniswood. 299.63
The Church and primitive peoples; the religiuos institutions and beliefs of the southern Bantu and their bearing on the problems of the Christian missionary, by Denys W. T. Shropshire...with a foreword by R. R. Marett... London, Society for promoting Christian knowledge; New York, The Macmillan company, 1938. xii, 466 p. 22 cm. Bibliography: p. 455-457. [BL2480.B3S4] 39-6952
1. Bantus. 2. Religion, Primitive. 3. Society, Primitive. 4. Missions—Africa, South. 5. Church of England—Missions. I. Title.

STOLEE, Michael J., 1871- 291
The genesis of religion, by Michael J. Stolee ... Minneapolis, Augsburg publishing house [c1930] x, 164 p. 20 1/2 cm. "Based on a thesis written as part requirement for the degree of doctor theologiae, Drew univeristy, Madison, New Jersey." Bibliography: p. 159-164. [BL430.S7] 30-25640
1. Religion, Primitive. I. Title.

SWANSON, Guy E. 291.2
The birth of the gods; the origin of primitive beliefs. Ann Arbor, Univ. of Mich. Pr. [1964, c.1960] ix, 260p tables. 21cm. (Ann Arbor paperback, AA93) Bibl. 4.95; 1.95 pap.,
1. Religion, Primitive. I. Title.

SWANSON, Guy E 291.2
The birth of the gods; the origin of primitive beliefs. Ann Arbor, University of Michigan Press [1960] ix, 260 p. tables. 22 cm. Bibliography: p. [244]-255. [GN470.S9] 60-9974
1. Religion, Primitive. I. Title.

TYLOR, Edward Burnett, Sir, 1832-1917
Religion in primitive culture, with an introd. by Paul Radin. New York, Harper [1958] xvii, 539 p. 21 cm. (The Library of religion and culture) Harper torchbooks, TB 34. "Originally published as chapters XI-XIX of Primitive culture" (London, J. Murray, 1871) Bibliographical footnotes.
1. Religion, Primitive. 2. Animism. 3. Mythology. 4. Society, Primitive. I. Title.

WALLIS, Wilson Dallam, 1886- 291
Religion in primitive society [by] Wilson D. Wallis... New York, F. S. Crofts & co., 1939. ix p., 1 l., 388 p. plates. 23 1/2 cm. [Crofts anthropology series; Alexander Goldenweiser, editor) Bibliography: p. 331-366. [GN470.W3] 39-21987
1. Religion, Primitive. I. Title.

WRIGHT, Julia (MacNair) Mrs., 1840-1903. 290
Bricks from Babel: a brief view of the myths, traditions and religious belief of races, with concise studies in ethnography. By Julia McNair Wright ... New York, J. B. Alden, 1885. 1 p. l., [5]-181 p. 19 1/2 cm. [BL85.W75] 30-23163
1. Religion, Primitive. 2. Ethnology. I. Title.

Religion, Primitive—Addresses, essays, lectures.

LEACH, Edmund Ronald. 291
Dialectic in practical religion; edited by E. R. Leach. London, published for the Department of Archaeology and Anthropology by Cambridge U.P., 1968. viii, 207 p. illus. 25 cm. (Cambridge papers in social anthropology, no. 5) Bibliography: p. 203-207. [GN470.L37] 67-21960 40/-
1. Religion, Primitive—Addresses, essays, lectures. I. Title. II. Series.

MARETT, Robert Ranulph, 1866-1943. 200'.9
Faith, hope, and charity in primitive religion. New York, B. Blom, 1972. 181 p. 21 cm. Reprint of the 1932 ed. "These lectures were originally given in Boston in the Fall of 1930 under the auspices of the Lowell Institution. They were then amplified and, as Gifford Lectures, were delivered before the University of St. Andrews during the academic year 1931-2." [GN470.M23 1972] 72-80150
1. Religion, Primitive—Addresses, essays, lectures. 2. Ethics, Primitive—Addresses, essays, lectures. I. Title.

MARETT, Robert Ranulph, 1866-1943. 291'.042
The threshold of religion / by R. R. Marett. 1st AMS ed. New York : AMS Press, 1979. xxxii, 223 p. ; 18 cm. Reprint of the 2d ed., rev. and enl., published in 1909 by Metheun, London. Includes bibliographical references and index. [BL430.M34 1979] 76-44755 ISBN 0-404-15950-8 : 18.00
1. Religion, Primitive—Addresses, essays, lectures. I. Title.

MIDDLETON, John, 1921- comp. 291'.042
Gods and rituals : readings in religious beliefs and practices / edited by John Middleton. Austin : University of Texas Press, [1976] c1967. p. cm. (Texas Press sourcebooks in anthropology ; 6) Reprint of the ed. published by the Natural History Press, Garden City, N.Y., in series: American Museum sourcebooks in anthropology. Includes index. Bibliography: p. [GN470.M48 1976] 75-44032 ISBN 0-292-72708-9 pbk. : 6.95
1. Religion, Primitive—Addresses, essays, lectures. I. Title. II. Series. III. Series: American Museum sourcebooks in anthropology.

MIDDLETON, John, 1921- comp. 291
Gods and rituals; readings in religious beliefs and practices. [1st ed.] Garden City, N.Y., Published for the American Museum of Natural History [New York, by] the Natural History Press, 1967. x, 468 p. illus. 22 cm. (American Museum sourcebooks in anthropology) Bibliography: p. [437]-450. [GN470.M48] 67-12870
1. Religion, Primitive—Addresses, essays, lectures. I. American Museum of Natural History, New York. II. Title. III. Series.

Religion. Primitive—Congresses.

CONFERENCE on Theravada Buddhism. University of Chicago 1962 294.391
Anthropological studies in Theravada Buddhism [papers, by] Manning Nash [and others. New Haven] Yale [dist. Cellar Bk. Shop. Detroit. 1966] xii, 223p. illus., map. 23cm. (Yale Univ. Southeast Asia studies) Title. (Series: Yale University. Graduate School. Southeast Asia Studies. Cultural report series, no. 13) Cultural report series no. 13. Held under the auspices of the Comm. on Southern Asian Studies of the Univ. of Chic. Bibl. [BL1400.C6 1962a] 66-19029 5.50
1. Religion. Primitive—Congresses. 2. Buddha and Buddhism—Asia, Southeastern—Congresses. 3. Hinavana Buddhism—Congresses. I. Nash. Manning. II. Chicago. University. Committee on Southern Asian Studies. III. Title. IV. Series.

Religion, Primitive—Juvenile literature.

BALDWIN, Gordon Cortis, 1908- 133.4
Schemers, dreamers, and medicine men; witchcraft and magic among primitive people [by] Gordon C. Baldwin. New York, Four Winds Press [1971, c1970] 176 p. illus. 24 cm. Bibliography: p. 169-171. Discusses the superstitions, customs, and magic of primitive and civilized people throughout the world. [GN470.B24] 76-124188 ISBN 0-7163-1001-5 4.88
1. Religion, Primitive—Juvenile literature. 2. Medicine, Primitive—Juvenile literature. 3. [Magic.] 4. [Superstition.] I. Title.

Religion — Psychology.

JURY, Paul, 1878-1953 253.2
Journal of a psychoanalyst-priest. Tr. [from French] by Albert R. Teichner. New York, Lyle Stuart [1965, c.1935, 1956] 158p. 21cm. [BX1765.2.J853] 64-13874 4.00 bds.,
I. Title.

PHILLIPS, William B. 248
... Letters to a convert--a psychological interpretation of the "first principles" of Christianity ... by William B. Phillips. [Vallejo, Calif., The Vallejo chronicle, c1919] cover-title, 50 p. 24 cm. (The Pureheart series) [BR123.P5] 19-18955
I. Title.

STALKER, James, 1848-1927.
Christian psychology, by the Rev. James Stalker ... New York and London, Hodder and Stoughton [pref. 1914] 281 p. 20 1/2 cm. (The James Sprunt lectures ... third series) A15
I. Title.

VETTER, George B 201
Magic and religion, their psychological nature, origin, and function. New York, Philosophical Library [1958] 555 p. illus. 22 cm. [BL53.V4] 58-59410
1. Religion — Psychology. 2. Magic. I. Title.

Religion—Quotations, maxims, etc.

THE Golden treasury of 230'.5'9
Puritan quotations / compiled by I. D. E. Thomas. Chicago : Moody Press, c1975. 321 p. ; 24 cm. Includes index. [PN6084.R3G6] 75-333021 ISBN 0-8024-3080-5 : 7.95
1. Religion—Quotations, maxims, etc. 2. Theology, Puritan. I. Thomas, Isaac David Ellis.

THE Great harmony : 200'.8
teachings and observations of the way of the universe / edited, with an introd., by S. Negrin. New York : Times Change Press, c1977. p. cm. Includes index. Bibliography: p. [PN6084.R3G7] 77-77387 ISBN 0-87810-533-6 : 8.00 ISBN 0-87810-033-4 pbk. : 3.00
1. Religion—Quotations, maxims, etc. I. Negrin, Su.

NEIL, William, 1909- 808.88'2
comp.
Concise dictionary of religious quotations. Grand Rapids, Eerdmans [1974] viii, 214 p. 24 cm. [PN6084.R3N4] 74-17470 8.95
1. Religion—Quotations, maxims, etc. I. Title.

ORIENTAL meditation / 291.4'4
edited by Harold Whalen ; ill. by Jeannee Wong. Mount Vernon, N.Y. : Peter Pauper Press, c1976. 62 p. : col. ill. ; 20 cm. [BL29.O73] 76-354802 1.95
1. Religion—Quotations, maxims, etc. I. Whalen, Harold.

SHEEN, Fulton John, 282'.0924
Bp., 1895-
The quotable Fulton J. Sheen. Comp., ed. by Frederick Gushurst and the staff of Quote. [1st ed.] Anderson, S.C., Droke House; dist. by Grosset, New York [1967] ix, 313p. 20cm. [BL29.S45] 4.95
1. Religion—Quotations, maxims, etc. I. Title.

SIMCOX, Carroll Eugene, 808.88'2
1912- comp.
A treasury of quotations on Christian themes / compiled by Carroll E. Simcox. New York : Seabury Press, [1975] p. cm. "A Crossroad book." Includes indexes. [PN6084.R3S5] 75-2229 ISBN 0-8164-0274-4 : 12.95
1. Religion—Quotations, maxims, etc. I. Title.

WOODS, Ralph Louis, 1904- ed. 208
The world treasury of religious quotations; diverse beliefs, convictions, comments, dissents, and opinions from ancient and modern sources, compiled and edited by Ralph L. Woods. [1st ed.] New York, Hawthorn Books [1966] xiv, 1106 p. 25 cm. [BL29.W6] 66-15355
1. Religion—Quotations, maxims, etc. I. Title.

Religion—Research—Handbooks, manuals, etc.

KENNEDY, James R. 200'.7'2
Library research guide to religion and theology : illustrated search strategy and sources / by James R. Kennedy, Jr. Ann Arbor, Mich. : Pierian Press, 1974. x, 53 p. : ill. ; 29 cm. (Library research guides series ; no. 1) Includes index. Bibliography: p. 43-51. [BL41.K45] 73-90317 ISBN 0-87650-038-6
1. Religion—Research—Handbooks, manuals, etc. 2. Reference books—Theology. 3. Libraries—Handbooks, manuals, etc. I. Title.

Religion—Societies, etc.—History.

BRAYBROOKE, Marcus. 291.1'72'06
Inter-faith organizations, 1893-1979 : an historical directory / by Marcus Braybrooke. New York : E. Mellen Press, c1980. xiii, 213 p. ; 23 cm. (Texts and studies in religion ; 6) Bibliography: p. 205-213. [BL11.A1B7] 19 79-91620 ISBN 0-88946-971-7 pbk. : 24.95
1. Religion—Societies, etc.—History. 2. Religion—Societies, etc.—Directories. I. Title. II. Series.

Religion — Study and teaching.

BOYER, Edward Sterling, 1888- 268
... *Religion in the American college;* a study and interpretation of facts, by Edward Sterling Boyer ... New York, Cincinnati [etc.] The Abingdon press [c1930] 105 p. 20 cm. (The Abingdon religious education monographs, J. W. Langdale, general editor) Bibliography: p. 104-105. [HV5072.B6] 30-8847
1. Religion—Study and teaching. 2. Universities and colleges—U. S. I. Title.

COMPENDIUM of first and 282.
second years academic religion, according to the requirements of the Catholic university, compiled from authentic sources by S. J. B. ... Cincinnati, O., St. Ursula convent and academy [c1924] 216, [2] p. front., illus. (map) 20 cm. Contains bibliographies. [BX904.C55] 25-1743
I. B. S. J. II. S. J. B.

EISTER, Allan W. 200'.7
Changing perspectives in the scientific study of religion, edited by Allan W. Eister. New York, Wiley [1974] xxii, 370 p. illus. 23 cm. (Contemporary religious movements) "A Wiley-Interscience publication." Includes bibliographies. [BL41.E37] 74-2092 ISBN 0-471-23476-1 14.50
1. Religion—Study and teaching. 2. Religion and sociology. I. Title.

ELIADE, Mircea, 1907- ed. 290.82
The history of religions; essays in methodology. Edited by Mircea Eliade and Joseph M. Kitagawa. With a pref. by Jerald C. Brauer. [Chicago] University of Chicago Press [1959] xi, 163 p. 23 cm. Bibliographical footnotes. [BL41.E5] 59-11621
1. Religion—Study and teaching. I. Kitagawa, Joseph Mitsuo, 1915- joint ed.

EVANS, John Henry, 1872-
How to teach religion, by John Henry Evans ... and P. Joseph Jensen ... Salt Lake City, Utah, The Deseret news, 1912. 160 p. 18 1/2 cm. 12-8883 0.75
I. Jensen, P. Joseph, joint author. II. Title.

HOLBROOK, Clyde A. 207
Religion, a humanistic field. Englewood Cliffs, N.J., Prentice-Hall [1963] xvi, 299 p. 22 cm. (The Princeton studies: humanistic scholarship in America) Bibliographical footnotes. [BL41.H6] 63-12269
1. Religion—Study and teaching. I. Title. II. Series.

*HOLM, Jean L. 207.1
Teaching religion in school; a practical approach, [by] Jean L. Holm. [London, New York] Oxford University Press 1975 200 p. 21 cm. (Oxford studies in education) Includes index. Bibliography: p. 178-197. [BV1534] ISBN 0-19-913224-0 3.50 (pbk.)
1. Religion—Study and teaching. 2. Theology—Study and teaching. 3. Religious—Education. I. Title.

KEITH, Noel Leonard. 200'.7
Religion; an introduction and guide to study [by] Noel Keith. [2d ed.] Dubuque, Iowa, W. C. Brown Book Co. [1967] xii, 467 p. illus., port. 24 cm. Includes bibliographies. [BL41.K4] 67-23296
1. Religion—Study and teaching. I. Title.

MOUNTCASTLE, William W., 200'.7
1925-
Religion in planetary perspective : a philosophy of comparative religion / William W. Mountcastle, Jr. Nashville : Abingdon, c1978. 208 p. ; 22 cm. Includes index. Bibliography: p. 201-205. [BL41.M64] 77-17111 ISBN 0-687-36023-4 : 5.95
1. Religion—Study and teaching. 2. Religion—Philosophy. I. Title.

RELIGIOUS studies in 377'.1
public universities, edited by Milton D. McLean. Carbondale, Central Publications, Southern Illinois University, 1967. xii, 266 p. 23 cm. Outgrowth of a conference sponsored by Southern Illinois University held November 1965. Contents.Contents.—A collection of papers on the study of religion in public universities.—An overview of courses and programs in religion in 135 public and 11 private colleges and universities. Bibliographical references included in "Notes" (p. 55-57) [BV1610.R42] 67-29053
1. Religion—Study and teaching. 2. Universities and colleges—United States. 3. Universities and colleges—Religion. I. McLean, Milton D., ed. II. Illinois. Southern Illinois University, Carbondale.

SISTERS of the Third Order of
St. Francis of Assisi.
Religion curriculum for the mentally handicapped. [Milwaukee, Dept. of Special Education, Cardinal Stritch College [1961] 146 p. Includes bibliography.
1. Religion — Study and teaching. 2. Mentally handicapped children — Education I. Title.

VRIES, Jan de, 1890-1964. 200'.7
Perspectives in the history of religions / Jan de Vries ; translated with an introd. by Kees W. Bolle. Berkeley : University of California Press, 1977, c1967. xxiii, 231 p. ; 21 cm. Translation of Godsdienstgeschiedenis in vogelvlucht. Includes bibliographical references and indexes. [BL41.V713 1977] 76-20154 ISBN 0-520-03300-0 pbk. : 3.95
1. Religion—Study and teaching. 2. Religion—Historiography. I. Title.

VRIES, Jan de, 1890-1964. 200'.9
The study of religion; a historical approach. Translated with an introd. by Kees W. Bolle. New York, Harcourt, Brace & World [1967] xxiii, 231 p. 21 cm. Bibliographical references included in "Notes" (p. 223-228) [BL41.V713] 67-19964
1. Religion—Study and teaching. 2. Religion—Historiography. I. Title.

*WEAVER, J. Bruce 268.434
Belonging to the people of God; a short-term study course for adults. Teacher's guide. By J. Bruce Weaver, Frank W. Klos. Philadelphia, Lutheran Church Pr. [1966] 127p. 21cm. price unreported pap.,
I. Title.

WEBB, Clement Charles Julian, 204
1865-
Religion and the thought of to-day, delivered before the University of Durham at Armstrong college, Newcastle-on-Tyne, on November 28th, 29th, and 30th, 1928, by C. C. J. Webb ... London, Oxford university press, H. Milford, 1929. 50 p., 1 l. 23 cm. (Riddell memorial lectures. 1st ser.) Contents.Contents.--The study of religion: problems and methods.--The debt of modern philosophy to the Christian religion.--The problem of religion in contemporary thought. [BL48.W3] 30-13249
1. Religion—Study and teaching. 2. Philsophy and religion. 3. Religious thought. I. Title.

WELCH, Claude. 377'.1
Graduate education in religion: a critical appraisal. Missoula, University of Montana Press [1971] xx, 279 p. illus. 24 cm. "Report of a study sponsored by the American Council of Learned Societies." Bibliography: p. 266-272. [BL41.W4] 70-181353
1. Religion—Study and teaching. I. American Council of Learned Societies Devoted to Humanistic Studies. II. Title.

WOODS, James Haughton, 291.13
1864-1935.
Practice and science of religion; a study of method in comparative religion, by James Haughton Woods ... New York, London [etc.] Longmans, Green, and co., 1906. viii p., 2 l., 3-123 p. 19 1/2 cm. (Half-title: The Paddock lectures, 1905-1906) "These lectures were delivered at the General theological seminary in New York during January and February of [1906]"--Pref. [BL41.W6] 6-22299
1. Religion—Study and teaching. 2. Religion, Primitive. I. Title.
Contents omitted.

Religion—Study and teaching—Addresses, essays, lectures.

THE History of religions; 200.9
essays on the problem of understanding, by Joachim Wach [and others] Edited by Joseph M. Kitagawa with the collaboration of Mircea Eliade and Charles H. Long. Chicago, University of Chicago Press [1967] xii, 264 p. 24 cm. (Essays in divinity v. 1) Most of the papers were presented at the Alumni Conference of the Field of History of Religions, Oct. 11-13, 1965, celebrating the 75th anniversary of the University of Chicago and the 100th anniversary of its Divinity School. Bibliographical footnotes. [BL41.H5] 67-20574
1. Religion—Study and teaching—Addresses, essays, lectures. 2. Religion—Historiography—Addresses, essays, lectures. I. Kitagawa, Joseph Mitsuo, 1915- ed. II. Wach, Joachim, 1898-1955. III. Chicago. University. Divinity School. IV. Title. V. Series.

THE Study of religion in 207'.73
colleges and universities. Edited by Paul Ramsey and John F. Wilson. With chapters by William A. Clebach [and others. Princeton, N.J.] Princeton University Press, 1970. ix, 353 p. port. 23 cm. Revised papers from a conference, held at Princeton University in 1968, in honor of G. F. Thomas. Bibliography: p. 347-352. [BL41.S78] 70-90957 10.00
1. Religion—Study and teaching—Addresses, essays, lectures. I. Ramsey, Paul, ed. II. Wilson, John Frederick, ed. III. Thomas, George Finger, 1899-

WAARDENBURG, Jean 200'.7'2
Jacques.
Reflections on the study of religion : including an essay on the work of Gerardus van der Leeuw / Jacques Waardenburg. The Hague, (Noordeinde 41) : Mouton, 1978. xi, 284 p. ; 24 cm. (Religion and reason ; 15) Includes indexes. Bibliography: p. [249]-253. [BL41.W29] 78-319077 ISBN 9-02-797604-X : 34.25
1. Leeuw, Gerardus van der, 1890-1950—Addresses, essays, lectures. 2. Religion—Study and teaching—Addresses, essays, lectures. I. Title.
Available from Mouton, New York.

Religion—Study and teaching—Africa.

KING, Noel Quinton. 200'.71'1
The queen of the sciences as a modern African professional woman; reflections on the place of religious studies in the tropical African university scene, by Noel King. [Nairobi] Published for Makerere University College by Oxford University Press [1967] 46 p. 25 cm. "An inaugural lecture delivered at Makerere University College (University of East Africa) Kampala, Uganda, on 14th July, 1966." Bibliography: p. 43-46. [BL41.K5] 68-89360
1. Religion—Study and teaching—Africa. 2. Universities and colleges—Africa. 3. Universities and colleges—Religion. I. Title.

Religion—Study and teaching—Collected works.

COMPENDIUM of third and 282.
fourth years high-school religion, according to the requirements of the Catholic university, including a particular study of the ten commandments and the virtues, compiled from authentic sources by S. J. B. ... Cincinnati, O., St. Ursula convent and academy [c1926] 5 p. l., [9]-622 p. front. 20 cm. Contains bibliographies. [BX904.C56] 26-9838
I. B., S. J. II. S. J. B.

WAARDENBURG, Jean Jacques. 200'.7
Classical approaches to the study of religion. Aims, methods and theories of research, by Jacques Waardenburg. The

Hague, Paris, Mouton, [1973- v. 23 cm. (Religion and reason, v. 3) Contents.Contents.—1. Introduction and anthology. Bibliography: v. 1, p. [667]-672. [BL41.W28] 70-152082
1. Religion—Study and teaching—Collected works. I. Title.
Distributed by Humanities; 20.00

Religion—Study and teaching—Congresses.

AMERICAN Academy of Religion. Academic Study of Religion Section. 200'.7
The academic study of religion : 1975 proceedings and Public schools religion-studies : 1975 proceedings / American Academy of Religion annual meeting, 1975. Missoula, Mont. : Distributed by Scholars Press, University of Montana, c1975. p. cm. "Preprinted papers for the Academic Study of Religion Section, compiled by Anne Carr, and the Public Schools Religion-Studies Group, compiled by Nicholas Piediscalzi." Includes bibliographical references. [BL41.A47 1975] 75-26653 ISBN 0-89130-023-6 : 2.00
1. Religion—Study and teaching—Congresses. 2. Religion in the public schools—Congresses. I. Carr, Anne. II. Piediscalzi, Nicholas. III. American Academy of Religion. Public Schools Religion-Studies Group. IV. Title. V. Title: Public schools religion studies.

Religion—Study and teaching—History.

DUDLEY, Guilford, 1932- 291'.092'4
Religion on trial : Mircea Eliade & his critics / Guilford Dudley III. Philadelphia : Temple University Press, 1977. 183 p. ; 22 cm. Includes bibliographical references and index. [BL43.E4D8] 77-77644 ISBN 0-87722-102-2 : 12.50
1. Eliade, Mircea, 1907- 2. Religion—Study and teaching—History. I. Title.

GLOCK, Charles Y. 200'.7
Beyond the classics? Essays in the scientific study of religion, edited by Charles Y. Glock and Phillip E. Hammond, with contributions by Norman Birnbaum [and others] New York, Harper & Row [1973] xvii, 422 p. 21 cm. (Harper torchbooks, HR 1751) Includes bibliographies. [BL41.G55 1973] 72-13909 ISBN 0-06-136105-4 12.00
1. Religion—Study and teaching—History. I. Hammond, Phillip E., joint author. II. Birnbaum, Norman. III. Title.

Religion—Study and teaching—United States.

HOLBROOK, Clyde A. 207'.73
Religion, a humanistic field / Clyde A. Holbrook. Westport, Conn. : Greenwood Press, 1978, c1963. xvi, 299 p. ; 23 cm. Reprint of the ed. published by Prentice-Hall, Englewood Cliffs, N.J., in series: The Princeton studies: humanistic scholarship in America. Includes bibliographical references and index. [BL41.H6 1978] 77-27448 ISBN 0-313-20214-1 lib.bdg. : 19.50
1. Religion—Study and teaching—United States. I. Title. II. Series: The Princeton studies : Humanistic scholarship in America.

MICHAELSEN, Robert. 207.73
The study of religion in American universities; ten case studies with special reference to State universities. New Haven, Society for Religion in Higher Education, 1965. x, 164 p. 23 cm. [BL41.M5] 65-5231
1. Religion — Study and teaching — U.S. I. Title.

RAMSEY, Paul, ed. 207.2
Religion [Essays by] Philip H. Ashby [others] Englewood Cliffs, N.J., Prentice [c.1965] x, 468p. 22cm. (Princeton studies: humanistic scholarship in Amer.) Bibl. [BL41.R3] 64-23553 8.95
1. Religion—Study and teaching—U. S. 2. Theology—Study and teaching—U.S. I. Title. II. Series.

RAMSEY, Paul, ed. 207.2
Religion. [Essays] [by] Philip H. Ashby [and others] Englewood Cliffs, N. J., Prentice-Hall [1965] x, 468 p. 22 cm. (The Princeton studies: humanistic scholarship in America) "Bibliographical note": p. 449-450. Bibliographical footnotes. [BL41.R3] 64-23553
1. Religion—Study and teaching—U.S. 2. Theology—Study and teaching—U.S. I. Title. II. Series.

WELCH, Claude. 200'.7'1173
Religion in the undergraduate curriculum; an analysis and interpretation. With essays contributed by Beverly A. Asbury [and others] Washington, Association of American Colleges, 1972. v, 129 p. 23 cm. Bibliography: p. 127-129. [BL41.W43] 72-182245
1. Religion—Study and teaching—United States. I. Asbury, Beverly A. II. Title.

Religion thought—History

TAWNEY, Richard Henry, 1880- 265.
Religion and the rise of capitalism; a historical study... by R. H. Tawney ... New York, Harcourt, Brace and company [c1926] x p. 2 l., 3-337 p. 22 1/2 cm. (Holland memorial lectures, 1922) [BR115.E3T3 1926a] 26-12446
1. Religion thought—Hist. 2. Sociology, Christian—Hist. 3. Gt. Brit.—Soc. condit. 4. Capitalism. I. Title.
Contents omitted.

Religion—United States—Biography.

AND a pair of warm socks 291 B
: five spiritual journeys / introduction, Frank Fennell. Sunspot, N.M. : Iroquois House, c1981. p. cm. Contents.Contents.—Pilgrimage without end / Ron Miller — And I contine / Annabeth McCorkle — Roots of return / Phyllis-Chana Sperber — Who is it that hurts? / Lorette Zirker — Full circle / Susanna Boesch. Includes bibliographies. [BL72.A73] 19 81-8370 ISBN 0-931980-05-4 : 10.00 ISBN 0-931980-06-2 pbk. : 6.50
1. Religion—United States—Biography. I. Miller, Ron.
Publisher's address: Box 15, Sunspot, NM 88349

Religion—Vocational guidance—United States.

HERRUP, Steven J., 1950- 200'.23
Your furure in religious work / by Steven J. Herrup. New York : Richards Rosen Press, 1980. xiv, 178 p. : port. ; 22 cm. Examines the advantages, disadvantages, and training requirements of a varity of careers in the field of religious work, including clergy, teaching, and religious social services. [BL42.5.U5H47] 19 79-25779 ISBN 0-8239-0507-1 : 5.58
1. Religion—Vocational guidance—United States. 2. [Religion—Vocational guidance.] 3. [Social service—Vocational guidance.] 4. [Vocational guidance.] I. Title.

Religions.

ADAM, Robert. 290
The religious world displayed; or, A view of the four grand systems of religion, Judaism, paganism, Christianity, and Mohammedism; and of the various existing denominations, sects, and parties, in the Christian world. To which is sub-joined, a view of deism and atheism... by the Rev. Robert Adam... Philadelphia; Published by Moses Thomas, no. 52 Chestnut street..... 1818. 3 v. 21 cm. First edition, Edinburgh, 1809. [BL80.A3] 30-12961
1. Religions. 2. Deism. I. Title.

ADAMS, William Henry Davenport, 1828-1891. 290
Curiosities of superstition, and sketches of some unrevealed religions. London, J. Masters, 1882. Detroit, Singing Tree Press, 1971. 328 p. 22 cm. Includes bibliographical references. [BL85.A3 1971] 76-155434
1. Religions. 2. Superstition. 3. Folk-lore. I. Title.

AFNAN, Ruhi. Effendi. 290
The great prophets: Moses, Zoroaster, Jesus. New York, Philosophical Library [1960] 457p. 22cm. [BL85.A4] 60-16205
1. Religions. 2. Civilization—Hist. I. Title.

AFNAN, Ruhi Muhsen.
The great prophets: Moses, Zoroaster, Jesus, by Ruhi M. Afnan. New York,, Philosophical Library [1960] 457 p. 22 cm.
1. Religions 2. Civilization—Hist. I. Title.

AMBERLEY, John Russell, viscount, 1842-1876. 200
An analysis of religious belief. New York, Arno Press, 1972. iv, 745 p. 23 cm. (The Atheist viewpoint) Reprint of the 1877 ed. [BL80.A6 1972] 76-161318 ISBN 0-405-03621-3
1. Religions. I. Title. II. Series.

AMBERLEY, John Russell, viscount, 1842-1876. 290
An analysis of religious belief. By Viscount Amberley ... From the late London ed. Complete. New York, D. M. Bennett, Liberal and scientific publishing house, 1877. xviii, [19]-745 p. 22 cm. (On cover: Truth seeker library) [BL80.A6 1877] 43-40340
1. Religions. I. Title.

ANDERSEN, William Niclaus. 290
What is new and old in religion; a book for the rationally minded. Philadelphia, Dorrance [1957] 168p. 20cm. [BL80.A63] 57-8484
1. Religions. I. Title.

ANDERSON, James A.
Religious unrest and its remedy, by James A. Anderson ... New York, Chicago [etc.] Flemming H. Revell company [c1913] 128 p. 20 cm. 13-4375 0.75
I. Title.

ANDERSON, James Norman Dalrymple, ed. 290
The world's religions. [2d ed.] Grand Rapids, Eerdmans [1953] 208p. 23cm. Bibliography (p. 197-203) [BL80] 54-1600
1. Religions. I. Title.
Contents omitted.

ANDERSON, James Norman Dalrymple, ed. 291
The world's religions / edited by Sir Norman Anderson. 4th ed., rev. Grand Rapids, Mich. : Eerdmans, 1976. 244 p. : ill. ; 21 cm. Includes bibliographies and index. [BL80.A64 1976] 75-26654 ISBN 0-8028-3001-3 pbk. : 3.95
1. Religions. 2. Christianity and other religions. I. Title.

ANSLEY, Delight. 290
The good ways. New rev. ed. Decorations by Robert Hallock. New York, Crowell [c1959] 214p. illus. 21cm. [BL82.A5 1959] 59-14674
1. Religions. I. Title.

ANSLEY, Delight. 290
The good ways. Decorations by Robert Hallock. New York, Crowell [1950] ix, 214 p. illus. 21 cm. Bibliography: p. 211. [BL82.A5] 50-13198
1. Religions. I. Title.

ARCHER, John Clark, 1881- 290
Faiths men live by. Rev. by Carl E. Purinton. 2d ed. New York, Ronald Press [1958] 553p. 22cm. Includes bibliography. [BL80.A7 1958] 58-7375
1. Religions. I. Title.

ARCHER, John Clark, 1881- 200
Faiths men live by [by] John Clark Archer... New York, T. Nelson and sons, 1934. ix p. 1 l., 497 p. 27 1/2-- (Half title: Nelson's religious series) "Collateral readings": p. 476-488. [BL80.A7] 34-37654
1. Religions. I. Title.

ARCHER, John Clark, 1881- 260
...Youth in a believing world; studies in living religions, by John Clark Archer. Tuxis in the Christian quest... Philadelphia, The Westminster press, 1931. 176 p. 20 cm. (Westminster departmental graded materials) At head of title: Senior elective. [BL82.A65] 31-7076
1. Religions. I. Title.

ARCHER, John Clark, 1881- 290
... Youth in believing world; studies in living religions, by John Clark Archer. Tuxis in the Christian quest ... Philadelphia, The Westminister press, 1931. 176 p. 20 cm. 43 p. 18 cm. (Westminister departmental graded materials) At head of title: Senior elective. --Suggestions to leaders of "Youth in a believing world" ... Philadelphia, The Westminster press, 1931. "Suggested reference": p. 3-5. [BL82.A65 Manual] [BL82.A65] 31-7076
1. Religions. I. Title.

ARCHER, John Clark, 1881-1957. 291
Faiths men live by. Freeport, N.Y., Books for Libraries Press [1971] ix, 497 p. 23 cm. (Essay index reprint series) Reprint of the 1934 ed. Includes bibliographical references. [BL80.A7 1971] 79-156606 ISBN 0-8369-2266-2
1. Religions. I. Title.

ASHBY, Philip H 290
The conflict of religions. New York, Scribner, 1955. 225p. 21cm. Includes bibliography. [BL85.A8] 55-9681
1. Religions. I. Title.

ASHBY, Philip H. 290
History and future of religious thought: Christianity, Hinduism, Buddhism, Islam. Englewood Cliffs, N.J., Prentice [c.1963] 171p. 21cm. (Spectrum bks. S-64) Bibl. 63-15411 4.25; 1.95 pap.,
1. Religions. I. Title.

ASHBY, Philip H. 290
History and future of religious thought; Christianity, Hinduism, Buddhism, Islam. Englewood Cliffs, N.J. Prentice-Hall [1963] 171 p. 21 cm. (A Spectrum book) "S-64." [BL80.2.A8] 63-15411
1. Religions. I. Title.

ATKINS, Gaius Glenn, 1868- 290
Procession of the gods, by Gaius Glenn Atkins and Charles Samuel Braden. [3d rev. ed.] New York, Harper [1948] xx, 586 p. 21 cm. Includes bibliographies. [BL80.A8 1948] 48-3314
1. Religions. I. Braden, Charles Samuel, 1887- joint author. II. Title.

ATKINS, Gaius Glenn, 1868- 290
Procession of the gods, by Gaius Glenn Atkins ... New York, R. R. Smith, inc., 1930. ix, p., 2 l., 3-577 p. 22 cm. Bibliography: p. 561-569. [BL80.A8] 30-28854
1. Religions. I. Title.

ATKINS, Gaius Glenn, 1868- 290
Procession of the gods, by Gaius Glenn Atkins ... and Charles Samuel Braden ... New York, London, Harper & brothers, 1936. xviii p., 1 l., 551 p. 22 cm. "Revised edition." Includes bibliographies. [BL80.A8 1936] 36-23901
1. Religions. I. Braden, Charles Samuel, 1887- joint author. II. Title.

ATKINS, Gaius Glenn, 1868- 290
Procession of the gods, by Gaius Glenn Atkins ... New York, R. R. Smith, inc., 1930. ix, p., 2 l., 3-577 p. 22 cm. Bibliography: p. 561-569. [BL80.A8] 30-28854
1. Religions. I. Title.

BACH, Marcus, 1906- 290
Had you been born in another faith; the story of religion as it is lived and loved by those who follow the path of their parental faith. Illustrated by Polly Bolian. Englewood Cliffs, N.J., Prentice-Hall [1961] 186 p. illus. 21 cm. [BL80.2.B28] 61-12979
1. Religions. I. Title.

BACH, Marcus, 1906- 290
Major religions of the world. Henry M. Bullock, general editor. Nashville, Graded Press [1959] 128p. 20cm. (Basic Christian books) [BL80.2.B3 1959] 59-16799
1. Religions. I. Title.

BACH, Marcus, 1906- 290
Major religions of the world. New York, Abingdon Press [1959] 128p. 20cm. [BL80.2.B3] 59-4175
1. Religions. I. Title.

BACH, Marcus, 1906- 209
Strange sects and curious cults. New York, Apollo [1962, c.1961] 277p. (A38) 1.75 pap.,
1. Religions. 2. Sects. I. Title.

BACH, Marcus, 1906- 209
Strange sects and curious cults. New York,

Dodd, Mead, 1961. 277p. 22cm. [BL85.B3] 61-7167
1. Religions, 2. Sects. I. Title.

BACH, Marcus, 1906- 200'.9
Strange sects and curious cults / by Marcus Bach. Westport, Conn. : Greenwood Press, 1977, c1961. viii, 277 p. ; 23 cm. Reprint of the 1962 ed. published by Dodd, Mead, New York. Includes index. [BL85.B3 1977] 76-52474 ISBN 0-8371-9457-1 lib.bdg. : 17.00
1. Religions. 2. Sects. I. Title.

BAHM, Archie J 290
The world's living religions, by Archie J. Bahm. [New York, Dell Pub. Co., 1964] 384 p. illus. 18 cm. (A Laurel original) Laurel edition 9704. Bibliography: p. [360]-369. [BL80.2.B35] 65-1136
1. Religions. I. Title.

BAKER, Joseph Baer, 1877-
Religious rheumatism, by J. B. Baker. Boston, Sherman, French & company, 1916. 3 p. l., 220 p. 21 cm. Contents.--Religious rheumatism.--Our besieging enemies.--The icy hand of God.--A sprig of evergreen.--How He sends us.--Little Samuel's coat.--Dungeons in the air.--The hopeless quest.--The dry brook.--Why we love the - church.--Heaven.--Boldness at the throne.--The resurrection body.--the stick and the axe.--Between two graves.--Finishing the unfinished. 16-20520 1.35
I. Title.

BANCROFT, Anne, 1923- 294
Religions of the East. New York, St. Martin's Press [1974] 256 p. illus. 26 cm. Bibliography: p. 250-252. [BL80.2.B36 1974] 72-97352 12.95
1. Religions. I. Title.

BARBER, John Warner, 1798-1885. 244
The book of similitudes; illustrated by a series of emblematic engravings; also The principal events connected with the religious history of the world from the earliest period to the present time: with a particular description of many remarkable events ... New Haven, Conn., J. H. Bradley, 1860. 524, iv p. col. front. (fold.) illus., col. pl. 12 degrees. [BV4515.B] 1--5174
1. Religions. I. Title.

BARING-GOULD, Sabine, 1834-1924. 290
The origin and development of religious belief. By S. Baring-Gould ... New York, D. Appleton and company, 1871. 2 v. 20 1/2 cm. First edition, London, 1889-70 Contents.pt. I. Heathenism and Mosaism.--pt.II. Christianity. [BL80.B25 1871] 16-3281
1. Religions. 2. Religion—Philosophy. 3. Christianity. I. Title.

BARTON, George Aaron, 1859- 290
The religions of the world by George A. Barton Chicago, Ill., The University of Chicago press [c1917] xi, 349 p. 20 cm. (Half-title: The University of Chicago publications in religious education ... Handbooks of ethics and religion) "Supplementary reading" at end of each chapter. "Additional books for the use of the teacher": p. 306-319. [BL80.B3] 17-20653
1. Religions. I. Title.

BARTON, George Aaron, 1859- 290
The religions of the world, by George A. Barton ... [2d ed.] Chicago, Ill., The University of Chicago press [c1919] xiii, 406 p. 20 cm. (Half-title: The University of Chicago publications in religious education ... Handbooks of ethics and religion) "Supplementary reading" at end of each chapter. "Additional books for the use of the teacher": p. 360-373. [BL80.B3 1919] 19-14330
1. Religions. I. Title.

BARTON, George Aaron, 1859- 290
The religions of the world, by George A. Barton ... Chicago, Ill., The University of Chicago press [c1929] xiii, 414 p. 20 cm. (Half-title: The University of Chicago publications in religious education ... Handbooks of ethics and religion) "Third edition." "Supplementary reading" at the end of each chapter. "Additional books for the use of the teacher": p. 360-380. [BL80.B3 1920] 29-25935
1. Religions. I. Title.

BARTON, George Aaron, 1859-1942. 200
The religions of the world. New York, Greenwood Press [1969, c1919] xiii, 414 p. 23 cm. Includes bibliographies. [BL80.B3 1969] 74-90469 ISBN 8-371-22163-
1. Religions. I. Title.

BAUM, Archie J
The world's living religions. New York, Dell Pub. Co. [1964] 384 p. 8o NUC66
I. Title.

BENEDICT, David, 1779-1874. 290
A history of all religions, as divided into paganism, Mahometanism, Judaism and Christianity, with an account of literary and theological institutions, and missionary, Bible, tract and Sunday school societies; with a general list of religious publications; accompanied with a frontispiece of six heads. By David Benedict, A. M. Providence, J. Miller, printer, 1824. 360, 96 p. front. (ports.) plates. 18 cm. [BL80.B45] 30-12964
1. Religious. I. Title.

BERRY, Gerald L. 1915- 290
Religions of the world. New York, Barnes & Noble [1956] 136p. 21cm. (Everyday handbooks, 224) [BL80.B478 1956] 56-12163
1. Religions. I. Title.

BERRY, Gerald L., 1915- 290
Religions of the world, from primitive times to the 20th century. New York, Barnes & Noble [1947] vi, 136 p. 21 cm. (Everyday handbook series) [BL80.B478] 47-11104
1. Religions. I. Series. II. Title.

BETTANY, George Thomas, 1850- 290
The world's religions; a comprehensive popular account of all the principal religions of civilized and uncivilized peoples; describing their doctrines, rites, priesthoods, sacred books, and moral teachings, together with lives of their founders, great teachers and reformers. By G. T. Bettany...with an introduction by the Rev. John Hall New York. The Christian literature company, 1891. xvii, 906 p. illus. (incl. ports.) fold. pl. 25 cm. "List of authorities": p. [xiii]-xvii. [BL80.B55] 30-12965
1. Religions. I. Title.

BETTANY, George Thomas, 1850-1891. 201
... *Primitive religions,* being an introduction to the study of religions, with an account of the religious beliefs of uncivilised peoples, Confucianism, Taosim (China), and Shintoism (Japan). By G. T. Bettany ... London, New York [etc.] Ward, Lock, Bowden & co., 1891. vii, 267 p. illus. 19 cm. ("The World's religions" series. [1]) Bibliographical foot notes. [BL80.B54] 44-14059
1. Religions. I. Title.

BIERER, Everard, 1827- 290
The evolution of religions, by Everard Bierer ... New York and London, G. P. Putnam's sons, 1906. xv p., 1 l., 385 p. 21 cm. [BL80.B6] 0-42349
1. Religions. I. Title.

BINDER, Louis Richard. 301.5'8
Modern religious cults and society; a sociological interpretation of a modern religious phenomenon. New York, AMS Press [1970] 213 p. 23 cm. Reprint of the 1933 ed. Originally presented as the author's thesis, Drew University, 1931. Bibliography: p. 203-205. [BL85.B5 1970] 77-113556 ISBN 4-04-008674-
1. Religions. 2. Religion and sociology. I. Title.

BINDER, Louis Richard. 289
Modern religious cults and society; a sociological interpretation of a modern religious phenomenon, by Louis Richard Biner ... Boston, R. G. Badger, The Gorham press [c1933] 3 p. l., v-viii, 9-213 p. 20 cm. Thesis (PH. D.)--Drew university, 1931. Without thesis note. Bibliography: p. 203-205. [BL85.B5 1931] 34-34769
1. Religions. 2. Religion and sociology. I. Title. II. Title: Religious cults and society.

BOA, Kenneth. 291
Cults, world religions, and you / Kenneth Boa. Wheaton, Ill. : Victor Books, c1977. 204 p. ; 20 cm. Bibliography: p. 204. [BL80.2.B6] 77-80442 pbk. : 2.50
1. Religions. 2. Christian sects—United States. 3. Occult sciences. 4. Cults—United States. I. Title.

BODIN, Jean, 1530-1596. 291
Colloquium of the seven about secrets of the sublime = colloquium heptaplomeres de rerum sublimium arcanis abditis / by Jean Bodin ; translation with introd., annotations, and critical readings, by Marion Leathers Daniels Kuntz. Princeton, N.J. : Princeton University Press, [1975] lxxxi, 509 p. ; 25 cm. Includes index. Bibliography: p. lxxiii-lxxxi. [B781.B33C6413 1975] 73-2453 ISBN 0-691-07193-4 : 25.00
1. Catholic Church—Relations. 2. Religions. 3. Religion—Philosophy. I. Title.

BOUQUET, Alan Coates, 1884- 290
Comparative religion, a short outline [New, rev.] London. Cassell [New York, Barnes & Noble, 1964, c.1961] 324p. 21cm. (Belle Sauvage lib.) Bibl. 62-41983 4.50
1. Religions. I. Title.

BOUQUET, Alan Coates, 1884- 290
... *Comparative religion,* a short outline, by A. C. Bouquet. Harmondsworth, Middlesex, Eng. New York, Penguin books [1941] x, 11-239 p. incl. front (port.) 18 1/2 cm. (Pelican books. [A89]) "First published 1941." "A list of books for further study": p. 229-234. [BL80.B625] 42-20882
1. Religions. I. Title.

BRACE, Charles Loring, 1826-1890. 290
The unknown God; or, Inspiration among pre-Christian races, by Loing Brace ... New York, A. C. Armstrong and son, 1890. 1 p. l., [v]-ix, [2], 336 p. 23 cm. [BL85.B75] 12-30872
1. Religions. 2. God. I. Title. II. Title: Inspiration among pre-Christian races.

BRADEN, Charles Samuel, 1887- 290
Modern tendencies in world religions, by Charles Samuel Braden ... New York, The Macmillan company, 1933. xi p., 2 l., 343 p. 20 cm. "Suggestions for further reading": p. 329-331. [BL96.B67] 33-11134
1. Religions. I. Title.

BRADEN, Charles Samuel, 1887- 290
The world's religions, a short history. Rev. Nashville, Abingdon Press [1954] 256 p. 21 cm. [BL80.B66 1954] 54-5510
1. Religions. I. Title.

BRADEN, Charles Samuel, 1887- 290
The world's religions; a short history [by] Charles Samuel Braden ... Nashville, Cokesbury press [c1939] 256 p. 20 cm. Maps on lining-papers. "Suggestions for further reading" at end of most of the chapters; "The sacred literature of the world's religions": p. 237-238; "Books of reference for the student of religions": p. 239-245. [BL80.B66] 39-27233
1. Religions. I. Title.

BRADLEY, David G. 291
Circles of faith; a preface to the study of the world's religious [by-) David G. Bradley. Nashville, Abingdon Press [1966] 239 p. 23 cm. Bibliographical footnotes. [BL80.2B69] 66-15491
1. Religions. I. Title.

BRIAULT, Maurice. 291
... *Polytheism and fetishism,* by the Rev. M. Briault, c.s.sp., translated by the Rev. Patrick Browne ... London, Sands & co.; St. Louis, Mo., B. Herder book co. [1931] xvi, 185, [1] p. illus. (maps) 19 cm. (Catholic library of religious knowledge, xviii) Bibliography: p. 185-[186] [BX880.C3 vol. 18] 282.082 34-12295
1. Religions. 2. Polythelsm. 3. Fetishism. 4. Religion, Primitive. I. Browne, Patrick William, 1864-1937, tr. II. Title.

BROWN, Opal Hartsell. 200
The cross, the cow, or the prayer rug. Philadelphia, Dorrance [1970] viii, 194 p. 22 cm. Bibliography: p. 193-194. [BL80.2.B76] 71-116752 4.95
1. Religions. 2. Voyages around the world. I. Title.

BROWNE, Lewis, 1897- 290
The believing world; a simple account of the great religions of mankind, by Lewis Browne ... with more than seventy illustrations and animated maps drawn by the author. New York, The Macmillan company, 1933. 347 p. illus. (incl. maps) 21 cm. "First reprinting, September, 1926 ... Seventeenth reprinting, Mar., 1932. Reissued in cheaper style, February, 1933." "Selected bibliography": p. 335-339. [BL80.B74 1933] 33-21168
1. Religions. I. Title.

BROWNE, Lewis, 1897- 290
This believing world; a simple account of the great religions of mankind, by Lewis Browne . . . with more than seventy illustrations and animated maps drawn by the author. New York, Macmillan, 1961 [c.1926, 1954] 347p. (Macmillan paperback, 83) 1.75
1. Religions. I. Title.

BROWNE, Lewis, 1897- 290
This believing world; a simple account of the great religions of mankind, by Lewis Browne ... with more than seventy illustrations and animated maps drawn by the author. New York, The Macmillan company, 1926. 347 p. illus. (incl. maps) 22 1/2 cm. Maps on lining-papers. "Selected bibliography": p. 335-339 [BL80.B74] 26-15042
1. Religions. I. Title.

BROWNE, Lewis, 1897- 290
This believing world; a simple account of the great religions of mankind, by Lewis Browne ... with more than seventy illustrations and animated maps drawn by the author. New York, The Macmillan company, 1928. 347 p. illus. (incl. maps) 22 cm. Maps on lining-papers. "Thirteenth reprinting, Nov., 1923.". "Selected bibliography": p. 335-339 [BL80.B74 1928] 29-4651
1. Religions. I. Title.

BUNGE, Martin Ludwig Detloff, 1876- 290
The story of religion, from caveman to superman, by Martin L. Bunge ... Pasadena, Calif., Fellowship publishing house [c1931] 2 p. l., 249 p. 21 cm. [BL80.B75] 31-20821
1. Religions. I. Title.

BUNSEN, Christian Karl Josias freiherr von, 1791-1860.
Chips from a German workshop. By Max Muller ... New York, C. Scribner's sons, 1889-91. 5 v. 20 cm. Vol. 1, 1891; v. 2, 4, 5, 1890; v. 3, 1889. "Letters from Bunsen to Max Muller in the years 1848 to 1859": v. 3, p. 391-492. On t.-p. of v. 3-5: By F. Max Muller. Contents.--v. 1. Essays on the science of religion.--v. 2. Essays on mythology, Traditions, and customs.--v. 3. Essays on literature, biography, and antiquities.--v. 4. Essays chiefly on the science of language With index to vols. iii and iv.--v. 5. Miscellaneous later essays. [PJ27.M73 1889] 17-30846
1. Religions. 2. Mythology. 3. Folk-lore—Addresses, essays, lectures. 4. Literature—Addresses, essays, lectures. 5. Philology, Comparative—Addresses, essays, lectures. I. Title.

BURDER, William. 290
A history of all religions, with accounts of the ceremonies and customs, or the forms of worship practised by the several nations of the known world from the earliest records to the year 1872. With a full account, historical, doctrinal, and statistical, of all the religious denominations. Philadelphia, W. W. Harding, 1872. ix. 807 p. ports. 28 cm. [BL80.B769] 50-51754
1. Religions. I. Title.

BURRELL, David James, 1844-1926. 290
The religions of the world. An outline of the great religious systems. By David James Burrell, D.D. Philadelphia, Presbyterian board of publication and Sabbath-school work [1888] 332 p. 19 1/2 cm. [BL80.B78] 30-13598
1. Religions. I. Title.

BURTT, Edwin Arthur, 1892- 290
Man seeks the divine; a study in the history and comparison of religions. 2d ed.

New York, Harper [c.1957, 1964] xii 514p. 22cm. Bibl. 64-12798 5.75
1. Religions. I. Title.

BURTT, Edwin Arthur, 1892- 290
Man seeks the divine; a study in the history and comparison of religions. New York, Harper [1957] 561p. 22cm. Includes bibliography. [BL80.B8] 56-13264
1. Religions. I. Title.

BURTT, Edwin Arthur, 1892- 290
Mann seeks the divine; a study in the history and comparison of religions [by] Edwin A. Burtt. 2d ed. New York, Harper & Row [1964] xii, 514 p. 22 cm. Bibliography: p. 495-498. [BL80.2.B8] 64-12798
1. Religions. I. Title.

BUSENBARK, Ernest, 1887- 291.37
Symbols, sex, and the stars, in popular beliefs; an outline of the origins of moon and sun worship, astrology, sex symbolism, mysticmeaning of numbers, the cabala, and many popular customs, myths, superstitions and religious beliefs. New York, Truth Seeker Co. [1949] xv, 396 p. illus. 24 cm. [BL85.B92] 50-312
1. Religions. 2. Symbolism. 3. Sex and religion. I. Title.

BUSHEY, Clinton Jay. 290
The superiority of Christianity, a comparative study of the great religions of the world [by] Clinton J. Bushey ... [Cleveland, Central publishing house, 1944] 240 p. fold. tab. 20 cm. "Suggested collateral readings" at end of most of the chapters. [BL82.B8] 44-32576
1. Religions. I. Title.

CAHIERS D'HISTOIRE MONDIALE 200.904
Religions and the promise of the twentieth century; readings in the history of mankind. Ed. for the Intl. Commn. for a Hist. of the Scientific and Cultural Development of Mankind, by Guy S. Metraux, Francois Crouzet. New York, New Amer. Lib. (c.1965] 277p. 18cm. (Mentor bk., MQ651; Readings in the hist. of mankind) Title. (Series: Readings in the history of mankind) These materials were used in the prep. of v.6 of the History of mankind: cultural and scientific development, and were orig. pub. in the Journal of World history. Bibl. [BL80.2C3] 65-22037 .95 pap.,
1. Religions. 2. Theology—20th cent. I. Metraux, Guy S., ed. II. Crouzet, Francois, 1922- ed. III. International Commission for a History of the Scientific and Cultural Development of Mankind. IV. Title. V. Series.

CARMODY, Denise Lardner, 291
1935-
Ways to the center : an introduction to the world religions / Denise Lardner Carmody, John Tully Carmody. Belmont, Calif. : Wadsworth Pub. Co., c1981. xiv, 408 p. : ill. ; 24 cm. Includes index. Bibliography: p. 385-389. [BL80.2.C34] 19 80-20257 ISBN 0-534-00890-9 : 17.95
1. Religions. I. Carmody, John, 1939- joint author. II. Title.

CARPENTER, Joseph Estlin, 1844-1927.
Comparative religion, by J. Estlin Carpenter ... New York, H. Holt and company; [etc., etc., 1913?] v. [1], 7-256 p. 18 cm. (Half-title: Home university library of modern knowledge, no. 60) Bibliography: p. 251-253. [BL2.C3] 13-7554
1. Religions. I. Title.

CARR, Burton W. 290
Gleanings of religion; ro A compilation containing the natural history of man--a true account of the different sects in the relitious world; toegthjer with much useful and instructive information on various subjects. By Burton W. Carr. Lexington, Ky., Printed by J. G. Norwood, 1828. viii, [9]-300 p. 21 cm. [BL80.C33] 23-5030
1. Religions. I. Title.

CATOIR, John T. 291
The way people pray; an introduction to the history of religions, by John T. Catoir. New York, Paulist Press [1974] v, 138 p. 18 cm. (Deus books) [BL80.2.C37] 73-91369 ISBN 0-8091-1805-X 1.45 (pbk.)
1. Religions. I. Title.

CAVENDISH, Richard. 291
The great religions / Richard Cavendish. New York : Arco Pub., 1980. p. cm. [BL80.2.C38 1980] 79-28659 ISBN 0-668-04929-4 : 16.95
1. Religions. I. Title.

CHAMPION, Selwyn Gurney, 290
comp.
The eleven religions and their proverbial lore, a comparative study by Selwyn Gurney Champion ... Foreword to the American edition by Rufus M. Jones ... A reference book to the eleven surviving major religions of the world, with introductions by thirteen leading authorities. New York, E. P. Dutton & co., inc., 1945. xix, 340 p. 22 1/2 cm. "First [American] edition." Bibliography: p. 336-340. [BL80.C337 1945] 45-6243
1. Religions. I. Title.

CHANLER, Julie (Olin) 1882- 290
His messengers went forth; illus. by Olin Dows. New York, Coward-McCann [1948] 64 p. illus. 21 cm. [BL80.C338 1948] 48-4600
1. Religious. I. Title.
Contents omitted.

CHANTEPIE de la Saussaye, 290
Pierre Daniel, 1848-1920.
Manual of the science of religion, by P. D. Chantepie de la Saussaye ... translated from the German by Beatrice S. Colyer-Fergusson (nee Max Muller) London and New York, Longmans, Green, and co., 1891. xiii p., 1 l., 672 p. 20 cm. Contains "Books of reference." [BL80.C35] 3-82467
1. Religions. 2. Religion—Hist. I. Fergusson, Beatrice Stanley (Max Buller) Coley, Mrs. d. 1902, tr. II. Title.

CHARLES, Robert Henry, 1855- 296
1931.
Religious development between the Old and the New Testaments, by R. H. Charles ... New York, H. Holt and company; [etc., etc.] 1914] v, 7-256 p. 17 cm. (Half-title: Home university library of modern knowledge. no. 88) [BM176.C5] 14-18109
I. Title.

CHILD, Lydia Maria (Francis) 290
Mrs., 1802-1880.
The progress of religious ideas. through successive ages. By L. Maria Child ... New York, C. S. Francis & co.; London, S. Low, son & co., 1855. 3 v. 20 1/2 cm. "List of books consulted": v. 3, p. [463]-464. [BL80.C38] 30-13600
1. Religions. I. Title.

CHRISTIAN, William A., 291.2
1905-
Oppositions of religious doctrines; a study in the logic of dialogue among religions [by] William A. Christian. [New York] Herder and Herder [1972] ix, 129 p. 22 cm. (Philosophy of religion series) Bibliography: p. 128. [BL80.2.C527] 76-173830 6.95
1. Religions. I. Title.

CLARKE, James Freeman, 1810- 290
1888.
Ten great religions: an essay in comparative theology. By James Freeman Clarke ... Boston, J. R. Osgood and company, 1871. x, 528 p. front. (diagr.) 20 1/2 cm. "Principal authors consulted": p. [511]-517. [BL80.C5 1871] 1-3765
1. Religions. 2. Christianity and other religions. I. Title.
Contents omitted.

CLARKE, James Freeman, 1810- 290
1888.
Ten great religions: an essay in comparative theology. By James Freeman Clarke ... Boston, Houghton, Mifflin and company, 1882. x, 528 p. front. (chart.) 21 cm. "Principal authorities consulted": p. [511]-517. [BL80.C5 1882] 6-24776
1. Religions. 2. Christianity and other religions. I. Title.
Contents omitted.

CLARKE, James Freeman, 1810- 290
1888.
Ten great religions: an essay in comparative theology, by James Freeman Clarke ... Boston and New York, Houghton, Mifflin and company, 1899['83] . 2 v. front. (diagr.) 20 1/2 cm. "Index of authors consulted": pt. i p. [511]-517. "Sources of information": pt. ii, p. x-xx. Contents.[pt. i] An essay in comparative theology. [New popular ed. 1899.-- pt. ii, A comparison of all religions. [22d impression, 1883]. [BL80.C5 1899] 4-5460
1. Religions. 2. Christianity and other religions. I. Title.

CLEMEN, Carl Christian, 1865- 290
ed.
Religions of the world, their nature and their history, by Professor Carl Clemen ... in collaboration with Franz Babinger, Leo Baeck, Heinrich Hackmann ... [and others] translated by the Rev. A. K. Dallas, M.A., with one hundred and thirty-five illustrations. New York, Chicago, Harcourt, Brace and company [c1931] xiv, 482 p. illus. (incl. ports.) 24 cm. "First edition." Bibliography at end of each chapter. [BL80.C66] 31-5199
1. Religions. 2. Religions—Hist. I. Babinger, Franz Carl Heinrich, 1891- II. Baeck, Leo, 1873- III. Hackmann, Heinrich Friedrich, 1864- Translation of Die religionen dererde. IV. Title.

CLEMEN, Carl Christian, 200'.9
1865-1940, ed.
Religions of the world; their nature and their history, by Carl Clemen, in collaboration with Franz Babinger [and others] Translated by A. K. Dallas. Freeport, N.Y., Books for Libraries Press [1969, c1931] xiv, 482 p. illus., ports. 24 cm. (Essay index reprint series) Translation of Die Religionen der Erde. Includes bibliographies. [BL80.C66 1969] 69-17570
1. Religions. 2. Religions—History. I. Babinger, Franz Carl Heinrich, 1891- II. Title.

CLODD, Edward, 1840-1930. 290
The childhood of religions; embracing a simple account of the birth and growth of myths and legends. By Edward Clodd... New York, D. Appleton and company, 1875. viii, 288 p. 18 cm. [BL85.C6 1875 a] 16-8278
1. Religions. I. Title.

CLODD, Edward, 1840-1930. 290
The childhood of religions; embracing a simple account of the birth and growth of myths and legends. By Edward Clodd... [New York, J. Fitzgerald, 1883] 51, [1] p. 23 1/2 cm. (Humboldt library of popular science literature, no. 47) Caption title. [BL85.C6 1883] 5-6396
1. Religions. I. Title.

COMPARATIVE religion,
a short outline. [5th ed. Baltimore] Penguin Books [1956] 320p. (A Pelican book) Bibliography: p. [307]-14.
1. Religions. I. Bouquet, Alan Coates, 1884-

COMPARATIVE religion,
a short outline. [5th ed. Baltimore] Penguin Books [1956] 320p. (A Pelican book) Bibliography: p. [307]-14.
1. Religions. I. Bouquet, Alan Coates, 1884-

COOMBS, J Vincent
Religious delusions; a psychic study, by J. V. Coombs ... Cincinnati, The Standard publishing company, [c1904] v p., 1 l., 185 p. 20 cm. 5-6302
I. Title.

CRANSTON, Ruth. 200
World faith; the story of the religions of the United Nations. Freeport, N.Y., Books for Libraries Press [1968, c1949] xi, 193 p. 23 cm. (Essay index reprint series) [BL80.C8 1968] 68-58782
1. Religions. I. Title.

CRANSTON, Ruth. 290
World faith; the story of the religions of the United Nations. New York, Harper [1949] xi, 193 p. 21 cm. [BL80.C8] 49-10464
1. Religions. I. Title.

CRAPSEY, Algernon Sidney, 290
1847-
The ways of the gods, by Algernon Sidney Crapsey ... [2d ed.] New York, The International press, 1921. vii, [3], x-xviii p., 1 l., 386, [4], 387-396 p. 21 cm. "Authorities adduced in this work": p. 387-396. [BL85.C78 1921] 22-4247
1. Religions. I. Title.
Contents omitted.

CUMONT, Franz, 1868-
... Astrology and religion among the Greeks and Romans, by Franz Cumont ... New York and London, G. P. Putnam's sons, 1912. xxvii, 208 p. 21 cm. (American lectures on the history of religious. Series of 1911-1912) [BF1674.C8] 12-2965 1.50
1. Religions. 2. Greece—Religion. 3. Rome—Religion. 4. Astrology. I. Title.

CUMONT, Franz Valery Marie, 292
1868-
... Astrology and religion among the Greeks and Romans, by Franz Cumont ... New York and London, G. P. Putnam's sons, 1912. xxvii, 208 p. 21 cm. (American lectures on the history of religions. Series of 1911-1912) [BL25.A6 vol. 9] [BL721.C8] (290.8) 12-2965
1. Religions. 2. Greece—Religion. 3. Rome—Religion. 4. Astrology. I. Title.

CUMONT, Franz Valery Marie, 292
1868-
The oriental religions in Roman paganism, by Franz Cumont; with an introductory essay by Grant Showerman. Authorized translation. Chicago, The Open court publishing company; [etc., etc.] 1911. 3 p. l., [iii]-xxiv p., 1 l., 298 p. 22 cm. [BL805.C8] 11-24148
1. Religions. 2. Rome—Religion. I. Showerman, Grant, 1870-1935. II. Title.

CUTTAT, Jacques Albert 291
The encounter of religions; a dialogue between the West and the Orient, with an essay on the prayer of Jesus. Translated [from the French] by Pierre de Fontnouvelle with Evis McGrew. Foreword by Dietrich von Hildebrand. New York, Desclee [1960] 159p., 22cm. (Bibl. notes) 60-10163 3.50
1. Religions. 2. Hesychasm. I. Title.

DABISTAN. 290
Oriental literature; or, The Dabistan, translated from the original Persian by David Shea and Anthony Troyer; introduction by A. V. Williams Jackson ... New York, Tudor publishing co., 1937. 6 p. l., 411 p. 24 cm. Authorship attributed to Muhammad Munsin, called Fanl. Abridged from the first edition of the translation begun by D. Shea, completed by A. Troyer, and published in 3 v. with title "The Dabistan. or School of manners ..." London. 1843 (Oriental translation fund of Great Britain and Ireland) In accordance with this title, "Dabistan ul-mazahab" (School of religious doctrines or institute) the work presents a sketch of many different kinds of doctrines and religious tenets, notably of Magism, Hinduism, Christianity, and Mohhamedanism. cf. "Special introduction." [BL1030.D3 1937] 37-37139
1. Religious. 2. Persia—Religion. I. Munsin, Fani, fl, 1618-1670. supposed author. II. Shea, David, 1777-1836. tr. III. Troyer, Anthony, d. 1865. tr. IV. Title.

DANIELOU, Jean 290.82
Introduction to the great religions [by] Jean Danielou [others] Tr. [from French] by Albert J. La Mothe. Jr. Notre Dame, Ind., Fides [1967, c.1964] 159p. 18cm. (Dome bk., D55) [BL80.2.D313] 64-16499 .95 pap.,
1. Religions. 2. Christionity and other religions. I. La Mothe, Albert' J., tr. II. Title. III. Title: The great religions.

DANIELOU, Jean. 290.82
Introduction to the great religions [by] Jean Danielou [and others] Translated by Albert J. LaMothe, Jr. Notre Dame, Ind., Fides Publishers, [1964] 142 p. 21 cm. [BL80.2.D313] 64-16499
1. Religions. 2. Christianity and other religions. I. LaMothe, Albert J., tr. II. Title. III. Title: Introduction to the great religions

DAWSON, Christopher Henry, 200'.9
1889-1970.
Religion and world history : a selection from the works of Christopher Dawson / edited by James Oliver and Christina Scott ; foreword by R. C. Zaehner. 1st ed. Garden City, N.Y. : Image Books, 1975. 351 p. ; 18 cm. (An Image book original) Includes bibliographical references and index. [BL80.2.D35 1975] 74-33612 ISBN 0-385-09551-1 pbk. : 2.45
1. Religions. 2. Church history. 3. Civilization, Modern. I. Title.

DEMERATH, Nicholas Jay.
Religious orientations and social class. [Berkeley, Calif., Survey Research Center, University of California 1961] xviii, 236 l. tables. 28 cm. Bibliography: leaves 231-236. 64-37507
I. Title.

DEVADUTT, Vinjamuri E
The Bible and the faiths of men. New York, Friendship Press [1967] 64 p. 18 cm. 68-44260
1. Religions. I. Title.

DICK, Kenneth C. 291
Man, father of the gods, by Kenneth C. Dick. [1st ed.] Brooklyn, T. Gaus' Sons, 1971. 550 p. 22 cm. (His Mighty pagan, v. 1) [BL80.2.D5] 76-148608 11.95
1. Religions. 2. Mysteries, Religious. 3. Sects. I. Title.

DIGGLE, John William, bp. of Carlisle, 1847-
Religious doubt; its nature, treatment, causes, difficulties, consequences, and dissolution, by the Rev. John W. Diggle ... London and New York, Longmans, Green, & co., 1895. xii, 371 p. 20 cm. 16-4821
I. Title.

DOBBINS, Frank Stockton, 1855-1916. 290
Error's chains: how forged and broken. A complete, graphic, and comparative history of the many strange beliefs, superstitious practices, domestic peculiarities, sacred writings, systems of philosophy, legends and traditions, customs and habits of mankind throughout the world, ancient and modern. By Frank S. Dobbins ... assisted by Hon. S. Wells Williams ... and Prof. Isaac Hall ... New York, Standard publishing house, 1883. xxii p., 1 l., 33-785 p. incl. illus., plates (part double) tab. 5 pl., map. 24 cm. Engraved half-title. Published also under titles: False gods: or, The idol-worship of the world, Philadelphia, 1881, and Story of the world's worship, Chicago, 1901. [BL80.D6 1883] 30-13606
1. Religions. 2. Mythology. 3. Idols and images—Worship. I. Williams, Samuel Wells, 1812-1884, joint author. II. Hall, Isaac Hollister, 1837-1896, joint author. III. Title. IV. Title: False gods.

DOBBINS, Frank Stockton, 1855-1916. 290
Errors chains: how forged and broken. A comparative history of the national, social and religious errors that mankind has fallen into and practised from the creation down to the present time. By Frank S. Dobbins ... assisted by Hon. S. Wells Williams ... and Prof. Isaac Hall ... 39th ed. New York. Willey brothers & co., 1886. xxii, 33-785 p. incl. illus., plates (part double) tab. 5 pl., map. 24 cm. Engraved half-title. Published also under titles: False gods: or, The idol-workship of the world. Philadelphia, 1881, and story of the world's worship, Chicago, 1901. [BL80.D6 1886] 30-13607
1. Religions. 2. Mythology. 3. Idols and Images—Worship. I. Williams, Samuel Wells 1812-1884 joint author. II. Hall, Isaac Hollister, 1837-1896 joint author. III. Title. IV. Title: Title: False gods.

DOBBINS, Frank Stockton, 1855-1916. 201
Error's chains: how forged and broken. A comparative history of the national, social and religious errors that mankind has fallen into and practised from the creation down to the present time. By Frank S. Dobbins ... assisted by Hon. S. Wells Williams and Prof. Isaac Hall ... 38th ed. New York city, Standard publishing house; Chicago, Ill., Empire publishing house; [etc., etc.] 1884. xxii, 33-785 p. incl. illus., plates (part double) front., plates, map. 24 1/2 cm. Published also under titles: False gods; or, The idol-worship of the world, Philadelphia, 1881, and Story of the world's worship, Chicago, 1901. [BL80.D6 1884] 43-38533
1. Religions. 2. Mythology. 3. Idols and images—Worship. I. Williams, Samuel Wells, 1812-1884, joint author. II. Hall, Isaac Hollister, 1837-1896, joint author. III. Title.

DOBBINS, Frank Stockton, 1855-1916. 290
False gods; or, The worship of idols. Ancient and modern--the world over ... by Rev. Frank S. Dobbins ... 53Philadelphia? c1880] 74 p. illus. 30 x 24 cm. Caption title. Published in greatly expanded form, 1883, under title: Error's chains. [BL80.D58] 30-17989
1. Religions. 2. Idols and images—Worship. I. Title.

DOBBINS, Frank Stockton, 1855-1916. 290
Story of the world's worship; a complete, graphic and comparative history of the many strange beliefs, superstitious practices, domestic preculiarities, sacred writings, systems of philosophy, legends and traditions, customs and habits of mankind throughout the world, ancient and modern. This dark and mystic picture strikingly compared with the beauty and purity of revealed religion, the whole forming the fascinating story of the world's worship from the birth of man to the present day, by Frank S. Dobbins ... Assisted by Hon. S. Wells Williams, LL., D., and Prof. Isaac Hall ... The whole profusely illustrated from authentic and trustworthy sources. Chicago, The Dominion company [1901] xxii, 33-785 p. incl. front., illus., plates. 25 cm. Published also with title: False gods; or, The idol-worship of the world, Philadelphia, 1881, , and: Error's chains: how forged and broken, New York, 1883, 1886. [BL80.D64] 3-5591
1. Religions. 2. Mythology. 3. Idols and images—Worship. I. Williams Samuel Wells, 1812-1884, joint author. II. Hall, Isaac Hollister, 1837-1896, joint author. III. Title. IV. Title: False gods.

DODSON, George Rowland, 1865- 290
The sympathy of religions, by George R. Dodson ... Boston, Mass., The Beacon press [1917] 5 p. l., 5-339 p. 20 cm. [The new Beacon course of graded lessons, W. I. Lawrence, F. Buck, editors] [BL80.D7] 17-13209
1. Religions. I. Title.

DUNLAP, Samuel Fales, 1825-1905. 290
The Ghebers of Hebron; an introduction to the Gheborim in the land of the Sethim, the Moloch worship, the Jews as Brahmans, the shepherds of Canaan, the Amorites, Kheta, and Azarielites, the sun-temples on the high places, the pyramid and temple of Khufu, the Mithramysteries, the Mithrabaptism, and successive oriental conceptions from Jordan fireworship to Ebionism, by Samuel Fales Dunlap ... [New York, The Trow printing company] 1894. vi p., 1 l., 1002 p. 24 cm. [BL85.D85 1894] 32-24186
1. Religions. 2. Asia Minor—Religion. 3. Ebionism. 4. Egypt.—Religion. 5. Fire-worshipers. I. Title.

DUNLAP, Samuel Fales, 1825-1905. 295
The Ghebers of Hebron, an introduction to the Gheborim in the lands of the Sethim, the Moloch worship, the Jews as Brahmans, the Shepherds of Canaan, the Amorites, Kheta, and Azarielites, the sun-temples on the high places, the pyramid and temple of Khufu, the Mithramysteries, the Mithrambaptism, and successive oriental conceptions from Jordan fireworship to Ebionism, by Samuel Fales Dunlaps, New and rev. ed. ... New York, J. W. Bouton; London, G. Redway, 1898. vi, [ix]-xv p., 1 l., 1017 p. 24 cm. [BL85.D85 1896] 32-15905
1. Religious. 2. Asia Minor—Religion. 3. Ebionism. 4. Egypt—Religion. 5. Fire. worshipers. I. Title.

DUNNE, John S., 1929- 200'.1
The way of all the earth; experiments in truth and religion [by] John S. Dunne. New York, Macmillan [1972] xiii, 240 p. 22 cm. [BL85.D87] 78-167928 6.95
1. Religions. 2. Spiritual life. I. Title.

DUNNE, John S., 1929- 200'.1
The way of all the earth : experiments in truth and religion / John S. Dunne. Notre Dame, Ind. : University of Notre Dame Press, 1978, c1972. p. cm. Reprint of the ed. published by Macmillan, New York. [BL85.D87 1978] 78-1575 ISBN 0-268-01927-4 : 12.95 ISBN 0-268-01928-2 pbk. : 3.95
1. Religions. 2. Spiritual life. I. Title.

DYER, Alvin Rulon. 291
This age of confusion; presaging the need for the restoration of the truth concerning life's great questions: Who am I? Whence am I? Whither am I going? By Alvin R. Dyer. Salt Lake City, Deseret Book Co., 1965. xxvi, 344 p. maps. 24 cm. Bibliography: p. [333]-336] [BL85.D9] 65-27486
1. Religions. I. Title.

EDKINS, Joseph, 1823-1905.
... The early spread of religious ideas especially in the Far East, by Joseph Edkins ... New York, Chicago, Fleming H. Revell company; London, The Religious tract society [1893] 144 p. 18 1/2 cm. (By-paths of Bible knowledge. XIX) A 41
1. Religions. 2. Persia—Religion. 3. China—Religion. I. Title.

EFFENDI, Shoghi 297.89
The faith of Baha'u'lah. a world religion. Wilmette, Illinois, Baha'i Publishing Trust, c.1959 20p. 22x10cm. apply pap.,
I. Title.

EINSTEIN, Morris. 290
Origin and development of religious ideas and beliefs, as manifested in history and seen by reason. By Morris Einstein. Titusville, Pa., Daily courier steam print., 1871. 2 p., l., 270 p. 20 cm. [BL80.E4] 30-18008
1. Religions. I. Title.

ELIADE, Mircea, 1907- 291
Patterns in comparative religion. Tr. [from French] by Rosemary Sheed. Cleveland, World [1963, c.1958] 484p. 21cm. (Meridian bk., M155) Bibl. 2.25 pap.,
1. Religions. I. Title.

ELIADE, Mircea, 1907-
Patterns in comparative religion. Translated by Rosemary Sheed. New York, Meridian Books [1963, c1958] xv, 484 p. 22 cm. Translation of Traite d'histoire des religion. Includes bibliographies. 68-87578
1. Religions. I. Title.

ELIADE, Mircea, 1907- 291
Patterns in comparative religion. Translated by Rosemary Sheed. New York, Sheed & Ward [1958] xv, 484 p. 22 cm. Translation of Traite d'histoire des religions. Includes bibliographies. [BL80.E513] 58-5885
1. Religions. I. Title.

ELLIOTT, Harvey Edwin, 1878- 290
The origin of religion as revealed by the chisel, the quill, and the spade. Cleveland, Herd Pub. Co. 1953] 309p. 22cm. Includes bibliography. [BL80.E55] 54-16317
1. Religions. I. Title.

ELLWOOD, Robert S., 1933- 291
Many peoples, many faiths : an introduction to the religious life of mankind / Robert S. Ellwood, Jr. Englewood Cliffs, N.J. : Prentice-Hall, c1976. xiii, 365 p. : ill. ; 24 cm. Includes index. Bibliography: p. 341-355. [BL80.2.E45] 75-37878 ISBN 0-13-555995-2 : 10.95
1. Religions. 2. Religion. I. Title.

EVANS, Allan Stewart, 1939- 200
What man believes: a study of the world's great faiths, by Allan S. Evans, Riley E. Moynes [and] Larry Martinello. Toronto, New York, McGraw-Hill Ryerson [1973] xvi, 421 p. illus. 24 cm. Bibliography: p. 410-418. [BL80.2.E82 1973] 73-7047 ISBN 0-07-077440-4
1. Religions. 2. Religion. I. Moynes, Riley E., joint author. II. Martinello, Larry, joint author. III. Title.

EVANS, Elizabeth Edson (Gibson) Mrs. 1832-1911. 290
A history of religions. Being a condensed statement of the results of scientific research and philosophical criticism. By Elizabeth E. Evans. New York, The Commonwealth company [1893] 128 p. 19 1/2 cm. (The Commonwealth library, no. 3] Original imprint covered by label. [BL82.E8] 30-17991
1. Religions. I. Title.

EVERETT, Charles Carroll, 1829-1900. 290
Religions before Christianity. A manual for Sunday schools. By C. C. Everett ... Boston, Unitarian Sunday school society, 1883. 62 p. 19 cm. "Books for reference": p. [57]-62. [BL82.E85] 30-17992
1. Religions. I. Title.

EVERETT, Charles Carroll, 1829-1900. 290
Religions before Christianity. A manual for Sunday schools. By C. C. Everett ... 7th ed. Boston, Unitarian Sunday-school society, 1892. 62 p. 19 cm. "Books for reference": p. [57]-62. [BL82.E85 1892] 33-1574
1. Religions. I. Title.

EVERETT, John Rutherford, 1918- 290
Religion in human experience, an introduction. New York, Holt [1950] xvii, 556 p. illus. 22 cm. Bibliography: p. 531-538. [BL80.E9] 50-8225
1. Religions. I. Title.

FAGLEY, Frederick Louis, 1879- 290.2
An outline of the religions of mankind, by Frederick L. Fagley ... Boston, Chicago, The Pilgrim press [c1936] vi, 81 p. diagrs. 20 cm. (Adult education series) "For further reading" at end of each chapter: Reference books": p. IV-V; "Acknowledgments" p. 81 [BL82.F3] 38-16779
1. Religions. I. Title.

FAIRCHILD, Johnson E., ed. 290
Basic beliefs; a simple presentation of the religious philosophies of mankind. New York, Hart [1965, c.1959] 192p. 21cm. [BL80.2.F26] 1.25 pap.,
1. Religions. I. Title.

FAIRCHILD, Johnson E ed.
Basic beliefs; a simple presentation of the religious philosophies of mankind. Ed. by Johnson E. Fairchild. New York, Hart Pub. Co. [1959] 192 p. tables. 21 cm. 68-84389
1. Religious. I. Title.

FAIRCHILD, Johnson E., ed. 290
Basic beliefs; the religious philosphies of mankind. New York, Sheridan House [1959] 190 p. 22 cm. (A Cooper Union forum) [BL80.2.F26] 59-8331
1. Religions. I. Title. II. Series.

FAITHS for a complex world.
[n. p., 1957] broadside (p. 459-465) 25x18cm. 'Offprinted from The American scholar, vol. 26, no. 4, Autumn, 1957. Copyright 1957 by the United chapters of Phi Beta Kappa.'
1. Religions. I. Cane, Melville, 1879-

AL FARUQI, Isma'il Ragi A., 1921- 912'.1'2
Historical atlas of the religions of the world. Isma'il Ragi al Faruqi, editor; David E. Sopher, map editor. New York, Macmillan [1974] xviii, 346 p. illus. 29 cm. Includes bibliographies. [BL80.2.F28] 73-16583 ISBN 0-02-336400-9
1. Religions. 2. Religions—Maps. I. Sopher, David Edward, joint author. II. Title.

FELLOWS, Ward J. 291
Religions east and west / Ward J. Fellows. New York : Holt, Rinehart, and Winston, c1979. xvi, 444 p. : ill. ; 25 cm. Includes bibliographies and index. [BL80.2.F44] 78-27721 ISBN 0-03-019441-5 : 14.95
1. Religions. 2. Religion. I. Title.

FERM, Vergilius Ture Anselm, 1896- ed. 290
Ancient religions (Orig. pub. as Forgotten religions; including some living primitive religions) New York, Citadel [1965, c.1950] xv, 392p. illus. 21cm. (C-209) Bibl. [BL80.F38] 2.25 pap.,
1. Religions. I. Title.

FERM, Vergilius Ture Anselm, 1896- ed. 290
Forgotten religions, including some living primitive religions. New York, Philosophical library [1950] xv, 392 p. illus. 24 cm. Includes bibliographies. [BL80.F38] 50-5099
1. Religions. I. Title.

FERM, Vergilius Ture Anselm, 1896- ed. 290
Living schools of religion (Religion in the twentieth century) Ames, Iowa, Littlefield, Adams, 1956 [c1948] 470p. 21cm. (Littlefield college outlines) New students outline series, 125. 'Originally published as

Religion in the twentieth century ... 1948.' [BL98] 56-13734
1. Religions. I. Title.

FERM, Vergilius Ture Anselm, 1896- ed. 291
Religion in the twentieth century. Edited by Vergilius Ferm. New York, Greenwood Press [1969, c1948] xix, 470 p. 23 cm. Includes bibliographies. [BL98.F4 1969] 74-90706
1. Religions. I. Title.

FERM, Vergilius Ture Anselm, 1896- ed. 290
Religion in the twentieth century. New York, Philosophical Library [1948] xix, 470 p. 22 cm. Each article preceded by biobibliographical sketch of the author. [BL98.F4] 48-5611
1. Religions. I. Title.

FITZGERALD, Thomas Edward, 1879- 290
Doctrines and descriptions of the present great religions of the world, by T. E. Fitzgerald. Animism, Brahmanism, Judaism, Buddhism, Confucianism, Christianity, Mohammedanism, Taoism, Shintoism and Zoroastrianism, together with some of the more important denominations of the Christian religion. [Deland, Fla, Printed by the E. O. Painter printing co., c1934] 150 p. 16 cm. [BL82.F5] 34-17345
1. Religions. 2. Sects. I. Title. II. Title: Present great religions of the world,

FOSS, Cyrus David, bp., 1834-1910. 252.
Religious certainties; sermons on special occasions [extemporaneously preached and stenographically reported.] By Bishop Cyrus D. Foss ... Cincinnati, Jennings and Graham; New York, Eaton and Mains [1905] 212 p. front. (port.) 20 cm. (Half-title: The Methodist pulpit) [BX8333.F6R4] 5-2581
I. Title.

FRADENBURGH, Jason Nelson, 1843- 200
Fire from strange altars. By Rev. J. N. Fradenburgh ... Cincinnati, Cranston & Stowe: New York, Hunt & Eaton [1891] 2 p. l., 7-324 p. illus. 20 cm. [BL96.F7] 30-23144
1. Religions. I. Title.

FRIEDMAN, Maurice S. 291
Touchstones of reality; existential trust and the community of peace [by] Maurice Friedman. [1st ed.] New York, Dutton, 1972. 341 p. 22 cm. Includes bibliographical references. [BL48.F75 1972] 74-165598 ISBN 0-525-22160-3 10.00
1. Religions. 2. Religion. I. Title.

FRIEDMAN, Maurice S. 1921- 291
Touchstones of reality; existential trust and the community of peace, [by] Maurice Friedman. New York, Dutton, 1974 341 p. 19 cm. [BL48.F75 1974] ISBN 0-525-47369-6 3.95 (pbk.)
1. Religious. 2. Religion. I. Title.
L.C. card no. for original ed.: 74-165598.

FRIESS, Horace Leland, 1900- 290
Religion in various cultures, by Horace L. Friess. Herbert W. Schenider. New York, Johnson Reprint [1966, c.1932, 1960] xxii, 586p. incl. illus., plates. facsims. 24cm. (Half-title: Studies in religion and culture) Bibl. [BL85.F7] 12.50
1. Religions. I. Schneider, Herbert Wallace, 1892- joint author. II. Title.

FRIESS, Horace Leland, 1900- 290
Religion in various cultures, by Horace L. Friess [and] Herbert W. Schneider ... New York, H. Holt and company [c1932] xxii, 586 p. incl. illus., plates, facsims. 25 cm. (Half-title: Studies in religion and culture) Bibliography: p. 497-556. [BL85.F7] 32-33278
1. Religions. I. Schneider, Herbert Wallace, 1892- joint author. II. Title.

GAER, Joseph, 1897- 290
How the great religions began. Wood engravings by Frank W. Peers. [New York] New American Library [1954] 240p. illus. 19cm. (A Signet key book, K308) [BL80] 54-2130
1. Religions. I. Title.

GAER, Joseph, 1897- 290
How the great religions began. [New York] Apollo Eds. [1968c.1956] 424p. 20cm. (A195) [BL80.G23 1956] 2.50 pap.,
1. Religions. I. Title.

GAER, Joseph, 1897- 290
How the great religions began. New and rev. ed. New York, Dodd, Mead, 1956. 424 p. 21 cm. [BL80.G23 1956] 56-5743
1. Religions. I. Title.

GAER, Joseph, 1897- 290
How the great religions began; wood engravings by Frank z W. Peers [New and rev. ed., Oct. 1935] New York, Dodd, Mead [1948] 424 p. illus. 21 cm. [BL80.G23 1948] 49-51
1. Religions. I. Title.

GAER, Joseph, 1897- 291
How the great religions began / by Joseph Gaer. New York : Dodd, Mead, [1981] c1956. 424 p. ; 20 cm. (A Dodd, Mead quality paperback) Includes index. [BL80.G23 1981] 19 81-7764 ISBN 0-396-08013-8 : 5.95
1. Religions. I. Title.

GAER, Joseph, 1897-
What the great religions believe. [New York, New American Library [c1963] xiv, 15-191 p. 18 cm. Includes bibliography. 68-88801
1. Religions. I. Title.

GAER, Joseph, 1897- 290
What the great religions believe. New York, Dodd, Mead [1963] 261 p. 21 cm. Includes bibliography. [BL80.2.G3] 63-16374
1. Religions. I. Title.

GARDNER, James. 290
The faiths of the world; an account of all religions and religious sects, their doctrines, rites, ceremonies, and customs. Compiled from the latest and best authorities, by the Rev. James Gardner ... London [etc.] A. Fullarton & co. New York, Fullarton, Macnab & co. [1858?-60?] 2 v. in 3. fronts., plates. 27 cm. Added title-pages, engraved. The plates are bound separately. [BL80.G25] 28-3080
1. Religions. 2. Sects. I. Title.

GLOVER, Terrot Reaveley, 1869- 200
Progress in religion to the Christian era, by T. R. Glover ... New York, George H. Doran company [1922] 350 p. 20 cm. [BL96.G5 1922 a] 22-23724
1. Religions. I. Title. II. Title: Religion, Progress in.

GOODING, Oliver Paul, 1835-
The people's God vs. the monarchic God; or, The true story of a world, by Gen. Oliver Paul Gooding ... Defends religion from the true standpoint, the republic of religion ... [St Louis, Mo.] The author, 1892. 413 [i. e. 405] p., 1 l. 23 cm. Error in paging; 338-346 omitted. Autobiography: p. 183-368. [BL95.G6] 30-23146
1. Religions. I. Title.

GRANT, Frederick Clifton, 1891- ed. 292
Hellenistic religions; the age of syncretism. New York, Liberal Arts Press [1953] 196p. 21cm. (The Library of religion, v. 2) [BL96.G7] 54-779
1. Religions. 2. Greece—Religion. I. Title.

GREAT religions of the world, by Herbert A. Giles ... [and others] New York and London. Harper & brothers. 1901. 4 p. l., 300, [1] p. 22 cm. [BL80.G7 1901] 1-25626 290
1. Religious. I. Giles, Herbert Allen, 1845-1935.
Contents omitted

GREAT religions of the world by Herbert A. Giles [and others] ... A new ed. with introductions. New York and London, Harper & brothers, 1912. 4 p. l., 3-300, [1] p. 22 cm. [BL80.G7 1912] 12-13459 290
1. Religions. I. Giles, Herbert Allen, 1845-1935.
Contents omitted

GROSS, Joseph B d.1891. 290
The heathen religion in its popular and symbolical development. By Rev. Joseph B. Gross. Boston, J. P. Jewett and company; New York, Sheldon, Lamport and Blakeman: [etc., etc.] 1856. xvi, 372 p. 20 cm. [BL80.G8] 30-18012
1. Religions. I. Title.

GUERANGER, Prosper Louis Paschal, 1806-1875.
... Religious and monastic life explained; authorized version from the French of Rt. Rev. Dom Prosper Gueranger, O. S. B., abbot of Solesmes, by Rev. Jerome Veth ... St. Louis, Mo., B. Herder; [etc., etc.] 1908. 4 p. l., 113 p. 18 cm. At head of title: U. I. O. G. D. 8-33423
I. Veth, Jerome, 1878- tr. II. Title.

HAM, Wayne. 290
Man's living religions; a course for adult study. [Independence, Mo., Herald Pub. House, c1966] 327 p. illus. 21 cm. [BL80.2.H27] 66-29091
1. Religions. I. Title.

HANSON, John Wesley, 1823-1901, ed. 290
The religions of the world the doctrines and creeds of mankind, stated in official documents by eminent representative expounders. Edited by J. W. Hanson... [Chicago! 1896] 720 p. front., illus., ports. 24 cm. Includes papers presented to the World's parliament of religions, Chicago 1898. [BL80.H25] 30-17996
1. Religions. I. World's parliament of religions, Chicago, 1893. II. Title.

HARDON, John A. 200
Religions of the Orient; a Christian view [by] John A. Hardon. Chicago, Loyola University Press [1970] viii, 212 p. 23 cm. Bibliography: p. 189-194. [BL80.2.H297] 71-108377 ISBN 8-294-01857-
1. Religions. 2. Christianity and other religions. I. Title.

HARDON, John A. 290
Religions of the world. Westminster, Md., Newman Press, 1963. x, 539 p. 24 cm. "Quoted references": p. 475-485. Bibliography: p. 487-505. [BL80.2.H3] 63-12236
1. Religions. I. Title.

HARDWICK, Charles, 1821-1859. 201
Christ and other masters: an historical inquiry into some of the chief parallelisms and contrasts between Christianity and the religious systems of the ancient world. With special reference to prevailing difficulties and objections. By Charles Hardwick ... 4th ed., edited by Francis Procter ... London and New York, Macmillan and co., 1886. xviii, 592 p. 19 cm. Contents.--pt. i. Introduction.--pt. ii. Religions of India.--pt. iii. Religions of China, America, and Oceanica.--pt. iv. Religions of Egypt and Medo-Persia. [BL80.H3 1886] 40-25665
1. Religions. 2. Christianity and other religions. I. Procter, Francis, 1812-1905, ed. II. Title.

HARTMAN, Louis O. 290
Popular aspects of oriental religions, by L. O. Hartman, PH. D. New York, Cincinnati, The Abingdon press [c1917] 255 p. front., plates. 21 cm. The first four chapters are based on articles which appeared in Zion's herald, 1915. cf. Foreword. "Reference books" at end of each chapter; "General reference books": p. 246. [BL1030.H3] 17-13234
1. Religions. I. Title.

HAWKRIDGE, Emma. 291
The wisdom tree. Illustrated with photos., line drawings by Theresa Garrett Eliot. Freeport, N.Y., Books for Libraries Press [1970, c1945] xvi, 504 p. illus. 23 cm. (Essay index reprint series) Bibliography: p. [487]-495. [BL80.H32 1970] 72-128257
1. Religions. I. Title.

HAWKRIDGE, Emma. 290
... The Wisdom tree, illustrated with photographs; line drawings, by Theresa Garrett Eliot. Boston, Houghton Mifflin company, 1945. xvi, 504 p. illus., plates. 20 cm. Folded table inserted. [Full name: Emma Lois Hawkridge] Bibliography: p. [487]-495. [BL80.H32] 45-8952
1. Religions. I. Title.

HAWLEY, John Savage, 1836- 290
Creeds and religious beliefs as they appear to a plain business man; by John S Hawley New York, W. B. Ketcham [1900] 4 p. l., 7-167 p. pl. 19 1/2 cm. [BL82.H4] 0-6642
1. Religions. 2. Sects. 3. Creeds. I. Title.

HAYDON, Albert Eustace, 1880- 291.211
Biography of the gods [by] A. Eustace Haydon. New York, Ungar [1967] xiii, 352p. 21cm. Reprint of the 1941 ed. Bibl. [BL80.H33 1967] 67-13617 5.75; 1.95 pap.,
1. Religious. 2. Gods. I. Title.

HAYDON, Albert Eustace, 1880- 290
Biography of the gods. Freeport, N.Y., Books for Libraries Press [1972] ix, 352 p. 23 cm. (Essay index reprint series) Reprint of the 1941 ed. [BL80.H33 1972] 74-37848 ISBN 0-8369-2595-5
1. Religions. 2. Gods. I. Title.

HAYDON, Albert Eustace, 1880- 290
Biography of the gods, by A. Eustace Haydon ... New York, The Macmillan company, 1941. xiii p., 1 l., 352 p. 21 cm. "First printing." Bibliography included in the "Notes": p. 331-342. [BL80.H33 1941] 41-5391
1. Religions. 2. Gods. I. Title.

HAYDON, Albert Eustace, 1880- 290
Man's search for the good life; an inquiry into the nature of religions, by A. Eustace Haydon. New York and London, Harper & brothers, 1937. viii p., 1 l., 269 p. 21 1/2 cm. "First edition." "Notes": p. 257-264. [BL80.H34] 37-8907
1. Religions. 2. Religion, Primitive. 3. Religion and sociology. I. Title.

HIRSCHOWITZ, Abraham Eber, 1845-
Religious duties of the Daughters of Israel. The three most important duties: viz. niddah, challah, hadlakah. We have also added laws concerning the salting of meat, prayers, meditations and duties for parents in training children. Comp. and rev. from authoritative sources, by Rabbi Abraham E. Hirschowitz ... New York [c1902] 3 p. l., [3]-77, [2] p. 18 1/2 cm. [BM726.H63 1902] 20-3270
I. Title.

HOOVER, William I. T., 1869- 290
Religionisms and Christianity, by W. I. T. Hoover... Boston, Mass., The Stratford co., 1924. 4 p. l., x, 225 p. 19 1/2 cm. [BL98.H6] 24-15085
1. Religions. 2. Christianity. I. Title.

†HOPFE, Lewis M. 291
Religions of the world / Lewis M. Hopfe. Beverly Hills, Calif. : Glencoe Press, c1976. xii, 308 p. : ill. ; 23 cm. Includes bibliographical references and index. [BL80.2.H66] 75-8425 ISBN 0-02-474810-2 pbk. : 7.95
1. Religions. I. Title.

HOPFE, Lewis M. 291
Religions of the world / Lewis M. Hopfe. 2d ed. Encino, Calif. : Glencoe Pub. Co., c1979. xiii, 368 p. : ill. ; 23 cm. Includes bibliographies and index. [BL80.2.H66 1979] 77-94769 ISBN 0-02-474820-X pbk. : 8.95
1. Religions. I. Title.

HOPKINS, Edward Washburn, 1857-1932. 290
The history of religions, by E. Washburn Hopkins... New York, The Macmillan company, 1918. 2 p. l., 6, [4], 624 p. 20 1/2 cm. Bibliography at end of each chapter. [BL80.H6] 18-22882
1. Religions. I. Title.

HUME, Robert Ernest, 1877- 261
... The world's living religions: an historical sketch, with special reference to their sacred scriptures and in comparison with Christianity, by Robert Ernest Hume ... New York, C. Scribner's sons, 1924. viii p., 2 l., 298 p. 17 cm. (Life and religion series) Bibliography: p. 279-295. [BL98.H8] 24-6750
1. Religions. 2. Christianity and other religions. I. Title.

HUME, Robert Ernest, 1877- 290
The world's living religions, an historical sketch with special reference to their sacred scriptures and in comparison with Christianity, by Robert Ernest Hume ... Revised. New York, C. Scribner's sons, 1936. viii p., 2 l., 312 p. 17 cm. [Life and religion series, by F. K. Sanders and H. A.

Sherman] "Published April, 1924 ... Revised edition, reprinted October, 1929 ... reprinted November, 1936." Bibliography: p. 279-285. [BL98.H8 1936] 37-4489
1. Religions. 2. Christianity and other religions. I. Title.

HUME, Robert Ernest, 1877-1948. 290
The world's living religions, with special reference to their sacred scriptures and in comparison with Christianity; an historical sketch. Completely rev. New York, Scribner [1959] 335 p. 20 cm. Includes bibliography. [BL98.H8 1959] 58-12515
1. Religions. 2. Christianity and other religions. I. Title.

HUME, Robert Ernest, 1877-1948. 291
The world's living religions, with special reference to their sacred scriptures and in comparison with Christianity; an historical sketch. Completely rev. New York, Scribner [1972, c1959] xii, 335 p. 21 cm. (The Scribner Library. Lyceum editions, SL 349) Bibliography: p. 291-311. [BL98.H8 1972] 72-175350 ISBN 0-684-31054-6 ISBN 0-684-12855-1 (pbk) 3.95
1. Religions. 2. Christianity and other religions. I. Title.

HUTCHISON, John Alexander, 1912- 291
Paths of faith / John A. Hutchison. 3d ed. New York : McGraw-Hill Book Co., c1981. xvii, 575 p. : ill. ; 24 cm. Edited by Rhona Robbin and Barry Benjamin. Includes bibliographies and index. [BL80.2.H78 1981] 80-14365 ISBN 0-07-031532-9 : 18.95
1. Religions. 2. Religion—History. I. Robbin, Rhona. II. Benjamin, Barry. III. Title.

HUTCHISON, John Alexander, 1912- 290
Ways of faith; an introduction to religion [by] John A. Hutchison [and] James Alfred Martin, Jr. 2d ed. New York, Ronald Press Co. [1960] 597p. 22cm. Includes bibliography. [BL80.2.H8 1960] 60-7770
1. Religions. I. Martin, James Alfred, 1917- joint author. II. Title.

THE illustrated book of all religions from the earliest ages to the present time. 290 Including the rise, progress, doctrines and government of all Christian denominations. Compiled from their own publications, and viewed from their own standpoint. Together with an account of the Jewish and all other systems of religion that have existed ... With nearly 300 illustrations. Philadelphia, J. E. Potter and company, ltd., 1897. xix, 17-592 p. illus. (incl. ports.) facsims. 21 cm. [BL80.I 3] 30-18013
1. Religions. 2. Christianity and other religions. I. Title: Book of all religions.

INMAN, Thomas, 1820-1876. 290
Ancient faiths and modern; a dissertation upon worships, legends and divinities in Central and Western Asia, Europe, and elsewhere, before the Christian era. Showing their relations to religious customs as they now exist. By Thomas Inman ... New York, J. W. Bouton; London, Trubner & co., 1876. xx, 478, xiv p. illus. 23 cm. Printed in Great Britain. [BL85.I 5] 30-19997
1. Religions. I. Title.

JACKSON, Herbert C 266
Man reaches out to God; living religions and the Christian missionary obligation. Valley Forge [Pa.] Judson Press [1963] 126 p; 20 cm. Includes bibliographies. [BV2063.J3] 63-13988
1. Religions. 2. Missions. I. Title.

JAMES, Edwin Oliver, 1886- 290
Comparative religion; an introductory and historical study. [Rev. ed.] London, Methuen; New York, Barnes & Noble [1962, c1961] 334p. 21cm. (University paperbacks, UP-37) Includes bibliography. [BL80.J3 1962] 62-855
1. Religions. 2. Religion, Primitive. I. Title.

JAMES, Edwin Oliver, 1886- 290
Comparative religions: an introductory and historical study. [Rev. ed.] London, Methuen; New York, Barnes & Noble [1963, c.1961] 334p. 21cm. (Univ. paperbacks, UP-37) Bibl. 62-855 4.50; 1.95 pap.,
1. Religions. 2. Religion, Primitive. I. Title.

JAMES, Edwin Oliver, 1886- 290
Myth and ritual in the ancient Near East; an archeological and documentary study. [New York, Barnes & Noble, 1961, c1958] 352p. map. Bibl. 6.50
1. Religions. 2. Mythology. 3. Ritual. I. Title.

JAMES, Edwin Oliver, 1886- 290
Myth and ritual in the ancient Near East; an archeological and Documentary study. New York, Praeger [1958] 352 p. illus. 23 cm. Includes bibliography. [BL96.J33 1958a] 58-11630
1. Religions. 2. Mythology. 3. Ritual. I. Title.

JEVONS, Frank Byron, 1858- 291
Comparative religion / by F. B. Jevons. Folcroft, Pa. : Folcroft Library Editions, 1976. vii, 154 p. ; 22 cm. Reprint of the 1913 ed. published at the University Press, Cambridge, Eng., in series: The Cambridge manuals of science and literature. Includes index. Bibliography: p. 145-146. [BL82.J48 1976] 76-57969 ISBN 0-8414-5326-8 lib. bdg. : 12.50
1. Religions. I. Title.

JEVONS, Frank Byron, 1858- 290
Comparative religion, by F. B. Jevons ... Cambridge [Eng.] The University press; New York, G. P. Putnam's sons, 1913. vii, 154 p., 1 l. 17 cm. (Half-title: The Cambridge manuals of sciences and literature) Title within ornamental borders. Bibliography: p. 145-146. [BL82.J6] 13-6304
1. Religions. I. Title.

JEVONS, Frank Byron, 1858- 291
Comparative religion / by F. B. Jevons. Philadelphia : R. West, 1978. vii, 154 p. ; 23 cm. Reprint of the 1913 ed. published at the University Press, Cambridge, Eng., in series: The Cambridge manuals of science and literature. Includes index. Bibliography: p. 145-146. [BL82.J48 1978] 78-1717 ISBN 0-8492-1342-8 lib. bdg. : 15.00
1. Religions. I. Title.

JOHNSON, Mary Parker. 290
The shortest path to heaven; a book dealing with the principal religions of the world and the chief religious cults and sects in the U. S. A. [1st ed.] New York, Exposition Press [1959] 203p. 21cm. Includes bibliography. [BL80.J58] 59-16016
1. Religions. 2. Sects—U. S. I. Title.

JOHNSON, Raynor Carey 210
A religious outlook for modern man. Foreword by Leslie D. Weatherhead. New York, McGraw [1964, c.1963] 220p. 23cm. Bibl. 64-19695 4.95
I. Title.

JOHNSTON, John Leslie, 1885-
Some alternatives to Jesus Christ; a comparative study of faiths in divine incarnation, by John Leslie Johnston, M. A. London, New York [etc.] Longmans, Green, and co., 1914. xvi, 215 [1] p. 20 cm. (Half-title: The layman's library, ed. by F. C. Burkitt, M. A., F. B. A. ... and the Rev. G. E. Newsom, M. A. ...) Series title also at head of verso of half-title. A 16
1. Religious. I. Title.

*JURJI, Edward J., ed. 290
The great religions of the modern world. Princeton. N.J., Princeton [1967, c.1946] 387p. 21cm. (Princeton paperbacks 81) Confucianism.--Taoism.--Hinduism.--Buddhism.--Shintoism.--Islam. --Judaism.--Eastern Orthodoxy.--Roman Catholicism.--Protestantism. Bibl. 2.95 pap.,
1. Religions. I. Title.

JURJI, Edward Jabra, 1907- 290
The phenomenology of religion. Philadelphia, Westminster Press [1963] ix, 308 p. 24 cm. Bibliographical footnotes. [BL80.2.J8] 63-12594
1. Religious. I. Title.

KALT, William J. 200
The religions of man [by] William J. Kalt and Ronald J. Wilkins. Chicago, Regnery [1967] v, 122 p. illus. 23 cm. (To live is Christ. Discussion booklet 2) Bibliographical footnotes. [BL80.2.K34] 67-29305
1. Religions. I. Wilkins, Ronald J., joint author. II. Title.

[KARG, George Adam] 1868- 248
The religious elevation of the human society. [Ozone Park, N. Y., G. A. Karg, c1934] cover-title, 102 p. illus. 20 cm. "... translated in English by George Hannes ..." Pref., signed: G. A. Karg, author. [BR126.K32] 34-16169
I. Hannes, George, tr. II. Title.

KARRER, Otto, 1888- 291
Religions of mankind, by Otto Karrer, translated by E. I. Watkins. New York, Sheed and Ward, 1945. ix, 291 p. 22 1/2 cm. Bibliography: p. 279-288. [BL85.K32 1945] 45-7014
1. Religions. 2. Religion. 3. Psychology, Religious. 4. Church. 5. Salvation—Comparative studies. I. Watkin, Edward Ingram, 1888-tr. II. Title.

KAUFMANN, Walter Arnold. 200
Religions in four dimensions : existential and aesthetic, historical and comparative / text and photos. by Walter Kaufmann. 1st ed. New York : Reader's Digest Press : distributed by Crowell, 1976. 490 p. : ill. ; 27 cm. Includes index. Bibliography: p. [475]-482. [BL80.2.K38 1976] 76-15367 30.00
1. Religions. 2. Arts and religion. I. Title.

KEDARA-NATHA DASA GUPTA. 290
Essence of religions, by Kedarnath Das Gupta ... compiled for the fifth World parliament of faiths, 1940-1941. New York, World fellowship of faiths, 1941. 208 p. 18 cm. [BL80.K4] 41-4705
1. Religions. 2. World fellowship of faiths. International congress. 5th, New York, etc., 1940-1941. I. Title.

KEGEL, Martin.
... The religious reformation of Ezra, by Martin Kegel ... Nashville, Tenn., Dallas, Tex. [etc.] Publishing house of the M. E. church, South, Lamar & Barton, agents, 1923. 2 p. l., 87-136 p. 20 cm. (The aftermath series ... pt. i, no. 3) [BS1355.K4] 23-13791
I. Title.

KELLEY, E G. 290
The philosophy of existence. The reality and romance of histories. In four books ... Including a brief history of angels and purgatory. By E. G. Kelley ... New York, J. W. Bouton; London, Chapman and Hall, 1878. xvi, 630 p. 23 cm. Printed in Great Britain. [BL85.K4] 18-12148
1. Religions. 2. Mythology. I. Title.
Contents omitted.

KELLOGG, Samuel Henry, 1839-1899. 291
A handbook of comparative religion. Grand Rapids, Eerdmans, 1951 [c1899] viii, 179p. 23cm. [BL85.K] A 53
1. Religions. 2. Religion 3. Christianity and other religions. I. Title. II. Title: Comparative religion.

KING, John H. 290
The supernatural: its origin, nature and evolution. By John H. King... London [etc.] Williams and Norgate; New York, G. P. Putnam's sons, 1892. 2 v. 22 1/2 cm. "Authorities referred to": v. 2. p. [281-296] [BL100.K5] [133] A 16
1. Religions. 2. Supernatural. 3. Superstition. I. Title.

KING, Ursula. 291.4'2
Towards a new mysticism : Teilhard de Chardin and Eastern religions / Ursula King. New York : Seabury Press, c1980. 318 p. ; 22 cm. "A Crossroad book." Includes index. Bibliography: p. 293-306. [BL80.2.K56] 80-17260 ISBN 0-8164-0475-5 : 14.95
1. Teilhard de Chardin, Pierre. 2. Religions. 3. Mysticism. I. Title.

KRETZMANN, Paul Edward, 1883- 290
The God of the Bible and other "gods," by P. E. Kretzmann ... St. Louis, Mo., Concordia publishing house [1943] 195, [1] p. 19 1/2 cm. "Works and books chiefly consulted": page at end. [BL80.K7] 43-97276
1. Religions. I. Title.

KUENEN, Abraham, 1828-1891. 201
National religions and universal religions, by A. Kuenen ... New York, C. Scribner's sons, 1882. 1 p. l., [v]-xii p., 1 l., 365 p. 19 1/2 cm. (The Hibbert lectures, 1882) Translated by Philip H. Wicksteed. cf. Pref. [BL80.K8 1882a] 43-39698
1. Religions. I. Wicksteed, Philip Henry, 1844-1927, tr. II. Title.

KUENEN, Abraham, 1828-1891. 291
National religions and universal religions / by A. Kuenen. 1st AMS ed. New York : AMS Press, 1979. xii, 339 p. ; 23 cm. Translation of Volksgodsdienst en wereldgodsdienst. Reprint of the 1882 ed. published by Williams and Norgate, London, which was issued as the 1882 Hibbert lectures. [BL80.K8 1979] 77-27169 ISBN 0-404-60403-X : 27.00
1. Religions. I. Title. II. Series: Hibbert lectures London ; 1882.

LANDIS, Benson Young, 1897- 290
World religions. New York, Dutton, 1960 (Dutton Everyman paperback) .95 pap.,
1. Religions. I. Title.

LANDIS, Benson Young, 1897- 290
World religions; a brief guide to the principal beliefs and teachings of the religions of the world and to the statistics of organized religion. [1st ed.] New York, Dutton, 1957. 158 p. 21 cm. [BL80.L3] 57-5344
1. Religions. I. Title.

LAZARON, Morris S. 1888-
Religious services for Jewish youth (designed for use in the assemblies of the high school department of Jewish religious and Sunday schools) written and arranged by Morris S. Lazaron ... Baltimore, Md. [Press of Meyer & Thalheimer] 1927. 275 p. 18 cm. [BM665.L32] 27-17671
I. Title.

LAZARON, Morris Samuel, 1888- 290
Bridges--not walls. [1st ed.] New York, Citadel Press [1959] 191p. 21cm. [BL85.L38] 59-14061
1. Religions. I. Title.

LENZ, Russell H
Religions. [Boston] Christian Science Publishing Society, 1964. map 25 x 44 cm. (World maps, 8) The Christian Science Monitor Map Series. Scale not given. 66-86097
1. Religions. 2. World maps. I. Title.

*LEWIS, H. D. 290
World religions: meeting points and major issues, by H. D. Lewis, Robert Lawson Slater. London. C. A. Watts, 1966. vii. 207p. 19cm. (New thinker's lib., 11) Bibl. 3.75 bds.
1. Religions. I. Slater, Robert Lawson. joint author. II. Title.
American distributor: Intl. Pubns. Serv., New York.

LEWIS, Hywel David. 290
The study of religions; meeting points and major issues [by] H. D. Lewis and Robert Lawson Slater. Baltimore, Penguin Books [1969, c1966] 221 p. 19 cm. (A Pelican book, A1011) First published in 1966 under title: World religions. Bibliography: p. 211-[213] [BL80.2.L47 1969] 72-3874 1.25
1. Religions. 2. East and West. I. Slater, Robert Henry Lawson, joint author. II. Title.

LIFE (Chicago) 290
The world's great religions [v.] by the edit. staff of Life. Special family ed. New York, Time [1963] 3v. (330p.) illus. (pt. col.) ports. (pt. col.) maps (pt. col.) 28cm. Contents.v.1. Religions of the East.--v.2. Religions of the West.--v.3. The glories of Christendom. 63-11285 1.39 ea.,
1. Religions. I. Title.

LIFE (Chicago) 290
The world's great religions. New York, Time, inc., 1957. 310 p. illus. (part col., part fold.) ports. 37 cm. Expansion of the material which originally appeared in six issues, from Feb-Dec. 1955. [BL80.L73] 57-13674
1. Religions. I. Title.

LIFE (Chicago) 200
The world's great religions, by the editorial staff of Life. Specially adapted for this

edition. New York, Golden Press [1967] 224 p. illus. (part col.) 21 cm. [BL80.2.L5 1967] 67-4288
1. Religions. I. Title.

LIFE (Chicago) 290
The world's great religions, by the editorial staff of Life. Life special ed. for young readers. New York, Simon and Schuster [1958] 192 p. illus. 29 cm. [A Deluxe golden book] [BL80.L74] 58-4280
1. Religions. I. Title.

LYON, Quinter Marcellus. 290
The great religions. [1st ed.] New York, Odyssey Press [1957] 732p. illus. 21cm. Includes bibliography. [BL80.L9] 57-1753
1. Religions. I. Title.

LYONE Quinter Marcellus 290
The great religions. [1st ed.] New York, Odyssey Press [1957] 732p. illus. 21cm. Includes bibliography. [BL80.L9] 57-1753
1. Religions. I. Title.

MCCAFFERTY, Lawrence M. 291.2
River of light; essays on Oriental wisdom and the meaning of Christ, by Lawrence M. McCafferty. New York, Philosophical Library [1969] 91 p. 22 cm. [BL80.2.M25] 69-14356 4.75
1. Religions. I. Title.

MCCASLAND, Selby Vernon, 200'.9 1896-
Religions of the world [by] S. Vernon McCasland, Grace E. Cairns [and] David C. Yu. New York, Random House [1969] xviii, 760 p. illus., maps. 25 cm. Includes bibliographies. [BL80.2.M27] 69-10524 8.50
1. Religions. I. Cairns, Grace Edith, 1908- joint author. II. Yu, Chien-shen, 1918- joint author. III. Title.

MCCROSSEN, Vincent A 290
The empty room. New York, Philosophical Library [1955] 156p. 23cm. [BL85.M185] 55-14870
1. Religions. 2. Catholic Church—Doctrinal and controversial works—Catholic authors. I. Title.

MAETERLINCK, Maurice, 1862- 290
The great secret, by Maurice Maeterlinck, tr. by Bernard Miall. New York, The Century co., 1922. 4 p. l., 3-268 p. 19 1/2 cm. $2.00 [BL85.M22] 22-11673
1. Religions. 2. Mysteries, Religious. 3. Agnosticism. 4. Occult sciences. 5. Theosophy. I. Miall, Bernard, tr. II. Title.

MAETERLINCK, Maurice, 128'.5 1862-1949.
The great secret. [Translated by Bernard Miall] New foreword by Leslie Shepard. New Hyde Park, N.Y., University Books [1969] xv, 267 p. 22 cm. ([Library of the mystic arts; a library of ancient and modern classics]) Reprint of the 1922 ed. [BL85.M22 1969] 69-16358 5.95
1. Religions. 2. Mysteries, Religious. 3. Agnosticism. 4. Occult sciences. 5. Theosophy. I. Title.

MALACHI, Martin. 200
The new castle; reaching for the ultimate. [1st ed.] New York, Dutton, 1974. x, 209 p. 22 cm. [BL80.2.M283 1974] 74-9663 ISBN 0-525-16553-3 7.95; 3.95 (pbk.).
1. Religions. 2. Civilization, Modern—1950- I. Title.

MALACHI, Martin. 200
The new castle; reaching for the ultimate. [by] Malachi Martin. [New York, Dell, 1975, c1974] 204 p. 18 cm. (A Laurel edition) [BL80.2M283 1975] 1.25 (pbk.)
1. Religions. 2. Civilization, Modern—1950- I. Title.
L.C. card number for original ed.: 74-9663.

MANCHESTER nonconformist 200 association for the promotion of religious equality.
Religious equality. Five lectures, delivered in the Free trade hall, Manchester ... Under the auspices of the Manchester nonconformist association. Manchester, Nonconformist association; [etc., etc.] 1872. [149] p. 21 1/2 cm. Various pagings. [BX5203.M3] 20-19109
1. Maclaren, Alexander, 1826-1910. II. Dale, Robert William, 1829-1895. III. Miller, Marmaduke. IV. Brown, James Baldwin, 1820-1884. V. Edmond, John, b. 1816. VI. Title.
Contents Omitted.

MARGOLIOUTH, David Samuel, 290 1858-1940.
Religions of Bible lands, by D. S. Margoliouth ... New York, A. C. Armstrong and son; London, Hodder and Stoughton, 1902. viii, 132 p. 18 cm. (Added t.-p.: Christian study manuals) [BL82.M35] 3-3543
1. Religions. I. Title.

MARSHALL, Edward Asaph, 1866- 290
Christianity and non-Christian religions compared, containing 800 library references to facilitate further study, by Edward A. Marshall ... Chicago, The Bible institute colportage association [1910] 79 p. illus. 21 cm. Bibliography: p. 78. [BL82.M4] 10-26777
1. Religions. I. Title.

MARTIN, Alfred Wilhelm, 1862- 201 1933.
Great religious teachers of the East, by Alfred W. Martin ... New York, The Macmillan company, 1911. ix, 268 p. 7 pl. 20 cm. Seven lectures of a series of twelve, delivered, "on successive Sunday evenings, in the winter of 1911, at the meeting-house of the Society for ethical culture of New York".--Prefatory note. [BL80.M195] 11-25329
1. Religions. I. Title.
Contents omitted.

MARTIN, Alfred Wilhelm, 1862- 290 1933.
The world's great religions and the religion of the future, by Alfred W. Martin ... New York, London, D. Appleton and company, 1921. vii, 230, [1] p. 20 cm. [BL80.M2] 21-20556
1. Religions. I. Title.

MAURICE, Frederick Denison, 290 1805-1872.
The religions of the world and their relations to Christianity. By Frederick Denison Maurice ... From the 3d rev. London ed. Boston, Gould and Lincoln, 1854. xxiv, [25]-262 p. 18 1/2 cm. [Boyle lectures, 1845-46] [BL80.M3 1854] 30-18014
1. Religions. 2. Christianity and other religions. I. Title.

MAYNARD, John Albert, 1884- 290
The living religions of the world, by John A. Maynard... Milwaukee, Wis., Morehouse publishing co.; [etc., etc., c1925] xiv, 146 p. 17 cm. (Half-title: Biblical and Oriental series) "Supplementary reading" at end of each chapter. [BL80.M35] 25-13861
1. Religions. I. Title. II. Series.

MENDELSOHN, Isaac, 1898- ed.
Religions of the ancient Near East; Sumero-Akkadian religious texts and Ugaritic epics. Indianapolis, Bobbs-Merrill [196-?] xxix, 284 p. (The Library of liberal arts, 136) Selected biliography: p. xxv-xxix.
I. Title.

MENZIES, Allan, 1845-1916. 290
History of religion; a sketch of primitive religious beliefs and practices, and of the origin and character of the great systems, by Allan Menzies ... New York, C. Scribner's sons, 1903. xiii, 438 p. 18 cm. (On cover: The university series) Bibliographical lists at end of most of the chapters. [BL80.M4] 4-11281
1. Religious. I. Title.

MENZIES, Allan, 1845-1916. 290
History of religion; a sketch of primitive religious beliefs and practices, and of the origin and character of the great systems, by Allan Menzies ... New York, C. Scribner's sons, 1927. xvii, 440 p. 19 cm. "First edition, April, 1895 ... fourth edition, September, 1911 ... reprinted, March, 1927." Bibliographical lists at end of most of the chapters. [BL80.M4 1927] 35-23146
1. Religious. I. Title.

MERCER, Lewis Pyle, 1847- 206. 1906.
Review of the world's religious congress of the World's congress auxiliary of the World's Columbian exposition. Chicago, 1893. By Rev. L. P. Mercer ... Chicago and New York, Rand, McNally & company, 1893. 334 p. ports. (incl. front.) 21 cm. [BL21.W8.M5] 9-5867
1. Religions. I. World's parliament of religions, Chicago, 1896. II. Title.

MILLER, Francis Trevelyan, 290 1877-
World's strange religions, by Francis Trevelyan Miller ... illustrations by Phillips Ward ... New York, London, The Thompson Barlow company [c1927] 6 v. fronts. 17 cm. [BL80.M45] 27-4082
1. Religions. I. Title.

MILLER, Milton G 290
Our religion and our neighbors; a study of comparative religion emphasizing the religions of the Western World, by Milton G. Miller and Sylvan D. Schwartzman. [Experimental ed.] New York, Union of American Hebrew Congregations [1959] 357p. illus. 23cm. Includes bibliography. [BL82.M58] 59-2451
1. Religions. 2. Judaism—Relations. I. Schwartzman, Sylvan David, joint author. II. Title.

MILLER, Milton G 290
Our religion and our neighbors; a study of comparative religion emphasizing the religions of the Western World by Milton G. Miller and Sylvan D. Schwartzman. Illustrated by William Steinel. New York, Union of American Hebrew Congregations [1963] xiv, 297 p. illus. (part col.) ports., maps (part col.) facsims. 27 cm. Includes bibliographies. [BL82.M58] 63-14742
1. Religions. 2. Judaism — Relations. I. Schwartzman, Sylvan David, joint author. II. Title.

MILLER, Orlando Dana, 1821- 200 1888.
Har-Moad; or The mountain of the assembly series of archaeological studies, chiefly from the standpoint inscriptions by Rev. O. D. Miller North Adams, Mass., S. M. Whipple, 1892. xxi, 445 p. front. (port.) 5 pl. 24 1/2 cm. "Sketch of the author's life", by S. M. Whipple: p. [xi]- xviii. "List of authors and their works": p. [441]-445. [BL96.M5] 30-23151
1. Religions. 2. Archaeology. 3. Cosmogony. 4. Chronology. I. Whipple, Stephen Munson, b. 1821. II. Title.

MILNER, Vincent L. 290
Religious denominations of the world; comprising a general view of the origin, history, and condition, of the various sects of Christians, the Jews and Mahometans, as well as the pagan forms of reglion existing in the different countries of the earth; with sketches of the founders of various religious sects. From the best authorities. By Vincent L. Milner. Philadelphia, J. W. Bradley, 1860. xxxiii, 35-512 p. front., ports. 22 1/2 cm. The introduction is from Hannah Adams View of religious cf. p. xxxiii. [BL80.M5 1860] 30-18017
1. Religious. I. Adams, Hannah, 1755-1831. II. Title.

MILNER, Vincent L. 290
Religious denominations of the world; comprising a general view of the origin, history, and ocndition of the various sects of Christians, the Jews, and Mahometans, as well as the pagan forms of religion existing ... with sketches of the founders of various religious sects. From the best authorities. By Vincent L. Milner. A new and improved ed., with an appendix brought up to the present time, by J. Newton Brown ... Philadelphia, Bradley & company, 1871. xxxiii, 35-609 p. front., ports. 20 1/2 cm. The introduction is from Hannah Adams View of religions. cf. p. xxxiii. [BL80.M5 1871] 30-18016
1. Religions. I. Brown, John Newton, 1803-1868. II. Adams. Hannah, 1755-1831. III. Title.

MILNER, Vincent L. 290
Religious denominations of the world; comprising a general view of the origin, history, and condition, of the various sects of Christians, the Jews, and Mahometans, as well as the pagan forms of religion existing ... with sketches of the founders of various religious sects, from the best authorities. By Vincent L. Milner. A new and improved ed., with an appendix brought up to the present time, by J. Newton Brown ... Philadelphia, Bradley, Garretson & co.; Galesburg, Ill. [etc.] W. Garretson & co., 1874. xxxiii, 35-629 p. front., ports. 20 1/2 cm. The introduction is from Hannah Adams View of religions. cf. p. xxxiii. [BL80.M5 1874] 30-18018
1. Religions. I. Brown, John Newton, 1803-1868. II. Adams, Hannah, 1755-1831. III. Title.

MOFFAT, James Clement, 1811- 290 1890.
A comparative history of religions: by James C. Moffat ... New York, Dodd & Mead, 1871-[74] 2 v. 19 cm. Contents.pt. I. Ancient scriptures.--pt. II. Later scriptures: progress, and revolutions of faith. [BL80.M55] 30-18019
1. Religions. I. Title.

MONDALE, Robert Lester, 1904- 290
Values in world religions. Boston, Starr King Press [1958] 109p. 21cm. [BL80.M58] 58-6339
1. Religions. I. Title.

MONTGOMERY, James Alan, 1866- 290 ed.
Religions of the past and present; a series of lectures delivered by members of the faculty of the University of Pennsylvania, ed. by James A. Montgomery ... Philadelphia and London, J. B. Lippincott company, 1918. 4 p. l., 3-425 p. 22 cm. Bibliography at end of each of the chapters. [BL80.M6] 18-5757
1. Religions. I. Title.

MOORE, George Foot, 1851- 290 1931.
The birth and growth of religion; being the Morse lectures of 1922, by George Foot Moore ... New York, C. Scribner's sons, 1923. viii p., 1 l., 178 p. 20 cm. "Eight lectures delivered in Union theological seminary."--Pref. [BL80.M68] 23-13669
1. Religions. I. Title.

MOORE, George Foot, 1851- 290 1931.
History of religions, by George Foot Moore ... New York, C. Scribner's sons, 1913-19. 2 v. 21 cm. (International theological library) "Literature": v. 2, p. 523-530. Contents.--i. China, Japan, Egypt, Babylonia, Assyria, India, Persia, Greece, Rome.--ii. Judaism, Christianity, Mohammedanism. [BL80.M7] 13-25397
1. Religions. I. Title.

MOORE, George Foot, 1851- 290 1931.
... History of religions, by George Foot Moore ... New York, C. Scribner's sons, 1929, '28. 2 v. 21 cm. (International theological library) Vol. 1; Rev. ed. with corrections and additions. "Literature": v. 2, p. 523-530. Contents.--i. China, Japan, Egypt, Babylonia, Assyria, India, Persia, Greece, Rome.--ii. Judaism, Christianity, Mohammedanism. [BL80.M7 1929] 30-31449
1. Religions. I. Title.

MOORE, George Foot, 1851- 290 1931.
... History of religions, by George Foot Moore ... New York, C. Scribner's sons, 1937,'32. 2 v. 21 cm. (International theological library) Vol. i: Rev. edition with corrections and additions. "Literature" at end of each volume. Contents.--i. China, Japan, Egypt, Babylonia, Assyria, India, Persia, Greece, Rome.--ii. Judaism, Christianity, Mohammedanism. [BL80.M7 1937] 38-33145
1. Religions. I. Title.

MULLER, Fried Max, 1823-1900.
Chips from a German workshop. By Max Muller ... New York, C. Scribner and company, 1871- v. 19 cm. Letters from Bunsen to Max Muller in the years 1848 to 1859: v. 3, p. [391]-492. [PJ27.M73 1871] CA 17
1. Religions. 2. Mythology. 3. Folk-lore—Addresses. essays, lectures. 4. Literature—Addresses, essays. lectures. I. Bunsen, Christian Karl Josias, freiherr von, 1791-1860. II. Title.

MULLER, Friedrich Max, 1823- 1900.
Chips from a German workshop. New York C. Scribner, 1869. 2 v. 19 cm. Contents.Essays on the science of religion.--Essays on mythology, traditions and customs. [PJ27.M73 1869] 48-37518
1. Religions. 2. Mythology. 3. Folk-lore—

Addresses, essays, lectures. 4. Literature—Addresses, essays, lectures. I. Title.

MULLER, Friedrich Max, 1823-1900.
Chips from a German workshop. By Max Muller ... New York, C. Scribner's sons, 1887-90. 5 v. 20 cm. First published 1867-75. Letters from Bunsen to Max Muller in the years 1848 to 1859: v. 3, p. [391]-492. Contents.--v. 1. Essays on the science of religion.--v. 2. Essay on mythology, traditions and customs.--v. 3. Essays on literature, biography and antiquities.--v. 4. Essays chiefly on the science of language. With index to vols. iii and iv.--v. 5. Miscellaneous later essays. [PJ27.M73 1890] 4-20731
1. Religions. 2. Mythology. 3. Folk-lore—Addresses, essays, lectures. 4. Literature—Addresses, essays, lectures. 5. Philology, Comparative—Addresses, essays, lectures. I. Bunsen, Christian Karl Josias freiherr von, 1791-1860. II. Title.

MULLER, Friedrich Max, 1823-1900. 290
Lectures on the science of religion; with a paper on Buddhist nihilsm, and a translation of the Dhammapada of "Path of virtue." By Max Miller ... New York, C. Scribner and company, 1872. iv, 300 p. 20 cm. [BL85.M86] 12-36943
1. Religions. I. Dhammapada II. Title.

MULLER, Friedrich Max, 1823-1900. 290
Theosophy; or, Psychological religion; the Gifford lectures delivered before the University of Glasgow in 1892, by F. Max Muller ... London and New York, Longmans, Green and co., 1893. xxiii, 585, 9 p. 20 cm. "Catalogue of principal works published by Professor F. Max Muller. Comp. by M. W.": 9 p. at end. [BL80.M8] 12-36947
1. Religions. 2. Religion—Philosophy. 3. Psychology, Religious. 4. Theism. I. W., M., comp. II. MW comp. III. Title.

MURPHY, John, 1876-1949. 200.9
The origins and history of religions. [New York] Philosophical Library [1952] 453p. 22cm. Bibliographical footnotes. [BL80.M] A 53
1. Religions. I. Title.

MURRELL, Ethel (Ernest) 1905- 290
The golden thread. [1st ed.] New York, Vantage Press [1956] 144p. 21cm. Includes bibliography. [BL80.M85] 56-6850
1. Religions. I. Title.

MYTH and ritual in the ancient Near East; an archeological and documentary study. New York, Barnes & Noble [c1958] 352p. illus. 23cm. Includes bibliography.
1. Religions. 2. Mythology. 3. Ritual. I. James, Edwin Oliver, 1886-

NATIONAL federation of religious liberals. 8th congress, Boston, 1917. 280
Religious liberals in council. Eight congress of the National federation of religious liberals at Boston, Mass. November 25 and 26, 1917. Proceedings and papers ... [Boston, 1917?] 96 p. 19 cm. [BX6.N4A5 1917 a] 19-15719
I. Title.

NATIONAL Geographic Society, Washington, D.C. Book Service. 291
Great religions of the world. Washington, National Geographic Society [1971] 420 p. illus. 27 cm. (The story of man library) Includes bibliographical references. [BL80.2.N347] 75-161575 ISBN 0-87044-103-5 11.95
1. Religions. I. Title.

NATIONAL Geographic Society, Washington, D.C. Book Service. 909 s
Great religions of the world. Washington : National Geographic Society, 1978. 419 p. : ill. ; 27 cm. (The Story of man ; 5) "A volume in the Story of man library prepared by National Geographic Book Service." Includes index. Bibliography: p. 419. [CB69.S86 vol. 5] [BL80.2] 291 79-103325 ISBN 0-87044-155-8 : 11.95
1. Religions. I. Title. II. Series.

NETTIS, Joseph 290
Man and his religions. Text, photos. by Joseph Nettis. Philadelphia, United Church Pr. [c.1963] 62p. 19cm. 1.00 pap.,
I. Title.

NEWPORT, John P., 1917- 248'.4
Christ and the new consciousness / John P. Newport. Nashville : Broadman Press, c1978. 180 p. ; 21 cm. Includes bibliographical references. [BL80.2.N45] 77-78621 ISBN 0-8054-6604-5 pbk. : 3.95
1. Religions. 2. Cults. 3. Christianity and other religions. I. Title.

NEWTON, Joseph Fort, 1876- 225
The religious basis of a better world order, an application of Christian principles to world affairs, by Joseph Fort Newton... New York, Chicago [etc.] Fleming H. Revell company [c1920] 183 p. 19 1/2 cm. [BR121.N5] 20-12137
I. Title.

NIELSEN, Niels Christian, 1921- 290
The layman looks at world religions. St. Louis, Bethany Press [1962] 112p. 21cm. [BL80.2.N5] 62-17915
1. Religions. I. Title.

NOBLE, Raymond Goodman, 1873- 290
The ABC of your religion and mine, by Raymond G. Noble ... Philadelphia, Dorrance & company [1945] vi, 7-121 p. 19 1/2 cm. "Bibliography of highly recommended readings":p. 117-118. [BL80.N56] 45-2489
1. Religions. I. Title.

NON-BIBLICAL systems of religion. 201
A symposium. By the Ven..Archdeacon Farrar, D.D., Rev. Canon Rawlinson, M. A., Rev. W. Wright, D. D., and others ... Cincinnati, Cranston and Curts. New York, Hunt and Eaton, 1893. iiv [i.e. vii], 232 p. 19 1/2 cm. "Reprinted from the Homiletic magazine."--Pref. [BL80.N6 1893] 46-38130
1. Religions. I. Rawlinson, George, 1812-1902. II. Farrar, Frederic William, 1831-1903.

NON-CHRISTIAN religions of the world, by Sir William Muir, Prof. Legge, LL.D., The Revs. J. Murray Mitchell, L.L.D., and H.R. Reynolds, D.D. Selected from the Living papers series. New York, Chicago [etc.] Fleming H. Revell company; London, The Religious tract society [1894] 2 p. l., 60, 36, 62, 64, 64, 63 p. 19 cm. A 40
1. Religions. 2. Christianity and other relgions. I. Muir, William Sir, 1819-1905. II. Legge, James, 1815-1897. III. Mitchell, John Murray, 1815-1904. IV. Reynolds, Henry Robert, 1825-1896.
Contents omitted.

NOSS, John Boyer 280
Living religions. Philadelphia, United Church [c.1957, 1962] 111p. 19cm. (Pilgrim bk.) 62-19786 1.45 pap.,
1. Religions. I. Title.

NOSS, John Boyer 290
Living religions [by] John B. Noss. Rev. ed. Philadelphia, United Church Pr. [1967] 121p. 19cm. Bibl. [BL95.N6 1967] 67-17925 1.95 pap.,
1. Religions. I. Title.

NOSS, John Boyer. 280
Living religions. Philadelphia, United Church Press [1962] 111 p. 19 cm. (A Pilgrim book) [BL95.N6] 62-19786
1. Religions. I. Title.

NOSS, John Boyer. 290
Living religions [by] John B. Noss. Rev. ed. Philadelphia, United Church Press [1967] 121 p. 19 cm. Bibliography: p. 119-121. [BL95.N6] 67-17925
1. Religions. I. Title.

NOSS, John Boyer. 290
Man's religions. Rev. ed. New York, Macmillan [1956] 784p. 25cm. Includes bibliographies. [BL80.N65 1956] 56-7326
1. Religions. I. Title.

NOSS, John Boyer. 200'.9
Man's religions [by] John B. Noss. 5th ed. New York, Macmillan [1974] xviii, 589 p. illus. 24 cm. Includes bibliographies. [BL80.2.N6 1974] 72-13972 ISBN 0-02-388440-1 9.95
1. Religions. I. Title.

NOSS, John Boyer. 290
Man's religions. 3d ed. New York, Macmillan [1963] 816 p. illus. 24 cm. [BL80.2.N6 1963] 63-8182
1. Religions. I. Title.

NOSS, John Boyer. 200'.9
Man's religions [by] John B. Noss. 4th ed. [New York] Macmillan [1969] xx, 598 p. illus. 24 cm. Includes bibliographical references. [BL80.2.N6 1969] 69-11587
1. Religions. I. Title.

NOSS, John Boyer. 291
Man's religions / John B. Noss. 6th ed. New York : Macmillan, c1980. xvi, 580 p. : ill. ; 25 cm. Includes bibliographies and index. [BL80.2.N6 1980] 79-1392 ISBN 0-02-388430-4 : 16.95
1. Religions. I. Title.

OSBORN, Arthur Walter, 1891- 290
The axis and the rim; the quest for reality in a modern setting. [1st American ed.] New York, T. Nelson [1963] 203 p. 23 cm. Includes bibliography. [BL80.2.O8] 63-2689
1. Religions. I. Title.

THE Outlook. 290
The message of the world's religions; reprinted from "The Outlook. New York [etc.] Longmans, Green, and co., 1898. 3 p. l., 125 p. 16 cm. [BL82.M5] 30-18001
1. Religions. I. Gotthell, Gustav, 1827-1903. II. Davids, Thomas William Rhys, 1843-1922. III. Smith, Arthur Henderson, 1845- IV. Washburn, George, 1833-1915. V. Lanman, Charles Rockwell, 1850- VI. Abbott, Lyman, 1835-1922. VII. Title.
Contents omitted.

OWEN, Ralph Albert Dornfeld, 1884- 204
Learning religion from famous Americans; a source book, by Ralph Dornfeld Owen ... New York, The Macmillan company, 1927. xvi, 279 p. 21 cm. [BR50.O8] 27-9590
I. Title.

PARKANY, Betty, 1927-
"Religious instruction" in the Washington Constitution. [Seattle, University of Washington] 1965. [100] l. typescript, photocopies, letters. "Legal Reference and Research, Law Librarianship 542, August 18, 1965." 67-54053
I. Title.

PARKER, Francis Marion.
Religious essays, by Francis Marion Parker; including a scientific exposition of the Mosaic story of creation and the fall of man. Louisville Ky., Pentecostal publishing company [c1911] 157 p. front. (port.) 20 cm. 11-19215 1.00
I. Title.
Contents omitted.

PARKES, James William, 1896- 290
Common sense about religion, by John Hadham [pseud.] New York, Macmillan, 1961. 176p. 22cm. (The Common sense series) [BL80.2.P3 1961a] 61-16727
1. Religions. 2. Theology, Doctrinal—Popular works. 3. Christianity—20th cent. I. Title.

PARKS, Mercer H. 291
The task worthy of travail / Mercer H. Parks. Houston, Tex. : Pacesetter Press, [1975] v, 522 p. ; 24 cm. Includes bibliographical references and index. [BL85.P34] 74-11835 ISBN 0-88415-784-9 : 15.00
1. Religions. 2. Creation (Literary, artistic, etc.) I. Title.

PARRINDER, Edward Geoffrey. 291
A book of world religions, by E. G. Parrinder. Chester Springs, Pa. Dufuor Editions, 1967. 176 p. illus., facsims., maps, ports. 26 cm. [BL80.2.P33] 67-15196
1. Religions. I. Title.

PARRINDER, Edward Geoffrey,
Comparative religion. New York, Macmillan, 1962. 130 p. 23 cm. 63-29730
1. Religions. I. Title.

PARRINDER, Edward Geoffrey. 291
Comparative religion / by Geoffrey Parrinder. Westport, Conn. : Greenwood Press, 1975, c1962. 130 p. ; 22 cm. Reprint of the ed. published by Allen & Unwin, London. Includes bibliographical references and index. [BL80.2.P34 1975] 73-19116 ISBN 0-8371-7301-9
1. Religions. I. Title.

PARRINDER, Edward Geoffrey. 200
Religions of the world, from primitive beliefs to modern faiths. General editor: Geoffrey Parrinder. [1st U.S. ed.] New York, Madison Square Press [1971] 440 p. illus. (part col.) 30 cm. Bibliography: p. 432-433. [BL80.2.P346 1971] 73-149816 ISBN 0-448-02128-5 14.95
1. Religions. I. Title.

PARRINDER, Edward Geoffrey 291
What world religions teach. London, Harrap [Mystic, Conn., Verry, 1966, c.1963] 223p. 22cm. Bibl. [BL80.2.P35] 64-36019 3.50 bds.,
1. Religions. I. Title.

PFLEIDERER, Otto, 1839-1908. 201
Religion and historic faiths, by Otto Pfleiderer ... translated from the German by Daniel A. Huebsch, PH. D. Aughotized ed. New York, B. W. Huebsch, 1907. 291 p. 19 cm. "The lectures here published were delivered at the University of Berlin during the last winter semester."--Pref., dated March, 1906. [BL80.P52] 7-29077
1. Religions. 2. Religion—Philosophy. I. Huebsch, Daniel Adolph, 1871- tr. II. Title.

PIKE, Samuel, 1717?-1773. 244
Religious cases of conscience answered in an evangelical manner, at the casuistical lecture, in little St. Helen's, Bishopsgate-street. By S. Pike and S. Hayward. To which is now added, The spiritual companion; or, The professing Christian tried at the bar of God's word: being some pious thoughts offered in answer to several practical questions, first published in the Spiritual magazine. And some free thoughts on the character of the happy man ... Philadelphia, Printed for Robert Campbell, 1794. viii, 527 p. 17 cm. "The spiritual companion ... To which is prefixed the touchstone of saving faith: by Samuel Pike": p. [333]-527. [BV4500.P5 1794] 17-31583
I. Hayward, Samuel, joint author. II. Title. III. Title: The spiritual companion.

POTTER, Charles Francis, 1885-1962.
The faiths men live by. Englewood Cliffs, N.J., Prentice-Hall [1960, c1954] 323 p. 68-14712
1. Religions. 2. Sects—U.S. I. Title.

POTTER, Charles Francis, 1885-1962. 280
The faiths men live by. New York, Prentice-Hall [1954] 323 p. 22 cm. [BL80.P59] 54-5679
1. Religions. 2. Sects—U.S. I. Title.

RADHAKRISHNAN. SARVEPALLI Sir 1888- 290
East and west in religion. London, G. Allen & Unwin [dist. New York, Barnes & Noble 1964] 146p. 1 l. 20cm. First pub. in 1933. 34-11195 2.00 bds.,
1. Religions. 2. Religion—Philosophy. I. Title.
Previously distributed by Macmillan.

RAMSEY, Ian T
Religious language; an empirical placing of theological phrases. New York, Macmillan [1963, 1957] 221 p. (Macmillan paperbacks, 129) 65-22256
I. Title.

RANDALL, John Herman, 1871- ed. 201
The unity of religions; a popular discussion of ancient and modern beliefs, edited by J. Herman Randall, D. D. and J. Gardner Smith, M. D. ... New York, T. Y. Crowell & co. [1910] ix, 362 p. 22 cm. [BL80.R23] 10-21150
1. Religions. I. Smith, J. Gardner, 1861- joint ed. II. Title.

RAWLINSON, George, 1812-1902. 290
... The religions of the ancient world, including Egypt, Assyria and Babylonia, Persia, India, Phoenicia, Eturia, Greece, Rome. By George Rawlinson ... New York, J. Fitzgerald [1884] cover-title, 95 p. 25 cm. (Humboldt library. no. 62) [BL96.R3 1884] 41-30616
1. Religions. I. Title.

REID, Gilbert, 1857-1927. 290
A Christian's appreciation of other faiths; a study of the best in the world's greatest religions, by Rev. Gilbert Reid ... Chicago, London, The Open court publishing company, 1921. 305 p. 20 1/2 cm. [BL80.R27] 21-15195
1. Religions. I. Title.

REID, John Morrison, 1820-1896, ed. 290
Doomed religious: a series of essays on great religions of the world; with a preliminary essay on primordial religion, and a supplemental essay on Lifeless and corrupt forms of Christianity. Ed. by Rev. J. M. Reid ... New York, Phillips & Hunt; Cincinnati, Walden & Stowe, 1884. 455 p. 19 cm. Contents.The primordial religion, by Rev. J. M. Reid.--Mohammedanism, by R. C. Bose.--Brahmanism, by Rev. T. J. Scott--Parseeism, by Rev. J. M. Thoburn.--Buddhism, by E. Wentworth.--Taoism, by Rev. V. C. Hart.--Shintoism, by Rev. R. S. Maclay.--Confucianism, by Rev. S. L. Baldwin.--Lifeless and corrupt forms of Christianity, by Rev. C. H. Fowler.--List of books on the subjects of the preceding essays (p. 452-455) [BL80.R28] 22-12522
1. Religions. I. Title.

REITMEISTER, Louis Aaron. 290
Paradise found; a philosophical history by Louis Aaron Reitmesiter. New York, F. H. Hitchcock, 1927. 5 p. l., ix-x, 311 p. 21 1/2 cm. "Author's autograph edition. This special edition has been printed for advance subscribers and each copy is numbered and signed by the author. This copy is number 88." [BL85.R35 1927] 27-17836
1. Religions. 2. History. I. Title.

RELIGIOUS progress on the Pacific slope; addresses and papers at the celebration of the semi-centennial anniversary of Pacific school of religion, Berkeley, California. Boston, Chicago, The Pilgrim press [c1917] vi p., 3 l., [3]-326 p. ports. (incl. front.) 21 cm. "Foreword" signed: Charles Sumner Nash, John Wright Buckham, editors. [BR550.R4] 17-29981
I. Nash, Charles Sumner, 1856-1926, ed. II. Buckham, John Wright, 1864- joint ed.

RELIGIOUS services and sermonettes around the year for children. [3rd ed.] New York, American Council for Judaism [1956] Various pagings, 28cm.
I. Baron, Samuel Halevi. II. American Council for Judaism.

RELIGIOUS systems of the world; a contribution to the study of comparative religion. A collection of addresses delivered at South Place institute, now rev. and in some cases rewritten by the authors, together with some others specially written for this volume. London, S. Sonnenschein & co., lim. New York, E. P. Dutton & co., 1902. viii, 824 p. 22 1/2 cm. (On cover: The half guinea international library) Preface signed: Wm. Sheowring, Conrad W. Thies, Hon. secs. Institute committee. [BL80.R35 1902] 4-4198 290
1. Religions. I. South Place institute, London.

RICE, Edward. 291
The five great religions. Photos. by the author. New York, Four Winds Press [1973] 180 p. illus. 26 cm. [BL80.2.R49] 72-87074 7.46
1. Religions. I. Title.

RIEPEN, Harry O 209
Mankind and religion: past, present, future. Kendall, Fla., Kendall Pub. Co. [c1959] 454p. 21cm. [BL80.2.R5] 60-20387
1. Religions. 2. Religion. I. Title.

[ROBBINS, Thomas] 1777-1856, comp. 201
All religions and religious ceremonies: in two parts. Pt. i. Christianity, Mahometanism, and Judaism. To which is added a Tabular appendix, by Thomas Williams. Exhibiting the present state of the world as to religion, population, religious toleration, government, &c. Pt. ii. A view of the history, religion, manners and customs of the Hindoos. By William Ward. Together with the religion and ceremonies of other pagan nations. Hartford, O. D. Cooke & sons, 1823. viii, [v]-viii, [9]-208, 29, [2], iv, 180 p. plates. 19 cm. Part ii has subtitle: A view of the idolatry of the Hindoos ... by William Ward, of serampore, abridged from his original work in 3 volumes. [BL80.R6] 30-23130
1. Religions. 2. Hindus. I. Ward, William, 1769-1823. II. Williams, Thomas. III. Title.

ROBERTSON, John Mackinnon, 1856-1933. 291.6'3
Pagan Christs. [Introd. by Hector Hawton] New Hyde Park, N.Y., University Books [1967] 171 p. 22 cm. [BL85.R6 1967] 66-23914
1. Religions. 2. Messiah—Comparative studies. I. Title.

ROBINSON, Frank A. 261
Religious revival and social betterment, by F. A. Robinson... Boston, The Gorham press, 1918. 54 p. 19 cm. (Lettered on cover: Library of religious thought) $0.75. [BV625.R6] 18-13282
I. Title.

ROMNEY, Thomas Cottam, 1876- 290
World religions in the light of Mormonism, by Thomas Cottam Romney ... [Independence, Mo., Press of Zion's printing and publishing company, 1946] xi, 427 p. 20 cm. Published serially in the "Liahona" over a period of two years. cf. Pref. [BL85.R66] 47-662
1. Religions. 2. Mormons and Mormonism. I. Title.

ROSS, Floyd Hiatt.
The great religions by which men live, by Floyd H. Ross and Tynette Hills. Greenwich, Conn., Fawcett Publications [1961] 192 p. (Premier book, d 120) Fawcett world library. "Former title: Questions that matter most asked by the world's religions." 63-63062
1. Religions. I. Hills, Tynette Wilson, 1926- joint author. II. Title.

ROSS, Floyd Hiatt. 290
Questions that matter most, asked by the world's religions, by Floyd H. Ross and Tynette W. Hills. With a foreword by Vergilius Ferm. Boston, Beacon Press [1954] Boston, Beacon Press [1954] 266p. illus. 22cm. 26p. 23cm. --A guide for teachers using Questions that matter most, asked by the world's religions, by Floyd H. Ross and Tynette Wilson Hills. [BL80.R65] 54-10685
1. Religions. I. Hills, Tynette Wilson, 1926 joint author. II. Title.

SABATIER, Auguste, 1839-1901. 280
Religions of authority and the religion of the spirit, by Auguste Sabatier...tr. by Louise Seymour Houghton New York, McClure, Phillips & co., 1904. xxxiii, 410 p. 23 1/2 cm. Prefactory note signed: Frankline Sabatier. "This volume forms a sequel to the work which the author published in 1897, under the title, 'Outlines of a philosophy of religion based upon psychology and history'."--Pref. [Full name: Louis Auguste Sabatier] Contents.Introduction: The problem.--book 1. The Roman Catholic dogma of authority. --book 2. The Protestant dogma of authority.--book 3. The religion of the spirit. [BR121.S24 1904] 4-2152
I. Houghton, Mrs. Louise (Seymour) 1838-1920, tr. II. Title.

SABATIER, Auguste i.e. Louis Auguste, 1839-1901.
Religions of authority and the religion of the spirit, by Auguste Sabatier...tr. by Louise Seymour Houghton New York, McClure, Phillips & co., 1903. xxxii, 410 p. 23 1/2 cm. Prefatory note signed: Frankline Sabatier. "This volume forms a sequel to the work which the author published in 1897, under the title, 'Outlines of a philosophy of religion based upon psychology and history'."--Pref. Contents.Introduction: The problem.--book 1. The Roman Catholic dogma of authority.--book 2. The Protestant dogma of authority.--book 3. The religion of the spirit. 13-9987
I. Houghton, Mrs. Louise (Seymour) 1838-tr. II. Title.

SALTUS, Edgar Everston, 1855-1921. 291
The lords of the ghostland; a history of the ideal. [1st AMS ed.] New York, AMS Press [1970] 215 p. 23 cm. Reprint of the 1907 ed. [BL85.S3 1970] 71-116003 ISBN 0-404-05539-7
1. Religions. I. Title.

SALTUS, Edgar Evertson, 1855-1921. 290
The lords of the ghostland; a history of the ideal, by Edgar Saltus... New York, M. Kennerley, 1907. 215 p. 19 cm. [BL85.S3] 7-14564
1. Religious. I. Title.
Contents. omitted.

SCHAFFLER, Albert. 239
First religious instructions for little ones; the Catholic faith simply explained to the youngest pupils, with particular view to their practical moral training. With an appendix: Instructions on first confession, by the Rev. Albert Schaffler. New York, J. F. Wagner [c1901] iv, 208, xxxiv p. 20 1/2 cm. [BX930.S3] 5-6907
I. Title.

SCHAFFLER, Albert. 239
First religious instructions for little ones; the Catholic faith simply explained to the youngest pupils, with particular view to their practical moral training. With an appendix: Instructions on first confession, by the Rev. Albert Schaffler. New York, J. F. Wagner [c1901] iv, 208, xxxiv p. 20 1/2 cm. [BX930.S3] 5-6907
I. Title.

SCHMIDT, Paul Frederic, 1925- 291.82
Religious knowledge. [Glencoe, Ill.] Free Press [c.1961] 147p. 60-10901 4.00
I. Title.

SCHMUCKER, Samuel Mosheim, 1823-1863. 290
History of all religions; containing a statement of the origin, development, doctrines, forms of worship and government of all the religious denominations in the world, by Samuel M. Schmucker, LL. D. New York, John W. Lovell company [c1881] vi, 7-350 p. 20 cm. (Lettered on cover: Lovell's universal series) First published in 1859. [BL82.S4 1881] 32-16340
1. Religions. I. Title.

SCHMUCKER, Samuel Mosheim, 1823-1863. 290
History of all religions; containing a statement of the origin, development, doctrines, forms of worship and government of all the religious denominations in the world, by Samuel M. Schmucker, LL. D. Philadelphia, New York [etc.] Cottage library publishing house [1882] vi p., 1 l., 7-350 p. front. (ports.) plates. 20 cm. (Lettered on cover: Cottage library) First published in 1859. [BL82.S4] 30-18005
1. Religions. I. Title.

SCHNEIDER, Delwin Byron. 290
No God but God; a look at Hinduism, Buddhism, and Islam, by Del Byron Schneider. Minneapolis, Augsburg Pub. House [1969] vii, 136 p. illus., maps, ports. 20 cm. Bibliographical footnotes. [BL80.2.S33] 74-84806 2.95
1. Religions. I. Title.

SCHURE, Edouard, 1841-1929. 291
From Sphinx to Christ; an occult history. Blauvelt, N.Y., R. Steiner Publications, 1970. 284 p. 22 cm. Translation of L'evolution divine. Includes bibliographical references. [BL80.S28 1970] 70-130818 10.00
1. Religions. I. Title.

SCHURE, Edouard, 1841-1929. 290
The great initiates; a study of the secret history of religions. Tr. from French by Gloria Rasberry. Introd. by Paul M. Allen. [Steiner, dist. Stamford, Conn., Herman Pub., 1962, c.1961] 526p. 22cm. (St. George bks.) 61-8623 8.50
1. Religions I. Title.

SCHURE, Edouard, 1841-1929. 291
The great initiates : a study of the secret history of religions / by Edouard Schure ; translated from the French by Gloria Rasberry ; introd. by Paul M. Allen. Blauvelt, N.Y. : Multimedia Pub. Corp., 1976, c1961. 526 p. : port. ; 21 cm. (Steinerbooks) Translation of Les grands inities. Includes bibliographical references and index. [BL80.S33 1976] 76-360634 6.95
1. Religions. I. Title.

SCHURE, Edouard, 1841-1929. 201
The great initiates; sketch of the secret history of religions, by Edouard Schure. Translated by Fred Rothwell ... Philadelphia, David M'Kay co., 1922. 2 v. 19 cm. Contents.--i. Rama. Krishua. Hermes. Moses. Orpheus.--ii. Pythdgoras. Plate. Jesus. [BL80.S33 1922] 23-15281
1. Religious. I. Rothwell, Fred, 1889- tr. II. Title.

SCHURE, Edouard, 1841-1929. 291
The great initiates : a study of the secret history of religions / by Edouard Schure ; translated from the French by Gloria Rasberry ; introd. by Paul M. Allen. San Francisco : Harper & Row, 1980. p. cm. Translation of Les grands inities. Includes bibliographical references and index. [BL80.S33 1980] 79-3597 ISBN 0-06-067125-4 pbk. : 8.95
1. Religions. I. Title.

[SCOTT, Walter, Sir bart.] 1771-1832.
Religious discourses. By a layman. Philadelphia, Carey, Lea and Carey, 1828. viii p., 1 l., [11]-79 p. 20 cm. [PR5322.R4 1828 a] 35-34192
I. Title.
Contents omitted.

SHEPHERD, Robert Perry.
Religious pedagogy in the modern Sunday school, by Robert Perry Shepherd ... St. Louis, Mo., Christian publishing company, 1911. 108 p. 19 cm. $0.25 (Advanced teacher-training course, vol. IV). On cover: Front rank teacher training series. vol. IV--Advanced standard course. 11-10196
I. Title.

SHOTWELL, James Thomson, 1874- 230
...The religious revolution of to-day, by James T. Shotwell... Boston and New York, Houghton Mifflin company, 1913. viii p., 1 l., 162 p. 19 1/2 cm. (Half-title: The William Brewster Clark memorial lectures, 1913) $1.10 [BR479.S5 1913] 13-23245
I. Title.

SHOTWELL, James Thomson, 1874- 230
The religious revolution of today, by James T. Shotwell... Boston and New York, Houghton Mifflin company, 1924. ix p., 2 l., 187 p. 19 cm. Second edition. [BR479.S5 1924] 24-26895
I. Title.

SIZOO, Joseph Richard, 1884- 232.9
The kingdom cometh; some aspects of the religion of Jesus, by Joseph Richard Sizoo, D.D. Washington, D. C. New York avenue Presbyterian church, 1930 5 p. l., [3]-184 p. front. (port.) 20 cm. Sermons. [BX9178.S522K5] 31-103
I. Title.

SMART, Ninian, 1927- 291
A dialogue of religions / Ninian Smart. Westport, Conn. : Greenwood Press, 1981, c1960. p. cm. Reprint of the ed. published by SCM Press, London, which was issued in series: The Library of philosophy and theology. Includes index. [BL425.S6 1981] 19 79-8730 ISBN 0-313-22187-1 lib. bdg. : 17.50
1. Religions. I. Title.

†SMART, Ninian, 1927- 291
The long search / Ninian Smart. 1st American ed. Boston : Little, Brown, c1977. 315 p. : ill. ; 26 cm. Includes index. Bibliography: p. [307] [BL80.2.S595 1977] 77-12285 ISBN 0-316-79875-4 : 17.50
1. Religions. 2. Religion. I. Title.

SMART, Ninian, 1927- 290
World religions: a dialogue. Harmondsworth, Penguin, 1966. 154 p. 18 1/2 cm. (Pelican books, A786) (B 66-10255) Originally published as A dialogue of religions. London, S. C. M. Press, 1960. [BL425.S6 1966] 66-75270
1. Religions. I. Title.

SMITH, Ann Eliza (Brainerd) "Mrs. J. G. Smith," 1818-1905. 290
From dawn to sunrise; a review, historical

and philosophical, of the religious ideas of mankind... By Mrs. J. Gregory Smith. Rouses Point, N.Y., Lovell printing and publishing co., 1876. 3 p. l., [9]-406 p. 19 1/2 cm. [BL80.S6] 30-23132
1. Religions. I. Title.

SMITH, Huston.
The religions of man. [New York] New American Library [1959] x, 336 p. 18 cm. (Mentor Book MD 253) Bibliographical footnotes: p. 323-332.
1. Religions. I. Title.

SMITH, Huston. 290
The religions of man. [1st ed.] New York, Harper [1958] 328 p. 22 cm. Includes bibliography. [BL80.S66] 56-11923
1. Religions.

*SMITH, Huston, 1919- 290
The religions of man. New York, Harper [1964, c.1958] 328p. 21cm. (CN/43) 1.95 pap.,
I. Title.

SMITH, James Ward, 1917-
... *Religious perspectives in American culture, culture.* Editors: James Ward Smith and A. Leland Jamison. Princeton, New Jersey, Princeton university press, 1961. 427 p. illus., plans. 23 cm. (Religion in American life. 2) "Princeton studies in American civilization. 5." Bibliographical footnotes.
I. Jamison, Albert Leland, 1911- II. Title.

SMITH, Robert Philip, 1863- 220
Religious optimism, by R. P. Smith... Boston, Mass., The Stratford company [c1922] 8 p. l., 189 p. 19 1/2 cm. [BR125.S65] 23-98
I. Title.

SMITH, Wilfred Cantwell, 290
1916-
The faith of other men. [New York] New American Library [1963] 140 p. 21 cm. [BL85.S5 1963] 63-21610
1. Religions. 2. Christianity and other religions. I. Title.

SODERBLOM, Nathan, Abp., 291
1866-1931.
The living God : basal forms of personal religion / by Nathan Soderblom ; with a biographical introd. by Yngve Brilioth. New York : AMS Press, 1979. p. cm. Translation of Den levande Guden. Reprint of the 1933 ed. published by Oxford University Press, London, which was issued as Gifford lectures, 1931. Includes index. Bibliography: p. [BL80.S6713 1979] 79-17706 32.50
1. Religions. 2. Religion—History. 3. Revelation. 4. Religion—Philosophy. 5. Christianity and other religions. I. Title. II. Series: Gifford lectures ; 1931.
Contents omitted

SODERBLOM, Nathan, Abp., 291
1866-1931.
The living God : basal forms of personal religion / by Nathan Soderblom ; with a biographical introd. by Yngve Brilioth. 1st AMS ed. New York : AMS Press, 1979. xxix, 398 p. : 23 cm. Translation of Den levande Guden. Reprint of the 1933 ed. published by Oxford University Press, London, which was issued as Gifford lectures, 1931. Includes index. Contents.Contents.—Training and inspiration in primitive religion.—Religion as method. Yoga.—Religion as psychology. Jinism and Hinayana.—Religion as devotion. Bhakti.—Religion with a salvation fact. Mahayana. Bhakti in Buddhism.—Religion as fight against evil. Zarathustra.—Socrates. The religion of good conscience.—Religion as revelation in history.—The religion of incarnation.—Continued revelation. Bibliography: p. [387]-392. [BL80.S6713 1979] 77-27196 32.50
1. Religions. 2. Religion—History. 3. Revelation. 4. Religion—Philosophy. 5. Christianity and other religions. I. Title. II. Series: Gifford lectures ; 1931.

SOPER, Edmund Davison, 1876- 290
... *The faiths of mankind,* by Edmund Davison Soper ... written under the direction of Sub-committee on college courses, Sunday school council of evangelical denominations, and Committee on voluntary study, Council of North American student movements. New York, Association press, 1918. viii, 165 p. 17 cm. (College voluntary study courses. 3d year--pt. II) [BL80.S7] 18-3456
1. Religions. I. Title.

SOPER, Edmund Davison, 1876- 290
The religions of mankind, by Edmund Davison Soper ... New York, Cincinnati, The Abingdon press [c1921] 2 p. l., [3]-344 p. 21 1/2 cm. "Suggestions for further study" at end of each chapter. [BL80.S75]
1. Religions. I. Title.

SOPER, Edmund Davison, 1876- 290
The religions of mankind [by] Edmund Davison Soper. Rev. ed., enl. and partly rewritten. New York, Cincinnati [etc.] The Abingdon press [c1938] 364 p. 21 1/2 cm. "First edition printed April, 1921 ... New edition, reset, 1938." "Suggestions for further study" at end of each chapter. [BL80.S75 1938] 38-30986
1. Religions. I. Title.

SOPER, Edmund Davison, 1876- 290
1961.
The religions of mankind. 3d ed., rev. New York, Abingdon-Cokesbury Press [1951] 253 p. 24 cm. [BL80.S75 1951] 51-13635
1. Religions.

SPICE, Marjorie.
Junior teacher's guide to accompany; the mysterious Mr. Cobb. New York, Friendship Press [1967] 64 p. 19 cm. Accompanied by: Myra Scovel, The mysterious Mr. Cobb; Myra Scovel, The World's children in pictures: ways they worship. 68-70211
1. Religions. I. Title.

SPIEGELBERG, Frederic, 1897- 290
Living religions of the world. Englewood Cliffs, N. J., Prentice-Hall, 1956. xii, 511p. illus. 22cm. Bibliography: p. 487-408. [BL80.S76] 56-11009
1. Religions. 2. Religion—Philosophy. I. Title.

SPITTLER, Russell P. 280
Cults and isms; twenty alternates to evangelical Christianity. Grand Rapids, Baker Bk. [1963, c.1962] 143p. 23cm. Bibl. 62-21702 2.95
1. Religions. I. Title.

SRIVASTAVA, Rama Shanker. 291
Comparative religion / by Rama Shanker Srivastava ; with a foreword by N. K. Devaraja. New Delhi : Munshiram Manoharlal Publishers, 1974, c1973. xv, 316 p. ; 23 cm. Includes index. Bibliography: p. [305]-311. [BL80.2.S67 1974] 74-904268 14.00
1. Religions. I. Title.
Distributed by South Asia Books.

STARKES, M. Thomas. 291
Today's world religions / by M. Thomas Starkes. New Orleans : Insight Press, c1978. 180 p. ; 22 cm. Includes bibliographies. [BL80.2.S69] 78-50683 ISBN 0-914520-11-3 : pbk. : 3.95
1. Religions. I. Title.
Publisher's address : P.O. Box 8369, New Orleans, LA 70182

STEVENS, Halsey R. 201
Faith and reason; heart, soul, and hand work. A concise account of the Christian religion, and of all the prominent religions before and since Christianity. By Halsey R. Stevens ... New York, C. P. Somerby, 1879. v, [7]-441 p. 20 cm. [BL80.S78] 30-23133
1. Religions. I. Title.

STILSON, Max 290
Major religions of the world. Grand Rapids, Mich., Zondervan [c.1964] 123p. 21cm. Bibl. 64-11951 1.95 bds.,
1. Religions. I. Title.

STILSON, Max. 221
Major religions of the world. Grand Rapids, Zondervan Pub. House [1964] 123 p. 21 cm. Bibliography: p. 113-123. [BL80.2.S74] 64-11951
1. Religions. I. Title.

STOWE, Harriet Elizabeth 170
(Beecher) Mrs., 1811-1896.
Religious poems. By Harriet Beecher Stowe ... Boston and New York, Houghton, Miffin and company, 1895. iv, 107 p. illus. 18 1/3 cm. [PS2954.R5] 12-39168
I. Title.

STOWE, Harriet Elizabeth
(Beecher) Mrs., 1811-1896.
Religious studies, sketches and poems, by Harriet Beecher Stowe. Boston and New York, Houghton, Mifflin and company, 1896. 3 p. l., [v]-xlll, 361. [3] p. front. (port.) 19 1/3 cm. (Half-title: Riverside edition. The writings of Harriet Beecher Stowe ... vol. xv) Added collective t.-p., engraved. [PS2950.E96 vol. 15] 12-39181
I. Title.

STREIKER, Lowell D. 200
The gospel of irreligious religion; insights for uprooted man from major world faiths [by] Lowell D. Streiker. New York, Sheed and Ward [1969] xix, 169 p. 21 cm. Includes bibliographical references. [BL85.S73] 75-82603 4.95
1. Religions. 2. Religion. I. Title.

SUMRALL, Lester Frank, 1913- 291
Where was God when pagan religions began? / By Lester Sumrall. Nashville : Nelson, c1980. 165 p. ; 21 cm. Includes bibliographical references. [BL80.2.S87] 80-17729 pbk. : 3.95
1. Religions. 2. Paganism. I. Title.

TANNER, Florice. 291
The mystery teachings in world religions. Wheaton, Ill., Theosophical Pub. House [1973] 192 p. 21 cm. (A Quest book original) Includes bibliographical references. [BL80.2.T29] 73-8887 ISBN 0-8356-0439-X 2.45 (pbk.)
1. Religions. I. Title.

THEBAUD, Augustus J., 1807- 290
1885.
Gentilism: religion previous to Christianity. By Rev. Aug. J. Thebaud, S.J. New York, D. & J. Sadlier & company, 1876. xv p., 1 l., 525 p. 24 cm. [BL85.T4] 30-23160
1. Religions. I. Title.

THOMPSON, Charles Lemuel, 277.
1839-1924.
The religious foundations of America; a study in national origins, by Charles Lemuel Thompson ... New York, Chicago [etc.] Fleming H. Revell company [c1917] 307 p. 21 cm. Bibliography: p. 301-302. [BR520.T4] 17-27668
I. Title.

TISDALL, William St. Clair
Towers.
Comparative religion, by W. St. Clair Tisdall... London, New York [etc.] Longmans, Green and co., 1909. 1 p. l., v-xiii, 15-132 p. 18 cm. A 11
1. Religions. I. Title.

TRAPP, Jacob, 1899- 200
The light of a thousand suns; mystery, awe, and renewal in religion. Photos. by Bruce Roberts. [1st ed.] New York, Harper & Row [1973] ix, 149 p. illus. 14 x 21 cm. Includes bibliographical references. [BL80.2.T7 1973] 72-78061 ISBN 0-06-068431-3 3.50
1. Religions. 2. Religion. I. Title.

TRUST, Josephine de Croix, 212
1886-
Superet atom aura science, light law and order; 12 lessons, class and home course [by] Scientist Dr. J. C. Trust ... [Los Angeles, Superet press, 1946] 98, [2] p. 21 1/2 cm. [BP605.T716] 47-17938
I. Aura. II. Title.

TRUST, Josephine de Croix, 212
1886-
Superet atom aura science, light law and order; 12 lessons, class and home course [by] Scientist Dr. J. C. Trust ... [Los Angeles, Superet press, 1946] 98, [2] p. 21 1/2 cm. [BP605.T716] 47-17938
I. Aura. II. Title.

[TRUST, Josephine de Croix] 212
1886-
Superet light doctrine; Jesus Christ's religion; fathomless love to God ... [Los Angeles] First Superet light doctrine church, c1944. 3 p. l., [9]-910 p., 5 l. col. plates. 17 cm. [BP605.T72] 45-18650
I. Los Angeles. First Superet light doctrine church. II. Title.

[TRUST, Josephine de Croix] 212
1886-
Superet light doctrine; Jesus Christ's religion; fathomless love to God ... [Los Angeles] First Superet light doctrine church, c1944. 3 p. l., [9]-910 p., 5 l. col. plates. 17 cm. [BP605.T72] 45-18650
I. Los Angeles. First Superet light doctrine church. II. Title.

VAIL, Albert Ross, 1880- 200
Transforming light; the living heritage of world religions [by] Albert Vail and Emily McClellan Vail. [1st ed.] New York, Harper & Row [1970] xvii, 451 p. 24 cm. [BL80.2.V3 1970] 70-85065 12.50
1. Religions. 2. Religion. I. Vail, Emily McClellan, joint author. II. Title.

VOS, Howard Frederic. 290.82
1925- ed.
Religions in a changing world, a presentation of world religion, in the mid-twentieth century facing the ouslaughts of rising nationalism, communism, and increasing mass communication. Chicago, Moody Press [1959] 441 p. illus., ports. 24 cm. Includes bibliographies. [BL80.2.V6] 59-3137
1. Religions. I. Title.

VOS, Johannes G. 261.2
A Christian introduction to religions of the world. Grand Rapids, Mich., Baker Bk. [c.] 1965. 79p. 19cm. [BL80.2.V63] 65-5709 1.50 pap.,
1. Religions. 2. Christianity and other religions. I. Title.

VOSS, Carl Hermann. 290
In search of meaning; living religions of the world. Illustrated by Eric Carle. Cleveland, World Pub. Co. [1968] 191 p. illus. 24 cm. (Excalibur books) Bibliography: p. 173-182. [BL80.2.V66 1968] 67-23356
1. Religions. I. Title.

WACH, Joachim, 1898-
Types of religious experience, Christian and non-Christian. Chicago, University of Chicago Press [1951] xvi, 275 p. 22 cm. Contents.CONTENTS. -- The place of the history of religions in the study of theology. -- Universals in religion. -- The concept of the 'classics' in the study of religions. -- The idea of man in the Near Eastern religions. -- Spiritual teachings in Islam with special reference to al-Hujwiri. -- The study of Mahayana Buddhism. -- Caspar Schwenckfeld: a pupil and a teacher in the school of Christ -- The role of religion in the social philosophy of Alexis de Tocqueville. -- Church, denomination and sect. -- Rudolf Otto and The idea of the holy. Bibliographical references included in "Notes" (p. 232-272) 51-9885
1. Religions. 2. Philosophy and religion. 3. Psychology, Religious. I. Title.

WACH, Joachim, 1898-1955 290
The comparative study of religions. Ed., introd. by Joseph M. Kitagawa. New York, Columbia [1961, c.1958] 231p. Bibl. 1.75 pap.,
1. Religious. I. Title.

WACH, Joachim, 1898-1955. 290
The comparative study of religions. Edited with an introd. by Joseph M. Kitagawa. New York, Columbia University Press, 1958. 231 p. 23 cm. (Lectures on the history of religions, sponsored by the American Council of Learned Societies, new ser., no. 4) Includes bibliography. [BL25.L4 no. 4] 58-9237
1. Religions. I. Title.

WARREN, William Fairfield, 290
1833-1929.
The religions of the world and the world-religion. An introduction to their scientific study. By William F. Warren. Boston, 1895. 135 p. forms. 21 1/2 x 18 cm. With blank leaves for notes, part of which are included in paging. [BL82.W3 1895] 30-18007
1. Religions. 2. Religion—Philosophy. I. Title.

WARREN, William Fairfield, 290
1833-1929.
The religions of the world and the world-religion; an outline for personal and class use, by William Fairfield Warren ... New York, Eaton & Mains; Cincinnati, Jennings & Graham [c1911] xiv, 103 p. incl. front. forms. 21 1/2 x 18 cm. [BL82.W3 1911] 11-26186

1. Religions. 2. Religion—Philosophy. I. Title.

WATTS, Harold Holliday, 1906- 290
The modern reader's guide to religions. New York, Barnes & Noble [1964] xi, 620 p. 24 cm. Bibliography: p. 587-597. [BL80.2.W3] 64-17645
1. Religions. I. Title.

WATTS. HAROLD HOLLIDAY., 1906- 290
The modern reader's guide to religions. New York, Barnes & Noble [1968] xi, 620p. 22cm. Bibl. [BL80.2.W3] 64-17645 3.50 pap.,
1. Religions. I. Title.

WETHERILL, Francis Macomb, 1883- 290
The heart's true home; appreciation of religious beliefs [by] Francis M. Wetherill ... Boston, R. G. Badger [c1930] 3 p. l., 9-136 p. 19 1/2 cm. Bibliography: p. 130-136. [BL82.W4] 30-12632
1. Religions. I. Title.

WHALEN, William Joseph. 291
Other religions in a world of change / William J. Whalen, Carl J. Pfeifer. Notre Dame, Ind. : Ave Maria Press, [1974] 127 p. : ill. ; 21 cm. Selected articles which appeared in the weekly NC News Service Know your faith columns in 1973. Includes index. Bibliography: p. 121-124. [BL80.2.W45] 74-81341 ISBN 0-87793-075-9 : 1.75
1. Religions. 2. Sects. I. Pfeifer, Carl J. II. Title.

WHAT the world believes, 201
the false and the true, embracing the people of all races and nations, their peculiar teachings, rites, ceremonies ... from the earliest pagan times to the present, to which is added an account of what the world believes to-day, by countries ... Written and prepared by Albert G. [i.e. L.] Rawson, esq., John Gilmary Shea, LL.D., Rev. C. M. Butler [etc.] ... George J. Hagar, editor. New York, Gay brothers & company [1886] v, [2], 9-629, [1], 85 p. front., illus., plates, ports. 23 cm. "Biographies": 85 p. at end. [BL80.W5 1886] 30-23136
1. Religions. I. Rawson, Albert Leighton, 1828-1902. II. Hagar, George Jotham, 1846-1921, ed.

WHAT the world believes, 201
the false and the true, embracing the people of all races and nations, their peculiar teachings, rites, ceremonies ... from the earliest pagan times to the present, to which is added an account of what the world believes today, by countries ... Written and prepared by Albert L. Rawson, esq., John Gilmary Shea, LL.D., Rev. C. M. Butler [etc.] ... George J. Hagar, editor. New York, Gay brothers & company [1888] v, [2], 9-647, [1], 85 p. front., illus., plates, ports. 23 cm. "Biographies": 85 p. at end. [BL80.W5 1888] 30-23137
1. Religions. I. Rawson, Albert Leighton, 1828-1902. II. Hagar, George Jotham, 1848-1921, ed.

WHITSON, Robley Edward. 291
The coming convergence of world religions. New York, Newman Press [1971] xiii, 209 p. 24 cm. Includes bibliographical references. [BL85.W47] 74-162344 6.50
1. Religions. 2. Theology. I. Title.

WIDGERY, Alban Gregory, 1887- 290
Living religions and modern thought, by Alban G. Widgery ... New York, Round table press, inc., 1936. ix, 306 p. 22 1/2 cm. Bibliographical references in "Notes" (p. 283-302) [BL85.W5] 36-22226
1. Religions. 2. Religion—Philosophy. I. Title.

WIDNEY, Joseph Pomeroy, 1841-1938. 290
The genesis and evolution of Islam and Judaeo-Christianity, by J. P. Widney ... Los Angeles, Calif., Pacific publishing company [c1932] xv, 238 p. front. (port.) 23 1/2 cm. "Companion [book to] 'The faith that has come to me'."--Foreword. [BL80.W63] 32-14993
1. Religions. 2. Religions (Proposed, universal, etc.) I. Title.

WILLIAMS, David Rhys, 1890- 290
World religions and the hope for peace; with a pref. by John Haynes Holmes. Boston, Beacon Press 1951. 221 p. 22 cm. [BL80.W65] 51-14426
1. Religions. I. Title.

WILSON, Howard A. 261.2
Invasion from the East / Howard A. Wilson. Minneapolis : Augsburg Pub. House, c1978. 160 p. ; 20 cm. Includes bibliographical references. [BL80.2.W56] 78-52203 ISBN 0-8066-1671-7 : 3.95
1. Religions. 2. Christianity and other religions. I. Title.

WINDLE, Bertram Coghill Alan, Sir 1858-1929. 201
Religions past & present; an elementary account of comparative religion, by Bertram C. A. Windle ... New York, London, The Century co. [c1927] x, 306 p. 20 1/2 cm. "Bibliographical note": p. 287-298. [BL80.W66] 27-18915
1. Religions. 2. Religion—Hist. I. Title.

WOLCOTT, Leonard T. 200
Religions around the world, by Leonard and Carolyn Wolcott. Nashville, Abingdon Press [1967] 191 p. col. illus. 25 cm. [BL92.W6] 67-17382
1. [Religions.] 2. Religions—Juvenile literature. I. Wolcott, Carolyn Muller, joint author. II. Title.

WOODWARD, Hugh McCurdy, 1881- 201
Humanity's greatest need; the common message of the world's great teachers, by Hugh McCurdy Woodward ... New York, London, G. P. Putnam's sons, 1932. xii p., 1 l., 15-326 p. 21 cm. "Books referred to in text and books suggested for reading": p. 323-326. [BL80.W7] 32-34912
1. Religions. 2. Religion—Philosophy. 3. Conduct of life. 4. Education—Philosophy. I. Title.

THE world's great religions,
by the editorial staff of Life. Life special ed. for young readers. New York, Golden Press [c1958] 192p. illus. 29cm. [A Deluxe golden book]
1. Religions. I. Life (Chicago)

WORLD'S parliament of religions, Chicago, 1893. 200.822
A chorus of faith as heard in the Parliament of religions, held in Chicago, Sept. 10-27, 1893, with an introduction by Jenkin Lloyd Jones. Chicago, The Unity publishing company, 1893. 333 p. 19 1/2 cm. [BL74.W6 1893] 33-15306
1. Religions. I. Jones, Jenkin Lloyd, 1842-1918, ed. II. Title.

WORLD'S parliament of religions, Chicago, 1893. 206.
The World's congress of religions; the addresses and papers delivered before the Parliament, and an abstract of the congresses held in the Art institute, Chicago ... August 25 to October 15, 1893, under the auspices of the World's Columbian exposition ... With marginal notes. Edited by J. W. Hanson ... Chicago, W. B. Conkey company, 1894. 1196 p. incl. front., illus., plates, ports. 24 x 18 1/2 cm. [BL21.W8H3] 9-5866
1. Religions. I. Hanson, John Wesley, 1823-1901, ed. II. Title.

WORLD'S religious parliament extension.
The World's parliament of religions and the Religious parliament extension; a memorial published by the Religious parliament extension committee. Popular edition, enlarged by the publication of the main responses received in acknowledgment of the memorial. Chicago, The Open court publishing company, 1899. 1 p. l., 56 p. front. 23 1/2 cm. 3-18356
I. Title.

YAGER, Thomas C. 1918- 291
The best in life / by Thomas C. Yager. [Los Angeles? : Yager?, 1975] vii, 101 p. : ports. ; 25 cm. Includes bibliographies and index. [BL80.2.Y25] 75-15008
1. Religions. I. Title.

ZAEHNER, Robert Charles. 291
At sundry times : an essay in the comparison of religions / by R. C. Zaehner. Westport, Conn. : Greenwood Press, 1977, c1958. 230 p. ; 22 cm. Reprint of the ed. published by Faber and Faber, London. Includes bibliographical references and index. [BL80.2.Z27 1977] 76-49621 ISBN 0-8371-9354-0 lib. bdg. : 15.00
1. Religions. 2. Christianity and other religions. I. Title.

ZAEHNER, Robert Charles. 290
The comparison of religions. With a new pref. by the author. Boston, Beacon Press [1962, c1958] 230 p. 21 cm. (Beacon paperback no. LR15) [BL80.2.Z28 1962] 62-51998
1. Religions. I. Title.

ZAEHNER, Robert Charles.
The Comparison of religions. With a new preface by the author. Boston, Beacon [1962] 230 p. 64-10469
1. Religions. 2. Christianity and other religions. I. Title.

ZAEHNER, Robert Charles, ed. 290.82
The concise encyclopedia of living faiths. Contributors: A. L. Basham [and others. 1st ed.] New York, Hawthorn Books [1959] 431 p. illus. (part col.) port. (1 col.) map. 26 cm. Includes bibliography. [BL80.2.Z3] 59-9601
1. Religions. I. Basham, Arthur Llewellyn. II. Title. III. Title: Living faiths.

ZEHAVI, A. M. 291
Handbook of the world's religions. Edited by A. M. Zehavi. New York, Watts, 1973. vii, 203 p. illus. 27 cm. Includes bibliographical references. [BL80.2.Z43] 73-9283 ISBN 0-531-02644-2 8.95
1. Religions. I. Title.

Religions—Addresses, essays, lectures.

AURORA, W. Va. Saint Paul's Lutheran Church. 284.1754
The Aurora documents: a accurate and complete translation and transcription of books i and ii of the original records of Saint Paul's Lutheran Church, Aurora, Preston Country, West Virgina, founded March 24, 1787, by Karl K. Gower. 1st ed. Oakland, Md., Sincell Pub. Co. [1957] 124p. illus. port. 23cm. [BX8076.A8S37] 57-8699
I. Gower, Karl K., ed. and tr. II. Title.

CONWAY, Moncure Daniel, 1832-1907. 290
Idols and ideals, with an essay on Christianity. By Moncure Daniel Conway ... New York, H. Holt and company, 1877. 5 p. l., [5]-214, 137 p. 19 1/2 cm. Erata slip inserted after p. 214. [BL87.C7] 30-23142
1. Religions—Addresses, essays, lectures. 2. Superstition. 3. Christianity. I. Title.

DAVISON, Phineas, d.1826.
[Phineas Davison's letter, to aged friends; and miscellaneous essays, in verse and prose; on divine and moral subjects ... Greenwich, Mass., Printed for the author by J. Howe, 1810] 2 v. in 1. 22 cm. Imperfect: t.-p. of v. 1 wanting. [PS1524.D2P5] A 32
I. Title.

ENELOW, Hyman, Gerson, 1876- 296
The diverse elements of religion, by H. G. Enelow. New York, The Bloch publishing co., 1924. 116 p. 18 1/2 cm. [BM565.E65] 24-10622
I. Title.

ENELOW, Hyman, Gerson, 1876- 296
The diverse elements of religion, by H. G. Enelow. New York, The Bloch publishing co., 1924. 116 p. 18 1/2 cm. [BM565.E65] 24-10622
I. Title.

FERM, Vergilius Ture Anselm, 1896- ed. 290
Forgotten religions, including some living primitive religions. Freeport, N.Y., Books for Libraries Press [1970, c1950] xv, 392 p. illus. 23 cm. (Essay index reprint series) Contents.Contents.—Editor's preface, by V. Ferm.—The dawn of religions, by P. Ackerman.—The religion of ancient Egypt, by S. A. B. Mercer.—Sumerian religion, by S. N. Kramer.—Assyro-Babylonian religion, by A. L. Oppenheim.—Hittite religion, by H. G. Guterbock.—The religion of the Canaanites, by T. H. Gaster.—Religion in prehistoric Greece, by G. E. Mylonas.—Mystery religions of Greece, by G. E. Mylonas.—The inhabited world, by C. A. Robinson, Jr.—Mithraism, by I. J. S. Taraporewala.—Manichaeism, by I. J. S. Taraporewala.—Mazdakism, by I. J. S. Taraporewala.—Old Norse religion, by M. Fowler.—Tibetan religion, by L. Anche.—The religion of the Australian aborigines, by A. P. Elkin.—South American Indian religions, by J. H. Steward.—Shamanism, by M. Eliade.—The religion of the Eskimos, by M. Lantis.—The religion of the Navaho Indians, by L. C. Wyman.—The religion of the Hopi Indians, by M. Titiev. Includes bibliographies. [BL87.F47 1970] 70-128240
1. Religions—Addresses, essays, lectures. I. Title.

HAYDON, Albert Eustace, 1880- ed. 290
Modern trends in world religions, edited by A. Eustace Haydon. Freeport, N.Y., Books for Libraries Press [1968] xiv, 255 p. 23 cm. (Essay index reprint series) Reprint of the 1934 ed. [BL80.H35 1968] 68-29214
1. Religions—Addresses, essays, lectures. I. Title.

HAYDON, Albert Eustace, 1880- ed. 290.4
Modern trends in world-religions; Haskell foundation institute: edited by A. Eustace Haydon. Chicago, Ill., The University of Chicago press, [1934] xiv, 255 p. 22 1/2 cm. (Half-title: The Haskell lectures in comparative religion) [BL80.H35] 35-192
1. Religions—Addresses, essays, lectures. I. Title.

HERVEY, James W. 290.81
Patterns in church history; essays on comparative religion, the Reformation, and John Wesley. [1st ed.] New York, Exposition Press [1963] 113 p. 21 cm. (An Exposition -- testament book) Includes bibliography. [BL87.114] 63-4295
1. Religions — Addresses, essays, lectures. I. Title.

JANES, George Milton, 1869- 261
The Pilgrim spirit, and other essays, by George Milton Janes. Pittsfield, Mass., Sun printing company, 1904. 95 p. 20 cm. [BR85.J37] 4-33393
I. Title.
Contents omitted.

KELLY, Cardinal Lyle. 200'.1
The role of the mind in the universe, by C. Lyle Kelly. Philadelphia, Dorrance [1969] 32 p. 22 cm. Bibliographical footnotes. [BL95.K43] 68-57733 3.00
1. Religions—Addresses, essays, lectures. I. Title.

LEAMING, Jeremiah, 1717-1804.
Dissertations upon various subjects, which may be well worth the attention of every Christian; and of real service to the sincere inquirer after true religion. By Jeremiah Leaming, A. M. rector of Christ's church, in Stratford ... Litchfield [Conn.] Reprinted by T. Collier, 1798. vi, [7]-68 p. 23 cm. [BX5929.L] A 33
I. Title.

LESSA, William Armand, ed. 200'.8
Reader in comparative religion : an anthropological approach / [edited by] William A. Lessa, Evon Z. Vogt ; with the assistance of John M. Watanabe. 4th ed. New York : Harper & Row, c1979. viii, 488 p. : ill. ; 26 cm. Includes index. Bibliography: p. 473-485. [BL80.2.L44 1979] 78-13409 ISBN 0-06-043991-2 pbk. : 16.95
1. Religions—Addresses, essays, lectures. I. Vogt, Evon Zartman, 1918- joint ed. II. Title.

MULLER, Friedrich Max, 1823-1900. 291
Introduction to the science of religion / Friedrich Max Muller. New York : Arno Press, 1978. ix, 403 p. ; 21 cm. (Mythology) Reprint of the 1873 ed. published by Longmans, Green, London. Includes bibliographical references. [BL87.M76 1978] 77-79145 ISBN 0-405-10554-1 lib bdg. : 24.00
1. Religions—Addresses, essays, lectures. I. Title. II. Series.

MULLER, Friedrich Max, 1823- 1900. 291
Theosophy : or, Psychological religion / by F. Max Muller. New York : AMS Press, [1975] p. cm. Reprint of the 1903 ed. published by Longmans, Green, London, which had originally been issued in series, Gifford lectures, 1892, and was reissued as no. 4 of the author's collected works in 1898. Includes index. Bibliography: p. [BL87.M765 1975] 73-18830 34.50
1. Religions—Addresses, essays, lectures. 2. Religion—Philosophy—Addresses, essays, lectures. 3. Psychology, Religious—Addresses, essays, lectures. 4. Theism—Addresses, essays, lectures. I. Title. II. Series: Gifford lectures, 1892.

PANIKKAR, Raymond, 1918- 291.1'72
The intrareligious dialogue / R. Panikkar. New York : Paulist Press, c1978. xxviii, 104 p. : ill. ; 24 cm. Includes bibliographical references and index. [BL87.P26] 78-58962 ISBN 0-8091-0273-0 : 5.95
1. Religions—Addresses, essays, lectures. 2. Christianity and other religions—Addresses, essays, lectures. I. Title.

PAUL Carus Memorial Symposium Peru, Ill., 1957 290.82
Modern trends in world religions. Edited by Joseph M. Kitagawa. La Salle, Ill., Open Court Pub. Co., [c.1959] 286p. 21cm. bibl. 60-1277 3.50
1. Religions—Addresses, essays, lectures. I. Kitagawa, Joseph Mitsuo, ed. II. Title.

PAUL Carus Memorial Symposium, Peru, Ill., 1957. 200'.8
Modern trends in world religions. Edited by Joseph M. Kitagawa. Freeport, N.Y., Books for Libraries Press [1972, c1959] xiv, 286 p. 22 cm. (Essay index reprint series) Bibliography: p. [283]-286. [BL87.P28 1957b] 72-5676 ISBN 0-8369-7294-5
1. Religions—Addresses, essays, lectures. I. Kitagawa, Joseph Mitsuo, 1915- ed. II. Title.

RADHAKRISHNAN, Sarvepalli, Sir 1888- 290
Eastern religions and western thought. 2d ed. London, Oxford University Press [1951] xiii, 906p. 23cm. 'Lectures ... gives in the years 1906-93 ... revised andslightly expanded.; [BL2003.R3 1951] 56-34044
1. Religions—Addresses, essays, lectures. 2. India—Religion. 3. Hinduism—Relations. 4. Philosophy, Comparative — Addresses, essays, lectures. I. Title.

RADHAKRISHNAN, Sarvepalli, Pres. India, 1888- 290
Eastern religions and Western thought. New York, Oxford University Press, 1959. 396p. 21cm. (A Galaxy book, GB27) 'Lectures ... given in the years 1936-38 ... revised and silghtly expanded.; Includes bibliography. [BL2003 R3 1959] 59-3890
1. Religions—Addresses, essays, lectures. 2. India—Religion. 3. Hinduism—Relations. 4. Philosophy, Comparative—Addresses, essays, lectures. I. Title.

RADHAKRISHNAN, Sarvepalli, Pres. India, 1888-
Eastern religions and western thought. 2d ed. [London] Oxford University Press [1958] 396 p. 23 cm. This ed. first published in 1940. 63-56311
1. Religions—Addresses, essays, lectures. 2. India—Religions. 3. Hinduism—Relations. 4. Philosophy, Comparative—Addresses, essays, lectures. I. Title.

RADHAKRISHNAN, Sarvepalli, Sir 1888- 290
Eastern religions and western thought, by S. Radhakrishnan. Oxford, The Claredon press, 1939. xiii, 394 p., 1 l. 23 cm. "Lectures ... given in the years 1936-8 ... revised and slightly expanded" -p. ix. [BL2003.R3] 39-8335
1. Religions—Addresses essays, lectures. 2. India—Religion. 3. Hinduism—Relations. I. Title.
Contens omitted.

A religion for the universal mind. New York, Comet Press Books, 1959. 70p. 20cm.
1. Religions—Addresses, essays, lectures. I. Johnson, Frend Irwin.

RENAN, Ernest, 1823-1892. 204
Studies of religious history and criticism. Authorized translation from the original French, by O. B. Frothingham. With a biographical introd. New York, Carleton, 1864. 394 p. 24 cm. On spine: Religious history and criticism. Most of the essays have been taken from the Etudes d'histoire religieuse. Full name: Joseph Ernest Renan. [BL27.R42] 49-32060
1. Religions—Addresses, essays, lectures. I. Frothingham, Octavius Brooks, 1822-1895, tr. II. Title.

ROSS, Robert, 1726-1799.
A plain address to the Quakers, Moravians, Separatists, Separate-Baptists, Rogerenes, and other enthuiasts; on immediate impulses and revelations, &c. By Robert Ross ... New Haven, Printed by Parker and comp. [1762] 213, [7] p. 19 cm. 11-31420
I. Title.

SLATER, Robert Henry Lawson. 290
World religions and world community. New York, Columbia University Press, 1963. 299 p. 23 cm. (Lectures on the history of religions, new ser., no. 6) [BL25.L4 no. 6] 63-9805
1. Religions — Addresses, essays, lectures. I. Title.

SMART, Ninian, 1927- 291.1'7
Beyond ideology, religion and the future of Western civilization / Ninian Smart. San Francisco : Harper & Row, c1981. p. cm. "Gifford lectures delivered in the University of Edinburgh, 1979-1980." Includes bibliographical references and index. [BL80.2.S593 1981] 19 81-47429 ISBN 0-06-067401-6 pbk. : 10.95 ISBN 0-06-067402-4 : 14.95
1. Religions—Addresses, essays, lectures. 2. Ideology—Addresses, essays, lectures. 3. Secularism—Addresses, essays, lectures. I. University of Edinburgh. II. Title.
Contents omitted.

SODERBLOM, Nathan, abp., 1866-1931. 290.4
The living God; basal forms of personal religion. The Gifford lectures, delivered in the University of Edinburgh in the year 1931, by Nathan Soderblom ... with a biographical introduction by Dr. Yngve Brilioth ... London, H. Milford, Oxford university press, 1933. xxix, 398 p., 1 l. front. (port.) 21 cm. "List of books quoted or referred to": p., [387]-392. [Full name: Lars Olof Jonathan Soderblom] Contents.--Training and inspiration in primitive religion.--Religion as method. Yoga.--Religion as psychology. Jinism and Hinayana.--Religion as devotion. Bhakti.--Religion with a 'salvation fact'. Mahayana. Bhakti in Buddhism.--Religion as fight against evil. Zarathushtra.--Socrates. The religion of good conscience.--Religion as revelation in history.--The religion of incarnation.--Continued revelation. [BL27.S55] 33-9561
1. Religions—Addresses, essays, lectures. 2. Religion—Hist. 3. Revelation. 4. Religion—Philosophy. 5. Christianity and other religions. I. Brilloth, Yngve Torgny, 1891- II. Title.

SODERBLOM, Nathan, [Lars Olaf Jonathan Soderblom.] abp. 1866-1931 290.4
The living God; basal forms of personal religion. The Gifford lectures, delivered in the Univ. of Edinburgh in the year 1931. [Gloucester, Mass., P. Smith, 1963] 398p. 21cm. (Beacon Pr. bk. rebound) Bibl. 4.50
1. Religions—Addresses, essays, lectures. 2. Religion—Hist. 3. Revelation. 4. Religion—Philosophy. 5. Christianity and other religions. I. Title.

SODERBLOM, Nathan [Lars Olof Jonathan Soderblom] abp., 1866-1931 290.4
The living God; basal forms of personal religion. The Gifford lectures, delivered in the Univ. of Edinburgh in the year 1931. Biographical introd. by Yngve Brilioth. Boston, Beacon [1962] 398p. 21cm. (LR 17) Bibl. 2.45 pap.,
1. Religions—Addresses, essays, lectures. 2. Religion—Hist. 3. Revelation. 4. Religion—Philosophy. 5. Christianity and other religions. I. Brilioth, Yngve Torgny, 1891. II. Title.

TIEBOUT, Harry M
Essays in comparative religion. Champaign, Ill., Stripes Pub. Co., c1961. 138 p. 28 cm. "Essays...designed as supplementary reading for Philosophy 110: World religions." 63-79235
1. Religions — Addresses, essays, lectures. I. Title.

WORDS of the world's religions : an anthology / Robert S. Ellwood, Jr. Englewood Cliffs, N.J. : Prentice-Hall, c1977. x, 421 p. ; 23 cm. Includes bibliographical references. Reading selections exploring the religious traditions of Judaism, Christianity, and Islam, in addition to Eastern religions and those of ancient Egypt and the Near East. [BL25.W67] 76-49545 ISBN 0-13-965004-0 pbk. : 7.95 291
1. Religions—Addresses, essays, lectures. 2. Religion—Addresses, essays, lectures. 3. [Religions.] I. Ellwood, Robert S., 1933-

Religions and science—1900—

HARPER, Samuel Alain, 1875- 215
Man's high adventure; with an introd. by A. J. Carlson. Chicago, R. F. Seymour [1955] 185p. 23cm. [BL240.H28] 56-4377
1. Religions and science—1900- I. Title.

Religions—Bibliography

ADAMS, Charles J., ed. 016.2
A reader's guide to the great religions. New York, Free Pr. [c.1965] xv, 364p. 24cm. [Z7833.A35] 65-15440 6.95
1. Religions—Bibl. I. Title.
Comprehensive, critical survey of the available literature on the history, beliefs, and institutions of Buddhism, Hinduism, Christianity, Judaism, and Islam. For the student, teacher, clergyman, and general reader.

ADAMS, Charles J., ed. 016.2
A reader's guide to the great religions / edited by Charles J. Adams. 2d ed. New York : Free Press, c1977. xvii, 521 p. ; 24 cm. Includes indexes. [Z7833.A35 1977] [BL80.2] 76-10496 ISBN 0-02-900240-0 : 14.95
1. Religions—Bibliography. I. Title.

HILLESHEIM, James W. 016.2
World religions; a selective bibliography [by] James W. Hillesheim. Anaheim, Calif., Yang-Yin Enterprises [1966] vi, 74 l. 28 cm. [Z7751.H6] 67-2189
1. Religions—Bibliography. I. Title.

NEWBERRY library, Chicago. 016.
... Religions: philosophy of religion, folklore, ethnic religions. Chicago [1925] x, 237 p. 26 cm. At head of title: The Newberry library. On verso of t.-p.: "150 copies multigraphed as manuscript 1925." Class B (Sections 7-9) [Z881.C525B] 26-15231
1. Religions—Bibl. 2. Religion—Philosophy—Bibl. 3. Folk-lore—Bibl. I. Title.

TAYLOR, Eugene. 016.291'095
An annotated bibliography in classical Eastern psychology; readily accessible paperback materials on the formative periods of India, Tibet, China, and Japan. Dallas, Essene Press [1973] vi, 28 p. 22 cm. [Z7751.T39] 74-165312
1. Religions—Bibliography. I. Title.

Religions Biography

ABBOTT, Benjamin, 1732-1796. 922.
Experience and gospel labors of the Rev. Benjamin Abbott; to which is annexed, a narrative of his life and death. By John Ffirth... New York, Carlton & Phillips, 1856. 264 p. 15 1/2 cm. [BX8495.A3A3 1856] 922
I. Ffirth, John, ed. II. Title.

ABBOTT, Benjamin, 1732-1796.
Experience and gospel labors of the Rev. Benjamin Abbott; to which is annexed a narrative of his life and death. By John Ffirth. New York, Pub. by T. Mason and G. Lane for the Methodist Episcopal church, 1836. 284 p. 14 1/2 cm. 8-36851
I. Ffirth, John. II. Title.

ABBOTT, Benjamin, 1732-1796. 922.773
The experience and gospel labours of the Rev. Benjamin Abbott. To which is annexed a narrative of his life and death: by John Ffirth ... Copy-right secured. Philadelphia: Printed by Solomon W. Conrad, for Ezekiel Cooper, no. 118, North Fourth-street, near the Methodist church. 1802. 240 p. 16 1/2 cm. [BX8495.A3A3 1802] 33-29257
I. Ffirth, John, ed. II. Title.

ABBOTT, Benjamin, 1732-1796. 922.773
The experience, and gospel labours, of the Rev. Benjamin Abbott; to which is annexed, a narrative of his life and death. by John Ffirth ... 4th ed. Copy-right secured. New York; published by Daniel Hitt andThomas Ware for the Methodist connection in the United States. John C. Totten, printer, 1813. iv, [5]-331 p. 14 cm. [BX8495.A3A3 1813] 30-29960
I. Ffirth, John, ed. II. Title.

ABBOTT, Benjamin, 1732-1796. 922.
The experience and gospel labours of the Rev. Benjamin Abbott; to which is annexed a narrative of his life and death. By John Ffirth... Harrisonburg: Printed by A. Davisson. for James A. Dillworth, Rockingham County, Virginia. 1820. 292 p. 17 1/2 cm. [BX8495.A3A3 1820] 8-25296
I. Ffirth, John, ed. II. Title.

ABBOTT, Benjamin, 1732-1796. 922.
Experience and gospel labours of the Rev. Benjamin Abbott; to which is annexed a narrative of his life and death. By John Ffirth ... New York, Pub. by J. Emory and B. Waugh for the Methodist Episcopal church, 1830. 211 p. 17 cm. On spine: Life of Abbott. [BX8495.A3A3 1830] 45-48152
I. Ffirth, John, ed. II. Title.

ABBOTT, Benjamin, 1782-1796. 922.773
Experience and gospel labours of the Rev. Benjamin Abbott; to which is annexed a narrative of his life and death. By John Ffirth... New York, Published by B. Waugh and T. Mason for the Sunday school union of the Methodist Episcopal church, 1838. 282 p. 14 cm. [BX8495.A3A3 1833] 12-17121
I. Ffirth, John, ed. II. Sunday-school union of the Methodist Episcopal church. III. Title.

ALLEN, Frank Gibbs, 1836-1887. 922.673
Autobiography of Frank G. Allen, minister of the gospel, and selections from his writings, Edited by Robert Graham ... Cincinnati, Guide printing & publishing co., 1887. xiii, 259 p. 21 1/2 cm. [BX7343.A6A3] 36-31086
I. Graham, Robert, 1822-1901, ed. II. Title.

ALLEN, Michael, 1927- 283'.0924
This time, this place. Indianapolis, Bobbs-Merrill [1971] viii, 170 p. 22 cm. Autobiographical. [BX5995.A54A3] 74-123221 4.95
I. Title.

ANDERSON, Edward M. 1886- 922
From ship to pulpit, an autobiography, by E. M. Anderson ... Forewords by Oswald J. Smith, D. D. [and] P. W. Philpott, D. D. Grand Rapids, Mich., Zondervan publishing house [1942] 134 p. 20 cm. Revised and enlarged edition of the author's From the ship to the pulpit published in 1922. [BV3785.A6A3 1942] 42-23499
I. Title.

ASHER, Jeremiah, b.1812. 286'.133'0924 B
Incidents in the life of the Rev. J. Asher. With an introd. by Wilson Armistead. Freeport, N.Y., Books for Libraries Press, 1971. 80 p. 23 cm. (The Black heritage library collection) Reprint of the 1850 ed. On spine: Life of Rev. J. Asher. [E185.97.A82 1971] 74-168506 ISBN 0-8369-8860-4
I. Title. II. Title: Life of Rev. J. Asher. III. Series.

ASHLEY, George Thomas. 230.
From bondage to liberty in religion; a

spiritual autobiography, by George T. Ashley. Boston, The Beacon press [c1919] 6 p. l., 226 p. 20 cm. [BX9841.A8] 20-446
I. Title.

ATKINS, Rebecca (Crittenden) Mrs. 1829- 920.7
"Truth stranger than fiction." Book of fate. Autobiography of Rebecca Atkins. Her life of fate ... Lincoln, Neb., 1896. 2 p. l., [3]-154 p. front. (port.) 19 x 15 cm. [BX8495.A85A3] 36-33595
I. Title.

BACUEZ, Louis.
Minor orders. By Rev. Louis Bacuez ... St. Louis, Mo. [etc.] B. Herder, 1912. x, 380 p. 16 cm. 13-1672 1.25
I. Title.

BAIRD, Charles Washington 1828-1887.
Memorials of the Rev. Charles W. Baird, D. D., for twenty-six years pastor of the Presbyterian church of Rye, New York, with a few selected sermons and sacred poems. New York and London, G. P. Putnam's sons, 1888. v, 235 p. front. (port.) pl. 23 cm. Prefatory note signed: M. E. B. (i. e. Margaret E. Baird) 5-5122
I. Baird, Margaret (Strang) Mrs. ed. II. Title.

BAIRD, Charles Washington 1828-1887.
Memorials of the Rev. Charles W. Baird, D. D., for twenty-six years pastor of the Presbyterian church of Rye, New York, with a few selected sermons and sacred poems. New York and London, G. P. Putnam's sons, 1888. v, 235 p. front. (port.) pl. 23 cm. Prefatory note signed: M. E. B. (i. e. Margaret E. Baird) 5-5122
I. Baird, Margaret (Strang) Mrs. ed. II. Title.

BANCROFT, Anne, 1923- 200'.92'2 B
Twentieth century mystics and sages / Anne Bancroft. Chicago : Regnery, 1976. p. cm. Includes bibliographical references and index. [BL72.B36] 76-153 ISBN 0-8092-8148-1. ISBN 0-8092-8237-2 pbk.
1. Religions—Biography. I. Title.

BAROODY, Anees Tannus, 1879-
Our man of patience, by Rev. Anees T. Broody, PH. D. Boston, New York [etc.] The Pilgrim press [c1915] 94 p. front., plates. 20 cm. Ornamental borders. 15-24852 1.00
I. Title.

BARRETT, Samuel, 1795-1866. 288
Memoir of the Rev. Samuel Barrett, D. D., with a selected series of his discourses. By Lewis G. Pray. Boston, W. V. Spencer, 1867. 4 p. l., 207 p. 18 cm. [BX9843.B2816M4] 34-4487
I. Pray, Lewis Glover, 1793-1882, ed. II. Title.

BARRETT, Samuel, 1795-1866. 288
Memoir of the Rev. Samuel Barrett, D. D., with a selected series of his discourses. By Lewis G. Pray. Boston, W. V. Spencer, 1867. 4 p. l., 207 p. 18 cm. [BX9843.B2816M4] 34-4487
I. Pray, Lewis Glover, 1793-1882, ed. II. Title.

BARROWS, Elijah Porter, 1807-1888. 922.573
Memoir of Everton Judson. By E. P. Barrows, jr. Boston, Crocker and Brewster, 1852. 212 p. front. (port.) 20 cm. [BX7260.J8B3] 36-2666
I. Judson, Everton, 1799-1848. II. Title.

BARROWS, Mary Eleanor. 285.
John Henry Barrows, a memoir, by his daughter, Mary Eleanor Barrows. Chicago, New York [etc.] Fleming H. Revell company, 1904. 4 p. l., [11]-450 p. front., ports. 21 cm. [BX9225.B39B3] 4-35740
I. Barrows, John Henry, 1847-1902. II. Title.

BARROWS, Mary Eleanor. 285.
John Henry Barrows, a memoir, by his daughter, Mary Eleanor Barrows. Chicago, New York [etc.] Fleming H. Revell company, 1904. 4 p. l., [11]-450 p. front., ports. 21 cm. [BX9225.B39B3] 4-35740
I. Barrows, John Henry, 1847-1902. II. Title.

BARRY, Joseph Gayle Hurd, 1858-1931. 922.342
Impressions and opinions, an autobiography, by J. G. H. Barry ... New York, E. S. Gorham, inc., 1931. vi p., 2 l., 302 p. front. (port.) 21 cm. [BX5995.B375A3] 32-877
I. Title.

BARRY, Joseph Gayle Hurd, 1858-1931. 922.342
Impressions and opinions, an autobiography, by J. G. H. Barry ... New York, E. S. Gorham, inc., 1931. vi p., 2 l., 302 p. front. (port.) 21 cm. [BX5995.B375A3] 32-877
I. Title.

BARRY, William Francis, 1849-1930. 922.
Memories and opinions, by William Barry ... London & New York, G. P. Putnam's sons, ltd. [1926] xiii p., 1 l., 302, [1] p. front. (port.) plates. 23 cm. [BX4705.B23A3] 27-18045
I. Title.

BARRY, William Francis, 1849-1930. 922.
Memories and opinions, by William Barry ... London & New York, G. P. Putnam's sons, ltd. [1926] xiii p., 1 l., 302, [1] p. front. (port.) plates. 23 cm. [BX4705.B23A3] 27-18045
I. Title.

BARTH, Karl, 1886- 230.420924
How I changed my mind. Introd., epilogue by John D. Godsey. Richmond, Knox [1966] 96p. ports. 21cm. Three autobiographical articles which first appeared in issues of the Christian Century. Bibl. [BX4827.B3A3] 66-17277 3.00
I. Title.

BAUER, Evelyn (Showalter) 922.654
Through sunlight and shadow. Scottdale, Pa., Herald Press, [1959] 221p. illus. 20cm. Autobiographical. [BV3269.B37A3] 59-11040
I. Title.

BECK, Vilhelm, 1829-1901 922.4489
Memoirs. Ed., introd. by Paul C. Nyholm. Tr. [from German] by C. A. Stub. Philadelphia, Fortress [c.1965] xi, 192p. 21cm. (Seminar eds.) On cover: A story of renewal in the Denmark of Kierkegaard and Grundtvig. Bibl. [BX8080.B359A35] 65-13376 2.25 pap.,
I. Nyholm, Paul C., 1895- ed. II. Title.

BECK, Vilhelm, 1829-1901 922.4489
Memoirs. Ed., introd. by Paul C. Nyholm. Tr. [from German] by C. A. Stub. Philadelphia, Fortress [c.1965] xi, 192p. 21cm. (Seminar eds.) On cover: A story of renewal in the Denmark of Kierkegaard and Grundtvig. Bibl. [BX8080.B359A35] 65-13376 2.25 pap.,
I. Nyholm, Paul C., 1895- ed. II. Title.

BECK, Vilhelm, 1829-1901. 922.4489
Memoirs, Edited and with an introd. by Paul C. Nyholm. Translated by C. A. Stub. Philadelphia, Fortress Press [1965] xi, 192 p. 21 cm. (Seminar editions) "An abridged translation of Erindringer fra mit liv." On cover: A story of renewal in the Denmark of Kierkegaard and Grundtvig. Bibliographical footnotes. "Selected bibliography of literature in Danish": p. 184-185. [BX8080.B359A35] 65-13376
I. Nyholm, Paul C., 1895- ed. II. Title.

BECK, Vilhelm, 1829-1901. 922.4489
Memoirs, Edited and with an introd. by Paul C. Nyholm. Translated by C. A. Stub. Philadelphia, Fortress Press [1965] xi, 192 p. 21 cm. (Seminar editions) "An abridged translation of Erindringer fra mit liv." On cover: A story of renewal in the Denmark of Kierkegaard and Grundtvig. Bibliographical footnotes. "Selected bibliography of literature in Danish": p. 184-185. [BX8080.B359A35] 65-13376
I. Nyholm, Paul C., 1895- ed. II. Title.

BERRY, Ruth Muirhead. 922.573
To enjoy God, a woman's adventure in faith. Philadelphia, Muhlenberg Press [1956] 228p. 22cm. [BR1725.B44A3] 56-9340
I. Title.

BICKERSTETH, Edward, 1786-1850. 922.
Memoirs of Simeon Wilhelm, a native of the Susoo country, West Africa; who died at the house of the Church Missionary Society, London, Aug. 29, 1817; aged 17 years. Together with some accounts of the superstitions of the inhabitants of West Africa. Pub. for the Yale College Society of Enquiry Respecting Missions. New-Haven, Printed by S. Converse, 1819. 108 p. 16 cm. Subsequently pub. under title: Life of Simeon Wilhelm. [BV3542.W5B5 1819] 48-32432
I. Wilhelm, Simeon, 1800 (ca)-1817. II. Title.

BICKERSTETH, Edward, 1786-1850. 922.
Memoirs of Simeon Wilhelm, a native of the Susoo country, West Africa; who died at the house of the Church Missionary Society, London, Aug. 29, 1817; aged 17 years. Together with some accounts of the superstitions of the inhabitants of West Africa. Pub. for the Yale College Society of Enquiry Respecting Missions. New-Haven, Printed by S. Converse, 1819. 108 p. 16 cm. Subsequently pub. under title: Life of Simeon Wilhelm. [BV3542.W5B5 1819] 48-32432
I. Wilhelm, Simeon, 1800 (ca)-1817. II. Title.

BINNS, Walter Pope. 286'.1'0924 B
My life story. [Wolfe City, Tex., Southern Baptist Press, 1968] 81 p. facsim., ports. 23 cm. Cover title. [BX6495.B49A3] 68-57708
I. Title.

BINNS, Walter Pope. 286'.1'0924 B
My life story. [Wolfe City, Tex., Southern Baptist Press, 1968] 81 p. facsim., ports. 23 cm. Cover title. [BX6495.B49A3] 68-57708
I. Title.

BOGIGIAN, Hagop.
In quest of the soul of civilization, by Hagop Bogigian; with a foreword by ex-Senator John Sharp Williams. Washington, D. C., H. Bogigian [c1925] 255 p. front. (port.) plates. 20 cm. Autobiography. [E170.5.B66] 26-2550
I. Title.

BOGIGIAN, Hagop.
In quest of the soul of civilization, by Hagop Bogigian; with a foreword by ex-Senator John Sharp Williams. Washington, D. C., H. Bogigian [c1925] 255 p. front. (port.) plates. 20 cm. Autobiography. [E170.5.B66] 26-2550
I. Title.

BOONE, Charles Eugene. 248
A new song [by] Pat Boone. [1st ed.] Carol Stream, Ill., Creation House [1970] 192 p. ports. 23 cm. [ML420.B7A3] 75-131441 4.95
I. Title.

BOUCHER, Sharon. 922.673
Luther Warren, man of prayer and power. Illustrated by Stanley Dunlap, Jr. Washington, Review and Herald Pub. Association [1959] 191p. illus. 22cm. [BX6193.W3B6] 59-37466
I. Warren, Luther Willis 1864- II. Title.

(BOUDINOT, Elias) 1740-1821.
A memoir of the Rev. William Tennent, minister of Freehold, Monmouth County, N.J. First published in the Evangelical magazine... Springfield, G. W. Callender; A. G. Tannatt & co., printers (1822) 67 p. 15 cm. 12-24839
I. Title.

(BOUDINOT, Elias) 1740-1821.
A memoir of the Rev. William Tennent, minister of Freehold, Monmouth County, N.J. First published in the Evangelical magazine... Springfield, G. W. Callender; A. G. Tannatt & co., printers (1822) 67 p. 15 cm. 12-24839
I. Title.

BOWDEN, Henry Warner. 209'.2'2 B
Dictionary of American religious biography / Henry Warner Bowden ; Edwin S. Gaustad, advisory editor. Westport, Conn. : Greenwood Press, 1976. p. cm. Includes bibliographies and index. [BL72.B68] 76-5258 ISBN 0-8371-8906-3 lib.bdg. : 29.95
1. Religions—Biography. 2. United States—Biography. I. Title.

BOWER, William Clayton, 1878- 922.673
Through the years; personal memoirs. Lexington, Ky., Transylvania College Press, 1957. 111p. illus. 24cm. [BX7343.B6A3] 57-22216
I. Title.

[BOYD, Andrew Kennedy Hutchinson] 1825-1899.
The recreations of a country parson. [1st series. 19th ed.] Boston, J. R. Osgood and company, 1874. vi, [7]-444 p. 19 cm. 7-36042
I. Title.

BRADY, H. Edgar.
In Christ, in Canaan. [Mattapan? Mass., 1900] 54 p. incl. front. (port.) 16 degree. 1-29650
I. Title.

BROWN, Burdette Boardman, 1871- 922.773
Brown goes, by Burdette Boardman Brown... New York, London [etc.] Fleming H. Revell company [c1936] 144 p. front., ports. 21 cm. Autobiography. [BX8495.B765A3] 36-20229
I. Title.

BROWN, Burdette Boardman, 1871- 922.773
Brown goes, by Burdette Boardman Brown... New York, London [etc.] Fleming H. Revell company [c1936] 144 p. front., ports. 21 cm. Autobiography. [BX8495.B765A3] 36-20229
I. Title.

BROWN, H E., Mrs.
...John Freeman and his family. By Mrs. H. E. Brown. Boston, American tract society [1864] iv, 5-96 p. front. 15 cm. (The freedman's library, no. 1) 3-23154
I. Title.

BROWN, H E., Mrs.
...John Freeman and his family. By Mrs. H. E. Brown. Boston, American tract society [1864] iv, 5-96 p. front. 15 cm. (The freedman's library, no. 1) 3-23154
I. Title.

BROWN, Willis M. 1856- 287.
From infidelity to Christianity; life sketches of Willis M. Brown. Written by himself. Moundsville, W. Va., Gospel trumpet company, 1904. 349 p. incl. front. ports. 18 1/2 cm. [BX7990.G7B7] 4-9951
I. Title.

BROWNSON, Orestes Augustus, 1803-1876. 133.
The spirit-rapper; an autobiography. By O. A. Brownson ... Boston, Little, Brown and company; [etc., etc.] 1854. xi, 402 p. 20 cm. [BF1251.B85] 6-17217
I. Title.

BRUCKBERGER, Raymond Leopold, 1907- 922.244
One sky to share, the French and American journals of Raymond Leopold Bruckberger; translated by Dorothy Carr Howell, Drawings by Jo Spier, New York, P. J. Kenedy [1952] 248 p. illus. 22 cm. [BX4705.B86A3] 52-11274
I. Title.

BULLARD, Asa, 1804-1888. 922.573
Incidents in a busy life. An autobiography. By Asa Bullard. Boston and Chicago, Congregational Sunday-school and publishing society [1888] 235 p. front. (port.) plates. 21 cm. "In memoriam. By M. C. Hazard": p. 215-235. [BX7260.B82A3] 35-37065
I. Hazard, Marshall Custiss, 1839-1929. II. Congregational Sunday-school and publishing society. III. Title.

BURROWS, Millar, 1889- 922
Founders of great religions; being personal sketches of famous leaders, by Millar Burrows ... New York, London, C. Scribner's sons, 1931. x p., 2 l., 3-243 p. 21 cm. "Suggestions for further reading": p. 239-240. [BL72.B8] 31-23684
1. Religions—Biog. I. Title.

BURROWS, Millar, 1889- 200'.92'2 B
Founders of great religions, being personal sketches of famous leaders. Freeport, N.Y., Books for Libraries Press [1973] p. (Essay index reprint series) Reprint of the 1931

ed. [BL72.B8 1973] 72-13272 ISBN 0-8369-8148-0
1. Religions—Biography. I. Title.

BUSHNELL, Katharine Caroline, 1855- 296
The reverend doctor and his doctor daughter, by Katharine C. Bushnell ... Oakland, Calif., Katharine C. Bushnell [c1927] 132 p. fold. diagr. 20 cm. "What the Bible teaches about women."--Introd. [BS680.W7B83] 28-9958
I. Title.

CACOPARDO, J. Jerry 922.573
Show me a miracle; the true story of a man who went from prison to pulpit [by] J. J. Cacopardo. Don Weldon. New York, Dutton [c.]1961. 220p. 61-6017 3.95 bds.,
I. Weldon, Don, joint author. II. Title.

CALLAGHAN, James Frederic, 1839-1899. 204
Memoirs and writings of the Very Reverend James F. Callaghan, D. D. comp. by his sister, Emily A. Callaghan ... Cincinnati, The Robert Clarke company, 1903. viii p., 1 l., 568 p. front. (port.) 23 cm. [BX890.C3] 3-11310
I. Callaghan, Emily A. comp. II. Title.

CALLAGHAN, James Frederic, 1839-1899. 204
Memoirs and writings of the Very Reverend James F. Callaghan, D. D. comp. by his sister, Emily A. Callaghan ... Cincinnati, The Robert Clarke company, 1903. viii p., 1 l., 568 p. front. (port.) 23 cm. [BX890.C3] 3-11310
I. Callaghan, Emily A. comp. II. Title.

CALVERT, John Betts, 1852- 232.
The impartial Christ, by John B. Calvert. 2d ed., enl. and rev. New York, Chicago [etc.] Fleming H. Bevell company [c1919] 54 p. 18 cm. [BT201.C2 1919] 19-16621
I. Title.

CAMPBELL, James Mann, 1840-1926. 922.
Transplanted heather; a Scotch preacher in America, by James M. Campbell, D.D.; edited by W. Douglas Mackenzie... Garden City, N.Y., Doubleday, Doran & company, inc., 1928. xv, 311 p. front. (port.) 20 cm. "First edition." "Books by the author": p. 310-311. [BX7260.C25A3] 28-28698
I. Mackenzie, William Douglas, 1859- ed. II. Title.

CARNEGIE, Amos Hubert, 1885- 922
Faith moves mountains, an autobiography. [1st ed.] Washington [1950- v. port. 21 cm. [BX8473.C3A3] 50-3933
I. Title.

CARNEGIE, Amos Hubert, 1885- 922
Faith moves mountains, an autobiography. [1st ed.] Washington [1950- v. port. 21 cm. [BX8473.C3A3] 50-3933
I. Title.

CARTER, John Franklin, 1897- 920.5
The rectory family [by] John Franklin Carter; with illustrations by Oscar Howard. New York, Coward-McCann, inc., 1937. 6 p. l., 3-275, [1] p. incl. front., illus. 21 cm. [PS3505.A7922R4 1937] 37-28725
I. Title.

CARVER, William Owen, 1868-1954. 922.673
Out of his treasure; unfinished memoirs. Nashville Broadman Press [1956] 158p. illus. 23cm. [BX6495.C36A3] 56-8673
I. Title.

CARVILLE, Joseph.
Tide, time and eternity; or, The great heavenly vision of Joseph Carville, by Joseph Carville. Chicago, 1903. 19 cm. (In his A peep through a knot hole in heaven's gate. Chicago, 1903. p. [205]- 3-30977
I. Title.

CAUGHEY, James, 1810?-1891. 922
The triumph of truth; and continental letters and sketches, from the journal, letters, and sermons of the Rev. James Caughey ... With an introduction by Rev. Jos. Castle, a. m. Philadelphia, higgins & Perkinpine; New York, Carlton & Porter; [etc., etc.] 1857. xxiii, 25-420 p. front. (port.) 19 cm. [BV3785.C3A4] 37-36530
I. Title.

CHAMBERLAIN, John, 1777-1821. 922.654
Memoirs of the early life of John Chamberlain, late missionary in India. With his diary of religious exercises. By William Yates ... Abridged from the Calcutta edition. Boston, J. Loring, 1831. 2 p. l., [iii]-vii, [1], [9]-204 p. front., plates (1 fold.) 16 cm. [BV3269.C35Y3] 33-16011
I. Yates, William, 1792-1845. II. Title.

CHAMBERLAIN, John, 1777-1821. 922.654
Memoirs of the early life of John Chamberlain, late missionary in India. With his diary of religious exercises. By William Yates ... Abridged from the Calcutta edition. Boston, J. Loring, 1831. 2 p. l., [iii]-vii, [1], [9]-204 p. front., plates (1 fold.) 16 cm. [BV3269.C35Y3] 33-16011
I. Yates, William, 1792-1845. II. Title.

CHANLER, Julie (Olin) 1882-1961. 291.6'3'0922 B
His messengers went forth. Illustrated by Olin Dows. Freeport, N.Y., Books for Libraries Press [1971, c1948] 64 p. illus. 23 cm. (Biography index reprint series) [BL72.C45 1971] 77-148209 ISBN 0-8369-8056-5
1. Religions—Biography. I. Title.

CHAPMAN, J. Wilbur, 1850-
The man who said he would, by the Rev. J. Wilbur Chapman ... Boston and Chicago, United society of Christian endeavor, 1902] vii, 9-87 p. 17 cm. 2-20326
I. Title.

[CHARLES, Elizabeth (Rundle)] "Mrs. Andrew Charles," 1828-1896.
Martyrs and saints of the first twelve centuries; studies from the lives of the Black letter saints of the English Calendar. By the author of Chronicles of the Schonberg-Cotta fam ily, pub. under the direction of the Tract committee. London, [etc.] Society for promoting Christian knowledge; New York, E. & J. B. Young & co., 1887. viii, 468 p. 19 cm. 10-12696
I. Society for promoting Christian knowledge. Tract committee. II. Title.

CHESTER, Samuel Hall, 1851- 922.573
Memories of four-score years; an autobiography by Samuel Hall Chester ... Richmond, Va., Priv. print. for the author by Presbyterian committee of publication, 1934. 235 p. front., ports. 21 cm. "Five hundred copies of this book have been printed, of which this copy is number 318." [BX9225.C525A3] 39-34139
I. Title.

CHESTER, Samuel Hall, 1851- 922.573
Memories of four-score years; an autobiography by Samuel Hall Chester ... Richmond, Va., Priv. print. for the author by Presbyterian committee of publication, 1934. 235 p. front., ports. 21 cm. "Five hundred copies of this book have been printed, of which this copy is number 318." [BX9225.C525A3] 39-34139
I. Title.

CLARK, Harriet Elizabeth (Abbott) "Mrs. Francis E. Clark," 1850- 920.7
The little girl that once was I, by Mrs. Francis E. Clark ("Mother Endeavor" Clark) [Worcester, Mass., Printed by the Commonwealth press, 1936] 2 p. l., vii-x, 52 p. ports. 20 cm. [BV1423.C63A3] 36-18435
I. Title.

CLARK, Isaac Newton, 1833-1917. 920.
Isaac Newton Clark, a personal sketch by himself, ed. by Philip Wendell Crannell. Kansas City, Kan., The Kansas City Baptist theological seminary, 1917. 167, [1] p. front. (port.) illus. (facsim.) 19 1/2 cm. [BX6495.C6A3] 17-14118
I. Crannell, Philip Wendell, 1861- ed. II. Title.

CLARK, Isaac Newton, 1833-1917. 920.
Isaac Newton Clark, a personal sketch by himself, ed. by Philip Wendell Crannell. Kansas City, Kan., The Kansas City Baptist theological seminary, 1917. 167, [1] p. front. (port.) illus. (facsim.) 19 1/2 cm. [BX6495.C6A3] 17-14118
I. Crannell, Philip Wendell, 1861- ed. II. Title.

CLARKE, James Freeman, 1810-1888. 922.
James Freeman Clarke; an autobiography, diary and correspondence, edited by Edward Everett Hale. Boston and New York, Houghton, Mifflin and company, 1891. 2 p. l., 430 p. front. (port.) 20 1/2 cm. [BX9869.C6A3] 4-16956
I. Hale, Edward Everett, 1822-1909, ed. II. Title.

CLEMENTS, Bernard, dam. 1880- 261
Members of Christ, by Bernard Clements... London, New York [etc.] Longmans, Green and co., 1932. 64 p. 18 cm. "The Mother of My Lord" was printed in Ave in 1924. 'Juxta crucem' was written specially for the All saints. Margaret street, parish paper in 1926." "The merchantman in Africa" was printed in several periodicals. cf. Note, p. [6] [secular name: William Dudley Clements] Contents.Members of Christ.--The mother of My Lord.--"Juxta crucem."--The merchantman in Africa. [BX5037.C53] 32-3782
I. Title.

CLEMMITT, Thomas, 1853- 286.6
Old Sycamore church and some other things; being memories, experiences and interpretations of one who has tried to live the Christian life without being either a pharisee or a puritan, by Thos. Clemmitt, jr... [Baltimore] Press of Fleet-McGinley, incorporated, 1932. 3 p. l., [9]-238 p. 2 port. (incl. front.) 20 cm. [BX7343.C6A3] 922.673 32-13659
I. Title.

COLE, Mary, 1853-
Trials and triumphs of faith, by Mary Cole ... Anderson, Ind., Gospel trumpet company [c1914] 300 p. incl. front. (port.) pl., ports. 18 1/2 cm. A narrative of the life and work of the author. 15-1816 1.00
I. Title.

COLES, George, 1792-1858. 922.742
Incidents of my later years ... By Rev. George Coles. New York, Carlton & Phillips, 1855. 315 p. 16 cm. Sequel to My youthful days. [BX8495.C613A35] 36-34012
I. Title.

COLLINS, Elizabeth (Ballinger) Mason, Mrs. 1755-1831. 922.8673
Memoirs of Elizabeth Collins, of Upper Evesham, New Jersey, a minister of the gospel of Christ, in the Society of Friends. Philadelphia, For sale at Friends' book store, 1859. 144 p. 16 cm. [BX7795.C664A3 1859] 33-25253
I. Title.

COLLINS, Elizabeth (Ballinger) Mason, Mrs. 1755-1831. 922.8673
Memoirs of Elizabeth Collins, of Upper Evesham, New Jersey, a minister of the gospel of Christ, in the Society of Friends. Philadelphia, For sale at Friends' book store, 1859. 144 p. 16 cm. [BX7795.C664A3 1859] 33-25253
I. Title.

COMBS, George Hamilton, 1864- 922.673
I'd take this way again, an autobiography by George Hamilton Combs. St. Louis, The Bethany press [1944] 256 p. front. (port.) 20 1/2 cm. [BX7343.C65A3] 44-47194
I. Title.

COMLY, John, 1773-1850. 922.
Journal of the life and religious labours of John Comly, late of Byberry, Pennsylvania. Published by his children. Philadelphia, T. E. Chapman, 1853. xvi, 645 p. 24 cm. [BX7795.C7A3 1853] 50-42700
I. Title.

COMLY, John, 1773-1850. 922.
Journal of the life and religious labours of John Comly, late of Byberry, Pennsylvania. Published by his children. Philadelphia, T. E. Chapman, 1853. xvi, 645 p. 24 cm. [BX7795.C7A3 1853] 50-42700
I. Title.

CONANT, Robert Warren 1852-
The manly Christ, a new view. By Dr. R. W. Conant ... Chicago, 1904. 157 p. 19 1/2 cm. 4-11202
I. Title.

COOME, Hannah (Grier) Mrs. 1837-1921.
A memoir of the life and work of Hannah Grier Coome, mother-foundress of the Sisterhood of St. John the divine, Toronto. Canada. London, Oxford university press, H. Milford, 1933. viii p., 1 l., 294, [1] p. front. (port.) 10 pl. 23 cm. [Full name: Mrs. Sarah Hannah Roberta (Grier) Coome] A 35
I. Sisterhood of St. John the divine, Toronto, Canada. II. Title.

COOME, Hannah (Grier) Mrs. 1837-1921.
A memoir of the life and work of Hannah Grier Coome, mother-foundress of the Sisterhood of St. John the divine, Toronto. Canada. London, Oxford university press, H. Milford, 1933. viii p., 1 l., 294, [1] p. front. (port.) 10 pl. 23 cm. [Full name: Mrs. Sarah Hannah Roberta (Grier) Coome] A 35
I. Sisterhood of St. John the divine, Toronto, Canada. II. Title.

COOPER, Mary (Hanson) 1786-1812. 920.
Memoirs of Mrs. Mary Cooper of London, who departed this life, June 22, 1812, in the twenty-sixth year of her age; extracted from her diary and epistolary correspondence. By Adam Clarke, LL.D. New York, B. Waugh and T. Mason, 1832. 240 p. 13 1/2 cm. [BR1725.C68A3 1832] 45-27333
I. Clarke, Adam, 1760?-1832, ed. II. Title.

COOPER, Mary (Hanson) 1786-1812. 920.
Memoirs of Mrs. Mary Cooper of London, who departed this life, June 22, 1812, in the twenty-sixth year of her age; extracted from her diary and epistolary correspondence. By Adam Clarke, LL.D. New York, B. Waugh and T. Mason, 1832. 240 p. 13 1/2 cm. [BR1725.C68A3 1832] 45-27333
I. Clarke, Adam, 1760?-1832, ed. II. Title.

CORNING, James Leonard, 1828-1903. 922
Recollections of a life [by] James Leonard Corning, sr. New York, The Knickerbocker press [1898?] iv p., 1 l., 100 p. 18 cm. [BL2790.C6A3] 33-31201
I. Title.

CRAIN, Clara (Moore) 1905- 922
We shall rise. New York, Pageant Press [1955] 68p. 21cm. Autobiography. [BR1725.C69A3] 55-12391
I. Title.

[CUSACK, Mary Frances] 1830-1899. 922.2415
The nun of Kenmare; an autobiography. Boston, Ticknor and company, 1889. xxi, [2], 558 p. front. (port.) 20 cm. "Works": p. 548-558. [BX4765.C798A3] 31-31291
I. Title.

[CUSACK, Mary Frances] 1830-1899. 922.2415
The nun of Kenmare; an autobiography. Boston, Ticknor and company, 1889. xxi, [2], 558 p. front. (port.) 20 cm. "Works": p. 548-558. [BX4765.C798A3] 31-31291
I. Title.

CUTHERS, John, 1876- 922.8373
... Autobiography of John Cuthers, 1876-1946, seventy years a Mormon, by John Cuthers ... [Glendale, Calif., The Church press, 1946] 160 p. front. (port.) 19 1/2 cm. [BX8695.C8A3] 47-18730
I. Title.

CUTLER, Helen R. 922.773
Jottings from life; or, Passages from the diary of an itinerant's wife. By Helen R. Cutler. Cincinnati, Poe & Hitchcock, 1864. 282 p. 18 cm. [BX8495.C8A3] 36-34751
I. Title. II. Title: Passages from the diary of an itinerant's wife.

CUTLER, Helen R. 922.773
Jottings from life; or, Passages from the diary of an itinerant's wife. By Helen R. Cutler. Cincinnati, Poe & Hitchcock, 1864. 282 p. 18 cm. [BX8495.C8A3] 36-34751

I. Title. II. Title: Passages from the diary of an itinerant's wife.

DARLINGTON, Charles Joseph, 1894-1966. 540.924
Memoirs by Charles J. Darlington. [Philadelphia? 1966-67] 2 v. illus., facsims, ports. 23 cm. Contents.Farm and school: 1894-1911, [aud] Swarthmore College: 1911-1916.--v. Wilmington: 1916-1925, [and] Woodstown: 1925-1965. [BX7795.D33A3] 66-29411
I. Title.

DARLINGTON, Charles Joseph, 1894-1966. 540.924
Memoirs by Charles J. Darlington. [Philadelphia? 1966-67] 2 v. illus., facsims, ports. 23 cm. Contents.Farm and school: 1894-1911, [aud] Swarthmore College: 1911-1916.--v. Wilmington: 1916-1925, [and] Woodstown: 1925-1965. [BX7795.D33A3] 66-29411
I. Title.

DARLINGTON, Charles Joseph, 1894-1966. 540.0924
Memoirs of Charles J. Darlington. [Philadelphia? 1966-67] 2 v. illus., facsims., ports. 23 cm. Contents.Contents.—v. 1. Farm and school: 1894-911, [and] Swarthmore College: 1911-1916.—v. 2. Wilmington: 1916-1925, [and] Woodstown: 1925-1965. [BX7795.D33A3] 66-29411
I. Title.

DARLINGTON, Charles Joseph, 1894-1966. 540.0924
Memoirs of Charles J. Darlington. [Philadelphia? 1966-67] 2 v. illus., facsims., ports. 23 cm. Contents.Contents.—v. 1. Farm and school: 1894-911, [and] Swarthmore College: 1911-1916.—v. 2. Wilmington: 1916-1925, [and] Woodstown: 1925-1965. [BX7795.D33A3] 66-29411
I. Title.

DAVENPORT, John Gaylord. 922.
Experiences and observations by the way; an autobiography published by special request, by John Gaylord Davenport, D. D. Boston, Chicago, The Pilgrim press [c1917] 5 p. l., 211 p. front., plates, ports. 19 cm. [BX7260.D3A3] 18-1010
I. Title.

DAVIS, George Thompson Brown, 1873-
Twice around the world with Alexander, prince of gospel singers, by George T. B. Davis. New York, The Christian herald [c1907] xv, [2], 18-382 p. incl. front., plates, ports. 20 cm. 7-40008
I. Title.

*DELAFIELD, D. A. 268.73
Elena G. de White y la Iglesia Adventista del Septimo Dia. Mountain View, Calif., Pacific Pr. Pub. Co. [c.1965] 96p. illus. (pt. col.) 18cm. Spanish tr. .50 pap.,
I. Title.

*DELAFIELD, D. A. 268.73
Elena G. de White y la Iglesia Adventista del Septimo Dia. Mountain View, Calif., Pacific Pr. Pub. Co. [c.1965] 96p. illus. (pt. col.) 18cm. Spanish tr. .50 pap.,
I. Title.

DENISON, George Anthony, 1805-1896. 922.
Notes of my life, 1805-1878. Oxford, J. Parker, 1878. viii, 415 p. 23 cm. [BX5199.D4A27] 49-40053
I. Title.

DENISON, George Anthony, 1805-1896. 922.
Notes of my life, 1805-1878. Oxford, J. Parker, 1878. viii, 415 p. 23 cm. [BX5199.D4A27] 49-40053
I. Title.

DICKINSON, Peard, 1758-1802.
Memoirs of the life of the Rev. Peard Dickinson, in which the dispensations of providence and grace towards individuals, are exemplified in some remarkable instances. Written by himself: rev. and cor. by Joseph Benson ... New York, Printed by John C. Totten, for the Methodist Episcopal church, and sold by Ezekiel Cooper and John Wilson at the book-room, 1804. 156 p. 16 cm. A34
I. Benson, Joseph, 1748-1821, ed. II. Title.

DOE, Walter P b.1813, comp.
Important religious truths. Comp. by Rev. Walter P. Doe. Providence, R. I., A. C. Green & son, printers, 1883. vii, 242, vi, 42 p. 20 cm. "A sketch of the life of Rev. Walter P. Doe": 42 p. at end. 6-25434
I. Title.

DOE, Walter P b.1813, comp.
Important religious truths. Comp. by Rev. Walter P. Doe. Providence, R. I., A. C. Green & son, printers, 1883. vii, 242, vi, 42 p. 20 cm. "A sketch of the life of Rev. Walter P. Doe": 42 p. at end. 6-25434
I. Title.

DON CARLOS, Thomas Boone, 1906- 922.4973
One man and God, by Thomas B. Don Carlos. 1st ed. Petaluma, Calif., T. B. Don Carlos, c1944. 4 p. l., 108, [2] p. illus. (port.) 17 1/2 cm. [BX6198.A7D6] 44-26412
I. Title.

DORNBLASER, Thomas Franklin, 1841- 922.473
My life-story for young and old, by Thomas Franklin Dornblaser ... [Philadelphia] Pub. for the author, 1930. 222 p. front. (port.) illus. (incl. ports.) 23 cm. [BX8080.D64A3] 30-30119
I. Title.

DORNBLASER, Thomas Franklin, 1841- 922.473
My life-story for young and old, by Thomas Franklin Dornblaser ... [Philadelphia] Pub. for the author, 1930. 222 p. front. (port.) illus. (incl. ports.) 23 cm. [BX8080.D64A3] 30-30119
I. Title.

DOWNING, James, b.1871. 920
A narrative of the life of James Downing, a blind man, late a private in His Majesty's 20th Regiment of Foot, containing historical, naval, military, moral, religious and entertaining reflections. Composed by himself in easy verse. From the 5th London ed. New York, Printed by J. C. Totten, 1821. 143 p. illus., port. 15 cm. [PR4613.D49N3] 49-34904
I. Title.

DRANE, Augusta Theodosia, 1823-1894. 922.
A memoir of Mother Francis Raphael, OS.D. (Augusta Theodosis Drane) ... with some of her spiritual notes and letters; edited by Rev. Father Bertrand Wilberforce ... New ed. London, New York [etc] Longmans, Green and co, 1923. xii, 572 p. front. (port.) 19 1/2 cm. "Works of Augusta Theodosia Drane": p. 569-572. [Name in religion: Francis Raphael, mother] [BX4705.D75A3] 23-9500
I. Wilberforce, Bertrand Arthur Henry, ed. II. Title.

DRANE, Augusta Theodosia, 1823-1894. 922.
A memoir of Mother Francis Raphael, OS.D. (Augusta Theodosis Drane) ... with some of her spiritual notes and letters; edited by Rev. Father Bertrand Wilberforce ... New ed. London, New York [etc] Longmans, Green and co, 1923. xii, 572 p. front. (port.) 19 1/2 cm. "Works of Augusta Theodosia Drane": p. 569-572. [Name in religion: Francis Raphael, mother] [BX4705.D75A3] 23-9500
I. Wilberforce, Bertrand Arthur Henry, ed. II. Title.

DU BOSE, Horace Mellard, bp., 1858- 922.772
Through two generations; a study in retrospect, by Horace Mellard Du Bose ... New York [etc.] Fleming H. Revell company [c1934] 160 p. 19 1/2 cm. Autobiography. [BX8495.D73A3] 34-37469
I. Title.

DUNGAN, David Roberts, 1837-
On the rock; or, Truth stranger than fiction. A story of souls whose pathway began in darkness, but brightened to the perfect day. By D. R. Dungan. Cincinnati O., The Standard publishing co., 1910. x, 340 p. 20 cm. 13-21324
I. Title.

DUNHAM, Samuel.
Retrospect of a happy ministry; the life story of half a century, including personal reminiscences, and a complete history from its first inception of the West Presbyterian church, Binghamton, N. Y., by Samuel Dunham ... with portraits of the successive pastors, and views of church edifices and parsonage, also an appendix. Binghamton and New York, Vail-Ballou company, 1914. 7 p. l., 259 p. front., plates, ports. 20 cm. 14-19728 1.00
I. Title.

DUVALL, C. H. 1858-
Twenty years in pulpit; or, The author's greatest secret, by C. H. Duvall ... Pittsburgh, Pa., The City mission publishing company, 1917. 69 p. front. (port.) port. group. 23 cm. 18-413
I. Title.

DYER, Heman, 1810-1900. 922.
Records of an active life, by Heman Dyer, D.D. New York, T. Whittaker, 1886. 2 p. l., x, [7]-422 p. front. (port.) 21 cm. [BX5995.D9A3] 2-26843
I. Title.

EARL, Sylvester, 1863- 922.8373
My life's philosophy, religio-politico and otherwise [by] Sylvester Earl. [Virgin, Utah, 1944] viii, 130 p. front. (ports.) 19 1/2 cm. [BX8695.E3A3] 44-39107
I. Title.

EASTMAN, Max, 1883-1969. 200'.922
Seven kinds of goodness. New York, Horizon Press [1967] 156 p. 22 cm. [BL72.E15] 67-17781
1. Religions—Biography. I. Title.

EDSON, Helen R.
My soul, thou hast much goods. By Helen R. Edson. Philadelphia, Presbyterian board of publication [1885] 64 p. 13 1/2 cm. In verse. [PS1568.E7] 24-24563
I. Title.

[ELY, Ezra Stiles] 1786-1861. 200
The second journal of the stated preacher to the hospital and almshouse in the city of New York, for a part of the year of Our Lord 1813. With an appendix... Philadelphia, Pub. by M. Carey, G. Palmer, printer, 1815. xi, [13]-255 p. 20cm. Preface signed: Ezra Stiles Ely. The first journal, for the year 1811, was pub. in New York in 1812, and repub. in London 1813 under title "Visits of mercy," after which there were several editions. The second journal was also issued under title "Visits of mercy." 15-24982
I. Title.

[ERHARD, Mary Alma, sister] 1907- 922.251
Grey dawns and red, by Marie Fischer [pseud.] New York and London, Sheed & Ward, 1939. xii, 102 p. illus. 22 cm. "First printing, April, 1939." [Secular name: Alma Mary Erhard] [BX4705.V43E7] 39-11738
I. Venard, Jean Theophane, 1829-1861. II. Title.

ESPEY, John Jenkins, 1913- 818.5
Minor heresies [by] John J. Espey. New York, A. A. Knopf, 1945. 5 p. l., 3-202 p., 1 l. 19 cm. Reminiscences. "First edition." [BV3427.E8A3] 45-1793
I. Title.

ESPEY, John Jenkins, 1913- 818.5
The other city. [1st ed.] New York, Knopf, 1950 [c1949] 211 p. 19 cm. Autobiographical. [BV3427.E8A32] 49-50395
I. Title.

EVANS, William, 1787-1867. 922.
Journal of the life and religious services of William Evans, a minister of the gospel in the Society of Friends. Philadelphia. For sale at Friends' book store, 1870. xv, 8-716 p. 24 cm. Preface signed: Charles Evans. [BX7795.E85A3] 9-2369
I. Evans, Charles, 1878-1879, ed. II. Title.

EVANS, William, 1787-1867. 922.
Journal of the life and religious services of William Evans, a minister of the gospel in the Society of Friends. Philadelphia. For sale at Friends' book store, 1870. xv, 8-716 p. 24 cm. Preface signed: Charles Evans. [BX7795.E85A3] 9-2369
I. Evans, Charles, 1878-1879, ed. II. Title.

EVENS, Tillie. 397
From darkness to light. The life story of Gypsy Tillie Evens together with songs used at her meetings. New York, Chicago, Fleming H. Revell company [1893] 60 p. 19 cm. [BV3785.E85A3] 37-33218
I. Title.

FAIRBROTHER, Lafayette I 922.99
The hand of God in my life; my story and sermon of a crusade for souls. Dayton, Ohio, Fay-Ma-Sha-Press, c1962. 63 p. illus. 23 cm. [BV3785.F27A3] 62-21920
I. Title.

*FAIRFIELD, James, ed. 289.7
The touch of God;; the personal story of eleven broadcasters and how they became 'new creatures in Christ,' as told to James Fairfield. Scottdale, Pa., Herald [c.1965] 64p. 20cm. .50 pap.,
I. Title.

FALES, William R. 1820-1850. 922
Memoir of William R. Fales, the Portsmouth cripple ... Philadelphia, Lindsay & Blakiston, 1851. 1 p. l., [xi]-xii, [43]-151 p. 16 cm. [BR1725.F27A3] 37-38004
I. Title.

FALES, William R. 1820-1850. 922
Memoir of William R. Fales, the Portsmouth cripple ... Philadelphia, Lindsay & Blakiston, 1851. 1 p. l., [xi]-xii, [43]-151 p. 16 cm. [BR1725.F27A3] 37-38004
I. Title.

FENELON, Francois de Salignac de La Mothe-, 1651-1715.
Extracts from the writings of Francis Fenelon, archbishop of Cambray. With some memoirs of his life. To which are added Letters, expressive of love and friendship. The writer not known. Recommended to the perusal and notice of the religiously disposed. By John Kendall. Philadelphia: Printed and sold by Kimber, Conrad, & co., no. 170, South Second street, 1804. xiii, [15]-223 p. 18 cm. A 18
I. Title.

FERRIS, David, 1707-1779. 922.
Memoirs of the life of David Ferris, an approved minister of the Society of Friends: late of Wilmington, in the state of Delaware. Revised and corrected from the original copy in manuscript. Philadelphia, J. Simmons, 1825. vi, [7]-99 p. 18 cm. [BX7795.F45A4 1825] 44-33208
I. Title.

FERRIS, David, 1707-1779. 922.
Memoirs of the life of David Ferris, an approved minister of the Society of Friends, late of Wilmington in the state of Dealware. Written by himself. Revised and corrected from the original copy in manuscript. Philadelphia, Merrihew & Thompson's press, 1855. 106 p. 17 cm. [BX7795.F45A4 1855] 3-29003
I. Title.

FINKELSTEIN, Louis, 1895- ed. 922
American spiritual autobiographies, fifteen self-portraits. [1st ed.] New York, Harper. [1948] xvi, 276 p. ports. 22 cm. [BL72.F5] 48-9493
1. Religions—Biog. 2. Spirituality. I. Title. Contents omitted.

FLAVEL, John, 1630?-1691.
A saint indeed, or The great work of a Christian opened and pressed from Proverbs, iv chap. 23d verse. Being a seasonable and proper expedient for the recovery of the much decayed power of Godliness, among the professors of these times. By John Flavel, minister of the gospel. Amherst, New-Hampshire: Printed and sold by Nathaniel Coverly and son, a little south of the Court-house, 1795. xiv, 15-180 p. 13 1/2 cm. A 32
I. Title.

FOWLER, James W., 1940- 291'.4'2 B
Trajectories in faith : five life stories / James W. Fowler & Robin W. Lovin, with Katherine Ann Herzog ... [et al.]. Nashville : Abingdon, c1980. 206 p. ; 20 cm. Includes bibliographical references. [BL72.F65] 79-20485 pbk. : 6.50
1. Religions—Biography. 2. Faith—Psychology—Case studies. I. Lovin, Robin W., joint author. II. Title.

FOX, Maria (Middleton) 1793- 922.
1844.
A brief memoir of Maria Fox, late of Tottenham. Philadelphia, Association of Friends for the Diffusion of Religious and Useful Knowledge, 1858. 157 p. 16 cm. "An abridgement of the [author's Memoirs] ... edited by her husband and published in 1846 ... Consists almost wholly of selections from her letters and extracts from her diary." [BX7795.F76A32] 50-42917
I. Title.

FOX, Maria (Middleton) 1793- 922.
1844.
A brief memoir of Maria Fox, late of Tottenham. Philadelphia, Association of Friends for the Diffusion of Religious and Useful Knowledge, 1858. 157 p. 16 cm. "An abridgement of the [author's Memoirs] ... edited by her husband and published in 1846 ... Consists almost wholly of selections from her letters and extracts from her diary." [BX7795.F76A32] 50-42917
I. Title.

FRANCK, Ira Stoner, 248.50924
1896-
My search for an anchor, by Ira S. Franck. Philadelphia, Dorrance [1966] 129 p. illus., ports. 21 cm. Autobiographical. [BX5995.F67A3] 66-18610
I. Title.

FREEHOF, Solomon Bennett, 922
1892-
Stormers of heaven, by Solomon B. Freehof. New York and London, Harper & brothers, 1931. viii p., 1 l., 225 p. 20 cm. "First edition." [BL72.F7] 31-25275
1. Religions—Biog. 2. Religion—Hist. I. Title.

FREMANTLE, Anne 200'.922
(Jackson) 1909-
Pilgrimage to people, by Anne Fremantle. New York, McKay [1968] viii, 231 p. 21 cm. [BL72.F73] 68-10539
1. Religions—Biography. I. Title.

FREMANTLE, William Henry, 922.
1831-1916.
Recollections of Dean Fremantle, chiefly by himself, edited by the Master of the Temple [W. H. Draper] With three illustrations. London, New York [etc.] Cassell and company, ltd., 1921. xi, 179, [1] p. 2 port. (incl. front.) pl. 22 cm. "Two appreciations", by the Rt. Rev. Lucius F. M. B. Smith and Rev. H. D. A. Major, respectively: p. 143-154. "'Excuses for war' (a sermon preached in Canterbury cathedral on July 12th, 1885)" by Dean Fremantle: p. 157-154. [BX5199.F73A3] 23-6733
I. Draper, William Henry, 1855- ed. II. Title.

FRIENDS, Society of. 922
Philadelphia. Yearly meeting. Book committee.
Quaker biographies. A series of sketches, chiefly biographical, concerning members of the Society of Friends, from the seventeenth century to more recent times ... Philadelphia, Pa., For sale at Friends' book store [1909]-16. 5 v. fronts., plates, ports. 21 cm. [BX7790.P45 1st ser.] 28-4427
I. Title.
Contents omitted.

GAER, Joseph, 1897- 922
Young heroes of the living religions. Drawings by Anne Marie Jauss. [1st ed.] Boston, Little, Brown [1953] 201p. illus. 22cm. [BL72.G28] 53-7323
1. Religions—Biog. I. Title.

GARRETT, Alfred Cope, 922.8673
1867-
One mystic, an autobiographical sketch by Alfred Cope Garrett. [Philadelphia, Harris & Partridge, inc., 1945] ix, 322 p. front., pl., ports. 23 cm. Bibliographical foot-notes. [BX7795.G33A3] 46-12866
I. Title.

GATES, Helen (Dunn) Mrs.
A consecrated life; a sketch of the life and labors of Rev. Ransom Dunn, D. D., 1818-1900, by his daughter Helen Dunn Gates. Boston, Mass., The Morning star publishing house, 1901. viii p., 1 l., 378 p. front., illus., plates, ports. 20 cm. 7-11188
I. Dunn, Ramsom, 1818-1900. II. Title.

GEIL, William Edgar, 1865- 232.
1925.
The Man of Galilee [by] William Edgar Geil ... Nine maps. New York, The International committee of Young men's Christian associations [c1906] vi, [2], 199 p. incl. ix maps. 17 cm. [BT301.G34] 6-23284
I. Title.

GIBBONS, James, cardinal, 204
1834-1921.
A retrospect of fifty years, by James cardinal Gibbons, archbishop of Baltimore ... Baltimore, New York, John Murphy company; [etc., etc., c1916] 2 v. 19 cm. [BX890.G47] 17-88
I. Title.

GIDADA Solon, 1901- 281'.7 B
The other side of darkness, by Gidada Solon. As told to and recorded by: Ruth McCreery and Martha M. Vandevort. Edited by: Marion Fairman. New York, Friendship Press [1972] 116 p. 23 cm. Bibliography: p. 114-116. [BX6510.B44G5] 75-187807
I. McCreery, Ruth. II. Vandevort, Martha M. III. Title.

GILLIAM, E[dward] W[inslow]
The rector of Hazlehurst, and some others of the cloth. By E. W. Gilliam ... Baltimore, J. Murphy company, 1903. 478 p. 19 cm. 5-5928
I. Title.

GILMAN, Bradley.
Ronald Carnaquay; a commercial clergyman, by Bradley Gilman ... New York, London, The Macmillan company, 1903. x p., 1 l., 374 p. 20 cm. 3-9332
I. Title.

GOODALL, Norman. 230.58
One man's testimony. New York, Harper [1949] 128 p. 20 cm. [BX7260.G568A3 1949a] 49-50420
I. Title.

GORRES, Ida Friederike 922.242
(Coudenhove) 1901-
Mary Ward, by Ida Goerres Coudenhove; English translation, by Elsie Codd. London, New York [etc.] Longmans, Green and co. [1939] viii, 260 p. 19 cm. "First issued by the Catholic book club, December 1939; general edition, February 1939." [BX4705.W29G62 1939] 39-19582
I. Title.

GORRES, Ida Friederike 922.242
(Coudenhove) 1901-
Mary Ward, by Ida Goerres Coudenhove; English translation, by Elsie Codd. London, New York [etc.] Longmans, Green and co. [1939] viii, 260 p. 19 cm. "First issued by the Catholic book club, December 1939; general edition, February 1939." [BX4705.W29G62 1939] 39-19582
I. Title.

GOSS, Cornelia A. Mrs. 1850- 922.
'Neath the waters, by Ensign Cornelia A. Goss. From modiste to Salvation army officer; a pen sketch of scenes in the life and labors of Mrs. Cornelia A. Goss. Cincinnati, O., Monfort & co., printers, 1923. 63 p. front., ports. 17 cm. [BX9743.G6A3] 23-13360
I. Title.

GOUGH, James, 1712-1780. 922.
Memoirs of the life. religious experiences, and labors in the gospel of James Gough of the city of Dublin, deceased. Compiled from his original mss. by his brother John Gough. Philadelphia, Friends' Book Store, 1886. 149 p. 19 cm. [BX7795.G55A3] 50-46983
I. Title.

GRAHAM, Balus Joseph 922.673
Winzer, 1862-
A ministry of fifty years, by B. J. W. Graham ... Atlanta, Ga., B. J. W. Graham [c1938] viii, 303 p. 23 cm. [BX6495.G66A3] 38-31978
I. Title.

GRAHAM, Henry, 1841- 251
Old truths newly illustrated, by Henry Graham, D. D. New York, Eaton & Mains; Cincinnati, Jennings & Graham [1904] xv, 229 p. 20 cm. "The truths illustrated are the old truths of the Gospel of Christ."--Pref. [BV4225.G7] 4-22842
I. Title.

GRATTON, John, 1641- 922.8642
1712.
A journal of the life of that ancient servant of Christ, John Gratton, giving an account of his exercises when young, and how he came to the knowledge of the truth, and was thereby raised up to preach the gospel; as also of his labors, travels, and sufferings for the same ... Stanford: (N. Y.) Printed by Daniel Lawrence for Henry Hull, and John F. Hull, 1805. xxvii, [29]-224 p. 17 cm. [BX7795.G6A3 1805] 32-19895
I. Title.

GRATTON, John, 1641- 922.8642
1712.
A journal of the life of that ancient servant of Christ, John Gratton, giving an account of his exercises when young, and how he came to the knowledge of the truth, and was thereby raised up to preach the gospel; as also of his labors, travels, and sufferings for the same ... Stanford: (N. Y.) Printed by Daniel Lawrence for Henry Hull, and John F. Hull, 1805. xxvii, [29]-224 p. 17 cm. [BX7795.G6A3 1805] 32-19895
I. Title.

GRATTON, John, 1641- 922.8642
1712.
A journal of the life of that ancient servant of Christ, John Gratton, giving an account of his exercises when young, and how he came to the knowledge of the truth, and was thereby raised up to preach the gospel; as also of his labors, travels, and sufferings for the same ... Stanford: (N. Y.) Printed by Daniel Lawrence for Henry Hull, and John F. Hull, 1805. xxvii, [29]-224 p. 17 cm. [BX7795.G6A3 1805] 32-19895
I. Title.

GRAY, Edna. Mrs. 920.7
One woman's life. The steppings of faith. Edna Gray's story. (Rev. ed.) Atlanta, Ga., The Franklin printing and publishing co., 1900. xii, 352 p. incl. plates. port. 21 cm. "The story is ... only unreal in the use of fictitions names ... except in a few instances. [BR1725.G83A3 1900] 36-21120
I. Title.

GREEN, John Edgar, 1856- 922.
John E. Green and his forty years in Houston, by Rev. John E. Green. Houston, Tex., Dealy-Adey-Elgin co., 1928. 176 p. front. (port.) 21 cm. [BX8495.G67A3] 28-22470
I. Title.

GREEN, John Edgar, 1856- 922.
John E. Green and his forty years in Houston, by Rev. John E. Green. Houston, Tex., Dealy-Adey-Elgin co., 1928. 176 p. front. (port.) 21 cm. [BX8495.G67A3] 28-22470
I. Title.

GRIBBLE, Florence Alma 922.667
(Newberry) 1879-1942.
Stranger than fiction, a partial record of answered prayer in the life of Dr. Florence N. Gribble. Winona Lake, Ind., Published for for the Foreign Missionary Society of the Brethren Church, by the Brethren Missionary Herald Co., 1949. xi, 249 p. illus., ports., maps. 24 cm. [BV3522.G7A3] 50-3972
I. Title.

GRONNIOSAW, James Albert 922
Ukawsaw.
A narrative of the most remarkable particulars in the life of James Albert. Akawsaw, Granwasa: as dictated by Himself. Second American edition. Catskill, [N. Y.]. Printed at the Eagle office, 1810. 96 p. 14 cm. Dedication signed: James Albert. [BV4935.G] A 33
I. Title.

GROSE, George Richmond, 275.
1869-
The new soul in China, by George Richmond Grose ... New York, Cincinnati, The Abingdon press [c1927] 152 p. 18 cm. [BV3415.G75] 27-13939
I. Title.

GUARESCHI, Giovanni, 1908-
Don Camillo and his flock; translated by Frances Frenaye. New York, All Saints Press [1961, c1952] 232 p. illus. 17 cm. 63-27173
I. Title.

GUGLIELMI, Francesco.
The Italian Methodist mission in the Little Italy of Baltimore, Md., by Rev. Francesco Guglielmi, B. D. Seven years of evangelical Christian work. [Baltimore, Md., Printed by W. V. Guthrie, c1912] 208 p. illus. 19 cm. 12-18338 0.50
I. Title.

GUGLIELMI, Francesco.
The Italian Methodist mission in the Little Italy of Baltimore, Md., by Rev. Francesco Guglielmi, B. D. Seven years of evangelical Christian work. [Baltimore, Md., Printed by W. V. Guthrie, c1912] 208 p. illus. 19 cm. 12-18338 0.50
I. Title.

GURNEY, Eliza Paul 922.
(Kirkbride) Mrs. 1801-1881.
Memoir and correspondence of Eliza P. Gurney. Edited by Richard F. Mott. Philadelphia, J. B. Lippincott & co., 1884. 377 p. front. (port.) plates, double facsim. 20 cm. [BX7795.G88A3] 42-5719
I. Mott, Richard F., b. 1825, ed. II. Title.

GURNEY, Eliza Paul 922.
(Kirkbride) Mrs. 1801-1881.
Memoir and correspondence of Eliza P. Gurney. Edited by Richard F. Mott. Philadelphia, J. B. Lippincott & co., 1884. 377 p. front. (port.) plates, double facsim. 20 cm. [BX7795.G88A3] 42-5719
I. Mott, Richard F., b. 1825, ed. II. Title.

-GURNEY, Priscilla, 1785- 922.
1821.
Memoir, ed. by Susanna Corder. Philadelphia, H. Longstreth, 1856. 228 p. 22 cm. [BX7795.G87A4] ISBN 49-32062
I. Corder, Susanna, 1787 or 8-1864 ed. II. Title.

-GURNEY, Priscilla, 1785- 922.
1821.
Memoir, ed. by Susanna Corder. Philadelphia, H. Longstreth, 1856. 228 p. 22 cm. [BX7795.G87A4] ISBN 49-32062
I. Corder, Susanna, 1787 or 8-1864 ed. II. Title.

GUYON, Jeanne Marie 922.244
(Bouvier de La Motte) 1648-1717.
Autobiography of Madame Guyon. Complete in two parts. New York, E. Jones, 1880. v, 346 p. 18 cm. [BX4705.G8A4 1880] 37-18192
I. Title.

GUYON, Jeanne Marie 922.
(Bouvier de La Motte) 1648-1717.
Autobiography of Madame Guyon... Chicago, Christian witness co. [c1917] v. [1] 346 p. 20 cm. Preface to 1917 edition signed: E. L. K. [i.e. Elmer L. Kletzing] [BX4705.G8A4 1917] 18-2988
I. Kletzing, Elmer L., ed. II. Title.

[HALES, Jacob Cecil] 1864-
"That they all may be one;" a plea for the reunion of Christians ... by a layman. Petersburg, Va., The Franklin press company, c1908. 183, [6] p. 19 1/2 cm. 8-20483
I. Title.

HALL, Manly Palmer. 922
Twelve world teachers; a summary of their lives and teachings, by Manly P. Hall. 1st ed. Los Angeles, Calif., The Philosophers press, 1937. 2 p. l., 3-237 p. illus. (ports.) 24 cm. [BL72.H3] 38-17808
1. Religions—Biog. 2. Philosophers. I. Title.

HALL, Rufus, 1744-1818. 922.
A journal of the life, religious exercises, and travels in the work of the ministry of Rufus Hall. Byberry [Philadelphia] J. and I. Comly, 1840. iv, 176 p. 18 cm. [BX7795.H353.A3] 50-42706
I. Title.

HALL, Rufus, 1744-1818. 922.
A journal of the life, religious exercises, and travels in the work of the ministry of Rufus Hall. Byberry [Philadelphia] J. and I. Comly, 1840. iv, 176 p. 18 cm. [BX7795.H353.A3] 50-42706
I. Title.

HALL, Rufus, 1744-1818. 922. *A journal of the life, religious exercises, and travels in the work of the ministry of Rufus Hall.* Byberry [Philadelphia] J. and I. Comly, 1840. iv, 176 p. 18 cm. [BX7795.H353.A3] 50-42706
I. Title.

HALL, Rufus, 1744-1818. 922. *A journal of the life, religious exercises, and travels in the work of the ministry of Rufus Hall.* Byberry [Philadelphia] J. and I. Comly, 1840. iv, 176 p. 18 cm. [BX7795.H353.A3] 50-42706
I. Title.

HALLIDAY, Jerry. 248'.83 *Spaced out and gathered in;* a sort of an autobiography of a Jesus freak. Old Tappan, N.J., F. H. Revell Co. [1972] 126 p. 18 cm. [BV4935.H26A3] 78-186536 ISBN 0-8007-0511-4 0.95 (pbk)
I. Title.

HALYBURTON, Thomas, 1674- 922.541 1712. *Memoirs of the Rev. Thomas Halyburton* ... with an introductory essay by Robert Burns ... and a preface by Archibald Alexander, D.D. Princeton, N. J., Baker & Connolly; New York, J. Leavitt; [etc.] 1833. xiix, [51]-299 p. 18 1/2 cm. [BX9225.H315.A3 1833] 33-17063
I. Burns, Robert, 1789-1869. II. Title.

HANSON, Miles. 922. *Out of old paths,* by Miles Hanson... Boston, Mass., The Beacon press [c1919] ix p., 1 l., 103 p. pl. 19 cm. Autobiographical, dealing especially with the author's changes of belief. [BX9869.H35A3] 19-11652
I. Title.

HARDING, Ulla Earl, 1882- 922 *Is the young man safe?* By Rev. U.E. Harding... West Salem, Ill. [Silent evangel society press, Indianapolis] 1911. 96 p. 2 port. (incl. front.) 19 cm. Autobiography. [BV3785.H345A3] 37-36771
I. Title.

HARDING, Ulla Earl, 1882- 922 *Is the young man safe?* By Rev. U.E. Harding... West Salem, Ill. [Silent evangel society press, Indianapolis] 1911. 96 p. 2 port. (incl. front.) 19 cm. Autobiography. [BV3785.H345A3] 37-36771
I. Title.

HAVEN, Erastus Otis, 922.773 bp., 1820-1881. *Autobiography of Erastus O. Haven...* Edited by The Rev. C. C. Stratton... With an introduction by the Rev. J. M. Buckley... New York, Phillips & Hunt; Cincinnati, Walden & Stowe, 1883. 329 p. incl. front. (port.) 19 cm. [BX8495.H27A3] 923.773 36-36940
I. Stratton, Charles Carroll, 1833-1910, ed. II. Title.

HAVNER, Vance, 286'.1'0924 B 1901- *Three-score & ten.* Old Tappan, N.J., F. H. Revell Co. [1973] 127 p. front. 21 cm. Autobiographical. [BX6495.H288A33] 72-10390 ISBN 0-8007-0578-5 4.95
I. Title.

HAWKER, Beatrice, 1910- 922 *Look back in love.* Illustrated by Rosemary Haughton. London, New York, Longmans, Green [1958] 149p. illus. 21cm. Autobiographical. [BR1725.H25A3] 59-2029
I. Title.

[HAWKINS, Anthony Hope] 1863- *Half a hero and Father Stafford,* by Anthony Hope [pseud.] ... New York, D. Appleton and company [c1902] vii, 264 p., 1 l., 187 p. front. 22 cm. (Half-title: Author's edition. Works of Anthony Hope...) "Baliol. Limited to one thousand sets." This copy not numbered. 3-24984
I. Title.

HAWLEY, Carrie Moss, Mrs. 131 *My soul and I,* by Carrie Moss Hawley. Boston, The Four seas company [c1926] 196 p. 20 1/2 cm. [BF639.H54] 26-10210
I. Title.

*HAYES, Wanda 232.9 *My Jesus book;* stories. Illus. by Frances Hook [Cincinnati, Ohio, Standard Pub. Co., 1964. c.1963] unpaged. col. illus. 31cm. (3046) cover title. 1.50 bds.,
I. Title.

HAYWARD, Helen (Harry). 253 *The other foot.* New York, Vantage Press [1951] 122 p. 23 cm. Autobiographical. [BR1725.H28A3] 51-8782
I. Title.

HAZARD, Thomas Benjamin, 920 1756-1845. *Nailer Tom's diary;* otherwise, The journal of Thomas B. Hazard of Kingstown, Rhode Island, 1778 to 1840, which includes observations on the weather, records of births, marriages and deaths, transactions by barter and money of varying value, preaching Friends and neighborhood gossip. Printed as written and introduced by Caroline Hazard ... Boston, The Merrymount press, 1930. xxiv, 808 p. 28 1/2 cm. "Four hundred copies printed." [F83.H42] 30-25828
I. Hazard, Caroline, 1856- ed. II. Title.

HAZARD, Thomas Benjamin, 920 1756-1845. *Nailer Tom's diary;* otherwise, The journal of Thomas B. Hazard of Kingstown, Rhode Island, 1778 to 1840, which includes observations on the weather, records of births, marriages and deaths, transactions by barter and money of varying value, preaching Friends and neighborhood gossip. Printed as written and introduced by Caroline Hazard ... Boston, The Merrymount press, 1930. xxiv, 808 p. 28 1/2 cm. "Four hundred copies printed." [F83.H42] 30-25828
I. Hazard, Caroline, 1856- ed. II. Title.

HEALY, Christopher, 1773- 922. 1851. *Memoir of Christopher Healy,* principally taken from his own memoranda. Philadelphia, Friends' Book Store, 1886. 258 p. 19 cm. [BX7795.H4A4] 49-32071
I. Title.

HENRICHSEN, Margaret. 922.773 *Seven steeples;* illustrated by William Barss. Boston, Houghton Mifflin, 1953. 238 p. illus. 22 cm. Autobiographical. [BX8495.H397A3] 53-9251
I. Title.

HENRY, George W., b.1801. 922. *Trials and triumphs (for a half a century) in the life of G. W. Henry* ... Together with the religious experience of his wife. To which are added, one hundred spiritual songs, with music ... 5th thousand. Enl. and stereotyped, and illustrated with a steel engraving of the author's whole family. Auburn, W. J. Moses, 1856. 349, 159, [1] p. front., illus. (music) ports. 15 cm. Title edition. Identical, except for title pages, with the 2d edition, New York, 1853. "One hundred spiritual songs" has special t.-p.: The golden harp; or, Camp meeting hymns, old and new. Set to music. Selected by G. W. Henry ... Auburn, 1856. [BX8495.H4A3 1856] 1-1081
I. Title.

HENRY, George W., b.1801. 922. *Trials and triumphs (for half a century) in the life of G. W. Henry ... Together with the religious experience of his wife. To which are added, one hundred spiritual songs, with music* ... 2d ed., enl. and stereotyped, and illustrated with a steel engraving of the author's whole family. New York, Pub. for the author, 1853. 349, 159, [1] p. front., illus. (music) ports. 15 cm. "One hundred spiritual songs" has special t.-p.: The golden harp; or, Camp meeting hymns, old and new. Set to music. Selected by G. W. Henry ... Auburn, W. J. Moses, 1855. Lettered on cover: Travels in Egypt, twilight & Beulah by a blind man. [BX8495.H4A3 1853] 29-30658
I. Title. II. Title: Travels in Egypt, twilight & Beulah.

HENRY, George W., b.1801. *Trials and triumphs for three score years and ten in the life of G. W. Henry ... together with the religious experience of his wife* ... [2d ed.] 11th thousand sold. Frankfort, N.Y., 1871. 1 p. l., 448 p. 15 1/2 cm. On cover: Travels in Egypt, twilight and Beulah by a blind man. 5-16547
I. Title.

HENSON, Herbert Hensley, 922.342 bp. of Durham, 1863- *Retrospect of an unimportant life* [by] Herbert Hensley Henson ... London, New York [etc.] Oxford university press, 1942-19- v. plates, ports. 22 cm. [BX5199.H45A4] 42-51083
I. Title.

HERVE-BAZIN, Marie Anne 922. Henriette Lucie, 1877-1901. *Marie de l'Agnus Dei;* a sketch of the life of Marie-Anne-Herve-Bazin, religious of the Society of Marie-Reparatrice, by Mme. S. S., with a preface by M. Rene Bazin ... translated from the fifth edition of Une religieuse reparatrice by Rev. Michael P. Hill, S. J. New York, The Macmillan company, 1923. xxi, 345 p. 21 cm. [Name in religion: Marie de l'Agnus Dei] [BX4705.H56A3] 23-9379
I. S., Mme. S. II. S. S., Mme. III. Hill, Michael Peter, 1855- tr. IV. Title.

HEUSER, Herman Joseph, 922.273 1851-1933, ed. *An ex-prelate's meditations,* edited by Herman J. Heuser ... New York [etc.] Longmans, Green and co., 1923. vi, 233 p. 20 cm. "Desultory reflection that embodys recollections, observations, experiences, and regrets of a long life in the ministry of the sanctuary."--Introd. [BX4705.H565A3] 23-18353
I. Title.

HEWITT, Arthur 253.0924 Wentworth, 1883- *The old brick manse.* New York, Harper [c.1966] vi, 246p. 22cm. Autobiography. [BX8495.H52A3] 66-10674 4.95
I. Title.

HEWITT, Arthur 253.0924 Wentworth, 1883- *The old brick manse.* [1st ed.]) New York, Harper & Row [c1966] vi, 246 p. 22 cm. Autobiography. [BX8495.H52A3] 66-10674
I. Title.

HILL, William B., b.1843. 230. *Experiences of a pioneer minister of Minnesota.* By Elder W. B. Hill. Minneapolis, Press of J. A. Folsom, 1892. 185 p. front. (port.) 20 cm. [BX6193.H5A3] 46-35627
I. Title.

HILLARD, Frederick Hadaway. 290 *The Buddha, the Prophet, and the Christ.* London, G. Allen & Unwin; New York, Macmillan [1956] 169p. 19cm. (Ethical and religious classics of East and West. no. 16) [BL72.H5] 57-202
1. Religions—Biog. 2. Buddha and Buddhism. 3. Muhammad, the prophet. 4. Jesus Christ—Divinity. I. Title.

HILLIARD, Frederick Hadaway. 290 *The Buddha,* the Prophet, and the Christ. London, G. Allen & Unwin; New York, Macmillan [1956] 169p. 19cm. (Ethical and religiuns classics of East and West, no. 16) [BL72.H5] 57-202
1. Religions—Biog. 2. Buddha and Buddhism. 3. Muhammad, the prophet. 4. Jesus Christ—Divinity. I. Title.

HOAG, Joseph, 1762-1846. *Journal of the life of Joseph Hoag,* an eminent minister of the gospel, in the Society of Friends ... Auburn, Knapp & Peck, printers, 1861. xiv, [9]-389 p. 18 1/2 cm. Errata slip at end. 8-25292
I. Title.

HOAG, Joseph, 1762-1846. *Journal of the life of Joseph Hoag,* an eminent minister of the gospel, in the Society of Friends ... Auburn, Knapp & Peck, printers, 1861. xiv, [9]-389 p. 18 1/2 cm. Errata slip at end. 8-25292
I. Title.

HOAG, Joseph, 1762-1846. *Journal of the life of Joseph Hoag,* an eminent minister of the gospel, in the Society of Friends ... Auburn, Knapp & Peck, printers, 1861. xiv, [9]-389 p. 18 1/2 cm. Errata slip at end. 8-25292
I. Title.

HOGG, Rena L. *A master-builder on the Nile;* being a record of the life and aims of John Hogg, D.D., Christian missionary, by Rena L. Hogg... New York, Chicago [etc.] Fleming H. Revell company [c1914] 304 p. plates, 2 port. (incl. front.) 21 1/2 cm. 14-11322 1.50
I. Title.

HOGG, Rena L. *A master-builder on the Nile;* being a record of the life and aims of John Hogg, D.D., Christian missionary, by Rena L. Hogg... New York, Chicago [etc.] Fleming H. Revell company [c1914] 304 p. plates, 2 port. (incl. front.) 21 1/2 cm. 14-11322 1.50
I. Title.

HOLDICH, Joseph, 1804- 922.773 1893. *The Wesleyan student;* or, Memoirs of Aaron Haynes Hurd, late a member of the Wesleyan university, Middletown, Conn. By Joseph Holdich ... Middletown, E. Hunt & co.; Boston, D. S. King, 1839. vii, [9]-281 p. 16 1/2 cm. [BR1725.H85H6] 38-3205
I. Hurd, Aaron Haynes, 1813-1836. II. Title.

HOLDICH, Joseph, 1804- 922.773 1893. *The Wesleyan student;* or, Memoirs of Aaron Haynes Hurd, late a member of the Wesleyan university, Middletown, Conn. By Joseph Holdich ... New York, G. Lane, for the Methodist Episcopal church, 1841. 288 p. 14 1/2 cm. Second edition. [BR1725.H85H6 1841] 38-3102
I. Hurd, Aaron Haynes, 1813-1836. II. Title.

HOLMES, John Haynes, 922.8173 1879-1964. *I speak for myself;* the autobiography of John Haynes Holmes. [1st ed.] New York, Harper [1959] 308 p. illus. 22 cm. [BX9869.H535A33] 59-5220
I. Title.

HORTON, James P., 922.773 b.1769. *A narrative of the early life, remarkable conversion and spiritual labours of James P Horton,* who has been a member of the Methodist Episcopal church upward of forty years. [n.p.] Printed for the author, 1839. 216 p. front. (port.) 15 cm. [BX8495.H57.A3] 36-36934
I. Title.

HORTON, James P., 922.773 b.1769. *A narrative of the early life, remarkable conversion and spiritual labours of James P Horton,* who has been a member of the Methodist Episcopal church upward of forty years. [n.p.] Printed for the author, 1839. 216 p. front. (port.) 15 cm. [BX8495.H57.A3] 36-36934
I. Title.

HOUSE, Abigail (Clark) Mrs., 1790-1861. *Memoirs of the religious experience and life of Abigail House,* late of Lenox, Ohio, and relict of the late Col. E. N. House. Pub. according to the last will of the author. Jefferson, O., Ashtabula sentinel steam press, 1861. iv, [5]-264 p. 18 1/2 cm. Advertisement signed: Josiah Atkins. 16-21899
I. Atkins, Josiah, ed. II. Title.

HOUTIN, Albert, 1867- *A married priest,* by Albert Houtin, tr. from the French, by John Richard Slattery. Boston, Sherman, French & company, 1910. 100 p. 20 cm. $0.70 10-4787
I. Slattery, John Richard, tr. II. Title.

HOUTIN, Albert, 1867- *A married priest,* by Albert Houtin, tr. from the French, by John Richard Slattery. Boston, Sherman, French & company, 1910. 100 p. 20 cm. $0.70 10-4787
I. Slattery, John Richard, tr. II. Title.

HUBBARD, Elbert, 1856- *The Man of sorrows,* by Elbert Hubbard. [East Aurora, N.Y., The Roycrofters,

1905] 5 p. l., 111, [1] p., 1 l. 22 1/2 cm. Illuminated t.-p. Colophon: So here endeth The Man of sorrows, being a little journey to the home of Jesus of Nazareth, by Elbert Hubbard. A sincere attempt to depict the life, times and teachings, and with truth limn the personality of the Man of sorrows. Done into a book by the Roycrofters at East Aurora, N.Y., 1905 years from the birth of the Man of sorrows. 5-12172
I. Title.

HUNT, Sarah (Morey) 1797-1889.
Journal of the life and religious labors of Sarah Hunt, (late of West Grove, Chester county, Pennsylvania) Philadelphia, Friends' book association, 1892. 1 p. l., 262 p. front. (port.) 19 1/2 cm. 11-21125
I. Title.

HUNT, Sarah (Morey) 1797-1889.
Journal of the life and religious labors of Sarah Hunt, (late of West Grove, Chester county, Pennsylvania) Philadelphia, Friends' book association, 1892. 1 p. l., 262 p. front. (port.) 19 1/2 cm. 11-21125
I. Title.

HUSE, Raymond Howard, 1880- 922.773
The autobiography of a plain preacher. Boston, Meador Pub. Co. [1949] 121 p. illus., ports. 21 cm. [BX8495.H86A3] 49-1307
I. Title.

HUTCHINSON, Forney, 1875- 922.773
My treasure chest, an indirect autobiography [by] Forney Hutchinson, D.D. Emory University, Ga., Banner press [c1943] 213 p. incl. front. (port.) 20 1/2 cm. [BX8495.H37A3] 44-3492
I. Title.

HUTCHINSON, Jonathan, 1760-1835. 922.
Memoir of Jonathan Hutchinson, with selections from his letters. Philadelphia, Assn. of Friends for the Diffusion of Religious and Useful Knowledge, 1860. 120 p. 16 cm. "Selected from a volume published in London, in 1841, entitled 'Extracts from the letters of Jonathan Hutchinson, with some brief notices of his life and character.'" [BX7795.H87A42] 48-42285
I. Title.

HYDE, Alvan, 1768-1833. 922
Memoir of Rev. Alvan Hyde, D. D., of Lee, Mass. Boston, Perkins, Marvin, & co.; Philadelphia, H. Perkins, 1835. vii, [13]-408 p. front. (port.) 19 cm. Diary and letters of Dr. Hyde. cf. p. [iii] [BX7260.H89A4] 36-8148
I. Title.

HYDE, Alvan, 1768-1833. 922
Memoir of Rev. Alvan Hyde, D. D., of Lee, Mass. Boston, Perkins, Marvin, & co.; Philadelphia, H. Perkins, 1835. vii, [13]-408 p. front. (port.) 19 cm. Diary and letters of Dr. Hyde. cf. p. [iii] [BX7260.H89A4] 36-8148
I. Title.

IMITATIO Christi. English. 242.1
Meditations from the following of Christ of Thomas a Kempis. Arr. from an old translation, by Ivah May Navaro. Illus. by Caroline Williams. [Burlington, Ky.] Penandhoe Press, 1954. 98p. illus. 16cm. [BV4821.N3] 54-39719
I. Navaro, Ivah May, 1906- ed. II. Title.

JACOBS, Bela, 1786-1836. 922.673
Memoir of Rev. Bela Jacobs, A. M., compiled chiefly from his letters and journals, by his daughter. With a sketch of his character, by Barnas Sears ... Boston, Gould, Kendall & Lincoln, 1837. vii, [9]-305 p. front. (port.) 17 cm. Signed: S. S. J. [i. e. Sarah Sprague Jacobs] [BX6495.J34A3] 36-24286
I. Jacobs, Sarah Sprague, b. 1813, ed. II. Sears, Barnas, 1802-1880. III. Title.

JACOBS, Bela, 1786-1836. 922.673
Memoir of Rev. Bela Jacobs, A. M., compiled chiefly from his letters and journals, by his daughter. With a sketch of his character, by Barnas Sears ... Boston, Gould, Kendall & Lincoln, 1837. vii, [9]-305 p. front. (port.) 17 cm. Signed: S. S. J. [i. e. Sarah Sprague Jacobs] [BX6495.J34A3] 36-24286
I. Jacobs, Sarah Sprague, b. 1813, ed. II. Sears, Barnas, 1802-1880. III. Title.

JAY, William, 1769-1853. 922.742
Memoirs of the life and character of the late Rev. Cornelius Winter; compiled and composed by William Jay ... 1st American ed. New-York: Published by Samuel Whiting & co. at their theological and classical book-store; no. 118 Pearlstreet. J. Seymour, printer, 1811. xi, [1], 371 p. 18 cm. [BX8495.W665J3 1811] 38-19133
I. Winter, Cornelius, 1742-1808. II. Title.

JEFFERYS, William Hamilton, 1871- 922.351
James Addison Ingle (Yin Teh-sen) first bishop of the missionary district of Hankow, China, by W. H. Jefferys ... New York, The Domestic and foreign missionary society, 1913. viii, 286 p. front. illus., plates. ports. 20 cm. [BV3427.I5J4] 14-14225
I. Ingle, James, Addison, bp., 1867-1903. II. Title.

JEFFERYS, William Hamilton, 1871- 922.351
James Addison Ingle (Yin Teh-sen) first bishop of the missionary district of Hankow, China, by W. H. Jefferys ... New York, The Domestic and foreign missionary society, 1913. viii, 286 p. front. illus., plates. ports. 20 cm. [BV3427.I5J4] 14-14225
I. Ingle, James, Addison, bp., 1867-1903. II. Title.

*JENSEN, Conrad S. 241
Twenty-six years on the losing side. Oradell, N.J., Amer. Tract. Soc., 660 Kinderkamack Rd. [1965, c.1964] 83p. 22cm. .85 pap.,
I. Title.

JESSOPP, Augustus, 1824-1914.
The trials of a country parson, by Augustus Jessopp ... New York, G. P. Putnam's sons; [etc., etc.] 1890. xxx p., 1 l., 295 p. 20 cm. "The first six essays have, in the main, appeared in the 'Nineteenth century': the seventh first saw the light in the 'North American review'." 12-34728
I. Title.
Contents omitted.

JEWELL, Earle B., 1896- 252.03
The rector's scrapbook, by Earle B. Jewell. Kansas City, Mo., Brown-White-Lowell press [1947] 238 p. 20 1/2 cm. [BX5845.J4] 47-17073
I. Title.

JOHN William Carter,
D. D. Sketches of his life, estimates of his character and work, selections from his sermons. [Charleston, W. Va., n. d.] 223p. illus. ports. O. 'The pastorate at Raleigh, N. C.,' by Thomas H. Briggs, pp. 43-45.
I. Johnson, T C II. Carter, John William, 1836-1907. III. Releigh, N. C. First Baptist Church. IV. Carter, John William, 1836-1907.

JOHN William Carter,
D. D. Sketches of his life, estimates of his character and work, selections from his sermons. [Charleston, W. Va., n. d.] 223p. illus. ports. O. 'The pastorate at Raleigh, N. C.,' by Thomas H. Briggs, pp. 43-45.
I. Johnson, T C II. Carter, John William, 1836-1907. III. Releigh, N. C. First Baptist Church. IV. Carter, John William, 1836-1907.

JONES, Abner, 1772-1841. 922.673
Memoir of Elder Abner Jones. By his son, A. D. Jones ... Boston, W. Crosby & company, 1842. viii, [9]-207 p. incl. front. (port.) 19 cm. [BX6793.J6A3] 36-32227
I. Jones, Abner Dumont, 1807-1872, ed. II. Title.

JONES, Eliza (Grew) Mrs. 1803-1838. 922.659
Memoir of Mrs. Eliza G. Jones, missionary to Burmah and Siam. Revised by the Committee of publication. Philadelphia, American Baptist publication and Sunday school society, 1842. 172 p. front. (port.) 16 cm. [BV3705.J6A3] 38-3100
I. American Baptist publication society. II. Title.

JONES, Eliza (Grew) Mrs. 1803-1838. 922.659
Memoir of Mrs. Eliza G. Jones, missionary to Burmah and Siam. Revised by the Committee of publication. Philadelphia, American Baptist publication and Sunday school society, 1842. 172 p. front. (port.) 16 cm. [BV3705.J6A3] 38-3100
I. American Baptist publication society. II. Title.

JONES, Jesse Henry, 1836-1904.
Joshua Davidson, Christian; the story of the life of one who, in the nineteenth century, was "like unto Christ;" as told by his body-servant; a parable by Jesse H. Jones; ed. by Halah H. Loud. New York, The Grafton press [c1907] 3 p. l., v-xviii p., 1 l., 308 p. front., ports. 21 cm. "Joshua Davidson is purely a fictitious character, who has been made to utter the teachings to which Mr. Jones devoted his life."--Editor's pref. 7-23698
I. Loud, Halah H., ed. II. Title.

JONES, Mary Alice, 1898- 268
Guiding children in Christian growth. C. A. Bowan, general editor. New York, Published for the Co-operative Pub. Association by Abingdon-Cokesbury Press [1949] 160 p. 19 cm. Bibliographies: p. 157-160. [BV1475.J533] 49-50011
1. Religious education of children. I. Title.

JONES, Mary Alice, 1898- 268
Guiding children in Christian growth. C. A. Bowan, general editor. New York, Published for the Co-operative Pub. Association by Abingdon-Cokesbury Press [1949] 160 p. 19 cm. Bibliographies: p. 157-160. [BV1475.J533] 49-50011
1. Religious education of children. I. Title.

JONES, Sylvester. 922.8673
Not by might, a little that is never too late, by Sylvester Jones. Elgin, Ill., Printed for the author by the Brethren publishing house, 1942. 4 p. l., [7]-159 p. illus. (map) 20 cm. Reminiscences. [BX7795.J57A3] 42-21915
I. Title.

JONES, Sylvester. 922.8673
Not by might, a little that is never too late, by Sylvester Jones. Elgin, Ill., Printed for the author by the Brethren publishing house, 1942. 4 p. l., [7]-159 p. illus. (map) 20 cm. Reminiscences. [BX7795.J57A3] 42-21915
I. Title.

JORDAN Of Saxony d.1237. 922.245
To heaven with Diana! A study of Jordan of Saxony and Diana d'Andalo, with a translation of the letters of Jordan, by Gerald Vann. [New York] Pantheon Books [1960] 160p. 22cm. [BX4705.J7A43] 60-11759
I. Diana de Andalc, 1201 (ca.)- 1236. II. Vann, Gerald, 1906- III. Title.

KAUFMANN, Walter Arnold.
The faith of a heretic. Garden City, New York, Doubleday [1963] viii, 414 p. (Anchor books A336) 65-37996
I. Title.

KAUFMANN, Walter Arnold.
The faith of a heretic. Garden City, New York, Doubleday [1963] viii, 414 p. (Anchor books A336) 65-37996
I. Title.

KEACH, Benjamin, 1640-1704. 248
The travels of True Godliness. By Rev. Benjamin Keach ... Revised and improved; with occasional notes, and a memoir of his life; by Howard Malcom, A.M. 2d ed. Boston, Lincoln & Edmands, 1831. 1 p. l., iv, [5]-212 p. 3 pl. (incl. front.) 16 1/2 cm. Added t.-p., engraved. [BV4515.K4 1831] 5-28766
I. Malcom, Howard, 1799-1879, ed. II. Title.

KEACH, Benjamin, 1640-1704.
The travels of True Godliness. By Benjamin Keach. Revised and improved. With a memoir of his life. By Howard Malcom ... Boston, Lincoln & Edmands, 1829. 1 p. l., vi, [7]-208 p. front. 17 cm. Added t.-p., engr. 5-28764
I. Malcom, Howard, 1799-1879, ed. II. Title.

KELLER, Helen 248
My religion. New York, Swedenborg Found. [1962] 208p. 18cm. 1.00
I. Title.

KELLER, Helen Adams 230.94
My religion. New York, Avon c.1927, 1960 157p. 17cm. (Bard bk. 7; Avon bk. T-07) .35 pap.,
I. Title.

KENDALL, Henry, b.1774. 922.673
Autobiography of Elder Henry Kendal, with an introduction by Prof. J. T. Champlin, Portland [Me.] The author, 1853. vi, [7]-201 p. front. (port.) 16 cm. [BX6495.K37A3] 36-29860
I. Title.

KERSEY, Jesse, 1768-1845. 922.
A narrative of the early life, travels, and gospel labors of Jesse Kersey. late of Chester county, Pennsylvania. Philadelphia, T. E. Chapman, 1851. iv, [5]-288 p. 19 1/2 cm. "Essays and letters": p. 179-288. [BX7795.K45A3] 46-44165
I. Title.

KERSEY, Jesse, 1768-1845. 922.
A narrative of the early life, travels, and gospel labors of Jesse Kersey. late of Chester county, Pennsylvania. Philadelphia, T. E. Chapman, 1851. iv, [5]-288 p. 19 1/2 cm. "Essays and letters": p. 179-288. [BX7795.K45A3] 46-44165
I. Title.

KETCHUM, Creston Donald. 266.585281
Bread upon the waters. [1st ed.] Rutland, Vt., C. E. Tuttle Co. [1964] 196 p. illus., ports. 22 cm. Autobiographical. Sequel to His path is in the waters. [BV3705.K47A33] 64-13267
I. Title.

KETCHUM, Creston Donald. 266.585281
Bread upon the waters. [1st ed.] Rutland, Vt., C. E. Tuttle Co. [1964] 196 p. illus., ports. 22 cm. Autobiographical. Sequel to His path is in the waters. [BV3705.K47A33] 64-13267
I. Title.

KILGORE, Elias Gaston, 1856- 922.
Trials and triumphs of a young preacher, with additional notes, by Rev. E. G. Kilgore ... Autobiography. Nashville, Tenn., Dallas, Tex., Publishing house of the M. E. church, South, Smith & Lamar, agents, 1908. 421 p. front. (port.) 19 cm. [BX8495.K53A3] 9-7927
I. Title.

KILGORE, Elias Gaston, 1856-
Trials and triumphs of a young preacher, with additional notes, by Rev. E. G. Kilgore...Autobiography. Nashville, Tenn., Dallas, Tex., Publishing house of the M.E. church, South, Smith & Lamar, agents, 1908. 421 p. front. (port.) 19 cm. 9-7927
I. Title.

KILLGORE, Robert Fansier.
Sparks from the burning bush. Thoughts that are original on special subjects. Sermons and letters. A short autobiographical sketch of the Rev. Robert Fansler Killgore... Olney, Ill. [c1901] 209, [1] p. front., port. 20 1/2 cm. Actual copyright entry, 1903. 3-13386
I. Title.

KING, William, abp. of Dublin, 1650-1729. 922.
A great archbishop of Dublin, William King, D.D., 1650-1729. His autobiography, family, and a selection from his correspondence. Ed. by Sir Charles Simeon King, bt. ... London, New York [etc.] Longmans, Green, and co., 1906. xii p., 1 l., 332 p. illus., 2 pl. 5 port. (incl. front.) 23 1/2 cm. Errata slip inserted before p. [1] [BX5595.K5A3] 8-3985
I. King, Sir Charles Simeon, 1840-1921, ed. II. Title.
Contents omitted.

KINGDON, Frank, 1894- 922.773
Jacob's ladder: The days of my youth, by Frank Kingdon. New York, L. B. Fischer [1943] vi p., 1 l., 312 p. 21 cm. "First edition." [BX8495.K57A3] 43-6958
I. Title.

KINGDON, Frank, 1894- 922.773
Jacob's ladder: The days of my youth, by Frank Kingdon. New York, L. B. Fischer [1943] vi p., 1 l., 312 p. 21 cm. "First edition." [BX8495.K57A3] 43-6958
I. Title.

KIRTON, John William, 1831-1892.
... Dr. Guthrie. Father Mathew. Elihu Burritt. Joseph Livesey. By John William Kirton ... London, New York [etc.] Cassell & company, limited, 1885. 128 p. front. (4 port.) 19 cm. (The world's workers) [HV5030.K6] 6-35780
I. Title.

KITTO, John, 1804-1854. 922
Memoirs of John Kitto ... compiled chiefly from his letters and journals. By J. E. Ryland ... With a critical estimate of Dr. Kitto's life and writings, by Professor Eadie ... New York, R. Carter & brother, 1857. 2 v. front. (port.) 19 cm. [BR1725.K5A3 1857] 38-3073
I. Ryland, Jonathan Edwards, 1798-1866, ed. II. Eadie, John, 1810-1876. III. Title.

KITTO, John, 1804-1854. 922
Memoirs of John Kitto ... compiled chiefly from his letters and journals. By J. E. Ryland ... With a critical estimate of Dr. Kitto's life and writings, by Professor Eadie ... New York, R. Carter & brother, 1857. 2 v. front. (port.) 19 cm. [BR1725.K5A3 1857] 38-3073
I. Ryland, Jonathan Edwards, 1798-1866, ed. II. Eadie, John, 1810-1876. III. Title.

KOGER, Nannie Elizabeth, 922.773
1862-
My life story, by Nan Elizabeth Koger. [Cincinnati, Printed by the Revivalist press, c1940] 70 p. front. (port.) 20 cm. [CT275.K83A3] 41-6963
I. Title.

KOGER, Nannie Elizabeth, 922.773
1862-
My life story, by Nan Elizabeth Koger. [Cincinnati, Printed by the Revivalist press, c1940] 70 p. front. (port.) 20 cm. [CT275.K83A3] 41-6963
I. Title.

[KUEGELE, Frederick]
Experimental religion; the experiences of Christophoros from his awaking to his falling asleep in Jesus. By F. K. Virginius [pseud.] ... Boston, Mass., J. H. Earle & co. [1903] 4 p. l., [13]-198 p. 20 cm. 3-29277
I. Title.

KUHN, Isobel. 922
In the arena. Chicago, Moody Press [1958] 222p. 22cm. Autobiographical. [BV3427.K8A3] 58-932
I. Title.

KUHN, Isobel. 922
In the arena. Chicago, Moody Press [1958] 222p. 22cm. Autobiographical. [BV3427.K8A3] 58-932
I. Title.

LAMB, George R. 920
Roman road. New York, Sheed and Ward, 1951. 125 p. 20 cm. Autobiography. [CT788.L28A3 1951] 51-2287
I. Title.

LAMB, George Robert. 920
Roman road. New York, Sheed and Ward, 1951. 125p. 20cm. Autobiography. [CT788.L28A3 1951] 51-2287
I. Title.

LANDAU, Rom. 922
God is my adventure; a book on modern mystics, masters and teachers, by Rom Landau. New York, A. A. Knopf [c1936] xii p., 2 l., 3-407, iv p., 1 l. front., ports. 23 cm. Biographical sketches and descriptions of the religious movements sponsored by Keyserling, Stefan George, Bo Yin Ra. Rudolf Steiner, Krishnamurti, Shri Meher Baba, George Jeffreys, Frank Buchman, P. D. Ouspensky and Gurdjieff. "First American edition." Bibliography: p. 397-407. [BL72.L3 1936] 36-7512
1. Religions—Biog. I. Title.

LANDAU, Rom, 1899- 200'.92'2 B
God is my adventure; a book on modern mystics, masters, and teachers. Freeport, N.Y., Books for Libraries Press [1972] viii, 407, iv p. ports. 22 cm. (Essay index reprint series) Reprint of the 1936 ed. Bibliography: p. 397-407. [BL72.L3 1972] 72-1265 ISBN 0-8369-2848-2
1. Religions—Biography. I. Title.

LAO-TZU. 299'.5148'2
A translation of Lao Tzu's Tao te ching and Wang Pi's commentary / by Paul J. Lin. Ann Arbor : Center for Chinese Studies, University of Michigan, 1977. xxvii, 198 p. ; 23 cm. (Michigan papers in Chinese studies ; no. 30) Appendices (p. 147-176): I. Ch'ien, S. The collective biography of Lao Tzu.—II. Shao, H. The biography of Wang Pi.—III. The major differences between Wang Pi's edition and the Ma-Wang-Tui editions A and B. Bibliography: p. 180-198. [BL1900.L26E5 1977] 77-623897 ISBN 0-89264-030-8 pbk. : 4.00
I. Wang, Pi, 226-249. II. Lin, Paul J. III. Title. IV. Series.

LARSEN, Caroline Dorothea 133
(Jensen) Mrs.
My travels in the spirit world, by Caroline D. Larsen. [Burlington, Vt., The Lane press, c1927] 57 p. incl. front. (port.) 24 cm. [BF1321.L3] 27-11187
I. Title.

LA TROBE-BATEMAN, William 922.
Fairbairn, 1845-1926.
Memories grave and gay of William Fairbairn La Trobe-Bateman ... with a foreword by the Right Rev. Bishop Gore; edited by Mildred La Trobe-Bateman. With four illustrations. London, New York [etc.] Longmans, Green and co., ltd., 1927. xix, 140 p. incl. front. (port.) plates. 19 cm. [BX5199.L25L3] 27-24915
I. La Trobe-Bateman, Mildred, 1871- ed. II. Title.

LA TROBE-BATEMAN, William 922.
Fairbairn, 1845-1926.
Memories grave and gay of William Fairbairn La Trobe-Bateman ... with a foreword by the Right Rev. Bishop Gore; edited by Mildred La Trobe-Bateman. With four illustrations. London, New York [etc.] Longmans, Green and co., ltd., 1927. xix, 140 p. incl. front. (port.) plates. 19 cm. [BX5199.L25L3] 27-24915
I. La Trobe-Bateman, Mildred, 1871- ed. II. Title.

LAUFER, Calvin Weiss.
The incomparable Christ, by Calvin Weiss Laufer. New York, Cincinnati, The Abingdon press [c1915] 228 p. 20 cm. 15-7261 1.00
I. Title.

LAWRENCE, Harold Gaines. 259
Marion Lawrence; a memorial biography, by his son, Harold G. Lawrence, with an introduction by Hugh S. Magill ... New York, Chicago [etc.] Fleming H. Revell company [c1925] 479 p. front., plates, ports. 23 cm. [BV1518.L3L3] 25-20511
I. Lawrence, Marion, 1850-1924. II. Title.

LEE, Ernest George, 1896- 248.2
The minute particular; one man's story of God [by] E. G. Lee. Boston, Beacon [1966] 191p. 21cm. [BX9869.L4A3] 67-14107 4.95 bds.,
I. Title. II. Title: One man's story of God.

LESCHER, Wilfrid.
St. Dominic and the rosary, by Wilfrid Lescher, O.P. London, R. & T. Washbourne; New York, Cincinnati [etc.] Benziger brothers, 1902. v, [1] 137 p. 17 cm. 4-5977
I. Title.

LIGHTON, William Beebay,
b.1805.
Narrative of the life and sufferings of William B. Lighton. (minister of the gospel.) Who was a solier, bound for life in th British army and in which is contained an account of its character, and the barbarous method practised in punishing their soldiers; with an interesting account of his escape from his regiment, his capture, imprisonment, trial, and condemnation to death; his subsequent sufferings, and final escape from captivity, and from the British dominious. Written by himself ... Rev. ed. ... Concord, N. H., The author, 1838. 228 p. front. (port.) plates. 16 cm. 8-25288
I. Title.

LIGHTON, William Beebay,
b.1805.
Narrative of the life and sufferings of William B. Lighton. (minister of the gospel.) Who was a solier, bound for life in th British army and in which is contained an account of its character, and the barbarous method practised in punishing their soldiers; with an interesting account of his escape from his regiment, his capture, imprisonment, trial, and condemnation to death; his subsequent sufferings, and final escape from captivity, and from the British dominious. Written by himself ... Rev. ed. ... Concord, N. H., The author, 1838. 228 p. front. (port.) plates. 16 cm. 8-25288
I. Title.

LILIENTHAL, Max, 1815-1882.
Max Lilienthal, American rabbi; life and writings, by David Philipson ... New York, The Bloch publishing co., 1915. vi p., 2 l., 498 p. 2 port. (incl. front.) 21 cm. 15-18982 1.50
I. Philipson, David, 1862- II. Title.

LILIENTHAL, Max, 1815-1882.
Max Lilienthal, American rabbi; life and writings, by David Philipson ... New York, The Bloch publishing co., 1915. vi p., 2 l., 498 p. 2 port. (incl. front.) 21 cm. 15-18982 1.50
I. Philipson, David, 1862- II. Title.

LOBSANG Rampa, pseud. 922.94
pseud.
Doctor from Lhasa. [1st U. S. ed] Clarksburg, W. Va, Saucerian Books [c1959] 239p. illus. 23cm. 'Continuation of ... [The author's] autobiography [The third eye]' [BL1490.L6A32 1959a] 60-8079
I. Title.

LONGO, Gabriel Anthony, 282.73
1926-
Spoiled priest; the autobiography of an ex-priest[by] Gabriel Longo. [1st ed.] New Hyde Park, N. Y., University Bks. [1966] 252p. illus., ports. 24cm. [BX4705.L717A3] 66-15077 5.95 bds.,
I. Title.

LONGO, Gabriel Anthony, 282.73
1926-
Spoiled priest; the authobiography of an expriest, by Gabriel Longo. New York, Bantam [1967, c.1966] 283p. 18cm. (N3512) [BX4705.L717A3] .95 pap.,
I. Title.

LOWRIE, Louisa Ann 922.544
(Wilson) Mrs. 1809-1833.
Memoir of Mrs. Louisa A. Lowrie, of the Northern India mission: by the Rev. Ashbel G. Fairchild. With an introduction, by the Rev. Elisha P. Swift, 2d ed., rev. and enl. Philadelphia, W. S. Martien, 1837. xxvii, [1], [19]-221 p. front. (port.) 16 cm. [BR1725.L67A4 1837] 38-9769
I. Fairchild, Ashbel Green, 1795-1864, ed. II. Title.

LOWRIE, Louisa Ann 922.544
(Wilson) Mrs. 1809-1833.
Memoir of Mrs. Louisa A. Lowrie, of the Northern India mission: by the Rev. Ashbel G. Fairchild. With an introduction, by the Rev. Elisha P. Swift, 2d ed., rev. and enl. Philadelphia, W. S. Martien, 1837. xxvii, [1], [19]-221 p. front. (port.) 16 cm. [BR1725.L67A4 1837] 38-9769
I. Fairchild, Ashbel Green, 1795-1864, ed. II. Title.

LOWRIE, Walter, 1784- 922.573
1868.
Memoirs of the Hon. Walter Lowrie, edited by his son. New York, The Baker & Taylor co., 1896. v p., 1 l., 192 p. front. (port.) 22 cm. [BV3705.L6A3] 923.273 38-3091
I. Lowrie, John Cameron, 1808-1900, ed. II. Title.

LOWRIE, Walter, 1784- 922.573
1868.
Memoirs of the Hon. Walter Lowrie, edited by his son. New York, The Baker & Taylor co., 1896. v p., 1 l., 192 p. front. (port.) 22 cm. [BV3705.L6A3] 923.273 38-3091
I. Lowrie, John Cameron, 1808-1900, ed. II. Title.

LOWRIE, Walter Macon, 922.573
1819-1847.
Memoirs of the Rev. Walter M. Lowrie, missionary to China. Edited by his father. New York, R. Carter & brothers; Philadelphia, W. S. Martien, 1849. viii, 500, [4] p. front. (port.) illus. (incl. map, plans) diagrs. 24 cm. "The editor ... has done little more than to select and arrange the papers of his ... son."--Pref. [BV3427.L6A3 1849] 38-19310
I. Lowrie, Walter, 1784-1868, ed. II. Title.

LOWRIE, Walter Macon, 922.573
1819-1847.
Memoirs of the Rev. Walter M. Lowrie, missionary to China. Edited by his father. New York, R. Carter & brothers; Philadelphia, W. S. Martien, 1849. viii, 500, [4] p. front. (port.) illus. (incl. map, plans) diagrs. 24 cm. "The editor ... has done little more than to select and arrange the papers of his ... son."--Pref. [BV3427.L6A3 1849] 38-19310
I. Lowrie, Walter, 1784-1868, ed. II. Title.

LOWRIE, Walter Macon, 922.573
1819-1847.
Memoirs of the Rev. Walter M. Lowrie, missionary to China. Edited by his father. 4th ed. New York, Board of foreign missions of the Presbyterian church, 1851. vii, 456, [4] p. front. (port.) illus. (incl. map, plans) diagrs. 24 cm. "The editor ... has done little more than to select and arrange the papers of his ... son."--Pref. [BV3427.L6A3 1851] 38-19308
I. Lowrie, Walter, 1784-1868, ed. II. Presbyterian church in the U. S. A. (Old school) Board of foreign missions. III. Title.

LOWRIE, Walter Macon, 922.573
1819-1847.
Memoirs of the Rev. Walter M. Lowrie, missionary to China. Edited by his father. 4th ed. New York, Board of foreign missions of the Presbyterian church, 1851. vii, 456, [4] p. front. (port.) illus. (incl. map, plans) diagrs. 24 cm. "The editor ... has done little more than to select and arrange the papers of his ... son."--Pref. [BV3427.L6A3 1851] 38-19308
I. Lowrie, Walter, 1784-1868, ed. II. Presbyterian church in the U. S. A. (Old school) Board of foreign missions. III. Title.

LOWRIE, Walter Macon, 922.573
1819-1847.
Memoirs of the Rev. Walter M. Lowrie, missionary to China. Edited by his father. Philadelphia, Presbyterian board of publication [1854] 405 p. front. (port.) 1 illus., diagr. 20 cm. "This edition ... is ... a selection from the letters and journals printed in the larger editions."--Pref. [BV3427.L6A3 1854] 38-19309
I. Lowrie, Walter, 1784-1868, ed. II. Presbyterian church in the U. S. A. (Old school) Board of publication. III. Title.

LOWRIE, Walter Macon, 922.573
1819-1847.
Memoirs of the Rev. Walter M. Lowrie, missionary to China. Edited by his father. Philadelphia, Presbyterian board of publication [1854] 405 p. front. (port.) 1 illus., diagr. 20 cm. "This edition ... is ... a selection from the letters and journals printed in the larger editions."--Pref. [BV3427.L6A3 1854] 38-19309
I. Lowrie, Walter, 1784-1868, ed. II. Presbyterian church in the U. S. A. (Old school) Board of publication. III. Title.

LOWRY, Anna M 1874-
The martyr in black; twenty years of convent life of "Sister Justina, O. S. B." ... By Miss Anna M. Lowry ("Sister Justina") in collaboration with H. George Buss ... Aurora, Mo., The Menace publishing co., ltd., 1912. x p., 1 l., [13]-80 p. incl. front. (port.) plates. 20 cm. 13-1723 0.25
I. Title.

LOWRY, Anna M 1874-
The martyr in black; twenty years of convent life of "Sister Justina, O. S. B." ... By Miss Anna M. Lowry ("Sister Justina") in collaboration with H. George Buss ... Aurora, Mo., The Menace publishing co., ltd., 1912. x p., 1 l., [13]-80 p. incl. front. (port.) plates. 20 cm. 13-1723 0.25
I. Title.

LUMPKIN, William Latane. 914.3'1
Doctor Sparks; a biography of Sparks White Melton, 1871 [i.e. 1870]-1957. Norfolk, Va., Phaup Print. Co. [c1963] [BX6495.M374L8] 63-23064
I. Title.

LUTZ, Henry Frey, 1868-
To infidelity and back; a truth-seeker's religious autobiography... by Evangelist

Henry F. Lutz... Cincinnati, O., The Standard publishing company, 1911. xvii p., 2 l., 231 p. 17 1/2 cm. 11-23404
I. Title.

MABIE, Henry Clay, 1847- 920.
From romance to reality; the merging of a life in a world movement, an autobiography, by Henry Clay Mabie ... Boston, Printed for the author, 1917. 396 p. front., plates, ports. 22 1/2 cm. $2.00. [BX6495.M2A3] 17-15174
I. Title.

MCCONNELL, Lela Grace, 1884- 922
Faith victorious in the Kentucky mountains; the story of twenty-two years of spirit-filled ministry, by Rev. Lela G. McConnell ... Winona Lake, Ind., Printed for the author by Light and life press, 1946. 237 p. front., plates, ports. 19 1/2 cm. [BX7990.H62M22] 47-18486
I. Title.

MCCULLOUGH, William 922.573
Wallace.
John McCullough, "grandfather," 1805-1870; pioneer Presbyterian missionary and teacher in the Republic of Texas. Galveston, 1944. 66, xviii l. plates, ports., map, facsims. 29 cm. Sources: leaves I-II. [BX9225.M195M3] 47-27309
I. McCullough, John, 1805-1870. II. Title.

MCCULLOUGH, William 922.573
Wallace.
John McCullough, "grandfather," 1805-1870; pioneer Presbyterian missionary and teacher in the Republic of Texas. Galveston, 1944. 66, xviii l. plates, ports., map, facsims. 29 cm. Sources: leaves I-II. [BX9225.M195M3] 47-27309
I. McCullough, John, 1805-1870. II. Title.

MCCULLOUGH, William 922.573
Wallace.
John McCullough, "grandfather," 1805-1870; pioneer Presbyterian missionary and teacher in the Republic of Texas. Galveston, 1944. 66, xviii l. plates, ports., map, facsims. 29 cm. Sources: leaves I-II. [BX9225.M195M3] 47-27309
I. McCullough, John, 1805-1870. II. Title.

MCCULLOUGH, William 922.573
Wallace.
John McCullough, "grandfather," 1805-1870; pioneer Presbyterian missionary and teacher in the Republic of Texas. Galveston, 1944. 66, xviii l. plates, ports., map, facsims. 29 cm. Sources: leaves I-II. [BX9225.M195M3] 47-27309
I. McCullough, John, 1805-1870. II. Title.

MACEOIN, Gary, 1909- 271.79
Nothing is quite enough. [1st ed.] New York, Holt [1953] 306p. 22cm. Autobiographical. [BX1777.M25A3] 53-5268
I. Title.

MACEOIN, Gary, 1909- 271.79
Nothing is quite enough. [1st ed.] New York, Holt [1953] 306p. 22cm. Autobiographical. [BX1777.M25A3] 53-5268
I. Title.

MCGINLEY, Gerard, 1906- 922.273
1955.
A Trappist writes home: letters of Abbot Gerard McGinley, O. C. S. O., to his family. Introd. by Father Raymond. Milwaukee. Bruce Pub. Co. [1960] 175p. illus. 22cm. [BX4705.M193A4] 60-10195
I. Title.

MCGRATTY, Arthur R, 1909- 818.5
I'd gladly go back; illustrated by Lloyd Ostendorf. Westminster, Md., Newman Press, 1951. 205 p. illus. 21 cm. Autobiographical. [BX4705.M214A3] 51-13092
I. Title.

MACKENZIE, Jean Kenyon, 285.
1874-1936.
The story of a fortunate youth; chapters from the biography of an elderly gentleman, by Jean Kenyon Mackenzie. Boston, The Atlantic monthly press [c1920] 5 p. l., 106 p. 18 1/2 cm. [BX9225.M25M3] 21-510
I. Title.

MACLEAN, Angus Hector, 266.509712
1892-
The galloping Gospel, by Angus H. MacLean. Boston, Beacon Press [1966] 174 p. illus., map. 22 cm. Autobiographical. [BX9969.M3A3] 66-15072
I. Title.

MCLEISTER, Clara, Mrs. 272
Men and women of deep piety, by Mrs. Clara McLeister; ed. and pub. by Rev. E. E. Shelhamer. Syracuse, N.Y., Wesleyan Methodist publishing association, 1920. 512 p. incl. ports. front. 19 1/2 cm. [BR1700.M3] 20-9146
I. Shelhamer, E. E., ed. II. Title.

MCLEOD, Malcolm James, 252.051
1867-
Seen from my pulpit, by Malcolm James McLeod... New York [etc.] Fleming H. Revell company [c1935] 191 p. front. (port.) 21 cm. Addresses. [BX9178.M27S4] 35-5086
I. Title.

MCPHERSON, Aimee Semple. Mrs. 922
In the service of the king; the story of my life, by Aimee Semple McPherson. New York, Boni and Liveright, 1927. 316 p. front., plates (1 double) ports. 19 1/2 cm. [BV3785.M28A3] 28-8629
I. Title.

MAGEE, James H., 286'.0924 B
1839-
The night of affliction and morning of recovery; an autobiography, by J. H. Magee. Cincinnati, 1873. Miami, Fla., Mnemosyne Pub. Co. [1969] 173 p. port. 23 cm. [E185.97.M2 1969] 77-89397
I. Title.

MAGUIRE, William 922.273
Augustus, 1890-
Rig for church, by William A. Maguire ... New York, The Macmillan company, 1942. xiv p., 1 l., 251 p. front. (port.) 20 1/2 cm. Autobiography. "First printing." [BX4705.M259A3] 42-13945
I. Title.

MAHOOD, John Wilmot, 1864- 253
Men of fire, by J. W. Mahood ... New York, Cincinnati, The Methodist book concern [c1920] 135 p. 17 1/2 cm. [BV3790.M32] 20-4089
I. Title.

MAINS, George Preston, 1844- 220
Mental phases in a spiritual biography, by George Preston Mains, with a foreword by Oscar L. Joseph. New York and London, Harper & brothers, 1928. xiii p., 1 l., 256 p. 21 1/2 cm. [BR125.M362] 28-8151
I. Title.

MALTER, Henry, 1864-1925. 922.
... *Saadia Gaon, his life and works,* by Henry Malter ... Philadelphia, The Jewish publication society of America, 1921. 446 p. 22 1/2 cm. (The Morris Loeb series [I]) The first volume issued under the Morris Loeb publication fund. Bibliography: p. [303]-419. [BM755.S2M3] 22-548
I. Saadiah ben Joseph, gaon, 892?-942. II. Title.

MARCHANT, James, Sir 1867- 920.
Dr. John Clifford, C. H.; life, letters and reminiscences, by Sir James Marchant ... with twelve half-tone illustrations. London, New York [etc.] Cassell and company, ltd. [1924] xv, [1], 311, [1] p. front., illus. (facsim.) plates, ports. 22 cm. "List of publications by Dr. Clifford": p. 291-293. [BX6495.C56M3] 24-18481
I. Clifford, John, 1836-1923. II. Title.

MARCUS, Jacob Rader, 1896- 296.
Israel Jacobson [by] Jacob Rader Marcus ... [n. p., 1928?] 120 p. 23 cm. "Reprinted from Yearbook, vol. xxxviii, Central conference of American rabbis, 1928." Bibliography: p. 117-120. [DS135.G5J3] 30-6950
I. Jacobson, Israel, 1768-1828. II. Title.

MARCUS, Jacob Rader, 1896- 296.
Israel Jacobson [by] Jacob Rader Marcus ... [n. p., 1928?] 120 p. 23 cm. "Reprinted from Yearbook, vol. xxxviii, Central conference of American rabbis, 1928." Bibliography: p. 117-120. [DS135.G5J3] 30-6950
I. Jacobson, Israel, 1768-1828. II. Title.

MARTIN, Isaac, 1758-1828. 922.
A journal of the life, travels, labours, and religious exercises of Isaac Martin. Philadelphia, Printed by W. P. Gibbons, 1834. 160 p. 19 cm. [BX7795.M333A3] 48-34206
I. Title.

MARTIN, Isaac, 1758-1828. 922.
A journal of the life, travels, labours, and religious exercises of Isaac Martin. Philadelphia, Printed by W. P. Gibbons, 1834. 160 p. 19 cm. [BX7795.M333A3] 48-34206
I. Title.

MARTIN, Isaac, 1758-1828. 922.
A journal of the life, travels, labours, and religious exercises of Isaac Martin. Philadelphia, Printed by W. P. Gibbons, 1834. 160 p. 19 cm. [BX7795.M333A3] 48-34206
I. Title.

MARTIN, Isaac, 1758-1828. 922.
A journal of the life, travels, labours, and religious exercises of Isaac Martin. Philadelphia, Printed by W. P. Gibbons, 1834. 160 p. 19 cm. [BX7795.M333A3] 48-34206
I. Title.

MARTIN, Isaac, 1758-1828. 922.
A journal of the life, travels, labours, and religious exercises of Isaac Martin. Philadelphia, Printed by W. P. Gibbons, 1834. 160 p. 19 cm. [BX7795.M333A3] 48-34206
I. Title.

MARTIN, Isaac, 1758-1828. 922.
A journal of the life, travels, labours, and religious exercises of Isaac Martin. Philadelphia, Printed by W. P. Gibbons, 1834. 160 p. 19 cm. [BX7795.M333A3] 48-34206
I. Title.

MARTIN DESCALZO, Jose 922.246
Luis, 1930-
A priest confesses. Translated by Rita Goldberg. [1st American ed. Fresno, Calif.] Academy Guild Press [1960] 218p. 22cm. Autobiography. [BX4705.M41242A33] 60-14624
I. Title.

MARTIQUE, L. F.
The scarlet mother on the Tiber; or, Trials and travels of Evangelist L. J. King, twenty-five years a Roman Catholic. Fifteen years a Protestant preacher and reformer. By L. F. Martique ... v. 1- St. Louis, Mo. [etc.] L. J. King, 1908- v. front., plates, ports. 20 cm. 8-24912
I. Title.

MASSEE, Jasper Cortenus 13-1074
1871-
Men and the kingdom, by J. C. Massee... New York, Chicago [etc.] Fleming H. Revell company [c1912] 157 p. 19 1/2 cm. 0.75
I. Title.

MATHEWS, Loulie (Albee) 922.97
Not every sea hath pearls. [Portsmouth N. H., 1951] 173 p. 20 cm. Autobiographical. [BP395.M3A3] 52-16005
I. Title.

MATHEWS, Loulie (Albee) 922.97
Not every sea hath pearls. [Portsmouth N. H., 1951] 173 p. 20 cm. Autobiographical. [BP395.M3A3] 52-16005
I. Title.

*MAYHEW, Christopher 920.92
Men seeking God. London, Allen & Unwin [Mystic, Conn., Verry, 1964, c.1955] 117p. illus. 23cm. Bibl. 3.75
I. Title.

M'CHEYNE, Robert Murray, 922.541
1813-1843.
Memoir and remains of the Rev. Robert Murray McCheyne, minister of St. Peter's church, Dundee. By the Rev. Andrew A. Bonar ... with an introductory letter by the Rev. Samuel Miller ... Philadelphia, Presbyterian board of publication [1844] xvii, 19-404 p. front.(port.) 20 cm. "Songs of Zion": p. 386-404. [BX9225.M17A3 1844] 32-30348
I. Bonar, Andrew Alexander, 1810-1892. II. Title.

M'CHEYNE, Robert Murray, 922.541
1813-1843.
Memoir and remains of the Rev. Robert Murray McCheyne, minister of St. Peter's church, Dundee. By the Rev. Andrew A. Bonar ... with an introductory letter by the Rev. Samuel Miller ... Philadelphia, Presbyterian board of publication [1844] xvii, 19-404 p. front.(port.) 20 cm. "Songs of Zion": p. 386-404. [BX9225.M17A3 1844] 32-30348
I. Bonar, Andrew Alexander, 1810-1892. II. Title.

MEADOWS, Denis. 271.5
Obedient men. New York, Appleton-Century-Crofts [c1954] 308p. 21cm. Autobiographical. [BX4705.M477A3] 53-10090
I. Title.

MEADOWS, Denis. 271.5
Obedient men. New York, Appleton-Century-Crofts [c1954] 308p. 21cm. Autobiographical. [BX4705.M477A3] 53-10090
I. Title.

MERCER, Edward Clifford 922
Anderson, 1873-
A tweintieth century miracle, by E. C. Mercer. Salisbury, Conn., E. C. Mercer [c1928] xv, 98 p. incl. front. (mounted port.) 19 cm. [BV3785.M45A3] 28-30461
I. Title.

MERRITT, Mary Carr.
Rev. J. W. T. McNiel; a brief biography comp. by Mary Carr Merritt ... Los Angeles, J. F. Elwell publishing company [c1909] 4 p. l., [13]-130 p., 1 l. incl. facsim. front. (port.) 22 cm. 10-2131 0.75
I. McNiel, John William Thomas, 1873-1907. II. Title.

MERTON, Thomas, 1915- 922.273
The seven storey mountain. New York, Harcourt, Brace [1948] 429 p. 21 cm. Autobiography. [BX4705.M542A3] 48-8645
I. Title.

MIEROW, Charles Christopher, 922
1883-
The hallowed flame. Evanston, Ill., Principia Press of Illinois [c1956] 255p. 24cm. Includes bibliography. [BL72.M5] 58-14652
1. Religions—Biog. I. Title.

MILLER, Lizzie E. 922
The true way. Life and evangelical work of Lizzie E. Miller, (of Fairview, West Va.) written by herself ... Los Angeles, Calif., Printed for the author, 1895. 326 p. front. (port.) 20 cm. [BV3785.M48A3] 37-36768
I. Title.

'MR. Baptist,'
a condensed biography of Pastor Clarence Walker. [St. Louis, 1956] 106p. illus., ports. 17cm. Cover title.
I. Beeny, Bill. II. Walker, Clarence O'Neil, 1890-

MOFFAT, John 266'.023'0924 B
Smith, 1835-1918.
John Smith Moffat, C.M.G. missionary; a memoir [compiled] by his son Robert U. Moffat. New York, Negro Universities Press [1969] xix, 388 p. illus., map, ports. 23 cm. Reprint of the 1921 ed. [DT776.M7A5 1969] 73-88443
I. Moffat, Robert Unwin, 1866-1947, comp.

MONOD, Frederic Joel 922.4489
Jean Gerard, 1794-1863.
Memoir of Julius Charles Rieu. From the French of Frederic Monod, jun. ... With introductory remarks by the Rev. A. Alexander, D. D. Philadelphia, French & Perkins, 1833. 65 p. 15 cm. [BX9459.R5M6] 36-22147
I. Rieu, Jules Charles, 1792-1821. II. Title.

MOORE, John Milton, 1871- 922.673
On the trail of truth; adventures in religion, by John Milton Moore ... introduction by Charles S. MacFarland, D. D. New York [etc.] Fleming H. Revell company [c1937] 187 p. 20 cm. "The story of John Milton Moore's intellectual and spiritual pilgrimage."--Introd. [BX6495.M58A3] 37-33394
I. Title.

MOORE, Kenneth Willoughby. 922.573
The romance of an orphan, Ken, by Kenneth Willoughby Moore. Trenton, N. J., The Smith press [c1941] viii, 296 p. 21 cm. Autobiography. [BX9225.M57A3] 42-901
I. Title.

MORRIS, Caspar, 1805-1884. 923.773
Memoir of Miss Margaret Mercer, by Caspar Morris ... 2d ed., with additions. Philadelphia, Lindsay & Blakiston, 1848. xii, [13]-268 p. front. (port.) 17 1/2 cm. [BR1725.M4M6 1848 a] 32-31807
I. Mercer, Margaret, 1792-1846. II. Title.

MORRIS, Caspar, 1805-1884. 923.773
Memoir of Miss Margaret Mercer, by Caspar Morris ... 2d ed., with additions. Philadelphia, Lindsay & Blakiston, 1848. xii, [13]-268 p. front. (port.) 17 1/2 cm. [BR1725.M4M6 1848 a] 32-31807
I. Mercer, Margaret, 1792-1846. II. Title.

MOSS, James E 1875- 922.8373
Jimmy Moss. Sal[t] Lake City, Deseret Book Co., 1963. 243 p. illus. 24 cm. Autobiography. [BX8695.M6A3] 63-5831
I. Title.

MULLINS, Eustace Clarence, 1923- 248
My life in Christ, by Eustace Mullins. Staunton, Va., Faith and Service Books, Aryan League of America [1968] 90 p. 22 cm. [CT275.M723A3] 68-25403
I. Title.

MULLINS, Eustace Clarence, 1923- 248
My life in Christ, by Eustace Mullins. Staunton, Va., Faith and Service Books, Aryan League of America [1968] 90 p. 22 cm. [CT275.M723A3] 68-25403
I. Title.

MY religion.
New York, Swedenborg Foundation, 1956. x, 208p. 18cm.
I. Keller, Helen Adams, 1880-

MY religion 204
[by] Arnold Bennett, Hugh Walpole, Rebecca West, J. D. Beresford, Israel Zangwill, Sir Arthur Conan Doyle, E. Phillips Oppenheim, Compton Mackenzie, H. de Vere Stacpole, Henry Arthur Jones. New York, D. Appleton and company, 1926. 4 p. l., 3-187 p. 19 cm. A series of articles which appeared in the London Daily express. [BR50.M8 1926] 26-8108
I. Bennett, Arnold, 1867-

A narrative of the travels of John Vandeleur, on the Western continent, Containing an account of the conversion of an Indian chief and his family to Christianity. Being a letter written by him to his uncle in Philadelphia, in the year 1796. Hallowell [Me.] Printed by E. Goodale, 1817. 87 p. 14 cm. 5-41099

[NEIL, Henry] 1863- ed.
Great achievements; an inspiration and guide to the highest attainments in life, prosperity and happiness, reflecting the lives of the most eminently successful men and women; ed. by Marshall Everett [pseud.] ... [Chicago?] 1902. vi, [v]-viii p., 1 l., [11]-606 p. front., ports. (partly col.) 26 cm. Each portrait has short biographical sketch on verso. 2-22202
I. Title.

NEMESIUS, William, Bp. of Emesa. 1886- ed. and tr. 281.4
on the nature of man in Telfer,On the nature of man in Telfer, 1886- ed. and tr. Philadelphia, Westminster Press [1955] [BR65.C93C45] 55-7709
I. Title. II. Title: Cyril of Jerusalem amd Nemesius of Emesa.

NEPVEU, Francois, 1639-1708.
Meditations for every day in the month, tr. from the "Reflexions chretiennes" of Rev. Francois Nepveu, S. J. by Francis A. Ryan. New York, Cincinnati [etc.] Benziger brothers, 1911. 176 p. front. 19 cm. 11-29825 0.75
I. Ryan, Francis Aloysius, 1887- tr. II. Title.

NEVIN, John Williamson, 1803-1886 922.473
My own life: the earlier years. Lancaster, Pa., Hist. Soc. of the Evangelical and Reformed Church, c/o Fackenthal Lib., Franklin & Marshall Coll., 1964. i, 160p. 23cm. (Paps. of the Eastern Chapter, Hist. Soc. of the Evangelical and Reformed Church, no. 1) (Evangelical and Reformed Church, Historical Society. Eastern Chapter. Papers, no.1) [BX9593.N4A3] 64-57065 1.75
I. Title. II. Series.

NEWELL, William, 1804-1881. 922.8171
Memoir of the Rev. Convers Francis, D.D. By the Rev. William Newell, D.D. Reprinted from the Proceedings of the Massachusetts historical society. Cambridge [Printed by J. Wilson and sons] 1866. 23 p. 24 cm. "List of the publications of Dr. Francis": p. 22-23. [BX9869.F688N4] 37-15503
I. Francis, Convers, 1795-1863. II. Title.

NEWELL, William, 1804-1881. 922.8171
Memoir of the Rev. Convers Francis, D.D. By the Rev. William Newell, D.D. Reprinted from the Proceedings of the Massachusetts historical society. Cambridge [Printed by J. Wilson and sons] 1866. 23 p. 24 cm. "List of the publications of Dr. Francis": p. 22-23. [BX9869.F688N4] 37-15503
I. Francis, Convers, 1795-1863. II. Title.

NIELSEN, Thomas Miller, 1875- 922.773
How a Dane became an American; or, Hits and misses of my life, byT. M. Nielsen. Cedar Rapids, Ia., The Torch press [c1935] 3 p. l., [5]-305 p. front., pl., ports. 21 cm. [BX8495.N45A3] 35-6851
I. Title.

NIELSEN, Thomas Miller, 1875- 922.773
How a Dane became an American; or, Hits and misses of my life, byT. M. Nielsen. Cedar Rapids, Ia., The Torch press [c1935] 3 p. l., [5]-305 p. front., pl., ports. 21 cm. [BX8495.N45A3] 35-6851
I. Title.

NIMETH, Albert J., tr. 922.245
To live the Gospel; tr. from French by Albert J. Nimeth. Chicago, Franciscan Herald [c. 1963] 51p. 18cm. .65 pap.,
I. Title.

NOALL, Matthew, 1864- 922.8373
To my children, an autobiographical sketch by Matthew Noall, in collaboration with Claire W. Noall. [Salt Lake City, 1947] 2 p. l., 3-110 p. incl. front., illus. (incl. ports., facsim.) 20 1/2 cm. [BX8695.N6A3] 47-26948
I. Noall, Claire Augusta (Wilcox) 1892- joint author. II. Title.

NORELIUS, Eric, 1833-1916 284'.1'0924
The journals of Eric Norelius, a Swedish missionary on the American frontier. Tr., ed., introd. by G. Everett Arden. Philadelphia, Fortress [1967] vii, 207p. 21cm. (Seminar eds) [BX8080.N6A 333] 67-11909 2.75 pap.,
I. Arden, Gothard Everett, 1905- ed. and tr. II. Title.

O'BRIEN, Isidore, father, 1895- 922.245
Enter Saint Anthony, by Father Isidore O'Brien, O. F. M.; illustrations by C. Bosseron Chambers. Paterson, N. J., St. Anthony guild press, Franciscan monastery, 1932. x p., 2 l., 174 p. front., plates. 22 cm. [Secular name: George O'Brien] [BX4700.A6O3] 32-35343
I. Antonio da Padova, Saint, 1195-1231. II. Title.

O'BRIEN, Isidore, father, 1895- 922.245
Enter Saint Anthony, by Father Isidore O'Brien, O. F. M.; illustrations by C. Bosseron Chambers. Paterson, N. J., St. Anthony guild press, Franciscan monastery, 1932. x p., 2 l., 174 p. front., plates. 22 cm. [Secular name: George O'Brien] [BX4700.A6O3] 32-35343
I. Antonio da Padova, Saint, 1195-1231. II. Title.

O'CONNELL, William Henry, cardinal, 1859- 922.273
Recollections of seventy years, by His Eminence William cardinal O'Connell... Boston and New York, Houghton Mifflin company, 1934. ix p., 2 l., 395 p. front., plates, ports. 24 cm. [BX4705.O3A42 1934a] 35-34781
I. Title.

O'CONNELL, William Henry, cardinal, 1859- 922.273
Recollections of seventy years, by His Eminence William cardinal O'Connell ... Boston and New York, Houghton Mifflin company, 1934. 4 p. l., [vii]-ix p., 2 l., 395 p. front., plates, ports. 25 cm. Title vignette in colors. "This first edition consists of five hundred and sixty-five copies printed and bound at the Riverside press, Cambridge, Massachusetts, in May, 1934, and autographed by the author." Issued in case. [BX4705.O3A42] 34-19155
I. Title.

ODHNER, Carl Th[eophilus] 1863-
Robert Hindmarsh; a biography, by Carl Th. Odhner. With three appendixes. Philadelphia, Academy book room, 1895. 1 p. l., 116 p. front. (port.) 20 cm. Appendix I has special t.-p. Appendices: I. Reasons for separating from the old church by the members of the New Jerusalem church, who assemble in Great East-Cheap, London. II. Principles of ecclesiastical government. By Robert Hindmarsh. III. The priesthood of the New church in Great Britain. A chronological list arranged by Carl Th. Odhner. 5-12184
I. Title.

ODHNER, Carl Th[eophilus] 1863-
Robert Hindmarsh; a biography, by Carl Th. Odhner. With three appendixes. Philadelphia, Academy book room, 1895. 1 p. l., 116 p. front. (port.) 20 cm. Appendix I has special t.-p. Appendices: I. Reasons for separating from the old church by the members of the New Jerusalem church, wwho assemble in Great East-Cheap, London. ii. Principles of eccelesiastical government. By Robert Hindmarsh. iii. The priesthood of the New church in Great Britain. A chronological list arranged by Carl Th. Odhner. 5-12184
I. Title.

OLIPHANT, John, 1771-1831. 922.
Memoirs and remains of John Oliphant, of Auburn, New York. To which is added his funeral sermon, by Rev. J. Hopkins ... Auburn, H. Ivison & co., 1835. 212 p. front. (port.) 14 cm. Edited by Matthew La Rue Perrine. cf. Ms. note at end of preface. [BX9225.O6A3] 22-12677
I. Hopkins, Josiah. II. Perrine, Matthew La Rue, 1777-1836, ed. III. Title.

OLIPHANT, John, 1771-1831. 922.
Memoirs and remains of John Oliphant, of Auburn, New York. To which is added his funeral sermon, by Rev. J. Hopkins ... Auburn, H. Ivison & co., 1835. 212 p. front. (port.) 14 cm. Edited by Matthew La Rue Perrine. cf. Ms. note at end of preface. [BX9225.O6A3] 22-12677
I. Hopkins, Josiah. II. Perrine, Matthew La Rue, 1777-1836, ed. III. Title.

OWEN, Epenetus, 1815- 922
Struck by lightning; a true and thrilling narrative of one who was struck by lightning; with incidents, experiences and anecdotes for old and young. By Rev. Epenetus Owen ... Cortland, Cortland co., N. Y., On sale by the author. [New York, J. W. Pratt, printer, 1878] 190, [1] p. 19 cm. [BV3785.O9A3] 37-37666
I. Title.

OYABE, Jenichiro, 1867- 922.
A Japanese Robinson Crusoe, by Jenichiro Oyabe ... Boston, Chicago, The Pilgrim press [c1898] 219 p. front. (port.) plates. 19 cm. [BV3457.O8A3] 3-19874
I. Title.

OYABE, Jenichiro, 1867- 922.
A Japanese Robinson Crusoe, by Jenichiro Oyabe ... Boston, Chicago, The Pilgrim press [c1898] 219 p. front. (port.) plates. 19 cm. [BV3457.O8A3] 3-19874
I. Title.

PAONE, Anthony J 1913- 242
My life with Christ. [1st ed.] Garden City, N. Y., Doubleday [1962] 310p. 22cm. esus Christ--Biog.--Meditations. [BT306.4.P3] 62-17359
I. Title. II. Series.

PAONE, Anthony J 1913- 242
My life with Christ. [1st ed.] Garden City, N. Y., Doubleday [1962] 310p. 22cm. esus Christ--Biog.--Meditations. [BT306.4.P3] 62-17359
I. Title. II. Series.

PARKE, Jean. 270
The immaculate perception, by Jean Parke; with seven drawings of the Christ by the author. New York, H. Vinal, 1927. 148 p., 1 l. incl. mounted front., mounted plates. 21 cm. "The first edition consists of one hundred copies printed on Georgian laid paper and one thousand copies printed on McMutirre laid." [BR125.P1735] 27-16444
I. Title.

PARKER, Theodore, 1810-1860. 922.8173
Theodore Parker's experience as a minister, with some account of his early life, and education for the ministry; contained in a letter from him to the members of the twenty-eighth Congregational society of Boston. Boston, R. Leighton, jr., 1859. v, [7]-182 p. 20 cm. [BX9869.P3A3] 33-402
I. Title.

PARKER, Theodore, 1810-1860. 204
The world of matter and the spirit of man; latest discourses of religion, by Theodore Parker, edited with notes by George Willis Cooke. Boston, American Unitarian association [c1907] 2 p. l., iii-iv p., 1 l., 428 p. 22 cm. [His Works. Centenary ed. v. 6] "The lecture and the sermons contained in the present volume have not appeared in any previous American edition of Theodore Parker's writings."--Pref. [BX9815.P3 1907 vol. 6] [BX9843.P3W8] 252. 7-39391
I. Cooke, George Willis, 1848-1923, ed. II. Title.
Contents omitted.

PARKS, Leighton, 1852- 922
Turnpikes and dirt roads, by Leighton Parks ... New York, London, C. Scribner's sons, 1927. xi p., 2 l., 3-334 p. front. (port.) 23 cm. "Reminiscences of a boyhood passed in the South and in territory of mixed allegiance."--Publisher's announcement. [BX5995.P33A3] 27-22937
I. Title.

PARRISH, Herbert. 232.
The mystery of character, by Herbert Parrish. New York, E. S. Gorham, 1917. 141 p. 20 cm. "This short study of the character of Christ if frankly and attempt to present and argument for belief in the divinity of Jesus."--Pref. [BT301.P3] 17-30019
I. Title.

[PARSONS, Julia (Warth) Mrs.
John Greenleaf, minister; or, The full stature of a man, by Julian Warth [pseud.] Boston, D. Lothrop company [c1888] 300 p. 19 cm. Published in 1886 under title: The full stature of a man. [PZ3.P254J] 7-34091
I. Title.

[PARSONS, Julia (Warth) Mrs.
John Greenleaf, minister; or, The full stature of a man, by Julian Warth [pseud.] Boston, D. Lothrop company [c1888] 300 p. 19 cm. Published in 1886 under title: The full stature of a man. [PZ3.P254J] 7-34091
I. Title.

PATON, John Gibson, 1824-1907. 922
John G. Paton, missionary to the New Hebrides. An autobiography edited by his brother. New and complete illustrated edition: 1824-1898. New York, Chicago [etc.] Fleming H. Revell company [c1898] 3 v. in l. front., plates, ports., map. 21 cm. Edited by Rev. James Paton. Cover-title: Pioneering in the New Hebrides. [BV3680.N6P2 1898] 4-19905
I. Paton, James, 1843-1906, ed. II. Title.

PATON, John Gibson, 1824-1907. 922
John G. Paton, missionary to the New Hebrides. An autobiography edited by his brother. New and complete illustrated edition: 1824-1898. New York, Chicago [etc.] Fleming H. Revell company [c1898] 3 v. in l. front., plates, ports., map. 21 cm. Edited by Rev. James Paton. Cover-title: Pioneering in the New Hebrides. [BV3680.N6P2 1898] 4-19905
I. Paton, James, 1843-1906, ed. II. Title.

PENINGTON, Isaac, 1616-1679. 922.
Memoirs of the life of Isaac Penington, to which is added a review of his writings by Joseph Gurney Bevan. Philadelphia, T. Kite, 1831. 208 p. 19 cm. (Friends' family library, v. 1) Bound with Grover, William. Selections from the letters and other papers of William Grover. Philadelphia, 1831. [BX7795.P35A3 1831a] 51-50910
I. Bevan, Joseph Gurney, 1753-1814, ed. II. Title. III. Series.

PENNINGTON, Levi Talbott, 1875- 289.6'0924 B
Rambling recollections of ninety happy years, by Levi T. Pennington. [1st ed.] Portland, Or., Metropolitan Press, 1967. xvi, 187 p. illus., ports. 23 cm. 500 copies printed. [BX7795.P43A3] 67-3486
I. Title.

PERINCHIEF, Octavius, 1829-1877. 922.373
Octavius Perinchief: his life of trial and supreme faith. By Charles Lanman ... Washington, J. Anglim, 1879. 2 p. l., 498 p. front. (port.) 24 cm. [BX5995.P37A3] 35-34808
I. Lanman, Charles, 1819-1895, ed. II. Title.

PETERSON, Daniel H 922.
The looking-glass; being a true report and narrative of the life, travels and labors of the Rev. Daniel H. Peterson, a colored clergyman; embracing a period of time from the year 1812 to 1854, and including his visit to western Africa. New York, Wright, printer, 1854. x [13]-150 p. illus. 16 cm. [BX8449.P4A3] 48-32666
I. Title.

PHILLIPS, Charles Henry, bp., 1858- 922.773
From the farm to the bishopric; an autobiography, by Bishop Charles Henry Phillips. Nashville, Tenn., Printed for the author by the Parthenon press [c1932] 308 p. 20 cm. [BX8409.P5A3] 33-1972
I. Title.

PIERSON, Arthur Tappan, 1837-1911.
Dr. Pierson and his message; a sketch of the life and work of a great preacher, together with a varied selection from his unpublished manuscripts. Ed. by J. Kennedy Maclean. New York, Association press, 1911. 4 p. l., 3-280 p. front. (port.) 22 1/2 cm. 14-6692
I. Maclean, J. Kennedy, ed. II. Title.

PILMORE, Joseph, 1734?-1825. 287'.0924
The journal of Joseph Pilmore, Methodist itinerant, for the years August 1, 1769, to January 2, 1774. With a biographical sketch of Joseph Pilmore by Frank B. Stanger. Editors: Frederick E. Maser [and] Howard T. Maag. Philadelphia, Printed by Message Pub. Co. for the Historical Society of the Philadelphia Annual Conference of the United Methodist Church, 1969. 262 p. illus., facsim., ports. 24 cm. [BX8495.P548A3] 79-11727 5.00
I. Title.

PILMORE, Joseph, 1734?-1825. 287'.0924
The journal of Joseph Pilmore, Methodist itinerant, for the years August 1, 1769, to January 2, 1774. With a biographical sketch of Joseph Pilmore by Frank B. Stanger. Editors: Frederick E. Maser [and] Howard T. Maag. Philadelphia, Printed by Message Pub. Co. for the Historical Society of the Philadelphia Annual Conference of the United Methodist Church, 1969. 262 p. illus., facsim., ports. 24 cm. [BX8495.P548A3] 79-11727 5.00
I. Title.

POLING, Daniel Alfred, 1884- 922.573
Mine eyes have seen. [1st ed.] New York, McGraw-Hill [1959] 297 p. illus. 22 cm. Autobiography. [BX9543.P62A3] 59-14960
I. Title.

POLING, Daniel Alfred, 1884- 922.573
Mine eyes have seen. [1st ed.] New York, McGraw-Hill [1959] 297 p. illus. 22 cm. Autobiography. [BX9543.P62A3] 59-14960
I. Title.

PORTER, Anthony Toomer, 1828-1902. 922.373
Led on! Step by step, scenes from clerical, military, educational, and plantation life in the South, 1828-1898; an autobiography by A. Toomer Porter, d. d. New York & London, G. P. Putnam's sons, 1898. xv p., 1 l., 462 p. front., plates. ports. 21 cm. [BX5995.P6A3] 35-29961
I. Title.

PORTER, Anthony Toomer, 1828-1902. 283'.0924 B
Led on! Step by step, scenes from clerical, military, educational, and plantation life in the South, 1828-1898; an autobiography. New York, Putnam, 1898. Miami, Fla., Mnemosyne Pub. Co. [1969] xv, 462 p. illus., ports. 23 cm. [BX5995.P6A3 1969] 75-89383
I. Title.

*POWERS, Robert Merrill. 922.777 B
Prairie preacher; a tale of our yesterdays along the middle border; memoirs. 1st. ed. [Jericho] N.Y. Exposition [1974] 165 p. 22 cm. [CT5500] ISBN 0-682-47854-7 7.00
1. Religions—Biography. I. Title.

PRATT, Magee.
The orthodox preacher and Nancy; being the tale of the misfortunes of a minister who tried to do as Jesus would; a story of ministerial life as it is. By the Rev. M. Pratt ... Hartford, Conn., Connecticut magazine co., 1901. 191 pp. port. 19 cm. Copyright by Magee Pratt, Hartford, Conn. Class A, XXc, no. 19548, Oct. 14, 1901; 2 copies rec'd Oct. 14, 1901. 1-24567
I. Title.

PRESCOTT, Jedediah Brown, 1784-1861. 922.
Memoir of Jedediah B. Prescott, late pastor of the Christian church in Monmouth. Monmouth, Me., 1861. viii, [9]-135 p. 18 cm. An autobiography. [BX6793.P7A3] 25-1457
I. Title.

PRICE, Phinehas, b.1789- 922.773
A narrative of the life and travels, preaching & suffering, with an account of the witnesses, defence and persecution of Phinehas Price, M. D. From 1789 to 1843 ... Philadelphia, 1843. 2 p. l., [3]-202 p. 19 cm. With this is bound the author's A sermon on the authenticity of the Holy Scriptures. Westchester, 1825. [BX8495.P66A3] 37-7028
I. Title.

PURCELL, William Ernest, 1909-
Onward Christian soldier, a life of Sabine Baring-Gould, parson, squire, novelist, antiquary 1834-1924. With an introduction by John Betjeman. London, New York [etc.] Longmans, Green and co. [1957] 188p. plates.
I. Title.

RAINSFORD, William Stephen, 1850-1933. 283'.0924 B
The story of a varied life; an autobiography. Freeport, N.Y., Books for Libraries Press [1970] 481 p. illus., ports. 23 cm. Reprint of the 1922 ed. [BX5995.R3A35 1970] 70-126249
I. Title.

RAINSFORD, William Stephen, 1850-1933. 922
The story of a varied life; an autobiography, by W. S. Rainsford ... Garden City, N. Y., Doubleday, Page & company, 1922. 6 p. l., 481 p. front. (port.) plates. 25 cm. [BX5995.R3A35] 22-21492
I. Title.

*RAMSAY, William M. 232
The meaning of Jesus Christ. Illus. by M. Milton Hull. Richmond, Va., CLC Pr. [dist. Knox, c.1964] 199p. 24cm. (Covenant Life Curriculum bk.) 2.95 pap.,
I. Title.

RAMSAY, William M
The meaning of Jesus Christ. Illustrated by M. Milton Hull. Richmond, Va., CLC Press [1964] 199 p. 24 cm. 85 p. 24 cm. (The Covenant Life Curriculum) (The Covenant Life Curriculum) Leaders' guide. Richmond, Va., CLC Press [1964] 65-99109
I. Title.

*RAMSEY, William M. 268.433
The meaning of Jesus Christ. [dist. Richmond, Va., John Knox, c.1964] CLC Press 200p. illus. (pt. col.) 24cm. (Convenant life curriculum, 9220) 2.95 pap.,
I. Title.

RAY, Emma J., 1859- 287'.873'0922 B
Twice sold, twice ransomed; autobiography of Mr. and Mrs. L. P. Ray. Introd. by C. E. McReynolds. Freeport, N.Y., Books for Libraries Press, 1971. 320 p. illus. 23 cm. (The Black heritage library collection) Reprint of the 1926 ed. [BX8473.R3A3 1971] 76-173613 ISBN 0-8369-8905-8
I. Ray, Lloyd P., 1860- II. Title. III. Series.

RAY, Emma J "Mrs. L. P. Ray," 1859- 922.
Twice sold, twice ransomed; autobiography of Mr. & Mrs. L. P. Ray, introduction by Rev. C. E. Reynolds. Chicago, Ill., The Free Methodist publishing house [c1926] 320 p. front., plates. ports. 20 cm. [BX8473.R3A3] 26-6278
I. Ray, Lloyd P., 1860- II. Title.

REICHARDT, E. Noel.
The significance of ancient religions in relation to human evolution and brain development, by E. Noel. Reichardt ... New York, Dodd, Mead and company; [etc., etc.] 1912. xiv, 456 p. plates, diagrs. 21 1/2 cm. $3.50 13-165
I. Title.

REITZEL, Charles F[rancis] 1869-
Robert Woodknow's difficulties in finding a church home. by Chas. F. Reitzel ... 2d ed.--Rev. and enl. (7th thousand) Harrisburg, Pa., Central printing and publishing house, Churches of God, 1903. 127 p. front., (port.) 18 1/2 cm. 4-1012
I. Title.

RELIGIONS of mission fields as viewed by Protestant missionaries ... 261
[New York] Student volunteer movement for foreign missions, 1905. ix, 309 p., 1 l. 19 cm. Contents.The religion of the African, by E. H. Richards.--Shinto, the way of the gods, by J. H. De Forest.--Hinduism, by C. A. R. Janvier.--Buddhism in southern Asia, by J. N. Cushing.--Buddhism in Japan, by A. D. Gring.--Taoism, by H. C. Du Bose.--Confucianism, by D. Z. Sheffield.--Judaism, by L. Meyer.--Mohammedanism, by S. M. Zwemer.--Roman Catholicism, by G. B. Winston. Bibliography at the beginning of each chapter. [BV2060.R4] 6-6

REZZORI, Gregor von. FIC
Memoirs of an anti-semite / Gregor von Rezzori. Harmondsworth, Middlesex, England ; New York, N.Y., U.S.A. : Penguin Books, 1982, c1981. 287 p. ; 20 cm. Translation of: Memoiren eines Antisemiten. [PT2635.E98M4513 1982] 833'.912 19 82-516 ISBN 0-14-006224-6 pbk. : 4.95
I. [Memoiren eines Antisemiten.] English II. Title.

REZZORI, Gregor von. FIC
Memoirs of an anti-semite / Gregor von Rezzori. Harmondsworth, Middlesex, England ; New York, N.Y., U.S.A. : Penguin Books, 1982, c1981. 287 p. ; 20 cm. Translation of: Memoiren eines Antisemiten. [PT2635.E98M4513 1982] 833'.912 19 82-516 ISBN 0-14-006224-6 pbk. : 4.95
I. [Memoiren eines Antisemiten.] English II. Title.

RHODES, Harrie Vernette, 1871- 920.9133
In the one spirit; the autobiography of Harrie Vernette Rhodes as told to Margueritte Harmon Bro. [1st ed.] New York, Harper [1951] 192 p. 20 cm. [BR1716.R5A3] 51-14400
I. Bro. Margueritte (Harmon) 1894- II. Title.

RICHARDS, Lucy, 1792-1837. 922.773
Memoirs of the late Miss Lucy Richards, of Paris, Oneida county, N.Y. Written by herself. Edited by another hand. Revised by the editor. New-York, G. Lane & P. P. Sandford, for the Methodist Episcopal church, 1842. 272 p. 14 cm. [BR1725.R52A3 1842] 38-7485
I. Title.

RICHARDSON, Simon Peter, 1818-1899. 922.
The lights and shadows of itinerant life: an autobiography of Rev. Simon Peter Richardson ... with an introduction by Rev. John B. Robins, D.D. Nashville, Tenn., Dallas, Tex., Barbee & Smith, 1901. xix, 288 p. ports. 19 cm. [BX8495.R5A3] 1-16628
I. Title.

RICKABY, Joseph John, 1845-1932. 204
An old man's jottings, by Joseph Rickaby... London, New York [etc.] Longmans, Green and co., 1925. xii, 247 p. 19 1/2 cm. [BX890.R5] 25-6337
I. Title.

RIEGEL, John Ira, 1871- 232.
Simon, son of man: a cognomen of undoubted historicity, obscured by translation and lost in the resplendence of a dual appellative, by John I. Riegel and John H. Jordan ... Boston, Sherman. French & company, 1917. xvi, [2] p., 1 l., 269 p. front., illus., map, double plan. 21 cm. [BT301.R5] 18-2619
I. Jordan, John H., joint author. II. Title.

RITTER, Jacob, 1757-1841. 922.
Memoirs of Jacob Ritter, a faithful minister in the Society of Friends. By Joseph Foulke ... Philadelphia, T. E. Chapman [etc.] N. York, Baker & Crane, 1844. viii, [9]-111 p. 15 1/2 cm. [BX7795.R55A3] 3-22484
I. Foulke, Joseph, ed. II. Title.

RITTER, Jacob, 1757-1841. 922.
Memoirs of Jacob Ritter, a faithful minister in the Society of Friends. By Joseph Foulke ... Philadelphia, T. E. Chapman [etc.] N. York, Baker & Crane, 1844. viii, [9]-111 p. 15 1/2 cm. [BX7795.R55A3] 3-22484
I. Foulke, Joseph, ed. II. Title.

RITTER, Jacob, 1757-1851.
Memoirs of Jacob Ritter, a faithful minister in the Society of Friends. By Joseph Foulke ... Philadelphia, T. E. Chapman [etc.] N. York, Baker & Crane, 1844. viii, [9]-111 p. 26 cm. 3-22484
I. Title.

RITTER, Jacob, 1757-1851.
Memoirs of Jacob Ritter, a faithful minister in the Society of Friends. By Joseph Foulke ... Philadelphia, T. E. Chapman [etc.] N. York, Baker & Crane, 1844. viii, [9]-111 p. 26 cm. 3-22484
I. Title.

ROBBINS, Thomas, 1777-1856. 920.
Diary of Thomas Robbins, D. D., 1796-1854. Printed for his nephew. Owned by the Connecticut historical society ... Ed. and annotated by Increase N. Tarbox ... Boston, T. Todd, printer, 1886-87. 2 v, fronts. (ports.) 28 cm. Contents.--i, 1796-1825.--ii. 1826-1854. [BX7260.R615A3] 13-6005
I. Tarbox, Increase Niles, 1815-1888, ed. II. Title.

ROBINSON, James Herman. 922.573
Road without turning, the story of Reverend James H. Robinson; an autobiography. New York, Farrar, Straus [1950] 312 p. 21 cm. [BX9225.R715A3] 50-9789
I. Title.

ROGERS, Ammi, 1770-1552. 922.373
Memoirs of the Rev. Ammi Rogers, A. M., a clergyman of the Episcopal church ...persecuted in the state of Connecticut, on account of religion and politics...and finally falsely accused and imprisoned in Norwich jaul, for two years...Also a

concise view of the authority, doctrine, and worship, in the Protestant Episcopal church, and a very valuable index to the Holy Bible. Composed, compiled and written by the said Ammi Rogers... 5th ed, with additions, omissions and alterations. Concord, N.H., Fisk & Chase, printers, 1833. 264 p. 16 1/2 cm. [BX5995.R6A3 1833] 35-29969
I. Title.

ROGERS, Ammi, 1770-1852. 922.
Memoirs of the Rev. Ammi Robers, A.M., a clergyman of the Episcopal church... persecuted in the state of Connecticut, on account of religion and politics...and finally, falsely accused and imprisoned in Norwich jail, for two years... Composed, compiled, and written by the said Ammi Rogers ...2d ed. Schenectady, Printed by G. Ritchie, jun. 1826. 272 p. 16 1/2 cm. [BX5995.R6A3 1826] 36-33251
I. Title.

ROGERS, Ammi, 1770-1852. 922.373
Memoirs of the Rev. Ammi Rogers, A.M., a clergyman of the Episcopal church ...persecuted in the state of Connecticut, on account of religion and politics...and finally, falsely accused and imprisoned in Norwich gaol for two years... Composed, compiled, and written by the said Ammi Rogers... [n. p.] Published for subscribers, by the author, 1824. 264 p. 18 cm. [BX5995.R6A3 1824] 36-2424
I. Title.

ROGERS, Ammi, 1770-1852. 922.373
Memoirs of the Rev. Ammi Rogers, A.M., a clergyman of the Episcopal church ...persecuted in the state of Connecticut, on account of religion and politics...and finally falsely accused and imprisoned in Norwich jail, for two years...Also, a concise view of the authority, doctrine, and worship, in the Protestant Episcopal church, and a very valuable index to the Holy Bible. Composed, compiled and written by the said Ammi Rogers... 11th ed., with additions, omissions, and alterations. Watertown, N.Y., Printed by Knowlton & Rice, for the author, 1846. 264 p. 18 cm. [BX5995.B6A3 1846] 35-29970
I. Title.

ROGERS, Ammi, 1779-1852. 922.373
Memoirs of the Rev. Ammi Rogers, A.M., a clergyman of the Episcopal church ...persecuted in the state of Connecticut, on account of religion and politics...and finally, falsely accused and imprisoned in Norwich jail, for two years...Also an index to the Holy Bible; and a concise view of the authority, doctrine, and worship, in the Protestant Episcopal church. Composed, compiled, and written by the said Ammi Rogers ...3d ed.; with additions, omissions and alterations. Middlebury, Vt. Printed by J. W. Copeland, 1830. 238 p. 17 1/2 cm. Error in paging: p. [43] numbered 34. [BX5995.R6A3 1830] 35-29968
I. Title.

ROGERS, Dale Evans. 248
My spiritual diary. [Westwood, N.J.] F. H. Revell Co. [1955] 144 p. 22 cm. [BR1725.R63A3] 55-5390
I. Title.

[ROGERS, George] fl.1838. 922.
Memoranda of the experience, labors. and travels of a Universalist preacher. Written by himself. Cincinnati, J. A. Gurley, 1845. 400 p. 20 cm. [BX9969.R6A3] 2-10430
I. Title.

ROGERS, Hester Ann, Mrs., 1756-1794. 922.742
Experience of Hester Ann Rogers; and her funeral sermon, by Rev. Dr. Coke. To which is added her religious correspondence... Cincinnati, Published by Swormstedt & Poe, for the Methodist Episcopal church, 1853. 295 p. 16 cm. [BX8495.R55A3 1853] 33-23864
I. Coke, Thomas, bp., 1747-1814. II. Title.

ROGERS, Samuel, 1789-1877. 922.673
Autobiography of Elder Samuel Rogers. Edited by his son, Elder John I. Rogers. 4th ed. Cincinnati, Standard publishing company [1909] xiii, 208 p. front., plates, ports. 20 cm. [BX7343.R55A3 1909] 9-28409
I. Rogers, John I., 1819-1896, ed. II. Title.

RONAYNE, E[dmond]
Ronayne's reminiscences; a history of his life and renunciation of Romanism and freemasonry. Chicago, Free Methodist pub. house, 1900. 445 p. port. 12 degrees. Feb
I. Title.

ROTROU, Jean, 1609-1650.
Jean Rotrou's Saint Genest and Venceslas; edited with introduction and notes by Thomas Frederick Crane ... Boston, New York [etc.] Ginn & company [c1907] ix, 433 p. front. 19 cm. (International modern language series) Bibliography: p. 403-413. [PQ1915.S3 1907] 7-20861
I. Crane, Thomas Frederick, 1844-1927, ed. II. Title.

ROTROU, Jean, 1609-1650.
Jean Rotrou's Saint Genest and Venceslas; edited with introduction and notes by Thomas Frederick Crane ... Boston, New York [etc.] Ginn & company [c1907] ix, 433 p. front. 19 cm. (International modern language series) Bibliography: p. 403-413. [PQ1915.S3 1907] 7-20861
I. Crane, Thomas Frederick, 1844-1927, ed. II. Title.

ROUNTREE, Horace G. 248.24
Thy will be done in all things; the story of a journey into faith. New York, Exposition [c.1963] 45p. 21cm. 2.50
I. Title.

ROUX, Joseph, 1834-
Meditations of a parish priest. Thoughts. By Joseph Roux. Introduction by Paul Marieton. Translated from the 3d French ed. by Isabel F. Hapgood. New York, T. Y. Crowell & co. [1886] 3 p. l., [iii]-xxx, 213 p. 19 cm. [PN6332.R6 1886] 8-751
I. Marieton, Paul, 1862-1911. II. Hapgood, Isabel Florence, 1850-1928, tr. III. Title. IV. Title: Thoughts. Translation of the Pension.
Contents omitted.

SAGE, Carleton M., 1904- 922.246
... Paul Albar of Cordoba; studies on his life and writings ... by Carleton M. Sage ... Washington, D.C., The Catholic university of America press, 1943. xil, 239 p. 23 cm. (The Catholic university of America. Studies in mediaeval history. New ser., vol. V) Thesis (PH.D.)--Catholic university of America, 1944. Bibliography: p. 231-236. [BX4705.A42S3] A 44
I. Albarus, Paulus, d. ca. 861. II. Title.

SCARLETT, John, 1830-1889. 922.773
The itinerant on foot; or, Life-scenes recalled. By John Scarlett ... With an introduction, by Rev. George Hughes ... New York, W. C. Palmer [1882] vii, 9-256 p. front. (port.) 17 cm. [BX8495.S34A35] 36-37400
I. Title. II. Title: Life-scenes recalled.

SCARLETT, John, 1830-1889. 922.773
The itinerant on foot; or, Life-scenes recalled. By John Scarlett ... With an introduction, by Rev. George Hughes ... New York, W. C. Palmer [1882] vii, 9-256 p. front. (port.) 17 cm. [BX8495.S34A35] 36-37400
I. Title. II. Title: Life-scenes recalled.

SCHAUFFLER, Adolphus Frederick, 1845-1919. 922.
Memories of a happy boyhood "long ago, and far away," by Adolph Frederick Schauffler ... New York, Chicago [etc.] Fleming H. Revell company [c1919] 96 p. front. (port.) plates. 19 1/2 cm. $0.75 [BX7260.S3A4] 19-9155
I. Title.

SCHAUFFLER, Adolphus Frederick, 1845-1919. 922.
Memories of a happy boyhood "long ago, and far away," by Adolph Frederick Schauffler ... New York, Chicago [etc.] Fleming H. Revell company [c1919] 96 p. front. (port.) plates. 19 1/2 cm. $0.75 [BX7260.S3A4] 19-9155
I. Title.

[SCHNITTKIND, Henry Thomas] 1888- 922
Living biographies of religious leaders, by Henry Thomas [pseud.] and Dana Lee Thomas [pseud.] Illustrations by Gordon Ross. Garden City, N.Y., Garden City publishing co., inc. [1942] viii, 297 p. front., illus., ports. 23 1/2 cm. "First edition." [BL72.S37] 42-22219
1. Religions—Biog. I. Schnittkind, Dana Arnold, 1918- joint author. II. Title.

[SCHNITTKIND, Henry Thomas] 1888- 922
Living biographies of religious leaders, by Henry Thomas [pseud.] and Dana Lee Thomas [pseud.] Illustrations by Gordon Ross. Garden City, N.Y., Blue ribbon books [1946] viii, 297 p. illus., ports. 21 cm. [BL72.S37 1946] 46-4978
1. Religions—Biog. I. Schnittkind, Dana Arnold, 1918- joint author. II. Title.

SCOTT, Jacob Richardson, 1815-1861. 922.673
To Thee this temple; the life, diary, and friends of Jacob Richardson Scott, 1815-1861, by Elizabeth Hayward and Roscoe Ellis Scott. Chester, Pa., American Baptist Historical Society, 1955. xiii, 405p. illus., port., facsims. 28cm. From family papers in the possession of the author's grandson, Roscoe Ellis Scott. Bibliography: p.379-380. [BX6495.S39A3] 55-18762
I. Hayward, Elizabeth (McCoy) 1901- ed. II. Scott, Roscoe Ellis, 1887- ed. III. Title.

SCOTT, Job, 1751-1793. 922.
A journal of the life, travels and gospel labours of that faithful servant and minister of Christ, Job Scott. Mountpleasant, Ohio, E. Bates, 1820. xi, 303 p. 18 cm. [BX7795.S4A5 1820] 49-57908
I. Title.

SCOTT, Job, 1751-1793. 922.
A journal of the life, travels and gospel labours of that faithful servant and minister of Christ, Job Scott. Mountpleasant, Ohio, E. Bates, 1820. xi, 303 p. 18 cm. [BX7795.S4A5 1820] 49-57908
I. Title.

SCOTT, Job, 1751-1793. 922.
A journal of the life, travels and gospel labours of that faithful servant and minister of Christ, Job Scott. Mountpleasant, Ohio, E. Bates, 1820. xi, 303 p. 18 cm. [BX7795.S4A5 1820] 49-57908
I. Title.

SCOTT, Job, 1751-1793. 922.
Journal of the life, travels and gospel labours of that faithful servant and minister of Christ, Job Scott. 4th ed. New-York, Printed and sold by Isaac Collins, no. 189, Pearl-street, 1798. 2 p. l., iii-xii, 360 p. 18 cm. [BX7795.S4A5 1798] 22-25337
I. Title.

SCOTT, Job, 1751-1793. 922.
Journal of the life, travels and gospel labours of that faithful servant and minister of Christ, Job Scott. 4th ed. New-York, Printed and sold by Isaac Collins, no. 189, Pearl-street, 1798. 2 p. l., iii-xii, 360 p. 18 cm. [BX7795.S4A5 1798] 22-25337
I. Title.

SCOTT, Job, 1751-1793. 922.
Journal of the life, travels and gospel labours of that faithful servant and minister of Christ, Job Scott. 4th ed. New-York, Printed and sold by Isaac Collins, no. 189, Pearl-street, 1798. 2 p. l., iii-xii, 360 p. 18 cm. [BX7795.S4A5 1798] 22-25337
I. Title.

SCOTT, Job, 1751-1793. 922.
Journal of the life, travels and gospel labours of that faithful servant and minister of Christ, Job Scott. 4th ed. New-York, Printed and sold by Isaac Collins, no. 189, Pearl-street, 1798. 2 p. l., iii-xii, 360 p. 18 cm. [BX7795.S4A5 1798] 22-25337
I. Title.

SCOTT, Job, 1751-1793. 922.
Journal of the life, travels, and gospel labours of that faithful servant and minister of Christ, Job Scott. Philadelphia: Printed for B. and T. Kite, No. 20, North Third Street. Griggs & Dickinsons, Printers. 1814. xii, [13]-323 p. 19 cm. [BX7795.S4A5 1814] 23-14325
I. Title.

SCOTT, Job, 1751-1793. 922.
Journal of the life, travels, and gospel labours of that faithful servant and minister of Christ, Job Scott. Philadelphia: Printed for B. and T. Kite, No. 20, North Third Street. Griggs & Dickinsons, Printers. 1814. xii, [13]-323 p. 19 cm. [BX7795.S4A5 1814] 23-14325
I. Title.

SCOTT, Job, 1751-1793. 922.
Journal of the life, travels, and gospel labours of that faithful servant and minister of Christ, Job Scott. Philadelphia: Printed for B. and T. Kite, No. 20, North Third Street. Griggs & Dickinsons, Printers. 1814. xii, [13]-323 p. 19 cm. [BX7795.S4A5 1814] 23-14325
I. Title.

SCOTT, Job, 1751-1793. 922.
Journal of the life, travels, and gospel labours of that faithful servant and minister of Christ, Job Scott. Philadelphia: Printed for B. and T. Kite, No. 20, North Third Street. Griggs & Dickinsons, Printers. 1814. xii, [13]-323 p. 19 cm. [BX7795.S4A5 1814] 23-14325
I. Title.

SCOTT, John, 1820-
Recollections of fifty years in the ministry: with numerous character sketches. By John Scott ... Introduction by Rev. J. J. Murray ... Pittsburgh, Pa., and Baltimore, Md., Methodist Protestant board of publication [c1898] 495 p. front. (port.) 21 cm. 12-38495
I. Title.

[SEELEY, Robert Benton] 1798-1886.
A memoir of the Rev. W. A. B. Johnson... With an introductory notice, by Stephen H. Tyng, D.D. New York, R. Carter & brothers, 1853. viii, [13]-385 p. 19 1/2 cm. 17-794
I. Johnson, William Augustine Bernard, d. 1823. II. Title.

[SEELEY, Robert Benton] 1798-1886.
A memoir of the Rev. W. A. B. Johnson... With an introductory notice, by Stephen H. Tyng, D.D. New York, R. Carter & brothers, 1853. viii, [13]-385 p. 19 1/2 cm. 17-794
I. Johnson, William Augustine Bernard, d. 1823. II. Title.

SELLECK, Alonzo Farrington, b.1806. 922.
Recollections of an itinerant life. By Rev. A. F. Selleck...Edited by his son. New York, Printed by Phillips & Hunt, 1836. 186 p. front. (port.) 16 1/2 cm. Preface signed: J. W. Selleck. [BX8495.S45A3] 4-13408
I. Selleck, James W. II. Title.

SHEARD, Charles. 250
The minister himself; or, The preacher's beacon light, with hints, incidents and admonitions; by the Rev. Charles Sheard ... [Cleveland, New York, F. M. Barton, 1900] 260 p. 19 1/2 cm. [BV4010.S47] 3-2212
I. Title.

SHEARDOWN, Thomas Simpson, b.1791. 922.673
Half a century's labors in the gospel, including thirty-five years of back-woods' mission work, and evangelizing, in New York and Pennsylvania. An autobiography, by Thomas S. Sheardown, as related, in his 74th year, to a stenographer. With an appendix, containing additional sketches, notices of Mrs. Esther G. Sheardown, histories, & c., & c., by other hands. [Lewisburg? Pa.] O. N. Worden and E. B. Case, 1865. 372 p. front. (phot.) 19 cm. [BX6495.S465A3 1865] 36-24267
I. Title.

SHEARDOWN, Thomas Simpson, b.1791.
Half a century's labors in the Gospel, including thirty-five years of back-woods' mission work, and evangelizing, in New York and Pennsylvania. An autobiography, by Thomas S. Sheardown, as related, in his 74th year, to a stenographer. With an appendix, containing additional sketches, notices of Mrs. Esther G. Sheardown, histories, & c., & c., by other hands. 2d thousand. [Philadelphia] O. N. Worden and E. B. Case, 1866. 372 p. front. (port.) 19 cm. [BX6595.S465A3 1866] 2-18691
I. Title.

SHERIDAN, William.
A consecrated life; or, The biography of Joh Sheridan. [Toledo, O.] The Andrew-Jones print co. [1898] 192, [2] p., 1 l. incl. front. (port.) 20 cm. Nov
I. Title.

SHERMAN, Eleazer, b.1795. 922.
The narrative of Eleazer Sherman, giving an account of his life, experience, call to the ministry of the gospel, and travels as such to the present time ... Providence, H. H. Brown, printer, 1832. 3 v. in 1. 18 1/2 cm. [BX6793.S45A8 1882] 27-472
I. Title.

SHOWALTER, Lewis Pendelton, 1868-
Jim Handy, the wandering preacher; or, Life among the lowly, by Lewis P. Showalter. [Eaton? O., c1909] 223 p. incl. plates. front. (port.) 23 1/2 cm. 9-13260
I. Title.

SHULTZE, David, 1717- 1797. 925.269
Journals and papers, translated and edited by Andrew S. Berky. ,531st ed.] Pennsburg, Pa., Schwenkfelder Library, 1952-53. 2v. maps., facsims. 25cm. Contents.v. 1. 1726-1760.--v. 2. 1761-1797. [BX9749.S47] 52-14356
I. Title.

SINGLETON, George A 922.773
The autobiography of George A. Singleton. Boston, Forum Pub. Co. [1964] 272 p. illus., ports. 22 cm. [BX8449.S5A3] 64-56507
I. Title.

SMIT, Erasmus. 266'.4'20924 B
The diary of Erasmus Smit. Edited by H. F. Schoon. Translated by W. G. A. Mears. Cape Town, C. Struik, 1972. x, 186 p. illus. 22 cm. Translation of Uit het dagboek van Erasmus Smit. [BX9595.S63S613] 72-189813 ISBN 0-86977-013-6 10.00
I. Title.
Available from Verry.

SMITH, Elbert A. 1871- 922.8373
On memory's beam, the autobiography of Elbert A. Smith. Independence, Mo., Herald publishing house, 1946. 350 p., 1 l. front., plates, ports. 20 cm. "Appeared in ... the Saints' herald, in the issues from April 29 to December 23, 1944 ... In preparing the material for book publication, the author has re-edited a number of parts, and has added some new chapters."--Introd. [BX8695.S48A3] 46-15779
I. Title.

SMITH, Jennie, 1842- 922
Ramblings in Beulah land. A continuation of experiences in the life of Jennie Smith... Philadelphia, Garrigues brothers, 1886-88. 2 v. front. (v. 2) 17 1/2 cm. [BV3785.S59A4] 37-36772
I. Title.

SMITH, Rodney, 1860- 922
Gipsy Smith; his life and work, by himself; introductions by G. Campbell Morgan and Alexander McLaren, D.D. Rev. ed. New York, Chicago [etc.] Fleming H. Revell company [c1925] 3 p. l., [5]-333 p. front., plates, ports. 21 cm. [BV3785.S6A4 1925] 25-4635
I. Title.

SMITH, Rodney, 1860- 922
My life story, by Gipsy (Rodney) Smith, evangelist, with an introduction by Rev. James R. Day... New York, A. Scott & co. [1892] 64 p. 18 1/2 cm. [BV3785.S6A3] 37-36516
I. Title.

SMITH, Rodney, 1860- 922
My life story, by Gipsy (Rodney) Smith, evangelist, with an introduction by Rev. James R. Day... New York, A. Scott & co. [1892] 64 p. 18 1/2 cm. [BV3785.S6A3] 37-36516
I. Title.

SMITH, Thomas, 1776-1844. 922.
Experience and ministerial labors of Rev. Thomas Smith ... compiled chiefly from his journal, by Rev. David Dailey ... George Peck, editor. New York, Lane & Tippett, 1848. 198 p. 16 cm. [BX8495.S6A3] 10-13339
I. Dailey, David, comp. II. Peck, George, 1797-1876, ed. III. Title.

SPALDING, Samuel Charles, 1878- 285'.092'4
I've had me a time! With autobiographical sketch, selected poems, and sermons. Great Barrington, Mass., Friends of Gould Farm, 1961. 72 p. port. 21 cm. "Limited edition of not more than one thousand copies, the first two hundred and fifty of which, at least, are to be numbered and autographed ... no. [C30]" [BX9225.S63A3] 285'.2'0924 78-230256
I. Title.

SPALDING, Samuel Charles, 1878- 285'.092'4
I've had me a time! With autobiographical sketch, selected poems, and sermons. Great Barrington, Mass., Friends of Gould Farm, 1961. 72 p. port. 21 cm. "Limited edition of not more than one thousand copies, the first two hundred and fifty of which, at least, are to be numbered and autographed ... no. [C30]" [BX9225.S63A3] 285'.2'0924 78-230256
I. Title.

SPALDING, Samuel Charles, 1878- 285'.092'4
I've had me a time! With autobiographical sketch, selected poems, and sermons. Great Barrington, Mass., Friends of Gould Farm, 1961. 72 p. port. 21 cm. "Limited edition of not more than one thousand copies, the first two hundred and fifty of which, at least, are to be numbered and autographed ... no. [C30]" [BX9225.S63A3] 285'.2'0924 78-230256
I. Title.

SPALDING, Samuel Charles, 1878- 285'.092'4
I've had me a time! With autobiographical sketch, selected poems, and sermons. Great Barrington, Mass., Friends of Gould Farm, 1961. 72 p. port. 21 cm. "Limited edition of not more than one thousand copies, the first two hundred and fifty of which, at least, are to be numbered and autographed ... no. [C30]" [BX9225.S63A3] 285'.2'0924 78-230256
I. Title.

SPARKS, Jacob B., 1886- 922
Jacob's well of life; a new sparks from Old Time Religion; the autobiography of Jacob B. Sparks. Royal Oak, Mich. [1948] 302 p. illus., ports. 24 cm. [BR1725.S68A3] 48-2501
I. Title.

SPARKS, Jacob B., 1886- 922
Jacob's well of life; a new sparks from Old Time Religion; the autobiography of Jacob B. Sparks. Royal Oak, Mich. [1948] 302 p. illus., ports. 24 cm. [BR1725.S68A3] 48-2501
I. Title.

SQUIRES, Walter Albion.
New Testament followers of Jesus ... by Walter Albion Squires ... Philadelphia, The Westminster press, 1923. xii, 274 p. front. (map) plates. 19 cm. (The Westminster textbooks of religious education for church schools having Sunday, week day, and expressional sessions, ed. by J. T. Faris. Intermediate department, 2d year, pt. I) [BS2435.S6] 24-18299
I. Title.

STACY, Nathaniel, 1778or9- 1868.
Memoirs of the life of Nathaniel Stacy preacher of the gospel of universal grace. Comprising a brief circumstan;ial history of the rise and progress of Universalism in the state of New York, as identified therewith ... Columbus, Pa., Pub. for the author by A. Vedder, 1850. xvi, [17]-523 p. front. (port.) 20 1/2 cm. [BX9909.S75A3] 9-30728
I. Title.

STALKER, Charles H[enry] 1876-
Twice around the world with the Holy Ghost; or, The impressions and convictions of the mission field, by Charles H. Stalker ... Columbus, O., C. H. Stalker, 1906. 237 p. front., plates, ports. 20 cm. 6-13348
I. Title.

STEPENS, John Vant, 1857- 922.573
Fourscore, life story (abridged) of John Vant Stephens ... Cincinnati, O., 1938. 5 p. l., 142 p. front. (ports.) illus. 20 cm. [BX9225.S74A3] 39-19719
I. Title.

STEURT, Marjorie Rankin. 266'.5'10924 B
Broken bits of old China. [1st ed.] Nashville, T. Nelson [1973] 152 p. 21 cm. Autobiographical. [BV3427.S814A3] 72-12986 ISBN 0-8407-6262-3 4.95
I. Title.

STEURT, Marjorie Rankin. 266'.5'10924 B
Broken bits of old China. [1st ed.] Nashville, T. Nelson [1973] 152 p. 21 cm. Autobiographical. [BV3427.S814A3] 72-12986 ISBN 0-8407-6262-3 4.95
I. Title.

STEVENS, William Bagshaw, 1756-1800 922.342
The journal of the Rev. William Bagshaw Stevens, ed. by Georgina Galbraith [New York] Oxford [c. 1965] xxvii, 550p. fold. geneal. table. map, port. 23cm. Bibl. [PR3717.S24Z5] 65-8452 10.10
I. Title.

STEVENS, William Bagshaw, 1756-1800 922.342
The journal of the Rev. William Bagshaw Stevens, ed. by Georgina Galbraith [New York] Oxford [c. 1965] xxvii, 550p. fold. geneal. table. map, port. 23cm. Bibl. [PR3717.S24Z5] 65-8452 10.10
I. Title.

[STEWART, W. G.] 922.
A memoir of the life and labors of the Rev. Thomas G. Stewart. By his son ... Philadelphia, Collins, printer, 1858. xvii p., 1 l., [13]-252 p. front. (port.) 20 cm. Introduction signed: S. Y. Monroe. [BX8495.S76S7] 7-29648
I. Stewart, Thomas G., 1790-1848. II. Title.

[STEWART, W. G.] 922.
A memoir of the life and labors of the Rev. Thomas G. Stewart. By his son ... Philadelphia, Collins, printer, 1858. xvii p., 1 l., [13]-252 p. front. (port.) 20 cm. Introduction signed: S. Y. Monroe. [BX8495.S76S7] 7-29648
I. Stewart, Thomas G., 1790-1848. II. Title.

STEWART, William, 1881- 922.773
Mindful of man; the chronicle of an octogenarian Methodist minister. Farmington, Mo., 1964. xiii, 139 p. illus., ports. 24 cm. [BX8495.S764A3] 65-1230
I. Title.

STEWART, William, 1881- 922.773
Mindful of man; the chronicle of an octogenarian Methodist minister. Farmington, Mo., 1964. xiii, 139 p. illus., ports. 24 cm. [BX8495.S764A3] 65-1230
I. Title.

STOCKING, Charles Francis, 1873-
The diary of Jean Evarts, by Charles Francis Stocking ... Freeport, Ill., The Standard publishing company, 1912. 352 p. 20 cm. [BV6947.S7] 12-23962
I. Title.

STODDARD, Charles Warren, 1843-1909. 922.
A troubled heart and how it was comforted at last. Notre Dame, Ind., J. A. Lyons, 1885. 178 p. 18 cm. [BX4705.S83A4] 12-39160
I. Title.

STONE, Darwell, 1859- 283
The faith of an English Catholic, by Darwell Stone ... London, New York [etc.] Longmans, Green and co., ltd., 1926. 4 p. l., 116 p. 19 cm. [BX5100.S7] 26-6201
I. Title.

*STOUDT, John Joseph, 1911- 230'.0924
Jacob Boehme: His life and thought. Foreword by Paul Tillich. New York, Seabury [1968, c. 1957] 317p. 20cm. (SP 46) Orig. pub. under the title Sunrise to eternity. Bibl. 2.75 pap.,
I. Title.

*STOUDT, John Joseph, 1911- 230'.0924
Jacob Boehme: His life and thought. Foreword by Paul Tillich. New York, Seabury [1968, c. 1957] 317p. 20cm. (SP 46) Orig. pub. under the title Sunrise to eternity. Bibl. 2.75 pap.,
I. Title.

STRATON, John Roach, 1875- 252.
The old gospel at the heart of the metropolis, by Rev. John Roach Straton ... New York, George H. Doran company [c1925] xi p., 2 l., 17-298 p. front., pl. 19 1/2 cm. $2.00. "An 'old-time religionist': an appreciation of the Reverend John Roach Straton, D. D., by William G. Shepherd": p. 291-298. [BX6333.S7303] 25-9083
I. Title.

STRINDBERG, August, 1849-1912.
The inferno, by August Strindberg ... tr. by Claud Field. New York, London, G. P. Putnam's sons, 1913. iv p., 1 l., 230 p. 20 cm. "His four autobiographical works, The son of a servant, The confessions of a fool, Inferno, and Legends, are four segments of an immense curve tracing his progress from the childish pletism of his early years, through a period of atheism and rebellion to the sombre faith in a 'God that punishes' of the sexagenarian." [Full name: John August Strindberg] A13
I. Field, Claud Herbert Alwyn, 1863- tr. II. Title.

STRINDBERG, August, 1849-1912.
The inferno, by August Strindberg ... tr. by Claud Field. New York, London, G. P. Putnam's sons, 1913. iv p., 1 l., 230 p. 20 cm. "His four autobiographical works, The son of a servant, The confessions of a fool, Inferno, and Legends, are four segments of an immense curve tracing his progress from the childish pletism of his early years, through a period of atheism and rebellion to the sombre faith in a 'God that punishes' of the sexagenarian." [Full name: John August Strindberg] A13
I. Field, Claud Herbert Alwyn, 1863- tr. II. Title.

STROUP, Herbert Hewitt, 1916- 200'.92'2 B
Founders of living religions, by Herbert Stroup. Philadelphia, Westminster Press [1974] 256 p. 21 cm. Bibliography: p. [241] -244. [BL72.S8] 74-10934 ISBN 0-664-24994-9 4.25
1. Religions—Biography. 2. Religions. I. Title.

[STUART, Henry Clifford] 1864- 133
A prophet in his own country, being the letters of Stuart X [pseud.] to many men on many occasions; ed. with an introduction and notes, by Aleister Crowley. Washington, D.C., The author [c1916] 499 p. front. (port.) 21 1/2 cm. [X3.S8] 16-13737
I. Crowley, Aleister, ed. II. Title.
Contents omitted.

STUART, William David, 1840- 1863. 285.
Memoir of William David Stuart. With copious extracts from his diary and letters. Together with an appendix. Philadelphia, Printed for private circulation, 1865. vi p., 2 l., [9]-375 p. mounted front. (phot.) 18 1/2 cm. Preface signed J. M'M. [BX9225.S79A3] 1-26876
I. M'M., J., ed. II. J., M'M., ed. III. Title.

STUART, William David, 1840- 1863. 285.
Memoir of William David Stuart. With copious extracts from his diary and letters. Together with an appendix. Philadelphia, Printed for private circulation, 1865. vi p., 2 l., [9]-375 p. mounted front. (phot.) 18 1/2 cm. Preface signed J. M'M. [BX9225.S79A3] 1-26876
I. M'M., J., ed. II. J., M'M., ed. III. Title.

SUMNER, John Daniel. 783.7 B
J. D. Sumner: Gospel music is my life [by] Bob Terrell. Nashville, Impact Books [1971] 208 p. illus. 22 cm. [ML420.S953A3] 77-182384 3.95
I. Terrell, Bob. II. Title: Gospel music is my life.

SUMNER, John Daniel. 783.7 B
J. D. Sumner: Gospel music is my life [by] Bob Terrell. Nashville, Impact Books [1971] 208 p. illus. 22 cm. [ML420.S953A3] 77-182384 3.95

I. Terrell, Bob. II. Title: Gospel music is my life.

SWARTZ, Joel, 1827-1914. 922.473
A short story of a long life; an autobiography. Written for the family, 1904. Edited and published by Philip Allen Swartz. [1st ed.] Poughkeepsie, N.Y. [1960] 224 p. illus. 23 cm. [BX7260.S875A3] 61-24999
I. Title.

TARDY, William Thomas, 1874- 208.
1919.
The man and the message, by William Thomas Tardy; with a foreword by Rev. J. B. Gambrell ... Marshall, Tex., Mrs. W. T. Tardy, 1920. 2 p. l., 200 p. front. (port.) 20 cm. [BX6217.T3] 20-15400
I. Title.

TARDY, William Thomas, 1874- 920.
1919.
Trials and triumphs, an autobiography, by Rev. W. T. Tardy, with a foreword by Rev. George W. Truett, D.D. Ed. by J. B. Cranfill, LL.D. Marshall, Tex., Mrs. W. T. Tardy [c1919] 5 p. l., 116 p. 2 port. (incl. front.) 19 1/2 cm. [BX6495.T3A3] 19-8641
I. Cranfill, James Britton, 1858- ed. II. Title.

TATHAM, Geoffrey Bulmer.
Dr. John Walker and the Sufferings of the clergy, by G. B. Tatham .. Cambridge, University press, 1911. vii, [1], 429 p. 19 cm. (Half-title: Cambridge historical essays. no. xx) The Prince Consort prize, 1910. 11-2378
I. Oxford. University. Bodleian library. Mss. (Walker collection) II. Title.
Contents omitted.

TAYLER Charles Benjamin, 1797-
1875.
The records of a good man's life. By the Rev. Charles B. Tayler ... Philadelphia, Protestant Episcopal book society [18--] 286 p. 19 1/2 cm. First published London, 1832. 9-30729
I. Title.

TAYLOR, Oliver Alden, 922.573
1801-1851.
Memoir of the Rev. Oliver Alden Taylor, A.M., late of Manchester, Massachusetts ... by Rev. Timothy Alden Taylor ... Boston, Tappan and Whittemore, 1853. xii, [13]-396 p. front. (port.) 19 1/2 cm. [BX7260.T34A3] 36-25700
I. Taylor, Timothy Alden, 1809-1858, ed. II. Title.

TAYLOR, Oliver Alden, 922.573
1801-1851.
Memoir of the Rev. Oliver Alden Taylor, A.M., late of Manchester, Massachusetts ... by Rev. Timothy Alden Taylor ... Boston, Tappan and Whittemore, 1853. xii, [13]-396 p. front. (port.) 19 1/2 cm. [BX7260.T34A3] 36-25700
I. Taylor, Timothy Alden, 1809-1858, ed. II. Title.

*THATCH, Harrell G. 248
God gets in the way of a sailor. Foreword by O. Hobart Mowrer. New York, Exposition [c.1964] 266p. 21cm. (EP42077) 4.50
I. Title.

THOMAS, Henry, 1886- 922
Living biographies of religious leaders, by Henry Thomas and Dana Lee Thomas. Garden City, N. Y., Perma Giants [1950, c1942] viii. 297p. 22cm. [BL72.T36 1950] 51-30711
1. Religions—Biog. I. Thomas, Dana Lee, 1918- joint author. II. Title.

THOMAS, Henry, 1886- 922
Living biographies of religious leaders, by Henry Thomas and Dana Lee Thomas. Garden City, N.Y., Garden City Books [1959] 298 p. illus. 22 cm. [BL72.T36 1959] 59-3053
1. Religions — Biog. I. Thomas, Dana Lee, 1918- joint author. II. Title.

THOMPSON, Lorne F. 286'.1'0924 B
The raw edge of courage [by] Lorne F. Thompson. Grand Rapids, Baker Book House [1970] 199 p. 21 cm. Autobiographical. [BX6495.T44A3] 70-141553 3.95
I. Title.

THOMPSON, Wilson, 286'.63'0924
1788-1866.
The autobiography of Elder Wilson Thompson; his life, travels, and ministerial labors. Springfield, Ohio, E. T. Aleshire, 1962. 363 p. illus. 23 cm. [BX6793.T54A3] 63-1325
I. Title.

THOREN, Herman H. 922
Lost and saved. A brief sketch of the experiences of Henry R. Baker. Written by Rev. H. H. Thoren ... Sterling, Ill., Bee hive publishing co. [1893] 47 p. illus. (ports.) 19 cm. Illustrated t.-p. [BV3785.B28T5] 37-33217
I. Baker, Henry R., 1858 II. Title.

TIPPETT, Edward D.
The experience and trials of Edward D. Tippett, preceptor; or, 44 years of his life: containing strange and mysterious events whilst the teacher of the Eastern free school, Washington, D.C.; also, singular and strange circumstances transpiring in Annapolis and Baltimore. Written for the information of his fellow citizens, by himself. Washington, D.C., Printed for the author [by] W. Freer, 1833. 120 p. 20 cm. 6-27368
I. Title.

TIRRELL, Mary Pierre. 922.246
Mary was her life; the story of a nun, Sister Maria Teresa Quevedo, 1930-1950. New York, Benziger Bros. [1960] 234 p. illus. 21 cm. Quevedo, Maria Teresa, 1930-1950. [BX4705.Q44T5] 60-9445
I. Title.

TIRRELL, Mary Pierre. 922.246
Mary was her life; the story of a nun, Sister Maria Teresa Quevedo, 1930-1950. New York, Benziger Bros. [1960] 234 p. illus. 21 cm. Quevedo, Maria Teresa, 1930-1950. [BX4705.Q44T5] 60-9445
I. Title.

TIRRELL, Mary Pierre. 922.246
Mary was her life; the story of a nun, Sister Maria Teresa Quevedo, 1930-1950. New York, Benziger Bros. [1960] 234 p. illus. 21 cm. Quevedo, Maria Teresa, 1930-1950. [BX4705.Q44T5] 60-9445
I. Title.

TIRRELL, Mary Pierre. 922.246
Mary was her life; the story of a nun, Sister Maria Teresa Quevedo, 1930-1950. New York, Benziger Bros. [1960] 234 p. illus. 21 cm. Quevedo, Maria Teresa, 1930-1950. [BX4705.Q44T5] 60-9445
I. Title.

TODD, John, 1800-1873. 922.573
John Todd, the story of his life, told mainly by himself. Compiled and edited by John E. Todd... New York, Harper & brothers, 1876. 529 p. incl. front. (port.) plates. 21 cm. [BX7260.T6A3] 36-25406
I. Todd, John Edwards, 1833-1907, ed. II. Title.

TODD, John, 1800-1873. 922.573
John Todd, the story of his life, told mainly by himself. Compiled and edited by John E. Todd... New York, Harper & brothers, 1876. 529 p. incl. front. (port.) plates. 21 cm. [BX7260.T6A3] 36-25406
I. Todd, John Edwards, 1833-1907, ed. II. Title.

TOLSTOI, Lev Nikolaevich, 241
graf, 1828-1910.
My religion. By Count Leo Tolstoi. Translated from the French. New York, T. Y. Crowell & co. [c1885] xii, 274 p. 19 cm. Translator's preface signed: Huntington Smith. [BR125.T7 1885] 12-39481
I. Smith, Huntington, 1857- tr. II. Title.

TOWSON, Hatton Dunica, 922.773
1892-1919.
Jap; the growth of a soul, the letters of Hatton Towson, student, soldier, and missionary, edited by Rev. J. O. J. Taylor. Nashville, Tenn., Publishing house of the Methodist Episcopal church, South [c1937] 169 p. 19 1/2 cm. [BR1725.T64A4] 38-7894
I. Taylor, James Oliver Jelks, 1893- ed. II. Title.

TOWSON, Hatton Dunica, 922.773
1892-1919.
Jap; the growth of a soul, the letters of Hatton Towson, student, soldier, and missionary, edited by Rev. J. O. J. Taylor. Nashville, Tenn., Publishing house of the Methodist Episcopal church, South [c1937] 169 p. 19 1/2 cm. [BR1725.T64A4] 38-7894
I. Taylor, James Oliver Jelks, 1893- ed. II. Title.

TRINE, Ralph Waldo, 1866- 130
My philosophy and my religion [by] Ralph Waldo Trine ... New York, Dodd, Mead & company, 1921. 130 p. front. (port.) 19 1/2 cm. (On cover: The life books) [BF639.T664] 21-18105
I. Title.

TUCKER, Irwin St. John, 922.373
1886-
Out of the hell-box, by Irwin St. John Tucker. New York, Morehouse-Gorham co., 1945. 3 p. l., 179 p. 21 cm. [BX5995.T73A3] 46-322
I. Title.

TUCKER, Sarah (Fish) 1779- 922.
1840.
Memoirs of the life and religious experience of Sarah Tucker, a minister of the Society of Friends. Providence, Moore & Choate, printers, 1848. 204 p. 19 cm. [BX7795.T79A3] 49-34830
I. Title.

*TURNBULL, Ralph G. 207'.773.11
A treasury of W. Graham Scroggie compiled by Ralph G. Turnbull. Grand Rapids, Baker Book House [1974] 220 p. 20 cm. Bibliography: p. 218-220. [BX6093] ISBN 0-8010-8822-4 3.95 (pbk.)
I. Title.

TURRENTINE, Francis M., 922.
1861-
My life story, biographical and historical. [n. p.] 1940. 124 l. 29 cm. Typewritten. [BX8495.T8A3] 50-42924
I. Title.

TURRENTINE, Francis M., 922.
1861-
My life story, biographical and historical. [n. p.] 1940. 124 l. 29 cm. Typewritten. [BX8495.T8A3] 50-42924
I. Title.

USSHER, Elizabeth, 1772?- 922
1796.
Extracts from the letters of Elizabeth, Lucy, and Judith Ussher, late of the city of Waterford, Ireland. Philadelphia, For sale at Friend's book store [W. H. Pile, printer] 1871 iv, [5]-148 p. 19 1/2 cm. [BR1725.U8A4] 38-7137
I. Ussher, Lucy, 1776?-1797. II. Ussher, Judith, 1780?-1798. III. Title.

VAIL, Albert Lenox, 1844-
Mary Webb and the mother socity, by Albert L. Vail ... Philadelphia, American Baptist publication society, 1914. 5 p. l., 110 p. 20 cm. 14-18103
I. Title.

VAIL, Albert Lenox, 1844-
Mary Webb and the mother socity, by Albert L. Vail ... Philadelphia, American Baptist publication society, 1914. 5 p. l., 110 p. 20 cm. 14-18103
I. Title.

VAILL, Joseph, 1751-1838. 920.
Memoir of the life and character of Rev. Joseph Vaill, late pastor of the church of Christ in Hadlyme. By Rev. Isaac Parsons ... New York, Taylor and Dodd, 1839. vii, [13]-236 p. front. 17 1/2 cm. [BX7260.V28H3]
I. Parsons, Isaac, 1790-1838, ed. II. Title.

VAILL, Joseph, 1751-1838. 920.
Memoir of the life and character of Rev. Joseph Vaill, late pastor of the church of Christ in Hadlyme. By Rev. Isaac Parsons ... New York, Taylor and Dodd, 1839. vii, [13]-236 p. front. 17 1/2 cm. [BX7260.V28H3]
I. Parsons, Isaac, 1790-1838, ed. II. Title.

VAN BUSKIRK, William 291.6'3 B
Riley.
The saviors of mankind. Freeport, N.Y., Books for Libraries Press [1969] xiv, 537 p. 23 cm. (Essay index reprint series) Reprint of the 1929 ed. Contents.Contents.—Lao-Tze.—Confucius.—Guatama.—Zoroaster.—Aakhnaton.—Moses.—Isaiah of Babylon.—Socrates.—Jesus of Nazareth.—Saul of Tarsus.—Mahomet. [BL72.V3 1969] 71-86790
1. Religions—Biography. 2. Prophets. I. Title.

VAN BUSKIRK, William Riley. 922
The saviors of mankind, by William R. Van Buskirk. New York, The Macmillan company, 1929. xiv p., 537 p. diagr. 22 1/2 cm. [BL72.V3] 29-20808
1. Religions—Biog. 2. Prophets. I. Title.
Contents omitted.

VAN DELLEN, Idzerd. 922.573
In God's crucible, an autobiography. Grand Rapids, Baker Book House, 1950 134 p. 22 cm. [BX6843.V3A3] 50-37398
I. Title.

VAN DELLEN, Idzerd. 922.573
In God's crucible, an autobiography. Grand Rapids, Baker Book House, 1950 134 p. 22 cm. [BX6843.V3A3] 50-37398
I. Title.

*VANN, Gerald 248.8940922
To heaven with Diana! A study of Jordan of Saxony and Diana d'Andalo, with a translation of the letters of Jordan. Chicago, Regnery [1965, c.1960] 160p. 18cm. (Logos bk., L707) 1.25 pap.,
I. Title.

VAN ZANDT, Grace Goodspeed. 248
The emergence of Emily, by Grace Goodspeed Van Zandt. Boston, The Christopher publishing house [c1930] 119 p. 20 1/2 cm. The story of a struggle for spiritual peace. [BV4935.Z9V3] 30-33551
I. Title.

VAN ZANDT, Grace Goodspeed. 248
The emergence of Emily, by Grace Goodspeed Van Zandt. Boston, The Christopher publishing house [c1930] 119 p. 20 1/2 cm. The story of a struggle for spiritual peace. [BV4935.Z9V3] 30-33551
I. Title.

VAN ZELLER, Hubert, 282.0924
1905-
One foot in the cradle; an autobiography. NewYork, Holt [1966, c.1965] xi, 282p. illus., ports. 22cm. [BX4705.V33A3 1966] 66-22064 5.95
I. Title.

VERKADE, Willibrord, 922.2492
pater, 1868-
In guest of beauty, by Dom Willbrord Verkade New York, P. J. Kenedy & sons [c1935] ix, 292 p. 20 1/2 cm. Sequel to the author's "Yesterdays of an artist-monk" being reminiscences of his life as a member of the Benedictine order. Translation of Der antrieb ins volkommene, orinnerungen elnom malermouchen. [Secular name: Jobannes Sixtue Gerhardus Verkade] [BX4705.V5A35] 36-5074
I. Title.

VERKADE, Willibrord, 922.2492
pater, 1868-
In guest of beauty, by Dom Willbrord Verkade New York, P. J. Kenedy & sons [c1935] ix, 292 p. 20 1/2 cm. Sequel to the author's "Yesterdays of an artist-monk" being reminiscences of his life as a member of the Benedictine order. Translation of Der antrieb ins volkommene, orinnerungen elnom malermouchen. [Secular name: Jobannes Sixtue Gerhardus Verkade] [BX4705.V5A35] 36-5074
I. Title.

VINCENT, Leon 287'.6'0924 B
Henry, 1859-1941.
John Heyl Vincent; a biographical sketch. Freeport, N.Y., Books for Libraries Press [1970] 319 p. port. 23 cm. Reprint of the 1925 ed. [BX8495.V5V5 1970] 71-124263 ISBN 8-369-54513-
I. Vincent, John Heyl, Bp., 1832-1920.

VINCENT, Leon 287'.6'0924 B
Henry, 1859-1941.
John Heyl Vincent; a biographical sketch. Freeport, N.Y., Books for Libraries Press [1970] 319 p. port. 23 cm. Reprint of the 1925 ed. [BX8495.V5V5 1970] 71-124263 ISBN 8-369-54513-
I. Vincent, John Heyl, Bp., 1832-1920.

VORN HOLZ, Miranda Morrow 922.773 (Locke) Mrs. 1823-
The old paths. By Miranda L. Vorn Holz. Edited by her daughter. Cincinnati, M. W. Knapp [1898] 371 p. 2 port. (incl. front.) 20 cm. [BX8495.V6A3] 98-964
I. Calkins, Mrs. Ida (Vorn Holz) ed. II. Title.

WAFFLE, Albert Edward, 1846-
If Christ were king; or, The kingdom of heaven on earth, by Albert E. Waffle ... Philadelphia, Boston [etc.] The Griffith & Rowland press [c1912] 352 p. 20 cm. $1.25 12-22005
I. Title.

WALKER, Doak, 1927- 227.9633
Dork Walker, three-time all-American, by Dorothy Kendall Bracken as told by Doak Walker. Austin, Tex., Steck Co., [1950] ix, 258 p. illus., ports. 24 cm. [GV939.W3A3] 50-9513
I. Bracken, Dorothy Kendall. II. Title.

WALLBROOK, William, 1864?- 922 1899.
Diary of, and poems, by the late Rev. Wm. Wallbrook. College Point, N.Y., A. K. Schultz, 1900. 2 p. l., 127 p. port. 16 cm. [BV3785.W27A3] 1-29404
I. Title.

WATSON, Eva Margaret 922. (Watson) Mrs., 1847-
Glimpses of the life and work of George Douglas Watson, by Eva M. Watson. Cincinnati, O., Pub. for the author by God's Bible school and revivalist [c1929] 169 p. front. (port.) 19 1/2 cm. [BX8495.W322W3] 29-19214
I. Watson, George Douglas, 1845-1924. II. Title.

WATT, Reed Loving 248.42
Memento; who am I, that you are? New York, Carlton [c.1962] 53p. 21cm. (Reflection bk.) 2.00
I. Title.

WAUGH, Lorenzo, b.1808. 922.
Autobiography of Lorenzo Waugh ...4th and enl. ed. San Francisco, Cal., Francis, Valentine & company, printers and engravers [etc.] 1888. xii, [13]-358 p. front., illus., pl., ports., facsim. 20 cm. [BX8495.W327A3 1888] 15-1353
I. Title.

WEAVER, George Sumner, 922.8173 1818-1908.
James Henry Chapin; a sketch of his life and work, by George Sumner Weaver ... New York, London, G. P. Putnam's sons, 1894. vii, 386 p. front., plates, port. 20 cm. Chapin, James Henry, 1832-1892. [BX9969.C6W4] 37-8725
I. Title.

WEAVER, George Sumner, 922.8173 1818-1908.
James Henry Chapin; a sketch of his life and work, by George Sumner Weaver ... New York, London, G. P. Putnam's sons, 1894. vii, 386 p. front., plates, port. 20 cm. Chapin, James Henry, 1832-1892. [BX9969.C6W4] 37-8725
I. Title.

WENDTE, Charles William, 288 1844-
The transfiguration of life by a modernist faith, by Charles William Wendte, D.D., 1844-1930. Boston, Mass., The Beacon press, inc., 1930. 4 p. l., 3-146 p. front., plates. 21 cm. [BX9841.W4] 31-5326
I. Title.

WESLEY, John, 1703-1791. 922.
An extract of the Rev. Mr. John Wesley's journals, Volume I. The 1st American ed. Philadelphia, Printed by Henry Tuckniss, no. 25, Churchvalley, and sold by John Dickins, no. 44, North Second street, near Arch street, MDCCXCV. 3 p. l., v-vi, 7-316 p. 17 cm. "It is our design to publish the whole of these journals, one volume at a time."--Advertisement. No more published. [BX8495.W5A2 1795] A34
I. Title.

WESLEY, John, 1703-1791. 922.742
The journal of the Rev. John Wesley... London & Toronto, J. M. Dent & sons, ltd.; New York, E. P. Dutton & co. [1922-30] 4 v. 17 1/2 cm. (Half-title: Everyman's library, ed. by Ernest Rhys. Biography. [no. 105-108]) First published in this edition, 1906: v. 1 reprinted, 1930; v. 2-4, 1922. Introduction by F. W. MacDonald. "Particulars of the death of Mr. Wesley": v. 4, p. [517]-531; "A short review of Mr. Wesley's character": v. 4, p. [532]-545. Bibliography: v. 1, p. [xv] [AC1.E8 no.105-108] 36-37442
I. Title.

WESLEY, John, 1703-1791. 922.
The journal of the Reverend John Wesley ... 1st complete and standard American ed. from the latest London ed., with the last corrections of the author, comprehending also numerous translations and notes by John Emory. New York, Pub. by T. Mason and G. Lane for the Methodist Episcopal Church, 1837. 2 v. 22 cm. [BX8495.W5A21837] 49-42894
I. Title.

WESLEY, John, 1703-1791. 922.
The journal of the Reverend John Wesley ... 1st complete and standard American ed. from the latest London ed., with the last corrections of the author, comprehending also numerous translations and notes by John Emory. New York, Pub. by T. Mason and G. Lane for the Methodist Episcopal Church, 1837. 2 v. 22 cm. [BX8495.W5A21837] 49-42894
I. Title.

WESTON, William, 1550- 922.242 1615.
The autobiography of an Elizabethan. Translated from the Latin by Philip Caraman; with a foreword by Evelyn Waugh. London, New York, Longmans, Green [1955] xxxi. 259p. illus., ports. 23cm. American ed. (New York, Farrar, Straus and Cudahy) has title: An autobiography from the Jesuit underground. Includes bibliographical references. [BX4705.W465A3 1955a] 56-1209
I. Title.

WEYLLAND, John Matthias.
The man with the Book; or, The Bible among the people. By John Matthias Weylland. Four illustrations. New York, Nelson & Phillips; Cincinnati, Hitchcock & Walden [188-?] 268 p. incl. front., plates. 18 cm. "An account of the labors of one of the ... home missionaries in the city of London ... originally written in detached papers for different English periodicals ... afterward collected and published in book form."--Pref. 9-22518
I. Title.

WHITE, Alma (Bridwell) 922.89 Mrs., 1862-
Looking back from Beulah, by Mrs. Mollie Alma White on the overruling and forming hand of God in the poverty and struggles of childhood, and the hardships of later years; the battles, victories and joys of the sanctified life ... Denver, Col., The Pentecostal union, 1902. 307, [1] p. front., illus. (incl. music) plates, ports. 20 cm. [Full name: Mrs. Mollie Alma (Bridwell) White] [BX8795.P5W47] 3-2232
I. Title.

WHITE, Alma (Bridwell) 922.89 Mrs., 1862-
Looking back from Beulah, by Bishop Alma White ... on the overruling and forming hand of God in the poverty and struggles of childhood and the hardships of later years; the battles, victories, and joys of the santified life ... Zarephath, N.J., Pillar of fire, 1929. vii, [1], 9-392 p. front., illus. (incl. music) plates, ports, 19 1/2 cm. [Full name: Mrs. Mollie Alma (Bridwell) White] [BX8795.P5W47 1929] 33-408
I. Title.

*WHITE, Elena G. de 226.2
El discurso maestro de Jesucristo. Mexico, Ediciones Interamericanas [dist. Mountain View, Calif., Pacific Pr. Pub. Assn., c.1964] 128p. illus. 20cm. 1.25 pap.,
I. Title.

WHITE, Joseph Blanco, 1775- 922. 1841.
...Extracts from Blanco White's Journal and letters... Boston, W. Crosby and H. P. Nichols, 1847. 52 p. 20 cm. (American Unitarian association. [Tracts] 1st ser., no. 237) [Name originally: Jose Maria Blanco y Crespo] [BX9869.W5A25 1847] 41-38428
I. Title.

WHITEHEAD, George, 1636?- 922. 1723.
Memoirs of George Whitehead, a minister of the gospel in the Society of Friends, being the substance of the account of his life written by himself and published after his decease, in the year 1725, under the title of "His Christian progress"; with an appendix containing a selection from his other works. Also introductory observations by Samuel Tuke. Philadelphia, N. Kite, 1832. 2 v. in 1. 18 cm. [BX7795.W43A4 1832] 50-43669
I. Title.

WHITEHEAD, George, 1636?- 922. 1723.
Memoirs of George Whitehead, a minister of the gospel in the Society of Friends, being the substance of the account of his life written by himself and published after his decease, in the year 1725, under the title of "His Christian progress"; with an appendix containing a selection from his other works. Also introductory observations by Samuel Tuke. Philadelphia, N. Kite, 1832. 2 v. in 1. 18 cm. [BX7795.W43A4 1832] 50-43669
I. Title.

WHITNEY, Orson Ferguson, 922.8373 1855-
Through memory's halls; the life story of Orson F. Whitney as told by himself... [Independence, Mo., Press of Zion's printing and publishing company. c1930] 424 p. front. (7 port.) illus. (coat of arms) 22 1/2 cm. [BX8695.W53A3] 31-506
I. Title.

WILLIAMS, Frank Chenhalls, 282. 1880-
Men who met Jesus, by F. Chenhalls Williams. London, New York [etc.] Longmans, Green and co., 1924. 3 p. l., ix-xiii, 112 p., 1 l. 19 cm. [BT309.W65] 24-23391
I. Title.

WILLS, Henry O. 922
Twice born; or, The two lives of Henry O. Wills, Evangelist. Being a narrative of Mr. Wills's remarkable experiences as a wharf-rat, a sneak-thief, a convict, a soldier, a bounty-jumper, a fakir, a fireman, a ward-heeler, and a plug-ugly. Also a history of his ... conversion ... Cincinnati, Printed for the author at the Western Methodist book concern, 1890. 223 p. incl. 1 illus., plates, ports. 19 cm. [BV3785.W6A3] 37-37124
I. Title.

WILSON, Arthur, 1888- 922.373
Thy will be done; the autobiography of an Episcopal minister. New York, Dial Press, 1960. 213 p. 21 cm. [BX5-95.W68A3] 59-15487
I. Title.

WIRT, Loyal Lincoln, 922.573 1863-
The world is my parish; an autobiographical odyssey. Introd. by Albert Wentworth Palmer. Los Angeles, W. F. Lewis [1951] 272 p. 22 cm. [BX7260.W563A3] 51-8683
I. Title.

WOLLASTON, John Ramsden, 922.394 1791-1856
Journals and diaries, 1841-1856; v.1. Coll. by Canon A. Burton. Ed., introd., notes by Canon Burton, Percy U. Henn [Perth, Australia, Paterson Brokensha; New Rochelle, N. Y., Australian Bk. Ctr., 1965] xxvi, 289p. illus., port. maps. 23cm. Contents.v.1. Picton journal, 1841-1844 [BX5700.W6A3] 50-19665 5.50
I. Title.

WOODROW, James, 1828-1907. 285.
Dr. James Woodrow ... Columbia, S.C., Printed by the R. L. Bryan company, 1909. xix, 973 p. front. (port.) 23 1/2 cm. [BX9225.W6] 24-7746
I. Woodrow, Marion Woodville, 1862- ed. II. Title.
Contents omitted.

WOODS, Margaret, 1748-1821. 922.
Extracts from the journal of the late Margaret Woods from the year 1771 to 1821. 3d ed. Philadelphia, H. Longstreth, 1850. 378 p. 21 cm. On spine: Journal of Margaret Woods. [BX7795.W65A3 1850] 49-42895
I. Title.

WRIGHT, Melton. 922
Giant for God; a biography of the life of William Ashley ("Billy") Sunday. Boyce, Va., Distributed by Carr Pub. Co. [c1951] 168 p. illus. 24 cm. [BV3785.S8W7] 52-378
I. U. Sunday, William Ashley, 1862-1935. II. Title.

WRIGHT, Ralph Justus 260
One man's views. New York, Carlton [c.1963] 58 p. 21 cm. (Reflection bk.) 2.00
I. Title.

WYCOTT, Sara Jean (Clark) 248 1924-1960
Everywhere God; a spiritual autobiography Comp. by her mother, Odessa Grist Clark. New York, Greenwich [1962, c.1961] 53p. 21cm. 61-17890 2.50
I. Title.

YOGANANDA, paramhansa, 921.9 1893-
Autobiography of a yogi, by Paramhansa Yogananda, with a preface by W. Y. Evans-Wentz ... New York, The Philosophical library [1946] xvi, 498 p. front., illus. (map, facsims.) plates, ports. 22 cm. [B133.Y63A3] 47-544
I. Title.

YOGANANDA, Paramhansa, 921.9 1893-1952.
Autobiography of a yogi, With a pref. by W. Y. Evans-Wentz. London, New York, Rider [1950] 403 p. plates, ports., map. 22 cm. [B133.Y63A3 1950] 58-18867
I. Title.

YOGANANDA, Paramhansa, 921.9 1893-1952.
Autobiography of a yogi. With a pref. by W. Y. Evans-Wentz. [7th ed.] Los Angeles, Self-Realization Fellowship, 1956 [c1946] 514 p. illus., map. 22 cm. "This 1956 American edition contains revision made ... in 1949 for the London, England edition and additional revision made ... in 1951." [B133.Y] A58
I. Title.

YOGANANDA, Paramhanse, 181'.45 B 1893-1952.
Autobiography of a Yogi. With a pref. by W. Y. Evans-Wentz. [9th ed.] Los Angeles, Self-Realization Fellowship, 1968 [c1946] xvi, 514 p. illus., map, ports. 22 cm. [BP605.S43Y6 1968] 68-17564
I. Title.

YOGANANDA, Paramahansa, 1893- 299 1952.
Autobiography of a Yogi. With a pref. by W. Y. Evans-Wentz. [8th ed.] Los Angeles, Self-Realization Fellowship, 1959 [c1946] xvi, 514 p. illus., map, ports. 22 cm. [BP605.S43Y6 1959] 68-39787
I. Title.

YOGANANDA, Paramhansa, 181'.45 B 1893-1952.
Autobiography of a Yogi. With a pref. by W. Y. Evans-Wentz. [10th ed.] Los Angeles, Self-Realization Fellowship, 1969 [c1946] xvi, 514 p. illus., map, ports. 22 cm. [BP605.S43Y6 1969b] 69-11377 5.00
I. Title.

YOGANANDA, Paramhansa, 181'.45 1893-1952.
Autobiography of a Yogi. With a pref. by W. Y. Evans-Wentz. [11th ed.] Los Angeles, Self-Realization Fellowship, 1971 [c1946] xv, 516 p. illus., map. 23 cm. [BP605.S43Y6 1971] 78-151319 ISBN 0-87612-075-3 5.00
I. Title.

YOUNG, Chester Smith. 922.773
Twenty-five years a country parson in Missouri, by Chester Smith Young... Barnard, Mo., Rush printing co., 1931. 111 p. pl. 20 cm. [BX8495.Y53A3] 31-17025
I. Title.

YOUNG, Dan, b.1783. 922.773
Autobiography of Dan Young, a New England preacher of the olden time. Edited by W. P. Strickland. New York, Carlton & Porter, 1860. 380 p. 19 1/2 cm. [BX8495.Y55A3] 37-12173

I. Strickland, William Peter, 1809-1884, ed. II. Title.

ZEIGLER, William Abraham, 1862- 922.573
On this side of Jordan, by Rev. W. A. Zeigler. Benton, La., c1945. 4 p. l., 177 p. port. 23 cm. [BX9225.Z4A3] 45-6824
I. Title.

ZELLE, Margaretha Geertruida, 1876-1917. 940.3
The diary of Mata Hari. Translated, and with a preface, by Mark Alexander. Introd. by Hilary E. Holt. North Hollywood, Calif. [Brandon House, 1967] xxi, 248 p. 17 cm. (A Brandon House book) [D639.S8Z413] 261.7'0941 67-66264
I. Title.

ZUNSER, Eliakum, 1840-1913.
A Jewish bard; being the biography of Eliakum Zunser, written by himself and rendered into English by Simon Hirsdansky. Ed. by A. H. Fromenson. New York, Zunser jubilee committee, 1905. 4 p. l., 9-44, 61 p. incl. port. 24 cm. Abridged translation, followed by Yiddish original with port. and special t.-p. The translation appeared first in the English department of the Jewish daily news; the original was first published serially in Der Morgee journal. 5-11832
I. Hirsdansky, Simon, tr. II. Fromenson, Abraham H., 1873- ed. III. Title.

Religions—Biography—Congresses.

ENCOUNTER with Erikson : historical interpretation and religious biography / edited by Donald Capps, Walter H. Capps, M. Gerald Bradford. Missoula, Mont. : Published by Scholars Press for the American Academy of Religion and the Institute of Religious Studies, University of California, Santa Barbara, c1977. xvi, 429 p. ; 24 cm. (Series on formative contemporary thinkers ; no. 2) Paper presented at a symposium to honor E. H. Erikson on the occasion of his seventieth birthday, held at La Casa de Maria Retreat Center near Santa Barbara, Calif., Feb. 17-19, 1972. "Erik Homburger Erikson: a bibliography of his books and articles": p. 421-429. [BL72.E5] 76-44434 200'.92'2 B
1. Erikson, Erik Homburger, 1902- — Congresses. 2. Religions—Biography—Congresses. 3. Psychohistory—Congresses. 4. Psychology, Religious—Congresses. I. Erikson, Erik Homburger, 1902- II. Capps, Donald. III. Capps, Walter H. IV. Bradford, Miles Gerald, 1938- V. American Academy of Religion. VI. California. University, Santa Barbara. Institute of Religious Studies. VII. Title. VIII. Series.

Religions—Biography—Juvenile literature.

BLOOM, Naomi, 1938- 209'2'2 B
Religion / by Naomi Bloom. Minneapolis : Dillon Press, c1978. 126, [1] p. : ill. ; 23 cm. (Contributions of women) Bibliography: p. [127] Six biographies of women who have made outstanding contributions to religion. Included are Anne Hutchinson, Ann Lee, Mary Baker Eddy, Amanda Smith, Henrietta Szold, and Dorothy Day. [BL72.B59] 920 77-20034 ISBN 0-87518-123-6 : 6.95
1. Religions—Biography—Juvenile literature. 2. Women—United States—Biography—Juvenile literature. 3. Reformers—United States—Biography—Juvenile literature. 4. Women in religion—Juvenile literature. 5. [Reformers.] I. Title.

HEIDERSTADT, Dorothy. 920
Ten torchbearers. Illustrated by Robert W. Arnold. New York, T. Nelson [1961] 192p. illus. 21cm. Includes bibliography [BR569.H4] 61-13831
1. —Religions biography —Juvenile literature. I. Title.

Religions—Classification.

PARRISH, Fred Louis. 291.14
The classification of religious, its relation to the history of religions [by] Fred Louis Parrish. [Scottdale, Pa., Printed by the Herald press, c1941] vii, 157, [1] p. maps, diagr 26c m. "The study is published in partial fulfilment of the requirements for the degree of doctor of philosophy in Yale university."--Pref. Bibliography: p. [137]-145. [BL350.P3 1941] 41-10314
1. Religions—Classification. I. Title.

Religions—Collected works.

EASTMAN, Roger, comp. 200'.1
The ways of religion / edited by Roger Eastman. San Francisco : Canfield Press, [1975] viii, 597 p. : ill. ; 23 cm. Includes bibliographies and indexes. [BL74.E18] 74-30211 ISBN 0-06-382595-3 pbk. : 8.95
1. Religions—Collected works. I. Title.

MAN'S religious quest : 291
a reader / edited by Whitfield Foy. New York : St. Martin's Press, 1977, c1978. 725 p. ; 23 cm. Includes bibliographical references and index. [BL74.M36 1978] 77-12266 ISBN 0-312-51254-6 : 22.00
1. Religions—Collected works. 2. Sacred books. I. Foy, Whitfield.

Religions—Collections.

LESSA, William Armand, ed. 291.082
Reader in comparative religion, an anthropological approach [ed. by] William A. Lessa, Evon Z. Vogt. 2d ed. New York, Harper [c.1958, 1965] xiii, 656p. illus. 27cm. Bibl. [BL80.2.L44] 65-12678 10.50
1. Religions—Collections. I. Vogt, Evon Zartman, 1918- joint ed. II. Title.

LESSA, William Armand, ed. 290.82
Reader in comparative religion, an anthropological approach; [edited by] William A. Lessa [and] Evon Z. Vogt. Evanston, Ill., Row, Peterson [1958] 508p. illus. 25cm. Includes bibliography. [BL80.L47] 58-13742
1. Religions—Collections. I. Vogt, Evon Zartman, 1918- joint ed. II. Title.

LESSA, William Armand, ed. 200'.8
Reader in comparative religion; an anthropological approach. [Edited by] William A. Lessa [and] Evon Z. Vogt. 3d ed. New York, Harper & Row [1972] xii, 572 p. illus. 26 cm. Bibliography: p. [559]-570. [BL80.2.L44 1972] 76-164691 ISBN 0-06-043992-0
1. Religions—Collections. I. Vogt, Evon Zartman, 1918- joint ed. II. Title.

Religions—Congresses.

MERCER, Louis P.
The world's religions in a nutshell; a religious symposium representing Christianity, Hinduism, Buddhism, Judaism, Mohammedanism, the Brahmo-Somaj, and woman. Chicago, Rand, McNally & co. [1898] 334 p. port. 12 degree. (Globe library, v. 2, no. 295) Oct
I. Title.

NEELY'S history of the 290.631
parliament of religions and religious congresses at the World's Columbian exposition. Compiled from original manuscripts and stenographic reports. Edited by a corps of able writers. Prof. Walter R. Houghton, editor in chief ... Chicago, 1893. 2 p. l., 6 p., 1 l., 7-1001 p. front., ports. 23 cm. Includes papers presented to the World's parliament of religions, Chicago, 1893. [BL21.W8N4] 38-13099
1. Religions—Congresses. I. World's parliament of religions, Chicago, 1893. II. Houghton, Walter Raleigh, ed.

THE Social impact of new 306'.6
religious movements / Bryan Wilson, editor ; [contributors, David Martin ... et al.]. 1st ed. Barrytown, N.Y. : Unification Theological Seminary ; New York, N.Y. : Distributed by Rose of Sharon Press, c1981. xix, 235 p. ; 23 cm. (Conference series / Union Theological Seminary ; no. 9) Papers presented at the Social Impact of New Religious Movements Conference held June 19-22, 1980, Berkeley, Calif. Includes bibliographical references. [BL21.S63] 19 81-51152 ISBN 0-932894-09-7 pbk. : 10.95
1. Religions—Congresses. 2. Sects—Congresses. 3. Religion and sociology—Congresses. I. Wilson, Bryan R. II. Martin, David A. III. Unification Theological Seminary. IV. Social Impact of New Religious Movements Conference Berkeley, Calif.) (1980 :
Distributor's address GPO Box 2432 New York, NY 10116.

WORLD fellowship of faiths. International congress. 1st, Chicago and New York, 1933-1934. 290.631
World fellowship; addresses and messages by leading spokesmen of all faiths, races and countries, edited by Charles Frederick Weller ... New York, Liveright publishing corporation [c1935] xviii, 986 p. 22 cm. "This book ... condenses and co-ordinates the 242 addresses delivered by 199 spokesmen ... in the 83 meetings held ... by the first International congress of the World fellowship of faiths."--p. v. [BL21.W6 1933-1934] 36-2382
1. Religions—Congresses. 2. Religions—Addresses, essays, lectures. I. Weller, Charles Frederick, 1870- ed. II. Title.

THE World's congress of 290
religions, with an introduction by Rev. Minot J. Savage ... Boston, Arena publishing company, 1893. vii, 1 l., 428 p. 20 cm. "The object of this publication is ... to give in a popular form the proceedings of the ... conference." (Publisher's preface, p. 2) The publication was undertaken by the Arena publishing co. with the sanction of the Parilament publishing co., publishers of the history of the World's parliament of religions, in 2 v. (cf. leaf following p. vii) [BL21.W8W6] 31-13893
1. Religions—Congresses. I. World's parliament of religions. Chicago, 1893. II. Savage, Minot Judson, 1841-1918.

Religions—Controversial literature.

BALDWIN, Harmon Allen, 1869- 248
The carnal mind; a doctrinal and experimental view of the subject, by Harmon A. Baldwin ... Chicago, Ill., Free Methodist publishing house [c1926] 183 p. 26 cm. [BT767.B22] 26-15534
I. Title.

GAYLOR, James Edward. 291
Universal wisdom / by James Edward Gaylor. 1st ed. Tucson, Ariz. : Gaylor, c1978. ix, 440 p. : ill. ; 23 cm. [BL2776.G38] 78-108188 9.95
1. Religions—Controversial literature. 2. Survival (Human ecology) 3. Birth control—Moral and religious aspects. I. Title.

Religions—Controversial literature—Collected works.

KIRBAN, Salem. 291'.08
Doctrines of devils; exposing the cults of our day. Huntingdon Valley, Pa., S. Kirban Inc. [1970- v. illus. (part col.), ports. 22 cm. Contents.Contents.—no. 1. Armstrong's Church of God.—no. 2. Mormonism. [BL85.K56] 75-124142
1. Religions—Controversial literature—Collected works. 2. Sects—Controversial literature—Collected works. I. Title.

Religions—Dictionaries.

A Dictionary of 291'.03
comparative religion. General editor: S. G. F. Brandon. New York, Scribner [1970] 704 p. 27 cm. Includes bibliographies. [BL31.D54 1970] 76-111390 17.50
1. Religions—Dictionaries. I. Brandon, Samuel George Frederick, ed.

PARRINDER, Edward Geoffrey. 290'.3
A dictionary of non-Christian religions, by Geoffrey Parrinder. Philadelphia, Westminster Press [1973, c1971] 320 p. illus. 24 cm. Bibliography: p. 318-320. [BL31.P36 1973] 73-4781 ISBN 0-664-20981-5 10.75
1. Religions—Dictionaries. I. Title.

RICE, Edward E., 1918- 290'.3
Eastern definitions : a short encyclopedia of religions of the Orient / Edward Rice. 1st ed. Garden City, N.Y. : Doubleday, 1978. x, 433 p., [16] leaves of plates : ill. ; 22 cm. "A guide to common, ordinary, and rare philosophical, mystical, religious, and psychological terms from Hinduism, Buddhism, Sufism, Islam, Zen, Taoism, the Sikhs, Zoroastrianism, and other major and minor Eastern religions." [BL31.R52] 77-19359 ISBN 0-385-08563-X : 10.00
1. Religions—Dictionaries. 2. Asia—Religion—Dictionaries. I. Title.

WEDECK, Harry Ezekiel, 1894- 290'.3
Dictionary of pagan religions, by H. E. Wedeck and Wade Baskin. [1st ed.] New York, Philosophical Library [1971] 363 p. 22 cm. [BL31.W4] 79-86508 10.00
1. Religions—Dictionaries. I. Baskin, Wade, joint author. II. Title.

Religions—Dictionaries—English.

GLASENAPP, Helmuth von [Otto Max Helmuth von Glasenapp] 1891- 290.3
Non-Christian religions A to Z. Based on the work of Helmuth von Glasenapp. Ed. under the supervision of Horace L. Friess. [Tr. from German by Eric Protter] New York, Grosset [1963, c.1957] 278p. illus., maps. 21cm. (Universal ref. lib.) Bibl. 63-3397 4.25
1. Religions—Dictionaries—English. I. Friess, Horace Leland, 1900- ed. II. Title.

Religions—Directories.

BUCK, Charles, 1771-1815.
... A theological dictionary, containing definitions of all religious terms ... By the late Rev. Charles Buck. Woodward's new ed. Published from the last London ed.; to which is added an appendix, containing an account of the Methodist Episcopal, and Presbyterian churches, in the United States, to the present period. Philadelphia, J. J. Woodward, 1831. 624 p. front. 22 cm. 4-23394
I. Title.

CUSHING, A. I. 133'.062
The international "mystery schools" directory. Compiled by A. I. Cushing. New 1970 ed. Boston, A.C. Publications [1970] 1 v. (unpaged) 29 cm. [BL35.C86] 70-16742
1. Religions—Directories. I. Title. II. Title: Mystery schools directory.

FRIEDLANDER, Ira. 200'.25'73
Year one catalog; a spiritual directory for the new age. Edited by Ira Friedlander. Introd. by Pir Vilayat Inayat Khan. [1st ed.] New York, Harper & Row [1972] 152 p. ports. 21 cm. [BP602.F74 1972] 73-150151 ISBN 0-06-063018-3 1.95
1. Religions—Directories. 2. Sects—Directories. I. Title.

Religions—Early works to 1800.

IBN Kammunah, Sa'd ibn Mansur, 13thcent. 291.2
Ibn Kammunah's Examination of the three faiths; a thirteenth-century essay in the comparative study of religion. Translated from the Arabic, with an introd. and notes by Moshe Perlmann. Berkeley, University of California Press, 1971. xi, 160 p. 23 cm. Translation of Tanqih al-abhath lil-milal al-thalath. Includes bibliographical references. [BL75.I213] 73-102659 ISBN 0-520-01658-0 8.50
1. Religions—Early works to 1800. I. Perlmann, Moshe, ed. II. Title: Examination of the three faiths.

IBN Kammunah, Sa'd ibn Mansur, 13thcent. 291
Sa d b. Mansar Ibn Kammuna's examination of the inquiries into the three faiths; a thirteenth-century essay in comparative religion. Ed. by Moshe Perlmann. Berkeley, Univ. of Calif. Pr. 1967. xii, 119p. 26cm. (Univ. of Calif. pubns. Near Eastern studies, v. 6) Added t. p. in Arabic. [BL75.12] 67-65689 4.00 pap.,
1. Religions—Early works to 1800. I. Perlmann, Moshe, ed. II. Title Examination of the inquiris into the three faiths. III. Title. IV. Series: California. University. Universty of Calforna publications. Near Eastern studies, v.6

Religions, Eastern—Sacred Books.

[ATKINSON, William Walker] 1862-
The arcane teaching; or, Secret doctrine of ancient Atlantis, Egypt, Childea and Greece, including the arcane aphorisms. 2d

ed. Chicago, Ill., The Arcane book concern, 1909. 2 p. l., 336 p. 18 cm. [BF1999.A73 1909] 9-17564
I. Title.

BENNETT, John Godolphin, 1897- 212
Approaching Subud; ten talks. And a discussion with Steve Allen. New York, dharma Book Co. [1962] 274p. 18cm. [BP605.B36] 62-5123
I. Title. II. Title: Subud.

BENNETT, John Godolphin, 1897- 212.5
Towards the true self, in the practice of Subud. New York, Dharma Book Co. [1963] xii, 229 p. 18 cm. [BP605.B377] 63-24380
I. Title.

BUCK, William. FIC
Ramayana : [King Rama's way] / by William Buck ; with an introd. by B. A. van Nooten ; illustrated by Shirley Triest. Berkeley : University of California Press, c1976. xxix, 432 p. : ill. ; 23 cm. Valmiki's Ramayana told in English prose. [PZ4.B9215Ram] [PS3552.U335] 294.5'922 78-153549 ISBN 0-520-02016-2 : 14.95
I. Valmiki. Ramayana. II. Title.

*MAZUMDAR, Shudha 294.5922
Ramayana. Foreword by S. Radhakrishnan. Bombay, Orient Longmans [S. Pasadena, Calif., Hutchins Oriental, 1965, c.1958] xx, 540p. 19cm. 6.00 bds.,
I. Title.

MILINDAPANHA 294.3
The questions of King Milinda; 2 pts. Tr. from Pali by T. W. Rhys Davids [Gloucester, Mass., P. Smith, 1964] 2v. 22cm. (Sacred bks. of the East, v.35-36) (Dover bks. rebound) 4.25 ea.,
I. Davids, Thomas William Rhys, 1843-1922; ed., and tr. II. Title. III. Series: The Sacred books of the East (New York) v.35-36

MILINDAPANHA. 294.3
The questions of King Milinda [2v.] Tr. from Pali by T. W. Rhys Davids. New York, Dover [1963] 2v. (various p.) 22cm. (Sacred bks. of the East, v. 35-6) 63-19514 2.25 pap., ea.,
I. Davids, Thomas William Rhys, 1843-1922, ed. and tr. II. Title. III. Series: The Sacred books of the East (New York)

MILINDAPANHA. 294.3
The questions of King Milinda, translated from the Pali by T. W. Rhys Davids. Oxford, The Clarendon press, 1890-94. 2 v. 23 cm. (Added t.-p.: The sacred books of the East ... vol. XXXV-XXXVI) [BL1010.S3 vol. 35-36] (290.8) [891.3701] 32-34312
I. Davids, Thomas William Rhys, 1843-1922, ed. and tr. II. Title.

**SACRED books of the East (The).* 290
Tr. by various Oriental scholars, Ed. by F. Max Muller [Delhi, Motilal Banarsidass, 1966] 50v. 23cm. (Sacred bks. of the East ser.) Unesco collection of representative works: Indian ser. First pub. in 1879 by the Clarendon Pr. Reprinted 1966. Contents.v. 1, 15. The Upanishads.--2, 14. The sacre laws of the Aryas.--3, 16, 27-28, 39-40. The sacred books of China.--4, 23. 31. The Zend-avesta.--5, 18, 24, 37, 47. Pahlavi texts.--6, 9. The Quar'an.--7. The Institutes of Visnu.--8. The Bhagavadgita.--10. The Dhammapada; Sutta-nipata.--11. Buddhist suttas.--12, 26, 41, 43-44. The Satapatha-Brahmana.--13, 17, 20. Vinaya texts.--19. The Fo-sho-hing-tsanking.--21. The Saddaharma-pundarika.--22, 45. Jaina sutras.--25. Manu.--29, 30. The Grihya-sutras.--32, 46. Vedic hymns.--33. The minor law-books.--34, 38. The Vedanta-sutras. 35-36. The questions of King Milinda.--42. Hymns of the Atharva-veda.--48. The Vedanta-Sutras.--49. Buddhist Mahayana texts.--50. Bibl. 250.00 6.00 Index. set, ea.,
1. Religions, Eastern—Sacred Books. I. Muller, F. Max, ed.
American distributor: Verry, Mystic, Conn.

SATAPATHABRAHMANA. 294.1
The Satapatha-brahmana, according to the text of the Madhyandina school, translated by Julius Eggeling ... Oxford, The Clarendon press, 1882-1900. 5 v. 23 cm. (Added t.-p.: The sacred books of the East ... vol. XII, XXVI, XLI, XLIII, XLIV) [BL1010.S3 vol.12,26,41,43,44] (290.8) 32-34308
I. Eggeling, Julius, 1842-1918, ed. and tr. II. Title.

SIVARAHASYA. English. Selections. 294.5'9
The heart of the Rihbu [i.e. Ribhu] gita. Edited, and with an introd., by Franklin Jones (Bubba Free John). Illustrated by Lydia Depole. [1st ed.] Los Angeles, Dawn Horse Press [1973] xi, 33 p. illus. 22 cm. Consists of chapter 26 of the Ribhu gita; and 6 verses selected from the whole text by Sri Ramana Maharshi. The Ribhu gita is pt. 6 of the Sivarahasya. [BL1146.S57213 1973] 73-88178 ISBN 0-913922-03-X 1.95
I. Ramana, Maharshi. II. Jones, Franklin, ed. III. Title.

[STUBBS, Ulysses] 213
Ramayana; the Egyptian priest's story of creation and the spirit world. [Everett, Wash., c1926] 2 p. l., 63 p. 18 1/2 cm. [BL225.S7] 26-13241
I. Title.

VALMIKI.
The Ramayana, and The Mahabharata, condensed into English verse by Romesh C. Dutt. London, J. M. Dent & sons, ltd.; New York, E. P. Dutton & co. [1910] xiv p., 1 l., 384 p. 17 1/2 cm. (Half-title: Everyman's library, ed. by Ernest Phys. Philosophy and theology. [no. 403]) "Note on the late Romesh C. Dutt", by S. K. Ratcliffe. Bibliography: p. xi-xii. A 10
I. Mahabharata. II. Dutt, Romesch Chunder, 1848-1909, tr. III. Title.

VIMALAKIRTINIRDESA. English. 294.3'8
The holy teaching of Vimalakirti : a Mahayana scripture / translated by Robert A. F. Thurman. University Park : Pennsylvania State University Press, c1976. ix, 166 p. ; 24 cm. Includes bibliographical references. [BQ2212.E5T47] 75-27196 ISBN 0-271-01209-9 : 14.50
I. Thurman, Robert A. F. II. Title.

Religions — Handbooks, manuals, etc.

BAIERL, Joseph John, 1884-
The holy sacrifice of the mass, explained in the form of questions and answers, by Rev. Joseph J. Baierl. Rev. ed., arranged and illustrated for school use. Rochester, N. Y. [Heindel, printer] 1913. ix p., 1 l., 144 p., 1 l. incl. front., illus. 16 cm. Bibliography: 1 l. following p. 144. 13-23211 0.50.
I. Title.

BAIERL, Joseph John, 1884-
The holy sacrifice of the mass, explained in the form of questions and answers, by Rev. Joseph J. Baierl. Rev. ed., arranged and illustrated for school use. Rochester, N. Y. [Heindel, printer] 1913. ix p., 1 l., 144 p., 1 l. incl. front., illus. 16 cm. Bibliography: 1 l. following p. 144. 13-23211 0.50.
I. Title.

IOWA. University. School of Religion.
Religion in human culture; a guide prepared by the teachers and assistants in the course "Religion in human culture", State University of Iowa, Iowa City, Iowa. Iowa City, Sernoll, Inc. [1965] 134 [i.e. 141] l. 28 cm. Mimeographed. 66-30441
1. Religions — Handbooks, manuals, etc. 2. Religion and sociology — Handbooks, manuals, etc. I. Title.

†JOHNSTONE, Patrick J. St. G. 200'.9'047
World handbook for the world Christian / by Patrick J. St. G. Johnstone. South Pasadena, Calif. : World Christian Book Shelf, c1976. 208 p. 15 p. ; 22 cm. [BL82.J64 1976] 76-15187 ISBN 0-87808-727-3 pbk. : 4.95
1. Religions—Handbooks, manuals, etc. 2. Geography—Handbooks, manuals, etc. I. Title.

LISTER, Louis, comp. 377.96
The religions school assembly handbook. New York, Union of Amer. Hebrew Cong. [c.1963] 258p. 28cm. illus 3.50 pap.,
I. Title.

*TREMMEL, William C. 259
A different drum, a manual on interreligious campus affairs. New York, Natl. Conf. of Christians & Jews [1964] 63p. 23cm. .50 pap.,
I. Title.

Religions — History

BRINTON, Daniel Garrison, 1837-1899. 299
Religions of primitive peoples. New York, Negro Universities Press [1969] xiv, 264 p. 23 cm. Reprint of the 1897 ed. Bibliographical footnotes. [GN470.B7 1969] 79-88423
1. Religions—History. 2. Religion, Primitive. 3. Mythology. I. Title.

BRINTON, Daniel Garrison, 1837-1899. 294.
...Religions of primitive peoples, by Daniel G. Brinton ... New York, London, G. P. Putnam's sons, 1897. xiv p., 1 l., 264 p. 20 1/2 cm. (American lectures on the history of religions, 2d series, 1896-1897) [BL25.A6 vol. 2] 4-4202
1. Religions—Hist. 2. Religion, Primitive. 3. Mythology. I. Title.

BURTON, Ormond Edward, 1893- 290
A study in creative history; the interaction of the eastern and western peoples to 500 B.C., by O. E. Burton. Port Washington, N.Y., Kennikat Press [1971] 320 p. 22 cm. (Kennikat classics series) Reprint of the 1932 ed. [BL96.B8 1971] 71-105821
1. Religions—History. 2. Civilization, Ancient. 3. History, Ancient. I. Title.

CAIRD, John, 1820-1898. 290
... Oriental religions, by John Carid, S. T. D. And other authors ... New York, J. Fitzgerald [1882] cover-title, 57 p. 24 cm. (Humboldt library, no. 35) Contents.--Religions of India: Brahmanism; Buddhism, by John Caird.--Religion of China: Confucianism, by George Matheson.--Religion of Persia: Zoroaster and the Zend Avesta, by John Milne. [BL80.C313] 41-30614
1. Religions—Hist. I. Matheson, George, 1842-1906. II. Milnes, John. III. Title.

CONERLY, Porter W. 290.9
Genealogy of the gods. New York, Monograph Press [1957] 218 p. 22 cm. [BL80.C68] 57-7906
1. Religions—History. 2. Civilization—History. I. Title.

ELIADE, Mircea, 1907- 291
Occultism, witchcraft, and cultural fashions : essays in comparative religions / Mircea Eliade. Chicago : University of Chicago Press, 1976. 148 p. ; 21 cm. Includes bibliographical references and index. [BL80.2.E43] 75-12230 ISBN 0-226-20391-3 : 6.95
1. Religions—History. 2. Occult sciences. I. Title.

FINEGAN, Jack, 1908-
The archeology of world religions. Princeton, Princeton University press [1965, c1952] 3 v. illus., maps, facsims. 21 cm. "First Princeton paperback edition, 1965." "The publishers have retained the original page, chapter, and illustration numbers, and have included in each of the three paperbound volumes the complete index to all ten religions that appeared in the original edition." Contents.-- v. 1. Primitivism, Zoroastrianism, Hinduism, Jainism. -- v. 2. Buddhism, Confucionism, Taoism. -- v. 3. Shinto, Islam, Sikhism. Bibliographical footnotes. 67-29159
1. Religions — Hist. I. Title.

FINEGAN, Jack, 1908- 290.9
The archeology of world religions; the background of primitivism, Zoroastrianism, Hinduism, Jainism, Buddhism, Confucianism, Taoism, Shinto, Islam, and Sikhism. Princeton, Princeton University Press, 1952. xi, 599 p. illus., maps, facsims. 25 cm. Bibliographical footnotes. [BL80.F5] 52-5839
1. Religions—History. I. Title.

FRADENBURGH, Jason Nelson, 1843-
History of Erie conference ... by Rev. J. N. Fradenburgh ... Published for the author. Oil City, Pa., Derrick publishing company, 1907. 2 v. fronts. (v. 1: port.) illus. 24 cm. "This work is published in a limited edition from type and will not re-published." 8-10302
I. Title.

GAER, Joseph, 1897- 290
How the great religions began, by Joseph Gaer; wood-engravings by Frank W. Peers. New York, R. M. McBride & company, 1929. x p., 2 l., 424 p. incl. front., illus., plates. 22 cm. [BL80.G23] 29-23904
1. Religions—hist. I. Title.

HINSHAW, Joseph Howard, 1890 291'.09
Elements of truth, by Joseph H. Hinshaw. New York, Philosophical Lib. [1967] xii, 144p. 22cm. Bibl. [BL80.2.H5] 67-13370 4.50
1. Religions—Hist. I. Title.

JAMES, Edwin Oliver, 1886- 290
The ancient Gods; the history and diffusion of religion in the ancient Near East and the eastern Mediterranean. [1st American ed.] New York, Putnam [1960] 359 p. illus., map. 24 cm. (The Putnam history of religion) Bibliography: p. 346-352. [BL96.J32 1960] 60-8472
1. Religions—History. 2. Near East—Religion. I. Title.

JAMES, Edwin Oliver, 1886- 290.9
History of religions. New York, Harper [1958, c1957] 237 p. illus. 19 cm. [BL80.J32 1958] 57-12934
1. Religions—History.

KELLET, Ernest Edward, 1864-1950 290
A short history of religions, by E. E. Kellett. [Baltimore] Penguin [1963] 605p. 18cm. (Pelican Bk. A576) Bibl. 1.65 pap.,
1. Religions—Hist. I. Title.

KELLETT, Ernest Edward, 1864- 290
A short history of religions, by E. E. Kellett. New York, Dodd, Mead & company, 1934. 602 p. 21 cm. [BL82.K4 1934] 34-6594
1. Religions—Hist. I. Title.

KELLETT, Ernest Edward, 1864-1950. 291
A short history of religions. Freeport, N.Y., Books for Libraries Press [1971] 602 p. 23 cm. (Essay index reprint series) Reprint of the 1934 ed. Includes bibliographical references. [BL80.K43 1971] 71-156671 ISBN 0-8369-2281-6
1. Religions—History. I. Title.

LECTURES on the history of religions ... 290
London, Catholic truth society; St. Louis, Mo., B. Herder, 1910-11. 5 v. 19 cm. Introduction signed: C. C. M. [ie. Cyril Charlie Martindale] Contents.I. The study of religions, by L. de Grandmaison. China, by L. Wieger. Celtic religions, by J. M'Neill. Buddhism by L. de la Vallee Poussin. Hinduism, by E. R. Hull. Babylonia and Arsyria, by A. Condamin. Ancient Syria, by G. S. Hitchcock. Egypt, by A. Mallon.--II. The great kings, by L. C. Casartelli. The avesta, by A. Cornoy. Ancient Greece, by J. Huby. The Athenian philosophers, by Henry Browne. Early Rome, by C. C. Martindale. Imperial Rome, by C. C. Martindale.--III. The Hebrew Bible, by G.S. Hitchcock. The Greek Testament, by C. C. Martindale. The early church, By C. Lattey. St. Augustine, by C. C. Martindale. Gregory VII, by A. Fortescue. Aquinas, by V. McNabb. The Council of Trent, by C. J. Cronin. The modern papcy, ed. by J. Rickaby.--IV. Eastern churches, by A. Fortescue. The Koran, by E. Power. The Thirty-nine articles, by A. H. Lang, Lutheranism, by J. Bourg. Wesleyanism, By A. Burbridge. Presbyterianism, by M. Power. Modern Judaism, By G. S. Hitchcock. Unitarianism, by G. S. Hitchcock.--V. The religion of "primitive" races, by A. Le Roy. The religions of Japan, by A. Dahlmann. Theosophy, by L. de Grandmaison. Spiritualism, by R. H. Benson. Christian science, by H. Thurston. The cults and Christianity; conclusion, by C. C. Martindale.--Index. Contains bibliographies. [BL80.L4] 12-35567
1. Religions—Hist. I. Martindale, Cyril Charlie, 1879- II. Catholic truth society, London.

LING, Trevor Oswald. 200'.9
A history of religion East and West; an introduction and interpretation [by] Trevor

Ling. New York, Harper & Row [1970, c1968] xxix, 464 p. maps. 21 cm. (Harper colophon books, CN 155) Bibliography: p. [431]-439. [BL80.2.L53 1970] 71-102219 3.45
1. Religions—History. I. Title.

MEAGHER, James L[uke]
The religions of the world, and how the fifty-eight grandsons of Noe and their descendants founded the nations after the flood. History of all the great empires of the earth. The religions of the Greeks and Romans, Celtic nations, Germans and Scandinavians, Medes and Persians, Assyrians and Babylonians, Chinese and Japanese, Mexicans and Peruvians, and of the Egyptians. Brahmanism, Buddhism, Mohammedanism, etc. By Rev. James L. Meagher... New York, Christian press association publishing co., 1896. 2 p. l., vii, 442 p. illus., plates. 19 1/2 cm. 3-22862
I. Title.

MULLER, Friedrich Max, 1823-1900. 294
Lectures on the origin and growth of religion as illustrated by the religions of India. Delivered in the chapter house, Westminster abbey, in April, May, and June, 1878. By F. Max Muller, M. A. New York, C. Scribner's sons, 1879. xvi, 382 p. 20 cm. (Half-title: The Hibbert lectures) [BL2003.M8] 12-36944
1. Religious—Hist. 2. India—Religion. I. Title.

REINACH, Salomon, 1858-1932. 290
Orpheus, a general history of religions, from the French of Salomon Reinach ... by Florence Simmonds. Revised by the author. London, W. Heinemann. New York, G. P. Putnam's sons, 1909. xiv, 430 p. col.front., 23 cm. [Full name: Salomon Hermann Reinach] Bibliography at end of each chapter. [BL80.R33] 10-8293
1. Religions—Hist. I. Simmonds, Florence, tr. II. Title.

REINACH, Salomon, 1858-1932. 290
Orpheus; a history of religions, from the French of Salomon Reinach by Florence Simmonds. Revised and partly rewritten by the author. New York, H. Liveright, inc., 1930. vii p., 2 l., 487 p. 24 cm. [Full name: Salomon Hermann Reinach] Bibliography at end of each chapter. [BL80.R33 1930] 30-5609
1. Religions—Hist. I. Simmonds, Florence, tr. II. Title.

REINACH, Salomon, 1858-1932. 290
Orpheus; a history of religions, by Salomon Reinach, newly revised and enlarged; translated by Florence Simmonds, illustrated by William Siegel. New York, Liveright, inc. [1933] vii p., 3 l., 487 p. plates 22 1/2 cm. [Black and gold library] [Full name: Salomon Hermann Reinach] Bibliography at end of each chapter. [BL80.R33 1933] 33-27123
1. Religions—Hist. I. Simmonds, Florence, tr. II. Title.

RING, George Cyril 1890- 290
Gods of the Gentiles; non-Jewish cultural religions of antiquity [by] George C. Ring ... Milwaukee, The Bruce publishing company [1938] xvi, 349 p. illus (incl. map, plans) plates, diagr. 23 cm. (Half-title: Science and culture series: Joseph Husslein ... general editor) Bibliography: p. 339-343. [BL96.R5] 38-39300
1. Religions—Hist. I. Title.

RINGGREN, Helmer, 1917- 200'.9
Religions of mankind today & yesterday, by Helmer Ringgren and Ake V. Strom. Edited by J. C. G. Greig; translated by Niels L. Jenson. [1st American ed.] Philadelphia, Fortress Press [1967] xlii, 426 p. 24 cm. Translation of Religionerna i historia och nutid. Includes bibliographies. [BL80.2.R5513 1967b] 67-11252
1. Religions—History. I. Strom, Ake V., joint author. II. Title.

ROBINSON, Theodore Henry, 1881-
An outline introduction to the history of religions, by Theodore H. Robinson ... London, Oxford university press, H. Milford, 1926. x, [2], 244 p. diagr. 19 1/2 cm. A 27
1. Religions—History. I. Title.
Contents omitted.

SAVAGE, Katharine. 209
The story of world religions. New York, H. Z. Walck, 1967 [c1966] 283 p. illus., maps. 21 cm. First published in 1966 under title: The history of world religions. A survey of the basic beliefs and historical background of man's diverse religions, from the nature worship of Early Sumeria and Egypt to the major religions and religious cultures active today. [BL82.S35 1967] AC 67
1. Religions—History. I. Title.

SCHOEPS, Hans-Joachim. 209
The religions of mankind. Tr. from German by Richard and Clara Winston. Garden City, N.Y., Doubleday [1968,c.1966] xiii, 343p. 18cm. (Anchor. A621) [BL80.2.S353] 66-14927 1.75 pap.,
1. Religions—Hist. I. Title.

SCHOEPS, Hans Joachim. 200'.9
The religions of mankind. Translated from the German by Richard and Clara Winston. [1st ed. in the U.S.A.] Garden City, N.Y., Doubleday, 1966. xiii, 320 p. illus., col. maps (on lining-papers) 24 cm. Translation of Religionen: Wesen und Geschichte. [BL80.2.S353] 66-14927
1. Religions—History. I. Title.

SMART, Ninian, 1927- 291
The religious experience of mankind / by Ninian Smart. 2d ed. New York : Scribner, c1976. xii, 594 p. : ill. ; 24 cm. Includes index. Bibliography: p. [563]-568. [BL80.2.S6 1976] 76-1437 ISBN 0-684-14647-9 : 17.50. ISBN 0-684-14648-7 pbk. : 6.95.
1. Religions—History. 2. Religion. 3. Experience (Religion) I. Title.

SMART, Ninian, 1927- 200'.9
The religious experience of mankind. New York, Scribner [1969] xii, 576 p. illus., maps, port. 25 cm. Bibliography: p. [545]-550. [BL80.2.S6] 68-12508 10.00
1. Religions—History. 2. Religion. 3. Experience (Religion) I. Title.

TOY, Crawford Howell, 1836-1919. 200'.9
Introduction to the history of religions. [1st AMS ed.] New York, AMS Press [1970] xix, 639 p. 23 cm. Reprint of the 1913 ed. Bibliography: p. 585-623. [BL80.T7 1970] 76-126655 ISBN 0-404-06498-1
1. Religions—History. 2. Religion—History. 3. Rites and ceremonies. 4. Mythology. I. Title.

TOY, Crawford Howell, 1836-1919. 290
... Introduction to the history of religions, by Crawford Howell Toy ... Boston, New York [etc.] Ginn and company [1913] xiv, 639 p. 21 1/2 cm. (Half-title: Handbooks on the history of religions, ed. by M. Jastrow, jr. ... vol. IV) "Selected list of books of reference": p. 585-623. [BL80.T7] 13-24168
1. Religions—Hist. 2. Religion—Hist. 3. Rites and ceremonies. 4. Mythology. I. Title.

VASSALL, William F 290
The origin of Christianity; a brief study of the world's early beliefs and their influence on the early Christian church, including an examination of the lost books of the Bible. [1st ed.] New York, Exposition Press [1952] 183 p. 21 cm. [BL80.V27] 52-10685
1. Religions...Hist. 2. Christianity — Origin. 3. Bible. N. T. Apocryphal books — Criticism, interpretation, etc. I. Title.

Religions—History—Juvenile literature.

APPLETON, Ernest Robert, 1891- 290
An outline of religion, by E. R. Appleton; with a foreword by the Reverend S. Parkes Cadman ... New York, H. C. Kinsey & company, inc., 1934. xi, 712 p. illus. 24 1/2 cm. London edition (Hodder and Stoughton) has title: An outline of religion for children. Bibliography included in preface. [BL82.A6 1934] 34-29165
1. Religions—Hist.—Juvenile literature. 2. Church history—Juvenile literature. I. Title.

SAVAGE, Katharine. 209
The history of world religions. [Maps by Richard Natkiel] New York, Walck [1973? c.1966] 283 p. plates, maps. 21 cm. Bibl.: p. 275-278. [BL82.S35] 66-18534 ISBN 0-8098-3401-4 pap., 1.95
1. Religions—History—Juvenile literature. I. Title.

Religions—History—Sources.

*ELIADE, Mircea. 291.09
Man and the sacred; a thematic source book of the history of religions New York, Harper & Row, [1974, c1967]. xiii, 173 p. 21 cm. Contains chapter 3 of From primatives to Zen. Bibliography: p. 171-172. [BL74.E4] 73-20950 ISBN 0-06-062137-0 2.25 (pbk.)
1. Religions—History—Sources. I. Title.

*ELIADE, Mircea, 1907- 291.09
Death, afterlife, and eschatology; a thematic source book of the history of religions. New York, Harper & Row [1974 c1967] xi., 109 p. 21 cm. Part 3 of From Primitives to Zen. Bibliography: 107-108. [BL74.E4] 73-20493 ISBN 0-06-062139-7 1.95 (pbk.)
1. Religions—History—Sources. I. Title.

ELIADE, Mircea, 1907- 291'.09
From primitives to Zen; a thematic sourcebook of the history of religions. [1st U.S. ed.] New York, Harper & Row [1967] xxv, 644 p. 24 cm. Bibliography: p. 635-643. [BL74.E4 1967] 66-20775
1. Religions—History—Sources. I. Title.

ELIADE, Mircea, 1907- 291.2
Gods, goddesses, and myths of creation; a thematic source book of the history of religions. New York, Harper & Row [1974] xiii, 162 p. 21 cm. First part, consisting of chapters 1 and 2, of the author's From primitives to Zen. Bibliography: p. 158-161. [BL74.E42 1974] 73-20949 1.95 (pbk.).
1. Religions—History—Sources. I. Eliade, Mircea, 1907- From primitives to Zen. Chap. 2. Myths of creation and of origin. II. Title.

Religions—History—Study.

MANUEL, Frank Edward 291.094
The eighteenth century confronts the gods. New York, Atheneum, 1966[c.1959] 336p. illus. 21cm. (97) Bibl. [BL41.M3] 59-10318 2.95 pap.,
1. Religions—Hist.—Study. 2. Religious thought—18th cent. 3. Enlightenment. I. Title.

MANUEL, Frank Edward. 291.094
The eighteenth century confronts the gods. Cambridge, Harvard University Press, 1959. 336p. illus. 25cm. Includes bibliography. [BL41.M3] 59-10318
1. Religious—Hist.—Study. 2. Religious thought—18th cent. 3. Enlightenment. I. Title.

MANUEL, Frank Edward.
The eighteenth century confronts the gods. New York, Atheneum, 1967 [c1959] 336 p. illus. 25 cm. (Atheneum paperbacks) "Originally published by Harvard University Press." Includes bibliography. 68-3951
1. Religions—Hist.—Study. 2. Religious thought—18th cent. 3. Enlightenment. I. Title.

Religions — Juvenile literature.

BAKER, Liva. 291
World faiths; a story of religion. New York, Abelard [1966, c.1965] x, 237p. illus. 23cm. Bibl. [BL92.B3] 65-23653 4.95
1. Religions—Juvenile literature. I. Title.

DOMINIC, Sister Mary. 922.2415
Little Nellie of Holy God. Pictures by Sister M. John Vianney. Milwaukee, Bruce [c.1961] unpaged. col. illus. .50 bds.,
I. Title.

EDUCATIONAL Research Council of America. Social Science Staff. 291
The human adventure, four world views / prepared by the Social Science Staff of the Educational Research Council of America. Learner-verified ed. 2. Boston : Allyn and Bacon, c1975. v, 154 p. : ill. (some col.) ; 26 cm. (Concepts and inquiry, the Educational Research Council social science program) Includes index. Explains the fundamentals of four classical approaches to life: the traditional Chinese, Buddhist, Hebrew, and Greek. [BL92.E37 1975] 74-4923 pbk. : 3.80
1. Religions—Juvenile literature. 2. [Religions.] 3. [Philosophy, Comparative.] I. Title. II. Title: Four world views. III. Series.

EDUCATIONAL Research Council of America. Social Science Staff. 372.8
The human adventure: four world views. Boston, Allyn and Bacon [1971] 154 p. illus. (part col.), col. maps. 26 cm. (Concepts and inquiry: the Educational Research Council social science program) Explains the fundamentals of four classic approaches to life: the traditional Chinese, Buddhist, Hebrew, and Greek. [BL92.E37 1971] 71-134008
1. Religions—Juvenile literature. 2. [Religions.] 3. [Philosophy, Comparative.] I. Title. II. Title: Four world views. III. Series.

HASKINS, James, 1941- 291
Religions. [1st ed.] Philadelphia, Lippincott [1973] 157 p. 21 cm. Bibliography: p. 152-154. Discusses the history, practices, and beliefs of the five major religions in the world today: Hinduism, Buddhism, Judaism, Christianity, and Islam. [BL92.H37] 72-11768 ISBN 0-397-31212-1 4.95
1. Religions—Juvenile literature. 2. [Religions.] I. Title.

KETTELKAMP, Larry. 200'.9
Religions, East and West. New York, Morrow, 1972. 128 p. illus. 23 cm. Discusses the similarities and differences of ten of the world's major religions. [BL92.K45] 72-75805 ISBN 0-688-20030-3 ISBN 0-688-30030-8 (lib. bdg.) 3.95
1. Religions—Juvenile literature. 2. [Religions.] I. Title.

LISTON, Robert A. 291'.02'4055
By these faiths : religions for today / Robert A. Liston. New York : J. Messner, c1977. 192 p. ; 22 cm. Includes index. Bibliography: p. 187. Discusses the attitudes, beliefs, and practices of the world's major religions and several minor sects and cults. [BL92.L57] 77-23324 ISBN 0-671-32836-0 lib. bdg. : 7.29
1. Religions—Juvenile literature. 2. Sects—Juvenile literature. 3. [Religions.] 4. [Sects.] I. Title.

MOSKIN, Marietta D. 291
In search of God / by Marietta Moskin. New York : Atheneum, 1979. p. cm. Includes index. Bibliography: p. Explains how and why different religions came about and what they provided their followers. Also discusses certain elements such as holy objects, religious laws, and the priesthood common to all faiths. [BL92.M67] 79-10493 ISBN 0-689-30719-5 : 9.95
1. Religions—Juvenile literature. 2. Religion—Juvenile literature. 3. [Religions.] I. Title.

RICE, Edward E., 1918- 291
Ten religions of the East / by Edward Rice. New York : Four Winds Press, c1978. p. cm. Includes index. Discusses ten faiths that have originated in the East: Bon, Sikhism, Taoism, Confucianism, Shinto, Cao Dai, Theosophy, the Baha'i Faith, Jainism, and Zoroastrianism. [BL92.R5] 78-6186 ISBN 0-590-07473-3 : 7.95
1. Religions—Juvenile literature. 2. [Religions.] I. Title.

Religions — lectures, illustrations, etc.

DRAKE, Durant, 1878- 230
Shall we stand by the church? a dispassionate inquiry, by Durant Drake... New York, The Macmillan company, 1920. 5 p. l., 181 p. 20 cm. "The following chapters have been given as lectures at various conferences and conventions. Most of them have been published in periodicals."--Acknowledgment. [BV600.D7] 20-21349
I. Title.

YEAR. 290.84
A picture-history of the Bible and Christianity in 1000 pictures, with the inspiring stories of all the world's great

religions. Introd. by Albert Schweitzer, forewords by leaders of the major faiths. [Wilton, Conn., 1957] 252 p. illus. 29 cm. [BL90.Y4 1956] 57-14504
1. Religions — lectures, illustrations, etc. I. Title. II. Title: Bible and Christianity.

Religions, Modern.

ATKINS, Gaius Glenn, 1868- 200
Modern religious cults and movements, by Gaius Glenn Atkins ... New York, Chicago [etc.] Fleming H. Revell company [c1923] 3 p. l., 5-359 p. 21 cm. [BL96.A8] 23-14364
1. Religions, Modern. 2. Faith-cure. 3. New thought. I. Title.

BACH, Marcus, 1906- 289
Faith and my friends. [1st ed.] Indianapolis, Bobbs-Merrill [1951] 302 p. 22 cm. [BL98.B2] 51-9823
1. Religions, Modern. I. Title.

COMBS, George Hamilton, 1864- 290
Some latter-day religions, by George Hamilton Combs. Chicago, New York [etc.] Fleming H. Revell company, 1899. 3 p. l., [9]-261 p. 19 cm. "Essays ... cast in part for platform uses."--Foreword. Contents.--Aesthetiucism.--Theosophy.--Otherism.--Faith cure--Pessimism.--Agnosticism.--Materialism.--Spiritualism.--Liberalism.-- Mormonism.--Christian sciences.--Soicialism. [BL98.C6] 99-5611
1. Religions, Modern. 2. Philosophy, Modern. I. Title.

DAVIES, Horton 209
The challenge of the sects. [Rev., enl. ed.] Philadelphia, Westminster [1962,c.1961] 176p. 19cm. First pub. in 1954 under title: Christian deviations. Bibl. 62-1216 1.45 pap.,
1. Religions, Modern. I. Title.

DAVIES, Horton. 290
Christian deviations; essays in defence of the Christian faith. New York, Philosophical Library [1954] 126p. 20cm. [BL98] 54-12269
1. Religions, Modern. I. Title.
Contents omitted.

DAVIES, Horton. 289
Christian deviations: the challenge of the new spiritual movements. Philadelphia, Westminster Press [1965] 144 p. 19 cm. "A revised edition of The challenge of the sects [first published in 1954 under title Christian deviations]" Includes bibliographies. [BL98.D3 1965] 65-21054
1. Religions, Modern. I. Title.

DAVIES, Horton. 209
Christian deviations: the challenge of the new spiritual movements. 3d rev. ed. Philadelphia, Westminster Press [1973, c1972] viii, 133 p. 22 cm. [BL98.D3 1973] 72-7365 ISBN 0-664-24966-3
1. Religions, Modern. I. Title.

GOBLET D'ALVIELLA, Eugene 290
Felicien Albert, comte, 1846-1925.
The contemporary evolution of religious thought in England America and India, by Count Goblet d'Alviella ... translated by J. Moden. New York, G. P. Putnam's sons, 1886. xv, 344 p. 23 cm. [BL98.G6 1886] 30-23145
1. Religious, Modern. 2. Philosophy, Modern. I. Moden, J., tr. II. Title.

Religions, Modern—Addresses, essays, lectures.

BECK, Frank B. 241
Questions on worldliness, what about--television, smoking. dancing, the theater, the lodge, gambling. Grand Rapids, Michigan, Zondervan [c.1960] 32p. 20cm. .35 pap.,
I. Title.

CLARKE, William B. 231
A more excellent way; a book concerning the provision made of God for a life in common between himself and man, by William B. Clarke. New York and London, G. P. Putnam's sons, 1904. vii, 227 p. 19 cm. [BT165.C5] 4-14160
I. Title.

DRESSER, Horatio Willis, 1866-
The religion of the spirit in modern life, by Horatio W. Dresser... New York and London, G. P. Putnam's sons, 1914. xi, 311 p. 19 1/2 cm. $1.50 "Further development of the theory of inner experience set forth in The philosophy of the spirit, 1908."-Pref. 14-15148
I. Title.

JACKSON, Henry Ezekiel, 1869-
The message of the modern minister, by Henry E. Jackson ... introduction by Amory H. Bradford ... New York, Chicago [etc.] F. H. Revell company [c1908] 63 p. 18 cm. 8-14317
I. Title.

THE New religious 301.5'8
consciousness / edited by Charles Y. Glock and Robert N. Bellah ; with contributions by Randall H. Alfred ... [et al.] ; foreword by P. J. Philip. Berkeley : University of California Press, c1976. xvii, 391 p. ; 25 cm. Includes bibliographical references and index. [BL98.N48] 75-17295 ISBN 0-520-03083-4 : 14.95
1. Religions, Modern—Addresses, essays, lectures. 2. Youth—Religious life—Addresses, essays, lectures. I. Glock, Charles Y. II. Bellah, Robert Neelly, 1927- III. Alfred, Randall H.

Religions—Outlines, syllabi, etc.

BRADLEY, David G. 290.2
A guide to the world's religions. Englewood Cliffs, N.J., Prentice [c.1963] 182p. 21cm. (Spectrum bk., S-51) Bibl. 63-191 3.95; 1.95 pap.,
1. Religions—Outlines, syllabi, etc. I. Title.

THOMPSON, Hugh Miller, 1830-
More "Copy"; a second series of essays from an editor's drawer on religion, literature and life, by Hugh Miller Thompson ... New York, T. Whittaker, 1897. 3 p. l., 17-244 p. 19 cm. 12-394742
I. Title.

Religions — Periods.

HISTORY of religions. v. 1-
[Chicago] University of Chicago Press, 1961. v. in illus. 24 cm. semi-annual. [BL1.H5] 64-1081
1. Religions — Periods.

Religions—Pictures, illustrations, etc.

FORMAN, Henry James, 1879- 290
Truth is one; the story of the world's great living religions in pictures and text [by] Henry James Forman and Roland Gammon. New York, Harper [1954] 224 p. illus. 29 cm. [BL90.F6] 54-8950
1. Religions—Pictures, illustrations, etc. I. Gammon, Roland, joint author. II. Title.

MOORE, Albert C. 704.94'8
Iconography of religions : an introduction / Albert C. Moore. 1st American ed. Philadelphia : Fortress Press, 1977. vi, 337 p. : ill. ; 26 cm. Includes index. Bibliography: p. [323]-325. [N7790.M65 1977] 76-62598 ISBN 0-8006-0488-1 : 25.00
1. Religions—Pictures, illustrations, etc. I. Title.

YEAR. 290.84
A picture history of the Bible and Christianity in 1000 pictures, with the inspiring stories of all the world's great religions. Introd. by Albert Schweitzer, forewords by leaders of the major faiths. [Los Angeles] [1952] 192 p. illus. 37 cm. [BL90.Y4] 52-13502
1. Religions—Pictures, illustrations, etc. I. Title. II. Title: Bible and Christianity.

ZOOK, Pat, 1956-1980. 811'.54
My spirit that lives after me : a collection of poems, drawings, paintings, and photographs / by Pat Zook. 1st ed. Raytown, MO : Avatar, 1981. 87, [3] p. : ill. ; 22 cm. [PS3576.O6M9 1981] 19 81-81421 ISBN 0-936040-01-7 (pbk.) : 3.95
Publisher's address: P.O. Box 16703, Raytown, MO 64133

Religions (Proposed, universal, etc.)

AIKEN, Janet (Rankin) 1892- 289.9
Commonsense religion [by] Janet Aiken ... Ridgefield, Conn., Quarry books, 1943. 3 p. l., 115 p. 21 cm. "First edition." [Full name: Janet Ruth (Rankin) Aiken] [BL390.A5] 43-13702
1. Religions (Proposed, universal, etc.) I. Title.

ALEKSANDR Mikhailovich grand 211
duke of Russia, 1866-1933.
The religion of love, by Alexander, grand duke of Russia; translated by Jean S. Proctor. New York, London, The Century co. [c1929] xx, p., 2 l., 3-310 p. 19 1/2 cm. [BL390.A55] 29-9636
1. Religions (Proposed, universal, etc.) 2. Soul. 3. Spiritual life. I. Proctor, Jean S., tr. II. Title.

ALEXANDER, grand duke of 290
Russia, 1866-1933.
The union of souls, by H. I. H. Alexander, grand duke of Russia, translated by Laura I. Finch... New York, Roerich museum press, 1931. 67 p. 19 cm. (Series: "Contemporary thought") [BL390.A62] 31-30097
1. Religions (Proposed, universal, etc.) 2. Soul. I. Finch, Mrs. Laura I., tr. II. Title.

BAGGS, Ralph L. 200.1
International brotherhood through service clubs; a practical path to peace, by Ralph L. Baggs. [1st ed.] New York, Exposition Press [1967] 80 p. 21 cm. [BL390.B27] 67-8439
1. Religions (Proposed, universal, etc.) 2. Associations, institutions, etc. I. Title.

BEELER, Olando Gillman. 212
Scientific spirituality, by O. G. Beeler, Ph.D. Knoxville, Tenn., Dr. O. G. Beeler [1940] 9 p. l., [21]-150 p. 20 1/2 cm. Page 147, advertising matter; pages 148-150 blank for "Notes." Contents.pt. 1. Explanation of scientific spirituality.--pt. 2. Searching the Scriptures.--pt. 3. Definition and explanation of God. [BL390.B37] 41-3891
1. Religions (Proposed, universal, etc.) I. Title.

BERG, Rebecka Carolina, 289.9
1872-
Life eternal and its work, revealed from the heavenly side, by Rebecka C. Berg. Every man's textbook. Los Angeles, Calif., De Vorss & co. [c1938] 4 p. l., [11]-101 p. 20 cm. [BL390.B4] 38-17813
1. Religions (Proposed, universal, etc.) I. Title.

BOOTH, Edwin Prince, 1898- 204
The greater church of the future. Foreword by Lyman V. Rutledge. Boston, Beacon Press [1951] 51 p. 22 cm. [BL390.B65] 52-6156
1. Religions (Proposed, universal, etc.) 2. Liberalism (Religion) 3. religions (Proposed, universal, etc.) 4. Liberalism (Religion) I. Title.

BRAUS, Irene Samuelson. 248
A new law for all living [by] Irene Samuelson Braus. Buffalo, N. Y., Sun publishing co. [c1941] 151 p. 20 cm. "First edition." [BL390.B7 1941] 41-12196
1. Religions (Proposed, universal, etc.) I. Title.

BROWN, Anton U 291.1
Dignitarian way. Orange, Calif [1960] 118p. 23cm. Includes bibliography. [BL390.B75] 60-44564
1. Religions (Proposed, universal, etc.) I. Title.

DEICH, Max, 1884- 289.9
Order out of chaos, by Max Deich; an approach to better understanding. [Atlanta, W. F. Melton, c1940] 1 p. l., [1], xvii, 113 p. 18 cm. [BL390.D4] 40-31756
1. Religions (Proposed, universal, etc.) I. Title.

DELORIA, Vine. 291.2
The metaphysics of modern existence / by Vine Deloria, Jr. San Francisco : Harper & Row, [1978] p. cm. Bibliography: p. [BL390.D43] 76-8708 ISBN 0-06-450250-3 : 8.95
1. Religions (Proposed, universal, etc.) 2. Religion and culture. 3. Indians of North America—Religion and mythology. 4. Civilization, Modern—Moral and religious aspects. I. Title.

DOLE, Charles Fletcher, 289.9
1845-1927.
The coming religion, by Charles F. Dole ... Boston, Small, Maynard & company [1910] 4 p. l., 200 p. 20 cm. [BL390.D6] 10-15384
1. Religions (Proposed, universal, etc.) I. Title.

DOLE, Charles Fletcher, 289.9
1845-1927.
A religion for the new day, by Charles F. Dole. New York, B. W. Huebsch, inc., 1920. xi p., 1 l., 297 p. 20 cm. [BL390.D62] 21-4337
1. Religions (Proposed, universal, etc.) I. Title.

ELIOT, Charles William, 1834- 204
1926.
The religion of the future, by Charles W.Eliot. Boston, J.W. Luce and company, 1909. 2 p. l., 63 p. front. (prot.) 19 1/2 cm. "From the Harvard theological review, October, 1909." "A lecture delivered at the close of the eleventh session of the Harvard summer school of theology, July 22, 1909." [BL390.E45] 9-31074
1. Religions (Proposed, universal. etc.) I. Title.

GRIGGS, Henry Septimus, 1848-
The book of truth, by Hon. Henry S. Griggs: a reasonable faith and the future religion of the world ... Brooklyn, N. Y., Henry S. Griggs company [c1914] 5 p. l., 3-284 p., 1 l. 21 cm. 14-19022 3.00
I. Title.

HARDMAN, Harvey. 289.9
Making your self the master, by Harvey Hardman. Denver, Col. H. Hardman, c1935. 1 p. l., [7]-196 p. 19 1/2 cm. [BL390.H32] 35-3899
1. Religions (Proposed, universal, etc.) 2. Religion and science- 1900- I. Title.

HAROLD, H J. 211
The knowledge of life, being a contribution to the study of religions, by H.J.Herald. New York, G.P. Putnam's sons; London, Archibald, Constable & co. [1896] vii, 353 p. 21 cm. [BL390.H3] 31-5274
1. Religions (Proposed, universal, etc.) I. Title.

HARRIS, Thomas Lake, 1823- 289.9
1906.
The breath of God with man: an essay on the grounds and evidences of universal religion. By Thomas Lake Harris ... New York and London, Brotherhood of the new life, 1867. 104 p. 20 cm. Republished, in part, in his "God's breath in man and in humane society", 1891 (314 p.) [BX9998.H26] 31-4572
I. Brotherhood of the new life. II. Title. III. Title: Universal religion.

HOCKING, William Ernest, 291
1873-1966.
Living religions and a world faith / by William Ernest Hocking. New York : AMS Press, 1976. 291 p. ; 23 cm. (Philosophy in America) Reprint of the 1940 ed. published by Macmillan, New York, issued in series: Hibbert lectures, 1938. Includes bibliograhical references and index. [BL410.H6 1976] 75-3187 ISBN 0-404-59189-2 : 20.50
1. Religions (Proposed, universal, etc.) 2. Religion. 3. Christianity and other religions. I. Title. II. Series: Hibbert lectures (New York) ; 1938.

HOCKING, William Ernest, 290
1878-
Living religions and a world faith, by William Ernest Hocking ... New York, The Macmillan company, 1940. 1p.e.,7-291p. diagrs. 21cm. [Hibbert lectures, 1938] [BL25.H52 1938] [BL410.H6] (208.2) 40-30439
1. Religious (Proposed, universal, etc.) 2. Religion. 3. Christianity and other religions. I. Title.

HOLY Spirit Association for
Unification of World Christianity, Seoul, Korea.
The divine principles, by Young Oon Kim. 3d ed. San Francisco [1963, c1960] xviii, 217 p. charts. 21 cm. 65-97399
1. Religions (Proposed, universal, etc.) I. Kim, Young Woon. II. Title.

JEFFERSON, Alpha, 1872- 211
The cosmic Chirst and the new ethical order, by Alpha jefferson. New York, Fortuny's [c1940] 95 p. front. 22 cm. "First edition." [BL390.J4] 40-8308
1. Religions (Proposed, universal, etc.) I. Title.

KEITH, W Holman, 1900- 291.14
Divinity as the eternal feminine. [1st ed.] New York, Pageant Press [1960] 194p. 21cm. [BL390.K43] 60-53292
1. Religions (Proposed, universal, etc.) I. Title.

KUENZLI, Alfred E., ed. 210
Reconstruction in religion; a symposium. Contributors: Ernest E. Bayles [others] Boston, Beacon [c.1961] xvi, 253p. Bibl. 61-13121 3.95
1. Religions (Proposed, universal, etc.) I. Bayles, Ernest Edward, 1897- II. Title.

LAWSON, Alfred William, 1869- 289.9
Lawsonian religion. Detriot, Humanity Benefactor Foundation [1949] 255 p. illus., ports. 21 cm. [BL390.L35] 49-25048
1. Religions (Proposed, Universal, etc.) I. Title.

LAWSON, Ernest, 1878- 289.9
The great revision; first book of the holy principalian religion, by Ernest Lawson. Boston, Meador publishing company, 1934. 154 p. 21 cm. [BR126.L365] 35-903
1. Religious (Proposed, universal, etc.) I. Title. II. Title: Holy principalian religion.

LUONGO, Anthony M. 291'.1
Let there be unity of religions within diversity; the way to go, by Anthony M. Luongo. [Chicago, Adams Press; distributed by Trans World Publications, Brooklyn, 1967] vii, 143 p. 23 cm. [BL390.L85] 67-19576
1. Religions (Proposed, universal, etc.) I. Title.

MORENO, Jacob L., 1892- 289.9
The words of the Father; preface and commentary by J. L. Moreno. New York, Beacon house, Alliance book corporation [c1941] xxi, 317 p. 24 cm. [BL390.M6] 42-5325
1. Religions (Proposed, universal, etc.) I. Title.

[NORTON, W. L.] 289.
Try-square, or, The church of practical religion. By reporter ... New York, The Truth-seeker company [1887] vii, 9-314 p. 20 cm. Dialogues. [BL390.N6] 39-411
1. Religions (Proposed, universal, etc.) I. Title. II. Title: The church of practical religion.

O'DONNELL, Francis Henry Etherington, 1862- 289.9
Our religion, by Francis H. E. and Florence D. O'Donnell. San Francisco, Calif., Phillips and Van Orden company, 1936. 32 p. 16 cm. [BL390.O3] 37-1968
1. Religions (Proposed, universal, etc.) I. O'Donnell, Florence Dunwell (Cowley) Mrs. 1862- II. Title.

[PATTERSON, James Herbert] 289.9
Now! Dedicated to Hon. Leland Stanford and associates, who are considering a proposition to start an undenominational church. By A Layman [pseud.] ... San Francisco, Press of the West end, 1889. 53 p. 18 cm. [BL390.P3] 31-6644
1. Religions (Proposed, universal, etc.) I. Title.

PATTON, Kenneth Leo, 1911- 201
A religion for one world: art and symbols for a universal religion. Charles R. McCormick, photographer. Boston, Beacon [c.1964] xii, 484p. illus. 24cm. 63-18732 7.50
1. Religions (Proposed, universal, etc.) I. Title.

PERSONS, Lee Chandler. 289.9
Alluring the soul along the pathway of nature's beauty, by Lee Chandler Persons ... Miami, Fla., Priv. print., [1929- v. 31 cm. Cover-title. [BL390.P38] 34-115086
1. Religions (Proposed, universal, etc.) I. Title.

PERSONS, Lee Chandler. 289.9
The religion of the beautiful: a development of Dr. Eliot's "Religion of the future", by Lee Chandler Persons ... A spiritual interpretation of natural beauty, using poetic symbolism as a means of representing emotional values ... Miami, Fla., Palm villa press [1932?- v. mounted col. fronts., illus. (mounted port.) mounted col. plates. 31 cm. Author's autograph on verso of t.-p. Parts 2- have imprint: Miami, Fla., The Hefty press, inc. [1933?]- [BL390.P4] 32-15462
1. Religions (Proposed, universal, etc.) I. Eliot, Charles William, 1834-1926. The religion of the future. II. Title.
Contents omitted.

PICTON, J[ames] Allanson, 1832-
The religion of the universe, by J. Allanson Picton ... London, New York, Macmillan and co., limited, 1904. x, 379, [1] p. 23 cm. 5-1996
I. Title.
Contents omitted.

REISNER, Edward Hartman, 1885- 289.9
Faith in an age of fact, a new religious outlook, by Edward H. Reisner. New York, Toronto, Farrar & Rinehart, incorporated [1937] 4 p. l., 3-117 p. 19 1/2 cm. [BL390.R36] 37-21631
1. Religious (Proposed, universal, etc.) 2. Religion—Philosophy. I. Title.

ROBERTS, Irene. 290
Let there be light. New York, Vantage Press [c1950) 119 p. 23 cm. [BL390.R52] 51-49
1. Religions (Proposed, universal, etc.) I. Title.

ROBINSON, Donald Fay, 1905- 289.9
In search of a religion [by] Donald Fay Robinson... Chester, Pa., 1938. 93 p. 23 cm. [BL390.R55] 38-18153
1. Religions (Proposed, universal, etc.) I. Title.

*ROSS, Floyd H. 209
The great religions by which men live [Reissue] (Title orig.: Questions that matter most asked by the world's religions) By Floyd H. Ross, Tynette Hills. Greenwich, Conn., Fawcett [1965, c.1956] 192p. 18cm. (Premier bk., R199) .60 pap.,
I. Title.

RUTHERFORD, James Walter. 230
The gospel of truth, by James Walter Rutherford... Boston, The Christopher publishing house [c1941] ix, 11-75 p. 19 cm. [BL390.R8] 41-17058
1. Religions (Proposed, universal, etc.) I. Title.

SALT, Henry Stephens, 1851- 301
The creed of kinship, by Henry S. Salt... New York, E. P. Dutton & co., inc., 1935. ix, 118 p. 19 1/2 cm. "First edition." [BL390.S3] 35-17210
1. Religious (Proposed, universal, etc.) 2. Social problems. 3. Animals, Treatment of. I. Title. II. Title: Kinship, The creed of.

SCALA, Jacob Israel, 1886- 200
The message to mankind under the view of eternity, by J. I. Scala. New York, Macoy publishing company, 1941. xvi, 147 p. 19 1/2 cm. [BL390.S35] 41-19941
1. Religious (Proposed, universal, etc.) I. Title.

SEMAAN, Andrew Nicola, 1876- 290
Religion and brotherhood of man; a manifestation of the spiriti-god in man. [1st ed.] Brooklyn [1950] 640 p. illus., ports. 25 cm. [BL390.S4] 50-3841
1. Religions (Proposed, universal, etc.) 2. Religions. 3. Brotherliness. I. Title.

SHAPIRA, Samuel S. 290
Your great awakening, by S. S. Shapira. Wilkinsburg, Pa., Eternal publishing co. [1941] 191 p. 21 1/2 cm. Portrait of author mounted on t.-p. [BL390.S43] 43-48460
1. Religions (Proposed universal, etc.) I. Title.

SHRIGLEY, Homer Theodore, 1889- 289.9
The unknown God, by H. T. Shrigley. Boston, The Christopher publishing house [c1941] xv, 17-199 p. front., diagrs. 19 1/2 cm. [BL390.S45] 41-19470
1. Religions (Proposed universal, etc.) I. Title.

SKINNER, Clarence Russell, 1881- 201
A religion for greatness, by Clarence R. Skinner ... Boston, Mass., The Murray press [1945] 3 p. l., 121 p. diagrs. 23 1/2 cm. Bibliographical foot-notes. [BL390.S55] 45-6379
1. Religions (Proposed, universal, etc.) I. Title.

[SMITH, Richard Morris] 1827-1896. 289.9
An outline of the future religion of the world, with a comsideration of the facts and doctrines on which it will probably be based. By T. Lloyd Stanley [pseud.]... New York, London, G. P. Putnam's sons, 1884. xi, 588 p. 22 1/2 cm. [BL390.S6] 31-6641
1. Religions (Prosed, universal, etc.) I. Title. II. Title: The future religion of the world, An outline of.

SMITH, Titus Keiper, 1859- 289.9
The allegion; or, New world religion, by Titus K. Smith; based upon a proposition affording a scientific fundament of thought as benevolently revolutionary as were the proposals of Copernicus and Galileo in astronomy, or of Dr. Joseph Priestly in chemistry. New York, Priv. print., 1932. 248, [1] p. 24 cm. "Of the first edition of twelve hundred fifty numbered copies designed and printed by the printing house of William Edwin Rudge, New York, this is number 397." [BL390.S63] 32-5364
1. Religions (Proposed, universal, etc.) I. Title.

SNARE, J P 1870- 280
A new look at religion. [1st ed.] New York, Greenwich Book Publishers [c1956] 60p. 21cm. [BL390.S64] 56-12843
1. Religions (Prop0sed, unlversal, etc.) I. Title.

SNARE, J P 3870- 280
A new look at religion. [1st ed.] New York, Greenwich Book Publishers [c1956] 60 p. 21 cm. [BL390.S64] 56-12843
1. Religious (Proposed, universal, etc.) I. Title.

STEELE, Wayne H. 201
The religion of beauty, by Rev. Wayne H. Steele. Chicago, Ill., The Hobbert press, 1940. 8 p. l., [3]-324 p. 23 cm. [BL390.S67] 41-620
1. Religions (Proposed, universal, etc.) 2. Cosmology. 3. Esthetics. I. Title.

[TABER, Clarence Wilbur] 1870- 289.9
Creative science; a scientific basis for a new religious philosophy, by a modern Job. Chicago, The Lake shore press [c1932] 6 p. l., vi, 382 p. 18 1/2 cm. [BL390.T3] 33-743
1. Religions (Proposed, universal, etc.) I. Title.

WIDNEY, Joseph Pomeroy, 1841-1938. 289.9
The faith that has come to me, by J. P. Widney ... Los Angeles, Calif., Pacific publishing company [c1932] xi, 272 p. front. (port.) 23 1/2 cm. [BL390.W5] 32-20957
1. Religions (Proposed, universal, etc.) I. Title.

WODEHOUSE, Ernest Armine, 1879-1936. 289.9
A world expectant; abridgement of A world expectant, by E. A. Wodehouse. Wheaton, Ill., The Theosophical press [c1938] 4 p. l., 78 p. 20 cm. [BL390.W6 1938] 44-18621
1. Religions (Proposed, universal, etc.) I. Title.

[WOLKENFELD, Aaron] 1910- 205
The American millennial message, by A. J. Welder [pseud.] New York, N.Y. Millennium publication [1941] 125, [1] p., 1 l. diagrs. 28 1/2 cm. "First edition." [BL390.W65] 42-7272
1. Religious (Proposed, universal, etc.) I. Title.

Religions—Relations.

*PARRINDER, Geoffrey. 291.2
Introduction to Asian religions / [by] Geoffrey Parrinder. New York Oxford Univ. Pr., 1976,c1957. 138p. ; 21 cm. Includes index. [BL85] 76-15098 ISBN 0-19-519858-1 pbk. : 2.50
1. Religions-Relations. 2. History-Theology. 3. Religion-History. I. Title.

TO Promote Good Will (Television program) 291
To promote good will [by] William Kailer Dunn, [others] Ed. by Lee Joyce Richmond, Mary E. Weller. Helicon [dist. New York, Taplinger, c.1965] 184p. 21cm. Transcribed from tape recordings of discussions between a rabbi, a Catholic priest, and a Protestant minister in the Baltimore interfaith program, sponsored by the American Legion. [BL410.T6] 65-24132 4.50 bds.,
1. Religions—Relations. I. Dunn, William Kailer. II. Richmond. Lee Joyce, ed. III. Weller, Mary Eileen, ed. IV. American Legion. V. Title.

Religions—Study and teaching.

BURKS, Thompson. 200'.7
Religions of the world; a study course for adults. Cincinnati, Standard Pub. [1972] [16], 112 p. 22 cm. The main work, also issued separately, is preceded by the author's "Instructor" with special t.p. Bibliography: p. 112 (2d group) [BL80.2.B78 1972] 72-188037
1. Religions—Study and teaching. I. Title.

GUNDRY, D. W. 200'.7
The teacher and the world religions, by D. W. Gundry. Cambridge, James Clarke, 1968. 160 p. 21 cm. (The Education and religion series) Includes bibliographical references. [BL41.G85] 75-538622 18/6
1. Religions—Study and teaching. 2. Religions—Historiography. I. Title.

Religions—Study and teaching—Great Britain.

CHRISTIAN Education Movement. Primary Dept. 372.8
World religions in the first and middle school / [produced by The Primary Department, Christian Education Movement]. [London : The Dept., 1976?] 8 p. ; 21 cm. Caption title. Bibliography: p. 4-7. [BL41.C48 1976] 76-382483
1. Religions—Study and teaching—Great Britain. I. Title.

Religions. Theology—20th century

SCOTT, Harvey W 1838-1910. 208.
Religion, theology and morals, by Harvey W. Scott, forty years editor-in-chief, Morning Orgenoian, of Portland, Oregon; selected editorial articles and public lectures comp. by Leslie M. Scott ... Cambridge, Printed at the Riverside press, 1917. 2 v. fronts. (ports.) 25 cm. [BR85.S3] 17-11561 5.00
I. Scott, Leslie M., ed. II. Title.

Religious and ecclesiastical institutions—Buildings.

CONTI, Flavio, 1943- 726'.09
Centers on belief / Flavio Conti ; translated by Patrick Creagh. Boston : HBJ Press, c1978. 168 p. : ill. (some col.) ; 31 cm. (His The grand tour) Translation of Il trionfo della fede. [NA4600.C6613] 78-54066 ISBN 0-15-003729-5 : 11.95
1. Religious and ecclesiastical institutions—Buildings. I. Title. II. Series.

Religious and ecclesiastical institutions—Management.

HENDRIX, Olan, 1927- 254
Management for the Christian worker / by Olan Hendrix. Libertyville, Ill. : Quill Publications, c1976. p. cm. Bibliography: p. [BV652.H39] 76-3510 ISBN 0-916608-01-8 : 6.95
1. Religious and ecclesiastical institutions—Management. 2. Church management. 3. Management. I. Title.

Religious and ecclesiastical institutions—United States.

WINTER, Gibson. 262
Religious identity; a study of religious

organization. New York, Macmillan [1968] ix, 143 p. 18 cm. (Studies in religion and society series) Part of the material included was previously published in v. 1. of The emergent American society, edited by W. Lloyd Warner. Bibliographical footnotes. [BR517.W55] 68-9701 1.45
1. Religious and ecclesiastical institutions—United States. 2. Institutionalism (Religion) 3. United States—Religion. I. Title. II. Series.

Religious Biography

ABRAMS, Julius H. 296
Out of the house of Judah; a story of conversion to Christianity by Commandant Julius H. Abrams...introduction by Bishop John W. Hamilton... New York, Chicago (etc.) Fleming H. Revell company (c1923) 215 p. front. (port) 19 1/2 cm. [BV2623.A2A3] 23-18243
I. Title.

ADLER, Cyrus, 1863-1940. 922.96
I have considered the days, by Cyrus Adler. Philadelphia, The Jewish publication society of America, 1941-5701. xiii, [1], 447. [1] p. front., plates, ports. 22 cm. Autobiography. [E184.J5A18] 41-11124
I. Title.

ANTHONY, Susanna, 1726-1791. 922.
The life and character of Miss Susanna Anthony, who died in New York, (R.I.) June 23, MDCCXCI, in the sixty fifth year of her age. Consisting chiefly in extracts from her writings, with some brief observations on them. Compiled by Samuel Hopkins ... Printed at Worcester, Massachusetts, by Leonard Worcester, MDCCXCVI 193 p. 17 1/2 cm. [BX7260.A6A3 1796] 1-2021
I. Hopkins, Samuel, 1721-1803 ed. II. Title.

BIBLE. N. T. English. 1906.
The New Testament of Our Lord and Saviour Jesus Christ, arranged in the order in which its parts came to those in the first century who believed in Our Lord. London, J. M. Dent & co. New York, E. P. Dutton & co. [1906] xxxii, 561, [1] p. 18 cm. (Half-title: Everyman's library, ed. by Ernest Rhys. Theology and philosophy) Title within ornamental border; illustrated end-papers. "First edition, March 1906; reprinted, May 1906." "Chronologicl arrangement by Principal Lindsay." "English translations of the New Testament": p. ix-xi. A 10
I. Lindsay, Thomas Martin, 1843-1914, ed. II. Title.

*BLOSE, Elcy Marie, 248.2'0924
1917-
Hello, God; the life story of Elcy Marie Blose. New York, Exposition [1968] 125p. 21cm. (EP46760) 4.50
I. Title.

BOUFFARD, Alma 920.7
I have chosen His glory; a personal testament. New York, Greenwich [1961, c.1960] 46p. 60-16675 2.00
I. Title.

BOWEN, Barbara (Macdonald) 922
1876-
God still guides. New York, Vantage Press [c1954] 57p. 23cm. Autobiography. [BV3785.B65A3 1954] 54-9128
I. Title.

BOWEN, Barbara (MacDonald) 922
Mrs. 1876-
God still guides. by Barbara M. Bowen ... Grand Rapids, Mich., Wm. B. Eerdmans publishing co., 1941. 88 p. 20 cm. Autobiography. [BV3785.B65A3] 41-26528
I. Title.

BRADLEY, Floyd N. 922
Ten years behind the sacred desk, by Floyd N. Bradley. [Cincinnati, Print by God's Bible school & revivalist, c1932] 5 p. l., 9-208 p. front. (3 port.) 20 cm. [BV3785.B68A3] 32-13795
I. Title.

BREWER, Elizabeth Luella
(Alexander) "Mrs. D. A. Brewer," 1856-
Stepping nearer; or, Life and lessons of Mrs. D. A. Brewer... Louisville, Ky., Pentecostal publishing company [c1911] 93 p. front. (port) 18 1/2 cm. 11-29875 0.50
I. Title.

COBER, Alvin Alonzo, 922.673
1861-
Telling on myself, by Rev. Alvin Alonzo Cober ... with introduction by Emmanuel Wilson Cober ... Berlin, Pa., Berlin publishing company, 1934. 3 p. l., [9]-298 p. incl. front. (port.) 19 cm. [BX6495.C66A3 1934] 34-41631
I. Title.

DAVIS, Jerome, 285'.80924 (B)
1891-
A life adventure for peace; an autobiography. Foreword by James A. Pike. [1st ed.] New York, Citadel Press [1967] xiii, 208 p. 21 cm. 67-18083
I. Title.

DRACH, George.
The Telugu mission of the General council of the Evangelical Lutheran church in North America, containing a biography of the Rev. Christian Frederick Heyer, M.D., by George Drach ... and Calvin F. Kuder ... Philadelphia, General council publication house, 1914. 1 p. l., 399 p. front., plates, ports., maps, plan. 24 cm. 15-2405
I. Kuder, Calvin F., 1864- joint author. II. Title.

DUTTON, Charles Judson, 922.8173
1888-
Saints and sinners, by Charles J. Dutton ... New York, Dodd, Mead & company, 1940. 7 p. l., 303 p. 23 cm. Autobiography. [BX9869.D8A3] 40-6836
I. Title.

FORSTER, Minnie Jane 920.7
(Wyatt), 1875-
He led me through the wilderness ... by Minnie Jane Forster. [Wichita, Kan., Preston printing company] c1947. 139 p. 2 port. (incl. front.) 17 1/2 cm. Autobiography. [CT275.F6824A3] 47-19954
I. Title.

FORSTER, Minnie Jane 920.7
(Wyatt), 1875-
He led me through the wilderness. [Wichita] c1947. 207 p. ports. 19 cm. Autobiography. [CT275.F6824A3 1947a] 17-6805
I. Title.

GUARESCHI, Giovanni, 1908-
Don Camillo and his flock; translated by Frances Frenaye. New York, All Saints Press [1961, c1952] 232 p. illus. 17 cm. 63-27173
I. Title.

HARE, William Hobart, bp., 922.
1838-1909.
The life and labors of Bishop Hare, apostle to the Sioux, by M. A. De Wolfe Howe. New York, Sturgis & Walton company, 1911. 6 p. l., 3-117 p. front., plates, ports. 23 cm. Largely drawn from the writings of Bishop Hare. cf. Note. [BX5995.H3A3] 11-29685
I. Howe, Mark Antony De Wolfe, 1864- II. Title.

HARRIS, John William, 1870- 922
Tears and triumphs; the life story of a pastor-evangelist. Louisville, Ky., Pentecostal Pub. Co., 1948. 445 p. illus., ports. 20 cm. [BV3785.H347A3] 48-4270
I. Title.

HEBER, Reginald, bp. of 922.
Calcutta, 1783-1826.
The life of Reginald Heber ... by his widow. With selections from his correspondence, unpublished poems, and private papers; together with a Journal of his tour in Norway, Sweden, Russia, Hungary, and Germany, and a History of the Cossacks. New York, Protestant Episcopal press, 1830. 2 v. front. (port.) 22 1/2 cm. [BX5199.H4A48] 40-22684
I. Heber, Mrs. Amelia (Shipley). II. Title.

HERR, Horace Dumont, 922.573
1852-
Harvey Vonore; or, The making of a minister; a story of old Lecompton and early Kansas, by Horace D. Herr; with an introduction by Rev. Charles M. Sheldon ... [Fort Myers, Fla., The Geddes printing co., 1934] 2 p. l., xi, 204 p. front., plates, ports. 22 cm. "First printing, December 1963, limited to an edition of 100 copies." "I adopted the plan of masking my personality under the story name of 'Harvey Vonore.'"--Explanatory note. [BX7260.H46A3] 34-1911
I. Title.

HESS, Thomas, 1863- 922.
Life and experience of the Rev. Thomas Hess, with ten sermons. [Reading, Pa., Miller printing company, c1920] 56 p. 18 cm. [BX8495.H5A3] 20-17597
I. Title.

LUMPKIN, William Latane. 914.3'1
Doctor Sparks; a biography of Sparks White Melton, 1871 [i.e. 1870]-1957. Norfolk, Va., Phaup Print. Co. [c1963] [BX6495.M374L8] 63-23064
I. Title.

MAFFITT, John Newland, 1794- 922.
1850.
Tears of contrition; or, Sketches of the life of John N. Maffitt: with religious and moral reflections. To which are appended several poetic effusions. Written by himself ... New-London, Printed by S. Green, 1821. vii, [9]-260, 40 p. 16 1/2 cm. [BX8495.M27A3] 44-26495
I. Title.

MOJICA, Jose, 1895-
I, a sinner ... autobiography. [Translated by Franchon Royer!! Chicago, Franciscan Herald Press [1963] v, 393 p. illus., ports., facsims. 22 cm.
I. Title.

MOORE, John Monroe, Bp., 922.773
1867-
Life and I; or, Sketches and comments. Nashville, Parthenon Press [1948] 222 p. port. 20 cm. [BX8495.M58A3] 48-2979
I. Title.

MORGAN, Lucy (Griscom) Mrs. 218
Finding his world; the story of Arthur E. Morgan, by Lucy Griscom Morgan. 2d ed. Yellow Springs [O.] Kahoe & company, 1928. 4 p. l., 108 p. front. (port.) 24 cm. [BD431.M88 1928] 28-6651
I. Morgan, Arthur Ernest, 1878- II. Title.

MURRAY, John, 1741-1815. 922.8173
The life of Rev. John Murray ... Written by Himself. The records contain anecdotes of the writers' infancy, and are extended to some years after the commencement of his public labors in America. To which is added a brief continuation to the closing scene ... 5th ed., stereotyped and improved, with notes and appendix, by Rev. L. S. Everett. Boston, Marsh, Capen and Lyon, 1833. 324 p. front. (port.) 20 cm. [Universalist library. v. 1] [BX9969.M8A3 1833] 37-8745
I. Everett, L. S., ed. II. Title.

MURRAY, John, 1741-1815. 922.8173
The life of Rev. John Murray ... Written by himself. The records contain anecdotes of the writer's infancy, and are extended to some years after the commencement of his public labors in America. To which is added a brief continuation to the closing scene ... 8th ed., stereotyped and improved, with notes and appendix, by Rev. L. S. Everett. Boston, A. Tompkins, 1860. 324 p. 20 cm. [BX9969.M8A3 1860] 33-35153
I. Everett, L. S., ed. II. Title.

NELSON, John, 1707-1774. 922.742
An extract from the journal of Mr. John Nelson, preacher of the gospel. Containing an account of God's dealings with him, form his youth to the forty-second year of his age. Written by himself ... Baltimore: Published by J. Kingston, bookseller, 164 Market-street. Magill and Clime, printers, 1810. 214 p. 14 cm. [BX8495.N34A3 1810] 36-37385
I. Title.

PERRIN, Henri 922.244
Priest and worker; the autobiography of Henri Perrin. Tr. [from French] introd. by Bernard Wall. Chicago, Regnery [1966, c.1958, 1964] v, 247p. 22cm. (Logos, 51L-711) [BX4705.P4334A43] 64-14356 1.95 pap.,
I. Title.

PERRIN, Henri. 922.244
Priest and worker; the autobiography of Henri Perrin. Translated and with an introd. by Bernard Wall. [1st ed.] New York, Holt, Rinehart and Winston [1964] v, 247 p. 22 cm. Translation of Itineraire d'Henri Perrin, pretre ouvrier, 1914-1954. [BX4705.P4334A43] 64-14356
I. Title.

RAPKING, Aaron Henry, 253'.0924
1886-
Stick to it farmer boy; an autobiography, by Aaron H. Rapking. Nashville, Parthenon Press, 1967. 188 p. 19 cm. [BX8495.R28A3] 67-8781
I. Title.

ROBBINS, Thomas, 1777-1856. 920.
Diary of Thomas Robbins, D. D., 1796-1854. Printed for his nephew. Owned by the Connecticut historical society ... Ed. and annotated by Increase N. Tarbox ... Boston, T. Todd, printer, 1886-87. 2 v, fronts. (ports.) 28 cm. Contents.--i, 1796-1825.--ii. 1826-1854. [BX7260.R615A3] 13-6005
I. Tarbox, Increase Niles, 1815-1888, ed. II. Title.

SCARLETT, John, 1803- 922.773
1889.
The life and experience of a converted infidel. By John Scarlett ... New-York, Carlton & Phillips, 1854. 274 p. 15 1/2 cm. Autobiography. [BX8495.S34A3 1854] 37-7030
I. Title.

SCHWARTZ, Samuel, 1880?- 922.96
Tell thy children; the autobiography of an American rabbi. Foreword by Leonard J. Mervis. [1st ed.] New York, Exposition Press [1959] 98p. illus. 21cm. [BM755.S36A3] 59-3892
I. Title.

SLATTERY, Sarah 248.2'5'0924 B
Lawrence, 1879-
I choose. Winchester, Mass., University Press, 1969. 161 p. illus., ports. 23 cm. Autobiography. [CT275.S5228A3] 72-93891 4.95
I. Title.

SMIT, Erasmus. 266'.4'20924 B
The diary of Erasmus Smit. Edited by H. F. Schoon. Translated by W. G. A. Mears. Cape Town, C. Struik, 1972. x, 186 p. illus. 22 cm. Translation of Uit het dagboek van Erasmus Smit. [BX9595.S63S613] 72-189813 ISBN 0-86977-013-6 10.00
I. Title.
Available from Verry.

SONO, Tel, Miss. 922.
Tel Sono, the Japanese reformer; an autobiography. New York, Printed by Hunt & Eaton, 1890. 66 p. incl. front. (port.) 18 1/2 cm. Introduction by Hester Alway. [BV3457.S6A3] 7-13764
I. Alway, Hester. II. Title.

[STERN, Elizabeth Gertrude 922.
(Levin) Mrs. 1890-
I am a woman--and a Jew, by Leah Morton [pseud.] ... New York, J. H. Sears & company, inc. [c1926] 3 p. l., 362 p. 22 cm. [BM755.S7A3] 26-20742
I. Title.

TILAK, Lakshmibai (Gokhale) 922
1873-1936.
I follow after, an autobiography. Translated by E. Josephine Inkster. [Madras, New York] Indian Branch, Oxford University Press [1950] 353p. ports. 20cm. (Champak library) Translation of the first three parts of Smrti citrem, published in Marathi, 1964-37. Geneal. tables and map on lining paper. [BV3269.T57A38] 52-6050
I. Title.

USSHER, Elizabeth, 1772?- 922
1796.
Extracts from the letters of Elizabeth, Lucy, and Judith Ussher, late of the city of Waterford, Ireland. Philadelphia, For sale at Friend's book store [W. H. Pile, printer] 1871 iv, [5]-148 p. 19 1/2 cm. [BR1725.U8A4] 38-7137
I. Ussher, Lucy, 1776?-1797. II. Ussher, Judith, 1780?-1798. III. Title.

WALKER, Doak, 1927- 227.9633
Dork Walker, three-time all-American, by Dorothy Kendall Bracken as told by Doak Walker. Austin, Tex., Steck Co., [1950] ix, 258 p. illus., ports. 24 cm. [GV939.W3A3] 50-9513

I. Bracken, Dorothy Kendall. II. Title.

WALLBROOK, William, 1864?- 1899. 922
Diary of, and poems, by the late Rev. Wm. Wallbrook. College Point, N.Y., A. K. Schultz, 1900. 2 p. l., 127 p. port. 16 cm. [BV3785.W27A3] 1-29404
I. Title.

WESLEY, John, 1703-1791. 922.
An extract of the Rev. Mr. John Wesley's journals, Volume I. The 1st American ed. Philadelphia, Printed by Henry Tuckniss, no. 25, Churchvalley, and sold by John Dickins, no. 44, North Second street, near Arch street, MDCCXCV. 3 p. l., v-vi, 7-316 p. 17 cm. "It is our design to publish the whole of these journals, one volume at a time."--Advertisement. No more published. [BX8495.W5A2 1795] A34
I. Title.

WHITE, Joseph Blanco, 1775- 1841. 922.
...Extracts from Blanco White's Journal and letters... Boston, W. Crosby and H. P. Nichols, 1847. 52 p. 20 cm. (American Unitarian association. [Tracts] 1st ser., no. 237) [Name originally: Jose Maria Blanco y Crespo] [BX9869.W5A25 1847] 41-38428
I. Title.

WISE, Stephen Samuel, 1874-1949. 296.6'1'0924
Stephen S. Wise: Servant of the people. Selected letters edited by Carl Hermann Voss. Foreword, by Justine Wise Polier and James Waterman Wise. [1st ed.] Philadelphia, Jewish Publication Society of America, 1969. xxi, 332 p. ports. 22 cm. [BM755.W53A42] 69-13549 5.50
I. Voss, Carl Hermann, ed. II. Title.

WOODS, Margaret, 1748-1821. 922.
Extracts from the journal of the late Margaret Woods from the year 1771 to 1821. 3d ed. Philadelphia, H. Longstreth, 1850. 378 p. 21 cm. On spine: Journal of Margaret Woods. [BX7795.W65A3 1850] 49-42895
I. Title.

ZELLE, Margaretha Geertruida, 1876-1917. 940.3
The diary of Mata Hari. Translated, and with a preface, by Mark Alexander. Introd. by Hilary E. Holt. North Hollywood, Calif. [Brandon House, 1967] xxi, 248 p. 17 cm. (A Brandon House book) [D639.S8Z413] 261.7'0941 67-66264
I. Title.

Religious communities—New Zealand—Maungapohatu.

BINNEY, Judith Mary Caroline Musgrove. 299'.92
Mihaia : the prophet Rua Kenana and his community at Maungapohatu / Judith Binney, Gillian Chaplin, Craig Wallace. Wellington, N.Z. : Oxford University Press, c1979. 208 p. : ill. (some col.) ; 30 cm. Includes index. Bibliography: p. 203-204. [BL632.5.N45B56] 80-491906 ISBN 0-19-558042-7 : 31.00
1. Rua Kenana, 1869-1937. 2. Religious communities—New Zealand—Maungapohatu. 3. Maungapohatu, N.Z.—Religious life and customs. I. Chaplin, Gillian, 1948- II. Wallace, Craig. III. Title.
Distributed by Oxford University Press, New York.

Religious communities—United States.

BENHAM Club, Princeton, N. J. 207.749
The Benham Club of Princeton, New Jersey, organized, October 1879, incorporated, May 1905. Princeton, 1930. 70 p. plate, port. 24 cm. "The Benham song" (words and music): p. [22] [BV4070.P75B4] 51-51421
I. Blair, Roy, ed. II. Title.

BIERSDORF, John E., 1930- 200'.973
Hunger for experience : vital religious communities in America / John E. Biersdorf. New York : Seabury Press, [1975] p. cm. "A Crossroad book." [BL632.5.U5B53] 75-28079 ISBN 0-8164-1198-0 : 7.95
1. Religious communities—United States. 2. Religious and ecclesiastical institutions—United States. I. Title.

FRACCHIA, Charles A., 1937- 291.4
Living together alone : the new American monasticism / Charles A. Fracchia. 1st ed. San Francisco : Harper & Row, c1979. 186 p. : ill. ; 20 cm. Bibliography: p. [185]-186. [BL632.5.U5F7] 78-3362 ISBN 0-06-063011-6 pbk. : 5.95
1. Religious communities—United States. 2. Monasticism and religious orders—United States. I. Title.

METROPOLITAN church association. 289.9
Discipline of the Metropolitan church assn. of Wisconsin, adapted Nov. 15, 1930. [Waukesha, Wis., c1931] 64 p. 19 cm. [BX8500.M3A5 1931] 31-24274
I. Title.

MUNTSCH, Albert, 1873- 248
Conferences for religious communities, by Albert Muntsch ... St. Louis, Mo. and London, B. Herder book co., 1928. 4 p. l., 249 p. 20 cm. [BX2385.M82] 28-20329
I. Title.

SKELLY, Andrew M. 271.
Conferences on the interior life for sisterhoods ... by the Rev. A. M. Skelly ... St. Louis, Mo., and London, B. Herder book co., 1928. 2 v. 19 1/2 cm. These volumes are in good part an adaptation and an abridgment of Theologie useetique et mystique, by Andrew Marie Maynard and Mystien theologia, by Thomas A. Vallgornera. cf. Foreword. [BX4210.S57] 28-12836
I. Title.

SKELLY, Andrew M. 271.
Conferences on the religious life for sisterhoods, by the Reverend A. M. Skelly, O.P. St. Louis, Mo., and London, B. Herder book co., 1927. viii, 271 p. 19 1/2 cm. [BX4210.S6] 27-9986
I. Title. II. Title: The religious life for sisterhoods, Conferences on.

Religious dance, Modern.

TAYLOR, Margaret Fisk. 246.7
The art of the rhythmic choir; worship through symbolic movement, by Margaret Palmer Fisk. Illus. by Lois-Louise Hines. [1st ed.] New York, Harper [1950] xi, 205 p. illus. 22 cm. Bibliography: p. 203-205. [GV1783.5.T28] 50-9694
1. Religious dance, Modern. I. Title. II. Title: The rhythmic choir.

TAYLOR, Margaret Fisk. 246.7
Look up and live, by Margaret Palmer Fisk. [1st ed.] Saint Paul, Macalester Park Pub. Co. [1953] 97, [2] p. illus. 29 cm. Includes hymns, with music. Bibliography: p. [99] [GV1783.T38] 54-36207
1. Religious dance, Modern. I. Title.

TAYLOR, Margaret Fisk. 246'.7
A time to dance; symbolic movement in worship. Philadelphia, United Church Press [1967] 180 p. illus., facsims. 21 cm. Bibliography: p. 177-180. [GV1783.5.T3] 67-21103
1. Religious dance, Modern. I. Title.

Religious drama.

AMMERMAN, Leila Tremaine 394.268
Programs for special days. Natick, Mass., Wilde [c.1961] 76p. 61-17635 2.00
1. Religious drama. 2. Schools—Exercises and recreations. I. Title.

AMMERMAN, Leila Tremaine. 394.268
Programs for speical days. Natick, Mass., W. A. Wilde Co. [1961] 76p. 20cm. [PN6120.R4A48] 61-17635
1. Religious drama. 2. Schools—Exercises and recreations. I. Title.

ATKINS, Alma Newell. Mrs. 792
Drama goes to church [by] Alma Newell Atkins. St. Louis, The Bethany press [c1931] 196 p. incl. front., illus. 19 cm. Bibliography at end of each chapter except chapter x. [BV1472.A8] 31-30535
1. Religious drama. 2. Drama in education. I. Title.

BIBLE. O. T. English. Selections. 1935. 792.1
Old Testament drama; or, Dramatic readings from Hebrew literature, selected and edited by M. W. Thomas ... London, New York [etc.] T. Nelson & sons, ltd. [1935] xi, 11-198 p. incl. front. 16 cm. (Half-title: The "Teaching of English" series: general ed., Richard Wilson. no. 112) "First published, July 1927; reprinted ... September 1935." [PN6120.R4B47 1935] 41-236
1. Religious drama. I. Thomas, M. W., ed. II. Bible. English. Selections. O. T. 1935. III. Title.

BROWN, Thelma Sharman, ed. 792.1
Treasury of religious plays. Introd. by Harold Ehrensperger. New York, Association Press [1947] xiii. 345 p. 22 cm. [PN6120.R4B82] 47-11234
1. Religious drama. I. Title.
Contents omitted.

CARUS, Paul, 1852-
The Buddha; a drama in three acts and four interludes, by Paul Carus ... Chicago, The Open court publishing co., 1911. iv, 68 p. 20 cm. 11-12509
I. Title.

CHILD, Charlotte Hoyt. 791.6
... Throughout all generations; a Whitsuntide drama, by Charlotte Hoyt Child. Hartford, Conn., Church missions publishing company, 1939. cover-title, 24 p. 19 cm. (The church in story and pageant, no. 62) [BR156.C45] 40-30001
I. Title.

COPENHAVER, Laura Scherer. 266
The way; a pageant of Japan, by Laura Scherer Copenhaver [and] Katharine Scherer Cronk. Philadelphia, Pa., Literature headquarters, Women's missionary society of the United Lutheran church in America [1923] 12 p. 23 cm. "Japanese national anthem" with music: p. 6. [BV2086.C6] ca 24
I. Cronk, Katherine (Scherer) Mrs. 1877- joint author. II. Title.

CURRY, Louise H. 792.1
Worship services using the arts. by Louise H. Curry, Chester M. Wetzel. Philadelphia, Westminster Pr. [c.1961] 251p. Bibl. 61-6230 4.50 bds.,
1. Religious drama. I. Wetzel, Chester M., joint author. II. Title.

EASTMAN, Fred, 1886-
Drama in the church; a manual of religious drama production, by Fred Eastman and Louis Wilson. New York, Samuel French [1960] xi, 187 p. illus. Includes bibliography. 67-86259
1. Religious drama. 2. Amateur theatricals. I. Wilson, Louis, 1899- II. Title.

EASTMAN, Fred, 1886- ed. 792.1
Ten one-act plays, selected and edited by Fred Eastman ... Chicago, New York, Willett, Clark & company, 1937. xii, 230 p. 20 1/2 cm. [PN6120.R4E28] 37-28748
1. Religious drama. 2. American drama (Collections) I. Title.

ECKARDT, Frances Dyer. 812.5
The kingdom of God; a missionary play in one acts, by Frances Dyer Eckardt. Boston, Mass., and Los Angeles, Cal., [Walter H. Baker company, c1936] 26 p. 19 cm. [BV2086.E35] CA36
I. Title.

EDLAND, Elisabeth. 264
The children's King and other plays for children, with chapters on dramatizing with children, by Elisabeth Edland. New York, Cincinnati, The Abingdon press [c1928] 78 p. 19 cm. Music: p. 42. Bibliography: p. 74-79. [BV1472.E15] 28-6204
1. Religious drama. 2. Children's plays. I. Title.

EDLAND, Elisabeth. 268.
... Principles and technique in religious dramatics, by Elisabeth Edland; approved by the Committee on curriculum of the Board of education of the Methodist Episcopal Church. New York, Cincinnati, The methodist book concern [c1926] 87 p. 19 cm. (Training courses for leadership) Bibliography: p. 85-87. [BV1575.E3] 26-17601
1. Religious drama. I. Title.

EDWARDS, Elizabeth 264
Sound his glories forth; religious programs for churches and schools. by Elizabeth Edwards, Gladys Besancon. Grand Rapids, Mich., Baker Bk. [c.]1965. 172p. 23cm. [PN6120.R4E37] 65-2258 3.95
1. Religious drama. I. Besancon, Gladys, joint author. II. Title.

HERON, Henrietia. ed. 268.
Christian Endeavor playlets, short, bright, different, edited by Henrietta Heron. Cincinnati, O., The Standard publishing company [c1928] 158 p. 23 cm. [BV1575.H37] 29-1038
1. Religious drama. I. Title.

HOENSHEL, Elmer Ulysses, 1864- 232.
The Bethlehem drama (in five acts) by Elmer U. Hoenshel... Staunton, Va., The McClure co., inc. [c1923] 32 p. incl. col. front. 20 1/2 cm. [BT315.H6] 24-3947
I. Title.

JONES, Henry Arthur, 1851-
Judah; an original play in three acts, by Henry Arthur Jones ... New York and London, Macmillan and co., 1894. xxiii, 104 p. 18 cm. [PR4827.J7 1894] 13-24219
I. Title.

LEONARD, Jim. 812'.54
The diviners : a play in two acts & elegies / by Jim Leonard, Jr. New York : S. French, c1981. 97 p. ; 19 cm. [PS3562.E559D5] 19 81-186012 ISBN 0-573-60837-7 pbk.: 3.00
I. Title.

LITCHFIELD, Grace Denio, 1849-
The nun of Kent; a drama in five acts, by Grace Denio Litchfield ... New York and London, G. P. Putnam's sons, 1911. 3 p. l., 125 p. 18 cm. 11-29629 1.00.
I. Title.

LOCKHART, Jennie Clare (Fagen) Mrs. d.1938. 792.1
Dramas for church services, by Jennie Clare Lockhart. Cincinnati, O., The Standard publishing company [c1939] 128 p. 24 cm. [PN6120.R4L56] 40-6167
1. Religious drama. I. Title.

METHODIST Episcopal church. Division of plays and pageants. 264
Seven dramatic services of worship, prepared by the Division of plays and pageants of the Methodist Episcopal church. New York, Cincinnati [etc.] The Methodist book concern [c1928] 63 p. diagrs. 23 cm. [BV1472.M4] 29-6963
1. Religious drama. I. Title.

MILLER, Sarah Walton 792.1
Acting out the truth; dramatic features for group worship. Nashville, Broadman [c.1961] 120p. 61-12415 2.50
1. Religious drama. I. Title.

MOODY, William Vaughn, 1869- 1910.
The faith healer; a play in four acts, by William Vaughn Moody. Boston and New York, Houghton Mifflin company, 1909. 4 p. l., [3]-160 p., 1 l. 21 cm. [PS2427.F3 1909] 9-1588
I. Title.

MOODY, William Vaughn, 1869- 1910.
The faith healer; a play in three acts, by William Vaughn Moody ... New York, The Macmillan company, 1910. 4 p. l., 3-164 p. 19 cm. [PS2427.F3] 10-5871
I. Title.

OGILVIE, Glencairn Stuart, 1858-
Hypatia, a play in four acts; founded on Charles Kingsley's novel of that name, by G. Stuart Ogilvie. First performed at the Theater Royal, Haymarket, London, January 2, 1893. Rahway, N. J., The Mershon company, 1894. 4 p. l., 63 p. 19 cm. [PR4842.H85O5] 25-24736
I. Kingsley, Charles, 1819-1875. II. Title.

OSGOOD, Phillips Endecott, 1882-
Pulpit dramas; a series of dramatizations for church, pulpit or parish house use, by Rev. phillips Endecott Osgood ... New York and London, Harper & brothers, 1929. xxxi p., 2 l., 3-191 [1] p. front., plates 19 cm. "First edition." [PN6120.R4O67] 29-9917
1. Religious drama. I. Title.

THE Prince of Peace;
a nativity play. [1st 1644-1718.
I. Peareth, V D

RAJA-SEKHARA, ca.880- ca.920. 294.
Raja-cekhara's Karpura-manjari; a drama by the Indian poet Rajacekhara (about 900 A.D.) critically edited in the original Prakrit, with a glossarial index, and an essay on the life and writings of the poet by Sten Konow ... and translated into English with notes by Charles Rockwell Lanman ... Cambridge, Mass., Harvard university, 1901. xxvi p., 1 l., 289 p. 26 1/2 cm. (Added t.-p.: Harvard Oriental series, vol. IV) "Chronological list of books and papers concerning Rajacekhara": p. 175-177. [PK2971.H3 vol. 4] 3-19856
I. Konow, Sten, 1867- ed. II. Lanman, Charles Rockwell, 1850-1941, ed. III. Title.

RELIGIOUS drama. 808.82
1- New York, Meridian Books, 1957- v. 18cm. (Living age books) Vols. 1- 'selected and introduced by Marvin Halverson.' [PN6120.R4A18] 57-6684
1. Religious drama. I. Halverson, Marvin.

RELIGIOUS drama 3. 808.82
The last word, The house by the stable, Grab and grace, Santa Claus, Let man live, It should happen to a dog, Billy Budd, The gospel witch. Selected and introduced by Marvin Halverson. [Gloucester, Mass., Peter Smith, 1960, c.1959] 314p. 19cm. (Meridian paperback rebound in cloth) 3.50
1. Religious drama. I. Halverson, Marvin.

RELIGIOUS drama 3, 808.82
New York, Meridian Books [c.1959] 314p. 19cm. (Living age books, LA27) Vols. 1- 'selected and introduced by Marvin Halverson.' 57-6684 1.45 pap.,
1. Religious drama. I. Halverson, Marvin.

ST. Clair, Robert, 1898- 812.52
Religious plays for amateur players. Minneapolis, Denison [c.1964] 390p. illus. 22cm. 64-22879 4.95
1. Religious drama. I. Title.

ST. Clair, Robert, 1898- 812.52
Religious plays for amateur players. Minneapolis, T.S. Denison [1964] 390 p. illus. 22 cm. [PN6120.R4S27] 64-22879
1. Religious drama. I. Title.

SHANNON, Mattie Bayly, 1885- ed. 792.1
Religious dramas for worship and service, edited by Mattie B. Shannon. Baltimore, Md, The stockton press [c1938] 216 p. 20 cm. [PN6120.R4S46] 38-15236
1. Religious drama. I. Title.

SMITH, John N. 245.
Ramanzo, the conscience stricken brigand. A tragic play. In five acts. By John N. Smith. New York, Printed for the author, 1840. 2 p. l., [7]-74 p. 16 cm. [PS2869.S265] 1-3840
I. Title.

SPENCER, Edna Earle Cole.
The Good Samaritan and other Biblical stories, dramatized by Edna Earle Cole Spencer. Illustrated with photographs by Harold Wagner. New York, Doran [c1915] xiii, [14]-126 p. front., 3 pl. 19 1/2 cm. A 22
1. Religious drama. 2. Children's plays. I. Title.

SWITZ, Theodore MacLean, ed. 808.82
Great Christian plays; a collection of classical religious plays in acting versions and of selected choral readings suitable for a worship service, edited by Theodore MacLean Switz and Robert A. Johnston. Greenwich, Conn., Seabury Press, 1956. xii, 306 p. illus. 25 cm. "Music [for piano] appropriate for these plays has been composed by Thomas Matthews." Errata slip inserted. Contents.PARTIAL CONTENTS. -- The Brome Abraham and Isaac. -- The York Resurrection. -- The Digby Conversion of St. Paul. -- Totentanz, a morality play. -- Everyman, a morality play. [PN6120.R4S94] 56-7971
1. Religious drama. 2. Choral recitations. I. Johnston, Robert A., joint ed. II. Matthews, Thomas, musician. III. Title.

WHEAT, Carl I.
The gods are good; a play in three acts and an epilogue, by Carl I. Wheat; written for and presented by the class of 1915, Pomona college, Greek theatre, Claremont, Cal., June 15, 1915. [Pomona, Cal., King printing company, c1915] 68 p. incl. front., plan, plates. 19 cm. [PS635.Z9W555] 15-17311 0.25
I. Title.

WHEELER, Lee. 244
They forgot the debt, three-act religious drama for amateur production, by Lee Wheeler ... Franklin, O., Denver, Colo., Eldridge entertainment house, inc., c1927. 11 p.19 1/2 cm. (On cover: Eldridge church entertainments) [PN6120.R4W4] 37-37268
I. Title.

WHITING, Isabel Kimball, Mrs. 268.
Dramatic services of worship, by Isabel Kimball Whiting; introduction by Samuel McChord Crothers... Boston, Mass., The Beacon press, inc., 1925. xiii, 220 p. front., pl. 23 1/2 cm. [BV1575.W45] 25-22769
1. Religious drama. I. Title.

WILLCOX, Helen Lida, 1883- 266
Tides of India; a pageant-play, by Helen L. Willcox. New York, Cincinnati, The Abingdon press [c1923] 24 p. illus. 23 cm. [BV2086.W67] 23-17701
I. Title.

WOOD, William Carleton, 1880- 268.67
... The dramatic method in religious education [by] W. Carleton Wood ... New York, Cincinnati [etc.] The Abingdon press [c1931] 344 p. illus., plates, diagrs. 20 cm. (The Abingdon religious education texts: J. W. Langdale, general editor. College series: G. H. Betts, editor) Bibliography: p. 319-330. [BV1575.W6] [792] 31-15434
1. Religious drama. 2. Religious education. 3. Drama in education. 4. Amateur theatricals. I. Title.

Religious drama, American.

JOHNSON, Albert. 792.102
Church plays and how to stage them. Introd. by R. H. Edwin Espy. Philadelphia, United Church Press [1966] xviii, 174 p. 21 cm. Part II (p. 87-174): Three church plays: Journey to judgment. The innocent. Everyman. [PN6120.R4J49] 66-17661
1. Religious drama, American. 2. Religious drama — Presentation, etc. I. Title.

JONES, Henry Arthur, 1851-1929.
The divine gift; a play in three acts, by Henry Arthur Jones. New York, George H. Doran company, 1913. 178 p., 1 l. 20 cm. [PR4827.D5 1913] 13-13544
I. Title.

JONES, Henry Arthur, 1851-1929.
The divine gift; a play in three acts, by Henry Arthur Jones. New York, George H. Doran company, 1913. 178 p., 1 l. 20 cm. [PR4827.D5 1913] 13-13544
I. Title.

JUDAH, Samuel Benjamin Herbert.
The Rose of Arragon; or, The vigil of St. Mark: a melo-drama, in two acts. By Samuel B. H. Judah ... As performed ... at the New-York theatre ... Music by Taylor. New-York, Printed and pub. by S. King, 1822. 38 p. 18 cm. On cover: 2d ed. [PS635.Z9J925] 1-1373
I. Title.

KELLY, Francis J. 791.6
A divine child is born, a nativity play in one act, seven scenes, by Rev. Francis J. Kelly, S.J., with a foreword by Rev. Francis L. Archdeacon, S.J. ... St. Louis, Mo., The Qusen's work [1945] 23, [1] p. 19 cm. "First printing." [PN6120.C5K36] 46-2954
I. Title.

KELLY, Francis J. 791.6
A divine child is born, a nativity play in one act, seven scenes, by Rev. Francis J. Kelly, S.J., with a foreword by Rev. Francis L. Archdeacon, S.J. ... St. Louis, Mo., The Qusen's work [1945] 23, [1] p. 19 cm. "First printing." [PN6120.C5K36] 46-2954
I. Title.

ME either ..... and other one-act plays : 812'.041
seven reflective dramas that invite new thought about old religious questions / edited by Jerry O'Malley. St. Louis : Bethany Press, c1976. 44 p. : ill. ; 23 cm. Contents.Contents.—Me either.—Time of the stranger.—A conversation on the way home.—A dialogue: black and white.—The Indian was restless.—Gr-r-eat!—The deserter. [PS627.R4M4] 76-40281 ISBN 0-8272-2311-0 pbk. : 1.95
1. Religious drama, American. 2. One-act plays, American. I. O'Malley, Jerry.

ROCKWELL, Ethel Theodora. 266
The apostles of light; a religious pageant-drama of the centenary movement, by Ethel Theodora Rockwell. Nashville, Tenn., Missionary centenary, Methodist Episcopal church, South [c1923] 54 p., 1 l. 24 1/2 cm. [BV2086.R6] 23-17329
I. Title.

YELVINGTON, Ramsey, 1913- ed.
Dramatic images [plays] for the church. 9 plays, 3 choral readings, edited by Ramsey Yelvington, with Mary Anna Branson, production, with Gene McKinney, advisor and Paul Baker, director. [Waco, Tex.] Baylor Theater, 1959. 1 v. (various pagings) 28 cm. (Baylor Theater church play series, v. 1)
1. Religious drama, American. I. Baylor University, Waco, Tex. Theater. II. Title. III. Series.

Religious drama — Bibliography

EHRENSPERGER, Harold Adam, 1897- 016.822
A dramatic calendar for churches; suggestions for dramatic programs for outstanding events in each month, compiled by Harold A. Ehrensperger ... Chicago, Ill, International council of religious education [c1937] 68 p. 23 cm. "Reprinted from the International journal of religious education for September, 1936 to July, 1937." [Z5784.R3E3] 37-33889
1. Religious drama—Bibl. I. Title.

ENTERLINE, Mildred Hahn. 016.7921
Best plays for the church. New ed. Philadelphia, Christian Education Press [c1959] 90 p. 22 cm. A62
1. Religious drama — Bibl. I. Title.

JOHNSON, Albert. 016.80882'9
Best church plays; a bibliography of religious drama. [Magnolia, Mass., Peter Smith, 1968] viii, 180p. 21cm (Pilgrim Pr. bk. rebound) [Z5784.R3J6] 6.00
1. Religious drama—Bibl. I. Title.

Religious drama-Collections.

RELIGIOUS plays that click.
[2d ed] Grand Rapids, Mich., Zondervan [1956, c1954] 91p.
1. Religious drama-Collections. I. Bryant, Al, 1926- comp.

Religious drama, German—Bibliography

RUDWIN, Maximilian Josef, 1885- 016.
... A historical and bibliographical survey of the German religious drama, by Maximilian J. Rudwin ... Pittsburgh, University of Pittsburgh, 1924. xxiii, 286 p. 24 cm. (University of Pittsburgh studies in language and literature) Preface in English, Einleitung and explanatory notes in German. [Z2234.D7R9] 25-320
1. Religious drama, German—Bibl. 2. German drama—Medieval—Bibl. 3. Mysteries and miracle-plays, German—Bibl. I. Title.
Contents omitted.

Religious drama—History and criticism

BLOOR, Robert Henry Underwood. 809.2'51
Christianity and the religious drama, by R. H. U. Bloor. Boston, The Beacon Press, 1930. [Folcroft, Pa.] Folcroft Library Editions, 1973. p. Original ed. issued as The Essex Hall lecture, 1928. [PN1880.B5 1973] 73-261 ISBN 0-8414-1425-4 (lib. bdg.)
1. Religious drama—History and criticism. 2. Drama, Medieval—History and criticism. I. Title. II. Series: The Essex Hall lecture, 1928.

HATFIELD, Louis Duane. 253.5
As the twig is bent; therapeutic values in the use of drama and the dramatic in the church. [1st ed.] New York, Vantage Press [1965] 166 p. 22 cm. Includes bibliographical references. [BV1534.4.H3] 65-4363
1. Religious drama — Hist. & crit. 2. Psychodrama. I. Title.

HAUGHTON, Rosemary, 1927- 809.2'51
The drama of salvation / Rosemary Haughton. New York : Seabury Press, [1975] x, 148 p. ; 22 cm. "A Crossroad book." [PN1880.H35] 75-14301 ISBN 0-8164-1201-4 : 6.95
1. Religious drama—History and criticism. 2. Salvation in literature. I. Title.

RELIGIOUS drama. 809.2'51
Editor-in-chief: Alfred Bates. Associate editors: James P. Boyd [and] John P. Lamberton. New York, AMS Press [1970] iii, 344 p. illus. 23 cm. Reprint of the 1903 ed., which was issued as v. 4 of The Drama. Includes the text of Belshazzar's feast, from the Spanish of Calderon; The ceremony of the printer's apprentice, a German morality play, by W. Blades; and Every-man, a morality, by Thomas Hawkins. [PN1880.R34 1970] 72-191945 ISBN 0-404-02194-8
1. Religious drama—History and criticism. I. Bates, Alfred, ed. II. Series: The Drama, v. 4.

SPEAIGHT, Robert, 1904- 809.25
Christian theatre. [1st ed.] New York, Hawthorn Books [1960] 140 p. 21 cm. (The Twentieth century encyclopedia of Catholicism, v. 124. Section 12: Catholicism and the arts) Includes bibliographies. [PM1880.S6] 60-13058
1. Religious drama — Hist. & crit. 2. Religion in drama. I. Title.

Religious drama—Presentation, etc.

[LANE, Margaret] 1874- 792
Through the Eye-gate into the city of Mansoul; a primer on the principles and the production of religious drama, by Mildred Welch [pseud.] Louisville, Ky., Department of Christian education of the Presbyterian church in the United States [c1927] 141 p. illus. 20 cm. Bibliography: p. 137-141. [BV1472.L3] 27-13840
1. Religious drama—Presentation, etc. 2. Amateur theatricals. I. Title.

Religious drama, Spanish-American.

CORREA, Gustavo. 330.972
The Native theatre in middle America. [By] Gustavo Correa [and others] New Orleans, 1961. 292 p. illus., port., map, facsims. 27 cm. (Tulane University. Middle American Research Institute. Publication 27) English or Spanish. Music for the Dance of the conquest, for piano: p. [267]-[280] Includes bibliographies. [F1421.T95] 63-24346
1. Religious drama, Spanish-American. 2. Folk-drama, Spanish-American. I. Title. II. Series: Tulane University of Louisiana. Middle American Research Institute. Publication 27
Contents omitted.

Religious education.

ACHESON, Edna Lucile, 1891- 268.
The construction of junior church school curricula by Edna Lucile Acheson... New York city, Teachers college, Columbia university, 1929. viii, 185 p. 23 1/2 cm. (Teachers college, Columbia university, Contributions to education, no. 331) Published also as thesis (PH. D.) Columbia university. "Summary of books examined": p. 7. [BV1546.A4] [LB5.C3 no. 331] 371. 29-11485
1. Religious education. 2. Bible—Study. I. Title. II. Title: Church school curricula, The construction of junior. III. Title: Junior church school curricula. The consturction of.

ADAMS, Rachel Swann 268.43
The small church and Christian education. Philadelphia, Westminster Press [c.1961] 75p. illus. Bibl. 61-8764 1.00 pap.,
1. Religious education. I. Title.

AMERICAN Sunday-school union.
The infant school teacher's assistant; embracing a course of moral and religious instruction, adapted to the minds of the children, and designed to draw answers from them. Prepared for the American Sunday-school union, and rev. by the Committee of publication. Philadelpnia, American Sunday-School union, 1833. 116 p. 22 cm. [LC361.A3] E 10
1. Religious education. I. Title.

ANDERSON, Arlene May 268.61
(Anderson) Mrs. 1895.
The kindergarten course for Sunday schools, by Arlene M. Anderson ... Minneapolis, Minn., Augsburg publishing house [c1935-36] 2 v. illus. (part col.) plates. 23 cm. "Prepared under the supervision of the Board of elementary Christian education."--Publishers' preface. Includes music. Contents.--[v. 1] Old Testament.--[v. 2] New Testament. [BV1540.A6] 38-29581
1. Religious education. I. Norwegian Lutheran church of America. Board of elementary Christian education. II. Title.

ANDERSON, Phoebe M. 268
Living and learning in the church school. Boston, Pub. for the Cooperative Pubn. Assn. [by] United Church Pr. [c.1965] viii, 102p. 19cm. (Cooperative ser.) Bibl. [BV1471.2.A5] 65-15198 1.25 pap.,
1. Religious education. I. Title.

ANDERSON, Phoebe M 268
Living and learning in the church school, by Phoebe M. Anderson. Boxton, Published for the Cooperative Publication Association [by] United Church Press [1965] viii, 102 p. 19 cm. (The Cooperative series) Bibliography: p. 100-102. [BV1471.2.A5] 65-15198
1. Religious education. I. Title.

ANDREWS, Matthew T 1865- 268.434
Adults and the art of learning, by Matthew T. Andrews, D.D. Nashville, Tenn., Broadman press [c1936] 123 p. 18 1/2 cm. [BV1550.A5] 37-1315
1. Religious education. 2. Education of adults. I. Title.

ANTHONY, Charles Volney.
The children's covenant, by C.V. Anthony, D.D. Cincinnati, Jennings & Pye; New York, Eaton & Mains, [1901.] 240 p. 19 cm. 2-1795
1. Religious education. 2. Education of children. I. Title.
Contents omitted.

ARNOLD, Helena. 133
Teachings on divine law, written for students of the plan by Helena Arnold. [Kansas City, Mo., Punton bros. pub. co., c1924] 305 p. 23 1/2 cm. [BF1999.A65] 24-12634
I. Title.

ASPER, Wallace J 268.4
How to organize the education program of your church: a planbook for the Committee on Parish Education. Minneapolis, Augsburg Pub. Co. [1959] 67p. illus. 20cm. Includes bibliography. [BV1471.A67] 59-12117
1. Religious education. I. Title.

ATHEARN, Clarence Royalty, 268.69
1895-
Discussing religion creatively, the use of the discussion method in religious education, by Clarence R. Athearn ... and Laura Armstrong Athearn ... New York [etc.] Fleming H. Revell company [c1939] 220 p. incl. forms. 21 cm. "Suggested references for further study" at end of each chapter. [BV1472.A77] 30-2573
1. Religious education. 2. Debates and debating. I. Athearn, Laura (Armstrong) Mrs. joint author. II. Title.

ATHEARN, Clarence Royalty, 268.69
1895-
Discussing religion creatively, the use of the discussion method in religious education, by Clarence R. Athearn ... and Laura Armstrong Athearn ... New York [etc.] Fleming H. Revell company [c1939] 220 p. incl. forms. 21 cm. "Suggested references for further study" at end of each chapter. [BV1472.A77] 30-2573
1. Religious education. 2. Debates and debating. I. Athearn, Laura (Armstrong) Mrs. joint author. II. Title.

ATHEARN, Walter Scott, 1872- 268
The church school, by Walter S. Athearn ... Boston, New York [etc.] The Pilgrim press [c1914] xv, 309 p. front. (plan) plates. 20 cm. Contains bibliographies. [BV1520.A67] 14-13408
1. Religious education. 2. Sunday-schools. I. Title.

ATHEARN, Walter Scott, 1872- 262.
The city institute for religious teachers, by Walter Scott Athearn ... Chicago, Ill., The University of Chicago press [c1915] xiv, 151 p. 18 cm. (Half-title: The University of Chicago publication in religious education) Contains bibliographies. [BV1533.A7] 15-6030
1. Religious education. I. Title.

ATHEARN, Walter Scott, 1872- 377.
... *The correlation of church schools and public schools,* by Walter S. Athearn ... [Malden, Mass., Malden school of religious education, c1917] 2 p. l., 3-59 p., 1 l. 19 cm. (Malden leaflets, no. 2) Contains bibliographies. [LC405.A7] 17-5147 0.25
1. Religious education. I. Title.

ATHEARN, Walter Scott, 1872- 377.
... *The correlation of church schools and public schools,* by Walter S. Athearn ... [Malden, Mass., Malden school of religious education, c1917] 2 p. l., 3-59 p., 1 l. 19 cm. (Malden leaflets, no. 2) Contains bibliographies. [LC405.A7] 17-5147 0.25
1. Religious education. I. Title.

ATHEARN, Walter Scott, 377.1
1872-
The minister and the teacher; an interpretation of current trends in Christian education by Walter Schoot Athearn ... New York, London, The Century co. [c1932] xiii, 274 p. 20 cm. "The Duncan lectures, in the Louisville Presbyterian theological seminary for the year 1930."--p. [v] "Notes": p. 253-266. [BV1471.A75 1932] 32-18849 2.00
1. Religious education. 2. Universities and colleges—U. S. 3. Theology, Pastoral. I. Louisville Presbyterian theological seminary (1901-) William G. Duncan lectureship in religious education. II. Title.

AYRE, G. B.
Suggestions for a syllabus in religious teaching, by G. B. Ayer; with an introduction by M. E. Sadler, Ll.D. London, New York [etc.] Longmans, Green and co., 1911. xv, 147, 28 p. 20 cm. "A suggested teachers reference library": p. 27, at end. [LC368.A7] E 11
1. Religious education. I. Title.

*BABIN, Pierre 238
Teaching religion to adolescents [by] Pierre Babin, J. P. Bagot. New York, Sadlier [1967] 99p. 21cm. Tr. and adaptation from French of two works by Pierre Babin & J. P. Bagot. 2.66 pap.,
1. Religious education. I. Bagot, J. P., joint author. II. Title.

BABINGTON, Thomas. 268.
A practical view of Christian education. From the 7th London ed. By T. Babington ...With a preliminary essay. By Rev. T. H. Gallaudet. 4th American ed. Hartford, Cooke and co., 1831. 1 p. l., 11, 212 p. 16 cm. [BV1475.B2 1831] 7-36689
1. Religious education. I. Gullaudet, Thomas Hopkins, 1787-1851. II. Title.

BABINGTON, Thomas. 268.
A practical view of Christian education in its earliest stages By T. Babington ... 1st American from the 3d London ed. To which are added translations of the Latin sentences and notes. Boston: Published by Cummings and Hilliard, Boston Bookstore, no. 1, Cornhill, 1818. viii, [13]-196 p. 19 cm. [BV1475.B2 1818] 10-9908
1. Religious education. I. Title.

BABINGTON, Thomas.
A practical view of Christian education in its earliest stages. By T. Babington ... 3d American from the 3d London ed. To which are added translations of the Latin sentences, and notes. Boston, Cummings and Hilliard, 1819. viii, [9]-188 p. 18 cm. [BV147.B2 1819] 7-36633
1. Religious education. I. Title.

BAIR, Hazel. 268.
A new way to teach juniors, captivating--stimulating--different, Hazel Bair ... Cincinnati, O., The Standard publishing company [c1929] 55 p. illus. 23 cm. [BV1546.B25] 29-8856
1. Religious education. I. Title.

BAKER, Clara Belle. 268.
... *Everyday lessons in religion* ... teacher's manual, by Clara Belle Baker. New York, Cincinnati, The Abingdon press [c1922] 196 p. front. 21 cm. (The Abingdon religious education texts, David J. Downey, general editor. Week-day school series, George Herbert Betts, editor) Bibliography: p. 191-196. [BV1534.B25] 22-17797
1. Religious education. 2. Sunday-schools. I. Title.
Contents omitted.

BALDWIN, Maud Junkin. 268.
... *The Heavenly Father and His children* ... by Maud Junkin Baldwin ... Philadelphia, Pa., The United Lutheran publication house [c1927] 160 p. 23 cm. (Religious education texts for vacation schools. First book) [BV1585.B3] 27-11510
1. Religious education. I. Title.

BALDWIN, Maud Junkin. 268.
... *Jesus and His lollowers* ... by Maud Junkin Baldwin ... Philadelphia, Pa., The United Lutheran publication house [c1929] 3 p. l., 5-175 p. 24 cm. (Religious education texts for vacation schools. Third book. Primary-third year) [BV1585.B315] 29-10664
1. Religious education. I. Title.

BALDWIN, Maud Junkin. 268.
... *Serving the Heavenly Father* ... by Maud Junkin Baldwin ... Philadelphia, Pa., The United Lutheran publication house [c1928] 174 p. 24 cm. (Religious education texts for vacation schools. Second book. Primary--second year) [BV1585.B32] 28-14560
1. Religious education. I. Title.

BALDWIN, Maud Junkin. 268.
... *Stories of early church heroes* ... by Maud Junkin Baldwin ... Philadelphia, Pa., The United Lutheran publication house [c1929] 189 p. illus. 24 cm. (Religious education texts for vacation schools. Sixth book. Junior-third year) Includes music. [BV1585.B285] 29-10661
1. Religious education. I. Title.

BALDWIN, Maud Junkin. 268.
... *Stories of Jesus* ... by Maud Jenkin Baldwin ... Philadelphia, Pa., The United Lutheran publication house [c1928] 189 p. illus. (incl. maps) 24 cm. (Religious education texts for vacation schools. Fifth book. Junior--second year) [BV1585.B34] 28-14561
1. Religious education. 2. Jesus Christ—Biog. I. Title.

BALDWIN, Maud Junkin. 268.
... *Stories of the early Hebrew heroes* ... by Maud Junkin Baldwin ... Philadelphia, Pa., The United Lutheran publication house [c1928] 191 p. illus. 24 cm. (Religious education texts for vacation schools. Fourth book. Junior-first year) [BV1585.B33] 28-12094
1. Religious education. 2. Bible. O. T.—Biog. I. Title.

BALL, Elsie. 377.1
... *Living to-day and to-morrow* [by] Elsie Ball. New York, Cincinnati [etc.] The Abingdon press [c1932] 143 p. 20 cm. (The Abingdon religious education texts, J. W. Langdale, general editor; Week-day school series, G. H. Betts, editor) [BV1583.B3] 32-22363
I. Title.

BALL, Elsie. 377.1
... *Living to-day and to-morrow;* teacher's manual [by] Elsie Ball. New York, Cincinnati [etc.] The Abingdon press [c1932] 128 p. 20 cm. (The Abingdon religious education texts, J. W. Langdale, general editor; Week-day school series, G. H. Betts, editor) Includes bibliographies. [BV1563.B32] 32-22964
1. Religious education. I. Title.

BAN, Joseph D. 268'.01
Education for change [by] Joseph D. Ban. Valley Forge, Pa., Judson Press [1968] 126 p. illus. 22 cm. Bibliography: p. 123-126. [BV1471.B23] 68-14562
1. Religious education. I. Title.

BARBOUR, Dorothy Dickinson 268
Mrs.
Making the Bible desired. by Dorothy Dickinson Barbour ... Garden City, N.Y., Doubleday, Doran & company, inc., 1928. xii, 146 p. 19 1/2 cm. "Classified list of books": p. 135-146. [BV1471.B25] 28-10408
1. Religious education 2. Missions—China. I. Title.

BARBOUR, Dorothy 268.61
(Dickinson) Mrs.
Working in the church; a third grade course, by Dorothy Dickinson Barbour. New York, Morehouse-Gorham co., 1938. 150 p. 22 cm. Includes bibliographies. [BV1545.B35] 38-34979
1. Religious education. I. Title.

BARCLAY, Wade Crawford, 268.
1874-
The principles of religious teaching, by Wade Crawford Barclay. New York, Cincinnati, The Methodist book concern [c1920] 132 p. 20cm. "References for supplementary reading" at end of each chapter. [BV1534.B3] 20-22022
1. Religious education. 2. Sunday schools. I. Title.

BARNES, Donald L. 370.114
Psychological considerations in religious education [by] Donald L. Barnes. Muncie, Ind., Ball State Univ., 1966. vi, 67p. illus. 23cm. (Ball State monograph no. 5) Title. (Series: Indiana. Ball State University, Muncie. Ball State monograph no. 5) Bibl. [BV1471.2.B36] 66-63894 price unreported pap.,
1. Religious education. I. Title. II. Series.

BARR, Margaret.
Great unity; a new approach to religious education. Boston, Beacon Press [1951] 95 p. 19 cm. a 53
1. Religious education. I. Title.

BARTHOLOMEW, Edward Fry, 268.
1864-
Biblical pedagogy; a handbook for Sunday school teachers and Bible students, by E. F. Bartholomew ... Rock Island, Ill., Augustana book concern [c1927] 131 p. 18 cm. [BV1475.B24] 26-3817
1. Religious education. I. Title.

BATES, Joshua, 1776-1854.
Christian education, as connected with baptism. By Joshua Bates, D.D. Written for the Massachusetts Sabbath school society, and approved by the Committee of publication. Boston, Massachusetts Sabbath school society [c1855] 54 p. incl. front. 16 cm. [LC361.B3] 7-36690
1. Religious education. I. Title.

BEARD, Frederica. 016.
Picture in religious education, by Frederica Beard... New York, George H. Doran company [c1920] xiv p., 1 l., 15-157 p. incl. front., plates. 19 1/2 cm. [BV1535.B45] 20-18236
I. Title.

BEECHER, Catherine Ester, 268.
1800-1878.
Religious training of children in the school, the family, and the church. By Catherine E. Beecher... New York, Harper & brothers, 1864. 2 p. l., [iii]-iv, 5-413 p. 20 cm. [LC331.B38] [BV1475.B3] 377. E 15
1. Religious education. I. Title.

BELL, George Charles.
Religious teaching in secondary schools suggestionst teachers and parents for lessons on the Old and New Testaments, early church history, Christian evidences, etc. By the Rev. George C. Bell ... London, New York, Macmillan and co., limited, 1897. xiv. 181 p. 19 cm. Bibliographical foot-notes. E10
1. Religious education. I. Title.

BENTON, Rita, 1881- 268.
... *The Bible play workshop,* by Rita Benton. New York, Cincinnati, The Abingdon press [c1923] 142 p. incl. front., illus. 21 cm. (The Abingdon religious

education texts, D. G. Downey, general editor, G. H. Betts, associate editor) Contains music. [BV1575.B4] 23-17491
1. Religious education. 2. Drama in education. 3. Children's plays. I. Title.

BERKOWITZ, Henry, 1857-
The new education in religion, with a curriculum of Jewish studies, by Henry Berkowitz ... Philadelphia, The Jewish Chautauqua society, 1913. 2 v. 20 cm. Vol. 2 has title: The new education in religion. Part ii. School organization admanaemnt. Contains bbliographies. [LC719.B35] A 17
1. Religious education. 2. Jews—Education. I. Title.

BETTS, Anna (Freelove) Mrs. 248
... The mother-teacher of religion, by Anna Freelove Betts. New York, Cincinnati, The Abingdon press [c1922] 290 p. front., illus. (incl. music) 21 cm. (The Abingdon religious education texts. D. G. Downey, general editor, G. H. Betts, associate editor) "bibliography of children's books": p. 286-290 [BV1590.B45] 22-3645
1. Religious education. I. Title.

BETTS, George Herbert, 1868-1934. 268.
... How to teach religion; principles and methods, by George Herbert Betts ... New York, Cincinnati, The Abingdon press [c1919] 223 p. 20 cm. The Abingdon serie--Religious education texts) [BV1475.B4] 19-13462
1. Religious education. I. Title.

BETTS, George Herbert, 1868-1934. 268.
... Method in teaching religion, by George Herbert Betts and Marion O. Hawthorne. New York, Cincinnati, The Abingdon press [c1925] 488 p. 21 cm. (The Abingdon religious education texts, D. G. Downey. general editor. College series, G. H. Betts, editor) "References" at end of each chapter. [BV1475.B43] 25-10898
1. Religious education. I. Hawthorne, Marion Olive, 1897- joint author. II. Title.

BETTS, George Herbert, 1868-1934. 268
... The new program of religious education, by George Herbert Betts. New York, Cincinnati, The Abingdon press [c1921] 107 p. 20 cm. (The Abingdon religious edation texts, D. G. Downey, general editor) [BV1471.B4] 22-451
1. Religious education. I. Title.

BETTS, George Herbert, 1868-1934. 286.6
Teaching religion to-day [by] George Herbert Betts ... New York, Cincinnati [etc.] The Abingdon press [c1934] 268 p. 20 cm. (The Abingdon religious education texts, J. W. Langdale, general editor; Guide to Christian leadership, P. H. Vieth, Editor] "References" at end of each chapter. [BV1534.B45] 34-12017
1. Religious education. I. Title.

BIBLE. N. T. Gospels. English. Harmonies. 1949. Revised standard. 226.1
Gospel parallels; a synopsis of the first three Gospels, with alternative readings from the manuscripts and non-canonical parallels. Text used is the Revised standard version, 1946: the arrangement follows the Huck-Lietzmann synopsis, 9th ed., 1936. New York, Nelson [1949] xi. 191 p. 26 cm. Prepared by a subcommittee of the American Standard Bible Committee. [BS2560.15] 49-48941
I. International Council of Religious Education. American Standard Bible Committee. II. Title.

BIGLER, Margaret K. Mrs. 268.432
A lantern to our children, by Margaret K. Bigler ... with foreword by the Right Reverend George Craig Stewart ... Milwaukee, Morehouse publishing co. [c1932] xii, 68 p. 1 l. incl. front., illus., pl. 24 cm. Includes bibliographies. [BV1537.B5] 32-4652
1. Religious education. I. Title.

BLAZIER, Kenneth L. 268
Planning Christian education in your church; a guide for boards or committees of Christian education [by] Kenneth D. [i.e. L.] Blazier [and] Evelyn M. Huber. Valley Forge [Pa.] Judson Press [1974] 32 p. illus. 22 cm. Bibliography: p. 31-32. [BV1471.2.B57] 73-19585 ISBN 0-8170-0633-8 1.00 (pbk.).
1. Religious education. I. Huber, Evelyn, joint author. II. Title.

BLICK, Ida S.
The adult department: its scope and opportunity, by Ida S. Blick... Philadelphia, Pa., The Westminster press, 1917. 92 p. 18 1/2 cm. Bibliography: p. 92. [BV1550B5] 19-2544
1. Religious education. I. Title.

BONSER, Edna Madison (MacDonald) Mrs. 268.
The golden rule city; a course in religious education based on activities (for children of nine to eleven) by Edna Madison Bonser ... Boston, Chicago, The Pilgrim press [c1927] xvi, 260 p. 20 1/2 cm. (Everyday Christian living series) Bibliography: p. [257]-260. [BV1534.B6] 28-8545
1. Religious education. I. Title.

BOWEN, Cawthon Asbury, 1885- 268.
... Lesson materials in the church school, by C. A. Bowen ... Nashville, Tenn., Cokesbury press, 1929. 213 p. diagr. 19 cm. (Leadership training series) "For reading and investigation" at end of most of the chapters. [BV1558.B6] 29-9122
1. Religious education. 2. Sunday schools. I. Title.

BOWER, William Clayton, 1878- 268
Christ and Christian education [by] William Clayton Bower ... New York, Nashville, Abingdon-Cokesbury press [1943] 128 p. 19 1/2 cm. "Originally delivered as lectures in the Harriet Drake Kirkham-Hay memorial lectureship of the College of the Bible of Drake university, in February of 1942.---Foreword. [BV1471.B6] 43-8662
1. Religious education. I. Title.

BOWER, William Clayton, 1878- 268.
The curriculum of religious education, by William Clayton Bower ... New York, C. Scribner's sons, 1925. xii p., 1 l., 283 p. 20 cm. Bibliography: p. 261-274. [BV1475.B57] 25-10897
1. Religious education. I. Title.

BOWER, William Clayton, 1878- 262.
The educational task of the local church, by William Clayton Bower ... a textbook in the Standard course in teacher training, outlined and approved by the Sunday school council of evangelical denominations. Third year specialization series. St. Louis, Pub. for the Teacher training publishing association, by the Front rank press [c1921] v, [1] 138 p. 17 cm. "References for reading" at end of each chapter. [BV1533.B6] 22-3037
1. Religious education. I. Title.

BOWER, William Clayton, 1878- 268.
Religious education in the modern church, by William Clayton Bower ... A textbook in the Standard leadership training curriculum outlined and approved by the International council of religious education. St. Louis, Mo., Printed for the Leadership training publishing association by the Bethany press [c1929] 270 p. 19 cm. "Sources" at end of each chapter. [BV1475.B58] 29-16507
1. Religious education. I. International council of religious education. II. Title.

BOWER, William Clayton, 1878- 268.
A survey of religious education in the local church, by William Clayton Bower ... Chicago, Ill., The University of Chicago press [c1919] xv, 177 p. 18 cm. (Half title: The University of Chicago publications in religious education ... Principles and methods of religious education) Contains "References for reading": Bibliography: p. 169-173. [BV1475.B6] 19-2201
1. Religious education. I. Title.

BOXRUD, Clara. 268.62
My second Sunday school book, grade two, by Clara Boxrud ... Minneapolis, Augsburg publishing house [1937] 115 p. incl. illus. (part col.) plates (part col.) map. col. front. 23 cm. Text and illustration on front lining-paper. "This volume is one in a series of graded Sunday school text books issued by the Board of elementary Christian education, Dr. Jacob Tanner, editor-in-chief." "First edition, September, 1937." [BV1545.B58] 37-29375
1. Religious education. I. Tanner, Jacob, 1865- ed. II. Title.

BRAITERMAN, Marvin. 377.1
Religion and the public schools. [New York] Commission on Social Action of Reform Judaism [1958] 73p. 18cm. (Issues of conscience) [LC111.B68] 59-33587
1. Religious education. I. Title.

BRALEY, Evelyn Foley, 1884- 268.6
The teaching of religion; a book of suggestions for the modern teacher, by E. F. Braley ... with a foreword by Sir Frederick Mander. London, New York [etc.] Longmans, Green and co. [1938] iv, 167, [1] p. illus. 7invl. maps) 19 cm. "First published, 1938." Includes bibliographies. [BV1534. B67] 39-9143
1. Religious education. I. Title.

BRETT, Jesse, 1858- 242
The life purposeful; considerations of practical religion, by Rev. Jesse Brett ... London, New York [etc.] Longmans, Green and co., 1924. ix, p., 1 l., 146 p. incl. front. 19 cm. [BV4832.B743] 24-1989
I. Title.

BROOKS, Nathan Covington, 1809-1898.
Scripture manual; or, Religious exercises for the morning and evening of each day in the month ... By N. C. Brooks ... New York, A. Hinds & co., 1890. 230 p. 16 cm. 16-4811
I. Title.

BROWN, Ario Ayres, 1883- 268.
...A history of religious education in recent times, by Ario Ayres Brown... New York, Cincinnati, The Abingdon press [c1923] 282 p. incl. front. (facsim.) 20 1/2 cm. (The Abingdon religious education texts, D. G. Downey, general editor. Community training school series, N. E. Richardson, editor) "Brief bibliography for special reference": p. 275-276. [BV1465.B7] 23-4815
1. Religious education. I. Title.

BROWN, Jeanette (Perkins), 1887- 268.69
The storyteller in religious education; how to tell stories to children and young people. Boston, Pilgrim Press [1951] x, 165 p. illus. 20 cm. A Co-operative book published for the Co-operative Publication Association. Bibliography: p. 157-163. [BV1472.B7] 51-3076
1. Religious education. 2. Story-telling. I. Title.

BROWN, Kenneth Irving, 1896- 377.1
Not minds alone; some frontiers of Christian education. [1st ed.] New York, Harper [c1954] 206p. 22cm. [LC368.B75] 53-11839
1. Religious education. I. Title.

BROWN, Mary Florence. 268.
Adventures in friendliness, programs for the primary department, prepared for use in the vacation church school, by M.F. Brown; John T. Faris, D.D., editor. Philadelphia, Board of Christian education of the Presbyterian church in the U.S.A., 1928. 209 p. front., illus. (music) plates. 23 1/2 cm. Bibliography: p. 188-192. [BV1585.B7] 28-0558
1. Religious education. I. Faris, John Thomason, 1871- ed. II. Title. III. Title: Vacation church school.

BROWN, Mary Florence. 268.
God the loving Father... by M. Florence Brown... Philadelphia, The Westminster press, 1921. x, 131 p. illus. (incl. music) 18 1/2 cm. (The Westminister textbooks for religious education for church schools having Sunday, week day, and expressional sessions, ed. by J. T. Faris. Primary department, 1st year, pt. 1.) [BV1561.B75] 22-4347
I. Title.

BRUMBAUGH, Martin Grove, 1862-1930. 268.37
The making of a teacher; a contribution to some phases of the problem of religious education, by Martin G. Brumbaugh ... New York and London, Harper & brothers, 1932. xvi p., 1 l., 223 p. 19 1/2 cm. [BV1533.B8 1932] 32-25978
1. Religious education. 2. Sunday-schools. I. Title.

BULTER, James Donald, 1908- 268
Religious education the foundations and practice nature. New York, Harper &Row [1962] 321p. 22cm. [BV147.1.2B8268] 62-10081
1. Religious education. I. Title.

BURGESS, Nellie V. Mrs. 268.6
A trail of everyday living; a manual for junior groups in vacation church schools, by Nellie V. Burgess; John T. Faris, editor, Elizabeth S. Whitehouse, assistant editor for children's publications. Philadelphia, Board of Christian education of the Presbyterian church in the U.S.A., 1932. 283 p. illus. 25 1/2 cm. Music: p. 180-181. "Books valuable for additional source materials and program ideas": p. 179. [BV1585.B8] 32-8288
1. Religious education. 2. Vacation schools. I. Faris, John Thomson, 1871- ed. II. Whitehouse, Elizabeth S., joint ed. III. Title.

BURKHART, Roy A., 1895- 268
Guiding individual growth: a discussion of personal counseling in religious education [by] Roy A. Burkhart. New York, Cincinnati [etc.] The Abingdon press [c1935] 205 p. incl. illus., forms. 20 cm. (Half-title: The Abington religious education texts ... Guides to Christian leadership) Music: p. 178. "Sources for the counselor": p. 183-189. "For further reading" at end of most of the chapters. [BV1523.B8] 35-10132
1. Religious education. 2. Psychology, Religious. I. Title. II. Title: Personal counseling in religious education.

BURKHART, Roy Abram, 1895- 268
Guiding individual growth; a discussion of personal counseling in religious education [by] Roy A. Burkhart. New York, Cincinnati [etc.] The Abingdon press [c1935] 205 p. incl. illus. forms. 20 cm. (Half-title: The Abingdon religious education texts ... Guides to Christian leadership) Music: p. 178. "Sources for the counselor": p. 183-189. "For further reading" at the end of most of the chapters. [BV1523.B8] 35-10132
1. Religious education. 2. Psychology, Religious. I. Title. II. Title: Personal counseling in religious education.

BUSHNELL, Horace, 1802-1876.
Christian nurture, Introd. by Luther A. Weigle. New Haven, Yale University Press [1967, c1916] xl, 351 p. 21 cm. 68-86385
1. Religious education. I. Title.

BUSHNELL, Horace, 1802-1876.
Christian nurture, by Horace Bushnell. Intro. by Luther A. Weigle. New Haven, Yale Univ. Pr. [1967 c1919] xl, 351 p. 21 cm. Contains biographical sketch of Horace Bushnell by Williston Walker. 68-61881
1. Religious education. I. Walker, Williston, 1860-1922. II. Title.

BUSHNELL, Horace, 1802-1876. 240
Christian nurture. Biographical sketch by Williston Walker; revision by Luther A. Weighle. New ed. New York, Scribner, 1916. xxx, 351 p. 20 cm. A portion of the work was published in 1847 under title: Views of Christian nurture. In its present form it first appeared in 1860. [BV1475.B9 1916] 16-22990
1. Religious education. 2. Children—Religious life. I. Title.

BUSHNELL, Horace, 1802-1876. 240
Christian nurture. By Horace Bushnell ... New York, C. Scribner, 1861. vi p., 1 l., [9]-407 p. 19 1/2 cm. A portion of the work was published in 1847 under title: Views of Christian nurture. In its present form it appeared first in 1860. [BV1475.B9 1861] 38-37407
1. Religious education. 2. Children—Religious life. I. Title.

BUSHNELL, Horace, 1802-1876. 240
Christian nurture. By Horace Bushnell ... New York, C. Scribner, 1863. vi p., 1 l., [9]-407 p. 19 1/2 cm. A portion of the work was published in 1847 under title: Views of Christian nurture. In its present

form it appeared first in 1860. [BV1475.B9 1863] 38-37402
1. Religious education. 2. Children—Religious life. I. Title.

BUSHNELL, Horace, 1802-1876. 240
Christian nurture. By Horace Bushnell ... New York, Scribner, Armstrong & co., 1876. vi p., 2 l., [9]-407 p. 19 1/2 cm. A portion of the work was published in 1847 under title: Views of Christian nurture. In its present form it appeared first in 1860. [BV1475.B9 1876] 38-37408
1. Religious education. 2. Children—Religious life. I. Title.

BUSHNELL, Horace, 1802-1876. 240
Christian nurture. By Horace Bushnell ... New York, C. Scribner's sons, 1890. vi p., 2 l., [9]-407 p. 19 1/2 cm. A portion of the work was published in 1847 under title: Views of Christian nurture. In its present form it appeared first in 1860. [BV1475.B9 1890] 38-37409
1. Religious education. 2. Children—Religious life. I. Title.

BUSHNELL, Horace, 1802-1876. 268.
Christian nurture; by Horace Bushnell ... Centenary ed. New York, C. Scribner's sons, 1903. 407 p. 20 1/2 cm. A portion of the work was published in 1847, but in its present form it first appeared in 1860. [BV1475.B9 1903] 4-10402
1. Religious education. I. Title.

BUSHNELL, Horace, 1802-1876. 268.
Christian nurture, by Horace Bushnell, biographical sketch by Williston Walker ... revision by Luther A. Weigle ... New ed. New York, C. Scribner's sons, 1916. xxx, 351 p. 20 cm. [BV1475.B9 1916] 16-22990
1. Religious education. I. Walker, Williston, 1860- II. Weigle, Luther Allan, 1880- ed. III. Title.

BUSHNELL, Horace, 1802-1876. 240
Views of Chrisitan nurture, and of subjects adjacent thereto, by Horace Bushnell. Hartford, E. Hunt, 1847. 251 p. 19 1/2 cm. On cover: Christian nurture. Published in 1860, in expanded form, under title: Christian nurture. [BV1475.B88] 38-37828
1. Religious education. 2. Children—Religious life. I. Title. II. Title: Christian nurture.

BUTTRICK, George Arthur 268
Biblical thought and the secular university. Baton Rouge, Louisiana State University Press [c. 1960] viii, 83p. 23cm. Bibl. notes: p.[69]-75 60-13168 2.50
1. Religious education. 2. Universities and colleges—Religion. I. Title.

BYRNE, Herbert W., 1917- 268
Christian education for the local church, an evangelical and functional approach. Grand Rapids, Mich., Zondervan [c.1963] 355p. illus. 23cm. 63-9310 5.95
1. Religious education. I. Title.

CABOT, Ella (Lyman) Mrs. 377.1
1866-
Our part in the world, by Ellan Lyman Cabot ... Rev ed. Boston, Mass., The Beacon press, inc., 1932. 4 p. l., vii-xiv, 187 p. 21 cm. (Half-title: The new Beacon course of graded lessons) [BV1475.C3 1932] 33-2055
I. Title.

CASTBERG, Leila Simon. 230.
Daily readings ... by Leila Simon Castberg ... Los Angeles, Church of divine power publishing company [c1924]- v. 21 cm. [BX6997.C35] 24-21353
I. Title.

CASTER, Marcel van. 238
God's word today; principles, methods, and examples of catechesis. New York, Benziger Bros., 1966. 144 p. 22 cm. 66-23491
1. Religious education. I. Title.

CASTER, Marcel van. 230.207
The structure of catechetics. [2d augum. ed., adapted by the author and translated by Edward J. Dirkswager, Jr., Olga Guedetarian, and Mother Nicolas Smith. New York] Herder and Herder [1965] 253 p. 22 cm. Translation of Dieu nous parie. 1. Structures de la catechese. Includes bibliographies. [BV1471.2.C312] 65-13487
1. Religious education. I. Title.

CASTER, Marcel van. 238.2
Themes of catechesis. [Translation by Olga Guedatarian. New York] Herder and Herder [1966] 207 p. 22 cm. Translation of Dieu nous parie. 2. Themes de la catechese. [BV1471.2.C3213] 66-13077
1. Religious education. I. Title.

CATHOLIC Church. National 230'.2
Conference of Catholic Bishops.
Basic teachings for Catholic religious education. Washington, Publications Office, U.S. Catholic Conference, 1973. 36 p. 22 cm. Includes bibliographical references. [BX1755.C34 1973] 73-172147
1. Catholic Church—Doctrinal and controversial works—Catholic authors. 2. Religious education. I. Title.

CHALMERS, William Everett, 268.
1868-
The church and the church school; a text-book study of the church organized for religious education ... by William Everett Chalmers. Philadelphia, Boston [etc.] The Judson press [c1927] 5 p. l., 186 p. 19 cm. (Keyston standard training course) Bibliography: p. 183-186. [BV1475.C45] 27-24567
1. Religious education. I. Title.

CHAMBERLIN, John Gordon 268
Freedom and faith; new approaches to Christian education. Philadelphia, Westminster [c.1965] 156p. 21cm. Bibl. [BV1471.2.C46] 65-11615 3.95
1. Religious education. I. Title.

CHAMBERLIN, John Gordon. 268
Freedom and faith; new approaches to Christian education, by J. Gordon Chamberlin. Philadephia, Westminster Press [1965] 156 p. 21 cm. Bibliographical references included in "Abbreviations" (p. 9) [BV1471.2.C46] 65-116152
1. Religious education. I. Title.

[CHAPIN, Clara Christiana 221.
(Morgan)] Mrs. 1852-
Mother and Betty; outline of truth teaching for children, by Clara English [pseud.] Los Angeles, J. F. Rowny press, 1921. 1 p. l. v. p., 1 l., 7-57 p. front. (2 port.) 18 cm. [BV4571.C4] 22-3717
1. Religious education. I. Title.

CHAPPELL, Edwin Barfield, 268
1853-
Building the kingdom; the educational ideal of the church, by E. B. Chappell ... Nashville, Tenn., Dallas, Tex. [etc.] Publishing house M. E. church, South, Smith and Lamar, agents, 1914. 382 p. 19 cm. [BV1471.C5] 14-10042
1. Religious education. 2. Sunday-schools. I. Title.

CHARTERS, Jessie Blount 268.434
(Allen) Mrs. 1880-
Young adults and the church [by] Jessie A. Charters. New York, Cincinnati [etc.] The Abingdon press [c1936] 153 p. 18 cm. [BV1550.C45] 36-9457
1. Religious education. I. Title.

CHAVE, Ernest John. 268.33
Supervision of religious education, by Ernest John Chave ... Chicago, Ill., The University of Chicago press [1931] xv, 352 p. 20 cm. (Half-title: The University of Chicago publications in religious education ... Handbooks of ethics and religion) [BV1520.C56] 377.1 32-128
1. Religious education. I. Title.

CHAVE, Ernest John, 1886- 268
A functional approach to religious education, by Ernest J. Chave. Chicago, Ill., The University of Chicago press [1947] ix, 168 p. 20 cm. "Notes and references": p. 162-166. [BV1471.C43] A47
1. Religious education. I. Title.

CHAVE, Ernest John, 268.0761
1886-
Measure religion; fifty-two experimental forms, by Ernest J. Chave. Chicago, Ill., Distributed by the University of Chicago bookstore [c1939] iv, 142, [26] p. incl. forms. 25 cm. Photoprinted. [BV1561.C47] 39-32152
1. Religious education. 2. Attitude (Psychology) I. Title.

CHRISTIAN education and the local church: history, principles, practice. [Rev. ed.] Cincinnati, Standard Pub. Co. [1958] 345p. illus., plans. 20cm. Bibliography: p. 328-334.
1. Religious education. I. Murch, James DeForest, 1892-

CHRISTIAN education 268.4
handbook; 157 outlines on various on various phases of the church's teaching program, organization, and personnel. Cincinnati, Standard Pub. Co., c.1960. 176p. 28cm. Includes bibl. 2.95 pap.,
1. Religious education. 2. Sunday-schools.

CHURCH educational 268'.07
agencies. [1st ed.] Wheaton, Ill., Evangelical Teacher Training Association [1968] 96 p. illus. 23 cm. (Advanced specialized certificate series) Includes bibliographical references. [BV1471.2.C53] 67-27288
1. Religious education. I. Evangelical Teacher Training Association.

CLARK, Francis Edward, 2-7292
1851-1927
Training the church of the future; Auburn seminary lectures on Christian nurture with special reference to the Young people's society of Christian endeavor as a training-school of the church, by Rev. Francis E. Clark... New York and London, Funk & Wagnalls co., 1902. 225 p. front. 19 1/2 cm.
1. Religious education. 2. International society of Christian endeavor. I. Title.

CLARK, James Everitt, 1868-
Education for successful living, by James E. Clarke. Philadelphia, The Westminster press, 1922. xiv p., 1 l, 152 p. incl. front., diagrs. 19 cm. [LC368.C6] 22-14700
1. Religious education. 2. Education, Higher. 3. Church and college. I. Title.

CLOWES, Amy. 268.
Seeking the beautiful in God's world; a course in religion for the third grade in the Sunday, week-day, or vacation church school, by Amy Clowes, edited by Blanche Carrier... New York, R. R. Smith, inc., 1930. xxxv, 208 p. illus., plates. 19 1/2 cm. "Books": p. xxi. [BV1545.C68] 30-3333
1. Religious education. I. Carrier, Blanche, 1895- ed. II. Title.

CLOYD, David Excelmons.
Religious education, the social teachings of Jesus, a study course, by David E. Cloyd... Des Moines, Ia., The Education publishing company, c1910. 64 p. 19 1/2 cm. Bibliography: p. 4. E11
1. Jesus Christ. 2. Religious education. I. Title.

COBB, Cora Stanwood. 268.
God's wonder world; a manual for religious instruction in junior grades, especially for pupils nine years old, by Cora Stanwood Cobb,A.B. Boston, Mass., The Beacon press [c1918] 6 p. l., ix-xxi, 335 p. 21 1/2 cm. (Half title: The Beacon press publications in religious education. The Beacon course of graded lessons, W. I. Lawrence, F. Buck, editors) [BV1561.C6] 19-1727
1. Religious education. 2. Nature study. I. Title.

COBER, Kenneth Lorne, 1902- 268
The church's teaching ministry [by] Kenneth L. Cober. Valley Forge [Pa] Judson Press [1964] 143 p. illus. 20 cm. Includes bibliographies. [BV1471.2.C6] 64-13123
1. Religious education. 2. Baptists — Education. I. Title.

COE, George Albert, 1862- 268.
A social theory of religious education, by George Albert Coe ... New York, C. Scribner's sons, 1917. xiii, 361 p. 19 1/2 cm. "Classified bibliography": p. 343-355. [BV1475.C6] 17-25741
1. Religious education. I. Title.

COE, George Albert, 1862- 268
What is Christian education? by George A. Coe. New York, London, C. Scribner's sons, 1929. xii, 300 p. 21 cm. [BV1471.C57] 29-21376
1. Religious education. I. Title. II. Title: Christian education.

COLE, Stewart Grant, 1892- 268
Character and Christian education, by Stewart G. Cole ... Nashville, Cokesbury press [c1936] 249 p. diagrs. 21 cm. Bibliography at end of each chapter. [BV1475.C62] 36-32091
1. Religious education. 2. Character. 3. Child study. I. Title.

COLLINS, Helen (clark) 268.62
Mrs. 1896-
We discover lights; units of experience for primary groups, by Helen Collins; music by Dorothy Broadbent; line drawings by Mary Marie Davis. Philadelphia, Pa., Friends general conference, 1936. 3 p. l., 190 p. incl. front., illus., charts, diagrs. 24 cm. Includes music. [BV1545.C64] 36-36750
1. Religious education. I. Title.
Contents omitted.

COLMAN, Marion. 268.
Rules of life for boys and girls; week-day lessons in religion (junior grades) by Marion Colman ... with introduction by Walter Scott Athearn ... New York, Chicago [etc.] Fleming H. Revell company [c1926] 2 p. l., 235 p. 20 cm. [BV1580.C55] 26-21877
1. Religious education. I. Title.

COMMITTEE on the war and the 268
religious outlook.
The teaching work of the church. The Committee on the war and the religious outlook (appointed by the Federal council of the churches of Christ in America) New York, Association press, 1923. ix, 309 p. 23 cm. "Classified bibliography": p. 297-304. [BV1471.C6] 24-2721
1. Religious education. I. Title.

CONNELLY, H. Walton. 268.86
Learning for living [by] H. Walton Connelly, Jr. Nashville, Convention Press [1967] xi, 129 p. 19 cm. Includes bibliographical references. [BV1471.2.C64] 67-10002
1. Religious education. I. Title.

CONNER, Miles Washington, 268
1888-
Leadership in religious education, by Miles W. Connor... Baltimore, Md. [The Garland press] 1947. vii, 59 p. 19 cm. [BV1471.C62] 47-19468
1. Religious education. I. Title.

COPE, Henry Frederick, 1870- 268.
1923.
Religious education in the church, by Henry Frederick Cope ... New York, C. Scribner's sons, 1918. viii p., 1 l., 274 p. 20 cm. References at end of each chapter. [BV1475.C65] 18-10285
1. Religious education. I. Title.

COPE, Henry Frederick, 1870- 268.
1923.
The school in the modern church, by Henry Frederick Cope ... New York, George H. Doran company [c1919] 1 p. l., v-x p., 1 l., 13-290 p. 20 cm. "A brief bibliography of religious education": p. 284-290. [BV1475.C67] 19-12301
1. Religious education. 2. Sunday-schools. I. Title.

COPE, Henry Frederick, 1870- 268.
1923, ed.
Week-day religious education; a survey and discussion of activities and problems, edited by Henry F. Cope ... published under the direction of the Religious education association. New York, George H. Doran company [c1922] 204 p. diagrs. 26 cm. [BV1580.C65] 23-7669
1. Religious education. I. Religious education association. II. Title.

CORSON, Fred Pierce, 1896- 268
The Christian imprint. New York, Abingdon Press [1955] 156p. 21cm. [BV1471.C68] 55-6761
1. Religious education. I. Title.

CORZINE, Jesse Lynn, 1892- 268.6
Looking at learning, by J. L. Corzine. Nashville, Tenn., The Sunday school board of the Southern Baptist convention [c1934] 126 p. diagr. 19 cm. [BV1534.C64] 35-1034
1. Religious education. 2. Learning, Psychology of. I. Title.

THE course of study in 268.61
religion ... Published by ecclesiastical authority ... Philadelphia, Pa., The Public press [c1936- v. illus. 20 cm. [BX930.C65] 36-13980
1. Religious education.

COX, Alva I. 268
Christian education in the church today. Henry M. Bullock, gen. d. Nashville, Graded Pr. [dist. Abingdon, 1966, c.1965] 160p. 19cm. d. Bibl. [BV1471.2.C68] 66-2940 1.75 pap.,
1. Religious education. I. Title.

CRANDALL, Edna M. 264
A curriculum of worship, for the junior church school, first year, by Edna M. Crandall; with an introduction by Luther A. Weigle. New York, London, The Century co. [c1925]- v. 20 cm. Includes hymns and responses with music. [BV10.C7] 25-15860
1. Religious education. 2. Sunday-schools. I. Title. II. Title: Worship, A curriculum of.

CROSSLAND, Weldon Frank, 1890- 268
How to build up your church school. Nashville, Abington-Cokesbury Press [1948] 144 p. 20 cm. [BV1475.C77] 48-2617
1. Religious education. 2. Sunday-schools. I. Title.

CRUM, Mason. 268.
The project method in religious education, by Mason Crum ... Nashville, Tenn., Cokesbury press [c1924] 2 p. l., iii-v, 157 p. diagr. 20 cm. Bibliography: p. 149-157. [BV1534.C7] 24-30199
1. Religious education. 2. Project method in teaching. I. Title.

CULLY, Kendig Brubaker 268
The teaching church, an introduction to Christian education for parents and teachers. Philadelphia, United Church [c.1963] 94p. 20cm. Bibl. 63-12579 2.50
1. Religious education. I. Title.

CULLY, Kendig Brubaker. 268
The teaching church, an introduction to Christian education for parents and teachers. Philadelphia, United Church Press [1963] 94 p. 20 cm. Includes bibliography. [BV1471.2.C8] 63-12579
1. Religious education. I. Title.

CUMMINGS, Oliver De Wolf, 1900- 268
Christian education in the local church, by Oliver de Wolf Cummings. Philadelphia, Chicago [etc.] The Judson press [1942] 159 p. incl. illus. (plans) diagrs., form. 19 cm. Bibliography: p. 155-159. [BV1471.C77] 43-11887
1. Religious education. 2. Church work. I. Title.

CUMMINGS, Oliver DeWolf. 268
Administering Christian education in the local church; a manual for the church board of Christian education, by Oliver DeWolf Cummings ... Philadelphia, Boston [etc.] The Judson press [1936] 106 p. incl. plans, diagrs., forms. fold. diagrs. 20 cm. Bibliography: p. 100-106. [BV1471.C75] 36-22224
1. Religious education. 2. Church work. I. Title.

THE Daily vacation church-school. 268.
... Program guide, no. i[-iii] ... New York, Cincinnati, The Methodist book concern [c1922] 3 v. illus. (incl. music) 21 x 21 cm. Contents.--i. The Heavenly Father and His helpers, for teachers of group i (children approximately 5 and 6 years old) prepared by Mina A. Clark.--ii. Learning how to live as God's children, for teachers of group ii, children 7 and 8 years old, prepared by Corinth C. Clausing.--iii. Playing the game, for teachers of group iii, juniors 9, 10, and 11 years old, prepared by Lois R. Robinson. Contains bibliographies. [BV1585.D3] 23-7054
1. Religious education. I. Clark, Mina A. II. Clausing, Corinth C. III. Robison, Lois R. IV. Title.

DANIELSON, Frances Weld, ed. 268.6
Teaching without textbooks; some experiments in teaching religion to children, edited by Frances Weld Daneilson and Jeanette E. Perkins. Boston, Chicago, The Pilgrim press [c1930] ix, 239 p. diagr. 21 cm. Music: p. 118. [BV1534.D3] 30-18034
1. Religious education. 2. Sunday-schools. 3. Education of children. I. Perkins, Jeanette Eloise, joint ed. II. Title.

DARSIE, Charles. 377.1
Adult religious teaching, by Charles Darsie ... St. Louis, Mo., The Bethany press, [c1930] 2 p. l., 3-186 p. 19 cm. [BV1550.D3] 30-14527
1. Religious education. 2. Education of adults. I. Title.

DAVIDSON, John, 1861-1947.
Means and methods in the religious education of the young with special reference to the Sunday school, by John Davidson ... London, New York [etc.] Longmans, Green and Co., 1917. viii, 152 p. 19 1/2 cm. E18
1. Religious education. 2. Sunday-schools. I. Title.

DAVIDSON, John, 1870-
Means and methods in the religious education of the young with special reference to the Sunday school, by John Davidson ... London, New York [etc.] Longmans, Green and co., 1917. xiii, 152 p. 20 cm. [LC381.D3] E 18
1. Religious education. 2. Sunday-schools. I. Title.

DAWSON, George Ellsworth. 268.
The child and his religion, by George E. Dawson ... Chicago, The University of Chicago press, 1909. ix, 124 p. diagrs. 20 cm. [BV1475.D3] 9-28188
1. Religious education. I. Title.

DE BLOIS, Austen Kennedy, 1866- 268
Christian religious education: principles and practice, by Austen Kennedyy de Blois ... and Donald R. Gorham ... New York [etc.] Fleming H. Revell company [c1939] 1 p. l., 5-385 p. 21 cm. Bibliography at end of each chapter. [BV1471.D4] 39-25419
1. Religious education. I. Gorham, Donald Rex, 1903- joint author. II. Title.

DESJARDINS, Lucile. 220.
... Discovering how to live, by Lucile Desjaridins. Pioneers in the Christian quest, Westminster department graded materials. Pupil's book. Philadelphia, The Westminster press, 1929. 241 p. front., plates. 21 cm. At head of title: Intermediate pupils in the week day church school. [BV1583.D4] 29-14874
1. Religious education. I. Title.

DESJARDINS, Lucile. 220.
... Discovering how to live, by Lucile Desjaridins. Pioneers in the Christian quest, Westminster department graded materials. Pupil's book. Philadelphia, The Westminster press, 1929. 198 p. front., plates, 21 cm. At head of title: Intermediate pupils in the week day church school. [BV1583.D43] 29-14875
1. Religious education. I. Title.

DESJARDINS, Lucile, 1892- 377
What boys and girls are asking; a guide for teachers including source materials and teaching procedures [by] Lucile Desjardins. New York, Cincinnati [etc.] The Abingdon press [c1936] 2 p. l., 3-176 p. 20 cm. [The Abingdon religious education texts, J. W. Langdale, general editor; Guides to Christian living, P. H. Vieth, editor] "Helpful books for teachers": p. 14-16: "Source materials for the browning table and the library book": p. 169-176. [BV1548.D4] 36-18439
1. Religious education. I. Title.

DIAZ, Abby (Morton) Mrs. 1821-1904. 268.
The religious training of children, by Abby Morton Diaz ... New York, The Metaphysical publishing company, c1895. 77 p. 22 cm. Reprinted from the Metaphysical magazine by special request. [BV1475.D5] 7-36692
1. Religious education. I. Title.

DILLINGHAM, John. 268
Making religious education effective; a new program for the church school today, by John Dillingham ... with an introduction by Robert Seneca Smith ... New York, N. Y., Association press [c1935] 203 p. diagrs. 20 cm. "References" at end of each chapter. [BV1520.D5] 36-5966
1. Religious education. I. Title.

DISCIPLES of Christ. National Church Program Coordinating Council.
Christian education [by Mabel Metze. Indianapolis, 1966] 64 p. 28 cm. (Church program guidance manuals for congregations of Christian Churches. Disciples of Christ) 68-31298
1. Religious education. 2. Disciples of Christ—Education. I. Metze, Mabel. II. Title. III. Series.

DOBBINS, Gaines Stanley, 1886- 268.
How to teach young people and adults in the Sunday school, by G. S. Dobbins ... Nashville, Tenn., Sunday school board of the Southern Baptist convention [c1930] 206 p. 19 cm. [BV1550.D6] E 41
1. Religious education. 2. Sunday-schools. I. Title.

DOBBINS, Gaines Stanley, 1886- 268.434
Teaching adults in the Sunday school [by] Gaines S. Dobbins ... Nashville, Tenn., Broadman press [c1936] 133 p. 19 cm. Bibliography: p. 101-104. [BV1550. D6] 37-4070
1. Religious education. 2. Sunday-schools. I. Title.

DRAWBRIDGE, C. L.
Religious education, how to improve it, by Rev. C. L. Drawbridge ... New ed. London, New York [etc.] Longmans, Green, and co., 1908. 3 p. l., 348 p. illus. 20 cm. E 8
1. Religious education. I. Title.

DRAWBRIDGE, Cyprian Leycester.
Religious education; how to improve it, by Rev. C. L. Drawbridge... London, New York and Bombay, Longmans, Green, and co., 1906. 4 p. l., 222 p. 20 cm. E 10
1. Religious education. I. Title.

DRAWBRIDGE, Cyprian Leycester.
The training of the twig (religious education of children), by the Rev. C. L. Drawbridge, M.A. New impression. London, New York and Bombay, Longmans, Green, and co., 1906. x, 191, [1] p. 19 1/2 cm. E 10
1. Religious education. 2. Children-Education. I. Title.

DRESSELHAUS, Richard L. 207
Teaching for decision [by] Richard L. Dresselhaus. Springfield, Mo., Gospel Pub. House [1973] 123, [1] p. 19 cm. Bibliography: p. [124] [BV1471.2.D73] 73-75502
1. Religious education. 2. Evangelistic work. I. Title.

DUBITSKY, Cora Marie. 230'.2
Building the faith community / by Cora Marie Dubitsky. New York : Paulist Press, [1974] vi, 177 p. ; 18 cm. (Deus books) [BV1471.2.D8] 74-12632 ISBN 0-8091-1848-3 pbk. : 1.95
1. Religious education. 2. Theology, Catholic. I. Title.

DURELL, Fletcher, 1859- 268
... A new life in education. By Fletcher Durell ... Philadelphia, The American Sunday school unions, 1894. 288 p. 20 cm. (Green fund book, no. 9a) [BV1471.D8] 7-34662
1. Religious education. I. Title.

DWIGHT, Benjamin Woodbridge, 1816-1889. 377.
The higher Christian education. By Benjamin W. Dwight ... New York, A. S. Barnes & Burr, 1859. 2 p. l., [vii]-xvii, iv p., 1 l., [7]-347 p. 22 cm. [LC383.D8] 7-36683
1. Religious education. I. Title.

EAKIN, Mildred Olivia (Moody) Mrs. 1890- 268.6
Exploring our neighborhood; a third and fourth grade church school enterprise; a guide for teachers [by] Mildred Moody Eakin. New York, Cincinnati [etc.] The Abingdon press [c1936] 252 p. illus. (plan) diagr. 20 cm. (Half-title: The Abingdon religious education texts, J. W. Langdale, general editor: Guides to Christian living. P. H. Vieth, editor) "Flag of our country" (words and music): p. 242. "Book list": p. 249-250; "Story-papers": p. 251. [BV1546.E27] 37-2210
1. Religious education. 2. Education of children. 3. Citizenship. I. Title.

EAKIN, Mildred Olivia (Moody) Mrs. 1890- 268.432
Teaching junior boys and girls [by] Mildred Moody Eakin; a textbook in the Standard course in leadership training, outlined and approved by the International council of religious education. New York, Cincinnati [etc.] Printed for the Leadership training publishing association by the Methodist book concern [c1934] 277 p. 17 1/2 cm. "Editor's introduction" signed: Erwin L. Shaver, chairman, Editorial and educational section. "Books to consult" at end of each chapter. [BV1546.E3] 34-22206
1. Religious education. I. Shaver, Erwin Leander, 1890- ed. II. International council of religious education. III. Title.

EAKIN, Mildred Olivia (Moody) 1890- 268
Your child's religion, by Mildred Moody Eakin and Frank Eakin. New York, The Macmillan company, 1942. xiii p., 1 l., 169 p. 19 1/2 cm. "First printing." "Reading suggestions": p. 152-164. [BV1475.E3] 42-22602
1. Religious education. I. Eakin, Frank, 1885- joint author. II. Title.

EBY, Frederick, 1874-
Christianity and education, by Frederick Eby... Dallas, Tex., Exective board of the Baptist general convention of Texas [c1915] 298 p. front., plates, ports. 21 1/2 cm. "Bibliography : p. 287-294. [LC368.E16] E16
1. Religious education. 2. Church and education. 3. Baptists—U.S.—Education. I. Title.

EDDY, Benjamin Lee, 1865- 268
...Christianity and education. New York, Fortuny's [c1940] 4 p. l., 11-82 p. 21 1/2 cm. At head of title: B. L. Eddy. "First edition." [BV1471.E3 1930] 40-31580
1. Religious education. I. Title.

EDWARDS, Paul M. 207
Inquiring faith; an exploration in religious education, by Paul M. Edwards. [Independence, Mo., Herald, 1967] 112p. 21cm. Bibl. [BV1471.2.E3] 67-4880 2.25; 1.50 pap.,
1. Religious education. I. Title.

EGGLESTON, Margaret (White) Mrs., 1878- 268.69
Use of the story in religious education (a revision) by Margaret W. Eggleston. New York and London, Harper & brothers, 1936. x p., 1 l., 76 p. 19 1/2 cm. "First edition." Bibliography: p. 74-76. [BV1472.E2 1936] 36-29589
1. Religious education. 2. Story-telling. I. Title.

ELIOT, William Greenleaf, 1811-1887. 268.
Early religious education considered as the divinely appointed way to the regenerate life. By William G. Eliot... Boston, Crosby, Nichols, & co., 1855. 3 p. l., 128 p. 18 1/2 cm. [BV1475.E6] 7-36684
1. Religious education. I. Title.

ELLIOTT, Harrison Sacket, 1882- 268
Can religious education be Christian? By Harrison S. Elliott. New York, The Macmillan company, 1940. x p., 2 l., 338 p. 21 cm. "The material on which the book is based was submitted as a dissertation...for the degree of doctor of philosophy at Yale university."--Pref. "First printing." Bibliography: p. 328-331. [BV1471.E4 1940a] 40-31202
1. Religious education. I. Title.

ELLIOTT, Harrison Sacket, 1882- 377.1
Group discussion in religious education, by Harrison Sacket Elliott... New York, Association press, 1930. vi p., 1 l., 100 p. 19 1/2 cm. Includes outlines illustrating group thinking procedure. [BV1472.E6] 31-2274
1. Religious education. 2. Debates and debating. 3. Association and associations. 4. Clubs. I. Title. II. Title: Discussion, Group.

EMME, Earle Edward, 1891- 268
An introduction to the principles of religious education, by Earle Edward Emme...and Paul Raymond Stevick... New York, The Macmillan company, 1926. 285

p. 19 1/2 cm. "References" at end of most of the chapters. [BV1471.E6] 26-2201
1. Religious education. I. Stevick, Paul Raymond, 1888- joint author. II. Title.

THE Encyclopedia of Sunday schools and religious education; giving a world-wide view of the hisotry and progress of the Sunday school and the development of religious education... Editors-in-chief: John T. McFarland...Benjamin S. Winchester...Canadian editor: R. Douglas Fraser...European editor: Rev. J. William Butcher... New York, London [etc.] T. Nelson & sons [c1915] 3 v. front., illus. (incl. maps, plans, forms) plates, ports., diagrs. 24 1/2 cm. Paged continuously. [BV1510.E5] 16-1651
I. McFarland, John Thomas, 1851-1913, ed. II. Winchester, Benjamin Severance, 1868- joint ed. III. Fraser, Robert Douglas, 1849- ed. IV. Butcher, James Williams, 1857- ed.

ERICKSEN, Mabel Natalie. 268.61
Listening to God; grade four, by Mabel Natalie Ericksen, illustrated by Stryker Ingerman. Minneapolis, Augsburg publishing house [c1938] 144 p. iilus. 22 cm. Text on lining-papers. "This volume is one in a series of graded Sunday school textbooks issued by the Board of elementary Christian education, Dr. Jacob Tanner, editor-in-chief." Also published in the teacher's manual. [BV1546.E7] 38-25496
1. Religious education. I. Tanner, Jacob, 1865- ed. II. Title.

ERICKSEN, Mabel Natalie. 268.61
Listening to God; grade four, teacher's manual, including the complete pupils' volume, by Mabel Natalie Ericksen. Minneapolis, Augsburg publishing house [c1938] ixx p., 1 l., 144 p. illus. 22 cm. Texts on lining-papers. "This volume is one in a series of graded Sunday school textbooks issued by the Board of elementary Christian education, Dr. Jacob Tanner, editor-in-chief." The pupils' volume is also published separately. [BV1546.E7 Manual] 38-25497
1. Religious education. I. Tanner, Jacob, 1865- ed. II. Title.

ESSEX, Herbert James, 1867-
The children in church; twenty-five addresses to young people, by the Rev. H. J. Essex ... Philadelphia, G. W. Jacobs & company [1919?] 1 p. l., v-vii, 119 p. 18 1/2 cm. E 20
1. Religious education. I. Title.

EUCHARISTIC Missionaries of St. Dominic. 268.6
Heralds of the good news [2d ed.] St. Paul, Minn., 55101, 262 E. Fourth St. Catechetical Guild Educational Soc., 1965 126p. illus. 23cm. Bibl. [BX921.E9] 65-28317 2.00
1. Religious education. I. Title.

FALLAW, Wesner 268
Church education for tomorrow. Philadelphia, Westminster Press [c.1960] 219p. 21cm. Bibl. and Bibl. notes p.[209]-215 60-9711 3.75
1. Religious education. 2. Religious education—Curricula. I. Title.

FENNER, Mable B. 220
God's good gifts ... by Mabel B. Fenner. Philadelphia, Pa., The United Lutheran publication house [c1928] (Religious education texts for [BS605.R35] 28-23212
I. Title. II. Title: (Religious education texts for weekday schools. Third book. Primary-third year. Teacher)

FERGUSSON, Edmund Morris, 1864-1934.
Teaching Christianity; a study in educational religion, by E. Morris Fergusson... New York, Chicago [etc.] Fleming H. Revell company [c1929] 168 p. 19 1/2 cm. [BV1471.F4] 29-19091
1. Religious education. I. Title.

FICKES, George Herman, 1878- 268
Principles of religious education, by George H. Fickes... New York [etc.] Fleming H. Revell company [c1937] 246 p. 1 illus. 21 cm. "References" at end of each chapter. [BV1471.F44] 37-2005
1. Religious education. I. Title.

FINN, Elizabeth M. 268.
Church work with intermediates, by Elizabeth M. Finn. Philadelphia, Boston [etc.] The Judson press [c1926] 4 p. l., 200 p. incl. diagrs., forms. 19cm. "Books for leaders and mothers": p. 198-199; "A few books for intermediates": p. 199. [BV1475.F45] 26-7357
1. Religious education. 2. Adolescence. I. Title.

FISKE, George Walter, 1872- 268.
Community forces for religious education, early adolescence, by G. Walter Fiske...a textbook in the Standard course in teacher-training, outlined and approved by the Sunday school council of Evangelical denominations. Third year specialization series. Nashville, Dallas [etc.] Pub. for the Teacher-training publication association, by the Publishing house of the M. E. church, South [c1922] 159 p. 17 cm. Contains bibliographies. [BV1475.F5] 23-8812
1. Religious education. I. Title.

FISKE, George Walter, 1872- 268.
Purpose in teaching religion, by George Walter Fiske ... New York, Cincinnati, The Abingdon press [c1927] 244 p. 20 cm. "Brief bibliography" at end of each chapter. [BV1475.F55] 27-24570
1. Religious education. I. Title.

FITZPATRICK, Edward Augustus, 1884- 377.1
The foundation of Christian education, by Edward A. Fitzpatrick... introduction by William M. Magee... Milwaukee, Wis., New York [etc.] The Bruce publishing company [c1930] 258 p. 18 1/2 cm. (Half-title: The Marquette monographs on education, no. 5) [BV1471.F5] 30-14399
1. Religious education. I. Title.

FLAQUE, Ferdinand Charles, 1901- 230.2
Catholic truth in survey; a textbook for the use of Confraternity of Christian doctrine classes at the secondary school level of learning, by Rev. Ferdinand C. Falque ... New York, Cincinnati [etc.] Benziger brothers, 1937- v. front. (v. 1) illus. (incl. map) 21 cm. (On cover: High school religion series) "Chief works consulted": p. xvii. [Full name: Ferdinand Charles Russel Falque] [BX930.F2] 37-31476
1. Religious education. I. Confraternity of Christian doctrine. II. Title.

FOLSOM, John Dana, 1842- 248
Religious education in the home, by John D. Folsom. New York, Eaton & Mains; Cincinnati, Jennings & Graham [c1912] 190 p. 19 cm. [BV1590.F6] 12-5827 0.75
1. Religious education. I. Title.

FOREST, Ilse, Mrs. 1896- 377.1
Child life and religion, by Ilse Forest. New York, R. R. Smith, inc., 1930. ix p., 2 l, 142 p. 19 1/2 cm. "Selected bibliography": p. 141-142. [BV1475.F65] 30-25832
1. Religious education. 2. Child study. I. Title.

FORSYTH, Nathaniel Frederick.
... *Training the junior citizen,* by Nathaniel F. Forsyth. New York, Cincinnati, The Abingdon press [c1923] 304 p. front. 20 cm. (The Abingdon religious education texts; D. G. Downey, general editor, G. H. Betts, editor) [BV1615.F6] 23-11343
1. Religious education. I. Title.

FOSTER, Virgil E. 268
Christian education where the learning is [by] Virgil E. Foster. Englewood Cliffs, N.J., Prentice-Hall [1968] xii, 147 p. 22 cm. [BV1471.2.F67] 68-15349
1. Religious education. I. Title.

FOSTER, Virgil E 268
How a small church can have good Christian education. [1st ed.] New York, Harper [1956] 127p. 20cm. [BV1520.F57] 56-7028
1. Religious education. 2. Sunday-schools. I. Title.

FOX, Henry Watson, 1872- 377.1
The child's approach to religion, by the Rev. H. W. Fox ... with an introduction by the Right Rev. the Lord Bishop of Liverpool. New York, R. R. Smith, inc., 1930. 95 p. 20 cm. [BV1475.F68] 30-28338
1. Religious education. I. Title.

FOX, Robert J. 377
Religious education; its effects, its challenges today [by] Robert J. Fox. [Boston] St. Paul Editions [1972] 86 p. illus. 18 cm. [BV1471.2.F68] 72-75561 0.95
1. Religious education. I. Title.

FRANCISCAN sisters of Christian charity 238.
Religion teaching plans, outline lessons based on modern principles of education as exemplified in practical class use, suggesting ways of developing, organizing and pplying the lesson in the Catechism, by the Franciscan sisters of Christian charity, Holy family convent, Manitowoc, Wisconsin; edited by Sister M. Inez, O. S. F.; with preface by Rev. George Johnson ... New York, Cincinnati [etc.] Benziger brothers, 1929. x, 245 p. illus. 19 cm. Contains bibliographies. [BX925.F7] 29-13310
1. Religious education. 2. Catholic church—Education. I. Inez, Sister Mary, 1878-ed. II. Title.

FRIENDS Council on Education. 377.1
Source book on religious education in Friends elementary schools. Philadelphia, 1951. 82 p. 19 cm. Includes bibliographies. [LC571.F8] 51-22669
1. Religious education. 2. Friends, Society of—Education. I. Title.

GABLE, Lee J
Christian nurture through the church. [New York] National Council of the Churches of Christ in the U. S. A. [1955] 126p. 20cm. Published for the Dept. of Administration and Leadership, Division of Christian Education, of the National Council. 'The outgrowth of the corporate thinking of seventy specialists in Christian education who gathered at Williams Bay, Wisconsin, in August, 1953.' Bibliography: p. 126. A56
1. Religious education. I. National Council of the Churches of Christ in the United States of America. Division of Christian Education. II. Title.

GAEBELEIN, Frank Ely, 1899- 377.1
The pattern of God's truth; problems of integration in Christian education. New York, Oxford University Press, 1954. 118p. 20cm. [LC368.G3] 54-6908
1. Religious education. I. Title.

GAEBELEIN, Frank Ely, 1899- 377.1
The pattern of God's truth; problems of integration in Christian education. Chicago, Moody, 1968, 118p. 18cm. (Christian forum bk. 30-6450) Orig. pub. in 1954 [LC368.G3] 1.25 pap.,
1. Religious education. I. Title.

GAILOR, Thomas Frank, bp. 1856-1935. 377.
The Christian church and education; the Bedell lectures, 1909, delivered at Kenyon college by the Rt. Rev. Thomas Frank Gailor ... New York, T. Whittaker, inc. [c1910] 104 p. 20 cm. [LC331.G3] 10-15377
1. Religious education. 2. Protestant Episcopal church in the U. S.—Education. 3. Church and education. I. Title.

GAINES, Robert Edwin, 1861- A 29-571
Guiding a growing life ... By Robert Edwin Gaines ... Nashville, Tenn., Sunday school board, Southern Baptist convention [c1927] vi p., 2 l., 11-128 p. 20 cm. (Holland lectures for 1926) [BV1475.G14]
1. Religious education. I. Title.

GALLOWAY, Thomas Walton, 1866-1929. 267
The dramatic instinct in religious education [by] Thomas Walton Galloway ... Boston, Chicago, The Pilgrim press [c1922] 5 p. l., 3-115 p. 19 cm. "Specimen Biblical dramas": p. [45]-115. [BV1472.G3] 22-23287
1. Religious education. I. Title.

GALLOWAY, Thomas Walton, 1866-1929. 268.
The use of motives in teaching morals and religion [by] Thomas Walton Galloway ... Boston, Chicago, The Pilgraim press [c1917] xi, 187 p. 20 cm. References at end of each of the chapters. [BV1534.G3] 18-1011

1. Religious education. 2. Sunday-schools. I. Title.

GENERAL council of the Congregational and Christian churches of the United States. Board of home missions. Division of Christian education. 268
A program of progress for Congregational and Christian churches, suggestions for building a parish program of Christian education, prepared by the Division of Christian education of the Board of home missions ... Boston, Mass., Chicago, Ill., The Pilgrim press [c1939] 2 p. l., 72, [4] p. 20 cm. Blank pages for "Memoranda" ([4] at end) Includes bibliographies. [BX7123.A5 1939] 39-14094
1. Religious education. I. Title.

GIFT, Foster U 1871- 268.
Week day religious education, by Rev. Foster U. Gift ... Philadelphia. Pa., The United Lutheran publication house [c1926] 96 p. diagrs. 20 cm. "Helps and materials needed": p. 96. [BV1580.G5] 26-9469
1. Religious education. I. Title.

GILBERT, W Kent.
The age group objectives of Christian education. Prepared in connection with the long-range program of Lutheran Boards of Parish Education. [Philadelphia] Boards of Parish Education of The American Evan. Luth. Church, The Augustana Luth. Church, The Suomi Synod, The United Lutheran Church in America. [c1958] 96 p. 25 cm. 64-25534
1. Religious education. I. Title.

GOD is with us. 268.432
Illus. by Kreigh Collins. Rev. teacher's manual replacing Wonder and faith in the first grade. Greenwich, Conn., Seabury [c.1955-1962] 105p. 27cm. (The church's teaching in the 1st grade) 2.00 pap.,

GODDARD, Carrie Lou.
God, the creator; a cooperative vacation church school text for use with primary boys and girls. Teacher's text. Nashville, Published for the cooperative Publication Association by Abingdon Press [1964] 111 p. 23 cm. 24 p. 23 cm. Pupil's book. Illustrated by Jim Padgett. [n.p., 1964?] 66-31304
I. Cooperative Publication Association. II. Title.

GOLDBRUNNER, Josef, ed. 268.6
New catechetical methods. Translated by M. Veronica Riedl. Notre Dame, Ind. University of Notre Dame Press, 1965. 134 p. illus. 18 cm. (Contemporary catechetics series) Translation of Katechetische Methoden heute. Bibliographical footnotes. [BX926.G643] 65-23518
1. Religious education. 2. Catechetics — Catholic Church. I. Title.

GORDON, Buford Franklin, 1894- 268
Teaching for abundant living; teaching through sharing and guiding experiences, by Buford Franklin Gordon ... Boston, The Christopher publishing house [c1936] 3 p. l., 5-188 p. 21 cm. [BV1534.G6] 36-11116
1. Religious education. I. Title.

GRAHAM, William (of Pittsburgh? Pa.)
Phases of the sacred passion; a Lenten course, by Rev. William Graham. New York, J. F. Wagner [1909] 58 p. 21 cm. 9-8425
I. Title.

GRIFFETH, Ross John. 286.6
... *Building the church of Christ as described in the New Testament* ... byRoss John Griffeth. Cincinnati, O., The Standard publishing company [c1931]- v. illus., diagr. 19 cm. (Standard elective series of special lessons) "Important reference-books": pt. 1, p. 6. [BX7314.G7] 270 31-3065
1. Religious education. 2. Church history. I. Title.

HAITHCOX, Henry C.
Schools and the Christian school, by Henry C. Haithcox, D.D. Boston, R. G. Badger, [c1919] 111, [1] p. 19 cm. (Lettered on cover: Library of religious thought) [LC368.H17] 19-12078
1. Religious education. I. Title.

HAKES, J Edward, 1917- 268.082
ed.
An introduction to evangelical Christian education. Edited by J. Edward Hakes. Chicago, Moody Press [1964] 423 p. illus. 24 cm. Includes bibliographies. [BV1471.2.H3] 64-20989
1. Religious education. I. Title.

HALL, Arthur Crawshay Alliston, bp., 1847-
Spiritual instructions, by the Rt. Rev. A. C. A. Hall... Milwaukee, The Young churchman co.; [etc., etc. 1913. 4 p. l., 3-80 p. 13 1/2 cm. $0.40 13-16144
I. Title.

HALL, Brian P. 207
Value clarification as learning process; a handbook for Christian educators, by Brian P. Hall [and] Maury Smith. Consultant authors: Gerald Conway, Michael J. Kenney [and] Joseph Osburn. [New York, Paulist Press, 1973] 270 p. illus. 26 cm. (Educator formation books) Bibliography: p. 258-265. [BV1464.H3] 73-81108 ISBN 0-8091-1797-5 7.95
1. Religious education. 2. Worth. I. Smith, Maury, joint author. II. Title.

HALL, Samuel Read, 1795- 268.
1877.
Practical lectures on parental responsibility, and the religious education of children. By S. R. Hall. Boston, Peirce and Parker, 1833. vii, [13]-176 p. 19 cm. [BV1475.H2] 7-34870
1. Religious education. I. Title.

HANSON, Helen Patten. 268.
...A travelbook for juniors, by Helen Patten Hanson. New York, Cincinnati, The Abingdon press [c1921] 4 p. l., 7-258 p. front., illus., amps. 20 cm. (The Abingdon religious education texts, D.G. Downey, general editor. Week-day school series, G.H. Betts, editor) [BV1546.H3] 22-445
I. Title.

HARNER, Nevin Cowger, 1901- 268
The educational work of the church [by] Nevin C. Harner. New York, Cincinnati [etc.] The Abington press [c1939] 257 p. diagrs. 20 cm. (Half-title: Abingdon religious education texts, J. W. Langdale, general editor; Guides to Christian leadership, P. H. Vieth, editor) [BV1471.H3] 39-27247
1. Religious education. I. Title.

HARNER, Nevin Cowger, 1901- 268
Religion's place in general education. Including The relation of religion to public education: the basic principles, a committee report of the American Council on Education. Richmond, John Knox Press [1949] 167 p. 21 cm. [LC107.H3] 49-2732
1. Religious education. I. American Council on Education. Committee on Religion and Education. The relation of religion to public education. II. Title.

HARPER, William Allen, 1880- 268.
An integrated program of religious education, by W. A. Harper ... New York, The Macmillan company, 1926. 7 p. l., 13-152 p. 20 cm. Bibliography at end of each chapter. [BV1475.H28] 26-16612
1. Religious education. I. Title.

HARPER, William Allen, 1880- 268
The minister of education, b W. A. Harper ... Ashland, O., The University post publishing company [c1939] 6 p. l., 11-159 p. 24 cm. "Some useful books": p. 155-159. [BV1532.H3] 39-16843
1. Religious education. I. Title.

HARRIS, George, of 268.
Baltimore.
The economy and policy of a Christian education. Adapted as a monitor and directory for all professors of Christianity; especially governors and directors of children and youth, in families and schools. By George Harris ... Baltimore, Printed by W. Wooddy, 1823. 282 p. 18 cm. [BV1475.H25] 7-34873
1. Religious education. I. Title.

HARRIS, Philip B 268.4
The training program of a church [by] Philip B. Harris and staff, Training Union Dept., Baptist Sunday School Board. Nashville, Convention Press [1966] xviii, 137 p. 20 cm. "Church study course [of the Sunday School Board of the Southern Baptist Convention] This book si number 1812 in category 18, section for adults and young people." Bibliography: p. 132-134. [BX6223.H3] 66-13313
1. Religious education. 2. Baptists. — Education. I. Southern Baptist Convention. Sunday School Board. Baptist Training Union Dept. II. Title.

HARTSHORNE, Hugh, 1885- 268.6
Case studies of present-day religious teaching, by Hugh Hartshorne ... and Elsa Lotz ... New Haven, Pub. for the Institute of social and religious research by the Yale university press; London, H. Milford, Oxford university press, 1932. vi p., 2 l., [3]-295 p. illus. (plans) 24 cm. (Half-title: Yale studies in religious education. vi) "The study was conducted ... as part of a more comprehensive investigation ... undertaken by the Institute of Soical and religion research."--Pref. [BV1534.H365] 32-34914
1. Religious education. 2. Sunday-schools. I. Lotz, Elsa, joint author. II. Institute of social and religious research. III. Title.

HARTSHORNE, Hugh, 1885- 268.
... Childhood and character; an introduction to the study of the religious life of children, by Hugh Hartshorne ... Boston, Chicago, The Pilgrim press [c1919] viii, 282 p. diagrs. 19 cm. (Manuals of religious education for parents and teachers) Bibliography: p. 268-275. [BV1475.H3] 19-15100
1. Religious education. 2. Child study. I. Title.

HARTSHORNE, Hugh, 1885- 268
Church schools of today, by Hugh Hartshorne ... and Earle V. Ehrhart ... London, H.Milford, Oxford university press, 1933 xiii p., 2 l., [3]-260 p. incl. diagrs., forms. 24 cm. (Half-title: Yale studies in religious education. vii) "The present volume ... is the fifth work issued by the Yale univeristy press on the Samuel B. Sneath memorial publication fund."--P. [v] [BV1516.A1H3] 33-11716
1. Religious education. 2. Sunday-schools. I. Ehrhart, Earle Vinton, 1887- joint author. II. Institute of social and religious research. III. Yale university. Samuel B. Sneath memorial publication fund. IV. Title.

HAWTHORNE, Marion Olive. 248
...Looking at life with boys and girls [by] Marion O. Hawthorne. New York, Cincinnati [etc.] The Abingdon press [c1932] 140 p. 20 1/2 cm. (The Abingdon religious education texts, J. W. Langdale, general editor; Week-day school series, G. H. Betts, editor) [BV4571.H385] 33-300
1. Religious education. 2. Youth. I. Title.

HAWTHORNE, Marion Olive. 248
...Looking at life with boys and girls. Teacher's manual [by] Marion O. Hawthorne. New York,Cincinnati [etc.] The Abingdon press [c1932] 127 p. 20 1/2 cm. (The Abingdon religious education texts, J. W. Langdale, general editor; Week-day school series, G. H. Betts, editor. Includes bibliographies. [BV4571.H385 Manual] 33-299
1. Religious education. 2. Youth. I. Title.

HAYWARD, Percy Roy, 1884- 377.1
The dream power of youth, young people of today and the religion of Jesus, by Percy R. Hayward ... New York and London, Harper & brothers, 1930. xv p., 1 l. 177 p. 19 1/2 cm. [BV1475.H38] 30-28470
1. Religious education. I. Title.

HAYWARD, Percy Roy, 1884- 268.423
Young people's method on the church [by] Percy R. Hayward and Roy A. Burkhart. New York, Cincinnati [etc.] The Abingdon press [c1933] 2 p. l. [8]-853 p. diagrs. 20 cm. (The Abingdon religious education texts. J. W. Langdale, general editor; Guides to Christian leadership, P. H. Vieth, editor) "Materials for use in a youth program": p. 236-282: Bibliography at end of each chapter. [BV1465.H3] 33-34000
1. Religious education. ' 2. Youth. I. Burkhart, Roy A., 1895- joint author. II. Title.

HEATHCOTE, Charles William, 268
1882-
The essentials of religious education, by Charles William Heathcote ... introduction by Russell H. Conwell ... Boston, Sherman, French & company, 1916. 5 p. l., 290 p. 21 cm. Bibliography: p. 279-284. [BV1471.H4] 16-22987
1. Religious education. I. Title.

HECKEL, Theodor, 1894- 268.6
How to teach evangelical Christianity with special reference to the word of God, by Theodor Heckel ... translated by Norman E. Richardson ... and Klaas Jacob Stratemeier ... Grand Rapids, Mich., Zondervan publishing house [1935] 121 p. 20 cm. [BV1534.H4] 36-13339
1. Religious education. 2. Bible—Study. I. Richardson, Norman Egbert, 1878- II. Stratemeier, Klass Jacob, joint tr. III. Title.

*HENDRICKS, William C. 207
Object lessons from sports and games, [by] William C. Hendricks and Merle Den Bleyker. Grand Rapids, Baker Book House, [1975] 106 p. 20 cm. [BV1471] [BV4227] ISBN 0-8010-4134-1 1.95 (pbk.)
1. Religious education. I. Bleyker, Merle Den. joint author. II. Title.

HENRY, Waights Gibbs. 268
The organization of personality, by Waights Gibbs Henry ... Birmingham, Ala., Birmingham printing co. [1922] 90 p. 21 cm. [BV1471.H45] 22-25623
1. Religious education. I. Title.

HENSLEY, John Clark, 1912- 268
The pastor as educational director. Kansas City, Kan., Central Seminary Press, 1946. 208 p. illus. 22 cm. "Revised from dissertation to faculty of Central Baptist Theological Seminary in partial fulfillment of the requirement for the degree, doctor of theology." Bibliography: p. 137-196. [BV4360.H4] 47-24768
1. Religious education. I. Title.

HERZOG, Charles G. 234.
... God the redeemer, the redemption from sin as wrought by Jesus Christ, the son of God: a textbook for colleges and universities, by Charles G. Herzog ... New York, Cincinnati [etc.] Benziger brothers, 1929. xvi, 230 p. 20 cm. (The truth of Christianity series) [BT775.H4] 29-19770
I. Title.

HOBEN, Allan, 1874- 268.
The church school of citizenship, by Allan Hoben... Chicago, University of Chicago press [c1918] ix 177 p., 18 cm. (Half-title: The University of Chicago publications in religious education...Principles and methods of religious education) "Reading recommended" at end of each chapter. [BV1475.H6] 18-17189
1. Religious education. 2. Citizenship. I. Title.

HOBENSACK, Alice (Bartow) 268.61
Mrs. 1904-
Riches to share; a guide for teachers including source manterials and teaching procedures [by] Alice Bartow Hobensack. New York, Cincinnati [etc.] The Abingdon press [c1937] 131 p. 20 cm. (Half-title: The Abingdon religious education texts, L. W. Langdale, general editor: Guides to Christian living, P. H. Vieth. editor) "Sharing" (words and music): p. 131. [Full name: Mrs. Alice Edwards (Bartow) Hobensack] Includes bibliographies. [BV1546.H6] 37-10139
1. Religious education. 2. Stewardship, Christian—Study and teaching I. Title.

HODGES, Edward Lewis. 230
Teachings of the secret order of the Christian brotherhood and school of Christian initiation, by Edward Lewis Hodges ... Los Angeles, Calif., Wetzel publishing co., inc [c1938] 243 p. illus., diagr. 20cm. "First edition." [BR126.H62] 39-12951
I. Title. II. Title: Secret order of the Christian brotherhood and school of Christian initiation.

HODGES, George, 1856-1919. 268.
The training of children in religion, by George Hodges ... New York and London, D. Appleton and company, 1911. 8 p. l., 828 p., 1 l. 20 cm. [BV1475.H63] 11-10757
1. Religious education. 2. Education of children. I. Title.

HOFINGER, Johannes. 207
Imparting the Christian message. [Notre Dame, Ind.] University of Notre Dame Press 1961. 119 p. 21 cm. "NDP 9." "Part I ... is a reprint of an interview with Father Hofinger, made at the historic Eichstatt Conference ... The interview is followed by a summary of the Eichstaff program. Part II [p. 21-119] ... is taken verbatim from his larger work. The art of teaching Christian doctrine." [BX921.H6 1961] 64-54537
1. Religious education. I. Title.

HOFINGER, Johannes.
Imparting the Christian message. [Notre Dame, Ind.] University of Notre Dame Press 1963 [c1961] 125 p. 21 cm. "NDP 9." "Part I ... is a reprint of an interview with Father Hofinger, made at the historic Eichstatt Conference ... The interview is followed by a summary of the Eichstatt program. Part II [p. 25-125] is taken verbatim from this larger work, The art of teaching Christian doctrine." 65-96880
1. Religious education. I. Title.

HOFINGER, Johannes, ed. 230.207
Pastoral catechetics edited by Johannes Hofinger and Theodore C. Stone. [New York Herder and Herder [1964] 287 p. 22 cm. Bibliographical footnotes. [BX921.H62] 64-19730
1. Religious education. I. Stone, Theodore C., joint ed. II. Title.

HOILAND, Richard.
Planning Christian education in the local church. Rev. ed. Chicago Judson Press [1962] 120 p. 64-15191
1. Religious education. I. Title.

HOLLENBACH, Blanche 268.6
(Schwartz) Mrs. 1889-
Teaching children; plans, suggestions and methods for junior and primary grades, by Blanche Schwartz Hollenbach; foreword by Will H. Houghton ... New York [etc.] Fleming H. Revell company [c1937] 83 p. 19 1/2 cm. [Full name: Mrs. Blanche Moore (Schwartz) Hollenbach] [BV1545.H64] 37-34654
1. Religious education. I. Title.

HOLMES, Harold.
Religious education in the state school; a South African study ... [Edinburgh] Nelson [c1962] vii, 284 p. 23 cm. Bibliography: p. 279-283. 64-15076
I. Title.

HOLY Family School dedication, Sunday, September 24, 1961. 100th anniversary, 1861-1961. [Latrobe, Pa., 1961] 69p. illus., ports. 29cm.
I. Latrobe, Pa. Holy Family Church.

HOLY Family School dedication, Sunday, September 24, 1961. 100th anniversary, 1861-1961. [Latrobe, Pa., 1961] 69p. illus., ports. 29cm.
I. Latrobe, Pa. Holy Family Church.

HORNBACK, Florence Mary, 374
1892-
Leadership manual for adult study groups, by Florence M. Hornback ... Paterson, N.J., St. Anthony guild press, Franciscan monastery [c1934] 2 p. l., vii-xii, 127 p. 25 cm. "A way of translating into concrete practice the recent pronouncements of the Holy see on Catholic action."--Introd. Encyclical letter of His Holiness Pope Plus xi on Christian education of youth: p. 83-112. [LC5215.H65] 35-741
1. Religious education. 2. Education of adults. 3. Catholic action. I. Catholic church. Pope, 1922- (Plus xi) Divinl illus magistri. II. Title.

HORNE, Herman Harrell, 1874- 268
The philosophy of Christian education, by Herman Harrell Horne ... New York [etc.] Fleming H. Revell company [c1937] 171 p. 1 illus. 19 1/2cm. [The James Sprunt lectures, 1937] [BV1471.H56] 37-2100
1. Religious education. I. Title.

HOWLETT, Walter Main, 1883- 268
ed.
Religion, the dynamic of education; a symposium on religious education, edited by Walter M. Howlett ... New York and London, Harper & brothers, 1929. xi, 172 p. 19 1/2 cm. [BV1471.H6] 29-4957
1. Religious education. 2. Bible in the schools. I. Title.

HOY, David. 268.6
Magic with a message. Illustrated by Sid

Couchey. [Westwood, N. J.] Revell [1956] 72p. illus. 23cm. [BV1472.H67] 56-5241
1. Religious education. 2. Conjuring. I. Title.

*HUTCHCROFT, Vera 207
Object lessons for church groups. Grand Rapids, Baker Book House, [1975] 95 p. 20 cm. (Object lesson series) [BV1471] [BV4227] ISBN 0-8010-4107-4 1.95 (pbk.)
1. Religious education. I. Title.

[HYDE, Charles]
Parental training; in a series of letters to Christian parents, on the religious education of their children. By a father. Wrtten for the Massachusetts Sabath school society and approved by the Committee of publications. Boston, Massachusetts Sabbath school society, 1849. xii, [13]-144 p. incl. front. 16 cm. [LC361.H99] E 9
1. Religious education. I. Title.

INTERNATIONAL council of religious education. 268
A century beckons; one hundred and ninety-two Christian citizens plead for extension and intensification of religious education, edited by Frances Dunlap Heron. Chicago, Ill., International council of religious education [1946] 60 p. 23 cm. "First printing." [BV1471.I48] 47-21957
1. Religious education. I. Heron, Frances Dunlap, ed. II. Title.

INTERNATIONAL council of religious education. 268.
Christian religion in growing life; the international curriculum guide for the development of a comprehensive program in Christian education ... Developed cooperatively by Protestant evangelical forces of the United States and Canada through the International council of religious education ... Chicago, Ill., The International council of religious education [c1932] v. 23 cm. Contents.bk. 1. Principles and objectives of Christian education with a prospectus of the total program. [LC368.I8] [BV1559.I58] E 34
1. Religious education. I. Title. II. Title: The international curriculum guide.

INTERNATIONAL council of religious education. 268.
The development of a curriculum of religious education; the origin, history, and purposes of the International curriculum of religious edjcation, the educational principles underlying it, and the program of work adopted for its construction, prepared by the Department of research and service of the International council of religious education, Paul H. Vieth, director. Chicago, The International council of religious education, 1928. 58, [2] p., 1 l. 23 cm. (Its Research service bulletin no. 5) Bibliography: p. [60] [BV1559.I6] 28-30465
1. Religious education. I. Vieth, Paul H. II. Title. III. Title: International curriculum of religious education.

INTERNATIONAL council of religious education. 268
The international curriculum guide for the development of a comprehensive program in Christian education ... Developed cooperatively by Protestant evangelical forces of the United States and Canada through the International council of religious education ... Chicago, Ill., The International council of religious education [c1935- v. 23 cm. "First edition, 1932. Reprinted, 1935." [BV1559.I632 1935] 36-6940
1. Religious education. I. Title.

INTERNATIONAL council of religious education. 268.3
... *Series courses of the New standard leadership curriculum* ... Ed. of 1935. Developed cooperatively by Protestant evangelical forces of the United States and Canada through the International council of religious education ... Chicago, Ill., The International council of religious education [c1935] v. 23 1/2 cm. (International bulletins in religious education. Educational bulletin, no. 502) Includes "Approved text materials" for each course. [BV1559.I64 1935] 36-6939
1. Religious education. I. Title.

INTERNATIONAL council of religious education. 268.3
... *Series courses of the Standard leadership curriculum* ... Ed. of 1938. Developed cooperatively by Protestant evangelical forces of the United States and Canada through the International council of religious education ... Chicago, Ill., The International council of religious education [c1938- v. 23 cm. (International bulletins in religious education. Educational bulletin no. 502) Includes "Recommended text material" for each course. [BV1559.I64 1938] 38-37484
1. Religious education. I. Title.

JACOBS, James Vernon, 1898-
Understanding your pupils. Grand Rapids, Mich., Zondervan [c1959] 64 p. (Sunday school know-how series) 64-47858
1. Religious education. I. Title.

JARRATT, Elizabeth Ann, 1895- 268.61
Home helpers far and near; a world friendship unit for primary children, by Elizabeth A. Jarratt. Nashville, Tenn., Cokesbury press [c1935] 79 p. 23 cm. Includes music. Bibliography: p. 77-79. [BV1545.J35] 35-20694
1. Religious education. I. Title. II. Title: World friendship unit for primary children.

JOHNSON, Raymond Burgeur, 1885- 268
What is happening in religious education. Boston, Beacon Press, 1948. 88 p. 20 cm. [BV1471.J58] 48-6733
1. Religious education. I. Title.

JONES, Mary Alice. 268.
... *Training juniors in worship,* by Mary Alice Jones ... Nashville, Dallas [etc.] Lamar & Barton, agents, Publishing house M. E. church, South, 1925. 200 p. 20 cm. (Training courses for leadership) References "for additional study" at end of each chapter) "Approved by the Committee on curriculum of the General Sunday school board of the Methodist Episcopal church, South." [BV1546.J6] 25-24785
1. Religious education. I. Title.

JONES, Mary Alice, 1898- 268
The church and the children, by Mary Alice Jones ... Nashville, Tenn., Cokesbury press [c1935] [BV1475.J53] 35-10115
1. Religious education. I. Title.

JONES, Mary Alice, 1898- 268.6
The faith of our children [by] Mary Alice Jones ... New York, Nashville, Abingdon-Cokesbury press [1943] 175 p. 19 1/2 cm. [BV1471.J6] 43-5495
1. Religious education. I. Title.

JONES, Olivia Mary, 1872- 268.432
Inspired children, by Olive M. Jones. New York and London, Harper & brothers, 1933. xiv, 186 p. 20 cm. "The first detailed description of the influence of the Oxford group movement ... upon the lives of children."--Introd. "First edition." Contents.--pt. 1. True stories of children's spiritual experience.--pt. 2. The way; how children learn to know God. [BV1475.J55] 248 33-34594
1. Religious education. 2. Oxford group. 3. Psychology, Religious. 4. Child study. I. Title.

JOY, Donald Marvin.
Introducing Aldersgate Biblical series. Specimen lessons by G. Herbert Livingston, Wilber T. Dayton. Winona Lake, Ind., Light and Life Press [1960] 49 p. 22 cm. 63-40127
I. Title.

JOY, Donald Marvin.
Introducing Aldersgate Biblical series. Specimen lessons by G. Herbert Livingston, Wilber T. Dayton. Winona Lake, Ind., Light and Life Press [1960] 49 p. 22 cm. 63-40127
I. Title.

KEACH, Benjamin, 1640-1704.
The travels of true godliness. From the beginning of the world to this pre[sent] day, in an apt and pleasant allegory, shewing, what true godliness is; also the troubles, [op]positions, reproaches, and persecutions he ha[th met] with in every age. Together with the danger and sad declining state he is in at this [pre]sent time, by errors, heresies, and ungodliness, or open prophaneness. The Tenth edition corrected, and with the ad[dition] of one whole chapter. By Benjamin Keach ... Boston, Printed by B. Green and company, for D. Gookin, over against the Old South meeting-house, 1745. 2 p. l., 151 p. front. (port.) 15 cm. Title-page mutilated: some words supplied from a later edition. 13-18894
I. Title.

KEACH, Benjamin, 1640-1704.
The travels of True Godliness: from the beginning of the world to this present day. In an apt and pleasing allegory. Shewing what True Godliness is, also the troubles, oppositions, reproaches, and persecutions, he hath met with in every age. Together with the danger and sad declining state he is in at this present time, by errors, heresies and ungodliness, or open prophaneness. By Benjamin Keach. New York, J. Tiebout, 1811. 144 p. incl. front., illus. 14 cm. 5-20025
I. Title.

KEACH, Benjamin, 1640-1704. 244
The travels of True Godliness and Ungodliness; abridged from the works of Mr. Benjamin Keach; showing the different success they met with, in their various journeyings amongst that race of fallen spirits, who are clothed for a season, with flesh and blood, and commonly called men and women. Schenectady: Printed and sold, wholesale and retail, by Cornelius P. Wyckoff, corner of State and Washington streets, 1796. iv, [5]-261 p. 18 cm. "The progress of sin: or, The travels of Ungodliness. Abridged from the works of Mr. Benjamin Keach" (with special t.-p.): p. [141]-261. Signatures: A-X6 (last leaf is advertising matter) [BV4515.K4 1796] 5-28765
I. Title.

KEACH, Benjamin, 1640-1704. 248
The travels of True Godliness: from the beginning of the world to this present day. In an apt and pleasing allegory. Shewing what True Godliness is, also the troubles, oppositions, reproaches, and persecutions, he hath met with in every age. Together with the danger and sad declining state he is in at this present time, by errors; heresies and ungodliness, or open prophaneness. By Benjamin Keach. New-York, Published by John Tiebout, no. 238. Water-street, 1811. G. Bunce, print. 144 p. incl. front., illus. 13 1/2 cm. [BV4515.K4 1811] 5-20025
I. Title.

KEEDY, John Lincoln, 1869- 232.
Teachers' book of the heroic Christ; a course of studies for classes in religious education, glorifying the heroic and kingly qualities in Jesus Christ, by John L. Keedy ... Lysander, N. Y., The author [c1905] 124 p. 18 cm. [BT307.K2] 5-40423
I. Title.

KENNGOTT, George Frederick, 1864-
Object-lessons and illustrated talks; a series ... for the use of superintendents of junior and intermediate societies, by Rev. George F. Kenngott. Boston and Chicago, United society of Christian endeavor [c1907] 3 p. l., 5-75, [1] p. 15 cm. 'Helpful books for junior and intermediate superintendents": 1 p. at end. 7-25714
I. Title.

KHOOBYAR, Helen 268.434
Facing adult problems in Christian education. Philadelphia, Westminster [c.1963] 140p. 21cm. Bibl. 63-15467 2.95
1. Religious education. I. Title.

KIRKPATRICK, Blaine E. 267.6
Adventures in Christian leadership, a guide to young people's work in church schools and the Epworth league, by Blaine E. Kirkpatrick. Chicago, Ill., The Board of education, Methodist Episcopal church [c1930] cover-title, 3 p. l., 97 p. 20 cm. [BV1475.K47] ca 30
1. Religious education. 2. Epworth league. I. Title.

KNOX, Edmund Arbuthnott, bp. of Manchester, 1847- 268
Pastors and teachers; six lectures on pastoral theology, delivered in the Divinity school, Cambridge, in the year 1902, by the Right Rev. Edmund Arbuthnott Knox ... with an introduction by the Right Rev. Charles Gore ... London, New York and Bombay, Longmans, Green, and co., 1902. xix, 300 p. 20 cm. The appendix contains the following catechisms: 1. Luther's. 2. Church of England. 3. Heidelberg. 4. The shorter catechism. 5. Russian catechism. 6. The penny catechism of the Roman church. 7. Catechism of the Free evangelical church. [BV1471.K6] 3-427
1. Religious education. 2. Catechisms. I. Title.

KOONS, William George. 268.
The child's religious life; a study of the child's religious nature and the best methods for its training and development, by Rev. William George Koons ... with an introduction by Thomas B. Neely ... New York, Eaton & Mains; Cincinnati, Jennings & Pye [c1903] xii, 270 p. 19 cm. "Selected list of books on this subject": p. 265. [BV1475.K6] 3-7783
1. Religious education. I. Title.

KRETZMANN, Paul Edward, 1883- 268.
The religion of the child and other essays, an inquiry into the fundamental errors of modern religious pedagogy and their correction, by Prof. P. E. Kretzmann ... St. Louis, Mo., Concordia publishing house, 1929. 152 p. 19 cm. [BV1475.K7] 29-17738
1. Religious education. 2. Lutheran church in the U. S.—Education. I. Title.

LAMBDIN, Ina (Smith) Mrs. 1894- 266.433
The art of teaching intermediates, by Ina S. Lambdin. Nashville, Tenn., The Sunday school board of the Southern Baptist convention [c1937] 160 p. 19 cm. "Books for further study" at end of most of the chapters. [BV1548.L3] 37-4069
1. Religious education. I. Title.

LAMOREAUX, Antoinette Abernethy, Mrs. 268.
The unfolding life; a story of development with reference to religious training, by Antoinette Abernethy Lamoreaux, with introduction by Marion Lawrence. Chicago, The Religious publishing company (not incorporated) [c1907] 6 p. l., [11]-188 p. 20 cm. [BV1475.L37] 8-16407
1. Religious education. I. Title.

LAMOREAUX, Antoinette Abernethy, Mrs.
The unfolding life; a study of development with reference to religious training, by Antoinette Abernethy Lamoreaux, with introduction by Marion Lawrence. New York, Chicago [etc.] F. H. Revell company [c1907] 6 p. l., [11]-188 p. 20 cm. [LC368.L2] 14-179
1. Religious education. 2. Child study. I. Title.

LANCE, Derek. 230.207
Teaching the history of salvation, an introduction for teachers. With study-club questions. [Rev. American ed.] Glen Rock, N.J., Paulist Press [1964] 127 p. 18 cm. (Insight series) First published in 1964 under title: Till Christ be formed. Bibliography: p. 125-127. [BX926.L3] 64-24522
1. Religious education. I. Title.

LAUX, John Joseph, 1878-1939. 230.2
A course in religion for Catholic high schools and academies... By Rev. John Laux... New York, Cincinnati [etc.] Benziger brothers, 1934-38. 4 v. illus. (incl., port., facsims.) plates, front. 20 1/2 cm. With this is bound his Teacher's manual to accompany A course in religion for Catholic high schools and academies, pt. I, III ... New York, Cincinnati [etc.] 1934. Bibliography at end of some of the chapters. [BX930.L3 1934] 34-23447
1. Religious education. 2. Christian ethics—Catholic authors. I. Title.

LAUX, John Joseph, 1878-1939. 230.2
A course in religion for Catholic high schools and academies ... by Rev. John Laux ... New York, Cincinnati [etc.] Benziger brothers, 1932. 4 v. 21 cm. "Readings" at the end of some of the chapters. Contents.--i. Chief truths of faith.--ii. Means of grace; the sacraments, the sacrifice of the mass, sacramentals, indulgences.--iii. Christian moral.--iv. God,

Christianity and the church; apologetics for high schools. [BX930.L3 1932] 32-16953
1. Religious education. 2. Christian ethics—Catholic authors. I. Title.

LAWRENCE, William Irvin, 1853- 268
The social emphasis in religious education, by William Irvin Lawrence, TH. D.; introduction by George Albert Coe, PH. D. Boston, Mass., The Beacon press [c1918] 9, 9-123, [1] p. 20 cm. [BV1475.L4] 19-95
1. Religious education. I. Title.

...LEARNING how to live with others. For use with grades three and four. Prepared by Ruth W. Rusell. Teacher's book. This text is for use in teaching religion through the week. Chicago, The Judson Press [1959] 157p. illus. 20cm.
1. Religious education. I. Russell, Ruth W

LE BAR, Lois Emogene, 1907- 268
Education that is Christian. [Westwood, N. J.] Revell [1958] 252p. 22cm. Includes bibliography. [BV1471.L4] 58-8602
1. Religious education. I. Title.

LE BAR, Lois Emogene, 1907- 268
Focus on people in church education [by] Lois E. LeBar. Westwood, N.J., Revell [1968] 256 p. illus. 21 cm. Includes bibliographies. [BV1471.2.L4] 68-17091
1. Religious education. I. Title.

LEBERMAN, Josephine Marie, 1892- 240
The Christian way, teacher's manual, by J. Marie Leberman; stories by E. May Munsell, and songs by Blanche D. Springer. Chicago, Ill., The University of Chicago press [c1929] xi, 124, [1] p. 20 cm. (Half-title: The University of Chicago publications in religious education ... Constructive studies) [BV1585.L4] 29-17515
1. Religious education. 2. Vacation schools. I. Munsell, Effe May. II. Springer, Blanche (Donahue) Mrs. III. Title.

LEDERACH, Paul M 268.6
Learning to teach, by Paul M. Lederach. Newton, Kan., Faith and Life Press [1964] 103 p. illus. 20 cm. 36 p. 20 cm. (Christian service training series) (Christian service training series) Leader's guide. [Newton, Kan., Faith and Life Press, 1964] Cover title. Bibliographical footnotes. [BV1475.2.L4] 64-24359
1. Religious education. 2. Mennonites — Education. I. Title.

LEDERACH, Paul M. 268
Reshaping the teaching ministry; toward relevant education in the local congregation, by Paul M. Lederach. Scottdale, Pa., Herald Press [1968] 125 p. 20 cm. Includes bibliographical references. [BV1471.2.L42] 68-22266
1. Religious education. I. Title.

LEE, James Michael. 268
The flow of religious instruction: a social-science approach. Dayton, Ohio, Pflaum/Standard [1973] 379 p. illus. 21 cm. Second vol. in a trilogy; the 1st of which is the author's The shape of religious instruction; and the 3d of which is his The content of religious instruction. Includes bibliographical references. [BV1471.2.L442] 72-97171 ISBN 0-8278-9058-3 4.95
1. Religious education. 2. Sociology, Christian. I. Title.

LEE, Mary Virginia. 268.433
Intermediate Sunday school work, by Mary Virginia Lee ... Nashville, Tenn., The Sunday school board of the Southern Baptist convention [c1937] 159 p. 19 cm. [BV1548.L42] 37-38550
1. Religious education. I. Title.

LEESON, Spencer, 1892- 377
Christian education; being eight lectures delivered before the University of Oxford, in the year 1944, on the foundation of the Rev. John Bampton, Canon of Salisbury. London, New York, Longmans, Green [1947] xvi, 258 p. 23 cm. Full name: Spencer Stottesbery Gwatkin Leeson. [BR45.B3 1944] 47-5621
1. Religious education. 2. Religious education—England. 3. Bampton lectures, 1944. I. Title.
Contents omitted.

LEESON, Spencer, 1892-1956.
Christian education reviewed. London, New York, Longmans, Green [1957] xii, 123p. 22cm. Bibliographical references included in footnotes. A58
1. Religious education. 2. Religious education—England. I. Title.

LEWIS, Edward Samuel, 1855- 268.
...The senior worker and his work, by Edward S. Lewis, authorized and issued by the Board of Sunday schools of the Methodist Episcopal church... [Chicago] Printed for the Board of Jennings and Graham [c1910] 285 p. diagr. 18 cm. (The worker and his work series; a correspondence study course for Sunday school workers. [v. 5]) Bibliography: p. 284-285. [BV1549.L4] 12-1323
1. Religious education. 2. Sunday-schools. I. Methodist Episcopal church. Board of Sunday schools. II. Title.

LEWIS, Hazel Asenath, 1886- 268.432
Planning for children in the local church, by Hazel A. Lewis ... St. Louis, The Bethany press [c1933] 90 p. 16 1/2 cm. "Approved as a textbook in leadership training by the Department of religious education. Disciples of Christ." "For further study" at end of each chapter. [BV639.C4L4] 34-6
1. Disciples of Christ. Dept. of religious education. 2. Religious education. 3. Sunday-schools. I. Title.

LEWIS, Hazel Asenath, 1886- 268.432
The primary church school, by Hazel A. Lewis. St. Louis, Mo., Printed for the Leadership training publishing association by the Bethany press [c1932] xi, 260 p. 20 cm. "Companion volume to ... Teaching primaries in the church school by Miss Ethel L. Smither."--Editor's introd., signed: Erwin L. Shaver. chairman. Bibliography: p. 260. [BV1545.L47] 33-1973
1. Religious education. 2. Sunday-schools. I. Title.

LIMOUZE, Arthur Henry, 1883- 240
Stories from the great library; Bible stories for use with children from six to twelve in the daily vacation Bible school, by Arthur Henry Limouze ... with a program of projects for boys and girls, arranged by George T. Arnold ... edited by John T. Faris, D. D. Phrladelphia, Board of Christian education of the Presbyterian church in the U. S. A., 1926. 143 p. illus. 24 cm. Bibliography: p. 143. [BV1585.L5] 26-9835
1. Religious education. I. Arnold, George T., joint author. II. Faris, John Thomson, 1871- ed. III. Title.

LINDHORST, Frank Atkinson. 268
The minister teaches religion [by] Frank A. Lindhorst ... New York, Nashville, Abingdon-Cokesbury press [1945] 125 p. 19 1/2 cm. Bibliography at end of each chapter. [BV1471.L54] 45-9815
1. Religious education. 2. Theology, Pastoral. I. Title.

LINK, Mark J., ed. 207
Faith and commitment; aim of religious education [by] Tilmann [others. Mark J. Link, ed.] Chicago, Loyola Univ. Pr. [c.] 1964. vii, 309p. 24cm. (Loyola pastoral studies) Bibl. 64-20940 3.50
1. Religious education. I. Title.

LINK, Mark J. 207
Faith and commitment; aim of religious education [by] Tilmann [and others. Mark J. Link, editor] Chicago, Loyola University Press, 1964. vii, 309 p. 24 cm. (Loyola pastoral studies) "Selected readings for busy teachers": p. 305-309. Bibliographical references included in footnotes. [BX926.L5] 64-20940
1. Religious education. I. Title.

LITTLE, Gertrude, 1911- 268
Understanding our pupils. Anderson, Ind., Warner Press [1950] 110 p. 19 cm. [BV1471.L56] 50-9995
1. Religious education. I. Title.

LITTLE, Lawrence Calvin, 1897- 268
Foundations for a philosophy of Christian education. [Nashville] Abingdon [c.1962] 240p. Bibl. 62-7440 4.00
1. Religious education. I. Title.

LOBINGIER, John Leslie, 1884- 268.
Projects in world-friendship, by John Leslie Lobingier ... Chicago, The University of Chicago press [1925] xv, 177 p. front., illus. 18 cm. (Half-title: The University of Chicago publications in religious education ... Principle and methods of religious education) "Reading suggestions": p. 168-171. [BV1475.L52] 25-9231
1. Religious education. I. Title.

LOONEY, Myrtle Owens. 268.432
Guiding junior boys and girls in the Sunday school [by] Myrtle Owens Looney. Nashville, Tenn., Broadman press [c1936] 127 p. 19 cm. "Editor's foreword" signed: P. E. Burroughs. [BV1546.L6] 36-32095
1. Religious education. I. Burroughs, Prince Emanuel, 1871- ed. II. Title.

LOTZ, Philip Henry, 1889- 268.
... Current week-day religious education, based on a survey of the field conducted under the supervision of the Department of religious education of Northwestern university, by Philip Henry Lotz ... New York, Cincinnati, The Abingdon press [c1925] 2 p. l., [3]-412 p. front. 21 cm. (The Abingdon religious education texts, D. G. Downey, general editor. College series, G. H. Betts, editor) The author's doctoral dissertation, Northwestern university, 1924, but not published as a thesis. Bibliography: p. 406-407. [BV1580.L6] 25-11011
1. Religious education. 2. Church schools. I. Title.

LOTZ, Philip Henry, 1889- ed. 377.1
Studies in religious education; a source and textbook for colleges, universities, seminaries, and discussion groups and for leaders and workers in the field of religious [!] education; the viewpoints of twenty-nine writers, each a specialist in his respective field. Philip Henry Lotz, editor ... L. W. Crawford, co-editor ... Nashville, Tenn., Cokesbury press [1931] 702 p. 23 cm. Bibliography at end of each chapter except chapters xx, xii-xxix; "A selected bibliography of religious education": p. 621-671. [BV1471.L6] 31-24867
1. Religious education. 2. Religious education—Bibl. I. Crawford, Leonidas Wakefield, 1877- joint ed. II. Title.

LOVE,
the motive principle and the motive power in the Christian nurture of children. In ten dialogues. By the author of "Home conversations on little things." New York, General Protestant Episcopal Sunday school union and church book society, 1855. 127 p. 16 cm. [LC361.L7] 7-34877
1. Religious education.

LOWRY, Oscar 243
Scripture memorizing for successful soul-winning. abridged. Grand Rapids, Mich., Zondervan, 1962 [c.1932, 1934] 140p. 21cm. 1.00 pap.,
I. Title.

MCDONALD, Osgoode Hamilton, 1897- 268
A church and only a church; a study in program unification, by Osgoode H. McDonald. Philadelphia, Boston [etc.] The Judson press [c1936] 67, [1] p. 19 1/2 cm. A brief bibliography": [1] p. at end. [BV1471.M25] 36-20697
1. Religious education. 2. Sunday-schools. 3. Church work. I. Title.

MCELHONE, James F. 242
Particular examen, by the Rev. J. F. McElhone, C.S.C. St. Louis, Mo. and London, B. Herder book co., 1929. vi, 216 p. 19 1/2 cm. [BX2182.M28] 29-14451
I. Title.

MACINNIS, John Murdoch, 1871- 268
The church as teacher, by John Murdock MacInnis ... Philadelphia, The Westminster press, 1936. 168 p. 17 1/2 cm. (On cover: Handybooks for church school leaders). "A brief chapter bibliography": p. 165-168. [BV1471.M27] 38-3602
1. Religious education. I. Title.

MCKIBBEN, Frank Melbourne, 1889- 268
Christian education through the church. Nashville, Abingdon-Cokesbury Press [1947] 158 p. 19 cm. Bibliographical references included in "Notes" (p. 157-158) [BV1471.M29] 47-11950
1. Religious education. I. Title.

MCKIBBEN, Frank Melbourne, 1889- 377.1
Improving religious education through supervision [by] Frank M. McKibben... a textbook in the Standard course in leadership training, outlined and approved by the International council of religious education. [Dobbs Ferry, N.Y.] Printed for the Leadership training publishing association by the Methodist book concern [c1931] 256 p. illus. 19 1/2 cm. "Editor's introduction" signed: Erwin L. Shaver. "Further reading" at end of each chapter. [BV1520.M32] 31-21720
1. Religious education. I. Shaver, Erwin Leander, 1890- ed. II. International council of religious education. III. Title.

MCKIBBEN, Frank Melbourne, 1889- 268.6
Improving your teaching, by Frank M. McKibben... Philadelphia, Boston [etc.] The Judson press [1934] 64 p. 19 1/2 cm. "A simple and practical treatment of some of the problems confronted by teachers and officers in church schools..."--Foreword. [BV1534.M23] 34-17636
1. Religious education. 2. Teaching. I. Title.

MCKINLEY, Charles Ethelbert, 1870-
Educational evangelism; the religious discipline for youth, by Charles E. McKinley. Boston, New York [etc.] The Pilgrim press [1905] 265 p. 19 cm. [BV147.M3] 5-10569
1. Religious education. I. Title.
Contents omitted.

MCKINNEY, Alexander Harris, 1858- 268.
Average boys and girls; a manual for parents, pastors, Christian workers and all others who are interested in the religious education of children and youth, by A. H. McKinney... New York, Chicago [etc.] Fleming H. Revell company [c1925] 110 p., 1 l. front. 19 cm. [BV1475.M3] 25-9229
1. Religious education. I. Title.

MCKINNEY, Alexander Harris, 1858- 262.
...Bible school pedagogy; outlines for normal classes, by A. H. McKinney, PH. D. With an introduction by Jesse Lyman Hurlbut, D.D. New York, Eaton & Mains; Cincinnati, Jennings & Pye [1900] 78 p. 20 cm. Bibliography: p. [77]-78. [BV1533.M32] 0-5240
1. Religious education. 2. Sunday-schools. I. Title.

MCKINNEY, Alexander Harris, 1858- 259
The child for Christ; a manual for parents, pastors and Sunday-school workers, interested in the spiritual welfare of children, by A. H. McKinney...with a prologue by A. F. Schauffler, D. D. New York, Chicago [etc.] Fleming H. Revell company [1902] 124 p. 19 1/2 cm. Bibliography: p. 112-116. [BV639.C4M3] 2-16951
1. Religious education. I. Title.

*MCLAREN, Rosemary Collyer, 1916- 268'.6
St. Michael the Archangel and the holy terror, memoirs, by Rosemary Collyer McLaren. [First ed.] New York, Exposition Press [1973] 61 p. 21 cm. [BV1471] ISBN 0-682-47828-8. 3.50
1. Religious education. I. Title.

MACLEAN, Angus Hector, 1892- 232.97
The new era in religious education; a manual for church school teachers, by Angus Hector MacLean. Boston, The Beacon press, inc., 1934. v, 270 p. 21 1/2 cm. "Suggestions for reading and study" at end of most of the chapters. [BV1534.M284] 34-8166
1. Religious education. 2. Sunday-schools. I. Title.

MCMILLIN, Joseph L. 268.6
How to make your teaching count. Nashville, Broadman [c.1965] 55p. 22cm. [BV1471.2.M3] 65-10337 .75 pap.,
1. Religious education. I. Title.

MADDEN, Ward Ellis, 1913- 377
Religious values in education. [1st ed.] New York, Harper [1951] 203 p. 22 cm. [LC368.M33] 51-6826
1. Religious education. I. Title.

MARIANISTS. 268.
Manual of Christian pedagogy, for the use of religious teachers. 1st ed. By The Brothers of Mary. Dayton, O., 1910. 3 p. l., 9-122 p. 20 cm. [BV1475.M33] 10-30164
1. Religious education. I. Title.

MARK, Harry Thiselton, 1862-
The teacher and the child; elements of moral and religious teaching in the day school, the home, and the Sunday school, by H. Thiselton Mark ... Introduction by Patterson Du Bois, [3d ed.] New York, Chicago [etc.] F. H. Revell company [19--?] 5 p. l., 5-165 p. 19 cm. [LC381.M3] E 12
1. Religious education. 2. Sunday schools—[Teaching] I. Title.

MARS, Flla May. Mrs. 201
Instructions how to enter the kingdom of God. [Long Beach, Calif.] Mrs. Ella M. Mars [c1926] 1 p. l., 52 p. 17 cm. [BF1999.M27] ca 26
I. Title.

MARTHALER, Berard L. 268'.6
Catechetics in context; notes and commentary on the General catechetical directory issued by the Sacred Congregation for the Clergy, by Berard L. Marthaler. Huntington, Ind., Our Sunday Visitor [1973] xxxi, 293 p. 23 cm. Includes bibliographical references. [BV1471.2.M347] 72-90557 ISBN 0-87973-842-1 pap. 4.95
1. Religious education. 2. Pastoral theology—Catholic Church. I. Catholic Church. Congregatio pro Clericis. Directorium catechisticum generale. English. 1973. II. Title.
Cloth 7.95; ISBN 0-87973-842-1.

MARTIN, Mary Grace. 268.6
Teaching primary children, by Mary Grace Martin. Philadelphia, Boston [etc.] The Judson press [c1937] 104 p. 19 1/2 cm. "Suggested reading" at end of each chapter. [BV1475.M35] 37-14724
1. Religious education. I. Title.

[MARVEL, Marie] 1899- 268.6
Teaching children in the small church ... Chicago, Ill., The Board of education, Methodist Episcopal church, c1938. 56 p. illus. (plans) 23 cm. On cover: By Marie Marvel. "Approved text for use in the first series leadership education courses." [Full name: Sadie Marie Marvel] Includes bibliographies. [BX8223.M3] 38-30974
1. Religious education. 2. Rural churches. I. Title.

MARY Agnesine, Sister, 1884- 268
Teaching religion for living. Milwaukee, Bruce Pub. Co. [1953, c1952] 184p. 23cm. [BX925.M33] 53-1999
1. Religious education. 2. Catholic Church— Education. I. Title.

MASON, Harold Carlton, 1888- 268
Abiding values in Christian education. [Westwood, N. J., F. H. Revell Co. [1955] 176p. 21cm. [BV1471.M37] 55-6629
1. Religious education. I. Title.

MASON, Harold Carlton, 1888- 268
The teaching task of the local church. Winona Lake, Ind., Light and Life Press [1960] 214p. 23cm. Includes bibliography. [BV1471.M372] 60-8218
1. Religious education. I. Title.

MAUS, Cynthia Pearl, 1880- 268.
Teaching the youth of the church: a manual on methods of teaching graded, elective and uniform lesson courses to intermediates, seniors and young people in the church's school, by Cynthia Pearl Maus ... New York, George H. Doran company [c1925] xiii, 17-211 p. 19 1/2 cm. Contains bibliographies. [BV1485.M3] 25-13426
1. Religious education. I. Title.

MAUS, Cynthis Pearl, 1880- 262.
Youth organized for religious education, by Cynthia Pearl Maus; a manual on the organization and administration of intermediate, senior, and young people's departments; a textbook in teacher training, conforming to the standard outlined and approved by the International council of religious education. Third year specialization series. St. Louis, Published for the Teacher training publishing association by the Bethany press [c1925] 2 p. l., [3]-190 p. 17 cm. Bibliography: p. 189-190. [BV1533.M35] 27-3825
1. Religious education. I. International council of religious education. II. Title.

MAYER, Herbert Carleton. 268
The church's program for young people; a textbook of adolescent religious education in the local church, by Herbert Carleton Mayer... New York & London, The Century co. [c1925] xix, 387 p. diagrs. 19 1/2 cm. Bibliography at end of most of the chapters. [BV1485.M35] 25-15691
1. Religious education. 2. Church work with youth. I. Title.

MEADE, William, bp., 1789-1862
Letters to a mother on the birth of a child, in which are set forth the feelings most proper on that occasion;--the private dedication--the public baptism--and future training of the child--With an appendix, in which the leading views of the baptismal service are considered ... By the Right Rev. William Meade, D.D. Philadelphia, King & Baird, printers, 1849. 101 p. 15 1/2 cm. 6-17195
I. Title.

MEREDITH, William V. 268.
... *Pageantry and dramatics in religious education,* by William V. Meredith. New York, Cincinnati, The Abingdon press [c1921] 212 p. front., illus., plates. 20 cm. (The Abingdon religious education texts, D. G. Downey, general editor. Community training school series, N. E. Richardson, editor) "Books for reference" at end of each chapter. [BV1575.M4] 22-3904
1. Religious education. 2. Drama in education. I. Title.

*MESSINGER, C. F. 268.43
Seeking meaning with junior highs in camp, by C. F. Messinger, J. E. Simpson, G. F. Ulrich. Philadelphia, Geneva Pr [Dist. Westminster, 1966] 192p. 23cm. 1.85 pap.,
I. Title.

METHODIST Church (United States) Board of Education. Editorial Division.
Outlines of curriculum (October 1964-September 1965) Published by the Editorial Division of the General Board of Education of the Methodist Church [1963] 436 p. 67-47762
1. Religious education. I. Title.

METHODIST Church (United States) Curriculum Committee. 268.6
Educational principles in the curriculum; a report to the Curriculum Committee of the Methodist Church. [Statement by Committee on Educational Principles in the Curriculum. Nashville, Pierce and Smith, c1951. 104 l. 28 cm. [BV1471.M4] 52-23366
1. Religious education. I. Title.

METHODIST Episcopal church. Board of education. 268.432
Planning for the nursery child in the church school. Chicago. Ill., Dept. of religious education of children, Division of religious education in the local church, Board of education, Methodist Episcopal church [c1935] 64 p. 23 cm. "Prepared by Mary Edna Lloyd for the Board of education, Methodist Episcopal church."--p. [2] Includes bibliographies. [BV1540.M4] 35-16615
1. Religious education. I. Lloyd, Mary Edna. II. Title.

MEYER, John Bleadon, 1875- 377.
Religion in the school curriculum; or, The sacramentalism of common things [by] John Bleadon Meyer ... Boston, R. G. Badger [c1927] 71 p. 21 cm. "Suggestion for further reading": p. 71. [LC405.M4] 27-24718
1. Religious education. I. Title.

MILLER, Randolph Crump, 1910- 268.6
The clue to Christian education. New York, Scribner, 1950. xi, 211 p. 21 cm. Bibliography: p. 203-204. [BV1471.M48] 50-11377
1. Religious education. I. Title.

MILLER, Randolph Crump, 1910- 268
Education for Christian living. 2d ed. Englewood Cliffs, N.J., Prentice, 1963[c.1956, 1963] 462p. 23cm. Bibl. 63-7923 10.60 bds.,
1. Religious education. I. Title.

MILLER, Randolph Crump, 1910- 268
Education for Christian living. Englewood Cliffs, N. J., Prentice-Hall, 1956. 418p. 22cm. [BV1471.M49] 56-6985
1. Religious education. I. Title.

MILLER, Randolph Crump, 1910- 268.6
A guide for church school teachers, by Randolph Crump Miller ... Louisville, The Cloister press, 1943. ix, 125 p. 21 cm. "A recommended list of lesson materials for the church school": p. 103 111. "Books for a church library": p. 112-121. [BV1471.M5] 43-8191
1. Religious education. 2. Protestant episcopal church in the U.S.A. Education. I. Title.

MINARD, Herbert Leslie, 1908- 268.433
A manual for leaders of intermediates. Herbert L. Minard, editor of young people's literature, Glenn McRae, editor-in-chief. St. Louis, Mo., Christian board of publication [c1937] 175 p. illus. 19 1/2cm. "This manual is based upon the outlines produced in cooperation with the Young people's section of the Curriculum committee of the United Christian missionary society."--p. 4. Includes bibliographies. [BV1548.M5] 37-35226
1. Religious education. I. United Christian missionary society. Dept. of religious education. Curriculum committee. II. Title.

MOORE, Henry Kingsmill.
The training of infants, with special reference to the Sunday school, by H. Kingsmill Moore ... London, New York [etc.] Longmans, Green and co., 1910. xii, 103 p. 20 cm. [LC381.M78] E 13
1. Religious education. 2. Children—Management. 3. Sunday schools. I. Title.

MOORE, Mary Anne. 220.
... *Senior method in the church school,* by Mary Anne Moore. New York, Cincinnati [etc.] The Abingdon press [c1929] xv, 360 p. 20 cm. (The Abingdon religious education texts, D. G. Downey, general editor. Community training school series, N. E. Richardson, editor) "References" at end of each chapter. [BV1583.M65] 29-15057
1. Religious education. 2. Sunday-schools. 3. Adolescence. I. Title.

*MORRIS, Colin. 207
The hammer of the Lord; signs of hope. Nashville, Abingdon [1974, c1973] 159 p. 20 cm. [BV1471.2] ISBN 0-687-16547-4 4.75
1. Religious education. 2. Evangelistic work. I. Title.
L.C. card number for original edition: 73-12234.

MORRISON, Eleanor Shelton. 268
Creative teaching in the church [by] Eleanor Shelton Morrison and Virgil E. Foster. Englewood Cliffs, N. J., Prentice-Hall [1963] 244 p. 22 cm. [BV1471.2.M6] 63-16578
1. Religious education. I. Foster, Virgil E., joint author. II. Title.

MORTON, Frances McKinnon. 377.1
First steps in religious education, by Frances McKinnon Morton. Nashville, Tenn., Cokesbury press, 1930. 203 p. 19 cm. "Selected bibliography." [BV1475.M6] 30-29811
1. Religious education. 2. Child study. I. Title.

MUNKRES, Alberta. 268.
... *Primary method in the church school,* by Alberta Munkres ... Revised and rewritten. New York, Cincinnati [etc.] The Abingdon press [c1930] 292 p. front., illus., plates. diagrs. 20 cm. (The abingdon religious education texts, J. W. Langdale, general editor. Community training school series, N. E. Richardson editor) "Reference list": p. 282-289: "Books for reference" at end of most of the chapters. [BV1545.M75 1930] 30-4126
1. Religious education. 2. Sunday-schools. I. Title.

MUNKRES, Alberta, 1886- 268
Which way for our children? A handbook in religious education for parents and teachers, by Alberta Munkres ... New York, C. Scribner's sons, 1936. xi p., 2 l., 3-198 p. illus. (music) 20 cm. "Books that help in further searching": p. [185]-198. [BV1475.M75] 36-8792
1. Religious education. I. Title.

MUNRO, Harry C. 377.1
The director of religious education, by Harry C. Munro; with an introduction by Luther A. Weigle ... Philadelphia, The Westminster press, 1930. ix 214 p. 20 cm. Bibliography: p. 208-214. [BV1531.M8] 268.333 30-16882
1. Religious education. I. Title.

MUNRO, Harry Clyde, 1890- 268
Christian education in your church, by Harry C. Munro ... St. Louis, Printed for the Leadership training publishing association by the Bethany press [c1933] 239 p. 17 cm. "Editor's introduction" signed: Erwin L. Shaver, chairman, Editorial and educational section. [BV1471.M75] 33-35465
1. Religious education. I. Shaver, Edwin Leander, 1890- ed. II. Title.

MUNRO, Harry Clyde, 1890- 268
The church as a school; a textbook and guidebook to be used in connection with a church school standard or program of work in making a first-hand study of church school administration, dealing particularly with the Sunday church school. By Harry C. Munro ... prepared for use in the Standard leadership training curriculum under direction of the Editorial and educational committee of the Leadership training publishing association. Approved by the International council of religious education. St. Louis, Mo., For the Leadership training publishing association, by the Bethany press [c1929] 270 p. incl. forms. 19 cm. "References" at end of each chapter. "General bibliography": p. 269-270. [BV1520.M8] 29-11488
1. Religious education. 2. Sunday-schools. I. Title.

MUNRO, Harry Clyde, 1890- 268.434
The effective adult class; a guide for improving the work of adult classes in the church or Sunday school, by Harry C. Munro ... prepared in co-operation with the Committee on religious education of adults and the Committee on leadership training of the International council of religious education. St. Louis, Mo., The Bethany press [c1934] 84 p. 17 cm. "References for further reading": p. 75-76. [BV1550.M8] 35-3451
1. Religious education. I. International council of religious education. Committee on religious education of adults. II. International council of religious education. Committee on leadership training. III. Title. IV. Title: Adult class.

MUNRO, Harry Clyde, 1890- 377.1
The pastor and religious education [by] Harry C. Munro ... New York, Cincinnati [etc] The Abingdon press [c1930] 227 p. 21 cm. Bibliography at end of each chapter. [BV4355.M8] 30-28584
1. Religious education. 2. Theology, Pastoral. I. Title.

MUNRO, Harry Clyde, 1890- 268
Protestant nurture; an introduction to Christian education. Englewood Cliffs, N. J., Prentice-Hall, 1956. 270p. 22cm. [BV1471.M76] 56-6111
1. Religious education. I. Title.

MURCH, James DeForest, 1892- 268
Christian education and the local church; history, principles, practice, by James DeForest Murch. Cincinnati, O., The Standard publishing company [1943] 416 p. incl. illus., plans, diagrs., forms. 20 cm. Bibliography: p. 395-402. [BV1471.M8] 43-6661
1. Religious education. I. Title.

MURCH, James DeForest, 1892- 268
Teach or perish! An imperative for Christian education at the localchurch level. Grand Rapids, Mich., Eerdmans [1962, c.1961] 1177p. 21cm. 62-11247 3.00
1. Religious education. I. Title.

MURRAY, Albert Victor, 1890- 268
Education into religion. New York, Harper [1953] xii, 230p. 22cm. [BV1471.M83] 54-7263
1. Religious education. I. Title.

MURRAY, Alfred Lefurgy, 1900- 268
Psychology for Christian teachers, by Alfred L. Murray. New York, Round table press, inc., 1938. ix, 245 p. 20 cm. [BV1523.M8] 38-33528
1. Religious education. 2. Educational psychology. I. Title.

MURRAY, Anna Florence, 1872- 268.
Handbook for primary teachers in church Sunday schools, by Anna F. Murray, with foreword by Charles Smith Lewis ... illustrations by Eleanor Hillman Barker. Milwaukee, The Young churchman company; London, A. R. Mowbray & co. [c1913] xii, 218 p., 1 l. illus. (incl. music) 20 cm. [BV1545.M8] 13-18499 0.75
1. Religious education. 2. Sunday-schools. I. Title.

MYERS, Alexander John William, 1877- 268
Horace Bushnell and religious education, by A. J. Wm. Myers ... Boston, Manthorne & Burack, inc., 1937. 5 p. l., 183 p. front. (port.) 20 cm. [BV1475.B92M85] 38-30990
1. Bushnell, Horace, 1802-1876. Christian nurture 2. Religious education. I. Title.

MYERS, Alexander John William, 1877- 268.432
Living stone; a record and interpretation of Riverside church explorations with boys and girls nine to twelve years of age, by A. J. William Myers ... and Alma N. Schilling; introduction by Harry Emerson Fosdick St. Louis Mo., The Bethany press [c1936] 191 p. front. (port.) plates. 24 cm. Bibliography: p. 187-191. [BV1546.M9] 36-18288
1. Religious education. I. Schilling, Alma Noretta, 1884-1933. II. Title.

NATIONAL Association of Evangelicals. 377.1
Christian education in a democracy; the report of the N. A. E. committee [by] Frank E. Gaebelein. New York, Oxford University Press, 1951. ix, 305p. 21cm. Includes bibliographical references. [LC368.N3] 51-10667
1. Religious education. I. Gaebelein, Frank Ely, 1899- II. Title.

NATIONAL Association of Evangelicals for United Action. 377.1
Christian education in a democracy; the report of the N. A. E. committee [by] Frank E. Gaebelein. New York, Oxford University Press, 1951. ix, 305 p. 21 cm. Includes bibliographical references. [LC368.N3] 51-10667
1. Religious education. I. Gaebelein, Frank Ely, 1890- II. Title.

NATIONAL education association of the United States.
The essential place of religion in education. Monograph pub. by National education association. Ann Arbor, Mich., 1916. 134 p. diagr. 23 cm. These essays are the result of a prize essay contest conducted by the National education association. Essays by Charles E. Rugh, Laura H. Wild, Frances Virginia Frisble, Clarence Reed and Anna B. West, printed in full. Synopsis of the remaining 427 essays was compiled by Sara Whedon. cf. Introd. [LC341.N2] E 16
1. Religious education. I. Rugh. Charles Edward. II. Wild, Laura Hulda, 1870- III. Frisble, Frances Virgina. IV. Reed, Clarence. V. West, Anna B. VI. Whedon, Sara. VII. Title.

NOLDE, Otto Fred. 268.372
My group sessions; a study of the church worker and his group sessions, by O. Fred Nolde and Paul J. Hoh. Prepared under the auspices of the Parish and church school board of the United Lutheran church in America. Philadelphia, Pa., The United Lutheran publication house [c1936] 94 p. 18 cm. [BV1533.N57] 36-178607
1. Religious education. 2. Leadership. I. Hoh, Paul Jacob, 1893- joint author. II. United Lutheran church in America. Parish and church school board. III. Title.

NOLDE, Otto Fred. 268.37
My pupils; a study of the church worker and his group, by O. Fred Nolde and Paul J. Hoh. Prepared under the auspices of the Parish and church school board of the United Lutheran church in America. Philadelphia, Pa., The United Lutheran publication house [c1934] 96 p. 18 cm. -- My pupils; a study of the churdh worker and his group; leader's guide, by O. Fred Nolde and Paul J. Hoh. Prepared under the auspieces of the Parish and church school board of the United Lutheran church in America. Philadelphia, Pa., The United Lutheran publication house [c1934] 15, [1] p. 18 cm. [BV1533.N6 Guide] 35-1918
1. Religious education. I. Hoh, Paul Jacob, 1893- joint author. II. United Lutheran church in America. Parish and church school board. III. Title.

NOLDE, Otto Frederick, 1899-. 268.37
My pupils; a study of the church worker and his group, by O. Fred Nolde and Paul J. Hoh. Prepared under the auspices of the Parish and church school board of the United Lutheran church in America. Philadelphia, Pa., The United Lutheran publication house [c1934] 96 p. 18 cm. My pupils; a study of the church worker and his group; leader's guide, by O. Fred Nolde and Paul J. Hoh. Prepared under the auspices of the Parish and church school board of the United Lutheran church in America. Philadelphia, Pa., The United Lutheran publication house [c1934] [BV1533.N6 Guide] 35-1918
1. Religious education. I. Hoh, Paul Jacob, 1896- joint author. II. United Lutheran church in America. Parish and church school board. III. Title.

NORDGREN, Rubye Patton. 268.
Beginner's course in the Sunday school; a manual for teachers and parents, by Rubye Patton Nordgren, B. S. Rock Island, Ill., Augustana book concern [c1927] 240 p. illus. 24 cm. "Part iv, Music": p. [213]-240. [BV1540.N6] 27-19145
1. Religious education. 2. Sunday-schools. I. Title.

NORDGREN, Rubye Patton. 268.
Primary course in the Sunday school ... a manual for teachers and parents, by Rubye Patton Nordgren, b. s. Rock Island, Ill., Augustana book concern [c1928] v. illus. 24 cm. "Music": Bk. i. pt. iii. [BV1545.N6] 28-24495
1. Religious education. 2. Sunday-schools. I. Title.

NOREM, Harian.
I believe . . . in the communion of teenage saints; for teachers of senior high. Division of Parish Education [of] the American Lutheran Church. Minneapolis, Augsburg Publishing House, 1966. 63 p. illus. 28 cm. 67-49469
1. Religious Education. 2. Youth. 3. Leadership education. I. American Lutheran Church (1961-) II. Title.

O'CONNELL, Cornelius Joseph, 1852- 370.
Christian education, by Very Rev. C. J. O'Connell... New York, Cincinnati [etc.] Benziger brothers, 1906. viii, 192 p. 18 cm. [LC473.O32] 6-45767
1. Religious education. I. Title.

O'CONNELL, Cornelius Joseph, 1852-
Christian education, by Very Rev. C. J. O'Connell ... New York, Cincinnati [etc.] Benziger brothers, 1906. viii, 192 p. 18 cm. [LC743.O32] 6-45767
1. Religious education. I. Title.

O'DONNELL, William Charles, jr. 377
Creed and curriculum; a discussion of the question, can the essentials of religious faith and practice be taught in the public schools of the United States? By William Charles O'Donnell, jr. ... New York, Eaton & Mains; Cincinnati, Jennings & Graham [c1914] 119 p. 19 cm. [LC111.O4] 14-7542
1. Religious education. I. Title.

O'DONNELL, William Charles, jr. 377.
Creed and curriculum; a discussion of the question, can the essentials of religious faith and practice be taught in the public schools of the United States? by William Charles O'Donnell, jr. ... New York, Eaton & Mains; Cincinnati, Jennings & Graham [c1914] 119 p. 19 cm. [LC111.O4] 14-7542
1. Religious education. I. Title.

OGLEVEE, Louise M. 268.
Plans and stories for the nursery class, by Louise M. Oglevee. A book for the teacher of the nursery class of the church school and for little children in the home; valuable material for every Sunday in the year. Cincinnati, O., The Standard publishing company [c1930[144 p. front., illus. 24 cm. "Books and magazines": p. 20-21. [BV1540.O55] 30-8846
1. Religious education. 2. Sunday-schools. 3. Nursery schools. I. Title.

OGLEVEE, Louise McAroy. Mrs. 268.432
Beginners and primary plan book; plans, stories, programs, and handwork patterns, for kindergaten and primary departments with home-made attendance cards, by Louis M. Oglevee. Cincinnati, O., The Standard publishing company [c1932] 100 p. illus. 23 cm. [Full name: Mrs. Louise Peletreau (McAroy) Oglevee] [BV1540.O56] 32-6903
1. Religious education. 2. Sunday-schools. I. Title.

OGLEVEE, Louise (McAroy) Mrs. 268.432
Junior plan book, by Louise M. Ogleves. Cincinnati, O., The Standard publishing company [c1932] 78 p. illus. 23 cm. Includes music. [Full name: Mrs. Louise Peletreau McAroy) Ogleves] [BV1546.O5] 32-8446
1. Religious education. 2. Sunday-schools. I. Title.

ORTON, Hazel V. 377.1
Out in the country; a junior course for rural groups, by Hazel V. Orton. New York, Friendship press [1931] 4 p. l., [3]-136 p. 20 cm. Bibliography: p. [129]-136. [BV1555.O7] 268.6 32-3277
1. Religious education. 2. Rural churches. I. Title.

OSBORN, Andrew R. 207
Schleiermacher and religious education, by Andrew R. Osborn. London, Oxford university press, H. Milford, 1934. 4 p. l., 226 p. 1 l. 20 cm. "In its original form this book was written as a thesis for the degree of doctor of theology in the Presbyterian theological college, Montreal." Bibliography: p. [203]-205. [BV1471.S4O82] 34-19096
1. Schleiermacher, Friedrich Ernst Daniel, 1768-1834. 2. Religious education. I. Title.

OSBORN, Andrew Rule, 1875- 268
Schleiermacher and religious education, by Andrew R. Osborn. London, Oxford university press, H. Milford, 1934. 4 p. l., 226 p., 1 l. 19 1/2 cm. "In its original form this book was written as a thesis for the degree of doctor of theology in the Presbyterian theological college, Montreal." Bibliography: p. [203]-205. [BV1471.S4O82] 34-19096
1. Schleiermacher, Friedrich Ernst Daniel, 1768-1834. 2. Religious education. I. Title.

OUDERSLUYS, Richard Cornelius, 1906- 268.61
Our Father in heaven; catechetical book for beginners, ages 5 and 6, by Rev. Richard Oudersluys ... 2d rev. ed. ... Grand Rapids, Mich., Zondervan publishing house [1935] 104 p. illus. 19 cm. [BV1545.O8 1935] 36-9161
1. Religious education. I. Title.

OUDERSLUYS, Richard Cornelius, 1906- 268.61
Stories of a people; a catechetical book for primary children, ages 7 to 8, by the Rev. Richard Oudersluys ... Grand Rapids, Mich., Zondervan publishing house, 1935. 87 (i. e. 90) p. illus. 19 cm. Part of the pages numbered as leaves. [BV1545.O63] 36-9151
1. Religious education. I. Title.

OUDERSLUYS, Richard Cornelius, 1906- 268.61
Stories of beginnings; a catechetical book for primary children, ages six and seven, by the Rev. Richard Oudersluys ... Grand Rapids, Mich., Zondervan publishing house, 1935. 89 p. illus. 20 cm. [BV1545.O82] 36-9157
1. Religious education. I. Title.

PALMER, Lala (Caldwell) Mrs., 1893- 268.61
...A guide for teachers and parents for use with... Christian living series, by Lala C. Palmer and Leon C. Palmer. New York, Milwaukee, Morehouse publishing co., 1935- v. 18 1/2 cm. [BX5874.P3 Guide] 41-19464
1. Religious education. I. Palmer, Leon Carlos, 1883- joint author. II. Title. III. Title: Christian living series.

PALMER, Leon Carlos, 1883- 268.6
The new religious education, by Leon C. Palmer...with foreword by John W. Suter, jr. ... Milwaukee, Wis., Morehouse publishing co. [c1932] xii, 130 p., 1 l. 19 cm. Bibliography at end of most of the chapters. [BV1471.P3] 32-6906
1. Religious education. I. Title.

PALMER, Leon Carlos, 1883- 268.
The religious education of adults, by Leon C. Palmer...with foreword by John Gardner Murray...and introduction by Theodore R. Ludlow... approved by the Teacher training commission of the Department of religious education as teaching material for methods and materials for adults. Milwaukee, Wis., Morehouse publishing co. [c1929] xvii, 115, [1] p. 19 1/2 cm. Contains bibliographies. [BV1550.P3] 29-8133
1. Religious education. I. Title.

THE Parsons year book ...
a book that visualizes college life at Parsons. Fairfield, Ia., Parsons college v. illus. (incl. ports.) 26 cm. [LD4471.P805] 21-13584
I. Parsons college, Fairfield, Ia.

PATTEE, Fred Lewis, 1863- 268.
Elements of religious pedagogy, a course in Sunday school teacher-training, by Fred Lewis Pattee ... Approved as an advanced standard course by the Committee on education, International Sunday school association. New York, Eaton & Mains; Cincinnati, Jennings & Graham [c1909] 224 p. 21 cm. "Books for supplementary reading and reference": p. 5-7. [BV1534.P35] 9-28226
1. Religious education. 2. Sunday-schools. 3. Teaching. I. Title.

PELL, Edward Leigh, 1861- 268.
Bringing up John. "How can I teach my children so that their religious faith will stand the tests of after years?" A book for mothers and other teachers of boys and girls, by Edward Leigh Pell ... New York, Chicago [etc.] Fleming H. Revell company [c1920] 192 p. 20 cm. [BV1475.P5] 20-12139
1. Religious education. I. Title.

PELL, Edward Leigh, 1861- 268
How can I lead my pupils to Christ? By Edward Leigh Pell ... New York, Chicago [etc.] Fleming H. Revell company [c1919] 160 p. 20 cm. [BV1520.P4] 19-18851
I. Title.

PERCEPTION and religious education. [Berkeley, Calif., 1960] vi, 244 l. 28cm. Bibliography: p. [236]-244.
I. Choate, Prentiss.

PERKINS, Jeanette Eloise, ed. 268.
At school with the great Teacher; a Sunday and weekday course ... By Jeanette Eloise Perkins, in editorial collaboration with Frances Weld Danielson ... Boston, Chicago, The Pilgrim press [c1924] v, 27 cm. (Everyday Christian living series) [BV1534.P47] 25-4672
1. Religious education. I. Danielson, Frances Weld, joint ed. II. Title.

PERKINS, Jeanette Eloise, 1887- ed. 268.
At school with the great Teacher; a Sunday and week-day course, complete in three parts, for children approximately eight years of age, by Jeanette Eloise Perkins, in editorial collaboration with Frances Weld Danielson ... Boston, Chicago, The Pilgrim press, [c1924] xiii. 78, iv p., 1 l., 79-149, iv p., 1 l., 151-208 p. front. 28 cm. (Everyday Christian living series) Each part has separate t.-p. Contains music. [BV1534.P47 1924 a] 25-12975

1. Religious education. I. Danielson, Frances Weld, joint ed. II. Title.

PERSON, Peter P 268
An introduction to Christian education. Grand Rapids, Baker Book House, 1958. 224p. 23cm. Includes bibliography. [BV1471.P4] 59-4465
1. Religious education. I. Title.

PERSON, Peter P 268
The minister in Christian education. Grand Rapids, Baker Book House, 1960. 134p. 20cm. Includes bibliography. [BV4360.P45] 60-10190
1. Religious education. 2. Pastoral theology. I. Title.

PETTEY, Emma. 268.
Guiding the primary child in the Sunday school [by] Emma Pettey. Nashville, Tenn., Broadman press [c1936] 138 p. 19 cm. [BV1545.P42] 37-418
1. Religious education. I. Title.

PIPER, David Roy. 232.9
How would Jesus teach? By David R. Piper. Elgin, Ill., David C. Cook publishing company [c1931] 106 p. plates. 19 cm. [BT590.T5P5] 32-8449
1. Jesus Christ. 2. Religious education. I. Title.

POTTS, Edwin James. 268.6
How to teach the word of God. Chicago, Harvest Publications [c1963] 104 p. illus. 20 cm. (A Harvest leadership training book) [BV1471.2.P6] 63-11151
1. Religious education I. Title.

POWELL, Marie (Cole) Mrs. 1882- 268.
... Junior method in the church school, by Marie Cole Powell. New York, Cincinnati, The Abingdon press [c1923] 320 p. front., plates. 20 cm. (The Abingdon religious education texts. D. G. Dewney, general editor. Community training school series. N. E. Richarson, editor) "For further reading" at end of each chapter. [Full name: Mrs. Marie Eldredge (Cole) Powell] [BV1516.P6] 23-11099
1. Religious education. 2. Sunday-schools. I. Title.

POWELL, Marie (Cole) Mrs. 1882- 268.432
... Junior method in the church school [by] Marie Cole Powell. Rev. and rewritten. New York, Cincinnati [etc.] The Abingdon press [c1931] 465 p. fronts., plates, diagr. 20 cm. (The Abingdon religious education texts, J. W. Langdale, general editor. Community training school series) "References" at the end of each chapter. [Full name: Mrs. Marie Eldredge (Cole) Powell] [BV1546.P6] 32-1089
1. Religious education. 2. Sunday-schools. I. Title.

POWELL, Wilfred Evans, 1893- 268
Education for life with God; a discussion of the meaning of religious education [by] Wilfred Evans Powell; introduction by L. A. Weigle. New York, Cincinnati [etc.] The Abingdon press [c1934] 264 p. 20 cm. Bibliography: p. [255]-259. [BV1471.P6] 34-40123
1. Religious education. I. Title.

POWELL, Wilfred Evans, 1893- 268.
The growth of Christian personality; a study of the pupil for teachers of religion in home and school, by Wilfred Evans Powell ... A textbook in the Standard leadership training curriculum outlined and approved by the International council of religious education. St. Louis, Mo., Printed for the Teacher-training publishing association by the Bethany press [c1929] 255 p. illus., diagrs. 19 cm. "References" at end of each chapter; Bibliography: p. 249-250. [BV1475.P6] 29-16568
1. Religious education. 2. Personality. 3. Educational psychology. I. International council of religious education. II. Title. III. Title: Christian personality, The growth of.

PRESBYTERIAN church in the U. S. A. General assembly. 285.
Report of the Committee of the General assembly, appointed to a draught a plan for disciplining baptized children. New-York, Published by Whiting and Watson, J. Seymour, printer, 1812. 56 p. 24 cm. [BX9190.A5] A 33
1. Religious education. 2. Presbyterian church in the U. S. A. Discipline. I. Title.

PRICE, John Milburn, 1884- ed. 377
Introduction to religious education; general editor, J. M. Price ... associate editors, L. L. Carpenter ... and J. H. Chapman ... New York, The Macmillan company, 1932. xi, 480 p. 23 cm. "A selected bibliography for class use" at the end of each chapter. [BV1471.P65] 32-23466
1. Religious education. I. Carpenter, Levy Leonidas, joint ed. II. Chapman, James H., joint ed. III. Title.

PRICE, John Milburn, 1884- 268
A survey of religious education [by] J. M. Price [and others] 2d ed. New York, Ronald Press Co. [1959] 466 p. 21 cm. Includes bibliography. [BV1471.P66 1959] 59-6624
1. Religious education.

PRICE, John Milburn, 1884- 268
A survey of religious education, by J. M. Price ... James H. Chapman ... A. E. Tibbs ... [and] L. L. Carpenter ... New York, T. Nelson and sons, 1940. x p., 1 l., 13-333 p. 21 cm. "Selected bibliography" at end of each part. [BV1471.P66] 40-7449
1. Religious education. I. Chapman, James Horton, 1881- II. Tibbs, Albert Ellias, 1901- III. Carpenter, Levy Leonidas, 1891. IV. Title.

... Principles of religious education; 268 a course of lectures delivered under the auspices of the Sunday-school commission of the diocese of New York; with an introduction by the Right Reverend Henry C. Potter ... New York [etc.] Longmans, Green, and co., 1900. xx, 292 p. 20 cm. At head of title: Christian knowledge lectures. Numerous errors in "Topical index". [BV1471.P7 1900] 0-6888
1. Religious education. 2. Sunday-schools. 3. Bible—Study. I. Title: Christian knowledge lectures.
Contents omitted.

... Principles of religious education; 268 a course of lectures delivered under the auspices of the Sunday-school commission of the diocese of New York; with an introduction by the Right Reverend Henry C. Potter ... New York [etc.] Longmans, Green, and co., 1901. xx, 292 p. 20 cm. At head of title: Christian knowledge lectures. Numerous errors in "Tropical index". "First ed., Nov., 1900; reprinted, Dec., 1900." [BV1471.P7 1901] 2-24238
1. Religious education. 2. Sunday-schools. 3. Bible—Study. I. Title: Christian knowledge lectures.
Contents omitted.

... Principles of religious education; 268.082 a course of lectures delivered under the auspices of the Sunday-school commission of the Diocese of New York; with an introduction by the Right Reverend Henry C. Potter ... New York [etc.] Longmans, Green, and co., 1901. xx, 292 p. 20 cm. At head of title: Christian knowledge lectures. "First ed., Nov., 1900; reprinted, Jan., 1901, Sept., 1901." Errors in "Topical index" made in previous editions are corrected in this edition. [BV1471.P7 1901 b] 4-14246
1. Religious education. 2. Sunday-schools. 3. Bible—Study. I. Title: Christian knowledge lectures.
Contents omitted.

RAFFETY, William Edward, 1876- 268.434
Religious education of adults; a practical manual for church-school leaders, by W. Edward Raffety ... New York, Chicago [etc.] Fleming H. Revell company [c1930] 214 p. 19 cm. [BV1550.R25] 30-31387
1. Religious education. 2. Education of adults. I. Title.

RANKIN, Mary Everett. 268.
A course for beginners in religious education, with lessons for one year for children five years of age, by Mary Everett Rankin ... with an introduction by Patty Smith Hill ... New York, C. Scribner's sons, [c1917] xi, 236 p. front., illus. (music) plates. 21 cm. "Reference books on story-telling and stories to tell": p. 18-19. [BV1540.R3] 17-24838
1. Religious education. I. Title.

REICHERT, Richard. 268'.6
A learning process for religious education / Richard Reichert. Dayton, Ohio : Pflaum Pub., [1974] c1975. vii, 151 p. ; 21 cm. Bibliography: p. 99-104. [BV1471.2.R43] 74-14308 ISBN 0-8278-0001-0 pbk. : 5.25
1. Religious education. I. Title.

THE Religious education association. Preliminary programme of the ... annual convention. v. 23 1/2 cm. 5-31553

RHODES, Bertha Marilda. 268.
My Sunday kindergarten book [by] Bertha Marilda Rhodes ... [Chicago, University of Chicago press, 1928] 1 v. illus. 27 cm. Contains music. Loose-leaf. [BV1540.R46] 29-8957
1. Religious education. I. Title.

RHODES, Bertha Marilda. 268.
Religion in the kindergarten; a course in religion for the beginners' department in the Sunday school or for use in the day school or the home, by Bertha Marilda Rhodes. Chicago, Ill., The University of Chicago press [c1924] xviii, 261 p. front., illus. 19 1/2 cm. (Half-title: The University of Chicago publications in religious education ... Constructive studies) "Songs and music": p. [211]-249. [BV1540.R5] 24-13490
1. Religious education. I. Title.

RICHARDSON, Norman Egbert, 1878- 232.9
The Christ of the class room; how to teach evangelical Christianity, by Norman E. Richardson ... New York, The Macmillan company, 1931. xviii, 372 p. diagrs. 20 1/2 cm. "General reference book list": p. 363-367. [BT590.T5R5] 31-19631
1. Jesus Christ. 2. Religious education. I. Title.

RICHARDSON, Norman Egbert, 1878- 232.9
The Christ of the class room; how to teach evangelical Christianity, by Norman E. Richardson ... New ed. New York, The Macmillan company, 1932. xxxiv, 372 p. diagrs. 20 1/2 cm. "General references book list": p. 363-367. [BT590.T5R5 1932] 32-11471
1. Jesus Christ—Teaching mentods. 2. Religious education. I. Title.

RICHARDSON, Norman Egbert, 1878- 268.
The religious education of adolescents, by Norman E. Richardson... including material contained in a pamphlet entitled: The government of adolescent young people, prepared by William Byron Forbush and rev. by Mary E. Moxcey... New York, The Abingdon press [c1918] x, 191 p. 17 cm. [BV1475.R5] 19-1666
1. Religious education. I. Forbush, William Byron, 1868-1927 II. Moxcey, Mary Eliza, 1875-ed. III. Title.

RITSCHL, Albrecht Benjamin, 1822-1889.
Instruction in the Christian religion. Translated, by permission, from the 4th German ed. by Alice Mead Swing. [Ann Arbor, University Microfilm, 1960] [169]-286 p. Xerox print reproduced from The theology of Albrecht Ritschl, by A. M. Swing, New York, 1901. 66-11029
1. Religious education. I. Title.

ROBERTS, Seldon L. 268.
Teaching in the church school; a manual of principles and methods for church school teachers. Keystone standard training course. By Seldon L. Roberts ... Philadelphia, Boston [etc.] The Judson press [c1927] 5 p. l., 148 p. diagr., fold. form. 19 cm. [BV1534.R5] 27-3250
1. Religious education. 2. Sunday-schools. I. Title.

ROBERTS, Seldon Low, 1871-1930. 268
Training lessons for church-school workers; a study of the church-school based on a survey problem solving plan, by Seldon L. Roberts ... introductory to the standard leadership training course. Philadelphia, Boston [etc.] The Judson press [c1930] 106 p. 19 cm. [BV1533.R62] 30-22735
1. Religious education. 2. Sunday-schools. I. Title.

*ROBERTSON, Betty B. 377
100 better ideas for children's workers [by] Betty B. Robertson. Grand Rapids, Baker Book House [1974, c1973] 80 p. 20 cm. Original title: A Galaxy of ideas for children's workers. [BV1471.2.] ISBN 0-8010-7621-8. 1.50 (pbk)
1. Religious education. I. Title.

ROCHESTER, Mich. North Central Christian College
Christian education; a series of Bible lectures by outstanding educators delivered at North Central Christian College, Rochester, Mich., October 11-15, 1959. Austin, Tex., Firm Foundation Pub. House [1960] 220 p. 21 cm. 63-3298
1. Religious education. 2. Church and college. I. Title.

RODEHEAVER, Homer Alvan, 1880- ed.
The second collection of penny object lessons, ed. by Homer A. Rodeheaver [and] Rev. C. H. Woolston... Philadelphia, Chicago, The Rodeheaver company [c1919] 93 p. illus. 20 cm. Portraits on cover. [BV1543.R6] 19-14542
I. Woolston, Clarence Herbert, joint ed. II. Title. III. Title: Penny object lessons.

ROOP, Geane A. 268.61
The junior and his church [by] Geane A. Roop. Nashville, Tenn., The Sunday school board of the Southern Baptist convention [c1937] 132 p. illus. 19 cm. [BV1546.R65] 37-21816
1. Religious education. I. Title.

ROPER, John Caswell, 1873- 377
Religious aspects of education, by John Caswell Roper ... Nashville, Tenn., Cokesbury press, 1926. 5 p. l., 196 p., 1 l. 20 cm. Bibliography: 1 p. at end. [LC311.R6] 26-9616
1. Religious education. 2. Education. I. Title.

ROWE, Henry Kalloch, 1869- 268.
... Landmarks in Christian history, by Henry K. Rowe ... New York, Charles Scribner's sons, c1911. vi, 289 p. 19 cm. (Bible study union lessons, the completely graded series) Charles F. Kent, George A. Coe, consulting editors. Each part has separate t.-p. Pupil's book. [BV1549.R] A 34
1. Religious education. 2. Church history. I. Title.
Contents omitted.

ROWE, Henry Kalloch, 1869- 268.
... Landmarks in Christian history, Prepared by Henry K. Rowe ... New York, Charles Scribner's sons, c1911. vi, 264 p. 19 cm. (Bible study union lessons, the completely graded series) At head of title: The Senior teacher. Charles F. Kent, George L. Coe, consulting editors. Each part has separate t.-p. Teacher's manual. [BV1549.R] A 34
1. Religious education. 2. Church history. I. Title.
Contents omitted.

*RUNK, Wesley T. 207
Challenging object lessons. Grand Rapids, Baker Book House [1974, c1971] 83 p., 20 cm. Formerly published under the title, Let's go to God's Party. [BV1471] ISBN 0-8010-7630-7 1.95 (pbk.)
1. Religious education. I. Title.

*RUNK, Wesley T. 207
Object lessons for christian growth. Grand Rapids, Baker Book House [1974, c1973] 104 p., 20 cm. Formerly published under the title, Growing up in God. [BV1471] ISBN 0-8010-7629-3 1.95 (pbk.)
1. Religious education. I. Title.

*RUNK, Wesley T. 207
Timely object lessons. Grand Rapids, Mich. Baker Book House. [1974, c1971] 95 p., 20 cm. [BV1471] ISBN 0-8010-7628-5 1.95 (pbk.)
1. Religious education. I. Title.

RUSK, Robert R.
The religious education of the child, with special reference to Sunday school work, by Robert R. Rusk ... London New York [etc.] Longmans, Green and co., 1915. x, 84 p. 19 cm. [LC381.R9] E 15
1. Religious education. I. Title.

RUSSELL, Letty M. 207
Christian education in mission, by Letty M. Russell. Philadelphia, Westminster Press [1967] 159 p. 19 cm. (Studies on the church for others) Bibliographical references included in "Notes" (p. [147]-159) [BV1471.2.R8] 67-10926
1. Religious education. I. Title.

RUTLEDGE, Loneta (Cessna) 268
"Mrs. Loyd N. Rutledge," 1899-
The church; the children, by Mrs. Loyd N. Rutledge, Miss Orlena Drennan, and Miss Davy Drennan... Austin, Tex., Firm foundation [!] publishing house [c1936] 2 p. l., [vii]-viii p., 1 l., 142 p. 19 cm. (On cover: Training for service series, by J. P. Sewell and H. E. Speck, editors) Bibliography at end of each chapter. [BV1534.R8] 36-29043
1. Religious education. 2. Child study. I. Drennan, Orlena. II. Drennan, Davy. III. Title.

RYBURN, W. M. 268
The theory and practice of Christian education, with special reference to India and the East, by W. M. Ryburn...With a foreword by Miss A. B. Van Doren... London, New York [etc.] Oxford university press, 1934. xii p., 1 l., 260 p. diagrs. 20 cm. "Books for further study": p. [255]-256. [BV1534.R9] 35-37253
1. Religious education. 2. Educational psychology. 3. Religious education—India. I. Title.

SCHIEFFELIN, Samuel 268
Bradhurst, 1811-1900.
A word to Christian teachers and students for the ministry. By Samuel B. Schieffelin... New York, Board of publication of the Reformed church in America, 1877. 1 p. l., 89 p. 15 1/2 cm. [BV1534.S33] 36-31904
1. Religious education. 2. Clergy—Office. I. Title.

SCHISLER, John Q. 268.876
The educational work of the small church, by John Q. Schisler; C. A. Bowen, D.D., general editor. Nashville, Tenn., Cokesbury press [c1932] 123 p. diagrs. 17 cm. On cover: For the Methodist Episcopal church, South. [BX8223.S4] 32-19479
1. Religious education. 2. Sunday-schools. I. Bowen, Cawthon Asbury, 1885- ed. II. Title.

SCHISLER, John Quincy. 268
Christian teaching in the churches. Nashville, Abingdon Press [1954] 173p. 21cm. [BV1471.S39] 54-5509
1. Religious education. I. Title.

SCHONHOVD, Hanna 268.62
Christine, 1876-
My first Sunday school book, grade one, by Hanna C. Schonhovd ... Minneapolis, Augsburg publishing house [1936] 104 p. incl. illus. (part col.) col. pl. pl. 23 cm. "This volume is one in a series of graded Sunday school text books issued by the Board of elementary Christian education, Dr. Jacob Tanner, editor-in-chief." "First edition, September, 1936." [BV1545.S28] 37-29876
1. Religious education. I. Tanner, Jacob, 1865- ed. II. Title.

SCHREYER, George M 1913- 268
Christian education in action. New York, Comet Press Books, 1957. 177p. 21cm. (A Reflection book) [BV1471.S415] 57-8111
1. Religious education. I. Title.

SCHREYER, George M 1913- 268
Christian education in theological focus. Philadelphia, Christian Education Press [1962] 211p. 21cm. [BV1471.2.S3] 62-19192
1. Religious education. I. Title.

SCHUMACHER, Matthew 268.62
Aloysius, 1879-
Learning my religion; the questions and answers of the catechism prepared and enjoined by the Third plenary council of Baltimore, graded and combined with an explanation and correlated with Bible history, etc., for the use of elementary schools according to modern teaching methods, by Rt. Rev. Msgr. M. A. Schumacher ... and Sister Mary Imelda ... New York, Cincinnati [etc.] Benziger brothers, 1935- v. col. illus. 19 cm. [BX930.S37] 36-9152
1. Religious education. I. Wallace, Mary Imelda, sister, 1884- joint author. II. Title.

SELL, Henry Thorne, 1854-
Studies in the life of the Christian, his faith and his service, by Henry T. Sell... New York, Chicago [etc.] Fleming H. Revell company [1905] 3 p. l., 9-169 p. 19 cm. (Lettered on cover: Sell's Bible study text books) [V1550.S35] 5-10558
1. Religious education. I. Title.

SETTLE, Myron C. 377.1
... The vacation church school ... for the guidance of churches and communities in the organization and administration of vacation church schools, prepared by Myron C. Settle ... Chicago, Ill., The International council of religious education, 1930. 55 p. illus., diagr. 23 cm. (On cover: International bulletins in religious education. Educational bulletin, no. 602) Series title in part also at head of t.-p. "Curriculum materials": p. 26-28. [BV1585.S4] 31-7939
1. Religious education. I. International council of religious education. II. Title.

SETTLE, Myron C. 377.1
... The weekday church school ... for the guidance of churches and communities in the organization and administration of weekday schools religious education, prepared by Myron C. Settle ... Chicago, Ill., The International council of religious education, 1930. 56 p. illus., diagrs. 23 cm. (International bulletins in religious education. Education bulletin, no. 601) Bibliography: p. 54-56. [BV1580.S45] 30-10031
1. Religious education. I. International council of religious education. II. Title.

SHACKFORD, John Walter, 377.1
1878-
Education in the Christian religion, by John W. Shackford... Nashville, Cokesbury press [c1931] 200 p. 19 cm. [BV1471.S5] 31-31136
1. Religious education. I. Title.

SHAMON, Albert J. 268'.6
Catching up on catechetics, by Albert J. Shamon. New York, Paulist Press [1972] 73 p. 18 cm. (Deus books) [BV1471.2.S48] 72-85698 ISBN 0-8091-1739-8 0.95 (pbk.)
1. Religious education. I. Title.

SHAVER, Erwin Leander, 1890- 268.
How to teach seniors; a discussion of materials and methods to be used in leading church-schools seniors in the Christian way of life [by] Erwin L. Shaver ... a text-book in the Standard leadership training curriculum outlined and approved by the International council of religious education ... Boston, Chicago, Printed for the Teacher training publishing association by the Pilgrim press [c1927] 7 p. l., [11]-213 p. 19 1/2 cm. Specialization series) "References" at end of each chapter except the last. [BV1549.S5] 27-21630
1. Religious education. 2. Sunday-schools. I. Title.

SHAVER, Erwin Leander, 1890- 268.
Present-day trends in religious education; lectures on the Earl foundation and other papers [by] Erwin L. Shaver. Boston, Chicago, The Pilgrim press [c1928] ix, 168 p. 19 1/2 cm. "For further study" at end of each chapter. [BV1475.S5P7] 28-21206
1. Religious education. I. Title.

SHAVER, Erwin Leander, 1890- 268.
Programs for teachers' meetins; suggested plans for the educational treatment of twenty-three problems commonly confronted by church-school officers and teachers, by Erwin L. Shaver ... Boston, Chicago, The Pilgrim press [c1928] 98 p. 19 cm. Contains bibliographies. [BV1534.S435] 28-25928
1. Religious education. 2. Sunday-schools. I. Title. II. Title: Teachers' meetings, Programs for.

SHAVER, Erwin Leander, 268.6
1890-
Programs for workers' conferences ... Tested guides for planning and conducting twelve or more meetings of the church-school teachers and officers, by Erwin L. Shaver. Boston, Chicago, The Pilgrim press [c1934] 2 v. 19 1/2 cm. Includes bibliographies. [BV1534.S436] 34-9900
1. Religious education. 2. Sunday-schools. I. Title.

SHAVER, Erwin Leander, 1890- 268.
A project curriculum for young people; a method guide and source plan book for leaders of young people's groups in the church, by Erwin L. Shaver. Chicago, Ill., The University of Chicago press [c1927] xvi, 222 p. 18 cm. (Half-title: The University of Chicago publications in religious education ... Principles and methods of religious education) "Reference and source material" at end of most of the chapters. [BV1534.S44] 27-23700
1. Religious education. 2. Project method in teaching. I. Title.

SHAVER, Erwin Leander, 377.1
1890-
Shall laymen teach religion? By Erwin L. Shaver ... New York, R. R. Smith, inc., 1931. x, 188 p. 19 1/2 cm. Bibliography: p. vii-viii. [BV1534.S47] 31-28912
1. Religious education. I. Title.

SHAVER, Erwin Leander, 1890- 268
The workers' conference manual [by] Erwin L. Shaver. New York, Cincinnati [etc.] The Abingdon press [c1938] 1 p. l., [5]-113 p. 20 cm. (The Abingdon religious education texts, J. W. Langdale, general editor: Guides to Christian leadership, P. H. Vieth, editor) Text on front lining paper. "References": p. 111-113. [BV1472.S5] 39-2880
1. Religious education. I. Title.

SHERIDAN, Alma Stanley. 268.
Teaching intermediates in the church school, by Alma Stanley Sheridan; a textbook in the standard leadership training curriculum, outlined and approved by the International council of religious education ... [New York] Printed for the Teacher training publishing association by the Methodist book concern [c1928] 215 p. 19 1/2 cm. (Specialization series) "References for supplementary reading" at end of each chapter. [BV1548.S5] 28-7762
1. Religious education. 2. Sunday-schools. I. Title.

SHERIDAN, Harold James, 377.1
1885-
... New tendencies in teaching religion [by] Harold J. Sheridan ... New York, Cincinnati [etc.] The Abingdon press [c1932] 112 p. 20 cm. (The Abingdon religious education monographs, J. W. Langdale, general editor) "A selected list of references for further reading": p. 110-111. [BV1534.S58] 32-11674
1. Religious education. I. Title.

SHERMAN, Homer Henkel, 1870- 377
ed.
Education and religion; vital messages on the home, the church, and the college, edited by Homer Henkel Sherman ... Nashville, Tenn., Cokesbury press, 1929. 194 p. 19 1/2 cm. Addresses delivered at a Conference on religion, and education, sponsored jointly by the Board of education, the Sunday school board, and the Epworth league board of the Methodist Episcopal church, South. The Conference was held at Lake Junaluska July 17-21, 1929. cf. Pref. [BV1463.M4 1929] 30-9629
1. Religious education. I. Methodist Episcopal church, South. Conference on religion and education, Lake Junaluska, 1929. II. Title.

SHERMAN, Homer Henkel, 1870- 377
ed.
Education and religion; vital messages on the home, the church, and the college, edited by Homer Henkel Sherman ... Nashville, Tenn., Cokesbury press, 1929. 194 p. 19 1/2 cm. Addresses delivered at a Conference on religion, and education, sponsored jointly by the Board of education, the Sunday school board, and the Epworth league board of the Methodist Episcopal church, South. The Conference was held at Lake Junaluska July 17-21, 1929. cf. Pref. [BV1463.M4 1929] 30-9629
1. Religious education. I. Methodist Episcopal church, South. Conference on religion and education, Lake Junaluska, 1929. II. Title.

SHERRILL, Lewis Joseph, 268.434
1892-
Adult education in the church, by Lewis Joseph Sherrill ... and John Edwin Purcell ... Richmond, Va., Presbyterian committee of publication [c1936] 290 p. 19 1/2 cm. [BV1550.S45] 36-7159
1. Religious education. 2. Education of adults. I. Purcell, John Edwin, joint author. II. Title.

SHERRILL, Lewis Joseph, 1892- 268
The gift of power. New York, Macmillan, 1955. 206p. illus. 22cm. [BV1471.S45] 55-13597
1. Religious education. 2. Church. 3. Psychology, Religious. I. Title.

SHERRILL, Lewis Joseph, 1892- 268
Religious education in the small church, by Lewis Joseph Sherrill ... Philadelphia, The Westminster press, 1932. 208 p. 17 1/2 cm. (On cover: Handybooks for church school leaders) "The international reading course": p. 205-206. [BV1471.S55] 32-10563
1. Religious education. 2. Sunday-schools. I. Title.

SHIELDS, Elizabeth McEwan. 268.
Beginners in God's world; programs for the beginners department; prepared for use in the vacation church school, by Elizabeth McE. Shields, John T. Faris, D.D., editor. Philadelphia, Board of Christian education of the Presbyterian church in the U.S.A., 1928. 141 p. illus. (incl. music) diagrs. 28 1/2 cm. "Hymns and songs": p. 133-141. [BV1540.S5] 28-7759
1. Religious education. 2. Education of children. I. Faris, John Thomson, 1871- ed. II. Title.

SHIELDS, Elizabeth 268.432
McEwen, 1879-
Guiding the little child in the Sunday school [by] Elizabeth McEwen Shields. Nashville, Tenn., Broadman press [c1936] 140 p. illus 19 cm. [BV1540.S52] 37-561
1. Religious education. I. Title.

SHINN, Roger Lincoln. 268.6
The educational mission of our church. Boston, United Church Press [1962] 176 p. 21cm. Includes bibliographies. [BX9884.A3S4] 62-13797
1. Religious education. 2. United Church of Christ — Education I. Title.

SLATTERY, Margaret. 268.
You can learn to teach, by Margaret Slattery. Boston, Chicago, The Pilgrim press [c1925] 7 p. l., [3]-223 p. pl. 18 1/2 cm. Bibliography: p. 222-223. [BV1534.S62] 25-22272
1. Religious education. I. Title.

SLOAN, Patrick James, 1874- 268.
The Sunday-school teacher's guide to success, by Rev. Patrick J. Sloan. New York, Cincinnati [etc.] Benziger brothers, 1908. xv, 187 p. 18 cm. "Books of interest": p. 183-187. [BV1534.S63] 8-4014
1. Religious education. 2. Sunday schools. I. Title.

SLOYAN, Gerard Stephen, 1919- 268
ed.
Modern catechetics: message and method in religious formation. New York, Macmillan [c.1960, 1963] 379p. 22cm. Bibl. 63-12401 5.95
1. Religious education. 2. Catechetics—Catholic Church. I. Title.

SLOYAN, Gerard Stephen, 1919- 268
ed.
Modern catechetics; message and method in religious formation. New York, Macmillan [1963] xi, 381 p. 22 cm. Bibliography: p. 361-367. [BX1968.S5] 63-14201
1. Religious education. 2. Catechetics — Catholic Church. I. Title.

SLOYAN, Gerard Stephen, 268.082
1919- ed.
Shaping the Christian message; essays in religious education. Abridged ed. Contribs.: Andre Boyer [others] Glen Rock, N. J., Paulist Pr. [c.1958, 1963] 256p. 18cm. (Deus bks) Bibl. 63-20215 .95 pap.,
1. Religious education. 2. Catholic Church—Education. I. Boyer, Andre, 1889- II. Title.

SLOYAN, Gerard Stephen, 268.082
1919- ed.
Shaping the Christian message; essays in religious education. Contributors: Andre

Boyer [and others] New York, Macmillan, 1958. 327 p. 22 cm. [BX925.S6] 58-11545
1. Religious education. 2. Catholic Church — Education. I. Boyer, Andre. II. Title.

SLOYAN, Gerard Stephen, 1919- ed. 268.082
Shaping the Christian message; essays in religious education. Abridged ed. Contributors: Andre Boyer [and others] Glen Rock, N.J. Paulist Press [1963] 256 p. 18 cm. (Deus books) Bibliography: p. 245. [BX921.S5 1963] 63-20215
1. Religious education. 2. Catholic Church — Education. I. Boyer, Andre 1889- II. Title.

SLUSSER, Gerald H 268
A dynamic approach to church education [by] Gerald H. Slusser. Illustrated by Paul Bogdanoff. Philadelphia, Geneva Press [c1968] 124 p. illus. 21 cm. (Decade books) [BV1471.2.S58] 68-10225
1. Religious education. I. Title.

SMART, James D 268
The teaching ministry of the church; an examination of the basic principles of Christian education. Philadelphia, Westminster Press [1954] 207p. 21cm. [BV1471.S57] 54-10569
1. Religious education. I. Title.

*SMITH, A. Richard 231.107
God and the universe. Ed.: Margaret J. Irvin. Illus.: Roland Shutts. Designer: William C. Kautz. Philadelphia, Lutheran Church Pr. [c.1965] 48p. col. illus. 22x28cm. (LCA vacation church sch. ser.) pap., .50; teacher's guide (to grades 5 & 6) pap., .90
I. Title.

SMITH, Cecil Daniel. 268.433
Administering the young people's department of the local church [by] Cecil Daniel Smith. Boston, Chicago, Printed for the Leadership training publishing association by the Pilgrim press [c1934] 219 p. diagrs., forms. 17 1/2 cm. "Editor's introduction" signed: Erwin L. Shaver, chairman, Editorial and educational section. Includes bibliographies. [BV1549.S6] 34-21477
1. Religious education. 2. Youth. I. Shaver, Erwin Leander, 1890- ed. II. Title. III. Title: The young people's department of the local church.

*SMITH, Doris J. 268.432
God loves me [pupil bk., nursery ed.] Margaret J. Irvin, ed. William C. Kautz, designer. Joy Troth Friedman, illus. Philadelphia, Lutheran Church Pr. [c.1965] 32p. col. illus. 22x28cm. (Vacation church sch. ser.) With teacher's guide God loves and plans for me. pupil's bk., pap., .50; teacher's guide, pap., .90
I. Title.

SMITH, Frank Webster, 1854-
Jesus--teacher, principles of education for both pupils and Bible school teachers [by] Frank Webster Smith ... New York, Sturgis & Walton company, 1916. ix p., 1 l., 58 p. 17 1/2 cm. $0.50 17-12033
I. Title.

SMITH, Henry Lester, 1876- 377.1
...A brief survey of present-day religious and moral education in the schools of countries other than the United States of America, by Henry Lester Smith, Robert Stewart McElhinney and George Renwick Steele. [Bloomington] Bureau of cooperative research, Indiana university [1935] 185 p. 22 1/2 cm. (Bulletin of the School of education; Indiana university. [vol. xi, no. 3]) Bibliography: p. 172-181. [LC107.S5] 35-28080
1. Religious education. 2. Moral education. I. McElhinney, Robert Stewart, joint author. II. Steele, George Renwick, joint author. III. Title.

SMITH, Henry Lester, 1876- 377
...The old world historical background of religious and moral education in schools, by Henry Lester Smith, Robert Stewart McElhinney and George Renwick Steele. [Bloomington] Bureau of cooperative research, Indiana university [1934] 144 p. 22 1/2 cm. (Bulletin of the School of education, Indiana university. [vol. x, no. 4]) Bibliography: 138-141. [LC268.S54] 34-27904
1. Religious education. 2. Moral education. 3. Education—Hist. I. McElhinney, Robert Stewart, joint author. II. Steele, George Renwick, Joint author. III. Title.

SMITH, Hilrie Shelton, 1893- 268
Faith and nurture, by H. Shelton Smith. New York, C. Scribner's sons, 1941. xii p., 1 l., 208 p. 21 cm. Bibliographical foot-notes. [BV1471.S58] 41-25774
1. Religious education. 2. Liberalism (Religion) I. Title.

SMITH, Juliet C.
My first duty; twelve short instructions on "my duty towards God" by Juliet C. Smith...With an introduction by George H. McGrew, D.D. New York, T. Whittaker [c1897] 2 p. l., vii-viii p., 1 l., 95 p. 18 1/2 cm. 12-38746
I. Title.

SMITH, Robert Seneca, 1880- 268.6
New trails for the Christian teacher; twelve studies for class use of personal reading, by Robert Seneca Smith...A text-book in the Standard leadership training, curriculum, outlined and approved by the International council of religious education. Philadelphia, The Westminster press, 1934. 260 p. diagr. 19 1/2 cm. "References" at end of each chapter. [BV1534.S65] 35-7221
1. Religious education. I. International council of religious education. II. Title.

SMITH, Robert Seneca, 1880- 268.
The use of the Old Testament in current curricula [by] Robert Seneca Smith... New York, London, The Century co., [c1929] xi, 337 p. incl. tables, diagrs. 20 1/2 cm. $2.25. "This book...in its present form...was offered to the faculty of the Yale graduate school in June, 1927, as a PH.D. dissertation."--Pref. A study fo Old Testament material in the most representaitve graded religious texts with a description and analysis of these courses. The graded curricula investigated are the following: The International graded series: The Constructive studies in religion; The Completely graded series: The Beacon course in religious education; The Christian nurture series: The Abingdon week-day religious education texts. Bibliography: p. 329-332; "The texts which have been examined": at the beginning of chap. III-VIII. [BV1485.S55 1927] 29-4960
1. Religious education. 2. Bible. O. T.—Study. 3. Bible. O. T.—Study—Bibl. 4. Bible—Study—O.T. 5. Bible—Study—Bibl.—O.T. I. Title.

SMITH, William Walter, 1868- 268.
The element of child study and religious pedagogy, in simple and practical form, fully illustrated, by the Rev. William Walter Smith ... With foreword by the Rev. Robert P. Kreitler. Milwaukee, The Young churchman co.; [etc., etc.] 1812. xiii, 277 p. illus., diagrs. 21 cm. "List of reference books suggested": p. [269]-271. [BV1534.S65] 12-21306
1. Religious education. 2. Sunday schools. I. Title.

SMITH, William Walter, 1868- 268
Religious education; a comprehensive text book, illustrated by the Rev. William Walter Smith ... with foreword by Charles William Stoughton. Milwaukee, The Young churchman co., 1909. xvi, 509 p. illus. 23 cm. "List of reference book suggested": p. [497]-500. [BV1471.S6] 9-8887
1. Religious education. I. Title.

SNEATH, Elias Hershey, 1857-1935. 268
Religious training in the school and home; a manual for teachers and parents, by E. Hershey Sneath ... George Hodges ... Henry Hallam Tweedy ... New York, The Macmillan company, 1917. 5 p. l., 341 p. 20 cm. "This manual is based on a similar one--Moral training in the school and home."--Pref. Contains bibliographies. [BV1475.S6] 17-24241
1. Religious education. I. Hodges, George, 1856-1919, joint author. II. Tweedy, Henry Hallam, 1868- joint author. III. Title.

SNOWDEN, James Henry, 1852-1936. 268
Outfitting the teacher of religion; a textbook on the principles and practice of religious education, by James H. Snowden. New York, the Macmillan company, 1929. x p., 1 l., 274 p. 21 cm. "Brief list of books for religious education workers": p. 269-270. [BV1475.S62] 29-19711
1. Religious education. I. Title.

SNYDER, Richard L
Leadership manual; administering the Christian Education Program in the local church. Boston, United Church Press [1964] 60 p. photos. 25 cm. 67-6913
1. Religious education. I. Title.

SOARES, Theodore Gerald, 1869- 268
Religious education, by Theodore Gerald Soares. Chicago, Ill., The University of Chicago press [c1928] xx, 336 p. 20 cm. (Half-title: The University of Chicago publications in religious education ... Handbooks of ethics and religion) Bibliography: p. 325-331. [BV1471.S7] 28-9382
1. Religious education. I. Title.

SOARES, Theodore Gerald, 1869- 268.
A study of adult life a textbook in the Standard course in teacher training outlined and approved by the Sunday school council of Evangelical denominations. by Theodore G. Soares, Third year specialization series Boston, Printed for the Teacher training publishing association by the Pilgrim press [c1923] xii p., 1 l., 114 p. 17 cm. "References for reading" at end of each chapter. [BV1550.S6] 23-12031
1. Religious education. I. Title.

SOULE, Ella Frances, Mrs. 248
Sunday afternoons for the children; a mother book, by E. Frances Soule. New York, Fords, Howard & Hulbert, 1900. 7, 11-162 p. 1 illus. 18 cm. [BV1590.S6] 0-2338
1. Religious education. I. Title. II. Title: A mother book.

SPOTTS, Charles Dewey, 1899- 268
Called to teach. Philadelphia, United Church [c.1963] 111p. 20cm. 63-10950 2.50 bds.,
1. Religious education. I. Title.

SPRING, Gardiner, 1785-1878.
Hints to parents on the religious education of children. By Gardiner Spring ... New York, Taylor & Gould, 1835. 130 p. front. 16 cm. [LC361.S7] 7-34878
1. Religious education. I. Title.

SQUIRES, Walter Albion, 1874- 268.
A parish program of religious education; suggestions for a church school designed to carry on a unified system of religious education consisting of a program of leadership training, a program of cooperation with the home, and a central program of information, worship and expression, by Walter Albion Squires ... with an introduction by Harold McA. Robinson ... Philadelphia, The Westminster press, 1923. 234 p. diagrs. 19 cm. [BV1475.S68] 23-17494
1. Religious education. I. Title.

SQUIRES, Walter Albion, 1874- 232.05
The pedagogy of Jesus in the twilight of to-day, by Walter Albion Squires, B.D., with an introduction by William Chalmers Covert, D.D. New York, George H. Doran company [c1927] xviii p., 1 l., 21-296 p. 19 1/2 cm. [BT590.T5865] 27-11603
1. Jesus Christ—Teaching methods. 2. Religious education. I. Title.

SQUIRES, Walter Albion, 1874- 268
Psychological foundations of religious education, by Walter Albion Squires ... with an introduction by A. Duncan Yocum, PH.D. New York, George H. Doran company [c1926] xvii p., 2 l., 23-153 p. 19 cm. [BV1471.S8] 26-9935
1. Religious education. 2. Psychology. I. Title.

SQUIRES, Walter Albion, 1874- 268.
The week day church schools; a historical sketch, brief analysis, and attempted evaluation of the organized efforts to furnish week day religious instruction to pupils of elementary and high school age in the United States, by Walter Albion Squires ... with an introduction by Harold McA. Robinson ... Philadelphia, Presbyterian board of publication and Sabbath school work, 1921. 168 p. front., illus. (charts) 19 cm. Contains bibliographies. [BV1580.S7] 22-3121
1. Religious education. I. Title.

STAGG, Samuel Wells. 248
... Home lessons in religion; a manual for mothers ... by Samuel Wells Stagg ... in collaboration with Mary Boyd Stagg. New York, Cincinnati, The Abingdon press [c1922- v. 21 cm. (The Abingdon religious education texts; D. G. Downey, general editor, G. H. Betts, associate editor) [BV1590.S7] 23-6876
1. Religious education. I. Stagg, Mrs. Mary Boyd, joint author. II. Title.

STARR, Homer Worthington, 1875- 377.1
Believing youth; a cheering experiment in creative teaching, by the Reverend Homer W. Starr ... with foreword by Rt. Rev. Frank A. Juhan ... and introductory note by Rev. John W. Suter, jr. ... Milwaukee, Wis., Morehouse publishing co. [c1931] x p., 1 l., 98 p., 1 l. 19 cm. Bibliography: p. [97]-98. [BV1485.S7] 81-8068
1. Religious education. I. Title.

STEEN, Inez. 268.6
God speaks to me; grade three, by Inez Steen ... Minneapolis, Augsburg publishing house [c1938] 168 p. incl. illus. (part col.) plates (part col.) 22 cm. Text and illustrations on lining-papers. "This volume is one in a series of graded Sunday school textbooks issued by the Board of elementary Christian education, Dr. Jacob Tanner, editor-in-chief." Also published as pt. ii of the teacher's manual. [BV1545.S75] 38-25299
1. Religious education. I. Tanner, Jacob, 1865- ed. II. Title.

STEEN, Inez. 268.61
God speaks to me; grade three, teacher's manual, including the complete pupils' volume, by Inez Steen. Minneapolis, Augsburg publishing house [c1938] 2 v. in 1 illus. (part col.) plates (part col.) 22 cm. Text and illustration on lining-papers. "This volume is one in a series of graded Sunday school textbooks issued by the Board of elementary Christian education, Dr. Jacob Tanner, editor-in-chief." Part ii, the pupil's volume, is also published separately. Included bibliographies. [BV1545.S75 Manual] 38-253000
1. Religious education. I. Tanner, Jacob, 1865- ed. II. Title.

STEPHEN college, Columbia, Mo.
The program of religious education at Stephens college. Issued from the Office of publications, Stephens college, Columbia, Missouri, March, 1937. [Columbia, Mo., 1937] 63 p. incl. illus., plates, ports. 25 cm. [The Stephen college bulletin, v. 18. no. 3, March 1937. Education service series, no. 2] Title vignette. Half-title: Report of the Burrall class commission. A 40
1. Religious education. I. Title.

STEPHENS, Thomas, d.1912, ed. 268.
The child and religion; eleven essays ... ed. by Thomas Stephens, B. A. New York, G. P. Putnam's sons; London, Williams and Norgate, 1905. 371 p. 19 cm. (Half-title: Crown theological library, vol. xi) [BV639.C4S75] 5-39579
1. Religious education. I. Title.
Contents omitted.

STEWART, Donald Gordon. 268
Christian education and evangelism. Philadelphia, Westminster Press [1963] 176 p. 21 cm. Bibliography: p. 173-176. [BV1471.2.S8] 63-13356
1. Religious education. 2. Kerygma. I. Title.

STEWART, George, 1892- 268
... Can I teach my child religion? Garden City, N. Y., Doubleday, Doran & company, inc., 1929. viii p., 2 l., 3-142 p. 20 cm. "Materials for religious instruction available for any home": p. 103-142. [BV1475.S685] 29-7093
1. Religious education. I. Title.

STILL, Florence Shirley (Swetnam) "Mrs. Owen Still," 1896- 268.433
Success with intermediates in an average church by Mrs. Owen Still. Cincinnati, O.,

The Standard publishing company [c1938] 159 p. 19 cm. [B1548.S8] 38-9158
1. Religious education. I. Title.

STILLMAN, Mildred (Whitney) Mrs. 204
The parson's garden, by Mildred Whitney Stillman. New York city, Duffield & Green [c1931] 5 p. l., 3-79, [1] p. 17 1/2 cm. Essays. [BR85.S787] 31-28909
1. Religious education. I. Title.

STILLZ, Eva M. 220
... *God's care of mankind...* by Eva M. Stilz. Philadelphia, Pa., The United Lutheran publication house [c1927] 69 p. front., illus. 20 cm. (Religious education texts for weekday schools. Fifth book. Junior-second year. For the pupil) [BS605.R35 book 5] 27-19717
1. Religious education. I. Title.

STILZ, Eva M. 268.
... *God working through mankind* ... by Eva M. Stilz. Philadelphia, Pa., The United Lutheran publication house [c1928] 120 p. front., illus. 20 cm. (Religious education texts for weekday schools. Sixth book. Junior--third year. For the teacher) [BV1580.S75] 28-23057
1. Religious education. I. Title.

STILZ, Eva M. 220
... *God's care of mankind...* by Eva M. Stilz. Philadelphia, Pa., The United Lutheran publication house [c1927] 109 p. front., illus. 20 cm. (Religious education texts for weekday schools. Fifth book. Junior-second year. For the teacher) [BS605.R35 book 5 a] 27-19718
1. Religious education. I. Title.

STILZ, Eva M. 220
... *God's great plan for mankind...* by Eva M. Stilz. Philadelphia, Pa., The United Lutheran publication house [c1926] 69 p. front., illus. 20 cm. (Religious education texts for weekday schools. Fourth book. Junior--first year) [BS605.R35 4th book] 37-5074
1. Religious education. I. Title.

STOCK, Harry Thomas. 259
Church work with young people [by] Harry Thomas Stock. Boston, Chicago, The Pilgrim press [c1929] vi p., 1 l., 236 p. 20 1/2 cm. Bibliography at end of each chapter. [BV4447.S7] 29-13701
1. Religious education. I. Title.

STORER, James W. 268
By ways to highways, by J.W. Storer. [Nashville] Broadman press [c1938] 121 p. 19 1/2 cm. "A revision of articles originally published in the Sunday school builder."--Foreword. [BV1520.S75] 38-31431
1. Religious education. 2. Sunday-schools. I. Title.

STORER, James Wilson. 268
By ways to highways, by J. W. Storer. [Nashville] Broadman press [1938] 121 p. 20 cm. "A revision of articles originally published in the Sunday school builder."--Foreword. [BV1520.S75] 38-31431
1. Religious education. 2. Sunday-schools. I. Title.

STOUT, John Elbert. 268.
... *Organization and administration of religious education* [by] John Elbert Stout ... New York, Cincinnati, The Abingdon press [c1922] 287 p. 20 cm. (The Abingdon religious education texts. D. G. Downey, general editor. Community training school series, N. E. Richardson, editor) [BV1475.S75] 22-3646
1. Religious education. I. Title.

STUHLMUELLER, Carroll 220.6
The Bible and college theology. Washington, D.C., 487 Michigan Ave., N.E., Thomist Pr., c.1962. 52p. 18cm. (Compact studies theology ser.) .35 pap.,
I. Title.

SUDLOW, Elizabeth (Williams) Mrs., 1878- 268.
All about the junior, by Elizabeth Williams Sudlow ... Philadelphia, The Union press [c1916] 143 p. 17 cm. [BV1546.S8] 16-19983
1. Religious education. 2. Sunday-schools. I. Title. II. Title: The junior. All about.

*SULLIVAN, Jessie P. 207
Object lessons and stories for children's church. Grand Rapids, Baker Book House [1974, c1973] 162 p., 20 cm. Formerly published under the title, Children's church programs. [BV1471] ISBN 0-8010-8037-1 2.50 (pbk.)
1. Religious education. I. Title.

SUTER, John Wallace, 1890- 268.
Creative teaching, letters to a church school teacher, by John Wallace Suter, jr. New York, The Macmillan company, 1924. 159 p. 20 cm. "Your reading"; list of books: p. 131-137. [BV1534.S89] 24-25306
1. Religious education. 2. Sunday-schools. I. Title.

SUTER, John Wallace, 1890- 268.6
Creative teaching; letters to a church school teacher, by John Wallace Suter, jr. Rev. ed. New York, The Macmillan company, 1934. 155 p. 10 1/2 cm. "Your reading": p. [129]-139. [BV1534.S89 1934] 34-11046
1. Religious education. 2. Sunday-schools. I. Title.

SUTER, John Wallace, 1890- 377.1
Open doors in religious education, by John Wallace Suter, jr. New York, R. R. Smith, inc., 1931. xiii, 128 p. 19 1/2 cm. [BV1471.S85] 31-22923
1. Religious education. I. Title.

SWEARINGEN, Tilford Tippett. 268.433
Planning for young people in the local church, by T. T. Swearingen ... St. Louis, The Bethany press [c1933] 96 p. 16 1/2 cm. "Apprived as a textbook in leadership training by the Department of religious education, Disciples of Christ." "For your library": p. 95-96. [BV1485.S35] 34-5
1. Religious education. I. Disciples of Christ. Dept. of religious education. II. Title.

TANNER, Jacob, 1865- 268.6
Ten studies in religious pedagogy, by Jacob Tanner ... published under the auspices of the Board of elementary Christian education of the Norwegian Lutheran church of America. Minneapolis, Minn., Augsbury publishing house, 1930. vii, 70 p. 20 1/2 cm. [BV1475.T3] 30-30003
1. Religious education. 2. Sunday-schools. I. Norwegian Lutheran church of America. Board of elementary Christian education. II. Title.

TANNER, Jacob, 1865- 268.6
Ten studies in religious pedagogy, one in a series of teachers' training course books, by Jacob Tanner ... Minneapolis, Augsburg publishing house, 1937. 4 p. l., 73 p. 19 1/2 cm. "Published under the auspices of the Board of elementary Christian education of the N.L.C.A." "Fourth edition, revised." [BV1475.T3 1937] 38-875
1. Religious education. 2. Sunday-schools. I. Title.

TATE, Edward Mowbray, 1902- 268.6
Church school curricula and education for Protestant church unity; an analysis of religious education materials used by six denominations in training children for church membership, in the light of denominational pronouncements favoring the movement for church unity, by Edward Mowbray Tate ... New York city, 1932. 94 p. 22 1/2 cm. Issued also as thesis (PH.D.) Columbia university. "List of textbooks": p. 11-14; Bibliography: p. 92-94. [BV1558.T3 1932 a] 33-301
1. Religious education. 2. Christian union. I. Title. II. Title: Education for Protestant church unity.

TAYLOR, Marvin J. 1921- ed. 268
An introduction to Christian education. Nashville, Abingdon [c.1966] 412p. 24cm. Bibl. [BV1471.2.T3] 66-11452 6.50
1. Religious education. I. Title. II. Title: Christian education.

TAYLOR, Marvin J 1921- ed. 268
An introduction to Christian education. Marvin J. Taylor, editor. Nashville, Abingdon Press [1966] 412 p. 24 cm. Includes bibliographies. [BV1471.2.T3] 66-11452
1. Religious education. I. Christian education. II. Title.

TAYLOR, Marvin J., 1921- ed. 268.082
Religious education: a comprehensive survey. New York, Abingdon Press [1960] 446 p. 24 cm. Includes bibliographies. [BV1471.T35] 60-5477
1. Religious education.

TAYLOR, Ruth B. 268.
Teacher's manual for the daily vacation Bible school, especially adapted to rural and village schools, by Ruth B. Taylor, Laura Merrihew Adams, and Elizabeth Hubbard Bonsall; James McConaughy, editor. 2d ed. Philadelphia, American Sunday-school union [c1927] 134 p. illus. 17 1/2 cm. [BV1585.T3 1927] 27-16739
1. Religious education. I. Adams, Mrs. Laura Merrihew, joint author. II. Bonsall, Elizabeth Hubbard, joint author. III. McConaughy, James, 1857- ed. IV. Title.

[THOMPSON, Louise Glenn] 1903- 268.62
Guide to child activity, for teachers and mothers, to be used with My first Bible lessons ... Nashville, Tenn., Gospel advocate company [1935] 256 p. 20 cm. By Louise G. Thompson. cf. p. 185. Songs, with music: p. [189]-[198] [BV1540.T55] 35-25806
1. Religious education. 2. Sunday-schools. 3. Bible—Study. 4. Bible stories, English. I. Thompson, Louise Glenn, 1903-ed. My first Bible lessons. II. Title.

TOOLS and techniques for the teaching of the Catholic religion in colleges and universities. [Huntington, Ind., Our Sunday Visitor, 1956- v. 23cm. Contents.- pt. 1. Foundations of the Catholic Church.
1. Religious education. 2. Universities and colleges—U. S. 3. Catholic Church in the U. S.— Education. I. National Association of Newman Club Chaplains.

TULPA, Leonid Vasilievich. 377
Religious education as character training; a study in the philosophy and psychology of religious education and character training, by Leonid V. Tulpa, ED. M. New York, 1935. xvi p. 1 l. 96 p. 22 cm. [BV1471.T8] 35-186653
1. Religious education. 2. Moral education. I. Title.

UNION University, Schenectady. Character Research Project.
Powerful learning tools in religion... Schenectady, N.Y. [c1958] 128 p. (Character research project workshop on powerful learning tools in religion) 65-74755
I. Title.

VACATION days with Jesus 268
... a manual for teachers of primary classes in vacation Bible schools ... Columbus, O., The Book concern [c1928- v. illus. 31 1/2 cm. Contains music. Contents.[v. 1] Primary, first year, by Marion Poppen Athy.--[v. 2] Primary, second year, by Eliatine Benson Schultz. [BV1585.V3] 28-17802
1. Religious education. 2. Vacation schools. I. Schulz, Ellatine Benson. II. Athy, Marion Peppen. III. Title: Vacation Bible schools.

VAN ORMER, Abraham Brower Bunn, 1869-
Studies in religious nurture, by A. B. Bunn Van Ormer. Philadelphia, Pa., Lutheran publication society [c1908] iv p., 1 l., 7-291 p., 1 l. 18 1/2 cm. Partly reprinted from various periodicals. 8-13668
I. Title.

VATICAN Council. 2d,1962-1965. 268
De educatione Christiana. The declaration on Christian education of Vatican Council II, promulgated by Pope Paul VI, October 28, 1965. Commentary by Mark J. Hurley. [Study-club ed.] Glen Rock, N.J., Paulist Press, 1966. 158 p. 18 cm. (Vatican II documents) Bibliographical footnotes. [BX830 1962.A45E33] 66-19151
1. Religious education. I. Hurley, Mark Joseph, 1917- II. Title. III. Title: The declaration on Christian education of Vatican Council II.

VATICAN COUNCIL. 2D, 1962-1965 268
De educatione Christiana. The declaration on Christian education of Vatican Council II, promulgated by Pope Paul VI. October 28, 1965. Commentary by Mark J. Hurley. [Study-club ed.] Glen Rock, N.J., Paulist, 1966. 158p. 18cm. (Vatican II docs.) Bibl. [BX8301962.A45E33] 66-19151 .75 pap.,
1. Religious education. I. Hurley. Mark Joseph, 1917. II. Title. III. Title: The declaration on Christian education of Vatican Council II.

VEACH, Robert Wells, 1871- 268
The meaning of the war for religious education, by Robert Wells Veach ... New York, Chicago, [etc.] Fleming H. Revell company [c1920] 254 p. 19 1/2 cm. [BV1471.V4] 20-4809
1. Religious education. 2. European war, 1914-1918—Religious aspects. I. Title.

VERKUYL, Gerrit.
Scripture memory work; a handbook containing fifty-two selections with helps for the leader, by Gerrit Verkuyl ... New York, Chicago [etc.] Fleming H. Revell company [c1918] 120 p. 19 1/2 cm. [BS610.V4] 18-19977
I. Title.

VERKUYL, Gerrit. 220
Scripture memory work (graded) a handbook containing fifty-two selections with helps for the leader, by Gerrit Verkuyl ... New York, Chicago [etc.] Fleming H. Revell company [c1924] 2 p. l. 120 p. 19 1/2 cm. [BS600.V4 1924] 24-19933
I. Title.

VIETH, Paul Herman, 1895- 268
The Church in its teaching work [by] Paul H. Vieth ... New York, Cincinnati [etc.] The Methodist book concern [c1937] 56 p. 19 1/2 cm. "Approved by the Committee on curriculum of the Board of education of the Methodist Episcopal church." "For further reading" at end of each chapter. [BV1471.V48] 37-21251
1. Religious education. 2. Sunday-schools. I. Methodist Episcopal church. Board of education. II. Title.

VIETH, Paul Herman, 1895- 268.6
How to teach in the church school; a simple introduction to the art of teaching for all those workers in the church school who want to learn more about what teaching is and how to do it more successfully, by Paul H. Vieth ... Philadelphia, The Westminster press, 1935. 173 p. 17 1/2 cm. "References": p. 172-173. [BV1534.V5] 35-13403
1. Religious education. 2. Sunday-schools. I. Title.

VIETH, Paul Herman, 1895- 207
Objectives in religious education, by Paul H. Vieth .... with an introduction by Luther A. Weigle ... New York and London, Harper & brothers, 1930. xiv, 331 p. 21 1/2 cm. "Sources on which the study in objectives was based": p. 295-316. [BV1471.V5] 30-13688
1. Religious education. I. Title.

WAHLQUIST, John Thomas, 1899- 268.6
Teaching as the direction of activities, by John T. Wahlquist, PH. D. Salt Lake City, Utah, Deseret Sunday school union, 1934. 214 p. 19 1/2 cm. "This text is written for the teacher-training classes conducted under the auspices of the Deseret Sunday school union."--Pref. Includes "Selected references". [BV1534.W3] 36-20226
1. Religious education. 2. Teaching. I. Title.

WALTERS, Dick H., 1907- 220
Our junior Bible course; a Bible course for catechetical work (a two-year course ... by Dick H. Walters ... Grand Rapids, Mich., Zondervan publishing house [c1937]- v. 26 1/2 cm. [BS605.W26] 38-3308
1. Religious education. I. Title.

WARDLE, Addie Grace. 268.
Handwork in religious education, by Addie Grace Wardle... Chicago, Ill., The University of Chicago press [c1916] xviii, 143 p. illus. 18 cm. (Half-title: The Univesity of Chicago publications in religious education) "Books for reference": p. 136-140. [BV1536.W3] 16-15072
I. Title.

WASHBURN, Alphonso V. 268.86
comp.
Reaching all prospects for the church. A. V.Washburn, compiler. Nashville, Convention Press [1964] xi, 145 p. 19 cm. [BV1471.2.W3] 64-17644
1. Religious education. 2. Baptists — Education. I. Title.

WATERSTON, Robert Cassie, 1812-1893.
Thoughts on moral and spiritual culture. By R. C. Waterston ... Boston, Crocker & Ruggles, etc., 1842. viii, 317 p. 18 cm. [BJ66.W3] 10-2422
1. Religious education. 2. Moral education. I. Title.

WATSON, Goodwin Barbour, 263
1899-
Case studies for teachers of religion [by] Goodwin B. Watson... Gladys H. Watson, A.M. New York, Association press, 1926. 296 p. 23 1/2 cm. "Source quotations": p. 127-293; "Typical stories by topics": p. 293-296. [BV1520.W3] 26-13055
1. Religious education. I. Watson, Mrs. Gladys (Hipple) 1898- joint author. II. Title.

WATSON, Goodwin Barbour, 268
1899-
Experimentation and measurement in religious education [by] Goodwin B. Watson... New York, Association press, 1927. xii, 295 p. incl. illus., tables, diagrs. 24 cm. [BV1475.W3] 27-25031
1. Religious education. 2. Mental tests. I. Title.

WATSON, James Fraughtman. 268
Basic principles of education and expression; a book for religious workers, training schools, professional and business men, women and children. By James Fraughtman Watson... [Atlanta, Printed by Walter W. Brown publishing co., c1929] 4 p. l., 11-128 p. diagrs. 20 cm. Advertising matter: p. 126-128. [BV1471.W3] 29-21278
1. Religious education. 2. Elocution. 3. Expression. I. Title.

WEIGLE, Luther Allan, 1880- 268
The pupil and the teacher, a leadership training text, by Luther A. Weigle ... Philadelphia, Pa., The United Lutheran publication house [c1929] 240 p. 19 1/2 cm. New suggestions for investigation and discussion and fresh bibliographies have been appended to each of the chapters. The text is unrevised. cf. Author's note. Bibliography at end of each chapter. [BV1520.W4 1929] 29-4590
1. Religious education. 2. Child study. 3. Education of children. I. Title.

WEIGLE, Luther Allan, 1880- 268.
Training the devotional life, by Luther Allan Weigle ... and Henry Hallam Tweedy ... Boston, Chicago, The Pilgrim press [c1919] 2 p. l., p. 261-352. 19 1/2 cm. Bibliography at end of each chapter. [BV1475.W4] 20-10546
1. Religious education. I. Tweedy, Henry Hallam, 1868- joint author. II. Title.

WENNER, George Unangst, 377.
1844-1934.
Religious education and the public school; an American problem, by George U. Wenner ... New York, Bonnell, Silver and co., 1907. ix, 163 p. 19 1/2 cm. [LC405.W4 1907] 7-16706
1. Religious education. I. Title.

WENNER, George Unangst, 268.
1844-1934.
Religious education and the public school: an American problem, by George U. Wenner ... New ed., rev. and enl., giving the action of the Federal council of the churches of Christ in America in 1912. New York, American tract society, [c1913] 4 p. l., vii-x, 191 p. 19 cm. [BV1580.W45] 13-20500
1. Religious education. I. Federal council of the churches of Christ in America. II. Title.

WESTPHAL, Arnold Carl. 268.76
Junior talks for special days, with surprise objects, by Arnold Carl Westphal... New York [etc.] Fleming H. Revell company [c1936] 142 p. illus. 23 1/2 cm. [BV4315.W43] [252] 36-18300
1. Religious education. 2. Object-teaching. 3. Sunday-schools—Exercises, recitations, etc. 4. Days. I. Title.

WHITE, Clara L. 377
Helpers in God's world, prepared for use with beginners in the vacation church school, by Clara L. White; John T. Faris, D.D., editor. Philadelphia, Board of Christian education of the Presbyterian church in the U.S.A., 1930. 207 p. front., illus., plates. 23 1/2 cm. "Music section": p. 183-205. Bibliography: p. 207. [BV1540.W5] 30-11744
1. Religious education. I. Faris, John Thomas, 1871- ed. II. Title.

WHITE, Ellen Gould (Harmon) 207
Mrs., 1827-1915.
Counsels to teachers, parents and students regarding Christian education, by Ellen G. White ... Mountain View, Cal., Portland, Or. [etc.] Pacific press publishing association [c1913] 2 p. l., 7-574 p. 19 cm. $1.00. [LC586.A3W5] 13-11695
1. Religious education. I. Title.

WHITE, James Asa, 1886- 377.108
ed.
Christian education objectives; a symposium assembled under the auspices of the California council of religious education, Berkley [!] Cal.; edited by James Asa White. New York [etc.] Fleming H. Revell company [c1932] 142 p. 19 1/2 cm. "The presentation in non-technical terms of the [seven] objectives for religious education as adopted by the International council of religious education."--Pref. "Selected bibliography" at end of each chapter. [BV1471.W35] 32-14308
1. Religious education. I. Northern California council of religious education, Berkeley. II. Title.

WHITWELL, Nevada (Miller) 268.7
Mrs. 1904-
Intermediate expressional services, a year of program materials for intermediates in church schools and young people's societies, by Nevada Miller Whitwell. Cincinnati, O., The Standard publishing company [c1938] 331 p. illus. 21 1/2 cm. "This book was planned for use in connection with my 'Intermediate worship services'."--p. 8. (Full name: Mrs. Nevada Gae (Miller) Whitwell) [BV1548.W5] 38-13172
1. Religious education. 2. Worship (Religious education) I. Title.

WILBUR, Mary Aronetta. 268.
A child's religion, by Mary Aronetta Wilbur... Boston and New York, Houghton Mifflin company, 1917. x p., 1 l., 141, [1] p. 18 cm. $1.00 Reprinted in part from the Churchman. [BV1475.W5] 17-9361
1. Religious education. I. Title.

WILLIAMS, Charles Bray, 1869- 268
The function of teaching in Christianity, by Charles B. Williams... Nashville, Tenn., Sunday school board, Southern Baptist convention [c1912] 260 p. 19 cm. [BV1471.W4] 12-18226
1. Religious education. I. Title.

WILLIAMS, Jessie (Tandy) 268.432
Mrs., 1876-
The junior workers' hand book; for junior workers in the Sunday school, the week-day religious school, the vacation Bible school, by Mrs. Jessie T. Williams. Butler, Ind., The Higley printing co. [c1934] 256 p. 20 cm. [Full name: Mrs. Jessie Martha (Tandy) Williams] Bibliography: p. 7. [BV1546.W5] 34-22217
1. Religious education. 2. Sunday-schools. I. Title.

WILLIAMS, John Paul, 1900- 268
The new education and religion, a challenge to secularism in education, by J. Paul Williams. New York, Association press, 1945. x, 198 p. 21 cm. [BV1475.W53] 45-4084
1. Religious education. I. Title.

WILM, Emil Carl, 1877- 268
The culture of religion; elements of religious education, by Emil Carl Wilm ... Boston, New York [etc.] The Pilgrim press [c1912] xi, 204 p. 20 cm. $0.75 Bibliography: p. 202-204. [BV1471.W5] 12-13254
1. Religious education. I. Title.

WILM, Emil Carl, 1877-1932. 377.
Religion and the school, by Emil Carl Wilm ... New York, Cincinnati, The Abingdon press [c1918] 53 p. 17 1/2 cm. Bibliography: p. 53. [LC268.W6] 18-7108
1. Religious education. 2. Moral education. I. Title.

WILSON, Caroline (Fry) Mrs. 268
1787-1846.
Scripture principles of education. By Caroline Fry ... Rev. from the London ed. Philadelphia, George, Latimer, & co., 1833. 100 p. 15 cm. [BV1475.W55] 7-36685
1. Religious education. I. Title.

WILSON, Dorothy Frances. 268
Child psychology and religious education, a book for parents and teachers, by Dorothy F. Wilson with a preface by Canon B. H. Streeter. Garden City, N.Y., Doubleday, Doran & company, inc., 1929. 158, [1] p. 19 1/2 cm. "Second edition." Printed in Great Britain. Bibliography: p. 154-157. [BV1475.W6 1929] 29-8645
1. Religious education. 2. Child study. I. Title.

WILSON, Mabel Aureola.
Love, light and life for God's little children. A course of instruction for primary Sunday schools. With a preface by C. M. Davis ... [St. Louis, Shallcross printing co., 1897] ix, 354 p. 8°. Jul
1. Religious education. 2. Sunday schools. I. Title.

WINCHESTER, Benjamin Severance,
1868-
Religious education and democracy, by Benjamin S. Winchester ... New York, Cincinnati, The Abingdon press [c1917] 298 p. fold tab. 21 1/2 cm. Bibliography: p. 277-280. [RV1475.W7] 17-24303
1. Religious education. 2. Democracy. 3. Church and state. I. Title.

WINCHESTER, Benjamin 268
Severance, 1868-
The teaching church, a discussion course for adults [by] Benjamin S. Winchester and Erwin L. Shaver. Boston, Chicago, The Pilgrim press [1925] v, 95 p. illus. 20 cm. Includes bibliographies. [BV1472.W5] 44-19796
1. Religious education. I. Shaver, Erwin Leander, 1890- joint author. II. Title.

WOOD, Irving Francis, 1861- 268.
1934.
... Adult class study, by Irving F. Wood Boston, New York [etc.] The Pilgrim press [c1911] vii 143 p. 19 1/2 cm. (Modern Sunday-school manuals, ed. by C. F. Kent) Contains bibliographies. [BV1550.W6] 11-15598
1. Religious education. I. Title.

WOOLSTON, Clarence Herbert.
Seeing truth; a book of object lessons with magical and mechanical effects ... by Rev. C. Herbert Woolston ... Philadelphia, Chicago, The Praise publishing co. [c1910] 207 p. front., illus., plates, ports., diagrs. 20 cm. $0.75 p. 206-207, advertising matter. 11-921
I. Title.

WORDEN, James Avery, 1841-1917.
The Westminster normal outlines; or, The Christian teacher in the Sabbath-school. Middle course. By the Rev. James A. Worden ... Philadelphia, Presbyterian board of publication [c1881] 283 p. front. (fold. map) illus. 19 cm. Bibliography: p. 253-260. [BX8923.W63] 3-15835
1. Religious education. 2. Bible. N. T. Acts, Epistles, and Revelation—Study—Text-books. 3. Bible—Study—Text-books—N. T. Acts, Epistles, and Revelation. I. Title.

WRIGHT, Kathryn S 268.6
Let the children paint; art in religious education [by] Kathryn S. Wright. New York, Seabury Press [1966] 168 p. illus. 22 cm. Includes bibliographies. [BV1536.W75] 66-16651
1. Religious education. 2. Object teaching. I. Title. II. Title: Art in religious education.

WYCKOFF, D. Campbell. 268
The gospel and Christian education; a theory of Christian education for our times. Philadelphia, Westminster Press [1958, c1959] 191 p. 21 cm. [BV1471.W88] 59-5128
1. Religious education. I. Title.

WYCKOFF, D. Campbell 268
How to evaluate your Christian education program. Philadelphia, Pub. for the Cooperative Pubn. Assn., by Westminster [c.1962] 103p. 28cm. (Cooperative ser.) Bibl. 62-8082 3.50 pap.,
1. Religious education. I. Title.

WYCKOFF, D Campbell. 268
How to evaluate your Christian education program. Philadelphia, Published for the Cooperative Publication Association, by Westminster Press [1962] 103 p. 28 cm. (The Cooperative series) Includes bibliography. [BV1471.2.W9] 62-8080
1. Religious education. I. Title.

WYCKOFF, D Campbell. 268
The task of Christian education. Philadelphia, Westminster Press [1955] 172p. 21cm. [BV1471.W9] 55-5074
1. Religious education. I. Title.

YEAXLEE, Basil Alfred, 377.1
1883-
The approach to religious education in Sunday school and day school, by Basil A. Yeaxlee ... New York, The Macmillan company, 1932. 143 [1] p. 19 1/2 cm. "A short course of lectures delivered in the University of Birmingham to day school and Sunday school teachers during the winter 1930-31."--Pref. "Bibliographical note": p. 9. [BV1471.Y4 1932] 32-2138
1. Religious education. I. Title.

YOUNG, Thomas Shields, 1863- 377.
Week-day church school methods, by Thomas S. Young... Philadelphia, Boston [etc.] The Judson press [c1924] 8 p. l., 112 p. front., diagrs. 19 1/2 cm. (Half-title: Judson training manuals for the school of the church...) [BV1580.Y6] 24-7539
1. Religious education. 2. Church schools. I. Title.

YOUNG, Warren Cameron, 1913-
The influence of John Dewey in religious education. Chicago, c1949 [Washington, Library of Congress, 1963] 54 l. 29 cm. Photocopy (positive) Bibliography: leaves [51]-54. 68-26926
1. Dewey, John, 1859- 2. Religious education. I. Title.

ZEIGLER, Earl Frederick, 377.1
1889-
Toward understanding adults, by Earl F. Zeigler. Philadelphia, The Westminster press, 1931. 164 p. 1 illus. 17 1/2 cm. (On cover: Handybooks for church school leaders) "Brief bibliography": p. 159-162. [BV1550.Z4] 31-20327
1. Religious education. 2. Education of adults. 3. Church work. 4. Theology, Pastoral. I. Title.

ZEIGLER, Earl Frederick, 268.434
1889-
The way of adult education, by Earl F. Zeigler...A text-book in the Standard leadership training curriculum, outlined and approved by the International council of religious education. Philadelphia, Printed for the Leadership training publishing association by the Westminster press [c1938] 320 p. 19 1/2 cm. "References for further study" at end of each chapter. [BV1550.Z43] 38-6781
1. Religious education. I. International council of religious education. II. Title.

ZUCK, Roy B 268
The Holy Spirit in your teaching. Wheaton, Ill., Scripture Press Publications [1963] xiii, 189 p. 24 cm. Bibliography: p. 171-179. [BV1471.2.Z8] 63-21391
1. Religious education. 2. Holy Spirit. I. Title.

Religious education—Addresses, essays, lectures.

CULLY, Kendig Brubaker. 207
The search for a Christian education since 1940. Philadelphia, Westminster Press [1965] 205 p. 21 cm. Bibliographical references included in "Notes" (p. [183]-197) [BV1471.2.C79] 65-15290
1. Religious education—Addresses, essays, lectures. I. Title.

DENDY, Marshall C. 268.081
Changing patterns in Christian education.

Richmond, Va., Knox Pr. [1965, c.1964] 96p. 21cm. Bibl. [BV1473.D4] 65-10715 1.50 pap.,
1. Religious education—Addresses, essays, lectures. I. Title.

HAVIGHURST, Robert James, 1900- 268
The educational mission of the church, by Robert J. Havighurst. Philadelphia, Westminster Press [1965] 150 p. 21 cm. "Stone lectures ... 1964 ... form the core of this book." Bibliographical references included in "Notes" (p. [153]-156) [BV1473.H3] 65-10538
1. Religious education — Addresses, essays, lectures. I. Princeton Theological Seminary. Stone lectures, 1964. II. Title.

JOHN, John Price Durbin, 1843-1916. 261
The worth of a man. Lectures and addresses, volume ii. By John P. D. John. Cincinnati, Jennings and Graham; New York, Eaton and Mains [c1907] 275 p. 20 cm. A companion volume to the author's "Signs of God in the world." [BR85.J55] 7-31232
I. Title.

MICHIGAN. Western Michigan College, Kalamasoo.
Focus on religion in teacher education, essays written at Western Michigan College, Kalamazoo, Michigan, for the Teacher Education and Religion Project. Oneonta, N. Y., American Association of Colleges for Teacher Education, 1955. v, 87p. 28cm. Bibliography: p. 80-87. A57
1. Religious education—Addresses, essays, lectures. I. American Association of Colleges for Teacher Education. Teacher Education and Religion Project Committee. II. Title.

MICHIGAN. Western Michigan University, Kalamazoo.
Focus on religion in teacher education, essays waritten at Western Michigan College, Kalamazoo, Michigan, for the Teacher Education and Religion Project. Oneonta, N. Y., American Association of Colleges for Teacher Education, 1955. v, 87p. 28cm. Bibliography: p. 80-87. A57
1. Religious education—Addresses, essays, lectures. I. American Association of Colleges for Teacher Education. Teacher Education and Regligion Project Committee. II. Title.

NIBLETT, William Roy 377.1
Christian education in a secular society. New York, Oxford University Press, 1960[ ]. 132p. 20cm. 60-1979 2.00
1. Religious education—Addresses, essays, lectures. I. Title.

SISEMORE, John T comp. 268.08
Vital principles in religious education, compiled by John T. Sisemore. Nashville, Broadman Press [c1966] 128 p. 21 cm. Includes bibliographies. [BV1473.S5] 66-10709
1. Religious education — Addresses, essays, lectures. I. Title.

SLATTERY, Margaret.
The seed, the soil and the sower, by Margaret Slattery. Cleveland, O., F. M. Barton company, 1910. 51 p. 19 cm. [BV1477.S6] 10-12317
1. Religious education—Addresses, essays, lectures. I. Title.

WHERE there's life 268'.8'2
[by] Gabriel Moran [others] Dayton, Ohio, Pflaum [1967] 126p. illus. 17cm. (Trends in religious educ., no. 1) Witness bks., 7. [BX921.W5] 67-20744 .75 pap.,
1. Religious education—Addresses, essays, lectures. 2. Catholic Church—Education—Addresses, essays,lectures. I. Moran, Gabriel.
Contents omitted.

WHO are we? : 207
In search of an identity / edited by John H. Westerhoff III on the occasion of the Religious Education Association's 75th anniversary. Birmingham, Ala. : Religious Education Press, [1978] p. cm. Includes bibliographical references. [BL42.W47] 78-12392 ISBN 0-89135-014-4 : 8.95
1. Religious education—Addresses, essays, lectures. I. Westerhoff, John H. II. Religious Education Association.

Religious education—Administration.

*KNIGHT, Cecil Bertie Howard. 268
Keeping the Sunday school alive, by Cecil B. Knight. Grand Rapids, Mich., Baker Book House [1972, c.1960] 118 p. 19 cm. (Sunday School Workers' Training Course) Bibl.: p. 117-118. [BV1471] ISBN 0-8010-5327-7 pap., 1.75
1. Religious education—Administration. 2. Sunday Schools—Administration. I. Title.

Religious education—Adult—Catholic.

*PANZARELLA, Andrew Brother 268.434
Growth in Christ. New York, Sadlier [1967] 371p. 22cm. (Life and light ser., bk. 3) 1.00 pap.,
1. Religious education—Adult—Catholic. I. Title. II. Series.

Religious education (Adult)—Lutheran.

**GOD'S Church and my life;* 268.434
student's book. Minneapolis, Augsburg [1967] v. illus. (pt. col.) 22cm. (Core curriculum--adult educ.) Prepd. for the Bd. of Parish Educ. and the Bd. of Pubn. of the Amer. Lutheran Church, based on materials provided by Orvis M. Hanson, others. 2.50;2.00 pap., teacher's guide.
1. Religious education—Adult—Lutheran.

**GOD'S grace and my need;* 268.434
student's book [Prepd. for the Bd. of Parish Educ., and the Bd. of Pubn. of the Amer. Lutheran Church, 1966. Minneapolis, Augsburg, 1966] 240p. illus. (pt. col) 22cm. (Core curriculum, adult educ.) pap., 2.50; teacher's guide, pap., 2.00
1. Religious education (Adult)—Lutheran.

Religious education—Adult—Presbyterian authors.

**FROM bondage to freedom.* 268.434
Richmond, Va., Covenant Life Curriculum, 1967. v. illus. 21cm. Contents.v. 4. God's varied voices. 2.95 pap.,
1. Religious education—Adult—Presbyterian authors.

Religious education—Africa.

BEAVER, Robert Pierce, 1906- ed. 377.096
Christianity and African education; the papers of a conference at the Univ. of Chic. Grand Rapids, Mich., Eerdmans [c.1966] 233p. 21cm. Conf. held Oct. 19-22, 1964, under the sponsorship of the Divinity Sch. of the Univ. of Chic. Bibl. [LC341.B35] 65-25184 2.65 pap.,
1. Religious education—Africa. 2. Missions—Educational work. 3. Missions—Africa. I. Chicago. University. Divinity School. II. Title.

BEAVER, Robert Pierce, 1906- ed. 377.096
Christianity and African education; the papers of a conference at the University of Chicago, edited by R. Pierce Beaver. Grand Rapids, W. B. Eerdmans Pub. Co. [1966] 233 p. 21 cm. Conference held October 19-22, 1964, under the sponsorship of the Divinity School of the University of Chicago. Bibliographical footnotes. [LC341.B35] 65-25184
1. Religious education — Africa. 2. Missions — Educational work. 3. Missions — Africa. I. Chicago. University. Divinity School. II. Title.

Religious education—Anecdotes, facetiae, satire, etc.

AASENG, Rolf E. 268
Anyone can teach (they said), by Rolf E. Aaseng. Illustrated by Janna Dory. Minneapolis, Augsburg Pub. House [1965] 108 p. illus. 20 cm. [BV1470.3.A2A3] 65-12137
1. Religious education — Anecdotes, facetiae, satire, etc. I. Title.

Religious education as a profession.

MCCOMB, Louise 268.069
D.C.E., a challenging career in Christian education. Richmond, Va., Knox [c.1963] 79p. 21cm. 63-12091 1.50 pap.,
1. Religious education as a profession. 2. Directors of religious education. I. Title.

MUELLER, Arnold Carl, 1891- 262
The ministry of the Lutheran teacher; a study to determine the position of the Lutheran parish school teacher within the public ministry of the church. St. Louis, Concordia [c.1964] 174p. front. 21cm. (12-2237) Bibl. 64-18882 3.00 pap.,
1. Religious education as a profession. 2. Clergy—Office. 3. Lutheran Church—Clergy. I. Title.

Religious education—Audio—visual aids.

AUDIO-VISUAL discussion guides. 377.078
no. 1 Philadelphia, Geneva Pr. [dist. Westminster, c.1961] 63p. illus. 28cm. 61-19302 1.75 pap.,
1. Religious education—Audio-visual aids.

AUDIO-VISUAL discussion guides. 377.078
no. 1- Philadelphia, Geneva Press [1961] v. illus. 28cm. [BV1535.A75] 61-19302
1. Religious education—Audio-visual aids.

AN experimental investigation of the effectiveness of selected motion pictures integrated with a unit of church school literature. Evanston, Ill., 1959. iv, 94p. 28cm.
1. Religious education—Audio—visual aids. 2. Audio—visual education. I. Perry, Paul Frederick, 1932-

FORD, LeRoy. 268'.635
Using audiovisuals in religious education / LeRoy Ford. Nashville : Convention Press, [1974] 128 p. : ill. ; 20 cm. "This book is the text for course 6912 of subject area 69, Program and Administrative Services of the Church Study Course [Sunday School Board, Southern Baptist Convention]" Bibliography: p. 121-125. [BV1535.F65] 75-302520
1. Religious education—Audio-visual aids. I. Southern Baptist Convention. Sunday School Board. II. Title.

HARRELL, John Grinnell, 1922- 268.635
Teaching is communicating; an audio-visual handbook for church use, by John Harrell. New York, Seabury Press [1965] 142 p. illus. 20 cm. [BV1535.H3] 64-19631
1. Religious education — Audio-visual aids. I. Title.

HUBBARD, Celia T ed.
Let's see, No. 1: Glen Rock, N.J., Paulist Press, 1966. 96 p. illus. 21 cm. 68-56168
1. Religious education—Audio-visual aids. I. Title. II. Title: The use and misuse of visual arts in religious education. III. Title: The use and misuse of visual art.

PARKER, Everett C 268.6353
Film use in the church, by Everett C. Parker [and others] New York, Broadcasting and Film Commission, National Council of the Churches of Christ in the United States [c1955] 78p. 28cm. (Studies in the mass media of communication) [BV1643.P3] 56-786
1. Religious education—Audio-visual aids. I. Title.

RUMPF, Oscar, 1903- 268.635
The use of audio-visuals in the church. Illustrated by Anna R. Atene. Philadelphia, Christian Education Press [1958] 150p. illus. 21cm. Includes bibliography. [BV1535.R8] 58-11703
1. Religious education—Audio-visual aids. I. Title.

WILLIAMS, Maxine. 268.084
The eyes have it; a handbook on the use of visual materials in Christian teaching. Springfield, Mo., Gospel Pub. House [1962] 145 p. 19 cm. [BV1535.W4] 62-15648
1. Religious education — Audio-visual aids. I. Title.

Religious education—Audio-visual aids—Addresses, essays, lectures.

THE Audio-visual man. 268'.635
Edited by Pierre Babin. Translated by C. Belisle [and others] Dayton, Ohio, Pflaum, 1970. v, 218 p. illus. 24 cm. Translation of Audio-visuel et foi. Bibliography: p. 216-217. [BV1535.A7613] 70-133407 5.95
1. Religious education—Audio-visual aids—Addresses, essays, lectures. 2. Audio-visual education—Addresses, essays, lectures. I. Babin, Pierre, ed.

Religious education—Audio-visual aids—Catalogs.

DALGLISH, William A. 268'.635
Media for Christian formation; a guide to audio-visual resources. William A. Dalglish, editor; Roger E. Beaubien [and] Walter R. Laude, associate editors. Dayton, Ohio, G. A. Pflaum, 1969. xix, 393 p. illus. 23 cm. [BV1535.Z9D3] 78-79711 7.50
1. Religious education—Audio-visual aids—Catalogs. I. Beaubien, Roger E., joint author. II. Laude, Walter R., joint author. III. Title.

Religious education—Biblical teaching.

HUDSON, Marshall Alonze, 1850- 268.
How to reach men, to hold men, to teach men, to win men ... a book about successful adult Bible classes, by Marshall A. Hudson ... Philadelphia, The Sunday school times company [c1908] 144 p. 18 1/2 cm. [BV1550.H8] 8-30152
I. Title.

MUIRHEAD, Ian A 225.826
Education in the New Testament, by Ian A. Muirhead. New York, Association Press [1965] 94 p. 22 cm. (Monographs in Christian education, no. 2) "The basis of this study was a working-paper contributed to the Church of Scotland Special Committee on Religious Education." Bibliographical references included in "Notes" (p. 89-94) [BV1465.M8] 65-11082
1. Religious education — Biblical teaching. I. Title.

Religious education — Bibliography

A bibliography of American doctoral dissertations, 1885 to 1959. [Pittsburgh] University of Pittsburgh, c1962. 215 p. 28 cm. Cover title: Bibliography of American doctor al dissertations in religious education, 1885 to 1959. 65-50182
1. Religious education — Bibl. 2. Dissertations — Bibl.

INTERNATIONAL council of religious education. 268
... *The Standard leadership training curriculum;* a bulletin describing the courses of the Standard leadership training curriculum, and providing information regarding approved texts and reference materials ... Chicago, Ill., The International council of religious education, 1930. 68 p. 23 cm. (International bulletins in religious education. Educational bulletin, no. 503) "International curricula of leadership training ... III." A bibliography of "approved textbooks" and "reference materials." [Z7849.I61] [016.268] 30-16970
1. Religious education—Bibl. I. Title.

INTERNATIONAL council of religious education. 268
... *The Standard leadership training curriculum;* a bulletin describing the courses of the Standard leadership training curriculum and providing information regarding approved texts and reference materials ... Chicago, Ill., The International council of religious education, 1932. 72 p. 23 cm. (International bulletins in religious education ... Educational bulletin, no. 503) "Includes all revisions made up to June 15, 1932."--Introd. A bibliography of "approved textbooks" and reference material." [Z7849.I61 1932] [016.268] 32-21477
1. Religious education—Bibl. I. Title.

KIRSCH, Felix Marie, 1884- 016.62 comp.
The religion teacher's library, a selected annotated list of books, pamphlets and magazines, compiled by Rev. Felix M. Kirsch ... and Rev. Claude Vogel ... Paterson, N. J., St. Anthony guild press, Franciscan monastery [c1938] v, 57 p. 23 cm. [Z7849.K62] 38-14674
1. Religious education—Bibl. 2. Catholic literature—Bibl. I. Vegel, Claude Lawrence, father, 1894- joint comp. II. Title.

LITTLE, Lawrence Calvin, 1897-
A bibliography of American doctoral dissertations, 1885 to 1959. [Pittsburgh] University of Pittsburgh, c1962. 215 p. 28 cm. Cover title: Bibliography of American doctor al dissertations in religious education, 1885 to 1959. 65-50182
1. Religious education — Bibl. 2. Dissertations — Bibl. I. Title.

LITTLE, Lawrence Calvin, 1897- 013.3784886
Researches in personality, Character and religious education; a bibliography of American doctoral dissertations, 1885 to 1959. Index prepared by Helen-Jean Moore. [Pittsburgh] Univ. of Pittsburgh Pr., 1962. iv, 215p. 28cm. 62-12625 6.00
1. Religious education—Bibl. 2. Dissertations, Academic—U.S.—Bibl. I. Title.

RELIGIOUS education association. 268
Graded text books for the modern Sunday school; a bibliography ... Chicago, The Religious education association [1914] 31 p. 23 1/2 cm. "Reprinted from Religious education for April, 1914." "The Religious education association published in its magazine, Religious education, for August, 1909, 'A selected list of text books available for use in the Sunday school,' compiled by Mr. Herbert Wright Gates ... Mr. Guy O. Carpenter, A.B., and Mr. Raymond F. Piper, A.B. ... prepared the following list of titles under the direction of Prof. N. S. Richardson, and the material has been edited and revised in the office of the association." [Z7849.R45] 14-9900
1. Religious education—Bibl. 2. Religious literature—Bibl. 3. Sunday school literature—Bibl. I. Carpenter, Guy O. II. Piper, Raymond F. III. Richardson, N. S. IV. Title.

Religious education—California.

NEWMAN, Louis Israel, 1893- 377
The sectarian invasion of our public schools, by Dr. Louis I. Newman...and Resolutions and opinions opposing the Miller bill. no. 128 in the California Assembly and similar legislation throughout the United States. San Francisco, 1925. 3 p. l., 3-55 p. 23 1/2 cm. Bibliography: p. 55. [LC111.N4] 26-3693
1. Religious education—California. 2. Public schools—California. 3. Religious education—U.S. 4. Public schools—U.S. I. Title. II. Title: Miller bill, no. 128 in the California Assembly.

Religious education—Catholic authors.

**YOUR responses to God.* 268.433
Co.-pub. by Priory Pr., & Webster-McGraw [1966] xi, 516p. illus. 24cm. Authors: Reginald Doherty, others. General ed.: Reginald Doherty (Challenge of Christ, 2) 5.24
1. Religious education—Catholic authors. I. Doherty, Reginald, ed.

Religious education—Collections.

CULLY, Kendig Brubaknnr, ed. 377.082
Basic writings in Christian education. Philadelphia, Westminster Press [c.1960] 350p. 60-9504 4.95
1. Religious education—Collections. I. Title.

SHAVER, Erwin L. 268.
The other fellow's religion; a suggested plan for a project for young people's groups, by Erwin L. Shaver. Chicago, Ill., The University of Chicago press [c1927] ix, 54 [4] p. 19 1/2 cm. (Half-title: The University of Chicago publications in religious education ... Constructive studies) Blank pages for "Notes" inserted between pages 25 and 26 and at end. "References and source material": p. 26-54. [BV1475.S5O7] 27-25794
I. Title.

Religious education—Colleges.

COURSE outlines in dogmatic theology for college students. [New York, La Salle Provincialate, 1958] 2v. 27cm.
1. Religious education—Colleges. I. Celestine Luke, Brother.

Religious education—Congresses.

BRICKMAN, Clarence W. ed. 377.83082
The church's ministry of reconciliation in the field of education; proceedings of the Washington conference, November 7-9, 1963, sponsored jointly by the Episcopal School Association and the Dept. of Christian Education of the National Council of the Protestant Episcopal Church. Edited by Clarence W. Brickman. [New York? 1964] 132 p. 29 cm. [BV1463.B7] 65-3590
1. Religious education — Congresses. 2. Protestant Episcopal Church in the U.S.A. — Education. I. Episcopal School Association. II. Protestant Episcopal Church in the U.S.A. National Council. Dept. of Christian Education. III. Title.

INTERNATIONAL congress on Christian education, Mexico, 1941. 268.0631
Christian education and world evangelization, with special reference to the implications for Christian education, today and tomorrow, of contemporary world conditions. Official report of the International congress on Christian education, Mexico, D. F., Mexico, July 16-20, 1941. New York, N.Y., World's Sunday school association [c1941] 144 p. illus. (map) plates, ports. 22 1/2 cm. [BV1463.I46 1941] 42-2837
1. Religious education—Congresses. I. World's Sunday school association. II. Title.

INTERNATIONAL convention of Christian education. 20th, Columbus, O., 1938. 268.0631
The Christian challenge to the modern world, with special reference to Christian education. The report of the International convention on Christian education, Columbus, Ohio, June 28 to July 3, 1938 ... Compiled by Forrest L. Knapp ... Chicago, Ill., The International council of religious education [c1938] ix, 263 p. illus. (incl. ports.(23 cm. Bibliography at end of most of the chapters. [BV1463.I5 1938a] 39-19183
1. Religious education—Congresses. I. Knapp, Forrest Lamar, 1899 comp. II. Title.

RELIGIOUS education association. 268.
... Proceedings of the first-annual convention ... Chicago, Executive office of the Association, 1903- v. 22 1/2 cm. Title varies slightly. [BV1460.R5] 4-1623
I. Title.

TRADITION and transformation in religious education / edited by Padraic O'Hare. Birmingham, Ala. : Religious Education Press, c1979. 114 p. ; 20 cm. Cover title: Transformation andd tradition in religious education. Includes bibliographical references and index. [BL42.T72] 78-27506 ISBN 0-89135-016-0 pbk. : 5.95 207
1. Religious education—Congresses. I. O'Hare, Padraic. II. Title: Transformation and tradition in religious education.

WORKSHOP on Home, Church, and School Relations in the Religious Education of Children and Youth, University of Chicago, 1954. 268
Home, church, and school relations in the religious education of children and youth; [lectures] Edited by Harold A. Anderson and Rolfe Lanier Hunt. [Chicago, 1963; 1 v. (unpaged) 28 cm. Sponsored by the Dept. of Education, University of Chicago, and the Dept. of Religion and Public Education, National Council of the Churches of Christ in the United States of America. "40 copies." Bibliographical footnotes. [BV1463.W6 1954] 66-7944
1. Religious education — Congresses. 2. Church and education — Congresses. I. Anderson, Harold A, ed. II. Hunt, Rolfe Lanier, 1903- ed. III. Chicago. University. Department of Education. National Council of the Churches of Christ in the United States of America. Office of Public Education. IV. Title.

WORLD Evaluation Conference on Christian Education, Geneva, 1969. 261
Christian education in a secular society. Gustav K. Wiencke, editor. [Philadelphia] Fortress Press [1970] 230 p. 23 cm. (Yearbooks in Christian education, v. 2) "A study document of the Commission on Education of the Lutheran World Federation, summarizing the results of a five-year consultation and study program, 1965-69." "Annotated listing of study papers, prepared by Dr. Herbert G. Schaefer": p. [209]-230. [BV1463.W63 1969b] 73-11416
1. Religious education—Congresses. 2. Secularism—Congresses. I. Wiencke, Gustav K., ed. II. Lutheran World Federation. Commission on Education. III. Title. IV. Series.

Religious education—Connecticut.

STEWART, George, 1892- 377.
A history of religious education in Connecticut to the middle of the nineteenth century, by George Stewart, jr., PH. D. New Haven, Yale university press; [etc., etc.] 1924. xiv p., 2 l., [3]-402 p. fold. front., facsims. 24 cm. (Half-title: Yale studies in the history and theory of religious education ...i) "The present volume is the first work published by the Yale university press on the Samuel B. Sneath memorial publication fund." "The present essay ... in-its original form was presented as a dissertation in partial fulfilment of the requirements for the degree of doctor of philosophy; and it was awarded the John Addison Porter prize in 1921."--Introd. Bibliography: p. [371]-384. [BV1468.C8S7] 24-24574
1. Religious education—Connecticut. I. Yale university. Samuel B. Sneath memorial publication fund. II. Title.

Religious education—Curricula.

BAKER City, Or. (Diocese) 268.62
A course of study in religion for the Catholic schools and academies of the diocese of Baker City, grades I.-VIII. and high school. Baker, Or., Diocesan board on catechetics, c1944. 93, [3] p. 25 1/2 cm. "List of texts": p. 87-91. [0X925.B33] 44-30241
1. Religious education—Curricula. 2. Catholic church—Education. I. Title.

BETTS, George Herbert, 1868-1934. 268.
... The curriculum of religious education, by George Herbert Betts New York, Cincinnati, The Abingdon press [c1924] 535 p. illus., fold tab. 21 cm. (The Abingdon religious education texts D. G. Downey, general editor. College series, G. H. Betts, editor) "References" at end of most of the chapters. [BV1475.B37] 24-28574
1. Religious education—Curricula. 2. Sunday-schools. I. Title.

CATHOLIC Church. Diocese of Green Bay, Wis. Dept. of Education. 268'.82
The Green Bay Plan. [Green Bay] 1971. 239 p. 29 cm. [BX929.A47] 77-175854
1. Religious education—Curricula. 2. Religious education—Philosophy. I. Title.

CLEVELAND (Diocese) Board of Catholic education.
Course of study in religion for grade three. Cleveland, O., Diocesan school board, 1940. 1 p. l., 55 p. diagrs. 28 1/2 cm. Photolithographed. "Reference books": p. 55 [A41-3128] A41
1. Religious education—Curricula. 2. Catholic church—Education. I. Title.

COLSON, Howard P., 1910- 268'.6
Understanding your church's curriculum, by Howard P. Colson [and] Raymond M. Rigdon. Nashville, Broadman Press [1969] 160 p. illus. 21 cm. Includes bibliographical references. [BV1558.C6] 77-93915
1. Religious education—Curricula. I. Rigdon, Raymond M., joint author. II. Title.

COOPERATIVE Curriculum Development 268'.6
Tools of curriculum development for the church's educational ministry; the work of Cooperative Curriculum Development. Anderson. Ind., Warner [1967] 224p. 24cm. Bibl. [BV1559.C66] 67-19936 10.50
1. Religious education—Curricula. I. Title.

COOPERATIVE Curriculum Project. 268'.6
A design for teaching-learning. St. Louis, Bethany Press [1967] xxxii, 317 p. 23 cm. "An abridged edition of The church's educational ministry: a curriculum plan." [BV1559.C672] 67-24194
1. Religious education—Curricula. I. Title.

DUCKERT, Mary. 268'.6
Tailor-made teaching in the church school. Illustrated by Lee DeGroot. Philadelphia, Westminster Press [1974] 124 p. illus. 21 cm. [BV1558.D82] 73-21904 ISBN 0-664-24985-X 2.85 (pbk.)
1. Religious education—Curricula. 2. Religious education. I. Title.

INTERNATIONAL Council of Religious Education. 268.6
The curriculum guide for the local church, developed cooperatively by Protestant evangelical forces of the United States and Canada through the International Council of Religious Education. [Rev.] Chicago [1950] 99 p. 23 cm. Bibliography: p. 86-87. [BV1558.I 5 1950] 51-862
1. Religious education—Curricula. I. Title.

INTERNATIONAL council of religious education. 268.6
The curriculum guide for the local church, developed cooperatively by Protestant evangelical forces of the United States and Canada through the International council of religious education... [Chicago 1946] 93 p. 23 cm. "First printing December, 1945. Second printing November, 1946." [BV1558.I5] 47-2984
1. Religious education—Curricula. I. Title.

INTERNATIONAL Council of Religious Education. 268.3
Standard leadership curriculum. Developed cooperatively by Protestant Evangelical forces of the United States and Canada through the International Council of Religious Education. Chicago, 1948- v. 23 cm. (International bulletin[s] in religious education. Educational bulletin no. 501-Contents.1st ser. courses. A plan for improving your work in the church.--2d ser. courses. A program of leadership education for all workers in the church and related agencies. [BV1559.I642] 49-5704
1. Religious education—Curricula. I. Title. II. Series.

JOINT Board of Christian Education of Australia and New Zealand. 268'.6
The Christian life curriculum; a plan for Christian education in local churches. Melbourne [1968] 48 p. diagrs., tables. 24 cm. [BV1559.J64] 76-494564 unpriced
1. Religious education—Curricula. I. Title.

METHODIST Church (United States) Curriculum Committee. 268.61
Outlines of curriculum. [Nashville?] Editorial Division of the General Board of Education of the Methodist Church. v. 23 cm. annual. "A supplement to the Report of the Curriculum Committee of the General Board of Education." [BX8219.A37] 52-36210
1. Religious education — Curricula. 2. Methodist Church — Education. I. Methodist Church (United States) Board of Education. Editorial Division. II. Methodist Church (United States) Curriculum Committee. Report. Supplement. III. Title.

PLANNING the curriculum for parish education in the Evangelical Lutheran Church; a report presented to the Division of Parish Education, the Board of Christian Education, the Evangelical Lutheran Church. [Minneapolis?] 1956. xix, 196p. 29cm. Includes bibliographies.
1. Religious education—Curricula. I. Narveson, Carl R II. Evangelical Lutheran

Church. Board of Christian Education. Division of Parish Education.

POWERS, Edward A. 268
Signs of shalom, by Edward A. Powers. Philadelphia, Published for Joint Educational Development [by] United Church Press [1973] 160 p. illus. 22 cm. (A Shalom resource) Bibliography: p. 152-156. [BV1558.P68] 73-6952
1. Religious education—Curricula. 2. Shalom (The word) 3. Christian life—United Church of Christ authors. I. Title.

SOUTHERN Baptist 268.6
Convention. Sunday School Board.
The curriculum guide. 1960- Nashville, Tenn., Convention Press. v. 20 cm. annual. Editors: 1960- C. J. Allen and W. I. Howse. Includes bibliography. [BV1559.S6] 60-9536
1. Religious education — Curricula. I. Allen, Clifton J. 1901- ed. II. Howse, William Lewis, 1965- ed. III. Title.

SOUTHERN Baptist 268.6
Convention. Sunday School Board.
The curriculum guide. 1960-1963/4. Nashville, Tenn., Convention Press. 4 v. 20 cm. annual. Edited by C. J. Allen and W. L. Howse. Superseded by Church program guidebook issued by the convention's Baptist Brotherhood Commission. [BV1559.S6] 60-9536
1. Religious education—Curricula. I. Allen, Clifton J., 1901- ed. II. Howse, William Lewis, 1905- ed. III. Title.

WEBER, Gerard P., 1918- 268'.6
Parents' guide; the word and worship program [by] Gerard P. Weber, James J. Killgallon [and] Sr. M. Michael O'Shaughnessy. [1st ed.] New York, Benziger Brothers, 1968. xii, 169 p. 18 cm. Bibliography: p. 161-164. [BX929.W4] 68-58714
1. Catholic Church—Education. 2. Religious education—Curricula. I. Killgallon, James J., 1914- joint author. II. O'Shaughnessy, Mary Michael, joint author. III. Title.

WYCKOFF, D Campbell. 268.6
Theory and design of Christian education curriculum. Philadelphia, Westminster Press [1961] 219 p. 22 cm. Includes bibliography. [BV1559.W9] 61-6103
1. Religious education-Curricula. I. Title. II. Title: Christian education curriculum.

Religious education—Dictionaries.

CULLY, Kendig Brubaker, 268.03
ed.
The Westminster dictionary of Christian education. Philadelphia, Westminster [c. 1963] 812p. 24cm. Bibl. 63-11083 6.00
1. Religious education—Dictionaries. I. Title. II. Title: Dictionary of Christian education.

CULLY, Kendig Brubaker, 268.03
ed.
The Westmister dictionary of Christian education. Philadelphia, Westminster Press [1963] 812 p. 24 cm. Bibliography: p. [756] -797. [BV1461.C8] 63-11083
1. Religious education — Dictionaries. I. Title. II. Title: Dictionary of Christian education.

Religious education—Elementary.

BAKER, Edna Dean, 1883- 268.
... The Beginner's book in religion, by Edna Dean Baker ... New York, Cincinnati, The Abingdon press [c1921] 271 p. front., plates diagrs. 21 cm. (The Abingdon religious eduycation texts, D. G. Downey, general editor. Week day school series, G. H. Betts, editor) [BV1475.B23] 21-5628
I. Title.

*HUTTAR, Leora W. 268.432
Jack and Jill stay for church; how to lead a churchtime nursery. Drawings by Doris L. Hedsten. Chicago, Moody [c.1965] 112p. illus. 28cm. (MP295) 2.95, pap., plastic bdg.
1. Religious education—Elementary. I. Title.

*RENFRO, Jean Marie 268.432
Sister
We are the people of God; grade 3, teacher's ed. [by] Sister Jean Marie Renfro. Jane Moore. Consultant: William J. Reedy. New York, Sadlier [1966] 112p. music. 22x21cm. (Summer sch. of religion ser., 048) .25 pap.,
1. Religious education (Elementary) I. Moore, Jane, joint author. II. Title. III. Series.

Religious education (Elementary) Catholic.

**COME to the Father;* 268.432
pupil's text, grade 1. Glen Rock, N.Y., Paulist [1966] 127p. col. illus. 23cm. (Come to the Father ser., 1) English version of the Catechism 'Viens vers le Pere,' written by the Office Catechistique Provincial, Montreal, Canada. 1.25 pap.,
1. Religious education (Elementary)—Catholic. I. Office Catechistique Provincial, Montreal, Canada.

ELIZABETH, Sister M. 268.432
The Lord Jesus says, by Sister M. Elizabeth, Sister M. Johnice. Confraternity ed. Consultant: Bernard J. Cooke. Illus. by A. and M. Provensen. Boston, Allyn, 1967. 126p. illus. (pt. col.) 23cm. (Bible, life, and worship ser.; bk. 3) Adapted from The Lord has said, by Andre Boyer, orig. pub. by Les Editions de 1 Ecole, Paris, in 1960. 1.20 pap.,
1. Religious education—Elementary (Catholic) I. Johnice, Sister M., joint author. II. Title. III. Series: Bible, life, and worship series. Book 3

*FRANCIS, Mary Grace 268.432
Sister
Christ in His church(grade 8, home workbook. New York, Sadlier, 1967. v. 22cm. (On our way ser.) .44; .14 pap.,keys,
1. Religious education—Elementary—Catholic. I. Title. II. Series.

*FRANCIS, Mary Grace 268.432
Sister
Fulfillment in Christ(grade 6, home workbook. New York, Sadlier, 1967. v. 22cm. (On our way ser.) .44 pap.,
1. Religious education—Elementary—Catholic. I. Title. II. Series.

*JOHNICE, M. Sister 268.432
Children of the kingdom, by Sister M. Johnice, Sister M. Elizabeth. Consultant: Bernard J. Cooke. Illus. by H. and R. Shekerjian. Boston, Allyn [1967] v. illus. (pt. col.) 23cm. (Bible, life, and worship ser., bk. 4, confraternity ed.) Adapted from Our history as children of God, by Andre Boyer. 1.32 pap.,
1. Religious education—Elementary (Catholic) I. Elizabeth, M., Sister joint author. II. Title.

*JOHNICE, M. Sister 268.432
Come, Lord Jesus, by Sister M. Johnice, Sister M. Elizabeth. Consultant: Bernard J. Cooke. Illus. by A. and M. Provensen. Confraternity ed. Boston, Allyn. 1967. 128p. p. illus. (pt. col.) 23cm. (Bible, life and worship ser.; bk. 2) Adapted from Come Lord, by Andre Boyer, orig. pub. by Les Editions de l'Ecole, Paris, in 1960. 1.20 pap.,
1. Religious education—Elementary (Catholic) I. Elizabeth, M., Sister joint author. II. Title. III. Series: Bible, life and worship series. Book 2

*JOHNICE, M. Sister 268.432
Growing as Christians, by Sister M. Johnice Sister M. Elizabeth. Consultant: Bernard J. Cooke. Illus. by Mary and Maurice Kirchoff. Boston, Allyn 1967. v. illus. (pt. col.) 23cm. (Bible, life, and worship ser., bk. 6) 2.04 pap.,
1. Religious education—Elementary (Catholic. I. Elizabeth, Mary, Sister joint author. II. Title.

*JOHNICE, M. Sister 268.432
Let us give thanks. By Sister M. Johnice, Sister M. Elizabeth, assistant, Barton & Joan DeMerchant consultants. Bernard J. Cooke. Boston, Allyn 1968. xvi. illus. (Bible, life and worship ser. bks.) guidebook, .56 pap.,
1. Religious education—Elementary (Catholic) I. Elizabeth, M. Sister Joint author. II. Title.

MARY Mauriana, Sister 268.432
Christ our Savior(grades 3, home workbook. New York, Sadlier, 1967. v. 22cm. (On our way ser.) .44; .14 pap.,key,
1. Religious education — Elementary — Catholic. I. Title. II. Series.

*PEIFFER, Marie Venard 268.432
Mother
God loves us; teacher's guide [for] grade 1. Advisory comm., Rev. John B. McDowell [others] New York, Sadlier [c.1965] 288p. 22x20cm. With 2 34 rpm phono-discs in pocket (Our life with God ser.; Vatican II ed., 011) Appended is Musical booklet entitled Sing to the Lord, by Mother Marie Venard, Margaret Land with words and piano accompaniment. 2.00 pap.,
1. Religious education (elementary) Catholic. I. Title.

**PEOPLE of God;* 268.432
grade 7. New York, Sadlier, 1967. v. (pt. col.) music. 21cm. (Our life with God ser., Vatican II ed.) Grade 7 by Sister Edward Mary Magill, Sister M. Celine Lhota. 1.44 pap.,
1. Religious education—Elementary—Catholic. I. Magill, Sister Edward Mary. II. Lotha, M. Celine, Sister joint author.

*PFEIFFER, Marie Venard 268.432
Sister
Christ with us; teacher's guide,by Sister Marie Venard Pfeiffer, Sister Mary Gerald Carroll. New York, Sadlier [1967] v. 22cm. (Out life with God ser., Vatican II ed.) Recording, Selections for Unit II, CSM 34 rpm in pocket on back cover. 2.00 pap.,
1. Religious education—Elementary—Catholic. I. Carroll, Mary Gerald, Sister joint author. II. Title. III. Series.

*PFEIFFER, Marie Venard 268.432
Mother
God's gifts to us; teacher's guide [for] gr. 2. Advisory comm.: Rev. John B. McDowell [others] New York, Sadlier [c.1965] 220p. illus. 22x20cm. With a 33 1/3 phonodisc in pocket. (Our life with God ser.; Vatican 22 ed., 012) Appended is music booklet entitled Sing joyfully to God, all the earth by Mother Marie Venard Pfeiffer, Margaret Lang with words and piano accompaniment. 2.00 pap.,
1. Religious education (Elementary) Catholic. I. Title.

*PFEIFFER, Marie Venard 268.42
Mother
In Christ Jesus, gr. 3. New York, Sadlier, c.1965. col. illus. music. 28cm. (Our life with God ser., Vatican II ed.) 1.08 pap.,
1. Religious education (Elementary) Catholic. I. Title.

*PFFIFFER, Marie Venard 268.432
Mother
Alive in Christ; Grade 5 [by] Marie Venard Mother Pfeiffer, Mother Mary Gerald Carrol. Advisory comm.: John B. McDowell [others] New York, Sadlier [1966] 191p. illus. (pt. col.) 22x21cm. Cover title. T. P. reads: It is no longer I who live, but Christ who lives in me (Our life with God ser.: Vatican II ed., 006) pap., 1.20; teacher58s ed., 2.00
1. Religious education (Elementary) Catholic. I. Carroll, Mother Mary Gerald, joint author. II. Title.

*POTTEBAUM, George A. 268.432
Little people's paperbacks [3v.] Illus. by Robert Strobridge. Dayton, Ohio, Pflaum. c.1965. 3v. (unpaged) chiefly col. illus. 18cm. (LPP13-15) .35 pap., ea.,
1. Religious education (Elementary)—Catholic. I. Title.
Contents omitted.

*POTTEBAUM, George A. 268.432
Little people's paperbacks [2v.] Illus. by Robert Strobridge. Dayton, Ohio, Pflaum [c.1964] 2v. (unpaged) col. illus. 18cm. (LPP—10) Contents.[1] The good samaritan.--[2] The king and the servant. (LPP9-10) .35 pap., ea.,
1. Religious education (Elementary)—Catholic. I. Title.

*POTTEBAUM, Gerard A. 268.432
Little people's paperbacks [3v.] Illus. by Robert Strobridge. Dayton, Ohio, Pflaum [c.1964] 3v. col. illus. 18cm. (LLP6-8) Contents.[1] The little grain of wheat.--[2] He obeyed.--[3] The Easter lamb. .35 pap., ea.,

1. Religious education (Elementary)—Catholic. I. Title.

*PRESENTINA, Mary Sister 268.432
Christ leads the way grade 4, home workbook. New York, Sadlier, 1967. v. 22cm. (On our way ser.) .44 pap.,
1. Religious education—Elementary — Catholic. I. Title. II. Series.

*PRESENTINA, Mary Sister 268.432
With Christ the Father; home workbook. New York, Sadlier, 1967. v. illus. 22cm. (On our way ser., Vatican II ed.) .52 pap.,
1. Religious education — Elementary — Catholic. I. Title. II. Series.

*PRESENTINA, Mary Sister 268.432
Witnessing Christ; grade 7, home workbook New York, Sadlier, 1967. v. 22cm. (On our way ser.) .44; .14 pap.,key,
1. Religious education — Elementary — Catholic. I. Title. II. Series.

PRFRANCIS, Mary Grace 268.432
Sister
One in Christ(grade 5, home workbook. New York, Sadlier, 1967, v. 22cm. (On our way ser.) .44; .14 pap.,key,
1. Religious education—Elementary — Catholic. I. Title. II. Series.

*RENFRD, Jean Marie 268.432
Sister
We are risen in the Lord; teacher's guide, [by] Sister Jean Marie Renfro, Jane Moore. Consultant: William J. Reedy. New York, Sadlier [1967] v. 22cm. (*summer sch. of religion ser., grade 5) .25 pap.,
1. Religious education—Elementary—Catholic. I. Moore, Jane, joint author. II. Title. III. Series.

*RENFRD. JEAN MARIE 268.432
Sister
Freedom in Christ; teacher's ed. [by] Sister Jean Marie Renfro, Jane Moore. Consultant: William J. Reedy. New York, Sadlier [1967] v. 22cm. (Summer sch. of religion ser., grade 6) .25 pap.,
1. Religious education—Elementary—Catholic. I. Moore, Jane, joint author. II. Title. III. Series.

*RENFRO, Sister Jean 268.432
Marie
Children of our Father; teacher's guide [for] grade 2 [by] Sister Jean Marie Renfro, Jean Moore. Consultant: William J. Reedy. New York, Sadlier [c.1965] 96p. music. 22cm. (Summer sch. of Religion ser., 047) .25 pap.,
1. Religious education (Elementary)—Catholic. I. Moore, Jean, joint author. II. Title.

*RENFRO, Sister Jean 268.432
Marie
Going to God our Father; teacher's guide [for] grade 1 [by] Sister Jean Marie Renfro, Jane Moore. Consultant: William J. Reedy. New York, Sadlier [c.1965] 96p. music. 22x20cm. (Summer sch. of religion ser., 046) .25 pap.,
1. Religious education (Elementary) Catholic. I. Moore, Jane, joint author. II. Title.

Religious education (Elementary) Lutheran.

**BOOK of good news* 268.434
(The): pupil's book grade 4, trimester A, weekday. Minneapolis, Augsburg 1967 v. illus. (pt. col.) 22x28cm. (Elementary curriculum, Amer. Lutheran Church) Prepd. for the Bd. of Parish Educ. and the Bd. of Pubn. of the Amer. Lutheran Church based on materials provided by Alice L. Schimpf and The Bible for all people. 1.25; 1.25 pap.,teacher's guide,
1. Religious education—Elementary—Lutheran.

**BOOK of the Convenant* 268.432
people (The). Illus. by Gordon Laite. Richmond, Va., CLC Pr. [dist. Knox, 1966] 95p. illus. (pt. col.) 21cm. (Covenant life curriculum, elementary; The Bible, year 2) 1.45 pap.,
1. Religious education (Elementary) — Lutheran.

*CURRIE, Stuart D. 268.432
The beginnings of the church. Illus. by Kathleen Elgin. Richmond, Va., CLC Pr.

dist. Knox [1966] 143p. illus. (pt. col.) 21cm. (Covenant life curriculum, elementary; the church year, 2) 1.95 pap.,
1. Religious education (Elementary)—Lutheran. I. Title.

*D becker, Pat 268.432
Finding out about God(teachings guide: kindergarten, age 4. Joseph W. Inslee, ed. Philadelphia, Lutheran Church Pr. [1966] 176p. 22cm. (LCA weekday church sch. ser.) 2.50
1. Religious education (Elementary)—Lutheran. I. Inslee, Joseph W., ed. II. Title.

FOUNTAIN, Rosanna B. 268.432
Learning from Jesus. Illus. by Huntley Brown. Richmond, Va., CLC Pr. [dist. Knox, 1966] 63p. illus. (pt. col.) 21cm. (Covenant life curriculum, elementary; The Christian life, year, 2) 1.25 pap.,
1. Religious education (Elementary)—Lutheran. I. Title.

**FRIENDS of Jesus;* 268.432
teacher's guide, grade 2. Philadelphia, Lutheran Church Pr. [1967] v. illus. 24cm. (LCA Sunday chruch sch. ser.) Teacher's guide grade 3, by Lawrie Hamilton, Evelyn Byerly, Kathryn Orso. 2.50
1. Religious edication—Elementary—Luthere I. Hamilton, Lawrie. II. Byerly, Evely oint author. III. Orso, Kathryn.

**GOD'S good news;*
pupil's book; grade 4, trimester A, Sunday. Minneapolis, Augsburg, 1967. v. illus. (pt. col.) 28cm. (Elementary curriculum, Amer. Lutheran church) Prepd. for the Bd. of Parish Educ. and the Bd. of Pubn. of the Amer. Lutheran Church based on materials provided by Bertha Meyer, others. [268.432] pap., 1.25; teacher's guide, 1.50
1. Religious education — Element1ry — Lutheran.

**GOD'S word for God's* 268.432
world; catechist's guide grade 7, trimester C, unit 9. Prepd. for the Bd. of Parish Educ., and the Bd. of Pubn. of the Amer. Lutheran Church. 1v. (unpaged) 28cm. (Amer Lutheran Church curriculum: junior-high confirmation) 1.35 pap.,
1. Religious education (Elementary) Lutheran.

*HAMILTON, Darlene 268.433
What God is like, by Darlene Hamilton, Beverly Schultz Mullins. Illus. by David K. Stone. Gustav K. Wiencke, ed. Philadelphia, Lutheran Church Pr. [1966] 128p. col. illus. 21cm. 1.25
1. Religious education (Elementary) Lutheran. I. Mullins, Beverly Schultz, joint author. II. Title.

*HAMILTON, Lawrie 268.432
Sunday church school for 4's; class activity packet for terms 2 & 3. Lawrie Hamilton, course author; Gisela Jordan, packet illustrator; Gustav K. Wiencke, ser. ed. Philadelphia. Lutheran Church Pr. [1967] v. col. illus. 26x34cm. (LCA Sunday church sch. ser.) pap., term 2, 5.25; term 3, 1.25
1. Religious education—Elementary—Lutheran. I. Title. II. Series.

*HURTY, Kathleen 268.432
God's children at work and play; teachers guide: kindergarten [by] Kathleen Hurty, Kathryn Swanson. Doris J. Smith, ed. Marjorie F. Garhart, ser. ed. Philadelphia, Lutheran Church Pr. [1967] 96p. 23cm. (LCA vacation church sch. ser.) Third year of three-year cycle: God and my life. .90 pap.,
1. Religious education (Elementary)—Lutheran. I. Swanson, Kathryn, joint author. II. Garhart, Marjorie F., ed. III. Title.

*HURTY, Kathleen 268.432
Michael Martin and his friends, by Kathleen Hurty, Kathryn Swanson. Illus. by June Goldsborough. 1v. (unpaged) col. illus. 22x28cm. (LCA vacation church sch. ser. Third year of 3-year cycle: God and my life.) .50 pap.,
1. Religious education—Elementary Lutheran. I. Swanson, Kathryn, joint author. II. Title.

*KIDD, Elizabeth 268.432
A Christian decides, by Elizabeth Kidd, Margaret. J. Irvin. Illus. by Tom Irons, Philadelphia, Lutheran Church Pr. [c.1966] 64p. illus. (pt. col.) 23cm. (LCA vacation church sch. ser.) With teacher's guide. .50; .90 pap., teacher's guide,
1. Religious education (Elementary)—Lutheran. I. Irvin, Margaret J., joint author. II. Title.

*MCFADYEN, Mary Jean 268.432
The earth is the Lord's; camp leader's guide, grades 5 and 6. Illus. by Ruth S. Ensign. Richmond, Va., CLC Pr. [dist. Knox, 1966] 158p. illus. 23cm. (Covenant life curriculum; camping and confs.) 3.00 pap.,
1. Religious education (Elementary)—Lutheran. I. Title.

*OSTWALT, Adeline Hill 268.432
God so loved the world. Illus. by Jo Polseno. Richmond, Va., CLC Pr. [dist. Knox, 1966] 128p. illus. (pt. col.) 21cm. (Covenant life curriculum, elementary, The Bible, year 2) 1.95 pap.,
1. Religious education (Elementary)—Lutheran. I. Title.

*PAULSON, Donna 268.432
The way of the Christian; teacher's guide: grades 5 & 6. Marjorie F. Garhart, ed. Philadelphia, Lutheran Church Pr. [1967] 86p. 23cm. (LCA vacation church sch. ser.) Third year of three-year cycle: God and my life. .90 pap.,
1. Religious education (Elementary)—Lutheran. I. Garhart, Marjorie F., ed. II. Title.

*PENNELL, Lucy 268.432
Our church at work in the world [by] Lucy Pennell, Jack Smith. Illus. by Don Bolognese. Richmond, Va., CLC Pr. [dist. Knox, 1966] 112p. illus. (pt. col.) 21cm. Covenant life curriculum elementary The Christian life, year 2) 1.45 pap.,
1. Religious education (Elementary)—Lutheran. I. Title.

*PRINZ, Harvey L. 286.433
They knew Jesus. Mariorie Garhart, ed. William Plummer, ed. Philadelphia, Lutheran Church Pr. [1966] 48p. illus. (pt. col.) 21x28cm. (LCA vacation church sch. ser.) .50 pap.,
1. Religious education (Elementary)—Lutheran. I. Title.

*PURDHAM, Betty Mae 268.342
Followers of Jesus. Ed. by Margaret J. Irvin. Illus. by John Gretzer. Philadelphia, Lutheran Church Pr. [c.1966] 32p. 23x28cm. (LCA vacation church sch. ser.) .50; .90 pap., teacher's ed., pap.,
1. Religious education—Elementary—Lutheran Church. I. Title.

*RINGLAND, Elinor 268.432
Loving others: grades 1 & 2: teacher's guide. Marjorie F. Garhart, ed. Philadelphia, Lutheran Church Pr. [1967] 86p. 23cm. (LCA vacation church sch. ser.) Third year of three-year cycle: God and my life. .90 pap.,
1. Religious education (Elementary)—Lutheran. I. Garhart, Marjorie F., ed. II. Title.

*RUDOLPH, L. C. 268.432
Story of the church. Illus. by Lewis Parker. Richmond, Va., CLC Pr. [dist. Knox, 1966] 191p. illus. (pt. col.) map (pt. col.) 21cm. (Covenant life curriculum, elementary; The church year 2) 2.45 pap.,
1. Religious education (Elementary)—Lutheran. I. Title.

*SMITH, Doris J. 268.432
God loves and plans for me: teacher's guide: nursery. Margaret J. Irvin, ed. William C. Kautz, designer. Philadelphia, Lutheran Church Pr. [1967] 96p. 23cm. (LCA vacation church sch. ser.) .90 pap.,
1. Religious education (Elementary)—Lutheran. I. Irvin, Margaret J., ed. II. Title.

Religious education (Elementary)—Presbyterian.

ANDREWS, Dorothy 268.432
Westlake.
A boy with a song. Illus. by Alex Kenne. Richmond, Va., CLC Pr. [dist. Knox] c.1965. 1v. (unpaged) col. illus. 22cm. 1.45 bds.,
1. Religious education (Elementary)—Presbyterian. I. Title.

ANDREWS, Dorothy 268.432
Westlake.
Everywhere I go [by] Dorothy Westlake Andrews, Virginia Barksdale Lancaster. Illus. by Robert William Hinds. Richmond, Va., CLC Pr. [dist. Knox] c.1965. 1v. (unpaged) col. illus. 22cm. 1.45 bds.,
1. Religious education (Elementary)—Presbyterian. I. Lancaster, Virginia Barksdale, joint author. II. Title.

*ANDREWS, Dorothy 268.432
Westlake
He has done marvelous things. Illus. by David K. Stone. Richmond, Va., CLC Pr. [dist. Knox] c.1965. 1v. (unpaged) col. illus. 22cm. 1.45 bds.,
1. Religious education (Elementary)—Presbyterian. I. Title.

*ANDREWS, Dorothy 268.432
Westlake
When I think of Jesus. Illus. by Elizabeth Dauber. Richmond, Va., CLC Pr. [dist. Knox] c.1965. 1v. (unpaged) col. illus. 22cm. 1.45 bds.,
1. Religious education (Elementary)—Presbyterian. I. Title.

*MEEK, Pauline Palmer 268.432
All day long. Illus. by Kelly Oechsli. Richmond, Va., CLC Pr. [dist. Knox] c.1965. 1v. (unpaged) col. illus. 22cm. 1.45 bds.,
1. Religious education (Elementary)—Presbyterian. I. Title.

*MEEK, Pauline Palmer 268.432
The broken vase. Illus. by Ati Forberg. Richmond, Va., CLC Pr. [dist. Knox] c.1965. 1v. (unpaged) col. illus. 22cm. 1.45 bds.,
1. Religious education (Elementary)—Presbyterian. I. Title.

*MEEK, Pauline Palmer 268.432
God sent his son. Illus. by Jo Polseno. Richmond, Va., CLC Pr. [dist. Knox] c.1965. 1v. (unpaged) col. illus. 22cm. 1.45 bds.,
1. Religious education (Elementary)—Presbyterian. I. Title.

*MEEK, Pauline Palmer 268.432
Hop, skip, hop. Illus. by June Goldsborough. Richmond, Va., CLC Pr. [dist. Knox] c.1965. 1v. (unpaged) col. illus. 22cm. 1.45 bds.,
1. Religious education (Elementary)—Presbyterian. I. Title.

*MEEK, Pauline Palmer 268.432
Knock!knock! Illus. by Richard Powers. Richmond, Va., CLC Pr. [dist. Knox] c.1965. 1v. (unpaged) col. illus. 22cm. 1.45 bds.,
1. Religious education (Elementary)—Presbyterian. I. Title.

*MEEK, Pauline Palmer 268.432
Who is Debbie? Illus. by. June Goldsborough. Richmond, Va., CLC Pr. [dist. Knox] c.1965. 1v. (unpaged) col. illus. 22cm. 1.45 bds.,
1. Religious education (Elementary)—Presbyterian. I. Title.

*SCHULZ, Florence 268.432
Families and friends. Illus. by Tom O'Sullivan. Richmond, Va., CLC Pr. [dist. Knox] c.1965. 1v. (unpaged) col. illus. 22cm. 1.45 bds.,
1. Religious education (Elementary)—Presbyterian. I. Title.

*SCHULZ, Florence 268.432
I am Andrew. Illus. by Lucy and John Hawkinson. Richmond, Va, CLC Pr. [dist. Knox] c.1965. 1v. (unpaged) col. illus. 22cm. 1.45 bds.,
1. Religious education (Elementary) Presbyterian. I. Title.

*SCHULZ, Florence 268.432
Sunday morning. Illus. by Erica Merkling. Richmond, Va., CLC Pr. [dist. Knox] c.1965. 1v. (unpaged) col. illus. 22cm. 1.45 bds.,
1. Religious education (Elementary)—Presbyterian. I. Title.

*SCHULZ, Florence 268.432
Who is Jesus? Illus. by Eleanor Mill. Richmond, Va., CLC Pr. [dist. Knox] c.1965. 1v. (unpaged) col. illus. 22cm. 1.45 bds.,
1. Religious education (Elementary)—Presbyterian. I. Title.

*CATON, Dorothy Webber 268.432
Light from my Bible for today. Teacher's guide. Nashville, Abingdon [1961] 128p. 23cm. (Co-op. ser.& Vacation Church sch. texts) A coop. vacation church sch. course for use with junior children. 1.25 pap.,
1. Religious education (Elementary)—Protestant. I. Title.

Religious education—England.

ARUNDALE, R. L. 377.1
Religious educatio in the senior school, by R. L. Arundale ... London, New York, [etc.] T. Nelson and sons ltd. [1944] vii, 100 p. 21 cm. "First published 1944." Bibliography at end of each chapter except the first. [LC410.G7A3] 44-51164
1. Religious educatonion—England. I. Title.

COX, Edwin 377.10942
Changing aims in religious education. London, Routledge & K. Paul; New York, Humanities, 1966. vi, 102p. 20cm. (Students lib. of educ.) Bibl. [BV1471.2.C69] 66-27377 3.50 bds.,
1. Religious education — England. I. Title.

SKEET, George William. 268
... Religious education in non-provided schools, by G. W. Skeet ... with a foreword by the Bishop of Manchester. London, New York [etc.] Oxford university press, 1939. 54 p. 16 1/2 cm. (Handbooks of religious education; general editor; G. W. Briggs) [BV1470.G7S55] 41-7438
1. Religious education—England. I. Title.

Religious education—France.

ELWELL, Clarence Edward, 377'.8'2
1904-
The influence of the Enlightenment on the Catholic theory of religious education in France, 1750-1850. New York, Russell & Russell [1967, c1944] x 335 p. 22 cm. (Harvard studies in education, v. 29) Bibliography: p. [305]-328. [LC506.F8E4] 66-27064
1. Religious education—France. 2. Church and education in France. I. Title. II. Series.

ELWELL, Clarence Edward, 268.82
1904-
The influence of the enlightenment on the Catholic theory of religious education in France. 1750-1850, by Clarence Edward Elwell ... Cambridge, Harvard university press, 1944. x, 335 p. 22 1/2 cm. (Half-title: Harvard studies in education, pub. under the direction of the Graduate school of education, vol. 29) Bibliography: p. [305]-328. [BX910.F8E4] A 44
1. Religious education—France. 2. Church and education in France. I. Title.

Religious education—Germany.

HELMREICH, Ernst 377.10943
Christian
Religious education in German schools: an historical approach. Cambridge, Mass., Harvard University Press [c.]1959[1960] xvi, 365p. 25cm. Bibliography: p.307-309; bibl. notes: p.321-353) 59-11509 7.50
1. Religious education—Germany. I. Title.

Religious education—Germany, West.

TERRY, W. Clinton. 377
Teaching religion : the secularization of religion instruction in a West German school system / W. Clinton Terry III. Lanham, MD : University Press of America, 1981. p. cm. Includes index. Bibliography: p. [LC410.G2T47] 19 80-5569 ISBN 0-8191-1366-2 lib. bdg. : 18.50 ISBN 0-8191-1367-0 (pbk.) : 9.50
1. Religious education—Germany, West. 2. Christian education—Germany, West. I. Title.

Religious education—Great Britain

CAMPAGNAC, Ernest Trafford, 1872-
Elements of religion and religious teaching, by E. T. Campagnac ... Cambridge, At the University press, 1918. ix, [2], 127 p. 19 1/2 cm. [LC116.G7C17] E19
1. Religious education—Gt. Brit. 2. Religion. I. Title.

KINLOCH, Tom Fleming, 1874- 377.
... *Religious education in provided schools,* by T. F. Kinloch ... London, New York [etc.] Oxford university press, 1938. 63, [1] p. 17 cm. (Handbooks of religious education: general editor: G. W. Briggs) "Bibliographical notes": p. 61-[64] [LC410.G7K6] E 40
1. Religious education—Gt. Brit. 2. Bible in the schools—[Gt. Brit.] I. Title.

RELIGIOUS education in the secondary modern school. Foreword by Basil A. Yeaxlee. Wallington [Eng.] Religious Education Press [1958] 128p. illus. Includes bibliography.
1. Religious education—Gt. Brit. 2. Theology—Study and teaching—Gt. Brit. I. Avery, Margaret, 1890-

SHEFFIELD, Eng. 377.10942
University. Institute of Education.
Religious education in secondary schools, a survey and a syllabus. London, New York, Nelson [1961] x. 85 p. illus. 25 cm. [LC410.G7S47] 66-50828
1. Religious education—Gt. Brit. 2. Church of England—Education. I. Title.

WAINWRIGHT, Joseph Allan. 377.10942
School and church, partners in Christian education; some suggestions for common action. London, New York, Oxford University Press, 1963. 107 p. 19 cm. Bibliographical references included in footnotes. [LC410.G7W3] 64-292
1. Religious education—Gt. Brit. I. Title.

WEDDERSPOON, Alexander G., ed. 377.10942
Religious education, 1944-1984. London, Allen & Unwin [New York, Humanities c.1966] 3-238p. tables. 20cm. Study conf. held in London in April 1965. [BV1470.G7W4] 66-70183 4.50 bds.,
1. Religious education—Gt. Brit. 2. Religion in the public schools—Gt. Brit. I. Title.

Religious education—Handbooks, manuals, etc.

BROTHERS of Mary, Dayton, O.
Manual of Christian pedagogy for the use of religious teachers. 1s. ed. By the Brothers of Mary ... Dayton, O., The Brothers of Mary, 1910 3 p., l., 9-122 p. 19 1/2 cm. $0.50 10-30164
I. Title.

CHICAGO. University. Press.
Religious education through graded instruction; a handbook for use in the selection of text and reference books, revised to October, 1911. Chicago, Ill., The University of Chicago press [c1911] cover-title, 152 p. illus., plates. 26 cm. 11-26492
I. Title.

CONFRATERNITY of Christian doctrine.
Manual of the Confraternity of Christian doctrine for priests, religious, seminarians and laity promoting confraternity activities Revised edition. The National center of the Confraternity of Christian doctrine ... [Paterson, N.J., Franciscan monastery, St. Anthony guild press 1937] viii, 76 p. 19 cm. "Second printing October, 1937. A40
1. Religious education—Handbooks, manuals, etc. I. Title.

HANSON, Helen Patten. 268.
...A travel book for juniors; teacher's manual, by Helen Patten Hanson. New York, Cincinnati, The Abingdon press c1923] 115 p. diagrs. 20 cm. [The Abingdon religious education texts; D.G. Downey general editor. Week-day school series; G.H. Betts, editor) Contains "References". [BV1546.H33] 24-3974
I. Title.

MILLER, Minor C. 221
... *Conquests for God,* a teacher's manual for juniors in week-day and vacation schools, by Minor C. Miller ... with an introduction by Luther A. Weigle ... Elgin, Ill., The Elgin press [c1924] 291 p. incl. maps. front. 20 cm. (The Elgin press religious education texts: week-day and vacation school series) Bibliography: p. 288-291. [BS1194.M45] 24-18184
I. Title.

PERKINS, Jeanette Eloise, 1887- 268.
Primary worship guide, of special value to schools using the closely graded church school courses; a bird's-eye view of the three primary classes, their objectectives, discussions, activities, and memory work, as suggested in the teachers' text-books; with material for workship brought together from text-book and folders; sample worship services and related story material for Sunday and the week day, prepared by Jeanette E. Perkins. Boston, Chicago, The Pilgrim press [c1929] xii, 307 p. 21 cm. [BV1545.P4] 29-32216
I. Title.

**WORK and worship.* 268.432
Rev. teacher's manual replacing Many messengers. New York, Seabury [1968] (Church's teaching in the third grade) 2.30 pap.,

Religious education—History

EAVEY, Charles Benton, 1889- 268.09
History of Christian education. Chicago, Moody [c.1964] 430p. illus., ports.24cm. Bibl. 5.50
1. Religious education—Hist. I. Title. II. Title: Christian education.

EAVEY, Charles Benton, 1889-
History of Christian education. Chicago, Moody Press [1964] 430 p. illus., ports. 24 cm. Includes bibliographies.
1. Religious education—Hist. I. Title.

EAVEY, Charles Benton, 1889- 268'.3
History of Christian education. Chicago, Moody Press [1964] 430 p. illus., ports. 24 cm. Includes bibliographies. [BV1465.E2] 64-1860
1. Religious education—Hist. I. Title. II. Title: Christian education.

GRASSI, Joseph A. 268'.3
The teacher in the primitive church and the teacher today [by] Joseph A. Grassi. Santa Clara, Calif., University of Santa Clara Press [1973] v, 132 p. 22 cm. Includes bibliographical references. [BV1465.G7] 73-78011 2.95
1. Religious education—History. 2. Teaching—History. I. Title.

KINLOCH, Tom Fleming, 1874- 268'.09
Pioneers of religious education, by T. F. Kinloch. With a foreword by J. S. Whale. Freeport, N.Y., Books for Libraries Press [1969] vii, 144 p. 22 cm. (Essay index reprint series) Reprint of the 1939 ed. Bibliography: p. 142-144. [BV1465.K5 1969] 69-18929
1. Religious education—History. I. Title.

KINLOCH, Tom Fleming, 1874- 268.09
Pioneers of religious education, by T. F. Kinloch ... with a foreword by J. S. Whale, D.D. London, New York [etc.] Oxford university press, 1939. vii, 144 p. 19 cm. (Half title: Handbooks of religious education; general editor: G. W. Briggs) Bibliography: p. 142-144. [BV1465.K5] 40-6773
1. Religious education—Hist. I. Title.

MOHLER, James A. 207'.1
The school of Jesus; an overview of Christian education yesterday and today [by] James Mohler. New York, Alba House [1973] xii, 279 p. illus. 22 cm. Bibliography: p. [267]-274. [BV1465.M6] 72-11835 ISBN 0-8189-0262-0 5.95
1. Religious education—History. I. Title.

POEHLER, Willy August, 1904- 377.09
Religious education through the ages. by William A. Poehler. [St. Paul? Minn.. 1966] 5a, 394p. illus. 22cm. Bibl. [BV1465.P6] 66-7074 3.95
1. Religious education—Hist. I. Title.
Available from Masters Church & School Supply, 4753 Chicago Ave., Minneapolis, Minn. 55407.

SHERRILL, Lewis Joseph, 1892- 268
The rise of Christian education, by Lewis Joseph Sherrill ... New York, The Macmillan company, 1944. xi p., 1 l., 349 p. 21 cm. "First printing." Bibliographical references included in "Notes" (p. 307-340) [BV1465.S5] 44-3780
1. Religious education—Hist. I. Title.

ULICH, Robert, 1890- 268'.09
A history of religious education; documents and interpretations from the Judaeo-Christian tradition. New York, New York University press, 1968. viii, 302 p. 24 cm. "Bibliographical references included in "Notes" (p. 283-298) [BV1465.U4] 68-29433
1. Religious education—History. I. Title.

Religious education—Home training.

CHURCH in Christian faith and life (The); 260
a study course to prepare local churches for the use of the curriculum Christian faith and life, a program for church and home. 3d ed. Pub. by the Bd. of Christian Educ. of the United Presbyterian Church in the United States of America. [dist. Philadelphia, Westminster, c.1962] 63p. Bibl. .60 pap.,

FOX, Henry Watson, 1872- 248
The child's approach to religion, by the Rev. H. W. Fox ... with an introduction by the Right Rev. the Lord Bishop of Liverpool. 2d ed. New York and London, Harper & brothers [1945] xiv p., 1 l., 80 p. 19 1/2 x 11 1/2 cm. [BV1590.F65 1945] 45-1959
1. Religious education—Home training. I. Title.

HASTINGS, Mary Louise Cutter (Jones) Mrs. 1875- comp. 242
Behold a sower! A book of religious teaching for the home, selected and arranged by M. Louise C. Hastings for the Committee on religion in the home... Boston, The Beacon press, 1919. xii, 211 p. 19 1/2 cm. [BV4810.H3] 19-18467
I. American unitorism association. Religious education department. Committee on religion in the home. II. Title.

JONES, Mary Alice, 1898- 230
Tell me about God, by Mary Alice Jones, illustrated by Pelagie Doane. New York, Chicago [etc.] Rand McNally & company [1943] 69, [3] p. incl. col. front., illus. (part col.) 26 1/2 x 20 1/2 cm. [BV1590.J6] 43-15119
1. Religious education—Home training. I. Doane, Pelagie, 1906- illus. II. Title.

LAPPIN, Samuel Strahl, 1870- 249
... *The home and family in the light of Bible teaching;* thirteen lessons prepared by S. S. Lappin, with additional material by Mrs. W. D. Van Voohris. E. W. Thornton, editor ... Cincinnati, O., The Standard publishing company, c1923. 110 p. 23 cm. (Standard elective series of special lessons) [BV4526.L3] 24-5907
I. Van Voorhis, W. D., Mrs. joint author. II. Thornton, Edwin William, 1863- ed. III. Title.

LOMAS, Margaret Dager. 221.95
Old Testament Bible lessons for the home [by] Margaret Dager Lomas. Philadelphia, The Westminster press [c1943] 220 p. illus. (incl. map) 21 cm. Map on lining-papers. Hymns (words and music): p. [213]-[216] [BV1590.L65] 44-2450
1. Religious education—Home training. 2. Bible stories, English—O.T. I. Title.

LORENSEN, Larry. 268
Spiritual home training for the child. Chicago, Moody Press [1954] 144p. 22cm. [BV1590.L67] 54-14780
1. Religious education—Home training. I. Title.

[MCGRATH, Marie Cecelia] 1896- 268
ABC religion; training the child in the home, by Sister Mary, I.H.M. ... Huntington, Ind., Our Sunday visitor press, 1940. 2 p. l., [7]-109 p. 19 cm. "Helpful books and pamphlets": p. [105]-109. [Name in religion: Mary, sister] [BV1590.M26] 41-22504
1. Religious education—Home training. I. Title.

MILLER, Randolph Crump, 1910- 649.7
Your child's religion. New York, Hawthorn Books [1975] xix, 164 p. 21 cm. Includes bibliographical references and index. [BV1590] 75-5034 ISBN 0-8015-9118-X 3.50 (pbk.)
1. Religious education—Home training. 2. Children—Religious life. I. Title.

MILLER, Randolph Crump, 1910- 268
Your child's religion. [1st ed.] Garden City, N.Y., Doubleday, 1962. 164 p. 22 cm. Includes bibliography. [BV1590.M52] 62-11445
1. Religious education—Home training. 2. Children—Religious life. I. Title.

NATIONAL school of correspondence, Quincy, Ill. 374.
... *Teachers' home series.* A normal course in six numbers. [no. 1- Quincy, Ill. [c1905- v. 20 cm. [LC6001.N7] 7-31571
I. Title.

NEWLAND, Mary (Reed) 268
We and our children; molding the child in Christian living. Garden City, N. Y., Doubleday [1961, c. 1954] 273p. (Image bk., D123) .85 pap.,
1. Religious education—Home training. 2. Children—Religious life. I. Title.

NEWLAND, Mary (Reed) 268
We and our children; molding the child in Christian living. New York, Kenedy [1954] 271p. 21cm. [BV1590.N4] 54-10067
1. Religious education—Home training. 2. Children—Religious life. I. Title.

RANWEZ, Pierre. 268
Together toward God; religious training in the family, by P. Ranwez, J. and M. L. Defossa and J. Gerard-Libois. Translated by Paul Barrett. Westminster, Md., Newman Press, 1959. 200p. 21cm. [BV1590.R313] 59-11339
1. Religious education —Home training. 2. Family—Religious life. I. Title.

STAGG, Samuel Wells. 268
... *Home lessons in religion,* a manual for mothers ... by Samuel Wells Stagg ... in collaboration with Mary Boyd Stagg. New York, Cincinnati, The Abingdon press [c1922- v. 21 cm. (The Abingdon religious education texts; D. G. Downey, general editor, G. H. Betts, associate editor) [BV1590.S7] 23-6876
1. Religious education—Home training. I. Stagg, Mary Boyd, joint author. II. Title.
Contents omitted.

STAPLES, Edward D
Hello toddler [a guidebook for Christian parents of nursery-infants, by] Edward D. and Ethlyne B. Staples. Nashville, Graded Press, 1964. 120 p. illus. 28 cm. 66-57674
1. Religious education—Home training. I. Title.

SUMMERBELL, Martyn, 1847- 248
Christian home training, by Martyn Summerbell ... Dayton, O., The Christian publishing association, 1917. 72 p. 19 1/2 cm. $0.75. [BV1590.S8] 17-17187
I. Title.

SWEET, Herman J., 1899- 266
Opening the door for God, a manual for parents, by Herman J. Sweet. Philadelphia, The Westminster press [c1943] 160 p. 19

1/2 cm. Bibliography: p. [143]-153. [BV1590.S9] 44-19246
1. Religious education—Home training. I. Title.

TAYLOR, Florence Marian (Tompkins) 1892- 268
Their rightful heritage; home and church working together for the Christian nurture of children [by] Florence M. Taylor ... Boston, Chicago, Printed for the Leadership training publishing association by the Pilgrim press [1942] xii, 120 p. 19 1/2 cm. Bibliography: p. 105-108. [BV1590.T3] 42-14604
1. Religious education—Home training. 2. Church work with children. I. Title.

TRENT, Robbie. 268
Your child and God, by Robbie Trent ... Chicago, New York, Willett, Clark & company, 1941. xi p., 1 l., 146 p. 20 cm. [BV1590.T7] 41-11837
1. Religious education—Home training. I. Title.

TRENT, Robbie, 1894- 268
Your child and God. [Rev. ed.] New York Harper [1952] 157 p. 20 cm. [BV1590.T7] 52-5476
1. Religious education — Home training. I. Title.

VAN METER, Harriet D 268.432
Hands, hands, hands, thank you, God for hands. Photos., music, and words by Harriet D. Van Meter. Richmond, John Knox Press [1958] unpaged. illus. 19 x 25 cm. [BV1590.V3] 58-9823
1. Religious education — Home training. I. Title.

WALPOLE, Ellen (Wales) 1907- 248
Why should I? Illustrated by Douglas Anderson. [New York] Harper [1949] xii, 102 p. illus. 25 cm. Full name: Grace Ellen (Wales) Walpole. [BV1590.W3] 49-11565
1. Religious education—Home training. I. Title.

WATERINK, Jan, 1890- 268
Leading little ones to Jesus; a book for mothers. Tr. from Dutch by Betty Vredvoogd. Grand Rapids, Mich., Zondervan [c.1962] 119p. illus. 22cm. 62-4374 2.50
1. Religious education—Home training. I. Title.

WHITE, Ellen Gould (Harmon) 1827-1915. 649.1
Child guidance; counsels to Seventh-Day Adventist parents as set forth in the writings of Ellen G. White. Nashville, Southern Pub. Association [1954] 616p. 18cm. (Christian home library) [BV1590.W5] 54-3554
1. Religious education— Home training. 2. Seventh-Day Adventists—Education. I. Title.

WRIGHT, James Roy, 1888- 269
Systematic personal work; a systematic presentation of New Testament Christianity. For use in house-to-house teaching, and in classes in personal evangelism and first principles, by J. Roy Wright ... Cincinnati, The Standard publishing company [c1922] 177 p. illus. 21 cm. [BV3790.W7] 22-6650
I. Title.

Religious education—India.

BROCKWAY, K Nora. 376.954
A larger way for women; aspects of Christian education for girls in south India, 1712-1948. [Madras, New York] Indian Branch, Oxford University Press [1949] viii, 189 p. illus., ports., maps. 19 cm. "References": p. [177]-184. [BV1470.I 5B7] 50-31284
1. Religious education—India. 2. Education of women—India. 3. Missions—India. I. Title.

Religious education—Indiana.

THE Indiana survey of religious education ... New York, George H. Doran company [c1923-24] 3 v. plates, tables, diagrs. 23 cm. "Made under the direction of Walter S. Athearn." Contents.- -v. 1. The religious education opf Protestants in an American commonwealth, by W. S. Athearn, E. S. Evenden, W. L. Hanson, W. R. Chalmers.- -v. 2. Measurements and standards in religious education ... by Walter S. Athearn. W. L. Hanson, E. S. Evenden ... [and others]--v. 3. Religious education survey schedules ... by Walter S. Athearn. [BV1468.I6I6] 23-16798 377.
1. Religious education—Indiana. I. Athearn, Walter Scott, 1872-

Religious education (Intermediate) — Lutheran.

*FOGELMAN, William J. 268.433
I live in the world, Art by Bill McKibben. Richmond, Va., CLC Pr. [dist. Knox, 1966] 223p. illus. (pt. col.) 24cm. (Covenant life curriculum, youth The Christan life, year3) 2.95pap.,
1. Religious education (Intermediate) — Lutheran. I. Title.

**IN communication with God;* student's book [Minneapolis] Augsburg [1967] v. illus. (pt. col.) 14x21cm. (Amer. Lutheran Church curriculum: Senior high sch.) Prepd. for the Bd. of Parish Educ. and the Bd. of Pubn. of the Amer. Lutheran Church based on materials provided by Norman Landvik. pap., 1.35; teacher's combined ed., 2.25 268.433
1. Religious education — Intermediate — Lutheran.

*NILSSEN, Jerome 268.433
Wise as serpents, innocent as doves, by Jerome Nilssen. John Kerr, ed. Andrew A. Snyder, illus. Philadelphia, Lutheran Church Pr. [1967] 126p. illus. 21cm. (LCA Sunday church sch. ser., 16-192) With accompanying teacher's guide, My world, my church and I, by Jerome Nilssen; John Kerr, ed. (LCA Sunday church sch. ser., 16-193) 1.00; 1.25 pap.,teach.guide, pap.,
1. Religious education — Intermediate — Lutheran. I. Title. II. Title: My world, my Church and I.

*PETERMAN, Richard 268.433
Who is Jesus? by Richard Peterman, John Kerr. Design/ illus.: Charles Light. Philadelphia, Lutheran Church Pr. [1967] 104p. illus. 21cm. (LCA Sunday church sch. ser.) 1.00 pap.,
1. Religious education (Intermediate)— Lutheran. I. Kerr, John, joint author. II. Title.

*SHRIVER, Donald W., Jr. 268.433
How do you do, and why? An introduction to Christian ethics. Illus. by Martha Meeks, Richmond, Va., CLC Pr. [dist. Knox, 1966] 224p. illus. 24cm. (Covenant life curriculum, youth; The Christian life, year 3) 2.95 pap.,
1. Religious education (Intermediate)— Lutheran. I. Title.

*WINN, Albert Curry 268.433
The worry and wonder of being human. Drawings by Jim Crane. Richmond, Va., CLC Pr. [dist. Knox, 1966] 224p. illus. 24cm. (Covenant life curriculum, youth; The Christian life, year 3) 2.95 pap.,
1. Religious education (Intermediate)— Lutheran. I. Title.

**WORLD religions and Christian mission;* senior high students book [Minneapolis, Augsburg, 1967] v. illus., maps. 21x29cm. (Amer. Lutheran Church curriculum) Prepd. for the Bd. of Parish Educ. and the Bd. of Pubn. of the Amer. Lutheran Church based on material prepd. by Lowell G. Almen, Waldemar Gies. Ed. by Lawrence W. Denef. pap., 1.75; teacher's guide, 1.75 268.433
1. Religious education—Intermediate Lutheran.

Religious education—Japan.

COMMISSION on Christian education in Japan 377.10952
Christian education in Japan; a study, being the report of a Co,, Commission on Christian education in Japan, representing the National Christian council of Japan, the National Christian education association of Japan, the Foreign missions conference of North America and the International missionary council. New York [etc.] The International missionary council, 1932. xi, 247 p. fold. maps. tables (part fold.) diagr. 24 cm. Kajinosuke Iboks, chairman. "Note": leaf inserted between p. [118] and 119. [LA1312.C6] 32-21487
1. Religious education—Japan. 2. Education—Japan. I. Ibuka, Kajinosuke. II. International missionary council. III. Title.

Religious education, Jewish.

BRILLIANT, Nathan. 296
Activities in the religious school, by Nathan Brilliant and Libbie L. Braverman. New York, Union of American Hebrew Congregations [1951] 258 p. illus. 21 cm. [BM103.B7] 51-33035
1. Religious education, Jewish. I. Title.

HEBREW union college, Cincinnati.
Catalog ... Cincinnati [18 -19 v. 23 cm. Title varies: 18 ... Catalogue of the three departments; preparatory, rabbinical, semitic. ... Prospectus. ... Catalog. [LC771.C5H3] ca5
I. Title.

LEVIN, Meyer, 1905- 296.6
The story of the synagogue, by Meyer Levin [and] Toby K. Kurzhand. Art. Behrman House [c1957] New York, -- Text-books for children. 156p. illus. (part col.) 24cm. (The Jewish heritage series, v. 1) [BM105.L48] 57-13093
1. Regligious education, Jewish editor; Stephen Kraft. Illus.: Robert Pous. 2. Synagogues. I. Kurband, Toby K., joint author. II. Title. III. Series.

NADEL, Max. 377'.9'6
Case studies in classroom teaching; teaching Jewish social studies in a Reform religious school. [New York] Jewish Education Committee of New York [1968] 110 p. 25 cm. [BM103.N24] 68-7086
1. Religious education, Jewish. 2. Social sciences—Study and teaching (Elementary) I. Jewish Education Committee of New York. II. Title. III. Title: Teaching Jewish social studies in a Reform religious school.

PARENTS are partners in Jewish religious education; parent activities at the Jewish community center, White Plains, N.Y. New York, Union of American Hebrew congregations [c1958] 85p. illus. 29cm. Reproduced from typewritten copy.
I. Kurzband, Toby K

Religious education, Jewish—Teacher training.

EDUCATION of American Jewish teachers (The) ed. by Oscar I. Janowsky. Foreword, by Abram Leon Sachar. Boston, Pub. for the Philip W. Lown Ctr. for Contemporary Jewish Studies by Beacon [1967] xvii, 352p. 21cm. Papers from a coloquium held at Brandies Univ. May 28-30, 1966. Bibl. [BM108.E37 1967] 67-25867 8.50 371.1
1. Religious education, Jewish—Teacher training. 2. Jews in the U. S.—Education. I. Janowsky, Oscar Isaiah, 1900- ed. II. Brandeis University, Waltham, Mass.

MARGOLIS, Isidor. 371.1
Jewish teacher training schools in the United States. New York, National Council for Torah Education of Mizrachi-Hapoel Hamizrachi, 1964. xvii, 349 p. 24 cm. Bibliography: p. 333-344. [BM108.M38] 68-189
1. Religious education, Jewish—Teacher training. I. Title.

Religious education, Jewish—Teaching methods.

CITRON, Samuel J 296.68
Dramatics for creative teaching. New York, United Synagogue Commission on Jewish Education, 1961. 405p. 26cm. [BM103.C5] 61-14855
1. Religious education, Jewish—Teaching methods. 2. Drama in education. I. Title.

Religious education, Jewish—Text books for children.

SCHWARTZMAN, Sylvan David. 296.68
Once upon a lifetime. Illustrated by Maurice Rawson. New York, Union of American Hebrew Congregations [1958] 134p. illus. 27cm. (Commission on Jewish Education of the Union of American Hebrew Congregations and the Central Conference of American Rabbis. Union graded series) [BM105.S43] 58-14445
1. Religious education, Jewish—Text books for children. I. Title.

SOLOFF, Mordecai Isaac. 933
The covenant people; the first 2000 years of Jewish life, from Abraham to Akiba, by Mordecai I. Soloff. Drawings by Chaya Burstein. Middle Village, N.Y., J. David Publishers [1973] 231 p. illus. 22 cm. Traces the ancient history of the Jews from their beginnings in Abraham's time to their revolt against the Romans. [DS118.S64] 72-97080 ISBN 0-8246-0154-8 3.95 (pbk.)
1. Jews—History—To 70 A.D.—Juvenile literature. 2. [Jews—History—To 70 A.D.] 3. Religious education, Jewish—Text-books for children. I. Burstein, Chaya M., illus. II. Title.
Work Book 1.95; ISBN 08246-0155-6

Religious education—Jews.

HERTZ, Richard C 296.6
The education of the Jewish child, a study of 200 Reform Jewish religious schools. New York, Union of American Hebrew Congregations, 1953. 185p. 22cm. [BM103.H4] 53-2391
1. Religious education—Jews. 2. Reform Judaism. I. Title.

A year's program of audio-visual units and projects, an illustrated manual for all grades of the religious school. New York, Union of American Hebrew Congregations [c1959] xvi, 226p. illus. 28cm.
1. Religious education—Jews. 2. Audiovisual education I. Bragman, Rae. II. Union of American Hebrew Congregations.

Religious education—Massachusetts.

SMITH, Sherman Meritt.
The relation of the state to religious education in Massachusetts. by Sherman M. Smith ... Syracuse, N. Y., Syracuse university book store, 1926. vii p., 1 l., 350 p. 20 cm. Bibliography: p. 323-339. [LC408.M4S6] 26-21477
1. Religious education—Massachusetts. 2. Education and state—Massachusetts. I. Title.

Religious education—Materials.

BUTLER, Alford Augustus, 1845-
The churchman's manual of methods; a practical Sunday school handbook for clerical and lay workers, by Alford A. Butler ... Milwaukee, The Young churchman co., 1906. 4 p. l., 227 p. front. 19 1/2 cm. "Helpful books and appliances": p. [214]-221. 6-18337
I. Title.

CABOT, Ella (Lyman) Mrs. 1866- 268.
Teachers' manual for Our part in the world, by Ella Lyman Cabot ... Boston, Mass., The Beacon press [c1918] xxiii, 93 p. 21 cm. (Half-title: The new Beacon course of graded lessons, W. I. Lawrence, F. Buck, editors) "Books for a teacher's library": p. xxii-xxiii. [BV1475.C32] 18-17916
I. Title.

CONNERY, John R, 1913- 222.16
Teacher's manual in Ferrell, William F. Loyalty, the Commandments in modern life. Chicago, Loyola University Press, 1949-51. [BV4655.F4 1949] 50-31748
I. Title.

CONNERY, John R, 1913- 222.16
Teacher's manual in Ferrell, William F. Loyalty, the Commandments in modern life. Chicago, Loyola University Press, 1949-51. [BV4655.F4 1949] 50-31748
I. Title.

EASTON, Burton Scott, 1877- 227
The teaching of St. Paul, by Burton Scott Easton ... New York, E. S. Gorham, 1919. 2 p. l., iv, 164 p. 19 1/2 cm. At head of title: Manuals for students of the Society

for the home study of Holy Scripture and church history. [BS2650.E3] 19-15950
I. Title.

ESSIG, Montgomery Ford, 1872-
The churchmember's guide and complete church manual; a handy volume prepared especially for the use of members of the Baptist, Christian, Methodist, Episcopal, and Presbyterian churches in their southern branches ... by Montgomery F. Essig ... Nashville, Tenn., Macon, Ga. [etc.] The Southwestern company (c1907) 287 p. incl. forms. front 21 cm. 7-15455
I. Title.

ESSIG, Montgomery Ford, 1872-
The churchmember's guide and complete church manual; a handy volume prepared especially for the use of members of the Baptist, Christian, Methodist, Episcopal, and Presbyterian churches in their southern branches ... by Montgomery F. Essig ... Nashville, Tenn., Macon, Ga. [etc.] The Southwestern company (c1907) 287 p. incl. forms. front 21 cm. 7-15455
I. Title.

LEADERSHIP education handbook;
a program of leadership education for church workers. [First and second series courses] 1956 ed. New York, Published for the Division of Christian Education, National Council of the Churches of Christ in the U. S. A., by the Office of Publication and distribution, c1956. 64p. 23cm. 'Formerly Educational bulletins 501, 502, and the Dean's manual.' Includes bibliographies.
1. Religious education—Materials. I. National Council of the Churches of Christ in the United States of America. Division of Christian Education.

MICHEL, Virgil George, 230.2
father, 1890-1938.
... Teachers' manual to accompany The redeeming sacrifice, The kingdom of God, With mother church, Through Christ Our Lord, by Dom Virgil Michel ... Dom Basil Stegmann ... and the Sisters of the Order of St. Dominic, Marywood, Grand Rapids, Michigan. New York, The Macmillan company, 1935. vii, 141 p. 18 1/2 cm. (The Christ-life series in religion) Includes bibliographies. [BX930.C5 book 5-8] (230.2) 43-21395
I. Stegmann, Basil Augustine, father, 1893- joint author. II. Sisters of the Order of St. Dominic, Marywood, Grand Rapids, joint author. III. Title.

NATIONAL Lutheran Council.
Advisory Committee for the Church in Town and Country.
The church's concern for communities with a rural nonfarm population in the northeast U.S.A. Chicago, National Lutheran Council, 1962. 127 p. 22 cm. 63-60484
I. Title.

RALL, Harris Franklin, 1870- 232.
... Teacher's manual for The Teachings of Jesus, by Harris Franklin Rall. New York, Cincinnati, The Abingdon press [c1918] 2 p. l., 7-79 p. 19 cm. (Kingdom of God series, ed. by H. H. Meyer and D. G. Downey) [BS2415.R35] 18-16713
I. Title.

TROUT, Ethel Wendell. 221
The beginning of a nation ... by Ethel Wendell Trout ... Philadelphia, The Westminster press, 19 v. illus., plates. 18 1/2 cm. (The Westminster textbooks of religious education for church schools having Sunday, week day, and expressional sessions, ed. by J. T. Faris. Junior department, 2d year, pt. [BS1194.T7] 24-18356
I. Title.

Religious education—New England.

FLEMING, Sandford, 377.10974
1888-
Children & Puritanism; the place of children in the life and thought of the New England churches, 1620-1847, by Sandford Fleming ... New Haven, Yale university press. London, H. Milford, Oxford university press, 1933. xii, 236 p. 23 1/2 cm. (On cover: Yale studies in religious education. [viii]) "The results of this study were presented to the faculty of the Yale Graduate school in partial fulfilment of the requirements for the degree of doctor of philosophy [1929]"--Acknowledgment. "The present volume is the sixth work published by the Yale university press on the Samuel B. Sneath memorial publication fund."--p. [v] Bibliography: p. [209]-220. [BV1467.F5 1933] 33-14951
1. Religious education—New England. 2. Puritans. 3. New England—Church history. 4. Congregational churches in New England. 5. Children in New England. 6. New England theology. I. Yale university. Samuel B. Sneath memorial fund. II. Title.

Religious education—New York (City)

PROTESTANT teachers 377.1062
association of New York city, inc.
The story of the Protestant teachers association of New York city, inc., compiled by Mary E. Lavers, Mary W. Newton [and] Amy J. Esty. New York, Chicago [etc.] Fleming H. Revell company [c1931] 80 p. front., plates. 20 cm. [BV1460.P7] 31-22922
1. Religious education—New York (City) I. Lavers, Mary Elizabeth, 1871- comp. II. Newton, Mary Wood, joint comp. III. Esty, Amy Janet, 1879- joint comp. IV. Title.

Religious education—New York (State)

HALL, Arthur Jackson. 377.
...Religious education in the public school of the state and city of New York; a historical study... by Arthur Jackson Hall. Chicago, Ill., The University of Chicago press [1914] x, 111 p. 24 1/2 cm. At head of title: The University of Chicago. Thesis (PH.D.)--University of Chicago, 1911. Bibliography: p. vii-x. [LC112.N7H2] 14-18546
1. Religious education—New York (State) I. Title.

MAHONEY, Charles 377.809747
Joseph, 1905-
... The relation of the state to religious education in early New York, 1633-1825 ... by Reverend Charles J. Mahoney, M.A. Washington, D.C., The Catholic university of America press, 1941. xiii, 225 p. 23 cm. Thesis (PH.D.)--Catholic university of America, 1941. Bibliography: p. 212-223. [LC406.N7M3] 41-13687
1. Religious education—New York (State) 2. Education and state—New York (State) I. Title.

Religious education of adolescents.

AUDINET, Jacques. 268'.6
Forming the faith of adolescents. Pref. by Gabriel Moran. [New York] Herder and Herder [1968] 88 p. 23 cm. Translation of Vers une catechese des adolescents. Bibliographical footnotes. [BV1475.9.A7813] 68-4530
1. Religious education of adolescents. I. Title.

AUGSBURGER, A. Don. 248.4897
Creating Christian personality, by A. Don Augsburger. Scottdale, Pa., Herald Press [1966] 128, [7] p. 21 cm. (Conrad Grebel lectures 1965) Bibliographical references included in "Footnotes" (p. 128-[135]) [BV1475.9.A8] 66-23905
1. Religious education of adolescents. I. Title. II. Series.

BABIN, Pierre. 268.433
Crisis of faith; the religious psychology of adolescence. [Translation and adaptation by Eva Fleischner. New York] Herder and Herder [1963] 251 p. 22 cm. Translation of Les jeunes et la foi. Bibliographical footnotes. [BV1475.9.B313] 63-18148
1. Religious education of adolescents. 2. Adolescence. I. Title.

BABIN, Pierre. 136.742
Faith and the adolescent. [Translated by David Gibson. New York] Herder and Herder [1965] 128 p. 21 cm. Translation of Dieu et l'adolescent. Bibliography: p. [124] [BV1475.9.B293] 65-13491
1. Religious education of adolescents. 2. Adolescence. I. Title.

BROWNING, Robert L. 268'.433
Communicating with junior highs [by] Robert L. Browning. Illus. by Tom Armstrong. Henry M. Bullock, general editor. Nashville, Graded Press [1968] 208 p. illus. 23 cm. Bibliography: p. 207-208. [BV1475.9.B7] 68-3726
1. Religious education of adolescents. 2. Communication (Theology) I. Title.

BRUNK, Ada Zimmerman. 268.433
The Christian nurture of youth; a guide for leaders of youth [by] Ada Zimmerman Brunk [and] Ethel Yake Metzler. Scottdale, Pa., Herald Press [1960] 158p. 21cm. Includes bibliography. [BV1547.B7] 60-5890
1. Religious education of adolescents. I. Metzler, Ethel Yake. II. Title.

BYRD, Annie Ward. 268.433
Better Bible teaching for intermediates. Nashville, Convention Press [1959] 127p. 19cm. Includes bibliography. [BV1548.B9] 59-9968
1. Religious education of adolescents. I. Title.

DESJARDINS, Lucile, 1892- 268.433
Building an intermediate program, by Lucile Desjardins. A textbook in the Standard leadership curriculum, outlined and approved by the International council of religious education. Philadelphia, Printed for the Leadership training publishing association by the Westminster press [c1939] x, 212 p. incl. diagrs., forms. 19 cm. Includes bibliographies. [BV1548.D36] 39-32151
1. Religious education of adolescents. I. International council of religious education. II. Title.

EGLY, Alan 268.433
So you work with junior highs. Anderson, Ind., Warner Press [Gospel Trumpet Press c.1960] 62p. 21cm. 60-10184 pap., apply
1. Religious education of adolescents. I. Title.

GARRISON, Karl Claudius, 268.433
1900-
Before you teach teen-agers. [Philadelphia, Lutheran Church. dist. Fortress, c.1962] 174p. illus. 22cm. (Leadership educ. ser.) Bibl. 63-799 1.50
1. Religious education of adolescents. I. Title.

GARRISON, Karl Claudius, 268.433
1900-
Before you teach teen-agers. [Philadelphia, Lutheran Church Press, 1962] Philadelphia, Lutheran Church Press [c1962] 174 p. illus. 22 cm. 64 p. 21 cm. (Leadership education series) (Leadership education series) [BV1547.G3] 63-799
1. Religious education of adolescents. I. Title. II. Title: Teacher's guide.

GRIFFITHS, Louise 268.433
(Benckenstein) 1908-
Junior high school boys and girls in the church, by Louise B. Griffiths. Boston and Chicago, The Pilgrim press [1944] vi, 64 p. illus. 23 1/2 cm. "Useful books for junior high workers": p. 61-64. [BV1548.G7] 45-1965
1. Religious education of adolescents. I. Title.

GRIFFITHS, Louise 268.433
(Benckenstein) 1908-
The teacher and young teens; illustrated by Chris Pearson. St. Louis, Bethany Press [1954] 176p. illus. 22cm. [BV1548.G73] 54-14350
1. Religious education of adolescents. I. Title.

*HILL, Dorothy La Croix 268.432
The church teaches nines to twelves. Illus. by Ann Doyle. Nashville, pub. for the Coop. Pub. Assn. by Abingdon [c.1965] 192p. 19cm. 1.75 pap.,
I. Title.

KIRK, Mary Virginia (Lee) 268.433
1888-
Effective work with intermediates in the Sunday school. [Rev. ed., 1955] Nashville, Convention Press [1959, c1952] 134p. 20cm. [BV1548.K55 1959] 60-53103
1. Religious education of adolescents. 2. Religious education—Teacher training. 3. Sunday-schools. I. Title.

KIRK, Mary Virginia (Lee) 268.433
1888-
Effective work with intermediates in the Sunday school. Nashville, Broadman Press [1952] 148 p. 20 cm. [BV1548.K55 1952] 52-4584
1. Religious education of adolescents. 2. Religious education — Teacher training. 3. Sunday-schools. I. Title.

KIRK, Mary Virginia (Lee) 268.433
1888-
Intermediate Sunday school work. Nashville, Sunday School Board of the Southern Baptist Convention [1937] 159 p. 19 cm. [BV1548.K56] 37-38550
1. Religious education of adolescents. I. Title.

THE Living light, 268'.8'2
helping adolescents grow up in Christ. Ed. by Mary Perkins ryan. New York, Paul 1st [1967] x, 246p. 18cm. (Deus bks.) Articles which orig. appeared in the Living light. Bibl. [BX926.L54] 67-15722 1.45 pap.,
1. Religious education of adolescents. 2. Catechetics—Catholic Church. I. Ryan, Mary Perkins, 1915- ed.

THE Living light.
Helping adolescents grow up in Christ. Edited by Mary Perkins Ryan. New York, Paulist Press [1967] x. 246 p. 18 cm. (Deus books) Articles which originally appeared in the Living light. Includes bibliographical references.
1. Religious education of adolescents. 2. Catechetics — Catholic Church. I. Ryan, Mary Perkins, 1915- ed. II. Title.

THE Living light. 268'.8'2
Helping adolescents grow up in Christ. Edited by Mary Perkins Ryan. New York, Paulist Press [1967] x. 246 p. 18 cm. (Deus books) Articles which originally appeared in the Living light. Includes bibliographical references. [BX926.L54] 67-15722
1. Religious education of adolescents. 2. Catechetics — Catholic Church. I. Ryan, Mary Perkins, 1915- ed. II. Title.

MCKIBBEN, Frank Melbourne, 268.
1889-
...Intermediate method in the church school, by Frank M. McKibben. New York, Cincinnati, The Abingdon press [c1926] 324 p. 20 cm. (The Abingdon religious education texts, D. G. Downey, general editor. Community training school series, N. E. Richardson, editor) "For further reading" at end of each chapter. [BV1548.M3] 26-17492
1. Religious education of adolescents. 2. Sunday-schools. I. Title.

MICHAEL, Sister, comp.
Readings in Christian education; a text for those preparing to teach in the CCD high school of religion; compiled by Sister Michael, O.L.V.M. and Sister Mary Lucille, O.L.V.M. Huntington, Ind., Our Sunday Visitor [c1961] 80 p. 28 cm. 66-94322
1. Religious education of adolescents. 2. Confraternity of Christian Doctrine. I. Mary Lucille, Sister, joint comp. II. Title.

MUNRO, Harry Clyde, 1890- 268.
Agencies for the religious education of adolescents, by Harry C. Munro; a textbook in the Standard course in teacher training, outlined and approved by the International council of religious education, Third year specialization series to be used as an elective. St. Louis, Pub. for the Teacher training publishing association by the Bethany press [c1925] 176 p. diagrs. 17 cm. Contains bibliographies. [BV1475.M8] 26-12885
1. Religious education of adolescents. I. Title.

PEARSON, Elaine Coleman. 268.433
The intermediate leadership manual [by] Elaine Coleman Pearson. Nashville, Tenn., The Sunday school board of the Southern Baptist convention [1944] 5 p. l., 157 p. incl. forms, diagrs. 19 cm. [BV1548.P4] 44-47765
1. Religious education of adolescents. I. Southern Baptist convention. Sunday school board. II. Title.

PROTESTANT Episcopal 268.432
Church in the U. S. A. National Council. Dept. of Christian Education.
Growing in faith; teacher's manual, grade 9. Greenwich, Conn., Seabury Press [1957] 88p. 28cm. (The Seabury series, F-9) [BV1548.P68] 57-8346
1. Religious education of adolescents. I. Title.

PROTESTANT Episcopal 268.432
Church in the U. S. A. National Council. Dept. of Christian Education.
What about us? Teacher's manual, grade 8. Greenwich, Conn., Seabury Press [1956] 103p. 28cm. (The Seabury series, T-8) [BV1548.P69] 56-7855
1. Religious education of adolescents. I. Title.

PROTESTANT Episcopal 268.433
Church in the U. S. A. National Council. Dept. of Christian Education.
Why should I? Teacher's manual, grade 7. Rev. ed. Greenwich, Conn., Seabury Press [1958] 106p. illus. 28cm. (The Seabury series, T-7B) Includes bibliography. [BV1548.P7 1958] 58-9263
1. Religious education of adolescents. I. Title.

REYNOLDS, Lillian 268.433
Richter.
A Pioneer handbook, for leaders of junior high school boys and girls. With illus. by Anne Newbold. Richmond, John Knox Press [1951] 109 p. illus. 23 cm. [BV1548.R4] 51-28813
1. Religious education of adolescents. I. Title.

SMITH, Barbara, 1922- 268.433
How to teach junior high. Philadelphia, Westminster [c.1965] 224p. 22cm. [BV1548.S55] 65-12101 3.95
1. Religious education of adolescents. I. Title.

SMITH, Barbara, 1922- 268.433
How to teach junior highs. Philadelphia, Westminster Press [1965] 224 p. 22 cm. [BV1548.S55] 65-12101
1. Religious education of adolescents. I. Title.

Religious education of adults.

APPS, Jerold W., 1934- 268'.434
How to improve adult education in your church [by] Jerold W. Apps. Minneapolis, Augsburg Pub. House [1972] 110 p. 20 cm. Includes bibliographical references. [BV1488.A65] 72-78560 ISBN 0-8066-1226-6 2.95
1. Religious education of adults. I. Title.

BARCLAY, Wade Crawford, 268.434
1874-
The church and a Christian society; a discussion of aims, content, and method of Christian education [by] Wade Crawford Barclay. New York, Cincinnati [etc] The Abingdon press [c1939] 428 p. 24cm. "References and notes": p. 383-398; Bibliography: p. 399-411 [BV1550.B32] 40-4928
1. Religious education of adults. I. Title.

BERGEVIN, Paul Emile. 268.434
Design for adult education in the church [by] Paul Bergevin [and] John McKinley. Greenwich, Conn., Seabury Press, 1958. 320p. 22cm. [BV1550.B4] 58-6061
1. Religious education of adults. I. McKinley, John, 1921- joint author. II. Title.

BREWBAKER, Charles Warren, 268.
1869-
The adult Bible teacher and leader, a twenty-hour course for teachers and officers of the adult department, by Charles W. Brewbaker. Cincinnati, O., The Standard publishing company, [1943] 128 p. 19 cm. [BV1550.B64] 43-16431
1. Religious education of adults. I. Title.

CALDWELL, Irene Catherine 268.61
(Smith) 1919-
Adults learn and like it; how to teach adults in the church. Anderson, Ind., Warner Press [1955] 112p. illus. 20cm. [BV1550.C3] 268.434 55-58705
1. Religious education of adults. I. Title.

CALDWELL, Irene Catherine 268.434
(Smith) 1919-
Responsible adults in the church school program. Anderson, Ind., Published for the Co-operative Publication Association [by] Warner Press [dist. Gospel Trumpet Press, c.1961] 96p. illus. Bibl. notes 61-5283 1.25 pap.,
1. Religious education of adults. I. Title.

*CALLEN, Barry. 268'.434
Where life begins! Anderson, Ind., Warner Press [1973] 128 p. 19 cm. Includes bibliographical references. [BV1488] ISBN 0-87162-146-0 2.50 (pbk)
1. Religious education of adults. 2. Religious education—Text-books for adults. I. Title.

CLEMMONS, Robert S
Adult education in The Methodist Church. [Prepared by Department of Christian Education of Adults. Nashville, Division of the Local Church, General Board of Education, The Methodist Church, 1961] 104 p. illus. 23 cm. Includes bibliography. 65-37381
1. Religious education of adults. I. Title.

CLEMMONS, Robert S
The Christian education of young adults. [Prepared by Department of Christian Education of Adults. Nashville, Division of the Local Church, Board of Education. The Methodist Church, 1958] 111 p. illus. 20 cm. Includes bibliography. 66-54637
1. Religious education of Adults. 2. Church work with young adults. I. Methodist Church (United States) Dept. of Christian Education of Adults. II. Title.

CLEMMONS, Robert S 268.434
Dynamics of Christian adult education. New York, Abingdon Press [1958] 143p. illus. 20cm. Includes bibliography. [BV1550.C53] 58-8122
1. Religious education of adults. I. Title.

CLEMMONS, Robert S 262.15
Education for churchmanship [by] Robert S. Clemmons Nashville, Abingdon Press [1966] 205 p. 22 cm. Includes bibliographies. [BV1488.C5] 66-21968
1. Religious education of adults. I. Title.

COLLINS, Joseph Burns, 1897-
We discuss the Creed: for religion discussion clugs. Paterson, N.J., Confraternity Publications, 1961. 95 p. 19 cm. 64-64227
1. Religious education of adults. 2. Apostles' creed — Catechisms, question-books, etc. I. Confraternity of Christian Doctrine. II. Title.

CONROY, Joseph P. 170
Talks to parents, by Rev. Joseph P. Conroy ... New York, Cincinnati [etc.] Benziger brothers, 1919. 173 p. 19 cm. [BJ1249.C6] 19-17101
I. Title.

DOBBINS, Gaines Stanley, 267.626
1886-
Meeting the needs of adults through the Baptist Training Union. Nashville, Sunday School Board of the Southern Baptist Convention [1947] 165 p. 20 cm. [BV1550.D57] 48-15931
1. Religious education of adults. 2. Baptist Training Union. I. Title.

DOBBINS, Gaines Stanley, 268.434
1886-
Understanding adults. Nashville, Broadman Press [1948] 147 p. 20 cm. [BV1550.D62] 48-8345
1. Religious education of adults. I. Title.

DOBLER, Walter E
Manuel for adults for administrators and leaders of adult study groups. Photos. by Sheldon Brody. Boston, United Church Press [c1963] 64 p. illus. 26 cm. [United Church curriculum. Adult. Administrators] Bibliography: p. 62-63 64-35822
1. Religious education of adults. 2. United Church of Christ-Education. I. Title. II. Series.

ERNSBERGER, David J. 248.4
Education for renewal, by David J. Ernsberger. Philadelphia, Westminster Press [1965] 174 p. 21 cm. Bibliographical references included in "Notes" (p. [170]-174) [BV1488.E8] 65-10578
1. Religious education of adults. I. Title.

FIFE, Earl Hanson. 268.434
Building a successful men's Bible class, by Earl Hanson Fife; foreword by Guy P. Leavitt. Cincinnati, O., The Standard publishing company [1940] 52 p. 16 1/2 cm. [BV1550.F5] 42-47980
1. Religious education of adults. I. Title.

FOREMAN, Kenneth Joseph, 1891-
Adults in the school, manual. Richmond, Va., The CLC Press [1963] 55 p. 22 cm. (The Covenant Life Curriculum) NUC64
1. Religious education of adults. I. Title. II. Series.

FRY, John R. 268.434
A hard look at adult Christian education. Philadelphia, Westminster Pr. [c.1961] 150p. 61-7708 3.50
1. Religious education of adults. I. Title.

GORHAM, Donald Rex, 1903- 268.434
Understanding adults. Philadelphia, Judson Press [1948] viii, 162 p. 20 cm. [BV1550.G65] 48-9000
1. Religious education of adults. I. Title.

A hand book of plans & programs for the community council. Under the auspices of Tuskegee Institute and The National Council of Churches of Christ in the United States of America. [2d ed.] iTuskegeb Institute, Ala., Tuskegee Institute Press, 1956. 87p. 23cm. Cover title.
1. Religious education of adults. 2. Rural churches. 3. Religious extension service—Alabama. I. Edwards, Vinsor, Allen. II. Tuskegee Institute. III. National Council of the Churches of Christ in the United States of America.

HANSON, Joseph John 268
Our church plans for adults; a manual on adult Christian education. Valley Forge, Pa., Judson [c.1962] 112p. illus. 19cm. Bibl. 62-16999 1.25 pap.,
1. Religious education of adults. I. Title.

HELD, John Adolf, 1869- 268.
The organized class; some principles and plans with a brief history of the adult class movement. [By] John A. Held... Nashville, Tenn., Sunday school board, Southern Baptist convention [c1915] 169, [7] p. incl. forms. 18 cm. [BV1550.H4] 42-28774
1. Religious education of adults. I. Southern Baptist convention. Sunday school board. II. Title.

IVERSON, Gerald D. 268'.434
Ways to plan & organize your Sunday school: adult [by] Gerald D. Iverson. Glendale, Calif., International Center for Learning [1973, c1971] 109 p. illus. 20 cm. (ICL teacher's/leader's success handbook) (An ICL insight book) Bibliography: p. 99-100. [BV1488.I9] 70-168841 ISBN 0-8307-0125-7 1.95
1. Religious education of adults. I. Title.

JONES, Idris W. 268.434
Our church plans for adult education; a manual on administration. Philadelphia, Judson Press [1952] 76 p. illus. 19 cm. Includes bibliography. [BV1550.J6] 52-10370
1. Religious education of adults. I. Title.

LEACH, Joan.
How to vitalize young adult classes. Cincinnati, Standard Pub. [c1965] 64 p. illus. Includes bibliographies. 66-86755
1. Religious education of adults. I. Title.

LEACH, Joan.
How to vitalize young adult classes. Cincinnati, Standard Pub. [c1965] 64 p. illus. Includes bibliographies. 66-86755
1. Religious education of adults. I. Title.

LENTZ, Richard E
Adult education in Christian Churches; a handbook for Disciples of Christ. St. Louis, Christian Board of Publication, 1961. 64 p. 66-24331
1. Religious education of adults. I. Title.

LENTZ, Richard E 268.434
Making the adult class vital; illustrated by Janice Lovett. St. Louis, Published for the Cooperative Publication Association by Bethany Press [1954] 112p. illus. 20cm. [BV1550.L4] 54-9472
1. Religious education of adults. I. Title.

LOESSNER, Ernest J. 268.434
Adults continuing to learn [by] Ernest J. Loessner. Nashville, Convention Press [1967] viii, 135 p. 19 cm. Includes bibliographical references. [BV1488.L6] 67-10001
1. Religious education of adults. I. Title.

LUTHERAN Education Association.
Toward adult Christian education; a symposium. With the assistance of Harry G. Coiner, Warren H. Schmidt, Roland H.A. Seboldt. River Forest, Ill., Lutheran Education Association, 1962. xii, 90 p. (Lutheran Education Association 19th yearbook, 1962) Edited by Donald Deffner. 65-30799
1. Religious education of adults. 2. Laity. 3. Church and social problems. I. Deffner,Donald, ed. II. Title. III. Series.

MCKINLEY, John 268.434
Creative methods for adult classes. St. Louis, Bethany Press [c.1960] 96p. illus. 20cm. 60-9919 1.50 pap.,
1. Religious education of adults. I. Title.

MINOR, Harold D., comp. 268'.434
Creative procedures for adult groups. Harold D. Minor, editor. Nashville, Abingdon Press [1968] 176 p. forms. 20 cm. Selected from Adult teacher. Bibliography: p. 173-176. [BV1534.M52] 68-27624 2.00
1. Religious education of adults. 2. Religious education—Teaching methods. I. Adult teacher. II. Title.

OSTERHELD, Dudley Oliver. 268.434
Training men for Bible teaching, by Dudley Oliver Osterheld ... Fourteen lessons. New York, N.Y., The Laymen's assembly [1945] 149 p. 20 1/2 cm. "Books to read and study" at the end of each chapter except one. [BV1550.O8] 45-18943
1. Religious education of adults. 2. Religious education—Teaching methods. I. Title.

PHILLIPS, William 268.434
Presley, 1882-
Adults in the Sunday school. Nashville, Sunday School Board of the Southern Baptist Convention [1947] [3] l., 3-175 p. illus., plans. 20 cm. [BV1550.P52] 47-29964
1. Religious education of adults. 2. Sunday-schools. I. Title.

PROCTOR, Robert A. 207
Too old to learn? [By] Robert A. Proctor. Nashville, Broadman Press [1967] 126 p. 21 cm. Includes bibliographical references. [BV1488.P7] 67-10307
1. Religious education of adults. I. Title.

PROTESTANT Episcopal 268.434
Church in the U. S. A. National Council.
Leading adult classes; a handbook. Greenwich, Conn., Seabury Press [1958] 80p. 21cm. (The Seabury series, P-L2) Includes bibliography. [BV1550.P78] 58-2642
1. Religious education of adults. I. Title.

PROTESTANT Episcopal Church in the U.S.A. National Council. Dept. of Christian Education.
Leading adult classes; a handbook. Materials for Christian education prepared at the direction of General Convention. Greenwich, Conn., Seabury Press [c1958] 80 p. 21 cm. Bibliography: p.79-80. 65-66581
1. Religious education of adults. I. Title.

REINHART, Bruce. 268.434
The institutional nature of adult Christian education. Philadelphia, Westminster Press [1962] 242p. 21cm. Includes bibliography. [BV1550.R4] 62-9809
1. Religious education of adults. I. Title.

SCHAEFER, James R. 268'.434
Program planning for adult Christian education, by James R. Schaefer. With a foreword by D. Campbell Wyckoff. New York, Newman Press [1972] x, 262 p. 23 cm. A revision of the author's thesis, Catholic University of America, 1971, with title: A proposed curriculum design for adult Christian education for use in Catholic dioceses. Bibliography: p. 232-251. [BV1488.S3 1972] 72-88324 ISBN 0-8091-0175-0 4.95
1. Religious education of adults. I. Title.

SHERRILL, Lewis Joseph, 1892- 268.
Adult education in the church, by Lewis Joseph Sherrill ... and John Edwin Purcell ... Rev. ed., 1939. Richmond, Va., J. Knox press [1939?] 290 p. 19 1/2 cm. "Selected bibliography on adult Christian education": p. 289-290. [BV1550.S] W 41
1. Religious education of adults. I. Purcell, John Edwin, joint author. II. Title.

SISEMORE, John T 268.434
The Sunday school ministry to adults. Nashville, Convention Press [1959] 148 p. 20 cm. Includes bibliography. [BV1550.S56] 59-5870
1. Religious education of adults. I. Title.

SNYDER, Alton G 268.434
Teaching adults. Philadelphia, Judson Press [1959] 96 p. illus. 20 cm. Includes bibliography. [BV1550.S58] 59-12888
1. Religious education of adults. I. Title.

WESTPHAL, Edward Pride, 1893- 268.434
The church's opportunity in adult education [by] Edward P. Westphal... Philadelphia, Printed for the Leadership training publishing association [by] The Westminster press [c1941] 6 p., 1 l., [11]-209 p. 19 cm. Bibliography: p. 197-209. [BV1550.W45] 41-19007
1. Religious education of adults. I. Title.

WORKSHOP on the Christian Education of Adults, University of Pittsburgh, 1958. 268.4341
Charting the future course of Christian adult education in America; selected addresses and papers. Lawrence C. Little, editor. [Pittsburgh] Dept. of Religious Education, University of Pittsburgh, c1958. 195 l. 20 cm. Bibliography:leaves 185-195. [BV1550.W67 1958] 59-17821
1. Religious education of adults. I. Little, Lawrence Calvin, 1897- ed. II. Title.

WORKSHOP on the Christian Education of Adults, University of Pittsburgh, 1958. 268.434
The future course of Christian adult education; selected addresses and papers. Editor: Lawrence C. Little. [Pittsburgh] University of Pittsburgh Press [1959] xi, 322 p. diagrs. 24 cm. Revision of "Charting the future course of Christian adult education in America." "A selected bibliography compiled by Lawrence C. Little": p. 300-322. [BV1550.W67 1958a] 59-11642
1. Religious education of adults. I. Little, Lawrence Calvin, 1897- ed. II. Title.

WORKSHOP on the Curriculum of Christian Education for Adults, University of Pittsburgh, 1961. 268
Wider horizons in Christian adult education; selected addresses and papers. Conducted by the Sch. of Educ., Univ. of Pittsurgh .Ed. by Lawrence C. Little. [Pittsburgh] Univ. of Pittsburgh Pr. [c.] 1962. x, 338p. illus. 24cm. Bibl. 62-14381 6.00
1. Religious education of adults. I. Pittsburgh. University. School of Education. II. Little, Lawrence Calvin, 1897- ed. III. Title.

ZEIGLER, Earl Frederick, 1889- 268.434
Christian education of adults. Philadelphia, Published for the Cooperative Pub. Association by Westminster Press [1958] 142 p. 21 cm. [BV1550.Z39] 58-5517
1. Religious education of adults. I. Title.

Religious education of adults — Abstracts.

LITTLE, Lawrence Calvin, 1897- comp.
Abstracts of selected doctoral dissertations on adult religious education. [Pittsburgh] Department of Religious Education, University of Pittsburgh, 1962. 322 l. Abstracts prepared by students in a graduated seminar at the University of Pittsburgh.
1. Religious education of adults — Abstracts. 2. Dissertations, Academic — U.S. — Abstracts. I. Pittsburgh. University. Dept. of Religious Education. II. Title.

LITTLE, Lawrence Calvin, 1897- comp.
Abstracts of selected doctoral dissertations on adult religious education. [Pittsburgh] Department of Religious Education, University of Pittsburgh, 1962. 322 l. Abstracts prepared by students in a graduated seminar at the University of Pittsburgh. 63-51014
1. Religious education of adults — Abstracts. 2. Dissertations, Academic — U.S. — Abstracts. I. Pittsburgh. University. Dept. of Religious Education. II. Title.

Religious education of adults, (children, etc.).

*NEWLAND, Mary Reed, comp. 268.
The resource guide: for adults religious education. Kansas City, Mo., National catholic Reporter, [1974]. 196 p. 28 cm. [BV1550] 9.95 (pbk.)
1. Religious education of adults, (children, etc.). I. Title.
Publisher's address: P.O. Box 281 Kansas City, Mo. 64141

Religious education of adults. Title.

CLEMMONS, Robert S. 262.15
Education for churchmanship [by] Robert S. Clemmon. Nashville, Abingdon [1966] 205 p. 22 cm (151) [bv1488.c5] 66-21968
1. Religious education of adults. Title. I. Title.

Religious education of children.

ACHESON, Edna Lucile, 1891- 268'.6
The construction of junior church school curricula. New York, Bureau of Publications, Teachers College, Columbia University, 1929. [New York, AMS Press, 1973, c1972] viii, 185 p. 22 cm. Reprint of the 1929 ed., issued in series: Teachers College, Columbia University. Contributions to education, no. 331. Originally presented as the author's thesis, Columbia. Includes bibliographical references. [BV1475.A33 1972] 73-176503 ISBN 0-404-55331-1 10.00
1. Religious education of children. 2. Religious education—Curricula. I. Title. II. Series: Columbia University. Teachers College. Contributions to education, no. 331.

ANDERSON, Vernon Ellsworth, 1908- 268
Before you teach children. Philadelphia, Lutheran Church [dist. Muhlenberg, c. 1962] 176p. illus. 22cm. (Leadership educ. ser.) 62-51866 1.50
1. Religious education of children. I. Title.

ANDERSON, Vernon Ellsworth, 1908- 268
Before you teach children. Philadelphia, Lutheran Church Press [1962] 176p. illus. 22cm. (Leadership education series) [BV1475.2.A5] 62-51866
1. Religious education of children. I. Title.

ARTHUR, Donald Ramsay. c6 268.432
The primary leadership manual by LaVerne Ashby and Doris Monroe Nashville, Convention Press [1959] 154p. illus. 19cm. Includes bibliography. [BV1545.A7] 59-3136
1. Religious education of children. 2. Religious education— Teaching methods. I. A II. Ashby, Laverne III. Monroe, Doris, joint author. IV. Title.

BABIN, Pierre 207
Options: approaches for the religious education of adolescents. Tr. & adapted by John F. Murphy. [New York] Herder & Herder [1967] Tr. of Options pour une education de la foi des jeuses. Bibl. [BX926.B313] 67-14140 3.95
1. Religious education of children. 2. Catechetics—Catholic Church. I.)0c173p. 21cm. II. Title.

BABIN, Pierre. 207
Options: approaches for the religious education of adolescents. Translated and adapted by John F. Murphy. [New York] Herder and Herder [1967] 173 p. 21 cm. Translation of Options pour une education de la foi des jeunes. Bibliographical footnotes. [BX926.B313] 67-14140
1. Religious education of children. 2. Catechetics—Catholic Church. I. Title.

BAKER, Dolores. 268.6
Teaching the Bible to primaries [by] Dolores Baker and Elsie Rives. Nashville, Convention Press [1964] vii, 150 p. 19 cm. [BV1475.2.B3] 64-24947
1. Religious education of children. I. Rives, Elsie, joint author. II. Title.

BALDWIN, Maud Junkin. 268.
The juniors; how to teach and train them, by Mayd Junkin Baldwin ... Philadelphia, The Westminster press, 1916. 107 p. front., illus. (plans) pl. 19 cm. Includes bibliographies. [BV1546.B37] 17-7481
1. Religious education of children. 2. Sunday-schools. I. Title.

THE Bible and the child, 268.
by The Very Rev. F. W. Farrar ... [and others] ... New York, The Macmillan company; London, Macmillan & co., ltd., 1896. vii, 171 p. 16 cm. [BS618.B5] 44-11319
1. Religious education of children. 2. Bible—Study. I. Farrar, Frederic William, 1831-1908.
Contents omitted.

BLANKENSHIP, Lois. 268.432
Our church plans for children; a manual on administration. Philadelphia, Judson Press, '1951. 94 p. illus. 20 cm. [BV1475.B53] 52-315
1. Religious education of children. I. Title.

BOLTON, Barbara J. 268'.432
Bible learning activities: children, grades 1 to 6 [by] Barbara J. Bolton and Charles T. Smith. Glendale, Calif., G/L Regal Books [1973] 154 p. illus. 20 cm. (ICL teacher's/leader's success handbook) (An ICL insight book) Bibliography: p. 151-152. [BV1475.2.B63] 73-85021 ISBN 0-8307-0240-7 2.25
1. Religious education of children. 2. Religious education—Text-books. I. Smith, Charles T., joint author. II. Title.

BOLTON, Barbara J. 268'.432
Ways to help them learn: children, grades 1 to 6 [by] Barbara J. Bolton. Glendale, Calif., International Center for Learning [1973, c1972] 149 p. illus. 20 cm. (ICL teacher's/leader's success handbook) (An ICL insight book) Bibliography: p. 149. [BV1475.2.B64] 77-168843 ISBN 0-8307-0119-2 1.95
1. Religious education of children. I. Title.

BOWMAN, Clarice M. 268-433
Guiding intermediates, by Claric M. Bowman. Lucius H. Bugbee, C. A. Bowen, editors. New York, Nashville, Abingdon-Cokesbury press [1943] 156 p. 19 cm. Bibliographical references included in "Notes" (p. 155-156) [BV1548.B6] 43-16562
1. Religious education of children. I. Bugbee, Lucius Hatfield, 1874- ed. II. Bowen, Cawthon Asbury, 1884- joint ed. III. Title.

BOWMAN, Clarice Margurette, 1910- 268.433
Guiding intermediates. Lucius H. Bugbee, C. A. Bowen, editors. New York, Abingdon-Cokesbury Press [1943] 156 p. 19 cm. Bibliographical references in "Notes" (p. 155-156) [BV1548.B6] 43-16562
1. Religious education of children. I. Bugbee, Lucius Hatfield, 1874- ed. II. Bowen, Cawthon Asbury, 1884- joint ed. III. Title.

BRADFORD, Ann. 268.432
Working with primaries through the Sunday school. Nashville, Convention Press [1961] 149p. illus. 19cm. [BV1545.B587] 61-11413
1. Religious education of children. 2. Religious education— Teacher training. 3. Sunday-schools. I. Title.

BRECK, Flora Elizabeth, 1886- 268.432
Church school chats for primary teaching. Boston, Wilde [1950] 155 p. 20 cm. Includes hymns. [BV1545.B59] 50-12736
1. Religious education of children. I. Title.

BREITIGAM, R R. 253
The challenge of child evangelism. Nashville, Southern Pub. Association [1950] 250 p. front. 21 cm. Bibliography: p. 238-242. [BV1475.B7] 51-22595
1. Religious education of children. 2. Evangelistic work. I. Title.

BROWN, Jeanette (Perkins) 1887- ed. 268.
At school with the great Teacher; a Sunday and week-day course, complete in three parts, for children approximately eight years of ages, by Jeanette Eloise Perkins, in editorial collabration with Frances Weld Danielson ... Boston Chicago, The Pilgrim press c194] xiii. 78, iv p., 1 l., 79-149, iv p., 1 l., 151-206 p. front. 28 cm. (Everyday Christian living series) Each part has separate t. p. Contains music. Full name: Jeanette Eloise (Perkins) Brown. [BV1545.B594 1924a] 25-12975
1. Religious edcation of children. I. Danielson, Frances Weld, joint ed. II. Title.

BROWN, Jeanette (Perkins) 1887- 268.6
Others call it God; a unit on how the world began, by Jeanette E. Perkins ... Enid Dearborn, teacher, Elizabeth Babcock, assistant; foreword by Frank W. Herriott. New York and London, Harper & brothers, 1934. xx. 141 p. plates. 20 cm. "First eition." Music: p. 113. Full name: Jeanette Elois (Perkis) Brown. Bibliograhy: p. 133-141. [BV1545.B596] 34-28594
1. Religious education of children. 2. Education—Experimental methods. 3. Man-Origin. I. Dearborn, Enid (Williams) 1895- II. Bacock, Elizabeth. III. Title.

BROWN, Jeanette (Perkins) 1887- 268.
Primary workship guide, of special value to schools using the closely graded church school courses; a bird's-eye view of the three primary classes, their objectives, discussions, activities, and memory work, as suggested in the teachers' textbooks with material for worship brought together from textbooks and folders; sample worship services and related story material for Sunday and the week day, prepared by Jeanette E. Perkins. Boston, Chicago, The Pilgrim press [1929] xii. 307 p. 21 cm. Full name: Jeanette Eloise (Perkins) Brown. [BV1545.B597] 29-22316
1. Religious education of children. I. Title.

BROWN, Mary Florence. 268.
Pleasing God by right-doing... by M. Florence Brown... Philadelphia, The Westminster press, 1923. xii, 417 p. 18 1/2 cm. (The Westminster textbooks of religious education for church schools having Sunday, week day, and expressional sessions, ed. by J.T. Faris. Primary department, 2d year) Contains music. Contains bibliographies. [BV1545.B6] 24-15087
I. Title.

CALDWELL, Irene Catherine (Smith) 1919- 268.432
Our concern is children. Anderson, Ind., Warner Press [1948] 180 p. 20 cm. Includes bibliographies. [BV1475.C33] 48-20935
1. Religious education of children. I. Title.

CATON, Dorothy Webber. 268.432
Let's teach through group relations; one of a series of guides on using the out-of-doors in Christian education, for leaders and parents of six- to twelve-year-olds. [Illus. by P. Nowell Yamron. New York, Published for the Division of Christian Education, National Council of the Churches of Christ in the U. S. A. by the Office of Publication and Distribution, 1959] 64p. illus. 23cm. Includes bibliography. [BV1538.C3] 59-11638
1. Religious education of children. 2. Social group work. I. Title.

CAVALLETTI, Sofia. 268.432
Teaching doctrine and liturgy, the Montessori approach [by] Sofia Cavalletti and Gianna Gobbi. [Translated by Sister M. Juliana] Staten Island, N.Y., Alba House [1964] 132 p. illus. 20 cm. Translation of Educazione religiosa, liturgia e metodo Montessori. [BX926.C343] 64-15370
1. Religious education of children. 2.

Catholic Church. Liturgy and ritual — Study and teaching (Elementary) I. Gobbi, Gianna, joint author. II. Title.

CHAMBERLAIN, Eugene. 268'.432
Children's Sunday school work [by] Eugene Chamberlain [and] Robert G. Fulbright. Nashville, Tenn., Convention Press [1969] 172 p. illus. 21 cm. [BV1475.2.C453] 79-98042
1. Religious education of children. I. Fulbright, Robert G., joint author. II. Title.

CHAMBERLIN, John Gordon. 268
Parents and religion; a preface to Christian education. Philadelphia, Westminster Press [1961] 111p. 21cm. Includes bibliography. [BV1475.2.C45] 61-5127
1. Religious education of children. 2. Theology, Doctrinal—Hist.—20th cent. I. Title.

CHAPIN, Lucy Stock. 268.
A year of primary programs, by Lucy Stock Chapin. New York, Cincinnati, The Abingdon press [c1924] 185 p. incl. front., illus. 26 cm. Music: p. 165-185. "Books of program material": p. 161-162. [BV1545.C5] 25-4417
1. Religious education of children. I. Title. II. Title: Primary programs.

CHAPLIN, Dora P. 268
Children and religion. With a foreword by Charles L. Taylor, Jr. Rev. ed. New York, Scribner [1961, c.1948, 1961] 238p. Bibl. 61-6029 3.95 half cloth,
1. Religious education of children. I. Title.

CHAPLIN, Dora P 268
Children and religion. With an introd. by Charles L. Taylor, Jr. New York, C. Scribner's Sons, 1948. ix, 230 p. 21 cm. [BV1475.C46] 48-7237
1. Religious education of children. I. Title.

CHILDHOOD education in 268'.432
the church / edited by Roy B. Zuck and Robert E. Clark. Chicago : Moody Press, [1975] p. cm. Includes bibliographical references and index. [BV1475.2.C47] 74-15350 ISBN 0-8024-1249-1 : 7.95
1. Religious education of children. I. Zuck, Roy B. II. Clark, Robert E.

COBB, Alice.
Who is my neighbor? A course for the third and fourth grades. Boston, United Church Press [c1964] 76 p. illus. 26 cm. (United Church curriculum. Lower Junior [Teachers. 13]) "Resources:" p. 74-75. 64-62849
1. Religious education of children. 2. United Church of Christ — Education. I. Title. II. Series.

COUDREAU, Francois 268.82
The child and the problem of faith. Tr. by Sister Gertrude. With discussion questions. Glen Rock, N.J., Paulist [1966] 92p. 18cm. (Deus bks.) [BX925.C6813] 66-22052 .75 pap.,
1. Religious education of children. 2. Catholic Church—Education. I. Title.

CULLY, Iris V. 268.432
Children in the church. Philadelphia, Westminster Press [c.1960] 204p. 21cm. (6p. bibl. and 2p. bibl. notes) 60-5125 3.75
1. Religious education of children. I. Title.

CULLY, Iris V 268.432
Ways to teach children, Ed. by Philip R. Hoh. Illus. by Harry Eaby. Philadelphia, Lutheran Church Pr. [c.1965] 136p. illus. 22cm. (Leadership educ. ser.) Bibl. [BV1475.2.C82] 65-2631 1.50; teacher's guide, pap., .50
1. Religious education of children. I. Title.

CULLY, Iris V. 268.432
Ways to teach children. by Iris V. Cully. Illus. by Harry Eaby. [Rev.] Philadelphia, Fortress [1966, c.1965] 135,[1]p. illus. 20cm. Bibl. [BV1475.2.C821966] 66-24201 2.50 bds.,
1. Religious education of children I. Title.

CULLY, Iris V 268.432
Ways to teach children, by Iris V. Cully. Edited by Philip R. Hoh. Illustrated by Harry Eaby. Philadelphia, Lutheran Church Press [1965] 136 p. illus. 22 cm. (Leadership education series) Teacher's guide, by Iris V. Cully. Edited by Philip R. Hoh, Philadelphia Lutheran Church Press [1965] 48 p. 21 cm. Leadership education series) Bibliography: p. 134-136. [BV1475.2.C82] 65-2631
1. Religious education of children. I. Title.

CULLY, Iris V 268.432
Ways to teach children, by Iris V. Cully. Illustrated by Harry Eaby. [Rev.] Philadelphia, Fortress Press [1966, c1965] 135, [1] p. illus. 20 cm. Bibliography: p. 134-[136] [BV1475.2C82 1966] 66-24201
1. Religious education of children. I. Title.

DEMAREE, Doris Clore. 268.432
Bethany junior department manual; a survey of the three junior graded lessons ... prepared by Doris Clore Demaree; Hazel A. Lewis, elementary editor. St. Louis, Mo., Christian board of publication [1945] 112 p. 23 cm. Includes bibliographies. [BV1546.D37] 46-12488
1. Religious education of children. 2. Religious education—Curricula. I. Lewis, Hazel Asenath, 1886- ed. II. Title.

DISCOVERING the holy fellowship: rev. teacher's manual, grade 5. Illus. by Beatrice and Leonard Derwinski. Greenwich, Conn., Seabury Press [1959] viii, 85p. 28cm. (The Seabury series [T-5B]) First published in 1956 under title: The goodly company. Pupil's resource book to be used with this work is: Protestant Episcopal Church in the U. S. A.--National Council--Dept. of Christian Education. Traveling the way. (BX5874 S438r5)
1. Religious education of children. I. Protestant Episcopal Church in the U. S. A. National Council. Dept. of Christian Education. II. Series.

DOEDERLEIN, Gertrude, 1903- 268.6
Living with our children, by Gertrude Doederlein, illustrated by Stryker Ingerman. Minneapolis, Minn., Augsburg publishing house [c1941] 2 p. l., 216, [4] p. illus. 22 cm. Songs with music: [4] p. at end. ----Teacher's manual. Minneapolis, Minn., Augsburg publishing house [1943] 2 p. l., 60 p. 21 cm. Bibliographies at end of some of the chapters. [BV1471.D6 Manual] 42-775
1. Religious education of children. I. Title.

DOMINGOS, Ann Maria. 268.432
Working with children in the small church. Issued by Dept. of Christian Education of Children [and] the Division of the Local Church, the General Board of Education of the Methodist Church. Nashville, Methodist Pub. House [1952] 63 p. illus. 20 cm. [BV1475.D64] 53-16589
1. Religious education of children. I. Title.

DREW, Louise C
Lower junior manual for administrators and leaders in the lower junior department of the church school. Photos. by Kenneth Thompson, Sheldon Brody, Peter C. Schaifer [and] Ronald Binks. Boston, United Church of Christ [c1963] 64 p. illus. 26 cm. [United Church curriculum. Lower junior. Administrators] "Resources for leaders in the lower junior department": p. 62-63. 64-34155
1. Religious education of children. 2. United Church of Christ — Education. I. Title. II. Series.

ERB, Alta Mae, 1891- 268
Christian education in the home. Scottdale, Pa., Herald Press [c1963] 92 p. 20 cm. Bibliography: p. 89-92. [BV1475.2F.7] 63-19648
1. Religious education of children. I. Title.

ERB, Alta Mae, 1891- 268.432
Christian nurture of children. [2d ed.] Scottdale, Pa. Herald Press [1955] 180 p. 21 cm. [BV1475.E8 1955] 55-7811
1. Religious education of children. I. Title.

FAHS, Sophia Blanche (Lyon), 268
1876-
Today's children and yesterday's heritage; a philosophy of creative religious development. With an introd. by Angus H. MacLean. Boston, Beacon Press [1952] 224 p. 22 cm. [BV1475.F3] 52-5242
1. Religious education of children. I. Title.

FARGUES, Marie. 268.432
Our children and the Lord; religious education for young children Translated by Geraldine McIntosh. Notre Dame, Ind., Fides Publishers [1965] Viii, 212 p. 20 cm. [BV1475.2.F313] 65-23117
1. Religious education of children. I. Title.

FARQUES, Marie 268.432
Our children and the Lord; religious education for young children. Tr. [from French] by Geraldine McIntosh. Notre Dame, Ind., Fides [c.1965] viii, 212p. 20cm. [BV1475.2.F313] 65-23117 2.95 pap.,
1. Religious education of children. I. Title.

FISK, Marian.
Children in the school, manual. Richmond, Va., The CLC Press [1963] 63 p. 22 cm. (The Covenant Life Curriculum) 65-6023
1. Religious education of children. I. Title.

FITZPATRICK, Edward 377.1
Augustus, 1884-
Methods of teaching religion in elementary schools [by] Edward A. Fitzpatrick...and Rev. Paul F. Tanner... Milwaukee, The Bruce publishing company [c1939] viii, 217 p. illus. 23 1/2 cm. Includes bibliographies. [BX925.B55] 39-21397
1. Religious education of children. I. Tanner, Paul Francis, 1905- joint author. II. Title.

FRITZ, Dorothy Bertolet.
The child and the Christian faith. Illus. by Ruth Singley Ensign. Richmond, CLC Press [1964] 226 p. illus. 21 cm. (The Covenant life curriculum. [Children. Administrators. Teachers. Parents]) Bibliography: p. 216-221. 65-77690
1. Religious education of children. 2. Presbyterian Church-Education. I. Title. II. Series.

FRITZ, Dorothy Bertolet.
The child and the Christian faith. Illus. by Ruth Singley Ensign. Richmond, CLC Press [1964] 226 p. illus. 21 cm. (The Covenant life curriculum. [Children. Administrators. Teachers. Parents]) Bibliography: p. 216-221. 65-77690
1. Religious education of children. 2. Presbyterian Church-Education. 3. Reformed churches — Education. 4. Moravian Church — Education. I. Title. II. Series.

GARDNER, Ann 268.432
Seek to serve, by Ann Gardner, Lois Burford. Murfreesboro, Tenn., DeHoff Pubns., 1963. 128p. illus. 21cm. Bibl. 63-12320 price unreported
1. Religious education of children. 2. Creative activities and seat work. I. Burford, Lois, joint author. II. Title.

GILLET, Edith Louise, 1899- 268
At work with children in the small church, by Edith L. Gillet. Philadelphia, Chicago [etc.] The Judson press [c1940] 102 p. 20 cm. Bibliography at end of each chapter. [BV1475.G5] 40-33091
1. Religious education of children. I. Title.

GODDARD, Carolyn E
Primary manual for administrators and leaders in the primary department of the church school. With photos by Robert Fulton, Peter C. Schlaifer, Sheldon A. Brody, Ronald Binks and drawing by Larry Channing. Boston, United Church Press [c1963] 64 p. illus. 26 cm. [United Church curriculum. Primary. Administrators] "Resources": p. 62-64. 64-23550
1. Religious education of children. 2. United Church of Christ-Education. I. Title. II. Series.

GOLDMAN, Ronald. 377'.1
Readiness for religion; a basis for developmental religious education. New York, Seabury Press [1968, c1965] ix, 238 p. 22 cm. Bibliographical references included in "Notes" (p. [225]-229) [BV1475.2.G6 1968] 68-11589
1. Religious education of children. I. Title.

GOULD, Josephine.
Growing with nursery and kindergarten children. Drawings by Jannette Spitzer. Boston, Beacon Press [c1960] 199 p. illus. 21 cm. "A Companion to Martin and Judy, Volumes I, II, III." Includes bibliographies. 63-13222
1. Religious education of children. I. Title.

HARRIS, Jane Bowerman. 268.432
When we teach junior; a junior guidance manual. Philadelphia, Board of Christian Education of the Presbyterian Church in the United States of America [1957] 89p. illus. 23cm. [BV1546.H344] 57-7594
1. Religious education of children. I. Title.

HARRIS, Jane Bowerman. 268.432
When we teach juniors; a junior guidance manual. Philadelphia, Baord of Christian Education of the Presbyterian Church in the United States of America [1957] 80p. illus. 23cm. [BV1546.H344] 57-7594
1. Religious education of children. I. Title.

HARRIS, William J. 268.432
Our priceless primaries; making child teaching more child reaching for primary leaders and teachers. Mountain View, Calif., Pacific Press Pub. Association [c.1959] 195p. illus. (part col.) 24cm. 59-13496 4.00
1. Religious education of children. I. Title.

HAUGHTON, Rosemary. 207
Beginning life in Christ; Gospel bearings on Christian education. Westminster, Md., Newman Press [1966] 192 p. 21 cm. Bibliography: p. 191-192. [BV1475.2.H38] 66-8856
1. Religious education of children. I. Title.

HAYNES, Marjorie. 268.432
When we teach primary children; a primary guidance manual. Philadelphia, Board of Christian Education of the Presbyterian Church in the United States of America [1957] 78p. illus. 23cm. Includes bibliography. [BV1545.H35] 57-8931
1. Religious education of children. I. Title.

HILDER, Enid. 268
Children of the font, by Enid Hilder ... London and Oxford, A. R. Mowbray & co. limited; New York, Morehouse-Gorham co., [1943] 63 p. 18 1/2 cm. "First published in 1942; second impression, 1943." [BV1475.H46] 44-47472
1. Religious education of children. I. Title.

HILL, Dorothy La Croix. 268.432
Working with juniors at church. Henry M. Bullock, general editor. Nashville, Abingdon Press [c1955] 160p. 20cm. [BV1546.H5] 55-6764
1. Religious education of children. I. Title.

HILL, Dorothy LaCroix. 268.432
The church teaches nines to twelves. Illus. by Ann Doyle. New York, Published for the Cooperative Publication Association by Abingdon Press [1965] 192 p. illus. 19 cm. (The Cooperative series) Bibliography: p. 187-188. [BV1475.2.H5] 65-8476
1. Religious education of children. I. Title.

HILLIS, Newell Dwight, 1858- 220
The home school; a study of the debt parents owe their children, by Newell Dwight Hillis... New York, Chicago [etc.] Fleming H. Revell company, 1902. 3 p. l., 9-126 p. 19 cm. "With a list of great chapters of the Bible and the twenty classic hymns, for memorizing." [BR125.H655] 2-19895
I. Title.

HOBBS, Charles R. 268.6
Teaching with new techniques. Illus. by Dick and Mary Scopes, Charles R. Hobbs. Salt Lake City, Utah, Deseret [c.]1964. xiv, 256p. illus., music. 24cm. Bibl. 64-5049 3.75
1. Religious education of children. I. Title.

HOBBS, Charles R 268.6
Teaching with new techniques. Illus. by Dick and Mary Scopes [and] Charles R. Hobbs. Salt Lake City, Utah, Deseret Book Co., 1964. xiv, 256 p. illus., music. 24 cm. "Teaching methods chart" (fold. leaf) in pocket. Bibliography: p. [248]-249. [BV1534.H58] 64-5019
1. Religious education of children. I. Title.

HOYLE, Frances P.
The complete speaker and reciter for home, school, church and platform; recitations, readings, plays, drills, tableaux, etc. ... By Frances P. Hoyle ... [Philadelphia? cc1905] 7 p. l. 27-484 p. incl. illus., plates. col. front., plates (partly col.) 25 cm. Issued also under title: The world's speaker, reciter and entertainer. 5-35684
I. Title.

**I believe in God* 268.43
[5 bxd. kits] Minneapolis, Augsburg [c.1962, 1965] 5 kits (unpaged) 29cm. (Vacation church school ser.) Series: Vacation church school series. [1] Nursery activities.--[2] Kindergarten activities.--[3]

Primary activities.--[4] Junior activities.--[5] Intermediate activities. .95 box, ea.,
1. Religious education of children. I. Series.

JEWETT, Susan W. Mrs.
The parent's gift; consisting of a series of poems and essays, on natural, moral, and religious subjects, strictly adapted to young persons, to which is prefixed a juvenile address, designed to encourage habits of observation, and awaken the love of truth and virtue. By Susan Jewett. New York, R. Martin & co., 1843- v. plates. 15 cm. Issued in parts. [JZ10.7.J555P] ca 7
I. Title.

JOHNSON, Tom, 1923- 201'.1
No tall buildings in Nazareth; parent-child conversations on religion. Drawings by Dan Marshall. [1st ed.] New York, Harper & Row [1973] viii, 101 p. illus. 21 cm. [BV1475.2.J56] 72-160640 ISBN 0-06-064193-2 4.95
1. Religious education of children. I. Title.

JONES, Jessie Mae (Orton) 268
The spiritual education of our children. New York, Viking Press [1960] 124p. 21cm. Includes bibliography. [BV1475.2.J6] 60-7673
1. Religious education of children. I. Title.

JONES, Mary Alice, 1898- 268
Guiding children in Christian growth. C. A. Bowan, general editor. New York, Published for the Co-operative Pub. Association by Abingdon-Cokesbury Press [1949] 160 p. 19 cm. Bibliographies: p. 157-160. [BV1475.J533] 49-50011
1. Religious education of children. I. Title.

KLEIN, Ernst E
God, creator and sustainer. Illus. by Alex Stein. Teacher's book. Valley Forge, Penn., The Judson Press, 1964. 128 p. illus. "A Cooperative vacation church school course for use with junior boys and girls." 68-60069
1. Religious education of children. 2. Vacation schools, Religious. I. Title.

KOONTZ, Ida Matilda. 244
Junior department organization and administration, by Ida M. Koontz; a textbook in the standard course in teacher training outlined and approved by the Sunday school council of evangelical denominations. Third year specialization series. Dayton, O., Printed for the Teacher training publishing association by the Otterbein press [c1922] 128 p. 17 cm. [BV1546.K6] 22-15903
1. Religious education of children. I. Title.

LAZARETH, William Henry, 1928- 268.43
Helping children know doctrine [by] William H. Lazareth, Marjorie F. Garhart. Philadelphia. Fortress [1963, c.1962] 176p. illus. 22cm. (Leadership educa. ser.) 63-1180 1.50
1. Religious education of children. I. Garhart, Marjorie F. II. Title.

LAZARETH, William Henry, 1928- 268.43
Helping children know doctrine [by] William H. Lazareth and Marjorie F. Garhart. Philadelphia, Lutheran Church Press, c1962. 176 p. illus. 22 cm. (Leadership education series) [BV1545.L3] 63-1180
1. Religious education of children. I. Garhart, Marjorie F. II. Title.

LE BAR, Lois Emogene, 1907- 268.432
Children in the Bible school; the how of Christian education. Westwood, N. J., Revell [1952] 382 p. illus. 21 cm. Includes bibliography. [BV1475.L43] 52-9635
1. Religious education of children. I. Title.

LEE, Florence B. 268.432
Primary children in the church. Illus. by Louis Segal. Philadelphia, Pub. for the Cooperative Pubn. Assn. by Judson Pr. [c.1961] 160p. illus. (Cooperative ser.) 61-11996 3.00
1. Religious education of children. I. Title.

LEWIS, Hazel Asenath, 1886- 268.432
The primary church school Rev. ed. St. Louis, Published for the Cooperative Publication Association by the Bethany Press [1951] 149 p. 20 cm. [BV1545.L47 1951] 51-11140
1. Religious education of children. 2. Sunday-schools. I. Title.

LINTHICUM, Blanche. 268.432
Junior Sunday school work, by Blanche Linthicum. Nashville, Tenn., The Sunday school board of the Southern Baptist convention [1941] 3 p. l., 5-134 19 cm. [BV1546.L5] 42-1152
1. Religious education of children. I. Southern Baptist convention. Sunday school board. II. Title.

**LIVING in the church.* 268.432
Rev. teacher's manual replacing Discovering the holy fellowship. Illus. by Frank Giusto. New York, Seabury [c.1964] 216p. illus. 21cm. (Church's teaching in the 5th gr.) 2.10 pap.,

LYON, Bernice E
Jesus, the teacher; a co-operative vacation church school text for use with kindergarten children. Based upon Children learn from Jesus. Teacher's text. St. Louis, Published for the Co-operative Publication Association by Bethany Press [1963] 126 p. 23 cm. 65-90791
I. Title.

MCARDLE, Mildred J. 268.432
The primary superintendent's manual; objectives, organization, procedures, lesson course, materials, prepared by Mildred J. McArdle. St. Louis, Mo., Christian board of publication [1931] 199 p. 22 1/2 cm. [BV1545.M27] 43-20469
1. Religious education of children. I. Title.

MCDANIEL, Elsiebeth. 268'.432
You and children, by Elsiebeth McDaniel, with Lawrence O. Richards. Chicago, Moody Press [1973] 125 p. 22 cm. (Effective teaching series) Bibliography: p. 124-125. [BV1475.2.M33] 72-95032 ISBN 0-8024-9831-0 1.95
1. Religious education of children. I. Richards, Lawrence O., joint author. II. Title.

MCDONNELL, Lois Eddy 268
The home and church; partners in the Christian education of children. Nashville, Pub. for the Co-operative Pubn. Assn. by Abingdon [1961] 160p. illus. (Cooperative ser.: leadership training texts) Bibl. 62-16020 1.50 pap.,
1. Religious education of children. 2. Religious education—Home training. I. Title.

MERJANIAN, Pepronia. 268.88
The joy of teaching. Philadelphia, United Church Press [1966] 143 p. 20 cm. Bibliography: p. 136-143. [BV1475.2.M45] 66-23991
1. Religious education of children. I. Title.

MERLAUD, Andre. 268'.4
Children and adolescents, our teachers. Translated by Theodore DuBois. Paramus, N.J. [Paulist Press, 1969] vii, 101 p. 19 cm. (Paulist Press Deus books) Translation of Enfants et adolescents, nos maitres. Bibliographical footnotes. [BV1475.2.M5613] 77-92043 1.25
1. Religious education of children. I. Title.

METHODS of teaching religion to children; for parents and teachers. [Rev. ed.] New York, The Macmillan Company 1956. x, 184p. 18cm.
1. Religious education of children. I. Clark, Marjocie Elizabeth Alice.

METHODS of teaching religion to children for parents and teachers. [Rev. ed.] New York, The Macmillan Company 1956. x, 184p. 18cm.
1. Religious education of children. I. Clark, Marjorie Elizabeth Alice.

MEYER, Fulgence. 262.
Jesus and his pets; mission and retreat talks to children, by Rev. Fulgence Meyer ... Cincinnati, O., St. Anthony monastery, 1925. 4 p. l., [7]-118 p. front. 17 cm. [BX2375.M4] 26-2583
I. Title.

MINARD, Herbert Leslie, 1908- 268.433
A manual for leaders of intermediates ... [By] Herbert L. Minard ... [and] Glenn McRae ... St. Louis, Mo., Christian board of publication [1941] 125, [3] p. illus. 19 cm. "Based upon the outlines produced in cooperation with the Young people's section of the Curriculum committee of the United Christian missionary society."--p. 4. "Revised." Includes bibliographies. [BV1548.M5 1941] 43-19469
1. Religious education of children. I. McRae, Glenn, 1887- joint author. II. United Christian missionary society. Dept. of religious education. Curriculum committee. III. Title.

MOLAN, Dorothy Lennon. 268.432
Teaching middlers. Valley Forge, Judson Press [1963] 94 p. illus. 22 cm. [BV1546.M6] 63-9447
1. Religious education of children. I. Title.

MORNINGSTAR, Mildred (Whaley) 268.6
Reaching children, by Mildred Morningstar. Chicago, Ill., Moody press [1944] 176 p. 20 cm. [BV1475.M58] 45-1997
1. Religious education of children. I. Title.

MOW, Anna B 268
Your child from birth to rebirth; how to educate a child to be ready for life with God, a book for parents and teachers. Grand Rapids, Zondervan Pub. House [1963] 152 p. 23 cm. Bibliography: p. 150-152. [BV1475.2.M6] 63-17741
1. Religious education of children. I. Title.

MOW, Anna B. 268
Your child from birth to rebirth; how to educate your child to be ready for a life with God. Grand Rapids, Mich., Zondervan [1972, c.1963] 186 p. 18 cm. Bibliography: p. 183-186. [BV1475.2.M6] 63-17741 pap., 0.95
1. Religious education of children. I. Title.

MUNSON, Helen.
The way of love; a course for first and second grades. Illus. by Susan R. Phelps. Boston, United Church Press [c1964] 75 p. illus., music. 26 cm. (United Church curriculum. Primary [Teachers. 23]) "References:" p. 73. 67-6869
1. Religious education of children. 2. United Church of Christ — Education. I. Title.

NARRAMORE, Clyde Maurice, 1916- 268.432
How to understand and influence children, ages five, six, seven, and eight. Illus. by by Sam Pollach. Grand Rapids, Zondervan Pub. House [1957] 93p. illus. 21cm. [BV1475.N3] 57-3369
1. Religious education of children. I. Title.

O'DOHERTY, Eamonn Feichin. 200'.7
The religious formation of the elementary school child [by] E. F. O'Doherty. New York, Alba House [1973] viii, 151 p. 22 cm. [BV1475.2.O33] 72-11911 ISBN 0-8189-0261-2 3.95
1. Religious education of children. I. Title.

O'SHAUGHNESSY, Mary Michael 377.82
The child and the Christian mystery; essays on the philosophy of elementary school religious education, by Mary Michael O'Shaughnessy, Gerard P. Weber, James J. Killgallon. New York, Benziger Bros., 1965. ix, 243p. illus. 21cm. [BX926.O8] 65-21766 2.75
1. Religious education of childern. I. Weber, Gerard P., 1918- II. Killgallon, James J., 1914- III. Title.

PECK, Kathryn (Blackburn) 1904- 268.432
Better primary teaching. Kansas City, Mo., Beacon Hill Press [1957] 128p. illus. 19cm. 'Text for first series unit 242a, 'Planning for primary children.'' Includes bibliography. [BV1545.P39] 57-3560
1. Religious education of children. I. Title.

PHILLIPS, Ethel M 1916- 268.432
So you work with primaries. Anderson, Ind., Warner Press [1960] 64p. 21cm. [BV1545.P5] 60-13192
1. Religious education of children. I. Title.

*PRIESTER, Gertrude 268.432
Teaching primary children in the church. Philadelphia, Geneva Pr. [dist.] Westminster [c.1964] 96p. 23cm. Bibl. 1.25 pap.,
I. Title.

PRIESTER, Gertrude Ann.
People who knew God. A coursebook for the third and fourth grades. Illus. by Susan R. Phelps. Boston, United Church Press [c1964] 124 p. illus., music. 26 cm. (United Church curriculum. Lower Junior. Teachers. 21]) 65-94126
1. Religious education of children. 2. United Church of Christ—Education. I. Title. II. Series.

PRIESTER, Gertrude Ann.
Teaching primary children in the church. Philadelphia, Geneva Pres [1964] 96 p. 23 cm. Bibliography: p. 93-96. 65-94013
1. Religious education of children. I. Title.

PROTESTANT Episcopal Church in the U. S. A. National Council. Dept. of Christian Education. 268.432
Apostles in the home; a manual for use with classes of parents and godparents, with special reference to church school grades 2, 5, and 8, and kindergarten (five-year-olds) Illustrated by Maurice Rawson. Greenwich, Conn., Seabury Press [1956] 179p. illus. 21cm. (The Seabury series, P-11) [BV1475.P7] 56-7856
1. Religious education of children. 2. Religious education—Home training. I. Title.

PROTESTANT Episcopal Church in the U. S. A. National Council. Dept. of Christian Education. 268.432
Deciding for myself; teacher's manual, grade 6. Illustrated by Susan Perl. Greenwich, Conn., Seabury Press [1957] 181p. illus. 21cm. (The Seabury series, T-6) Includes bibliography. [BV1546.P68] 57-8344
1. Religious education of children. I. Title.

PROTESTANT Episcopal Church in the U. S. A. National Council. Dept. of Christian Education. 268.432
God's world and mine, revised teacher's manual, grade 2. Prepared at the direction of General Convention. Greenwich, Conn., Seabury Press [1960] 121p. illus. 28cm. (The Seabury series, T-2B) First published in 1956 under title: My place in God's world. Includes bibliography. [BV1545.P699 1960] 60-2707
1. Religious education of children. I. Title.

PROTESTANT Episcopal Church in the U. S. A. National Council. Dept. of Christian Education. 268.432
The goodly company; teacher's manual, grade 5. Illustrated by William Sharp. Greenwich, Conn., Seabury Press [1956] 182p. illus. 21cm. (The Seabury series, T-5) [BV1546.P69] 56-7854
1. Religious education of children. 2. Protestant Episcopal Church in the U. S. A.—Education. I. Title.

PROTESTANT Episcopal Church in the U. S. A. National Council. Dept. of Christian Education. 268.432
My place in God's world; teacher's manual, grade 2. Illustrated by Mary Stevens. Greenwich, Conn., Seabury Press [1956] 87p. illus. 28cm. (The Seabury series, T-2) [BV1545.P699] 56-7853
1. Religious education of children. I. Title.

PROTESTANT Episcopal Church in the U. S. A. National Council. Dept. of Christian Education. 268.61
Right or wrong? Teacher's manual, grade 4. Rev. ed. Illus. by Gregor Thompson Goethals. Greenwich, Conn., Seabury Press [1958] 157p. illus. 21cm. (The Seabury series, T-4B) Includes bibliographies. [BV1546.P7 1958] 268.432 58-9261
1. Religious education of children. I. Title.

PROTESTANT Episcopal Church in the U. S. A. National Council. Dept. of Christian Education. 268.432
Throughout the whole wide earth: teacher's manual, grade 3. Illustrated by Beatrice and Leonard Derwinski. Greenwich, Conn., Seabury Press [1957] 83p. illus. 28cm. (The Seabury series, T-3) [BV1545.P6993] 57-8342
1. Religious education of children. I. Title.

PROTESTANT Episcopal Church in the U. S. A. National Council. Dept. of Christian Education. 268.432
Wonder and faith in the first grade; revised teacher's manual, grade 1. Illustrated by Randolph Chitwood. Greenwich, Conn., Seabury Press [1958] 89p. illus. 28cm.

(The Seabury series, T-1B) Includes bibliography. [BV1545.P6995 1958] 58-9259
1. Religious education of children. I. Title.

PROTESTANT Episcopal Church in the U.S.A. National Council. Dept. of Christian Education.
Keeping the covenant. New York. Seabury Press [1963] vii, 200 p. 21 cm. (The Church's teaching, T-4C) "Revised teacher's manual replacing Right or wrong." 65-66467
1. Religious education of children. I. Title. II. Series.

PROTESTANT Episcopal Church in the U.S.A. National Council. Dept. of Christian Education.
Sons and heirs. Illustrated by Maurice Rawson. Greenwich, Conn., Seabury Press [c1962] 222 p. The Seabury series, T-6B) "Revised teacher's manual replacing Deciding for Myself." 65-66509
1. Religious education of children. I. Title.

REED, William Wellington, 1912- 268
Teaching the church's children; a handbook for teachers and parents. New York, Morehouse-Gorham Co., 1958. 183p. 21cm. Includes bibliography. [BV1475.R4] 58-6842
1. Religious education of children. I. Title.

RICE, Lillian (Moore) 268.433
Better Bible teaching for juniors in the Sunday school. Nashville, Broadman Press [1952] 143 p. illus. 20 cm. [BV1546.R48] 52-13859
1. Religious education of children. 2. Bible — Study. 3. Sunday-schools. I. Title.

RICE, Lillian (Moore) 268.432
How to work with juniors in the Sunday school. Nashville, Convention Press [1956] 143p. 19cm. [BV1546.R485] 56-42688
1. Religious education of children. I. Title.

RITTENHOUSE, Laurence.
Understanding ourselves; a course for the third and fourth grades. Photos. by Ronald Binks, Sheldon Brody, Peter Schlaifer [and] Kenneth Thompson. Illus. by Oliver Balf. Boston, United Church Press [c1963] 128 p. illus. 26 cm. (United Church curriculum. Lower junior. Teachers. 1) "Resource: p. 125-126. 66-10772
1. Religious education of children. 2. United Church of Christ — Education. I. Title. II. Series.

*RUDOLPH, Mary Baine 268.432
The church teaching children grades one through six. [dist.] Richmond, Va. [Knox, CLC Pr. c.1964] 104p. 28cm. (Covenant life curriculum) 2.00 pap.,
I. Title.

RUDOLPH, Mary Baine.
The Church teaching children grades one through six. Richmond, CLC Press, 1964. 101 p. (The Covenant life curriculum) 67-61026
1. Religious education of children. I. Title.

SANDT, Eleanor E., comp. 268'.8'3
Variations on the Sunday church school, edited by Eleanor E. Sandt. New York, Seabury Press [1967] 89 p. illus. 24 cm. Consists chiefly of articles adapted from the magazine Christian education findings. [BV1475.2.S25] 68-1300
1. Religious education of children. 2. Sunday-schools. I. Christian education findings. II. Title.

SHARP, Margaret. 268.432
A church training juniors. Nashville, Convention Press [1966] xiv, 145 p. 20 cm. "Church study course [of the Sunday School Board of the Southern Baptist Convention] This book is number 1816 in category 18, section for adults and young people." [BV1547.S5] 66-13317
1. Religious education of children. I. Southern Baptist Convention. Sunday School Board. II. Title.

SHERRILL, Lewis Joseph, 1892- 268.6
The opening doors of childhood [by] Lewis Joseph Sherrill ... New York, The Macmillan company, 1939. xi p., 1 l., 198 p. 20 1/2 cm. "First printing." "Books which might be of interest": p. 191-198. [BV1475.S56] 39-23875
1. Religious education of children. I. Title.

SMITH, Clarence T. 268'.432
Ways to plan & organize your Sunday school: children, grades 1 to 6 [by] Charles T. Smith. Glendale, Calif., International Center for Learning [1973, c1971] 127 p. illus. 20 cm. (ICL teacher's/leader's success handbook) (An ICL insight book) Bibliography: p. 125-127. [BV1475.2.S63] 71-168839 ISBN 0-8307-0123-0 1.95
1. Religious education of children. I. Title.

SMITHER, Ethel Lisle. 268.432
Primary children learn at church [by] Ethel L. Smither. New York, Nashville, Printed for the Leadership training publishing association by Abingdon-Cokesbury press [1944] 170 p. 19 1/2 cm. "For further study" at end of each chapter. Replaces the author's Teaching primaries in the church school. cf. p. 8. [BV1545.S58] 44-8719
1. Religious education of children. I. Smither, Ethel Lisle. Teaching primaries in the church school. II. Title.

SMITHER, Ethel Lisle. 268.6
Teaching primaries in the church school [by] Ethel L. Smither, a textbook in the Standard course in leadership training, outlined and approved by the International council of religious education. [Dobbs Ferry, N. Y.] Printed for the Leadership training publishing association by the Methodist book concern [c1930] 251 p. 20 cm. "A reference library for the primary teacher": p. 249-251. Bibliography at end of each chapter. [BV1545.S6] 31-89
1. Religious education of children. 2. Religious education—Teacher training. 3. Sunday-schools. I. International council of religious education. II. Title.

SPRAGUE, Ruth L
Junior manual for those who plan for and work with junior-age boys and girls in the church. Boston, United Church Press [c1963] 64 p. illus. 26 cm. (United Church curriculum. Junior. Administrator) Bibliography: p. 60-61. 66-57366
1. Religious education — children. 2. United Church of Christ — Education. I. Title. II. Series.

STEELE, Eileen Aultman. 268'.6
In behalf of children: a guide to challenge the bit of God in us. Philadelphia, Dorrance [1974] 85 p. 22 cm. [BV1475.2.S77] 73-87873 ISBN 0-8059-1948-1 4.95
1. Religious education of children. I. Title.

SUMMERS, Jester. 268.432
God loves everybody; leadership material. A unit to use with primary children. Nashville, Convention Press [1963] 84 p. illus. 19 cm. Hymns, with music (p. 77-84) [BV1545] 63-8380
1. Religious education of children. I. Title.

SWEET, Helen (Firman) Mrs. 268.
Exploring religion with eight year olds, by Helen Firman Sweet and Sophia Lyon Fahs; illustrations by Dorothy Harewood Smedley. New York, H. Holt and company [c1930] xvi, 288 p. illus., plates. 19 1/2 cm. Bibliography: p. 280-288. [BV1545.S87] 30-7210
1. Religious education of children. 2. Sunday-schools. I. Fahs, Mrs. Sophia Blanche (Lyon) joint author, 1876- II. Title.

TAYLOR, Margaret Fisk 268.6
Time for discovery. Illus. by Ruth Baldwin. Philadelphia, United Church [1964] 76p. illus. 28cm. Includes hymns, with music. Bibl. 64-24444 3.25, pap., plastic bdg.
1. Religious education of children. 2. Dancing (in religion, folklore, etc.) I. Title.

TRENT, Robbie, 1894- 268.432
A year of junior programs. Nashville, Broadman Press [1950] ix, 201 p. illus., music. 21 cm. [BV1546.T75] 50-12072
1. Religious education of children. 2. Worship (Religious education) I. Title.

WELKER, Edith Frances. 268.432
Friends with all the world; illustrated by Janet Smalley. New York, Friendship Press [1954] 167p. illus. 22cm. [BV1475.W44] 54-6188
1. Religious education of children. I. Title.

WESTON, Sidney A. 268.433
Jesus' teachings for young people: a discussion unit for high school ages and young adults. [rev. ed.] Boston, Whittemore [c.]1962. 93p. 19cm. .75 pap.,
I. Title.

*WHITE, Marian 268.432
Through the Bible with finger plays. Illus. by Robert Winter. Grand Rapids, Mich., Baker Bk. [c.]1965. 60p. illus. 22cm. 1.00 pap.,
I. Title.

WHITEHOUSE, Elizabeth Scott, 1893- 268
The children we teach. [1st ed.] Philadelphia, Judson Press [1950] 304 p. 21 cm. Includes bibliographies. [BV1475.W47] 50-9200
1. Religious education of children. I. Title.

WHITLEY, Mary Theodora, 1878-
A study of the primary child for primary teachers, by Mary Theodora Whitley; a textbook in the Standard course in teacher training, outlined and approved by the Sunday school council of evangelical denominations, Third year specialization series. Philadelphia, Printed for the Teachers training publishing association by the Westminister press [c1922] 114 p. 17 cm. "A good reference bibliography": p. 114. [BV1545.W45] 23-11367
1. Religious education of children. 2. Child study. 3. Educational psychology. I. Sunday school council of evangelical denominations. II. Title.

WILLIAMS, Jessie (Tandy) 1876-1948. 268.432
The junior workers' manual, including helps for Bible study, worship themes, projects, special selections for junior workers in Sunday school, worship services, vacation Bible schools, week-day religious schools [and] the home circle. Butler, Ind., Higley Press [1950] 160 p. 20 cm. [BV1546.W52] 50-13813
1. Religious education of children. Full name: Jessie Martha (Tandy) Williams Earhart. I. Title.

WILSON, Lewis Gilbert, 1858- 248
The little red wonder book a first book of religion for little children, by Lewis Gilbert Wilson. Pictures by Clara E. Atwood. Boston, The Beacon press [c1917] 61 p. incl., front., illus. 16 cm. $0.50. [BV4571.W5] 18-2728
I. Title.

A year of junior programs and activities. Drawings by Adalin Wichman. Cincinnati, Standard Publishing Foundation [1956] 176p. illus. 28cm.
1. Religious education of children. I. Buerger, Jane.

A year of junior programs and activities. Drawings by Adalin Wichman. Cincinnati, Standard Publishing Foundation [1956] 176p. illus. 28cm.
1. Religious education of children. I. Buerger, Jane.

YOUNG, Helen.
Sunday school work with four's and five's. Nashville, Tennessee, Covention Press [1962] 147 p. 68-53925
1. Religious education of children. 2. Religious education—Teacher training. 3. Sunday schools. I. Title.

ZINK, Heidi. 649'.7
Will my dog go to heaven? How to answer your child's religious questions [by] Heidi and Jorg Zink. Translated by William Oyler. Minneapolis, Augsburg Pub. House [1973] 175 p. illus. 20 cm. Translation of Kriegt ein Hund im Himmel Flugel? [BV1475.2.Z5613] 72-90267 ISBN 0-8066-1315-7 3.50 (pbk.)
1. Religious education of children. I. Zink, Jorg, joint author. II. Title.

ZINK, Heidi. 649'.7
Will my dog go to heaven? How to answer your child's religious questions [by] Heidi and Jorg Zink. Translated by William Oyler. Notre Dame, Ind., Fides Publishers [1973, c.1972] 175 p. illus. 20 cm. Translation of Kriegt ein Hund im Himmel Flugel? [BV1475.2.Z5613] 3.50 (pbk)
1. Religious education of children. I. Zink, Jorg, joint author. II. Title.
L.C. card no. for Augsburg Pub. House edition: 72-90267

Religious education of children—Bruderhof Communities.

BRUDERHOF Communities. 268
Children in community. [By the Society of Brothers. Photography & art editor Roswith Arnold. New York, Plough Pub. House, 1963] 103 p. 25 cm. [BX8129.B62A4] 63-19099
1. Religious education of children — Bruderhof Communities. 2. Children — Religious life. I. Title.

Religious education of children, Buddhist.

FUJIMOTO, Hogen.
A guide to better teaching in the Buddhist Sunday school. San Francisco, Buddhist Churches of America, Sunday School Dept. 1961. 115 p. 22 cm. Includes bibliography. [BL1418.F8] 63-5950
1. Religious education of children, Buddhist. I. Title. II. Title: Better teaching in the Buddhist Sunday school.

Religious education of children, Islamic.

UNION of Muslim Organisations of United Kingdom and Eire. 297.7
Guidelines and syllabus on Islamic education / [Union of Muslim Organisations of United Kingdom and Ireland]. London : The Union, 1976. 28 p. ; 22 cm. [BP44.U54 1976] 76-372771 ISBN 0-9504335-1-9
1. Religious education of children, Islamic. I. Title.

Religious education of children, Jewish.

CHANOVER, Hyman.
Teaching the Haggadah. [New York] Jewish Education Committee [c1964] 135 p. 25 cm. Each chapter includes "Aids and resources" listing filmstrips, slides, and recordings. "Selected resources": p. 124-132. 67-80347
1. Religious education of children, Jewish. 2. Jews. Liturgy and ritual. Hagadah. I. Jewish Education Committee of New York. II. Title.

Religious education of children, Jewish—Curricula.

SKOLNICK, Irving H. 377'.9'6
A guide to curriculum construction for the religious school, by Irving H. Skolnick. Chicago, College of Jewish Studies Press [1969] vii, 143 p. 25 cm. Includes bibliographical references. [BM103.S56] 74-106196
1. Religious education of children, Jewish—Curricula. I. Title.

Religious education of children—Lutheran

*BORAAS, Roger S. 268.432
A letter from Paul. Philip R. Hoh, ed. Karl Wurzer, ed. Philadelphia, Lutheran Church Pr. [c.1965] 102p. illus. 21cm. (LCA Sunday Church sch. ser.) With a teacher's guide. pap., 1.00; teacher's guide, pap., 1.25
1. Religious education of children—Lutheran I. Title.

MULLINS, Beverly Schultz 268.432
Why Jesus came, by Beverly Schultz Mullins. Bonny Vaught. Illus. by Isa Barnett. Gustav K. Wiencke, ed. Philadelphia, Lutheran Church Pr. [c.1966] 126p. illus. (pt. col.) 21cm. 1.25
1. Religious education of children—Lutheran Church. I. Title.

SMITH, Arthur Harms, 1867-
...The Lutheran church and child-nurture, by Arthur H. Smith, D.D. Philadelphia, Pa., The Lutheran publication society [c1911] vi p., 1 l., 9-135 p. 19 1/2 cm. (Lutheran teacher-training series for the Sunday school...book 4) $0.50 12-34
I. Title.

Religious education of children—Occupations and busy work.

KEISER, Armilda Brome. 268.6
Here's how and when; illustrated by Janet Smalley. New York, Friendship Press [1952] 174 p. illus. 22 cm. [BV1536.K4] 52-7624
1. Religious education of children—Occupations and busy work. I. Title.

LOBINGIER, Elizabeth Erwin 268.68 (Miller) 1889-
Activities in child education for the church school teacher. With drawings by children. Boston, Pilgrim Press [1950] xiv, 226 p. illus. 23 cm. Bibliography: p. 221-224. [BV1535.L55] 50-79466
1. Religious education of children—Occupations and busy work. I. Title.

Religious education of children—Presbyterian.

*LUCKHARDT, Mildred Corell 268.85
The church at work and worship; teacher's book. Philadelphia, pub. for the Cooperative Pubn. Assn. by Westminster [c.1965] 111p. 23cm. (Coop. ser., Vacation church sch. texts) A vacation church sch. course for junior groups. Accompanied by Pupil's book, and Activity sheets. pap., 1.25; pupil's bk., pap., .35; activity sheets, .45 per packet.
1. Religious education of children—Presbyterian. I. Title.

Religious education of exceptional children.

NEFF, Herbert B. 268'.432
Meaningful religious experiences for the bright or gifted child [by] Herbert B. Neff. New York, Association Press [1968] 160 p. 21 cm. Bibliography: p. 158-160. [BV1475.2.N4] 68-17777
1. Religious education of exceptional children. I. Title.

Religious education of girls.

REORGANIZED Church of Jesus 268 of Latter Day Saints. Children's Division
Skylark ways; a handbook for Skylark Girls. Independence, Mo., Herald Pub., c.1966. 72p. illus. 28cm. [BX8671.A549] 66-17863 1.95 pap.,
1. Religious education of girls. I. Title.

Religious education of mentally handicapped.

JOHNSON, Jerry Don.
Learning to know God; a resource book for use with retarded persons, by Jerry Don Johnson and Martha Jones. St. Louis, Bethany Press [1966] 128 p. illus. 67-42486
1. Religious education of mentally handicapped. I. Jones, Martha, joint author. II. Title.

Religious education of mentally handicapped children.

BOGARDUS, LaDonna 268.6
Christian education for retarded children and youth. Illus. by Pat Roper. Nashville Pub. for the Cooperative Pubn. Assn. by Abingdon, [c.1963] 108p. illus. 19cm. (Cooperative ser.: Leadership training texts) Bibl. 63-23612 1.25 pap.,
1. Religious education of mentally handicapped children. I. Title.

BOGARDUS, LaDonna. 268.6
Christian education for retarded children and youth. Illus. by Pat Roper. New York, Published for the Cooperative Publication Association by Abingdon Press [c1963] 108 p. illus. 19 cm. (The Cooperative series: Leadership training texts) Bibliography: p. 105-108. [BV1615.M4B6] 63-23612
1. Religious education of mentally handicapped children. I. Title.

Religious education of pre-school children.

ADAIR, Thelma C. 268.432
When we teach 4's & 5's, by Thelma C. Adair, Rachel S. Adams. Philadelphia, Geneva Pr. [dist. Westminster, 1963, c.1962] 96p. illus. 23cm. 63-598 1.25 pap.,
1. Religious education of pre-school children. I. Adams, Rachel Swann, joint author. II. Title.

ANDERSON, Phoebe M 268.432
Religious living with nursery children in church and home. Boston, Published for the Co-operative Publication Association [by] Pilgrim Press [1956] 179p. 20cm. [BV1540.A62] 56-9758
1. Religious education of pre-school children. I. Title.

ANDERSON, Phoebe M 268.432
3's in the Christian community; a course for the church school nursery. Photos. by Sheldon Brody. Illustrated by Lawrence Scott. Boston, United Church Press [c1960] 320 p. illus. (part col.) 26 cm. Includes music. Bibliography: p. 294-295. [BV1475.7.A5] 60-5690
1. Religious education of pre-school children. I. Title.

ARNOTE, Thelma. 268.432
Understanding nursery children. Nashville, Convention Press [1963] viii, 103 p. illus. 19 cm. "Church study course [of the Sunday School Board of the Southern Baptist Convention] This book is number 1505 in category 15, section for adults and young people." Bibliography: p. 96-99. [BV1475.7.A7] 63-13396
1. Religious education of pre-school children. I. Southern Baptist Convention. Sunday School Board. II. Title.

BAKER, Cosette. 268'.432
God's outdoors; a unit for use with nursery children in the church study course. [Nashville, Convention Press, 1968] x, 78 p. illus. 19 cm. Includes melodies with words. [BV1475.7.B3] 68-11675
1. Religious education of preschool children. I. Title.

BARTLETT, Margaret J
Training for service in the preschool department, by Margaret Bartlett. Cincinnati, Standard Pub. [c1964] 112 p. illus., charts, diagr. (Training for service) "To read" at end of each chapter. NUC66
1. Religious education of pre-school children. I. Title. II. Series.

BLANKINSHIP, Carribel. 268.432
Programs and plans for the Cradle Roll department. Nashville, Sunday School Board of the Southern Baptist Convention [1954] 51p. illus. 26 cm. [BV1537.B55] 55-18043
1. Religious education of pre-school children. 2. Sunday-schools. I. Title.

BRECK, Flora Elizabeth, 268.432 1886-
Success with beginners [by] Flora E. Breck. Cincinnati, O., The Standard publishing company [c1939] 163 p. 1 illus. 19 cm. [BV1540.B7] 39-23630
1. Religious education of pre-school children. I. Title.

CARLSON, Jessie B 268.432
Guiding children in the nursery class. Philadelphia, Judson Press [1948] 111 p. 20 cm. "For further reading and study": p. 110-111. [BV1540.C3] 48-2916
1. Religious education of pre-school children. I. Title.

CARLSON, Jessie B 268.432
The nursery department of the church. St. Louis, Bethany Press [1958] 128p. illus. 20cm. Includes bibliography. [BV1540.C315] 58-14386
1. Religious education of pre-school children. I. Title.

CARLSON, Jessie B 268.432
Teaching nursery children. Philadelphia, Judson Press [c1957] 112p. illus. 20cm. Includes bibliography. [BV1540.C32] 58-1134
1. Religious education of pre-school children. I. Title.

CARLSON, Jessie B. 268.432
Toddlers at church. Illus. by Dorothy Grider. St. Louis, Bethany [c.1961] 80p. illus. Bibl. 61-11104 1.00 pap.,
1. Religious education of pre-school children. I. Title.

CHRISTIAN *nurture for the nursery school child* by Maggie May Burrow and Mary Edna Lloyd. Nashville, Graded Press [1959] 240p. illus. 23cm. Teacher's textbook for use with three-year-old children.
1. Religious education of pre-school children. I. Burrow, Maggie May. II. Lloyd, Mary Edna, joint author. III. Series: Methodist Church (U.S.) Board of Education. [Closely graded material]

DES MARAIS, Louise M.
For goodness sake; the virtues of the preschool child. Paterson, N.J., Confraternity Publications [1966] vii, 119 p. 23 cm. Contains bibliographies. 67-93082
1. Religious education of pre-school children. I. Confraternity of Christian Doctrine. II. Title.

DREW, Louise C 268.432
Nursery manual; a manual for administrators in the church school nursery department, by Louise C. Drew. Photos. by Sheldon Brody. Illustrated by Walter Lorraine. Boston, United Church Press [c1960] 63 p. illus. 26 cm. "One of a series of administrative manuals for use with the United Church Curriculum." Bibliography: p. 61-62. [BV1475.7.D7] 6010301
1. Religious education of pre-school children. I. Title.

DREW, Louise C. 268'.432
Nursery manual; a manual for administrators in the church school nursery department, by Louise C. Drew. Photos. by Sheldon Brody. Illustrated by Walter Lorraine. [Rev. ed.] Boston, United Church Press [1969] 63 p. illus. 26 cm. Bibliography: p. 60-62. [BV1539.D7 1969] 68-10417
1. Religious education of pre-school children. I. Title.

FENNER, Mabel B. 268.432
Guiding the nursery class; edited by Theodore K. Finck. Philadelphia, Muhlenberg Press [1950] viii, 248 p. illus. 20 cm. Includes music. Bibliography: p. 244-245. [BV1540.F38] 50-9483
1. Religious education of pre-school children. 2. Sunday-Schools. I. Title.

FRITZ, Dorothy Bertolet.
Christian teaching of kindergarten children. Richmon, CLC Press [1964] 96 p. illus. 28 cm. (The Covenant life curriculum. Kindergarten [Administrators and Teacher]) "Books for additional reading": p. 91-93. 65-77689
1. Religious education of pre-school children. 2. Presbyterian Church — Education. 3. Reformed churches — Education. 4. Moravian Church — Education. I. Title. II. Series.

FRITZ, Dorothy Bertolet.
Christian teaching of kindergarten children. Richmon, CLC Press [1964] 96 p. illus. 28 cm. (The Covenant life curriculum. Kindergarten [Administrators and Teacher]) "Books for additional reading": p. 91-93. 65-77689
1. Religious education of pre-school children. 2. Presbyterian Church — Education. 3. Reformed churches — Education. 4. Moravian Church — Education. I. Title. II. Series.

GALE, Elizabeth Wright 268.432
Have you tried this? Activities for preschool groups at church. Photos. by M. Edward Clark. Philadelphia, Judson Press [c.1960] 64p. illus. 28cm. 60-4518 pap., apply
1. Religious education of pre-school children. I. Title.

GARDNER, Elizabeth. 268.432
Teaching kindergarten children. Philadelphia, Judson Press [1949] 94 p. 20 cm. "Helpful books and pamphlets": p. 93-94. [BV1540.G3] 50-713
1. Religious education of pre-school children. I. Title.

GARDNER, Elizabeth.
Teaching plans for 3's. Philadelphia, Geneva Press [1962] 127 p. illus. 20 x 28 cm. [Christian faith and life; a program for church and home, Nursery. Teachers] 64-26505
1. Religious education of pre-school children. I. Title. II. Series.

GARDNER, Elizabeth. 268.432
The 2's at church; teaching material for the year for use with two-year-olds Philadelphia, Judson Press [1953] 132p. illus. 23cm. (Judson graded series. Judson nursery series) [BV1540.G33] 53-3853
1. Religious education of pre-school children. I. Title.

HARGIS, Pauline. 268.432
Teaching the beginner child [by] Pauline Hargis and others. Nashville, Sunday School Board of the Southern Baptist Convention [1948] 128 p. illus. 19 cm. [BV1540.H27] 48-7638
1. Religious education of pre-school children. I. Title.

HAXTON, Jennie Norman. 268.432
The two-year-old at home; a quarterly guide for parents of two-year-olds. Parents' manual. Nashville, The Graded Press ['1950- v. illus. 23 cm. "Closely graded courses." Bibliography: v. 1, p. 46. [BV1540.H33] 51-3349
1. Religious education of pre-school children. I. Title.

HAXTON, Jennie Norman. 268.432
When the two-year-old comes to church; a teachers' guide for use in church schools where two-Year-olds meet in separate groups. C. A. Bowen, general editor. Nashville. Graded Press ['1950] 128 p. illus. 20 cm. "Listening music [for piano]": p. 127. "Closely graded courses." Bibliography: p. 128. [BV1540.H34] 51-3350
1. Religious education of pre-school children. I. Title.

HAYSTEAD, Wesley. 268'.432
Ways to plan & organize your Sunday school: early childhood, birth to 5 yrs. Glendale, Calif., International Center for Learning [1973, c1971] 127 p. illus. 20 cm. (ICL teacher's/leader's success handbook) (An ICL insight book) Bibliography: p. 127. [BV1475.8.H38] 78-168838 ISBN 0-8307-0122-2 1.95 (pbk.)
1. Religious education of preschool children. I. Title.

HAYSTEAD, Wesley. 649'.7
You can't begin too soon. Glendale, Calif., International Center for Learning [1974] 130 p. illus. 20 cm. Bibliography: p. 129-130. [BV1475.8.H383] 74-176193 ISBN 0-8307-0281-4 2.25 (pbk.)
1. Religious education of preschool children. 2. Children—Religious life. I. Title.
Available from Regal Books.

HEATON, Ada Beth, 1918- 268.432
The 3's at church; teaching material for the year for use with three-year olds in the church school. With methods sections by Helen Cann Rounds. Philadelphia, Judson Press [1953] 296p. illus. 23cm. (Judson graded series, Judson nursery series) [BV1540.H4] 53-3852
1. Religious education of pre-school children. I. Title.

HEMPHILL, Martha Locke. 268'.432
Weekday ministry with young children. Valley Forge [Pa.] Judson Press [1973] 95 p. music. 22 cm. Includes bibliographies. [BV1475.7.H45] 72-7594 ISBN 0-8170-0573-0 2.50
1. Religious education of preschool children. I. Title.

HERON, Frances Dunlap. 268.432
Kathy Ann, kindergartner. Illustrated by Janet Smalley. New York, Abingdon Press [1955] 128 p. illus. 20 cm. [BV1540.H45] 55-6763
1. Religious education of pre-school children. I. Title.

HILLS, Hannah Brummitt. 268.432
The cradle roll department visitor. Nashville, Convention Press [c1959] 137p. 20cm. Includes bibliography. [BV1537.H5] 59-14358
1. Religious education of pre-school

children. 2. Visitations (Church work) 3. Sunday-schools. I. Title.

HUNTER, Elizabeth M. 268.432
Learning to live with others; a course for the church school kindergarten. Photos. by Sheldon Brody. Philadelphia, United Church [c.1962] 64p. illus. 23cm. Bibl. 62-7222 .75 pap.,
1. Religious education of pre-school children. I. Title.

JONES, Elizabeth Norton. 268.432
Nursery children and our church; nursery superintendent's book. Philadelphia, Judson Press [1955] 96p. illus. 23cm. (Judson nursery series) 'An official publication of the Board of Education and Publication of the American Baptist Convention.' [BV1540.J56] 56-4677
1. Religious education of pre-school children I. Title.

KEYSER, Wilma (Sudhoff) 268.432
Mrs., 1904-
Planning for nursery children, by Wilma Sudhoff Keyser. Philadelphia, Boston [etc.] The Judson press [1939] 95 p. 19 1/2 cm. "Published January, 1939." [Full name:Mrs. Wilma Jane]Sudhoff: Keyser] Bibliography at end of each chapter. [BV1540.K45] 39-17792
1. Religious education of pre-school children. I. Title.

KLEIN, Sarah Guss, 1911- 268.432
When they are three; nursery children in the church and home, by Sara G. Klein and Elizabeth C. Gardner. Illustrated by Jacqueline C. Stone. Philadelphia, Westminster Press [c1956] 255p. illus. 24cm. [BV1540.K57] 56-11766
1. Religious education of pre-school children. I. Gardner, Elizabeth, joint author. II. Title.

LEACH, Joan.
First steps; helps for workers in the church nursery, by Joan Leach . . . [and] Patricia Elliott . . . Cincinnati, Standard Pub. [c1964] 128 p. illus., charts. Songs with music: p. 77-80. Includes bibliography.
1. Religious education of pre-school children. I. Title.

LEACH, Joan.
First steps; helps for workers in the church nursery, by Joan Leach . . . [and] Patricia Elliott . . . Cincinnati, Standard Pub. [c1964] 128 p. illus., charts. Songs with music: p. 77-80. Includes bibliography. 66-86522
1. Religious education of pre-school children. I. Elliott, Patricia, joint author. II. Title.

LE BAR, Mary E 1907- 268.432
Patty goes to the nursery class; a year's course in twelve units for 2- and 3-year-old children, illus. by Faith McNaughton. [Chicago, Pub. by Scripture Press, 1948] 300 p. illus. 22 cm. (The All Bible graded series of Sunday school lessons) [BV1540.L4] 48-4341
1. Religious education of pre-school children. I. Title. II. Series.

LE BAR, Mary Evelyn, 1910- 268.61
Patty goes to the nursery class; a year's course in twelve units for 2- and 3-year-old children. Illustrated by Faith M. Lowell. Chicago, Scripture Press, c1952. 256p. illus. 22cm. [All-Bible graded series of Sunday school lessons] [BV1540.L4 1952] [BV1540.L4 1952] 268.432 53-1723 53-1723
1. Religious education of pre-school children. I. Title.

LEFEBVRE, Xavier 268.432
Bringing your child to God; the religious education of the pre-school child [by] Xavier Lefebvre, Louis Perin. Tr. [from French] by Marta Gondos. New York, Kenedy [c.1963] 178p. 21cm. 63-20401 3.95 bds.,
1. Religious education of pre-school children. 2. Children—Religious life. I. Perin, Louis, joint author. II. Title.

LEFEBVRE, Xavier. 268.432
Bringing your child to God; the religious education of the pre-school child [by] Xavier Lefebvre and Louis Perin. Translated by Marta Gondos. New York, P. J. Kenedy [1963] 178 p. 21 cm. Translation of L'enfant devant Dieu. [BV1475.8.L413] 63-20401
1. Religious education of pre-school children. 2. Children — Religious life. I. Perin, Louis, joint author. II. Title.

LUMB, John Reginald. 268.432
The next three years; talks to modern parents and teachers of infants, by Reginald Lamb ... London and Oxford, A. R. Mowbray & co. limited; New York, Morehouse-Gorham co. [1944] 61 p. 18 cm. "First published in 1944. Second impression, October, 1944." [Full name: John Reginald Bertrand Bradley Lumb] [BV1475.L8] A 45
1. Religious education of pre-school children. I. Title.

MCCALLUM, Eva Beatrice 268.432
(McNown) 1892-
Learning in the nursery class, by Eva B. McCallum. St. Louis, The Bethany press [1944] 256 p. illus. (plans) 20 cm. "Songs" (unaccompanied melodies): p. 247-255. [BV1540.M315] 44-12814
1. Religious education of pre-school children. I. Title.

MCDANIEL, Elsiebeth. 268'.432
You and preschoolers / by Elsiebeth McDaniel and Lawrence O. Richards. Chicago : Moody Press, 1976 126 p. : ill. ; 22 cm. (Effective teaching series) Bibliography: p. 125-126. [BV1475.8.M3] 74-15353 ISBN 0-8024-9834-5 : 1.95
1. Religious education of preschool children. I. Richards, Lawrence O., joint author. II. Title.

MUELLER, Arnold Carl, 268.432
1891-
Growing up with Jesus, a nursery manual for parents and teachers. St. Louis, Concordia Pub. House, 1948. xiv, 166 p. illus. 23 cm. [BV1540.M8] 48-1580
1. Religious education of pre-school children. I. Title.

NICHOLSON, Dorothy. 268.432
So you work with kindergartners. Anderson, Ind., Warner Press [1960] 64p. 21cm. [BV1540.N53] 60-13193
1. Religious education of pre-school children. I. Title.

ODELL, Mary (Clemens) 268.61
Mrs., 1904-
Our little child faces life, by Mary Clemens Odell. Nashville, Cokesbury press [c1939] 64 p. port. 22 1/2 cm. [Full name: Mrs. Mary Ruth (Clemens) Odell] [BV1475.04] 39-23518
1. Religious education of pre-school children. I. Title.

OPENING doors of faith; 268.61
guidance for the Kansian home children are one to five. Kansas City, Mo., Beacon Hill Press [1953] 154p. illus. 19cm. (Christian home series) [BV1590] [BV1590] 268.432 55-2957 55-2957
1. Religious education of pre-school children. I. Edwards, Mildred Speakes, 1904-

PROTESTANT Episcopal 268.432
Church in the U. S. A. National Council. Dept. of Christian Education.
Five-year-olds in the church; revised kindergarten teacher's manual. Prepared at the direction of General Convention. Greenwich, Conn., Seabury Press [1960] 122p. illus. 28cm. (The Seabury series, T-KB) First published in 1956 under title: Receiving the five-year-old. Includes bibliography. [BV1540.P7 1960] 60-2708
1. Religious education of pre-school children. I. Title.

PROTESTANT Episcopal 268.432
Church in the U. S. A. National Council. Dept. of Christian Education.
Receiving the five- year-old; kindergarten teacher's kit. Illustrated by Alice Golden; flannelboard section by Dellwyn Cunningham. Greenwich, Conn., Seabury Press [1956] 85p. illus. 28cm. (The Seabury series, T-K1) [BV1540.P7] 56-7852
1. Religious education of pre-school children. I. Title.

PROTESTANT Episcopal 268.432
Church in the U. S. A. National Council. Dept. of Christian Education.
Receiving the nursery child; a manual for teaching children three and four years old. Illustrated by Sally Michel. Greenwich, Conn., Seabury Press [1957] 92p. illus. 28cm. (The Seabury series, T-N) Includes bibliography. [BV1540.P72] 57-8340
1. Religious education of pre-school children. I. Title.

PROTESTANT Episcopal Church in the U.S.A. National Council. Dept. of Christian Education.
The nursery child in the church. New York, Seabury Press [1963] viii, 152 p. illus. 28 cm. (The Church's teaching, T-NB) "Revised teacher's manual replacing Receiving the nursery child." 65-66472
1. Religious education of pre-school children. I. Title. II. Series.

REEVES, Katherine 268.432
When we teach 3's. Philadelphia, Geneva [dist. Westminster, c.1962] 63-836 1.25 pap.,
1. Religious education of pre-school children. I. Title.

RIVES, Elsie. 268.432
My family, a unit for use with nursery children in the Church study course. [By] Elsie Rives and Hazel Rowe Luck. [Nashville, Convention Press, c1962] 79 p. illus. 19 cm. "B.S.S.B. [1. i.e. the Sunday School Board of the Southern Baptist Convention] Church nursery program." [BV1539.R5] 62-21681
1. Religious education of pre-school children. I. Luck, Hazel Rowe, joint author. II. Southern Baptist Convention. Sunday School Board. III. Title.

ROORBACH, Rosemary K 268.432
Religion in the kindergarten. [1st ed.] New York, Harper [1949] 218 p. 20 cm. Bibliography: p. 217-218. [BV1540.R6] 49-11461
1. Religious education of pre-school children. I. Title.

ROWEN, Dolores. 268'.432
Ways to help them learn: early childhood, birth to 5 yrs. Glendale, Calif., International Center for Learning [1973, c1972] 152 p. illus. 20 cm. (ICL Teacher's/leader's success handbook) (An ICL insight book) Bibliography: p. 151-152. [BV1475.8.R68 1973] 73-168842 ISBN 0-8307-0118-4 1.95
1. Religious education of preschool children. I. Title.

SCHOONMAKER, Hazel K 268.432
Kindergarten manual for administrators and teachers in the church school kindergarten. With photos by Sheldon Brody and drawings by Shirley Hirsch. Boston, United Church Press [1961]*0p. illus. 26cm. Includes bibliography. [BV1540.S3] 61-9724
1. Religious education of pre-school children. I. Title.

SCHOONMAKER, Hazel K. 268'.432
Kindergarten manual for administrators and teachers in the church school kindergarten [by] Hazel K. Schoonmaker. With photos. by Sheldon Brody and drawings by Shirley Hirsch. [Rev. ed.] Boston, United Church Press [1969] 80 p. illus. 26 cm. Bibliography: p. 76-78. [BV1540.S3 1969] 68-13123
1. Religious education of pre-school children. I. Title.

SCHULZ, Florence. 268.432
Growing in the fellowship; a course for the church school kindergarten. Phtos. by Sheldon Brody; drawings by Laurence Scott. Boston, United Church Press [c1960] 128p. illus. 26cm. Includes singing games (unace.) [BV1540.S32] 60-53133
1. Religious education of pre-school children. I. Title.

SCHULZ, Florence. 268.432
Living in the Christian community, a course for the church school kindergarten. Photos. by Sheldon Brody. Drawings by Shirley Hirsch. Boston, United Church Press [1962] 128p. illus. 26cm. [BV1475.8.S3] 61-17818
1. Religious education of pre-school children. I. Title.

SHIELDS, Elizabeth 268.432
McEwen, 1879-
Guiding kindergarten children in the church school. Rev. by Dorothae G. Mallard. Richmond, Published for the Co-operative Pub. Association by John Knox Press [1955] 174p. illus. 19cm. (A Cooperative text) [BV1540.S518 1955] 54-10894
1. Religious education of pre-school children. 2. Religious education—Teacher training. I. Title.

SHIELDS, Elizabeth 268.432
McEwen, 1879-
Guiding kindergarten children in the church school, by Elizabeth McE. Shields; a textbook in the standard course in leadership training, outlined and approved by the International council of religious education. Richmond, Va., Printed for the Leadership training publishing association by the Onward press [c1931] 7 p. l., [13]-224 p. 19 1/2 cm. Includes music. "Intended as a guide and source book for students pursuing course-unit number 23, 'Beginners' department administration'."--Editor's introduction, signed: Erwin L. Shaver, chairman, Editorial and educational section. Includes bibliographies. [BV1540.S518] 42-35842
1. Religious education of pre-school children. 2. Religious education—Teacher training. I. Shaver, Erwin Leander, 1890- ed. II. International council of religious education. III. Title.

SMITH, Velma 268.432
So you work with nursery children. Anderson, Ind., Warner Press [dist. Gospel Trumpet Press, c.1960] 64p. 21cm. 60-13194 1.00 pap.,
1. Religious education of pre-school children. I. Title.

SMITH, Velma. 268.432
So you work with nursery children. Anderson, Ind., Warner Press [1960] 64 p. 21 cm. [BV1540.S6] 60-131947
1. Religious education of pre-school children. I. Title.

STRANG, Ruth May, 1895- 268.432
A study of young children, by Ruth Strang PH.D. Lucius H. Bugbee, C. A. Bowen, editors. New York, Nashville, Abingdon-Cokesbury press. 1944 160 p. 19 cm. Bibliographical references in "Notes" (p. 149-151) "Selected books for further reading": p. 151-152. "Selected books for children's reading": p. 156-160. [BV1540.S73] 44-8579
1. Religious education of pre-school children. 2. Child study. I. Bugbee, Lucius Hatfield, 1874- ed. II. Bowen, Cawthon Asbury, 1885- joint ed. III. Title.

STRIPLIN, Clara M 268.432
Those tiny tots; a manual for leaders and teachers in the Cradle Roll and Kindergarten Divisions of the Sabbath School. Rev. ed. Mountain View, Calif., Pacific Press Pub. Association [1954] 268p. illus. 24cm. [BV1537.S75 1954] 54-12717
1. Religious education of pre-school children. I. Title.

STRIPLIN, Clara M 268.432
Those tiny tots; a manual for leaders and teachers in the Cradle Roll and Kindergarten Divisions of the Sabbath School. Pub. by the Sabbath School Dept. of the General Conference of Seventh-Day Adventists. Mountain View, Calif., Pacific Press Pub. Assn., [1948] 253 p. illus. 24 cm. [BV1537.S75] 48-28132
1. Religious education of pre-school children. I. Seventh-Day Adventists. General conference. II. Title.

SWEDBURG, Melva.
Training for service in the nursery class. Cincinnati, Standard Pub. [c1964] 112 p. illus. (Training for service) Includes bibliographies. 66-59890
1. Religious education of pre-school children. I. Title. II. Title: Nursery class, Training for service in the. III. Series.

THOMPSON, Jean A 268.432
Before they are three; infants and two-year-olds in the home and church, by Jean A. Thompson, Sara G. Klein [and] Elizabeth Cringan Gardner. Illustrated by Janet Smalley. Philadelphia, Westminster Press [1954] 217p. illus. 24cm. Bibliography: p. 213-216. [BV1540.T53] 54-7370
1. Religious education of pre-schoolchildren. I. Title.

TOBEY, Kathrene 268.432
McLandress.
The church plans for kindergarten children. Philadelphia, Published for Cooperative Publication Association by Westminster Press [1959] 192 p. 20 cm. Includes bibliography. [BV1540.T57] 59-13436
1. Religious education of pre-school children. I. Title.

TOBEY, Kathrene 268.432
McLandress.
When we teach kindergarten children; a kindergarten guidance manual. Philadelphia, Board of Christian Education of the Presbyterian Church in the United States of America [1957] 70p. illus. 23cm. [BV1540.T58] 57-8942
1. Religious education of pre-school children. I. Title.

TRIMMER, Ellen McKay 268.432
Tiny tales 'n tunes. Pictures by Joanne Brubaker. Chicago, Moody [c.1963] 55p. illus. 28cm. 1.50, pap., plastic bdg.
1. Religious education of pre-school children. I. Title.

VON HAGEN, Elizabeth W. 268.432
The cradle roll department of the Sunday school, by Elizabeth W. Von Hagen. Nashville, Tenn., The Sunday school board of the Southern Baptist convention [1947] 6 p. l., 132 p. illus. 19 cm. [BV1537.V6] 47-4384
1. Religious education of pre-school children. 2. Sunday-schools. I. Title.

WELLER, Katharine J. 268.432
Here am I; primary leader's guide. Minneapolis, Augsburg [c.1963] 63p. 22cm. 1.25 pap.,
1. Religious education of pre-school children. I. Title.

ZIMMERMAN, Eleanor. 268.432
Doctrine for 3's to 5's. [Philadelphia, Lutheran Church Press, 1963] 160 p. illus. 21 cm. (LCA leadership education series) Includes bibliography. [BV1475.8.Z5] 63-6199
1. Religious education of pre-school children. I. Title.

ZIMMERMAN, Eleanor. 268.432
Now we are three. Joseph W. Inslee, editor. Philadelphia, Muhlenberg Press [1960] 252 p. illus. 24 cm. Includes bibliography. [BV1540.Z5] 60-51022
1. Religious education of pre-school children. I. Title.

Religious education of preschool children, Jewish.

BESSLER, Helen. 377'.9'6
Beresheet; a kindergarten guide. New York, Union of American Hebrew Congregations [1969] xvi, 111 p. illus. 28 cm. Bibliography: p. 109-111. [BM103.B48] 68-30816
1. Religious education of preschool children, Jewish. I. Title.

Religious education of primary children.

CHURCH-TIME for four's and five's. Learning God's Word. Leader's and worker's guide for one year. Beginner Church. Wheaton, Ill., Scripture Press Foundation, 1960. 150p.
1. Religious education of primary children. 2. Sunday—schools—Teaching— Primaries. I. LeBar, Mary Evelyn, 1910-

Religious education of socially handicapped children.

EBERSOLE, Eleanor 268
Christian education for socially handicapped children and youth; a manual for chaplains and teachers of persons under custody. Philadelphia. Pub. for the Coop. Pubn. Assn. by United Church [c.1964] 96p. 19cm. (Cooperative ser.: Leadership training texts) [BV1615.S6E2] 64-25579 1.25 pap.,
1. Religious education of socially handicapped children. I. Title.

Religious education of young people.

BILLINGS, Sherrard. 252.
Talks to boys in the chapel of Groton school, by Sherrard Billings ... Boston and New York, Houghton Mifflin company, 1928. 5 p. l., 175, [1] p. 19 cm. [BV4310.B53] 28-18163
I. Title.

BOWMAN, Clarice 268.433
Margurette, 1910-
Ways youth learn. [1st ed.] New York, Harper [1952] 189 p. 20 cm. [BV1600.B6] 52-8462
1. Religious education of youth. I. Title.

BOWMAN, Locke E. 268.433
How to teach senior highs. Philadelphia, Westminister Press [1963] 191 p. 21 cm. [BV1549.78.B6] 63-8065
1. Religious education of young people. I. Title.

CALFEE, John Edward, 1875- 252.
Doing the impossible; chaple talks to young men and women, by John E. Calfee ... New York, Chicago [etc.] Fleming H. Revell company [c1925] 116 p. 20 cm. [BV4310.C27] 25-20510
I. Title.

CARTER, Carlton, 1926- 268.433
A church training young people. Nashville, Convention Press [1966] x. 118 p. 20 cm. "Church study course [of the Sunday School board of the Southern Baptist Convention] This book is number 1814 in category 18, section for adults and young people." "Replaces Baptist young people's union administration by Arthur Flake." Bibliography: p. 116-118. [BV1549.2.C3] 66-13315
1. Religious education of young people. I. Southern Baptist Convention. Sunday School. Board. II. Title.

CASSILLY, Francis Bernard, 1860-
Shall I be a daily communicant? A chat with young people, by Rev. Francis Cassilly ... Chicago, Ill., Loyola university press, 1915. 80 p. front. pl. 20 cm. 15-14097 0.30
I. Title.

CHURCH school methods ... 268.
New York, Cincinnati, The Methodist book concern [1926- v. forms 20 cm. Contents.pt. I. An introduction, a syllabus for discussion by E. R. Bartlett--pt. II. A working program, a syllabus for discussion by H. M. Le Sourd. Includes bibliographies. [BV1485.C53] 44-39106
1. Religious education of young people. I. Bartlett, Edward Randolph, 1889- II. Le Sourd, Howard Marion, 1889-

COBER, Kenneth Lorne, 268.453
1902-
Teaching seniors, by Kenneth L. Cober and Esther Stricker. Philadelphia, Chicago [etc.] The Judson press [1940] 88 p. incl. 1 illus., forms. 20 cm. Includes bibliographies. [BV1549.C6] 42-5463
1. Religious education of young people. I. Stricker, Esther, joint author. II. Title.

CONFREY, Burton, 1898- 248
Faith and youth; experiences in the religious training of Catholic youth as a phase of pastoral theology, by Burton Confrey ... with and introduction by Rev. William J. Kerby ... New York, Cincinnati [etc.] Benziger brothers, 1932. X [2], 225, [1] p. 19 1/2 cm. [B X903. C58] 32-17072
I. Title.

CUMMINGS, Oliver De Wolf, 268.433
1900--
Guiding youth in Christian growth. Philadelphia, Published for the Cooperative Publication Association by the Judson Press [1954] 192p. 20cm. [BV1600.C8] 54-6177
1. Religions education of young people. I. Title.

CUTTON, George Leon, 268.433
1892-
Teaching young people, by George L. Cutton. Philadelphia, Chicago [etc.] The Judson press [1941] 95 p. 20 cm. Includes bibliographies. [BV1485.C8] 41-10082
1. Religious education of young people. I. Title.

DEWEY, Robert D
Youth ministry manual; a manual for adults who work with youth in the local church. Illus. by Susan Phelps. Photos. by Peter C. Schlaifer [and] Kenneth Thompson. Boston, United Church Press [c1963] 96 p. illus. 26 cm. (United Church curriculum. Youth. Administrators) "Resources. p. 89-92. 64-37641
1. Religious education of young people. 2. United Church of Christ — Education. I. Title. II. Series.

DOHERTY, Mary Michael. 377'.1
Electives for revitalizing high school religion [by] M. Michael. Staten Island, N.Y., Alba House [1972] vii, 256 p. 22 cm. Includes bibliographical references. [BV1485.D64] 72-299 ISBN 0-8189-0244-2 4.95
1. Religious education of young people. I. Title.

EZELL, Mancil. 268'.6
Youth in Bible study/new dynamics. Nashville, Convention Press [1970] 126 p. illus. 20 cm. Includes bibliographical references. [BS592.E95] 77-110747
1. Bible—Study—Outlines, syllabi, etc. 2. Religious education of young people. I. Title.

FARLEY, Claude J. 207'.12'79777
"Be-attitudes"; an involvement approach to teaching Christian values [by] Claude J. Farley. Staten Island, N.Y., Alba House [1973] xx, 130 p. illus. 19 cm. [BV1485.F37] 72-6753 ISBN 0-8189-0260-4 pap. 1.35
1. Religious education of young people. I. Title.

GLOVER, Gloria (Diener) 268.433
Mrs. 1902-
Letters to a young people's leader [by] Gloria Diener Glover. New York, Cincinnati [etc.] The Abingdon press [c1940] 135 p. 18 cm. [Full name: Mrs. Gloria Opal (Idener) Glover] [BV1485.G55] 40-14745
1. Religious education of young people. I. Title.

*GRIMES. HOWARD 260
The church and my life; a course for junior high youth in vacation church schools. youth week programs, and other settings [2v] Nashville, Pub. for the Cooperative Pubn. Assn. by Abingdon [c.1965] 2v. (128; 48p.) illus. 23cm. 1.25, 40 pap., teacher's ed., pupil's ed.,
I. Title.

HALL, Kenneth, 1926- 268.433
So you work with senior high youth. Anderson, Ind., Warner Press [1959] 64p. 21cm. [BV1480.H3] 59-1115
1. Religious education of young people. I. Title.

HALL, Kenneth F 1926- 268.433
So you work with senior high youth. Anderson, Ind., Warner Press [1959] 64 p. 21 cm. [BV1480.H3] 59-1115
1. Religious education of young people. I. Title.

HOWSE, William Lewis, 268.433
1905-
Teaching young people in the Sunday school [by] W. L. Howse, jr. ... Nashville, Tenn., The Sunday school board of the Southern Baptist convention [c1939] 137 p. 19 1/2 cm. "List of books quoted in the manuscript": p. [12]; "Suggested books": p. 78-80. [BV1549.H6] 40-896
1. Religious education of young people. I. Title.

JOHNSON, Rex E. 268'.433
Ways to plan & organize your Sunday school; youth, grades 7 to 12 [by] Rex E. Johnson. Glendale, Calif., International Center for Learning [1972] 104 p. illus. 20 cm. (ICL teacher's/leader's success handbook) (An ICL insight book)) Bibliography: p. 103-104. [BV1485.J64] 76-168840 ISBN 0-8307-0124-9 1.95
1. Religious education of young people. I. Title.

LACKEY,James Vernon. 268.433
Understanding and developing young people. Nashville, Convention Press [1959] 146p. 20cm. Includes bibliography. [BV1485.L3] 59-5626
1. Religious education of young people. I. Title.

LACKEY, James Vernon. 268.433
Young people and the Sunday school challenge. Nashville, Convention Press [1960] 144p. illus. 19cm. 'Church study course for teaching and training ... number 1771 in category 17, section B.' [BV1485.L33] 60-97435
1. Religious education of young people. 2. Sunday-schools. I. Title.

LAZARETH, William Henry, 268.433
1928-
Helping youth and adults know doctrine [by] William H. Lazareth and Ralph O. Hjelm. Philadelphia, Lutheran Church Press, c1963. 176 p. illus. 22 cm. (Leadership education series) Teacher's guide [by] Ralph O. Hjelm and William H. Lazareth. Philadelphia, Lutheran Church Press, c1963. 48 p. 21 cm. (Leadership education series) [BV1549.2.L3] 63-3305
1. Religious education of young people. I. Hjelm, Ralph O. II. Title.

LOSH, Apul T
Teaching senior highs. Philadelphia, Judson Press [c1959] 72 p. 20 cm. Bibliography: p. 71-72. A 63
1. Religious education of young people. I. Title.

LOSH, Apul T
Teaching senior highs. Philadelphia, Judson Press [c1959] 72 p. 20 cm. Bibliography: p. 71-72. A 63
1. Religious education of young people. I. Title.

MARY Vincenza, Sister, 268'.6
S.S.N.D.
Creative religion involvement programs [by] M. Vincenza. Staten Island, N.Y., Alba House [1973] viii, 169 p. 21 cm. Bibliography: p. [145]-162. [BV1485.M28] 73-10212 ISBN 0-8189-0277-9 2.95 (pbk)
1. Religious education of young people. I. Title.

MIX, Rex. 268'.433
Toward effective teaching; youth, by Rex and Susan Mix. Anderson, Ind., Warner Press [1970] 112 p. (p. 110-112 blank and advertisements) 26 cm. (Foundations for teaching) Includes bibliographical references. [BV1485.M55] 70-99936
1. Religious education of young people. 2. Religious education—Text-books. I. Mix, Susan, joint author. II. Title.

MOON, Alleen. 268.433
The Christian education of older youth [by] Alleen Moon. Lucius H. Bugbee, C. A. Bowen, editors. New York, Nashville, Abingdon-Cokesbury press [1943] 160 p. 18 1/2 cm. "War edition." [BV1485.M6] 43-16978
1. Religous education of young people. I. Bowen, Cawthon Asbury, 1885- ed. II. Bugbee, Lucius Hatfield, 1874- joint ed. III. Title.

MURPHY, John F., 1922- 377'.8'2
The catechetical experience [by] John F. Murphy. [New York] Herder and Herder [1968] 126 p. 21 cm. [BV1485.M75] 68-19479
1. Religions education of young people— Personal narratives. I. Title.

OATES, Wayne Edward, 268'.433
1917-
On becoming children of God, by Wayne E. Oates. Philadelphia, Published for the Cooperative Publication Association by Westminster Press [1968, c1969] 124 p. 22 cm. Bibliographical references included in "Notes" (p. [121]-124) [BV1475.9.O2] 68-20149 ISBN 0-664-21281-6
1. Religious education of young people. 2. Child study. I. Cooperative Publication Association. II. Title.

PRIME, Mary Ellen.
In His image. Conferee's source book. Illustrated by John Koehne. St. Louis, Christian Board of Publication [c1963] 64 p. illus. 67-51916
1. Religious education of young people. I. Title.

PRIME, Mary Ellen.
In His image. Curriculum area guide. St. Louis, Christian Board of Publication

[c1963] 128 p. Includes bibliography. 67-51740
1. Religious education of young people. I. Title.

*RUSSELL, Wylie H. 248.8'3
Life values for young America. Berkeley, Calif., McCutcheon [1967] 58p. port. 23cm. 3.15 pap.,
I. Title.

SCRIBNER, Frank J. 253
The portion for the children; a pastor's talks with the children of his congrgation, by Frank J. Scribner. New York, The Macmillan company, 1927. 182 p. 20 cm. [BV4315.S38] 27-4079
I. Title.

SEGER, Doris Louise 259
Ten teen programs. Chicago, Moody [c.1963] 95p. illus. 22cm. 1.35, pap., plastic bdg.
I. Title.

SHAVER, Erwin L. 268.
Christianizing our community; a suggested plan for a project for young people's groups, by Erwin L. Shaver. Chicago, Ill., The University of Chicago press [c1927] ix, 61 [5] p. 19 1/2 cm. (Half-title: The University of Chicago publications in religious education ... Constructive studies) Blank pages for "Notes" inserted between pages 34 and 35 and at end. "Reference and source material": p. 35-61. [BV1475.S5C54] 27-25561
I. Title.

STOOP, David A. 268'.433
Ways to help them learn: youth, grades 7 to 12 [by] David A. Stoop. Glendale, Calif., International Center for Learning [1973, c1971] 141, [3] p. illus. 20 cm. (ICL teacher's/leader's success handbook) (An ICL insight book) Bibliography: p. [143]-[144] [BV1485.S77] 70-168844 ISBN 0-8307-0120-6 1.95
1. Religious education of young people. I. Title.

TAYLOR, Bob R 1935- 268.433
A church training intermediates, by Bob R. Taylor. Nashville, Convention Press [1966] xii, 145 p. illus. 19 cm. "Church study course [of the Sunday School Board of the Southern Baptist Convention]. This book is numbered 1815 in category 18, section for adults and young people." Includes bibliographical references. [BV1548.T3] 66-13316
1. Religious education of young people. 2. Baptist training union. I. Southern Baptist Convention. Sunday School Board. II. Title.

YOUNG adolescent in the church (The) 268.433
a guide for workers with Junior Highs. Geneva Pr. [dist. Philadelphia, Westminster, 1963, c.1962] 96p. 22cm. 1.00 pap.,

Religious education—Ohio—Cincinnati.

MAYO, Amory Dwight, 1823-1907. 377.
Religion in the common schools. Three lectures delivered in the city of Cincinnati, in October, 1869. By Rev. A. D. Mayo. Cincinnati, R. Clarke & co., printers, 1869. 51 p. 23 1/2 cm. [LC113.C5M3] 8-6612
1. Religious education—Ohio—Cincinnati. 2. Catholic church in the U.S.—Education. 3. Bible in the schools. I. Title.
Contents omitted.

Religious education—Outlines, syllabi, etc.

LINDBORG, Olga E. 268.
... Departmental teachers' manual for the elementary school. Beginners' department, Primary department, by Olga E. Lindborg. Intermediate department, history department, Supplemental outline of Young people's Bible school and Post graduate school, by G. F. Hedstrand. Prepared for the Covenant Sunday school committee. Chicago, The Covenant book concern [c1923] 239 p. 20 cm. At head of title: The Covenant graded lessons. [BV1538.L5] 24-1279
I. Hedstrand, G. F. II. Swedish evangelical mission covenant of America. III. Title. IV. Title: Covenant graded lessons.

SPEEDY, Graeme W. 268
Education for Christian living, by Graeme W. Speedy. [Melbourne, Joint Board of Christian Education of Australia and New Zealand, 1968] 40 p. illus. 21 cm. (Christian life curriculum) [BV1471.2.S59] 74-388603 0.30
1. Religious education—Outlines, syllabi, etc. I. Title.

Religious education—Periodicals

KNEELAND, Abner, 1774-1844, ed. 230.
The Columbian miscellany; containing a variety of important, instructive, and entertaining matter, chiefly selected out of the Philadelphia magazines, published in London in the years 1788 and 1789, calculated to promote true religion and virtue. Compiled for the use and benefit of the followers of Christ. By Abner Kneeland ... Keene, Newhampshire. Printed by John Prentiss, for the editor, 1804. xix, [20]-408 p. 18 cm. [BX9913.K5] 28-3074
I. The Philadelphia magazine. II. Title.

RESEARCH service in religious education 268.
... published by Department of research and service of the International council of religious education. v. 1 (no. 1-3/4); Jan.-July/Oct. 1926. Chicago, Ill. [1926] 20, 31, 64 p. illus. 26 cm. quarterly. No more published? [BV1460.I65] 29-6817
1. Religious education—Period. I. International council of religious education.

Religious education—Philosophy.

CULLY, Iris V. 268
Change, conflict, and self-determination; next steps in religious education, by Iris V. Cully. Philadelphia, Westminster Press [1972] 191 p. 21 cm. Includes bibliographical references. [BV1464.C85] 72-5582 ISBN 0-664-20954-8 5.95
1. Religious education—Philosophy. I. Title.

HOLLEY, Raymond. 200'.7
Religious education and religious understanding : an introduction to the philosophy of religious education / Raymond Holley. London ; Boston : Routledge & K. Paul, 1978. x, 180 p. ; 23 cm. Includes bibliographical references and indexes. [BL42.H64] 78-40590 ISBN 0-7100-8995-3 : 15.50
1. Religious education—Philosophy. I. Title.

LO, Samuel E. 268'.01
Tillichian theology and educational philosophy, by Samuel E. Lo. New York, Philosophical Library [1970] 126 p. 22 cm. Bibliography: p. 117-126. [BX4827.T53L6] 70-124516 6.95
1. Tillich, Paul, 1886-1965. 2. Religious education—Philosophy. I. Title.

WILLIAMSON, William Bedford, 1918- 268'.01
Language and concepts in Christian education. Philadelphia, Westminster Press [1969, c1970] 173 p. 21 cm. Based on the author's thesis, Temple University, 1966. Bibliography: p. [165]-169. [BV1464.W5 1970] 72-85859 6.50
1. Religious education—Philosophy. 2. Religion and language. I. Title.

Religious education—Pre-school.

*TINY thoughts books 268.432
[4v.] Written by Ruth McNaughton Hinds. Illus. by Richard Mlodock, Faith McNaughton Hinds [Wheaton, Ill.] Scripture Pr., c.1963. [4v.] col. illus. 20cm. (Tiny thoughts bks. for pre-schoolers, 71x2029-2032) Contents.[1] God gives us night-time.--[2] God gives us sunlight.--[3] God gives us water.--[4] God gave us Jesus .50 pap., ea.,
1. Religious education—Pre-school. I. Hinds. Ruth McNaughton. Tiny thought books.

Religious education—Programming.

BERG, Mary Kirkpatrick. 268.
Primary story worship programs, by Mary Kirkpatrick Berg. New York, George H. Doran company [c1924] x p., 2 l., 15-195 p. front., plates. 20 cm. [BV1545.B45] 24-28377 1.75
I. Title.

**IT'S a great time to be a Christian;* 268.1
experiences and experiments with parish programs of lay Christian eduction. New York. Seabury [1968] 71p. illus. 21cm. 1.50 pap.,
1. Religious education—Programming.

Religious education—Protestant Episcopal.

*CHENEY, Ruth G. 268.433
Transition; an overview of twelve- to fourteen-year-olds in the church. Illus. by Randolph Chitwood. New York, Seabury [1967] 127p. 21cm. Prepd. under the auspices of the Dept. of Chritian Educ.,Executive Council of the Protestant Episcopal Church. 1.95 pap.,
1. Religious education—Protestant Episcopal. I. Title.

Religious education—Psychology.

BOEHLKE, Robert R. 268
Theories of learning in Christian education. Philadelphia, Westminister Press [1962] 221 p. 21 cm. [BV1471.2.B6] 62-14049
1. Religious education — Psychology. I. Title.

GODIN, Andre, ed. 201.6
From religious experience to a religious attitude. Ed. by A. Godin. Chicago, Loyola [c.]1965. viii, 210p. illus. 24cm. (Loyola pastoral ser.: Lumen vitae studies) Bibl. [BX926.G6] 65-12553 4.00
1. Religious education—Psychology. 2. Psychology, Religious. I. Title.

HARPER, Albert Foster, 1907- 268.01
... The story of ourselves, a study in the growth of personality for teachers and parents, by Albert F. Harper... Kansas City, Mo., Nazarene publishing house [1944] 214 p. diagrs. 19 cm. (On cover: Christian service training course) At head of title: Understanding our pupils. "Designed for use as a textbook in the Christian service training second series unit 14lb. 'Understanding our pupils'."--Foreowrd. "Some interesting reading" at enf of each chapter. [BV1475.H22] 44-30562
1. Religious education—Psychology. 2. Personality. I. Title.

LOVE or constraint?
Translated by Una Morrissey. New York, Paulist Press, 1961. 160p. 18cm. (Deus books) Originally published by P. J. Kennedy in 1959 as a translation of Amour ou constrainte? uContents omitted.
1. Religious education—Psychology. I. Oraison, Marc.

MCLESTER, Frances Cole. 268
A growing person, by Frances Cole McLester. Lucius H. Bugbee, C. A. Bowen, editors. New York, Nashville, Abingdon-Cokesbury press [1942] 160 p. 18 1/2 cm. Bibliography: p. 156-160. [BV1475.M32] 42-2352
1. Religious education—Psychology. 2. Child study. I. Bugbee, Lucius Hatfield, 1874- ed. II. Bowen, Cawthon Asbury, 1885- joint ed. III. Title.

ORAISON, Marc M. D. 268.01
Love or constraint? Some psychological aspects of religious education. Tr. from French. New York, Paulist Pr. [c.1959, 1961] 160p. (Deus bks.) 95 pap.,
1. Religious education—Psychology. I. Title.

ORAISON, Marc. 268.01
Love or constraint? Some psychological aspects of religious education. Translated from the French by Una Morrissy. New York, P. J. Kenedy [1959] 172 p. 21 cm. [BV1471.O543] 59-12899
1. Religious education—Psychology. I. Title.

PEACHEY, Laban. 268
Learning to understand people. Scottdale, Pa., Herald Press [1965] 109 p. illus. 20 cm. (Christian service training series) Includes bibliographical references. [BV1471.2.P4] 65-18237
1. Religious education—Psychology. I. Title.

RYBURN, William Morton. 268
The theory and practice of Christian education, with special reference to India and the East, by W. M. Ryburn ... With a foreword by Miss A. B. Van Doren ... London, New York [etc.] Oxford university press, 1934. xii, p., 1 l., 260 p. diagrs. 20 cm. "Books for further study": p. [255]-256. [BV1471.R9] 35-37253
1. Religious education—Psychology. 2. religious education—India. I. Title.

SHERIDAN, Harold James, 1885- 268.
Growth in religion; an introduction to psychology for teacers of religion, by Harold J. Sheridan ... Nashville, Tenn., Cokesbury press, 1929. 192 p. diagrs. 19 1/2 cm. [Leadership training series. Standard training series] Series title in part on t.-p. "For further reading": p. 191-192. [BV1475.S55] 29-19462
1. Religious education—Psychology. 2. Educational psychology. I. Title.

ZIEGLER, Jesse H. 268
Psychology and the teaching church. Nashville, Abingdon [c.1962] 125p. illus. 20cm. 62-16813 2.75
1. Religous education—Psychology. I. Title.

ZIEGLER, Jesse H 268
Psychology and the teaching church. New York, Abingdon Press [1962] 125 p. illus. 20 cm. [BV147.Z5] 62-16813
1. Religious education—Psychology. I. Title.

Religious education—Psychology—Addresses, essays, lectures.

GRIFFIN, Dale E., comp. 268'.01'9
The subject is persons; psychological perspectives in Christian education. Edited by Dale E. Griffin. Saint Louis, Concordia Pub. House [1970] 85 p. 19 cm. (Church teachers library) [BV1471.2.G67] 78-107423
1. Religious education—Psychology—Addresses, essays, lectures. I. Title.

Religious education—Sermons.

MURRAY, Andrew, 1828-1917. 268
The children for Christ. Chicago, Moody Press [1952] 191p. 20cm. 'A condensation of the author's original work of this title.' [BV1477.M8] 53-30883
1. Religious education—Sermons. 2. Religious education—Home training. I. Title.

Religious education—Societies.

RELIGIOUS education association. 268.
Monograph[s] [Chicago, Religious education association, 1927- v. diagrs. 25 1/2 cm. Reprinted from Religious education, 1926- [BV1460.R53] 28-19522
1. Religious education—Societies. I. Title.

Religious education—Study and teaching.

ALBERT, Hubert.
Training lay teachers for the parish high school of religion; a book of methods for the use of instructors. Chicago, Confraternity of Christian Doctrine, 1960. 127 p. 27 cm. NUC66
1. Religious education—Study and teaching. I. Title.

ARENTROUT, James Sylvester, 1887- 377.85173
... Effectiveness of Prebyterian college programs in developing leadership for religious education, by James Sylvester Armentrout ... Scottdate, Pa., Printed by the Mennonite press, 1936. 67, [1] p. 25 1/2 cm. (Yale studies in religion. no. 10) Based on thesis (PH.D.)--Yale university.

Bibliography: p. [65]-[68] [BX8917.A8] 37-17373
1. Religious education—Study and teaching. 2. Presbyterian church in the U.S.A.—Education. 3. Church and college in the U.S. 4. Leadership. I. Title.

ATHEARN, Walter Scott, 1872- 268
An adventure in religious education; the story of a decade of experimentation in the collegiate and professional training of Christian workers, by Walter Scott Athearn, dean of Boston university School of religious education and social service, 1918-1929. New York and London, The Century co. [c1930] xxi, 505 p. incl. tables. diagrs. 21 cm. Contains bibliographies. [BV1610.A7] 30-8106
1. Religious education—Study and teaching. 2. Universities and colleges—U. S. 3. Boston university, School of religious education and social service. I. Title.

DE WOLF, Lotan Harold, 1905- 268
Teaching our faith in God. Nashville, Abingdon [1963] 188p. 23cm. Bibl. 63-7480 3.75
1. Religious education—Study and teaching. 2. Theology—Study and teaching. I. Title.

DE WOLF, Lotan Harold, 1905- 268
Teaching our faith in God. New York, Abingdon Press [1963] 188 p. 23 cm. [BV1534.D4] 63-7480
1. Religious education — Study and teaching. 2. Theology — Study and teaching. I. Title.

FOSTER, Eugene Clifford, 1867- 220
Starting to teach, for those who lead Bible classes of boys [by] Eugene C. Foster ... 2d revision. New York, Association press, 1924. vii, 104 p. 18 cm. [BS603.F6 1924] 24-32098
I. Title.

GILBERT W Kent. 268
As Christians teach. Philadelphia, Lutheran Church Press [1962] 160 p. illus. 21 cm. (Leadership education series) Teacher's guide. [n.p., c1962] 32 p. illus. 29 cm. and phonodisc (2 s., 7 in., 33 1/3 rpm) in pocket. (Leadership education series) [BV1475.2.G5] 62-53282
1. Religious education — Study and teaching. 2. Lutheran Church — Education. I. Title.

GILBERT, W Kent. 268
As Christians teach [by] W. Kent Gilbert. Philadelphia, Fortress Press [1964, c1962] 167 p. illus. 21 cm. Includes bibliographies. [BV1475.2.G5] 64-23270
1. Religious education — Study and teaching. 2. Lutheran Church — Education. I. Title.

NATIONAL Council of the Churches of Christ in the United States of America. Division of Christian Education.
Handbook for the leadership education curriculum. For interdenominational leadership classes and schools. Edition for 1963 and 1964. New York Pub. for the Division of Christian Education National Council of Churches of Christ in the U.S.A. by the Office of Publication and Distribution, c1963. 64 p. 23 cm. Earlier eds. pub. under title: Leadership education handbook. 64-51415
1. Religious education-Study and teaching. 2. Leadership. I. Title.

A primary teacher's guide on the church's mission in town and country. New York, Friendship Press, 1959. 63p. 21cm.
I. McDowell, Elizabeth Tibbals.

SISTERS of Saint Joseph, Chestnut Hill, Philadelphia. 265.
The objective teaching of the Holy sacrifice of the mass, by the Sisters of St. Joseph of Philadelphia. Philadelphia, American ecclesiastical review, 1918. 74 p. illus. 15 cm. $0.25 [BX2230.S6] 18-19131
I. Title.

Religious education study and teaching, (Elementary)—Catholic.

*PFEIFFER, Mother Marie 268.432
Love the Lord, with all your heart, and with all your soul, and with all your mind [by] Mother Marie Pfeiffer, Mother Mary Laiiatte. New York, Sadlier, 1966. 191p. illus. (pt. col.) 21cm. (Our life with God ser., Vatican II ed., Grade 4) 1.20 pap.,
1. Religious education study and teaching, (Elementary)—Catholic. I. Carroll, Mary, Mother jipoint author. II. Title. III. Series.

Religious education—Study and teaching (Intermediate)—Catholic.

*PETULLA, Joseph 268.433
The friendship of Christ, by Joseph Petulla. William J. Reedy. New York, Sadlier [1966] 94p. 22cm. (Life & light ser., bk. 2) 1.00 pap.,
1. Religious education—Study and teaching (Intermediate)— Catholic. I. Reedy, William J., joint author. II. Title. III. Series.

*REEDY, William J. 268.433
The story of salvation [by] William J. Reedy. Consultants: Brother Bartholomew Albert [others] New York. Sadlier [1966] 449p. illus. 22cm. (Life & light ser., bk. 2) pap., 2.16; teacher's guide, pap., 1.50
1. Religious education—Study & teaching (Intermediate)—Catholic. I. Title. II. Series.

Religious education—Sunday schools.

BREWBAKER, Charles Warren, 1869- ed. 268.
Progressive training course for Sunday-school workers (forty lessons) ed. by Chas. W. Brewbaker ... Dayton, O., The Otterbein press, 1923. 223 p. illus. (plans) 20 1/2 cm. Bibliography at end of each part. [BV1561.B65] 23-5377
I. Batdorf, Grant D. II. Weber, William A. III. Title.

*GREATER Chicago Sunday School Association (The) 268.6
The key to Sunday school achievement, ed. by Lawrence O. Richards. Chicago, Moody [c.1965] 110p. diagrs. 28cm. 2.95 pap., plastic bdg.
1. Religious education—Sunday schools. I. Richards, Lawrence O., ed. II. Title.

KING, Henry Churchill, 1858-
Letters to Sunday-school teachers on the great truths of our Christian faith, by Henry Churchill King ... Boston, New York [etc.] The Pilgrim press, 1906. vi, 199 p. 19 1/2 cm. "Reprinted from the Pilgrim teacher and Sunday school outlook." 6-23080
I. Title.

MASSACHUSETTS Universalist Sabbath School Association.
Report. Boston. v. 23cm. annual. [BX9918.M3] 61-57502
I. Title.

PARK, Charles Edwards, 1873-
... Jesus of Nazareth, by Charles Edwards Park. Boston, Chicago, Unitarian Sunday-school society [c1909] 2 p. l., 72 p. 21 cm. (The Beacon series; a graded course of study for the Sunday school) 9-25425 Cloth, $0.40
I. Title.

[PHELPS, Amos Augustus] 1805-1847. 922
Letters to little children; or, The history of little Sarah. Written for the Massachusetts Sabbath school society, and revised by the Committee of publication. Boston, Massachusetts Sabbath school society, 1833. viii, [9]-52 p. incl. front. 15 cm. [BR1715.Z9P45] 37-38006
I. Massachusetts Sabbath school society. Committee of publication. II. Title.

PHILLIPS, Grace Darling. 259
Far peoples, by Grace Darling Phillips. Chicago, Ill., The University of Chicago press [c1929] xxii, 274 p. 20 cm. (Half-title: The University of Chicago publications in religious education ... Principles and methods of religious education) Stories, songs with music, poetry, games, etc., representing India, China, Korea, Japan, the Philippines, Brazil, Africa and Russia, adapted to program building for Sunday school classes and young peoples' and missionary societies. List of plays and pagents: p. 251-265. [BV2086.P45] [M1627.P6] 812. 29-11359
I. Title.

RIDGWAY, William H.
Ridgway's religion for folks who don't have any. Being some notes on John as taught to the Iron Rose Bible class, by Wm. H. Ridgway ... Philadelphia, Chicago [etc.] The Griffith & Rowland press [1909] 135 p. 20 cm. 9-19055
I. Title.

TROUT, Ethel Wendell. 232.
Jesus the light of the world ... by Ethel Wendell Trout ... Philadelphia, The Westminster press, 1921. xxviii, 127 p. front., illus. (incl. maps, plans) plates, 18 1/2 cm. (The Westminster textbooks of religious education for church schools having Sunday, week day, and expressional sessions, ed. by J. T. Faris. Junior department, 1st year, pt. I) [BT307.T7] 22-4346
I. Title.

TROUT, Ethel Wendell. 232.
Jesus the light of the world ... by Ethel Wendell Trout ... Philadelphia, The Westminster press, 1924. 2 v. fronts., illus. (incl. maps, plans) plates. 18 1/2 cm. (The Westminster textbooks of religious education for church schools having Sunday, week day, and expressional sessions, ed. by J. T. Faris. Junior department, 1st year, pt. I) Paged continuously. Contains bibliographies. [BT307.T7 1924] 24-23633
I. Title.

THE United Norwegian Lutheran church of America.
The church and Sunday school hymnal. By authority of the United Norwegian Lutheran church of America. Minneapolis, Augsburg pub. house, 1898. lxii, 337 p. 19 x 14 cm. 3-8272
I. Title.

WILSON, Mabel Aureola.
Love, light, and life for God's little children; a course of instruction for primary Sunday schools, by Mabel A. Wilson ... with a preface by the Very Reverend Carroll M. Davis ... Rev. ed. Twenty-seven new illustrations by Elizabeth Souther. [St. Louis, Mo., Shallcross printing co., c1912] xv, 348 p. illus. 24 cm. $2.50. 12-13932
I. Title.

Religious education—Teacher recruitment.

SCOTFORD, John Ryland, 1888- 268.3
How to recruit and keep Sunday school teachers. [Westwood, N. J.] Revell [c.1962] 62p. 22cm. (Revell's better church ser.) 62-17110 1.00 pap.,
1. Religious education—Teacher recruitment. I. Title.

Religious education—Teacher training.

*ALVES, Colin 220.07
The Scriptures; a supplement for teachers [New York] Cambridge [c.1964] 77p. 19cm. cover title. 1.50 pap.,
I. Title.

BASICS for teaching in the church 268'.3 [by] T. Franklin Miller [and others] Study guidance by Kenneth F. Hall. Anderson, Ind., Warner Press [1968] 224 p. illus. 26 cm. (Foundations for teaching) Bibliographical footnotes. [BV1533.B36] 68-23026
1. Religious education—Teacher training. I. Miller, T. Franklin.

BENSON, Erwin George, 1905- 268.6
Planning church school workers' conferences. Boston, W. A. Wilde Co. [1952] 104 p. 20 cm. [BV1533.B43] 52-12580
1. Religious education—Teacher training. 2. Sunday-schools. I. Title.

BROWN, Ario Ayres, 1833- 262.
Primer of teacher training, by Ario Ayres Brown; outline approved by the Committee on cirriculum of the Board of Sunday schools, Henry H. Meyer, editor. New York, Cincinnati, The Methodist book concern [1916] 168 p. 17 1/2 cm. "Books for references": p. 168. [BV1533.B75] 16-15890
1. Religious education—Teacher training. I. Meyer, Henry Herman, 1874- ed. II. Title.

CHAPLIN, Dora P. 268
A leader's guide for use with The privilege of teaching. Prepared by the Rev. Robert W. Renouf. New York, Morehouse [c.1963] 112p. 21cm. 1.75 pap.,
1. Religious education—Teacher training. I. Title.

CHAPLIN, Dora P. 268
The privilege of teaching, its dimension and demand for all who teach the Christian faith. Foreword by Stephen F. Bayne, Jr. New York, Morehouse-Barlow [c.1962] 295p. illus. Bibl. 62-9800 4.50 bds.,
1. Religious education—Teacher training. I. Title.

CHURCH of God (Cleveland, Tenn.) 268
Workers training course. Cleveland, Tenn., Pathway Press [19 v. 20cm. 'Prepared under the auspices of the Church of God, National Sunday School and Youth Board.' [BV1533.C45] 58-40611
1. Religious education—Teacher training. I. Title.

DUNN, Paul H
You too can teach; a how to book for the lay teacher on methods and techniques of teaching the gospel, by Paul H. Dunn in collaboration with Cherie B. Parker. With illus. by Hal T. Sperry. Salt Lake City, Bookcraft [1962] 226 p. illus. 24 cm.
1. Religious education — Teacher training. I. Title.

DUNN, Paul H 268.6
You too can teach; a how to book for the lay teacher on methods and techniques of teaching the gospel, by Paul H. Dunn in collaboration with Cherie B. Parker. With illus. by Hal T. Sperry. Salt Lake City, Bookcraft [1962] 226 p. illus. 24 cm. [BV1534.D84] 62-53281
1. Religious education — Teacher training. 2. Mormons and Mormonism.-Education. I. Title.

FEUCHT, Oscar E. 268.6
Building better Bible classes. St. Louis, Concordia Pub. House [1951] iv, 117 p. 19 cm. "Practical library for Bible teachers": p. 45-50. [BV1533.F4] 51-5178
1. Religious education—Teacher training. 2. Sunday-schools. I. Title.

FIDLER, James E. 268.3
Our church plans for leadership education; a manual on enlisting and developing workers. Valley Forge [Pa.] Judson [c.1962] 112p. illus. 20cm. 62-17001 1.25 pap.,
1. Religious education—Teacher training. 2. Leadership. 3. American Baptist Convention—Education. I. Title.

GOODYKOONTZ, Harry G. 268.07
Training to teach, a basic cource in Christian education [by]. Harry G. and Betty L. Goodykoontz. Philadelphia, Westminster Pr. [c. 1961] 141p. illus. Bibl. 61-10293 3.50
1. Religious education—Teacher training. I. Goodykoontz, Betty L., joint author. II. Title.

GROGG, Evelyn Leavitt. 268.442
The beginner Bible teacher and leader; a twenty-hour course for teachers and workers of the beginner department, by Evelyn Leavitt Grogg. Cincinnati, O., The Standard publishing company [1942] 2 p. l., 3-119 p. 19 cm. "Book references" at end of some of the chapters. [BV1540.G7] 42-22630
1. Religious education—Teacher training. 2. Religious education of pre-school children. I. Title.

GROTON, William Mansfield, 1850-1915, ed. 268.
The Sunday-school teacher's manual, designed as an aid to teachers in preparing

Sunday-school lessons. Edited by the Rev. William M. Groton ... Philadelphia, G. W. Jacobs & company [1909] 391 p. 21 cm. "Published January, 1909." Bibliography at end of each chapter. [BX5870.G7 1909] 9-2533
1. Religious education—Teacher training. 2. Sunday-schools. I. Title.

GWYNN, Price Henderson, 1892- 268.3
Leadership education in the local church. Philadelphia, Published for the Cooperative Publishing Association by the Westminster Press [1952] 157 p. 21 cm. [BV1533.G8] 52-7051
1. Religious education—Teacher training. I. Title.

HAMMACK, Mary L. 268.3
How to train the Sunday school Grand Rapids, Mich., Zondervan [c.1961] 63p. illus. (Sunday school 'Know-how' ser.) Bibl. 62-1132 1.00 pap.,
1. Religious education—Teacher training. I. Title.

HAMMACK, Mary L 268.3
How to train the Sunday school teacher. Grand Rapids, Zondervan Pub. House [1961] 63p. illus. 21cm. (Sunday school 'Know-how' series) Includes bibliography. [BV1533.H28] 62-1132
1. Religious education—Teacher training. I. Title.

HASSKARL, Gottlieb Christopher Henry, 1855-
The teacher's compendium of first principles of Christian pedagogy in analysis and outlines ethico-psychological, illustrated by the various stages of growth from childhood to adolescence with blackboard demonstrations, by G. C. H. Hasskarl... [Williamsport, Pa.,] F. Hasskarl [c1910] [iii]-viii, [9]-111 p. 2 fold. tab. (incl. front.) 19 1/2 cm. 10-10237
I. Title.

HENDERSON, Caroline D 268.6
Sunday school training plans and recognitions. Nashville, Convention Press [1957] unpaged. illus. 22cm. [BV1533.H43] 57-8662
1. Religious education—Teacher training. I. Title.

HOPKINS, Granville Shelby, 1878- 268.433
Tomorrow you lead. Nashville, Sunday School Board of the Southern Baptist Convention [1947] [7] l., 3-127 p. 19 cm. [BV1533.H65] 47-26952
1. Religious education—Teacher training. 2. Sunday-schools. 3. Southern Baptist Convention—Education I. Title.

HORTON, Gilmer Ayers.
Elementary grade children in the school manual. Richmond, The CLC Press [1967] 85 p. 22 cm. (The Covenant Life Curriculum) 68-56141
1. Religious education—Teacher training. I. Title. II. Series.

HURLBUT, Jesse Lyman, 1843-1930. 268.07
Outline normal lessons for normal classes, assemblies, Bible students, and Sunday-school teachers. By Rev. J. L. Hurlbut, D. D. New York, Phillips & Hunt; Boston, Congregational publishing house; [etc., etc.] 1885. 107 p. illus. (maps) 20 cm. Published later under title: Revised normal lessons. [BV1533.H85] 40-37721
1. Religious education—Teacher training. 2. Sunday-schools. I. Title.

HURLBUT, Jesse Lyman, 1843-1930. 268.07
Revised normal lessons, by Jesse Lyman Hurlbut. New York, Hunt & Eaton; Cincinnati, Cranston & Curts, 1893. 111 p. illus. (incl. maps, plans) 20 cm. "This book is a revision of Outline normal lessons, first printed as leaflets, and afterwards, in 1885, gathered into a book."--Pref. "Books for further study": p. [9]-10. [BV1533.H36 1893] 40-37722
1. Religious education—Teacher training. 2. Sunday-schools. I. Title.

HURLBUT, Jesse Lyman, 1843-1930. 262.
Revised normal lessons, by Jesse Lyman Hurlbut. New York, Eaton & Mains; Cincinnati, Jennings & Graham [c1907] 121 p. illus. 20 cm. "This book is a later revision of Outline normal lessons, first printed as leaflets, and afterwards, in 1885, gathered into a book."--Pref. [BV1533.H86 1907] 7-31969
1. Religious education—Teacher training. 2. Sunday-schools. I. Title.

HYDE, Floy (Salls). 268.3
Protestant leadership education schools. New York, Bureau of Publications, Teachers College, Columbia University, 1950. viii, 164 p. tables. 24 cm. (Columbia University. Teachers College. Contributions to education, no. 965) Issued also as thesis, Columbia University. Bibliography: p. [149]-153. [BV1533.H94] 50-9189
1. Religious education—Teacher training. I. Title. II. Series.

HYDE, Floy (Salls) 262'.1'07
Protestant leadership education schools, by Floy S. Hyde. New York, Bureau of Publications, Teachers College, Columbia University, 1950. [New York, AMS Press, 1972, i.e. 1973] viii, 164 p. 22 cm. Reprint of the 1950 ed., issued in series: Columbia University. Teachers College. Contributions to education, no. 965. Originally presented as the author's thesis, Columbia. Bibliography: p. 151-153. [BV1533.H94 1972] 70-176892 ISBN 0-404-55965-4 10.00
1. Religious education—Teacher training. I. Title. II. Series: Columbia University. Teachers College. Contributions to education, no. 965.

JAHSMANN, Allan Hart 268.6
How you too can teach, reading text of a basic training course for church school teachers. St. Louis, Concordia [c.1963] 85p. 21cm. (Concordia leadership training ser.; 22-1177) Bibl. 63-18733 pap., .75; Trainers manual, pap., 1.50
1. Religious education—Teacher training. I. Title.

JAHSMANN, Allan Hart. 268.6
How you too can teach, reading text of a basic training course for church school teachers. St. Louis, Concordia Pub. House [1963] St. Louis, Concordia Pub. House, 1963. 85 p. 21 cm. 40 p. 28 cm. (Concordia leadership training series) "22-1177." "22-1179." BV1533.J3 Manual Includes bibliography. [BV1533.J3] 63-18733
1. Religious education—Teacher training. I. Title. II. Title: Trainer's manual.

KLYVER, Faye Huntington, 1893- 370'.733
The supervision of student-teachers in religious education. New York, Bureau of Publications, Teachers College, Columbia University, 1925. [New York, AMS Press, 1972] viii, 186 p. 22 cm. Reprint of the 1925 ed., issued in series: Teachers College, Columbia University. Contributions to education, no. 198. Originally presented as the author's thesis, Columbia. Bibliography: p. 185-186. [BV1533.K6 1972] 79-176952 ISBN 0-404-55198-X 10.00
1. Religious education—Teacher training. I. Title. II. Series: Columbia University. Teachers College. Contributions to education, no. 198.

MCKIBBEN, Frank Melbourne, 1889- 268.372
Guiding workers in Christian education. Nashville, Published for the Cooperative Publication Association by Abingdon-Cokesbury Press [1953] 160p. 20cm. (The Cooperative series leadership training textbooks) [BV1533.M32] 53-5397
1. Religious education—Teacher training. I. Title.

MCLAUGHLIN, Henry Woods, 1869- 268
The gospel in action, by Henry W. McLaughlin ... Richmond, Va., John Knox press [1944] 135, [1] p. 20 cm. "Advance with Christ" (words and music): page at end. Bibliography: p. [134]-135. [BV1533.M323] 44-14429
1. Religious education—Teacher training. 2. Sunday-schools. I. Title.

MCMASTER, Vernon Cochrane. 268.6
Tips to teachers, by Vernon McMaster. New York, Morehouse-Gorham co., 1946. 5 p. l., 99 p. 21 cm. [BV1534.M2874] 46-6460
1. Religious education—Teacher training. I. Title.

MICHAEL, Sister.
Communicating the mystery; a textbook for training CCD catechists for the elementary school of religion. Huntington, Ind., Our Sunday Vistor [1963] 128 p. illus. 23 cm. "Related readings" at end of each chapter. 67-41524
1. Religious education — Teacher training. 2. Catechetics. 3. Confraternity of Christian Doctrine. I. Title.

MONINGER, Herbert, 1876-1911. 262.
Fifty lessons in training for service, by Herbert Moninger... Rev. ed., for use in teacher-training classes, young people's societies, mid-week prayer-meetings, adult Bible classes, etc. Cincinnati, O., The Standard publishing co., c1907. viii, 136 p. illus. 20 1/2 cm. [Full name: Henry Herbert Moninger] [BV1533.M65 1907a] 8-6993
1. Religious education—Teacher training. I. Title.

NOLDE, Otto Frederick, 1899- 268.372
God's master builders; methods of leading group sessions, by O. Frederick Nolde and Paul J. Hoh. Philadelphia, Muhlenberg Press [1950] 95 p. illus. 18 cm. "Based on an earlier book, My group sessions, by the same authors." Bibliography: p. 94. "Audio-visual aids": p. 95. [BV1533.N55] 50-1757
1. Religious education — Teacher training. I. Hoh, Paul Jacob, 1893- joint author. II. Title.

NOLDE, Otto Frederick, 1899-. 268.392
My group sessions; a study of the church worker and his group sessions, by O. Fred Nolde and Paul J. Hoh. Prepared under the auspices of the Parish and church school board of the United Lutheran church in America. Philadelphia, Pa., The United Lutheran publication house [c1936] 94 p. 18 cm. [BV1533.N57] 36-17860
1. Religious education—Teacher training. 2. Leadership. I. Hoh, Paul Jacob, 1898- joint author. II. United Lutheran church in America. Parish and church school board. III. Title.

NOLDE, Otto Frederick, 1899-. 268.372
My materials; a study of the church worker and his materials, by O. Fred Nolde and Paul J. Hoh. Prepared under the auspices of the Parish and church school board of the United Lutheran church in America. Philadelphia, Pa., The United Lutheran publication house [c1936] 93 p. 17 1/2 cm. [BV1533.N58] 36-4283
1. Religious education—Teacher training. 2. Leadership. I. Hoh, Paul Jacob, 1893- joint author. II. United Lutheran church in America. Parish and church school board. III. Title.

NOLDE, Otto Frederick, 1899-. 268.372
My preparation; a study of the church worker and his preparation, by O. Fred Nolde and Paul J. Hoh. Prepared under the auspices of the Parish and church school board of the United Lutheran church in America. Philadelphia, Pa., The United Lutheran publication house [c1935] 96 p. 18 cm. [BV1533.N59] 36-4286
1. Religious education—Teacher training. 2. Leadership. I. Hoh, Paul Jacob, 1893- joint author. II. United Lutheran church in America. Parish and church school board. III. Title.

PROTESTANT Episcopal Church in the U. S. . National Council. Dept. of Christian Education. 262.
Standard course in teacher training, Unit 1- Milwaukee, Morehouse Pub. Co. [c1918- v. illus. 19 cm. No. 1- issued by the General Board of Religious Education; no. by the dept. under its earlier name: Dept. of Religious Education. [BV1533.P75] 51-30754
1. Religious education—Teacher training. I. Title.

RENOUF, Robert W 248
A leader's guide. New York, Morehouse-Barlow Co. [1963] 112 p. 21 cm. "For use with The privilege of teaching, by Dora Chaplin." [BV1533.R4] 64-1962
1. Religious education — Teacher training. I. Chaplin, Dora P. The privilege of teaching. II. Title.

SEBALY, Avis Leo, 1912- ed. 377.1
Teacher education and religion [by] A.L. Sebaly [and others] Oneonta, N.Y., American Association of Colleges for Teacher Education, 1959. xiii, 292p. 24cm. 'Notes and bibliography :p. 245-285. [LC379.S4] 59-5143
1. Religious education—Teacher training. I. Title.

STEEL, Robert.
The Christian teacher in Sunday schools. By the Rev. Robert Steel ... London and New York [etc.] T. Nelson and sons, 1867. 249 p. 18 cm. [BV1530.S75] 40-36611
1. Religious education—Teacher training. 2. Sunday-schools. I. Title.

SWAIN, Dorothy G 268.6
Teach me to teach [by] Dorothy G. Swain. Valley Forge [Pa.] Judson Press [1964] 127 p. 20 cm. Bibliography: p. 123-127. [BV1533.S8] 64-13125
1. Religious education — Teacher training. I. Title.

TEACHING the teacher; 268.
a first book in teacher training. Section I, The development of the church in Old Testament times, by James Oscar Boyd ... section II, The life of Christ and the development of the church in apostolic times and in post apostolic times, by John Gresham Machen, D.D.; section III, An introduction to the study of the mind, by Walter Scott Athearn; section IV, The church as a teaching institution, by Harold McA. Robinson, D.D. Philadelphia, The Westminster press, 1921. 4 p., 2 l., 7-214 p. front., maps. 19 cm. [BV1534.T43] 22-3122
I. Boyd, James Oscar, 1874- II. Machen, John Gresham, 1881- III. Athearn, Walter Scott, 1872- IV. Robinson, Harold McAfee, 1881-

THAT men may live in Christ; a course on Why we teach, by Elaine Tracy, Harlen Norem. Minneapolis, Augsburg, c.1963. 48p. 28cm. (Leadership educ. ser. course 11a. 5; senior high school dept.) 1.25 pap., 268.3
1. Religious education—Teacher training. I. Tracy, Elaine. II. Norem, Harlan.

U.S. Dept. of Defense. Armed Forces Chaplains' Board. 268
Teaching in the Armed Forces; Protestant religious education program. Rev. [Washington, U.S. Govt. Print. Off., 1967] 73 p. 24 cm. Cover title. Bibliography: p. 66-73. [BV1533.U53 1967] 68-61133
1. Religious education—Teacher training. I. Title.

VINCENT, John Heyl, bp., 1832-1920. 268.02
The Chautauqua normal guide. A series of lessons for the use of Sabbath-school normal and training classes. By J. H. Vincent, D.D. New York, Phillips & Hunt. Cincinnati, Hitchcock & Walden, 1880. 149 p. illus. (incl. maps) 19 cm. [BV1533.V5] 40-37723
1. Religious education—Teacher training. I. Chautauqua literary and scientific circle. II. Title.

Religious education—Teaching methods.

ANDERSEN, Karen. 268.6
Ways of teaching. Philadelphia, Muhlenberg Press [c1952] 144p. illus. 20cm. [BV1534.A63] 52-11416
1. Religious education—Teaching methods. 2. Sunday-schools. I. Title.

BENSON, Clarence Herbert, 1879- 268.6
The Christian teacher. Chicago, Moody Press [1950] 288 p. 21 cm. Bibliography: p. 287-288. [BV1534.B35] 50-9203
1. Religious education—Teaching methods. 2. Sunday schools. I. Title.

BERKELEY, James Percival, 1879- 266.6
You can teach, by James Percival Berkeley. Philadelphia, Chicago [etc.] The Judson press [1941] 94 p. diagr. 20 cm. [BV1534.B42] 41-10225

1. Religious education—Teaching methods. I. Title.

BOWMAN, Locke E. 268'.6
Straight talk about teaching in today's church, by Locke E. Bowman, Jr. Philadelphia, Westminister Press [1967] 151 p. 21 cm. Bibliographical references included in "Notes" (p. 149-151) [BV1534.B6] 67-11764
1. Religious education — Teaching methods. I. Title.

BROWN, Marianna Catherine, d.1916.
How to plan a lesson, and other talks to Sunday-school teachers, by Marianna C. Brown... New York, Chicago [etc.] Fleming H. Revell company [1904] 93 p. 19 cm. [BV1584.B7] 4-33205
1. Religious education—Teaching methods. 2. Sunday-schools. I. Title.

BRUMBAUGH, Martin Grove, 262. 1862-1930.
The making of a teacher; a contribution to some phases of the problem of a religious education, by Martin G. Brumbaugh ... Philadelphia, The Sunday school times company, 1905. xv, 351 p. 20 1/2 cm. [BV1533.B8] 5-34005
1. Religious education—Teaching methods. 2. Sunday-schools. I. Title.

BURKHARDT, Edward C. 268'.6
Guidelines for high school CCD teachers [by] Edward C. Burkhardt. [1st ed.] New York, Benziger Bros., 1968. 45 p. 28 cm. [BX926.B8] 68-18699
1. Confraternity of Christian Doctrine. 2. Religious education—Teaching methods. 3. Catechetics—Catholic Church. I. Title.

CALDWELL, Irene Catherine 268'.6 (Smith) 1919-
Basics for communication in the church, by Irene S. Caldwell, Richard A. Hatch [and] Beverly Welton. Anderson, Ind., Warner Press [1971] 224 p. illus. 26 cm. (Foundations for teaching) [BV1534.C237] 78-150370 ISBN 0-87162-121-5
1. Religious education—Teaching methods. I. Hatch, Richard A. II. Welton, Beverly. III. Title.

CALDWELL, Irene Catherine 268.6 (Smith) 1919-
Teaching that makes a difference. [Rev. ed.] Anderson, Ind., Warner [c.1958, 1962] 95p. illus. 21cm. 62-13334 1.25 pap.,
1. Religious education—Teaching methods. I. Title.

CALDWELL, Irene Catherine 220'.07 (Smith) 1919-
Teaching that makes a difference. [Rev. ed.] Anderson, Ind., Warner Press [1962] 95p. illus. 21cm. [BV1534.C24 1962] 62-13334
1. Religious education—Teaching methods. I. Title.

CALDWELL, Irene Catherine 268.6 (Smith), 1919-
Teaching that makes a difference. Anderson, Ind., Warner Press [1950] 111 p. 19 cm. Includes bibliographies. [BV1534.C24] 50-9989
1. Religious education—Teaching methods. I. Title.

CAMPBELL, Doak Sheridan, 268.6 1888-
When do teachers teach? Nashville, Convention Press [1958, c1935] 107p. 20cm. [BV1534.C25 1958] 58-10181
1. Religious education—Teaching methods. 2. Sunday-schools. I. Title.

CARLTON, Anna Lee. 268.6
Blessed are they who teach. Anderson, Ind., Warner Press [1961] 112p. 21cm. [BV1534.C28] 61-9719
1. Religious education—Teaching methods. 2. Sunday -schools. I. Title.

CARRIER, Blanche, 1895- 268.6
How shall I learn to teach religion? Teaching through the experience of the pupil, by Blanche Carrier ... New York and London, Harper & brothers, 1930. ix p., 1 l., 216 p. 20 cm. "First edition." "Books you will enjoy" at end of part of the chapters. [BV1475.C345] 30-20139
1. Religious education—Teaching methods. 2. Sunday-schools. I. Title.

COLE, Clifford A. 232
Jesus the Christ; senior high teacher's manual, course A--October, November, December [Independence, Mo., Herald Pub. House, c.1961] 62p. (T) .40 pap.,
I. Title.

COLLINS, Joseph Burns, 268.6 1897.-
CCD methods in modern catechetics for use in leadership courses in the catechetical renewal S. 103: Catechetical procedures in CCD elementary school. S. 104: Catechetical procedures in CCD high school. [By] Joseph B. Collins. Milwaukee. Bruce [1966] xi, 139p. forms. 23cm. Bibl. [BV1534.C58] 66-22584 2.95
1. Religious education—Teaching methods I. Confraternity of Christian Doctrine. II. Title.

CORZINE, Jesse Lynn, 1892- 268.6
Teaching to win and develop. Nashville, Sunday School Board of the Southern Baptist Convention [1954] 152p. 20cm. [BV1534.C66] 54-36206
1. Religious education—Teaching methods. I. Title.

DE OVIES, Raimundo, 1877- 268.6
The church and the children, by Raimundo de Ovies ... New York, Morehouse-Gorham co., 1941. 213 p. front. (group port.) 21 cm. [BV1471.D45] 42-1021
1. Religious education—Teaching methods. 2. Children's sermons. I. Title.

DOUTY, Mary Alice. 259
How to work with church groups. Nashville, Abingdon Press [1957] 170p. illus. 21cm. Includes bibliography. [BV1534.D67] 57-5076
1. Religious education— Teaching methods. 2. Leadership. 3. Discussion. I. Title. II. Title: Church groups.

DRIGGS, Howard Roscoe, 268.6 1873-
The Master's art, an activity course in gospel teaching, by Howard R. Driggs. [Salt Lake City] Deseret Sunday school union of the Church of Jesus Christ of latter-day saints [1946] xiv, 325 p. illus. 20 cm. "General references": p. 317-320. [BV1534.D7] 47-15362
1. Jesus Christ—Teaching methods. 2. Religious education—Teaching methods. I. Title.

EAKIN, Mildred Olivia 268.6 (Moody) 1890-
The church-school teacher's job, by Mildred Moody Eakin and Frank Eakin. New York, Macmillan Co., 1949. xi, 233 p. 21 cm. "Reading suggestions": p. 225-228. [BV1534.E25] 49-7698
1. Religious education—Teaching methods. I. Eakin, Frank, 1885- joint author. II. Title.

EAVEY, Charles Benton, 268.6 1889-
Principles of teaching for Christian teachers [by] C. R. Eavey...introduction by Clarence H. Benson... Grand Rapids, Mich., Zondervan publishing house [c1940] 346 [5] p. 19 1/2 cm. "References" at end of most of the chapters. [RV1534.E3] 40-31667
1. Religious education—Teaching methods. I. Title.

EDGE, Findley B 1916- 268.6
Teaching for results. Nashville, Broadman Press [1956] 230p. 22cm. [BV1534.E34] 56-1640
1. Religious education—Teaching methods. 2. Sunday-schools. I. Title.

EDWARDS, Charlotte 268'.432 Walrath.
Let yourself go; try creative Sunday school. New York, Morehouse-Barlow Co. [1969] 122 p. 21 cm. [BV1534.E36] 77-88121
1. Religious education—Teaching methods. I. Title.

EGGLESTON, Margaret (White) 267 Mrs., 1878-
The use of the story in religious education, by Margaret W. Eggleston ... New York, George H. Doran company [c1920] x p., 2 l., 15-181 p. 20 cm. Bibliography: p. 175-181. [BV1472.E2] 20-4125
1. Religious education—Teaching methods. 2. Story-telling. I. Title.

FORD, LeRoy. 268'.632
Using the lecture in teaching and training. Illustrated by Doug Dillard. Nashville, Broadman Press [1968] 127 p. illus. 21 cm. [BV1534.F6] 68-20673
1. Religious education—Teaching methods. 2. Lecture method in teaching. I. Dillard, Samuel D., illus. II. Title.

GANGEL, Kenneth O. 268'.6
Understanding teaching, by Kenneth O. Gangel. [1st ed.] Wheaton, Ill., Evangelical Teacher Training Association [1968] 95 p. illus. 22 cm. (E.T.T.A. preliminary (foundational) certificate series) Includes bibliographical references. [BV1534.G33] 68-24579
1. Religious education—Teaching methods. I. Title.

HALL, Arlene Stevens 268
Teaching children in your church. Rev. ed. Anderson, Ind., Warner [1962] 96p. 21cm. 62-13336 1.25 pap.,
1. Religious education—Teaching methods. I. Title.

HALL, Arlene Stevens. 268
Teaching children in your church. Anderson, Ind., Warner Press [1951] 118 p. 19 cm. [BV1534.H27] 51-5371
1. Religious education—Teaching methods. I. Title.

HARPER, Albert Foster, 268.6 1907-
The Sunday-school teacher. Kansas City, Mo., Beacon Hill Press [1956] 115p. illus. 19cm. (Christian service training course) [BV1534.H358] 56-2200
1. Religious education- -Teaching methods. 2. Sunday-schools. I. Title.

HARTLEY, Gertrude. 268.
The use of projects in religious education, by Gertrude Hartley. Philadelphia, Boston [etc.] The Judson press [c1921] 91 p. plates. 19 cm. (Half-title: Judson training manuals for the school of the church, ed. by W. E. Raffety, H. E. Traile, W. E. Chaimeres) [BV1534.H36] 21-15413
1. Religious education—Teaching methods. 2. Project method in teaching. I. Title.

HAWTHORNE, Marion Olive. 232.
...Jesus among His neighbors. Teacher's manual. By Marion O. Hawthorne. New York, Cincinnati [etc.] The Abingdon press [c1929] 117 p. 20 cm. (The Abingdon religious education texts, J. W. Langdale, general editor; Week-day school series, G. H. Betts, editor) [BT307.H36] 29-24358
I. Title.

HOAG, Frank Victor, 1891- 268.6
It's fun to teach; a book for folks who wish to help children in the church school, but don't know how to start. [Abridged ed.] New York, Morehouse-Gorham Co., 1951. 150 p. 21 cm. [BV1534.H57] 51-8611
1. Religious education—Teaching methods. 2. Sunday-schools. I. Title.

HOAG, Frank Victor, 1891- 268.6
It's fun to teach; a book for folks who wish to help children in the church school, but don't know how to start. New York, Morhouse-Gorham Co., 1949. xiii, 199 p. 21 cm. "Most of the material appeared originally in the Living Church in the department "Talks with teachers," but has been largely re-written," [BV1534.H56] 49-10150
1. Religious education—Teaching methods. 2. Sunday-schools. I. Title.

HOAG, Frank Victor, 1891- 268.6
The ladder of learning; new ways of teaching in the church school. Greenwich, Conn., Seabury Press, 1960. 152p. 22cm. [BV1534.H58] 60-11085
1. Religious education— Teaching methods. I. Title.

HOBBS, Charles R. 371.3
The power of teaching with new techniques, by Charles R. Hobbs. [2d ed., rev. and enl.] Salt Lake City, Utah, Deseret Book Co., 1972. xxii, 357 p. illus. 24 cm. Published in 1964 under title: Teaching with new techniques. Bibliography: p. [343]-347. [BV1534.H583 1972] 72-92037 ISBN 0-87747-267-X 5.95
1. Religious education—Teaching methods. I. Title.

HOLCOMB, Jerry. 268'.6
Team teaching with the Scotts and Bartons. Valley Forge [Pa.] Judson Press [1968] 127 p. illus. 20 cm. [BV1534.H59] 68-22753 2.50
1. Religious education—Teaching methods. 2. Teaching teams. I. Title.

HOWARD, Philip Eugene, 1870- 268.
A little kit of teachers' tools, by Philip E. Howard ... Philadelphia, The Sunday school times company [c1921] 2 p. l., 72 p. 19 cm. [BV1534.H7] 22-693
I. Title.

HOWSE, William Lewis, 268.61 1905-
Guiding young people in Bible study. Nashville, Convention Press [1955] 144p. 20cm. [BV1534.H73] 268.433 55-14855
1. Religious education—Teaching methods. 2. Bible— Study. I. Title.

JEEP, Elizabeth. 268'.4
Classroom creativity; an idea book for religion teachers. [New York] Herder and Herder [1970] vii, 148 p. illus. 28 cm. Includes bibliographies. [BV1534.J4] 73-114150 2.45
1. Religious education—Teaching methods. I. Title.

JESUS went about doing good;
a course for primary groups in the vacation church school. Teacher's book... New York, Nashville Published for the Cooperative publication association by Abingdon press [c1957] 95p. illus. 23cm. (The cooperative series: vacation church school texts) Includes music.
I. Hanson, Olaf.

KIRKENDALL, Norma Anne. 268.6
Let's do something about our teaching. Independence, Mo., Herald House [1958] 237p. 18cm. At head of title: Reorganized Church of Jesus Christ of Latter Day Saints. [BX8672.K5] 58-8200
1. Religious education—Teaching methods. 2. Reorganized Church of Jesus Christ of Latter-Day Saints—Education. I. Title.

KUEHNERT, Theodore. 268.6
Directing the learner; an introduction to the study of method, by Theo. Kuehnert ... St. Louis, Mo., Concordia publishing house, 1939. viii, 102 p. diagr. 19 cm. (Condcordia teacher training series) [BV1534.K8] 40-1914
1. Religious education—Teaching methods. I. Title.

LEAVITT, Guy P 268.6
Teach with success. Illustrated by Robert E. Huffman. Cincinnati, Standard Pub. Foundation [1956] 160p. illus. 28cm. [BV1534.L43] 66-47552
1. Religious education—Teaching methods. I. Title.

LITTLE, Sara. 268.6
Learning together in the Christian fellowship. Richard, John Knox Press [1956] 104p. illus. 21cm. [BV1534.L5] 56-9220
1. Religious education—Teaching method I. Title.

LOBINGIER, John Leslie, 268.6 1884-
If teaching is your job. Boston, Pilgrim Press [1956] 154p. 21cm. [BV1534.L6] 56-8212
1. Religious education—Teaching methods. I. Title.

LWIN, Esther.
A church school teacher's guide for youth in Burma (ages twelve through fourteen) vii, 308 l. 28 cm. Bibliography: p. 303-308. 66-90174
I. Title.

LWIN, Esther.
A church school teacher's guide for youth in Burma (ages twelve through fourteen) [Berkeley, Calif.] 1963. vii, 308 l. 28 cm. Bibliography: p. 303-308. 66-90174
I. Title.

MCINTYRE, Marie, comp. 268'.432
Aids for grade school religion teachers: organization and procedures, edited by Marie McIntyre. Huntington, Ind., Our Sunday Visitor [1972] 128 p. 18 cm. [BV1534.M18] 72-84253 ISBN 0-87973-756-5 pap., 1.25

1. Religious education—Teaching methods. I. Title.

MCKINNEY, Alexander Harris, 1858- 250
Human nature in Christian work; a manual for ministers, directors of religious education, church school workers, club leaders and all who work with or for people, by A. H. McKinney... Boston, W. A. Wilde company [c1928] 216 p. 19 1/2 cm. [BV4400.M35] 29-4954
I. Title.

MCLESTER, Frances Cole. 268.6
Teaching in the church school. Henry M. Bullock, general editor. Rev. ed. New York, Abingdon Press [1961] 158p. 19cm. Includes bibliography. [BV1534.M286 1961] 61-2653
1. Religious education—Teaching methods. I. Title.

MCLESTER, Frances Cole. 268.6
Teaching in the church school, by Frances Cole McLester. C. A. Bowen, general editor. Nashville, Cokesbury press [c1940] 160 p. 18 1/2 cm. "Notes": p. 156-160. [BV1534.M286] 40-10025
1. Religious education—Teaching methods. I. Bowen, Cawthon Asbury, 1885- ed. II. Title.

MCLESTER, Frances Cole. 268.6
What is teaching? Suggestions on how to teach in the church school. 3d ed., rev. Nashville, Abingdon-Cokesbury Press [1953] 125p. 19cm. [BV1534.M287 1953] 52-13758
1. Religious education—Teaching methods. 2. Sunday-schools. 3. Teaching. I. Title.

MCLESTER, Frances Cole. 377.1
What is teaching? An introduction to principles of teaching, for officers and teachers in church schools of the Methodist Episcopal church, South, by Frances C. McLester; C. A. Bowen, D.D., general editor. Nashville, Tenn., Cokesbury press, 1932. 128 p. 17 cm. Bibliography: p. 128. [BV1534.M287] 32-19481
1. Religious education—Teaching methods. 2. Sunday-schools. 3. Teaching. I. Bowen, Cawthon Asbury, 1885- ed. II. Title.

MCRAE, Glenn, 1887- 268.6
Teaching youth in the church. [Rev. ed.] St. Louis, Bethany Press [1957, c1940] 119p. 18cm. [BV1534.M288 1957] 56-12428
1. Religious education—Teaching methods. I. Title.

MCRAE, Glenn, 1887- 268.6
Teaching youth in the church, by Glenn McRae. Authorized and approved as a textbook in leadership education by the Curriculum committee of the United Christian missionary society... St. Louis, Mo., The Bethany press [c1940] 109, [1] p. 16 1/2 cm. Bibliography at end of each chapter. [BV1534.M288] 41-6830
1. Religious education—Teaching methods. I. Title.

MEAGHER, James Luke, 1848-1920. 232.
Teaching truth by signs and ceremonies; or, The church, its rites and services, explained for the people. By Rev. Jas. L. Meagher. New York, Russell brothers, 1882. viii, 289 p. incl. front., illus., plates. 19 1/2 cm. [BX1754.M4] 12-36708
I. Title.

[MOGRIDGE, George] 1787-1854. 268.
Ephraim Holding's homely hints. Chiefly addressed to Sunday-school teachers. By Old Humphrey [pseud.] Revised by Thomas O. Summers, D.D. Nashville, Tenn., E. Stevenson & F. A. Owen, for the Methodist Episcopal church, South, 1855. 241 p. 16 cm. [BV1534.M57] 43-46026
1. Religious education—Teaching methods. 2. Christian life. I. Summers, Thomas Osmond. 1812-1882, ed. II. Methodist Episcopal church, South. III. Title.

MUNKRES, Alberta. 268.
... Primary method in the church school, by Alberta Munkres ... New York, Cincinnati, The Abingdon press [c1921] 243 p. front., illus., plates. diagrs. 20 cm. (The Abingdon religious education texts, D. G. Downey, General editor Community training school series, N. E. Richardson, editor) "Books for reference" at end of most of the chapters. [BV1545.M75] 21-4243
I. Title.

MYERS, Alexander John William, 1877- 268.
Teaching religion, by A. J. William Myers, PH. D.; a text-book in the standard leadership training curriculum, outlined and approved by the International council of religious education. Philadelphia, Printed for the Teacher training published association by the Westminster press, 1928. 224 p. diagrs. 20 cm. [BV1485.M8] 28-21076
1. Religious education—Teaching methods I. Title.

MYERS, Alexander John William, 1877- 268.6
Teaching religion creatively, by A. J. Wm. Myers New York [etc.] Fleming H. Revell company [c1932] 239 p. illus. (music) 20 cm. Includes bibliographies. [BV1534.M9] 33-821
1. Religious education—Teaching methods. I. Title.

OLSON, Ove Sigfrid, 1892- 266.6
... Methods of teaching in the church school, by Ove S. Olson ... Recommended by the Board of Christian education and literature of the Augustana synod. Rock Island, Ill., Augustana book concern [1940] 102 p. 20 cm. (The Augustana teacher training course) [BV1534.O4] 40-8920
1. Religious education—Teaching methods. sSreligious education—Teaching methods. 2. Sunday-schools. I. Evangelical Lutheran Augustan synod of North Amerca. Board of Christian education and literature. II. Title.

REYNOLDS, Ferris E 268.6
An adventure with people; the 'reading, writing, and arithmetic' of teaching religion. Philadelphia, Christian Education Press [1954] 96p. 20cm. [BV1534.R4] 54-7072
1. Religious education—Teaching methods. I. Title.

ROADS, Charles, 1855- 268.
Child study for teacher-training, by Rev. Charles Roads ... New York, Eaton & Mains; Cincinnati, Jennings & Graham [c1907] 107 p. 20 cm. "This text-book is the companion of the author's Bible studies for teacher training and together ... they have been called the Comprehensive normal course."--Pref. "Helpful books for further study": p. 107. [BV1533.R6 1907] 7-21543
1. Religios education—Teaching methods. 2. Sunday-schools. I. Title.

ROOD, Wayne R. 268'.07
The art of teaching Christianity; enabling the loving revolution [by] Wayne R. Rood. Photos. by Robert D. Fitch. Nashville, Abingdon Press [1968] 224 p. illus. 20 cm. [BV1534.R627] 68-11472
1. Religious education—Teaching methods. I. Title.

ROORBACH, Rosemary K 268.432
Teaching children in the church. New York, Abingdon Press [1959] 159p. 19cm. Includes bibliography. [BV1534.R63] 59-1746
1. Religious education—Teaching methods. I. Title.

ROZELL, Ray 268.6
Talks on Sunday school teaching, [3d ed.] Grand Rapids, Zondervan Pub. House [1960, c.1956] 150p. 21cm. 60-4132 1.50 pap.,
1. Religious education—Teaching methods. 2. Sunday-schools. I. Title.

SAPP, Phyllis Woodruff, 1908- 268'.432
Creative teaching in the church school. Nashville, Broadman Press [1967] vi, 120 p. illus. 22 cm. [BV1534.S2] 67-22033
1. Religious education—Teaching methods. 2. Religious education of children. I. Title.

SEE, Edwin Francis, 1861-1906. 268.6
The teaching of Bible classes, principles and methods: with special reference to classes of young men and boys [by] Edwin F. See. New York, The International committee of Young men's Christian associations, 1905. viii p., 1 l., 180 p. 19 1/2 cm. "References for reading" at end of each chapter. [BS600.S4 1905] 5-17297
1. Religious education—Teaching methods. 2. Religious education of young people. I. Title. II. Title: Bible classes, The teaching of.

SEVENTH-DAY Adventists. General Conference. Sabbath School Dept. 268.4
Teaching teachers to teach; especially prepared for teachers of the primary, junior, earliteen, and youth divisions of our Sabbath schools, by the General Conference, Sabbath School Department. Rev. ed. Nashville, Southern Pub. Association [c1964] 406 p. illus. 22 cm. [BV1534.S42 1964] 63-21240
1. Seventh-Day Adventists—Education. 2. Religious education—Teaching methods. I. Title.

SHARP, John Kean, 1892- 238.
Aims and methods in teaching religion; a text-book for use in seminaries, novitiates, normal schools and by all who teach religion to the young, by Rev. John K. Sharp ... foreword by Rt. Rev. Thomas E. Molloy ... New York, Cincinnati [etc.] Benziger brothers, 1929. xvi, 407 p. illus., diagrs. 20 cm. "Further reading references" at end of each chapter. [Full name: John Joseph Kean Sharp] [BX925.S5] 29-12696
1. Religious education—Teaching methods. 2. Catholic church—Education. I. Title.

SISEMORE, John T. 268.6
Blueprint for teaching. Nashville, Broadman [c.1964] 103p. forms. 21cm. Bibl. 64-12413 1.95 bds.,
1. Religious education—Teaching methods. I. Title.

SPILMAN, Bernard Washington, 1871- 268.
A study in religious pedagogy; based on Our Lord's interview with the woman of Samaria, by Bernard Washington Spilman ... New York, Chicago [etc.] Fleming H. Revell company [c1920] 88 p. 19 1/2 cm. [BV1534.S7] 21-4242
I. Title.

TAYLOR, Margaret Fisk. 372.82
Time for wonder. Illus. by Ruth Baldwin. Philadelphia, Christian Education Press [1961] 70 p. illus. 28 cm. Includes bibliography. [BV1534.4.T35] 61-17682
1. Religious education — Teaching methods. 2. Drama in education. I. Title.

VIETH, Paul Herman, 1895- 268.
Teaching for Christian living; a practical discussion on the principles and practice of making a curriculum for the church school which shall center in life experience, by Paul H. Vieth ... St. Louis, Mo., The Bethany press [c1929] 272 p. incl. diagr., forms. 20 1/2 cm. "General bibliography": p. 272. [BV1475.V5] 29-16509
1. Religious education—Teaching methods. 2. Sunday-schools. I. Title.

YOUNG, Lois Horton. 268'.6
Dimensions for happening. Valley Forge [Pa.] Judson Press [1971] 96 p. illus. 22 cm. Bibliography: p. 77-82. [BV1536.Y68] 76-144081 ISBN 0-8170-0506-4
1. Bible—Study. 2. Religious education—Teaching methods. I. Title.

Religious education—Teaching methods—Addresses, essays, lectures.

GRIFFIN, Dale E., comp. 268'.07
New ways to learn; practical methods for Christian teaching. Edited by Dale E. Griffin. Saint Louis, Concordia Pub. House [1970] 91 p. illus. 19 cm. (Church teachers library) [BV1534.G73] 74-107422
1. Religious education—Teaching methods—Addresses, essays, lectures. I. Title.

Religious education — Text-books.

BECKWITH, C. M.
The teacher's companion to the Trinity course of church instruction; the Book of common prayer: the text book of the Sunday-school, by Rev. C. M. Beckwith. Grades I, II, III. New York, E. S. Gorham, 1902. 139 p. 20 cm. Subject entries: Church of England--Book of common prayer--Calendar and lectionaires. 2-17013
I. Title.

DELL, Edward Thomas.
A leader's guide for use with The rough years by Chad Walsh. Prepared by Edward T. Dell, Jr. New York, Morehouse-Barlow Co. [1962, c1960] 133 p. 21 cm. "M-B." Includes bibliographies. 66-23011
1. Walsh, Chad, 1914- The rought years. 2. Religious education — Text-books. I. Title.

EGGLESTON, George Teeple, 1906- ed. 268.6
A treasury of Christian teaching. [1st ed.] New York, Harcourt, Brace [1958] 306 p. 22 cm. [BV1561.E4] 58-10912
1. Religious education—Text-books. I. Title.

EVANS, J. J., comp. 200'.71
Guard our unbelief: passages for discussion; selected by J. J. Evans. London, Oxford University Press, 1971. xii, 180 p. 21 cm. [BV1561.E83] 78-591485 ISBN 0-19-913035-3 £0.75
1. Religious education—Text-books. 2. Readers—Religion. I. Title.

HODGSON, Natalie. 268'.432
Pieces of the puzzle. St. Louis, Published for the Cooperative Publication Association by Bethany Press [1969] 191 p. 22 cm. (The Cooperative through-the-week series) "One of two courses available for grades 7 and 8. Teacher's book." Bibliography: p. 189-191. [BV1559.H6] 69-20438
1. Religious education—Text-books. I. Cooperative Publication Association. II. Title.

JESUS, our best friend,
by Kate Chenault Maddry. A teacher's book...to be used only in 1958, 1961, 1964, 1967. Nashville, Convention Press, 1958. [Nashville, Convention Press, 1958] 116p. illus., music. 24, [1] p. illus., music. (Vacation Bible school textbooks. Primary book B) Convention press series.
I. Title: —Pupils book.

A primary teacher's guide on Bible lands today. New York, Friendship Press, 1958. 64p. music. For use with: The thirsty village, by Dorothy Blatter.
I. Hoke, Blanche.

SCHUMAKER, Albert Jesse Ringer, 1882-
The Union lesson guide and golden text book for 1917, prepared by A. J. R. Schumaker ... Philadelphia, American Sunday-school union [c1916] 64 p. 13 cm. 16-22789 0.06
I. American Sunday-school union. II. Title.

SQUIRES, Walter Albion. 225.
Paul, the traveler and missionary ... by Walter Albion Squires ... Philadelphia, The Westminster press, 1923. xii, 291 p. front. (map) illus., plates. 19 cm. (The Westminster textbooks of religious education for church schools having Sunday, week day, and expressional sessions, ed. by J. T. Faris. Intermediate department, 2d year, pt. II) [BS2507.S7] 24-18353
I. Title.

TROUT, Ethel Wendell. 221
The downfall of the Hebrew nation ... by Ethel Wendell Trout ... Philadelphia, The Westminster press, 1924. x, xlix-lxxxiii, 201-406 p. illus. (incl. maps) plates. 18 1/2 cm. (The Westminster textbooks of religious education for church schools having Sunday, week day, and expressional sessions, ed. by J. T. Faris. Junior departments, 3d year, pt. 11) Contains bibliographies. [BS1194.T72] 24-18298
I. Title.

TYNDALL, John William, 1877- 220
Special lessons for Bible schools, by John W. Tyndall ... [Charlotte, N.C., Southern printing co., c1922] 133 p. 22 1/2 cm. [BS605.T93] 23-2155
I. Title.

VERSTEEG, John M. 220
... Christianity at work, by John M. Versteeg. New York, Cincinnati, The Abingdon press [c1925] 307 p. 20 1/2 cm. (The Abingdon religious education texts, D. G. Downey, general editor. Week-day

school series, G. H. Betts, editor) "Suggested readings" at end of each chapter. Bibliography: p. 307. [BR125.V4] 25-20148
I. Title.

YORKE, P[eter] C., ed.
Text-books of religion for parachial and Sunday schools. By Rev. P. C. Yorke... San Francisco, The Text-book pub. co., 1901. 304 p. incl. illus., maps. 12 cm. 1-20365
I. Title.
Contents omitted.

Religious education—Text-books—Anglican.

EXPANDING life in the 268'.433
Christian faith with junior highs. Nancy B. Geyer, editor. New York, Seabury Press [1972] 80 p. illus. 28 cm. "Prepared from materials developed under the direction of Robert G. Nesbit at St. Mary's Episcopal Church, Park Ridge, Ill." [BX5875.E9] 75-189103 ISBN 0-8164-5697-6
1. Religious education—Text-books—Anglican. I. Geyer, Nancy, ed.

Religious education—Text-books—Catholic.

BOTHWELL, Mary de 377'.8'2
Angelis.
God cares for us; teacher's manual for perform-a-text 2 [by] Sister Mary de Angelis Bothwell, Sister Mary Margarette Harwood, and other sisters of Notre Dame of Chardon, Ohio. Theological advisor: John A. Hardon. Consultant: Daniel L. Flaherty. Chicago, Loyola University Press [1973] 416 p. illus. 23 cm. (Christ our life series) Includes bibliographical references. [BX930.B6424] 73-12708 ISBN 0-8294-0222-5 4.95 (pbk.)
1. Religious education—Text-books—Catholic. I. Harwood, Mary Margarette, joint author. II. Title. III. Series.

BOTHWELL, Mary de Angelis. 230'.2
God guides us; teacher's manual for perform-a-text 3 [by] Mary de Angelis Bothwell [and] Mary Margarette Harwood. Theological advisor: John A. Hardon. Consultant: Vincent G. Horrigan. Chicago, Loyola University Press [1974] 32, 435 p. illus. 23 cm. (Christ our life series, 3) [BX930.B64245] 74-167306 ISBN 0-8294-0226-8 4.95; 2.00 (for text without manual)
1. Religious education—Text-books—Catholic. I. Harwood, Mary Margarette, joint author. II. Title.

BOTHWELL, Mary de 377'.8'2
Angelis.
God is good; teacher's manual for perform-a-text 1 [by] Sister Mary de Angelis Bothwell and other Sisters of Notre Dame. Theological adviser, John A. Hardon; consultant, Daniel L. Flaherty. Chicago, Loyola University Press [1973] 448 p. illus. 23 cm. (Christ our life series, 1) [BX930.B6425] 73-5752 ISBN 0-8294-0219-5 4.95
1. Religious education—Text-books—Catholic. I. Title.

DISCOVERY patterns 268'.61
[edited by] Robert J. Heyer [and] Richard J. Payne. Paramus, N.J., Paulist Press [1969] 3 v. illus., facsims., ports. 28 cm. Contents.Contents.—book 1. Patterns of situations.—book 2. Patterns of dynamics and strategies.—book 3. Patterns of techniques. [BX930.D53] 77-103003
1. Religious education—Text-books—Catholic. I. Heyer, Robert J. II. Payne, Richard J., ed.

HENNESSY, Nancy. 260
Decision; church, teacher's introduction with idea-lines [by] Nancy Hennessy and Carol White. [New York] Herder and Herder [1970] 95 p. 21 cm. [BX930.H42] 75-87756 1.95
1. Religious education—Text-books—Catholic. I. White, Carol, joint author. II. Title.

LARSEN, Earnest. 265'.6'07
Will morality make sense to your child? [by] Earnest Larsen [and] Patricia Galvin. Liguori, Mo., Liguori Publications [1971] 165, [4] p. col. illus. 18 cm. Bibliography: p. [167] [BX930.L27] 73-160694 1.75
1. Religious education—Text-books—Catholic. 2. Confession of children. I. Galvin, Patricia, joint author. II. Title.

LIFE in God's love 268.6
series; Catholic programmed instruction. Program ed.: Julian May. Content ed.:Louis B. Antl. Chicago, Franciscan Herald [1963] 28cm. 63-17251 teacher's ed., 2.95; student's ed., 1.50
1. Religious education—Text-books—Catholic Church. I. May, Julian, ed.

PODSIADLO, Jack, comp. 268'.433
Discovery in celebration; a teacher source book [by] Jack Podsiadlo and Robert Heyer. Designed by Judith Savard and Marion Faller. New York, Paulist Press [1970] 124 p. illus. (part col.) 20 cm. (Discovery series) [BX930.P6] 75-133470 4.50
1. Religious education—Text-books—Catholic. I. Heyer, Robert J., joint comp. II. Title.

TEACHING with Witness 268'.433
junior high: handbook for use in 1969-1970. [Dayton, Ohio, G. A. Pflaum, 1969] 72 p. illus. 21 cm. Cover title. Intended for use with the "Witness program—student magazine, filmstrips, guide, resources, and doctrinal topics." "Resource guide": p. 61-72. [BX930.T38] 75-95906
1. Religious education—Text-books—Catholic. I. Title: Witness junior high.

*WERR, Donald F. 261.83
Today's world; a textual guide for the college course in Catholic and modern problems [dist. Berkeley, Calif., 94704, McCutchan] 1966. 128p. 28cm. Bibl. price unreported pap.,
I. Title.

Religious education—Text-books—Congregational.

RUSSELL, Howard H., 268'.432
1934-
Growing in love; a course for the first and second grades, by Howard H. Russell. Philadelphia, United Church Press [1972] 128 p. illus. 26 cm. "Part of the United Church curriculum, prepared and published by the Division of Christian Education and the Division of Publication of the United Church Board for Homeland Ministries." Bibliography: p. 125-126. [BX9884.A3R87] 72-7378 2.20
1. Religious education—Text-books—Congregational. I. United Church Board for Homeland Ministries. Division of Christian Education. II. United Church Board for Homeland Ministries. Division of Publication. III. Title.

Religious education—Text-books for adolescents.

ADVANCED course for Catholic living; teacher's manual. [Huntington, Ind., Our Sunday Vistor Press, 1959] [Huntington, Ind., Our Sunday Visitor Press, 1959] 4 v. illus. 28cm. 4v. 23p. Cover title.
1. Religious education—Textbooks for adolescents. I. Mission Helpers of the Sacred Heart, Baltimore, Md. II. Title: — Student's memo pages.

COBB, Margaret Brown. 268.6
... Everything counts; Christian adventures in learning and living, by Margaret Brown Cobb. New York, Friendship press [1943] 127 p. illus. 18 1/2 cm. At head of title: A course for junior high school groups. [BV1548.C6] 44-25602
1. Religious education—Text-books for adolescents. I. Title.

HOYER, George W. 268
I think I'll be . . . ; a workbook for young people in the church. St. Louis, Concordia, c.1961. 65p. illus. 28cm. .85 pap.,
I. Title.

LIVING with the Church;
a teacher's guide in presenting devotional religion. Detroit, Parochial School Publications, c1959. iii, 66p. 26cm. Ninth grade text.
1. Religious education—Textbooks for adolescents.

MCCLELLAND, Margaret 268.433
Tyrrell.
Intermediates in action, through the Sunday school. [Teacher's ed.] Nashville, Convention Press [c1960] 104p. illus. 19cm. [BV1549.65.M25] 60-15526
1. Religious education—Text-books for adolescents. I. Title.

NALL. FRANCES (MAHAFFIE) 268.61
1902-
It happened this way. Illustrated by John Gretzer. New York, Friendship Press [1956] 117p. illus. 21cm. [BV1548N3] 268.433 56-6580
1. Religious education—Text-books for adolescents. I. Title.

REICHERT, Richard. 377'.8'2
The real thing. Notre Dame, Ind., Ave Maria Press [1972] 125 p. 21 cm. [BX930.R43] 72-76480
1. Religious education—Text-books for adolescents. 2. Religious education—Catholic Church. I. Title.

SAILER, Thomas Henry Powers, 268.
1868-
What does Christ expect of young people today? A series of questions for discussion for girls and boys, thirteen to sixteen years of age [by] T. H. P. Sailer ... Teacher's complete manual, including pupil's assignments. Boston, Chicago, The Pilgrim press [1926] 2 p. l., 113 p. 18 1/2 cm. [BV1561.S3] 26-4288
1. Religious education—Text-books for adolescents. I. Title.

Religious education—Text-books for adolescents—Anglican.

PROTESTANT Episcopal 268.432
Church in the U. S. A. National Council. Dept. of Christian Education.
What is Christian Education. Greenwich, Conn., Seabury Press [1956] 177p. illus. 22cm. (The Seabury series, R-8) [BV1548.P694] 56-7851
1. Religious education—Text-books for adolescents—Anglican. I. Title. II. Title: What is Christian courage?

Religious education—Text-books for adolescents—Baptist.

BIBY, Mary Alice, 1887- 268.433
comp.
Sunday school programs for intermediates, compiled by Mary Alice Biby ... Nashville, Tenn., Broadman press [1946] 276 p. diagr. 19 1/2 cm. "The material for the programs ... was taken from the Intermediate counselor."--Pref. [BV1548.B5] 46-7974
1. Religious education—Text-books for adolescents.—Baptist. I. Title.

BURKHALTER, Frank Elisha, 268.433
1880-
Intermediate fishers. Nashville, Broadman Press [1951] 104 p. illus. 20 cm. [BV1548.B8] 51-3472
1. Religious education—Text-books for adoiescents—Baptist. 2. Evangelistic work—Study and teaching. I. Title.

CAMMACK, James C 1918- 248.5
Yours to share [by] James C. Cammack. [Teacher's ed.] Nashville, Convention Press [1966] vii, 72 p. illus. 19 cm. [BX6225.C3] 66-10255
1. Religious education—Text-books for adolescents—Baptist. I. Title.

MCKAY, Richard W. 268'.8'6
Helping people in need [by] Richard W. McKay. [Teacher's ed.] Nashville, Convention Press [1968] xii, 78 p. illus. 19 cm. "Church study course [of the Sunday School Board of the Southern Baptist Convention] This book is number 0483 in category 4, section for intermediates." Includes bibliographical references. [BX6225.M33] 68-11672
1. Religious education—Text-books for adolescents—Baptist. I. Title.

OLSON, Virgil A 268.433
Church history, by Virgil A. Olson. Chicago, Harvest Publications [1955] 115 p. illus. (part col.) 26 cm. ("Tell me, please," book 2) [BX6225.O4] 65-25400
1. Religious education — Text-books for adolescents — Baptist. 2. Church history. I. Title.

PINSON, William M. 268'.433
No greater challenge [by] William M. Pinson, Jr. [Teacher's ed.] Nashville, Convention Press [1969] xiii, 82 p. 19 cm. "Church study course [of the Sunday School Board of the Southern Baptist Convention] This book is number 1484 in category 4, section for intermediates." "Teacher's helps": [16] p. bound in between p. 34-35. Bibliography: p. 76-79. [BX6225.P5] 69-10015
1. Religious education—Text-books for adolescents—Baptist. I. Southern Baptist Convention. Sunday School Board. II. Title.

SHERWICK, Winston M 268.432
Bible doctrine, by Winston M. Sherwick. Chicago, Harvest Publications [c1964] 103 p. illus. (part col.) 26 cm. ("Tell me, please," book 1) [BX6225.S5] 64-8448
1. Religious education—Textbooks for adolescents—Baptist. I. Title.

TAYLOR, Bob R., 1935- 268'.8'6132
Intermediates in training [by] Bob R. Taylor. [Teacher's ed.] Nashville, Convention Press [1968] vi, 106 p. illus. 19 cm. "Church study course [of the Sunday School Board of the Southern Baptist Convention] This book is number 1882 in category 18, section for intermediates." Includes bibliographies. [BX6225.T35] 68-11674
1. Religious education—Text-books for adolescents—Baptist. I. Southern Baptist Convention. Sunday School Board. II. Title.

Religious education—Text-books for adolescents—Catholic.

BROWNSON, Josephine Van 230.2
Dyke.
To the heart of the child; or, Learn of Me, viii, by Josephine Van Dyke Brownson. Detroit, Mich., The Catholic instruction league [1936] vii, 248 p. illus. (incl. maps) diagrs. 19 cm. (Her Learn of Me. viii) "Second revised edition, November, 1936." Pages 237-248 blank for "Notes". [BX930.B8 1936] 40-25704
1. Religious education—Text-books for adolescents—Catholic. I. Title.

BROWNSON, Josephine Van 230.2
Dyke.
To the heart of the child, or book eight in the Learn of me series, by Josephine Van Dyke Brownson ... in collaboration with Rev. Leo De Barry ... Illustrations by the author. Huntington, Ind., Our Sunday visitor press [c1940] 5 p. l., 254 p. illus. (incl. maps) diagrs. 19 cm. [BX930.B8 1940] 40-34452
1. Religious education—Text-books for adolescents—Catholic. I. De Barry, Leo, joint author. II. Title.

CATHOLIC catechism. 238'.2
Grades five and six. Huntington, Ind., Our Sunday Visitor, inc. [1971] x, 262 p. col. illus. 19 cm. A rev. ed. for use in North America of a work originally issued as "Book one" in 1962 for use in the Catholic schools of Australia by the Australian hierarchy. [BX930.C34 1971] 71-27774
1. Religious education—Text-books for adolescents—Catholic.

FLYNN, Anthony J. 232.9
... The way, the truth and the life [by] Reverend Anthony J. Flynn ... Sister Vincent Loretto ... [and] Mother Mary Simeon ... New York, Chicago, W. H. Sadlier, inc [c1943] ix, 277 p. illus., diagrs. 23 1/2 cm. (The Catholic high school religion series. Book 1) [BX930.F63] 44-4059
1. Religious education—Text-books for adolescents—Catholic. I. Vincent Loretto, sister, 1893- joint author. II. Mary Simeon, mother, 1894- joint author. III. Title.

KALT, William J. 268'.61
The emerging church [by] William J. Kalt and Ronald J. Wilkins. With the special assistance of Raymond Schmandt. Chicago, Regnery [1968] 2 v. (v, 243 p.) illus., maps, ports. 23 cm. (To live is Christ. Dicusssion booklet 4-5) Includes

bibliographical footnotes. [BX930.K25] 68-55750
1. Religious education—Text-books for adolescents—Catholic. I. Wilkins, Ronald J., joint author. II. Title.

KEVANE, Eugene, ed. 268.6
Divine providence and human progress series. General editor: Eugene Kevane. Washington, Christian Culture Press [c1963- v. 25 cm. Contents.-- v. 4. Christian social living in the modern world, by J. P. Ashton. [BV1549.9D5] 64-28475
1. Religious education — Text-books for adolescents — Catholic. I. Title.

MURRAY, Jane Marie, 1896- 268.433
The Christian life series. Chicago, Fides Publishers Association [1957- v. illus. 24cm. [BX930.M8] 57-11577
1. Religious education—Text-books for adolescents—Catholic. I. Title.
Contents omitted.

O'KEEFE, Thomas. 268'.433
The signs of the times. North Easton, Mass., Holy Cross Press [1969] 76 p. illus. 22 cm. [BX930.O45] 74-89845 2.25
1. Religious education—Text-books for adolescents—Catholic. I. Title.

PRETE, Anthony. 268'.61
Witness catechist's handbook; theme material. Dayton, Ohio, G. A. Pflaum [1968] xvii, 78 p. illus. 21 cm. "Teacher material for Witness-Plus a doctrinal course 'The life of the Church—today and tomorrow' combined with Witness junior high 1968-1969." Bibliographical references included in "Weekly resource guide" (p. 69-78) [BV1549.77.P7] 68-55340
1. Religious education—Text-books for adolescents—Catholic. I. Title.

WILKINS, Ronald J. 268'.433
Focus on life [by] Ronald J. Wilkins and John T. Bettin. Dubuque, Iowa, W.C. Brown Co. [1971] 204 p. illus. (part col.) 16 x 23 cm. (To live is Christ. Focus book 3) [BX930.W485] 72-160431
1. Religious education—Text-books for adolescents—Catholic. I. Bettin, John T., joint author. II. Title.

Religious education—Text-books for adolescents—Congregational.

ALPENFELS, Ethel Josephine. [261]
Brothers all, a course for the junior high age; illus. by John Leamon. Teacher's ed. Boston, Pilgrim Press [1950] xiv, 54, v-vi, 88 p. illus. 21 cm. (Pilgrim series) The "Pupil's book" (v-vi, 88 p.) is preceded by the "Teacher's guide" (xiv, 54 p.) Bibliography: p. xiii. [BV1548.A4] 268.433 50-2139
1. Religions education—Text-books for adolescents—Congregational. 2. Church and social problems—Study and teaching. I. Title.

MCKENDRY, James Banford. 268.433
God revealed through His world, a course for thejunior high age; illus. by Matthew William Boyhan. Boston, Pilgram Press [1948] 72 p. illus. 21 cm. (Pilgram series) [BV1548.M26] 48-11074
1. Religious education—Text-books for adolescents—Congregational. I. Title.

MCKENDRY, James Banford. 268.433
God revealed through His world, a course for the junior high age; illus. by Matthew William Boyhan. Boston, Pilgram Press [1948] x. 54, 72 p. illus. 21 cm. (Pilgrim series) The main work (72 p.) also issued separately, is preceded by a manual for the teacher (x. 54 p.) [BV1548.M265] 48-11161
1. Religious education—Text-books for adolescents—Congregational. I. Title.

Religious education—Text-books for adolescents—United Church of Christ.

DODDER, G. Clyde 268.432
Becoming a Christian person, a course for ninth and tenth grades. Illus. by Mark Kelley. Philadelphia, United Church [c.1963] 127p. illus. 26cm. 62-15302 1.50 pap.,
1. Religous education—Text-books for adolescents—United Church of Christ. I. Title.

DODDER, G Clyde. 268.432
Becoming a Christian person, a course for ninth and tenth grades. Illus. by Mark Kelley. Boston, United Church Press [1963] 127 p. illus. 26 cm. [BX9884.A3D6] 62-15302
1. Religious education — Text-books for adolescents — United Church of Christ. I. Title.

HULL, Eleanor (Means)
Through the secret door. Illus. by Gilbert Riswold. Boston, United Church Press [c1963] 96 p. illus. 22 cm. (United Church curriculum. Junior High. Pupils. 1') 64-19733
1. Religious education—Text-books for adolescents—United Church of Christ. I. Title.

PRICHARD MARIANNA (NUGENT) 268.433
My Christian heritage; a course for ninth and tenth grades. by Marianna Nugent Prichard and Norman Young Prichard. Boston, United Church Press,[1964] 124 p. illus., col., maps. 26 cm. "Part of the United Church curriculum, prepared and published by the Division of Christian Education and the Division of Publication of the United Church Board for Homeland Ministries." Bibliography: p. 122-123. [BX9884.A3P7] 64-19463
1. Religious education—Textbooks for adolescents—United Church of Christ. I. Prichard, Norman Young, joint author. II. United Church Board for Homeland Ministries. Division of Christian Education. III. United Church Board for Homeland Ministries. Division of Publications. IV. Title.

REID, Clyde H 260.7
I belong, a course for seventh and eighth grades, by Clyde Reid. Boston, United Church Press [c1964] 124 p. illus. (part col.) fold. col. map. 26 cm. "Part of the United Church Curriculum prepared and published by the Division of Christian Education and the Division of Publication of the United Church Board for Homeland Ministries." Bibliography: p. 122-123. [BX9884.A3R4] 64-19462
1. Religious education — Test-books for adolescents — United Church of Christ. I. United Church Board for Homeland Ministries. Division of Christian Education. II. United Church Board for Homeland Ministries. Division of Publication. III. Title.

Religious education—Text-books for adults.

ADKINS, Edward T. 260
Study-action manual for "Mission: the Christmas calling", by Edward T. Adkins. New York, Friendship Press [1965] 96 p. 19 cm. "Program for adults, for use with Voices of protest and hope: The Word with power: Mission as decision; Babylon by choice; [and] Realms of our calling." [BV1561.A2] 65-11420
1. Religious education — Text-books for adults. 2. Missions — Study and teaching I. Title.

CULLY, Kendig Brubaker. [261]
We can live together; a reading and study guide for older young people and adults. Boston, Pilgrim Press [1950] 96 p. 21 cm. (Pilgrim series) [BV1550.C8] 268.434 50-2138
1. Religions education —Textbooks for adults—Congregational. 2. Church and social problems—Study and teaching. I. Title.

FOUNDATIONS of Catholic theology. Gerald S. Sloyan, editor. Englewood Cliffs, N.J., Prentice-Hall, 1963- v. 23 cm.
1. Religious education — Textbooks for adults. 2. Theology — Textbooks — 20th cent.

JACKSON, Edgar Newman.
Facing outselves; an elective unit for adults. With Leader's guide by Robert S. Clemmons and Russell L. Dicks. New York, Abingdon [1960?] 124 p. 63-21865
1. Religious education — Textbooks for adults. 2. Psychology, Religious. I. Title.

JOHNSTON, Howard Agnew, 1860-1936.
Studies in God's methods of training workers, by Howard Agnew Johnston. New York, International committee of Young men's Christian associations, 1900. xi, 2-171 p. 22 cm. [BV4401.J6] 0-6654
1. Religious education—Text-books for adults. 2. Bible—Study—Text-books. I. Title.

SHANNON, Robert, 1930- 248.4
Belonging; a key to closer fellowship with the God of the universe and those who belong to Him in the deepest sense. Cincinnati, Ohio, Standard Pub. [1971, c1968] 96 p. 18 cm. (Fountain books) [BV1561.S48] 78-164741
1. Religious education—Text-books for adults. I. Title.

SLOYAN, Gerald Stephen, 1919- ed.
Foundations of Catholic theology. Gerald S. Sloyan, editor. Englewood Cliffs, N.J., Prentice-Hall, 1963- v. 23 cm. 65-48390
1. Religious education — Textbooks for adults. 2. Theology — Textbooks — 20th cent. I. Title.

STEVENSON, Dwight Eshelman, 1906-
The church -- what and why. St. Louis, Christian Board of Publication [c1962] 164 p. (Christian Discipleship series, v. 1, parts 1-2) Includes bibliography. 63-75276
1. Religious education — Textbooks for adults. 2. Church. I. Title. II. Series.

TRENT, Robbie, 1894-
Basic Christian beliefs. Nashville, Sunday school board of the SBC, 1964. 50 p. Teacher's ed. by Howard P. Colson [and] Robbie Trent. 68-18139
1. Religious education—Text-books for adults. I. Colson, Howard P., 1910- II. Title.

Religious education—Text-books for adults—Anglican.

PARTRIDGE, Edmund B., 1932- 268'.434
The church in perspective; standard lay readers' training course, by Edmund B. Partridge. New York, Morehouse-Barlow Co. [1969] 142 p. 24 cm. [BX5875.P3] 68-56918
1. Religious education—Text-books for adults—Anglican. 2. Lay readers. I. Title.

PROTESTANT Episcopal Church in the U. S. A. National Council. Dept. of Christian Education. 268.434
Faith is a family affair; a manual for use with classes of parents and godparents with special reference to church school grades 3, 6, and 9, and nursery children three and four years old. Illustrated by Seymour Fleishman. Greenwich, Conn., Seabury Press [1957] 151p. illus. 21cm. (The Seabury series, P-3) Includes bibliography. [BV1550.P8] 57-8347
1. Religious education—Text-books for adults—Anglican. I. Title.

Religious education—Text-books for adults—Baptist.

BURROWS, Lansing.
How Baptists work together; for use as textbook in study courses either with the individual, with the church B. Y. P. U., or as supplemental studies in the church Sunday school [by] Lansing Burrows ... Nashville, Tenn., Sunday school board, Southern Baptist convention [c1911] 138 p. 17 1/2 cm. $0.50 11-12254
I. Title.

EUTING, George L. 268.86
Missionary education for Baptist men; a guide for organizing and operating a Baptist men's unit, by George L. Euting. [Memphis, Brotherhood Commn., 1966] 154p. 20cm. [BX6225.E9] 66-27808 1.00
1. Religious education—Text-books for adults—Baptist. 2. Southern Baptists Convention—Education. I. Title.
548 Poplar Ave., Memphis, Tenn. 38104

GRAYUM, H. Frank. 230.6
Bible truths for today. H. Frank Grayum, editor. Nashville, Convention Press [1970] 69 p. 20 cm. "Reprinted from Baptist adults, January, February, March, 1964." "This book is the text for course number 3301 of subject area Christian theology in the New church study course." [BX6225.G67] 71-118304
1. Religious education—Text-books for adults—Baptist. I. Title.

ISHEE, John A. 268'.61
Adults in church training [by] John A. Ishee. Nashville, Convention Press [1969] ix, 131 p. illus. 20 cm. "Text for course 6403 of subject area 64, Christian leadership series, New church study course." Bibliography: p. 113-114. [BX6225.I8] 79-85882
1. Religious education—Text-books for adults—Baptists. 2. Church group work. I. Title.

THE 70's: opportunities for your church. Edited by James Daniel and Elaine Dickson Nashville, Convention Press [1969] 160 p. illus. 21 cm. Includes 6 resource papers from intensive studies conducted by the Southern Baptist Convention. [BX6225.S43] 69-17890 261
1. Religious education—Text-books for adults—Baptist. I. Daniel, James H., ed. II. Dickson, Elaine, ed. III. Southern Baptist Convention.

TRENTHAM, Charles Arthur, 1919- 268'.434
Daring discipleship [by] Charles A. Trentham. Nashville, Convention Press [1969] xiii, 123 p. 20 cm. "Church study course [of the Sunday School Board of the Southern Baptist Convention] This book is number 0412 in category 4, section for adults and young people." Includes bibliographies. [BV4511.T7] 69-10013
1. Religious education—Text-books for adults—Baptist. 2. Christian life—Baptist authors. I. Southern Baptist Convention. Sunday School Board. II. Title.

Religious education—Text-books for adults—Catholic.

COONEY, Eugene J. 268.8'2
A murmur within me; theological themes of Come to the Father, by Eugene J. Cooney. New York, Paulist Press [1973] 134 p. 23 cm. Bibliography: p. 131-134. [BX930.C64] 72-94110 ISBN 0-8091-1762-2 4.50
1. Religious education—Text-books for adults—Catholic. I. Title.

GALLAGHER, Joseph Vincent, 1923- 238
A parish catechumenate; materials and format for adult catechesis, by Joseph V. Gallagher. Westminster, Md., Newman Press [1967] vii, 183 p. 22 cm. Includes bibliographies. [BX930.G3] 67-18461
1. Religious education—Text-books for adults—Catholic Church. I. Title.

SEMMELROTH, Otto 268.82
The church and Christian belief. Tr. by Thomas R. Milligan. Study-club questions. Glen Rock, N. J., Paulist [1966] 156p. 19cm. (Deus bks.) Tr. of articles which were orig. pub. separately. [BX930.S4] 66-26962 .95 pap.,
1. Religious education—Text-books for adults—Catholic. I. Title.

VATICAN Council. 2d, 1962-1965. 238
The catechism of modern man; all in the words of Vatican II. Compiled by a group of priest specialists of the Roman province of the Society of St. Paul. Editing of the English edition, addition of the latest implementing documents, arrangement and documentation for study and discussion, topic index, and bibliographical lists, by the Daughters of St. Paul. [Boston] St. Paul Editions [1967] 533 p. 21 cm. National Catholic Welfare Conference translation. Includes bibliographies. [BX830 1962.A517] 67-31725
1. Catholic Church—Doctrinal and controversial works. 2. Religious education—Text-books for adults—Catholic. I. Pious Society of St. Paul. II. Daughters of St. Paul. III. Title.

VATICAN Council. 2d, 1962-1965. 238
The catechism of modern man; all in the words of Vatican II and related documents. Compiled and edited by a team of

Daughters of St. Paul. [Boston] St. Paul Editions [1968] 803 p. 22 cm. Includes bibliographical references. [BX830 1962.A5172 1968b] 78-627 5.95
1. Catholic Church—Doctrinal and controversial works. 2. Religious education—Text-books for adults—Catholic. I. Daughters of St. Paul. II. Title.

WIGAL, Donald. 268'.434
A presence of love. Edited by Donald Wigal and Charles Murphy. [New York] Herder and Herder [1969] 127 p. illus., ports. 21 cm. (Experiences in faith, book 2) Bibliography: p. 126-127. [BX930.W48] 72-87774 1.95
1. Religious education—Text-books for adults—Catholic. I. Murphy, Charles, joint author. II. Title. III. Series.

WIGAL, Donald. 917.3'03'924
A way of community; a program for an adult church. Edited by Donald Wigal and Charles Murphy. [New York] Herder and Herder [1970] 94 p. illus., map, ports. 21 cm. (Experiences in faith, book 3) Cover title. [BX930.W485] 78-13737
1. Religious education—Text-books for adults—Catholic. I. Murphy, Charles, joint author. II. Title. III. Series.

WILLIAM, Franz Michel, 1894- 230.2
Our way to God; a book of religious self-education. Translated by Ronald Walls. Milwaukee, Bruce Pub. Co. [1964] xv, 400 p. 23 cm. [BX930.W513] 64-22859
1. Religious education — Text-books for adults — Catholic. I. Title.

Religious education—Text-books for adults—Lutheran.

BERTRAM, Martin H ed. 230.41
Stimmen der Kirche. St. Louis, Concordia Pub. House, 1961. 240p. illus. 23cm. [BX8015.B45] 61-66363
1. Religious education—Text-books for adults—Lutheran. 2. German language—Chrestomathies and readers. I. Title.

HUNT, Joel Ransom Eallis, 1876-
The Lutheran Sunday-school handbooks, by Rev. J. R. E. Hunt, B.D. Rock Island, Ill., Augustana book concern, 1911. 9 p. l., [11]-291 p. 19 1/2 cm. 11-26485 1.00
I. Title.

Religious education — Text-books for adults — Methodist.

CHILCOTE, Thomas F. 268.61
Man's spiritual pilgrimage; an adventure into elementary theology for laymen, by Thomas F. Chilcote, Jr. Nashville, Methodist Evangelistic Materials, [1965] 88 p. col. front. 14 x 22 cm. Bibliography: p. 86-87. [BX8225.C5] 65-20492
1. Religious education — Text-books for adults — Methodist. I. Title.

Religious education—Text-books for adults—Presbyterian.

BRUERE, John, 1903- 268.434
How to use the Bible for help today, by John Bruere; a series of studies for older young people and adults. Philadelphia, The Westminster press [1941] cover-title, 96 p. illus. 19 cm. "Originally appeared as a part of the periodically issued Westminster departmental graded lessons." "Copyright by the Board of Christian education of the Presbyterian church in the United States of America." [BV1550.B69] 44-15408
1. Religious education—Text-books for adults—Presbyterian. 2. Bible—Use. I. Presbyterian church in the U.S.A. Board of Christian education. II. Title.

Religious education — Text-books for adults — United Church of Christ.

FACKRE, Gabriel J. 268'.8'5834
Conversation in faith; a resource and discussion book for adults, by Gabriel Fackre. Illustrated by Reed Champion. Boston, United Church Press [1968] 92 p. illus. 22 cm. (Confirmation education series) "Part of the United Church curriculum, prepared and published by the Division of Christian Education and the Division of Publication of the United Church Board for Homeland Ministries." Bibliography: p. 90-91. [BV4501.2.F27] 68-10312
1. Christian life—United Church of Christ authors. 2. Religious education—Textbooks for adults—United Church of Christ. I. United Church Board for Homeland Ministries. Division of Christian Education. II. United Church Board for Homeland Ministries. Division of Publication. III. Title.

GIBB, Robert E 248
Armed for crisis; a coursebook for leaders of adults [by] Robert E. Gibb. Boston, United Church Press [c1965] 124 p. illus., ports. 21 cm. Includes bibilographical references. [BX9884.A3G5] 65-14277
1. Religious education — Text-books for adults — United Church of Christ. I. Title.

WETZEL, Willard W 268.434
The Christian view of man. Boston, United Church Press [c1963] 234 p. illus. 21 cm. [BX9884.A3W4] 63-19207
1. Religious education — Text-books for adults — United Church of Christ. I. Title.

Religious education—Text-books for children.

ATHY, Marion (Poppen) Mrs. 1898- 268.62
... Doing as God wants [by] Marion Poppen Athy. A primary unit, ages 6, 7 and 8. Leader's book. [Philadelphia, The United Lutheran publication house, c1941] 63 p. illus. 22 cm. (The children of the church series) "Prepared under the auspices of the Parish and church school board of the United Lutheran church in America." [BV1545.A75] 42-477
1. Religious education—Text-books for children. I. United Lutheran church in America. Parish and church school board. II. Title.

ATHY, Marion (Poppen) Mrs. 1898- 268.62
... Doing as God wants [by] Marion Poppen Athy. A primary unit, ages 6, 7 and 8. Leader's book. [Philadelphia, The United Lutheran publication house, c1941] 63 p. illus. 22 cm. (The children of the church series) "Prepared under the auspices of the Parish and church school board of the United Lutheran church in America." [BV1545.A75] 42-477
1. Religious education—Text-books for children. I. United Lutheran church in America. Parish and church school board. II. Title.

ATHY, Marion (Poppen) Mrs. 1898- 268
Telling others [by] Marion Poppen Athy. A primary unit, ages 6, 7 and 8. Leader's book. [Philadelphia, The United Lutheran publication house, c1939] 63 p. 22 cm. (The children of the church series) "Prepared under the auspices of the Parish and church school board of the United Lutheran church in America." Includes songs with music. "Materials": p. 9-10. [BX8015.A8] 40-85631
1. Religious education—Text-books for children. I. United Lutheran church in America. Parish and church school board. II. Title.

ATHY, Marion (Poppen) 1898- 268.62
... We learn of a wonderful world [by] Marion Poppen Athy. A primary unit, ages 6, 7 and 8. Leader's book. [Philadelphia, The United Lutheran publication house, c1941] 63 p. 22 cm. (The Children of the church series) "Prepared under the auspices of the Parish and church school board of the United Lutheran church in America." [BV1545.A78] 42-15435
1. Religious education—Text-books for children. I. United Lutheran church in America. Parish and church school board. II. Title.

AUS, George. 266.62
Forward with Christ, by George Aus; illustrations by William Hole, R. S. A. Minneapolis, Augsburg publishing house [c1940] 176 p. incl. front., illus. (incl. maps; part col.) 22 cm. Text and colored illustrations on lining-papers. "This volume is one in a series of graded Sunday school textbooks issued by the Board of elementary Christian education, Dr. Jacob Tanner, editor-in-chief." "Luther's small catechism": p. [9]-24. [BX8015.A9] 42-33355
1. Religious education—Text-books for children. I. Tanner, Jacob, 1865-.ed. II. Hole, William, 1846-1917, illus. III. Luther, Martin. Catechismus, Kleiner. IV. Title.

AUS, George. 266.62
Forward with Christ; teacher's manual for grade vii by George Aus. Minneapolis, Augsburg publishing house [1941] 286 p. illus. (incl. maps) diagrs. 22 cm. Includes bibliographies. [BX8015.A92] 42-13321
1. Religious education—Text-books for children. I. Title.

BARNHOUSE, Donald Grey, 1895- 268.62
Teaching the word of truth, by Donald Grey Barnhouse ... Philadelphia, Pa., Revelation book service [c1940] 189 p. illus. 26 cm. [BV1561.B27] 40-12456
1. Religious education—Text-books for children. I. Title.

CLARK, Lillian Rosaria, 1883- 230.
I belong to God; great truths in simple stories for children and the lovers of children, by Lillian Clark...drawings by Clarie Armstrong. New York (etc.] Longmans, Green and co., 1928. xviii, 124 p. illus. 22 cm. "As a series these story-meditations will form a three-day retreat." [BX2371.C7] 28-15196
I. Title.

A Confraternity school year religion course; the adaptive way. For teachers of children attending public schools. Developed under the auspices of the Confraternity of Christian Doctrine. Based on the original School year religious instruction manual of the Confraternity of Christian Doctrine and the Adaptive way manual of the Mission Helpers of the Sacred Heart. [2d ed.] Washington, Confraternity of Christian Doctrine [1956-57] 3v. 21cm. Contents.[1] Grades 1 and 2.-[2] Grades 3, 4 and 5.-[3] Grades 6, 7, 8. Includes bibliographies.
1. Religious education-Textbooks for children. 2. Confraternity of Christian Doctrine. I. Rosalia, Sister, 1896- II. Mission Helpers of the Sacred Heart, Baltimore, Md.

DALE, Mary E
Come unto me [a religion manual and workbook for teachers and parents of the mentally handicapped child, in collaboration with Henry Bedessen. Original art drawings by Mary Jane Hamerski. Appleton, Wis., Come Publishing Co., 1963] 64 p. illus., music. 22 x 28 cm. 68-46252
1. Religious education—Textbooks for children. 2. Church work with mentally handicapped children. I. Bedessen, Henry. II. Title.

DESJARDINS, Lucile, 1892- 268.433
What boys and girls are asking; a guide for teachers including source materials and teaching procedures [by] Lucile Desjardins. New York, Cincinnati (etc.] The Abingdon press [1936] 2 p. l. 3-176 p. 20 cm. (The Abingdon religious education texts, J. W. Langdale, general editor: Guides to Christian living, P.H. Vieth, editor] "Helpful books for teachers": p. 14-16. "Source materials for the browsing table and the library nook": p. 160-176. Vacation church school guide, prepared for use with What boys and girls are asking ... New York, Cincinnati [etc.] The Abingdon press [1937] 24 p. 19 cm. [BV1548.D412] 36-18439
1. Religious education—Text-books for children. 2. Vacation schools, Religious—Teachers' manuals. I. Desjardins, Lucile, 1892- Vacation church school guide. II. Title.

EAKIN, Mildred Olivia (Moody) Mrs. 1890- 268.62
In anybody's town (Exploring our neighborhood, pupil's work book II [by] Mildred Moody Eakin. New York, Cincinnati [etc.] The Abingdon press [c1937] 76 p. illus. 21 1/2 cm. (Half-title: The Abingdon religious education texts, J. W. Langdale, general editor; Guides to Christian living, P. H. Vieth, editor) [BV1546.E28] A41
1. Religious education—Text-books for children. I. Title. II. Title: Exploring our neighborhood, pupil's work book II.

HUNTER, Edith Fisher, 1919- 268.432
Conversation with children. Boston, Beacon Press [1961] 192p. illus. 23cm. Includes bibliography. [BX9821.H8] 61-10571
1. Religious education—Text-books for children. I. Title.

LAMBERTSON, Floyd Wesley, 1891- 220.
... The rules of the game, by Floyd W. Lambertson. New York, Cincinnati, The Abingdon press [c1920] 208 p. plates, map. 20 cm. (The Abingdon religious education texts. D. G. Downey, general editor. Week-day school series. G. H. Betts, editor) [BV1583.L3] 21-1447
I. Title.

LAMBERTSON, Floyd Wesley, 1891- 220.
... The rules of the game; teacher's manual, by Floyd W. Lamberson. New York, Cincinnati, The Abingdon press [c1920] 77 p. 20 cm. (The Abingdon religious education texts. D. G. Dewney, general editor. Week-day school series. G. H. Betts, editor) [BV1583.L35] 21-1448
I. Title.

LOCKER, Mabel Elsie, 1890- 266
... What difference does it make? [By] Mabel Elsie Locker. A junior unit, ages, 9, 10, 11. Leader's book. [Philadelphia, The United Lutheran publication house, c1939] 63 p. 22 cm. (The children of the church series) "Prepared under the auspices of the Parish and church school board of the United Lutheran church in America." Includes bibliographies. [BX8015.L6] 40-35632
1. Religious education—Text-books for children. I. United Lutheran church in America. Parish and church school board. II. Title.

LOCKER, Mabel Elsie, 1890- 268.62
... World Christians worshiping [by] Mabel Elsie Locker. A junior unit, ages 9, 10, 11. Leader's book. [Philadelphia, The United Lutheran publication house, c1941] 62 p., 1 l. 22 cm. (The children of the church series) Illustrated t.-p. "Prepared under the auspices of the Parish and church school board of the United Lutheran church in America." Bibliography: p. 6-7. [BV1546.L57] 42-478
1. Religious education—Text-books for children. I. United Lutheran church in America. Parish and church school board. II. Title.

MEEK, Pauline Palmer. JUV
God speaks to me. Illustrated by Ati Forberg and Hans Zander. Richmond, Va., John Knox Press [1973, c1972] 95 p. illus. 21 cm. (Covenant life curriculum) An original short story, two Bible stories, and a brief biography of missionary Ida Scudder illustrate how God can direct one's life. [BV1561.M44] 248'.42 73-160570 1.95
1. Religious education—Text-books for children. 2. [Christian life.] I. Forberg, Ati, illus. II. Zander, Hans, 1937- illus. III. Title.

METCALFE, Richard Lee, 1861-
"Of such is the kingdom," a school reader, by Richard L. Metcalfe; illustrations by Franklin Booth. Lincoln, Neb., The Woodruff-Collins press, 1909. 288 p. incl. front., illus. 21 cm. 9-17213
I. Title.

PHELPS, Frances Brown. 268.432
Let's get to know God, by Frances Brown Phelps, illustrated by Marie-Ann Phelps and Doreen Penson. New York, Morehouse-Gorham co., 1944. 7 p. l., 3-129 p. incl. plates. 21 cm. [BV1561.P48] 44-10226
1. Religious education—Text-books for children. I. Title.

PRUGH, Marcella. 268.62
... Discovering our church; a program in Christian education for the third grade, by Marcella Prugh; foreword by Katharine Smith Adams. Teacher's book. Louisville,

Ky., The Cloister press [c1940] 2 p. l., vii, 138 p. illus. 20 cm. (The Cloister series [of church school courses] Rev. Maurice Clarke ... editor) Includes bibliographies. [BV1545.P7] 40-12959
1. Religious education—Text-books for children. I. Title.

RUDOLPH, L C
Story of the Church. Illustrated by Lewis Parker. Richmond, Va., CLC Press [1966] 191 p. illus. 21 cm. (Covenant Life Curriculum) 68-63214
1. Religious education—Text-books for children. 2. Church history. I. Title. II. Series.

STEEN, Inez. 268.62
The march of faith, by Inez Steen. Illustrated by John Ellingboe ... Grade six. Minneapolis, Augsburg publishing house [c1939] 215, [1] p. illus. (part col., incl. port., maps, facsims, music) diagrs., form. 22 cm. Text on lining-papers. "This volume is one in a series of graded Sunday school textbooks issued by the Board of elementary Christian education, Dr. Jacob Tanner, editor-in-chief." [BX8015.S65] 284.1 39-34129
1. Religious education—Text-books for children. I. Tanner, Jacob, 1865- ed. II. Title.

STEEN, Inez. 268.62
The march of faith; grade six--teacher's manual, by Inez Steen; illustrated by John Ellingboe ... Minneapolis, Augsburg publishing house [c1940] xxxvi, [5], 205 p. incl. illus., tables. 22 cm. "This volume is one in a series of graded Sunday school textbooks issued by the Board of elementary Christian education, Dr. Jacob Tanner, editor-in-chief." Includes bibliographies. [BX8015.S65] 40-13352
1. Religious education—Text-books for children. I. Tanner, Jacob, 1865- ed. II. Title.

TROUT, Ethel Wendell. 268.
Stories of the beginnings ... by Ethel Wendell Trout ... Philadelphia, The Westminster press, 1923. ix, 432 p. illus. (incl. maps) plates. 18 1/2 cm. (The Westminster textbooks of religious education for church schools having Sunday, week day, and expressional sessions, ed. by J. T. Faris. Junior department, 2d year) [BV1546.T8] 24-16948
I. Title.

WHITE, Mary (Chapin) Mrs. 1888- 221
...The Old Testament and you; a program in religious education for the seventh grade, by Mary Chapin White. Teachers guide. Louisville, Ky., The Cloister press [c1939] v, 37 p. diagr. 19 1/2 cm. (The Cloister series [of church school courses] Rev. Maurice Clarke ... editor) "Reading list": p. [35]-37. [Full name: Mrs. Mary Whitney (Chapin) White. [BS1194.W37] 40-4917
1. Religious education—Text-books for children. 2. Bible—Study—Text-books. I. Title.

Religious education—Text -books for children—Anglican.

INGRAM, Tolbert Robert, 1913- 268.432
Sacred studies; foundations of our common heritage. [Bellaire, Tex.] St. Thomas Press, 1958. 124p. 24cm. [BX5875.I5] 58-14390
1. Religious education—Text -books for children—Anglican. I. Title.

Religious education—Text-books for children—Baptist.

GREEN, Joseph Franklin, 1924- 230.61
God wants you [by] Joe and Janie Green. [Teacher's ed.] Nashville, Convention Press [1966] 84 p. forms. 19 cm. "Church study course [of the Sunday School Board of the Southern Baptist Convention] This book is number 0792 in category 7, section for juniors." "Helps for the teacher": [19] p. bound in. [BX6225.G7] 66-10256
1. Religious education—Text-books for children—Baptist. I. Green, Janie, joint author. II. Southern Baptist Convention. Sunday School Board. III. Title.

MCELRATH, William N. 268'.8'6
Me, myself, and others, by William N. McElrath. [Teacher's ed.] Nashville, Convention Press [1968] vi, 93 p. illus. 19 cm. [BX6225.M3] 68-11673
1. Religious education—Text-books for children—Baptist. I. Title.

MCKEE, Rose Knisley. 268'.61
The Christian way. Nashville, Tenn., Broadman Press [1969] 96 p. illus. 21 cm. (The Weekday Bible study series) "Student's book." [BX6225.M35] 69-10831
1. Religious education—Text-books for children—Baptist. I. Title.

ROOP, Geane Alice, 1890- 268.61
The junior and his church [by] Geane A. Roop. Nashville, Tenn., The Sunday school board of the Southern Baptist convention [c1937] 132 p. illus. 19 cm. [BV1546.R65] 37-21816
1. Religious education—Text-books for children—Baptist. I. Title.

RYAN, Roberta. 268.432
Keep telling the story. [Teacher's ed.] Nashville, Convention Press [1963] 102 p. illus. 19 cm. "Helps for the teacher": 16 p. bound in. [BX6225.R9] 63-8379
1. Religious education—Text-books for children—Baptists. 2. Baptists—Missions—Juvenile literature. I. Title.

SHARP, Margaret. 268'.8'6
Juniors in training. [Teacher's ed.] Nashville, Convention Press [1968] 104, [16] p. illus. 19 cm. "Church study course [of the Sunday School Board of the Southern Baptist Convention] This book is number 1893 in category 18, section for juniors." "Helps for the teacher": [16] p. (2d group) [BX6225.S45] 69-10016
1. Religious education—Text-books for children—Baptist. I. Southern Baptist Convention. Sunday School Board. II. Title.

STINSON, Roddy. 268.432
My church helps me learn. [Teacher's ed.] Nashville, Convention Press [1967] vi, 89 p. illus. 19 cm. [BX6225.S7] 67-10004
1. Religious education — Text-books for children — Baptist. I. Title.

YOUNG, Lois Horton. 268.432
Kindergarten story time. Illus. by Alcy Kendrick., Cover by James Koscis. Valley Forge [Pa.] Judson Pr. [1962] 269p. illus. 27cm. 62-52107 3.95
1. Religious education—Text-books for children—Baptists. I. Title.

Religious education — Text-books for children — Catholic.

BROWNSON, Josephine Van Dyke. 268.432
Come and see ... by Josephine Van Dyke Brownson ... in collaboration with Rev. Leo De Barry ... Huntington, Ind., Our Sunday visitor press [c1939] 137 p. illus. 19 cm. (Her Learn of Me series. Book 3) [BX930.B766] 43-45140
1. Religious education—Text-books for children—Catholic. I. De Barry, Leo, joint author. II. Title.

BROWNSON, Josephine Van Dyke. 268.433
I am the vine ... by Josephine Van Dyke Brownson ... in collaboration with Rev. Leo De Barry ... Huntington, Ind., Our Sunday visitor press [c1939] 377 p. illus. 19 cm. (Her Learn of Me series. Book 7) [BX930.B773] 43-45139
1. Religious education—Text-books for children—Catholic. I. De Barry, Leo, joint author. II. Title.

BROWNSON, Josephine Van Dyke. 268.432
Keep my commandments ... by Josephine Van Dyke Brownson ... in collaboration with Rev. Leo De Barry ... Huntington, Ind., Our Sunday visitor press [1938] 223 p. illus. 19 cm. (Her Learn of Me series. Book 4) Maps on p. [2] and [3] of cover. [BX930.B775] 43-45138
1. Religious education—Text-books for children—Catholic. I. De Barry, Leo, joint author. II. Title.

BROWNSON, Josephine Van Dyke. 268.432
Living water ... by Josephine Van Dyke Brownson ... in collaboration with Rev. Leo De Barry ... Huntington, Ind., Our Sunday visitor press [c1939] 345 p. illus. (incl. maps) 19 cm. (Her Learn of Me series. Book 6) [BX930.B777] 43-45032
1. Religious education—Text-books for children—Catholic. I. De Barry, Leo, joint author. II. Title.

CONNOLE, Roger Joseph. 268'.432
The Christian inheritance. Book 1- [Authors: Roger J. Connole, Sister Judith Stodola, and Sister Aline Baumgartner. Illus.: Sister Angsar Holmberg. Rev. ed.] Saint Paul, North Central Pub. Co.; distributed by the Liturgical Press, Collegeville, Minn. [1968- v. illus. (part col.) 26 cm. [BX930.C6332] 68-55351
1. Religious education—Text-books for children—Catholic. I. Stodola, Judith, joint author. II. Baumgartner, Aline, joint author. III. Holmberg, Ansgar, illus. IV. Shields, Kathleen Marie. V. Confraternity of Christian Doctrine. VI. Title.

MIRIAM Auxilium, sister.
My Holy Child book; a book of simple instruction in religion prepared for handicapped children. [2d ed.] San Francisco, Holy Family College [1958] 20 p. 22 cm. 67-55242
1. Religious education — Text-books for children — Catholic. 2. Handicapped children — Religious education. I. Title.

MONTREAL (Ecclesiasti cal Province) Office catechistique provincial. 238
Come to the Father series. [Pupils text. New York, Paulist Press, 1966- v. col. illus. 22 cm. Title from p. [4] of cover of y. 1. "English version of the cathechism...written by the Office catechistique provincial, Montreal, Canada." Commentaries on doctrinal themes according to the catechetical program of Come to the Father series. grades 1 and 2- New York, Paulist Press [1967- v. 21 cm. Contents.- grade Come to the Father.--grade Celebrate God's mighty deeds. Includes bibliograaphies. BX930.V42 [BX930.V4] 66-24234
1. Religious education—Text-books for children—Catholic. I. Title.

MONTREAL (Ecclesiastical Province) Office catechistique provincial. 268.61
Come to the Father series. 1- New York, Paulist Press [1966-] v. illus. 23 cm. Prepared by the Office catechistique provincial, Montreal. [BX930.C59] 66-24234
1. Religious education — Text-books for children — Catholic. I. Title.

PHILIPPS, Martin, 1853-1924. 220.
Sunday school instructions for every Sunday of the year, with a short sketch of eminent saints, followed by prayers of the mass and hymns; compiled by Rev. M. Philipps. [Buffalo, 1910] 432 p. 21 x 11 /1/2 cm. [BX930.P5] 10-20507
1. Religious education—Text-books for children—Catholic. I. Title.

[SCHORSCH, Alexander Peter] 1882-
A course in religion. Work book one-[eight] Unit plan ... [Chicago, Ill., Archdiocese of Chicago school board, 1937-38] 3 v. illus. 28 cm. Cover-title. Each volume includes hymns, with music. [A 41-2971]
1. Religious education—Text-books for children—Catholic. I. Schorsch, Dolores, sister, 1896- joint author. II. Catholic univ. of America. Library. III. Title.
Contents omitted.

SCHORSCH, Alexander Peter, 1882-
A course in religion for the elementary schools. Teacher's guidebook ... by Rev. Alexander P. Schorsch ... and Sister M. Dolores Schorsch ... Chicago, Ill., Archdiocese of Chicago school board [c1934-38] 8 v. 24 cm. Cover-title: A course in religion. Guidebook one-[eight] Unit plan. Includes hymns, with music. Bibliographical foot-notes. [A 41-2970]
1. Religious education—Text-books for children—Catholic. I. Schorsch, Dolores, sister, 1896- joint author. II. Title.
Contents omitted.

SCHUMACHER, Magnus Ambrose, 1885- 268.62
Learning my religion; the questions and answers of the catechism prepared and enjoined by the Third plenary council of Baltimore, graded and combined with an explanation and correlated with Bible history, etc., for the use of elementary schools according to modern teaching methods; by Rt. Rev. Msgr. M. A. Schumacher... and Sister Mary Imelda... New York, Cincinnati [etc.] Benziger brothers, 1935- v. col. illus. 18 1/2 cm. [BX930.S37] 36-9152
1. Religious education—Text-books for children—Catholic. I. Wallace, Mary Imelda, sister, 1884- joint author. II. Title.

WHITLOCK, Pamela, ed. 268.432
The open book; a collection of stories, essays, poems, songs and music for girls and boys and every member of all Christian families. Drawings by Marcia Lane Foster. New York, P. J. Kenedy [1956] xii, 222p. illus. map. 22cm. 'Songs to sing' (for 1-4 voices): p.[187]-222. [BX930.W47] 56-10357
1. Religious education—Text-books for children—Catholic. 2. Children's songs. I. Title.

Religious education—Text-books for children (Elementary)

**BIBLE, life and worship series;* bks. 2 & 3. Boston, Allyn [c.]1965. 268.432
2v. (160; 174p.) col. illus. 23cm. Bk. 2.--Come, Lord Jesus, by Sister M. Johnice, Sister M. Elizabeth. Illus. by A. and M. Provensen.--Bk. 3. The Lord Jesus says, by Sister M. Elizabeth, Sister M. Johnice. Illus. by A. and M. Provenson. pap., bk. 2, 1.40; bk. 3, 1.60
1. Religious education—Text-books for children (Elementary) I. Johnice, M. II. Elizabeth, M., joint authors.

**BIBLE, life and worship series;* bk.4 Boston, Allyn, 1966 [c.1960, 1966] 191p. col. illus. 23cm. 1.64 pap., 268.432
1. Religious education—Textbooks for children (Elementary) I. Johnice, M. II. Elizabeth, M., joint author. III. Cooke, Bernard J., joint author. IV. Title: Children of the Kingdom.
Contents omitted.

Religious education — Text-books for children — Lutheran.

BORENMANN, Robert E
Spokesmen for God. Teacher's guide. Philadelphia, Lutheran Church Press [1966] 63 p. 20 cm. (LCA school of religion series) 68-47547
I. Title.

BORNEMANN, Robert E.
Spokesmen for God. Artist, Robert McGovern. Philadelphia, Lutheran Church Press[c1966] 152 p. illus. 20 cm. (LCA school of religion series) 68-47546
I. Title.

*HORN, William M. 268.433
I believe in God the Father. Ed. by Frank W. Klos. Illus. by Rey Abruzzi. Philadelphia, Lutheran Church Pr. [c.1964] 191p. illus. 22cm. (LCA week day sch. ser., gr. 7) 2.00; 2.50 teacher's guide,
I. Title.

IRVIN, Donald F. 268.433
What's in the catechism? We obey and we believe. By Donald F. Irvin. Study book. Intermed, 1st quarter. Philadelphia, Columbus [etc.] Christian growth press [1944] 68 p. illus. (part col.) 22 cm. [The Christian growth series of Sunday school lessons] Cover-title: We obey and we believe. Teacher's guide ... Philadelphia, Columbus [etc.] Christian growth press [1944] 64 p. 22 cm. [The Christian growth series of Sunday school lessons] Bibliography: p. 7. [BX8015.I7 Guide] 44-37033
1. Religious education—Text-books for children—Lutheran. I. Title. II. Title: We obey and we believe.

LUTHERAN Church. Missouri Synod. Board for Parish Education 268.62
Graded memory course for Lutheran Sunday-schools and other institutions. Dr. Martin Luther's Small catechism with correlated Bible-passages, hymn stanzas, prayers, and Bible-story references. Published by the Board of Christian St. Louis, Mo., Concordia publishing house,

1933. 63 p. 18 1/2 cm. [BX8015.L8] 39-1484
1. Religious education — Text books for children — Lutheran. I. Title.

LUTHERAN Church. Missouri 268.62
Synod. Board for Parish Education
Graded memory course for Lutheran Sunday-schools and other institutions. Dr. Martin Luther's Small catechism with correlated Bible-passages, hymn stanzas, prayers, and Bible-story references. Published by the Board of Christian education of the Evangelical Lutheran synod of Missouri, Ohio, and other states. St. Louis, Mo., Concordia publishing house, 1933. 63 p. 18 1/2 cm. [BX8015.L8] 39-1484
1. Religious education — Text books for children — Lutheran. I. Title.

LUTHERAN Church -- Missouri
Synod. Board for Parish Education.
Memory book for Lutheran schools, published under the auspices of the Board of Christian Education, Evangelical Lutheran Synod of Missouri, Ohio, and Other States. St. Louis, Mo., Concordia Pub. House, 1944. 172 p. illus. 19 cm. At head of title: Grades I to VIII, number 18. "Source books used": p.8.
1. Religious education — Text-books for children — Lutheran. I. Title.

LUTHERAN Church -- 268.432
Missouri Synod. Board for Parish Education.
Memory book for Lutheran schools, published under the auspices of the Board of Christian Education, Evangelical Lutheran Synod of Missouri, Ohio, and Other States. St. Louis, Mo., Concordia Pub. House, 1944. 172 p. illus. 19 cm. At head of title: Grades I to VIII, number 18. "Source books used": p.8. [BX8015.A3 1944b] 62-56774
1. Religious education — Text-books for children — Lutheran. I. Title.

*PURDHAM, Betty Mae 268.342
Followers of Jesus. Ed. by Margaret J. Irvin. Illus. by John Gretzer. Philadelphia, Lutheran Church Pr. [c.1966] 32p. 23x28cm. (LCA vacation church sch. ser.) .50; .90 pap., teacher's ed., pap.,
1. Religious education—Elementary—Lutheran Church. I. Title.

SWAN, Able Bernhardt, 268.62
1891-
My second Sunday school book, grade two. Teacher's manual, including the complete pupils' volume. Pupils' volume by Clara Boxrud. Teacher's manual by A.B. Swan ... Minneapolis, Augsburg publishing house [1937] cxx p., 1 l., 115 p. incl. illus. (part col.) plates (part col.) map. col. pl. 22 1/2 cm. The "pupils' volume" (115 p.) has special t.-p., "My second Sunday school book, grade two, by Clara Boxrud," and was also published separately. "This volume is one in a series of graded Sunday school text books issued by the Board of elementary Christian education, Dr. Jacob Tanner, editor-in-chief." "First edition, September, 1937." [BV1545.S86] 44-25657
1. Religious education—Text-books for children—Lutheran. I. Boxrud, Clara. II. Tanner, Jacob, 1865- ed. III. Norwegian Lutheran church of America. Board of elementary Christian education. IV. Title.

Religious education - Text-books for children - Men nonite.

GLASS, Esther Eby. 268.61
Our city neighbors; children's mission study. Illustrated by Charles F. Ellis. Scottdale, Pa., Herald Press [1966] 96, L-32 p. illus., map, ports. 22 cm. Includes hymns, with music. "Leader's guide": L-32 p. inserted. [BX8114.G5] 66-25427
1. Religious education — Text-books for children — pmennonite. 2. City missions. I. Title.

Religious education—Text-books for children—Methodist.

SMITHER, Ethel Lisle. 268.432
They help along with me; child helpers around the world, by Ethel L. Smither. A unit of work for primary children for use in additional sessions, with suggestions for ten monthly meetings. C. A. Bowen, editor ... Baltimore, New York [etc.] The Methodist publishing house [1944] 62, [2] p. 23 cm. Includes songs with music. [BV1545.S62] 44-49927
1. Religious education—Text-books for children—Methodist. I. Bowen, Cawthon Asbury, 1885- ed. II. Title.

Religious education—Text-books for children—Mormon.

CROWTHER, Jean Decker. 289.3
Growing up in the church. Illustrated by Carol Niederhauser [and] Roger Matkin. Salt Lake City, Deseret Book Co., 1965. ix. 76 p. illus. 24 cm. [BX8610.C7] 65-28861
1. Religious education — Text-books for children — Mormon. I. Title.

REORGANIZED Church of Jesus 289.3
Christ of Latter-Day Saints. Children's Division.
Learning God's way; a book for children who want to become church members. Illustrated by Beverly Logan. [Independence, Mo., Herald Pub. House, 1964] 85 p. col. illus. 22 cm. [BX8610.A49] 64-18779
1. Religious education — Text-books for children — Mormon. I. Title.

SCHOENFELD, Elizabeth. 268.432
Please tell me; answers to gospel questions children ask [by] Elizabeth Schoenfeld and J. Stanley Schoenfeld. Salt Lake City, Deseret Book Co., 1966. 168 p. illus. 24 cm. [BX8610.S34] 66-20707
1. Religious education—Text-books for children—Mormon. I. Schoenfeld, J. Stanley, joint author. II. Title.

Religious education—Text-books for children—Reformed.

GOSSELINK, Henrietta E. 268.61
(Plasman)
How things began, by Henrietta E. Gosselink. Approved and supervised by the Curriculum committee of the Reformed church in America. A third grade course. Grand Rapids, Mich., Wm. B. Eerdmans publishing company, 1944. 91 p. 19 1/2 cm. [BV1545.G7] 44-13198
1. Religious education—Text-books for children—Reformed. I. Reformed church in America. Curriculum committee. II. Title.

Religious education— Text-books for children—Seventh-Day Adventists.

SEVENTH-DAY Adventists. 268.61
General Conference. Dept. of Education.
Witness s for Jesus; Bible lessons for grades 7 and 8. [Teacher's ed.] Mountain View, Calif., Pacific Press Pub. Association for the Dept. of Education, General Conference of Seventh-Day Adventists [1952] 134, 520p. illus. 24cm. 'Series IV degree, odd year.' The main work, also issued separately, is preceded by 'Teacher's guide and key for Witnesses for Jesus,' with special t.p. [BX6155.S45 1952a] [BX6155.S45 1952a] 268.432 56-17682 56-17682
1. Religious education— Text-books for children—Seventh-Day Adventists. I. Title.

Religious education—Text-books for children—Unitarian.

FAHS, Sophia Blanche Lyon, 291.13
1876-
Beginnings: earth, sky, life, death; stories, ancient and modern, by Sophia Lyon Fahs and Dorothy T. Spoerl. Boston, Starr King Press [1958] 217 p. illus. 24 cm. "A combination and revision of Beginnings of earth and sky, by Sophia L. Fahs...and Beginnings of life and death, by Sophia L. Fahs and Dorothy T. Spoerl." Includes bibliography. [BV1561.F2] 58-11973
1. Religious education—Text-books for children—Unitarian. 2. Mythology—Juvenile literature. 3. [Mythology.] 4. [Religion.] I. Spoerl, Dorothy T., joint author. II. Title.

Religious education — Text-books for children — United Church of Christ.

LIBBEY, Scott 268.433
God's restless servants, a course for seventh and eighth grades. Illus. by Larry Channing [Philadelphia] United Church [1964] 124p. illus. (pt. col.) 26cm. Pt. of the United Church curriculum, prepared, pub. by the Div. of Christian Educ. and the Div. of Pubn. of the United Church Bd. for Homeland Ministries. Bibl. 64-14493 2.25
1. Religious education—Text-books for children—United Church of Christ. I. United Church Board for Homeland Ministries. Division of Christian Education. II. United Church Board for Homeland Ministries. Division of Publication. III. Title.

LLOYD, Sarah, pseud.
Claimed by God, a course for seventh and eighth grades, by Sarah Lloyd [pseud.] & Jane Evans [pseud.] Boston, United Church Press [1963] 128 p. illus. 26 cm. "JH I-1."
1. Religious education — Text-books for children — United Church of Christ. I. Title.

LLOYD, Sarah, pseud. 268.432
Claimed by God, a course for seventh and eighth grades, by Sarah Lloyd [pseud.] & Jane Evans [pseud.] Boston, United Church Press [1963] 128 p. illus. 26 cm. "JH I-1." [BX9884.A3L55] 63-7420
1. Religious education — Text-books for children — United Church of Christ. I. Evans, Jane, pseud. joint author. II. Title.

RITTENHOUSE, Laurence 268.432
God created me. Illus. by Trina Schart Hyman. Philadelphia, United Church [c.1963] 95p. col. illus. 23cm. Part of the United Church curriculum. 63-4252 1.50
1. Religious education—Text-books for children—United Church of Christ. I. Title.

TRICKEY, Edna Butler 268.432
Our Christian community; a course for the first and second grades. Illus. by Robert Hanson. Philadelphia, United Church [1964] 124p. illus. (pt. col.) 26cm. Pt. of the United Church curriculum, prepared, pub. by the Div. of Christian Educ. and the Div. of Pubn. of the United Church Bd. for Homeland Ministries. Bibl. 64-14492 price unreported
1. Religious education—Text-books for children—United Church of Christ. I. United Church Board for Homeland Ministries. Division of Christian Education. II. United Church Board for Homeland Ministries. Division of Publication. III. Title.

Religious education—Text-books for mentally handicapped children.

ADVENTURES in Christian 268'.432
living and learning; a resource book for use with retarded persons, ages 6-10. Jessie B. Carlson, editor. Martha Jones, supervisory editor. St. Louis, Published for the Cooperative Publication Association, by the Bethany Press [1969- v. illus. 22 cm. (The Cooperative series: Curriculum materials for the mentally retarded) Includes music. Includes bibliographical references. [BV1615.M4A36] 78-86154
1. Religious education—Text-books for mentally handicapped children. I. Carlson, Jessie B., ed. II. Cooperative Publication Association.

AYCOCK, Martha B., 268'.432 s
1920-
Understanding: a resource book for use with persons who have learning difficulties. Martha B. Aycock, editor. Richmond, Va., Published for Cooperative Publication Association by John Knox Press [1972] 107 p. music. 23 cm. (Exploring life, ages 7-12, pt. 2) "The resources for use with this teacher's guide ... include pupil's books: Hey, somebody look. God created it all. My big friends. We remember Jesus." Includes bibliographies. [BV1615.M4A9] [BV1615.M4] 248'.82'07 72-519 ISBN 0-8042-1195-7
1. Religious education—Text-books for mentally handicapped children. I. Title. II. Series: Exploring life.

EXPLORING life. 268'.432 s
Richmond, Va., Published for Cooperative Publication Association by John Knox Press [197 p. Curriculum materials for persons who have learning difficulties. Includes bibliographies. [BV1615.M4E9] 72-520
1. Religious education—Text-books for mentally handicapped children. I. Cooperative Publication Association.

Religious education—Text-books for pre-school children.

BARBOUR, Dorothy 268.61
(Dickinson)
Living with other people; a Christian education unit for kindergarten, by Dorothy Dickinson Barbour ... New York, N.Y., The National council, Protestant Episcopal church, [1942] 31, [1] p. 21 1/2 cm. [Christian education units] "Source materials": p. 13-21. [BV1540.B33] 42-19737
1. Religious education—Text-books for pre-school children. I. Title.

FARIS, Lillie Anne, 1868- 268.432
Lights aglow, a teachers' manual; standard Bible course for preschool children, by Lillie A. Faris ... Cincinnati, O., The Standard publishing company [c1940] 220 p. incl. illus., pl. 22 cm. Includes bibliographies. [BV1540.F3] 40-5098
1. Religious education—Text-books for pre-school children. I. Title.

KEYSER, Wilma (Sudhoff) 266
Mrs., 1904-
... Jesus wants them all [by] Wilma Sudhoff Keyser. A beginner unit, ages 4 and 5. Leader's book. [Philadelphia, The United Lutheran publication house, c1939] 63 p. 21 1/2 cm. (The children of the church series) "Prepared under the auspices of the Parish and church school board of the United Lutheran church in America." Includes songs with music. [Full name:Mrs. Wilma Jane]Sudhoff: Keyser] Includes bibliographies. [BX8015.K4] 40-35630
1. Religious education—Text-books for pre-school children. I. United Lutheran church in America. Parish and church school board. II. Title.

MARAMARCO, Phyllis 268.62
Newcomb.
... Finding God in our homes; a program in Christian education for kindergarten A, by Phyllis Newcomb Maramarco. Parent's and pupil's book. Louisville, Ky., The Cloister press [c1940] 4 p. l., 67 p. 20 cm. (The Cloister series [of church school courses] Rev. Maurice Clarke ... editor) "Mary's lullaby" (with music): p. 18. Includes bibliographies. [BV1540.M352] 40-13561
1. Religious education—Text-books for pre-school children. I. Title.

OGLEVEE, Louis (McArot) 268.
1872-
Cradle roll lessons, by Louise M. Oglevee; a book for the cradle roll class of the Sunday school and for little children in the home, a program for every Sunday in the year, including the Bible story, a finger-play, handwork, picture and cut-out suggestions and songs, both words and music. Cincinnati, O., The Standard publishing company. c1924. 144 p. illus., pl. 23 1/2 cm. Music: p. 139-144. [BV1540.O5] 24-9559
1. Religious education—Text-books for pre-school children. I. Title. II. Title: [Full name: Louise Peletreau (McAroy) Oglevee]

SAMUEL, Sallie (Brummal) 268.432
Mrs., 1862-
Steps to heaven via the true kindergarten, by Sallie B. Samuel. Boston, The Christopher publishing house [c1940] 2 p. l., vii-xi, 13-177 p. front. 19 1/2 cm. [BV1540.S27] 40-11770
1. Religious education—Text-books for pre-school children. I. Title.

WALTON, Thelma. 268.6
... Bible stories for a little child ... prepared by Thelma Walton, edited by Henrietta C. Mears. Hollywood, Calif., The Gospel light press, c1937- v. illus. 21 1/2 cm. (Gospel light series for beginners) At head of title: Beginners teacher's text book. [BV1540.W25] 45-45159

1. Religious education—Text-books for pre-school children. 2. Sunday-schools. I. Mears, Henrietta Cornelia, 1890- ed. II. Title.

Religious education—Text-books for pre-school children—Catholic.

LACHAPELLE, Dolores. 268'.432
First steps in faith ... [by] Dolores LaChapelle, Janet Bourque, and Pat McCauley. [New York] Herder and Herder [1969] 3 v. illus., music. 28 cm. Contents.Contents.—[1] First steps in faith; an introduction for parents and teachers.—[2] Learning about God's world; first steps in faith for four-year olds.—[3] Learning to love God; first steps in faith for five-year olds. Bibliographical footnotes. [BX930.L18] 69-12678 5.95 (v. 1) 4.95 (v. 2) 6.95 (v. 3)
1. Religious education—Text-books for pre-school children—Catholic. I. Bourque, Janet, joint author. II. McCauley, Pat, 1940- joint author. III. Title. IV. Title: Learning about God's world. V. Title: Learning to love God.

Religious education—Text-books for pre-school children—United Church of Christ.

HUNTER, Elizabeth M 268.432
God's wonderful world, a course for the church school kindergarten. Photos. by Sheldon Brody. Drawings by Calvin Burnett. Boston, United Church Press [1963] 64 p. illus. 26 cm. [BX9884.A3H8] 63-7295
1. Religious education — Text-books for pre-school children — United Church of Christ. I. Title.

Religious education—Text-books for young people.

BELL, Bernard Iddings, 1886- 268.62
Understanding religion; an introductory guide to the study of Christianity, by Bernard Iddings Bell. New York, Morehouse-Gorden co., 1941. xiv p., 1 l., 249 p. 20 cm. Bibliography: p. xiii-xiv. [BV1605.B4] 41-11138
1. Religious education—Text-books for young people. I. Title.

FAULSTICH, John. 248.8'3
For man's sake; a resource book on theology for youth. Philadelphia, United Church Press [1971] 64 p. illus. 21 cm. [BV1561.F35] 74-152646
1. Religious education—Text-books for young people. I. Title.

HABEL, Norman C. 222.1206
Wait a minute, Moses! [Reissue] St. Louis, Concordia [c.1965] 97p. illus. 20cm. (Current perspectives of life for Christian youth, 2) [BV1549.2.H2] 65-23701 1.00 pap.,
1. Religious education—Text-books for young people. 2. Exodus, The—Study and teaching. I. Title.

HATHAWAY, Lulu. 268'.432
Partners in teaching older children. Valley Forge [Pa.] Judson Press [1971] 55 p. illus. 28 cm. "Manual for middler and junior workers." Bibliography: p. 55. [BV1475.9.H38] 74-147849 ISBN 0-8170-0531-5 2.50
1. Religious education—Text-books for youth. I. Title.

HEYER, Robert J., comp. 261
Discovery in politics: humanizing the world and its structures [compiled by] Robert J. Heyer, Richard J. Payne [and] Mary E. Tierney. New York, Paulist Press [1971] 160 p. illus. 21 cm. (Discovery series) [BV1561.H46] 70-152574 2.50
1. Religious education—Text-books for young people. I. Payne, Richard J., joint comp. II. Tierney, Mary E., joint comp. III. Title.

HOLMES, Almira F.
The building of the Kingdom; a discussion course by Almira F. Holmes. New York, The Womans press, 1919. 53 p. 23 cm. Bibliography: p. 58. [BV1603.H6] 19-18856
1. Religious education—Text-books for young people. I. Title.

KATHAN, Boardman. 261'.071'2
Youth—where the action is, by Boardman and Joyce Kathan. Grades 7 and 8. Philadelphia, Published for the Cooperative Publication Association by United Church Press [1970] 2 v. illus. 22 cm. (The Cooperative through-the-week series) Consists of a teacher's book with outlines and study guides and a student's book with reading material. Bibliography: v. [1] p. 184-186. [BV1561.K3] 71-122924 ISBN 0-8298-0161-8 (teacher's book) ISBN 0-8298-0162-6 (student's book)
1. Religious education—Text-books for young people. I. Kathan, Joyce, joint author. II. Cooperative Publication Association. III. Title.

SKOGLUND, John E 268.433
Come and see, a cooperative text; an invitation to older youth and young adults. Philadelphia, Published for the Cooperative Publication Association by the Judson Press [1956] 96p. 19cm. (Faith for life series) [BV1603.S5] 57-44912
1. Religious education — Text-books for young people. 2. Jesus Christ—Biog.—Study. I. Title.

SKOGLUND, John E 268.433
Come and see, a cooperative text; an invitation to older youth and young adults. Philadelphia, Published for the Cooperative Publication Association by the Judson Press [1956] 96 p. 19 cm. (Faith for life series) [BV1603.S5] 57-44912
1. Religious education — Text-books for young people. 2. Jesus Christ — Biog. — Study. I. Title.

STOCK, Harry Thomas, 1891- 259
Christian life problems for young people's classes and societies [by] Harry Thomas Stock ... Boston, Chicago, The Pilgrim press [c1927] 58, [5] p. 19 1/2 cm. Five blank pages at end "For notes." [BV4447.S68] A 41
1. Religious education—Text-books for young people. 2. Youth—Religious life. I. Title.

WEBB, K. L. 373
Four minute talks for superintendents; excellent, also, for superintendents of junior and intermediate departments of graded schools and for leaders of junior and intermediate Endeavor societies, by K. L. Webb. Cincinnati, O., The Standard publishing company [c1926] 110 p. 20 cm. [BV4315.W35] 26-17501
I. Title.

Religious education — Text-books for young people — Baptist.

AMERICAN Baptist Publication Society. 267.626
Topic; the quarterly for young people's meetings. [Philadelphia, American Baptist Publication Society] v. in 19 cm. [BX6225.T6] 51-31805
1. Religious education — Text-books for young people — Baptist. I. Title.

HASTINGS, Robert J. 268.433
The Christian faith and life. Teacher's bk. for use with 15- and 16-year-olds, may be adapted for other ages. Nashville, Broadman [c.1964, 1965] 192p. 21cm. (Weekday Bible study ser.) [BV1549.2.H3] 65-16572 pap., 2.75; student's bk., pap., 1.00
1. Religious education—Text-books for young people—Baptist. I. Title.

JENKINS, David L. 268'.62
Openings to understandings; (student's book for use primarily by older youth) Writers: David L. Jenkins, Floyd A. Craig, and Val Harvey. Editor: Thomas L. Clark. Nashville, Convention Press, c1971. 98 p. illus. 28 x 11 cm. At head of title: Learning at home and church. [BX6225.J45] 72-185016
1. Religious education—Text-books for young people—Baptist. I. Craig, Floyd A. II. Harvey, Val. III. Title.

LIFE and work lesson annual. 268.434
1966/67- Nashville, Convention Press. v. 21 cm. [BX6225.L5] 66-19916
1. Religious education — Text-books for young adults — Baptist. 2. Religious education — Text-books for adults — Baptist.

RESPOND; 268'.4
a resource book for youth ministry [edited by] Keith L. Ignatius. Valley Forge [Pa.] Judson Press [1971-73] 3 v. illus., music. 28 cm. Vol. 2 edited by J. M. Corbett; v. 3 by M. L. Brown. Includes bibliographies. [BX6225.R47] 77-159050 ISBN 0-8170-0542-0 (v. 1) 3.95 per vol.
1. Religious education—Text-books for young people—Baptist. I. Ignatius, Keith L., ed. II. Corbett, Janice M., ed. III. Brown, Mason L., ed.

Religious education—Text books for young people Catholic.

*BOTHWELL, Sister Mary de Angelis. 268'.432
Good is good [by] Sister Mary de Angelis Bothwell and other Sisters of Notre Dame. Art: Sister Mary Megan Dull [&] Sister Mary Leon Wilhelmy. Theological advisor: John A. Hardon. Consultant: Daniel L. Flaherty. Chicago, Loyola University Press [1973] 138 p. col. illus. 28 cm. (Christ our life series: perform-a-text, 1) [BX930] ISBN 0-8294-0218-7 1.48 (pbk.)
1. Religious education—Textbooks for young people—Catholic. I. Hardon, John A. II. Flaherty, Daniel L. III. Title. IV. Series.

BUETOW, Harold A 268.433
Joy to my youth; a religious guide for Catholic youth, with instructions for altar servers. Illustrated by Carl Pfeufer. [1st ed.] New York, Dutton [1961] 208p. illus. 22cm. [BX930.B86] 61-6010
1. Religious education—Text-books for young people—Catholic. 2. Altar boys. I. Title.

CAMPION, Raymond James, 1896- 282
... *Religion, a secondary school course* ... by Rev. Raymond J. Campion ... foreword by Very Rev. Msgr. Joseph V. S. McClancy ... New York, Chicago, W. H. Sadlier, incorporated [1930- v. illus. 21 cm. (Catholic action series) [BX930.C25 1930] [230.2] 30-11388
1. Religious education—Text-books for young people—Catholic. I. Title.

CATHOLIC catechism. 238'.2
Grades seven and eight. Huntington, Ind., Our Sunday Visitor, inc. [1971] xii, 356 p. col. illus. 19 cm. A rev. ed. for use in North America of a work originally issued as "Book two" in 1963 for use in the Catholic schools of Australia by the Australian hierarchy. [BX930.C342 1971] 76-27743
1. Religious education—Text-books for young people—Catholic.

THE Christian in the world. 268.61
General editor: Reginald Doherty. [Authors: Francis Kelly and others] Dubuque, Iowa, Priory Press [1963] viii, 527 p. maps. 24 cm. (The Challenge of Christ, no. 4) [BV1549.94.C5] 63-21761
1. Religious education — Text-books for young people — Catholic. I. Doherty, Reginald, ed. II. Series.

THE Christian in the world. 268'.61
General editor, Reginald Doherty. Rev. ed. Chicago, Priory Press [1968] 536 p. illus., maps. 24 cm. (The Challenge of Christ, 4) [BV1549.94.C5 1968] 68-7269
1. Religious education—Text-books for young people—Catholic. I. Doherty, Reginald, ed. II. Title. III. Series.

CHRISTIAN in the world. (The) 261
General ed.: Reginald Doherty. [Authors: Francis Kelly, others] Dubuque, Iowa, Priory [c.1963] viii, 527p. maps. 24cm. (Challenge of Christ, no. 4) 63-21761 3.95
1. Religious education—Text-books for young people—Catholic. I. Doherty, Reginald, ed. II. Series.

CLEVELAND (Diocese) Board of Catholic education. 282.02
Our quest for happiness... Cleveland, Board of Catholic education. Dept. of high schools and academies, Diocese of Cleveland, 1941 4v. diagrs. 23 cm. Reproduced from type written copy. A revised outline of the Course of study, religion for high school students. Contents.T. 1. Our goal and guides--pt. 2. Through Christ our Lord--pt. 3. The ark and the dove.--pt. 4 Toward the eternal commencement. [BX930C54] 41-20368
1. Religious education—Text books for young people—Catholic. I. Cleveland (Diocese) Board of Catholic education. Course of study is religion. II. Title.

COME alive. 268'.433
[Editor. Sister M. St. Thomas. North American ed. Huntington, Ind., Our Sunday Visitor, 1971- v. illus. (part col.) 28 cm. Cover title. Contents.Contents.—v. 1. To be a man.—v. 2. Patterns.—v. 3. I am not a rock.—v. 4. Life's like that.—v. 5. Wide angle.—v. 6. Turned off.—v. 7. The now.—v. 8. The shape of things to come.—v. 9. The big rethink. [BX930.C58] 74-153781
1. Religious education—Text-books for young people—Catholic. I. St. Thomas, Sister, R.S.M., ed.

FLYNN, Anthony J. 268.433
... *Faith in action* [by] Reverend Anthony J. Flynn ... Sister Vincent Loretto ... [and] Mother Mary Simeon ... Contributing editors: Rev. James Donnelly ... [and] Rev. William Ferree ... Problems and tests: Rev. Alfred J. Schnepp ... New York, Chicago, W. H. Sadlier, inc. [1946] vii, 312 p. illus. (incl. ports., facsims.) diagrs. 23 1/2 cm. (The Catholic high school religion series, book 4) "Readings on related topics" at end of each unit. [BX930.F615] 47-1491
1. Religious education—Text-books for young people—Catholic. 2. Christian life—Catholic authors. I. Vincent Loretto, sister, 1893- joint author. II. Mary Simeon, mother, 1895- joint author. III. Title.

FLYNN, Anthony J. 268.433
... *Living our faith* [by] Reverend Anthony J. Flynn ... Sister Vincent Loretto ... [and] Mother Mary Simeon ... New York, Chicago, W. H. Sadlier, inc. [1945] 315 p. illus., diagrs. 23 cm. (The Catholic high school religion series. Book 3) "Readings on related topics" at end of each unit except one. [BX930.F62] 46-2863
1. Religious education—Text-books for young people—Catholic. 2. Christian life—Study and teaching. I. Vincent Loretto, sister, 1893- joint author. II. Mary Simeon, mother, 1894- joint author. III. Title.

FLYNN, Anthony J. 268.433
... *The triumph of faith* [by] Reverend Anthony J. Flynn ... Sister Vincent Loretto ... [and] Mother Mary Simeon ... New York, Chicago, W. H. Sadlier, inc. [1945] 364 p. illus. (incl. ports., maps) diagrs. 23 1/2 cm. (The Catholic high school religion series. Book 2) Includes bibliographies. [BX930.F627] 46-6818
1. Religious education—Text-books for young people—Catholic. 2. Church history. 3. Sacraments—Catholic church. I. Vincent Loretto, sister, 1893- joint author. II. Mary Simeon, mother, 1894- joint author. III. Title.

[JOHN Berchmans, Sister] 282.
Compendium of first and second years academic religion, according to the requirements of the Catholic University, comp. from authentic sources by S. J. B. Cincinnati, St. Ursula Convent and Academy [c1924] 216 p. front., map. 20 cm. Includes Bibliographies. [BX904.J6] 25-1743
1. Religious education—Text-books for young people—Catholic. I. Title.

[JOHN Berchmans, Sister] 282.
Compendium of third and fourth years high-school religion, according to the requirements of the Catholic University, including a particular study of the Ten commandments and the virtues. comp. from authentic sources by S. J. B. Cincinnati, St. Ursula Convent and Academy [1926] [5] l., [9]-622 p. front. 20 cm. Includes bibliographies. [BX904.J62] 26-9838
1. Religious education—Text-books for young people—Catholic. I. Title.

KALT, William J 268'.61
To live is Christ [by] William J. Kalt and Ronald J. Wilkins. Chicago, Regnery [1965- v. 23 cm. Contents.--v. 1. An overview.--v. 2. The mystery of Christ. Bibliographical footnotes. [BX930.K26] 65-21900
1. Religious education—Text-books for youth—Catholic Church. I. Wilkins, Ronald J., joint author. II. Title.

LAUX, John Joseph, 1878-1939. 239
A course in religion for Catholic high schools and academies ... By Rev. John Laux, M. A. New York, Cincinnati [etc.] Benziger brothers, 1928- v. 20 cm. Contents.pt. 1. Chief truths of faith.--pt. ii. The sacraments.--pt. iii. Christian morals.--pt. iv. God, Christianity and the church apologetics for high schools.--pt. v. Church history. [BX930.L3 1928] 28-19671
1. Religious education—Text-books for young people—Catholic. 2. Christian ethics—Catholic authors. I. Title.

LINK, Mark J 220.6
Christ teaches us today. Chicago, Loyola University Press [1964] xi, 277 p. illus. 24 cm. [BX930.L485] 64-2920
1. Religious education — Text-books for young people — Catholic. I. Title.

LINK, Mark J 230.2
We are God's people [by] Mark J. Link. Chicago, Loyola University Press [1966] ix. 226 p. illus. 24 cm. [BX930.L4858] 66-5787
1. Religious education — Text-books for youth — Catholic. I. Title.

LINK, Mark J 265
We live in Christ [by] Mark J. Link. Chicago, Loyola University Press [1965] xi, 239 p. illus. 24 cm. [BX930.L486] 65-3098
1. Religious education — Text-books for young people — Catholic. I. Title.

LINK, Mark J. 268'.61
Youth in the modern world; literature, friends, Christ, action [by] Mark J. Link. Chicago, Loyola University Press [1969] xi, 243 p. illus. 23 cm. [BX930.L4863] 73-3337 2.80
1. Religious education—Text-books for young people—Catholic. I. Title.

[LUCIAN Alphonsus, 268.433
brother] 1913-
Living with Christ. High school religion, course 1- Wonona, Minn., St. Mary's college, 1943- v. illus, diagrs. 23 cm. "A Christian brothers publication." Developed from Brother John Joseph's Religion outlines, published in 1832. cf. Acknowledgments. [BX930.L8] 44-26827
1. Religious education—Text-books for young people—Catholic. I. St. Mary's college. Winona, Minn. II. John Joseph, brother, 1874-1942. Religious outlines. III. Title.

[LUCIAN Alphonsus, 268.433
brother] 1913-
Living with Christ. High school religion, course 1- 2d ed. ... Winona, Minn., St. Mary's college press, 1945- v. illus. (incl. maps) diagrs. 22 cm. "A Christian brothers publication." Developed from Brother John Joseph's Religion outlines, published in 1932. cf. Acknowledgments. [Secular name: Raymond Jacob Pluth] [BX930.L8 1945] 45-20170
1. Religious education—Text-books for young people—Catholic. I. John Joseph, brother, 1874-1942. Religion outlines. II. Title.

LUCIAN ALPHONSUS, 268.433
Brother, 1913-
Living with Christ. High school religion, course 1- 2d ed. Winona, Minn., St. Mary's College Press, 1945- v. illus., ports., maps, diagrs. 22 cm. "A Christian Brothers publication." Developed from Brother John Joseph's Religion outlines, published in 1932. Teacher's handbook. Winona, Minn., St. Mary's College Press, 1947- v. 20 cm. Rev. ed. [BX930.L82] 45-20170
1. Religious education—Text-books for young people—Catholic. I. John Joseph, Brother, 1874-1942. Religion outlines. II. Title.

MICHEL, Virgil George, 282
father, 1890-1938.
Life in Christ ... by Dom Virgil Michel ... Minneapolis, Minn., Burgess publishing company, mimeoprint publishers, c1934. 1 p. l., 105 numb. l. 29 cm. (The Christ-life series. 2d ser. vol. i) [Secular name: George F. Michel] Bibliography at end of most of the chapters. [BX930.M47 1934] 40-4060
1. Religious education—Text-books for young people—Catholic. I. Title.

MICHEL, Virgil George, 282
father, 1890-1938.
Life in Christ ... by Dom Virgil Michel ... Minneapolis, Minn., Burgess publishing company, mimeoprint, publishers, c1935. 1 p. l., ii, 193 (i. e. 194) numb. l. 28 cm. (The Christ-life series. 2d ser. v. 3) Includes extra numbered leaf 5a. [Secular name: George F. Michel] Bibliography at end of most of the chapters. [BX930.M47 1935] 40-4061
1. Religious education—Text-books for young people—Catholic. I. Title.

MICHEL, Virgil George, 282
father, 1890-1938.
... Our life in Christ, by Dom Virgil Michel, O. S. B., in collaboration with monks of St. John's abbey, Collegeville, Minnesota, and Sisters of St. Dominic, Marywood, Grand Rapids, Michigan. Collegeville, Minn., The Liturgical press [c1939] vi, 240 p. 23 cm. (The Christian religion series) "Printed as ms." Published previously, 1935, under title: Life in Christ. [Secular name: George F. Michel] Includes bibliographies. [BX930.M47 1939] 40-4062
1. Religious education—Text-books for young people—Catholic. I. Collegeville, Minn. St. John's abbet. II. Sisters of the Order of St. Dominic, Marywood, Grand Rapids. III. Title.

OUR goal and our guides 268.433
... A textbook series for high school religion ... by Rev. Clarence E. Elwell ... Rev. Anthony N. Fuerst ... Sister Mary St. Therese Dunn ... [and others] Chicago, Mentzer, Bush & company, c1945- v. front., illus., col. plates. 21 cm. Includes bibliographies. [BX930.O83] 45-10166
1. Religious education—Text-books for young people—Catholic. I. Elwell, Clarence Edward, 1904- II. Fuerst, Anthony Norman, 1904-
Contents omitted.

OUR quest for 268.433
happiness; the story of divine love. High school religion. By ClarenceE. Elwell [and others] Chicago, Mentzer, Bush, 1955- v. illus. 23cm. [BX930.O866] 55-28233
1. Religious education—Text-books for young people—Catholic. I. Elwell, Clarence Edward, 1904-

OUR quest for 268.433
happiness; the story of divine love. High school religion. [By] Clarence E. Elwell [and others. Rev.] Chicago, Mentzer, Bush, 1955-58. 4 v. illus. 23cm. [BX930.O866] 55-28233
1. Religious education—Text-books for young people—Catholic. I. Elwell, Clarence Edward, 1904-

ROENSCH, Roger C 282
The Mass and sacraments for teenagers, by Roger C. Roensch. Glen Rock, N.J., Paulist Press [1966] 224 p. 18 cm. (Deus books] [BX930.R57] 66-16554
1. Religious education—Text-books for young people—Catholic. I. Title.

ROSENBERGER, Edward Glen, 230.2
1898-
Outlines of religion for Catholic youth A course of weekly instruction for high school students, prepared for the Archcon fraternity of Christian doctrine under the authority of His Excellency the Most Rev. Maurice F. McAuliffe ... By Rev. E. G. Rosenberger ... New York, N. Y., G. Grady press, 1940- v. 24 cm. Bibliography: v. 1, p. [307]-310. [BX930.R6] 40-35914
1. Religios education—Text-books for young people—Catholic. I. Confraternity of Christian doctrine. II. Title.

WEGER, Hilary R. 268.433
Studies in religion for high school and adult groups ... by Rev. Hilary R. Weger ... New York, Chicago, W. H. Sadlier, inc. [1938-39] 3 v. 25 1/2 cm. Loose-leaf in portfolios; title from cover. Vol. 1 by Rev. Hilary R. Weger in collaboration with Rev. Paul J. Brissel. Rev. Francis L. Fate, Rev. Robert E. Gallagher and others. Contents.[v. 1] Catholic morality. [1939]--[v. 2] The means of grace. [1938]--[v. 3] Catholic doctrine. [1939] [BX930.W4] (230.2) 43-19228
1. Religious education—Text-books for young people—Catholic. 2. Religious education—Text-books for adults—Catholic. I. Title.

Religious education—Text-books for young people—Congregational.

KINNEY, Dorothy W 268.61
Sore spots in society, a course for young people [by] Dorothy W. Kinney and Charles B. Kinney, Jr. Drawings by Allen M. Johson. Teacher's ed. Boston, Pilgrim Press [1953] 74p, 84p. illus. 19cm. (Pilgrim series) [BV1549.K5 1953] 268.433 53-20860
1. Religious education—Text-books for young people—Congregational. 2. Church and social problems—Study and teaching. I. Kinney, Charles B., joint author. II. Title.

Religious education—Text-books for young people—Lutheran.

GRAF, Arthur E. 268'.433
God's claim on you; a Bible study guide on the dedicated life, by Arthur E. Graf. Jefferson City, Mo., Faith Publications [1969] 41 p. 19 cm. Includes bibliographies. [BX8015.G72] 70-81748 0.40
1. Religious education—Text-books for young people—Lutheran. I. Title.

HOH, Philip Richard, 1921- 268.6
Called to be Christian. Terence Y. Mullins, editor. Roland Shutts, artist. Philadelphia, Muhlenberg Press [1961] Philadelphia, Muhlenberg Press [1961] 192p. illus. 23cm. 80p. 23cm. [BX8015.H6] 61-19961
1. Religious education—Text-books for young people—Lutheran. I. Title. II. Title: —Teacher's guide.

Religious education—Text-books for young people—Methodist.

BIBLE lessons for 268.433
youth; teacher's quarterly. [Cincinnati, Methodist Pub. House, etc.] v. 23 cm. Prepared by the Editorial Division of the General Board of Education of the Methodist Church. [BX8225.A1B5151] 51-17109
1. Religious education—Text-books for young people—Methodist. I. Methodist Church (United States) Board of Education. Editorial Division.

Religious education—Text-books for young people—Mormon.

REORGANIZED Church of 230.933
Jesus Christ of Latter-Day Saints. Dept. of Religious Education.
Facing today's frontiers; a foundational guide to the theological thinking of older youth, young adults and adults in the Reorganized Church of Jesus Christ of Latter Day Saints. Ed. by the Dept. of Religious Educ. [Independence, Mo.] Herald House [c.]1965 112p. 21cm. [BX8610.A493] 65-21327 1.50 bds.,
1. Religious education—Text-books for young people—Mormon. I. Title.

Religious education—Text-books for young people—Salvation Army.

AGNEW, Milton S., 1905- 268'.61
Manual of salvationism, by Milton S. Agnew. [New York] Salvation Army [1968] 72, 72a-b p. illus., map. 22 cm. Includes bibliographies. [BX9714.A37] 68-22790
1. Religious education—Text-books for young people—Salvation Army. I. Title.

Religious education—Text-books for young people—Unitarian.

ELIOT, Frederick May, 1889- 268
The unwrought iron; an introduction to religion, by Frederick May Eliot... Boston, Mass., The Beacon press [c1920] xii p. 2 l. 3-243 p. 19 cm. (Half-title: The Beacon course of graded sermons. W. I. Lawrence, Florence Buck, editors) "Suggestions for reading" at end of each chapter. [BX9821.E6] 20-20095
1. Religious education—Text-books for young people—Unitarian. I. Title.

ELIOT, Frederick May, 1889- 268
The unwrought iron; an introduction to religion, by Frederick May Eliot... [Teachers' ed.] Boston Mass., The Beacon press [c1920] xii p., 2 l., 3-274 p. 19 cm. (Half-title: The Beacon course of graded lessons. W. I. Lawrence, Florence Buck, editors) "Suggestions for reading" at end of each chapters. [BX9821.E6 1920a] 20-20095
1. Religious education—Text-books for young people—Unitarian. I. Title.

Religious education — Text-books for young people — United Church of Christ.

BRUEGGEMANN, Walter. 268'.61
Confronting the Bible; a resource and discussion book for youth. [Rev. ed. New York] Herder and Herder [1968] 75 p. illus. 22 cm. (Christian commitment series) Bibliography: p. 73-75. [BS605.2.B78] 68-29888 1.20
1. Bible—Study—Text-books. 2. Religious education—Text-books for young people—United Church of Christ. I. Title.

CHASE, Loring D. 238
Words of faith; a resource and discussion book for youth [by] Loring D. Chase. Illustrated by Micaela Myers. Boston, United Church Press [1968] 92 p. illus. 22 cm. (Confirmation education series) "Part of the United Church curriculum, prepared and published by the Division of Christian Education and the Division of Publication of the United Church Board for Homeland Ministries." [BX9884.A3C49] 68-10038
1. United Church of Christ—Catechisms and creeds. 2. Religious education—Text-books for young people—United Church of Christ. I. United Church Board for Homeland Ministries. Division of Christian Education. II. United Church Board for Homeland Ministries. Division of Publication. III. Title.

GILLIOM, James O. 266'.5'834
Sent on a mission; a resource and discussion book for youth, by James O. Gilliom. Illustrated by Carol Bachenheimer. [Rev. ed. New York] Herder and Herder [1968] 59 p. illus. 22 cm. (Christian commitment series) Includes bibliographical references. [BX9884.A3G54 1968b] 68-29890 1.20
1. Religious education—Text-books for young people—United Church of Christ. 2. Mission of the church. I. Bachenheimer, Carol, illus. II. Title.

KINNEY, Dorothy W.
The Christian in the world, by Dorothy W. and Charles B. Kinney, Jr. Photos. by Peter C. Schlaifer. Boston, United Church Press [c1963] 128 p. illus. 21 cm. (United Church curriculum. Senior High. Pupils. 1') Bibliographical references included in "Notes and acknowledgements" (p. 126-128) 65-4314
1. Religious education — Text-books for young people — United Church of Christ. I. Kinney. Charles B., joint author. II. Title. III. Series.

VANGUARDS for change; 268'.433
an action-reflection handbook. Robert L. Burt, editor. Philadelphia, United Church Press [1971] 95 p. illus. 26 cm. [BX9884.A3V35] 70-151862
1. Religious education—Text-books for young people—United Church of Christ. I. Burt, Robert L., ed.

Religious education—Text-books—Lutheran.

ALPERS, Kenneth P
God's grace and my need, teacher's guide by Kenneth P. Alpers and Robert G. Konzelman. Course design by Robert G. Konzelman. Minneapolis, Augsburg Publishing House,1966. 80 p. 27 cm. 240 p. illus. 21 cm. 68-68445
1. Part of the core curriculum and the program of adult Christian education (Pace) of the American Lutheran Church. It is correlated with the eighth grade junior high confirmation curriculum.—Student's book. [Illustrated by Joseph Bergeron. n.p., 1966?] 2. Christian doctrine. 3. Confirmation. I. Title.

EICKMANN, Paul E. 268'.434
The wonderful works of God, by Paul E. Eickmann. Milwaukee, Northwestern Pub.

House [1970] 88 p. 27 cm. [BX8015.E34] 70-123728
1. Religious education—Text-books—Lutheran. I. Title.

Religious education — Text-books — Methodist.

METHODIST Church (United States) Dept. of Children's Publications. 268.61
Resources for leaders of children. [Nashville, Methodist Pub. House] v. 23 cm. annual. Prepared by the Department of Children's Publications and the Department of Christian Education of Children. [BX8225.A1M38] 64-5644
1. Religious education — Text-books — Methodist. I. Methodist Church (United States) Dept. of Christian Education of Children. II. Title.

Religious education—Text-books—Mormon.

HOOLE, Daryl (Van Dam) 268.893
With sugar 'n spice, by Daryl V. Hoole, Donette V. Ockey, Illus. by Aurelia P. Richards. Salt Lake City, Deseret, 1966. vii, 146p. illus., ports. 27cm. [BX8610.H69] 65-28862 price unreported.
1. Religious education—Text-books—Mormon. I. Ockey, Donette V., joint author. II. Title.

Religious education—Text-books—Protestant.

OLSON, Bernhard Emmanuel. 290
Faith and prejudice; intergroup problems in Protestant curricula, New Haven, Yale University Press, 1963. 451 p. illus. 24 cm. (Yale publications in religion, 4) Bibliography: p. 423-435. [DS145.O4] 61-15000
1. Religious education—Text-books—Protestant. 2. Antisemitism. 3. Judaism—Relations—Christianity. 4. Christianity and other religions—Judaism. I. Title.

Religious education—Text-books—Reorganized Church of Jesus Christ of Latter-Day Saints.

SPENCER, Geoffrey F. 230'.9'33
The burning bush : revelation and Scripture in the life of the church / by Geoffrey F. Spencer. Independence, Mo. : Herald Pub. House, [1975] 224 p. : ill. ; 27 cm. Adapted from the author's We have these books. Includes bibliographical references. [BX8672.S67] 74-84762 ISBN 0-8309-0129-9
1. Bible—Study—Text-books. 2. Religious education—Text-books—Reorganized Church of Jesus Christ of Latter-Day Saints. 3. Revelation—Study and teaching. I. Title.

Religious education—Text-books—Series.

CHURCH of Jesus Christ of latter-day saints. Deseret Sunday school union. 268.893
Sunday school lessons. Salt Lake city, v, illus. 23-27 1/2 cm. annual. Binder's title. Each volume is a compilation of lesson manuals which are published separately. [BX8610.A1C5] 42-16081
1. Religious education—Text-books—Series. 2. Mormons and Mormonism—Education. I. Title.

EVANGELICAL Sunday school 268.61
lesson commentary on the Uniform Bible lesson series of the National Sunday School Association for 1960; 8th annual volume. Butler, Ind., Higley Press. c.1959 320p. maps 22cm. 53-33415 2.50
1. Religious education—Text-books—Series.

KRAMER, William Albert, 1900- ed. 268.433
Units in religion [for Lutheran schools. (Intermediate and upper grades)] Saint Louis, Concordia Pub. House, c19 v. illus. 28cm. [BX8015] 57-4029
1. Religious education—Text-books—Series. 2. Religious education—Text-books—Lutheran. I. Concordia Publishing House, St. Louis. II. Title.

Contents omitted.

NATIONAL Sunday School Association. 268.4
Annual lesson commentary [on the] National Sunday School Association uniform lessons. Springfield, Mo., Gospel Publishing House. v. illus. 23 cm. Began publication in 1958. [BV1561.A65] 64-28482
1. Religious education — Text-books — Series. I. Title.

PROTESTANT Episcopal Church in the U. S. A. National Council. Dept. of Christian Education. 268.432
Christian nurture series. Course J-2: Adventures in church worship, by Maurice Clarke. Milwaukee, Morehouse Pub. Co. [1933] 2 v. 20 cm. Contents.[1] Pupil's book.--[2] Teacher's book. [BX5874.A32] 52-45397
1. Religious education—Text-books—Series. I. Clarke, Maurice, 1882- II. Title. III. Title: Adventures in church worship.

PROTESTANT Episcopal Church in the U. S. A. National Council. Dept. of Christian Education. 268.61
Christian nurture series, leader's manual. Revision of 1936-[38] New York, Morehouse Pub. Cp., 1936- v. illus. 19 cm. Published, 1938- by Morehouse-Gorham Co. Includes bibliographies. [BX5874.A4] 52-16996
1. Religious education—Text-books—Series. I. Title.
Contents omitted.

PROTESTANT Episcopal Church in the U. S. A. National Council. Dept. of Christian Education. 268.
Christian nurture series, teacher's manual. Milwaukee, Young Churchman Co., 19 v. illus., col. maps. 19 cm. Vols., 1918- published by Morehouse Pub. Co. Includes bibliographies. [BX5874.A35] 17-28085
1. Religious education—Text-books—Series. I. Title.
Contents omitted.

PROTESTANT Episcopal Church in the U. S. A. National Council. Dept. of Christian Education. 268.
Christian nurture series, teacher's manual; a supplement to the instruction in the kindergarden grade A [-senior high school] for the public schol [and for students in colleges] Revision of [1923-1925] Milwaukee, Morehouse Pub. Co., 1923- [v. 1, 1925] v. illus., maps. 19 cm. --From sheepfold to throne: David the valorous; a course for summer instruction adapted to the grammar grades of the public schools. Milwaukee, Morehouse Pub. Co., 1925. xviii, 92 p. illus., maps. 19 cm. BX5874.A3522 Includes bibliographies. [BX5874.A352] 52-16061
1. Religious education—Text-books—Series. I. Title.
Contents omitted.

PROTESTANT Episcopal Church in the U. S. A. National Council. Dept. of Christian Education. 268.61
Christian nurture series, teacher's manual. Revision of 1930. Milwaukee, Morehouse Pub. Co. [1930- v. illus., col. maps. 19 cm. Includes bibliographies. [BX5874.A353] 52-15611
1. Religious education—Text-books—Series. I. Title.

PROTESTANT Episcopal church in the U.S.A. National council. Dept. of religious education. 268.
... Christian nurture series, course ... Prepared for the General board of religious education ... Milwaukee, the Young churchman co., 19 v. 19 cm. At head of title: Teacher's manual. Vols. 5-6 have imprint: Milwaukee, The Morehouse publishing co. Includes bibliographies. [BX5874.A4] 17-28085
1. Religious education—Text-books—Series. I. Title.

Religious education — Textbooks.

*HAZZARD, Lowell Brestel 268.433
Come, follow me; a course for junior high youth in vacation church schools, youth week programs, and other settings [by] Lowell Brestel [and] Stella Tombaugh Hazzard. Illus. by Murray McKeehan. Nashville, Abingdon [c.1957, c.1963] 48p. illus. (pt. col.) music. 23cm. Rev. of Fairest Lord Jesus, pub. 1957. .40; 1.25 pap., teacher's ed.,
1. Religious education—Textbooks. I. Hazzard, Stella Tombaugh, joint author. II. Title.

KERSTEN, John C.
Bible catechism; the Catholic faith presented through the Bible and the liturgy. New York, Catholic Book Publishing Co. [1964] 288 p. illus. 21 cm. "A Saint Joseph Edition." 66-81485
1. Religious education — Textbooks. I. Title.

MISSION Helpers of the Sacred Heart, Baltimore, Md.
Religion lessons for Catholic living. Second grade manual for teachers and parents. Rev. ed. Baltimore [1962] x, 276 p. illus. 28 cm. 63-28364
1. Religious education — Textbooks. I. Title.

REYNOLDS, Lillian Richter 268.433
How big is your world: a text for leaders of young people of Junior high school age . . . usable in vacation church schools, youth week programs, and other settings. Teacher's bk. Pub. for the Cooperative Pubn. Assn. by Richmond, Va., Knox [c.1962] 99p. 23cm. 1.25 pap.,
I. Title.

*TILLEY, Ethel 268.433
He was called Jesus; a vacation Church school course for junior groups: teacher's bk. Philadelphia, Pub. for the Cooperative Pubn. Assn. by Westminster [c.1963] 96p. illus. 23cm. Based on Jesus in his name. Pupil's bk. illus. by Robert Jefferson. With activities packet. pap., 1.25; pupil's bk., pap., .35; activities packet, .35
1. Religious education—Textbooks. I. Title.

Religious education — Textbooks for children — Catholic.

**IN Christ Jesus;* 230.2076
gr. 3, teacher's ed. New York, Sadlier, c. 1965. 224p. music 22x21cm. (Our life with God ser., Vatican II ed.) 2.00 pap.,

NAUGHTON. IRENE MARY 268.432
Make ready the way of the Lord. Milwaukee. Bruce [1966] xxv. 267p. 23cm. Music appendix: p.263-267 [BX930.N3] 66-19972 3.95
1. Religious education—Textbooks for children—Catholic. 2. Church year—Study and teaching. I. Title.

SCHOOL Sisters of Notre Dame, Milwaukee. 238.2
Living my religion series... Newly rev. ed. by the School Sisters of Notre Dame, Milwaukee, under the direction of Edmund J. Goebel. [New York, Benziger Bros., 1960-62 8 v. illus. 23 cm. These textbooks for the lower, middle, and upper grades contain questions and answers of The new Baltimore first communion catechism and The new Baltimore catechism no. 1 and no. 2, Official rev. Confraternity editions, with text explanations. [BX1961.L52] 60-14608
1. Religious education — Textbooks for children — Catholic. 2. Baltimore catechism. I. Title.

Religious education—Textbooks for children (Elementary)

**BIBLE, life and worship* 268.432
series; bk.4 Boston, Allyn, 1966 [c.1960, 1966] 191p. col. illus. 23cm. 1.64 pap.,
1. Religious education—Textbooks for children (Elementary) I. Johnice, M. II. Elizabeth, M., joint author. III. Cooke, Bernard J., joint author. IV. Title: Children of the Kingdom.
Contents omitted.

Religious education—Textbooks for children—Lutheran Church.

*ANDERSON, Marbury E. 268.433
I believe in Jesus Christ, by Marbury E. Anderson, Frank W. Klos. Illus. by Albert Machini. Philadelphia, Lutheran Church Pr. [c.1965] 207p. illus. (pt. col.) 22cm. (LCA weekday church sch. ser.) With teacher's guide. 2.25; 2.50 teacher's ed.,
1. Religious education— Textbooks for children—Lutheran Church. I. Klos, Frank W., joint author. II. Title.

*GARHART, Marjorie 268.432
The book of the promises of God; term 1, work-book. Illus. by Bert Marsh. Gustave K. Wiencke, ed. Philadelphia, Lutheran Church Pr., c.1965. 48p. illus. (pt. col.) map. 28cm. (LCA Sunday church sch. ser.) Flexible vinyl 34 record, 'a talking book of Psalms and prayers' in pocket on back cover. .70 pap.,
1. Religious education—Textbooks for Children—Lutheran Church. I. Title.

*GARHART, Marjorie 268.432
The book of the promises of God; term 4. Illus. by Tom Irons. Gustav K. Wiencke, ed. Philadelphia, Lutheran Church Pr., c.1965. 304p. 21cm. (LCA Sunday church sch. ser.) With teacher's guide and workbook. bds., 2.50; teacher's guide, 2.50; workbook, pap., .70
1. Religious education—Textbooks for children—Lutheran Church. I. Title.

*STACKEL, Robert W. 268.43
I believe in the holy spirit and the church. Philadelphia, Lutheran Church Pr. [c.1966] 191p. col. illus. music. 22cm. (LCA weekday church sch. ser.) 2.25; 2.50 teacher's ed.,
1. Religious education—Textbooks for children—Lutheran Church. I. Title.

Religious education — Textbooks for children — United Church of Christ.

DUNCAN, Cleo. 268.432
The mark of Christians; a course for the first and second grades. Boston, United Church Press [1964] 124 p. illus. 26 cm. "Part of the United Church curriculum, prepared and published by the Division of Christian Education and the Division of Publication of the United Church Board for Homeland Ministries." Bibliography: p. 123. []bX9884.A3D8] 64-19458
1. Religious education — Textbooks for children — United Church of Christ. I. United Church Board for Homeland Ministries. Division of Christian Education. II. United Church Board for Homeland Ministries. Division of Publication. III. Title.

EAKIN, Mildred Olivia (Moody) Mrs. 1890- 268.62
In anybody's town, (exploring our neighborhood, pupil's work book I) by Mildred Moody Eakin. New York, Cincinnati [etc.] The Abingdon press [c1936] 74 p. 21 1/2 cm. (Half-title: The Abingdon religious education texts, J. W. Langdale, general editor; Guides to Christian living, p. H. Vieth, editor) [BV1546.E32] A 41
1. Religious education—Texts-books for children. I. Title.

FROHNE, Marydel D 268.432
Understanding the church; a course for the third and fourth grades, by Marydel D. and Victor M. Frohne. Boston, United Church Press [1964] iii, 124 p. illus. (part col.) 26 cm. "Part of the United Church curriculum, prepared and published by the Division of Christian Education and the Division of Publication of the United Church Board for Homeland Ministries." Bibliography: p. 122-123. [BX9884.A3F7] 64-19459
1. Religious education — Textbooks for children — United Church of Christ. 2. Church — Study and teaching. I. Frohne, Victor M., joint author. II. United Church Board for Homeland Ministries. Division of Christian Education. III. United Church Board for Homeland Ministries. Division of Publication. IV. Title.

TOWER, Grace Storms. 268.432
What is the church? A course for fifth and sixth grades. Boston, United Church Press [1964] 124 p. illus. (part col.) 26 cm. "Part of the United Church curriculum prepared and published by the Division of Christian Education and the Division of Publication of the United Church Board for Homeland Ministries." Bibliography: p. 123. [BX9884.A3T6] 64-19460
1. Religious education — Textbooks for children — United Church of Christ. 2. Church — Study and teaching. I. United

Church Board for Homeland Ministries. Division of Christian Education. United Church Board for Homeland Ministries Division of Publication. II. Title.

Religious education — Textbooks for young people.

BAILEY, James Martin, 248.8'3
1929-
From wrecks to reconciliation, by J. Martin Bailey. Illustrated by Jim Crane. New York, Friendship Press [1969] 192 p. illus. 18 cm. Includes bibliographical references. [BV1561.B24] 68-57230
1. Religious education—Textbooks for young people. I. Title.

COLE, Orma Jeanne.
Day by day. Ray L. Henthorne, George S. Caroland, youth editors. Illustrated by Donald Keuker. St. Louis, Christian Board of Publication [c1957] 143 p. col. illus. ([Bethany graded youth books] v. 8, pt. 4) 65-43487
1. Religious education — Textbooks for young people. I. Henthorne, Ray L., ed. II. Caroland, George S., ed. III. Kueker, Donald, illus. IV. Title. V. Series.

COLE, Orma Jeanne.
Day by day. Ray L. Henthorne, George S. Caroland, youth editors. Teacher's ed. St. Louis, Christian Board of Publication [c1957] 128 p. (Bethany graded youth books, v. 8, pt. 4; teacher's ed.) 65-43489
1. Religious education — Textbooks for young people. I. Henthorne, Ray L., ed. II. Caroland, George S., ed. III. Title. IV. Series.

Religious education—Textbooks for young people—Catholic.

*BOTHWELL, Sister Mary 268'.432
de Angelis.
Good is good [by] Sister Mary de Angelis Bothwell and other Sisters of Notre Dame. Art: Sister Mary Megan Dull [&] Sister Mary Leon Wilhelmy. Theological advisor: John A. Hardon. Consultant: Daniel L. Flaherty. Chicago, Loyola University Press [1973] 138 p. col. illus. 28 cm. (Christ our life series: perform-a-text, 1) [BX930] ISBN 0-8294-0218-7 1.48 (pbk.)
1. Religious education—Textbooks for young people—Catholic. I. Hardon, John A. II. Flaherty, Daniel L. III. Title. IV. Series.

Religious education — United States

AMERICAN Association of 377.0973
School Administrators. Commission on Religion in the Public Schools
Religion in the public schools, a report. New York, Harper [1965, c.1964] x, 68p. 21cm. (Harper chapel bks., CB13) [LC111.A75] 65-2563 .85 pap.,
1. Religious education—U.S. I. Title.

AMERICAN Association of School
Administrators. Commission on Religion in the Public Schools.
Religion in the public schools, a report. New York, Harper & Row [1965, 1964] x, 68 p. 21 cm. (Harper chapel books, OB13)
1. Religious education — U.S. I. Title.

AMERICAN Council on 377.1
Education. Committee on Religion and Education.
The function of the public schools in dealing with religion; a report on the exploratory study made by the Committee on Religion and Education. Washington [1953] xiv, 145p. 22cm. Bibliography: p. [125]-145. [LC405.A55] 53-5772
1. Religious education—U. S. I. Title.

ATHEARN, Walter Scott, 1872- 377.
Character building in a democracy, by Walter Scott Ahearn ... New York, The Macmillan company, 1924. xii p., 2 l., 17-163 p. diagrs. 20 cm. (The Washington Gladden lectures for the year 1924) [BV1467.A7] 24-28238
1. Religious education—U. S. I. Title.
Contents omitted.

ATHEARN, Walter Scott, 1872- 377.
Character building in a democracy, by Walter Scott Ahearn ... New York, The Macmillan company, 1924. xii p., 2 l., 17-163 p. diagrs. 20 cm. (The Washington Gladden lectures for the year 1924) [BV1467.A7] 24-28238
1. Religious education—U. S. I. Title.
Contents omitted.

ATHEARN, Walter Scott, 1872- 377.
Religious education and American democracy, by Walter Scott Athearn ... Boston, Chicago, The Pilgrim press [c1917] xi p., 1 l., 384 p. illus. 20 cm. Contains references. "Chapters i, ii, and iii were published during the past year as the Maiden leaflects ... A portion of chapter v has previously appeared in the columns of Religious education."--Foreword. [LC405.A75] 17-27657
1. Religious education—U. S. I. Title.

BEMAN, Lamar Taney, 1877- 377.
comp.
... Religious teaching in the public schools, compiled by Lamar T. Beman ... New York, The H. W. Wilson company, 1927. 170 p. 20 cm. (The reference shelf, v. 5, no. 2) Bibliography: p. [21]-33. [LC405.B4] 27-14630
1. Religious education—U. S. 2. Bible in the schools. I. Title.

BOWER, William Clayton, 377.8
1878-
Church and state in education, by William Clayton Bower. Chicago, Ill., The University of Chicago press [1944] v, 102, [1] p. 19 1/2 cm. "Originally given as the James R. Richard lectures in Christian religion at the University of Virginia in November, 1943." "A selected bibliography": p. 93-99. [LC111.B6] A 44
1. Religious education—U.S. 2. Church and education in the U.S. I. Title.

BYRNES, Lawrence, 1940- 377'.1
Religion and public education. New York, Harper & Row [1974] p. cm. (Critical issues in education) Bibliography: p. [LC111.B97] 74-4530 ISBN 0-06-041119-8 3.95 (pbk.)
1. Religious education—United States. I. Title.

CIARLANTINI, Lino Aldo, 377.1
1906-
The liberty of the school and family education. New York, Educational Publishers [1954] 253 p. 21 cm. [LC368.C5] 54-4084
1. Religions education—U. S. I. Title.

COX, Claire. 377'.1'0973
The fourth R; what can be taught about religion in the public schools. [1st ed.] New York, Hawthorn Books [1969] ix, 179 p. 22 cm. [LC111.C69] 69-16030 4.95
1. Religious education—U.S. I. Title.

DE FOREST, Ernest Grant. 377'.1
God in the American schools : religious education in a pluralistic society / Ernest Grant De Dorest. Albuquerque, N.M. : American Classical College Press, [1979] p. cm. Bibliography: p. [BL42.5.U5D43] 79-23466 22.75
1. Religious education—United States. I. Title.

EDWARDS, Frances Rose, 268.83
1898-
Children and the church; a study of information and attitudes in the Protestant Episcopal church, by Frances Rose Edwards ... New York, N.Y., The National council, Department of religious education, 1936. 211, [1] p. fold. tab. 19 cm. Thesis (ph. d.)--Columbia university, 1936. Vita. "Some books and materials used in this study": p. 202-203. [BX5870.E3 1936] 37-3642
1. Religious education—U.S. 2. Protestant Episcopal church in the U.S.A.—Education. 3. Sunday schools. I. Title.

FLEMING, William 377.10973
Sherman, 1865-
God in our public schools, by W. S. Fleming ... With introduction by Luther A. Weigle ... Pittsburgh, Pa., The National reform association [1942] 246 p. 20 cm. [LC111.F5] 42-22445
1. Religious education—U.S. 2. Public schools—U.S. 3. Bible in the schools I. National reform association. II. Title.

FLEMING, William Sherman, 377.1
1865-
God in our public schools, by W. S. Fleming, D.D. With introduction by Luther A. Weigle ... Pittsburgh, Pa., The National reform association [1944] 248 p. diagrs. 19 cm. "First edition, July, 1942. Second edition, July, 1944." Biliography at end of most of the chapters. [LC111.F5 1944] 44-7034
1. Religous education—U.S. 2. Public schools. 3. Bible in the schools. I. National reform association. II. Title.

FLEMING, William Sherman, 377.1
1865-
God in our public schools, by W. S. Fleming, D.D. With introduction by Luther A. Weigle ... Pittsburgh, Pa., The National reform association [1947] 248 p. diagrs. 19 1/2 cm. "First edition, July, 1942 ... Third edition, January, 1947." Bibliography at end of most of the chapters. [LC111.F5 1947] 47-19758
1. Religious education—U.S. 2. Public schools—U.S. 3. Bible in the schools. I. National reform association. II. Title.

GAUSS, Christian Frederick, 377.1
1878- ed.
The teaching of religion in American higher education, by Christian Gauss [and others] New York, Ronald Press Co. [1951] viii, 158 p. 21 cm. [LC391.G3] 51-11129
1. Religious education—U. S. I. Title.

GLENVILLE, N. Y. Second Reformed
church.
Memorial volume of the semicentennial anniversary of the Second Reformed church of Glenville, N. Y., November 21, 1868. By Rev. F. F. Wilson. Scotia, N. Y., 1868. 61 p. 25 cm. 9-17942
I. Wilson, Fred F., 1830- II. Title.

HARTSHORNE, Hugh, 1885- 377.10973
Community organization in religious education, by Hugh Hartshorne ... and J. Quinter Miller ... with the assistance of Willard E. Uphaus ... and Charles G. Chakerian ... New Haven, Pub. for the Institute of social and religious research by the Yale university press; London, H. Milford, Oxford university press, 1932. xxvi, 250 p. maps, diagrs. 24 cm. (Half-title: Yale studies in a religious education. v) "The original monography upon which this report is based ... is a dissertation presented [by J. Q. Miller] for the degree of doctor of philosophy in Yale university under the title 'A functional study of community cooporation in religious education."--p. vi, foot-notes. "New Haven was selected as the community to be used as a test case."--Introd., p. xxvi. Bibliography: p. [249]-250. [BV1467.H3] 32-18848
1. Religious education—U. S. 2. Religious education—Societies. 3. Protestant churches—U. S. 4. Church work. 5. Sociology, Christian. 6. Religious education—Connecticut—New Haven. I. Miller, Joseph Quinter, joint author. II. Uphaus, Willard Edwin. III. Chakerian, Charles Garabed. IV. Institute of social and religious research. V. Title.

HARTSHORNE, Hugh, 1885- 377.1
Standards and trends in religious education, by Hugh Hartshorne ... Helen R. Stearns ... and Willard E. Uphaus ... New Haven, Pub. for the Institute of social and religious research by the Yale university press; London, H. Milford, Oxford university press, 1933. xv, [1], 230 p. diagrs. 24 cm. (Half-title: Yale studies in religious education. ix) "The present volume ... is the seventh work issued by the Yale university press on the Samuel B. Sneath memorial publication fund."--p. [v] "The Institute of social and religious research ... is responsible for this publication."--p. [ii] "Part one ... based on a monography by Miss Helen R. Stearns, which was presented as a dissertation for the degree of doctor of philosophy in Yale university, under the title 'An empirical study of standardization in church schools'."--Pref. "References": p. [227]-230. Contents.--pt. 1. In church schools.--pt. 2. In American colleges. [BV1467.H33] 33-18904
1. Religious education—U. S. 2. Sunday-schools. 3. Church and college in the U. S. 4. Students—U. S. 5. Universities and colleges—U. S. 6. Universities and colleges—Religion. I. Stearns, Helen Rachel, joint author. II. Uphaus, Willard Edwin, joint author. III. Yale university, Samuel B. Sneath memorial publication fund. IV. Institute of social and religious research. V. Title.

HARTWICK seminary, Brooklyn. 207.
Memorial volume of the semi-centenial anniversary of Hartwick seminary, held August 21, 1866. Albany, J. Munsell, 1867. 2 p. l., 201 p. incl. illus., facsims. front., ports. 24 1/2 cm. L.C. copy imperfect: frontispiece and portraits wanting. [BV4070.H3065 1867] 7-14047
I. Title.

HAUSER, Conrad 377.10973
Augustine, 1872-
Teaching religion in the public school, by Conrad A. Hauser... New York, Round table press, 1942. xv, 300 p. 20 cm. "Sequel to Latent religious resources in public school education."--p. vii. [LC405.H32] 42-18333
1. Religious education—U.S. 2. Public schools—U.S. I. Title.

HAY, Clyde Lemont, 1874- 377.1
The blind spot in American public education; with introd, by Herbert B. Mulford. New York, Macmillan, 1950. xvi, 110 p. 21 cm. [LC405.H35] 50-9702
1. Religious education—U. S. I. Title.

HEALEY, Robert M. 322'.1
Jefferson on religion in public education, by Robert M. Healey. [Hamden, Conn.] Archon Books, 1970 [c1962] xi, 294 p. 22 cm. "A dissertation presented for the degree of doctor of philosophy at Yale University ... somewhat revised." Bibliography: p. [277]-284. [LC111.H4 1970] 73-114422
1. Jefferson, Thomas, Pres. U.S., 1743-1826. 2. Religious education—U.S. 3. Church and education in the United States. I. Title.

HEALEY, Robert M. 322
Jefferson on religion in public education. New Haven, Yale University Press, 1962. xi, 294 p. 23 cm. (Yale publications in religion, 3) "A dissertation presented for the degree of doctor of philosophy at Yale University...somewhat revised." Bibliography: p. [277]-284. [LC111.H4] 62-16233
1. Jefferson, Thomas, Pres. U.S., 1743-1826. 2. Religious education—U.S. 3. Church and education in the U.S. I. Series.

HENRY, Virgil. 377.1
The place of religion in public schools, a handbook to guide communities. [1st ed.] New York, Harper [1950] x, 164 p. 21 cm. Bibliography: p. 151-160. [LC405.H4] 50-5278
1. Religious education—U. S. I. Title.

JACKSON, Jerome Case, 377
d.1927.
Religious education and the state, by Jermoe K. [!] Jackson ... and Constantine F. Malmberg ... Garden City, N. Y., Doubleday, Doran & company, inc., 1928. xxii p., 1 l., 195 p. diagrs. 20 cm. Bibliography: p. 189-195. [LC111.J3] 28-27757
1. Religious education—U. S. 2. Bible in the schools. 3. Public schools—U. S. I. Malmberg, Constantine Frithiof, joint author. II. Title.

KELLER, James Gregory, 377.1
1900-
All God's children: what your schools can do for them. Garden City, N. Y., Hanover House [1953] 292 p. 22 cm. [LC111.K43] 53-12979
1. Religious education—U.S. 2. Church and education in the U.S. I. Title.

KIENEL, Paul A. 370.11'4
What this country needs / Paul A. Kienel ; foreword by Tim F. LaHaye. San Diego : Beta Books, [1977], c1976. p. cm. First published in 1976 under title: America needs Bible centered families and schools. [LC368.K53 1977] 77-340 ISBN 0-89293-015-2 : 1.95
1. Religious education—United States. I. Title.

KLYVER, Faye Huntington, 371.
1893-
The supervision of student-teachers in

religious education, by Faye Huntington Klyver ... New York city, Teachers college, Columbia university, 1925. viii, 186 p. 24 cm. (Teachers college, Columbia university. Contributions to education, no. 198) Published also as thesis (PH. D.) Columbia university, 1926. Bibliograpy: p. 185-186. [BV1533.K6 1925] [LB5.C8 no. 198] 262. 26-10212
1. Religious education—U. S. I. Title.

LOTZ, Philip Henry, 1889- ed. 268
Orientation in religious education. New York, Abingdon-Cokesbury Press [1950] 618 p. 24 cm. Includes bibliographies. "A selected bibliography of religious education [by] Leonard A. Stidley": p. 567-583. [LC427.L6] 50-7274
1. Religious education—U. S. I. Title.

MCKIBBEN, Frank Melbourne. 377.
A series of six radio talks on the renaissance in religious education (with select bibliography) by Frank M. McKibben...with a foreword by Grover H. Alderman... [Pittsburgh] 1929. 68 p. 22 1/2 cm. (University of Pittsburgh. Radio publication no. 46) "Broadcast from the University of Pittsburgh studio of KDKA, Westinghouse electric and manufacturing company, Pittsburgh, Pennsylvania. "Select bibliography": p. 64-65. [LC405.M3] 29-13158
1. Religious education—U.S. I. Title. II. Title: The renaissance in religious education.

MARTIN, Renwick Harper, 1872- 377.1
The fourth R in American education, With foreword by the author. Pittsburgh [c1957] 106p. 21cm. [LC111.M28] 58-7017
1. Religious education—U. S. I. Title.

MARTIN, Renwick Harper, 1872- 377.1
Our public schools,Christian or secular; with introd. by Luther A. Weigle. Pittsburgh, National Reform Association [1952] 132 p. 21 cm. [LC111.M3] 52-27122
1. Religious education—U. S. 2. Education and state—U. S. I. Title.

MATTOX, Fount William, 1909- 377.1
The teaching of religion in the public schools. Nashville, George Peabody College for Teachers, 1948 [i.e. 1949] vii, 133 p. 24 cm. (George Peabody College for Teachers [Nashville] Contri4ution to education no. 396) Bibliography: p. 130-133. [LC405.M35] 49-1098
1. Religious education—U.S. I. Title. II. Series.

NATIONAL council on religion in higher education. 268.
Bulletin. 1st- [New Haven, 1923- v. 23 cm. Publication irregular. Title varies: i, Bulletin of the Council of schools of religion. ii-iii, Bulletin of the National council of schools of religion. iv-Bulletin of the National council on religion in higher education. Contents.i. The origin, organization and aims of the council. [1923]-ii. Filling the gap in modern education, by C. F. Kent. [1923]-iii. Religion at a great state university, by C. F. Kent. [1924]--iv. The undergraduate courses in religion at the tax-supported colleges and universitiesof America, by C. F. Kent. [1924]--v. State constitutional and legislative provisions and Supreme court decisions relating to sectarian religious influence in tax-supported universities, colleges and public schools, by H. L. Searles. [1924] [BV1460.N3] 25-27697
1. Religious education—U. S. I. Title.

NOLL, John Francis, bp., 1875-. 377
Our national enemy number one: education without religion, by John F. Noll. Huntington, Ind., Our Sunday visitor press, 1942. 8 p. l., 312 p. 19 cm. [LC111.N6] 43-9674
1. Religious education—U.S. 2. Church and education in the U.S. 3. Public schools—U.S. 4. Catholic church in the U.S.—Education. I. Title.

O'NEILL, James Milton, 1881- 377'.0973
Religion and education under the Constitution, by J. M. O'Neill. New York, Da Capo Press, 1972 [c1949] xii, 338 p. 22 cm. (Civil liberties in American history) Bibliography: p. 319-325. [LC405.O5 1972] 72-171389 ISBN 0-306-70228-2
1. Religious education—United States. 2. Religion in the public schools. I. Title.

O'NEILL, James Milton, 1881- 377.1
Religion and education under the Constitution. [1st ed.] New York, Harper [1949] xii, 338 p. 22 cm. Bibliography: p. 319-325. [LC405.O5] 49-8342
1. Religious education—U. S. 2. Bible in the schools. I. Title.

PHENIX, Philip Henry, 1915- 377.10973
Education and the worship of God, by Philip H. Phenix. Philadelphia, Westminster Press [1966] 192 p. 21 cm. [LC405.P5] 66-10142
1. Religious education—U. S. I. Title.

PHENIX, Philip Henry, 1915- 377.10973
Religious concerns in contemporary education; a study of reciprocal relations. New York, Bureau of Publications. Teachers College, Columbia University, 1959. 108p. 22cm. [LC111.P5] 59-11329
1. Religious education—U. S. I. Title.

QUINN, Mary Antonina. Sister. 375.2
... Religious instruction in the Catholic high school, its content and method from the viewpoint of the pupil ... by Sister Mary Antonina Quinn ... Washington, D. C., The Catholic university of America, 1930. x, 147 p. 23 cm. At head of title: The Catholic university of America. Thesis (PH. D.)--Catholic university of America, 1960. Bibliography: p. 143-147; "Helpful books and magazines suggested by pupils": p. 69-75. [BX925.Q5 1930] 377.82 30-15901
1. Religious education—U. S. 2. Catholic church in the U. S.—Education. 3. High schools. I. Title.

SEARLES, Herbert Leon, 1891- 207
The study of religion in state universities, by Herbert Leon Searles, PH. D. Iowa City, The University [1927] 91 p. 23 cm. (University of Iowa. Studied in character. vol. 1, no. 3) University of Iowa studies. First series no. 141. Thesis (PH D.)--University of Iowa, 1925. Without thesis note. Bibliography: p. 89-91. [BV1610.S4 1927] 28-27344
1. Religious education—U. S. 2. Universities and colleges—U. S. I. Title. II. Title: State universities, The study of religion in.

SELLERS, Horace B 377.1
The Constitution and religious education. Boston, Christopher Pub. House [1950] 146 p. 21 cm. Bibliographical footnotes. [LC111.s4] 50-11321
1. Religious education — U.S. I. Title.

SPEAR, Samuel Thayer, 1812-1891.
Religion and the state; or, The Bible and the public schools. By Samuel T. Spear, D.D. New York, Dodd, Mead & company, 1876. 2 p. l., 9-393 p. 19 cm. "Originally pub. as a series of articles in the correspondence columns of the Independent."--Pref. E 10
1. Religious education—U.S. 2. Bible in schools—U.S. I. Title.

TAYLOR, Marvin J., 1921- 377.0973
Religious and moral education [by] Marvin J. Taylor. New York, Center for Applied Research in Education [1965] x, 118 p. 24 cm. (The Library of education) Bibliography: p. 113. Bibliographical footnotes. [LC428.T3] 65-25729
1. Religious education—United States. 2. Moral education. 3. Church and education in the United States. I. Title.

THAYER, Vivian Trow, 1886- 377.1
... Religion in public education. New York, The Viking press, 1947. xi, 212 p. 21 cm. At head of title: V. T. Thayer. "First published ... in January 1947." Bibliographical foot-notes. [LC111.T5] 47-1127
1. Religious education—U.S. 2. Church and education in the U.S. I. Title.

THAYER, Vivian Trow, 1886- 377'.1
Religion in public education / V. T. Thayer. Westport, Conn. : Greenwood Press, 1979, c1947. xi, 212 p. ; 23 cm. Reprint of the ed. published by Viking Press, New York. Includes bibliographical references and index. [LC111.T5 1979] 78-12385 ISBN 0-313-21212-0 lib. bdg. : 16.25
1. Religious education—United States. 2. Church and education in the United States. I. Title.

THORNE, Charles Greenwood. 377'.1
Word or words; a view of religion in independent schools. Edited by Peter C. Moore. [Wallingford, Conn.] Council for Religion in Independent Schools [1971] 19 p. 22 cm. Cover title. [LC368.T45] 72-184512 0.50
1. Religious education—United States. 2. Private schools—United States. I. Title.

VAN DUSEN, Henry Pitney, 1897- 377.1
God in education; a tract for the times. New York, Scribner, 1951. 128 p. 21 cm. (The Rockwell lectures delivered at the Rice Institute) Bibliography: p. [119]-128. [LC391.V3] 51-3202
1. Religious education — U.S. 2. Universities and colleges — Religion. I. Title. II. Series: Rockwell lectures

VERKUYL, Gerrit, 1872- 377.10973
Christ in American education, by Gerrit Verkuyl ... New York [etc.] Fleming H. Revell company [c1934] 192 p. 19 1/2 cm. "Preparatory reading" at end of most of the chapters. [BV1467.V4] 34-13525
1. Religious education—U. S. 2. Public schools—U.S. I. Title.

WARD, Leo Richard, 1893- 375.2
Religion in all the schools. Notre Dame, Ind., Fides Publishers [1960] 195 p. 21 cm. [LC111.W37] 60-15438
1. Religious education — U.S. I. Title.

*WESTON, Sidney A. 230
Life problems in a changing world [a discussion unit for high school ages and young adults. Rev. ed.] Boston, Whittemore Assocs. [c.1964] 96p. illus. 17cm. .75 pap.,
I. Title.

WILDER, Amos Niven, 1895- ed. 377.1
Liberal learning and religion. [1st ed.] New York, Harper [1951] xi, 338 p. 22 cm. "The contributors . . . are all fellows or officers of the National Council on Religion in Higher Education." [LC391.W56] 51-11012
1. Religious education—U.S. 2. Church and college in the U.S. I. National Council on Religion in Higher Education. II. Title.

WILDER, Amos Niven, 1895- ed. 377'.1
Liberal learning and religion, edited by Amos N. Wilder. Port Washington, N.Y., Kennikat Press [1969, c1951] xi, 338 p. 23 cm. (Essay and general literature index reprint series) "The contributors ... are all fellows or officers of the National Council on Religion in Higher Education." Bibliographical footnotes. [LC391.W56 1969] 77-86072
1. Religious education—U.S. 2. Church and college in the United States. I. National Council on Religion in Higher Education. II. Title.

Religious education—United States—Addresses, essays, lectures.

PUBLIC education religion studies : an overview / by Paul J. Will, ed., Nicholas Piediscalzi, assoc. ed., Barbara Ann DeMartino Swyhart, assoc. ed. Missoula, Mont. : Published by Scholars Press for the American Academy of Religion, c1980. p. cm. (Aids for the study of religion ; no. 7) Bibliography: p. [LC405.P82] 80-12237 ISBN 0-89130-401-0 : 17.50 ISBN 0-89130-402-9 pbk. : 12.00 377
1. Religious education—United States—Addresses, essays, lectures. I. Will, Paul J. II. Piediscalzi, Nicholas. III. Swyhart, Barbara Ann DeMartino. IV. Title. V. Series.

TEACHING about religion in public schools / edited by Nicholas Piediscalzi and William E. Collie. 1st ed. Niles, Ill. : Argus Communications, c1977. xii, 258 p. ; 23 cm. Includes bibliographies. [BL42.5.U5T42] 77-80623 ISBN 0-913592-79-X : 3.95 200'.7'1073
1. Religious education—United States—Addresses, essays, lectures. 2. Church and state in the United States—Addresses, essays, lectures. I. Piediscalzi, Nicholas. II. Collie, William E.

Religious education—United States—History.

PARKER, Inez Moore. 377'.8'5133
The rise and decline of the program of education for Black Presbyterians of the United Presbyterian Church, U.S.A., 1865-1970 / by Inez Moore Parker. San Antonio : Trinity University Press, c1977. 319 p. ; 24 cm. (Presbyterian Historical Society publication series ; 16) Includes index. Bibliography: p. [307]-312. [LC580.P37] 76-49248 ISBN 0-911536-66-3 : 10.00
1. United Presbyterian Church in the U.S.A.—History. 2. Religious education—United States—History. 3. Presbyterians, Afro-American—United States—History. I. Title: The rise and decline of the program of education ... II. Series: Presbyterian Historical Society. Publications ; 16.

Religious education—[Universities and colleges]

WORLD'S student Christian federation.
Religious forces in the universities of the world; four years of progress in the World's student Christian federation; presented at the tenth conference of the federation held at Lake Mohonk, June 2-8, 1913. Rev. ed. [New York?] World's student Christian federation, 1914. 74 p. front., plates (part. fold.) diagr. 23 cm. [LC351.W88A4] E 14
1. Religious education—[Universities and colleges] 2. Universities and colleges. I. Title.
Contents omitted.

Religious education—[Universities and colleges]—United States

TEXAS. University.
... Religious activities at the University of Texas. [Austin] The University of Texas [1909] 53 p. plates, plan. 28 cm. (Bulletin of the University of Texas. no. 129. General ser. no. 17) [BR561.T4A2] 10-33264
I. Title.

WILLIAMS, Wolcott B. 377.
Christian and secular education, by the Rev. Wolcott B. Williams ... Introduction by E. C. Ray, D.D. The Presbyterian board of aid for colleges and academies, 30 Montauk block, Chicago, 1894. Chicago, R. R. Donnelley & sons company, printers, 1894. 82 p. 19 cm. [LC405.W67] E 9
1. Religious education—[Universities and colleges]—U.S. 2. Church schools. I. Presbyterian board of aid for colleges and academies. II. Title.

Religious education—Virginia.

BELL, Sadie. 377.8
The church, the state, and education in Virginia [by] Sadie Bell. Philadelphia [The Science press printing company] 1930. xii, 796 p. 24 cm. Published also as thesis (PH. D.) University of Pennsylvania. Half-title: An explanation of present day attitudes toward religion in education from the point of view of their historical development. Bibliography: p. 661-735. [LC428.V8B41930] 30-31706
1. Religious education—Virginia. 2. Education and state—Virginia. 3. Church and education 4. Church and state in Virginia. 5. Bible in the schools. I. Title.

VIRGINIA council of religious education, inc. 377.109755
The churches in cooperation, a digest of cooperative church activity in religious education in Virginia, approved by the Educational committee of the Council, January 20, 1931, and publication authorized by the Virginia council of religious education, inc., January 21, 1931 ... Bridgewater, Va., Virginia council of religious education, inc. [c1931] 5 p. l.,

[13]-94 p. incl. illus., ports., maps, diagrs. 23 cm. Prepared by Rev. M. C. Miller, executive secretary, cf. Introd. Bibliography at end of some of the chapters. [BV1468.V8V5 1931] 31-22128
1. Religious education—Virginia. I. Miller, Minor Cline, 1889- ed. II. Title.

Religious education—Year-books.

COUNCIL of church boards of education. 377.058
... *Handbook* ... 1931- New York, N. Y., The Council of church boards of education in the United States of America [1931- v. 24 cm. Issued as a number of Christian education, v. 14-(1930/31-) On cover: Christian education handbook ... Includes sections "Educational foundations" and "Educational associations and agencies." [BV1460.C62] 31-27198
1. Religious education—Year-books. I. Title.

INTERNATIONAL council of religious education. 268.
... *Year book. 1st* 1924- Chicago [1924- v. illus. (ports.) 23 cm. At head of title, 1924- : International Sunday school council of religious education. Cover-title, 1924- : International year book of religious education. [BV1460.I7] 24-16339
1. Religious education—Year-books. 2. Sunday-schools. I. Title. II. Title: International year book of religious education.

NATIONAL council on religion in higher education. 268.
Year book. 1923/24- [New Haven, 1924- v. 23 cm. [BV1460.N25] 25-27693
1. Religious education—Year-books. 2. Religious education—U. S. I. Title.

Religious education (Young adults)—Lutheran.

*DAEHLING, Edythe 268.433
Together: doing our part as Christians. Writers: Edy-the Daehling, Marjorie F. Garhart, John Stevens Kerr. Designer: Peggy Powell. Photos: John Kerr [others] Philadelphia, Lutheran Church Pr., 1967. 49p. illus. 28cm. (Vacation church sch. ser.) Third year of three-year cycle: God and my life. .50 pap.,
1. Religious education (Young adults)—Lutheran. I. Garhart, Marjorie F. II. Kerr, John Stevens. III. Title.

*HEIN, Lucille E. 268.433
Living in Christ, by Lucille E. Hein, Walter A. Kortrey. Art. by Jeff Zinggler. Philadelphia, Lutheran Church Pr. [1967] 49p. illus. 21cm. (LCA church camp ser.) .65 pap.,
1. Religious education (Young adults)—Lutheran. I. Kortrey, Walter A., joint author. II. Title.

*HORN, William M. 268.433
Challenge and witness. Ed. by Wilbur G. Volker. Illus. by Stan Tusan. Philadelphia, Lutheran Church Pr. [c.1966] 320p. illus. (pt. col.) 24cm. (LCA Sunday church sch. ser.) Accompanied by a Teacher's guide. 2.25; 2.50 text, teacher's guide,
1. Religous education (Young adults)—Lutheran. I. Title.

**IT'S my congregation, too!* 268.433
Student's book [Minneapolis, Augsburg, c.1965] 80p. 22cm. [Based on material prep. by Clifton Anderson, others] (Amer. Lutheran Church curriculum: senior high) With teacher's guide. pap., 1.00; teacher's guide, pap., 2.00
1. Religious education (Young adults) Lutheran.

*MASHECK, Charles L. 268.433
We serve. Art by Frank P. Grobelny. Walter A. Kortery, ed. Philadelphia, Lutheran Church Pr. [1967] 61p. illus. 19cm. (LCA church camp ser.) .85 pap.,
1. Religious education (Young adults)—Lutheran. I. K. Kortrey, Walter A., ed. II. Title.

*MATHEWS, Eleanor Muth 268.432
Lives that praise God; teacher's guide: grades 3 8 4. Marjorie F. Garhart, ed. Philadelphia, Lutheran Church Pr. [1967] 80p. 23cm. (LCA vacation church sch. ser.) Third year of three-year cycle: God and my life. .90 pap.,
1. Religious education (Young adults)—Lutheran. I. Garhart, Mrrjorie F., ed. II. Title.

*NORQUIST, N. Leroy. 286.433
The church in the New Testament and today. Philip R. Hoh, ed., Mae Gerhard, illus. Philadelphia, Lutheran Church Pr. [c1966] 112p. illus. 21 cm. (LCA Sunday church sch. ser.) 1.00 pap., teacher's guide, pap., 1.25
1. Religious education (young adults) Lutheran. I. Title.

**QUESTIONS about the Bible;* 268.433
student's bk. Minneapolis, Minn., Augsburg [c.1965] 22cm. (Amer. Lutheran Church curriculum: senior high) pap., 1.25 Teacher's guide, pap., 1.75
1. Religious education (Young adults) Lutheran.

**RIGHT and wrong; student's book.* 268.433
Minneapolis, Augsburg, 1966. 72p. illus. (pt. col.) 22cm (Amer. Lutheran Church curriculum: senior high student's bk.) 1.00; 2.00 pap., teacher's guide,
1. Religious education (Young adults) Lutheran.

**WHY doesn't God . . .?* 268.433
student's book. Minneapolis, Augsberg, c.1965. 64p. illus. (pt. col.) 28cm. Prep. for the Bd. of Parish Educ., and the Bd. of Pubn. of the Amer. Lutheran Church. Based on material prep. by Paul Gabrielsen, Lena Seidel, Janet Woodcock (Amer. Lutheran church curriculum; senior high students bk.) With teacher's guide. pap., 1.50;teacher's guide, pap., 1.75
1. Religious education (young adults) Lutheran. I. Gabrielsen, Paul. II. Deidel, Lena, joint author.

Religious education—Youth.

KEMBLE, Duston.
The teaching of the Holy Scriptures, for young people's classes in all evangelical churches; an outline study, by Duston Kemble. Philadelphia, American Sunday school union, 1908. 186 p., 1 l. 18 cm. 8-26395
I. Title.

LAYMON, Charles M. 220.07
The use of the Bible in teaching youth. Nashville, Abingdon [1963, c.1962] 175p. maps. 19cm. 1.50 pap.,
I. Title.

LOBINGIER, John Leslie. 261
Our church; a course of study for young people of the highschool age, by John Leslie Lobingier. Chicago, Ill., The University of Chicago press [c1927] 4 p. l., vii-viii, 121 p. illus. (maps) 20 cm. (Half-title: The University of Chicago publications in religious education ... Constructive studies) Part of pages blank for "Notes", etc. Contains bibliographies. [BV602.L6] 27-25560
I. Title.

WELSHIMER, Mildred, 1902- 268.6
The young people's Bible teacher and leader, a ten-hour course for teachers and officers of the young people's department, by Mildred Welshimer. Cincinnati, O., The Standard publishing company [c1939] 137 p. 19 cm. "Supplementary reading" at end of some of the chapters. [Full name: Mildred Katherine Welshimer] [BV1533.W4] 39-6773
1. Religious education—Youth. I. Title.

WILSON, Lewis Gilbert, 1858- 252.
The uplifted hands and other sermons, by Lewis Gilbert Wilson ... [Hopedale, Mass.] The Women's alliance of the Hopedale memorial church [192-?] 2 p. l., 136 p. front. (port.) 2 pl. 18 1/2 cm. [BX9843.W75U6] 24-13110
I. Title.
Contents omitted.

Religious ethics.

SWYHART, Barbara Ann DeMartino. 241
Bioethical decision-making : releasing religion from the spiritual / by Barbara Ann DeMartino Swyhart. Philadelphia : Fortress Press, c1975. x, 130 p. ; 23 cm. Includes bibliographical references. [BJ1188.S9] 75-13040 ISBN 0-8006-0418-0 : 6.50
1. Religious ethics. 2. Bioethics. 3. Abortion—Religious aspects. I. Title.

Religious ethics—Comparative studies.

LITTLE, David. 291.5
Comparative religious ethics / David Little, Sumner B. Twiss. 1st ed. San Francisco : Harper & Row, c1978. p. cm. Includes index. Bibliography: p. [BJ1188.L57 1978] 76-10003 ISBN 0-06-065254-3 : 10.95
1. Religious ethics—Comparative studies. I. Twiss, Sumner B., joint author. II. Title.

Religious experience.

BURLING, Nettie (Van Asselt) Mrs. 248
The joy of revelations, by Nettie Van Asselt Burling. Seattle, Wash. [Pigott Washington ptg. co.] 1930. 4 p. l., 7-66 p. 2 port. (incl. front.) 19 cm. [BV4510.B77] 31-4697
I. Title.

CHANDLER, Arthur, bp. of Bloemfontein, 1860- 201
Christian religious experience, by Arthur Chandler ... London, New York [etc.] Longmans, Green and co., 1929. viii p., 2 l., 115 p. 20 cm. (Half-title: Anglican library of faith and thought, edited by Leonard Prestige) [BR110.C4] 29-19469 1.35
I. Title.

FERGUSON, Delseanure. Mrs. 248
The journey from sense to soul, by Delseanure Ferguson... New York, N.Y., Delseanure Ferguson, 1935. 2 p. l., ix-xiii, 15-90 p. 17 1/2 cm. [Full name: Mrs. Delseanure-Maxwell Ferguson] [BR126.F35] 35-30035
I. Title.

FORRER, Samuel Henry, 1876- 201
Some cognitive elements of religious experience, by Samuel H. Forrer. Boston, The Gorham press; [etc., etc., c1917] 57 p. 19 cm. (Lettered on cover: Library of religious thought) $0.75 [BR110.F6] 17-25248
I. Title.

GILBERT, James Eleazer 1839-
Religious experience: adult probationer's first book, by Rev. J. E. Gibert ... New York, Eaton & Mains; Cincinnati, Jennings & Pye [1904] 67 p. 18 cm. 4-3571
I. Title.

GILL, William Icrin, 1831-1902. 225
Christian conception and experience. By Rev. William I. Gill ... New York, The Author's publishing company, 1877. viii p., 1 l., 11-238 p. 20 cm. [BR121.G45] 25-13629
I. Title.

GRAFTON, Charles Chapman, bp., 1830-
A journey Godward of a servant of Jesus Christ by Charles C. Grafton Milwaukee, The Young churchman co., etc., etc., 1910. viii p., 1 l., 316 p. front., plates, ports. 23 cm. 10-4609 2.50
I. Title.

HICKMAN, Franklin Simpson, 1886- 250
Christian vocation: a study in religious experience, by Frank S. Hickman ... Nashville, Tenn., Cokesbury press, 1930. 239 p. 19 cm. (The Belk lectures, second series, Wesleyan college [1930]) [BV660.H5] 30-25516
I. Title.

LEE, Jarena, Mrs., b.1783. 922
Religious experience and journal of Mrs. Jarena Lee; giving an account of her call to preach the gospel. Rev. and cor. from the original manuscript, written by herself. Philadelphia, Pub. for the author, 1849. 97 p. front. (port.) 19 cm. Published Philadelphia, 1836, under title: The life and religious experience of Jarena Lee. [E185.97.L46] 12-20711
I. Title.

LIVERMORE, Harriet, 1788-1868. 922
A narration of religious experience. In twelve letters. By Harriet Livermore. With an appendix, containing her religious belief, and an original poem ... In two volumes ... vol. i. Concord [N. H.] Printed by Jacob. B. Moore, for the author, 1826. iv, [5]-282 p. 15 cm. No more published? [BR1725.L5A3] 38-4811
I. Title.

MIEL, Charles Francis Bonaventure, 1817-1902. 922.
A soul's pilgrimage; being the personal and religious experiences of Charles F. B. Miel, D.D. Philadelphia, G. W. Jacobs & co., 1899. 190 p. front. (port.) 19 1/2 cm. [BX5995.M6A3] 99-1331
I. Title.

RICHELSEN, John. 243
The joy of discovery, and other addresses by John Richelsen ... with an introduction by G. B. F. Hallock ... New York, Chicago [etc.] Fleming H. Revell company [c1925] 160 p. 19 1/2 cm. [BX9178.R5J6] 26-3613
I. Title.

*ROTHACKER, Viola. 248.2
Walking with the master. New York, Vantage Press, [1974] 135 p. 21 cm. [BV4520] ISBN 0-533-00948-0. 3.95.
1. Religious experience. 2. Spiritual life. I. Title.

SCOTT, Samuel, 1719-1788. 922.
A diary of some religious exercises and experience. Philadelphia, Kimber & Conrad, 1811. xi, 264 p. 19 cm. [BX7795.S415A3 1811] 50-43535
I. Title.

SMITH, Roy Lemon, 1887- 204
Four-wheel brakes, and other essays by Roy L. Smith ... New York, Chicago [etc.] Fleming H. Revell company [c1925] 135 p. 20 cm. [BX8333.S575F6] 26-3147
I. Title.

STEINER, Edward Alfred, 1866- 248
The eternal hunger, vivid moments in personal experience, by Edward A. Steiner ... New York, Chicago [etc.] Fleming H. Revell company [c1925] 150 p. 20 cm. "Most of these sketches were written for the Christian century and the Christian advocate." [BV4935.S67A3] 25-20956
I. Title.

STEINER, Edward Alfred, 1866- 248
The eternal hunger, vivid moments in personal experience, by Edward A. Steiner ... New York, Chicago [etc.] Fleming H. Revell company [c1925] 150 p. 20 cm. "Most of these sketches were written for the Christian century and the Christian advocate." [BV4935.S67A3] 25-20956
I. Title.

[TAYLOR, Jeremiah Humphre] 1797-1882.
Sketches of the religious experience and labors of a layman. With an appendix. Hartford, Press of Case, Lockwood and company, 1860. 171, [1] p. 17 cm. 15-25660
I. Title.

TERRY, Milton Spenser, 1840-1914. 225
The new and living way, an orderly arrangement and exposition of the doctrines of Christian experience according to the Scriptures, by Milton S. Terry ... New York, Eaton & Mains; Cincinnati, Jennings & Pye [c1901] 134 p. front. (port.) 19 1/2 cm. [BR121.T44] 2-14457
I. Title.

*UHRIG, Gilbert R. 236.24
The journey beyond. New York, Exposition [1966] 53p. 21cm. 3.00
I. Title.

VANCE, James Isaac, 1862-
The eternal in man, by James I. Vance ... New York, Chicago [etc.] F. H. Revell company [c1907] 240 p. 20 cm. 7-13923

I. Title.

VANCE, James Isaac, 1862-
The eternal in man, by James I. Vance ... New York, Chicago [etc.] F. H. Revell company [c1907] 240 p. 20 cm. 7-13923
I. Title.

Religious Experience Research Unit—History.

HARDY, Alister Clavering, Sir. 291.4'2
The spiritual nature of man : a study of contemporary religious experience / by Alistair Hardy. Oxford : Clarendon Press ; New York : Oxford University Press, 1979. viii, 162 p. ; 24 cm. Includes index. Bibliography: p. [154]-157. [BL53.H297] 79-41143 ISBN 0-19-824618-8 : 19.95
1. Religious Experience Research Unit—History. 2. Experience (Religion) 3. Spirituality. I. Title.

Religious instruction—Catholic authors.

BROWNSON, Josephine Van Dyke. 239
To the heart of a child, by Josephine Van Dyke Brownson, with preface by Rev. John J. Wynne, S. J. New York, The Encyclopedia press, inc [c1918] xii p., 1 l., 193 p. illus. 19 1/2 cm. Religious instruction for Catholics. [BX930.B8] 19-1274
I. Title.

BROWNSON, Josephine Van Dyke. 230.2
To the heart of the child; or, Learn of Me, viii, by Josephine Van Dyke Brownson. Detroit, Mich., The Catholic instruction league [c1934] vii, 248 p. illus. (incl. maps) diagrs. 19 cm. "No. viii in the Learn of Me series."--Foreword. "Revised edition." Blank pages for records (237-248) [BX930.B8 1934] 34-40708
I. Title.

*GLYNN, Jeanne Davis 268.82
If I were an angel. Pictures by Irene Otani. New York, Guild, c.1965. 1v. (unpaged) col. illus. 19cm. (Little angel bk., 30910) .25 pap.,
1. Religious instruction—Catholic authors. I. Title.

**LITTLE children praise the Lord.* Adapted from the Book of Daniel, chapter 3. Pictures by Idellette Dordigoni. New York, Guild, c.1965. 1v. (unpaged) col. illus. 19cm. (Little angel bk., 30905) .25 pap., 268.82
1. Religious instruction—Catholic authors.

NICOLAY, Helen, 1866- 226.
Peter and Paul and their friends; a manual for religious instruction, by Helen Nicolay. Boston, Mass., The Beacon press [c1922] 2 p. l., 284 p. 20 1/2 cm. (On verso of half-title: The Beacon course of graded lessons. W. I. Laurence, Florence Buck, editors) "Books which teachers may find useful": p. 5-6. [BS2619.N5] 22-20658
I. Title.

O'CONNOR, Joseph P. 239
A course in religious instruction for grammar grades and high school by Rev. Joseph P. Oconnor, M A Buffalo, N.Y., Catholic union store [c1924] 167, [5] p. 22 cm. [BX930.O3] 24-22018
I. Title.

O'CONNOR, Joseph P. 220.
A course in religious instruction for grammar grades and high school, by Rev. Joseph P. O'Connor, M. A. Buffalo, N. Y., Catholic union store [c1924] 167, [5] p. 22 cm. [BX930.O3] 24-22018
I. Title.

*ROUKE, Eve 268.82
I like Christmas. Pictures by Betsy J. Roosen. New York, Guild, c.1965. 1v. (unpaged) col. illus. 19cm. (Little angel bk., 30906) .25 pap.,
1. Religious instruction—Catholic authors. I. Title.

SMARIDGE, Norah 268.82
I do my best. Pitcures by Trina Hyman. New York, Guild, c.1965. 1v. (unpaged) col. illus. 19cm. (Little angel bk., 30908) .25 pap.,
1. Religious instruction—Catholic authors. I. Title.

*VAL, Sue 268.82
Why? Pictures by Christiane Cassan. New York, Guild, c.1965. 1v. (unpaged) col. illus. 19cm. (Little angel bk., 30907) .25 pap.,
1. Religious instruction—Catholic authors. I. Title.

Religious liberty.

BAINTON, Roland Herbert, 1894- 272
The travail of religious liberty. New York, Harper [1958] 272p. illus., ports. 21cm. (Harper torchbooks TB30) Bibliography: p. [261]-265. [BV741.B] A59
1. Religious liberty. 2. Christian biography. I. Title.

BAINTON, Roland Herbert, 1894- 261.7'2'0922
The travail of religious liberty; nine biographical studies, by Roland H. Bainton. [Hamden, Conn.] Archon Books, 1971 [c1951] 272 p. illus. 23 cm. Bibliography: p. [261]-266. [BV741.B26 1971] 76-122412 ISBN 0-208-01085-8 8.50
1. Religious liberty. 2. Christian biography. I. Title.

BAINTON, Roland Herbert, 1894- 272
The travail of religious liberty; nine biographical studies. Philadelphia, Westminster Press [1951] Philadelphia, Westminster Press [1951] 272 p. illus. 21 cm. 272 p. illus. 21 cm. [BV741.B26] 51-11705
1. Religious liberty. 2. Christian biography. I. Title.

BATES, Miner Searle, 1897- 261.7
Religious liberty: an inquiry [by] M. Searle Bates ... New York, London, International missionary council, 1945. xviii p., 1 l., 604 p. 24 cm. "This study has been accomplished under the auspices of a joint committee appointed by the Foreign missions conference of North America and the Federal council of the churches of Christ in America and is published for the committee." "List of publications cited": p. 583-596. [BV741.B3] 45-7079
1. Religious liberty. I. International missionary council. II. Title.

BATES, Miner Searle, 1897- 323.44'2
Religious liberty: an inquiry, by M. Searle Bates. New York, Da Capo Press, 1972 [c1945] xviii, [2], 604 p. 23 cm. (Civil liberties in American history) Bibliography: p. 583-596. [BV741.B3 1972] 77-166096 ISBN 0-306-70235-5
1. Religious liberty. I. Title. II. Series.

BYRD, Valois. 261.72
Pioneers of religious liberty. Nashville, Convention Press [1963, c1964] 101 p. 19 cm. Bibliographical footnotes. [BV741.B9] 63-22242
1. Religious liberty. 2. Baptists—Doctrinal and controversial works. I. Title.

CARLYLE, Alexander James, 1861-1943. 261.7'2
The Christian Church and liberty. New York, B. Franklin [1968] 159 p. 19 cm. (Selected essays in history & social science, 24) (Burt Franklin Research & source works, 214.) Reprint of the 1924 ed. [BV741] 68-56734
1. Religious liberty. I. Title.

CARRILLO DE ALBORNOZ, Angel Francisco, 1905- 261.72
The basis of religious liberty. New York, Association Press [1963] 182 p. 23 cm. Includes bibliography. [BV741.C34] 63-16047
1. Religious liberty. I. Title.

CARRILLO DE ALBORNOZ, Angel Francisco 1905- 262.12
Religious liberty, by A. F. Carrillo de Albornoz. Translated by John Drury. New York, Sheed and Ward [1967] xiii, 209 p. 22 cm. Translation of La libertad religiosa y el Concilio Vaticano II. Bibliography: p. 201-209. [BX830.1962.A45L523] 67-21903
1. Vatican Council. 2d, 1962-1965. Declaratio de libatate religiosa. 2. Religious liberty. I. Title.

CROOKER, Joseph Henry, 1850-1931. 261.
The winning of religious liberty, by Joseph Henry Crooker ... Boston, Chicago, The Pilgrim press [c1918] xiv, 269 p. 20 cm. [BV741.C8] 18-17462
1. Religious liberty. I. Title.

DALRYMPLE, Gwynne. 261.7
The fight for freedom, by Gwynne Dalrymple ... Washington, D. C., Review and herald publishing association [c1941] 96 p. incl. front., illus. 20 cm. [BV741.D25] 41-6827
1. Religious liberty. I. Title.

HUGHES, John, Abp., 1797-1864. 261.7
A discussion: Is the Roman Catholic religion inimical to civil or religious liberty? Is the Presbyterian religion inimical to civil or religious liberty? By John Hughes and John Breckinridge. New York, Da Capo Press, 1970 [c1836] 546 p. 24 cm. (Civil liberties in American history) Facsim. of original t.p. has title: A discussion of the question, Is the Roman Catholic region, in any or in all its principles or doctrines, inimical to civil or religious liberty? And of the question, Is the Presbyterian religion, in any or in all its principles or doctrines, inimical to civil or religious liberty? On spine: A discussion on civil and religious liberty. [BV741.H78 1970] 76-122167
1. Catholic Church—Doctrinal and controversial works—Debates, etc. 2. Presbyterian Church—Doctrinal and controversial works—Debates, etc. 3. Religious liberty. I. Breckinridge, John, 1797-1841. II. Title. III. Title: Is the Roman Catholic religion inimical to civil or religious liberty? IV. Title: Is the Presbyterian religion inimical to civil or religious liberty? V. Title: A discussion on civil and religious liberty. VI. Series.

INGERSOLL, Robert Green, 1833-1899. 211
Trial of C. B. Reynolds for blasphemy, at Morristown, N. J., May 19th and 20th, 1887. Defence by Robert G. Ingersoll ... New York, C. P. Farrell, 1888. iv, [3]-84 p. 20 cm. Lettered on cover: Ingersoll on blasphemy. "Stenographically reported by I. N. Baker, and revised by the author." [BL2725.B5] 33-37367
1. Reynolds, Charles B., 1832- 2. Religious liberty. 3. Liberty of speech. 4. Blasphemy. I. Title.

INTERNATIONAL congress of free Christians and other religious liberals. 4th, Boston, 1907. 280
Freedom and fellowship in religion. Proceedings and papers of the fourth International congress of religious liberals, held at Boston, U. S. A., September 22-27, 1907; edited by Charles W. Wendte ... With fifty-five portraits. Boston, Mass., International council [1907?] 1 p. l., vii, 651 p. front., pl., ports. 24 cm. Held under the auspices of the International council of Unitarian and other liberal religious thinkers and workers. cf. Foreword. [BX6.I 6A5 1907] 8-13947
I. Wendte, Charles William, 1844- ed. II. Title.

JOHNS, Varner Jay, 1890- 261.7
Forty centuries of law and liberty; a history of the development of religious liberty, by Varner J. Johns ... Mountain View, Calif., Portland, Or. [etc.] Pacific press publishing association [c1940] 223 p. 20 cm. (Ministerial reading course selection for 1941, Ministerial association of Seventh-day Adventists) Bibliography: p. 223. [BV741.J575] 41-4189
1. Religious liberty. I. Title.

JONES, Alonzo Trevier.
The divine right of individuality in religion; or, Religious liberty complete [by] Alonzo Trevier Jones ... [Battle Creek! Mich., c1908] 153 p. 17 cm. 8-18415
I. Title.

JONES, Alonzo Trevier.
The divine right of individuality in religion; or, Religious liberty complete [by] Alonzo Trevier Jones ... [Battle Creek! Mich., c1908] 153 p. 17 cm. 8-18415
I. Title.

KING, Henry Melville, 1838-
Religious liberty, an historical paper, by Henry Melville King ... Providence, R.I., Preston & Rounds co., 1903. vii, 132 p. 19 1/2 cm. 4-53
I. Title.

KING, Henry Melville, 1838-1919. 261.
Religious liberty, an historical paper, by Henry Melville King ... Providence, R.I., Preston & Rounds co., 1903. vii, 132 p. 19 1/2 cm. [BV741.K5] 4-53
1. Religious liberty. I. Title.

KRISHNASWAMI, Arcot. 261.72
Study of discrimination in the matter of religious rights and practices. New York, United Naions, 1960. x, 79p. 23cm. (United Nations. [Document] E/CN.4/sub.2/200/rev.1) 'United Nations publication. Catalogue no.: 60. XIV. 2.' Bibliographical footnotes. [JX1977.A2 E/CN.4/sub.2/200/rev.1] 61-2431
1. Religious liberty. I. Title. II. Series.

KRISHNASWAMI, Arcot. 261.74
Study of discrimination in the matter of religious rights and practices; report. [New York] 1959. 95p. 28cm. (United Nations. [Document] E/CN.4/Sub.2/200) [JX1977.A2 E/CN.4/Sub.2/200] 60-1252
1. Religious liberty. I. Title.

*LOEWEN, M. E. 286.7
Religious liberty and the seventh-day adventist. Nashville, Tenn., Southern Pub. [c.1964] 62p. 18cm. 1.35 pap.,
I. Title.

LUZZATTI, Luigi, 1841-1927. 261.7
God in freedom; studies in the relations between church and state, by the late Luigi Luzzatti ... translated from the Italian by Alfonso Arbid-Costo, with American supplementary chapters by President William H. Taft, Hon. Irving Lehman...[and others]... New York, The Macmillan company, 1930. xxxix, 794 p. front. (port.) 24 cm. Editor's preface: Max J. Kohler. "Issued in commemoration of the one hundred and fiftieth anniversary of the constitutional establishment of religious liberty." "Luigi Luzzatti's Dio nella liberta...was published in its original form in Italian in 1909 under the title La liberta di conscienza e di scienza...In 1926 the distinguished author enlarged it to about double its original size, to constitute the second volume of his collected Italian works. It is this edition which is here presented in English garb."--Editor's pref. "The life and owrk of Luigi Luzzatti, by Dr. Dora Askewith": p. xvii-xxv. [BF741.L85] 30-25515
1. Religious liberty. 2. Liberty of conscience. 3. Church and state. 4. Religion and science—1900- I. Arbib-Costa, Alfonso, 1869- tr. II. Kohler, Max James, 1871-1934, ed. III. Askowith, Dora., 1884- IV. Title.

MCDONAGH, Enda. 261.7'2
Freedom or tolerance? The Declaration on religious freedom of Vatican Council II, the text with commentary in the context of the church-state discussion. [New York] Magi Books [1967] 155 p. 19 cm. First published under title: The Declaration on religious freedom of Vatican Council II. Bibliographical footnotes. [BX830.1962.A45L55 1967b] 67-21467
1. Religious liberty. I. Vatican Council. 2d, 1962-1965. The Declaration on religious freedom. II. Title.

MIEGGE, Giovanni. 233.7
Religious liberty. New York, Association Press [1957] 94p. 20cm. (World Christian books) [BV741.M5] 57-6882
1. Religious liberty. I. Title.

MURRAY, John Courtney 261.72
The problem of religious freedom. Westminster, Md., Newman [c.]1965. 112p. 22cm. (Woodstock papers; occasional essays for theology, no. 7) Appeared orig. in Theological studies, 25, 1964. Bibl. [BV741.M86] 65-19454 1.50 pap.,
1. Religious liberty. I. Title. II. Series.

NORTHCOTT, William Cecil, 1902- 261.7
Religious liberty. New York, Macmillan Co., 1949 [c1948] 127 p. 20 cm. [BV741.N6 1949] 49-1352
1. Religious liberty. I. Title.

O'CONNELL, David A 261.73
Christian liberty. Westminster, Md., Newman Press [c1952] 142p. 22cm. (Thomlstic studies, no. 5) Includes bibliography. [BV741.O25] 53-1550
1. Religious liberty. I. Title.

O'LEARY, Arthur, 1729-1802. 261.
An essay on intolerance, or Arthur O'Leary's plea for the liberty of conscience ... Albany, J. Leslie, 1834. 36 p. 18 cm. Preface signed: J. Coleman. [BV741.O5] 41-38414
1. Religious liberty. I. Coleman, J., ed. II. Title.

PEEL, Albert, 1887- 285.8
Christian freedom; the contribution of Congregationalism to the church and to the world, by Albert Peel ... New York, N. Y., The General council of the Congregational and Christian churches [1939] 131 p. 19 cm. "Lectures ... delivered to the General council of the Congregational and Christian churches at its assembly at Beloit, Wisconsin, in June, 1938."--Pref. [BX7231.P38] 39-30119
1. Religious liberty. 2. Congregationalism. I. General council of the Congregational and Christian churches of the United States. II. Title.

PIONEERS of religious liberty 922
in America; being the Great and Thursday lectures delivered in Boston in nineteen hundred and three. Boston, American Unitarian association, 1903. x, 396 p. 21 cm. [BR569.P5] 3-15557
I. American Unitarian association.
Contents omitted.

POLISHOOK, Irwin H. 261.7'2'08
Roger Williams, John Cotton, and religious freedom; a controversy in new and old England [by] Irwin H. Polishook. Englewood Cliffs, N.J., Prentice-Hall [1967] vi, 122 p. 21 cm. (American historical sources series: research and interpretation) Includes bibliographical references. [F82.W792] 67-20229
1. Williams, Roger, 1604?-1683. 2. Cotton, John, 1584-1652. 3. Religious liberty. I. Title.

[POND, Enoch] 1791-1882. 261.
Review of Mr. Whitman's letters to Professor Stuart, on religious liberty. 2d ed. With an appendix not before published. Boston, Pierce & Parker, 1831. 84 p. 23cm. [BV741.S7W5 1831] 45-43900
1. Whitman, Bernard, 1796-1834. Two letters to the Reverend Moses Stuart. 2. Religious liberty. 3. Unitarianism—Controversial literature. I. Title.

RELIGION & freedom of 261
thought, by Perry Miller [and others] Foreword by Henry P. Van Dusen. Freeport, N.Y., Books for Libraries Press [1971, c1954] 64 p. 24 cm. (Essay index reprint series) Addresses, given at the one-day conference on "The relation between religion and freedom of the mind" which was held by the Union Theological Seminary as a tribute to Columbia University on the occasion of its bicentennial. Contents.Contents.—The location of American religious freedom, by P. Miller.—The historical relations between religion and intellectual freedom, by R. L. Calhoun.—Religion's role in liberal education, by N. M. Pusey.—The commitment of the self and the freedom of the mind, by R. Niebuhr. [BV741.R42 1971] 78-128296 ISBN 0-8369-2199-2
1. Religious liberty. 2. Church and education. I. Miller, Perry, 1905-

RINGGOLD, James Trapier, 1852-1898.
The legal Sunday, its history and character. By James T. Ringgold ... [Battle Creek, Mich.] International religious liberty association, 1894. viii, 252 p. 20 cm. (On cover: Religious liberty library. no. 22) p. 1-2 wanting. 6-44455
I. Title.

RUFFINI, Francesco, 1863- 261.
Religious liberty, by Francesco Ruffini ... tr. by J. Parker Heyes, with a preface by J. B. Bury ... London, Williams & Norgate; New York, G. P. Putnam's sons, 1912. xxiv, 536 p. 22 cm. (Half-title: Theological translation library, vol. xxxii) "Bibliographical note": p. 523-525. [BV741.R78] A 13
I. Heyes, J. Parker, tr. II. Title.

RUMBLE, Leslie, 1892-
Religious liberty and tolerance. [St. Paul, Minn., Radio Replies Press Society, n.d.] 94 p. 17 cm. 66-17908
1. Religious liberty. I. Title.

RUSSELL-SMITH, Hugh Francis.
The theory of religious liberty in the reigns of Charles ii and James ii, by H. F. Russell Smith... Thirlwall dissertation, 1911. Cambridge [Eng.] The University press, 1911. vi p., 1 l., 143 p. 20 cm. (Half-title: Cambridge historical essays. no. xxi) Bibliography: p. [135]-140. [BR756.R9] 11-27931
1. Religious liberty. 2. Toleration. 3. Church and state in Great Britain. I. Title.

SNOW, Charles Miles, 1868-
Religious liberty in America [by] Charles M. Snow ... Washington, D. C., Review & herald publishing association, 1914. 448 p. illus. (incl. ports.) 20 cm. 14-6263 1.00
I. Title.

STEINER, Franklin. 261.
Religious treason in the American republic. By Franklin Steiner ... Chicago, Ill., The American rationalist association [1927?] 62 p. 23 cm. [BV741.S7] 28-3275
1. Religious liberty. I. Title.

STRAUS, Roger Williams, 1891- 204
Religious liberty and democracy; writings and addresses, [by] Roger Williams Straus. Chicago, New York, Willett, Clark & company, 1939. x p., 1 l., 115 p. 19 1/2 cm. [BV741.S67] 39-31038
1. Religious liberty. 2. Jews in the U.S. 3. Toleration. 4. Democracy. I. Title.

STUART, Moses, 1780-1852. 261.
A letter to William E. Channing, D.D., on the subject of religious liberty. By Moses Stuart ... 2d ed. Boston, Perkins & Marvin, 1830. 52 p. 24 cm. Cover-title: Prof. Stuart's letter to Dr. Channing on religious liberty. [BV741.S7 1830] 45-43786
1. Religious liberty. 2. Unitarianism—Controversial literature. I. Channing, William Ellery, 1780-1842. II. Title.

SWANK, Harold Allen. 261.
The glory of a nation, by Harold Allen Swank. Greensboro, N.C., H. A. Swank company, c1921. 8 p. l., [9]-125 p. incl. front., illus., plates, ports. 19 1/2 cm. [BV741.S9] 21-7045
1. Religious liberty. I. Title.

SWIDLER, Leonard J. 261.7'2
Freedom in the church [by] Leonard Swidler. Dayton, Ohio, Pflaum Press, 1969. x, 142 p. 21 cm. (Themes for today) Bibliographical footnotes. [BV741.S94] 76-93013 2.95
1. Catholic Church—Doctrinal and controversial works—Catholic authors. 2. Religious liberty. I. Title.

VATICAN Council. 2d,1962- 261.7'2
1965.
Declaration on religious freedom of Vatican Council II. Promulgated by Pope Paul VI, December 7, 1965, Commentary by Thomas F, Stransky New York, Paulist Press [1967] 190 p. 19 cm. (Vatican II documents) Contents.CONTENTS. -- Commentary, by T. F. Stransky. -- Study club questions. -- Outline of the declaration. -- Declaration on religious freedom. -- Appendix I: Bishop de Smedt's report on religious liberty. -- Appendix II: The method and principles of the declaration (Relatio, issued by the Secretariat for Promoting Christian Unity). -- Appendix III: The Declaration on religious freedom, by J. C. Murray. -- Appendix IV, part one: The declaration and the World Council of Churches. -- Appendix IV, part two: Religious freedom and the World Council of Churches, by L. Vischer. -- Selected bibliography (p. 187-190) [BX830 1962.A45D415] 67-16718
1. Religious liberty. I. Stransky, Thomas F., ed. II. Title.

WEAVER, Rufus Washington, 261.7
1870-
Champions of religious liberty; a summoning of Baptist youth to the Christian reconstruction of the world, by Rufus W. Weaver. Nashville, Tenn., The Sunday school board of the Southern Baptist convention [1946] 7 p. l. 154 p. front. (port.) 19 cm. "For further study" at end of each chapter. Bibliography: p. 149-152. [BV741.W37] 47-517
1. Religious liberty. 2. Baptists—Doctrinal and controversial works. I. Southern Baptist convention. Sunday school board. II. Title.

WHITMAN, Bernard, 1796-1834. 261.
Two letters to the Reverend Moses Stuart; on the subject of religious liberty. By Bernard Whitman. Boston, Gray and Bowen, 1830. 165, [1] p. 23 1/2 cm. Cover-title: Mr. Whitman's letters to Professor Stuart, on religious liberty. [BV741.S7W4 1830] 45-43784
1. Stuart, Moses, 1780-1852. A letter to William E. Channing. 2. Religious liberty. 3. Unitarian churches—Doctrinal and controversial works. I. Title.

WHITMAN, Bernard, 1796-1834. 261.
Two letters to the Reverend Moses Stuart; on the subject of religious liberty. By Bernard Whitman. 2d ed. Boston, Gray and Bowen, 1831. 1 p. l., [v]-vi, 162, [v]-vi p. 23 1/2 cm. Cover-title: Mr. Whitman's letters to Professor Stuart, on religious liberty. [BV741.S7W4 1831] 44-28895
1. Stuart, Moses, 1780-1852. A letter to William E. Channing. 2. Religious liberty. 3. Unitarian churches—Doctrinal and controversial works. I. Title.

WILLIAMS, Chester Sidney, 261.7
1907-
Religious liberty, by Chester S. Williams...illustrated by Everett Shinn. Evanston, Ill., New York [etc.] Row, Peterson and company [c1941] 72 p. illus. (part col.) 23 cm. [Our freedoms series) [BV741.W47] 41-10224
1. Religious liberty. I. Title. II. Series.

WOGAMAN, J. Philip 261.7'2
Protestant faith and religious liberty [by] Philip Wogaman. Nashville, Abingdon [1967] 254p. 23cm. Bibl. [BV741.W65] 67-14993 4.75
1. Religious liberty. 2. Theology, Protestant. I. Title.

WOOD, Herbert George, 1879- 261.7
Religious liberty to-day. Cambridge [Eng.] University Press, 1949. vii, 149 p. 18 cm. (Current problems, 31) [BV741.W68] 49-11732
1. Religious liberty. I. Title. II. Series.

WOOD, Herbert George, 261.7'2
1879-1963.
Religious liberty to-day. New York, Octagon Books, 1973. viii, 149 p. 19 cm. Reprint of the 1949 ed. published by University Press, Cambridge, Eng., which was issued as no. 31 of Current problems. Includes bibliographical references. [BV741.W68 1973] 73-17441 ISBN 0-374-98716-5 8.00
1. Religious liberty. I. Title. II. Series: Current problems, 31.

WOOLLEY, Davis C 1908- 261.72
Champions of religious freedom. Rev. in 1963 from the book Champions of religious liberty by Rufus W. Weaver. Nashville, Convention Press [1964] xiv, 125 p. 20 cm. "Church study course of the Sunday School Board of the Southern Baptist Convention] This book is number 0871 in category 8, section for young people." Bibliographical footnotes. [BV741.W69] 63-22241
1. Religious liberty. 2. Baptists — Doctrinal and controversial works. I. Weaver, Rufus Washington, 1870-1947. Champions of religious liberty. II. Southern Baptist Convention. Sunday School Board. III. Title.

Religious liberty—Addresses, essays, lectures.

[BACKUS, Isaac] 1724-1806.
An appeal to the public for religious liberty, against the oppressions of the present day ... Boston: Printed by John Boyle in Marlborough-street, 1773. 62 p. 19 cm. Signed (p. 61): Issac Backus. 6-29163
I. Title.

BASEBALL, popcorn, apple 261.7'2
pie, and liberty / compiled by Roland R. Hegstad. Washington : Review and Herald Pub. Association, c1979. p. cm. Articles and stories from the July-Aug. 1963 issue through the Nov.-Dec. 1977 issue of Liberty. Includes bibliographical references. [BV741.B29] 78-26289 6.95
1. Religious liberty—Addresses, essays, lectures. I. Hegstad, Roland R. II. Liberty.

BRENT, Charles Henry, bp., 1862-
Liberty, and other sermons, by the Rt. Rev. Charles H. Brent ... New York, London [etc.] Longmans, Green, and co., 1906. 6 p. l., 3-190 p. 1 l., 19 1/2 cm. 6-24148
I. Title.

FREE religious association,
Boston.
Free religious. Report of addresses at a meeting held in Boston, May 30, 1867, to consider the conditions, wants, and prospects of free religion in America. Together with the constitution of the Free religious association there organized. Boston, Adama & co. [1867] 55 p. 23 cm. [BR21.F845] 38-33112
I. Title.

RELIGIOUS freedom, canon 262.9
law. [Edited by Neophytos Edelby and Teodoro Jimenez-Urresti] New York, Paulist Press [1966] viii, 183 p. 24 cm. (Concilium, v. 18) "Religious freedom, a bibliographical survey": p. 111-139. Includes bibliographical footnotes. [BV741.R43] 66-29261
1. Catholic Church—Discipline—Addresses, essays, lectures. 2. Religious liberty—Addresses, essays, lectures. I. Edelby, Neophytos, Abp. 1920- ed. II. Jimenez Urresti, Teodoro Ignacio, ed. III. Series: Concilium (New York) v. 18.

Religious liberty—Canada.

PENTON, M. James, 1932- 289.9
Jehovah's Witnesses in Canada : champions of freedom of speech and worship / M. James Penton. Toronto : Macmillan of Canada, c1976. xi, 388 p. ; 24 cm. Includes index. Bibliography: p. [370]-373. [BX8525.8.C2P46] 77-356230 ISBN 0-7705-1340-9
1. Jehovah's Witnesses—Canada. 2. Religious liberty—Canada. I. Title.

Religious liberty—Congresses.

RELIGIOUS freedom, 1965 261.7'2
and 1975 : a symposium on a historic document / edited by Walter J. Burghardt New York : Paulist Press, 1976, c1977. v, 74 p. ; 21 cm. (Woodstock studies ; 1) Includes bibliographical references. [BX830 1962.A45L584] 76-45938 ISBN 0-8091-1993-5 pbk. : 2.45
1. Vatican Council. 2d, 1962-1965. Declaratio de libertate religiosa—Congresses. 2. Religious liberty—Congresses. I. Burghardt, Walter J. II. Title. III. Series.

Religious liberty—England.

LYON, Thomas, 1912- 261.7'0942
The theory of religious liberty in England, 1603-39 / by T Lyon New York : Octagon Books, 1976. viii, 241 p. ; 20 cm. Reprint of the 1937 ed. published by University Press, Cambridge, Eng., which was issued as the Thirlwall prize essay, 1937. Includes index. [BR757.L96 1976] 76-6526 ISBN 0-374-95212-4 : 12.00
1. Religious liberty—England. 2. Great Britain—Politics and government—1603-1625. 3. Church and state in England. I. Title. II. Series: Thirlwall prize essay ; 1937.

Religious liberty—Europe.

COCKBURN, James Hutchison, 261.73
1882-
Religious freedom in eastern Europe. Richmond, John Knox Press [1953] 140p. 21cm. [BR735.C6] 53-6969
1. Religious liberty—Europe. I. Title.

Religious liberty—Great Britain

LOANE, Marcus L., Bp. 261.72
Makers of religious freedom in the seventeenth century: Henderson,

Rutherford, Bunyan, Baxter. [1st ed.] Grand Rapids, Eerdmans [1961] 240 p. illus. 23 cm. Includes bibliography. [BR757.L68] 59-6951
1. Religious liberty—Gt. Brit. 2. Henderson, Alexander, 1583-1646. 3. Rutherford, Samuel, 1600?-1661. 4. Bunyan, John, 1628-1688. 5. Baxter, Richard, 1615-1691. I. Title.

LYON, Thomas, 1912- 261.70942
The theory of religious liberty in England, 1603-39, by T. Lyon... Cambridge [Eng.] The University press, 1937. viii p., 1 l., 241, [1] p. 19 cm. (Half-title: The Thirlwall prize essay, 1937) [BV741.L87] 38-12283
1. Religious liberty—Gt. Brit. 2. Gt. Brit.—Pol. & govt.—1603-1625. 3. Church and state in Great Britain. I. Title.

THE Palladium of 323.44'2'0942
conscience; or, The foundation of religious liberty displayed, asserted and established, agreeable to its true and genuine principles, above the reach of all petty tyrants, who attempt to lord it over the human mind. Containing Furneaux's Letters to Blackstone, Priestley's Remarks on Blackstone, Blackstone's Reply to Priestley, and Blackstone's Case of the Middlesex-election; with some other curious tracts, worthy of high rank in every gentleman's literary repository, being a necessary companion for every lover of religious liberty. And an interesting appendix to Blackstone's Commentaries on the laws of England. New York, Da Capo Press, 1974. p. cm. (Civil liberties in American history) Each part has special t.p. Also published under title: An interesting appendix to Sir William Blackstone's Commentaries on the laws of England. Reprint of the 1773 ed. printed by R. Bell, Philadelphia. [BR758.P33 1974] 74-122161 12.50
1. Religious liberty—Great Britain. 2. Dissenters, Religious—England. 3. Great Britain—Parliament—Elections. I. Furneaux, Philip, 1726-1783. II. Priestley, Joseph, 1733-1804. III. Blackstone, William, Sir, 1723-1780. IV. Blackstone, William, Sir, 1723-1780. Commentaries on the laws of England. V. Title. VI. Series.

THE palladium of conscience;
or, The foundation of religious liberty displayed, asserted, and established, agreeable to its true and genuine principles, above the reach of all petty tyrants, who attempt to lord it over the human mind, containing Furneaux's Letters to Blackstone. Priestly's remarks on Blackstone. Blackstone's Reply to Priestley. And Blackstone's Case of the Middlesex-election; with some other curious tracts, being a necessary companion for every lover of religious liberty. And An interesting appendix to Blackstone's Commentaries on the laws of England. America: Printed for the subscribers by Robert Bell, at the late Union library, in Third-street; Philadelphia, 1773. 2 p. l., iv, [5]-119, xii, 155 p. 22 1/2 cm. Each part has special t.-p. Also published with title: An interesting appendix to Sir William Blackstone's Commentaries on the laws of England...Philadelphia, 1773. [RV741.P3] 22-24305
1. Religious liberty—Gt. Brit. 2. Dissenters—England. 3. Gt. Brit.—Parliament—Elections. I. Blackstone, Sir William, 1723-1780. II. Priestley, Joseph, 1733-1804. III. Furneaux, Philip, 1726-1783. IV. Foster, Sir Michael, 1689-1763. V. Mansfield, William Murray, 1st earl of 1705-1793
Contents omitted.

UNDERHILL, Edward Bean, 261.70942
1813-1901.
Struggles and triumphs of religious liberty. An historical survey of controversies pertaining to the rights of conscience, from the English reformation to the settlement of New England. By Edward B. Underhill ... With an introduction by Sewall S. Cutting. New York, L. Colby, 1851. 1 p. l., [v]-vi p., 1 l., xii p., 1 l., [15]-242 p. 20 cm. Taken from the introductions of the following works, edited by the author, and published by the Hanserd Knollys society, London: Tracts on liberty of conscience and persecution, 1614-1661: The records of a church of Christ, meeting in Broadmead, Bristol, 1640-1687, and Roger Williams' The bloudy tenent persecution for cause of conscience discussed. cf. Pref. [BV741.U7] 36-2831
1. Religious liberty—Gt. Brit. 2. Church and state in Great Britain. 3. Baptists—Hist. I. Title.

WARD, Nathaniel, 1578?- 274.2
1652.
The simple cobler of Aggawam in America. Edited by P. M. Zall. Lincoln, University of Nebraska Press [1969] xviii, 81 p. map (on lining papers) 22 cm. Bibliographical footnotes. [PS858.W2S5 1969] 69-19107 3.95
1. Religious liberty—Gt. Brit. 2. Gt. Brit.—Church history—17th century. 3. Gt. Brit.—Politics and government—1642-1649. I. Zall, Paul M., ed. II. Title.

WILLIAMS, Roger, 261.7'2'0942
1604?-1683.
The fourth paper presented by Major Butler, with other papers edited and published by Roger Williams in London, 1652. With an introd. and notes by Clarence Saunders Brigham. New York, B. Franklin [1968] xxiii, 49 p. 24 cm. (Burt Franklin research & source works series, 312) (American classics in history & social science, 60.) On spine: Roger Williams on Major Butler's Fourth paper on religious tolerance. "Mr. Goads letter to Maior Butler" (p. [5]-10) signed Christopher Goad. Reprint of 1903 ed. which included a facsim. (p. 1-23) of the 1652 ed. [BV741.W6 1968] 68-57125
1. Religious liberty—Gt. Brit. 2. Gt. Brit.—Politics and government—1649-1660. I. Butler, William, 17th cent. II. Goad, Christopher, fl. 1651. III. Brigham, Clarence Saunders, 1877-1963, ed. IV. Title.

Religious liberty—India.

GHOUSE, Mohammad. 323.44'2'0954
Secularism, society, and law in India. Delhi, Vikas Pub. House [1973] vii, 254 p. 22 cm. Bibliography: p. [241]-250. [LAW] 73-903452
1. Religious liberty—India. 2. Secularism—India. I. Title.
Distributed by International Scholarly Book Service; 12.00.

Religious liberty—Levant.

DAVIS, Helen Clarkson 261.70956
(Miller) Mrs. comp.
Some aspects of religious liberty of nationals in the Near East, a collection of documents, compiled by Helen Clarkson Miller Davis ... New York, London, Harper & brothers, 1938. xviii, 182 p. incl. front. (map) 1 illus. 24 cm. [BL1060.D3] 38-12723
1. Religious liberty—Levant. 2. Religious law and legislation—Lavant. I. Title.

MORRISON, Stanley A 261.7
Religious liberty in the Near East. London, New York, World Dominion Press [1948] 50 p. 22 cm. (Post war survey series, no. 1) "Postscript on Egypt": leaf inserted. [BR1070.M6] 48-27428
1. Religious liberty—Levant. I. Title.

MORRISON, Stanley Andrew. 261.7
Religious liberty in the Near East. London, New York, World Dominion Press [1948] 50p. 22cm. (Post war survey series, no. 1) 'Postacript on Egypt': leaf inserted. [BR1070.M6] 48-27428
1. Religious liberty—Levant. I. Title. II. Series.

Religious liberty—Rome.

DORRIES, Hermann. 261.72
Constantine and religious liberty. Translated from the German by Roland H. Bainton. New Haven, [Conn.] Yale University Press [c.] 1960. xi, 141 p. 21 cm. (The Terry lectures) (Bibl. note 133-134 & Bibl. footnotes) 60-7823 4.00
1. Constantinus I, the Great, Emperor of Rome, d. 337. 2. Religious liberty—Rome. I. Title.

Religious liberty—Russia—Addresses, essays, lectures.

RELIGIOUS liberty in 322'.1'0947
the Soviet Union : WCC and USSR ; a post-Nairobi documentation / edited by Michael Bourdeaux, Hans Hebly and Eugen Voss. [Keston] : Keston College, Centre for the Study of Religion and Communism, 1976. [7], 96 p. : ill., ports. ; 30 cm. (Keston book ; no. 7) Errata slip inserted. [BR936.R46] 77-354247 £1.50 ($3.50 U.S.)
1. World Council of Churches—Addresses, essays, lectures. 2. Religious liberty—Russia—Addresses, essays, lectures. I. Bourdeaux, Michael. II. Hebly, Hans. III. Voss, Eugen.

Religious liberty—Salvador.

UNITED States. 323.44'2'097284
Congress. House. Committee on International Relations. Subcommittee on International Organizations.
Religious persecution in El Salvador : hearings before the Subcommittee on International Organizations of the Committee on International Relations, House of Representatives, Ninety-fifth Congress, first session, July 21 and 29, 1977. Washington : U.S. Govt. Print. Off., 1977. vi, 85 p. ; 24 cm. (International human rights) [KF27.I5494 1977g] 77-604330
1. Religious liberty—Salvador. 2. Persecution—Salvador. I. Title. II. Series.

Religious liberty—South America.

LEE, John. 278
Religious liberty in South America, with special reference to the recent legislation in Peru, Ecudor, and Bolivia, By John Lee ... With an introduction by Bishop John H. Vincent ... Cincinnati, Jennings and Graham; New York, Eaton and Mains [1907] vii, 266 p. 20 cm. [BR660.L4] 7-11041
1. Religious liberty—South America. I. Title.

LEE, John, 1867-
Religious liberty in South America, with special reference to recent legislation in Peru, Ecuador, and Bolivia. By John Lee ... With an introduction by Bishop John H. Vincent ... Cincinnati, Jennings and Graham; New York, Eaton and Mains [c1907] vii, 266 p. 20 cm. 7-11041
I. Title.

Religious liberty—Spain.

HUGHEY, John David. 261.7'2'0946
Religious freedom in Spain: its ebb and flow. Freeport, N.Y., Books for Libraries Press [1970] xi, 211 p. 23 cm. Reprint of the 1955 ed. A revision of the author's thesis, Columbia University. Bibliography: p. 201-207. [BR1023.H8 1970] 77-119935
1. Religious liberty—Spain. 2. Protestants in Spain. 3. Church and state in Spain. I. Title.

Religious liberty—Spanish America.

HOWARD, George Parkinson, 261.7
1882-
Religious liberty in Latin America? [By] George P. Howard. Foreword by John A. Mackay. Philadelphia, The Westminster press [1944] xxii, 170 p. 21 cm. Bibliographical foot-notes. [BR600.H6] 44-40208
1. Religious liberty—Spanish America. I. Title.

Religious liberty-United States

BLAU, Joseph Leon. 1909- 322.0973
ed.
Cornerstones of religious freedom in America. Ed., introd., interpretations, by Joseph L. Blau. Rev., enl. ed. New York, Harper [1964] xiii,344, 9p. 21cm. (Harper torchbks. The Cloister lib., CL/TB-118) Bibl. 64-6727 2.25 pap.,
1. Religious liberty—U.S. 2. U.S.—Hist.—Sources. I. Title.

BLAU, Joseph Leon, 1909- 261.7
ed.
Cornerstones of religious freedom in America. Boston, Beacon Press, 1949. viii. 250 p. 22 cm. (Beacon Press studies in freedom and power) Bibliographical references included in "notes" (p. 240-245) "List of sources": p. 246-247. [BR516.B55] 49-10649
1. Religious liberty—U. S. 2. U. S.—Hist.—Sources. I. Title.

CARLSON, Carl Emanuel, 261.72
1906-
Religious liberty; case studies in current church-state issues [by] C. Emanuel Carlson and W. Barry Garrett. Nashville, Convention Press [1964] ix, 149 p. 20 cm. Bibliography: p. 146-149. [BR516.C3] 63-22243
1. Religious liberty—U.S. I. Garrett, Wilkins Barry, 1915- joint author. II. Title.

CLINCHY, Everett Ross, 261.70973
1896-
All in the name of God, by Everett R. Clinchy; with an introduction by Newton D. Baker. New York, The John Day company [1934] 3 p. l., 194 p. 19 1/2 cm. Bibliography: p. 181-189. [BR516.C6] 34-39193
1. Religious liberty—U.S. 2. Toleration. 3. Jews in the U.S. 4. Catholics in the U.S. 5. Protestants in the U.S. I. Title.

COBB, Sanford 261.7'2'0973
Hoadley, 1838-1910.
The rise of religious liberty in America; a history. New York, Cooper Square Publishers, 1968. xx, 541 p. 24 cm. Reprint of the 1902 ed. Includes bibliographical references. [BR515.C6 1968] 68-27517
1. Religious liberty—United States. 2. Church and state in the United States. I. Title.

COBB, Sanford 261.7'2'0973
Hoadley, 1838-1910.
The rise of religious liberty in America; a history. New York, B. Franklin [1970] xx, 541 p. 23 cm. (American classics in history and social science 140) (Burt Franklin research and source works series 529.) Reprint of the 1902 ed. Includes bibliographical references. [BR516.C66 1970b] 70-129031
1. Religious liberty—U.S. 2. Church and state in the United States. I. Title.

COBB, Sanford 261.7'2'0973
Hoadley, 1838-1910.
The rise of religious liberty in America; a history. With a new introd. by Paul L. Murphy. New York, Johnson Reprint Corp., 1970. xviii, xx, 541 p. 23 cm. (Series in American studies) Reprint of the 1902 ed. Bibliography: p. xviii (1st group) [BR516.C66 1970] 76-105360
1. Religious liberty—U.S. 2. Church and state in the United States. I. Title. II. Series.

COBB, Sanford Hoadley, 261.7'2
1838-1910.
The rise of religious liberty in America. New introd. by Leo Pfeffer. New York, Da Capo Press, 1973. p. (Civil liberties in American history) Reprint of the 1902 ed. published by Macmillan, New York. Bibliography: p. [BR516.C66 1973] 70-164514 ISBN 0-306-70289-4
1. Religious liberty—United States. 2. Church and state in the United States. I. Title.

COBB, Sanford Hoadley, 1838- 284
1910.
The rise of religious liberty in America; a history, by Sanford H. Cobb ... New York, The Macmillan company; London, Macmillan & co., ltd., 1902. xx p., 1 l., 541 p. 23 cm. "Authorities": p. xvii-xx. [BR515.C6] 2-13240
1. Religious liberty—U.S. 2. Church and state. 3. U.S.—Religion. 4. U.S.—Pol. & govt. I. Title.

CUNINGGIM, Merrimon, 1911- 261.73
-
Freedom's holy light. [1st ed.] New York, Harper [1955] 192p. 22cm. Includes bibliography. [BR516.C9] 54-11660
1. Religious liberty—U. S. 2. Church and state in the U. S. I. Title.

GREGG, Lucy Corliss 261.7
(Phinney) "Mrs. Abel J. Gregg."
New relationships with Jews and Catholics; discussion outlines for Protestant groups, by Mrs. Abel J. Gregg. New York city, Association press, c1934. 64 p. 20 cm. "The six areas ... for discussion ... have been suggested by Dr. E. R. Clinchy ... in his ... book, 'All in the name of God'."--Foreword. "The material was prepared under the auspices of the national conference of Jews and Christians, and at the recommendation of the Committee on the religious education of youth of the International council of religious education for use in discussions on inter-faith relationships in the new united youth program, 'Christian youth building a new world'."--p. [2] Includes bibliographies. [BR516.G7] 35-13949
1. Religious liberty—U. S. 2. Toleration. 3. Jews in the U. S. 4. Catholics in the U. S. 5. Protestants in the U. S. I. National conference of Jews and Christians. II. International council of religious education. Committee on religious education of youth. III. Title.

HISTORY of bigotry in the United States. Edited and revised by Henry M. Christman. New York, Capricorn [1960] xii, 474p. 19cm. (Capricorn Books, CAP 42) Revision with three added chapters bringing work to 1960 Presidential nominations.
1. Religious liberty-U. S. 2. U. S.-Race questions. I. Myers, Gustavus, 1872-1942. II. Christman, Henry M. III. Title: Bigotry in the United States.

KATZ, Wilber Griffith, 1902- 322
Religion and American constitutions. Evanston, Ill., Northwestern University Press [1964] vii, 114 p. 21 cm. (Rosenthal lectures, 1963) Bibliographical references included in "Notes" (p. 105-112) 64-13704
1. Religious liberty — U.S. 2. Church and state in the U.S. I. Title. II. Series.

KAUPER, Paul G 322
Religion and the Constitution [by] Paul K. Kauper. [Baton Rouge] Louisiana State University Press, 1964. ix. 137 p. 22 cm. Based on the Edward Douglass White lectures delivered at Louisiana State University in the spring of 1964. Bibliography: p. 131-134. 64-7898
1. Religious liberty — U.S. 2. Church and state in the U.S. I. Title.

LINDSTROM, David Edgar, 261.7
1899-
American foundations of religious liberty. Champaign, Ill., Garrard Press, 1950. xii, 107 p. 20 cm. (Rauschenbusch lectures, 1950) Bibliographical footnotes. [BR516.L6] 51-1464
1. Religious liberty—U. S. 2. Rural churches—U. S. I. Title. II. Series: Rauschenbusch lectures, Colgate Rochester Divinity School Rochester, N. Y., 1950

MILLER, Glenn T., 1942- 323.44'2
Religious liberty in America : history and prospects / by Glenn T. Miller. Philadelphia : Westminster Press, c1976. 156 p. ; 21 cm. Bibliography: [153]-156. [BR516.M54] 75-33000 ISBN 0-664-24785-7 pbk. : 4.25
1. Religious liberty—United States. 2. Church and state in the United States. I. Title.

MYERS, Gustavus, 1872-1942 272.9
History of bigotry in the United States, by Gustavus Myers. Edited and revised by Henry M. Christman. New York, Capricorn Books [dist. Putnam, 1960, c.1943, 1960] xii, 474p. 19cm. (A Putnam Capricorn bk. CAP42) (Bibl. footnotes) 1.65 pap.,
1. Religious liberty—U. S. 2. Persecution. 3. Toleration. 4. U. S.—Race question. I. Title. II. Title: Bigotry in the United States.

MYERS, Gustavus, 1872-1942. 272.9
History of bigotry in the United States, by Gustavus Myers. New York, Random house [1943] viii, 504 p. 22 1/2 cm. "First printing." Bibliographical foot-notes. [BR516.M9] 43-9842
1. Religious liberty—U.S. 2. Persecution. 3. Toleration. 4. U.S.—Race question. I. Title. II. Title: Bigotry in the United States.

RAY, Mary 301.15'43'28273
Augustina, Sister, 1880-
American opinion of Roman Catholicism in the eighteenth century. New York, Octagon Books, 1974 [c1936] 456 p. 23 cm. Reprint of the ed. published by Columbia University Press, New York, which was issued as no. 416 of Studies in history, economics, and public law. Bibliography: p. 397-444. [BX1406.R35 1974] 74-5254 ISBN 0-374-96723-7 15.50
1. Religious liberty—United States. 2. Catholics in the United States. 3. United States—History—Colonial period, ca. 1600-1775. 4. Public opinion—United States. 5. Religious tolerance. 6. Prejudices and antipathies. I. Title. II. Series: Columbia studies in the social sciences, no. 416.

RAY, Mary Augustina, 282.73
sister, 1880-
American opinion of Roman Catholicism in the eighteenth century, by Sister Mary Augustina (Ray) ... New York, Columbia university press; London, P. S. King & sons, ltd., 1936. 456 p. 1 illus. 23 cm. (Half-title: Studies in history, economics and public law, ed. by the Faculty of political science of Columbia university. no. 416) Issued also as thesis (PH. D.) Columbia university. b"Bibliographical notes": p. 397-444. [Secular name: Ethel Agnes Ray] [H31.C7 no. 416] [BX1406.R35] 308.2 37-6398
1. Religious liberty—U. S. 2. Catholics in the U. S. 3. U. S.—Hist.—Colonial period. 4. Public opinion—U. S. 5. Toleration. 6. Antipathies and prejudices. I. Title.

RELIGIOUS liberty. 261.7'2'0973
[New York] Board of Social Ministry, Lutheran Church in America, 1968. vi, 88 p. 20 cm. On cover: Christian social responsibility. Contents.Contents.—Christian freedom and religious liberty, by G. W. Forell.—Legal aspects of religious liberty, by P. G. Kauper.—Religious liberty and current tensions: problems beyond the constitution, by D. Oberholtzer. Includes bibliographical references. [BR516.R38] 68-3836
1. Religious liberty—United States. I. Lutheran Church in America. Board of Social Ministry. II. Title: Christian social responsibility.

RELIGIOUS liberty 261.7
association. Washington, D.C.
Freedom of religion, the heritage of liberty and the dangers facing America today, a symposium prepared by the religious liberty association. Mountain View, Calif., Brookfield, Ill. [etc.] Pacific press publishing association [1944] 96 p. incl. front., illus. 19 1/2 cm. [BR516.R4] 44-47517
1. Religious liberty—U.S. I. Title.
Contents omitted.

SECULARISM and 342*.73*085
religious freedom. Law and religious pluralism. [Villanova, Pa.] Villanova School of Law [1963] 166 p. 22 cm. (Institute of Church and State. Proceedings, 3-4) Proceedings of 2 meetings held in 1959 and 1960, sponsored by the Institute of Church and State. [BR516.S4] 72-188930
1. Religious liberty—United States. 2. Religion and law. I. Title: Law and religious pluralism. II. Series: Villanova University, Villanova, Pa. Institute of Church and State. Proceedings, 3-4.

SMITH, Elwyn Allen, 1919- 261.7'2
Religious liberty in the United States; the development of church-state thought since the Revolutionary era [by] Elwyn A. Smith. Philadelphia, Fortress Press [1972] xiv, 386 p. 24 cm. Includes bibliographical references. [BR516.S57] 70-178093 ISBN 0-8006-0071-1 10.95
1. Religious liberty—United States. 2. Church and state in the United States. I. Title.

SWANCARA, Frank.
Obstruction of justice by religion; a treatise on religious barbarities of the common law, and a review of judicial oppressions of the non-religious in the United States, by Frank Swancara ... Denver, Col., W. H. Courtright publishing company, 1936. 296 p. 19 1/2 cm. 40-8505
1. Religious liberty—U.S. 2. Law—U.S. 3. Free thought. I. Title.

THORNING, Joseph Francis, 261.7
1896-
Religious liberty in transition; a study of the removal of constitutional limitations on religious liberty as part of the social progress in the transition period... by Joseph Francis Thorning, S.J. Washington, D.C., The Catholic university of America, 1931- v. 23 cm. "1st series: New England" issued as thesis (PH.D.) Catholic university of America, 1931. Vita. "Select bibliography": [v. 1] p. 232-242. [Full name: Joseph Francis Xavier Thorning] [BR516.T57 1931] [277.3] 31-15531
1. Religious liberty—U.S. 2. Constitutions, State—U.S. 3. U.S.—Constitutional history. 4. Church and state—U.S. I. Title.

WILLIAMS, Michael, 261.70973
1878-
The shadow of the pope, by Michael Williams. New York and London, Whittlesey house, McGraw-Hill book company, inc., 1932. xi, 329 p. front., illus., plates, facsims. 23 1/2 cm. "First edition." [Full name: Charles Michael Williams] [BR516.W5] 32-5124
1. Religious liberty—U.S. 2. Church and state in the U.S. 3. Catholic church in the U.S. 4. Presidents—U.S.—Election—1928. I. Title.

Religious liberty—United States—History.

CORD, Robert L. 342.73'0852
Separation of church and state : historical fact and current fiction / Robert L. Cord. New York : Lambeth Press, c1982. xv, 307 p. ; 23 cm. Includes bibliographical references and index. [KF4783.C67 1982] 347.302852 19 81-20705 ISBN 0-931186-03-X : 16.95
1. Religious liberty—United States—History. I. Title.
Publisher's address: Box 21, Essex Sta., Boston, MA 02112

KRAFT, Virgil A. 322'.2'0973
The freedom story : a survey of the origin and meaning of the American experiment with civilization's basic freedom, freedom of religion / by Virgil A. Kraft. Tujunga, Calif. : Parthenon Books, c1977. x, 152 p. ; 22 cm. Includes bibliographical references. [BR516.K67] 76-44994 4.00
1. Religious liberty—United States—History. 2. Church and state in the United States—History. I. Title.

MODE, Peter George. 261.
The frontier spirit in American Christianity, by Peter G. Mode ... New York, The Macmillan company, 1923. x p., 1 l., 196 p. 19 1/2 cm. [BR516.M6] 28-15143
I. Title.

Religious liberty—United States—Juvenile literature.

GELFAND, Ravina. 323.44'2'0973
The freedom of religion in America. Minneapolis, Lerner Publications Co. [1969] 86 p. illus., facsims., ports. 24 cm. (In America series) Traces the history of religion in the United States and its relationship to government concentrating on the development and interpretation of constitutional guarantees of tolerance and freedom of worship. [BR516.G4] 68-31502 ISBN 8-225-02194-
1. Religious liberty—U.S.—Juvenile literature. 2. [Religious liberty—U.S.] I. Title.

HANFF, Helene 261.7
Religious freedom; the American story. Pictures by Charles Waterhouse.Consultant and co-author: Lloyd L. Smith. New York, Grosset [c.1966] 61p. illus. 24cm. (Who, when, where bk.) [BR516.H3] 66-14290 1.95
1. Religious liberty—U. S.—Juvenile literature. I. Smith, Lloyd Lowell, 1929- joint author. II. Title.

WORTON, Stanley N., 323.44'2
comp.
Freedom of religion / [compiled by] Stanley N. Worton. Rochelle Park, N.J. : Hayden Book Co., [1975] 150 p. ; 23 cm. (American issues in perspective, a documentary approach) Includes bibliographies. Considers important historical documents leading to the establishment of the Bill of Rights and major recent events refining its interpretation, particularly in regards to religious freedom. [BR516.W67] 74-32381 ISBN 0-8104-6010-6 pbk. : 4.06
1. Religious liberty—United States—Juvenile literature. 2. [Religious liberty.] 3. [United States—Constitutional law.] I. Title.

Religious liberty—Virginia.

JAMES, Charles 323.44'2'09755
Fenton, 1844-1902.
Documentary history of the struggle for religious liberty in Virginia. New York, Da Capo Press, 1971 [c1899] 272 p. 23 cm. (Civil liberties in American history) [BR555.V8J3 1971] 70-121101
1. Religious liberty—Virginia. 2. Virginia—Church history. I. Title. II. Title: Struggle for religious liberty in Virginia. III. Series.

JAMES, Charles Fenton, 1844- 261.
1902.
Documentary history of the struggle for religious liberty in Virginia. By Charles F. James ... Lynchburg, Va., J. P. Bell company, 1900. 272 p. 20 cm. [BR555.V8J3] 1-29332
1. Religious liberty—Virginia. 2. Virginia—Church history. I. Title.

Religious life.

BITTINGER, Lucy Forney, 1859 277.
German religious life in colonial times, by Lucy Forney Bittinger... Philadelphia and London, J. B. Lippincott company, 1906. 146 p. 20 cm. [BR563.G3B6] 7-12674
I. Title.

*BOLLINGER, J. W. 248.4
Lightning flash! A practical guide to a God-centered and God-directed life. New York, Exposition [c.1966] 80p. 21cm. 3.00
I. Title.

CARPENTER, Newton Cleveland.
"Steps unto heaven," by N. C. Carpenter ... with an introduction by T. S. Tinsley ... Owingsville, Ky., The author [c1912] 5 p. l., [9]-131 p. incl. illus., pl., ports. 20 cm. 12-23691 1.00
I. Title.

CARPENTER, Newton Cleveland.
Steps unto heaven, by N. C. Carpenter, with an introduction by T. S. Tinsley ... Rev. ed. Boston, Sherman, French & company, 1915. 5 p. l., 177 p. 21 cm. 15-19306 1.25
I. Title.

CARTER, Jesse Benedict, 1872-
1917.
The religious life of ancient Rome; a study in the development of religious consciousness, from the foundation of city until the death of Gregory the Great, by Jesse Benedict Carter ... Boston and New York, Houghton Mifflin company, 1911. viii p., 1 l., 270 p., 1 l. 23 cm. "Eight chapters ... originally eight lectures delivered before the Lowell institute in Boston, during January, 1911."--Pref. [BR874.C3] 11-29882
I. Title.

COHAUSZ, Otto, 1872- 248
Light and shadow in religious life, by Rev. Otto Cohausz... translated by Rev. Laurence P. Emery... New York, Cincinnati [etc.] Benziger brothers, 1930. viii p., 1 l., 458 p. front. 17 cm. [BX2385.C55] 30-4877
I. Emery, Laurence Peter Ernest, tr. II. Title.

*DEETER, Walter Wells. 234
Eternal life, how attained, how and where served. New York, Vantage [1968] 65p. 21 cm. 2.50
I. Title.

*DEETER, Walter Wells. 234
Eternal life, how attained, how and where served. New York, Vantage [1968] 65p. 21 cm. 2.50
I. Title.

ESTEP, William. 133
Eternal wisdom and health, with light on the Scriptures, by Professor Wm. Estep ...

founder of Super mind science churches, U.S.A. Excelsior Springs, Mo., Super mind science publications [c1932] 4 p. l., [13]-742 p. front. 24 cm. [BF1999.E68] 32-10094
I. Title. II. Title: Super mind science churches.

ESTEP, William. 133
Eternal wisdom and health, with light on the Scriptures, by Professor Wm. Estep ... founder of Super mind science churches, U.S.A. Excelsior Springs, Mo., Super mind science publications [c1932] 4 p. l., [13]-742 p. front. 24 cm. [BF1999.E68] 32-10094
I. Title. II. Title: Super mind science churches.

THE eternal security of the believer. Dallas, American Guild Press [c1956] 173p.
I. Anderson, Earl.

THE eternal security of the believer. Dallas, American Guild Press [c1956] 173p.
I. Anderson, Earl.

EVANS, Thomas, 1798-1868.
Examples of youthful piety; principally intended for the instruction of young persons, by Thomas Evans ... Philadelphia, For sale at Friends book store, 1847. 296 p. 19 cm. Short biographies of members of the Society of Friends. 16-19330
I. Title.

EVANS, Thomas, 1798-1868.
Examples of youthful piety; principally intended for the instruction of young persons, by Thomas Evans ... Philadelphia, For sale at Friends book store, 1847. 296 p. 19 cm. Short biographies of members of the Society of Friends. 16-19330
I. Title.

FRIGERIO, Costanzo.
Practical manual for the superiors of religious houses, by Father Costanzo Frigerio, S. J.; tr. from the Italian by F. Loughnan. New York, P. J. Kenedy & sons, 1912. 81 p. 16 cm. 13-687 0.46
I. Loughnan, Frances, 1847- tr. II. Title.

GENERAL principles of the religious life. By O., S. J. Based on the German translation of Rev. August Meer. By Very Rev. Boniface F. Verheyen ... New York, Cincinnati [etc.] Benziger brothers, 1892. 154 p. 12 cm. First published in French over two hundred years ago under title: Les secrets de la vie religieuse decouverts a une novice fervente par son pere spirituel. 13-18879
I. O., S. J. II. Meer, August, 1841-1895. III. Verheyen, Boniface F., tr.

GREEN, Edward Michael Bankes.
The archbishop's test. [2nd ed.] New York, Morehouse-Barlow, 1960. 94 p. 64-22565
I. Title.

GREEN, Emma Martha, 1858-
The archbishop's test, by E. M. Green. London, J. M. Dent & sons ltd.; New York, E. P. Dutton & co., 1914. 3 p. l., 106 p. 19 cm. 15-3043
I. Title.

GREEN, Emma Martha, 1858-
The archbishop's test, by E. M. Green. New York, E. P. Dutton & company [c1915] 3 p. l., 107 p. 20 cm. 15-4657 1.00
I. Title.

HILL, John Godfrey, 1870- 248
... *An everyday Christian;* an elective course for young people, by John Godfrey Hill ... New York, Cincinnati, The Methodist book concern [c1928] 160 p. 19 cm. (Studies in Christian living) "References for further reading" at end of each chapter. [BV4501.H49] 28-3696
I. Title.

HILL, John Godfrey, 1870- 248
... *An everyday Christian;* an elective course for young people, by John Godfrey Hill ... New York, Cincinnati, The Methodist book concern [c1928] 160 p. 19 cm. (Studies in Christian living) "References for further reading" at end of each chapter. [BV4501.H49] 28-3696
I. Title.

HODGES, George, 1856-1919.
Everyman's religion, by George Hodges. New York, The Macmillan company, 1913. v, 297 p. 19 cm. (On cover: The Macmillan standard library) A 13 0.50
I. Title.

HODGES, George, 1856-1919.
Everyman's religion, by George Hodges. New York, The Macmillan company, 1913. v, 297 p. 19 cm. (On cover: The Macmillan standard library) A 13 0.50
I. Title.

HODGES, George, 1856-1919. 252.
The path of life, by George Hodges ... New York, T. Whittaker, 1900. v, 248 p. 19 1/2 cm. [BX5937.H6P3] 1-29827
I. Title.

THE law of Christ; moral theology for priests and laity. Translated by Edwin G. Kaiser. Westminster, Md., Newman Press, 1961- v. 24cm. Includes bibliography.
I. Haring, Bernhard, 1912-

THE life of perfection; points of view on the essence of the religious state. Translated by Leonard J. Doyle. Collegeville, Minn., Liturgical Press [1961] xi, 125p. 22cm. Bibliographical footnotes.
1. Religious life. I. Leclercq, Jean, 1911-

MASSEE, Jasper Cortenus, 1871- 227
Eternal life in action; an illustrated exposition of the first Epistle of John: being the substance of messages delivered to Tremont temple, Boston, congregation, and to many thousands who listened in on the radio, by J. C. Massee... New York, Chicago [etc.] Fleming H. Revell company [c1925] 205 p. 19 1/2 cm. [BS2805.M3] 25-4303
I. Title.

MASSEE, Jasper Cortenus, 1871- 227
Eternal life in action; an illustrated exposition of the first Epistle of John: being the substance of messages delivered to Tremont temple, Boston, congregation, and to many thousands who listened in on the radio, by J. C. Massee... New York, Chicago [etc.] Fleming H. Revell company [c1925] 205 p. 19 1/2 cm. [BS2805.M3] 25-4303
I. Title.

NEWTON, Joseph Fort, 1876-1950. 252.091
Everyday religion. New York, Abingdon-Cokesbury Press [1950] 240 p. 16 cm. [BX9943.N4E9] 50-7150
I. Title.

NEWTON, Joseph Fort, 1876-1950. 252.091
Everyday religion. New York, Abingdon-Cokesbury Press [1950] 240 p. 16 cm. [BX9943.N4E9] 50-7150
I. Title.

REMLER, Francis Joseph, 1874- 248
The eternal inheritance; an explanation of man's supernatural destiny and the means he must use to attain it, adapted especially for young men and young women and members of sodalities, with an introduction by the Right Reverend C. E. Byrne ... By F. J. Remler ... St. Louis, Mo., The Vincentian press [c1924] 4 p. l., 136 p. 19 cm. [BX2355.R4] 24-3623
I. Title.

REMLER, Francis Joseph, 1874- 248
The eternal inheritance; an explanation of man's supernatural destiny and the means he must use to attain it, adapted especially for young men and young women and members of sodalities, with an introduction by the Right Reverend C. E. Byrne ... By F. J. Remler ... St. Louis, Mo., The Vincentian press [c1924] 4 p. l., 136 p. 19 cm. [BX2355.R4] 24-3623
I. Title.

[SERLE, Ambrose] 1742-1812. 248
The Christian remembrancer; or, Short reflections upon the faith, life, and conduct, of a real Christian. In three parts. Second American edition ... Chambersburg [Pa.] From the press of Snowden & M'Corkle, March 30, 1799. iv, 272 p. 16 1/2 cm. By Ambrose Serle. cf. Brit. mus. Catalogue. [BV4501.S] A 33
I. Title.

SMOOT, Thomas Arthur, 1871- 267.
The evolution of a churchman, by Thomas A. Smoot. Nashville, Tenn., Cokesbury press, 1926. v p., 2 l., 3-163 p. 20 cm. [BX8332.S63] 26-23667
I. Title.

SMOOT, Thomas Arthur, 1871- 267.
The evolution of a churchman, by Thomas A. Smoot. Nashville, Tenn., Cokesbury press, 1926. v p., 2 l., 3-163 p. 20 cm. [BX8332.S63] 26-23667
I. Title.

SOCIETY of the sons of St. George, Philadelphia.
An historical sketch of the origin and progress of the Society of the Sons of St. George, also the charter, bylaws, and permanent resolutions, together with an alphabetical list of the members and associates, list of officers, etc., from April 23d, 1772, to April 23d, 1872. Philadelphia, W. W. Bates & co., printers, 1872. 112 p. col. front. 25 cm. Prepared by the secretary, William Uderdown. [HS1804.P5S64 1873] 18-2904
I. Underdown, William. II. Title.

SOCIETY of the sons of St. George, Philadelphia.
An historical sketch of the origin and progress of the Society of the Sons of St. George, also the charter, bylaws, and permanent resolutions, together with an alphabetical list of the members and associates, list of officers, etc., from April 23d, 1772, to April 23d, 1872. Philadelphia, W. W. Bates & co., printers, 1872. 112 p. col. front. 25 cm. Prepared by the secretary, William Uderdown. [HS1804.P5S64 1873] 18-2904
I. Underdown, William. II. Title.

STONE, John Timothy, 1868- 261
Everyday religion; a book of applied Christianity, by John Timothy Stone ... Boston, Mass., W. A. Wilde company [c1927] 267 p. 19 cm. [BR123.S79] 28-19273
I. Title.

STONE, John Timothy, 1868- 261
Everyday religion; a book of applied Christianity, by John Timothy Stone ... Boston, Mass., W. A. Wilde company [c1927] 267 p. 19 cm. [BR123.S79] 28-19273
I. Title.

VAN ZELLER, Hubert, 1905-
The yoke of Divine Love; a study of conventual perfection. Springfield, Ill., Templegate [1957] xii, 238 p. 23 cm.
1. Religious life. 2. Perfection, Christian. I. Title.

WAITE, Richard Alfred, jr., 1874-
The gospel in athletic phrases [by] R. A. Waite, jr. ... New York, Young men's Christian association press, 1907. vii, 101 p. 18 cm. 7-37976
I. Title.

WOODS, Edward Sydney, 1877- 248
Every-day religion, by Edward S. Woods ... New York, The Macmillan company, 1923. xi, 253 p. 19 1/2 cm. Printed in Great Britain. [BV4501.W678] 24-4549
I. Title.

WOODS, Edward Sydney, 1877- 248
Every-day religion, by Edward S. Woods ... New York, The Macmillan company, 1923. xi, 253 p. 19 1/2 cm. Printed in Great Britain. [BV4501.W678] 24-4549
I. Title.

Religious life (Buddhism)

BULLEN, Leonard A. 294.3'4'44
A technique of living : based on Buddhist psychological principles / Leonard A. Bullen. New York : Schocken Books, 1978, c1976. p. cm. [BQ5395.B84 1978] 77-14722 ISBN 0-8052-0591-8 pbk. : 4.95
1. Religious life (Buddhism) I. Title.

KIRK, Edward Norris, 1802-1874.
Useful and happy. An address to the young, by Rev. E. N. Kirk; The pleasantness of early piety, by J. G. Pike; and The pleasures of a religious life, by J. A. James. New York, Dayton & Saxton, 1841. 101 p. 15 1/2 cm. [BX4531.K6] 18-8648
I. Pike, John Gregory. II. James, John Angell, 1785-1859. III. Title.

NAGARJUNA, Siddha. 294.3'4'44
Nagarjuna's letter : Nagarjuna's "Letter to a friend" with a commentary by the venerable Rendawa, Zhonnu Lo-dro / translated by Geshe Lobsang Tharchin and Artemus B. Engle. Howell, N.J. : Rashi Gempil Ling, First Kalmuk Buddhist Temple, c1977. xi, 262 p. ; 28 cm. Includes index. [BQ5385.N3313 1977] 77-156251
1. Religious life (Buddhism) 2. Priests, Buddhist—Correspondence. I. Red-mda'-ba Gzon-nu-blo-gros, 1349-1412. II. Title.

RICHARDS, Harriet M. 294.3'4'44
Light your own lamp, by Harriet M. Richards. New York, Philosophical Lib. [1967] xi, 158p. 22cm. [BL1478.54.R5] 66-26971 4.00
1. Religious life (Buddhism) I. Title.

Religious life for women.

SISTER Formation Conferences.
Program for progress; proceedings and communications of regional meetings of the Sister-Formation Conferences, 1965. Editor: Sister Mary Hester Valentine, S.S.N.D. Foreword [by] Edwin A. Quain, S.J. New York, Fordham University Press [1966] xi, 287 p. 24 cm. (The Sister Formation series) 68-17311
1. Religious life for women. I. Valentine, Mary Hester, Sister, S.S.N.D., ed. II. Title.

ZORN, Carl Manthey, 1846- 248
Eunice, Letters of a fatherly friend to a young Christian mother ... Adapted from the German of C. M. Zorn. St. Louis, Mo., Concordia publishing house, 1921. 98 p. front. (ports.) illus. 19 1/2 cm. [BV4529.Z63] 21-9862
I. Title.

Religious life for women — Addresses, essays, lectures.

NELSON, Joseph A
The sisterhoods and the apostolate. Pref.by John Cardinal O'Hara. Philadelphia, P. Reilly [c1959] 62 p. 23 cm. 63-28612
1. Religious life for women — Addresses, essays, lectures. I. Title.

Religious life (Hinduism)

MAHESH YOGI, Maharishi. 294.5'4'4
The science of being and art of living. [New York] New Amer. Lib. [1968,c.1963] 320p. 22cm. [LB1146.M3S35 1968] 68-25334 5.95; bds., .95 pap.,
1. Religious life (Hinduism) I. Title.

Religious life (Islam)

NIYAZI, Kausar. 297'.4'4
Islam, our guide / Kausar Niazi ; [translated by Mohammad Mazharuddin Siddiqi]. 1st ed. Lahore : Sh. Muhammad Ashraf, 1976. xi, 221 p. ; 21 cm. Translation of Islam hamara rahnuma hai. [BP188.N5313] 77-930040 Rs30.00
1. Religious life (Islam) I. Title.

Religious life (Jainism)—Meditations.

CHANDRAPRABHSAGAR, Muni, 1922- 294.4'4'3
The psychology of enlightenment : meditations on the seven energy centers / by Gurudev Shree Chitrabhanu ; edited by Lyssa Miller. New York : Dodd, Mead, c1979. xix, 91 p. : ill. : 22 cm. [BL1378.6.C46] 79-795 ISBN 0-396-07676-9 : 6.95
1. Religious life (Jainism)—Meditations. I. Miller, Lyssa. II. Title.

Religious life (Mahayana Buddhism)

NAGARJUNA, Siddha. 294.3'4'4
Golden zephyr / translated from the Tibetan and annotated by Leslie

Kawamura. Emeryville, Calif. : Dharma Pub., c1975. xx, 165 p. : ill. ; 21 cm. (Tibetan translation series) Translation of Suhrllekha, by S. Nagarjuna, and of Bse sprin gi mchan 'grel Padma-dkar-po'i phren ba, by 'Jam-mgon 'Ju Mi-pham-rgya-mtsho. Includes indexes. Contents.Contents.—Nagarjuna, S. A letter to a friend.—Mi-pham-rgya-mtsho, 'Jam-mgon 'Ju. The garland of white lotus flowers, a commentary on Nagarjuna's A letter to a friend. Bibliography: p. [154]-157. [BQ5385.N3313] 75-5259 ISBN 0-913546-22-4 : 7.95. ISBN 0-913546-21-6 pbk. : 4.75
1. Religious life (Mahayana Buddhism) I. Mi-pham-rgya-mtsho, 'Jam-mgon 'Ju, 1846-1912. Bse sprin gi mchan 'grel Padma-dkar-po'i phren ba. English. 1975. II. Title. III. Series.
Contents omitted.

Religious life (Pure Land Buddhism)—Shin authors.

FUJIMURA, Bunyu, 1910- 294.3'444
Wet sleeves / by Benyu Fijimura. Los Angeles : Nembutsu Press, 1980. 178 p. ; 22 cm. [5bQ8736.F83] 19 79-90653 7.95
1. Religious life (Pure land Buddhism)-Shin authors. I. Title.

KIMURA, Gibun, 1906- 294.3'4'4
Why pursue the Buddha? / By Gibun Kimura ; edited by Sosuke Nishimoto. Los Angeles : Nembutsu Press, c1976. 160 p. ; 23 cm. [BQ968.I487A35] 75-14981 ISBN 0-912624-00-0 5.95
1. Kimura, Gibun, 1906- 2. Religious life (Pure Land Buddhism)—Shin authors. I. Title.

Religious life (Sikhism)

KIRPAL Singh, 1894-1974. 294.6'4'4
The night is a jungle, and other discourses of Kirpal Singh. 1st ed. Tilton, N.H. : Sant Bani Press, 1975. xiii, 358 p. : ports. ; 21 cm. "The discourses, except the first four ... are translations from the Hindi." "Originally published in the monthly magazine Sat sandesh ... October 1969 ... April 1971." Contents.Contents.—Introduction.—God and man.—The higher values of life.—The kingdom of God.—The most natural way.—Guru, gurudev, and satguru.—Let us reform ourselves.—Oh mind! Listen for once.—Thief of your life's breath.—Chastity and forgiveness.—Change your habits now.—Gurubhakti: a lesson in love.—To gain His pleasure.—Protector and protection.—The night is a jungle. [BL2018.37.K6 1975] 75-9244
1. Religious life (Sikhism) I. Sat sandesh. II. Title.

Religious life (Zen Buddhism)

BRANDON, David. 294.3'4'44
Zen in the art of helping / David Brandon. London ; Boston : Routledge & K. Paul, 1976. vii, 124 p. ; 20 cm. Includes bibliographical references. [BQ9286.B73] 78-301779 ISBN 0-7100-8428-5 : 7.50
1. Religious life (Zen Buddhism) 2. Compassion (Buddhism) 3. Zen Buddhism. I. Title.

MITCHELL, Elsie P., 1926- 294.3'927
Sun Buddhas, moon Buddhas : a Zen quest. by Elsie P. Mitchell. With a foreword by Aelred Graham. [1st ed.] New York, Weatherhill [1973] 214 p. 22 cm. Includes bibliographical references. [BQ972.I87A37 1973] 73-4037 ISBN 0-8348-0083-7 7.50
1. Mitchell, Elsie P., 1926- 2. Religious life (Zen Buddhism) I. Title.

SEUNG Sahn. 294.3'927
Only don't know : the teaching letters of Zen Master Seung Sahn. San Francisco : Four Seasons Foundation ; Eugene, OR : Distributed by the Subterranean Co., 1982. p. cm. (Wheel series ; 3) [BQ9286.S45 1982] 19 82-17380 ISBN 0-87704-054-0 : 6.50
1. Religious life (Zen Buddhism) 2. Priests, Zen—United States—Correspondence. 3. Zen Buddhists—United States—Correspondence. I. Title. II. Series.

Religious literature.

ABOTH. English. 1964. 296.12
Pirke Aboth. Sayings of the Fathers. Edited with translations and commentaries by Isaac Unterman. New York, Twayne Publishers, 1964. 408 p. 21 cm. Bibliography: p. 387-397. [BM506.A2E5 1964] 63-9782
I. Unterman, Isaac, 1889- ed. II. Title. III. Title: Title: Sayings of the Fathers.

ABOTH. 1969 296.1'23
Pirke Aboth [Pirke avot] (romanized form) in etchings, by Saul Raskin. New York, Bloch [1969] 136 p. illus. 35 cm. Hebrew, Yiddish, and English. [BM506.A2 1969] 69-15987 12.50
I. Raskin, Saul, 1878-1966, illus. II. Aboth. III. Aboth. IV. Title.

*ACKER, Julius W., ed. 242.1
A thought for today. New ed. [St. Louis] Concordia [1966] iv. (unpaged) 11cm. 1.95
I. Title.

ALBANY religious spectator.
A family paper devoted to religion and general intelligence. v. 1; Nov. 2, 1844-Oct. 25, 1845. Albany, N.Y., E. H. Pease, 1844-45. [208] p. 51 cm weekly. Unpaged. No more published? 14-15346

ALBERTSON, Charles Carroll, 1865- 220
The reality of religion, by Charles Carroll Albertson ... New York, Chicago [etc.] Fleming H. Revell company [c1928] 127 p. 19 1/2 cm. Bibliography: p. 126-127. [BR125.A38] 28-15517
I. Title.

ALDRICH, Thomas Bailey, 1836-1907.
...*Friar Jerome's beautiful book,* etc., selected from Cloth of gold and Flower and thorn. Boston, Houghton, Mifflin and company, 1881. 94 p. 17 x 10 cm. At head of title: T. B. Aldrich. [PS1024.F7 1881] 18-20195
I. Title.

ALLEN, Walter Smith. 220
A voice from the pew. An uncertain sound. By Walter Smith Allen. Brooklyn, The author, 1887. 1 p. l., 169 p. 20 cm. [BR125.A43] 1-5116
I. Title.

AMERICAN church union.
Publications. New York, Pott & Amery, 1868. 2 v. 8. 0-7069
I. Title.

AMERICAN church union.
Publications. New York, Pott & Amery, 1868. 2 v. 8. 0-7069
I. Title.

THE American year-book and national register for 1869. Astronomical, historical, political, financial, commercial, agricultural, educational, and religious. A general view of the United States, including every department of the national and state governments: together with a brief account of foreign states. Embracing educational, religious and industrial statistics; facts relating to public institutions and societies; miscellaneous essays; important events; obituaries; etc. Edited by David N. Camp. v. 1. Hartford, O. D. Case & company, 1869. 842 p. illus. 22 cm. 6-8087
I. Camp, David Nelson, 1820-1916, ed.

ANDERSON, Charles Palmerston, bp., 1863-
Letters to laymen, by Charles Palmerston Anderson ... Milwaukee, The Young churchman co., 1913. 4 p. l., 120 p. 20 cm. 13-18039
I. Title.

ANDERSON, Uell Stanley, 1917-
The other Jesus, a novel. Philadelphia, Muhlenberg Press [c1960] 314p.
I. Title.

ANSTADT, Peter, 1819-1903.
Recognition of our friends in heaven, with extracts from distinguished authors and selections from the poets [by] P. Anstadt ... 4th ed. York, Pa., P. Anstadt & sons [c1907] 256 p. incl. front., 15 pl. 20 cm. 3-1403
I. Title.

BAKER, Emilie Kip. JUV
Out of the Northland; stories from the northern mytha, by Emilie Kip Baker. New York, The Macmillan company; London, Macmillan & co., ltd., 1904. ix, 165 p. front. 15 cm. (Macmillan's pocket American and English classics] [PZ8.1.B1730] .293 4-32297
I. Title.

BALFOUR, Walter, 1776-1852. 237.
Letters on the immortality of the soul, the intermediate state of the dead, and a future retribution, in reply to Mr. Charles Hudson ... By Walter Balfour. Charlestown (Mass.) G. Davidson, 1829. xii, [13]-359, [1] p. 19 cm. [BT921.B27] 21-9100
I. Title.

BALLOU, Robert Oleson, 1892- 211
This I believe, a letter to my son, by Robert O. Ballou. New York, The Viking press, 1938. 285 p. 21 cm. "First published in June 1938 under the title, The glory of God." [BL2775.B32 1938a] 39-530
I. Title.

BARBER, John Warner, 1798-1885.
Royal road to happiness; or, The picture preacher. A book of pictures, fables, allegories and anecdotes ... Philadelphia, Hubbard bros., 1882. 511 p. 1 l. front., illus. 8 degrees. 0-7137
I. Title.

BARBER, Walter Lanier. 248
Show me the way to go home, by Red Barber. Philadelphia, Westminster Press [1971] 192 p. 22 cm. [BX5995.B373A3] 72-150993 ISBN 0-664-20901-7 4.95
I. Title.

BARRETT, Edward John Boyd, 1883- 922.273
A shepherd without sheep. Milwaukee, Bruce Pub. Co. [c1956] 143p. 21cm. Autobiographical. [BX8495.B327A3] 56-6719
I. Title.

BEACH, David N.
The Annie Laurie mine; a story of love, economics and religion, By David N. Beach; with illustrations by Charles Copeland. Boston, Chicago, The Pilgrim press [c1902] 397 p. front., 6 pl. 20 cm. 3-13015
I. Title.

BEATTIE, Robert Brewster, 1875- 242
In the fulness of time [by] Robert Brewster Beattie. [Rumson, N.J., 1944] xvi, 200 p. 21 1/2 cm. Verse and prose. [BR85.B52] 45-720
I. Title.

BECKETT, Lemuel Morgan, 1854- 231
Rational thoughts concerning the Supreme Being of the universe, and the true primitive religion, by Rev. L. M. Beckett, S.D. Washington, D.C., 1919. 3 p. l., 5-182 p. front (port.) 19 cm. [BT101.B28] 19-16092
I. Title.

BELL, Hermon Fiske, 1880- comp. 208
Religion through the ages; an anthology, assembled by Hermon F. Bell. Edited and interpreted by Charles S. MacFarland. New York, Greenwood Press, 1968 [c1948] xlvi, 445 p. 23 cm. [BL29.B4 1968] 68-23275
1. Religious literature. I. Title.

BELL, Robert Bloomer Hare, 1872- 265.
The life abundant; a manual of living, by Rev. Robert B. H. Bell, M. A. 5th ed., rev. and rewritten. Milwaukee, Wis., Morehouse publishing co. [c1928] xiii, 186 p. front. (port.) 19 cm. [BR115.H4B4 1928] 28-12033
I. Title.

BENSON, Robert Hugh, 1871-1914.
Christ in the church; a volume of religious essays, by Robert Hugh Benson ... St. Louis, Mo., B. Herder, 1911. 3 p. l., v-vi, 231 p. 20 cm. 11-5721
I. Title.

BENTZ VAN DEN BERG, John Cato, 1903- 204
Themes to ponder; religious essays. [1st ed.] New York, Vantage Press [1957] 135p. 21cm. [BR126.B38] 57-9294
I. Title.

BEST, Nolan Rice.
Beyond the natural order; essays on prayer, miracles and the incarnation, by Nolan Rice Best ... New York, Chicago [etc.] F. H. Revell company [c1908] 149 p. 20 cm. 8-11093
I. Title.

BEST, Nolan Rice, 1871-
Applied religion for every man, by Nolan R. Best ... introduction by William P. Merrill, D. D. New York, Chicago [etc.] Fleming H. Revell company [c1916] 188 p. 20 cm. 17-862 1.00
I. Title.

BEVAN, Philip.
Adalia; the sinless world. By Philip Beven ... Louisville, Ky., N. H. White, 1861. 154 p. 21 cm. [PS1096.B413] 20-8575
I. Title.

BIBLE. N. T. English. 1962. Authorized. 225
The personal worker's New Testament. With notes and marked plan of salvation arr. and compiled [sic] by Clifton W. Brannon using the edition of 1611 A.D. commonly known as the Authorized King James version Longview, Tex., Clift Brannon Evangelistc Association, 1962. vii, 585p. 12cm. [BS2085 1962.L6] 62-4749
I. Brannon, Clifton Woodrow, comp. II. Title.

BIDWELL, Barnabas, 1763-1833. 264
The mercenary match, a tragedy. By Barna Bidwell ... New-Haven: Printed by Meigs, Bowen and Dana, in Chapel-Street [1784?] 57, [1] p. 18 cm. [Wolcott pamphlets, v. 71, no. 6] Imperfect: p. 33-36, 57, [1] wanting. cf. Photostat copy made by Harvard college library, 1922. [AC901.W7 vol. 71] 25-15087
I. Title.

[BIGLOW, William] 1773-1844. 264
Re-re-commencement; a kind of a poem: calculated to be recited before an "Assemblage" of New-England divines, of all the various denominations; but which never was so recited, and in all human probability never will be. By a friend of everybody and every soul... Salem, Printed by Thomas C. Cushing, 1812. 8 p. 24 cm. [PS1098.B46R4 1812] [AC901.M5 vol.852] 20-13423
I. Title.

BLACK, Campbell. FIC
Raiders of the lost ark : novel / by Campbell Black ; adapted from a screenplay by Lawrence Kasdan ; based on a story by George Lucas and Philip Kaufman. 1st ed. New York : Ballantine Books, 1981. 181 p. ; 18 cm. [PR6052.L25R3 1981] 823'.914 19 80-69250 ISBN 0-345-29548-X (pbk.) : 2.50
I. Kasdan, Lawrence. II. Lucas, George. III. Raiders of the lost ark. IV. Title.

BLACK, James.
The pilgrim ship [by] James Black ... New York, The Christian herald [c1911] 345 p. front. 20 1/2 cm. $1.25 11-28396
I. Title.

BLANKENSHIP, William D. FIC
Brotherly love : a novel / by William D. Blankenship. New York : Arbor House, c1981. 345 p. ; 24 cm. [PS3552.L366B7 1981] 813'.54 19 80-70212 ISBN 0-87795-301-5 : 12.95
I. Title.

BOAT, Reverend William J. 922.273
With gun and cross; a soldier and his angel advance and defend the eternal truths of the church militant. New York, Exposition [c.1962] 511p. (Expositiontestament bk.) 6.00
I. Title.

BOWIE, Walter Russell, 1882- 221.
The armor of youth, talks to children, by Walter Russell Bowie ... New York, Chicago, Fleming H. Revell company [c1923] 175 p. 20 cm. [BV4571.B6] 23-10934
I. Title.

BRAMBLETT, Agnes Cochran. 222
With lifted heart. Boston, Branden Press

[1965] 64 p. 21 cm. Poems. [PS3503.R2555255] 65-26246
I. Title.

BROCKMAN, William Frasier. 234
The day star of salvation, by William Frasier Brockman ... Cedar Rapids, Ia., Press of the Advance publishing co., [1923] cover-title, 1 p. l., 24, [2] p. 21cm. "Initial edition 1000 copies. [BT753.B7] 23-6724
I. Title.

BROOKS, Mary Wallace, ed.
The magic ladder, and other stories, by the pupils of Washington seminary;cover design and illustrations by Harriet Clark Scott; ed. by Mary Wallace Brooks ... [Washington, Pa., Press of H. F. Ward, c1905] 2 p., l., 63 p., 1 l., front. 21 cm. 5-42527
I. Title.

BROUGHTON, Leonard Gaston.
The plain man and his Bible; with suggestions for the formation and conduct of a popular Bible class, by Len G. Broughton ... Philadelphia, Boston [etc.] American Baptist publication society [1909] 116 p. 29 cm. 9-14069
I. Title.

BROWN, Clinton C. 220
Thoughts towards sunset, by C. C. Brown, D.D. Greenville, S.C., The Courier printing co. [c1920] xii, 316 p. front. (port.) 19 1/2 cm. [BR125.B75] 20-22175
I. Title.

BUCK, Pearl (Sydenstricker) 222
1892-
Laba zeme; romans. No anglu valodas tulkojusi Anna Kalnina. [New York] Gramatu draugs, 1953. 264p. 22cm. [PS3503.U198G644] 53-39682
I. Title.

BUNYAN, John, 1628-1688.
Every child's Pilgrim's progress; a new, simplified version of John Bunyan's famous story by Derek McCulloch. Illustrated by Geoffrey Fletcher. Richmond, Va., John Knox Press [1957] xv, 127 p. illus., col. plates. 20 cm. 67-22383
I. McCulloch, Derek. II. Fletcher, Geoffrey, S., illus. III. Title. IV. Title: Pilgrim's progress

BUNYAN, John, 1628-1688.
Every child's Pilgrim's progress; a new, simplified version of John Bunyan's famous story by Derek McCulloch. Illustrated by Geoffrey Fletcher. Richmond, Va., John Knox Press [1957] xv, 127 p. illus., col. plates. 20 cm. 67-22383
I. McCulloch, Derek. II. Fletcher, Geoffrey, S., illus. III. Title. IV. Title: Pilgrim's progress

BUNYAN, John, 1628-1688. 252.
The riches of Bunyan; selected from his works, for The American tract society, by Rev. Jeremiah Chaplin. With an introductory notice by Rev. William R. Williams, D.D. New York, American tract society [1850] 488 p. 19 1/2 cm. [BR75.B75C4] 26-12112
I. Chaplin, Jeremiah, 1813-1886, ed. II. American tract society. III. Title.

BURD, Charlotte.
The silent hour, by Charlotte Burd. New York, Barse & Hopkins [c1917] 285 p. 21 cm. [BV225.B8] 17-16184
I. Title.

BYRUM, Isabel Coston, 1870- 220
The poorhouse waif and his divine teacher; a true story, by Isabel C. Byrum. Anderson, Ind., Kansas City, Mo., Gospel trumpet company [c1919] 223 p. 19 cm. [BR125.B97] 19-19375 0.60
I. Title.

CALLAN, Charles Jerome, 1877-
The Shepherd of my soul, by Rev. Charles J. Callan of the Order of preachers. Baltimore, Md., John Murphy company [c1915] 215 p. front. 20 cm. "We have taken as our guide ... the Psalm of the Good Shepherd."--Pref. 15-25525 1.00
I. Title.

CAMPION, Sidney Ronald, 1801-
Reaching high heaven, by Sidney R. Campion; a story of adventures: physical, mental, spiritual, emotional, thrilling and fascinating for men and women of all ages. London, New York [etc.] Rich & Cowan [1944] 183 p. front. (port.) 21 1/2 cm. A companion volume to Sunlight on the foothills and Towards the mountains. A 45
I. Title.

CARTWRIGHT, Thomas.
... The seven champions of Christendom; by Thos. Cartwright. New York, E. P. Dutton and company [1908] 4 p. l., 119, [1] p. illus., 8 col. pl. (incl. front.) 17 cm. (Every child's library) Title within ornamental border. Series note at head of title and of caption title. "Printed in England." W 8
I. Title.

CASE, Elizabeth York. Mrs.
Faith and reason; a poem, by Elizabeth York Case. New York, I. Somerville & company [c1907] 8 17 x 14 cm. Added title and first page of text within ornamental border. Printed on one side of leaf only. 7-37241
I. Title.

CHANGEY, Eugene 248.42
The thinker and the hare. New York, Carlton [c.1963] 76p. 21cm. (Reflection Bk.) 2.50
I. Title.

CHARLTON, Emanuel Carlson, 1849-
Ragged Hill; a rural church record, by Emanuel C. Charlton. [Spencer, Mass., Printed by W. J. Hefferman, 1913] 115 p. incl. illus., ports. 17 cm. 14-3308 1.00
I. Title.

CHIPMAN, Charles.
Honolulu: the greatest pilgrimage of the Mystic shrine, by Charles Chipman... [n. p.] c1901. 4 p. l., [13]-327, [1] p. front., illus., port. 24 cm. 2-9901
I. Title.

THE Christian library. 208.2
A reprint of popular religious works ... New York, T. George, jr., 1836. 6 v. illus., diagrs. 24 1/2 cm. Vols. ii-vi. "Under the supervision of the following clergymen: Rev. Jonathan Going ... Rev. J.F. Schroeder ... Rev. J.M. Krebs ... Agrees in contents with v. 3-8 of a periodical of the same name published 1834-36. Contents.I. The Life of the Rev. John Wesley, by Richard Watson. The life of William Cowper, by Thomas Taylor. The life of the Rev. Thomas Spencer, by Thomas Raffles. The life of Mclancthon, by F.A. Cox. Memoirs of the late Rev Samuel Pearce, by Andrew Fuller.--II. Martha [Reed] by Rev. Andrew Reed. Thoughts on religion, by Blaise Pascal. A new translation, and a memoir of his life, by the Rev. Edward Craig. A narrative of the visit to the American churches, by Andrew Reed and James Matheson. A discourse of natural theology, by Henry, lord Brougham.--III. The Christian contemplated, by William Jay. Memoirs of the Rev. Christian Frederick Swartz, by Hugh Pearson. The Marys, by Rev. Robert Phillip. The complete duty of man, by Rev. Henry Venn.--IV. Christian charity explained, The family monitor, The Christian father's present to his children, by Rev. J. A. James. Mental illumination and moral improvement of mankind, by Thomas Dick. Sacra privata: or, The private prayers and meditations of the Rev. Thomas Wilson.--V. Travels in the Holy Land, by Rev. R. S. , Hardy, Travels on the continent of Europe, by Daniel Wilson. Narrative of a journey to the Zoolu country, in South Africa, by Capt. A. F. Gardiner. Christian researches in Syria and Palestine, by Rev. William Jowett.--VI. The Marthas, The love of the Spirit, by Rev. Robert Philip. The reasonableness of Christianity, by John Locke. Lives of the apostles, by William Cave. Remains of Rev. Richard Cecil, to which is prefixed, A view of his character, by Josiah Pratt. [BR83.C5] 33-6292
1. Religious literature 2. Christian biography. I. Going, Jonathan, 1786-1844, ed.

CLARK, Glenn, 1882- 220
The though farthest out, by Glenn Clark... St. Paul, Minn., Macalester park publishing co., [1930] 2 p. l., 91, [1] p. 19 1/2 cm. [BR125.C528] 30-8912
I. Title.

CLARKE, Thomas, fl.1830-1872.
The two angels, or, Love-led; a story of either paradise; in six cantos; by Thomas Clarke ... Chicago, Clarke & Bouron, 1867. vi, [7]-194 p. 19 1/2 cm. [PS1299.C65T8] 22-184
I. Title.

CLAY, Lucretia Hart. 232.
Art thou the Christ? art thou he that cometh or look we for another? [by] Lucretia Hart Clay. Boston, R. G. Badger [c1925] 230 p. pl., 2 port. (incl. front.) 20 1/2 cm. [BT205.C6] 25-8613
I. Title.

COBBE, Frances Power, 1822-1904.
The hopes of the human race, hereafter and here. By Frances Power Cobbe. New York, J. Miller, 1876. 270 p. 19 1/2 cm. 15-28219
I. Title.

COMSTOCK, William Charles, 133.
1847-1924.
Thought for help, from those who know men's need; William C. Comstock, amanuensis; with a foreword by Rev. Joseph A. Milburn... Boston, R. G. Badger [1913] 3 p. l., 5-227 p. 23 cm. [BF1301.C687 1913] 14-255
I. Title.

COMSTOCK, William Charles, 133.
1847-1924.
Thought for help from those who know men's need, William C. Comstock, amanuensis, with a foreword by Rev. Joseph A. Milburn... Boston, R. G. Badger [1918] 474 p. 19 cm. [BF1301.C687 1918] 18-12367
I. Title.

COOLEY, Charles Horton, 1864- 218
1929.
Life and the student; roadside notes on human nature, society, and letters, by Charles Horton Cooley ... New York, London, A. A. Knopf, 1927. viii, 273, [1] p. 20 cm. [BD431.C68] 27-18005
I. Title.

COSGROVE, Eugene Milne, 1886- 133
Letters to a disciple, by Eugene Milne Cosgrove ... Chicago, Ashram press, 1935. x p., 1 l., 257 p. 1 illus. 24 cm. [BF1999.C6967] 159.961 35-8811
I. Title.

CRAGIN, Laura Ella. 268.
Kindergarten stories for the Sunday school and home, by Laura Ella Cragin. [2d ed.] Chicago, Ill., The Winona publishing company [1903] 2 p. l., ix-xxx, 316 p. front., illus. 20 cm. "First edition January, 1903. Second edition September, 1903." [BV1540.C7 1903a] 3-29293
I. Title.

CRAGIN, Laura Ella. 268.
Kindergarten stories for the Sunday school and home, by Laura Ella Cragin. Chicago, Ill., The New era publishing co. [1903] 2 p. l., ix-xxx, 316 p. front., illus. 20 cm. [BV1540.C7 1903] 3-12279
I. Title.

*CUNNINGHAM, Sam L. 236
Beware of these days, light your lamps. New York, Exposition [c.1964] 333p. 21cm. (EP42116) 4.00
I. Title.

CUSHING, Richard James, 248.482
Cardinal 1895-
The purpose of living. [Boston, Daughters of St. Paul, 1960] 12p. 19cm. .15 pap.,
I. Title.

DAWSON, William Harrison, 922.
1841-1908.
"The life beautiful"; being extracts from the diary of W. H. Dawson. Owensboro, Ky., Messenger job printing co., 1908. x, 157 p. front., plates, ports. 19 cm. [BX6495.D4A45] 43-47996
I. Title.

DENTON, J. A. 220
The ship of light, with "The little white-top kingdom" (an allegory) by Dr. J. A. Denton. Boston, Mass., The Stratford co., 1924. 3 p. l., vi, 422 p. front., illus., plates, port. 21 cm. [BR125.D47] 24-3978
I. Title.

DETLING, William Colbert.
The three circles; the home, the church, and the heavenly circle, or the home, the church, and the immortal life. By Rev. Wm. Colbert Detling ... Cleveland, O., 1904. 213, [11] p. front. (port.) illus., plates. 21 cm. 4-216259
I. Title.

DICKINSON, Mary Lowe, ed.
A treasury of the world's brightest gems of thought, song and story, on the three themes dearest to the human heart, heaven, home and happiness; ed. by Mary Lowe Dickinson and Myrta Lockett Avary, introduction by Rev. T. De Witt Talmage, D. D. New York, The Christian herald, 1901. xxxii, [33]-416 pp. incl. front. (port.) illus. 23 cm. 2-218
I. Title.

[DOW, Lorenzo] 1777-1834. 922.
Quintescence of Lorenzo's works. History of Cosmopolite; or, The four volumes of Lorenzo's journal, concentrated in one; containing his experience and travels, from childhood to 1815, being upwards of thirty-seven years. Also, his polemical writings: consisting of his Chain, with five links, two books and a swivel. Reflections on matrimony. Hints on the fulfillment of prophecy. Dialogue between the curious and singular. Analects upon the rights of man. A journey from Babylon to Jerusalem. &c. ... 2d ed., cor. and enl. Philadelphia: Printed and sold by Joseph Rakestraw, no. 256, North third street. Where may be had the "Journey of life", by Peggy Dow, being as an appendix to this work, 1815. vi, [7]-554 p. front. (port.) 18 1/2 cm. [BX8495.D57A3 1815] 6-29131
I. Title. II. Title: History of Cosmopolite.

DUFFIELD, T Ewing. 237.
Life after death, by T. Ewing Duffield ... Altoona, Pa., Commercial printing company, 1921. 4 p. l., 7-77 p. 18 cm. [BT921.D76] 21-16441
I. Title.

DYE, James W., comp. 291
Religions of the world; selected readings [compiled by] James W. Dye [and] William H. Forthman. New York, Appleton Century Crofts [1967] xi, 636 p. 24 cm. (The Century philosophy series) Includes bibliographies. [BL29.D9] 67-18207
1. Religious literature. I. Forthman, William H., joint comp. II. Title.

EAKIN, Frank. 291
Revaluing Scripture, by Frank Eakin... New York, The Macmillan company, 1928. 249 p. 19 1/2 cm. Contents.pt. I. Bibles in general.--pt. II. Other great bibles compared with the Jewish-Christian Bible.--pt. III. The influence of bibles. [BL71.E3] 28-11412
1. Religious literature. 2. Christianity and other religions. 3. Bible—Criticism, interpretation, etc. I. Title.

EBELING, Gerhard, 1912- 230
Theology and proclamation; dialogue with Bultmann. Tr. byJohn Riches. Philadelphia, Fortress [1966] 186p. 21cm. Bibl. [BX4827.B78E213] 66-7851 3.95 bds.,
1. Bultmann, Rudolf Karl, 1884- 2. Theology—Methodology. I. Title.

EDDY, George Sherwood, 1871- 922
A pilgrimage of ideas; or, The re-education of Sherwood Eddy, by Sherwood Eddy; illustrated with photographs. New York, Farrar & Rinehart, incorporated [c1934] xiii, 336 p. front., ports. 21 1/2 cm. [BV1085.E3A3] 34-27293
I. Title.

ELLERTON, John, 1826-1893.
John Ellerton: being a collection of his writings on hymnology, together with a sketch of his life and works, by Henry Housman... Pub. under the direction of the Tract committee. London [etc.] Society for promoting Christian knowledge; New York, E. & J.B. Young & co., 1896. xiii, [15]-427, [1] p. front. (port.) illus. 19 cm. "List of Canon Ellerton's hymns, translations, and poems": p. [419]-421. 16-9646
I. Housman, Henry, ed. II. Title.
Contents omitted.

ELLIS, John William, 1839-1910.
The life mission. By J. W. Ellis. Read at

the twenty-fifth annual commencement of Christian college, Columbia, Mo. St. Louis, C. E. Ware & co., printers, 1876. 42 p. 19 1/2 cm. In verse. [PS1589.E5] 24-24568
I. Columbia, Mo. Christian college. II. Title.

ELVY, Cora. 244
The apple is my symbol. [1st ed.] New York, Pageant Press [1957] 114p. 21cm. [BR126.E53] 57-8304
I. Title.

EVA, Mary Mother, 1862-1928. 244
Transfigured tales; talks to children in the chapel of the Transfiguration, Glendale, Ohio, by Reverend Mother Eva Mary, C.J. Boston, The Stratford company [c1930] 3 p. l., 5-27 p. 25 cm. (The Stratford booklets) [PS3509.V2T7 1930] [[813.5]] 30-21629
I. Title.

FENWICK, Malcolm C. 266
Life in the cup, by Malcolm C. Fenwick, W.S. Mesa Grande, Cal., Church of Christ in Corea extension [c1917] 236 p. 20 cm. [BV2063.F4] 17-15444 1.00
I. Title.

FIELDS, William, jr;, comp.
The literary and miscellaneous scrap book; consisting of tales and anecdotes--biographical, historical, patriotic, moral, religious, and sentimental pieces in prose and poetry. Comp. by William Fields, jr. Knoxville, Tenn., W. Fields, jr., 1837. 600 p. 22 1/2 cm. 9-16544
I. Title.

FIGGIS, John Neville, 1866-1919 261.7
The political aspects of St. Augustine's 'City of God', Gloucester, Mass., Peter Smith 1963[c.1921] 132p. 22cm. Bibl. 3.00
I. Title.

FOULKES, William Hiram, 1877- 171.
Sunset by the lakeside, vesper messages to young people, by William Hiram Foulkes ... New York, Chicago [etc.] Fleming H. Revell company [c1917] 94 p. 20 cm. [BV4531.F7] 17-27954
I. Title.

FRITZ, William Grant. 220
Rubies and diamonds, by W. Grant Fritz, missionary to Ecuador, S. A., and Philippine islands. Milwaukee, Wis., W. G. Fritz, 1908. 236, [4] p. illus. 23 cm. "The aim [of this volume] is to awaken a deeper heart-felt interest in the principal portions of God's Word, forth his warnings, his love, and his promises for the present as well as the future life."--Pref. [BS530.F7] 8-18557
I. Title.

FROTHINGHAM, Octavius Brooks, 1822-1895. 922.8173
Recollections and impressions, 1822-1890. [By] Octavius Brooks Frothingham ... New York, London, G. P. Putnam's sons, 1891. iii, 305 p. 20 cm. [BX9869.F83A3] 37-16461
I. Title.

FULLERTON, Arthur Grey, 1878- 266.3'0924 B
Sunset at midnight; autobiography. [1st ed.] Portland, Or., Professional Pub. Print., inc. [1969] 111 p. illus., ports. 22 cm. Includes Mrs. Fullerton's notebook: p. 78-105. [CT275.F824A3] 74-93479
I. Fullerton, Annie Elizabeth, 1878-1968. II. Title.

GALT, John, 1779-1839.
Annals of the parish; The Ayrshire legatees [by] John Galt. London, J. M. Dent & sons, ltd.; New York, E. P. Dutton & co., inc. [1926] xv, 310 p. 18 cm. (Half-title: Everyman's library, ed. by Ernest Rhys. Fiction. [no. 427]) "First published in this edition, 1910; reprinted ... 1926." "List of the works of John Galt": p. xiv. 36-37313
I. Title. II. Title: The Ayrshire legatees.

GARDNER, John, 1868- 248
Letters to a soldier on religion, by John Gardner. New York, George H. Doran company [c1918] vi p., 1 l., 9-95 p. 19 1/2 cm. $0.75 [BV4588.G3] 19-3613
I. Title.

GIBRAN, Kahlil, 1883-1931. 892.78
Spirits rebellious; tr. from the Arabic, and with an introd., by H. M. Nahmad. [1st American ed.] New York, A. A. Knopf, 1948. ix. 139 p. illus. 22 cm. "Illustrations ... reproduced from original drawings by the author." "In a way, a continuation and extension of Gibran's Nymphs of the valley." Contents.--Warde al-Hani.--The cry of the graves.--The bridal couch.--Khaill the heretic. [BR1616.G5 1948] 48-7942
I. Nahmad, H. M., tr. II. Title.

GIBRAN, Kahlil, 1883-1931. 892.78
Spirits rebellious, by Kahlil Gibran; translated from the Arabic by Anthony Rizcallah Ferris, edited by Martin L. Wolf. New York, Philosophical library [1946] vi, 120, [1] p. 23 1/2 cm. "Copyright, 1947." [BR1616.G5] 47-1274
I. Ferris, Anthony Rizcallah, tr. II. Wolf, Martin L., ed. III. Title.

GLADDEN, Washington, 1836-1918. 922.
Recollections, by Washington Gladden. Boston and New York, Houghton Mifflin company, 1909. vi p., 1 l., 445, [1] p. front. (port.) 21 cm. "Books by Washington Gladden": p. [433]-434. [BX7260.G45A3] 9-28138
I. Title.

GLADSTONE, William Ewart, 1809-1898. 252.
Studies subsidiary to the Works of Bishop Butler, by the Right Hon. W. E. Gladstone. New York, Macmillan & co.; [etc., etc., c1896] vii, 370 p. 20 cm. Issued as an additional volume to the Works of Joseph Butler, edited by W. E. Gladstone. [BR75.B9 1896 a] 12-32583
I. Butler, Joseph, bp. of Durham, 1692-1752. II. Title.

GOLLANCZ, Victor, 1893-1967, comp. 208.2
Man and God; passages chosen and arranged to express a mood about the human and divine. Boston, Houghton Mifflin, 1951 [c1950] 576 p. music. 21 cm. First published in London in 1950 under title: A year of grace; passages chosen & arranged to express a mood about God and man. Bibliography: p. 560-572. [PN6071.R4G6 1951] 51-11493
1. Religious literature. I. Title.

GREENE, Reynolds W., Jr. 248.42
Between an atom and a star. Grand Rapids, Mich., Eerdmans [c.1963] 89p. 20cm. 2.50 bds.,
I. Title.

GROSSMANN, Louis, 1863- 170
The real life, by Rabbi Louis Grossmann, D. D. New York, The Bloch publishing co., 1914. 4 p. l., 103 p. 20 cm. [BJ1581.G83] 14-11590
I. Title.

HALDEMAN, Isaac Massey, 1845- 252.
The signs of the times, by I. M. Haldeman... 2d thousand. New York, C. C. Cook, 1910. 455 p. 19 1/2 cm. [BX6333.H3S5] 12-22011
I. Title.

HALFYARD, Samuel Follet, 1871-
Cardinal truths of the Gospel, by Samuel F. Halfyard ... New York, Cincinnati, The Methodist book concern [c1915] 252 p. 19 1/2 cm. $1.00 "This book is a companion volume to the author's Fundamentals of the Christian religion."--Pref. 15-18642
I. Title.

HALL, Bolton, 1854- 220
Life, and love and peace, by Bolton Hall ... with introduction by the late bishop Huntington. New York, The Arcadia press, 1909. 293 p. 20 cm. [BR125.H28] 9-16973
I. Title.

[HALL, Bolton, 1854-
Life, and love and peace, by Bolton Hall...with introduction by the late Bishop Huntington. New York, The Arcadia press, 1909. 203 p. 20 cm. Sep
I. Title.

HARRINGTON, Gardner. 922.
A short epitome of the life suffering and travels, of Gardiner! Harrington, of Stephentown,Resselaer co., N.Y., Commencing at the termination of the second volume of the history of his life. Pittsfield, Printed by Axtel, Bull and Marsh, 1849. 51 p. incl. port. 14 cm. [BX6495.H27A32 1849] 44-12816
I. Title.

HARRINGTON, Gardner. 920.
A short epitome of the life, sufferings and travels, of Gardner Harrington, of Stephentown, Rennsselaer co., N. Y., commencing at the termination of the second volume of the history of his life. Pittsfield, Axtel & Marsh, printers, 1851. 1 p. l., [5]-50 p. 14 cm. [BX6495.H27A32] 41-31783
I. Title.

HARRIS, Thomas Lake, 1823-1906. 289.9
A lyric of the morning land. New York, Patridge and Brittan, 1854. 256 p. 10 cm. [PS1819.H6L9] 65-59679
I. Title.

HARRIS, W[illiam] S[huler]
Life in a thousand worlds, by Rev. W. S. Harris ... Cleona, Pa., G. Holzapfel [1905] 344 p. incl. front. (port.) 18 pl. 22 cm. 5-4549
I. Title.

HART, Henry Martyn, 1838- 922.
Recollections and reflections, by Henry Martyn Hart ... [New York, Gibb bros. & Moran, printers] c1917. 205 p. front., plates, ports. 20 cm. [BX5995.H35A3] 17-13403 1.00
I. Title.

HASTINGS, Horace Lorenzo 232.6
The church not in darkness [3rd ed.] New York 25 Box 87 Cathedral Station People's Christian Bulletin, 28p. 19cm. .10 pap.,
I. Title.

HENRY, G[eorge] W.
Shouting; genuine and spurious, in all ages of the church, from the birth of creation ... until the shout of the archangel: with numerous extracts from the Old and New Testament ... By G. W. Henry ... Chicago, Metropolitan church association [1903] 305 p. front., plates, ports. 20 cm. 3-14729
I. Title.

HEYNE, William P. 261
This is our destiny. Boston, Christopher Pub. House [1952] 210 p. 21 cm. [BR126.H47] 52-946
I. Title.

HOLCOMBE, William Henry, 1825-1893.
Letters on spiritual subjects in answer to inquiring souls. By William H. Holcombe ... Philadelphia, Porter & Coates, 1885. 1 p. l., v-xiv, 15-405 p. 19 cm. 12-34374
I. Title.

*HOSTETTER, Charles, B. 248.42
Life at its best. Chicago, Moody [c.1966] 128p. 17cm. (Colportage lib., 523) .39 pap.,
I. Title.

HOUSE, Elwin Lincoln, 1861- 220
The glory of going on and other life studies, by Elwin Lincoln House... New York, Chicago [etc.] Fleming H. Revell company [c1920] 256 p. 21 cm. [BR125.H725] 21-3503
I. Title.

HOWARD, Burt Estes, 1862-1913.
The shepherd's question, by Burt Estes Howard. Boston, American Unitarian association, 1906. 3 p. l., 9-62 p. 20 cm. Title within ornamental border. 6-42944
I. Title.

HUNT, Elsie Denean. 920
The ship of peace. [1st ed.] New York, Pageant Press [1957] 178p. 21cm. [CT275.H7535A3] 57-7926
I. Title.

HUSE, Raymond Howard, 1880- 232.
Letters on the atonement, by Raymond H. Huse, introduction by Bishop Edwin H. Hughes. New York, Cincinnati, The Methodist book concern [c1917] 79 p. 18 cm. [BT265.H8] 17-23445
I. Title.

INGERSOLL, Caroline E Lawrence.
"In His name" (poetry and prose) ... By Caroline E. Lawrence Ingersoll ... Waynesburg, Pa., Independent job printing office, 1903. 182 p. 23 cm. On cover: Vol. i. 4-6079
I. Title.

JAMES, Henry, 1811-1882. 201
The literary remains of Henry James. With an introd. by William James. Upper Saddle River, N.J., Literature House [1970] 471 p. port. 23 cm. Reprint of the 1884 ed. Contents.Contents.—Introduction.—Immortal life: an autobiographical sketch.—Spiritual creation.—Some personal recollections of Carlyle.—Bibliography (p. [469]-471) [B921.J2 1970] 73-104495
I. James, William, 1842-1910, ed.

JAMES, Stanley Bloomfield, 1869- 922.
The adventures of a spiritual tramp, by Stanley B. James; with a preface by the Rev. Ronald A. Knox. London, New York [etc.] Longmans, Green and co., 1925. xv, 167, [1] p. 20 cm. "The bulk of these chapters appeared first in the Catholic world (U. S. A.)" [BX4705.J33A3] 25-11097
I. Title.

JOHNSON, Frances Simington 248.42
The horizon of light. New York, Vantage [1962, c.1961] 109p. 2.95 bds.,
I. Title.

JOHNSON, Sarah Eliza, called Saint Sarah, 1913- 922
Wilderness to Eden, by Saint Sarah. Philadelphia, Printed by the Patterhannan Print. Co. [1953] 112p. illus. 23cm. [BR1725.J63A3] 53-36889
I. Title.

JOHNSON, Sarah Eliza, called Saint Sarah, 1913- 922
Wilderness to Eden, by Saint Sarah. Philadelphia, Printed by the Patterhannan Print. Co. [1953] 112p. illus. 23cm. [BR1725.J63A3] 53-36889
I. Title.

JONES, John Daniel, 1865- 252.
The hope of the gospel, by J. D. Jones ... [3d ed.] London, New York [etc.] Hodder and Stoughton [1919] viii, 312 p. 20 cm. [BX7233.J6H6] 20-4627
I. Title.

[JUDSON, Edward Zane Carroll] 1823-1886.
Ella Adams: or, The demon of fire. A tale of the Charleston conflagration. By Ned Buntline [pseud.] New York, F. A. Brady [1862] 84 p. incl. plates. 24 1/2 cm. [Mercury stories] [PS2156.J2E4] 44-53365
I. Title.

[JUDSON, Edward Zane Carroll] 1823-1886.
Mermet Ben; or, The astrologer king. A story of magic and wonderful illusions. New York, Hilton & co., 1865. 96 p. front. 24 1/2 cm. (On cover: Ned Buntline's own series. No. 3) "A sequel to Rose Seymour." [PS2156.J2M4] 44-53375
I. Title.

KEANE, John Joseph, abp., 1839-
Emmanuel, by John the beloved; Christi servulus, John Joseph Keane ... being his scribe. Philadelphia, J. J. McVey, 1915. ix, 10-221 p. front. 21 cm. p. 219-221 blank for notes. 15-5394 1.00
I. Title.

KEDDIE, Nikki R. 297'.0924
An Islamic response to imperialism; political and religious writings of Sayyid Jamal ad-Din "al-Afghani", by Nikki R. Keddie. Including a translation of the Refutation of the materialists from the original Persian by Nikki R. Keddie and Hamid Algar. Berkeley, University of California Press, 1968. xii, 212 p. 24 cm. Bibliography: p. [191]-200. [BP80.A45K4] 68-13224
I. al-Afghani, Jamal al-Din, 1838-1897. II. Title.

KELMAN, John, 1864- 243
Things eternal, by Rev. John Kelman ... New York, George H. Doran company [1920] 2 p. l., vii-xii p., 1 l., 13-271 p. 21 cm. [BX9178.K3T5] 20-8019
I. Title.

KENTUCKY Baptist historical society.
Publications of the Kentucky Baptist historical society. Louisville, Ky., Baptist world publishing co. v. 22 1/2 cm. Editor: no. 3, W. J. McGlothlin. 13-26469
I. McGlothlin, William Joseph, 1867- ed. II. Title.

KIMBALL, Warren Young 232
These are God's sons. Dedham, Mass., 302 Mt. Vernon St., Author, c.1959. 133p. 22cm. 3.50
I. Title.

KIRLIN, Joseph Louis J 1868-
With Him in mind, by the Very Reverend Monsignor J. L. J Kirlin ... New York, The Macmillan company, 1926. 5 p. l., 13-146 p. 20 cm. [BX218.K53] 26-17603
I. Title.

LAGERKVIST, Par, 1891-1974. FIC
The Holy Land / Par Lagerkvist ; translated from the Swedish by Naomi Walford ; illustrated by Emil Antonucci. 1st Vintage Books ed. New York : Vintage Books, 1982, c1966. 85 p. : ill. ; 19 cm. Translation of: Det Heliga landet. Originally published: New York : Random House, 1966. [PT9875.L2H3813 1982] 839.7'372 19 81-16147 ISBN 0-394-70819-9 pbk. : 2.95
I. [Heliga landet.] English II. Title.

LAGERKVIST, Par, 1891-1974. FIC
The Holy Land / Par Lagerkvist ; translated from the Swedish by Naomi Walford ; illustrated by Emil Antonucci. 1st Vintage Books ed. New York : Vintage Books, 1982, c1966. 85 p. : ill. ; 19 cm. Translation of: Det Heliga landet. Originally published: New York : Random House, 1966. [PT9875.L2H3813 1982] 839.7'372 19 81-16147 ISBN 0-394-70819-9 pbk. : 2.95
I. [Heliga landet.] English II. Title.

LANYON, Walter Clemow, 20-19871 1887-
And it was told of a certain potter [by] Walter C. Lanyon ... [Milwaukee] North American press, 1920] 1 p. l., 5-62 p. 20 cm. Contents.--Abd Allah, the potter.--Prayer.--The perfect man.--Abd Allah's philosophy.--The man who resisted.--The woman who was poor.--Jethro's song.--The power of silence.--The house that stood in darkness.--Love. --The man who lost a friend. [PS3523.A65A8 1920]
I. Title.

LARCOM, Lucy, 1824-1893. 242
As it is in heaven, by Lucy Larcom. Boston and New York, Houghton, Mifflin and company, 1891. vi p., 1 l., [9]-157 p. 17 cm. [BV4832.L3] 12-34982
I. Title.

LAW, Robert, 1860- 230
The hope of our calling, by Robert Law ... New York, George H. Doran company [c1918] 185 p. 20 cm. [BT820.L3] 18-23051 1.50
I. Title.

LEICESTERSHIRE Education 208 Committee.
Gathered together: readings on religious themes [by Leicestershire Education Authority] London, Oxford University Press, 1971. v, 91 p. 19 cm. First published as a section of Gathered together: a service book for senior schools. [BL29.L44] 73-28821 ISBN 0-19-233414-X £0.62
1. Religious literature. I. Title.

LETTERS to a ministerial son,
by a man of the world. Boston, The Pilgrim press; [etc., etc.] 1911. 221, [1] p. 19 cm. Printed in Great Britain. 11-35817

LEUSCHNER, Albert Edward, 220.7 1875-
Rambling along through the Scriptures; basic truths gone over, for regenerate men; a book for mature believers... [by] A. E. Leuschner... Los Angeles, Calif., 1944. 1 p. l., 100 p. 17 1/2 cm. [BR126.L43] 44-47090
I. Title.

LEWIS, Clive Staples, 283'.0924 1898-1963.
Letters to an American lady. Edited by Clyde S. Kilby. Grand Rapids, Mich., W. B. Eerdmans Pub. Co. [1967] 121 p. facsims. (on lining papers) 23 cm. [BX5199.L53A42] 67-30853
I. Title.

LEWIS, Matthew Gregory, 1775- 264 1818.
Raymond and Agnes; or, The bleeding nun of the castle of Lindenberg. By the late M. G. Lewis ... New York, Printed for S. King [1821?] 38 p. incl. col. front. 21 cm. [Miscellaneous pamphlets, v. 1004, no. 11] [AC901.M5 vol. 1004] 5-5234
I. Title.

LEWIS, Matthew Gregory, 1775- 1818.
Raymond and Agnes; or, The bleeding nun or [read of] the castle of Lindenberg. By the late G. M. Lewis ... New York, S. King, 1828. 38 p. col. front. 19 1/2 cm. 5-18462
I. Title.

LIM, Catherine. FIC
Or else, the lightning god & other stories / Catherine Lim. Singapore : Heinemann Educational Books (Asia), 1980. 194 p. ; 18 cm. (Writing in Asia series) [PR9570.S53L48] 823 19 81-182207 ISBN 9-9716401-4-7 pbk. : 4.50
I. Title. II. Series.
Distributed by Heinemann Educational Books Inc., 4 Front St., Exeter, NH 03833

*LINDSAY, S. B. 232.958
The three hours' vigil. New York, Vantage [c.1965] 57p. 21cm. 2.50 bds.,
I. Title.

LIPPINCOTT, Haines Hallock, 270 1891-
Thoughts concerning things eternal [by] Chaplain Haines Hallock Lippincott ... Boston, The Roxburgh publishing company, inc., 1922. 291 p. 20 cm. [BR125.L735] 22-13010
I. Title.

LLOYD, Marjorie Lewis. 244
The way back. Washington, Review and Herald Pub Assn. [1949] 128 p. 20 cm. Verse and prose. [PS3523.L67W3] 49-24270
I. Title.

LORD, Daniel Aloysius, 271.9 1888-
Everynun; a modern morality play. Illus. by Lee Hines. St. Louis, Eucharistic Crusade of the Knights and Handmaids of the Blessed Sacrament [1952] 163p. 22cm. [BX4205.L65] 52-66377
I. Title.

LORD, Daniel Aloysius, 271.9 1888-
Everynun; a modern morality play. Illus. by Lee Hines. St. Louis, Eucharistic Crusade of the Knights and Handmaids of the Blessed Sacrament [1952] 163p. 22cm. [BX4205.L65] 52-66377
I. Title.

LOREDANO, Giovanni 221.92'4 Francesco, 1606-1661
The life of Adam (1640). A facsim. reproduction of the English tr. of 1659 with an introd. by Roy C. Flanagan with John Arthos. Gainesville, Fla., Scholars' Facsimiles, 1967. xxi, 86p. illus. 20cm. Tr. of L'Adamo. [BS580.A4L613 1659a] 67-26617 6.00
I. Roy C. ed. II. Orthos, John, 1908- ed. III. Title.

LUCCOCK, George Naphtali, 248 1857-
The home God meant, by George N. Luccock ... Philadelphia, The Westminster press, 1922. 205 p. 20 cm. [BV4501.L8] 22-14224
I. Title.

LYTTON, Edward George Earle Lytton Bulwer-Lytton, 1st baron, 1803-1873.
The lost tales of Miletus. By the Right Hon. Sir Edward Bulwer Lytton ... New York, Harper and brothers, 1872. xiv, [2], [17]-182 p. 19 1/2 cm. Contents.The secret way.--Death and Sisyphus.--Corinna: or, The grotto of Pan at Ephesus.--The fate of Calchas.--The Oread's son: a legend of Sicily.--The wife of Miletus.--Bridals in the spirit land.--Cydippe; or, The apple. [PR4922.L6 1872] 12-36427
I. Title.

LYTTON, Edward George Earle Lytton Bulwer-Lytton, 1st baron, 1803-1873.
The lost tales of Miletus: by Sir Edward Bulwer Lytton. New York, Sturgis & Walton company, 1909. xv, 219 p. 18 1/2 cm. Contents.The secret way.--Death and Sisyphus.--Corinna: or, The grotto of Pan at Ephesus.--Fate of Calchas.--The Oread's son: a legend of Sicily.--The wife of Miletus.--Bridals in spirit land.--Cydippe; or, The apple. W 9
I. Title.

MCDOWALL, Stewart Andrew. 215
Seven doubts of a biologist, by Stewart A. McDowall... London, New York [etc.] Longmans, Green and co., 1917. 64 p. 18 1/2 cm. "The first, second, and fifth papers appeared originally in the Challenge."--Foreword. [BL263.M3] 17-24842
I. Title.

MCLAREN, William E[dward].
The holy priest. Milwaukee and London, The young churchman co., 1899. 176 p. 12 cm. Feb
I. Title.

MCLAREN, William E[dward].
The holy priest. Milwaukee and London, The young churchman co., 1899. 176 p. 12 cm. Feb
I. Title.

MCMINN, Edwin.
Thrilling scenes in the Persian kingdom. The story of a scribe, by Edwin MacMinn. New York, Hunt & Eaton. Cincinnati, Cranston & Curts, 1892. 321 p. 19 cm. 5-41081
I. Title.

MAMREOV, Anna F.
A day with the Good Shepherd, by Anna F. Mamreov. New York, Eaton & Mains; Cincinnati, Jennings & Graham [c1910] 84 p. front., 3 pl. 19 cm. 10-22990
I. Title.

MASON, John, 1646?-1694. 242
Select remains of the Rev. John Mason ... Recommended by the Rev. Isaac Watts, D.D. With a preface giving some account of the author. Brookfield [Mass.] Printed by E. Merriam, & co. for G. Merriam [1800] 15, [4], [17]-237 p. 14 1/2 cm. Edited by his grandson John Mason. [BV4831.M3 1800] 11-2591
I. Mason, John, 1706-1763, ed. II. Title.

MASSON, Thomas Lansing, 1866- 220
Ascensions, by Thomas L. Masson. New York, London, The Century co. [c1929] ix p., 2 l., 3-371 p. 19 1/2 cm. [BR125.M4715] 29-4956 2.50
I. Title.

MAUD, John Primatt, bp. of 248 Kensington, 1860-
Applied religion, by the Rt. Rev. J. P. Maud, D.D., lord bishop of Kensington. With a preface by the Rev. H. R. L. Sheppard ... London, New York [etc.] Longmans, Green and co., 1925. 4 p. l., 111, [1] p. 19 cm. "The addresses that are printed in this book were given in the church of S. Martin-in-the-Fields."--Pref. [BV4501.M44] 25-20518
I. Title.

MAUD, John Primatt, bp. of 248 Kensington, 1860-
Life in fellowship, by John P. Maud ... with an introduction by the Lord Bishop of Manchester. New York, The Macmillan company, 1924. 88 p. 20 cm. [BV4501.M46 1924a] 24-22470
I. Title.

MAURO, Philip. 220
Life in the Word ... by Philip Mauro ... New York, Chicago [etc.] Fleming H. Revell company [c1909] 110 p. 19 1/2 cm. $0.50 [BS538.M3] 9-5138
I. Title.

MAXWELL, William Babington. 218
Life a study of self, by W. B. Maxwell ... Garden City, N.Y., Doubleday, Page & company, 1925. 3 p. l. 269 p. 21 1/2 cm. "First edition." [BD431.M46] 26-944
I. Title.

MEAD, Warren B 248.42
Life in the balance. New York, Carlton [c.1966] 130 p. 21 cm (reflection bk.) 3.00
I. Title.

MEHER BABA, 1894- 294.56
Life at its best. Edited by Ivy O. Duce. [Mt. Vernon, N.Y., Printed at the Peter Pauper Press, 1957] 78p. 19cm. [BL1270.M3787] 57-14432
I. Title.

MELTON, William Walter, 252. 1879-
Sifted but saved, by W. W. Melton ... Philadelphia, Boston [etc.] The Judson press [c1925] 5 p. l., 180 p. 20 cm. [BX6333.M39S5] 25-17963
I. Title.

MERRILL, William Pierson, 201 1867-
Liberal Christianity, by William Pierson Merrill ... New York, The Macmillan company, 1925. 170 p. 20 cm. [BR1615.M4] 25-17962
I. Title.

MILK for babes;
or, A text and verse of a hymn for every day in the year. New York, American tract society, [18--] 128 p. 8 cm. 10-21438
I. American tract society, New York.

MILLER, W. H. B. 225.
Sweetest stories ever told, by W. H. B. Miller ... Mountain View, Calif., Portland, Ore. [etc.] Pacific press publishing association [c1927] 5 p. l., 9-91 p. illus. 22 cm. [BS2401.M5] 27-24907
I. Title.

THE mind of God:
to meet today's challenge; thoughts in verse, with scriptural annotations, for folk of discernment. New York, Exposition press [1959] 64p. 21cm.
I. Harris, Mildred (Versoy) 1896-

MITCHELL, Elizabeth Ann 922.89 (Oldacre) 1876-
Anchored to the Rock. Anderson, Ind., Printed for the author by Gospel Trumpet Co. [1950] 142 p. 20 cm. [BX7094.C678M5] 50-31157
I. Title.

MOISE, Penina, 1797-1880.
Secular and religious works of Penina Moise, with brief sketch of her life. Comp. and pub. by Charleston section Council of Jewish women. Charleston, S.C., N. G. Duffy, printer, 1911. 4 p. l., xi, 313 p. 20 1/2 cm. $1.25 Cover-title: Poems of Penina Moise. 11-20897
I. Council of Jewish women. Charleston section. II. Title.

MORGAN, George Campbell, 922.542 1863-1945.
This was his faith; the expository letters of G. Campbell Morgan, compiled and edited by Jill Morgan. Westwood, N. J., Revell [1952] 319p. illus. 21cm. [BX7260.M555A4] 53-2018
I. Title.

MORRIS, Otho Anderson, 248.20924 1891-
Shining my light, by Otho A. Morris. San Antonio, Naylor [1966] ix, 29p. ports. 22cm. [BR1725.M53A3] 66-26722 2.95
I. Title.

MUDGE, James, 1844-
The riches of His grace; a portion for every Sunday, by James Mudge ... New York, Eaton & Mains; Cincinnati, Jennings & Graham [c1909] 316 p. 20 cm. 9-25190 1.00
I. Title.

MULLER, Friedrich Max, 1823- 261 1900.
Life and religion; an aftermath from the writings of the Right Honorable Professor F. Max Muller. By his Wife. New York. Doubleday. Page & company, 1905. viii, 237 p. 21 cm. [BR85.M75] 5-33230
I. Muller, Georgina Adelaide (Grenfell) "Mrs. Max Muller," ed. II. Title.

NEIGHBOUR, Robert Edward, 239 1872-
The rider on the white horse, and other prophecy sermons, by R. E. Neighbour ... Cleveland, O., Union gospel printing co. [c1921] 263 p. 20 cm. [BS647.N4] 21-15357
I. Title.

NEWMAN, John Henry, cardinal, 1801-1890.
... Selections from the prose writings of John Henry, cardinal Newman; for the use of schools. New York, Maynard, Merrill, & co. [c1906] 233 p. front. (port.) 17 cm. (Maynard's English classic series--Special number) [PR5106.M3] 7-3189
I. Title.

NEWTON, Joseph Fort, 1876- 922.373
River of years, an autobiography by Joseph Fort Newton... Philadelphia, New York, J. B. Lippincott company [1946] 6 p. l., 11-390 p. front. (port.) 22 cm. "First edition." Bibliography: p. 375-377. [BX5995.N39A3] 46-3126
I. Title.

NOIT, Dean.
Inspired words for the inspired life and man's privilege as to its physical duration and twentieth century field of endeavor, with an appendix, by Dean Noit; illustrated from paintings by the great masters. Chicago, C. A. Welch & company [c1909] 576 p. front., plates. 24 cm. 9-31454 4.75
I. Title.

NOIT, Dean.
Inspired words for the inspired life and man's privilege as to its physical duration and twentieth century field of endeavor, with an appendix, by Dean Noit; illustrated from paintings by the great masters. Chicago, C. A. Welch & company [c1909] 576 p. front., plates. 24 cm. 9-31454 4.75
I. Title.

NORRIS, W[illiam] E[dward]
His Grace, by W. E. Norris ... New York, Street & Smith [1901] 278 pp. 19 cm. A novel. 1-26199
I. Title.

NORRIS, W[illiam] E[dward]
His Grace, by W. E. Norris ... New York, Street & Smith [1901] 278 pp. 19 cm. A novel. 1-26199
I. Title.

NORWOOD, Frederick William. 922.542
Adventures of a preacher, by F. W. Norwood ... New York and London, Harper and brothers, 1932. 287 p. incl. front. (port.) 2 pl. 19 cm. Published also under title: Indiscretions of a preacher. [BX7260.N6A3] 33-11722
I. Title.

O'KEEFFE, Henry E. 204
Thoughts and memories, by Rev. Henry E. O'Keeffe ... New York, The Paulist press, 1920. ix, 197 p. 19 cm. [BX890.O4] 21-294
I. Title.

OLIVER, Edmund Henry, 1882- 208.1
Tracts for difficult times; Christian literature of comfort, challenge and reconstruction, by Edmund S. [!] Oliver ... New York, Round table press, inc., 1933. xii, 212 p. 19 cm. [BR117.O4] 34-1015
1. Religious literature. 2. Church history. I. Title. II. Title: Christian literature of comfort, challegne and reconstrcution.

O'NEILL, Arthur Barry, 1858- 250
Sacerdotal safeguards; casual readings for rectors and curates, by Arthur Barry O'Neill ... Notre Dame, Ind., University press [c1918] 304 p. 20 cm. [BX1912.O55] 18-23137
I. Title.

O'REILLY, John Boyle, 1844-1890.
... Selections from the writings of John Boyle O'Reilly and Reverend Abram J. Ryan; ed. with an introduction and notes and questions. Chicago, Ainsworth & company, 1904. 71 p. incl. front. ports. 18 cm. (The Lakeside series of English readings [no. 103]) 5-4211
I. Ryan, Abram Joseph, 1839-1886. II. Title.

OXENDEN, Ashton, bp., 1808-1892. 922.371
The history of my life; an autobiography, by the Right Reverend Ashton Oxenden ... London and New York, Longmans, Green, & co., 1891. x, 264 p. 20 cm. [BX5620.O8A3] 36-25145
I. Title.

OXENDEN, Ashton, bp., 1808-1892. 922.371
The history of my life; an autobiography, by the Right Reverend Ashton Oxenden ... London and New York, Longmans, Green, & co., 1891. x, 264 p. 20 cm. [BX5620.O8A3] 36-25145
I. Title.

OXLEY, J[ames] MacDonald, 1855-
L'hasa at last. Philadelphia, American Baptist publication society [c1900] 269 p. front., pl. 12°. 1-18542
I. Title.

PARK, Olga 237
Between time and eternity. New York, Vantage Press [c.1960] 105p. 21cm. 2.75 bds.,
I. Title.

PARMON, Kon 248.42
This we shall do, how God's fundamental truths assure survival in today's world. New York, Exposition [c.1962] 69p. 21cm. 2.75
I. Title.

[PATMORE, Conventry Kersey Dighton] 1823-1896.
The angel in the house. The betrothal ... Boston, Ticknor and Fields, 1858. x p., 1 l., [13]-201 p. 19 cm. [PR5142.A4 1858] 40-23541
I. Title. II. Title: The betrothal.

[PATMORE, Coventry Kersey Dighton] 1823-1896.
The angel in the house. The betrothal ... Boston, Ticknor and Fields, 1856. x p., 1 l., [13]-201 p. 19 cm. [PR5142.A4 1856 a] 15-23459
I. Title.

PERCIVAL, Harold Waldwin, 1868- 212
Thinking and destiny, with a brief account of the descent of man into this human world, and, how he will return to the eternal order of progression, by Harold W. Percival. Symbols, illustrations and charts, and definitions and explanations of terms and phrases, as used in this book. New York, N. Y., The World publishing company [1946] xxxi, 1014 p. diagrs. 25 cm. "First edition." [BP605.P4] 47-1811
I. Title.

PORRITT, Arthur, 1872- 274.
The best I remember, by Arthur Porritt ... New York, George H. Doran company [1923] x, 253, [1] p. 21 cm. Printed in Geat Britain. "Memories stored up during ... years of London journalism--especially religious journalism."--Pref. [BR759.P6] 23-6046
I. Title.

PORTER, Edward, 1935- illus.
They came to Bethlehem. Philadelphia, 1966. 1 v. "This edition of 200 copies has been commissioned by Christ Church, Philadelphia." 68-61699
I. Title.

POWELL, Lewis. 261
Life and service, by Rev. Lewis Powell ... Nashville, Tenn., Dallas, Tex. [etc.] Publishing house of the M. E. church, South, Smith & Lamar, agents, 1918. 208 p. front. (port.) 20 cm. [BR85.P6] 18-18973
I. Title.

PRATT, Lillian Louise 248.42
There is a way. New York, Carlton [c.1963] 117p. 21cm. (Reflection bk.) 2.75
I. Title.

QUEEN, Charles Nicholas.
The threshold of the kingdom, by Charles Nicholas Queen. Dayton, O., United brethren publishing house, 1907. 2 p. l., [3]-109 p. 20 cm. 7-29075
I. Title.

RANDALL, George Maxwell, bp., 1810-1873.
Why I am a churchman. The Pitts street chapel lecture, in answer to the question. "Why I am a churchman." By the Rt. Rev. Geo. M. Randall ... New York, E. P. Dutton & company, 1887. 106 p. 15 cm. On cover: 140th thousand. 10-699
I. Title.

RANDALL, George Maxwell, bp., 1810-1873.
Why I am a churchman. The Pitts street chapel lecture, in answer to the question. "Why I am a churchman." By the Rt. Rev. Geo. M. Randall ... New York, E. P. Dutton & company, 1887. 106 p. 15 cm. On cover: 140th thousand. 10-699
I. Title.

A real treasure for the pious mind. 242
Compiled by a lady of Connecticut. From the collections and writings of the Countess of Huntingdon, Mrs. Rowe, Miss Harvey, Dr. Watts, Mr. Perin, Mr. Smith, and others. Second edition ... Hartford, Printed by John Babcock, 1799. 96 p. 17 cm. [BV4831.R4] A 32
I. A lady of Connecticut, comp.

REILLY, Thomas a Kempis.
Messages of truth in rhymes and story. By Rev. Thomas a Kempis Reilly Philadelphia, J. J. McVey, 1911. 7 p., p., ix, 127 p. front. 18 cm. Partly reprinted from "The Rosary magazine" and "The Young eagle." 11-10193 0.50
I. Title.
Contents omitted.

REYNES-MONLAUR, Marie 282.
The ray; a story of the time of Christ. By R. Monlaur. Translated from the French by Rev. J. M. Leleu. St. Louis, Mo., B. Herder, 1904. 203 p. 16 cm. [BT309.R43] 5-615
I. Leleu, John Mary, 1873- tr. II. Title.

ROBERTS, Evelyn Harvey.
The purse causeway [a religious story] Chicago, C. H. Kerr & co. [1899] 263, [1] p. 16 degree. Jul
I. Title.

ROBERTS, Kenneth J., 1930- 271'.53'024 B
Playboy to priest [by] Kenneth J. Roberts. Staten Island, N.Y., Alba House [1971] ix, 290 p. 22 cm. [BX4705.R58A3] 78-169145 ISBN 0-8189-0234-5 4.95
I. Title.

ROBINSON, Forbes, 1867-1904. 922.
Letters to his friends, by Forbes Robinson...edited with an introductory notice by his brother Charles. 7th impression. New York, Longmans, Green, and co., 1911. 4 p. l., 210 p. 3 port. (incl. front.) 18 1/2 cm. "First edition, July 1904. Reprinted October 1904, June 1905, May 1906, October 1907, April 1909, April 1911." Printed in Great Britain. [BX5199.R72A3 1911] 12-137
I. Robinson, Charles Henry, 1861-1925, ed. II. Title.

ROGERS, Hester Ann, Mrs., 1756-1794. 922.
A short account of the experience of Mrs. Hester Ann Rogers. Written by herself. With a brief extract from her diary. To which are now added, her Spiritual letters... New York, Published by Daniel Hitt, for the Methodist connection in the United States. Paul & Thomas, printers, 1811. 256 p. 17 1/2 cm. "A funeral sermon preached in Spitalfields chpael, London, on Sunday October 26, 1794, on the death of Mrs. Hester Ann Rogers. By the Rev. Thomas Coke, LL.D. Also, an appendix..." (p. [65]-156) and "Spiritual letters" (p. [157]-256) have special title-pages. [BX8495.R55A3 1811] 31-14810
I. Coke. Thomas, 1747-1814. II. Title.

ROWLEY, Charles E. 922.
Apples of gold, by Rev. C. E. Rowley ... Findlay, O., C. E. Rowley [c1925] vi p., 2 l., 11-257 p. front., 1 illus. (music) pl., ports. 20 cm. [BX8495.R6A3] 25-15539
I. Title.

RUNES, Dagobert David, 1902- 242
Letters to my God. New York, Philosophical Library [1958] 58p. 21cm. [B945.R83L39] 58-14857
I. Title.

RUSKIN, John, 1819-1900.
... Sesame and lilies; The ethics of the dust ... London, New York [etc.] H. Milford, Oxford university press, 1925. 188 p., 4 l., 11-224 p. 16 cm. (The works of Ruskin) Half-title: The world's classics. [145] "Ruskin house edition." [PR5250.E25 vol. 1] 33-27218
I. Title. II. Title: The ethics of the dust.

RUTHERFORD, Joseph F., 1869- 289.
Life; the infallible proof from the Word of the Creator that He has provided the way for man to enjoy everlasting life upon earth and that the earth is to be transformed into a paradise. By J. F. Rutherford... 1,000,000 ed. Brooklyn, N.Y. [etc.] International Bible students association, Watch tower Bible and tract society [c1929] 358 p. incl. front., plates (part col.) map, facsim. 18 1/2 cm. [BX8526.R868] 29-15938
I. Title.

ST. Botolph's town and other stories ... New York, Akron, O. [etc.] The Werner co., 1899. [36] p. illus., pl. 13°. Jul

SANTAYANA, George, 1863-
Lucifer; a theological tragedy, by George Santayana. Chicago and New York, H. S. Stone and company, 1899. 4 p. l.,187 p., 1 l. 17 1/2 cm. [PS2772.L8 1899] 99-2599
I. Title.

SANTAYANA, George, 1863-
Lucifer; or, The heavenly truce; a theological tragedy, by George Santayana. Cambridge, Mass., Dunster house, 1924. 2 p. l., xiii-xxi, 128 p., 1 l. 31 cm. "The first edition of Lucifer was published in 1890 ... This, the second edition--the first with the author's preface and revised text, consists of four hundred and fifty copies. The head-pieces, initial letters, and end-papers have been designed and the typography has been arranged by Pierre de Chaignon la Rose, and the printing, under his direction, has been done at Portland, Maine, by the Southworth press." [PS2772.L8 1924] 25-440
I. Title.

SAY, Thomas, 1709-1796. 922.
A short compilation of the extraordinary life and writings of Thomas Say, in which is faithfully copied from the original manuscript the uncommon vision which he had when a young man, his son. Philadelphia, Budd and Bartram, 1796. 34, 144 p. 16 cm. [BX7795.S2A3 1796] 50-44285
I. Title.

*SCHREINER, Samuel A., Jr. FIC
Thine is the glory. New York, Arbor House [1975] 476 p., 21 cm. 74-18163 ISBN 0-87795-101-2 8.95
I. Title.

SHARP, William, 1855-1905.
Vistas, The Gypsy Christ, and other prose imaginings, by William Sharp; selected and arranged by Mrs. William Sharp. New York, Duffield & company, 1912. 4 p. l., 3-484 p. 20 1/2 cm. (Half-title: Selected writings of William Sharp. Uniform ed., arranged by Mrs. William Sharp, vol. V) [PR5350.F12 vol. 5] 12-24267
I. Sharp, Elizabeth Amelia (Sharp) "Mrs. William Sharp," 1856- ed. II. Title.

SHAW, Henry B., Rt. Rev. Msgr. 242
Approaches to the true church. Derby, N.Y., St. Paul Pubns., Queen of Apostles Seminary [1962] 84p. 18cm. .80 pap.,
I. Title.

SHEEHAN, Patrick Augustine, 1852-1913.
Under the cedars and the stars; reflections, literary and philosophical [by] P. A. Sheehan, D.D. ... Philadelphia, Pa., American ecclesiastical review, 1903. 1 p. l., 282 p. 25 cm. [PR5377.S5N5 1903] 3-25768
I. Title.

SHEEHAN, Patrick Augustine, 1852-1913.
Under the cedars and the stars, by the Rev. P. A. Sheehan ... New York, Cincinnati [etc.] Benziger brothers, 1904. 1 p. l., iv, 287 p. 23 cm. Issued in serial form in the Dolphin. Published in 1903 under title: Under the cedars and the stars, reflections literary and philosophical. [PR5377.S5U5 1904] 4-9352
I. Title.

SHEPARD, Thomas, 1605-1649. 252.
Three valuable Pieces. Viz. Select Cases Resolved; First Principles Of the Oracles of God; or, Sum of Christian Religion; Both corrected by Four several Editions:

And A private Diary; Containing Meditations and Experiences Never before Published. By Thomas Shepard ... With some account of the Rev. Author ... Boston: Printed and Sold by Rogers and Fowle in Queen-street, 1747. [183] p. 16 1/2 cm. Each piece has special t.p. and separate paging. "A general preface giving some account of the author, and the following pieces" signed: Thomas Prince. "Books sold by Rogers and Fowle in Boston": [3] p. at end. [BR75.S5] 28-20391
I. Prince, Thomas. 1687-1758, ed. II. Title.

SLOAN, Patrick James, 1874-
With Christ my friend, by Patrick J. Sloan... New York, Cincinnati [etc.] Benziger brothers, 1912. 190 p. front. 18 1/2 cm. 12-2212 0.75
I. Title.

SLOAN, Patrick James, 1874-
With Christ my friend, by Patrick J. Sloan... New York, Cincinnati [etc.] Benziger brothers, 1912. 190 p. front. 18 1/2 cm. 12-2212 0.75
I. Title.

SMITH, Francis Shubael, b.1819. 245.
The young Magdalen; and other poems. By Francis S. Smith ... With a portrait of the author. Philadelphia, T. B. Peterson & brothers [1874] 280 p. front. (port.) 21 cm. [PS2869.S153] 30-19351
I. Title.

SMITH, Hoder. 222.
The dawn of light, by Hoder Smith; interpretations of the garden of Eden, the "flood", the land of Nod. Do these interpretations answer Ingersoll? [San Francisco, Enterprise printing company] 1922. 2 p. l., 9-130, [4] p. 1 l., map. 19 1/2 cm. [BS1235.S6] 22-20375
I. Title.

*SMITH, Mabel G. 252
Honey out of the rock. New York, Vantage [1967] 318p. 21cm. 4.95 bds.,
I. Title.

*SMITH, Robert Ora 248
Life and the Bible. New York, Pageant [c.1964] 209p. 21cm. 3.00
I. Title.

SMITH, Sara (Henderson) Mrs. d.1884.
Up to the light, with other religious and devotional poems. By Sara Henderson Smith. New York, A. D. F. Randolph & company [1884] 108 p. front. (port.) 16 cm. Frontispiece is mounted photograph. [PS2875.S53] 30-29691
I. Title.

SMYTH, Newman, 1843-1925. 920.
Recollections and reflections, by Newman Smyth, with commemorative addresses by Benjamin W. Bacon ... Rev. Peter Ainslie, Rt. Rev. James De Wolf Perry, jr. New York, C. Scribner's sons, 1926. 5 p. l., 244 p. 20 cm. [Full name: Samuel Phillips Newman Smyth] [BX7260.S63A3] 26-16411
I. Bacon, Benjamin Wisner, 1860- II. Ainslie, Peter, 1867- III. Perry, James De Wolf, bp., 1871- IV. Title.

SNIPES, A. M. 215.24
This holy thing. Sparta, N. C., Cosmic Pr. P. O. Box 6, c.1965. iv, 145p. 21cm. Bibl. [BF1999.S56] 65-25325 2.50 pap.,
I. Title.

SNIPES, A M 215.24
This holy thing, by A.M. Snipes. [1st ed.] Sparta, N.C., Cosmic Press [1965] iv, 145 p. 21 cm. Bibliography: p. 141-145. [BF1999.S56] 65-25325
I. Title.

[SPALDING, Baird Thomas] 1857- 133
Life and teaching of the masters of the Far East... San Francisco, Calif., California press [c1924-35] 3 v. 19 1/2 cm. (Sun series) Foreword signed: Baird T. Spalding. Vol. III has imprint: Los Angeles, Calif., De Vorse & co. [BF1999.S6 1924] [159.961] 24-5329
I. Title.

SPENCER, Anna (Garlin) Mrs., 1851-1931. 922.
Bell street chapel discourses, by Anna Garlin Spencer; containing selections from the writings of James Eddy ... 1889-1899. Providence, R.I. [Printed by Journal of commerce co., 1899] viii, 110 p., 1 l. 19 1/2 cm. [BX9999.P9B42] 16-4810
I. Eddy, James, 1806-1888. II. Title.

STANLEY, Theodore P. 211
Putting devils and hells out of existence by destroying the God of the Bible, the God of the Jews, the Christian God ... [by] Stanley. [Collingswood, N.J., c1925] [521] p. illus. 22 cm. Title on front lining-paper. [BL2775.S685 1925] 25-17468
I. Title.

STONE, James Samuel, 1852- 236.
The hope of the ages: an Easter message, by the Rev. James S. Stone, D.D. Chicago, Daughaday & company, 1924. 6 p. l., 78 p. 19 1/2 cm. [BT871.S8] 24-16947
I. Title.

SUNDAR, Singh, 1889- 248
At the Master's feet, by Sadhu Sundar Singh, tr. from the Urdu by Rev. Arthur and Mrs. Parker. New York, Chicago [etc.] Fleming H. Revell company [c1922] 90 p. 20 cm. [BV5082.S8] 23-5962
I. Parker, Arthur, tr. II. Parker, Rebecca J., Mrs. Arthur Parker," joint tr. III. Title.

TABAK, Israel, 1904-
Heine and his heritage; a study of Judaic lore in his work. New York, Twayne, 1956. 338 p. 24 cm. Contains extensive quotations and translations from Heine's works.
I. Title.

THEOCRITUS. 281
Theocritus. Idyls; translations by Dryden, Polwhele, Calverley, Fawkes, and Lang; with illustrations by M. Meaulle. Philadelphia, G. Barrie & son [c1901] 7 p. l., [xi]-xiv, 545 p. illus. (part col.) 22 1/2 cm. (Half-title: Antique gems from the Greek and Latin, v. 1) Added title in Greek: Greek and English on opposite pages. Limited edition of 1,000 numbered copies on Japanese vellum paper. This copy not numbered. Pink ornamental borders. "Bibliographical note": p. 523-543. [PA3606.A7 vol. 1] 1-27601
I. Dryden, John, 1631-1700, tr. II. Polwhele, Richard, 1760-1838, tr. III. Calverley, Charles Stuart, 1831-1884, tr. IV. Fawkes, Francis, 1720-1777, tr. V. Lang, Andrew, 1844-1912, tr. VI. Title.

THIRLWALL, Connop, bp. of St. David's, 1797-1875. 922.
Letters to a friend, by Connop Thirlwall, late lord bishop of St. David's; ed. by the Very Rev. Arthur Penrhyn Stanley ... Boston, Roberts brothers, 1883. xxiv, 399 p. 18 1/2 cm. [BX5199.T45A3 1883] 6-26576
I. Stanley, Arthur Penrhyn, 1815-1881, ed. II. Title.

THOMPSON, James Westfall, 1869-
The lost oracles; a masque, by James Westfall Thompson ... Chicago, W. M. Hill [c1921] xi, 143 p. 24 1/2 cm. "This edition consists of five hundred numbered and signed copies." This copy not numbered. [PS3539.H673L7 1921] [812] 21-10700
I. Title.

THORLEY, Enoch.
Showers of blessing. The story of God's faithfulness to His promises. By Enoch Thorley... [Cleveland?] The author [c1909] 240 p. 4 port. 18 1/2 cm. $0.75. 9-28385
I. Title.

TICHENOR, Henry Mulford, 1858-
The life and exploits of Jehovah, by Henry M. Tichenor. St. Louis, Mo., P. Wagner [c1915] 222 p. incl. front. (port.) 20 cm. $1.00. 15-25368
I. Title.

TOLSTIO, Lev Nikolaevich, graf, 1828-1910.
...Resurrection, translated by Archibald J. Wolfe... New York, International book publishing company, 1920. 2 v. plates. 19 1/2 cm. (Russian authors' library) At head of title: Leo Tolstoy. 21-5362
I. Wolfe, Archibald John, 1878, tr. II. Title.

TOLSTOI, Lev Nikolaevich, graf, 1828-1910.
Resurrection, a novel by Leo Tolstoy; translated by Louise Maude, with an introduction by Aylmer Maude. New York, Oxford university press [1956] xiii, 499 p. 16 cm. (Half-title: The world's classics, CCIX) Translation of Voskresen'e.
I. Maude, Louise (Shanks) 1855-1939. tr. II. Title.

TOLSTOI, Lev Nikolaevich, graf, 1828-1910.
Resurrection. Translated by Louise Maude. Garden City, N.Y., Doubleday [1961] 477 p. 18 cm. (Dolphin books C152)
I. Title.

TOLSTOI, Lev Nikolaevich, graf, 1828-1910.
Resurrection. Translated by Vera Traill. With a foreword by Alan Hodge. [New York] New American Library [1961] viii, 430 p. (Signet classics, CT 63)
I. Title.

TOOLE, Isaac N. 234.
Three great facts, by Isaac N. Toole. Indianapolis,Ind., Pierson & Lantz co. [c1919] 3 p. l., [5]-138 p. front. (port.) 18 1/2 cm. [BT775.T6] 19-13064
I. Title.

*TURNBULL, Ralph G. 251.027
Letters to Christian leaders. Grand Rapids, Mich., Baker Bk. [c.1964] 96p. 22cm. 1.00 pap.,
I. Title.
Contents omitted.

VAN DYKE, Henry, 1852-
The reality of religion, by Henry J. Van Dyke, jr.... New York, C. Scribner's sons, 1884. xii p., 2 l., [3]-146 p. 18 1/2 cm. 12-39686
I. Title.

VANSANT, Nicholas, 1823- 922.
Sunset memories, by Rev. Nicholas Vansant ... With an introduction by General James F. Rusling. New York, Eaton & Mains; Cincinnati, Curts & Jennings, 1896. 271 p. incl. front. (port.) 19 cm. [BX8495.V3A3] 12-39700
I. Title.

[VARNER, W. I.]
The day of wrath. Athens, Ga., J. B. Vaughan, c1910. 2 p. l., 3-253 p. 20 1/2 cm. Cover-title: Day of wrath. Varner's reply to the Millennial dawn. 11-1525 1.25
I. Title.

VINCENT, Edgar La Verne, 1851-
Without sound of hammer, by Edgar L. Vincent. Cincinnati, Jennings & Graham. New York, Eaton & Mains [c1914] 135 p. 16 cm. (Lettered on cover: Devotional classics) $0.25. 14-3912
I. Title.

VIRGINIA religious tract society.
The publications, of the Virginia religious tract society ... Harrisonburg, Davidson & Bourne, 1813. [178] p. 16 cm. Various paging. Lettered: Religious tracts. 5-21282
I. Title.
Contents omitted.

WALSTON, Marie. 286'.1'0924 B
These were my hills. Valley Forge [Pa.] Judson Press [1972] 128 p. 24 cm. [BX6495.W3A3] 72-189436 ISBN 0-8170-0563-3
I. Title.

WALTERS, James A. 220
The purpose of life, by James A. Walters; pub. for the Welden book co. [Chicago, W. B. Conkey company] 1922. 57 p. 19 1/2 cm. [BR125.W28] 22-24992
I. Title.

WARN, Charles Lathrup, 1882- 226.9
"Thine is the kingdom," by Charles Lathrup Warn. Los Angeles, Calif., Walton & Wright [1942] 5 p. l., 15-164 p. 23 cm. [BF1999.W25] 42-12080
I. Title.

WARREN, Meta (Hullihen) 242.4
It is always spring! Philadelphia, Dorrance [1955] 164p. 20cm. 'Forty-two religious and inspirational articles.'--Dust jacket. [PS3545.A747317] 54-12869
I. Title.

WATSON, Tom, J.r. 231
The will of my father. Chicago, Moody [c.1963] 153p. 18cm. (Moody pocket bk., 85) .59 pap.,
I. Title.

WATSON, Tom, J.r. 231
The will of my father. Chicago, Moody [c.1963] 153p. 18cm. (Moody pocket bk., 85) .59 pap.,
I. Title.

WATTS, Isaac, 1674-1748. 201.1
Miscellaneous thoughts. New York, Garland Pub., 1971. xx, 350 p. 21 cm. Facsimile reprint. Original t.p. reads: Reliqviae juveniles: miscellaneous thoughts in prose and verse on natural, moral, and divine subjects; written chiefly in younger years, by I. Watts, D.D. London: Printed for Richard Ford at the Angel, and Richard Hett at the Bible and Crown, both in the Poultry, 1734. [BX5200.W36 1734a] 72-112259
I. Title.

WATTS, Isaac, 1674-1748. 208.1
Miscellaneous thoughts, in prose and verse, on natural, moral and divine subjects; written chiefly in younger years. By I. Watts... 1st American ed. Elizabeth-town: Printed and sold by Shepard Kollock. M,DCC,XCVI. vii, [9]-240, [3] p. 17 cm. Published also under title: Reliquiae juveniles. [BX5200.W36 1796] 33-11049
I. Title.

WHATELY, Richard, abp. of Dublin, 1787-1863.
Thoughts and apophthegms from the writings of Archbishop Whately... Philadelphia, Lindsay & Blakiston, 1856. 1 p.l., ix-xii, 13-442 p. 19 1/2 cm. 15-24176
I. Title.

WHIPPLE, Nellie Agatha (Downs) Mrs., 1880- 200
America's mission; a book of the hour, by Mrs. J. T. Whipple. Meinrad, Ind., Abbey press [c1925] 4 p. l., 98 p. 16 1/2 cm. [BR115.S6W43] 25-7408
I. Title.

WHITE, Prescott [Cushing] 1864-
Honesty with the Bible, by Prescott White... Morgantown, W. Va., Acme pub. co., printers [c1903] 245p. 18 1/ 2 cm. 4-22271
I. Title.

WHITEHOUSE, Elizabeth S. 220.
Kingdom stories for juniors; stories of the Kingdom of Israel, arranged for story-tellers, by Elizabeth S. Whitehouse ... with introductions by Alberta Munkres and Neilson C. Hannay ... New York, Chicago [etc.] Fleming H. Revell company [c1828] 221 p. 19 1/2 cm. [BS551.W56] 28-24615
I. Title.

WHITON, James Morris, 1833- 231
The life of God in the life of His world, by James Morris Whiton, PH.D. New York and London, Funk & Wagnalls company, 1918. xii p., 1 l., 15-69 p. 17 cm. A revised and amplified edition of an essay first published in the Homilectic review. cf. Prefatory. [BT111.W5] 18-11432
I. Title.

WHYTE, Alexander, 1837-1921. 252
With mercy and with judgment, by Alexander Whyte ... New York, George H. Doran company [1925] xiii, 285 p. 20 cm. Preface signed: J. M. E. Ross. Sermons. [BX9178.W55W5] 25-9423
I. Title.

WICKER, Evelyn Lowes. Mrs. 133
Life and its forces, by Evelyn Lowes Wicker. Stockton, Calif., A. D. Klump publishing co. [c1922] 75 p. incl. front. (port.) 19 1/2 cm. [BF1999.W55] 23-4575
I. Title.

WIGGS, Lewis D 1888- 922.673
Thirty-nine years with the great I am. [Chapel Hill? N. C.] 1952. 154p. illus. 23cm. [BX7343.W5A3] 53-16398
I. Title.

WILKIN, Esther 264
The Christ child missal. Pictures by John Johnson. New York, Guild [dist. Golden] c.1963. 29p. col. illus. 20cm. (Catholic child's read-with-me bk.) 1.00 bds.,
I. Title.

WILLEY, John Heston, 1854- 236
Between two worlds; the new day and the old questions [by] John Heston Willey. New York, Association press, 1919. 5 p. l., 3-160 p. 19 1/2 cm. [BT821.W6] 19-12349
I. Title.

WILLIAMS, Michael, ed. 922.2
They walked with God. Newly rev., abridged ed. of The book of Christian classics. Greenwich, Conn., Fawcett [c.1962] 192p. 18cm. (Premier bk. d60) .50
I. Title.

WILLIAMS, William Carlos, 1883-
Adam & Eve & The city [by] William Carlos Williams. Peru, Vt., Alcestis press, 1936. 5 p. l., 15-69 p. 24 cm. Poems. "This first edition ... is strictly limited to 167 copies signed by the author ... This is number 29." A 39
I. Title.

WILSON, Philip Whitwell, 1875- 232.
Two ancient Red cross tales, by P. Whitwell Wilson ... New York, Chicago [etc.] Fleming H. Revell company [c1918] 64 p. front. 19 cm. "The first story is based on the second chapter of St. Mark's Gospel, while the sequel may be found in the tenth chapter of St. Luke." Contents.A paralyzed life.--A case for first aid. [BT309.W5] 8-16715
I. Title.

WILSON, Waitman.
The pilgrim's teacher; or, Bible key to practical doctrine, written by Waitman Wilson ... 1st ed. 1st thousand. Portsmouth, O., U. G. Drake, c1906. 5 p. l., 17-272 p. 2 fold. pl. 19 1/2 cm. 6-12842
I. Title.

WOOD, J[ohn] Al[len] 1828-
Sunset echoes, by Rev. J. A. Wood ... Chicago and Boston, The Christian witness company, 1904. 179 p. front. (port.) 19 1/2 cm. 5-295
I. Title.

WRIGHT, Bruce S. 270
The life in the Spirit, by Bruce S. Wright ... Nashville, Tenn., Cokesbury press, 1927. 118 p. front. 19 1/2 cm. [BR125.W825] 27-15637
I. Title.

YOST, Martha England Murphey. 245.2
With song and timbrel, a book of sacred verse, by Martha England Murphey Yost. Bethlehem, Pa., The Rockford studio, 1930. 3 p. l., 9-60 p. front. (port.) 18 cm. [PS3547.O43W3] CA 31
I. Title.

YOUNG, Lucinda (Smith) Mrs.
The seven seals. "A sinner's dream," "Conversion," "Daniel in the lions' den," "Meditation," "Distance of falling," "Vision of the judgement," "Vision of after the judgement." By Madame Lucinda Smith-Young. Philadelphia, Pa., J. G. Baugh, jr., 1903. 199 p. front., pl., ports. 19 cm. 3-18205
I. Title.

Religious literature—Authorship.

ANDERSON, Margaret J. 808'.02
The Christian writer's handbook [by] Margaret J. Anderson. [1st ed.] New York, Harper & Row [1974] x, 270 p. illus. 22 cm. Bibliography: p. [260]-262. [BR44.A5 1974] 73-18706 ISBN 0-06-060191-4 8.50
1. Religious literature—Authorship. I. Title.

*ARNELLOS, Gabriel J. 201
Arising call for every man and every nation. Tr. from Greek by George S. Vournas [Chicago, Adams Pr.] 1966. 100p. ports. 23cm. 3.75 pap.,
I. Title.

BELL, Arthur Donald. 808.06'6'2
Dimensions of Christian writing, by A. Donald Bell and John C. Merrill. Grand Rapids, Zondervan Pub. House [1970] 96 p. 21 cm. Bibliography: p. 94-96. [BR44.B44] 73-120034
1. Religious literature—Authorship. I. Merrill, John Calhoun, 1924- joint author. II. Title.

CHRISTIAN Writers Institute. 808'.066'24
Handbook for Christian writers. [6th ed.] Carol Stream, Ill., Creation House [1974] 155 p. 21 cm. [BR44.C47 1974] 73-92316 ISBN 0-88419-074-9 3.95
1. Religious literature—Authorship. I. Title.

COX, James H. 808'.02
Confessions of a moonlight writer : a freelancer's guide to the church market / James H. Cox. [Brentwood, Tenn. : JM Productions ; Middletown, KY (202 S. Evergreen Rd., Middletown 40243) : Available from the author, c1981. 97 p. : forms ; 22 cm. Bibliography: p. 93-97. [BR44.C69] 19 80-70315 ISBN 0-939298-00-7 (pbk.) : 4.95
1. Religious literature—Authorship. I. Title.

MOORE, John Allen. 808'.0662
Write for the religion market / by John A. Moore. Palm Springs, Calif. : ETC Publications, c1981. p. cm. Includes index. Bibliography: p. [BR44.M66] 19 80-25607 ISBN 0-88280-084-1 : 9.95
1. Religious literature—Authorship. I. Title.

SCHELL, Mildred. 808'.066'2021
Wanted, writers for the Christian market / Mildred Schell. Valley Forge, Pa. : Judson Press, [1975] 160 p. ; 22 cm. Includes index. Bibliography: p. 154-158. [BR44.S33] 75-6556 ISBN 0-8170-0682-6 pbk. : 4.95
1. Religious literature—Authorship. I. Title.

WIRT, Sherwood Eliot. 808'.066'2
You can tell the world : new directions for Christian writers / Sherwood Eliot Wirt, with Ruth McKinney. Minneapolis : Augsburg Pub. House, [1975] 127 p. ; 20 cm. [BR44.W54] 75-2834 ISBN 0-8066-1479-X pbk. : 3.50
1. Religious literature—Authorship. I. McKinney, Ruth, joint author. II. Title.

WOLSELEY, Roland Edgar, 1904- ed. 808.06
Writing for the religious market, the co-authors: Henry B. Adams [and others] New York, Association Press [c1956] 304p. 21cm. [BR44.W6] 56-6451
1. Religious literature—Authorship. I. Title.

WOLSELEY, Roland Edgar, 1904- ed. *808.06
Writing for the religious market, the co-authors: Henry B. Adams [and others] New York Association Press [c1956] 304 p, 21 cm. [BR44.W6] 56-6451
1. Religious literature — Authorship. I. Title.

Religious literature—Bibliography

AMERICAN Library Association. Religious Books Committee. 016.2
Fifty outstanding religious books; a selection from books submitted by the publishers. [Chicago?] v. 28 cm. annual. Report year ends May 1. Cover title, Outstanding religious books. [Z7751.A6] 50-11305
1. Religious literature—Bibl. I. Title.

AMERICAN Library Association. Religious Books Round Table. 016.2
A list of outstanding religious books. Chicago. v. 28cm. annual. Report year ends May 1. Title vaires: Fifty outstanding religious books (cover title, :Outstanding religious books) Compiled by the round table's Book Selection Committee (called Religious Books Committee) [Z7751.A6] 50-11305
1. Religious literature—Bibl. I. Title.

DOHENY, William Joseph, 1898- 016.2
A spiritual reading list; a list intended for lay persons as well as for priests, seminarians and religious. Westminster, Md., Newman Press, 1950 ['1951] 64 p. 17 cm. [Z7751.D6] 51-2034
1. Religious literature—Bibl. I. Title.

[HONLINE, Moses Alfred] 1873. 268
... A reference library for community training schools. Chicago, Ill., International Sunday school association [c1918] 57 p. 23 cm. (Educational bulletin, 1918, no. 6) "Compiled by Moses Alfred Honline ... and Walter Scott Athearn." [Z7849.H73] 19-3238
1. Religious literature—Bibl. 2. Religious education—Bibl. I. Athearn, Walter Scott, 1872- joint author. II. Title.

INTERNATIONAL council of religious education. Committee on religious education of youth. 016.268
Classified bibliography of youth materials that can be used by youth groups and their leaders in the church and in the field of informal education in other social and fellowship groups, prepared by Subcommittee of Committee on religious education of youth for compilation of bibliography of youth materials of the International council of religious education. Chicago, Ill. [1943] 1 p. l., 7-82 p. 19 1/2 cm. Cover-title: Youth publications: classified bibliography... [Z7751.I5] 43-5808
1. Religious literature—Bibl. 2. Youth—Religious life—Bibl. 3. Social problems—Bibl. I. Title. II. Title: Youth publications.

Religious literature—Collected works.

LIN, Timothy Tian-min, comp. 200'.8
Readings in the world's living religions. Dubuque, Iowa, Kendall/Hunt Pub. Co. [1974] vii, 253 p. 23 cm. [BL29.L56] 74-76460 ISBN 0-8403-0913-9 6.50 (pbk.)
1. Religious literature—Collected works. I. Title.

[MAHAN, William Dennes] 1824-1906. 232.
The archko library; translated from ancient manuscripts at the Vatican of Rome, and the Seraglio library at Constantinople, by Drs. McIntosh and Twyman. 20th century ed. Five volumes in one. Topeka, Kan., W. C. Fisk [c1904] 3 p. l., [5]-126 p. 17 1/2 cm. Also issued at part of the volume published under the title The archko volume. This work is considered a forgery by Dr. Montague R. James in his Apocryphal New Testament, Oxford, 1924, p. 90. [BT441.A2M4] 5-3712
I. McIntosh, M. II. Twyman, T. H. III. Title.
Contents omitted.

Religious literature, English-Bibliography

KANSAS. State University of Agriculture and Applied Science, Manhattan. Library. 016.2
A descriptive catalogue of seventeenth-century English religious literature in the Kansas State University Library, by William P. Williams. Manhattan, Kansas State University Library, 1966. [26] p. facsims. 28 cm. (Kansas State University Library. Bibliography series, no. 3) [Z7755.K35] 67-63307
1. Religious literature, English—Bibliography. I. Williams, William P. II. Title. III. Series: Kansas. State University of Agriculture and Applied Science, Manhattan. Library. Bibliography series, no. 3

WILLIAMS, William Proctor.
A descriptive catalogue of seventeenth century English religious literature in the Kansas State University library, by William P. Williams. Manhattan, Kansas State University Library, 1966. v. (unpaged) facsims. 28 cm. (Bibliography series, no. 3) 68-71303
1. Religious literature, English-Bibl. 2. Literature, Modern-17th cent.—Bibl. I. Title.

Religious literature—History and criticism

BARRY, George Duncan. 220.
... The inspiration and authority of Holy Scripture; a study in the literature of the first five centuries, by George Duncan Barry ... London, Society for promoting Christian knowledge; New York, The Macmillan company, 1919. vii, [9]-146 p. 19 cm. (Handbooks of Christian literature) [BS480.B355] 22-2248
I. Title.

HURST, George Leopole. 261
An outline of the history of Christian literature, by George Leopold Hurst, B. D. New York, The Macmillan company, 1926. ix p., 1 l., 547 p. 23 cm. [BR117.H8] 26-8107
1. Religious literature—Hist. & crit. 2. Theology—Hist. I. Title. II. Title: Christian literature.

KRANZ, Gisbert. 208.2
Modern Christian literature. Translated from the French by J. R. Foster. [1st ed.] New York, Hawthron Books [1961] 174p. 21cm. (Twentieth century encyclopedia of Catholicism, v. 119. Section 11. Catholicism and literature) Includes bibliography. [BR117.K713] 61-9460
1. Religious literature—Hist. & crit. I. Title.

MCNEILL, John Thomas, 1885- 261
Books of faith and power. [1st ed.] New York, Harper [1947] viii, 183 p. 20 cm. Interpretive comments on Martin Luther's On Christian liberty, John Calvin's institutes of the Christian religion, Robert Hooker's The laws of ecclesiastical polity, John Bunyan's The pilgrim's progress, William Law's A serious call to a devout and holy life, and John Wesley's Journal. [BR117.M2] 48-5057
1. Religious literature—Hist. & crit. I. Title.

MARTIN, Hugh, 1890- 240
Great Christian books [by] Hugh Martin. Philadelphia, The Westminister press [1946] 3 p. l., [9]-118 p. illus. (facsims.) 19 1/2 cm. [BR117.M3 1946] 46-6760
1. Religious literature—Hist. & crit. I. Title.

REILLY, Robert James, 1925- 820.9'009'12
Romantic religion; a study of Barfield, Lewis, Williams and Tolkien [by] R. J. Reilly. Athens, University of Georgia Press [1971] x, 249 p. 24 cm. Bibliography: p. [227]-237. [BR117.R4] 70-145886 ISBN 0-8203-0267-8 9.00
1. Religious literature—History and criticism. 2. Romanticism. I. Title.

SMITH, Wilbur Moorehead, 1894- 016.2
Chats from a minister's library. Boston, Wilde [1951] 283 p. 21 cm. Includes ten talks broadcast by the author on the radio program, Chats from a minister's library, sponsored by the Radio Dept. of the Moody Bible Institute. [BR117.S6] 51-9193
1. Religious literature—Hist. & crit. 2. Apologetics—20th cent. I. Chats from a minister's library (Radio program) II. Title.

Religious literature, Jewish—History and criticism.

GERSH, Harry. 296.1
The sacred books of the Jews. New York, Stein and Day [1968] 256 p. 25 cm. [BM496.5.G4 1968] 68-17320 8.95
1. Religious literature, Jewish—History and criticism. I. Title.

Religious literature — Publication and distribution.

BETHER Consultation on Christian Literature, 1962
Record of proceedings: Oct. 8-13, 1962. London [Published by] S.P.C.K. [for the Division of World Mission and Evangelism of the World Council of Churches] 1963. xiii, 122 p. NUC64
1. Religious literature — Publication and distribution. I. World Council of Churches. Commission on World Mission and Evangelism. II. Title.

CAMPBELL, Roy G 266.67
Adverturing with gospel literature. Washington*eview and Herald Pub. Association [c1955] 247p. 18cm. [BV2369.C35] 55-19728
1. Religious literature—Publication and distribution. 2. Seventh-Day Adventists. I. Title.

MCADAMS, Daniel A 259
Ringing doorbells for God. Washington, Review and Herald Pub. Association

[1958] 192p. illus. 18cm. [BV2369.M27] 58-22709
1. Religious literature—Publication and distribution. 2. Seventh-Day Adventists—Missions. I. Title.

MCADAMS, Daniel A 259
Successful leadership. Washington, Review and Herald Pub. Association [c1954] 320p. 18cm. [BV2369.M28] 55-18137
1. Religious literature—Publication and distribution. 2. Booksellers and bookselling—Colportage, subscription trade, etc. 3. Seventh-Day Adventists. I. Title.

SEVENTH-DAY Adventists. 259
General Conference. Publishing Dept.
Essentials of Christian salesmanship, a compilation of principles and procedures by Publishing Dept. leaders. Washington, Review and Herald Pub. Association [1956] 316p. 18cm. [BV2369.S4] 56-28909
1. Religious literature—Publication and distribution. 2. Booksellers and bookselling—Colportage, subscription trade, etc. I. Title.

URE, Ruth. 655.5
The highway of print, a world-wide study of the production and distribution of Christian literature. New York, Pub. for the Committee on World Literacy and Christian Literature of the Foreign Missions Conference of North America, by Friendship Press [1946] ix, 277 p. 20 cm. (Studies in the world mission of Christianity no. 7) Bibliographical footnotes. Bibliography: p. [257]-262 [BV2369.U7] 48-248
1. Religious literature—Publication and distribution. I. Title. II. Series.

Religious literature (Selections: Extracts, etc.)

ABERNETHY, George L. ed. 291.43
Living wisdom from the world's religions; 365 daily readings of insight and inspiration. New York, Holt [c.1965] ix, 237p. 22cm. Bibl. [BL29.A2] 65-22447 4.95 bds.,
1. Religious literature (Selections: Extracts, etc.) 2. Devotional calendars. I. Title.

ABERNETHY, George L ed. 291.43
Living wisdom from the world's religions; 365 daily readings of insight and inspiration, edited by George L. Abernethy. [1st ed.] New York, Holt, Rinehart and Winston [1965] ix, 237 p. 22 cm. "Sources and bibliography": p. 227-237. [BL29.A2] 65-22447
1. Religious literature (Selections: Extracts, etc.) 2. Devotional calendars. I. Title.

BERTHOLD, Fred, 1922- ed. 208.2
Basic sources of the Judaeo-Christian tradition. Editors: Fred Berthold, Jr. [and others] Englewood Cliffs, N. J., Prentice-Hall, 1962. xi, 444 p. illus. 26 cm. Includes bibliographies. [BR53.B4] 62-9946
1. Religious literature (Selections: Extracts, etc.) 2. Judaism—Collections. I. Title.

... Bible stories and 221.
religious classics, with an introduction, by Anson Phelps Stokes, jr.; illustrated by Beatrice Stevens. New York. P. F. Collier & son, 1903. 2 p. l., viii, 620 p. col. front., col. pl. 21 cm. (Added t.-p: Library for young people ... [vol. ii]) Illustrated lining-papers. Series title also at head of t.-p. [BS551.B443] 3-17973
1. Religious literature (Selections: Extracts, etc.) 2. Children's literature. 3. Bible stories, English.

BLACKBURN, Emmeline 240.82
Alethea, 1910- ed.
A treasury of the Kingdom; an anthology compiled by E. A. Blackburn and others. New York, Oxford University Press, 1954. 280p. 20cm. [BR53.B55] 54-10012
1. Religious literature (Selections: Extracts, etc.) 2. Religious poetry. I. Title.

BOTHEM, J. W.
...Earthly stories with heavenly meanings, by J. W. Bothem...with introduction by Rev. D. M. Stearns. Philadelphia, J.M. Armstrong, 1902. 118 p. 18 1/2 x 10 1/2 cm. At head of title: A book of new and original illustrations. 2-21884
I. Title.

BRANTL, George, ed. 208.2
The religious experience. New York, G. Braziller [1964] 2 v. (1144 p.) 24 cm. Contents.CONTENTS. -- v. 1. The image and the idol: the God of immanence. -- v. 1. Beyond the gods: the God of transcendence. In place of God: from nihilism to affirmation. A gift of presence: the God of dialogue. Includes bibliographical references. [PN6071.R4B7] 64-23163
1. Religious literature (Selections: Extracts, etc.) 2. Theology — Collections. I. Title.

BULLETT, Gerald William, 808.8
1894- ed.
The testament of light; an anthology. Boston, Beacon Press, 1954. 229p. 20cm. [PN6071.R4B8 1954] 54-1420
1. Religious literature (Selections: Extracts, etc.) I. Title.

COUPLAND, William Chatterton, 242
1838-1915 ed.
Thoughts and aspirations of the ages; selections in pross and verse from the religious writings of the world, edited by William Chatterton Coupland ... London, S. Sonnenschain & co.; New York, Macmillan & co., 1895. 2 p. l., [vii]-xiii, [3] , 715 p. 23 cm. (Lettered on cover: Half guinea international library) [BL29.C7] 1-1628
1. Religious literature (Selections: Extracts, etc.) I. Title.

CUMMINGS, Samuel, comp. 808.83
Golden legends; great religious stories from ancient to modern times. Introd. by Alson J. Smith. New York, Pellegrini & Cudahy [1948] 541 p. 22 cm. [BL29.C85] 48-8644
1. Religious literature (Selections: Extracts, etc.) I. Title.

DANA, John Monroe, ed. 208
The wider view; a search for truth ... Collected and edited by John Monroe Dana. New York and London, G. P. Putnam's sons, 1899. xxvii, 261 p. 20 cm. [BR53.D3] 99-5616
1. Religious literature (Selections: Extracts, etc.) I. Title.

GRIERSON, Herbert John 232.96082
Clifford, Sir 1865- ed.
And the third day ... a record of hope and fulfilment. Pictures chosen by John Rothenstein. New York, Macmillan Co., 1948. xxviii, 297 p. plates (part col.) 22 cm. [BT540.G7] 49-7295
1. Jesus Christ in literature. 2. Jesus Christ—Resurrection. 3. Religious literature (Selections: Extracts, etc. I. Title.

HALE, Edward Everett, 208.22
1822-1909, ed.
The rosary of illustrations of the Bible. Edited by Rev. Edward E. Hale ... Boston, Phillips & Sampson, 1849. 3 p. l., [v]-vi, [13]-298 p. front., 5 pl. 24 1/2 cm. Prose and poetry. [BR53.H25] 36-25142
1. Religious literature (Selections: Extracts, etc.) I. Title.

HARDESTY, H.H., publisher. 208.2
Illustrated Bible scenes and studies; containing...the Bible verified by its geography and history; the religions of the world in all ages; the...Exodus; Job ... the creation, the fall and the flood ... Our Saviour's life and labors ... origin and growth of Sunday schools...Illustrated with...original engravings... New York, Chicago [etc.] H. H. Hardesty [1887?] 4 p. l., [13]-386 p. front., illus. (incl. maps) 20 cm. [BR53.H35] 36-25141
1. Religious literature (Selections: Extracts, etc.) I. Title.

HOWE, Henry, 1816-1893, comp. 244
The Sunday book of pleasing and comforting literature, prose and poetry, from the best writers. By Henry Howe ... Cincinnati, O., The Howe subscription book concern [1866] vi, 7-100 p. col. front. 20 1/2 x 16 cm. [BR53.H6] [BV4515.B25 1866] 208. 1-1778
1. Religious literature (Selections: Extracts, etc.) 2. Religious poetry. I. Title.

KING, Grace Hamilton, 270.082
1903- ed.
An anthology of Christian literature. Glendale, Calif. [1951] 223 l. 29 cm. [BR53.K63] 51-6860
1. Religious literature (Selections: Extracts, etc.) I. Title.

LAI, Chaman, ed. 208
Mysteries of life and death. [Fort Lauderdale, Fla.] 1965. xvi, 237 p. 21 cm. [BL29.L3] 66-54962
1. Religious literature (Selections: Extracts, etc.) I. Title.

LUNDQUIST, Amos Theodore, 240.82
1896- comp.
Inspiration for today; readings for church and home. Rock Island, Ill., Augustana Book Concern [1950] xi, 244 p. 20 cm. Verse and prose. [PN6071.R4L8] 50-58178
1. Religious literature (Selections: Extracts, etc.) I. Title.

LUNDQUIST, Amos Theodore, 240.82
1896- comp.
Inspirational readings for church and home, compiled by Amos T. Lundquist. Rock Island, Ill., Augustana book concern [c1938] 252 p. 19 cm. Prose and verse. [BR53.L8] 38-10316
1. Religious literature [Selections: Extracts, etc.) 2. Religious poetry. I. Title.

LYON, Quinter Marcellus. 291.43
Meditations from world religious [by] Quinter M. Lyon. New York, Abingdon Press [1966, c1960] xi, 234 p. 20 cm. (Apex books) First published in 1960 under title: Quiet strength from world religions. "Acknowledgments and bibilography of sources": p. 229-232. [BL29.L93 1966] 66-210
1. Religious literature (Selections:Extracts, etc) 2. Meditations. I. Title.

MARTIN, Alfred Wilhelm, 1862- 208
comp.
Ideals of life; selections from the sacred scriptures of the world's great religions, Egyptian, Hindu, Buddhist, Zoroastrian, Confucian, Greek, Roman, Jewish, Christian, Mohammedan, with an introductory lecture on the symphony of religions, by Alfred W. Martin ... New York, Press of the Lent & Graff co. [1915] 3 p. l., 5-104 p. 19 cm. Published, 1925, under title: The fellowship of faiths. "The first edition of this anthology appeared in 1895 ... Third edition."--Prefatory note. [BL29.M3 1915] 31-7154
1. Religious literature (Selections: Extracts, etc.) I. Title.

MARTIN, Alfred Wilhelm, 1862- 242
1933, comp.
The fellowship of faiths, by Alfred W. Martin; selections from the world's great religions, Egyptian, Hindu, Buddhist, Zoroastrian, Confucian, Greek, Roman, Jewish, Christian, Mohammedan, together with forewords by Rabindranath Tagore, Mahatma Gandhi, Swami Paramananda, Channing Pollock, John Haynes Holmes, Rabbi Rudolph Grossman. New York, Roland publishing company, for the Fellowship of faiths, 1925. xxviii, 93 p. 18 cm. Published, 1915, under title: Ideals df life. [BL29.M3 1925] 25-23436
1. Religious literature (Selections: Extracts, etc.) I. Title.

PARENTE, Pascal P. 1890- 220.52
comp.
The well of living waters; excerpts on spiritual topics from the Bible, the Fathers, and the masters of the spirit. St. Louis, B. Herder Book Co., 1948. viii, 335 p. 22 cm. Bibliographical footnotes. [BR53.P33] 48-1848
1. Religious literature (Selections: Extracts, etc.) 2. Bible. English. Selections. 1948. Doual. I. Title.

REUTER, Frederick A.
Readings and reflections for the Holy hour; the manifestations of the Divine Presence, by Rev. Frederick A. Reuter ... New York, Cincinnati, F. Pustet & co., 1917. xiv, 482 p. front. 15 1 /2 cm. $1.25. [BX2185.R5] 17-31682
I. Title.

[ROBBINS, Chandler] 1810- 204
1882, comp.
Our pastors' offering. A compilation from the writings of the pastors of the Second church. For the Ladies' fair to assist in furnishing the new church edifice. Boston, Printed by G. Coolidge, 1845. 126, [2] p. 18 cm. Preface signed: C. R. [i. e. Chandler Robbins] [BR50.R6] 5-26739
1. Religious literature (Selections: Extracts, etc.) I. Title.

RUTER, Martin, 1785-1838, 208
comp.
A collection of miscellaneous pieces, in prose and verse, on subjects moral and religious. By Rev. Martin Ruter. Concord, N.H., Printed by Isaac and Walter R. Hill, 1811. 84 p. 18 cm. [BR53.R8] 41-31802
1. Religious literature (Selections: Extracts, etc.) I. Title.

SMITH, Ruth, ed. 290.82
The tree of life; selections from the literature of the world's religions, edited by Ruth Smith, with an introduction by Robert O. Ballou, and fourteen drawings by Boris Artzybasheff. New York, The Viking press, 1942. 496 p. illus. 24 1/2 cm. "First published November 1942." "Sources of texts": p. 469-475. [BL29.S5] 42-50181
1. Religious literature (Selections: Extracts, etc.) I. Artzybasheff, Boris, 1899- illus. II. Title.

SPENCE-JONES, Henry Donald 208.
Maurice, 1836-1917, ed.
Thirty thousand thoughts, being extracts covering a comprehensive circle of religious and allied topics, gathered from the best available sources, of all ages and all schools of thought; with suggestive and seminal headings and homiletical and illuminative framework: the whole arranged upon a scientific basis. With classified and thought-multiplying lists, comparative tables, and elaborate indices, alphabetical, topical, textual, and Scriptural. Edited by the Rev. Canon H. D. Spence, M.A., Rev. Joseph S. Exell, M.A., Rev. Charles Neil ... With introduction by the Very Rev. J. S. Howson ... New York, Funk & Wagnalls, 1885-88. 6 v. 26 1/2 cm. [BR53.S65] 5-17093
1. Religious literature (Selections: Extracts, etc.) 2. Homiletical illustrations. I. Exell, Joseph Samuel, 1849- joint ed. II. Neil, Charles, 1841- joint ed. III. Title.

STEBBINS, Giles Badger, 1817- 208
1900.
Chapters from the bible of the ages ... Compiled and edited by G. B. Stebbins. Detroit, Mich., The editor, 1872. 2 p. l., 400 p. 20 cm. [BL29.S8] 30-12953
1. Religious literature (Selections: Extracts, etc.) I. Title.

STUBER, Stanley Irving, 208.2
1903- ed.
Treasury of the Christian faith; an encyclopedic handbook of the range and witness of Christianity. Ed. by Stanley I. Stuber and Thomas Curtis Clark; foreword by Charles Clayton Morrison. New York, Association Press, 1949. 832 p. 22 cm. [BR53.S73] 49-6956
1. Religious literature (Selections: Extracts, etc.) 2. Homiletical illustrations. I. Clark, Thomas Curtis, 1877- joint ed. II. Title.

VOSS, Carl Hermann, ed. 208.2
The universal God, the eternal quest in which all men are brothers; an interfaith anthology of man's search for God. Boston, Beacon [1961, c.1953] 326p. (Beacon LR 14) Bibl. 1.75 pap.,
1. Religious literature (Selections: Extracts, etc.) 2. God. I. Title.

VOSS, Carl Hermann, ed. 208.22
The universal God, the eternal quest in which all men are brothers; an interfaith anthology of man's search for God. [Gloucester, Mass., Peter Smith, 1962, c..1953] 326p. (Beacon paperback rebound) Bibl. 3.75
1. Religious literature (Selections: Extracts, etc.) 2. God. I. Title.

VOSS, Carl Hermann, ed. 208.2
The universal God, the eternal quest in which all men are brothers; an interfaith anthology of man's search for God. [1st ed.] Cleveland, World Pub. Co. [1953] 306p. 22cm. [BL29.V6] 53-6645
1. Religious literature (Selections: Extracts, etc.) 2. God. I. Title.

WILLIAMS, Michael, 1878-1950.
They walked with God. Newly rev. ed., edited by D. E. Wheeler. Greenwich, Conn., Fawcett Publications [1957, c1933] 192 p. 18 cm. Originally published, 1933, under title: The book of Christian classics. 67-24632
1. Religious literature (Selections: Extracts, etc.) I. Title.

Religious newspapers and periodicals—Directories

ASSOCIATED Church Press. 016.22592
Directory. New York. v. 23cm. [Z7753.A7] 56-40660
1. Religious newspapers and periodicals—Direct. I. Title.

ASSOCIATED Church Press. 016.22592
Directory. New York. v. 23cm. [Z7753.A7] 56-40660
1. Religious newspapers and periodicals—Direct. I. Title.

BATTEN, firm, advertising agents, New York. (1892. George Batten) 016.
George Batten's directory of the religious press of the United States. A list of all religious periodicals with their denomination; frequency of issue; number of pages; size of pages; whether illustrated; subscription price; circulation; distribution; editor and publisher ... 1892. New York, G. Batten [1892] 167 p. 22 cm. [Z7753.B33 1892] 0-7128
1. Religious newspapers and periodicals—Direct. 2. Advertising. I. Title.

BATTEN, firm advertising agents, New York. (1897. George Batten & co.) 016.
... Directory of the religious press of the United States ...[3d ed.] New York, G. Batten & co., 1897. 211 p. 21 cm. (In Our wedge, New York, 1897. v. 1, no. 3) [Z7753.B33 1897] 4-23017
1. Religious newspapers and periodicals—Direct. 2. Advertising. I. Title.

RELIGIOUS press directory. 1943- New York, J. F. Wagner inc. [1943- v. 23 1/2 cm. Editor: 1943- C. J. Wagner. [Z7753.R42] 44-2778 016.205
1. Religious newspapers and periodicals—Direct. I. Wagner, Clement J., ed.

Religious newspapers and periodicals—Southern States—Bibliography

STROUPE, Henry Smith. 016.205
The religious press in the South Atlantic States, 1802-1865; an annotated bibliography with historical introduction and notes. Durham. N. C. Duke University Press, 1956. viii, 172p. 23cm. (Historical papers of the Trinity College Historical Society, ser. 32) Bibliography: p.[160]-163. [F251.D83 ser.31] 55-12244
1. Religious newspapers and periodicals—Southern States—Bibl. I. Title. II. Series: Duke University. Durham, N. C. Trinity College Historical Society. Historical papers. ser. 32

STROUPE, Henry Smith. 016.205
The religious press in the South Atlantic States, 1802-1865; an annotated bibliography with historical introduction and notes. Durham, N.C., Duke University Press, 1956. vii. 172 p. 23 cm. (Historical papers of the Trinity College Historical Society, ser. 32) Bibliography: p. [160]-165. [F251.D83 ser. 31] 55-12244
1. Religious newspapers and periodicals — Southern States — Bibl. 2. (Series: Duke University, Durham, N.C. Trinity College Historical Society. Historical papers, ser. 32) I. Title.

Religious of Our Lady of the cenacle.

LYNCH, Helen M. 271.97
In the shadow of Our Lady of the cenacle, by Helen M. Lynch ... Published in commemoration of the first half century of the Cenacle in America 1892-1942. Introduction by the Very Reverend Edward J. Walsh ... New York, The Paulist press [1941] xiii, 249, [1] p. plates, ports. 22 cm. Bibliographical references included in "Notes" (p. 229-235) [BX4430.R4L9] 41-24298
1. Religious of Our Lady of the cenacle. I. Title.

SURLES, Eileen. 922.244
Surrender to the Spirit; the life of Mother Therese Couderc, foundress of the Society of Our Lady of the Retreat in the Cenacle, 1805-1885. New York, P. J. Kenedy [1951] xxi, 243 p. port. 21 cm. Bibliography: p. 243. [BX4705.C7794S8] 51-3428
1. Couderc, Therese, Mother, 1805-1885. 2. Religious of Our Lady of the Cenacle. I. Title.

Religious of the Cenacle.

PERROY, Henry, d.1925. 922.244
A great and humble soul, Mother Therese Couderc, foundress of the Society of Our Lady of the retreat in the Cenacle (1805-1885) translated from the French of the Reverend Henry Perroy ... by the Reverend John J. Burke ... New York, The Paulist press, 1933. 3 p. l., v-viii, 241 p. front. (port.) 20 cm. [BX470.C7794P4] 33-35469
1. Couderc, Therese, mere, 1805-1885. 2. Religious of the Cenacle. I. Burke, John Joseph, 1875- tr. II. Title.

RELIGIOUS of the cenacle. 239
The spiritual way, twenty carefully prepared inductive lessons, presenting more than 150 statements of the catechism, a preparation for confession, communion, confirmation, written by the Religious of the cenacle; original illustrations by Claire Armstrong. [New York, c1928] 4 p. l., 278 p. illus. 23 1/2 cm. [BX930.R4] 28-13137
I. Title.

Religious orders — Meditations.

DEAN, George, comp.
Digest of the decisions of the Grand lodge of the Independent order of odd fellows of the state of Michigan, from its organization to and including the annual session in October 1905 now in force; together with the constitution, by laws, rules of order of and Grand lodge ... as amended to the close of the annual session in October, 1905. Comp. by George Dean ... Published by order of the Grand lodge. [Lansing. Mich., Press of Wynkoop, Hallenbeck, Crawford co., c1906] 311 p. 23 cm. 6-7388
I. Title.

DOYLE, Charles Hugo.
Leaven of holiness; conferences for religious. Westminster, Md., Newman, 1957. vii, 242 p. 21 cm. 66-79574
1. Religious orders — Meditations. I. Title.

HOYT, Lucius W.
Digest of the decisions and legislation of the Grand lodge, Grand encampment and Rebekah assembly of the Independent order of Odd fellows of Colorado, from their organization to 1904; together with the annotated constitutions, by-laws and rules of order of those bodies and their subordinates. By Lucius W. Hoyt ... [Denver?] By authority of the Grand lodge of Colorado, 1905. 2 p. l., v, 5-417 p. 23 cm. 5-7373
I. Odd fellows, Independent order of. Colorado. Grand lodge. II. Title.

KNIGHTS of Pythias. Buffalo, N. Y. William McKinley lodge, no. 399.
Report. Buffalo, 1905- v. 20 cm. Lodge instituted, June 24, 1903. ca 5
I. Title.

KNIGHTS of Pythias. Iowa. Grand lodge.
Grand constitution and grand statutes of the Grand lodge, Knights of Pythias, domain of Iowa, adopted at Council Bluffs, August 13, 1903. [Cedar Rapids, Ia., Press of the Republican, 1903] 155, xivii p. 23 cm. [HS1225.I8A3 1903] 17-6281
I. Title.

KNIGHTS of Pythias. Iowa. Grand Lodge.
Grand constitution and grand statutes of the Grand lodge, Knights of Pythias, domain of Iowa. Adopted at Council Bluffs, August 13, 1903. [Cedar Rapids, Ia., Press of the Republican, 1903] 155, xivii p. 20 cm. [With its Journal of proceedings. 1902-03] [HS1253.I8A2 1902] 17-11182
I. Title.

KNIGHTS of Pythias. Iowa. Grand lodge.
Grand constitution and grand statutes of the Grand lodge, Knights of Pythias, domain of Iowa. Revised grand statutes adopted at Sioux City, August 13, 1909. [Oskaloosa, Ia., Presses of the Globe, 1909] 189 p. 21 cm. [With its Journal of preceedings. 1909] [HS1253.I8A2 1909] 17-11183
I. Title.

KNIGHTS of Pythias. Iowa. Grand Lodge.
Grand constitution and grand statutes of the Grand lodge, Knights of Pythias, domain of Iowa. Revised grand statutes adopted at Sioux City, August 13, 1909. [Oskaloosa, Ia., Presses of the globe, 1909] 189 p. 23 cm. [HS1225.I8A3 1909] 17-6282
I. Title.

KNIGHTS of Pythias. Iowa. Grand lodge.
Grand constitution and grand statutes of the order of Knights of Pythias as adopted by the Grand lodge of Iowa at the convention of 1895. Pub. by order of the Grand lodge. Des Moines, Conaway & Shaw, printers, 1895. 137 p. illus. 22 cm. [HS1225.I8A3 1895] [HS1253.I8A2 1895] 17-11181
I. Title.

KNIGHTS of Pythias. Pennsylvania. Grand lodge.
A digest of the laws of the order of Knights of Pythias in the state of Pennsylvania. Comp. and pub. by authority of the Grand lodge of Pennsylvania, by William Blancbois, P. G. C. Philadelphia, Knights of Pythias journal print, 1872. iv p., 2 l., 13-190 p. illus. 16 cm. [HS1225.P4A3 1873] 9-18097
I. Blancbois, William. II. Title.

KNIGHTS of Pythias, Wisconsin Grand Lodge
Grand constitution and grand status, adopted at the 47th Annual Convention, Sheboygan, Wisconsin, June 18 and 19, 1918. [Milwaukee?] 1918. 95 p. 24 cm. [HS1253.W6A32] 51-49594
I. Title.

KNIGHTS of Tabor.
A manual of the Knights of Tabor, and Daughters of the tabernacle, including the ceremonies of the order, constitutions, installations, dedications, and funerals, with forms, and the Taborian drill and tactics. By Moses Dickson ... St. Louis, Mo. [Press of G. I. Jones and company] 1879. 255 p. incl. plates, port., plans, diagrs. front. 21 cm. L. C. copy imperfect: p. 55-58 (including portrait) wanting. [HS2259.T33K5] 45-52410
I. Dickson, Moses. II. Daughters of Tabor. III. Title.

ODD-FELLOWS, Independent order of . Illinois. Grand lodge.
Digest of the laws of the I.O.O.F. for Illinois. By Samuel Willard ... Pub. by the R.W. Grand lodge of Illinois. [Peoria, Ill., Printed by N. C. Nason] 1864. viii, 244 p. 15 1/2 cm. [HS1003.I 3A5 1864] 9-13749
I. Willard, Samuel, comp II. Title.

ODD-FELLOWS, Independent order of. Illinois. Grand lodge.
Digest of the laws of the I. O. O. F. for Illinois. By Samuel Willard ... Pub. by the R. W. Grand lodge of Illinois. [Peoria, Ill., Printed by N. C. Nason] 1864. viii, 244 p. 16 cm. [HS1003.I 3A5 1864] 9-13749
I. Willard, Samuel, comp. II. Title.

ODD-FELLOWS, Independent order of. Nebraska. Grand lodge.
Digest of the proceedings, laws, decisions and enactments of the Grand lodge of Nebraska, I.O.O.F., from its organization in 1858 to 1891, inclusive ... By George N. Beels ... [Fremont, Neb., Fremont tribune print, 1892] 141 p. 22 cm. [HS1003.N2A5] 9-13753
I. Beels, George N. II. Title.

ODD-FELLOWS, Independent order of. Nebraska. Grand lodge.
Digest of the proceedings, laws, decisions and enactments of the Grand lodge of Nebraska, I. O. O. F., from its organization in 1858 to 1891, inclusive ... By George N. Beels ... [Fremont, Neb., Fremont tribune print, 1892] 141 p. 22 cm. [HS1003.N2A5] 9-13753
I. Beels, George N. II. Title.

ODD-FELLOWS, Independent order of. New York (State) Grand lodge.
The digest of the Grand lodge, I.O.O.F., of the state of New York, from 1866 to 1893 inclusive ... New York, J. Medole & son, printers, 1894. iv, 228 p. 24 cm. [HS1003.N7A5 1893] 9-13868
I. Title.

ODD-FELLOWS, Independent order of. New York (State) Grand lodge.
The digest of the Grand lodge, I. O. O. F., of the state of New York, from 1866 to 1893 inclusive ... New York, J. Medole & son, printers, 1894. iv, 228 p. 24 cm. [HS1003.N7A5 1893] 9-13868
I. Title.

ODD-FELLOWS, Independent order of. Pennsylvania. Grand lodge.
A digest of the laws of the Independent order of Odd fellows of the state of Pennsylvania ... Philadelphia, Printed by authority of the Grand lodge of Pennsylvania 1861. 198 p. 18 cm. [HS1003.P3A4 1861] 9-15698
I. Title.

ODD-FELLOWS, Independent order of. Pennsylvania. Grand lodge.
A digest of the laws of the Independent order of Odd fellows of the state of Pennsylvania ... Philadelphia, Printed by authority of the Grand lodge of Pennsylvania, 1861. 198 p. 18 cm. [HS1003.P3A4 1861] 9-15698
I. Title.

ROYAL order of Tibet fraternity. 212
... Questions and answers, by The Royal order of Tibet ... [Laguna Beach, Calif., 1936] 1 p. l., 67 p. illus. 20 cm. (On cover: Wisdom of the masters of the Far East, vol. i) "Compiled by Professor G. Adamski." Advertising matter: p. 67. [BP600.R6] 36-25826
I. Adamaki, George, 1891- comp. II. Title.

Religious orders of women — Education — Bibliography

DEHEY, Elinor Tong.
Religious orders of women in the United States: accounts of their origin and of their most important institutions, interwoven with brief histories of many famous convents, especially prepared (with illustrations) from authentic sources and comp, by Elinor Tong Dehey. 1st ed. Hammond, Ind., New York [etc.] W. B. Conkey company [c1913] 366 p. incl. front. plates, ports. 23 cm. 13-17005 3.00
I. Title.

LONG, Brideen.
An annotated bibliography of research studies on the education of sisters, by Sister M. Brideen Long, O.S.F. Washington, Sister Formation Conference, 1964. 48 p. 23 cm. 67-99277
1. Religious orders of women — Education — Bibl. I. Title.

LONG, Brideen.
An annotated bibliography of research studies on the education of sisters, by Sister M. Brideen Long, O.S.F. Washington, Sister Formation Conference, 1964. 48 p. 23 cm. 67-99277
1. Religious orders of women — Education — Bibl. I. Title.

Religious Poetry

[ALDINGTON, Hilda (Doolittle)] 1886-
Tribute to the angels, by H. D. London, New York [etc.] Oxford university press, 1945. 3 p. l., 9-42 p. 21 cm. "Certain of these poems have already appeared in Life and letters today."--p. [7] A 45
I. Title.

ARISTOCRACY. 252.
An epic poem ... [Bk. I-II] Philadelphia, Printed for the editor, 1795. 2 v. 20 1/2 cm. [Wolcott pamphlets, v. 3, nos. 9 and 10] Manuscript note on t.-p. of book I: Richard Alsop--reputed author. [AC901.W7] [PS700.A1A7] [AC901.D8] 252. 22-11709
I. Alsop, Richard, 1761-1815.

BARLOW, Warren Sumner.
Immortality inherent in nature. By Warren Sumner Barlow... New York, Fowler & Wells co., 1885. 40 p. front. (port.) 19 cm. Poem. Advertising matter: . [39]-40. [PS1065.B9 I S 1885] 18-23999
I. Title.

BARRETT, Roxanna Mae (Stephens) Mrs.
Evening meditations. A book of poems, by Roxie M. Barrett ... Gainesville, Ga., The Baptist sun publishing company [c1888] 1 p. l., 95 p. 22 cm. [PS1074.B25E7 1888] 18-23977
I. Title.

BARRETT, Roxanna Mae (Stephens) Mrs.
Evening meditations. A book of poems, by Roxie M. Barrett ... Gainesville, Ga., The Baptist sun publishing company [c1888] 1 p. l., 95 p. 22 cm. [PS1074.B25E7 1888] 18-23977
I. Title.

BECKER, Frederick W.
St. Hilda & other poems [by] Frederick W. Becker. New York, The Grafton press [1904] 51 p. 19 1/2 cm. 4-34544
I. Title.

BENTON, Patricia. 222
Love is. New York, F. Fell [1963] 45 p. 21 cm. Poems. [PS3503.E585L6] 63-1743
I. Title.

BETHUNE, George Washington, 1805-1862.
Lays of love and faith, with other fugitive poems. By Geo. W. Bethune. Philadelphia, Lindsay & Blakiston [1847?] viii. [13]-184 p. 23 cm. [PS1096.B3L3 1847] 20-11040
I. Title.

BETTNER, George.
Harmoniae caelestes, or Christian melodies: and other poems. By George Bettner. New York, McElrath, Bangs & co., 1833. x. [11]-147 p. 20 cm. [PS1096.B366] 20-8574
I. Title.

BHARAVI.
Bharavi's peom Kiratarjuniya; or, Arjuna's combat with the Kiranta; tr. from the original Sanskrit into Germau and explained by Carl Cappeller ... Cambridge, Mass., Harvard university, 1912. xxv, [1] p., 1 l., 206 p. 26 cm. (Added t.-p.: Harvard oriental series ... v. 15) "Printed from type at the printing-office of W. Kohlhammer, Stuttgart, Wurttemberg, Germany." "First edition, 1912, one thousand copies." "Bibliographisches [1]": p. [xxii]-xxv. 14-4048
I. Cappeller, Carl, 1840- tr. II. Title. III. Title: Kiratarjuniya.

BLACKIE, John Stuart, 1809-1895.
Songs of religion and life, by John Stuart Blackie ... New York, Scribner, Armstrong & company, 1876. x, [1], 242 p. 17 1/2 cm. A13
1. Religious poetry. I. Title.

BREWER, Wilmon, 1895- 222
Still more adventures; [poems] Illus. in color from paintings by Polly Thayer Starr and Mrs. William Armistead Falconer. Francestown, N. H., M. Jones [1966] 436 p. col. illus., col. ports. 21 cm. [PS3503.R513S7] 66-31781
I. Title.

BRINGS, Erik. 222
Golden arrows. Philadelphia, Dorrance [1962] 32 p. 20 cm. (Contemporary poets of Dorrance, 562) [PS3503.R557G6] 62-21888
I. Title.

BRINGS, Erik. 222
Golden arrows. Philadelphia, Dorrance [1962] 32 p. 20 cm. (Contemporary poets of Dorrance, 562) [PS3503.R557G6] 62-21888
I. Title.

BRITT, Bertha Marie. 248
Ashes of tomorrow. Philadelphia, Dorrance [1955] 94p. 20cm. Prose and poems. [PS3503.R5765A7] 55-7594
I. Title.

[BROCKWAY, Thomas, 1714-1807.
The gospel tragedy: an epic poem. In four books ... Published according to act of Congress. Worcester, Massachusetts, Printed by James R. Hutchin. mdccxcv. iv p. 1 l., [7]-119 p. front. 18cm. Frontispiece engraved by Doolittle: Published by Isaiah Thomas, jun. 1795. A 31
I. Title.

BROPHY, Dennis P.
G. A. R. patriotic and semi-religious poems. Written and pub. by D. P. Brophy ... Nokomis, Ill., D. P. Brophy [1894] 53 p. illus. 26 cm. [PS1124.B13B6 1894] 21-15776
I. Title.

BULMER, Agnes (Collinson) Mrs 1775-1836.
Messiah's kingdom. A poem. In twelve books. By Agnes Bulmer ... New York, B. Waugh and T. Mason, 1833. 1 p. l., [ix]-xv, [16]-364 p. 15 cm. [PS1199.B4M4 1833] 21-17398
I. Title.

BURTON, Richard, 1861-
From the book of life, poems, by Richard Burton... Boston, Little, Brown, and company, 1909. ix, 94 p. 20 cm. Partly reprinted from various periodicals. [BS1229.B6F7 1909] 9-24977 1.25
I. Title.

CARMINA coeli; 808.1
or, Songs on heaven. Boston, H. Hoyt [c1870] 2 p. l., 3-151, [1], p. front. 18 cm. Edited by Elias Nason. [PR1191.C15] 245 30-17232
1. Religious poetry. 2. Hymns, English. 3. Heaven. I. Nason, Elias, 1811-1887, ed.

CHALLIS, Gordon. 133.1
Building; poems. Christchurch, Caxton Press, 1963. 41 p. 23 cm. [PR6053.H27B8] 66-33484
I. Title.

CHAMBERS, Moses Leonard, 1880- 245
Diamonds in the rough, by Rev. Moses Leonard Chambers. Rockwood, Tenn. [c1929] cover-title, 68 p. incl. port. 22 cm. Poems. [PS3505.H27D5 1929] 811.5 ca 30
I. Title.

CLAFLIN, Sumner Franklin, 1862-
Thoughts in verse that I have gathered by the pathway of life, if anything herein is true, 'tis God's, all else is mine, pub. for and at the request of friends by Sumner F. Claflin... 2d ed. Manchester, N.H., Printed by the John B. Clarke company, 1893. 90 p. front. (port.) 21 1/2 cm. [PS1299C153T5] 14-16635
I. Title.

COBLENTZ, Stanton Arthur 1896- comp. 808.81
Poems to change lives. New York, Association Press [1960] 124p. 160cm. (An Association Press reflection book) [PN6110.R4C6] 60-6568
1. Religious poetry. I. Title.

COLGAN, Harold V. 245.22
Little buds for Jesus' garden, written and compiled by Rev. H. V. Colgan. New York, The Edward J. O'Toole co., inc. [c1930] 4 p. l., 178 p. illus. 14 cm. [PS3505.O29L5 1930] 30-33771
1. Religious poetry. I. Title.

CONLON, Anastasia E. 245.2
A tribute to the Little flower of Jesus, and other poems, by Anastasia E. Conlon. [Baltimore, "Read-Taylor"] 1930. 61, [1] p. mounted port. 18 1/2 cm. [PS3505.O479T7 1930] 31-852
I. Title.

COYLE, Henry.
The promise of morning [poems] Boston, Angel guardian press, 1899. 142 p. 16 cm. May
I. Title.

[DELTWYN, Agnes Procter] 1854- 133.
Believest thou this, by A. P. D. ... [Chicago, M. A. Donohue & co., c1913] 117 p. front. (port.) 19 cm. "These poetic messages were received clairaudiently from a source external to the writer, claiming to be the soul of Adah Issacs Menken, and are the sequelze to a volume of poems issued before the demise of that writer, under the title "Infelicia."--Pref. First published in 1900 under the title Ehoes from shadowland, by Agnes Proctor. [BF1301.D3] 13-11994 0.75
I. Menken, Adah Isaacs, 1835-1868. II. Title.

DEPENNING, George Alfred Guelph.
God and man. [Poem] by George Alfred Guelph Depenning ... New York, The Kinsella press, 1904. 2 p. l., v, 63 p. 27 cm. 5-1986
I. Title.

EDMOND, Amanda M. (Corey) Mrs. 1824-1862.
Religious and other poems. By Amanda M. Edmond. Boston, Gould and Lincoln, 1872. 263 p. 19 1/2 cm. "Mrs. Amanda M. Edmond": p. 250-263. "Note of introduction" signed: J. E. "Introduction by S. F. Smith." [PS1568.E52] 25-1916
I. Title.

ELIOT, George, pseud. 25-4923
i.e. Marian Evans, afterwards Cross, 1819-1880.
The legend of Jubal and other poems, old and new; The Spanish gypsy; by George Eliot. New York, T. Y.Corwell & co. (189-) 356 p. 18 1/2 cm. Publisher's lettering: George Eliot's poems. [PR4666.L4 1830]
I. Title. II. Title: Spanish gypsy.

EMMONS, Charles Ashbury, 1840-
Incarnated and redemmed; or, Rocktown reveries, and other poems, by Chas A. Emmons. [Sedalia, Mo., Sedalia printing co., 1906] 227, [1] p. 21 cm. 6-43924
I. Title.

FAITH triumphant and others poems; a collection of inspirational poems. Minneapolis, T. S. Denison [c1956] 62p. 22cm.
I. Haglund, Otto Engelbert.

[FINN, Mary Paulina] Sister 1842-.
Sacred poems, by M.S. Pine [pseud.] ... Washington, D.C., Pub. for Georgetown visitation convent, 1924. 4 p. l., 7-320 p. front., plates, ports. 20 1/2cm. "First edition (1000)." [PS1672.F46] 25-3109
I. Title.

FITGERALD, Robert David, 1902- 220'.07
Of some country; 27 poems. With drawings by Sister Mary Corita. [Austin] University of Texas [c1963] 46 p. illus. 23 cm. (Tower series, no. 4) [PR6011.I85O4] 63-63491
I. Title. II. Series.

FRY, John, d.1775.
Select poems, containing religious epistles, &c. occasionally written on various subjects. To which is now added, The history of Elijah and Elisha. By John Fry. Stonington Port, Connecticut, Printed by Samuel Trumbull, 1800. iv, [5]-144 p. 16 cm. A 35
I. Title.

[FULLER, Richard Frederick] 1821-1869. 204
Visions in verse; or, Dreams of creation and redemption ... Boston, Lee and Shepard; [etc., etc.] 1864. 282 p. 18 cm. [PS1729.F34] 25-128031
I. Title.

GARNETT, Emmeline, 1924- comp. 808.815
Seasons; a cycle of verse. New York, Farrar [1966, c.1965] xvii, 235p. 20cm. (Bell bks.) [PN6110.R4G29] 66-14152 3.95
1. Religions poetry (Collections) I. Title.

GAVAN, Duffy Thomas, 1888- 811.5
... *Wayfarer for Christ,* by T. Gavan Duffy. St. Louis, Mo., The City house alumnae, Convent of the Sacred heart [c1939] 4 p. l., 11-66 p. 16 1/2 cm. (His The new Hope series) Verse. [BV2175.G32W3] [PS3513.A92W35 1939] [266.2] 40-6511
I. Title.

GILES, Charles, 1783-1867.
The triumph of truth; or, The vindication of divine Providence. A poem; in which philoisophy, theology, & description are combined. In fourteen books ... By Rev. Charles Giles. New York, Harper & brothers, printers, 1838. vii, [13]-276 p. front. (port.) 16 cm. Man's fall and redemption. [PS1744.G113 1838] 27-22262
I. Title.

GILES, Charles, 1783-1867.
The triumph of truth; or, The vindication of divine Providence. A poem; in which philosophy, theology, and description are combined. In fourteen books. By Rev. Charles Giles ... 2d ed., rev. and improved by the author. New York, Published by G. Lane & P. P. Sandford for the Methodist Episcopal church, 1843. 288 p. 16 cm. Man's fall and redemption. [PS1744.G113 1843] 27-22263
I. Title.

GOUDGE, Elizabeth, 1900- ed. 808.81
A book of comfort; an anthology. Illus. by Gloria Kamen. [1st American ed.] New York, Coward-McCann [1964] 384 p. illus. 23 cm. "Acknowledgments" (bibliographical): p. 7-12. [PN6110.R4G6 1964] 64-25767
1. Religious poetry. 2. Poetry. I. Title.

GREGORY, Horace, 1898- ed. 808.81
The Mentor book of religious verse, edited by Horace Gregory [and] Marya Zaturenska. [New York] New American Library [1957, c1956] 238p. 19cm. (A Mentor book, MD 189) [PN6110.R4G65] 57-6280
1. Religious poetry. I. Zaturenska, Marya, 1902- joint ed. II. Title.

GUTHRIE, Kenneth Sylvan.
Voices of prayer and praise; hymns and poems [by] Kenneth Sylvan Guthrie. New York, Theosophical publishing co.; [etc., etc., c1905] [208] p. 20 cm. 5-21458
I. Title.

HANSCOM, Beatrice. 2-23974
Love, laurels & laughter, by Beatrice Hanscom; with a frontispiece by William J. Hurlbut. New York, Frederick A. Stokes company [1902] xi, 156 p. front. 19 cm. Poems. [PS3515.A532L8 1902]
I. Title.

HARKNESS, Georgia Elma, 1891-
The glory of God; poems and prayers for devotional use. New York, Nashville, Abingdon Press [1963] 125 p. 16 cm. (Apex books, M4) 64-19768
I. Title.

HAYNES, Louise Marshall.
Through the church door, verses by Louise Marshall Haynes, pictures by Clara Atwood Fitts. Boston, Wright & Potter printing co., c1924. 53, [1] p. illus. 23 1/2 cm. [PZ8.3.H3336Th] 25-114
I. Title.

HILL, Caroline (Miles) 1866-1951, ed. 808.81'5
The world's great religious poetry. Westport, Conn., Greenwood Press [1973] xxxix, 836 p. 22 cm. Reprint of the 1938 ed. published by Macmillan, New York. [PN6110.R4H5 1973] 70-137058 ISBN 0-8371-5521-5
1. Religious poetry. I. Title.

HITCHCOCK, David, 1773-1849
The shade of Plato: or, A defence of religion, morality & government. A poem in four parts. By David Hitchcock. To which is prefixed a sketch of the author's life ... Hudson [N.Y.,] Printed at the Balance-press ... 1805. xvi, [17]-107 p. 15 1/2 cm. [PS1929.H83S5] 26-21939
I. Title.

HOFFMAN, Charles Fenno, 1806-1884.
The vigil of faith, and other poems. By Charles Fenno Hoffman. 4th ed. New York, Harper & brothers, 1845. vi, 7-164 p. 16 cm. [PS1934.V4 1845] 17-21091
I. Title.

IRONSIDE, Henry Allan, 1876-1951.
Poems and hymns of H. A. Ironside. Grand Rapids, Singspiration Inc., 1962. 32 p. 65-2412
1. Religious poetry. I. Title.

ISAACS, Evelyn 248.42
Inchristed men; spiritual nuggets and poems. New York, Exposition [c.1965] 80p. 21cm. 3.00
I. Title.

JUAN de la Cruz Saint, 1542-1591.
The poems of St. John of the Cross. Original Spanish texts and new English versions by John Frederick Nims. New York, Grove Press [1959] 147 p. 22 cm. (Evergreen original, E158) 64-52775
I. Nims, John Frederic, 1913- tr. II. Title. III. Series.

JUAN de la Cruz, Saint, 1542-1591. 248'.22'0924
The poems of St. John of the Cross. Original Spanish texts and English versions newly revised and rewritten by John Frederick Nims. With an essay, A lo divino, by Robert Graves. [Rev. ed.] New York, Grove Press [1968] 151 p. 21 cm. [PQ6400.J8A17 1968] 67-27891
I. Title.

KAUFFMAN, Donald T., comp. 808.81
The treasury of religious verse. New York, Pyramid [1966, c.1962] xii, 371p. 18cm. (N-1384) [PN6110.R4 K36] .95 pap.,
1. Religious poetry. 2. Religious poetry, English. 3. Religious poetry, American. I. Title.

[KEBLE, John] 1792-1866. 245.
Lyra innocentium; thoughts in verse on Christian children, their ways, and their privileges ... New York, Wiley and Putnam, 1846. xv, 360 p. 16 cm. [PR4839.K15L8 1846] 12-34895
1. Religious poetry. I. Title.

KEEGSTRA, Jean Connie, 1922- comp. 808.81
101 inspirational poems that cheer the soul, a compilation by Jean Connie Keegstra. Illustrated by Frances Elizabeths McNeil, Grand Rapids, Mich., Zondervan publishing house [1946] 7 p. l., 11-92 p. illus. 19 cm. [PN6110.R4K4] 46-8029
1. Religious poetry. I. Title.

KLOPSTOCK, Friedrich Gottlieb, 1724-1803.
The Messiah, attempted from the German of Mr. Klopstock, by Joseph Collyer ... New York, Printed by G. Forman for E. Duyckinck & co., 1795. xvi, [2], [19]-403 p. 17 cm. A prose translation of "Der Messias, i-xv. gesang", begun by Mary Collyer, and after her death completed by her husband, Jospeh Collyer. cf. Translator's pref. [PT2381.Z3C6] 18-1075
I. Collyer, Mary (Mitchell) Mrs. d. 1763, tr. II. Collyer, Joseph, d. 1776, tr. III. Title.

KNIFFIN, Evelyn Gage.
Guide-posts on the foot-path to peace; a book of religious verse, by Evelyn Gage Kniffin ... Brooklyn, N. Y., The author, 1910. x, 96 p. front. (port.) 17 cm. 10-29736 1.00
I. Title.

LLOYD, Marjorie Lewis. 269 243
Love on fire. Decorations by Iris Johnson. Washington Review and Herald Pub. Association [1952] 127 p. illus. 18 cm. Prose and poems. [PS3523.L67L6] 52-32440
I. Title.

LO! He is coming!
Awake and prepare! [1st ed.] New York, Pageant Press [c1958] 67p. 21cm. Poetry and prose.
I. Jeffers, Merritt J

MCGOVERN, Margaret. 29-21598
The lost year, by Margaret McGovern; with a foreword by Rollo Walter Brown. New York, Conward-McCann, inc., 1929. xiii, 95 p. 19 1/2 cm. Poems. [PS3525.A239L6 1929]
I. Title.

MACK, Alexander, 1712-1803.
The religious poetry of Alexander Mack, jr. [ed. and tr. by] Samuel B. Heckman ... Elgin, Ill., Brethren publishing house, 1912. 268 p. 20 1/2 cm. German and English on opposite pages. Works consulted: p. 268. [PS793.M3 1912] 12-12004
I. Heckman, Samuel B., 1870- ed. and tr. II. Title.

MANIKKA-VACAGAR.
The Tiruvacagam; or, 'Sacred utterances' of the Tamil poet, saint, and sage Manikka-Vacagar; the Tamil text of the fifty-one poems, with English translation, introductions, and notes, to which is prefixed a summary of the life and legends of the sage, with appendices illustrating the great South-Indian system of philosophy and religion called the Caiva Siddhantam; with Tamil lexicon and concordance, by the Rev. G. U. Pope... Oxford, Clarendon press, 1900. 1 p. l., xcvii p., 1 l., 354 p., 1 l., 84 p. 25 cm. Added t.-p. in Tamil. "...Presented in substance to the members of the Victoria philosophical society ...and printed by them...Now reprinted in a considerably enlarged form..." 3-7859
I. Pope, George Uglow, 1820-1908, ed. II. Title.
Contents omitted.

MARTIN, Ellen.
Faith walks with me. Dexter, Mo., Candor Press [c1967] 32 p. 21 cm. Poems. 68-95518
I. Title.

MARTIN, Philip Montague.
Mastery and mercy; a study of two religious poems: The wreck of the Deutschland by G. M. Hopkins and Ash Wednesday by T. S. Eliot. London, Oxford University Press, 1957. 149p.
I. Title.

MARVIN, Dwight Edwards, 1851- 811.5
Knowing God, a collection of religious poems, by Dwight Edwards Marvin. New York, Trinity press, 1931. 7 p. l., 168, [5] p. 20 cm. [PS3525.A773K6 1931] [245] 31-19110
I. Title.

MERRICK, James, 1720-1769.
Poems on sacred subjects. Viz., The benedicite, paraphrased. The Lord's prayer, paraphrased ... &c. By James Merrick ... Oxford, The Clarendon press, sold by R. and J. Dodsley, London, 1763. 1 p. l., 30 p. 27 cm. Signatures: 1 leaf (t.-p.) unsigned; A-C;D. [PR3548.M75 1763] 27-8518
I. Title.

MITCHELL, Silas Weir, 1829-1914.
A psalm of deaths and other poems, by S. Weir Mitchell ... Boston and New York, Houghton, Mifflin and company, 1890. 3 p. l., 70 p. 22 1/2 cm. [PS2414.P7] 24-18235
I. Title.

MONTGOMERY, James, 1771-1854.
Sacred poems and hymns, for public and private devotion, by James Montgomery ... With the author's latest corrections, and an introduction by John Holland. New York, D. Appleton and company, 1854. lvi, 390 p. 19 cm. [PR5032.S2 1854] 16-23910
I. Holland, John, 1794-1872. II. Title.

MOREHOUSE, Carrie Warner, Mrs.
...Legend of Psyche, and other verses. Holiday ed. St. Johnsbury [Vt.] C. T. Walter, 1889. 2 p. l., [7]-98 p. 18 x 14 1/2 cm. [PS2433.M25] 24-7036
I. Title.

MORGAN, Angela.
God prays. Answer, world! Two poems by Angela Morgan... New York, The Baker & Taylor company, 1917. 4-24, [1] p. 16 cm. A 20
I. Title.

MORRISON, James Dalton, 1893- ed. 808.81
Masterpieces of religious verse. [1st ed.] New York, Harper [1948] xiv, 706 p. 27 cm. [PN6110.R4M6] 48-8937
1. Religious poetry. I. Title.

MULLER, Albert Arney.
Gospel melodies, and other occasional poems. By the Rev. Albert A. Muller ... Charleston, J. R. Schenck, 1823. viii p., 1 l., [7]-104 p. 20 cm. In original boards. [PS2448.M6] 24-21721
I. Title.

NEIHARDT, J[ohn] G[neisenau]
The divine enchantment; a mystical poem, by J. G. Neihardt. New York, J. T. White & co., 1900. 46 pp. 19 cm. 2-4684
I. Title.

NEIHARDT, J[ohn] G[neisenau]
The divine enchantment; a mystical poem, by J. G. Neihardt. New York, J. T. White & co., 1900. 46 pp. 19 cm. 2-4684
I. Title.

OLDS, Barbara Moses, ed. 808.81
Favorite poems faith and confort, edited by Barbara Moses Olds. New York, Triangle books [1942] 320 p. 20 cm. [PN6110.R4O5] 42-7555
1. Religious poetry. I. Title.

OLDS, Barbara Moses, ed. 808.81
Favorite poems of faith and comfort. Garden City, N. Y., Garden City Pub. Co. [1947] 320 p. 21 cm. [PN6110.R4O5 1947] 48-2404
1. Religious poetry. I. Title.

PALM, Edith Cling. JUV
Little folks' hour, stories and poems for children, by Edith Cling Palm... Rock Island, Ill., Augustana book concern [c1931] 40 p. front., illus. 21 1/2 cm. [PZ7.P1802Li] 244 31-30612
I. Title.

PALMER, Ray, 1808-1887.
Hymns and sacred pieces, with miscellaneous poems... By Ray Palmer. New York, A. D. F. Randolph, 1865. ix, [7]-195 p. 19 cm. [PS2519.P6H7 1865] 24-15563
I. Title.

PALMER, Ray, 1808-1887.
The spirit's life; a poem; delivered before the Literary fraternity, Waterville college, and the Porter rhetorical society, Theological seminary, Andover, at their anniversaries, August and September, 1837. By Rev. Ray Palmer. Boston, Whipple and Damrell, 1837. 16 p. 22 cm. [PS2519.P6S6 1837] 24-30048
I. Title.

PARR, Margaret S Linn comp.
God; and other poems, tr. by Sir John Bowring, comp. by Margaret S. LinnParr. Boston, R. G. Badger [c1912] 96 p. 20 cm. Mostly translation from the Russian. "Biographical notes: Lomonosov, Derzhaven, Zhukovsky, Rogdanovich": p. 76-96. 12-18148
I. Bowring, John, Sir 1792-1872, tr. II. Title.

PEGUY, Charles Pierre, 1873-1914.
God speaks; religious poetry. Translation and introduction by Julian Green. [New York] Pantheon [1965, 1945] 82 p. At head of title: Charles Peguy. "The whole text is quoted from Charles Peguy's 'Cahiers de la quinzaine', Paris 1900-1914." - Editor's note. "Sources": leaf at end. 66-33069
I. Green, Julian, 1900- ed. and tr. II. Cahiers de la quinzaine. III. Title.

PERKINS, R. L. 1863-
Shadows of poetry ... Containing a collection of sacred poems, hymns, acrostics, etc. Written by R. L. Perkins ... Pensacola, Fa., Florida sentinel publishing co., 1896. 2 pt. in 1 v. incl. 1 illus., 3 port. 18 cm. Paged continuously. [PS2544.P76S5] 24-17854
I. Title.

PHELPS, Samuel Merrick, 1770-1841.
The triumphs of devine grace, a poem in three parts. By Samuel M. Phelps, A. M. Part i. The history of a penitent sinner. Part ii. A description of the millennial reign of Jesus Christ on earth, by a converted Israelite. To which are added promiscuous pieces, by Harriette E. Phelps. New York, Craighead and Allen, printers, 1835. 2 p. l., [7]-132 p. 19 cm. [PS2558.P3] 24-18678
I. Gilbert, Harriette Eliza (Phelps) Mrs. II. Title.

PIERCE, David Rand, 1869-
The heavenly pilgrim, and other poems, by Rev. D. Rand Pierce ... 40th anniversary ed. Fitchburg, Mass., The author, 1909. 114 p. front. (port.) illus. 19 1/2 cm. $1.00 10-2563
I. Title.

PIERSON, Johnson.
The Judaid; a poem detailing the rise and decline of the Jews from the exodus from Egypt to the destruction of their temple by the Romans. St. Louis, Printed by D. Davies, 1844. ix, 248 p. 19 cm. [PS2584.P78J5] 50-50653
I. Title.

PREUSS, Henry Clay.
... God save our noble Union! and other poems for the times; also, Metropolitan notes of men and things at Washington, and A reply to charges of disloyalty by the Potter investigating committee. By H. Clay Preuss ... [Washington, D. C., c1862] 8 p. 24 cm. Caption title. [PS2664.P15G6] 16-19999
I. Title.

RAY, Randolph, 1886- ed. 808.81
100 great religious poems. [1st ed.] Cleveland, World Pub. Co. [1951] 160 p. 20 cm. [PN6110.R4R39] 51-12039
1. Religious poetry. I. Title.

RAY, Randolph, 1886- ed. 808.81'9'3
100 great religious poems. Freeport, N.Y., Books for Libraries Press [1969, c1951] 160 p. 21 cm. (Granger index reprint series) [PN6110.R4R39 1969] 78-80378
1. Religious poetry. I. Title.

RINEER, Harriet Snyder. Mrs. 811.5
The hand of a child and other poems ... by Harriet Synder Rineer. Lancaster, Pa., 1932. 2 p. l., iii-v, 69 p. 21 cm. [PS3535.I716H3 1932] 245.2 32-35904
I. Title.

ROBERTSON, William. Rev.
Sacred harmony; or Council of peace. A divine poem, in two books. By Rev. William Robertson. 2d ed. New York, Printed at the Greenwich printing office, 1831. 36 p. 18 cm. [PS2719.R39S3 1831] 24-12065
I. Title.

ROBINSON, Phinehas, d.,1871.
Immortaility: a poem, in ten cantos ... By Rev. Phinehas Robinson ... New-York, Leavitt, Trow & company, 1846. 411, [1] p. 20 cm. [PS2719.R67] 1-2744
I. Title.

ROWE, M. F. Mrs.
The Master's messenger; or, Gospel truths in rhyme. Collection of spiritual songs and short poems, principally devoted to the subject of scriptural holiness. By Mrs. M. F. Rowe ... San Francisco, J. Winterburn & co., printers, 1884. 97 p. 18 cm. Introduction signed: M. D. Buck. [PS2735.R7] 30-7579
I. Title. II. Title: Gospel truths in rhyme.

SANBURN, Isabella.
The touch of the Master's hand; religious poetry. [1st ed.] New York, Vantage Press [c1967] 64 p. 21 cm. 68-71364
I. Title.

SCHAFF, Philip, 1819-1893, ed. 808.81
A library of religious poetry; a collection of the best poems of all ages and tongues, with biographical and literary notes. Ed. by Philip Schaff ... and Arthur Gilman ... New York [etc.] Funk & Wagnalls company [c1889] xxxi, [1], 1004 p. 13 port. (incl. front.) 26 cm. First edition, 1881. [PN6110.R4S2 1889] 4-5613
1. Religious poetry. I. Gilman, Arthur, 1837-1909, joint ed. II. Title.

[SCUDDER, Eliza] 1821-1896.
Hymns and sonnets, by E. S. Boston, Lockwood, Brooks, and company, 1880. vi p., 1 l., 50 p. 14 cm. [PS2794.S5 1880] 20-10792
I. Title.

SCUDDER, Eliza, 1821-1896.
Hymns and sonnets, by Eliza Scudder. Boston and New York, Houghton, Mifflin and company, 1896. xxiii p., 1 l., 54 p. 19 cm. [PS2794.S5 1896] 12-38487
I. Title.

SELECT poems for the silent hour. 245.2
Chicago, New York [etc.] Fleming H. Revell company [1895] 125 p. 19 cm. Edited by Arthur P. Fitt. [PN6110.R4S3] 31-1029
1. Religious poetry. I. Fitt, Arthur Percy, ed.

SHIPPEY, Josiah, b.1778.
Specimens; or Leisure hours poetically

employed on various subjects; moral, political & religious ... By Josiah Shippey, A.B. With notes critical and explanatory; also, A brief history of the life of the author, from the year 1778 to the year 1841; to which is added a Synopsis of all the parts of learning. By Samuel Johnson ... New-York, Printed by J. B. Allee, 1841. 1 p. l., [ix]-xi, [13]-238 p. 19 cm. "Subscribers' names": p. [285]-238. [PS2826.S325S4] 30-11995
I. Johnson, Samuel, 1696-1772. II. Title.

SIEBENMANN, Paul J
Songs of the soul; poems for pastors and Christian workers. [1st ed.] New York, Vantage Press [c1963] 95 p. 21 cm. 66-52342
I. Title.

SLOANE, James Robinson, 1857- comp.
Golden gleanings to comfort the afflicted and help the toiler; select poems, quotations, verses, comp.by James R. Sloane. Minneapolis, The Western architect, 1908. vi, [7]-78 p. 17 1/2 cm. 8-37717
I. Title.

SLOANE, James Robinson, 1857- comp.
Golden gleanings to comfort the afflicted and help the toiler; select poems, quotations, verses, comp.by James R. Sloane. Minneapolis, The Western architect, 1908. vi, [7]-78 p. 17 1/2 cm. 8-37717
I. Title.

SMITH, Mary (Riley) Mrs., 1842?- 245.
Tired mothers, by May Riley Smith... New York, A. D. F. Randolph & company, 1887. 6 numb. l. 9 x 11 1/2 cm. Printed on one side of leaf only. In verso. [Full name: Mrs. Mary Louise (Riley) Smith] [PS2869.S3T5 1887] 30-19357
I. Title.

SONGS of deliverance.
London, New York [etc.] Longmans, Green and co., 1923. vii, 92 p. 19 1/2 cm. $1.75. [PR6000.A1S6] 24-150
1. Religious poetry.

STICKNEY, Henry Elmer.
The holy flower, by Henry Elmer Stickney. New York, The Walter Morris publishing company, 1890. [21] p. illus. 28 1/2 cm. Illustrated covers. In verse. 30-28378
I. Title.

STICKNEY, Henry Elmer.
The holy flower, by Henry Elmer Stickney. New York, The Walter Morris publishing company, 1890. [21] p. illus. 28 1/2 cm. Illustrated covers. In verse. 30-28378
I. Title.

STRYKER, Peter, 1826-1900.
Words of comfort, By Rev. Peter Stryker, D.D. ... New York, G. L. Shearer, [1893] 96 p. front. (port.) 19 cm. Religious verse. [PS2959.B65] 31-2640
I. Title.

TAYLOR, Emily, 1795-1872, comp.
Sabbath recreations; or, Select poetry of a religious kind, chiefly taken from the works of modern poets; with original pieces never before published. By Miss Emily Taylor. First American ed.; in which many pieces have been withdrawn from the English copy, and others substituted, by John Pierpont. Boston, Bowles & Dearborn, 1829. x, 278 p. 14 1/2 cm. [DN6110.R4T3 1829] 3-20158
1. Religious poetry. I. Pierpont, John, 1785-1866, ed. II. Title.

THOMPSON, Edward John, 1886- comp. 808.81
O world invisible; anthology of religious poetry, compiled by Edward Thompson. New York, E. P. Dutton & co., inc. [c1932] vii, 135, [1] p. 21 1/2 cm. "First edition." "Notes": p. 123-130. [PN6110.R4T67] [245] 32-5740
1. Religious poetry. I. Title.

THORNE, J[ohn] J[ulius] 1871-
Humble hours of solitude. Poems by J. J. Thorne... Wilson, N.C., P. D. Gold publishing co., 1904. x, [1],-198 p. 22 cm. 4-14133
I. Title.

TILTON, Theodore, 1835-1907.
The true church. By Theodore Tilton. Illustrated from designs by Granville Perkins. Philadelphia, J. B. Lippincott & co., 1867. 3 p. l., [9] p. 1 illus., 8 col. pl. 23 1/2 cm. Poem. [PS3069.T5T7 1867] 31-16747
I. Perkins, Granville, illus. II. Title.

UNDERHILL, Evelyn, 1875-
Immanence: a book of verses, by Evelyn Underhill. London, J. M. Dent & sons, ltd.; New York, E. P. Dutton & co. [c1914] x. 83 p. 19 cm. A 14
I. Title.

[WADE, George N.]
Dominion rhymes. Malden [Mass.?] E. B. Blen & co., printers, 1882. 106, [1] p. 16 1/2 cm. Poems. [PS3129.W295D6] 31-21602
I. Title.

WALLIS, Charles Langworthy, 1921- comp. 242
Holy Holy Land; a devotional anthology, edited by Charles L. Wallis. Photos. by Archie Lieberman. [1st ed.] New York, Harper & Row [1969] 224 p. illus. 29 cm. [BS483.5.W3] 79-85046
1. Bible—Meditations. 2. Bible—Devotional literature. 3. Religious poetry. I. Lieberman, Archie, illus. II. Title.

WELLS, Amos R[ussel] 1862-
Just to help; some poems for every day. Boston & Chicago, United society of Christian endeavor [1900] 45 p. front. 12 degree. 0-5855
I. Title.

WESLEY, Charles, 1707-1788. 245
Sacred poetry. Selected from the works of the Rev. Charles Wesley ... edited by a lay member of the Protestant Episcopal church ... New-York, D. Appleton & co., 1864 xxii, 465, xiii p., 1 l., [483]-709 p. 20 cm. "Selections from a poetical version of the Psalms of David ... ": p. i-xiii, 1 l., p. [483] -595. [PR3763.W4A6 1864] 32-19992
1. Religious poetry. I. Title.

WHEELER, Glen, comp. 808.88
1010 illustrations, poems and quotes Cincinnati, Standard Pub. [1967] 288 p. 24 cm. [PN6110.R4W46] 67-9537
1. Religious poetry. 2. Quotations, English. I. Title.

WHEELER, Glen, comp. 808.88
1010 illustrations, poems, and quotes. Cincinnati, Standard Pub, [1967] 288 p. 24 cm. [PN6110.R4W46] 67-9537
1. Religious poetry. 2. Quotations, English. I. Title.

WILD, Laura Hulda, 1870- comp. 808.81
Meditations. suggested by Biblical and other poetry [by] Laura H. Wild. New York, Cincinnati [etc.] The Abingdon press [c1937] 150 p. 17 1/2 cm. Selections from the Bible and from religious poems. [PN6110.R4W5] 37-11132
1. Religious poetry. 2. Nature in poetry. 3. Nature in the Bible. 4. Poetry—Collections. I. Bible. English. Selections. 1937. II. Title.

WILKERSON, Pauline DeGarmo.
The window of prayer, and other poems. [1st ed.] New York, Exposition Press [c1962] 72 p. 21 cm. 67-25935
I. Title.

WILKERSON, Pauline DeGarmo.
The window of prayer, and other poems. [1st ed.] New York, Exposition Press [c1962] 72 p. 21 cm. 67-25935
I. Title.

WILKINSON, William Cleaver, 1833-
The epic of Moses, a poem in two parts... [by] William Cleaver Wilkinson... New York and London, Funk & Wagnalls company [c1910?] 2 v. front. (port.) 21 1/2 cm. Contents.--i. The exodus.--ii. The wandering in the wilderness. 10-24050
I. Title.

WOODS, Ralph Louis, 1904- ed. 808.81
Poems of prayer. [1st ed.] New York, Hawthorn Books [1962] 287 p. 24 cm. [PN6110.R4W75] 62-10888
1. Religious poetry. I. Title.

Religious poetry, American.

BROUGHTON, James Richard, 1913- 222
Tidings, [poems at the land's edge] San Francisco, Pearce & Bennett [c1965] 57 p. 25 cm. "500 copies" [PS3503.R759T5] 65-28768
I. Title.

BURROUGHS, Charles, 1787-1868.
The poetry of religion, and other poems. By Rev. Charles Burroughs ... Printed for private circulation. Boston, Ticknor, Reed & Fields, 1851. 101 p. 18 cm. [PS1219.B8P6 1851] 21-17425
I. Title.

CARNEY, William Harrison Bruce, 1870- ed.
Lutheran lyrics; an anthology of aesthetic, moral and religious poems for use in church and house. Edited and compiled by W. H. Bruce Carney ... with the co-operation of Harry Tennyson Domer ... [and] W. H. Greever ... Philadelphia, Pa., The United Lutheran publication house [c1938] 279 p. 21 cm. A 40
1. Religious poetry, American. I. Domer, Harry Tennyson, joint ed. II. Greever, Walton Harlowe, 1870- joint ed. III. Title.

DAVIDSON, Alice Joyce. 811'.54
Reflections of love / Alice Joyce Davidson. Old Tappan, N.J. : F.H. Revell, 1982, c1983. 128 p. : ill. (some col.) ; 27 cm. [PS3554.A922R4 1983] 19 82-10211 ISBN 0-8007-1327-3 : 10.95
1. Religious poetry, American. I. Title.

DE FLEURY, Maria.
Divine poems and essays, on various subjects. In two parts. By Maria De Fleury ... New-York; Printed and sold by Dears and Andrews, 12, cedar-street, 1804. x p., 1 l., [13]-288 p. 18 cm. "Eternal love: an ode, by Richard Lee": p. [263]-275. Recommendatory preface signed: John Towers, Clerkenwell. [PR4526.D37D5] 22-9815
I. Lee, Richard. II. Title.

DE FLEURY, Maria.
Divine poems and essays, on various subjects. In two parts. By Maria De Fleury ... New-York; Printed and sold by Dears and Andrews, 12, cedar-street, 1804. x p., 1 l., [13]-288 p. 18 cm. "Eternal love: an ode, by Richard Lee": p. [263]-275. Recommendatory preface signed: John Towers, Clerkenwell. [PR4526.D37D5] 22-9815
I. Lee, Richard. II. Title.

[DE WITT, Susan (Linn) Mrs.] 1778-1824.
The pleasures of religion; a poem ... New-York; Published by Wiley and Halsted. C. S. Van Winkle, printer, 1820. 72 p. 15 cm. [PS1537.D4] 24-24132
I. Title.

FURMAN, Charles Edwin, 1801- 1880. 204
Home scenes. Divine songs, and other poems, by the Rev. C. E. Furman, A. M. Rochester [N. Y.] E. Darrow, 1874. 156 p. 19 cm. [PS1729.F7]
I. Title.

HILLER, Oliver Prescott, 1814- 1870.
The pleasures of religion, a poem: in two parts. With other poems. By O. Prescott Hiller. London, W. White; Boston, O. Clapp, 1856. vi p., 1 l., 136 p. 18 cm. [Name originally: Thomas Oliver Prescott] [PS1929.H672] 26-21929
I. Title.

THE hymn of hate and The law of love... Poems. Emory University Station, Atlanta, Banner Press [1960?] 66p. 21cm. 'A Banner book.' 'Based in part upon 'The tide of time' with additional material.'
I. Neff, Lawrence Wilson, 1879- II. Title: The law of love.

HYMNS to St. Geryon, and other poems. San Francisco, Auerhahn Press, 1959. 54p.
I. McClure, Michael.

LEE, William James.
Poems. Adrift and anchored. By Rev. William J. Lee. Kansas City, Mo., Ramsey, Millett & Hudson, 1875. v, [7]-304 p. front. 20 cm. [PS2236.L35] 28-2220
I. Title.

LEE, William James.
Poems. Adrift and anchored. By Rev. William J. Lee. Kansas City, Mo., Ramsey, Millett & Hudson, 1875. v, [7]-304 p. front. 20 cm. [PS2236.L35] 28-2220
I. Title.

LORBEER, Floyd Irving.
Religious poems for an age of science, especially written for those who are searching for a better integration of science and religion than that which prevails at the present time. Lancaster, Calif., Laurel Foundation [1966] 92 p. 21 cm. 68-73462
1. Religious poetry, American. 2. Science—Poetry. I. Title.

NEVE, Frederick William, 1855- 811.5
The house of God and the child, and other poems, by Frederick W. Neve ... Richmond, Va., Richmond press, inc., 1930. 2 p. l., [3]-62 p. pl. 20 cm. [PS3527.E74H6 1930] 245 30-21759
I. Title.

NIELD, Thomas, 1834-1913.
The human brotherhood and a Psalm of faith. Two poems. By ThomasNield. Indianapolis, Ind., The Church at work pub. co. [c1888] 165 p. 18 cm. [PS2466.N3H8] 24-9067
I. Title.

NIENDORFF, John.
Divine adventures; a book of verse, by John Niendorff. Boston, R. G. Badger, 1907. 70 p. 20 cm. 7-22086
I. Title.

NIENDORFF, John.
Divine adventures; a book of verse, by John Niendorff. Boston, R. G. Badger, 1907. 70 p. 20 cm. 7-22086
I. Title.

PERCY, Frances Coan. Mrs.
An illuminated way, and other poems, by Frances Coan Percy. Boston, R. G. Badger, 1907. 5 p. l., 9-123 p. 20 cm. [PS353.E36 I 6 1907] 8-249
I. Title.

PIKE, Albert, 1809-1891.
Hymns to the gods, and other poems, by Gen. Albert Pike, ed. by Mrs. Lilian Pike Roome ... Little Rock, Ark., F. W. Allsopp, 1916. 269 p. plates. 20 1/2 cm. [PS2585.H8 1916] 16-24598
I. Roome, Mrs. Lilian (Pike) ed. II. Title.

POMFRET, John, 1667-1702.
Poems upon several occasions By the Reverend Mr. John Pomfret. Viz. i. The choice. ii. Love triumphant over reason. iii. Cruelty and lust. iv. On the divine attributes. v. A prospect of death. vi. On the conflagration and last judgment. The eleventh edition, corrected. With some account of his life and writings. To which are added, his Remains. Boston: Reprinted and Sold by Zechariah Fowle in Queen-Street, 1751. viii, 136 p. 17 cm. "Some account of Mr. Pomfret, and his writings" (p. 119-123) signed: Philalethes. [PR3619.P7 1751] 28-17218
I. Title.

POMFRET, John, 1667-1702.
Poems upon several occasions. By the Reverend Mr. John Pomfret. Viz: i. The choice. ii. Love triumphant over reason. iii. Cruelty and lust. iv. On the divine attributes. v. A prospect of death. vi. On the conflagration, and last judgment. The 12th ed., cor. With some account of his life and writings. To which are added, his remains. London, Printed: New York, Reprinted by Hugh Gaine, at the Bible, in Hanover-Square, 1785. vi, 98, iv, 12 p., 1 l. 17 cm. Catalogue of books, &c sold by Hugh Gaine": [3]-10, [2] p., at end. "Some account of Mr. Pomfret, and his writings" signed: Philalethes. [PB3619.P7 1785] 6-30060
I. Title.

POMFRET, John, 1667-1702.
Poems upon several occasions, by the Reverend Mr. John Pomfret. To which are added, his remains, with some account of his life and writings. From an accurate London ed. Philadelphia, Printed and sold

by Parry Hall, no. 149 Chestnut street, 1791. 1 p. l., [v]-x, [11]-158 p., 1 l. 14 cm. "The life of Mr. John Pomfret" signed: Philalethea. Extra illustrated; woodcuts mounted also on fly-leaves, end-papers and covers. [PR3619.P7 1791] 19-11407
I. Title.

POMFRET, John, 1667-1702.
Poems upon several occasions, by the Reverend Mr. John Pomfret. To which are added, his remains, with some account of his life and writings. From an accurate London edition. Boston, Printed by Samuel Etheridge, and sold by the booksellers, 1794. vii, [9]-158 p., 1 l. 14 cm. [PR3619.P] A 33
I. Title.

RICHARDSON, Charlotte (Smith) Mrs., 1775-1850?
Poems written on different occasions, by Charlotte Richardson. To which is prefixed some account of the author, together with the reasons which have led to their publication. By Catherine Cappe. Philadelphia: Printed and sold by Kimber, Conrad, & co. no. 93, Market street, and no. 170, South second street, 1806. xxii, [23]-125, [2] p. 19 1/2 x 11 cm. [Full name: Mrs. Charlotte Caroline (Smith) Richardson] [PR5226.R25P6] 30-998
I. Cappe, Mrs. Catherine (Harrison) 1744-1821, ed. II. Title.

RUSSELL, John X.
Romocanto; an original poem in honor of the "American federation of Catholic societies" ... by John X. Russell. [Milwaukee, The Standard printing co., c1915] 32 p. 17 cm. 15-14844 0.10
I. Title.

SHAW, John K.
Poems on religious subjects. By John K. Shaw ... New York, Printed for the author, 1821. 107, [1] p. 15 cm. [PS2809.S33] 30-13026
I. Title.

SHEPARD, Isaac Fitzgerald, 1816-1889.
Poetry of feeling, and spiritual melodies. By Isaac F. Shepard. Boston, Lewis and Sampson, 1844. vii, [8]-128 p. 11 1/2 cm. [PS2809.S575P6] 30-13039
I. Title.

SMITH, Benjamin. 245
Poems, moral and religious. By Benjamin Smith... Pittsburgh, 1842. 128 p. 18 1/2 cm. [PS2859.S46] 30-23843
I. Title.

[SMITH, Jane Luella (Dowd), 245. Mrs.] 1847-
Wayside leaves, by J. Luella Dowd... New York, G. P. Putnam's sons, 1879. vii, 201 p. 17 1/2 cm. Poems. Preface signed: J. L. D. S. [PS2869.S22W3] 22-17107
I. Title.

[TITTERINGTON, Sophie 245 (Bronson) Mrs.] 1846- comp.
Folded hands. "They also serve, who only stand and wait." New York, American tract society [c1878] 306 p. 17 cm. Poems. Prefatory note signed: S. B. T. [PR1191.F55] 20-13622
1. Religious poetry, American. 2. Religious poetry, English. I. Title.

UNITY School of Christianity.
Best-loved Unity poems; an anthology compiled from the Unity periodicals. Lee's Summit, Mo., 1956. 220 p. illus. 17 cm. "First published in 1946. ... Fourth printing." 66-94091
1. Religious poetry, American. I. Title.

VAILL, Joseph, 1751-1838.
Noah's flood: a poem. In two parts. Part I. Contains an historical account of the deluge, taken from the Bible; interspersed with conjectural observations. Part II. Is designed as a moral improvement of the subject. To which are added the following pieces in poetry, viz. Youth cautioned against vice. On happiness. A New Year's hymn ... By Joseph Vail, A.M., pastor of the Third church in East-Haddam. New-London: --Printed by Samuel Green. 1796. 28 p. 22 cm. [PS855.V3N6 1796] 24-8197
I. Title.

WATTS, Isaac, 1674-1748. 245
Horse lyricae. Poems, chiefly of the lyric kind, in three books. Sacred I. To devotion and piety. II. To virtue, honour and friendship. III. To the memory of the dead. By I. Watts, D.D. The 10th ed., cor. ... New York, Printed and sold by Hugh Gaine, 1762. xxiii, [1] 212, [4] p. 16 1/2 cm. [PR3763.W2A7 1762] 14-18231
I. Title.

WATTS, Isaac, 1674-1748. 245
Horse lyricae. Poems, chiefly of the lyric kind. In three books. Sacred I. To devotion and piety. II. To virtue, honour and friendship. III. To the memory of the dead. By I. Watts, D.D. The 12th ed., cor. Boston, Printed by Daniel Kneeland for Thomas Leverett, 1772. xxii, [12], 3-250, [4] p. 16 1/2 cm. [PR3763.W2A7 1772] 14-18232
I. Title.

WATTS, Isaac, 1674-1748. 245
Horse lyricae. Poems, chiefly of the lyric kind. In three books. Sacred. I. To devotion and piety. II. To virtue, honour, and friendship. III. To the memory of the dead. By I. Watts ... Boston, Printed by S. Hall for B. Larkin, J. White, D. West, and E. Larkin, 1790. xxxviii, 252 p. incl. front. (port.) 18 cm. [PR3763.W2A7 1790] 13-33887
I. Title.

WATTS, Isaac, 1674-1748. 245
Horse lyricae. Poems, chiefly of the lyric kind. In three books. Sacred I. To devotion and piety. II. To virtue, honour, and friendship. III. To the Memory of the dead. By I. Watts ... Exeter [N.H.] Printed by H. Ranlet, for I. Thomas and E. T. Andrews, Boston, 1795. xxii, [23]-204 p. 15 1/2 cm. [PR3763.W2A7 1795] 14-17392
I. Title.

WATTS, Isaac, 1674-1748. 245
Horse lyricae. Poems, chiefly of the lyric kind. In three books. Book I. Sacred to devotion and piety. Book II. To virtue, honor and friendship. Book III. To the memory of the dead. By Isaac Watts, D.D. ... Printed at Windham, (Connecticut) by John Byrne, M,DCC,XCVIII. xxi, [23]-208 p. 17 1/2 cm. [PR3763.W] A 34
I. Title.

WATTS, Isaac, 1674-1748. 245
Horse lyricae. Poems, chiefly of the lyric kind: in three books. Sacred I. To devotion and piety. II. To virtue, honour, and friendship. III. To the memory of the dead. By I. Watts... Haverhill, Printed by Galen H. Fay, for Angier March, bookseller. Newburyport, 1802. xxiv, [25]-287 p. 15 cm. [PR3763.W2A7 1802] 14-18234
I. Title.

WATTS, Isaac, 1674-1748. 245
Horse lyricae. Poems, chiefly of the lyric kind. In three books. Sacred I. To devotion and piety. II. To virtue, honor and friendship. III. To the memory of the dead. By Isaac Watts, D.D. ... Vergennes [Vt.] Published by Jepthah Shedd and co. Wright & Sibley, printers, 1813. 216 p. 17 cm. [PR3763.W] A 31
I. Title.

WATTS, Isaac, 1674-1748. 245
Horse lyricae, by Isaac Watts. To which are added the Divine songs and Moral songs, for children. With a life of the author, by Robert Southey. Boston, Little, Brown and company, 1864. cviii, 368 p. 17 cm. [British poets, ed. by F. J. Child] [PR3763.W2A7 1864] 15-7882
I. Southey, Robert, 1774-1843. II. Title.

WHEATLEY, Phillis, afterwards Phillis Peters, 1753?-1784.
Poems on various subjects, religious and moral. By Phillis Wheatley, negro servant to Mr. John Wheatley, of Boston, in New-England. Philadelphia: Printed by Joseph James, in Chesnut-street, 1787. 55, [2] p. 16 1/2 cm. Book plate: Thomas Hornsby, 1793. [PS866.W5 1787] 26-374
I. Title.

WHEATLEY, Phillis, afterwards Phillis Peters, 1753?-1784.
Poe[ms] on various su[bjects] religious and [moral] By Phillis Wheat[ley,] negro servant to Mr. John W[heatley,] of Boston, in New-England. Dedicated to the Countess of Huntingdon. Walpole, N.H., Printed for Thomas & Thomas, by David Newhall, 1802. 86 p. 15 cm. Signatures: B4, B-G6, leaf (contents) unsigned. Imperfect: p. 39-46 wanting; t.-p. mutilated, missing parts supplied from Heartman's Bibliography of Phillis Wheatley. [Ps866.W5 1802] 30-20913
I. Title.

WHEATLEY, Phillis, afterwards Phillis Peters, 1753?-1784.
Poems of various subjects, religious and moral. By Phillis Wheatley, negro servant to Mr. John Wheatley of Boston, in New-England. London, Printed, Philadelphia, Re-printed, and sold by Joseph Crukshank in Market-street, between Second and Third-streets, 1786. vi, [2], [9]-66, [2] p. 15 1/2 cm. [PS866.W5 1786] 26-376
I. Title.

WHEATLEY, Phillis, afterwards Phillis Peters, 1753?-1784.
Poems on various subjects, religious and moral. By Phillis Wheatley, Negro servant to Mr. John Wheatley, of Boston, in New England. London; Printed for A. Bell, bookseller, Aldgate; and sold by Messrs. Cox and Berry, King-street, Boston, MDCCLXXIII. v, [1] p., 1 l., [9]-124, [3] p. front. (port.) 17 1/2 cm. Signatures: (A)-Q4. [PS866.W5 1773] 30-20911
I. Title.

WHEATLEY, Phillis, afterwards Phillis Peters, 1753?-1784.
Poems on various subjects, religious and moral. By Phillis Wheatley, negro servant to Mr. John Wheatley, of Boston, in New-England. London: Printed. Philadelphia: Re-printed, and sold by Joseph Crukshank, in Market-street, between Second and Third-streets, 1789. vi, [2], [9]-66, [2] p. 16 1/2 cm. [PS866.W5 1789] 26-375
I. Title.

WHEATLEY, Phillis, afterwards Phillis Peters, 1753?-1784.
Poems on various subjects, religious and moral. By Phillis Wheatley, negro servant to Mr. John Wheatley, of Boston, in New-England. Albany; Re-printed, from the London edition, by Barber & Southwick, for Thomas Spencer, book-seller, Market-street, 1793. viii, 9-89, [3] p. 15 1/2 cm. Signatures: (A)-L4, M2. [PS866.W5 1793] 30-20912
I. Title.

WHEATLEY, Phillis, afterward Phillis Peters, 1753?-1784.
Poems on various subjects, religious and moral. By Phillis Wheatley, negro servant to Mr. John Wheatley, of Boston, in New England. With memoirs, by W. H. Jackson. Denver, Colo., W. H. Lawrence & co., 1887. 149 p. front. (port.) 17 1/2 cm. Includes sketches of Phillis Wheatley, Benjamin Banneker, Thomas Fuller and James Durham (p. 117-149) [PS866.W5 1887] 30-20916
I. Jackson, W. H. II. Title.

[WHEELER, Alfred] 1822-1903.
Immortality, or, The pilgrim's dream; and other poems... New-York, Saxton & Miles, 1844. 88 p. 22 cm. "Immortality, or, The pilgrim's dream, delivered on the...first anniversary of 'The New-York society of literature'...Jan. 11, 1844." [PS3165.W85] 31-30142
I. New-York society of literature. II. Title.

Religious poetry, Celtic.

GRAVES, Alfred Perceval, 1846-1931.
A Celtic psaltery, being mainly renderings in English verse from Irish & Welsh poetry, by Alfred Perceval Graves. New York, The F. A. Stokes company [1917] xvii, 176, [1] p. 20 cm. "Mainly consists of close and free translations from Irish, Scotch Gaelic, and Welsh poetry of a religious or serious character."--Pref. Printed in Great Britain. "Published in England by the Society for promoting Christiau knowledge ... London, 1917".--Note on verso of t.-p. Without music. [PB1100.G7] 18-26405
1. Religious poetry, Celtic. 2. Welsh poetry—Translations into English. 3. English poetry—Translations from Welsh. 4. Irish poetry—Translations into English. 5. English poetry—Translations from Irish. I. Title.
Contents omitted.

Religious poetry, English.

ARMSTRONG, Iscar Vance, 1876- comp.
Prayer poems, complied by O. V. and Helen Armstrong. New York, Abingdon Press [196? c1942] i v. NUC63
1. Religious poetry, English. I. Armstrong, Helen, joint comp. II. Title.

CLARK, Thomas Curtis, 821.06 1877- comp.
The golden book of faith; an anthology of verse, compiled by Thomas Curtis Clark. New York, R. R. Smith, inc., 1931. 5 p. l., 3-273 p. 19 1/2 cm. [PR1191.C553] 245.2 31-11938
1. Religious poetry, English. 2. Religious poetry, American. I. Title.

CLARK, Thomas Curtis, 821.0822 1877- comp.
The golden book of religious verse; the golden book of faith, compiled by Thomas Curtis Clark. Garden City, N.Y., Garden City publishing co., inc. [1937] 5 p. l., 3-273 p. 21 cm. Published also under title: The golden book of faith. [PR1191.C553 1937] 245.2 37-12092
1. Religious poetry, English. 2. Religious poetry, American. I. Title.

COMPER, Frances M M ed. 821.0822
Spiritual songs from English mss. of fourteenth to sixteenth centuries, edited by Frances M. M. Comper; with a preface by Herbert J. C. Grierson. London, Society for promoting Christian knowledge; New York, The Macmillan company [1936] xxii, 293, [1] p. 19 cm. "First published in 1936." [PR1191.C58] 245.2 37-5778
1. Religious poetry, English. 2. English poetry—Middle English (Modernized) I. Society for promoting Christian knowledge, London. II. Title.

DOUGHTY, William 821'.4'093 Lamplough.
Studies in religious poetry of the seventeenth century, by W. L. Doughty. Port Washington, N.Y., Kennikat Press [1969] xiv, 199 p. 18 cm. Reprint of the 1946 ed. Includes bibliographical references. [PR545.R4D6 1969] 68-26278
1. Religious poetry, English. 2. English poetry—Early modern, 1500-1700. I. Title. II. Title: Religious poetry of the seventeenth century.

GIBSON, H. S. 28-8669
A collection of miscellaneous poems, moral, religious, sentimental, and amusing. By H. S. Gibson ... Philadelphia, J. Crissy, 1834. iv, [5]-156 p. 18 x 10 cm. The author's "Vision of War," 1835 has half-title: Poems, by H. S. Gibson, vol. ii. The present volume probably is "vol. i." "List of subscribers": p. [153]-156. [PS1739.G56 1834]
I. Title.

GRIBBLE, Leonard R. ed. 821.08
The Jesus of the poets: an anthology selected and edited by Leonard R. Gribble ... New York, R. R. Smith, inc. [1930] 157 p. 17 cm. "First published October 1930." Printed in Great Britain. [PR1191.G67] 245.2 31-11088
1. Jesus Christ—Poetry. 2. Religious poetry, English. I. Title.

GRISWOLD, Rufus Wilmot, 245.2 1815-1857, ed.
The illustrated book of Christian ballads and other poems. Edited by Rev. Rufus W. Griswold. Philadelphia, Lindsay & Blakiston [1844] 1 p. l., 164 p. front., plates, 27 cm. Added t.-p. in colors; initials; title and text within ornamental borders. [PR1191.G68] 30-33063
1. Religious poetry, English. 2. English poetry (Collections) 3. Ballads, English. I. Title.

HILL, Caroline (Miles) 808.81 Mrs. 1866- ed.
The world's great religious poetry, edited by Caroline Miles Hill, PH. D. New York, The Macmillan company, 1938. xxxix p., 1 l., 836 p. 22 cm. "First edition published January 1923. New edition with corrections, June 1923. Reprinted ... September, 1938." [PN6110.R4H5 1938 a] 40-31228
1. Religious poetry, English. I. Title.

LEWIS, Clifford, 1909- comp. 808.81
235 precious poems, compiled by Cliffrod Lewis ... Grand Rapids, Mich., Zondervan publishing house [1946] 263 p. 20 cm. [Full name: John Clifford Lewis] [PN6110.R4L43] 47-15809
1. Religious poetry, English. I. Title.

NICHOLSON, Norman, 1914- ed.
An anthology of religious verse designed for the times, edited by Norman Nicholson. Harmondsworth, Middlesex, Eng., New York, Penquin books [1942] xii p., 1 l., 15-106 p. 1 l. illus. (port.) 18 cm. (Pelican books [A96]) "First published 1942." A 43
1. Religious poetry, English. I. Title.

[PEIRCE, Bradford Kinney] 1819-1889, comp. 821.0822
At the cross ... Cliftondale, Mass., Coates brothers [186-?] 1 p. l., v-xiv, 17-258 p. 16 cm. Poems. Preface signed: B. K. P. [i. e. Bradford Kinney Peirce] [PN6110.R4P4] 245.2 38-11292
1. Religious poetry, English. 2. Religious poetry, American. I. Title.

PRIME, Samuel Irenaeus, 1812-1885, comp. 808.81
Songs of the soul, gathered out of many lands and ages. By Samuel Irenaeus Prime ... [New York] New York observer [1873] viii, 661 p. 21 cm. [PN6110.R4P7] 35-29799
1. Religious poetry, English. I. Title.

[RANDOLPH, Anson Davies Fitz] 1820-1896, comp. 245
At the beautiful gate, and other religious poems. Comp. by the editor of "The changed cross"; "The shadow of the rock"; "The chamber of peace", etc. New York, A. D. F. Randolph & company, 1880. 176 p. 15 cm. [PR1191.R2] 14-7851
1. Religious poetry, English. I. Title.

[RANDOLPH, Anson Davies Fitz] 1820-1896, ed. 245
The chamber of peace, and other religious poems. Selected and edited by the compiler of "The changed cross", "The shadow of the rock", etc. ... New York, A. D. F. Randolph & co. [1874] 288 p. 15 cm. [PR1191.R23] 40-23517
1. Religious poetry, English. I. Title.

[RANDOLPH, Anson Davies Fitz] 1820-1896, comp. 245
The changed cross, and other religious poems. New and enl. ed. New-York, A. D. F. Randolph, 1866. 228 p. 14 cm. "Mainly waifs, gathered from magazines and newspapers."--p. [3] [PR1191.R24 1866] 28-19722
1. Religious poetry, English. I. Title.

[RANDOLPH, Anson Davies Fitz] 1820-1896, comp. 245
The changed cross, and other religious poems. New and enl. ed. New-York, A. D. F. Randolph, 1868. 228 p. 14 cm. "Mainly waifs, gathered from magazines and newspapers."--p. [3] [PR1191.R24 1868] 40-22288
1. Religious poetry, English. I. Title.

[RANDOLPH, Anson Davies Fitz] 1820-1896, comp. 245
The changed cross, and other religious poems. Philadelphia, H. Altemus [c1897] 2 p. l., iv, 5-192 p. front., pl. 16 cm. [PR1191.R24 1897 a] 98-455
1. Religious poetry, English. I. Title.

[RANDOLPH, Anson Davies Fitz] 1820-1896, comp. 245
The changed cross, and other religious poems. 2d enl. ed. New York, A. D. F. Randolph [1872] 288 p. 15 cm. 'Mainly waifs, gathered from magazines and newspapers." [PR1191.R24 1872] 13-7982
1. Religious poetry, English. I. Title.

RANDOLPH, Anson Davies Fitz, 1820-1896, comp. 245
The changed cross, and other religious poems, compiled by Anson D. F. Randolph. New York, A. D. F. Randolph co., 1897. 1 p. l., 5-288 p. 17 cm. [PR1191.R24 1897] 13-7992
1. Religious poetry, English. 2. Religious poetry, American. I. Title.

[RANDOLPH, Anson Davies Fitz] 1820-1896, comp. 821.0822
The changed cross, and The shadow of the rock. Religious poems selected from many sources. New York, A. D. F. Randolph & co. [1865] 3 p. l., [5]-228 p., 2 l., 7-224 p. 17 cm. [PR1191.R24 1865] 245.2 38-11298
1. Religious poetry, English. 2. Religious poetry, American. I. Title. II. Title: The shadow of the rock.

[RANDOLPH, Anson Davies Fitz] 1820-1896, comp. 245
The changed cross, and The shadow of the rock. Religious poems selected from many sources. New and enl. ed. New York, A. D. F. Randolph & co. [1872] 3 p. l., [5]-288, 288 p. 16 cm. [PR1191.R24 1872 a] 13-7983
1. Religious poetry, English. I. Title. II. Title: The shadow of the rock.

[RANDOLPH, Anson Davies Fitz] 1820-1896, comp. 821.0822
The changed cross, and The shadow of the rock. Religious poems selected from many sources. New and enl. ed. New York, A. D. F. Randolph & co. [1872] 3 p. l., [5]-288, 288 p. 16 cm. [PR1191.R24] [245.2] 13-7983
1. Religious poetry, English. 2. Religious poetry, American. I. Title. II. Title: The shadow of the rock.

[RANDOLPH, Anson Davies Fitz] 1820-1896, comp. 245
The shadow of the rock, and other religious poems. New York, A. D. F. Randolph, 1866. 224 p. 14 cm. "Designed as a companion-book to "The changed cross." [PR1191.R27 1866] 3-7981
1. Religious poetry, English. I. Title.

[RANDOLPH, Anson, Davies Fitz,] 1820-1896, comp. 245
The shadow of the rock, and other religious poems. New and enl. ed. New York, A. D. F. Randolph & co. [1872] 288 p. 15 cm. "Designed as a companion book to 'The changed cross'." [PR1191.R27 1872] 13-7991
1. Religious poetry, English. I. Title.

[RANDOLPH, Anson Davies Fitz] 1820-1896, comp. 245.2
Unto the desired haven, and other religious poems Compiled by the editor of "The changed cross" ... New York, A. D. F. Randloph & company, 1880. 174 p. 15 cm. [PR1191.R3] 31-20571
1. Religious poetry, English. I. Title.

SACRED gems from the English poets, Chaucer to Tennyson; with biographical notices of the authors ... New York, The American news co. [188-?] xvii, 411 p. 19 cm. [PR1191.S145] 20-16542 245
1. Religious poetry, English. 2. Hymns, English.

STEWART, George, 1892- ed. 821.08
Dedication; an anthology of the will of God, collected and edited by George Stewart ... New York, Association press, 1931. xxxvi, 142 p. 21 cm. Poems, with introductory discussion by the editor on "The will of God." [PR1191.S63] 245 31-17557
1. Religious poetry, English. 2. Religious poetry, American. 3. Providence and government of God. I. Title. II. Title: The will of God, An anthology of.

THOMAS, Ronald Stuart. ed. 808.81
The Penguin book of religious verse [Gloucester, Mass., P. Smith 1964, c.1963] 191p. 19cm. (Penguin poets. D66 rebound) 2.85
1. Religious poetry, English. 2. Religious poetry, American. I. Title.

THOMAS, Ronald Stuart, ed. 808.81
The Penguin book of religious verse. Baltimore, Penguin [c.1963] 191p. 19cm. (Penguin poets, D66) 63-3983 .85 pap.,
1. Religious poetry, English. 2. Religious poetry, American. I. Title.

[THOMPSON, Augustus Charles] 1812-1901, comp. 245.2
Songs in the night: or, Hymns for the sick and suffering ... Boston, B. Perkins, 1845. xvi, 271 p. 17 1/2 cm. [PN6110.R4T65 1845] 38-3468
1. Religious poetry, English. 2. Hymns, English. 3. Consolation—Poetry. I. Title.

TUTTLE, Emma (Rood) Mrs. 1839-
From soul to soul. By Emma Rood Tuttle. New York, M. L. Holbrook & co., 1890. x, [17]-222 p. front. (port.) 19 cm. Poems. Contains music. [PS3109.T56] 12-39557
I. Title.

WORDSWORTH, William, 1770-1850.
The Ecclesiastical sonnets of William Wordsworth; a critical edition by Abbie Findlay Potts. New Haven, Yale university press; [etc., etc.] 1922. x, 316 p. pl., facsims. 23 cm. (Half-title: Cornell studies in English ...) Thesis (PH.D.)--Cornell university, 1920. Bibliography: p. 305-307. [PR5866.P6] 23-5009
I. Potts, Abbie Findlay, ed. II. Title.

Religious poetry, English—18th century—History and criticism.

HORNING, Mary Eulogia, Sister. 821'.6'09
Evidences of romantic treatment of religious elements in late eighteenth-century minor poetry (1771-1800). New York, Haskell House Publishers, 1972. ix, 103 p. 23 cm. Thesis—Catholic University of America, 1932. Bibliography: p. 96-102. [PR575.R4H6 1972] 72-3719 ISBN 0-8383-1542-9
1. Religious poetry, English—18th century—History and criticism. 2. Romanticism—England. I. Title.

Religious poetry, English—Early modern, 1500-1700.

CATTERMOLE, Richard, 1795?-1858, ed. 821'.4'0803
Sacred poetry of the seventeenth century; including the whole of Giles Fletcher's Christ's victory and triumph, with copious selections from Spenser [and others] With an introductory essay and critical remarks by R. Cattermole. New York, B. Franklin [1969] 2 v. illus., port. 19 cm. (Burt Franklin research and source works series, 346) (Essays in literature and criticism, 24.) Reprint of the 1835 ed. [PR1191.C3 1969] 75-80223
1. Religious poetry, English—Early modern, 1500-1700. I. Fletcher, Giles, 1588?-1623. Christ's victory and triumph. II. Title.

Religious poetry, English—Early modern, 1500-1700—History.

ROSS, Malcolm Mackenzie. 821'.4'093
Poetry & dogma; the transfiguration of eucharistic symbols in seventeenth century English poetry. New York, Octagon Books, 1969 [c1954] xii, 256 p. 23 cm. Bibliographical footnotes. [PR545.R4R6 1969] 78-86284
1. Religious poetry, English—Early modern, 1500-1700—History. 2. Lord's Supper in literature. 3. Symbolism in literature. I. Title.

Religious poetry, English — History and criticism

KERR, Hugh Thomson, 1871-
The Gospel in modern poetry, by Hugh Thomson Kerr... New York, Chicago [etc.] Fleming H. Revell company [c1926] 187 p. 19 1/2 cm. [PR506.R4K4] 26-14939
1. Religious poetry, English—Hist. & crit. 2. Religious poetry, American—Hist. & crit. I. Title.

LEBOWITZ, Regina, ed.
John Donne and the metaphysical poets; analytic notes and reviews with critical commentary. New York, American R.D.M. Corp. [1964] 54 p. 21 cm. (Study master, 216) Bibliography: p. 53-54. 67-52244
1. Donne, John, 1573-1631. 2. Religious poetry, English — Hist. & crit. 3. English poetry — Early modern (to 1700) — Hist. & crit. I. Title.

MARTZ, Louis Lohr. 821.409
The paradise within; studies in Vaughan, Traherne, and Milton, by Louis L. Martz. New Haven, Yale University Press, 1964. xix, 217 p. col. illus., facsims. 21 cm. Bibliography: p. 203-205. [PR549.R4M316] 64-20926
1. Vaughan, Henry, 1622-1695. 2. Traherne, Thomas, d. 1674. 3. Milton, John, 1608-1674. 4. Religious poetry, English—History and criticism. I. Title.

Religious poetry, English—Middle English (1100-1500)—Bibliography.

BROWN, Carleton Fairchild, 1869-1941. 016.821'1'08031
A register of Middle English religious & didactic verse. Freeport, N.Y., Books for Libraries Press [1973] p. Reprint of the 1916-20 ed., issued in series: Bibliographical Society, London, publications. Contents.Contents.—pt. 1. List of manuscripts.—pt. 2. Index of first lines and index of subjects and titles. [Z2014.P7B772] 73-2885 ISBN 0-8369-7155-8
1. Religious poetry, English—Middle English (1100-1500)—Bibliography. 2. Didactic poetry, English—Bibliography. I. Title. II. Series: Bibliographical Society, London. Publication, 1916-20.

Religious poetry, Hebrew.

IBN Gabirol, Solomon ben Judah, ca.1021-ca.1058. 892.4'1'2
Selected religious poems of Solomon Ibn Gabirol. From a critical text edited by Israel Davidson. New York, Arno Press, 1973 [c1923] lix, 123, 123, [125]-247 p. 21 cm. (The Jewish people: history, religion, literature) Original title in Hebrew: Mahberet mi-shire kodesh. English and Hebrew. English translation by Israel Zangwill. Reprint of the ed. published by the Jewish Publication Society, Philadelphia, in series: The Schiff library of Jewish classics. [PJ5050.13M3 1973] 73-2210 22.00
1. Religious poetry, Hebrew. I. Zangwill, Israel, 1864-1926, tr. II. Title. III. Series. IV. Series: The Schiff library of Jewish classics.

Religious poetry—History and criticism

BURGESS, George, bp., 1809-1866.
The poets of religion. A poem, delivered before the House of convocation of Trinity college, in Christ church, Hartford, August 4, 1847. By the Rev. George Burgess...Published by the House of convocation. Hartford, Press of Case, Tiffany & Burnham, 1847. 27 p. 22 1/2 cm. [PS1206.B7P7 1847] 21-17409
1. Religious poetry—Hist. & crit. 2. Religious poetry, English—Hist. & crit. I. Title.

SAUNDERS, Frederick, 1807-1902.
Evenings with the sacred poets: a series of quiet talks about the singers and their songs. By Frederick Saunders ... Rev. and enl. New York, A. D. F. Randolph and company [1885] vi, [2] p., 1 l., [11]-574 p. 21 cm. [PN1385.S28] 11-20081
1. Religious poetry—Hist.& crit. I. Title.

Religious poetry, Latin.

DREVES, Guido Maria, 1854-1909, ed.
Hymnographi latini. Lateinische Hymnendichter des Mittelalters. Leipzig, 1905-1907. New York, Reprinted by Johnson Reprint Corporation, 1961. 2 v. 21 cm. (Analecta hymnica medii aevii, 48, 50) 63-9514
1. Religious poetry, Latin. 2. Hymns, Latin — Bio-bibliography. I. Title. II. Series.

Religious poetry, Latin—History and criticism

RABY, Frederic James Edward, 1888- 879.109
A history of Christian-Latin poetry from the beginnings to the close of the Middle Ages. 2d ed. Oxford, Clarendon Press, 1953. xii, 494p. 25cm. Bibliography: p.[461]-489. [PA8056.R3 1953] 53-4223
1. Religious poetry, Latin—Hist. & crit. 2. Latin poetry, Medieval and modern—Hist. & crit. I. Title. II. Title: Christian-Latin poetry.

RABY, Frederic James Edward, 1888-
A history of Christian-Latin poetry from the beginnings to the close of the middle ages, by F.J. E. Raby. Oxford, Clarendon press, 1927. xii, 491, [1] p. 26 cm. Bibliography: p. [461]-485. [PA8056.R3] 28-11851
1. Religious poetry, Latin—Hist. & crit. 2. Latin poetry, Medieval and modern—Hist. & crit. I. Title.

Religious text-books for children.

ADAMS, Katherine (Smith) 268.432
... *Now we are going to school;* an activity program in religious education for the first grade, by Katherine Smith Adams ... Louisville, Ky., The Cloister press [1938] 2 v. 19 1/2 cm. (Cloister series [of church school courses] Rev. Maurice Clarke, editor) [Full name: Katherine Carter (Smith) Adams] Contents.[v. 1] Parents and pupils book.--[v. 2] Teachers book. Includes bibliographies. [BV1545.A27] 43-19991
1. Religious text-books for children. I. Title.

Religious thought.

BEACH, Arthur Granville, 1870-
Endeavors after the spirit of religion, by Arthur G. Beach. Boston, Sherman, French & company, 1912. 2 p. l., 124 p. 19 1/2 cm. 12-16442
I. Title.

BLACK, Samuel Charles, 1869-
Plain answers to religious questions modern men are asking, by Samuel Charles Black ... with an introduction by Howard Agnew Johnston, D.D. Philadelphia, The Westminster press, 1910. 203 p. incl. front. (port.) 19 1/2 cm. $0.75 10-28033
I. Title.

BRASHER, John Lakin, 1868- 287
Reckoning with the eternals, and other themes, by Rev. John Lakin Brasher, D. D.; introduction by President Joseph Rev. John Owen ... University Park, Ial., John Fletcher college press [c1927] 144 p. 21 cm. [BX8333.B65R4] 27-16456
I. Title.

CHRISTIANITY and modern thought. Boston, American Unitarian association, 1873. 5 p. l., [3]-304 p. 20 cm. "Discourses ... delivered in Boston at Hollis street church ... during the winter of 1871-72."--Introd. Contents.The break between modern thought and ancient faith and worship. By Henry W. Bellows.--A true theology the basis of human progress. By James Freeman Clarke.--The rise and decline of the Romish church. By Athanase Coquerel, fils.--Selfhood and sacrifice. By Orville Dewey.--The relation of Jesus to the present age. By Charles Carroll Everett.--The mythicale element in the New Testament. By Frederic Henry Hedge.--The place of mind in nature and intuition in man. By James Martineau.--The relations of ethics and theology. By Andrew P. Peabody.--Christianity: what it is not and what it is. By G. Vance Smith.--The aim and hope of Jesus. By Oliver Stearns. 16-7479
I. Bellows, Henry Whitney, 1814-1882. II. Clarke, James Freeman, 1810-1883. III. Coquerel, Athanase Josue, 1820-1875. IV. Dewey, Orville, 1794-1882. V. Everett, Charles Carroll, 1829-1900. VI. Hedge, Frederic Henry, 1805-1890. VII. Martineau, James, 1805-1900. VIII. Peabody, Andrew Preston, 1811-1893. IX. Smith, George Vance, 1816-1902. X. Stearns, Oliver, 1807-1885.

CHRISTIANITY and modern thought. Boston, American Unitarian association, 1880. 5 p. l., [3]-304 p. 19 1/2 cm. Contents.Introduction.--Break between modern thought and ancient faith and worship, by Henry W. Bellows.--A true theology the basis of human progress, by James Freeman Clarke.--The rise and decline of the Romish church, by Athanase Coquerel, fils.--Selfhoos and sacrifice, by Orville Dewey.--The relation of Jesus to the present age, by Charles Carroll Everett.--The mythical element in the New Testament, by Frederic Henry Hedge.--The place of mind in nature and intuition in man, by James Martineau.--The relations of ethics and theology, by Andrew P. Peabody.--Christianity: what it is not, and what it is, by G. Vance Smith.--The aim and hope of Jesus, by Oliver Stearns. 15-28232
I. American Unitarian association. II. Bellows, Henry Whitney, 1814-1882. III. Clarke, James Freeman, 1810-1880. IV. Coquerel, Athanase Josue, 1820-1875. V. Dewey, Orville, 1794-1882. VI. Everett, Charles Carroll, 1829-1900. VII. Hedge, Frederic Henry, 1805-1890. VIII. Martineau, James, 1805-1900. IX. Peabody, Andrew Preston, 1811-1893. X. Smith, George Vance.

DARLING, Charles David.
Doubters and their doubts, by Charles David Darling, PH. D. Boston, Sherman, French & company, 1916. 2 p. l., 117 p. 20 cm. 17-1171 1.10
I. Title.

GORDON, James Logan, 1858- 252.
The weight of a word; addresses on some of life's great issues, by James L. Gordon ... New York, Chicago [etc.] Fleming H. Revell company [c1925] 191 p. 20 cm. [BX7233.G73W4] 25-20615
I. Title.
Contents omitted.

GORDON, Samuel Dickey, 1859- 236
Quiet talks about life after death, by S. D. Gordon ... New York, Chicago [etc.] Fleming H. Revell company [c1920] 197 p. 19 cm. [BT901.G65] 21-3699
I. Title.

HAAS, John Augustus William, 1862-
Trends of thought and Christian truth, [by] John A. W. Haas... Boston, R. G. Badger; [etc., etc. c1915] 5 p. l. 9-329 p. 19 1/2 cm. (Lettered on cover: Library of religious thought) $1.50 15-11892
I. Title.

HUMBOLDT, Wilhelm, von, freiherr 1767-1835.
Religious thoughts and opinions. By William von Humboldt ... Boston, W. Crosby and H. P. Nichols, 1851. 171 p. 17 1/2 cm. The English edition of this work has title: Thoughts and opinions of a statesman. [Full name: Friedrich Wilhelm Christian Karl Ferdinand, freiherr von Humboldt] [DD422.H8A6 1851] 16-4342
I. Title.

JOHNSTON, Howard Agnew, 1860- 220
Scientific Christian thinking for young people, by Howard Agnew Johnston ... New York, George H. Doran company [c1922] xiv p., 1 l., 17-238 p. 20 cm. [BR125.J53] 23-1226 1.25
I. Title.

LAMB, Alexander Mackenzie.
Twilight, the sign of His coming, by Alexander Mackenzie Lamb. Boston, The Gorham press; [etc., etc., c1916] 87 p. 20 cm. (Lettered on cover: Library of religious thought) 17-1165 0.50
I. Title.
Contents omitted. Contents omitted.

LANKARD, Frank Glenn, 1892- 248
Difficulties in religious thinking [by] Frank Glenn Lankard. New York, Cincinnati [etc.] The Abingdon press [c1933] 271 p. 20 cm. Bibliography: p. 265-271. [BR125.L28] 33-4709
1. Religious thought. 2. Christianity. I. Title. II. Title: Religious thinking, Difficulties in.

LODGE, Oliver Joseph, Sir 261 1851-
Reason and belief, by Sir Oliver Lodge. New York, George H. Doran company [1920] ix p., 2 l., 3-166 p. 22 cm. [BR85.L8 1920] 20-26578
I. Title.

MCILVAINE, Edwin Linton, 220 1873-
The compass, by Edwin L. McIlvaine. Boston, The Gorham press; [etc., etc., c1918] 130 p. 19 1/2 cm. (Lettered on cover: Library of religious thought) $1.00. [BR125.M3] 18-6038
I. Title.
Contents omitted.

MCLEISTER, Luther H., comp. 208.
Christian thoughts for the journey of life, comp. and arranged by Rev. L. H. McLeister ... Butler, Ind., Higley printing co., c1921] viii, [9]-196 p. 19 1/2 cm. [BR53.M3] 22-5620
I. Title.

MARTIN, Samuel Albert, 1853-
The oracles of God ... [by] Samuel A. Martin ... Boston, R. G. Badger; [etc., etc., c1916- v. 19 1/2 cm. (Lettered on cover: Library of religious thought) 17-4486
I. Title.

MASSEE, Jasper Cortenus, 252. 1871-
Sunday night talks, by J. C. Massee... Chicago, The Bible institute colportage ass'n [c1926] 124 p. 19 cm. [BX6333.M37S8] 26-20257
I. Title.

REIMENSNYDER, John Milton, 1847-
Reason, history and religion, by Rev. J. M. Reimensnyder ... Philadelphia, Pa., For the author by the Lutheran publication society [c1907] vii, [1], 9-94 p. 19 1/2 cm. 7-16357
I. Title.

RELIGIOUS thought at the University of Michigan; being addresses delivered at the Sunday morning services of the Students' Christian association. Ann Arbor, Mich., The Register publishing company, 1893. xii, 247 p. 20 cm. E 13
I. Michigan. University. Students' Christian association.

SCHOFIELD, Alfred Taylor, 1846-
Studies in the highest thought, by A. T. Schofield ... New York, Hodder & Stoughton, George H. Doran company [c1911] vi p., 1 l., xi-xviii, 150 p. 20 cm. 11-25331
I. Title.

SIRRELL, Lawrence N. 220
As He said, by Lawrence N. Sirrell ... Philadelphia, Dorrance and company, 1925. 115 p. 19 1 / 2 cm. [Contemporary religious thought series, 4] [BR125.S515] 25-16109
I. Title.

SIRRELL, Lawrence N. 232.
The seven words; a study of the great accomplishment at Jerusalem for Holy week, by Lawrence N. Sirrell ... Philadelphia, Dorrance and company [c1927] xv p., 2 l., 21-95 p. front. (port.) 19 1/2 cm. (Half-title: Contemporary religious thought, 5) [BT455.S5] 27-7158
I. Title.

STERRETT, James Macbride 1847-
Reason and authority in religion, by J. Macbride Sterrett ... New York, T. Whittaker, 1891. xiii, [15]-184 p. 19 cm. 5-28779
I. Title.
Contents omitted.

STRAIN, John Newton.
The unpardonable sin, by John Newton Strain. Boston, The Gorham press; [etc., etc., c1916] 83 p. front. (port.) 19 1/2 cm. (Lettered on cover: Library of religious thought) $1.00. 16-23975
I. Title.

STUDIES in current religious thought ... [Philadelphia] The Booklovers library [1901] cover-title, 5-167 p. front., port. 23 cm. (Course XVII, Booklovers reading club hand-book) The information usually found on the t.-p. is distributed over 5 prelinary leaves paged 5-13. 2-1804
Contents omitted.

TILLICH, Paul, 1886- 270.8
The religious situation, by Paul Tillich ... translated by H. Richard Niebuhr. New York, H. Holt and company [c1932] xxv, 182 p. 19 1/2 cm. [BR479.T53] 32-35034
1. Religious thought. I. Niebuhr, Helmut Richard, 1894- tr. II. Title.

VEDDER, Henry Clay, 1853-1935.
The recent movement toward Christian unity, by Henry C. Vedder ... Chester, Pa., The Seminary bookstore, 1910. 57 p. 18 cm. A 21
1. Christian union. I. Title.

Religious thought—18th century

CREED, John Martin, ed. 204
Religious thought in the eighteenth century, illustrated from writers of the period, by John Martin Creed ... & John Sandwith Boys Smith ... Cambridge [Eng.] The University press, 1934. xl, 301 p. 23 cm. Includes biographical sketches. "Index of authors and passages": p. [299]-301. [BL25.C7] 35-3219
1. Religious thought—18th cent. 2. Natural theology. 3. Rationalism. 4. Church and state. 5. Gt. Brit.—Biog. I. Boys Smith, John Sandwith, joint ed. II. Title.
Contents omitted.

Religious thought—19th century

HUTTON, John Alexander, 270. 1868-
The winds of God; five lectures on the intercourse of thought with faith during the nineteenth century, by the Rev. John A. Hutton, M. A. London, New York [etc.] Hodder and Stoughton [1911] v p., 1 l., 108, [1] p. 20 cm. "The five lectures ... were spoken, with additions, at Mundesley in Norfold."--p. v. [BR477.H8] 12-18835
1. Religious thought—19th cent. I. Title.

MACKAY, James Hutton.
Religious thought in Holland during the nineteenth century, by James Hutton Mackay... London, New York [etc.] Hodder and Stoughton, 1911. xvi, 225 p., 1 l. 20 1/2 cm. 12-4947
I. Title.

REARDON, Bernard M. G. 230.09034 ed.
Religious thought in the nineteenth century [by] Bernard M. G. Reardon. Illus. from writers of the period. London, Cambridge 1966. ix, 406p. 24cm. Bibl. [BR477.R4] 66-10542 11.00; 3.95 pap.,
1. Religious thought—19th cent. 2. Theology—Collections. I. Title.
Available from the Publisher's New York office.

Religious thought—20th century

CARVER, William Owen, 1868- 204
... *The re-discovery of the spirit,* by William Owen Carver ... New York [etc.] Fleming H. Revell company [c1934] 160 p. 20 cm. (Norton lectures (1963-4) Southern Baptist theological seminary) [BR479.C35] 34-38175
1. Religious thought—20th cent. I. Title.

THE Christian century. 208.2
How my mind has changed [by] John C. Bennet [and others] Edited and introduced by Harold E. Fey. Cleveland, Meridian Books [1961] 191p. 18cm. (A Living age book, LA33) 'The contributions ... were first published as articles [in the Christian century] during the 1959-60 publishing year.' [BR481.C48] 61-15600
1. Religious thought—20th cent. 2. Theology—20th cent. I. Fey, Harold Edward, 1898- ed. II. Title.

CHRISTIAN Century (The) 208.2
How my mind has changed [by] John C. Bennet [others] Ed. introd. by Harold E. Fey, [Magnolia, Mass., P. Smith, 1967. c.1961] 191p. 19cm. (Meridian Living age bk., LA33 rebound) [BR481.C48] 61-15600
1. Religious thought—20th cent. 2. Theology—20th cent. I. Fey, Harold Edward, 1898- ed. II. Title.

DE WOLF, Lotan Harold, 1905- 230
Trends and frontiers of religious thought. Nashville, National Methodist Student Movement [1955] 139p. 20cm. [BT28.D48] 55-14429
1. Religious thought—20th cent. 2. Theology, Doctrinal—Hist.—20th cent. I. Title.

DUDLEY, George W. 252.
Compendium of religious and scientific reflections, by Geo. W. Dudley, D. D. Chicago, 1929. 96 p. front. (port.) 20 cm. [BX6452.D8] 29-10304
I. Title.

FEY, Harold E., ed. 208.2
How my mind has changed. Cleveland, Meridian Bks. [dist.] World Pub. Co.

[c.1960, 1961] 191p. (Living age bk., LA33) 61-15600 1.25 pap.,
1. Religious thought—20th cent. 2. Theology—20th cent. I. Fey, Harold Edward, 1898- ed. II. Title.

FORSTER, Arthur Haire. 290
Four modern religious movements, by Arthur Haire Forster. Boston, R. G. Badger [c1919] 95 p. 19 1/2 cm. (Lettered on cover: Library of religious thought) Reprinted in part from the Teachers' assistant, Toronto, and Church life. [BL98.F7] 19-8087
I. Title.
Contents omitted.

HARTSOCK, Donald E., comp. 230'.08
Contemporary religious issues, edited by Donald E. Hartsock. Belmont, Calif., Wadsworth Pub. Co. [1968] ix, 422 p. 23 cm. (Wadsworth continuing education series) [BL25.H33] 68-29159
1. Religious thought—20th century. I. Title.

HROMADKA, Josef Lukl, 1889- 230
... Doom and resurrection, with an introduction by John A. Mackay. Richmond, Va., Madrus house [1945] 122 p., 1 l. 20 cm. At head of title: Joseph L. Hromadka. [BR479.H7] 45-1857
1. Masaryk, Tomas Garrigue, pres. Czechoslovak republic, 1850-1937. 2. Religious thought—20th cent. 3. Civilization, Modern. 4. World war, 1939—-Religious aspects. 5. Dialectic (Theology) I. Title.

PADOVANO, Anthony T. 230.2
The estranged God; modern man's search for belief, by Anthony T. Padovano. New York, Sheed [1966] xviii, 300p. 22cm. Bibl. [BT28.P25] 66-14154 6.00
1. Religious thought—20th cent. 2. Existentialism. 3. Theology—20th cent. I. Title.

PAUL, Leslie Allen, 1905- 190
Alternatives to Christian belief; a critical survey of the contemporary search for meaning [by] Leslie Paul. [1st ed.] Garden City, N.Y., Doubleday, 1967. x, 227 p. 22 cm. Bibliographical references included in "Notes" (p.[207]-220) [BR479.P3] 67-10448
1. Religious thought—20th century. 2. Philosophy, Modern—20th century. I. Title.

SHEEN, Fulton John, 1895- 204
Moods and truths. Garden City, N.Y., Garden City Pub. Co. [1950, c1932] ix, 237 p. 21 cm. A continuation of the author's Old errors and new labels. [BX1395.S5 1950] 51-1975
1. Religious thought—20th cent. I. Title.

SHEEN, Fulton John, Bp., 1895- 201
Moods and truths, by Fulton J. Sheen. Port Washington, N.Y., Kennikat Press [1970, c1932] ix, 238 p. 21 cm. (Essay and general literature index reprint series) A continuation of the author's Old errors and new labels. [BX1395.S5 1970] 77-91054
1. Religious thought—20th century. I. Title.

SHEEN, Fulton John, 1895- 204
Moods and truths, by Fulton J. Sheen ... New York & London, The Century co. [c1932] ix, 238 p. 19 cm. "This work ... is a continuation of the previously published 'Old errors and new labels'." [BX1395.S5] 32-11012
1. Religious thought—20th cent. I. Title.

TILLICH, Paul, 1886- 270.8
The religious situation. Translated by H. Richard Niebuhr. New York, Meridian Books, 1956 [c1932] 219p. 19cm. (Living age books, LA6) Translation of Die religlose Lage der Gegenwart. [BR479] 56-9242
1. Religious thought—20th cent. I. Title.

YOUR cosmic destiny.
[1st ed.] New York, Vantage Press [c1958] 261p.
1. Religious thought—20th cent. I. Chapman, W A

Religious thought—Ancient periodicals

FRANKFORT, Henri, 1897- 200'.956
Before philosophy, the intellectual adventure of ancient man; an essay on speculative thought in the ancient Near East, by H. and H. A. Frankfort [and others] Harmonds-worth, Middlesex, Penguin Books [1951] 275p. 18cm. (Pelican books, A 198) 'An Oriental Institute essay.' Originally published under title: The intellectual adventure of ancient man. [BL96.F] A54
1. Religious thought—Ancient period. 2. Civilization, Ancient. 3. Philosophy, Ancient. I. Frankfort, Henriette Antonia (Groenewegen) 1806- joint author. II. Title.
Contents omitted.

FRANKFORT, Henri, 1897- 200'.956
Before philosophy, the intellectual adventure of ancient man; an essay on speculative thought in the ancient Near East, by B. and B. A. Frankfort [and others] Harmondsworth, Middlesex, Penguin Books [1951] 275 p. 18 cm. (Pelican books, A 198) "An Oriental Institute essay." Originally published under title: The intellectual adventure of ancient man. Contents.CONTENTS.—Introduction: Myth and reality, by H. and B. A. Frankfort.—Egypt: The nature of the universe. The function of the state. The values of life. By J. A. Wilson.—Mesopotamia: The cosmos of the state. The function of the state. The good life. By T. Jacobsen. Conclusion: The emancipation of thought from myth, by H. and H. A. Frankfort. [BL96.F] A54
1. Religious thought—Ancient period. 2. Civilization, Ancient. 3. Philosophy, Ancient. I. Frankfort, Henriette Antonia Groenewegen, 1896- joint author. II. Title.

FRANKFORT, Henri, 1897- 290
The intellectual adventure of ancient man; an essay on speculative thought in theancient Near East, by H. and H. A. Frankfort, John A. Wilson, Thorkild Jacobsen [and] William A. Irwin. Chicago, The University of Chicago press [1946] vii, 401 p. 23 1/2 cm. "An Oriental institute essay." "Contains lectures given as a public course in the Division of the humanities of the University of Chicago."--Pref. Includes bibliographies. [BL96.F8] 47-1318
1. Religious thought—Ancient period. 2. Civilization, Ancient. 3. Philosophy, Ancient. I. Frankfort, Henriette Antonia (Groenewegen) 1896- joint author. II. Wilson, John Albert, 1899- III. Jacobsen, Thorkild, 1904- IV. Irwin, William A., 1884- V. Title.
Contents omitted.

LOEW, Cornelius Richard. 290
Myth, sacred history, and philosophy; the pre-Christian religious heritage of the West [by] Cornelius Loew. New York, Harcourt, Brace & World [1967] ix, 284 p. 21 cm. Bibliography: p. [277]-282. [BL96.L6] 67-16822
1. Religious thought — Ancient period. I. Title.

WORKMAN, Herbert Brook, 1862- 230'.09
Christian thought to the Reformation. Freeport, N.Y., Books for Libraries Press [1973] p. Reprint of the 1911 ed., issued in series: Studies in theology. Bibliography: p. [BR162.W8 1973] 72-10865 ISBN 0-8369-7127-2
1. Religious thought—Ancient period. 2. Religious thought—Middle Ages. I. Title. II. Series: Studies in theology (London).

Religious thought—England.

COCKSHUT, A. O. J., ed. 230.3
Religious controversies of the nineteenth century: selected documents. Lincoln, Univ. of Neb. Pr. [c.1966] v,246p. 23cm. Bibl. [BR759.C57] 66-18225 5.50
1. Religious thought—England. 2. Religious thought—19th cent. I. Title.
Contents omitted.

COCKSHUT, A. O. J. 209.42
The unbelievers; English agnostic thought, 1840-1890 [by] A. O. J. Cockshut. [New York] New York University Press, 1966 [c1964] 191 p. 22 cm. [BR759.C603] 66-13549
1. Religious thought—England. 2. Religious thought—19th cent. I. Title.

CURTIS, Lewis Perry, 1900- 274.2
Anglican moods of the eighteenth century, by L. P. Curris. [Hamden Conn.] Archon Books, 1966. 84 p. 22 cm. Bibliographical footnotes. [BR756.C8] 66-19325
1. Religious thought — England. 2. Religious thought — 18th cent. 3. Church of England — Parties and movements. I. Title.

MCLACHLAN, Herbert, 1876- 201'.1
The religious opinions of Milton, Locke, and Newton / by H. McLachlan. Folcroft, Pa. : Folcroft Library Editions, 1974. vii, 221 p. ; 23 cm. Reprint of the 1941 ed. published by Manchester University Press, Manchester, Eng., which was issued as Publications no. 276, theological series no. 6, of the University of Manchester. Includes index. [BR756.M32 1974] 74-20740 ISBN 0-8414-5930-4 lib. bdg. : 11.95.
1. Milton, John, 1608-1674—Religion and ethics. 2. Locke, John, 1632-1704. 3. Newton, Isaac, Sir, 1642-1727. 4. Religious thought—England. I. Title. II. Series: Victoria University of Manchester. Publications. Theological series ; no. 6.

MCLACHLAN, Herbert, 1876- 201'.1
The religious opinions of Milton, Locke, and Newton / by H. McLachlan. Norwood, Pa. : Norwood Editions, 1976. vii, 221 p. ; 23 cm. Reprint of the 1941 ed. published by the Manchester University Press, Manchester, which was issued as no. 276 of Publications of the University of Manchester and as no. 6 of Publications of the University of Manchester Theological series. Includes bibliographical references and index. [BR756.M32 1976] 76-2350 ISBN 0-88305-532-5 : 15.00
1. Milton, John, 1608-1674—Religion and ethics. 2. Locke, John, 1632-1704. 3. Newton, Isaac, Sir, 1642-1727. 4. Religious thought—England. I. Title. II. Series: Victoria University of Manchester. Publications ; no. 276. III. Series: Victoria University of Manchester. Publications : Theological series ; no. 6.

MCLACHLAN, Herbert, 1876- 201'.1
The religious opinions of Milton, Locke, and Newton / by H. McLachlan. Folcroft, Pa. : Folcroft Library Editions, 1974. vii, 221 p. ; 23 cm. Reprint of the 1941 ed. published by Manchester University Press, Manchester, Eng., which was issued as Publications no. 276, theological series no. 6, of the University of Manchester. Includes index. [BR756.M32 1974] 74-20740 ISBN 0-8414-5930-4 lib. bdg.
1. Milton, John, 1608-1674—Religion and ethics. 2. Locke, John, 1632-1704. 3. Newton, Isaac, Sir, 1642-1727. 4. Religious thought—England. I. Title. II. Series: Victoria University of Manchester. Publications. Theological series ; no. 6.

STROMBERG, Ronald N 1916- 274.2
Religious liberalism in eighteenth-century England. [London] Oxford University Press, 1954. xi, 192p. 23cm. Bibliography: p.[175]-185. [BR758.S85] 54-2970
1. Religious thought—England. 2. Liberalism (Religion) I. Title.

Religious thought—England—London.

SMITH, Warren Sylvester, 1912- 200'.9421
The London heretics, 1870-1914 New York, Dodd, Mead [1968] xvii, 319 p. illus., ports. 22 cm. Bibliography: p. 299-307. [BR764.S6 1968] 68-2791
1. Religious thought—England—London. 2. Religious thought—19th century. 3. London—Religion. I. Title.

Religious thought—France.

CATHOLICS & unbelievers in eighteenth century France. [2d ed.] New York, Cooper Square Publishers, 1961 [c1939] 236p. Includes bibliography.
1. Religious thought—France. 2. Religious thought—18th cent. 3. Apologetics—18th cent. I. Palmer, Robert Roswell, 1909-

PALMER, Robert Roswell, 1909- 230.0944
Catholics & unbelievers in eighteenth century France. [2d ed.] New York, Cooper Square Publishers, 1961 [c1939] 236 p. 24 cm. Includes bibliography. [[BR845]] 61-13266
1. Religious thought — France. 2. Religious thought — 18th cent. 3. Apologetics — 18th cent. I. Title.

PALMER, Robert Roswell, 1909- 230.0944
Catholics & unbelievers in eighteenth century France, by R. R. Palmer. Princeton, Princeton university press, 1939. 6 p. l., [3]-236 p. 23 1/2 cm. "First edition." "Bibliographical note": p. [225]-227. [BR845.P3] 39-32300
1. Religious thought—France. 2. Religious thought—18th cent. 3. Apologetics—18th cent. I. Title.

Religious thought—Great Britain.

MCCONNELL, Francis John, bp., 1871- 922
Evangelicals, revolutionists and idealists; six English contributors to American thought and action, by Francis John McConnell. New York, Nashville, Abingdon-Cokesbury press [1942] 184 p. 19 1/2 cm. [Drew lectureship in biography. 1942] [BR758.M3] 43-849
1. Oglethrope, James Edward, 1696-1765. 2. Wesley, John, 1703-1791. 3. Whitefield, George, 1714-1770. 4. Paine, Thomas, 1737-1809. 5. Berkeley, George, bp. of Cloyne, 1685-1753. 6. Wilberforce, William, 1759-1883. 7. Religious thought—Gt. Brit. 8. Religious thought—U.S. I. Title.

MCCONNELL, Francis John, Bp., 1871-1953. 201'.1'0922 B
Evangelicals, revolutionists, and idealists; six English contributors to American thought and action. Port Washington, N.Y., Kennikat Press [1972, c1942] 184 p. 21 cm. (Essay and general literature index reprint series) Contents.Contents.—James Edward Oglethorpe.—John Wesley.—George Whitefield.—Thomas Paine.—George Berkeley.—William Wilberforce. [BR758.M3 1972] 75-153252 ISBN 0-8046-1505-5
1. Oglethorpe, James Edward, 1696-1785. 2. Wesley, John, 1706-1791. 3. Whitefield, George, 1714-1770. 4. Paine, Thomas, 1737-1809. 5. Berkeley, George, Bp. of Cloyne, 1685-1753. 6. Wilberforce, William, 1759-1833. 7. Religious thought—Gt. Brit. 8. Religious thought—U.S. I. Title.

MOSSNER, Ernest Campbell. 922.342
Bishop Butler and the age of reason; a study in the history of thought, by Ernest Campbell Mossner. New York, The Macmillan company, 1936. xv, 271 p. 22 1/2 cm. Bibliography: p. 241-261. [BX5199.B9M6] 36-34559
1. Butler, Joseph, bp. of Durham, 1692-1752. 2. Religious thought—Gt. Brit. I. Title.

MOSSNER, Ernest Campbell, 1907- 283'.0924 B
Bishop Butler and the age of reason; a study in the history of thought. New York, B. Blom, 1971. xv, 271 p. 21 cm. Reprint of the 1936 ed. Bibliography: p. 241-261. [BX5199.B9M6 1971] 69-13247
1. Butler, Joseph, Bp. of Durham, 1692-1752. 2. Religious thought—Gt. Brit. I. Title.

TULLOCH, John, 1823-1886. 230'.0942
Movements of religious thought in Britain during the nineteenth century. With an introd. by A. C. Cheyne. New York, Humanities Press, 1971. 34, xi, 338 p. 20 cm. (The Victorian library) Reprint of the London, 1885 ed. Includes bibliographical references. [BR759.T8 1971] 72-178660 ISBN 0-7185-5017-X 9.75
1. Religious thought—Great Britain. I. Title.

TULLOCH, John, 1823-1886. 274.2
Movements of religious thought in Britain during the nineteenth century. St. Giles lectures. By John Tulloch ... New York, C. Scribner's sons, 1885. xi, 888 p. 20 cm. [BR759.T8 1885] 37-21107
1. Religious thought—Gt. Brit. I. Title.

WEBB, Clement Charles 274.2
Julian, 1865-
A study of religious thought in England from 1850; being the Olaus Petri lectures, delivered at Upsala in 1932, by Clement C. J. Webb ... Oxford, The Clarendon press, 1933. viii, 192 p. 19 1/2 cm. [BR759.W4] 33-24877
1. Religious thought—Gt. Brit. I. Title.

WOOD, Herbert George, 1879- 260
1963.
Living issues in religious thought, from George Fox to Bertrand Russell. Freeport, N.Y., Books for Libraries Press [1966] 187 p. 22 cm. (Essay index reprint series) Reprint of the 1924 ed. Contents.Contents.—Religion and the unknown.—Logic and pessimism.—The moral scepticism of today.—A disciple of Spinoza.—Liberal Protestantism and modernist criticism.—The attitude of Mr. H. G. Wells towards Jesus Christ.—G. Bernard Shaw and religion.—The next revival of religion.—Quakerism.—Personal religion and social progress, a study of John Woolman. [BR85.W6 1966] 67-22128
1. Religious thought—Great Britain. I. Title.

Religious thought — History

LUND, Harold Woodhull.
Four steps in the evolution of religious thought. Bridgeport, Conn., 1964. 44 p. 24 cm.
I. Title.

RICHARDS, George Warren, 230
1869-
Creative controversies in Christianity, by George W. Richards ... New York [etc.] Fleming H. Revell company [c1938] 223 p. 21 cm. [The James Sprunt lectures, 1933] "Footnotes" at end of each chapter. [BR148.R53] 38-13643
1. Religious thought—Hist. 2. Theology, Doctrinal—Hist. I. Title.

SELWYN, Edward Gordon, 1885- 270
ed.
History of Christian thought; a volume of essays, edited by Edward Gordon Selwyn... London, J. Heritage, The Unicorn press [1937] 2 p. l., 3-190 p. 19 cm. [BR148.S4] 38-11534
1. Religious—thought—Hist. 2. Theology, Doctrinal—Hist. I. Title.
Contents omitted.

TAWNEY, Richard Henry, 1880- 261
Religion and the rise of capitalism, a historical study. Gloucester, Mass., Peter Smith [1963, c.1926] 337p. 21cm. (Holland memorial lects., 1922) Bibl. 4.00
1. Religious thought—Hist. 2. Christianity and economics—Hist. 3. Gt. Brit.—Soc. condit. 4. Capitalism. I. Title.

TAWNEY, Richard Henry, 1880-
Religion and the rise of capitalism; a historical study. [New York] The New American Library [1958] 280 p. 18 cm. (Holland Memorial lectures, 1922)
1. Religious thought — Hist. 2. Gt. Brit. — Soc. condit. 3. Capitalism. 4. Christianity and economics — Hist. I. Title. II. Series: Oxford University. Henry Scott Holland memorial lectures, 1922

TAWNEY, Richard Henry, 1880- 261
Religion and the rise of capitalism; a historical study. New York, Harcourt, Brace [pref. 1937, c1926] xix, 337 p. 22 cm. (Holland memorial lectures, 1922) Contents.--The medieval background.--The continental reformer--The Church of England.--The Puritan movement. [BR115.E3T3 1937] 48-30312
1. Religious thought—Hist 2. Christianiy and economics—Hist. 3. Gt. Brit.—Soc. condit. 4. Capitalism. I. Title. II. Series.

TAWNEY, Richard Henry, 1880- 261
Religion and the rise of capitalism, a historical study. New York, Penguin Books [1947] 280 p. 18 cm. (Holland memorial lectures, 1922) Pelican books, i'22. Bibliographical references included in "Notes" (p. 237-270) [BR115.E3T3 1947] 48-593
1. Religious thought—Hist. 2. Christianity and economics—Hist. 3. Gt. Brit.—Soc. condit. 4. Capitalism. I. Title. II. Series.

TAWNEY, Richard Henry, 261.85
1880-1962
Religion and the rise of capitalism; a historical studv. London, E. Murray [Mystic, Conn., Verry, 1965] 339p. 23cm. [BR115.E3T3] 6.00 bds.,
1. Religious thought—Hist. 2. Christianity and economics—Hist. 3. Gt. Brit.—Soc. condit. 4. Capitalism. I. Title.

TAWNEY, Richard Henry, 261.85
1880-1962.
Religion and the rise of capitalism; a historical study. Gloucester Mass., P. Smith, 1962, [c1926] 337 p. 21 cm. (Holland memorial lectures, 1922) [BR115.E3T3] 63-1429
1. Religious thought—Hist. 2. Christianity and economics—Hist. 3. Gt. Brit.—Soc. condit. 4. Capitalism. I. Title.

Religious thought—History—Addresses, essays, lectures.

COBB, John B. 260
Can the church think again? / John B. Cobb, Jr. [Nashville, TN] : United Methodist Board of Higher Education and Ministry, 1976. 11 p. ; 28 cm. (Occasional papers - United Methodist Board of Higher Education and Ministry ; v. 1, no. 12) Caption title. [BR148.C6] 77-356708
1. Religious thought—History—Addresses, essays, lectures. I. Title. II. Series: United Methodist Church (United States). Board of Higher Education and Ministry. Occasional papers — United Methodist Board of Higher Education and Ministry ; v. 1, no. 12.

WESTCOTT, Brooke Foss, bp. of
Durham, 1825-1901.
Essays in the history of religious thought in the West. By Brooks Foss Westcott ... London and New York, Macmillan and co., 1891. vi, [2], 397, [3] p. 18 1/2 cm. [BL690.W5] 6-25885
I. Title.
Contents omitted.

Religious thought—India.

MEHTA, Phirozshah Dorabji 294
Early Indian religious thought; an introduction and essay. London, Luzac [dist. Mystic, Conn., Verry, 1965] 532p. 23cm. Bibl. [BL2003.M4] 58-2912 8.50
1. Religious thought—India. 2. India—Religion. I. Title.

Religious thought—Kentucky.

SONNE, Niels Henry, 1907- 211
Liberal Kentucky, 1780-1828, by Niels Henry Sonne. New York, Columbia university press, 1939. viii, [1] p., 1 l., 286, [1] p. 23 1/2 cm. (Half-title: Columbia studies in American culture. No. 3) Issued also as thesis (PH.D.) Columbia university. Bibliography: p. 263-273. [BR555.K4S6 1939 a] 39-20412
1. Religious thought—Kentucky. 2. Liberalism (Religion) 3. Kentucky—Intellectual life. 4. Transylvania university, Lexington Ky. I. Title.

Religious thought—Middle ages.

MELLONE, Sydney Herbert, 270.3
1869-
Western Christian thought in the middle ages; an essay in interpretation. Edinburgh and London, W. Blackwood [Mystic, Conn., Verry, 1965] viii p., 1 1,304p. 19cm. [BR252.M4] 3.00 bds.,
1. Religious thought—Middle ages. 2. Philosophy, Medieval. 3. Middle ages—Hist. I. Title.

Religious thought—Modern period, 1500-

GROFF, Warren F. 230
The shaping of modern Christian thought, by Warren F. Groff and Donald E. Miller. Cleveland, World Pub. Co. [1968] xii, 489 p. 24 cm. Bibliographical footnotes. [BR450.G7] 68-23018
1. Religious thought—Modern period, 1500- I. Miller, Donald Eugene, joint author. II. Title.

KAUFMANN, Walter Arnold, 208.2
ed. ed.
Religion from Tolstoy to Camus. New York, Harper [1961] 450 p. 25 cm. Bibliographical footnotes. [BL25.K35] 61-12838
1. Religious thought—Modern period, 1500- I. Title.

SPINKA, Matthew, 1890-1972. 190
Christian thought from Erasmus to Berdyaev / Matthew Spinka. Westport, Conn. : Greenwood Press, 1979, c1962. x, 246 p. ; 23 cm. Reprint of the ed. published by Prentice-Hall, Englewood Cliffs, N.J. Includes index. Bibliography: p. 232-237. [BR290.S8 1979] 78-11967 ISBN 0-313-21122-1 : 22.50
1. Religious thought—Modern period, 1500- 2. Religious thought—Europe. I. Title.

[YOUNG, Edward] 1683-1765.
The complaint: or, Night-thoughts on life, death, and immortality. To which are added, The last day, a poem. And A paraphrase on part of the Book of Job... Philadelphia, Printed and sold by Prichard & Hall, in Market street, between Front and Second streets, 1787. xii, [13]-300 p. 16 1/2 cm. [PR3782.N5 1787] 14-5678
I. Title. II. Title: Night-thoughts.

[YOUNG, Edward] 1683-1765.
The complaint: or, Night-thoughts on life, death, and immortality. To which is prefixed, the life of the author... New-York, Printed by John Tiebout for N. Bell, 1796. 1 p. l., [v]-xii, 268 p. 17 cm. [PR3782.N5 1796] 14-5680
I. Title. II. Title: Night-thoughts.

YOUNG, Edward, 1683-1765.
The complaint: or, Night thoughts. By Edward Young, D.D. Hartford, S. Andrus, 1823. 3 p. l., [5]-324 p. plates. 15 cm. Added t.-p. (engr., with vignette) and plates have imprint: New York, Johnston and Van Norden, 1823. [PR3782.N5 1823] 17-10499
I. Title. II. Title: Night thoughts.

YOUNG, Edward, 1683-1765.
The complaint; or, Night thoughts. By Edward Young. D.D. In two volumes... Hartford, Published by Silas Andrus, 1824. 2 v. front. 15 1/2 cm. Paged continuously. Vol. 1 has added t.-p., engraved with vignette, and imprint: New-York, Published by Johnston and Van Norden, 1823. [PR3782.N] A 32
I. Title. II. Title: Night thoughts.

YOUNG, Edward, 1683-1765.
The complaint: or, Night thoughts. By Edward Young, D.D. Hartford, S. Andrus, 1824. 3 p. l., [5]-325 p. plates. 17 cm. Added t.-p., engraved, with vignette and plates, has imprint: New-York, Johnston and Van Norden, 1823. [PR3782.N5 1824] 14-5683
I. Title. II. Title: Night thoughts.

YOUNG, Edward, 1683-1765.
The complaint: or, Night thoughts. By Edward Young, D.D. Baltimore, N. Hickman, 1837. 296 p. 15 cm. [PR3782.N5 1837] 41-38915
I. Title. II. Title: Night thoughts.

YOUNG, Edward, 1683-1765.
The complaint: or, Night thoughts. By Edward Young, D.D. Hartford, S. Andrus and son, 1847. 324 p. 16 cm. [PR3782.N5 1847] 39-18239
I. Title. II. Title: Night thoughts.

Religious thought — Modern periodicals

KAUFMANN, Walter, ed. 208.2
Religion from Tolstoy to Camus [Selected, introd., prefaces by Walter Kaufmann] New York, Harper [c.1961, 1964] 450p. 21cm. (CL/TB-123) 2.95 pap.,
1. Religious thought—Modern period. I. Title.

KAUFMANN, Walter Arnold, ed.
Religion from Tolstoy to Camus. New York, Harper [1961] 479 p. Harper torchbooks, TB 123. The Cloister library. Bibliographical footnotes. 65-91819
1. Religious thought — Modern period. I. Title.

MCGIFFERT, Arthur Cushman, 230
1861-1933
Protestant thought before Kant [Gloucester, Mass., Peter Smith, 1962, c.1961] 265p. 21cm. (Harper torchbks. Cloister lib., TB93 rebound) Bibl. 3.50
1. Religious thought—Modern period. 2. Theology, Doctrinal—Hist.—Modern period. 3. Rationalism—Hist. I. Title.

MCGIFFERT, Arthur Cushman, 230
1861-1933.
Protestant thought before Kant, by Arthur Cushman McGiffert ... New York, C. Scribner's sons, 1936. 8 p. l., 261 p. 19 cm. (On cover: Studies in theology) Bibliography: p. 255-261. [BX4817.M3] 37-8552
1. Religious thought—Modern period. 2. Theology, Doctrinal—Hist.—Modern period. 3. Rationalism. I. Title.

Religious thought—Netherlands.

YOUNG, William, 1918- 230.04
Toward a reformed philosophy; the development of a Protestant philosophy in Dutch Calvinistic thought since the time of Abraham Kuyper. Grand Rapids, Piet Hein Publishers, 1952. 155p. 24cm. Includes bibliography. [BT30.N5Y6] 54-35628
1. Religious thought—Netherlands. 2. Theology, Doctrinal—Hist.—Netherlands. 3. Philosophy, Dutch. 4. Calvinism. I. Title. II. Title: Protestant philosophy.

Religious thought—New England.

HATCH, Nathan O. 261.7'0974
The sacred cause of liberty : republican thought and the millennium in Revolutionary New England / Nathan O. Hatch. New Haven : Yale University Press, 1977. p. cm. Includes index. Bibliography: p. [BR520.H34] 77-6626 ISBN 0-300-02092-9 : 12.50
1. Religious thought—New England. 2. Political science—New England. 3. Millennialism. 4. Clergy—New England. I. Title.

NEWLIN, Claude Milton. 277.4
Philosophy and religion in colonial America [by] Claude M. Newlin. New York, Greenwood Press, 1968 [c1962] ix, 212 p. 22 cm. [BR520.N4 1968] 68-23317
1. Religious thought—New England. 2. Philosophy and religion. I. Title.

NEWLIN, Claude Milton. 277.3
Philosophy and religion in colonial America. New York, Philosophical Library [1962] 212 p. 22 cm. [BR520.N4] 61-15245
1. Religious thought—New England. 2. Philosophy and religion. I. Title.

Religious thought—Russia.

FEDOTOV, Georgii Petrovich 281.9
The Russian religious mind, by George P. Fedotov [Gloucester, Mass., Peter Smith. 1960, c.1946] xvi, 431p. 'Selected literature'; v. 1, p.[413]-422. 21cm. (Harper Torchbook/The Cloister library, rebound in cloth) Contents.[1] Kievan Christianity. The tenth to the thirteenth centuries. 4.00
1. Religious thought—Russia. 2. Russia—Church history. 3. Orthodox Eastern church, Russian—Hist. 4. Spirituality. I. Title.

FEDOTOV, Georgii Petrovich 281.9
The Russian religious mind; Kievan Christianity: the 10th to the 13th centuries. New York, Harper [1960, c.1946] xvi, 431p. Bibl.: p.413-422 21cm. (Harper Torchbooks/The Cloister Library/TB 70) 1.95 pap.,
1. Religious thought—Russia. 2. Russia—Church history. 3. Orthodox Eastern church, Russian—Hist. 4. Spirituality. I. Title.

FEDOTOV, Georgii Petrovich, 281.9
1886-1951
The Russian religious mind; 2v. Cambridge, Mass., Harvard [c.1946, 1966] 2v. (431; 423) 24cm. Contents.v.1. Kievan Christianity.--v2. The Middle Ages. Bibl. [BX485.F4] A47 v.1, 10.00; v.2, 12.00
1. Orthodox Eastern church, Russian—Hist. 2. Religious thought—Russia. 3.

Russia—Church history. 4. Spirituality. I. Title.

FEDOTOV, Georgii Petrovich, 1886-1951. 281.947
The Russian religious mind. Cambridge, Harvard University Press, 1946-66. 2 v. 13 1/2 cm. "Selected literature": v. 1. p. [413]-424. "Bibliography of the writings of George P. Fedotov (1886-1951) compiled and edited by Thomas E. Bird": v. 2, p. [397]-413. Bibliographical footnotes. Contents.[I] Klevan Christianity--II. The Middle Ages, the thirteenth to the fifteenth centuries, edited, with a foreword, by John Meyendorff. [BX485.F4] A 47
1. Religious thought—Russia. 2. Russia—Church history. 3. Orthodox Eastern church, Russian—Hist. 4. Spirituality. I. Title.

GORODETZKY, Nadejda, 1904- 200'.947
The humiliated Christ in modern Russian thought, by Nadejda Gorodetzky. London, Society for Promoting Christian Knowledge, 1938. [New York, AMS Press, 1973] xiii, 185 p. 23 cm. Includes bibliographical references. [BR936.G57 1973] 79-168159 ISBN 0-404-02883-7 10.00
1. Religious thought—Russia. 2. Incarnation—History of doctrines. I. Title.

GORODETZKY, Nadejda, 1904- 232
The humiliated Christ in modern Russian thought, by Nadejda Gorodetzky ... London, Society for promoting Christian knowledge; New York, The Macmillan company, 1938. xiii p., 1 l., 185, [1] p. 22 cm. [BR936.G57] 891.70903 39-12135
1. Religious thought—Russia. 2. Incarnation. I. Society for promoting Christian knowledge, London. II. Title.

ZERNOV, Nicolas. 209'.47
Three Russian prophets: Khomiakov, Dostoevsky, Soloviev. 3d ed., with a pref. by the author. [Gulf Breeze, Fla.] Academic International Press, 1973. xiii, 8-171 p. ports. 24 cm. (Russian series, v. 23) "The basis of a course of lectures ... delivered at the School of Slavonic Studies in Oxford and London in 1942." Bibliography: p. [169]-171. [BX595.Z4 1973] 72-97040 ISBN 0-87569-050-5
1. Khomiakov, Aleksei Stepanovich, 1804-1860. 2. Dostoevskii, Fedor Mikhailovich, 1821-1881. 3. Solov'ev, Vladimir Sergeevich, 1853-1900. 4. Religious thought—Russia. I. Title.

Religious thought—Russia—19th century.

KLINE, George Louis, 1921- 209'.47
Religious and anti-religious thought in Russia [by] George L. Kline Chicago, University of Chicago Press [1968] 179 p. 21 cm. (The Weil lectures) Bibliographical footnotes. [BR936.K55] 68-54484
1. Religious thought—Russia—19th century. 2. Religious thought—Russia—20th century. 3. Atheism—Russia. I. Title. II. Series.

Religious thought—U.S.

CASKEY, Marie, 1945- 285'.8'0922 B
Chariot of fire : religion and the Beecher family / Marie Caskey. New Haven : Yale University Press, 1978. xv, 442 p. : ill. ; 24 cm. (Yale historical publications : Miscellany ; 117) Includes index. Bibliography: p. 417-434. [BR525.C38] 77-5291 ISBN 0-300-02131-3 : 25.00
1. Beecher family. 2. Religious thought—United States. 3. Theology, Doctrinal—United States—History. 4. Liberalism (Religion)—United States. I. Title. II. Series.

COFFIN, Henry Sloane, 1877- 204
Religion yesterday and today, by Henry Sloane Coffin ... Nashville, Cokesbury press [c1940] 183 p. 20 1/2 cm. "These six lectures were delivered on the Charles F. Deems foundation in New York university in the autumn of 1939 and on the Jarrell foundation in Emory university, Atlanta, Georgia, in January, 1940."--Pref. "Reference": p. 174-183. [BR525.C58] 40-27567
1. Religious thought—U.S. I. Title.

COFFIN, Henry Sloane, 1877-1954. 201
Religion yesterday and today. Freeport, N.Y., Books for Libraries Press [1970, c1940] 183 p. 23 cm. (Essay index reprint series) Contents.Contents.—Evolutionary science.—The divine immanence.—Biblical criticism.—Religious experience.—The social conscience.—The church. Includes bibliographical references. [BR525.C58 1970] 75-117769 ISBN 8-369-17901-
1. Religious thought—U.S. I. Title.

COWING, Cedric B. 917.3'03'2
The Great Awakening and the American Revolution: colonial thought in the 18th century [by] Cedric B. Cowing. Chicago, Rand McNally [1971] ix, 260 p. 21 cm. (The Rand McNally series on the history of American thought and culture) [BR520.C68] 74-126834
1. Religious thought—U.S. I. Title.

*GAUSTAD, Edwin Scott. 200.9'73
Dissent in American religion. Chicago, University of Chicago Press [1973] xii, 184 p. 21 cm. (Chicago history of American religion.) Bibliography: p. 161-176. [BR515] 73-77131 ISBN 0-226-28436-0 6.95
1. Religious thought—U.S. 2. U.S.—Religion. I. Title.

HEIMERT, Alan E. 261.70973
Religion and the American mind, from the Great Awakening to the Revolution [by] Alan Heimert. Cambridge, Harvard University Press, 1966. x, 668 p. 25 cm. "Biographical glossary": p. 555-563. Bibliographical references included in "Sources" & "Notes" (p. 564-639) [BR520.H4] 66-14444
1. Religious thought—United States. 2. United States—Church history. I. Title.

MARTY, Martin E., 1928- 277.3
The infidel; freethought and American religion. Cleveland, World Pub. Co. [c.1961] 224p. (Meridian Living Age bk., LA34) 61-15604 3.75; 1.45 pap.,
1. Religious thought—U. S. 2. Free thought—Hist. 3. U. S.—Church history. I. Title.

MARTY, Martin E., 1928- 277.3
The infidel; free thought and American religion [Magnolia, Mass., P. Smith, 1967, c.1961] 244p. 20cm. (Living age bk., LA34: Meridian bk. rebound) Bibl. [BR515.M3] 3.50
1. Religious thought—U. S. 2. Free thought—Hist. 3. U. S.—Church history. I. Title.

MARTY, Martin E 1928- 277.3
Infidel free thought and American religion Cleveland, Meridian Books [1961] 224p. 19cm. (Living age books, LA34) Includes bibliography. [BR515.M3] 61-15604
1. Religious thought—U. S. 2. Free thought—Hist. 3. U. S.—Church history. I. Title.

SMITH, James Ward, 1917-
... The shaping of American religion. Editors: James Ward Smith and A. Leland Jamison. Princeton, New Jersey, Princeton university press, 1961. 514 p. 23 cm. (Religion in American life. 1) "Princeton studies in American civilization. 5." Bibliographical footnotes.
I. Jamison, Albert Leland, 1911- II. Title.

Religious thought—United States—Addresses, essays, lectures.

NEW World metaphysics : 261
readings on the religious meaning of the American experience / edited by Giles Gunn. New York : Oxford University Press, 1981. xxi, 464 p. ; 25 cm. [BR515.N48] 19 80-20233 ISBN 0-19-502873-2 : 17.00 ISBN 0-19-502874-0 (pbk.) : 9.00
1. Religious thought—United States—Addresses, essays, lectures. 2. Religious thought—Modern period, 1500- — Addresses, essays, lectures. 3. United States—Civilization—Addresses, essays, lectures. I. Gunn, Giles B.

Religious tolerance.

ACONCIO, Giacomo, 1492?-1566? 261.7'2
Darkness discovered : (Satans stratagems) / by Jacobus Acontius ; a facsim. reproduction with an introd. by R. E. Field. Delmar, N.Y. : Scholars' Facsimiles & Reprints, 1978. p. cm. Translation of books 1-4 of Satanae stratagemata. Reprint of the 1651 ed. printed by J. Macock, London, and sold by J. Hancock. Reproduction of Wing A442. Bibliography: p. [BR1610.A35213 1978] 78-9490 ISBN 0-8201-1313-1 : 30.00 30.00
1. Religious tolerance. 2. Religious liberty. I. Title. II. Title: Satans stratagems.

SEATON, Alexander Adam. 274.2
The theory of toleration under the later Stuarts, by A. A. Seaton. New York, Octagon Books, 1972. vii, 364 p. 23 cm. Reprint of the 1911 ed., which was issued as no. 19 of the Cambridge historical essays. Bibliography: p. [346]-350. [BR757.S4 1972] 72-7443 ISBN 0-374-97233-8 12.25
1. Religious tolerance. 2. Great Britain—Church history—Modern period. 3. Religious liberty—Great Britain. I. Title. II. Series: Cambridge historical essays, no. 19.

Religious tolerance—Addresses, essays, lectures.

WATSON, Adam, 1914- 261.7
Toleration in religion & politics / Adam Watson on behalf of Sir Herbert Butterfield ; in symposium with Adam Watson, Abraham Bargman ... [et al.]. New York, N.Y. : Council on Religion and International Affairs, c1980. vii, 55 p. ; 22 cm. (Distinguished CRIA lecture on morality & foreign policy ; 2d) [BR1610.W37] 19 80-65746 ISBN 0-87641-218-5 pbk. : 4.00
1. Religious tolerance—Addresses, essays, lectures. 2. Toleration—Addresses, essays, lectures. I. Butterfield, Herbert, Sir, 1900- II. Title. III. Series: Council on Religion and International Affairs. Distinguished CRIA lecture on morality & foreign policy ; 2d.

Religiousness.

CARDWELL, Jerry Delmas. 306'.6
The social context of religiosity / Jerry D. Cardwell. Lanham, MD : University Press of America, 1980. p. cm. Includes index. [BL60.C36] 19 80-67216 ISBN 0-8191-1136-8 (pbk.) : 8.75 ISBN 0-8191-1135-X : 17.50
1. Religiousness. 2. Religion and sociology. I. Title.

KNUDSEN, Harold F. 201
To know or not to be; an arraignment of the religiously oriented attitude, by Harold F. Knudsen. New York, William-Frederick Pr., 1966. 120p. 22cm. [BV4509.5.K58] 65-28153 2.50 pap.,
1. Religiousness. I. Title.

Remads, 1608-1681.

DEMING, Wilbur Stone, 1889- 294.55
... Ramdas and the Ramdasis, by Wilbur S. Deming ... Calcutta, Association press (Y. M. C. A.); London, New York [etc.] H. Milford, Oxford university press, 1928. xii, p. 2 l. 223 [1] p. front., plates, ports. 19 cm. (The religious life of India) Thesis (PH. D.)-Hartford seminary foundation, Kennedy school of missions, 1927. Without thesis note. Bibliography: leaf proceding p. [1] [BL1175.R3D4 1927] 36-20102
1. Remads, 1608-1681. I. Title.

Remarriage (Hindu law)

VIDYASAGAR, Iswar Chandra, 1820-1891. 294.5'94
Marriage of Hindu widows / Isvarachandra Vidyasagara ; with an introd. by Arabinda Podder. Calcutta : K. P. Bagchi, 1976. xvi, ii, 144 p. ; 23 cm. Includes bibliographical references. [LAW] 76-900930 ISBN 0-88386-738-9 : 8.00
1. Remarriage (Hindu law) 2. Widows (Hindu law) I. Title.
Distributed by South Asia Books

Remarriage—Moral and religious aspects.

RICHARDS, Larry, 1931- 241'.63
Remarriage, a healing gift from God / Larry Richards. Waco, Tex. : Word Books, c1981. 144 p. ; 23 cm. [BV835.R53] 19 80-54548 ISBN 0-8499-0265-7 : 7.95
1. Remarriage—Moral and religious aspects. 2. Remarriage—Biblical teaching. I. Title.

Rembrandt Hermanszoon van Rijn, 1606-1669.

VISSER 't Hooft, William Adolph, 1900- 755.5
Rembrandt and the Gospel. [Magnolia, Mass., P. Smith, 1967] 192p. plates. 19cm. (Meridian living age bk. rebound) Tr. by K. Gregor Smith from the German, Rembrandt's Weg zum Evangelium [a tr. of Rembrandt et la Bible] rev. by the author. [ND653.R4V5713] 3.50
1. Rembranot Hermanszoon van Rijn, 1606-1669. 2. Bible—Pictures, illustrations, etc. I. Title.

VISSER'T Hooft, Willem Adolph, 1900- 755.5
Rembrandt and the Gospel. Philadelphia, Westminster Press [1958?] 192 p. plates. 23 cm. "Translated by K. Gregor Smith from the German, Rembrandt's Weg zum Evangelium [a translation of Rembrandt et la Bible] ... and revised by the author." [ND653.R4V5713] 58-5487
1. Rembrandt Hermanszoon van Rijn, 1606-1669. 2. Bible — Pictures, illustrations, etc. I. Title.

VISSER'T HOOFT, Willem Adolph 755
Rembrandt and the Gospel. Translated by K. Gregor Smith from the German text, revised by the author. New York, Meridian Books [1960] 192p. Bibl. notes: p.117-128. illus. 19cm. (Living Age Books, LA30) 1.25 pap.,
1. Rembrandt Hermanszoon van Rijn, 1606-1669. 2. Bibl—Pictures, illustrations, etc. I. Title.

VISSER 'T HOOFT, Willem Adolph, 1900-
Rembrandt and the Gospel [by] W. A. Visser 't Hooft. New York, Meridian Books [1960] 192 p. plates. 18 cm. (Living age books, LA30) Translation of Rembrandts Weg zum Evangelium. 67-69759
1. Rembrandt Hermanszoon van Rijn, 1606-1669. 2. Bible—Pictorial illustrations. I. Title.

Remington, Stephen, 1805-1860.

BISHOP, William P. 265.
Review of Remington's Reasons for being a Baptist. By William P. Bishop...To which is appended a vocabulary of the Greek particles involved in the controversy, taken from the books fo the New Testament. Nashville, Tenn., Printed for the author at the Southern Methodist publishing house, 1859. iv, 5-104 p. 19 cm. "The Review was published in the Holston Christian advocate."--Pref. [BV813.R45B5] 39-1464
1. Remington, Stephen, 1805-1860. Reasons for becoming a Baptist. 2. Baptism. I. Title.

Remnant (Theology)—Biblical teaching.

HASEL, Gerhard F. 296.3
The remnant : the history and theology of the remnant idea from Genesis to Isaiah / by Gerhard F. Hasel. 2d ed. Berrien Springs, Mich. : Andrews University Press, c1974. x, 478 p. ; 24 cm. (Andrews University monographs ; v. 5) (Studies in religion) Revised version of the author's thesis, Vanderbilt University, 1970, which was presented under title: The origin and early history of the remnant motif in ancient Israel. Includes index. Bibliography: p. 408-432. [BS1199.R37H37 1974] 76-351607
1. Bible. O.T.—Criticism, interpretation, etc. 2. Remnant (Theology)—Biblical teaching. 3. Remnant (Theology)—History of doctrines. I. Title. II. Series. III. Series: Andrews University. Monographs ; v. 5.

Renaissance.

ALLEN, Don Cameron, 1904- 273.0903
Doubt's boundless sea: skepticism and faith in the Renaissance. Baltimore Johns Hopkins Press, 1964. xi, 272 p. 22 cm. Bibliography: p. 244-261. [CB361.A48] 64-10939
1. Renaissance. 2. Religious thought — 16th cent. 3. Skepticism. I. Title.

ALLEN, Don Cameron, 1904- 211'.8'094
Doubt's boundless sea / Don Cameron Allen. New York : Arno Press, 1979, c1964. xi, 272 p. ; 23 cm. (Johns Hopkins University Press reprints) Reprint of the ed. published by the Johns Hopkins Press, Baltimore. Includes index. Bibliography: p. 244-261. [CB361.A48 1979] 78-19267 ISBN 0-405-10577-0 : 22.00
1. Renaissance. 2. Religious thought—16th century. 3. Skepticism. I. Title.

BLAYNEY, Ida Walz. 270.6
The age of Luther; the spirit of Renaissance-humanism and the Reformation. [1st ed.] New York, Vantage Press [1957] 499p. illus. 21cm. Includes bibliography. [BR280.B5] 56-12321
1. Luther, Martin, 1483-1586. 2. Renaissance. 3. Humanism. 4. Reformation. I. Title.

DANNENFELDT, Karl H. 270.6
The church of the Renaissance and Reformation; decline and reform from 1300 to 1600, by Karl H. Dannenfeldt. Saint Louis, Concordia Pub. House [1970] 145 p. 21 cm. (Church in history series) Includes bibliographical references. [BR280.D33] 77-98300
1. Renaissance. 2. Reformation. I. Title. II. Series.

GIRALDI, Lilio Gregorio, 1479-1552. 292'.2'11
De deis gentium : Basel, 1548 / Lilio Gregorio Giraldi. New York : Giraldi, 1976. p. cm. (The Renaissance and the gods ; no. 8) Reprint of the 1548 ed. [PA8520.G58D4 1976] 75-27850 ISBN 0-8240-2057-X : 40.00
I. Title. II. Series.

GUNSAULUS, Frank Wakeley, 1856-
Martin Luther and the morning hour in Europe: two lectures delivered at the University of Chicago, October 16 and 17, 1917, by Frank Wakeley Gunsaulus. Chicago, Ill., The University of Chicago press [c1917] 1 p. l., 50 p. 24 cm. Bibliography, Emma B. Hodge collection: p. 47-50. [BR326.G8] 18-411
1. Luther, Martin, 1483-1546. 2. Renaissance. I. Title.

HYMA, Albert, 1893-
Christian renaissance: a history of "Devotio moderna", by Albert Hyma. Grand Rapids, Mich., The Reformed press, 1924. xviii, 501 p. facsims. 23 cm. First three chapters published as thesis (PH. D.) University of Michigan, 1922, under title: The "Devotio moderna" or Christian renaissance (1380-1520) "The original constitution of the Brethren of the common life at Deventer": p. 440-474. Bibliography: p. 477-494. [BR270.B8 1924] 25-6901
I. Title. II. Title: "Devotio moderna."

HYMA, Albert, 1893- 270.5
Renaissance to Reformation. Grand Rapids, Eerdmans, 1951. 591 p. 24 cm. Bibliographical footnotes. [BR280.H9] 51-11560
1. Renaissance. 2. Reformation. I. Title.

Renaissance—Bibliography—Catalogs.

CHRISTENSEN, Niels. 016.09
Renaissance & Reformation; books for libraries, scholars & booklovers; manuscripts, incunabula, humanists, neo-Latin authors & related books from famous presses, fifteenth to twentieth centuries. Bloomfield, N. J. [194-] 217 p. 23 cm. [Catalogue 1] [Z6207.R4C5] 48-41800
1. Renaissance—Bibl.—Catalogs. 2. Reformation—Bibl.—Catalogs. I. Title.

Renan, Ernes, 1823-1892.

[HARRISSE, Henry] 1829-1910. 204
M. Ernest Renan. [New York, Carleton, 1864] xxxvi p. 23 cm. Caption title. Signed: F. H. [i.e. Henry Harrisse] Biographical introduction to Ernest Renan's Studies of religious history and criticism; authorized translation from the original French by O. B. Frothingham, with t. p., translator's pref., and table of contents of complete work. Holograph letters addressed to the author, clippings, etc., inserted. [BL27.R43H3] 50-45014
1. Renan, Ernes, 1823-1892. I. Renan, Ernest, 1823-1892. Etudes d'histoire religieuse. II. Title.

LAGRANGE, Marie Joseph, 1855-1938.
Christ and Renan; a commentary on Ernest Renan's "The life of Jesus", by M. J. Lagrange, O. P.; translated by Maisie Ward. New York, Cincinnati [etc.] Benziger brothers [1928] 3 p. l., 127 p. 20 cm. "Printed in Great Britain." A 40
1. Renan, Ernest, 1823-1892. Vie de Jesus. 2. Jesus Christ—Biography. I. Ward, Maisie, 1889- tr. II. Title.

RENAN, Ernest, 1823-1892. 232.
The life of Jesus, by Ernest Renan ... Tr. from the original French by Charles Edwin Wilbour ... New York, Carleton; [etc., etc.] 1874. 1 p. l., [v]-viii, [9]-376 p. 18 cm. [Full name: Joseph Ernest Renan] [BT301] 15-16168
I. Wilbour, Charles Edwin, 1833-1896, tr. II. Title.

RENAN, Ernest i.e. Joseph Ernest, 1823-1892. 928.
Renan's letters from the Holy Land; the correspondence of Ernest Renan with M. Berthelot while gathering material in Italy and the Orient for "The life of Jesus"; tr. by Lorenzo O'Rourke ... New York, Doubleday, Page & company, 1904. xxxiv, 313 p. front. (port.) 23 1/2 cm. [BR139.R4A27 1904] 4-27344
I. O'Rourke, Lorenzo, tr. II. Title.

Rensselaerville, N. Y. Trinity church.

FULLER, Samuel, 1802-1895. 922.
Early days of the church in the Helderberg. Two sermons preached in trinity church, Rensselaerville, N. Y. Sunday, April 24, 1842, on the death of its founder and first rector. the Rev. Samuel Fuller, who died on the ninth in the 75th year of his age, and 50th of his ministry. By his son, the Rev. Samuel Fuller ... Andover, Printed by Allen, Morrill and Wardwell, 1843. 52 p. 23 cm. [BX5995.F8F8] 10-7617
1. Fuller, Samuel, 1767-1842. 2. Rensselaerville, N. Y. Trinity church. I. Title. II. Title: Helderberg. Early days of the church in the.

Renty, Gaston Jean Baptiste, baron de, 1611-1648.

SAINT JURE, Jean Baptiste de, 1588-1657. 922.244
An extract of the life of Monsieur de Renty, a late nobleman of France. Published by John Wesley. 1st American ed. Philadelphia, Printed by H. Tuckniss and sold by J. Dickins, 1795. 70 p. 19 cm. "Extracted from 'The holy life of Monr. de Renty...Written in French by John Baptist S. Jure...translated into English by E. S. Gent. London...1958.' "--Richard Green. The works of John and Charles Wesley. 2d ed. 1906. [BX4705.R44S322] 65-58543
1. Renty, Gaston Jean Baptiste, baron de, 1611-1648. I. Wesley, John, 1703-1791, ed. II. Title.

[SAINT Jure, Jean Baptiste de] 1588-1657. 922.244
Nobility at the cross. Life of Monsieur de Renty. Revised by Rev. W. McDonald. Boston, J. Bent & co., 1873. 4, iv, 5-139 p. 18 cm. Edited and translated by Rev. John Wesley. [BX4705.R44S32] 37-21098
1. Renty, Gaston Jean Baptists, baron de, 1611-1648. I. Wesley, John, 1703-1791, ed. and tr. II. McDonald, William, 1820-1901, ed. III. Title.

Reorganized Church of Jesus Christ of Latter-Day Saints.

HOWARD, Richard P. 289.3'2
Restoration scriptures; a study of their textual development, by Richard P. Howard. [Independence, Mo.] Dept. of Religious Education, Reorganized Church of Jesus Christ of Latter Day Saints [1969] 278 p. facsims. 23 cm. Includes bibliographical references. [BX8627.H67] 73-85800
1. Reorganized Church of Jesus Christ of Latter Day Saints. Book of doctrine and covenants. 2. Book of mormon. 3. Bible—Criticism, Textual. I. Reorganized Church of Jesus Christ of Latter Day Saints. Dept. of Religious Education. II. Title.

JUDD, Peter A., 1943- 265
The sacraments : an exploration into their meaning and practice in the Saints Church / by Peter A. Judd. Independence, Mo. : Herald Pub. House, c1978. 174 p. ; 20 cm. Includes bibliographical references. [BX8655.J83] 78-12776 ISBN 0-8309-0225-2 : 5.75
1. Reorganized Church of Jesus Christ of Latter Day Saints. 2. Sacraments—Reorganized Church of Jesus Christ of Latter Day Saints. I. Title.

OAKMAN, Arthur A. 289.3
The call of Christ in an age of dilemma; six studies based upon the Apostolic epistle of 1964, by Arthur A. Oakman. Independence, Mo., Herald Pub. House [1964] 64 p. 22 cm. Includes bibliographies. [BX8675.O2] 64-9183
1. Reorganized Church of Jesus Christ of Latter-Day Saints. I. Title.

REIMANN, Paul E. 289.3
The Reorganized church in the light of court decisions, by Paul E. Reimann ... [Salt Lake city, Harper brothers, printers, 1942] 1 p l., 102 p. 23 cm. [BX8671.R4] 42-5721
1. Reorganized church of Jesus Christ of latter-day saints. I. Title.

REORGANIZED Church of Jesus Christ of Latter-Day Saints. 289.3
Zionic problems, a close-up view; lectures and discussions at the Business and Professional Men's Institute, February, 1953. [Independence, Mo., 1953] 162p. illus. 28cm. [BX8671.A547] 54-28239
1. Reorganized Church of Jesus Christ of Latter-Day Saints. I. Title.

WIDTSOE, John Andreas, 1872-1952. 289.3
The message of the Doctrine and covenants. Edited and arranged with a foreword by G. Homer Durham. Salt Lake City, Bookcraft, 1969. xii, 179 p. 24 cm. The transcript of lectures delivered by the author at the University of Southern California, April-June, 1936. [BX8628.W53 1969] 74-77460 3.50
1. Reorganized Church of Jesus Christ of Latter Day Saints. Book of doctrine and convenants. I. Title.

YARRINGTON, Roger 289.3
The auditorium; world headquarters building of the Reorganized Church of Jesus Christ of Latter Day Saints. Independence, Mo., Herald House [c.1962] 90p. illus. (pt. col.) 26cm. 62-9963 2.95
1. Reorganized Church of Jesus Christ of Latter-Day Saints. 2. Independence, Mo. Auditorium. I. Title.

Reorganized Church of Jesus Christ of Latter-Day Saints—Addresses, essays, lectures.

RESTORATION studies, 1980 289.3'3
/ Maurice L. Draper,editor, Clare D. Vlahos, assistant editor. Independence, Mo. : Herald Pub. House, c1980. p. cm. [BX8674.A454] 19 80-19346 ISBN 0-8309-0292-9 : 12.00
1. Reorganized Church of Jesus Christ of Latter-Day Saints—Addresses, essays, lectures. I. Draper, Maurice L. II. Vlahos, Clare D.

Reorganized Church of Jesus Christ of Latter-Day Saints—Biography

CHEVILLE, Roy Arthur, 1897- 289.3'0922 B
They made a difference, by Roy Cheville. [Independence, Mo., Herald Pub. House, 1970] 350 p. ports. 21 cm. "A roster of thirty persons whose participation made significant impact upon the Latter Day Saint Movement: The Early Church, 1820-1844; the Reorganized Church, 1853-1970." [BX8678.A2] 78-101568 6.95
1. Reorganized Church of Jesus Christ of Latter-Day Saints—Biography. I. Title.

LIVING saints witness 289.3'3 B
at work / compiled by T. Ed Barlow. Independence, Mo. : Herald Pub. House, c1976. 126 p. : ill. ; 21 cm. [BX8678.A28] 76-27227 ISBN 0-8309-0153-1
1. Reorganized Church of Jesus Christ of Latter-Day Saints—Biography. 2. Christian life—Mormon authors. I. Barlow, T. Ed, 1931-

PHILLIPS, Emma M 922.83
33 women of the restoration Independence, Mo., Herald House [1960] 197p. 21cm. Includes bibliography. [BX8678.A43] 60-14176
1. Reorganized Church of Jesus Christ of Latter-Day Saints—Biog. 2. Woman—Biog. I. Title.

REORGANIZED Church of Jesus Christ of Latter- Day Saints. 289.33
Pioneer helpers; 52 selected stories about some of Jesus' helpers in the restoration. Independence, Mo., Herald Pub. House [1959] 79p. 26cm. [BX8678.A3] 59-8310
1. Reorganized Church of Jesus Christ of Latter-Day Saints—Biog. I. Title.

RUOFF, Norman D. comp. 289.3/0922
Witness to the world; a collection of testimonies and inspirational writings from the pages of the Resforation witness, ed., comp. by Norman D. Ruoff. [Independence, Mo., Herald Pub., 1967] 216p. 20cm. [BX8678.A46] 67-30460 3.50
1. Reorganized Church of Jesus Christ of Latter-Day Saints—Biog. 2. Restoration witness. I. Title.

WHO'S who in service—a 289.3'3 B
look at areas of service participation by members of the Reorganizaed Church of Jesus Christ of Latter Day Saints. Independence, Mo. : Herald Pub. House, c1977. 164 p. ; 26 cm. [BX8678.A48] 76-29064 ISBN 0-8309-0173-6 : 12.00
1. Reorganized Church of Jesus Christ of Latter Day Saints—Biography. I. Herald Publishing House.

Reorganized Church of Jesus Christ of Latter-Day Saints. Board of Publication.

REORGANIZED Church of Jesus Christ of Latter-Day Saints.
Book of Doctrine and Covenants carefully selected from the revelations of God, and given in the order of their dates. [The board of publications of] the Reorganized Church of Jesus Christ of Latter Day Saints. Enl. and improved ed. Independence, Mo., Herald Pub. House, 1960. 387, 39 p. 19 cm. Topical index paged separately. 68-41112
1. Reorganized Church of Jesus Christ of Latter-Day Saints. Board of Publication. I. Title.

Reorganized church of Jesus Christ of latter-day saints. Book of doctrine and covenants.

BUTTERWORTH, F. Edward. 289.3'22
The sword of Laban, by F. Edward Butterworth. Illustrated by Don Wagler. Independence, Mo.] Reorganized Church of Jesus Christ of Latter Day Saints [1969- v. illus., map. 21 cm. Paraphrased from the Book of Mormon. Bibliography: p. 120. [BX8627.A2B87] 70-101571
I. Reorganized Church of Jesus Christ of Latter Day Saints. II. Book of Mormon. III. Title.

EDWARDS, Francis Henry, 1897- 230.93
... A commentary on the Doctrine and covenants (sections 1 to 131) by F. Henry

Edwards; a brief historical treatment of each section, stating the conditions under which it was given, its import for the time it was given, and its application to the problems and needs of the church today. Independence, Mo., Herald publishing house, 1946. 447, [1] p. 20 1/2 cm. (The Priesthood library) "First edition, August 1938. Revised edition, September 1946." [BX8628.E3] 47-16470
1. Smith, Joseph, 1805-1844. Doctrine and covenants. 2. Reorganized church of Jesus Christ of latter-day saints. Book of doctrine and covenants. I. Title.

EDWARDS, Francis Henry, 1897- 230'.9'3
A new commentary on the Doctrine and covenants / by F. Henry Edwards. Independence, Mo. : Herald Pub. House, 1977. 565 p. ; 21 cm. "An introduction to the Book of doctrine and covenants (Reorganized Church) plus a brief historical treatment of each section, stating the conditions under which it was given, its import for the time it was given, and its application to the problems and needs of the church today." [BX8628.E33] 77-7385 ISBN 0-8309-0187-6 : 15.00
1. Reorganized Church of Jesus Christ of Latter-Day Saints. Book of doctrine and covenants. 2. Smith, Joseph, 1805-1844. Doctrine and covenants. I. Title.

HARTSHORN, Chris Benson. 289.3
A survey of the doctrine and covenants. Independence, Mo., Herald House, 1961. 168p. 21cm. Includes bibliography. [BX8628.H3] 61-17863
1. Reorganized Church of Jesus Christ of Latter-Day Saints. Book of doctrine and covenants. I. Title.

Reorganized Church of Jesus Christ of Latter-Day Saints—Collected works.

EDWARDS, Francis Henry, 1897- 289.3
For such a time. Independence, Mo., Herald Pub. House, 1963. 351 p. 21 cm. Chiefly selections from the author's editorials, articles, sermons, etc. [BX8674.E32] 62-22193
1. Reorganized Church of Jesus Christ of Latter-Day Saints—Collected works. I. Title.

SMITH, Frederick Madison, 1874-1946. 230'.9'33
The writings of President Frederick M. Smith / edited by Norman D. Ruoff. Independence, Mo. : Herald Pub. House, c1978- v. : ill. ; 20 cm. Articles first published in the Saints herald. Contents.Contents.—v. 1. His theology and philosophy.—v. 2. Educating, nurturing, and upholding. [BX8674.S63 1978] 78-6428 ISBN 0-8309-0215-5 pbk. : 6.50
1. Reorganized Church of Jesus Christ of Latter-Day Saints—Collected works. 2. Theology—Collected works—20th century. I. Ruoff, Norman D.

Reorganized Church of Jesus Christ of Latter-Day Saints—Congresses.

REORGANIZED Church of Jesus Christ of Latter-Day Saints. 289.3'3
Highlights of the 968 World Conference. [Independence, Mo., Herald Pub. House? 1968] 124 p. illus. 23 cm. [BX8605.A5] 68-6769
1. Reorganized Church of Jesus Christ of Latter-Day Saints—Congresses. I. Title.

Reorganized Church of Jesus Christ of Latter-Day Saints — Directories

REORGANIZED Church of Jesus Christ of Latter-Day Saints. 289.3
Church directory; locations of branch and missions in all countries. Independence, Mo. v. 16 cm. [BX8606.A35] 52-29973
1. Reorganized Church of Jesus Christ of Latter-Day Saints — Direct. I. Title.

Reorganized Church of Jesus Christ of Latter-Day Saints—Doctrinal and controversial works.

BROCKWAY, Esther. 248'.5
Toward better witnessing / by Esther Brockway. Independence, Mo. : Herald Pub. House, c1976. 210 p. ; 21 cm. [BX8674.4.B76] 74-82511 ISBN 0-8309-0123-X
1. Reorganized Church of Jesus Christ of Latter Day Saints—Doctrinal and controversial works. 2. Witness bearing (Christianity) I. Title.

CHEVILLE, Roy Arthur, 1897- 230.93
By what authority? A series of lectures delivered to the Melchisedec priesthood of Independence, Missouri, January 8-13, 1956. Reorganized Church of Jesus Christ of Latter Day Saints. [Independence] Herald House [c1956] 96p. 21cm. [BX8674.C48] 56-12878
1. Reorganized Church of Jesus Christ of Latter-Day Saints—Doctrinal and controversial works. 2. Authority (Religion) I. Title.

CHEVILLE, Roy Arthur, 1897- 230.93
The field of theology; an introductory study. [Independence, Mo.] Dept. of Religious Education, Reorganized Church of Jesus Christ of Latter Day Saints [1959] 144p. 21cm. (Restoration theology series) [BX8674.C5] 59-11403
1. Reorganized Church of Jesus Christ of Latter-Day Saints— Doctrinal and controversial works. 2. Theology. I. Title.

COLE, Clifford Adair, 1915- 234.2
Faith for new frontiers. Independence, Mo., Herald House [1956] 156p. 21cm. [BX8674.C6] 56-12023
1. Reorganized Church of Jesus Christ of Latter-Day Saints—Dectrinal and controversial works. 2. Faith. I. Title.

A Compendium of the faith and doctrine of the Reorganized Church of Jesus Christ of Latter Day Saints, for its ministry, church schools, and members, including texts of the standard books of the church and a historical appendix. Based on the Stebbins-Walker compendium as revised by S. A. Burgess. Edited, rearranged, and enlarged by A. B. Phillips. Independence, Mo., Herald Pub. House, 1947. 315&p. 21 cm. (The Priesthood library) [BX8671.C6] 47-2955 230.93
1. Reorganized Church of Jesus Christ of Latter-Day Saints—Doctrinal and controversial works. I. Stebbins, Henry A., 1844-1920. II. Phillips. Arthur Bernicie, 1873- ed. III. Series.

EDWARDS, Francis Henry, 1897- 289.3
Authority and spiritual power: Reorganized Church of Jesus Christ of Latter Day Saints. Independence, Mo., Herald House [1956] 125p. 21cm. [BX8674.E3] 56-11958
1. Reorganized Church of Jesus Christ of Latter-Day Saints— Doctrinal and controversial works. I. Title.

EVANGELISM, the ministry of the Church : an introduction to the Faith to grow program / edited by Richard Hughes and Joe Serig (Program Services Division, Reorganized Church of Jesus Christ of Latter Day Saints). Independence, Mo. : Herald Pub. House, c1981. 299 p. ; 21 cm. Includes bibliographical references. [BV3.E93] 19 80-26010 ISBN 0-8309-0304-6 : 12.00 253
1. Reorganized Church of Jesus Christ of Latter-Day Saints—Doctrinal and controversial works—Addresses, essays, lectures. 2. Theology, Practical—Addresses, essays, lectures. I. Hughes, Richard, 1938- II. Serig, Joe. III. Reorganized Church of Jesus Christ of Latter-Day Saints. Division of Program Services.

FARROW, Percy, E., 1902- 236
God's eternal design / by Percy E. Farrow. Independence, Mo. : Herald Pub. House, c1980. 316 p. ; 20 cm. Bibliography: p. 312-316. [BT821.2.F3] 79-26277 ISBN 0-8309-0272-4 pbk. : 10.00
1. Reorganized Church of Jesus Christ of Latter-Day Saints—Doctrinal and controversial works. 2. Eschatology. 3. Prophecy. 4. Kingdom of God. I. Title.

HIELD, Charles R 265.1
Baptism for the dead, by Charles R. Hield and Russell F. Ralston. [Rev. Independence, Mo., Herald Pub. House 1960. 56p. 18cm. [BX8675.H5 1960] 60-4213
1. Reorganized Church of Jesus Christ of Latter-Day Saints—Doctrinal and controversial works. 2. Baptism for the dead. 3. Mormons and Mormonism—Doctrinal and controversial works. I. Ralston, Russell F., joint author. II. Title.

HOLMES, Reed M 230.93
Seek this Christ; the Reorganized Church of Jesus Christ of Latter Day Saints. [Independence, Mo., Herald Pub. House, 1954] 112p. 18cm. [BX8671.H6] 54-11778
1. Reorganized Church of Jesus Christ of Latter-Day Saints—Doctrinal and controversial works. I. Title.

JUDD, Peter A., 1943- 230'.9'33
An introduction to the Saints Church : including user's guide / by Peter A. Judd and A. Bruce Lindgren. Independence, Mo. : Christian Education Office, Reorganized Church of Jesus Christ of Latter Day Saints, c1976. 228, 108 p. ; 21 cm. Includes bibliographical references and index. [BX8674.J82] 75-35763 ISBN 0-8309-0154-X
1. Reorganized Church of Jesus Christ of Latter Day Saints—Doctrinal and controversial works. I. Lindgren, A. Bruce, joint author. II. Title.

KOURY, Aleah G. 289.3
The truth and the evidence; a comparison between doctrines of the Reorganized Church of Jesus Christ of Latter Day Saints and the Church of Jesus Christ of Latter-Day Saints, by Aleah G. Koury. [Independence, Mo., Herald Pub. House. 1965] 112 p. 18 cm. Bibliographical footnotes. [BX8674.K6] 65-26287
1. Reorganized Church of Jesus Christ of Latter-Day Saints—Doctrinal and controversial works. 2. Church of Jesus Christ of Latter-Day Saints—Doctrinal and controversial works. I. Title.

LANDON, Donald D. 262'.22
For what purpose assembled; a study of the congregation and mission [by] Donald D. Landon & Robert L. Smith. New York, Family Library [1973, c.1969] 141 p. 19 cm. Bibliography: p. 140-141. [BX8675.L3] ISBN 0-515-03230-1 0.95 (pbk.)
1. Reorganized Church of Jesus Christ of Latter-Day Saints—Doctrinal and controversial works. I. Smith Robert L., joint author. II. Title.
L.C. card no. for the hardbound edition: 72-13619.

LANDON, Donald D. 262'.22
For what purpose assembled; a study of the congregation and mission, by Donald D. Landon and Robert L. Smith. [Independence, Mo., Herald Pub. House, 1969] 188 p. illus. 18 cm. Bibliography: p. 187-188. [BX8675.L3] 72-13619 2.95
1. Reorganized Church of Jesus Christ of Latter-Day Saints—Doctrinal and controversial works. I. Smith, Robert L., joint author. II. Title.

NJEIM, George A. 264'.09'3
The sacrament of the Lord's Supper in the fullness of the Gospel / by George A. Njeim. Independence, Mo. : Herald Pub. House, c1978. 260 p. ; 20 cm. Includes bibliographical references. [BX8655.2.N56] 77-7649 ISBN 0-8309-0182-5 : 7.50
1. Reorganized Church of Jesus Christ of Latter-Day Saints—Doctrinal and controversial works. 2. Lord's Supper—Mormonism. I. Title.

OAKMAN, Arthur A. 230.93
God's spiritual universe. Independence, Mo., Herald House [c.1961] 188p. Bibl. 61-9684 2.50
1. Reorganized Church of Jesus Christ of Latter-Day Saints—Doctrinal and controversial works. I. Title.

OAKMAN, Arthur A 289.3081
Resurrection and eternal life; a series of lectures delivered to the Melchisedec priesthood of Independence, Missouri. January 5-12, 1958. [Independence. Mo.] Herald House. Reorganized Church of Jesus Christ of Latter Day Saints [1959] 256p. 21cm. [BX8674.O2] 59-8361
1. Reorganized Church of Jesus Christ of Latter-Day Saints—Doctrinal and controversial works. 2. Resurrection. 3. Future life. I. Title.

PACKER, Athol B 289.3
An open door; a study of the basic teachings of Christ and His church. Independence, Mo., Herald House [1959] 191p. 21cm. [BX8674.P2] 58-14400
1. Reorganized Church of Jesus Christ of Latter-Day Saints—Doctrinal and controversial works. I. Title.

PHILLIPS, Arthur Bernicie, 1873- 230.93
... A compendium of the faith and doctrine of the Reorganized church of Jesus Christ of latter day saints; for its ministry, church schools, and members, including texts of the standard books of the church and a historical appendis. Based on the Stebbins-Walker compendium as revised by S. A. Burgess. Edited, rearranged, and enlarged by A. B. Phillips. Independence, Mo., Herald publishing house, 1947. 315 p. 20 1/2 cm. (The Priesthood library) [BX8671.P5] 47-2955
1. Reorganized church of Jesus Christ of latter-day saints—Doctrinal and controversial works. I. Stebbins, Henry A., 1844-1920. II. Title.

RALSTON, Russell F. 230.93
Fundamental differences between the Reorganized Church and the Church in Utah; a series of lects. delivered to the Melchidesec priesthood of Independence, Mo., Jan. 4-11, 1959, Reorganized Church of Jesus Christ of Latter Day Saints [Rev. ed. Independence, Mo.] Herald House, 1963. 328p. 21cm. Bibl. 63-25860 price unreported
1. Reorganized Church of Jesus Christ of Latter-Day Saints—Doctrinal and controversial works. 2. Mormons and Mormonism—Doctrinal and controversial works. I. Title.

REORGANIZED Church of Jesus Christ of Latter-Day Saints. Committee on Basic Beliefs. 230.93'3
Exploring the faith; a series of studies in the faith of the Church, prepared by a Committee on Basic Beliefs. [Independence, Mo., Herald Pub. House, 1970] 248 p. 21 cm. Includes bibliographical references. [BX8674.R43] 76-101570
1. Reorganized Chruch of Jesus Christ of Latter-Day Saints—Doctrinal and controversial works. I. Title.

RUOFF, Norman D. 248'.5
1974 yearbook of testimony : testimonies from the general officers and staff of the leading departments and commissions of the world church with supporting testimonies of state and regional officers / compiled by Norman D. Rvoff Independence, Mo. : Herald Pub. House, [1974] 189 p. ; 21 cm. [BX8674.R86] 74-84192 ISBN 0-8309-0122-1 : 5.50
1. Reorganized Church of Jesus Christ of Latter-Day Saints—Doctrinal and controversial works. 2. Christian life—Mormon authors. I. Title.

SALYARDS, Christiana. 230.93
The enduring word; the gospel in all ages, by Christiana Salyards. Gospel lesson studies, adult grade, the Department of religious education, the Reorganized church of Jesus Christ of latter-day saints. Independence, Mo., Herald publishing house [1942] 368 p. 22 1 /2 cm. Includes "Reference material." [BX8671.S3] 42-25390
1. Reorganized church of Jesus Christ of latter-day saints—Doctrinal and controversail works. I. Reorganized church of Jesus Christ of latter-day saints. Dept of religious education. II. Title.

SMITH, Elbert A., 1871- 289.3
Restoration:a study in prophecy, by Elbert

A. Smith. Independence, Mo., Herald publishing house [1945] 240 p. front. 20 1/2 cm. (The Priesthood library) "References" at end of each chapter. [BX8671.S58] 45-10021
1. Reorganized church of Jesus Christ of latter-day saints—Doctrinal and controversial works. I. Title.

TOWNSEND, Janice M. 230'.933
Joy before us / by Janice M. Townsend. Independence, Mo. : Herald Pub. House, c1982. 151 p. ; 21 cm. Bibliography: p. 151. [BX8674.T68] 19 81-7198 ISBN 0-8309-0327-5 : Write for information
1. Reorganized Church of Jesus Christ of Latter-Day Saints—Doctrinal and controversial works—Addresses, essays, lectures. I. Title.

WELLINGTON, Paul A., comp. 261
Challenges to kingdom building; a symposium on contemporary issues, edited and compiled by Paul A. Wellington. [Independence, Mo., Herald Pub. House, 1968] 380 p. 21 cm. A selection of articles which originally appeared in the Saints' herald. [BX8674.W4] 68-15216
1. Reorganized Church of Jesus Christ of Latter-Day Saints—Doctrinal and controversial works. I. The Saints' herald. II. Title.

WELLINGTON, Paul A. 230'.9'33
Readings on concepts of Zion, edited by Paul A. Wellington. [Independence, Mo., Herald Pub. House, 1973] 316 p. 21 cm. Includes bibliographical references. [BX8674.W44] 73-81076 ISBN 0-8309-0102-7 7.95
1. Reorganized Church of Jesus Christ of Latter-Day Saints—Doctrinal and controversial works. I. Title. II. Title: Concepts of Zion.

Reorganized Church of Jesus Christ of Latter-day Saints—Doctrine.

REORGANIZED Church of Jesus Christ of Latter-Day Saints. Dept. of Religious Education. Youth Division.
Follow thou Me, junior high course of study. Independence, Mo., Herald Publishing House, 1963. 52 p. 25 cm. 68-4972
1. Reorganized Church of Jesus Christ of Latter-day Saints—Doctrine. I. Title.

Reorganized Church of Jesus Christ of Latter-day Saints—Education.

REORGANIZED Church of Jesus Christ of Latter-Day Saints. Dept. of Religious Education.
Jesus speaks to me; a vacation church school unit for use with primary children, by Peggy Hajicek, Grace Emma Church, and Katherine Howell. Craft ideas by Barbara Jobst. [Independence, Mo., Herald Publishing House, c1963] 125 p. illus. 23 cm. 68-4912
1. Reorganized Church of Jesus Christ of Latter-day Saints—Education. I. Hajicek, Peggy. II. Church, Grace Emma. III. Howell, Katherine. IV. Title.

REORGANIZED church of 267.8293 Jesus Christ of latter day saints. Dept. of religious education.
The Oriole girls' handbook ... Independence, Mo., 1946. 136 p. illus. 20 cm. "Second edition."--Foreword. [BX8671.A65 1946] 47-4197
I. Title.

VAUGHAN, John Elwyn, 1918-
The future growth and development of higher education in the Reorganized Church of Jesus Christ of the Latter Day Saints. [n.p.] 1960. xxiv, 291 p. Final document (Ed. D.) -- N.Y.U., School of Education, 1960. Bibliography: p. [166]-177.
1. Reorganized Church of Jesus Christ of Latter-Day Saints — Education. I. Title.

Reorganized Church of Jesus Christ of Latter-Day Saints—Finance.

STEWARDSHIP opportunities and responsibilities; prepared under the direction of the presiding bishopric. [Rev.] Independence Mo., Herald Publishing House [1957, c1956] 78p. (Its Aaronic priesthood studies)
1. Reorganized Church of Jesus Christ of Latter-Day Saints—Finance. I. Reorganized Church of Jesus Christ of Latter-Day Saints.

Reorganized Church of Jesus Christ of Latter-Day Saints—Government.

REORGANIZED Church of Jesus 289.3 Christ of Latter Day Saints.
Rules and resolutions. Independence, Mo., Herald House, 1952. 215 p. 18 cm. [BX8671.A5445] 52-43441
1. Reorganized Church of Jesus Christ of Latter Day Saints — Government. I. Title.

REORGANIZED Church of 262'.09'33 Jesus Christ of Latter Day Saints.
Rules and resolutions / Reorganized Church of Jesus Christ of Latter Day Saints. Independence, Mo. : Herald House, 1975. 304 p. ; 18 cm. (Pastors reference library) Includes index. [BX8671.A5445 1975] 74-84765 ISBN 0-8309-0136-1
1. Reorganized Church of Jesus Christ of Latter-Day Saints—Government. I. Title.

SMITH, Herman Conoman
True succession in church presidency of the church of Jesus Christ of Latter day saints. Being a reply to...B. H. Roberts on "Succession in the presidency of the church." Lamoni, Ia., Board of publication of the reorganized church of Jesus Christ of Latter day saints, 1898. 1 p. l., 167 p. 16°. 0-1747
I. Title.

Reorganized Church of Jesus Christ of Latter-Day Saints—Government—Addresses, essays, lectures.

THE Patriarchs / 253.7
edited by Reed M. Holmes. Independence, Mo. : Herald Pub. House, 1978. p. cm. [BX8675.P37] 78-1895 ISBN 0-8309-0205-8 pbk. : 6.75
1. Reorganized Church of Jesus Christ of Latter-Day Saints—Government—Addresses, essays, lectures. 2. Patriarchs (Mormonism)—Addresses, essays, lectures. I. Holmes, Reed M.

Reorganized Church of Jesus Christ of Latter-Day Saints — Handbooks, manuals, etc.

REORGANIZED Church of Jesus 289.3 Christ of Latter-Day Saints. Committee on Ministry to College People.
A quest for meaning; handbook for college students. Prep. under the direction of the Comm. on Ministry to College People, Reorganized Church of Jesus Christ of Latter Day Saints [Independence, Mo., Herald Pub., c.1965] 175p. illus. (pt. col.) 18cm. Bibl. Includes bibliographies. [BX8674.A45] 65-18297 2.00 pap.,
1. Reorganized Church of Jesus Christ of Latter-Day Saints—Handbook, manuals, etc. 2. Religious education—Text-books for young people—Mormon. I. Title.

Reorganized Church of Jesus Christ of Latter Day Saints—History.

BRYANT, Verda Evelyn 289.3 (Bilger)
Between the covers of the Doctrine and covenants. Independence, Mo., Herald House, 1958. 272p. illus. 21cm. [BX8673.B7] 58-8199
1. Reorganized Church of Jesus Christ of Latter-Day Saints—Hist. 2. Smith, Joseph, 1805-1844. Doctrine and covenants. I. Title.

THE History of the 289.3'3
Reorganized Church of Jesus Christ of Latter Day Saints. Independence, Mo. : Herald House, 1967- , c1896- v. : ill. ; 23 cm. Authors' name in publisher's pref. of v. 1: Joseph Smith and Heman C. Smith; v. 2: Heman Smith; v. 5-7: pref. signed: F. Henry Edwards. Includes indexes. Contents.Contents.—v. 1. 1805-1835.—v. 2. 1836-1844.—v. 3. 1844-1872.—v. 4. 1873-1890.—v. 5. 1890-1902.—v. 6. 1903-1915.—v. 7. 1915-1925. [BX8673.H57] 75-302471 ISBN 0-8309-0075-6 (v. 7)
1. Reorganized Church of Jesus Christ of Latter Day Saints—History. I. Smith, Joseph, 1832-1914. II. Smith, Heman Conoman, 1850- III. Edwards, Francis Henry, 1897-

REORGANIZED Church of Jesus Christ of Latter-Day Saints. Board of Publication.
The history of the Reorganized Church of Jesus Christ of Latter Day Saints. Independence, Missouri, Herald House, 1967- v. 23 cm. First published, 1896. Contents.V.1. 1805-1835.- 68-71368
1. Reorganized Church of Jesus Christ of Latter Day Saints—History. I. Title.

SMITH, Joseph Fielding, 1876-
Origin of the "reorganized" church, and the question of succession, by Elder Joseph F. Smith, jr. Salt Lake City, The Deseret news, 1909. 139 p. 20 cm. $0.50 9-27434
I. Title.

STEWART, Georgia Metcalf. 289.3
How the church grew; Reorganized Church of Jesus Christ of Latter Day Saints. Independence, Mo., Herald House [1959] 342 p. 21 cm. [BX8673.S8] 59-11404
1. Reorganized Church of Jesus Christ of Latter-Day Saints — Hist. I. Title.

WILCOX, Pearl. 289.3'778
The Latter Day Saints on the Missouri frontier. [Independence? Mo., 1972] 367 p. illus. 21 cm. Bibliography: p. 351-355. [BX8615.M8W5] 72-83317
1. Reorganized Church of Jesus Christ of Latter-Day Saints—History. 2. Mormons and Mormonism in Missouri. I. Title.

Reorganized Church of Jesus Christ of Latter-Day Saints—Hymns.

THE hymnal [of the] reorganized Church of Jesus Christ of Latter Day Saints. Independence, Missouri, Herald Publishing House [1957] 508 p. 23 cm.
I. Church of Jesus Christ of Latter-Day Saints.

REORGANIZED Church of Jesus 783.9 Christ of Latter-Day Saints.
The hymnal. Independence, Mo., Herald Pub. House [1956] 508p. 23cm. [M2129.R4H9] 56-11867
1. Reorganized Church of Jesus Christ of Latter-Day Saints—Hymns. 2. Hymns, English. I. Title.

Reorganized Church of Jesus Christ of Latter-Day Saints—Hymns—History and criticism

WEDDLE, Franklyn S 245.2093
How to use the hymnal. Independence, Mo., Herald House [1956] 96p. 22cm. [BV420.A1W4] 56-12877
1. Reorganized Church of Jesus Christ of Latter-Day Saints—Hymns— Hist. & crit. I. Title.

Reorganized Church of Jesus Christ of Latter-Day Saints—Juvenile literature.

MAPLES, Evelyn. 289.3'3
Norman learns about the Scriptures. Illus. by Garry R. Hood. [Independence, Mo., Herald Pub. House, 1972] 36 p. illus. 21 cm. A brother and sister learn about the Scriptures and the teachings of the Reorganized Church of Jesus Christ of Latter-Day Saints. [BX8674.M36] 72-189295 ISBN 0-8309-0060-8
1. Reorganized Church of Jesus Christ of Latter-Day Saints—Juvenile literature. 2. [Reorganized Church of Jesus Christ of Latter-Day Saints.] 3. Bible—Juvenile literature. I. Hood, Garry R., illus. II. Title.

Reorganized Church of Jesus Christ of Latter-Day Saints. Liturgy and ritual.

HARTSHORN, Chris Benson. 264.093
Let us worship, by Chris B. Hartshorn... Independence, Mo., Herald publishing house [1946] 190 p., 1 l. front., illus., plates. 20 1/2 cm. "Bibliography of worship literature": p. 181-184. [BX8671.H3] 46-15318
1. Reorganized church of Jesus Christ of latter-day saints. Liturgy and ritual. 2. Public worship. I. Title.

WEDDLE, Franklyn S 264.093
O worship the King; a manual of helps and materials for priesthood, ministers of music, and others who assist in worship . . . prepared by Franklyn S. Weddle and Arthur A. Oakman. Independence, Mo., Herald House, Reorganized Church of Jesus Christ of Latterday Saints [1952] 203 p. 21 cm. Appendices (p. [148]-203): A. Bibliography. -- B. Music for weddings. -- C. Music for the prayer meeting. -- D. A selected list of organ music suitable for the church service. -- E. Worship music for the piano. -- F. Graded anthem list. -- G. Epochal hymns. [BX8671.W4] 52-27458
1. Reorganized Church of Jesus Christ of Latter-Day Saints. Liturgy and ritual. 2. Church music — Reorganized Church of Jesus Christ of Latter-Day Saints. I. Oakman, Arthur A., joint author. II. Title.

Reorganized Church of Jesus Christ of Latter-Day Saints—Membership.

REORGANIZED Church of Jesus 289.3 Christ of Latter-Day Saints.
Church member's manual; duties and privileges of members. [2d revision] Independence, Mo., Herald House, 1957. 128p. 16cm. [BX8675.A4 1957] 57-8433
1. Reorganized Church of Jesus Christ of Latter-Day Saints— Membership. I. Title.

REORGANIZED Church of 289.3'02'02 Jesus Christ of Latter-Day Saints.
Church member's manual; duties and privileges of members. [3d revision] Independence, Mo., Herald House, 1969. 120 p. 16 cm. [BX8675.A4 1969] 77-80872
1. Reorganized Church of Jesus Christ of Latter-Day Saints—Membership. I. Title.

REORGANIZED Church of Jesus 289.3 Christ of Latter-Day Saints.
A church member's manual; duties and privileges of members. First comp. by Charles A. Davies for use and pub. in the Australasian Mission. Rev. under the direction of the First Presidency. Independence, Mo., Herald Pub. House, 1947. 112 p. 16 cm. Bibliography: p. 111-112. [BX8671.A4] 47-28912
1. Reorganized Church of Jesus Christ of Latter-Day Saints—Membership. I. Davies, Charles A. II. Title.

Reorganized Church of Jesus Christ of Latter-Day Saints—Missions.

BUTTERWORTH, F. 266'.9'396 Edward.
Roots of the reorganization : French Polynesia / by F. Edward Butterworth. Independence, Mo. : Herald Pub. House, c1977. 266 p. : ill. ; 20 cm. Sequel to The adventures of John Hawkins. Includes bibliographical references. [BV3678.5.B87] 77-944 ISBN 0-8309-0176-0 : 8.00
1. Reorganized Church of Jesus Christ of Latter-Day Saints—Missions. 2. Missions—Polynesia. I. Title.

RUSSELL, Naomi. 266'.93'3
Light from the Valley / by Naomi Russell. Independence, Mo. : Herald Pub. House, c1979. 200 p. : ill. ; 20 cm. [BV2843.H6R87] 79-12302 ISBN 0-8309-0235-X : 7.00
1. Reorganized Church of Jesus Christ of Latter-Day Saints—Missions. 2. Missions—Honduras. I. Title.

WIGHT, Maxine C. 266'.9'30924 B
A story about light / by Maxine C. Wight. Independence, Mo. : Herald Pub. House, c1979. p. cm. [BV2616.W53] 79-14691 ISBN 0-8309-0236-8 : 4.00
1. Reorganized Church of Jesus Christ of

Latter-Day Saints—Missions. 2. Wight, Maxine C. 3. Church work with children—Peru. 4. Missions—Peru. I. Title.

Reorganized Church of Jesus Christ of Latter-Day Saints—Parliamentary practice.

REORGANIZED Church of Jesus Christ of Latter-Day Saints. 289.3
Parliamentary procedure in the church, by Fred L. Young [general church secretary] Independence, Mo., Herald House, 1960. 101p. 18cm. (Pastors' reference library) 'Based on Roberts Rules of order.' [BX8671.A542] 60-9002
1. Reorganized Church of Jesus Christ of Latter-Day Saints— Parliamentary practice. I. Young, Fred L. II. Title.

Reorganized Church of Jesus Christ of Latter-Day Saints—Periodicals.

SMITH, H. Alan. 289.3'3
Our heritage of humor : humor in the Reorganized Church of Jesus Christ of Latter Day Saints / by H. Alan Smith. Independence, MO : Herald Pub. House, c1982. 320 p. ; 20 cm. [BX8670.S64 1982] 19 81-7229 ISBN 0-8309-0330-5 pbk. : 12.00
1. Reorganized Church of Jesus Christ of Latter-Day Saints—Periodicals. 2. Christianity and humor—History. I. Title.

Reorganized Church of Jesus Christ of Latter-Day Saints—Prayer-books and devotions—English.

CONGREGATIONAL 261'.09'33
readings from the Scriptures ..., hymns, inspirational writings / compiled by Cecil R. Ettinger. Independence, Mo. : Herald Pub. House, [1975] p. cm. Includes index. [BX8675.C66] 75-8596 ISBN 0-8309-0145-0
1. Reorganized Church of Jesus Christ of Latter-Day Saints—Prayer-books and devotions—English. 2. Responsive worship. I. Ettinger, Cecil Ray, 1922-

HOWARD, Barbara, 1930- 249
Be swift to love / by Barbara Howard. Independence, Mo. : Herald Pub. House, [1974] 186 p. : ill. ; 21 cm. Bibliography: p. 185-186. [BX8675.H68] 74-82423 ISBN 0-8309-0128-0 : 7.00
1. Reorganized Church of Jesus Christ of Latter-Day Saints—Prayer-books and devotions—English. 2. Family—Prayer-books and devotions—English. I. Title.

Reorganized Church of Jesus Christ of Latter-Day Saints—Sermons.

CASE, Oscar, 1872- 252.093
My book of acts; missionary experiences and short sermons . . . [Independence? Mo.] c1956. 198p. illus. 20cm. [BX8678.C3A3] 56-32561
1. Reorganized Church of Jesus Christ of Latter-Day Saints—Sermons. I. Title.

ETTINGER, Cecil Ray, 1922- 252.093
Thy kingdom come, a study in Christian ethics. Independence, Mo., Herald House [c.1965] 96p. 18cm. Bibl. [BX8676.E8] 65-18921 1.75 bds.,
1. Reorganized Church of Jesus Christ of Latter-Day Saints—Sermons. 2. Sermons, American. I. Title.

ETTINGER, Cecil Ray, 1922- 252.093
Thy kingdom come, a study in Christian ethics [by] Cecil R. Ettinger. Independence, Mo., Herald Pub. House [1965] 96 p. 18 cm. Includes bibliographies. [BX8676.E8] 65-18921
1. Reorganized Church of Jesus Christ of Latter-Day Saints — Sermons. 2. Sermons, American. I. Title.

FRY, Evan, 1902-1959. 252'.09'33
Evan Fry : illustrations from radio sermons / edited and compiled by Norman D. Ruoff. [Independence, Mo.] : Herald House, c1975. 160 p. ; 21 cm. Compiled from the author's radio sermons delivered under the title: Hear ye Him. [BX8676.F67 1975] 74-84763 ISBN 0-8309-0131-0 : 6.50
1. Reorganized Church of Jesus Christ of Latter-Day Saints—Sermons. 2. Sermons, American. I. Title: Illustrations from radio sermons.

FRY, Evan Anselm, 1902-1959 252.093
The restoration faith. Independence, Mo., Herald House [c.1962] 377p. 21cm. 62-12901 3.75
1. Reorganized Church of Jesus Christ of Latter Day Saints—Sermons. 2. Sermons, American. I. Title.

LANDON, Donald D. 252.0933
To be the salt of the earth: messages on the nature of Christ, the church. and discipleship [Independence, Mo.] Dept. of Religious Education, Reorganized Churchof Jesus Christ of Latter Day Saints [dist. Herald House, c.1965] 214p. 21cm. [BX8676.L3] 65-26305 2.25; 1.50 pap.,
1. Reorganized Church of Jesus Christ of Latter Day Saints—Sermons. 2. Sermons, American. I. Reorganized Church of Jesus Christ of Latter Day Saints. Dept. of Religious Education. II. Title.

OAKMAN, Arthur A. 252'.09'33
Arthur A. Oakman : themes from his radio sermons / edited by Stephen Gregson. Independence, Mo. : Herald Pub. House, 1978. 199 p. ; 20 cm. [BX8676.O29A77] 78-7712 ISBN 0-8309-0216-3 : 6.50
1. Reorganized Church of Jesus Christ of Latter-Day Saints—Sermons. 2. Sermons, American. I. Gregson, Stephen.

OAKMAN, Arthur A. 252.093
He who is. Independence, Mo., Herald Pub. [c.1963] 136p. 20cm. 63-22369 2.00
1. Reorganized Church of Jesus Christ of Latter-Day Saints—Sermons. 2. Sermons, American. I. Title.

REORGANIZED Church of Jesus Christ of Latter-Day Saints. 252.093
The kingdom of heaven is like . . . A symposium of nineteen sermons. Independence, Mo., Herald Pub. House [1954] 231p. 21cm. [BX8671.A46] 55-16794
1. Reorganized Church of Jesus Christ of Latter-Day Saints—Sermons. 2. Sermons, American. I. Title.

REORGANIZED Church of Jesus Christ of Latter-Day Saints. Council of Twelve Apostles. 252'.093'3
Twelve sermons. Independence, Mo., Herald Pub. House, 1972] 151 p. 18 cm. [BX8676.A2] 76-182436 ISBN 0-8309-0069-1 3.00
1. Reorganized Church of Latter-Day Saints—Sermons. 2. Sermons, American. I. Title.

RUSSELL, William D., 1938- comp. 252.09'3'3
The word became flesh; sermons on New Testament texts, edited by William D. Russell. [Independence, Mo.] Herald Pub. House [1967] 284 p. 21 cm. Bibliographical footnotes. [BX8676.R8] 67-26969
1. Reorganized Church of Jesus Christ of Latter-Day Saints—Sermons. 2. Sermons, American. I. Title.

Reorganized Churh of Jesus Christ of Latter-Day Saints—Doctrinal and controvers

HAM, Wayne. 230'.9'33
More than burnt offerings : a study course on theology for adults / by Wayne Ham. Independence, Mo. : Herald Pub. House, c1978. p. cm. [BV4020.H35] 78-17646 ISBN 0-8309-0217-1 pbk. : 6.50
1. Reorganized Church of Jesus Christ of Latter-Day Saints—Doctrinal and controversial works—Study and teaching. 2. Theology—Study and teaching.

Repentance.

ARNAUD, Francois Thomas Marie de Baculard d', 1718-1805.
Fanny; or, The happy repentance. From the French of M. d'Arnaud. The 1st American ed. Printed at Worcester, Massachusetts, By Isaiah Thomas, and sold at his bookstore. MDCCLXXXV. 139 p. 15 cm. Signatures: A-D8, E-K4, L2 "Books sold by I. Thomas, in Worcester, Massachusetts": verso of p. 139. [PQ1954.A7A625 1785] 14-1826
I. Title.

BETHUNE, George Washington, 1805-1862. 234.
The history of a penitent. A guide for the inquiring: in a commentary on the One hundred and thirtieth psalm. By Geo. W. Bethune ... Philadelphia, H. Perkins; Boston, B. Perkins & co., 1848. 264 p. 16 1/2 cm. [BT800.B5 1848] 45-47051
1. Repentance. 2. Bible. O. T. Psalms cxxx—Commentaries. I. Title.

BETHUNE, George Washington, 1805-1862. 234.
The history of a penitent. A guide for the inquiring: in a commentary on the One hundred and thirtieth psalm. By Geo. W. Bethune ... 3d (rev.) ed. New York, Board of publication of the Reformed Protestant Dutch church, 1859. 260 p. 15 1/2 cm. [BT800.B5 1859] 45-47052
1. Repentance. 2. Bible. O.T. Psalms cxxx-Commentaries. I. Reformed church in America. Board of publication. II. Title.

BOOKWALTER, Lewis, 1846-
Repentance, by Lewis Bookwalter ... Dayton, O., United brethren publishing house, 1902. xv, 17-64 p. 17 cm. (Doctrinal series) 2-21566
I. Title.

CHAMBERLAIN, William Douglas, 1890- 234.5
The meaning of repentance [by] William Douglas Chamberlain ... Philadelphia, The Westminster press [1943] xii p., 1 l., 15-258 p. 21 cm. "Consist[s] largely of the Smyth lectures delivered at Columbia theological seminary, 1941."--Pref. [BT800.C45] 43-11769
1. Repentance. I. Title.

GALLAUDET, Thomas Hopkins, 1787-1851. 221.
The child's book on repentance; designed, also, for older person. By Rev. T. H. Gallaudet ... New York, American tract society, [1834] 147 p. front. 15 x 9 cm. [BV4571.G3] 11-33690
1. Repentance. I. Title.

HALL, Newman, 1816-1902. 234.
A parting word. By Newman Hall, LL.B. New York, Sheldon and company, 1868. 88 p. 16 cm. Full name: Christopher Newman Hall. [BT800.H3] 29-1471
1. Repentance. I. [Full name: Christopher Newman Hall] II. Title.

IRONSIDE, Henry Allan, 1876- 234.5
Except ye repent, by Harry A. Ironside ... New York, American tract society [c1937] 191 p. 19 1/2 cm. Awarded the prize of one thousand dollars in a recent contest of the American tract society, cf. Publisher's pref. [BT800.I7] 37-8541
1. Repentance. I. Title.

IRONSIDE, Henry Allan, 1876-1951 234.5
Except ye repent. Grand Rapids, Mich., Zondervan [1963, c.1937] 191p. 21cm. Reprinted by special arrangement with the Amer. Tract Soc. 63-17745 2.50 bds.,
1. Repentance. I. Title.

KINSEY, Robert Baldwin, 1848- 234.
A serious question, what is true repentance, by R. B. Kinsey ... Reading, Pa. [Press of Reading eagle co., c1908] 215 p. front. (port.) 19 cm. [BT800.K56] 9-25193
1. Repentance. I. Title.

KINSEY, Robert Baldwin, 1848-
A serious question, what is true repentance, by R. B. Kinsey ... Reading, Pa. [Press of Reading eagle co., c1908 215 p. front. (port.) 19 cm. $1.00 9-25193
I. Title.

RITCHER, Stephan.
Metanoia; Christian penance and confession. Translated by Raymond T. Kelly. New York, Sheed and Ward [1966] 126 p. 21 cm. Translation of Metanoia; von der Busse und Beichte des Christen Ueberlegung und Einuebung. 67-62689
1. Repentance. I. Title.

SCHLINK, Basilea. 234'.5
Repentance—the joy-filled life [by] M. Basilea Schlink. Translated by Harriet Corbin with Sigrid Langer. Grand Rapids, Zondervan [1968] 63 p. 21 cm. [BT800.S33] 68-56090
1. Repentance. I. Title.

SEYMOUR, Richard A. 234'.5
All about repentance [by] Richard A. Seymour. Hollywood, Fla., Harvest House Publishers [1974] 180 p. 18 cm. Bibliography: p. 167-171. [BT800.S47] 74-81381 1.50
1. Repentance. I. Title.

SOBOSAN, Jeffrey G., 1946- 234'.5
Act of contrition : personal responsibility and sin / Jeffrey Sobosan. Notre Dame, Ind. : Ave Maria Press, c1979. 127 p. ; 21 cm. [BT800.S62] 79-54695 ISBN 0-87793-189-5 (pbk.): 2.95
1. Repentance. 2. Sin. 3. Penance. I. Title.

UPDIKE, L. Wayne. 234.5
Whosoever repenteth; a series of lectures delivered to the Melchisedec priesthood of Independence, Missouri, January 6-11, 1957. [Independence, Mo.] Herald House [c1957] 111 p. illus. 21 cm. [BX8674.U62] 57-14408
1. Repentance. 2. Reorganized Church of Jesus Christ of Latter-Day Saints — Doctrinal and controversial works. I. Title.

[WALKER, Charles] 1791-1870. 234.
Repentance explained to the understanding of children. By a pastor ... Windsor, Vt., Richards and Tracy, 1833. vi, [7]-87 p. 15 1/2 cm. [BT800.W2] 45-47954
1. Repentance. I. Title.

WIGHT, Fred Hartley, 1899- 234.5
If my people; repentance and revival. Butler, Ind., Higley Press, 1959. 148 p. 23 cm. [BT800.W46] 60-45
1. Repentance. 2. Revivals. I. Title.

WINES, Enoch Cobb, 1806-1879. 234.
The true penitent portrayed in a practical exposition of the Fifty-first psalm; to which is added the doctrine of repentence, as declared in Acts xvii. 30 By E. C. Wines ... Philadelphia, Presbyterian board of publication [1864] 119 p. 18 cm. [BT800.W5] 45-47053
1. Repentance. 2. Bible. O. T. Psalms li-Commentaries. I. Presbyterian church in the U. S. A. (Old school) Board of publication. II. Title.

Repentance—Biblical teaching.

SALICO, Dale Vincent. 234'.5
New birth—new life : what the bible says about repentance / Dale Vincent Salico. Valley Forge, PA : Judson Press, c1980. 93 p. ; 22 cm. [BS680.R36S24] 80-16761 ISBN 0-8170-0887-X pbk. : 3.95
1. Repentance—Biblical teaching. I. Title.

Repentance—History of doctrines.

DUKKER, Chrysostomus 922.245
The changing heart; the penance-concept of St. Francis of Assisi. Translated [from the German] by Bruce Malina. Chicago, Franciscan Herald Press [c.1959] 156p. (10p. bibl. notes) 22cm. 59-14705 3.00
1. Francesco d'Assisi, Saint, 1182-1226. 2. Repentance—History of doctrines. I. Title.

MEYER, Charles R., 265.61
The Thomistic concept of justifying contrition. Mundelein, Ill., Apud Aedes Seminarii Sanctae Mariae ad Lacum, 1949. 236 p. 23 cm. (Pontificia Facultas Theologica, Seminarii Sanctae Mariae ad Lacum. Dissertationes ad lauream, 18) Bibliography: p. 223-236. [BX1749.T7M4] 51-28816
1. Thomas Aquinas, Saint, 1225?-1274. 2. Repentance—History of doctrines. I. Title. II. Series: St. Mary of the Lake Seminary, Mundelein, Ill. Dissertationes ad lauream. 18

Repentance (Judaism)

KOOK, Abrahahm Isaac, 1865-1935. 296.3'2
Rabbi Kook's Philosophy of repentance a

translation of Orot ha-teshuvah / by Alter B. Z. Metzger. New York : Yeshiva University Press, Dept. of Special Publications : selling agents, Bloch Pub. Co., 1968. 132 p. ; 23 cm. (Studies in Torah Judaism ; 11) Caption title: Orot ha-teshuvah. Lights of repentance. Includes bibliographical references. [BM645.R45K613] 74-192553
1. Repentance (Judaism) I. Title. II. Series.

Repentance—Popular works.

SKINNER, Craig. 234'.5
Back where you belong / Craig Skinner ; [foreword by Ernest E. Mosley]. Nashville, Tenn. : Broadman Press, c1980. 136 p. ; 20 cm. [BT800.S58] 79-53819 ISBN 0-8054-5332-6 pbk. : 3.50
1. Repentance—Popular works. 2. Salvation—Popular works. 3. Christian life—Baptist authors. I. Title.

Requiems—History and criticism.

ROBERTSON, Alec. 783.2'2
Requiem : music of mourning and consolation / by Alec Robertson. Westport, Conn. : Greenwood Press, 1976. p. cm. Reprint of the 1968 ed. published by Praeger, New York. Includes bibliographical references and index. [ML3088.R62 1976] 75-32462 ISBN 0-8371-8552-1 lib.bdg. : 19.50
1. Requiems—History and criticism. 2. Holy-Week music—History and criticism. 3. Funeral music—History and criticism. I. Title.

ROBERTSON, Alec. 783.2'9
Requiem: music of mourning and consolation. New York, F. A. Praeger [1968, c1967] xii, 300 p. music. 26 cm. [ML3088.R62 1968] 68-19860
1. Requiems—History and criticism. 2. Holy-Week music—History and criticism. 3. Funeral music—History and criticism. I. Title.

Res Shamra.

HABEL, Norman C 291
Yahweh versus Baal: a conflict of religious cultures; a study in the relevance of Ugaritic materials for the early faith of Israel, by Norman C. Habel. New York, Published for the School for Graduate Studies, Concordia Seminary, St. Louis [by] Bookman Associates, 1964. 128 p. 21 cm. (Concordia Theological Seminary, St. Louis Graduate study no. 6) Revised and shortened ed. of the author's thesis, Concordia Theological Seminary. Bibliography: p. 119-121. [BL1670.H3] 64-14448
1. Res Shamra. 2. Palestine — Religion. 3. Bible. O.T. — Criticism, interpretation, etc. I. Title. II. Series: Concordia Theological Seminary, St. Louis. School for Graduate Studies. Graduate study no. 6

Rescripts, Papal.

O'NEILL, William Henry, 262.13
1900-
... *Papal rescripts of favor* ... by the Reverend William H. ONeill ... Washington, D. C., The Catholic university of America, 1930. vii, 28 p., 1 l., 23 cm. (The Catholic university of America. Canon law studies, no. 57) Thesis (J. C. D.)--Catholic university of America, 1980. Vita. Bibliography: p. 206-213. [BX1939.B5O6 1930] 30-33942
1. Rescripts, Papal. 2. Catholic church. Codex juris canonici. C. 36-62: De rescripts. I. Title. II. Title: Rescripts of favor, Papal.

Research—Bibliography.

WATSON, Goodwin Barbour, 377.
1899-
A year of research--1927. Some investigations published between January 1, 1927 and January 1, 1928, bearing upon the program of religious, educational and social agencies, by Goodwin B. Watson and Delia H. Biddle ... [Chicago] The Religious education association, 1929. v, 82 p. 25 1/2 cm. (Religious education monograph, no. 4) "Annotated bibliography": p. 25-82. [BV1460.R53 no. 4] E 32
1. Research—Bibliography. 2. Research, Educational—Bibliography. I. Biddle, Delia H., joint author. II. Title.

Resep (Canaanite deity)

FULCO, William J. 299'.3'1
The Canaanite god Resep / by William J. Fulco. New Haven : American Oriental Society, 1976. 71 p. : ill. ; 26 cm. (American Oriental series : Essay ; 8) Includes bibliographical references. [BL1672.R47F84] 77-150163
1. Resep (Canaanite deity) I. Title. II. Series.

Reser, Stanley.

BACH, Marcus, 1906- 133.4
Strange altars. [New York] New Amer. Lib. [1968, c.1952] 176p. 18cm. (Signet, T 3484) [BL2490.B2] .75 pap.,
1. Reser, Stanley. 2. Voodooism. 3. Folk-lore—Haiti. I. Title.

BACH, Marcus, 1906- 133.4
Strange altars. [1st ed.] Indianapolis, Bobbs-Merrill [1952] 254 p. illus. 23 cm. [BL2490.B2] 52-10690
1. Reser, Hanley. 2. Voodooism. 3. Folk-lore—Haiti. I. Title.

Reserve (Christian theology)—History of doctrines.

SELBY, Robin C. 230'.2'0924
The principle of reserve in the writings of John Henry Cardinal Newman / by Robin C. Selby. London ; New York : Oxford University Press, 1975. 108 p. ; 23 cm. (Oxford theological monographs) Includes indexes. Bibliography: p. [106]-108. [B1745.S44] 75-322798 ISBN 0-19-826711-8 : 16.00
1. Newman, John Henry, Cardinal, 1801-1890. 2. Reserve (Christian theology)—History of doctrines. I. Title. II. Series.

Responsa.

AGUS, Irving, Abraham, 1910- 296
Rabbi Meir of Rothenburg, his life and his works and sources for the religious, legal, and social history of the Jews of Germany in the thirteenth century, by Irving A. Agus. Philadelphia, Dropsie College for Hebrew and Cognate Learning, 1947. 2v.(xxxxiii, 749 p.) 24 cm. Bibliography: v 2. p. 703 719. [BM522.62.B34A4] 48-96
1. Meir ben Baruch, of Rothenburg, d 1298. 2. Responsa. 3. Jews in Germany. I. Title.

FREEHOF, Solomon Bennett 296.834
Reform responsa. Cincinnati, Hebrew Union College Press [c.]1960. xi, 226p. 21cm. Bibl. p.218-222 60-12708 6.00
1. Responsa. 2. Reform Judaism. I. Title.

FREEHOF, Solomon Bennett, 296.834
1892-
Recent Reform responsa. Cincinnati, Hebrew Union Col. Pr., 1963. xi, 232p. 21cm. 63-15720 6.00
1. Responsa. 2. Reform Judaism. I. Title.

FREEHOF, Solomon Bennett, 296.1
1892-
The responsa literature. Philadelphia, Jewish Publication Society of America, 1955. 304p. 22cm. [BM646.F68] 55-6706
1. Responsa. I. Title.

KLASS, Sholom. 296.74
Responsa of modern Judaism; a compilation of questions and answers on past and present day Halacha as presented in the Jewish press. [Brooklyn, Jewish Press] 1965-66. 2 v. 24 cm. [BM522.59.L26] 66-927
1. Responsa. I. Title.

Responsa—1040-1600.

BAZAK, Jacob, comp. 296.1'79
Jewish law and Jewish life : selected Rabbinical responsa / compiled, annotated, and arr. by Jacob Bazak ; translated, annotated, and edited by Stephen M. Passamaneck. New York : Union of American Hebrew Congregations, c1977-1978. v. ; 23 cm. Translation of Mishpat va-halakhah. Contents.Contents.—book 1. The judiciary, attorneys and their ethics, civil and criminal procedure, and civil rights. Includes bibliographical references. [BM522.A1B3813] 78-303638 ISBN 0-8074-0036-X (bks. 5 & 6) pbk. : 3.00 ISBN 0-8074-0037-8 (bks. 7 & 8) pbk. : 3.00
1. Responsa—1040-1600. I. Passamaneck, Stephen M. II. Title.

Responsa—1800-

FREEHOF, Solomon Bennett, 296.1'8
1892-
Contemporary Reform responsa / by Solomon B. Freehof. [Cincinnati] : Hebrew Union College Press, 1974. ix, 309 p. ; 22 cm. Includes index. [BM522.36.R368] 74-23748 ISBN 0-87820-108-4 : 10.00
1. Responsa—1800- 2. Reform Judaism. I. Title.

FREEHOF, Solomon 296.8'346
Bennett, 1892-
Current Reform responsa, by Solomon B. Freehof. [Cincinnati] Hebrew Union College Press, 1969. viii, 259 p. 21 cm. Bibliography: p. 251-254. [BM522.36.R37] 68-57979 7.50
1. Responsa—1800- 2. Reform Judaism. I. Title.

FREEHOF, Solomon 296.8'34
Bennett, 1892-
Modern Reform responsa, by Solomon B. Freehof. [Cincinnati?] Hebrew Union College Press, 1971. x, 319 p. 21 cm. [BM522.36.R375 1971] 72-151008 7.50
1. Responsa—1800- 2. Reform Judaism. I. Title.

FREEHOF, Solomon Bennett, 296.1'8
1892-
New Reform responsa / by Solomon B. Freehof. [Cincinnati, Ohio] : Hebrew Union College Press, c1980. 282 p. ; 22 cm. (Alumni series of the Hebrew Union College Press ISSN 0192-2904s) Includes index.I[BM522.36.R376]V80-18218 ISBN 0-87820-110-6 : 12.50
1. Responsa—1800- 2. Reform Judaism—Ceremonies and practices. I. Title.

FREEHOF, Solomon 296.1'79
Bennett, 1892-
Reform responsa; and, Recent Reform responsa [by] Solomon B. Freehof. [New York] Ktav Pub. House, 1973 [c1963] 2 v. in 1. 23 cm. Bibliography: p. [219]-222 (2d group) [BM522.36.R383] 72-12300 ISBN 0-87068-203-2 15.00
1. Responsa—1800- 2. Reform Judaism. I. Freehof, Solomon Bennett, 1892- Recent Reform responsa. 1973. II. Title. III. Title: Recent Reform responsa.

FREEHOF, Solomon 296.1'79
Bennett, 1892-
Reform responsa for our time / by Solomon B. Freehof. [Cincinnati] : Hebrew Union College Press, 1977. xxvii, 320 p. ; 22 cm. Includes index. [BM522.36.R385] 77-24078 ISBN 0-87820-111-4 : 12.50
1. Responsa—1800- 2. Reform Judaism. I. Title.
Available from KTAV Publishing House

KLEIN, Isaac. 296.1'79
Responsa and halakhic studies / by Isaac Klein. New York : Ktav Pub. House, 1975. vii, 190 p. ; 24 cm. Includes bibliographical references and index. [BM52259.L37] 75-25634 ISBN 0-87068-288-1 : 10.00
1. Responsa—1800- 2. Jewish law—Addresses, essays, lectures. I. Title.

NOVAK, David, 1941- 296.1'79
Law and theology in Judaism. Foreword by Louis Finkelstein. New York, Ktav Pub. House [1974] xvi, 176 p. 24 cm. Includes bibliographical references. [BM522.74.O9] 74-806 ISBN 0-87068-245-8 10.00
1. Responsa—1800- I. Title.

Responsa—Collections.

FREEHOF, Solomon Bennett, 296.1
1892-
A treasury of responsa. Philadelphia, Jewish Pubn. Soc. [1963, c.1962] 313p. 22cm. 62-12951 4.50
1. Responsa—Collections. 2. Judaism—Collections. I. Title.

Responsa—History and criticism.

FREEHOF, Solomon 296.1'79
Bennett, 1892-
The responsa literature and A treasury of responsa [by] Solomon B. Freehof. [New York] KTAV Pub. House, 1973. 304, xiv, 313 p. 22 cm. Reprint of the 1955 ed. of The responsa literature and the 1963 ed. of A treasury of responsa, both published by the Jewish Publication Society, Philadelphia. Includes bibliographies. [BM523.F72] 72-12301 ISBN 0-87068-202-4 15.00
1. Responsa—History and criticism. 2. Responsa—Collections. I. Freehof, Solomon Bennett, 1892- A treasury of responsa. 1973. II. Title. III. Title: A treasury of responsa.

JACOBS, Louis. 296.1'79
Theology in the Responsa / [by] Louis Jacobs. London ; Boston : Routledge and Kegan Paul, 1975. xi, 378 p. ; 23 cm. (The Littman library of Jewish civilization) Includes index. Bibliography: p. 357-362. [BM523.J3] 75-315923 ISBN 0-7100-8010-7 : 18.75
1. Responsa—History and criticism. 2. Jewish theology—Addresses, essays, lectures. I. Title.

JACOBS, Louis. 296.1'79
Theology in the Responsa / [by] Louis Jacobs. London ; Boston : Routledge and Kegan Paul, 1975. xi, 378 p. ; 23 cm. (The Littman library of Jewish civilization) Includes index. Bibliography: p. 357-362. [BM523.J3] 75-315923 ISBN 0-7100-8010-7 : £6.00
1. Responsa—History and criticism. 2. Jewish theology—Addresses, essays, lectures. I. Title.

Responsa—To 1040.

MANN, Jacob, 1888-1940. 296.1'79
The responsa of the Babylonian geonim as a source of Jewish history. New York, Arno Press, 1973. 1 v. (various pagings) 23 cm. (The Jewish people: history, religion, literature) Reprint of the 1917-21 ed. published by Dropsie College for Hebrew and Cognate Learning, Philadelphia, of articles originally published in the Jewish quarterly review. New series. [BM501.5.M36 1973] 73-2215 ISBN 0-405-05278-2 15.00
1. Responsa—To 1040. 2. Geonic literature—History and criticism. 3. Jews in Babylonia. I. Jewish quarterly review. New series. II. Title. III. Series.

Responses (Music)

KETTRING, Donald D., ed. 783.24
Choral responses. Philadelphia, Westminster. c.1962. 64p. 26cm. For mixed chorus; in part with organ acc. 62-10579 1.10 pap.,
1. Responses (Music) I. Title.

Responsibility.

BONHOEFFER, Dietrich, 1906- 208
1945
I loved this people. Testimonies of responsibility. Introd. by Hans Rothfels. Tr. [from German] by Keith R. Crim. Richmond, Va., Knox [c.1965] 62p. 19cm. (Chime paperbacks) [BX8080.B645A53] 65-15715 1.00 pap.,
I. Title.

JONSEN, Albert R. 241
Responsibility in modern religious ethics, by Albert R. Jonsen. Foreword by James M. Gustafson. Washington, Corpus Books [1968] xiv, 249 p. 21 cm. Includes bibliographical references. [BJ1451.J57] 68-25761 6.95
1. Responsibility. 2. Christian ethics. I. Title.

Responsive worship.

BIBLE. English. Selections. 264.4
1865.
Scripture readings for devotion and study

in seminaries, Sabbath schools, and families. By L. D. Barrows ... Boston, Chase and Nichols [etc.] 1865. 160 p. 16 cm. [BS391.B35] 37-16441
1. Responsive worship. I. Barrows,Lorenzo Dow, 1817-1878, comp. II. Title.

BIBLE. English. Selections. 1922. 783.
Selections from the Scriptures, edited by Charles Carroll Albertson, D.D. New York, The Century co., 1922. 2 p. l., 51 p. 21 1/2 cm. [With as issued: Goucher college, Baltimore. Goucher college hymnal. New York, 1916] [M2117.G73G6] 46-33452
1. Responsiye worship. I. Albertson, Charles Carroll, 1865- ed. II. Title.

BIBLE. English. Selections. 1942. Authorized. 264.4
"Thus saith the Lord," compiled by George F. Tibbitts ... Park-of-the-Palms, Keystone Heights, Fla., The Gospel volunteers of the world (incorporated) [1942] 2 p. l., 3-398 p. 21 cm. Colored illustration on t.-p. [BV199.R5T5] 42-10931
1. Responsive worship. I. Tibbitts, George F., ed. II. Gospel volunteers of the world, inc. III. Title.

BIBLE. English. Selections. 1955. Revised standard. 264.4
Choral readings from the Bible; [selections for groups of all ages] Edited by Helen A. Brown and Harry J. Heltman. Philadelphia, Westminster Press [1955] 63p. 23cm. [BV199.R5B77] 55-8597
1. Responsive worship. 2. Choral speaking. I. Brown, Helen Ada, 1914- ed. II. Heltman, Harry Joseph, 1885- ed. III. Title.

BIBLE. N. T. Gospels. English. Lessons, Liturgical. 1882. 264.4
Words of the Lord Jesus, arranged for responsive reading in the home, the school, and the church. By William Salter ... Burlington, Ia., J. Love, 1882. 61 p. 18 cm. [BT306.S3] 35-33473
1. Jesus Christ—Words. 2. Responsive worship. I. Bible. English. Lessons. Liturgical. N. T. Gospels. 1882. II. Salter, William, 1821-1910, comp. III. Title.

BIBLE. O.T. Psalms. English. Selections. 18--. Authorized.
The Psalter; or, Selections from the book of Psalms. Arranged to be used in public worship. New York, The Century co. [18--] vi, 94 p., 1 l. 21 1/2 cm. [BS1436.C38] 45-47344
1. Responsive worship. I. Title.

BIBLE. O. T. Psalms. English. Selections. 1934. 223.5
A book of Psalms arranged for use in a college chapel, by Eliza Hall Kendrick ... [Wellesley, Mass.] Wellesley college, c1934. 1 p. l., 114 p. 22 cm. [BS1436.K4] 34-33441
1. Responsive worship. 2. Universities and colleges—Chapel exercises. I. Bible. English. Selections. O. T. Psalms. 1934. II. Kendrick, Eliza Hall, 1863- ed. III. Title.

BREWSTER, Edward Thomson. 268.
Scripture responses for worship, arranged from the authorized version by Edward T. Brewster, M.A. With an introduction by Rev. John Pearson, D.D. Dayton, O., Union publishing company [1898] x, 11-158 p. 20 cm. [BV199.R5B7] C-305
1. Responsive worship. I. Title.

BROWN, Helen Ada, 1914- ed. 264.4
Choral reading for worship and inspiration. [Graded selections for groups of all ages] Edited by Helen A. Brown and Harry J. Heltman. Philadelphia, Westminster Press [1954] 64 p. 23 cm. [BV199.R5B76] 53-12916
1. Responsive worship. 2. Choral speaking. I. Heltman, Harry Joseph, 1885- joint ed. II. Title.

CONGREGATIONAL readings from the Scriptures ..., hymns, inspirational writings / compiled by Cecil R. Ettinger. Independence, Mo. : Herald Pub. House, [1975] p. cm. Includes index. [BX8675.C66] 75-8596 ISBN 0-8309-0145-0 261'.09'33
1. Reorganized Church of Jesus Christ of Latter-Day Saints—Prayer-books and devotions—English. 2. Responsive worship. I. Ettinger, Cecil Ray, 1922-

[TAYLOR, Kenneth Nathaniel] 264'.4
Responsive readings from the Living Bible. Wheaton, Ill., Tyndale House Publishers [1973] 1 v. (unpaged) 20 cm. [BV199.R5T32] 72-97658 ISBN 0-8423-5480-8
1. Responsive worship. I. Title.

WILLIAMS, L. Griswold, 1893- comp. 264.4
Antiphonal readings for free worship, arranged by L. Griswold Williams. Boston, The Murray press, 1933. [232] p. 22 1/2 cm. "First edition." [BV199.R5W55] 33-16862
1. Responsive worship. I. Title.

Restitutio in integrum (Canon law)

FEENEY, Thomas John, 1912- 348
... Restitutio in integrum; an historical synopsis and commentary ..; by Rev. Thomas John Feeney ... Washington, D.C., The Catholic university of America press, 1941. vi, 169 p. 22 1/2 cm. (The Catholic university of America. Canon law studies, no. 129) Thesis (J.C.D.)--Catholic university of America, 1941. "Biographical note": p. [157] Bibliography: p. [149]-156. [BX1939.R52F4] A 41
1. Restitutio in integrum (Canon law) 2. Catholic church. Codex juris canonici. C. 1687-1689. 3. Catholic church. Codex juris canonici. C. 1905-1907. I. Title.

Restitution.

QUILL, James E. 230'.2
Restitution to the poor: its origin, nature, and extent. Milwaukee, Bruce Pub. Co. [1961] 141 p. 23 cm. [BX1753.Q57] 281'.5 74-240619
1. Restitution. I. Title.

TACK, Theodoro V 922.246
Fray Pedro de Aragon, O. S. A.; his life, works, and doctrine on restitution. Chicago, 1957. viii, 156 p. 23 cm. Diss. --Pontificia Universita gregoriana, Rome. Includes bibliographies. [BX4705.A666T3] 59-24150
1. Aragon, Pedro de, ca. 1544-ca. 1592. 2. Restitution. I. Title.

Restorationism.

CREEL, James Cowherd 1846-
The plea to restore the apostolic church, by James C. Creel ... Cincinnati, O., The Standard publishing company, 1902. xvi, 142 p. incl. front. (port.) 21 cm. 2-30062
I. Title.

DAVIS, Morrison Meade, 1850-
The restoration movement of the nineteenth century, by M. M. Davis ... Cincinnati, O., The Standard publishing company, 1913. x, 294 p. groups of ports. 20 cm. A brief history of the Disciples of Christ cf. Pref. 13-25063
I. Title.

DEAN, Paul, 1789-1860. 289
A course of lectures in defence of the final restoration. Delivered in the Bulfinch street church, Boston, in the winter of eighteen hundred and thirty two. By Paul Dean ... Boston, E. M. Stone, 1832. viii, [9]-190 p. 24 cm. [BX9941.D4] 41-33878
1. Restorationism. I. Title.

DOWLING, Enos E. 268.433
The restoration movement; study course for youth and adults. Cincinnatti, Standard [c.1964] 128p. 22cm. Bibl. pap., price unreported.
I. Title.

JOHNSTON, Joseph S. 220
Christ victorious over all ... by Joseph S. Johnston ... Chicago, Ill. [c1921] 233 [1] p. iv diagr. 23 cm. [BR125.J55] 21-5404
1. Restorationism. I. Title.

PRIDGEON, Charles Hamilton, 1863-1932. 237
Is hell eternal; or, Will God's plan fail? by Rev. Charles H. Pridgeon ... New York and London, Funk & Wagnalls company, 1920. ix, 11-333 p. diagrs. 19 cm. [BT836.P7] 20-21212
1. Restorationism. I. Title.

RUTHERFORD, Thomas G. 234
The extent of salvation: a treatise showing the compatibility of a state of punishment beyond the grave with universal salvation. By T. G. Rutherford... Philadelphia, The author, 1846. iv, 5-96 p. 18 1/2 cm. [BX9941.R8] 41-41815
1. Restorationism. I. Title.

WIDTSOE, Osborne J. P.
The restoration of the gospel, by Osborne J. P. Widtsoe ... with an introduction by Joseph F. Smith, jr. ... Salt Lake City, Utah, The Deseret news, 1912. xix, 243 p. 20 cm. $0.75. 12-16578
I. Title.

Resurrection.

ADDAMS, James Lawrence. 236.8
Asleep in Jesus. by J.L. Addams. [Louisville, Ky., c1938] cover-title 2 p. l., 75 p. 19 1/2 cm. [BT871.A3] 38-39351
1. Resurrection. I. Title.

*ARMERDING, Carl 232.6
Signs of Christ's coming, as son of man. Chicago, Moody [1965] 79p. 18cm. (Compact bks., no. 53. MP29) .29 pap.,
I. Title.

BARTH, Karl, 1886-1968. 227'.2'06
The resurrection of the dead / by Karl Barth ; translated by H. J. Stenning. New York : Arno Press, 1977, c1933. 213 p. ; 23 cm. (The Literature of death and dying) Translation of Die auferstehung der toten. Reprint of the ed. published by Revell, New York. [BS2675.B32 1977] 76-19559 ISBN 0-405-09555-4 : 15.00
1. Jesus Christ—Resurrection. 2. Bible. N.T. 1 Corinthians XV—Commentaries. 3. Resurrection. I. Title. II. Series.

BIBLE. Selections. English. 1914.
Resurrection of the dead; visions of God's revelations to man as found in the Old and New Testaments ... Martinsville, Ind., M. Dickson. 1914. 201p. (Half-title: Classified subjects of the Bible) 14-9294
I. Title.

BOUNDS, Edward McKendree, 1835-1913. 236.
The ineffable glory; thoughts on the resurrection, by Rev. Edward M. Bounds ... with an introduction by Rev. Homer W. Hodge. New York, George H. Doran company [c1921] xii, p., 1 l, 15-142 p. 19 1/2 cm. First published in 1907 under title: The resurrection. [BT871.B75 1921] 21-15198 1.25.
I. Title.

BOUNDS, Edward McKendree, 1835-1913. 236.
The ineffable glory; thoughts on the resurrection, by Rev. Edward M. Bounds ... with an introduction by Rev. Homer W. Hodge. New York, George H. Doran company [c1921] xii, p., 1 l, 15-142 p. 19 1/2 cm. First published in 1907 under title: The resurrection. [BT871.B75 1921] 21-15198 1.25.
I. Title.

BOUNDS, Edward McKendree, 1835-1913. 236.
The resurrection, [by] E. M. Bounds ... Nashville, Tenn., Dallas, Tex., Publishing house of the M. E. church, South, Smith & Lamar, agents, 1907. 172 p. 15 1/2 cm. (Series on heaven). [BT871.B75] 7-28289
I. Title.

BURGE, Hubert Murray bp. of Oxford 1862- 236.
The doctrine of the resurrection of the body; documents of relating to the question of heresy raised against the Rev. H. D. A. Major, Ripon hall, Oxford, issued by the Right Rev. H. M. Burge. London [etc] A. R. Mowbray & co., ltd; Milwaukee, The Morehouse publishing co. [1922] 2 p. l., 75, [1] p. 21 1/2 cm. Contains the Rev. C. E. Douglas' formal charge against Mr. Major, Mr. Major's reply, the Bishop of Oxford's decision, and opinions by Rev. A. C. Headlan, Rev. W. Lock, and Rev. E. W. Watson. [BT871.B785] 22-12416
I. Title.

BURRELL, David James, 1844- 236.
The resurrection and the life beyond, by David James Burrell ... New York, American tract society [c1920] 3 p., l., 241 p. 19 1/2 cm. [BT871.B79] 20-6441
I. Title.

BUSH, George, 1796-1859. 236.
Anastasis; or, The doctrine of the resurrection of the body, rationally and scripturally considered... By George Bush... 2d ed. New York & London, Wiley and Putnam, 1845. xii, [13]-396 p. 19 cm. [BT871.B8] 20-23093
1. Resurrection. I. Title.

CAMP, Norman Harvey, 1867- 236.8.
The resurrection of the human body, by Norman H. Camp Chicago, The Bible institute colportage association [1937] 127 p. 19 cm. [BT871.C18] 38-1805
1. Resurrection. 2. Jesus Christ—Resurrection. I. Title.

CHARLES, Robert Henry, 1855- 252.0
The resurrection of man and other sermons preached in Westminster Abbey by the Ven. R. H. Charles ... New York, C. Scribner's sons [1929] xi, 264 p. 21 cm. (Half-title: "The scholar as preacher." 5th ser.) Printed in Great Britain. List of volumes to be consulted by the reader: p. vii. [BX5133.C5R4] 30-13862
1. Resurrection. 2. Future life. I. Title.

CLARK, Neville. 232'.5
Interpreting the resurrection. Philadelphia, Westminster Press [1967] 128 p. 20 cm. [BT481.C55 1967b] 67-20612
1. Jesus Christ—Resurrection. 2. Resurrection. I. Title.

†CRIBB, C. C. 236
The horrified and the glorified / C. C. Cribb. Raleigh, N.C. : Manhattan, c1977. 139 p. ; 18 cm. Selections from the author's From now till eternity. [BT872.C68] 77-70214 1.75
1. Resurrection. 2. Judgment Day. 3. Heaven. 4. Hell. I. Title.
Publisher's address: P .O. Box 18601, Raleigh, NC 27609

DARRAGH, John Thomas.
The resurrection of the flesh, by the Rev. John T. Darragh ... London, Society for promoting Christian knowledge; New York, Macmillan, 1921. xi, 324 p. 22 cm. A 22
1. Resurrection. I. Title.

DOWNIE, Robert Mager, 1853-
The resurrection and its implications; an examination of the reason why so many consider it a thing incredible that God should raise the dead. By R. M. Downie ... Boston, The Roxburgh publishing company, inc. [c1924] 2 p. l., [7]-236 p. 20 cm. Lettered on cover: R. L. Downie. [BT371.D6] 24-24719
1. Resurrection. I. Title.

DREW, Samuel, 1765-1833. 236.
An essay on the identity and general resurrection of the human body; in which the evidences in favour of these important subjects are considered, in relation both to philosophy and Scripture. By Samuel Drew... Brooklyn, Printed by T. Kirk, for the publisher, 1811. xvi, [xxix]-xxxii, 439 p. 22 1/2 cm. [BT871.D7 1811] 42-26089
1. Resurrection. I. Title. II. Title: The identity and general resurrection of the human body.

DREW, Samuel, 1765-1833. 236.8
An essay on the identity and general resurrection of the human body; in which the evidences in favour of these important subjects are considered, in relation both to philosophy and Scripture. By Samuel Drew... Philadelphia, J. Whetham, 1837. 1 p. l., [vii]-xx, [21]-364 p. 19 1/2 cm. [BT871.D7 1837] 36-25162
1. Resurrection. I. Title. II. Title: The identity and general resurrection of the human body.

ECKMAN, George Peck, 1860-
The return of the Redeemer, by George P. Eckman. New York,Cincinnati, The Abingdon press [c1920] 275 p. 17 cm. [DT885.E25] 21-464
I. Title.

*EKERHOLM, H. E. 231
Hope beyond the darkness. New York, Vantage [1967] 134p. 21cm. 2.95 bds.

I. Title.

FOLK, David Henry, 1850-
Infallibility and the resurrection, by Eld. D. H. Folk... Teague [Tex., Printed by D. H. Folk, 1916] cover-title, 86 p. 23 cm. 16-15894 0.50
I. Title.

FOLK, David Henry, 1850-
Infallibility and the resurrection, by Eld. D. H. Folk... Teague [Tex., Printed by D. H. Folk, 1916] cover-title, 86 p. 23 cm. 16-15894 0.50
I. Title.

FOLK, David Henry, 1850- 236.
Resurrection and other truths explained, by Eld. D. H. Folk. Teague, Tex. [c1919] cover-title, 50 p. 22 cm. [BR126.F67] 20-1132
I. Title.

FUDGE, Edward. 232'.5
Resurrection! Essays in honor of Homer Hailey. Edited by Edward Fudge. [Athens, Ala.] C.E.I. Pub. Co. [1973] 131 p. port. 23 cm. Includes bibliographies. [BT481.F78] 73-80555 ISBN 0-88407-003-4 4.95
1. Jesus Christ—Resurrection. 2. Hailey, Homer, 1904- 3. Resurrection. I. Hailey, Homer, 1904- II. Title.
Publisher's Address: 1005 Jefferson, Athens, Ala. 35611

HANNA, William, 1808-1882. 236.
The resurrection of the dead. By William Hanna, D. D. New York, R. Carter and brothers, 1873. 222 p. 19 1/2 cm. [BT871.H3] 26-5874
1. Resurrection. I. Title.

HARDMAN, Oscar, 1880- 236.8
The resurrection of the body, by Oscar Hardman ... The White lectures, delivered in St. Paul's cathedral in 1933. London, Society for promoting Christian knowledge; New York, The Macmillan co. [1934] v. [1], 7-96 p. 19 cm. "First published 1934." [BT871.H35] 34-41837
1. Jesus Christ—Resurrection. 2. Resurrection. I. White lectures. 1933. II. Title.

HOSKINS, Sarah Bartlett.
Why two resurrections? A strictly non-sectarian production, by Sarah Bartlett Hoskins ... Upper Alton, Ill., 1901. 76 pp. 19 1/2 cm. 2-1215
1. Resurrection. I. Title.

KERR, William Henry, 1852- 236
Radio messages from paradise, revealing the glorious condition, priveleges [!] immunities and blessings of the redeemed in the great beyond, by W. H. Kerr... Crawfordsville, Ind., The Indiana book concern [c1923] 2 p. l., [iii]-xvii, 211 p. 20 cm. [BT821.K4] 23-7053
1. Resurrection. 2. Future life. I. Title.

KESICH, Veselin, 1921- 232'.5
The first day of the new creation : the resurrection and the Christian faith / Veselin Kesich. Crestwood, N.Y. : St. Vladimir's Seminary Press, 1981. p. cm. Includes index. Bibliography: p. [BT481.K42] 19 81-21516 ISBN 0-913836-78-8 : 7.95
1. Jesus Christ—Resurrection. 2. Resurrection. I. Title.
Publisher's address: 575 Scarsdale Rd., Crestwood, NY 10707

KINGSLEY, Calvin, 1812-1870. 236.
The resurrection of the dead: a vindication of the literal resurrection of the human body; in opposition to the work of Professor Bush. By Calvin Kingsley ... George Peck, editor. New York, Carlton & Phillips, 1853. 159 p. 15 1/2 cm. [BT871.K5 1853] 27-17491
1. Bush, George, 1796-1859. Anastasis: or, The doctrine of the resurrection of the body. 2. Resurrection. I. Peck, George, ed. II. Title.

KINGSLEY, Calvin, 1812-1870. 236.
The resurrection of the dead: a vindication of the literal resurrection of the human body; in opposition to the work of Professor Bush. By Calvin Kingsley ... George Peck, editor. New-York, Carlton & Phillips, 1856. 159 p. 15 1/2 cm. [BT871.K5 1856] 20-16828
1. Bush, George, 1796-1859. Anastasis: or, The doctrine of the resurrection of the body. 2. Resurrection. I. Peck, George, ed. II. Title.

MCCANN, Justin, 1882- 236.
The resurrection of the body, by the Rev. Dom Justin McCann, M.A.; introduction by Jas. J. Walsh, M.D. New York, The Macmillan company, 1928. ix, 96 p. 17 cm. (Half-title: The treasury of the faith series: 34) [Full name: Philip Justin McCann] [Full name: Philip Justin McCann] [BT871.M15 1928a] 28-27963
1. Resurrection. I. Title.

MORICE, Charles, 1861-
The re-appearing (Il est ressuscite!); a vision of Christ in Paris, by Charles Morice; tr. by John N. Raphael; with an introduction by Coningsby Dawson. New York, Hodder & Stoughton, George H. Doran company [c1911] 211 p. 19 1/2 cm. $1.20 11-14549
I. Raphael, John N., tr. II. Title.

OBERG, John Ulrick.
The false and the true; a psychic phantasmagoria of the resurrection in epic verse, with sub-headings, illustrations and comments, by John Ulrick Oberg... Berkeley, Cal., J. U. Oberg, 1902. 175 p. illus. 18 cm. 2-20256
I. Title.

OBERG, John Ulrick.
The false and the true: a psychic phantasmagoria of the resurrection in epic verse, with sub-headings, illustrations and comments, by John Ulrick Oberg ... Berkeley, Cal., J. U. Oberg, 1902. 175 p. illus. 18 cm. 2-20256
I. Title.

ORDAL, Zakarias Johannesen, 1875- 252.
The resurrection of Jesus, an historical fact, by Rev. Z. J. Ordal ... Minneapolis, Minn., Augusburg publishing house, 1923. 2 p. l., [7]-128 p. 20 cm. [BT480.O7] 23-17149
I. Title.

RIGGENBACH, Eduard, 1861-
The resurrection of Jesus, by Eduard Riggenbach ... New York, Eaton & Mains; Cincinnati, Jennings & Graham [c1907] 74 p. 18 cm. (On cover: Foreign religious series) 8-262
I. Title.

SIMPSON, William John Sparrow, 1859- 236.
The resurrection and modern thought, by W. J. Sparrow Simpson ... London, New York [etc.] Longmans, Green, and co., 1911. ix, 462, [2] p. 23 1/2 cm. Bibliography: 2 p. at end. [BT871.S6] 12-852
1. Jesus Christ—Resurrection. 2. Resurrection. I. Title.

SIMPSON, William John Sparrow, 1859-1952. 232'.5
The Resurrection and the Christian faith. Grand Rapids, Zondervan Pub. House [1968] ix, 462 p. 23 cm. Reprint of the 1911 ed., published under the title: The Resurrection and modern thought. Includes bibliographical references. [BT480.S53 1968] 68-13317
1. Jesus Christ—Resurrection. 2. Resurrection. I. Title.

SISSON, Elizabeth, 1848-
Foregleams of glory; Ressurrection papers; Faith reminiscences; In Trinity college, by Elizabeth Sisson. Chicago, Ill., The Evangel publishing house, 1912. 3 p. l., 9-201 p. 19 1/2 cm. $1.00. 13-1391
I. Title.

SPIVEY, Thomas Sawyer, 1856- 133
The resurrection, by Thomas Sawyer Spivey; gnosticism, the basis of ecclesiasticism ... a sequel to The Revelation ... Beverly Hills, Calif., The author [c1925] 3 p. l., 9-414 p. illus., diagrs. 20 1/2 cm. [X3.S57] 25-8018
I. Title.

STAUDT, Calvin Klopp. 236.8
The idea of the resurrection in the ante-Nicene period, by Calvin Klopp Staudt, PH. D. Chicago, The University of Chicago press, 1909. 90 p. 25 cm. (On cover: The University of Chicago ... Historical and linguistic studies in literature related to the New Testament ... 2d ser. ... v. 1. pt. viii) Published also as the author's thesis (PH. d.) University of Chicago. [BT871.S7 1909] 30-33847
1. Resurrection. 2. Jesus Christ—Resurrection. I. Title.

STEWART, George, 1892- 232.
The resurrection in our street, by George Stewart ... Garden City, N. Y., Doubleday, Doran & company, inc., 1928. viii, 124 p. 20 cm. [BT871.S75] 28-8153
1. Resurrection. I. Title.

STUTENROTH, Allen Wert, 1875-
The hope and resurrection of the dead, both of the just and the unjust. Practical Christianity, a reason of the hope that is in you. By Allen W. Stutenroth ... Chicago, Ill., The author [c1911] 236 p. 21 1/2 cm. $1.50. 11-20316
I. Title.

TORREY, Reuben Archer, 1856-
The return of the Lord Jesus; the key to the Scripture, and the solution of all our political and social problems; or, The golden age that is soon coming to the earth, by R. A. Torrey. [Los Angeles, Printed by Grant's publishing house, c1913] 160 p. 18 1/2 cm. $0.25. 13-24875
I. Title.

WHITE, Wilbert Webster, 1863- 232.
The resurrection body "according to the Scriptures", by Wilbert W. White... New York, George H. Doran company [c1923] x p., 2 l., 15-90 p. 19 1/2 cm. $1.00 [BT871.W5] 23-6852
I. Title.

WILLIAMS, Harry Abbot. 236'.8
True resurrection [by] H. A. Williams. New York, Holt, Rinehart and Winston [1972] x, 182 p. 22 cm. Includes bibliographical references. [BT872.W53] 72-78108 ISBN 0-03-091994-0 6.95
1. Resurrection. I. Title.

WILLIAMS, Harry Abbott. 236'.8
True resurrection. New York, Harper & Row [1974, c1972] x, 182 p. 20 cm. (Colophon books, CN332) [BT872.W53] ISBN 0-06-090332-5 2.45 (pbk.)
1. Resurrection. I. Title.
L.C. card no. for the hardbound edition: 72-78108.

WILLIS, Frederick Milton, 1868- 212
The return of the world-teacher; Purifying Christianity: The common voice of religion, by F. Milton Willis ... New York, E. P. Dutton & company [c1924] ix, 121 p. 19 1/2 cm. (Half-title: Sacred occultism series) [BP565.W56] 24-5835
I. Title.

Resurrection—Addresses, essays, lectures.

CORNELIS, Humbert, 1915- 236.8082
The resurrection of the body, by H. Cornelis [others] Tr. [from French] by Sister M. Joselyn. Notre Dame. Ind., Fides [c.1964] 278p. 20cm. (Themes of theology) 64-16497 4.50
1. Resurrection—Addresses, essays, lectures. I. Title.

FRICK, Philip Louis, 1874-
The resurrection and Paul's argument: a study of First Corinthians, fifteenth chapter, by Philip L. Frick ... Cincinnati, Jennings and Graham; New York, Eaton and Mains, [1912] 348 p. 20 cm. 12-20649 1.25
I. Title.

LILLEY, James Samuel.
Was the resurrection a fact? and other essays, by James Samuel Lilley. Boston, R. G. Badger; [etc., etc., c1916] 61 p. 20 cm. Contents.--Was the resurrection a fact?--A crisis in the church.--Is the infinite knowable?--The Holy Book.--A purpose in life. 16-18759 1.00
I. Title.

LOCKTON, William. 225.
The resurrection and other Gospel narratives and The narratives of the virgin birth; two essays by W. Lockton ... London, New York [etc.] Longmans, Green and co., 1924. x, 184 p. 20 cm. [BS2555.L55] 24-16780
I. Title.

SUFFIN, Arnold.
Resurrection; an offering. [1st ed.] New York, Exposition Press [1963] 64 p. 21 cm. Poems. NUC67
I. Title.

Resurrection—Biblical teaching.

BOWEN, Clayton Raymond, 1877-1934. 236.
The resurrection in the New Testament; an examination of the earliest references to the rising of Jesus and of Christians from the dead, by Clayton R. Bowen ... New York and London, G. P. Putnam's sons, 1911. viii p., 1 l., 492 p. 19 cm. (On cover: Crown theological library) "List of works most frequently cited": p. 481-485. Bible--Theology--N.T. [BT871.B78] 11-29880
1. Resurrection—Biblical teaching. 2. Bible. N.T.—Theology. I. Title.

GAFFIN, Richard B. 234
The centrality of the resurrection : a study in Paul's soteriology / Richard B. Gaffin, Jr. Grand Rapids : Baker Book House, c1978. 155 p. ; 22 cm. (Baker Biblical monograph) A revision of the author's thesis, Westminster Theological Seminary, 1969, under title: Resurrection and redemption: a study in Pauline soteriology. Includes indexes. Bibliography: p. 145-146. [BS2655.R35G33 1978] 78-57894 ISBN 0-8010-3726-3 : 4.95
1. Bible. N.T. Letters of Paul—Theology. 2. Resurrection—Biblical teaching. 3. Salvation—Biblical teaching. I. Title. II. Series.

LADD, George Eldon, 1911- 232'.5
I believe in the resurrection of Jesus / by George Eldon Ladd. Grand Rapids : Eerdmans, 1975. 156 p. ; 21 cm. (I believe ; 2) Includes bibliographical references and index. [BT481.L25] 75-14148 ISBN 0-8028-1611-8 pbk. : 2.95
1. Jesus Christ—Resurrection. 2. Resurrection—Biblical teaching. I. Title.

SCHEP, J A 220.82368
The nature of the resurrection body, a study of the Biblical data, by J. A. Schep. Grand Rapids, W. B. Eerdmans Pub. Co. [1964] 252 p. 23 cm. Bibliography: p. 230-241. [BT872.S3] 64-16586
1. Resurrection—Biblical teaching. I. Title.

WILCKENS, Ulrich, 1928- 236'.8
Resurrection : Biblical testimony to the Resurrection : an historical examination and explanation / Ulrich Wilckens ; translated by A. M. Stewart. Atlanta : John Knox Press, 1978, c1977. vi, 134 p. ; 22 cm. Translation of Auferstehung. Bibliography: p. 133-134. [BS680.R37W513 1978] 77-15752 ISBN 0-8042-0396-2 : 6.95
1. Jesus Christ—Resurrection. 2. Resurrection—Biblical teaching. I. Title.

Resurrection Church, Chicago.

CHICAGO. Resurrection Church.
Golden Anniversary 1910-1960. [Chicago, 1960] 1 v. (unpaged) illus., ports. 23 cm. 68-35467
1. Resurrection Church, Chicago. I. Title.

Resurrection—Early works to 1800.

MULLINS, William Ritcherdson, 1886- 232.
The first resurrection and the reign of Christ with his saints on earth, by W. R. Mullins ... [Knoxville, Tenn.] 1923. 142 p. incl. front. (port.) illus. 18 cm. "Addenda" (1 leaf) laid in. [BT885.M75] 24-2269
I. Title.

PEEL, Malcolm Lee. 236
The Epistle to Rheginos; a Valentinian letter on the resurrection; introduction, translation, analysis, and exposition. Philadelphia, Westminster Press [1969] xv, 208 p. 23 cm. (The New Testament library) Based on the author's thesis, Yale. Bibliography: p. [181]-183. [BT870.P4 1969] 70-89686 ISBN 0-664-20877-0 10.00
1. Resurrection—Early works to 1800. 2. Eschatology—Early works to 1800. 3.

Gnosticism. I. Treatise concerning the resurrection. II. Title.

Resurrection — Sermons.

KELLEMS, Jesse Randolph, 1892- 252
The resurrection Gospel, and other sermons delivered at the First Christian church, Long Beach, Cal., January, 1922, by Jesse R. Kellems ... with introduction by George P. Taubman ... Cincinnati, O., The Standard publishing company [c1924] 368 p. incl. front. 20 cm. [BX7327.K35K4] 24-9558
I. Title.

MANN, Stella Terrill. 133.8
Beyond the darkness; three reasons why I believe we live after death. New York, Dodd, Mead [1965] ix, 178 p. 21 cm. [BF648.M3A3] 65-11667
I. Title.

TENNEY, Merrill Chapin, 1904- 232.5
Resurrection realities. "Now is Christ risen." [By] Merrill C. Tenney ... Foreword by V. Raymond Edman ... Los Angeles, Calif., Bible house of Los Angeles [1945] 96 p. 21 cm. [BT871.T37] 46-1420
1. Resurrection—Sermons. 2. Jesus Christ—Resurrection—Sermons. 3. Baptists—Sermons. 4. Sermons, American. I. Title.

TENNEY, Merrill Chapin, 1904- .
The vital heart of Christianity [by] Merrill C. Tenney. Foreword by V. Raymond Edman. Grand Rapids, Zondervan Pub. House [1964, c1945] 96 p. 21 cm. First published in 1945 under title: Resurrection realities. [BT871.T37] 66-364
1. Resurrection — Sermons. 2. Jesus Christ — Resurrection — Sermons. 3. Baptists — Sermons. 4. Sermons, American. I. Title.

WHITWORTH, John Ford, 1854-
Legal and historical proof of the resurrection of the dead; with an examination of the evidence in the New Testament, by John F. Whitworth ... Harrisburg, Pa., Publishing house of the United Evangelical church, 1912. 3 p. l., 5-70 p. 21 cm. $0.60 13-359
I. Title.

Retreat.

WEEK end with God; 242.3
the authentic account of a forty-eight hour period spent at a typical retreat house for men. Recorded with candid photos. [By] Hugh Morley and John Jewell. New York, D. McKay Co. [c1953] 80p. illus. 26cm. [BX2375.M6] 269 53-13299
1. Retreat. I. Morley, Hugh M II. Jewell, John, joint author.

Retreats.

BROWN, Stephen James Meredith, 1881- 242
Alone with God; meditations for a retreat. New York City, Wagner [1956] 310p. 21cm. [BX2375.B77] 56-3334
1. Retreats. 2. Meditations. I. Title.

CASTEEL, John Laurence, 1903- 269.6
Renewal in retreats. New York, Association Press [1959] 250p. 20cm. [BV5068.R4C3] 59-12107
1. Retreats. I. Title.

DAVID, John Baptist Maria, bp., 1761-1841. 242
A spiritual retreat of eight days. By the Right Rev. John M. David ... Edited, with additions, and an introduction, by M. J. Spalding ... Louisville, Webb and Levering, 1864. x, 9-307 p. 18 cm. "Biographical notice of Bishop David": p. 9-32. "Bishop David's Manual of the religious life": p. 281-307. [BX2375.D3] 32-11968
1. Retreats. 2. Meditations. I. Spalking, Martin John abp., 1810-1872 II. Title.

DIGNAM, Augustus, 1833-1894. 262.
Retreats given by Father Dignam of the Society of Jesus, with letters and notes of spiritual direction and a few conferences and sermons; with a preface by Father Gretton, S. J. ... London, Burns & Oates, limited; New York Cincinnati [etc.] Benziger brothers [1896] xxxvi, 409 p. 19 cm. [BX2375.D5] 41-3756
1. Retreats. I. Title.

DOLAN, Albert Harold. 922.244
Roses fall where rivers meet; a description and explanation of the showers of roses of the Little Flower, by the Reverend Albert H. Dolan ... Englewood, N. J., Chicago, Ill., The Carmelite press [c1937] 4 p. l., 11-167 p. 19 cm. [BX4700.T5D62] 37-33932
1. Therese, Saint, 1873-1897. 2. Retreats. I. Title.

GABRIEL, Henry Albert, 1860- 242
An eight days' retreat for religious, by Henry A. Gabriel, S. J. St. Louis, Mo. [etc.] B. Herder, 1914. 6 p. l., [3]-393, [1] p. 20 cm. "Little more than an adaptation of the Spiritual exercises of St. Ignatiua."--Prefatory note. "Books recommended for retreat reading": 1 p. at end. [BX2375.G2 1914] 15-1477
1. Retreats. 2. Meditations. I. Loyola, Ignacio de, Saint, 1491-1556. Exercitia spiritulla. II. Title.

GABRIEL, Henry Albert, 1860- 242
An eight days' retreat for religious, by Henry A. Gabriel, S. F J 3d ed., rewritten and enl. St. Louis, Mo and London, B. Herder book co., 1925. 6 p. l., 3-451 p. 21 cm. "A practical adapation of the wonderfull little treatise of our holy founder."--Pref. "Books recommended for retreat reading": p. 451. [BX2375.G2 1925] 25-5492
1. Retreats. 2. Meditations. I. Loyola, Ignacio de, Saint, 1491-1556. Exercitia spiritualia. II. Title.

GABRIEL, Henry Albert, 1860- 242
An eight days retreat for religious, by Henry A. Gabriel, S. J. New ed. New York, P. J. Kenedy & sons [c1937] 422 p., 1 l., 21 cm. "A practical adaptation of the wonderful little treatise of our holy founder."--Pref. "New edition." "Books recommended for retreat reading": 1 leaf at end. [BX2375.G2 1937] 37-16012
1. Retreats. 2. Meditations. I. Loyola, Ignacio de, Saint, 1491-1556. Exercitia spiritualia. II. Title.

GARRETT, Constance, 1894- 269.6
I give myself unto prayer; addresses and meditations for a retreat, together with a timetable, prayers and readings. [Cincinnati, Literature Headquarters, Woman's Division of Christian Service, Board of Missions of the Methodist Church, 1962] 64 p. 20 cm. [BV5068.R4G3] 62-16513
1. Retreats. I. Title.

GEIERMANN, Peter, 1870-1929. 242
A private retreat for religious, enriched with reflections and select readings taken from the spiritual writings of St. Alphonsus, by Rev. Peter Geiermann ... New York, Cincinnati [etc.] Benziger brothers, 1909. 479 p. 21 cm. [BX2375.G4] 9-17337
1. Retreats. 2. Meditations. I. Liguori, Alfonso Maria de', Saint, 1696-1787. II. Title.

GRANDMAISON, Leonce de [Septime Leonce de Grandmaison] 1868-1927 242
Tongues of fire. Tr. [from French] by M. Angeline Bouchard. Notre Dame. Ind., Fides [1965, c.1961] 214p. 20cm. (Spire bk.,) [BX2375.B673] 61-17234 1.95 pap.,
1. Retreats. 2. Meditations. I. Title.

GRANNAN, Dick. 269'.6'3
Youth quake; a radical restructuring of the high school retreat ... Dayton, Ohio, G. A. Pflaum [1969] 55 p. 28 cm. (What's happening) Based on a program conducted by staff members of the Renewal Centre, Windsor, Ont. [BX2376.S7G7] 78-82522 2.50
1. Retreats. 2. Students—Religious life. I. Renewal Centre. II. Title.

GREEN, Andrew, 1865- 262.
A retreat for religious, by Rev. Andrew Green, O.S.B. ... St. Louis, Mo., and London, B. Herder book co., 1945. iii, 191 p. 22 cm. [BX2375.G7] 45-5166
1. Retreats. 2. Catholic church—Sermons. 3. Sermons, American. I. Title.

HAMMER, Bonaventure, 1842-1917. 242
The spiritual exercises of an eight days' retreat. Arranged for general use by the Rev. Bonaventure Hammer ... St. Louis, Mo., B. Herder, 1895. 259 p. 19 1/2 cm. "Method of assisting at holy mass. By Saint Leonard of Port Maurice": p. 233-237; "Three methods of prayer, recommended by St. Ignatius in his book of Spiritual exercises": p. 238-242; "St. Bonaventure's maxims of piety": p. 243-258; "St. Bonaventure's exhortation on the imitation of Christ": p. 258-259. [BX2375.H3] 32-11967
1. Retreats. 2. Meditations. I. Leonardo, of Porto Maurisio, Saint, 1676-1751. II. Loyola, Ignacio de, Saint, 1491-1556. Exercitis spiritualia. III. Bonaventura, Saint, cardinal, 1221-1274. IV. Title.

HARRINGTON, Wilfrid J. 269'.6
Come, Lord Jesus; a Biblical retreat [by] Wilfrid J. Harrington. Staten Island, N.Y., Alba House [1968] 207 p. 22 cm. [BX2375.H35] 68-31512 4.95
1. Retreats. 2. Meditations. I. Title.

HAVEY, Francis Patrick, 1864- 250
Retreat companion for priests, by Very Reverend Francis P. Havey ... Baltimore, Md., St. Mary's seminary [1946] 3 p. l., 113 p. 13 1/2 cm. [BX2375.H36] 46-18457
1. Retreats. 2. Clergy—Religious life. I. St. Mary's seminary, Baltimore. II. Title.

HENNESSY, Thomas C. ed. 269.6
The inner crusade; the closed retreat in the United States. Foreword by John J. Wright. Chicago, Loyola Univ. Pr. [c.] 1965. x, 207p. 23cm. Bibl. [BX2375.H38] 65-28325 3.00 pap.,
1. Retreats. I. Title.

HENNESSY, Thomas C ed. 269.6
The inner crusade; the closed retreat in the United States. Thomas C. Hennessy, editor. With a foreword by John J. Wright. Chicago, Loyola University Press, 1965. x, 207 p. 23 cm. Bibliographical footnotes. [BX2375.H38] 65-28325
1. Retreats. I. Title.

HENNRICH, Kilian Joseph, 1880- 242
Readings and meditations for retreats and spiritual renewals [by] Fr. Kilian J. Hennrich, O.M. CAP. Paterson, N.J., St. Anthony guild press, Franciscan monastery, 1936. vii, 77 p. incl. front. 16 cm. Half title: Retreats. Adapted and selected from "Mit Gott" by Rev. Athanasius Bierbaum. cf. Foreword. [BX2375.H4] 36-9156
1. Retreats. 2. Meditations. I. Bierbaum, Athanasius. Mit Gott. II. Title.

HOWARD, Roy J 1925- 265.1
Liturgical retreat. New York, Sheed and Ward [1959] 145p. 21cm. [BX2375.H66] 59-10657
1. Retreats. I. Title.

IPARRAGUIRRE, Ignacio. 269.6
How to give a retreat; practical notes. [Translation by Angelo Benedetti] Westminster, Md., Newman Press, 1959. 188p. 19cm. [BX2375.A3I63] 61-484
1. Retreats. I. Title.

JUD, Gerald John. 269'.6
Training in the art of loving; the church and the human potential movement [by] Gerald J. and Elisabeth Jud. Philadelphia, Pilgrim Press [1972] 191 p. 22 cm. Bibliography: p. 190-191. [BV5068.R4J83] 79-184455 ISBN 0-8298-0223-1 7.95
1. Retreats. 2. Love. I. Jud, Elisabeth, joint author. II. Title.

KEARNEY, John, 1865-1941. 242
My spiritual exercises: materials for meditation on the principal exercises of piety, by John Kearney, C.S. SP. New York, P. J. Kenedy & sons [1945] xiv, 272 p. 19 1/2 cm. Edited, with additions, by Bernard Fennelly, cf. Foreword. Bibliographical foot-notes. [BX2375.K4] 46-1277
1. Retreats. 2. Meditations. 3. Spiritual life—Catholic authors. I. Fennelly, Bernard, ed. II. Title.

KNOX, Ronald Arbuthnott, 1888-1957.
A retreat for lay people. New York, Paulist Press, 1963 [c1955] 256 p. 18 cm. (Deus books) 68-2486
1. Retreats. I. Title.

LEEN, James abp., 1888- 242
By Jacob's well, a planned retreat, by Most Rev. James Leen ... translated from the French by Rev. Edward Leen ... New York, P. J. Kenedy & sons [c1940] x, 419 p. 22 cm. [BX2375.L42] 41-683
1. Retreats. I. Leen, Edward, 1885- tr. II. Title.

LONERGAN, William I. 269
Laymen's retreats explained, by Rev. William I. Lonergan ... New York, N. Y., The America press [c1930] 104 p. 19 cm. [BX2375.L6] 30-16884
I. Title.

MCNAMARA, William. 269.2
Manual for retreat masters. Milwaukee, Bruce Pub. Co. [1960] 94p. 20cm. [BX2375.W5] 60-12649
1. Retrents. I. Title.

MAGEE, Raymond J., ed. 269'.6
Call to adventure; the retreat as religious experience, edited by Raymond J. Magee. Nashville, Abingdon Press [1967] 160 p. 20 cm. Bibliography: p. 153-155. [BX2375.A3M2] 67-11013
1. Retreats. I. Title.

MARTINI, Prosdocimus, 1893- 242.3
Be ye renewed; an eight-day retreat for missionary priests. Translated from the Latin by Valerian Schott. Chicago, Franciscan Herald Press [c1956] 473p. 19cm. [BX2375.M272] 269 57-1697
1. Retreats. I. Title.

MEDITATIONS for monthly 242
retreats, for the use of religious, with preface by Rev. H. C. Semple, S. J. New York, Cincinnati [etc.] Benziger brothers, 1907. xxvi, 232 p. front. 16 cm. [BX2375.M35] 7-42086
1. Retreats. 2. Meditations. I. Semple, Henry Churchill, 1853-1925.

MEYER, Fulgence, father, 1876- 269
Conferences for married men, by Rev. Fulgence Meyer ... St. Louis, Mo., and London, B. Herder book co., 1936. ix, 196 p. 20 cm. [Secular name: Alphonse Meyer] [BX2375.M38] 36-9454
1. Retreats. 2. Men. I. Title.

MEYER, Fulgence, father, 1876- 269
Waiting for the Paraclete; retreat lectures for religious and other pious souls, by Rev. Fulgence Meyer ... Cincinnati, O., St. Francis book shop, 1930. 2 v. fronts. 17 cm. "A sequel to 'Uni una'."--Foreword. [Secular name: Alphonse Meyer] [BX2182.M42] 35-5129
1. Retreats. 2. Monasticism and religious orders for women. I. Title.

MEYER, Fulgence, father, 1876-1938. 269
In God's sacred cave, a retreat book for nuns and other persons a thirst for personal perfection, holiness and salvation, by Rev. Fulgence Meyer ... Cincinnati, O., St. Francis book shop, 1938. viii p., 1 l., 408 p. front. 17 cm. [Secular name: Alphonse Meyer] [BX4214.M4] 39-2318
1. Retreats. 2. Monasticism and religious orders for women. I. Title.

OWEN, Aloysius J. 269'.6
The Holy Spirit, your retreat director / Aloysius J. Owen. New York : Alba House, c1979. p. cm. Work is based on the Spiritual exercises of St. Ignatius. [BX2375.A3O93] 79-14945 ISBN 0-8189-0387-2 pbk. : 3.50
1. Loyola, Ignacio de, Saint, 1491-1556. Exercitia spiritualia. 2. Retreats. I. Loyola, Ignacio de, Saint, 1491-1556. Exercitia spiritualia. II. Title.

PETIT, Adolphe.
My bark; a souvenir of retreats given by the Rev. P. Adolphe Petit, S. J.; tr. from the French by Marian Lindsay. St. Louis, Mo. [etc.] B. Herder, 1914. 4 p. l., 148 p. 19 cm. 14-7287 0.60
I. Lindsay, Marian, tr. II. Title.

PLANUS, Romain Louis, 1838-1916. 242
The priest; a retreat for parish priests,

translated from the French of Abbe Planus by Rev. John L. Zoph; with a preface by His Excellency, Most Rev. John J. Mitty ... New York, Cincinnati [etc.] Benziger brothers, 1937. x, 310 p. 20 1/2 cm. Translation of "Le pretre", t. x. "Use retraite pastorale." [BX2375.P62] 37-8522
1. Retreats. 2. Catholic church—Clergy. 3. Meditations. I. Zoph, John Lawrence, 1908- tr. II. Title.

RETREATS for adults. 269.6'08 s
New York : Paulist Press, c1976. xix, 265 p. ; 28 cm. (Retreat resources ; v. 2) Includes bibliographies and index. [BX2375.A3R47 vol. 2] 269'.6 76-372449 ISBN 0-8091-1911-0 : 11.50
1. Retreats. I. Series.

RETREATS for clergy 269'.6'08 s *and religious.* New York : Paulist Press, [1975] x, 181 p. : ill. ; 28 cm. (Retreat resources ; v. 1) Includes bibliographies and indexes. [BX2375.A3R47 vol. 1] 269'.6'9 74-83719 ISBN 0-8091-1850-5 : 9.50
1. Retreats. I. Title. II. Series.

SCHRYVERS, Joseph, 1876- 242
Our Divine Friend; meditations on divine love, readings for a retreat and for all times, by Rev. Joseph Schryvers ... Rev. English ed. by Rev. John F. Coll. St. Louis, Mo., Redemptorist fathers [c1932] viii, 424 p. 15 cm. [BX2183.S4 1932] 33-589
1. God—Worship and love. 2. Retreats. 3. Meditations. I. Coll, John Francis, 1900- ed. II. Title.

SCHRYVERS, Joseph, 1876- 269
With the divine retreat Master; a message from Jesus to His priest, by Jos. Schrijvers, C. SS. R., translated and adapted from the French by Edwin V. O'Hara. Paterson, N. J., St. Anthony guild press, Franciscan monastery, 1939. vii, 156 p. incl. front. 17 cm. Translation of Message de Jesus a son pretre. [BX2375.S37] 39-15051
1. Retreats. 2. Clergy—Religious life. 3. Catholic church—Clergy. I. O'Hara, Edwin Vincent, 1881- tr. II. Title. III. Title: A message from Jesus to His priest.

SIMONS, Joseph B. 269'.6
Retreat dynamics [by] Joseph B. Simons. Notre Dame, Ind., Fides Publishers [1967] 189 p. 23 cm. Includes bibliographies. [BX2375.A3S5] 67-24812
1. Retreats. I. Title.

SMETANA, Rudolph von. 242
Spirtual exercises for a ten days' retreat, for the use of religious congregations. By Very Rev. Rudolph v. Smetana... New York, Cincinnati [etc.] Benziger brothers, 1898. 280 p. 18 cm. [BX2375.S55] 32-11966
1. Retreats. 2. Meditations. I. Title.

A spiritual retreat for 242 *religious persons* ... Philadelphia, H. L. Kilner & co. [c1891] 286 p. 14 cm. "A rule of life, by Bossuet, bishop of Meaux": p. 275-266. [BX2375.S6] 32-11965
1. Retreats. 2. Meditations. I. Bossuet, Jacques Bonigne, bp. of Meaux, 1627-1704.

STEERE, Douglas Van, 1901- 269
Time to spare. New York, Harper [1949] 187 p. 20 cm. Includes bibliographies. [BV5068.R4S8] 49-9557
1. Retreats. I. Title.

WILLIAM, Father 269.2
Manual for retreat masters. Milwaukee, Bruce Pub. Co. [1961, c.1960] 94p. 60-12649 1.50 pap.,
1. Retreats. I. Title.

Retreats—Addresses, essays, lectures.

HALL, Arthur Crawshay 280
Alliston, bp, 1847-
The sevenfold unity of the Christian church, by the Rt. Rev. A. C. A. Hall... New York [etc.] Longmans, Green, and co., 1911. vii 63 p. 19 1/2 cm. $0.75 "This book contains the substance of addresses given at retreats in the autumn of 1910"--Pref. 11-2009
I. Title.

HOGAN, Joseph F 1910- 242.3
A do-it- yourself retreat; how to bring out the real good in you. Chicago, Loyola University Press [c1961] 274p. illus. 19cm. [BX2376.5.H6] 61-15688
1. Retreats—Addresses, essays, lectures. I. Title.

KNOX, Ronald Arbuthnott, 242.3
1888-1957.
The layman and his conscience: a retreat. New York, Sheed & Ward [1961] 218p. 21cm. [BX2375.K5] 61-11797
1. Retreats—Addresses, essays, lectures. I. Title.

KNOX, Ronald Arbuthnott, 269.6
1888-1957.
Retreat for beginners. New York, Sheed and Ward [c.1960] 234p. 21cm. 60-11680 3.50
1. Retreats—Addresses, essays, lectures. 2. Boys—Religious life. I. Title.

KNOX, Ronald Arbuthnott, 269.6
1888-1957
Retreat for beginners. Glen Rock, N.J., Paulist [1964, c.1960] 192p. 18cm. (Deus bks.) 64-20246 .95 pap.,
1. Retreats—Addresses, essays, lectures. 2. Boys—Religious life. I. Title.

MATULICH, Silvano, Father, 269
1893-
"Show me they face!" Exodus 33, 13; retreat conferences. Paterson, N.J., Saint Anthony Guild Press, 1948. ix, 99 p. 19 cm. Secular name: George Joseph Matulich. [BX2375.M3] 49-7259
1. Retreats—Addresses, essays, lectures. I. Title.

WALCHARS, John. 269.6
The call from beyond; thoughts for a retreat. St. Paul, North Central Pub. Co., 1960. 172 p. 23 cm. [BX2375.W3] 60-40203
1. Retreats — Addresses, essays, lectures. I. Title.

Retreats—Collected works.

RETREAT resources : 269'.6'08
designs and strategies for spiritual growth / general editor, Maury Smith ; assistant editor, E. Jackie Kenney. New York : Paulist Press, [1975- v. : ill. ; 28 cm. Includes bibliographies and indexes. [BX2375.A3R47] 75-307051
1. Retreats—Collected works. I. Smith, Maury. II. Kenney, E. Jackie.

Retreats for clergy.

*GEARON, Patrick J. 242.6
'I have chosen you': retreat talks for priests. Chicago, Carmelite Third Order Pr. [1964] 210p. 19cm. 2.50
I. Title.

GEARON, Patrick J 1980-
I have chosen you; retreat talks for priests. Chicago, 1964. 210 p. 19 cm. 64-68146
1. Retreats for clergy. I. Title.

JOHN Paul II, Pope, 1920- 242'.6'9
Sign of contradiction / by Karol Wojtyla (Pope John Paul II). New York : Seabury Press, 1979. p. cm. "A Crossroad book." Translation of Segno di contraddizione. [BX1912.5.J6313] 79-4606 8.95
1. Retreats for clergy. 2. Clergy—Catholic Church—Religious life. I. Title.

MEYER, Fulgence. 242
Uni una! To the one God my one soul! Retreat lectures and readings for religious and priests, by Rev. Fulgence Meyer ... with a foreword by His Lordship, the Right Rev. Joseph Chartrand ... Cincinnati, O., St. Anthony monastery, 1925. 4 p. l., 719 p. front. 18 cm. [BX2182.M4] 25-10228
I. Title.

MURPHY, John Baptist Tuohill, 242
bp., 1854-1926.
A retreat for the clergy, by the Right Rev. J. T. Murphy ... St. Louis, Mo., and London, B. Herder book co., 1926. vi, 239 p. 20 cm. [BX2182.M8] 26-17487
I. Title.

RIHN, Roy J. 242.6
The priestly amen. by Roy Rhin [sic] New York, Sheed [c.1965] x, 180p. 22cm. [BX1912.5.R46] 65-12202 3.95
1. Retreats for clergy. 2. Catholic Church—Clergy—Religious life. I. Title.

Retreats for members of religious orders.

BRINKMEYER, Henry, 1854- 269
A retreat for sisters; meditations and conferences, by Rev. Henry Brinkmeyer ... 2d rev. ed. Grand Rapids, Mich., Convent of the good shepherd, 1924. 4 p. l., [7]-284 p. 19 1/2 cm. [BX4214.B7] 24-31822
I. Title.

DUBAY, Thomas. 271.9069
Sisters' retreats, a guide for priests and sisters. Westminster, Md., Newman Press, 1963. 226 p. 22 cm. [BX4214.D8] 62-21501
1. Retreats for members of religious orders. I. Title.

EDWIN, B. 242.3
Retreat conferences for religious. Milwaukee, Bruce [1964] 150p. 22cm. 64-24742 price unreported
1. Retreats for members of religious orders. I. Title.

GEARON, Patrick J., 1890- 242.3
Rest a while retreat talks. Pref. from Kilian Healy. Chicago, 6415 Woodlawn Ave. Carmelite Third Order Pr., [1963] 315p. 19cm. 63-6663 3.50 bds.,
1. Retreats for members of religious orders. I. Title.

SKELLY, Andrew Maria, 1855- 269
Retreat conferences for religious sisterhoods, by the Rev. A. M. Skelly, o. p. St. Louis, Mo. and London, B. Herder book co., 1927. x, 223 p. 20 cm. [BX4214.S5] 27-3334
I. Title.

Retreats for young men.

DIRECTING boys and students; retreats, mediations, conferences. Paterson, N. J., St. Anthony Guild Press, 1957. xxi, 201p. front. 17cm. Bibliographical references: p. 193-194.
1. Retreats for young men. 2. Students—Religious life. I. Mackey, Ernest.

Retreats for youth.

RETREATS for youth / 269.6'08 s
general editor, Maury Smith, assistant editor, E. Jackie Kenney. New York : Paulist Press, c1976. xix, 202 p. ; 28 cm. (Retreat resources ; v. 3) Includes index. [BX2376.Y73] [BX2375.A3R47 vol. 3] 269'.6'3 76-360813 ISBN 0-8091-1910-2 : 10.50
1. Retreats for youth. I. Smith, Maury. II. Kenney, E. Jackie. III. Series.

STIEGELE, Paul, 1847-1903. 243
Retreats for Catholic girls and women, by the V. Rev. Paul Stieglee; adapted from the German by the Rev. Charles F. Keyser; edited by Arthur Preuss. St. Louis, Mo., and London, B. Herder book co., 1930. vi, 158 p. 19 cm. $1.50 "This is the second part of ... 'Exerzitienvortrage', the first having been given to the English-reading public ... under the title, 'Retreat matter for priests'."--Pref. [BX2184.S72] 30-20257
I. Keyser, Charles F., tr. II. Preuss, Arthur, 1871- ed. III. Title.

Retreats—Handbooks, manuals, etc.

NELSON, Virgil. 269'.6'0202
Retreat handbook : a-way to retreat making / Virgil and Lynn Nelson. Valley Forge, Pa. : Judson Press, c1976. 129 p. : ill. ; 28 cm. Includes bibliographical references. [BV5068.R4N44] 75-23468 ISBN 0-8170-0694-X : 5.95
1. Retreats—Handbooks, manuals, etc. I. Nelson, Lynn, joint author. II. Title.

Retreats. Meditations

GARESCHE, Edward Francis, 262.
1876-
Retreat readings; some thoughts for those making retreats, by Rev. Edward F. Garesche ... with preface by Most Rev. S. G. Messmer ... New York, Cincinnati [etc.] Benziger brothers, 1929. xiii, 185 p. 14 1/2 cm. [BX2375.G3] 29-16565
I. Title.

SAINT PAUL, mother, 1861- 242
Societas Christi; an eight days' retreat founded on the Spiritual exercises of St. Ignatius, by Mother St. Paul ... preface by the Rev. Joseph Rickaby ... London, New York [etc.] Longmans, Green and co., 1924. xii, 244 p. 19 1/2 cm. [Secular name: Emily Gyles] [BX2375.S3] 24-21953
1. Loyola, Ignacio de, Saint, 1491-1556. Exercitia spiritualla. 2. Retreats. Meditations I. Title.

STIEGELE, Paul, 1847-1903. 242
Retreat matter for priests, by the Very Rev. Paul Stiegele; adapted into English by the Rev. C. F. Keyser, edited by Arthur Preuss. St. Louis, Mo. and London, B. Herder book co., 1926. viii, 140 p. 19 cm. [BX2184.S7] 26-7190
I. Keyser, Charles F., tr. II. Preuss, Arthur, 1871-1884, ed. III. Title.

TOUSSAINT, Johann Peter, 242
1833-1906.
Retreat discourses and meditations for religious, by the Rev. J. P. Toussaint...from the German by the Rev. J. P. Miller... St. Louis, Mo., and London, B. Herder book co., 1929. vi, 394 p. 21 cm. [BX2184.T6] 29-18426
I. Miller, John Peter, 1874- tr. II. Title.

Retreats, Religious.

STEUART, Robert Henry Joseph,
1874-1948.
Spiritual teaching of Father Steuart, S. J. Notes of his retreats and conferences, collected and arranged by Katherine Kendall, with an introduction by Fr. H. P. C. Lyons, S.J. London, Burns Oates; (Westminster, Md., Newman) 1957. xiv, 148 p. 22 cm. (Catholic paperbacks, 2) Reprint of the 1952 edition.
1. Retreats, Religious. 2. Spiritual life. I. Kendall, Katharine, ed. II. Title.

Reu, Johann Michael, 1869-1943.

IN remembrance of 384'.1'0924 B *Reu :* an evaluation of the life and work of J. Michael Reu, 1868-1943, on the 100th anniversary of his birth by some of his friends and former students / edited by Robert C. Wiederaenders. Dubuque : Wartburg Seminary Association, 1969. 31 leaves : port. ; 28 cm. Cover title. Consists of presentations made at a luncheon sponsored by the Wartburg Seminary (Alumni) Association held Nov. 12, 1961. "Writings about J. Michael Rue": leaf 31. [BX8080.R3815] 75-316286
1. Reu, Johann Michael, 1869-1943. 2. Reu, Johann Michael, 1869-1943—Bibliography. I. Reu, Johann Michael, 1869-1943. II. Wiederaenders, Robert C. III. Wartburg Seminary Association.

Revel, Bernard, 1885-1940.

HOENIG, Sidney 296'.0924
Benjamin.
Rabbinics and research; the scholarship of Dr. Bernard Revel, by Sidney B. Hoenig. New York, Yeshiva University Press, 1968. 167 p. 24 cm. (Studies in Judaica, 2) Bibliography: p. 129-135. [BM755.R44H6] 71-19636
1. Revel, Bernard, 1885-1940. I. Title. II. Series.

ROTHKOFF, Aaron. 296.8'32'0924 B
Bernard Revel: builder of American Jewish orthodoxy. [1st ed.] Philadelphia, Jewish Publication Society of America, 1972. xiv, 378 p. illus. 22 cm. Bibliography: p. 343-359. [BM755.R44R67] 71-188582 6.00
1. Revel, Bernard, 1885-1940.

Revelation.

ABRAHAM, William J. 1947- 231.7'4
(William James)
Divine revelation and the limits of historical criticism / William J. Abraham. Oxford [Oxfordshire] ; New York : Oxford University Press, 1982. 222 p. ; 23 cm.

Includes bibliographical references and index. [BT127.2.A27 1982] 19 81-22441 ISBN 0-19-826665-0 : 24.95
1. Revelation. 2. History (Theology) I. Title.

ANDREWS, Samuel James, 1817-1906. 231.74
God's revelations of Himself to men as successively made in the patriarchal, Jewish, and Christian dispensations and in the Messianic kingdom, by Samuel J. Andrews ... New York, C. Scribner's sons, 1886. xiv p., 1 l., 391 p. 21 1/2 cm. [BT127.A5 1886] 40-23718
1. Revelation. I. Title.

ANDREWS, Samuel James, 1817-1906. 231.
God's revelations of himself to men as successively made in the patriarchal, Jewish, and Christian dispensations and in the Messianic kingdom, by Samuel J. Andrews ... 2d ed., rev. and enl. New York and London, G. P. Putnam's sons, 1901. xxi p., 1 l., 421 p. 23 1/2 cm. [BT127.A5 1901] 1-24631
1. Revelation. I. Title.

ATWOOD, Isaac Morgan, 1838-1917. 281.74
... Relation. By Isaac M. Atwood ... Boston, Universalist publishing house, 1889. 3 p. l., [5]-90 p. 18 cm. (Added t. p.: Manuals of faith and duty. Ed. by J. S. Cantwell. no. iii) Series title in part at head of t.p. [BT127.A7] 88-11179
1. Revelation. I. Title.

BAIERL, Joseph John, 1884- 231.74
The theory of revelation ... by Rev. Joseph J. Baierl, S.T.D., for the use of the students of St. Bernard's seminary. Rochester, N. Y., The Seminary press, 193. v. 23 cm. [BT127.B23] CA34
1. Revelation. 2. Miracles. 3. Prophecies. I. Title.

BAILLIE, John, 1886- 231.74
The idea of revelation in recent thought. New York, Columbia [1964, c.1956] 151p. 21cm. (Bampton lects. in Amer., no. 7. 54) Bibl. 1.45 pap.,
1. Revelation. I. Title.

BARRY, Joseph Gayle Hurd, 1858-
The self-revelation of Our Lord. By the Reverend J. G. H. Barry, D.D. 2d ed., rev. and cor. [New York] E. S. Gorham, 1914. 4 p. l., 334 p. 19 cm. 14-10041
I. Title.

BAVINCK, Herman, 1854-1921. 231.74
The philosophy of revelation. Grand Rapids, Eerdmans, 1953. x, 349p. 23cm. (The Stone lectures for 1908-1909 Princeton Theological Seminary) Bibliographical references included in 'Notes' (p. 317-349: sRevelation. [BT127] 54-6234
I. Title. II. Series: Princeton Theological Seminary. Stone lectures, 1908-9

BAVINCK, Herman, 1854-1921. 231.
The philosophy of revelation; the Stone lectures for 1908-1909, Princeton theological seminary, by Herman Bavinck ... New York [etc.] Longmans, Green, and co., 1909. x, 349 p. 21 1/2 cm. [BT127.B3] 9-2534
1. Revelation. I. Title.

BEA, Augustin, Cardinal, 1881- 231'.74
The word of God and mankind. Chicago, Franciscan Herald Press [1967] 318 p. 23 cm. Translation of La parola di Dio et l'umanita. Commentary on Constitution on divine revelation of Vatican Council II. Includes bibliographical references. [BX830 1962.A45C772 1967b] 68-17560
1. Vatican Council. 2d, 1962-1965. Constitutio dogmatica de divina revelatione. 2. Revelation. I. Title.

BEEGLE, Dewey M. 220.1'3
Scripture, tradition, and infallibility [by] Dewey M. Beegle. Grand Rapids, Eerdmans [1973] 332 p. 21 cm. Published in 1963 under title: The inspiration of Scripture. Bibliography: p. 313-320. [BS480.B363 1973] 73-78218 ISBN 0-8028-1549-9 4.95 (pbk.)
1. Bible—Inspiration. 2. Revelation. 3. Bible and tradition. I. Title.

BENDER, Harold Stauffer 231.74
Biblical revelation and inspiration. [Scottdale, Pa., Mennonite Pub. House, c.1959] 20p. 20cm. (Focal pamphlet series, no. 4) 59-15635 .35 pap.,
1. Revelation. 2. Bible—Inspiration. I. Title.

BERKOUWER, Gerrit Cornelis, 1903- 231.74
General revelation. Grand Rapids, W. B. Eerdmans Pub. co., 1955. 336p. 23cm. (His Studies in dogmatics) [BT127.B435] 53-8142
1. Revelation. 2. Theology, Doctrinal. I. Title.

BIBLE. N. T. Revelation. English. 1916.
The analysis of Revelation. Mabton, Wash., N. J. Beckner [c1916] 1 p. l., [5]-134 p. 20 cm. On cover: Authored and compiled by Noah J. Beckner. 16-18036 0.50
I. Beckner, Noah J., comp. II. Title.

BOWNE, Borden Parker, 1847-1910. 231.74
The Christian revelation [by] Borden P. Bowne. Cincinnati, Curts & Jennings; New York, Eaton & Mains [1898] 107 p. 18 x 9 cm. "This discussion is a paper, somewhat enlarged, which I read last summer before the University of Syracuse."--p. 3. [BT127.B7] 40-24456
1. Revelation. I. Title.

BREWSTER, Chauncey Bunce, bp. 1848- 231.
Aspects of revelation; being the Baldwin lectures for 1900, by Chauncey B. Brewster... New York, London [etc.] Longmans, Green, and co., 1901. xxviii, 275 p. 19 1/2 cm. [BT127. B8] 1-15238
1. Revelation. I. Title.

BRING, Ragnar, 1895- 231.74
How God speaks to us; the dynamics of the living word. Philadelphia, Muhlenberg Press [1962] 120p. 21cm. [BT127.2.B7] 62-15699
1. Revelation. I. Title.

BRUCE, Alexander Balmain, 1831-1899. 231.74
The chief end of revelation. By Alexander Balmain Bruce ... New York, A. D. F. Randolph & company [1881] 278 p. 19 1/2 cm. "Portions of ... this volume were recently delivered as lectures at the Presbyterian college, London."--Pref. [BT127.B83] 36-25376
1. Revelation. 2. Bible—Evidences, authority, etc. I. Title.

BRUNNER, Heinrich Emil, 1889- 231.74
Revelation and reason; the Christian doctrine of faith and knowledge, by Emil Brunner, translated by Olive Wyon. Philadelphia, The Westminster press [1946] xii, 440 p. 23 1/2 cm. [BT127.B842] 46-7404
1. Revelation. I. Wyon, Olive, tr. II. Title.

[BRUNS, Henry Arnold]
The science of Revelation in modern English ... Cleveland, H. A. Bruns, 1913. [92] p. 19 cm. 13-14804 1.00
I. Title.

[BRUNS, Henry Arnold]
The science of revelation in modern English, 2d ed. Cleveland, O. Minneapolis, Minn., H. A. Bruns [c1915] [130] p. 19 cm. 16-1706 1.00
I. Title.

BRUNS, Henry Arnold.
The science of revelation in modern English ... 5th ed. ... copyright 1918 by Henry A. Bruns ... Cleveland, O., c1918. [168] p. fold. chart. 20 cm. Text on front lining-paper. 18-9444
I. Title.

BUIST, Werner. 231.74
Revelation. Translated by Bruce Vawter. New York, Sheed and Ward [1956] 158 p. 21 cm. Includes bibliographical references. [BT127.1.B813] 65-12200
1. Revelation. I. Title.

BULST, Werner 231.74
Revelation. Tr. [from German] by Bruce Vawter. New York, Sheed [c.1965] 158p. 21cm. Bibl. [BT127.2.B813] 65-12200 3.95
1. Revelation. I. Title.

CHANDLER, George, 1779?-1859. 231.7
The scheme of divine revelation considered, principally in its connection with the progress and improvement of human society; in eight sermons preached before the University of Oxford in the year mdccccxxv. at the lecture founded by the late Rev. John Bampton ... Bythe Rev. George Chandler ... Oxford, The University press for the author; [etc., etc.] 1825. xxviii, 300 p. 22 cm. Binder's title: Bampton lectures. 1825. [BR45.B3 1825] 230.082 38-16173
1. Revelation. 2. Providence and government of God. I. Title.

CORBON, Jean, 1924- 220.6'3
God's Word to men [by] Michael Bouttier, Jean Corbon [and] George Khodre. Translated by Agnes Cunningham. Techny, Ill., Divine Word Publications [1969] ix, 142 p. 18 cm. (Churches in dialogue, DWP 111) Translation of La Parole de Dieu. Bibliographical footnotes. [BS476.C613] 69-20419 1.95
1. Bible—Hermeneutics. 2. Revelation. I. Bouttier, Michel, 1921- II. Khodre, Georges, 1923- III. Title.

CUMMINGS, Ephraim Chamberlain, 1825-1897. 231.74
Nature in Scripture. A study of Bible verification in the range of common experience. By E. C. Cummings ... Boston, Cupples and Hurd, 1887. xiii, 357 p. 21 cm. "Second edition." [BT127.C8 1887] 37-30806
1. Revelation. 2. Providence and government of God. 3. Christianity—Philosophy. I. Title.

CUMMINGS, Ephraim Chamberlain, 1825-1897. 281.74
Nature in Scripture. A study of Bible verification in the range of common experience. By E. C. Cummings ... Portland, Me., Hoyt, Fogg, and Donham, 1885. xi, 348 p. 21 cm. [BT127.C8 1885] 37-30807
1. Revelation. 2. Providence and government of God. 3. Christianity—Philosophy. I. Title.

DEMAREST, Bruce A. 231.7'4
General revelation : historical views and contemporary issues / Bruce A. Demarest ; foreword by Vernon C. Grounds. Grand Rapids, Mich. : Zondervan Pub. House, 1982. 301 p. : ill. ; 25 cm. Includes indexes. Bibliography: p. 285-293. [BT127.2.D4 1982] 19 81-16221 ISBN 0-310-44550-7 : 12.95
1. Revelation. I. Title.

DICKEY, Edgar Primrose. 239
Revelation and response, by Edgar P. Dickie ... New York, C. Scribner's sons, 1938. vii, [1], 278 p. 238 cm. "Some of the lectures ... were delivered in Trinity college, Glassgow, under the Kerr trust, in ... 1937: others in [1938] ... in Union theological seminary, New York", and elsewhere: parts have appeared in Religion and life and the Evangelical quarterly. cf. Pref. [BT127.D5 1938 a] 39-9784
1. Revelation. 2. Apologetics—20th cent. I. Title.

DORONZO, Emmanuel, 1903- 231'.74
The channels of revelation. Middleburg, Va., Notre Dame Institute Press [1974] vii, 77 p. 22 cm. (His The science of sacred theology for teachers, book 3) Bibliography: p. iv. [BT127.2.D583] 74-76099 2.00 (pbk.)
1. Revelation. 2. Dogma. 3. Theology, Catholic. I. Title.

DORONZO, Emmanuel, 1903- 231'.74
The channels of revelation. Middleburg, Va., Notre Dame Institute Press [1974] vii, 77 p. 22 cm. (His The science of sacred theology for teachers, book 3) Bibliography: p. iv. [BT127.2.D583] 74-76099
1. Revelation. 2. Dogma. 3. Theology, Catholic. I. Title.

DORONZO, Emmanuel, 1903- 231'.74
Revelation. Middleburg, Va., Notre Dame Institute Press [1974] ix, 120 p. 22 cm. (His The science of sacred theology for teachers, book 2) Bibliography: p. iv-v. [BT127.2.D584] 74-76098 4.00 (pbk.)
1. Revelation.

DOWNER, William Arthur.
The hand of God on the wall; or, Revelations explained, by William Arthur Downer. Glassboro, N.J., The author, 1906. 335 p. front. (port.) illus. 21 cm. 6-32411
I. Title.

DOWNING, Francis Gerald. 231.74
Has Christianity a revelation? [By] F. Gerald Downing. Philadelphia, Westminster Press [c1964] 315 p. 23 cm. Includes bibliographical references. [BT127.2.D6 1964a] 67-12282
1. Revelation. I. Title.

DULLES, Avery Robert, 1918- 231'.74
Revelation and the quest for unity, by Avery Dulles. With a foreword by Robert McAfee Brown. Washington, Corpus Books [1968] 325 p. 21 cm. Bibliographical references included in "Notes" (p. 284-312) [BT127.2.D8] 68-10450
1. Revelation. 2. Christian union—Catholic Church. 3. Bible and Christian union. I. Title.

ESTEP, William. 133
The great revelation: or, The white prophecy, by Prof. Wm. Estep ... Washington [The Library press] 1927- v. 18 1/2 cm. [BF1999.E7] 28-1576
I. Title.

FICHTE, Johann Gottlieb, 1762-1814. 231'.74
Attempt at a critique of all revelation / by Johann Gottlieb Fichte ; translated, with an introd., by Garrett Green. Cambridge ; New York : Cambridge University Press, 1978. viii, 186 p. ; 22 cm. Translation of Versuch einer Kritik aller Offenbarung. Includes index. Bibliography: p. 181-182. [B2833.E5] 77-77756 ISBN 0-521-21707-5 : 15.95
1. Revelation. I. Title.

FINEGAN, Jack, 1908- 230
The three R's of Christianity. Richmond, Va., Knox [c.1964] 125p. 20cm. Bibl. 64-10078 1.75 pap.,
1. Revelation. 2. Redemption. I. Title.

FINEGAN, Jack, 1908- 230
The three R's of Christianity. Richmond, John Knox Press [1964] 125 p. 20 cm. Bibliographical references included in "Notes" (p. [119]-125) [BT127.2.F5] 64-10078
1. Revelation. 2. Redemption. I. Title.

FISHER, George Park, 1827-1909. 226
The nature and method of revelation, by George Park Fisher... New York, C. Scribner's sons, 1890. xiii p., 1 l., 291 p. 19 cm. The first part of this volume is composed of articles published in the Century magazine, now "carefully revised and somewhat enlarged." cf. Introd. [BT127.F5] 39-32773
1. Revelation. 2. Bible, N.T. Gospels—Criticism, interpretation, etc. 3. Bible—Criticism, Interpretation, etc.—N.T. Gospels I. Title.

FRIES, Heinrich. 231'.74
Revelation. [New York] Herder and Herder [1969] 96 p. 22 cm. (Mysterium salutis) (Series: Feiner, Johannes. Mysterium salutis. English) Translation of Die Offenbarung, originally published in 1965 as p. [159]-234 of Die Grundlagen heilsgeschichtlicher Dogmatik, edited by H. U. von Balthasar. Bibliographical footnotes. [BT127.2.F73] 68-55085 3.95
1. Revelation. I. Series.

GOODWIN, Benjamin Thelston, 1873- 228
An interpretation of the symbols of the book of Revelation ... by B. T. Goodwin ... in collaboration with James Starbridge Wise ... Waco, Tex., The Gayle printing company [1923] 220 p. 21 cm. [BS2825.G5] 23-13306
I. Wise, James Starbridge, joint author. II. Title.

GOODWIN, Benjamin Thelston, 1873- 228
An interpretation of the symbols of the book of Revelation ... by B. T. Goodwin ... in collaboration with James Starbridge

Wise ... Waco, Tex., The Gayle printing company [1923] 220 p. 21 cm. [BS2825.G5] 23-13306
I. Wise, James Starbridge, joint author. II. Title.

GORDON, George Angier, 1853-1929. 231.
Revelation and the ideal, by George A. Gordon ... Boston and New York, Houghton Mifflin company, 1913. x p., 1 l., 427, [1] p. 20 cm. [BT127.G6] 13-21783
1. Revelation. 2. Idealism. I. Title.

GRATACAP, Louis Pope, 1851-1917. 220
The world's prayer (revelatio revelata) by L. P. Gratacap ... New York, T. Benton, 1915. 250 p. 23 cm. [BR125.G7195] 15-13176
1. Revelation. I. Title.

GREENE, Lemuel Austin, 1854- 236
Dawning of the great day of revelations, by L. A. Greene. Greenville, S.C., 1925. 7 p. l., 161 p. illus., plates. 19 cm. [BT885.G73] 25-3979
I. Title.

GREENE, Oliver B.
Revelation. Greenville, S.C., The Gospel Hour, Inc. [n.d.] 296 p. 67-39468
1. Revelation. I. Title.

GUTH, William Wesley, 1871- 231.
Revelation and its record, by William W. Guth ... Boston, Sherman, French & company, 1912. viii p., 2 l., 255 p. 20 cm. [BT127.G8] 12-16444 1.25
I. Title.

HANNA, Emmanuel Elkouri. 282.
The pearl of revelation; the real presence of Christ in the holy eucharist from the beginning of time, by Rev. Emmanuel Elkouri Hanna... New York, N. Y., The author, [c1929] xii, 228 p. front., ports. 19 1/2 cm. At head of title: A. M. D. G. [Full name: Emmanuel Joseph Elkouri Hanna] [BX2215.H3] 30-1516
I. Title.

HARDINGE, Leslie. 231'.74
Dove of gold, and other signposts of the spirit. Nashville, Southern Pub. Association [1972] 191 p. 21 cm. [BT127.2.H28] 72-80771
1. Revelation. I. Title.

HARRINGTON, Wilfrid J. 231'.74
Vatican II on revelation [by] Wilfrid Harrington and Liam Walsh. Dublin, Chicago, Scepter Books [1967] 191 p. 22 cm. "Constitutio dogmatica de divina revelatione," and its English translation: p. [156]-185. Bibliography: p. [186]-187. [BX830 1962.H36] 76-261381
1. Vatican Council. 2d, 1962-1965. Constitutio dogmatica de divina revelatione. 2. Bible—Study—Catholic Church. 3. Revelation. I. Walsh, Liam. II. Vatican Council. 2d, 1962-65. Constitutio dogmatica de divina revelatione. 1967. III. Vatican Council. 2d, 1962-65. Constitutio dogmatica de divina revelatione. English. 1967. IV. Title.

HARRISON, Joshua H. 231.74
The doctrine and function of revelation, and its relation to the doctrines of physical science. By Joshua H. Harrison ... Nashville, Tenn., Printed for the author. Publishing house of the M. E. church, South, J. D. Barbee, agent, 1889. 183 p. 20 cm. [BT127.H3] 40-23721
1. Revelation. 2. Religion and science—1860-1899. I. Title.

HART, Ray L. 218
Unfinished man and the imagination; toward an ontology and a rhetoric of revelation [by] Ray L. Hart. [New York] Herder and Herder [1968] 418 p. 22 cm. Includes bibliographical references. [BT127.2.H285] 68-8354
1. Revelation. 2. Imagination. I. Title.

HATT, Harold E. 231.74
Encountering truth; a new understanding of how revelation, as encounter, yields doctrine, by Harold E. Hatt. Nashville, Abingdon Press [1966] 208 p. 23 cm. Bibliographical footnotes. [BT127.2H3] 66-22917
1. Revelation. I. Title.

HAVNER, Vance, 1901- 922.673
"That I may know Him," a personal testimony. New York, F. H. Revell Co., [1948] 94 p. 20 cm. Full name: Vance Houston Havner. [BX6495.H288A3] 48-9365
I. Title.

HENRY, Carl Ferdinand Howard, 1913- ed. 220.1
Revelation and the Bible; contemporary evangelical thought [by] G. C. Berkouwer [and others] Grand Rapids, Baker Book House [1958] 413 p. 24 cm. ([Contemporary evangelical thought]) Includes bibliography. [BS413.H45] 58-59822
1. Bible—Addresses, essays, lectures. 2. Bible—Evidences, authority, etc. 3. Revelation. 4. Evangelicalism. I. Title.

HERSEY, Harry Greenlief, 1872- 230
The new revelation, by H. G. Hersey ... [Doverfoxcroft, Me.] c1929. 105 p. 23 cm. "The word of God spoken not in proverbs but in plain speech, fulfilling the promise of Jesus in the 16th chapter and 25th verse of St. John." [BR126.H44] ca 30
I. Title.

HOOD, Gwenyth. FIC
The coming of the demons / Gwenyth Hood. 1st ed. New York : Morrow, 1982. 288 p. ; 24 cm. [PS3558.O54C6] 813'.54 19 81-11263 ISBN 0-688-00794-5 : 10.95
I. Title.

HUGHES, Jasper Seaton, 1843-
The Revelation, by Jasper Seaton Hughes. [Holland? Mich.] The author [c1910] 4 p. l., 7-177 p. 20 cm. 11-10622
I. Title.

HYDE, Gordon M. 231'.74
God has spoken / by Gordon M. Hyde. Nashville, Tenn. : Southern Pub. Association, c1976. 94 p. ; 21 cm. Bibliography: p. 93-94. [BT127.2.H9] 75-40913 ISBN 0-8127-0109-7
1. Bible—Evidences, authority, etc. 2. Revelation. I. Title.

JONES, Charles Robert Stansfeld, 1886- 135.4
The anatomy of the body of God, being the supreme revelation of cosmic consciousness, explained and depicted in graphic form by Frater Achad, with designs showing the formation, multiplication, and projection of the Stone of the Wise by Will Ransom. New York, S. Weiser, 1969. xv, 111 p. illus. (part col.) 24 cm. Originally published in 1925. [BF1999.J55 1969] 79-16549 10.00
I. Title.

JONES, John (Archdeacon of Merioneth) 231.74
The moral tendency of divine revelation asserted and illustrated, in eight discourses preached before the University of Oxford in the year mdcccxxi, at the lecture founded by the late Rev. John Bampton ... By the Rev. John Jones ... Oxford, The University press for the author; [etc., etc.] 1821. xv, 431 p. 22 cm. Binder's title: Bampton lectures. 1821. [BR45.B3 1821] 230.082 38-16170
1. Revelation. 2. Christian ethics—Anglican authors. I. Title.

JONES, Rufus Matthew, 1863- 226
The eternal gospel, by Rufus M. Jones ... New York, The Macmillan company, 1938. vi p., 2 l., 235 p. 21 cm. (Great issues of life series) "First printing." [BT127.J65] 38-7152
1. Revelation. 2. Mysticism. I. Title.

KEAN, Charles Duell, 1910- 231.74
God's Word to His people. Philadelphia, Westminster Press [1956] 187p. 21cm. [BT127.K4] 56-8421
1. Revelation. 2. Bible—Influence. 3. Jews—Election, Doctrine of. I. Title.

LATOURELLE, Rene, 1918- 232
Christ and the church; signs of salvation. Translated by Sr. Dominic Parker. Staten Island, N.Y., Alba House [1972] viii, 324 p. 22 cm. Translation of Le Christ et l'eglise, signes du salut. Includes bibliographical references. [BT202.L3713] 73-39673 ISBN 0-8189-0241-8 9.50
1. Jesus Christ—Person and offices. 2. Vatican Council. 2d, 1962-1965. 3. Revelation. 4. Church. I. Title.

LEWIS, Edwin, 1881- 231.73
A philosophy of the Christian revelation, by Edwin Lewis... New York, London, Harper & brothers [c1940] xii, 346 p. 22 1/2 cm. "First edition." "Notes and references": p. [307]-342. [BT127.L4] 40-34100
1. Revelation. 2. Christianity—Philosophy. I. Title.

LILLEY, Alfred Leslie, 1860- 231.74
Religion and revelation; a study of some moments in the effort of Christian theology to define their relations, being the Paddock lectures for 1931, by A. L. Lilley ... London, Society for promoting Christian knowledge; New York. The Macmillan company [1932] xiv, 146 p. 19 cm. "First published 1932." [BT127.L5] 34-2529
1. Revelation. 2. Religion—Philosophy. I. Title.

MCKAY, Lucinda E., 1840- 220
A few thoughts on Revelation; a few thoughts on some of the Old Testament types. A brief history of the people of God under the gospel dispensation and the second coming of Christ. By Lucinda E. McKay. 2d ed. Cincinnati, Printed for the author by the Abingdon press [c1919] 304 p. front. (port.) 22 1/2 cm. [BR125.M32 1919] 20-14834
I. Title.

MCKAY, Lucinda E., 1840-
A few thoughts on Revelation; a few thoughts on some of the Old Testament types. A brief history of the people of God under the gospel dispensation and the second coming of Christ. By Lucinda E. McKay. Cincinnati, Printed for the author by Jennings and Graham [c1913] 286 p. front. (port.) 22 cm. 13-25471
I. Title.

MACKENSEN, Herman, 1869- 231.
Revelation in the light of history and experience; an effort to think straight, by Herman Mackensen, with an introduction by Professor Henry Offermann... Boston, Mass., The Stratford company, 1926. 7 p. l., 3-208 p. 19 cm. [BT127.M3] 26-8566
1. Revelation. I. Title.

MARQUAM, Philip A. 236.
The Saviour's Bible. A divine revelation. By Philip A. Marquam. Marquam, Or., 1899. 126 p. 21 cm. [BR126.M37] 99-3598
I. Title.

*MARTIN, Oliver S. 228.06
A study in the Revelation. New York, Exposition [c.1964] 209p. 22cm. (EP 42101) 4.00
I. Title.

MONSMA, Peter Halman, 1902- 922.4494
Karl Barth's idea of revelation, by Peter Halman Monsma ... Somerville, N. J., Somerset press, inc., 1937. 5 p. l., [3]-218 p., 1 l. 24 cm. Vita. Issued also as thesis (PH. D.) Columbia university. Bibliography: p. 213-218. [BX4827.B3M6 1937 a] 38-5236
1. Barth, Karl, 1886- 2. Revelation. 3. Dialectical theology. I. Title.

MORAN, Gabriel. 231'.74
The present revelation; the search for religious foundations. [1st ed.] New York Herder and Herder [1972] 318 p. 22 cm. [BT127.2.M597] 72-2307 ISBN 0-07-073787-8 8.95
1. Revelation. 2. Experience (Religion) I. Title.

MORAN, Gabriel. 231.74
Theology of revelation. [New York] Herder and Herder [1966] 223 p. 22 cm. (Studies in religious education) Bibliography: p. 189-201. [BT127.2.M6] 66-16578
1. Revelation. I. Title.

MORRIS, Leon, 1914- 231'.74
I believe in revelation / by Leon Morris. (1st American ed.) Grand Rapids, Mich. : Eerdmans, 1976. 159 p. ; 21 cm. (I believe) Includes bibliographical references. [BT127.2.M64 1976] 75-45349 ISBN 0-8028-1637-1 pbk. : 2.95
1. Revelation. I. Title.

NEWBERRY, Frederick B.
The voice of Christianity; or, The theocratic philosophy of revelation ... By Frederick B. Newberry ... Hannibal, Mo., Standard printing co., 1897. 226, [2] p. 18 1/2 cm. 3-4210
I. Title.

NIEBUHR, Helmut Richard 231.74
The meaning of revelation. New York, Macmillan 1960[c.1941] 196p. (Macmillan paperbacks, 27) 'Contains, with some additions and revisions, the Nathanael W. Taylor lectures given at the Divinity School of Yale University in April, 1940.'—Pref. 1.25 pap.,
1. Revelation. I. Title.

NIEBUHR, Helmut Richard, 1894-
The meaning of revelation. New York, Macmillan, 1962 [c1941] xi, 196 p. 21 cm. (Macmillan paperback, 27) "Macmillan paperback edition, 1960." 67-37011
1. Revelation. I. Title.

NIEBUHR, Helmut Richard, 1894- 261.74
The meaning of revelation, by H. Richard Niebuhr ... New York, The Macmillan company, 1941. x p., 2 l., 196 p. 20 cm. "First printing." "Contains, with some additions and revisions, the Nathanael W. Taylor lectures given at the Divinity school of Yale university in April, 1940."--Pref. [BT127.N5 1941] 41-5080
1. Revelation. I. Title.

O'COLLINS, Gerald. 231'.74
Theology and revelation. Notre Dame, Ind., Fides Publishers [1968] 96 p. 18 cm. (Theology today, no. 2) Bibliography: p. 95-96. [BT127.2.O3] 79-358 0.95
1. Revelation. I. Title.

OLSSEN, William Whittingham, 1827-1917. 231.74
Revelation, universal and special, by the Rev. William W. Olssen ... New York, T. Whittaker, 1885. 259 p. 20 cm. [BT127.O5] 40-23722
1. Revelation. I. Title.

ORR, James, 1844-1913. 231'.74
Revelation and inspiration. Grand Rapids, Baker Book House [1969] xii, 224 p. 20 cm. (Twin brooks series) Reprint of the 1910 ed. Bibliography: p. 219. [BT127.O7 1969] 74-100535 2.95
1. Revelation. 2. Inspiration. I. Title.

PACKER, James Innell. 220.1'3
God has spoken / J. I. Packer. Downers Grove, Ill. : InterVarsity Press, c1979. 156 p. ; 21 cm. Bibliography: p. 154-156. [BT127.2.P3] 19 80-7789 ISBN 0-87784-656-1 (pbk.) : 3.95
1. Bible.—Evidences, authority, etc. 2. Revelation. I. Title.

PETTINGILL, William Leroy, 1866- 228
Simple studies in the Revelation, by William L. Pettingill. 4th ed. 17th thousand. Harrisburg, Pa., F. Kelker, 1916. 132 p. 17 cm. [BS2825.P4 1916] 18-17193
I. Title.

PINK, Arthur Walkington, 1886-1952. 231'.74
The doctrine of revelation / A. W. Pink. Grand Rapids, Mich. : Baker Book House, c1975. 259 p. ; 23 cm. [BT127.2.P56 1975] 74-15575 ISBN 0-8010-6964-5 : 6.95
1. Revelation. I. Title.

PINK, Arthur Walkington, 1886-1952. 231'.74
The doctrine of revelation / A.W. Pink. Grand Rapids, Mich. : Baker Book House, 1977,c1975. 267p. ; 22 cm. Includes indexes. [BT127.2P56 1975] ISBN 0-8010-7024-4 pbk. : 3 .95
1. Revelation. I. Title.
L.C. card no. for hardcover ed.: 74-15575.

PITTS, F. E. 224.
A defence of Armageddon, or Our great country foretold in the Holy Scriptures. In two discourses. Delivered in the Capitol of the United States, at the request of several members of Congress, on the anniversary of Washington's birthday, 1857. By F. E. Pitts ... Baltimore, J. W. Bull, 1859. viii, [9]-116 p. 19 cm. First edition, 1857. [BS649.U6P6 1859] 15-22797
I. Title.

RAHNER, Karl, 1904- 231.74
Revelation and tradition [by] Karl Rahner [and] Joseph Ratzinger. [Translated by W. J. O'Hara. New York] Herder and Herder [1966] 78 p. 21 cm. (Quaestiones disputatae, 17) Bibliographical references included in "Notes" (p. 69-78) [BT127.2.R2813 1966a] 66-18747
1. Revelation. 2. Tradition (Theology) I. Ratzinger, Joseph. II. Title.

RAMM, Bernard, 1916- 231.74
Special revelation and the word of God. Grand Rapids, Eerdmans [1961] 220 p. 22 cm. Includes bibliography. [BT127.2.R3] 61-10854
1. Revelation. I. Title.

REVELATION and the life to come, ed., with an introduction, in two parts by the author of "The way: the nature and means of revelation." New York and London, G. P. Putnam's sons, 1916. v, 216 p. 18 1/2 cm. $1.00. "The writings in part III ... were printed for private distribution in 1894, under title 'The kingdom of heaven'"--Pref. 16-13650
I. The way: the nature and means of revelation, Author of.

RIFFEL, Herman H. 231'.74
Voice of God / Herman H. Riffel. Wheaton, Ill. : Tyndale House Publishers, 1978. 165 p. ; 21 cm. Includes bibliographical references and index. [BT127.2.R53] 78-55979 ISBN 0-8423-7803-0 : 3.95
1. Bible—Inspiration. 2. Revelation. 3. Word of God (Theology) 4. Dreams. 5. Visions. 6. Private revelations. I. Title.

ROBINSON, Lemuel King, 1855-
Beasts and sevens of Revelations, by L. K. Robinson ... [La Grande, Or., La Grande evening observer] c1917. 1 p. l., 118 p. 21 cm. $1.00 17-13267
I. Title.

SCHILLEBEECKX, Edward Cornelius Florentinius Alfons, 1914- 231'.74
Revelation and theology, by E. Schillebeeckx. Translated by N. D. Smith. New York, Sheed and Ward [1967- v. 22 cm. (His Theological soundings) "Originally published as parts 1 and 2 of Openbaring en Theologie ... 1964. This translation is based on the second revised edition of 1966." Bibliographical footnotes. [BT127.2.S3313] 67-21907
1. Revelation. 2. Theology, Doctrinal. I. Title.

SCHILLEBEECKX, Edward Cornelius Florentius Alfons, 1914- 231.74
Revelation and theology, by E. Schillebeeckx. Tr. by N. D. Smith. New York, Sheed [1968- v. 22cm. (Theological soundings) Orig. pub. as parts 1 & 2 of Openbaringen Theologie . . . 1964. This tr. is based on the second rev. ed. of 1966. Bibl. [BT127.2.S3313] 67-21907 4.95
1. Revelation. 2. Theology, Doctrinal. I. Title.

SCHILLEBEEKX, Edward Cornelius Florentinius Alfons, 1914- 231'.74
Revelation and theology, by E. Schillebeeckx. Translated by N. D. Smith. New York, Sheed and Ward [1967- "Originally published as parts 1 and 2 of Openbaring en Theologie ... 1964. This translation is based on the second revised edition of 1966." Bibliographical footnotes. [BT127.2.S3313] 67-21907
1. Revelation. 2. Theology, Doctrinal. I. Title.

SCHUTZ, Roger. 231'.74
Revelation, a Protestant view; the Dogmatic Constitution on divine revelation, a commentary, by Roger Schutz and Max Thurian. Pref. by Henri de Lubac. Westminster, Md., Newman Press [1968] v, 104 p. 21 cm. "The dogmatic constitution on divine revelation": p. [81]-102. Bibliography: p. 103-104. [BX830 1962.A45C774] 68-21453
1. Vatican Council, 2d. 1962-1965. Constitutio dogmatica de divina revelatione. 2. Revelation. I. Thurian, Max, joint author. II. Vatican Council, 2d, 1962-1965. Constitutio dogmatica de divina revelatione. English. 1968. III. Title.

SCOTT, Ernest Findlay, 1868- 231.74
The New Testament idea of revelation, by Ernest Findlay Scott ... New York London, C. Scribner's sons, 1935. vi p., 2 l., 255 p. 19 cm. [BT127.S3] 35-4712
1. Revelation. 2. Bible. N. T.—Theology. 3. Bible—Theology—N. T. I. Title.

*SHERMAN, Alva W. 228.07
The analysis of revelation. New York, Vantage [c.1964] 211p. 21cm. 4.50
I. Title.

SIBLEY, Julian Scales 232
The climax of revelation, by Julian Scales Sibley... New York, Chicago, [etc.] Fleming H. Revell company [c1932] 175 p. 19 1/2 cm. [BT201.S47] 32-4094
1. Jesus Christ. 2. Revelation. I. Title.

SODERBLOM, Nathan, Abp., 1866-1931. 231.74
The nature of revelation. Edited and with an introd. by Edgar M. Carlson. Translated by Frederic E. Pamp. Philadelphia, Fortress Press [1966] vii, 163 p. 21 cm. (Seminar editions) Translation of Uppenbarelsereligion. Bibliographical footnotes. [BT127.S6 1966] 66-23224
1. Revelation. 2. Religion—Philosophy. I. Title.

SODERBLOM, Nathan, abp., 1866-1931. 231
The nature of revelation, by Nathan Soderblom; authorized translation from the second edition of 1930 by Frederic E. Pamp; with an introduction by Edward, Caldwell Moore ... New York, Oxford university press, 1933. xiv p., 2 l., 205 p. 20 cm. [Full name: Lars Olof Jonathan Soderblom] [BT127.S6] 34-485
1. Revelation. 2. Religion—Philosophy. I. Pamp, Frederic Ernest, tr. II. Title. III. Title: Translation of Uppenbarelsereligion.

STEIGER, Brad. 291.4'2
Revelation : the divine fire / Brad Steiger. New York : Berkley Publishing Corporation, 1981, c1973. 291 p. ; 18 cm. Includes bibliographical references and index. [BL53.S675 1973] ISBN 0-425-04615-X pbk. : 2.50
1. Revelation. 2. Religion, Psychology. I. Title.
L.C. card no. for 1973 Prentice-Hall edition: 72-10243

STEIGER, Brad. 291.4'2
Revelation: the divine fire. Englewood Cliffs, N.J., Prentice-Hall [1973] 316 p. 24 cm. Bibliography: p. 311-312. [BL53.S675 1973] 72-10243 ISBN 0-13-779322-7 7.95
1. Revelation. 2. Religion, Psychology. I. Title.

STOKES, Mack B 231.74
The epic of revelation; an essay in Biblical theology. [1st ed.] New York, McGraw-Hill [1961] 240 p. 22 cm. Includes bibliography. [BT127.2.S8] 61-11655
1. Revelation. I. Title.

SWEENEY, Joseph W
Those distant years; or, Revelation in stories. More than sixty episodes from the Old Testament text, told in readable prose. With foreword by His Excellency, The Most Rev. Thomas E. Molloy. [New York, Press of Loughlin Bros., c1956] 197 p. 21 cm.
I. Title.

TENNEY, Merrill Chapin, 1904- 220.1
The Bible; the living word of revelation, edited by Merrill C. Tenney. With essays by John H. Gerstner [and others] Grand Rapids, Zondervan Pub. House [1968] 228 p. ports. 23 cm. (An Evangelical Theological Society publication. Monograph no. 6) Includes bibliographical references. [BS480.T4] 69-11632 5.95
1. Bible—Evidences, authority, etc. 2. Revelation. I. Gerstner, John H. II. Title. III. Series: Evangelical Theological Society. Monograph no. 6

THORNTON, Lionel Spencer, 1884-
The form of the servant. Westminster [London] Dacre Press [1950-1956] 3 v. 23 cm. Contents.Revelation and the modern world.--The dominion of Christ.--Christ and the church. Bibliographical footnotes.
1. Revelation. 2. Bible—Theology. I. Title.

THOSE distant years;
or, Revelation in stories. More than sixty episodes from the Old Testament text, told in readable prose. With foreword by His Excellency, The Most Rev. Thomas E. Molloy. [New York, Press of Loughlin Bros., c1956] 197p. 21cm.
I. Sweeney, Joseph W

TILLEY, Charles J 231.74
Religion with revelation. Boston, Christopher Pub. House, [1963] 323 p. 21 cm. Includes bibliography. [BT127.2.T5] 63-13311
1. Revelation. I. Title.

TORRANCE, Thomas Forsyth, 1913- 231.7'4
Reality and evangelical theology / by T.F. Torrance. 1st ed. Philadelphia : Westminister Press, c1982. 174 p. ; 21 cm. (The 1981 Payton lectures) Includes bibliographical references and indexes. [BT127.2.T67 1982] 19 81-19811 ISBN 0-664-24401-7 pbk. : 8.95
1. Revelation. 2. Religion and science—1946- 3. Truth (Christian theology) I. Title.

THE triumph of the crucified;
a survey of historical revelation in the New Testament... Translated by G. H. Lang, with a foreword by A. Rendle Short... Grand Rapids, Michigan, Wm. B. Eerdmans Publishing Company, 1957. 207p. 23cm.
I. Sauer, Erich. II. Title: Translated from the German Der Triumph des Gelreuzigten.

UNOPULOS, James J., 1919- 230'.93'
Reasoning, fevelation, and you! 'Project Temple' principles of sMormons and Mormonism--Doctrinal and controversial works. [Bx8635.2.U5] 67-21352
I. Title.

UNOPULOS, James J., 1919- 230'.93'3
Reasoning, revelation, and you- Project Temple principles of [BX8635.2.U5] 67-21352
I. Title.

VATICAN Council. 2d,1962-1965. 231.74
De divina revelatione: the dogmatic Constitution on divine revelation of Vatican Council II, Promulgated by Pope Paul VI, November 18, 1965. Commentary and translation by GeorgeH. Tavard. [Study-club ed.] Glen Rock, N.J., Paulist Press, 1966. 94 p. 19 cm. (Vatican II documents) Bibliography: p. 93-94. [BX830 1962.A45C33] 66-19148
1. Revelation. 2. Bible — Study — Catholic Church. I. Tavard, Georges Henri, 1922- II. Title.

WALKER, Thomas Hamilton B., 1873-
Revelation, trial and exile of John in epics... by Thos. H. B. Walker.... Gainesville, Fla. [Pepper pub. & ptg. co., 1912- v. illus. port. 17 1/2 cm. 12-17525
I. Title.

WEIR, John Ferguson, 1841-1926. 231.74
The way: the nature and means of revelation, by John F. Weir ... Boston and New York, Houghton, Mifflin and company, 1889. xvi, 430 p. 20 cm. [BT127.W4] 40-24459
1. Revelation. I. Title.

WOODMAN, J. M. 215
God in nature and revelation. By Rev. J. M. Woodman ... New York, S[an] F[rancisco, etc.] J. G. Hodge & co., 1875. xi, [1], [13]-542, [1] p. front., plates. 22 1/2 cm. [BS651.W73] 39-424
1. Revelation. 2. Natural theology. 3. Bible and science. 4. Religion and science—1860-1899. I. Title.

WOODMAN, J. M. 215
God in nature and revelation. By Rev. J. M. Woodman ... New York, S[an] F[rancisco, etc.] J. G. Hodge & co., 1875. xi, [1], 10, [13]-624 p. front., plates. 22 cm. [With his The Neptunian, or water theory of creation. San Francisco, 1888] "The song of cosmology: or, The voice of god in the science of nature. Completed by eighty thousand years in star-dates of human history. By Rev. J. M. Woodman" (with special t.-p.): p. [545]-624. Publisher's lettering: God in nature and revelation: or, The grand march of time complete ... vol. I-IV [i.e. III?] [BS651.W75 1888a] 39-410
1. Revelation. 2. Natural theology. 3. Bible and science. 4. Religion and science—1860-1899. 5. Cosmology—Curiosa and miscellany. I. Title. II. Title: The song of cosmology.

Revelation—Addresses, essays, lectures.

COLES, George, '1792-1858. 231
The antidote, or Revelation defended, and infidelity repulsed; in a course of lectures, by George Coles ... Hartford, Printed by P. Canfield, 1836. 365 p. 22 cm. [BT1101.C65] 26-22112
I. Title. II. Title: Revelation defended, and infidelity repulsed.

NORMAN, Ruth, 1900- 133.9'1
Bridge to Heaven; revelations of Ruth Norman. [Glendale, Calif., Unarius, 1969] 506 p. ports. 23 cm. [BF1999.N67] 76-10224
I. Title.

O'COLLINS, Gerald. 231'.74
Foundations of theology. Chicago, Loyola University Press [1971] x, 211 p. 23 cm. Includes bibliographical references. [BT127.2.O28] 70-153756 ISBN 0-8294-0201-2
1. Revelation—Addresses, essays, lectures. 2. Theology—Addresses, essays, lectures. I. Title.

REVELATION and experience 231'.8
/ edited by Edward Schillebeeckx and Bas van Iersel. New York : Seabury Press, 1979. ix, 132 p. ; 23 cm. (Concilium : religion in the seventies ; 113) "A Crossroad book." Includes bibliographical references. [BT127.2.R45] 78-66133 ISBN 0-8164-2609-0 pbk. : 4.95
1. Revelation—Addresses, essays, lectures. 2. Experience (Religion)—Addresses, essays, lectures. I. Schillebeeckx, Edward Cornelius Florentius Alfons, 1914- II. Iersel, Bastiaan Martinus Franciscus van. III. Series: Concilium (New York) ; 113.

SIMPSON, William John Sparrow, 1859- 283.
The revelation of God, and other sermons, by W. J. Sparrow Simpson, D.D. London, Society for promoting Christian knowledge; New York and Toronto, The Macmillan company, 1925. v, 120 p., 1 l. 19 cm. [BX5133.S54R4] 25-15260
I. Title.

Revelation Bible-Study-Catholic Church.

VATICAN Council, 2d, 1962-1965 231.74
De divina releatione the dogmatic constitution on divine revelation of Vatican II, promulgated by Pope Paul VI, November 18, 1965 Glen Rock, N.J. Paulist [c.]1966 94 p. 19 cm (Vatican ii docs.) Commentary and tr. by George H. Tavard [study club. ed.] bibl. [bx8301962.a45c33] 6619148 pap .75
1. Revelation Bible-Study-Catholic Church. I. Title.

Revelation—Biblical teaching.

BIBLE. N. T. Revelation. English. 1914.
The Revelation, a students' handbook, by Iva Durham Vennard ... Chicago, Ill., Chicago evangelistic institute press [c1914] 112 p. 16 x 23 cm. "Part of pages blank for "Notes." 15-1804 1.00
I. Vennard, Iva May (Durham) Mrs. 1871- II. Title.

ROOSEN, P A 231.74
The Bible on revelation, by P. A. Roosen. Translated by F. Vander Heijden. De Pere, Wis., St. Norbert Abbey Press, 1966. 139 p. 17 cm. Translation of De Bijbel over openbaring en overlevering. Bibliography: p. [138]-139. [BT126.R613] 66-22822
1. Revelation — Biblical teaching. I. Title.

SALGUERO, Jose. 231'.74
Biblical revelation : the history of salvation / by J. Salguero ; translated by Judith Suprys. Arlington, Va. : Christian Culture Press, 1976. vii, 202 p. ; 22 cm.

Translation of La rivelazione biblica. Includes bibliographical references and index. [BS646.S2313] 76-100100 8.95
1. Revelation—Biblical teaching. 2. Revelation—History of doctrines. I. Title.

THOMSON, James G. S. S. 221
The Old Testament view of revelation. Grand Rapids, Mich., Eerdmans [c.1960] 107p. Bibl. 60-10095 2.50
1. Revelation—Biblical teaching. 2. Bible. O. T.—Theology. I. Title.

Revelation—Biblical teaching—Addresses, essays, lectures.

CASE, Shirley Jackson, 1872- 228
The Revelation of John; a historical interpretation, by Shirley Jackson Case ... Chicago, Ill., The University of Chicago press [c1919] xii, 419 p. 20 cm. [BS2825.C35] 19-17329
I. Title.

CUSTANCE, Arthur C. 230 s
Hidden things of God's revelation / Arthur C. Custance. Grand Rapids : Zondervan Pub. House, c1977. p. cm. (His The doorway papers ; v. 7) Bibliography: p. [BS543.A1C87 vol. 7] [BS540] 231'.74 77-22036 ISBN 0-310-23020-9 : 8.95
1. Bible—Criticism, interpretation, etc.—Addresses, essays, lectures. 2. Revelation—Biblical teaching—Addresses, essays, lectures. I. Title.

FARNSWORTH, Edward Clarence. 228
The Revelation of John, explained by Edward Clarence Farnsworth. Portland, Smith & Sale, printers, 1919. xii, 189, [1] p. 20 cm. [BS2825.F3] 19-9458
I. Title.

WHITING, Charles C. 228
The Revelation of John; an interpretation of the book with an introduction and a translation by Charles C. Whiting... Boston, The Gorham press, 1918. 259 p. 19 1/2 cm. $1.50 [BS2825.W4] 18-17617
I. Title.

Revelation—Collections.

BUNGER, Fred S. 231'.74
A new light shines out of present darkness, by Fred S. Bunger and Hans N. von Koerber. Philadelphia, Dorrance [1971] xii, 337 p. 22 cm. [BX9998.B85] 77-132428 ISBN 0-8059-1501-X 6.95
1. Revelation—Collections. I. Koerber, Hans Nordewin von, joint author. II. Title.

HAYWOOD, Garfield Thomas. 236.
Before the foundation of the world; a revelation of the ages ... copyrighted by G. T. Haywood. [Indianapolis] 1923. 2 p. l. 76 p. fold. col. front., illus. 19 cm. "Enlarged and revised edition of the little booklet formerly called A revelation of the ages'." [BR126.H35] ca 24
I. Title.

Revelation—Commentaries.

BARKER, C L
The Revelation; analyzed and made plain. New York, Carlton Press [1964] 179 p. 68-81495
1. Revelation—Commentaries. I. Title.

BRIGGS, Henry Clay, 1872- 228
Revelation symbolism [by] Rev. Henry C. Briggs ... Brooklyn, N.Y., The author [c1923] 1 p. l., iii p., 1 l., 104 p. 18 1/2 cm. [BS2825.B67] 23-10803
I. Title.

[BURR, William Henry] 1819-
Revelations of Antichrist, concerning Christ and Christianity ... Boston, J. P. Mendum; New York, D. M. Bennett, 1879. xiv, 432 p. 21 cm. Published anonymously. 3-25913
I. Title.

CHALMERS, Thomas, 1780-1847. 215
A series of discourses on the Christian revelation, viewed in connection with the modern astronomy. By Thomas Chalmers ... New York, American tract society [185-?] 263 p. 20 cm. [BL253.C5 1850] 18-15955
I. Title.

EMERSON, Laura B. Payne. Mrs. 215
Revelation vs. evolution; or, God's kingdom on earth, by Laura Payne Emerson ... Encanto, San Diego, Calif., c1925. 53 p. front. (port.) 19 1/2 cm. [BL263.E5] 25-18796
I. Title.

GAEBELEIN, Arno Clemens, 1861-1945. 228.07
The Revelation; an analysis and exposition of the last book of the Bible. New York, Loizeaux Bros. [1961] 225 p. 21 cm. Bible. N.T. Revelation -- Prophecies. [BS2825.G3 1961] 61-17225
I. Title.

MYLAND, David Wesley.
The Revelation of Jesus Christ; a comprehensive harmonic outline and perspective view of the book, by Rev. D. Wesley Myland. Chicago, Ill., The Evangel publishing house, 1911. xiv, 15-255 p. illus. (map) 20 cm. 11-29052
I. Title.

WHITE, Sam Jordan. 228
Revelation made easy, by Sam Jordan White. [Detroit, Northwestern printing co.] c1924. 74 p. 23 cm. [BS2825.W38] 24-7610
I. Title.

Revelation—History of doctrines.

DULLES, Avery Robert, 1918- 231'.74
Revelation theology; a history [by] Avery Dulles. [New York] Herder and Herder [1969] 192 p. 22 cm. Bibliography: p. 183-187. [BT126.5.D84] 70-81381 5.95
1. Revelation—History of doctrines. 2. Theology, Catholic—History. I. Title.

FAIRWEATHER, Alan M. 231'.74
The word as truth : a critical examination of the Christian doctrine of revelation in the writings of Thomas Aquinas and Karl Barth / by A. M. Fairweather. Westport, Conn. : Greenwood Press, 1979. xvi, 147 p. ; 24 cm. Reprint of the 1944 ed. published by Lutterworth Press, London, which was issued as v. 18 of the Lutterworth library. Includes bibliographical references. [BT127.F3 1979] 78-26040 ISBN 0-313-20808-5 lib. bdg. : 15.00
1. Thomas Aquinas, Saint, 1225?-1274—Theology. 2. Barth, Karl, 1886-1968. 3. Revelation—History of doctrines. I. Title.

LATOURELLE, Rene. 231.74
Theology of revelation, including a commentary on the constitution "Dei verbum" of Vatican II. Staten Island, N.Y ., Alba House [1966] 508 p. 24 cm. Bibliography: p. [491]-508. [BT126.5.L313] 65-15734
1. Revelation — History of doctrines. 2. Vatican Council. 2d, 1962-1965. Constitutio de divina revelatione. I. Title.

MCDONALD, Hugh Dermot. 231.74
Ideas of revelation; an historical study, A. D. 1700 to A. D. 1860. London, Macmillan; New York, St. Martin's Press, 1959. 300p. 23cm. [BT126.5.M3] 59-2449
1. Revelation —History of doctrines. I. Title.

MCDONALD, Hugh Dermot 231.74
Theories of revelation; an historical study, 1860-1960. London, G. Allen & Unwin [dist. New York, Humanities, c.]1963. 384p. 22cm. A continuation of the author's Ideas of revelation, 1700-1860. Bibl. 63-4467 7.50
1. Revelation—History of doctrines. I. Title.

PANNENBERG, Wolfhart, 1928- 231'.74
Revelation as history. Edited by Wolfhart Pannenberg, in association with Rolf Rendtorff, Trutz Rendtorff, & Ulrich Wilkens. Translated from the German by David Granskou. New York, Macmillan [1968] x, 181 p. 22 cm. Translation of Offenbarung als Geschichte. Bibliographical footnotes. [BT126.5.P313 1968] 67-20185
1. Revelation—History of doctrines. I. Rendtorff, Rolf, 1925- II. Rendtorff, Trutz. III. Wilkens, Ulrich. IV. Title.

PERSSON, Per Erik, 1923- 230.20924
Sacra doctrina; reason and revelation in Aquinas. Translated by Ross Mackenzie. Philadelphia, Fortress Press [1970] xii, 317 p. 23 cm. Bibliography: p. 299-312. [BT126.5.P47 1970] 69-12992 9.75
1. Thomas Aquinas, Saint, 1225?-1274—Theology. 2. Revelation—History of doctrines. 3. Reason. I. Title.

SALM, Celestine Luke.
The problem of positive theology. Washington, Catholic University of America Press, 1955. 73p. 24cm. (Catholic University of America. Studies in sacred theology, 2d ser., no. 88) Abstract of thesis-Catholic University of America. Bibliography: p. 71-73. Bibliographical footnotes. A 59
1. Revelation—History of doctrines. I. Title. II. Title: Positive theology. III. Series: Catholic University of America. School of Sacred Theology. Studies in sacred theology, 2d ser., no.88

WALLACE, Ronald S 230.42
Calvin's doctrine of the Word and sacrament. Grand Rapids, W. B. Eerdmans Pub. Co., 1957. xii, 253 p. 23 cm. Bibliographical footnotes. [BX9418.W314] 57-14162
1. Calvin, Jean, 1509-1564 — Theology. 2. Revelation — History of doctrines. 3. Sacraments — History of doctrines. I. Title.

Revelation—History of doctrines—20th century.

POTTER, Frederic James 232
Revelation of Jesus and his teachings; as revealed in the Scriptures. New York, Vantage [c.1961] 64p. 2.00 bds.,
I. Title.

SICA, Joseph F. 231.7'4
God so loved the world / Joseph F. Sica. Washington, D.C. : University Press of America, c1981. p. cm. Includes index. [BT127.2.S53] 19 81-40441 ISBN 0-8191-1677-7 : 16.50 ISBN 0-8191-1678-5 (pbk.) : 7.50
1. Rahner, Karl, 1904- 2. Niebuhr, Helmut Richard, 1894-1962. 3. Revelation—History of doctrines—20th century. I. Title.

Revelation (Mohammedanism)

ARBERRY, Arthur John, 1905- 297.2
Revelation and reason in Islam. London, Allen & Unwin [dist. Mytic, Conn., Verry, 1964] 122p. 19cm. (Forwood lects., 1956) A57 3.00 bds.,
1. Revelation (Mohammedanism) I. Title. II. Series.

REVELATION and reason in Islam. London. Allen & Unwin; New York, Macmillan [1957] 122p. 19cm. (Forwood lectures. 1956) Includes bibliographical references.
1. Revelation (Mohammedanism) I. Arberry, Arthus John, 1905- II. Series.

Revelation (Mormonism)

HARMER, Lewis J 289.3
Revelation. Salt Lake City, Bookcraft [1957] 297p. 24cm. [BX8643.R4H3] 58-15187
1. Revelation (Mormonism) I. Title.

Revelation (Mormonism)—Controversial literature.

MCELVEEN, Floyd. 230'.9'3
The Mormon revelations of convenience / Floyd McElveen. Minneapolis : Bethany Fellowship, c1978. 108 p. ; 18 cm. Bibliography: p. 107-108. [BX8643.R4M32] 78-72945 ISBN 0-87123-385-1 pbk. : 1.75
1. Church of Jesus Christ of Latter-day Saints—Doctrinal and controversial works. 2. Revelation (Mormonism)—Controversial literature. I. Title.

Revelation—Study and teaching.

KRATZER, Glenn Andrews, 1869-
Revelation interpreted, by Rev. G. A. Kratzer ... 1st ed. Chicago, Ill., The Central Christian science institute, c1915. 4 p. l., 396 p. fold. tables. 21 cm. Blank pages interspersed for "Notes by the reader." 15-15029 3.00
I. Title.

MORAN, Gabriel 231.74
Catechesis of revelation. [New York] Herder & Herder [1966] 174p. 22cm. (Studies in relig. educ.) Bibl. [BT127.2.M59] 66-22607 4.50
1. Revelation—Study and teaching. I. Title.

WILLIAMS, Henry Clay, 1871-
The Revelation of Jesus Christ, a study of Apocalypse, by H. C. Williams... Cincinnati, The Standard publishing company [c1917] 370 p. 20 cm. $1.50. 17-12375
I. Title.

Revelation Title.

HATT, Harold E 231.74
Ecountering truth; a new understanding of how revelation, as encounter, yields doctrine by Harold E. Hatt. Nashville, Abingdon [1966] 208 p. 23 cm [bt127.2h3] 66-22197 4.50
1. 1. Revelation Title I. Title.

Revenge in literature.

MROZ, Mary Bonaventure, Sister, 1906- 822.3'3
Divine vengeance; a study in the philosophical backgrounds of the revenge motif as it appears in Shakespeare's chronicle history plays. New York, Haskell House Publishers, 1971. x, 168 p. 22 cm. Thesis—Catholic University of America. Reprint of the 1941 ed. Bibliography: p. 142-158. [PR2982.M7 1971] 77-120130 ISBN 0-8383-1091-5
1. Shakespeare, William, 1564-1616—Histories. 2. Revenge in literature. I. Title.

Revere, Paul, 1702-1754.

DOUGLAS, Donald. 284.573
The Huguenot; the story of the Huguenot emigrations, particularly to New England, in which is included the early life of Apollos Rivoire, the father of Paul Revere. With an introd. by C. C. Little. [1st ed.] New York, Dutton, 1954. 384 p. 22 cm. Includes bibliography. [BX9459.R4D6] 54-5035
1. Revere, Paul, 1702-1754. 2. Huguenots. I. Title.

Review of hints on evangelical preaching.

WEBSTER, Noah, 1758-1843. 230
The peculiar doctrines of the gospel explained and defended. In a letter from Noah Webster, esq., to a friend in Boston. 3d ed. Portland: Published and sold by A. Lyman & co. Insurance-buildings, Exchange-street, J. M'Kown, printer. -- 1811. 50 p. 15 cm. A discussion of "Review of hints on evangelical preaching." cf. p. [3] [BT80.R42W4 1811] 40-36595
1. Review of hints on evangelical preaching. 2. Evangelicalism. I. Title.

Revivals.

ALLEN, Stanton P. 1849-1901. 922.773
A summer revival and what brought it about, by Stanton P. Allen... New York, Hunt & Eaton; Cincinnati, Cranston & Curts [1894]. 7, [3], [13]-200 p. front., illus. (incl. ports.) 19 cm. [BV3785.A45A3] 37-33220
1. Revivals. I. Title.

BEARDSLEY, Frank Grenville.
A history of American revivals, by Frank Grenville Beardsley, S.T.D. 2d ed., rev. and enl. New York, American tract society [c1912] 3 p. l., 352 p. 20 cm. $0.50 12-23138
I. Title.

BEARDSLEY, Frank Grenville.
A history of American revivals, by Frank Grenville Beardsley, S.T.D. 2d ed., rev. and enl. New York, American tract society [c1912] 3 p. l., 352 p. 20 cm. $0.50 12-23138
I. Title.

BEECHER, Lyman, 1775-1863. 289
Letters of the Rev. Dr. Beecher and Rev. Mr. Nettleton, on the "new measures" in conducting revivals of religion. With a review of a sermon, by Novanglus... Published at the request of several gentlemen of the city of New York. New York, G. & C. Carvill, 1828. viii, [9]-104 p. 21 1/2 cm. "Review. A sermon preached in the Presbyterian church, Troy, March 4, 1827, by the Rev. Charles G. Finney": p. 44-80. [BV3790.B45] 37-37683
1. Revivals. 2. Finney, Charles Grandison, 1789-1875. I. Novangius, pseud. II. Title.

BIEDERWOLF, William Edward, 1867- 253
Evangelism; its justification, its operation and its value, by William E. Biederwolf ... New York, Chicago [etc.] Fleming H. Revell company [c1921] 5 p. l., 9-254 p. diagr. 20 cm. [BV3790.B47] 21-12248
1. Revivals. 2. Evangelistic work. I. Title.

BLAKEMORE, William Barnett, 1912- ed.
The revival of the churches. St. Louis, Bethany Press, 1963. 368 p. 23 cm. (Panel of Scholars. The renewal of church, v. 3) Includes bibliography. NUC67
I. Title.

BRADLEY, Joshua, 1773-1855. 260
Accounts of religious revivals in many parts of the United States from 1815 to 1818. Collected from numerous publications, and letters from persons of piety and correct information. By Joshua Bradley ... Albany: Printed by G. J. Loomis & co. State-street. 1819. xii, [13]-300 p. 15 cm. [BV3773.B7] 32-34066
1. Revivals. I. Title.

BROUGHTON, Leonard Gaston, 1864-
The revival of a dead church. Chicago, The Bible institute colportage assoc. [1900] 131 p. 12° (The colportage library. v. 6, no. 85) 0-2061
I. Title.

BUELL, Samuel, 1716-1798. 277.
A faithful narrative of the remarkable revival of religion, in the congregation of Easthampton, on Long-island, in the year of Our Lord, 1764: with some reflections. By Samuel Buell. D. D. late minister of the gospel in that place. To which are added, sketches of the author's life--memoirs of his daughter. Mrs. Conklin [!] and his son, Samuel buell, which were annexed to the sermons published on the occasion of their death. And, also, An account of the revival of religion in Bridgehampton & Easthampton, in the year 1800. Sag-Harbor: Printed by Alden Spooner, 1808. 144 p. front. (port.) 18 cm. [BR560.E25B8 1808] 9-3794
1. Conkling, Mrs. Jerusha (Buell) 1749-1782. 2. Buell, Samuel, 1771-17879 3. Revivals. 4. Easthampton. N. Y.—Church history. 5. Revivals 6. East Hampton, N.Y.—Church history I. Title.

CARRADINE, Beverly.
Revival incidents, by Beverly Carradine ... Chicago, Christian witness co., 1913. iv, 245 p. 19 cm. 13-14975 1.00
I. Title.

CAUGHEY, James, 1810?-1891. 922
Methodism in earnest: being the history of a great revival in Great Britain; in which twenty thousand souls were justified, and ten thousand sanctified, in about six years, through the instrumentality of Rev. James Caughey; including an account of those mental and spiritual exercises which made him so eminent a revivalist. Selected and arranged from "Caughey's letters", by Rev. R. W. Allen, and edited by Rev. Daniel Wise ... 2d thousand. Boston, C. H. Peirce, 1850. xii, [9]-456 p. 20 cm. [BV3785.C3A3 1850] 30-13580
1. Revivals. I. Allen, Ralph William, 1812- ed. II. Wise, Daniel, 1813-1898, ed. III. Title.

CAUGHEY, James, 1810?-1891. 922
Methodism in ernest; the history of a revival in Great Britain in which twenty thousand souls professed faith in Christ, and ten thousand professed sanctification in connection with the labors of the Rev. James Caughey. With an introduction by Thomas O. Summers, d. d. Richmond and Louisville, J. Early, for the Methodist Episcopal church, South, 1852. xvii, 9-456 p. 20 cm. "Selected and arranged from the Letters of Mr. Caughey, by Rev. R. W. Allen, and edited by the Rev. D. Wise."--p. ix. [BV3785.C3A3 1852] 30-13581
1. Revivals. I. Allen, Ralph William, 1912- ed. II. Wise, Daniel, 1813-1898, ed. III. Title.

CAUGHEY, James, 1810?-1891. 922
Showers of blessing from clouds of mercy; selected from the journal and other writings of the Rev. James Caughey; containing most stirring scenes and incidents, during great revivals in Birmingham, Chesterfield, Macclesfield, and other places in England, under his ministry; several of Mr. Caughey's awakening addresses and sermons; thoughts on holiness; notes of personal experience, and observations upon persons and places visited ... 6th thousand. Boston, J. P. Magee, 1860. 413, [397]-404 p. 20 cm. Editor's preface signed: R. W. A. [i. e. R. W. Allen] [BV3785.C3A37 1860] 33-17084
1. Revivals. I. Allen, Ralph William, 1812- ed. II. Title.

CHAPMAN, John Wilbur Chapman ... 269
Revivals and missions, by Rev. J. Wilbur Chapman ... New York, Lentilhon & company [1900] ix, ii, 220 p. 17 cm. ([Hand-books for practical workers in church and philanthropy: ed. by S. M. Jackson]) [BV3790.C55] 0-3430
1. Revivals. 2. Evangelistic work. 3. Parish missions. I. Title.

THE Church journal. 269
The revival system and the Paraclete. A series of articles from the Church journal. New York, D. Dana, jr., 1858. 90 p. 19 cm. [BV3790.C563] 38-35104
1. Revivals. I. Title.

DAVENPORT, Frederick Morgan, 1866- 253
Primitive traits in religious revivals, a study in mental and social evolution, by Frederick Morgan Davenport ... New York, The Macmillan company; London, Macmillan & co., ltd., 1905. xii p., l., 323 p. 20 cm. "This book is the expansion of a dissertation, which was originally submitted in partial fulfilment of the requirements for the degree of doctor of philosophy in the faculty of political science at Columbia university."--Pref. [BV3790.D4] 5-13529
1. Revivals. 2. Psychology, Religious. I. Title.

DAVENPORT, Frederick Morgan, 1866-1956. 269'.2
Primitive traits in religious revivals; a study in mental and social evolution. New York, Negro Universities Press [1968, c1905] 323 p. 23 cm. Thesis—Columbia University. Bibliographical footnotes. [BV3790.D4 1968] 68-58053
1. Revivals. 2. Psychology, Religious. I. Title.

DAVENPORT, Frederick Morgan, 1866-1956. 269'.2
Primitive traits in religious revivals; a study in mental and social evolution. New York, Macmillan, 1905. [New York, AMS Press, 1972] xii, 323 p. 19 cm. Expansion of the author's thesis, Columbia, 1905. Includes bibliographical references. [BV3790.D4 1972] 72-163669 ISBN 0-404-01929-3 15.00
1. Revivals. 2. Psychology, Religious. I. Title.

DEAN, Horace F. 269
Christ for America, a nation-wide campaign for union evangelistic meetings by cities, by Horace F. Dean ... New York, London [etc.] Fleming H. Revell company [1943] 80 p. diagr. 19 cm. [BV3790.D472] 43-14536
1. Revivals. 2. Evangelistic work. I. Appleman, Hyman, 1902- II. Davis, George Thompson Brown, 1873- III. Title. Contents omitted.

DIMOND, Sydney George. 287
The psychology of the Methodist revival, an empirical & descriptive study, by Sydney G. Dimond, M. A. London, Oxford university press, H. Milford, 1926. xv, 296 p. 23 cm. Bibliography: p. 280-289. [BX8331.D5] 27-16743
1. Revivals. 2. Methodism. 3. Psychology, Religious. I. Title.

EATON, Charles Aubrey, 1868- 253
The old evangel & the new evangelism, by Charles Aubrey Eaton. Chicago, New York [etc.] Fleming H. Revell company, 1901. 162 p. 29 1/2 cm. [BV3790.E28] 1-10347
1. Revivals. I. Title.

*FINNEY, Charles Grandison 269.2'0974
Finney on revival the highlights of the sermons on revival Minneapolis, Dimension Books, [1974] v., 120 p. 18 cm. [BV3774] ISBN 0-87123-151-4 0.95 (pbk.)
1. Revivals. I. Title.

FINNEY, Charles Grandison. 1792-1875. 253.7
Lectures on revivals of religion. Edited by William G. McLoughlin. Cambridge, Mass., Belknap Press of Harvard University Press [c.]1960. lix. 470p. 25cm. (The John Harvard library) (Bibl. footnotes) 60-11558 5.95
1. Revivals. 2. Evangelistic work. 3. Sermons, American. I. Title.

FINNEY, Charles Grandison, 1792-1875. 253
Lectures on revivals of religion. By Charles G. Finney. From notes by the editor of the N.Y. evangelist, revised by the author. New York, Leavitt, Lord & co.; Boston, Crocker & Brewster, 1835. viii, [9]-438 p. 19 1/2cm. [BV3790.F5 1835] 33-20563
1. Revivals. 2. Evangelistic work. 3. Sermons, American. I. Title.

FINNEY, Charles Grandison, 1792-1875. 253
Lectures on revivals of religion. By Charles G. Finney. From notes by the editor of the N.Y. evangelist, revised by the author. 6th ed., each 2000 copies. New York, Leavitt, Lord & co.; Boston, Crocker & Brewster, 1835. viii, [9]-438 p. 21cm. [BV3790.F5 1835a] 33-20564
1. Revivals. 2. Evangelistic work. 3. Sermons, American. I. Title.

FINNEY, Charles Grandison, 1792-1875. 253
Lectures on revivals of religion. By Rev. Charles G. Finney ... A new ed., rev. and enl. by the author. Oberlin, O., E.J. Goodrich [1868] viii, [9]-445 p. 19 1/2cm. [BV3790.F5 1868] 33-20562
1. Revivals. 2. Evangelistic work. 3. Sermons, American. I. Title.

FINNEY, Charles Grandison, 1792-1875 253.7
Revivals of religion. Chicago, Moody [1963, c.1962] 352p. 18cm. (MP129) Condensation of the author's Lectures on revivals of religion, first publ. in 1835. 63-1685 .89 pap.,
1. Revivals. 2. Evangelistic work. 3. Sermons, American. I. Title.

FOSTER, Allyn King, 1868- 220
The coming revival of religion, by Allyn K. Foster. Philadelphia, Boston [etc.] The Judson press [1929] 5 p. l., 146 p. 20 cm. [BR125.F63] 29-10042
I. Title.

HEADLEY, Phineas Camp, 1819-1903. 922
The reaper and the harvest; or, Scenes and incidents in cnnection with the work of the Holy Spirit in the life and labors of Rev. Edward Payson Hammond, M.A. Edited by Rev. P. C. Headley ... With an introduction by Rev. A. H. Burlingham ... New York, London, Funk & Wagnalls, 1884. xi, [13]-550 p. front., illus. (incl. port.) 20cm. [BV3785.H3H4] 37-36521
1. Hammond, Edward Payson, 1831-1910. 2. Revivals. I. Title.

HILL, Francis Constantine, 1823- 922.773
Robed and crowned. A memorial of Mrs. Nettie Hill Weeden. By Rev. Francis C. Hill. With selections from her writings and sketches and papers from Rev. B. M. Adams, D.D., Rev. A. C. Bowdish, D.D. ... and others. New York, Printed by Hunt & Eaton, 1891. 272 p. front., ports., plates. 19 cm. Includes songs with music. [BV3785.W45H5] 37-36757
1. Weeden, Mrs. Nettie (Hill) 1844-1889. 2. Revivals. I. Title.

HINDSON, Edward E. 269'.2
Glory in the church : the coming Bicentennial revival / by Edward E. Hindson. New York : T. Nelson, [1975] p. cm. [BV3790.H48] 75-17883 ISBN 0-8407-5600-3 pbk.
1. Revivals. I. Title.

HOWARD, Greenbery B.
Twenty years of revival effort; with supplementary chapters by ministerial brethren. Comp. by A. P. Lineard and E. S. Higgins. Syracuse, N.Y., A. W. Hall 1899. 218 p. port 12°. Sep
I. Title.

LEE, Luther, 1800-1889. 269
The revival manual. By Luther Lee ... New York, Wesleyan Methodist book room, 1850. viii, [9]-108 p. 15 1/2 cm. [BV3790.L28] 37-39311
I. Title.

LEWIS, J. D. 253
Revival hand book; or, Worker's guide setting forth the plan of salvation, how obtained and how lived, as taught in the word of God. By the Rev. J. D. Lewis ... Merced, Cal., J. D. Lewis, 1918. 125 p. 16 1/2 cm. [BV3790.L4] 19-13410
I. Title.

MACDONALD, James Henry, 1864- ed. 243
The revival; a symposium ... collected and edited by Rev. J. H. MacDonald ... Cincinnati, Jennings and Graham; New York, Eaton and Mains [1905] 147 p. 19 cm. "These addresses were first delivered before the Chicago preachers' meeting." [BV3760.M3] 5-32519
1. Revivals. I. McDowell, William Fraser, bp., 1858- II. Crawford, Edward B. III. Little, Charles Joseph, 1840-1911. IV. Thompson, John. V. Tilroe, William Edwin, 1861- VI. Swift, Polemus Hamilton, 1855- VII. Title.
Contents omitted.

MCKAY, William Alexander, 1842- 269
Outpourings of the spirit; or, A narrative of spiritual awakenings in different ages and countries. By Rev. W. A. McKay... Philadelphia, Presbyterian board of publication and Sabbath-school work [1890] 141 p. 14 1/2 cm. [BV3770.M3] 38-3099
1. Revivals. I. Presbyterian church in the U.S.A. Presbyterian board of publication. II. Title.

MALLALIEU, Willard Francis, bp., 1828-1911. 253
The why, when, and how of revivals, by Bishop W. F. Mallalieu. New York, Eaton & Mains; Cincinnati, Jennings & Pye [1901] 160 p. 18 cm. [BV3790.M34] 1-19615
1. Revivals. I. Title.

*MALONE, Tom 252.061
With Jesus after sinners. 12 Bible messages as blessed of God in conferences on revival and soul winning. Introd. by John R. Rice. Murfreesboro, Tenn., Sword of the Lord Pubs. [c.1966] 200p. ports. 21cm. 2.75
I. Title.

MATTHEWS, Charles Evert, 1887- 269.2
A church revival. Nashville, Broadman Press [c1955] 119p. illus. 20cm. [BV3790.M445] 55-14118
1. Revivals. I. Title.

OLFORD, Stephen F. 243
Heart-cry for revival; expository sermons on revival. [Westwood, N.J.] Revell [c.1962] 128p. 20cm. 62-10738 2.50
1. Revivals. I. Title.

ORR, James Edwin, 1912- 269'.2
The fervent prayer: the worldwide impact of the Great Awakening of 1858, by J. Edwin Orr. Chicago, Moody Press [1974] xx, 236 p. 24 cm. Bibliography: p. 225-233. [BV3770.O67] 74-2938 ISBN 0-8024-2615-8 5.95
1. Revivals. I. Title.

ORR, James Edwin, 1912- 269
Good news in bad times: signs of revival. Grand Rapids, Zondervan Pub. House [1953] 259p. 20cm. [BV3770.O7] 54-743
1. Revivals. I. Title.

PEARCE, William P[eter] 1867-
The revival thermometer; or Gauging one's spiritual worth, by William P. Pearce ... Introduction by A. C. Dixon ... Dayton, o., United Brethern publishing house, W. R. Funk, agent [c1905] xvi, 17-311 p. front. (port.) 20 cm. 5-34190
I. Title.

PETTIT, Hermon. 227'.87'077
Hebrews handbook for world revival / Hermon Pettit and Helen Wessel. Fresno, Calif. : Bookmates International, [1979] 146 p. ; 21 cm. Includes the text of the book of Hebrews, with commentary. [BS2775.2.P44] 78-73585 ISBN 0-933082-01-0 pbk. : 2.95
1. Bible. N.T. Hebrews—Criticism, interpretation, etc. 2. Revivals. I. Wessel, Helen Strain, 1924- joint author. II. Bible. N.T. Hebrews. English. New international. 1978. III. Title. IV. Title: Handbook for world revival.

PORTER, Ebenezer, 1772-1834. 269
Letters on the religious revivals which prevailed about the beginning of the present century By E. Porter ... Boston, Congregational board of publication, 1858. iv, 174 p. 20 cm. "The following letters were addressed to the Revivals association in the Theological seminary, Andover, in A. D. 1832."--Pref. [BV3773.P6] 37-7761
1. Revivals. 2. Evangelistic work. I. Congregational board of publication, Boston. II. Title.

PORTER, James, 1808-1888. 269
Revivals of religion; their theory, means, obstructions, uses and importance; with the duty of Christians in regard to them, By Rev. James Porter ... 5th ed. New-York, Lane & Scott, 1850. viii, [9]-260 p. 17 cm. [BV3790.P65 1850] 15-16166
1. Revivals. I. Title.

PORTER, James, 1808-1888. 269
Revivals of religion, revised and enlarged, showing their theory, means, obstructions, importance, and perversions; with the duty of Christians in regard to them. By Rev. James Porter ... New York, Nelson & Phillips; Cincinnati, Hitchcock & Walden, 1877. xii, [9]-285 p. 18 cm. [BV3790.P65 1877] 37-37655
1. Revivals. I. Title.

PRESBYTERIAN church in the U. S. A. Presbytery of Oneida. 285.174762
A narrative of the revival of religion in the county of Oneida; particularly in the bounds of the Presbytery of Oneida, in the year 1826. Utica, Printed by Hastings & Tracy, 1826. Princeton, N. J., Reprinted by D. A. Borrenstein, 1827. viii, [9]-67 p. 22 cm. Signed: John Frost, Moses Gillet, Noah Coe, committee. [BX8958.O55A5 1827 a] 21-18636
1. Revivals. 2. Oneida county, N. Y.—Church history. I. Frost, John, 1783-1842. II. Title.

RENDALL, Ted S. 269'.2
Fire in the church / Ted S. Rendall ; foreword by Theodore H. Epp. Chicago : Moody Press, [1974] 160 p. ; 22 cm. Bibliography: p. 152-160. [BV3790.R4] 74-193336 ISBN 0-8024-2635-2 pbk. : 2.95
1. Revivals. I. Title.

THE revival and its lessons 243
... New-York, A. D. F. Randolph, 1858- v. 15 cm. [BV3760.R4] 41-40823
1. Revivals.
Contents omitted.

*RHODES, Rev. D. L. 269
Revival now. New York, Vantage [c.1964] 78p. 22cm. 2.00 bds.,
I. Title.

ROLLER, Henry B.
The twentieth century revival; a call to prayer. Get ready for the great awakening. by Rev. Henry B. Roller... Cincinnati, Jennings and Graham; New York, Eaton and Mains [c1911] 115 p. 17 1/2 cm. $0.40 11-10044
I. Title.

SHAW, Solomon Benjamin 1854-
... *Old time religion,* including an account of the greatest revivals since Pentecostal days, and telling how to bring about an old time revival, by Rev. S. B. Shaw ... [Abridged ed.] Chicago, Ill., S. B. Shaw [1904] 285 p. 20 1/2 cm. 4-35756
I. Title.

SKINNER, Otis Ainsworth, 1807-1861. 269
Letters to Rev. B. Stow, R. H. Neale, And R. W. Cushman, on modern revivals. By Otis A. Skinner. Boston, A. Tompkins, 1842. iv, [7]-144 p. 19 1/2 cm. [BV3790.S6] 37-39293
1. Stow, Baron, 1801-1869. 2. Neale, Rollin Heber, 1808-1879. 3. Cushman, Robert Woodward, 1800-1868. 4. Revivals. I. Title.

SMITH, Oswald J. 243
The revival we need, by Oswald J. Smith... New York, N.Y., Christian alliance publishing co. [c1925] 2 p. l., 7-125 p. 18 cm. [BV3797.S48] 25-14850
I. Title.

SMITH, Wilbur Moorehead, 1894- 269
The glorious revival under King Hezekiah, by Wilbur M. Smith ... Grand Rapids, Mich., Zondervan publishing house [c1937] 54 p. 20 cm. Bibliography: p. 49-54. [BV3770.S6] 37-9462
1. Revivals. 2. Hezekiah, king of Judah. I. Title.

SPRAGUE, William Buell, 1795-1876. 269
Lectures on revivals of religion; by William B. Sprague ... with an introductory essay by Leonard Woods ... also an appendix, consisting of letters from the Reverend Doctors Alexander, Wyland ... [and others] Albany, Webster & Skinners; New-York, J. P. Haven; [etc., etc.] 1832. 1 p. l., xxxii, 287, 165 p. 23 1/2 cm. [BV3790.S75 1832] 34-6013
1. Revivals. I. Woods, Leonard, 1774-1854. II. Title.

SPRAGUE, William Buell, 1795-1876. 269
Lectures on revivals of religion; by William B. Sprague ... with an introductory essay, by Leonard Woods ... also, an appendix, consisting of letters from the Rev. Doctors Alexander, Wayland ... [and others] 2d ed., with additional letters. New York, D. Appleton & co., 1833. xxviii, 400 p. 20 cm. [BV3790.S75 1833] 34-6014
1. Revivals. I. Woods, Leonard, 1774-1854. II. Title.

STEPHENS, George T 1884?-1956. 269.2
True revival; six messages With a message on revival and the home and a biographical sketch of the author by his wife. [Abington, Pa.] Bible Evangelism [1961] 134 p. 21 cm. [BV3790.S766] 61-17479
1. Revivals. I. Title.

THE story of the Welsh revival as told by eyewitnesses, together with a sketch of Evan Roberts and his message to the world, by Arthur Goodrich, B.A., Rev. G. Campbell Morgan, D.D., W. T. Stead ... Rev. W. W. Moore, M.A., Rev. Evan Hopkins, and others. To which is added a number of incidents of this most remarkable movement. New York, Chicago [etc.] Fleming H. Revell company [c1905] 3 p. l., [5]-98 p. 2 port. (incl. front.) 19 cm. [BV3777.G85S73] 5-9282 269
1. Revivals. 2. Wales—Church history. I. Roberts, Evan. II. Goodrich, Arthur. III. Morgan, George Campbell, 1863- IV. Stead, William Thomas, 1849-1912. V. Hopkins, Evan. VI. Moore, Edward William.

TAYLOR, Charles Forbes, 1899- 243
The riveter's gang, and other revival addresses, by Charles Forbes Taylor (known as the English boy evangelist) New York, Chicago [etc.] Fleming H. Revell company [c1921] 3 p. l., 9-144 p. 19 1/2 cm. [BV3797.T3] 21-3687
I. Title.

TAYLOR, Jack R. 222'.806
When revival comes / Jack Taylor & O. S. Hawkins. Nashville, Tenn. : Broadman Press, c1980. 170 p. ; 19 cm. [BS1365.2.T39] 19 80-66956 ISBN 0-8054-6226-0 pbk. : 4.25
1. Bible. O.T. Nehemiah—Criticism, interpretation, etc. 2. Revivals. I. Hawkins, O. S., joint author. II. Title.

TENNESSEE Temple College, Chattanooga. 269.2058
Annual lecture on revival and evangelism, Tennessee Temple schools, Chattanooga, Tennessee. 1st-1954- Wheaton, Ill., Sword of the Lord Publishers. v. 21cm. [BV3760.T4] 55-374548
1. Revivals. 2. Evangelistic work. I. Title.

TORREY, Reuben Archer, 1856- ed. 253
How to promote & conduct a successful revival, with suggestive outlines, edited by R. A. Torrey... Chicago, New York [etc.] Fleming H. Revell company [1901] 336 p. 21 cm. [BV3790.T6] 1-30845
1. Revivals. 2. Evangelistic work. I. Title.

TYSON, William Ainsworth, 1891- 253
The revival, by Rev. W. A. Tyson. Nashville, Tenn., Cokesbury press, 1925. 287 p. 19 1/2 cm. [BV3790.T8] 25-23239
1. Revivals. I. Title.

VALLOWE, Ed. F. 252
Revival or ruin. Grand Rapids, Mich., Baker Bk. [c.1963] 91p. 22cm. 1.00 pap.,
I. Title.

VINCENT, John Heyl, bp., 1832-1920. 269
The revival and after the revival. By J. H. Vincent. New York, Phillips & Hunt; Cincinnati, Walden & Stowe, 1883. 74 p. 15 1/2 cm. Text on lining-papers. [BV3790.V45] 42-43674
1. Revivals. I. Title.

WEISER, Reuben, 1807-1885. 269
... *The mourner's bench.* By R. Weiser ... [Bedford? Pa.] W. T. Chapman, jr., pr. [pref. 1844] cover-title, 32 p. 21 cm. At head of title: A tract for the people. Caption title: The mourner's bench; or, An humble attempt to vindicate new measures. A reply to John W. Nevin's The anxious bench. [BV3790.N38W4] 44-25660
1. Nevin, John Williamson, 1803-1886. The anxious bench. 2. Revivals. I. Title.

WELLS, Robert J., ed. 269
How to have a revival, by evangelists Hyman J. Appleman ... Joe Henry Hankins ... Jesse Hendley ... [and others] Compiled and edited by evangelists Robert J. Wells ... [and] John R. Rice ... Wheaton, Ill., Sword of the Lord publishers [1946] 399 p. 20 1/2 cm. [BV3790.W46] 46-20756
1. Revivals. I. Rice, John R., 1895- joint author. II. Appelman, Hyman, 1902- III. Title.

WILSON, Henry Blauvelt, 1870-
The revival of the gift of healing, by Rev. Henry B. Wilson ... including suitable prayers and an office for the anointing of the sick. Milwaukee, The Young churchman co.; [etc., etc.] 1914. viii, 78 p. 17 cm. $0.60. 14-14794
I. Title.

WOODS, Grace Winona (Kemp) 1871- 269
Preparing the way. Copyright ... by Mrs. Henry M. Woods. [Atlantic City, The World wide revival prayer movement, c1941] 163 p. illus. (port.) 18 1/2 cm. [BV3770.W575] 43-17720
1. Revivals. 2. Prayer. I. World wide revival prayer movement. II. Title.

[WOODS, Grace Winona (Kemp)] 1871-
With signs multiplying. Atlantic City, World Wide Revival Prayer Movement [c1945] 134 p. (p. 131-134 advertisements) illus., ports. 18 cm. A 48
1. Revivals. 2. Prayer. I. World Wide Revival Prayer Movement. II. Title.

[WOODS, Grace Winona (Kemp) "Henry M. Woods"] Mrs., 1871- 269
The half can never be told. Atlantic City, N.J., The World wide revival prayer movement [1933] 102 p. illus. (facsims.) 19 cm. Foreword signed: Grace W. Woods. "Publish abroad. Words and music by Helen Howarth Lemmel": p. 14-15. [BV3770.W56] 38-18171
1. Revivals. I. World wide revival prayer movement. II. Title.
Contents omitted.

WOODWARD, William W., comp. 269
Surprising accounts of the revival of religion in the United States of America, in different parts of the world, and among different denominations of Christians with a number of interesting occurences of divine Province. Collected by the publisher. [Philadelphia] Printed and published by William W. Woodward, no. 52, South Second street; at the book-store lately occupied by Mr. William Young, 1802. 255 p. 17 1/2 cm. [BV3770.W6] 36-28605
1. Revivals. 2. Conversion. I. Title.

Revivals—Addresses, essays, lectures.

FINNEY, Charles Grandison, 1792-1875. 269'.2
Reflections on revival / by Charles G. Finney ; compiled by Donald W. Dayton. Minneapolis : Bethany Fellowship, c1979. 160 p. ; 21 cm. First published in 1845 under title: Letters on revivals. [BV3790.F514 1979] 78-26527 ISBN 0-87123-157-3 pbk. : 3.50
1. Revivals—Addresses, essays, lectures. I. Dayton, Donald W. II. Title.

MCLEOD, Malcolm James, 1867- 220
The revival of wonder, and other addresses, by Malcolm James McLeod... New York, Chicago [etc.] Fleming H. Revell company [c1923] 3 p. l., 9-187 p. 19 1/2 cm. [BR125.M337] 23-11528
I. Title.

SMITH, Constance Penswick.
The revival of Mothering Sunday, being an account of the origin, development, and significance of the beautiful customs which have entwined themselves around the fourth Sunday in Lent, the true and ancient day in praise of mothers, by C. Penswick Smith. London, Society for promoting Christian knowledge; New York, The Macmillan co, [1921] vii p., 1 l., 84 p. front., plates. 18 1/2 cm. [BV135.M5S6] 22-5557
I. Title. II. Title: Mothering Sunday.

Revivals—Africa.

MCMAHAN, Tom. 269.2096
Safari for souls: with Billy Graham in Africa. Columbia, S. C., State-Record Co. [1960] 111p. illus. 22cm. [BV3785.G69M33] 60-14979
1. Graham, William Franklin, 1918- 2. Revivals—Africa. I. Title.

Revivals—Africa, Sub-Saharan—History.

ORR, James Edwin, 1912- 269'.2'0967
Evangelical awakenings in Africa / J. Edwin Orr. Rev. and expanded. Minneapolis : Bethany Fellowship, [1975] x, 245 p. ; 22 cm. Published in 1970 under title: Evangelical awakenings in South Africa. Includes index. Bibliography: p. 231-242. [BV3777.A4O77 1975] 74-32018 ISBN 0-87123-128-X pbk. : 2.95
1. Revivals—Africa, Sub-Saharan—History. I. Title.

Revivals—Anaheim, Calif.

KOOIMAN, Helen W. 269'.2
Transformed; behind the scenes with Billy Graham [by] Helen W. Kooiman. Wheaton, Ill., Tyndale House Publishers [1970] 145 p. illus., port. 22 cm. [BV3775.A5K6] 70-112663 3.95
1. Graham, William Franklin, 1918- 2. Revivals—Anaheim, Calif. I. Title.

Revivals—Anderson, Ind.

TARR, Charles R., 1932- 269'.2'0924 B
A new wind blowing! [by] Charles R. Tarr. [Anderson, Ind.] Warner Press [1972] 123 p. illus. 19 cm. Includes bibliographical references. [BV3775.A53T37] 72-10912 ISBN 0-87162-147-9 2.50 (pbk.)
1. Revivals—Anderson, Ind. 2. Revivals—Wilmore, Ky. I. Title.

Revivals—Appalachian Mountains, Southern.

DICKINSON, Eleanor, 1931- 269'.2'0974
Revival. Text by Barbara Benziger. Introd. by Walter Hopps. [1st ed.] New York, Harper & Row [1974] p. cm. [BV3774.A66D5] 73-18697 ISBN 0-06-061920-1. 7.95
1. Revivals—Appalachian Mountains, Southern. I. Benziger, Barbara. II. Title.
Pbk. 5.95, ISBN 0-06-061921-X.

Revivals-Asia.

BURNHAM, George. 922
To the far corners, with Billy Graham in Asia, including excerpts from Billy Graham's diary. [Westwood, N. J.] Revell [1956] 160p. 22cm. [BV3785.G69B82] 56-10891
1. Graham, William Franklin, 1918- 2. Revivals-Asia. I. Title.

Revivals—Australia.

BABBAGE, Stuart Barton 269.2
Light beneath the Cross, by Stuart Barton Babbage and Ian Siggins. Garden City, N. Y., Doubleday [c.]1960. 161p. illus. 22cm. 60-11374 2.95 half cloth,
1. Graham, William Franklin. 2. Revivals—Australia. 3. Revivals—New Zealand. I. Siggins, Ian, joint author. II. Title.

BABBAGE, Stuart Barton. 269.2
Light beneath the Cross, by Stuart Barton Babbage and Ian Siggins. [1st ed.] Garden City, N. Y., Doubleday, 1960. 161p. illus. 22cm. [BV3785.G69B23] 60-11374
1. Graham. William Franklin. 1918- 2. Revivals— Australia. 3. Revivals—New Zealand. I. Siggins, Ian. joint author. II. Title.

Revivals—Canada.

KOCH, Kurt E. 269'.2'0971
Revival fires in Canada, by Kurt E. Koch. [1st ed.] Grand Rapids, Kregel Publications [1973] 102 p. 18 cm. Translation of Die Erweckung in Kanada. [BV3777.C36K613] 72-93352 ISBN 0-8254-3015-1 pap. 1.00
1. Revivals—Canada. I. Title.

WIRT, Sherwood Eliot. 269'.2'0924 B
Afterglow : the excitement of being filled with the spirit / by Sherwood Eliot Wirt. Grand Rapids, Mich. : Zondervan Pub. House, c1975. p. cm. [BR1725.W56A32] 75-21122 4.95 pbk. : 2.95
1. Wirt, Sherwood Eliot. 2. Revivals—Canada. I. Title.

Revivals—Connecticut.

[MITCHELL, Mary (Hewitt) Mrs.] 277.46
...*Great awakening* and other revivals in the religious life of Connecticut... [New Haven] Published for the Tercentenary commission by the Yale university press, 1934. cover-title, 59, [3] p. 23 cm. (Connecticut. Tercentenary commission. Committee on historical publications. [Tercentenary pamphlet series xxvi]) By Mary Hewitt Mitchell. cf. p. 1. "Publications of the Tercentenary commission of the state of Connecticut": [2] p. at end. [Full name: Mrs. Mary Cornwell (Hewitt) Mitchell] "Bibliographical note": p. 58, 59. [BV3774.C8M5] 34-27657
1. Revivals—Connecticut. 2. Great awakening. 3. Connecticut—Church history. I. Title.

Revivals—East (Far East)—History.

ORR, James Edwin, 1912- 269'.2'095
Evangelical awakenings in Eastern Asia / J. Edwin Orr. Minneapolis : Bethany Fellowship, [1975] x, 180 p. ; 22 cm. Includes index. Bibliography: p. 175-178. [BV3777.E18O77] 74-30353 ISBN 0-87123-126-3 pbk. : 2.95
1. Revivals—East (Far East)—History. I. Title.

Revivals—Europe.

FOSTER, Dave. 269'.2'094
Billy Graham, Euro '70; eight days when the miracle of modern technology projected the Christian message across Europe. [Minneapolis, World Wide Publications, 1971] 138 p. illus. (part col.), col. map, ports. (part col.) 28 cm. [BV3785.G69F67] 71-150990
1. Graham, William Franklin, 1918- 2. Revivals—Europe. I. Title.

Revivals—Great Britain.

CLARK, Rufus Wheelwright, 1813-1886. 922
The work of God in Great Britain: under Messrs. Moody and Sankey, 1873 to 1875. With biographical sketches. By Rufus W. Clar... New York, Harper & brothers, 1875. 371 p. incl. front., pl., port. 19 1/2 cm. [BV3785.M7C6] 269 37-37094
1. Moody, Dwight Lyman, 1837-1899. 2. Sankey, Ira David, 1840-1908. 3. Revivals—Gt. Brit. I. Title.

MITCHELL, Curtis. 269'.2'0942
The all-Britain crusade of 1967. Minneapolis, World Wide Publications [1968] 139 p. illus., ports. 28 cm. [BV3785.G69M46] 68-5661
1. Graham, William Franklin, 1918- 2. Revivals—Great Britain. I. Title.

Revivals—Greenville, S.C.

BRABHAM, Lewis F. 269'.2'0924
A new song in the South; the story of the Billy Graham Greenville, S.C. Crusade [by] Lewis F. Brabham. Introd. by Billy Graham. Grand Rapids, Zondervan Pub. House [1966] 155 p. illus., ports. 21 cm. [BV3785.G69B66] 66-29033
1. Graham, William Franklin, 1918- 2. Revivals—Greenville, S.C. I. Title.

Revivals—History

AUTREY, C. E. 269'.2'09
Renewals before Pentecost [by] C. E. Autrey. Nashville, Broadman Press [1968] 144 p. 20 cm. 1960 ed. published under title: Revivals of the Old Testament. Bibliographical references included in "Notes" (p. 141-144) [BV3770.A8 1968] 68-9025
1. Bible. O.T.—History of Biblical events. 2. Revivals—History. I. Title.

AUTREY, C E 269.2
Revivals of the Old Testament. Grand Rapids, Zondervan Pub. House [1960] 160p. 23cm. Includes bibliography. [BV3770.A8] 60-147
1. Revivals—Hist. 2. Bible. O. T.—History of Biblical events. I. Title.

BEARDSLEY, Frank Grenville, 1870- 269
Religious progress through religious revivals, by Frank Grenville Beardsley ... New York city, American tract society [1943] viii p., 1 l., 181 p. 19 1/2 cm. [BV3770.B4] 43-7078
1. Revivals—Hist. I. American tract society. II. Titie.

BURNS, James, 1865-1948. 269.209
Revivals, their laws and leaders. Two additional chapters by Andrew W. Blackwood, Sr. Grand Rapids, Baker Book House, 1960. 353p. 21cm. [BV3770.B8 1960] 60-2791
1. Revivals— Hist. 2. Reformers. I. Title.

FISCHER, Harold Arthur. 269
Reviving revivals [by] H. Arthur Fischer. [Sheboygan, Wis., The Gospel print shop, 1943] cover-title, 4 p. l., 5-140 p. illus. (ports.) 21 cm. [BV3770.F5] 44-25565
1. Revivals—Hist. I. Title.

GLASCOCK, James Luther, 1852-
Revivals of religion; before they occur, how to promote them, while they are in progress, and after they are over, by the Rev. J. L. Glascock ... with an introduction by Rev. H. C. Morrison ... Louisville, Ky., Pentacostal pub. co. [c1911] 109 p. front. (port.) 20 cm. 11-19587 0.50
I. Title.

LACY, Benjamin Rice, 1886- 269
Revivals in the midst of the years, by Benjamin Rice Lacy, jr. ... Richmond, Va., John Knox press, 1943. 3 p. l., 9-167 p. 21 cm. [BV3770.L3] 44-169
1. Revivals—Hist. I. Title.

ORR, James Edwin, 1912- 269'.2'09034
The eager feet : Evangelical awakenings, 1790-1830 / by J. Edwin Orr. Chicago : Moody Press, [1975] viii, 248 p. ; 24 cm. Includes index. Bibliography: p. 230-244. [BV3770.O66] 75-315875 ISBN 0-8024-2287-X : 5.95
1. Revivals—History. I. Title.

ORR, James Edwin, 1912- 269'.2
The flaming tongue; the impact of twentieth century revivals, by J. Edwin Orr. Chicago, Moody Press [1973] xiv, 241 p. 24 cm. Bibliography: p. 231-237. [BV3770.O68] 72-95016 ISBN 0-8024-2801-0 4.95
1. Revivals—History. I. Title.

Revivals—Huntington, W. Va.

HERNDON, Bob. 286'.1'0924 B
Eight days with Bob Harrington; "chaplain of Bourbon Street" hits sawdust trail. Written and photographed by Bob Herndon. Produced by Bill Faulkner. New Orleans, B. Harrington [1972] 273 p. illus. 23 cm. [BV3785.H346H47] 72-195221 5.00
1. Harrington, Bob, 1927- 2. Revivals—Huntington, W. Va. I. Title.

Revivals—Hymns.

ALBRIGHT, Isaac H 783.
Revival hymns and choruses. 4th ed. York, Pa., Crider, 1891. [88] p. 15 cm. Without music. [M2198.A35R4 1891] 50-40337
1. Revivals—Hymns. I. Title.

BLISS, Philip Paul, 1838-1876, ed. 245.
Gospel hymns and sacred songs. (Words only.) By P. P. Bliss and Ira D. Sankey, as used by them in gospel meetings ... New York, Biglow & Main; Cincinnati, J. Church & co.; [etc., etc., c1875] 95 p. 12 cm. [BV460.B48] 45-41236
1. Revivals—Hymns. 2. Hymns, English. I. Sankey, Ira David, 1840-1908, joint ed. II. Title.

[BLISS, Philip Paul] 1838-1876, ed. 245.
Gospel hymns combined, embracing volumes no. 1, 2 and 3, as used in gospel meetings and other religious services. Words only. New York, Chicago, Biglow & Main; Cincinnati, New York, J. Church & co. [1879] 228 p. 12 cm. "Embraces ... 'Gospel hymns and sacred songs' (vol. 1,) 'Gospel hymns, no. 2' compiled by P. P. Bliss and Ira D. Sankey, and 'Gospel hymns, no. 3,' by Ira D. Sankey, James McGranahan and George C. Stebbins."--Pref. [BV460.B4815 1879] 45-41135
1. Revivals—Hymns. 2. Hymns, English. I. Sankey, Ira David, 1840-1908, joint ed. II. McGranahan, James, 1840-1907, joint ed. III. Stebbins, George Coles, 1846- joint ed. IV. Title.

[BLISS, Philip Paul] 1838-1876, ed. 245.
Gospel hymns combined. Embracing volumes nos. 1, 2, and 3. As used in gospel meetings and other religious services. Words only. Cincinnati, New York, J. Church & co.; New York, Chicago, Biglow & Main [1880] 256 p. 17 1/2 cm. "Embraces ... 'Gospel hymns and sacred songs' (vol. 1); 'Gospel hymns, no. 2,' compiled by P. P. Bliss and Ira D. Sankey; and 'Gospel hymns, no. 3,' by Ira D. Sankey, James McGranahan, and George C. Stebbins."--Pref. [BV460.B4815 1880] 45-41134
1. Revivals—Hymns. 2. Hymns, English. I. Sankey, Ira David, 1840-1908, joint ed. II. McGranahan, James, 1840-1907, joint ed. III. Stebbins, George Coles, 1846- joint ed. IV. Title.

[BLISS, Philip Paul] 1838-1876, ed. 245.2
Gospel hymns consolidated, containing all the hymns in Gospel hymns, numbers 1, 2, 3 and 4. Duplicates omitted. New York, Biglow & Main; Cincinnati, J. Church & co., c1884. cover-title, [3]-126 p. 13 x 10 cm. Without music. "Embraces ... 'Gospel hymns and sacred songs,' (vol. 1,) 'Gospel hymns no. 2,' compiled by P. P. Bliss and Ira D. Sankey, 'Gospel hymns no. 3,' and 'Gospel hymns no. 4,' by Ira D. Sankey, James McGranahan, and George C. Stebbins."--Pref. [BV460.B4817 1884] 40-15491
1. Revivals—Hymns, 2. Hymns, English. I. Sankey, Ira David, 1840-1908, joint ed. II. McGranahan, James, 1840-1907, joint ed. III. Stebbins, George Coles, 1846- joint ed. IV. Title.

BLISS, Philip Paul, 1838-1876, Ed. 783.
Gospel hymns no. 2. By P. P. Bliss and Ira D. Sankey, as used by them in gospel meetings. New York, Biglow & Main; Cincinnati, J. Church & co.; [etc., etc., c1876] 112 p. 20 1/2 cm. With music. [M2198.B66G7] 46-34475
1. Revivals—Hymns. 2. Hymns, English. I. Sankey, Ira David, 1840-1908, joint ed. II. Title.

EARLE, Absalom Backas, comp. 783.
Revival hymns. Compiled by Rev. A. B. Earle. Rev. ed. Boston, J. H. Earle, 1874. 96 p. 12 cm. Principally without music: some of the tunes indicated by title. [M2198.E18R3 1874] 44-51857
1. Revivals—Hymns. I. Title.

FLEHARTY, J. Q. A. comp. 245.2076
The revivalist; a collection of popular hymns for revival occasions. By J. Q. A. Fleharty ... Galesburg, C. Faxon, printer, 1859. 96 p. 15 cm. Without music. [BV460.F55]
1. Revivals—Hymns. 2. Methodist Episcopal church—Hymns. 3. Hymns, English. I. Title.

REVIVAL melodies, 783.
or Songs of Zion ... Boston, J. Putnam, 1842. 2 v. in 1. 14 1/2 x 12 cm. [M2198.R327] 3-31560

SANKEY, Ira David, 1840-1908, ed.
Christian endeavor edition of Gospel hymns no. 6, by Ira D. Sankey, James McGranahan and Geo. C. Stebbins. Words only. Boston, Mass., United society of Christian endeavor; New York and Chicago, The Biglow & Main co.; [etc., etc., 1891] 192 p. 12 1/2 cm. "Contains sixteen pages more than the regular edition ... embracing ... Christian endeavor hymns ... the motto, pledge, and benediction of the society."--Pref. [BV465.C4S3] 45-41325
1. Revivals—Hymns. 2. Hymns. English. I. McGranahan, James, 1840-1907, joint ed. II. Stebbins, George Coles, 1846- joint ed. III. International society of Christian endeavor. IV. Title.

SANKEY, Ira David, 1840-1908, ed. 245.
Gospel hymns no. 3. (Words only.) By Ira D. Sankey, James McGranahan, and Geo C. Stebbins, as used by them in gospel meetings. New York, Biglow & Main; Cincinnati, J. Church & co.; [etc., etc. 1878] 96 p. 12 cm. [BV460.S32] 45-41136
1. Revivals—Hymns. 2. Hymns, English. I. McGranahan, James, 1840-1907, joint ed. II. Stebbins, George Coles, 1846- joint ed. III. Title.

SANKEY, Ira David, 1840-1908, ed. 245.
Gospel hymns no. 4. (Words only.) By Ira D. Sankey, James McGranahan, and Geo. C. Stebbins, as used by them in gospel meetings. New York, Biglow & Main; Cincinnati, J. Church & co.,; [etc., etc., c1881] 96 p. 12 cm. [BV460.S33] 45-41137
1. Revivals—Hymns. 2. Hymns, English. I. McGranahan, James, 1840-1907, joint ed. II. Stebbins, George Coles, 1840- joint ed. III. Title.

SANKEY, Ira David, 1840-1908, ed. 245.
Gospel hymns no. 5, with standard selections, by Ira D. Sankey, James McGranahan, and George C. Stebbins. Words only. New York, Biglow & Main; Cincinnati, The John Church co. [1887] 78 p. 13 x 10 1/2 cm. [BV460.S34] 45-41138
1. Revivals—Hymns. 2. Hymns, English. I. McGranahan, James, 1840-1907, joint ed. II. Stebbins, George Coles, 1846- joint ed. III. Title.

SANKEY, Ira David, 1840-1908, ed. 245.
Gospel hymns no. 6 By Ira D. Sankey, James McGranahan and Geo. C. Stebbins. For use in gospel meetings and other religious services. (Words only.) New York, Chicago, The Biglow & Main co.; Cincinnati, O., New York, The John Church co. [1891] 173 p. 12 1/2 cm. [BV460.S36] 45-41140
1. Revivals—Hymns. 2. Hymns, English. I. McGranahan, James, 1840-1907, joint ed. II. Stebbins, George Coles, 1846- joint ed. III. Title.

SANKEY, Ira David, 1840-1908, ed. 783.
Gospel hymns nos. 1 to 6, by Ira D. Sankey, James McGranahan and Geo C. Stebbins. [Excelsior ed.] New York, Chicago, The Biglow & Main co.; Cincinnati, New York [etc.] The John Church co. [1895] 512 p. 19 1/2 cm. With music. "Gospel hymns nos. 1 and 2, by P. P. Bliss and Ira D. Sankey; nos. 3, 4, 5, and 6, by Ira D. Sankey. James McGranahan, and Geo. C. Stebbins, are ... compiled in this volume."--Pref. [M2198.S232G58] 46-34481
1. Revivals—Hymns. 2. Hymns, English. I. McGranahan, James, 1840-1907, joint ed. II. Stebbins, George Coles, 1846-1945, joint ed. III. Bliss, Phillip Paul, 1838-1876, joint ed. IV. Title.

SANKEY, Ira David, 1840-1908, ed. 245.
Gospel hymns nos. 5 and 6 combined. By Ira D. Sankey, James McGranahan, and Geo. C. Stebbins. Words only. New York and Chicago, The Biglow & Main co.; Cincinnati and New York, The John Church co. [1892] cover-title, [3]-139 p. 13 x 10 1/2 cm. Text on p. [2] of cover; p. 139 is 3d page of cover. [BV460.S35] 45-41139
1. Revivals—Hymns. 2. Hymns, English. I. McGranahan, James, 1840-1907, joint ed. II. Stebbins, George Coles, 1846- joint ed. III. Title.

[SANKEY, Ira David] 1840-1908, comp. 245.
100 select gospel hymns from Gospel hymns consolidated, embracing Gospel hyms nos. 1,2,3 and 4. Words only... New York, Chicago, Biglow & Main; Cincinnati, New York, J. Church & co. [1883] 64 p. 12 1/2 cm. "Selections ... made by Ira D. Sankey, Jas. McGrahahan, and Geo. C. Stebbins."--Pref. [BV460.S363] 45-46422
1. Revivals—Hymns. 2. Hymns, English. I. McGrahahan, James, 1840-1907, joint. comp. II. Stebbins, George Coles, 1846- joint comp. III. Title.

SCOTT, Orange, 1800-1847, comp. 245.
The new and improved camp meeting hymn book; being a choice selection of hymns from the most approved authors. Designed to aid in the public and private devotion of Christians, by Orange Scott ... 2d ed. Published by the compiler. Brookfield [Mass.] E. and G. Merriam, printers, 1831. iv, [5]-192 p. 11 cm. Without music. [BV460.S39 1831] 45-22340
1. Revivals—Hymns. 2. Hymns, English. I. Title.

SPALDING, Joshua.
The Lord's songs, a collection of composures in metre, such as have been most used in the late glorious revivals; Dr. Watts's Psalms and hymns excepted. By Joshua Spalding... Salem, Printed by J. Cushing, 1805. 10 p. l., 291, [1] p. 14 1/2 cm. 5-2937
I. Title.

Revivals—Hymns—History and criticism.

SIZER, Sandra S., 1946- 264'.2
Gospel hymns and social religion : the rhetoric of nineteenth-century revivalism / Sandra S. Sizer. Philadelphia : Temple University Press, c1978. p. cm. (American civilization) Based on the author's thesis, University of Chicago. Includes bibliographical references and index. [BV460.S58] 78-10165 15.00
1. Revivals—Hymns—History and criticism. 2. Revivals—United States. 3. Sociology, Christian—United States. I. Title. II. Series.

Revivals—India—History.

ORR, James Edwin, 1912- 269'.2'0954
Evangelical awakenings in southern Asia / J. Edwin Orr. Minneapolis : Bethany Fellowship, [1975] x, 240 p. ; 22 cm. Published in New Delhi, 1970, under title: Evangelical awakenings in India. Includes index. Bibliography: p. 227-236. [BV3777.I4O77 1975] 74-32019 ISBN 0-87123-127-1 pbk. : 2.95
1. Revivals—India—History. 2. Revivals—South Asia—History. I. Title.

Revivals—Indonesia.

CRAWFORD, Don, 1929- 269'.2'09598
Miracles in Indonesia; God's power builds his church! Wheaton, Ill., Tyndale House Publishers [1972] 160 p. illus. 18 cm. [BV3777.I5C7] 72-75962 ISBN 0-8423-4350-4 1.25 (pbk.)
1. Revivals—Indonesia. I. Title.

Revivals—Kentucky.

MCNEMAR, Richard, 1770-1839. 289.8'09769
The Kentucky revival; or, A short history of the late extraordinary outpouring of the spirit of God in the western states of America, agreeably to Scripture promises and prophecies concerning the latter day, with a brief account of the entrance and progress of what the world call Shakerism among the subjects of the late revival in Ohio and Kentucky. Presented to the true Zion traveler as a memorial of the wilderness journey. New York, E. O. Jenkins, 1846. [New York, AMS Press, 1974] 156 p. 19 cm. (Communal societies in America) "Observations on church government, by the Presbytery of Springfield" (p. [133]-156) has special t.p. [BX9767.K4M3 1974] 72-2990 ISBN 0-404-10752-4 9.00
1. Shakers. 2. Revivals—Kentucky. 3. Church polity. I. Springfield (Ohio). Presbytery. Observations on church government. 1974. II. Title.

MCNEMAR, Richard, 1770-1839. 289.
The Kentucky revival; or, A short history of the late extraordinary outpouring of the spirit of God in the western states of America, agreeably to Scripture promises and prophecies concerning the latter day; with a brief account of the entrance and progress of what the world call Shakerism among the subjects of the late revival in Ohio and Kentucky. Presented to the true Zion-traveler as a memorial of the wilderness journey. By Richard McNemar... New York, Preprinted by E. O. Jenkins, 1846- 156 p. 10 cm. First edition published 1807. "Observations on church government, by the presbytery of Springfield" (p. [133]-156) has special t.-p. [BX9767.K4M3 1846] 24-19718
1. Shakers. 2. Revivals—Kentucky. I. Shakers. Springfield (Ohio) Presbytery. II. Title.

Revivals—Korea.

KOCH, Kurt E. 269'.2'09519
Victory through persecution, by Kurt Koch. Translated by Anthea Bell. With a foreword by Billy Graham. [1st American ed.] Grand Rapids, Kregel Publications [1972, c1971] 62 p. 18 cm. Translation of Koreas Beter. [BV3777.K6K613 1972] 72-77231 ISBN 0-8254-3009-7 1.00
1. Revivals—Korea. I. Title.

Revivals—Latin America—History.

ORR, James Edwin, 1912- 269'.2'098
Evangelical awakenings in Latin America / J. Edwin Orr. Minneapolis : Bethany Fellowship, c1978. x, 216, [38] p. ; 22 cm. Includes index. Bibliography: p. [247]-251. [BV3777.L3O77] 77-16148 ISBN 0-87123-130-1 : 3.95
1. Revivals—Latin America—History. I. Title.

Revivals—London.

MITCHELL, Curtis. 269'.2'0924
The Billy Graham London crusade. Official photographer: Vincent Hayhurst. [Minneapolis? c1966] 128 p. illus., ports. 28 cm. [BV3785.G69M48] 67-5692
1. Graham, William Franklin, 1918- 2. Revivals—London. I. Title.

Revivals—Massachusetts.

CONRAD, Arcturus Z., 1855- ed.
Boston's awakening, ed. by Rev. Arcturus Z. Conrad ... A complete account of the great Boston revival under the leadership of J. Wilbur Chapman and Charles M. Alexander, January 26th to February 21st, 1909. Boston, Mass., The King's business publishing company [c1909] 290 p. ports. 19 cm. 9-30855
I. Title.

EDWARDS, Jonathan, 1703-1758. 277.
A faithful narrative of the surprising work of God in the conversion of many hundred souls in Northampton, and the neighbouring towns and villages in the county of Hampshire, in the province of the Massachusetts bay in New-England. In a letter to the Reverend Dr. Benjamin Colman, of Boston, Written by the Rev. Mr. Edwards, minister of Northampton. Nov. 6, 1736. Published with a large preface by the Rev. Dr. Watts and Dr. Guyse of London: to which a shorter is added by some of the reverend ministers of Boston. Together with an attestation from some of the reverend ministers of Hampshire. The 3d ed. Boston: N. E. Printed by S. Kneeland and T. Green, for D. Henchman, in Cor,-Hill, 1738. 1 p. l., viii, v. [1], 79 p. 15 1/2 cm. [BR520.E4 1738] 21-18452
1. Revivals—Massachusetts. I. Watts, Isaac, 1674-1748. II. Guyse, John, 1680-1761. III. Title.

Revivals—New England.

TYLER, Bennet, 1783-1858, comp. 269
New England revivals, as they existed at the close of the eighteenth, and the beginning of the nineteenth centuries. Compiled principally from narratives first published in the Conn. evangelical magazine. By Bennet Tyler ... Prepared for the Massachusetts Sabbath school society, and revised by the Committee of publication. Boston, Massachusetts Sabbath school society, 1846. xvi, [17]-328 p. 16 1/2 cm. [BV3773.T9] 38-3204
1. Revivals—New England. I. Massachusetts Sabbath school society. Committee of publication. II. Title.

YALE, Cyrus, 1786-1854. 922.573
The godly pastor. Life of the Rev. Jeremiah Hallock, of Canton, Conn., to which is added a Sketch of the life of the Rev. Moses Hallock, of Plainfield, Mass. ... By Rev. Cyrus Yale ... A new edition of the memoir, revised by the author, and enlarged, under his sanction, by the sketch from another hand. New York, Boston, American tract society [1854?] 389 p. front. 19 1/2 cm. [BX7260.H15Y3] 36-2819
1. Hallock, Jeremiah, 1758-1826. 2. Hallock, Moses, 1760-1837. 3. Revivals—New England. I. American tract society. II. Title.

Revivals—New York (City)

BURNHAM, George. 922
Billy Graham and the New York crusade, by George Burnham and Lee Fisher. Grand Rapids, Zondervan Pub. House [1957] 192p. plates. group port. 22cm. [BV3785.G69B813] 57-59532
1. Graham, William Franklin, 1918- 2. Revivals—New York (City) I. Fisher, Lee, joint author. II. Title.

MITCHELL, Curtis. 922
God in the Garden; the story of the Billy Graham New York crusade. [1st ed.] Garden City, N. Y., Doubleday [1957] 195p. illus. 22cm. [BV3775.N5M5] 57-13496
1. Graham, William Franklin, 1918— 2. Revivals—New York (City) 3. New York. Madison Square Garden. I. Title.

Revivals—New York (State)—Rochester.

JOHNSON, Paul E., 1942- 269'.2'0974789
A shopkeeper's millenium : society and revivals in Rochester, New York, 1815-1837 / Paul E. Johnson. 1st ed. New York : Hill and Wang, 1978. ix, 210 p. : maps ; 22 cm. (American century series) Includes bibliographical references and index. [BV3775.R62J63 1978] 78-10533 ISBN 0-8090-8654-9 : 10.00. ISBN 0-8090-0136-5 pbk. : 3.95
1. Revivals—New York (State)—Rochester. 2. Rochester, N.Y.—History. 3. Rochester, N.Y.—Church history. I. Title.

Revivals—North Carolina.

HALL, James, 1744-1826.
A narrative of a most extraordinary work of religion in North Carolina. by the Rev. James Hall. Also a collection of interested letters from the Rev. James Hall. Also a collection of interesting letters from the Rev. James McCorkel. To which is added the agreeable intelligence of a revival in South Carolina. Philadelphia, Printed and published by Willaim W. Woodward, 1802. 52 p. 22 cm. [With Fuller, Andrew, Socinianism...London, 1797] "Annexed to the above is an astonishing instance of the power of conscience--The folly of atheism, and a poem written by a young Lady of Philadelphia, after the death of her father." "Collection of letters communicated to the editor by the Rev. Samuel MCorkle": p. 19-38. "True account of a great meeting held in the district of Spartanburgh, South Carolina [by] Ebenzer H. Cummins": p. 39-47. A35
1. Revivals—North Carolina. 2. Revivals—South Carolina. I. McCorkie, James. II. Cummins, Ebenezer Harlow. III. Title.

Revivals—Nova Scotia.

STEWART, Gordon, 1945- 277.16
A people highly favoured of God; the Nova Scotia Yankees and the American Revolution [by] Gordon Stewart and George Rawlyk. [Hamden, Conn.] Archon Books [1972] xxii, 219 p. map. 24 cm. "A revised version of Gordon Stewart's doctoral dissertation, 'Religion and the Yankee mind of Nova Scotia during the American Revolution' ... Queen's University." Includes bibliographical references. [BV3777.N6S73 1972] 78-38968 ISBN 0-208-01283-4 13.00
1. Alline, Henry, 1748-1784. 2. Revivals—Nova Scotia. 3. Nova Scotia—History. 4. United States—History—Revolution, 1775-1783—Foreign public opinion. 5. New Englanders in Nova Scotia. I. Rawlyk, George A., joint author. II. Title.

Revivals—Oceanica—History.

ORR, James Edwin, 1912- 269'.2'099
Evangelical awakenings in the South Seas

/ by J. Edwin Orr. Minneapolis : Bethany Fellowship, c1976. p. cm. Includes index. Bibliography: p. [BV3777.O26O77] 76-26966 ISBN 0-87123-129-8 pbk. : 2.95
1. Revivals—Oceanica—History. 2. Revivals—Madagascar—History. I. Title.

Revivals—Oneida Co., N.Y.

PRESBYTERIAN Church in the U.S.A. Presbyteries. 285.174762
A narrative of the revival of religion in the county of Oneida, particularly in the bounds of the Presbytery of Oneida, in the year 1826. Princeton, N.J., Reprinted by D. A. Borrenstein, 1827. 67 p. 22 cm. [BX8958.O55A5 1827a] 21-18636
1. Revivals—Oneida Co., N.Y. I. Title.

PRESBYTERIAN Church in the U.S.A. Presbyteries. Oneida. 266.
A narrative of the revival of religion in the county of Oneida, particularly in the bounds of the Presbytery of Oneida, in the year 1826. Utica, Printed by Hastings & Tracy, 1826. 88 p. 21 cm. [BX8958.O55A5 1826] 49-40202
1. Revivals—Oneida Co., N.Y. I. Title.

Revivals—Patchogue, N.Y.

GAMMAGE, Smith P. 1810-1893. 922
Fact not fiction: or, The remarkable history of Mrs. Louisa Liscum. With an appendix. By S. P. Gammage. New York, W. C. Martin, printer, 1840. viii, [9]-71 p. 16 cm. "Times of refreshing; or, A narrative of a revival of religion at Patchogue, L. I. in 1834 & 1835": p. [47]-71. [BR1725.L48G3] 38-3078
1. Liscum, Mrs. Louisa, 1808-1834. 2. Revivals—Patchogue, N.Y. I. Title.

Revivals—Pennsylvania—Philadelphia.

BELL, Marion L. 269'.2'0974811
Crusade in the city : revivalism in nineteenth-century Philadelphia / Marion L. Bell. Lewisburg, Pa. : Bucknell University Press, c1977. p. cm. "The original version of this work was a doctoral dissertation at Temple University." Includes index. Bibliography: p. [BV3775.P5B44 1977] 76-759 ISBN 0-8387-1929-5 : 15.00
1. Revivals—Pennsylvania—Philadelphia. 2. Philadelphia—Social life and customs. I. Title.

Revivals — San Francisco.

WIRT, Sherwood Eliot. 269.20979461
Crusade at the Golden Gate. Foreword and keynote sermon by Billy Graham. [1st ed.] New York, Harper [1959] 176 p. illus. 21 cm. A report on Billy Graham's evangelistic campaign in San Francisco, April 27-June 22, 1958. [BV3785.G69W5] 59-7163
1. Graham, William Franklin, 1918- 2. Revivals — San Francisco. I. Title.

Revivals—Sandy Creek, N.Y.

HOWE, Cora E. 269
Before and after; or, the work of grace in Sandy Creek, by Cora E. Howe ... 1st ed. Sandy Creek, N.Y., News print., 1898. 73 p. front. (port.) 15 1/2 cm. [BV3775.S38H6] 98-77
1. Revivals—Sandy Creek, N.Y. I. Title.

Revivals—Sermons.

*APPELMAN, Hyman 252
Revival sermons. Grand Rapids, Mich., Baker Bk. [c.1966] 85p. 22cm. ((1.00 sermon lib.) 1.00 pap.,
I. Title.

BANKS, Louis Albert, 1855- 287
Sermons for reviving, on the table talk of the Master, by Louis Albert Banks ... New York, Chicago [etc.] Fleming H. Revell company [c1928] 160 p. 19 cm. [BX8333.B3S35] 28-29457
I. Title.

CHAPMAN, J Wilbur, 1859-
Revival sermons, by J. Wilbur Chapman ... New York, Chicago [etc.] Fleming H. Revell company [c1911] 237 p. 20 cm. 11-26767 1.00
I. Title.

FIFE, Clyde Lee. 243
Fife's revival sermons, by Clyde Lee Fife... Louisville, Ky., Pentecostal publishing company [c1922] 239 p. front. (port.) 19 1/2 cm. [BV3797.F5] 22-21268
I. Title.

JOHNSON, Samuel Lee, 1866-
Revival sermons, by the Rev. Samuel L. Johnson ... ed. by the Rev. Matthew W. Gilbert ... New York, Press of the Fleming H. Revell company [c1909] 192 p. front. (port.) 20 cm. 10-387 1.00
I. Gilbert, Matthew W., ed. II. Title.

MASSEE, Jasper Cortenus, 1871- 243
Revival sermons, by J. C. Massee... New York, Chicago [etc.] Fleming H. Revell company [c1928] 156 p. 19 1/2 cm. [BV3797.M34] 28-12452
I. Title.

NOWLIN, William Dudley. 252.
Does religion pay? Revival sermons, by William Dudley Nowlin ... Philadelphia, Boston [etc.] The Judson press [c1923] 6 p. l., 132 p. 20 cm. [BX6333.N6D6] 23-8626
I. Title.

OLFORD, Stephen F. 269
Lord, open the heavens! : A heart-cry for revival / by Stephen F. Olford. Wheaton, Ill. : H. Shaw Publishers, c1980. 144 p. ; 21 cm. Published in 1962 under title: Heart-cry for revival. [BV3790.O47 1980] 19 80-52053 ISBN 0-87788-335-1 pbk. : 4.95
1. Revivals—Sermons. 2. Sermons, American. 3. Baptists—Sermons. I. Title.

RILEY, William Bell, 1861- 243
Revival sermons; essentials in effective evangelism, by William Bell Riley ... New York, Chicago [etc.] Fleming H. Revell company [c1929] 190 p. 20 cm. [BV3797.R45] 29-4474
I. Title.

Revivals—Shantung, China.

CULPEPPER, C. L., 1895- 269'.2'095114
The Shantung revival, by C. L. Culpepper. [Dallas, Tex., Crescendo Book Publications, c1971] 79 p. illus. 21 cm. Cover title. [BV3777.C5C8] 73-81143
1. Revivals—Shantung, China. I. Title.

Revivals—Southern States.

BOLES, John B. 269'.2'0975
The Great Revival, 1787-1805: the origins of the Southern evangelical mind [by] John B. Boles. [Lexington] University Press of Kentucky [1972] xiii, 236 p. illus. 24 cm. Bibliography: p. [205]-221. [BV3773.B65] 77-183349 ISBN 0-8131-1260-5 10.00
1. Revivals—Southern States. I. Title.

Revivals—Timor.

TARI, Mel. 269'.2'095986
The gentle breeze of Jesus [by] Mel and Nona Tari. Carol Stream, Ill., Creation House [1974] 191 p. illus. 23 cm. [BV3777.I5T37] 74-82507 ISBN 0-88419-057-9 4.95
1. Revivals—Timor. I. Tari, Nona, joint author. II. Title.

Revivals—Tokyo.

A Lantern in Tokyo. 269'.2'0952135
[Reporting and editing: J. D. Douglas and others; photography: Russell Busby] Minneapolis, World Wide Publications [1968] 79 p. illus. (part col.), ports. 21 cm. On cover: The Billy Graham Tokyo crusade. [BV3785.G69L3] 68-4524
1. Graham, William Franklin, 1918- 2. Revivals—Tokyo. I. Douglas, James Dixon. II. Title: The Billy Graham Tokyo crusade.

Revivals—United States

[AITCHISON, Estella Viola (Sutton)] Mrs., 1868- 269
The true story of a revival; how one town arranged for special evangelistic meetings with a record of the outcome; by a pastor's wife. Chicago, New York & Toronto, Fleming H. Revell company, 1901. 174 p. incl. front. plates, ports. 19 cm. Author's name given on p. [6] [BX3785.W5A4] 1-6704
1. Revivals—U.S. I. Title.

AMERICA'S hour of decision; 922
featuring a life story of Billy Graham, and stories of his evangelistic campaigns in Portland, Ore., Minneapolis, Atlanta, Fort Worth, Shreveport, La., Memphis, and the Rose Bowl, Pasadena, California. Includes four of the evangelist's sermons. Wheaton, Ill., Van Kampen Press [1951] 158 p. illus. 20 cm. [BV3785.G69A5] 51-6987
1. Graham, William Franklin, 1918- 2. Revivals—U. S. 3. Evangelistic sermons. I. Graham, William Franklin, 1918-

BEARDSLEY, Frank Grenville, 1870- 260
A history of American revivals, by Frank Grenville Beardsley, S.T.D. Boston, New York [etc.] American tract society [c1904] 3 p., l., 324 p. 20 1/2 cm. [BV3773.B4 1904] 4-27155
1. Revivals—U.S. I. Title.

BELMAN, J. C. 269
The great revival at Roberts Park M. E. church and other churches, by Rev. J. C. Belman. Indianapolis, Journal company, printers, 1881. 309 p. plates, 2 port. (incl. front.) 20 cm. [BV3785.H35B4] [922.773] 37-36523
1. Revivals—U. S. I. Title.

BLODGETT, Harvey Alvaro, 1869- comp. 269
Times of refreshing; story of the Mills revival in St. Paul, Minn., May 10th to May 30th, 1893. Compiled and published by H. A. Blodgett and J. J. Symes ... St. Paul, Minn. [1893] 122 p. front., illus. (ports.) 20 cm. Mills, Benjamin Fay, 1857-1916. [BV3785.M5B6] 37-37095
1. Revivals—U.S. I. Symes, John J., joint comp. II. Title.

CAMPBELL, Robert Clifford, 1888- 269
The coming revival [by] R. C. Campbell... Nashville, Broadman press, [c1939] 176 p. 19 1/2 cm. [BV3773.C27] 39-16401
1. Revivals—U.S. I. Title.

CANNON, William S. 269'.2'0973
The Jesus revolution; new inspiration for evangelicals [by] William S. Cannon. Nashville, Tenn., Broadman Press [1971] 144 p. illus., ports. 21 cm. [BV3773.C33] 76-172423 ISBN 0-8054-5516-7 4.95
1. Revivals—United States. 2. Jesus People—United States. I. Title.

COLTON, Calvin, 1789-1857. 269'.2'0973
History and character of American revivals of religion. London, F. Westley and A. H. Davis, 1832. [New York, AMS Press, 1973] xvi, 294 p. 19 cm. On spine: American revivals of religion. [BV3773.C6 1973] 72-1008 ISBN 0-404-00018-5 12.00
1. Revivals—United States. I. Title. II. Title: American revivals of religion.

CREIGHTON, Charles Frisbie, 1849- 922.773
Noise it abroad: or, Bitler and his methods, together with remarkable events attenting some of the revivals in which he has labored. By Rev. C. F. Creighton ... With an introduction. by Rev. S. A. Keen ... Columbus, O. W. G. Hubbard, 1885. 293 p. incl. pl. front. (port.) pl. 19 cm. [BV3785.B5C7] 37-36520
1. Bitler, James Summerfield, 1852- 2. Revivals—U. S. I. Title.

DAVIES, Edward, b.1830. 922
The boy preacher; or, The life and labors of Rev. Thomas Harrison, together with sketches of the most remarkable revivals in which he has been engaged. Reading, Mass., Holiness Book Concern [1881] 290 p. port. 20 cm. [BV3785.H35D3 1881a] 48-35813
1. Harrison, Thomas, 1854- 2. Revivals—U. S. I. Title.

FRANCIS, John Junkin, ed. 269
Mills' meetings memorial volume. An account of the great revival in Cincinnati and Covington, January 21st to March 6th, 1892, under the leadership of the distinguished evangelist, Rev. B. Fay Mills, assisted by the eminent gospel singer, Mr. Lawrence B. Greenwood; andl also, for a part of the time by Rev. J. Wilbur Chapman, D. D., and Mr. Geo. C. Stebbins ... with over one hundred illustrations. Edited by John Junkin Francis, D. D., assisted by Charles B. Morrell, D. D. Cincinnati, Standard publishing company [1892] xxii, 354 p., 3 l., 3-26 p. front., illus., pl., ports. 22 cm. "Prepared and published by authority of the 'Mills meetings executive committee'." Hymns (with music): leaf following p. 354. [BV3785.M5F7] 37-36751
1. Mills, Benjamin Fay, 1857-1916. 2. Chapman, John Wilbur, 1859-1918. 3. Stebbins, George Coles, 1846- 4. Greenwood, Lawrence B. 5. Revivals—U. S. I. Morrell, Charles B., 1859- joint ed. II. Mills meetings executive committee. III. Title.

GRAHAM, William Franklin, 1918- 269
Revival in our time [by Billy Graham and others] The story of the Billy Graham evangelistic campaigns, including six of his sermons. Wheaton, Ill., Van Kampen Press [1950] 140 p. illus., ports. 20 cm. [BV3785.G69A3] 50-7766
1. Revivals—U. S. 2. Evangelistic sermons. 3. Sermons, American. I. Title.

THE great awakening in the middle colonies. Gloucester, Mass., P. Smith, 1958. vii, 158p. 21cm. First published in 1920. Bibliography: p. 152-158.
1. Revivals—U. S. I. Maxson, Charles Hartshorn, 1864-

HARRELL, David Edwin. 269'.2'0973
All things are possible : the healing and charismatic revivals in modern America / David Edwin Harrell, Jr. Bloomington : Indiana University Press, [1975] p. cm. Bibliography: p. [BV3773.H37 1975] 75-1937 ISBN 0-253-10090-9 : 10.95
1. Revivals—United States. 2. Faith-cure—History. 3. Pentecostalism—History. I. Title.

HOFFMAN, Fred W 269.2
Revival times in America. Boston, W. A. Wilde Co. [1956] 189p. 20cm. [BV3773.H6] 56-11245
1. Revivals— U. S. I. Title.

HUNTER, Charles, 1920- 269'.2
Since Jesus passed by, by Charles [and] Frances Hunter. Old Tappan, N.J., F. H. Revell Co. [1974, c1973] 148 p. 18 cm. (Spire books) [BV3785.H78A37 1973] 74-155357 1.45
1. Revivals—United States. 2. Faith-cure. 3. Pentecostalism. I. Hunter, Frances Gardner, 1916- joint author. II. Title.

JORSTAD, Erling, 1930- 269'.2
That new-time religion; the Jesus revival in America. Minneapolis, Augsburg Pub. House [1972] 143 p. 20 cm. Bibliography: p. 139-141. [BV3773.J67] 72-78553 ISBN 0-8066-1221-5 2.95
1. Revivals—United States. 2. Jesus People—United States. I. Title.

KIRK, Edward Norris, 1802-1874. 269
Lectures on revivals. By Edward Norris Kirk ... Edited by Rev. David O. Mears. Boston, Congregational publishing society, 1875. viii, 333 p. 20 cm. Lectures delivered at the Theological seminary, Andover, in the winter of 1888. cf. Pref. [BX3790.K53] 35-33975
1. Revivals—U.S. I. Mears, David Otis, 1842-1915, ed. II. Title.

KNIGHT, Walker L., 1924- comp. 269'.2
Jesus people come alive. Compiled by Walker L. Knight. Wheaton, Ill., Tyndale House Publishers [1971] 127 p. illus. 18 cm. Contents.Contents.—"It's so wild ... praise the Lord!" By E. Hullum, Jr., and D. Lee.—The Jesus explosion, by B. Price and E. Hullum, Jr.—Communes for Christ, by W. L. Knight.—Stirrings in the churches, by D. Lee.—Reverberations from Asbury, by F. Ashley.—Coast-to-coast

echoes, by T. Druin.—The new sound, by M. V. Burns.—Faddists or disciples? By W. L. Knight. [BV3773.K58] 75-179070 1.25
1. Revivals—United States. 2. Jesus People—United States. I. Title.

LOWDEN, Joseph D. 269
The story of the revival; a narrative of the Mills meetings, held in Elizabeth, N. J., from December 29, 1891, to January 15, 1892, conducted by Rev. B. Fay Mills and Mr. L. B. Greenwood. Compiled from reports in the Elizabeth Daily journal, by Joseph D. Lowden, city editor. [Elizabeth, 1892] 111, [1] p. front., illus., port. 18 cm. [BV3785.M5L6] 37-37125
1. Mills, Benjamin Fay, 1857-1916. 2. Greenwood, Lawrence B. 3. Revivals—U. S. I. Title.

MCLOUGHLIN, William Gerald. 269.20973
Modern revivalism: Charles Grandison Finney to Billy Graham. New York, Ronald Press Co. [1959] 551p. 22cm. Includes bibliography. [BV3773.M3] 58-12959
1. Revivals—U. S. I. Title.

MCLOUGHLIN, William Gerald. 269'.2'0973
Revivals, awakenings, and reform : an essay on religion and social change in America, 1607-1977 / William G. McLoughlin. Chicago : University of Chicago Press, 1978. p. cm. (Chicago history of American religion) Includes index. Bibliography: p. [BV3773.M32] 77-27830 ISBN 0-226-56091-0 : 12.50
1. Revivals—United States. 2. United States—Church history. 3. United States—Civilization. I. Title.

SMITH, R. S. 269
Recollections of Nettleton, and the great revival of 1820, By Rev. R. Smith. Albany, E. H. Pease & co., 1848. 150 p. 15 cm. [BV3785.N36S5] 37-37664
1. Nettleton, Asabel, 1783-1844. 2. Revivals—U.S. I. Title.

STRICKLAND, Arthur Barsalou, 1879- 269
The great American revival; a case study in historical evangelism, with implications for today [by] Arthur B. Strickland. Cincinnati O., Standard press [1934] 235 p. 20 cm. "A selected bibliography": p. 233-235. [BV3773.S7] 34-31084
1. Revivals—U. S. 2. U. S.—Church history. I. Title.

STRICKLAND, Arthur Barsazou. 269
The great American revival; a case study in historical evangelism, with implications for today [by] Arthur B. Strickland. Cincinnati, O., Standard press [c1934] 235 p. 20 cm. "A selected bibliogrpahy": p. 233-235. [BV3773.S7] 34-31084
1. Revivals—U.S. 2. U.S.—Church history. I. Title.

SWAN, Jabez Smith, 1800- 922.673
The evangelist: or, Life and labors of Rev. Jabez S. Swan. Being an autobiographical record of this far-famed preacher, and of his wonderful success in the conversion of more than ten thousand souls in the New England and middle states; with accounts of scores of remarkable revivals ... Also papers contributed by distinguished divines and members of different denominations. Illustrated with steel plate portrait and engravings ... Edited by Rev. F. Denison ... Waterford, Conn., W. L. Peckham [1873] 466 p. incl. illus., plates. front. (port.) 20 1/2 cm. [BV3786.S85A3] 37-36770
1. Revivals—U.S. I. Denison, Frederic, 1819-1901, ed. II. Title.

SWEET, William Warren, 1881-
Revivalism in America, its origin, growth and decline, by William Warren Sweet. New York, C. Scribner, 1944. [i.e., 1965] 4 p.l., xi-xv p., 1 l., 192 p. 20 cm. "Selected bibliography: p. 183-188. 68-18719
1. Revivals—U.S. I. Title.

SWEET, William Warren, 1881- 269
Revivalism in America, its origin, growth and decline, by William Warren Sweet. New York, C. Scribner's sons, 1944. 4 p. l., xi-xv p., 1 l., 192 p. 20 cm. "Selected bibliography": p. 183-188. [BV3773.S8] 44-6536
1. Revivals—U.S. I. Title.

VAN COTT, Maggie (Newton) Mrs., 1830- 922.773
The harvest and the reaper, Reminiscences of revival work of Mrs. Maggie N. Van Cott. The first lady licensed to preach in the Methodist Episcopal church in the United States. Introduction by Bishop Haven. New York, G. A. Sparks [1883] xxxix, 360 p. 19 cm. Portrait on cover. [BV3785.V3A3] 37-36758
1. Revivials—U.S. I. Title.

WEISBERGER, Bernard A., 1922- 269.2
They gathered at the river; the story of the great revivalists and their impact upon religion in America [Magnolia, Mass., Peter Smith, 1968,c.1958] xi, 345p. (Quadrangle paperback rebound) Bibl. [BU3773.W4] 5.00
1. Revivals—U.S. 2. Evangelists. I. Title.

WEISBERGER, Bernard A., 1922- 269.2
They gathered at the river; the story of the great revivalists and their impact upon religion in America. [1st ed.] Boston, Little, Brown [1958] 345 p. illus. 22 cm. Includes bibliography. [BV377.W4] 58-7848
1. Revivals—United States. 2. Evangelists. I. Title.

WEISBERGER, Bernard A., 1922- 269'.2'0922
They gathered at the river : the story of the great revivalists and their impact upon religion in America / by Bernard A. Weisberger. New York : Octagon Books, 1979, c1978. xii, 3345 p., [4] leaves of plates : ill. ; 21 cm. Reprint of the ed. published by Little, Brown, Boston. Includes bibliographical references and index. [BV3773.W4 1979] 78-27278 ISBN 0-374-98338-0 lib.bdg. : 17.50
1. Revivals—United States. 2. Evangelists. I. Title.

WILLIAMS, R. E. 922
George K. Little, and his revival work; comprising a history of his life, conversion, and six years of evangelistic work. By Rev. R. E. Williams... Dayton, O., United brethren publishing house, 1887. xii, 9-172 p. front., 1 illus., port. 20 cm. [BV3785.L53W5] 37-36526
1. Little, George Kirkley, 1860- 2. Revivals—U.S. I. Title.

[WOODWARD, William Wallis] 269
Increase of piety; or, The revival of religion in the United States of America; containing several interesting letters not before published. Together with three remarkable dreams, in succession, as related by a female in the Northern Liberties of Philadelphia, to several Christian friends, and handed to the press by a respectable minister of the gospel. Collected by the publisher. Newburyport [Mass.]; Printed by Angier March ... 1802. vi, [7]-128 p. 19 cm. Compiled by W. W. Woodward. cf. Sabin, v. 29, no. 105172. Most of this work is included in Woodward's Surprising accounts of the revival of religion. [BV3773.W6 1802] A 34
1. Revivals—U.S. I. Title.

WOODWARD, William Wallis, comp. 269
Increase of piety, or, The revival of religion in the United States of America; containing several interesting letters not before published. Together with three remarkable dreams, in succession, as related by a female in the northern liberties of Philadelphia, to several Christian friends, and handed to the press by a respectable minister of the gospel. Collected by the publisher. Philadelphia: Printed and published by W. W. Woodward, no. 52, corner of Second and Chestnut-street ... 1802. 3 p. l., 5-114 p. 19 1/2 cm. Most of this work is included in Woodward's Surprising accounts of the revival of religion. [BV3773.W6 1802a] 38-11649
1. Revivals—U.S. I. Title.

Revivals—United States—History.

CARWARDINE, Richard. 269'.2'0973
Transatlantic revivalism : popular evangelicalism in Britain and America, 1790-1865 / Richard Carwardine. Westport, Conn. : Greenwood Press, 1979. xviii, 249 p. : ill. ; 25 cm. (Contributions in American history ; no. 75 ISSN 0084-9219s) Includes index.IBibliography: p. [231]-236. [BV3773.C35] 77-94740 ISBN 0-313-20308-3 : 18.95
1. Revivals—United States—History. 2. Revivals—Great Britain—History. 3. Evangelicalism—Great Britain—History. 4. Evangelicalism—United States—History. 5. United States—Church history. 6. Great Britain—Church history. I. Title.

LOVELACE, Richard F. 269'.2
Dynamics of spiritual life : an evangelical theology of renewal / Richard F. Lovelace. Downers Grove, Ill. : Inter-Varsity Press, c1979. 455 p. ; 21 cm. Includes bibliographical references and index. [BV3773.L63] 78-24757 ISBN 0-87784-626-X : 8.95
1. Revivals—United States—History. 2. Church renewal. 3. Evangelicalism—United States. 4. Spiritual life—History of doctrines. I. Title.

SMITH, Timothy Lawrence, 1924- 269'.24'0973
Revivalism and social reform : American Protestantism on the eve of the Civil War / Timothy L. Smith ; with a new afterword by the author. Baltimore : Johns Hopkins University Press, 1980. 269 p. ; 20 cm. Originally published in 1957 by Abingdon Press, New York, under title: Revivalism and social reform in mid-nineteenth-century America. Includes index. Bibliography: p. 263-264. [BV3773.S6 1980] 19 80-8114 ISBN 0-8018-2477-X pbk. : 5.95
1. Protestant churches—United States. 2. Revivals—United States—History. 3. United States—Church history—19th century. 4. Church and social problems—United States. I. Title.

SWEET, William Warren, 1881- 269
Revivalism in America [its origin, growth and decline] Nashville, Abingdon [1965, c.1944] xv, 192p. 19cm. (Apex bks., V3) [BV3773.S8] 1.50 pap.,
I. Title.

Revivals—United States—Juvenile literature.

COHEN, Daniel. 269'.2'0973
The spirit of the Lord : revivalism in America / Daniel Cohen. New York : Four Winds Press, [1975] 220 p. : ill. ; 23 cm. Includes index. Bibliography: p. 210-212. Traces the causes and progression of revival movements in the United States from the eighteenth century to the present. [BV3773.C56] 74-28056 ISBN 0-590-07292-7 : 7.95
1. Revivals—United States—Juvenile literature. 2. [Revivals.] I. Title.

Revivals—Virginia.

GEWEHR, Wesley Marsh, 1888- 269.09755
The great awakening in Virginia, 1740-1790. Gloucester, Mass., P. Smith [1966, c.1930] vii, 292p. maps, ports. 21cm. (Duke Univ. pubns.) Orig. pub. by Duke in 1930 Bibl. [BR555.V8G4] 66-1635 4.50
1. Revivals—Virginia. 2. Great awakening. 3. Virginia—Church history. I. Title.

GEWEHR, Wesley Marsh, 1888- 269.09755
The great awakening in Virginia, 1740-1790, by Wesley M. Gewehr. Gloucester, Mass., P. Smith, 1965 [c1930] viii, 292 p. maps, ports. 21 cm. (Duke University publications) Bibliography: p. 263-279. [BR555.V8G4 1965] 66-1635
1. Revivals — Virginia. 2. Great awakening. 3. Virginia — Church history. I. Title. II. Series.

GEWEHR, Wesley Marsh, 1888- 261.
The great awakening in Virginia, 1740-1790, by Wesley M. Gewehr. Durham, N. C., Duke university press, 1930. viii p., 2 l., 3-292 p. front., ports., maps. 24 cm. (Half-title: Duke university publications) "This work was first undertaken as a doctoral dissertation [University of Chicago, 1922]"--Pref. Bibliography: p. 263-279. [BR555.V8G4] 30-7517
1. Revivals—Virginia. 2. Great awakening. 3. Virginia—Church history. I. Title.

Revivals—Wales.

MATTHEWS, David. 269
I saw the Welsh revival. Chicago, Moody Press [1951] 126 p. 17 cm. (Colportage library, 205) [BV3777.G85M3] 51-9654
1. Revivals—Wales. I. Title.

SHAW, Solomon Benjamin, 1854- 269
The great revival in Wales, also an account of the great revival in Ireland in 1859, by Rev. S. B. Shaw ... Chicago, Ill., S. B. Shaw [1905] 191, [225]-285 p. front. (port.) 20 cm. "The great revival in Ireland" (p. [225]-285) reprinted from the author's "Old time religion", retains the paging, chapter heading and running title of that book. [BV3777.G85S5] 5-13531
I. Title.

Revolution (Theology)

BROWN, Dale W., 1926- 261.8
The Christian revolutionary [by] Dale W. Brown. Grand Rapids, Eerdmans [1971] 147 p. 21 cm. Includes bibliographical references. [BT738.3.B76] 77-142903 2.45
1. Revolution (Theology) 2. Theology—20th century. I. Title.

DAVIES, John Gordon, 1919- 261.7
Christians, politics and violent revolution / [by] J. G. Davies. London : S.C.M. Press, 1976. vii, 216 p. ; 22 cm. Includes index. Bibliography: p. 203-211. [BT738.3.D38] 76-362839 ISBN 0-334-00287-7 : £2.50
1. Revolution (Theology) 2. Christianity and politics. 3. Violence—Moral and religious aspects. I. Title.

EPPSTEIN, John, 1895- 261.1
The cult of revolution in the church. New Rochelle, N.Y., Arlington House [1974] 159 p. 23 cm. Includes bibliographical references. [BT738.3.E66] 73-18470 ISBN 0-87000-241-4 6.95
1. Revolution (Theology) 2. Violence—Moral and religious aspects. 3. Social ethics. I. Title.

GISH, Arthur G. 261.8
The New Left and Christian radicalism, by Arthur G. Gish. Grand Rapids, Mich., Eerdmans [1970] 158 p. 20 cm. Bibliography: p. 143-151. [BT738.3.G55] 75-107618 2.45
1. Revolution (Theology) 2. Radicalism—U.S. 3. Anabaptists. I. Title.

GROUNDS, Vernon C. 261.7
Revolution and the Christian faith / Vernon C. Grounds. 1st ed. Philadelphia : Lippincott, 1971. 240 p. ; 21 cm. (Evangelical perspectives) "A Holman book." Bibliography: p. [231]-240. [BT738.3.G76] 75-156368 4.95
1. Revolution (Theology) 2. Revolutions. I. Title.

GUNNEMANN, Jon P. 261.7
The moral meaning of revolution / Jon P. Gunnemann. New Haven : Yale University Press, 1979. p. cm. Includes index. [BT738.3.G86 1979] 79-10219 ISBN 0-300-01997-1 : 15.00
1. Revolution (Theology) 2. Revolutions—Moral and religious aspects. I. Title.

HENGEL, Martin. 232
Was Jesus a revolutionist? Translated by William Klassen. Philadelphia, Fortress Press [1971] xviii, 46 p. (p. 45-46 advertisements) 19 cm. (Facet Books. Biblical series, 28) Translation of War Jesus Recolutionar? Includes bibliographical references. [BT202.H4313] 77-157545 ISBN 0-8006-3066-1 1.00
1. Jesus Christ—Person and offices. 2. Revolution (Theology) I. Title.

MCCARTHY -Shulz, 248.42
Handbook of the revolution; phase 1: back to discipline. New York, Pageant [c.1962] 109p. 21cm. 2.50
I. Title.

NOVAK, Michael. 261.7
A theology for radical politics. [New York] Herder and Herder [1969] 128 p. 21 cm. Includes bibliographical references. [BT738.3.N68] 69-17073 1.95
1. Revolution (Theology) 2. Students—United States—Conduct of life. I. Title.

RUETHER, Rosemary Radford. 261.8
The radical Kingdom; the Western

experience of Messianic hope. New York, Paulist Press, [1975 c1970] viii, 304 p. 21 cm. Includes bibliographical references and index. [BT738.3.R8] ISBN 0-8091-1860-2 3.95 (pbk.)
1. Revolution (Theology). 2. Sociology, Christian. 3. Messianism. I. Title.
L.C. card no. for original edition: 70-109080.

RUETHER, Rosemary Radford. 261.8
The radical kingdom; the Western experience of Messianic hope. [1st ed.] New York, Harper & Row [1970] viii, 304 p. 22 cm. Includes bibliographical references. [BT738.3.R8 1970] 70-109080 7.50
1. Revolution (Theology) 2. Messianism. 3. Sociology, Christian. I. Title.

VERKUYL, Johannes. 261.8'3
Responsible revolution; means and ends for transforming society, by Johannes Verkuyl and H. G. Schulte Nordholt. Translated and edited by Lewis Smedes. Grand Rapids, Eerdmans [1974] 101 p. 21 cm. Translation of Verantwoorde revolutie. [BT738.3.V413] 73-13560 ISBN 0-8028-1546-4 1.95 (pbk.).
1. Revolution (Theology) 2. Revolution. I. Schulte Nordholt, H. G. II. Title.

Revolution (Theology)—Addresses, essays, lectures.

IS revolution change? 261.1
Edited by Brian Griffiths. Downers Grove, Ill., Inter-Varsity Press [1972] 111 p. 18 cm. Includes bibliographical references. [BT738.3.I8] 74-186350 ISBN 0-87784-545-X
1. Revolution (Theology)—Addresses, essays, lectures. 2. Church and social problems—Addresses, essays, lectures. I. Griffiths, Brian, ed.

MARXISM and radical 261.8
religion; essays toward a revolutionary humanism. Edited by John C. Raines and Thomas Dean. Philadelphia, Temple University Press, 1970. xvi, 176 p. 22 cm. "This book grows out of a two-day conference ... held at Temple University in April 1969 under the sponsorship of the Department of Religion." Includes bibliographical references. [BT738.3.M35] 78-119903
1. Revolution (Theology)—Addresses, essays, lectures. 2. Communism and religion—Addresses, essays, lectures. I. Raines, John C., ed. II. Dean, Thomas, 1938- ed. III. Philadelphia. Temple University. Dept. of Religion.

WHEN all else fails; 261.8'3
Christian arguments on violent revolution. Edited by IDO-C. Philadelphia, Pilgrim Press [1970] vi, 230 p. 22 cm. "Based on a book published originally ... as Vangelo, violenza, rivoluzione." Contents.Contents.—The Gospels and the Church as a revolutionary force, by H. D. Wendland.—Revolution and violence, by A. Bezerra de Melo.—A theological perspective on human liberation, by R. Shaull.—Why the Gospels are revolutionary, by V. Borovoj.—Christianity and the socialist revolution, by J. M. Gonzalez-Ruiz.—The Christian faith and Marxism in revolution, by P. Blanquart.—Search for a phenomenology of revolution, by P. L. Geschiere and H. G. Schulte Nordholt.—The stages of the revolution in the Third World, by A. P. Lentin.—Latin America - land of revolution, by the IDO-C Staff, et al.—Violence or nonviolence in the transformation of society, by the IDO-C Staff. Includes bibliographical references. [BT738.3.W48] 74-131205 ISBN 8-298-01871- 7.95
1. Revolution (Theology)—Addresses, essays, lectures. 2. Revolutions—Addresses, essays, lectures. I. Idoc. II. Vangelo, violenza, rivoluzione.

Revolution (Theology)—History of doctrines.

KIRK, J. Andrew. 261.7
Theology encounters revolution / J. Andrew Kirk. Downers Grove, Ill. : InterVarsity Press, c1980. 188 p. ; 21 cm. (Issues in contemporary theology) Includes bibliographical references and index. [BT738.3.K57] 80-7471 ISBN 0-87784-468-2 (pbk.) : 4.95
1. Revolution (Theology)—History of doctrines. 2. Liberation theology. I. Title. II. Series.

Revolutions.

ADORATSKILL, Vladimir 335
Viktorovich, 1878-
Dialectic materialism; the theoretical foundation of Marxism-Leninism. by V. Adoratsky. New York, International publishers [c1934] 96 p. 19 1/2 cm. "Reference notes": p. 94-96. [BX314A36] 34-40284
1. Lenin, Nikolai, 187001940. 2. Marx, Karl, 1818-1883. 3. Revolutions. 4. Communism. I. Title.

DICKEY, Samuel, 1872- 248
The constructive revolution of Jesus; a study of some of his social attitudes, by Samuel Dickey ... London, The Swarthmore press ltd.; New York, George H. Doran company [1923] 160 p. 19 cm. (Half-title: Christian revolution series. no. xvi) [BS2417.S7D5] 24-12636
I. Title.

Reward (Theology)

BARNES, Woodruff L. 233.4
Retribution; or, Heaven and hell. By Woodruff L. Barnes. The Bible doctrine of rewards and punishments, and its consonance with human reason: pictorially illustrated. New York, Hall & company, 1883. vi, 210 p. front. 24 cm. [BT940.B2] 37-37115
1. Reward (Theology) I. Title.

KROLL, Woodrow Michael, 1944- 234
It will be worth it all : a study in the believer's rewards / by Woodrow Michael Kroll. Neptune, N.J. : Loizeaux Bros., [1977] p. cm. [BT940.K76] 76-30438 ISBN 0-87213-475-X
1. Reward (Theology) 2. Salvation. I. Title.

NELSON, Thomas Hiram, 1863- 233.
The gospel of cause and effect: or, The philosophy of rewards and punishments here and hereafter. By Thos. H. Nelson ... Indianapolis, Ind., Grace publishing co. [c1903] 4 p. l., [3]-258 p. 20 cm. [BT940.N4] 3-28850
1. Reward (Theology) I. Title.

[WILLIAMS, Edward C.] 233.4
The world to come. Bible teachings concerning its rewards and punishments. By a layman... Oakland, Cal., The author, 1884. vi, 7-130 p. 19 cm. Copyrighted by E. C. Williams. [BT940.W7] 37-30615
1. Reward (Theology) I. Title.

Reward (Theology)—Biblical teaching.

RANKIN, Oliver Shaw. 223
Israel's Wisdom literature; its bearing on theology and the history of religion [by] O. S. Rankin. New York, Schocken Books [1969] xvi, 270 p. 21 cm. Reprint of the 1936 ed. Bibliographical footnotes. [BS1455.R27 1969] 69-19620 2.45
1. Bible. O.T. Wisdom literature—Theology. 2. Reward (Theology)—Biblical teaching. 3. Immortality (Judaism) I. Title.

Reyes, Antonio de los, Bp., 1729-1786.

STAGG, Albert. 266'.2'0924 B
The first Bishop of Sonora : Antonio de los Reyes / Albert Stagg. Tucson : University of Arizona Press, c1976. ix, 109 p. : ill. ; 24 cm. Includes index. Bibliography: p. 103-106. [F1219.3.M59R497] 76-379189 ISBN 0-8165-0549-7 : 8.50. ISBN 0-8165-0486-5 pbk. :
1. Reyes, Antonio de los, Bp., 1729-1786. 2. Indians of Mexico—Missions. 3. Franciscans in Mexico. 4. Missionaries—Mexico—Biography. 5. Missionaries—Spain—Biography. I. Title.

Reynolds, Bede, 1892-

REYNOLDS, Bede, 271'.1'024 B
1892-
A rebel from riches : the autobiography of an unpremeditated monk / Bede Reynolds (ne Kenyon L. Reynolds). Canfield, Ohio : Alba Books, [1975] 150 p., [11] leaves of plates : ill. ; 18 cm. [BX4705.R446A34] 74-27608 pbk. : 1.65
1. Reynolds, Bede, 1892- I. Title.

Reynolds, Charles B., 1832-

INGERSOLL, Robert Green, 211
1833-1899.
Trial of C. B. Reynolds for blasphemy, at Morristown, N. J., May 19th and 20th, 1887, Defence by Robert G. Ingersoll. New York city, C. P. Farrell, 1899. iv, [3]-84 p. 21 cm. (On cover: The agnostic library. v. 1, no. 5) On cover: Only authorized edition. "Stenographically reported by I. N. Baker, and revised by the author." [BL2725.B5 1899] 34-14487
1. Reynolds, Charles B., 1832- 2. Blasphemy. 3. Religious liberty. 4. Liberty of speech. I. Baker, Isaac Newton, 1838- II. Title.

INGERSOLL, Robert Green, 211
1833-1899.
Trial of C. B. Reynolds for blasphemy, at Morristown, N. J., May 19th and 20th, 1887. Defence by Robert G. Ingersoll ... New York, C. P. Farrell, 1888. iv, [3]-84 p. 20 cm. Lettered on cover: Ingersoll on blasphemy. "Stenographically reported by I. N. Baker, and revised by the author." [BL2725.B5] 33-37367
1. Reynolds, Charles B., 1832- 2. Religious liberty. 3. Liberty of speech. 4. Blasphemy. I. Title.

Reynolds, George.

CANNON, George, Quayle, 1827-
1901.
A review of the decision of the Supreme court of the United States, in the case of Geo. Reynolds vs. the United States. by George Q.Cannon. Salt Lake City, Utah, Deseret news printing and publishing establishment, 1879. v, 57 p. 24 cm. [BX8641.R4] 9-8716
1. Reynolds, George. 2. Polygamy. 3. Mormons and Mormonism. I. Title.

Rhea, Claude H.

RHEA, Claude H. 783.7'092'4 B
With my song I will prasie Him / Claude H. Rhea. Nashville : Broadman Press, c1977. 156 p. : ill. ; 21 cm. [ML420.R43A3] 76-17946 ISBN 0-8054-5571-X : 4.95
1. Rhea, Claude H. 2. Gospel musicians—United States—Biography. I. Title.

Rhetoric, Ancient.

MAAT, William Anthony, 262.14
1907-
... A rhetorical study of St. John Chrysostom's De sacerdotio, by William A. Maat ... Washington, D.C., The Catholic university of America press, 1944. vi, 85 p. incl. tables. 23 cm. (The Catholic university of America. Patristic studies, vol. LXXI) Thesis (PH.D.)--Catholic university of America, 1944. "Select bibliography": p. vi. [BV4009.C525M3] A 44
1. Chrysostomus, Joannes, Saint, patriarch of Constantinople, d. 407. De sacerdotio. 2. Rhetoric, Ancient. I. Title.

STOWERS, Stanley Kent. 227'.1066
The diatribe and Paul's letter to the Romans / Stanley Kent Stowers. Chico, Calif. : Scholars Press, c1981. p. cm. (Dissertation series / Society of Biblical Literature ; no. 57) Bibliography: p. [BS2665.2.S86] 19 81-5314 ISBN 0-89130-493-2 : 13.50
1. Bible. N.T. Romans.—Language, Style. 2. Rhetoric, Ancient. I. Title.
Publisher's address: 101 Salem St., Chico, CA 95926.

Rhinelander, Philip Mercer, Bp., 1869-1939.

WASHBURN, Henry Bradford, 922.373
1869-
Philip Mercer Rhinelander, seventh Bishop of Pennsylvania, first warden of the College of Preachers. New York, Morehouse-Gorham Co., 1950. ix, 210 p. illus., port. 21 cm. [BX5995.R48W3] 50-10776
1. Rhinelander, Philip Mercer, Bp., 1869-1939. I. Title.

Rhoads, Bert.

ROTH, Don A., 1927- 286'.7'0924 B
The individualist; a biography of Bert Rhoads, by Don A. Roth. Nashville, Southern Pub. Association [1968] 126 p. port. 22 cm. A biography of the man who overcame poverty and ill health to serve most of his ninety-six years as an educator and writer for the Seventh-Day Adventist Church. [BX6193.R45R6] 92 AC 68
1. Rhoads, Bert. I. Title.

ROTH, Don A., 1927- 286.7'0924 B
The individualist; a biography of Bert Rhoads, by Don A. Roth. Nashville, Southern Pub. Association [1968] 126 p. port. 22 cm. [BX6193.R45R6] 68-20844
1. Rhoads, Bert. I. Title.

Rhode Island—Church history.

CONLEY, Patrick T. 282'.745
Catholicism in Rhode Island : the formative era / Patrick T. Conley, Matthew J. Smith. [Providence] : Diocese of Providence, 1976. xiv, 173 p. : ill. ; 30 cm. Includes index. Bibliography: p. 153-162. [BX1415.R5C6] 76-62863
1. Catholic Church in Rhode Island—History. 2. Rhode Island—Church history. I. Smith, Matthew J., joint author. II. Title.

WILSON, Arthur Edward. 277.45
Weybosset Bridge in Providence Plantations, 1700-1790, being an account of a quest for liberty, with portraits of many saints and sinners, and a special study of the Rev'd Joseph Snow, Jun'r. Boston, Pilgrim Press [1947] xi, 275 p. map (on lining-papers) 22 cm. Bibliography: p. 261-267. [BR555.R4W5] 47-12123
1. Snow, Joseph, 1715-1803. 2. Rhode Island—Church history. I. Title.

Rhode Island—History—Colonial periodicals

CALLENDER, John, 1706-1748. 295
An historical discourse, on the civil and religious affairs of the colony of Rhode-Island. By John Callender, M. A. With a memoir of the author; biographical notices of some of his distinguished contemporaries: and annotations and original documents, illustrative of the history of Rhode-Island and Providence Plantations, from the first settlement to the end of the first century. By Romeo Elton ... [2d ed.] Providence, Knowles, Vose & company, 1838. 270, [2] p. 23 cm. (Added t.-p.: Collections of the Rhode-Island historical society. vol. iv) First edition, Boston, 1739. [F76.R47 vol. 4] Rc-2943
1. Rhode Island—Hist.—Colonial period. 2. Rhode Island—Church history. I. Elton, Romeo, 1790-1870, ed. II. Title.

Rhodesia, Southern—Religion.

BHEBE, Ngwabi. 266'.0096891
Christianity and traditional religion in western Zimbabwe, 1859-1923 / Ngwabi Bhebe. London : Longman, 1979. xiv, 190 p. : map ; 23 cm. Revision of the author's thesis. Includes index. Bibliography: p. [174]-183. [BL2470.R5B48 1979] 79-322844 ISBN 0-582-64237-X : 21.50
1. Rhodesia, Southern—Religion. 2. Christianity—Rhodesia, Southern. 3. Missions—Rhodesia, Southern. I. Title.
Available from Longman, NY, NY

Rhys, Morgan John, 1760-1804.

GRIFFITH, John Thomas, 1845- 922.
1917.
Rev. Morgan John Rhys. "The Welsh Baptist hero of civil and religious liberty of the 18t century." By John T. Griffith ... Lansford, Pa., Leader job print, 1899. 4 p. l., [7]-126 p. 19 x 15 cm. "Family records: Rhees family, Loxley family, Lowry

family": p. 74-80. [BX6495.R53G7] 99-2414
1. Rhys, Morgan John, 1760-1804. 2. Rhees family. 3. Loxley family. 4. Lowry family. I. Title.

Ricci, Matteo, 1552-1610.

CRONIN, Vincent. 922.251
The wise man from the West. Garden City, N. Y., Image Books [1957, (1955] 276 p. 18 cm. (A Doubleday image book, D44) Includes bibliography. [BV3427] 57-273
1. Ricci, Matteo, 1552-1610. I. Title.

CRONIN, Vincent. 922.251
The wise man from the West. [1st American ed.] New York, Dutton, 1955. 300 p. illus. 22 cm. [BV3427.R46C7 1955a] 55-8331
1. Ricci, Matteo, 1552-1610. I. Title.

Rice, John Holt, 1777-1831.

MAXWELL, William, 1784-1857. 922.573
A memoir of the Rev. John H. Rice, D.D., first professor of Christian theology in Union theological seminary, Virginia. By William Maxwell. Philadelphia, J. Whetham; Richmond, R. I. Smith, 1835. vii, 412 p. front. (port.) 19 1/2 cm. [BX9225.R5M3] 36-24296
1. Rice, John Holt, 1777-1831. I. Title.

PRICE, Philip B. 922.573
The life of the Reverend John Holt Rice, D.D. Richmond, Lib. of Union Theological Seminary in Virginia, 1963. ix, 144 1. facsim. 28cm. Reprinted from the Central Presbyterian, 1886-1887. 63-23592 price on request
1. Rice, John Holt, 1777-1831. I. Title.

Rice, John R., 1895-

SUMNER, Robert Leslie, 1922-
Man sent from God; a biography of Dr. John R. Rice. Grand Rapids, Eerdmans [1959] c.262 p. illus. 23 cm.
1. Rice, John R., 1895- I. Title.

Rice, Luther, 1783-1836.

THE dreamer cometh.
Atlanta, Home Mission Board, Southern Baptist Convention [1960] 104p. 22cm. (Southern Baptist Convention. Home Mission studies. 1961 graded series)
1. Rice, Luther, 1783-1836. 2. Southern Baptist Convention. I. Carleton, William A II. Series.

GEORGE Washington University, Washington, D.C. Office of the University Historian. 286'.1'0924
Luther Rice, founder of Columbian College [by Elmer Louis Kayser] Washington, 1966. 32 p. 22 cm. "Bibliographical note": p. 31-32. [BX6495.R55G4] 67-6661
1. Rice, Luther, 1783-1836. I. Kayser, Elmer Louis, 1896-

POLLARD, Edward Bagby, 1864-1927. 922.
Luther Rice, pioneer in missions and education, by Edward B. Pollard ... edited and completed by Daniel Gurden Stevens ... Philadelphia, Boston [etc.] The Judson press [1928] 7 p. l., 125 p., 1 l. front. plates, fold. facsim. 20 cm. Bibliography: p. [127] [BX6495.R55P6] 28-30087
1. Rice, Luther, 1783-1836. I. Stevens, Daniel Gurden, 1869- II. Title.

TAYLOR, James Barnett, 1804-1871. 922.673
Memoir of Rev. Luther Rice, one of the first American missionaries to the East, by James B. Taylor. 2d ed. Nashville, Tenn., Broadman press [1937] 306 p. 20 1/2 cm. [BX6495.R55T3 1937] 37-21929
1. Rice, Luther, 1783-1836. I. Title.

TAYLOR, James Barnett, 1804-1871. 922.673
Memoir of Rev. Luther Rice, one of the first American missionaries to the East. By James B. Taylor. Baltimore, Armstrong and Berry, 1840. ix, [9]-344 p. 19 1/2 cm. [BX6495.R55T3] 37-24338
1. Rice, Luther, 1783-1836. I. Title.

THOMPSON, Evelyn Wingo. 286.0924 (B)
Luther Rice: believer in tomorrow. Nashville, Broadman Press [c1967] 234 p. 22 cm. Bibliography: p. 226-228. [BX6495.R55T5] 67-100345
1. Rice, Luther, 1783-1836. II. Title.

THOMPSON, Evelyn Wingo 286.0924 (B)
Luther Rice: believer in tomorrow. Nashville, Broadman [c.1967] 234p. 22cm. Bibl. [BX6495.R55T5] 67-10034
1. Rice, Luther, 1783-1836. I. Title.

Rice, Luther, 1783-1836— Juvenile literature.

CARVER, Saxon Rowe. 92
Ropes to Burma; the story of Luther Rice. Illustrated by Edward Shenton. Nashville, Broadman Press [1961] 183p. illus. 21cm. [BX6495.R55C3] 61-7552
1. Rice, Luther, 1783-1836— Juvenile literature. I. Title.

Rice, Merton Stacher, 1872-1943.

CHABUT, Elaine (Rice) 1910- 922.773
Preacher Mike; the life of Dr. Merton S. Rice. [1st ed.] New York, Citadel Press [1958] 226p. illus. 22cm. [BX495.R466C5] 58-7309
1. Rice, Merton Stacher, 1872-1943. I. Title.

RICE, Merton Stacher, 1872- 287
Preachographs; a series of crisp sermonettes, by M. S. Rice ... New York, Chicago [etc.] Fleming H. Revell company [c1925] 212 p. front. (port.) 19 1/2 cm. [BX8333.R5P7] 25-9222
I. Title.

Rich, Charles Coulson, 1809-1883.

ARRINGTON, Leonard J. 289.3'092'4 B
Charles C. Rich, Mormon general and Western frontiersman [by] Leonard J. Arrington. Provo, Utah, Brigham Young University Press [1974] xvii, 386 p. illus. 24 cm. (Studies in Mormon history, v. 1) Includes bibliographical references. [BX8695.R46A77] 74-13624 ISBN 0-8425-1051-6 7.50
1. Rich, Charles Coulson, 1809-1883. I. Title. II. Series.

EVANS, John Henry, 1872- 922.8373
Charles Coulson Rich; pioneer builder of the West, by John Henry Evans. New York, The Macmillan company, 1936. xv p., 2 l., 400 p. front., illus. (map) plates, ports. 22 1/2 cm. "First printing." Bibliography: p. 391-392. [BX8695.R46E8] 36-13440
1. Rich, Charles Coulson, 1809-1883. 2. Mormons and Mormonism. I. Title.

Rich fool (Parable)—Juvenile literature.

KRAMER, Janice 226
The rich fool: Luke 12: 16-21 for children. Illus. by Sally Mathews. St. Louis, Concordia, c.1964 [32]p. col. illus. 21cm. (Arch bks., Quality religious bks. for children, 59-1109) 64-16984 .35 pap.,
1. Rich fool (Parable)—Juvenile literature. I. Title.

Richard de la Vergne, Francois Marie Benjamin, cardinal, 1819-1908.

LA VERGNE, Yvonne de, 1888- 922.244
Good Cardinal Richard, archbishop of Parish, by Yvonne de la Vergne, translated by Rev. Newton Thompson, S. T. D. St. Louis, Mo. and London, B. Herdedr book co., 1942. 2 p. l., 235 p. 21 cm. [BX4705.R47L3] 42-1797
1. Richard de la Vergne, Francois Marie Benjamin, cardinal, 1819-1908. I. Thompson, Newton Wayland, 1882- tr. II. Title.

Richard. Gabriel, 1767-1832.

MAST, Dolorita 277.740924
Always the priest; the life of Gabriel Richard, S.S. Helicon [dist New York, Taplinger, c.1965] 368p. 21cm. Bibl. [F574.D4R517] 64-20229 6.95
1. Richard. Gabriel, 1767-1832. I. Title.

Richard I, King of England, 1157-1199.

SABATINI, Rafael, 1875-1950. 920.02
Heroic lives; Richard I: Saint Francis of Assisi: Joan of Arc: Sir Walter Ralegh: Lord Nelson: Florence Nightingale. Freeport, N.Y., Books for Libraries Press [1971, c1934] 416 p. 23 cm. (Essay index reprint series) [D106.S28 1971] 70-99648 ISBN 0-8369-2071-6
1. Richard I, King of England, 1157-1199. 2. Francesco d'Assisi, Saint, 1182-1226. 3. Jeanne d'Arc, Saint, 1412-1431. 4. Raleigh, Walter Sir, 1552?-1618. 5. Nelson, Horatio Nelson, Viscount, 1758-1805. 6. Nightingale, Florence, 1820-1910. I. Title.

Richard, Saint, Bp. of Chichester, 1197-1253.

RICHARDSON, Mary Kathleen, 1903- 922.242
Richard. Drawings by Apolloni. New York, Sheed & Ward [1959] unpaged. illus. 21cm. (A Patron saint book) [BX4700.R44R5] 58-14456
1. Richard, Saint, Bp. of Chichester, 1197-1253. I. Title.

Richards, Ceri, 1903-1971.

LIVERPOOL. Public Libraries, Museums, and Art Gallery. Walker Art Gallery. 726'.595
Ceri Richards and the Metropolitan Cathedral of Christ the King : [catalogue of an exhibition held at the] Walker Art Gallery, Liverpool, 1975-6. [Liverpool] : [Walker Art Gallery], [1976] 15 p. : ill. ; 25 cm. [NC242.R52L58 1976] 77-355315 ISBN 0-901534-34-X : £0.50
1. Richards, Ceri, 1903-1971. 2. Liverpool. Metropolitan Cathedral of Christ the King. 3. Artists' preparatory studies—England—Exhibitions. I. Richards, Ceri, 1903-1971. II. Title.

Richards, Franklin Dewey, 1821-1899.

WEST, Franklin Lorenzo Richards, 1885- 922.
Life of Franklin D. Richards, president of the Council of the twelve apostles, Church of Jesus Christ of latterday saints, by Franklin L. West ... Salt Lake City, Deseret news press [c1924] 75 p. 2 port. (incl. front.) 24 cm. [BX8695.R5W4] 24-13363
1. Richards, Franklin Dewey, 1821-1899. I. Title.

Richards, Harold Marshall Sylvester, 1894-

CASON, Virginia. 286'.73 B
H. M. S. Richards, man alive / [Virginia Cason]. [Sacramento, Calif.] : Freedom House, [1974] ca. 200 p. : ill. (some col.), ports. (some col.) ; 29 cm. [BX6193.R5C37] 74-81143
1. Richards, Harold Marshall Sylvester, 1894- I. Title.

Richards, Henry Livingston, 1814-1903.

RICHARDS, Joseph Havens, 1851-1923. 922.273
A loyal life; a biography of Henry Livingston Richards, with selections from his letters and a sketch of the Catholic movement in America, by Joseph Havens Richards... St. Louis, Mo., Freiburg (Baden) [etc.] B. Herder, 1913. 2 p.l., ix, 397 p. front., ports. 21 1/2 cm. "Books consulted in the preparation of this work": p. i-ii. [BX4705.R48R5] 13-23188
1. Richards, Henry Livingston, 1814-1903. I. Title.

RICHARDS, William, 1819-1899. 922.273
On the road to Rome, and how two brothers got there. By William Richards. New York, Cincinnati [etc.] Benziger brothers, 1895. 117 p. 16 1/2 cm. Autobiography. [BX4668.R5] 37-17428
1. Richards, Henry Livingston, 1814-1903 2. Converts, Catholic. I. Title.

Richards, Miriam, 1885-1894.

[RICHARDS, James A.] 922
Miriam: a Christ-child. Being glimpses of the short stream of a little girl's life. Its spring was in Christ, and it flowed in love, in fun, in tears, in joy, in poetry, and in music through eight years until the ocean of God's love received it. New York, Chicago [etc.] Fleming H. Revell company [1895] 40 p. front. (port.) facsim. (music) 17 1/2 cm. "My God" (hymn with music): p. 33. [BR1715.R5R5] 37-19929
1. Richards, Miriam, 1885-1894. I. Title.

Richards, Theodore, 1867-1948.

ALLEN, Gwenfread Elaine, 1904- 285'.8'0922 B
Bridge builders; the story of Theodore and Mary Atherton Richards, by Gwenfread E. Allen. [Honolulu] Hawaii Conference Foundation, 1970. 260 p. illus. 24 cm. [BV3680.H4R4762] 75-131598
1. Richards, Theodore, 1867-1948. 2. Richards, Mary (Atherton) I. Title.

Richards, Willard, 1804-1854.

NOALL, Claire Augusta (Wilcox) 1892- 922.8373
Intimate disciple; a portrait of Willard Richards, apostle to Joseph Smith, cousin of Brigham Young, by Claire Noall. [Salt Lake City] University of Utah Press, 1957. xi, 630 p. illus., maps., ports. 24 cm. Bibliography: p. 621-630. [BX8695.R53N6] 64-57118
1. Richards, Willard, 1804-1854. I. Title.

Richards, William, 1793-1847.

WILLISTON, Samuel, 1861- 922
William Richards, by Samuel Williston ... Cambridge, Mass., Priv. print, 1938. 91 p. 20 1/2 cm. "Books cited in the notes": p. 80-91. [BV3680.H4R5] 40-1492
1. Richards, William, 1793-1847. 2. Hawaiian islands—Hist. 3. Missions—Hawaiian islands. I. Title.

Richardson, Richard Higgins, 1823-1892.

MEMORIALS of Richard H. Richardson, D. D. New York, A. D. F. Randolph and company [1893] 133 p. front. (mounted phot.) 23 cm. Contents.--Biographical sketch.--The Chicago pastorate.--The Newburyport pastorate.--The Trenton pastorate.--Funeral services and public tributes.-- Letters of sympathy.--Sermons by Dr. Richard H. Richardson. [BX9225.R52M4] 36-31461 922.573
1. Richardson, Richard Higgins, 1823-1892. 2. Presbyterian church—Sermons. 3. Sermons, American.

Richardson, Robert. 1806-1876.

GOODNIGHT, Cloyd, 1881or2-1932. 922.673
Home to Bethphage, a biography of Robert Richardson, by Cloyd Goodnight and Dwight E. Stevenson. St. Louis, Christian Board of Publication [1949] 255 p. 21 cm. Bibliography: p. 243-246. [BX7343.R48G6] 49-9781
1. Richardson, Robert. 1806-1876. I. Stevenson, Dwight Eshelman, 1906- joint author. II. Title.

Richardson, Samuel, 1689-1761.

POVEY, Charles, 1652?-1743. 823'.6
The virgin in Eden, 1741 / by Charles Povey. Memoirs of the life of Lady H., 1741? / Anonymous. New York : Garland Pub., 1975. 118, 67 p. ; 23 cm. (The Life

& times of seven major British writers) (Richardsoniana ; 10) Reprint of 2 works, the 1st of which was the 5th ed. printed by J. Roberts, London, and the 2d, "from the British Museum, the only copy known, which lacks the title page." [PR3667.R5 vol. 10] [BR75.P6] 75-5728 ISBN 0-8240-1312-3 lib.bdg. : 28.00
1. Richardson, Samuel, 1689-1761. Pamela. 2. Mary II, Queen of Great Britain, 1662-1694. 3. Caroline, consort of George II, 1683-1737. I. Memoirs of the life of Lady H. 1975. II. Title. III. Series.

Richelieu, Armand Jean du Plessis, cardinal, duc de, 1585-1642.

AUCHINCLOSS, Louis. 944'.032'0924 B
Richelieu. New York, Viking Press [1972] 263 p. illus. (part col.) 26 cm. (A Studio book) [DC123.9.R5A84 1972] 72-81676 ISBN 0-670-59755-4 16.95
1. Richelieu, Armand Jean du Plessis, Cardinal, duc de, 1585-1642.

BELLOC, Hilaire, 1870- 920.
Richelieu; a study, by Hilaire Belloc; with 7 illustrations and 4 maps. Philadelphia & London, J. B. Lippincott company, 1929. 392 p. front., plates, ports., maps. 25 cm. "Second edition." [Full name: Joseph Hilaire Pierre Belloc] [DC123.9.R5B4 1929] 29-28658
1. Richelieu, Armand Jean du Plessis, cardinal, duc de, 1585-1642 2. France—Hist.—Louis xiii, 1610-1643. I. Title.

BELLOC, Hilaire, 1870-1953. 944'.032'0924 B
Richelieu; a study. Westport, Conn., Greenwood Press [1972, c1929] 392 p. 22 cm. [DC123.9.R5B4 1972] 77-114466 ISBN 0-8371-4762-X
1. Richelieu, Armand Jean du Plessis, Cardinal, duc de, 1585-1642. 2. France—History—Louis XIII, 1610-1643.

CHURCH, William Farr, 1912- 944'.032'0924
Richelieu and reason of state, by William F. Church. Princeton, N.J., Princeton University Press [1973, c1972] 554 p. 25 cm. Bibliography: p. 515-547. [DC123.9.R5C5] 76-181518 ISBN 0-691-05199-2 20.00
1. Richelieu, Armand Jean du Plessis, Cardinal, duc de, 1585-1642. 2. France—Politics and government—1610-1643. I. Title.

ERLANGER, Philippe, 1903- 944'.032'0924 B
Richelieu. Translated by Patricia Wolf. New York, Stein and Day [1968- v. illus., ports. 25 cm. Contents.Contents.—The thrust for power. Bibliography: v. 1, p. 243-245. [DC123.9.R5E713] 68-31678 6.95
1. Richelieu, Armand Jean du Plessis, Cardinal, duc de, 1585-1642.

FEDERN, Karl, 1868- 920.
Richelieu, by Karl Federn with twenty-six illustrations and one facsimile, translated by Bernard Miall. New York, Frederick A. Stokes company [1928] 253 p. front. (port.) illus., plates, ports., facsim. 23 1/2 cm. [DC123.9.R5F5] 28-24401
1. Richelieu, Armand Jean du Plessis, cardinal, duc de, 1585-1642. I. Miall, Bernard, tr. II. Title.

FEDERN, Karl, 1868-1942. 944'.032'0924
Richelieu. Translated by Bernard Miall. New York, Haskell House, 1970. 253 p. illus., facsim., ports. 23 cm. Reprint of the 1928 ed. [DC123.9.R5F413 1970] 72-132440
1. Richelieu, Armand Jean du Plessis, Cardinal, duc de, 1585-1642.

LODGE, Richard, Sir 1855- 920.
The life of Cardinal Richelieu, by Richard Lodge ... with explanatory notes by Henry Ketcham ... New York, A. L. Burt company [1903] viii, 328 p. front. (port.) plates. 20 cm. "The chief books on the period": p. 325-326. First published London, 1896. [DC123.9.R5L9] 3-14560
1. Richelieu, Armand Jean du Plessis, cardinal, duc de, 1585-1642. I. Ketcham, Henry, ed. II. Title.

LODGE, Richard, Sir, 1855-1936. 944'.032'0924 B
Richelieu. Port Washington, N.Y., Kennikat Press [1970] x, 235 p. 21 cm. Reprint of the 1896 ed. Bibliography: p. [232]-233. [DC123.9.R5L8 1970] 77-112812
1. Richelieu, Armand Jean du Plessis, Cardinal, duc de, 1585-1642.

LODGE, Richard, Sir 1855-1936. 920.
Richelieu, by Richard Lodge ... London, Macmillan and co., ltd.; New York, Macmillan & co., 1896. x, 235 p. 20 cm. (Half-title: Foreign statesmen) "The chief books on the period": p. [232]-233. [DC123.9.R5L8] 4-620
1. Richelieu, Armand Jean du Plessis, cardinal, duc, de, 1585—1642. I. Title.

MASSON, Gustave i. e. Goerge Joseph Gustave, 1819-1888. 920.
...Richelieu. by Gustave Masson...Published under the direction of the tract committee. London [etc.] Society for promoting Christian knowledge. New York, E. & J. B. Young and co. [1884] xv, 350 p. 18 1/2 cm. (The home library) [DC123.9.R5M4] 4-621
1. Richelieu, Armand Jean du Plessis, cardinal, duc de, 1585-1642. I. Title.

O'CONNELL, Daniel Patrick. 944'.032'0924 B
Richelieu [by] D. P. O'Connell. Cleveland, World Pub. Co. [1968] 509 p. illus., map, ports. 22 cm. Bibliography: p. 449-484. [DC123.9.R5O25 1968b] 68-27612 10.00
1. Richelieu, Armand Jean du Plessis, Cardinal, duc de, 1585-1642.

PERKINS, James Breck, 1847-1910. 920.
France under Mazarin, with a review of the administration of Richelieu, by James Breck Perkins ... New York and London, G. P. Putnam's sons, 1886. 2 v. 4 port. (incl. fronts.) 23 cm. [DC123.P44] 4-609
1. Richelieu, Armand Jean du Plessis, cardinal, duc de, 1585-1642. 2. Mazarin, Jules, Cardinal, 1602-1661. 3. France—Hist.—Louis xiii, 1610-1643. 4. France—Hist.—Louis xiv, 1643-1715. I. Title.

PERKINS, James Breck, 1847-1910. 944'.032'0924
Richelieu and the growth of French power. Freeport, N.Y., Books for Libraries Press [1971] xiii, 359 p. illus., map, ports. 23 cm. Reprint of the 1900 ed. [DC123.9.R5P4 1971] 70-157353 ISBN 0-8369-5814-4
1. Richelieu, Armand Jean du Plessis, Cardinal, duc de, 1585-1642. 2. France—History—Louis XIII, 1610-1643. I. Title.

TREASURE, Geoffrey Russell Richards. 944'.032'0924 B
Cardinal Richelieu and the development of absolutism [by] G. R. R. Treasure. New York, St. Martin's Press [1972] 316 p. map. 23 cm. Bibliography: p. 288-297. [DC123.9.R5T7] 76-183397 10.95
1. Richelieu, Armand Jean du Plessis, Cardinal, duc de, 1585-1642. I. Title.

WILKINSON, Burke, 1913- 944.0320924
Cardinal in armor. Illus. by Arthur Shilstone. New York, Macmillan [c.1966] 178p. illus., 2 col. maps. 21cm. Bibl. [DC123.9.R5W53] 66-16108 3.95
1. Richelieu, Armand Jean du Plessis, Cardinal, ducde, 1585-1642. I. Title.

Richey, Raymond Theodore, 1893-

RICHEY, Eloise May. Mrs. 265.
What God hath wrought in the life of Raymond T. Richey, by Eloise May Richey. Houston, Tex., The Full gospel advocate [c1925] 2 p. l., 172 p. front., plates, ports. 19 1/2 cm. [BR115.H4R5] 26-8207
1. Richey, Raymond Theodore, 1893- 2. Faith-cure. I. Title.

Richland Baptist Church, Richland, Miss.

FARR, Eugene Ijams. 286'.1762'59
A history of Richland Baptist Church, Richland, Mississippi / by Eugene Ijams Farr. [s.l. : s.n.], c1976 (Florence, MS. : Messenger Press) xv, 358 p. : ill. ; 22 cm. [BX6480.R493R523] 77-358468
1. Richland Baptist Church, Richland, Miss. I. Title.

Richland Baptist Church, Twiggs Co., Ga.

FAULK, Lanette (O'Neal). comp. 286.1758
Historical collections of Richland Baptist Church. Macon, Ga., Printed by J. W. Burke Co. [1950] xi, 92 p. illus., group port. 24 cm. [BX6480.R49F3] 50-3244
1. Richland Baptist Church, Twiggs Co., Ga. I. Title.

Richland Center, Wis.—Biography.

SCOTT, Margaret Helen. 287'.6775'75
Glory to Thy name; a story of a church. Richland Center, Wis., Richland County Publishers, 1973. 110, xiv p. illus. 26 cm. Bibliography: p. 107-110. [BX8481.R43T747] 73-76879
1. Trinity United Methodist Church, Richland Center, Wis. 2. Richland Center, Wis.—Biography. I. Title.

Richmond. All Saints Episcopal Church.

HUGHES, Jennie. 283.755451
All Saints Episcopal Church, Richmond, Virginia, 1888-1958. Richmond, 1960. 69p. illus. 26cm. [BX5980.R5A45] 60-16745
1. Richmond. All Saints Episcopal Church. I. Title.

Richmond. Cathedral of the Sacred heart of Jesus.

RICHMOND (Diocese) Catholic historical society. 282.755451
A guide book for the Sacred heart cathedral, Richmond, Virginia. [Richmond, The Catholic historical society of the diocese, 1939. xiv p., 1., 62 p. incl. front., illus., plates. 20 1/2 cm. Introduction signed: Rev. Vincent S. Waters, executive secretary of the Historical society. [BX4603.R52C3] 40-5296
1. Richmond. Cathedral of the Sacred heart of Jesus. I. Waters, Vincent Stanislaus, 1904- II. Title.

Richmond. Centenary Methodist Church.

WHITE, Edith Denny. 287.6755451
The elect ladies of Centenary; the story of the organization and development of the woman's work in Centenary Methodist Church, Richmond, Virginia, through one hundred and fifty years, 1810-1960, by Edith Denny White (Mrs. Roscoe M. White) [Richmond? 1964] ix, 154 p. 23 cm. [BX8481.R45C385] 64-24099
1. Richmond. Centenary Methodist Church. 2. Women in church work — Richmond. I. Title.

Richmond. First Baptist church, South Richmond.

RANSOME, William Lee, 1879- 286.1755451
History of the First Baptist church and some of her pastors, South Richmond, Va. By W. L. Ransome, assisted by the following committee: C. H. Munford, Mary V. Binga, Mary V. Nelson [and others] ... [Richmond] 1935. 6 p. l., [7]-308 p., 2 l. illus. (incl. ports.) 23 cm. [BX6445.R5F5] 36-30349
1. Richmond. First Baptist church, South Richmond. 2. Negroes—Biog. 3. Negroes—Richmond. I. Title.

Richmond Hill, N.Y. Union Congregational Church and Society.

HAUSER, Raymond C. 285.8747
The story of Union Congregational Church, commemorating sixty years of progress and achievement, by Raymond C. Hauser and George F. Hagerman. [Richmond Hill, N.Y., 1947] 102 p. plates, ports. 23 cm. Bibliography: p. 96. [BX7255.R48U5] 47-7893
1. Richmond Hill, N.Y. Union Congregational Church and Society. I. Hagerman, George F., joint author. II. Title.

Richmond, Ky. first Methodist Church.

DORRIS, Jonathan Truman, 1883- 287.6769
Methodism and the home church; the First Methodist Church, Richmond, Kentucky. An anniversary publication by Jonathan Truman Dorris and Maud Weaver Dorris. Nashville, Printed for the authors by the Methodist Pub. House, 1952. 128 p. illus. 20 cm. [BX8481.R46D6] 52-30633
1. Richmond, Ky. first Methodist Church. I. Title.

Richmond, Legh, 1772-1827.

BEDELL, Gregory Townsend, 1793-1934 922.342
Life of Legh Richmond ... Prepared for the American Sunday school union, from the most recent memoirs, by Gregory T. Bedell ... Revised by the Committee of publication, Am. S. s.u. Philadelphia, American Sunday school union, [1829.] iv, [5]-211 p. front. (port.) 15 cm. [BX5199.R4B4] 33-32828
1. Richmond, Legh, 1772-1827. I. American Sunday-school union. II. Title.

GRIMSHAWE, Thomas Shuttleworth, 1778-1850. 922.342
A memoir of the Rev. Legh Richmond ... by the Rev. T. S. Grimshawe ... Abridged by the Rev. William Patton, A. M. New York, J. Leavitt; Boston, Crocker & Brewster, 1829. viii, 364 p. front. (port.) 19 cm. [BX5199.R4G8 1829 a] 39-25950
1. Richmond, Legh, 1772-1827. I. Patton, William, 1798-1879 ed. II. Title.

GRIMSHAWE, Thomas Shuttleworth, 1778-1850. 922.342
Memoir of the Rev. Legh Richmond ... By the Rev. T. S. Grimshawe ... 3d American, from the 3d London ed. Boston, Crocker and Brewster; New York, J. Leavitt, 1829. vii, [9]-371 p. 19 cm. [BX5199.R4G8 1829 b] 39-24027
1. Richmond, Legh, 1772-1827. I. Title.

GRIMSHAWE, Thomas Shuttleworth, 1778-1850. 922.342
A memoir of the Rev. Legh Richmond ... by the Rev. T. S. Grimshawe ... 3d American, from the last London ed. New York, G. & C. & H. Carvill, 1829. 4, [vii]-viii, [9]-362 p. front. (port.) 21 cm. [BX5199.R4G8 1829] 33-16425
1. Richmond, Legh, 1772-1827. I. Title.

GRIMSHAWE, Thomas Shuttleworth, 1778-1850. 922.
A memoir of the Rev. Legh Richmond ... by the Rev. T. S. Grimshawe ... 8th American, from the last London ed. New York, M. W. Dodd, 1845. viii, [9]-362 p. incl. front. (port.) 19 cm. [BX5199.R4G8 1845] 40-25723
1. Richmond, Legh, 1772-1827. I. Title.

GRIMSHAWE, Thomas Shuttleworth, 1778-1850. 922.342
A memoir of the Rev. Legh Richmond ... by the Rev. T. S. Grimshawe ... 8th American, from the last London ed. New York, M. W. Dodd, 1851. 2 p. l., [vii]-viii, [9]-362 p. 20 cm. [BX5199.R4G8 1851] 35-22773
1. Richmond, Legh, 1772-1827. I. Title.

RICHMOND, Legh, 1772-1827. 268
Domestic portraiture; or, The successful application of the religious principle in the education of a family, exemplified in the memoirs of three of the deceased children of the Rev. Legh Richmond. New York, Jonathan Leavitt; Boston, Crocker & Brewster, 1833. xii, 292 p. 19 1/2 cm. Compiled from Mr. Richmond's letters and writings by Rev. T. Fry. cf. Dict. nat. biog. [BV1471.R5] 21-2999
1. Richmond, Legh, 1772-1827. I. Fry, Thomas, 1775?-1860, ed. II. Title.

Richmond, Mrs. Cora L. v. (Scott) 1810-

BARRETT, Harrison Delivan, 1863-1911? ed. 133.
Life work of Mrs. Cora L. V. Richmond, Comp. and ed. by Harrison D. Barrett. Published under the auspices of the National spiritualists association of the U.S.A. Chicago, Hack & Anderson, printers, 1895. xvii, 759 p. 3 port. (incl. front.) 21 cm. [BF1283.R45B3] 14-15342
1. Richmond, Mrs. Cora L. v. (Scott) 1810- 2. Spiritualism. I. Title.

Richmond, N. Y.—Statistics, Vital.

DAVIS, William Thompson, 1862- 283.74726
The church of St. Andrew, Richmond, Staten island; its history, vital records, and gravestone inscriptions, by William T. Davis, Charles W. Leng [and] Royden Woodward Vosburgh ... Staten island, N. Y., Published under the auspices of the Staten island historical society by W. T. Davis, 1925. 266 p. front., 1 illus., plates. 26 cm. [BX5980.R45A6] 31-14795
1. Richmond, N. Y.—Statistics, Vital. 2. Epitaphs—Richmond, N. Y. I. Leng, Charles William, 1859- joint author. II. Vosburgh, Royden Woodward, joint author. III. Richmond, N. Y. St. Andrew's church. IV. Staten island historical society. V. Title.

Richmond. St. James's Church.

MCGUIRE, Murray Mason, 1872- 283.755451
St. James's church, 1835-1935; a centennial address delivered at St. James's church, Richmond, Virginia, November 3, 1935, by Murray M. McGuire ... [Richmond?] Printed by direction of the vestry [1935?] 51 p. 22 1/2 cm. [BX5980.R5J3] 36-12146
1. Richmond. St. James's church. I. Title.

ST. James's Church, 1835-1957.
A centennial address delivered at Saint James's Church, Richmond, Virginia, November 3, 1935, by Murray M. McGuire; A supplemental history in 1957, by John B. Mordecai. With an appendix prepared under the direction of the vestry. [Richmond?] 1958. 71p. 23cm.
1. Richmond. St. James's Church. I. McGuire, Murray Mason, 1872-1945. II. Mordecai, John Brooke, 1878-

Richmond. St. Paul's church (Protestant Episcopal)

WEDDELL, Elizabeth Wright. 283.755451
St. Paul's Church, Richmond, Virginia, its historic years and memorials, by Elizabeth Wright Weddell, with a foreword by the Reverend Beverley Dandridge Tucker, jr. ...with twenty-six illustrations... Richmond, Va., The William Byrd press, inc., 1931. 2 v. fronts, (1 col.) plates, ports., facsims. (1 fold.) 22 cm. Paged continuously. "Limited edition of one thousand copies." This copy not numbered. [BX5980.R5P3] 31-11715
1. Richmond. St. Paul's church (Protestant Episcopal) I. Title.

Richmond, St. Peter's Church.

BAILEY, James Henry 282.755451
History of St. Peter's Church, Richmond, Virginia: 125 years, 1834-1959. [Richmond, Va., 1107 E. Cary St. Lewis Printing Co., 1959] 81p. illus. 21cm. (3p. bibl.) 59-3861 pap., gratis
1. Richmond, St. Peter's Church. I. Title.

Richmond. Second Presbyterian church.

BLANTON, Wyndham Bolling, 1890- 285.1755
The making of a downtown church, the history of the Second Presbyterian church, Richmond, Virginia, 1845-1945, by Wyndham B. Blanton. Richmond, Va., John Knox press [1945] 526 p. front., illus., plates, ports., maps, facsims., diagrs. 23 1/2 cm. "Principal source material": p. [479]-492. [BX9211.R48S4] 45-3656
1. Richmond. Second Presbyterian church. I. Title.

Richmond. Union station Methodist church.

WILTSHIRE, Mollie (Roberson) 287.6755
A century of service; the history of Union station Methodist church, 1843-1943, by Mrs. J. L. Wiltshire. Published for the centennial celebration in 1943. [Richmond, Printed by Whittet & Shepperson, 1943] 143 p. illus., (incl. ports., facsim.) 24 cm. [BX8481.R45U5] 44-13185
1. Richmond. Union station Methodist church. I. Title.

Richmond, Va. First Baptist Church. Woman's Missionary Society-History

DECKER, Florence Frazer (Boston) 1893- comp.
A continuing light; history of the Woman's Missionary Society, First Baptist Church, 1813-1963. Richmond, Va., Woman's Missionary Society, First Baptist Church [1963] 54 p. 2 cm. Bibliography: p. 54. 64-42812
1. Richmond, Va. First Baptist Church. Woman's Missionary Society-Hist. 2. Baptists — Missions. 3. Missionaries, American. I. Title.

Richmond, Va. Monumental church.

FISHER, George D. 283.
History and reminiscences of the Monumental church, Richmond, Va., from 1814 to 1978. By Geo. D. Fisher. Richmond, Whittet & Shepperson, 1880. xvi, 508 p., 2 l., front., ports. 21 cm. [BX5980.R5M7] 6-24673
1. Richmond, Va. Monumental church. I. Title.

Richter, Don.

BARLOW, Sanna Morrison. 266.0847
Arrows of His bow. Chicago, Moody Press [1960] 208p. illus. 22cm. [BV2082.A8B3] 60-16877
1. Richter, Don. 2. Phonorecords in missionary work. 3. Gospel Recordings, inc. I. Title.

Rico, Jose Maria.

ROBERTS, Verne D.
Life begins for a Jesuit priest. [Plainfield? N.J.] Bolivian Indian Mission [196-?] 80 p. 19 cm. 64-56586
1. Rico, Jose Maria. 2. Catholic Church — Doctrinal and controversial works — Protestant authors. I. Title.

Ridderhof, Joy.

BARLOW, Sanna Morrison. 279.14
Mountains singing; the story of Gospel Recordings in the Philippines. Chicago, Moody [1968,c.1952] 352p. illus. 17cm. [BV3380.B3] 53-2338 1.29 pap.,
1. Gospel Recordings, inc. 2. Ridderhof, Joy. 3. Missions—Philippine Islands. 4. Phonorecords in missionary work. I. Title.

Ridderhof, Joy. a Missions—Philippine Islands.

BARLOW, Sanna Morrison. 266
Mountains singing; the story of Gospel Recordings in the Philippines. Chicago, Moody Press, 1952. 352p. illus. 22cm. [BV3380.B3] [BV3380.B3] 279.14 53-2338 53-2338
1. Ridderhof, Joy. a Missions—Philippine Islands. 2. Gospel Recordings. inc., Los Angeles. I. Title.

Riddles—History and criticism.

GRENSHAW, James L. 222'.32'077
Samson : a secert betrayed, a vow ignored / James L. Crenshaw. Atlanta : John Knox Press, c1978. 172 p. ; 21 cm. Includes indexes. Bibliography: p. [167]-170. [BS1305.2.C73] 77-15748 ISBN 0-8042-0170-6 : 7.95
1. Samson, Judge of Israel. 2. Bible. O.T. Judges XIII, 1-XVI, 31—Criticism interpretation, etc. 3. Riddles—History and criticism.

Ridgecrest Baptist Conference Center.

MCANEAR, Kenneth. 286'.175688
Ridgecrest, mountain of faith / Kenneth McAnear. Nashville, Tenn. : Broadman Press, [c1982] 96 p. : ill. ; 20 cm. Includes bibliographical references. [BX6207.S68M3 1982] 19 81-67325 ISBN 0-8054-6566-9 pbk. : 3.50
1. Ridgecrest Baptist Conference Center. I. Title.

Ridgecrest. N. C. Southern Baptist Assembly.

[FALLIS, William J]ed. 286.175
The Ridgecrest story. Nashville, Broadman Press [1933] 64p. illus. 23cm. [BX6476.R5F3] 56-33679
1. Ridgecrest. N. C. Southern Baptist Assembly. I. Title.

MIDDLETON, Robert Lee, 1894- 286.175
A drama come true; a history, Ridgecrest Baptist Assembly, 50th anniversary, 1907-1957. Nashville, Convention Press [1957] 72p. illus. 23cm. [BX6476.R5M5] 57-10107
1. Ridgecrest, N. C. Southern Baptist Assembly. I. Title.

MIDDLETON, Robert Lee, 1894- 286.175
A dream come true; a history, Ridgecrest Baptist Assembly, 50th anniversary, 1907-1957. Nashville, Convention Press [1957] 72p. illus. 23cm. [BX6476.R5M5] 57-10107
1. Ridgecrest, N. C. Southern Baptist Assembly. I. Title.

Ridgefield, Conn. First Congregational Church.

HANSON, Muriel R 285'.8758'231
A history of the First Congregational Church of Ridgefield 1712-1962 [Ridgefield, Conn., First Congregational Church, 1962] 53 p. illus. 26 cm. [BX7255.R49F5] 63-412
1. Ridgefield, Conn. First Congregational Church. I. Title.

Ridgewood, N.J.—History.

OLD Paramus Reformed Church, Ridgewood, N.J. Historical Committee. 285'.7749'21
Old Paramus Reformed Church in Ridgewood, New Jersey, the years 1725-1975 / [prepared for the 250th anniversary of Old Paramus Reformed Church by the Historical Committee]. Ridgewood, N.J. : Old Paramus Reformed Church, c1975. 64 p. : ill., facsims. ; 29 cm. Cover title. [BX9531.R55O4 1975] 75-322483
1. Old Paramus Reformed Church, Ridgewood, N.J. 2. Ridgewood, N.J.—History.

Ridley, Nicholas, Bp. of London, 1500?-1555.

RIDLEY, Jasper Godwin. 922.342
Nicholas Ridley, a biography. London, New York, Longmans, Green [1957] 453p. illus. 21cm. Includes bibliography. [BX5199.R5R53] 57-13904
1. Ridley, Nicholas, Bp. of London, 1500?-1555. I. Title.

Ridpath, George, d. 1726.

THE Stage acquitted. 792'.013
Anonymous. With a pref. for the Garland ed. by Arthur Freeman. New York, Garland Pub., 1972. 185 p. 18 cm. (The English stage: attack and defense, 1577-1730) Reprint of the 1699 ed. "Wing S5160." [PN2047.R52S7 1972] 77-170448 ISBN 0-8240-0614-3 22.00
1. Ridpath, George, d. 1726. The stage condemn'd. 2. Theater—Moral and religious aspects. 3. Theater—England. I. Title. II. Series.

Rienzo, Cola di, d. 1354.

ADAMS, William Henry Davenport, 1828-1891. 920
Wrecked lives; or, Men who have failed. By W.H. Davenport Adams. 1st series. Published under the direction of the Committee of general literature and education appointed by the Society for promoting Christian knowledge. London, Society for promoting Christian knowledge; New York, Pott, Young and co., 1880. vi p., 1 l., 365 p. 19 cm. "Authorities" at end of each chapter. Contents.Cola di Rienzi.--Thomas Wolsey.--Dean Swift--Richard Savage.-- Thomas Chatterton. [CT105.A26] 3-9176
1. Rienzo, Cola di, d. 1354. 2. Wolsey, Thomas, cardinal, 1475?-1530. 3. Swift, Jonathan, 1667-1745. 4. Savage, Richard. 1698-1743. 5. Chatterton, Thomas, 1752-1770. 6. Biography. I. Society for promoting Christian knowledge. General literature committee. II. Title.

Rifredo, Italy. Santa Marie (Cistercian convent)

BOYD, Catherine Evangeline, 1904- 271.97
A Cistercian nunnery in medieval Italy; the story of Rifreddo in Saluzzo, 1220-1300, by Catherine E. Boyd ... Cambridge, Harvard university press, 1943. 5 p. l., [3]-189 p. front. (map) 20 1/2 cm. (Half-title: Harvard historical monographs. XVIII) Bibliography: p. [173]-180. [BX4330.C5B6] A 43
1. Rifreddo, Italy. Santa Marie (Cistercian convent) 2. Cistercians in Italy. I. Title.

Right and wrong.

BODLEY, Homer S. 268.
The fourth "R", the forgotten factor in education. by Homer S. Bodley. New York, Chicago [etc.] Fleming H. Revell company [c1923] 271 p. 21 cm. "Believing that ... the fourth 'R', righteousness, or right relations. should find a place in our school system, the writer has undertaken to point out some of the higher ideals of life which should be taught without infringing upon any creed or sect."--Pref. [BV1475.B55] 23-18008
I. Title.

FIELD, David, 1936- 248'.4
Free to do right. Downers Grove, Ill., InterVarsity Press [1973] 111 p. 18 cm. Includes bibliographical references. [BJ1411.F53 1973] 73-81577 ISBN 0-87784-549-2 1.25
1. Right and wrong. I. Title.

GRAEBNER, Theodore Conrad, 1876-1950.
The borderland of right and wrong. Revised by the Literature Board, 1956. St. Louis, Concordia [1957] xiii, 185 p. 64-23325
I. Title.

Right to die—Law and legislation—United States—Addresses, essays, lectures.

LEGAL and ethical aspects of treating critically and terminally ill patients / edited by A. Edward Doudera, J. Douglas Peters. Ann Arbor, Mich. : Published in cooperation with the American Society of Law and Medicine [by] AUPHA Press, 1982. xiv, 344 p. ; 24 cm. Papers derived from 4 conferences sponsored by the American Society of Law and Medicine, and held in Detroit (Nov. 1979), Los Angeles (Apr. 1980), Minneapolis (May 1980), and Chicago (Oct. 1980) Includes index. Bibliography: p. [334]-339. [KF3827.E87L43 1982] 347.304419 19 81-20523 ISBN 0-914904-76-0 : 27.00 344.73'0419
1. Right to die—Law and legislation—United States—Addresses, essays, lectures. 2. Terminal care—Law and legislation—United States—Addresses, essays, lectures. 3. Right to die—Addresses, essays, lectures. 4. Terminal care—Moral and ethical aspects—Addresses, essays,

lectures. I. Doudera, A. Edward, 1949- II. Peters, J. Douglas, 1948- III. American Society of Law and Medicine.
Publisher's address: 1021 E. Huron St., Univ. of Michigan, Ann Arbor, MI 48109

Right to die—Law and legislation—United States—Bibliography.

COOK, Earleen H. 016.34473'0419
Euthanasia and the right to die : the medical and legal viewpoint / Earleen H. Cook. Monticello, Ill. : Vance Bibliographies, [1982] 36 p. ; 28 cm. (Public administration series—bibliography,) ISSN 0193-970X ; P-961) Cover title. "May 1982." [KF3827.E87A123 1982] 016.347304419 19 82-157266 5.25 (pbk.)
1. Right to die—Law and legislation—United States—Bibliography. 2. Euthanasia—United States—Bibliography. 3. Right to die—Bibliography. I. Title. II. Series.

Righter, Chester Newell, 1824-1856.

PRIME, Samuel Irenaeus, 1812-1885. 220
The Bible in the Levant; or, The life and letters of the Rev. C. N. Righter, agent of the American Bible society in the Levant. By Samuel Irenaeus Prime. New York, Sheldon & company; Boston, Gould & Lincoln, 1859. vi, [7]-336 p. front. (port.) 18 cm. [BV2369.P7] 15-16187
1. Righter, Chester Newell, 1824-1856. I. Title.

Riley, James, 1843-

RILEY, James Whitcomb, 1849-1916.
The prayer perfect, and other poems, by James Whitcomb Riley; with pictures by Will Vawter. Indianapolis, The Bobbs-Merrill company [c1912] 1 p. l., 7-29 p. front., illus. 19 cm. [PS2704.P7 1912] 12-24024 0.50
I. Title.

VLEREBOME, Abraham, 1843- 133.
The life of James Riley, commonly called Farmer Riley, one of the world's greatest psychics; a complete and accurate account of the wonderful manifestations produced through his mediumship, at his home, and in different parts of the United States. And the author's twenty-two years' experience in the investigation of psychic phenomens. A. Vlerebome, author. [Akron, O., The Werner company, c1911] 5 p. l., 9-296 p. pl., 2 port. (incl. front.) 20 cm. $1.00. [BF1283.R6V6] 11-5722
1. Riley, James, 1843- 2. Spiritualism. I. Title.

Rileyville, Va. Rileyville Baptist Church.

BALDWIN, Judson D
The story of a village church in a village of churches. Rileyville, Va., Rileyville Baptist Church, 1960. 56 p. 21 cm. Cover title. NUC64
1. Rileyville, Va. Rileyville Baptist Church. I. Title.

Rinker, Rosalind.

RINKER, Rosalind. 283'.092'4 B
Ask me, Lord, I want to say yes / Rosalind Rinker. Plainfield, N.J. : Logos International, c1979. 105 p. ; 18 cm. Bibliography: p. 105. [BX5995.R5A32] 79-53030 ISBN 0-88270-381-1 pbk. : 1.95
1. Rinker, Rosalind. 2. Episcopalians in the United States—Biography. 3. Baptism in the Holy Spirit. I. Title.

RINKER, Rosalind. 248'.092'4 B
Within the circle. Grand Rapids, Zondervan Pub. House [1973] 120 p. illus. 21 cm. Bibliography: p. [119]-120. [BV3427.R526A33] 72-83867 1.95
1. Rinker, Rosalind. 2. Christian life—1960- I. Title.

Rinzai (Sect)—Addresses, essays, lectures.

THE Original face : 294.3'927
an anthology of Rinzai Zen / translated and edited by Thomas Cleary. 1st ed. New York : Grove Press : distributed by Random House, 1978. 158 p. ; 20 cm. [BQ9366.O74] 77-91354 ISBN 0-394-17038-5 : 4.95
1. Rinzai (Sect)—Addresses, essays, lectures. I. Cleary, Thomas.

Rinzai (Sect)—Controversial literature.

HAU Hoo. 294.3'927
The sound of the one hand : 281 Zen koans with answers / translated, with a commentary by Yoel Hoffmann ; foreword by Zen Master Hirano Sojo ; introd. by Ben-Ami Scharfstein. New York : Basic Books, c1975. p. cm. Translation of Gendai soji Zen hyoron. Bibliography: p. [BQ9369.H3813] 75-7274 ISBN 0-465-08078-2 : 10.00 ISBN 0-465-08079-0 pbk. : 4.95
1. Rinzai (Sect)—Controversial literature. I. Hoffmann, Yoel. II. Title.

Rio Grande college, Rio Grande, O.

HOUF, Horace Thomas, 1889- 261
Real living and God's help, by Horace Thomas Houf... Rio Grande, O., Rio Grande college, 1925. 52 p. 23 1/2 cm. [BR85.H58] 27-10774
1. Rio Grande college, Rio Grande, O. I. Title.

Riordan, Patrick William, Abp., 1841-1914.

GAFFEY, James P. 282'.092'4 B
Citizen of no mean city: Archbishop Patrick Riordan of San Francisco (1841-1914) [by] James P. Gaffey. [Washington, Catholic University of America Press, 1974] p. cm. Includes bibliographical references. [BX4705.R555G33] 74-5435 ISBN 0-8132-0537-9
1. Riordan, Patrick William, Abp., 1841-1914. I. Title.

Riou, Roger, 1909-

RIOU, Roger, 1909- 266'.2'0924 B
The island of my life : from petty crime to priestly mission / Roger Riou ; translated from the French by Martin Sokolinsky. New York : Delacorte Press, [1975] 300 p., [7] leaves of plates : ill. ; 22 cm. [R722.R56A3313] 75-4980 ISBN 0-440-04559-2 : 7.95
1. Riou, Roger, 1909- 2. Missionaries, Medical—Correspondence, reminiscences, etc. 3. Missions, Medical—Haiti. I. Title.

Rippetoe, Karen.

RIPPETOE, Odessa B., 1913- 248.8'6'0924 B
While heaven waited, by Odessa B. Rippetoe. Philadelphia, Dorrance [1970] 233 p. ports. 22 cm. [RC263.R5] 77-83701 ISBN 0-8059-1378-5 5.95
1. Rippetoe, Karen. 2. Cancer—Personal narratives. I. Title.

Rishell, Charles Wesley, 1850-1908, tr.

SOHM, Rudolf, 1841-
A history of Christianity. From the German of Prof. Rudolph Sohm ... by Charles W. Rishell, M. A. With revisions, notes, and additions. Cincinnati, Cranston & Stowe; New York, Hunt & Eaton, 1891. 1 p. l., 370 p. 18 cm. 14-6791
1. Rishell, Charles Wesley, 1850-1908, tr. I. Title.

Rita da Cascia, Saint, 1381?-1457.

THE Augustinian manual of 264.
Saint Rita of Cascia, O.S.A. (revised) with a short life of the saint, compiled from approved sources by Augustinian fathers attached to Saint Rita's shrine, Chicago, Illinois. Chicago, Ill., D. B. Hansen & sons, 1926. cix, 351, 168 p. front. 12 cm. [BX2110.A8] 26-12881
1. Rita da Cascia, Saint, 1381?-1457. I. Augustiniana, Chicago. St. Rita's shrine. II. Catholic churhc. Liturgy and ritual.

THE Augustinian manual of Saint Rita of Cascia, O.S.A.; with a short life of the saint, comp. from approved souves by Augustinian fathers attached to Saint Rita's shrine Chicago, Illinois. Chicago, Ill., The Augustinian community, 1913. 4 p. l., v-lvii, [1] 322, 119, [7] p. front. 12 cm. 13-12886 1.50
I. Augustinians, Chicago. St. Rita's shrine. II. Catholic church. Liturgy and ritual.

CORCORAN, Matthew J. 922.
Our own St. Rita; a life of the saint of the impossible, by Rev. M. J. Corcoran, O. S. A. New York, Cincinnati [etc.] Benzinger brothers, 1919. vii, 9-187 p. front., plates, ports. 19 cm. [BX4700.R5C6] 19-9258
1. Rita da Cascia, Saint, 1381-1457. I. Title.

MOSIER, Bernardine, Brother, 1908- 922.245
Saint of the impossible; a story of St. Rita. Illus. by Brother Bernard Howard. Notre Dame, Ind., Dujarie Press [1953] 93p. illus. 24cm. [BX4700.R5M6] 53-34339
1. Rita da Cascia, Saint, 1381?-1457. I. Title.

SICARDO, Jose, 1643-1715. 922.
Life of Sister St. Rita of Cascia, of the Order of St. Augustine, Advocate of the impossible. Model of maidens, wives, mothers, widows and nuns. Translated by the Rev. Dan J. Murphy, O.S.A., from the Spanish of Rev. Joseph Sicardo, O.S.A. Chicago, D. B. Hansen & sons [c1916] vi, 9-176 p. front. (port.) 19 1/2 cm. [BX4700.R5S53] 16-13629
1. Rita da Cascia, Saint, 1381?-1457. I. Murphy, Daniel Joseph, 1856-1919, tr. II. Title.

SPENS, Willy de, 1911- 922.245
Saint Rita. Translated by Julie Kerman. [1st ed.] Garden City, N.Y., Hanover House [1962] 144 p. 22 cm. Includes bibliography. [BX4700.R5S73] 62-8295
1. Rita de Cascia, Saint, 1381?-1457. I. Title.

Rita da Cascia, Saint, 1381?-1457—Prayer-books and devotions—English.

CATHOLIC church. Liturgy and ritual. Augustinian.
The Augustinian manual of Saint Rita of Cascia, O.S.A. (revised) with a short life of the saint, compiled from approved sources by Augustinian fathers attached to Saint Rita's shrine, Chicago, Illinois. Chicago, Ill., D. B. Hansen & sons, 1926. ix, 351, 168 p. front. 12 cm. [BX2167.R5A3 1926] 26-12881
1. Rita da Cascia, Saint, 1381?-1457—Prayer-books and devotions—English. I. Augustinians, Chicago. St. Rita's shrine. II. Title.

KLARMANN, Andrew F.
Saint Rita's treasury; a book of pious exercises in the spirit of St. Rita of Cascia, by Rev. Andrew Klarmann, A. M. Ratisbon, New York [etc.] F. Pustet & co., 1913. 270 p. front. 14 cm. 13-18729 1.25
I. Title.

MCGRATH, Thomas Sylvester, 1878-
Little manual of St. Rita; prayers and devotions, with the story of her life, by Rev. Thomas S. McGrath. New York, Cincinnati [etc.] Benziger brothers, 1915. 302 p. front., plates. 13 1/2 cm. 15-14380
I. Title.

Ritchie, George G., 1923-

FORTESCUE, Adrian, 1874-1923.
The ceremonies of the Roman rite described [by] Adrian Fortescue & J.B. O'Connell. With a pref. by the Archibishop of Birmingham and an appendix on The ceremonies of the ritual in the U.S.A. by Frederick R. McManus. [12th rev. ed.] Westminster, Md., Newman Press, 1962. 423 p. illus. 64-64487
I. Title.

RITCHIE, George G., 1923- 248'.2'0924 B
Return from tomorrow / George G. Ritchie, with Elizabeth Sherrill. Waco, Tex. : Chosen Books : distributed by Word Books, c1978. 124 p. ; 21 cm. [BR1725.R58A37] 77-27543 ISBN 0-912376-23-6 : 5.95
1. Ritchie, George G., 1923- 2. Christian biography—United States. 3. Psychiatrists—United States—Biography. 4. Death, Apparent—Case studies. I. Sherrill, Elizabeth, joint author. II. Title.

Rites and ceremonies.

BLACK, Algernon David, 1900- 301.2'1
Without burnt offerings; ceremonies of humanism [by] Algernon D. Black. New York, Viking Press [1974] xxi, 231 p. 22 cm. [BL600.B55 1974] 73-15020 ISBN 0-670-77676-9 10.00
1. Rites and ceremonies. I. Title.

BRIGHAM, Amariah, 1798-1849. 291.3'8
Observations on the influence of religion upon the health and physical welfare of mankind. New York, Arno Press, 1973 [c1835] 331 p. 22 cm. (Mental illness and social policy: the American experience) Reprint of the ed. published by Marsh, Capen & Lyon, Boston. Includes bibliographical references. [BL65.M4B7 1973] 73-2389 ISBN 0-405-05197-2 15.00
1. Rites and ceremonies. 2. Nervous system—Hygiene. 3. Revivals. I. Title. II. Series.

BRIGHAM, Amariah, 1798-1849. 200.
Observations on the influence of religion upon the health and physical welfare of mankind. By Amariah Brigham, M.D. Boston, Marsh, Capen & Lyon, 1835. xxiv, [25]-331 p. 19 1/2 cm. [BL65.H4B7] 30-9664
1. Rites and ceremonies. 2. Nervous system—Hygiene. 3. Revivals. I. Title. II. Title: Health, Influence of religion upon the.

BURDICK, Lewis Dayton. 264
Foundation rites with some kindred ceremonies; a contribution to the study of beliefs, customs, and legends connected with buildings, locations, landmarks, etc., etc., by Lewis Dayton Burdick... New York [etc.] The Abbey press, 1901. 258 p. 20 1/2 cm. Bibliography: p. 233-238. [BL600.B8] 1-31705
1. Rites and ceremonies. 2. Sacrifice. I. Title.

BURRELL, Percy Jewett, 1877- 791.6
Watchers of the world, a dramatic ritual in honor of the living who serve and in tribute to the fallen in the cause of the United nations, a ceremonial for dedication of service flag, honor roll and for memorial day, by Percy Jewett Burrell. Boston, Mass., Los Angeles, Calif., Baker's plays [1944] 32 p. incl. front. 21 1/2 cm. [BV199.P3B8] 44-36901
I. Title.

COOKE, Allan Worthington, 1872- 264
Sacraments and society; a study of the origin and value of rites in religion [by] Allan Worthington Cooke. Boston, B. Badger [c1924] 243 p. 22 cm. "The manuscript was prepared in June, 1915, and submitted to the faculty of the Graduate school of arts and literature of the University of Chicago in candidacy for the degree of doctor of philosophy."--Pref. [BL600.C6] 25-9798
1. Rites and ceremonies. 2. Sacraments. I. Title.

FORSE, Edward John George. 208.1
Ceremonial curiosities and queer sights in foreign churches; ecclesiological and other notes from the travel diaries of Edward J. G. Forse ... with twenty pen-and-ink sketches by the author and a foreword by the Lord Bishop of Winchester ... London, The Faith press, ltd.; New York & Milwaukee, Morehouse publishing co., [c1938] vii [1], 176 p. front. (port.) illus. 19 cm. "First published, January, 1938." [BR735.F6] 38-23356
1. Rites and ceremonies. 2. Churches. 3. Voyages and travels. I. Title.

FOSTER, Steven, 1938(Aug.13)- 291.3'8
The book of the vision quest / by Steven Foster with Meredith Eaton Little. Covelo, Calif. : Island Press, [1980] p. cm. [BL600.F67] 19 80-22810 ISBN 0-933280-03-3 : 8.00
1. Rites and ceremonies. 2. Visions. I. Little, Meredith Eaton, 1951- joint author. II. Title.

FRERE, Walter Howard, bp. of Truro, 1863-1938. 264
The principles of religious ceremonial; by the Rev. Walter Howard Frere ... London, New York [etc.] Longmans, Green, and co., 1906. xii, 324 p. 20 cm. (Half-title: The Oxford library of practical theology; ed. by the Rev. W. C. E. Newbolt ... and the Rev. Darwell Stone ...) [BV175.F8] W 6
1. Rites and ceremonies. I. Title.

GIANT oaks.
Ritual of the Giant oaks; containing the opening and closing ceremonies, degree work, anniversary, instituting, and installation ceremonies, unveiling of monuments, funeral and burial services. Kansas City, Mo., Hailman printing co., 1899. 61 p. diagr. 8 degree. Jan
I. Title.

GIRARD, Rene, 1923- 291.3'4
Violence and the sacred / Rene Girard ; translated by Patrick Gregory. Baltimore : Johns Hopkins University Press, c1977. vii, 333 p. ; 24 cm. Translation of La violence et le sacre. Includes index. Bibliography: p. 319-323. [BL600.G5413] 77-4539 ISBN 0-8018-1963-6 : 17.50
1. Rites and ceremonies. 2. Sacrifice. I. Title.

GIRARD, Rene, 1923- 291.3'4
Violence and the sacred / Rene Girard ; translated by Patrick Gregory. Baltimore : Johns Hopkins University Press, c1977. vii, 333 p. ; 24 cm. Translation of La violence et le sacre. Includes index. Bibliography: p. 319-323. [BL600.G5413] 77-4539 ISBN 0-8018-1963-6 : 17.50
1. Rites and ceremonies. 2. Sacrifice. I. Title.

ISERLOH, William O. 133
Exoteric philosophy presents the rhythmic rite, by William O. Iserloh. Los Angeles, Calif., W. O. Iserloh, 1940. xiii, [1] 105, [1] p. 23 cm. "First edition." [B68.18] 40-8736
I. Title. II. Title: Rhythmic rite of exoteric philosophy presents the.

JAMES, Edwin Oliver, 1886- 264
Christian myth and ritual; a historical study [Gloucester, Mass., P. Smith, 1965] xv, 345p. 21cm. (Living age bks., Meridian bk., La43 rebound) Bibl. [BV175.J3] 4.25
1. Rites and ceremonies. 2. Christianity and other religions. 3. Catholic Church. Liturgy and ritual—History. I. Title.

OLSSON, Karl A. 248'.4
When the road bends : a book about the pain and joy of passage / Karl A. Olsson. Minneapolis : Augsburg Pub. House, c1979. 234 p. ; 20 cm. Includes bibliographical references. [BV178.O47] 78-66948 ISBN 0-8066-1695-4 : 7.95 ISBN 0-8066-1674-1 (pbk.) : 4.95
1. Rites and ceremonies. 2. Christian life—1960- I. Title.

ORDER American plowmen.
Ritual for the use of all councils ... containing opening and closing ceremonies, gleaner, plowmen and plowmen's amplified degrees. [Logansport, Ind.] 1900. 67 p. 8 degrees. Nov
I. Title.

REIK, Theodor, 1888- 291.37
Ritual; psycho-analytic studies, by Theodor Reik; with a preface by Sigm. Freud; translated from the second edition by Douglas Bryan. New York, W. W. Norton & Company, inc. [1931] 1 p. l., 5-307 p. 23 1/2 cm. Printed in Great Britain. [GN473.R4] 32-117
1. Rites and ceremonies. 2. Jews—Rites and ceremonies. 3. Psychoanalysis. I. Bryan, Douglas Tr. II. Title.

REIK, Theodor, 1888-1969. 296.4'01'9
Ritual : psycho-analytic studies / by Theodor Reik ; with a preface by Sigm. Freud ; translated from the 2d German ed. by Douglas Bryan. Westport, Conn. : Greenwood Press, 1975, c1946. 367 p. ; 22 cm. At head of title: The psychological problems of religion, I. Translation of Probleme der Religionspsychologie, v. 1. Reprint of the ed. published by Farrar, Straus, New York. Includes bibliographical references and index. [GN473.R4 1975] 73-2645 ISBN 0-8371-6814-7 lib.bdg. : 18.25
1. Jews—Rites and ceremonies. 2. Rites and ceremonies. 3. Psychoanalysis. I. Title.

Rites and ceremonies—Addresses, essays, lectures.

LITURGY and human passage / 265
edited by David Power and Luis Maldonado. New York : Seabury Press, 1979. viii, 128 p. ; 23 cm. (Concilium: religion in the seventies ; 112) "A Crossroad book." Includes bibliographical references. [BV178.L57] 78-66050 pbk. : 4.95.
1. Rites and ceremonies—Addresses, essays, lectures. 2. Liturgics—Catholic Church—Addresses, essays, lectures. I. Power, David Noel. II. Maldonado Arenas, Luis, 1930- III. Series: Concilium (New York) ; 112.

Rites and ceremonies—Africa, Sub-Saharan.

JULES-ROSETTE, Bennetta. 269'.2
African apostles : ritual and conversion in the Church of John Maranke / Bennetta Jules-Rosette. Ithaca, N.Y. : Cornell University Press, 1975. 302 p. : ill. ; 22 cm. (Symbol, myth, and ritual series) Includes index. Bibliography: p. [290]-298. [BX6194.A63J84] 75-8437 ISBN 0-8014-0846-6
1. Apostolic Church of John Maranke. 2. Jules-Rosette, Bennetta. 3. Rites and ceremonies—Africa, Sub-Saharan. I. Title.

Rites and ceremonies—India.

BHATTACHARYYA, Narendra Nath. 294
Ancient Indian rituals and their social contents / Narendra Nath Bhattacharyya. Delhi : Manohar Book Service, 1975. xvi, 184 p. ; 23 cm. Includes index. Bibliography: p. [165]-176. [BL2003.B4] 75-903622 12.75
1. Rites and ceremonies—India. 2. Cultus—India. 3. India—Religion. I. Title.
Dist. by Rowman & Littlefield

GRIHYASUTRAS. 274.1
The Grihya-sutras, rules of Vedic domestic ceremonies, translated by Hermann Oldenberg... Oxford, The Clarendon press, 1886-92. 2 v. 23 cm. (Added t.-p.: The sacred books of the East ... vol. xxix-xxx) Each text preceded by introduction. Contents.--pt. i. Sankhayana-Grihya-sutra. Asvalayana-Grihya-sutra. Paraskara-Grihya-sutra. Khadira-Grihyra-sutra.--pt. ii. Gobhila-Grihya-sutra. Hiranyajesin-Grihya-sutra. Apastamba-Grihyra-sutra. Apastamba's Yagna-Paribhasha-sutras, translated by F. Max Muller. [BL1010.S3] 290.8 32-34339
1. Rites and ceremonies—India. I. Oldenberg, Hermann, 1854-1920, ed. and tr. II. Muller, Friedrich Max, 1853-1900, ed. and tr. III. Title.

Rites and ceremonies—Indonesia—Bali (Island)

MERSHON, Katharane Edson. 294.5'38'095986
Seven plus seven; mysterious life-rituals in Bali. [1st ed.] Illustrated with photos. New York, Vantage Press [1971] 368 p. illus. 21 cm. [GN473.M4] 79-32163 7.50
1. Rites and ceremonies—Indonesia—Bali (Island) 2. Bali (Island)—Social life and customs. I. Title.

Rites and ceremonies—New Guinea—Sepik Valley.

NEWTON, Douglas, 1920- 299'.9
Crocodile and cassowary; religious art of the upper Sepik River, New Guinea. New York, Museum of Primitive Art; distributed by New York Graphic Society, Greenwich, Conn., 1971. 112 p. illus., map. 22 x 27 cm. Bibliography: p. 111-112. [GN473.N48] 70-145914 ISBN 0-912294-42-6 12.95
1. Rites and ceremonies—New Guinea—Sepik Valley. 2. Art—Sepik Valley. 3. Ethnology—New Guinea—Sepik Valley. I. Title.

Rites and ceremonies—Palestine.

LUKE, Harry Charles Joseph, Sir 1884- 275.69
Ceremonies at the holy places, by Harry Charles Luke ... with illustrations from paintings by Philippa A. F. Stephenson, O.B.E. London. The Faith press, ltd.; Milwaukee, The Morehouse publishing co. [1932] 3 p. l., 74 p. col. front., illus. (maps, plan, music) col. plates. 19 cm. "First published. October, 1932." Descriptions originally "scattered through several volumes and periodical publications." cf. Pref. [Name originally: Harry Charles Joseph Lukach] Contents.The Christian communities in the Holy Sepulchre.--The Church of the Holy Sepulchre and the holy fire.--Easter in Jerusalem.--Christmas in Bethlehem.--The Samaritans and their passover.--The "great burnings" of Meiron. [BL2340.L77] (231.73) 33-21606
1. Rites and ceremonies—Palestine. 2. Fasts and feasts. 3. Shrines—Palestine. 4. Jerusalem. Church of the Holy Sepulcher. I. Title.

Ritschl, Albrecht Benjamin, 1822-1889.

HEFNER, Philip J 230.0924
Faith and the vitalities of history: a theological study based on the work of Albrecht Ritschl [by] Philip Hefner. [1st ed.] New York, Harper & Row [1966] xi, 192 p. port. 22 cm. (Makers of modern theology) Bibliography: p. 187-190. [BX4827.R5H4] 66-15038
1. Ritschl, Albrecht Benjamin, 1822-1889. 2. Theology — Methodology. 3. History (Theology) 4. Theology — 20th cent. I. Title.

HERRMANN, Wilhelm, 1846-1922. 248
Faith and morals. i.--Faith as Ritschl defined it. ii.--The moral law as understood in Romanism and Protestantism; by Wilhelm Herrmann ... tr. from the German by Donald Matheson, M. A., and Robert W. Stewart ... London, Williams & Norgate; New York, G. P. Putnam's sons, 1904. xii, 415 p. 19 cm. (Half-title: Crown theological library, vol. vi) "Appendix: Two replies by Adolff and Mausbach contrasted": p. 194-407. [BT771.H4] 5-10564
1. Ritschl, Albrecht Benjamin, 1822-1889. 2. Adolff, Joseph, 1865—Katholische moral und sittlichkelt. 3. Mausbach, Joseph, 1861-1981. Die katholische moral. 4. Faith. 5. Ethics. I. Matheson, Donald, tr. II. Stewart, Robert W., joint tr. III. Title.

MUELLER, David Livingstone, 1929- 230.4'0924
An introduction to the theology of Albrecht Ritschl, by David L. Mueller. Philadelphia, Westminster Press [1969] 214 p. 24 cm. Bibliographical references included in "Notes" (p. 181-214) [BX4827.R5M8] 77-80978 ISBN 6-642-08738- 8.50
1. Ritschl, Albrecht Benjamin, 1822-1889. I. Title.

ORR, James, 1814-1913.
Ritschlianism; expository and critical essays, by James Orr... London, Hodder and Stoughton, 1903. Cleveland, Bell & Howell [1967] xii, 283, [1] p. 22 cm. Reproduced by Duopage Process. 68-58606
1. Ritschl, Albrecht Benjamin, 1822-1889. 2. Ritschlianism. I. Title.

RICHMOND, James, 1931- 230'.4'0924
Ritschl, a reappraisal : a study in systematic theology / [by] James Richmond. London ; New York : Collins, 1978. 319 p. ; 22 cm. Includes bibliographical references and index. [BX4827.R5R45 1978] 78-69701 ISBN 0-529-05622-4 (U.S.) : 18.95 (U.S.)
1. Ritschl, Albrecht Benjamin, 1822-1889. I. Title.

RITSCHL, Albrecht Benjamin, 1822-1889. 230'.4
Three essays. Translated and with an introd. by Philip Hefner. Philadelphia, Fortress Press [1972] 301 p. 24 cm. Contents.Contents.—Theology and metaphysics.—"Prolegomena" to The history of pietism.—Instruction in the Christian religion. Includes bibliographical references. [B85.R58] 72-75654 ISBN 0-8006-0224-2 10.50
1. Ritschl, Albrecht Benjamin, 1822-1889. 2. Pietism. 3. Christianity—Philosophy. 4. Theological, Doctrinal. I. Title.

SCHWAB, Laurence Harry, 1857-1911. 231.7
The kingdom of God; an essay in theology ... By Laurence Henry Schwab ... New York, E. P. Dutton and company, 1897. xii, 276 p. 20 cm. (The Bohlen lectures, 1897) "The main trend of thought and the method are Ritzchlian."--Pref. [BT94.S35] 40-20166
1. Ritschi, Albrecht Benjamin, 1822-1889. 2. Kingdom of God. 3. Christian life. 4. Theology, Doctrinal. I. Title.

SCOTT, Hugh McDonald, 1848-1909. 238.1
Origin and development of the Nicene theology, with some reference to the Ritschlian view of theology and history of doctrine ... By Hugh M. Scott ... Chicago, Chicago theological seminary press, 1896. 2 p. l., ix, 5-390 p. 23 cm. Lectures delivered on the L. P. Stone foundation at Princeton theological seminary, in January, 1896. [BT999.S4] 38-31387
1. Ritschi, Albrecht Benjamin, 1822-1889. 2. Jesus Christ—History of doctrines. 3. Nicene creed. 4. Theology, Doctrinal—Hist. I. Title.

SWING, Albert Temple, 1849-1925. 260
The theology of Albrecht Ritschl, by Albert Temple Swing, A.M... together with Instruction in the Christian religion by Albrecht Ritschl; translated by permission from the 4th German ed., by Alice Mead Swing, A.B. New York, London [etc.] Longmans, Green and co., 1901. xiv, 296 p. 19 1/2 cm. Bibliography: p. xiii-xiv. [BT75.R6S8] 1-7262
1. Ritschl, Albrecht Benjamin, 1822-1889. I. Ritschl, Albrecht Benjamin, 1822-1889. II. Swing, Alice Mead, tr. III. Title.

WENLEY, Robert Mark, 1861-1929.
Contemporary theology and theism, by R. M. Wenley ... New York, C. Scribner's sons, 1897. x p., 1 l., 202 p. 19 1/2 cm. [BT28.W4] 45-40060
1. Ritschi, Albrecht Benjamin, 1822-1889. 2. Theology, Doctrinal—Hist. 3. Theism. I. Title.

Ritschlianism.

ORR, James, 1814-1913.
Ritschlianism; expository and critical essays, by James Orr... London, Hodder and Stoughton, 1903. Cleveland, Bell & Howell [1967] xii, 283, [1] p. 22 cm. Reproduced by Duopage Process. 68-58606
1. Ritschl, Albrecht Benjamin, 1822-1889. 2. Ritschlianism. I. Title.

Rittman, Ohio—Biography.

LEHMAN, James O. 289.7'771'61
Crosswinds : from Switzerland to Crown Hill / James O. Lehman. Rittman, Ohio : Crown Hill Mennonite Church, 1975. 112 p. : ill. ; 22 cm. Includes bibliographical references and index. [BX8131.R573L43] 75-323612
1. Crown Hill Mennonite Church, Rittman, Ohio. 2. Rittman, Ohio—Biography. I. Crown Hill Mennonite Church, Rittman, Ohio. II. Title.

Ritual.

BURNETT, Charles Phillip Augustus, 1849-
A ritual and ceremonial commentary on the occasional offices of holy baptism, matrimony, penance, communion of the

sick, and extreme unction, by the Rev. Charles P. A. Burnett ... New York [etc.] Longmans, Green, and co., 1907. xi, 288 p. 20 1/2 cm. 7-40005
I. Title.

FISK, Stephen.
The ritual and manual of the Temperance temple, by Stephen Fisk, LL. D. Jacksonville, Fla., The Vance-Garrett printing co., 1893. 1 p. l., 54 p., 2 l. front. (port.) 22 cm. 6-2868
I. Title.

FRATERNITY sons of Osiris. 299
Ritual, Second temple, Fraternity sons of Osiris [Allentown? Pa.] The Supreme exalted temple, c1909. 1 p. l., 70. [2] p. illus. 16 cm. [BF1613.R607] 10-1674
I. Title.

FRATERNITY sons of Osiris. 299
Ritual. Temple of "Osiris-Isis." Eighteenth to twenty-first degree, eighth to eleven degree of an arcane fraternity which has been in existence 2000 B. C., and which is now teaching humanity the old truth ... Issued under authority of the Supreme exalted temple. By instructions of the Royal fraternity association. [Allentown, Pa., The Philosophical publishing co., c1909] 65 p. 16 cm. [BF1623.R6075] 10-1676
I. Title.

GAY, Volney Patrick. 200'.1'9
Freud on ritual ; reconstruction and critique / Volney Patrick Gay. Missoula, Mont. : Scholars Press, c1979. ix, 212 p. ; 23 cm. (Dissertation series - American Academy of Religion ; no. 26 ISSN 0145-272Xs) Originally presented as the author's thesis, University of Chicago, 1976. Bibliography: p. 193-207. [BL600.G36 1979] 79-11385 ISBN 0-89130-282-4 : 12.00 ISBN 0-89130-282-4 pbk. : 7.50
1. Freud, Sigmund, 1856-1939. 2. Ritual. I. Title. II. Series: American Academy of Religion. Dissertation series — American Academy of Religion ; 26.

JEWS. Liturgy and ritual.
The American Jewish ritual; as instituted in Temple Israel, Brooklyn, by Raphael D'C. Lewin. New York L. H. Frank, 1870 vii, 273 p. 20 cm. Hebrew and English. [BM665.A3B7 1870] 51-50914
I. Lewin, Raphael De Cordova, 1844-1886, ed. II. Title.

KNIGHTS of the mystic chain.
Supreme lodge.
Ritual ... containing the opening and closing ceremonies, degrees of knighthood, mystery and chivalry, and installation. Adopted by the Supreme lodge, July 1900. Lynchburg, Va. [1900] 63 p. 12 degree. Nov
I. Title.

ORDER of the amaranth.
The authorized ritual of the Order of the amaranth as written by William J. Duncan ... Rev. by Committee on ritual of the Supreme council, Order of the amaranth, 1915. New York, 1918. 199, [1] p. illus. 15 cm. "Fifth edition." [HS853.5.A5 1918] 19-3693
I. Duncan, William J. II. Title.

ORDER of the amaranth.
The authorized ritual of the Order of the amaranth, inc., by Arthur H. Ziegler ... [San Francisco] 1923. 4 p. l., [11]-174 p. illus. 16 cm. On verso of t.-p.: "Edition for the states of New York and New Jersey, Series of 1923; sixth edition." Two syllabi laid in. [HS859.A7N7] 24-1843
I. Ziegler, Arthur Herman. II. Title.

ORDER of the amaranth.
The authorized ritual of the Order of the amaranth, inc., by Arthur H. Ziegler ... [San Francisco] 1923. 4 p. l., [11]-174 p. illus. 16 cm. On verso of t.-p.: Series of 1923; sixth edition. [HS859.A6A5] 24-1844
I. Ziegler, Arthur Herman. II. Title.

ORDER of the golden seal.
Ritual for use in local camps of the Order of the golden seal. [Roxbury? N. Y.] The Supreme council, 1907. 72 p. diagr. 23 cm. 7-17293
I. Title.

THE Roots of ritual. 264
Edited by James D. Shaughnessy. Grand Rapids, Mich., Eerdmans [1973] 251 p. 21 cm. Most of the contributions were first presented at a conference at the University of Notre Dame. Bibliography: p. 235-245. [BL600.R64] 72-96405 ISBN 0-8028-1509-X 3.95
1. Ritual. I. Shaughnessy, James D., ed.

SONS and daughters of Jacob of Florida and America, incorporated.
Ritual of the independent order of the Sons and daughters of Jacob of Florida and America (incorporated) headquarters at Jacksonville, Fla. Rev. ed. [Jacksonville] Hall bros. print., 1917. 75 p. 15 1/2 cm. [HS2259.J32 1917] 18-15610
I. Title.

UNITED sons of America.
Ritual for subordinate lodges ... adopted by the cabinet pursuant to section 16, article 10 of the constitution. Humboldt, Ia., Independent print, 1899. 73 p. 8°. Nov
I. Title.

Ritual murder.

LEESE, Arnold Spencer, 1878- 296
My irrelevant defence; being meditations inside gaol and out on Jewish ritual murder, by Arnold S. Leese... London, The I. F. L. printing and publishing co., 1938. Chicago, Ill., Reprinted by Pioneer news service, 1945. 3 p. l., 57 p. 21 1/2 cm. "Bibliography of works supporting the blood accusation": p. 56-57. [BM717.L35 1945] 46-29653
1. Ritual murder. I. Title.

TAGER, Aleksandr 296.0947
Semenovich, 1888-
The decay of czarism; the Beiliss trial, a contribution to the history of the political reaction during the last years of Russian czarism. Based on unpublished materials in the Russian archives, by Alexander B. [!] Tager. Translated from the Russian original. Philadelphia, The Jewish publication society of America, 1935. xxi, 297, [1] p. facsims. 23 1/2 cm. Mendel Beilis was tried in the Kiev Circuit court (Okruzhuol sud) September-October 1913, for the murder of Andrei Iuschinskif. "This book has appeared in the Russian language [Tsarakaif Russian I delo Bellsa. Moskva, 1938] The Russian edition differs from this one in two respects: first, it contains more details about the czaristic regime and the Beiliss case, and second, it has a complete list of the sources upon which this work is based."--p. 285. "Archive cases ... which served as the foundation of this book": p. 235-250. Translation of Llapcgas Pocchi Russia I delo Bellia) 35-25779
1. Beilis, Mendel, 1873-1934, defendant. 2. Iushchinskif, Andrei, 1900-1911. 3. Ritual murder. 4. Jews in Russia. 5. Jews—Persecutions. I. Jewish publication society. II. Title. III. Title: The Beiliss trial.

Ritualism.

BENTLEY, James. 261.7'0941
Ritualism and politics in victorian Britain : the attempt to legislate for belief / by James Bentley. Oxford [Eng.] ; New York : Oxford University Press, 1978. xii, 162 p. : ill. ; 23 cm. (Oxford theological monographs) Includes text of the Public worship regulation act. Includes index. Bibliography: p. [143]-154. [BX5123.B38] 77-30353 ISBN 0-19-826714-2 : 15.50
1. Ritualism. 2. Great Britain—Church history—19th century. 3. Church and state—Church of England. 4. Ecclesiastical law—Great Britain. I. Great Britain. Laws, statutes, etc. Public worship regulation act, 1874. II. Title. III. Series.

GRATACAP, Louis Pope, 1851- 264
1917.
Philosophy of ritual; apologia pro ritu, by L. P. Gratacap, A. M. New York, J. Pott & co., 1887 v p., 3 l., [3]-290 p. 20 cm. Running title: Apologia pro ritu. [BL600.G7] 31-11649
1. Ritualism. 2. Christian art and symbolism. I. Title. II. Title: Apologia pro ritu.

HENKE, Frederick Goodrich.
... A study in the psychology of ritualism ... Chicago, Ill., The University of Chicago press [1910] vii, 96 p. 24 cm. $0.50 Thesis (PH.D)--University of Chicago. Bibliography: p. 94-96. 10-25126
I. Title.

Robb, James Henry.

CARVER, Saxon Rowe.
James Robb, pioneer. Illustrated by William Moyers. Atlanta, Home Mission Board, Southern Baptist Convention [1963] 75 p. illus. 20 cm. (Southern Baptist Convention. Home Mission Board. Home Mission studies. 1964 graded series) [Supplement] Teacher's guide [by] Margaret Sharp. [Atlanta, Home Mission Board, Southern Baptist Convention, 1963] 27 p. illus. 28 cm. 65-7967
1. Robb, James Henry. 2. Southern Baptist Convention — Missions. 3. Missions, Home — Juvenile literature. I. Title. II. Series.

Robbins, Philemon, d. 1781.

[TODD, Jonathan] 1713-1791.
A defence of the doings of the reverend Consociation and association of New-Haven county, respecting Mr. Philemon Robbins of Branford: or, An answer to Mr. Robbins's Plain narrative and the remarks annexed thereunto. Wherein many of the false representations of that narrative are corrected, the plain truth is faithfully declared; and the insufficiency of the remarker's essay to vindicate Mr. Robbins is discovered. By a member of the Consociation and association of New-Haven county ... [New London] Printed for the Consociation & association of New Haven county, 1748. 1 p. l., 118 p. 19 cm. [BX7243.R6T6] 44-21104
1. Robbins, Philemon, d. 1781. A plain narrative of the proceedings of the reverend Association and consociation of New-Haven county, against the Rev. Mr. Robbins. 2. Congregational churches in Connecticut. Consociation and association of New Haven county. I. Title.

Robbins, Shawn.

ROBBINS, Shawn. 133.3'092'4 B
Ahead of myself : confessions of a professional psychic / Shawn Robbins, as told to Milton Pierce. Englewood Cliffs, N.J. : Prentice-Hall, c1980. p. cm. Includes index. [BF1027.R56A32] 19 80-20486 ISBN 0-13-004002-9 : 9.95
1. Robbins, Shawn. 2. Psychical research—United States—Biography. I. Pierce, Milton, joint author. II. Title.

Robert-Houdin, Jean Eugene, 1805-1871.

EVANS, Henry Ridgely, 1861- 920.9
A master of modern magic; the life and adventures of Robert-Houdin, by Henry Ridgely Evans ... New York, Macoy publishing company, 1932. 58 p. front., illus. (incl. facsims.) plates, ports. 24 cm. [GV1545.R7E8] 32-5010
1. Robert-Houdin, Jean Eugene, 1804-1871. 2. Conjuring. I. Title.

HOUDINI, Harry, 1874-1926. 920.
The unmasking of Robert-Houdin, by Harry Houdini. New York, The Publishers printing co., 1908. 319 p. front., illus., ports. 21 cm. [GV1545.R7H8] 8-12145
1. Robert-Houdin, Jean Eugene, 1805-1871. 2. Conjuring—Hist. I. Title.

HOUDINI, Harry, 1874-1926. 920.9
The unmasking of Robert-Houdin, by Harry Houdini. New York, The Publishers printing co., 1908. 319. v. 321-333 p. front., illus. (incl. ports. facsims.) 21 cm. "Illustrations" (v. p.) and "Index" (p. 321-333) inserted at end of this edition. [GV1545.R7H8 1908a] 33-83316
1. Robert-Houdin, Jean Eugene, 1805-1871. 2. Conjuring—Hist. I. Title.

[MANNING, William] 920.9
d.1905.
Recollections of Robert Houdin, clockmaker, electrician, conjuror. [Chicago, C. L. Burlingame & co., c1898] cover-title, 74 p. illus., port. 18 cm. Originally published as no. 24 of Privately printed opuscula. Issued to the members of the Sette of odd volumes. London, 1891. This edition omits the part devoted to the minute explanation of Houdin's electrical clock. Advertising matter: p. 30-74. Bibliography of Robert-Houdin's published works: p. 29. [GV1545.R7M3] 34-14370
1. Robert-Houdin, Jean Eugene, 1805-1871. 2. Conjuring. I. Title.

Roberts, Benjamin Titus, 1823-1893.

ZAHNISER, Clarence 922.773
Howard.
Earnest Christian; ;life and works of Benjamin Titus Roberts. [n. p., 1957] 349 p. illus. 24 cm. [BX8419.R6Z2] 57-38376
1. Roberts, Benjamin Titus, 1823-1893. I. Title.

Roberts, Bill.

DODSON, Kenneth. 248'.24 B
From make-believe to reality: the Bill Roberts story. Old Tappan, N.J., F. H. Revell Co. [1973] 154 p. 21 cm. [BV4935.R57D62] 73-8802 ISBN 0-8007-0614-5 4.95
1. Roberts, Bill. 2. Conversion. I. Title.

Roberts, Brigham Henry, 1857-1933.

MADSEN, Truman G. 289.3'3 B
Defender of the faith : the B. H. Roberts story / Truman G. Madsen. Salt Lake City, Utah : Bookcraft, c1980. xiv, 455 p., [3] leaves of plates : ill. ; 23 cm. Includes index. Bibliography: p. [441]-443. [BX8695.R58M29] 19 79-54895 ISBN 0-88494-395-X : 9.50
1. Roberts, Brigham Henry, 1857-1933. 2. Mormons and Mormonism in the United States—Biography. I. Title.

SMITH, Heman Conoman, 1850- 267.
True succession in church presidency of the Church of Jesus Christ of latter day saints. Being a reply to Elder B. H. Roberts on "Succession in the presidency of the church." By Elder Heman C. Smith... 2d ed. Lamoni, Ia., Board of publication to the Reorganized church of Jesus Christ of latter day saints, 1900. 1 p. l., 234 p. 17 1/2 cm. [BX8671.S6 1900] 38-20547
1. Roberts, Brigham Henry, 1857-1933. Succession in the presidency of the church. 2. Mormons and Mormonism—Doctrinal and controversial works. I. Title.

Roberts, Evelyn, 1917-

ROBERTS, Evelyn, 269'.2'0924 B
1917-
His darling wife, Evelyn : the autobiography of Mrs. Oral Roberts / by Evelyn Roberts. New York : Dial Press, 1976. x, 273 p., [8] leaves of plates : ill. ; 22 cm. "A Damascus House book." [BX8495.R52A3] 76-23429 ISBN 0-8037-3601-0 : 6.95
1. Roberts, Evelyn, 1917- 2. Roberts, Oral. I. Title.

ROBERTS, Evelyn, 269'.2'0924 B
1917-
His darling wife, Evelyn : the autobiography of Mrs. Oral Roberts / Evelyn Roberts. Boston : G. K. Hall, 1977, c1976. 418 p. ; 25 cm. Large print ed. [BX8495.R52A3 1977] 77-1416 ISBN 0-8161-6469-X lib.bdg. : 11.95
1. Roberts, Evelyn, 1917- 2. Roberts, Oral. 3. Methodist Church—Clergy—Biography. 4. Clergymen's wives—Oklahoma—Tulsa—Biography. 5. Tulsa, Okla.—Biography. 6. Clergy—Oklahoma—Tulsa—Biography. 7. Large type books. I. Title.

ROBERTS, Evelyn, 269'.2'0924
1917-
His darling wife Evelyn : the autobiography of Mrs. Oral Roberts / by Evelyn Roberts. New York : Dell Pub. Co., 1978,c1976. 256p., 8 l. of plates : ill. ; 18 cm. (A Dell Book) [BX8495.R52A3] ISBN 0-440-13660-1 pbk. : 1.95
1. Roberts, Evelyn, 1917- 2. Roberts, Oral. I. Title.
L.C. card no. for 1976 Dial Press ed.:76-23429.

Roberts, Jane, 1929-

ROBERTS, Jane, 1929- 133.9'3
The God of Jane : a psychic manifesto / Jane Roberts. Englewood Cliffs, N.J. : Prentice-Hall, c1981. x, 262 p. ; 24 cm. Includes index. [BF1029.R6] 19 81-321 ISBN 0-13-357517-9 : 10.95
1. Roberts, Jane, 1929- 2. Psychical research—Case studies. I. Title.

Roberts, John, 1623?-1684.

ROBERTS, Daniel, 1658-1727. 922.
Some accont of the persecutions and sufferings of the people called Quakers in seventeenth century exemplified in the memoirs of the life of John Robets. 1665. Philadelphia, Kinber & Sharpless, 1840. 72 p. 15 cm. [BX7795.R6R58] 50-42935
1. Roberts, John, 1623?-1684. I. Title.

ROBERTS, Daniel, 1658-1727. 922.
Some memoirs of the life of John Roberts. Written by his son Daniel Roberts. The 5th ed. ... London and Bristol: Printed Philadelphia: Reprinted by Henry Miller. And sold by James Der Kinderen, in Strawberry-Alley, 1766. [BX7795.R6R6 1766] 23-1326
1. Roberts, John, 1623?-1684. I. Title.

ROBERTS, Daniel, 1658-1727. 922.
Some memoirs of the life of John Roberts. Written by his son Daniel Roberts. The 7th ed. ... Philadelphia: Printed and sold by Joseph Cruskshank, in Market-street, between Second and Third-streets, m dcc xc. 66 p. 16 cm. First edition Exon, 1746. [BX7795.R6R6 1790] 2-28628
1. Roberts, John, 1623?-1684? I. Title.

ROBERTS, Daniel, 1658-1727. 922.
Some memoirs of the life of John Roberts. Written by his son, Daniel Roberts. Philadelphia, Friends' book-store [188-?] 1 p. l., 5-86 p. 16 cm. First edition, Exon, 1746. [BX7795.R6R6 1880] 2-28630
1. Roberts, John, 1623-1684? I. Title.

Roberts, John E. Spiritualism.

CLYMER, Reuben Swinburne, 1878-
True spiritualsim; also, a contradiction of the work of John E. Roberts, entitled "Spiritualism; or, Bible salvation vs. modern spiritualsim"... by Rev. R. Swinburne Clymer... Allentown, Pa., The Philosophical publishing company [c1906] 190 p. 20 cm. [BF1201.C65] 7-2066
1. Roberts, John E. Spiritualism. 2. Spiritualism. I. Title.

Roberts, Oral.

ARMSTRONG, D. Wade, ed.
California state evangelistic-stewardship conference seromsn, Memorial Auditorium, Fresno, California, January 9-11, 1961. Over 40 sermons and addresses. Fresno, Department of Evangelism, SBGCC [1961] 237 p. NUC65
I. Title.

HUTCHINSON, Warner. 269'.2'0924 B
The Oral Roberts scrapbook / by Warner A. Hutchinson. New York : Grosset & Dunlap, c1978. 124 p., [2] leaves of plates : ill. ; 28 cm. Bibliography: p. 124. [BX8495.R528H87] 78-58611 ISBN 0-448-16257-1 : 14.95 ($16.95 Can) pbk. : 5.95
1. Roberts, Oral. 2. Methodist Church—Clergy—Biography. 3. Clergy—United States—Biography. I. Title.

ROBERTS, Oral. 269'.2'0924 B
The call; an autobiography. [1st ed.] Garden City, N.Y., Doubleday, 1972 [c1971] 216 p. 22 cm. [BV3785.R58A23] 79-139057 4.95
I. Title.

ROBERTS, Oral.
... The 4th man, and other famous sermons exactly as Oral Roberts preached them from the revival platform. [4th ed.] Tulsa, Okla. [1958, c1951] 139 p. 20 cm. 67-70333
I. Title.

ROBERTS, Oral.
My twenty years of a miracle ministry. [Tulsa, Okla., 1967] 96 p. illus. (part col.) ports. (part col.) 28 cm. 68-62744
1. Roberts, Oral. 2. Evangelists—Correspondence, reminiscences, etc. I. Title.

ROBERTS, Oral. 269'.2'0924 B
Twelve greatest miracles of my ministry / by Oral Roberts. 1st published ed. [Tulsa, Okla. : Pinoak Publications], 1974. 174 p. : ill. ; 21 cm. [BV3785.R58A35] 75-308770
1. Roberts, Oral. 2. Miracles. 3. Faith-cure. I. Title.

ROBINSON, Wayne, 1937- 269'.2'0924 B
Oral : the warm, intimate, unauthorized portrait of a man of God / Wayne A. Robinson. Los Angeles : Acton House, c1976. xi, 154 p. ; 23 cm. [BX8495.R528R62] 76-151756 ISBN 0-89202-003-2 : 5.95
1. Roberts, Oral. 2. Methodist Church—Clergy—Biography. 3. Clergy—Oklahoma—Tulsa—Biography. 4. Tulsa, Okla.—Biography. I. Title.

SHOLES, Jerry. 269'.2'0924 B
Give me that prime-time religion : an insider's report on the Oral Roberts Evangelistic Association / by Jerry Sholes. 1st ed. [s.l.] : Oklahoma Book Pub. Co., c1979. xvi, 208 p. ; 20 cm. [BX8495.R528S48] 79-116733 5.75
1. Roberts, Oral. 2. Oral Roberts Evangelistic Association. I. Title.
Publisher's address: 5272 South Lewis, Tulsa, Ok.

Roberts, Robert Richford, Bp., 1778-1843.

ELLIOTT, Charles, 1792-1869. 922.773
The life of the Rev. Robert R. Roberts, one of the bishops of the Methodist Episcopal church. By Rev. Charles Elliott, D.D. New York, Published by G. Lane & C.B. Tippett, for the Methodist Episcopal church, 1844. 407, [1] p. incl. 1 illus., plates, facsims. front. (port.) 18 1/2 cm. [BX495.R53E6] 35-38359
1. Roberts, Robert Richford, 1778-1843. I. Title.

FRY, Benjamin St. James, 1824-1892. 922.773
The life of Robert R. Roberts, one of the bishops of the Methodist Episcopal church. By Benjamin St. James Fry. New-York, Carlton & Phillips, 1856. 126 p. 16 cm. [BX8495.R53F7] 37-7031
1. Roberts, Robert Richford, bp., 1778-1843. I. Title.

TIPPY, Worth Marion, 1867- 922.773
Frontier bishop; the life and times of Robert Richford Roberts. New York, Abingdon Press [1958] 207 p. illus. 23 cm. Includes bibliography. [BX8495.R53T5] 58-5394
1. Roberts, Robert Richford, Bp., 1778-1843. I. Title.

Robertson, Archibald Thomas, 1863-1934.

GILL, Everett, 1869- 920.
A. T. Robertson, a biography by Everett Gill ... New York, The Macmillan company, 1943. xvi, 250 p. front., pl., ports. 21 cm. "First printing." "The Robertson shelf of books": p. 143-145. [BX6495.R65G5] 43-4036
1. Robertson, Archibald Thomas, 1863-1934. I. Title.

ROBERTSON, Archibald Thomas, 1863- 171.
The new citizenship; the Christian facing a new world order, by A. T. Robertson ... New York, Chicago [etc.] Fleming H. Revell company [c1919] 157 p. 20 cm. [BR115.P7R7] 19-5503 1.00
I. Title.
Contents omitted.

ROBERTSON, Archibald Thomas, 1863-1934. 225.
The minister and his Greek New Testament, by A. T. Robertson ... New York, George H. Doran company [c1923] 3 p. l., ix-xi p., 1 l., 15-139 p. 21 cm. [BS1938.R6] 23-12802
I. Title.

Robertson, Charles Franklin, 1835-1886.

HARRISON, John A. 1850-
Courts of appeal in causes ecclesiastical; their necessity illustrated by the history of the case of Rev. Henry D. Jardine (deceased), containing Dr. Fulton's letters, the "vindication" of Bishop Robertson, and observations on the case by John A. Harrison, esq. St. Louis, Nixon-Jones printing co., 1886. 66 p. 24 cm. 16-24127
1. Robertson, Charles Franklin, 1835-1886. 2. Jardine, Henry D., d. 1886. 3. Ecclesiastical law—U. S. I. Fulton, John, 1834-1907. II. Title.

Robertson, Dede.

ROBERTSON, Dede. 248'.2 B
My God will supply : how the Lord provides in times of shortage / Dede Robertson, with John Sherrill. Lincoln, Va. : Chosen Books ; Waco, Tex. : distributed by Word Books, c1979. 172 p. ; 22 cm. [BR1725.R616A35] 79-16126 ISBN 0-912376-48-1 : 5.95
1. Robertson, Dede. 2. Christian biography—United States. 3. Soybean as food. 4. Cookery (Soybeans) I. Sherrill, John, joint author. II. Title.

Robertson, Frederick William, 1816-1853.

BLACKWOOD, James Russell. 922.342
The soul of Frederick W. Robertson, the Brighton preacher, by James R. Blackwood, with an introduction by Andrew Watterson Blackwood, sr. New York and London, Harper & brothers [1947] xiii, 201 p. front. (port.) 20 cm. "First edition." "A selected Robertson bibliography": p. 191-193. [BX5199.R7B5] 47-3909
1. Robertson, Frederick William, 1816-1853. I. Title.

ROBERTSON, Frederick William, 1816-1853. 922.
Life and letters of Frederick W. Robertson ... Edited by Stopford A. Brooke ... Boston, Ticknor and Fields, 1865. 2 v. front. (port.) 19 cm. [BX5199.R7A3 1865] 12-38041
I. Brooke, Stopford Augustus, 1832-1916. II. Title.

ROBERTSON, Frederick William, 1816-1853. 922.
Life and letters of Frederick W. Robertson ... Edited by Stopford A. Brooke ... Boston, Ticknor and Fields, 1866. 2 v. front. (port.) 20 cm. "Third edition." [BX5199.R7A3 1866] 25-23357
I. Brooke, Stopford Augustus, 1832-1916, ed. II. Title.

Robertson, Hector Menteith.

BRODRICK, James, 1891- 261
The economic morals of the Jesuits; an answer to Dr. H. M. Robertson. New York, Arno Press, 1972. 158 p. 23 cm. (The Evolution of capitalism) Reprint of the 1934 ed. [BR115.E3R623 1972] 76-38248 ISBN 0-405-04113-6
1. Robertson, Hector Menteith. Aspects of the rise of economic individualism. 2. Jesuits. 3. Christianity and economics. I. Title. II. Series.

Robertson, Noralie, tr.

SAGE, Michel, 1863-1931. 920.
Mrs. Piper & the Society for psychical research; translated & slightly abridged from the French of M. Sage by Noralie Robertson, with a preface by Sir Oliver Lodge. New York, Scott-Thaw co., 1904. xxiv, 187, [1] p. 19 cm. [BF1283.P6S2] 4-16274
1. Robertson, Noralie, tr. 2. Spiritualism. 3. Piper, Mrs. Leonora E. I. Title.

Robertson, Pat.

ROBERTSON, Pat. 269'.2'0924 B
Shout it from the housetops, by Pat Robertson, with Jamie Buckingham. Plainfield, N.J., Logos International, 1972. xi, 238 p. 22 cm. [BR1725.R62A3] 72-76591 ISBN 0-912106-30-1 4.95
1. Robertson, Pat. 2. Mass media in religion. I. Buckingham, Jamie. II. Title.

Robin, 1944-1975.

ROBIN, 1944-1975. 286'.1'0924 B
Don't bury me 'til I'm dead / Robin. Denver : Accent Books, c1977. 128 p. ; 21 cm. [BX6495.R655A32] 76-50299 ISBN 0-916406-61-X : 2.95
1. Robin, 1944-1975. 2. Baptists—Georgia—Biography. 3. Cancer—Biography. 4. Death. I. Title.

Robinson, Edward, 1794-1863.

†HITCHCOCK, Roswell Dwight, 1817-1887. 285'.8'0924 B
The life, writings, and character of Edward Robinson / Henry Boynton Smith and Roswell D. Hitchcock. New York : Arno Press, 1977, [c1863]. 100 p. ; 21 cm. (America and the Holy Land) Reprint of the ed. published by A. D. F. Randolph, New York. [BX7260.R62H5 1977] 77-70744 ISBN 0-405-10290-9 : 12.00
1. Robinson, Edward, 1794-1863. 2. Congregationalists—United States—Biography. I. Smith, Henry Boynton, 1815-1877, joint author. II. Title. III. Series.

ROBINSON, Edward, 1794-1863. 220.9'1
Biblical researches in Palestine, Mount Sinai, and Arabia Petraea / Edward Robinson. New York : Arno Press, 1977. p. cm. (America and the Holy Land) Also authored by E. Smith. Reprint of the 1841 ed. published by Crocker & Brewster, Boston. Includes bibliographical references. [DS107.R664 1977] 77-70738 ISBN 0-405-10281-Xlib.bdg. : 120.00
1. Robinson, Edward, 1794-1863. 2. Smith, Eli, 1801-1857. 3. Bible—Geography. 4. Palestine—Description and travel. 5. Sinaitic Peninsula—Description and travel. 6. Palestine—Antiquities. 7. Sinaitic Peninsula—Antiquities. I. Smith, Eli, 1801-1857, joint author. II. Title. III. Series.

Robinson, Elsie Anne (LeBeau)

KNOX, Olive Elsie. 920.7
Mrs. Minister. Philadelphia, Westminster Press [1956] 190p. 21cm. [CT275.R735K6] 56-5248
1. Robinson, Elsie Anne (LeBeau) I. Title.

Robinson, George Livingston, 1864-

FROM the pyramids to Paul; 204
studies in theology, archaeology and related subjects, prepared in honor of the seventieth birthday of George Livingstone Robinson, PH. D., D. D., LL., D., S. T. D., professor of Biblical literature and English Bible in the Presbyterian theological seminary, Chicago, Illinois, by Former pupils, colleagues, and friends; edited by Lewis Gaston Leary. New York, T. Nelson and sons, 1935. xi p., 2 l., 306 p. front. (port.) illus., plates. 21 cm. [BS413.R6] 35-6283
1. Robinson, George Livingston, 1864- 2. Bible—Addresses, essays, lectures. 3. Semitic phsiology—Collections. I. Leary, Lewis Gaston, 1877- ed.
Contents omitted.

Robinson, Jay, 1930-

ROBINSON, Jay, 1930- 248'.24 B
The comeback / Jay Robinson, as told to Jim Hardiman. Lincoln, Va. : Chosen Book ; Waco, Tex. : distributed by Word Books, c1979. 251 p. : ill. ; 24 cm. [BV4935.R573A32] 78-31489 ISBN 0-912376-45-7 : 59.50
1. Robinson, Jay, 1930- 2. Converts—United States—Biography. I. Hardiman, James W., joint author. II. Title.

Robinson, John, 1575?-1625.

GEORGE, Timothy. 285'.9'0924
John Robinson and the English separatist tradition / by Timothy George. Macon, Ga. : Mercer University Press, c1982. p. cm. (NABPR dissertation series ; no. 1) Originally presented as the author's thesis (D.D.)—Harvard Divinity School. Includes

index. Bibliography: p. [BX9339.R55G46 1982] 19 82-14201 ISBN 0-86554-043-8 : 16.95
1. Robinson, John, 1575?-1625. 2. Theology, Doctrinal—England—History—17th century. 3. Separatists—History—17th century. 4. Theology, Puritan—England—History—17th century. I. Title. II. Series.

Robinson, John Arthur Thomas, Bp., 1919-

BILDSTEIN, Walter J. 201'.1
Radical response / Walter J. Bildstein. 2d ed. Hicksville, N.Y. : Exposition Press, [1974] xvi, 144 p. ; 21 cm. (An Exposition-testament book) First ed. published in 1972 under title: Secularization: the theology of John A. T. Robinson, a radical response. Bibliography: p. [131]-144. [BX5199.R722B54 1974] 74-186984 ISBN 0-682-47931-4 : 6.50
1. Robinson, John Arthur Thomas, Bp., 1919- 2. Secularization (Theology) I. Title.

CLARKE, Oliver Fielding 230
For Christ's sake; a reply to the Bishop of Woolwich's book Honest to God, and a positive continuation of the discussion [2d ed.] New York, Morehouse [c.1963] 103p. 18cm. Bibl. 63-25421 1.50 pap.,
1. Robinson, John Arthur Thomas, Bp., 1919-Honest to God. 2. Christianity—Essence; genius, nature. I. Title.

CLARKE, Oliver Fielding. 230
For Christ's sake; a reply to the Bishop of Woolwich's book Honest to God, and a positive continuation of the discussion. [2d ed.] New York, Morehouse-Barlow Co. [1963] 103 p. 18 cm. Bibliographical footnotes. [BT55.R63C5 1963] 63-25421
1. Robinson, John Arthur Thomas, Bp. 1919- Honest to God. 2. Christianity — Essence, genius, nature. I. Title.

CLARKE, Oliver Fielding. 230
For Christ's sake; a reply to the Bishop of Woolwich's book Honest to God and a positive continuation of the discussion. [3d American ed.] New York, Morehouse-Barlow [1964, c1963] 103 p. 19 cm. Bibliographical footnotes. [BT55.R63C5 1964] 64-2099
1. Robinson, John Arthur Thomas, Bp., 1919- Honest to God. 2. Christianity — Essence, genius, nature. I. Title.

EDWARDS, David Lawrence, ed. 230
The "Honest to God" debate; some reactions to the book "Honest to God." With a new chapter by its author, John A. T. Robinson. Philadelphia, Westminster Press [1963] 287 p. 18 cm. Bibliographical footnotes. [BT55.R63E4 1963a] 63-22614
1. Robinson, John Arthur Thomas, Bp., 1919- Honest to God. I. Title.

MCBRIEN, Richard P. 262.000924
The church in the thought of Bishop John Robinson [by] Richard P. McBrien. Philadelphia, Westminster [1966] xv, 160p. 23cm. Bibl. [BX5199.R722M3 1966a] 66-23087 3.95
1. Robinson, John Arthur Thomas, Bp., 1919- 2. Church—History of doctrines—20th cent. I. Title.

MASCALL, Eric Lionel, 1905- 230
The secularization of Christianity; an analysis and a critique [by] E. L. Mascall. New York, Holt [1966, c.1965] xiii, 286p. 23cm. Bibl. [BT28.M28 1966] 66-15656 6.00
1. Robinson, John Arthur Thomas, Bp., 1919- Honest to God. 2. Van Buren, Paul Matthew, 1924- The secular meaning of the Gospel. 3. Christianity — 20th cent. 4. Death of God theology. I. Title.

NILES, Daniel Thambyrajah 231
We know in part. Philadelphia, Westminster [c.1964] 158p. 19cm. 64-18685 1.95 pap.,
1. Robinson, John Arthur Thomas, Bp., 1919-Honest to God. I. Title.

PARRINDER, Edward Geoffrey. 294
The Christian debate: light from the East, by Geoffrey Parrinder. [1st ed. in the U. S. A.] Garden City, N. Y., Doubleday, 1966 [c1964] 159, [1] p. 22 cm. "For further reading": p. [160] [BR128.H5P36 1966] 66-10516
1. Robinson, John Arthur Thomas, Bp., 1919- Honest to God. 2. Christianity and other religions—Hinduism. 3. Hinduism—Relations—Christianity. I. Title.

Robinson, Ras B.

ROBINSON, Ras B. 248'.48'61
Before the sun goes down : the spiritual journey of a layman / Ras B. Robinson, Jr. Nashville : Broadman Press, c1976. 137, [3] p. ; 20 cm. Bibliography: p. [139]-[140] [BV4501.2.R6175] 76-4243 ISBN 0-8054-8510-4 : 2.50
1. Robinson, Ras B. 2. Baptists—Biography. 3. Christian life—Baptist authors. I. Title.

Robinson, Reuben, 1860-1942.

MILLER, Basil William, 1897- 922
Bud Robinson, miracle of grace. Kansas City, Mo., Beacon Hill Press, 1947. 207 p. 20 cm. [BV3785.R6M5] 49-250478
1. Robinson, Reuben, 1860-1942. I. Title.

ROBINSON, Reuben.
"Honey in the rock," by Bud Robinson ... Cincinnati, O., Office of "God's revivalist," c1913. 3 p. l., 3-288 p. front. (4 port.) 19 1/2 cm. $1.00 14-579
I. Title.

WISE, George C. 922
Rev. Bud Robinson. Louisville, Ky., Pentecostal Pub. Co. [1946] 96 p. 20 cm. [BV3785.R6W5] 47-28900
1. Robinson, Reuben, 1860-1942. I. Title.

Robinson, Theodore Henry, 1881-

SOCIETY for Old Testament Study.
Studies in Old Testament prophecy. Presented to Theodore H. Robinson on his sixty-fifth birthday, Aug. 9th, 1946. Edited by H. H. Rowley. Edinburgh, Clark [1957] 206 p. 22 cm.
1. Robinson, Theodore Henry, 1881- 2. Bible — Prophecies. 3. Bible. O.T. Prophets — Criticism, interpretation, etc. I. Rowley, Harold Henry, 1890- ed. II. Title.

SOCIETY for Old Testament Study.
Studies in Old Testament prophecy. Presented to Theodore H. Robinson on his sixty-fifth birthday, August 9th, 1946. Edited by H. H. Rowley. New York, Scribner, 1950. xi, 206 p. 22 cm. Errata slip inserted. A 51
1. Robinson, Theodore Henry, 1881- 2. Bible — Prophecies. 3. Bible. O.T. Prophets — Criticism, Interpretation, etc. I. Rowley, Harold Henry, 1890- ed. II. Title.
Contents omitted.

Rochester, Eng. (Dioceser)—History

PEARMAN, Augustus John.
... Rochester, by the Rev. A. I. Pearman ... With map. Published under the direction of the Tract committee. London [etc.] Society for promoting Christian knowledge; New York, E. & J. B. Young & co., 1897. iv p., 1 l., [5]-340 p. front. (fold. map) 17 cm. (Diocesan histories) [BX5107.R6P4] 3-31890
1. Rochester, Eng. (Dioceser)—Hist. I. Society for promoting Christian knowledge. Tract committee. II. Title.

Rochester, N.Y.—Biography.

MI-CHA-EL : 282'.747'89
a history of St. Michael's Parish, the Diocese of Rochester, from 1874 to 1974. [Rochester, N.Y. : s.n., 1974] 48 p. : ill. ; 28 cm. Cover title: Michael, who is like God? [BX4603.R58S245] 75-329964
1. St. Michael's Parish, Rochester, N.Y. 2. Rochester, N.Y.—Biography. I. Title: Michael, who is like God?

Rochester, N.Y. Brighton Presbyterian church.

PAGE, Joseph R. 1816or7- 285.
1884.
History of the Brighton church. Five discourses, delivered in January, February and March, 1877, by Rev. Joseph R. Page, D.D. Published by the society. Rochester, N.Y., Evening express printing company, 1877. 60 p. 23 cm. [BX9211.R6B7] 44-29708
1. Rochester, N.Y. Brighton Presbyterian church. I. Title.

Rochester, N.Y. (Diocese)—History.

MCNAMARA, Robert 282.747'8
Francis, 1910-
The Diocese of Rochester, 1868-1968, by Robert F McNamara. with a foreword by Fulton J. Sheen [Rochester, N.Y.] Diocese of Rochester, 1968. xx, 618 p. illus., maps (on lining papers), ports. 24 cm. Bibliographical references included in "Notes" (p. 539-603) [BX1417.R6M3] 68-19638
1. Rochester, N.Y. (Diocese)—History. I. Title.

Rochester, N.Y. Lake Avenue Memorial Baptist Church.

NELSON, William Rhame, 262'.06
1930-
Journey toward renewal [by] William R. Nelson [and] William F. Lincoln. Valley Forge [Pa.] Judson Press [1971] 158 p. 22 cm. [BV600.2.N43] 71-163579 ISBN 0-8170-0543-9 3.50
1. Rochester, N.Y. Lake Avenue Memorial Baptist Church. 2. Church renewal—Case studies. I. Lincoln, William F., joint author. II. Title.

Rochester, N.Y. Sacred Heart Cathedral.

MCNAMARA, Robert 277.47*89
Francis, 1910-
History of Sacred Heart Cathedral, Rochester, New York, 1911-1961; a historical sketch, by Robert F. McNamara. Rochester, The Cathedral, 1961. 78 p. illus. 23 cm. Cover title: History of Sacred Heart Parish. [BX4603.R58S24] 72-204321
1. Rochester, N.Y. Sacred Heart Cathedral. I. Title. II. Title: History of Sacred Heart Parish.

Rochester, N.Y. St. Luke's church.

ANSTICE, Henry, 1841- 283.
Centennial annals of St. Luke's church, Rochester, N.Y., 1817-1917, the Rev. Henry Anstice ... Rochester, Scranton, Wetmore & co., 1917. 142. [4] p. front., 5 pl. (incl. ports.) 20 cm. [BX5980.R6L8] 17-30398
1. Rochester, N.Y. St. Luke's church. 2. Rochester, N.Y.—Church history. I. Title.

Rochester theological seminary, Rochester, N.Y.—Bibliography.

ROCHESTER theological seminary, Rochester, N.Y.
General catalogue 1850 to 1900 together with the Historical discourse delivered as a part of the semi-centennial exercises, May the ninth, 1900 by President Augustus H. Strong. Rochester, E. R. Andrews, printer, 1900. xi, 354 p. 24 cm. At head of title: Rochester theological seminary. E 9
1. Rochester theological seminary, Rochester, N.Y.—Bibliography. I. Strong, Augustus Hopkins, 1836- II. Title.

Rochester theological seminary, Rochester, N.Y.—Biography

ROCHESTER theological seminary, Rochester, N.Y.
... Rochester theological seminary; general catalogue 1850 to 1910. [5th ed.] Rochester, N.Y., E. R. Andrews printing co., 1910. xxii, 326 p. 25 cm. "Previous editions appeared in 1869, 1876, 1889 and 1900." E 10
1. Rochester theological seminary, Rochester, N.Y.—Biog. I. Title.

Rock Hill, S.C. First Presbyterian Church.

WHITE, William 285'.1'0975743
Boyce, 1929-
History of the First Presbyterian Church of Rock Hill, South Carolina, 1869-1969, by William Boyce White, Jr. [Richmond] Printed by order of the Session in commemoration of the centenary of the church [by Whittet & Shepperson] 1969. 134 p. illus., ports. 24 cm. Bibliographical references included in "Notes" (p. 131-134) [BX9211.R64F57] 73-96802
1. Rock Hill, S.C. First Presbyterian Church. I. Title.

Rock Island, Ill. Monastery of the Visitation.

BURTON, Katherine (Kruz) 271.975
1890-
Bells on two rivers; the history of the Sisters of the Visitation of Rock Island, Illinois [by] Katherine Burton. Milwaukee,Burce Pub. Co. [1965] viii, 118 p. illus. 23 cm. [BX4549.R6M63] 66-6381
1. Rock Island, Ill. Monastery of the Visitation. I. Title.

Rock, John Charles, 1890-

MCLAUGHLIN, 613.9'432'0924 B
Loretta.
The pill, John Rock, and the church : the biography of a revolution / by Loretta McLaughlin. 1st ed. Boston : Little, Brown, c1982. p. cm. Includes index. [RG137.5.M38 1982] 19 82-16187 ISBN 0-316-56095-2 : 12.95
1. Rock, John Charles, 1890- 2. Oral contraceptives—United States—History. 3. Oral contraceptives—Religious aspects—Catholic Church. 4. Gynecologists—United States—Biography. 5. Medical research personnel—United States—Biography. I. Title.

Rockbridge Co., Va.—Genealogy.

DIEHL, George West. 285'.1755'852
Old Oxford and her families. [Verona, Va.] McClure Press [1971] ix, 217 p. illus. 24 cm. Includes bibliographical references. [BX9211.V38O433] 79-160702 7.50
1. Old Oxford Presbyterian Church. 2. Rockbridge Co., Va.—Genealogy. I. Title.

Rockwell, Orrin Porter, 1813-1878.

KELLY, Charles, 1889- 922.8373
Holy murder; the story of Porter Rockwell, by Charles Kelly and Hoffman Birney. New York, Minton, Balch & company [c1934] ix, [3], 313 p. front., plates, ports. 23 cm. Bibliography: p. 301-306. [BX8695.R6K4] 34-10303
1. Rockwell, Orrin Porter, 1813-1878. 2. Mormons and Mormonism. I. Birney, Hoffman, 1891- joint author. II. Title.

SCHINDLER, Harold, 289.3'0924
1929-
Orrin Porter Rockwell: man of God, son of thunder. Illustrated by Dale Bryner. Salt Lake City, University of Utah Press, 1966. 399 p. illus., maps, ports. 26 cm. Bibliography: p. 366-385. [BX8695.R6S32] 66-29846
1. Rockwell, Orrin Porter, 1813-1878.

Rocky River Church, Cabarrus Co., N. C.

SPENCE, Thomas Hugh, 285.1756
1899-
The Presbyterian congregation on Rocky River. Concord, N. C., Rocky River Presbyterian Church, 1954. 238p. illus. 25cm. [BX9211.C14R6] 55-19724
1. Rocky River Church, Cabarrus Co., N. C. I. Title.

Rocky Springs Baptist Church, Claiborne Parish, La.

HEMPHILL, Annie Mae 286'.1763'94
Tooke.
A brief history of Rocky Springs Baptist Church, organized 1845. Rev. Lisbon, La., 1968. 16 p. 22 cm. Cover title. Bibliography: p. 16. [BX6480.C448R63 1968] 74-165053
1. Rocky Springs Baptist Church, Claiborne Parish, La. I. Title.

Rocthaan, Joannes Phillippus, 1785-1853.

NORTH, Robert Grady, 1916- 922.2492
The general who rebuilt the Jesuits [by] Robert G. North, S.J. Milwaukee, The Bruce Publishing company [1944] xii, 292 p. illus. (maps) plates, ports. 22 cm. (Half-title: Science and culture series: Joseph Husslein ... general editor) Bibliography: p. 273-278. [BX4705.R715N6] 44-7309
1. Rocthaan, Joannes Phillippus, 1785-1853. 2. Jesuits—Hist. I. Title.

Rodgers, John, 1727-1811.

MILLER, Samuel, 1769-1850. 922.573
Memoir of the Rev. John Rodgers, D.D., late pastor of the Wall-street and Brick churches, in the city of New York. By Samuel Miller ... Abridged from the original edition of 1813. Philadelphia, Presbyterian board of publication, 1840. 240 p. 15 1/2 cm. [BX9225.R72M5 1840] 36-31463
1. Rodgers, John, 1727-1811. I. Presbyterian church in the U.S.A. (Old school) Board of publication. II. Title.

MILLER, Samuel, 1769-1850. 922.573
Memoirs of the Rev. John Rodgers, D.D., late pastor of the Wall- street and Brick churches in the city of New-York. By Samuel Miller ... New-York: Published by Whiting and Watson, theological and classical book sellers. J. Seymour, printer, 1813. 432 p. front. (port.) 22 cm. "A sermon, preached in the city of New-York, May 12th, 1811, occasioned by the death of the Rev. John Rodgers ... By Samuel Miller": p. [351]-395. [BX9225.R72M5 1813] 36-34774
1. Rodgers, John, 1727-1811. I. Title.

Rodrigues, Joao, 1561 (ca.)-1634.

COOPER, Michael, S.J. 271'.53'024 B
Rodrigues the interpreter; an early Jesuit in Japan and China. [1st ed.] New York, Weatherhill [1974] 416 p. illus. 24 cm. Bibliography: p. 385-395. [BX4705.R619C66] 73-88466 ISBN 0-8348-0094-2 13.50
1. Rodrigues, Joao, 1561 (ca.)-1634. I. Title.

Rodriguez, Alonso, Saint, 1531-1617.

FARNUM, Mabel Adelaide, 1887- 922.246
The wood merchant of Segovia (St. Alphonsus Rodriguez) [by] Mabel Farnum. Milwaukee, The Bruce publishing company [1945] x, 202 p. front. (group port.) 20 1/2 cm. [BX4700.R56F3] 45-9080
1. Rodriguez, Alonso, Saint, 1531-1617. I. Title.

Rodriguez, Alonso, Saint, 1531-1617 — Juvenile literature.

DALY, Marco. 92
The wool merchant's son; a story of St. Alfonso Rodriguez. Illus. by Carolyn Lee Jagodits. Notre Dame, Ind., Dujarie Press [c1962] 94 p. illus. 24 cm. [BX4700.R56D3] 63-32427
1. Rodriguez, Alonso, Saint, 1531-1617 — Juvenile literature. I. Title.

Roethke, Theodore, 1908-1963.

SCOTT, Nathan A. 246
The wild prayer of longing; poetry and the sacred [by] Nathan A. Scott, Jr. New Haven, Yale University Press, 1971. xix, 124 p. 23 cm. Includes bibliographical references. [BL65.C8S36 1971] 72-140538 ISBN 0-300-01389-2 6.75
1. Roethke, Theodore, 1908-1963. 2. Religion and culture. 3. Holy, The. 4. Religion and poetry. I. Title.

Roger, Bp. of Worcester, d. 1179.

CHENEY, Mary Gwendolen. 282'.092'4
Roger, Bishop of Worcester, 1164-1179 / Mary G. Cheney. Oxford : Clarendon Press ; New York : Oxford University Press, 1980. xvi, 397 p., [1] leaf of plates : ill. ; 23 cm. (Oxford historical monographs) Includes index. Books and articles cited, with abbreviations": p. [ix]-xiv. [BX4705.R647C45] 79-41665 ISBN 0-19-821879-6 : 49.50
1. Roger, Bp. of Worcester, d. 1179. 2. Catholic Church—Bishops—Biography. 3. Bishops—England—Worcester—Biography. 4. Worcester, Eng.—Biography. I. Title.

Rogers, Ammi, 1770-1852.

CAMERON, Kenneth Walter, 1908- comp. 283'.092'4 B
Ammi Rogers and the Episcopal Church in Connecticut, 1790-1832; his Memoirs and documents illuminating historical, religious, and personal backgrounds. Hartford, Transcendental Books [1974] 138 l. illus. 29 cm. "Memoirs of the Rev. Ammi Rogers, A.M.": leaves 15-91. [BX5995.R6C35] 74-173629
1. Rogers, Ammi, 1770-1852. 2. Protestant Episcopal Church in the U.S.A.—Connecticut—History—Sources. I. Rogers, Ammi, 1770-1852. Memoirs of the Rev. Ammi Rogers, A.M. 1974. II. Title.

Rogers, Carl Ransom, 1902-

ODEN, Thomas C 253.5
Kerygma and counseling; toward a covenant ontology for secular psychotherapy, by Thomas C. Oden. Philadelphia, Westminster Press [1966] 186 p. 21 cm. Bibliographical references included in "Notes" (p. [171]-186) [BV4012.O27] 66-11516
1. Rogers, Carl Ransom, 1902- 2. Barth, Karl, 1886- 3. Pastoral psychology. 4. Psychotherapy. I. Title.

Rogers, Charles Bolles—Art collections.

MCKENZIE, A Dean. 704.948'4'074094183
Greek and Russian icons and other liturgical objects in the Collection of Mr. Charles Bolles Rogers [by] A. Dean MacKenzie. Milwaukee, University of Wisconsin [1965] 44, 35 p. illus. (part col.) 28 cm. Catalog of an exhibition held Nov. 15 to Dec. 10, 1965, Dept. of Art History Gallery, University of Wisconsin, Milwaukee. Bibliography: p. 22. [N7827.M3] 66-65270
1. Rogers, Charles Bolles—Art collections. 2. Icons, Greek. 3. Icons, Russian. I. Wisconsin. University, Milwaukee. Dept. of Art History. II. Title.

Rogers, Dale Evans.

DAVIS, Elise Miller. 927.92
The answer is God; the inspiring personal story of Dale Evans and Roy Rogers. New York, McGraw-Hill [1955] 242 p. illus. 22 cm. [BR1725.R63D3] 55-9539
1. Rogers, Dale Evans. 2. Rogers, Roy, 1912- I. Title.

GARRISON, Maxine. 244
The Angel spreads her wings. [Westwood, N. J.] Revell [1956] 159 p. 22 cm. [BR1715.R6R65] 55-8762
1. Rogers, Dale Evans Angel unaware. 2. Rogers, Robin Elizabeth, 1950-1952. 3. Rogers, Roy, 1911- I. Title.

LANE, Carlie. 248
I walk a joyful road [Introd. by Dale Evans Rogers] Westwood, N.J., F. Revell [1967] 110 p. 21 cm. [BV4935.L3] 67-22571
I. Title.

ROGERS, Dale Evans. 234.2
To my son: faith at our house. [Westwood, N. J.] Revell [1957] 142p. 22cm. The author's letters to her son Tom. [BR1725.R63A4] 57-6856
I. Fox, Thomas Frederick. II. Title.

ROGERS, Dale Evans. 209'.2'4 B
Trials, tears, and triumph / Dale Evans Rogers. Old Tappan, N.J. : F. H. Revell Co., c1977. 128 p., [4] leaves of plates : ill. ; 21 cm. [BR1725.R63A324] 76-51293 ISBN 0-8007-0847-4 : 4.95
1. Rogers, Dale Evans. 2. Christian biography—California. I. Title.

ROGERS, Dale Evans. 209'.2'4 B
Trials, tears, and triumph / Dale Evans Rogers. Boston : G. K. Hall, 1977. 157 p. ; 24 cm. Large print ed. [BR1725.R63A324 1977a] 77-12656 ISBN 0-8161-6523-8 lib.bdg. : 8.95
1. Rogers, Dale Evans. 2. Christian biography—California. 3. Large type books. I. Title.

ROGERS, Dale Evans. 248'.4
Where He leads. Old Tappan, N.J., F. H. Revell Co. [1974] 126 p. 21 cm. [BR1725.R63A327] 74-1225 ISBN 0-8007-0648-X 3.95
1. Rogers, Dale Evans. I. Title.

ROGERS, Dale Evans. 248'.4
Where He leads / Dale Evans Rogers. Boston : G. K. Hall, 1975, c1974. p. cm. Large print ed. [BR1725.R63A327 1975] 75-20039 ISBN 0-8161-6321-9 lib.bdg. : 8.95
1. Rogers, Dale Evans. 2. Sight-saving books. I. Title.

ROGERS, Dale Evans. 248.8'43
Woman / Dale Evans Rogers, with Carole C. Carlson. Old Tappan, N.J. : F. H. Revell Co., c1980. 127 p. ; 22 cm. [BV4527.R63] 79-27090 ISBN 0-8007-1115-7 : 7.95
1. Rogers, Dale Evans. 2. Women—Religious life. 3. Women—Conduct of life. I. Carlson, Carole C., joint author. II. Title.

ROGERS, Dale Evans. 784'.092'4 B
The woman at the well. Boston, G. K. Hall, 1973 [c1970] 304 p. 25 cm. Large print ed. [BR1725.R63A33 1973] 73-9912 ISBN 0-8161-6135-6 8.95 (lib. bdg.)
1. Rogers, Dale Evans. 2. Sight-saving books. I. Title.

Rogers, Deborah Lee, 1952-1964.

ROGERS, Dale Evans 927.92
Dearest Debbie: In Ai Lee. Westwood, N.J., Revell [c.1965] 62p. 20cm. [BV4907.R6] 65-14798 1.95 bds.,
1. Rogers, Deborah Lee, 1952-1964. 2. Children—Death and future state. I. Title.

ROGERS, Dale Evans. 927.92
Dearest Debbie: In Ai Lee. Westwood, N.J., F. H. Revell Co. [1965] 62 p. 20 cm. [BV4907.R6] 65-14798
1. Rogers, Deborah Lee, 1952-1964. 2. Children—Death and future state. I. Title.

Rogers, Harold, 1907-

ROGERS, Harold, 1907- 248'.3
A handful of quietness / Harold Rogers. Waco, Tex. : Word Books, c1977. 140 p. ; 23 cm. [BJ1533.Q5R63] 77-75463 ISBN 0-8499-0010-7 : 5.95
1. Rogers, Harold, 1907- 2. Quietude. 3. Spiritual life—Methodist authors. I. Title.

ROGERS, Harold, 1907- 248'.3
A handful of quietness / Harold Rogers. Boston : G. K. Hall, 1979, c1977. xi, 218 p. ; 24 cm. Large print ed. [BJ1533.Q5R63 1979] 79-11192 ISBN 0-8161-6696-X : 9.95
1. Rogers, Harold, 1907- 2. Quietude. 3. Spiritual life—Methodist authors. 4. Large type books. I. Title.

Rogers, Jack Bartlett.

ROGERS, Jack Bartlett. 269'.2'0924 B
Confessions of a conservative Evangelical, by Jack Rogers. Philadelphia, Westminster Press [1974] 144 p. 20 cm. [BX9225.R73A33] 74-12249 ISBN 0-664-24996-5 2.65 (pbk.)
1. Rogers, Jack Bartlett. 2. Evangelicalism. I. Title.

WOODBRIDGE, John D., 1941- 220.1'3
Biblical authority : a critique of the Rogers/McKim proposal / John D. Woodbridge. Grand Rapids, Mich. : Zondervan Pub. House, c1982. p. cm. Includes bibliographical references and index. [BS500.R633W66 1982] 19 82-8592 ISBN 0-310-44751-8 pbk. : 8.95
1. Rogers, Jack Bartlett. Authority and interpretation of the Bible. 2. Bible—Criticism, interpretation, etc.—History. 3. Bible—Evidences, authority, etc.—History. 4. Theology, Reformed Church—History. I. Title.

Rogers, Mary Joseph, 1882-1955.

LYONS, Jeanne Marie, 1904- 922.273
Maryknoll's first lady. New York, Dodd, Mead [1964] xi, 327 p. illus., ports. 24 cm. [BV2300.M45L9] 64-12763
1. Rogers, Mary Joseph, 1882-1955. 2. Maryknoll Sisters of St. Dominic. I. Title.

LYONS, Jenne Marie, 1904- 922.275
Maryknoll's first lady, by Sister Jeanne Marie. Garden City, N.Y., Doubleday [1967, c.1964] 319p. 19cm. (Echo bk., E39) .95 pap.,
1. Rogers, Mary Joseph, 1882-1955. 2. Mary-knoll Sisters of St. Dominic. I. Title.

Rogers, Peter V.

ROGERS, Peter V. 282'.092'4 B
Tragedy is my parish : working for God in the streets of New Orleans / Peter V. Rogers. New York : Macmillan, c1979. xii, 159 p., [6] leaves of plates : ill. ; 22 cm. p. cm. Autobiography. [BX4705.R648A34 1979] 78-25896 ISBN 0-02-604390-4 : 7.95
1. Rogers, Peter V. 2. Catholic Church—Clergy—Biography. 3. Clergy—Louisiana—New Orleans—Biography. 4. New Orleans—Biography. 5. Chaplains, Police—Louisiana—New Orleans—Biography. I. Title.

Rogers, Robin Elizabeth, 1950-1952.

ROGERS, Dale Evans. 244
Angel unaware. [Westwood, N. J.] Revell [1953] 63 p. 20 cm. [BR1715.R6R6] 53-7446
1. Rogers, Robin Elizabeth, 1950-1952. I. Title.

ROGERS, Dale Evans [Orig. name: Frances Octavia Smith] 244
Angel unaware. New York, Pyramid [1963, c.1953] 64p. 18cm. (R826) .50 pap.,
1. Rogers, Robin Elizabeth, 1950-1952. I. Title.

Rogers, Sandy.

ROGERS, Dale Evans. 248
Salute to Sandy. Westwood, N. J., F. H. Revell Co. [1967] 117 p. illus., ports. 20 cm. [BR1725.R63A32] 67-19296
1. Rogers, Sandy. I. Title.

Rogo, D. Scott.

ROGO, D. Scott. 133.1'4
The poltergeist experience / D. Scott Rogo. New York : Harmondsworth, Eng. ; Penguin Books, 1979. 301 p. ; 19 cm. Includes index. Bibliography: p. [285]-291. [BF1483.R63] 78-31465 ISBN 0-14-004995-9 pbk. : 2.95
1. Rogo, D. Scott. 2. Poltergeists. I. Title.

Rogues and vagabonds—Biography.

BODO, John R. 225.9'22 B
A gallery of New Testament rogues : from Herod to Satan / by John R. Bodo. 1st ed. Philadelphia : Westminster Press, c1979. 151 p. ; 19 cm. [BS2448.R63B63] 78-13984 ISBN 0-664-24227-8 pbk. : 5.95
1. Bible. N.T.—Biography. 2. Rogues and vagabonds—Biography. I. Title.

Rohner, Karl, 1904-

SHEPHERD, William C. 230.2'0924
Man's condition; God and the world process [by] William C. Shepherd. [New York] Herder and Herder [1969] 266 p. 22 cm. Bibliographical footnotes. [BT761.2.S5] 68-55091

1. Rohner, Karl, 1904- 2. Natural theology—History of doctrines. 3. Grace (Theology)—History of doctrines. I. Title.

Roiphe, Anne Richardson, 1935- — Religion and ethics—Addresses, essays, lectures.

ROIPHE, Anne Richardson, 1935- 973'.04924
Generation without memory : A Jewish journey through Christian America / Anne Roiphe. New York : Linden Press/Simon and Schuster, 1981. p. cm. [BM205.R56] 19 81-1611 ISBN 0-671-41455-0 : 11.95
1. Roiphe, Anne Richardson, 1935- — Religion and ethics—Addresses, essays, lectures. 2. Judaism—United States—Addresses, essays, lectures. 3. Jews—United States—Cultural assimilation—Addresses, essays, lectures. 4. Jews—United States—Identity—Addresses, essays, lectures. 5. Novelists, American—20th century—Biography—Addresses, essays, lectures. I. Title.

ROIPHE, Anne Richardson, 1935- 973'.04924
Generation without memory : a Jewish journey in Christian America / Anne Roiphe. Boston : Beacon Press, 1982, c1981. 221 p. ; 21 cm. [BM205.R56 1982] 19 82-70567 ISBN 0-8070-3601-3 pbk. : 7.95
1. Roiphe, Anne Richardson, 1935- — Religion and ethics—Addresses, essays, lectures. 2. Roiphe, Anne Richardson, 1935- —Biography—Addresses, essays, lectures. 3. Judaism—United States—Addresses, essays, lectures. 4. Jews—United States—Cultural assimilation—Addresses, essays, lectures. 5. Jews—United States—Identity—Addresses, essays, lectures. 6. Novelists, American—20th century—Biography—Addresses, essays, lectures. I. Title.

Rollins, Wallace Eugene, 1870-

ZABRISKIE, Alexander Clinton, 1898- ed. 283
Anglican evangelicalism, edited by Alexander C. Zabriskie, dean of the Virginia theological seminary. With foreword by the presiding bishop ... Philadelphia, The Church historical society [1943] xiv p., 1 l., 288 p. 24 cm. ([Church historical society, Philadelphia] Publication no. 13) "These essays have been written and are published as a testimonial to Dr. Wallace E. Rollins."--Foreword. [BX5125.Z3] 43-15973
1. Rollins, Wallace Eugene, 1870- 2. Evangelicalism—Church of England. 3. Evangelicalism—Protestant Episcopal church in the U.S.A. I. Alexandria, Va. Protestant Episcopal theological seminary in Virginia. II. Title.
Contents omitted.

Roloff, Lester, 1918-

ROLOFF, Marie Brady. 269'.2'0924 B
Lester Roloff : living by faith / by Marie Brady Roloff. Nashville : Action Press, c1978. 192 p., [4] leaves of plates : ill. ; 21 cm. [BX6495.R664R64] 78-3654 ISBN 0-8407-9506-8 pbk. : 3.95
1. Roloff, Lester, 1918- 2. Baptists—Texas—Biography. 3. Evangelists—Texas—Biography. 4. Texas—Biography.

Roman Catholic Church.

THE end of Roman Catholicism; 176 one great essential is to create a state of human affairs wherein more people will live a normal human life. Chicago, Ill., The Ashland publishing company [c1925] 2 p. l., 7-139 p. 19 cm. [HQ63.E5] 25-7048

JAN, Father, C.S.C. 282'.0924 B
When dreams come true, by Father Jan (Sigmund A. Jankowski). Notre Dame, Ind., 1970. 189 p. illus., ports. 19 cm. [BX4705.J333A3] 77-105320
I. Title.

LIEBLER, H. B. 282
When we look around us; a little book about God and what he has done for us. Illus., Gertrude Van Allen. New York, Exposition Press [c.1960] 86p. (Exposition-Testament bk.) 2.50
1. Roman Catholic Church. I. Title.

MCNALLY, Augustin Francis, 1876- 282.
The Catholic centenary, 1808-1908, as a newspaper man saw it, by Augustin McNally. With an introduction by ex-Chief Justice Morgan H. O'Brien, an article on the ancient glories of the Roman Catholic church and a closing word by William Winter, the editorial remarks of the principal New York newspapers; also eight full page and four double page illustrations. New York, Moffat, Yard & company, 1908. 3 p. l., ix-xxxii, 170 p. 1 l. front., illus. (coat of arms) 4 double pl., ports. 19 1/2 cm. [BX1417.N4M3] 8-17905
I. Winter, William, 1836-1917. II. Title.

MELVILLE, Thomas. 282'.0922 [B]
Whose heaven, whose earth? By Thomas and Marjorie Melville. New York, Pocket Books [1973, c.1971] xii, 274 p. ports. 18 cm. [BX4705.M4847A3] ISBN 0-671-78347-5 1.25 (pbk)
I. Melville, Marjorie, 1929- II. Title.
L.C. card no. for the hardbound edition: 70-118719.

MELVILLE, Thomas. 282'.0922 B
Whose heaven, whose earth? [By] Thomas and Marjorie Melville. [1st ed.] New York, Knopf, 1971 [c1970] 303 p. illus., ports. 22 cm. [BX4705.M4847A3 1971] 70-118719 6.95
I. Melville, Marjorie, 1929- II. Title.

MILLER, Charles R. 230.2
A dominant Romanism; its religious and political significance. New York, Vantage Press [c.1959] 112p. 21cm. (bibl.) 2.75 bds.,
I. Title.

MUSSER, Benjamin Francis.
Outside the walls, tributes to the principle and practice of Roman Catholicism from our friends fuori le mura, by Benjamin Francis Musser. St. Louis, Mo., B. Herder, 1914. viii p., 1 l., 362 p. 21 cm. 14-15424 1.25
I. Title.

RYAN, Archie Lowell, 1881- 282
... When we join the church, by Archie Lowell Ryan, in collaboration with George Herbert Betts. New York, Cincinnati [etc.] The Abingdon press [c1928] 118 p. front., port., double map. 17 cm. (The Abingdon religious education texts...Week-day school series) [BV600.R8 1928] 28-28853
I. Betts, George Herbert, 1868- joint author. II. Title.

TICHENOR, Henry Mulford, 1858-
The Roman religion; a short history of how the holy humbug was hatched, by Henry M. Tichenor ... St. Louis, Mo., The Melting pot, c1913. 64 p. illus. (incl. ports.) 24 1/2 cm. $0.25. 13-21318
I. Title.

WILLIAMSON, Benedict, 1868- 242
The triumph of live, by Benedict Williamson, with a foreword by the Lord Bishop of Plymouth. London, K. Paul, Trench. Trubner & co.; St. Louis, B. Herder book company, 1923. xxiii, 230 p. 22 1/2 cm. [BX2182.W5] 23-8630
I. Title.

YARBROUGH, Caesar Augustus. 282
The Roman Catholic church challenged in the discussion of thirty-two questions with the Catholic layman's association of Georgia, by Dr. C. A. Yarbrough ... Macon, Ga., The Patriotic societies of Macon, 1920. v. [1] 7-411 p. 20 cm. [BX1765.Y3] 20-9417
I. Catholic laymen's association of Georgia. II. Title.

YOUNG Christian Workers. 267'.62'2
Time for living. [Melbourne, Young Christian Worker's Movement (Aust.) 1967] 47 p. illus. 21 cm. Cover title. [BX809.Y62A28] 78-444453 unpriced
I. Title.

Roman Catholic church in the United States — Biography

CODE, Joseph Bernard, 1899-
Dictionary of the American hierarchy, 1789-1964. With a preface by Egidio Vagnozzi. New York, J. F. Wagner [c1964] 452 p. 26 cm. 65-57970
1. Roman Catholic church in the U.S. — Biog. 2. Bishops — U.S. I. Title.

EVANS, Hiram Wesley. 282.73
The rising storm; an analysis of the growing conflict over the political dilemma of Roman Catholics in America, by Dr H. W. Evans. Atlanta, Buckhead publishing co. [c1930] xviii, 345 p. 23 cm. "Principal publications cited": p. xvii-xviii. [BX1770.E8] 30-10517
I. Title.

WATSON, Thomas Edward, 1856-
Is Roman Catholicism in America identical with that of the popes? Or, Open letters to Cardinal James Gibbons, by Thos. E. Watson... Thomson, Ga., The Jeffersonian publishing co., 1914. v, [1], 147 p. illus. 23 cm. 14-14519
I. Title. II. Title: Open letters to Cardinal James Gibbons.

Roman Catholic Church—Religious orders—Franciscans.

WROBLEWSKI, Sergius 271.3
Following Francis; commentary on the Third Order general constitutions. Chicago, Franciscan Herald Pr., c.1961. 63p. .50 pap.,
1. Roman Catholic Church—Religious orders—Franciscans. 2. Roman Catholic Church—The Third Order. 3. Third Order. I. Title.

Roman Catholic Church—Religious orders—Jesuits.

MCGLOIN, Joseph T. 271.5
I'll die laughing! New York, All Saints Pr. [1962, c.1955] 145p. illus. (Bruce paperback, AS215) .50 pap.,
1. Roman Catholic Church—Religious orders—Jesuits. 2. Roman Catholic Church—Clergy—Humor. I. Title.

Roman law.

BURR, Alexander George, 1871- 225.
The Apostle Paul and the Roman law, by A. G. Burr ... foreword by Chief Justice Birdzell ... [Bismarck, N.D., Quick print, inc., c1928] c.88 [4] p. 20 cm. Bibliography: p. [3] at end. [BS2505.B785] 28-8825
1. Paul, Saint, apostle. 2. Roman law. I. Title.

CICERO, Marcus Tullius. 24-16682
Select orations of Marcus Tullius Cicero, with explanatory notes, and a special dictionary. By Albert Harkness ... Rev. ed. New York [etc.] D. Appleton and company, 1877. xii, 319 p. front., plates. 19cm. [PA6279.A4H3 1877]
I. Harkness, Albert, 1822-1907, ed. II. Title.

RODDY, Irving Gaines. 225.92
Paul before Caesar from the legal viewpoint [by] Irving Gaines Roddy... Philadelphia, Boston [etc.] The Judson press [c1936] 6 p. l., 3-148 p. 20 cm. Bibliography: p. [145]-148. [BS2505.R62] 922.1 36-18290
1. Paul, Saint, apostle—Trial. 2. Roman law. I. Title.

ROMAN, LuLu. 248'.24 B
LuLu / LuLu Roman. Old Tappan, N.J. : F. H. Revell, c1978. 173 p. : ill. ; 22 cm. [BR1725.R65A34] 78-15510 ISBN 0-8007-0956-X : 6.95
1. Roman, LuLu. 2. Christian biogrphy—United States. 3. Entertainers—United States—Biography. I. Title.

Roman question.

CIVIS romanus, pseud. 261.
The pope is king, by Civis romanus; with 17 illustrations. New York, London, G.P. Putnam's sons, 1929. xii, 323 p. front., plates, ports. map. facsims. 22 1/2 cm. Frontispiece accompanied by guard sheet with descriptive letterpress. [BX1545.C5 1929a] 29-20534
1. Roman question. 2. Catholic church. Pope, 1922- (Pius xi) 3. Concordat of 1929. I. Title.

Romances.

COX, George William, 1827-1902. 293
Popular romances of the middle ages, by Sir George W. Cox ... and Eustace Hinton Jones. 1st American, from the 2d English ed. New York, H. Holt and company, 1882. 1 p. l., [v]-viii, 514 p. 21 cm. [PN683.C6 1882] 16-18433
1. Romances. 2. Arthur, King. I. Jones, Eustace Hinton, ed. II. Title.

Romances, English.

EBBUTT, Maud Isabel, 1867- 293
Hero-myths & legends of the British race; by M. I. Ebbutt. With sixty-four full-page illustrations by J. H. F. Bacon... Ryam Shaw, W. H. Margetson...Patten Wilson, and Gertrude Demain Hammond... New York; T. Y. Crowell & company, [1910] 3 p. l., ix-xxix, 374, [1] p. 64 pl. (incl. front.) 22 cm. Title in brown and black. [(PN683.E)] W10
1. Romances, English. 2. Heroes. I. Title.

EBBUTT, Maud Isabel, 1867- 293
Hero-myths & legends of the British race, by M. I. Ebbutt, M.A., with fifty-one full-page illustrations by J. H. F. Bacon... Byam Shaw, W. H. Margetson...Gertrude Demain Hammond and others. New York, Farrar & Rinehart, [1931] 2 p. o., ix-xxvil, [1], 374,[1] p. col. front., plates. 22 cm. (Lettered on cover: The myths series) Printed in Great Britain. Popular adaptations. [PN683.E3 1931] 31-28230
1. Romances, English. 2. Heroes. I. Title.

Romanes, Ethel Georgina, 1880-1914.

ROMANES, Ethel (Duncan), Mrs. 922.
The story of an English sister (Ethel Georgina Romanes--Sister Etheldred) by Ethel Romanes...With three portraits. London, New York [etc.] Longmans, Green and co., 1918. xii, 293, [1] p. 3 port. (incl. front.) 22 1/2 cm. [BX5199.R75R7] 19-6508
1. Romanes, Ethel Georgina, 1880-1914. I. Title.

Romano, Juanita Napoles.

ROMANO, Juanita Napoles. 286'.7'0924 B
The wind blows free on Cupcake Hill. Mountain View, Calif., Pacific Press Pub. Association [1973] 112 p. 22 cm. (A Destiny book, D-141) The author recalls her childhood in Hawaii, her growing-up years in the Philippines as the daughter of Seventh Day Adventist missionaries, and her marriage and battle with disease in the United States. [BX6193.R65A37] 73-85875
1. Romano, Juanita Napoles. 2. [Romano, Juanita Napoles.] 3. [Seventh-Day Adventists.] I. Title.

Romanticism—Germany.

WERNAER, Robert Maximilian, 1865- 830.93
Romanticism and the romantic school in Germany. New York, Haskell House, 1966. xv, 373 p. 22 cm. First published in 1910. Bibliography: p. 335-350. [PT361.W5 1966] 230'.092'4 68-681
1. Romanticism—Germany. I. Title.

Rome Baptist Church.

GARDNER, Robert Grosvenor. 286'.1758'35
The Rome Baptist Church, 1835-1865 / Robert G. Gardner Rome, Ga. : First Baptist Church, 1975. 75 p. : ill. ; 23 cm. Bibliography: p. 75. [BX6480.R65R654] 75-318794
1. Rome Baptist Church.

Rome—Churches.

SHARP, Mary, 1903- 726.5'09'45632
A guide to the churches of Rome. Philadelphia, Chilton Books [1966] xi, 260 p. illus., maps. 23 cm. "A project of Dimension Books." Bibliography: p. 260. [DG816.3.S5] 66-22875
1. Rome—Churches. I. Title. II. Title: The churches of Rome.

Rome (City)—Church history.

BARNES, Arthur Stapylton, 1861-1936. 270.1
Christianity at Rome in the apostolic age; an attempt at reconstruction of history. Westport, Conn., Greenwood Press [1971] xiii, 222 p. 23 cm. Reprint of the 1938 ed. Includes bibliographical references. [BR165.B285 1971] 72-114462 ISBN 0-8371-4760-3
1. Peter, Saint, apostle. 2. Paul, Saint, apostle. 3. John, Saint, apostle. 4. Rome (City)—Church history. 5. Church history—Primitive and early church, ca. 30-600. I. Title.

EDMUNDSON, George, 1848-1930. 230
The church in Rome in the first century, an examination of various controverted questions relating to its history, chronology, literature and traditions; eight lectures preached before the University of Oxford in the year 1913 on the foundation of the late Rev. John Bampton ... by George Edmundson ... London, New York [etc.] Longmans, Green and co., 1913. xiii, 296 p. 23 1/2 cm. [The Bampton lectures for 1913] [BR45.B3 1913] 14-63
1. Rome (City)—Church history. 2. Church history—Primitive and early church. I. Title.

MACGRAIL, Joseph F.
The curse of Rome. A frank confession of a Catholic priest, and a complete expose of the immoral tyranny of the Church of Rome. By Very Rev. Canon Joseph F. Mac Grail, former chaplain United States navy. [New York, Printed by the Nyvall press, c1907] 95, [1] p. front. (port.) 19 cm. 7-13930
I. Title.

Rome (City)—Churches.

BREWYN, William, fl.1470. 282'.45632
A XVth century guide-book to the principal churches of Rome / compiled c. 1470 by William Brewyn ; translated from the Latin, with introd. and notes, by C. Eveleigh Woodruff. New York : AMS Press, [1980] p. cm. Reprint of the 1933 ed. published by the Marshall Press, London. "XVth cent. English poems" : p. Includes index. [BX1548.R6B73 1980] 78-63451 ISBN 0-404-16375-0 : 14.50 14.50
1. Rome (City)—Churches. I. Woodruff, Charles Eveleigh, 1855 or 6- II. Title.

LANCIANI, Rodolfo Amedeo, 1847-1929. 726.
Wanderings through ancient Roman churches, by Rodolfo Lanciani ... Boston and New York, Houghton Mifflin company, 1924. xiv p., 1 l., 325 p. incl. illus., plates. front. (port.) 25 cm. Contains references at end of some of the chapters. [NA5620.A1L3] 24-27654
1. Rome (City)—Churches. 2. Rome (City)—Antiq. 3. Christian antiquities—Rome. I. Title.
Contents omitted.

MALE, Emile 726.582
The early churches of Rome. Translated [From the French] by David Buxton. Chicago, Quadrangle Books, 1960[ ] 253p. (bibl. footnotes) illus. 29cm. 60-7082 2.50
1. Rome (City)—Churches. I. Title.

SHARP, Mary, 1903- 726'.5'0945632
A guide to the churches of Rome. Philadelphia, Chilton Books [1966] xi, 260 p. illus., maps. 23 cm. "A project of Dimension Books." London ed. (Evelyn) has title: A traveller's guide to the churches of Rome. Bibliography: p. 260. [DG816.3.S5 1966] 66-22875
1. Rome (City)—Churches. I. Title. II. Title: The churches of Rome.

THYNNE, Roger.
The churches of Rome, by Roger Thynne ... London, K. Paul, Trench, Trubner & co., ltd. Neu York, E. P. Dutton & co., 1924. xxxii, 460 p. 48 pl. (incl. front.) on 36 l., fold. plan. 17 cm. [BX4634.R6T5] 25-3760
1. Rome (City)—Churches. 2. Christian antiquities—Rome. 3. Art—Rome. I. Title.

Rome (City) Collegio americano degil Stati Uniti.

BRANN, Henry Athanasius 1837-1921 ed. 307.
History of the American college of the Roman Catholic church of the United States Rome, Italy, by Rev. Henry A. Brann ... New York, Cincinnati [etc.] Benziger brothers, 1910. 2 p. l., 3-570 p. front., plates, ports. 21 cm. [BX920.R66B7] 10-11865
1. Rome (City) Collegio americano degil Stati Uniti. I. Title.

Rome (City). Collegio anglico.

GASQUET, Francis Aidan, cardinal, 1846-1929. 207.
A history of the venerable English college, Rome; an account of its origins and work from the earliest times to the present day, by Cardinal Gasquet ... London, New York [etc.] Longmans, Green and co., 1920. xii, 291, [1] p. front., plates, ports. 23 cm. [BX920.R76G3] 20-20215
1. Rome (City) Collegio angelico. I. Title.

MUNDAY, Anthony, 1553-1633. 207'.45'632
The English Roman life / Anthony Munday ; edited by Philip J. Ayres. Oxford : Clarendon Press ; New York : Oxford University Press, 1980. xxvii, 114 p., [1] leaf of plates : ill. ; 23 cm. (Studies in Tudor and Stuart literature) Originally published as the English Romayne Lyfe, London, 1582. Includes bibliographical references and index. [BX920.R76M86 1980] 19 79-40268 ISBN 0-19-812635-2 : 22.00
1. Rome (City). Collegio anglico. 2. Catholic Church in Italy. 3. British in Rome (City) I. Ayres, Philip J. II. Title. III. Series.

Rome (City) San Pietro in Vaticano (Church)

MCNALLY, Augustin Francis, 1876- 726.509456
St. Peter's on the Vatican; the first complete account in our English tongue of its origins and reconstruction, by Augustin McNally... New York city, Strand press [1939] xii, 216 p. illus. (ports., plan) plates. 23 1/2 cm. "Partial list of authorities": p. ix. [NA5620.S9M3] 40-9653
1. Rome (City) San Pietro in Vaticano (Church) I. Title.

Rome. Exposizione missionaria vaticana.

CONSIDINE, John J.
The Vatican mission exposition; a window on the world, by Reverend John J. Considine ... New York, The Macmillan company, 1925. 177 p. incl. front., illus., ports. double diagrs. 19 1/2 cm. [BV2165.R6 1925] 25-27775
1. Rome. Esposizlone missionaria vaticana. 2. Catholic church—Missions. I. Title.

CONSIDINE, John Joseph, 1897-
The Vatican mission exposition; a window on the world, by Reverend John J. Considine... New York, The Macmillan company, 1925. 177 p. incl. front., illus., ports. double diagrs. 19 1/2 cm. [BV2165.R6 1925] 25-27775
1. Rome. Exposizione missionaria vaticana. 2. Catholic church—Missions. I. Title.

Rome—History—Empire, 30 B.C.-476 A.D.

CICERO, Marcus Tullius. 281
The three dialogues of M.T. Cicero on the orator, tr. into English, by W. Guthrie. Rev. and cor., with notes, 2d American ed. New York, Harper & brothers, 1847. 346 p. front. 16cm. (Lettered on cover: [Harper's] classical library. no. 37) [PA3606.H4 no. 37] 28-19709
I. Guthrie, William, 1706-1770, ed. and tr. II. Title.

HAARHOFF, Theodroe Johannes. 1802-. 292.211
Roman life and letters; studies presented to H. J. Haarhoff, professor of classics at the University of the Witwatersrand, 1922-1957. Cape Town, A. A. Balkeman, 1959. 178 p. port. 24 cm. Latin literature--Addresses, essays, lectures. (Acta classica, v. 1) Contents.Professor T. J. Haarhoff, an appreciation. by A. Petrie.--De praepositionis apud poetas Latinos loco scripalt H. Wagenvoort.--A lost manuscript of Lucretius, by G. P. Goold.--Vergil's Latin, by W. F. Jackson Knight.--Vergil and Lucretius, by B. Farrington.--Vergil's debt to Catullus, by R. E. H. Westendorp Boerina.--Boerma.--Humanitas Horatiana, a.p. 1-37, von K, Bilchner.--Lo Hercules Octacus e di Seneca ed e anteriore al Furens, dl E. Paratore.--The dream of Pompey, by H. J. Rose.--A propos d'Apulee, par P. J. Enk.--Battles and sieges in Ammianus Marcellinus, by C. P. T. Naude.--Stoisynse invioed op Tiberius Gracchus, deur F. Smuts.--The death of Marius, by T.F. Carney,--The policy of Augustus in Greece, by J. A. O. Larsen.--The frontier policy of the Roman emperors down to a.p. 200, by M. Cary.--Writing and the epic, by S. Davis.--Die probleem van de oorsprong van die groot Alexandrynse bibiloteek, deur C. A. van Rooy.--A list of publications by T. J. Haarhoff. [PA25.A2] 64-41695
I. Title. II. Series.

HARDY, Ernest George, 1852-1925. 937'.06
Christianity and the Roman government; a study in imperial administration. New York, B. Franklin [1971] xv, 208 p. 19 cm. (Burt Franklin: research & source works series, 874. Selected essays in history, economics & social science, 318) Reprint of the 1894 ed. Includes bibliographical references. [BR170.H3 1971] 70-171514 ISBN 0-8337-4158-6
1. Rome—History—Empire, 30 B.C.-476 A.D. 2. Church history—Primitive and early church, ca. 30-600. I. Title.

HARDY, Ernest George, 1852-1925. 225.
Christianity and the Roman government, a study in imperial administration, by E. G. Hardy... London and New York, Longmans, Green, and co., 1894. xv, 208 p. 19 1/2 cm. Reprinted from stereotyped plates in 1925; second and third editions, with additional essays, were published in 1908 and 1910, respectively under title: Studies in Roman history. [1st series] Appendix on two "Acta martyrum", one of them relating to the trial of the martyrs of Scili, in Numidia, under proconsul Saturninus in 181 A.D., the other to the trial of Apoilonius in Rome between 180 and 184 A.D.: p. 196-208. [BR170.H3 1894] 3-4988
1. Rome—Hist.—Empire, B.C. 30-A.D. 476. 2. Church-history—Primitive and early church. I. Title.

HARDY, Ernest George, 1852-1925. 225.
Christianity and the Roman government, a study in imperial administration, by E.G. Hardy... London, G. Allen & Unwin, ltd.; New York, The Macmillan company [1925] xiii, 161, [1] p. 19 cm. Half-title: Studies in Roman history. A reprint of the 1st edition, published in 1894; 2d and 3d editions, with additional essays were published in 1905 and 1910, respectively, under title: Studies in Roman history. [1st series] [BR170.H3 1925] 25-27649
1. Rome—Hist.—Empire, B.C. 30-A.D. 476. 2. Church history—Primitive and early church. I. Title.

Rome (Italy)—Churches.

BENY, Roloff. 726'.5'0945632
The churches of Rome / Roloff Beny and Peter Gunn. New York : Simon & Schuster, c1981. p. cm. Includes index. [NA5620.A1B46] 19 81-5255 ISBN 0-671-43447-0 : 35.00
1. Rome (Italy)—Churches. 2. Christan art and symbolism—Italy—Rome. I. Gunn, Peter. II. Title.

Rome—Libri pontificum.

PREIBISCH, Paul, 1851- 292'.6'1
Two studies on the Roman pontifices. New York : Arno Press, 1975. 48, 47 p. ; 24 cm. (Ancient religion and mythology) Reprint of Fragmenta librorum pontificiorum, first published 1878 by J. Reylander, Tilsit, in Programm des koniglichen Gymnasiums zu Tilsit; and of Quaestiones de libris pontificiis, first published in 1874 by W. Friedrich, Bratislava. Latin or German. [DG135.9.P73 1975] 75-10647 ISBN 0-405-07271-6
1. Rome—Libri pontificum. 2. Cultus, Roman. 3. Rome—Religious life and customs. I. Preibisch, Paul, 1851- Quaestiones de libris pontifciis. 1975. II. Title. III. Series.

Rome, Pa. Presbyterian church.

DETTY, Victor Charles. 285.1748
History of the Presbyterian church of Rome, Pennsylvania 1844-1942, by Victor Charles Detty ... Wysox, Pa., The author, 1942. 4 p. l., [11]-234 p. front., plates, ports., maps. 21 cm. "Books and records consulted": p. [201]-202. [BX9211.R72D4] 43-11788
1. Rome, Pa. Presbyterian church. I. Title.

Rome—Religion.

AXTELL, Harold Lucius, 1876-
... The deification of abstract ideas in Roman literature and inscriptions ... by Harold L. Axtell. Chicago, The University of Chicago press, 1907. 4 p. l., 7-100 p. 24 cm. Thesis (PH.D.)--University of Chicago, 1907. Bibliography: 3d prelim. leaf. [DG121.A8] 7-33567
1. Rome—religion. 2. Cultus, Roman. I. Title.

BAILEY, Cyril, 1871- 292
Phases in the religion of ancient Rome, by Cyril Bailey. Berkeley, Calif., University of California press, 1932. ix, 340 p. 23 cm. (half-title: Sather classical lectures, v. 10, 1932) "Notes": p. 277-323. [BL801.B25] 32-17778
1. Rome—Religion. 2. Cultus, Roman. I. Title.

BAILEY, Cyril, 1871-1957. 292'.07
Phases in the religion of ancient Rome. Westport, Conn., Greenwood Press [1972] ix, 340 p. 22 cm. Original ed. issued 1932 as v. 10 of Sather classical lectures. Includes bibliographical references. [BL801.B25 1972] 75-114460 ISBN 0-8371-4759-X
1. Rome—Religion. 2. Cultus, Roman. I. Title. II. Series: Sather classical lectures, v. 10.

BARRY, William Francis, 1849-1930. 204
Roma sacra, essays on Christian Rome, by William Barry ... London, New York [etc.] Longmans, Green & co., ltd., 1927. vi, [2], 250 p. 23 cm. [BX890.B33] 27-21251
I. Title.
Contents omitted.

BURRIS, Eli Edward. 292
Taboo, magic, spirits; a study of primitive elements in Roman religion, by Eli Edward Burriss ... New York, The Macmillan company, 1931. x p. 2 l., 250 p. 19 1/2 cm. Bibliography included in preface. [BL805.B8] 31-23315
1. Rome—Religion. 2. Cults, Roman. 3. Religion, Primitive. 4. Taboo. 5. Magic, Roman. I. Title.

BURRISS, Eli Edward. 292'.07
Taboo, magic, spirits; a study of primitive elements in Roman religion. Westport, Conn., Greenwood Press [1972] x, 250 p. 22 cm. Reprint of the 1931 ed. Includes bibliographical references. [BL805.B8 1972] 72-114489 ISBN 0-8371-4724-7 11.25
1. Rome—Religion. 2. Cultus, Roman. 3. Religion, Primitive. 4. Taboo. 5. Magic, Roman. I. Title.

CARTER, Jesse Benedict, 1872-1917. 292
The religion of Numa, and other essays on the religion of ancient Rome; by Jesse Benedict Carter. London, Macmillan and

co., limited; New York, The Macmillan company, 1906. viii p., 1 l., 189 p. 20 cm. "References to the more recent literature ... have been given in connection with the appropriate topics in ... [the] index." Contents.The religion of Numa.--The reorganization of Servius.--The coming of the sibyl.--The decline of faith.--The Augustan renaissance. [BL801.C3] 6-16617
1. Numa Pompilius, king of Rome. 2. Augustus, emperor of Rome, B.C. 63-A.D. 14. 3. Rome—Religion. I. Title.

CONWAY, Robert Seymour, 1864-1933. 292
Ancient Italy and modern religion; being the Hibbert lectures for 1932, by Robert Seymour Conway ... New York The Macmillan company; Cambridge, Eng., The University press, 1933. xiv, 150 p. plates, facsims. 22 1/2 cm. [BL25.H5 1932] (208.2) 34-2532
1. Rome—Religion. 2. Culture—Italy. 3. Christianity and other religions. I. Title.

CUMONT, Franz [Valery Marie] 292.23
After life in Roman paganism; lectures delivered at Yale University on the Silliman Foundation. New York, Dover Publications [1959 i.e., 1960] xv, 224p. 21cm. (Yale University. Mrs. Hepsa Ely Silliman memorial lectures, T573) 'An unabridged and unaltered republication of the first edition published by Yale University Press in 1922.' (Bibl. Footnotes) 59-65210 1.35 pap.,
1. Rome—Religion. 2. Future life. I. Title.

CUMONT, Franz Valery Marie, 1868- 292
After life in Roman paganism; lectures delivered at Yale university on the Silliman foundation, by Franz Cumont. New Haven, Yale university press; [etc., etc.] 1922. xv. 224, [2] p. 24 cm. (Half-title: Yale university. Mrs. Hepsa Ely Silliman memorial lectures) Bibliographical foot-notes. [BL815.F8C9] 22-24887
1. Rome—Religion. 2. Future life. I. Title.

CUMONT, Franz Valery Marie, 1868-1947 292.23
After life in Roman paganism; lectures delivered at Yale University on the Silliman Foundation. [Gloucester, Mass., Peter Smith, 1962] 224p. (Yale Univ. Mrs. Hepsa Ely Silliman memorial lectures. Dover bk. rebound) Bibl. 3.35
1. Rome—Religion. 2. Future life. I. Title.

CUMONT, Franz Valery Marie, 1868-1947. 292
The Oriental religions in Roman paganism. Introductory essay by Grant Showerman. Authorized tr. [from French. Gloucester, Mass., Peter Smith, 1962] 298p. (Dover bk. rebound) Bibl. 3.75
1. Rome—Religion. 2. Religions. I. Title.

CUMONT, Franz Valery Marie, 1868-1947. 292
The Oriental religions in Roman paganism. With an introductory essay by Grant Showerman. Authorized translation. New York, Dover Publications [1956] 298 p. 21 cm. "An unabridged and unaltered republication of the first English translation published in 1911." [BL805.C8 1956] 58-259
1. Rome—Religion. 2. Religions. I. Title.

DOCUMENTS study of the Gospels / David R. Cartlidge, David L. Dungan. Cleveland : Collins, 1980, c1979. p. cm. Includes bibliographical references. [BS2555.5.D62 1980] 79-21341 ISBN 0-529-05683-6 : 14.95 ISBN 0-529-05726-3 (pbk.) : 8.95 226'.06
1. Bible. N.T. Gospels—Extra-canonical parallels. 2. Rome—Religion. I. Cartlidge, David R. II. Dungan, David L.

DU CHOUL, Guillaume, 16th cent. 292'.07
Discours de la religion des anciens Romains illustre : Lyon, 1556 / Guillaume du Choul. New York : Garland, 1976. p. cm. (The Renaissance and the gods : no. 9) Reprint of the 1556 ed. published by G. Rouille, Lyon. [BL800.D8 1976] 75-27851 ISBN 0-8240-2058-8 : 40.00
1. Rome—Religion. I. Title. II. Series.

DUMEZIL, Georges, 1898- 292'.07
Archaic Roman religion, with an appendix on the religion of the Etruscans. Translated by Philip Krapp. Foreword by Mircea Eliade. Chicago, University of Chicago Press [1970] 2 v. (xxx, 715 p.) 24 cm. Translation of La religion romaine archaique. Includes bibliographies. [BL802.D813] 76-116981 ISBN 0-226-16968-5 25.00
1. Rome—Religion. I. Title.

EVANS, Elizabeth Cornelia, Mrs. 292
The cults of the Sabine territory by Elizabeth C. Evans. New York, N.Y., American adademy in Rome, 1939. xiv p., 1 l., 254 p. vii pl. incl. fold. map, plans 23 cm. (Half-title: Papers and monographs of the American academy in Rome. vol. xi) Printed in Germany "Select bibliography": p. [xiii] xiv. [BL813.S3E5] 39-25699
1. Rome—Religion. 2. Sabines. I. Title.

FERGUSON, John, 1921- 200'.937
The religions of the Roman Empire. Ithaca, N.Y., Cornell University Press [1970] 296 p. illus. 23 cm. (Aspects of Greek and Roman life) Bibliography: p. [244]-274. [BL802.F45 1970] 71-110992 8.50
1. Rome—Religion. I. Title. II. Series.

FOWLER, William Warde, 1847-1921. 292'.07
The religious experience of the Roman people, from the earliest times to the age of Augustus. New York, Cooper Square Publishers, 1971. xviii, 504 p. 22 cm. (Gifford lectures, 1909-10) Reprint of the 1911 ed. Includes bibliographical references. [BL801.F7 1971] 71-145870 ISBN 0-8154-0372-0
1. Rome—Religion. 2. Cultus, Roman. I. Title. II. Series.

FOWLER, William Warde, 1847-1921. 292'.2'11
Roman ideas of Deity in the last century before the Christian era; lectures delivered in Oxford for the common university fund. Freeport, N.Y., Books for Libraries Press [1969] vii, 167 p. 22 cm. (Select bibliographies reprint series) Reprint of the 1914 ed. Bibliographical footnotes. [BL805.F75 1969] 75-102236
1. Rome—Religion. 2. Monotheism. I. Title.

GRANT, Frederick Clifton, 1891- 292'.07
Ancient Roman religion. New York, Liberal Arts Press [1957] 252p. 21cm. (The Library of religion, no. 8) [BL801.G7] 57-3661
1. Rome—Religion. I. Title.

LAING, Gordon Jennings, 1869- 292
Survivals of Roman religion, by Gordon J. Laing ... New York, Longmans, Green and co., 1931. xiii, 257 p. 19 cm. (Half-title: Our debt to Greece and Rome; editors, G. D. Hadzsits ... D. M. Robinson) "First edition." Bibliography: p. 253-257. [BL805.L3] 31-25514
1. Rome—Religion. 2. Christianity and other religions. I. Title.

LAING, Gordon Jennings, 1869-1945. 292
Survivals of Roman religion. New York, Cooper Square Publishers, 1963. xiii, 257 p. 19 cm. (Our debt to Greece and Rome) Bibliography: p. 253-257. [BL805.L3 1963] 63-10280
1. Rome—Religion. 2. Christianity and other religions. I. Title. II. Series.

LIEBESCHUETZ, John Hugo Wolfgang Gideon. 292'.07
Continuity and change in Roman religion / J. H. W. G. Liebeschuetz. Oxford : Clarendon Press ; New York : Oxford University Press, 1979. xv, 359 p. ; 23 cm. Includes index. Bibliography: p. [310]-342. [BL802.L53] 78-40499 ISBN 0-19-814822-4 : 49.00
1. Rome—Religion. I. Title.

MACMULLEN, Ramsay, 1928- 200'.937
Paganism in the Roman Empire / Ramsay MacMullen. New Haven : Yale University Press, c1981. xiii, 241 p. : ill. ; 24 cm. Includes index. Bibliography: p. 207-234. [BL802.M32] 19 80-54222 ISBN 0-300-02655-2 : 23.00
1. Rome—Religion. I. Title.

OGILVIE, Robert Maxwell. 292'.07
The Romans and their gods in the age of Augustus [by] R. M. Ogilvie. New York, Norton [1970, c1969] 135 p. illus., facsim., map, plan. 21 cm. (Ancient culture and society) Bibliography: p. 129-130. [BL802.O36 1970] 75-95886 5.00
1. Rome—Religion. I. Title.

PALMER, Robert E. A. 292'.07
Roman religion and Roman Empire : five essays / Robert E. A. Palmer. Philadelphia : University of Pennsylvania Press, [1974] xii, 291 p. : ill. ; 24 cm. (The Haney Foundation series ; 15) Includes index. Bibliography: p. [277]-280. [BL802.P34] 73-89289 ISBN 0-8122-7676-0 : 25.00
1. Rome—Religion. I. Title.

PLUTARCHUS. 292'.07
The Roman questions of Plutarch : a new translation with introductory essays & a running commentary / by H. J. Rose. New York : Arno Press, 1975. p. cm. (Ancient religion and mythology) Reprint of the 1924 ed. published by the Clarendon Press, Oxford. Includes bibliographies. [DG121.P5 1975] 75-14267 ISBN 0-405-07272-4 : 12.00
1. Rome—Religion. 2. Rome—Social life and customs. I. Rose, Herbert Jennings, 1883-1961. II. Title. III. Series.

PLUTARCHUS.
The Roman questions of Plutarch; a new translation with introductory essays & a running commentary / by H. J. Rose ... Oxford, The Clarendon press, 1924. 219 [1] p. 23 cm. Bibliography: p. 44-45, 113. [DG121.P5] 25-7219
1. Rome—Religion. 2. Rome—Soc. life & cust. I. Rose, Herbert Jennings, 1883- II. Title.

ROSE, Herbert Jennings, 1883- 292
Ancient Roman religion. London, New York, Hutchinson's University Library [1948] 164 p. 19 cm. (Hutchinson's university library. World religions, no. 27) Bibliography: p. 158. [BL801.R6] 50-711
1. Rome—Religion. I. Title.

SHIELDS, Emily Ledyard, 1883- 292
Juno; a study in early Roman religion, by Emily Ledyard Shields ... Northampton, Mass., 1926. 3 p. l., 74 p. 22 1/2 cm. (Smith college classical studies. no. 7) [BL820.J6S4] 26-14699
1. Juno. 2. Rome—Religion. 3. Cultus, Roman. I. Title.
Contents omitted.

SMITH, John Holland. 292'.07
The death of classical paganism / John Holland Smith. New York : Scribner, c1976. vii, 280 p. ; 24 cm. Includes index. Bibliography: p. [269]-274. [BL802.S6] 76-28906 ISBN 0-684-14449-2 : 12.95
1. Rome—Religion. 2. Paganism. 3. Church and state in Rome—History. 4. Rome—History—Empire, 30 B.C.-476 A.D. I. Title.

STRONG, Eugenie (Sellers) 709'.37
Apotheosis and after life; three lectures on certain phases of art and religion in the Roman Empire, by Mrs. Arthur Strong. Freeport, N.Y., Books for Libraries Press [1969] xx, 293 p. illus. 23 cm. (Select bibliographies reprint series) Reprint of the 1915 ed. Includes bibliographical references. [DG121.S7 1969] 78-103668 ISBN 8-369-51689-
1. Rome—Religion. 2. Art, Roman. I. Title.

STRONG, Eugenie (Sellers) "S. A. Strong., Mrs."
Apotheosis and after life; three lectures on certain phases of art and religion in the Roman empire, by Mrs. Arthur Strong ... New York, E. P. Dutton & company [1916] xx, 293 p. XXXII pl. (incl. front.) 24 1/2 cm. Printed in Great Britain. [DG121.S7] 16-17716
1. Rome—Religion. 2. Art, Roman. I. Title.

VARRO, Marcus Terentius. 292'.07
M. Terenti Varronis Antiquitatum rerum divinarum libri I, XIV, XV, XVI / edited by Reinholdo Agahd. New York : Arno Press, 1975. 381 p. ; 23 cm. (Ancient religion and mythology) Reprint of the 1898 ed. (Lipsiae, In aedibus B. G. Teubneri) which was issued as an offprint from Jahrbucher fur classische Philologie, supplement 24. "Quaestionse Varronianae": p. [7]-136. Includes bibliographical references and indexes. [BL800.V372 1975] 75-10661 ISBN 0-405-07268-6
1. Rome—Religion. I. Agahd, Reinhold. II. Title. III. Title: Antiquitates rerum divinarum. IV. Series.

Rome—Religion—Addresses, essays, lectures.

THE Catacombs and the Colosseum; the Roman Empire as the setting of primitive Christianity [edited by] Stephen Benko [and] John J. O'Rourke. Valley Forge, Judson Press [1971] 318 p. illus., maps. 23 cm. Most of the papers originally presented at meetings of the Philadelphia Seminar on Christian Origins (PSCO) Includes bibliographies. [BL810.C38] 78-129486 ISBN 0-8170-0455-6 6.95 913.7'036
1. Rome—Religion—Addresses, essays, lectures. 2. Rome—History—Empire, 30 B.C.-284 A.D.—Addresses, essays, lectures. I. Benko, Stephen, 1924- ed. II. O'Rourke, John J., ed.

DOMASZEWSKI, Alfred von, 1856-1927. 292'.07
Abhandlungen zur romischen Religion / Alfred von Domaszewski. New York : Arno Press, 1975. vii, 240 p. [1] fold. leaf of plates : ill. ; 23 cm. (Ancient religion and mythology) Reprint of the 1909 ed. published by B. C. Teubner, Leipzig. Includes bibliographical references and index. [BL810.D65 1975] 75-10633 ISBN 0-405-07008-X
1. Rome—Religion—Addresses, essays, lectures. I. Title. II. Series.

Rome-Religion—Relations—Judaism.

FORMBY, Henry, 1817-1884. 292
Monotheism, in the main derived from the Hebrew nation and the law of Moses, the primitive religion of the city of Rome. An historical investigation, by the Rev. Henry Formby ... ... London and Edinburgh, William & Norgate New York Scibner, Welford & Co.: [etc, etc] 1877 xxxvi. 360 p. fold. front., illus. 23 cm. Illustrated t.-p. [BL805.F7] 291.1422 31-35045
1. Rome-Religion—Relations—Judaism. 2. Jews—Religion—Relations—Roman. 3. Monotheism. I. Title.

Rome—Religious life and customs.

DOMASZEWSKI, Alfred von, 1856-1927. 292'.07
Die Religion des romischen Heeres / Alfred von Domaszewski. New York : Arno Press, 1975. 121 p., [3] leaves of plates : ill. ; 24 cm. (Ancient religion anc mythology) Reprint of the 1895 ed. published by F. Lintz, Trier, which was also issued as v. 14 of Westdeutsche Zeitschrift fur Geschichte und Kunst. Includes bibliographical references. [DG135.D65 1975] 75-10634 ISBN 0-405-07012-8
1. Rome—Religious life and customs. 2. Soldiers—Rome—Religious life. I. Title. II. Series.

Rome—Religious life and customs—Addresses, essays, lectures.

WISSOWA, Georg, 1859-1931. 292'.07
Gesammelte Abhandlungen zur romischen Religions- und Stadtgeschichte / Georg Wissowa. New York : Arno Press, 1975. vi, 329 p. : ill. ; 23 cm. (Ancient religion and mythology) Reprint of the 1904 ed. published by C. H. Beck, Munchen. Includes bibliographical references and indexes. [BL810.W57 1975] 75-10663 ISBN 0-405-07279-1
1. Rome—Religious life and customs—Addresses, essays, lectures. 2. Rome—Civilization—Addresses, essays, lectures. I. Title. II. Series.

Romero, Oscar A. (Oscar Arnulfo), 1917-1980.

BROCKMAN, James R. 282'.092'4 B
The word remains : a life of Oscar Romero / by James R. Brockman. Maryknoll, NY : Orbis Books, c1982. viii, 241 p. : ill., maps,

ports. ; 24 cm. Includes bibliographical references and index. [BX4705.R669B76 1982] 19 82-3607 ISBN 0-88344-364-3 pbk. : 11.95
1. Romero, Oscar A. (Oscar Arnulfo), 1917-1980. 2. Catholic Church—Bishops—Biography. 3. Bishops—El Salvador—Biography. I. Title.

ERDOZAIN, Placido. 282'.092'4 B
Archbishop Romero, martyr of Salvador / Placido Erdoza in and priests of the church in El Salvador ; foreword by Jorge Lara-Braud ; translated by John McFadden and Ruth Warner. Maryknoll, N.Y. : Orbis Books, c1981. p. cm. Translation of: Monsenor Romero, Marti de la Iglesia popular. [BX4705.R669E7213] 19 81-2007 ISBN 0-88344-019-9 pbk. : 4.95
1. Romero, Oscar A. (Oscar Arnulfo), 1917-1980. 2. Catholic Church—Bishops—Biography. 3. Bishops—El Salvador—Biography. I. [Monsenor Romero, Marti de la Iglesia popular.] English II. Title.

Romeyn, Theodore Bayard, 1827-1885.

HACKENSACK, N. J. First Reformed church.
A memorial of Theodore Bayard Romeyn, D.D., late pastor of the First Reformed (Dutch) church, Hackensack, N. J. [New York] Pub. by the consistory, 1885. 62 p.incl. front. (port.) 24 cm. 9-19764
1. Romeyn, Theodore Bayard, 1827-1885. I. Title.

Ronchamp, France. Notre-Dame du Haut (Chapel)

JEANNERET-GRIS, Charles Edouard, 1887- 726.41
The chapel at Ronchamp [by] Le Corbuster [pseud.] New York, Praeger [1957] 135p. illus., 21cm. (Books that matter) [NA5551.R55J4] 57-12654
1. Ronchamp, France. Notre-Dame du Haut (Chapel) I. Title.

Rondthaler, Edward, Bp.,

ALLEN, Walser Haddon, 1898-
Recollections of Bishop Edward Rondthaler (1842-1931) a distinguished leader of the Moravian Church. [Bethlehem, Pa., 1966] 69 p. illus., ports. 20 cm. 68-77283
1. Rondthaler, Edward, Bp., I. Title.

Ronning, Nils Nilsen, 1870- joint author.

RONNING, Halvor Nilson, 1862- 922.473
The gospel at work, by Rev. H. N. Ronning, D.D., in cooperation with N. N. Ronning. Minneapolis, Minn., N.N. Ronning [c1943] iii-x, 11-127 p. ports. 20 cm. The life of Halvor Nilson Ronning. [BX8080.R62A2] 44-19794
1. Ronning, Nils Nilsen, 1870- joint author. I. Title.

Ronsisvalle, Daniel.

HUIE, William Bradford, 1910- 289.9 B
It's me O Lord! / William Bradford Huie. Nashville : T. Nelson, c1979. 189 p., [4] leaves of plates : ill. ; 21 cm. [BX8762.Z8R653] 79-403 ISBN 0-8407-5141-9 7.95
1. Ronsisvalle, Daniel. 2. Pentecostal churches—Clergy—Biography. 3. Clergy—United States—Biography. I. Title.

Roosevelt, Franklin Delano, Pres. U.S., 1882-1945.

FLYNN, George Q. 282'73
Roosevelt and romanism : Catholics and American diplomacy, 1937-1945 / George Q. Flynn. Westport, Conn. : Greenwood Press, 1976. xx, 268 p. ; 22 cm. (Contributions in American history ; no. 47) Includes bibliographical references and index. [E806.F55] 75-35343 ISBN 0-8371-8581-5 lib.bdg. : 13.95
1. Roosevelt, Franklin Delano, Pres. U.S., 1882-1945. 2. United States—Foreign relations—1933-1945. 3. Catholics in the United States—History. I. Title.

FLYNN, George Q. 282'73
Roosevelt and romanism : Catholics and American diplomacy, 1937-1945 / George Q. Flynn. Westport, Conn. : Greenwood Press, 1976. p. cm. (Contributions in American history ; no. 47) Includes bibliographical references and index. [BX1406.2.F58] 75-35343 ISBN 0-8371-8581-5 : 13.95
1. Roosevelt, Franklin Delano, Pres. U.S., 1882-1945. 2. Catholics in the United States—History. 3. United States—Foreign relations—1933-1945. I. Title.

Roosevelt, Theodore, pres. U.S., 1858-1919.

BEERS, Henry Augustin, 1847-1926.
Four Americans: Roosevelt, Hawthorne, Emerson, Whitman, by Henry A. Beers ... New Haven, Conn., Pub. for the Yale review by the Yale university press, 1919. 90 p. 19 1/2 cm. Reprinted from the Yale review. Contents.Roosevelt as a man of letters.--Fifty years of Hawthorne.--A pilgrim in Concord.--A wordlet about Whitman. [PS203.B4] 19-16752
1. Roosevelt, Theodore, pres. U.S., 1858-1919. 2. Hawthorne, Nathaniel, 1804-1864. 3. Concord school of philosophy. 4. Whitman, Walt, 1819-1892. I. Title.

[WILCOXON, Mitchell Haney] 1852-
Roosevelt steam rolled by the Bible. Washington, D.C., M. H. Wilcoxon, c1910. 272 p. 23 cm. $1.00. 10-3633
I. Title.

WILSON, Amos Lincoln. 220
Roosevelt and the money kings, by Amos Lincoln Wilson ... [Oklahoma City, Okla., Printed by N. D. Warner] c1918. cover-title, 2 p. l., 180 p. illus. (incl. port.) 18 1/2 cm. (Epochal series, book 2) [BS647.W52 1918] 18-17918
I. Title.
Contents omitted

Root, Helen Isabel, 1873-1945.

TAPPER, Ruth M 922.754
The full years; the life story of Helen I. Root. Winona Lake, Ind., Young People's Missionary Society, 1948. 96 p. illus., ports. 20 cm. [BV3705.R6T3] 48-22834
1. Root, Helen Isabel, 1873-1945. I. Title.

Roper River Mission.

COLE, Edmund Keith, 1919- 266.3'0994'29
A short history of the C.M.S. Roper River Mission, 1908-1969, by E. K. Cole. [Melbourne, Church Missionary Historical Publications Trust, 1969?] 28 p. illus. 24 cm. Cover title: Roper River Mission. [BV3660.N6C64] 71-859347
1. Roper River Mission. 2. Church of England in Australia—Missions. 3. Missions—Northern Territory, Australia. I. Title.

Rore, Sasa.

HEDGES, Ursula M. 266.0230995
Sasa Rore—Little Warrior, by Ursula M. Hedges. Cover painting by Thomas Dunbebin. Washington, Review and Herald Pub. Association [1966] 96 p. illus., ports. 22 cm. [BV3680.N52R6] 66-19420
1. Rore, Sasa. 2. Seventh-Day Adventists—Missions. 3. Missions—New Guinea. I. Title.

Rosa, of Lima, Saint, 1586-1617.

HANSEN, Leonhard, d.1685. 922.285
...The life of Saint Rose of Lima... Edited by the Rev. F.W. Faber D.D. 4th American ed. Philadelphia, P.F. Cunningham & son [1855] 264 p. 17 1/2 cm. (The saints and servants of God) "A translation of J.B. Feuillet's French versio of Gonzalez de Acudin's abridgment of L.H.'s Vitn...b. Rose."--Brit. mus. Catalogue. [BX4700.R6H22 1855]
1. Rosa, of Lima, Saint, 1586-1617 I. Gonzales de Acuffa, Antonio, bp., d. 1682, tr. II. Feuillet, Jean Baptise, f. 1670, tr. III. Faber, Frederick William, 1814-1863, ed. and tr. IV. Title.

KEYES, Frances Parkinson (Wheeler) 1885-1970. 922.285
The Rose and the Lily; the lives and times of two South American saints. [1st ed.] New York, Hawthorn Books [1961] 253 p. illus. 22 cm. Includes bibliography. [BX4700.R6K4] 61-6704
1. Rosa, of Lima, Saint, 1586-1617. 2. Paredes y Flores, Marians de Jesus, Saint, 1618-1645. I. Title.

MARY Alphonsus, Sister, O.SS.R. 271'.972'0924 B
St. Rose of Lima, patroness of the Americas. St. Louis, Herder [1968] xiii, 304 p. 21 cm. (Cross and crown series of spirituality, no. 36) [BX4700.R6M27] 68-8925 5.50
1. Rosa, of Lima, Saint, 1586-1617. I. Title. II. Series.

MAYNARD, Sara Katherine (Casey) 922.285
... Rose of America, illustrated by Richard Bennett. New York, Sheed & Ward, 1943. 4 p. l., 143 p. col. plates. 19 cm. At head of title: Sara Maynard. [BX4700.R6M3] 43-16161
1. Rosa, of Lima, Saint, 1586-1617 I. Bennett, Richard, 1892- illus. II. Title.

RICHARDSON, Mary Kathleen 922.285
Linda. Drawings by R. M. Sax. New York, Sheed &Ward [c.1960] (part col.) illus. 21cm. (A Patron saint book) 60-6287 2.00 bds.,
1. Rosa, of Lima, Saint, 1586-1617 I. Title.

ROBERTO, Brother, 1927- 922.285
The girl who laughed at Satan; a story of St. Rose of Lima. Illus. by Elaine Smith. Notre Dame, Ind., Dujarie Press [1956] 94p. illus. 24cm. [BX4700.R6R6] 56-42846
1. Rosa of Lima, Saint, 1586-1617. I. Title.

STORM, Marian. 922.285
... The life of Saint Rose, first American saint & only American woman saint. Santa Fe, N.M., Writers' editions, 1937. 216 p., 1 l. 24 1/2 cm. "Works studied": p. 213-216. [Full name: Marian Isabel Storm] [BX4700.R6S8] 37-21364
1. Rosa, of Lima, Saint, 1586-1617. I. Title.

WINDEATT, Mary Fabyan, 1910- 922.285
Angel of the Andes; the story of Saint Rose of Lima, by Mary Fabyan Windeatt, Illustrated by Sister M. Jean, O. P. Paterson, N. J., Saint Anthony guild press, 1943. ix, [3], 133 p. incl. front., illus. 21 cm. "The greater part of this book first appeared in ... the Torch." [BX4700.R6W5] 43-18218
1. Rosa, of Lima, Saint, 1586-1617. I. Title.

Rosalie, soeur, 1787-1856.

LHOTTE, Celine. 922.244
White wings and barricades, a story of great adventure; from the French of Celine Lhotte and Elizabeth Dupeyrat, by a daughter of charity of St. Vincent de Paul, Emmitsburg, Md. New York, Boston [etc.] Benziger brothers, inc., 1939. ix, 178 p. front. (port.) illus. 19 cm. Translation of Cornette et barricades. [BX4705.R72L47] 39-31934
1. Rosalle, saeur, 1787-1856. I. Dupeyrat, Elizabeth, joint author. II. Steele, Delphine, 1880-tr. III. Title.

THE life of Soeur 922.224
Rosalie, of the Daughters of St. Vincent de Paul, born September 8, 1787; died February 7, 1856. Baltimore, J. Murphy & co., 1859. vii, [1], [9]-141 p. incl. front. (port.) 15 x 12 cm. [BX4705.R72L5] 137
1. Rosalie, soeur, 1787-1856.

Rosaries—Meditations.

GENOVESE, Mary Rosalia, Sister. 248.36
The Rosary and the living word. Baltimore, Helicon [1965] 222 p. (chiefly illus.) 16 cm. "Pictures illustrating the mysteries of the Rosary." Includes bibliographical references. [BX2163.G4] 64-22969
1. Rosaries—Meditations. I. Title.

GENOVESE, Mary Rosalia, Sister 248.36
The Rosary and the living word. Helicon [dist. New York, Taplinger. c.1965] 222p. (chiefly illus.) 16cm. Pictures illus. the mysteries of the Rosary. Bibl. [BX2163.G4] 64-22969 4.95
1. Rosaries—Meditations. I. Title.

Rosary.

BEEHAN, Martin Aloysius, 1893- 248
Virgin most powerful; spiritual growth through the rosary, by Martin A. Beehan, LL.B. New York, P. J. Kenedy & sons [1935] xv, [1], 158 p. 17 cm. [BX2163.B35] 36-4282
1. Rosary. 2. Christian life—Catholic authors. I. Title.

BIBLE. English. Selections. 1954. Douai. 232.9
The story in the Rosary. Text from the Douay-Rheims translation of the Holy Bible selected and illustrated by Katharine Wood. New York, McKay [1954] unpaged. illus. 29 cm. [BX2163.W6] 54-11998
1. Rosary. I. Wood, Katharine Marie, 1910- comp. and illus. II. Title.

BLUNT, Hugh Francis, 1877- 232.931
Mary's garden of roses, by the Rev. Hugh F. Blunt,... New York, P. J. Kenedy & sons [c1939] 6 p. l., 3-239 p. 21 cm. [BX2163.B5] 39-31823
1. Rosary. I. Title.

CALLAN, Charles Jerome, father, 1877- 264.02
Our Lady's rosary, by Fathers Callan and McHugh ... illustrations from Fra Angelico. New York, P. J. Kenedy & sons [c1939] xxv, [1], 164 p. incl. front., illus. 17 cm. [Scoular name: Charles Louis Callan] [BX2163.C3] 39-6771
1. Rosary. I. McHugh, John Ambrose, father 1880 joint author. II. Title.

CALLAN, Charles Jerome, 1877- 248
Spiritual riches of the Rosary mysteries, by Charles J. Callan and John F. McConnell. New York, J. F. Wagner [c1957] 106p. illus. 21cm. [BX2163.C32] 58-1174
1. Rosary. I. McConnell, John F., joint author. II. Title.

CATHOLIC church Pope, 1878-1903 Leo XIII)
The rosary of Mary. Translations of the encyclical and apostolic letters of Pope Leo XiII, collected by William Raymond Lawler ... Paterson, N.J., St. Anthony guild press, 1944. xvii p., 1 l., 220 p. 20 cm. A 44
1. Rosary. I. Lawler, William Raymond, comp. II. Title.

DONNELLY, Francis Patrick, 1869- 264
Heart of the rosary [by] Francis P. Donnelly, S. J., illustrated by Charles Sander. Ozone Park, N. Y., Catholic literary guild [c1941] 126 p. illus. 20 cm. [BX2163.D243] 30-10715
1. Rosary. I. Title.

ESCRIVA, Jose Maria. 248
Holy rosary. [1st American ed.] Chicago, Scepter, 1953. 157p. illus. 16cm. [BX2163.E813] 53-29341
1. Rosary. I. Title.

FAGES, Pierre Henri, pere, 1839-1915. 242
A month of roses; or, Thirty-one meditations on the rosary, by P. H. Fages, O. P. Milwaukee, The Bruce publishing company [1944] xiv, 116 p. incl. front. plates. 19 1/2 cm. "The Dominican sisters of the perpetual rosary ... publish the collection ... in honor of their golden jubilee year 1941."--Pref. Bibliographical foot-notes. [BX2163.F32] 44-47050
1. Rosary. I. Congregation of the Dominican sisters of the perpetual rosary. II. Title.

FRINGS, M J.
The excellence of the rosary; conferences for devotions in honor of the Blessed Virgin, by Rev. M. J. Frings. New York, J. F. Wagner [c1912] 2 p. l., 75 p. 19 cm. 13-169 0.75
I. Title.

FRINGS, M J.
The excellence of the rosary; conferences for devotions in honor of the Blessed Virgin, by Rev. M. J. Frings. New York, J. F. Wagner [c1912] 2 p. l., 75 p. 19 cm. 13-169 0.75
I. Title.

FRINGS, Math Josef, 1819-1895. 232.
The excellence of the rosary; conferences for devotions in honor of the Blessed Virgin, by Rev. M. J. Fings. New York, J. F. Wagner [1912] 2 p. l., 75 p. 19 cm. Translated from the German by Minna Bachem. [BX2163.F7] 13-169
1. Rosary. I. Bachem, Minna (Sieger) 1870- tr. II. Title.

FUERST, Anthony, 1904- 247.9
This rosary [by] Rev. Anthony N. Fuerst ... Rev. and enl. ed. Milwaukee, The Bruce Publishing company [1943] 146 p. 19 cm. Bibliography: p. 139-141. [BX2163.F8 1943] 43-8736
1. Rosary. I. Title.

FUERST, Anthony Norman, 1904- 247.9
This rosary [by] Anthony N. Fuerst. Milwaukee, The Bruce Publishing company [1942] 112 p. 19 cm. Bibliography: p. 105-107. [BX2163.F8 1942] 43-11325
1. Rosary. I. Title.

GOLDEN wreath for the 232.961
month of Mary; composed of daily considerations on the triple crown of Our Blessed Lady's joys, sorrows, and glories; with examples, and hymns set to music. New ed., 1938. Notre Dame, Ind., The Ave Maria press [1938] vii, 9-232 p. 18 cm. "A meditation for each mystery of the rosary."--p. vi, [BX2161.G6 1938] 40-16260
1. Mary, Virgin—May devotions. 2. Rosary.

GRASHOFF, Raphael. 248
The joys, sorrows, and glories of the Rosary. St. Meinrad, Ind., Grail [1954] 173p. 14cm. [BX2163.G7] 54-37564
1. Rosary. I. Title.

GUARDINI, Romano, 1885- 248
The rosary of Our Lady. Translated by H. von Schuecking. New York, Kenedy [1955] 94p. illus. 20cm. [BX2163.G8] 55-6637
1. Rosary. I. Title.

HARRINGTON, Wilfrid J. 242'.742
The Rosary : a Gospel prayer / W. J. Harrington. Canfield, Ohio : Alba Books, c1975. xii, 146 p. : ill. ; 18 cm. Bibliography: p. [145]-146. [BX2163.H34] 75-44676 ISBN 0-8189-1129-8 pbk. : 1.65
1. Rosary. I. Title.

HAUGG, Donatus. 243
The rosary and the soul of woman, by Donatus Haugg [translated by] Sister Mary Aloysi Kiener... [New York, Frederick Pustet co., inc., 1941] 115 p. 19 1/2 cm. [BX2163.H37] 41-6910
1. Rosary. I. Klener, Mary Aloysi, sister, 1882- tr. II. Title.

JOHNSON, John Sevier, 1899- 247.9
The rosary in action. With a foreword by Robert W. Barron. St. Louis, Herder [1954] 271p. 21cm. [BX2163.J57] 54-8388
1. Rosary. I. Title.

KENNEDY, Maurice B. 247.9
The complete Rosary; with foreword by Samuel Cardinal Stritch. Chicago, Ziff-Davis Pub. Co., [1949] xi, 194 p. front. 21 cm. [BX2163.K4] 49-9202
1. Rosary. I. Title.

MCKENNA, Charles Hyacinth, 1835-
The treasures of the rosary, by the Very Rev. Charles Hyacinth McKenna...introduction by His Eminence James cardinal Gibbons... New York, P. J. Kenedy & sons [c1913] 271 p. 19 1/2 cm. 14-2219 1.00
I. Title.

[MCKENNA, Charles Hyacinth] 264.
1835-1917.
The rosary, the crown of Mary; by a Dominican father. Cincinnati, New York, F. Pustet & co. [1900] 147 p. illus. 14 1/2 cm. [BX2163.M3 1900] 0-3231
1. Rosary. I. Title.

[MCKENNA, Charles Hyacinth] 264.
1835-1917.
The rosary, the crown of Mary. By a Dominican father. New and rev. ed. New York, The Apostolate of the rosary [c1922] 159 p. incl. front., illus. 15 cm. [BX2163.M3 1922] 22-23130
1. Rosary. I. Title.

[MCKENNA, Charles Hyacinth] 248
1835-1917.
The rosary, the crown of Mary. By a Dominican father. New and rev. ed. New York, N.Y., The Apostolate of the rosary [c1935] 171 p. incl. front., illus. 14 1/2 cm. Manual of the Confraternity of the most holy rosary. [BX2163.M3 1935] 36-6351
1. Rosary. I. Confraternity of the most holy rosary. II. Title.

MEYER, Wendelin, 1882- 248
Rosary thoughts for priests, by Rev. Wendelin Meyer, O. F. M.; done into English by Sr. M. Liguori. Stella Niagara, N. Y., Sisters of St. Francis [c1934] 108, [2] p., 1 l. pl. 16 cm. Translation of Die kostbare perle; rosenkranzgedanken fur priester. [BX2163.M4] 34-20730
1. Rosary. 2. Meditations. I. Mary Ligouri, sister, 1863- tr. II. Title.

MOFFATT, John Edward, 1894- 248
Ave Maria; thoughts on the mysteries of the holy rosary. Milwaukee, Bruce Pub. Co. [1957] 64p. 18cm. [BX2163.M55 1957] 57-543
1. Rosary. I. Title.

MOFFATT, John Edward, 1894- 248
Ave Maria; thoughts on the mysteries of the holy rosary, by Rev. J. E. Moffatt, S.J. Milwaukee, The Bruce publishing co. [c1932] 100 p. 14 cm. [BX2163.M55] 32-30290
1. Rosary. I. Title. II. Title: Thoughts on the mysteries of the holy rosary.

O'BRIEN, James Bernard, 1876- 248
Christ in the rosary, by Rev. James B. O'Brien. New York, Cincinnati [etc.] Benziger brothers, 1934. 240 p. incl. front., illus. plates. 19 cm. [BX2163.O34] 34-36419
1. Rosary. I. Title.

PARSONS, Thomas William, 1819-1892.
The rosary. By T. W. Parsons ... Cambridge, Mass., J. Wilson and sons, 1865. 2 p. l., [7]-46 p. 4 cm. Poems. "Eighty copies printed." [PS25239.P8R6 1865] 24-19172
I. Title.

[SCHUEMACHER, Simone] 248
Your way. Translated from the French by a sister of Notre Dame de Namur. Milwaukee, Bruce Pub. Co. [1955] 78p. 17cm. [BX2163.S333] 56-968
1. Rosary. I. Julie du St. Esprit. Sister, 1808- tr. II. Title.

SCHWERTNER, Thomas Maria, 248
1883-1933.
The rosary, a social remedy. 2d ed. prepared by Vincent M. Martin. Milwaukee, Bruce [1952] 137 p. 21 cm. (Science and culture series) [BX2163.S35 1952] 52-2365
1. Rosary. I. Title.

SCHWERTNER, Thomas Maria, 248
1883-1933.
The rosary; a social remedy [by] Thomas Schwertner ... New York, Milwaukee [etc.] The Bruce publishing company [c1934] vii, 140 p. 21 cm. (Half-title: Religion and culture series, J. Huselein ... general editor) [BX2163.S35] 34-16383
1. Rosary. I. Title.

SHAW, James Gerard. 247.9
The story of the rosary. Milwaukee, Bruce [1954] 175p. 21cm. [BX2310.R7S47] 54-9337
1. Rosary. I. Title.

SISTERS of the Order of St. 242
Dominic, Great Bend, Kan.
The day with Jesus and Mary, notes gathered from approved sources for the spiritual consideration of Sisters. Milwaukee, Bruce Pub. Co. [1949] 143 p. 20 cm. [BX2163.S53] 49-5286
1. Rosary. I. Title.

SISTERS of the Order of St. 248
Dominic, Great Bend, Kan.
Reflections on the rosary for Martha sisters, by Dominican sisters. Great Bend, Kan., Congregation of the immaculate conception [1941] 136 p. incl. front. 16 x 9 1/2 cm. [BX2163.S54] 41-23454
1. Rosary. I. Title.

SISTERS of the Order of St. 248
Dominic, Great Bend, Kan.
Reflections on the rosary for nursing sisters, by Dominican sisters ... Great Bend, Kan., Congregation of the immaculate conception [c1940] 126 p. incl. front. 16 x 9 1/2 cm. Head-pieces. [BX2163.S55] 40-31747
1. Rosary. I. Title.

SISTERS of the Order of St. 248
Dominic, Great Bend, Kan.
Reflections on the rosary for teaching sisters, by Dominican sisters ... Great Bend, Kan., Congregation of the immaculate conception [c1940] 148 p. incl. front. 16 cm. Head-pieces. [BX2163.S56] 40-35915
1. Rosary. I. Title.

SLAVES of the Immaculate 248.3
Heart of Mary.
Hail Mary, full of grace. Still River [Mass] 1958. 116 p. illus. 22 cm. [BX2163.S6] 58-14484
1. Rosary. I. Title.

SLAVES of the Immaculate 242'.742
Heart of Mary.
Hail Mary, full of grace. Still River [Mass., 1972] 116 p. illus. 21 cm. [BX2163.S6 1972] 72-93984
1. Rosary. I. Title.

SOCIETY of the rosary 267.442
altar.
The Rosarian's handbook of the Society of the rosary altar, edited by the Reverend Dominic Dolan ... [New York, The Apostolate of the rosary, 1942] xiv p., 1 l., 152 p. plates, 1 illus. 17 cm. [BX810.S63A3] 42-50731
1. Rosary. I. Apostolate of the rosary. II. Dolan, Dominic, ed. III. Title.

THORNTON, Francis 248.36
Beauchesne. 1898-
This is the Rosary. Introd. by Pope John XXIII. Drawings by Alex Ross. New York, Hawthorn [c.1961] 190p. 26cm. Bibl. 61-13234 4.95 bds.,
1. Rosary. I. Title.

THORNTON, Francis 248.36
Beauchesne, 1898-
This is the Rosary. With an introd. by Pope John xxiii. Original drawings by Alex Ross. [1st ed.] New York, Hawthorn Books [1961] 190 p. illus. 26 cm. [BX2310.R7T5] 61-13234
1. Rosary. I. Title.

VIAU, Arthur M. 922.244
The rosary in union with Saint Bernadette at the shrine of Loudres [i.e. Lourdes] at Lafargeville, New York, by Rev. Arthur M. Viau. [Watertown, N.Y., Printed by A. M. Phillips, 1942] 176 p. 15 1/2 cm. [BX2163.V5] 43-10603
1. Rosary. 2. Soubirous, Bernadette, Saint, 1844-1879. I. Title.

WANSBROUGH, Elizabeth. 248
The Rosary: the joyful mysteries. Pictures by Cecilia Pollen. [New York] Sheed and Ward [c1951] 1 v. illus. 21 cm. [BX2163.W27] 51-14578
1. Rosary I. Title.

WARD, Joseph Neville. 242'.742
Five for sorrow, ten for joy; a consideration of the Rosary [by] J. Neville Ward. [1st ed.] Garden City, N.Y., Doubleday, 1973 [c1971] 164 p. 22 cm. Includes bibliographical references. [BX2163.W29 1973] 72-96263 ISBN 0-385-03805-4 4.95
1. Rosary. 2. Christian life—Methodist authors. I. Title.

WARD, Joseph Neville. 242'.742
Five for sorrow, ten for joy; a consideration of the Rosary [by] J. Neville Ward. Garden City, N.Y., Image Books, 1974 [c1971] 197 p. 18 cm. [BX2163.W29 1974] 74-3378 ISBN 0-385-09544-9 1.45 (pbk.).
1. Rosary. 2. Christian life—Methodist authors. I. Title.

WARD, Maisie, 1889- 264.02
The rosary. New York, Sheed and Ward [1957?] 96p. 18cm. (Canterbury books) 'An abridged version of The splendor of the rosary.' [BX2163.W32] 57-4635
1. Rosary. I. Title.

WARD, Maisie, 1889- 264.02
The rosary. New York, Sheed and Ward [1957?] 96 p. 18 cm. (Canterbury books) "An abridged version of The splendor of the rosary." [BX2163.W32] 57-4635
1. Rosary. I. Title.

WARD, Maisie, 1889- 264.02
... *The splendor of the rosary,* with prayers by Caryll Houselander, with pictures by Fra Angelico. New York, Sheed and Ward, 1945. 5 p. l., 164 p., 1 l. fold. front., plates. 22 cm. [Full name: Mary Josephine (Ward) Sheed] [BX2163.W3] 45-8382
1. Rosary. I. Houselander, Frances Caryll. II. Fiesole, Giovannida, called Era Angelico, 1387-1455 illus III. F IV. Fiesole, Giovannida, called Fro Angelica, 1887-1455 illus. V. Title.

WILKINS, Eithne. 246'.5
The rose-garden game; a tradition of beads and flowers. [New York] Herder and Herder [1969] 239 p. illus. (part col.) 24 cm. (An Azimuth book) Includes bibliographical references. [BX2310.R7W5 1969] 70-87776 7.50
1. Rosary. 2. Rosary in art. I. Title.

WILLAM, Franz Michel, 232.931
1894-
The Rosary: its history and meaning. Translated by Edwin Kaiser. New York, Benziger Bros. [1953] 216p. 21cm. Translation of Die Geschichte und Gebetsschule des Rosenkranzes. [BX2163.W513] 53-1421
1. Rosary. I. Title.

WILLAM, Franz Michel, 232.931
1894-
The Rosary in daily life; translated by Edwin Kaiser. New York, Benziger Bros. [1953] 238p. 21cm. Translation of Der Rosenkranz und das Menschenleben. [BX2163.W5312] 54-188
1. Rosary. I. Title.

Rosary—Bibliography

AUTH, Charles Robert. 016.24836
Rosary bibliography: English language works. Washington, Dominican House of Studies, 1960. ix, 112p. 24cm. '500 copies ... Number 46.' [Z7838.R7A8] 60-3577
1. Rosary—Bibl. I. Title.

Rosary — Early works to 1800.

GRIGNON de Montfort, Louis Marie
Saint, 1673-1716.
The secret of the rosary, by Saint Louis Mary de Montfort. Translator: Mary Barbour, T.O.P. Bay Short, N.Y., Montfort Fathers Publications. [Rockford, Ill., Christ and Country Books, 1965] 125 p. 18 cm. 67-50200
1. Rosary — Early works to 1800. I. Title.

Rosary—Juvenile literature.

GEARON, Patrick J. 248.36
The Rosary for boys and girls. Chicago, 6415 Woodlawn Ave., Carmelite Third Order Press, 1961 201p. 2.00
I. Title.

GEARON, Patrick J., 1890- 248.36
The Rosary for children. Chicago, Carmelite Third Order Pr. [c.1961] 150p. 2.00 bds.,
I. Title.

JOYFUL mysteries of the 248.36
Rosary: pictures to punch out and assemble [New York, Golden Press] c.1960. unpaged col. illus. 36cm. (A Guild

punchout for Catholic boys and girls 30201) .50 pap.,

MCGRADE, Francis. 248
The Rosary for little Catholics; illustrated by Bruno Frost. St. Paul, Catechetical Guild Educational Society, c1952. unpaged. illus. 17cm. [BX2163.M26] 53-15935
1. Rosary—Juvenile literature. I. Title.

Rosary—Meditations.

BRICKEY, Janice. 242'.742
The triumphant way; rosary meditations. Foreword by Patrick J. Peyton. Pictures by Fra Angelico. St. Louis, Herder [1962] 95p. illus. 18cm. [BX2163.B68] 61-18371
1. Rosary—Meditations. I. Title.

A Dominican tertiary. 248
Simple rosary meditations, by a Dominican tertiary. Westminster, Md., Newman Press [1951] 164 p. 17 cm. [BX2163.S52] 52-928
1. Rosary—Meditations. I. Title.

FERRARO, John 248.36
Ten series of meditations on the mysteries of the Rosary. [dist. Boston, Daughters of St. Paul [c.1964] 229p. illus. 19cm. Cover title: Mysteries of the Rosary. 64-21600 2.25; 1.25 pap.,
1. Rosary—Meditations. I. Title. II. Title: Mysteries of the Rosary.

HAMMES, John A. 248.36
To help you say the Rosary better; practical Rosary meditations from scripture, the liturgy and the writings of the saints. Paterson, N.J. St. Anthony Guild Pr. [c.1962] 143p. 2.00; 1.50 pap.,
I. Title.

HAMMES, John A
To help you say the rosary better; practical rosary meditations from Scripture, the liturgy and the writings of the Saints. Paterson, N.J., St. Anthony Guild Press [1962] 143 p. illus. 17 cm. 63-18133
1. Rosary—Meditations. I. Title.

SCRIPTURAL Rosary Center. 242'.742
Scriptural Rosary; a modern version of the way the Rosary was once prayed throughout Western Europe in the late Middle Ages. Chicago [1963, c1961] 80 p. col. illus. 13 cm. [BX2163.S37] 64-66463
1. Rosary—Meditations. I. Title.

WALLACE, W J 242
Meditations for five Saturdays devotion; spiritual reflections for public and private use. [1st ed.] New York, Exposition Press [1955] 83p. 21cm. [BX2163.W25] 55-10307
1. Rosary—Meditations. I. Title.

WALLS, Ronald. 242
Christ who lives in me : Rosary meditations / Ronald Walls. Huntington, Ind. : Our Sunday Visitor, c1978. 144 p. ; 16 cm. [BX2163.W26] 78-62341 ISBN 0-87973-853-7 : 4.95
1. Rosary—Meditations. I. Title.

Rosary—Papal documents.

CATHOLIC Church. Pope. 242'.74
The Holy rosary / selected and arr. by the Benedictine monks of Solesmes ; translated by Paul J. Oligny. Boston, Ma. : St. Paul Editions, c1980. p. cm. (Papal teachings) Includes indexes. [BX2310.R7C3 1980] 79-28718 5.50
1. Rosary—Papal documents. I. Solesmes, France. Saint-Pierre (Benedictine abbey) II. Title.
Publisher's address: 50 St. Paul's Ave., Boston, MA 02130

Rosati, Joseph, Bp., 1789-1843.

EASTERLY, Frederick John, 1910- 922.273
... The life of Rt. Rev. Joseph Rosati, C.M., first bishop of St. Louis, 1789-1843 ... By Reverend Frederick John Easterly ... Washington, D.C., The Catholic university of America press, 1942. xi, 203 p., 1 l. 23 cm. (The Catholic university of America. Studies in American church history ... vol. XXXIII) Thesis (PH.D.)--Catholic university of America, 1942. Vita. "Essay on the sources": p. 191-197. [BX4705.R723E3] A 43
1. Rosati, Joseph, bp., 1789-1843. 2. St. Louis, Mo. (Archdiocese)—Hist. 3. Catholic church in St. Louis—Hist. I. Title.

EASTERLY, Frederick John, 1910- 282'.092'4 B
The life of Rt. Rev. Joseph Rosati, C.M., first bishop of St. Louis, 1789-1843. Washington, Catholic University of America Press, 1942. [New York, AMS Press, 1974] xi, 203 p. 23 cm. Reprint of the author's thesis, Catholic University of America, 1942, which was issued as v. 33 of the Catholic University of America. Studies in American church history. Bibliography: p. 191-197. [BX4705.R723E3 1974] 73-3587 ISBN 0-404-57783-0 9.00
1. Rosati, Joseph, Bp., 1789-1843. 2. Catholic Church in St. Louis—History. 3. St. Louis, Mo. (Archdiocese)—History. I. Series: Catholic University of America. Studies in American church history, v. 33.

Rose, Horace William, 1874-1901.

HICKS, Harry Wade. 922
A memorial of Horace William Rose, by Harry Wade Hicks. New York, The International committee of Young men's Christian associations, 1904. v, [3], 7-146 p. front. (port.) 19 cm. [BV1085.R6H5] 4-16329
1. Rose, Horace William, 1874-1901. I. Young men's Christian associations. International committee. II. Title.

Rose, Robert, 1704-1751.

ROSE, Robert, 1704-1751. 283'.092'4 B
The diary of Robert Rose : a view of Virginia by a Scottish colonial parson, 1746-1751 / edited and annotated by Ralph Emmett Fall ; map prepared and drawn by Murray Fontaine Rose. Verona, Va. : McClure Press, 1977. xxii, 400 p. : ill. ; 24 cm. Includes bibliographical references and indexes. [BX5995.R65A33] 77-88039 15.00
1. Rose, Robert, 1704-1751. 2. Church of England—Clergy—Biography. 3. Clergy—Virginia—Biography. I. Fall, Ralph Emmett. II. Title.

Rosemont, Pa. Church of the Good Shepherd.

COATES, Edward Osborne, 1889- 283.74812
An historical sketch of the Church of the Good Shepherd, Rosemont, Pennsylvania, 1869-1934, by E. Osborne Coates... [Philadelphia, 1935] 68 p. incl. front., illus. (incl. ports.) 23 cm. "Errata" slips inserted. [BX5980.R65C5] 35-10685
1. Rosemont, Pa. Church of the Good Shepherd. I. Title.

Rosen, Kopul, 1913-1962.

MEMORIES of Kopul Rosen, 296.6'1'0924 B edited by Cyril Domb. Wallingford (Berks.), Carmel College, 1970. 267 p., 23 plates. illus., facsims., plans, ports. 26 cm. Includes Dear David by K. Rosen, Wallingford, Carmel College (p. [191]-267) with special t.p. [BM755.R545M4] 75-520950 42/-
1. Rosen, Kopul, 1913-1962. 2. Judaism. I. Rosen, Kopul, 1913-1962. II. Domb, Cyril, ed. III. Rosen, Kopul, 1913-1962. Dear David. 1970.

Rosen, Moishe.

ROSEN, Moishe. 248'.246
Jews for Jesus [by] Moishe Rosen with William Proctor. Old Tappan, N.J., Revell [1974] 126 p. 21 cm. [BV2623.R58A34] 73-22169 ISBN 0-8007-0638-2 3.95
1. Rosen, Moishe. 2. Missions to Jews. 3. Converts from Judaism. I. Proctor, William, joint author. II. Title.

Rosenberg, Alfred, 1893-1946.

WHISKER, James B., 1939- 943.086'092'4
The social, political, and religious thought of Alfred Rosenberg : an interpretive essay / James Biser Whisker. Washington, D.C. : University Press of America, c1982. 141 p. ; 22 cm. Bibliography: p. 138-141. [DD247.R58W48 1982] 19 81-40652 ISBN 0-8191-2023-5 : 19.00 ISBN 0-8191-2024-3 (pbk.) : 8.25
1. Rosenberg, Alfred, 1893-1946. I. Title.

Rosenblatt, Samuel, 1902-

ROSENBLATT, Samuel, 1902- 296.6'1 B
The days of my years : an autobiography / by Samuel Rosenblatt. New York : Ktav Pub. House, 1976. 207 p., [7] leaves of plates : ill. ; 22 cm. [BM755.R565A33] 76-47616 ISBN 0-87068-494-9 : 10.00
1. Rosenblatt, Samuel, 1902- 2. Rabbis—United States—Biography. I. Title.

Rosenthal, Erwin Isak Jacob, 1904- — Addresses, essays, lectures.

INTERPRETING the Hebrew Bible : 221.6 essays in honour of E.I.J. Rosenthal ... / edited by J.A. Emerton and Stefan C. Reif. Cambridge [Cambridgeshire] ; New York : Cambridge University Press, 1982. xv, 318 p. : ill. ; 23 cm. (University of Cambridge oriental publications ; no. 32) Includes bibliographical references and indexes. [BS1188.I57 1982] 19 81-21668 ISBN 0-521-24424-2 : 39.50
1. Rosenthal, Erwin Isak Jacob, 1904- — Addresses, essays, lectures. 2. Bible. O.T.—Criticism, interpretation, etc.—Addresses, essays, lectures. 3. Bible. O.T.—Criticism, interpretation, etc., Jewish—Addresses, essays, lectures. I. Rosenthal, Erwin Isak Jacob, 1904- II. Emerton, John Adney. III. Reif, Sefan C., 1944- IV. Title. V. Series.

Rosenzweig, Franz, 1886-1929.

FREUND, Else, 1898- 296.3
Franz Rosenzweig's philosophy of existence : an analysis of The star of redemption / by Else-Rahel Freund ; [translated into English from the German rev. ed. by Stephen L. Weinstein and Robert Israel ; edited by Paul R. Mendes-Flohr]. The Hague ; Boston : M. Nijhoff ; Higham, MA : distribution for the U.S. and Canada, Kluwer Boston, 1979. viii, 189 p. ; 25 cm. (Studies in philosophy and religion ; v. 1) Translation of Die Existenzphilosophie Franz Rosenzweigs. Includes bibliographical references. [BM565.R6193F7313] 78-11983 ISBN 9-02-472091-5 : 35.30
1. Rosenzweig, Franz, 1886-1929. Stern der Erlosung. 2. Judaism. 3. Cosmology. 4. Religion—Philosophy. I. Mendes-Flohr, Paul R. II. Title. III. Series: Studies in philosophy and religion (Hague) ; v. 1.
Dist. by Kluwer, Boston, Mass.

Roseveare, Helen.

BURGESS, Alan. 266'.023'0924 B
Daylight must come; the story of a courageous woman doctor in the Congo. New York, Delacorte Press [1975, c1974] vi, 297 p. illus. 22 cm. [BV3625.C63R633 1975] 74-5479 ISBN 0-440-03365-9 6.95
1. Roseveare, Helen. I. Title.

BURGESS, Alan. 266'.023'0924 B
Daylight must come : the story of a courageous woman doctor in the Congo / Alan Burgess. Boston : G. K. Hall, 1975, c1974. 520 p. ; 25 cm. Originally published under title: Hostage. Large print ed. [BV3625.C63R633 1975b] 75-6727 ISBN 0-8161-6281-6 lib.bdg. : 12.95
1. Roseveare, Helen. 2. Sight-saving books. I. Title.

ROSEVEARE, Helen. 248.4
Living faith / by Helen M. Roseveare. Chicago : Moody Press, 1981, c1980. 158 p. ; 22 cm. [BV4637.R67 1981] 19 80-27923 ISBN 0-8024-4941-7 pbk. : 3.95
1. Rosevere, Helen. 2. Bible. N.T. Hebrews XI—Criticism, interpretation, etc. 3. Faith. I. Title.

ROSEVEARE, Helen. 266'.0092'4 B
Living sacrifice / by Helen M. Roseveare. Chicago : Moody Press, 1979. p. cm. Bibliography: p. [BV3625.C63R6433] 79-14831 ISBN 0-8024-4943-3 pbk. : 3.95
1. Roseveare, Helen. 2. Missionaries—Zaire—Biography. 3. Missionaries—United States—Biography. I. Title.

Rosh ha-Shanah.

ARZT, Max. 296.431
Justice and mercy: commentary on the liturgy of the new year and the day of Atonement. [1st ed.] New York, Holt, Rinehart and Winston [1963] 298 p. 21 cm. Bibliography: p. [297]-298. [BM695.N5A8] 63-11872
1. Rosh ha-Shanah. 2. Yom Kippur. I. Title.

GOODMAN, Philip, 1911- comp. 394.2'6829'6
The Rosh Hashanah anthology. [1st ed.] Philadelphia, Jewish Publication Society of America, 1970. xxx, 379 p. illus., facsims., music. 22 cm. Bibliography: p. 361-379. [BM695.N5G6] 74-105069 6.00
1. Rosh ha-Shanah. I. Title.

Rosh ha-Shanah—Juvenile literature.

CONE, Molly 296.4
The Jewish New Year. Illus. by Jerome Snvder New York, Crowell [1966] 1v. (unpaged) col. illus. 23cm. (Crowell holiday bk.) [BM695.N5C6] 66-7314 2.95 bds.,
1. Rosh ha-Shanah—Juvenile literature. 2. Rosh ha-Shanah—Juvenile literature I. Title.

SIMON, Norma. 296.431
Rosh Hashanah. Illus. by Ayala Gordon. [New York] United Synagogue Commission on Jewish Education, c1959 unpaged. illus. 25 cm. [BM695.N5S5] 59-12528
1. Rosh ha-Shanah — Juvenile literature. I. Title.

Rosicrucians.

ANDREA, Raymund. 212
The technique of the disciple, by Raymund Andrea ... San Jose, Calif., Supreme grand lodge of AMORC, Printing and publishing dept. [c1935] 184 p. 20 1/2 cm. (Rosicrucian library, vol. XVI) "First edition." Advertising matter: p. 170-184. [BF1623.R7R65 vol. 16] (133.082) [(159.961082)] 36-35
1. Rosicrucians. I. Title.

ANDREA, Raymund. 212
The technique of the master; or, The way of cosmic preparation, by Raymund Andrea ... San Jose, Calif., Rosicrucian press, Amorc college [c1932] 187 p. 20 1/2 cm. (Rosicrucian library, vol. XIII) "First edition." Advertisements: p. 175-187. [BF1623.R7R65 vol. 13] (133.082) [(159.961082)] 32-34356
1. Rosicrucians. I. Title.

ANDREA, Raymund. 212
The technique of the master; or, The way of cosmic preparation, by Raymund Andrea ... San Jose, Calif., Rosicrucian press, Amorc college [1934] 188 p. 20 1/2 cm. (Rosicrucian library, vol. XIII) "Second edition." Advertisements: p. 175-188. [BF1623.R765 vol.13 a] (133.082) [159.961082)] 35-11449
1. Rosicrucians. I. Title.

BOND, Frederick Clifton. 212
The demonstrating Christ, by Frederick Clifton Bond. Los Angeles, Printed by the Catterlin publishing co. [c1933] 210 p. front. 19 1/2 cm. [BF1623.R7B58] 33-14658
1. Rosicrucians. I. Title.

BOND, Frederick Clifton. 212
God, nature, man, by Frederick Bond. Los Angeles, Calif., Printed by Catterlin publishing company [c1933] 1 p. l., [7]-77 p. front. (port.) 18 1/2 cm. [BF1623.R7B6] 83-4922
1. Rosicrucians. I. Title.

[BROOKSMITH, Clifford Edgar] 1899- 212
The secret doctrine of the Rosicrucians, by Magnus Incognito [pseud.] Illus. with the secret Rosicrucian symbols. Chicago,

Occult Press [1949] 256 p. illus. 20 cm. [BF1623.R7B7] 49-5513
1. Rosicrucians. I. Title.

CARRINGTON, Ulrich Steindorff, 1888- tr. 212
Of Gods and miracles; wondrous tales of the ancient Egyptians. [1st ed.] San Jose, Calif., Supreme Grand Lodge of AMORC [1954] 189p. illus: 20cm. (Rosicrusion library, v. 24) [BF1623.R7C28] 53-9733
1. Rosichucians. I. Title.

CASE, Paul Foster. 212
The true and invisible Rosicrucian order; an interpretation of the Rosicrucian allegory and an explanation of the ten Rosicrucian grades, by Paul Foster Case. 3d ed. rev. and enl. [San Marino, Calif.] c1933. 1 p. l., 147 numb. l. front., illus., diagrs. 28 cm. Mimeographed. [BF1623.R7C3 1933] ca 34
1. Rosicrucians. I. Title.

CLYMER, Reuben Swinburne, 1878- 133
A compendium of occult laws; the selection, arrangement and application of the most important of occult laws taught by the masters on initiation of the great secret schools of the past and present--Hermetic, Rosicrucian, alchemic and Aeth priesthood, and the practice of the laws in the development of the fourfold nature of man in attaining success and mastership on all planes of activity: interpretation, arrangement and application by R. Swinburne Clymer... Quakertown, Penna., The Philosophical publishing company [c1938] 1 p. l., 5-269, [1] p. 23 1/2 cm. (On cover: Rosicrucian series) [BF1623.R7C55] [159.961 39-2587
1. Rosicrucians. I. Title. II. Title: Occult laws.

CLYMER, Reuben Swinburne, 1878- 299
The Fraternitatis Rosae Crucis; an attempt to harmonize the spirit of the writings of those who are known to have been Rosicrucians and a comparison of the statements of those recognized as authorities, with extensive analysis and annotations, by R. Swinburne Clymer. Quakertown, Pa., The Philosophical publishing co. [c1929] 3 p. l., [ix]-xxiv, 221 p. incl. front., illus. 23 1/2 cm. [BF1623.R7C57] 29-13243
1. Rosicrucians. 2. Secret societies. I. Title.

CLYMER, Reuben Swinburne, 1878- 299
The fraternity of the Rosicrucians, their teachings and mysteries according to the manifestoes issued at various times by the fraternity itself. Also, some of thier secret teachings and the mystery of the order explained... By Rev. Dr. R. Swinburne Clymer... Allentown, Pa., The Philosophical publishing co. [c1906] 304 p. front. 20 1/2 cm. [BF1623.B7C6] 6-45110
1. Rosicrucians. I. Title.

CLYMER, Reuben Swinburne, 1878- ed. 299
The Rose cross order; a short sketch of the history of the Rose cross order in America, together with a sketch of the life of Dr. P. B. Randolph, the founder of the order... Introduction and notes by Dr. R. Swinburne Clymer... Allentown, Pa., The Philosophical publishing co., 1916. 208 p. illus. 20 1/2 cm. [BF1623.R7C67] 17-3898 1.00
1. Randolph, Paschal Beverly, b. 1825. 2. Rosicrucians. I. Title.

CLYMER, Reuben Swinburne, 1878- 299
The Rosicrucians, their teachings... by R. Swinburne Clymer... Quakertown, Pa., The Philosophical publishing company [c1923] 4 p. l., [11]-238 p. illus. 23 1/2 cm. "Third edition." [BF1623.R7C7 1923] 23-17130
1. Resicrucians. I. Title.

CLYMER, Reuben Swinburne, 1878- 299
The Rosicrucians, their teachings and mysteries according to the manifestoes issued at various times by the fraternity itself. Also, some of their secret teachings and the mystery of the order explained... By Rev. Dr. R. Swinburne Clymer ... 2d. ed. Allentown, Pa., The Philosophical publishing co. [c1910] 212 p. illus. 23 1/2 cm. [BF1623.R7C7] 10-14179
1. Rosicrucians. I. Title.

CLYMER, Reuben Swinburne, 1878- 212
The Rosicrucians--their teachings, the Fraternitas Rosae Crucis, American section; the manifestoes issued by the Brotherhood, order, temple and fraternity of the Rosicrucians since its foundation in America have been edited and the teachings made applicable to modern conditions and the needs of the new age. By R. Swinburne Clymer... Quakertown, Penna., The Philosophical publishing company, Beverly hall foundation [c1941] xvi, 275, [1] p. 23 1/2 cm. "Completely revised edition." "The first edition was issued under the title: Fraternity of the Rosicrucians."--Introd. [BF1623.R7C6 1941] 42-5323
1. Rosicrucians. I. Title.

DORCHEFF, George, 1893- 135.43
Evolution of the earth. Illustrated with diagrs. by the author. [1st ed.] New York, Vantage Press [1967, c1966] 271 p. 21 cm. [BF1623.R7D6] 66-21110
1. Rosicrucians. I. Title.

[DOWD, Freeman Benjamin] 218
Evolution of immortality, by Rosicrucise [pseud.] ... Salem, Mass., Eulian publishing company [1900] 145 p. 20 1/2 cm. [BF1623.R7D65] 3-3544
1. Rosicrucians. I. Title.

DOWD, Freeman Benjamin. 133
The temple of the rosy cross. The soul: its powers, migrations, and transmigrations. By F. B. Dowd ... Philadelphia, J. R. Rue, jr., printer, 1882. vi, [7]-253 p. 16 cm. [BF1623.R7D7 1882] 1-21017
1. Rosicrucians. I. Title.

DOWD, Freeman Benjamin. 133
The temple of the rosy cross. The soul: its powers, migrations, and transmigrations. 2d ed. Rev. and enl. by F. B. Dowd ... San Francisco, Cal., Rosy cross publishing co., 1888. 240 p. 19 cm. [BF1623.R7D7 1888] 1-21018
1. Rosicrucians. I. Title.

DOWD, Freeman Benjamin. 133
The temple of the rosy cross. The soul: its powers, migrations, and transmigrations. 4th ed., rev. and enl. By F. B. Dowd ... Salem, Mass., Eulian publishing co., 1901. 323 p. front. (port.) 19 cm. [BF1623.R7D7 1901] 1-22084
1. Rosicrucians. I. Title.

DOWD, Freeman Benjamin. 133
The way; a text book for the student of Rosicrucian philosophy, by Freeman B. Dowd ... Quakertown, Pa., c1917. 160 p. 23 cm. [BF1623.R7D75] 18-1513
1. Rosicrucians. I. Title.

HEINDEL, Mas, 1865-1919. 133
The Rosicrucian philosophy in questions and answers, by Max Heindel. 1st ed. ... Seattle, Rosicrucian fellowship; Chicago, M. A. Donohue & co. [c1910] 430 p. diagrs. 20 cm. [BF1623.R7H5] 10-24184
1. Rosicrucians. I. Title.

HEINDEL, Mas; d.1919. 133
The Rosicrucian cosmo--conception; or, Mystic Christanity; an elementary treatise upon man's past evolution, present constitution and future development, by Max Heindel ... 3d ed., rev. enl. and indexed ... Ocean Park, Calif., Rosicrucian fellowship [c1911] 602 p. front., col. pl., diagrs. 20 cm. 1.50 [BF1623.R7H43] 11-
1. Rosicrucians. I. Title.

HEINDEL, Max. 133
The Rosicrucian cosmo--conception; or, Christian occult science; an elementary treatise upon man's past evolution, present constitution and future development, by Max Heindel ... 2d ed., rev. and enl. Seattle, Wash., Rosicrucian fellowship; Chicago, M. A. Donahue & co. [c1910] 542 p. front., illus., col. pl. 20 cm. [BF1623.R7H42] 10-24315
1. Rosicrucians. I. Title.

HEINDEL, Max.
The Rosicrucian cosmo--conception; or, Christian occult science, an elementary treatise upon man's past evolution, present constitution and future development, by Max Heindel ... 1st ed. ... Seattle, Wash., Rosicrucian fellowship; Chicago, Ill., Independent book co. [c1909] 536, [6] p. col. front., illus., diagrs. (partly col.) 19 1/2 cm. $1.00 9-29803
1. Rosicrucians. I. Title.

HEINDEL, Max, 1864-1919. 133
Freemasonry and Catholicism [by] Max Heindel, an exposition of the cosmic facts underlying these two great institutions as determined by occult investigation. 1st ed. Oceanside, Calif., International headquarters Rosicrucian fellowship; [etc., etc. c1919] 96 p. front. (port.) fold. pl. 20 cm. [BF1623.R7H3 1919] 20-
1. Rosicrucians. I. Title.

HEINDEL, Max, 1865-1919. 212
The desire body. 1st ed. Oceanside, Calif., Rosicrucian Fellowship [1953] 160p. illus. 20cm. [BF1623.R7H28] 53-36888
1. Rosicrucians. 2. Desire. I. Title.

HEINDEL, Max, 1865-1919. 133
Gleanings of a mystic, by Max Heindel, a series of essays on practical mysticism. 1st ed. Oceanside, Calif., The Rosicrucian fellowship; [etc., etc, c1922] 196 p. 19 1/2 cm. [BF1623.R7H35] 23-
1. Rosicrucians. I. Title.

HEINDEL, Max, 1865-1919. 133
The Rosicrucian cosmo--conception; or, Mystic Christianity, an elementary treatise upon man's past evolution, present constitution and future development, by Max Heindel ... 8th ed., twenty--seventh thousand. Oceanside, Calif., Rosicrucian fellowship; [etc., etc., c1922] 616 p. front. (port.) illus., plates (1 col.) diagrs. 19 1/2 cm. [BF1623.R7H43 1922] 23-7735
1. Rosicrucians. I. Title.

HEINDEL, Max, 1865-1919 212
The Rosicrucian cosmo--conception; or, Mystic Christianity; an elementary treatise upon man's past evolution, present constitution and future development, by Max Heindel ... 11th ed. Oceanside, Calif., The Rosicrucian fellowship; London, L. N. Fowler & co. [c1929] 702 p. front. (port.) illus., plates (part col.) diagrs. 19 1/2 cm. [BF1623.R7H43 1929] 37-8453
1. Rosicrucians. I. Title.

HEINDEL, Max, 1865-1919. 212
The Rosicrucian cosmo--conception; or, Mystic Christianity; an elementary treatise upon man's past evolution, present constitution and future development, by Max Heindel ... 14th ed. Oceanside, Calif., Mrs. Max Heindel; London, L. N. Fowler & co. [c1931] 702 p. front. (port.) illus., plates (part col.) diagrs. 19 1/2 cm. [BF1623R7H43 1931 a] 32-
1. Rosicrucians. I. Title.

HEINDEL, Max, 1865-1919. 133
The Rosicrucian mysteries; an elementary exposition of their secret teachings, by Max Heindel ... Ocean Park, Cal., Rosicrucian fellowship [c1911] 198 p. 20 cm. [BF1623.R7H45] 11-
1. Rosicrucians. I. Title.

HEINDEL, Max, 1865-1919. 299
The Rosicrucian philosophy in questions and answers. 1st ed. Seattle, Rosicrucian Fellowship [1910]-48. 2 v. illus. 20 cm. Vol. 2 comp. from magazine articles pub. 1913-1919 in Rays from the Rose Cross. Vol. 2 pub. in Oceanside, Calif. [BF1623.R7H5] 10-24184
1. Rosicrucians I. Title.

HEINDEL, Max, 1865-1919. 212
The vital body. 1st ed. Oceanside, Calif., Rosicrucian Fellowship [1951, '1950] 198 p. port. 20 cm. [BF1623.R7H57] 51-20324
1. Rosicrucians. I. Title.

HEINDEL, Max, 1865-1919. 299
The web of destiny; how made and unmade, also The occult effect of our emotions. Prayer--a magic invocation. Practical methods of achieving success. [By] Max Heindel; a series of lessons upon the hidden side of life, showing the occult forces which shape our destiny. 1st ed. Oceanside, Calif., Roscicrucian fellowship; [etc., etc., c1920] 175 p. front. (port.) 20 cm. [BF1623.R7H6] 21-
1. Roscicrucians. I. Title.

HEINDEL, Max, d.1919. 299
Mas Heindel's letters to students, Dec. 1910 to Jan. 1919, inclusive, 1st ed. Oceanside, Calif., The Rosicrucian fellowship; [etc., etc., c1925] 237 p. front. (port.) 19 1/2 cm. [BF1623.R7H37 1925] 26-1199
1. Rosicrucians. I. Title.

HEINDEL, Max, d.1919. 212
The Rosicrucian cosmo--conception; or, Mystic Christianity; an elementary treatise upon man's past evolution, present constitution and future development, by Max Heindel ... 13th ed., fifty--one thousand. Oceanside, Calif., The Rosicrucian fellowship; London, L. N. Fowler & co. [c1931] 603 p. illus., plates (part col., 1 fold.) diagrs. 19 cm. [BF1623.R7H43 1931] 31-19973
1. Rosicrucians. I. Title.

HENRY, Alfred Hylas, 1865- 299
Ex oriente lux: lecture outlines for those seeking initiation into the hidden house of masonry; a discussion of the method of approach, to the fundamental principles of Rosicrucian doctrine, on the part of those who have become habituated to western ideas and modes of thinking, by Alfred H. Henry ... Boston, Mass., The Stratford company, 1924. 4 p. l., x p., 1 l., 248 p. 19 1/2 cm. [BF1623.R7H7] 24-4128
1. Rosicrucians. I. Title.

JENNINGS, Hargrave, 1817?-1890. 212
The Rosicrucians, their rites and mysteries. 4th ed., rev., by Hargrave Jennings ... Illustrated by upwards of three hundred engravings and twelve full-page plates. London, G. Routledge & sons, limited; New York, E. P. Dutton & co. [1907] xvi, 464 p. illus., 12 pl. on. 6 l. 23 cm. [BF1623.R7J4 1907] 32-32113
1. Rosicrucians. I. Title.

LEWIS, Harve Spencer, 1883- 366.4
Rosicrucian manual, prepared under the supervision of H. Spencer Lewis ... San Jose, Calif., Rosicrucian press, Amore college [c1932] viii, 194 p. incl. illus., plates, ports., facsim., diagrs. 23 1/2 cm. (Rosicrucian library, v. no. 8) Pages 191-194, advertisements. [BF1623.R7R65 vol. 8] (133.082) 32-33004
1. Rosicrucians. I. Title.

LEWIS, Harve Spencer, 1883- 299
Rosicrucian principles for the home and business, by Dr. H. Spencer Lewis. San Jose, Calif., AMORC [c1929] 2 p. l., 7-170 p. 17 cm. [BF1623.R7L4] 29-18992
1. Rosicrucians. 2. Psychology, Applied. I. Ancient and mystical order rosae crucis. II. Title.

LEWIS, Harve Spencer, 1883- 299
Rosicrucian questions and answers, with complete history of the Rosicrucian order, by H. Spencer Lewis ... San Jose, Calif., Rosicrucian press, AMORC college [c1929] 300 p. illus. 20 cm. (Rosicrucian library, v. no. 1) Pages 294-300, advertisements. Bibliography: p. 60-68. [BF1623.R7R65 vol. 1] 29-30689
1. Rosicrucians. I. Title.

LEWIS, Harve Spencer, 1883- 299
Self mastery and fate, with the cycles of life, by H. Spencer Lewis ... San Jose, Calif., Rosicrucian press, AMORC college [1929] 261 p. diagrs. 20 cm. (Rosicrucian library, v. no. 7) Pages 256-261, advertising matter. [BF1623.R7R65 vol. 7] 30-7514
1. Rosicrucians. 2. Success. I. Title.

LEWIS, Harve Spencer, 1883- 913.32
The symbolic prophecy of the Great pyramid, by Dr. H. Spencer Lewis ... San Jose, Calif., Supreme grand lodge of AMORC [c1936] 208 p. incl. illus., plates, plans. 20 cm. (Rosicrucian library, vol. xiv) "First edition." Pages 193-208, advertising matter. [BF1623.R7R65 vol. 14bis] (133.082) [(159.961082)] 37-3808
1. Rosicrucians. 2. Pyramids—Curiosa and miscellany. I. Title.

LEWIS, Harve Spencer, 1883-1939. 133.4'3
Essays of a modern mystic, from the writings of H. Spencer Lewis. [1st ed.] San Jose, Calif., Supreme Grande Lodge of AMORC, Print. and Pub. Dept. [1962] 214 p. illus. 20 cm. (Rosicrucian library, v. 27) [BF1623.R7R65 vol. 27] 63-32873
1. Rosicrucians. I. Title.

LEWIS, Harve Spencer, 1883-1939.
Rosicrucian manual, prepared under the supervision of H. Spencer Lewis. [16th ed] San Jose, Calif., Supreme Grand Lodge of AMORC [1961, c1941] x. 217 p. llus. 23 cm. (Rosicrucian library, v. no. 8) 63-50874
1. Rosicrucians. I. Title. II. Series.

LEWIS, Harve Spencer, 1883-1939.
Rosicrucian manual, prepared under the supervision of H. Spencer Lewis [17th ed] San Jose, Calif. Supreme Grand Lodge of AMORC Print. and Pub. Dept. [1963] x, 217 p. illus., ports. 23 cm. (Rosicrucian library, v. 8) 66-94007
1. Rosicrucians. I. Title. II. Series.

LEWIS, Harve Spencer, 1883- 366.4
1939.
Rosicrucian manual, prepared under the supervision of H. Spencer Lewis ... San Jose, Calif., Rosicrucian press, printing and publishing department, for the Supreme grand lodge AMORC [1941] viii, 211 p. incl. illus., plates, ports., facsims., diagrs. 23 cm. (Rosicrucian library, v. 8) "First edition, 1918 ... eighth edition, 1941." [BF1623.R7R65] (133.082) [(159.961082)] 41-16452
1. Rosicrucians. I. Title.

LEWIS, Harve Spencer, 1883- 366.4
1939.
Rosicrucian questions and answers; with complete history of the Rosicrucian order, by H. Spencer Lewis ... San Jose, Calif., Supreme grand lodge of AMORC [1941] 340 p. incl. group port., facsims. 20 cm. (Rosicrucian library, vol. i) "Third edition, July 1941." Pages 321-340, advertising matter. [BF1623.R7R65 vol. 1b] (133.082) [(159.961082)] 41-23465
1. Rosicrucians. I. Title.

LEWIS, Harve Spencer, 1883- 212
1939.
Self mastery and fate, with the cycles of life. [14th ed.] San Jose, Calif., Supreme Grand Lodge of AMORC [1954] 271p. illus. 20cm. (Rosicrucian library, v. 7) [BF1623.R7R65 vol.7 1954] 55-16785
1. Rosicrucians. 2. Success. I. Title.

LEWIS, Harve Spencer, 1883-1939.
Self mastery and fate, with the cycles of life. [20th ed.] San Jose, Calif., Supreme Grand Lodge of AMORC [1963] 271 p. illus. 20 cm. (Rosicrucian library, v, 7) "Guide for use with self mastery and fate coin" (11 p.) in pocket. 68-80316
1. Rosicrucians. 2. Success. I. Title. II. Series.

LEWIS, Ralph M. 133
Along civilization's trail, by Ralph M. Lewis... San Jose, Calif., Supreme grand lodge of AMORC, Printing and publishing department [c1940] 216 p. illus. 23 1/2 cm. (Rosicrucian library. vol. xix) Pages 208-216, advertising matter. [BF1623.R7R65 vol. 19] [159.961] (133.062) [(159.961082)] 41-11764
1. Rosicrucians. 2. Occult sciences. 3. Voyages and travels. I. Title.

LEWIS, Ralph Maxwell, 1904- 212
The conscious interlude. [1st ed.] San Jose, Calif., Supreme Grand Lodge of AMORC [1957] 390p. illus. 20cm. (Rosicrucian library, v. 26) [BF1623.R7R65 vol.26] 57-8541
1. Rosicrucians. I. Title. II. Series.

LEWIS, Ralph Maxwell, 1904-
The sanctuary of self. [7th ed.] San Jose, Calif., Supreme Grand Lodge of AMORC, Print. and Pub. Dept. [1966, c1948] 367 p. 20 cm. (Rosicrucian library, v. 22) 68-3702
1. Rosicrucians. I. Title.

LITTLEFIELD, George Elmer. 212
Illumination and love, by Ariel, George Elmer Littlefield. Santa Barbara, Calif., The Red rose press [1928] 3 p. l., iv p., 1 l., [13]-96 p. illus. 21 cm. [BF1623.R7L5] 38-10410
1. Rosicrucians. I. Title.

†MAIER, Michael, 1568?- 135.4'3
1622.
Laws of the Fraternity of the Rosie Crosse (Themis aurea) / by Michael Maier ; introductory preface by Manly P. Hall. Los Angeles : Philosophical Research Society, c1976. [39], 136 p. ; 19 cm. Reprint of the 1656 ed. Printed for N. Brooke, London, under title: Themis aurea. [BF1623.R7M21313 1976] 76-9613 10.00
1. Rosicrucians. I. Title.

MYSTIC Americanism 135.4'3'0973
: or, The spiritual heritage of America revealed : from the works of R. S. Clymer and Grace Kincaid Morey / edited by Paul P. Ricchio ; authorization by Emerson M. Clymer. Quakertown, Pa. : Philosophical Pub. Co., c1975. xxv, 328 p. : ill. ; 24 cm. [BF1623.R7M82] 75-39512
1. Rosicrucians. 2. United States—History—Miscellanea. I. Clymer, Reuben Swinburne, 1878- II. Morey, Grace Kincaid. III. Ricchio, Paul P.

MYSTIC Americanism 135.4'3'0973
: or, The spiritual heritage of America revealed : from the works of R. S. Clymer and Grace Kincaid Morey / edited by Paul P. Ricchio ; authorization by Emerson M. Clymer. Quakertown, Pa. : Philosophical Pub. Co., c1975. xxv, 328 p. : ill. ; 24 cm. [BF1623.R7M82] 75-39512
1. Rosicrucians. 2. United States—History—Miscellanea. I. Clymer, Reuben Swinburne, 1878- II. Morey, Grace Kincaid. III. Ricchio, Paul P.

NUTHALL, Beatrice. 133.9'092'4
The triumph of life. London, New York, Regency Press, 1971. 93 p. 23 cm. [BF1623.R7N88] 72-185242 ISBN 0-7212-0134-2 £1.20
1. Rosicrucians. I. Title.

PARCHMENT, Samuel Richard, 212
1881-
The just law of compensation, by S. R. Parchment. A labor of love in the cause of universal brotherhood. 1st ed. ... San Francisco, Calif., San Francisco center, Roiscrucian fellowship [c1932] 126 p. 16 cm. [BF1623.R7P3] 32-34915
1. Rosicrucians. I. Title.

[PLUMMER, George Winslow] 133
1876-
Rosicrucian fundamentals; an exposition of the Rosicrucian synthesis of religion, science and philosophy in fourteen complete instructions, by Khei [pseud.] ... authorized by the High council of the Societas rosicruciana in America. New York city, Flame press, 1920. 7 p. l., 398 p., 1 l. col. front., illus. 23cm. [BF1623.R7P5] 20-18412
1. Rosicrucians. I. Title.

[PLUMMER, George Winslow] 299
Rosicrucian symbology a treatise wherein the discerning ones will find the elements of constructive symbology and certain other things, by Khei, F. . R. . C. . 0°-X° [pseud.] ... New York, Macoy pvblishing and masonic svpply co., 1916. 4 p. l., 66 p. illus., pl., diagrs. 24cm. $1.50. [BF1623.R7P6] 16-22327
1. Rosicrucians. 2. Symbolism. I. Title.

PLUMMER, George Winslow, 133
1876-
Hermetic fundamentals, by Dr. George Winslow Plummer ... [New York, Mercury publishing company] c1924. cover-title, 104 p. 21 1/2cm. In 12 lessons, each with caption title: Societas rosicruciana in America ... Occult sciences, liber Hermetic series, nos. [1-12] Serial number, 13[-24] [BF1623.R7P45] 25-10628
1. Rosicrucians. I. Title.

PLUMMER, George Winslow, 299
1876-
Rosicrucian manual for the instruction of postulants in the associate membership neophytes, and fraters of duly instituted colleges of the Societas rosicrusians in America. written and compiled by Dr. George Winslow Plummer ...Authorized by the High council S. R. A. ...3d ed. New York, Done into print and publisht for the S. . R. . I. . A. ., by the Mercury publishing co., 1927. 2 p. l., [9]-131, [1] p. front., illus. 23cm. Lettered on cover: S. . R. . I. . A. . First edition has title: Rosicrucian fundamentals. [BF1623.R7P5 1927] 27-20142
1. Rosicrucians. I. Title.

PLUMMER, George Winslow, 299
1876-
Rosicrucian manual for the instruction of postulants in the congregation of the outer, neophytes, and fraters of duly instituted colleges of the Societas rosicruciana in America. written and compiled by Dr. George Winslow Plummer ... 2d ed. Authorized by the High council, S. R. I. A. ... New York, Published for the S. . R. . I. . A. ., by the Mercury publishing co., 1923. 2 p. l., [9]-131, [1] p. front., illus. 23 1/2cm. Lettered on cover: S. . R. . I. . A. . manual. First edition has title: Rosicrucian fundamentals. [BF1623.R7P5 1923] 25-9447
1. Rosicrucians. I. Title.

PLUMMER, Goerge Winslow.
The master's word; a short treatise on the word, the light and the self. Addressed to Rosicrucians and Freemasons whereever they may be dispersed, by George Winslow Plummer, F.R.C. New York, Goodyear book concern, 1913. 116 p. 17 1/2cm. $0.50. 14-274
I. Title.

POOLE, Cecil A. 135.4'3
The eternal fruits of knowledge / by Cecil A. Poole. 1st ed. San Jose, Calif. : Supreme Grand Lodge of AMORC, Print. and Pub. Dept., 1975. 162 p. ; 20 cm. (Rosicrucian library ; v. 33) [BF1623.R7R65 vol. 33] 76-352583
1. Rosicrucians. I. Title. II. Series.

REGARDIE, Israel. 135.4
Twelve steps to spiritual enlightenment. [Dallas, Sangreal Foundation, c1969] 92 [4] p. 22 cm. Bibliography: p. [94-95] [BF1623.R7R36] 73-20622
1. Rosicrucians. I. Title.

ROSICRUCIAN questions and answers; with complete history of the Rosicrucian order. [6th ed.] San Jose, Calif., Supreme Grand Lodge of AMORC [1959] 315p. illus. 20cm. (Rosicrucian library, v. 1)
1. Rosicrucians. I. Lewis, Harve Spencer, 1883-1939. II. Series.

SCOTT, John Pinckney. 226
The four Gospels esoterically interpreted, by John P. Scott ... [Oceanside, Calif., The Langford press, c1937] 3 p. l., 169 p. 29 cm. [BS2891.S35] 37-4481
1. Rosicrucians. 2. Bible. N. T. Gospels—Commentaries. 3. Bible—Commentaries—N. T. Gospels. I. Title.

SCOTT, John Pinckney. 220.7
The hidden Bible ... by John P. Scott ... [Oceanside, Calif., c1935- v. 23 cm. Cover-title. [BS534.S37] 35-14703
1. Rosicrucians. 2. Bible—Criticism, interpretations, etc. I. Title.

WAITE, Arthur Edward, 1857-1942.
The Brotherhood of the Rosy Cross, being records of the House of the Holy Spirit in its inward and outward history. New Hyde Park, N.Y., University Books [1961] 649 p. illus. 24 cm.
1. Rosicrucians. I. Title.

WEED, Joseph J. 135.43
A Rosicrucian speaks [by] Joseph J. Weed. New York, Chatsworth Pr. [1966, c.1965] 216p. 21cm. [BF1623.R7W4] 66-7903 4.95
1. Rosicrucians. I. Title.

WEED, Joseph J. 135.4'3
Wisdom of the mystic masters [by] Joseph J. Weed. West Nyack, N.Y., Parker Pub. Co. [1968] xii, 208 p. 24 cm. [BF1623.R7W42] 68-24130
1. Rosicrucians. I. Title.

Rosicrucians—Bibliography

BIRDSONG, Robert E 016.212
Rosicrucian literature listed in Union Catalog and not to be found in Library of Congress comp. 1946-1948. $53n. p., 1948] [65] 1. 21 x 27 cm. Typewritten. [Z6878.R7B53] 49-5032
1. Rosicrucians—Bibl. 2. U. S. Library of Congress. National Union Catalog. I. Title.

Rosicrucians—Bibliography—Catalogs.

BIRDSONG, Robert E 016.
Check list of Rosicrucian literature in the Library of Congress, comp. 1937-1947. [n. p., 1947] v. (unpaged) 27 cm. Typewritten. [Z6878.R7B5] 49-3796
1. Rosicrucians—Bibl.—Catalogs. I. U. S Library of Congress. National Union Catalog. II. Title.

Rosicrucians—History.

YATES, Frances 135.4'3'094
Amelia.
The Rosicrucian enlightenment, [by] Frances A. Yates. London, Boston, Routledge and Kegan Paul, 1972. xv, 269, [31] p. illus., facsims., map, ports. 23 cm. Includes bibliographical references. [BF1623.R7Y38 1972] 72-90113 ISBN 0-7100-7380-1
1. Rosicrucians—History. I. Title.

Rosicrucians—Manuscripts.

CODEX rosae crucis; 135.4'3
a rare and curious manuscript of Rosicrucian interest, now published for the first time in its original form. Introd. and commentary, by Manly Hall. [Rev. and enl. ed. Los Angeles] Philosophical Research Society, 1971. 113 p. illus. 36 cm. [BF1623.R7C78 1971] 72-176826
1. Rosicrucians—Manuscripts. I. Hall, Manly Palmer, 1901-

Rosmini Serbati, Antonio, 1797-1855.

LEETHAM, Claude Richard Harbord.
Rosmini, Priest, philosopher and patriot. With an introd. by Giuseppe Bozzetti. [1st ed.] London, New York, Longmans, Green [1957] xxiii, 508p. port., facsim., map. 28cm. Bibliography: p. 483-485.
1. Rosmini Serbati, Antonio, 1797-1855. I. Title.

LEETHAM, Claude Richard 921.5
Harbord.
Rosmini: priest, philosopher, and patriot. With an introd. by Giuseppe Bozzetti. Baltimore, Helicon Press [1958] 508p. illus. 23cm. [B3646.L4 1958] 58-10748
1. Rosmini Serbati, Antonio, 1797-1855. I. Title.

Ross, Eliza Scott, 1838-1846.

MANN, Thomas. 922
Eliza Scott Ross, who died at Huntley, Aberdeenshire, August 19th, 1846, aged eight years, and two months. By Thomas Mann ... From the London edition. Approved by the Committee of publication. Boston, Massachusetts Sabbath school society, 1849. iv, [5]-108 p. 15 1/2 cm. English edition, 1847, has title: Letters to children. A narrative of the life and death of Eliza Scott Ross. [BR1715.R65M3 1849] 37-20252
1. Ross, Eliza Scott, 1838-1846. I. Massachusetts Sabbath school society. Committee of publication. II. Title.

Ross, Mrs. Elizabeth (Williams) 1852-1926.

WEAVER, Gustine Nancy 922.673
(Courson) Mrs. 1873-
Our guest, by Gustine Courson Weaver (Mrs. Clifford Selden Weaver) ... St. Louis, Mo., The Bethany press, 1928. 289 p. front., pl., ports. 19 1/2 cm. [BX7343.R58W4] 30-33482
1. Ross, Mrs. Elizabeth (Williams) 1852-1926. I. Title.

Ross, Xavier, Mother, 1813-1895.

GILMORE, Julia, Sister. 922.273
Come north! The life-story of Mother Xavier Ross, foundress of the Sisters of Charity of Leavenworth. Illus. by Patricia De Buck. New York, McMullen Books, 1951. 310 p. illus. 21 cm. [BX4705.R7252G5] 52-6153
1. Ross, Xavier, Mother, 1813-1895. 2. Sisters of Charity of Leavenworth (Kansas) I. Title.

Rossello, Maria Giuseppa, Saint, 1811-1880.

BURTON, Katherine (Kurz) 922.245
Wheat for this planting; the biography of Saint Mary Joseph Rossello, foundress of the Daughters of Our Lady of Mercy. Milwaukee, Bruce Pub. Co. [c.1960] ix, 158p. illus. 22cm. (Catholic life publications) 60-50092 3.50
1. Rossello, Maria Giuseppa, Saint, 1811-

1880. 2. Daughters of Our Lady of Mercy. I. Title.

Roswell Street Baptist Church, Marietta, Ga.

PRICE, Nelson L. 286'.1758'245
I've got to play on their court / Nelson L. Price. Nashville, Tenn. : Broadman Press, c1975. 140 p. : ill. ; 20 cm. [BX6480.M25R676] 75-8326 ISBN 0-8054-5554-X : 4.95
1. Roswell Street Baptist Church, Marietta, Ga. I. Title.

Roth, Leon, 1896-1963.

LOEWE, Raphael, ed. 296.08
Studies in rationalism, Judaism & universalism; in memory of Leon Roth. London, Routledge & K. Paul; New York, Humanities P., 1966. xiii, 357 p. front. (port.) 22 1/2 cm. 50/- Bibliography: p. 323-336. [BM42.L6] 67-70094
1. Roth, Leon, 1896-1963. 2. Judaism — Addresses, essays, lectures. I. Roth, Leon, 1896-1963. II. Title.

Roth, Sid.

ROTH, Sid. 248'.246'0924 B
Something for nothing / by Sid Roth as told to Irene Burk Harrell. Plainfield, N.J. : Logos International, c1976. vii, 133 p. ; 22 cm. [BV2623.R63A35] 75-31396 ISBN 0-88270-145-2 : 5.95. ISBN 0-88270-146-0 pbk. :
1. Roth, Sid. 2. Converts from Judaism. I. Harrell, Irene Burk. II. Title.

Round Top, Tex. Bethlehem Lutheran Church.

GRASTY, Sue Watkins, ed. 284'.173
Our God is marching on; a centennial history of Bethlehem Lutheran Church, Round Top, Texas, by Martin H. Obst, John G. Banik, and other contributors. Austin, Tex., Printed by Von Boeckmann-Jones [1966] 120 p. illus., map (on lining papers) music, ports. 24 cm. Bibliographical footnotes. [BX8076.R65B4] 67-7368
1. Round Top, Tex. Bethlehem Lutheran Church. I. Obst, Martin H. II. Banik, John G. III. Title.

Rounds, James Burley, 1876-

SAPP, Phyllis. 922.673
The ice cutter; the life of J. B. Rounds, missionary to the Indians. Atlanta, Home Mission Board, Southern Baptist Convention [1948] 99 p. illus., ports. 20 cm. (Graded series on frontiers) [E98.M6S2] 48-1931
1. Rounds, James Burley, 1876- 2. Indians of North America—Missions. 3. Baptists—Missions. I. Title. II. Series.

Rouner, Arthur Acy.

ROUNER, Arthur Acy. 248.2
Receiving the spirit at Old First Church / Arthur A. Rouner, Jr. New York : Pilgrim Press, c1982. viii, 86 p. ; 21 cm. [BR1644.R68] 19 81-19959 ISBN 0-8298-0492-7 pbk. : 5.95
1. Rouner, Arthur Acy. 2. Colonial Church of Edina (Minneapolis, Minn.) 3. Pentecostalism. I. Title.

Rountree Church, Pitt Co., N.C.

WARE, Charles Crossfield, 1886- 286.6756
Rountree chronicles, 1827-1846, documentary primer of a Tar Heelfaith Wilson, N.C., North Carolina Christian Missionary Convention, 1947. 64 p. plate, ports., facsims. 24 cm. [BX7331.P5R68] 47-31191
1. Rountree family (Jesse Rountree, 1765-1831) 2. Rountree Church, Pitt Co., N.C. I. Title.

Rountree family (Jesse Rountree, 1765-1831)

WARE, Charles Crossfield, 1886- 286.6756
Rountree chronicles, 1827-1846, documentary primer of a Tar Heelfaith Wilson, N.C., North Carolina Christian Missionary Convention, 1947. 64 p. plate, ports., facsims. 24 cm. [BX7331.P5R68] 47-31191
1. Rountree family (Jesse Rountree, 1765-1831) 2. Rountree Church, Pitt Co., N.C. I. Title.

Rousseau, Jean Jacques, 1712-1778.

CASSIRER, Ernst, 1874-1945. 190
Rousseau, Kant, Goethe; two essays. Translated from the German by James Gutmann, Paul Oskar Kristeller, and John Herman Randall, Jr. Hamden, Conn., Archon Books, 1961 [c1945] 98 p. 21 cm. (History of ideas series, no. 1) [B802.C362 1961] 61-4985
1. Rousseau, Jean Jacques, 1712-1778. 2. Kant, Immanuel, 1724-1804. 3. Goethe, Johann Wolfgang von, 1749-1832.

COMPAYRE, Gabriel, 1843-1913.
... Jean Jacques Rousseau and education from nature, by Gabriel Compayre ... tr. by R. P. Jago. New York, T. Y. Crowell & co. [1907] 2 p. l., iii-viii, 129 p. front. (port.) 20 cm. (Pioneers in education) [Full name: Jules Gabriel Compayre] Bibliography: p. 119-120. [LB517.C7] 7-32037
1. Rousseau, Jean Jacques, 1712-1778. 2. Education. I. Jago, R. P., tr. II. Title. III. Title: Nature, Education from.

GRIMSLEY, Ronald. 201
Rousseau and the religious quest. Oxford, Clarendon P., 1968. xiv, 148 p. 23 cm. Bibliography: p. [143]-144. [B2138.R4G7] 68-142344 ISBN 0-19-815380-5 25/-
1. Rousseau, Jean Jacques, 1712-1778. I. Title.

LETTERS of an Italian nun and an English gentleman. Tr. from the French of J. J. Rousseau ... 6th ed. Harrisburgh, Printed for M. Carey. Philadelphia, by J. Wyeth, 1809. ix, [11]-144 p. 14 1/2 cm. [PR3991.A1L4] 5-2460
I. Rousseau, Jean Jacques, 1712-1778.

Rowan, Frederica Maclean, 1814-1882, tr.

ZSCHOKKE, Heinrich, 1771-1848. 149.
Meditations on life, death, and eternity. By Johann Heinrich Daniel Zschokke. Translated from the German by Frederica Rowan. Compiled by Rev. L. R. Dunn ... New York, Phillips & Hunt; Cincinnati, Cranston & Stowe, 1884. 2 v. 16 cm. [Full name: Johann Heinrich Daniel Zschokke] [BV4834.Z86 1884] 12-40308
1. Rowan, Frederica Maclean, 1814-1882, tr. I. Dunn, Lewis Romaine, 1822- comp. II. Title.

Rowden, Paul D.

CARTER, John T. 266.6'1'0924 B
Witness in Israel; the story of Paul Rowden [by] John T. Carter. Nashville, Broadman Press [1969] 64 p. illus., ports. 19 cm. [BV3202.R6C3] 69-19023
1. Rowden, Paul D. 2. Missions—Israel. I. Title.

Rowe, Peter Trimble, bp., 1856-1942.

JENKINS, Thomas, bp., 1871- 922.373
The man of Alaska, Peter Trimble Rowe, by the Right Reverend Thomas Jenkins, D.D., retired bishop of Nevada. New York, Morehouse-Gorham co., 1943. xvi p., 1 l., 340 p., 1 l. col. front., plates, ports. 22 1/2 cm. Map on lining-papers. [BX5995.R67J4] 43-18399
1. Rowe, Peter Trimble, bp., 1856-1942. I. Title.

Rowland, Henry Augustus, 1804-1859.

MEMORIAL of the life and services of the late Rev. Henry A. Rowland, D D., 922.573 Pastor of the parl Presbyterian church, Newark, New Jersey. With the sermon preached at his huneral, by E. R. Fairchild, D. D. New York, M. W. Dodd, 1860. 191 p. front. (port.) 19 cm. [BX9225.R78M4] 36-31937
1. Rowland, Henry Augustus, 1804-1859. 2. Funeral sermons. I. Fairchild Elias Riggs, 1808-1878.

Roxbury, Mass. Church of Our Lady of perpetual help.

BYRNE, John F. 282.
The glories of Mary in Boston; a memorial history of the Church of Our Lady of perpetual help (Mission church) Roxbury, Mass., 1871-1921, by the Rev. John F. Byrne ... Boston, Mass., Mission church press [c1921] 4 p. l., [3]-584 p. front., plates, ports. 23 cm. "Sources of information": 4th prelim. leaf. [BX4603.B7O8] 22-3493
1. Roxbury, Mass. Church of Our Lady of perpetual help. I. Title.

Roy, Dilipkumar, 1897

ROY, Dilip Kumar, 1897- 294.5'61'0922 B
Pilgrims of the stars [by] Dilip Kumar Roy and Indira Devi. New York, Macmillan [1973] xiii, 362 p. 21 cm. [BL1175.R6A3] 72-93632 7.95
1. Roy, Dilip Kumar, 1897- 2. Indira Devi, 1920- I. Indira Devi, 1920- II. Title.

ROY, Dilip Kumar, 1897- 294.5.61.0922 B
Pilgrims of the stars [by] Dilip Kuman Roy and Indira Devi. [New York Dell Books 1974, c1973] 362 p. 20 cm. (A Delta Book.) [BL1175.R6A3] 3.25 (pbk.)
1. Roy, Dilipkumar, 1897 2. Indira Devi, 1920- I. Indira Devi, 1920- II. Title.
L.C. card number for original ed.: 72-93632.

Royal Oak, Mich. First Presbyterian Church.

COLE, Maurice F 285.477438
The First Presbyterian Church of Royal Oak, Michigan: the first fifty years [by] Maurice F. Cole. [Royal Oak? Mich., 1964] 115 p. illus., ports. 23 cm. [BX9211.R76F5] 65-1542
1. Royal Oak, Mich. First Presbyterian Church. I. Title.

Royal Oak, Mich. Saint John's Methodist Church.

FANSLOW, Mrs. Robert H.
The history of Saint John's Methodist Church, 1922-1960... Compiled and edited by Mrs. Robert H. Fanslow and Mrs. W. C. Fritzley. [Royal Oak? Mich., 1960?] 1 v. (unpaged) illus., ports. 64-69078
1. Royal Oak, Mich. Saint John's Methodist Church. I. Fritzley, Mrs. W. C. II. Title.

Royal Oak, Mich. Shrine of the Little Flower.

HUTTING, Albert M. 1903- 726.50977438
Shrine of the Little Flower, souvenir book, dedicatory volume, prepared by Reverend A. M. Hutting ... [Royal Oak., Mich., Radio league of the Little Flower, c1936] 3 p. l., ix-xx p., 1 l., 105, [1] p. incl. front., illus., ports., plan. 25 cm. [NA5235.R6S5] 36-25226
1. Royal Oak, Mich. Shrine of the Little Flower. I. Title.

Royal supremacy (Church of England)

DAVIES, Ebenezer Thomas. 262'.12
Episcopacy and the royal supremacy in the Church of England in the XVI century / by E. T. Davies. Westport, Conn. : Greenwood Press, [1978] p. cm. Reprint of the 1950 ed. published by B. Blackwell, Oxford. [BX5157.D3 1978] 78-13202 ISBN 0-313-20626-0 lib.bdg. : 15.00
1. Church of England—Government. 2. Royal supremacy (Church of England) 3. Episcopacy. I. Title.

Royce, Josiah, 1855-1916.

FUSS, Peter Lawrence, 1932- 171
The moral philosophy of Jewish Royce [by] Peter Fuss. Cambridge, Mass., Harvard University Press. xv, 272 p. 22 cm. "Revised version of [the author's] doctoral dissertation at Harvard University in 1962." Bibliography: p. [265]-268. [B945.R64F8] 65-11590
1. Royce, Josiah, 1855-1916. I. Title.

FUSS, Peter Lawrence, 1932- 171
The moral philosophy of Josiah Royce. Cambridge, Mass., Harvard [c.]1965. xv. 272p. 22cm. Bibl. [B945.R64F8] 65-11590 6.95
1. Royce, Josiah, 1855-1916. I. Title.

MARCEL, Gabriel, 1889-1973. 110'.92'4
Royce's metaphysics / Gabriel Marcel ; translated by Virginia and Gordon Ringer. Westport, Conn. : Greenwood Press, 1975, c1956. xix, 180 p. ; 22 cm. Translation of La metaphysique de Royce. Reprint of the ed. published by H. Regnery Co., Chicago. Includes bibliographical references. [B945.R64M33 1975] 74-33746 ISBN 0-8371-7978-5 lib.bdg. : 11.50
1. Royce, Josiah, 1855-1916. 2. Metaphysics. I. Title.

Royersford Baptist Church.

SCHOONMAKER, Paul D. 253.7'5
The prison connection : a lay ministry behind bars / Paul D. Schoonmaker. Valley Forge, Pa. : Judson Press, c1978. 110 p. ; 21 cm. Includes bibliographical references. [BV4465.S36] 77-17158 pbk. : 3.95
1. Royersford Baptist Church. 2. Church work with prisoners—Pennsylvania—Graterford. I. Title.

Rua Kenana, 1869-1937.

BINNEY, Judith Mary Caroline Musgrove. 299'.92
Mihaia : the prophet Rua Kenana and his community at Maungapohatu / Judith Binney, Gillian Chaplin, Craig Wallace. Wellington, N.Z. : Oxford University Press, c1979. 208 p. : ill. (some col.) ; 30 cm. Includes index. Bibliography: p. 203-204. [BL632.5.N45B56] 80-491906 ISBN 0-19-558042-7 : 31.00
1. Rua Kenana, 1869-1937. 2. Religious communities—New Zealand—Maungapohatu. 3. Maungapohatu, N.Z.—Religious life and customs. I. Chaplin, Gillian, 1948- II. Wallace, Craig. III. Title.
Distributed by Oxford University Press, New York.

Rubenstein, Richard L.

RUBENSTEIN, Richard L. 296.3'092'4 B
Power struggle [by] Richard L. Rubenstein. New York, Scribner [1974] x, 193 p. 24 cm. Autobiographical. [BM755.R83A36] 73-1354 ISBN 0-684-13757-7 7.95
1. Rubenstein, Richard L. I. Title.

Rudisill, Abraham, 1811-1899.

RUDISILL, James Jefferson, 1900- 922.473
The day of our Abraham, 1811-1899 [by] James Jefferson Rudisill ... York, Pa., The printing company, 1936. 3 p. l., 9-14, [2] p., 1 l., 13-335, [2], 336-530 p. incl. front. (port.) illus., facsim. plates, ports., maps, facsims., coat of arms, fold geneal. tab. 24 cm. Maps on lining-papers.; folded genealogical table mounted on back lining-papers. "There have been 200 copies ... printed--after which the type was destroyed. Theis is copy no. 199." [BX9877.R8R8] 36-7984
1. Rudisill, Abraham, 1811-1899. 2. U. S.—Hist.—Civil war—Personal narratives. I. Title.

Rudolph, Erwin Paul, 1947-1969.

RUDOLPH, Erwin Paul, 1916- 242.4
Good-by, my son. Grand Rapids, Zondervan [1975 c1971] 150 p. 17 cm. [BV4905.2] 1.50 (pbk.)

1. Rudolph, Erwin Paul, 1947-1969. 2. Consolation. I. Title.
L.C. card number for original edition: 72-153463.

RUDOLPH, Erwin Paul, 1916- 242'.4
Good-by, my son. Grand Rapids, Zondervan Pub. House [1971] 150 p. facsims., port. 22 cm. [BV4905.2.R83] 72-153463 3.95
1. Rudolph, Erwin Paul, 1947-1969. 2. Consolation. I. Title.

Ruetenik, Herman Julius, 1826-1914.

STEPLER, John Henry, 922.473
1841-
Herman J. Ruetenik, D. D., LL. D.; his services as pastor, editor, author, publisher, educator. By J. H. Stepler. Cleveland, O., Central publishing house [1922] 250 p. incl. front., plates, ports. 19 cm. "Sources": p. 7. [BX9593.R83S8] 33-405
1. Ruetenik, Herman Julius, 1826-1914. I. Title.

Ruether, Rosemary Radford.

RUETHER, Rosemary 282'.092'4
Radford.
Disputed questions : on being a Christian / Rosemary Radford Ruether. Nashville, Tenn. : Abingdon, c1982. 142 p. ; 21 cm. (Journeys in faith) [BX4705.R7277A33] 19 81-12718 ISBN 0-687-10950-7 : 9.95
1. Ruether, Rosemary Radford. 2. Christian life—Catholic authors. 3. Theology, Doctrinal—History—20th century. I. Title. II. Series.

Ruffin, Charles Edward.

WORTHINGTON, Anne, 286'.1'0924 B
1943-
Pop. Bowie, Md., Golden Triangle Pub. Co., 1972. 245 p. illus. 19 cm. [BX6495.R75W67] 76-188929 8.98
1. Ruffin, Charles Edward. I. Title.

Rufinus Tyrannius, Aquileiensis, 345] ca:—410.

MURPHY, John J. S.J. 242
June prayers; a flower for each day of the month of June, by John J. Murphy, S.J. Philadelphia, The Peter Reilly company, 1943. 3 p. l., 113 p. 17 cm. [BX2158.M85] 43-14355
1. Rufinus Tyrannius, Aquileiensis, 345] ca:—410. 2. Rufinus Tyrannius, Aquileiensis, 345 (ca)—410 3. Sacred heart, Devotion to. I. Title.

Ruggles, Thomas, 1704-1770.

TODD, Jonathan, 1713-1791. 252
Judgment and mercy: or, Aaron dead and lamented, and Eleazar in his office. Two sermons, delivered in the first society of Guilford, on the next Lord's-day, after the much lamented death, of the Reverend, Mr. Thomas Ruggles, senior pastor of the church there. Who departed this life, November 19, 1770; in the sixty-sixth year of his life, and forty-second of his ministry ... By Jonathan Todd ... New Haven, Printed by Thomas & Samuel Green [1770] 52 p. 19 1/2 cm. [BX7260.R77T6] 46-41663
1. Ruggles, Thomas, 1704-1770. I. Title.

[Runaways—Fiction.]

SHREVE, Susan Richards. JUV
The revolution of Mary Leary / Susan Shreve. New York : Knopf : Distributed by Random House, c1982. 185 p. ; 22 cm.
During the summer before her senior year, a Catholic girl runs away from her well-meaning but narrow-minded mother and finds a job as a mother's helper. [PZ7.S55915Re 1982] [Fic] 19 82-185 ISBN 0-394-84776-8 : 9.95 ISBN 0-394-94776-2 lib. bdg. : 9.99
1. [Runaways—Fiction.] 2. [Mothers and daughters—Fiction.] 3. [Baby sitters—Fiction.] I. Title.

Ruotsalainen, Paavo,1777-1852

ARDEN, Gothard Everett, 922.448
1905-
Four northern lights; men who shaped Scandinavian churches. Illus. by Jordan Lang. Minneapolis, Augsburg [c.1964] 165p. ports. 21cm. Bibl. 64-21502 3.75
1. Ruotsalainen, Paavo,1777-1852 2. Hauge, Hans Nielsen, 1771-1824. 3. Grundtvig, Nikolai Frederik Severin, 1783-1872. 4. Rosenius, Carl Olof, 1816-1868. I. Title.

ARDEN, Gothard Everett, 922.448
1905-
Four northern lights; men who shaped Scandinavian churches, by G. Everett Arden. Illus. by Hordan Lang. Minneapolis, Augsburg Pub. House [1964] 165 p. ports. 21 cm. "Originally presented as a series of lectures in connection with the twenty-fourth Luther Academy, held at Wartburg Theological Seminary, Dubuque, Iowa, during the summer of 1963." Includes bibliographies. [BX8079.A7] 64-21502
1. Ruotsalainen, Paavo, 1777-1852. 2. Hauge, Hans Nielsen, 1771-1824. 3. Grundtvig, Nikolai Frederik Severin, 1783-1872. 4. Rosenius, Carl Olof, 1916-1868. I. Title.

Rural churches.

ADULT guide on the Churche's mission town and country. New York, Friendship Press, 1959. 64p. 19cm. (Friendship Press book 1959.) Guide to People, land and churches by R. C. Smith and On good soil, by W. Bockelman.
1. Rural churches. 2. Religious education of adults. I. Belcher, Richard. II. Smith, Rockwell Carter, 1908- People, land and churches. III. Bockelman, Wilfred, On Good soil. IV. Series.

ASHENHURST, James Oliver, 261
1861-
The day of the country church, by J. O. Ashenhurst. New York and London, Funk & Wagnalls company, 1910. 208 p. 19 1/2 cm. [BV638.A7] 10-23636
1. Rural churches. I. Title. II. Title: Country church, The day of the.

BEMIES, Charles Otis, 1867- 261
The church in the country town, by Charles O. Bemies ... Philadelphia, Boston [etc.] American Baptist publication society [c1912] 72 p. 21 cm. (On cover: Social service series) Published for the Social service commission of the Northern Baptist convention. [BV638.B4] 12-23428 0.15
I. Title.

BOCKELMAN, Wilfred. 254.24097
On good soil. New York, Friendship Press [1959] 173p. 21cm. [BV638.B6] 59-6036
1. Rural churches. I. Title.

BRICKER, Garland Armor. 261
The church in rural America, by Garland A. Bricker ... Cincinnati, The Standard publishing company [c1919] 193 p. illus., diagrs. 20 cm. [BV638.B82] 19-14902
I. Title.

BRICKER, Garland Armor, 1881- 261
Solving the country church problem, by Garland A. Bricker ... in cooperation with fourteen collaborators. Cincinnati, Jennings and Graham; New York, Eaton and Mains [c1913] 296 p. incl. front., illus. (incl. ports., plans, music) fold. map. 19 1/2 cm. "A select bibliography on the country church": p. 287. [BV638.B83] 13-21319
1. Rural churches. I. Title.

BRUNNER, Edmund de 261
Schweinitz, 1889-
Industrial village churches, by Edmund de S. Brunner ... New York, Institute of social and religious research [c1930] xii, 196 p. incl. tables, diagr. 20 cm. [BV638.B855] 30-25240
1. Rural churches. 2. Sociology, Rural. I. Institute of social and religious research. II. Title.

BUTT, Edmund Dargan, 1898- 254.2
Preach there also; a study of the town and country work of the Episcopal Church. With a foreword by Alden Drew Kelley. Evanston, Ill., Seabury- Western Theological Seminary, 1954. 140p. 24cm. [BV638.B867] 261 54-2361
1. Rural churches. 2. Protestant Episcopal Church in the U. S. A. I. Title.

BUTTERFIELD, Kenyon Leech, 261
1868-1935.
A Christian program for the rural community, by Kenyon L. Butterfield ... Nashville, Tenn., Publishing house M. E. church, South, 1923. 188 p. 20 cm. (Half-title: The Fondren lectures for 1923, delivered before the School of theology of Southern Methodist university) [BV638.B87] 24-1661
I. Title.

CARR, James McLeod. 922.773
Glorious ride; the story of Henry Woods McLaughlin. 'Little jet' sketches by the author. Atlanta, Church and Community Press [1958] 156p. illus. 21cm. [BX9225.M2549C3] 58-8225
1. McLaughlin, Henry Woods, 1869-1950. 2. Rural churches. I. Title.

DOWD, Matthew Hamilton, 1859- 261
The rural church and the farmer. Copyright ... [by] Matthew H. Dowd ... Moira, N.Y., M. H. Dowd, c1912. [94] p. incl. front., pl. 15 1/2 cm. [BV638.D6] 45-26977
1. Rural churches. 2. Country life. I. Title.

FEDERAL council of the 261
churches of Christ in America. Commission on church and country life.
The church and country life; report of conference held by the Commission on church and country life under the authority of the Federal council of churches of Christ in America. Columbus, Ohio. December 8-10, 1915. Edited by Paul L. Vogt ... New York, Missionary education movement of the United States and Canada, 1916. xi, 273 p. 20 cm. [BV638.F4] 16-13054
1. Rural churches. I. Vogt, Paul Leroy, 1878- ed. II. Title.

FELTON, Ralph Almon 254.24
The pulpit and the plow. New York, Friendship Press [c.1960] viii, 168p. 20cm. 60-8323 2.95; 1.75 half cloth, pap.,
1. Rural churches. I. Title.

FELTON, Ralph Almon, 1882- 261
... A Christian in the countryside, by Ralph A. Felton. Approved by the Committee on curriculum of the Board of Sunday schools of the Methodist Episcopal church. New York, Cincinnati, The Methodist book concern [c1925] 134 p. 18 1/2 cm. (Rural life series, H. H. Meyer, editor; W. C. Barclay, associate director) [BV638.F44] 25-10932
1. Rural churches. 2. Country life. 3. Sociology, Christian. I. Title.

FELTON, Ralph Almon, 1882- 261
Our templed hills, a study of the church and rural life, by Ralph A. Felton ... New York, Council of women for home missions and Missionary education movement [c1926] x, 11-240 p. incl. plates. 19 1/2 cm. Bibliography: p. 237-240. [BV638.F443] 26-9174
1. Farm life—U.S. 2. Rural churches—U.S. I. Title.

FREEMAN, John Davis, 1884- 250
Country church; its problems and their solution, by John D. Freeman. Atlanta, Ga., Home mission board, Southern Baptist convention [1943] 127 p. incl. illus. (maps, plans) forms. 19 1/2 cm. [BV638.F67] 43-16835
1. Rural churches. I. Southern Baptist convention. Home mission board. II. Title.

FREY, Leibert Garland, 1893- 260
Romance of rural churches. Nashville, Executive Board, Tennessee Baptist Convention [1947] 177 p. port. 20 cm. "Books for a country preacher": p. 176-177. [BV638.F68] 47-23930
1. Rural churches. I. Title.

GALPIN, C J.
Types of rural churches; a bulletin on the problems of the rural church, by C. J. Galpin. Philadelphia, Boston [etc.] American Baptist publication society, c1917. cover-title, 5-84 p. illus. 23 cm. 17-13269
I. Title.

GREENE, Shirley Edward 254.24
Ferment on the fringe; studies of rural churches in transition. Philadelphia, Christian Education Press [c.1960] 174p. 60-53027 2.00 pap.,
1. Rural churches. I. Title.

HERZEL, Frank Benton. 260
More than bread, an analysis of rural life. Philadelphia, Muhlehberg Press [1949] 280 p. 20 cm. [BV638.H38] 50-6390
1. Rural churches. I. Title.

HEWITT, Arthur Wentworth, 250
1883-
God's back pastures, a book of the rural parish, by Arthur Wentworth Hewitt. Chicago, New York, Willett, Clark & company, 1941. xii p., 144 p. 20 cm. Bibliographical references included in "Notes" (p. 138) [BV638.H4] 41-26256
1. Rural churches. I. Title.

HOOKER, Elizabeth Robbins, 277.3
1872-
Hinterlands of the church, by Elizabeth R. Hooker... New York, Institute of social and religious research [c1931] xvi, 314 p. incl. front., maps, diagrs. 22 1/2 cm. [BV638.H6] 31-16852
1. Rural churches. I. Institute of social and religious research. II. Title.

JENT, John William, 1877- 261
Rural church development; a manual of methods, by John William Jent ... Shawnee, Okl., Oklahoma Baptist university [c1928] 2 p. l., v p., 2 l., 298 p. maps, form. 21 cm. "Rural life literature": p. 295-298. [BV638.J45] 28-23810
1. Rural churches. I. Title.

JENT, John William, 1877- 261
Rural church problems, by John William Jent ... Shawnee Okl., Oklahoma Baptist university press, 1935. 6 p. l., [9]-140 p. port. 20 cm. "Rural life literature": p. [137] -140. [BV638.J47] 35-8815
1. Rural churches. I. Title.

*JOHNSON, Daniel E. 266.022
Building with buses [by] Daniel E. Johnson Grand Rapids, Baker Book House [1974] [138 p.] illus. 20 cm. [BV638.7] ISBN 0-8010-5059-6 2.95 (pbk.)
1. Rural Churches. I. Title.

LONGENECKER, Harold. 254.2'4
Building town and country churches. [Rev. ed.] Chicago, Moody Press [1973] 122 p. 22 cm. Published in 1961 under title: The village church: its pastor and program. Includes bibliographical references. [BV638.L6 1973] 73-7333 ISBN 0-8024-0997-0 1.95 (pbk.)
1. Rural churches. 2. Rural clergy. I. Title.

LONGENECKER, Harold. 254.24
The village church; its pastor and program. Chicago, Moody Press [1961] 192p. 26cm. []wBV638.L6] 61-19635
1. Rural churches. 2. Rural clergy. I. Title.

MYERS, Alexander John 261
William, 1877-
The country church as it is; a case study of rural churches and leaders, by A. J. Wm. Myers ... and Edwin E. Sundt ... New York, Chicago [etc.] Fleming H. Revell company [c1930] 189 p. 20 cm. "A brief bibliography":p. 185. [BV638.M8] 31-8068
1. Rural churches. 2. Theology, Pastoral. I. Sundt, Edwin Elnar, 1891- joint author II. Title.

NATIONAL convocation on the 260
church in town and country. Columbus, O., 1943.
What emphasis for the church in town and country? A report of the National convocation on the church in town and country. Columbus, Ohio, September 6-8, 1943. New York, N.Y., Committee on town and country, Home missions council of North America and the Federal council of the churches of Christ in America, 1943. 4 p. l., 106 p. 20 cm. [BV638.N36 1943] 44-11304
1. Rural churches. 2. Church and social problems—U.S. I. Committee on town and country. II. Title.

PROTESTANT parish; 254.2
a case study of rural and urban parish patterns, by Earl D. C. Brewer [and others] Atlanta, Communicative Arts Press [1967] viii, 129 p. 22 cm. Project sponsored by

the National Division of the Board of Missions of the Methodist Church. Bibliography: p. 124-129. [BV637.P7] 67-28402
1. Rural churches. 2. City churches. I. Brewer, Earl D. C. II. Methodist Church (United States). Board of Missions. National Division.

RICH, Mark. 261
Rural prospect. New York, Friendship Press [1950] viii, 183 p. illus. 20 cm. Bibliography: p. [173]-176. [BV638.R45] 50-8260
1. Rural churches. 2. Interdenominational cooperation. I. Title.

ROADMAN, Earl A. 261
... The country church and its program, by Earl A. Roadman; approved by the committee on curriculum of the Board of Sunday schools of the Methodist Episcopal church. New York, Cincinnati, The Methodist book concern [c1925] 143 p. 19 cm. (Rural life series, H. H. Meyer, editor, W. C. Barclay, associate editor) Contains "Books for reference". [BV638.R55] 25-8493
1. Rural churches. I. Title.

ROADS, Charles, 1855- 261
... Rural Christendom; or, The problems of Christianizing country communities, by Charles Roads ... a prize book. Philadelphia, American Sunday-school union, 1909. 322 p. 20 cm. (Green fund book no. 15) [BV638.R6] 9-28124
I. Title.

RURAL churches in 254.2
transition. Nashville, Broadman Press [1959] 145p. 21cm. [BV638.C546] 261 59-5853
1. Rural churches. I. Clark, Carl Anderson, 1905-

SCHNUCKER, Calvin. 254.2
How to plan the rural church program. Philadelphia, Westminster Press [1954] 158 p. 21 cm. [BV638.S35] 261 54-5281
1. Rural churches. 2. Church work. I. Title.

SMITH, Rockwell Carter, 254.2
1908-
The church in our town; a study of the relationship between the church and the rural community. Rev. and enl. ed. New York, Abingdon Press [1955] 220p. illus. 23cm. [BV638.S6 1955] [BV638.S6 1955] 261 55-8612 55-8612
1. Rural churches. 2. Sociology, Rural. I. Title.

SMITH, Rockwell Carter, 1908- 261
The church in our town; a study of the relationship between the church and the rural community, by Rockwell C. Smith ... New York, Nashville, Abingdon-Cokesbury press [1945] 190 p. diagrs. 19 1/2 cm. Bibliography: p. 185-188. [BV638.S6] 45-9408
1. Rural churches. 2. Sociology, Rural. I. Title.

SMITH, Rockwell Carter, 254.24
1908-
People, land and churches. New York, Friendship Press [1959] 164 p. 20 cm. Includes bibliography. [BV638.S617] 59-6035
1. Rural churches. 2. U.S. — Rural conditions. I. Title.

SMITH, Rockwell Carter, 254.2
1908-
Rural church administration. Nashville, Abingdon-Cokesbury Press [1953] 176p. 20cm. [BV638.S62] [BV638.S62] 261 53-5402 53-5402
1. Rural churches. I. Title.

SMITH, Rockwell Carter, 254.2'4
1908-
Rural ministry and the changing community [by] Rockwell C. Smith. Nashville, Abingdon Press [1971] 206 p. 21 cm. Includes bibliographical references. [BV638.S623] 73-158671 ISBN 0-687-36661-5 4.75
1. Rural churches. I. Title.

TAYLOR, Key W 287.656
Roots, religion, and revival, in the interest of an enterprise of spiritual and organic development of the rural churches, and of rural church extension, and of rural evangelism by the North Carolina Annual Conference, Se. J., the Methodist Church. By Key W. Taylor. [Raleigh, N.C.] Commission on Town and Country Work, North Carolina Annual Conference, Southeastern Jurisdiction, Methodist Church, 1965. 117 p. illus., map, group port. 23 cm. Bibliography: p. 115-116. [BX8248.N8T3] 65-29071
1. Rural churches. 2. Methodist Church (United States) Conferences. North Carolina. I. Title.

THORNTON, Martin. 261
Rural synthesis; the religious basis of rural culture. Foreword by R. Hanson. London, New York, Skeffington [1948] 124 p. 20 cm. [BV638.T5] 48-25171
1. Rural churches. I. Title.

WILL, Theodore St. Clair, 261
1886-
The rural parish, by Theodore St. Clair Will...with foreword by John G. Murray... Milwaukee, Wis., Morehouse publishing co. [c1926] xi, p., 1 l., 140 p., 1 l., diagr. 19 cm. [BV638.W4] 26-9085
1. Rural churches. 2. Protestant Episcopal church in the U.S.A. I. Title.

WILSON, Warren Hugh, 1867- 261
The farmer's church, by Warren Hugh Wilson ... New York & London, The Century co. [c1925] 5 p. l., 3-264 p. 19 1/2 cm. [The Century rural life books] [BV638.W55] 25-8803
1. Rural churches. I. Title.

WINTERMEYER, Herbert Herman 264
Henry, 1912-
Rural worship, by Herbert H. Wintermeyer. Philadelphia, St. Louis, The Christian education press [1947] 99 p. illus. 23 cm. "The worship library": p. 95-99. [BV638.W6] 47-5619
1. Rural churches. 2. Worship programs. I. Title.

WITTE, Raymond Philip, 1911- 261
Twenty-five years of crusading; a history of the National Catholic Rural Life Conference. Des Moines, National Catholic Rural Life Conference, 1948. xviii, 274 p. ports., diagrs. 24 cm. Bibliography: p. 255-264. [BX1407.R8W5] 51-2079
1. Rural churches. 2. Catholic Church in the U. S. I. National Catholic Rural Life Conference. II. Title.

YOUNG men's Christian 267.
associations. International committee.
The country church and rural welfare, edited by the International committee of Young men's Christian associations. New York [etc.] Association press, 1912. 4 p. l., 152 p. 19 1/2 cm. [BV1210.A4 1911] 12-17264
1. Rural churches. 2. Sociology, Rural. I. Title.

Rural churches—Southern States.

BRUNNER, Edmund de 254.2'4'0975
Schweinitz, 1889-
Church life in the rural South; a study of the opportunity of Protestantism based upon data from seventy counties, by Edmund deS. Brunner. New York, Negro Universities Press [1969] 117 p. illus., maps. 24 cm. At head of title: Committee on Social and Religious Surveys, Town and Country Department. Reprint of the 1923 ed. Bibliography: p. 117. [BV638.B844 1969] 70-90129
1. Rural churches—Southern States. 2. Social surveys—Southern States. I. Title.

BRUNNER, Edmund de 277
Schweinitz, 1889-
Church life in the rural South; a study of the opportunity of Protestantism based upon data from seventy counties. New York, G. H. Doran Co. [1923] 117 p. illus., maps. 24 cm. (Unique studies of rural America; town and country series, 4) Bibliography: p. 117. [BR535.B7] 23-10324
1. Rural churches—Southern States. 2. Social surveys—Southern States. I. Title. II. Series.

CARR, James McLeod. 254.2
Bright future a new day for the town and country church. Illustrated by Ruth S. Ensign. Richmond, Published for Board of Church Extension, Presbyterian Church in the United States, by John Knox Press [1956] 162p. illus. 21cm. [BV638.C3] [BV638.C3] 261 56-10740 56-10740
1. Rural churches—Southern States. 2. Presbyterian Church in the U.S.—Missions. I. Title.

CLARK, Elmer Talmage, 1886- 261
The rural church in South, by Elmer T. Clark... Nashville, Dallas [etc.] The Cokesbury press [c1924] 51 p. illus., diagr. 19 1/2 cm. (The homeland series, no. 1) "Reprinted from 'Healing ourselves, the first task of the church in America'." [BV638.C6] 24-30196
I. Title.

METHODIST Episcopal 261.0975
church, South. Rural work commission.
Report ... of the Rural work commission of the Methodist Episcopal church, South. [Nashville, Tenn.] Pub. by authority of the Commission by the Board of Missions of the Methodist Episcopal church, South [c1936- v. 23 cm. [BX8241.A4] 287.675 36-9308
1. Rural churches—Southern states. 2. Methodist Episcopal church, South. 3. Social surveys. I. Title.

Rural churches—Stories.

BAILEY, James Martin, 254.24
1929-
Windbreaks; six stories of the rural church in action. Illustrated by Brinton Turkle. New York, Friendship Press [1959] 111p. illus. 23cm. [BV638.8.B3] 59-6039
1. Rural churches—Stories. I. Title.

COCHRAN, Jean Carter.
Church street: stories of American village life, by Jean Carter Cochran ... Philadelphia. The Westminster press, 1922. vii, 227 p. front., plates. 19 1/2 cm. Contents.Home. Oral traditions.--Old John.--Clerical notes.--Neighbors.-- Poverty and riches.--The day we celebrate.--A billtop idyl.--Our mother's passlon.--Peculiar people.--An evergreen woman.--Everybody's uncle.--Dooryards.--His own people. [PZ3.C6415.5Ch] 23-8757
I. Title.

Rural churches—United States

BUTTERFIELD, Kenyon Leech, 261
1868-1935.
The Christian enterprise among rural people, by Kenyon L. Butterfield ... Nashville, Cokesbury press [c1933] 247, [1] p. 20 cm. (The Cole lectures for 1932 delivered before Vanderbilt university) [BV638.B869] 33-6580
1. Rural churches—U. S. 2. Sociology, Rural. 3. Sociology, Christian. 4. Missions, Foreign. I. Title.

BUTTERFIELD, Kenyon Leech, 261
1868-1935.
The country church and the rural problem; the Carew lectures at Hartford theological seminary, 1909, by Kenyon L. Butterfield ... Chicago, Ill., The University of Chicago press 1911] ix, 153 p. 20 cm. [BV638.B88] 11-2041
1. Rural churches—U. S. I. Carew lectures. II. Title.

EARP, Edwin Lee, 1867- 261
The rural church movement, by Edwin L. Earp ... New York, Cincinnati, The Methodist book concern [c1914] 177 p. front. 19 1/2 cm. "Select bibliography": p. 172-173. [BV638.E28] 14-10371
1. Rural churches—U.S. I. Title.

FELTON, Ralph Almon, 1882- 261
One foot on the land; stories of sixteen successful rural churches, by Ralph A. Felton. Madison, N.J., Dept. of the Rural church, Drew theological seminary [1947] 2 p. l., 3-94 p. 23 cm. Reprinted from the Farm journal and the Progressive farmer. [BV638.F442] 47-24766
1. Rural churches—U.S. I. Title.

FELTON, Ralph Almon, 1882- 260
What's right with the rural church; an application of Christian principles to the new rural life, by Ralph A. Felton. Philadelphia, Presbyterian board of Christian education, 1930. 150 p., incl. front., illus. 19 1/2 cm. "Helpful books" at the end of each chapter. [BV638.F47] 30-16881
1. Rural churches—U.S. I. Title.

FRY, Charles Luther, 1894- 261
Diagnosing the rural church, a study in method by C. Luther Fry, with a foreword by Professor Franklin H. Giddings; with tables. charts and maps. New York, George H. Doran company [c1924] xxvi p., 1 l., 29-234 p. incl. tables, diagrs. 20 cm. (Half-title: Institute of social and religious research. Town and country series, E. de S. Brunner, director) Published also as thesis (PH. D.) Columbia university, 1924. [BV638.F7] 24-13482
1. Rural churches—U. S. I. Title. II. Title: Rural church, Diagnosing the.

GALPIN, Charles Josiah, 1864- 261
Types of rural churches; a bulletin on the problems of the rural church, by C. J. Galpin. Philadelphia, Boston [etc.] American Baptist publication society, c1917. cover-title, 5-84 p. illus. 23 cm. [BV638.G3] 17-13269
1. Rural churches—U.S. 2. Churches—U.S. I. Title.

GEBHARD, Anna Laura (Munro) 261
1914-
Rural parish/ A year from the journal of Anna Laura Gebhard. Illus. by Janet Smalley. New York, Abingdon-Cokesbury Press [1947] 121 p. illus. 20 cm. [BV638.G4] 47-12450
1. Rural churches—U. S. I. Title.

HOSTETLER, John Andrew, 1918-
Participation in the rural church; a summary of research in the field, by John A. Hostetler and William G. Mather. State College, Pennsylvania State College, School of Agriculture, Agricultural Experiment Station, Dept. of Agricultural Economics and Rural Sociology, 1952. 64p. tables. 28cm. (Pennsylvania. Agricultural Experiment Station, State College. Journal series. Paper no. 1762) A61
1. Rural churches—U. S. I. Mather, William Green, 1901- II. Title. III. Series: Pennsylvania. Agricultural Experiment Station, University Park. Journal series. Series: Pennsylvania. Agricultural Experiment Station, University Park. Paper no. 1762

HUNTER, Edwin Alfred. 1886- 260
The small town and country church. Nashville, Abingdon-Cokesbury Press 1947 143 p. 20 cm. [BV638.H8] 47-11826
1. Rural churches—U.S. I. Title.

ISRAEL, Henry, 1877- ed.
The country church and community cooperation, ed. by Henry Israel ... New York [etc.] Association press, 1913. 179 p. 19 1/2 cm. This conference is the third of a series issued by the International committee of the Young men's Christian associations. The first was purlished in 1911 under the title "The rural church and community letterment": the second in 1912 under the title "The country church and rural welfare". cf. Introd. [BV1210.A4 1912] 13-9805
1. Rural churches—U.S. 2. Sociology, Christian. I. Young men's Christian association. International committee. II. Title.

LINDSTROM, David Edgar. 261
The church in rural life, by David Edgar Lindstrom ... 1st ed. Champaign, Ill., The Garrard press, 1939. xiv, 145 p. 19 cm. "First edition." "Readings" at end of each chapter. [BV638.L5] 39-31173
1. Rural churches—U. S. 2. Sociology, Rural. I. Title.

LINDSTROM, David Edgar, 1899- 261
Rural life and the church, by David Edgar Lindstrom ... A revision of The church in rural life. Champaign, Ill., The Garrard press, 1946. xiv, 205 p. 20 cm. Errata slip inserted. "Readings" at end of each chapter. [BV638.L5 1946] 46-21429
1. Rural churches—U.S. 2. Sociology, Rural. I. Title.

MCBRIDE, Clarence Ralph 254.24
Protestant churchmanship for rural America. Valley Forge [Pa.] Judson [c.1962] 334p. 23cm. Bibl. 61-8938 4.95
1. Rural churches—U.S. I. Title.

MCCONNELL, Charles Melvin. 254.2
High hours of Methodism in town-country

communities. [1st ed.] New York, Editorial Dept., Joint Section of Education and Cultivation, Board of Missions of the Methodist Church, 1956. 109p. illus. 20cm. [BV638.M15] 261 56-10362
1. Rural churches—U. S. 2. Methodist Church—Missions. I. Title.

MCLAUGHLIN, Henry Woods, 1869- ed. 260
The country church and public affairs, edited by Henry W. McLaughlin ... New York, The Macmillan company, 1930. 260 p. front. (port.) 20 1/2 cm. "The twenty chapters in this volume are the outgrowth of the open forum and round table studies and discussions ... in the 1929 Institute of public affairs [University of Virginia]"--Pref. "A pageant 'Along the highway of the king'": p. [251]-260. [BV638.M2] 30-11743
1. Rural churches—U.S. 2. Sociology, Rural. I. Institute of public affairs, University of Virginia. II. Title.

MCLAUGHLIN, Henry Woods, 1869- 268
Religious education in the rural church, by Henry W. McLaughlin ... New York, Chicago [etc.] Fleming H. Revell company [c1932] 220 p. front. (port.) 19 1/2 cm. Results of the discussions at the round table in the Institute of public affairs at the University of Virginia, 1930 and 1931. cf. Pref., p. 10. [BV1555.M3] 32-13915
1. Rural churches—U.S. 2. Religious education. I. Institute of public affairs. University of Virginia. II. Title.

MUELLER, Elwin W. 1908- ed. 261.8082
The silent struggle for mid-America; the church in town and country today. E. W. Mueller and Giles C. Ekola, editors. Minneapolis, Augsburg Pub. House [c1963] xi, 167 p. map. 22 cm. Lectures and findings of a workshop on "The church's concern for town and country communities in mid-America" sponsored by the office of Church in Town and Courtry of the Division of American Missions, National Lutheran Council. Bibliography: p. 165-167. [BV638.M77] 63-16602
1. Rural churches — U.S. 2. Sociology, Christian (Lutheran) I. Ekola, Giles C., joint ed. II. National Lutheran Council. Division of American Missions. Church in Town and Country. III. Title.

NATIONAL conference on the rural church. 1st, Washington, D. C., 1936. 261
The rural church, today & tomorrow; a report of the National conference, on the rural church. Under the auspices of the Home mission council and the Council of women for home missions ... [New York! 1936] 90 p. 23 cm. Bibliography: p. 83-85. [BV638.N35 1936] 36-30057
1. Rural churches—U. S. I. Home missions council. II. Council of women for home missions. III. Title.

NATIONAL conference on the rural church. 2d, Ames, Ia., 1936. 261
The church and the agricultural situation; a report of the National conference on the rural church, Iowa state college, Ames, Iowa, November 23-25, 1936. Under the auspices of the Home missions council and the Council of women for home missions ... with the cooperation of the Agricultural extension service of the Iowa state college. [New York! 1936!] 85 p. 23 cm. [BV638.N35 1936 b] 38-12282
1. Rural churches—U. S. I. Home missions council II. Council of women for home missions. III. Iowa. State college of agriculture and mechanic arts, Ames. Agricultural extension service. IV. Title.

NATIONAL conference on the rural church. 2d, Ames, Ia., Nov. 1936. 261
The church and the agricultural situation; a report of the National conference on the rural church, Iowa state college, Ames, Iowa, November 23-25, 1936. Under the auspices of the Home missions council and the Council of women for home missions ... with the cooperation of the Agricultural extension service of the Iowa state college. [New York? 1936?] 85 p. 23 cm. [BV638.N35 1936b] 38-12282
1. Rural churches—U.S. I. Home missions council. II. Council of women for home missions. III. Iowa. State college of agriculture and mechanic arts. Ames. Extension service in agriculture and home economics. IV. Title.

O'HARA, Edwin Vincent, Bp., 1881- 282'.73
The church and the country community / Edwin V. O'Hara. New York : Arno Press, 1978 [c1927] 115 p. ; 21 cm. (The American Catholic tradition) Reprint of the ed. published by Macmillan, New York. Includes index. [BX1407.R8O36 1978] 77-11304 ISBN 0-405-10846-X : 10.00
1. Catholic Church in the United States. 2. Rural churches—United States. I. Title. II. Series.

ORMOND, Jesse Marvin, 1878- 261
By the waters of Bethesda, by J. M. Ormond ... Nashville, Tenn., Department of education and promotion, Board of missions, Methodist Episcopal church, South, 1936. 153 p. 19 cm. [BV638.O7] 38-1810
1. Rural churches—U. S. 2. Missions, Home. 3. Missions—Study and teaching. I. Methodist Episcopal church, South. Board of missions. II. Title.

PEPPER, Clayton. 286'.173
Streams of influence; an historical evaluation of the Town and Country Church Movement within the American Baptist Convention [by] Clayton A. Pepper. Illustrated by Betty B. Janssen. Valley Forge, Pa., Division of Parish Development and Missions, American Baptist Churches in the U.S.A. [1973] 160 p. illus. 22 cm. Includes bibliographical references. [BV638.P4] 73-1463
1. American Baptist Convention. 2. Rural churches—United States. I. Title.

RANDOLPH, Henry S
Orientation to the town and country church; a discussion of United Presbyterian philosophy, organization, and methods [by] Henry S. Randolph and Betty Jean Patton. [Philadelphia] Board of National Missions, United Presbyterian Church in the U.S.A., 1961. [xviii]) 228 p. 23 cm. illus. 63-53095
1. Rural churches — U.S. I. Title.

RAPKING, Aaron Henry, 1886- 261
Building the kingdom of God in the countryside ... [by] Aaron H. Rapking. New York, Cincinnati [etc.] The Methodist book concern [c1938] 3 p. l., 5-60 p. diagr. 20 cm. Portrait on t.-p. "Approved by the Committee on curriculum of the Board of education of the Methodist Episcopal church." Bibliography: p. 59-60. [BV638.R3] 38-24878
1. Rural churches—U. S. 2. Sociology, Christian—Study and teaching. 3. Sociology, Rural. 4. Kingdom of God. I. Title.

RICH, Mark. 254.2
The rural church movement. Columbia, Mo., Juniper Knoll Press, 1957. ii, 251p. 28cm. Includes bibliographies. [BV638.R44] A58 261
1. Rural churches—U. S. 2. Interdenominational cooperation. I. Title.

SUNDT, Edwin Einar, 1891- 261
The country church and our generation, by Edwin E. Sundt ... New York, Chicago [etc.] Fleming H. Revell company [c1932] 160 p. diagr. 19 1/2 cm. Bibliography: p. 156-160. [BV638.S8] 32-3766
1. Rural churches—U.S. I. Title.

WILSON, Warren H.
The church of the queen country; a study of the church for the working farmer, by Warren H. Wilson. New York, Missionary education movement of the United States and Canada, 1911. xiv, 238 p. plates, 3 port. (incl. front.) 19 1/2 cm. (Half-title: Forward mission study courses ...) Bibliography: p. 220-226. 11-31908
I. Title.

WILSON, Warren Hugh, 1867- 261
Rural religion and the country church, by Warren H. Wilson ... New York, Chicago [etc.] Fleming H. Revell company [c1927] 141 p. 19 1/2 cm. [BV638.W57] 27-23325
1. Rural churches—U.S. I. Title.

YOUNG men's Christian associations. International committee. County work dept. 267.
The rural church and community betterment, edited by County work department. New York, Association press, 1911. 136 p. 19 1/2 cm. "Minutes of the rural church of conference held under the auspices of the County work department of the International committee of Young men's Christian associations...in New York city, Thursday, December first, 1910." [BV1210.A4 1910] 11-13748
1. Rural churches—U.S. I. Title.

YOUTH work in the rural church, by Mark Rich, Mossie Allman Wyker, Mary Heald Williamson [and others]...Authorized and approved as a textbook in leadership education by the Curriculum committee of the United Christian missionary society, a board of missions and education. St. Louis, Mo., The Bethany press [c1940] 112 p. illus. (plan) 17 cm. "To read" at end of each chapter. "Sources of information": p. 107-112. [BV4447.Y6] 40-31204 259
1. Rural churches—U.S. 2. Church work with youth. I. Rich, Mark. II. United Christian missionary society.

Rural churches—United States—Case studies.

BYERS, David M. 261.8'0973
New directions for the rural church : case studies in area ministry / by David M. Byers and Bernard Quinn. New York : Paulist Press, c1978. v, 186 p. ; 20 cm. [BX1407.R8B93] 77-14799 ISBN 0-8091-2085-2 pbk. : 3.50
1. Rural churches—United States—Case studies. I. Quinn, Bernard, 1928- joint author. II. Title.

Rural clergy—Great Britain

HART, Arthur Tindal 253
The country priest in English history. London, Phoenix House [1959, i.e.,1960 dist., Hollywood-by-the-Sea, Fla., Transatlantic Arts] 176p. Bibl.: p.163-167. illus., ports. 23cm. 60-2015 6.25
1. Rural clergy—Gt. Brit. 2. Clergy—Gt. Brit. I. Title.

Rusch, Harley G., 1947-

RUSCH, Harley G., 1947- 248.4
Dudley's dog days : joining faith to life / Harley G. Rusch. Philadelphia : Fortress Press, c1981. p. cm. [BV4501.2.R84] 19 81-43074 ISBN 0-8006-1610-3 : 3.95
1. Rusch, Harley G., 1947- 2. Christian life—1960- I. Title.

Rusch, Paul, 1897-

HEMPHILL, Elizabeth Anne. 266.3'0924 B
The road to KEEP; the story of Paul Rusch in Japan. With a foreword by Edwin O. Reischauer. [1st ed.] New York, Walker/Weatherhill [1970, c1969] ix, 195 p. illus., ports. 24 cm. Bibliography: p. 190. [BV3457.R8H4 1970] 78-96053 4.95
1. Rusch, Paul, 1897- 2. Protestant Episcopal Church in the U.S.A.—Missions. 3. Missions—Japan. I. Title.

Rushmore, Jane Palen,

JOHNSON, Emily (Cooper) 922.8673
Under Quaker appointment: the life of Jane P. Rushmore. Philadelphia, University of Pennsylvania, 1953. 211p. illus. 21cm. [BX7795.R8J6] 53-10517
1. Rushmore, Jane Palen, I. Title.

Ruskin, John, 1819-1900.

CHRISMAN, Lewis Herbert, 1883-
John Ruskin, preacher, and other essay, by Lewis H. Chrisman ... New York, Cincinnati, The Abingdon press [c1921] 187 p. 19 1/2 cm. Contents.John Ruskin, preacher.--Jonathan Edwards.--Radiant vigor.--The spiritual message of Whittier.--The art of being human.--The white water lily.--The fundamental teaching of Thomas Carlyle.--Cross-eyed souls.--The American heritage.--Permanent values in the Biglow papers.--Leasening the denominator. [P83505.H82A16 1921] 21-18406
I. Title.

HARRISON, Frederic, 1831-1923. 928.2
... John Ruskin, by Frederic Harrison. New York, The Macmillan company; London, Macmillan & co., ltd., 1902. vi p., 1 l., 216 p. 19 cm. (Half-title: English men letters, ed. by J. Morley) Series title also at head of t.-p. [BR5263.H3] 2-22009
1. Ruskin, John, 1819-1900. I. Title.

RUSKIN, John, 1819-1900.
... John Ruskin; The two boyhoods, The slave ship, The mountain gloom, The mountain glory, Venice, St. Mark's, Art and morals, The mystery of life, Peace. New York, Doubleday, Page & company, 1909. 3 p. l., v-ix p., 1 l., 191 p. front. (port.) 16 cm. (Little masterpieces, ed. by Bliss Perry) [PR5252.P3 1909] 14-7494
I. Title.

RUSKIN, John, 1819-1900.
Precious thoughts moral and religious. Gathered from the works of John Ruskin, A. M. By Mrs. L. C. Tuthill ... New York, J. Wiley & son, 1866. x, 349 p. 21 cm. [PR5252.T8] 28-14892
I. Tuthill, Louisa Caroline (Huggins) Mrs. 1798-1879, comp. II. Title.

RUSKIN, John, 1819-1900.
The religion of Ruskin. The life and works of John Ruskin; a biographical and anthological study, by William Burgess ... New York, Chicago [etc.] Fleming H. Revell company [c1907] xi, 449 p. 24 cm. Selections arranged by subject, "with a brief history of his life and work" (p. 3-72) prefixed. Bibliography: p. 424. [PR5267.R4A3] 10-9841
I. Burgess, William, 1843-1922, ed. II. Title.

RUSKIN, John, 1819-1900.
The true and the beautiful in nature, art, morals, and religion, selected from the works of John Ruskin ... With a notice of the author, by Mrs. L. C. Tuthill ... 3d ed. New York, J. Wiley, 1860. xxxi, 452 p. incl. front. (port.) 20 cm. [PR5252.T82] 28-13632
I. Tuthill, Louisa Caroline (Huggins) Mrs. 1798-1879, ed. II. Title.

Russell, Bertrand Russell, 3d earl, 1872-

AIKEN, Lillian Woodworth. 170
Bertran Russell's philosophy of morals. New York, Humanities Press, 1963. 172 p. 24 cm. Includes bibliography. [B1649.R94A47] 62-21320
1. Russell, Bertrand Russell, 3d earl. 1872- I. Title.

AIKEN, Lillian Woodworth 170
Bertrand Russell's philosophy of morals. New York, Humanities [c.]1963. 172p. 24cm. Bibl. 62-21320 5.00
1. Russell, Bertrand Russell, 3d earl, 1872- I. Title.

OUR knowledge of the external world. [New York] The New American Library [1960] 191p. 18cm. (A Mentor book [MD28]) 'First printing.'
I. Russell, Bertrand Russell, 3d earl, 1872-

RUSSELL, Bertrand Russell, 3d earl, 1872-
An inquiry into meaning and truth. Baltimore, Penguin Books [1962] 332 p. 18 cm. (The William James lectures for 1940, delivered at Harvard University) Pelican books, A590. "These lectures formed the basis for seminar courses at the University of Chicago in 1938-9 and the University of California at Los Angeles in 1939-40."--Pref. 63-57472
I. Title.

RUSSELL, Bertrand Russell, 3d earl, 1872-
An inquiry into meaning and truth. Baltimore, Penguin Books [1962] 332 p. 18 cm. (The William James lectures for 1940, delivered at Harvard University) Pelican books, A590. "These lectures formed the basis for seminar courses at the University of Chicago in 1938-9 and the University of California at Los Angeles in 1939-40."--Pref. 63-57472
I. Title.

Russell, Charles Taze, 1852-1916.

BROWN, John Elward. 289.
"In the cult kindgom" Mormonism, Eddyism, Russellism, by John Elward Brown ... Chicago, Siloam Springs, Ark. [etc.] International federation publishing company [1918] 124 p. 19 cm. [BX8645.B8] 18-3542
1. Russell, Charles Taze, 1852-1916. 2. Mormons and Mormonism. 3. Christian Science. I. Title.

EATON, Ephraim Llewellyn, 1846-
The millennial dawn heresy; an examination of Pastor Charles T. Russell's teaching concerning the purpose of the second advent and the millennium, as set forth in his published books and papers--"The divine plan of the ages," and others of similar import. By E. L. Eaton, D.D. Cincinnati, Jennings and Graham New York, Eaton and Mains [1911] iv p. 1 l., [2], 3-153 p. diagr. 19 cm. 11-20630 0.50
I. Title.

FORREST, James Edward, 1875-
Errors of Russellism; a brief examination of the teachings of Pastor Charles T. Russell, as set forth in his "Studies in the Scriptures," by J. E. Forrest. Anderson, Ind., Gospel trumpet company [c1915] 277 p. incl. double plan. 19 cm. 15-24925 0.50
I. Title.

JOHNSON, Thomas Cary, 1859- 290
Some modern isms, by Thos. Cary Johnson ... Richmond, Va., Presbyterian committee of publication [c1919] 192 p. illus. (port. group) 20 cm. "The lectures in this volume, on Mormonism, on Christian science, and on Russellism, were delivered to the senior class in Union theological seminary in Virginia, in January, 1918."--Pref. "Literature on Mormonism": p. [9]; "Literature on Christian science": p. 45; "Literature on Russellism": p. 97; "Literature on Nietzscheism": p. 158. Contents.--Mormonism.--Eddyism, or Christian science.--Wayward children of Mother Eddy: or The new thought people's ism; and the ism of the Unity school of Christianity.--Russellism.--Nietzscheism. [BL98.J6] 19-8309
1. Russell, Charles Taze, 1852-1916. 2. Nietzsche Friedrich Wilhelm, 1844-1900. 3. Mormons and Mormonism. 4. Christian science. 5. New thought. I. Title.

RUSSELL, Charles Taze, 1852-1916. 289.
What Pastor Russell said, his answers to hundreds of questions. [Chicago, Ley-Cross printing co., c1917] cover-title, 776 p. port. 20 cm. [BX8526.R8] 17-13486
I. Title.

[WISDOM, William M.]
The Laodicean messenger, being the memeirs of the life, works and character of that faithful and wise servant of the most high God. Chicago, Ill., The Bible students book store [c1923] 6 p. l., 332 p. front., illus., plates (1 col.) ports. 19 1/2 cm. A memoir of Charles Taze Russell. [BX8527.R8W5] 24-6985
1. Russell, Charles Taze, 1852-1916. I. Title.

Russell, George William, 1867-1935.

[RUSSELL, George William] 1867-
The divine vision, and other poems, by A. E. New York, The Macmillan company; London, Macmillan & co., ltd., 1904. 123 p. 20 cm. [PR6065.U7D5 1904] 4-1582
I. Title.

RUSSELL, George William, 1867-1935. 291.4'2
The candle of vision, by AE (George William Russell). Introd. by Leslie Shepard. Wheaton, Ill., Theosophical Pub. House [1974, c1965] xiv, 175 p. 21 cm. (A Quest book) Autobiographical. "A bibliography of 'AE'": p. [xii] [PR6035.U7Z52 1974] 73-17195 ISBN 0-8356-0445-4 2.25 (pbk.)
1. Russell, George William, 1867-1935. I. Title.

Russell, Mary Baptist, 1829-1898.

MCARDLE, Mary Aurelia. 922.273
California's pioneer Sister of Mercy, Mother Mary Baptist Russell, 1829-1898. Fresno, Calif., Academy Library Guild, 1954. 204p. illus. 23cm. [BX4705.R74M3] 56-36570
1. Russell, Mary Baptist, 1829-1898. I. Title.

RUSSELL, Matthew, S. J.
The life of Mother Mary Baptist Russell, sister of mercy, by her brother ... New York, The Apostleship of prayer, 1901. 187 p. front., pl., port. 12 degree. Apr
I. Title.

Russia—Church history.

BIGG-WITHER, Reginald Fitz Hugh, 1842-
A short history of the church of Russia, its teaching & its worship, by the Rev. Reginald F. Bigg-Wither ... With 14 illustrations and 4 appendices. London, Society for promoting Christian knowledge; New York, Macmillan, 1920. 112 p. front., 13 pl. 22 cm. A 20
1. Russia—Church history. I. Title.

CASEY, Robert Pierce, 1897- 274.
Religion in Russia, by Robert Pierce Casey ... New York, London, Harper & brothers, [1946] viii p., 1 l., 196 p. 19 1/2 cm. "First edition." "Contains the Lowell lectures, delivered at King's chapel in Lent, 1945."--Pref. [BR932.C3] 46-3423
1. Russia—Church history. 2. Orthodox Eastern church, Russian—Hist. I. Title.

ISWOLSKY, Helene. 274.7
Soul of Russia, by Helen Iswolsky. New York, Sheed & Ward, 1943. xiii, 200 p. front., plates, ports. 19 1/2 cm. "Sources": p. ix-x. Bibliography: p. 187-196. [BR932.I8] 43-16644
1. Russia—Church history. 2. Orthodox Eastern church, Russian—Hist. 3. Religious thought—Russia. I. Title.

LATIMER, Robert Sloan.
Under three tsars: liberty of conscience in Russia, 1856-1909. by Robert Sloan Latimer ... with illustrations. New York Chicago [etc.] F. H. Revell company [1909] xii, 244 p. front., plates, ports., fold map. 21 cm. W 10
1. Russia—Church history. 2. Russia—Pol. & govt. I. Title.

SALOFF-ASTAKHOFF, Nikita Ignatievich, 1893- 274.7
Christianity in Russia, by N. I. Saloff-Astakhoff... New York, Loizeaux brothers [1941] 149 p. 19 cm. "First edition...November, 1941." [BR932.S3] 42-3051
1. Russia—Church history. 2. Protestant churches—Russia. I. Title.

ZERNOV, Nicolas. 274.7
Moscow, the third Rome, by Nicolas Zernov... London, Society for promoting Christian knowledge; New York, The Macmillan company [1937] 94 p. 19 cm. "First published, 1937." A history of the Russian Orthodox Eastern church. [BR932.Z4] 38-11611
1. Russia—Church history. 2. Orthodox Eastern church, Russian. I. Society for promoting Christian knowledge, London. II. Title.

ZERNOV, Nicolas. 281.9'47
Moscow, the third Rome. New York, AMS Press [1971] 94 p. 19 cm. Reprint of the 1938 ed. A history of the Russian Orthodox Eastern church. [BR932.Z4 1971] 76-149664 ISBN 0-404-07075-2
1. Orthodox Eastern Church. Russian. 2. Russia—Church history. I. Title.

Russia—Church history—1917—

BOURGEOIS, Charles, 1887- 922.247
A priest in Russia and the Baltic. With an introd. by Sir David Kelly, translated from the French by the Earl of Wicklow. Dublin, Clonmore and Reynolds [1953] 146p. illus. 20cm. [BX4705.B728A32] 55-16784
1. Russia—Church history—1917- I. Title.

COOKE, Richard Joseph, bp., 1853-1931. 281.
Religion in Russia under the Soviets, by Richard J. Cooke ... New York, Cincinnati, The Abingdon press [c1924] 311 p. 19 cm. Bibliography: p. 308-305. [BX492.C6] 24-28984
1. Russia—Church history—1917- 2. Church and state in Russia—1917- 3. Bolshevism—Russia. I. Title.

EMHARDT, William Chauncey, 1874- 281.
Religion in soviet Russia; anarchy, by William Chauncey Emhardt...together with an essay on the Living church, by Sergius Troitsky...with an introduction by Clarence A. Manning... Milwaukee, Wis., Morehouse publishing co.; London, A. R. Mowbray & co. [c1929] xix, 386, [2] p. 24 cm. "The translation of Professor Troitsky's articles was made in Paris by associates of the Russian theological seminary, and placed in the hands of the author of this volume to edit and revise without restrictions. It has been carefully revised by Mr. Alexis Wiren of the Young men's Christian association."--Pref. [BX492.E6] 29-13572
1. Russia—Church history—1917- 2. Church and state in Russia—1917- 3. Bolshevism—Russia. 4. Greek church in Russia. 5. Russian Orthodox Greek Catholic church of North America. I. Troitskii, Sergiei Viktorovich. II. Wiren, Alexis. III. Title. IV. Title: The Living church.

GEORGE, Father, pseud. 274.7
God's underground, by Father George as told to Gretta Palmer. New York, Appleton-Century-Crofts [1949] xix, 296 p. 21 cm. A story of the fight for Christianity in Soviet Russia. [BR936.G4] 49-7196
1. Russia—Church history—1917- I. Palmer, Gretta. II. Title.

GRUNWALD, Constantin de 274.7
The churches and the Soviet Union. Tr. by G. J. Robinson-Paskevsky. New York, Macmillan, 1962 [c.1961] 255p. illus. Bibl. 62-1974 4.00
1. Russia—Church history—1917- 2. Russia—Religion—1917- I. Title.

HEARD, Albert F.
The Russian church and Russian dissent, comprising orthodoxy, dissent, and erratic sects, by Albert F. Heard ... New York, Harper & brothers, 1887. ix, 310 p. 21cm. "List of books consulted": p. [vii]-ix. [BX510.H4] 17-14844
I. Title.

JACKSON, Joseph Harrison, 1900- 266.6
The eternal flame; the story of a preaching mission in Russia. Philadelphia, Christian Education Press [1956] 125p. illus. 22cm. [BR936.J3] 274.7 56-43423
1. Russia—Church history—1917- 2. Baptists—Russia. I. Title.

JACKSON, Joseph Harrison, 1900- 266.6
The eternal flame; the story of a preaching mission in Russia. Philadelphia, Christian Education Press [1956] 125p. illus. 22cm. [BR936.J3] 274.7 56-43423
1. Russia—Church history—1917- 2. Baptists—Russa. I. Title.

ORTHODOX Eastern church, Russian. 281.947
The truth about religion in Russia, issued by the Moscow patriarchate (1942) Editorial committee: Nicholas (Yarushevich) ... Gregory Petrovich Georgievsky ... [and] Alexander Pavlovich Smirnov ... English translation under the supervision of the Rev. E. N. C. Sergeant. London, New York [etc.] Hutchinson & co., ltd. [1944] 175 p. front., illus. (facsims.) plates, ports. 22 cm. Translation of (transliterated: Pravda o religii v Rossii) [BX492.O712] 45-11301
1. Russia—Church history—1917- I. Sergeant, Ernest Noel Copland. II. Title.

ORTHODOX Eastern church, Russian. Patriarch. 281.947
The truth about religion in Russia, issued by the Moscow patriarchate (1942) Editorial committee: Nicholas (Yarushevich) ... Gregory Petrovich Georgievsky ... [and] Alexander Pavlovich Smirnov ... English translation under the supervision of the Rev. E. N. C. Sergeant. London, New York [etc.] Hutchinson & co., ltd. [1944] 175 p. front., illus. (facsims.) plates. ports. 22 cm. [BX192.A452] 45-11301
1. Russia—Church history—1917- I. Sergeant, Ernest Noel Copland. II. Title.

SPINKA, Matthew, 1890- 281.
The church and the Russian revolution, by Matthew Spinka ... New York, The Macmillan company, 1927. xii p., 1 l., 330 p. 19 1/2 cm. Bibliography: p. 327-330. [BX492.S6] 27-23319
1. Russia—Church history—1917- 2. Church and state in Russia—1917- 3. Russia—Hist.—Revolution, 1917- 4. Communism—Russia. I. Title.

SZCZESNIAK, Boleslaw ed. and tr. 274.7
The Russian revolution and religion; a collection of docuemnts concerning the suppression of religion by the Communists, 1917-1925. With introductory essays, appendices, and a selective bibliography. [Ntre Dame, Ind. University of Notre Dame Press 1959. xx, 289 p. 24 cm. (International studies of the Committee on International Relations, University of Notre Dame) Notre Dame, Ind. University. Committee on International Relations. International studies) Bibliography: p. 253-269. Bibliographical footnotes. [BR936.S94] 58-14180
1. Russia — Church history — 1917- I. Title. II. Series.

TELEPUN, L. M., pseud. 282.47
The bloody footprints. New York, Vantage Press [1954] 145p. illus. 23cm. [BR936.T4] 53-12143
1. Russia—Church history—1917- I. Title.

ZERNOV, Nicolas 274.7
The Russian religious renaissance of the twentieth century. New York, Harper [1964, c.1963] xi, 410p. ports. 23cm. Bibl. 64-10768 7.00
1. Russia—Church history—1917- I. Title.

Russia—Description and travel

PAUL, of Aleppo, archdeacon, fl.1654-1666. 914.7
The travels of Macarius, extracts from the diary of the traveles of Macarius, patriarch of Antioch, written in Arabic by his son Paul, archdeacon of Aleppo, in the years of their journeying, 1652-1660. Translated into English and printed for the Oriental translation fund. 1836. Selected and arranged by Lady Laura Ridding. London, Oxford university press, H. Milford, 1936. xi, 125, [1] p. 20 cm. "Translated ... by F. C. Reifour."--p. v. [BX395.M3P3] 36-31753
1. Macarius iii. patriarch of Antioch, fl. 1636-1666. 2. Russia—Descr. & trav. 3. Balkan peninsula—Descr. & trav. 4. Orthodox Eastern church. I. Belfour, Francis Cunningham, tr. II. Ridding, Laura Elizabeth (Palmer) Lady 1849 III. Title.

PAUL, of Aleppo, Archdeacon, fl.1654-1666. 914.7'03'4
The travels of Macarius, 1652-1660. Selected and arranged by Lady Laura Ridding. New York, Arno Press, 1971. xi, 125 p. 23 cm. (Russia observed) Reprint of the 1936 ed. "Extracts from the diary of the travels of Macarius ... written in Arabic." [BX395.M3P3 1971] 77-115577 ISBN 0-405-03089-4
1. Macarius III, Patriarch of Antioch, fl. 1636-1666. 2. Orthodox Eastern Church. 3. Russia—Description and travel. 4. Balkan Peninsula—Description and travel. I. Title.

Russia—Economic conditions—1918-

PERLO, Victor. 330.947
Dynamic stability : the Soviet economy today / Victor and Ellen Perlo. New York : International Publishers, c1980. 343 p., [32] leaves of plates : ill. ; 20 cm. (New World paperbacks) (Impressions of the USSR) [HC335.P3456 1980] 80-18105 ISBN 0-7178-0577-8 (pbk.) : 4.75
1. Russia—Economic conditions—1918- I. Perlo, Ellen, joint author. II. Title. III. Series.

Russia—Foreign relations—Catholic Church.

POSSEVINO, Antonio, 1533or4-1611. 327.45'634
The Moscovia of Antonio Possevino, S.J. / translated, with critical introd. and notes by Hugh F. Graham. Pittsburgh : University Center for International Studies, University of Pittsburgh, c1977. 180 p. : ill. ; 26 cm. (UCIS series in Russian & East European studies ; no. 1) Includes bibliographical references. [BX1780.P5813] 77-12648 ISBN 0-916002-27-6 : 20.00
1. Catholic Church—Doctrinal and controversial works—Catholic authors. 2. Catholic Church—Relations (diplomatic) with Russia. 3. Russia—Foreign relations—Catholic Church. I. Title. II. Series: Pittsburgh. University. Center for International Studies. UCIS series in Russian and East European studies ; no. 1.

Russia—History—Revolution, 1917—Outlines, syllabi, etc.

ERICSON, Eston Everett, 1890- 947-084
Modern Russia, by Eston Everett Ericson and Ervid Eric Ericson. Chapel Hill, N.C., University of North Carolina press [c1932] 58 p. 22 1/2 cm. ([North Carolina. University. University extension division] University of North Carolina extension bulletin. vol. XII, no. 1) "Special reference bibliography: p. [48]-50; "Additional reference bibliography": p. [52] [LC6301.N43 vol. 12, no. 1] [DK266.E7] (378.13] 32-21488
1. Russia—Hist.—Revolution, 1917—Outlines, syllabi, etc. 2. Russia—Hist.—Revolution, 1917—Bibl. 3. Russia—Pol. & govt.—1917- I. Ericson, Ervid Eric, joint author. II. Title.

Russia—Religion.

CHYZHEVS'KYI, Dmytro, 1894- 001.2'0947
Russian intellectual history / Dmitrij Tschizewskij ; translated by John C. Osborne ; edited by Martin P. Rice. Ann Arbor : Ardis, c1978. 283 p., [13] leaves of plates : ill. ; 24 cm. Translation of th 1959-1961 ed. of Russische Geistesgechichte. Includes index. Bibliography: p. 253-259. [BR932.C4513] 78-110675 ISBN 0-88233-219-8 : 22.95
1. Russia—Religion. 2. Russia—Church history. 3. Russia—Intellectual life. I. Rice, Martin P. II. Title.

HECKER, Julius Friedrich, 1881- 274.
Religion under the soviets, by Julius F. Hecker ... New York, Vanguard press [1927] xvii, 207 p. 18 1/2 cm. (Vanguard studies of soviet Russia) "Selected bibliography": p. 204-207. [BR936.H3] 27-
1. Russia—Religion. 2. Greek church in Russia. I. Title.

IAROSLAVSKII, Emel'ian, 1878- 274.7
Religion in the U. S. S. R., by E. Yaroslavsky ... New York, International publishers [c1934] 64 p. 19 cm. [Name originally: Minel Israllevich Gubel'man] [BR966.I 3] 34-11418
1. Russia—Religion. 2. Church and state in Russia. 3. Atheism. I. Title.

PASCAL, Pierre, 1890- 209'.47
The religion of the Russian people / P. Pascal ; translated by Rowan Williams. London : Mowbrays, 1976. ix, 130 p. ; 22 cm. Translation of La religion du peuple russe, being v. 2 of the author's Civilisation paysanne en Russie. Includes bibliographical references. [BR932.P37213 1976b] 76-374983 £2.95
1. Russia—Religion. 2. Persecution—Russia. I. Title.

POWELL, David E. 301.15'4
Antireligious propaganda in the Soviet Union : a study of mass persuasion / David E. Powell. Cambridge, Mass. : The MIT Press, [1975] x, 206 p. : ill. ; 23 cm. Includes index. Bibliography: p. [197]-201. [BR936.P64] 74-34127 ISBN 0-262-16061-7
1. Russia—Religion. 2. Communism and Christianity—Russia. 3. Propaganda, Russian. I. Title.

READ, Christopher, 1946- 947.08
Religion, revolution, and the Russian intelligentsia, 1900-1912 : the Vekhi debate and its intellectual background / Christopher Read. Totowa, N.J. : Barnes & Noble, c1979. ix, 221 p. ; 23 cm. Includes index. Bibliography: 199-216. [BL980.R8R4] 79-13453 ISBN 0-06-495822-1 : 25.00
1. Russia—Religion. 2. Russia—Intellectual life—1801-1917. 3. Revolutionists—Russia. 4. Vekhi. I. Title.

RELIGION and the search for new ideals in the USSR, edited by William C. Fletcher and Anthony J. Strover. New York, Published for the Institute for the Study of the USSR [by] Praeger [1967] vi, 135 p. 25 cm. (Praeger publications in Russian history and world communism, no. 187) Papers presented at an international symposium, Munich, Germany, April 25-27, 1966, sponsored by the Institute for the Study of the USSR. Contents.Contents.—Communism and the problem of intellectual freedom, by G. Wetter.—The problem of alienation; life without spiritual or religious ideals, by P. B. Anderson.—Orthodoxy and the younger generation in the USSR, by D. Konstantinov.—The rejuvenation of the Russian Orthodox clergy, by N. Teodorovich.—Pseudo-religious rites introduced by the party authorities, by N. Struve.—Changes in Soviet medical ethics as an example of efforts to find stable moral values, by H. Schulz.—Protestant influences on the outlook of the Soviet citizen today, by W. C. Fletcher.—The search for new ideals in the USSR: some first-hand impressions, by P. B. Reddaway.—The tenacity of Islam in Soviet central Asia, by G. von Stackelberg.—Jews and Judaism in the Soviet Union, by H. Lamm.—The significance of religious themes in Soviet literature, by Z. Shakhovskaya.—Summary, by M. Hayward. Bibliographical footnotes. [BR932.R38] 67-16683 200'.9'47
1. Russia—Religion. 2. Russia—Social life and customs. I. Fletcher, William C., ed. II. Strover, Anthony J., ed. III. Institut zur Erforschung der UdSSR. IV. Title.

Russia-Religion-1917-

BACH, Marcus, 1906- 274.7
God and the Soviets. [New York 16, 425 Park Ave., S., Apollo Editions, Inc., 1961, c.1958] 214p. (Apollo ed. A-2) 1.25 pap.,
1. Russia—Religion—1917- 2. Communism and religion. I. Title.

BACH, Marcus, 1906- 274.7
God and the Soviets. New York, Crowell [1958] 214 p. illus. 21 cm. [BR936.B15] 58-12287
1. Russia—Religion—1917- 2. Communism and religion. I. Title.

BAKER, Alonzo Lafayette, 1894- 200.9'47
Religion in Russia today, by Alonzo L. Baker. Nashville, Southern Pub. Association [1967] 141 p. illus. (part col.), ports (part col.) 24 cm. Bibliography: p. 139-141. [BR936.B2] 67-28907
1. Russia—Religion—1917- I. Title.

BOURDEAUX, Michael. 274.7
Opium of the people; the Christian religion in the U.S.S.R. Indianapolis, Bobbs-Merrill [1966] 244 p. illus., map, ports. 22 cm. "Notes for further reading": p. 235-240. [BR936.B65] 66-15532
1. Russia — Religion — 1917- . 2. Church and state in Russia — 1917- . I. Title. II. Title: The Christian religion in the U.S.S.R.

BRAUN, Leopold L S 209.47
Religion in Russia, from Lenin to Khrushchev; an uncensored account. Paterson, N. J., St. Anthony Guild Press [1959] 88p. 18cm. [BR936.B67] 59-35890
1. Russia—Religion—1917- I. Title.

CONQUEST, Robert. 274.7
Religion in the U.S.S.R. New York, Praeger [1968] 135 p. 23 cm. (Praeger publications in Russian history and world communism, no. 201.) (The Contemporary Soviet Union series: institutions and policies) Bibliography: p. 128-135. [BR936.C6 1968] 68-17377
1. Russia—Religion—1917- I. Title. II. Series.

FLETCHER, William C. 306'.6
Soviet believers : the religious sector of the population / William C. Fletcher. Lawrence : Regents Press of Kansas, c1981. p. cm. Includes index. Bibliography: p. [BL980.R8F53] 19 80-25495 ISBN 0-7006-0211-9 : 27.50
1. Russia—Religion—1917- I. Title.

HARRIS, Thomas Leonard, 1901- 274.7
Unholy pilgrimage, by Thomas L. Harris. New York, Round table press, inc., 1937. ix, 185 p. 20 cm. [BR936.H25] 37-21921
1. Russia—Religion—1917- I. Title.

HECKER, Julius Friedrich, 1881- 274.7
Religion and communism; a study of religion and atheism in Soviet Russia, by Julius F. Hecker. Westport, Conn., Hyperion Press [1973] p. Reprint of the 1934 ed. published by Wiley, New York. [BR936.H28 1973] 73-842 ISBN 0-88355-037-7 14.75
1. Russia—Religion—1917- 2. Church and state in Russia—1917- 3. Communism and religion. I. Title.

KANIA, Ladislao. 274.7
Bolshevism and religion. Tr. by R. M. Dowdall. New York, Polish Library [1946] xvi, 96 p. 22 cm. [BR936.K] A 49
1. Russia—Religion—1917- 2. Communism and religion. I. Dowdall, R. M., tr. II. Title.

KOLARZ, Walter. 209.47
Religion in the Soviet Union. [New York] St. Martin's Press, 1961 [i. e. 1962] xii, 518 p. illus., ports., maps, facsims. 23 cm. Bibliographical footnotes. [BR936.K58 1962] 62-323
1. Russia—Religion—1917- 2. Russia—Church history—1917- I. Title.

RELIGION in the Soviet Union. London, Macmillan. New York, St. Martin's Press, 1961 [i. e. 1962] xii, 518p. illus., ports., maps, facsims. 23cm. Bibliographical footnotes.
1. Russia-Religion-1917- 2. Russia-Church history-1917- I. Kolarz, Walter.

TIMASHEFF, Nicholas Sergeyevitch, 1886- 274.7
Religion in soviet Russia, 1917-1942, by N. S. Timasheff ... New York, Sheed & Ward, 1942. xii, 171 p., 2 l., 171 p. 21 cm. Bibliographical notes at end of each chapter. "Selected bibliography": p. ix. [BR936.T5] 42-36332
1. Russia—Religion—1917- I. Title.

VAN PAASSEN, Pierre, 1895- 274.7
Visions rise and change. New York, Dial Press, 1955. 400 p. 22 cm. [BR936.V34] 55-11199
1. Russia—Religion—1917- I. Title.

Russia—Religion—1917- —Addresses, essays, lectures.

RELIGION and the Soviet State: a dilemma of power, edited by Max Hayward and William C. Fletcher. New York, Published for the centre de recherches et d'etude des institutions religieuses by Praeger [1969] x, 200 p. 22 cm. Papers of a conference sponsored by the Centre de recherches et d'etude des institutions religieuses in Geneva, in Sept. 1967. Bibliographical footnotes. [BR936.R43] 73-85539 6.50 200'.947
1. Russia—Religion—1917- —Addresses, essays, lectures. I. Hayward, Max, ed. II. Fletcher, William C., ed. III. Centre de recherches et d'etude des institutions religieuses.

Russia—Religion—1917- —Congresses.

RELIGION and modernization in the Soviet Union / edited by Dennis J. Dunn. Boulder, Colo. : Westview Press, 1977. x, 414 p. : ill. ; 24 cm. (A Westview replica edition) Papers from an international symposium organized by the American Association for the Advancement of Slavic Studies at Southwest Texas State University in Mar. 1976. Includes bibliographical references and index. [BR936.R42] 77-86372 ISBN 0-89158-241-X lib.bdg. : 21.75 200'.947
1. Russia—Religion—1917- —Congresses. 2. Russia—Civilization—1917- —Congresses. I. Dunn, Dennis J. II. Southwest Texas State University. III. American Association for the Advancement of Slavic Studies.

Russia—Religion—Addresses, essays, lectures.

ASPECTS of religion in the Soviet Union, 1917-1967. Edited by Richard H. Marshall, Jr. Associate editors: Thomas E. Bird and Andrew Q. Blane. Chicago, University of Chicago Press [1971] xv, 489 p. port. 24 cm. Bibliography: p. [465]-470. [BL980.R8A9] 70-115874 ISBN 0-226-50700-9 200'.947
1. Russia—Religion—Addresses, essays, lectures. I. Marshall, Richard H., 1897- ed.

THE Religious world of Russian culture / Andrew Blane, editor. The Hague : Mouton, 1976 359 p. ; 25 cm. (Russia and Orthodoxy ; v. 2) English, French, German or Russian. Includes bibliographical references and index. [BX250.R87 vol. 2] [BR932] 281.9'47 72-94520 40.00 281.9 s
1. Florovskii, Georgii Vasil'evich, 1893- 2. Russia—Religion—Addresses, essays, lectures. I. Blane, Andrew. II. Series. III. Slavistic printings and reprintings ; 260/2
Distributed by Humanities

Russia—Religious life and customs.

DEYNEKA, Anita. 209'.47
Christians in the shadow of the Kremlin / Anita and Peter Deyneka, Jr. Elgin, Il. : D. C. Cook Pub. Co., c1974. 96 p., [8] leaves of plates : ill. ; 18 cm. [BR936.D38] 74-17730 ISBN 0-912692-48-0 : 1.50
1. Russia—Religious life and customs. I. Deyneka, Peter, 1931- joint author. II. Title.

KOVALEVSKY, Pierre. 281.9'3 B
Saint Sergius and Russian spirituality / by Pierre Kovalevsky ; translation by W. Elias Jones. Crestwood, N.Y. : St. Vladimir's Seminary Press, 1976. p. cm. Translation of Saint Serge et la spiritualite russe. Includes index. Bibliography: p. [BX597.S45K6913] 76-13018 ISBN 0-913836-24-9 : 5.50
1. Sergii Radonezhskii, Saint, 1314?-1392. 2. Russia—Religious life and customs. I. Title.

Russian Orthodox Greek Catholic Church of America—Government.

TREMPELAS, Panagiotes Nikolaou, 1886- 262'.01'93
The autocephaly of the Metropolia in America / by Panagiotes N. Trempelas ; translated and edited by George S. Bebis, Robert G. Stephanopoulos, N. M. Vaporis. Brookline, Mass. : Holy Cross Theological School Press, 1973, c1974. 80 p. ; 21 cm. Includes bibliographical references. [BX496.T7313] 75-329980
1. Russian Orthodox Greek Catholic Church of America—Government. I. Title.

Russian Orthodox Greek Catholic church of North America.

KOHANIK, Peter G 1880- 230.19
The most useful knowledge for the Orthodox Russian-American young people. Compiled by: V. Rev. Peter G. Kohanik ... [Passiac? N. J.] 1934. 800 p. illus. (incl. ports.) diagr. 24 cm. [BX496.K6] 41-25507
1. Russian Orthodox Greek Catholic church of North America. I. Title.

Russkaia pravoslavnaia tserko

MAYER, Fred, 1933- 281.9'3
The Orthodox Church of Russia : a millennial celebration / photographed by Fred Mayer ; texts by Monseigneur Piririm ... [et al.]. New York : Vendome Press ; Zurich : Orell Fussli Verlag, 1982. p. cm. [BX510.M39] 19 82-6933 ISBN 0-86565-029-2 : 65.00

1. Russkaia pravoslavnaia tserko . I. Pitirim, Archbishop of Volokolamsk. II. Title.
Distributed by Viking Press, New York, NY 10022.

Russkaia pravoslavnaia tserkov'—History—20th century.

CUNNINGHAM, James W. 281.9'47
A vanquished hope, the church in Russia on the eve of the revolution / James W. Cunningham. Crestwood, N.Y. : St. Vladimir's Seminary Press, 1981. p. cm. Includes index. Bibliography: p. [BX491.C78] 19 81-9077 ISBN 0-913836-70-2
1. Russkaia pravoslavnaia tserkov'—History—20th century. 2. Church renewal—Russkaia pravoslavnaia tserkov'. 3. Soviet Union—Church history. I. Title.
Publisher's address: 575 Scarsdale Rd., Crestwood, NY 10707

Russkaia pravoslavnaia tserkov' zagranitsei.

HOLY Transfiguration Monastery. 281.9'3'09
A history of the Russian Church abroad and the events leading to the American Metropolia's autocephaly. Seattle, Wa., St Nectarios Press, c1976. 210 p. 24 cm. Bibliography: p. 210. [BX495.5.H64] 72-79507 ISBN 0-913026-04-2
1. Russkaia pravoslavnaia tserkov' zagranitsei. 2. Avtokefal'naia Amerikanskaia pravoslavnaia tserkov'. 3. Orthodox Eastern Church, Russian. I. Title.

RODZIANKO, M. 281.9'3
The truth about the Russian Church abroad : the Russian Orthodox Church outside of Russia / by M. Rodzianko ; translated from the Russian by Michael P. Hilko. [Jordanville, N.Y. : Holy Trinity Monastery], 1975. 48 p. : ports. ; 24 cm. [BX495.5.R613] 74-29321 ISBN 0-88465-004-9 pbk. : 1.50
1. Russkaia pravoslavnaia tserkov' zagranitsei. I. Title.

Rust, Eric Charles—Addresses, essays, lectures.

SCIENCE, faith, and revelation : an approach to Christian philosophy / edited by Bob E. Patterson. Nashville : Broadman Press, c1979. xi, 371 p. ; 24 cm. Festschrift in honor of Eric Charles Rust. "Publications by Eric C. Rust": p. 369-371. [BR50.S26] 79-50751 ISBN 0-8054-1809-1 pbk. : 8.95 230
1. Rust, Eric Charles—Addresses, essays, lectures. 2. Theology—Addresses, essays, lectures. I. Patterson, Bob E. II. Rust, Eric Charles.

Rutgers University, New Brunswick, N.J.

THE British Open University in the United States : adaptation and use at three universities / Rodney T. Hartnett ... [et al.]. Princeton, N.J. : Educational Testing Service, 1974. 112, [34] p. ; 28 cm. Includes bibliographical references. [LC6576.B74] 75-324326 5.00 378.1'554
1. Rutgers University, New Brunswick, N.J. 2. Maryland. University. 3. Houston, Tex. University. 4. Open University. 5. University extension—United States. I. Hartnett, Rodney T.

Ruth (Biblical character)

[ALCOTT, William Andrus] 1798-1859. 221.92
Story of Ruth the Moabitess. By the author of the "First foreign mission"...Written for the Massachusetts Sabbath school society, and revised by the Committee of publication. Boston, Massachusetts Sabbath school society, 1835. xvi, [19]-158 p. incl. front. 15 1/2 cm. Introduction signed: W. A. A. [i.e. William Alexander Alcott] [BS580.R8A43] 37-12154
1. Ruth. I. Massachusetts Sabbath school society. II. Title.

GARDINER, George E. 222'.35'0924 B
The romance of Ruth / by George E. Gardiner. Grand Rapids : Kregel Publications, [1977] p. cm. [BS580.R8G37] 77-79187 ISBN 0-8254-2718-5 pbk. : 1.50
1. Bible. O.T.—Biography. 2. Ruth (Biblical character) I. Title.

MCGEE, J. Vernon. 222.3
Ruth; the romance of redemption, by J. Vernon McGee ... Grand Rapids, Mich., Zondervan publishing house [1943] 195 p. 20 cm. "Printed and published by permission of Dallas theological seminary, Dallas, Texas." Bibliography: p. 194-195. [BS580.R8M3] 43-10140
1. Ruth. 2. Redemption—Biblical teaching. I. Dallas theological seminary and graduate school of theology. II. Title.

MCGEE, John Vernon, 1904- 221.92'4
In a barley field, by J. Vernon McGee. Glendale, Calif., G/L Regal Books [1968] 192 p. 18 cm. On cover: Ruth's romance of redemption. 1943 and 1954 editions published under title: Ruth: the romance of redemption. Bibliography: p. 192. [BS580.R8M3 1968] 68-22387
1. Ruth (Biblical character) 2. Redemption—Biblical teaching. I. Title.

MCGEE, John Vernon, 1904- 222.3
Ruth: the romance of redemption. 2d ed. Wheaton, Ill., Van Kampen Press, 1954. 158p. 20cm. [BS580.R8] 54-2978
1. Ruth (Biblical character) 2. Redemption—Biblical teaching. I. Title.

MARSHALL, Effie Lawrence, 1873- 221.92
Ruth, the world's most famous love story. Portland, Me., Falmouth Pub. House [1949] 195 p. front. 21 cm. "Based on the King James version of the story of Ruth." [BS580.R8M38] 49-8840
1. Ruth. I. Title.

MAURO, Philip. 222.
Ruth: The satisfied stranger, by Philip Mauro ... New York, Chicago [etc.] Fleming H. Revell company [c1920] 220 p. 19 1/2 cm. [BS1315.M3] 20-4811
I. Title.

MAURO, Philip, 1859- 222.3506
Ruth: the satisfied stranger. Swengel, Pa., Bible Truth Depot [1963, c.1920] 220p. 19cm. 1.95 pap.,
1. Ruth. I. Title.

PETERSHAM, Maud (Fuller) 1890- 221.92
Ruth; from the story told in the book of Ruth [by] Maud and Miska Petersham. New York, Macmillan, 1958 [c1938] [32] p. illus. 24 cm. Presents the Old Testament tale of Ruth who, when her husband died, returned with her mother-in-law to Bethlehem to work in the fields of Boaz. [BS580.R8P45 1958] AC 68
1. Ruth (Biblical character) 2. Bible stories—Old Testament. I. Petersham, Miska, 1888- joint author. II. Title.

TAYLOR, William Mackergo, 1829-1895. 221.92
Ruth the gleaner and Esther the queen, by William M. Taylor ... New York, Harper & brothers, 1891. 3 p. l., 369 p. illus. (plan) 19 1/2 cm. [BS580.R8T3] 37-7011
1. Ruth. 2. Esther, queen of Persia. I. Title.

TYNG, Stephen Higginson, 1800-1885. 221.92
The rich kinsman The history of Ruth the Moabitess. By Stephen H. Tyng ... New York, R. Carter & brothers, 1855. vii, [9]-425 p. 17 1/2 cm. [BS580.R879] 37-7010
1. Ruth. I. Title.

Ruth (Biblical character) — Drama.

BROWNE, Frances Elizabeth, Mrs.
Ruth; a sacred drama, and original lyrical poems, by Frances Elizabeth Browne. New York, Wynkoop & Hallenbeck, 1871. 2 p. l., (vii)-viii, 121 p. 18 1/2 cm. [PS1144.B3R8 1871] 13-33889
I. Title.

LENCH, Charles Harris.
The love story of Ruth & Boaz; a dramatic verse version of the Biblical story, by Charles H. de Lench. [1st ed.] New York, Exposition Press [c1966] 71 p. 21 cm. 66-95591
1. Ruth (Biblical character) — Drama. I. Title.

Ruth (Biblical character)-Fiction.

LARSEN, Beverly 221.9505
Damsel from afar; the story of Ruth. Illus. by Melva Mickelson. Minneapolis, Augsburg [c.1965] 96p. illus. 21cm. [BS580.R8L3] 65-22834 2.95
1. Ruth (Biblical character)—Fiction. I. Title.

MALVERN, Gladys.
The foreigner; the story of a girl named Ruth. Decorations by Corinne Malvern. New York, D. McKay [1967] 214 p. illus. 27 cm. 68-80692
1. Ruth (Biblical character)-Fiction. I. Title.

Ruth (Biblical character)—Juvenile literature.

GRIFFITHS, Kitty Anna. 222'.35'09505
Come, meet Ruth : the story of the book of Ruth / Kitty Anna Griffiths ; illustrated by "Willy". 1st Zondervan ed. Grand Rapids : Zondervan Pub. House, 1978, c1976. 95 p. : ill. ; 21 cm. (Come, meet series) Retells the story of Ruth which describes her devotion and commitment to God. [BS580.R8G74 1978] 78-16723 ISBN 0-310-25261-X : 1.95
1. Ruth (Biblical character)—Juvenile literature. 2. [Ruth (Biblical character)] 3. Bible. O.T.—Biography—Juvenile literature. 4. Bible stories, English—O.T. Ruth. 5. [Bible stories—O.T.] I. Willy. II. Title.

POLLARD, Josephine, 1834-1892.
Ruth, A Bible heroine, and other stories; told in the language of childhood. New York, Akron, O. [etc.] The Werner co., 1899. [105] p. illus., pl. 8 degrees. Duplicate of chaps. 10-20 in her History of the Old Testament, issued simultaneously with the above. 99-3644
I. Title.

Ruthenia—Church history.

LACKO, Michael. 281.9'47'71
The Union of Uzhorod / Michael Lacko. Cleveland : Slovak Institute, 1966 [i.e. 1969?] 190 p., [2] leaves of plates : ill., maps ; 25 cm. "This dissertation appeared in Slovak studies vol. VI with the same pagination." Translation of Unio Uzhorodensis Ruthenorum Carpaticorum cum Ecclesia Catholica, by Joseph Gill. Bibliography: p. 11-14. [BX4711.62.L313] 75-316503
1. Catholic Church. Byzantine rite (Ruthenian) 2. Ruthenia—Church history. I. Title.

Ryall, Edward W., 1902-

RYALL, Edward W., 1902- 133.9'013 B
Born twice : total recall of a seventeenth-century life / by Edward W. Ryall ; with an introd. and appendix by Ian Stevenson. 1st U.S. ed. New York : Harper & Row, [1975] c1974. 214 p., [4] leaves of plates : ill. ; 22 cm. Includes index. [BL515.R9 1975] 74-20412 ISBN 0-06-013713-4 : 8.95
1. Ryall, Edward W., 1902- 2. Reincarnation. 3. [Parapsychology—Personal narratives.] I. Title.

Ryan, Edward, d. 1819. Analysis of Ward's Errata of the Protestant Bible.

WARD, Thomas, 1652-1708. 220.52
Errata of the Protestant Bible; or, The truth of the English translations examined; in a treatise, showing some of the errors that are to be found in the English translations of the Sacred Scriptures, used by Protestants...in which also, from their mistranslating the twenty-third verse of the fourteenth chapter of the Acts of the Apostles, the consecration of Dr. Matthew Parker...is occasionally considered. By Thomas Ward, esq. A new ed., carefully rev. and cor. To which are added, the celebrated preface of the Rev. Dr. Lingard in answer to Ryan's "Analysis", and a vindication, by the Right Rev. Doctor Milner, in answer to Grier's "Reply" ... New York, D. & J. Sadlier, 1844. 2 p. l., 118 p. 19 1/2 cm. Published also under title: Errata to the Protestant Bible. [BS410.W3 1844] 37-18498
1. Ryan, Edward. d. 1819. Analysis of Ward's Errata of the Protestant Bible. 2. Grier, Richard, fl. 1820. An answer to Ward's Errata of the Protestant Bible. 3. Bible—Versions. Catholic vs. Protestant. I. Lingard, John, 1771-1851. II. Milner, John, bp., 1752-1826. III. Title.

WARD, Thomas, 1652-1708.
Errata of the Protestant Bible; or, The truth of the English translations examined; in a treatise, showing some of the errors that are to be found in the English translations of the Sacred Scriptures, used by Protestants...in which also, from their mistranslating the twenty-third verse of the fourteenth chapter of the Acts of the Apostles, the consecration of Dr. Mathew Parker...is occasionally considered. By Thomas Ward, esq. A new ed., carefully rev. and cor. To which are added, the celebrated preface of the Rev. Doctor L...in answer to Ryan's "Analysis", and a vindication, by the Right Rev. Doctor Milner, in answer to Grier's "Reply" ... New York, D. & J. Sadlier, 1814. 2 p. l., 118 p. 29 1/2 cm. [With Bible. English 1845. Donal. The Holy Bible. [1845]) [BS180.1845.N4] 31-19028
1. Ryan, Edward, d. 1819. Analysis of Ward's Errata of the Protestant Bible. 2. Grier, Richard, fl. 1820. An answer to Ward's Errata of the Protestant Bible. 3. Bible—Versions, Catholic vs. Protestant. I. Lingard, John, 1771-1851. II. Milner, John, bp., 1752-1826. III. Title.

Ryan, John Augustine, 1869-1945.

BRODERICK, Francis L 922.273
Right Reverend New Dealer, John A. Ryan. New York, Macmillan [1963] 290 p. illus. 25 cm. [BX4705.R83B7] 62-19419
1. Ryan, John Augustine, 1869-1945. I. Title.

RYAN, John Augustine, 1869- 922.273
Social doctrine in action, a personal history, by Rt. Rev. Msgr. John A. Ryan... New York and London, Harper & brothers, 1941. vii p., 1 l., 297 p. front. (port.) 22 1/2 cm. "First edition." [BX4705.R83A3 1941] 41-6305
I. Title.

Ryan, Mary Perkins, 1915- Are parochial schools the answer?

DEFERRARI, Roy Joseph, 1890- 377.8273
A complete system of Catholic education is necessary [Boston] St. Paul Eds. [dist. Daughters of St. Paul, c.1964] 72p. 22cm. Cover title: Catholic education is necessary. 64-22429 2.25; 1.25 pap.,
1. Ryan, Mary Perkins, 1915- Are parochial schools the answer? 2. Catholic Church in the U.S.—Education. I. Ryan, Mary Perkins, 1915- Are parochial schools the answer? II. Title. III. Title: Catholic education is necessary.

DEFERRARI, Roy Joseph, 1890- 377.8273
A complete system of Catholic education is necessary, by Roy J. Deferrari. [Boston] St. Paul Editions [1964] 72 p. 22 cm. Cover title: Catholic education is necessary. "A reply to 'Are parochial schools the answer?' by Mary Perkins Ryan." [BX926.R93D4] 64-22429
1. Ryan, Mary Perkins, 1915- Are parochial schools the answer? 2. Catholic Church in the U.S. — Education. I. Ryan, Mary Perkins, 1915- Are parochial schools the answer? II. Title. III. Title: Catholic education is necessary.

Ryan, Patrick John, abp., 1831-1911.

[COWLEY, Richard F] 922.273
d.1926, comp.
The episcopal silver-jubilee of the Most Reverend Patrick John Ryan ... A full and concise account of the celebration of the episcopal silver jubilee of His Grace, the Archbishop of Philadelphia, together with two biographical sketches, and much other matter written for the occasion ... Philadelphia, Pa., Published at St. Dominic's rectory [1897] 264 p. incl. front., illus. (incl. ports.) 26 cm. [BX4705.R84C6] 37-18216
1. Ryan, Patrick John, abp., 1831-1911. I. Title.

Ryan, Stephen Vincent, bp., 1825-1896.

CRONIN, Patrick, 1835- 922.273
1905.
Memorial of the life and labors of Rt. Rev. Stephen Vincent Ryan ... second bishop of Buffalo, N.Y. By Rev. Patrick Cronin ... Buffalo, N. Y., Buffalo Catholic publications company, 1896. xi, [1] p. 1 l., 141 p. front., illus. (incl. port.) 24 cm. [BX4705.R85C7] 37-18504
1. Ryan, Stephen Vincent, bp., 1825-1896. I. Title.

Ryckman, Harold.

RYCKMAN, Lucile 266'.7'97 B
Damon.
Paid in full : the story of Harold Ryckman, missionary pioneer to Paraguay and Brazil / by Lucile Damon Ryckman. Winona Lake, Ind. : Light and Life Press, c1979. 128 p. : ill. ; 21 cm. [BV2853.P3R927] 79-112549 ISBN 0-89367-033-2 pbk. : 3.75
1. Ryckman, Harold. 2. Missionaries—Paraguay—Biography. 3. Missionaries—Brazil—Biography. 4. Missionaries—United States—Biography. I. Title.

Ryder, James, 1800-1860.

[POLK, Josiah F. 220.
A defence of the Protestant Bible, as published by the Bible societies, against the charge raised against it by the Rev. Dr. Ryder ... during a course of theological lectures, delivered in March and April, 1844, in the city of Washington: that it does not contain the whole of the written word of God--or sacred Scripture--by 139 chapters, and, that consequently it is a book which all Catholics detest and abhor. By Akroatees [pseud.] ... New-York, Leavitt, Trow, & co.; Washington, D. C., W. M. Morrison, 1844. 68 p. 22 cm. [BS470.P6] 12-24396
1. Ryder, James, 1800-1860. 2. Bible—Canon. 3. Bible—Verstona Catholic. 4. Catholic church—Doctrinal and controversial works—Protestant. I. Title.

Rye, N. Y. Rye Presbyterian Church.

MCKAY, Ellen Cotton. 285.1747
A history of the Rye Presbyterian Church; a documentary story of presbyterianism in. rye, new york, from the date of its settlement in 1660 until the present time. Rye, N. Y., Presbyterian Church [1957] 260p. illus: 24cm. Includes bibliography. [BX9211.R9R9] 57-45930
1. Rye, N. Y. Rye Presbyterian Church. I. Title.

Ryken, Theodore James, 1797-1871.

AUBERT, Brother. 189.4
March on! God will provide. Boston, E. L. Grimes Co. [1961] 196p. illus. 17cm. 'Synopsized version of a full-length biography of Theodore James Ryken . . . not ready for publication.' [BX4705.R9A8] 61-46755
1. Ryken, Theodore James, 1797-1871. I. Title.

Rylaarsdam, John Coert, 1906-—Addresses, essays, lectures.

†SCRIPTURE in history & theology : essays in honor of J. Coert Rylaarsdam / edited by Arthur L. Merrill 220.6 and Thomas W. Overholt. Pittsburgh : Pickwick Press, 1977. ix, 413 p. ; 22 cm. (The Pittsburgh theological monograph series ; 17) "The writings of J. Coert Rylaarsdam, Arthur L. Merrill": p. [BS540.S36] 77-12106 ISBN 0-915138-32-8 : 8.95
1. Rylaarsdam, John Coert, 1906-—Addresses, essays, lectures. 2. Rylaarsdam, John Coert, 1906-—Bibliography. 3. Bible—Criticism, interpretation, etc.—Addresses, essays, lectures. I. Rylaarsdam, John Coert, 1906- II. Merrill, Arthur L. III. Overholt, Thomas W., 1935- IV. Series.

Ryle, Gilbert, 1900- The concept of mind.

AUSTRALASIAN Association 128'.2
of Philosophy
The identity theory of mind. Ed. by C. F. Presley. [St. Lucia, Brisbane] Univ. of Queensland Pr. [1967] xix, 164p. 22cm. Papers presented at the Annual Cong. of the Australasian Assn. of Phil. held at the Univ. of Queensland in 1964- Bibl. [BF161.A9] 68-31940 6.75
1. Ryle, Gilbert, 1900- The concept of mind. 2. Smart, John Jamieson Carswell. 1920- 3. Mind and body—Addresses, essays, lectures. I. Presley, Charles Frederick, 1920- ed. II. Queensland. University, Brisbane. III. Title.
Distributed by Tri-Ocean, San Francisco.

Ryle, John Charles, Bp. of Liverpool, 1816-1900.

TOON, Peter, 1939- 283'.092'4 B
John Charles Ryle : evangelical bishop / by Peter Toon and Michael Smout. Cambridge : J. Clarke, 1976. 123 p., plate : port. ; 24 cm. "Selected list of tracts and books by J. C. Ryle": p. 121. [BX5199.R9T66 1976b] 77-358597 ISBN 0-227-67826-5 : £3.75
1. Ryle, John Charles, Bp. of Liverpool, 1816-1900. 2. Church of England—Bishops—Biography. 3. Bishops—England—Biography. I. Smout, Michael, 1937- joint author.

Rymer, J. Sykes.

RYMER, J. Sykes. 133.9'092'4
Stepping stones : from orthodoxy to a new understanding / by A. Pilgrim (Rev. J. Sykes Rymer). [Onchan] : [Barbara M. Rymer], [1976] 152 p. : ports. ; 21 cm. [BF1283.R94A34] 77-369511 ISBN 0-9505509-0-6 : £1.30
1. Rymer, J. Sykes. 2. Spiritualists—England—Biography. I. A. Pilgrim. II. Title.

Ryukyu Islands—History.

ROSS, William 248.2'46'0924 B
Gordon, 1900-
Why to ... Okinawa? By W. Gordon Ross. North Quincy, Mass., Christopher Pub. House [1971] 137 p. illus. 21 cm. [BR1317.K55R68] 72-171074 4.95
1. Kina, Shosei. 2. Ryukyu Islands—History. I. Title.

Ryukyu Islands—Religion.

ROBINSON, James C. 299'.56
Okinawa; a people and their gods, by James C. Robinson. [1st ed.] Rutland, Vt., C. E. Tuttle [1969] 110 p. illus., maps. 22 cm. Bibliography: p. 103-104. [BL2215.R9R6] 69-16179 3.75
1. Ryukyu Islands—Religion. I. Title.

m (Cistercian abbey), Aarhus, Denmark (Province)

MCGUIRE, Brian 271'.12'04895
Patrick.
Conflict and continuity at m abbey : a Cistercian experience in medieval Denmark / Brian Patrick McGuire. Copenhagen : Museum Tusculanum : [Institut for klassisk filologi, Fiolstrade 10], 1976. 151 p., [4] leaves of plates : ill. ; 23 cm. (Opuscula Graecolatina ; v. 8) Includes index. Bibliography: p. [137]-141. [BX2644.O4M32] 77-457250 kr35.00
1. m (Cistercian abbey), Aarhus, Denmark (Province) I. Title. II. Series.

Saadiah ben Joseph, gaon, 892?-942.

AMERICAN academy for 922.96
Jewish research.
...Saadia anniversary volume. New York [Philadelphia, Press of the Jewish publication society] 1943. 346 p. 23 1/2 cm. (Its Texts and studies. Vol. II) "Essays on Rabbi Saudia ben Joseph, a native of Fayyum, Egypt, and gaon of Sura, the thousandth anniversary of whose death was commemorated by Jews in the year gone by ... edited by Professor Boux Cohen."--Editorial statement. Bibliographical footnotes. [DS101.A343 vol. 2] 44-6513
1. Saadiah ben Joseph, gaon, 892?-942. I. Cohen, Boaz, 1899- ed. II. Title.
Contents omitted.

DRUCK, David, 1883- 922.96
Saadya Gaon, scholar, philosopher champion of Judaism, by David Druck, translated from the Yiddish by M. Z. R. Frank. New York, Bloch publishing company, 1942. 2 p. l., 96 p. 19 1/2 cm. [BM755.S2D7] 42-17725
1. Saadish ben Joseph, gaon, 392-942. I. Frank, M.Z.R., tr. II. Title.

EFROS, Israel Isaac, 1890- 181'.3
Studies in medieval Jewish philosophy, [by] Israel Efros. New York, Columbia University Press, 1974. 269 p. 23 cm. Substantially the same material as originally published in the author's ha-Filosofyah ha-yehudit bi-yeme ha-benayim. Contents.Contents.—The philosophy of Saadia Gaon.—Three essays.—Studies in pre-Tibbonian philosophical terminology. Includes bibliographical references. [B755.E33] 73-12512 ISBN 0-231-03194-7
1. Saadiah ben Joseph, gaon, 892?-942. al-Amanat wa-al-i'tiqadat. 2. Judah, ha-Levi, 12th cent. Kitab al-Hujjah. 3. Moses ben Maimon, 1135-1204. Dalalat al-ha'irin. 4. Abraham bar Hiyya, ha-Nasi, 12th cent. 5. Philosophy, Jewish. 6. Philosophy, Medieval. I. Title.

THE Jewish quarterly 922.96
review. New series.
Saadia studies, published by the Jewish quarterly review in commemoration of the thousandth anniversary of the death of Saadia Gaon, edited by Abraham A. Neuman and Solomon Zeitlin. Philadelphia, The Dropsie college for Hebrew and cognate learning, 1943. 2 p. l., 293 p. 24 1/2 cm. Bibilographical footnotes. [BM755.S2J4] 43-5670
1. Saadiah ben Joseph, gaon, 892-942. I. Neuman, Abraham Aaron, 1890- ed. II. Zeitlin, Solomon, 1892- joint ed. III. Title.

JEWISH theological 922.96
seminary of America.
Rab Saadia gaon: studies in his honor, edited by Louis Finkelstein. [New York] Jewish theological seminary of America, 1944. xi p., 1 l., 191 p., 10 l. 21 cm. "Virtually all the material ... was prepared in connection with meetings held in honor of Rab Saadia gaon at the Jewish theological seminary of America, or under its auspices."--Pref. [BM755.S2J43] 44-24282
1. Saadiah ben Joseph, gaon, 892?-942. I. Finkelstein, Louis, 1895- ed. II. Title.
Contents omitted.

MALTER, Henry, 1864- 296.6'1'0924
1925.
Saadia Gaon; his life and works. New York, Hermon Press [1969] 446 p. 23 cm. "First Edition: New York, 1926." Bibliography: p. [303]-419. [BM755.S2M3 1969] 77-82475
1. Saadiah ben Joseph, gaon, 892?-942. 2. Saadiah ben Joseph, gaon, 892?-942—Bibliography.

MALTER, Henry, 1867-1925. 922.
...Saadia Gaon, his life and works, by Henry Malter... Philadelphia, The Jewish publication society of America, 1921. 446 p. 22 1/2 cm. (The Morris Loeb series. [I]) The first volume issued under the Morris Loeb publication fund. Bibliography: p. [303]-419. [BM755.S2M3] 22-548
1. Saadish ben Joseph, gaon, 892-942. I. Title.

Saadiah ben Joseph, gaon, 892?-942—Addresses, essays, lectures.

AMERICAN Academy for 296.6'1'0924
Jewish Research.
Saadia anniversary volume / edited by Boaz Cohen. New York : Arno Press, 1980, c1943. 346 p. ; 23 cm. (Jewish philosophy, mysticism, and the history of ideas) Reprint of the ed. published by the American Academy for Jewish Research, New York, which was issued as v. 2 of the Academy's Texts and studies. Includes bibliographical references and index. [BM755.S2A84 1980] 79-7168 ISBN 0-405-12244-6 : 25.00
1. Saadiah ben Joseph, gaon, 892?-942—Addresses, essays, lectures. I. Cohen, Boaz, 1899-1968. II. Title. III. Series. IV. Series: American Academy for Jewish Research. Texts and studies ; v. 2.
Contents omitted Contents omitted

Saadiah ben Joseph, gaon, 892?-942—Congresses.

JEWISH Theological 296.6'1'0924
Seminary of America.
Rab Saadia Gaon : studies in his honor / edited by Louis Finkelstein. New York : Arno Press, 1980 [c1944] xi, 191 p. : music ; 23 cm. (Jewish philosophy, mysticism, and the history of ideas) Reprint of the ed. published by the Jewish Theological Seminary of America, New York. "Virtually all the material ... was prepared in connection with meetings held in honor of Rab Saadia Gaon at the Jewish Theological Seminary of America, or under its auspices." Contents.Contents.—Marx, A. Rab Saadia Gaon.—McKeon, R. P. Saadia Gaon.—Compton, A. H. Freedom.—Halkin, A.S. Saadia's exegesis and polemics.—Bokser, B. Z. Saadia as a philosopher of Judaism.—Gordin, R. Saadia in the light of today.—Appendices: I. Cohen, B. Selected bibliography of Rab Saadia Gaon.—II. Hymn by Frederick Jacobi: words by Saadia Gaon (882-942), for men's chorus.—III. Program of the assembly commemorating the life and works of Rabbi Saadia Gaon (882-942), held at the Jewish Theological Seminary of America, March 24, 1942.—IV. Programs of the convocation to commemorate the life and works of Rab Saadia Gaon (882-942), held at Mandel Hall of the University of Chicago, April 20, 1942. [BM755.S2J43 1980] 79-7169 ISBN 0-405-12250-0 : 16.00
1. Saadiah ben Joseph, gaon, 892?-942—Congresses. I. Saadiah ben Joseph, gaon, 892?-942. II. Finkelstein, Louis, 1895- III. Title. IV. Series.

Saadiah ben Joseph, gaon, 892-942. Kitab al-amanat.

HESCHEL, Abraham, 1907- 181.3
The quest for certainty in Saadia's philosophy, by Abraham Heschel. New York, N.Y., P. Feldheim [1944] 1 p. l., 67 p. 23 cm. "Reprinted from the Jewish quarterly review, vol. XXXIII, nos. 2 and 3, vol. XXVIV, no. 4." [B759.S24H4] 44-12391
1. Saadish ben Joseph, gaon, 892?-942. Kitab al-amanat. I. Title.

HESCHEL, Abraham Joshua, 181.3
1907-
The quest for certainty in Saadia's philosophy. New York, Feldheim [1944] 67p. 23cm. 'Reprinted from the Jewish quarterly review, vol. XXXIII, nos. 2 and 3, vol. XXXIV, no. 4. [B759.S24H4] 44-12391
1. Saadiah ben Joseph, gaon, 892-942. Kitab al-amanat. I. Title.

Saadiah ben Joseph, gaon, 892 -942. Kutub al-lughah.

SKOSS, Solomon Leon, 1884- 492.45
1953.
Saadia Gaon, the earliest Hebrew grammarian. Philadelphia, Dropsie College Press, 1955. 66p. illus. 24cm. (volumes xxi, xxii and xxiii).' 'Appeared originally in serial form in the Proceedings of the American Academy for Jewish Research [PJ4556.S33S5] 55-8787

1. Saadiah ben Joseph, gaon, 892 -942. Kutub al-lughah. I. Title.

Sabbatarians—Biography.

WUST, Klaus German, 1925- 289.9 B
The saint-adventurers of the Virginia frontier : southern outposts of Ephrata / Klaus Wust. Edinburg, Va. : Shenandoah History Publishers, 1977. 125 p. : ill. ; 22 cm. "An exacted relation on the appearance of a disembodied spirit: translation of the Relation of 1761": p. 87-101. Includes index. Bibliography: p. 104-120. [BX9680.S3W87] 76-48566 ISBN 0-917968-04-2 : 8.00
1. Eckerlin, Samuel, 1703-1781. 2. Eskerlin, Israel, b. 1710 or 11. 3. Eckerlin, Gabriel. 4. Sabbatarians—Biography. 5. Sabbatarians—Virginia. 6. Ephrata Community. I. Abgeforderte Relation der Erscheinung eines entleibten Geists. English. 1977. II. Title.

Sabbath.

ANDREASEN, Milian Lauritz, 1876- 263.2
The Sabbath, which day and why! By M. L. Andreasen. Takoma Park, Washington, D. C., Review and herald publishing association [1942] 255 p. 21 cm. [BV125.A5] 42-19849
1. Sabbath. 2. Seventh-day Adventists—Doctrinal and controversial works. I. Title.

ANDREWS, John Nevins, 1829-1883. 263
History of the Sabbath and first day of the week, by J. N. Andrews and L. R. Conradi. 4th ed., rev. and enl. Washington, D.C., New York, N.Y. [etc.] Review & herald publishing association [c1912] 864 p. 22 cm. Bibliographical foot-notes. [BV110.A5 1912] 12-18158
1. Sabbath. 2. Sunday. I. Conradi, Ludwig Richard, joint author. II. Title.

BESSE, Henry True, 1823-
The Sabbath; a memorial of different events, with the corresponding changes of the day, and the manner of its observance. By Rev. H. T. Besse ... Cincinnati, Printed for the author, by Jennings and Graham, 1914. 82 p. 23 cm. 14-9775 0.35
I. Title.

BIBLE Sabbath Association. 280'.4
Directory of Sabbath-observing groups. 4th ed. Fairview, Okla. : Bible Sabbath Association, 1974. 258 p. ; 21 cm. Previously published under title: Sabbath handbook and directory of Sabbath-observing organizations. Includes indexes. [BV125.B5 1974] 74-196036
1. Sabbath. 2. Sunday. 3. Sabbatarians. 4. Sects—Directories. I. Title.

BRIN, Ruth Firestone. 296.7
The Shabbat catalogue / by Ruth F. Brin ; illustrated by Ruthann Isaacson. New York : Ktav Pub. House, [1978] p. cm. [BM685.B66] 78-11981 ISBN 0-87068-636-4 : 4.00
1. Sabbath. 2. Family—Religious life (Judaism) I. Title.

BROWN, John Newton, 1803-1868. 263
The obligation of the Sabbath: a discussion between Rev. J. Newton Brown, and Wm. B. Taylor... Philadelphia, A. Hart, 1853. xi [13]-300 p. 20 cm. On cover: By Wm. B. Taylor. [BV110.B73] 33-22265
1. Sabbath. 2. Sunday. I. Taylor, William Bower, 1821-1895. II. Title.

BUTLER, George Ide, 1834- 263
The change of the Sabbath, was it by divine or human authority? By Geo. I. Butler. Nashville, Tenn., Fort Worth, Tex., Southern publishing association [1904] 196 p. illus. 20 cm. [BV125.B8 1904] 4-35760
1. Sabbath. I. Title.

CENTRAL Conference of American Rabbis. 296.4'1
[Tadrikh le-Shabat (romanized form)] a Shabbat manual. [New York] Published for the Central Conference of American Rabbis, by Ktav Pub. House, 1972. 104 p. 22 cm. Part of text in English and Hebrew. Includes unacc. melodies. [BM685.C44] 72-10299 ISBN 0-87068-199-0 2.50
1. Sabbath. I. Title. II. Title: A Shabbat manual.

CULLMANN, Oscar.
Early Christian worship. Translated by A. Stewart Todd and James B. Torrance. Chicago, Regnery, 1953. 124p. 21cm. (Studies in Biblical theology, no. 10) 'A translation of the second edition of Urchristeutum und Gottesdienst ... and contains also an extra chapter on 'Jesus and the day of rest' from the French translation of part 2. which appeared under the title Les sacrements dans Pevangile Johannique' Bibliographical footnotes. A55
1. Sabbath. 2. Worship—Early church. 3. Bible. N. T. John—Commentaries. I. Title. II. Series.

DUGGER, Andrew Nugent, 1884- 263.2
The Dugger-Porter debate, a written discussion on the Sabbath and the Lord's day ... Austin, Tex., Firm foundation publishing house [c1942] 233 p. 2 front. (ports.) 23 cm. [BV125.D8] 43-16985
1. Sabbath. 2. Sunday. I. Porter, W. Curtis. II. Title.

FLASKERUD, Ole E. 263
Christianity or Christ, by Ole E. Flaskerud... Chicago, Ill., The Author [c1940] 162 p. 24 cm. "A song for the Sabbath day" (words and music): p. 149-162. [BV110.F57] 40-29544
1. Sabbath. I. Title.

FLINK, Eugene, comp. 296.4'1
Yavneh shiron. Editor: Eugene Flink. Associate editor: Tom Ackerman. [New York, Yavneh, 1969] 221, [1] p. illus. 22 cm. Added to t.p.: Shiron Yavneh (romanized form) Selections (p. 86-[222]) from Z'mirot, Tanach, Talmud, Liturgy, Songs of the land (In Hebrew and English) Contents.Contents.—Prologue: The Sabbath-faith through action, by C. Keller.—Around the Sabbath table, by Y. Vainstein.—Birkhat Hamazon, by Z. Schachter.—The Sabbath-meaning and spirit, by S. Spero.—Sabbath rest, by N. Lamm.—The Sabbath ritual, by E. Fromm.—Sabbath and creation, by W. Wurtzburger.—Work on the Sabbath.—Living the Sabbath, by Z. Schachter.—Sabbath in Moscow, by B. Poupko. [BM685.F55] 76-16847
1. Sabbath. I. Ackerman, Tom, joint comp. II. Jews. Liturgy and ritual. Zemirot. III. Jews. Liturgy and ritual. Zemirot. English. IV. Yavneh (Association) V. Title. VI. Title: Shiron Yavneh.

FLOODY, Robert John, 1859- 263
Scientific basis of Sabbath and Sunday; a new investigation after the manner and methods of modern science, revealing the true origin and exact nature of the Jewish Sabbath and the Lord's day, for the purpose of ascertaining their real significance and proper observance, by the Rev. Robert John Floody... Boston, Mass., Cupples & Schoenhof [1901] 2 p. l., iii-xi, 354 p. 20 1/2 cm. "This work had its origin in an article entitled The Seventh Day of heathens, Hebrews, and Christians, presented to the New Testament history seminar of Boston university in the fall of 1895."--Pref. [BV110.F64 1901] 1-26259
1. Sabbath. 2. Sunday. I. Title.

FREDRICK, William.
Three prophetic days; or, Sunday the Christian's Sabbath ... Clyde, O., The author [1900] 230 p. 12 degree. 0-3191
I. Title.

[GRAHAME, James] 1765-1811.
The Sabbath: a poem, The 1st American ed. To which are now added, Sabbath walks ... New York, Ronalds and Loudon, 1805. 168 p. 16 degree. 1-835
I. Title.

[GRAY, George Seaman] 1835-1885. 263
Eight studies of the Lord's day. Boston, New York, Houghton, Mifflin and company, 1885. xiv, 292 p. 20 cm. [BV110.G7 1885] 24-8992
1. Sabbath. I. Title. II. Title: The Lord's day.

HAYNES, Carlyle Boynton, 1882- 263
The Christian Sabbath, is it Saturday or Sunday? A careful study of this important religious question from the standpoint of the Scriptures of truth. By Carlyle B. Haynes. Nashville, Tenn., Fort Worth, Tex. [etc.] Southern publishing association, 1916. 128 p. incl. front., illus. 19 1/2 cm. [BV125.H3] 26-3277
1. Sabbath. 2. Seventh-day Adventists. I. Title.

HESCHEL, Abraham, Joshua, 1907- 296
The sabbath: its meaning for modern man. With wood engravings by Ilya Schor. New York, Farrar, Straus and Young [1951] 118p. illus. 24cm. [BM685.H4] 51-8400
1. Sabbath. I. Title.

HESCHEL, Abraham Joshua, 1907- 296
The Sabbath: its meaning for modern man. With wood engravings by Ilya Schor. New York, Farrar, Straus and Young [1951] 118 p. illus. 24 cm. [BM685.H4] 51-8400
1. Sabbath.

JEWETT, Paul King. 263'.3
The Lord's day; a theological guide to the Christian day of worship [by] Paul K. Jewett. Grand Rapids, Mich., W. B. Eerdmans Pub. Co. [1971] 174 p. 21 cm. Bibliography: p. 170-171. [BV111.J48] 77-162038 2.95
1. Sabbath. 2. Sunday. I. Title.

KUBO, Sakae, 1926- 232'.6
God meets man : a theology of the Sabbath and the Second Advent / Sakae Kubo. Nashville : Southern Pub. Association, c1978. 160 p. ; 21 cm. Bibliography: p. 157-160. [BV125.K8] 78-6616 ISBN 0-8127-0171-2 : write for information.
1. Seventh-Day Adventists—Doctrinal and controversial works. 2. Sabbath. 3. Second Advent. I. Title.

LEWIS, Abram Herbert, 1836-1908. 263
Biblical teachings concerning the Sabbath and the Sunday, by A. H. Lewis... To which is added an important chapter on "The origin of the week." Alfred Centre, N.Y., The American Sabbath tract society, 1884. 2 p. l., [3]-159, 6 p. 17 cm. First published in 1870, under title: The Sabbath and the Sunday. [BV125.L43 1884] 41-28170
1. Sabbath. 2. Sunday. 3. Seventh-day Baptists. 4. Seventh-day Adventists. I. American Sabbath tract society. II. Title.

LEWIS, Abram Herbert, 1836-1908. 263
A critical history of the Sabbath and the Sunday in the Christian church. By A. H. Lewis... Alfred Centre, N.Y., The American Sabbath tract society, 1886. viii, 583 p. 16 1/2 cm. [BV125.L4 1886] 41-28168
1. Sabbath. 2. Sunday. I. American Sabbath tract society. II. Title. III. Title: The Sabbath and the Sunday.

LEWIS, Abram Herbert, 1836-1908. 263
A critical history of the Sabbath and the Sunday in the Christian church (2d ed., rev.) By A. H. Lewis... Plainfield, N.J., The American Sabbath tract society, 1903. v, 412 p. 18 cm. "Index of books and authors": p. 406-412. [BV110.L63 1903] 3-25303
1. Sabbath. 2. Sunday. I. Title.

LEWIS, Abram Herbert, 1836-1908 263
The Sabbath and the Sunday. Part i, Argument Part ii, History. By Rev. A. H. Lewis, A. M. Alfred Centre, N.Y., American Sabbath tract society, A. H. Lewis, gen'l agent, 1870. 268 p. 17 1/2 cm. A new edition published in 1884 under title: Biblical teachings concerning the Sabbath and the Sunday. [BV125.L43 1870] 41-28169
1. Sabbath. 2. Sunday. 3. Seventh-day Baptists. 4. Seventh-day Adventists. I. American Sabbath tract society. II. Title.

LEWIS, Abram Herbert, 1836-1908.
Spiritual Sabbathism, by the late Abram Herbert Lewis... Plainfield, N.J., The American Sabbath tract society, 1910. xvi, 223 p. front. (port.) 22 cm. "The work of revision has been completed by...E. H. Lewis."--Editorial note. 10-12318 1.50
I. Lewis, Edwin Herbert, 1866- ed. II. Title.

LEWIS, Abram Herbert, 1836-1908. 263.
Swift decadence of Sunday. What next? By Abram Herbert Lewis... Plainfield, N.J., American Sabbath tract society, 1899. 1 p. l., vi p., 1 l., 273 p. 18 1/2 cm. [BV125.L45] 99-2430
1. Sabbath. 2. Sunday. I. American Sabbath tract society. II. Title.

LEWIS, Richard Burton, 1906- 230.67
The Protestant dilemma; how to achieve unity in a completed reformation. Mountain View, Calif., Pacific Press Pub. Association [1961] 106p. 20cm. [BV125.L47] 61-6481
1. Sabbath. 2. Seventh-Day Adventists—Doctrinal and controversial works. I. Title.

LITTLEJOHN, Wolcott H. 263.
The constitutional amendment; or, The Sunday, the Sabbath, the change, and restitution, by W. H. Littlejohn. Battle Creek, Mich., Steam press of the Seventh day Adventist publishing association, 1873. iii, 4-79 p. 17 1/2 cm. [BV125.L5] 45-40601
1. Sabbath. 2. Sunday. 3. Seventh-day Adventists—Doctrinal and controversial works. 4. Sunday legislation—U.S. I. Title.

LITTLEJOHN, Wolcott H. 263.
The constitutional amendment; or, The Sunday, the Sabbath, the change, and restitution. A discussion between W. H. Littlejohn ... and the editor of the Christian statesman. Battle Creek, Mich., Steam press of the Seventh day Adventist publishing association, 1873. 384 p. 18 cm. [BV125.L53] 43-40597
1. Sabbath. 2. Sunday. 3. Seventh-day Adventists—Doctrinal and controversial works. 4. Sunday legislation—U.S. I. Christian statesman. II. Title.

LOGAN, Maurice S 1859-
Sabbath theology; a reply to those who insist that Saturday is the only true Sabbath day, by Maurice S. Logan ... New York city, Pub. under the auspices of the New York Sabbath committee [c1913] xvii, [2], 20-451 p. front., illus. 20 cm. 13-25393 1.50
I. Title.

LOGAN, Maurice S 1859-
Sabbath theology; a reply to those who insist that Saturday is the only true Sabbath day, by Maurice Logan ... New York, Lord's day alliance of the U. S. [c1913] xvii, [2], 20-451, [1] p. front., illus. 20 cm. 16-8264
I. Title.

MCMASTER, William H., 1841-
Modern Sabbath questions for the people, by Rev. W. H. McMaster ... Raleigh, N.C., Edwards & Broughton printing company, 1910. 106 p. 19 cm. 13-16740
I. Title. II. Title: Sabbath questions for the people.

MAIN, George Arthur. 263
The Sabbath in divine revelation and human history ... by Geo. A. Main, B.S. Rev. Alva L. Davis, M.A., editor ... 1st ed. Stanberry, Mo., Bible advocate publishing company, 1928. viii, 107 p. 22 1/2 cm. [BV110.M4] 28-19261
1. Sabbath. I. Davis, Alva L., ed. II. Title.

MILLGRAM, Abraham Ezra, 1901- 296
Sabbath, the day of delight, by Abraham E. Millgram. Philadelphia, The Jewish publication society of America, 5705--1944. xxx p., 1 l., 495 p. plates. 22 1/2 cm. Includes songs with Hebrew and Yiddish words (transliterated) with music. Bibliography: p. 479-486. Bibliographical references included in "Notes" (p. 487-495) [BM685.M47] 44-51032
1. Sabbath. I. Jewish publications society of America. II. Jewish publication society of America. III. Title.
Contents omitted.

ODOM, Robert Leo, 1901- 263
The Lord's day on a round world. Rev. ed. Nashville, Southern Pub. Association [1970]. 254 p. illus., map. 22 cm. Bibliography: p. 229-241. [BV125.O3 1970] 71-126040
1. Sabbath. I. Title.

ODOM, Robert Leon, 1901- 263
The Lord's day on a round world; a discussion of Sabbath observance as it is related to natural time measurement, the length of the days of creation, the beginning and ending of the natural day, the international date line ... by Robert Leo Odom ... Nashville, Tenn., The Southern publishing association [1946] 180p. incl. front. illus (ind. map) diagrams 20 cm Bibliography: p. 181-189. [BV125.O3] 47-15256
1. Sabbath. I. Title.

PARSONS, James B. 263
His deity hence His day; or, How the Christian Sabbath was changed, by James B. Parsons, D. D. Dayton, O., The Otterbein press, 1927. 95 p. 20 cm. [BV110.P35]
I. Title.

PARSONS, James B. 263
His deity hence His day; or, How the Christian Sabbath was changed, by James B. Parsons, D. D. Dayton, O., The Otterbein press, 1927. 95 p. 20 cm. [BV110.P35]
I. Title.

PHELPS, Amos Augustus, 1805- 263
1847.
An argument for the perpetuity of the Sabbath. By Rev. A. A. Phelps. Boston, D. S. King, 1841. 164 p. 19 cm. [BV110.P5] 33-29252
1. Sabbath. I. Title.

RIGGLE, Herbert McClellan, 263
1872-
The Sabbath and the Lord's day by H. M. Riggle. (6th ed., rev.) Anderson, Ind., Gospel trumpet company [c1928] xii, 13-263 p. 20 cm. [BV110.R5] 28-13233
1. Sabbath. I. Title.

ROSMARIN, Trude (Weiss) Mrs. 296
1908- ed.
The Oneg Shabbath book, compiled and edited by Trude Weiss Rosmarin, PH. D. New York, The Jewish book club [c1940] 96 p. 19 cm. Prose and verse. "Songs" (words and music): p. [77]-92. Bibliography: p. [93]-95. [BM685.R6] 40-34687
1. Sabbath. I. Title.

THE Sabbath;
a guide to its understanding and observance. [3d ed.] New York Feldheim, 1959. 96p.
1. Sabbath. I. Grunfeld, Isidor, 1900-

SAUNDERS, Herbert E. 263
The Sabbath: symbol of creation and re-creation [by] Herbert E. Saunders. Plainfield, N.J., American Sabbath Tract Society [1970] 111 p. 22 cm. "Series of lectures delivered at the Seventh Day Baptist Ministers Conference." Includes bibliographical references. [BV111.S37] 73-120460 2.50
1. Sabbath. I. Title.

SCRIVEN, Charles. 263
Jubilee of the world / by Charles Scriven. Nashville : Southern Pub. Association, [1978] p. cm. Includes bibliographical references. [BV125.S37] 78-15456 ISBN 0-8127-0188-7 pbk. : 0.75
1. Sabbath. I. Title.

SEGAL, Samuel Michael, 296.4
1904-
The Sabbath book. [New ed.] New York, T. Yoseloff [1957] 238p. 25cm. [BM685.S4 1957] 57-13823
1. Sabbath. I. Title.

SEGAL, Samuel Michael, 263.1
1904-
The Sabbath book, by Samuel M. Segal. New York, Behrman's Jewish book house, 1942. 3 p. l., ix-xv, 238 p. 24 cm. "Bibliography for home and school": p. 229-232. [BM685.S4] 42-9438
1. Sabbath. I. Title.

SHULER, John Lewis, 1887- 263
God's everlasting sign, by J. L. Shuler. Nashville, Southern Pub. Association [1972] 124 p. 21 cm. [BV125.S58] 72-80770
1. Sabbath. I. Title.

STRICKLAND, Robert G. 263.2
Verdure Valley, by Robert G. Strickland. Takoma Park, Washington, D.C., South Bend, Ind. [etc.] Review and herald publishing association [c1930] 2 p. l., 7-222 p. 20 cm. [BV125.S75] 30-28059
1. Sabbath. 2. Seventh-day Adventists. I. Title.

THOMSEN, Russel J. 263
Latter-day Saints and the Sabbath, by R. J. Thomsen. Mountain View, Calif., Pacific Press Pub. Association [1971] 150 p. illus., facsims., map, ports. 22 cm. (Dimension 110) Bibliography: p. 147-150. [BX8643.S2T48] 74-130031
1. Church of Jesus Christ of Latter-Day Saints—History. 2. Sabbath. I. Title.

THE way of Judaism:
the Sabbath as idea and experience. [New York?] B'nai B'rith Hillel Foundations [1951?] 69p. 24cm.
1. Sabbath. 2. Judaism—Addresses, essays, lectures. I. National Hillel Summer Institute. 15th, Camp B'nai B'rith, Pa., 1960. II. B'nai B'rith Hillel Foundations.

WEBSTER, John Robinson, 1851-
The sign of the covenant, ten papers on the Sabbath, by John R. Webster ... Cincinnati, The Standard publishing company [c1916] 277 p. front. (port.) 20 cm. $1.25 17-251
I. Title.

WILLISTON, Seth, 1770-1851. 248
Five discourses on the Sabbath, preached at Durham, N. Y. by Seth Williston ... Albany, Printed by E. & E. Hosford, 1813. iv, [5]-144 p. 14 1/2 cm. [BX9178.W64F5] [BV110.W] 263 A 32
1. Sabbath. I. Title.

WILSON, Gilbert Lord, 1856- 232.9
Christ in chronology and science of the Sabbath. By Rev. Gilbert Lord Wilson ... Chicago, Scroll publishing co. [1902] 1 p. l., [vii]-xx, [21]-220 p. front. (port.) tables, diagrs. 18 1/2 cm. Blank pages for "Notes on the text" (192-200) [BT309.W45] 3-1873
1. Jesus Christ—Chronology. 2. Sabbath. 3. Calendar. I. Title.

YOST, Frank H. 263
The early Christian Sabbath. Mountain View. Calif., Pacific Press Pub. Assn. [1948, c1947] 96 p. illus. 20 cm. [BV125.Y6] 48-15923
1. Sabbath. I. Title.

Sabbath—Addresses, essays, lectures.

ANTI-SABBATH Convention, 263'.3
Boston,
Proceedings. Reported by Henry M. Parkhurst. Port Washington, N.Y., Kennikat Press [1971] 168 p. 21 cm. (Kennikat Press scholarly reprints. Series on literary America in the nineteenth century) "Held in the Melodeon, March 23d and 24th." "First published in 1848." [BM685.A55 1971] 79-122662
1. Sabbath—Addresses, essays, lectures. 2. Sabbath legislation—U.S.—Addresses, essays, lectures. I. Parkhurst, Henry Martyn, 1825-

MORTON, Eliza Happy. 263
Rays of light on the Sabbath question, by Eliza H. Morton ... [South Lancaster, Mass., South Lancaster printing co., c1924] 3 p. l., [5]-135 p. incl. front., illus., plates. 20 1/2 cm. [BV110.M7] 25-7867
I. Title.

Sabbath—Biblical teaching.

ANDREASEN, Niels-Erik A. 263'.1
The Old Testament Sabbath; a tradition-historical investigation, by Niels-Erik A. Andreasen. [Missoula, Mont.] Published by Society of Biblical Literature for the Form Criticism Seminar, 1972. xii, 301 p. 22 cm. (Dissertation series, no. 7) Originally presented as the author's thesis, Vanderbilt University, 1971. Bibliography: p. 275-301. [BS1199.S18A5 1972] 72-88671
1. Bible. O.T.—Criticism, interpretation, etc. 2. Sabbath—Biblical teaching. I. Title. II. Series: Society of Biblical Literature. Dissertation series, no. 7.

Sabbath—History.

BARACK, Nathan A. 296.41
A history of the Sabbath, by Nathan A. Barrack. New York, J. David [1965] xvii, 202 p. 23 cm. Bibliography: p. 199-202. [BM685.B3] 64-8425
1. Sabbath—History. I. Title.

BOND, Ahva John Clarence. 263
Sabbath history ... by Ahva John Clarence Bond ... Plainfield, N. J., American Sabbath tract society, c1922. x. 19 1/2 cm. [BV110.B65] 23-3168
I. Title.

MORGAN, Louis Krafft, 1867-
Divine law and the Sabbath in all ages [by] L. K. Morgan. Anderson, Ind., Gospel trumpet company [c1912] 255 p. 18 1/2 cm. $0.50 12-6248
I. Title.

MORGAN, Louis Krafft, 1867-
Divine law and the Sabbath in all ages [by] L. K. Morgan. Anderson, Ind., Gospel trumpet company [c1912] 255 p. 18 1/2 cm. $0.50 12-6248
I. Title.

ODOM, Robert Leo, 1901- 263
Sabbath and Sunday in early Christianity / Robert L. Odom. Washington : Review and Herald Pub. Association, 1978. 304 p. ; 21 cm. Includes bibliographical references. [BV111.O33] 75-41893 12.95
1. Sabbath—History. 2. Sunday—History. I. Title.

SOLBERG, Winton U. 263'.0973
Redeem the time : the Puritan Sabbath in early America / Winton U. Solberg. Cambridge : Harvard University Press, 1977. xii, 406 p. ; 24 cm. (A Publication of the Center for the Study of the History of Liberty in America, Harvard University) Includes index. Bibliography: p. 367-383. [BV111.S64] 76-26672 ISBN 0-674-75130-2 : 18.50
1. Sabbath—History. 2. Sunday—History. 3. Puritans. I. Title. II. Series: Harvard University. Center for the Study of the History of Liberty in America. Publication.

Sabbath—History—Addresses, essays, lectures.

STRAND, Kenneth Albert, 1927- 263
The early Christian Sabbath : selected essays and a source collection / by Kenneth A. Strand. Enl. ed. Worthington, Ohio : Ann Arbor Publishers, 1979. 80 p. ; 23 cm. Edition of 1972 published under title: Essays on the Sabbath in early Christianity. Includes bibliographical references. [BV111.S7 1979] 79-105210 ISBN 0-89039-140-8 bpk. : 4.80
1. Sabbath—History—Addresses, essays, lectures. I. Title.

Sabbath, Jewish.

CARROLL, Wesley Philemon.
The Sabbath as an American war day. "The Carroll theory." Three great mysteries solved ... Cheyenne Sun-Leader printing house, 1899. 130 p. 8 cm. 99-5196
I. Title.

*FOSTER, Iris. FIC
The Sabbath quest. New York, Lancer Books [1973] 383 p. 18 cm. 1.50 (pbk)
I. Title.

FRANK, Edgar.
Shabbath, the time of its beginning and termination; a halachic-astronomic investigation. With foreword by Leo Jung, pref. by Immanuel Jakobovits, postscript by Simon Schwab, bibliographical sketch by Ernest Mainz. Edited by Abbie Goldstein. New York, P. Feldheim, 1964. x, 62 p. illus. 25 cm. Bibliography: p. ix-x. 65-29903
1. Sabbath, Jewish. 2. Sabbath. I. Title.

FRANK, Edgar.
Shabbath, the time of its beginning and termination; a halachic-astronomic investigation. With foreword by Leo Jung, pref. by Immanuel Jakobovits, postscript by Simon Schwab, bibliographical sketch by Ernest Mainz. Edited by Abbie Goldstein. New York, P. Feldheim, 1964. x, 62 p. illus. 25 cm. Bibliography: p. ix-x. 65-29903
1. Sabbath, Jewish. 2. Sabbath. I. Title.

JUNGREIS, Theodore.
Oneg Shabbat manual. North Woodmere, N.Y., [c1965] 146 p. 24 cm. Songs in romanized Hebrew or Yiddish with English translation without the music. Contents.-- pt. Cavalcade of songs. -- pt. Basic Jewish in information. 67-95029
1. Sabbath, Jewish. 2. Songs, Jewish. 3. Sabbath. 4. Songs. I. Title.

MILLGRAM, Abraham Ezra, 1901-
Sabbath, the day of delight, by Abraham E. Millgram. Philadelphia, The Jewish Publication Society of America, 5705-1944, 1965. xxx p., 1 l., 495 p., plates. Includes songs with Hebrew and Yiddish words (transliterated) with music. Bibliography: p. 479-486. Bibliographical references included in "Notes" (p. 487-495) 67-44898
I. Title.

PUNSHON, William Morley, 1824-
1881.
Sabbath chimes; or, Meditations in verse for the Sundays of a year. By W. Morley Punshon, M. A. New York, Carlton & Lanahan, 1868. 223, [1] p. incl. front. (port.) illus., plates. 20 cm. [PS2669.P5] 12-37991
I. Title.

Sabbath—Juvenile literature.

CONE, Molly 296.4
The Jewish Sabbath. Illus. by Ellen Raskin. New York, Crowell [c.1966] 1v. (unpaged) col. illus. 22cm. (Crowell holiday bk.) [BM685.C66] 65-27292 2.95
1. Sabbath—Juvenile literature. I. Title.

KNOCHE, Vikki. 248.4'8673
Keith and the cactus patch / Vikki Knoche. Mountain View, CA : Pacific Press, [1981] p. cm. A young boy eventually learns the consequences of not obeying his mother and promptly preparing for the Sabbath. [BX6154.K6] 19 81-1084 ISBN 0-8163-0426-2 pbk. : 1.75
1. [Seventh-Day Adventists.] 2. Sabbath—Juvenile literature. 3. Children—Religious life—Juvenile literature. 4. [Sabbath.] 5. [Christian life.] I. Title.
Distributed by the Greater New York Bookstore, 12 W. 40th St., New York, NY

KOLATCH, Mollie. 296.4
Sabbath is special. Story by Mollie Kolatch. Pictures by Evelyn Urbanowich. New York, Behrman House [c1956] unpaged. illus. 21cm. (The Play-and-learn library) [BM685.K6] 57-1543
1. Sabbath—Juvenile literature. I. Title.

RAU, Lois E., 1943- 263'.1
A very special day / by Lois E. Rau ; illustrated by Lynn Turigliatto Inlow. Mountain View, Calif. : Pacific Press Pub. Association, c1982. [32] p. : col. ill. ; 22 cm. At head of title: Book III. Discusses the origin of the Sabbath, the meaning of the fourth commandment, and ways to observe the Sabbath. [BV125.R38 1982] 79-24933 ISBN 0-8163-0447-5 pbk. : 1.75
1. Sabbath—Juvenile literature. 2. [Sabbath.] I. Inlow, Lynn Turigliatto, ill. II. Title.

SCHARFSTEIN, Sol, 1921- 296.4
A wonderful Shabbos, story by Robert Sol [pseud.] Pictures by Lili Cassel. [New York] Ktav Pub. House [1954] unpaged. illus. 22cm. [BM685.S2] 54-28240
1. Sabbath—Juvenile literature. I. Title.

WENGROV, Charles. j296.4
The book of the Sabbath; story and traditions, songs and music; being the heartwarming account of Friday evening and Saturday in the life of one Jewish family, interwoven with stories of adventure about the Sabbath in days long gone, written and illustrated especially for children, together with a full collection of beloved z'mirot and songs for the entire Sabbath, from beginning to end. Illustrated by Siegmund Forst. Music edited by Samuel Bugatch. New York. At the Press of Shulsinger Bros. [1962] 128 p. illus. 32 cm. [BM685.W39] 63-1968
1. Sabbath — Juvenile literature. I. Bugatch, Samuel, ed. II. Title.

Sabbath — Programs.

UNITED Synagogue of America.
Program materials for Sabbath observances 1956-5716. [n.p., 1956?] 1 v. 30 cm. Materials in folder.
1. Sabbath — Programs. I. Title.

Sabbathaians.

SCHOLEM, Gershom 296.6'1 B
Gerhard, 1897-
Sabbatai Sevi; the mystical Messiah, 1626-1676. [Translated by R. J. Zwi Werblowsky. Princeton, N.J.] Princeton University Press [1973] xxvii, 1000 p. illus. 24 cm. (Bollingen series, 93) Rev. and augm. translation of Shabtai Tsevi vehatenu'ah ha-shabta'it bi-yeme hayav. Bibliography: p. [931]-956. [BM199.S3S3713 1973] 75-166389 ISBN 0-691-09916-2 25.00
1. Shabbethai Zebi, 1626-1676. 2. Sabbathaians. I. Title. II. Series.

Sabbatical year (Judaism)

ZUCKERMANN, Benedict, 296.4'3
1818-1891.
A treatise of the Sabbatical cycle and the Jubilee : a contribution to the archaeology and chronology of the time anterior and subsequent to the captivity : accompanied by a table of Sabbatical years / translated from the German of B. Zuckermann by A. Lowy. New York : Hermon Press, 1974. 64 p. ; 24 cm. Translation of Uber Sabbathjahrcyclus und Jubelperiode. Reprint of the 1866 ed. printed for the Chronological Institute of London. Includes index. Bibliography: p. 4-6. [BM720.S2Z913 1974] 74-78326 ISBN 0-87203-044-X : 6.75
1. Sabbatical year (Judaism) 2. Jubilee (Judaism) I. Title.

Sabetha, Kan. First Congregational Church.

FAITH of our fathers. A centennial history of the First Congregational Church of Sabetha, Kansas, 1858-1958. [Sabetha, Kan., 1958] vii, 118p. illus. ports., facsims. 23cm.
1. Sabetha, Kan. First Congregational Church. I. Sabetha, Kan. First Congregational Church. Centennial Committee.

Sabian Assembly.

JONES, Marc Edmund, 1888- 133.062
The ritual of living; an occult manual, by Marc Edmund Jones ... Los Angeles, J. F. Rowny press, 1930. 5 p. l., 13-132 p., 1 l. 24 cm. Manual of the Sabian assembly. [BF1995.S25] 30-33467
1. Sabian assembly. 2. Occult sciences. I. Title.

JONES, Marc Edmund, 1888- 133
The Sabian book of letters to aspirants [by] Marc Edmund Jones. Selection and commentary by Helen Rentsch and Helen Hill. Stanwood, Wash., Sabian Pub. Society, 1973. ix, 389 p. 22 cm. [BF1995.S25J66] 73-76920 ISBN 0-87878-013-0
1. Sabian Assembly. 2. Meditations. I. Rentsch, Helen, ed. II. Hill, Helen, ed. III. Title.

Sabine, James, 1774-1845. Universal salvation indefensible upon Mr. Balfour's ground.

BALFOUR, Walter, 1776-1852. 237.
A reply to Mr. J. Sabine's lectures on the Inquiry into the Scriptural import of the words Sheol, Hades, Tartarus and Gehenna. In two parts: 1st. A defence of the inquiry. 2d. His proofs of a future retribution considered. Boston, Howe & Norton, printer, 1825. 136 p. 24 cm. [BT837.B22S3] 50-52415
1. Sabine, James, 1774-1845. Universal salvation indefensible upon Mr. Balfour's ground. 2. Balfour, Walter, 1776-1852. An inquiry into the Scriptural import of the words Sheol, Hades, Tartarus and Gebenna. 3. Future punishment—Controversial literature. 4. Hell. I. Title.

Sacheverell, Henry, 1674?-1724.

SCUDI, Abbie (Turner) 922.342
Mrs. 1907-
The Sacheverell affair, by Abbie Turner Scudi, PH. D. New York, Columbia university press; London, P. S. King & son, ltd., 1939. 170 p. 23 cm. (Half-title: Studies in history, economics and public law, ed. by the Faculty of political science of Columbia university. no. 456) Issued also as thesis (PH. D.) Columbia university. [Full name: Mrs. Abbie Janet (Turner) Scudi] Bibliography: p. 139-164. [H31.C7 no. 456] [DA497.S3S35 1939 a] 942.069 308.2 39-20004
1. Sacheverell, Henry, 1674?-1724. I. Title.

Sacramentals.

GUARDINI, Romano, 1885- 264.9
Sacred signs. Translated by Grace Branham; drawings by Wm. V. Cladek. St. Louis, Pio Decimo Press [1956] 106p. 19cm. Translation of Von helligen Zeichen. [BX2295.G817] 56-58164
1. Sacramentals. I. Title.

LAMBING, Andrew Arnold, 264.
1842-1918.
The sacramentals of the holy Catholic church. By Rev. A. A. Lambing ... New York, Cincinnati [etc.] Benziger brothers, 1892. 356 p. 20 cm. "Nearly all the essays contained in this volume originally appeared in the Ave Maria or in the American ecclesiastical reviews."--Pref. [BX2295.L3 1892] 3-2632
1. Sacramentals. I. Title.

LAMBING, Andrew Arnold, 264.
1842-1918.
The sacramentals of the holy Catholic church. By Rev. A. A. Lambing ... New York, Cincinnati [etc.] Benziger brothers, 1896. 325 p. front., plates. 16 cm. First edition published 1892. "Nearly all the essays contained in this volume originally appeared in the Ave Maria or in the American ecclesiastical review."--Pref. [BX2295.L3 1896] 3-3103
1. Sacramentals. I. Title.

MCCLOUD, Henry J. 264.9
The sacramentals of the Catholic church [by] Rev. Henry J. McCloud, A.B. Brooklyn, N.Y., International Catholic truth society [1940] 63, [1] p. 19 cm. Bibliography: p. 63. [BX2295.M27] 41-5091
1. Sacramentals. I. Title.

MCNEILL, Charles James, 264.9
1912-
The sacramentals, a study of the origin, nature, and proper use of the sacramentals of the church by Charles J. McNeill...with an introduction by Rev. Leon A. McNeill... Wichita, Kan., Catholic action committee [c1938] cover-title, 52 p. 23 cm. (The Catholic action series of discussion-club textbooks, vol. 1, no. 4) "First printing August 1938." "Reference list": p. [3] of cover. [Full name: Charles James Stanislaus McNeill] [BX2295.M3] 39-5692
1. Sacramentals. I. Title.

TONNE, Arthur, 1904- 265
Talks on the sacramentals. [Emporia? Kan., 1950] 126 p. 24 cm. [BX2295.T6] 51-37804
1. Sacramentals. I. Title.

Sacramentaries.

MORETON, Bernard. 264'.02
The eighth-century Gelasian sacramentary : a study in tradition / Bernard Moreton. London; New York Oxford University Press 1976 xii, 222 p. ; 23 cm. (Oxford theological monographs) Includes indexes. Bibliography: p. [206]-218. [BX2037.A3G435] 76-361685 ISBN 0-19-826710-X : 22.00
1. Sacramentaries. I. Title. II. Series.

Sacraments.

AMBROSIUS, Saint, Bp. of Milan.
On the sacraments; the Latin text edited by Henry Chadwick. Chicago, Loyola university press [1961, c 1960] 54p. 22cm.
1. Sacraments. I. Chadwick, Henry, 1920- ed. II. Title.

AN approach to the theology of the sacraments. Chicago, A. R. Allenson [1956] 96p. 22cm. (Studies in biblical theology, no. 17) Bibliography.
1. Sacraments. I. Clark, Neville. II. Series.

BAILLIE, Donald Macpherson, 265
1887-1954.
The theology of the sacraments, and other papers. With a biographical essay by John Baillie. New York, Scribner [1957] 158p. 22cm. [BV800.B3] 57-7580
1. Sacraments. 2. Free will and determinism. 3. Preaching. I. Title.

BERKOUWER, Gerrit Cornelis, 265
1903-
The sacraments, by G. C. Berkouwer. [Translated by Hugo Bekker] Grand Rapids, Eerdmans [1969] 304 p. 23 cm. (His Studies in dogmatics) Translation of De Sacramenten. Bibliographical footnotes. [BV800.B4713] 66-27410 7.50
1. Sacraments.

A book of common prayer and administration of the sacraments and other rites and ceremonies of the church togther with the form and manner of making, ordaining and consecration of bishops, priests and deacons. Set forth by authority for use in the Church of the Province of South Africa. London, Capetown, Oxford University Press London, Johannesbu-g, Salisbury, Society for Promoting Christian Knowledge [1956] xlvii, 711p. 15cm.
I. Church of England. Book of Common Prayer. English. 1956.

BRO, Bernard. 265
The spirituality of the sacraments; doctrine and practice for today. Translated by Theodore DuBois. New York, Sheed and Ward [1968] 250 p. 22 cm. Translation of Faut-il encore pratiquer? Includes bibliographical references. [BV800.B6813] 68-26034 5.00
1. Sacraments. I. Title.

BROMILEY, Geoffrey William. 265
Sacramental teaching and practice in the Reformation churches. Grand Rapids, Eerdmans [1957] 111p. 19cm. (Pathway books) [BV800.B7] 57-14944
1. Sacraments. I. Title.

BROWNSON, Josephine Van Dyke. 265
Living forever, by Josephine Van Dyke Brownson ... New York, The Macmillan company, 1928. x p., 1 l, 290 p. front., illus. 20 1/2 cm. A study of the sacraments. [BX2200.B7] 28-30464
1. Sacraments. I. Title.

CATHOLIC Church. Liturgy 264.025
and ritual. Missal. English.
Blessed Sacrament missal; an extra-large type Sunday missal with complete new Holy Week services, in conformity with the new decree simplifying the Mass rubrics. Edited by the Fathers of the Blessed Sacrament Raymond A. Tartre, editorial director. With Confraternity text of Old and New Testaments. New York, Benziger Bros. [1958] 608p. illus. 17cm. [BX2015.A4F3] 59-29211
I. Fathers of the Blessed Sacrament. II. Title.

CHAPMAN, Michael Andrew. 265
The Saviour's fountains; a book for children on the seven sacraments, by Michael Andrew Chapman; with illustrations by Father Raphael, O. S.B. Huntington, Ind., Our Sunday visitor, 1921. [40] p. illus. 31 cm. [BX2200.C4] 21-20140
I. Title.

CHRIST acts through the Sacraments. Translated by Carisbrooke Dominicans. Collegeville, Minn., Liturgical Press, 1957. 162p.
I. Roguet, A M 1906-

CHRIST in his sacraments; by a group of theologians; translated by Angeline Bouchard. Chicago, Ill., Fides [1958] xv, 466p. 20cm. (Theology Library, 6) Includes bibliography.
I. Henry, Antonin Marcel, 1911- ed.

CHURCH of England. Book of 264.06
common prayer.
The Book of common prayer and administration of the sacraments and other rites and ceremonies of the church, according to the use of the Church of England; together with the Psalter or Psalms of David, pointed as they are to be sung or said in churches; and the form and manner of making, ordaining, and consecrating of bishops, priests and deacons. London, Oxford university press, H. Milford [1926?] viii, 5-575 p. 18 1/2 cm. "Pica 12 mo." "Extract from an Order in Council of the 31st January, 1936, prescribes the changes now to be made in the Book of common prayer": leaf mounted on p. iii. [BX5145.A4 1926] 37-8747
I. Title.

CHURCH of England. Book of 264.02
common prayer.
The Book of common prayer with the additions and deviations proposed in 1928. Book of common prayer with the additions and deviations proposed in nineteen twenty-eight Oxford, The University press; London, Oxford university press, H. Milford [1928] iv, 506 p., 1 l. 12 1/2 cm. [BX5145.A4 1928] 30-33153
I. Title.

CULLY, Kendig Brubaker 265
Sacraments: a language of faith. Philadelphia, Christian Educ. Pr. [c.1961] 83p. Bibl. 61-13243 2.00
1. Sacraments. I. Title.

ELLER, Vernard. 234'.161
In place of sacraments; a study of Baptism and the Lord's Supper. Grand Rapids, Mich., Eerdmans [1972] 144 p. 21 cm. [BV800.E46] 72-75570 ISBN 0-8028-1476-X 2.95
1. Sacraments. 2. Baptism. 3. Lord's Supper. I. Title.

EMMONS, Nathanael, 1745- 286.
1840.
A candid reply to the Reverend Doctor Hemmenway's Remarks on a dissertation on the Scriptural qualifications for admission and access to the Christian sacraments. By Nathanael Emmons, A.M., pastor of the church in Franklin... Printed at Worcester, Massachusetts. By Leonard Worcester. MDCCXCV. 36 p. 20 1/2 cm. [BV820.E53] 30-7917
1. Hemmenway, Moses, 1735-1811. Remarks on the Reverend Mr. Emmon's Dissertation on the Scriptural qualifications for admission and access to the Christian sacraments. 2. Sacraments. I. Title.

GALLAGHER, John F
Significando causant. A study of scramental efficiency. Fribourg, University Press, 1965. xxi, 264 p. 24 cm. (Studia Friburgensia, N. F. 40) 65-108764
1. Thomas Aquinas, Saint. 1225?-1274 — Criticism and Interpretations. 2. Sacraments. I. Title.

GAVIN, Frank Stanton Burns, 265
1890-
The Jewish antecedents of the Christian sacraments, by F. Gavin ... London, Society for promoting Christian knowledge; New York and Toronto, The Macmillan co., 1928. viii, 120 p. 19 cm. "These chapters were given in substance as [Chapman] lectures in September, 1927, at the S. P. C. K. house, London."--P. [ii] [BV800.G35] 28-25257
1. Sacraments. 2. Christianity and other religions—Judaism. 3. Jews—Religion. I. Chapman lectures, 1927. II. Title.

GAVIN, Frank Stanton 291.3'8
Burns, 1890-1938.
The Jewish antecedents of the Christian sacraments. New York, Ktav Pub. House, 1969. viii, 120 p. 24 cm. Reprint of the 1928 ed. Bibliographical footnotes. [BV800.G35 1969] 68-56890 6.95
1. Jews. Liturgy and ritual. Benedictions. 2. Sacraments. 3. Proselytes and proselyting, Jewish. 4. Conversion—Comparative studies. 5. Lord's Supper. I. Title.

GUZIE, Tad W. 234'.16
The book of sacramental basics / Tad Guzie. New York : Paulist Press, c1981. 140 p. : ill. ; 21 cm. Bibliography: p. 139-140. [BV800.G88] 19 81-83189 ISBN 0-8091-2411-4 (pbk.) : 5.95
1. Sacraments. I. Title.

HALL, Francis Joseph, 1857- 260
1932.
The sacraments. by the Rev. Francis J. Hall... New York, London [etc.]

Longmans, Green and co., 1921. xv, 331 p. 19 1/2 cm. (On cover: Dogmatic theology. [v. 9]) Bibliographical foot-notes. [BT75.H3 vol. 9] 21-20212
1. Sacraments. I. Title.

HELLWIG, Monika. 234'.16
The meaning of the sacraments. Foreword by Robert W. Hovda. Dayton, Ohio, Pflaum/Standard, 1972. ix, 102 p. 21 cm. Bibliography: p. 101-102. [BV800.H45] 78-178840 1.50
1. Sacraments. I. Title.

HENRY VIII. king of England, 1491-1547 265
Assertio septem sacramentorum; or, Defence of the seven sacraments, by Henry VIII, king of England, re-edited, with an introduction, by Rev. Louis O'Donovan, S. T. L., preceded by a preface by His Eminence James, cardinal Gibbons... New York, Cincinnati [etc.] Benziger brothers, 1908. 479 p. 20 1/2 cm. Bibliography: p. [136]-143. [BX2200.H4 1908] 8-5572
1. Sacraments. I. O'Donovan, Louis, ed. II. Title.

HERZOG, Charles G. 265
... Channels of redemption; the sacraments, their instruction, nature and effect: a textbook for colleges and universities, by Charles G. Herzog ... New York Cincinnati [etc.] Benziger brothers, 1931. xii, 246 p. 20 cm. (The truth of Christianity series) [BX2200.H55] 31-30332
1. Sacraments. I. Title.

JENSON, Robert W. 234'.16
Visible words : the interpretation and practice of Christian sacraments / Robert W. Jenson. Philadelphia : Fortress Press, c1978. xi, 212 p. ; 24 cm. Includes bibliographical references and indexes. [BV800.J45] 77-78631 ISBN 0-8006-0507-1 : 10.95
1. Sacraments. I. Title.

KERR, Hugh Thomson, 1871- 265
The Christian sacraments, a source book for ministers [by] Hugh Thomson Kerr. Philadelphia, The Westminster press [1944] 179 p. 21 cm. (Half-title: The Westminster source books for ministers) Bibliographical references included in "Notes" (p. 169-175) [BV800.K4] 44-9996
1. Sacraments. I. Title.

KNOWLES, Archibald Campbell.
The church and the greater sacraments. With a sketch concerning early church buildings. By Archibald Campbell Knowles. Milwaukee, The Young churchman co., 1894. 69 p. fold. tab. 17 cm. 3-1875
I. Title.

LASANCE, Francis Xavier, 1860-
Blessed sacrament book, by Rev. F. X. Lasance ... New York, Cincinnati [etc.] Benziger brothers, 1913. xi p., 1 l., 27-1227 p. front., plates. 16 cm. 13-15547 1.50
I. Title.

LEADBEATER, Charles Webster, 1847- 265
The science of the sacraments, by Charles W. Leadbeater ... Los Angeles, Sydney [etc.] The St. Alban press, 1920. 560 p. fold. col. front., illus., plates, plans. 19 cm. Printed in Sydney. [BV800.L4] 21-18943
1. Sacraments. I. Title.

LEWIS, William Henry, 1803-1877. 265
Confession of Christ, By the Rev. Wm. H. Lewis... New-York, Stanford & Swords, 1852. 1 p. l., 124 p. 19 cm. [BX5949.A1L4] 33-28661
1. Sacraments. 2. Confirmation. I. Title.

LILLEY, Alfred Leslie, 1860- 265
Sacraments; a study of some moments in the attempt to define their meaning for Christian worship, by A. L. Lilley ... New York, The Macmillan company, 1929. 159 p. 21 cm. [BV800.L5] 29-1097
1. Sacraments. I. Title.

MCNEILL, Leon Aloysius, 1902- 265
The means of grace, by Rev. Leon A. McNeill...and Madeleine Aaron ...with a foreword by His Excellency, Most Rev. Edwin V. O'Hara... Paterson, N.J., St. Anthony guild press, 1935. xi p., 1 l., 250 p. incl. front. 22 cm. (The mystical body of Christ series of religion textbooks) [Full name: Leon Aloysius Michael McNeill] [BX2200.M32] 35-6471
1. Sacraments. 2. Catholic church—Education. I. Aaron Madeleine, 1895- joint author. II. Title.

MARTINDALE, Cyril Charlie, 1879- 265
The sacramental system, by the Reverend C. C. Martindale, S.J.; introduction by Neil McNeil ... New York, The Macmillan company, 1928. ix p., 1 l., 83 p. 17 cm. (Half-title: The treasury of the faith series: 21) [BX2200.M35 1928] 28-6540
1. Sacraments. I. Title.

POHLE, Joseph, 1852-1922. 265
The sacraments; a dogmatic treatise, by the Reverend Joseph Pohle ... authorized English version, based on the 5th German ed., with some abridgment and additional references, by Arthur Preuss ... St. Louis, Mo. [etc.] B. Herder, 1915-17. 4 v. 21 cm. (Half-title: [His] Dogmatic theology, viii-xi) Contents.--1. The sacraments in general. Baptism. Confirmation.--ii. The holy eucharist.--iii. Penance.--iv. Extreme unction. Holy orders. Matrimony. Contains bibliographies. [BX2200.P6] 15-26945
1. Sacraments. I. Preuss, Arthur, 1871-1934, tr. II. Title.

POURRAT, Pierre, 1871- 265
Theology of the sacraments; a study in positive theology, by the Very Rev. P. Pourrat ... Authorized translation from the 3d French ed. St. Louis, Mo. and Freiburg (Baden) B. Herder, 1910. xv, 417 p. 21 cm. Bibliographical foot-notes. [BX2200.P7] 10-4596
1. Sacrements. I. Title.

PROTESTANT Episcopal church in the U. S. A. Book of common prayer. 264.03
The Book of common prayer and administration of the sacraments, and other rites and ceremonies of the church, according to the use of the Protestant Episcopal church in the United States of America; together with the Psalter, or Psalms of David. Philadelhia, J. B. Lippincott & co., 1847. 1 p. l., 680 p. 16 cm. Added t.-p., in colors. With this is bound: Selections from the Psalms of David in metre; with hymns ... Philadelphia, 1847. [BX5943.A1 1847] 31-13882
I. Title.

PROTESTANT Episcopal church in the U. S. A. Book of common prayer. 264.
The Book of common prayer and administration of the sacraments and other rites and ceremonies of the church according to the use of the Protestant Episcopal church in the United States of America, together with the Psalter or Psalms of David. Oxford, Printed at the University press; New York, T. Nelson & sons [1892] xxviii, 566 p. 19 cm. [BX5943.A1 1892] 15-20500
I. Title.

PROTESTANT Episcopal church in the U. S. A. Book of common prayer. 264.03
The Book of common prayer and administration of the sacraments and other rites and ceremonies of the church, according to the use of the Protestant Episcopal church in the United States of America. Together with the Psalter, of Psalms of David. Chicago, The Chicago prayer book society, 1893. 1 p. l., xxviii, 566 p. 14 cm. [BX5943.A1 1893 c] 33-23866
I. Title.

PROTESTANT Episcopal church in the U. S. A. Book of common prayer. 264.
The Book of common prayer and administration of the sacraments and other rites and ceremonies of the Church according to the use of the Protestant Episcopal church in the United States of American; together with the Psalter or Psalms of David. [Vignette] New York: Printed for the Committee [by the De Vinne press] mdcccxciii. 14 p. l., 566, [2] p. 37 cm. Eighth standard edition. Printed on "American hand-made paper ... at the De Vinne press in the city of New York. The plan of symbolism and method of decoration were arranged by Mr. Daniel Berkeley Updike: the preparatory studies of plants were made by Mr. William Wells Bosworth: the designes for the borders and cover by Mr. Bertram Grosvenor Goodhue, and the final drawings for reproduction by Mr. Joseph Eliot Hill. [no.] 19." Title and text within floral borders. In white vellum, elaborately gilt, with claps. Book-plate of Washington cathedral library. [BX5943.A1 1893] 30-20808
I. Title.

PROTESTANT Episcopal church in the U. S. A. Book of common prayer. 264.
The Book of common prayer and administration of the sacraments and other rites and ceremonies of the church. According to the use of the Protestant Episcopal church in the United States of America. Together with the Psalter of Psalms of David. New York, T. Nelson & sons, 1896. xxviii, 556 p. 20 cm. [BX5943.A1 1896] 15-3373
I. Title.

PROTESTANT Episcopal church in the U. S. A. Book of common prayer. 264.03
The Book of common prayer and administration of the sacraments and other rites and ceremonies of the church, according to the use of the Protestant Episcopal church in the United States of America; together with the Psalter, or Psalms of David. New York, Oxford university press [1929] xxxviii, 598 p. 15 cm. [BX5943.A1 1929 a] 35-23136
I. Title.

PROTESTANT Episcopal church in the U. S. A. Book of common prayer. 264.
The Book of common prayer and administration of the sacraments and other rites and ceremonies of the church, according to the use of the Protestant Episcopal church in the United States of America, together with the Psalter or Psalms of David. New York, J. Pott & company [1929] xli, 584 p. 20 cm. [BX5943.A1 1929] 29-30656
I. Title.

PROTESTANT Episcopal church in the U. S. A. Book of common prayer. 264.03
The Book of common prayer and administration of the sacraments and other rites and ceremonies of the church according to the use of the Protestant Episcopal church in the United States of American: together with the Psalter or Psalms of David. Printed for the Commission A. D. mdccccxxviii. [Boston, Printed by D. B. Updike, The Merrymount press, 1930] xli, 611 p. 1 l. 36 cm. "Five hundred copies were printed by D. B. Updike, The Merrymount press, Boston, Massachusetts, A. D. mdccccxxx." "This edition ... conforms to the text of the standard Book accepted by the church in General convention in the month of October, 1928." [BX5943.A1 1930] 31-7854
I. Title.

PROTESTANT Episcopal church in the U. S. A. Book of common prayer. 264.03
The Book of common prayer and administration of the sacraments and other rites and ceremonies of the church according to the use of the Protestant Episcopal church in the United States of American: together with the Psalter or Psalms of David. Printed for the Commission A. D. mdccccxxviii. [Boston, Printed by D. B. Updike, The Merrymount press, 1930] xli, 611 p. 1 l. 36 cm. "Five hundred copies were printed by D. B. Updike, The Merrymount press, Boston, Massachusetts, A. D. mdccccxxx." "This edition ... conforms to the text of the standard Book accepted by the church in General convention in the month of October, 1928." [BX5943.A1 1930] 31-7854
I. Title.

PROTESTANT Episcopal church in the U. S. A. Book of common prayer.
The Book of common prayer and administration of the sacraments; and other rites and ceremonies of the church, according to the use of the Protestant Episcopal church in the United States of America. Together with the Psalter, or Psalms of David; New York, H. W. Hewet, 1843. xxv, 621 p. illus. 28 cm. Initials; head and tail pieces. Added ornamental t.-p.: The illustrated Book of common prayer, ed. by Rev. J. M. Wainwright, D. D. Issued in 21 numbers. 15-3397
I. Wainwright, Jonathan Mayhew, bp., 1793-1854, ed. II. Title.

QUICK, Oliver Chase, 1885- 265
The Christian sacraments, by Oliver Chase Quick ... New York and London, Harper & brothers, 1927. xv, 264 p. 22 cm. (Half-title: The library of constructive theology) Printed in Great Britian. [BV800.Q5] 28-13144
1. Sacraments. I. Title.

REUTER, Frederick A. 264.
Moments divine before the blessed sacrament; historic and legendary readings and prayers, by Rev. Frederick A. Reuter ... Philadelphia, H. L. Kilner & co. [c1922] xiv, 320 p. incl. front. 15 cm. [BX2169.R4] 22-23725
I. Title.

ROBISON, William Ferretti, 1871- 265
The seven-fold gift; a study of the seven sacraments, by William F. Robison ... St. Louis, Mo., and London, B. Herder book co., 1922. vii, [4], 225 p. 19 cm. [BX2200.R55] 22-15528
I. Title.

ROLFUS, Herman, 1821-1896. 265
Illustrated explanation of the holy sacraments. A complete exposition of the sacraments and the sacramentals of the church. Adapted from the original of Rev. H. Rolfus, D.D., with a reflection and practice on each sacrament, by Very Rev. Ferreol Girardey... New York, Cincinnati [etc.] Benziger bros., 1898. 307 p. 7 pl. 17 cm. [Full name: Hermann Ludwig Rolfus] [BX2200.R65] 98-1657
1. Sacraments. 2. Sacramentals. I. Girardey, Ferreol, 1839-1930. II. Title.

THE sacraments; a dogmatic treatise. Adapted and edited by Arthur Preuss. St. Louis, Mo., B. Herder [1955-1957. vol. 1, 1957] 4v. 20cm. (His, Dogmatic theology, 8-11) Printings vary. Contents.1. The sacraments in general. Baptism. Confirmation.--2. The holy eucharist.--3. Penance.--4. Extremeunction. Holy orders. Matrimony. Includes bibliographies.
1. Sacraments. I. Pohle, Joseph, 1852-1922. II. Preuss, Arthur, 1871-1934, ed.

SKELLY, Andrew M. 265
The sacraments and the commendments; discourses on various occasions, by the Rev. A. M. Skelly, O.P. St. Louis, Mo. and London, B. Herder book co., 1929. vi, 306 p. 19 1/2 cm. [BX2200.S5] 29-20812
1. Sacraments. 2. Commendments, Ten. I. Title.

TAIT, Arthur James, 1872- 265
The nature and functions of the sacraments, by Arthur J. Tait ... London, New York [etc.] Longmans, Green, and co., 1917. xiii, 104 p. 19 1/2 cm. [BV800.T3] 18-14209
I. Title.

VAN LOAN, Samuel Dies.
Thoughts on the church and the sacraments ... by Samuel Dies Van Loan ... New York, E. S. Gorham, 1916. 5 p. l., 121 p. 19 1/2 cm. $0.75 16-8257
I. Title.

WADHAMS, Gordon Butler, 1904-
To his soul's health, by the Reverend Gordon B. Wadhams [and] the Reverend Thomas J. Bigham, jr. ... Hartford, Conn., Church congress in the United States, 1944. cover-title, 58 p. 21 cm. On cover: Lenton booklet, 1944. "Instructions given by the clergy of the Church of the Resurrection, New York city, in ... 1943."--Pref. A 44
1. Sacraments. I. Bigham, Thomas James, 1911- II. Title.

WILLIAMS, Granville Mercer, 1889- 265
The touch of Christ; lectures on the Christian sacraments, by Granville Mercer Williams... New York, E. S. Gorham, inc. [c1928] 4 p. l., vii-viii, 109 p. 19 1/2 cm. [BV800.W5] 28-13798
1. Sacraments. I. Title.

WORLD conference on faith and order. 2d, Edinburgh, 1937. Commission on the ministry and sacraments. 265
The ministry and the sacraments; report of the Theological commission appointed by the Continuation committee of the Faith and order movement, under the chairmanship of the Right Rev. Arthur Cayley Headlam ... edited by the Rev. Roderic Dunkerley ... New York, The Macmillan company, 1937. viii, [1], 559 [1] p. 22 1/2 cm. "Printed in Great Britain." [BX6.W75 1937h] 38-18420
1. Sacraments. 2. Clergy—Office. 3. Apostolic succession. 4. Christian union. I. Headlam, Arthur Cayley, bp. of Gloucester, 1862- II. Dunkerley, Roderic, ed. III. Title.

WRIGHT, John, 1836-1919.
The restoration of the reservation of the blessed sacrament for the sick, by the Rev. John Wright ... Milwaukee, Wis., The Young churchman co.; London, W. Walker [1904] 101 p. front., plates. 19 1/2 cm. 4-21077
I. Title.

Sacraments—Addresses, essays, lectures.

BEECK, Frans Jozef van. 234'.16
Grounded in love : sacramental theology in an ecumenical perspective / Frans Jozef van Beeck. Washington, D.C. : University Press of America, c1981. x, 151 p. ; 23 cm. Includes bibliographical references and index. [BV800.B43 1981] 19 81-40117 ISBN 0-8191-2040-5 : 19.50 ISBN 0-8191-2041-3 (pbk.) : 9.25
1. Sacraments—Addresses, essays, lectures. I. Title.

*HILLIS, Don W. 265.8
Where is the gift of healing. Chicago, Moody [c.1964] 63p. 18cm. (Compact bk., no.47) (Twentieth century encyclopedia of Catholicism v. 55) .29 pap.,
I. Title.

WYLIE, Samuel J. 265
Sacramental living. Prepared under the auspices of the Dept. of Christian Educ., Protestant Episcopal Church. New York, Seabury [c.1965] 61p. 21cm. Bibl. (Senior-High-Sch. Unit) price unreported pap.,
I. Title.

Sacraments and Christian union.

FIEDLER, Ernest J. 265
The sacraments; an experiment in ecumenical honesty [by] Ernest J. Fiedler [and] R. Benjamin Garrison. Nashville, Abingdon Press [1969] 144 p. 21 cm. Bibliography: p. 137-139. [BX9.5.S2F5] 70-87027 ISBN 0-687-36726-3 3.50
1. Sacraments and Christian union. I. Garrison, R. Benjamin, joint author. II. Title.

THE Sacraments: 265
an ecumenical dilemma. New York, Paulist Press [1967, c1966] x, 178 p. 24 cm. (Concilium theology in the age of renewal: Ecumenical theology, v. 24) Contents.Contents.—Preface, by H. Kung; translated by T. L. Westow.—Articles: Why Baptists do not baptize infants, by J. McClendon. What can Catholics learn from the infant baptism controversy? By M. Hurley. Confession in the Evangelical churches, by M. Thurian; translated by D. Wharton. Confession outside the confessional, by W. Kasper; translated by P. Burns. Ecumenically significant aspects of New Testament eucharistic doctrine, by D. Stanley. Notes on the Orthodox understanding of the Eucharist, by J. Meyendorff. Understanding Protestant teaching on the Lord's Supper, by R. Bertalot; translated by A. M. Buono. Is the Eucharist a sacrifice? By J. Ratzinger; translated by J. Drury. Transubstantiation: how far is this doctrine historically determined? By P. Schoonenberg; translated by T. L. Westow.—Bibliographical survey: Eucharistic developments in the Evangelical church, by W. L. Boelens; translated by T. L. Westow. Divorce and remarriage: east and west, by O. Rousseau; translated by A. M. Buono. Yes, no, and nevertheless, by J. M. Oesterreicher.—DO-C: Documentation concilium: Some results of Catholic education in the United States, by A. Greeley.—Biographical notes. Bibliographical footnotes. [BX9.5.S2S2] 67-23612
1. Sacraments and Christian union. I. Kung, Hans, 1928- II. Series: Concilium (New York) v. 24

Sacraments—Anglican Communion.

CHALMERS, Robert Scott, 1882-1935. 265
Privileges of the Christian sacraments ... by the Rev. Robert S. Chalmers ... New York, Milwaukee, Morehouse publishing co., 1935. vi, 232 p. 20 cm. (The pastoral series--course 3) Bibliography: p. 18. [BX5148.C45] 35-17207
1. Sacraments—Anglican communion. I. Title.

LANDON, Harold R., ed. 265
Living thankfully; the Christian and the sacraments. Greenwich, Conn., Seabury Pr. [c.]1961. 215p. (Cathedral bk.) Bibl. 61-18037 3.75 bds.,
1. Sacraments—Angelican Communion. I. Title.

MONTGOMERY, David Kemble, 1905- 265
The tree of life. New York, Morehouse-Gorham, 1950. xi, 172 p. front. 21 cm. Bibliographical footnotes. [BX5949.A1M6] 50-6365
1. Sacraments — Angilican Communion. I. Title.

PARMELEE, Alice. 265
The fellowship of the church; a work book based on The privileges of the Christian sacraments, by R. S. Chalmers, course iii of The pastoral series, prepared by Alice Parmelee; illustrated by Catherine Graeff Barton. New York, Morehouse-Gorham co., 1941. 139 p. illus. 20 cm. Bibliography: p. 5. [BX5148.C46] 41-12879
1. Sacraments—Anglican communion. 2. Sacraments—Study and teaching. I. Chalmers, Robert Scott, 1882-1935. Priveleges of the Christian sacraments. II. Title.

SIMCOX, Carroll Eugene, 1912- 265
Understanding the sacraments. New York, Morehouse-Gorham, 1956. 104p. 21cm. [BX5949.A1S5] 56-12154
1. Sacraments—Anglican Communion. I. Title.

VAUX, William, 1874?-1844. 265
The benefits annexed to a participation in the two Christian sacraments, of baptism and the Lord's supper, considered in eight sermons preached before the University of Oxford, in the year MDCCXXVI., at the lecture founded by the late Rev. John Bampton ... By William Vaux ... Oxford, The University press for the author; [etc., etc.] 1826. x, 343 p. 22 cm. Binder's title: Bampton lectures 1826. [BR45.B3 1826] (230.082) 38-16174
1. Sacraments—Anglican communion. I. Title.

Sacraments (Canon law)

AYRINHAC, Henry Amans, 1867-1930. 265
Legislation on the sacraments in the new Code of canon law [lib. iii, Can. 726-1011, 1144-1153] by Very Rev. H. A. Ayrinhac ... New York, London, Longmans, Green and co., 1928. xxv p., 1 l., 416 p. 20 cm. "The legislation on the sacraments in the new Code forms the first part of the third book De rebus."--Pref. [BX2200.A8] 28-3812
1. Sacraments (Canon law) 2. Catholic church. Codex juris canonici. I. Title.

Sacraments (Canon law)—Addresses, essays, lectures.

THE Sacraments in theology and canon law. 262.9'33
Edited by Neophytos Edelby, Teodoro Jimenez-Urresti [and] Petrus Huizing. New York, Paulist Press [1968] viii, 183 p. 24 cm. (Concilium: theology in the age of renewal. Canon law, v. 38) Bibliographical footnotes. [LAW] 68-58308 4.50
1. Catholic Church—Government—Addresses, essays, lectures. 2. Sacraments (Canon law)—Addresses, essays, lectures. I. Edelby, Neophytos, Abp., 1920- ed. II. Jimenez Urresti, Teodoro Ignacio, ed. III. Huizing, Petrus, 1911- ed. IV. Series: Concilium (New York) v. 38

Sacraments—Catholic Church.

ALEXANDER, Anthony F., rev. 1920- 265
College sacramental theology. Chicago, Regnery [c.] 1961. 270 p. Bibl. 61-11083 3.00
1. Sacraments—Catholic Church. I. Title.

ALEXANDER, Anthony F 1920- 265
College sacramental theology. Chicago, Regnery, 1961. 270p. 22cm. Includes bibliography. [BX2200.A47] 61-11083
1. Sacraments—Catholic Church. I. Title.

BAIERL, Joseph John, 1884- 265
The sacraments explained according to the Munich or psychological method, for children of the intermediate and higher grades; based on the Baltimore catechism (no. 2) an aid to catechists, by Rev. Joseph J. Baierl. Rochester, N. Y., The Seminary press, 1921. 3 p. l., v-vii p., 2 l., 3-434 p. 21 cm. Bibliography: p. vi. [BX2200.B3] 22-1468
I. Title.

BAUSCH, William J. 264'.02
A new look at the sacraments / William J. Bausch. Notre Dame, Ind. : Fides/Claretian, c1977. vii, 237 p. ; 20 cm. Includes bibliographical references. [BX2200.B37] 77-2975 ISBN 00-8190-0619-X pbk. : 4.95
1. Sacraments—Catholic Church. I. Title.

CHAMPLIN, Joseph M. 234'.16
The sacraments in a world of change [by] Joseph M. Champlin. Notre Dame, Ind., Ave Maria Press [1973] 141 p. 21 cm. An outgrowth of the author's syndicated column, Workship and the world, in the NC News Service Know your faith series. [BX2200.C38] 73-83347 ISBN 0-87793-085-6 1.65 (pbk.)
1. Sacraments—Catholic Church. I. Title.

COOKE, Bernard J. 265
Christian sacraments and Christian personality. Introd. by Frederick R. McManus. Garden City, N.Y., Doubleday [1968, c.1965] 278p. 18cm. (Image bk. D246) Bibl. [BX2200.C6] 65-23937 1.25 pap.,
1. Sacraments—Catholic church. I. Title.

COOKE, Bernard J. 265
Christian sacraments and Christian personality [by] Bernard J. Cooke. New York, Holt, Rinehart and Winston [1965] ix, 181 p. 24 cm. Includes bibliographies. [BX2200.C6] 65-23937
1. Sacraments—Catholic Church. I. Title.

COOKE, Bernard J. 265
Christian sacraments and Christian pesonality. New York, Holt [c.1965] ix, 181p. 24cm. Bibl. [BX2200.C6] 65-23937 4.95
1. Sacraments—Catholic Church. I. Title.

CROCK, Clement. 265
... Discourses on grace and the sacraments, by the Rev. Clement Crock ... New York city, J. F. Wagner, inc.; London, B. Herder [c1936] x, 203 p. 24 cm. Bibliography: p. v-vi. [BX2200.C7] 37-1733
1. Sacraments—Catholic church. 2. Sacraments—Sermons. Catholic church—Sermons. 3. Sermons, American. I. Title.

CROCK, Clement Henry. 265
... Discourses on grace and the sacraments, by the Rev. Clement Crock ... New York city, J. F. Wagner, inc.; London, B. Herder [c1936] x, 293 p. 23 1/2 cm. Bibliography: p. v-vi. [BX2200.C7] 37-1733
1. Sacraments—Catholic church. 2. Sacraments—Sermons. 3. Catholic church—Sermons. 4. Sermons, American. I. Title.

CUSHING, Richard James, cardinal 265
The Sacraments, seven channels of grace for every state in life. [Boston, Daughters of St. Paul, 1960] 218 p. 22 cm. (st. paul editions) 60.50066 3.00; pap., 2.00
1. Sacraments—Catholic Church. I. Title.

CUSHING, Richard James, Cardinal, 1895- 265
The Sacraments: seven channels of grace for every state in life. [Boston, Daughters of St. Paul, 1961] 218 p. 22 cm. [BX2200.C85 1961] 61-17251
1. Sacraments — Catholic Church. I. Title.

*DAUGHTERS of St. Paul 265
In Christ we live; grade 5. Written by the Daughters of St. Paul under the direction of James Alberione. Illus. by the Daughters of St. Paul under the direction of Guy R. Pennisi. St. Paul Catechetical Ctr. [1966, i.e. 1967] 96p. illus. (pt. col.) 21cm. (The St. Paul way, truth and life ser., 5) Each lesson contains: Sacred scripture, litergy, catechism. .45 pap.,
1. Sacraments—Catholic Church. I. Aberione, James. II. Title.
Available from Daughters of St. Paul, Boston.

DE REEPER, John 265
The Sacraments on the missions a pastoral theological supplement for the missionary. [2d ed.] Dublin, Browne Nolan [dist. Mystic, Conn., Lawrence Verry, 1964] xxiii, 531p. 22cm. Bibl. 64-9586 8.00
1. Sacraments—Catholic Church. 2. Sacraments (Canon law) 3. Missions (Canon law) I. Title.

DE SALVO, Raphael, 1919- 265
The dogmatic theology on the intention of the minister in the confection of the sacraments. Washington, Catholic Univ. of America Press, 1949. xi, 115 p. 23 cm. (Catholic University of America. Studies in sacred theology, 2d ser., no. 26) Snynopsis of thesis--Catholic Univ. of America. Vita. Bibliography: p. 107-112. [BX2203.D4] A 49
1. Sacraments—Catholic Church. 2. Sacraments (Liturgy) I. Title. II. Series: Catholic University of America. School of Sacred Theology. Studies in sacred theology, 2d ser., no. 26

DIDIER, Jean Charles, 1905- 265.8
Death and the Christian. Tr. from French by P. J. Hepburne-Scott. New York, Hawthorn Books [c.1961] 106p. (Twentieth century encyclopedia of Catholicism, v.55) Bibl. 61-9459 3.50
1. Sacraments—Catholic Church. 2. Church work with the sick. I. Title.

DILLENSCHNEIDER, Clement 265
The dynamic power of our sacraments. Tr. by Sister M. Renelle. St. Louis, B. Herder [1966] vi. 161p. 24cm. BBibl. [BX2200.D513] 66-17098 4.25
1. Sacraments—Catholic Church. I. Title.

DOYLE, Francis X., 1886-1928. 265
The wonderful sacraments, what they are and what they do, by Francis X. Doyle ... New York, Cincinnati [etc.] Benziger brothers, 1924. 252 p. 19 cm. [BX2200.D6] 24-31077
1. Sacraments—Catholic church. I. Title.

ELLARD, Gerald, 1894- 265
Power: the supernatural powers and helps conferred on man, by Gerald Ellard and John R. Gleason. Chicago, Loyola Univ. Press, 1947. vi, 306 p. 21 cm. (Religion essentials series) [BX220.E63] 48-15767
1. Sacraments—Catholic Church. I. Title. II. Series.

ELLARD, Gerald, 1894- 265
Power; the supernatural powers and helps conferred on man, by Gerald Ellard and John R. Gleason. Chicago, Loyola University Press [1948] Chicago,Loyola University Press, 1949. vi, 346 p. illus. 21 cm. vi, 265 p. 24 cm. (Religion essentials series (book 1)) Teacher's manual, by Austin G. Schmidt. [BX2200.E63 1948] 48-8649
1. Sacraments—Catholic Church. I. Gleason, John R., 1903- II. Schmidt, Austin Guildford, 1883- III. Title. IV. Series.

EVELY, Louis, 1910- 265
Love your neighbor. Translated by Imelda L'Italien. Garden City, N.Y.: Image Books, 1975 [c1969] 114 p.; 18 cm. Translation of L'Eglise et les sacrements. [BX2200.E7613] ISBN 0-385-06256-7 1.45 (pbk.)
1. Sacraments—Catholic Church. I. Title.

EVELY, Louis, 1910- 265
Love your neighbor. Translated by Imelda L'Italien. [New York] Herder and Herder [1969] 92 p. 21 cm. Translation of L'Eglise et les sacrements. [BX2200.E7613] 79-81745 3.95
1. Sacraments—Catholic Church. I. Title.

EVERETT, Lawrence Patrick, 1917- 265
The nature of sacramental grace, by the Rev. Lawrence P. Everett, c. 88. r. Washington, Catholic Univ. of America Press, 1948. ix,151 p. 21 cm. (The Catholic University of America. Studies in sacred theology, 2d ser., no. 7) Thesis--Catholic Univ. of America. Biographical note. [BX2200.E78] A48
1. Sacraments—Catholic Church. 2. Grace (Theology)—History of doctrines. I. Title. II. Series: Catholic University of America. School of Sacred Theology. Studies in sacred theology, 2d ser., no. 7

FARRELL, Christopher. 234'.16
The sacraments today : their meaning and celebration / Christopher Farrell and Thomas Artz. Liguori, Mo. : Liguori Publications, c1978. 143 p. : ill. ; 22 cm. [BX2200.F37] 78-108848 ISBN 0-89243-087-7 pbk. : 2.95
1. Sacraments—Catholic Church. I. Artz, Thomas, joint author. II. Title.

FEARON, John. 265
Graceful living; a course in the appreciation of the sacraments. Westminster, Md., Newman Press, 1955. 160p. 21cm. [BX2200.F4] 55-9037
1. Sacraments—Catholic Church. I. Title.

FOLEY, Leonard, 1913- 265
Signs of love. [Cincinnati, St. Anthony Messenger Press, 1971] vii, 168 p. illus. 19 cm. [BX2200.F65] 71-170370 ISBN 0-912228-04-0 1.25
1. Sacraments—Catholic Church. I. Title.

GRENTE, Georges, Abp., 1872- 265
The power of the sacraments; translated by Sister Mary Madonna. New York, P. J. Kenedy [1951] 236 p. 21 cm. Translation of La magnificence des sacrements. [BX2200.G713] 51-10748
1. Sacraments—Catholic Church. I. Title.

GUMAYON Parado, Cornelio.
An Expository analysis of the various systems of sacramental causality; an abstract of a dissertation. Baltimore, St. Mary's University, 1960. xiii, 59 p. 23 cm. At head of title: Pontifical Theological Faculty of St. Mary's University. Bibliography: p. 53-59. 68-8294
1. Sacraments—Catholic Church. I. Title.

HALLIGAN, Francis Nicholas, 1917- 265
The administration of the sacraments; some practical guides for priest and seminarians. [Staten Island] N.Y., Alba House [1963] xxi, 585p. 24cm. Bibl. 63-12676 9.75
1. Sacraments—Catholic Church. 2. Casuistry. 3. Sacraments (Canon law) I. Title.

HARING, Bernhard, 1912- 265
A sacramental spirituality [Tr. from German by R. A. Wilson] New York, Sheed, c.1962,1965] xi, 281p. [BX2203.H253] 65-20859 5.00
1. Sacraments—Catholic Church. 2. Spiritual life—Catholic authors. I. Title.

HARING, Bernhard, 1912- 265
A sacramental spirituality [by] Bernard Haring. New York ., Sheed and Ward [1965] xi, 281 p. 22 cm. Translation of Gabe und Auftrage der Sakramente. [BX2203.H253 1965] 65-20859
1. Sacraments — Catholic Church. 2. Spiritual life — Catholic authors. I. Title.

HARING, Bernhard, 1912- 264'.02
The sacraments and your everyday life / Bernard Haring. Liguori, Mo. : Liguori Publications, 1976. 192 p. ; 22 cm. Includes index. Bibliography: p. 186-187. [BX2200.H23 1976] 76-7824 ISBN 0-89243-053-2 pbk. : 2.95
1. Sacraments—Catholic Church. I. Title.

HARING, Bernhard, 1912- 234'.16
The sacraments in a secular age : a vision in depth on sacramentality and its impact on moral life / [by] Bernard Haring. Slough : St. Paul Publications, 1976. [8], 253 p. ; 21 cm. Includes index. Bibliography: p. 246-247. [BX2200.H24] 76-374949 ISBN 0-85439-122-3 : £3.50
1. Jesus Christ—Person and offices. 2. Sacraments—Catholic Church. 3. Church. I. Title.

HASTINGS, Cecily 265
The sacraments. New York, Sheed & Ward [c.1961] 217p. 61-11793 3.50 bds.,
1. Sacraments—Catholic Church. I. Title.

HASTINGS, Cecily. 265
The sacraments. London, New York, Sheed and Ward [1961] 217p. 18cm. (Canterbury books, 15) [BX2200.H3 1961a] 61-66075
1. Sacraments—Catholic Church. I. Title.

HEALY, Edwin F 1897- 265
Christian guidance; the moral aspects of the sacraments, matrimony excepted. Chicago, Loyola University Press [1958] 240p. 21cm. Includes bibliography. [BX2200.H35 1958] 58-3549
1. Sacraments—Catholic Church. I. Title.

HEALY, Edwin F. 1897- 265
Christian guidance; the moral aspects of the sacraments, matrimony excepted. Chicago, Loyola Univ. Press, 1949. ix, 245 p. 21 cm. Includes bibliographies. [BX2200.H35] 49-6525
1. Sacraments—Catholic Church. I. Title.

HORNYOLD, John Joseph, bp., 1706-1778.
The commandments and sacraments explained in fifty-two discourses, by the Right Rev. Bishop Hornihold ... New York, Christian press association publishing co., c1910. iv, 560 p. 19 1/2 cm. $0.75. [1910; A 261963;] 10-11647
I. Title.

HOWELL, Clifford, 1902- 265
Of sacraments and sacrifice. Collegeville, Minn., Liturgical Press [1953, c1952] 171p. illus. 23cm. (Popular liturgical library) [BX2200.H73] 53-712
1. Sacraments—Catholic Church. 2. Catholic Church. Liturgy and ritual. I. Title.

HUGHSON, Shirley Carter, 1867- 265
The seven sacraments. West Park, N. Y., Holy Cross Press, 1950. iv, 73 p. 19 cm. [BX2200.H8] 51-37193
1. Sacraments—Catholic Church. I. Title.

JACOBS, Joseph, 1879- 265
The sacramentary teachings of the church, by Rev. Joseph Jacobs ... Boston, Meador publishing company, 1936. 248 p. 21 cm. [BX2200.J3] 36-16888
1. Sacraments—Catholic church. I. Title.

JANSEN, G. M. A. 265
The sacramental we; an existential approach to the sacramental life [by] G. M. A. Jansen. Milwaukee, Bruce Pub. Co. [1968] xiii, 134 p. 22 cm. (Impact books) "All Biblical citations are taken from the Jerusalem Bible (New York, Doubleday, 1966)" [BX2200.J34] 68-28443
1. Sacraments—Catholic Church. I. Title. II. Title: An existential approach to the sacramental life.

KAISER, Edwin G. 265.
Our spiritual service to the sick and dying; a guide to prepare the sick and dying for the reception of the last sacraments, containing the ceremonies of the church according to the "Rituale Romanum" (the book used by the priest), together with other useful blessings and prayers. By Rev. Edwin G. Kaiser ... with pictures and diagrams after special drawings in accordance with the ceremonial and usage of the church ... New York, Cincinnati, etc., Benziger brothers, 1929. 128 p. incl. front., illus. 13 cm. An adaptation of Sei engel am krankenbett, by Emil Kofier. cf. Pref. [BX2292.K3] 29-14653
I. Title.

KEENAN, Alan. 265
Neuroses and sacraments. New York, Sheed and Ward, 1950. xi, 163 p. 20 cm. [BX2203.K4] 50-9858
1. Sacraments—Cathol'c Church. 2. Psychology, Pastoral. 3. Theology, Pastoral—Catholic Church. I. Title.

KELLY, Bernard J. 265
The Sacraments of daily life, by Bernard J. Kelly, C. S. SP. New York, Sheed & Ward, 1943. ix p., 1 l., 291 p. 19 1/2 cm. [BX2200.K4] 43-15284
1. Sacraments—Catholic church. I. Title.

KILLEEN, B. D. 264'.02
Sacraments in the new liturgy / B. D. Killeen. Huntington, Ind. : Our Sunday Vistor, c1976. 159 p. ; 21 cm. [BX2203.K54] 76-23698 ISBN 0-87973-801-4 pbk. : 3.50
1. Catholic Church. Liturgy and ritual. 2. Sacraments—Catholic Church. I. Title.

LEEMING, Bernard.
Principles of sacramental theology. London, New York, Longmans, Green and Co. [1956] lviii, 690p.
1. Sacraments—Catholic Church. I. Title. II. Title: Sacramental theology.

LEEMING, Bernard. 265
Principles of sacramental theology. Westminster, Md. Newman Press, 1956. 600p. 23cm. [BX2200.L43] 56-7382
1. Sacraments—Catholic Church. I. Title. II. Title: Sacramental theology.

LOUVEL, Francois, 1907- ed. 265
Signs of life [by]Francois Louvel and Louis J. Putz. Chicago, Fides Publishers Association [1953] 134p. 21cm. 'Essays from the current Fides albums ... [with] new material ... added ... Orginally edited under the direction of Father Francois Louvel ... [and] published in French ... Put into English and adapted to the American scence under the direction of Father Louis J. Puts.'--Dust jacket. [BX2200.L68] 53-10870
1. Sacraments—Catholic Church. I. Puts, Louis J. II. Title.

MCAULIFFE, Clarence R. 265
De sacramentis in genere. St. Louis, Mo., B. Herder [c.1960] 224p. 21cm. In Latin Bibl.: p.199-209 60-11797 4.00
1. Sacraments—Catholic Church. I. Title.

MCAULIFFE, Clarence R 265
Sacramental theology; a textbook for advanced students. St. Louis, Herder Herder [1958] 457p. 22cm. Includes bibliography. [BX2200.M27] 58-11740
1. Sacraments—Catholic Church. I. Title.

MARGERIE, Bertrand de. 261.8
The sacraments and social progress. Translated by Malachy Carroll. Chicago, Franciscan Herald Press [1974] p. Bibliography: p. [BX2203.M3713] 74-1451 ISBN 0-8199-0499-6 5.50
1. Sacraments—Catholic Church. 2. Sociology, Christian (Catholic) I. Title.

MARTOS, Joseph, 1943- 234'.16
Doors to the sacred : a historical introduction to sacraments in the Catholic Church / Joseph Martos. 1st ed. Garden City, N.Y. : Doubleday, 1981. xiii, 531 p. ; 22 cm. [BX2200.M355] 19 80-626 ISBN 0-385-15738-X : 14.95
1. Sacraments—Catholic Church. I. Title.

MAYNOOTH Union Summer School, 1963. 265.082
Sacraments; the gestures of Christ; [papers] Edited by Denis O'Callaghan. New York, Sheed and Ward [c1964] xii, 194 p. 22 cm. Sponsored by the Maynooth Union. Bibliography: p. [193]-194. [BX2200.M38] 65-12207
1. Sacraments—Catholic Church. I. O'Callaghan, Denis, 1931- ed. II. Maynooth Union. III. Title.

MILLER, John H. 1925- 265
Signs of transformation in Christ. Englewood Cliffs, N.J., Prentice-Hall [1963] x, 117 p. 24 cm. (Foundations of Catholic theology series) Bibliography: p. 103-112. [BX2200.M5] 63-21440
1. Sacraments — Catholic Church. 2. Jesus Christ — Person and offices. I. Title.

MORK, Wulstan 265
Led by the spirit; a primer of sacramental theology. Milwaukee, Bruce [c.1965] ix, 181p. 22cm. Bibl. [BX2200.M658] 65-18574 3.95
1. Sacraments—Catholic Church. I. Title.

MORRISON, Bakewell. 265
In touch with God; prayer, mass, and the sacraments [by] Bakewell Morrison ... Milwaukee, The Bruce publishing company [1943] vii, 184 p. 22 1/2 cm. (Half-title: Religion and culture series: Joseph Husslein, general editor) "References": p. 178-182. [BX2200.M67] 43-14266
1. Sacraments—Catholic church. 2. Mass. 3. Prayer. I. Title.

O'CALLAGHAN, Denis, 1931- ed. 265.082
Sacraments; the gestures of Christ. New York, Sheed [1965, c.1964] xii, 194p. 22cm. (Paps. of the Maynooth Union Summer Schl., 1963) Bibl. [BX2200.O33] 65-12207 4.00
1. Maynooth Union Summer School, 1963. 2. Sacraments—Catholic Church. I. Title.

O'NEILL, Colman E 265
Meeting Christ in the sacraments [by] Colman E. O'Neill. Staten Island, New York, Alba House [1964] 371 p. illus. 22 cm. [BX2200.O6] 64-20111
1. Sacraments — Catholic Church. I. Title.

OTTEN, Bernard John, 1862-1930. 265
The sacramental life of the church, by Rev. Bernard J. Otten ... St. Louis, Mo. and Freiburg (Baden), B. Herder, 1907. 239 p. 15 cm. [BX2200.O8] 7-42087
1. Sacraments—Catholic church. 2. Catholic church—Doctrinal and controversial works—Catholic authors. I. Title.

PALMER, Paul F., ed. 265.6
Sacraments and forgiveness; history and doctrinal development of penance, extreme unction and indulgences. Edited with commentary by Paul F. Palmer. Westminster, Md., Newman Press [1960, c.1959] 410p. (Sources of Christian theology, v. 2) 59-14809 6.00
1. Sacraments—Catholic Church. 2. Sacraments—History of doctrines. I. Title.

PALMER, Paul F ed. 265
Sacraments and worship; liturgy and doctrinal development of baptism, confirmation, and the Eucharist. Westminster, Md., Newman Press, 1955. xxii, 227p. 23cm. (Sources of Christian theology, v. 1) Includes bibliographical references. [BX1749.S6 vol.1] 54-7546
1. Sacraments—Catholic Church. 2. Sacraments—History of doctrines. I. Title. II. Series.

PENNOCK, Michael. 234'.16
The sacraments & you : living encounters with Christ / Michael Pennock. Notre Dame, Ind. : Ave Maria Press, c1981. 269 p. : ill. ; 23 cm. [BX2200.P38] 19 81-65227 ISBN 0-87793-221-2 (pbk.) : 3.95
1. Catholic Church—Doctrinal and controversial works—Catholic authors. 2. Sacraments—Catholic Church. I. Title.

PHILIPON, Marie Michel, 1898- 263
The sacraments in the Christian life; translated by John A. Otto. Westminster, Md., Newman Press, 1954. 304p. 22cm. [BX2200.P476] 54-9606
1. Sacraments—Catholic Church. I. Title.

PIAULT, Bernard 265
What is a sacrament? Tr. from French by A. Manson. New York, Hawthorn [c.1963] 174p. 21cm. (Twentieth cent. ency. of Catholicism, v.49, sec.5:The life of faith) Bibl. 63-20975 3.50 bds.,
1. Sacraments—Catholic Church. I. Title. II. Series:The Twentieth century encyclopedia of Catholicism, v.49

PRINCIPLES of sacramental theology. London, New York, Longmans, Green and Co. [1956] lviii, 690p.
1. Sacraments— Catholic Church. I. Leeming, Bernard. II. Title: Sacramental theology.

QUINN, John Richard, 1921- 265
The sacraments of growth and renewal [by] J. Richard Quinn. New York, Bruce Pub. Co. [1969] xv, 196 p. 24 cm. (Contemporary college theology series. Ecclesial theology) Bibliographical footnotes. [BX2200.Q5] 70-78972
1. Catholic Church. Liturgy and ritual. 2. Sacraments—Catholic Church. I. Title.

RAHNER, Karl, 1904- 265
The Church and the sacraments Tr. from German by W. J. O Hara. NewYork] Herder & Herder [1963] 116p. 22cm.

(Quaestiones disputatae, 9) 63-10786 2.25 pap.,
1. Sacraments—Catholic Church. 2. Church. I. Title.

RICHARDS, Hubert J 1921- 265
Christ in our world; a study of baptism, Eucharist, penance, and marriage [by] Hubert J. Richards [and] Peter De Rosa. Milwaukee, Bruce Pub. Co. [1966] xi, 208 p. 23 cm. [BX2200.R5] 66-17274
1. Sacraments — Catholic Church. I. De Rosa, Peter, joint author. II. Title.

RIGA, Peter J. 234'.16
Sign and symbol of the invisible God: essays on the sacraments today [by] Peter J. Riga. Notre Dame, Ind., Fides Publishers [1971] v, 89 p. 18 cm. (A Fides dome book, D-79) Includes bibliographies. [BX2200.R53] 72-166155 ISBN 0-8190-0495-2 1.25
1. Sacraments—Catholic church. I. Title.

ROGUET, A M 1906-
Christ acts through the sacraments. Translated by Carisbrooke Dominicans. Collegeville, Minn., Liturgical Press [1953] 162p. 19cm. Translation of Les sacrements, signes de vie. A 55
1. Sacraments—Catholic Church. I. Title.

ROGUET, A M 1906-
Christ acts through the sacraments. Translated by Carisbrooke Dominicans. Collegeville, Minn., Liturgical Press [1962] 183 p. 64-11198
1. Sacraments—Catholic Church. I. Title.

SCHANZ, John P 265
The sacraments of life and worship [by] John P. Schanz. Milwaukee, Bruce Pub. Co. [1966] xxii, 310 p. 23 cm. (Contemporary college theology series. Ecclesial theology section) Bibliography: p. 301-306. [BX2200.S33] 66-19748
1. Sacraments—Catholic Church. I. Title.

SCHILLEBEECKX, Edward Cornelis Florentius Alfons, 1914-
Christ, the sacrament of encounter with God [by] E. Schillebeeckx. [Translation by Paul Barrett. English text rev. by Mark Schoof and Laurence Bright] London, New York, Sheed and Ward [1965, c1963] xix, 276 p. 18 cm. Translation of Christus, Sacrament van de Godsontmoeting. Bibliographical footnotes. 68-22929
1. Sacraments—Catholic Church. I. Title.

SCHILLEBEECKX, Edward 265
Cornelius Florentius Alfons, 1914-
Christ, the sacrament of the encounter with God, by E. Schillebeeckx. [Translation by Paul Barrett. English text rev. by Mark Schoof and Laurence Bright] New York, Sheed and Ward [1963] xvii, 222 p. 22 cm. Bibliographical footnotes. [BX2200.S4143] 63-17144
1. Sacraments—Catholic Church. I. Title.

SCHLITZER, Albert L. 1902- 265
Our life in Christ [2v.] the realization of redemptive incarnation. Notre Dame, Ind., Univ. of Notre Dame Pr. [c.]1962. 2v., 500; 134p. 22cm. (Univ. theology ser.) Bibl. 61-18651 6.50 set,
1. Sacrements—Catholic Church. 2. Christian ethics Catholic authors. 3. Incarnation. I. Title.

SEGUNDO, Juan Luis. 230'.2 s
The sacraments today, by Juan Luis Segundo, in collaboration with the staff of the Peter Faber Center in Montevideo, Uruguay. Translated by John Drury. Maryknoll, N.Y. [Orbis Books, 1974] vi, 154 p. 24 cm. (His A theology for artisans of a new humanity, v. 4) (Series: Segundo, Juan Luis. Teologia abierta para el laico adulto. English, v. 4.) Translation of Los sacramentos hoy. Includes bibliographical references. [BX1751.2.A1S413 vol. 4] [BX2200] 234'.16 73-77359 ISBN 0-88344-484-4 6.95
1. Sacraments—Catholic Church. I. Centro Pedro Fabro de Montevideo. II. Title. III. Series.
Pbk. 3.95, ISBN 0-88344-490-9.

SEMMELROTH, Otto. 265
Church and sacrament. Translated by Emily Schossberger. Notre Dame, Ind., Fides Publishers [c1965] 111 p. 19 cm. Translation of Vom Sinn der Sakramente. [BX2200.S4513] 65-13801
1. Sacraments—Catholic Church. I. Title.

SHEEN, Fulton John, Bp., 264.025
1895-
These are the sacraments, as described by Fulton J. Sheen, as photographed by Yousuf Karsh. New York, Hawthorn [c.1962] 159p. illus. (pt. col.) 26cm. 62-9037 4.95 bds.,
1. Sacraments—Catholic Church. I. Karsh, Yousuf, 1908- illus. II. Title.

SHEEN, Fulton John, Bp., 264.025
1895-
These are the sacraments, as described by Fulton J. Sheen, as photographed by Yousuf Karsh. Garden City, N. Y., Doubleday [1964, c.1962] 196p. illus. 19cm. (Image bk., D174) .95 pap.,
1. Sacraments—Catholic Church. I. Karsh, Yousuf, 1908—illus. II. Title.

SHEEN, Fulton John Bp., 264.025
1895- 1895-
These are the sacraments, as described by Fulton J. Sheen, as photographed by Yousuf Karsh. New York, Hawthorn Books [1962] 159 p. illus. 26 cm. [BX2200.S46] 62-9037
1. Sacraments—Catholic Church. I. Karsh, Yousuf, 1908- illus. II. Title.

SHEEN, Fulton John, Bp., 1895-
These are the sacraments, as described by Fulton J. Sheen, as photographed by Yousuf Karsh. Garden City, N. Y., Doubleday [1964, c1962] 196 p. illus. (Image books) 66-52586
1. Sacraments—Catholic Church. I. Karsh, Yousuf, 1908- illus. II. Title.

STONE, Darwell, 1859-
The reserved sacrament. By Darwell Stone ... London, R. Scott. Milwaukee,Wis., Young churchman co., 1917. 143 p. 18 1/2 cm. (Half-title: Handbooks of Catholic faith and practice, ed. by W. J. Sparrow Simpson, D.D.) A 17
I. Title.

TAYMARIS d'Expernon Fr 265
The Blessed Trinity and the sacraments. Westminster, Md., Newman Press [1961] 150 p. 21 cm. [BX2200.T313 1961] 60-14821
1. Sacraments — Catholic Church. I. Title.

VAILLANCOURT, Raymond. 234'.16
Toward a renewal of sacramental theology / Raymond Vaillancourt ; translated by Matthew J. O'Connell. Collegeville, Minn. : Liturgical Press, c1979. v, 126 p. ; 22 cm. Translation of Vers un renouveau de la theologie sacramentaire. Bibliography: p. 125-126. [BX2200.V3413] 79-12621 ISBN 0-8146-1050-1 pbk. : 4.95
1. Sacraments—Catholic Church. I. Title.

WORGUL, George S. 234'.16
From magic to metaphor : a validation of Christain sacraments / George S. Worgul ; with a foreword by Piet Fransen. New York : Paulist Press, c1980. xv, 232 p. ; 24 cm. Includes bibliographical references. [BX2200.W67] 79-56753 ISBN 0-8091-2280-4 pbk. : 8.95
1. Sacraments—Catholic Church. 2. Sacraments. I. Title.

Sacraments—Catholic Church—Addresses, essays, lectures.

THE Sacraments : 234'.16
readings in contemporary sacramental theology / edited by Michael J. Taylor. New York, N.Y. : Alba House, c1981. xiv, 274 p. ; 21 cm. Includes bibliographical references. [BX2200.S24] 19 80-39534 ISBN 0-8189-0406-2 pbk. : 7.95
1. Catholic Church—Doctrinal and controversial works—Catholic authors—Addresses, essays, lectures. 2. Sacraments—Catholic Church—Addresses, essays, lectures. I. Taylor, Michael J.

THE Sacraments in general: 265
a new perspective. Edited by Edward Schillebeeckx [and] Boniface Willems. New York, Paulist Press [1968] viii, 166 p. 24 cm. (Concilium. Dogma, v. 31) Bibliographical footnotes. [BX2200.S23] 68-20451
1. Sacraments—Catholic Church—Addresses, essays, lectures. I. Schillebeeckx, Edward Cornelis Florentius Alfons, 1914- ed. II. Willems, Boniface A., 1926- ed. III. Series: Concilium (New York) v. 31

SCHILLEBEECKX, Edward 265
Cornelius Florentius Alfons, 1914-
The sacraments in general: a new perspective. Edited by Edward Schillebeeckx [and] Boniface Willems. New York, Paulist Press [1968] viii, 166 p. 24 cm. (Concilium theology in the age of renewal: Dogma, v. 31) Bibliographical footnotes. [BX2200.S4145] 68-20451
1. Sacraments—Catholic Church—Addresses, essays, lectures. I. Willems, Boniface A., 1926- joint author. II. Title. III. Series: Concilium: theology in the age of renewal, v. 31

SULLIVAN, C. Stephen, ed. 265.082
Readings in sacramental theology. Englewood Cliffs, N.J., Prentice [c.1964] viii, 236p. 21cm. Bibl. 64-18183 2.95 pap.,
1. Sacraments—Catholic Church—Addresses, essays, lectures. I. Title.

Sacraments—Catholic Church—Collected works.

HALLIGAN, Francis 264'.02'008
Nicholas, 1917-
The ministry of the celebration of the sacraments [by] Nicholas Halligan. New York, Alba House [1973-74] 3 v. 22 cm. Includes bibliographical references. [BX2200.H25] 73-4203 ISBN 0-8189-0271-X 3.95
1. Sacraments—Catholic Church—Collected works. I. Title.

Sacraments—Catholic Church—Meditations.

DONNELLY, Francis Patrick, 242
1869-
Watching an hour; a book for the blessed sacrament [by] Francis P. Donnelly. New York, P. J. Kenedy & sons, 1914. xiii, 262 p. 18 cm. [BX2182.D63] 14-8717
I. Title.

RAHNER, Karl, 1904- 234'.16
Meditations on the Sacraments / Karl Rahner. New York : Seabury Press, c1977. p. cm. Translation of Die siebenfaltige Gabe. "A Crossroad book." [BX2200.R3313] 76-52938 ISBN 0-8164-0344-9 : 7.95
1. Sacraments—Catholic Church—Meditations. I. Title.

Sacraments—Catholic Church—Study and teaching.

REICHERT, Richard. 265'.07
Teaching Sacraments to youth / by Richard Reichert. New York : Paulist Press, [1975] 136 p. ; 19 cm. [BX2200.R4] 75-9121 ISBN 0-8091-1880-7 pbk. : 1.65
1. Sacraments—Catholic Church—Study and teaching. I. Title.

Sacraments—Early works to 1800.

HUGO, of Saint Victor, 265
1096or7-1141.
On the sacraments of the Christian faith (De sacramentis) English version by Roy J. Deferrari. Cambridge, Mass., Mediaeval Academy of America, 1951. xx, 486 p. 27 cm. (The Mediaeval Academy of America. Publication no. 58) "Selected works on Hugh of Saint Victor": p. xx. [BX2200.H843] 51-7939
1. Sacraments—Early works to 1800. I. Title. II. Series.

PSEUDO-DIONYSIUS, the 265
Areopagite.
The ecclesiastical hierarchy / Dionysius, the Pseudo-Areopagite ; translated and annotated by Thomas L. Campbell. Washington, D.C. : University Press of America, c1981. v, 230 p. ; 22 cm. Translation made from Corderius' Greek text. Originally presented as Thomas L. Campbell's thesis (S.T.D.)—Catholic University of America, 1955. Bibliography: p. 215-230. [BR65.D64E513 1981] 19 81-40140 ISBN 0-8191-1798-6 : 20.25 ISBN 0-8191-1799-4 (pbk.) : 10.25
1. Sacraments—Early works to 1800. 2. Chrism—Early works to 1800. 3. Monasticism and religious orders—Early works to 1800. 4. Funeral service—Early works to 1800. I. Campbell, Thomas L. II. [Ecclesiastical hierarchy.] English III. Title.

Sacraments—History of doctrines.

HOLIFIELD, E. Brooks. 234'.16
The covenant sealed : the development of Puritan sacramental theology in old and New England, 1570-1720 / E. Brooks Holifield. New Haven : Yale University Press, 1974. xi, 248 p. ; 25 cm. Includes index. Bibliography: p. 233-242. [BV800.H64] 73-92695 ISBN 0-300-01733-2 : 12.50
1. Sacraments—History of doctrines. 2. Puritans. I. Title.

MCLELLAND, Joseph C 265
The visible words of God; an exposition of the sacramental theology of Peter Martyr Vermigli, A. D. 1500-1562. Grand Rapids, Eerdmans [1957] ix, 291p. 23cm. Bibliography: p. 261-266. [BX9419.V4M35] 58-9551
1. Vermigli, Pietro Martire, 1500-1562. 2. Sacraments—History of doctrines. I. Title.

PALMER, Paul F 265
Sacraments of healing and of vocation. Englewood Cliffs, N.J., Prentice-Hall, 1963. 118 p. 23 cm. (Foundations of Catholic theology series) Bibliography: p. 109-110. [BV803.P3] 63-10939
1. Sacraments — History of Doctrines. 2. Sacraments — Catholic Church. I. Title.

PAYNE, John Barton, 234'.16'0924
1931-
Erasmus: his theology of the sacraments [by] John B. Payne. [Richmond, Va., John Knox Press, 1970] 341 p. 21 cm. (Research in theology) A revision of the author's thesis, Harvard University, 1966. Bibliography: p. [338]-341. [BV800.P38 1970] 70-82938
1. Erasmus, Desiderius, d. 1536. 2. Sacraments—History of doctrines. 3. Theology, Doctrinal—History—16th century. I. Title.

ROGERS, Elizabeth 234'.16'09
Frances, 1892-
Peter Lombard and the sacramental system / Elizabeth Frances Rogers. Merrick, N.Y. : Richwood Pub. Co., 1976. 250 p. ; 24 cm. Reprint of the 1917 ed. published in New York. Originally presented as the author's thesis, Columbia University, 1917. Vita. Bibliography: p. 247-250. [BX2200.R6 1976] 76-20688 ISBN 0-915172-22-4 lib.bdg. : 18.50
1. Petrus Lombardus, Bp of Paris, 12th cent. 2. Sacraments—History of doctrines. I. Title.

Sacraments (Liturgy)

BRINGING the sacraments 264*.02
to the people; a guide to the fruitful use of the English ritual by priests and teachers. Collegeville, Minn., Liturgical Press [1966] 200 p. 24 cm. Bibliography: p. 191-192. [BX2200.B66] 72-177002
1. Sacraments (Liturgy) I. Catholic Church. Liturgy and ritual. Ritual (U.S.). English. Selections.

ELLARD, Gerald, 1894- 264.025
Christian life and workship. Illus. by Ade' de Bethune. [Rev. and enl.] Milwaukee, Bruce Pub. Co. [1953] 426p. illus. 24cm. cScience and culture series) [BX2200.E6 1953] 53-4356
*1. Sacraments (Liturgy) 2. Catholic Church. Liturgy and ritual. 3. Christian life—*catholic authors. I. Title.*

ELLARD, Gerald, 1894- 264.025
Christian life and worship. Illus. by Ade' De Bethune. [Rev. and enl.] Milwaukee, Bruce Pub. Co. [1956] 432p. illus. 24cm. [BX2200.E6 1956] 56-58823
1. Sacraments (Liturgy) 2. Catholic Church. Liturgy and ritual. 3. Christian life—Catholic authors. I. Title.

ELLARD, Gerald, 1894- 264.025
Christian life and worship. Illus. by Ade De Bethune. [Rev. and enl.] Milwaukee, Bruce [1950] xxi, 418 p. illus. 24 cm. (Science and culture series) Includes bibliographies. [BX2200.E6 1950] 51-788
1. Sacraments (Liturgy) 2. Catholic Church. Liturgy and ritual. 3. Christian life—Catholic authors. I. Title.

ELLARD, Gerald, 1894- 264.025
Christian life and worship; a religion text for colleges, by Rev. Gerald Ellard... New

York, Milwaukee [etc.] The Bruce publishing company [c1933] xxiv, 379 p. incl. front., illus., diagrs. (1 double) 22 cm. (Half-title: Science and cultural texts, J. Husselein..general editor) "Select bibliography: p. xvii-xviii; "Readings" at end of most of the chapters. [BX2200.E6] 33-31105
1. Sacraments (Liturgy) 2. Catholic church. Liturgy and ritual. 3. Christian life. I. Title.

ELLARD, Gerald, 1894- 264.025
Christian life and worship, by Rev. Gerald Ellard... New York, Milwaukee [etc.] The Bruce publishing company [c1934] xxvi, 358 p. front., illus., plates, port., diagrs. (1 fold.) 22 cm. (Half-title: Religion and culture series, J. Husselein...general editor) First edition published 1933 as a volume of the "Science and culture texts." Includes bibliographies. [BX2200.E6 1934] 34-16382
1. Sacraments (Liturgy) 2. Catholic church. Liturgy and ritual. 3. Christian life. I. Title. II. Series.

ELLARD, Gerald, 1894- 264.025
Christian life and worship [by] Gerald Ellard...with original illustrations by Ade de Bethune. Milwaukee, The Bruce publishing company [c1940] xxi p., 1 l., 420 p. incl. front., illus. (incl. music) plans, diagrs. (1 double) 23 1/2 cm. (Half-title: Religion and culture series; Joseph Husselein...general editor]) "Revised and enlarged." "Select bibliography": p. 402-405; "Readings" at end of each chapter. [BX2200.E6 1940] 40-6019
1. Sacraments (Liturgy) 2. Catholic church. Liturgy and ritual. 3. Christian life. I. De Bethune, Adelaide, 1914- illus. II. Title. III. Series.

ELLARD, Gerald, 1894-1963. 248'.3
Christian life and worship / Gerald Ellard ; with an introd. by Leo Klein. Reprint ed. New York : Arno Press, 1978 [c1940]. xxi, 420 p. : ill. ; 24 cm. (The American Catholic tradition) Reprint of the 1948 rev. and enl. ed. published by Bruce Pub. Co., Milwaukee, issued in Science and culture series. Includes bibliographies and index. [BX2200.E6 1978] 77-11282 ISBN 0-405-10819-2 : 26.00
1. Catholic Church. Liturgy and ritual. 2. Sacraments (Liturgy) 3. Christian life—Catholic authors. I. Title. II. Series.

Sacraments—Lutheran Church.

KRAABEL, Alf M 265
Ten studies on the sacraments. Minneapolis, Augsburg Pub. House [1954] 116p. 20cm. (Ten-week teacher-training course books) [BX8072.K7] 54-4026
1. Sacraments—Lutheran Church. I. Title.

MISCA, Frederica E. 265
The love of Jesus. A discourse upon the spiritual uses of baptism, confirmation, and the Lord's supper. From the German of Frederica Misca. Boston, Printed for the author, 1836. vi, [7]-90 p. 16 cm. Another edition, translated by A. W. McClure, published the same year at Andover. [BV800.M6 1836a] 38-24324
1. Sacraments—Lutheran church. I. Title.

MISCA, Frederica E. 265
The love of Jesus. A treatise upon baptism, confirmation, and the Lord's supper. From the German of F. E. Misca. Translated by Rev. A. W. M'Clure... Andover [Mass.] Printed for the author, 1836. 3 p. l., [3]-4, [9]-94 p. front. 15 1/2 cm. [BV800.M6] 38-24323
1. Sacraments—Lutheran church. I. M'Clure, Alexander Wilson, 1808-1865, tr. II. Title.

Sacraments-Methodist Church.

GOODLOE, Robert Wesley, 1888- 265
The sacraments in Methodism. Nashville, Methodist Pub. House [1953] 160p. 20cm. [BX8338.A1G6] 52-13755
1. Sacraments-Methodist Church. I. Title.

Sacraments—Mormons and Mormonism—Juvenile literature.

MAPLES, Evelyn 265
Norman learns about the sacraments. Illus. by Beverly Logan. Independence, Mo., Herald House. [c.]1961. 40p. illus. 61-9685 1.25
1. Sacraments—Mormons and Mormonism—Juvenile literature. I. Title.

ZOLLINGER, Camma Larsen. 234'.163
Sacrament. Illustrated by William Kuhre. Salt Lake City, Bookcraft [1973] [24] p. col. illus. 31 cm. Discusses the sacrament in the Mormon church as a reminder of the friendship and love of Jesus. [BX8655.A1Z64] 73-88613
1. [Church of Jesus Christ of Latter-Day Saints.] 2. Sacraments—Mormons and Mormonism—Juvenile literature. 3. [Sacraments—Mormonism.] 4. [Christian life.] I. Kuhre, William, illus. II. Title.

Sacraments—Orthodox Eastern Church.

SILIGARDAKIS, Titus. 265
The seven sacraments. Brooklyn, Greek Orthodox Community Kimisis Theotokou, 1963. 63 p. illus. 24 cm. [BX377.S5] 63-38386
1. Sacraments—Orthodox Eastern Church. I. Title.

Sacraments—Reorganized Church of Jesus Christ of Latter-Day Saints.

BROCKWAY, Charles Edward, 1917- 264.0935
Ordinances and sacraments of the church [by] Charles E. Brockway and Alfred H. Yale, Independence, Mo., Herald House, 1962. 184p. 21cm. [BX8675.B7] 62-15950
1. Sacraments—Reorganized Church of Jesus Christ of Latter-Day Saints. I. Yale, Alfred H., joint author. II. Title.

JUDD, Peter A., 1943- 265
The sacraments : an exploration into their meaning and practice in the Saints Church / by Peter A. Judd. Independence, Mo. : Herald Pub. House, c1978. 174 p. ; 20 cm. Includes bibliographical references. [BX8655.J83] 78-12776 ISBN 0-8309-0225-2 : 5.75
1. Reorganized Church of Jesus Christ of Latter Day Saints. 2. Sacraments—Reorganized Church of Jesus Christ of Latter Day Saints. I. Title.

Sacraments—Sermons.

CROOKSTON, Joseph Claude. 264.031
The wells of salvation; addresses of the three hours of Good Friday, by Father Joseph (Rev. Joseph Claude Crookston) ... Milwaukee, Wis., Morehouse publishing co. [c1933] ix, 118 p. 19 cm. Sermons about the sacraments. [Name in religion, Joseph, father] [BX5949.AiC7] 33-6201
1. Sacraments—Sermons. 2. Good Friday. 3. Protestant Episcopal church in the U. S. A.—Sermons. 4. Sermons, American. I. Title.

KUIPER, Henry J 1885- ed. 265
Sermons on baptism and the Lord's supper, Lord's days: xxv-xxxi ... by ministers of the Reformes and Christian Reformed churches. Edited by Henry J. Kuiper ... Grand Rapids, Mich., Zondervan publishing house [c1938] 136 p. 20 cm. (Half-title: Sermons on the Heldelberg catechism, vol. iii) [BX9426.A1K8 no. 3] [BV800.K8] 238.41 38-29579
1. Sacraments—Sermons. 2. Reformed church—Sermons. 3. Sermons, American. I. Title.

LIPTAK, David Q. 252'.02
Sacramental and occasional homilies / David Q. Liptak. New York : Alba House, c1981. xiv, 96 p. ; 21 cm. [BX1756.L56S22] 19 80-29287 ISBN 0-8189-0408-9 pbk. : 4.95
1. Catholic Church—Sermons. 2. Sacraments—Sermons. 3. Occasional sermons. 4. Sermons, American. I. Title.

MAC DONALD, Alexander, bp., 1858- 265
The sacraments; a course of seven sermons, by Very Rev. Alexander Mac Donald, D.D. New York, J. F. Wagner [c1906] 82 p. 20 1/2 cm. [BX2200.M3] 7-6729
1. Sacraments—Sermons. 2. Catholic church—Sermons. 3. Sermons, English—Canada. I. Title.

Sacraments—Study and teaching.

LINK, Mark J., ed. 268
Teaching the sacraments and morality [by] Stenzel [others. Mark J. Link, ed.] Chicago, Loyola Univ. Pr. [c.]1965. ix, 214p. illus. 24cm. (Loyola pastoral ser.: Lumen vitae studies) Bibl. [BX2203.L5] 64-8102 3.50
1. Sacraments—Study and teaching. 2. Religious education. I. Stenzel, Alois. II. Title.

Sacred books.

EVERTS, William Wallace, 1814-1890, comp.
The Scripture school reader, consisting of selections of sacred Scriptures for the use of schools ... Comp. and arranged by W. W. Everts ... and Wm. H. Wyckoff ... New York, Nafis & Cornish: St. Louis, Nafis, Cornish & co., 1847. vi, [7]-348 p. 19 cm. 15-13514
I. Title.

FROST, S. E., 1899- ed. 291.8'2
The sacred writings of the world's great religions. Selected and edited by S. E. Frost, Jr. New York, McGraw-Hill [1972, c1943] vi, 410 p. 21 cm. [BL70.F7 1972] 72-192672 ISBN 0-07-022520-6
1. Sacred books. I. Title.

GOLDBRUNNER, Josef 265
Teaching the sacraments. [New York] Herder & Herder [c.1961] 140p. illus. 1.75 pap.,
I. Title.

TURNBULL, Grace Hill, 1880- 291.8'2
Tongues of fire : a bible of sacred scriptures of the pagan world / Grace H. Turnbull. New York : Arno Press, 1979, c1941. xxvi, 416 p. ; 21 cm. (Johns Hopkins University Press reprints) Reprint of the 1929 ed. published by Macmillan, New York. Includes bibliographical references. [BL70.T7 1979] 78-19278 ISBN 0-405-10634-3 : 28.00
1. Sacred books. 2. Oriental literature—Translations into English. 3. English literature—Translations from Oriental languages. 4. Classical literature—Translations into English. 5. English literature—Translations from Oriental languages. 6. Philosophy, Ancient. I. Title.

VEDAS, Rigveda. Selections. English. 294.1
Vedic hymns, translated by F. Max Muller ... Oxford, The Clarendon press, 1891-97. 2 v. 23 cm. (Added t.p.: The sacred books of the East ... vol. XXXII, XLVI. Part II: Vedic hymns, translated by Hermann Oldenberg. Part I published in 1899 with title: Rig-veda sanhita. The sacred hymns of the Brahmans. Contents.pt. I. Hymns to the Maruts, Rudra, Vayu, and Vata.--pt. II. Hymns to Agni (Mandalas I-V) "A bibliographical list of the more important publications on the Rig-veda": pt. I, p. [540-549] [BL1010.S3 vol. 32, 46] (290.8) 891.21 32-11950
I. Miller Friedrich, 1823-1900, ed. and tr. II. Oldenberg, Hermann, 1854-1920, joint tr. III. Title.

VEDAS. Regveda. English. Selections. 294.1
Vedic hymns translated by F. Max Muller. Oxford, The Clarendon press, 1891-97. 2 v. 23 cm. (Added t.-p.: The Sacred books of the East ... vol. xxxiii, xlvi) Part 2: Vedic hymns, translated by Hermann Oldberg. Part 1 published in 1869 with title: Rig-veda-sanhita. The sacred hymns of the Brahmans. "A bibliographical list of the more important publications on the Rig-veda": pt. 1. p. [540]-549. Contents.pt. I. Hymns to the Maruts, Ruda, Vayu, and Vata.--pt. II. Hymns to Agni (Mandalas I-v) [BL1010.S3 vo;. 32, 46 (290.8) [891.21]] 32-11950
I. Miller, Friedrich Max, 1823-1900. ed. and tr. II. Oldenberg, Hermann. 1854-1920, joint tr. III. Title.

THE world's great scriptures
an anthology of the sacred books of the tenprincipal religions, compiled and annotated with historical introductions and interpretive comments by Lewis Browne... With decorations and maps by the editor. New York, the Macmillan company, 1961. xvi, 559p. illus. (incl. maps), diagr. 24cm.
1. Sacred books. I. Browne, Lewis, 1879-1949, ed.

Sacred books—Addresses, essays, lectures.

HOLY Book and holy tradition. 291.8
Edited by F. F. Bruce and E. G. Rupp. Grand Rapids, Eerdmans [1968] viii, 244 p. illus. 23 cm. Papers presented at an international colloquium held in November 1966 in the Faculty of Theology of Manchester University. Bibliographical footnotes. [BL71.H6 1968b] 70-3048 5.95
1. Sacred books—Addresses, essays, lectures. 2. Tradition (Theology)—Addresses, essays, lectures. I. Bruce, Frederick Fyvie, 1910- ed. II. Rupp, Ernest Gordon, ed. III. Victoria University of Manchester. Faculty of Theology.

Sacred books—Collected works.

PREBISH, Charles S. 291.8'2
Introduction to religions of the East : reader / edited by Charles S. Prebish and Jane I. Smith. Dubuque, Iowa : Kendall/Hunt Pub. Co., [1974]. xiii, 182 p. : ill. ; 23 cm. [BL70.P73] 74-82806 ISBN 0-8403-0985-6 : 7.50
1. Sacred books—Collected works. I. Smith, Jane I., joint comp. II. Title. III. Title: Religions of the East.

Sacred books—Comparative studies.

PARRINDER, Edward Geoffrey. 291.8'2
Upanishads, Gita, and Bible; a comparative study of Hindu and Christian scriptures, by Geoffrey Parrinder. New York, Harper & Row [1972, c1962] 136 p. 21 cm. (Harper torchbooks, TB 1660) Includes bibliographical references. [BR128.H5P37 1972] 72-188029 ISBN 0-06-131660-1 2.25
1. Sacred books—Comparative studies. 2. Christianity and other religions—Hinduism. I. Title.

PARRINDER, Edward Geoffrey. 291.82
Upanishads, Gita and Bible; a comparative study of Hindu and Christian Scriptures. [New York] Association Press [1963, c1962] 136 p. 23 cm. Bibliographical footnotes. [BR128.H5P37 1963] 63-8884
1. Sacred books—Comparative studies. 2. Christianity and other religions—Hinduism. I. Title.

Sacred books—Criticism, Textual—Addresses, essays, lectures.

THE Critical study of sacred texts / 291.8'2
edited by Wendy Doniger O'Flaherty. [Berkeley] : Graduate Theological Union, 1979. xiii, 290 p. ; 23 cm. (Berkeley religious studies series ; 2) "Product of a series of seminars held at the Graduate Theological Union in Berkeley." Includes index. Bibliography: p. 279-280. [BL71.C74] 79-120598 ISBN 0-89581-101-4 : 16.00
1. Sacred books—Criticism, Textual—Addresses, essays, lectures. I. O'Flaherty, Wendy Doniger. II. Graduate Theological Union. III. Series.

Sacred books—History and criticism

BRADEN, Charles Samuel, 1887- 291.8
The scriptures of mankind, an introduction. New York, Macmillan, 1952. 496 p. 22 cm. Includes bibliography. [BL71.B7] 52-10590
1. Sacred books—Hist. & crit. I. Title.

HURST, George Leopold. 809'.935'2
Sacred literature, by George L. Hurst. [Folcroft, Pa.] Folcroft Library Editions, 1974. p. cm. Reprint of the 1905 ed. published by J. M. Dent, London. Bibliography: p. [BL71.H8 1974] 74-3454 10.00 (lib. bdg.).
1. Sacred books—History and criticism. I. Title.

MARTIN, Alfred Wilhelm, 1862-1933. 291.8'2
Seven great Bibles; the sacred Scriptures of Hinduism, Buddhism, Zoroastrianism, Confucianism (Taoism), Mohammedanism, Judaism, and Christianity. New York, Cooper Square Publishers, 1975. xx, 277 p. 23 cm. Reprint of the 1930 ed. published by F. A. Stokes Co., New York, in series: World unity library. [BL71.M3 1975] 74-11849 ISBN 0-8154-0495-6 7.50
1. Sacred books—History and criticism. I. Title. II. Series: World unity library.

MARTIN, Alfred Wilhelm, 1862-1933. 291
... *Seven great Bibles,* the sacred Scriptures of Hinduism, Buddhism, Zoroastrianism, Confucianism (Taoism), Mohammedanism, Judaism and Christianity, by Alfred W. Martin ... New York, Frederick A. Stokes company [c1930] xx p., 1 l., 277 p. 20 cm. (World unity library) [BL71.M3] 30-30518
1. Sacred books—Hist. & crit. I. Title.

Sacred books—History and criticism—Addresses, essays, lectures.

LITERATURE of belief : 291.8'2
sacred scripture and religious experience / edited with a preface by Neal E. Lambert ; introduction by M. Gerald Bradford. [Provo, Utah] : Religious Studies Center, Brigham Young University, c1981. xiii, 274 p. : ill. ; 24 cm. (Religious studies monograph series ; v. 5) Includes bibliographical references and index. [BL71.L57] 19 80-70038 ISBN 0-88494-409-3 : 8.95
1. Sacred books—History and criticism—Addresses, essays, lectures. I. Lambert, Neal E., 1934- II. Brigham Young University. Religious Studies Center. III. Series.

Sacred books—Introductions.

LANCZKOWSKI, Gunter 291.82
Sacred writings; a guide to the literature of religions. Tr. [from German] by Stanley Godman. New York, Harper [1966, c.1956, 1961] 147p. illus. 21cm. (Harper chapel bk., CB21H) Bibl. [BL71.L313] 66-2996 1.45 pap.,
1. Sacred books—Introductions. I. Title.

Sacred books (Selections; Extracts, etc.)

BALLOU, Robert Oleson 1892- ed.
The Bible of the world; edited by Robert O. Ballou in collaboration with Friedrich Spiegelberg ... and with the assistance and advice of Horace L. Friess ... New York, Viking press [1961 1939]. xxl, 1415 p. illus. 24 cm. "The scriptual essence of eight great living source religions. "-Introd. "First published in October 1939." Bibliographical references in "Notes": p. [1343]-1379; "Condensed bibliography": p. 1380-1384. 68-88669
1. Sacred books (Selections: Extracts, etc.) I. Spiegelberg, Frederic, 1897- ed. II. Friess, Horace Leland, 1900- ed. III. Title.

THE Bible of the world; 290
edited by Robert O. Ballou in collaboration with Friedrich Spiegelberg ... and with the assistance and advice of Horace L. Friess ... New York, The Viking press, 1939. xi, 1415 p. illus. 24 cm. "The scriptural essence of eight great living source religious."--Introd. "First published in October 1969." Bibliographical references in "Notes": p. [1343]-1379; "Condensed bibliography": p. 1880-1884. [BL70.B5] 39-27953
1. Sacred books (Selections: Extracts, etc.) I. Ballou, Robert Oleson, 1892- ed. II. Spiegelberg, Friedrich, 1897- joint ed. III. Friess, Horace Leland, 1900- joint ed.

BOUQUET, Alan Coates, 1884- ed. 290.82
Sacred books of the world. London, Cassell [dist. New York, Barnes & Noble, 1964, c.1954 342p. 21cm. (Belle sauvage lib.) Companion source-book to the author's Comparative religion. 63-22884 3.75
1. Sacred books (Selections: Extracts, etc.) I. Title.

BOUQUET, Alan Coates, 1884- ed. 290.82
Sacred books of the world. [An anthology with full commentary, illustrating the development from the formulas and invocations of primitive magic to the hymns and revelations of the twentieth century] London, Baltimore, Penguin Books [1954] 343p. 18cm. (Pelican books, A283) A companion source-book to Comparative religion. [BL70.B6] 54-3069
1. Sacred books (Selections: Extracts, etc.) I. Title.

BOUQUET, Alan Coates, 1884- 291.8'2
Sacred books of the world: a companion source-book to comparative religion, by A. C. Bouquet. Harmondsworth, Penguin, 1967. 345 p. 18 cm. (Pelican books, A253) 8/6 (B67-24457) [BL70.B6] 68-112466
1. Sacred books (Selections: Extracts, etc.) I. Title.

BROWNE, Lewis, 1897- ed. 291.82
The world's great scriptures; an anthology of the sacred books of the ten principal religions, comp. and annotated with historical introductions and interpretative comments by Lewis Browne. With decorations and maps by the ed. New York, Macmillan [1961, c.1946] 559p. (Macmillan paperback, MP54) 2.95 pap.,
1. Sacred books (Selections: Extracts, etc.) I. Title.

BROWNE, Lewis, 1897- ed. 290.82
The world's great scriptures; an anthology of the sacred books of the ten principal religions, compiled and annotated with historical introductions and interpretive comments by Lewis Browne ... With decorations and maps by the editor. New York, The Macmillan company, 1946. xvi, 559 p. illus. (incl. maps) diagr. 24 cm. "First printing." [BL70.B7] 46-8512
1. Sacred books (Selections: Extracts, etc.) I. Title.

CHAMPION, Selwyn Gurney, comp. 208.2
Readings form world religions, complied by Selwyn Gurney Champion and Dorothy Short. Greenwich, Conn., Fawcett Pubns. [1959, c.1951] 319p. (bibl. p. 317-319) 19cm. (Premier bk. d85) .50 pap.,
1. Sacred books (Selections: Extracts, etc.) 2. Religions. I. Short, Dorothy (Field) joint comp. II. Title.

CONWAY, Moncure Daniel, 1832-1907. 291
The sacred anthology; a book of ethnical Scriptures, collected and edited by Moncure Daniel Conway ... New York, H. Holt and company, 1874. viii, 480 p. 23 cm. "Principal authorities": p. [461]-465. [BL1010.C6 1874] 5-18842
1. Sacred books (Selections: Extracts, etc.) 2. Oriental literature. I. Title.

CONWAY, Moncure Daniel, 1832-1907 comp. 291
The sacred anthology (oriental); a book of ethnical scriptures, collected and edited by Moncure Daniel Conway ... 5th ed. New York, H. Holt and co., 1889. xviii, 530 p. 19 1/2 cm. "Principal authorities": p. 507-511. [BL1010.C6 1889] 2-988
1. Sacred books (Selections: Extracts, etc.) 2. Oriental literature. I. Title.

FROST, S. E., 1899- ed. 291.8
The sacred writings of the world's great religions. New York, Perma Giants [1949, c1943] 410 p. 21 cm. [BL70.F7 1949] 49-48174
1. Sacred books (Selections: Extracts, etc.) 2. Religious literature (Selections: Extracts, etc.) I. Title.

FROST, S. E., 1899- ed. 291.8
The sacred writings of the world's great religions, selected and edited by S. E. Frost, jr. ... New York, The New home library [1943] ix, 410 p. 21 cm. [BL70.F7] 43-13666
1. Sacred books (Selections: Extracts, etc.) 2. Religious literature (Selections: Extracts, etc.) I. Title.
Contents omitted.

HUME, Robert Ernest, 1877- comp. 290.822
Treasure-house of the living religions; selections from their sacred scriptures, compiled and edited by Robert Ernest Hume ... New York, London, C. Scribner's sons, 1932. xviii p., 1 l., 3-493 p. 21 1/2 cm. Bibliography: p. 405-443. [BL70.H8] 33-2132
1. Sacred books (Selections: Extracts, etc.) I. Title.

IKBAL 'Ali Shah, Sirdar, ed. 290.822
The spirit of the East; an anthology of the scriptures of the East, with an explanatory introduction [by] the Sirdar Ikbal Ali Shah. London, New York [etc.] T. Nelson and sons, ltd. [1939] vi, 7-277 p. 19 cm. "First published, June, 1939." [BL1010.I 4] 40-7908
1. Sacred books (Selections: Extracts, etc.) 2. Religious literature (Selections: Extracts, etc.) 3. Oriental literature—Translations into English. 4. English literature—Translations from Oriental literature. I. Title.

MARTIN, William Wallace, 1851- 220.52
Ancient religious cults; the cult of Amen, the cult of Aten, the cult of the chosen people, the cult of the crucified, by William Wallace Martin. Nashville, Tenn., The Parthenon press [c1943] ix, 178 p. 16 cm. [BL70.M37] 44-1209
1. Sacred books (Selections: Extracts, etc.) I. Title.

RILEY, Frank Lawrence, 1870- comp. 270
The bible of bibles; a source book of religions, demonstrating the unity of the sacred books of the world, compiled by Frank L. Riley, M. D. Los Angeles, J. F. Rowny press, 1928. 3 p. l., 5-432 p. 25 cm. "A list of the sacred books": p. 33-36. [BL70.R5] 28-20853
1. Sacred books (Selections: Extracts, etc.) I. Title. II. Title: The sacred books of the world.

SACRED books of the world;
a companion source book to Comparative religion. [Harmonds worth, Middlesex, Baltimore] Penguin Books [1959] 345p. (Pelican books, A283) 'First published 1954; reprinted 1955, 1959.' Bibliography: p. [15]-17.
1. Sacred books (Selections; Extracts, etc.) 2. Religious literature (Selections Extracts, etc. I. Bouquet, Alan Coates, 1884- II. Bouquet, Alan Coates, 1884- Comparative relition.

... *Sacred writings* ... 238
with introductions, notes and illustrations. New York, P. F. Collier & son [c1910] 2 v. fronts., plates (part col.) 22 1/2 cm. (The Harvard classics ed. by C. W. Eliot. [vol. XLIV-XLV]) Contents.v. 1. Confucian, Hebrew, Christian (part I)--v. 2. Christian (part II) Buddhist, Hindu, Mohammedan. [BL70.S25] [AC1.A4] 878. 10-20198
1. Sacred books (Selections: Extracts, etc.)

SCHERMERHORN, Martin Kellogg, 1841- comp. 290
Sacred scriptures of the world; being selections of the most devotional and ethical portions of the ancient Hebrew and Christian scriptures, to which have been added kindred selections from other ancient scriptures... compiled, edited, and in part retranslated by Rev. Martin K. Schermerhorn... New York, G. P. Putnam's sons, 1883. xxxi, 406 p. 24 1/2 cm. [BL70.S3 1883] 30-14962
1. Sacred books [Selections: Extracts, etc.] 2. Religious literature [Selections: Extracts, etc.] I. Title.

SCHERMERHORN, Martin Kellogg, 1841- comp. 290
Sacred scriptures of world-religion. 3rd ed., entirely rev., re-translated and re-arranged, with numerous additions from the scriptures of ethnic religions in place of numerous omissions of less important portions of the Jewish and the Christian scriptures; compiled, re-translated, adapted and arranged, by Martin Kellogg Schermerhorn. Cambridge, Mass. [Caustic-Claflin co., printers] 1914. xx, 247 [xxl]-xxiv p. incl. pl. 25 1/2 cm. Published 1913. [BL70.S3 1914] 13-23246
1. Sacred books [Selections: Extracts, etc.] 2. Religious literature [Selections: Extracts, etc.] I. Title.

SOHRAB, Mirza Ahmad, 1891- comp. 290
The Bible of mankind, compiled and edited by Mirza Ahmad Sohrab. New York, Universal publishing co., 1939. xxx, 31-743 p. 25 cm. "First edition April, 1939." "Acknowledgment": p. vii-viii; "Sources" at beginning of each book. Contents.--Hinduism.--Zoroastrianism.--Buddhism.--Confucianism.-- Taoism.--Judaism.--Christianity.--Islam.--The Bahal cause. [BL70.S6] 39-16324
1. Sacred books (Selections: Extracts, etc.) 2. Religions. I. Title.

TURNBULL, Grace Hill, 1880- comp. 290
Tongues of fire; a bible of sacred scriptures of the pagan world, compiled by Grace H. Turnbull ... New York, The Macmillan company, 1929. xxvi, 416 p. 22 1/2 cm. Bibliography: p. 407-416. [BL70.T7] 29-5091
1. Sacred books (Selections: Extracts, etc.) 2. Religious literature (Selections: Extracts, etc.) 3. Oriental literature—Translations into English. 4. English literature—Tranlations from oriental literature. 5. Classical literature—Translations into English. 6. English literature—Translations from classical literature. 7. Philosophy, Ancient. I. Title. II. Title: A bible of sacred scriptures of the pagan world.

TURNBULL, Grace Hill, 1880- comp. 290
Tongues of fire; a bible of sacred scriptures of the non-Christian world, compiled by Grace H. Turnbull ... Baltimore, The Johns Hopkins press, 1941. xxvi, 422 p. 22 cm. "Published January, 1929 ... Second printing June 1941." Bibliography: p. 407-416. [BL70.T7 1941] 42-4099
1. Sacred books (Selections; Extracts, etc.) 2. Religious literature (Selections; Extracts, etc.) 3. Oriental literature—Translations into English. 4. English literature—Translations from oriental literature. 5. Classical literature—Translations into English. 6. English literature—Translations from classical literature. 7. Philosophy, Ancient. I. Title. II. Title: A bible of sacred scriptures of the non-Christian world.

... *World Bible,* 290
edited by Robert O. Ballou. New York, The Viking press, 1944. xviii, 605 p. illus. 17 cm. (The Viking portable library) "The gist of each of the world's eight most influential religious faiths, as revealed by their basic scriptures."--General introd., p. 13. "Condensed from The Bible of the world." Bibliography: p. xv-xviii. [BL70.W6] 44-4542
1. Sacred books (Selections: Extracts, etc.) I. Ballou, Robert Oleson, 1892- ed.

The Sacred harp, a collection of psalm and hymn tunes, odes, and anthems.

COBB, Buell. 783.6'7
The sacred harp : a tradition and its music / Buell Cobb. Athens : University of Georgia Press, c1978. p. cm. Includes index. [ML3111.C6] 77-6323 ISBN 0-8203-0426-3 : 10.00
1. The Sacred harp, a collection of psalm and hymn tunes, odes, and anthems. 2. Hymns, English—History and criticism. 3. Church music—Southern States. I. Title.

Sacred Heart Church, Alamosa, Colo.

CARTER, Carrol Joe. 282'.788'36
Rocky Mountain religion : a history of Sacred Heart Parish, Alamosa, Colorado / by Carrol Joe Carter. Alamosa, Colo. : Sangre de Cristo Print., c1976. 106 p. : ill. ; 25 cm. [BX4603.A58S222] 76-375228 6.00
1. Sacred Heart Church, Alamosa, Colo. I. Title.

Sacred Heart Church, Hebron, Neb.

A Bicentennial centennial history, Sacred Heart Church, Hebron, Nebraska, 1876-1976. 282'.782'335
Hebron, Neb. : Sacred Heart Church, c1976. vi, 205 p. : ill. ; 28 cm. Cover title: The bell of Sacred Heart Church. Includes index. [BX4603.H38S22] 76-24301

1. Sacred Heart Church, Hebron, Neb. 2. Hebron, Neb.—Biography. I. Title: The bell of Sacred Heart Church.

Sacred Heart, Devotion to.

APOSTLESHIP of prayer.
League devotions especially adapted for members of the Apostleship of prayer in league with the sacred heart, with choral service for the first Friday of the month. New York, Central office of the Apostleship of prayer, [1914.] 152 p. 12 cm. "Revised edition." 14-12460
I. Title.

ARCHCONFRATERNITY of the Guard of honor of the Sacred heart of Jesus. 264.02
...Manual of the Archconfraternity of the Guard of honor of the Sacret heart of Jesus. Translated from the French. 1st ed... Brooklyn, N.Y., Monastery of the visitation, 1885. xxvii, 365 p. incl. front., plates (1 col.) 15 1/2 cm. At head of title: Hail Jesus. Compiled by Soeur Marie du Sacre Cocur. [BX2055.G8 1895] 39-8729
1. Sacred heart, Devotion to. 2. Catholic church—Prayer books and devotions—English. 3. Marie du Sacre Cocur, Soeur, 1826-1903. comp. I. Title.

ARCHONFRATERNITY of the Guard of honor of the Sacred heart of Jesus. 264.02
...Manual and other approved prayers of the Arch-confraternity of the Guard of honor of the Sacred heart of Jesus. Translated from the French. 3d ed., rev... Brooklyn, N. Y., Monastery of the visitation 1894? xxvii, 385 p. incl. front. plates (1 col.) 15 1/2 cm. At head of title: Hail Jesus. Compiled by Soeur Marie du Sacre Cocur. [BX2055.G8 1894] 39-3958
1. Sacred heart, Devotion to. 2. Catholic church—Prayer-books and devotions—English. I. Marie du Sacre Cocur, soeur, 1825-1903. comp. II. Title.

ARNOUDT, Pierre, 1811-1865. 242
The imitation of the Sacred heart of Jesus. By Rev. F. Arnoudt, S.J. Translated from the Latin by I. M. Fastre. New ed., with morning and evening prayers, devotions for mass, confession, communion, etc. New York, Cincinnati [etc.] Benziger brothers, 1904. 734 p. front. 15 cm. [Full name: Pierre Jean Arnoudt] [BX2157.A7 1904] 4-13638
1. Sacred heart. Devotion to. I. Fastre, Joseph, 1823-1878 tr. II. Title.

ARNOUDT, Pierre, 1811-1865. 242
The limitation of the Sacred heart of Jesus. By Rev. F. Arnoudt, S. J. Translated from the Latin by I. M. Fastre. New ed., with morning and evening prayers, devotions for mass, confession, communion, etc. New York, Cincinnati [etc.] Benziger brothers, 1896. xxii, 810 p. 15 1/2 cm. [Full name: Pierre Jean Arnoudt] [BX2157.A7 1896] 38-11661
1. Sacred heart, Devotion to. I. Fastre, Joseph, 1823-1878 tr. II. Title.

ARNOUDT, Pierre, 1811-1865. 242
Of the imitation of the Sacred heart of Jesus. Four books. By the Rev. P. J. Arnoudt ... translated from the Latin by the Rev. J. A. M. Fastre ... Cincinnati, J. P. Walsh, 1865. 2 p. l., iii-xxii, 774 p. front. 19 cm. [Full name: Pierre Jean Arnoudt] [BX2157.A7 1865] 38-11660
1. Sacred heart, Devotion to. I. Fastre, Joseph, 1823-1878 tr. II. Title.

BECHARD, Henri. 922.246
The visions of Bernard Francis de Hoyos, S. J., apostle of the Sacred Heart in Spain a biography. [1st ed.] New York, Vantage Press[1959] 178p. illus. 21cm. Includes bibliography. [BV5095.H6B4] 59-8423
1. Hoyos, Bernardo Francisco de, 1711-1735. 2. Sacred Heart, Devotion to. 3. Visions. I. Title.

BERRY, L Claude.
The favorite and favors of the Sacred heart of Jesus, tr. from the French of l'Abbe L. C. Berry, by a sister of mercy. New York, Christian press association publishing company, 1908. 243 p. 19 cm. 8-8277
I. Title.

BIERBAUM, Ewald. 264.021
Six sermons on devotion to the Sacred heart. By Rev. Ewald Bierbaum, D. D. Translated from the German by Miss Ella Mcmahon. New York, Cincinnati [etc.] Benziger brothers, 1888. 106 p. 18 cm. [BX2157.B55] 37-23892
1. Sacred heart. Devotion to. 2. Catholic church—Sermons. 3. Sermons, German—Translations into English. 4. Sermons, English—Translations from German. I. McMahon, Ella, tr. II. Title.

BLUNT, Hugh Francis, 1877- 242
The heart aflame, thoughts on devotion to the Sacred heart, by the Rt. Rev. Hugh F. Blunt, LL.D. Milwaukee, The Bruce publishing company [1947] ix p., 1 l., 127 p. 20 1/2 cm. (Half-title: Religion and culture series; Joseph Husslein, general ed.) [BX2157.B63] 47-23430
1. Sacred heart, Devotion to. I. Title.

BOUGAUD, Emile, 1824-1888 922.
Life of Saint Margaret Mary Alacoque by Rt. Rev. E. Bougaud... New York, Cincinnati [etc.] Benziger brothers [1920] 2 p. l., 7-339 p. front., plates, port, facsim. 21 cm. (Full name: Louis Victor Emile Bougaud) [BX4700.A37B6 1920] 20-23035
1. Alacoque, Marguerite Marie, Saint, 1647-1690. 2. Sacred heart, Devotion to. I. Title.

CARTHUSIANS. 264.02
Ancient devotions to the Sacred Heart of Jesus by Carthusian monks of the XIV-XVII centuries. [4th ed.] Westminster, Md., Newman Press [1954] 232p. illus. 16cm. [BX2158.C3 1954] 54-9088
1. Sacred Heart, Devotion to. I. Title.

CATHOLIC Church. Pope (Pius XII), 1939-1958, Haurietis Aquas (15 may, 1956) English. 264.021
The Sacred Heart; a commentary on Haurietis aquas [by] Alban J. Dachauer. Milwaukee, Bruce Pub. Co. [1959] 209p. 23cm. 'The translation of Haurietis aquas is taken ... from the Catholic mind of October, 1956.' [BX2157.A45D3] 59-10966
1. Sacred Heart, Devotion to. I. Dachauer, Alban J. II. Title.

CHARMOT, Francois. 242
In retreat with the Sacred Heart; translated by Sister Maria Constance. Westminster, Md., Newman Press, 1956. 221p. 24cm. In verse. [BX2157.C553] 56-9985
1. Sacred Heart, Devotion to. I. Title.

CRAWLEY-BOEVEY, Mateo. 264.021
... Jesus, King of love, by Rev. Mateo Crawley-Boevey, ss, cc. 2d ed., rev. and enl. Translated from the Spanish. Fairhaven, Mass., The National center of the enthronement [c1933] 2 p. l., vii-xvi, 365 p. 18 cm. [BX2157.C75 1933] 33-9372
1. Sacred heart, Devotion to. I. Title.

CRAWLEY-BOEVEY, Mateo, 1875- 264.021
... Jesus, king of love, by Father Mateo Crawley-Boevey, SS.CC. 4th ed., rev. and enl. Fairhaven, Mass., The National center of the enthronement [1945] xiii, 301 p. 18 cm. [BX2157.C75 1945] 45-5227
1. Sacred heart, Devotion to. I. Title. II. Title: Translation of Vers le Roi d'amour.

CRAWLEY-BOEVEY, Mateo, 1875-1960. 264.025
Jesus, King of Love. 5th ed., rev. and enl. Pulaski, Wis., Franciscan Publishers [1963] 318 p. 20 cm. Translation of Versle Roi d'amour. [BX2157.C75 1963] 63-10258
1. Sacred Heart, Devotion to. I. Title.

CRAWLEY-BOEVEY, Mateo, 1875-1960 264.025
Jesus, King of Love [Tr. from French] 5th ed., rev. and enl. Pulaski, Wis., Franciscan [c.1963] 318p. 20cm 63-10258 2.50; 1.25 pap.,
1. Sacred Heart, Devotion to. I. Title.

DEHON, Leon Gustave, 1843-1925. 242
The life of love towards the Sacred Heart of Jesus; thirty-three meditations for the month of the Sacred Heart, tr. from the French by Sister M. Jocelyn. [n.p., c1945] ix, 229 p. 16 cm. [BX2158.D4] 47-29989
1. Sacred heart, Devotion to. I. Jocelyn, Sister, tr. II. Title.

DEVINE, Arthur.
The Sacred heart, the source of grace and virtue; sermons for the devotion of the Sacred heart, by Rev. Arthur Devine, C. P. New York, J. F. Wagner [c1912] 122 p. 20 cm. 13-8870 0.75
I. Title.

DONNELLY, Francis Patrick, 1869- 264.
The heart of revelation, further traits of the Sacred heart [by] Francis P. Donnelly ... Rev. ed. New York, P. J. Kenedy & sons, 1917. v p. 1 l., 267 p. 17 cm. "Companion volume to "The heart of the Gospel.'" [BX2157.D62] 18-15269
1. Sacred heart, Devotion to. I. Title.

DONNELLY, Francis Patrick, 1869- 264.02
The heart of the church; the Sacred heart in the liturgy [by] Francis P. Donnelly, S. J. New York city, W. J. Hirten co., inc. [1937] 206 p. incl. front. 15 cm. [BX2158.D6] 40-9399
1. Sacred heart, Devotion to. 2. Catholic church—Prayer-book and devotions—English. I. Title.

DONNELLY, Francis Patrick, 1869- 264.
The heart of the Gospel, traits of the sacred heart [by] Francis P. Donnelly ... Rev. ed. New York, P. J. Kenedy & sons, 1917. x p., l., 237 p. 17 cm. [BX2157.D6] 18-15266
I. Title.

DOOLEY, Lester M., 1898- 264.021
The love of the Sacred Heart. Milwaukee, Bruce Pub. Co. [1947] x, 108 p. 21 cm. [BX2157.D65] 47-5000
1. Sacred Heart, Devotion to. I. Title.

ENTHRONEMENT of the Sacred Heart of Jesus. St. Paul Minn., Catechetical Guild Educational Society, 1956. 384p. front. (port) 17 cm.
1. Crawley-Boevey, Mateo, 1875- 2. Sacred Heart, Devotion to. I. Larkin, Francis.

ENTRHONEMENT of the Sacred Heart of Jesus. St. Paul, Minn., Catechetical Guild Educational Society, 1956. 384p. front. (port.) 17cm.
1. Sacred Heart, Devotion to. 2. Crawley—Boevey, Mateo, 1875- I. Larkin, Francis.

EUDES, Jean, Saint, 1601-1680. 242
The Sacred heart of Jesus, by Saint John Eudes, translated by Dom. Richard Flower ... With an introduction by the Reverend Gerald B. Phelan ... New York, P. J. Kennedy & sons, 1946. xxx p., 1 l., 183 p. front. (port.) pl. 21 cm. [BX2157.E82] 46-4658
1. Sacred heart, Devotion to. I. Flower, Richard, 1890- tr. II. Title. III. Title: Translation of Le coeur admirable de la tres sacree Mere de Dieu.

GARESCHE, Edward Francis, 1876- 264.
The Sacred heart and the Catholic home [by] Edward F. Garesche ... Milwaukee, Wis., The Bruce publishing company [c1927] 126 p. front. 20 cm. [BX2157.G3] 28-951
I. Title.

THE glories of the Sacred Heart, by Henry Edward. 5th ed. Longon, Burns & Oates; New York, Catholic Publication Society Co. [19-?] xii, 302p. 20cm.
1. Sacred Heart, Devotion to. I. Manning, Henry Edward, Cardinal, 1808-1892.

HAUSHERR, Melchior, 1830-1888. 248
The glories of the sacred heart of Jesus ...instructions and exhortations taken from or composed in the spirit of the writings of Blessed Margaret Mary, together with an enumeration of the various devotions to the sacred heart of Jesus, from the original of Rev. M. Hausherr, S.J., with preface by Rev. John J. Wynne, S.J. New York, Cincinnati, [etc.] Benziger brothers, 1906. iv, 8, v-xv p., 1 l., 28-544 p. front. 15 1/2 cm. [BX2158.M35 1906] 6-38884
1. Sacred heart, Devotion to. 2. Catholic church—Prayer-books and devotions—English. I. Alacoque, Marqurite Marie, Saint, 1647-1699. II. Title.

KELLER, Joseph A.
The Sacred Heart. Anecdotes and examples to assist in promoting the devotion to the Sacred Heart. From the original of Rev. Dr. Joseph Keller. New York, Cincinnati [etc.] Benziger bros., 1899. 256 p. 16 cm. [BX2157.K3] 99-1987
1. Sacred Heart, Devotion to. I. Title.

KONZ, F. 242
The Sacred heart of Christ. spiritual readings, by Rev. F. Knoz, o. M. I. New York, Chicago [etc.] Benziger brothers, 1936. xiv, 258 p. front. 20 cm. [BX2158.K6] 36-37287
1. Sacred heart, Devotion to. 2. Devotional exercises. 3. Meditations. I. Title.

LARKIN, Francis 242
Enthronement of the sacred heart. [2d rev. angm. ed.] New York, Guild Press; distributed by Golden Press [c.1956, 1960] 416p. (Angelus books) Bibl.: 60-4950 .408-412 front. 17cm. .95 bds.,
1. Crawley-Boevey, Mateo, 1875- 2. Sacred Heart, Devotion. 3. Sacred Heart of Mary, Devotion to. I. Title.

LARKIN, Francis. 242
Enthronement of the Sacred Heart. [2d rev. augm. ed.] New York, Guild Press; distrubuted by Golden Press [1960] 416p. illus. 17cm. (Angelus books) Includes bibliography. [BX2157.L33 1960] 60-4950
1. Sacred Heart, Devotion to. 2. Sacred Heart of Mary, Devotion to. I. Crawley-Boevey, Mateo, 1875- II. Title.

LEPICIER, Alexis Henri Marie, cardinal, 1863-1936. 264.
Jesus Christ, The King of our hearts; elevations on the most Sacred heart of Jesus, by Very Rev. Alexis M. Lepicier... New York, Cincinnati [etc.] Benziger brothers 1921. 264 p. front. 19 cm. [BX2157.L4] 21-19599
1. Sacred heart, Devotion to. I. Title.

LEVY, Rosalie Marie, comp. 242
Heart talks with Jesus. Fifth series. Compiled and edited by Rosalie Marie Levy. New York, N.Y., Rosalie M. Levy [c1935] 6 p. l., 180 p. illus. 14 cm. Prose and verse. Advertising matter: p. 176-180. [BX2158.L4 5th ser.] 35-20276
1. Sacred Heart, Devotion to. 2. Catholic church—Prayer-books and devotions—English. I. Title.

LEVY, Rosalie Marie, 1889- comp. 248
Heart talks with Jesus. Fifth series. Compiled and edited by Rosalie Marie Levy. (2d ed.) [New York. Catholic book publishing company, 1944] 6 p. l., 179 p. illus. 13 1/2 cm. Verse and prose. [BX2158.L4 1944] 44-46886
1. Sacred heart, Devotion to. 2. Catholic church—Prayer-books and devotions—English. I. Title.

THE Little manual of devotion, to the Sacred heart of Jesus. 242
A.M.D.G. Cincinnati, J. P. Walsh, 1867. 171 p. 11 1/2 cm. With this is bound, as issued: Spiritual bouquet, offered by pious souls, to the Sacred heart of Jesus. By a father of the Society of Jesus ... Cincinnati, 1867. [BX2158.L6] 43-49160
1. Sacred heart, Devotion to. 2. Catholic church—Prayer-books and devotions—English. I. Title: Manual of devotion, to the Sacred heart of Jesus.

LITTLE manual of the Sacred heart. 242
A collection of instructions, prayers, hymns, and various practices of piety. In honor of the Sacred heart of Jesus. Compiled and adapted from approved sources ... New York, Sullivan & Schaefer, 1883. 2 p. l., [iii]-ix, [1], [11]-124 p. front., illus., plates. 12 1/2 cm. [BX2158.L65] 43-49157
1. Sacred heart, Devotion to. 2. Catholic church—Prayer-books and devotions—English.

MACDONALD, Alexander, bp., 1858- 264.
The mercies of the Sacred heart; twelve sermons for the first Fridays, by the Very Rev. Alex. MacDonald, D.D. New York, J. F. Wagner [1904] 2 p. l., 56 p. 21 cm. [BX2157.M2] 4-6093
1. Sacred heart, Devotion to. 2. Catholic church—Sermons. 3. Sermons, American. I. Title.

MCGRATTY, Arthur R, 1909- 264.021
The Sacred Heart yesterday and today; with a supplement containing prayers and devotions to the Sacred Heart. New York, Benziger, 1951. xiv. 306 p. col. front. 21 cm. Bibliography: p. 300-302. [BX2157.M25] 51-4497
1. Sacred Heart, Devotion to. I. Title.

MANUAL of the Sacred Heart. 242
Compiled and translated from approved sources. New rev. ed. Philadelphia, H. L. Kilner & co. [c1904] v, 6-355 p. illus. 13 cm. Cover-title: New Manual of the Sacred Heart. [BX2158.M3 1904] 43-49156
1. Sacred heart, Devotion to. 2. Catholic church—Prayer-books and devotions—English.

MARY Emmanuel, sister, 264.021
1873-
Month of the Sacred heart, by Sister Mary Emmanuel ... St. Louis, Mo. and London, B. Herder book co., 1930. vi, 294 p. 19 1/2 cm. [Secular name: Mary Josephine Irwin] Bibliography included in preface. [BX2158.M45] 31-1506
1. Sacred heart. Devotion to. I. Title.

[MARY MILDRED, Sister] 1876- 242
The heart of the King, by a Sister of Mercy. [n.p.] St. Paul Editions [c1956] 140p. 20cm. [BX2157.M27] 59-25206
1. Sacred Heart, Devotion to. I. Title.

MATULICH, Silvano, father. 232
The heart of the King [by] Silvano Matulich, O.F.M. Milwaukee, The Bruce publishing company [c1935] xiv p., 2 l., 3-133 p. incl. front. 19 cm. [Secular name: George Joseph Matulich] [BT205.M38] 36-226
1. Jesus Christ—Person and offices. 2. Sacred heart, Devotion to. I. Title.

MURPHY, John J. S.J. 242
June prayers; a flower for each day of the month of June, by John J. Murphy, S.J. Philadelphia, The Peter Reilly company, 1943. 3 p. l., 113 p. 17 cm. [BX2158.M85] 43-14355
1. Rufinus Tyrannius, Aquileiensis, 345] ca:—410. 2. Rufinus Tyrannius, Aquileiensis, 345 (ca)—410 3. Sacred heart, Devotion to. I. Title.

NEW manual of the Sacred Heart. Containing the most approved prayers and devotions. New York, Cincinnati [etc.] Benziger bros. [1900] 398 p. incl. front. mar. 24 degrees. 0-6945

NOLDIN, Hieronymus, 1838- 232.
1922.
The devotion to the Sacred heart of Jesus. Intended specially for priests and candidates for the priesthood. By the Rev. H. Noldin ... Authorized translation from the German. Revised by the Rev. W. H. Kent, O. S. C. New York, Cincinnati [etc.] Benziger brothers, 1905. 272 p. 19 cm. [BX2157.N7] 5-8082
1. Sacred heart, Devotion to. I. Kent, William Henry, 1857- II. Title.

PESCH, Christian, 1853- 232.9
1925.
Our best Friend, translated by Bernard A. Hausmann from the German. Milwaukee, Bruce Pub. Co. [1953] 220p. 23cm. [BX2157.P35 1953] 53-2238
1. Sacred Heart, Devotion to. I. Title.

PESCH, Christian, 1853- 232.9
1925.
Our best Friend; from the German by Christian Pesch, S. J., translated by Bernard A. Hausmann, S. J. Milwaukee, The Bruce publishing company [c1931] x, 265 p. 21 cm. [BX2157.P35] 31-3789
1. Jesus Christ. 2. Sacred heart, Devotion to. I. Hausmann, Bernard Andrew, tr. II. Title.

SCHMID, Max, 1875- 264.021
Guide for victim souls of the Sacred heart, compiled by Very Rev. Joseph Kreuter ... New York, Boston [etc.] Benziger brothers, 1939. xiv, 236 p. incl. front., port. pl. 17 cm. "In 1920 the first 'Manual for victim souls of the Sacred heart' was published in Germany by the Rev. Max Schmid."--Pref. [BX2157.S37 1939] 39-14089
1. Sacred heart, Devotion to. 2. Association of victim souls in union with the sacred hearts of Jesus and Mary. I. Kreuter, Joseph, 1888- comp. II. Title. III. Title: Victim souls of the Sacred heart, Guide for.

SCHMID, Max, 1875- 264.021
Manual for victim souls of the Sacred heart, by Rev. Max Schmid, S. J.; translated from the ninth German edition. [Chicago, Ill., Loyola university press, c1932] xxx, 522 p. 14 cm. "Preface to English edition" signed: R. B. [i. e. Richard Brunner] [BX2157.S35] 33-8766
1. Sacred heart, Devotion to. I. Brunner, Richard, tr. II. Title. III. Title: Victim souls of the Sacred heart, Manual for.

SCHOENHERR, Irenaeus Martin, 242
father, 1879-
Sacred heart manual. The spirit of the first Friday, honor for dishonor, gratitude for ingratitude, fervor for coldness, by Rev. Irenaeus Schoenherr, O. F. M. 2d ed. rev. New York, N. Y., Catholic book publishing co. [c1936] xii p., 1 l., 259 p. col. front., illus., col. plates. 12 cm. [Secular name: William Schoenherr] [BX2158.S35 1936] 36-18295
1. Sacred heart, Devotion to. 2. Catholic church—Prayer-books and devotions—English. I. Title.

SPIRITUAL bouquet, offerec by pious souls, to the Sacred heart of Jesus. 242
By a father of the Society of Jesus. Tranlated from the French ... Cincinnati, J. P. Walsh, 1867. 71 p. 11 1/2 cm.]With, as issued: The Little manual of devotion, to the Sacred heart of Jesus...Cincinnati, 1867: [BX2158.L6] 43-49382
1. Sacred heart, Devotion to. I. A father of the Society of Jesus.

STIERLI, Josef, ed. 264.021
Heart of the Saviour; a symposium on devotion to the Sacred Heart. With contributions by Richard Gutzwiller, Hugo Rahner and Karl Rahner. English translation by Paul Andrews. [New York] Herder and Herder [1958] ix, 267 p. 23 cm. Translation of Cor Salvatoris. Bibliography: p. 261-262. [BX2157.S75] 58-5868
1. Sacred Heart, Devotion to. I. Gutzwiller, Richard. II. Title.

VERHEYLEZOON, Louis. 248
Devotion to the Sacred Heart: object, ends, practice, motives. With a foreword by C. C. Martindale. Westminster, Md., Newman Press [1955] 280p. 23cm. [BX2157.V43] 55-14740
1. Sacred Heart, Devotion to. I. Title.

VON HILDEBRAND, Dietrich, 248
1889-
The heart : an analysis of human and divine affectivity / Dietrich von Hildebrand. Chicago : Franciscan Herald Press, c1977. 182 p. ; 22 cm. Published in 1965 under title: The sacred heart. Includes bibliographical references. [BX2157.V6 1977] 76-52744 ISBN 0-8199-0665-4 : 6.95
1. Sacred Heart, Devotion to. I. Title.

VON HILDEBRAND, Dietrich, 248
1889-
The sacred heart; an analysis of human and divine affectivity. Helicon [dist. New York, Taplinger, c.1965] 182p. 21cm. [BX2157.V6] 65-24130 4.50
1. Sacred Heart, Devotion to. I. Title.

VON HILDEBRAND, Dietrich, 248
1889-
The sacred heart; an analysis of human and divine affectivity. Baltimore, Helicon [1965] 182 p. 21 cm. [BX2157.V6] 65-24130
1. Sacred Heart, Devotion to. I. Title.

WILLIAMS, Margaret Anne, 264.021
1902-
The Sacred Heart in the life of the church. New York, Sheed and Ward [1957] 248 p. 22 cm. [BX2157.W5] 57-10176
1. Sacred Heart, Devotion to. I. Title.

Sacred heart, Devotion to—Meditations.

ARCHONFRATERNITY of the Guard of honor of the Sacred heart of Jesus. 242
...The holy year of the Guards of honor and friends of the Sacred heart of Jesus. Translated from the French. Revised by the Sisters of the visitation... Brooklyn, Monastery of the visitation [1892] xxix, 363 p. illus. 19 1/2 cm. Compiled by Soeur Marie du Sacre Cocur. At head of title: Vive Jesus "The following pages first appeared in the Monthly bulletin of the Guard of honor under the Salesian form of cartels."--p. vii. [BX2055.G8 1892] 39-8721
1. Sacred heart, Devotion to—Meditations. I. Marie du Sacre Cocur, sorur, 1825-1906, comp. II. Sisters of the visitation, Brooklyn, N.Y., ed. III. Title.

BRANSIET, Phillipe, frere, 232.9
1792-1874.
Meditations on the Sacred heart of Jesus, by Brother Philip ... New and rev. ed. Authorized English version. New York, La Salle bureau, 1911. iii p., 1 l., 153 p. 19 cm. [Secular name: Matthieu Bransiet] [BX2157.B66 1911] 12-6666
1. Sacred heart, Devotion to—Meditations. I. Title.

LANZI, Father.
Short discourses and considerations on the sacred heart of Jesus, and the sacred heart of Mary. Translated from the Italian of Father Lanzi. New ed. New York, Christian press association, 1906. 1 p. l., [xiii]-xvi, 333 p. 13 cm. 7-6730
I. Title.

LASANCE, Francis Xavier.
The sacred heart book. By Rev. F. X. Lasance ... New York, Cincinnati [etc.] Benziger brothers, 1903. 638 p. front., pl. 14 x 9 cm. 3-8453
I. Title.

MOFFATT, John Edward, 1894- 232.9
... Thoughts on the heart of Jesus, by Rev. J. E. Moffatt, S.J. Milwaukee, The Bruce publishing co. [c1933] 3 p. l., 5-91 p. incl. front. 14 cm. (Minute meditations. ser. II) [BX2158.M6] 242 33-15116
1. Sacred heart, Devotion to—Meditations. I. Title.

NAUER, Lorenz, 1875- 242
First Fridays with the Sacred heart, by the Rev. L. Nauer, M. S. C., adapted from the German by the Rev. B. Greifenberg, M. S. C. Aurora, Ill., Sacred heart monastery [c1937] 380, [3] p. incl. front., illus. 13 cm. "Meditations ... [and] devotions for holy communion."--Pref. Translation of Die andachtige feier des Herz-Jesu-freitags. [BX2158.N47] 38-6778
1. Sacred heart, Devotion to—Meditations. 2. Lord's supper—Prayer-books and devotions—English. I. Greifenberg, Bineaus Bernard, father, 1885- tr. II. Title.

Sacred Heart, Devotion to—Miscellanea.

LARKIN, Francis. 232
Understanding the Heart / by Francis Larkin. 2d, rev. ed. San Francisco : Ignatius Press, c1980. 127 p. ; 19 cm. [BX2157.L335 1980] 19 80-81066 ISBN 0-89870-007-8 pbk. : Price Unreported
1. Sacred Heart, Devotion to—Miscellanea. 2. Sacred Heart of Mary, Devotion to—Miscellanea. I. Title.

Sacred Heart, Devotion to—Study and teaching.

DIEHL, Thomas, ed. 248
Teaching the devotion to the Sacred Heart. Eds.: Thomas Diehl, John Hardon. Chicago, Loyola [c.]1963. 242p. 24cm. Bibl. 63-3368 4.00
1. Sacred Heart, Devotion to—Study and teaching. I. Hardon, John A., joint ed. II. Title.

DIEHL, Thomas, ed. 248
Teaching the devotion to the Sacred Heart. Editors: Thomas Diehl [and] John Hardon. Chicago, Loyola University Press, 1963. 242 p. 24 cm. [BX2157.D5] 63-3368
1. Sacred Heart, Devotion to — Study and teaching. I. Harden, John A., joint ed. II. Title.

Sacred Heart of Mary, Devotion to.

BAINVEL, Jean Vincent, 232.931
1858-1937.
And the light shines in the darkness; a way of life through Mary. Translated by John J. Sullivan. New York, Benziger Bros [1953] 239p. 21cm. Translation of Le saint coeur de Marie. [BX2160.3.B253] 53-9641
1. Sacred Heart of Mary, Devotion to. I. Title.

ENDES, Jean, Saint, 1601- 232.931
1680.
The admirable Heart of Mary, tr. from the French by Charles di Targiani and Ruth Hauser, with a foreword by Richard J. Cushing. New York, P. J. Kenedy, 1948. xxi, 365 p. plates, port. 22 cm. (Selected works of Saint Joha Eudes) [BX2160.3.E82] 48-10713
1. Sacred Heart of Mary, Devotion to. I. Title.

MURPHY, John F 1922- 232.931
Mary's Immaculate Heart; the meaning of the devotion to the Immaculate Heart of Mary. Milwaukee, Bruce [1951] xiii, 127 p. 20 cm. Bibliography: p. 121-127. [BX2160.3.M8] 51-2735
1. Sacred Heart of Mary, Devotion to. I. Title.

STRATER, Paul. 232.931
The heart of Mary, sacrificial altar of Christ's love. Translated by Mother Mary Aloysi Kiener. New York, F. Pustet Co., 1957. 170p. 22cm. [BX2160.3.S8] 57-31387
1. Sacred Heart of Mary, Devotion to. I. Title.

STRATER, Paul. 232.931
The heart of Mary, sacrificial altar of Christs' love, Translated by Mother Mary Aloysi Kiener. New York, F. Pustet Co., 1957. 170 p. 22 cm. [BX2160.3.S8] 57-31387
1. Sacred Heart of Mary, Devotion to. I. Title.

Sacred literature (Selections: Extracts, etc.)

ORIENTAL treasures. 291.8/2
[Ed. by Edward Lewis, Robert Myers] With reprods. from the oriental collection of the William Rockhill Nelson Gallery of Art-Atkins Museum. [Kansas City, Mo.] Hallmark Eds. [1967] 62p. col. illus. 20cm. [BL1010.O7] 67-17882 2.50 bds.,
1. Sacred literature (Selections: Extracts, etc.) I. Lewis, Edward W. ed. II. Myers, Robert J. ed. III. William Rockhill Nelson Gallery of Art and Mary Atkins Museum of Fine Arts, Kansas City. Mo.
Contents Omitted.

Sacred meals.

DROWER, Ethel Stepana 291.3
(Stevens) Lady
Water into wine; a study of ritual idiom in the Middle East. London, Murray [Mystic, Conn., Verry, 1965] 273p. illus. 23cm. [BL619.S3D7] 56-4507 6.00
1. Sacred meals. 2. Lord's Supper. I. Title.

Sacred songs.

BARBER, Edward, 1878-1914.
Sacred Scripture in song and story, by Edward Barber ... introductory by Dr. James Crutchfield ... Baltimore, Williams & Wilkins company, 1914. ix. 158 p. front. (port.) 19 1/2 cm. 15-538 1.25
I. Title.

EVERFLOWING streams : 783.9'52
songs of worship / Ruth C. Duck, Michael G. Bausch, editors. New York : Pilgrim Press, 1981. p. cm. For 1-4 voices; in part with keyboard acc. and/or chord symbols. Includes index. [M2198.E915] 19 81-701 ISBN 0-8298-0428-5 (pbk.) : 3.95
1. Sacred songs. 2. Hymns, English. I. Duck, Ruth C., 1947- II. Bausch, Michael G., 1949-

PORTSMOUTH, N. H. South parish.
A collection of sacred music for the use of the South parish in Portsmouth. Exeter [N. H.] Printed by C. Norris & co., 1814. 134 p., 1 l. 10 x 26 cm. [M2116.C7] 17-5213
I. Title.

WHARTON, Morton Bryan.
Sacred songs composed to popular airs. A collection of original hymns, consecrating

to the service of God the most beautiful and familiar secular tunes known to the world. By Morton Bryan Wharton ... Atlanta, Ga., The Franklin printing & publishing co., 1904. v. 120 p. 12 1/2 cm. 5-4059
I. Title.

Sacred songs (Medium voice) with organ.

FISHER, William Arms, 1861-
Bible songs, by Wm. Arms Fisher. Op. 2 ... New York, Luckhardt & Belder; [etc., etc., 1895] 4 v. 34 x 27 cm. Publisher's plate nos.: L. & B. 179-182. For solo voice with organ accompaniment: v. 1 contains violin obbligato part. Contents.no. 1. Hide not Thou Thy face.--no. 2. Save me O God--no. 3. The Lord is my light.--no. 4. I have not the Lord always before me. [M2113.F] 44-44617
1. Sacred songs (Medium voice) with organ. I. Title.

FISHER, William Arms, 1861-
Bible songs, by Wm. Arms Fisher ... Op. 6. For fetal use ... New York, Luckhardt & Belder; [etc., etc., c1896] 3 v. 34 x 27 cm. Publisher's plate nos.: L. & B. 300-302. For solo voice with organ accompaniment. Contents.no. 1. O give thanks unto the Lord.--no. 2. There were shepherds abiding in the field.--no. 3. The first day of the week cometh Mary Magdalene. [M2113.F] 44-44618
1. Sacred songs (Medium voice) with organ. I. Title.

Sacred songs (Medium voice) with piano.

HARRELL, Mack, 1909- ed. and arr.
The sacred hour of song, a collection of sacred solos suitable for Christians science services, compiled, edited and arranged by Mack Harrell. New York, Boston [etc.] C. Fischer inc. [1939] 67 p. 30 1/2 cm. On cover: Medium voice. Publisher's plate no.: 28754. With piano accompaniment. [M2110.H3S3] 44-44444
1. Sacred songs (Medium voice) with piano. I. Title.

NOEL: The Joan Baez 783.65
Christmas songbook. Illus. by Eric von Schmidt. Arrangements by Peter Schickele. Ed. by Maynard Solomon. Designed by Jules Halfant. [1st ed.] New York, Ryerson Music Pubs. [1967] 64p. col. illus. 28cm. Arrangements for voice and piano ... with complete chord progressions and capo-key indications for the guitarist. [M2110.N69] 67-125511 2.50 pap.,
1. Sacred songs (Medium voice) with piano. 2. Carols. 3. Christmas music. I. Schickele, Peter. arr. II. Solomon, Maynard. ed. III. Title: The Joan Baez Christmas songbook.
Distributed by Crown, New York.

Sacred songs with organ—Bibliography.

ESPINA, Noni. 016.7836'75'1
Vocal solos for Protestant services: a descriptive reference of solo music for the church year, including a bibliographical supplement of choral works; sacred repertoire for concert and teaching. 2d ed., rev. and enl. New York, Vita d'Arte [1974] xvii, 218 p. 22 cm. "A list of choral music": p. 133-144. [ML128.V7E8 1974] 74-169256
1. Sacred songs with organ—Bibliography. 2. Choral music—Bibliography. I. Title.

Sacred songs with piano.

ARNOLD, Jay, arr.
Sacred songs the people sing, compiled and arranged by Jay Arnold. New York, N. Y., Manhattan publications, c1941. 96 p. 31 cm. For solo voice with piano accompaniment; words in English, or in original language with English translation. [M2110.A77S3] 45-47425
1. Sacred songs with piano. I. Title.

EHRET, Walter, comp. 783.9'5'2
The international book of sacred song [by] Walter Ehret, Melinda Edwards [and] George K. Evans. Woodcuts by Fritz Kredel. Englewood Cliffs, N.J., Prentice-Hall [1969] xiv, 270 p. illus. 29 cm. With easy piano accompaniments and chord indications. "Some notes about the hymns": p. 244-264. [M2110.E43I5] 78-76456 ISBN 0-13-471656-6 12.95
1. Sacred songs with piano. 2. Hymns, English. I. Edwards, Melinda, joint comp. II. Evans, George K., joint comp. III. Kredel, Fritz, 1900- illus. IV. Title.

HILES, John, 1810-1882, ed.
Sacred songs, ancient and modern, a complete collection of sacred vocal music by celebrated composers, suitable for home use. Edited by John Hiles. London and New York, Boosey and co. [188-?] iv, 252 p. 25 1/2 cm. For solo voice with piano accompaniment. [M2110.H64S3] 46-28275
1. Sacred songs with piano. I. Title.

LA BERTE, Paul A., comp.
... The finest album of religious songs ... compiled by Paul A. La Berte. New York, N.Y., E. Schuberth & co., inc. [1945] cover-title, 96 p. 30 cm. ("The Finest" series, no. 10) With piano accompaniment. [M2110.L15F5] 46-2439
1. Sacred songs with piano. I. Title.

Sacred vocal music — Discography.

RELIGIOUS Record 016.7899'12 Index, Dayton, Ohio.
Official religious record index. Dayton, Ohio, 1961. 132 p. 24 cm. v. 24 cm. Supplement. 1962- Dayton, Ohio. [ML156.4.R4R4] 61-42109
1. Sacred vocal music — Discography. I. Title.

Sacred vocal music—To 1800.

ASTON, Hugh. b.ca.1485. 783
[Works, vocal] Hugh Aston, 1485 (?)-(?) John Marbeck, 1510 (?)-85(?) Osbert Parsley, 1511-85. London, New. Published for the Carnegie United Kingdom Trust by the Oxford University Press, 1929. xxiii p. score (293 p.) facsim. (Tudor church music, v. 10) For 3-7 voices, principally unacc. [M2.T9 vol. 10] A 51
1. Scared vocal music—To 1800. I. Marbeck, John, ca. 1510-ca. 1585. Works, vocal. Selections. II. Parsley, Osbert, 1511-1585. Works, vocal. Selections. III. Title. IV. Series.
Contents omitted.

SCHOLASTICA, Mary, Sister, 1893- ed.
Treasury of sacred polyphony, comp. and ed. by Sister M. Scholastica and Theodore Marier. Boston, McLaughlin & Reilly Co. [1948] v. 28 cm. Latin words with English translations. Secular name: Emily Veronica Chainey. Contents.v. 1. Four mixed voices [M2012.S3T7] 49-14665
1. Sacred vocal music—To 1800. I. Marier, Theodore N., 1912- joint ed. II. Title.

Sacrifice.

BUSHNELL, Horace, 1802-1876. 232.3
The vicarious sacrifice, grounded in principles of universal obligation, by Horace Bushnell. New York, C. Scribner & co., 1866. xii, [13]-552 p. 22 1/2 cm. [BT265.B93 1836] 35-31068
1. Sacrifice. 2. Jesus Christ—Person and offices. 3. Atonement. I. Title.

BUSHNELL, Horace, 1802-1876. 232.3
The vicarious sacrifice, grounded in principles interpreted by human analogies. By Horace Bushnell. New York, Scribner, Armstrong, 1877. 2 v. 19 1/2 cm. Contents.Vol. 1 contains the whole text of the work published in 1866 with title: The vicarious sacrifice grounded in principles of universal obligation. Vol. 2 is additional matter which the author intended "should eventually take the place of parts III and IV of his treatise." of. vol. II Advertisement. [BT265.B93 1877] 35-31067
1. Sacrifice. 2. Jesus Christ—Person and offices. 3. Atonement. I. Title.

CHYTRAEUS, David, 1531-1600. 291.34
On sacrifice; a Reformation treatise in Biblical theology. De sacrificiis of 1569 tr. for the first time into a modern language and ed. in tr. by John Warwick Montgomery. St. Louis, Concordia [c.] 1962. 151p. 21cm. Bibl. 61-18224 2.75 pap.,
1. Sacrifice. I. Montgomery, John Warwick, ed. and tr. II. Title.

GRAY, George Buchanan, 1865-1922. 296
Sacrifice in the Old Testament, its theory and practice, by George Buchanan Gray ... Oxford, The Clarendon press, 1925. xiv p., 1 l., 434 p. 23 cm. "List of works published by Dr. G. Buchanan Gray": p. [ix]-xi. Bibliography: p. [xiii]-xiv. [BM715.G7] 26-10538
1. Sacrifice. 2. Fasts and feasts. 3. Cultus, Jewish. I. Title.

GREEN, Will S., 1832- 223
Sacrifice; or, The living dead. By Will S. Green ... Colusa [Cal.] Addington & Green, 1882. 225 p. 22 1/2 cm. [PS1764.G259S3] 6-45552
I. Title.

HUBERT, Henri, 1872-1927 291.34
Sacrifice: its nature and function [by] Henri Hubert, Marcel Mauss. Tr. [from French] by W. D. Halls. Foreword by E. E. Evans-Pritchard [Chicago] Univ. of Chic. Pr. [c.1964] iv, 165p. 23cm. Bibl. 64-12260 3.25
1. Sacrifice. I. Mauss, Marcel, 1872-1950, joint author. II. Title.

HUBERT, Henri, 1872-1927. 291.34
Sacrifice: its nature and function [by] Henri Hubert and Marcel Mauss. Translated by W.D. Halls. Foreword by E.E. Evans-Pritchard. [Chicago] University of Chicago Press [1964] ix, 165 p. 23 cm. Translation of Essai sur la nature et le fonction du sacrifice. Bibliographical references included in "Notes" (p. 104-156) [BL570.H813] 64-12260
1. Sacrifice. I. Mauss, Marcel, 1872-1950, joint author. II. Title.

IRONSIDE, Henry Allan, 1876-1951.
Lectures on the Levitical offerings. New York, Loizeaux Bros. [1951] 78p. 19cm. [BM715.I7] 55-42342
1. Sacrifice. 2. Cultus, Jewish. I. Title. II. Title: The Levitical offerings.

JAMES, Edwin Oliver, 1886- 291.34
Sacrifice and sacrament. New York, Barnes & Noble [1962] 319p. 23cm. [BL570.J32] 62-6074
1. Sacrific —Hist. I. Title.

KRUEGER, Arthur F. 281.4
Synthesis of sacrifice according to Saint Augustine; a study of the sacramentality of sacrifice. Mundelein, Ill., Apud Aedes Seminarii Sanctae Mariae ad Lacum, 1950. 171 p. 23 cm. (Poutificia Facultas Theologica Seminaril SanctaeMariae ad Lacum. Dissertationes ad lauream, 19) Bibliography: p. 165-171. [BR65.A9K7] 50-32946
1. Sacrifice. 2. Augustinus, Aurelius, Saint, Bp. of Hippo. I. Title. II. Series: St. Mary of the Lake Seminary, Mundelein, Ill. Dissertationes ad lauream, 19

LEIGHTON, John, D.D. 232.
The Jewish altar; an inquiry into the spirit and intent of the expiatory offerings of the Mosaic ritual. With special reference to their typical character. By John Leighton ... New York, London, Funk & Wagnalls, 1886. viii, [9]-126 p., 1 l. 19 1/2 cm. [BT265.L45] 3-15814
1. Sacrifice. 2. Typology (Theology) 3. Jews—Rites and ceremonies. I. Title.

SMYTH, Frederic Hastings, 1888- 232.4
Sacrifice; a doctrinal homily. New York, Vantage Press [c1953] 149p. illus. 22cm. [BT265.S68] 53-10308
1. Sacrifice. I. Title.

SPENCER, Bonnell.
Sacrifice of Thanksgiving. West Park, N.Y., Holy Cross Publications [c1965] 175 p. 21 cm. 66-39063
1. Sacrifice. I. Title.

STEWART, George Craig, 1879- 247.
Six altars, studies in sacrifice, by George Craig Stewart. Milwaukee, Wis., Morehouse publishing co. [c1930] 4 p. l., 83, [1] p. front. 19 cm. [BV195.S7] 30-6185
I. Title.

WRIGHT, Walter Coleman, 1877- 296
The sacrificial system of the Old Testament [by] Walter C. Wright ... Cleveland, O., Union gospel press [c1942] 3 p. l., [5]-175 p.20 cm. [BM715.W7] 41-1703
1. Sacrifice. 2. Cultus, Jewish. I. Title.

YOUNG, Frances Margaret. 234
Sacrifice and the death of Christ / by Frances M. Young ; foreword by Maurice Wiles. Philadelphia : Westminster Press, [1978] c1975. p. cm. Includes indexes. Bibliography: p. [BL570.Y68 1978] 78-2889 ISBN 0-664-24210-3 pbk. : 5.95
1. Sacrifice. I. Title.

Sacrifice—Biblical teaching.

DALY, Robert J., 1933- 230
Christian sacrifice : the Judaeo-Christian background before Origen / by Robert J. Daly. Washington : Catholic University of America Press, [1978] p. cm. (The Catholic University of America studies in Christian antiquity ; no. 18) Includes indexes. Bibliography: p. [BS680.S2D33] 78-12004 ISBN 0-8132-0530-1 : 20.00
1. Sacrifice—Biblical teaching. 2. Sacrifice—History of doctrines. I. Title. II. Series: Catholic University of America. Studies in Christian antiquity ; no. 18.

DALY, Robert J., 1933- 232'.4
The origins of the Christian doctrine of sacrifice / by Robert J. Daly. Philadelphia : Fortress Press, c1977. p. cm. Includes indexes. [BS680.S2D34] 77-78628 ISBN 0-8006-1267-1 : pbk. : 5.95
1. Sacrifice—Biblical teaching. 2. Sacrifice—History of doctrines. I. Title.

HORVATH, Tibor, 1927(July28)- 232'.4
The sacrificial interpretation of Jesus' achievement in the New Testament : historical development and its reasons / by Tibor Horvath. New York : Philosophical Library, c1979. vii, 100 p. ; 22 cm. Includes bibliographical references. [BS2545.S24H67] 19 79-83604 ISBN 0-8022-2240-4 : 8.50
1. Jesus Christ—Person and offices. 2. Bible. N.T.—Criticism, interpretation, etc. 3. Sacrifice—Biblical teaching. I. Title.

MILGROM, Jacob, 1923- 296.4
Cult and conscience : the Asham and the priestly doctrine of repentance / by Jacob Milgrom. Leiden : Brill, 1976. xiii, 173 p. ; 25 cm. (Studies in Judaism in late antiquity ; v. 18) Includes indexes. Bibliography: p. [144]-150. [BS1199.S2M54] 76-375991 ISBN 9-00-404476-0 : fl 64.00
1. Sacrifice—Biblical teaching. 2. Repentance—Biblical teaching. 3. Asham (The Hebrew word) I. Title. II. Series.

MOORE, Marvin, 1937- 234'.1
Sacrifice / Marvin Moore. Nashville : Southern Pub. Association, c1979. 32 p. ; 18 cm. [BS680.S2M58] 78-21712 ISBN 0-8127-0214-X pbk. : 0.75
1. Sacrifice—Biblical teaching. I. Title.

MORGAN, Richard. 233
The Biblical theology of sacrifice. Nashville, Printed by Parthenon Press [1969] 85 p. 24 cm. [BS680.S2M6] 72-100635 2.00
1. Sacrifice—Biblical teaching. I. Title.

RINGGREN, Helmer [Karl Vilhelm Helmer Ringgren] 1917- 220.82324
Sacrifice in the Bible. New York, Association [1963] 80p. 19cm. (World Christian bks., no. 42, 2d ser.) 63-3228 1.00 pap.,
1. Sacrifice—Biblical teaching. I. Title.

VAUX, Roland de, 1903- 232.4
Studies in Old Testament sacrifice. Cardiff, Univ. of Wales Pr. [Mystic, Conn., Verry, 1966] x, 120p. 23cm. Contains in a somewhat expanded form the Four Elizabeth James lects. given at Univ. Coll.

Cardiff, in Oct. 1961. Bibl. [BS1199.S2V3] 65-6513 3.50
1. Sacrifuie—Biblical teaching. 2. Bible. O. T.—Rites and ceremonies. I. Title.

Sacrifice—Comparative studies.

JAMES, Edwin Oliver, 1886- 291.3'4
Origins of sacrifice; a study in comparative religion, by E. O. James. Port Washington, N.Y., Kennikat Press [1971] xv, 313 p. 22 cm. Reprint of the 1933 ed. Bibliography: p. 291-309. [BL570.J3 1971] 299'.21 75-118530
1. Sacrifice—Comparative studies. 2. Christianity and other religions. I. Title.

Sacrifice—Congresses.

SACRIFICE / 291.3'4
edited by M.F.C. Bourdillon, Meyer Fortes. London : Published by Academic Press for the Royal Anthropological Institute of Great Britain and Ireland, 1980. xix, 147 p. ; 24 cm. "Based on the proceedings of a Conference on Sacrifice held at Cumberland Lodge, Windsor, England from February 23rd to 25th, 1979." Includes index. Contents.Contents.—On understanding sacrifice / J.H.M. Beattie — Sacrifice in the Old Testament / J.W. Rogerson — Sacrifice in the New Testament and Christian theology / S.W. Sykes — Ritual in performance and interpretation / Suzanne Campbell-Jones — A commensal relationship with God / Audrey Hayley — Postscript, a place for sacrifice in modern Christianity? / S. Barrington-Ward and M.F.C. Bourdillon. Bibliography: p. [137]-143. [BL570.S24] 19 80-40424 ISBN 0-12-119040-4 : 21.00
1. Sacrifice—Congresses. I. Bourdillon, M. F. C. II. Fortes, Meyer. III. Conference on Sacrifice Cumberland Lodge) (1979 :

Sacrifice (Hinduism)—History.

AGUILAR, H. 294.5'3'4
The sacrifice in the Rgveda : doctrinal aspects / H. Aguilar ; with a pref. by R. Panikkar. Delhi : Bharatiya Vidya Prakashan, 1976. ix, 222 p. ; 23 cm. Includes bibliographical references and index. [BL1215.S2A34] 76-902122 Rs50.00
1. Vedas. Rgveda—Criticism, interpretation, etc. 2. Sacrifice (Hinduism)—History. I. Title.

Sacrifice, Human.

GREEN, Alberto Ravinell Whitney. 299'.21
The role of human sacrifice in the ancient Near East / by Alberto Ravinell Whitney Green. Missoula, Mont. : Published by Scholars Press for the American Schools of Oriental Research, c1975. xvi, 383 p. ; 22 cm. (Dissertation series ; no. 1) Bibliography: p. 361-383. [BL570.G7] 75-43709 ISBN 0-89130-069-4 : 4.00
1. Sacrifice, Human. 2. Rites and ceremonies—Near East. I. Title. II. Series.

Sacrifice (Judaism)

GRAY, George Buchanan, 1865-1922. 296.4
Sacrifice in the Old Testament; its theory and practice. Prolegomenon by Baruch A. Levine. New York, Ktav Pub. House, 1971. liii, 434 p. 23 cm. (The Library of biblical studies) Reprint of the 1925 ed. [BS680.S2G7 1971] 72-105753 ISBN 0-87068-048-X
1. Sacrifice (Judaism) 2. Priests, Jewish. 3. Fasts and feasts—Judaism. I. Title. II. Series.

THOMPSON, R J
Penitence and sacrifice in early Israel outside the Levitical law; an examination of the fellowship theory of early Israelite sacrifice, by R. J. Thompson. With a foreword by H. H. Rowley. Leiden, E. J. Brill, 1963. xii, 287 p. 25 cm. Bibliography: p. [256]-272. [BM715.T45] 66-6731
1. Sacrifice (Judaism) 2. Sacrifice — Biblical teaching. 3. Atonement (Judaism) I. Title.

Sacrilege (Canon law)

GULCZYNSKI, John Theophilus, 1911- 265.9
... The desecration and violation of churches; an historical synopsis and commentary, by John Theophilus Gulczynski ... Washington, D.C., The Catholic university of America, 1942. ix, 126 p. 23 cm. (The Catholic university of America. Canon law studies, no. 150) Thesis (J.C.D.)--Catholic university of America, 1942. "Biographical note": p. [115] Bibliography: p. [109]-114. [BX1939.S27G8] A 44
1. Sacrilege (Canon law) I. Title.

Saddharmapundarika.

SADDHARMAPUNDARIKA 294.32
Saddharma-Pundarika; or, The lotus of the true law. Tr. by H. Kern [Gloucester, Mass., P. Smith, 1964] xlii, 454p. 22cm. (Sacred bks. of the East, v.21) Tr. based on a Sanskrit ms. on palm leaves, in the D. Wright collection, Univ. of Cambridge Lib. (Dover bk. rebound) 4.50
I. Kern, Hendrik, 1833-1917, tr. II. Cambridge. University. Library. Mss. (Add. 1682) III. Title. IV. Title: The lotus of the true law. V. Series: The Sacred books of the East (New York) v.21

SADDHARMAPUNDARIKA 294.32
Saddharma--Pundarika; or, The lotus of the true law. Tr. by H. Kern. New York, Dover [1963] xlii, 454p. 22cm. (Sacred bks. of the East, v.21) Unaltered republication of the work first pub., Oxford, 1884. Tr. based on a Sanskrit ms. on palm leaves, in the D. Wright Collection, Univ. of Cambridge Lib. 63-19509 2.45 pap.,
I. Kern, Hendrik, 1833-1917, tr. II. Cambridge. University. Library. Mss. (Add. 1682) III. Title. IV. Title: The lotus of the true law. V. Series: The Sacred books of the East (New York) v.21

SADDHARMAPUNDARIKA. 294.32
The Saddharma-pundarika; or, The lotus of the true law. Translated by H. Kern. Oxford, The Clarendon press, 1884. xiii, 454 p. 22 1/2 cm. (Added t.-p.: The sacred books of the East ... vol. XXI) Translation based on a Sanskrit manuscript on palm leaves, in the D. Wright collection, University of Cambridge library. [BL1/10.S3 vol. 21] (290.8) 32-19888
I. Kern, Hendrik, 1833-1917, tr. II. Cambridge, University. Library. Mss. (Add. 1682) III. Title. IV. Title: The lotus of the true law.

THE Threefold lotus sutra / translated by Bunno Kato, Yoshiro Tamura, and Kojiro Miyasaka ; with revisions by W. E. Soothill, Wilhelm Schiffer, and Pier P. Del Campana. 1st ed. New York : Weatherhill, 1975. xviii, 383 p. ; 23 cm. Contents.Contents.—Innumerable meanings.—The Lotus flower of the wonderful law.—Meditation on the Bodhisattva universal virtue. [BQ2052.E5K37 1975] 74-23158 ISBN 0-8348-0105-1 : 19.00. ISBN 0-8348-0106-X pbk. : 10.00 294.3'82
1. Saddharmapundarika. 2. Mahayana Buddhism—Sacred books. I. Kato, Bunno, tr. II. Soothill, William Edward, 1861-1935. III. Wu liang i ching. English. 1975. IV. Saddharmapundarika. English. 1975. V. Kuan p'u hsien P'u-sa hsing fa ching. English. 1975.
Contents omitted.

Saddharmapundarika—Commentaries.

HSUAN-HUA, 1908- 294.3'823
The wonderful Dharma lotus flower sutra : translated into Chinese by Tripitaka Master Kumarajiva of Yao Ch'in / with the commentary of Tripitaka Master Hua ; translated by the Buddhist Text Translation Society ; [edited by Kuo-lin Lethcoe]. San Francisco : Buddhist Text Translation Society, 1977- v. ; 22 cm. Cover title: The Dharma flower sutra. Includes index. Contents.Contents.—v. 1. Introduction. [BQ2057.H77] 77-87782 ISBN 0-917512-162 pbk. : 3.95 (v. 1)
1. Saddharmapundarika—Commentaries. I. Lethcoe, Kuo-lin. II. Title. III. Title: The Dharma flower sutra.

NIWANO, Nikkyo, 1906- 294.3'8
Buddhism for today : a modern interpretation of The threefold lotus sutra / Nikkyo Niwano ; [translation by Kojiro Miyasaka]. 1st English ed. New York : Weatherhill ; Tokyo : Kosei, 1976, 1980 printing. xxvii, 472 p. ; 23 cm. Translation of Hokekyo no atarashii kaishaku. Includes index. [BQ2057.N57813 1976b] 79-22383 ISBN 0-8348-0147-7 pbk. : 10.95
1. Saddharmapundarika—Commentaries. 2. Amitarthasutra—Commentaries. 3. Kuan P'u-hsien p'u sa hsing faching—Commentaries. I. Title.

TU-LUN, Shih, 1908- 294.3'8
The essentials of the Dharma blossom sutra [by] Tripitaka Master Tu Lun. Translated by Bhikshu Heng Ch'ien. San Francisco, Buddhist Text Translation Society; distributed in the United States by the Sino-American Buddhist Association, 1974- v. illus. 22 cm. The commentary was originally delivered as a series of lectures. The text of the sutra is a translation of Kumarajiva's version entitled Miao fa lien hua ching. [BQ2057.T84] 74-171025
1. Saddharmapundarika—Commentaries. I. Heng Ch'ien, Bhikshu, tr. II. Saddharmapundarika. English. 1974- III. Title.

Saddharmapundarika—Criticism, interpretation, etc.

THE Lotus Sutra : 294.3'8
its history and practice today. Santa Monica, Calif. : World Tribune Press, c1977. 78 p. : ill., [1] leaf of plates ; 18 cm. [BQ2057.L67] 77-152891
1. Soka Gakkai—Prayer-books and devotion—English. 2. Saddharmapundarika—Criticism, interpretation, etc.

Saddharmasmrtiupasthanasutra.

MATSUNAGA, Daigan. 294.3'4'23
The Buddhist concept of hell, by Daigan and Alicia Matsunaga. New York, Philosophical Library [1971, c1972] 152 p. illus. 22 cm. Bibliography: p. 145-147. [BL1456.68.M38] 73-145466 ISBN 0-8022-2048-7 4.95
1. Saddharmasmrtiupasthanasutra. 2. Hell (Buddhism) I. Matsunaga, Alicia, joint author. II. Title.

Sadhus.

ALLISON, Walter Leslie, 1889- 294.55
...The Sadhs, by W. L. Allison ... Calcutta, Y.M.C.A. publishing house. London, New York [etc.] H. Milford, Oxford university press, 1935. 11 p., 5 l., [3]-127 [1] p., 1 l. 19 cm. (The religious life of India) Bibliography: p. [128] [BL1245.S17A6] 36-10315
1. Sadhs. I. Title.

Sadhus—India.

BOYD, Doug. 181'.4
Swami / Douglas Boyd. 1st ed. New York : Random House, c1976. xx, 330 p. ; 22 cm. [BL2003.B6] 75-40566 ISBN 0-394-49603-5 : 10.00
1. Rama, Swami, 1925- 2. Boyd, Doug. 3. Sadhus—India. 4. India—Religion. I. Title.

OMAN, John Campbell, 1841-1911. 294.5
The mystics, ascetics, and saints of India : a study of Sadhuism, with an account of the Yogis, Sanyasis, Bairagis, and other strange Hindu sectarians / by John Campbell Oman ; with ill. by William Campbell Oman. New York : Gordon Press, 1980. p. cm. Reprint of the 1903 ed. published by T. F. Unwin, London. [BL1226.85.O45 1980] 80-10129 ISBN 0-8490-0698-8 lib. bdg. : 70.00
1. Sadhus—India. I. Title.

Sadoleto, Jacopo, Cardinal, 1477-1547.

DOUGLAS, Richard M. 922.245
Jacopo Sadoleto, 1477-1547: humanist and reformer. Cambridge, Harvard University Press, 1959. xvi, 307 p. illus., port. 22 cm. Bibliography: p. 229-242. [BX4705.S13D6] 58-12965
1. Sadoleto, Jacopo, Cardinal, 1477-1547.

Sadr al-Din Shirazi, Muhammad ibn Ibrahim, d. 1641.

MORRIS, James Winston, 1949- 297'.2
The wisdom of the throne : an introduction to the philosophy of Mulla Sadra / James Winston Morris. Princeton, N.J. : Princeton University Press, c1981. p. cm. (Princeton library of Asian translations) Includes a translation of: al-Hikmah al-'arshiyah. Includes index. Bibliography: p. [B753.M83H5435] 19 81-47153 ISBN 0-691-06493-8 : 22.50
1. Sadr al-Din Shirazi, Muhammad ibn Ibrahim, d. 1641. Hikmah al-'arshiyah. 2. Transcendence (Philosophy) 3. Philosophy, Islamic—Early works to 1800. I. Sadr al-Din Shirazi, Muhammad ibn Ibrahim, d. 1641. Hikmah al-'arshiyah. English. 1981. II. Title. III. Series. IV. UNESCO collection of representative works. Arabic series

Sa'eed, 1863-1942.

RASOOLI, Jay M 922
The life story of Dr. Sa'eed of Iran, Kurdish physician to princes and peasants, nobles and nomads, by Jay M. Rasooli and Cady H. Allen. Grand Rapids, Grand Rapids International Publications, 1957. 188p. illus. 23cm. [BV3217.S3R3] 57-13245
1. Sa'eed, 1863-1942. 2. Missions—Persia. I. Allen, Cady Hews, 1886- joint author. II. Title.

Safford, Daniel, 1792-1856.

[SAFFORD, Ann Eliza (Bigelow) Turner] Mrs. 922.573
A memoir of Daniel Safford, by his wife ... Boston, The American tract society [c1861] 384 p. front., plates, port. 19 1/2 cm. [BX7260.S15S3] 36-16656
1. Safford, Daniel, 1792-1856. 2. The American tract society. I. Title.

Sahajiya.

DIMOCK, Edward C 294.55
The place of the hidden moon; erotic mysticism in the Vaisnavasahajiya cult of Bengal [by] Edward C. Dimock, Jr. Chicago, University of Chicago Press [1966] xix, 299 p. 22 cm. Much of the material in this book was presented as part of the author's thesis, Harvard University, 1959. Bibliography: p. 271-283. [BL1245.S2D5] 66-13865
1. Sahajiya. 2. Sex and religion. I. Title.

Sa'id, khan, 1862-

YONAN, Isaac Malek, 1869- 266.
The beloved physician of Teheran; the miracle of the conversion of Dr. Sa'eed, khan, Kurdistani, Lokman-il-mulk, the man who walks and talks with God, by Issac Malek Yonan ... Nashville, Cokesbury press [c1934] 217 p. plates. ports. 19 1/2 cm. [BV3217.S3Y6] 34-29169
1. Sa'id, khan, 1862- 2. Missions—Persia. I. Title.

St. Aloysius church (Catholic) Grant township, Crawford, co., Kan.

GRAVES, William Whites, 1871- 282.78198
The legend of Greenbush; the story of a pioneer country church, by W. W. Graves ... St. Paul, Kan., The Journal press, c1937. 1 p. l., 78 p. illus. (incl. ports.) 24 cm. [BX4603.S26G7] 37-20299
1. St. Aloysius church (Catholic) Grant township, Crawford, co., Kan. I. Title.

St. Alphonsus Church, Chicago, Ill.

CHICAGO. St. Alphonsus Church.
Diamond Jubilee of St. Alphonsus Church, 1882-1957. [Chicago, Ill., 1957] 1 v. (unpaged) illus. ports. 28 cm. 68-34182

1. St. Alphonsus Church, Chicago, Ill. I. Title.

St. Andrew's Parish, Cambridge, N.Z.

CARTER, Harry Garlin. 283'.9312'2
Parish of Saint Andrew Cambridge; centennial chronicle, 1871-1971, based on the text of Harry G. Carter, edited and arranged by Lilian M. Hanton and George N. Marshall. [Cambridge, N.Z.] Printed by the Cambridge Independent, 1971. 55 p. illus. ports. 22 cm. [BX5720.5.Z7C35] 74-162574
1. St. Andrew's Parish, Cambridge, N.Z. I. Hanton, Lilian May, ed. II. Marshall, George Nairn, ed. III. Title.

St. Andrews, Scot. Church of the Holy Trinity.

RANKIN, William Eric Kilmorack.
The parish church of the Holy Trinity, St. Andrews, pre-Reformation. Edinburgh, Oliver and Boyd [1955] xii, 153p. illus. 23cm. (St. Andrews University publications, no. 52) Bibliographical footnotes. A58
1. St. Andrews, Scot. Church of the Holy Trinity. I. Title. II. Series: St. Andrews, Scot. University.Publications, no. 52

Saint Andrews, Scotland.

[BOYD, Andrew Kennedy 285.
Hutchinson] 1825-1899.
St. Andrews and elsewhere; glimpses of some gone and of things left, by the author of 'Twenty-five years of St. Andrews,' 'The recreations of a country parson,' &c. London and New York, Longmans, Green and co., 1894. xiii, 384 p. 23 cm. Reminiscencesm including chapters on Archbishop Tait, Dean Stanley, and Canon Pearson. [BX9225.B7A5] 18-14720
1. SaintAndrews, Scotland. I. Tait, Archibasld Campbell, abp. of Canterbury, 1811-1882. II. Stanley, Arthur Penrhyn, 1815-1881. III. Pearson, Hugh, 1817-1882. IV. Title.

St. Andrews. University.

[BOYD, Andrew Kennedy 285.
Hutchinson] 1825-1899.
Twenty-five years of St. Andrews, September 1865 to September 1890, by the author of 'The recreations of a country parson' ... London and New York, Longmans, Green, and co., 1892. 2 v. 23 cm. Vol. 2, 2d edition. Slip pasted on cover: Mudie's select library ... [BX9225.B7A3] 3-13663
1. St. Andrews. University. I. Title.

St. Anne's schools, London.

CARDWELL, John Henry, 1882-
The story of a charity school, two centuries of popular education in Soho, 1699-1899, by J. H. Cardwell ... with a preface by the dean of Saint Paul's. London and New York, Truslove, Hanson and Comba, 1899. 6 p. l., 126 p. front., plates (1 fold.) ports. 23 cm. [LC4096.G7C2] E 10
1. St. Anne's schools, London. I. Title.

*GEARON, Patrick J. 242.62
Chats with St. Anne for children. [Downers Grove, Ill.] Carmelite Third Order Pr., Aylesford [1965] 64p. illus. 19cm. .75 pap.,
I. Title.

St. Ann's Church, Dublin.

POYNTZ, S. G. 283'.418'35
St. Ann's : the church in the heart of the city / S. G. Poyntz. [Dublin : Representative Church Body Library, 1976] 105 p. : ill. ; 23 cm. Author's note, 1976. Includes bibliographical references. [BX5570.D8S246] 77-358422
1. St. Ann's Church, Dublin. I. Title.

St. Anthony's Church, Detroit, Michigan.

ONE hundred years for God and county, county, The story of St. Anthony Parish, Detroit, Michigan, 1857-1957. Compiled and edited by Sister Mary Charitas, S. S. N. D. Detroit, 1957. 132p. illus. 24cm.
1. St. Anthony's Church, Detroit, Michigan. I. Mary Charitas, Sister, 1893-

St. Anthony's Church, Lancaster, Pa.

MUSSER, Edgar A., 917.48'15'03 s
1903-
Church of St. Anthony of Padua, 1870-1919, by Edgar A. Musser. Lancaster, Pa., Lancaster County Historical Society, 1970. [141]-252 p. illus. 23 cm. (Journal of the Lancaster County Historical Society, v. 74, no. 4) Cover title. [F157.L2L5 vol. 74, no. 4] [BX4603.L25] 282'.748'15 74-153878 1.50
1. St. Anthony's Church, Lancaster, Pa. I. Series: Lancaster Co., Pa. Historical Society. Journal, v. 74, no. 4.

St. Asaph, Wales (Diocese)

THOMAS, David Richard, 1833-
1916.
... *St. Asaph.* By the Venerable D. R. Thomas ... Pub. under the direction of the Trace committee. London, Society for promoting Chrisitan knowledge; New York, E. & J. B. Young & co., 1888. 2 p. l., 140 p. front. (fold. map) 17 cm. (Dioceasan histories) [BX5107.S3T5] 4-202
1. St. Asaph, Wales (Diocese) 2. Gt. Brit.—Church history. I. Title.

St. Augustine Cathedral, Tucson, Ariz.

CHAMBERS, George W. 917.91'77
San Agustin, first cathedral church in Arizona, by George W. Chambers, and C. L. Sonnichsen. [Tucson] Arizona Historical Society [1974] 55 p. illus. 27 cm. [BX4603.T8S243] 74-620037 7.50
1. St. Augustine Cathedral, Tucson, Ariz. I. Sonnichsen, Charles Leland, 1901- joint author.

St. Augustine (Diocese)—History

GANNON, Michael V 922.273
Rebel bishop; the life and era of Augustin Verot, by Michael V. Gannon. With a foreword by John Tracy Ellis. Milwaukee, Bruce Pub. Co. [1964] xvii, 267 p. illus., map. ports. 22 cm. Bibliographical footnotes. [BX4705.V4G3] 64-23895
1. Verot, Augustine, Bp., 1804-1876. 2. St. Augustine (Diocese) — Hist. I. Title.

St. Augustine, Fla.—History—Drama.

GREEN, Paul, 1894-
Cross and sword; a symphonic outdoor drama commemorating the four-hundredth anniversary of the founding of St. Augustine, Florida. By Paul Green; musical arrangements by Isaac van Grove. Rehearsal script only (to be cut some twenty or thirty pages) [n.p., 1965] [6], 148 p. 28 cm.
1. St. Augustine, Fla.—History—Drama. I. Title.

Saint Augustine of Canterbury Parish, Hecker, Ill.

WITTENAUER, Josephine 282'.773'91
Carole.
History of Saint Augustine of Canterbury Parish, 1824-1974. Hecker, Ill. : St. Augustine of Canterbury Church, [1974] xxii, 194 p. : ill. ; 23 cm. Bibliography: p. 188-189. [BX4603.H4S248] 75-304583
1. Saint Augustine of Canterbury Parish, Hecker, Ill. 2. Hecker, Ill.—Biography. I. Title.

St. Augustine's Church. Rensselaer, Ind.

THE story of Saint Augustine's from pioneer days, 1868, 1882, 1958. Carthagena, Ohio, Messenger Press, 1958. 102p. illus. 27cm.
1. St. Augustine's Church. Rensselaer, Ind. I. Kaiser, Edwin G 1893-

St. Benedict's Abbey, Atchison, Kan.

BECKMAN, Peter, 1911- 271.1
Kansas monks; a history of St. Benedict's Abbey. Atchison, Kan, Abbey Student Press [1957] 362p. illus. 24cm. (American Benedictine Academy. Historical studies. Monasteries and convents, 3) [BX2525.A8S22] 57-44042
1. St. Benedict's Abbey, Atchison, Kan. 2. St. Benedict's College, Atchison, Kan. I. Title.

St. Bernard's Seminary, Rochester, N.Y.

[MCNAMARA, Robert 207.747
Francis] 1910-
St. Bernard's Seminary, 1893-1943. Golden jubilee ed. [Rochester, N.Y.] Alumni Assn., 1943. 61 p. illus., ports. 23 cm. [BX915.R66M3] 44-51469
1. St. Bernard's Seminary, Rochester, N.Y. I. St. Bernard's Seminary, Rochester, N.Y. Alumni Association. II. Title.

Saint Catherine (Monastery : Mount Sinai)

CHARLESWORTH, James H. 091
The new discoveries in St. Catherine's Monastery : a preliminary report on the manuscripts / by James Hamilton Charlesworth, assisted by George Themelis Zervos ; with a foreword by David Noel Freedman. Cambridge, MA : American Schools of Oriental Research ; Winona Lake, IN : Distributed by Eisenbrauns, 1982, c1981. xv, 45 p. : ill. ; 28 cm. (Monograph series ; no. 3) Includes bibliographical references. [Z6605.G7C53 1981] 19 81-10992 ISBN 0-89757-403-6 pbk. : 6.00
1. Saint Catherine (Monastery : Mount Sinai) 2. Manuscripts, Greek. I. Zervos, George. II. Title.

HEUSER, Herman Joseph, 1851- 248
The chaplain of St. Catherine's, by Herman J. Heuser ... New York [etc.] Longmans, Green and co., 1925. x, 305 p. 20 cm. [BX2350.H4] 25-8074
I. Title.

WEITZMANN, 704.9'482'07409531
Kurt, 1904-
Studies in the arts at Sinai : essays / by Kurt Weitzmann. Princeton, N.J. : Princeton University Press, c1982. 449 p. : ill. ; 29 cm. (Princeton series of collected essays) Includes bibliographical references and index. [N7988.A1W44 1982] 19 81-47959 ISBN 0-691-03993-3 : 35.00 ISBN 0-691-00342-4 (pbk.) : 16.50
1. Saint Catherine (Monastery : Mount Sinai) 2. Christian art and symbolism—Medieval, 500-1500—Egypt. 3. Icons, Byzantine—Egypt. 4. Icons, Medieval—Egypt. 5. Christian antiquities—Egypt. I. Title. II. Series.

St. Columban's Foreign Mission Society—History.

FISCHER, Edward. 266'.2591
Mission in Burma : the Columban Fathers' forty-three years in Kachin country / by Edward Fischer. New York : Seabury Press, 1980. vi, 164 p., [9] leaves of plates ; 24 cm. "A Crossroad book." [BV3270.F57] 80-16897 ISBN 0-8164-0464-X : 9.95
1. St. Columban's Foreign Mission Society—History. 2. Catholic Church—Missions. 3. Missions—Burma. 4. Missions to Kachin tribes. I. Title.

St. Davids, Eng. (Diocese)

BEVAN, William Latham, 1821-
1908.
... *St. David's.* By W. L. Bevan ... With map. Published under the direction of the Tract committee. London, Society for promoting Christian knowledge; New York, E. & J. B. Young & co., 1888. x, 254, 11, [1] p. front. (fold. map) 17 cm. (Diocesan histories) "Appendix: On the parish-names of the diocese of St. David's": 11 p. [BX5107.S4B4] 4-208
1. St. Davids, Eng. (Diocese) I. Title.

Saint Denis Church, Havertown, Pa.

BARRETT, Joseph P. 282'.748'11
The sesquicentennial history of Saint Denis Parish, 1825-1975 : an Augustinian suburban parish with roots deep in the past / by Joseph P. Barrett, in cooperation with Edwin T. Grimes. Devon, Pa. : W. T. Cooke Pub. Co., [1975] xii, 212 p. : ill. ; 32 cm. Cover title: Saint Denis sesquicentennial, 1825-1975. Includes index. Bibliography: p. 209-210. [BX4603.H35S242] 74-29440
1. Saint Denis Church, Havertown, Pa. I. Grimes, Edwin T., joint author. II. Title. III. Title: Saint Denis sesquicentennial, 1825-1975.

Saint-Denis, France (Benedictine abbey).

SUGER, abbot of Saint 726.582
Denis, 1081-1151,
Abbot Suger on the abbey church of St.-Denis and its art treasures. Edited, translated and annotated by Erwin Panofsky. Princeton, N.J., Princeton university press, 1946. xiv, 250 p. illus., plates, fold. plan. 24 cm. Latin and English. "Abbreviations" (bibliography): p. 141-142 [NA5551.S2S8 1946] A46
1. Saint-Denis, France (Benedictine abbey) I. Panofsky, Erwin, 1892- ed. and tr. II. Title.

SUGER, Abbot of 726'.5'0944362
Saint Denis, 1081-1151.
Abbot Suger on the Abbey Church of St.-Denis and its art treasures / edited, translated, and annotated by Erwin Panofsky. 2d ed. / by Gerda Panofsky-Soergel. Princeton, N.J. : Princeton University Press, c1978. p. cm. Latin and English. Includes index. Bibliography: p. [NA5551.S2S8 1978] 78-51186 ISBN 0-691-03936-4 : 22.50. ISBN 0-691-10068-3 pbk. : 9.95
1. Saint-Denis, France (Benedictine abbey). 2. Architecture—Early works to 1800. 3. Art—Early works to 1800. I. Panofsky, Erwin, 1892-1968. II. Panofsky-Soergel, Gerda, 1929- III. Title.

Saint-Denis, France (Benedictine abbey). Apostle Bas-relief.

CROSBY, Sumner McKnight, 731'.54
1909-
The apostle bas-relief at Saint-Denis [by] Sumner McK. Crosby. New Haven, Yale University Press, 1972. xvi, 116 p., 86 p. of illus. 26 cm. (Yale publications in the history of art, 21) Bibliography: p. [98]-110. [NB543.C7] 71-179471 ISBN 0-300-01504-6 10.00
1. Saint-Denis, France (Benedictine abbey). Apostle Bas-relief. I. Title. II. Series.

Saint-Denis, France. Eglise abbatiale de Saint-Denis.

SMITH, Katharine Lawrence, 282.44
1874-
People, pomp & circumstance in Saint Denis and Notre Dame, Paris. [1st ed.] New York, Blackmore Press [1955] 117p. 21cm. [BX4629.P3S55] 55-30111
1. Saint-Denis, France. Eglise abbatiale de Saint-Denis. 2. Paris. Notre-Dame (Cathedral) I. Title.

Saint Edward Church, Providence.

WALSH, Richard A. 282'.745'2
The centennial history of Saint Edward Church, Providence, Rhode Island, 1874-1974, by Richard A. Walsh. With an introd. by Louis E. Gelineau. [Providence? R.I., 1974] 242 p. illus. 24 cm. Bibliography: p. [240]-242. [BX4603.P7S258] 74-163508
1. Saint Edward Church, Providence. 2. Providence—Biography. I. Title.

St. Felicitas Church, Chicago, Ill.

CHICAGO. St. Felicitas Church.
Dedication Ceremonies, April 29, 1956 by His Eminence Samuel Cardinal Stritch. [Chicago, Ill., 1956] 1 v. (unpaged) illus., ports., 28 cm. 68-34124
1. St. Felicitas Church, Chicago, Ill. I. Title.

St. Ferdinand Church, Chicago, Ill.

CHICAGO. St. Ferdinand Church.
Solemn dedication of the new St. Ferdinand Church and the fortieth anniversary of Rt. Rev. Msgr. Matthew A. Cunning, pastor; 1919-1959. [Chicago, 1959] 1 v. (unpaged) ports. 25 cm. 68-33526
1. Canning, Matthew A., Msgr. 1894- 2. St. Ferdinand Church, Chicago, Ill. I. Title.

Saint Francis De Sales Parish, Chicago.

CHICAGO. Saint Francis De Sales Parish.
The anniversary of Saint Francis de Sales Parish 1889-1964. Chicago, Norman King Co., Inc. [1964] 108 p. illus. ports, plates, 29 cm. 68-38923
1. Saint Francis De Sales Parish, Chicago. I. Title.

St. Francis Seminary, St. Francis, Wis.

JOHNSON, Peter Leo. 207.775
Halcyon days; story of St. Francis Seminary, Milwaukee, 1856-1956. Foreword by Albert G. Meyer. Milwaukee, Bruce Pub. Co. [1956] 416p. illus. 23cm. [BX915.Si6J6] 56-59133
1. St. Francis Seminary, St. Francis, Wis. I. Title.

St. Francis Xavier Church-St. Mary's County, Md.

BEITZEIL, Edwin Warfield, 1905-
A history of St. Francis Xavier Roman Catholic Church (Old Newtown) the Manor of Little Bretton, St. Mary's County, Maryland [1662-1962. Leonardtown? 1962] 75 p. illus. Title page on verso of page 1. NUC64
1. St. Francis Xavier Church-St. Mary's County, Md. 2. Manor of Little Bretton-St. Mary's County, Md. I. Title.

Saint Francis Xavier Church, Warwick, Md.

CANN, Joseph C. 282'.752'38
History of Saint Francis Xavier Church and Bohemia Plantation, now known as Old Bohemia, Warwick, Maryland / researched by the Old Bohemia Historical Society's History Committee, Joseph C. Cann, chairman ... [et al.] ; compiled and edited by Joseph C. Cann. [s.l.] : The Society, c1976. xxii, 271 p., [1] leaf of plates : ill. (some col.) ; 24 cm. Bibliography: p. 263. [BX4603.W3S342] 76-151886
1. Saint Francis Xavier Church, Warwick, Md. 2. Bohemia Plantation, Md. 3. Church records and registers—Maryland—Warwick. I. Old Bohemia Historical Society. History Committee. II. Title.

Saint Francis Xavier, Sister, 1816-1856.

COULTON, George Gordon, 1858- 220
Christ, St. Francis and to-day, by G. G. Coulton ... Cambridge, The University press, 1919. 4 p. l., 203 p. 23 cm. "Lectures ... delivered ... at Cambridge during the Michaelmas term of 1918." [BR125.C815] 20-641
I. Title.

[JULIANA, sister] 1901- 922.273
Irma, wirtten and illustrated by a sister of providence. Saint Mary-of-the-Woods, Ind., 1942. 4 p. l., 218 p. incl. front., illus. 21 1/2 cm. [Secular name: Florence Terstegge] [BX4705.S15J8] 42-50623
1. Saint Francis Xavier, sister, 1816-1856. I. Title.

LACORBINIERE, Clementine 922.273
(Le Fer de la Motte) de, Mme. 1829-
An apostolic woman; or, The life and letters of Irma Le Fer de la Motte, in religion Sister Francis Xavier, who died at St. Mary's of the Woods, Vigo county, Ind. Published by one of her sisters, with a preface by M. Leon Aubineau. Translated from the French. New York, The Catholic publication society co., 1882. 1 p. l., [vii]-xii, [13]-416 p. front. (port.) 20 cm. [BX4705.S15L35 1882] 37-16279
1. Saint Francis Xavier, sister, 1816-1856. I. Catholic publication society co., New York. II. Title.

LA CORBINIERE, Clementine 922.
(Le Fer de la Motte) de, Mme 1829-
The life and letters of Sister St. Francis Xavier (Irma Le Fer de la Motte) of the Sisters of Providence of Saint Mary-of-the-Woods, Indiana, by one of her sisters, Mme. Clementine de la Corbiniere; tr. from the French by the Sisters of Providence. Rev. and enl. ed. St. Louis, Mo., and London, B. Herder book co., 1917. xxix, 416 p. front., ports. 24 cm. "First published in France in 1879 ... English translation appeared in 1882."--Foreword. [BX4705.S15L35 1917] 17-30907
1. Saint Francis Xavier, Sister, 1816-1856. I. Sisters of Providence, Saint Mary-of-the-Woods, Ind., tr. II. Title.

LA CORBINIERE, Clementine 922.273
(Le Fer de la Motte) de, Mme. b.1829.
The life and letters of Sister St. Francis Xavier (Irma Le Fer de la Motte) of the Sisters of Providence of Saint Mary-of-the-Woods, Indiana, by one of her sisters, Mme. Clementine de La Corbiniere; translated from the French by the Sisters of Providence. Rev. and enl. ed. Saint Mary-of-the-Woods, Ind., Providence press, 1934. xxviii, 459 p. 24 cm. "First published in France in 1879."--Foreword. "First translation, 1882, revised and enlarged edition, 1917, reprint with addenda, 1934." [BX4750.S15L35 1984] 41-30963
1. Saint Francis Xavier, sister, 1816-1856. I. Sisters of Providence, Saint Mary-of-the-Woods, Ind., tr. II. Title.

St. Fursy (Church), Peronne, France—History—Sources.

ST. Fursy (Church), 282'.44'26
Peronne, France.
Charters of St-Fursy of Peronne / edited by William Mendel Newman, with the assistance of Mary A. Rouse ; pref. by John F. Benton. Cambridge, Mass. : Mediaeval Academy of America, 1977. xxiv, 173 p. : ill. ; 27 cm. English or Latin. Includes indexes. Bibliography: p. 16-17. [BX4629.P47S247] 75-36479 ISBN 0-910956-59-6 : 16.00
1. St. Fursy (Church), Peronne, France—History—Sources. 2. Cartularies. I. Newman, William Mendel, 1902- II. Rouse, Mary A. III. Title.

Saint Gabriel's Episcopal Church, Marion, Mass.

LOVELL, Daisy 283'.744'82
Washburn.
Glad tidings; centennial history of Saint Gabriel's Episcopal Church, Marion, Massachusetts, 1871-1971. Marion, Mass., Saint Gabriel's Episcopal Church [1973] 288 p. illus. 26 cm. [BX5980.M313S344] 73-82234
1. Saint Gabriel's Episcopal Church, Marion, Mass. I. Title.

Saint Gall Church, Chicago, Ill.

CHICAGO. St. Gall Church.
Dedication, April 13, 1958. [Chicago, Leander Co., 1958] 160 p. illus. ports. 27 cm. 68-35466
1. Saint Gall Church, Chicago, Ill. I. Title.

St. Gall, Switzerland (Benedictine abbey)

CLARK, James Midgley, 1888-
The abbey of St. Gall as a centre of literature & art, by J. M. Clark... Cambridge [Eng.] The University press, 1926. vi, [2] 322 p. illus. (incl. plans) facsims. 23 cm. Appendices: A. The nationality of Tuotilo--B. A list of the insular manuscripts in the St. Gall abbey library--C. St. Gall manuscripts in other libraries. Bibliography: p. [305]-313. [DQ549.4.C6] 26-23229
1. St. Gall, Switzerland (Benedictine abbey) I. Title.

St. George's Episcopal Chapel, Long Cove, Me.

NEESON, Margaret 283'.741'53
Graham.
On solid granite; the story of St. George's Church, its village, priests, and people. Modern photos. by Jack Neeson. Old photos. reproduced by Charles Gifford. Long Cove, Me., St. George's Episcopal Chapel [1974] 154 p. illus. 22 cm. Bibliography: p. 144-148. [BX5980.L7S246] 74-77660
1. St. George's Episcopal Chapel, Long Cove, Me. I. Title.

Saint-Germain, comte de, d. 1784?

COOPER-OAKLEY, 133'.0924 B
Isabel.
The Comte de St. Germain; the secret of kings. New York, S. Weiser, 1970. xvi, 249 p. illus., facsims., port. 22 cm. Reprint of the 1912 ed. Bibliography: p. 243-249. [BF1598.S3C6 1970b] 72-132187 ISBN 0-87728-026-6 7.50
1. Saint-Germain, comte de, d. 1784?

COOPER-OAKLEY, 133'.0924 B
Isabel.
The Count of Saint Germain. Introd. by Paul M. Allen. Blauvelt, N.Y., R. Steiner Publications, 1970. viii, 248 p. 22 cm. First published in 1912 under title: The Comte de St. Germain, the secret of kings. Bibliography: p. 243-248. [BF1598.S3C6 1970] 70-137422 7.95
1. Saint-Germain, comte de, d. 1784?

Saint-Germain-des-Pres (Paris, France)

ULTEE, Maarten, 271'.1'044361
1949-
The abbey of St. Germain des Pres in the seventeenth century / Maarten Ultee. New Haven : Yale University Press, c1981. p. cm. Includes index. Bibliography: p. [BX2615.P3U44] 19 81-2265 ISBN 0-300-02562-9 : 20.00
1. Saint-Germain-des-Pres (Paris, France) I. Title.

St. Gregory's Abbey, Shawnee, Okla.

MURPHY, Joseph F. 271'.1'0766
Tenacious monks : the Oklahoma Benedictines, 1875-1975 : Indian missionaries, Catholic founders, educators, agriculturists / by Joseph F. Murphy. Shawnee, Okla. : Benedictine Color Press, [1974] x, 465 p. : ill. ; 25 cm. Includes bibliographical references. [BX3009.O5M87] 74-84770
1. St. Gregory's Abbey, Shawnee, Okla. 2. Benedictines in Oklahoma. 3. Indians of North America—Oklahoma—Missions. I. Title.

St. Gregory's Church, Deerfield, Ill.

KELLEY, Hugh N., 1911- 262'.001
The profile of a parish, by H. N. Kelley. New York, Morehouse-Barlow Co. [1973] xiii, 111 p. 19 cm. Pages 48 and 49 misplated. [BX5980.D394S334] 73-84096 ISBN 0-8192-1163-X 3.50 (pbk.)
1. St. Gregory's Church, Deerfield, Ill. 2. Church renewal—Case studies. I. Title.

St. Hugh's Church, Lewsey, Eng.

URQUHART, Colin. 248'.2'0924 B
When the Spirit comes / Colin Urquhart. 1st U.S. ed. Minneapolis : Bethany Fellowship, 1975, c1974. 127 p. ; 18 cm. (Dimension books) [BX5195.L44S348 1975] 75-21165 ISBN 0-87123-645-1 pbk. : 1.50
1. St. Hugh's Church, Lewsey, Eng. 2. Urquhart, Colin. 3. Pentecostalism. I. Title.

St. Ignatius Church, Hickory, Md.

JOERNDT, Clarence V., 282'.752'74
1898-
St. Ignatius, Hickory, and its missions, by Clarence V. Joerndt. [Baltimore, Printed by Publication Press, 1972] xii, 536 p. illus. 24 cm. Includes bibliographical references. [BX4603.H52S344] 72-92408 11.00
1. St. Ignatius Church, Hickory, Md. 2. Hickory, Md.—Biography. I. Title.

St. Ignatius Church, Oxon Hill, Md.

ST. Ignatius Church, 282'.752'51
Oxon Hill, Md.
St. Ignatius Church, Oxon Hill, Maryland. [White Plains, N.Y.] : Monarch Pub., c1974. [32] p. : ill. ; 28 cm. [BX4603.O93S344 1974] 74-17834
1. St. Ignatius Church, Oxon Hill, Md.

St. James Catholic Church, Seguin, Tex.

ST. James Catholic 282'.764'34
Church, Seguin, Tex.
The centennial story, 1873-1973. Seguin, Tex. : St. James Catholic Church, [1973?] 64 p. : ill. ; 28 cm. Cover title. [BX4603.S63S347 1970z] 75-331288
1. St. James Catholic Church, Seguin, Tex. 2. Seguin, Tex.—Biography. I. Title.

Saint James Episcopal Church, Farmington, Conn.

HEWES, Philip. 283'.746'2
St. James Parish, Farmington, Connecticut: centennial history, 1873/1973. [Farmington, Conn., 1973] viii, 66 p. illus. 24 cm. Bibliography: p. 58-59. [BX5980.F35S344] 73-178391
1. Saint James Episcopal Church, Farmington, Conn. I. Title.

St. James United Methodist Church, Miamisburg, Ohio.

SMITH, Jean Herron. 287'.6771'72
Four churches, one church / by Jean Herron Smith. [s.l. : s.n.], c1975 (Miamisburg, Ohio : Miamisburg News) 72, ix p. : ill. ; 22 cm. [BX8481.M48S63] 75-32342
1. St. James United Methodist Church, Miamisburg, Ohio. I. Title.

Saint John Evangelical Lutheran Church, Meyersville, Tex.

HISTORY and 284'.1764
rededication of Saint John Evangelical Lutheran Church of 1867 on October 26th, 1958, Meyersville, Texas. [Meyersville? Tex., 196-?] 24 p. illus. 22 cm. [BX8076.M43S255] 74-151150
1. Saint John Evangelical Lutheran Church, Meyersville, Tex.

St. John, Harold, 1876-1957.

ST. John, Patricia Mary, 1920- 922

Harold St. John, a portrait by his daughter. New York, Loizeaux Bros, [c1961] 182p. illus. 19cm. [BV3705.S3S3] 62-3910
1. St. John, Harold, 1876-1957. I. Title.

St. John River.

METHODIST Episcopal church.
Conferences. St. Johns River.
Minutes and year book, St. Johns River conference ... Annual session ... Melbourne, Fla. [etc.] v. port. fold. tab. 22 cm. 6-578
I. Title.

NEW Brunswick Historical 922.271
Society.
Champlain and the St. John, 1604-1954, edited by George MacBeath: assistant editors: Jessie I. Lawson, Wm. D. F. Smith, William F. Ryan. With an introd. by A. G. Bailey. [St. John] 1954. 80p. illus. 31cm. [F1030.1.N4] 59-37505
1. Champlain, Samuel de, 1567-1635. 2. St. John River. 3. New Brunswick—Hist. I. MacBeath, George B., ed. II. Title.

St. John the Baptist church, Franklin co., Mo.

CENTENNIAL,
St. John the Baptist congregation, Jefferson, Wisconsin. 66p. illus. 23cm. Cover-title.
1. Jefferson, Wis. St. John the Baptist Catholic Church. II. Title: [Jefferson, Wis.,

HILDNER, George John, 1881- 282.77863
One hundred years for God and country, St. John's, the church and community, 1839-1940, historical sketches by George J. Hildner ... Washington, Mo., Printed by the Washington Missourian, 1940. 128 p. front., plates, ports. 22 cm. [BX4603.F72S34] 42-45050
1. St. John the Baptist church, Franklin co., Mo. I. Title.

St. John the Evangelist Catholic Church, New York.

KELLY, George Anthony, 1916- 282'.747'1
The parish, as seen from the Church of St. John the Evangelist, New York City, 1840-1973, by George A. Kelly. New York, St. John's University [1973] xii, 163 p. illus. 26 cm. Bibliography: p. 157-160. [BX4603.N6S374] 73-4567 ISBN 0-87075-067-4 10.00
1. St. John the Evangelist Catholic Church, New York. I. Title.

St. John's Abbey, Collegeville, Minn.

BARRY, Colman James, 1921- 271.1
Worship and work; Saint John's Abbey and University, 1856-1956. Collegeville, Minn., Saint John's Abbey, 1956. 447p. illus. 27cm. (American Benedictine Academy. Historical studies, no. 11) [BX2525.C6S3] 56-10530
1. St. John's Abbey, Collegeville, Minn. 2. St. John's University, Collegeville, Minn. I. Title.

DEEGAN, Paul J., 1937- 255'.1'00977647
The monastery: life in a religious community, by Paul J. Deegan. Photos. by Bruce Larson. Mankato, Minn., Creative Educational Society [1970] 79 p. illus. 28 cm. "An Amecus Street book." [BX2525.C65D4] 70-125912 ISBN 0-87191-043-8
1. St. John's Abbey, Collegeville, Minn. I. Title.

STODDARD, Whitney S 726.771
Adventure in architecture; building the new Saint John's. Text and pictures by Whitney S. Stoddard, plans by Marcel Breuer. [1st ed.] New York, Longmans, Green, 1958. 127 p. illus., ports., diagrs., plans. 29 cm. [NA5235.C6S8] 57-13215
1. St. John's Abbey, Collegeville, Minn. I. Title.

St. John's Abbey, Collegeville, Minn.—History.

BARRY, Colman James, 1921- 282'.776'47
Worship and work : Saint John's Abbey and University, 1856-1980 / Colman J. Barry. Collegeville, Minn. : Liturgical Press, 1980. 526 p. : ill. ; 24 cm. Includes bibliographical references and index. [BX2525.C65S33] 80-10753 ISBN 0-8146-1123-0 : 12.50
1. St. John's Abbey, Collegeville, Minn.—History. 2. St. John's University, Collegeville, Minn.—History. 3. Collegeville, Minn.—Church history. 4. Collegeville, Minn.—History. I. Title.

Saint John's Church, Keokuk, Iowa.

TALBOT, William L. 283'.777'99
Saint John's Church in Keokuk : a history, 1850-1975 / by William L. Talbot ; with The stained glass of Saint John's by Alice Bowers. Keokuk, Iowa : The Church, 1975. 202 p., [29] leaves of plates : ill. ; 24 cm. Includes bibliographical references and index. [BX5980.K36S247] 75-38945
1. Saint John's Church, Keokuk, Iowa. 2. Keokuk, Iowa—Biography. I. Title.

Saint John's Church, Peterborough, Ont.

JONES, Elwood H. 283'.713'67
St. John's, Peterborough : the sesquicentennial history of an Anglican parish, 1826-1976 / by Elwood H. Jones. Peterborough, [Ont.] : Maxwell Review, 1976. 110 p. : ill. ; 23 cm. [BX5617.P47S244] 77-361693
1. Saint John's Church, Peterborough, Ont. I. Title.

St. John's diocesan seminary, Wonersh.

HOOLEY, Thomas. 207.
A seminary in the making; being a history of the foundation and early years of St. John's diocesan seminary, Wonersh, 1889 to 1903, compiled by the Rev. Thomas Hooley... With an introductory letter from His Eminence Cardinal Bourne... With eight illustrations. London, New York [etc.] Longmans, Green and co., ltd., 1927. xii p., 2 l., 195 p. front., illus. (music) plates, ports. 22 cm. "The Right Reverend John Butt, fourth bishop of Southwark, by Edward canon St. John": p. [167]-195. [BX920.W66H6] 27-23242
1. Butt, John, bp., 1826-1899. 2. Bourne, Francis, cardinal, 1861- 3. St. John's diocesan seminary, Wonersh. I. Title.

St. John's Episcopal Church, Knoxville, Tenn.—History.

ST. John's Bicentennial Committee. 283'.768'85
St. John's Episcopal Church in Knoxville, Tennessee, 1946-1976 / prepared and edited by St. John's Bicentennial Committee. Knoxville : Vestry of St. John's Parish, 1977. x, 100 p. : ill. ; 25 cm. Cover title: St. John's Church, Knoxville, 1946-1976. Includes index. [BX5980.K64S347] 77-155375
1. St. John's Episcopal Church, Knoxville, Tenn.—History. I. Title. II. Title: St. John's Church, Knoxville, 1946-1976.

St. John's Evangelical Lutheran Church, Wythe Co., Va.

KEGLEY, Frederick Bittle, 1877-
St. John's Evangelical Lutheran Church, Wythe County, Virginia, its pastors and their records 1800-1924. With its branches, Lebanon -- 1851, Holy Trinity -- 1876, St. Luke's -- 1888, and Holy Advent -- 1912 and tombstone inscriptions from St. John's Cemetery By F. B. Kegley and Mary B. Kegley. [Wytheville, Va.] Printed privately by Gestetner Duplicator Process, 1961. 420, 48 p. 28 cm. 63-40985
1. St. John's Evangelical Lutheran Church, Wythe Co., Va. I. Title.

St. John's Parish, Wynberg, South Africa.

VOS, K. 283'.68'2
The church on the hill; St. John's Parish, Wynberg [by] K. Vos. Cape Town, Struik, 1972. 174 p. illus. 22 cm. [BX5700.6.Z7W8678] 73-162705 ISBN 0-86977-022-5
1. St. John's Parish, Wynberg, South Africa. I. Title.
Distributed by Verry; 6.25

Saint John's seminary, Brighton, Mass.

SEXTON, John Edward. 207.744
History of Saint John's seminary, Brighton, by John E. Sexton and Arthur J. Riley, with a foreword by His Excellency Richard James Cushing ... Boston, Roman Catholic archbishop of Boston, 1945. 320 p. incl. front., illus. (incl. ports.) 21 1/2 cm. "Priests-alumni of St. John's seminary, Brighton, Mass., 1884-1945." p. [149]-319. [BX915.B76S4] 45-9873
1. Saint John's seminary, Brighton, Mass. I. Riley, Arthur Joseph, 1905- joint author. II. Title.

St. John's Seminary, Carmarillo, Calif.

WEBER, Francis J. 207.79492
A guide to Saint John's Seminary, Camarillo, California, by Francis J. Weber. [Los Angeles] Westernlore Pr., 1966. 32p. illus., col. port. 21cm. Issued to commemorate the silver episcopal jubilee of James Francis Cardinal McIntyre. [BX915.C342W44] 66-23590 3.00
1. St. John's Seminary, Carmarillo, Calif. I. McIntyre, James Francis, Cardinal. II. Title.

St. John's Seminary of San Antonio, Tex.

ST. John's and Assumption Seminaries Alumni Association. 207.764'35
Priest forever; history of St. John's Seminary, San Antonio, Texas, 1915-1965. San Antonio, 1966. 129 p. illus., ports. 24 cm. [BX915.S476] 67-3890
1. St. John's Seminary of San Antonio, Tex. 2. Seminary of the Assumption of the Blessed Virgin Mary of SanAntonio, Tex. I. Title.

ST. John's and Assumption Seminaries Alumni Association. 207.764'35
Priest forever; history of St. John's Seminary, San Antonia, Texas, 1915-1965. San Antonio, 1966. 129 p. illus., ports. 24 cm. [BX915.S476] 67-3890
1. St. John's Seminary of San Antonio, Tex. 2. Seminary of the Assumption of the Blessed Virgin Mary of San Antonio, Tex. I. Title.

St. Johnsbury, Vt.—History—Civil war.

CHADWICK, Albert G comp. 920
Soldiers record of the town of St Johnsbury, Vermont, in the war of the rebellion, 1861-5. Comp. by Hon. Albert G. Chadwick. St. Johnsbury, Vt., C. M. Stone & co., printers, 1883. iv, [5]-215, [1] p. 23 cm. Authorized by vote of the town, Mar. 7, 1865. [F59.S12C4] 13-18451
1. St. Johnsbury, Vt.—Hist.—Civil war. 2. St. Johnsbury, Vt.—Biog. I. St. Johnsbury, Vt. II. Title.

Saint Joseph, mere, 1756-1838.

LEBEURIER, Pierre Francois, 1819- 922.244
Life of Rev. Mother Saint Joseph, foundress of the Congregation of Sisters of St. Joseph of Bordeaux. By L'abbe P. F. Lebeurier ... Translated from the French by a Sister of St. Joseph. New York, Montreal, D. & J. Sadlier & co., 1876. 365 p. 20 cm. [BX4705.S163L4] 37-11168
1. St. Joseph, mere, 1795-1854. I. A Sister of St. Joseph, tr. II. Title.

LEGENDS of Saint Joseph, patron of the universal church by Abbe ... New York [etc.] D. & J. Sadlier, 1872. 2 p. l., [iii]-x, [11]-340 p. front. 16 1/2 cm. 12-38301
I. ..., II. ...Abbe III. Sadlier, Mary Anne (Madden) "Mrs. James Sadlier," 1820-1903, tr.

THE life of Mere St. Joseph (Marie Louise Francoise Blin de Bourdon) co-fondress and second superior general of the Institute of Sisters of Notre Dame of Namur, by a member of the same institute ... London, New York [etc.] Longmans, Green and co., 1923. x, 285, [1] p. front., plates, ports. 22 1/2 cm. "Based ... on the French edition published in 1920."--Note, p.v. Adapted and translated by Sister Frances de Chantal, S.N.D. [BX4705.S16L52] 23-18952 922.2493
1. Saint Joseph, mere, 1756-1838. 2. Sisters of Notre Dame de Namur. I. Frances de Chantal, sister, 1875- ed. and tr.

St. Joseph, Minn. Convent of St. Benedict.

MCDONALD, Grace. 271.9
With lamps burning. Saint Joseph, Minn., Saint Benedict's Priory Press, 1957. 329p. illus. 24cm. (American Benedictine Academy. Historical studies. Monasteries and convents, 4) [BX4278.S25M27] 57-13066
1. St. Joseph, Minn. Convent of St. Benedict. I. Title.

Saint Joseph, Mother, 1756-1838.

MCMANAMA, Mary Fidelis, 1886- 922.2493
Treasure in a field; the life of Venerable Mother St. Joseph, cofoundress of the Sisters of Notre Dame de Namur, nee Viscountess Marie Louise Francoise Blin de Bourdon, heiress of the Barony de Gezaincourt. Milwaukee, Bruce Pub. Co. [1960] 215p. illus. 22cm. [BX4485.3.Z8S25] 60-15480
1. Saint Joseph, Mother, 1756-1838. 2. Sisters of Notre Dame de Namur. I. Title.

MCMANAMA, Mary Fidelis 922.2493
[Secular name: Maude E. McManama] 1886-
Treasure in a field; the life of Venerable Mother St. Joseph, confoundress of the Sisters of Notre Dame de Namur, nee Viscountess Marie Louise Francoise Blin de Bourdon, heiress of the Barony de Fezaineourt. Milwaukee, Bruce Pub. Co. [c.1960] 215p. illus. 60-15480 3.95
1. Saint Joseph, Mother, 1756-1838. 2. Sisters of Notre Dame de Namur. I. Title.

St. Joseph's college, Philadelphia.

TALBOT, Francis Xavier, 1889-
Jesuit education in Philadelphia; Saint Joseph's college, 1851-1926, by Francis X. Talbot, S.J., with a foreword by Wilfrid Parsons, S.J. Philadelphia, Pa., Saint Joseph's college, 1927. xvii p., 1 l., 146 p. incl. front. plates, ports. 23 1/2 cm. [LD4814.S72T3] 27-14569
1. St. Joseph's college, Philadelphia. I. Title.

St. Joseph's College, Princeton, N. J. Queen of the Miraculous Medal Chapel.

DIRVIN, Joseph I. 726.41
The queen of the Miraculous Medal Chapel, Saint Joseph's College, Princeton, New Jersey. Philadelphia, Central Association of the Miraculous Medal, 1951. 125 p. illus. 17 cm. [NA5235.P75D5] 52-21730
1. St. Joseph's College, Princeton, N. J. Queen of the Miraculous Medal Chapel. I. Title.

St. Joseph's convent, Emmittsburg, Md.

BUNKLEY, Josephine M. 271.9760975
...The testimony of an escaped novice from the Sisterhood of St. Joseph, Emmettsburg, Maryland, the mother-house of the Sisters of charity in the United States. By Josephine M. Bunkley. New York, Harper & brothers, 1855. xii, [13]-338 p. incl. illus. (plans) pl. 20 1/2 cm. At head of title: Miss Bunkley's book. [BX4216.B8A2] 31-9986
1. St. Joseph's convent, Emmittsburg, Md. 2. Sisters of charity of St. Vincent de Paul, Emmittsburg, Md. I. Title.

St. Joseph's foreign missionary advocate. American supplement.

ST. Joseph's advocate,
organ of the Josephite fathers. An illustrated quarterly in the interests of missions to the colored races. v. 1- ([1st]-year) Jan. 1884- Baltimore, Md. [1883- v. illus. 25 cm. No.1-4 (1883) have title: American supplement to St. Joseph's foreign missionary advocate. Ed. and pub. by the Fathers of St. Joseph's foreign missionary society of the Sacred Heart. CA 10
1. St. Joseph's foreign missionary advocate. American supplement.

St. Joseph's provincial seminary, Troy, N. Y.

GABRIELS, Henry, bp., 1838-1921. 207.
... Historical sketch of St. Joseph's provincial seminary, Troy. N. Y., by the Right Rev. Henry Gabriels ... With an

introduction: i. Life of Bishop Henry Gabriels, ii. Early New York seminaries. by Charles George Herbermann ... and an epilogue by by Rev. Thomas F. Myhan, A. M. New York, The United States Catholic historical society, 1905. 4 p. l., 5-188 p. front., 1 illus. (music) pl., ports. 24 cm. (United States Catholic historical society. Monograph series. iii) [BX915.T76G2] 5-40424
1. St. Joseph's provincial seminary, Troy, N. Y. I. Herbermann, Charles George, 1840-1916. II. Title.

St. Joseph's seminary and college, Yonkers, N.Y.

SOUVENIR of the blessing of the corner-stone of the new Seminary of St. Joseph, by the Most Rev. Michael Augustine Corrigan, p.p., archbishop of New York, at Valentine hill, Pentecost Sunday, May 17, 1891. New York, The Cathedral library association, 1891. 117 p. front. (port.) plates, 3 maps (1 fold., 2 double) 20 1/2 cm. E10
1. St. Joseph's seminary and college, Yonkers, N.Y.

St. Joseph's seminary, Dunwoodie, N.Y.

SCANLAN, Arthur J. 207.
... St. Joseph's seminary, Dunwoodie, New York, 1896-1921, with an account of the other seminaries of New York; historical sketch by the Rev. Arthur J. Scanlan, S.T.D., with a foreword by the Most Rev. Patrick J. Hayes, D.D., and a chapter on the seminarian's life at Dunwoodie, by the Rev. Francis P. Duffy, D.D. New York, The United States Catholic historical society, 1922. xv, 237 p., 1 l. front., plates, ports. 24 cm. (United States Catholic historical society. Monograph series. vii) Bibliography: p. viii. [BX915.D86S3] 22-13427
1. St. Joseph's seminary, Dunwoodie, N.Y. 2. Catholic church—Education. 3. Duffy, Francis Patrick, 1871-1932. I. Title.

St. Joseph's Ursuline academy, Daviess Co., Ky.

MARY Agnes, Sister, originally Mary Agnes O'Flynn, 1872- comp.
A souvenir of Mount St. Joseph's Ursuline academy, "Maple Mount," Daviess County, Kentucky. Comp. by an Ursuline. 1880-1905. Boston, Mass., Angel guardian press, 1907. 8 p. l., 200 p. front., plates, ports. 23 1/2 cm. [LD7521.S16M3] 7-39407
1. St. Joseph's Ursuline academy, Daviess Co., Ky. I. Title.

St. Kilda Hebrew Congregation.

ROSENTHAL, Newman Hirsch. 296.8'3'09945
Look back with pride; the St. Kilda Hebrew Congregation's first century [by] Newman Rosenthal. [Melbourne, Thomas] Nelson [(Australia) 1971] xv, 182 p. illus. 23 cm. [BM445.M43R68] 73-859578 ISBN 0-17-001955-1
1. St. Kilda Hebrew Congregation. 2. Jews in Melbourne. I. Title.

Saint Leo, Fla. (Benedictine abbey)- Anniversaries, etc.

[DRESSMAN, Aloysius] 1898-
Saint Leo golden jubilee, 1890-1940. History and illustrations commemorating the founding and activities of the Order of Saint Benedict of Florida at Saint Leo, Florida. Issued by and with the authority of Right Reverend Abbot Francis Sadlier... [Saint Leo, Fla., The Abbey press, 1940] xiv p., 1 l., 126 p. plates, ports. 28 cm. Prepared by Aloysius Dressman, O.S.B. cf. p. ix. Pages 97-128, advertising matter. A41
1. Saint Leo, Fla. (Benedictine abbey)- Anniversaries, etc. I. Sudlier, Francis, 1889- II. Title.

St. Louis (Archdiocese)

FAHERTY, William Barnaby. 282'.778'86
Dream by the river; two centuries of Saint Louis Catholicism, 1766-1967. Saint Louis, Piraeus [1973] ix, 246 p. illus. 32 cm. Includes bibliographical references. [BX1417.S2F35] 73-77204 ISBN 0-88273-213-7 12.95
1. St. Louis (Archdiocese) I. Title.
Available from Forum House.

St. Louis (Archdiocese)—History

ROTHENSTEINER, John Ernest, 1860- 282.
History of the archdiocese of St. Louis in its various stages of development from A. D. 1673 to A. D. 1928, by Rev. John Rothensteiner ... St. Louis, Mo. [Printed by Blackwell Wielandy co.] 1928. 2 v. fronts., plates, ports., maps, facsims. 24 cm. Bibliography: vol. ii, p. 769-799. [BX1417.S2R6] 29-5191
1. St. Louis (Archdiocese)—Hist. 2. Catholic church in Missouri. I. Title.

St. Louis. Centenary Methodist church.

WILLIAMS, Francis Emmett, 1877- comp. 287.677866
Centenary Methodist church of St. Louis, the first hundred years, 1839-1939. Compiled for the Centenary Methodist church in St. Louis, Missouri, in commemoration of the inception of its organization one hundred years ago, and in honor of the beginning of Methodism in England two hundred years ago, and including the program of the one hundredth anniversary celebration of Centenary Methodist church in October, 1939. By Mr. and Mrs. Francis Emmett Williams. St. Louis, Mo., Mound City press, inc., 1939. 5 p. l., 9, [5] 11-294 p. front., pl., ports., facsims. 19 1/2 cm. [BX8481.S3C4] 39-31166
1. St. Louis. Centenary Methodist church. 2. Methodists in St. Louis. I. Williams, Anna Belle (Donnell) "Mrs. Francis Emmett Williams," 1887- joint comp. II. Title.

St. Louis. Christ church cathedral.

RODGERS, Eugene L. 283'.778'66
And then a cathedral; a history of Christ Church Cathedral, St. Louis, Missouri, by Eugene L. Rodgers. [St. Louis, Christ Church Cathedral, 1970] 93 p. illus., ports. 23 cm. Bibliography: p. 92-93. [BX5980.S2C48] 70-19302
1. St. Louis. Christ Church Cathedral. I. Title.

SCHUYLER, Montgomery, 1814-1896.
Historical discourse delivered at the semi-centennial celebration of Christ church, St. Louis, on All-saints' day, 1869, by the Rev. Montgomery the Rev. Montgomery Schuyler... St. Louis, Mo;, Printed by G. Knapp & co., 1870. 85 p. 22 cm. [BX5980.S2C5] 2-8977
1. St. Louis. Christ church cathedral. I. Title.

St. Louis Church, Castroville, Tex.

ST. Louis Church, Castroville; a history of the Catholic Church in Castroville, Texas. Written and compiled by Ted Gittinger [and others. Castroville, Tex., St. Louis Catholic Church, 1973] 137 p. illus. 24 cm. Bibliography: p. [123]-[124] [BX4603.C37S276] 74-155414 282'.764'42
1. St. Louis Church, Castroville, Tex. I. Gittinger, Ted.

St. Louis—Church history.

RELIGIONS in St. Louis : a strong heritage / edited by Robert P. Jacobs. Saint Louis, Mo. : Interfaith Clergy Council, c1976. 152 p. : ill. ; 23 cm. [BR560.S2R44] 76-50368 3.95 200'.9778'66
1. St. Louis—Church history. 2. St. Louis—Religion. I. Jacobs, Robert P.

St. Louis. Church of St. Louis of France.

SCHULTE, Paul Clarence, bp., 1890- 282.77866
The Catholic heritage of Saint Louis: a history of the Old Cathedral parish, St. Louis, Mo., compiled by Paul C. Schulte. St. Louis, Mo. Printed by The Catholic herald] 1934. 4 p. l., 274 p. front. plates, facsims. 23 cm. [BX4603.S36C57] 38-16300
1. St. Louis. Church of St. Louis of France. 2. Catholic church in St. Louis. I. Title.

St. Louis. Church of St. Louis of France—History.

FRANZWA, Gregory M. 282'.77866
The Old Cathedral / by Gregory M. Franzwa. Gerald, Mo. : Patrice Press, 1980. p. cm. Includes index. [BX4603.S36C53] 80-15885 ISBN 0-935284-18-4 : 14.95 ISBN 0-935284-17-6 (deerskin) : 100.00
1. St. Louis. Church of St. Louis of France—History. I. Title.

St. Louis. Church of the Messiah (Unitarian)

SWISHER, Walter Samuel, 1882- 288.77866
A history of the Church of the Messiah, 1834-1934, by Walter Samuel Swisher... [St. Louis? 1934?] 56 p. front., illus. 20 1/2 cm. Illustrated t.-p. Bibliogrraphy: p. 5-7. [BX9861.S28C5] 35-10684
1. St. Louis. Church of the Messiah (Unitarian) I. Title.

St. Louis—Churches.

DOUGLASS, Harlan Paul, 1871- 277.
The St. Louis church survey; a religious investigation with a social background, by H. Paul Douglass ... New York, George H. Doran company [c1924] xxi p., 1 l., 27-327 p. front., plates, diagrs. 22 1/2 cm. "The Institute of social and religious research ... shares responsibility for this publication with the Church federation of St. Louis." [BR560.S2D6] 24-18271
1. St. Louis—Churches. 2. St. Louis—Soc. condit. I. Institute of social and religious research. II. Church federation of St. Louis. III. Title.

St. Louis, Mo. (Archdiocese)—History.

EASTERLY, Frederick John, 1910- 922.273
... The life of Rt. Rev. Joseph Rosati, C.M., first bishop of St. Louis, 1789-1843 ... By Reverend Frederick John Easterly ... Washington, D.C., The Catholic university of America press, 1942. xi, 203 p., 1 l. 23 cm. (The Catholic university of America. Studies in American church history ... vol. XXXIII) Thesis (PH.D.)--Catholic university of America, 1942. Vita. "Essay on the sources": p. 191-197. [BX4705.R723E3] A 43
1. Rosati, Joseph, bp., 1789-1843. 2. St. Louis, Mo. (Archdiocese)—Hist. 3. Catholic church in St. Louis—Hist. I. Title.

EASTERLY, Frederick John, 1910- 282'.092'4 B
The life of Rt. Rev. Joseph Rosati, C.M., first bishop of St. Louis, 1789-1843. Washington, Catholic University of America Press, 1942. [New York, AMS Press, 1974] xi, 203 p. 23 cm. Reprint of the author's thesis, Catholic University of America, 1942, which was issued as v. 33 of the Catholic University of America. Studies in American church history. Bibliography: p. 191-197. [BX4705.R723E3 1974] 73-3587 ISBN 0-404-57783-0 9.00
1. Rosati, Joseph, Bp., 1789-1843. 2. Catholic Church in St. Louis—History. 3. St. Louis, Mo. (Archdiocese)—History. I. Series: Catholic University of America. Studies in American church history, v. 33.

St. Louis. Pilgrim Congregational Church.

HACKETT, Allen, 1905- 261.83
For the open door. Philadelphia, United Church [c.1964] 110p. 19cm. Bibl. 64-25363 1.45 pap.,
1. St. Louis. Pilgrim Congregational Church. 2. Church and race problems—St. Louis. I. Title.

HACKETT, Allen, 1905- 261.83
For the open door. Philadelphia, United Church Press [1964] 110 p. 19 cm. Bibliographical footnotes. [BX7255.S28P5] 64-25363
1. St. Louis. Pilgrim Congregational Church. 2. Church and race problems — St. Louis. I. Title.

St. Louis—Religious life and customs—Statistics.

DOUGLASS, Harlan Paul, 1871-1953. 280'.4'0977866
The St. Louis church survey. New York, Arno Press, 1970 [c1924] 327 p. illus., forms, maps. 23 cm. (The Rise of urban America) [BR560.S2D6 1970] 77-112540 ISBN 4-05-024495-
1. St. Louis—Religious life and customs—Statistics. 2. St. Louis—Social conditions—Statistics. I. Title. II. Series.

St. Louis. St. Paul's Episcopal Church.

KLEINE, Glen. 283'.778'66
St. Paul's Episcopal Church, 1866-1966, [by G. Kleine. St. Louis? 1967] 22 p. illus., ports. 22 x 28 cm. Cover title. [BX5980.S2S25] 71-13703
1. St. Louis. St. Paul's Episcopal Church. I. Title.

St. Louis. Third Baptist Church.

NYGAARD, Normal Eugene, 1897- 286.1778
Where cross the crowded ways; the story of the Third Baptist Church of St. Louis, Missouri, and its minister, Dr. C. Oscar Johnson. New York, Greenberg [1950] viii, 240 p. illus., ports. 21 cm. "Where cross the crowded ways of life" (words and music): verse of frontispiece. [BX6480.S27T47] 50-4729
1. Johnosn, Charles Oscar, 1886- 2. St. Louis. Third Baptist Church. I. Title.

PAYNE, Alex Wesley, 1856- 286.177866
What mean these stones! ... The Third Baptist church, St. Louis, for eighty-three years, by A. W. Payne; foreword by Pastor C. Oscar Johnson, D. D.; introduction by S. E. Ewing, D. D. St. Louis, The author, 1934. 237, [3] p. incl. front., illus., ports. fold. tab. 24 cm. Table mounted on back lining-paper. [BX6480.S27T5] 34-40310
1. St. Louis. Third Baptist church. 2. Baptists—St. Louis. I. Title.

St. Louis university—Bibliography

ST. Louis university. 016.
Publications of the faculty and graduate students of St. Louis university in the five years, 1923-1927, with an index according to subjects, comp. by the Reverend James B. Macelwane, S. J., and the Misses M. Ruth Morgan and Kathleen A. Dougherty. [St. Louis] Saint Louis university, 1929. 102 p. 22 cm. (On cover: Bulletin of St. Louis university. vol. XXV. Special number) [Z5055.U5S3] 29-23156
1. St. Louis university—Bibl. I. Macelwane, James Bernard, 1883- II. Morgan, Mary Ruth, 1905- III. Dougherty, Kathleen A. IV. Title.

St. Margaret's School for Girls, Waterbury, Conn.

OHMANN, Carol Burke. 377.837467
Saint Margaret's School, 1865-1965. [Waterbury? Conn.] Saint Margaret's Alumnae Association [1965] vi, 109 p. illus., ports. 22 cm. [LD7251.W487O34] 65-15382
1. St. Margaret's School for Girls, Waterbury, Conn. I. Title.

St. Mark's Chuch, Worsley, Eng.

MILLIKEN, Harold Turner. 942.7'32
Changing scene : two hundred years of

church and parish life in Worsley / by H. T. Milliken ; [photography Peter Tillotson]. [Worsley] : [Worsley Parochial Church Council], 1976. 48 p. : ill., plan, port. ; 23 cm. [BX5195.W86S245] 76-379254 ISBN 0-9505113-0-7 : £0.75
1. St. Mark's Chuch, Worsley, Eng. 2. Worsley, Eng.—Church history. I. Title.

St. Martha's Catholic Parish, Sarasota, Fla.

ST. Martha's Catholic 282'.759'61 Parish, Sarasota, Fla. History Committee. *The story of St. Martha's Catholic Parish* : Sarasota, Florida, 1912-1977 / compiled by the Parish History Committee. [Sarasota, Fla.] : St. Martha's Catholic Parish, 1977. vii, 325 p. : ill. ; 22 cm. Bibliography: p. 291. [BX4603.S59S157] 78-100726
1. St. Martha's Catholic Parish, Sarasota, Fla. I. Title.

Saint-Martin, Louis Claude de, 1743-1808.

WAITE, Arthur Edward, 1857- 922
Three famous mystics; Saint-Martin, by Arthur Edward Waite ... Jacob Boehme, by W. P. Swainson; Swedenborg, by W. P. Swainson. Philadelphia, The David McKay company [1940] 192 p. 19 cm. "Printed in Great Britain." "Jacob Boehme" was published separately in London, 1921: "Emanual Swedenborg" in 1920. [BV5095.A1W28] 40-8924
1. Saint-Martin, Louis Claude de, 1743-1808. 2. Boeheme, Jakob, 1575-1624. 3. Swedenborg, Emanuel, 1688-1772. I. Swainson, William Perkes, 1851- II. Title.

St. Martin, O. Immaculate heart of Mary (Ursuline convent)

[BAPTISTA, sister] 271.97409771796
Fifty years in Brown county convent, by a member of the community. Cincinnati, McDonald & co., 1895. xvi p., 2 l., 294 p. incl. front., illus. plates, ports., facsim. 24 1/2 cm. [Secular name: Susan Fraener] [BX4544.S3B3] 34-16724
1. St. Martin, O. Immaculate heart of Mary (Ursuline convent) I. Title. II. Title: Brown county convent, Fifty years in.

St. Martin, O. School of Brown county Ursulines.

MONICA, sister, 1892- 922.2
The cross in the wilderness; a biography of pioneer Ohio, by Sister Monica ... London, New York [etc.] Longmans, Green and co., 1930. xii p., 1 l., 290 p. front., plates, ports., facsims. 23 cm. "First edition." The life of Mother Julia Chatfield. [BX4705.C463M6] 30-12244
1. Chatfield, Julia, d. 1878. 2. St. Martin, O. School of Brown county Ursulines. 3. Education—Ohio. 4. Frontier and pioneer life—Ohio. I. Title.

St. Mary-of-the-Angels Song School, Addlestone, Eng.

MORSE-BOYCOTT Desmond Lionel, 1892- 258
A golden legend of the slums, being the true tale of life as lived there and the beautiful vision seen there and the wonderous thing that came about there. London. New York, Skeffington [1952] 200 p. illus. 24 cm. [HV4088.L8M58] 52-33536
1. St. Mary-of-the-Angels Song School, Addlestone, Eng. 2. London — Soc. condit. 3. London — Poor. I. Title.

St. Mary the Virgin Church, Linton, Eng.

NOCKOLDS, Hilda. 942.6'57
The early history of Linton Church / by Hilda Nockolds. [Linton] : [St Mary's Church], [1976] [1], 13 p. ; 21 cm. [BX5195.L53S246] 77-351031 ISBN 0-9505286-0-9 : £0.10
1. St. Mary the Virgin Church, Linton, Eng. I. Title.

St. Mary's Armenian Apostolic Church, Washington, D.C.

ST. Mary's Armenian 281'.62'09753 Apostolic Church, Washington, D.C. Booklet Committee.
Saint Mary's Armenian Apostolic Church; commemorative booklet. [Washington] 1968. 64 p. illus. 28 cm. Cover title. [BX128.W37S347 1968] 75-303574
1. St. Mary's Armenian Apostolic Church, Washington, D.C.

St. Mary's Church, Fairfax Station, Va.

RODRIGUES, Jeanne. 282'.755'291
St. Mary's, Fairfax Station, Virginia : the beginnings and growth of a community / by Jeanne Rodrigues with William Hammond. Fairfax Station, Va. : St. Mary's Church, [1975] 48 p. : ill. ; 21 cm. Bibliography: p. 44-48. [BX4603.F26S247] 75-13488 2.00
1. St. Mary's Church, Fairfax Station, Va. I. Hammond, William, joint author.

St. Mary's Church, Garforth, Eng.

PICKLES, Walter. 942.8'19
The history of St Mary's Church, Garforth / by W. Pickles. [New ed.]. [Garforth] : The author, [1976] 24 p. ; 21 cm. Cover title: St Mary's Church, Garforth. "An updating and revision of the late G. E. Kirk's booklet 'The Parish Church of Garforth.'" [BX5195.G377P52] 77-360728 ISBN 0-9502870-1-6 : £0.50
1. St. Mary's Church, Garforth, Eng. I. Kirk, George Edward. The parish church of Garforth. II. Title. III. Title: St. Mary's Church, Garforth.

St. Mary's Church, Great Bealings, Eng.

BROWN, Cynthia. 746.9'5
Hassocks for your church : how we made them at Great Bealings / [by] Cynthia Brown. [Great Bealings] : [St. Mary's Church], [1976] 36 p. : ill. ; 12 x 19 cm. [NK9310.B77] 77-364716 ISBN 0-9505054-0-4 : £0.95
1. St. Mary's Church, Great Bealings, Eng. 2. Ecclesiastical embroidery—England—Great Bealings. 3. Canvas embroidery. 4. Kneelers (Church furniture)—England—Bealings. I. Title.

St. Mary's-in-Tuxedo.

CROFUT, Doris. 283'.747'31
St. Mary's-in-Tuxedo, 1888-1975 / by Doris Crofut. Tuxedo Park, N.Y. : Printed by Library Research Associates for St. Mary's-in-Tuxedo, 1975. 58 p. : ill., ports. ; 23 cm. [BX5980.T89S243] 76-350022
1. St. Mary's-in-Tuxedo. 2. Tuxedo, N.Y.—Biography. I. Title.

St. Mary's Mission. Omak, Wash.

RAUFER. MARIA ILMA 266.20979728
Black robes and Indians on the last frontier, a story of heroism. Milwaukee. Bruce [1966] xiv. 489p. illus,. maps, ports. 23cm. Bibl. [E78.W3R17] 65-29168 7.50
1. St. Mary's Mission. Omak, Wash. 2. Indians of North America—Washington (State)—Hist. 3. Indians of North America—Missions. I. Title.

Saint Mary's Parish, Hagerstown, Md.

HUTZELL, Rita Clark. 282'.752'92
Mother of churches : a history of St. Mary's Church, Hagerstown, Maryland / by Rita Clark Hutzell. [Hagerstown, Md.] : Saint Mary's Parish, 1976. 84 p. : ill. ; 27 cm. Includes bibliographical references. [BX4603.H26S344] 76-24141
1. Saint Mary's Parish, Hagerstown, Md. I. Title.

St. Mary's Parish, Stevensville, Mont.

EVANS, Lucylle H. 266'.2'78689
St. Mary's in the Rocky Mountains : a history of the cradle of Montana's culture / by Lucylle H. Evans. [Stevensville? Mont. : s.n., 1975] viii, 249 leaves ; 28 cm. Bibliography: leaves 245-249. [E99.S2E93] 75-309850
1. St. Mary's Parish, Stevensville, Mont. 2. Salish Indians—Missions. 3. Jesuits—Missions. I. Title.

Saint Matthew's Parish, Black Brook, N.Y.

GAUTHIER, Jeffrey A. 282'.747'54
The heritage of Saint Matthew's Parish of Black Brook, New York, 1832-1876-1976 / by Jeffrey A. Gauthier. [Black Brook? N.Y. : Gauthier?, c1977] 44 p. : ill. ; 27 cm. Cover title. Bibliography: p. 43. [BX4603.B52S243] 77-150937
1. Saint Matthew's Parish, Black Brook, N.Y. I. Title.

Saint Maurice, Switzerland (Augustinian abbey)

ANTON, Hans Hubert. 128'.3
Studien zu den Klosterprivilegien der Papste im fruhen Mittelalter : unter bes. Berucks. d. Privilegierung von St. Maurice d'Agaune / von Hans Hubert Anton. Berlin ; New York : de Gruyter, 1975. x, 172 p. ; 25 cm. (Beitrage zur Geschichte und Quellenkunde des Mittelalters ; Bd. 4) Errata slip inserted. Originally presented as the author's Habilitationsschrift, Bonn, 1970. Includes index. Bibliography: p. [150]-161. [LAW] 75-516225 ISBN 3-11-004686-5 : DM80.00
1. Saint Maurice, Switzerland (Augustinian abbey) 2. Privileges and immunities, Ecclesiastical. I. Title. II. Series.

St. Melnrao Arch. anney, Meinrao, Ind.

ESSAYS on the priesthood [offered to St. Meinrad Archabbey on the occasion of its centenary (1854-1954) by members of the alumni. St. Meinrad, Ind., St. Meinrao Seminary, 1954. 100p. port. 23cm. (St. Meinrad essays, v.11, no.1) Cover title. Bibliographical footnotes. A55
1. St. Melnrao Arch. anney, Meinrao, Ind. 2. Theology, Pastoral—Addresses, Eassays, lectures. 3. [Priesthood] I. Series.
Contents omitted.

St. Michael and All Angels (Church), Kerry, Wales.

JERMAN, H. Noel. 942.9'51
Kerry : the church and the village / by H. Noel Jerman ; line drawings by Kate Mellor. [Kerry, Montgomeryshire] : [The author], [1976] [1], 44, [1] p. : ill., map ; 21 cm. Caption title. [NA5494.K47J47] 77-363473 ISBN 0-9505399-0-2 : £0.50
1. St. Michael and All Angels (Church), Kerry, Wales. 2. Kerry, Wales. I. Title.

St. Michael's Parish, Rochester, N.Y.

MI-CHA-EL : 282'.747'89
a history of St. Michael's Parish, the Diocese of Rochester, from 1874 to 1974. [Rochester, N.Y. : s.n., 1974] 48 p. : ill. ; 28 cm. Cover title: Michael, who is like God? [BX4603.R58S245] 75-329964
1. St. Michael's Parish, Rochester, N.Y. 2. Rochester, N.Y.—Biography. I. Title: Michael, who is like God?

St. Michael's Parish, Talbot Co., Md.

HARPER, Anna Ellis. 283.752
History of St. Michael's Parish. [St. Michaels? Md., 1956] 62p. illus. 20cm. [BX5980.S27H3] 56-44832
1. St. Michael's Parish, Talbot Co., Md. I. Title.

St. Michael's United Church of Christ, Rockingham Co., Va.

HUFFMAN, Charles Herbert. 285.875592
The St. Michaels story, 1764-1964: the United Church of Christ; two centuries of church history. [Staunton Va, 1964] 66 p. illus., facsims., ports. 23 cm. Bibliography: p. 64. [BX9886.Z7S34] 65-1161
1. St. Michael's United Church of Christ, Rockingham Co., Va. I. Title.

Saint, Nathanael, 1923-1956.

HITT, Russell T. 922.6866
Jungle Pilot, the life and witness of Nate Saint. Photos by Nate Saint, other missionaries and Cornell Capa. Grand Rapids, Mich., Zondervan Publishing House [1973, c1959] 263 p. illus. 18 cm. [BV2853.E3S3] pap. 1.25
1. Saint, Nathanael, 1923-1956. 2. Missions—Ecuador. I. Title.
L.C. card no. for original ed. 59-10335

St. Patrick's day.

DOCTER, Kathryn. 394.268
Celebrating St. Patrick's day, a real Irish collection, by Kathryn Docter ... Lebanon, O., March brothers publishing co. [c1936] 110 p. 19 cm. [PN4305.H7D6] 38-29742
1. St. Patrick's day. I. Title.

IRISH, Marie. 394.268
... St. Patrick's day; plays and pieces, by Marie Irish and Willis N. Bugbee ... Syracuse, N.Y., The Willis N. Bugbee co., c1932. 32 p. 18 1/2 cm. (Bugbee's entertainments) [PN4305.H71743] 37-31735
1. St. Patrick's day. I. Bugbee, Willis Newton, 1870- joint author. II. Title.

IRISH, Marie. 394.268
Shamrocks for St. Patrick's day, by Marie Irish ... New York, Fitzgerald publishing corporation [c1932] 187 p. illus., diagrs. 19 cm. (Playhouse plays) [PN4305.H71744] 32-32287
1. St. Patrick's day. I. Title.

St. Patrick's Day—Juvenile literature.

BARTH, Edna. 394.2'6
Shamrocks, harps, and shillelaghs : the story of the St. Patrick's Day symbols / by Edna Barth ; illustrated by Ursula Arndt. New York : Seabury Press, c1977. 95 p. : col. ill. ; 26 cm. "A Clarion book." Includes index. Bibliography: p. 94-95. Explores the origin and meaning of the symbols and legends associated with St. Patrick's Day. [GT4995.P3B37] 77-369 ISBN 0-8164-3195-7 : 7.95
1. St. Patrick's Day—Juvenile literature. I. Arndt, Ursula. II. Title.

CANTWELL, Mary. 394.268 (J)
St. Patrick's Day. Illustrated by Ursula Arndt. New York, Crowell [1967] [40] p. illus. (part col.) 22 cm. (Crowell holiday books) [GT4995.S3C35] 67-846
1. St. Patrick's Day—Juvenile literature. I. Title.

St. Paul (Archdiocese)—History

REARDON, James Michael. 282.776
The Catholic Church in the Diocese of St. Paul, from earliest origin to centennial achievement; a factual narrative. St. Paul, North Central Pub. Co., 1952. xv. 726p. illus. ports. 25cm. Bibilographical references: p. 691-707. [BX1417.S3R4] 53-82
1. St. Paul (Archdiocese)—Hist. I. Title.

St. Paul catechism of Christian doctrine.

ALEXANDER, Sidney Arthur, 1866-
The Christianity of St. Paul, by S. A. Alexander ... London, New York [etc.] Longmans, Green, and co., 1899. viii, 216 p. 20 cm. 12-30188
I. Title.

THE Christianity of St. Paul; ten lectures, October. December 1955. [Washington? D. C.] Published by the organizing committee, Christianity and modern man [1956] iv, 113p. (Christianity and modern man)
I. Mollegen, Albert T

THE Christianity of St. Paul; ten lectures, October-December 1955. [Washington? D. C.] Published by the organizing committee, Christianity and

modern man [1956] iv, 113p. (Christinity and modern man)
I. Mollegen, Albert T

DAUGHTERS OF ST. PAUL.
Guide to the revised Baltimore catechism . . . according to the St. Paul catechism of Christian doctrine . . . [Boston] St. Paul Editions [1957-1962] 6 v. illus. 22 cm. Contents.[no. 1] First Communion. -- no. 2-4. Grades 1-3. -- no. 5. Grades 4-6. -- [no. 6] Grades 7-8. 63-7915
1. Daughters of St. Paul-St. Paul catechism of Christian doctrine. 2. St. Paul catechism of Christian doctrine. 3. Baltimore catechism. 4. Religious education — Textbooks. I. Title.

St. Paul. Mount Zion Hebrew Congregation.

PLAUT, W Gunther, 1912- 296.6509776581
Mount Zion, 1856-1956; the first hundred years. [St. Paul, Minn., 1957] 152p. illus. 23cm. Includes bibliography. [BM225.S28M6] 59-28918
1. St. Paul. Mount Zion Hebrew Congregation. I. Title.

St. Paul the Apostle Church, Greencastle, Ind.

PORTER, Jack W., 1927- 282'.772'49
The Catholic Church in Greencastle, Putnam County, Indiana, 1848-1978 / by Jack W. Porter and William F. Stineman. Greencastle, Ind. : Saint Paul the Apostle Church, c1979. 93 p. : ill. ; 29 cm. Includes bibliographical references. [BX4603.G744S246] 78-65724 ISBN 0-9602352-0-5 : 14.95
1. St. Paul the Apostle Church, Greencastle, Ind. I. Stineman, William Frederick, 1925- joint author. II. Title.

St. Paul United Methodist Church, Ninety Six, S.C.

OWEN, Fred Colley. 287'.6757'33
St. Paul United Methodist Church, Ninety Six, South Carolina: church history, 1875-1972. Greenwood, S.C., Drinkard Print. Co. [1974] 61 p. illus. 24 cm. Cover title: History of St. Paul United Methodist Church, 1875-1972. [BX8481.N55S35] 74-172782
1. St. Paul United Methodist Church, Ninety Six, S.C.

St. Paul. Unity Church.

OTTO, Elinor Sommers. 288'.776'58
The story of Unity Church, 1872-1972. St. Paul, Unity Church of St. Paul, 1972. viii, 130 p. illus., ports. 26 cm. Bibliography: p. 125. [BX9861.S29O8] 72-179644
1. St. Paul. Unity Church. I. Title.

St. Paul's Church, Alverthorpe, Eng.

SPEAK, Harold. 283'.428'15
St Paul's Church, Alverthorpe : parish and people, 1825[-]1975 : an outline history / by Harold Speak and Jean Forrester. Ossett : The authors [for] the Parochial Church Council, Alverthorpe St Paul's Church, 1976. [1], 26 p. : ill., ports. ; 21 cm. Cover title. [BX5195.A55S367] 76-382450 ISBN 0-902829-04-1 : £0.35
1. St. Paul's Church, Alverthorpe, Eng. 2. Alverthorpe, Eng.—History. I. Forrester, Jean F., joint author. II. Title.

St. Paul's Church, Grosse Pointe Farms, Mich.

MECKE, Theodore H. 282'.774'33
A brief history of St. Paul's Parish, Grosse Pointe Farms, Michigan [by Theodore H. Mecke. 1st ed. Grosse Pointe Farms, Mich., 1973] 34, [1] p. 19 cm. Bibliography: p. [35] [BX4603.G76S345] 73-80650
1. St. Paul's Church, Grosse Pointe Farms, Mich. I. Title.

St. Paul's Church, Heaton Moor, Eng.

OPENSHAW, Eunice M. 283'.427'34
The story of S. Paul's Church, Heaton Moor / written by Eunice M. Openshaw. [Stockport] : [The author], 1976. 55 p., [8] p. of plates : ill., facsim., ports. ; 21 cm. Cover title: S. Paul's Church Heaton Moor, 1877-1976. [BX5195.H38S366] 77-364636 ISBN 0-9505582-0-6 : £0.90
1. St. Paul's Church, Heaton Moor, Eng. I. Title.

St. Paul's Church (Rome, Italy)

MILLON, Judith Rice, 1934- 726'.5'0945632
St. Paul's within the walls, Rome : a building history and guide, 1870-1980 / Judith Rice Millon. Dublin, N.H. : W.L. Bauhan, c1982. 117 p., [8] p. of plates : ill. (some col.) ; 22 cm. Includes index. Bibliography: p. 108-110. [NA5620.S98M5 1982] 19 81-8055 ISBN 0-87233-058-3 : 8.95
1. St. Paul's Church (Rome, Italy) I. Title.
Publisher's address: Old Country Rd., Dublin, NH 03444.

Saint Peter.

*COSGROVE, John. 282'.092'4
Upon this rock : a tale of Peter / John Cosgrove. Huntington, IN : Our Sunday Visitor 1978. 298p. ; 20 cm. [BS2575] 77-94404 ISBN 0-87973-775-1 pbk. : 4.95
1. Saint Peter. 2. Popes. I. Title.

St. Peter, Minn. Scandian Grove Evangelical Lutheran Church.

SCANDIAN Grove;
a history of the Scandian Grove Evangelical Lutheran church, St. Peter,Minnesota, 1858-1958. St. Peter, Minnesota, 1858-1958. St. Peter, Centennial Committee of Scandian Grove Lutheran Church [1958] 151p. illus. (incl. ports.) 22cm. Includes bibliography.
1. St. Peter, Minn. Scandian Grove EvangelicalLutheran Church. I. Johnson, Emercy.

St. Peter's Church, London—Organs.

GOULDEN, Colin. 786.6'2421'32
The organs of All Souls Church, Langham Place, London and St. Peter's Church, Vere Street, London / by Colin Goulden. London : All Souls Church, 1976. [4], 15 p. : ill. ; 21 x 18 cm. [ML594.L62S35] 77-358093
1. St. Peter's Church, London—Organs. 2. All Souls Church, London—Organs. I. Title: The organs of All Souls Church ...

St. Peter's Church, Wymondham, Eng. (Leicestershire)

TAYLOR, Ralph Penniston. 914.25'48
St Peter's Church, Wymondham, Leicestershire : a history and description / [by] Ralph Penniston Taylor ; modern photographs by Trevor Hickman. Wymondham : T. Hickman : [Distributed by Brewhouse Private Press], 1976. 88 p. : ill., facsims. ; 21 cm. Limited ed. of 120 signed copies. No. 67. Ill. on lining papers. Bibliography: p. 87. [BX5195.W94S257] 77-357779 ISBN 0-900190-38-8 : £6.90
1. St. Peter's Church, Wymondham, Eng. (Leicestershire) I. Title.

St. Peter's Episcopal church, East Whiteland township, Chester co., Pa.

EBERLEIN, Harold Donaldson. 283.748
The Church of Saint Peter in the Great valley, 1700-1940, the story of a colonial country parish in Pennsylvania, by Harold Donaldson Eberlein & Cortlandt Van Dyke Hubbard. Richmond, Va., Printed by A. Dietz and his son, 1944. 4 p. l., [iii]-iv, 167 p. front., plates, facsims. 25 cm. [BX5980.E2C5] 46-4212
1. St. Peter's Episcopal church, East Whiteland township, Chester co., Pa. I. Hubbard, Cortlandt Van Dyke, joint author. II. Title.

St. Petersburg, Fla. Pasadena Community Church.

ALDRICH, Guy V 287.675963
Seven miles out; the story of Pasadena Community Church, St. Petersburg, Florida, 1924-1960 [by] Guy V. Aldrich. [Tampa, Fla. [1965?] [BX8481.S315P32] 66-6973
1. St. Petersburg, Fla. Pasadena Community Church. I. Title.

Saint, Philip.

SAINT, Philip. 266'.0092'4
Amazing Saints, by Phil Saint. Plainfield, N.J., Logos International, 1972. vii, 211 p. illus. 21 cm. Autobiographical. [BV3785.S15A3] 71-124480 ISBN 0-912106-24-7 4.95
1. Saint, Philip. I. Title.

St. Philip's Church, Bemidji, Minn.

SCHUILING, Walter John, 1953- 282'.776'82
History of St. Philip's Parish, 1897-1975 / Walter John Schuiling. [Bemidji, Minn. : s.n.], c1977. vii, 283 p., [5] leaves of plates : ill. ; 28 cm. Thesis (M.A.)—Bemidji State University. Vita. Bibliography: p. 211-217. [BX4603.B48S247] 77-151715
1. St. Philip's Church, Bemidji, Minn. I. Title.

St. Rose Church, Proctor, Minn.

SCHUMACHER, Claire W. 282'.776'77
This is our St. Rose Church in Proctor, Minnesota : a Catholic's viewpoint of history / researched, written, and designed by Claire W. Schumacher. 1st ed. Proctor : The Church, c1976. 84 p. : ill. ; 27 cm. [BX4603.P65S347] 76-22312 ISBN 0-917378-01-6
1. St. Rose Church, Proctor, Minn. I. Title.

Saint Rose (Dominican priory)

ST. Rose (Dominican Priory) 271.2
The first two Dominican priories in the United States: Saint Rose's priory, near Springfield, Kentucky; Saint Joseph's priory, near Somerset, Ohio, by Victor Francis O'Daniel and James Reginald Coffey. New York, National Headquarters of the Holy Name Society [1947] xiv, 301 p. illus., ports. 24 cm. [BX2525.S27O2] 48-12625
1. Saint Rose (Dominican priory) 2. Saint Joseph (Dominican priory) I. St. Joseph (Dominican Priory) II. Coffey, James Reginald, 1908- joint author. III. St. Joseph (Dominican Priory) IV. Coffey, James Reginald, 1908- joint author. V. Title.

St. Rose's Home.

BERRIGAN, Daniel. 362.1'96029
We die before we live / Daniel Berrigan. New York : Seabury Press, 1980. p. cm. "A Crossroad book." [BT825.B455] 80-16835 ISBN 0-8164-0462-3 : 8.95
1. St. Rose's Home. 2. Berrigan, Daniel. 3. Catholic Church—Clergy—Biography. 4. Death. 5. Terrinal care—Moral and religious aspects. 6. Clergy—United States—Biography. I. Title.

Saint Sauveur (Colony)

BROWN, Lenard E. 266.2'741'45
Significance of St. Sauveur Mission, established 1613, Mount Desert Island, by Lenard E. Brown. Washington, Office of History and Historic Architecture, Eastern Service Center, 1970. iv, 57 l. 8 plates (incl. maps) 27 cm. At head of title: Acadia National Park, Maine. Bibliography: leaves 54-56. [F22.B85] 71-612223
1. Saint Sauveur (Colony) I. Title. II. Title: Acadia National Park, Maine.

Saint-Savin, Frances (Vinne) Eglise.

GILLARD, Georges. 751.73
The frescoes of Saint-Savin. New York, Studio Publications [1944- v. illus., col. plates. 34 cm. (Romanesque painting) Issued in portfolio. Bibliographie": v. 1,p. 9. [NA5551.S45G] A 48
1. Saint-Savin, Frances (Vinne) Eglise. 2. Mural painting and decoration. I. Title. II. Series.
Contents omitted.

St. Saviour's, Claremont, South Africa.

LANGHAM Carter, R. R. 283'.68'7
Under the mountain; the story of St. Saviour's, Claremont [by] R. R. Langham-Carter. [Claremont, S.A., Southern Press, 1973] 31 p. illus. 23 cm. [BX5983.C55S34] 73-178981
1. St. Saviour's, Claremont, South Africa. I. Title.

St. Stanislaus Church, Cleveland.

A People: 100 years. 282'.771'32
[Editor in chief: Jean Jagelewski. Cambridge, Md., Western Pub. Co., c1973] 300 p. illus. 29 cm. Cover title. On spine: St. Stanislaus, 1873-1973. English or Polish. [BX4603.C65S336] 73-90634
1. St. Stanislaus Church, Cleveland. I. Jagelewski, Jean, ed.

St. Stephen Baptist Church, Kansas City, Mo.

ST. Stephen Baptist Church, Kansas City, Mo. History Committee. 286'.1778'411
Symbols of God's grace; seventy years history. St. Stephen Baptist Church, Kansas City, Missouri. [Thelma M. Dumas, chairman. 2d ed. Kansas City, St. Stephen Baptist Church, 1974, c1973] 538 p. illus. 26 cm. Edition for 1963 published under title: Meeting the challenge of change. [BX6480.K3S3 1973] 74-176286
1. St. Stephen Baptist Church, Kansas City, Mo. 2. Kansas City, Mo.—Biography. I. Dumas, Thelma M. II. Title.

St. Thomas Christians.

BROWN, Leslie, 1912- 281.9'3
The Indian Christians of St. Thomas : an account of the ancient Syrian Church of Malabar / by Leslie Brown. Reissued with additional chapter. Cambridge [Cambridgeshire] ; New York : Cambridge University Press, 1982. xii, 327 p., 7 p. of plates : ill. ; 23 cm. Includes index. Bibliography: p. 318-324. [BX163.2.B76 1982] 19 81-21766 ISBN 0-521-21258-8 : 34.50
1. St. Thomas Christians. I. Title.

BROWN, Leslie Wilfrid, Bp., 1912- 281.63
The Indian Christians of St. Thomas; an account of the ancient Syrian Church of Malabar. Cambridge [Eng.] University Press, 1956. 315p. illus. 22cm. [BX163.B7] 57-544
1. St. Thomas Christians. I. Title.

POTHAN, S. G., 1905- 281.5
The Syrian Christians of Kerala. New York, Asia Pub. [dist. Taplinger, c.1963] 119p. illus. 23cm. 63-1869 6.50
1. St. Thomas Christians. 2. Kerala—Church history. I. Title.

POTHAN, S. G. 1905- 281.5
The Syrian Christians of Kerala. Bombay, New York, Asia, Pub, House [1963] 119 p. illus., plates. 23 cm. Bibliography: p. 111-112 [BX163.2] 63-4051
1. St. Thomas Christians. 2. Kerala—Church history. I. Title.

POTHAN, S G 1905- 281.5
The Syrian Christians of Kerala. New York, Asia Pub. House [1963] 119 p. illus. 23 cm. [BX163.2.P6] 63-1869
1. St. Thomas Christians 2. Kerala—Church history. I. Title.

St. Thomas' parish, Orange co., Va.

ORANGE, Va. St. Thomas' church. 283.75537
Bi-centennial, St. Thomas' parish and centennial, St. Thomas' church,October 20-21, 1933. Historical notes, printed by order of thevestry. Prepared by H. C. Warren; introduction by the rector. [Gordonsville, Va., Printed by Bibb & co., 1933] 77 p. front., plates. 22 cm. Folded map attached to inside of back cover. Lettered on cover: St. Thomas' Episcopal church, 1730, 1833, 1933.Historic statement. Orange, Virginia. [BX5980.O7T5] 34-8551
1. St. Thomas' parish, Orange co., Va. I. Warren, Henry Crew, 1879- II. Title.

St. Thomas' seminary, Nelson co., Ky.

HOWLETT, William Joseph, 1848-1936. 207.
Historical tribute to St. Thomas' seminary at Poplar Neck, near Bardstown, Kentucky. By Rev. Wm. J. Howlett ... St. Louis, Mo., B. Herder, 1906. 197 p. front., illus., plates, ports. 20 cm. [BX915.B46H7] 6-45766
1. St. Thomas' seminary, Nelson co., Ky. I. Title.

HOWLETT, William Joseph, 1848-1936. 207.
Historical tribute to St. Thomas' seminary at Poplar Neck, near Bardstown, Kentucky. By Rev. Wm. J. Howlett ... St. Louis, Mo., B. Herder, 1906. 197 p. front., illus., plates, ports. 20 cm. [BX915.B46H7] 6-45766
1. St. Thomas' seminary, Nelson co., Ky. I. Title.

St. Urban, mother, 1857-1933

WILLIAMS, Thomas David, 1872- 922.273
The life of Mother St. Urban of the Congregation of the sisters of bon secours of Paris, by Rev. Thomas David Williams ... Baltimore, Md., John Murphy company, 1936. 336 p. front. (port.) 20 cm. [BX4705.S185W5] 36-8791
1. St. Urban, mother, 1857-1933 2. Sisters of bon secours of Paris. I. Title.

St. Valentine's Day.

BULLA, Clyde Robert. 394.268
St. Valentine's Day. Illus. by Valenti Angelo. New York, Crowell [1965] [38] p. illus. 22 cm. (A Crowell holiday book) Relates briefly the history of St. Valentine's Day, originally celebrated by the Romans thousands of years ago. [GT4925.B8] AC 68
1. St. Valentine's Day. I. Angelo, Valenti, 1897- illus. II. Title.

St. Valentine's Day—Juvenile literature.

BARTH, Edna. 394.2'683
Hearts, cupids, and red roses; the story of the valentine symbols. Illustrated by Ursula Arndt. New York, Seabury Press [1974] 64 p. illus. 26 cm. Bibliography: p. 62-63. The history of Valentine's Day and the little-known stories behind its symbols. [GT4925.B32] 73-7128 ISBN 0-8164-3111-6 5.50
1. St. Valentine's Day—Juvenile literature. 2. [St. Valentine's Day.] I. Arndt, Ursula, illus. II. Title.

BULLA, Clyde Robert 394.2
St. Valentine's Day. Illus. by Valenti Angelo. New York, Crowell [c.1965] 1v. (unpaged) illus. 23cm. (Crowell holiday bk.) [GT4925.B8] 65-11643 2.95 bds.,
1. St. Valentine's Day—Juvenile literature. I. Angelo, Valenti, 1897- illus. II. Title.

BULLA, Clyde Robert. 394.2
St. Valentine's Day. Illus. by Valenti Angelo. New York, Crowell [1965] 1 v. (unpaged) illus. 22 cm. (A Crowell holiday book) [GT4925.B8] 65-11643
1. St. Valentine's Day—Juvenile literature. 2. [St. Valentine's Day.] I. Angelo, Valentine 1897- illus.

GUILFOILE, Elizabeth JUV
Valentine's Day. Illus. by Gordon Laite. Champaign, Ill., Garrard [c.1965] 62p. col. illus. 25cm. (Holiday bk.) [PZ9.G923Val] 394.2 65-10086 2.12
1. St. Valentine's Day—Juvenile literature. I. Title.

Saint Vibiana's Cathedral, Los Angeles.

WEBER, Francis J. 282'.794'94
Saint Vibiana's Cathedral : a centennial history / by Francis J. Weber. Los Angeles : Weber, 1976. 73 p. : ill. ; 25 cm. Includes bibliographical references. [BX4603.L27S258] 74-21935
1. Saint Vibiana's Cathedral, Los Angeles.

Saints.

ALACOQUE, Marguerite Marie, Saint, 1647-1690. 242
Gems of thought from Saint Margaret Mary; revised and edited by a religious of the Visitation. New York, Cincinnati [etc.] Benziger brothers, 1931. xviii p. 1 l., 165 p. front. 14 cm. [BX2179.A6A25] 31-21815
I. Lefbell, Jane Frances, sister 1877- ed. II. Title.

ATTWATER, Donald, 1892- 922.1
The golden book of Eastern saints [by] Donald Attwater ... Milwaukee, The Bruce publishing company [c1938] xx. 166 p., 1 l. front., plates, ports. 23 cm. (Half-title: Religion and culture series, Joseph Husslein ... general editor) [BX303.A8] 38-9006
1. Saints. I. Title. II. Title: Eastern saints, The golden book of.

ATTWATER, Donald, 1892- 922.22
Saints of the East. New York, P. J. Kenedy [1963] 190 p. illus. 22 cm. [BX393.A83] 63-11328
1. Saints. I. Title.

BALCH, Stephen Bloomer, 1747-1833.
Two sermons, on the certain and final perseverance of the saints. By Stephen Bloomer Balch, A. M., pastor of the Presbyterian congregation, Georgetown ... Georgetown, Printed for the author, by M. Day and W. Hancock, 1791. iv, [5]-63 p. 20 cm. "Said to be the first book printed in the District of Columbia." Imperfect: Original t.-p. and seven lines at end wanting, but replaced by a facsimile of the t.-p. and p. 63, photostatted and rephotostatted from the copy in the possession of W. H. Lowdermilk & co., Washington. 16-1208
I. Title.

BALCH, Stephen Bloomer, 1747-1833.
Two sermons on the certain and final perseverance of the saints. By Stephen Bloomer Balch, A.M., pastor of the Presbyterian congregation, George-town ... George-town, Printed, for the author, by M. Day and W. Hancock, 1791. [Philadelphia, Reprinted 1907?] p. 125-176. 2 pl. (incl. front., port.) 27 cm. Reprinted from "Balch genealogica, by Thomas Willing Balch. Philadelphia, Allen, Lane and Scott, 1907." "Said to be the first book printed in the District of Columbia." 10-19576
I. Title.

BALSKUS, Pat. 282'.092'4 B
Mary's pilgrim; life of St. Peregrine. Illustrated by the Daughters of St. Paul. [Boston] St. Paul Editions [1972] 92 p. illus. 22 cm. (Encounter books) The life of the thirteenth-century Italian priest who became the patron against cancer after being miraculously cured of that disease. [BX4700.L43B34] 92 68-58160 1.50
1. Laziosi, Pellegrino, Saint, 1265-1345—Juvenile literature. 2. [Laziosi, Pellegrino, Saint, 1265-1345.] 3. [Saints.] I. Daughters of St. Paul. II. Title.

BARCLAY, Vera C 1893- 922.2
Saints by firelight; stories for guides and rangers, by Vera Barclay. New York, The Macmillan company, 1931. xi p., 2 l., 17-206 p. 19cm. "Printed in Great Britain." [BX4658B3] 32-14931
1. Saints. I. Title.

Contents omitted.

BARING-GOULD, Sabine, 1834-1924.
Virgin saints and martyrs, by S. Baring-Gould. With sixteen full-page illustrations by F. Anger. New York, T. Y. Crowell & co., 1901. 400 p. front., plates. 19 cm. A 11
1. Saints. 2. Martyrs. I. Title.

BATES, Arlo, 1850-
The diary of a saint, by Arlo Bates ... Boston and New York, Houghton, Mifflin and company, 1902. 3 p. l., 310 p., 1 l. 20 cm. 2-17856
I. Title.

BLOCKER, Hyacinth.
Walk with the wise. Cincinnati, St. Francis Book Shop, 1950. 240 p. 21 cm. A 52
1. Saints. 2. Spiritual life—Catholic authors. I. Title.

THE book of saints; 922.2
a dictionary of servants of God canonised by the Catholic church; extracted from the Roman & other martyrologies. Compiled by the Benedictine monks of St. Augustine's abbey, Ramsgate. 3d ed., with appendix of additional names and a calendar of saints. New York, The Macmillan company. London, A & C. Black, ltd., 1934. 2 p. l., vii-xi [1]-327, [1] p. 22 1/2 cm. [BX4655.B6 1934] 34-23291
1. Saints. I. Saint Augustine's abbey. Ramsgate.

BOUQUET, John Alexander, 1875- 922
A people's book of saints, by J. Alick Bouquet, with sixteen illustrations. London, New York [etc.] Longmans, Green and co., 1930. 3 p. l., 5-299 p. front., plates. 19 1/2 cm. [BX4655.B65] 30-12393
1. Saints. I. Title.

BOWDEN, Henry Sebastian, 1836-1919, comp. 922.22
The following of the saints; miniature lives of the saints for daily meditation. Edited and rev. by Donald Attwater. New York, Kenedy [1959] 802 p. illus. 18 cm. Published in 1877 under title: Miniature lives of the saints for every day in the year. [BX4655.B68 1959] 59-7524
1. Saints. 2. Catholic Church—Prayer-books and devotions. 3. Devotional calendars—Catholic Church. I. Title.

BREWSTER,H. Pomeroy, d.1906. 922
Saints and festivals of the Christian church, by H. Pomeroy Brewster... New York, Frederick A. Stokes company [1904] 2 p. l., xiv, 556 p. illus. 21 cm. "A considerable part of the matter presented in the following pages was printed [as] a series of articles in the Union and advertiser of Rochester, N.Y." [BR1710 B7] 4-28224
1. Saints. 2. Fasts and feasts. I. Title.

BRODRICK, James, 1891- 270 B
A procession of saints. Freeport, N.Y., Books for Libraries Press [1972, c1949] p. (Biography index reprint series) Includes bibliographical references. [BX4655.B7 1972] 72-5436 ISBN 0-8369-8134-0
1. Saints. I. Title.

BRODRICK, James, 1891- 922.242
A processionof saints [1st ed.] New York, Longmans, Green, 1949. ix, 198 p. 22 cm. Bibliographical footnotes. [BX4655.B7 1949] 49-7983
1. Saints. I. Title.

BROWN, Beverly Holladay, 1912- 235.2
Mary communes with the saints, by Raphael Brown [pseud.] St. Meinrad, Ind. [1955] 147p. illus. 20cm. (A Grall publication) [BX4657.B76] 55-9130
1. Saints. 2. Mary, Virgin—Apparitions and miracles (Modern) I. Title.

BURGHARDT, Walter J 248.0922 (B)
Saints and sanctity [by] Walter J. Burghardt. Englewood Cliffs, N.J., Prentice-Hall [1965] xiv, 239 p. illus. 22 cm. Bibliographical footnotes. [BX4655.2.B8] 65-8828
1. Saints. 2. Exempla. I. Title.

BUTLER, Alban, 1711-1773. 235.20922
Lives of the saints. Edited, rev., and supplemented by Herbert Thurston and Donald Attwater. Complete ed. [New York. P. J. Kenedy, 1965, c1963] 4 v. 24 cm. Includes bibliographies. [BX4654.B8] 67-5269
1. Saints. 2. Devotional calendars. I. Thurston, Herbert, 1856-1939. II. Attwater, Donald, 1892- III. Title.

BUTLER, Alban, 1711-1773. 922.22
Lives of the saints; edited, rev., and supplemented by Herbert Thurston and Donald Attwater. Complete ed. New York, Kenedy [1956] 4 v. 24 cm. Includes bibliographical references. [BX4654.B8 1956] 56-5383
1. Saints. 2. Devotional calendars. I. Thurston, Herbert, 1856-1939. II. Attwater, Donald, 1892- III. Title.

BUTLER, Alban, 1711-1773. 922.22
Lives of the saints. Edited, rev., and supplemented by Herbert Thurston and Donald Attwater. Complete ed. [New York] [Kenedy] [1962] 4 v. 24 cm. Includes bibliographical references. [BX4654.B8 1962] 62-51171
1. Saints. 2. Devotional calendars. I. Thurston, Herbert, 1856-1939. II. Attwater, Donald, 1892- III. Title.

BUTLER, Alban, 1711-1773.
Lives of the saints, with reflections for every day in the year, compiled from the "Lives of the saints", by Rev. Alban Butler, to which are added lives of the American saints placed on the calendar for the United States by special petition of the third plenary council of Baltimore. New York, Cincinnati [etc.] Benziger brothers, 1913. 406 p. 19 cm. [BX4654.B95] 13-24457
1. Saints. 2. Caldendars. I. Title.

BUTLER, Alban, 1711-1773. 922.22
Lives of the saints, with reflections for every day in the year; compiled from the "Lives of the saints" by Alban Butler, with new saints and those whose feasts are special to the United States. New York, Benziger [1953] 390 p. 19 cm. [BX4654.B95 1953] 53-27731
1. Saints. 2. Calendars. I. Title.

CANTON, William, 1845-1926.
A child's book of saints, by William Canton... London, J.M. Dent & co. New York, E.P. Dutton & co. [1906] x p. 1 l., [2], 258 p. illus. 17 1/2 cm. (Half-title: Everyman's library, ed. by Ernest Rhys. For young people. (no. 61]) W6-345
I. Title.

CHAVEZ, Angelico, 1910- 271'.3'024 B
The song of Francis. Illus. by Judy Graese. [1st ed.] Flagstaff, Ariz., Northland Press [1973] 59 p. illus. (part col.) 21 cm. Recounts the life of St. Francis of Assisi, who gave all his riches to the poor and devoted the rest of his life to the service of Lady Poverty. [BX4700.F69C47] 92 73-75205 ISBN 0-87358-105-9 6.50
1. Franceso d'Assisi, Saint, 1182-1226—Juvenile literature. 2. [Francis of Assisi, Saint, 1182-1226.] 3. [Saints.] I. Graese, Judy, illus. II. Title.

CLARKE, Charles Philip Stewart, 1871-
Everyman's book of saints, by C.P.S. Clarke ... London, A.R. Mowbray & co., ltd.; New York, Morehouse publishing co. [1960] xvi, 357 p. plates. 19 cm. "First published in 1914; new impressions, 1915 ... 1933." "List of authorities": p. 356-357. 68-34523
1. Saints. I. Title.

CLARKE, Charles Philip Stewart, 1871- 922.3
Everyman's book of saints, by C. P. S. Clarke... London and Oxford, A. R. Mowbray & co., ltd.; Milwaukee, Morehouse publishing co. [1933] xvi, 357 p. plates. 19 cm. "First published in 1914: new impressions, 1915...1933." "List of authorities": 356-357. [PB41710.C6 1963] 36-872
1. Saints. I. Title.

CLUNY, Roland 922.22
Holiness in action. Pref. by Henri Daniel-Rops. Tr. from French by D. A. Askew. New York, Hawthorn [c.1963] 128p. 22cm. (Twentieth cent. encyclopedia of Catholicism, v.98. Section 9: The church and the modern world) Bibl. 63-14885 3.50 bds.,

1. Saints. I. Title.

CLUNY, Roland. 922.22
Holiness in action. Pref. by Henri Daniel-Rops. Translated from the French by D. A. Askew. [1st ed.] New York, Hawthorn Books [1963] 128 p. 22 cm. (The Twentieth century encyclopedia of Catholcism, v. 98. Section 9: The church and the modern world) Translation of L'Eglise agit par ses saints. Includes bibliography. [BX4657.C533] 63-14885
1. Saints. I. Title.

COMMINS, Marie C 922.22
Be a saint in spite of yourself. Milwaukee, Bruce Pub. Co. [1956] 118p. 22cm. [BX4657.C63] 56-9642
1. Saints. I. Title.

CORLEY, Francis J. 271.5
Wings of eagles; the Jesuit saints and blessed, by Francis J. Corley, S. J. and Robert J. Willmes, S. J. Milwaukee, The Bruce publishing company [c1941] xiv p., 1 l., 206 p. 29 cm. (Half-title: Science and culture series, Joseph Husslein ... general editor.) Portraits on lining-papers. "Readings" at end of most of the chapters. [BX4655.C6] 41-5092
1. Saints. 2. Jesuits—Biog. I. Willmes, Robert J., joint author. II. Title. III. Title: Jesuit saints.

CORLEY, Francis Joseph, 1909- 922.2
Wings of eagles; the Jesuit saints and blessed [by]Francis J. Corley, Robert J. Willmes [Reissue] Chicago, Loyopa Univ. Pr., 1965 [c.1941, 1965] xvii, 206p. 24cm. (Loyola request reprint ser.) Bibl. [BX4655.C6] 65-2581 3.50
1. Saints. 2. Jesuits—Biog. I. Willmes, Robert Joseph. 1909- joint author. II. Title. III. Title: Jesuit saints and blessed.

CORLEY, Francis Joseph, 1909- 271.5
Wings of eagles; the Jesuit saints and blessed, by Francis J. Corley, S.J. and Robert J. Willmes, S.J. Milwaukee, The Bruce publishing company [1941] xiv p., 1 l., 206 p. 23 1/2 cm. (Half-title: Science and culture series, Joseph Husslein...general editor) Portraits on lining-papers. "Readings" at end of most of the chapters. [BX4655.C6] 41-5092
1. Saints. 2. Jesuits—Biog. I. Willmes, Robert Joseph, 1909- joint author. II. Title. III. Title: Jesuit saints.

CURTISS, Anthony. 922
Further lives of the saints, by Anthony Curtiss. [Brooklyn, Guide printing company, inc., c1936] 73 p. 20 cm. [BX4658.C8] 36-9654
1. Saints. I. Title.

DABOVICH, Sebastian. 922
The lives of the saints, and several lectures and sermons. Compiled and translated by Rev. Sebastian Dabovich for devotional family reading and school practice ... San Francisco, The Murdock press, 1898. 3 p. l., [5]-217 p. 17 cm. [BX393.D3] 99-1106
1. Saints. 2. Sermons, American. I. Title.

DANIEL-ROPS, Henry 922.22
Golden legend of young saints. New York, Kenedy [c.1960] 192p. illus. 22cm. 60-7790 2.95
I. Saints—Juvenile literature. II. Title.

DANIEL-ROPS, Henry 922.22
Golden legend of young saints. New York, Kenedy [c.1960] 192p. illus. 22cm. 60-7790 2.95
I. Saints—Juvenile literature. II. Title.

DELANY, Selden Peabody, 1874-1935. 922.2
Married saints, by Selden P. Delany. New York, Toronto, Longmans, Green and co., 1935. x p., 1 l., 338 p. 20 cm. "First edition." [BX4661.D38] 35-17208
1. Saints. 2. Catholic church—biog. I. Title.

DIONYSIUS, of Alexandria, Saint, d.265. 265.
... *St. Dionysius of Alexandria:* letters and treatises, by Charles Lett Feltoe, D. D. London, Society for promoting Christian knowledge; New York, The Macmillan company [1918] vii, 9-110 p. 19 cm. (Translations of Christian literature. ser. i, Greek texts) Title within ornamental border. [BR65.D5F4] 19-10547
I. Feltoe, Charles Lett, tr. II. Title.

DOUILLET, Jacques Marie Joseph 235.2
What is a saint? Tr. from French by Donald Attwater. New York, Paulist Pr. [1963, c.1958] 115p. 19cm. (Deus bks.) Bibl. .95 pap.,
1. Saints. 2. Saints—Cultus. I. Title.

EIMER, Robert. 235
Tilted haloes. Milwaukee, Bruce Pub. Co. [1964] xv, 126 p. 21 cm. Bibliographical footnotes. [BX4661.E5] 64-15487
1. Saints. 2. Wit and humor. I. Title.

ELEANORE, sister, 1890- 235
Troubadours of Paradise, by Sister M. Eleanore ... New York and London, D. Appleton & company, 1926. xvi p., 1 l., 282 p. front. 19 1/2 cm. [Secular name: Katherine Mary Broanahan] [BX2325.E6] 26-14998
1. Saints. I. Title.

ELEANORE, Mary, Sister 1890- 235
Troubadours of Paradise, by Sister M. Eleanore... New York and London, D. Appleton & company, 1926. xvi p., 1 l., 282 p. front. 19 1/2 cm. [Secular name: Katherine Mary Brennahan] [BX2325.E6] 26-14998
1. Saints. I. Title.

FADIMAN, Edwin. 248'.22'0924
The feast day, by Edwin Fadiman, Jr. Illustrated by Charles Mikolaycak. [1st ed.] Boston, Little, Brown, [1973] 93 p. illus. 25 cm. Bibliography: p. 93. Describes the events of the Feast Day on which twelve-year-old Joan of Arc receives the vision which influences the course of her life. [DC103.5.F3] 92 74-182256 ISBN 0-316-27300-7 5.95
1. Jeanne d'Arc, Saint, 1412-1431—Juvenile literature. 2. [Jeanne d'Arc, Saint, 1412-1431.] 3. [Saints.] I. Mikolaycak, Charles, illus. II. Title.

FARJEON, Eleanor, 1881-1965. 920
Ten saints. With illus. by Helen Sewell. [Catholic ed.] New York, H. Z. Walck [1958, c1936] 124 p. illus. 25 cm. Brief biographical sketches of Saints Christopher, Martin, Dorothea, Bridget, Patrick, Hubert, Giles, Simeon Stylites, Nicholas, and Francis. [BR1711.F3 1958] AC 68
1. Saints. I. Sewell, Helen, 1896-1957, illus. II. Title.

FOSTER, John, 1898- 922.1
Five minutes a saint. Richmond, Va., Knox [1964, c.1963] 112p. 19cm. 64-15239 1.25 pap.,
1. Saints. 2. Nicholas, Saint, Bp of Myra—Juvenile literature. I. Title.

GARRETT, Randall 922.22
A gallery of the saints. Derby, Conn., Monarch [c.1963] 238p. 19cm. (Monarch select bk. MS9) .75 pap.,
I. Title.

GOODIER, Alban, abp., 1869-1939. 922.2
Saints for sinner, by the Most Reverend Alban Goodier ... New York, London [etc.] Longmans, Green and co., 1930. 4 p. l., [11]-223, [1] p. 19 cm. Printed in Great Britain. "Three studies ... have already appeared in the Month."--Pref. [BX4655.G6] 31-14644
1. Saints. I. Title.
Contents omitted

GOODSELL, Buel.
Animadversions on a pamphlet, entitled "A series of letters on this question. Whether true saints are liable finally to fall from an estate of grace...?" Being a full refutation of the various arguments... and a vindication of the sentiment...in a tract, written by ...John Wesley...Addressed to the Rev. Elisha Andrews Plattsburgh, F. P. Allen, 1822. 77 p. 16 degree. 1-19586
I. Title.

-GUMBLEY, Walter, 1887- 922.2
Parish priests among the saints, cannonized or beatified parish priests. Forword by Father Vincent McNabb. Westminster, Md., Newman Bookshop, 1947. 90 p. 20 cm. [[BX4657.G]] A48
1. Saints. 2. Clergy—Religious life. I. Title.

HALL, Grace. 922
Stories of the saints for children, young and old, by Grace Hall. Garden City, New York [etc.] Doubleday, Page & company, 1920. xv, 332 p., 1 l., 19 1/2 cm. [BR1711.H3] 20-7585
1. Saints. I. Title.

HARNEY, Martin Patrick, 1896- 922.22
Boother and sister saints. [1st ed.] Paterson, N. J., St. Anthony Guild Press [1957] 128p. 20cm. Includes bibliography. [BX4657.H3] 58-26550
1. Saints. I. Title.

HARTON, Sibyl, 1898- 922.22
Stars appearing; lives of sixty-eight saints of the Anglican calendar. New York, Morehouse-Gorham [1954] 237p. 19cm. [BR1710] 55-42
1. Saints. I. Title.

HAUGHTON, Rosemary 922.22
Six saints for parents. New York, Sheed [1963, c.1962] 249p. 22cm. 63-8538 3.95
1. Saints. I. Title.

HODGES, George, 1856-1919. 922
The human nature of the saints, by George Hodges ... New York, T. Whitaker [c1904] iii, 244 p. 19 cm. [BR1710.H6] 4-31292
1. Saints. I. Title.

HOGAN, John Gerard, 1896- 923.2
Heralds of the King, by the Reverend John G. Hogan. Boston, Mass., The Stratford company [c1934] 6 p. l., ii, 190 p. 19 1/2 cm. [BX4655.H55] 34-18162
1. Saints. 2. Catholic church—Biog. I. Title.
Contents omitted.

HOLWECK, Frederick George, 1856- 922
A biographical dictionary of the saints, with a general intro- duction on hagiology, by the Rt. Rev. F. G. Holweck... St. Louis, Mo., and London, B. Herder book co., 1924. 1 p. l., xxix, 1053 p. 23 1/2 cm. [BX4655.H6] 24-20782
1. Saints. I. Title.

HUTCHINSON, R A 922.22
Diocesan priest saints. St. Louis, Herder [1958] 219p. 21cm. [BX4657.H8] 58-7062
1. Saints. I. Title.

JACOBUS de Varagine. 282'.092'2 B
The golden legend; or, Lives of the saints, as Englished by William Caxton. London, J. M. Dent, 1900-39. [v. 1, 1931. New York, AMS Press, 1973] 7 v. cm. Original ed. issued in series: The Temple classics. [BX4654.J33 1973] 76-170839 ISBN 0-404-06770-0 92.50
1. Saints. I. Caxton, William, ca. 1422-1491, tr. II. Title.

JAMESON, Anna Brownell (Murphy) Mrs. 1794-1860. 704.
Legends of the monastic orders, as represented in the fine arts. Forming the second series of Sacred and legendary art. By Mrs. Jameson. Cor. and enl. ed. Boston, Ticknor and Fields, 1865. xv, 489 p. front. (port.) 15 cm. [N8080.J4 1865] 10-2266
1. Saints. 2. Saints—Art. 3. Monasticism and religious orders. 4. Christian art and symbolism. I. Title.

JAMESON, Anna Brownell (Murphy) Mrs. 1794-1860. 704.
Legends of the monastic orders, as represented in the fine arts. Forming the second series of sacred and legendary art. By Mrs. Jameson. Cor. and enl. ed. Boston, Ticknor and Fields, 1866. xv, 489 p. 17 cm. [N8080.J4 1866] 15-11724
1. Saints. 2. Saints—Art. 3. Monasticism and religious orders. 4. Christian art and symbolism. I. Title.

JAMESON, Anna Brownell (Murphy) Mrs. 1794-1860. 704.
Legends of the monastic orders, by Anna Jameson; ed., with additional notes, by Estelle M. Hurll, and abundantly illustrated with designs from ancient and modern art. Boston and New York, Houghton, Mifflin and company, 1896. xxvi, 467 p. front., illus., plates. 21 cm. (Half-title: The writings on art of Anna Jameson ... vol. iii) "Authorities": p. [xxii]-xxvi. [N8080.J4 1896] 10-12601
1. Saints. 2. Saints—Art. 3. Monasticism and religious orders. 4. Christian art and symbolism. I. Hurll, Estelle May, 1863- ed. II. Title.

JAMESON, Anna Brownell (Murphy) Mrs. 1794-1860. 755
Legends of the monastic orders, by Anna Jameson; ed., with additional notes, by Estelle M. Hurll ... Boston and New York, Houghton, Mifflin and company, 1901. xxvi, 467 p. front., illus., plates. 21 cm. (Half-title: The writings on art of Anna Jameson ... vol. iii) "Authorities": p. [xxii]-xxvi. [N8080.J4 1901] 4-13471
1. Saints. 2. Saints—Art. 3. Monasticism and religious orders. 4. Christian art and symbolism. I. Hurll, Estelle May, 1863,- ed. II. Title.

JAMESON, Anna Brownell (Murphy) Mrs. 1794-1860. 704.
Legends of the monastic orders as represented in the fine arts, forming the second series of Sacred and legendary art, by Mrs. Jameson. Cor. and enl. ed. Boston and New York, Houghton Mifflin company [1911?] 1 p. l., [v]-xv, 489 p. 1 8 cm. [N8080.J4 1911] 12-26197
1. Saints. 2. Saints—Arts. 3. Monasticism and religious orders. 4. Christian art and symbolism. I. Title.

JAMESON, Anna Brownell (Murphy) Mrs. 1794-1860. 704.
Legends of the monastic orders as represented in the fine arts, forming the second series of Sacred and legendary art, by Mrs. Jameson. Cor. and enl. ed. Boston and New York, Houghton, Mifflin and company [n. d.] xv, 489 p. 18 cm. First published 1850. [N8080.J4] 4-20546
1. Saints. 2. Saints—Art. 3. Monasticism and religious orders. 4. Christian art and symbolism. I. Title.

JOLY, Henri, 1839-1925. 200
The psychology of the saints, by Henri Joly, with preface and notes by G. Tyrrell, S. J. London, Duckworth & co.; New York [etc.] Benziger bros.; [etc., etc.] 1898. xv, 184 p. 19 cm. [Full name: Jules Charles Henri Joly] [BF798.J64] E 15
1. Saints. I. Title.

KINGSTON, William Henry Giles, 1814-1880. 922
The seven champions of Christendom, comp. from the most ancient chronicles and records and all other authentic and reliable sources of information. With coloured illus. by C. O. Murray. London, New York, G. Routledge, 1879. 250 p. illus. 19 cm. Copy imperfect: illustrations wanting. [BX4655.K5] 49-43573
1. Saints. I. Title.

KINNIBURGH, L B. 248
Lessons on the life of St. Paul. New York, Vantage Press [1952] 67 p. 22 cm. [BR126.K54] 52-9687
I. Title.

LANG, Leonora Blanche, "Mrs. Andrew Lang." 922
The book of saints and heroes, by Mrs. Lang; edited by Andrew Lang. With 12 coloured plates and numerous other illustrations by H. J. Ford. London, New York [etc.] Longmans, Green, and co., 1912. xii, 351, [1] p. incl. plates. col. front., col. plates. 22 cm. [BR1710.L3 1912] 12-22791
1. Saints. 2. Heroes. I. Lang, Andrew, 1844-1912, ed. II. Title.

LANG, Leonora Blanche, "Mrs. Andrew Lang." 922
The book of saints and heroes, by Mrs. Lang; edited by Andrew Lang; with 12 coloured plates and numerous other illustrations by H. J. Ford. New York [etc.] Longmans, Green, and co., 1912. xii, 351 p. incl. plates. col. front., col. plates. 22 cm. [BR1710.L3 1912a] 12-24314
1. Saints. 2. Heroes. I. Lang, Andrew, 1844-1912, ed. II. Title.

LANG, Leonora Blanche, "Mrs. Andrew Lang." 922
The book of saints and heroes, by Mrs. Lang; ed. by Andrew Lang; with 12 coloured plates and numerous other illustrations by H. J. Ford. New impression. London, New York [etc.] Longmans, Green and co., 1918. xii, 351 p. incl. plates. col. front., col. plates. 19 cm. (On verso of half-title: The fairy book

series, ed. by A. Lang) [BR1710.L3 1918] 20-9310
1. Saints. 2. Heroes. I. Lang, Andrew, 1844-1912, ed. II. Title.

LECKIE, Robert. 235.2
These are my heroes; a study of the saints. New York, Random House [1964] 177 p. 22 cm. Bibliography: p. 175-177. [BX4655.2.L4] 64-20039
1. Saints. I. Title.

LETTS, Winifred M., 1882-
The mighty army, by W. M. Letts; illustrated by Stephen Reid ... New York, F. A. Stokes co. [1912] xii, 115, [1] p. col. mounted front., illus., col. mounted pl. 28 cm. Illustrated cover. A 13
1. Saints. I. Title.

LEVY, Rosalie Marie, 1889- 922.22
Heavenly friends. [Boston] St. Paul Educations c1958] 484p. illus. 22cm. [BX4655.L4] 59-25199
1. Saints. I. Title.

LIPTAK, David Q 922.22
101 saints. Milwaukee, Bruce Pub. Co. [c1963] xvii, 170 p. 17 cm. "Sermonlike essays." Bibliography: p. xi-xii. [BX4657.L47] 63-21342
1. Saints. I. Title.

LIVES of saints. 922.22
with excerpts from their writings. Introd. by Father Thomas Plassmann; editorial supervision by Father Joseph Vann. Roslyn, N. Y., Published for the Classics Club by W. J. Black [1953] 426p. 20cm. [BR1710.L5] 54-17181
1. Saints. 2. Religi0s literature (Selections: Extracts, etc() I. Vann, Joseph, Father, 1907- ed.

LIVES of saints, 922.22
with excerpts from their writings. New York, J. J. Crawley [1954- v. col. illus., col. ports. 22 cm. [BR1710.L52] 54-37560
1. Saints. 2. Religious literature (Selections: Extracts, etc.)

LIVES of saints, with 922.22
excerpts from their writings. Introd. by Father Thomas Plassmann; editorial supervision by Father Joseph Vann. New York, J. J. Crawley [1954] xv, 527p. col. illus. 22cm. [BR1710.L5 1954] 54-37560
1. Saints. 2. Religious literature (Selections: Extracts, etc.) I. Vann, Joseph, Father. 1907- ed.

THE Lives of the saints 922.22
for every day of the year; a new, illustrated collection, offering the modern reader the inspiration and example of God's heroes through twenty centuries. Chicago, Catholic Press [1959] 3v. illus. 19cm. [BX4655.L5] 59-3270
1. Saints. 2. Devotional calendars—Catholic church

LUCAS, Barbara, 1911-
Great saints and saintly figures. With illus. by Anne Linton. [1st ed.] New York, Hawthorn Books [1963] 417-512 p. illus., ports. (part col.) 26 cm. (The New library of Catholic knowledge, v. 5) Bibliography: p. 512. 65-63879
1. Saints. 2. Christian biog. 3. Catholic Church — Biog. I. Title.

LUCE, Clare (Boothe) 1903- 922.22
ed.
Saints for now. New York, All Saints [1963, c.1952] 311p. illus. 17cm. (AS704) .75 pap.,
1. Saints. I. Title.

LUCE, Clare (Boothe) 1903- 922.22
ed.
Saints for now. New York, Sheed & Ward, 1952. 312 p. illus. 22 cm. [BX4655.L8] 52-10608
1. Saints. I. Title.

MCCANN, Paul, 1909- 922.2
The circle of sanctity, by Paul McCann. St. Louis, Mo. and London, B. Herder book co., 1939. 4 p. l., 271 p. 22 1/2 cm. Bibliography: p. [247]-258. [BX4655.M23] 39-3537
1. Saints. I. Title.

MCGILL, Mary E 922.22
Introducing the saints. Silhouettes by Gertrud Januzewski. St. Meinrad, Ind. [1952] 2v. illus. 21cm. 'A Grall publication.' 'Sketches . . . first published in Our Sunday visitor.' [BX4657.M2] 52-13551
1. Saints. I. Title.

MCGINLEY, Phyllis, 1905- 235'.2
Saint-watching. Garden City, N.Y., Doubleday, 1974 [c1969] 239 p. 18 cm. (Image books.) [BR1710.M23] ISBN 0-385-09537-6 1.75 (pbk.)
1. Saints. 2. Heroes. I. Title.
L.C. card number for original ed.: 79-83242.

MCGINNIS, Charles Francis, 1877-
The communion of saints, by Rev. Charles F. McGinnis ... with an introduction by the Most Reverend John Ireland, D.D. ... St. Louis, Mo. [etc.] B. Herder, 1912. 3 p. l., v-xiv, [3], 395 p. 20 1/2 cm. 12-27876
I. Title.

MARTINDALE, Cyril Charlie, 922.2
1879-
What are saints? Fifteen chapters in sanctity, broadcast by C. C. Martindale, S.J. London and New York, Sheed & Ward, 1933. 157 p. 19 cm. Biographical sketches. "These 'talks' were broadcast ... on fifteen Sundays, from January 24th to May 8th, 1932." "First published May, 1932 ... Seventh impression April, 1933." [BX4655.M35 1933] 33-25045
1. Saints. I. Title.

MATIMORE, Patrick Henry, 922.2
1891-
Heroes of God's church, by Reverend P. Henry Matimore...illustrated by Carle Michel Boog. New York, The Macmillan company, 1931. xii p., 1 l., 286 p. col. front., illus. 19 1/2 cm. (Half-title: The Madonna series) [BX4658.M45] 31-19210
1. Saints. 2. Catholic church—Biog. I. Title.

[MAYNARD, Laurens] 1866- comp.
The book of Saint Valentine. Boston, Small, Maynard & company, 1908. ix, 83, [1] p., 1 l. 18 cm. 8-11416
I. Title.

MAYNARD, Theodore, 1890- 922.22
Saints for our times. Garden City, N. Y., Image Books [1955, c1952] 304p. 18cm. (A Doubleday image book, D 12) [BX4651] 55-824
1. Saints. I. Title.

MAYNARD, Theodore, 1890- 922.22
1956.
Saints for our times. New York, Appleton-Century-Crofts [1952] 296 p. 22 cm. [BX4651.M382] 52-6723
1. Saints. I. Title.

MECKLIN, John Moffatt, 1871- 235
The passing of the saint; a study of a cultural type, by John M. Mecklin. Chicago, Ill., The University of Chicago press [1941] ix, 205, [1] p. 21 cm. [BX2325.M4] 41-3755
1. Saints. 2. Sociology, Christian—Hist. I. Title.

MOLINARI, Paolo, 1912- 235.2
Saints: their place in the church, by Paul Molinari. Pref. by Cardinal Larraona. Translated by Dominic Maruca. New York. Sheed and Ward [1965] xv, 240 p. 22 cm. Translation of I santi e il loro culto. Bibliographical references included in "Notes" (p. 176-233) [BN2325.M613] 65-20853
1. Saints. 2. Saints — Cultus. I. Title.

MONRO, Margaret Theodora, 922.2
1896-
A book of unlikely saints, by Margaret T. Monro. London, New York [etc.], Longmans, Green and co. [1943] 2 p. l., 220 p. 22 cm. "Note on sources": p. 9-12. "First [American] edition." [BX4652.M6 1943 a] 43-16158
1. Saints. I. Title.

THE Month. 922.22
Saints and ourselves; personal studies. [1st] - ser. New York, P. J. Kenedy [1953- v. 23cm. 'First published in the Month.' Editor: v. 1- P. Caraman. [BX4657.M66] 53-11510
1. Saints. I. Caraman, Philip, 1911- ed. II. Title.

MORETTI, Girolamo Maria 922.22
The saints through their handwriting. Tr. [from Italian] by Serge Hughes [New York] Macmillan [c.1964] xv, 269p. facsims. 22cm. 64-15463 6.00
1. Saints. 2. Graphology. I. Title.

MURPHY, Edward Francis, 922.2
1892-
Hand clasps with the holy, by Rev. Edward F. Murphy, S. S. J. Ozone Park, N. Y., Catholic literary guild [c1941] 246 p. 20 cm. [BX4655.M77] 41-19014
1. Saints. I. Title.

MURRAY, Desmond P 922.22
A saint of the week; short lives of English, Irish, Scottish, and universal saints taken from the calendar of saints, followed by practical lessons. Chicago, H. Regnery Co., 1955. 294p. illus. 22cm. [BX4655.M79] 55-13790
1. Saints. I. Title.

MURRAY, John O'Kane, 1847- 922.2
1885.
Little lives of the great saints. By John O'Kane Murray ... New York, P. J. Kenedy, 1880. 2 p. l., 9-513 p. front., plates. 18 cm. "Hints on religious reading": p. 512-513. [BX4655.M8] 39-20425
1. Saints. I. Title.

MURRAY, John O'Kane, 1847- 922.2
1885.
Little lives of the great saints, by John O'Kane Murray ... [New York] P. J. Kenedy & sons [1939?] 2 p. l., 9-511, [1] p. front. 19 cm. [BX4655.M8] 39-21200
1. Saints. I. Title.

MURRAY, Verona. 920
The saint of the week [by] Sister M. Verona Murray. Illustrated by Harold Schmitz. Milwaukee, Bruce Pub. Co. [1966] viii, 158 p. illus. 22 cm. Brief sketches of the lives of twenty-nine saints, for inspirational reading during the weeks of the Catholic school year. [BX4658.M8] AC 67
1. Saints. I. Schmitz, Harold, illus. II. Title.

NEWTON, Joseph Fort, 1876- 922
Life victorious, a testament of faith. New York, F. H. Revell Co. [1948] 111 p. 20 cm. "First appeared, in shorter form, under the title What have the saints to teach us? in 1914." [BR1710.N515] 49-7061
1. Saints. I. Title.

O'CONOR, John Francis Xavier, 922
1852-
Sacred scenes and mysteries, by Rev. J. F. X. O'Conor... New York, London and Bombay, Longmans, Green, & co., 1898. 5 p. l., [5]-138, [5] p. front., plates. 20 cm. "Jesus, the all beautiful" (with music): plate facing p. [143] Contents.Devotion to the Sacred heart.--Paray-le-Monial.--Our Lady of Oostacker.--The home and heart of a saint.--Clairefontaine.--The childhood of Mary.--Some of Our Mother's sorrow.--Our Blessed Lady's assumption.--Christmastide art.--The glory of Jerusalem.--St. Ursula and the eleven thousand virgins.--The holy robe of Treves.--St. Peter Claver.--St. Alphonsus Rodriguez.--Thoughts on the Good Shepard.--Dear Lord!--The guardian angels.--I stand at the door and knock.--A birthday.--Jesus, the all beautiful. [BR1710.O3] 37-21104
1. Saints. I. Title.

*ONGARO, A. Cremonini 922.22
Saint Pancratius. Illus. by G. de Luca. Boston, Daughters of St. Paul, c.1964. 28p. col. illus. 21cm. (St. Paul eds.) .50;.35 pap.,
I. Title.

PAINTING, Norman. 922.22
Stories of the saints. Edited by Michael Day. With a foreword by Peggy Bacon. Chicago, Franciscan Herald Press [1958?] 185p. 19cm. [BR1710.P3] 58-14609
1. Saints. I. Title.

THE patron saints.
Canfield, Society of St. Paul [1958] 60p. 21cm.
1. Saints. I. Immerso, John. II. Society of St. Vincent de Paul.

PECK, George Clarke, 1865- 811.
Side-stepping saints, by George Clarke Peck. New York, Cincinnati, The Methodist book concern [c1918] 329 p. 20 cm. "Some of the flesh and blood saints of the Bible." [BS571.P4] 18-6439
I. Title.

THE people of the way; 290
from a saint to the saints. Swengel, Pa., Bible Truth Depot, 1961. 278p. 20cm. [BX9998.P45] 61-11026

QUADFILEG, Josef, 1924- 922.22
The saints and your name. Illustrated by Johannes Grueger. Translated from the German by Margaret Goldsmith. [New York] Pantheon [1958] 159p. illus. 21cm. Translation of Das Buch von den heiligen Namenspatronen. [BX4657] 58-8263
1. Saints. 2. Names, Personal. I. Title.

READINGS for the Saints' days,
by F. E. C. Printed for private circulation only. [Cambridge, Printed at the University press] 1865. 2 p. l., 87, [1] p. 25 cm. First published in 1864 in the successive numbers of the Magazine for the young. [BV65.C2] 24-16060
1. Saints. I. C., F. E. II. F. E. C.

*REES, Jean A. 248
Saints at work. Grand Rapids, Mich., Zondervan [1964, c.1958] 121p. illus. 21cm. 1.25 pap.,
I. Title.

ROEDER, Helen, 1909- 922.22
Saints and their attributes; with a guide to localities and patronage. Chicago, H. Regnery Co. [1956, c1955] xxviii, 391p. illus. 18cm. Billiography: p. xiv. [BX4661] 56-13630
1. Saints. 2. Patron saints. I. Title.

RUEMMER, Franz. 235
The great secret of the saints, by Franz Ruemmer, translated from the German by Isabel Garahan, B. A. St. Louis, Mo., and London, B. Herder book co., 1926. xi, 119 p. 20 cm. [BX2325.R8] 26-3511
1. Saints. I. Garahan, Isabel, tr. II. Title.

THE saints; 922.22
a concise biographical dictionary, edited by John Coulson. With an introd. by C.C. Martindale. 1st ed. New York, Hawthorn Books [1958] 496p. plates (part col.) 26cm. Bibliography: p. 489-491. [BX4655.S28] 58-5626
1. Saints. I. Coulson, John, 1919- ed.

SAINTS and ourselves;
personal portraits of favorite saints by twenty-four outstanding Catholic authors. Edited by Philip Caraman. 1st and 2d ser. Garden City, N.Y., Doubleday [1958, c1953] 311p. (Image books, D61)
1. Saints. I. The Month. II. Caraman, Philip, 1911- ed.

SAINTS and ourselves,
third series; personal studies by Walter Starkie [and others] New York, P. J. Kenedy [c1958] 140p. 23cm.
1. Saints. I. The Month. II. Caraman, Philip, 1911- ed.

SAINTS (The); 922.22
a concise biographical dictionary, ed. by John Coulson. Introd. by C. C. Martindale. New York, Guild [1966, c.1958] 496p. plates (pt. col.) 26cm. (Angelus bk., 31181) Bibl. [BX4655.S28] .95 pap.,
1. Saints. I. Coulson, John, 1919- ed.

SANGSTER, William Edwin, 235.2
1900-
The pure in heart; a study in Christian sanctity. Nashville, Abingdon Press [1954] 254p. 23cm. (The Cato lecture of 1954) [BR1710.S35] 54-13191
1. Saints. 2. Holiness. 3. Piety. I. Title.

SCHAMONI, Wilhelm, 1905- 922.22
... The face of the saints. Translation by Anne Fremantle. [New York] Pantheon [1947] 5 p. l., 13-278, [1] p. illus. (incl. ports.) 23 1/2 cm. In this edition, sketches of five European saints found in the German edition have been omitted; and sketches of five western hemisphere saints have been substituted. cf. Translator's note. Translation of Das wahre gesicht der heiligen. [BX4655.S342] 47-2808
1. Saints. 2. Saints—Art. I. Fremantle, Anne, tr. II. Title.

SHARKEY, Donald C. 1912- 922.22
Popular patron saints [by] Don Sharkey and Sister Loretta Clare. Milwaukee, Bruce Pub. Co. [1960] 283 p. 24 cm. [BR1710.S46] 60-7175
1. Saints. I. Felertag, Loretta Clare 1890- joint author. II. Title.

SHEA, John [Dawson] Gilmary, 1824-1892, ed. 235.2
Pictorial lives of the saints. With reflections for every day in the year. Comp. from Butler's Lives" and other approved sources. To which are added lives of the American saints ... Ed. by John Gilmary Shea, L L. D. New ed. New York, Cincinnati [etc.] Benziger brothers. 1902. 618 p. front., illus. 24 cm.
I. Title.

[SHEA, John Dawson Gilmary] 1824-1892, ed. 922
Pictorial lives of the saints, with reflections for every day in the year, compiled from "Butler's lives" and other approved sources, to which are added Lives of certain saints contained in the calendar of special feasts for the United States and of some others recently canonized. New York, Cincinnati [etc.] Benziger brothers [c1922] 624 p. front., illus. 23 1/2 cm. Cover-title: Lives of the saints. [BX4655.S5 1922] 24-5909
I. Title. II. Title: Lives of the saints.

SHEA, John Dawson Gilmary, 1824-1892, ed. 922.
Pictorial lives of the saints. With reflections for every day in the year. Compiled from "Butler's Lives" and other approved sources. To which are added lives of the American saints ... Edited by John Gilmary Shea, LL.D. New ed. New York, Cincinnati [etc.] Benziger brothers, 1902. 618 p. front., illus. 24 cm. [BX4655.S5 1902 a] 2-23626
1. Saints. I. Title.

SHEED, Francis Joseph, 1897- comp. 922
Saints are not sad; forty biographical portraits. New York, Sheed & Ward, 1949. 441 p. 22 cm. [BX4655.S52] 49-11681
1. Saints. I. Title.

SIMON, Edith, 1917- 270.1
The saints. [New York, Delacorte Press [1969, c1968] 127 p. illus. 22 cm. (Pageant of history series) Bibliography: p. [123] [BR1710.S52 1969] 70-75098 3.95
1. Saints. 2. Church history—Primitive and early church.

SLAVES of the Immaculate Heart of Mary. 282'.0922 B
The communion of saints: sanctity through the centuries. Still River [Mass., 1967] v, 121 p. illus. (part col.) 24 cm. [BX4655.2.S54] 72-191281
1. Saints. I. Title.

SYNGE, J. M. 1871-1909. (John Millington), 822'.912
The well of the saints / J.M. Synge ; edited with an introduction and notes by Nicholas Grene. Washington, D.C. : Catholic University of America Press, c1982. ix, 80 p. ; 23 cm. (Irish dramatic texts) Includes bibliographical references. [PR5532.W4 1982] 19 82-4367 ISBN 0-8132-0571-9 : 11.95 ISBN 0-8132-0570-0 pbk. : 5.95
I. Grene, Nicholas. II. Title. III. Series.

VITAE patrum. 922
The Desert Fathers. Translations from the Latin with an introd. by Helen Waddell. [Ann Arbor] University of Michigan Press 1957] 309 p. 21 cm. (Ann Arbor books, AA8) Translated from Rosweyde's 2d rev. ed. of the Vitae Patrum, published in 1628. [[BR1705]] 57-731
1. Saints. 2. Hermits. I. Waddell, Helen Jane, 1889- II. Title.

WADDELL, Helen Jane, 1889- tr. 922.2
Beasts and saints; translations by Helen Waddell; woodcuts by Robert Gibbings. New York, H. Holt and company [c1934] xx, 151 p. incl. front., illus. 21 cm. "Stories of ... saints and beasts, from the end of the fourth to the end of the twelfth century ... translated ... from the original Latin."--Translator's note. "Sources": p. 149-151. [BX4658.W3 1934a] 34-40130
1. Saints. 2. Animals, Legends and stories of. 3. Legends. I. Gibbings, Robert, 1889- II. Title.

WALSH, William Thomas, 1891-1949 922.22
Saints in action. Garden City, N. Y., Hanover House [c.1961] 359p. Bibl. 61-12567 4.95
1. Saints. I. Title.

WALSH, William Thomas, 1891-1949. 922.22
Saints in action. [1st ed.] Garden City, N.Y., Hanover House, 1961. 359 p. 22 cm. [BX4655.2.W25] 61-12597
1. Saints. I. Title.

WARD, Maisie, full name. Mary Josephine Ward Sheed 922.22
Saints who made history: the first five centuries. New York, Sheed and Ward [1960, c.1959] xiv, 377p. (6p. bibl.) 22cm. 60-7310 4.50 bds.,
1. Saints. I. Title.

WATERS, Clara (Erskine) Clement, Mrs., 1834-1916. 755
Saints in art, by Clara Erskine Clement ... Boston, L. C. Page and company, 1899. viii, 8-428 p. incl. 32 pl. front. 19 1/2 cm. [Art lovers' series] [N8080.W32] 99-3705
1. Saints. 2. Christian art and symbolism. I. Title.

WATSON, George Douglas.
The bridehood saints, treating of the saints who are the "Selection from the selection," those saints who are to make up the bride of Christ, by George D. Watson... Cincinnati, O., Office God's revivalist [c1913] 3 p. l., 287 p. 19 1/2 cm. $1.00 14-678
I. Title.

WATSON, George Douglas, 1845- 270
God's eagles; or, Complete testing of the saints, by George D. Watson... Cincinnati, O., God's revivalist office [c1927] 268 p. 19 1/2 cm. [BR125.W345] 28-20149
I. Title.

WEDGE, Florence. 922.22
Holiness is where you find it. Pulaski, Wis. Franciscan Publishers, 1958. 192 p. 22 cm. [BX4657.W4] 57-12618
1. Saints I. Title.

[WEIGEL, Edward]
Novenas in honor of St. Alphonsus, doctor of the church, bishop of Saint Agatha, and founder of the congregation of the Most holy Redeemer; and blessed Clement, vicar-general of the same congregation ... Translated from the German by a priest of the congregation of the Most holy Redeemer. Ilchester, Md., Printed at the Redemptorist college, 1899. viii p., 1 l., 7-146 p. 12°. Published anonymously. Sep *I. Title.*

WESCOTT, Glenway, 1901- 922
A calendar of saints for unbelievers, by Glenway Wescott. New York and London, Harper & brothers, 1933. 1 p. l., v-ix, 215 p. 21 1/2 cm. "First edition." Bibliography included in foreword. [BR1710.W4 1933] 33-15276
1. Saints. 2. Calendars. I. Title.

WIGHT, Francis Asa, 1854- 236.
The rapture; or, The translation of the saints, by Francis Asa Wight ... Harrisburg, Pa., The Evangelical press [c1929] 93 p. 19 cm. [BT890.W6] 29-10660
I. Title.

WILLIAMSON, Claude Charles H. 1892- comp.
Letters from the saints; early renaissance and reformation periods from St. Thomas Aquinas to Bl. Robert Southwell. New York, Philosophical Library [c1958] x, 214 p. 22 cm. Bibliography: p. 213-214.
1. Saints. I. Title.

Saints—Art.

BREESE, Frances, illus. 704.948'2'09789
New Mexico santos: how to name them. Illus. by Frances Breese. Foreword and captions by E. Boyd. Santa Fe, N. M., Museum of New Mexico [and] International Folk Art Foundation, 1966. 1 v. (chiefly illus.) 26 cm. [NK835.N5N4] 68-6768
1. Saints—Art. 2. Folk art—New Mexico. I. Hall, Elizabeth Boyd (White) 1903- II. International Folk Art Foundation. III. Santa Fe, N. M. Museum of New Mexico. IV. Title.

HUSENBETH, Frederick Charles, 1796-1872. 704.
Emblems of saints: by which they are distinguished in works of art. By the late Very Rev. F. C. Husenbeth ... 3d ed., edited by Augustus Jessopp ... Norwich, Printed for the Norfolk and Norwich archaeological society by A. H. Goose and co., 1882. 1 p. l., xiii, [1], 426 p., 36 numb. l. col. illus. (coats of arms) pl. 23 cm. [N8080.H8] 11-28930
1. Saints—Art. 2. Emblems. 3. Sibyls—Art. 4. Heraldry, Sacred. I. Jessopp, Augustus, II. Blackburne, Edward Lushington. III. Marsh, William. IV. Title.
Contents omitted.

MILBURN, Robert Leslie Pollington. 704.9486
Saints and their emblems in English churches. London, Oxford Univ. Press, 1949. xxxviii, 283 p. illus. 17 cm. Erratum slip inserted. [N8080.M5] 49-9265
1. Saints—Art. 2. Christian art and symbolism. 3. Church decoration and ornament—England. I. Title.

TINTORI, Leonetto, 1908- 704.9486
The painting of The life of St. Francis in Assisi, with notes on the Arena Chapel, by Leonetto Tintori, Millard Meiss. [New York] N.Y. Univ. Pr. [c.]1962 xv, 205p. illus. 25cm. At head of title: Conservation Ctr., Inst. of Fine Arts, New York Univ. Bibl. 62-10308 12.50
1. Francesco d'Assisi, Saint, 1182-1226. 2. Saints—Art. 3. Assisi. San Francesco (Church) 4. Padua. Madonna dell' Arena (Chapel) 5. Mural painting and decoration, Italian. I. Meiss, Millard, joint author. II. Title.

TINTORI, Leonetto, 1908- 704.9486
The painting of the life of St. Francis in Assisi. With notes on the arena chapel, and a 1964 appendix, by Leonetto Tintori, Millard Meiss. New York, Norton, [1967,c.1962] xv, 207p. illus. 20cm. (Norton lib., N393) Bibl. [N8080.T55] 1.95 pap.,
1. Francesco d'Assisi, Saint 1182-1226. 2. Assisi, San Francesco (Church) 3. Padua. Madonna dell' Arena (Chapel) 4. Saints—Art. 5. Mural painting and decoration. I. Meiss, Millard, joint author. II. Title.

TINTORI, Leonetto, 1908-
The painting of the life of St. Francis in Assisi; with notes on the Arena Chapel and a 1964 appendix, by Leonetto Tintori and Millard Meiss. New York, Norton [1967] xv, 207 p. illus. (The Norton Library, N 393) "First published in the Norton Library by arrangement with the New York University Press." Includes bibliographical references. 68-17604
1. Francesco d'Assisi, Saint, 1782-1226. 2. Saints—Art. 3. Assisi. San Francesco (Church) 4. Padua. Madonna dell'Arena (Chapel) 5. Mural painting and decoration, Italian. I. Meiss, Millard. II. Title.

TINTORI, Leonetto, 1908- 704.9486
The painting of The life of St. Francis in Assisi, with notes on the Arena Chapel, by Leonetto Tintori and Millard Meiss. [New York] New York University Press, 1962. xv, 205 p. illus. 25 cm. At head of title: Conservation Center, Institute of Fine Arts, New York University. Erratum slip inserted. "Selective list of technical studies": p. 187-188. Includes bibliographical references. [N8080.T55] 62-10308
1. Francesco d'Assisi, Saint, 1182-1226. 2. Saints—Art. 3. Assisi. San Francesco (Church) 4. Padua. Madonna dell'Arena (Chapel) 5. Mural painting and decoration, Italian. I. Meiss, Millard, joint author. II. Title.

WHAYMAN, Horace W. 755
A manual of emblems of the saints by which they are distinguished in works of art, and represented in the decoration of churches, by Horace W. Whayman... Columbus, O., 1897. 4 p.l., [3]-52 p. front., illus., plates. 23 cm. [N8080.W55] 10-2268
1. Saints—Art. 2. Emblems. 3. Christian art and symbolism. I. Title.

Saints—Biography

CLARA, of Assisi, Saint, d.1253. Legend. 922.
The life and legend of the Lady Saint Clare, translated from the French version (1563) of Brother Francis Du Puis, by Charlotte Balfour; with an introduction by Father Cuthbert, O.S.F.C. With 24 illustrations. London, New York [etc.] Longmans, Green and co., 1910. xi, 154 p. front., 23 pl. (incl. ports., facsims.) 20 1/2 cm. "The Legend here rendered into English is the primitive legend of St. Clare, written about the time of her canonisation ... At one time it was attributed to St. Bonaventure, but more recently and generally to Thomas of Celano...The authorship, however, is very doubtful...The present English version has been made from a French translation of the sixteenth century." [BX4700.C6A3 1910] 11-28305
I. Balfour, Mrs. Charlotte (Cornish) tr. II. DuPuis, Francois, 16th cent. III. Cuthbert, Father 1866- IV. Thomas, of Celano, fl. 1257, supposed author. V. Title.
Contents omitted.

DAVIS, Muriel Orlidge.
Saints & heroes of the western world, by Muriel O. Davis ... Oxford, The Clarendon press, 1921. 2 p. l., 140 p. illus. 19 cm. [D115.D3] 22-4444
I. Title.

FULOP-MILLER, Rene, 1891-
The saints that moved the world: Anthony, Augustine, Francis, Ignatius, Theresa. Translated by Alexander Gode and Erika Fulop-Miller. New York, Collier books [1962] 511 p. 18 cm.
I. Title.

FULOP-MILLER, Rene, 1891-
The saints that moved the world: Anthony, Augustine, Francis, Ignatius, Theresa. Translated by Alexander Gode and Erika Fulop-Miller. New York, Collier books [1962] 511 p. 18 cm. Bibliography: p. 485-494. 63-17620
I. Title.

THE lives of the fathers, martyrs, and other principal saints; compiled from original moments, and other authentic records; illustrated with the remarks of judicious modern critics and historians. New York, D. & J. Sadlier [n. d.] 4 v. illus. (Part Col.) 29cm. 'Published with the approbation of the Most Rev. John Hughes, Archbishop of New York.' Issued in 55 parts. Text within ornamental border.
1. Saints—Biog. I. Butler, Alban, 1711-1773.

RADEGONDE, Saint. Legend.
The lyfe of Saynt Radegunde, ed. from the copy in Jesus college library by F. Brittain ... Cambridge [Eng.] The University press, 1926. xxiii, 53, 2 p., incl. 1 illus., pl. 18 cm. Middle English poem, from the edition printed by Pynson between 1508 and 1529, with facsimiles of original t.-p. and printer's mark. Has been ascribed to Henry Bradshaw because of its similarity to his "The lyfe of Saynt Werburge". Follows chiefly Antoninu's account of the saint; about half the poem is original. cf. Introd. [PR2120.R25A15] 27-18651
I. Bradshaw, Henry, d. 1513, supposed author. II. Brittain, Fred, ed. III. Title.

THERESE Saint 1873-1897. 922.244
The story of a soul; the autobiography of Saint Therese of Lisieux, in a new and rev. translation by Michael Day. With a foreword by Vernon Johnson. Westminster, Md., Newman Press, 1952. x. 208 p. 19 cm. [BX4700.T5A5] 52-9637
I. Title.

Saints, British.

WEBB, J. F. ed. and tr. 922.22
Lives of the saints. Tr., introd. by J. F. Webb. Baltimore, Penguin [c.1965] 206p. 19cm. (Penguin classics, L153) [BX4659.G7W43] 65-4003 .95 pap.,
1. Saints, British. I. Brendan, Saint. Legend. II. Beda Venerabilis, 673-735. Life of Cuthbert. III. Eddi, fl. 669. Life of Wilfrid. IV. Title. V. Title: V. Life of Cuthbert. VI. Title: Life of Wilfrid.
Contents omitted.

Saints—Calendar.

BITTLE, Berchmans, 1887- 922.22
A saint a day, according to the liturgical

calendar of the church. Milwaukee, Bruce Pub. Co. [1958] 356p. 23cm. [BX4655.B5] 58-6926
1. Saints—Calendar. I. Title.

[CLARKE, William Kemp Lowther] 1879- 264.031
Saints' days as observed by the churches of the Anglican communion. London, Society for promoting Christian knowledge. New York, The Macmillan company [1941] viii, 9-96 p. 17 cm. Preface signed by author. First published 1941. [BX5145.C55] 42-25201
1. Church of England. Book of common prayer—Calendar and lectionaries. 2. Saints—Calendar. 3. Anglican communion. I. Title.

CRONIN, Vincent, comp. 922.22
A calendar of saints. Westminster, Md., Newman Press [1963] xvi, 368 p. ports. 22 cm. [BX4655.2.C7] 63-12230
1. Saints—Calendar. I. Title.

CRONIN, Vincent, comp. 922.22
A calendar saints. Westminster, Md., Newman [c.1963] xvi, 368p. ports. 22cm. 63-12230 10.50
1. Saints—Calendar. I. Title.

DAUGHTERS of St. Paul 922.2
Saints for young people for everyday of the year; v.2 [Boston] St. Paul Eds. [dist.] Author [c.1964] 337p. illus. ,pt. col.) ports. (pt. col.) 22cm. Contents.v.2. July-Dec. 63-19997 2.50 pap.,
1. Saints—Calendar. 2. Saints—Juvenile literature. I. Title.

ELICK, Eva Marie. 922.22
Everyday saints. New York, Vantage Press [c1954] 493p. 23cm. Poems. [BX4655.E45] 54-10238
1. Saints—Calendar. 2. Saints—Poetry. I. Title.

ENGLEBERT, Omer, 1893- 922.22
The lives of the saints. Translated by Christopher and Anne Fremantle. New York, D. McKay Co. [1951] xi, 532 p. 23 cm. Translation of Les saints. [BX4655.E513] 51-11328
1. Saints—Calendar. I. Title.

*FOLEY, Leonard, ed. 242'.37
Saint of the day. Cincinnati, St. Anthony Messenger Press [1974] 161 p. illus. 18 cm. Includes index Contents.Contents: Vol. 1: January-June [BR1710] ISBN 0-912228-16-4 1.95 (pbk.)
1. Saints—Calendar. 2. Christian saints—Calendar. I. Title.

SLAVES of the Immaculate Heart of Mary. 922.22
Saints to remember from January to December. Still River [Mass., 1961] 121 p. illus. 24 cm. [BX4655.2.S55] 61-10149
1. Saints — Calendar. I. Title.

Saints, Cornish.

[MARY Catherine, sister, of the English Dominican congregation of Saint Catherine of Siena] 922.242
Once in Cornwall, being an account of Friar Peter's journey in search of the saint and dragon legends of the land, by S. M. C., of the English Dominican congregation of Saint Catherine of Siena. New York, Toronto, Longmans, Green and co., 1944. viii p., 1 l., 179 p. 21 1/2 cm. "First edition." [Secular name: Kathleen Agnes Cicely Anderson] [BX4659.G7M3] 44-40078
1. Saints, Cornish. I. Title.

Saints—Correspondence, reminiscences, etc.

FRANCOIS de Sales Saint,bp. of Geneva 1567-1622 242
Selections from the letters of S. Francis de Sales. Translated from the French by Mrs. C. W. Bagot. Revised by a priest of the English church. 4th ed. London, J. Masters; New York, Pott and Amery, 1871. 1 p. l., x, 93 p. 16 cm. [BX2179.F8L5 1871] 4-183
I. Bagot, Charles Walter, Mrs. tr. II. Title.

LETTERS from the saints., 208.2
arr., selected by a Benedictine of Stanbrook Abbev. Illus. by Vivian Berger. New York, Hawthorn [c.1964] ix, 302p. illus., facsims. 22cm. Bibl. 64-19205 4.95
1. Saints—Correspondence, reminiscences, etc. I. A Benedictine of Stanbrook Abbey, ed.

SHEA, John [Dawson] Gilmary, 1824-1892, ed.
Lives of the saints. With reflections for every day in the year. Comp. from "Butler's Lives" and other approved sources. To which are added lives of the American saints ... Ed. by John Gilmary Shea, LL.D. New ed. New York, Cincinnati [etc.] Benziger brothers, 1902. 430 p. front., pl., port. 24 cm. 3-1129
I. Title.

VINCENTIUS Lerinensis, 5thcent. 281.
... *The Commonitory of St. Vincent of Lerins,* translated into English by T. Herbert Bindley ... London [etc.] Society for promoting Christian knowledge; New York, E. S. Gorham, 1914. xviii, 19-128 p. 17 cm. (Early church classics) [BR00.E3V5] 22-6507
I. Bindley, Thomas Herbert, 1861-1931, tr. II. Title.

Saints—Cultus.

BACIGALUPA, Andrea, 1923- 759.13
Santos and saints' days. [1st ed.] Santa Fe, N.M., Sunstone Press, 1972. 32 p. illus. 22 cm. [BX2333.B3] 73-154725 ISBN 0-913270-09-1 2.95
1. Mary, Virgin—Cultus. 2. Saints—Cultus. 3. Santos (Art) I. Title.

BROWNSON, Orestes Augustus, 1803-1876 235.2
Saint-worship [and] The worship of Mary. Ed., abridged by Thomas R. Ryan. Paterson, N.J., St. Anthony Guild [c.1963] ix, 122p. 23cm. 63-18551 2.50
1. Saints—Cultus. 2. Mary, Virgin—Cultus. I. Ryan, Thomas Richard, 1898- ed. II. Title. III. Title: The worship of Mary.

BROWNSON, Orestes Augustus, 1803-1876 235.2
Saint-worship[and] The worship of Mary, Edited and abridged by Thomas R. Ryan. Paterson, N.J., St. Anthony Guild Press [1963] ix, 122 p. 23 cm. [BX2333.B76] 63-18551
1. Saints — Cultus. 2. Mary, Virgin — Cultus. I. Ryan, Thomas Richard, 1898- ed. II. Title. III. Title: The worship of Mary.

Saints—Dictionaries.

ATTWATER, Donald, 1892- 922.22
A dictionary of saints; based on Butler's Lives of the saints, complete ed. New York, P. J. Kenedy [1958] vii, 280 p. front. 24 cm. "With each entry ... an index reference is given to the fuller treatment in 'Butler' [published in 1956]" [BX4654.B8 1958 Index] 58-12556
1. Saints—Dictionaries. I. Butler, Alban, 1711-1773. The lives of the saints. New York, 1956. II. Title.

ATTWATER, Donald, 1892- 235.20922
The Penguin dictionary of saints. Baltimore, Penguin Books [1965] 362 p. 19 cm. (Penguin reference books, R30) [BX4655.8.A8] 65-5009
1. Saints—Dictionaries. I. Title. II. Title: Dictionary of saints.

ATTWATER, Donald, 2)1892- 235.20922
The Penguin dictionary of saints [Magnolia, Mass., P. Smith, 1967, c.1965] 362p. 19cm. (Penguin ref. bk., R30 rebound) [BX4655.8.A8] 3.50
1. Saints—Dictionaries. I. Title. II. Title: Dictionary of saints.

THE Book of saints; 235.203
a dictionary of persons canonized or beatified by the Catholic Church. Compiled by the Benedictine monks of St. Augustine's Abbey, Ramsgate. 5th ed., entirely rev. and re-set. New York, Crowell [1966] xii, 740 p. 24 cm. [BX4655.B6 1966] 66-22140
1. Saints—Dictionaries. I. St. Augustine's Abbey, Ramsgate, Eng.

THE book of saints; 922.2
a dictionary of servants of God canonized by the Catholic church; extracted from the Roman & other martyrologies. Comp. by the Benedictine monks of St. Augustine's Abbey, Ramagate. 4th ed., rev. and enl., with a calendar of saints. New York, Macmillan co., 1947. xviii, 706 p. 22 cm. [BX4655.B6 1947] 47-11914
1. Saints—Dictionaries. I. Saint Augustine's Abbey, Ramagate.

BOOK of saints (The); 235.203
a dictionary of persons canonized or beatified by the Catholic Church. Comp. by the Benedictine monks of St. Augustine's Abbey, Ramsgate. 5th ed., entirely rev., re-set. New York, Crowell [1966] xii, 740p. 24cm. [BX4655.B6 1966] 66-22140 8.95
1. Saints—Dictionaries. I. St. Augustine's Abbey, Ramsgate, Eng.

SHARP, Mary 922.22
A traveller's guide to saints in Europe. London, H. Evelyn [dist. Wilkes-Barre, Pa., Dimension Bks., c.1964] xv, 251p. 23cm. Bibl. 64-7696 5.95 bds.,
1. Saints—Dictionaries. I. Title. II. Title: Saints in Europe.

Saints, Egyptian.

O'LEARY, De Lacy Evans, 1872- 922.1
The saints of Egypt, by De Lacy O'Leary ... Published for the Church historical society, saints of Egypt London, Society for promoting Christian knowledge; New York, The Macmillan company, 1937. vii p., 1 l., 286 p. 23 cm. "Printed in India." "The following pages aim at providing a compendium o informatin about the martyrs and other saints honoured in the Coptic church, for the most part following the biographies given in the Jacobite (Egyptian Synaxarium."--Foreword. [BX4659.E4O6] 38-14248
1. Saints, Egyptian. 2. Martyrs—Egypt. 3. Church history—Primitive and early church. I. Church historical society. II. Society for promoting Christian knowledge, London. III. Title.

Saints, English.

ALBERTSON, Clinton, comp. 235.20922
Anglo-Saxon, saints and heroes [ed., tr. by] Clinton Albertson. [Bronx, N.Y.] Fordham [1967] xv, 347p. illus. 24cm. Bibl. [BX4659.G7A5] 67-16652 7.50
1 Saints, English. I. Title.
Contents omitted.

WINDHAM, Joan. 922.242
Saints who spoke English, by Joan Windham; illustrated by E. Benedict Davies. New York, Sheed & Ward, 1939. 3 p. l., 11-147 p. front., illus. 22 1/2 cm. "Printed in Great Britain." [BX4659.G7W5] 40-3543
1. Saints, English. 2. Saints—Juvenile literature. I. Title.

Saints, Ethiopian.

MASHAFA, senkesar.
The book of the saints of the Ethiopian church; a translation of the Ethiopic synaxarium ... made from the manuscripts Oriental 660 and 661 in the British museum, by Sir E. A. Wallis Budge ... Cambridge [Eng.] The University press, 1928. 4 v. 23 cm. "Three hundred copies only of this work have been printed: of these two hundred and fifty are for sale." [BX149.A1M3] 29-11616
1. Saints, Ethiopian. 2. Martyrs—Ethiopia. 3. Church history—Primitive and early church. I. Budge, Sir Ernest, Alfred Thompson Wallis, 1857- tr. II. Title.

Saints,Georgian.

LANG, David Marshall, ed. and tr. 922.1479
Lives and legends of the Georgian saints, selected and translated from the original texts by David Marshall Lang. London, Allen & Unwin; New York, Macmillan [1956] 179p. illus. 20cm. (Ethical and religious classics of East and West, no. 15) Includes bibliography. [BX669.A1L3] 57-3831
1. Saints, Georgian. I. Title.

LANG, David Marshall, ed. and tr. 922.1479
Lives and legends of the Georgian saints, selected and translated from the original texts by David Marshall Lang. London, Allen & Unwin; New York, Macmillan [1956] 179p. illus. 29cm. (Ethical and religious classics of East and West, no. 15) Includes bibliography. [BX669.A1L3] 57-3831
1. Saints,Georgian. I. Title.

LIVES and legends of the Georgian saints; selected and translated from the original texts. New York, Macmillan [1956] 179p.
I. Lang, David Marshall, ed. and tr.

LIVES and legends of the Georgian saints, selected and tr. from the original texts. London, G. Allen & Unwin; New York, Macmillan [1956] 179p. (Ethical and religious classics of East and West, no. 15) 'Select bibliography' :p. 173-174.
I. Land, David Marshal, tr.

LIVES and legends of the Georgian saints; selected and translated from the original texts. New York, Macmillan [1956] 179p.
I. Lang, David Marshall, ed. and tr.

Saints—Great Brit

KNOWLES, David [Secular name: Michael Clive Knowles] 1896- 922.22
Saints and Scholars; twenty-five medieval portraits. [New York] Cambridge [c]1962. 207p., illus. 21 cm. 62-4142 3.95; pap., 1.65
1. Saints—Gt. Brit 2. Scholars, English. I. Title.

SAMSON, Saint, bp. of Dol, d.565.Legend. 230
The life of St. Samsom of Dol, by Thomas Taylor... London, Society for promoting Christian knowledge; New York and Toronto, The Macmillan co., 1925. xli, [1], 82 p., 1 l. front., 2 illus. (maps) 19 cm. (Half-title: Translations of Christian literature, series V: Lives of the Celtic saints) Bibliography: p. [xiii] [BR45.T65S3] 25-14251
I. Taylor, Thomas, 1858- ed. and tr. II. Title.

Saints, Irish.

CURTAYNE, Alice. 922.22
More tales of Irish saints. Illustrated by Brigid Rynne. New York, Sheed and Ward [1957] 139p. illus. 21cm. [BX4659.I7C79] 57-10187
1. Saints, Irish. I. Title. II. Title: Tales of Irish saints.

CURTAYNE, Alice. 922.22
Twenty tales of Irish saints; with illus. by Johannes Troyer. New York, Sheed and Ward [1955] 178p. illus: 21cm. [BX4659.I7C8] 55-9458
1. Saints. Irish. I. Title.

LYNCH, Patricia, 1898- 922.22
Knights of God stories of the irish saints Chicago, H. Regnery Co., 1955. 216p. 22cm. [BX4659.I7L9] 55-6413
1. Saints, Irish. I. Title.

PLUMMER, Charles, 1851-1927. 922.
Bethada naem nErenn. Lives of Irish saints, edited from the origianl mass. with introduction, translations, notes, glossary and indexes, by Charles Plummer ... Oxford, The Clarendon press, 1922. 2 v. 22 1/2cm. "List of abbreviations used, and of works cited": v. 1, p. [xii]-xliv. [BX4659.I7P8] 23-6732
1. Saints, Irish. I. Title. II. Title: Lives of Irish saints.

SANDERSON, Joseph, 1823-
The story of Saint Patrick; embracing a sketch of the condition of Ireland before the time of Patrick, during his life, at his death, and immediately after it, by Joseph Sanderson ... New York, W. B. Ketcham publishing company [1902] 286 p. 21 cm. 2-20490

I. Title.

Saints, Irish—Juvenile literature.

LYNCH, Patricia, 1898- 274.15 B
Knights of God; tales and legends of the Irish saints. Illustrated by Victor Ambrus. [1st ed.] New York, Holt, Rinehart and Winston [1969] xix, 219 p. illus. 24 cm. Contents.Contents.—Introduction.—Saint Ciaran, the first of them all.—Saint Patrick, the Roman slave.—Enda of Aran.—Saint Brigid, the light of Kildare.—Brendan the voyager.—Columcille, dove of the church.—Kevin of Glendalough.—Lawrence O'Toole, captive prince.—There were other saints.—List of books (p. 219) [BX4659.I7L9 1969] 920 69-11811 4.50
1. Saints, Irish—Juvenile literature. 2. [Saints, Irish.] 3. [Folklore—Ireland.] I. Ambrus, Victor G., illus. II. Title.

REILLY, Robert T. 922.22
Irish saints. Illus. by Harry Barton. New York, Farrar [c.1964] xvii, 172p. illus., map. 22cm. (Vision bk., 63) 64-19806 2.25
1. Saints, Irish—Juvenile literature I. Title.

REILLY, Robert T 922.22
Irish saints, by Robert T. Reilly. Illustrated by Harry Barton. New York, Vision Books [1964] xvii, 172 p. illus., map. 22 cm. "63." [BX4659.I7R4] 64-19806
1. Saints, Irish — Juvenile literature. I. Title.

Saints, Italian.

CATERINA da Siena, Saint, 1347-1380.Legend.
The little flowers of Saint Catherine of Siena; culled from old munscripts by Innocenzo Taurisano, of the Order of preachers; translated from the Italian by Charlotte Dease. Saint Paul, Minn., The E. M. Lohman co. [1929] 3. l., 5-153, [1] p. incl. front. (port.) 17. (Half-title: Home and cloister books, general editor, E. Vincent Wareing) "Printed in Great Britan." Title vignette; head and tail pieces; initials. A 40
I. Taurisano, Innocenzo M., 1877- ed. II. Deseas, Charolotte, tr. III. Title. IV. Title: His translation is based chiefy on the first of the two editions of the Floretti di Santa Caterian. cf. p. l., 3.

GREGORIUS I, the Great, Saint, Pope, 540(ca.)-604.
Li Dialoge Gregoire lo Pape. Altfranzosische Uebersetzung des XII. Jahrhunderts der Dialogen des Papstes Gregor, mit dem lateinischen Original, einem Anhang: Sermo de Sapientia und Moralium in Iob Fragmenta, einer grammatischen Einleitung, erklarenden Anmerkungen und einem Glossar. Zum ersten Male hrsg. von Wendelin Foerster. Amsterdam, RODOPI, 1965- . v. 23 cm. Added t.p. in French (facsim. of 1876 ed.) Contents.Contents. -- T.1. Text. 67-36697
1. Benedictus, Saint, abbot of Monte Cassino. 2. Saints, Italian. 3. Miracles — Early works to 1800. 4. Immortality. I. Foerster, Wendelin, 1844-1915, ed. II. Title.

GREGORIUS I, the Great, Saint, Pope, 540(ca.)-604. 281.4
Dialogues; translated by Odo John Zimmerman. New York, Fathers of the Church, inc., 1959. xvi, 287 p. 22 cm. (The Fathers of the church, a new translation, v. 39) Bibliography: p. viii. [BR60.F3G7] 59-4637
1. Benedictus, Saint, Abbot of Monte Cassino. 2. Saints, Italian. 3. Miracles—Early works to 1800. 4. Immortality. I. Title. II. Series.

Saints — Juvenile literature.

BARCLAY, Vera Charlesworth, 1893- 922.2
Saints by fire light; stories for guides and rangers, by Vera Barclay. New York, The Macmillan company, 1931. xi p., 2 l., 17-206 p. 19 cm. "Printed in Great Britain." [BX4658.B3] 32-14931
1. Saints—Juvenile literature. I. Title.
Contents omitted.

BEEBE, Catherine, 1898- 922.22
Saints for boys and girls; stories. Pictures by Robb Beebe. Milwaukee, Bruce Pub. Co. [1959] 147p. illus. 21cm. [BX4658.B43] 59-13571
1. Saints—Juvenile literature. I. Title.

BURTON, Doris. 922.22
The girls' book of saints. Illustrated by T. J. Bond. St. Louis, Herder [1958] 149p. illus. 23cm. [BX4658.B8 1958] 59-2322
1. Saints—Juvenile literature. 2. Saints, Women. I. Title.

BURTON, Doris.
Saints and heroes for boys. Illustrated by Rosemary de Souza. Springfield, Ill., Templegate [n.d.] 118 p. illus. 22 cm. 67-12297
1. Saints — Juvenile literature. I. Title.

CANTON, William, 1845-1926. 922
A child's book of saints [by] William Canton. London, J.M. Dent & sons, ltd.; New York, E.P. Dutton & co., inc. [1933] x p., 1 l., 343, [1] p. incl. plates. 17 1/2 cm. (Half-title: Everyman's library, ed. by Ernest Rhys. For young people. (no. 61]) "First published in this edition, 1906; reprinted...1963." Bibliography: p. vii. [AC1E8 no.. 61] 30-37434
1. Saints—Juvenile literature. I. Title.

CHADWICK, Enid M. 920
Saints who loved animals, written, illus. by Enid M. Chadwick. London. A. R. Mowbrav [dist. Westminster, Md., Canterbury, 1963, c.1962] 61p. 21cm. 63-802 1.95 bds.,
1. Saints—Juvenile literature. I. Title.

CHAPMAN, Michael Andrew. 922
A garland of saints for children, by the Reverend Michael Andrew Chapman. New York and Cincinnati, Frederick Pustet co. (inc.) [c1929] 4 p. l., 11-130 p. incl. front., illus. 22 cm. [BX4658.C45] 29-25932
1. Saints—Juvenile literature. I. Title.

CHENOWETH, Caroline (Van Dusen) Mrs., 1846- 922
Stories of the saints. by Mrs. C. Van D. Chenoweth ... Boston, J. R. Osgood and company, 1880. 162 p. front., plates (1 double) 19 cm. [BR1711.C5] 37-21090
1. Saints—Juvenile literature. I. Title.

CHENOWETH, Caroline (Van Dusen) Mrs., 1846- 922
Stories of the saints, by Mrs. C. Van D. Chenoweth. New and enl. ed., with illustrations. Boston and New York, Houghton, Mifflin and company, 1907. 6 p. l., (7)-239 (1) p. front., 7 pl. 19 1/2cm. [BX4658.C5] 7-33563
1. Saints—Juvenile literature. I. Title.

CONWAY, E. Carolyn 922.22
The little ways. Illustrated by Astrid Walford. Baltimore, Helicon Press, 1960 [ ] 114p. illus. 20cm. 6 -9509 2.50 bds.
1. Saints—Juvenile literature. I. Title.

CONWAY, E. Carolyn 922.22
More little ways. Illustrated by Astrid Walford. Baltimore, Helicon Press, 1960[ ] u12p. ill1s. 20cm. 6 -9508 2.50 bds.
1. Saints—Juvenile literature. I. Title. II. Title: Little ways.

COOK, Frederick. 922.22
Young girl of France, and other stories. Paterson, N.J., St. Anthony Guild Press, 1956. 118p. illus. 21cm. [BX4658.C57] 56-14269
1. Saints—Juvenile literature. I. Title.

COUSINS, Mary 922.22
More about the saints. Illustrated by Margery Gill. Westminister, Md., Newman Press, 1960.[ ] 158p. illus. (part col.) 22cm. 60-16074 2.75 bds.,
1. Saints —Juvenile 9iterature. I. Title.

COUSINS, Mary 920
The saints in history. Illus. by Sally Mellersh. New York, Kenedy [1963, c.1962] 125p. illus. map. 3cm. 62-22117 2.95
1. Saints—Juvenile literature.s8 I. Title.

CRISS, Mildred, 1890- 922.22
A book of saints. New York, Dodd, Mead, 1956. 156 p. illus. 22 cm. [BX4658.C6] 56-6800
1. Saints—Juvenile literature. I. Title.

DAUGHTERS of St. Paul. 920
57 stories of saints for for boys and girls. Written, illus. by the Daughters of Saint Paul [Boston] St. Paul Eds. [dist. daughter of St. Paul.] c.1963] 581p. col. illus. 22cm. 63-19996 4.00 5.00 pap.,
1. Saints —Juvenile literature. I. Title.

DAUGHTERS of St. Paul 922.2
Saints for young people for everyday of the year; v.2 [Boston] St. Paul Eds. [dist.] Author [c.1964] 337p. illus. ,pt. col.) ports. (pt. col.) 22cm. Contents.v.2. July-Dec. 63-19997 2.50 pap.,
1. Saints—Calendar. 2. Saints—Juvenile literature. I. Title.

DORCY, Mary Jean, sister, 1914- 922.2
Truth was their star [by] Sister Mary Jean Dorcy, O.P. Milwaukee, The Bruce publishing company [1947] 124 p. illus. 23 1/2 cm. [BX4653.D6] 47-2300
1. Saints—Juvenile literature. I. Title.
Contents omitted.

EASTWOOD, Edna, 1894- 922.2
Saints courageous, stories for boys and girls; illus. by Emma Gaard. New York, Morehouse-Gorham Co., 1948. 189 p. illus. 21 cm. [BX4653.E3] 48-9701
1. Saints—Juvenile literature. I. Title.

ELEANORE, Mary, Sister 1890- 922
Through the lane of stars, by Sister M. Eleanore...foreword and afterword by Daniel A. Lord, S. J., illustrated by Karl S. Woerner. New York and London, D. Appleton and company, 1928. xvi p., 1 l., 3-266 [1] p. illus. 19 1/2 cm. [BX4658.E6] 28-4499
1. Saints—Juvenile literature. I. Title.

FARJEON, Eleanor, 1881- 922
Ten saints, by Eleanor Farjeon; with illustrations by Helen Sewell. London, New York [etc.] Oxford university press, 1936. 124 p. incl. col. front., col. plates. 25 cm. "First edition." [BR1711.F3] 36-28542
1. Saints—Juvenile literature. I. Sewell, Helen, 1896- illus. II. Title.

FLAHIVE, Robert F. 922.22
Saints for Scouts. Milwaukee, Bruce Pub. Co., [c.1960] ix, 149p. illus. 22 cm. 60-10657 2.75
1. Saints—Juvenile literature. I. Title.

FLAHIVE, Robert F. 922.22
Saints for servers. Illus. by Arnie Kohn. Milwaukee, Bruce [c.1961] 62p. 61-17438 1.25
1. Saints—Juvenile literature. I. Title.

FOX, Frances Margaret, 1870- 922.2
Gay legends of the saints, by Frances Margaret Fox, illustrated by Jill Elgin. New York, Sheed & Ward, 1942. 5 p. l., 3-169, [1] p. illus. 22 cm. [BX4658.F6] 42-50006
1. Saints—Juvenile literature. 2. Saints. I. Title.

GALES, Louis A 1896- 922.22
A first book of saints for little Catholics; illustrated by Gertrude Elliott Espenscheid. St. Paul, Catechetical Guild Educational Society, c1954. unpaged. illus. 17cm. (First books for little Catholics) [BX4653.G3] 54-27105
1. Saints—Juvenile literature. I. Title.

HASKELL, Arnold Lionel, 1903- 922.22
Saints alive; a study of six saints for young people. With a foreword by Barbara Ward. New York Roy Publishers [1953] 148 p. illus. 20 cm. [BX4658.H28] 54-7908
1. Saints—Juvenile literature. 2. [Saints.] I. Title.

HERBST, Winfrid. 922.2
Follow the saints: a series of readings on the lives and virtues of some saints, with a reflection to encourage imitation, by Rev. Winfrid Herbst, S.D.S. New York, Cincinnati [etc.] Benziger brothers, 1933. 2 p. l., iii, 253 p. 19 cm. [BX4658.H4] 33-33466
1. Saints—Juvenile literature. I. Title.

LAHEY, Thomas Aquinas, 1886- 922.2
God's heroes; a study of the saints for children, and Teacher's aid, a supplement to "God's heroes" (combined in one book) by Rev. Thomas A. Lahey ... Notre Dame, Ind., The Ave Maria press [c1936] 287 p. 20 cm. "Third printing." [BX4653.L3 1936] 36-11944
1. Saints—Juvenile literature. 2. Saints—Study and teaching. I. Title.

LOVASIK, Lawrence George, 1913- j 920
New picture book of saints; illustrated lives of the saints for young and old. Saint Joseph ed. New York, Catholic Book Pub. Co. [c1962] 116 p. col. illus. 24 cm. [BX4658.L6] 63-4966
1. Saints — Juvenile literature. I. Title. II. Title: Picture book of saints.

MARY, Charitas Sister, 1893- 922
Faith and a fishhook. Milwaukee, Bruce Pub. Co. [1949] ix, 164 p. illus. 20 cm. Secular name: Catherine Krieter. [BX4658.M418] 49-3771
1. Saints—Juvenile literature. I. Title.

MARY Charitas, sister, 1893- 922
The man who built the secret door [by] Sister Mary Charitas ... Milwaukee, The Bruce publishing company [1945] ix p., 1 l., 130 p. incl. front., illus. 20 cm. [BX4658.M42] 45-11395
1. Saints—Juvenile literature. 2. Christian biography—Juvenile literature. I. Title.

MARY Cornelius, Sister, 1901- 922.22
Saints to know. Milwaukee, Bruce Pub. Co. [1954] 128p. illus. 23cm. [BX4658.M424] 54-10664
1. Saints—Juvenile literature. I. Title.

MARY Fidelis, sister, 1891- 242
A character calendar, by Sister Mary Fidelis and Sister Mary Charitas ... New York, Milwaukee [etc.] The Bruce publishing company [c1931] viii p., 1 l., 236 p. 18 1/2 cm. "Catholic school journal reprint."--p. [iv] [Secular name: Mary Krieter] [BX4658.M43] 32-23463
1. Saints—Juvenile literature. 2. Calendars. I. Mary Charitas, sister, 1893- joint author. II. Title.

MOORE, Margaret R 922.22
Big saints, by Margaret and John Travers Moore. Illus. by Gedge Harmon. St. Meinrad, Ind., Grail [c1954] 77p. illus. 22cm. [BX4658.M6] 55-14066
1. Saints—Juvenile literature. I. Moore, John Travers, joint author. II. Title.

MORRISS, Frank 235
Saints for the small. Illus. by Robert Poppert. Milwaukee, Bruce [c.1964] 112p. illus. 22cm. 64-23894 2.50
1. Saints—Juvenile literature. I. Title.

MOSELEY, Daisy Haywood. 922.2
Sunshine and saints, by Daisy Haywood Moseley; illustrated by Da Osimo. New York, P. J. Kenedy & sons [c1935] vii, 181 p. incl. front., illus. 24 cm. [BX4653.M6] 36-143
1. Saints—Juvenile literature. I. Title.

O'NEILL, Mary 920
Saints: adventures in courage. Illus. by Alex Ross. Garden City, N. Y., Doubleday [c.1963] 186p. col. illus. 29cm. 63-17278 4.95
1. Saints—Juvenile literature. I. Title.

O'NEILL, Mary (Le Duc) 1908- 920
Saints: adventures in courage. Illustrated by Alex Ross. [1st ed.] Garden City, N.Y., Doubleday [1963] 186 p. illus. 29 cm. [BX4658.O5] 63-17278
1. Saints — Juvenile literature. I. Title.

PAULI, Hertha Ernestine, 1909- 232.92
Christmas and the saints. Illustrated by Rus Anderson. New York, Farrar, Straus and Cudahy [1956] 190 p. illus. 22 cm. (Vision books, 16) [BX4658.P3] 56-11060
1. Saints—Juvenile literature. 2. Christmas. 3. [Saints.] 4. [Christmas.]

PETERS, Caroline 920
Lives of the saints, for boys and girls, Drawings by Mitzi Young. Paterson. N. J., St. Anthony Guild Pr [c.1966] vi, 130p. illus. 25cm. [BX4658.P4] 66-17973 3.00
1. Saints—Juvenile literature. I. Title.

PETERS, Caroline. 920
Lives of the saints, for boys and girls. Drawings by Mitzi Young. Paterson, N. J., St. Anthony Guild Press [1966] vi. 130 p. illus. 25 cm. [BX4658.P4] 66-17973

1. Saints—Juvenile literature. I. Title.

ROSES, Anthony. 920 (j)
The golden man. Illustrated by Mary Taylor. Westminster, Md., Newman Press [1955] 99p. illus. 19cm. Stories adapted from Legenda aurea by Jacobus de Varagine. [BX4658.R6] 55-8662
1. Saints—Juvenile literature. I. Jacobus de Varagine. Legenda aurea. II. Title.

ROSS Williamson, Hugh, 1901- 922.22
The young people's book of saints; sixty-three saints of the Western church from the first to the twentieth century. Illustrated by Sheila Connelly. New York, Hawthorn Books. [1960] 239 p. illus. 22 cm. [BX4653.R65] 60-10338
1. Saints—Juvenile literature. 2. [Saints.] I. Title.

STEEDMAN, Amy. 922.2
In God's garden; stories of the saints for little children, by Amy Steedman; with sixteen reproductions from Italian masterpieces. London, New York [etc.] T. Nelson and sons, ltd. [1936] xii, 142 p., 1 l. col. front., col. plates. 21 cm. [BX4658.S75] 40-15778
1. Saints—Juvenile literature. I. Title.
Contents omitted.

STIRLING, John. 232.9
For a little child like me, by John Stirling; with illustrations by Horace J. Knowles. New York, C. Scribner's sons, 1934. 52 p. front., illus. 21 1/2 cm. [BT302.S875] 34-40703
1. Jesus Christ—Biog.—Juvenile literature. 2. Saints—Juvenile literature. I. Title.

THOMPSON, Blanche Jennings 922.22
When saints were young. Illustrated by John Lawn. New York, Farrar, Straus and Cudahy [c.1960] 188p. illus. 22cm. (Vision books, 46) 60-6139 1.95
1. Saints—Juvenile literature. I. Title.

THOMPSON, Blanche Jennings, 1887- 922.244
A candle burns for France, by Blanche Jennings Thompson, illustrated by Kate Seredy. Milwaukee, The Bruce publishing company [1946] 80 p. col. front., illus. 20 1/2 cm. [BX4658.T5] 46-6458
1. Saints—Juvenile literature. 2. Saints, French. I. Seredy, Kate, illus. II. Title.

THOMPSON, Blanche Jennings, 1887- 922
Saints of the Byzantine world. Illus. by Donald Bolognese. New York, Vision Bks. [dist. Farrar, c.1961] 192p. (Vision bks., 52) 61-11325 1.95
1. Saints—Juvenile literature. I. Title.

THOMPSON, Blanche Jennings, 1887- 922.22
When saints were young. Illustrated by John Lawn. New York, Vision Books [1960] 188 p. illus. 22 cm. (Vision books, 46) [BX4658.T52] 60-6139
1. Saints — Juvenile literature. I. Title.

TWIGG-PORTER, George. 920 (j)
Caves, conversions, and creatures. [Boston] St. Paul Editions [1967] 74 p. illus. 19 cm. Bibliographical footnotes. [BX4658.T87] 67-29165
1. Saints—Juvenile literature. I. Title.

WEDGE, Florence. 922.22
Saints without wrinkles; thirteen saints for teen-agers. Pulaski, Wis., Franciscan Printery, 1956. 173 p. 22 cm. [BX4658.W4] 57-36861
1. Saints — Juvenile literature I. Title.

WEDGE, Florence. 920
Sixty shining halos. Pulaski, Wis., Franciscan Publishers [1963] 187 p. illus. 22 cm. [BX4658.W42] 63-10259
1. Saints — Juvenile literature. I. Title.

WINDHAM, Joan. 922.2
... Heaven on earth, adapted from the French, Sur la terre comme au ciel by Camille Melloy; with illustrations by Jeanne Hebbelynck. [London and New York] Sheed & Ward, 1937. 2 p. l., 7-47 p. incl. col. plates. 22 1/2 x 22 1/2 cm. "Made in Belgium." [BX4658.W52] 38-39361
1. Saints—Juvenile literature. I. Melloy, Camille. Sur la terre comme au ciel. II. Title.

WINDHAM, Joan. 922
More saints for six o'clock, by Joan Windham; illustrations by Marigold Hunt. New York, Sheed & Ward, inc., 1935. vii, 110 p. illus. 22 cm. "Printed in Great Britain." [BR1711.W52 1935] 36-13140
1. Saints—Juvenile literature. I. Title.

WINDHAM, Joan. 922.2
New Six o'clock saints, by Joan Windham, with illustrations by Caryll Houselander. New York, Sheed & Ward, inc., 1945. 3 p. l., 104 p. illus. 22 cm. [BX4653.W5] 45-8366
1. Saints—Juvenile literature. I. Houselander, Frances Caryll, illus. II. Title.

WINDHAM, Joan. 922
Saints by request, by Joan Windham. New York, Sheed & Ward, 1937. vii, 125 p. illus. 22 1/2 cm. "Printed in Great Britain." [BR1711.W54] 38-3042
1. Saints—Juvenile literature. I. Title.

WINDHAM, Joan. 922.2
Six o'clock saints, by Joan Windham; with illustrations by Marigold Hunt. New York, Sheed & Ward, inc., 1934. vii, 107 p. illus. 22 cm. "Printed in Great Britain." [BR1711.W5 1934a] 35-10327
1. Saints—Juvenile literature. I. Title.

WINDHAM, Joan, 1904- 922.2
Here are your saints; with illus. by Frank Russell. New York, Sheed & Ward [1948] vi, 104 p. illus. 23 cm. Contents.--St. Alexander.--St Felix.--St. Beatrice.--St Monica.--St. Grace.--St. Alan.--St Gwen.--St. Maude.--St. Harold.--St. Guy.-- St. Angela.--St. Jane.--St. Vincent. [BX4658.W53] 48-2642
1. Saints—Juvenile literature. I. Title.

WINDHAM, Joan, 1904- 922.22
Saints upon a time; illustrated by Kurt Werth. New York, Sheed and Ward [1956] 160p. illus. 21cm. [BX4658.W55] 56-6133
1. Saints—Juvenile literature. I. Title.

WINDHAM, Joan, 1904- 922
Sixty saints for boys; with illus. by Mona Doneux. New York, Sheed & Ward, 1948. x, 404 p. illus., 23 cm. Contents.:A Joan Windham ominbus [!] [BX4653.W517] 48-9290
1. Saints—Juvenile literature. I. Title.

Saints—Legends.

HOLE, Christina. 398.22
Saints in folklore. Illustrated by T. Every-Clayton. New York, M. Barrows, 1965. xiv, 159 p. illus. 21 cm. Bibliography: p. 151-153. [BX4661.H64] 65-20959
1. Saints—Legends. I. Title.

SOUTH English legendary. 270 B
The South English legendary. Edited from Corpus Christi College, Cambridge, MS. 145 and British Museum MS. Harley 2277, with variants from Bodley MS. Ashmole 43 and British Museum MS. Cotton Julius D. IX, by Charlotte D'Evelyn and Anna J. Mill. London, New York, Published for the Early English Text Society by the Oxford University Press [1967- v. facsims. 23 cm. (Early English Text Society. [Publications. Original series] no. 235) Reprint of the 1956-59 ed. [PR1119.A2 no. 235, etc., 1967] 77-825 50/- per vol.
1. Saints—Legends. I. D'Evelyn, Charlotte, 1889- ed. II. Mill, Anna Jean, ed. III. Series: Early English Text Society. Publications. Original series, no. 235 [etc.]

Saints, Muslim.

FARID AL-DIN ATTAR 13thcent. 297.6
Muslim saints and mystics; episodes from the Tadhkirat al-auliya' ('Memorial of the saints'). Tr. [from Arabic] by A. J. Arberry. [Chicago] Univ. of Chic. Pr. [c.1966] xii, 287p. 23cm. (UNESCO collec. of representative works: Persian heritage ser.) Bibl. [BP189.4.F323 1966] 65-27758 6.00
1. Saints, Muslim. I. Arberry, Arthur John, 1905- tr. II. Title. III. Title: Memorial of the saints. IV. Series. V. UNESCO collec. of representative works: Persian heritage ser.

FARID AL-DIN 'ATTAR, 13thcent. 297.6
Muslim saints and mystics; episodes from the Todhkirat al-auliya' ("Memorial of the saints"). Translated by A. J. Arberry. [Chicago, University of Chicago Press [1966] xii, 287 p. 23 cm. (UNESCO collection of representative works: Persian heritage series) Includes bibliographies. [BP189.4.F323 1966] 65-27758
1. Saints, Muslim. I. Arberry, Arthur John, 1905- tr. II. Title. III. Title: Memorial of the saints. IV. Series.

Saints, Norwegian.

UNDSET, Sigrid, 1882- 922.2481
Saga of saints, by Sigrid Undset; translated by E. C. Ramsden. New York, Longmans, Green and co., 1934. xii, 321 p. front., plates, port., map. 19 1/2 cm. "First edition." [BX4569.N8U7 1934 a] 34-33258
1. Saints, Norwegian. 2. Norway—Church history. I. Ramsden, Evelyn Charlotte, 1898- tr. II. Title.
Contents omitted.

UNDSET, Sigrid, 1882-1949. 282'.0922
Saga of saints. Translated by E. C. Ramsden. Freeport, N.Y., Books for Libraries Press [1968, c1934] xii, 321 p. illus., map, ports. 22 cm. (Essay index reprint series) Translation of Norske helgener. Contents.Contents.—The coming of Christianity.—St. Sunniva and the Seljemen.—St. Olav, Norway's king to all eternity.—St. Hallvard.—St. Magnus, Earl of the Orkney Islands.—St. Eystein, Archbishop of Nidaros.—St. Thorfinn, Bishop of Hamar.—Father Karl Schilling, Barnabite. [BX4659.N8U7 1968] 68-22952
1. Saints, Norwegian. 2. Norway—Church history. I. Title.

Saints—Poetry.

METCALFE, James J 1906- 922.22
Poem portraits of the saints; lives of the saints in verse. [1st ed.] Garden City, N. Y., Hanover House [1956] 119p. 22cm. [BX4657.M4] 56-5589
1. Saints—Poetry. I. Title.

PAULINUS, Saint, Bp. of Nola, 353-431. 281'.08 s
The poems of St. Paulinus of Nola / translated and annotated P. G. Walsh. New York : Newman Press, 1975. vi, 443 p. ; 23 cm. (Ancient Christian writers : The works of the Fathers in translation ; no. 40) Includes bibliographical references and indexes. [BR60.A35 no. 40] [PA6554.P5] 871'.1 74-77484 12.95
I. Title. II. Series.

Saints — Quotations.

JOHNSTON, Francis W. ed.
Voice of the saints; counsels from the saints to bring comfort and guidance in daily living. Springfield, Ill., Templegate [1965] ix, 150 p. 17 cm. 67-101864
1. Saints — Quotations. I. Title.

Saints, Russian.

GRUNWALD, Constantin de. 922.147
Saints of Russia. Translated by Roger Capel. New York, Macmillan, 1960. 180p. 22cm. Translation of Quand la Russie avait des saints. [BX596.G713 1960] 60-12977
1. Saints, Russian. I. Title.

Saints, Serbian.

... Lives of the Serbian saints, by Voyeslav Yanich, D. D., and C. Patrick Hankey, M. A. London, Society for promoting Christian knowledge; New York, The Macmillan company, 1921. xx, 108 p. front., pl., ports. 19 cm. (Translations of Christian literature, series vii) Translated from a martyrology issued in the middle of the last century, for the use of the church throughout Serbia. cf. Introd. [BR45.T6.L5] 21-21906 230
1. Saints, Serbian. I. Janie, Vojislav, 1890- ed. and tr. II. Hankey, Cyril Patrick, joint ed.

Saints, Women.

FARLEY, Luke A., 1919 922.22
Saints for the modern woman; a united nations of holiness for the woman of today. Written, illus. by Luke A. Farley. 53Boston] St. Paul Eds. [dist. Daughters of St. Paul, c.1961] 276p. Bibl. 61-18635 3.95; 2.50 pap.,
1. Saints, women. I. Title.

HOME, Georgina. 922.2
The immortal garland; a book of women saints, by Georgina Home. London and Oxford, A. R. Mowbray & co., ltd.; Milwaukee. vii, 175. [1] p. 19 cm. "First published in 1934." [BX4656.H6] 35-9869
1. Saints, Women. I. Title. II. Title: Morehouse publishing co.

MARGARET PATRICE, sister, 1900- 922.2
Up the shining path [by] Sister Margaret Patrice, illustrated by Eleanore Barte. Milwaukee, The Bruce publishing company [1946] 173 p. illus. 20 1/2 cm. [Secular name: Ellen Josephine Donovan] [BX4656.M35] 47-1162
1. Saints, Women. I. Title.

MARTINDALE, Cyril Charlie, 1879- 922.22
The Queen's daughters, a study of women saints. New York, Sheed & Ward, 1951. 252 p. 22 cm. [BX4656.M43] 51-13726
1. Saints, Women. I. Title.

MARY Cornelius, Sister, 1901- 922.2
Fifteen saints for girls. Milwaukee, Bruce [1951] 133 p. illus. 23 cm. [BX4656.M44] 51-8945
1. Saints, Women. I. Title.

MENZIES, Lucy. 922.
Mirrors of the holy; ten studies in sanctity, by Lucy Menzies ... London [etc.] A. R. Mowbray & co. ltd.; Milwaukee, The Morehouse publishing co. [1929] xxviii, 308 p. mounted front., mounted ports. 22 cm. Bibliography at end of each study. [BX4656.M5] 29-14042
1. Saints, Women. I. Title.
Contents omitted.

WINDHAM, Joan, 1904- 922.22
Sixty saints for girls; a Joan Windham omnibus. Illus. by Renee George. New York, Sheed [1962] 376p. illus. 22cm. 62-15288 3.95
1. Saints, Women. I. Title.

Saints—Worship.

PERCIVAL, Henry Robert, 1854-1903.
The invocation of saints treated theologically and historically, by Henry R. Percival ... London, New York [etc.] Longmans, Green, & co., 1896. xix, 265 p. 20 cm. [BX2333.P4] 3-32832
1. Saints—Worship. I. Title.

Sakkara—Antiquities

GHUNAIM, Muhammad Zakariya. 932
The lost pyramid. New York, Rinehart [1956] 175p. illus. 22cm. [DT73.S3G5] 913.32 56-11024
1. Sekhem-khet, King of Egypt. 2. Sakkara—Antiq. 3. Pyramids. I. Title.

LAUER, Jean Philippe, 1902- 932'.01
Saqqara : the royal cemetery of Memphis : excavations and discoveries since 1850 / Jean-Philippe Lauer. New York : Scribner, c1976. 248 p. : ill. (some col.) ; 26 cm. Includes index. Bibliography: p. 231-240. [DT73.S3L38 1976b] 75-33508 ISBN 0-684-14551-0 : 25.00
1. Sakkara—Antiquities. 2. Egypt—Antiquities. I. Title.

Sakti (Hindu deity)—Poetry.

RAMAPRASADA Sena, 1718-1775. 891'.4413
Grace and mercy in her wild hair : selected poems to the Mother Goddess / by Ramprasad Sen ; translated by Leonard Nathan and Clinton Seely. Boulder, Colo. : Great Eastern Book Co., 1982. p. cm. Translation from Bengali. Bibliography: p.

[PK1718.R2514A26] 19 82-904 ISBN 0-87773-761-4 (pbk.) : 7.00
1. Sakti (Hindu deity)—Poetry. I. Nathan, Leonard, 1924- II. Seely, Clinton B. III. Title.

Saktism.

PAYNE, Ernest Alexander, 1902- 294.551
... *The Saktas;* an introductory and comparative study, by Ernest A. Payne ... Calcutta, Y. M. C. A. publishing house; London, New York [etc.] H. Milford, Oxford university press, 1933. ii p., 6 l., 153 p. front., plates. 19 cm. (The religious life of India) Bibliography: p. [141]-147. [BL1245.S3P3] 34-35485
1. Saktism. I. Title.

Sala, Darlene.

SALA, Darlene. 266'.0092'4 B
Bugs, floods, and fried rice : one mom's journal / Darlene Sala. Grand Rapids : Baker Book House, c1978. 96 p. ; 21 cm. [BV3382.S24A32] 78-102972 ISBN 0-8010-8128-9 pbk. : 2.95
1. Sala, Darlene. 2. Missionaries—Philippines—Biography.—Anecdotes, facetiae, satire, etc. 3. Missionaries—United States—Biography—Anecdotes, fasetiae, satire, etc. 4. Missions—Philippines—Anecdotes, facetiae, satire, etc. I. Title.

Saladin, Sultan of Egypt and Syria, 1137-1193.

ABU Shamah, 'Abd al-Rahman ibn Isma'il, 1203-1267. 909.07
Arabische Quellenbeitrage zur Geschichte der Kreuzzuge / ubers. u. hrsg. von E. P. Goergens. Machdr. d. Ausg. Berlin 1879. Bd. 1. Zur Geschichte Salah ad-din's. Hildesheim ; New York : Olms, 1975. xxiii, 295 p. ; 19 cm. No more published. Reprint of the ed. published by Weidmann'sche Buchhandlung. Includes bibliographical references. [D152.A2 1975] 76-459998 ISBN 3-487-05590-2 : DM49.80
1. Saladin, Sultan of Egypt and Syria, 1137-1193. 2. Crusades—Sources. I. Goergens, E. P. II. Title.

LANE-POOLE, Stanley, 1854-1931 909.07
Saladin and the fall of the Kingdom of Jerusalem. Beirut, Khayats [Mystic, Conn., Verry, 1965] xxiv, 416p. illus., maps (pt. fold.) plans. 23cm. (Khayats oriental reprints, no. 8) Bibl. [D198.4.S2L3] 65-6309 5.50
1. Saladin, Sultan of Egypt and Syria, 1137-1193. 2. Jerusalem—Hist.—Latin kingdom, 1099-1244. I. Title.

Salcation—Sermons.

BAXTER, James Sidlow. 234
God so loved; an expository series on the theology and evangel of the best-known text in the Bible. Grand Rapids, Zondervan Pub. House [1960] 206p. 23cm. First published in London in 1949 under title: The best word ever. [BT753.B35 1960] 60-50189
1. Salcation—Sermons. 2. Baptists—Sermons. 3. Sermons, English. I. Title.

Salem Baptist Church. Chesterfield Co., Va.

PANKEY, William Russell.
The history of Salem Baptist Church. Organized 1794, Chesterfield, Virginia. [Richmond?, 1965] 72 p. 22 cm. Cover title. 67-58820
1. Salem Baptist Church. Chesterfield Co., Va. I. Title.

Salem Church, Spotsylvania County, Va.

HAPPEL, Ralph. 975.5'365
Old Salem Church, Fredericksburg and Spotsylvania National Military Park. [Washington] Division of History, Office of Archeology and Historic Preservation, 1968. viii, 134 l., [62] p. illus. 27 cm. (Historic structures report) "Historic structures report—part II, historical data section." Bibliography: leaves 130-134. [BX6480.S8S25] 73-601803
1. Salem Church, Spotsylvania County, Va. I. Title. II. Series.

Salem Co., N.J.—Churches.

JACQUETT, Josephine.
Churches of Salem County, New Jersey. Author: Josephine Jaquett. Photography: Josephine Jaquett, Stephen S. Joseph. [Salem, N.J.] Published by the Salem County Tercentenary Committee, 1964. 2 p.l., 49 p., 1 l. illus. 18 x 28 cm. 68-100947
1. Salem Co., N.J.—Churches. I. Salem County Tercentenary Committee. II. Title.

Salem co., N. J.—Social conditions

BRUNNER, Edmund de Schweinitz, 1889- ed. 261.
A church and community survey of Salem county, New Jersey, made under the direction of Edmund de S. Brunner ... New York, George H. Doran company [c1922] ix p., 1 l., 13-92 p. illus. (incl. maps) fold. tab., diagrs. 23 cm. (Committee on social and religious surveys. [Unique studies of rural American, town and country series, no. 1]) [BR555.N5583] 23-7453
1. Salem co., N. J.—Soc. condit. 2. Churches—New Jersey—Salem co. I. Title.

Salem, Mass.—Biography

SALEM, Mass. North church. 289
The first centenary of the North church and society, in Salem, Massachusetts. Commemorated July 19, 1872. Salem, Printed for the Society, 1873. vii, 222 p. front., illus., ports. 23 1/2 cm. "Proprietors and occupants of pews in the first meeting house.": p. 197-222. [BX9861.S3N58] 41-35250
1. Salem, Mass.—Biog. I. Title.

Salem, Mass. First church.

UPHAM, Charles Wentworth, 1802-1875. 288.
Principles of Congregationalism. The second century lecture of the First church. By Charles Wentworth Upham ... Salem, Foote & Brown, 1829. 72 p. 21 1/2 cm. No. 6 in a volume lettered: Sermons. [BX9843.A1S4 no. 6] [BX9861.S3F52] 252. 45-52222
1. Salem, Mass. First church. 2. Congregationalism. I. Title.

Salem, Mass. — History

BENTLEY, William, 1759-1819. 922.8173
The diary of William Bentley, D. D., pastor of the East Church, Salem, Massachusetts. Gloucester, Mass., P. Smith, 1962. 4 v. illus., ports 21 cm. Contents.CONTENTS. -- v. 1. 1784-1792. -- v. 2. 1703-1802. -- v. 3. 1803-1810. -- v. 4. 1811-1819, including subject index to volumes 1-4. "Bibliography, complied by Alice G. Waters": v. 1, p. xxxvii-xi. [F74.S1B462] 63-1100
1. Salem, Mass. — Hist. 2. Salem, Mass. East Church. I. Essex Institute, Salem, Mass. II. Title.

Salem, Mass. St. Peter's church.

TAPLEY, Harriet Silvester, 1870-
St. Peter's church in Salem, Massachusetts, before the revolution, by Harriet Silvester Tapley. Salem, Mass., The Essex institute, 1944. iv, 92 p. front., illus. (incl. plan) ports., facsims. 23 1/2 cm. "Reprinted from the Essex institute historical collections, volume LXXX." Bibliographical foot-notes. A 45
1. Salem, Mass. St. Peter's church. I. Essex institute, Salem, Mass. II. Title.

Salem, Mass. Tabernacle church.

WORCESTER, Samuel Melanchthon, 1801-1866. 285.
A memorial of the old and new Tabernacle, Salem, Mass., 1854-5. By Samuel M. Worcester ... Boston, Crocker and Brewster; Salem, H. Whipple and son, 1855. 84 p. front., pl. 19 cm. "Pastors of the Tabernacle church": p. 8-9. [BX7255.S3T3] 5-26564
1. Salem, Mass. Tabernacle church. I. Title.

Salem, N.C. Home Moravian church. Sunday school.

A brief history of the Moravian church, prepared by teachers and friends of the Salem Home Sunday school, Winston-Salem, N.C., January 1909. Raleigh, N.C., Edwards & Boughton printing co. [1909] 146, 23 p. 23 cm. "Funeral chorals of the Unitas fratrum or Moravian church," German and English text, with music, 23 p. at end. 9-10968
1. Salem, N.C. Home Moravian church. Sunday school.

Salem, N.J. First Presbyterian church.

VAN METER, Anna Hunter, 1851-1923. 285.
The history of the First Presbyterian church, Salem, New Jersey, between the years 1821 and 1921 with some antecedent facts about earlier churches in Salem County and elsewhere, by Anna Hunter Van Meter. Salem, N.J. Sunbeam publishing co., 1924. 81 p. front. (port.) 23 cm. [BX9211.S35FS] 24-8802
1. Salem, N.J. First Presbyterian church. I. Title.

Salem, N. Y. Methodist Episcopal church.

BROWN, Frank C. 287.
Annals of loyalty; the Methodist Episcopal church, Salem, New York, 1845-1925, with a brief sketch of early Methodists in the town of Salem, 1770-1845, by Frank C. Brown. Salem, N.Y., The Salem press, 1925. 56 p. front., illus. 20 1/2 cm. [BX8481.S32B8] 25-10424
1. Salem, N. Y. Methodist Episcopal church. I. Title.

Salem, Or. Methodist Episcopal church.

ODELL, Margaretta (Grubb) W. H. Odell." "Mrs d.1908. 287.
... *A semi-centennial offfering to the members and friends of the Methodist Episcopal church Salem, Oregon.* By Mrs. W. H. Odell. [Salem, Or.] 1884. 4 p. l., [5] -109 p. plates, ports. (incl. front.) 21 cm. At head of title: 1784-1834. [BX8481.S34O3] 24-4658
1. Salem, Or. Methodist Episcopal church. I. Title.

ODELL, Margaretta (Grubbs) "W. H. Odell, Mrs." d.1908. 287.
... *A semi-centennial offering* to the members and friends of the Methodist Episcopal church, Salem, Oregon. By Mrs. W. H. Odell. [Salem, Or.] 1884. 4 p. l., [5] -109 p. plates, ports. (incl. front.) 21 cm. At head of title: 1784-1834. [BX8481.S34O3] 24-4658
1. Salem, Or. Methodist Episcopal church. I. Title.

Salem United Methodist Church, Honey Creek, Wis.

MUELLER, Erhart. 287'.6775'76
The history of the Salem Church of Honey Creek; 1844-1946, Salem Evangelical Church, 1946-1969, Salem Evangelical United Brethren Church, 1969, Salem United Methodist Church. [Honey Creek? Wis., 1969?] 153 p. illus. 22 cm. On cover: Salem Church, 1844-1969. [BX8481.H77S35] 74-152494
1. Salem United Methodist Church, Honey Creek, Wis. 2. Honey Creek, Wis.—Biography. I. Title.

Salesians.

DOHERTY, Edward Joseph. 1890- 922.245
Lambs in wolfskins; the conquering march of Don John Bosco. New York, Scribner, 1953. 228p. 22cm. [BX4700.B75D57] 53-9435
1. Bosco, Giovanni, Saint, 1815-1888. 2. Salesians. I. Title.

FORBES, Frances Alice Monica, 1869- 922.245
Saint John Bosco, a seeker of souls; founder of the Salesian Society, of the Nuns of Mary, Help of Christians, and of the Salesian Co-operators. Tampa, Fla., Salesian Press, 1941. 197 p. front. 21 cm. [BX4700.B75F6] 50-42069
1. Bosco, Giovanni, Saint, 1815-1888. 2. Salesians. I. Title.

Salette, Notre-Dame de la.

BLOY, Leon, 1846-1917. 231.73
She who weeps: Our Lady of La Salette; an anthology of Leon Bloy's writings on La Salette, translated and edited with an introd. by Emile La Douceur. Fresno, Calif., Academy Library Guiide, 1956. 167p. illus. 22cm. [BT660.S33B58] 56-14096
1. Salette, Notre-Dame de la. I. Title.

THE Catholic digest. 232.9317
Notre Dame de la Salette in France. St. Paul [1959] 64p. illus. 21cm. (Shrines of the world) [BT660.S33S3] 60-23457
1. Salette, Notre-Dame de la. I. Title.

COX, Michael J 231.73
Rain for these roots; the Mother of Grace and the modern world. Milwaukee, Bruce Pub. Co. [1956] 210p. 22cm. [BT650.C6] 56-13331
1. Salette, Notre-Dame de la. 2. Lourdes, Notre-Dame de. 3. Fatima, Nossa Senhora da. I. Title.

ERNEST, Brother, 1897- 231.73
Our Lady comes to La Salette. Illus. by Brother Bernard Howard. Notre Dame, Ind., Dujarie Press [1953] 85p. illus. 24cm. [BT660.S33E7] 53-35198
1. Salette, Notre-Dame de la. I. Title.

KENNEDY, John S 231.73
Light on the mountain; the story of La Salette. Garden City, N. Y., Image Books [1986] 197p. 18cm. .A Doubleday image book, D33) [BT660.S33K4 1956] 56-13665
1. Salette. Notre-Dame de la. I. Title.

KENNEDY, John S 231.73
Light on the mountain; the story of La Salette. New York, McMullen Books [1953] 205p. 21cm. [BT660.S33K4] 53-122988
1. Salette, Notre-Dame de la. I. Title.

KENNEDY, John S 231.73
Light on the mountain; the story of La Salette. Garden City, N. Y., Image Books [1956] 197p. 18cm. (A Doubleday image book, D33) [BT660.S33K4 1956] 56-13665
1. Salette, Notre- Dame de la. I. Title.

LADOUCEUR, Emile. 231.73
The vision of La Salette: the children speak. New York, Vantage Press [1956] 145p. illus. 21cm. [BT660.S33L3] 56-10542
1. Calvat, Melanie, 1831-1904. 2. Giraud, Maximin, 1835-1875. 3. Salette, Notre-Dame de la. I. Title.

O'REILLY, James P 1913- 232.931
The story of La Salette; Mary's apparition, its history and sequels. Chicago, J. S. Paluch Co. [1953] 167p. illus. 18cm. (Lumen books, 526) [BT660.S33O7] 54-30228
1. Salette, Notre Dame de la. I. Title.

WINDEATT, Mary Fabyan, 1910- 231.73
The children of La Salette; illustrated by Gedge Harmon. [St. Meinrad, Ind., 1951] 188 p. illus. 22 cm. "A Grail publication." [BT660.S33W5] 52-221
1. Salette, Notre-Dame de la. I. Title.

Salimbene, Ognibene di Guido di Adamo, Brother, b. 1221.

COULTON, George Gordon, 1858-1947. 271'.3'024 B
From St. Francis to Dante; translations from the chronicle of the Franciscan Salimbene (1221-1288), with notes and illustrations from other medieval sources.

2d ed., rev and enl. Philadelphia, University of Pennsylvania Press [1972] xlii, 446 p. 21 cm. Reprint of the 1907 ed., with a new introd. by Edward Peters. Bibliography: p. [414]-415. [BX4705.S24C7 1972] 73-150704 ISBN 0-8122-7672-8 15.00
1. Salimbene, Ognibene di Guido di Adamo, Brother, b. 1221. I. Salimbene, Ognibene di Guido di Adamo, Brother, b. 1221. II. Title.

COULTON, George Gordon, 1858-1947. 271'.3'0924 B
From St. Francis to Dante; translations from the chronicle of the Franciscan Salimbene, 1221-1288, with notes and illus. from other medieval sources, by G. G. Coulton. 2d ed., rev. and enl. New York, Russell & Russell [1968] xiv, 446 p. front. 23 cm. A reprint of the 1907 ed. Bibliography: p. [414]-415. [BX4705.S24C7 1968] 68-10910
1. Salimbene, Ognibene di Guido di Adamo, Brother, b. 1221. I. Salimbene, Ognibene di Guido di Adamo, Brother, b. 1221. II. Title.

Salisbury, N.C. St. Luke's Episcopal Church.

POWELL, William Stevens, 1919- 283.756
St. Luke's Episcopal Church, 1753-1953. Salisbury, N.C., St. Luke's Episcopal Church, 1753. 76p. illus. 23cm. [BX5980.S23S3] 53-39479
1. Salisbury, N.C. St. Luke's Episcopal Church. I. Title.

Salish Indians—Missions.

EVANS, Lucylle H. 266'.2'78689
St. Mary's in the Rocky Mountains : a history of the cradle of Montana's culture / by Lucylle H. Evans. [Stevensville? Mont. : s.n., 1975] viii, 249 leaves ; 28 cm. Bibliography: leaves 245-249. [E99.S2E93] 75-309850
1. St. Mary's Parish, Stevensville, Mont. 2. Salish Indians—Missions. 3. Jesuits—Missions. I. Title.

Sallee, William Eugene, 1878-1961.

SALLEE, Annie (Jenkins) Mrs. 922.651
W. Eugene Sallee, Christ's ambassador, by Annie Jenkins Sallee. Nashville, Tenn., Sunday school board, Southern Baptist convention [c1933] viii, 256 p. front., pl., ports., facsim. 21 1/2 cm. Maps on lining-papers. [BV3427.S3S3] 34-33084
1. Sallee, William Eugene, 1878-1961. 2. Baptists—Missions. 3. Missions—China. I. Title.

Salome.

HEYWOOD, Joseph Converse, d.1900.
Salome. A dramatic poem. By J. C. Heywood. New York, Hurd and Houghton, 1867. 222 p. 18 cm. An entirely different play from the author's "Salome, the daughter of Herodias," Published anonymously in 1862, and reissued in 1867 under title: Herodias. [PS1924.H64S2 1867] 17-20157
I. Title.

HEYWOOD, Joseph Converse, d.1900.
Salome, the daughter of Herodias. A dramatic poem. New York, Putnam, 1862. 251 p. 19 cm. Reissued in 1867 under title: "Herodias. A dramatic poem. By J. C. Heywood." The author's "Salome. A dramatic poem," also issued in 1867, is and entirely different play. [PS1924.H64S3 1862] 17-20159
I. Title.

HOSPODAR, Blaise, 1893- 225.92
Salome: virgin or prostitute? [1st ed.] New York, Pageant Press [1953] 79p. 24cm. [BS2520.S6H6] 53-7032
1. Salome. I. Title.

LOOS, Isaac K. 225.92
Salome the dancer. By Rev. Isaac K. Loos. Philadelphia, S. R. Fisher & co. [1869] vi, 7-96 p. front. 17 cm. [BS2520.S6L6] 39-11839
1. Salome. I. Title.

WILDE, Oscar, 1854-1900.
Salome [by] Oscar Wilde. New York and Boston, H. M. Caldwell co. [c1907] 4 p. l., v-xviii, 117 p. front. 14 1/2 cm. [Full name: Oscar Fingall O'Flahertie Wills Wilde] [PR5820.S2 1907] 7-15140
I. Title.

WILDE, Oscar, 1854-1900.
Salome, by Oscar Wilde, illustrations by Aubrey Beardsley. New York, Illustrated editions company [1931] 120, [1] p. incl. plates, double facsim. front. 24 1/2 cm. [Full name: Oscar Fingall O'Flahertie Wills Wilde] [PR5820.S] A 33
I. Beardsley, Aubrey Vincent, 1872-1898, illus. II. Title.

WILDE, Oscar, 1854-1900.
Salome, a tragedy in one act; translated from the French of Oscar Wilde: pictured by Aubrey Beardsley. London, E. Mathews & John Lane; Boston, Copeland & Day 1894. 5 p. l., 66, [2] p. front., illus., plates. 21 1/2 cm. "500 copies have been printed." Translated by Alfred Bruce Douglas. [Full name: Oscar Fingall O'Flahertie Wills Wilde] [PR5820.S2 1894] 44-10195
I. Douglas, Lord Alfred Bruce, 1870- tr. II. Beardsley, Aubrey Vincent, 1872-1898, illus. III. Title.

WILDE, Oscar, 1854-1900.
Salome; a tragedy in one act, by Oscar Wilde; inventions by John Vassos. New York, E. P. Dutton & company [c1927] 6 p. l., 3-57 p., 1 l. front., plates. 27 cm. Each plate accompanied by leaf with descriptive letterpress. "This edition is limited to five hundred numbered copies of which this is no. 158." [Full name: Oscar Fingall O'Flahertie Wills Wilde] [PR5820.S2 1927] 27-23798
I. Vassos, John, illus. II. Title.

WILDE, Oscar [Fingall O'Flahertie Wills] 1856-1900.
Salome, a play, by Oscar Wilde. New York, F. M. Buckles & company, 1906. 60 p. 19 1/2 cm. [With his The Duchess of Padua. New York, 1906] 6-32393
I. Title.

Salomoni, Giacomo, 1231-1314.

DESMOND, Cecelia. 271'.2'00924 B
Blessed James Salomoni; patron of cancer patients apostle of the afflicted. [Boston] St. Paul Editions [1971] 76, [1] p. illus. 20 cm. Bibliography: p. [77] [BX4705.S142D4] 70-150719 2.00
1. Salomoni, Giacomo, 1231-1314. I. Title.

Salt Lake City. First Unitarian Church.

HANCE, Irma Watson.
In commemoration of the seventy-fifth anniversary of the founding of the First Unitarian Church, Salt Lake City, Utah, 1891-1966. Church historians: Irma Watson Hance [and] Virginia Hendrickson Picht. Art work by Ranch Kimball. Cover design by Dorothy Kyremes. [Salt Lake City] 1966. v, 265 p. illus., facsims., ports. 29 cm 68-43859
1. Salt Lake City. First Unitarian Church. 2. Church history—Utah—Unitarian Church. I. Picht, Virginia Hendrickson. II. Title.

Salt lake City — History

MORGAN, Nicholas Groesbeck, 1884- comp.
The old fort, historic Mormon bastion; the Plymouth Rock of the West. Salt Lake City, Utah, 1964. 108 p. illus. 24 cm. 66-95633
1. Salt lake City — Hist. 2. Mormons and Mormonism in Utah. I. Title.

SMITH, Ruby Kate, 1888-
One hundred years in the heart of Zion; a narrative history of the Eighteenth ward. [Salt Lake City, Deseret news press, 1961] 113 p. illus., ports. 24 cm. Bibliography, p. [112]-113. 65-60302
1. Salt Lake City — Hist. 2. Mormons and Mormonism. I. Title.

TULLIDGE, Edward Wheelock. 289.
The history of Salt Lake City and its founders. By Edward W. Tullidge. Incorporating a brief history of the pioneers of Utah ... By authority of the City council and under supervision of its committee on revision ... Salt Lake City, Utah, E. W. Tullidge [1883-84] 336 p. ports. 25 cm. [With Tullidge's quarterly magazine ... Salt Lake City, 1885. v. 3] Issued with Tullidge's quarterly magazine, v. 3 no. 1-3 Oct, 1883- July 1884. [F821.T91] 4-27771
1. Salt Lake City—Hist. 2. Salt Lake City—Biog. I. Title.

Salt Lake City. Tabernacle.

GROW, Stewart L 289.3792
A tabernacle in the desert. Salt Lake City, Deseret Book Co., 1958. 101p. illus. 23cm. [BX8685.S35G7] 58-35742
1. Salt Lake City. Tabernacle. I. Title.

Salt Lake City. Tabernacle. Choir.

CALMAN, Charles Jeffrey. 783.8'09792'25
The Mormon Tabernacle Choir / by Charles Jeffrey Calman ; illus. prepared by William I. Kaufman. New York : Harper & Row, 1979. p. cm. Includes index. [ML200.8.S18T23] 79-1656 ISBN 0-06-010624-7 : 14.95
1. Salt Lake City. Tabernacle. Choir. I. Kaufman, William I. II. Title.

PETERSEN, Gerald A., 1933- 783.8'09792'25
More than music : the Mormon Tabernacle Choir / Gerald A. Petersen. Provo, Utah : Brigham Young University Press, c1979. xiii, 103 p. : ill. ; 28 cm. Includes bibliographical references. [ML200.8.S18T28] 79-21122 ISBN 0-8425-1736-7 pbk. : 5.95
1. Salt Lake City. Tabernacle. Choir. I. Title.

THOMAS, Warren John. 783.8
Salt Lake Mormon Tabernacle Choir goes to Europe, 1955. [1st ed.] Salt Lake City, Deseret News Press, 1957. 277p. illus. 20cm. [ML200.8.S18T3] 57-41518
1. Salt Lake City. Tabernacle. Choir. I. Title.

THOMAS, Warren John. 783.8
Salt Lake Mormon Tabernacle Choir goes to Europe, 1955. [1st ed.] Salt Lake City, Deseret News Press, 1957. 277 p. illus. 20 cm. [ML200.8.S18T3] 57-41518
1. Salt Lake City. Tabernacle. Choir. I. Title.

Salt Lake City. Temple.

RAYNOR, Wallace Alan. 726.5893
The everlasting spires; a story of the Salt Lake Temple. Salt Lake City, Deseret Book Co. [c1965] 203 p. illus., facsims., plans. 24 cm. Bibliography: p. [193]-196. [BX8685.S35R3] 65-28864
1. Salt Lake City. Temple. I. Title.

Salt Lake City, Utah. First Unitarian Church.

HANCE, Irma Watson.
Statistics of First Unitarian Church, Salt Lake City, Utah 1891-1966. [Salt Lake City, c1967] vii, 175 p. 28 cm. 68-105770
1. Salt Lake City, Utah. First Unitarian Church. I. Title.

Salt Lake Stake.

HILTON, Lynn M. 289.3'792'25
The story of Salt Lake Stake of the Church of Jesus Christ of Latter-Day Saints; 125 year history, 1847-1972. Lynn M. Hilton, editor. Salt Lake City, Utah, Salt Lake Stake [1972] x, 336 p. illus. 24 cm. Includes bibliographical references. [BX8611.H57] 72-89166
1. Salt Lake Stake. I. Title.

Salter, William, 1821-1910.

[HILL, James Langdon] 1848-
Rev. William Salter, D.D., 1821-1910, minister of the Congregational church and society of Burlington, Iowa, 1846-1910. [Des Moines, 1911] 2 p. l., p. [560]-644, 63-66. front., pl., ports., geneal. tab. 23 cm. A memorial tribute by the Rev. James L. Hill, reprinted from the Annals of Iowa, vol. IX, no. 8, 3d ser., and an editorial, "William Salter," reprinted from vol. X, no. 1, 3d ser., p. 63-64. "Published works by Dr. Salter": p. 64-66 at end. 16-14524
1. Salter, William, 1821-1910. 2. Salter family. I. Title.

JORDAN, Philip Dillon, 1903- 922.573
William Salter, western torch-bearer, by Philip D. Jordan ... Oxford, O., The Mississippi valley press, 1939. x, [11]-273 p. front. (port.) 23 cm. (Half-title: Men of America series. vol. i) "Author's notes": p. 223-243; "Essay on authorities": p. 245-260. [BX7260.S2J6] 40-3335
1. Salter, William, 1821-1910 I. Title.

SALTER, William, 1821-1910. 252.
Sixty years, and other discourses, with reminiscences, by William Salter... Boston, Chicago, The Pilgrim press [c1907] vii, 326 p. front., illus., pl., ports. 20 cm. [BX7233.S3S5] 7-39396
I. Title.

Salvado, Rosendo, Bp., 1814-1900.

SALVADO, Rosendo, Bp., 1814-1900. 266'.2'0924 B
The Salvado memoirs : historical memoirs of Australia and particularly of the Benedictine mission of New Norcia and of the habits and customs of the Australian natives / by Dom Rosendo Salvado ; translated and edited by E. J. Stormon. Nedlands, W.A. : University of Western Australia Press, [1977.] xx, 300 p., [7] leaves of plates : ill. ; 25 cm. Aus Translation of Memorie Storiche dell' Australia. Sold by International Scholarly Book Services, Forest Grove, Or. Includes bibliographical references and index. [BV3667.S25A3513] 77-559483 ISBN 0-85564-114-2 : 23.00
1. Salvado, Rosendo, Bp., 1814-1900. 2. Missionaries—Australia—Western Australia—Biography. 3. Missionaries—Spain—Biography. 4. Missions to Australian aborigines—Australia—Western Australia. 5. Australian aborigines—Australia—Western Australia. 6. Western Australia. I. Title.
Distributed by ISBS.

Salvation.

AMIOT, Francois 227
The key concepts of St. Paul. [Tr. by John Dingle. New York] Herder & Herder [c.1944, 1962] 297p. 21cm. Bibl. 61-17458 4.95
1. Salvation. 2. Bible. N. T. Epistles of Paul—Theology I. Title.

AMIOT, Francois. 227'.8'06
The key concepts of St. Paul. [Translated by John Dingle. New York] Herder and Herder [1962] 297 p. 21 cm. Translation of Les idees maitresses de saint Paul. [BS2651.A643] 61-17458
1. Bible. N.T. Epistles of Paul—Theology. 2. Salvation. I. Title.

ANDERSON, Robert, Sir 1841-1918. 234
The gospel and its ministry, a handbook of evangelical truth. 17th ed. Grand Rapids, Kregel Publications, 1956. 213p. 20cm. [BT751.A6 1956] 55-8176
1. Salvation. I. Title.

ANDERSON, Robert, Sir, 1841-1918. 234
The gospel and its ministry / by Robert Anderson. Grand Rapids : Kregel Publications, c1978. x, 212 p. ; 19 cm. (His Sir Robert Anderson library) Reprint of the 18th ed. published by Pickering & Inglis, London. Includes bibliographical references and indexes. [BT751.A6 1978] 78-9539 ISBN 0-8254-2126-8 : pbk. : 3.50
1. Salvation. I. Title. II. Series.

ANDERSON, Robert, Sir, 1841-1918. 234
Redemption truths / by Sir Robert Anderson. Grand Rapids, Mi. : Kregel Publications, c1980. viii, 185 p. ; 19 cm.

Reprint of the ed. published by Gospel Publishing House, New York under title: "For us men." "Sir Robert Anderson library." Includes index. [BT751.A58 1980] 80-16161 ISBN 0-8254-2131-4 : 3.95 (pbk.)
1. Salvation. I. Title.

BAINVEL, Jean Vincent. 1858- 234
Is there salvation outside the Catholic church? An authorized translation from the French of Rev. J. Bainvel, S. J., by the Rev. J. L. Weidenhan, S. T. L. St. Louis, Mo., and London, B. Herder book co., 1917. vi p., 2 l., 68 p. 20 cm. [BT755.B2] 284 17-23055
1. Salvation. 2. Catholic church—Doctrinal and controversial works. I. Weldenhan, Joseph L. tr. II. Title.

BANVARD, Joseph, 1810-1887. 220
A topical question book, on subjects connected with the plan of salvation, arranged in consecutive order; with hints for the assistance of teachers. Designed for Sabbath schools and Bible classes. By Rev. Joseph Banvard. 20th ed. Boston, New England Sabbath school union [1841] vi, [4], [7]-122 p. 15 cm. [BS613.B3 1841] 41-35213
1. Salvation. I. New England Sabbath school union. II. Title.

BARRY, Henry Aloysius, d.1907. 234
Am I of the chosen. The same being a series of conferences spoken by the Rev. Henry Aloysius Barry, to the nuns and the public in the Carmelite chapel in the city of Boston. Boston, Angel guardian press, 1897. 288 p. front. 22 cm. [BT751.B3] 41-82810
1. Salvation. 2. Election (Theology) 3. Penance. 4. Catholic church—Doctrinal and controversial works. I. Title.

BAXTER, James Sidlow. 232
The master theme of the Bible; grateful studies in the comprehensive Saviorhood of Our Lord Jesus Christ [by] J. Sidlow Baxter. Wheaton, Ill., Tyndale House Publishers [1973] 336 p. 22 cm. [BT202.B35] 73-88678 ISBN 0-8423-4185-4 4.95
1. Jesus Christ—Person and offices. 2. Jesus Christ—Crucifixion. 3. Salvation. I. Title.

BLANEY, John C. 234
Salvation from sin, by John C. Blaney. Anderson, Ind., Gospel trumpet company [c1934] iii, 5-95 p. 17 1/2 cm. [BX7990.G7B6] 36-9344
1. Salvation. I. Title.

[BLIVEN, Ransom] 1898- 234
Leaving dark valleys behind. Written and published by Ransom for the King. Minneapolis, Minn. [c1938] 96 p. 20 cm. "Copyright ... by Ransom Bliven." [Full name: Ransom Marion Bliven] [BT753.B6] 38-10007
1. Salvation. I. Title.

BLOESCH, Donald G., 1928- 234
The Christian life and salvation, by Donald G. Bloesch. Grand Rapids, W. B. Eerdmans Pub. Co. [1967] 164 p. 23 cm. Bibliographical footnotes. Bibliographical references included in "Explanatory notes" (p. 141-153) [BT751.2.B5] 66-27406
1. Salvation. I. Title.

BONNER, David Findley.
Saving the world; what it involves and how it is being accomplished, by the Rev. David Findley Bonner ... Middletown, N.Y., Hanford and Horton, 1902. iv, 259 p. 19 cm. 2-21130
I. Title.

BOOTH, Abraham, 1734-1806. 243
Glad tidings to perishing sinners: or, The genuine gospel, a complete warrant for the ungodly to believe in Jesus... By Rev. Abraham Booth. Philadelphia, S. Taylor, 1833. viii p., 1 l., [9]-162 p. 17 1/2 cm. [BV4920.B6] 1-2565
1. salvation. 2. Conversion. I. Title.

BOSTON, Thomas, 1676-1732. 233
Human nature in its fourfold state, of primitive integrity, entire depravation, begun recovery, and consummate happiness or misery. Subsisting in the parents of mankind in paradis. The unregenerate. The regenerate. All mankind in the future state. In several practical discourses, by the eminently pious and learned Mr. Thomas Boston, late minister of the Gospel at Etterick. First American edition... Exeter [N.H.] Printed by H. Ranlet, for Thomas and Andrews, Fausts' statue, no. 45, Newbury-street, Boston, 1796. xvi, [17]-386 (i.e. 384) p. 16 1/2 cm. Numbers 161-162 omitted in paging. [BT700.B] A 31
1. Salvation. I. Title.

†BRANDT, Robert L. 234
One way / Robert L. Brandt. Springfield, Mo. : Gospel Pub. House, c1977. 128 p. (p. 127-128 blank) ; 18 cm. (Radiant books) Includes bibliographical references. [BT751.2.B67] 77-75601 ISBN 0-88243-909-X : pbk. : 1.50
1. Salvation. I. Title.

BRANSON, William H. 248
The way to Christ; or, How can a bad man become good? By William H. Branson ... Washington, D. C., South Bend, Ind. [etc.] Review and herald publishing association [c1928] 128 p. incl. front., illus. 20 cm. [BV4915.B7] ca 28
I. Title.

BRANSON, William Henry, 1887- 234
How men are saved; the certainty, plan, and time for man's salvation, by William Henry Branson ... Nashville, Tenn., Southern publishing association [c1941] 128 p. pl. 17 cm. [BT751.B77] 42-4336
1. Salvation. I. Title.

BRENTS, T. W. 234
The gospel plan of salvation. By T. W. Brents ... Cincinnati, Bosworth, Chase & Hall, 1874. vi, 7-667 p. 20 cm. [BT751.B83] 40-25505
1. Salvation. I. Title.

BRENTS, Thomas W., 1823-1905. 234
The gospel plan of salvation. By T. W. Brents ... Cincinnati, Bosworth, Chase & Hall, 1874. vi, 7-667 p. 20 cm. [BT751.B83] 40-25505
1. Salvation. I. Title.

BROOKES, James Hall, 1830-1897 234
The way made plain [an ancient classic rev., adapted for modern use] by James H. Brookes. D. D. Grand Rapids. Mich., Baker Bk. [1967, c.1937] 305p. 19cm. [BT751.B86 1937] 3.50
1. Salvation. 2. Evangelistic work. 3. Sunday-schools. 4. Bible. N. T. Romans x, 1-13—Criticism, interpretation, etc. I. Title.

BROOKES, James Hall, 1830-1897. 234
The way made plain. By the Rev. James H. Brookes ... Philadelphia, American Sunday-school union [1871] 490 p. front. 17 cm. [BT751.B86] 38-11663
1. Salvation. 2. Evangelistic work. 3. Sunday-schools. 4. Bible. N.T. Romans x, 1-13—Criticism, interpretation, etc. I. American Sunday-school union. II. Title.

BROOKES, James Hall, 1830-1897. 234
The way made plain, an ancient classic revised and adapted for modern use [by] James H. Brookes, D.D. Nashville, Tenn., The Sunday school board of the Southern Baptist convention [c1937] 111 p. 19 cm. "Editor's foreword" signed: P.E. Burroughs. [BT751.B86 1937] 38-7565
1. Salvation. 2. Evangelistic work. 3. Sunday-schools. 4. Bible. N.T. Romans x, 1-13—Criticism, interpretation, etc. I. Burroughs, Prince Emanuel, 1871- ed. II. Title.

BROWN, Charles Ewing, 1883- 234
The meaning of salvation, by Charles Ewing Brown ... Anderson, Ind., Gospel trumpet company [1944] xvii, 18-202 p. 19 1/2 cm. Bibliography: p. 201-202. [BT751.B89] 44-6294
1. Salvation. I. Title.

BULLOCK, James R., 1910- 234
Whatever became of salvation? / James R. Bullock. Atlanta : John Knox Press, c1979. p. cm. [BT751.2.B84] 78-71049 ISBN 0-8042-1468-9 : 8.95
1. Salvation. I. Title.

CHAFER, Lewis Sperry. 233
Salvation, by Lewis Sperry Chafer ... New York, C. C. Cook [c1917] ix, 139 p. 20 cm. [BT751.C5] 17-30236
I. Title.

CHAFER, Lewis Sperry, 1871-1952. 234
Salvation. Grand Rapids, Zondervan Pub. House [1972, c1917] ix, 149 p. 21 cm. "A Dunham publication." [BT751.C5 1972] 73-150623 3.50
1. Salvation.

CHAPMAN, Clifford Thomas. 234.3
The conflict of the kingdoms; the Christian message of salvation, its history and significance. London, New York, Hutchinson's University Library, 1951. 144p. 19cm. (Hutchinson's university library: Christian religion) Includes bibliography. [BT751.2.C5] 60-40636
1. Salvation. I. Title.

CLARKE, Catherine Goddard. 234
The Loyolas and the Cabots, the story of the Boston heresy case. Boston, Ravengate Press, 1950. xi, 301 p. 21 cm. [BT755.C6] 50-8321
1. Salvation. 2. St. Benedict Center, Cambridge, Mass. 3. Catholic Church—Doctrinal and controversial works—Miscellaneous authors. I. Title.

COLLINS, Almer M. 234
The contradictions of orthodoxy; or, "What shall I do to be saved?" As answered by several representative orthodox clergymen of Chicago; with sermons on the same subject by Prof. David Swing, Rev. D. L. Moody, and others. All of which is carefully examined and critically reviewed in the light of the Sacred Scriptures. By Almer M. Collins, M. D. Chicago, Ill., Central book concern, 1880. xi, 13-160 p. 17 cm. [BT751.C7] 40-38469
1. Salvation. I. Swing, David, 1830-1894. II. Moody, Dwight Lyman, 1837-1899. III. Title.

COLLINS, Mahlon D. 233
The common sense of Bible salvation, by M. D. Collins. Philadelphia, Pa., Christian standard company, ltd. [c1899] 60 p. front. (port.) 18 cm. [BT751.C74]
1. Salvation. I. Title.

COMBLIN, Joseph, 1923- 232.97
The resurrection in the plan of salvation. Translated by Sister David Mary. Notre Dame, Ind., Fides Publishers [1966] 176 p. 20 cm. Translation of La resurrection de Jesus-Christ. Bibliographical reference included in "Notes" (p. 176) [BT481.C613] 65-24102
1. Jesus Christ—Resurrection. 2. Salvation. I. Title.

CONE, Orello, 1835-1905. 234
...Salvation, By Orello Cone ... Boston, Universalist publishing house, 1889. 3 p. l., [5]-101 p. 17 1/2 cm (Added t.-p.: Manuals of faith and duty. Ed. by J. S. Cantwell no. V) Series title in part at head of t. p. [BT751.C75] 38-11186
1. Salvation. I. Title.

COOPER, David Lipscomb, 1886- 233
Man, his creation, fall, redemption, and glorification. (Chapter one, revised and enlarged) Los Angeles, Biblical Research Society ['1950] xi, 164 p. 21 cm. Bibliography: p. 164. [BT751.C753 1950] 51-3637
1. Salvation. 2. Bible. N. T. Hebrews I-II—Commentaries. I. Title.

COOPER, David Lipscomb, 1886- 233
Man, his creation, fall, redemption, and glorification. Los Angeles, Biblical Research Society [1948] xi, 131 p. diagrs. 21 cm. The material in this volume will appear in "Messiah: His historical appearance," the fifth volume of the author's "Messianic series." Bibliography: p. 131. [BT751.C753] 48-4690
1. Salvation. 2. Bible. N. T. Hebrews i-ii—Commentaries. I. Title.

CRIBB, C. C. 234
Getting ready for heaven / C. C. Cribb. Raleigh, N.C. : Manhattan, c1979. 109 p. (p. 106-109 advertisements) ; 18 cm. (If God has it I want it! Series) [BT751.2.C74] 78-60614 ISBN 0-932046-13-4 pbk. : 2.75
1. Salvation. 2. Christian life—1960- I. Title.
Publisher's address: PO Box 18601, Raleigh, NC.

CUMMING, Alexander. 234
"Sirs, what must I do to be saved?" By Rev. Alexander[Cumming ... Danville, Ill., O. Freese, printer, 1889. 112 p. 16 cm. [BT751.C8] 40-25507
1. Salvation. I. Title.

CUTTING, George. 234
Light for anxious souls in some of their difficulties, by Geo. Cutting. New York, Loizeaux Bros. [1954?] 90 p. 19 cm. [BT753.C88] 75-304255
1. Salvation. 2. Christian life. I. Title.

DART, John Lovering Campbell. 234
God's plan of salvation. London, Faith Press; New York, Morehouse-Gorham [1952] 129 p. 19 cm. [BT751.D3] 52-8881
1. Salvation. I. Title.

DEACON, Samuel, 1746-1816. 234
An attempt to answer the important queston, What must I do to be saved! A poem, in three dialogues, between Prudens and Evangelicus. With an introduction, on the worth of the soul, and the importance of religion. By S. Deacon ... Pittsburgh, Printed for L. Thomas by Johnston and Stockton, 1826. x, [11]-84 p. 17 x 10 cm. [PR3398.D4A8 1828] 24-22080
1. Salvation. I. Title.

DICKIE, Edgar Primrose, 1897- 234
God is light; studies in revelation and personal conviction. New York, Scribner, 1954. 261p. 23cm. [BT751] 54-8545
1. Salvation. 2. Revelation. I. Title.

DOUTY, Norman Franklin, 1899- 234
Union with Christ [by] Norman F. Douty. Swengel, Pa., Reiner Publications, 1973. 274 p. 23 cm. [BT751.2.D68] 73-160672 7.95
1. Salvation. I. Title.

DU BOIS, Patterson, 1847-1917. 233
The practice of salvation; trailing a word to a world ideal, by Patterson Du Bois ... New York, Chicago [etc.] Fleming H. Revell company [c1913] 215 p. 20 cm. [BT751.D8] 13-24811
1. Salvation. I. Title.

DUN, Angus, Bp., 1892- 234
The Saving Person. [1st ed.] New York, Harper [1957] 127p. 20cm. [BT751.D85] 56-12065
1. Salvation. I. Title.

DUTY, Guy, 1907- 234
If ye continue. Minneapolis, Bethany Fellowship [c.1966] 186p. 21cm. Bibl. [PT751.2.D8] 66-3086 2.95
1. Salvation. I. Title.

EARY, T. M. 234
Rightly dividing the word of truth; or, A key to the study of the Bible. By Rev. T. M. Eary. Wichita, Kan., Press of the Wichita eagle, 1897. 135 p. 20 cm. [BT752.E3] 31-2095
1. Salvation. 2. Perfection. I. Title.

EDWARDS, Dan Luther. 234
... So great salvation ... Kansas City, Mo., Burton publishing company [c1941] 3 p. l., 9-206 p. 20 1/2 cm. [BT751.E3] 41-23095
1. Salvation. I. Title.

EDWARDS, Walter Ross, 1910- 234
Have you been saved? [By] W. Ross Edwards. Nashville, Broadman Press [1973] 128 p. 21 cm. [BT751.2.E35] 73-78215 ISBN 0-8054-8121-4
1. Salvation. I. Title.

ERICKSON, Millard J. 234
Salvation : God's amazing plan / Millard J. Erickson. Wheaton, Ill. : Victor Books, c1978. 131 p. ; 21 cm. (The Victor know & believe series) Bibliography: p. 131 [BT751.2.E74] 78-55263 ISBN 0-88207-772-4 pbk. : 2.95
1. Salvation. I. Title. II. Series.

EZZELL, S R. 234
The great legacy: a presentation of the gospel plan of salvation, under the similitude of a will. By S. R. Ezzell ... St. Louis, Mo., J. Burns, 1878. viii, [9]-316 p. 19 cm. [BT751.E9] 40-25510
1. Salvation. I. Title.

FABER, Frederick William 234
The Precious Blood: The price of our salvation. New ed. Philadelphia, P. Reilly Co. [1959] 278 p. 24 cm. 59-16917 3.95
1. Salvation. 2. Precious Blood, Devotion to. I. Title.

FAHS, Sophia Blanche (Lyon) 234
1876-
The old story of salvation. Boston, Starr King Press; distributed by the Beacon Press [1955] 191p. illus. 25cm. [BT751.F3] 55-9360
1. Salvation. I. Title.

FEATHERSTUN, Henry Walter, 234
1849-
Whiter than snow. By the Rev. H. Walter Featherstun ... Nashville, Tenn., Southern Methodist publishing house, 1881. 75 p. 12 1/2 cm. [BT753.F4] 42-33854
1. Salvation. I. Title.

FEENEY, Leonard, 1897- 234
Bread of life. Cambridge, Mass., Saint Benedict Center, 1952. 204p. illus. 19cm. [BT755.F4] 53-15579
1. Salvation. 2. Salvation outside the Catholic Church. I. Title.

FRELIGH, Harold 234.0202
Meredith, 1891-
Newborn; a basic handbook on salvation for personal or group study [by] Harold M. Freligh. Minneapolis, Bethany Fellowship [1975 c1962] 123 p. 18 cm. [BT751.2F7] 75-5444 ISBN 0-87123-120-4 1.25 (pbk.)
1. Salvation. I. Title.

GARTH, John Goodall, 1871- 234
The little Gospel, a popular study of John 3: 16. [Charlotte? N. C., 1952] 158 p. 24 cm. [BT751.G25] 52-24897
1. Salvation. 2. Bible. N. T. John III, 16—Criticlsm, interpretation, etc. I. Title.

GETHSEMANE: 234
or, Thoughts on the sufferings of Christ. By the author of "The refuge" ... 1st American, from the second enlarged London edition. Philadelphia: Published by Anthony Finley, at the White-house, n. e. corner of Chesnut and Fourth streets. William Fry, printer, 1817. xxvi, [27]-208 p. 18 cm. [BT751.G4 1817] 40-37152
1. Salvation.

GORDON, Adoniram Judson, 234
1836-1895.
The two fold life; or, Christ's work for us and Christ's work in us. By A. J. Gordon ... Boston, H. Gannett, 1883. 259 p. 18 cm. [BT751.G6] 40-25511
1. Salvation. 2. Christian life. I. Title. II. Title: Christ's work for us and Christ's work in us.

GORHAM, B Weed. 234
God's method with man; or, Sacred scenes along the path to heaven. By Rev. B. Weed Gorham ... Cincinnati, Hitchcock and Walden, for the author, 1879. 281 p. 18 cm. [BT751.G62] 37-23900
1. Salvation. 2. Methodist Episcopal church—Doctrinal and controversial works. I. Title.

*GORRIE, Ron 234
Man's greatest question; precisely how good does a man have to be before God will let him pass into heaven.? New York, Exposition [c.1965] 225p. 22cm. 4.00
I. Title.

GRAEF, Paul Hubert, 1870- 234
"Eye to "aye", by Paul H. Graef ... with introduction by Will H. Houghton ... Harrisburg, Pa., Christian publications, inc., c1934. 127 p. col. plates. 21 cm. [BT753.G67] 40-1727
1. Salvation. 2. Sin. 3. Visual instruction. I. Title.

GREEN, Edward Michael Bankes 234
The meaning of salvation. Philadelphia, Westminster [1966,c.1965] 255p. 23cm. Bibl. [BT751.2.G67] 66-11090 4.50
1. Salvation. I. Title.

GRITZMACHER, Victor J. 234
Out of the night; the way of salvation. Anderson, Ind., Warner Press [dist. Gospel Trumpet Press, c.1961] 160p. 61-7027 2.95
1. Salvation. I. Title.

GROMACKI, Robert Glenn. 234
Salvation is forever. Chicago, Moody Press [1973] 188 p. 22 cm. [BT751.2.G74] 73-7331 ISBN 0-8024-7506-X 2.50
1. Salvation. I. Title.

GUTHRIE, William, 1620-1665. 234
The Christian's great interest. In two parts: i. The trial of a saving interest in Christ. ii. The way how to attain it. By the Rev. William Guthrie ... To which are prefixed memoirs of the author; a preface by the Rev. Mr. Robert Traill, and other recommendatory introductions ... New-York, Printed for Samuel Whiting, and co., A. Niven, printer, 1811. 253 p. 18 cm. [BT750.G8] [BV4914.G] A 32
1. Guthrie, William, 1620-1665. 2. Salvation. I. Title.

GUTZKE, Manford 222'.12'06
George.
Plain talk on Exodus / Manford George Gutzke. Grand Rapids : Zondervan Pub. House, [1974] 244 p. : ill. ; 21 cm. [BS1245.2.G87] 74-4954 pbk. : 2.95
1. Bible. O.T. Exodus—Criticism, interpretation, etc. 2. Salvation. I. Title.

HAMMEL, W. W., 1900- 234
How shall we escape if we neglect... so great salvation; a scriptural study with poems and chart [by] W. W. Hammel. [1st ed.] Cleveland, Tenn., Pathway Press [1972] 95 p. 21 cm. [BT751.2.H28] 72-86758
1. Salvation. I. Title. II. Title: So great salvation.

HARRIS, John William, 1870- 262
God's plan; The plan of God for man's restoration to the holy state. A worker's manual for Holiness workers. By John W. Harris ... Indianapolis, Ind., Pub. for the author by Grace publishing co. [1904] x, 11-110 p. front. (port) 15 1/2cm. [BT751.H25] 45-51715
1. Salvation. 2. Holiness. I. Title.

HARTMANN, Marcus Kristian, 234
1878-
We have found the Messiah [by] M. K. Hartmann ... Minneapolis, Augsburg publishing house [c1936] vii, 105 p. 20 cm. [BT753.H3] 36-18294
1. Salvation. I. Title.

HAZEN, Edward Adams, 1824- 234
Salvation to the uttermost. A work written by Rev. E. A. Hazen ... Lansing, Mich., D. D. Thorp, printer, 1892. x, 340 p. front. (port.) 19 1/2 cm. [BT751.H3] 33-37527
1. Salvation. I. Title.

HEPPENSTALL, Edward. 234
Salvation unlimited; perspectives in righteousness by faith. Washington, Review and Herald Pub. Association [1974] 256 p. 21 cm. Bibliography: p. 255-256. [BT751.2.H46] 73-91425 6.95
1. Salvation. I. Title.

HEWIT, Augustine Francis, 280.2
father, 1820-1897.
The king's highway; or, The Catholic church the way of salvation, as revealed in the Holy Scriptures ... By the Rev. Augustine F. Hewit ... New York, The Catholic publication society, 1874. xv, 17-292 p. 18 cm. [Secular name: Nathaniel Augustus Hewit] [BX1751.H6 1874] 41-40827
1. Salvation. 2. Catholic church—Doctrinal and controversial works—Catholic authors. I. Title. II. Title: The Catholic church the way of salvation.

HEWIT, Augustine Francis, 230.2
father, 1820-1897.
The king's highway; or, The Catholic church the way of salvation as revealed in the Holy Scriptures ... By the Very Rev. Augustine F. Hewit ... 3d ed. New York, The Catholic book exchange, 1893. xv, 17-292 p. 17 cm. [Secular name: Matheniel Augustus Hewit] [BX1751.H6 1803] 2-6221
1. Salvation. 2. Catholic church—Doctrinal and controversial works—Catholic authors. I. Title. II. Title: The Catholic church the way of salvation.

HODGES, Zane Clark. 248'.4
The hungry inherit; refreshing insights on salvation, discipleship, and rewards. Chicago, Moody Press [1972] 128 p. 22 cm. [BT751.2.H57] 72-175491 ISBN 0-8024-3800-8 3.95
1. Salvation. 2. Christian life—1960- I. Title.

HOEKSEMA, Herman. 234
"Whosoever will," by Herman Hoeksema ... Grand Rapids, Mich., Wm. B. Eerdmans publishing company, 1945. 164 p. 20 cm. [BT751.H7] 45-7012
1. Salvation. 2. Grace (Theology) 3. Free will and determinism. I. Title.

HORNE, Charles M. 234
Salvation, by Charles M. Horne. Chicago, Moody Press [1971] 128 p. illus. 22 cm. (A Handbook of Bible doctrine) Includes bibliographies. [BT751.2.H67] 72-143477 1.95
1. Salvation.

HOW to be saved; 234
or, The sinner directed to the Saviour, by J. H. B. ... St. Louis, J. W. McIntyre, bookseller, 1865. 1 p. l., 5-126 p. 15 1/2 cm. "Fortieth thousand." [BT751.H8] 40-25514
1. Salvation. I. B., J. H. II. J. H. B.

HOWELL, Robert Boyte 234
Crawford, 1801-1868.
The way of salvation. By Robert Boyte C. Howell ... 4th ed. Charleston, S.C., Southern Baptist publication society. Richmond, Va., Virginia Baptist S.s. and publication society, 1854. 331 p. 19 cm. [BT751.H84] 40-25515
1. Salvation. I. Southern Baptist publication society. II. Title.

JENKINS, Mary Jane. 922.
Saved for service, by Mary Jane Jenkins. [n. p., c1928] 1 p. l., 5-128 p. 19 cm. [BV3705.J4A3] 29-6879
I. Title.

JOHNSON, Albinus Alonzo, 233
1852-
Steps to salvation. A compendium of essential doctrines. By A. A. Johnson ... foreword by Henry Augustus Buchtel ... Cincinnati, Jennings & Pye; New York, Eaton & Mains [c1901] 112 p. 15 cm. (On cover: Little books on doctrine) [BT751.J6] 2-1797
1. Salvation. I. Title.

JOHNSON, Edward H. 234
For a time like this; studies on salvation today and mission today [by] E. H. Johnson. New York, Friendship Press [1973] 128 p. 21 cm. Includes bibliographical references. [BT751.2.J63] 73-3087 ISBN 0-377-03001-5 pap. 1.95
1. Salvation. 2. Missions. I. Title.

JOHNSON, James Wager, 1863- 234
The great awakening, by James W. Johnson ... New York [etc.] Fleming H. Revell company [c1938] 61 p. 20 cm. [BT753.J63] 38-13648
1. Salvation. I. Title.

KAISER, Edwin G., 1893- 234
The everlasting covenant; theology of the Precious Blood [by] Edwin G. Kaiser. Carthagena, Ohio, Messenger Press [1968] x, 303 p. illus. 23 cm. Includes bibliographical references. [BT751.2.K3] 68-6134
1. Salvation. 2. Atonement. 3. Precious Blood, Devotion to. I. Title.

[KATHERINE EDITH, sister] 234
1848-1919.
The new creation. By the author of "Our family ways." Milwaukee, Wis., The Young churchman company, 1891. 128 p. 18 cm. On cover: Sister Katherin Edith. [Secular name: Katherine Edith Peirce] [BT752.K3] 265 37-33224
1. Salvation. 2. Sacraments—Anglican commission. I. Title.

KEMPER, Earskine Gault. 234
The light of the truth. Am I an infidel? By Dr. Earskine G. Kemper ... [Dallas, Tex.] Priv. print. [Globe book agency] 1937. 75 p. incl. front. (port.) 21 cm. [BT753.K37] 38-1425
1. Salvation. I. Title.

KENYON, Essek William, 1867- 233
1948.
The Father and His family; or, A restating of the plan of redemption. Spencer, Mass., Reality Press [1916] 272 p. port. 20 cm. (Its Bulletin, v. 22, no. 1) [BT751.K44] 17-258
1. Salvation. 2. Public schools—Kentucky—Princeton. 3. Public schools—Kentucky—Caldwell Co. I. Title. II. Series.

KERSWILL, William Dean, 234
1863?-1905.
The Old Testament doctrine of salvation; or, How men were saved in Old Testament times, by William Dean Kerswill... Philadelphia, Presbyterian board of publication and Sabbath school work, 1904. vii, 215 p. 20 1/2 cm. [BT752.K4] 4-13644
1. Salvation. 2. Bible. O.T.—Theology. 3. Bible—Theology—O.T. I. Title.

KEVAN, Ernest Frederick, 234
1903-
Salvation. Grand Rapids, Mich., Baker Bk. [c.]1963. 130p. 21cm. (Christian faith ser.) Bibl. 63-13774 2.50 bds.,
1. Salvation. I. Title.

KILLINGER, John. 234
The salvation tree. [1st ed.] New York, Harper & Row [1973] xxii, 169 p. 22 cm. Includes bibliographical references. [BT751.2.K54 1973] 72-11357 ISBN 0-06-064583-0 5.95
1. Salvation. 2. Christianity—20th century. I. Title.

KLOPPENBURG, Boaventura, 234
1919-
Christian salvation and human temporal progress / by Bonaventura Kloppenburg ; translated by Paul Burns. Chicago : Franciscan Herald Press, [1979] p. cm. Translation of Salvacion cristiana y progreso humano temporal. [BT752.K513] 79-21361 ISBN 0-8199-0778-2 : 7.50
1. Salvation. 2. Progress. 3. Liberation theology. I. Title.

KRAMER, Alice Bishop. Mrs. 234
God's reach for man, by Alice Bishop Kramer [and] Albert Ludlow Kramer ... New York city, A. L. Kramer [c1938] 163 p. 20 cm. [BT751.K7] 38-39118
1. Salvation. I. Kramer, Albert Ludlow, joint author. II. Title.

KRAMER, Alice Bishop. Mrs. 234
I bring you joy; including "A business man's search for god" and "How he found him", by Alice Bishop Kramer [and] Albert Ludlow Kramer ... New York city, A. L. Kramer [c1937] 88 p. 20 cm. [BT753.K7] 37-35142
1. Salvation. I. Kramer, Albert Ludlow, joint author. II. Title.

KRAMER, Paul Stevens, 1895- 234
The doctrine of our salvation; an introduction to the theology of atonement, of the church, and of the sacraments. New York, Exposition Press [1951] 165 p. 22 cm. Bibliography: p. [163]-165. [BT751.K73] 51-4896
1. Salvation. 2. Protestant Episcopal Church in the U. S. A.—Doctrinal and controversial works. I. Title.

KUIPER, Herman. 234
By grace alone; a study in soteriology. Grand Rapids, Eerdmans, 1955. 165p. 23cm. [BT751.K8] 55-13836
1. Salvation. I. Title.

KURTZ, Johann Heinrich, 1809- 234
1890.
Manual of sacred history: a guide to the understanding of the divine plan of salvation according to its historical development. By John Henry Kurtz ... Translated from the sixth German edition, by Charles F. Schaeffer, D. D. Philadelphia, Lindsay & Blakiston, 1855. xx, 21-436 p. 19 cm. [BT752.K8 1855] 33-11040
1. Salvation. 2. Bible—Theology. 3. Bible—History of Biblical events. I. Schaeffer, Charles Frederick, 1807-1879, tr. II. Title.

KURTZ, Johann Heinrich, 1809- 234
1890.
Manual of sacred history: a guide to the understanding of the divine plan of salvation according to its historical development. By John Henry Kurtz ... Tr. from the sixth German edition, by Charles F. Schaeffer ... 3d ed. Philadelphia, Lindsay & Blakiston, 1857. 2 p. l., vii-xx, 21-436 p. 20 cm. [BT752.K8 1857] 22-15346
I. Schaeffer, Charles Frederick, 1807-1879, tr. II. Title.

KURTZ, Johann Heinrich, 1809-1890. 234
Manual of sacred history: a guide to the understanding of the divine plan of salvation according to its historical development. By John Henry Kurtz ... Tr. from the 6th German ed., by Charles F. Schaeffer ... 6th ed. Philadelphia, Lindsay & Blakiston, 1860. xx, 21-436 p. 20 cm. [BT752.K8 1860] 22-15357
1. Schaeffer, Charles Frederick, 1807-1879, tr. II. Title.

LAMONT, Thomas Johnston, 1842-1900. 234
The joy of salvation. By Rev. T. Johnston Lamont ... Rockford, Ill., Monitor publishing company, 1892. 128 p. 19 cm. [BT751.L2] 40-37291
1. Salvation. I. Title.

LAPSLEY, James N. 234
Salvation and health; the interlocking processes of life, by James N. Lapsley. Philadelphia, Westminster Press [1972] 174 p. 21 cm. Includes bibliographical references. [BT732.L33] 79-188383 ISBN 0-664-20936-X
1. Salvation. 2. Hygiene. 3. Mental hygiene. I. Title.

LEGTERS, Leonard Livingston, 1873- 234
Partakers, by L. L. Legters ... Philadelphia, Pa., Pioneer mission agency [c1936] 2 p. l., 7-95 p. 18 1/2 cm. [BT751.L4] 36-29042
1. Salvation. I. Title.

LINDSEY, Hal. 218
The liberation of planet earth / Hal Lindsey. Grand Rapids : Zondervan Pub. House, c1974. 236 p. : ill. ; 21 cm. [BT751.2.L49] 73-13075 5.95
1. Lindsey, Hal. 2. Salvation. I. Title.

LINEBERRY, John, 1926- 234
Salvation is of the Lord; topical and word studies in the plan of salvation, its need, meaning, source, blessing, and assurance. Foreword by Kenneth S. Wuest. Grand Rapids, Zondervan Pub. House [1959] 96p. 20cm. [BT751.2.L5] 59-38172
1. Salvation. I. Title.

LIPSCOMB, David.
... Salvation from sin, by David Lipscomb ... Ed. by J. W. Shepherd ... Nashville, Tenn., McQuiddy printing company, 1913. x, 440 p. 24 cm. 13-3848 1.50
I. Shepherd, James Walton, 1861- ed. II. Title.

LLOYD-JONES, David Martyn 234
The plight of man and the power of God [by] D. Martyn Lloyd-Jones [2d ed.] Grand Rapids, Mich., Eerdmans [1966] 93p. 21cm. Reprint of the 1945 London ed. [BT751.L55 8] 66-18724 2.50 bds.,
1. Salvation. I. Title.

LLOYD-JONES, David Martyn. 234
The plight of man and the power of God [by] D. Martyn Lloyd-Jones. [2d ed.] Grand Rapids, W. B. Eerdmans Publ. Co. [1966] 93 p. 21 cm. Reprint of the 1945 ed. [BT751.L55 1966] 66-18724
1. Salvation. I. Title.

LLOYD-JONES, David Martyn. 234
The plight of man and the power of God [by] D. Martyn Lloyd-Jones ... New York, Nashville, Abingdon-Cokesbury press [1943] 120 p. 19 1/2 cm. [BT751.L55] 43-3145
1. Salvation. I. Title.

LOCHMAN, Jan Milic. 234
Reconciliation and liberation : challenging a one-dimensional view of salvation / Jan Milic Lochman ; translated from the German by David Lewis. 1st American ed. Phildelphia : Fortress Press, 1980. p. cm. Translation of Versohnung und Befreiung. [BT751.2.L6213 1980] 19 80-24060 ISBN 0-8006-1340-6 pbk. : 6.95
1. Salvation. I. Title.

LOVETT, W Davis, 1856- 234
The penalty of a broken law; or, Law and penalty, by Dr. W. Davis Lovett ... Newland, N. C. [c1926] 87 p. 19 cm. [BT753.L6] 41-33825
1. Salvation. I. Title.

LUTZER, Erwin W. 234
You're richer than you think / Erwin W. Lutzer. Wheaton, Ill. : Victor Books, c1978. 128 p. ; 18 cm. [BT751.2.L82] 78-56619 ISBN 0-88207-765-1 pbk. : 1.75
1. Salvation. I. Title.

MCDANIEL, Mabel C. 248
God's great plan of salvation. New York, Pageant [c.1963] 164p. 21cm. 2.50
I. Title.

MCDONALD, William, b.1820. 248
Saved to the uttermost, by W. McDonald ... Chicago, The Christian witness co. [1921] 76 p. front. (port.) 20 cm. Preface dated 1885. [BT767.M24 1921] 21-16442
I. Title.

MACON, Leon Meertief, 1908- 234
Salvation in a scientific age. Grand Rapids, Zondervan Pub. House [1955] 121p. 21cm. [BT751.M26] 55-39576
1. Salvation. I. Title.

MADRIGAL, Jose A., 1945- 291.2'2
El salvaje y la mitologia, el arte y la religion / Jose A. Madrigal. Miami, Fla. : Ediciones Universal, 1975. 55 p. ; 21 cm. (Coleccion Polymita) "500 ejemplares." Bibliography: p. 51-54. [BL476.M3] 75-1692
1. Salvation. I. Title.

*MARTIN, Harold S. 234
Simple messages on Romans, by Harold S. Martin. Elgin, Ill., Brethren Press, [1974] 123 p. 21 cm. [BT751] 3.95
1. Salvation. 2. Theology. I. Title.

MASSABKI, Ch. 232
Christ, liberation of the world today / by Charles Massabki ; [translated from the French by Eloise Therese Mescall]. Staten Island, N.Y. : Alba House, c1979. p. cm. Translation of Le Christ, liberation du monde aujourd'hui. Includes bibliographical references. [BT202.M37713] 78-12998 ISBN 0-8189-0374-0 : 6.95
1. Jesus Christ—Person and offices. 2. Salvation. 3. Spiritual life—Church authors. I. Title.

MAXWELL, L. E. 234
Crowded to Christ. Grand Rapids, Mich., Eerdmans [1965, c.1950] 354p. 22cm. [BT751.M4] 2.25 pap.,
1. Salvation. I. Title.

MAXWELL, L E 234
Crowded to Christ. Grand Rapids, Eerdmans, 1950. 354 p. 22 cm. [BT751.M4] 50-14781
1. Salvation. I. Title.

MERRILL, Stephen Mason, bp., 1825-1905. 233
Doctrinal aspects of Christian experience. By S. M. Merrill ... Cincinnati, Curts & Jennings; New York, Eaton & Mains [c1882] 297 p. 18 cm. [BT751.M5] 40-38471
1. Salvation. I. Title.

MORRIS, Frederick M 234
Power to save. Greenwich, Conn., Seabury Press, 1960. 64p. 21cm. [BT751.2.M6] 60-5885
1. Salvation. I. Title.

MOSER, Kenney Carl, 1893- 234
The way of salvation, being an exposition of God's method of justification through Christ, by K. C. Moser ... Nashville, Tenn., Gospel advocate company, 1932. 174 p. 19 1/2 cm. [BT751.M85] 32-12097
1. Salvation. I. Title.

MULLER, Michael, 1825-1899. 234
The Catholic dogma ... by Michael Muller, C. SS. R. New York, Cincinnati and Chicago, Benziger brothers [1888] xiv, [5]-292 p. 20 cm. [BT755.M8] 40-38477
1. Salvation. 2. Catholic church—Doctrinal and controversial works—Catholic authors. I. Title.

NELSON, Henry Addison, 1820-1906. 234
Sin and salvation. By Henry A. Nelson. New York, A. D. F. Randolph & company [1881] vi, 7-215 p. 20 cm. [BT751.N4] 40-25518
1. Salvation. 2. Sin. I. Title.

NIES, Richard, 1928- 234
Security of salvation / by Richard Nies. Nashville : Southern Pub. Association, c1978. p. cm. Includes bibliographical references. [BT751.2.N53] 78-17523 pbk. : 0.95
1. Seventh-Day Adventists—Doctrinal and controversial works. 2. Salvation. I. Title.

NUNEZ C., Emilio Antonio. 234
Caminos de renovacion / Emilio Antonio Nunez C. Grand Rapids, Mich. : Editado por Publicaciones Portavoz Evangelico para Outreach Publications, c1975. 218 p. ; 18 cm. Includes bibliographical references. [BT751.2.N86] 76-459912 ISBN 8-439-94101-3
1. Salvation. 2. Church renewal. I. Title.

[OLIVER, John]
The salvation of the little child. Cincinnati, Press of Jennings and Graham [c1909] 96 p. 18 cm. 9-12078
I. Title.

OLIVER, John.
The salvation of the little child, by John Oliver. 2d ed., rev. Cincinnati and Denver, The Movement for the salvation of the Little child [c1915] 64 p. 18 cm. 15-18413 0.10
I. Title.

OSGOOD, Anna Ripley. 233
Grace and judgment; or, The plan of salvation, by Anna Ripley Osgood ... [Binghamton, Binghamton Republican printery] c1905. 3 p. l., [9]-128 p. 18 cm. [BT751.O8] 5-16616
1. Salvation. I. Title.

OTTEN, Bernard John, 1862-1930. 233
The business of salvation, by Bernard J. Otten ... St. Louis, Mo., Freiburg (Baden) [etc.] B. Herder, 1911. ix, 377 p. 20 cm. [BT751.O86] 11-31170
1. Salvation. I. Title.

PALMER, Agnes Lizzie (Page) Mrs., 1874-
The salvage of men; stories of humanity touched by divinity, by Agnes L. Palmer. New York, Chicago [etc.] Fleming H. Revell company [c1913] 214 p. 19 1/2 cm. 14-2139 1.00
I. Title.
Contents omitted.

PARKER, John, 1800-1878. 234
The upward path; or, Brief thoughts on Christian salvation, as revealed to us in the Holy Scriptures, and as understood and taught by the great body of Methodists throughout the world. By The Rev. John Parker ... Rochester [N. Y.] E. Darrow & brothers, 1857. 123 p. 18 cm. [BT751.P25] 40-37154
1. Salvation. I. Title.

PERDELWITZ, George.
Spiritual starlight on earth and road to heavenly bliss, by G. Perdelwitz. Boston, Mass., Meador publishing company, [c1929] 130 p. incl. front. (ports.) illus. pl. 21 cm. [BX3.P4] 29-595
I. Title.

PETERS, Henry Harrison, 1867- 234
Salvation light, by H. H. Peters, a railroad conductor. Louisville, Ky., Pentecostal publishing company [c1915] 188 p. 20 cm. 16-5636 1.00
I. Title.

PIERSON, Arthur Tappan, 1837-1911. 233
In Christ Jesus; or, The sphere of the believer's life, by Arthur T. Pierson ... New York and London, Funk & Wagnalls company, 1898. xv, 17-197 p., 1 l. 17 cm. Each epistle followed by leaf with summary of teachings. [BT751.P6] 98-1354
1. Salvation. 2. Christian life. I. Title.
Contents omitted.

PIETERS, Albertus, 1869- 234
Divine Lord and Saviour; the meaning and method of salvation. With an introd. by Samuel M. Zwemer. New York, F. H. Revell Co. [1949] 187 p. 20 cm. [BT751.P63] 49-8055
1. Salvation. I. Title.

PINK, Arthur Walkington, 1886-1952. 234
The doctrine of salvation / A. W. Pink. Grand Rapids, Mich. : Baker Book House, c1975. 164 p. ; 24 cm. [BT751.2.P53] 75-18228 ISBN 0-8010-6980-7 : 5.95
1. Salvation. I. Title.

PINK, Arthur Walkington, 1886-1952. 234
The doctrine of salvation / A.W. Pink. Grand Rapids, Mich. : Baker Book House, 1977,c1975. 169p. ; 22 cm. Includes indexes. [BT751.2P53] ISBN 0-8010-7026-0 pbk. : 2.95
1. Salvation. I. Title.
L.C. card no. for hardcover ed.: 75-18228.

*PINK, Arthur Walkington 1886-1952 234
Eternal security [by] Arthur W. Pink. Grand Rapids, Guardian Press, [1974] 126 p. 21 cm. [BT751] ISBN 0-89086-001-7 2.95 (pbk.)
1. Salvation. I. Title.
Distributed by Baker Book House, Grand Rapids, Michigan

†PRESSAU, Jack Renard, 1933- 248'.48'51
I'm saved, you're saved—maybe / Jack Renard Pressau. Atlanta : John Knox Press, c1977. 146 p. ; 24 cm. Includes bibliographical references and indexes. [BT751.2.P73] 76-12401 ISBN 0-8042-0832-8 : 6.95
1. Salvation. 2. Christian life—Presbyterian authors. I. Title.

QUERRY, B F. 234
A debate held at Lena, Ind., May 24, 25 and 26, 1892, between Elder B. F. Query, of Raymond, Ill., and Elder W. H. Williams, of Lena, Ind. ... Indianapolis, W. B. Burford, printer, 1892. 233 p. 20 cm. [BT751.Q4] 40-37292
1. Salvation. 2. Election (Theology) 3. Faith. I. Williams, W. H. II. Title.

RALL, Harris Franklin, 1870- 234
Religion as salvation. Nashville, Abingdon-Cokesbury Press [1953] 254p. 24cm. [BT751.R25] 53-5400
1. Salvation. I. Title.

REID, William, 1814-1896. 233
The blood of Jesus. By the Rev. William Reid ... Boston, The American tract society [1863] iv, 5-138 p. 15 cm. [BT751.R35 1863] 38-33148
1. Salvation. I. American tract society. II. Title.

REID, William, 1814-1896. 234
The blood of Jesus. By the Rev. William Reid ... 120th thousand. Philadelphia, American Baptist publication society [187-?] vi, 7-122 p. 15 cm. [BT751.R35 1870] 33-24541
1. Salvation. I. American Baptist publication society. II. Title.

REID, William, 1814-1896. 234
The blood of Jesus. By the Rev. William Reid, M.A. With an introduction by the Rev. Edward Payson Hammond ... New York, Funk & Wagnalls, 1882. 115 p. 18 cm. (On cover: The standard series. no. 75) Advertising matter: p. 109-115. [BT751.R35 1882] 39-2993
1. Salvation. I. Title.

REM, Oscar, 1901- 234
God's architecture, by Oscar Rem. Minneapolis, Augsburg publishing house [c1937] viii p., 2 l., [3]-157 p. 20 1/2 cm. [BT751.R36] 37-24787
1. Salvation. I. Title.

RICE, John R., 1895- 234
A know- so salvation. Wheaton, Ill., Sword of the Lord Publishers [1953] 187p. 21cm. [BT751.R49] 53-30193
1. Salvation. I. Title.

ROGERS, William Hubert, 1883- 234
Sinners yet saints, by W. H. Rogers, D.D. New York, American tract society [c1940] 225 p. 20 1/2 cm. [BT751.R62] 40-11603
1. Salvation. I. American tract society. II. Title.

ROYER, W M 234
The mystery of God; or, There is a spiritual body. [1st ed.] New York, Greenwich Book Publishers [c1958] 54p. 21cm. [BT751.2.R6] 58-14372
1. Salvation. I. Title.

[RUTHERFORD, Joseph Franklin] 1869- 234
Salvation; disclosing God's provision for man's protection from disaster and salvation to life everlasting in complete happiness; a text book for the Jonadabs.

[Brooklyn, etc., Watchtower Bible and tract society, inc., International Bible students association, c1939] 381 p. incl. front. (facsim.) illus. col. plates. 18 1/2 cm. On verso of t.-p.: By J. F. Rutherford. "1,000,000 edition." [BX8526.R8818 1939] 39-17800
1. Salvation. I. Title.

SAUER, Erich. 234
From eternity to eternity, an outline of the divine purposes' translated by G. H. Lang. Grand Rapids, Eerdmans, 1954. 207p. illus. 23cm. Translation of Der gottliche Erlosungsplan von Ewigkeit su Ewigkeit. [BT751.S273] 54-4153
1. Salvation. I. Title.

SAVAGE, Henry Harold, 1887- 234
Facts concerning salvation, by H. H. Savage ... Hoytville, O., Fundamental truth store [c1934] 63 p. 18 1/2 cm. [BT753.S3] 34-5955
1. Salvation. I. Title.

SCHER, Bertha. 242
The seen and the unseen; solace and light for those who hunger and thirst for more than bread alone. New York, William-Frederick Press, 1949. 87 p. 21 cm. [BR126.S347] 49-7360
I. Title.

SCULL, David. 234
Salvation in a two-fold aspect. The gospel: is it merely an addition to the "law", or is it in truth the "glad tidings" of an infinite love! By David Scull. Philadelphia, J. C. Winston & co., 1897. 148 p. 18 cm. [BT51.S43] 40-37298
1. Salvation. 2. Law and gospel. I. Title.

SEARCY, William Everard Hamilton, 1847-
The way to the kingdom of heaven and what to do to be saved in it, by W. E. H. Searcy ... Griffin, Ga., Searcy publishing company, 1908. 176 p. front. (port.) illus. 20 cm. 8-29857
I. Title.

SHELNUTT, James Bunkett.
The plan of salvation, by J. B. Shelnutt. Nashville, Tenn., McQuiddy printing co., 1916. 177 p. 19 cm. 16-14643
I. Title.

SHELNUTT, James Bunkett, 262 1863-
The plan of salvation, by J. B. Shelnutt. Nashville, Tenn., McQuiddy printing co., 1916. 177 p. 19 cm. [BT751.S5] 16-14643
1. Salvation. I. Title.

SHERIN, Henry, 1850- 234
Why many preacher's hobby horses fail to win the (human) race, by Henry Sherin ... Wilmington, Del., H. Sherin [c1933] 80 p. 18 1/2 cm. "Errata" slip mounted on p. [1] [BT753.S5] 33-20693
1. Salvation. I. Title.

SHINN, Asa, 1781-1853.
An essay on the plan of salvation; in which the several sources of evidence are examined, and applied to the interesting doctrine of redemption, in its relation to the government and moral attributes of the Diety. By Asa Shinn ... Baltimore, Neal, Wills and Cole, 1813. 4 p. l., [v]-ix, 11-416, [3] p. 23 cm. 16-24019
I. Title.

SHULER, John Lewis, 1887- 234
Are you saved? / J. L. Shuler. Washington : Review and Herald Pub. Association, c1978. 63 p. : ill. ; 18 cm. [BT751.2.S525] 78-4186 pbk. : 0.85
1. Salvation. I. Title.

SMITH, William Edward, 1881- 234
How to be saved; miscellaneous writings. Boston, Meador Pub. Co. [1950] 622 p. 21 cm. [BT751.S67] 50-10773
1. Salvation. I. Title.

SOVIK, Arne. 234
Salvation today. Foreword by Philip Potter. Minneapolis, Augsburg Pub. House [1973] 112 p. 20 cm. [BT751.2.S6] 73-78252 ISBN 0-8066-1318-1 2.95
1. Salvation. I. Title.

SPANGLER, Bob. 234
Marked! / Bob Spangler. Washington, D.C. : Review and Herald Pub. Association, c1981. p. cm. [BT751.2.S63] 19 81-8598 ISBN 0-8280-0079-4 : 1.25
1. Salvation. I. Title.

SPENCER, Ichabod Smith, 1798- 234 1854.
A pastor's sketches; or, Conversations with anxious inquirers respecting the way of salvation. By Ichabod S. Spencer ... New York, M. W. Dodd, 1850. x, 414 p. 19 cm. [BT751.S7] 35-22743
1. Salvation. 2. Conversion. I. Title.

SPENCER, Ichabod Smith, 1798- 234 1854.
A pastor's sketches; or, Conversations with anxious inquirers, respecting the way of salvation ... By Ichabod S. Spencer ... Second series. New York, M. W. Dodd, 1853. ix, [11]-430 p., 1 l., 18 1/2 cm. [BT751.S73] 35-22744
1. Salvation. 2. Conversion. I. Title.

SPENCER, Ichabod Smith, 1798- 233 1854.
A pastor's sketches; or, Conversations with anxious inquirers, respecting the way of salvation ... By Ichabod S. Spencer ... Second series. 6th thousand. New York, M. W. Dodd, 1857. ix, 11-430 p., 1 l., 20 cm. [BT751.S7 2d ser. 1857] 30-18087
1. Salvation. 2. Conversions. I. Title.

SPENCER, Ichabod Smith, 1798- 234 1854.
The young Irshman. From A pastor's sketches; or Conversation with anxious inquirers respecting the way of salvation." By I. S. Spencer, D.D. New York, M. W. Dodd [185-?] 1 p. l., [v]-vi, 64 p. 19 cm. [BT751.S73] 35-31066
1. Salvation. 2. Conversion. I. Title.

SPRENG, Samuel P., 1858-
... The sinner and his Savior; the way of salvation, made plain, by Samuel P. Spreng ... Cleveland, O., Publishing house of the Evangelical association, J. H. Lamb, agent [c1906] 130 p. 19 cm. (The Albright. series) 7-7182
I. Title.

STEPS to Jesus / 230'.673
by Ellen G. White ; adapted. Nashville, Tn. : Review and Herald Pub. Association, c1981. p. cm. [BT751.2.S67] 19 80-22225 ISBN 0-8127-0316-2 : 3.95 ISBN 0-8127-0318-9 pbk. : 1.95
1. Salvation. I. White, Ellen Gould Harmon, 1827-1915.

STEVENS, George Bakers. 1854- 262 1906.
... The Christian doctrine of salvation, by George Barker Stevens ... New York, C. Scribner's sons, 1905. xi, 546 p. 22 cm. (Half-title: The international theological library) Series title in part at head of t.-p. [BT751.S8] 5-32666
1. Salvation. I. Title.
Contents omitted.

STOCK, Augustine. 234
Lamb of God, the promise and fulfillment of salvation. [New York] Herder & Herder [1963] 175p. 21cm. 63-9554 3.95
1. Salvation. I. Title.

STROMBECK, John Frederick, 234 1881-
So great salvation, by J. F. Strombeck ... Moline, Ill., Strombeck agency, inc., 1940. 152 p. 19 1/2 cm. [BT751.S85] 40-12880
1. Salvation. I. Title.

*SZOPKO, Emey J. 234
Jesus: his mission on earth; a book of salvation. New York, Carlton [1968] 84p. 21cm. (Hearthstone bk.) 2.75
1. Salvation. I. Title.

TAPSCOTT, Betty. 248'.86
Set free through inner healing / by Betty Tapscott. Houston : Hunter Ministries Pub. Co., c1978. 176 p. ; 21 cm. [BT751.2.T36] 77-94460 ISBN 0-917726-24-3 : pbk. : 2.95
1. Salvation. 2. Mental healing. I. Title.
Publisther's address : 1600 Townthurst, Houston, TX 77043

TILLETT, Wilbur Fisk, 1854- 262
Personal salvation; studies in Christian doctrine pertaining to the spiritual life [by] Wilbur F. Tillett ... Ninth thousand. Nashville, Tenn., Cokesbury press, 1924. xx, 536 p. 20 1/2 cm. [BT751.T5 1924] 25-2799
1. Salvation. 2. Theology, Doctrinal. I. Title.

TILLETT, Wilbur Risk, 1854- 262 1938.
Personal salvation; studies in Christian doctrine pertaining to the spiritual life. By Wilbur F. Tillett ... Nashville, Tenn., Dallas, Tex., Publishing house of the M. E. church, South, Barbee & Smith, agents, 1902. xx, 586 p. 20 1/2 cm. [BT751.T5] 2-18352
1. Salvation. 2. Theology, Doctrinal. I. Title.

TORREY, Reuben Archer, 1856- 233 1928.
Real salvation and whole-hearted service, by R. A. Torrey. New York, Chicago [etc.] Fleming H. Revell company [1905] 3 p. l., [9]-267 p. 20 cm. [BT751.T6] 5-5420
1. Salvation. 2. Evangelistic work. I. Title.

TRIBBLE, Harold Wayland, 234 1899-
Salvation [by] Harold W. Tribble ... Nashville, Tenn., The Broadman press [c1940] viii, [9]-91 p. 19 1/2 cm. (My Covenant series. book 1) Text on lining-paper. [BT751.T7] 40-8894
1. Salvation. I. Title.

TROEGER, Thomas H., 1945- 234
Are you saved? : Answers to the awkward question / Thomas H. Troeger. 1st ed. Philadelphia : Westminster Press, c1979. 131 p. ; 21 cm. [BT751.2.T76] 79-14402 ISBN 0-664-24267-7 pbk. : 5.95
1. Salvation. I. Title.

[TYLER, John] 1742-1823.
Universal damnation and salvation clearly proved by the Scriptures, of the Old and New Testament, specially recommended to the perusal of those who believe in the salvation of all mankind ... From a Boston edition. Buffalo, Printed and sold by H. A. Salisbury, 1819. 59 p. 20 cm. [BX9943.T] A 32
1. Salvation. I. Title.

VENN, Henry, 1725-1797 234
Mistakes in religion exposed; an essay on the prophecy of Zacharias. By the late Rev. H. Venn ... New York; Published by Williams and Whiting, at their Theological & classical bookstore, no. 118 Pearl-street; also, by B. B. Hopkins & co. Philadelphia; J. Simpson & co. New-Brunswick; D. Farrand & Green. Albany; Nathan, Elliott, Catskill; Asshel Seward, Utica; Beers & Howe; New-Haven; and Swift & Chipman; Middlebury, Vt., Paul & Thomas, printers, 1810. xvi, [17]-206 p. 18 1/2 cm. [BT750.V4] 33-20560
1. Salvation. 2. Bible. N.T. Luke I. 68-79—Prophecies. 3. Zacharias, the priest, father of John the Baptist. I. Title.

VERKUYL, Johannes. 234
The message of liberation in our age, by J. Verkuyl. Translated by Dale Cooper. Grand Rapids, Mich., W. B. Eerdmans Pub. Co. [1972] 110 p. 21 cm. Translation of De boodschap der bevrijding in deze tijd. [BT751.2.V4413 1972] 75-180786 ISBN 0-8028-1437-9 2.45
1. Salvation. I. Title.

[WALKER, James Barr] 1805- 233 1887.
Philosophy of the plan of salvation. A book for the times. By an American citizen... 2d ed. New-York, M. W. Dodd, and R. Carter; Boston, Tappan & Dennett; [etc., etc.] 1843. x, [11]-239 p. 18 1/2 cm. [BT751.W2 1843] 24-19618
1. Salvation. I. Title.

[WALKER, James Barr] 1805- 233 1887.
Philosophy of the plan of salvation. A book for the times. By an American citizen. With an introductory essay by Calvin E. Stowe...8th thousand. Boston, Gould, Kendall and Lincoln; Cincinnati, G. L. Weed, 1848. xvi, [5]-239 p. 20 cm. [BT751.W2 1848] 27-25539
1. Salvation. I. Title.

[WALKER, James Barr] 1805- 234 1887.
Philosophy of the plan of salvation. A book for the times. By an American citizen. With an introductory essay by Calvin E. Stowe...Ninth thousand. Boston, Gould, Kendall and Lincoln; Cincinnati, G. L. Weed, 1850. xi, [ix]-xvi, [5]-239 p. 20 cm. [BT751.W2 1850] 24-11624
1. Salvation. I. Title.

[WALKER, James Barr] 1805- 233 1887.
Philosophy of the plan of salvation. A book for the times; by an American citizen. With an introductory essay, by Calvin E. Stowe... Boston, Gould and Lincoln, 1851. xxii, [5]-239 p. 18 1/2 cm. [BT751.W2 1851] 25-27729
1. Salvation. I. Title.

[WALKER, James Barr] 1805- 234 1887.
Philosophy of the plan of salvation. A book for the times, by an American citizen. With an introductory essay, by Calvin E. Stowe... Boston, Gould and Lincoln, 1853. xxii, [5]-239 p. 19 1/2 cm. [BT751.W2 1853] 35-24721
1. Salvation. I. Title.

WALKER, James Barr 1805- 24-19619 1887.
Philosophy of the plan of salvation. A book for the times. By Rev. James B. Walker... Cincinnati, Hitchcock and Walden; New York, Phillips and Hunt [c1855] xiv, [25]-286 p. 18 cm. First published anonymously in 1841. [BT751.W2 1855a]
1. Salvation. I. Title.

[WALKER, James Barr] 1805- 233 1887.
Philosophy of the plan of salvation. A book for the times. By an American citizen. With an introductory essay by Calvin E. Stowe... A new ed., with a supplementary chapter by the author. Boston, Gould and Lincoln; New York, Sheldon, Lamport & Blakeman, 1855. 4, [iii]-xxii, [25]-286 p. 20 cm. [BT751.W2 1855] 24-19612
1. Salvation. I. Title.

[WALKER, James Barr] 1805- 234 1887.
Philosophy of the plan of salvation. A book for the times. By an American citizen. With an introductory essay by Calvin E. Stowe... A new ed., with a supplementary chapter by the author. Boston, Gould and Lincoln; New York, Sheldon, Blakeman & co.; [etc., etc.] 1856. 4, [iii]-xxii, [25]-286 p. 19 1/2 cm. [BT751.W2 1856] 34-40560
1. Salvation. I. Title.

[WALKER, James Barr] 1805- 234 1887.
Philosophy of the plan of salvation. A book for the times. By an American citizen. With an introductory essay by Calvin E. Stowe... A new ed., with a supplementary chapter by the author. Boston, Gould and Lincoln; New York, Sheldon and company, [etc., etc.] 1860. xxii, [25]-286 p. 19 1/2 cm. [BT751.W2 1860] 38-10393
1. Salvation. I. Title.

[WALKER, James Barr] 1805- 234 1887.
Philosophy of the plan of salvation. A book for the times. By an American citizen. With an introductory essay, by Calvin E. Stowe... A new ed., with a supplementary chapter by the author. Boston, Gould and Lincoln; New York, Sheldon and company; [etc., etc.] 1866. 4, [iii]-xxii, [25]-286 p. 20 cm. [BT751.W2 1866] 33-33623
1. Salvation. I. Title.

WALKER, James Barr, 1805- 234 1887.
Philosophy of the plan of salvation. A book for the times. By Rev. James B. Walker... Cincinnati, Walden and Stowe; New York, Phillips & Hunt [1881?] xiv, [15]-276 p. 18 cm. First published anonymously in 1841. [BT751.W2] 39-10492
1. Salvation. I. Title.

WALKER, James Barr, 1805- 234 1887.
The philosophy of the plan of salvation / by James B. Walker. Minneapolis, Minn. : Bethany Fellowship, 1980. 264 p. ; 21 cm. Reprint. Originally published: Cranston &

Stowe, 1887. [BT751.W2 1980z] 19 80-69727 ISBN 0-87123-469-6 pbk. : 5.95
1. Salvation. I. Title. II. Title: Plan of salvation.

WALSH, John Tomline. 234
Salvation from sin; or, What must I do to be saved? In six discourses, by Dr. John Tomline Walsh. Rev. and enl. St. Louis, Mo., J. Burns, 1880. iv, [5]-69 p. 17 1/2 cm. [BT753.W2] 40-36601
1. Salvation. I. Title.

WARFIELD, Benjamin Breckinridge, 1851-1921. 234
The plan of salvation, by Benjamin R. Warfield ... New, rev. ed. Grand Rapids, Mich., Wm. B. Eerdmans publishing co., 1935. 142 p. 20 cm. [BT751.W24 1935] 35-35400
1. Salvation. I. Title.
Contents omitted.

WATERS, Plummer. 234
Salvation for the chief of sinners, by Elder Plummer Waters, at Hammond's Branch and New Lisbon churches, Anne Arundel county. Baltimore, Printed by J. W. Woods, 1838. xxi p., 1 l., [25]-228 p. 19 cm. [BT751.W3] 40-37298
1. Salvation. I. Title.

THE way of salvation familiarly explained, in a conversation between a father and his children. Philadelphia, Presbyterian board of publication of tracts and Sabbath school books, 1839. 49 p. 16 1/2 cm. [BT753.W3] 41-328145 234
1. Salvation. I. Presbyterian church in the U.S.A. (Old school) Board of publication.

WEST, Anson. 234
The old and the new man; or, Sin and salvation. By the Rev. Anson West ... Nashville, Tenn., Southern Methodist publishing house, 1885. 385 p. 19 1/2 cm. [BT751.W5] 40-37299
1. Salvation. 2. Sin. I. Title.

WHITE, Ellen Gould (Harmon) 1827-1915. 234
Love unlimited: combining Steps to Christ, and Thoughts from the Mount of Blessing. Mountain View, Calif., Pacific Press Pub. Association [c1958] 313 p. illus. 18 cm. [BX6111.W513] 59-6403
1. Salvation. 2. Sermon on the Mount. I. Title.

WHITE, Ellen Gould (Harmon) Mrs., 1827-1915. 234
Steps to Christ, by Ellen G. White ... Mountain View, Calif., Portland Or. [etc.] Pacific press publishing association [1938] 2 p. l., [9]-122 p. illus. 16 cm. [BX6111.W598 1938] 40-3806
1. Salvation. I. Title.

WHITE, Ellen Gould (Harmon) Mrs., 1827-1915.
Steps to Christ, by Ellen G. White ... Battle Creek, Mich., Washington, D.C., Review and herald publishing assn.; Mountain View, Cal., Pacific press pub. co.; [etc., etc., c1908] 144 p. illus. 19 cm. [BX6111.W598 1903] 8-13943
1. Salvation. I. Title.

WHITEHEAD, John. 234
The pious Christian's faith and hope. From the hand of John Whitehead ... New-York, J. S. Taylor, 1851. vii, [9]-220 p. 16 cm. "Mail edition." [BT751.W57] 40-37301
1. Salvation. I. Title.

WIDNEY, Joseph Pomeroy, 1841-1938. 234
The way of life. Holiness unto the Lord. The indwelling Spirit. Three essays. [By] J. P. Widney. Los Angeles, Cal., Commercial printing house, 1900. 5 p. l., [9]-152 p. 19 1/2 cm. "After the title-page had been printed two further essays, The baptism with the Holy Ghost and with fire, The enduement with power, were added to the book." [BT753.W55] 0-4636
1. Salvation. 2. Holiness. 3. Holy Spirit. 4. Christian life. I. Title. II. Title: Holiness unto the Lord. III. Title: The indwelling Spirit.

WIGLE, E[li].
"How may I win my unsaved friend to Christ?" By Rev. E. Wigle. Grand Rapids, Mich., Continental publishing co. [1904] 128 p. front. (port.) 19 1/2 cm. Advertising matter: p. 126-128. 4-28972
I. Title.

WILLIAMS, D. L. 234
The way of salvation. Being a series of short articles on subjects, pertaining to salvation as revealed in the word of God. By D. L. Williams... Nashville, Tenn., Gospel advocate publishing co., 1892. viii, 9-262 p. 19 cm. [BT751.W7] 40-37302
1. Salvation. I. Title.

[WILSON, James Patriot] 1769-1830. 262
An essay, on the probation of fallen men: or, The scheme of salvation, founded in sovereignty, and demonstrative of justice ... Philadelphia, Printed by W. F. Geddes, 1827. v, [7]-111, [1] p. front. (port.) 23 cm. "To the members of the First Presbyterian church in the city of Philadelphia" signed: James P. Wilson. [BT751.W75] 45-40051
1. Salvation. I. Title.

WRIGHTON, William Hazer. 234
A philosopher's victory through Christ, by William Hazer Wrighton ... New York [etc.] Fleming H. Revell company [c1938] 90 p. 19 1/2 cm. A companion volume to A philosopher's love for Christ. cf. Pref. [BT751.W93] 38-13644
1. Salvation. I. Title.

WYMAN, Edwin Allen, 1834- 234
Acquaintance with God; or, Salvation and character. By Rev. E. A. Wyman, PH.D. With an introduction by Rev. James Upham ... Springfield, Mass., C. W. Bryan and company, printers, 1876. 3 p. l., [v]-xvi, 198 p. 19 cm. [BT751.W95] 40-37306
1. Salvation. I. Title.

WYNKOOP, Elizabeth W. 234
... *Wages of sin is death* but the gift of God is eternal life, through Jesus Christ--Romans 6:23. By Elizabeth W. Wynkoop ... Millville, Pa., Weekly tablet print., 1894. cover-title, 58, [4] p. 22 1/2 cm. [BT753.W9] 41-30189
1. Salvation. 2. Annihilationism. I. Title.
Contents omitted.

Salvation—Addresses, essays, lectures.

BREWER, Charles Louis.
Stepping-stones to Heaven; three lectures, by C. L. Brewer ... Chicago, Ill., To-morrow publishing co. [1908?] 82 p. 18 cm. (Lettered on cover: Dawn thought series) 15-28242
I. Title.

HASTINGS, H.L. 234
Will all men be saved? New York 25, Box 87, Cathedral Station, People's Christian Bulletin, 1960. 22p. .25 pap.,
I. Title.

KNOTT, Lucy Pierce, Mrs. 1856-
Salvation life lines and spiritual life preservers ... Arranged by Lucy P. Knott. [Los Angeles, Cal., Nazarene pub. house, 1899] 3 p. l., [6]-76 p. 16 cm. 0-6416
I. Title.

*LANTERMAN, Wilmer D. 233
Will man live again? The Name whereby we are saved. New York, Carlton [1967] 69p. 21cm. 2.00
I. Title.

MARCHBANKS, John B., 1914- 234
Great doctrines relating to salvation, by John B. Marchbanks. Neptune, N.J., Loizeaux Bros. [1970] 96 p. 21 cm. [BT753.M29] 73-123612 1.50
1. Salvation—Addresses, essays, lectures. I. Title.

PORTER, John William, 1863- 252.
Assurance of salvation and other evangelistic addresses, by J. W. Porter ... New York, Chicago [etc.] Fleming H. Revell company [c1921] 4 p. l., 7-141 p. 20 cm. [BX6333.P7A8] 21-21712
I. Title.

Salvation army.

BEGBIE, Harold, 1871-1929. 266
The life of General William Booth, the founder of the Salvation army, by Harold Begbie ... New York, The Macmillan company, 1920. 2 v. fronts., plates, ports., facsim. 22 1/2 cm. [HV4334.B7B4 1920 a]
1. Booth, William, 1829-1912. 2. Salvation army. I. Title.

BISHOP, Edward 922.89
Blood and fire! The story of General William Booth and the Salvation Army. Chicago, Moody [1965, c.1964] 114p. illus. ports. 20cm. Bibl. [BX9743.B7B5] 65-4089 2.50 bds.,
1. Booth, William, 1829—1912. 2. Salvation Army. I. Title.

BOOTH, Maud Ballington (Charlesworth) Mrs., 1865. 267.
Beneath two flags. By Maud 0. Booth ... New York, London, Bunk & Wagnalls, 1889. ix. [1] [11]-288 p. front., illus (music) plates. 19 1/2cm. A history of Salvation army life. [BX9715.B6] 12-30828
1. Salvation army. I. Title.

BRENGLE, Elizabeth (Swift) Mrs. 1849-
The Army drum, by Mrs. Colonel Brengle. London, New York [etc.] The Salvation army book department, 1909. 179 p. 19 cm. [HV4337.B8] 9-17331
1. Salvation army. I. Title.
Contents omitted.

CARPENTER, Minnie Lindsay (Rowell) 922.
The angel adjutant of "twice born men," by Minnie L. Carpenter; introduction by General Bramwell Booth, foreword by Commander Evangeline Booth. New York, Chicago [etc.] Fleming H. Revell co. [c1922] 190 p. 19 1/2 cm. [BX9743.L4C3] 23-483
1. Lee, Kate. 2. Salvation army. I. Title.

COATES, Thomas F. G. 205
The prophet of the poor; the life-story of General Booth, by Thomas F. G. Coates ... New York, E. P. Dutton and company, 1906. xii, 354 p., 1 l. front. (port.) 20 1/2 cm. [HV4334.B7C6] 6-10889
1. Booth, William, 1829-1912. 2. Salvation army. I. Title.

DAVIS, Morrison Meade, 1850-
... *How to be saved;* a study of first principles, by M. M. Davis ... Cincinnati, The Standard publishing company [c1914] 206 p. 20 cm. (Phillips Bible institute series of efficiency text-books for Bible schools and churches) "This book is both an abbreviation and expansion of the author's work on 'First principles.'"--Foreword. 15-4964
I. Title.

FRIEDERICHS, Hulda.
The romance of the Salvation army, by Hulda Friederichs. With a preface by General Booth ... London, New York [etc.] Cassell and company, limited, 1907. 5 p. l., 215, [1] p. front. (port.) 7 pl. 21 cm. "First edition October 1907, reprinted November 1907." [HV4386.F88] 8-9033
1. Salvation army. I. Booth, William, 1829-1912. II. Title.

GULLEY, Samuel Samson, 1859-
Happy Sam, the converted miner. The reminiscences of a Salvation army captain. Samuel S. Gulley. Louisville, Ky., Pentecostal publishing company [c1918] 68 p. 19 cm. [BV9743.G8A3] 19-13065
I. Title.

HAGGARD, Henry Rider, Sir, 1856-1925.
The poor and the land; being a report on the Salvation army colonies in the United States and at Hadleigh, England, with scheme of national land settlement and an introduction; by H. Rider Haggard... With twelve illustrations. London, New York [etc.] Longmans, Green, and co., 1905. xii, 157 p. 12 illus. on 6 pl. (incl. front.) 19 1/2 cm. [HF1516.G7H32] 5-42512
1. Salvation army. 2. Agricultural colonies—U.S. 3. Hadleigh, Eng. 4. Agricultural colonies. I. Title.

HAGGARD, Henry Rider, Sir, 1856-1925.
Regeneration; being an account of the social work of the Salvation army in Great Britain, by H. Rider Haggard. New York, London [etc.] Longmans, Green & co., 1910. 264 p. incl. tables. front., pl., ports. 20 cm. [HV4386H] A 11
1. Salvation army. 2. Gt.Brit.—Soc. condit. I. Title.

HALL, Clarence Wilbur, 1902- 922.89
Our of the depths the life-story of Henry F. Milans, by Ensign Clarence W. Hall;foreword by Evangeline C. Booth... New York, Chicago [etc.] Fleming H. Revell company [c1930] 224 p. front. (port.) pl. 19 1/2 cm. [BV4935.M5H3] [[920.5]] 31-1112
1. Milanes, Henry Fetter, 1961- 2. Salvation army. I. Title.

HARRIS, William G 267.15
Stuff that makes an army. [New York] Salvation Army Supplies, Print. and Pub. Dept. [1962] 157 p. 23 cm. [BX9721.2H3] 62-21024
1. Salvation Army. I. Title.

LEE, Porter Raymond, 1879-
Social salvage; a study of the central organization and administration of the Salvation army. [By] Porter R. Lee and Walter W. Pettit ... New York, National information bureau, 1924. 124 p. incl. tables, diagrs. 23 1/2 cm. A 27
1. Salvation army. 2. Social service. I. Pettit, Walter William, 1882- II. Title.

MACKENZIE, Frederick Arthur, 1869-
The clash of the cymbals; the secret history of the revolt in the Salvation army, by F. A. Mackenzie. New York, London [etc.] Brentano's, ltd. [1929] 223, [1] p. front., ports. 19 1/2 cm. "Printed in Great Britain." [BX9726.M25] 29-14113
1. Booth, Bramwell, 1856-1929. 2. Booth, Evangeline Cory, 1865- 3. Salvation army. I. Title.

MANSON, John.
The Salvation army and the public; a religious, social, and financial study, by John Manson. London, G. Routledge and sons limited; New York, E. P. Dutton and co., 1906. xix, 376 p. 19 1/2 cm. [HV4337.M3] 7-15897
1. Salvation army. I. Title.

NELLER, Earl.
"You Brutus" if you please, by Earl Neller ... St. Louis, Mo., Mound city press, inc. [c1929] 1 p. l., 238 p. 20 cm. "One example of what happens frequently in the Salvation army."--Foreword. [BX9723.N4] 29-1096
1. Salvation army. I. Title.

NELSON, William Hamilton, 1878- 922.
Blood & fire: General William Booth, by William Hamilton Nelson. New York, London, The Century co. [c1929] xv p., 2 l., 3-269 p. front., ports. 21 cm. Bibliography; p. 269. [BX9743.B7N4] 29-23812 2.50
1. Booth, William, 1823-1912. 2. Salvation army. I. Title.

OTTMAN, Ford Cyrinde, 1859-1929. 922.
Herbert Booth; a biography, by Ford C. Ottman. Garden City, N. Y., Doubleday, Doran & company, inc., 1928. xiii p., 1 l., 477 p. front. (port.) 21 cm. [BX9743.B65O8] 28-20541
1. Booth, Herbert, 1882-1926. 2. Salvation army. I. Title.

PALMER, Agnes Lizzie (Page) Mrs., 1874-
1904-1926. The time between; reviewing the progress of the Salvation army in the United States under the leadership of Commander Evangeline Booth, by Agnes L. Palmer. [New York, S. A. print., 1926] 123, [1] p. illus. (incl. ports.) 26 cm. Cover-title: Twenty-two. [BX9716.P3] 27-21549
1. Booth, Evangeline Cory, 1865- 2. Salvation army. I. Title. II. Title: The time between 1904 and 1926.

REDWOOD, Hugh. 267.150942
God in the shadows, by Hugh Redwood ... New York [etc.] Fleming H. Revell company [c1932] 127 p. 20 cm. "Autobiographical, but it is not autobiography."--Pref. [HV4387.R35 1932 a] 32-25105
1. Salvation army. I. Title.

REDWOOD, Hugh. 267.150942
God in the slums, by Hugh Redwood, introduction by Evangeline C. Booth ... New York, Chicago [etc.] Fleming H. Revell company [c1931] 167 p. 19 cm. [HV4387.R4] 31-5179
1. Salvation army. 2. Poor—Gt. Brit. I. Title.

SALVATION army. 267.150973
Service, an exposition of the Salvation army in America. New York city, National headquarters [1937] 155 p., 1 l. incl. illus. (incl. map) ports. 19 cm. "Printed...1937." [BX9721.A5 1937] 38-34322
1. Salvation army. I. Title.

SALVATION army. 267.15
What is the Salvation army? An interpretation of its aims, methods and activities. New York city, Eastern territorial headquarters [1924] 82, [5] p. 19 cm. "Publications--list of books and pamphlets for reference and study": p. 78-82. [BX9721.A5 1924] 35-84756
1. Salvation army. I. Title.

SALVATION army. 267.
What is the Salvation army? An interpretation of its aims, methods and activities. New York city, Eastern territorial headquarters [1926] 82, [5] p. 18 1/2 cm. On cover: Sequi-centennial edition. [BX9721.A5] 28-1578
1. Salvation army. I. Title.

SEARCH, Pamela. 267.15
Happy warriors; the story of the social work of the Salvation Army. [1st ed.] London, New York, Arco Publishers [1956] 173p. illus. 23cm. [HV4337.S4] 56-3510
1. Salvation Army. I. Title.

SEARCH, Pamela. 267.15
Happy warriors: the story of the social work of the Salvation Army. 1st ed. London, New York, Arco Publishers [1956] 173p. illus. 23cm. [HV4337.S4] 56-3510
1. Salvation Army. I. Title.

STEAD, William Thomas, 1849-1912.
Life of Mrs. Booth, the founder of the Salvation army, by W. T. Stead ... New York, Chicago [etc.] Fleming H. Revell company [c1900] 256 p. front. (port.) 20 cm. [HV4334.B6S7] 0-6965
1. Booth, Catherine (Mumford) "Mrs. William Booth." 1829-1890. 2. Salvation army. I. Title.

STEELE, Harold C 922.89
I was a stranger; the faith of William Booth, founder of the Salvation Army. With a foreword by B. O. Williams. [1st ed.] New York, Exposition Press [1954] 183p. illus. 21cm. 'Exposition-Banner book. [BX9743.B7S7] 54-5558
1. Booth, William, 1829-1912. 2. Salvation Army. I. Title.

TORREY, Reuben Archer, 1856- 248
How to be saved, and how to be lost; the way of salvation and the way of condemnation made as plain as day, by R. A. Torrey... New York, Chicago [etc.] Fleming H. Revell company [c1923] 218 p. 19 1/2 cm. [BV4915.T6] 23-18242
I. Title.

WILLIAMS, Stephen Bassanno, 1882-
The Salvation army today, by S. B. Williams ... an exposure revealing an unholy and unethical condition of affairs not suspected by the American public. [2d ed.] Chicago, Ill., G. W. Perry; Lincoln, Neb., The Church press, c1915. 51 p. incl. front. (port.) 18 1/2 cm. [HV4344.W5 1915] 15-7409
1. Salvation army. I. Title.

WILSON, Philip Whitwell, 922.89 1875-
General Evangeline Booth, by P. Whitwell Wilson ... New York [etc.] Fleming H. Revell company [c1935] 127 p. front. (port.) 19 1/2 cm. London edition (Hodder and Stoughton) has title: The General: the story of Evangeline Booth. [BX9743.B63W5 1935b] 35-15286
1. Booth, Evangeline Cory, 1865- 2. Salvation army. I. Title.

WILSON, Philip Whitwell, 922.89 1875-
General Evangeline Booth of the Salvation Army. New York, C. Scribner's Sons, 1948. 264 p. ports. 22 cm. [BX9743.B63W52] 48-3749
1. Booth, Evangeline Cory, 1865- 2. Salvation Army. I. Title.

Salvation Army—Charities.

SANDALL, Robert. 267'.15'09 s
Social reform and welfare work; 1883-1953 1883-1953. London, New York, T. Nelson, 1955. xiv, 369 p. illus. 23 cm. (His The History of the Salvation Army, v. 3) Bibliography: p. 361-364. [BX9715.S3 vol. 3] [BX9727.3] 361.7'5 74-171957
1. Salvation Army—Charities. I. Title. II. Series.

Salvation Army—Doctrinal and controversial works.

COUTTS, John James. 230
This we believe : a study of the background and meaning of Salvation Army doctrines / by John J. Coutts. London : Salvation Army International Headquarters, 1976. 133 p. ; 19 cm. (Challenge books) Includes bibliographical references. [BX9721.2.C68] 76-373787 ISBN 0-85412-282-6 : £0.60
1. Salvation Army—Doctrinal and controversial works. I. Title.

Salvation Army—Doctrinal and controversial works—Addresses, essays, lectures.

†*HERITAGE of holiness :* 234'.1
a compilation of papers on the historical background of holiness teaching. New York : Salvation Army, c1977. 110 p. : ill. ; 20 cm. "This compilation ... is the result of the combined efforts of the Salvation Army's Eastern Territorial Historical Commission and the Literary Board. Five of these papers originally were presented at the first Historical Commission Congress." Includes bibliographical references. [BX9721.2.H4] 78-113630 ISBN 0-89216-013-6 : 3.50
1. Salvation Army—Doctrinal and controversial works—Addresses, essays, lectures. 2. Holiness—Addresses, essays, lectures. I. Salvation Army. Eastern Territorial Historical Commission. II. Salvation Army. Literary Board.

Salvation Army—Exeter, Eng.—Biography.

BRADDICK, Muriel. 362.4'092'4 B
Born for a purpose / [by] Muriel Braddick. St. Ives, Cornwall : United Writers Publications, 1976. 158 p. ; 22 cm. [BX9743.B845A33] 76-374950 ISBN 0-901976-34-2 : £1.95
1. Salvation Army—Exeter, Eng.—Biography. 2. Braddick, Muriel. 3. Church work with the handicapped. I. Title.

Salvation Army—History

NEAL, Harry Edward, 267.1509 1906-
The Hallelujah Army. Philadelphia, Chilton [c.1961] 261 p. illus. 61-16619 4.95
1. Salvation Army—Hist. I. Title.

NYGAARD, Norman Eugene, 922.89 1897-
Trumpet of salvation: the story of William and Catherine Booth. Grand Rapids, Zondervan Pub. House [1961] 180p. 21cm. [BX9743.B7N9] 61-1590
1. Booth, William, 1829-1912. 2. Booth, Catherine (Mumford) 1829-1800. 3. Salvation Army—Hist. I. Title.

SANDALL, Robert. 267.15
The history of the Salvation Army. Foreword by General Orsborn. London, New York, T. Nelson [1947- v. illus., ports. 22 cm. Bibliography: v. 1. p. 295-296. [BX9715.S3] 47-6828
1. Salvation Arym—Hist. I. Title.
Contents omitted.

Salvation Army—History—Juvenile literature.

FELLOWS, Lawrence. 267'.15
A gentle war : the story of the Salvation Army / by Lawrence Fellows ; photos. by Janet Beller. New York : Macmillan, c1979. 88 p. : ill. ; 24 cm. Includes index. Bibliography: p. [83]-84. Examines the history, goals, and work of the Salvation Army. [BX9715.F44] 79-14622 ISBN 0-02-734430-4 : 7.95
1. Salvation Army—History—Juvenile literature. 2. [Salvation Army—History.] I. Beller, Janet. II. Title.

Salvation Army—Puerto Rico—History.

CHESHAM, Sallie. 267'.15'097295
One hand upon another / by Sallie Chesham. New York : Salvation Army, c1978. 160 p. : ill. ; 22 cm. Includes index. Bibliography: p. 153-154. [BX9719.P9C46] 78-113254 ISBN 0-89216-016-0 : 2.95
1. Salvation Army—Puerto Rico—History. I. Title.
Pub. address : 145 W. 15th St. NY,NY 10011

Salvation army—Sermons.

MILANS, Henry Foster, 1861- 243
Sermons without texts, by Henry F. Milans. Chicago, Ill., The Salvation army, inc. [c1940] 1 p. l., 5-191 p. 19 cm. "Appeared from week to week in the Chicago War cry."--Foreword. [BX9727.M5S4] 40-14011
1. Salvation army—Sermons. 2. Sermons, American. I. Title.

Salvation Army—United States

BOOTH Tucker, 267'.15'0973 Frederick St. George de Lautour, 1853-1929.
The Salvation Army in America; selected reports, 1899-1903. New York, Arno Press, 1972. 983-1005, [85], 37, 32 p. illus. 24 cm. (Religion in America, series II) Contents.Contents.—Farm colonies of the Salvation Army [first published in 1903]—The Salvation Army in the United States [first published in 1899]—The social relief work of the Salvation Army in the United States [first published in 1900]—The Salvation Army as a temperance movement. [BX9716.B68 1972] 79-38439 ISBN 0-405-04060-1
1. Salvation Army—United States. I. Title.

BOOTH TUCKER, Frederick St. George de Lautour, 1853-1929.
The Salvation army in the United States Christmas, 1899. [New York, The Salvation army printing and engraving dept., 1899] [85] p. illus. 17 1/2 x 23 cm. [BX9716.B7] 45-51265
1. Salvation army—U.S. I. Title.

CHESHAM, Sallie. 267.150973
Born to battle; the Salvation Army in America. Chicago, Rand McNally [1965] 286 p. illus., ports. 22 cm. [BX9716.C5] 65-18586
1. Salvation Army—U.S. I. Title.

SALVATION Army. Men's Social Service.
Handbook of standards, principles and policies. New York, 1960. 263 p. 22 cm. 66-32434
1. Salvation Army—U. S. I. Title.

WISBEY, Herbert Andrew, 267.15 1919-
Soldiers without swords; a history of the Salvation Army in the United States. New York, Macmillan, 1955. 242 p. illus. 22 cm. [BX9716.W5] 55-13783
1. Salvation Army—U.S. I. Title.

Salvation Army—United States—History.

MCKINLEY, Edward H. 267'.15'0973
Marching to glory : the history of the Salvation Army in the United States of America, 1880-1980 / Edward H. McKinley. 1st ed. San Francisco : Harper & Row, c1980. xviii, 286 p., [4] leaves of plates : ill. ; 21 cm. Includes bibliographical references and index. [BX9716.M32 1980] 79-2997 ISBN 0-06-065538-0 : 7.95
1. Salvation Army—United States—History. I. Title.

Salvation — Biblical teaching.

GORRIE, Ron, 1908-
Man's greatest question; precisely how good does a man have to be before God will let him pass into heaven? Startling new light on Christianity. New York, Exposition Press [c1965] 225 p. diag. (fold.) 20 cm. 67-39207
1. Salvation — Biblical teaching. I. Title.

GROOT, A de, S.V.D.
The Bible on the salvation of nations. Trans. by F. Vander Heijden. De Pere, Wisc., St. Norbert Abbey Press, 1966. 149 p. 17 cm. 67-91150
1. Salvation — Biblical teaching. I. Title.

RUST, Eric Charles 234
Salvation history; a Biblical interpretation. Richmond, Knox [c.1962] 325p. 21cm. Bibl. 62-19459 6.00
1. Salvation—Biblical teaching. 2. Eschatology—Biblical teaching. I. Title.

SAWYER, John F. A. 234
Semantics in Biblical research; new methods of defining Hebrew words for salvation [by] John F. A. Sawyer. Naperville, Ill., A. R. Allenson [1972] xii, 146 p. 22 cm. (Studies in Biblical theology, 2d ser., 24) "Revised version of a thesis submitted to the Faculty of Divinity in the University of Edinburgh in 1968 under the title, Language about salvation." Bibliography: p. [130]-136. [BT752.S28 1972] 72-75901 ISBN 0-8401-3074-0
1. Bible. O.T.—Language, style. 2. Salvation—Biblical teaching. 3. Ysh' (Hebrew root) I. Title. II. Series.

WARD, Ronald Arthur. 234
The pattern of our salvation : a study of New Testament unity / Ronald A. Ward. Waco, Tex. : Word Books, c1978. 433 p. ; 24 cm. Includes indexes. Bibliography: p. 410-422. [BS2617.8.W37] 77-75454 ISBN 0-8499-0002-6 : 12.95
1. Bible. N.T. Acts, Epistles, and Revelation—Theology. 2. Salvation—Biblical teaching. I. Title.

Salvation—Caricatures and cartoons.

CHICK, Jack T. 234'.02'07
The battle, by Jack T. Chick. Chino, Calif., Chick Publications [1972] 96 p. illus. 13 cm. [BT753.C48] 72-84847 1.25
1. Salvation—Caricatures and cartoons. I. Title.

Salvation—Comparative studies.

BRADEN, Charles Samuel, 1887- 291
Man's quest for salvation; an historical and comparative study of the idea of salvation in the world's great living religions, by Charles Samuel Braden ... Chicago, New York, Willett, Clark & company, 1941. xii p., 1 l., 274 p. 20 cm. Bibliography: p. 261-263. Bibliographical foot-notes. [BL85.B76] 41-26723
1. Salvation—Comparative studies. I. Title.

BRANDON, Samuel George 291.22082 Frederick, ed.
The saviour god; comparative studies in the concept of salvation, presented to Edwin Oliver James, professor emeritus in the Univ. of London, by colleagues and friends to commemorate his seventy-fifth birthday. New York, Barnes & Noble [c.1963] xxii, 242p. port. 23cm. Bibl. 63-25478 7.50
1. James, Edwin Oliver, 1886- 2. Salvation—Comparative studies. I. Title.

BRAUNTHAL, Alfred. 291.2'2
Salvation and the perfect society : the eternal quest / by Alfred Braunthal. Amherst : University of Massachusetts Press, 1979. p. cm. [BL476.B7] 79-4705 ISBN 0-87023-273-8 lib. bdg. : 25.00
1. Salvation—Comparative studies. 2. Utopias. 3. Religions. 4. Humanism. I. Title.

DE ROPP, Robert S. 234
Science and salvation, a scientific appraisal of religion's central theme. New York St. Martin's [c.1962] 308p. 22cm. Bibl. 62-11103 5.00
1. Salvation—Comparative studies. 2. Religion and science—1946- I. Title.

PADOVANO, Anthony T. 291.2'2
American culture and the quest for Christ, by Anthony T. Padovano. New York, Sheed & Ward [1970] x, 309 p. 22 cm. Includes bibliographical references. [BL85.P26] 77-82597 6.95
1. Salvation—Comparative studies. 2. U.S.—Civilization. I. Title.

THIBAULT, B[enoit] C[lovis] 1854-
... *Salvation and sanctification;* will Protestants be saved? By Rev. B. C. Thibault ... New York, Christian press association publishing company, 1906. 232 p. 12 cm. 6-22288
I. Title.

Salvation—Comparative studies—Addresses, essays, lectures.

BRANDON, Samuel George 291.2'2 Frederick, ed.
The saviour god : comparative studies in the concept of salvation / presented to Edwin Oliver James by colleagues and friends to commemorate his seventy-fifth birthday ; edited by S. G. F. Brandon. Westport, Conn. : Greenwood Press, 1980, c1963. xxii, 242 p., [1] leaf of plates : port. ; 22 cm. Reprint of the ed. published by Manchester university Press, Manchester, England. English, Italian, or French. "A list of the principal published writings of E. O. James: p. [BL475.B7 1980] 80-14924 ISBN 0-313-22416-1 lib. bdg. : 22.50
1. James, Edwin Oliver, 1886- — Addresses, essays, lectures. 2. Salvation—Comparative studies—Addresses, essays, lectures. I. James, Edwin Oliver, 1886- II. Title.

BROUGHTON, Leonard Gaston.
Salvation and the old theology; pivot points in Romans by Rev. Len G. Broughton ... New York, Chicago [etc.] F. H. Revell company [c1908] 188 p. 29 cm. "Salvation and the old theology, or pivot points in Romans' consists of a series of Friday night talks given before the Tabernacle Bible school, and revised with much care for publication."--Pref. 8-9520
I. Title.

LIVING faiths and 291.2'2
ultimate goals : salvation and world religions / edited by S. J. Samartha. 1st U.S. ed. Maryknoll, N.Y. : Orbis Books, c1974. xvii, 119 p. ; 24 cm. Result of the world conference on mission and evangelism held at Bangkok from Dec. 29, 1972 to Jan. 8, 1973 on the theme: Salvation today. Includes bibliographical references. [BL476.L58] 75-7610 ISBN 0-88344-297-3 pbk. : 3.95
1. Salvation—Comparative studies—Addresses, essays, lectures. I. Samartha, Stanley J.

Salvation—Early works to 1800.

BUNYAN, John, 1628- 230'.044 s 1688.
Instruction for the ignorant ; Light for them that sit in darkness ; Saved by grace ; Come, & welcome, to Jesus Christ / John Bunyan ; edited by Richard L. Greaves. Oxford : Clarendon Press ; New York : Oxford University Press, 1979. lv, 413 p., [4] leaves of plates : ill. ; 22 cm. (The Miscellaneous works of John Bunyan ; v. 8) Bibliography: p. [xv]-xvi. [BR75.B73 1976 vol. 8] [BT750] 230'.044 77-30369 ISBN 0-19-812736-7 : 49.00
1. Salvation—Early works to 1800. 2. Christian life—Miscellanea. I. Greaves, Richard L. II. Title.

FISHER, Edward, fl. 1627- 234 1655, supposed author.
The marrow of modern divinity. Touching the covenant of works, and the covenant of grace: with their use and end, both in the time of the Old Testament, and in the time of the New. Clearly describing the way to eternal life by Jesus Christ. In a dialogue "betwixt: Evangelista, a minister of the gospel. Nomista, a legalist. Antinomists, an antinomian. And, Neophytus, a young Christian. By E. Fisher. The 10th ed. With the commendatory epistles of divers divines of great esteem in the city of London. Boston, Printed by Green, Bushell, and Allen, for D. Henchman in Cornhil, 1743. 2 p. l., 3, [13], 279 p. 14 1/2 cm. First published in 1645 under the initials E. F. Tanner's edition of Wood's "Athene", 1721, identified the author with "Edward Fisher, M.A., of Oxford", and the identification has been accepted by many. According to the Dict. of nat. biog. "Internal evidenne completely disproves It." [BT750.F5 1743] 8-25629
1. Salvation—Early works to 1800. 2. Covenants (Theology) 3. Antinomiauism. I. Title.

HALYBURTON, Thomas, 1674- 234 1712.
The great concern of salvation. In three parts. I. A discovery of man's natural state; or, The guilty sinner convicted. II. Man's recovery by faith in Christ; or, The convinced sinner's case and cure. III. The Christian's duty, with respect to both personal and family religion. By the late Rev. Thomas Halyburton ... 2d Elizabeth town ed. Elizabeth town, N.J. Published by Mervin Hale. J. & E. Sanderson, printers. 1815. ix, [11]-428 p. 18 cm. [BT750.H2 1815] 41-31259
1. Salvation—Early works to 1800. I. Title.

HALYBURTON, Thomas, 1674- 234 1712.
The great concern of salvation. By the Rev. Thomas Halyburton ... Philadelphia, Presbyterian board of publication [1838] 176 p. 15 1/2 cm. "Advertisement" signed: Charles C. Corse. [BT750.H2 1838] 40-25512
1. Salvation—Early works to 1800. I. Corss, Charles C., 1804?—1896, ed. II. Presbyterian church in the U.S.A. (Old school) Board of publication. III. Title.
Contents omitted.

HALYBURTON, Thomas, 1674- 234 1712.
The great concern of salvation in three parts. or, The convinced sinner's case and cure. III. The Christian's duty, with respect to both personal and family religion. By the late Rev. Thomas Halyburton ... Elizabeth town [N.J.] Published by Mervin Hale, R. and P. Canfield, printers, 1814. viii, [9]-139, [1], 198, 127, [1] p. 18 cm. [BT750.H2 1814] 44-25374
1. Salvation—Early works to 1800. I. Title.

HAMMOND, William, 1718-1783. 234
The marrow of the church. The doctrines of Christ's righteousness imputed, and regeneration, fairly stated and clearly demonstrated from the homilies, Articles and liturgies, of the Church of England. Confirmed by apposite texts of Scripture, with proper reflections, inferences, and instructions annexed to each head. Being the substance of several discourses delivered at Cambridge, Bristol, & c., by William Hammond ... London--Printed: New York, Reprinted and published by Isaac Riley. 1816. xxii, 274 p., 1 l. 20 1/2 cm. A continuation of the author's Medulla ecclesiac. The doctrines of original sin, justification by faith, and the Holy Spirit. 1744. [BT750.H25] 41-36239
1. Salvation—Early works to 1800. 2. Church of England—Doctrinal and controversial works. I. Title.

JOHNSON, John, 1706-1791. 234
A mathematical question, propounded by the vicegerent of the world; answered by the King of glory. Enigmatically represented, and demonstratively opened by John Johnson ... The 1st Exeter ed. Exeter [N.H.]: Printed and sold by Henry Ranley, M,DCC,LXXXIX. 1 p. l., 116 p. 18 cm. [BT750.J6 1789] 43-38096
1. Salvation—Early works to 1800. I. Title.

JOHNSON, John, 1706-1791. 234
A mathematical question, propounded by the vicegerent of the world; answered by the King of glory: enigmatically represented, and demonstratively opened. By John Johnson ... Amherst [N.H.] Printed by Samuel Preston, and sold at his printing-office. 1797. 132 p. 16 cm. [BT750.J6 1797] 43-30405
1. Salvation—Early works to 1800. I. Title.

Salvation—History of doctrines.

BLOESCH, Donald G., 1928- 234
Jesus is victor! : Karl Barth's doctrine of salvation / Donald G. Bloesch. Nashville : Abingdon, c1976. 176 p. ; 19 cm. Includes bibliographical references and index. [BT751.2.B54] 76-14360 ISBN 0-687-20225-6 pbk. : 5.95
1. Barth, Karl, 1886-1968. 2. Salvation—History of doctrines. I. Title.

MINEAR, Paul Sevier, 1906- 234.09
... *And great shall be your reward:* the origins of Christian views of salvation, by Paul S. Minear. New Haven, Yale university press, London, H. Milford, Oxford university press, 1941. vii, 74 p. 25 1/2cm. (Yale studies in religion, no. 12) "Based upon a dissertation presented to the faculty of the Graduate school of Yale university ... for the degree of doctor of philosophy. The title of that dissertation was 'The development of ethical sanctions in Judaism, Hellenism, and early Christianity'."--Pref. [BT752.M5] 41-10222
1. Salvation—History of doctrines. 2. Salvation—Comparative studies. 3. Bible. N.T.—Theology. 4. Bible—Theology—N.T. I. Title.

MURRMAN, Warren 234'.092'4 Daniel.
The significance of the human nature of Christ and the Sacraments for salvation according to William Estius. Latrobe, Pa., Saint Vincent Archabbey, c1970. xvii, 259 p. 23 cm. Inaug. Diss.—Munich, 1967. Includes bibliographical references. [BT198.M87] 74-158340
1. Jesus Christ—History and doctrines—17th century. 2. Estius, Guilielmus, 1542-1613. 3. Salvation—History of doctrines. 4. Sacraments—History of doctrines. I. Title.

PFURTNER, Stephanus 234
Luther and Aquinas on salvation. Tr. [from German] by Edward Quinn. Introd. by Jaroslav Pelikan. New York, Sheed [1965, c.1964] 160p. 21cm. Bibl. [BT752.P453] 65-12206 3.50
1. Luther, Martin, 1483-1546—Theology. 2. Thomas Aquinas, Saint, 1225?-1274—Theology. 3. Salvation—History of doctrines. 4. Assurance (Theology)—History of doctrines. I. Title.

ROGERS, Jack Bartlett. 232'.09
Case studies in Christ and salvation / by Jack Rogers, Ross Mackenzie, Louis Weeks. Philadelphia : Westminster Press, c1977. 176 p. ; 23 cm. Includes bibliographies. [BT198.R63] 76-53765 ISBN 0-664-24133-6 pbk. 7.95
1. Jesus Christ—History of doctrines. 2. Salvation—History of doctrines. I. Mackenzie, Ross, 1927- joint author. II. Weeks, Louis, 1941- joint author. III. Title.

WEBB, Robert Alexander, 1856- 262 1919.
Christian salvation, its doctrine and experience, by Robert Alexander Webb ... Richmond, Va., Presbyterian committee of publication, 1921. 437 p. front. (port.) 23 cm. [BT751.W4] 21-18506
I. Title.

WELLS, David F. 234
The search for salvation / David F. Wells. Downers Grove, Ill. : InterVarsity Press, c1978 176 p. ; 21 cm. (Issued in contemporary theology) Includes bibliographical references and index. [BT751.2.W42 1978] 78-2076 ISBN 0-87784-706-1 : 3.95
1. Salvation—History of doctrines. I. Title. II. Series.

WIEDERKEHR, Dietrich. 234'.09
Belief in redemption : concepts of salvation from the New Testament to the present time / Dietrich Wiederkehr ; translated by Jeremy Moiser. Atlanta : J. Knox Press, c1979. 109 p. ; 22 cm. Translation of Glaube an Erlosung. Includes bibliographical references and indexes. [BT751.2.W4813 1979] 78-24088 ISBN 0-8042-0476-4 pbk. : 5.95
1. Salvation—History of doctrines. I. Title.

Salvation—Meditations.

LIGUORI, Alfonso Maria de', 234 Saint, 1696-1787.
The way of salvation, to which is added A Christian's rule of life. Meditations for every day in the year, tr. from the Italian. New York, Catholic Book Pub. Co. [1948] 318 p. 16 cm. [BT750.L52] 48-9457
1. Salvation—Meditations. 2. Christian life—Catholic authors. I. Title. II. Title: A Christian's rule of life.

LIGUORI, Alfonso Maria de', 242 Saint, 1696-1787.
The way of salvation and of perfection. Meditations--pious relections--spiritual treatises, by St. Alphonsus de Liguori ... edited by Rev. Eugene Grimm ... Brooklyn, St. Louis [etc.] Redemptorist fathers [c1926] 512 p. 19 cm. (Half-title: The complete works of Saint Alphonsus de Liguori ... tr. from the Italian. Ed. by Rev. Eugene Grimm ... The ascetical works. Vol. ii) [BX890.L5 1926 vol. 2] 26-7841
1. Salvation—Meditations. 2. Spiritual life—Catholic authors. I. Grimm, Eugene, 1835-1891, ed. II. Title.

Salvation—Miscellanea.

BEALL, James Lee. 234
Laying the foundation / James Lee Beall, Marjorie Barber. Plainfield, N.J. : Logos International, c1976. xvii, 389 p. ; 21 cm. [BT753.B39] 76-42084 ISBN 0-88270-198-3 pbk. : 4.95
1. Salvation—Miscellanea. I. Barber, Marjorie, joint author. II. Title.

Salvation outside the Catholic Church.

CAMPBELL, Robert Edward, 234 1924-
Catholic theology and the human race. [Maryknoll, N. Y.] Maryknoll Publications [1956?] 54p. 24cm. (World horizon reports, report no. 17) Includes bibliography. [BT755.C3] 58-22513
1. Salvation outside the Catholic Church. I. Title.

CLARKE, Catherine Goddard. 234
Gate of Heaven. Cambridge, Mass., Saint Benedict Center [1951] 145 p. 19 cm. [BT755.C58] 52-349
1. Salvation outside the Catholic Church. 2. St. Benedict Center. Cambridge, Mass. 3. Catholic Church—Doctrinal and controversial works—Miscellaneous authors. I. Title.

CLARKE, Catherine Goddard. 234
Gate of heaven. Boston, Ravengate Press, 1952 ['1951] 141 p. 20 cm. [BT755.C58 1951a] 52-7634
1. Salvation outside the Catholic Church. 2. St. Benedict Center, Cambridge, Mass. 3. Catholic Church—Doctrinal and controversial works—Miscellaneous authors. I. Title.

CONGAR, Marie Joseph, 234 [Secular name: Georges Yves Congar] 1904-
The wide world my parish; salvation and its problems [by] Yves Congar. Tr. [from French] by Donald Attwater. Baltimore, Helicon Pr. [c.1961] 188p. Bibl. 61-14675 4.50 bds.,
1. Salvation outside the Catholic Church. I. Title.

CONGAR, Yves Marie Joseph, 234 1904-
The wide world my parish; salvation and its problems [by] Yves Congar. Translated by Donald Attwater. Baltimore, Helicon Press [1961] 188 p. 21 cm. [BT755.C653] 61-14675
1. Salvation outside the Catholic Church. I. Title.

EMINYAN, Maurice, 1922- 234
The theology of salvation. [Boston] St. Paul Editions [dist. Daughters of St. Paul, c.1960] 233p. Bibl. 60-53304 4.00; 3.00 pap.,
1. Salvation outside the Catholic Church. I. Title.

LOMBARDI, Riccardo. 234
The salvation of the unbeliever. [Translation from the Italian by Dorothy M. White] Westminster, Md., Newman Press [1956] 376p. 23cm. [BT755.L62] 56-11424
1. Salvation outside the Catholic Church. I. Title.

PROSPER, Tiro, Aquitanus, Saint. Spurious and doubtful works. 234
The call of all nations; translated and annotated by P. de Letter. Westminster, Md., Newman Press, 1952. 234 p. 23 cm. (Ancient Christian writers; the works of the Fathers in translation, no. 14) Variously ascribed to St. Prosper, St. Ambrose, and St. Leo the Great. Translation of De vocatione omnium gentium. Bibliographical references included in "Notes" (p. [155]-219) [BR60.A35 no. 14] 52-9014
1. Salvation outside the Catholic Church. 2. Semi-Pelagianism. I. Ambrosius, Saint, Bp. of Milan. Spurious and doubtful works. The call of all nations. II. Leo I, the Great, Saint, Pope, d. 461. Spurious and doubtful works. The call of all nations. III. Letter, Prudentius de, ed. and tr. IV. Title. V. Title: De vocatione omnium gentium. VI. Series.

Salvation outside the church.

KENNY, John Peter, 1916- 291.2'2
Christ outside Christianity: the supernatural in non-Christian religions [by] J. P. Kenny. Melbourne, Spectrum, 1971. viii, 64 p. 18 cm. Bibliography: p. 62-64. [BT759.K45] 73-155503 ISBN 0-909837-09-0 1.50
1. Salvation outside the church. 2. Religions. I. Title.

ROPER, Anita, 1908-
The anonymous Christian. Translated by Joseph Donceel. With an afterword: The anonymous Christian according to Karl Rahner, by Klaus Riesenhuber. New York, Sheed and Ward [1966] ix, 179 p. 22 cm. Bibliographical references for the afterword included in "Notes" (p. 172-179) [TB759.R613] 66-12269
1. Salvation outside the church. I. Title.

ROPER, Anita, 1908- 234
The anonymous Christian. Translated by Joseph Donceel. With an afterword: The anonymous Christian according to Karl Rahner, by Klaus Riesenhuber. New York, Sheed and Ward [1966] ix, 179 p. 22 cm. Bibliographical references for the afterword included in "Notes" (p. 172-179) [BT759.R613] 66-12269
1. Salvation outside the church. I. Title.

WIDMER, R. Rubin. 234
Jesus, the light of the world; a study of contemporary views, by R. Rubin Widmer. Nashville, Southern Pub. Association [1967] 142 p. 22 cm. Bibliography: p. 135-142. [BT759.W5] 67-28845
1. Salvation outside the church. I. Title.

Salvation — Popular works.

ADAMS, Fred Baird, 1883- 234
The way to God and holiness; a study of Bible doctrines. St. Joseph, Mo. [1947] 92 p. 18 cm. [BT751.A3] 47-29558
1. Salvation—Popular works. 2. Holiness. I. Title.

BATES, Maurice L. 234
Saved forever. [By] Maurice L. Bates. Nashville, Broadman Press [1968] 63 p. 19 cm. [BT753.B33] 68-26917
1. Salvation—Popular works. I. Title.

BREED, David Riddle, 1848-1931. 234
Plain progressive talks upon the way of salvation. By Rev. David R. Breed ... New York, American tract society [1878] 56 p. 15 cm. [BT751.B8] 40-25504
1. Salvation—Popular works. I. American tract society. II. Title.

BYRUM, Enoch Edwin, 1861- 234
The secret of salvation, how to get it: and how to keep it. Showing the way of salvation, giving the reader the key with which to unlock its great storehouse of peace and happiness. By E. E. Byrum ... Grand Junction, Mich., Gospel trumpet publishing company, 1896. 4 p. l., 7-408, [1] p. incl. plates. 19 cm. [BT751.B9] 40-25508
1. Salvation—Popular works. I. Title.

COTTRELL, Jack. 234
Being good enough isn't good enough : God's wonderful grace / by Jack Cottrell. Cincinnati : New Life Books, c1976. 96 p. ; 18 cm. [BT751.2.C67] 75-44590 ISBN 0-87239-060-8
1. Salvation—Popular works. 2. Justificaton—Popular works. I. Title.

DE ROSA, Peter. 234
God our Savior; a study of the atonement. Milwaukee, Bruce Pub. Co. [1967] ix, 230 p. 22 cm. (Impact books) Bibliographical footnotes. [BT751.2.D4] 67-28213
1. Salvation—Popular works. I. Title.

DE ROSA, Peter. 234
God our Saviour; a study of the atonement. Milwaukee, Bruce Pub. Co. [1967] ix, 230 p. 22 cm. (Impact books) Bibliographical footnotes. [BT751.2.D4] 67-28213
1. Salvation — Popular works. I. Title.

GREATHOUSE, Josephine A. 234
Calvary life insurance. Santa Monica, Calif., Wesco Publications [1951] 210 p. illus. 24 cm. [BT751.G67] 51-38722
1. Salvation—Popular works. I. Title.

GUIDE to the Savior. 233
Written for the American Sunday School Union and rev. by the Committee of Publication. Philadelphia, American Sunday School Union [1948] 157 p. 16 cm. [BT751.G8] 48-41761
1. Salvation—Popular works. 2. American Sunday School Union.

HARSHA, John W. 234
The song of the redeemed, salvation to God, and to the Lamb. By Rev. J. W. Harsha ... New York, Sheldon & co., 1861. vii, 446 p. front. (port.) 19 cm. [BT751.H27] 40-25513
1. Salvation—Popular works. I. Title.

HARTMAN, A Lincoln. 234
The gospel according to the Scriptures; unique outline method of Bible study. A Course of study comprising twenty-three lessons or examinations, which may be competed in from three to five months. [Rev. ed.] Boston, Christopher Pub. House [1952] 86 p. illus. 21 cm. [BT753.H29] 52-4541
1. Salvation—Popular works. I. Title.

HEGRE, Theodore A
The cross and sanctification, formerly published as Three aspects of the Cross. Minneapolis, Bethany Fellowship [1960] 176 p. illus. 66-24637
1. Salvation — Popular works. 2. Perfection. I. Title.

HEGRE, Theodore A 234
Three aspects of the Cross. Minneapolis, Bethany Fellowship Press [c1960] 276p. illus. 20cm. [BT751.2.H4] 61-45612
1. Salvation—Popular works. 2. Perfection. I. Title.

JAMES, John Angell, 1785-1859. 233
The anxious enquirer after salvation, directed and encouraged. New York, D. Appleton [pref. 1834] 176 p. 16 cm. [BT751.J2 1834] 48-40423
1. Salvation—Popular works. I. Title.

JAMES, John Angell, 1785-1859 234
The anxious inquirer after salvation. By Rev. John Angell James ... Revised under the saction of the author. New York, American tract society [186-!] 199 p. 15 cm. [BT751.J2] 40-25516
1. Salvation—Popular works. I. American tract society. II. Title.

JOHNSON, Early Ashby, 1917- 234
Saved, from what? By E. Ashby Johnson. Richmond, Va., Knox [1966] 79p. 19cm. (Chime paperbacks) [BT751.2.J6] 66-11687 1.00 pap.,
1. Salvation—Popular works. I. Title.

KEAN, Charles Duell, 1910- 234
Christ in our hearts. New York, Abingdon [1957] 109p. 20cm. Bibliographical references included in 'Notes' (p. 107-109) [BT751] 56-10148
1. Salvation—Popular works. I. Title.

MCCOMB, John Hess, 1898- 234
Wondrous truths from the Word, by John Hess McComb ... New York, London [etc.] Fleming H. Revell company [1943] 128 p. 19 cm. [BT753.M23] 48-14428
1. Salvation—Popular works. I. Title.

MCCORD, William J., 1810?-1888. 234
Salvation; or, The sinner directed in the way of life. By The Rev. William J.McCord. Philadelphia, Presbyterian board of publication [1846] vi, 7-113 p. 15 1/2 cm. [BT751.M25] 40-25517
1. Salvation—Popular works. I. Presbyterian chruch in the U.S.A. (Old school) Board of publication. II. Title.

MACGUIRE, Meade. 234
Lambs among wolves. Nashville, Southern Pub. Association [1957] 136p. 18cm. [BT751.M254] 57-29530
1. Salvation—Popular works. I. Title.

MCLEAN, Robert Norris, 1882- 234
... Christianity's compelling conviction, by Robert N. McLean. Philadelphia, The Westminster press, 1941. 72 p. 18 1/2 cm. At head of title: Learning for life. "Issued as a part of the 'Learning for life' plan of guided adult study." [BT753.M25] 41-9626
1. Salvation—Popular works. I. Title. II. Title: Learning for life.

MARTIN, Thomas Theodore, 1862- 262
God's plan with men, by T. T. Martin ... New York, Chicago [etc.] Fleming H. Revell company [1912] 197 p. 19 1/2 cm. "A brief list ... of books that will be helpful to skeptical readers": p. 14-15. [BT751.M29] 12-17652
1. Salvation—Popular works. I. Title.

MURRAY, Ferne H. 231'.7
A journey into His presence : a story of God-man encounters from the beginning to the end of time / by Ferne H. Murray ; [foreword by Morris Cerullo]. San Diego, CA : Day Star Publishers, c1978. 164 p. ; 21 cm. [BT753.M86] 78-73439 ISBN 0-932994-00-8 pbk. : 3.95
1. Salvation—Popular works. I. Title.

NEWBIGIN, James Edward Lesslie, Bp. 234
Sin and salvation. Philadelphia, Westminster Press [1937] 128p. 20cm. [BT751] 57-5901
1. Salvation—Popular works. I. Title.

NEWBIGIN, James Edward Lesslie, Bp. 234
Sin and salvation. Philadelphia, Westminster Press [1957] 128p. 20cm. [BT751] 57-5901
1. Salvation—Popular works. I. Title.

OLESEN, Albert H. 234.3
The golden chain; or, The process of redemption. Mountain View, Calif., Pacific Press Pub. Association [c.1960] 103p. 23cm. 60-10105 3.00
1. Salvation—Popular works. I. Title.

PALMER, Phoebe (Worrell) Mrs. 1807-1874. 234
Incidental illustrations of the economy of salvation, its doctrines and duties. By Mrs. Phoebe Palmer... Boston, H. V. Degen; Binghamton, N.Y., B. W. Gorham, 1855. x, [11]-380 p. front. (port.) 20 cm. [BT751.P2] 40-37153
1. Salvation—Popular works. 2. Homiletical illustrations. I. Title.

PAXSON, Ruth. 234
War in your heart. Chicago, Moody Press [1952] 180 p. 20 cm. [BT751.P35] 52-44403
1. Salvation — Popular works. I. Title.

RHOADS, Samuel G., 1832?-1876. 234
The old way, and only method of salvation. By S. G. Rhoads ... Philadelphia, Perkinpine & Higgins, 1869. xi, 13-240 p. front. 27 cm. [BT751.R4] 40-37155
1. Salvation—Popular works. I. Title.

RING, John.
I am; or, A narrative of creation and salvation through redemption and restoration. By John Ring ... Chicago, Ill., S. B. Shaw, 1906. 141 p. 20 cm. 6-19426
I. Title.

SARLES, John Wesley, 1817-1903. 233
Man's peerless destiny in Christ, "but little lower than God." By John W. Sarles ... New York and London, Funk & Wagnalls company, 1901. 230 p. 19 cm [BT751.S25] 1-10355
1. Salvation—Popular works. I. Title.

SHULER, John Lewis, 1887- 234
Give your guilt away, by J. L. Shuler. Mountain View, Calif., Pacific Press Pub. Association [1972] 62 p. 19 cm. [BT753.S53] 72-79605
1. Salvation—Popular works. I. Title.

THE sinner saved: 234
or, The divine law and saving faith ... By the author of "Child assisted in giving his heart to God." Written for the Massachusetts Sabbath school society, and revised by the Committee of publication. Boston, Massachusetts Sabbath school society, 1845. vi, 7 90 p. incl. front. 15 1/2 cm. [BT753.S6] 42-46485
1. Salvation—Popular works. I. "Child assisted in giving his heart to God." Author of. II. Massachusetts Sabbath school society. Committee of publication. III. Title: The divine law and saving faith.

SIWEL, Hplour, 1940- 234
Society in rebellion. Philadelphia, Dorrance [1973] 22 p. 22 cm. [BT751.2.S54] 73-78155 ISBN 0-8059-1862-0 2.95
1. Salvation—Popular works. I. Title.

STACKPOLE, Everett Schermerhorn, 1850- 234
The evidence of salvation; or, The direct witness of the Spirit, by Rev. Everett S. Stackpole, D.D. New York, Boston, Thomas Y. Crowell & company [1894] viii, 115 p. 17 cm. [BT751.S77] 40-37296
1. Salvation—Popular works. 2. Holy Spirit. I. Title.

SUMMERS, Thomas Osmond, 1812-1882. 234
The way of salvation. By Thos. O. Summers, D.D. Nashville, Tenn., Southern Methodist publishing house, 1879. 176 p. 18 cm. [BT751.S9] 40-37297
1. Salvation—Popular works. I. Title.

WORDSWORTH, Ephraim Edward 1887- 234
Steps to heaven. Kansas City, Mo., Beacon Hill Press [1955] 103p. 19cm. [HF753] 55-14618
1. Salvation—Popular works. I. Title.

*WOYCHUCK, N. A. 234
The incomparable salvation. St. Louis, Mo., Miracle Pr. [1968,c.1967] 112p. 20cm. 1.75 bds.,
1. Salvation—Popular works. I. Title.
Publisher's address: 5410 Kerth Rd., St. Louis, Mo. 63128.

YLVISAKER, Nils Martin, 1882- 243
Trumpets of God, by N. M. Ylvisaker. Minneapolis, Augsburg publishing house [1945] vi p., 1 l., 176 p. 20 1/2 cm. [BT751.Y4] 45-16479
1. Salvation—Popular works. I. Title.

Salvation—Sermons.

BACON, William, 1789-1863. 234
Salvation sought in earnest; a series of sermons, showing the way and the wisdom of securing eternal life. By Rev. William Bacon. New York, Miller, Orton & co., 1857. x, [11]-397 p. 19 cm. [BT751.B23] 40-37151
1. Salvation—Sermons. 2. Presbyterian church—Sermons. 3. Sermons, American. I. Title.

BARNARD, John, 1681-1770. 234
Janua coelestis, Or, The mystery of the gospel in the salvation of a sinner, opened and explained ... in several discourses on Acts xvi. 30. By John Barnard ... Boston, New-England, Printed and sold by Rogers and Fowle in Queen street, and D. Gookin near the South-meeting. 1750 442 [1] p. 20 1/2 cm. [BT750.B25] 31-11696
1. Salvatios. sermons, American. I. Title.

BARNES, Albert, 1798-1870. 233
The way of salvation illustrated in a series of discourses. By Albert Barnes. Philadelphia, Parry & McMillan; London, Knight and sons, 1855. 1 p. l., [v]-xii, 474 p. 20 cm. [BT751.B27] 40-33463
1. Salvation—Sermons. 2. Presbyterian church—Sermons. 3. Sermons, American. I. Title.

BOLTON, Robert, 1572-1631. 234
A discourse about true happinesse /

Robert Bolton. Amsterdam : Theatrum Orbis Terrarum ; Norwood, N.J. : W. J. Johnson, 1979. 156 p. ; 22 cm. (The English experience, its record in early printed books published in facsimile ; no. 909) Photoreprint of the 1611 ed. printed by F. Kyngston for E. Weaver, London. STC 3228. [BT750.B64 1979] 19 79-84089 ISBN 90-221-2109-7 : 14.00
1. Church of England—Sermons. 2. Salvation—Sermons. 3. Happiness—Sermons. 4. Sermons, English. I. Title. II. Series: English experience, its record in early printed books published in facsimile ; no. 909.

DICKSON, Andrew Flinn, 1825-1879. 234
Lessons about salvation; from the life and words of the Lord Jesus. Being a second series of plantation sermons. By the Rev. A. F. Dickson ... Philadelphia, Presbyterian board of publication [c1860] 264 p. 18 cm. [BT751.D5] 40-25508
1. Salvation—Sermons. 2. Presbyterian church in the U. S. A.—Sermons. 3. Sermons, American. I. Presbyterian church in the U. S. A. (Old school) Board of publication. II. Title. III. Title: Plantation sermons.

GARRETT, Willis Edward. 234
The life that wins; salvation sermonettes. [1st ed.] New York, Exposition Press [1954] 56p. 21cm. [BT753.G3] 54-10336
1. Salvation—Sermons. 2. Presbyterian Church—Sermons. 3. Sermons, American. I. Title.

MAST, Russell L. 234
Lost and found. Scottdale, Pa., Herald [c.1963] 102p. 20cm. 63-7537 2.50
1. Salvation—Sermons. 2. Bible. N. T. Luke xv—Sermons. 3. Mennonite Church—Sermons. 4. Sermons, American. I. Title.

SIMPSON, Albert B., 1844-1919. 243
Salvation sermons, by Rev. A. B. Simpson, D.D., with an introduction by Rev. Walter M. Turnbull, D.D. New York, Christian alliance publishing company [c1925] 123 p. 18 cm. (On cover: The Alliance colportage series) [BV3797.S45] 25-10235
I. Title.

SMITH, Butler Kennedy. 234
A series of discourses on various subjects, embodying a brief synopsis of the divine scheme of human redemption and recovery from sin. By Butler Kennedy Smith... Indianapolis, Printing and publishing house print., 1874. vii, 320 p. front. (port.) 19 cm. With this is bound the author's An earnest inquiry into the true Scriptural organization of the Churches of God in Christ Jesus... Indianapolis, Ind., 1871. [BT751.S64] 40-37294
1. Salvation—Sermons. 2. Churches of God in Christ Jesus—Sermons. 3. Sermons, American. I. Title.

VAN GORDER, John Jay, 1881- 234
ABC's of salvation, by John J. Van Gorder ... Chicago, Ill., Moody press [1946] 175 p. 19 1/2 cm. [BX6333.V3A2] 47-15587
1. Salvation—Sermons. 2. Baptists—Sermons. 3. Sermons, American. I. Title.

WILLIAMS, William R., 1804-1885. 234
God's rescues; or, The lost sheep, the lost coin, and the lost son. Three discourses on Luke xv. By William R. Williams. New York, A. D. F. Randolph & co., 1871. 95 p. 19 cm. [BT751.W73] 40-37303
1. Salvation—Sermons. 2. Bible. N.T. Luke xv—Sermons. I. Title. II. Title: The lost sheep, the lost coin, and the lost son.

WOODRUFF, Hezekiah. 234
Familiar discourses on the way of salvation. By Hezekiah Woodruff ... Ithaca [N.Y.] Mack, Andrus, & Woodruff, 1841. viii, [9]-226 p. front. (port.) 23 cm. [BT751.W8] 40-37304
1. Salvation—Sermons. 2. Sermons, American. I. Title.

Salvation—Sermons—Outlines.

COMPTON, W. H. comp. 234
Salvation sermon outlines. [Westwood, N. J.] Revell Co. [c.1961] 64p. (Revell's sermon outline ser.) 61-9247 1.00 pap.,
1. Salvation—Sermons—Outlines. I. Title.

Salvation—Study and teaching.

ALLEN, Hattie Bell (McCracken), 1896- 234
Jesus saves. Drawings by Mariel Wilhoite Turner. Nashville, Broadman Press [1951] 107 p. illus. 19 cm. Includes hymns, with music. [BT751.A55] 51-3529
1. Salvation—Study and teaching. 2. Religious education—Text. books for adolescents—Baptist. I. Title.

CROSS, George, 1862- 233
Christian salvation, a modern interpretation by George Cross. Chicago, Ill., The University of Chicago press [c1925] x, 254 p. 20 cm. [BT751.C78] 25-10791
I. Title.

**IN God's care;* 220.9
the way of salvation in the Old and New Testaments, for religious instruction in the junior school [Illus. by Albert Burkart. New York, Herder & Herder, 1965, c.1964] 166p. 19cm. 1.50 pap.,

Salvationists—Biography.

TROUTT, Margaret. 267'.15'0924 B
The general was a lady : the story of Evangeline Booth / by Margaret Troutt. Nashville : A. J. Holman, c1980. 325 p., [4] leaves of plates : ports. ; 23 cm. Includes index. Bibliography: p. 307-311. [BX9743.B63T76] 80-117590 ISBN 0-87981-141-2 : 9.95 ISBN 0-87981-139-0 pbk. : 5.95
1. Booth, Evangeline Cory, 1865-1950. 2. Salvationists—Biography. I. Title.

Salvationists—England—Biography.

ROBINSON, Virgil E. 267'.15'0924 B
William Booth and his Army / Virgil Robinson. Mountain View, Calif. : Pacific Press Pub. Association, c1976. 112 p. : ill. ; 22 cm. (A Destiny book ; D-163) [BX9743.B7R62] 75-25226 pbk. : 3.50
1. Booth, William, 1829-1912. 2. Salvation Army. 3. Salvationists—England—Biography. I. Title.

Salvationists—Germany—Biography.

LINNETT, Arthur. 267'.15'0924 B
Radiant rebel : the story of Ernst Schmidtke / by Arthur Linnett. London : Salvationist, 1976. 97 p. ; 19 cm. [BX9743.S3L56] 77-366233 ISBN 0-85412-292-3
1. Schmidtke, Ernst, 1908- 2. Salvationists—Germany—Biography. 3. Missionaries—China—Biography. 4. Missionaries—Germany—Biography. I. Title.

Salvations.

ZOLLARS, Ely Vaughan, 1847-1916. 234
The great salvation, by Ely V. Zollars ... Cincinnati, The Standard publishing company [1898] viii, 272 p. 23 cm. [BT751.Z8] 40-37307
1. Salvations. I. Title.

Salvatorians.

JORDAN, Franziskus Maria vom Kreuze, pater, 1848-1918. 271.79
Exhortations and admonitions of our venerable father and founder, Father Francis Mary of the Cross Jordan, translated by Father Winfrid Herbst, S.D.S. St. Nazianz, Wis., The Society of the Divine Savior, 1939. x, 221 p. 17 1/2 cm. Compiled by Father Guerricus Buerger. cf. Pref. [Secular name: Johann Baptist Jordan] [BX4040.S28J62] 44-5042
1. Salvatorians. I. Herbst, Winfrid, father, 1891- tr. II. Buerger, Guerricus, father, comp. III. Title.

Salve Regina.

COLLINS, John H. 232.9318
Hail, holy Queen; reflections on a well-known prayer. [Boston] St. Paul Eds. [c.1963] 69p. col. illus. 22cm. 63-22754 2.00; 1.00 pap.,
1. Salve Regina. I. Title.

JARRETT, Bede, father, 1881-1934. 232.931
Lourdes, interpreted by the Salve Regina; meditations given by Father Bede Jarrett, O.P., during the novena preached in they Church of Our Lady of Lourdes in preparation for the celebration of the seventy-fifth anniversary of the apparitions at Lourdes, February 2nd-February 10th, 1933. Westminster, Md., The Newman bookshop, 1943. 4 p. l., 97 p. 17 1/2 cm. Title on spine: Our Lady of Lourdes. English edition (London, Burns, Oates & Washbourne, ltd.) has title: Our Lady of Lourdes. [Secular name: Cyril Beaufort Jarrett] [BV469.S3J] A 44
1. Salve Regina. 2. Mary, Virgin—Meditations. I. Title. II. Title: Our Lady of Lourdes.

Salvery.

WOOLMAN, John, 1720-1772.
Considerations on keeping Negroes; Recommended to the Professors of Christianity, of every Denomination, Part second. By John Woolman ... Philadelphia: Printed by B. Franklin, and D. Hall, 1762. 52 p. 18 cm. Part first published under title "Some considerations on the keeping of Negroes," Philadelphia, 1754. [HT871.W6] 9-37
1. Salvery. I. Title.

Salzburgers—Emigration. 1731-1735.

SOCIETY for Promoting Christian Knowledge, London. 274.363
Henry Newman's Salzburger letterbooks. Transcribed, ed. by George Fenwick Jones. Athens, Univ. of Ga. Pr. [1966] xi, 626p. illus., maps. 25cm. (Wormsloe Found. Pubns., no. 8) Based on Xerox copies from microfilms of letterbks., preserved in the archives of the soc., consisting of correspondence, chiefly between Henry Newman, secretary, & Samuel Urlsperger about the soc. efforts to aid Protestant exiles from Salzburg who wished to settle in colonial Ga. Bibl. [BR817.S3S6] 66-25848 12.00
1. Salzburgers—Emigration. 1731-1735. I. Newman, Henry, 1670-1743. II. Urlsperger, Samuel, 1685-1772. III. Jones, George Fenwick, 1916- ed. IV. Title. V. Title: Salzburger letterbooks. VI. Series.

Salzmann, Joseph, 1819-1874.

RAINER, Joseph, Rev. 1845- 922
A noble priest: Joseph Salzmann, D. D., founder of the Salesianum; by Very Rev. Joseph Rainer ... Translated from the German by Rev. Joseph William Berg ... Milwaukee, Olinger & Schwartz, 1903. 254 p. front. (port.) 6 pl. 20 cm. [BX4705.S27R3] 3-20994
1. Salzmann, Joseph, 1819-1874. I. Berg, Joseph William, tr. II. Title.

Samaritan language—Texts.

SAMARITANS. Liturgy and ritual. 290
The Samaritan liturgy, edited by A. E. Cowley... Oxford, Clarendon press, 1909. 2 v. 23 cm. Paged continuously. Contents.1. Text; Common prayers (Defter) Passover series. Pentecost series. Services of the seventh month.--v. 2. Introduction. Glossary. Index of first lines. Index of authors. Corrigenda. Text: Services of the seventh month (cont.) Occasional prayers: Marriage and circumcision. Burial. Appendix. [BM175.S3A3] 11-29944
1. Samaritan language—Texts. I. Cowley, Sir Arthur Ernest, 1861-1931, ed. II. Title.

Samaritans.

GASTER, Moses, 1856-1939. 296
... *The Samaritans;* their history, doctrines and literature. With six appendices and nineteen illustrations. By Moses Gaster ... London, Pub. for the British academy by H. Milford, Oxford university press, 1925. vi p., 1 l., 206 p. incl. plan. 18 pl. (incl. front. (map) ports., facsims.) 25 cm. (The Schweich lectures, 1923) At head of title: The British academy. [BM175.S3G3] 26-6683
1. Samaritans. I. British academy, London. II. Title.

JOSHUA, the son of Nun.
The Samaritan chronicle or The book of Joshua the son of Nun; tr. from the Arabic, with notes by Oliver Turnbull Crane ... New York, J. B. Alden, 1890. v, [7]-178 p. 20 cm. A compilation of legends of the 13th century. cf. James Alan Montgomery, "The Samaritans", p. 303. [DS129.S3] 24-20448
1. Samaritans. I. Crane, Oliver Turnbull, tr. II. Title.

JOSHUA, son of Nun.
The Samaritan chronicle or The book of Joshua the son of Nun; tr. from the Arabic, with notes by Oliver Turnbull Crane ... New York, J. B. Alden, 1890. v, [7]-178 p. 20 cm. A compilation of legends of the 13th century. cf. James Alan Montgomery, "The Samaritans," p. 308. [DS129.S3] 24-20448
1. Samaritans. I. Crane, Oliver Turnbull, tr. II. Title.

MACDONALD, John 296.81
The theology of the Samaritans. Philadelphia, Westminister [1965, c.1964] 480p. front. 23cm. (New Testament lib.) Bibl. [BM945.M3] 65-10060 10.00
1. Samaritans. 2. Jewish theology. I. Title.

THE modern Samaritan;
a handbook on Christian social action. [n.p.] Board of Social Economic Relations of the Methodist Church, c1956. 80p. Bibliography: p. 72-77.
I. Cook, Clair Marvin.

MONTGOMERY, James Alan, 1866-
... *The Samaritans,* the earliest Jewish sect; their history, theology and literature, by James Alan Montgomery ... Philadelphia, The J. C. Winston co., 1907. 2 p. l., vii-xiv p., 2 l., 358 p. front., plates, 2 maps (1 fold.) facsims. 23 cm. (The Bohien lectures for 1906) "Samaritan bibliography": p. 322-346. [DS129.M8] 7-15492
1. Samaritans. I. Title.

MONTGOMERY, James Alan, 1866-1949. 296.8'1
The Samaritans; the earliest Jewish sect: their history, theology, and literature. Introd. by Abraham S. Halkin. New York, Ktav Pub. House [1968] xxx, 358 p. illus., map, plan, ports. 24 cm. (The Bohlen lectures, 1906) "First published in 1907." Bibliography: p. 322-346. [DS129.M8 1968] 67-30121
1. Samaritans. I. Title. II. Series.

PURVIS, James D. 222'.1'06
The Samaritan Pentateuch and the origin of the Samaritan sect [by] James D. Purvis. Cambridge, Mass., Harvard University Press, 1968. xiv, 147 p. 22 cm. (Harvard Semitic monographs, v. 2) Based on the author's thesis, Harvard, 1962. Bibliography: p. [130]-142. [BS1225.2.P8] 68-17631 6.00
1. Bible. O.T. Pentateuch—Criticism, interpretation, etc. 2. Samaritans. I. Title. II. Series.

STEUART, John Alexander, 1861-
The Samaritans; a tale of to-day, by John Alexander Steuart ... New York, London [etc.] F. H. Revell company, 1903. 6, [9]-405 p. 20 cm. 3-12962
I. Title.

STEUART, John Alexander, 1861-
The Samaritans, a tale of to-day, by John Alexander Steuart ... New York, London [etc.] F. H. Revell company [1903] 6, [9]-405 p. 19 cm. 3-10722
I. Title.

Samaritans — Bibliography

MAYER, Leo Ary, 1895- 016.910091749229
Bibliography of the Samaritans. Ed. by Donald Broadribb. Leiden, E. J. Brill [New York, Humanities, 1966, c.1964] vi, 49p.

25cm. (Supps. to Abr-Nahrain, v.1) Title. (Series: Abr-Nahrain. Supplements, v.1) Appeared in a prelim. form under title 'Outline of a bibliography of the Samaritains,' in Eretz-Israel, 1956. [Z3478.S3M3] 66-1249 2.75 pap.,
1. Samaritans — Bibl. I. Broadribb, Donald, ed. II. Title. III. Series.

Samaritans—Religion.

BOWMAN, John, 1916- 296.8'1
The Samaritan problem : studies in the relationships of Samaritanism, Judaism, and early Christianity / by John Bowman ; translated by Alfred M. Johnson, Jr. Pittsburgh : Pickwick Press, 1975. p. cm. (Pittsburgh theological monograph series ; no. 4) (Franz Delitzsch lectures ; 1959) Translation of Samaritanische Probleme. Includes bibliographical references. [BM935.B6413] 75-20042 ISBN 0-915138-04-2 : 5.95
1. Samaritans—Religion. 2. Christianity and other religions—Samaritanism. 3. Qumran community. I. Title. II. Series. III. Series: Pittsburgh theological monograph series ; no. 4.

Samaritans—Religion—Sources.

BOWMAN, John, 1916- 296.8'1
Samaritan documents : relating to their history, religion, and life / translated and edited by John Bowman. Pittsburgh : Pickwick Press, 1977. vii, 370 p. ; 22 cm. (Pittsburgh original texts and translation series ; 2) Includes index. Bibliography: p. 367-370 [BM917.B68] 77-4949 ISBN 0-915138-27-1 pbk. : 7.95
1. Samaritans—Religion—Sources. I. Title.

Samford University, Birmingham, Ala. Extension Division for Christian training.

HELMBOLD, F. Wilbur, ed. 378.7'61'781
"Born of the needs of the people"; the extension ministry of Samford University. F. Wilbur Helmbold, editor. Birmingham, Ala., Published for Samford University by Banner Press, 1967. vii, 71 p. 23 cm. [BR561.S3H4] 67-1980
1. Samford University, Birmingham, Ala. Extension Division for Christian training. 2. Samford University, Birmingham, Ala.—Religion. I. Title. II. Title: The extension ministry of Samford University.

Sampey, John Richard, 1863-

DUGGAR, Elsie (Sampey) Mrs. 922.673
Laughing and loving with John Richard Sampey, by Elsie Sampey Duggar. [Tuscaloosa, Ala., Weatherford printing company, c1937] 4 p. l., 95 p. front. (port.) 20 cm. "What others say": p. 61-95. [BX6495.S28D8] 38-1807
1. Sampey, John Richard, 1863- I. Title.

LOUISVILLE, Ky. Southern Baptist theological seminary. 016.
Southern Baptist theological seminary. The first thirty years. 1859-1889. [Edited by] John R. Sampey ... Baltimore, Wharton, Barron & co., 1890. 217 p. 19 cm. [BV4070.L76A3 1890] 25-25470
I. Sampey, John Richard, 1863- II. Title.

SAMPEY, John Richard, 1863-1946. 922.673
Memoirs of John R. Sampey ... Nashville, Tenn., Broadman press [1947] xi, 286 p. front., ports. 23 cm. [BX6495.S28A3] 47-4320
I. Title.

Sampson, Francis Smith, 1814-1854.

DABNEY, Robert Lewis, 1820-1898. 922.
A memorial of the Christian life and character of Francis S. Sampson, D.D., by Robert L. Dabney, D.D. Richmond, Va., Enquirer book and job press, 1855. viii, 122 p. 22 cm. [BX9225.S26D3] 43-30407
1. Sampson, Francis Smith, 1814-1854. I. Title.

Samson, judge of Israel.

CARUS, Paul, 1852-1919. 221.93
The story of Samson and its place in the religious development of mankind, by Paul Carus ... Chicago, The Open court publishing company; [etc., etc.] 1907. viii, 183 p. front., illus. 20 cm. [BS580.S15C3] 7-14568
1. Samson, judge of Israel. I. Title.

GRENSHAW, James L. 222'.32'077
Samson : a secert betrayed, a vow ignored / James L. Crenshaw. Atlanta : John Knox Press, c1978. 172 p. ; 21 cm. Includes indexes. Bibliography: p. [167]-170. [BS1305.2.C73] 77-15748 ISBN 0-8042-0170-6 : 7.95
1. Samson, Judge of Israel. 2. Bible. O.T. Judges XIII, 1-XVI, 31—Criticism interpretation, etc. 3. Riddles—History and criticism.

HALL, Joseph, Bp. of Norwich, 1574-1656. 221.9'24 B
Samson; selections from a contemplation on an historical passage in the Old Testament. With drawings by Fritz Kredel. [Lexington, Ky., Stamperia del Santuccio, 1972] a-c, xix p. illus. 29 cm. Selections from Book 10 in the part dealing with the Old Testament of the work first published 1612-26 under title: Contemplations upon the principall passages of the Holy Storie. [BS580.S15H34] 73-151450
1. Samson, Judge of Israel.

PALMER, Abram Smythe. 291.1'3
The Samson-saga and its place in comparative religion / Abram Smythe Palmer. New York : Arno Press, 1977. xii, 267 p., [2] leaves of plates : ill. ; 21 cm. (International folklore) Reprint of the 1913 ed. published by I. Pitman, London. Includes index. Bibliography: p. x. [BS580.S15P34 1977] 77-70613 ISBN 0-405-10112-0 : 17.00
1. Samson, Judge of Israel. 2. Sun (in religion, folk-lore, etc.) I. Title. II. Series.

SCOTT, William Anderson, 1813-1885. 221.92
The giant judge, or, The story of Samson. By Rev. W. A. Scott ... Philadelphia, Presbyterian board of publication [1858] 240 p. front., illus. 19 cm. [BS580.S15S3 1858] 33-24804
1. Samson, judge of Israel. I. Presbyterian church in the U. S. A. Board of publication. II. Title.

SCOTT, William Anderson, 1813-1885. 221.92
The giant judge: or, The story of Samson, the Hebrew Hercules. By Rev. W. A. Scott ... San Francisco, Whitton, Towne & co., 1858. xviii p., 1 l., [21]-324 p. front., illus. plates. 20 cm. [BS580.S15S3 1858 a] 33-24803
1. Samson, judge of Israel. I. Title.

SMITH, Daniel, 1806-1852. 221.92
The life of Samson. By Rev. Daniel Smith...Revised by the editors. New York, Published by T. Mason and G. Lane, for the Sunday school union of the Methodist Episcopal church, 1840. 94 p. incl. front. 14 cm. (On cover: S[unday] s[chool] & y[ouths] library. 294) [BS580.S15S6] 37-15511
1. Samson, judge of Israel. I. Sunday school union of the Methodist Episcopal church. II. Title.

Samson, Judge of Israel—Juvenile literature.

LAPPIN, Peter. 221.9
Mightly Samson. Garden City, N. Y. [1961] 63p. illus. 21cm. (The Catholic know-your-Bible program) [BS580.L15L3] 61-65885
1. Samson, Judge of Israel—Juvenile literature. I. Title.

ROSE, Anne K. 92 (j)
Samson and Delilah [by] Anne K. Rose. Illustrated by Richard Powers. New York, Lothrop, Lee & Shepherd [1968] 1 v. (unpaged) col. illus. 26 cm. [BS580.S15R62] 68-27713 3.50
1. Samson, Judge of Israel—Juvenile literature. I. Powers, Richard, illus. II. Title.

WALSH, Bill. 221.9'24 B
The secret of Samson / by Bill Walsh ; with an afterword for parents and teachers by Andrew Greely. Kansas City [Kan.] : Sheed Andrews and McMeel, c1978. 77 p. : ill. ; 27 cm. (A Cartoon Bible story) [BS580.S15W34] 78-4938 ISBN 0-8362-4302-1 pbk. : 1.95
1. Samson, Judge of Israel—Juvenile literature. 2. Bible. O.T.—Biography—Juvenile literature. I. Title.

Samson, judge of Israel—Poetry.

MILTON, John, 1608-1674. 821.47
Milton's Samson Agonistes; with introduction, notes, glossary and indexes, by A. W. Verity ... Cambridge [Eng.] University press, 1932. lxvi p., 1 l., 170, [2] p. 17 cm. (Half-title: Pitt press series) "First edition 1892; reprinted ... 1932." "The text ... is based upon that of the first edition (1671), compared with the second edition (1680)."--Note. [PR3566 1932] 33-6657
1. Samson, judge of Israel—Poetry. I. Verity, Arthur Wilson, 1863- ed. II. Title.

MILTON, John, 1608-1674 821.4
Samson Agonistes; the poem and materials for analysis, selected, ed. by Ralph E. Hone. San Francisco, Chandler [c.1966] viii, 284p. illus. 22cm. Bibl. [PR3566] 66-11621 2.95 pap.,
1. Samson, judge of Israel—Poetry. I. Home, Ralph E., ed. II. Title.

MILTON, John, 1608-1674 821.4
Samson Agonistes, and the shorter poems. Ed. by Isabel Gamble MacCaffrey. New York, New Amer. Lib. [c.1966] 216p. 18cm. (Signet classic poetry ser., CT323) Bibl. [PR3566 1966a] 66-23613 .75 pap.,
1. Samson. judge of Israel—Poetry. I. MacCaffrey, Isabel Gamble, ed. II. Title.

Samuel bar Abba, 179 (ca.)-257.

BOKSER, Baruch M. 296.1'2307
Post Mishnaic Judaism in transition : Samuel on Berakhot and the beginnings of Germara / by Baruch M. Bokser. Chico, CA : Scholars Press, c1980. xxxi, 543 p. ; 23 cm. (Brown Judaic studies ; no. 17) Includes indexes. Bibliography: p. 493-520. [BM502.3.S3B63] 19 80-19702 ISBN 0-89130-433-9 pbk. : 15.00
1. Samuel bar Abba, 179 (ca.)-257. 2. Mishnah. Berakot—Commentaries. I. Title. II. Series.

Samuel, judge of Israel.

BIBLE. O. T. Historical Books. English. Harmonies. 1951. Revised.
A harmony of the books of Samuel, Kings and Chronicles; the books of the Kings of Judah and Israel, by William Day Crockett. An introd. by William Judson Beecher. Grand Rapids, Mich., Baker Book House, 1951. x, 365p. 21cm. A53
I. Crockett, William Day, 1869-1930. II. Title.

DEANE, William John, 1823-1895. 221.92
... Samuel and Saul, their lives and times, by Rev. William J. Deane ... New York, Chicago [etc.] Fleming H. Revell company [189-?] vii, 213 p. 20 cm. (Men of the Bible) [BS580.S2D4] 37-10887
1. Samuel, judge of Israel. 2. Saul, king of Israel. I. Title.

DOUGLAS, George Cunninghame Monteath, 1826-1904. 221.
Samuel and his age; a study in the constitutional history of Isreal. By George C. M. Douglas ... London, New York [etc.] Eyre and Spottiswoode, 1901. xxiii, 276 p. front. 19 1/2 cm. (On cover: The Bible student's library, 10) [BS580.S2D6] 3-12901
1. Samuel, judge of Israel. 2. Bible, O.T. Samuel—Criticism, interpretation, etc. 3. Bible—Criticism, interpretation, etc.—O.T. Samuel. I. Title.

ROYER, Galen Brown, 1862- 221.
Samuel, the judge. By Galen B. Royer ... Elgin, Ill., Brethren publishing house, 1900. 136 p. front., 1 illus., plates. 16 cm. (Bible biographies for the young, v. 2) [BS580.S2R6] 1-30380
1. Samuel, judge of Israel. I. Title.

WEE, Mons Olson, 1871- 224
Men who knew God: Samuel, Amos, Haggai; prophets and their times, prophetism, and "the schools of prophets" in the Old Testament, by M. O. Wee. Minneapolis, Minn., Augsburg publishing house [c1932] xiii, 122 p. 20 1/2 cm. "Works for reference": p. 122. [BS1505.W4] 32-20843
1. Samuel, judge of Israel. 2. Amos, the prohpet. 3. Haggai, the prophet. 4. Prophets. I. Title.

Samuel, judge of Israel—Juvenile literature.

MONCURE, Jane Belk. 222'.43'0924 B
The little boy Samuel / by Jane Belk Moncure ; illustrated by Paul Karch. Elgin, Ill. : Child's World ; Cincinnati : distributed by Standard Pub., c1979. 31 p. : col. ill. ; 25 cm. Retells the Bible story of how the child Samuel opened the doors of the House of the Lord so all kinds of people could come in. [BS580.S2M6] 79-12174 ISBN 0-89565-084-3 : 4.95
1. Samuel, judge of Israel—Juvenile literature. 2. [Samuel, judge of Israel.] 3. Bible. O.T.—Biography—Juvenile literature. 4. [Bible stories—O.T.] I. Karch, Paul. II. Title.

WHALEY, Richie. 222'.43'09505
Samuel, prophet and judge / Richie Whaley ; illustrated by Dean Shelton. Nashville : Broadman Press, c1978. 48 p. : col ill. ; 24 cm. (Biblearn series) Tells of the Hebrew prophet, priest, judge, and ruler who selected Saul as the first king of Israel and chose David to succeed him. [BS580.S2W46] 78-317387 ISBN 0-8054-4242-1 : 3.95
1. Samuel, Judge of Israel—Juvenile literature. 2. [Samuel, Judge of Israel.] 3. Bible. O.T.—Biography—Juvenile literature. 4. [Bible stories—O.T.] I. Shelton, Dean. II. Title.

Samuel, Maurice, 1895-1972—Addresses, essays, lectures.

SAMUEL, Maurice, 1895-1972. 296'.092'4 B
The gentleman and the Jew : twenty-five centuries of conflict in manners and morals / Maurice Samuel. New York : Behrman House, 1978. viii, 325 p. ; 22 cm. (A Jewish legacy book) Autobiographical. [BM755.S243A3 1977] 77-6666 ISBN 0-87441-264-1 : 4.95
1. Samuel, Maurice, 1895-1972—Addresses, essays, lectures. 2. Bible. O.T.—Criticism, interpretation, etc.—Addresses, essays, lectures. 3. Jews in the United States—Biography—Addresses, essays, lectures. 4. Judaism—20th century—Addresses, essays, lectures. 5. Zionism—Addresses, essays, lectures. I. Title.

Samyutta-nikaya.

BUDDHAGHOSA. 294.31
... Sarattha-ppakasini, Buddhaghosa's commentary on the Sanyutta-nikaya, edited by F. L. Woodward ... London, Pub. for the Pali text society by H. Milford, Oxford university press, 1929- v. 23 cm. (Pali text society. [Publications, Pali text transliterated. [PK4541.P4] 891.3701 31-24175
1. Samyutta-nikaya. I. Woodward, Frank Lee, ed. II. Title.

San Antonio de Padua mission.

ENGELHARDT, Zephyrin, father, 1851- 979.
San Antonio de Padus, the mission in the Sierras, by Fr. Zephyrin Engelhardt... Santa Barbara, Calif., Mission Santa Barbara, 1929. 4 p. l., [3]-140 p. front., illus. 22 cm. (Missions and missionaries of California. New series. Local history) [Secular name: Charles Anthony Engelhardt] [F864.E584] [F869.S176E5] 271. 30-4546
1. San Antonio de Padua mission. I. Title.

San Antonio—History—Sources.

GUIDELINES for a 266'.2'764351 *Texas Mission* : instructions for the missionary of Mission Concepcion in San Antonio, ca. 1760 : transcript of the Spanish original and English translation, with notes / by Benedict Leutenegger. San Antonio, Tex. : Old Spanish Missions Historical Research Library at San Jose Mission, 1976. 61 leaves ; 29 cm. ([Documentary series] - Old Spanish Missions Historical Research Library ; 1) English and Spanish. [F394.S2G93] 76-379353
1. Nuestra Senora de la Purisima Concepcion de Acuna Mission. 2. San Antonio—History—Sources. 3. Indians of North America—Missions. 4. Missions—San Antonio. I. Leutenegger, Benedict. II. Series: Old Spanish Missions Historical Research Library. Documentary series — Old Spanish Missions Historical Research Library ; 1.

San Antonio. Madison Square Presbyterian Church.

HATLEY, Roy O. 285'.14764'351
A ninety-year record of Madison Square Presbyterian Church: 1882-1972. Compiled by Mr. and Mrs. Roy O. Hatley. Church Editing Committee: Marg-Riette Hamlett [and others. Special ed. San Antonio, Tex., Printed by Munguia Printers, 1972] 248 p. illus. 24 cm. [BX9211.S37M334] 72-181179
1. San Antonio. Madison Square Presbyterian Church. I. Hatley, Roy O., Mrs., joint author. II. Title.

San Antonio, Tex. Laurel Heights Methodist Church.

A crowning decade, 1949-1959: Laurel Heights Methodist Church, 50th Anniversary [by] C. Stanley Banks [and] Pat Ireland Nixon. San Antonio, 1959. 58p. illus. 24cm.
1. San Antonio, Tex. Laurel Heights Methodist Church. I. Banks, Clinton Stanley, 1892- II. Nixon, Patrick Ireland, 1883- joint author.

San Augustine, Tex. First Baptist Church.

JONES, Eva 286'.1'764175
McDaniel.
From darkness to light; the story of the First Baptist Church of San Augustine, Texas. Researched by the Business Women's Missionary Society. Illus. by Raye McGilbery Wise. San Antonio, Tex., Naylor [1970] xxii, 106 p. illus., facsims., ports. 22 cm. [BX6480.S366F55] 78-131482 6.95
1. San Augustine, Tex. First Baptist Church. I. San Augustine, Tex. First Baptist Church. Business Women's Missionary Society. II. Title.

San Augustine, Tex. First Methodist Church.

HANKS, Mrs. Casset.
The Methodist Church, San Augustine, Texas. [San Augustine, 1963] Caption title. 64-17492
1. San Augustine, Tex. First Methodist Church. I. Title.

San Buenaventura mission.

ENGELHARDT, Zephyrin, 277.9492
father, 1851-1934.
San Buenaventura, the mission, by the sea by Fr. Zephyrin Engelhardt... Santa Barbara, Calif., Mission Santa Barbara, 1930. ix, [1], 166, [6] p. incl. front., illus., ports., map, plan, facsims. 22 cm. (Missions and missionaries of California. New series. Local history) "The missions of California (correct dates of their founding)": p. [5] at end. [F864.E586] [F869.S187E5] 266.2 31-4512
1. San Buenaventura mission. I. Title.

San Carlos Borromeo mission.

ENGELHARDT, 271.30979469
Zephyrin, father, 1851-1934.
Mission San Carlos Borromeo (Carmelo). The father of the missions. By Fr. Zephyrin Engelhardt...edited by Fr. Felix Pudlowski... Santa Barbara, Calif., Mission Santa Barbara, 1934. xii, 264, [10] p. incl. front. (port.) illus. 22 cm. (Missions and missionaries of California. New series. Local history) Includes music. [Secular name: Charles Anthony Engelhardt] [F864.E563] 34-24136
1. San Carlos Borromeo mission. 2. Serra, Junipero, fray, 1713-1784. I. Pudiowski, Felix, ed. II. Title.

San Diego, Calif. St. Paul's Church.

BARNES, Calvin 283'.794'98
Rankin, 1891-
The Parish of Saint Paul, San Diego, California: its first hundred years, by C. Rankin Barnes. [San Diego] Published by the Parish, 1969. 62 p. illus., ports. 23 cm. [BX5980.S34S32] 72-182743
1. San Diego, Calif. St. Paul's Church. I. Title.

San Diego mission.

JAYME, Luis, 1740- 266.2'794'98
1775.
Letter of Luis Jayme, O.F.M., San Diego, October 17, 1772. Translated and edited by Maynard Geiger. Los Angeles, Published for San Diego Public Library by Dawson's Book Shop, 1970. 66 p. facsim. 23 cm. (Baja California travels series, 22) Includes the original Spanish letter in facsimile. Includes bibliographical references. [F869.S22J3813] 77-127978
1. San Diego mission. I. Geiger, Maynard J., 1901- ed. II. Title. III. Series.

San Francisco. Church for the Fellowship of All Peoples.

THURMAN, Howard, 1899- 289.9
Footprints of a dream; the story of the Church for the Fellowship of All Peoples. New York, Harper [1959] 157 p. illus. 20 cm. [BN9999.S3C5] 59-11412
1. San Francisco. Church for the Fellowship of All Peoples. I. Title.

San Francisco. Corpus Christi Church.

CORPUS Christi
[Catholic Church. Arch. 2N, Sec. 2., Jan. 12, 1959. Berkeley, Calif., 1959] 1 v. (unpaged, chiefly mounted illus. (part col.)) 16x39cm. Cover title.
1. San Francisco. Corpus Christi Church. I. Leonard, King P

San Francisco el Grande (Basilica) Madrid.

ST. Francis the Great. 914.6'41
Madrid ; New York : British American Pub. Co., 1953. 32 p. : ill. ; 17 cm. [NA5810.S3S25] 75-315848
1. San Francisco el Grande (Basilica) Madrid.

San Francisco. Grace Cathedral.

ALI, Bader Salem.
Cathedral. [The architecture of faith] Arch. 2N, Mr. Prestini. [Berkeley, Calif., 1961] 1v. (unpaged, chiefly mounted plates) plan. Cover title.
1. San Francisco. Grace Cathedral. I. Title.

San Francisco. Holy cross church.

CARROLL, Luke Michael, 282.79461
1848-
Holy cross parish and Lone mountain district of San Francisco, by Luke M. Carroll; published in honor of golden jubilee, October, 1937. San Francisco 1937 64 p. incl. plates, ports fold pl, double map. 24 cm. [BX4603.S5H6] 39-7820
1. San Francisco. Holy cross church. I. Title. II. Title: Lone mountain district of San Francisco.

San Francisco. St. Mary's Cathedral. California Street.

MCSWEENEY, Thomas Denis. 282.794
Cathedral on California Street; the story of St. Mary's Cathedral, San Francisco, 1854-1891, and of Old St. Mary's, a Paulist church, 1894-1951. Fresno, Academy of California Church History, 1952. 94p. illus. 23cm. (Academy of California Church History. Publication no.4) [BX4603.S5S33] 56-38596
1. San Francisco. St. Mary's Cathedral. California Street. 2. San Francisco. St. Mary's Church. I. Title.

San Francisco Theological Seminary, San Anselmo, Calif.

BAIRD, Jesse Hays, 207.79462
1889-
The San Anselmo story; a personalized history of San Francisco Theological Seminary. Stockton, California Lantern Press, 1963. 124 p. 21 cm. [[BV4070.S26B3]] 63-5403
1. San Francisco Theological Seminary, San Anselmo, Calif. I. Title.

San Francisco. University.

MCGLOIN, John 271'.53'079461
Bernard.
Jesuits by the Golden Gate; the Society of Jesus in San Francisco, 1849-1969. [San Francisco] University of San Francisco, 1972. 309 p. illus. 24 cm. Includes bibliographical references. [BX3710.S36M36] 74-173134 8.50
1. San Francisco. University. 2. Jesuits in San Francisco. I. Title.

RIORDAN, Joseph W. 207.
The first half century of St. Ignatius church and college, by Joseph W. Riordan, S.J. San Francisco, Cal. [H. S. Crocker company] 1905. 3 p. l., 5-380 p. front., plates (part col.) ports., plan, facsims. 25 cm. [BX915.S556R5] 6-1082
1. San Francisco. University. 2. San Francisco. St. Ignatius church. 3. Jesuits in San Francisco. I. Title.

San Gabriel mission.

ENGELHARDT, Zephyrin, 798.
father, 1851-1934.
San Gabriel mission and the beginnings of Los Angeles, by Fr. Zephyrin Engelhardt... San Gabriel, Cal., Mission San Gabriel, 1927. xiv, 369 p. incl. front., illus. 22 cm. (The missions and missionaries of California. New series. Local history) [Secular name: Charles Anthony Engelhardt] Bibliographical foot-notes. [F364.E594] [F309.S312E5] [F869.S312E5] 979. 271. 27-3158
1. San Gabriel mission. 2. Los Angeles—Hist. I. Title.

San Jose de Aguayo mission.

[ILG, John, father] 1877- 917.64
San Jose, queen of the missions. [San Antonio, Tex., c1936] 64 p. illus. (incl. port.) 24 cm. On cover: Text by Rev. John Ilg. O. P. M., by H. L. Summerville. [Secular name: Frank Leo Ilg] [NA5235.S24 I 5] [F395.M6 I5] 36-36606
1. San Jose de Aguayo mission. 2. Spanish missions of Texas. I. Title.

[ILG, John, father] 1877- 917.64
San Jose, Queen of the missions. [San Antonio, Tex., Printed by Artes graficas, c1938] 68 p. illus., plan. 23 cm. Illustrated half-title. On cover: ... 29 full page illustrations: text by Rev. John Ilg, O. F. M., photos by H. L. Summerville. "Fourth edition." [Socular name: Frank Leo Ilg] [NA5234.S24 I5 1938] [F395.M6 I 5 1938] 39-8536
1. San Jose de Aguayo mission. 2. Spanish missions of Texas. I. Title.

San Leandro, Calif. First Methodist Church.

STUART, Reginald Ray, 1882- 287
How firm a foundation; a centennial history of the First Methodist Church, San Leandro, California, by Reginald R. Stuart & Grace D. Stuart. [San Leandro] FirstMethodist Church, 1953. 112p. illus. 28cm. [BX8481.S42F5] 53-30050
1. San Leandro, Calif. First Methodist Church. I. Stuart, Grace Dell, 1889- joint author. II. Title.

San Sebastian de Garabandal.

LAFFINEUR, M., 246'.9'0946351
1897-
Star on the mountain, by M. Laffineur [and] M. T. le Pelletier. Translated by Service de traduction Champlain, ENR [and] Shelia Laffan Lacouture. Newtonville, N.Y., Our Lady of Mount Carmel of Garabandal, inc. [1967, c1968] xi, 284 p. illus. 21 cm. Translation of L'Etoile dans la montagne. [BT660.S343L313] 68-28493
1. San Sebastian de Garabandal. I. Le Pelletier, M. T., 1901- joint author. II. Title.

SANCHEZ-VENTURA y 248.2'2
Pascual, Francisco.
The apparitions of Garabandal [by] F. Sanchez-Ventura y Pascual. Translated from the Spanish by A. de Bertodano. Detroit, San Miguel Pub. Co. [1966] 205 p. illus., maps, ports. 22 cm. Translation of Las apariciones no son un mito. [BT660.S343S2] 68-2667
1. San Sebastian de Garabandal. I. Title.

San Xavier del Bac Mission.

AHLBORN, Richard E. 731'.88'6
The sculpted saints of a borderland mission : los bultos de San Xavier del Bac : with notes on the statues of Tumacacori / by Richard Eigme Ahlborn ; photos. by Helga Teiwes-French. Tucson, Ariz. : Southwestern Mission Research Center, 1974. 124 p. : ill. ; 29 cm. Cover title: Saints of San Xavier. Bibliography: p. 121-124. [NB230.A6A34] 74-18171 ISBN 0-915076-03-9
1. San Xavier del Bac Mission. 2. Christian saints in art. 3. Sculpture, Baroque—Arizona. 4. Sculpture, Spanish American—Arizona. I. Title. II. Title: Saints of San Xavier.

NEWHALL, Nancy (Wynne) 726.773
Mission San Xavier del Bac. Photos. by Ansel Adams; drawings by Edith Hamlin. San Francisco, 5 Associates, 1954. 71p. illus. (part col.) port. 31cm. Bibliography: p.71. [NA5235.S25N4] 55-19187
1. San Xavier del Bac Mission. I. Adams, Ansel Easton, 1902- illus. II. Title.

TEIWES-FRENCH, Helga. 917.91'77
Mission San Xavier del Bac; a photographic essay on the desert people and their church, by Helga Teiwes-French. Text by Bernard L. Fontana. Tucson, University of Arizona Press [1973] [32] p. illus. (part col.) 23 x 31 cm. [BX4603.B27S267] 73-163822 3.00
1. San Xavier del Bac Mission. I. Fontana, Bernard L.

WRITERS' program, 793.34 1-7431
Arizona.
Mission San Xavier del Bac, Arizona; a descriptive and historical guide, compiled by workers of the Writers' program of the Work projects administration in the state of Arizona. Sponsored by Arizona pioneers' historical society. New York, Hastings house, [1940] 57 p incl. plates, plan. front. 21 cm. [American guide series] Illustrated t.-p. and lining-papers. "First published in March 1940." Bibliography: p. 33-54. [NA5235.Wn] 726.509791 40-27588
1. San Xavier del Bac mission. I. Title.

Sancho VII, King of Navarre, 1160 (ca.)-1234.

THE Pamplona Bibles; 220.4'7
a facsimile compiled from two picture Bibles with martyrologies commissioned by King Sancho el Fuerte of Navarra (1194-1234): Amiens manuscript Latin 108 and Harburg MS. 1, 2, Lat. 4 , 15. By Francois Bucher. New Haven, Yale University Press, 1970 [i.e. 1971] 2 v. illus., geneal. table, 4 maps, 570 plates (part col.) 32 cm. Contents.Contents.—v. 1. Text.—v. 2.

Facsimile. Bibliography: v. 1, p. 153-161. [ND3355.P3] 73-99820
1. Sancho VII, King of Navarre, 1160 (ca.)-1234. 2. Bible—Pictures, illustrations, etc. 3. Illumination of books and manuscripts, Medieval. I. Bucher, Francois. II. Amiens. Bibliotheque municipale. MSS. (Lat. 108) III. Furstlich Oettingen-Wallerstein'sche Bibliothek. MSS. (1, 2, Lat. 4 , 15 IV. Bible. Latin. King Sancho's Bible. V. Bible. Latin. Harburg Bible.

Sanctification.

ADAMS, John Quincy pres. 234.8
U. S., 1825-1881, ed.
Experiences of the higher Christian life in the Baptist denomination; being the testimony of a number of ministers and private members of Baptist churches to the reality and blessedness of the experience of sanctification, through faith in the blood of Jesus Christ. Edited by John Q. Adams... New York Sheldon & company; Boston, Gould & Lincoln; [etc., etc.,] 1870. 267 p. 19 cm. [BT765.A2] 41-31261
1. Sanctification. I. Title.

ADOLPH, Paul Ernest, 1901- 248.4
Triumphant living. Chicago, Moody Press [1959] 127p. 22cm. [BT765.A28] 59-978
1. Sanctification. 2. Bible—Biog. I. Title.

ARNOLD, John Motte, 1824- 922.773
1884.
Selections from the autobiography of Rev. J. M. Arnold, D.D., and from his editorial writings on the doctrine of sanctification. Compiled and arranged by M. A. Boughton, PH.D. Ann Arbor, Mich., Index publishing house, 1885. iv p., 1 l., 7-113 p. front. (port.) 20 cm. [BX8495.A7A3 1885] 36-33995
1. Sanctification. I. Boughton, Mrs. Martha Elizabeth (Arnold) 1857-1928, ed. II. Title.

ASBURY Theological Seminary,
Wilmore, Ky.
The Distinctive emphasis of Asbury Theological Seminary. [Wilmore, Ky., 1963] 100 p. Published as part of a triology to commemorate the fortieth anniversary of Asbury Theological Seminary, 1963. Spine title: The Doctrinal Distinctives of Asbury Theological Seminary. Contains bibliography. NUC64
1. Sanctification. 2. Atonement. I. Title.

BALDWIN, Harmon Allen, 1869-
Objections to entir-sanctification considered. By H. A. Baldwin ... Pittsburgh, Pa., For the author [c1911] 63 p. 18 cm. 11-25154 0.35
I. Title.

BARNARD, Allison F. 234.8
Plain paths to the land of promise; or, Sanctification made clear. A series of simple and concise statements of truth for those seeking true holiness, by Allison F. Barnard ... Anderson, Ind., Gospel trumpet company [c1933] V, 7-128 p. 17 1/2 cm. [BX7990.B7G3] 34-2624
1. Sanctification. I. Title.

BAXTER, James Sidlow. 234'.1
Christian holiness restudied and restated / J. Sidlow Baxter. Grand Rapids : Zondervan Pub. House, c1977. 206 p. ; 23 cm. Contents.Contents.—A new call to holiness.—His deeper work in us.—Our high calling. [BT765.B34] 76-52939 ISBN 0-310-20600-6 : 12.95
1. Sanctification. 2. Holiness. 3. Holiness—Biblical teaching. I. Title.

BAXTER, James Sidlow. 234'.8
A new call to holiness; a restudy and restatement of New Testament teaching concerning Christian sanctification [by] J. Sidlow Baxter. Grand Rapids, Zondervan Pub. House [1973] 257 p. 21 cm. [BT765.B35 1973] 73-13058 2.95 (pbk.)
1. Sanctification. 2. Holiness. I. Title.

BAXTER, James Sidlow. 234'.8
Our high calling : a series of devotional and practical studies in the New Testament doctrine of personal sanctification / J. Sidlow Baxter. Grand Rapids, Mich. : Zondervan Pub. House, 1975, c1967. 206 p. ; 21 cm. [BT765.B36 1975] 75-323761 pbk. : 2.95
1. Sanctification. I. Title.

BOARDMAN, Henry Augustus, 234.8
1808-1880.
The "higher life" doctrine of sanctification, tried by the word of God. By Henry A. Boardman ... Philadelphia, Presbyterian board of publication [1877] 286 p. 18 cm. [BT765.B6] 41-30211
1. Sanctification. I. Presbyterian church in the U.S.A. Board of publication. II. Title.

BOURDEAU, Daniel T. 234'.8
Sanctification; or, Living holiness, by D. T. Bourdeau. Battle Creek, Mich., Steam Press, 1864. [Nashville, Tenn., Printed by Southern Pub. Association, 1970] 144 p. 21 cm. [BT767.B68 1970] 74-19705
1. Sanctification. 2. Holiness. 3. Sabbath. I. Title: Living holiness.

BOYNTON, Jeremy, 1824-1883. 234.
Sanctification practical: a book for the times. By Rev. J. Boynton. With an introduction and an appendix by Mrs. Palmer. New York, Foster and Palmer, jr., 1867. 2 p. l., iii-iv, 3-142 p. 17 cm. [BT765.B7] 234 41-30212
1. Sanctification. I. Palmer, Phoebe (Worrell) Mrs. 1807-1874. II. Title.

BROOKS, John Rives, 1836- 248
Scriptural sanctification; an attempted solution of the holiness problem. By Jno. R. Brooks ... With an introduction by Jno. J. Tigert ... 9th thousand. Nashville, Tenn., Dallas, Tex., Publishing house of the M. E. church, South Smith & Lamar, agents, 1904. xv, 413 p. front. (port.) 19 cm. [BT767.B85] 5-1988
1. Sanctification. I. Title.

CAROL, Angela 248.482
Ways of sanctity. Pulaski, Wis., Franciscan Pubs. [c.1963] 64p. 19cm. .25 pap.,
I. Title.

CARRADINE, Beverly.
The sanctified life, by Rev. B. Carradine ... Cincinati, O., Office of the Revivalist, c1897. 286 p. front. (port.) 19 cm. 16-24754
I. Title.

CARRADINE, Beverly, 1848- 234.8
Sanctification. By Rev. B. Carradine, D.D. Introduction by Rev. L. L. Pickett. Nashville, Tenn., Publishing house of the M. E. church, South, Barbee & Smith, agents, 1891. 227 p. 19 cm. Pages 223-227, advertising matter. [BT765.C3] 41-30213
1. Sanctification. I. Title.

CHURCH, John Robert, 1899- 234.3
Earthen vessels; or, The human element in holiness, by John R. Church ... Introduction by Dr. Paul S. Rees. Grand Rapids, Mich., Zondervan publishing house [1942] 56 p. 20 cm. [BT765.C48] 42-16482
1. Sanctification. I. Title.

COLLINS, J H. 234.8
Sanctification: what it is, when it is, how it is. By Rev. J. H. Collins ... Nashville, Tenn., Southern Methodist publishing house, printed for the author, 1885. 30 p. 16 cm. [BT765.C7] 41-30214
1. Sanctification. I. Title.

DANE, Charles W.
Why, when and how of sanctification, by Charles W. Dane ... Chicago and Boston, The Christian witness company, 1904. 92 p. 17 cm. 4-8305
I. Title.

DANE, Charles W.
Why, when and how of sanctification, by Charles W. Dane ... Chicago and Boston, The Christian witness company, 1904. 92 p. 17 cm. 4-8305
I. Title.

FAIRBAIRN, Charles Victor, 234.8
bp., 1890-
Purity and power; or, The baptism with the Holy Ghost, by Charles V. Fairbairn ... with introduction by Rev. David Anderson. Chicago, Ill., The Christian witness company [c1930] 256 p. 20 1/2 cm. Bibliography: p. 18. [BT767.F25] 31-3088
1. Sanctification. 2. Holy Spirit. 3. Regeneration (Theology) I. Title.

GLASCOCK, James Luther, 284.8
1852-
Some grapes from Eshcol. A sermon on perfect love--what it is, and how to obtain it. By the Rev. J. L. Glascock, and also his Christian experience. With introductions by Rev. E. I. D. Pepper and Rev. John Thompson ... Cincinnati, O., M. W. Knapp, [1896] 53 p. front. (port.) 19 cm. [BT766.G45] 41-31265
1. Sanctification. 2. Methodist Episcopal church—Sermons. I. Title.

GOLZ, L. 248.4
Walking as He walked. Chicago, Moody [c.1963] 63p. 18cm. (Compact bks., 26) .29 pap.,
I. Title.

GREGORY, John.
Sanctification, a gift for this life, by John Gregory. Detroit, Mich., The Truth press association, c1914. 1 p. l., 244 p. illus., pl. 24 cm. 14-22325 1.00
I. Title.

GUARDINI, Romano, 1885- 234.8
The saints in daily Christian life. Philadelphia, Chilton Books [1966] 110 p. illus. 21 cm. "A project of Dimension Books." [BX2350.2.G8] 66-17193
1. Sanctification. 2. Christian life—Catholic authors. I. Title.

HEGRE, Theodore A
"The will of God ...you sanctification." Minneapolis, Bethany Fellowship [1962, c1961] 110 p. 64-16605
1. Sanctification. I. Title.

HOLLENBACK, Roy L
True holiness. [2d ed.] Oroville, Calif., Oro Dam Publishers [1966] 81 p. port. 68-900391
1. Sanctification. I. Title.

HOPE, Ludvig, 1871- 234.12
Sanctification: a discussion of evangelical Christian living, by Ludvig Hope ... A translation by John A. Houkom ... Minneapolis, Minn., The Lutheran free church publishing company [c1933] 64 p. 21 1/2 cm. "The treatise here made available in English constitutes a chapter of a book entitled 'I liv og ded' recently published in Norway."--Forward. [BT765.H57] 33-17138
1. Sanctification. 2. Justification. 3. Christian life. I. Houkom, John Asbjorn, 1890- tr. II. Title.

HUEGEL, Frederick Julius. 234.8
Fairest flower, by F. J. Huegel ... Grand Rapids, Mich., Zondervan publishing house [1945] 85 p. 20 cm. [BT765.H8] 46-14
1. Sanctification. I. Title.

HULME, William Edward, 234.8
1920-
The dynamics of sanctification [by] William E. Hulme. Minneapolis, Augsburg Pub. House [1966] iv. 194 p. 22 cm. Bibliographical footnotes. [BT765.H84] 66-13052
1. Sanctification. I. Title.

LAVELLE, Louis, 1883-1951 235.2
Four saints. Introd. by Illtyd Trethowan [Tr. from French by Dorothea O'Sullivan. Notre Dame, Ind.] Univ. of Notre Dame Pr. [c.1963] xiv, 113p. 18cm. (ndp 33) 64-78 1.25 pap.,
1. Sanctification. 2. Saints. I. Title.

LAVELLE, Louis, 1883-1951. 235.2
Four saints. With an introd. by Illtyd Trethowan. [Translation by Dorothea O'Sullivan. Notre Dame, Ind.] University of Notre Dame Press [c1963] xiv, 113 p. 18 cm. [BT765.L313 1963] 64-78
1. Sanctification. 2. Saints. I. Title.

LAVELLE, Louis, 1883-1951.
The meaning of holiness [as exemplified in four saints: St. Francis of Assisi, St. Teresa of Avila, St. John of the Cross, and St. Francis de Sales] New York, Pantheon Books, 1954. vi, 113p. 23cm. 'This translation of Quatre saints was made by Dorothea O'Sullivan.' A55
1. Francesco d Assisi, Saint, 2. Teresa, Saint, 1515- 1582. 3. Juan de la Cruz, Saint, 1542-1591. 4. Francois de Sales, Saint, Bp. of Geneva, 1567-1622. 5. Sanctification. I. Title.

LOWREY, Asbury, 1816-1898. 234.
Possibilities of grace. By Rev. Asbury Lowrey ... New York, Phillips & Hunt; Cincinnati, Cranston & Stowe, 1884. 472 p. front. (port.) 20 cm. [BT765.L6] 41-33832
1. Sanctification. I. Title.

LOWREY, Asbury, 1816-1898. 234.8
... Possibilities of grace [by] Asbury Lowrey, D.D., abridged by John Paul, D.D. Kansas City, Mo., Beacon hill press, 1944. 121 p. 20 1/2 cm. (Abridged holliness classics) [BT765.L62] 45-9950
1. Sanctification. I. Paul, John Haywood, 1877- II. Title.

MCCUMBER, W. E. 234.8
Our sanctifying God. Kansas City, Mo., Beacon Hill Press [1956] 124p. 20cm. [BT765.M23] 57-1206
1. Sanctification. I. Title.

MARSHALL, Walter, 1628-1680. 234.
The gospel-mystery of sanctification, opened, in sundry practical directions: suited especially to the case of those who labour under the guilt and power of indwelling sin. To which is added a sermon on justification. By Mr. Walter Marshall ... Philadelphia: N. Wiley, southwest corner of Market and Third streets, F. W. Scott, printer, 1804. xvi, [17]-287 p. 16 cm. [BT765.M3 1804] 26-21530
1. Sanctification. I. Title.

MARSHALL, Walter, 1628-1680. 234.
The gospel-mystery of sanctification, opened, in sundry practical directions: suited especially to the case of those who labour under the guilt and power of indwelling sin. To which is added a sermon on justification. By Mr. Walter Marshall ... Lexington: (K.) Printed by Joseph Charless, and sold at his bookstore, where may be had a great variety of books on different subjects. 1804. xvi, [17]-287 p. 16 cm. [BT765.M3 1804 a] 26-21527
1. Sanctification. I. Title.

MARSHALL, Walter, 1628- 234.8
1680.
The gospel-mystery of sanctification opened in sundry practical directions Suited especially to the case of those who labour under the guilt and power of indwelling-sin. To which is added, a sermon on justification. By Walter Marshall ... To which is prefixed, a recommendation by eleven divines ... From the 12th European ed. New-York: Printed and published by Southwick and Pelsue no. 3, New-street. 1811. xi, [1], 13-312 p 19 cm. [BT765.M3 1811] 33-24561
1. Sanctification. I. Title.

MARSHALL, Walter, 1628- 234.8
1680.
The gospel-mystery of sanctification, opened, in sundry practical directions: suited especially to the case of those who labor under the guilt and power of indwelling sin. To which is added a sermon on justification. By Mr. Walter Marshall ... New York, R. Carter & brothers, 1859. xv, [17]-320 p. 16 cm. [BT765.M3 1859] 20-23086
1. Sanctification. I. Title.

MATTISON, Hiram, 1811-1868. 922.
An answer to Dr. Perry's Reply to the Calm review. By H. Mattison ... New-York, 1856. ix, [3]-96 p. 22 1/2 cm. [BX8495.P26P38] 38-20509
1. Perry, James H., 1811-1862. Reply to Professor Mattison's Calm review. 2. Palmer, Mrs. Phoebe (Worrell) 1807-1874. 3. Sanctification. 4. Methodist Episcopal church—Doctrinal and controversial works. I. Title.

MAXWELL, L. E. 232.3
Born crucified, by L. E. Maxwell ... Chicago, Ill., Moody press [1945] 191 p. 20 1/2 cm. Appeared originally in the Sunday school times as a series of articles on "The cross in the life of the believer." cf. Acknowledgments. [BT765.M37] 45-13786
1. Sanctification. 2. Atonement. I. Title.

MERRILL, Stephen Mason, 234.8
bp., 1825-1905.
Sanctification; right views and other views, by S. M. Merrill. Cincinnati, Jennings & Pye; New York, Eaton & Mains [1901] 105 p. 15 cm. (On cover: Little books on doctrine) [BT765.M5] 1-23126
1. Sanctification. I. Title.

MITCHELL, Thomas, Rev. 234.
The old paths: a treatise on sanctification. Scripture the only authority. By Rev. Thomas Mitchell ... Albany, C. Van Benthuysen & sons, print., 1869. 258 p. 17 1/2 cm. [BT765.M55] 41-33063
1. Sanctification. I. Title.

PALMER, Phoebe (Worrell) 1807-1874. 234.
Present to my Christian friend on entire devotion to God. By Mrs. P. Palmer ... 25th thousand. Boston, H. V. Degen, 1857. 192 p. 12 cm. On spine: Entire devotion. [BT765.P3] 43-29159
1. Sanctification. I. Title.

PERRY, James H 1811-1862. 923.773
Reply to Prof. Mattison's "Answer", etc.; being the summing up to the case of Professor Mattison against Mrs. Palmer. By J. H. Perry ... New-York, J. A. Gray's Salamander printing-office, 1856. 106, [1] p. 24 cm. [BX8495.P26P4] 36-37395
1. Mattison, Hiram, 1811-1868. Answer to Dr. Perry's Reply to the Calm review. 2. Palmer, Mrs. Phoebe (Worrell) 1807-1874. 3. Sanctification. 4. Methodist Episcopal church—Doctrinal and controversial works. I. Title.

PINK, Arthur Walkington, 1886-1952. 234.8
The doctrine of sanctification. Grand Rapids. Baker Book House, 1955. 206p. 22cm. [BT765.P5] 55-8587
1. Sanctification. I. Title.

PINK, Arthur Walkington, 1886-1952. 234.8
The doctrine of sanctification [by] Arthur W. Pink. Swengel, Pa., Reiner Publications, 1966. 206 p. 21 cm. [BT765.P5 1966] 67-1476
1. Sanctification. I. Title.

PLUS, Raoul. 234.8
... Holiness in the church, by the Rev. Raoul Plus, S. J.; translated from the original by Mother Mary St. Thomas. London and Edinburgh, Sands & company; St. Louis, Mo., B. Herder book company [1930] 3 p. l., 140 p. 19 cm. (Catholic library of religious knowledge. xi) Translation of La saintete catholique. [BX880.C3 vol. 11] 282.082 35-29374
1. Sanctification. 2. Saints. I. Mary St. Thomas, Mother, 1867- tr. II. Title.

PRICE, Walter K. 234'.8
Channels for power; [how Christians today can know the power of the Holy Spirit in daily living. By Walter K. Price. Nashville, Broadman Press [1966] 63 p. 21 cm. Bibliography: p. 62-63. [BT765.P86] 67-12174
1. Sanctification. I. Title.

PRIOR, Kenneth Francis William 234.8
The way of holiness; the Christian doctrine of sanctification, by Kenneth F. W. Prior. Chicago, Inter-Varsity [1967] 128p. 19cm. (Great doctrines of the Bible) Bibl. [BT765.P7 1967b] 67-27067 1.50 pap.,
1. Sanctification. I. Title.

PRIOR, Kenneth Francis William. 234'.8
The way of holiness: the Christian doctrine of sanctification, by the Rev. Kenneth F. W. Prior. 128 p. 18 1/2 cm. (Great doctrines of the Bible) 6/- (B67-8934) [BT765.P7] 67-90498
1. Sanctification. I. Inter-Varsity Fellowship of Evangelical Unions. II. Title. III. Title: London,

PRIOR, Kenneth Francis William. 234'.8
The way of holiness : a study in Christian growth / Kenneth Prior. Rev. ed. Downers Grove, Ill. : InterVarsity Press, c1982. 172 p. ; 21 cm. Includes bibliographical references. [BT765.P7 1982] 19 82-16214 ISBN 0-87784-380-5 : 4.95
1. Sanctification. I. Title.

RUTH, C[hristian] W[ismer] 1865-
Entire sanctification, a second blessing, together with life sketch, Bible readings and sermon outlines, by Rev. C. W. Ruth. Chicago and Boston, Christian witness co., 1903. 192 p. front. (port.) 20 cm. 3-32543
I. Title.

SCHELL, William Gallio. 234.
Sanctification and holiness, the false and the true, by Rev. Wm. G. Schell ... Chicago, Ill., Herald publishing company, c1922. 1 p. l., [7]-208 p. 19 1/2 cm. [BT765.S4] 23-5963
I. Title.

SPOOLMAN, Jacob. 248
The will to be Christian, by Jacob Spoolman ... Boston, Meador publishing company, 1942. 232 p. 20 cm. [BT765.S65] 42-21914
1. Sanctification. 2. Free will and determinism I. Title.

TAYLOR, Jesse Paul, Bp., 1895- 234.8
Holiness, the finished foundation. Winona Lake, Ind., Light &Life Pr. [c.1963] 216p. 23cm. 63-35498 2.95; 1.95 pap.,
1. Sanctification I. Title.

VAN ZELLER, Hubert 1905- 234.8
Sanctity in other words; presentation for beginners. Springfield, Ill., Templegate [1963] 94 p. 20 cm. [In other words series] [BX2350.2.V3] 63-1969
1. Sanctification. I. Title.

VAN ZELLER, Hubert [Secular name: Claude Van Zeller] 1905- 234.8
Sanctity in other words; a presentation for beginners. Springfield, Ill., Templegate [c.1963] 94p. 20cm. (In other words ser.) 63-1969 2.95
1. Sanctification. I. Title.

WHITAKER, C. B., 1855- 234.8
Entire sanctification a second work of grace. By Rev. C. B. Whitaker ... Grand Rapids, Mich., S. B. Shaw, 1887. viii, [2], [11]-167 p. 15 cm. [BT765.W5] 33-32830
1. Sanctification. I. Title.

WHITE, Ellen Gould (Harmon) Mrs., 1827-1915. 286.7
The sanctified life, by Mrs. E. G. White ... Washington, D.C., South Bend, Ind. [etc.] Review and herald publishing assn. [c1937] 69 p. 19 1/2 cm. "Selections from the writings of Ellen G. White, compiled by the Trustees of the Ellen G. White estate of the United States." [BX6111.W8] 37-16527
1. Sanctification. 2. Seventh-day Adventists—Doctrinal and controversial works. I. Trustees of the Ellen G. White estate of the United States. II. Title.

WINCHESTER, Olive May, 1880-1947. 234.8
Crisis experiences in the Greek New Testament; an investigation of the evidence for the definite, miraculous experiences of regeneration and sanctification as found in the Greek New Testament, especially in the figures emphasized and in the use of the aorist tense. Edited throughout, with final chapter and appendix, by Ross E. Price. Kanss City, Mo., Beacon Hill Press, 193)053. 110p. 20cm. Includes bibliography. [BT765.W53] 53-11007
1. Sanctification. 2. Regeneration (Theology) 3. Greek language. Biblical—Tense. I. Title.

ZEPP, Arthur C.
Progress after entire sanctification, by Rev. Arthur C. Zepp. Chicago and Boston, The Christian witness company, 1909. viii, [2], 9-108 p. 20 cm. $0.50 9-28748
I. Title.

ZEPP, Arthur C.
Walking as He walked; or, Holiness in action; designed to show the practical side of sanctification in its outworking and application to daily life, by Arthur C. Zepp... Chicago and Boston, The Christian witness company, 1912. 134 p. front. (port.) 20 cm. $0.50 12-14726
I. Title.

Sanctification — Addresses, essays, lectures.

SPANN, John Richard, 1891- ed. 230
Fruits of faith. New York, Abingdon-Cokesbury Press [1950] 240 p. 23 cm. Lectures of 18 scholars at the 30th Annual Conference on Ministerial Training. Evanston, Ill., rev. and adapted to book form. [BT765.S63] 50-9179
1. Sanctification — Addresses, essays, lectures. I. Title.

Sanctification— Early works to 1800.

MARSHALL, Walter, 1628-1680. 234.8
The gospel-mystery of sanctification. Grand Rapids, Zondervan Pub. House [1954] viii, 264p. 23cm. Includes Marshall's sermon, The doctrine of justification opened and applied. [BT765.M3 1954] 55-14089
1. Sanctification— Early works to 1800. I. Title.

Sanctification—History of doctrines—Congresses.

OXFORD Institute on Methodist Theological Studies, 6th, 1977. 261.8
Sanctification & liberation : liberal theologies in the light of the Wesleyan tradition / edited by Theodore Runyon ; prepared under the direction of the World Methodist Council. Nashville : Abingdon, c1981. 255 p. ; 20 cm. Papers presented at the conference held under the auspices of the World Methodist Council. Bibliography: p. 245-251. [BT765.O93 1977] 19 80-20287 ISBN 0-687-36810-3 pbk. : 6.95
1. Wesley, John, 1703-1791—Congresses. 2. Sanctification—History of doctrines—Congresses. 3. Liberation theology—Congresses. I. Runyon, Theodore. II. World Methodist Council. III. Title.

Sanctuary doctrine (Seventh-Day Adventists)

FRAZEE, Willmonte Doniphan, 1906- 234
Ransom and reunion through the sanctuary / W. D. Frazee. Nashville : Southern Pub. Association, c1977. 124 p. ; 20 cm. [BX6154.F67] 77-76135 ISBN 0-8127-0138-0 pbk. : 3.95
1. Seventh-Day Adventists—Doctrinal and controversial works. 2. Sanctuary doctrine (Seventh-Day Adventists) I. Title.

FRAZEE, Willmonte Doniphan, 1906- 234
Ransom and reunion through the sanctuary / W. D. Frazee. Nashville : Southern Pub. Association, c1977. 124 p. ; 20 cm. [BX6154.F67] 77-76135 ISBN 0-8127-0138-0 pbk. : 3.95
1. Seventh-Day Adventists—Doctrinal and controversial works. 2. Sanctuary doctrine (Seventh-Day Adventists) I. Title.

Sandeman, Robert, 1718-1771.

FULLER, Andrew, 1754-1815.
Strictures on Sandemanianism. In twelve letters to a friend [!] By Andrew Fuller. New-York: Published by Richard Scott, no. 276 Pearl-street, and sold by all the booksellers in town and country. Largin & Thompson, printers, 1812. 162 (i. e. 216) p. 15 cm. Page 216 incorrectly numbered 162. [BX9747.F8] [BX9747.F8] A 32
1. Sandeman, Robert, 1718-1771. 2. [Sandemanians] I. Title.

[Sandemanians]

FULLER, Andrew, 1754-1815.
Strictures on Sandemanianism. In twelve letters to a friend [!] By Andrew Fuller. New-York: Published by Richard Scott, no. 276 Pearl-street, and sold by all the booksellers in town and country. Largin & Thompson, printers, 1812. 162 (i. e. 216) p. 15 cm. Page 216 incorrectly numbered 162. [BX9747.F8] [BX9747.F8] A 32
1. Sandeman, Robert, 1718-1771. 2. [Sandemanians] I. Title.

Sanders, Alex.

JOHNS, June. 133.4'0924
King of the witches; the world of Alex Sanders. With photos. by Jack Smith. [1st American ed.] New York, Coward-McCann [1970, c1969] 154 p. illus., ports. 22 cm. [BF1408.2.S25J6 1970] 77-104689 5.00
1. Sanders, Alex. I. Title.

Sanders, Billington McCarter, 1789-1854.

MALLARY, Charles Dutton, 1801-1864. 922.673
Living and dying unto the Lord. A discourse in commemoration of the life, services and death of Elder Billington M. Sanders; delivered before the Georgia Baptist convention, at Washington, Wiles co., on Lord's day, April 23, 1854. By C. D. Mallary. Published by request of the convention. Charleston [S.C.] Southern Baptist publication society, 1854. 106 p. port. 15 1/2 cm. [BX6495.S3M3] 36-24284
1. Sanders, Billington McCarter, 1789-1854. I. Title.

Sanderson, Robert, bp. of Lincoln, 1587-1663.

LEWIS, George, 1848- 922.
... Robert Sanderson, chaplain to King Charles the First, regius professor of divinity, Oxford, and bishop of Lincoln, by the Rev. George Lewis ... London, Society for promoting Christian knowledge; New York and Toronto, The Macmillan co., 1924. xiv, 196 p. 20 cm. (English theologians) "Chief writings": p. xiii-xiv. [BX5199.S25L4] 26-5381
1. Sanderson, Robert, bp. of Lincoln, 1587-1663. I. Title.

Sandford, Frank W., 1862-1948.

ABRAM, Victor P. 232.6
The restoration of all things. Amherst, N. H., Chestnut Hill Rd. Kingdom Pr., [c.1962] 149p. 21cm. 62-18059 2.00
1. Sandford, Frank W., 1862-1948. 2. Second Advent. I. Title.

SANDFORD, Frank W., 1862-1948. 910'.45
The golden light upon the two Americas / Frank W.Sandford. Amherst, N.H. : Kingdom Press, [1974] 256 p., [3] leaves of plates (1 fold.) : ill. ; 21 cm. [BV3785.S18A29] 74-192044 ISBN 0-910840-18-0 : 5.00
1. Sandford, Frank W., 1862-1948. 2. Latin America—Description and travel. I. Title.

Sandpaintings.

FOSTER, Kenneth E. 299'.7
Navajo sandpaintings, by Kenneth E. Foster. Window Rock, Ariz., Navajo Tribal Museum, 1964. 34 p. illus. 22 cm. (Navajoland publications, ser. 3) Cover title. Bibliography: p. 33-34. [E99.N3F63] 74-151619
1. Sandpaintings. 2. Navaho Indians—Rites and ceremonies. I. Title. II. Series.

REICHARD, Gladys Amanda, 1893-1955. 299'.7
Navajo medicine man : sandpaintings / by Gladys A. Reichard. New York : Dover Publications, 1977. x, 83 p., [25] leaves of plates : ill. (some col.) ; 31 cm. Reprint of the 1939 ed. published by J. J. Augustin, New York. [E99.N3R37 1977] 77-73298 ISBN 0-486-23329-4 : 6.95
1. Miguelito, Navaho Indian, 1865 (ca.)-1936. 2. Sandpaintings. 3. Navaho Indians—Relgion and mythology. 4. Navaho Indians—Biography. I. Title.

Sandusky, O. St. Mary's church.

[REYNOLDS, Thomas Edward] 1898- 282.771221
St. Mary's church, 1855-1930, Sandusky, Ohio. [Toledo, F. J. Wenzel printing co., 1930] 240 p. illus. (incl. ports.) 28 cm. Illustrated lining-papers. Advertising matter: p. [207]-240. [BX4603.S56S36] 32-2705
1. Sandusky, O. St. Mary's church. I. Title.

Sandwich Islands mission.

BOND, Elias, 1813-1896. 922
Father Bond of Kohala, a chronicle of pioneer life, in Hawaii, put together by Ethel M. Damon. Honolulu, The Friend, 1927. ix, 284 p. illus. (incl. faxsims) plates ports. 25 cm. [BV3680.H4B6] 28-13324
1. Sandwich Islands mission. 2. Missions—

Hawaiian Islands. I. Damon, Ethel M., ed. II. Title. III. Title: A chronicle of pioneer life in Hawaii.

Sandy Spring, Md. Friends Meeting House.

SESQUICENTENNIAL 289.6*0975284 *Sandy Spring Friends Meeting House, 1817-1967.* [Sandy Spring? Md., 1967?] 88 p. illus. 24 cm. Organized by the Sandy Spring Friends Monthly Meeting. [BX7780.S25S47] 72-260115
1. Sandy Spring, Md. Friends Meeting House. I. Sandy Spring, Md. Friends Meeting House. II. Friends, Society of. Sandy Spring Monthly Meeting.

Sandys, Sir John Edwin, 1844-1922.

HAMMOND, Nicholas Geoffrey Lempriere. JUV
Sir John Edwin Sandys, 1844-1922, by N. G. L. Hammond ... Cambridge [Eng.] The University press, 1933. viii, 126, [1] p. front., port. 22 1/2 cm. [PA85.S2ZH3] 924.8 34-11445
1. Sandys, Sir John Edwin, 1844-1922. I. Title.

Sanford, Agnes Mary (White)

SANFORD, Agnes Mary (White) 266'.5'10924 B
Sealed orders [by] Agnes Sanford. Plainfield, N.J., Logos International, 1972. 313 p. 25 cm. Autobiographical. [BR1725.S27A37] 72-76592 ISBN 0-912106-37-9 5.95
1. Sanford, Agnes Mary (White) I. Title.

Sanford, Charlotte, 1936-

SANFORD, Charlotte, 1936- 285'.1'0924 B
Second sight : a miraculous story of vision regained / Charlotte Sanford and Lester David. New York : M. Evans, c1979. 203 p. ; 22 cm. [BX9225.S278A36] 79-10282 ISBN 0-87131-287-5 : 7.95 7.95
1. Sanford, Charlotte, 1936- 2. Presbyterians—United States—Biography. 3. Blind—Biography. I. David, Lester, joint author. II. Title.

Sanford, Joseph, 1797-1831.

BAIRD, Robert, 1798-1863. 922.573
Memoir of the Rev. Joseph Sanford A. M., pastor of the Second Presbyterian church Philadelphia. By Robert Baird ... Philadelphia, H. Perkins; Boston, Perkins & Marvin, 1836. vi, 268 p. front. (port.) 20 cm. [BX9225.S28B3] 36-31800
1. Sanford, Joseph, 1797-1831. I. Title.

Sanger, Tex. First Methodist Church.

HISTORY of First Methodist Church, Sanger, Texas. Denton District, North Texas Conference. Bishop William C. Martin, Rev. T. H. Minga, district superintendent, Rev. Richard T. Perry, pastor. [Sanger? Tex., 1956] 80p. illus., ports. 23cm.
1. Sanger, Tex. First Methodist Church. I. Chambers, Alma (Lain)

Sanhedrin.

MANTEL, Hugo, 1908- 296.6
Studies in the history of the Sanhedrin. Cambridge, Harvard University Press, 1961. xv, 374p. 24cm. (Harvard Semitic series, 17) 'An elaboration of a doctoral dissertation submitted to... Harvard University in 1952.' Bibliography: p. 322-345. [BM655.4.M3 1961] 61-7391
1. Sanhedrin. 2. Sanhedrin, Great. I. Title. II. Series.

Sankaracarya.

DAVIS, Roy Eugene. 126
The path of soul liberation / by Roy Eugene Davis. Lakemont, Ga. : CSA Press, [1975] 79 p. ; 21 cm. Includes Atmabodha by Shankaracharya. Includes bibliographical references. [B132.A8D39] 75-2507 ISBN 0-87707-152-7 pbk. : 1.95
1. Sankaracarya. 2. Atman. 3. Self-knowledge, Theory of. 4. Self-realization. I. Sankaracarya. Atmabodha. English. 1975. II. Title.

MENON, Y Keshava. 181.482
The pure principle; an introduction to the philosophy of Shankara, by Y. Keshava Menon and Richard F. Allen. [East Lansing] Michigan State University Press [1960] xii, 127p. 22cm. [B133.S5M4] 59-11690
1. Sankaracarya. I. Allen, Richard F., 1908- joint author. II. Title.

SIVARAM, Mysore, 1905- 294.5'4
Ananda and the three great acharyas / M. Sivaram. New Delhi : Vikas Pub. House, c1976. [10], 165 p. ; 22 cm. Bibliography: p. [7] (1st group) [BL1228.S588] 76-901494 Rs35.00
1. Sankaracarya. 2. Ramanuja, founder of sect. 3. Madhva, 13th cent. 4. Spiritual life (Hinduism)—History. I. Title.

Sankaracarya. Vivekacudamani.

WOOD, Ernest, 1883-1965 181'.482
The pinnacle of Indian thought; being a new. independent tr. of the Viveka Chudamani (Crest jewel of discrimination) with commentaries. Wheaton, Ill., Theosophical Pub. House [1967] 161p. 18cm. (Quest bk.) [B133.S4V58 1967] 67-5144 1.25 pap.,
1. Sankaracarya. Vivekacudamani. I. Title.

Sankaradeva, 1449-1569.

SREENIVASA Murthy, H. V. 294.5'512
Vaisnavism of Samkaradeva and Ramanuja; a comparative study [by] H. V. Sreenivasa Murthy. [1st ed.] Delhi, Motilal Banarsidass [1973] viii, 254 p. 23 cm. A revision of the author's thesis, Gauhati University. Bibliography: p. [236]-244. [BL1245.V3S64 1973] 73-900571
1. Sankaradeva, 1449-1569. 2. Ramanuja, founder of sect. 3. Vaishnavism. I. Title.
Distributed by Verry, 7.50

Sankey, Ira David, 1840-1908.

LAWRENCE county historical society, New Castle, Pa. 922
The Ira D. Sankey centenary; proceedings of the centenary celebration of the birth of Ira D. Sankey, together with some hitherto unpublished Sankey correspondence. New Castle, Pa., The Lawrence county historical society, 1941. 4 p. l., 109 p. incl. illus., ports. 24 cm. "First edition." Cover-title: Sankey centenary celebration, 1840-1940. Bibliography: p. 108. [BV3785.S2L3] 42-5026
1. Sankey, Ira David, 1840-1908. I. Title.

LUDWIG, Charles, 1918- 922
Sankey still sings, by Charles Ludwig ... Anderson, Ind., The Warner press [1947] vii, 9-164 p. 19 cm. Bibliography: p. 163-164. [BV3785.S2L8] 47-4582
1. Sankey, Ira David, 1840-1908. I. Title.

MOODY, Dwight Lyman, 1837-1899. 243
Dwight Lyman Moody's life work and gospel sermons as delivered by the great evangelist in his revival work in Great Britain and America. Together with a biography of his colaborer, Ira David Sankey. Handsomely illustrated from Gustav Dore. Edited by Richard S. Rhodes. Chicago, Rhodes & McClure publishing co., 1900. 1 p. l., 6, [2], liv, 17-443 p. incl. plates. plates. ports. 20 cm. [BV3797.M7L5] 1-30134
1. Sankey, Ira David, 1840-1918. 2. Evangelistic work. I. Rhodes, Richard S., ed. II. Title.

SANKEY, Ira David, 1840-1908. 783.9
My life and the story of the Gospel hymns and of sacred songs and solos. With an introd. by Theodore L. Cuyler. Philadelphia, Sunday School Times Co., 1907. [New York, AMS Press, 1974] 410 p. illus. 19 cm. [BV330.S4A3 1974] 72-1682 ISBN 0-404-08332-3
1. Sankey, Ira David, 1840-1908. 2. Hymns, English—History and criticism. I. Title.

Sankhya.

ANIRVAN, 1896- 294.5'4
To live within [comp. by] Lizelle Reymond. Foreword by Jacob Needleman. Translated from French by Nancy Pearson & Stanley Spiegelberg. Baltimore, Penguin [1973, c.1971] x 245, [27] p. 18 cm. (Penguin metaphysical library) Translation of La vie dans la vie. [B132.S3A713] 0-14 pap., 1.75
1. Sankhya. I. Reymond, Lizelle, comp. II. Title.
Contents omitted.

ANIRVAN, 1896- 294.5'4
To live within. [Compiled by] Lizelle Reymond. Foreword by Jacob Neddleman. Translated from the French by Nancy Pearson and Stanley Spiegelberg. [1st ed.] Garden City, N.Y., Doubleday, 1971. x, 245 p. illus., port. 22 cm. Translation of La vie dans la vie. Contents.Contents.—Life in a Himalayan hermitage, by L. Reymond.—Talks on samkhya, by Shri Anirvan.—The Bauls of Bengal, by Shri Anirvan.—Mystic songs. [B132.S3A713] 79-147361 6.95
1. Sankhya. I. Reymond, Lizelle, comp. II. Title.

KAPILA. 181'.41
The Samkhya philosophy, containing (1) Samkhya-pravachana sutram, with the vritti of Aniruddha, and the bhasya of Vijnana Bhiksu and extracts from the vritti-sara of Mahadeva Vedantin (2) Tatva samasa (3) Samkhya karika (4) Panchasikha sutram. Translated by Nandalal Sinha. Allahabad, Panini Office, 1915. [New York, AMS Press, 1974] 1 v. (various pagings) 23 cm. Added t.p., dated 1912: The Samkhya-pravachana-sutram. Also includes Narendra's commentary on Kapila's Tattvasamasa. Isvarakrsna's Sankhyakarika and Pancasikha's Pancasikhasutra form appendices 6-7. Original ed. issued as v. 11, of The Sacred books of the Hindus. Texts of Kapila, Isvarakrsna, and Pancasikha in English and Sanskrit; introductory matter and commentaries in English. [B133.K38S313 1974] 73-3799 ISBN 0-404-57811-X
1. Sankhya. I. Narendra. II. Sinha, Nandalal, ed. III. Kapila. Tattvasamasa. English & Sanskrit. 1974. IV. Aniruddha. Sankhyasutravrtti. English. 1974. V. Vijhanabhiksu, fl. 1550. Sankhyapravacanabhasya. English. 1974. VI. Mahadeva Vedantin. Sankhyavrttisara. English. 1974. VII. Isvarakrsna. Sankhyakarika. English & Sanskrit. 1974. VIII. Pancasikha. Pancasikhasutra. English & Sanskrit. 1974. IX. Title. X. Title: The Samkhya-pravachana-sutram. XI. Series: The Sacred books of the Hindus, v. 11.

Sankt Jakob (Monastery), Wurzburg.

DILWORTH, Mark. 271'.1'04333
The Scots in Franconia : a century of monastic life / Mark Dilworth. Totowa, N.J. : Rowman and Littlefield, 1974. 301 p. : ill. ; 23 cm. Includes index. Bibliography: p. 282-289. [BX2618.S3117D54 1974b] 74-195058 ISBN 0-87471-453-2 : 13.50
1. Sankt Jakob (Monastery), Wurzburg. 2. Scotch in Franconia. I. Title.

Sanskirt drama—Bibliography

SCHUYLER, Montgomery, 1877-
A bibliography of the Sanskirt drama, with an introductory sketch of the dramatic literature of India, by Montgomery Schuyler, jr. ... New York, The Columbia university press, the Macmillan company, agents, 1906. xi, 105 p. 22 cm. (Added t.-p.: Columbia university Indo-Iranian series ... vol. iii) [Z7090.S35] 6-13672
1. Sanskirt drama—Bibl. I. Title.

Sanskrit drama—History and criticism

KEITH, Arthur Berriedale, 1879-
The Sanskrit drama in its origin, development, theory & practice, by A. Berriedale Keith ... Oxford, The Clarendon press, 1924. 405, [1] p. 23 cm. [PK2931.K4] 24-24835
1. Sanskrit drama—Hist. & crit. I. Title.

Sanskrit drama—Technique.

DHAMAMJAYA.
... *The Dasarupa;* a treatise on Hindu dramaturgy, by Dhanamjaya, now first translated from the Sanskrit with the text and an introduction and notes, by George C. O. Haas ... New York [Lancaster, Pa., Press of the New era printing company] 1912. xiv, 169 p., 1 l. 23 cm. (Columbia university Indo-Iranian series, v. 7) Thesis (PH.D.)--Columbia university, 1909. Vita. Text transliterated. Published also without thesis note. "Conspectus of editions of texts": p. xiv-xvii. Bibliography: p. xiii. [PK4131.D62] 13-1325
1. Sanskrit drama—Technique. I. Haas, George Christian Otto, 1883- II. Title.

DHANAMJAYA.
The Dasarupa; a treatise on Hindu dramaturgy, by Dhanamjaya, now first translated from the Sanskrit with the text and an introduction and notes, by George C. O. Haas ... New York, Columbia university press, 1912. xiv, 169 p. 23 cm. (Added t.-p. Columbia university Indo-Iranian series, ed. by A. V. Williams Jackson ... vo. 7) Text transliterated. "Conspectus of edition of texts": p. xiv-xvii. Bibliography: p. xiii. [PK4131.D6] 12-22978 1.50
1. Sanskrit drama—Technique. I. Hass, George Christian Otto. II. Title.

Sanskrit language—Dictionaries—English.

MACDONELL, Arthur Anthony, 1854-1930.
A practical Sanskrit dictionary with transliteration, accentuation, and etymological analysis throughout, by Arthur Anthony Macdonell... London, Oxford university press H. Milford, 1924. ix, [3], 382 p. 20 1/2 cm. "The original edition of this dictionary was published by Messers. Longmans, Green & co., and has been reproduced photographically with their consent." [PK933.M3] 24-31889
1. Sanskrit language—Dictionaries—English. 2. English language—Dictionaries—Sanskrit. I. Title.

MONIER-WILLIAMS, Monier, Sir. 1819-1889.
A Sanskrit-English dictionary etymologically and philologically arranged with special reference to cognte Indo-European languages, by Sir Monier Monier-Williams ... New ed., greatly enl. and improved, with the collaboration of Professor E. Leumann ... Professor C. Chappeller ... and other scholars. Oxford, The Clarendon press, 1899. xxxiv, [2], 1333 p. 31 cm. [PK933.M6 1899] 11-24167
1. Sanskrit language—Dictionaries—English. 2. English language—Dictionaries—Sanskrit. I. Leumann, Ernst, 1859-1931. II. Chappeller, Carl, 1840-1925. III. Title.

MONIER-WILLIAMS, Monier, Sir. 1819-1899.
A Sanskrit-English dictionary etymologically and philologically arranged with special reference to Greek, Latin, Gothic, German, Anglo-Saxon, and other cognate Indo-European languages, by Monier Williams ... Oxford, The Clarendon press; [etc., etc.] 1872. xxv, [3], 1186 p. 28 cm. [PK933.M6 1872] 11-24168
1. Sanskrit language—Dictionaries—English. 2. English language—Dictionaries—Sanskrit. I. Title.

Sanskrit language—Terms and phrases.

TYBERG, Judith. 212
Sanskrit keys to the wisdom-religion; an exposition of the philosophical and religious teachings imbodied in the Sanskrit terms used in theosophical and occult literature [by] Judith Tyberg ... Point Loma, Calif., Theosophical university press, 1940. xvi p., 1 l., 163 p. diagr. 23 cm. Includes blank pages for "Notes". "References for further study": p. [149]-154. [Full name: Judith Marjorie Tyberg] [BP527.T9] 41-1893

1. Sanskrit language—Terms and phrases. 2. Theosophy—Terminology. I. Title.

Sanskrit literature—History and criticism.

ASVAGHOSA. 294.3'82
The awakening of faith, attributed to Asvaghosha. Translated, with commentary, by Yoshito S. Hakeda. New York, Columbia University Press, 1967. xi, 128 p. 24 cm. "Prepared for the Columbia College program of translations from the oriental classics." Translation of the Chinese version of the Sanskrit manuscript: Mahayanasraddhotpadasastra. Bibliography: p. 119-122. [BL1416.A7M33] 67-13778
I. Hakeda, Yoshito S., tr. II. Title.

WINTERNITZ, Moriz, 1863-1937. 294
A history of Indian literature. Translated from the original German by S. Ketkar, and rev. by the author. New York, Russell & Russell [1971] 2 v. 25 cm. Reprint of the 1927-33 ed. Vol. 2 translated by S. Ketkar and H. Kohn. Translation of Geschichte der indischen litteratur. Includes bibliographical references. [PK2903.W63 1971] 73-151559
1. Sanskrit literature—History and criticism. 2. Indic literature—History and criticism. 3. Pali literature—History and criticism. 4. Jaina literature—History and criticism. I. Title.

Sanskrit literature—Translations into English.

HINDU literature ...
with critical and biographical sketches by Epiphanius Wilson, A. M. Limited ed. de luxe. London, New York [etc.] The Colonial press [1902] 2 p. l., v p., 1 l., 467 p. col. front., 2 pl., port., facsim. 24 cm. (Added t.-p.: Literature of the Orient. Byzantine ed.) "Limited to five hundred copies." This copy not numbered. Added t.-p., illuminated: Literature of the Orient. Byzantine ed. Edited, grouped & classified, with introduction & translations by Sir Edwin Arnold, Max Muller, LL. D., Rene Basset, PH. D., Richard Gotthell, PH. D., & other oriental scholars. Epiphanius Wilson, A. M., literary editor; Clarence Cook, art editor. [PJ302.L5 vol. 5] 2-21966
1. Sanskrit literature—Translations into English. 2. English literature—Translations from Sanskrit. I. Histopadesa. II. Mahabharata. Nalopakhyanam. III. Valmiki. Ramayana. English. IV. Kalidasa. Sakuntala. English. V. Dutt, Toru, 1856-1877. VI. Arnold, Edwin, Sir 1832-1904, tr. VII. Monier-Williams, Monler, Sir 1819-1899, tr. VIII. Wilson, Epiphanius, 1845-1916, ed.
Contents omitted.

HITOPADESA, English.
Fables and proverbs from the Sanskrit; being the Hitopadesa translated by Charles Wilkins. With an introduction by Henry Morley... 2d ed. London, New York, G. Routledge and sons, 1886. 277 p. 20 cm. (Half-title: Morley's universal library [v. 30]) [PK3741.H6E5 1886] 41-40996
I. Morley, Henry, 1822-1894, ed. II. Wilkins, Sir Charles, 1740?-1836, tr. III. Title.

HITOPADESA, English.
Fables and proverbs from the Sanskrit, being the Hitopadesa translated by Charles Wilkins. With an introduction by Henry Morley... 3d ed. London, New York [etc.] G. Routledge and sons, 1888. 277 p. 20 cm. (Half-title: Morley's universal library [v.30]) [PK3741.H6E5 1888] 1-18409
I. Morley, Henry, 1822-1894, ed. II. Wilkins, Sir Charles, 1749?-1836., tr. III. Title.

Sanskrit poetry—History and criticism

SIDHANTA, Nirmal Kumar.
The heroic age of India; a comparative study, by N. K. Sidhanta ... London, K. Paul, Trench, Trubner & co., ltd.; New York, A. A. Knopf, 1929. viii, 224 p. 24 1/2 cm. (Half-title: The History of Civiliation. [Pre-history and antiquity]) [PK2919.S5 1929] 29-29955
1. Sanskrit poetry—Hist. & crit. 2. Epic poetry—Hist. & crit. 3. Literature, Comparative. 4. India—Civiliation. 5. Civilization—Hist. I. Title.

SIDHANTA, Nirmal Kumar.
The heroic age of India, a comparative study, by N. K. Sidhanta ... London, K. Paul, Trench, Trubner & co., ltd.; viii, 232 p. 24 1/2 cm. (Half-title: The History of civilization ... [Pre-history and antiquity]) Bibliographical foot-notes. [PK2919.S5 1929a] 46-33480
1. Sanskrit poetry—Hist. & crit. 2. Epic poetry—Hist. & crit. 3. Literature, Comparative. 4. India—Civilization. 5. Civilization—Hist. I. Title.

Sant Mat.

DARSHAN Singh, Maharaj. 299
The secret of secrets : spiritual talks / Darshan Singh. 1st ed. Bowling Green, Va. : Sawan Kirpal Publications, 1978. x, 255 p. : ports. ; 21 cm. [BL2018.7.S3D35] 78-69930 ISBN 0-918224-06-3 : 2.50
1. Sant Mat. I. Title.

Sant Nirankari Mandal.

GARGI, Balwant, 1916- 294
Nirankari Baba. [Delhi] Thomson Press (India), Publication Division, 1973,[i.e.1974] 172 p. illus. 23 cm. [BP605.S12G37] 73-906699
1. Sant Nirankari Mandal. 2. Singh, Gurbachan, 1930- I. Title.
Distributed by International Publications Service; 9.00.

Santa Barbara Mission.

ENGELHARDT, Zephyrin, father, 1851-1934. 271.
Santa Barbara mission, by Fr. Zephyrin Engelhardt... San Francisco, Cal., The James H. Barry company, 1923. xviii, 470 p. incl. front., illus. 22 cm. (The Missions and missionaries of California. New series. Local history) Includes music. [Secular name: Charles Anthony Engelhardt] [F364.E65] [F869.S45E6] [F869.S45E5] 979. 979. 22-10910
1. Santa Barbara mission. I. Title.

GEIGER, Maynard J 1901- 266.27949
Mission Santa Barbara, 1782-1965, by Maynard Geiger. Santa Barbara, Calif. [Franciscan Fathers of California] 1965. 285 p. illus., ports. 24 cm. Bibliography: p. [265]-272. [F869.S45G4] 66-6613
1. Santa Barbara Mission. I. Title.

GEIGER, Maynard J., 1901- 726.41
A pictorial history of the physical development of Mission Santa Barbara, from brush hut to institutional greatness, 1786-1963. [Oakland, Calif., Franciscan Fathers of California, c1963] x, 180 p. illus., plans. 28 cm. 500 copies. Copy no. 213. [NA5235.S26G4] 64-911
1. Santa Barbara Mission. I. Title.

Santa Clara Mission.

SPEARMAN, Arthur Dunning, 1899-
The five Franciscan churches of Mission Santa Clara, 1777-1825; a documentation. Palo Alto, Calif., National Press[c1963] xiv, 164 p. illus., facsims., maps (part fold.) ports. 27 cm. Bibliography: p. 153-157.
1. Santa Clara Mission. I. Title.

Santa Claus.

[CHURCH, Francis Pharcellus] 1839-1906. 394.2'68282
Yes, Virginia. Illustrated by Suzanne Hausman. New York, Elizabeth Press [1972] [31] p. illus. (part col.) 22 x 24 cm. Contains chiefly the text of the editorial by F. P. Church which appeared in the New York Sun, September 21, 1897 under title: Is there a Santa Claus? The text of the well-known editorial explaining that Santa Claus exists despite rumors to the contrary. [GT4985.C545 1972] 72-87236 3.95
1. O'Hanlon, Virginia—Juvenile literature. 2. Santa Claus. 3. [Santa Claus.] 4. [Christmas.] I. O'Hanlon, Virginia. II. Hausman, Suzanne, illus. III. Title.

EBON, Martin. 282'.092'4 B
Saint Nicholas : life and legend / Martin Ebon. 1st ed. New York : Harper & Row, [1975] p. cm. Bibliography: p. [BX4700.N55E26 1975] 75-9329 ISBN 0-06-062113-3 : 8.95
1. Nicholas, Saint, Bp. of Myra. 2. Santa Claus.

WALSH, William Shepard, 1854- 394.
The story of Santa Klaus; told for children of all ages from six to sixty, by William S. Walsh, and illustrated by artists of all ages from Fra Angelico to Henry Hutt. New York, Moffat, Yard and company, 1909. 4 p. l., 13-222 p. incl. plates. front., plates. 20 1/2 cm. [GT4985.W3] 9-30036
1. Santa Claus. I. Title.

WALSH, William Shepard, 1854-1919. 394.268
The story of Santa Klaus; told for children of all ages from six to sixty, and illustrated by artists of all ages from Fra Angelico to Henry Hutt. Detroit, Gale Research Co., 1970. 222 p. illus. 23 cm. Reprint of the 1909 ed. [GT4985.W3 1970] 68-58166
1. Santa Claus. I. Title.

Santa Fe, N. M. Cathedral of San Francisco de Asis.

CHAVEZ, Angelico, 1910- 978.9
Al Conquistadora; the autobiography of an ancient statue. Paterson, N. J., St. Anthony Guild Press, 1954. 134p. illus. 23cm. [BT660.S45C5] 54-8231
1. Santa Fe, N. M. Cathedral of San Francisco de Asis. La Conquistadora (Statue) 2. Santa Fe, N. M.—Church history. I. Title.

CHAVEZ, Angelico, Father, 1910- 282.789
The Cathedral of the Royal City of the Holy Faith of Saint Francis. Santa Fe, c1947. [52] p. illus., ports. 20 cm. Cover title: The Santa Fe Cathedral. Secular name: Manuel Chaves. [BX4603.S58C3] 48-12355
1. Santa Fe, N. M. Cathedral of San Francisco de Asis. I. Title.

Santa Fe, N.M. San Miguel (Church)

B Lewis Brother, F.S.C., 1906- 917.89'56
Oldest church in U.S., the San Miguel Chapel, Santa Fe, New Mexico [by] Brother B. Lewis, F. S. C. [Santa Fe? N.M.] 1968. [60] p. illus. 19 cm. Reprint of the 1957 ed. On cover: Story of the San Miquel, oldest chapel in the U.S., Santa Fe, New Mexico. "Published as a guide to the San Miguel Church." [BX4603.S58S262 1968] 73-176787
1. Santa Fe, N.M. San Miguel (Church) I. Title. II. Title: Story of the San Miquel.

Santa Maria Maddalena dei Pazzi (Church), Florence.

LUCHS, Alison. 726'.5'094551
Cestello, a Cistercian church of the Florentine renaissance / Alison Luchs. New York : Garland Pub. Co., 1977. xix, 443 p. : ill. ; 21 cm. (Outstanding dissertations in the fine arts) Originally presented as the author's thesis, Johns Hopkins University, 1975. Bibliography: p. 421-443. [NA5621.F748L8 1977] 76-23642 ISBN 0-8240-2706-X lib.bdg. : 45.00
1. Santa Maria Maddalena dei Pazzi (Church), Florence. 2. Architecture, Cistercian—Italy—Florence. 3. Art, Italian—Italy—Florence. 4. Art, Renaissance—Italy—Florence. I. Title. II. Series.

Santa Ynes mission.

ENGELHARDT, Zephyrin, father, 1851- 271.30979491
Mission Santa Ines, virgen y martir,and its ecclesiastical seminary, by Fr. Zephyrin Engelhardt... Santa Barbara, Calif., Mission Santa Barbara, 1932. ix, [1], 194, [7] p. incl. front., illus., ports., map, plans. 22 cm. (Missions and missionaries of California. New series. Local history) With this is bound the author's Mission La Concepcion Purisima de Maria Santisima. Santa Barbara, Calif., 1932. Includes music. [Secular name: Charles Anthony Engelhardt] [F864.E569] [F370.M6E45] 979.40082 33-29510
1. Santa Ynes mission. I. Title.

Santals.

GAUSDAL, Johannes. 291.211
The Santal khuts; contribution to animistic research. Oslo, Aschehoug; Cambridge, Harvard University Press, 1960. 218 p. illus., facsims., tables. 24 cm. (Institutte for sammenlignende kulturforskning. Serie B: Skrifter, 50) [GN471.G3 1960] 63-4260
1. Santals. 2. Animism. I. Title. II. Series. III. Series: Instituttet for sammenlignende kulturforskning, Oslo. Serie B: Skrifter, 50

Santayana, George, 1863-1952.

BUTLER, Richard, 1918- 921.1
The life and world of George Santayana. Chicago, H. Regnery Co. [1960] 205p. 28cm. [B945.S24B78] 60-7924
1. Santayana, George, 1863-1952. I. Title.

CORY, Daniel, 1904- 921.1
Santayana: the later years; a portrait with letters. New York, Braziller [c.1963] 330p. 24cm. Bibl. 63-19573 7.50
1. Santayana, George, 1863-1952. I. Title.

HOWGATE, George Washburne, 1903- 921.1
George Santayana, by George W. Howgate. Philadelphia, University of Pennsylvania press; London, H. Milford, Oxford university press, 1938. viii p., 1 l., 363 p. 24 cm. Bibliography: p. 349-352. [B945.S24H6] 39-787
1. Santayana, George, 1863- I. Title.

HOWGATE, George Washburne, 1903- 921.1
George Santayanna, by George W. Howgate. Philadelphia, University of Pennsylvania press; London, H. Milford, Oxford university press, 1938. viii p., 1 l, 363 p. 23 1/2 cm. Bibliography: p. 349-352. [B945.S24H6] 39-787
1. Santayna, George, 1863- I. Title.

KIRKWOOD, Mossie May (Waddington) 921.1
Santayana: saint of the imagination. [Toronto] University of Toronto Press, 1961. 240p. illus. 24cm. [B945.S24K54] 61-65164
1. Santayana, George, 1863-1952. I. Title.

THE moral philosophy of
Santayana. New York, Humanities Press, 1958. vii, 116p. Issued also as thesis, Columbia University, 1939.
1. Santayana, George, 1863-1952. 2. Ethics. I. Munitz, Milton Karl, 1913-

PELLINO, Michael William, 1915- 149'.73
George Santayana and the endless comedy, by Michael W. Pellino. New York, Carlton Press [1968] 63 p. 21 cm. (A Hearthstone book) [B945.S24P4] 68-6531
1. Santayana, George, 1863-1952. Skepticism and animal faith. I. Title.

Santayana, George, 1863-1952—Aesthetics.

ASHMORE, Jerome 111.850924
Santayana, art, and aesthetics. [Cleveland] Pr. of Western Reserve Univ. [c.]1966. xii, 139p. 24cm. (Case Inst. of Tech. bk. in the humanities and social scis.) Bibl. [B945.S24A85] 66-16889 5.00
1. Santayana, George, 1863-1952—Aesthetics. I. Title.

SINGER, Irving. 111.8'5
Santayana's aesthetics; a critical introduction. Westport, Conn., Greenwood Press [1973, c1957] ix, 235 p. 22 cm. Includes bibliographical references. [B945.S24S55 1973] 72-12317 ISBN 0-8371-6696-9 11.25
1. Santayana, George, 1863-1952—Aesthetics. I. Title.

Santeria (Cultus)

GONZALEZ-WIPPLER, Migene. 299'.6
Santeria; African magic in Latin America. Garden City, N.Y., Doubleday [1975

c1973] 178 p. illus. 18 cm. (Anchor books) Bibliography: p. 167-168. [BL2532.S3G66] ISBN 0-385-09696-8 2.95 (pbk.)
1. Santeria (Cultus) I. Title.
L.C. card no. for original ed.: 73-82439

GONZALEZ-WIPPLER, Migene. 299'.6
Santeria; African magic in Latin America. New York, Julian Press [1973] 181 p. illus. 22 cm. Bibliography: p. 172-173. [BL2532.S3G66] 73-82439 ISBN 0-87097-055-0 6.50
1. Santeria (Cultus) I. Title.

Santiago de Compostela.

STARKIE, Walter Fitzwilliam, 1894- 248.29
The road to Santiago: pilgrims of St. James [by] Walter Starkie. Berkeley, University of California Press, 1965. x, 339 p. illus., fold. map, music 23 cm. Partly autobiographical. Bibliographical footnotes. [BX2321.S3S68] 65-5668
1. James, Saint, apostle. 2. Santiago de Compostela. 3. Pilgrims and pilgrimages—Spain. 4. Spain—Descr. & trav. I. Title.

STARKIE, Walter Fitzwilliam, 1894- 248
The road to Santiago; pilgrims of St. James. New York, Dutton, 1957. x, 339 p. illus., map, music. 22 cm. Bibliographical footnotes. [BX2321.S3S68] A 58
1. James, Saint, Apostle. 2. Santiago de Compostela. 3. Pilgrimages—Spain. 4. Spain—Description and travel. I. Title.

Santiago de Compostela, Cathedral.

CONANT, Kenneth John.
The early architectural history of the cathedral of Santiago de Compostela, by Kenneth John Conant. Cambridge, Harvard university press. 1926. xi, [1] 81, [1], p., 1 l., incl. viii pl. front.. plates col. fold. plan. 32 cm. [NA5811.S46C6] 26-14242
1. Santiago de Compostela, Cathedral. I. Title.

Santification.

TAYLOR, Jesse Paul, Bp., 1895- 234'.1
Holiness, the finished foundation. Winona Lake, Ind., Light and Life Press [1963] 216 p. 28 cm. [BT765.T3] 63-35498
1. Santification. I. Title.

Santo Nino Jesus de Cebu (Statue)

TENAZAS, Rosa C. 246.3
The Santo Nino of Cebu [by] Rosa C. P. Tenazas. Manila, Catholic Trade School: foreign dist. by the Cellar Bk. Shop, Detroit, 1965. vii, 122p. illus. 23cm. (San Carlos pubns. Ser. A. Humanities, no. 4) On verso of t.p.: 'Series A: Humanities, number 5. [BX2159.C4T4] 66-6769 3.25 pap.,
1. Santo Nino Jesus de Cebu (Statue) I. Title. II. Series.

Santos (Art)

ESPINOSA, Jose Edmundo, 1900- 704.948'4
Saints in the valleys; Christian sacred images in the history, life and folk art of Spanish New Mexico [by] Jose E. Espinosa. Rev. ed. [Albuquerque] University of New Mexico Press [1967] xiii, 122 p. illus., map (on lining paper) 28 cm. Bibliography: p. 101-108. [N8080.E8 1967] 67-2675
1. Santos (Art) 2. Folk art—New Mexico. 3. Art, Latin American. I. Title.

MILLS, George Thompson. 704.948'6
The people of the saints [by] George Mills. Colorado Springs, Taylor Museum [1967] 71 p., 32 col. plates. 16 x 17 cm. "Illustrated ... from the collection of the Taylor Museum of the Colorado Springs Fine Arts Center." Bibliographical references included in "Footnotes" (p. 63-65) [NK835.N5M5] 68-1617
1. Santos (Art) 2. Folk art—New Mexico. 3. Art, Latin-American. I. Colorado Springs. Fine Arts Center. Taylor Museum. II. Title.

NEW Mexico 704.948'2'09789
santos: how to name them. Illus. by Frances Breese. Foreword and captions by E.Boyd. Santa Fe, N.M., Museum of New Mexico [and] International Folk Art Foundation, 1966. 1 v. (chiefly illus.) 26 cm. [NK835.N5N4] 68-6768
1. Santos (Art) 2. Folk art—New Mexico. I. Breese, Frances, illus. II. Hall, Elizabeth Boyd (White) 1903- III. International Folk Art Foundation. IV. Santa Fe., N.M. Museum of New Mexico.

Santos (Art)—New Mexico.

HALL, Elizabeth Boyd (White) 1903- 704.948'2'09789
The New Mexico santero, by E. Boyd. [Santa Fe, Museum of New Mexico Press, 1969] 23, [1] p. illus. 28 cm. Bibliography: p. [24] [N7910.N6H2] 73-628661
1. Santos (Art)—New Mexico. I. Title.

STEELE, Thomas J. 704.948'2'09789
Santos and saints : essays and handbook / by Thomas J. Steele. 1st ed. Albuquerque : Calvin Horn, 1974. viii, 220 p. : ill. ; 24 cm. Includes bibliographical references and index. [N7910.N6S8] 74-75452 ISBN 0-910750-30-0 : 10.00
1. Santos (Art)—New Mexico. 2. Art, Spanish-American—New Mexico. I. Title.

WILDER, Mitchell A. 704.948'2
Santos : the religious folk art of New Mexico : text and photographs / by Mitchell A. Wilder, with Edgar Breitenbach. New York : Hacker Art Books, 1976. 49, [64] p., [32] leaves of plates : ill. ; 32 cm. Reprint of the 1943 ed. published by Taylor Museum of the Colorado Springs Fine Arts Center, Colorado Springs, Colo. Bibliography: p. 48-49 (1st group) [N7910.N6W5 1976] 75-11066 ISBN 0-87817-169-X lib.bdg. : 30.00
1. Santos (Art)—New Mexico. 2. Folk art—New Mexico. 3. Art, Spanish-American—New Mexico. I. Breitenbach, Edgar, joint author. II. Title.

Santos (Art)—Southwest, New—Catalogs.

DENVER. Art Museum. 704.948'2'074018883
Santos of the Southwest; the Denver Art Museum collection. [Text prepared by Mary Jane Downing. Florence B. Haslett, photographer. Denver, Lithography by A. B. Hirschfeld Press, 1969?] 72 p. illus. 26 cm. Bibliography: p. 70. [N7822.D4A75] 72-25362
1. Santos (Art)—Southwest, New—Catalogs. I. Downing, Mary Jane. II. Title.

Sanvitores, Diego Luis de, 1627-1672.

[LEDESMA, Andres de] d.1684. 266'.2'967
Mission in the Marianas : an account of Father Diego Luis de Sanvitores and his companions, 1669-1670 / translated, with commentary by Ward Barrett. Minneapolis : University of Minnesota Press, c1975. vii, 62 p. : ill. ; 23 cm. (A publication from the James Ford Bell Library at the University of Minnesota) Translation of Noticia de los progressos de nuestra Santa Fe, en las Islas Marianas ... desde 15 de mayo de 1669 ... Includes bibliographical references and index. [BV3680.G8L413] 74-27258 ISBN 0-8166-0747-8 : 8.50
1. Sanvitores, Diego Luis de, 1627-1672. 2. Missions—Mariana Islands. 3. Jesuits—Missions. 4. Mariana Islands—History. I. Barrett, Ward J. II. Jesuits. Letters from missions. III. Title. IV. Series: James Ford Bell Library. A publication from the James Ford Bell Library at the University of Minnesota.

Sarada Devi, 1853-1920.

NIKHILANANDA, Swami. 921.9
Holy mother; being the life the life of Sri Sarada Devi, wife of Sri Ramakrishna and helpmate in his mission. New York 28, Ramakrishna-Vivekananda ctr., 17 E. 94th St. [c.]1962. 334p. illus. 21cm. 62-13423 4.50
1. Sarada Devi, 1853-1920. I. Title.

NIKHILANANDA, Swami. 921.9
Holy mother; being the life of Sri Sarada Devi, wife of Sri Ramakrishna and helpmate in his mission. [1st ed.] New York, Ramakrishna-Vivekananda Center, 1962. 334p. illus. 21cm. [B133.S62N5] 62-13423
1. Sarada Devi, 1853-1920. I. Title.

Saranac, N. Y. First Methodist Episcopal church.

BULL, Henry J. 287.
A history of the First Methodist Episcopal church of Saranac, Clinton County, N. Y. By Henry J. Bull, September, 1912. [n. p., 1912] 54 p., 1 l. front., plates, port. 24 cm. [BX8481.S43F5] 22-13796
1. Saranac, N. Y. First Methodist Episcopal church. I. Title.

Sarcophagi.

HANFMANN, George Maxim Anossov, 1911- 733.176
The Season sarcophagus in Dumbarton Oaks. Cambridge, Harvard University Press, 1951 [i. e. 1952] 2 v. plates. 30 cm. (Dumbarton Oaks studies, 2) "A catalogue of the representations of the Horae and the Seasons in ancient art": v. 2, p. [129]-192. Includes bibliographies. [NB1810.H3] 52-7580
1. Sarcophagi. 2. Seasons in art. 3. Art, Roman. I. Title. II. Series.

LAWRENCE, Marion, 1901-
The sarcophagi of Ravenna. [New York] College Art Assn. of America in conjunction with the Art Bulletin, 1945. x, 53 p. plates. 31 cm. (Monographs on archaeology and fine arts, 2) Bibliographical footnotes. A 48
1. Sarcophagi. 2. Tombs—Italy—Ravenna. 3. Christian art and symbolism. I. Title. II. Series.

Sardica, Synod of, 343-344.

HESS, Hamilton. 262.3
The Canons of the Council of Sardica, A. D. 343; a landmark in the early development of Canon law. Oxford, Clarendon Press, 1958. viii, 170p. 22cm. (Oxford theological monographs, v. 1) Bibliography: p. 159-163. 58-1441
1. Sardica, Synod of, 343-344. 2. Bishops (Canon law) I. Title. II. Series.

Sargeant, Genevieve (Gildersleeve)

HENDRICKSON, Albert L 1893- 922.673
Life in a floating city, by Albert L. Hendrickson. Nashville, Southern Pub. Association [1964] 166 p. illus. 21 cm. [BX6193.S3H4] 64-18174
1. Sargeant, Genevieve (Gildersleeve) I. Title.

Sarles, Mrs. Mary Elizabeth (Smalley) 1834-1866.

SARLES, John Wesley, 1817-1903. 922.673
Memorial of Mary E. Smalley, late the wife of John W. Sarles, pastor of the Central Baptist church, Brooklyn. By her husband. New York, Holman, printer, 1867. vi p., 1 l., 217 p. front. (port.) 19 cm. [BX6495.S35S3] 36-24287
1. Sarles, Mrs. Mary Elizabeth (Smalley) 1834-1866. I. Title.

Sarpi, Paolo, 1552-1623.

LIEVSAY, John Leon. 282'.092'4 B
Venetian Phoenix: Paolo Sarpi and some of his English friends (1606-1700) Lawrence, University Press of Kansas [1973] 262 p. 23 cm. Bibliography: p. 235-250. [BX4705.S36L53] 73-6818 ISBN 0-7006-0108-2 11.00
1. Sarpi, Paolo, 1552-1623. I. Title.

Sartre, Jean-Paul, 1905-

KING, Thomas Mulvihill, 1929- 200'.1
Sartre and the sacred / Thomas M. King. Chicago : University of Chicago Press, 1974. xii, 200 p. ; 22 cm. Includes index. Bibliography: p. 193-196. [B2430.S34K44] 73-87304 ISBN 0-226-43612-8
1. Sartre, Jean Paul, 1905- 2. Holy, The. I. Title.

MARCEL, Gabriel, 1889-
The philosophy of existentialism. [7th ed.] New York, Citadel Press [1966] 128 p. 68-78698
1. Sartre, Jean-Paul, 1905- 2. Marcel, Gabriel, 1887- 3. Existentialism. I. Title.

Sartre, Jean Paul, 1905- — Ethics.

WARNOCK, Mary. 171
Existentialist ethics. London, Macmillan; New York, St. Martin's p., 1967. [6], 58 p. 22 cm. (New studies in ethics) 7/6 (B 67-10790) Includes chapters on Klerkegaard and Heidegger. Bibliography: p. 58. [B2430.S34W28] 67-11399
1. Sartre, Jean Paul, 1905- — Ethics. 2. Heidegger, Martin, 1889- — Ethics. 3. Klerkegaard, Sgren Aabye, 1813-1855 — Ethics. I. Title.

Sarvastivadins.

PATIMOKKHA. English. 294.3'822
Buddhist monastic discipline: the Sanskrit Pratimoksa sutras of the Mahasamghikas and Mulasarvastivadins. [Edited by] Charles S. Prebish. University Park, Pennsylvania State University Press [1975] 156 p. 24 cm. "The Mahasamghika and Mulasarvastivadin Pratimoksa sutras presented face to face for easy comparison." Bibliography: p. [151]-156. [BQ2272.E5P73] 74-10743 ISBN 0-271-01171-8
1. Sarvastivadins. 2. Mahasanghikas. 3. Monasticism and religious orders, Buddhist—Rules. I. Prebish, Charles S., ed. II. Title.

Satanism.

BROOKS, Thomas, 1608-1680.
Precious remedies against Satan's devices with the Covenant of grace. [Ann Arbor] Sovereign Grace publishers, 1960. 316 p. 65-27951
I. Title.

COLMAN, Benjamin, 1673-1747. 235
The case of Satan's fiery darts in blasphemous suggestions and hellish annoyances; as they were considered in several sermons, heretofore preach'd to to the congregation in Brattlestreet, Boston, May 1711. and lately repeated to them May 1743. By Bejamin Colman, D. D., pastor of said church. And now publish'd at the desire of some, who having suffer'd by such temptations, would thus (by the will of God) minister to the direction and support of others in like spiritual trouble and distress ... Boston, Printed by Rogers and Fowle, for J. Edwards in Cornhill. 1714. 1 p. l., [5]-95 p. 22 cm. Half-title (?) wanting. [BT980.C6]
I. Title.

GOLDSTON, Robert 133.4
Satan's disciples New York, Ballantine [c.1962] 189 p. (f581) Bibl. pap., .50
1. Satanism. 2. Witchcraft. 3. Occult sciences. I. Title.

HARRIS, Thomas Lake, 1823-1906. 289.9
Arcana of Christianity: an unfolding of the celestial sense of the divine word, through T. L. Harris. Vol. i, pt. i, [iii] New York, New church publishing association, 1858-67. 2 v. 22 cm. Vol. i, pt. iii has imprint: New York & London, Brotherhood of the new life, 1867. No more published. -- Appendix to the Arcana of Christianity. The song of Satan: a series of poems, originating with a society of infernal spirits, and received, during temptation combats. [By] T. L. Harris ... New York, New church publishing association, 1858. 2 p. l., iii-lxxxvii p. 23 cm. Contents.--vol. i, pt. i. Genesis--1st chapter. pt. iii. The Apocalypse. lypse. [BX9998.H25 Appendix] 31-4581
I. Brotherhood of the new life. II. Title. III. Title: Song of Satan.

LYONS, Arthur. 133.4'22
The second coming; Satanism in America. New York, Dodd, Mead [1970] 211 p. illus., ports. 22 cm. Bibliography: p. 205-207. [BF1548.L9] 70-129954 ISBN 3-9606252-0- 6.95
1. Satanism. I. Title.

SALTUS, Edgar Evertson, 1855-1931.
The pomps of Satan, by Edgar Saltus ... New York, M. Kennerley, 1906. vii, 251, [1] p. 19 1/2 cm. [PS2752.P6 1906] 23-15919
I. Title.

SMITH, Hershel. 248'.2 B
The devil and Mr. Smith [by] Hershel Smith, with Dave Hunt. Old Tappan, N.J., F. H. Revell Co. [1974] 192 p. 21 cm. Autobiographical. [BV4935.S63A33] 74-3043 ISBN 0-8007-0662-5 2.95
1. Smith, Hershel. 2. Satanism. 3. Conversion. I. Hunt, Dave, joint author. II. Title.

STEIGER, Brad. 133.4'22
Sex and Satanism. New York, Ace Pub. Corp. [1969] 187 p. 18 cm. (An Ace book) (An Ace star book.) Bibliography: p. 185-187. [BF1548.S8] 72-19726 0.95
1. Satanism. 2. Sex and religion. I. Title.

ZACHARIAS, Gerhard P., 1923- 299
The Satanic cult / Gerhard Zacharias ; translated by Christine Trollope. London ; Boston : Allen & Unwin, 1980. 181 p., [5] p. of plates : ill. ; 23 cm. Translation of: Satanskult und Schwarze Messe. Includes bibliographical references and index. [BF1550.Z313] 19 79-41557 ISBN 0-04-133008-0 : 22.50
1. Satanism. I. [Satanskult und Schwarze Messe.] English II. Title.

Satanism—Case studies.

ROUMANE, Norman Morand, 1870-
Satan in society and his modern methods of winning victims, the sins and follies of the world exposed. Comp. by Norman Morand Roumane ... Introduced by Russell H. Conwell ... Beaver Springs, Pa., American publishing company [1903] 1 p. l., xxv, [2], 34-499, [1] p. incl. illus., plates. ports. front. 22 cm. 4-2667
I. Title.

SMITH, Michelle. 133.4'22'0926
Michelle remembers / by Michelle Smith and Lawrence Pazder. New York : Congdon & Lattes : distributed by St. Martin's Press, c1980. p. cm. [BF1548.S65 1980] 80-67862 ISBN 0-312-92531-X (St. Martin's) : 12.95
1. Smith, Michelle. 2. Satanism—Case studies. I. Pazder, Lawrence, joint author. II. Title.

Satanism—Rituals.

LA VEY, Anton Szandor, 1930- 133.4'22
The Satanic rituals. [New York] Avon [1972] 220 p. 18 cm. [BL480.L34] 73-154234 1.25 (pbk)
1. Satanism—Rituals. I. Title.

Satchidananda, Swami.

SRI Swami 294.5'6'1 B
Satchidananda : a decade of service : commemorative volume. [Pomfret Center, Ct. : Satchidananda Ashram-Yogaville], c1976. vii, 96 p. : ill. ; 22 x 29 cm. Issued as a special issue to v. 7, no. 3 and 4, of the Integral yoga magazine. [BL1175.S38S67] 76-376786
1. Satchidananda, Swami. 2. Hindus—Biography. I. Integral yoga.

WIENER, Sita. 294.5'61'0924 B
Swami Satchidananda; his biography. [1st ed.] San Francisco, Straight Arrow Books; [distributed by the World, New York, 1970] 194 p. illus., ports. 22 cm. [BL1175.S38W5] 70-141477 7.95
1. Satchidananda, Swami.

Sathya Sai Baba, 1926-

SAI Baba and his 294.5'6'2
message : a challenge to behavioural sciences / edited by Satya Pal Ruhela, Duane Robinson. 1st. Bell Books ed. Delhi : Vikas Pub. House, 1976. xx, 330 p., [5] leaves of plates : ill., map ; 20 cm. Bibliography: p. [323]-325. [BL1175.S385S24] 76-900490 Rs9.70
1. Sathya Sai Baba, 1926- Addresses, essays, lectures. I. Ruhela, Satya Pal, 1935- II. Robinson, Duane.

SANDWEISS, Samuel H. 294.5'6'2
Sai Baba, the holy man ... and the psychiatrist / Samuel H. Sandweiss. San Diego, Calif. : Birth Day Pub. Co., c1975. 240 p. : ill. ; 23 cm. Includes bibliographical references. [BL1175.S385S26] 75-28784 4.25
1. Sathya Sai Baba, 1926- 2. Psychology, Religious. I. Title.

SCHULMAN, Arnold. 294.5'6'20924
Baba. New York, Pocket Bks. [1973, c.1971] 174 p. illus., maps. 18 cm. [BL1175.S385S38 1971] ISBN 0-671-78260-6 pap., 1.25
1. Sathya Sai Baba, I. Title.

SCHULMAN, Arnold. 294.5'6'20924
Baba. New York, Viking Press [1971] 177 p. illus., map, ports. 22 cm. [BL1175.S385S38 1971] 77-151261 ISBN 0-670-14343-X 5.95
1. Sathya Sai Baba, 1926- I. Title.

Satipatthana sutta—Commentaries.

SONI, R. L. 294.3'823
The only way to deliverance / R. L. Soni. Boulder : Prajna Press, 1978. p. cm. Consists of a commentary, accompanied by the author's translation of Satipatthana sutta. Bibliography: p. [BQ1320.S257S66] 78-13237 ISBN 0-87773-744-4 pbk. : 4.95
1. Satipatthana sutta—Commentaries. 2. Meditation (Buddhism) I. Satipatthana sutta. English. 1978. II. Title.

Satmar Hasidim.

RUBIN, Israel, 1923- 309.1'747'2304
Satmar; an island in the city. Chicago, Quadrangle Books, 1972. x, 272 p. 22 cm. Includes bibliographical references. [BM198.R8 1972] 79-182505 ISBN 0-8129-0245-9 8.95
1. Satmar Hasidim. 2. Jews in Brooklyn. I. Title.

Satmon, George, 1819-1904.

BUTLER, Basil Christopher. 262.8
The church and infallibility; a reply to the abridged 'Salmon.' New York, Sheed and Ward, 1954. 230p. 22cm. [BT91.S33B8] 54-6145
1. Satmon, George, 1819-1904. The infallibility of the church. 2. Church—Infallibility. 3. Catholic Church—Infallibility. I. Title.

Satre, Ellen.

SATRE, Elizabeth Dahl. 248'.2 B
The story of Ellen : how love transforms a troubled child / Elizabeth Dahl Satre. Minneapolis : Augsburg Pub. House, c1979. 110 p. ; 20 cm. [BR1725.S3S27] 78-66952 ISBN 0-8066-1691-1 pbk. : 2.95
1. Satre, Ellen. 2. Christian biography—United States. 3. Problem children—United States—Biography. I. Title.

Satterlee, Churchill, 1867-1904.

SCHUYLER, Hamilton, 1862- 922
A fisher of men: Churchill Satterlee, priest and missionary--an interpretation of his life and labors by Hamilton Schuyler. New York, E. S. Gorham, 1905. 202 p., 1 l. front. (port.) plates. 20 cm. [BX5995.S25S3] 5-15536
1. Satterlee, Churchill, 1867-1904. I. Title.

Satterlee, Henry Yates, bp., 1843-1908.

BRENT, Charles Henry, bp., 1862-1929 922.
A master builder, being the life and letters of Henry Yates Satterlee, first bishop of Washington, by Charles H. Brent ... New York, London [etc.] Longmans, Green and co., 1916. xvi, 477 p. front., 1 illus. plates, ports. 23 1/2 cm. [BX5995.S26B8] 16-4588
1. Satterlee, Henry Yates, bp., 1843-1908. I. Title.

Saturn (PLanet)(in religion, folklore, etc.)

TALBOTT, David N. 291.2'12
The Saturn myth / David N. Talbott. 1st ed. Garden City, N.Y. : Doubleday, 1980. 419 p. : ill. ; 22 cm. Includes index. Bibliography: p. [385]-392. [BL325.S37T34] 19 76-51986 ISBN 0-385-11376-5 : 14.95
1. Saturn (PLanet)(in religion, folklore, etc.) I. Title.

Satya Bharti, Ma.

SATYA Bharti, Ma. 299'.93
Death comes dancing : celebrating life with Bhagwan Shree Rajneesh / Ma Satya Bharti. London ; Boston : Routledge & Kegan Paul, 1981. viii, 183 p. ; 22 cm. [BL624.S28] 19 80-41144 ISBN 0-7100-0705-1 pbk. : 9.95
1. Satya Bharti, Ma. 2. Rajaneesh, Acharya, 1931- 3. Spiritual life. I. Title.

Saudi Arabia—Addresses, essays, lectures.

STATE, society, and 953'.8053
economy in Saudi Arabia / edited by Tim Niblock. New York : St. Martin's Press, c1982. 314 p. : ill. ; 23 cm. Includes bibliographical references and index. [DS204.S72 1982] 19 81-14444 ISBN 0-312-75617-8 : 27.50
1. Saudi Arabia—Addresses, essays, lectures. I. Niblock, Tim.

Saudi Arabia—Economic conditions.

FARSY, Fouad, 1946- 330.953'8053
Saudi Arabia : a case study in development / Fouad Al-Farsy. London ; Boston : Kegan Paul International, 1982. 224 p., [8] p. of plates : ill. ; 23 cm. Originally presented as the author's thesis (doctoral—Duke University) Includes index. Bibliography: p. [205]-218. [HC415.33.F37 1982] 19 81-19376 ISBN 0-7103-0005-0 : 17.50
1. Saudi Arabia—Economic conditions. 2. Saudi Arabia—Politics and government. I. Title.

Saul, king of Israel.

CULVER, Samuel Wightman, 1825-1906. 221.92
Crowned and discrowned; or, The rebel king and the prophet of Ramah. By Rev. S. W. Culver, A. M. With an introduction, by Rev. G. W. Eaton ... Boston, Gould and Lincoln; New York, Sheldon and company, 1870. xiv p., 1 l., 17-149 p. 18 cm. [BS580.S3C7] 37-15512
1. Saul, king of Israel. 2. Samuel, judge of Israel. I. Title. II. Title: The rebel king. III. Title: The prophet of Ramah.

GOLDIN, Hyman Elias, 1881- 811.
Three kings; the story of Saul, David and Solomon, by Hyman E. Goldin ... New York, The Jordan publishing co., inc., 1929. 144 p. incl. plates. 19 cm. [BS571.G6] 30-6069
1. Saul, king of Israel. 2. David, king of Israel. 3. Solomon, king of Israel. I. Title.

NEWCOMB, Harvey, 1803-1863. 221.
The Benjamite king: or, The history of Saul, the first king of Israel. By Harvey Newcomb ... Boston, Massachusetts Sabbath school society, 1839. viii, [9]-198 p. incl. front., illus. 15 1/2 cm. Some of the illustrations are signed by Anderson. [BS580.S3N4] 21-7935
1. Saul, king of Israel. I. Anderson, Alexander, 1775-1870, illus. II. Title.

PETERSEN, Mark E. 222'.40922 B
Three kings of Israel / Mark E. Petersen. Salt Lake City, Utah : Deseret Book Co., 1980. p. cm. Includes index. [BS579.K5P47] 19 80-36697 ISBN 0-87747-829-5 : 6.95
1. Saul, King of Israel. 2. David, King of Israel. 3. Solomon, King of Israel. 4. Jews—Kings and rulers—Biography. 5. Bible. O.T.—Biography. I. Title.

WILKINSON, William Cleaver, 1833-
The epic of Saul, by William Cleaver Wilkinson... New York and London, Funk & Wagnalls company [1910?] 4 p. l., [7]-390 p. 21 1/2 cm. 10-24049
I. Title.

Saul, King of Israel—Juvenile literature.

MCCALL, Yvonne Holloway. 222'.43'0905
The angry king : 1 Samuel 18-2 Samuel 5 for children / written by Yvonne Holloway McCall ; illustrated by Jim Roberts. St. Louis : Concordia Pub. House, c1976. p. cm. (Arch books ; ser. 14) Retells in rhyme how David came to replace Saul as king of Israel with emphasis on the meaning of love, trust in God, and handling competition in a Christian way. [BS580.S3M3] 76-27365 ISBN 0-570-06110-5 pbk. : 0.59
1. Saul, King of Israel—Juvenile literature. 2. David, King of Israel—Juvenile literature. 3. [Saul, King of Israel.] 4. [David, King of Israel.] 5. Bible. O.T.—Biography—Juvenile literature. 6. [Bible. O.T. 1 Samuel XVIII-2 Samuel V—Poetry.] 7. [Bible stories—O.T.] 8. [Christian life.] I. Roberts, Jim. II. Title.

Sauma, Rabban, d. 1293?

THE Monks of 281'.8'0922 B
Kublai Khan, Emperor of China; or, The history of the life and plenipotentiary of Rabban Sawma, envoy and plenipotentiary of the Mongol khans to the kings of Europe, and Markos who as Mar Yahbh-Allaha III became Patriarch of the Nestorian Church in Asia. Translated from the Syriac by E. A. Wallis Budge. With 16 plates and 6 illus. in the text. London, Religious Tract Society, 1928. [New York, AMS Press, 1973] xvi, 335 p. illus. 23 cm. Translation of Yish'iata demar Yahbalaha vderaban Sauma. Bibliography: p. [307]-313. [DS752.Y5513 1973] 71-38051 ISBN 0-404-56905-6 20.00
1. Sauma, Rabban, d. 1293? 2. Yabhalaha III, Patriarch of the Nestorians, 1244?-1317. 3. Voyages and travels. 4. Nestorians. I. Budge, Ernest Alfred Thompson Wallis, Sir, 1857-1934, tr.

Saunders, Albert Edward.

MACNAIR, John Van, 1915- 922.373
Chaplain on the waterfront; the story of Father Saunders. New York, Seabury [c.] 1963. 141p. 22cm. 63-19451 3.50
1. Saunders, Albert Edward. 2. Longshoremen—New York (City) I. Title.

Saunders, Mrs. Eliza (Morton) 1824-1863.

SAUNDERS, William Trebell, d.1889. 922.373
The pastor's wife; or, Memoirs of E. M. S. ... New York, Little, Rennie & co., 1867. 198 p. front. (port.) 18 1/2 cm. [BX5995.S27S3] 35-35422
1. Saunders, Mrs. Eliza (Morton) 1824-1863. I. Title.

Sauniere, Berenger, 1852-1917.

FANTHORPE, P. A. 001.9'4
The Holy Grail revealed : the real secret of Rennes-le-Chateau / by Patricia and Lionel Fanthorpe ; edited by R. Reginald. San Bernardino, Calif. : Borgo Press, 1982. p. cm. [BF1434.F8F36 1982] 19 82-4303 ISBN 0-89370-660-4 : 12.95
1. Sauniere, Berenger, 1852-1917. 2. Occult sciences—France—Rennes-le-Chateau. 3. Rennes-le-Chateau (France)—Miscellanea. 4. Treasure-trove—France—Rennes-le-Chateau. I. Fanthorpe, R. Lionel. II. Reginald, R. III. Title.

FANTHORPE, P. A. 001.9'4
The Holy Grail revealed : the real secret of Rennes-le-Chateau / Patricia & Lional Fanthorpe ; edited and with an introduction by R. Reginald ; line drawings by Patrick Kirby. 1st ed. North Hollywood, Calif. : Newcastle Pub. Co., 1982. 143 p. : ill. ; 22 cm. [BF1434.F8F36 1982b] 19 82-6315 ISBN 0-87877-060-7 (pbk.) : 5.95

1. Sauniere, Berenger, 1852-1917. 2. Occult sciences—France—Rennes-le-Chateau. 3. Rennes-le-Chateau (France)—Miscellanea. 4. Treasure-trove—France—Rennes-le-Chateau. I. Fanthorpe, R. Lionel. II. Reginald, R. III. Title.

Sava, Saint, Abp. of Serbia, 1169-1237.

MATEJIC, Mateja. 282'.092'4 B
Biography of Saint Sava / Mateja Matejic. Columbus, Ohio : Kosovo Pub. Co., 1976. 128 p. : ill. ; 23 cm. Bibliography: p. 127-128. [BX719.S35M37] 77-366931
1. Sava, Saint, Abp. of Serbia, 1169-1237. 2. Christian saints—Serbia—Biography. I. Title.

NIKOLAJ, Bp. of Ohrid, 1880- 922.1497
The life of St. Sava. Libertyville, Ill., Serbian Eastern Orthodox Diocese for United States of America and Canada [1951] 233p. illus. 21cm. [BX719.S35N49] 51-35108
1. Sava, Saint, Abp., of Serbia, 1169-1237. I. Title.

Savage, Mrs. Sarah (Henry) 1664-1752.

WILLIAMS, John Bickerton, Sir, 1792-1855. 922
Memoirs of the life and character of Mrs. Sarah Savage, eldest daughter of the Rev. Philip Henry, A.M., and an appendix. By J. B. Williams. With a preface by the Rev. William Jay... 1st American ed. Boston, S. T. Armstrong, and Crocker & Brewster, 1821. xxviii, [19]-240 p. 15 1/2 cm [BR1725.S32W5 1821] 38-7489
1. Savage, Mrs. Sarah (Henry) 1664-1752 I. Title.

Savannah—Atlanta (Diocese)—Directories

THE Catholic directory for the dioceses of Savannah-Atlanta; 282.758 comprises all of Georgia. Savannah, Ga., St. Thomas vocational school [c19 v. illus. (incl. port.) 24 cm. [BX1417.S37A14] 40-9692
1. Savannah—Atlanta (Diocese)—Direct. 2. Catholic church in Georgia.

Savannah. First African Baptist church.

LOVE, Emanuel King, 1850-1900. 286.
History of the First African Baptist church. from its organization, January 20th, 1788, to July 1st. 1888. Including the centennial celebration, addresses, sermons, etc. By Rev. E. K. Love ... Savannah, Ga., The Morning news print., 1888. 7 p. l., iii-v, 300 p. front., illus. 21 cm. [BX6480.S45F5] 26-5886
1. Savannah. First African Baptist church. I. Title.

THOMAS, Edgar Garfield, 1880- 286.
The first African Baptist church of North America, by Rev. Edgar Garfield Thomas ... Savannah, Ga. [c1925]. 144 p. front., illus. 19 cm. [BX6480.S45F6] 26-4814
1. Savannah. First African Baptist church. I. Title.

Savannah. First Bryan Baptist church.

SIMMS, James Meriles. 286'.1758'724
The first Colored Baptist church in North America. Constituted at Savannah, Georgia, January 20, A.D. 1788. With biographical sketches of the pastors. Written for the church by James M. Simms. New York, Negro Universities Press [1969] 264 p. illus. 23 cm. Reprint of the 1888 ed. [BX6480.S45F55 1969] 70-82074 ISBN 0-8371-1561-2

1. Savannah. First Bryan Baptist Church. I. Title.

SIMMS, James Meriles. 286.
The first colored Baptist church in North America. Constituted at Savannah, Georgia, January 20, A.D. 1788. With biographical sketches of the pastors. Written for the church by Rev. James M. Simms. Philadelphia, J. B. Lippincott company, 1888. 264 p. front., plates, ports. 19 1/2 cm. [BX6480.S45F55] 3-14432

1. Savannah. First Bryan Baptist church. I. Title.

Savelli, Troilo, d. 1592.

BIONDO, Giuseppe. 230'.2 s
A relation of the death of ... Troilo Savelli / [by] Giuseppe Biondo ; [and] Holy philosophy / [by] Guillaume Du Vair ; [translated from the French by J. H.]. Ilkley [etc.] : Scolar Press, 1976. 464 p. (in various pagings) ; 20 cm. (English recusant literature, 1558-1640 ; v. 293) (Series: Rogers, David Morrison, comp. English recusant literature, 1558-1640 ; v. 293.) Biondo's work reprinted from a copy in the library of Downside Abbey of the 1620 ed.; references: Allison and Rogers 112; STC 3134. Du Vair's work reprinted from a copy in the library of Heythrop College of the 1636 ed.; reference: Allison and Rogers 290. [BX1750.A1E5 vol. 293] [BX4705.S367] 248'.246 B 77-356063 ISBN 0-85967-294-8 : £10.00

1. Savelli, Troilo, d. 1592. 2. Christian martyrs—Italy—Rome (City)—Biography. 3. Rome (City)—Biography. 4. Christian life—Catholic authors. I. Du Vair, Guillaume, 1556-1621. De la sainte philosophie. English. 1976. II. Title. III. Series.

Savery, William, 1750-1804.

TAYLOR, Francis Richards, 1884- 922.
Life of William Savery of Philadelphia, 1750-1804, by Francis R. Taylor ... New York, The Macmillan company, 1925. x p., 2 l., 474 p. 2 port. (incl. front.) plates. 22 1/2 cm. [BX7795.S15T3] 25-11965

1. Savery, William, 1750-1804. I. Title.

Saville, Jonathan, 1759-1842.

WEST, Francis Athow, 1801-1869. 922.742
Memoir of Jonathan Saville; of Halifax, Eng. Including his autobiography. By Francis A. West. From the London edition. New-York, G. Lane & C. B. Tippett, for the Sunday school union of the Methodist Episcopal church, 1845. 90 p. 15 1/2 cm. [BX8495.S33W4] 37-7032

1. Saville, Jonathan, 1759-1842. I. Sunday-school union of the Methodist Episcopal church. II. Title.

Savio, Domenico, Saint, 1842-1857.

BOSCO, Giovanni, Saint, 1815-1888. 922.245
Life of Blessed Dominic Savio; slightly abridged from the Italian by Roderic Bright. Paterson, N. J., Salesiana Publishers [c1950] 155p. illus. 22cm. Translation of Vita del giovanetto Dom. Savio. [BX4700.S35B62] 55-36994

1. Savio, Domenico, Saint, 1842-1857. I. Title.

BOSCO, Giovanni, Saint, 1815-1888. 922.245
The life of Saint Dominic Savio. 1st American ed., complete and unabridged, translated from the 5th Italian ed., with introd. and notes, by Paul Aronica. Paterson, N. J., Salesiana Publishers, 1955. 112p. illus. 22cm. Translation of Vita del giovanetto Dom. Savio. [BX4700.S35B616] 56-4539

1. Savio, Domenico, Saint, 1842-1857. I. Title.

BOSCO, Giovanni, Saint, 1815-1888. 282'.092'4 B
St. Dominic Savio / by Saint John Bosco ; translated, with notes by Paul Aronica ; foreword by Humberto Cardinal Medeiros. 2d ed. New Rochelle, N.Y. : Don Bosco Publications, c1979. ix, 169 p. : ill. ; 19 cm. (A Patron book) Translation of Vita del giovanetto Dom. Savio. First American ed. published in 1955 under title: The life of Saint Dominic Savio. [BX4700.S35B63 1979] 78-112476 ISBN 0-89944-033-9 pbk. : 2.75
1. Savio, Domenico, Saint, 1842-1857. 2. Christian saints—Italy—Biography.

ERNEST, Brother, 1897- 922.245
A story of Saint Dominic Savio. Pictures by Carolyn Lee Jagodits. Notre Dame, Ind., Dujarie Press [c1957] unpaged. illus. 21cm. [BX4700.S35E7] 57-27079
1. Savic, Domenico, Saint, 1842-1857. I. Title.

Savio, Domenico, Saint, 1842-1857 — Juvenile literature.

ROBERTO Brother, 1927- 92
Boy in a hurry; a story of Saint Dominic Savio. Notre Dame, Ind., Dujarie [c.1966] 95p. illus. 24cm. [BX4700.S35R54] 66-12758 2.25

1. Savio, Dominico, Saint, 1842-1857—Juvenile literature. I. Title.

Savitri (Hindu deity)—Poetry.

GHOSE, Aurobindo, 1872-1950. 821
Savitri unveiled : a selection / [edited with commentary and notes by] Syed Mehdi Imam. 1st ed. Delhi : Motilal Banarsidass, 1980. xi, 144 p., [2] leaves of plates : ports. ; 22 cm. (Savitri series) [PR9499.3.G52S22 1980] 19 81-900324 10.00
1. Savitri (Hindu deity)—Poetry. I. Imam, Syed Mehdi. II. [Savitri.] Selections III. Title. IV. Series.
Distributed by Lawrence Verry, Inc., Box 98, Mystic, CT 06335

Savonarola, Girolamo Maria Francesco Matteo, 1452-1498.

CLARK, William Robinson, 1829-1912. 922.245
Savonarols, His life and times, by William Clark... Chicago, A. C., McClurg and company, 1890. 352 p. 20 cm. [DG737.97.C5] 6-25656
1. Savonarola, Girolamo Maria Francesco Matteo, 1452-1496. I. Title.

MISCIATTELLI, Piero, marchese, 1882- 922.245
Savonarola, by Piero Misciattelli; translated by M. Peters-Roberts. New York, D. Appleton and company, 1930. xi, 273, [1] p. front., plates, ports. 21 1/2 cm. [DG737.97.M5 1930] 30-4733
1. Savonarola, Girolamo Maria Francesco Matteo, 1452-1498. I. Peters-Roberts, Mrs. Margaret, tr. II. Title.

POWELL, Edward Lindsay, 1860- 265.
Savonarola; or, The reformation of a city. With other addresses on civic righteousness. By E. L. Powell, LL. D. Louisville, Sheltman & company, 1903. 156 p. front. (port.) 21 cm. [BR115.P7P7] 3-29858
1. Savonarola, Girolamo Maria Francesco Matteo, 1452-1498 2. Citizenship. I. Title. II. Title: Civic righteousness.

RENNER, R Richard, 1896- 282.0924
Savonarola, the first great Protestant, by R. Richard Renner. [1st ed.] New York, Greenwich Book Publishers [c1965] 153 p. 21 cm. Bibliography: p. 153. [DG737.97.R4] 65-24258
1. Savonarola, Girolamo Maria Francesco Matteo, 1452-1498. I. Title.

RIDOLFI, Roberto, 1895- 922.245
The life of Girolamo Savonarola. Translated from the Italian by Cecil Grayson. [1st American ed.] New York, Knopf, 1959. 325 p. illus. 24 cm. "The extensive documentation of the original has been omitted." [DG737.97.R533 1959] 58-9668
1. Savonarola, Girolamo Maria Francesco Matteo, 1452-1498.

RIDOLFI, Roberto, 1899- 271'.2'00924 B
The life of Girolamo Savonarola / by Roberto Ridolfi ; translated from the Italian by Cecil Grayson. Westport, Conn. : Greenwood Press, 1976, c1959. x, 325 p., [1] leaf of plates : port. ; 24 cm. Reprint of the ed. published by Knopf, New York. Translation of Vita di Girolamo Savonarola. Includes index. [DG737.97.R533 1976] 76-8001 ISBN 0-8371-8873-3 lib.bdg. : 21.00
1. Savonarola, Girolamo Maria Francesco Matteo, 1452-1498.

ROEDER, Ralph. 922.245
Savonarola; a study in conscience, by Ralph Roeder. New York, Brentano's, 1930. 5 p.l., 3-307 p. front., plates, ports. 24 1/2 cm. Bibliography: p. 307. [DG737.97.R6] 30-25503
1. Savanarola, Girolame Maria Francesco Matteo, 1452-1498. I. Title.

VAN PAASSEN, Pierre, 1895- 922.245
A crown of fire; the life and times of Girolamo Savonarola. New York, Scribner [1960] 330 p. illus. 22 cm. [DG737.97.V34] 60-6335

1. Savonarola, Girolamo Maria Francesco Matteo, 1452-1498. I. Title.

VILLARI, Pasquale, 1827-1917. 271'.2'024 B
Life and times of Girolamo Savonarola. Translated by Linda Villari. New York, Scribner and Welford, 1888. St. Clair Shores, Mich., Scholarly Press, 1972. 2 v. illus. 22 cm. Translation of La storia di Girolamo Savonarola e de suoi tempi. Includes bibliographical references. [DG737.97.V7 1972] 79-115284 ISBN 0-403-00265-6 25.00
1. Savonarola, Girolamo Maria Francesco Matteo, 1452-1498. I. Title.

VILLARI, Pasquale, 1827-1917. 271'.2'0924 B
Life and times of Girolamo Savonarola. Translated by Linda Villari. New York, Haskell House Publishers, 1969. 2 v. illus., facsim., plates, ports. 23 cm. Translation of La storia di Girolamo Savonarola e de suoi tempi. Reprint of the 1888 ed. Bibliographical footnotes. [DG737.97.V7 1969] 68-25276
1. Savonarola, Girolamo Maria Francesco Matteo, 1452-1498. I. Title.

WEINSTEIN, Donald, 1926- 236'.3
Savonarola and Florence; prophecy and patriotism in the Renaissance. Princeton, N.J., Princeton University Press, 1970. viii, 399 p. illus., port. 25 cm. Includes bibliographical references. [DG737.97.W4] 76-113013 13.50
1. Savonarola, Girolamo Maria Francesco Matteo, 1452-1498. 2. Florence—History—Prophecies. 3. Millennialism—Italy—Florence. I. Title.

Savoy, Gene.

SAVOY, Gene. 001.9
Project X : the search for the secrets of immortality / by Gene Savoy ; ill. by Nicholas A. Nush. Indianapolis : Bobbs-Merrill, c1977. p. cm. [BF1999.S3423] 76-44670 ISBN 0-672-52181-4 : 11.95
1. Savoy, Gene. 2. Occult sciences. I. Nush, Nicholas A. II. Title.

Sawyer, Thomas Jefferson, 1804-1899.

EDDY, Richard, 1828-1906. 922.8173
The life of Thomas J. Sawyer ... and of Caroline M. Sawyer. By Richard Eddy, S. T. D. Boston and Chicago, Universalist publishing house, 1900. xii, 458 p. front., plates, ports. 21 1/2 cm. [BX9969.S35E4] 1-29689
1. Sawyer, Thomas Jefferson, 1804-1899. 2. Sawyer, Mrs. Caroline Mehetabel (Fisher) 1812-1894. I. Title.

Saxton, William Randall, 1814-1837.

TORREY, Charles Turner, 1813-1846. 923.773
Memoir of William Randall Saxton, of Lebanon, Conn. With the funeral sermon. By Charles T. Torrey... Salem [Mass.] W. & S. B. Ives, 1838. 130 p. 16 cm. [BR1725.S35T6] 38-7487
1. Saxton, William Randall, 1814-1837. 2. Funeral sermons. I. Title.

Sayville, N.Y.—Churches.

BROOKS, Rachel Gleason. 277.
Our international house (the religion of an American town) by Rachel Brooks. Sayville, N.Y., The Sayville press, inc., 1927. 61 [3] p. 23 cm. Vita. "The particular community which is the subject of this study is Sayville, New York." [BR560.S4B7] 28-28760
1. Sayville, N.Y.—Churches. 2. Social surveys. I. Title.

Sayville, N. Y. St. Ann's Church—History

STEVENSON, Charles Goldsmith, 1903- 917.47'25
But as yesterday; the early life and times of St. Ann's Church, Sayville, Long Island, New York, 1864-1888, by Charles G. Stevenson. Sayville, N.Y., 1967. vii, 169 p. illus., maps, ports. 24 cm. On spine: A history of St. Ann's Church. Bibliography: p. 165-169. [BX5980.S36S35] 68-722
1. Sayville, N.Y. St. Ann's Church—History. I. Title. II. Title: A history of St. Ann's Church.

Scalabrini, Giovanni Battista, Bp., 1839-1905.

CALIARO, Marco. 282'.092'4 B
John Baptist Scalabrini, apostle to emigrants / Marco Caliaro and Mario Francesconi ; [translation by Alba I. Zizzamia]. 1st ed. New York : Center for Migration Studies, 1977. xi, 555 p. : ill. ; 24 cm. Translation of L'apostolo degli emigranti. Includes indexes. Bibliography: p. 453-469. [BX4705.S38C313] 76-44922 ISBN 0--913256-24-2 : 15.00
1. Scalabrini, Giovanni Battista, Bp., 1839-1905. 2. Catholic Church—Bishops—Biography. 3. Bishops—Italy—Biography. 4. Church work with emigrants—Italy. I. Francesconi, Mario, joint author. II. Title.

FELICI, Icilio, 1892- 922.245
Father to the immigrants, the servant of God: John Baptist Scalabrini, Bishop of Piacenza. Translated by Carol Della Chiesa. New York, P. J. Kenedy [1955] 248p. illus. 22cm. Translation of G. B. Scalabrini, vescovo insigne. [BX4705.S38F415] 55-11371
1. Scalabrini, Giovanni Battista, Bp., 1839-1905. I. Title.

Scandella, Domenico, 1532-1601.

GINZBURG, Carlo. 230'.2'0924
The cheese and the worms : the cosmos of a sixteenth-century miller / Carlo Ginzburg ; translated by John and Anne Tedeschi. Baltimore : Johns Hopkins University Press, 1980. xxvii, 177 p. : ill. ; 24 cm. Translation of Il formaggio e i vermi. Includes bibliographical references and index. [BR877.F74G5613] 79-3654 ISBN 0-8018-2336-6 : 14.00
1. Scandella, Domenico, 1532-1601. 2. Friuli—Religious life and customs. 3. Friuli—Civilization. 4. Peasantry—Italy—Friuli. 5. Heresies and heretics—Italy—Friuli. 6. Heresies and heretics—Modern period, 1500- 7. Friuli—Church history. I. Title.

Scandinavia—Religion.

DAVIDSON, Hilda Roderick (Ellis) 293
Pagan Scandinavia [by] H. R. Ellis Davidson. New York, F. A. Praeger [1967] 214 p. illus. 21 cm. (Ancient peoples and places, v. 58) Bibliography: p. 149-159. [BL860.D38 1967b] 67-24530
1. Scandinavia—Religion. 2. Scandinavia—Antiquities. I. Title.

HUNTER, Leslie Stannard, Bp. of Sheffield, 1890- ed. 274.48
Scandinavian churches; a picture of the development and life of the churches of Denmark, Finland, Iceland, Norway, and Sweden. [London, Faber &Faber] Minneapolis, Augsburg [1966, c.1965] 200p. illus., ports. 23cm. Bibl. [BR973.H8] 66-3693 4.50
1. Scandinavia—Religion. 2. Sects—Scandinavia. I. Title.

TURVILLE-PETRE, Edward Oswald Gabriel. 293
Myth and religion of the North; the religion of ancient Scandinavia. [1st ed.] New York, Holt, Rinehart and Winston [1964] ix, 340 p. illus. 25 cm. Bibliography: p. 321-329. [BL860.T8] 64-11276
1. Scandinavia—Religion. 2. Mythology, Norse. I. Title.

Scandinavian alliance mission of North America.

GRAUER, Otto Christopher, 1859- 266
Fifty wonderful years, missionary service in foreign lands ... compiled and edited by Rev. O. C. Grauer, D.D. Chicago, Ill., Scandinavian alliance mission [1940] 333, [3,) p. illus. (incl. ports.) 23 1/2 cm. On spine: Foreign mission service. [BV2417.S4G7] 42-47689
1. Scandinavian alliance mission of North America. I. Title.

Scapulars

CARMELITES. Third Order. 2d National Conference, Chicago and Englewood, N. J., 1949 271.73
Take this scapular! Commemorating the seventh centenary of the brown scapular given to St. Simon Stock, prior general of the Carmelites, on July16, 1251. [Conferences given April 23, 24, 30, and May 1, 1949] by Carmelite fathers and tertiaries. Chicago, Carmelite Third Order Press, 1949. 270 p. illus. 19 cm. Biblioigraphy: p. 266-270. [BX2310.S3C3 1949] 50-286337
1. Simon Stock, Saint, 1165?-1265. 2. Mary, Virgin. 3. Scapulars. I. Title.

LYNCH, Edward Kilian, 1902- 271.73
Your brown scapular; with a preface by Francis Cardinal Spellman. Westminster, Md., Newman Press, 1950. xv, 141 p. 20 cm. [BX2310.S3L9] 50-9760
1. Scapulars I. Title.

Scarritt Bible and training school, Kansas City, Mo.

GIBSON, Maria Layng, 1845-1927. 016.
Memories of Scarritt, by Maria Layng Gibson, edited and completed by Sara Estelle Haskin. Nashville, Tenn., Cokesbury press, 1928. 188 p. front., plates, ports. 19 cm. [BV4070.S356G5] 28-8543
1. Scarritt Bible and training school, Kansas City, Mo. I. Haskin, Sara Estelle, ed. II. Title.

Schaeffer, Francis August.

MORRIS, Thomas V. 239
Francis Schaeffer's apologetics : a critique / by Thomas V. Morris. Chicago : Moody Press, c1976 128 p. ; 22 cm. Bibliography: p. 126-128. [BT1102.M69] 75-43866 ISBN 0-8024-2873-8 pbk. : 2.50
1. Schaeffer, Francis August. 2. Apologetics—20th century. I. Title.

SCHAEFFER, Edith. 267'.13'0922 B
The tapestry : the life and times of Francis and Edith Schaeffer / Edith Schaeffer. Waco, Tex. : Word Books, c1981. 650 p. : ill. ; 24 cm. [BR1725.S355S3] 19 81-51009 ISBN 0-8499-0284-3 : 17.95
1. Schaeffer, Francis A. (Francis August) 2. Schaeffer, Edith. 3. Christian biography. I. Title.

Schaff, Philip, 1819-1893.

JANEWAY, Jacob Jones, 1774-1858. 282
Antidote to the poison of popery. In the publications of Professor Schaff. First in his essay and then in his history. By J. J. Janeway, D.D. New-Brunswick, N.J., Press of J. Terhune and son, 1854. 50 p. 22 1/2 cm. [BR139.S4J3] 43-18956
1. Schaff, Philip, 1810-1893. Das princip des protestantismus. 2. Catholic church—Doctrinal and controversial works—Protestant authors. I. Title.

NICHOLS, James Hastings, 1915- 230.0973
Romanticism in American theology; Nevin and Schaff at Mercersburg. [Chicago] University of Chicago Press [1961] 322 p. illus. 22 cm. [BT30.U6N5] 61-5609
1. Schaff, Philip, 1819-1893. 2. Nevin, John Williamson, 1803-1886. 3. Mercersburg theology. 4. Theology, Doctrinal—History—United States. I. Title.

SCHAFF, David Schley, 1852- 928.
The life of Philip Schaff, in part autobiographical, by David S. Schaff ... New York, C. Scribner's sons, 1897. xv, 526 p. 2 port. (incl. front.) 23 cm. "List of Dr. Schaff's writings": p. 511-518. [BR139.S4S3] 28-22529
1. Schaff, Philip, 1819-1893. I. Title.

...THE semi-centennial of 928.
Philip Schaff. New York, Priv. print., 1893. 2 p. l., [iii]-vi, 66 p. front. (port.) 23 1/2 cm. At head of title: Berlin 1842--New York 1892. [BR139.S4S4] 9-16890
1. Schaff, Philip, 1819-1893.
Contents omitted.

Schall von Bell, Johann Adam, 1952?-1666.

ATTWATER, Rachel. 266.251
Adam Schall, a Jesuit at the court of China, 1592-1666. Adapted from the French of Joseph Duhr. Milwaukee, Bruce Pub. Co. [c1963] 163 p. illus., ports., maps, plans. 21 cm. "Much of the material ... was first published in Un jesuite en Chine, Adam Schall, by Joseph Duhr ... in 1936." [BV3427.S35A8] 63-22843
1. Schall von Bell, Johann Adam, 1952?-1666. 2. Missions — China. I. Duhr, Joseph. Un jesuite en Chine, Adam Schall. II. Title.

Schauffler College of Religious and Social Work, Cleveland.

SCHAUFFLER, Grace Leavitt, 1894- 207.771
Fields of the Lord; the story of Schauffler College, 1886-1957. [Oberlin? Ohio, 1957] 99p. illus., ports. 24cm. [BV4176.S45S4] 57-41481
1. Schauffler College of Religious and Social Work, Cleveland. 2. Oberlin College. Schaufflier Division of Christian Education. I. Title.

Schechter, Solomon, 1847-1915.

BENTWICH, Norman De Mattos, 1883- 922.96
Solomon Schechter, a biography, by 3 Norman Bentwich. A golden jubilee volume. Philadelphia, The Jewish publication society of America, 1938. xvi p., 1 l., 373, [1] p. front., pl., ports., facsims. 22 cm. "Bibliography of the principal writings of Solomon Schechter": p. 351-352. [BM90.J589S2] 38-29999
1. Schecter, Solomon, 1847-1915. I. Title.

EISENBERG, Azriel Louis, 1903- 92
Fill a blank page; a biography of Solomon Schechter. New York, United Synagogue Comm., 218 E. 70th St. [c.]1965. x, 114p. illus., ports. 22cm. [BM755.S27E39] 65-17216 2.95
1. Schechter, Solomon, 1847-1915. I. Title.

Scheeben, Matthias Joseph, 1835-1888.

BURKE, Thomas Patrick, 1934- 234'.2'0924
Faith and the human person; an investigation of the thought of Scheeben [by] Patrick Burke. Chicago, John XXIII Institute [1968] xi, 176 p. 23 cm. Includes bibliographical references. [BX1751.S257B8] 68-9724
1. Scheeben, Matthias Joseph, 1835-1888. 2. Faith—History of doctrines. I. Title.

Scheler, Max Ferdinand, 1874-1928—Ethics.

DEEKEN, Alfons. 171'.2
Process and permanence in ethics; Max Scheler's moral philosophy. New York, Paulist Press [1974] ix, 282 p. 23 cm. Bibliography: p. 259-273. [B3329.S484D36] 73-87476 ISBN 0-8091-0179-3 7.95
1. Scheler, Max Ferdinand, 1874-1928—Ethics. I. Title.
Pbk. 5.95, ISBN 0-8091-1800-9.

Schellenberger, Bernardin, 1944-

SCHELLENBERGER, Bernardin, 1944- 271'.125'024
Nomad of the spirit : reflections of a young monastic / Bernardin Schellenberger ; translated from German by Joachim Neugroschel ; with a foreword by Basil Pennington. New York : Crossroad, 1981, c1980. p. cm. Translation of: Ein anderes Leben. [BX2435.S3613 1981] 19 81-5363 8.95
1. Schellenberger, Bernardin, 1944- 2. Monastic and religious life. I. [Anderes Leben.] English II. Title.

Schelling, Friedrich Wilhelm Joseph von, 1775-1854.

BROWN, Robert F., 1941- 292'.2'11
Schelling's treatise on "The deities of Samothrace" : a translation and an interpretation / by Robert F. Brown. Missoula, Mont. : Published by Scholars Press for American Academy of Religion, c1977. viii, 65 p. ; 24 cm. (Studies in religion ; no. 12) Bibliography: p. 64-65. [BL793.S3S332 1977] 76-42239 ISBN 0-89130-087-2 : 4.20
1. Schelling, Friedrich Wilhelm Joseph von, 1775-1854. Ueber die Gottheiten von Samothrace. 2. Mythology, Greek. 3. Samothrace—Religion. I. Schelling, Friedrich Wilhelm Joseph von, 1775-1854. Ueber die Gottheiten von Samothrace. English. 1976. II. Title. III. Series: American Academy of Religion. AAR studies in religion ; no. 12.

Schenectady, N. Y. First Reformed Church.

BIRCH, John Joseph, 1894- 285.7747
The pioneering church of the Mohawk Valley; de banbreckende kerk van de Mohawk Vallei. Schenctady, N. Y., The Consistory, First Reformed Church, 1955. 204p. illus. 24cm. [BX9531.S48F53] 56-21480
1. Schenectady, N. Y. First Reformed Church. I. Title.

SCHENECTADY, N. Y. First Reformed church.
... Two hundredth anniversary of the First Reformed Protestant Dutch church, of Schenectady, N.Y., June 20th and 21st ... 1880. [Schenectady, Daily and weekly union steam printing house, 1880. 264 p. front. 23 cm. At head of title: 1680. 15-9182
I. Title.

Schereschewsky, Samuel Isaac Joseph, bp., 1831-1906.

MULLER, James Arthur, 1884- 922.351
Apostle of China, Samuel Isaac Joseph Schereschewsky, 1831-1906, by James Arthur Muller ... New York, Milwaukee, Morehouse publishing co., 1937. 279 p. front., plates, ports. 22 cm. "Research in the cellar": p. 11-22: "Dates of first publication of Schereschewsky's translations": p. 263-264. [BV3427.S36M8] 37-35143
1. Schereschewsky, Samuel Isaac Joseph, bp., 1831-1906. I. Title.

Schervier, Franziska, 1819-1876.

GOSSENS, Bruno. 922.243
The Venerable servant of God, Mother Frances Schervier, foundress of the congregation of the Sisters of the poor of St. Francis; from the German of Bruno Gossens ... by Ferdinand B. Gruen ... New York, P. J. Kenedy & sons [c1935] 64 p. illus. 16 cm. [BX4705.S51G62] 35-7508
1. Schervier, Franziska, 1819-1876. 2. Sisters of the poor of St. Francis. I. Gruen, Ferdinand Bernard, 1882- tr. II. Title. III. Title: Translation of Die gottselige mutter Franziska Schervier.

JEILER, Ignatius, 1823-1904. 922.243
The Venerable Mother Frances Schervier, foundress of the congregation of the Sisters of the poor of St. Francis. A sketch of her life and character. By the Very Rev. Ignatius Jeiler ... Authorized translation. By Rev. Bonaventure Hammer, O. S. F. With a preface by the Rt. Rev. C. M. Maes ... St. Louis, Mo., B. Herder, 1895. xxvi, 492, [3] p. front. (port.) 20 cm. [BX4705.S51J4] 37-18476
1. Schervier, Franziska, 1819-1876. 2. Sisters of the poor of St. Francis. I. Hammer, Bonaventure, 1842-1917, tr. II. Title.

MAYNARD, Theodore, 1890- 922.243
Through my gift: the life of Frances Schervier. New York, P. J. Kenedy [1951] 318 p. port. 21 cm. "Bibliographical note": p. 315-318. [BX4705.S51M3] 51-11216
1. Schervier, Franziska, 2. Sisters of the Poor of St. Francis. I. Title.

PAULINE, sister. 922.243
Frances Schervier, mother of the poor, by Sister Pauline, St. Clare convent, Cincinnati, Ohio. [Cincinnati] Congregation of the Sisters of the poor of St. Francis [1946] 89, [2] p. col. front. (port.) illus. 20 1/2 cm. Bibliography: p. 88. [BX4705.S51P3] 46-22181
1. Schervier, Franziska, 1819-1876. I. Title.

SCHERVIER, Franziska, 1819-1876. 248
Words of Frances Schervier, selected and arranged by Sister Pauline. [Hartwell, Cincinnati] Congregation of the Sisters of the poor of St. Francis [1946] 95 p. col. front. (port.) 20 1/2 cm. "A calendar of thoughts from the writings of Mother Frances Schervier, foundress of the Congregation of the Sisters of the poor of St. Francis."--p. [1] [BX890.S383] 46-20752
I. Pauline, sister, ed. II. Sisters of the poor of St. Francis. Cincinnati. III. Title.

Scheuring, Tom.

SCHEURING, Tom. 248.4'82
God longs for family : family evangelization / by Tom and Lyn Scheuring ; foreword by our children, Maria, Malissa, and Paul. Huntington, Ind. : Our Sunday Visitor, c1980. 149 p. ; 21 cm. [BX2351.S33] 19 79-92535 ISBN 0-87973-533-3 pbk. : 2.95
1. Scheuring, Tom. 2. Scheuring, Lyn. 3. Family—Religious life. 4. Marriage—Catholic Church. I. Scheuring, Lyn, joint author. II. Title.

SCHEURING, Tom. 282'.092'2 B
Two for joy : spirit-led journey of a husband and wife through Jesus to the Father / by Tom and Lyn Scheuring. New York : Paulist Press, c1976. v, 183 p. : ill. ; 21 cm. [BX2350.2.S32] 76-28274 ISBN 0-8091-1985-4 pbk. : 4.95
1. Scheuring, Tom. 2. Scheuring, Lyn. 3. Spiritual life—Catholic authors. 4. Christian communities. 5. Catholics in the United States—Biography. I. Scheuring, Lyn, joint author. II. Title.

Schiffman, Steve.

SCHIFFMAN, Steve. 248'.246
Once a thief ... / Steve Schiffman. Old Tappan, N.J. : F. H. Revell Co., c1978. 63 p. ; 18 cm. (New life ventures) [BV4935.S35A34] 77-18711 ISBN 0-8007-9007-3 pbk. : 0.95
1. Schiffman, Steve. 2. Converts—United States—Biography. I. Title.

Schild, Friedrich Kienholz, 1868-1933.

SHIELD, Frederic K. 285'.732'0922 B
Lillie Helena Kull and Friedrich Kienholz Schild: a tribute [by Frederic K. Shield] Winter Park [Fla.] 1967. 47 l. 2 ports. 29 cm. [BX9543.S33S47] 72-299114
1. Schild, Friedrich Kienholz, 1868-1933. 2. Schild, Lillie Helena Kull, 1869-1957. I. Title.

Schillebeeckx, Edward Cornelis Florentius Alfons, 1914- — Jezus.

SCHILLEBEECKX, Edward Cornelis Florentius Alfons, 1914- 232
Interim report on the books Jesus & Christ / Edward Schillebeeckx. New York : Crossroad, 1981. 151 p. ; 24 cm. Translation with revisions of Tussentijds verhaal over twee Jezus boeken. Includes bibliographical references. [BT202.S335313] 19 80-26708 ISBN 0-8164-0477-1 : 9.95
1. Schillebeeckx, Edward Cornelis Florentius Alfons, 1914- —Jezus. 2. Schillebeeckx, Edward Cornelis Florentius Alfons, 1914- —Gerechtigheid en liefde. 3. Jesus Christ—Person and officers. I. Title.

Schiller, Johann Christoph Friedrich von, 1759-1805.

FLORER, Warren Washburn, 1869-
German liberty authors, by Warren Washburn Florer... Boston, R.G. Badger [c1918] 109 p. 19 1/2 cm. (Lettered on cover: Studies in literature) Contents.The spirit of 1776 and Schiller's conception of liberty.--The attitude of the modern German novelists toward religion.--Gustav Frenssen.--Herman Sudermann.--Hilligeniel.--Frenssen's Hilligeniel and Rosegger's I.N.R.I. [PT137.L5F6] 18-12189 1.00
1. Schiller, Johann Christoph Friedrich von, 1759-1805. 2. Frenssen, Gustav, 1863- 3. Sudermann, Herman, 1857-1928. 4. Rosegger, Peter, 1843- 5. German fiction—19th cent.—Hist. & crit. 6. Religion in literature. I. Title. II. Title: Liberty authors.

Schiotz, Frederik Alex, 1901-

SCHIOTZ, Fredrik Axel, 1901- 284.1'31'0924 B
One man's story / Fredrik A. Schiotz. Minneapolis : Augsburg Pub. House, c1980. 189 p. ; 20 cm. [BX8080.S264A36] 19 80-67790 ISBN 0-8066-1851-5 (pbk.) : 7.95
1. Schiotz, Frederik Alex, 1901- 2. Lutheran Church—Clergy—Biography. 3. Clergy—United States—Biography. I. Title.

Schism.

DAWSON, Christopher Henry 270.6
The dividing of Christendom. Foreword by Douglas Horton. New York, Doubleday [1967, c.1965] 237p. 18cm. (Image bks. R229) Bibl. [BR148.D3] .95 pap.,
1. Schism. 2. Reformation—Addresses, essays, lectures. 3. Church history—Addresses, essays, lectures. I. Title.

DAWSON, Christopher Henry, 1889- 270.6
The dividing of Christendom [by] Christopher Dawson. Foreword by Douglas Horton. New York, Sheed and Ward [1965] x, 304 p. 22 cm. "Drawn, in considerable part, from the lectures which . . . [the] author gave while occupying the Charles Chauncey Stillman Chair of Roman Catholic Theological Studies at the Divinity School of Harvard University." Bibliographical footnotes. [BR148.D3] 65-12208
1. Schism. 2. Reformation — Addresses, essays, lectures. 3. Church history — Addresses, essays, lectures. I. Title.

GREENSLADE, Stanley Lawrence. 270.3
Schism in the early church. New York, Harper [1953] 247p. 23cm. (Edward Cadbury lectures, 1949-50) Bibliography: p. [231]-235. [BT1317.G7] 53-1118
1. Schism. 2. Church history—Primitive and early church. 3. Theology, Doctrinal—Hist.—Early church. I. Title. II. Series.

KELCHER, James P 281.3
Saint Augustine's notion of schism in the Donatist controversy. Mundelein, Ill., Saint Mary of the Lake Seminary, 1961. 147 p. 23 cm. (Pontificia Facultas Theologica Seminarii Sanctae Marise ad Lacum. Dissertationes ad lauream, 34) Bibliography: p. 141-147. [BR1720.A9K44] 63-3918
1. Augustinus, Aurelius, Saint, Bp. of Hippo. 2. Schism. 3. Donatists. I. Title. II. Series. III. Series: St. Mary of the Lake Seminary, Mundelein, Ill. Dissertationes ad lauream, 34

Schism—Eastern and Western Church.

CONGAR, Yves Marie Joseph, 1904- 270.3
After nine hundred years; the background of the schism between the Eastern and Western churches [by] Yves Congar. New York, Fordham University Press [1959] 150 p. 23 cm. "A translation of Neuf cents ans apres, originally published as part of 1054-1954, l Eglise et les Eglises." Includes bibliography. [BX303.C613] 59-15643
1. Schism—Eastern and Western Church. I. Title.

CONGAR, Yves Marie Joseph, 1904- 270.3'8
After nine hundred years : the background of the schism between the Eastern and Western churches / Yves Congar. Westport, Conn. : Greenwood Press, 1978, c1959. ix, 150 p. ; 23 cm. Translation of Neuf cents ans apres, originally published as v. 1, pt. 1 of L'Eglise et les eglises, 1054-1954. Reprint of the ed. published by Fordham University Press, New York. Includes bibliographical references and index. [BX303.C613 1978] 78-6154 lib.bdg. : 14.00
1. Schism—Eastern and Western Church. I. Title.

EVERY, George. 281.9
The Byzantine patriarchate, 451-1204 / [by George Every]. New York : AMS Press, 1980 [c1962] p. cm. Reprint of the 2d ed., rev. published by S.P.C.K., London. Includes index. [BX300.E8 1980] 78-63340 ISBN 0-404-17015-3 : 21.50
1. Orthodox Eastern Church—History. 2. Schism—Eastern and Western Church. I. Title.

EVERY, George 270.38
Misunderstandings between East and West. Richmond, Va., Knox [1966, c.1965] 70p. 22cm. (Ecumenical studies in hist., no. 4) Bibl. [BX303.E9] 66-12355 1.75 pap.,
1. Schism—Eastern and Western Church. I. Title. II. Series.

GEANAKOPLOS, Deno John 270.3'8
Byzantine east and Latin west: two worlds of Christendom in Middle Ages and Renaissance; studies in ecclesiastical and cultural history [by] Deno J. Geanakoplos. New York, Harper [1966] x, 206, 6p. illus., maps. 21cm. (Harper torchbks.) Bibl: [BX303.G4 1966] 66-29030 1.95 pap.,
1. Schism—Eastern and Western Church. 2. Ferrara- Florence, Council of 1438-1439. 3. Byzantine Empire—Relations (general) with Europe. 4. Europe—Relations (general) with the Byzantine Empire. I. Title.

GEANAKOPLOS, Deno John. 270.3'8
Byzantine East and Latin West : two worlds of Christendom in Middle Ages and Renaissance : studies in ecclesiastical and cultural history / Deno J. Geanakoplos. Hamden, Conn. : Archon Books, 1976, c1966. xii, 206 p., [8] leaves of plates : ill. ; 23 cm. Reprint of the ed. published by Blackwell, Oxford. Includes index. Bibliography: p. [194]-200. [BX303.G4 1976] 76-20685 ISBN 0-208-01615-5 : 10.00
1. Ferrara-Florence, Council of 1438-1439. 2. Byzantine Empire—Relations (general) with Europe. 3. Schism—Eastern and Western Church. 4. Europe—Relations (general) with the Byzantine Empire. I. Title.

GEANAKOPLOS, Deno John. 270.38
Byzantine East and Latin West: two worlds of Christendom in Middle Ages and Renaissance; studies in ecclesiastical and cultural history [essays, by] Deno J. Geanakoplos. New York, Barnes & Noble, 1966. x, 206 p. illus., maps (part fold.) ports. 22 cm. Bibliography: p. [194]-200. [BX303.G4] 66-31413
1. Ferrara-Florence, Council of, 1438-1439. 2. Schism—Eastern and Western Church. 3. Byzantine Empire—Relations (general) with Europe. 4. Europe—Relations (general) with the Byzantine Empire. I. Title.

SHERRARD, Philip. 270.38
The Greek East and the Latin West; a study in the Christian tradition. London, New York, Oxford University Press, 1959. 202 p. 22 cm. Includes bibliography. [BX303.S5] 59-65256
1. Schism — Eastern and Western church. 2. Religious thought — Hist. 3. Philosophy — Hist. I. Title.

Schism, The great western, 1378-1417.

BRUCE, Herbert, 1877- 270.
The age of schism; being an outline of the history of the church from A. D. 1304 to A. D. 1503, by Herbert Bruce ... New York, The Macmillan company, 1907. viii, 279 p. 18 1/2 cm. (On cover: The church

universal [v. 5]) "A short bibliography": p. 272-273. [BR141.C5 vol. 5] 8-5813
1. Schism, The great western, 1378-1417. 2. Church history—Middle ages. I. Title.

GAIL, Marzieh. 270.3'8
The three Popes; an account of the great schism when rival Popes in Rome, Avignon, and Pisa vied for the rule of Christendom. New York, Simon and Schuster [1969] 320 p. illus. 25 cm. Bibliography: p. 307-310. [BX1301.G25] 79-75861 7.95
1. Schism, The Great Western, 1378-1417. I. Title.

JORDAN, George Jefferis, 1890- 282'.09'023
The inner history of the Great Schism of the West; a problem in Church unity, by G. J. Jordan. New York, B. Franklin [1972] 216 p. 23 cm. (Burt Franklin research and source works series. Philosophy & religious history monographs, 105) Reprint of the 1930 ed. Bibliography: p. 210-211. [BX1301.J6 1972] 72-80392 ISBN 0-8337-4193-4 13.50
1. Schism, The Great Western, 1378-1417. I. Title.

LOCKE, Clinton, 1829-1904. 270.
... The age of the great western schism, by Clinton Locke, D. D. New York, The Christian literature co., 1896. x, 314 p. 20 cm. (Ten epochs of church history. [vol. viii]) [Full name: James Dewitt Clinton Locke] [BR141.T4 vol. viii] 28-28080
1. Schism, The great western, 1378-1417. I. Title.

SMITH, John Holland. 270.5
The Great Schism, 1378. New York, Weybright and Talley [1970] vii, 280 p. illus., ports. 23 cm. (Turning points in history) [BX1301.S6 1970b] 75-99006 7.50
1. Schism, The Great Western, 1378-1417. I. Title.

ULLMANN, Walter, 1910- 270.5
The origins of the Great Schism; a study in fourteenth-century ecclesiastical history. [Hamden, Conn.] Archon Books, 1967. xiii, 244 p. illus., ports. 22 cm. Reprint of the 1948 ed. Bibliographical footnotes. [BX1301.U55 1967] 67-12982
1. Schism, The Great Western, 1378-1417. I. Title.

ULLMANN, Walter, 1910- 282'.09'023
The origins of the great schism; a study in fourteenth-century ecclesiastical history. With a 1972 pref. by the author. [Hamden, Conn.] Archon Books, 1972. xxvii, 244 p. illus. 22 cm. Reprint of the 1948 ed. published by Burns, Oates, & Washbourne, London. Includes bibliographical references. [BX1301.U55 1972] 79-39365 ISBN 0-208-01277-X
1. Schism, The Great Western, 1378-1417. I. Title.

Schizophrenia.

BAYNES, Helton Godwin, 1882-1943. 270
Mythology of the soul; a research into the unconscious from schizophrenic dreams and drawings. New York, Humanities Press, 1955. xiii, 939p. illus., plates (part col.) 23cm. [RC628.B] A 56
1. Schizophrenia. 2. Subconsciouness. 3. Dreams. I. Title.

Schlamm, Vera, 1923-

SCHLAMM, Vera, 1923- 248'.246'0924 B
Pursued, by Vera Schlamm as told to Bob Friedman. Glendale, Calif., G/L Regal Books [1972] 212 p. 18 cm. [D810.J4S317] 72-77800 ISBN 0-8307-0153-2 1.25
1. Schlamm, Vera, 1923- 2. World War, 1939-1945—Personal narratives, Jewish. 3. Converts from Judaism. I. Friedman, Bob. II. Title.

Schlatter, Francis, 1856-1896?

[MAGILL, Harry Byron] 1872- 920.9
Biography of Francis Schlatter, the healer, with his life, works and wonderings. Denver, Col., Schlatter publishing co., 1896. 206 p. plates, port. 19 cm. "Copyrighted...by Harry B. Magill." Portrait on cover. [BR1716.S35M3 1896] 34-14282
1. Schlatter, Francis, 1856-1896? 2. Faith-cure. I. Title.

[MAGILL, Harry Byron] 1872- 922
Biography of Francis Schlatter, the healer, with his life, works and wanderings. Denver, Col., Schlatter publishing co., 1896. 198 p. plates, port. 19 cm. "Copyrighted...by Harry B. Magill." Portrait on cover. [BR1716.S35M3] 37-25850
1. Schlatter, Francis, 1856-1896? 2. Faith-cure. I. Title.

Schlatter, Michael, 1716-1790.

REFORMED church in the United States. Synod of the Potomac. 922.
Michael Schlatter: memorial addresses at the sesquicentennial services held in Hagerstown, Md., by the Synod of the Potomac, October 20, A.D. 1897, in honor of the pioneer organizer of Reformed churches in America. Prepared for the occasion by Rev. Cyrus Cort, D.D., General John E. Roller and Rev. E. R. Eschbach, D.D., and pub. by request of Synod, January 1900 ... Reading, Pa., D. Miller, printer, 1900. 61 p. front., illus., ports. 22 cm. [BX9593.S3R4] 17-19425
1. Schlatter, Michael, 1716-1790. I. Cort, Cyrus, 1834- II. Roller, John Edwin, 1844- III. Eschbach, Edmund Rishel, 1835-1910. IV. Title.

Schleiermacher, Friedrich Ernst Daniel, 1768-1834.

BRASTOW, Lewis Orsmond, 1834-1912. 251.
Representative modern preachers, by Lewis O. Brastow ... New York, The Macmillan company; London, Macmillan & co., ltd., 1904. xv, 423 p. 20 cm. [BV4207.B7] 4-4064
1. Schleiermacher, Friedrich Ernst Daniel, 1768-1834. 2. Robertson, Frederick William, 1816-1853. 3. Beecher Henry Ward, 1813-1887. 4. Bushnell, Horace, 1802-1876. 5. Mozley, James Bowling 1813-1878. 6. Guthrie, Thomas, 1803-1873. 7. Spurgeon, Charles Haddon, 1834-1892. 8. Brooks, Phillips, 1835-1893. 9. Newman, John Henry, cardinal, 1801-1890. I. Title.
Contents omitted.

CHRISTIAN, C. W. 193
Friedrich Schleiermacher / by C. W. Christian. Waco, Tex. : Word Books, c1979. 157 p. ; 23 cm. (Makers of the modern theological mind) Bibliography: p. 153-157. [BX4827.S3C47] 78-65806 ISBN 0-8499-0132-4 : 7.95
1. Schleiermacher, Friedrich Ernst Daniel, 1768-1834.

JOHNSON, William Alexander 201
On religion: a study of theological method in Schleiermacher and Nygren. Leiden, E. J. Brill [New York, Humanities, 1966, c.1964] x, 167p. 25cm. Bibl. [BR118.J6] 65-4258 5.00
1. Schleiermacher, Friedrich Ernst Daniel, 1768-1834. 2. Nygren, Anders, Bp., 1890- 3. Theology — Methodology. I. Title.

NEIBUHR, Richard R 230.4
Schleiermacher on Christ and religion, a new introduction [by] Richard R. Niebuhr. New York, Scribner [1964] xv, 267 p. 24 cm. Bibliograpical footnotes. [BX4827.S3N5] 64-22393
1. Schleiermacher, Friedrich Ernst Daniel, 1768-1834. I. Title.

OSBORN, Andrew R. 207
Schleiermacher and religious education, by Andrew R. Osborn. London, Oxford university press, H. Milford, 1934. 4 p. l., 226 p. 1 l. 20 cm. "In its original form this book was written as a thesis for the degree of doctor of theology in the Presbyterian theological college, Montreal." Bibliography: p. [203]-205. [BV1471.S4O82] 34-19096
1. Schleiermacher, Friedrich Ernst Daniel, 1768-1834. 2. Religious education. I. Title.

OSBORN, Andrew Rule, 1875- 268
Schleiermacher and religious education, by Andrew R. Osborn. London, Oxford university press, H. Milford, 1934. 4 p. l., 226 p., 1 l. 19 1/2 cm. "In its original form this book was written as a thesis for the degree of doctor of theology in the Presbyterian theological college, Montreal." Bibliography: p. [203]-205. [BV1471.S4O82] 34-19096
1. Schleiermacher, Friedrich Ernst Daniel, 1768-1834. 2. Religious education. I. Title.

REDEKER, Martin, 1900- 193 B
Schleiermacher: life and thought. Translated by John Wallhausser. Philadelphia, Fortress Press [1973] 221 p. 20 cm. Translation of Friedrich Schleiermacher; Leben und Werk. Bibliography: p. 214-218. [BX4827.S3R413] 72-91526 ISBN 0-8006-0149-1 4.50
1. Schleiermacher, Friedrich Ernst Daniel, 1768-1834. I. Title.

SELBIE, William Boothby, 1862-
Schleiermacher; a critical and historical study by W. B. Selbie... New York, E. P. Dutton & co., 1913. ix, 271, [1] p. 22 1/2 cm. (Half-title: The Great Christian theologies; ed. by Rev. Henry W. Clark) Bibliography: p. 268-269. A 13
1. Shcleiermacher, Friedrich Ernst Daniel, 1768-1834. I. Title.

SPIEGLER, Gerhand 230'.0924
The eternal covenant; Schleiermacher's experiment in cultural theology. [1st ed.] New York, Harper [1967] xvii, 205p. port. 22cm. (Makers of modern theol.) Bibl. [BX4827.S3S65] 67-21553 5.50
1. Schleiermacher, Friedrich Ernst Daniel, 1768-1834. I. Title.

STRAUSS, David Friedrich, 1808-1874. 232.9'01
The Christ of faith and the Jesus of history : a critique of Schleiermacher's Life and Jesus / by David Friedrich Strauss ; translated, edited, and with an introduction by Leander E. Keck. Philadelphia : Fortress Press, c1977. cxii, 169 p. ; 19 cm. (Lives of Jesus series) Translation of Der Christus des Glaubens und der Jesus der Geschichte. Bibliography: p. cvii-cxii. [BT301.S363S813] 75-37152 ISBN 0-8006-1273-6 pbk. : 9.95
1. Schleiermacher, Friedrich Ernst Daniel, 1768-1834. Das Leben Jesu. 2. Jesus Christ—Biography. I. Title.

SYKES, Stephen. 230'.0924 B
Friedrich Schleiermacher. Richmond, John Knox Press [1971] viii, 51, [1] p. 19 cm. (Makers of contemporary theology) Bibliography: p. [52] [BX4827.S3S85 1971] 75-158145 ISBN 0-8042-0556-6
1. Schleiermacher, Friedrich Ernst Daniel, 1768-1834.

WILLIAMS, Robert R. 231
Schleiermacher the theologian : the construction of the doctrine of God / Robert R. Williams. Philadelphia : Fortress Press, c1978. xiii, 196 p. ; 24 cm. Includes bibliographical references and index. [BT101.S144W54] 77-78650 ISBN 0-8006-0513-6 : 11.95
1. Schleiermacher, Friedrich Ernst Daniel, 1768-1834. 2. God—History of doctrines. I. Title.

WOBBERMIN, Georg, 1869- 201
The nature of religion, by Georg Wobbermin ... translated by Theophil Menzel ... and Daniel Sommer Robinson ... with an introduction by Douglas Clyde Macintosh ... New York, Thomas Y. Crowell company [c1933] xvi, 379 p. front. (port.) 22 1/2 cm. An interpretation of religion based upon Schleiermacher's conception. Translation of "Systematische theologie nach religionspsychologischer methode". pt. 2, "Das wesen der religion". [BL51.W73] 33-39320
1. Schleiermacher, Frederick Ernst Daniel, 1768-1834. 2. Religion—Philosophy I. Menzel, Theophil, tr. II. Robinson, Daniel Sommer, 1888- joint tr. III. Title.

Schleiermacher, Friedrich Ernst Daniel, 1768-1834—Bibliography.

TICE, Terrence N. 012
Schleiermacher bibliography. With brief introds., annotations, and index, by Terrence N. Tice. Princeton, N.J., Princeton Theological Seminary, 1966. 168 p. 23 cm. (Princeton pamphlets, no. 12) [BV4070.P713 no. 12] 66-29801
1. Schleiermacher, Friedrich Ernst Daniel, 1768-1834—Bibliography. I. Title.

Schlink, Basilea.

SCHLINK, Basilea. 271'.97 B
I found the key to the heart of God : my personal story / Basilea Schlink. Minneapolis : Bethany Fellowship, 1975. 412 p., [8] leaves of plates : ill. ; 18 cm. (Dimension books) Translation of Wie ich Gott erlebte. [BX8080.S248A3613 1975] 75-23920 ISBN 0-87123-239-1 pbk. : 2.95
1. Schlink, Basilea. I. Title.

Schlosser, George, 1875-1936.

SCHERER, Frances Schlosser, 1912- 266'.7'60922 B
George and Mary Schlosser : ambassadors for Christ in China / by Frances Schlosser Scherer. Winona Lake, Ind. : Light and Life Press, c1976. xiv, 189 p. : ill. ; 21 cm. [BX8419.S35S34] 76-371953 3.95
1. Schlosser, George, 1875-1936. 2. Schlosser, Mary, 1885-1955. 3. Missionaries—United States—Biography. 4. Missionaries—China—Biography. I. Title: Ambassadors for Christ in China.

Schmauk, Theodore Emanuel, 1860-1920.

SANDT, George Washington, 1854- 922.
Theodore Emanuel Schmauk, D.D., LL.D., a biographical sketch, with liberal quotations from his letters and other writings, by George W. Sandt. Philadelphia, United Lutheran publication house, 1921. xiii, [1], 291 p. incl. front. (port.) plates, ports. 22 1/2 cm. [BX8080.S25S3] 22-207
1. Schmauk, Theodore Emanuel, 1860-1920. I. Title.

Schmelzenbach, Elmer, 1910-

SCHMELZENBACH, Elmer, 1910- 266'.99 B
Sons of Africa : stories from the life of Elmer Schmelzenbach / as told to Leslie Parrott. Kansas City, Mo. : Beacon Hill Press of Kansas City, c1979. 217 p. : ill. ; 21 cm. [BV3625.S92S357] 79-122616 ISBN 0-8341-0601-9 : 9.95
1. Schmelzenbach, Elmer, 1910- 2. Missionaries—Swaziland—Biography. 3. Missionaries—United States—Biography. I. Parrott, Leslie, 1922- II. Title.

Schmidt, Elisabeth, 1908-

SCHMIDT, Elisabeth, 1908- 284'.23 B
When God calls a woman : the struggle of a woman pastor in France and Algeria / by Elisabeth Schmidt ; translated, with notes, by Allen Hackett. New York : Pilgrim Press, c1981. p. cm. Translation of: Quand Dieu appelle des femmes. Includes bibliographical references. [BX9459.S35A3613] 19 81-12009 ISBN 0-8298-0430-7 pbk. : 7.95
1. Schmidt, Elisabeth, 1908- 2. Reformed Church—Clergy—Biography. 3. Clergy—France—Biography. 4. Clergy—Algeria—Biography. I. [Quand Dieu appelle des femmes.] English II. Title.

Schmidtke, Ernst, 1908-

LINNETT, Arthur. 267'.15'0924 B
Radiant rebel : the story of Ernst Schmidtke / by Arthur Linnett. London : Salvationist, 1976. 97 p. ; 19 cm. [BX9743.S3L56] 77-366233 ISBN 0-85412-292-3
1. Schmidtke, Ernst, 1908- 2. Salvationists—Germany—Biography. 3. Missionaries—China—Biography. 4.

Missionaries—Germany—Biography. I. Title.

Schmucker, Samuel Simon, 1799-1873.

ANSTADT, Peter, 1819-1903. 922.473
Life and times of Rev. S.S. Schmucker ... By P. Anstadt ... York, Pa., P. Anstadt & sons, 1896. viii, [9]-902 p. front. (port.) plates. 21 1/2 cm. "Family record of S.S. Schmucker ...": p. 24-37. "A complete list of his publications": p. 203-365. [BX8080.S3A6] 36-33085
1. Schmucker, Samuel Simon, 1799-1873. 2. Schmucker family. I. Title.

SCHMUCKER, Samuel Simon 1799-1873.
The church of the Redeemer, as developed within the General synod of the Lutheran church in America. With a historic outline from the apostolic age. To which is appended a plan for restoring apostolic union between all orthodox denominations. By S. S. Schmucker ... Baltimore, T. N. Kurtz; Philadelphia, E. W. Miller; [etc., etc.] 1867. xxii, [23]-281 p. 19 cm. 3-29254
I. Title.

WENTZ, Abdel Ross, 1883- 284'.13
Pioneer in Christian unity: Samuel Simon Schmucker. Philadelphia, Fortress Press [1967] xi, 372 p. port. 24 cm. Bibliographical footnotes. "Published writings of Samuel Simon Schmucker, 1799-1873": p. 355-364. [BX8080.S3W4] 67-10596
1. Schmucker, Samuel Simon, 1799-1873. I. Title.

Schneder, Charles Bauman, 1861-1931.

WIEST, William James. 922.
A good minister of Jesus Christ; an interpretation of the Reverend Charles Bauman Schneder, D.D. Published on the occasion of the centenary of St. John's church, Evangelical and Reformed, Shamokin, Pennsylvania, October, 1939 ... By William James Wiest. [Shamokin, Pa.] 1939. 102 p. front., pl., ports., facsim. 20 cm. [BX9593.S33W5] 922 ISBN 39-31930
1. Schneder, Charles Bauman, 1861-1931. I. Title.

Schneider, Delano Douglas.

SCHNEIDER, Delano Douglas. 266'.5'8340924 B
Deep the roots of hope / by D. Douglas Schneider. 1st ed. Muskegon, Mich. : Creative Design Books, c1976. xii, 264 p., [16] leaves of plates : ill. ; 22 cm. Autobiographical. [BV3269.S295A3] 75-21171
1. Schneider, Delano Douglas. 2. Missions—Kalahandi, India. 3. Missions—Agricultural work. I. Title.

Schoenbrunn, O.

WEINLAND, Joseph E.
The romantic story of Schoenbrunn, the first town in Ohio; a brief account of the founding of the town, its destruction, and the finding of the lost town site after 146 years. Also a short description of the rebuilding of the town, and the founding of Schoenbrunn memorial park as a memorial to our pioneers. By Rev. Joseph E. Weinland ... Dover, O., Seibert printing company, 1928. 3-56 p. illus. (incl. port., maps, facsims.) 22 1/2 cm. [F449.S36W42] 29-19836
1. Schoenbrunn, O. 2. Zelsberger, David, 1721-1808. 3. Moravians in Ohio. I. Title.

Scholars, Buddhist.

PEIRIS, William. 294.3
The Western contribution to Buddhism. With a foreword by H. Saddhatissa Maha Thera. [1st ed.] Delhi, Motilal Banarsidass [1973] xxviii, 287 p. 48 ports. 23 cm. Includes bibliographical references. [BQ164.P44] 73-91127 ISBN 0-842-60537-1
1. Scholars, Buddhist. 2. Buddha and Buddhism—Study and teaching. I. Title.
Distributed by Verry, 15.00

Scholars, Buddhist—United States—Biography.

WINKLER, Ken. 291.6'4 B
Pilgrim of the clear light / Ken Winkler ; [foreword by Lama Anagarika Govinda]. 1st ed. Berkeley, Calif. : Dawnfire Books, c1982. xvi, 114 p. : ill. ; 22 cm. "The biography of Dr. Walter Y. Evans-Wentz"—Cover. Includes bibliographical references and index. [BQ952.V367W56 1982] 19 81-70183 ISBN 0-942058-00-3 pbk. : 4.50
1. Evans-Wentz, W. Y. (Walter Yeeling), 1878-1965. 2. Scholars, Buddhist—United States—Biography. I. Title.
Publisher's address: 1804 Grant, Berkeley, CA 94703.

Scholars, Jewish—Germany—Biography.

BIALE, David, 1949- 296.7'1 B
Gershom Scholem : Kabbalah and counter-history / David Biale. Cambridge, Mass. : Harvard University Press, 1979. vi, 279 p. : port. ; 25 cm. Includes index. Bibliography: p. [217]-226. [BM755.S295B5] 78-23620 ISBN 0-674-36330-2 : 16.50
1. Scholem, Gershom Gerhard, 1897- 2. Scholars, Jewish—Germany—Biography. 3. Scholars, Jewish—Israel—Biography.

SCHOLEM, Gershom Gerhard, 1897- 296.8'2 B
From Berlin to Jerusalem : memories of my youth / Gershom Scholem ; translated from the German by Harry Zohn. New York : Schocken Books, 1980. 178 p., [2] leaves of plates : ill. ; 21 cm. Translation of Von Berlin nach Jersualem. Includes index. [BM755.S295A3413] 79-25678 ISBN 0-8052-3738-0 : 10.95
1. Scholem, Gershom Gerhard, 1897- 2. Scholars, Jewish—Germany—Biography. 3. Scholars, Jewish—Israel—Biography. 4. Jews in Germany—Intellectual life. I. Title.

Scholars, Jewish—Italy—Biography.

MARGOLIES, Morris B. 296.6'1'0924 B
Samuel David Luzzatto, traditionalist scholar / by Morris B. Margolies. New York : Ktav Pub. House, 1979. xv, 253 p. ; 24 cm. Includes indexes. Bibliography: p. 211-222. [BM755.L8M37] 79-23472 ISBN 0-87068-696-8 : 15.00
1. Luzzatto, Samuele Davide, 1800-1865. 2. Scholars, Jewish—Italy—Biography. I. Title.

Scholars, Jewish—United States—Biography.

STERN, Ellen Norman. 221.9'3 B
Dreamer in the desert : a profile of Nelson Glueck / by Ellen Norman Stern. New York : KTAV Pub. House, c1980. viii, 158 p., [5] leaves of plates : ill. ; 24 cm. Includes index. Bibliography: p. 152-153. [BM755.G56S74] 79-23707 ISBN 0-87068-656-9 : 8.95
1. Glueck, Nelson, 1900- 2. Scholars, Jewish—United States—Biography. I. Title.

Scholasticism.

BRUNI, Gerardo, 1896- 111
Progressive scholasticism, by Gerardo Bruni, PH. D. Authorized translation from the Italian by John S. Zybura ... St. Louis, Mo, and London, B. Herder book co., 1929. xxxviii, 185 p. 20 cm. "A contribution to the commemoration of the fiftieth anniversary of the encyclical'Aeternal partris." [B839.B7] 29-1036
1. Scholasticism. I. Zybura. John S., tr. II. Title.

DAY, Sebastian J 189.4
Intuitive cognition; a key tothe significance of the later scholastics. St. Bonaventure, N. Y.,Francscan Institute, 197. xiii, 217 p. 23 cm. (Franciscan Institute publications. Philosophy series, no 4) Seris: St. Bonaventure's College, St. Bonaventure, N. Y. Franciscan Institute. Publications. Bibliographical footnotes. [B734.D3] 48-892
1. Scholasticism. 2. Intutition. I. Title. II. Series. III. Series: St. Bonaventure's College St. Bonaventure, N. Y. Franciscan Institute. Philosophy series, no. 4.

FAIRWEATHER, Eugene Rathbone, ed. and tr. 189.4
A scholastic miscellany: Anselm to Ockham. Philadelphia, Westminster Press [1956] 457p. 24cm. (The Library of Christian classics, v. 10) Includes bibliographies. [B734.F3] 56-5104
1. Scholasticism. I. Title. II. Series.

HILL, James Langdon, 1848- 204
The scholar's larger life. by James L. Hill ... Boston, Mass., The Stratford company, 1920. 5 p. l., 201 p. front. (port.) 19 1/2 cm. [BX7117.H5] 21-1295
I. Title.

KLAUDER, Francis J. 111
The wonder of the real; a sketch in basic philosophy, by Francis J. Klauder. North Quincy, Mass., Christopher Pub. House [1973] 114 p. illus. 21 cm. Includes bibliographical references. [B765.T54K553] 72-94706 4.95
1. Thomas Aquinas, Saint, 1225?-1274—Ontology. 2. Scholasticism. I. Title.

MARITAIN, Jacques, 1882- 922.245
The angelic doctor: the life and thought of Saint Thomas Aquinas, by Jacques Maritain ... translated by J. F. Scanlan. New York, L. MacVeagh The Dial press; Toronto, Longmans, Green & co., 1931. xviii p., 2 l., 23-300 p. 21 cm. [BX4700.T6M35] 31-9121
1. Thomas Aquinas, Saint, 1225?-1274. 2. Scholasticism. I. Scanlan, James Fr., tr. II. Title.

MARITAIN, Jacques, 1882- 922.245
St. Thomas Aquinas. [Newly translated and rev. by Joseph W. Evans and Peter O'Reilly] New York, Meridian Books [1958] 281p. 19cm. (Merdian books, M55) Includes bibliography. [BX4700.T6M345] 57-10837
1. Thomas Aquinas, Saint, 1225?-1274. 2. Scholasticism. I. Title.

PEGIS, Anton Charles, 1905- 189.4
The Middle Ages and philosophy; some reflections on the ambivalence of modern scholasticism. Chicago, H. Regnery Co., 1963. xiv, 102 p. 21 cm. (James Roosevelt Bayley lecture, Seton Hall University, 1) Bibliographical references included in "Notes" (p. 94-102) [B839.P37] 63-20522
1. Scholasticism. 2. Philosophy and religion. 3. Philosophy, Medieval. I. Title. II. Series.

PERRIER, Joseph Louis, 1874-
The revival of scholastic philosophy in the nineteenth century. New York, AMS Press, 1967. viii, 344 p. Reprint of 1909 ed. Bibliography of neo-scholastic philosophy: p. 249-336. 68-64691
1. Scholasticism. 2. Scholasticism—Bibl. 3. Metaphysics. 4. Philosophy—Hist. I. Title.

PHILLIPS, Richard Percival.
Modern Thomistic philosophy; an explanation for students. Westminster, Md., Newman Press, 1962-64. 2 v. Contents.v.l. The philosophy of nature.--v.2. Metaphysics. 68-21670
1. Thomas Aquinas, Saint, 1225?-1274—Philosophy. 2. Scholasticism. I. Title.

PIEPER, Josef, 1904- 189.4
Scholasticism; personalities and problems of medieval philosophy. [Tr. [from German] by Richard and Clara Winston] New York, McGraw [1964, c.1960] 192p. 21cm. (49930) Bibl. 1.95 pap.,
1. Scholasticism. I. Title.

PIEPER, Josef, 1904- 189.4
Scholasticism; personalities and problems of medieval philosophy. [Translated by Richard and Clara Winston. New York] Pantheon Books [1960] 192p. 21cm. Includes bibliography. [B734.P513] 60-11766
1. Scholasticism. I. Title.

SCHOLASTICISM and politics. Translation ed. by Mortimer J. Adler. Garden City, N. J. Doubleday [1960] 233p. 18cm. (Image books)
1. Scholasticism. 2. Political sciences. I. Maritain, Jacques, 1882-

SERTILLANGES, Antonin Gilbert, 1863- 180.4
... Foundations of Thomistic philosophy, by A. D. Sertillanges, O.P.; translated by Godfrey Anstruther, O.P. London, Sands & co. St. Louis, Mo., B. Herder book co. [1931] 3 p. l., 254, [1] p. 19 cm. (Catholic library of religious knowledge. xx) [Name in religion: Dalmatius Sertillanges] [BX890.C3 vol. 20] (282.082) 35-14135
1. Thomas Aquinas, Saint, 1225?-1274. 2. Scholasticism. I. Anstruther, Godfrey, 1903- tr. II. Title.

SERTILLANGES, Antonin Gilbert, 1863-1948.
Foundations of Thomistic philosophy. Translated by Godfrey Anstruther, O.P. Springfield, Ill., Templegate [1956] 254p. 20cm.
1. Scholasticism. 2. Thomas Aquinas, Saint, 1225?-1274—Philosophy. I. Anstruther, Godfrey, 1903- tr. II. Title.

SERTILLANGES, Antonin Gilbert, 1863-1948.
Foundations of Thomistic philosophy. Translated by Godfrey Anstruther, O.P. Springfield, Ill., Templegate [1956] 254 p. 20 cm.
1. Scholasticism. 2. Thomas Aquinas, Saint, 1225?-1274 — Philosophy. I. Anstruther, Godfrey, 1903- tr. II. Title.

STAUNTON, John Armitage, 1864-
Scholasticism, the philosophy of common sense, by the Rev. John A. Staunton; with a foreword by the Rev. Charles C. Miltner ... [Garrison, N. Y., 1937] 3 p. l., 65, [1] p. diagr. 18 cm. Bibliography: p. [66] A 40
1. Scholasticism. I. Title.

WUELLNER, Bernard. 189.4
Summary of scholastic principles. Chicago, Loyola University Press, 1956. 164 p. 24 cm. [BS39.W8] 56-10903
1. Scholasticism. I. Title.

WULF, Maurice Marie Charles Joseph de, 1867-1947. 189.4
An introduction to scholastic philosophy, medieval and modern. Scholasticism old and new. Translated by P. Coffey. New York, Dover Publications [1956] 327 p. 21 cm. "An unabridged republication of the English edition published under the title Scholasticism old and new." [(B734)] 57-3219
1. Scholasticism. 2. Neo-scholasticism. I. Title.

WULF, Maurice Marie Charles Joseph de, 1867-1947. 189.4
An introduction to scholastic philosophy, medieval and modern. Scholasticism old and new. Translated by P. Coffey. New York, Dover Publications [1956] 327 p. 21 cm. "An unabridged republication of the English edition published under the title Scholasticism old and new." [B734.W905 1956] 57-3219
1. Scholasticism. 2. Neo-scholasticism.

Scholasticism— Dictionaries.

DICTIONARY of scholastic philosophy. Milwaukee, Bruce Pub. Co. [1956] xvi, 138p. 24cm. Bibliography: p. 138. [B50.S35W8] [B50.S35W8] 149.2 56-7043 56-7043 189.4
1. Scholasticism— Dictionaries. 2. Philosophy—Dictionaries. I. Wuellner, Bernard.

WUELLNER, Bernard. *189.4 149.2
Dictionary of scholastic philosophy. Milwaukee, Bruce Pub. Co. [1956] xvi, 138 p. 24 cm. Bibliography: p. 138. [B50.S35W8] 56-7043
1. Scholasticism — Dictionaries. 2. Philosophy — Dictionaries. I. Title.

WUELLNER, Bernard. 189.403
A dictionary of scholastic philosophy. 2d ed. Milwaukee, Bruce Pub. Co. [1966] xviii, 330 p. illus. 21 cm. [B50.S35W8 1966] 66-24259
1. Scholasticism — Dictionaries. 2. Philosophy — Dictionaries. I. Title.

Scholasticism—History.

RIEDE, David Charles, 1925- comp. 189'.4
Scholasticism, humanism, and reform [compiled by] David C. Riede [and] J. Wayne Baker. Dubuque, Iowa, Kendall/Hunt Pub. Co. [1972] vi, 151 p. 29 cm. [B734.R5] 70-180506 ISBN 0-8403-0555-9
1. Scholasticism—History. 2. Philosophy, Renaissance. 3. Humanism—History. 4. Reformation. I. Baker, J. Wayne, joint comp. II. Title.

Scholem, Gershom Gerhard, 1897-

BIALE, David, 1949- 296.7'1 B
Gershom Scholem : Kabbalah and counter-history / David Biale. Cambridge, Mass. : Harvard University Press, 1979. vi, 279 p. : port. ; 25 cm. Includes index. Bibliography: p. [217]-226. [BM755.S295B5] 78-23620 ISBN 0-674-36330-2 : 16.50
1. Scholem, Gershom Gerhard, 1897- 2. Scholars, Jewish—Germany—Biography. 3. Scholars, Jewish—Israel—Biography.

BIALE, David, 1949- 296.7'1 B
Gershom Scholem : Kabbalah and counter-history / David Biale. 2nd ed. Cambridge, Mass. : Harvard University Press, 1982. p. cm. Includes index. Bibliography: p. [BM755.S295B5 1982] 19 82-9295 ISBN 0-674-36332-9 pbk. : 7.95
1. Scholem, Gershom Gerhard, 1897- 2. Mysticism—Judaism—Historiography. 3. Scholars, Jewish—Germany—Biography. 4. Scholars, Jewish—Israel—Biography. I. Title.

SCHOLEM, Gershom Gerhard, 1897- 296.8'2 B
From Berlin to Jerusalem : memories of my youth / Gershom Scholem ; translated from the German by Harry Zohn. New York : Schocken Books, 1980. 178 p., [2] leaves of plates : ill. ; 21 cm. Translation of Von Berlin nach Jersualem. Includes index. [BM755.S295A3413] 79-25678 ISBN 0-8052-3738-0 : 10.95
1. Scholem, Gershom Gerhard, 1897- 2. Scholars, Jewish—Germany—Biography. 3. Scholars, Jewish—Israel—Biography. 4. Jews in Germany—Intellectual life. I. Title.

School, Choice of.

PRAETZ, Helen Margaret. 301.15'43'3778294
Where shall we send them? : the choice of school for a Catholic child / [by] Helen Praetz. Melbourne : Hawthorn Press, 1974. x, 117 p. : tables ; 22 cm. Includes index. Bibliography: p. 110-115. [LC509.P72] 75-501899 ISBN 0-7256-0119-1 : 2.95
1. Catholic Church in Australia—Education. 2. School, Choice of. I. Title.

School ethics.

MARCHBANKS, Eleanor. 377.
School ethics, by Eleanor Marchbanks, with selections for reading ... Boston, The Four seas company, 1913. 6 p. l., 11-178 p. 18 cm. Contents.--To teachers--Martha and Mary.--Teaching kindness.--A flower lesson.--Memory gems.--Cheerfulness.--Nationality.--Manners.--Selections for reading. [LC268.M2] 14-6837
1. School ethics. I. Title.

PUBLIC schools, religion, and values; a series of addresses on the teaching of moral and spiritual values in public schools Lexington, Ky., 1956. 51p.
I. Kentucky. University. College of Education.

School management and organization.

BROTHERS of the Christian schools. 807
Management of Christian schools. By the Brothers of the Christian schools. New York, P. O'Shea, 1893. xiii, 3-263 p. pl., plan. fold, form. 19 cm. [LC485.B86] E10
1. School management and organization. I. Title.

BROTHERS of the Christian schools.
Management of Christian schools. By the Brothers of the Christian schools, 2d ed. New York, O'Shea, 1907. xiii, 3-263 p. pl., plan. fold. forms. 19 cm. E10
1. School management and organization. I. Title.

CAMPBELL, Paul Edward, 1890- 377.8273
Parish school administration, by the Reverend Paul E. Campbell... New York city, J. F. Wagner, inc. [c1937] xi p., 1 l., 177 p. 20 1/2 cm. [LC485.C3] 38-3162
1. School management and organization. 2. Church schools—U.S. 3. Catholic church in the U.S.—Education. I. Title.

MARY Mildred, Sister. 807
Supervision in the Catholic elementary school, by Sister Mary Mildred ... Glen Riddle, Pa., 1925. 170 p. 23 cm. "list of books recommended": p. 165-168; Bibliography: p. 168-170. [LC485.M3] 26-13400
1. School management and organization. 2. Teaching. 3. Catholic church—Education. I. Title.

School personnel management.

BRUBAKER, J. Lester. 377'.8
Personnel administration in the Christian school / J. Lester Brubaker. Winona Lake, Ind. : BMH Books, c1980. 165 p. : forms ; 22 cm. Includes bibliographical references. [LB2831.5.B78] 19 80-149441 ISBN 0-88469-130-6 (pbk.) : 5.95
1. School personnel management. 2. Church schools—Administration. I. Title.

School Sisters of Notre Dame.

[DYMPNA, sister] 1855- 271.97
Mother Caroline and the School sisters of Notre Dame in North America, by a School sister of Notre Dame... Saint Louis, Woodward & Tiernan co., 1928. 2 v. fronts., plates, ports. 23 1/2 cm. [Secular name: Margaret Teresa Flynn] [BX4443.U6D88] 34-2441
1. Caroline, mother, 1824-1892. 2. School sisters of Notre Dame. I. Title.

MARY Hester, Sister, 1909- 271.97
Canticle for the harvest, New York, Kenedy [1951] 196 p. 21 cm. Includes bibliographies. [BX4443.U6M3] 51-4895
1. School Sisters of Notre Dame. I. Title.

School Sisters of St. Francis (Milwaukee, Wis.)

MARY Francis Borgia, Sister, 1922- 271.973
He sent two; the story of the bargaining of the School Sisters of St. Francis. Bruce in coop. with Seraphic Pr. [dist.] Milwaukee, Bruce [c.]1965. xiii, 224p. illus., ports. 24cm. Bibl. [BX4446.M3] 65-6845 5.00
1. Alexia, Mutter, 1839-1918. 2. Alfons, Mutter, d. 1929. 3. School Sisters of St. Francis, Milwaukee, Wis. I. Title.

ROTHLUEBBER, Francis Borgia, 1922-
He sent two; the story of the beginning of the School Sisters of St. Francis. Milwaukee, Bruce, 1965. xiii, 224 p. plates, ports, 23 cm. 67-19888
1. School Sisters of St. Francis (Milwaukee, Wis.) I. Title.

School song-books.

DICKIE, Mary Stevens, Mrs. comp. 783
Singing pathways; hymns and songs and worship material for junior and senior high school age (12 to 18 years) compiled and arranged by Mary Stevens Dickie ... Cincinnati, O., Powell & White [c1929] xxiii, [2], 275 p. illus. 22 cm. "A few sources for stories and poetry": p. 270-271. [M2193.D5] 30-4713
1. School song-books. 2. Sunday-schools—Hymn-books. I. Title.

FORD, Stephen van Rensselaer, 1835?-1910. 783
Recitations, song and story for Sunday and day schools, primary and intermediate departments; material for anniversary and holiday programs, church and parlor sociables and entertainments, by Stephen V. R. Ford... New York, Eaton & Mains; Cincinnati, Jennings & Pye [1900] 160 p. 20 1/2 cm. [M2193.F711] 0-4275
1. School song-books. 2. Sunday-schools—Hymn-books. 3. Sunday-schools—Exercises, recitations, etc. I. Title.

Schooley, Frank Budd, 1905-

SCHOOLEY, Frank Budd, 1905- 242'.4
Spiritual traveler / by Frank Budd Schooley. [Dallas? Pa.] : Schooley, 1976. 319 p. : ill. ; 24 cm. Includes index. [F159.D14S36] 76-365508
1. Schooley, Frank Budd, 1905- 2. Dallas, Pa.—History—Miscellanea. 3. Meditations. I. Title.

Schools—Dubuque, Iowa (Archdiocese)

DRISCOLL, Justin Albert, 1920- 377'.8'209777
With faith and vision; schools of the Archdiocese of Dubuque, 1836-1966 [by] Justin A. Driscoll. Dubuque, Iowa, Bureau of Education, Archdiocese of Dubuque [1967] xxviii, 409 p. illus., maps (on lining papers), ports. 25 cm. [LC502.I8D7] 67-8464
1. Catholic Church in Iowa. 2. Schools—Dubuque, Iowa (Archdiocese) I. Title.

Schools—Furniture, equipment, etc.

ADAIR, Thelma. 268.2
How to make chruch school equipment: it's easier than you think! By Thelma Adair and Elizabeth McCort. Philadelphia, Westminster Press [1955] 96p. illus. 23cm. [BV1528.A3] 55-7707
1. Schools—Furniture, equipment, etc. 2. Religious education. I. McCort, Elizabeth, joint author. II. Title.

ADAIR, Thelma C 268.2
How to make church school equipment: it's easier than you think! By Thelma Adair and Elizabeth McCort. Philadelphia, Westminster Press [1955] 96 p. illus. 23 cm. [BV1528.A3] 55-7707
1. Schools — Furniture, equipment, etc. 2. Religious education. I. McCort, Elizabeth, joint author. II. Title.

Schools, Jewish — Exercises and recreations.

LISTER, Louis, comp.
The religious school assembly handbook. New York, Union of American Hebrew Congregations [c1963] v, 258 p. illus. 28 cm. 65-27132
1. Schools, Jewish — Exercises and recreations. I. Union of American Hebrew Congregations. II. Title.

LISTER, Louis, comp.
The religious school assembly handbook. New York, Union of American Hebrew Congregations [c1963] v, 258 p. illus. 28 cm. 65-27132
1. Schools, Jewish — Exercises and recreations. I. Union of American Hebrew Congregations. II. Title.

Schools, Jewish—United States—Curricula.

KUSELEWITZ, David. 377.96
Teaching Israel; a guide for curriculum development. New York, Herzl Press [1965, c1964] 140 p. 21 cm. Includes bibliographical references. [LC724.K8] 64-24384
1. Schools, Jewish — U.S. — Curricula. I. Title.

*SEGAL, Abraham 377.96
Teacher's guide to Israel today. New York, Union of Amer. Hebrew Congregations [1966] 61p. 28cm. 2.00 pap.,
1. Schools, Jewish—U.S.—Curricula. I. Title.

Schools, Jewish—United States—Religious instruction—Curricula.

*FISCHMAN, Joyce 377.96
Bible work and play; bk. 3 [New York] Union of Amer. Hebrew Congregations, 1966. 78p. illus. (pt. col.) 28cm. (Union graded ser.) Bibl. 1.25 pap.,
1. Schools, Jewish—U.S.—Religious instruction—Curricula. I. Title.

Schools, Jewish—United States—Social studies—Curricula.

*FIELDS, Harvey J. 377.96
Modern Jewish problems: teacher's guide. New York, Union of Amer. Hebrew Congregations [1966] vi, 122p. Bibl. 2.25 pap.,
1. Schools, Jewish—U.S.—Social studies—Curricula. I. Title.

Schools—Prayer-books and devotions—English.

KRAMER, William Albert, 1900- 264.1
Devotions for Lutheran schools, by Wm. A. Kramer. St. Louis, Mo., Concordia publishing house, 1934. 7. 107 p. 19 cm. [BV283.S3K7] 34-37972
1. Schools—Prayer-books and devotions—English. 2. Lutheran church—Prayer-books and devotions—English. I. Title.

KRAMER, William Albert, 1900- 264.1
Devotions for Lutheran schools, by Wm. A. Kramer. Saint Louis, Concordia publishing house, 1946. 286 p. 19 cm. "Revised and enlarged edition." Bibliographical references included in the foreword. [BV283.S3K7 1946] 46-19426
1. Schools—Prayer-books and devotions—English. 2. Lutheran church—Prayer-books and devotions—English. I. Title.

Schools—Prayers.

FISHER, Arthur Stanley Theodore. 264.1
An anthology of prayers, compiled for use in school and home, by A. S. T. Fisher... London, New York [etc.] Longmans, Green and co., 1934. xiv, 144, [2] p. 17 cm. Blank pages for additional prayers at end. "Biographical notes": p. [119]-132. [BV283.S3F5] 34-33264
1. Schools—Prayers. 2. Family—Prayer-books and devotions.—English. I. Title.

Schools—Sermons.

COIT, Henry Augustus, 1830-1895. 252.
School sermons, by Henry Augustus Colt ... New York, Moffat, Yard & company, 1909. 3 p. l., v-xiv, 362 p. 20 cm. [BV4310.C68] 9-5886
1. Schools—Sermons. 2. Protestant Episcopal church in the United States of America—Sermons. 3. Sermons, American. I. Title.

EDWARDS, Boyd, 1876- 252.5
Boys will be men; Mercersburg addresses, by Boyd Edwards ... New York [etc.] Fleming H. Revell company [c1936] 191 p. 19 1/2 cm. [Full name: Franklin Boyd Edwards] [BV4310.E35] 36-11678
1. Schools—Sermons. 2. Baccalaureate addresses. I. Mercersburg academy, Mercersburg, Pa. II. Title.

HERRICK, Cheesman Abiah, 1866- 252.5
More first things, by Cheesman A. Herrick ... Philadelphia, Printed in Girard college Mechanical school, 1936. viii, 213 p. 22 cm. "The following essays supplement a series which appeared in 1924 under the title First things." They were developed from addresses delivered in Girard college chaple. cf. Pref. [BV4310.H446] 37-2629
1. Schools—Sermons. 2. Christian life. I. Title.

Schools, Ukrainian—U.S.—History.

CZUBA, Natalie Ann. 377.82
History of the Ukrainian Catholic parochial schools in the United States. Chicago,

1956. xi, 71 p. map. 23 cm. Cover title: Ukrainian Catholic parochial schools. Thesis (M.A.)—De Paul University. Bibliography: p. 69-71. [LC501.C9] 70-211580
1. Catholic Church. Byzantine rite (Ukrainian)—Education. 2. Schools, Ukrainian—U.S.—History. I. Title. II. Title: Ukrainian Catholic parochial schools.

Schopenhauer, Arthur, 1788-1860.

DAUER, Dorothea W., 1917- 181'.04'3
Schopenhauer as transmitter of Buddhist ideas. By Dorothea W. Dauer. Berne, Lang, 1969. 39 p. 21 cm. (European University papers. Series 1: German language and literature, v. 15) Bibliographical footnotes. [B3148.D3] 76-427548 10.00
1. Schopenhauer, Arthur, 1788-1860. 2. Philosophy, Buddhist. I. Title. II. Series: Europaische Hochschulschriften. Reihe 1: Deutsche Literatur und germanistik, Bd. 15

MCGILL, Vivian Jerauld, 1897- 921.3
Schopenhauer; pessimist and pagan, by V. J. McGill. New York, Brentano's [c1931] 6 p. l., 312 p. front., pl., ports. 22 1/2 cm. Bibliography: p. 307-308. [B3147.M3] 31-7940
1. Schopenhauer, Arthur, 1788-1860. I. Title.

THE philosophy of Schopenhauer. Edited with an introd. by I. Edman. New York, Modern Library [c1956] xiv, 376p. (The modern library of the world's best books, 52)
I. Schopenhauer, Arthur, 1788-1860.

SCHOPENHAUER, Arthur, 1788-1860.
Philosophy of Arthur Schopenhauer; translated by Belfort Bax and Bailey Saunders. With a special introduction by James Gibson Hume ... New York, Tudor publishing co., 1933. 1 p. l., v-xii, 332 p. 25 cm. [B3108.S] A 34
I. Bax, Ernest Belfort, 1854-1926, tr. II. Saunders, Thomas Bailey, 1860-1928, joint tr. III. Hume, James Gibson. IV. Title.

Schreiber Moses. 1762-1839.

SPERO, Shubert. 922.96
... The story of Chasam Sofer ... Cleveland, Spero foundation; [etc., etc., 1946] 76 p. illus., ports. 21 cm. "Published works of the Chassam Sofer": p. [4] [BM755.S33S6] 47-20891
1. Schreiber Moses. 1762-1839. I. Title.

Schubert, Paul, 1900-

KECK, Leander E., ed. 226.406
Studies in Luke-Acts; essays presented in honor of Paul Schubert, edited by Leander E. Keck [and] J. Louis Martyn. Nashville, Abingdon Press [1966] 316 p. port. 24 cm. Contents.Contents.—Paul Schubert at Yale, by R. L. Calhoun.—Luke-Acts, a storm center in contemporary scholarship, by W. C. van Unnik.—On the Paulinism of Acts, by P. Vielhauer.—The perspective of Acts, by E. R. Goodenough.—Interpreting Luke-Acts in a period of existentialist theology, by U. Wilckens.—Four features of Lucan style, by H. J. Cadbury.—In search of the original text of Acts, by A. F. J. Klikn.—Luke's use of the birth stories, by P. S. Minear.—On preaching the Word of God, by W. C. Robinson, Jr.—The story of Abraham in Luke-Acts, by N. A. Dahl.—The Christology of Acts, by C. F. D. Moule.—The concept of the Davidic Son of God in Acts and its Old Testament background, by E. Schweizer.—The missionary stance of Paul in I Corinthians 9 and in Acts, by G. Bornkamm.—Concerning the speeches in Acts, by E. Schweizer.—The address of Paul on the Aeropagus, by H. Conzelmann.—Jewish Christianity in Acts in light of the Qumran scrolls, by J. A. Fitzmyer.—The Book of Acts as source material for the history of early Christianity, by E. Haenchen.—Acts and the Pauline letter corpus, by J. Knox.—Ephesians and Acts, by E. Kasemann.—Luke's place in the development of early Christianity, by H. Conzelmann. Includes bibliographies. [BS2589.Z72K4] 66-14998
1. Schubert, Paul, 1900- 2. Bible. N.T. Luke and Acts—Addresses, essays, lectures. I. Schubert, Paul, 1900- II. Martyn, James Louis, 1925- joint ed. III. Title.

KECK, Leander E., ed. 226'.4'06
Studies in Luke-Acts / edited by Leander E. Keck, J. Louis Martyn. 1st Fortress Press ed. Philadelphia : Fortress Press, 1980. 316 p. ; 22 cm. Essays presented in honor of P. Schubert. Includes bibliographical references. [BS2589.K42 1980] 79-8886 ISBN 0-8006-1379-1 pbk. : 7.95
1. Schubert, Paul, 1900- 2. Bible. N.T. Luke and Acts—Addresses, essays, lectures. I. Schubert, Paul, 1900- II. Martyn, James Louis, 1925- joint ed. III. Title.

Schuller, Robert Harold.

COLEMAN, Sheila Schuller. 285.7'32'0924 B
Robert Schuller, my father & my friend / by Sheila Schuller Coleman. Milwaukee, Wis. : Ideals Pub. Corp., c1980. 191 p. : ill. ; 21 cm. [BX9543.S36C64] 19 80-126499 ISBN 0-89542-025-2 pbk. : 3.95
1. Schuller, Robert Harold. 2. Reformed Church—Clergy—Biography. 3. Clergy—United States—Biography. I. Title.

Schultz, Samuel J.—Addresses, essays, lectures.

THE Living and active word of God : studies in honor of Samuel J. Schultz / edited by Morris Inch and Ronald Youngblood. Winona Lake, Ind. : Eisenbrauns, c1982. p. cm. Includes bibliographical references and index. [BS540.L58 1982] 19 82-9376 ISBN 0-931464-10-2 : 15.00 220.6
1. Schultz, Samuel J.—Addresses, essays, lectures. 2. Bible—Criticism, interpretation, etc.—Addresses, essays, lectures. I. Schultz, Samuel J. II. Inch, Morris A., 1925- III. Youngblood, Ronald F.
Publisher's address: P. O. Box 275, Winona Lake, IN 46590

Schutz, Heinrich, 1585-1672.

MOSER, Hans Joachim, 1889- 783'.0924 (B)
Heinrich Schutz; a short account of his life and works. Translated and edited by Derek McCulloch. New York, St. Martin's Press [1967] 120 p. map, music, port. 23 cm. Originally published under title Kleines Heinrich-Schutz-Buch. Discography: p. 111-116. [ML410.S35M652 1967b] 67-25262
1. Schutz, Heinrich, 1585-1672. I. Title.

Schutz, Heinrich, 1585-1672—Bibliography.

SKEI, Allen B. 783'.092'4 B
Heinrich Schutz, a guide to research / Allen B. Skei. New York : Garland, 1981. p. cm. (Garland composer resource manuals ; v. 1) Includes index. [ML134.S412S5] 19 80-9028 ISBN 0-8240-9310-0 lib. bdg. : 20.00
1. Schutz, Heinrich, 1585-1672—Bibliography. I. Title. II. Series. III. Garland reference library of the humanities ; v. 272.

Schutz, Roger.

SCHUTZ, Roger. 282'.092'4 B
Festival / Brother Roger ; translated by Brethren of the Taize community. New York : Seabury Press, [1974] c1973. 174 p. ; 18 cm. Translation of Ta fete soit sans fin. "A Crossroad book." [BR1725.S39A313 1974] 73-17913 ISBN 0-8164-2583-3 : 2.95
1. Schutz, Roger. I. Title.

SCHUTZ, Roger. 282'.092'4 B
Struggle and contemplation; journal, 1970-2 [by] Brother Roger. New York, Seabury Press [1974] p. cm. "A Crossroad book." Translation of Lutte et contemplation. [BR1725.S39A2813] 74-13954 ISBN 0-8164-2106-4 2.95 (pbk.)
1. Schutz, Roger. 2. Contemplation. I. Title.

Schwarzenau, Ger.

SHULTZ, Lawrence W 289.92
Schwarzenau yesterday and today, where the Brethren began in Europe. Told in picture and storyt Milford, Ind. [1954] 111p. illus. 22cm. [BX7819.G4S4] [BX7819.G4S4] 286.5 54-28242 54-28242
1. Schwarzenau, Ger. 2. Church of the Brethreu—Hist. I. Title.

Schweitzer, Albert, 1875-1965.

THE Albert Schweitzer jubilee book, edited by A. A. Roback. With the co-operation of J. S. Bixler [and] George Sarton. Westport, Conn., Greenwood Press [1970] 508 p. illus., facsims., ports. 23 cm. Reprint of the 1945 ed. "A tentative bibliography of Albert Schweitzer": p. [467]-483. [CT1098.S45A5 1970] 79-97392 ISBN 0-8371-2670-3 266'.025'0924
1. Schweitzer, Albert, 1875-1965. I. Roback, Abraham Aaron, 1890-1965, ed.

ANDERSON, Erica. 922.443
Albert Schweitzer. [1st ed.] Philadelphia, Chilton Co., Book Division [1961] 122p. illus. 21cm. (Meet your great contemporaries series, 633) [CT1098.S45A62] 61-9023
1. Schweitzer, Albert, 1875- I. Title.

ANDERSON, Erica 922.443
Albert Schweitzer's gift of friendship New York, Harper [c.1964] viii, 152p. illus., ports. 24cm. 64-19496 4.95
1. Schweitzer, Albert, 1875- I. Title.

ANDERSON, Erica. 362.10924
The Schweitzer album; a portrait in words and pictures. Additional text by Albert Schweitzer. [1st ed.] New York, Harper & Row [1965] 176 p. illus. (part col.) facsims., maps, ports. 30 cm. [BV3625.G3S422 1965] 65-20444
1. Schweitzer, Albert, 1875-1965. I. Title.

ANDERSON, Erica. 922.443
The world of Albert Schweitzer, a book of photographs by Erica Anderson. With text and captions by Eugene Exman. New York, Harper [c1955] 144p. illus. 26cm. [CT1098.S45A63] 54-12197
1. Schweitzer, Albert, 1875- I. Exman, Eugene. II. Title.

BERRILL, Jacquelyn 922.443
Albert Schweitzer: man of mercy. Illus. with drawings by the author and with photos. 90th birthday ed. New York, Dodd [1965] 202p. illus., ports. 21cm. [CT1098.S45B4] 65-2217 3.25
1. Schweitzer, Albert, 1875- I. Title.

BERRILL, Jacquelyn. 922.443
Albert Schweitzer, man of mercy; illustrated with drawings bythe author and with photos. New York, Dodd, Mead [1956] 200p. illus. 21cm. [CT1098.S45B4] 56-5188
1. Schweitzer, Albert, 1875- I. Title.

BRABAZON, James. 266'.025'0924 B
Albert Schweitzer : a biography / by James Brabazon. New York : Putnam, [1975] 509 p., [8] leaves of plates : ill. ; 24 cm. Includes index. Bibliography: p. 485-488. [CT1098.S45B7 1975] 74-30545 ISBN 0-399-11421-1 : 12.50
1. Schweitzer, Albert, 1875-1965. I. Title.

BRABAZON, James. 266'.025'0924 B
Albert Schweitzer : a biography / James Brabazon. London : Gollancz, 1976. 509 p., [16] p. of plates : ill., plan, ports. ; 24 cm. Includes index. [CT1018.S45B72 1976] 76-383118 ISBN 0-575-02035-0 : £6.95
1. Schweitzer, Albert, 1875-1965. 2. Missionaries, Medical—Gabon—Biography. 3. Theologians—Europe—Biography. 4. Musicians—Europe—Biography.

COUSINS, Norman. 922.443
Dr. Schweitzer of Lambarene. With photos. by Clara Urquhart. New York, Harper [1960] 254 p. illus. 22 cm. [CT1098.S45C6] 60-9134
1. Schweitzer, Albert, 1875-1965.

COUSINS, Norman. 266'.025'092'4 B
Dr. Schweitzer of Lambarene. With photos. by Clara Urquhart. Westport, Conn., Greenwood Press [1973, c1960] 254 p. illus. 22 cm. Reprint of the ed. published by Harper, New York. [CT1098.S45C6 1973] 73-7075 ISBN 0-8371-6902-X
1. Schweitzer, Albert, 1875-1965. I. Title.

COUSINS, Norman. 266'.025'092'4 B
Dr. Schweitzer of Lambarene. With photos. by Clara Urquhart. Westport, Conn., Greenwood Press [1973, c1960] 254 p. illus. 22 cm. Reprint of the ed. published by Harper, New York. [CT1098.S45C6 1973] 73-7075 ISBN 0-8371-6902-X 12.50
1. Schweitzer, Albert, 1875-1965. I. Title.

DANIEL, Anita. 922.443
The story of Albert Schweitzer. Illustrated with photos. by Erica Anderson, and drawings by W. T. Mars. New York, Random House [1957] 179 p. illus. 22 cm. (World landmark books, W-33) [CT1098.S45D3] 57-7517
1. Schweitzer, Albert, 1875-1965.

FESCHOTTE, Jacques. 922.443
Albert Schweitzer, an introduction. With two addresses by Albert Schweitzer. [Translated from the French by John Russell. 1st ed.] Boston, Beacon Press [1955] 130p. port. 21cm. [CT1098.S45F43] 54-13056
1. Schweitzer, Albert, 1875- I. Schweitzer, Albert, 1875- II. Title.

FRANCK, Frederick, 1909- 266'.025'0924 B
Days with Albert Schweitzer; a Lambarene landscape. Illustrated by the author. Westport, Conn., Greenwood Press [1974, c1959] xii, 178 p. illus. 22 cm. Reprint of the ed. published by Holt, Rinehart and Winston, New York. [CT1098.S45F68 1974] 73-22636 ISBN 0-8371-7341-8 9.50
1. Schweitzer, Albert, 1875-1965. I. Title.

HAGEDORN, Hermann, 1882- 922.443
Albert Schweitzer; prophet in the wilderness. New rev ed. New York, Collier Books [1962] 224p. 19cm. (Collier books, AS150) Previous editions published under title: Prophet in the wilderness. [CT1098.S45H3 1962] 61-18561
1. Schweitzer, Albert, 1875- I. Title.

HAGEDORN, Hermann, 1882- 922.443
Albert Schwitzer; prophet in the wilderness. New rev. ed. New York, Collier Bks. [c.1947-1962] Previous eds. pub. under title: Prophet in the wilderness 61-18561 .95 pap.,
1. Schweitzer, Albert, 1875- I. Title.

HAGEDORN, Hermann, 1882- 922.443
Prophet in the wilderness; the story of Albert Schweitzer. Rev. ed. New York, Macmillan, 1954. 240p. illus. 21cm. [CT1098.S45H3 1954] 54-13060
1. Schweitzer, Albert, 1875- I. Title.

HAGEDORN, Hermann, 1882- 922.443
Prophet in the wilderness; the story of Albert Schweitzer. New York, Macmillan Co., 1947. 221 p. port. 21 cm. Bibliographical references included in "Acknowledgments" (p. 214-221) [CT1098.S45H3] 47-11858
1. Schweitzer, Albert, 1875- I. Title.

HASSOLD, Ernest Christopher, 1896- 266'.025'0924
Albert Schweitzer, E. R. Hagemann, editor. [Louisville, Ky., University of Louisville, 1969] [33] p. facsims., ports. 22 x 28 cm. "The occasion for this symposium, December 6, 1965, was to commemorate Albert Schweitzer (1875-1965) as part of the faculty lectures in the humanities at the University of Louisville." Contents.Contents.—Schweitzer's philosophy of culture, by E. C. Hassold.—Schweitzer and Indian philosophy, by D. P. Patnaik.—Schweitzer, the musician/personal recollections, by G. Herz. Includes bibliographical references. [CT1098.S45H35] 79-230389
1. Schweitzer, Albert, 1875-1965. I. Hagemann, Edward R., ed. II. Louisville, Ky. University. III. Patnaik, Deba Prasad. Schweitzer and Indian philosophy. 1969. IV. Herz, Gerhard, 1911- Schweitzer, the musican/personal recollections. 1969.

JOY, Charles Rhind, 1885- 922.443
The Africa of Albert Schweitzer [by] Charles R. Joy & Melvin Arnold; with a concluding essay by Albert Schweitzer. Photos by Charles R. Joy. New York, Harper [1948] [160] p. illus., ports., map (on lining-papers) 24 cm. [BV3625.G315S35] 48-9372
1. Schweitzer, Albert, 1875- 2. Missions, Medical. 3. Lambarene, Gabon. I. Arnold, Melvin, joint author. II. Title.

JOY, Charles Rhind, 1885- 922.443
The Africa of Albert Schweitzer [by] Charles R. Joy & Melvin Arnold. Photos. by Charles R. Joy. New [i. e. 2d] ed., rev. London, A. & C. Black; New York, Harper [1958] 159p. illus. 24cm. [BV3625.G315S35 1958] 59-1239
1. Schweitzer, Albert. 1875- 2. Missions, Medical — Gabon. 3. Lambarene Gabon. I. Arnold, Melvin, joint author. II. Title.

JUNGK, Robert, 1913- 922.443
Albert Schweitzer; the story of his life, by Jean Pierhal [pseud.] New York, Philosophical Library [c1957] 100 p. illus. 23 cm. "A version of [the author's] Albert Schweitzer; das Leben eines guten Menschen." [CT1098.S45.J83] 57-13702
1. Schweitzer, Albert, 1875- I. Title.

KIK, Richard 922.443
With Schweitzer in Lambarene. Translated [from the German] by Carrie Bettelini. Philadelphia, Christian Education Press [c.1959] 87p. illus. 18cm. 59-14778 2.00 bds.,
1. Schweitzer, Albert, 1875- I. Title.

KRAUS, Oskar, 1872-1942 922.443
Albert Schweitzer; his work and his philosophy [tr. from German by E. G. McColman] Introd. by A. D. Lindsay. London, A. & C. Black [Chester Springs, Pa., Dufour, 1966] x, 75p. front. (port.) 22cm. First pub. in the Jahrbuch fur charakterologie. Bibl. [CT1098.S45K72] A44 2.50
1. Schweitzer, Albert, 1875- I. McCalman, E. G., tr. II. Title.

MCKNIGHT, Gerald. 922.443
Verdict on Schweitzer, the man behind the legend of Lambarene. New York, John Day Co. [1964] 254 p. illus., plan, ports. 23 cm. Bibliography: p. 247. [CT1098.S45M24 1964a] 64-20467
1. Schweitzer, Albert, 1875-1965. I. Title.

MANTON, Jo, 1919- 922.443
The story of Albert Schweitzer. Illustrated by Astrid Walford. New York, Abelard-Schuman [1955] 223 p. illus. 22 cm. [CT1098.S45M3 1955a] 55-8542
1. Schweitzer, Albert, 1875-1965.

MARSHALL, George. 266'.025'0924 B
Schweitzer a biography [by] George Marshall and David Poling. New York, Pillar Books [1975 c1971] 346 p., illus. 18 cm. Includes index. [CT1098.S45M34] 71-130888 ISBN 0-89129-020-6 1.95 (pbk.)
1. Schweitzer, Albert, 1875-1965. I. Poling, David, joint author II. Title.

MARSHALL, George N. 362.10924
An understanding of Albert Schweitzer. New York, Philosophical Lib. [c.1966] 180p. illus., ports. 22cm. Bibl [BV3625.G3S43] 65-28763 4.00
1. Schweitzer, Albert, 1875-1965. I. Title.

MURRY, John Middleton, 1889- 194
1957.
The challenge of Schweitzer. [Folcroft, Pa.] Folcroft Press, 1970. 133 p. 23 cm. "Limited to 150 copies." Reprint of the 1948 ed. [BX4827.S35M87 1970] 72-190328
1. Schweitzer, Albert, 1875-1965. I. Title.

OSTERGAARD Christensen, 922.443
Lavrids 1896-
At work with Albert Schweitzer. Translated from the Danish by F. H. Lyon. Boston, Beacon Press [1962] 117p. illus. 21cm. Translation of Dansk laege hos Albert Schweitzer. [CT1098.S45O43 1962] 61-4345
1. Schweitzer, Albert, 1875- I. Title.

PAYNE, Pierre Stephen 922.443
Robert, 1911-
The three worlds of Albert Schweitzer. Bloomington, Indiana Univ. Press [1961, c.1957] 252p. (Midland bk. MB29) 1.75 pap.,
1. Schweitzer, Albert, 1875- I. Title.

PAYNE, Pierre Stephen 922.443
Robert, 1911-
The three worlds of Albert Schweitzer. New York, T. Nelson [1957] 252p. 21cm. [CT1098.S45P3] 57-11896
1. Schweitzer, Albert, 1875- I. Title.

PICHT, Werner Robert 922.443
Valentin, 1887-
The life and thought of Albert Schweitzer. Tr. from German by Edward Fitzgerald. New York, Harper [1965, c.1960, 1964] 288p. ports. 22cm. Bibl. [CT1098.S45P493] 65-10373 6.50
1. Schweitzer, Alb ert, I. Title.

PIERHAL, Jean. 922.443
Albert Schweitzer; the story of his life. New York, Philosophical Library [c1957] 160p. illus. 23cm. [CT1098.S45P513] 57-13702
1. Schweitzer, Albert, 1875- I. Title.

RATTER, Magnus C. 922.443
Albert Schweitzer, life and message. Boston, Beacon Press, 1950. 214 p. group port. 20 cm. [CT1098.S45R3 1950] 50-5266
1. Schweitzer, Albert, 1875-1965.

REGESTER, John Dickinson. 922-443
Albert Schweitzer, the man and his work [by] John Dickinson Regester. New York, Cincinnati [etc] The Abingdon press [c1931] 145 p. 19 cm. Bibliography: p. 139-140. [CT1098.S45R4] 31-6722
1. Schweitzer, Albert, 1875- I. Title.

RICHARDS, Kenneth 266'.025'0924 B
G., 1926-
Albert Schweitzer, by Kenneth G. Richards. Chicago, Childrens Press [1968] 94 p. illus. 29 cm. (People of destiny: a humanities series) Bibliography: p. 90-91. Photographs, drawings, and text trace the life of the famous doctor whose dedicated service to suffering humanity in French Equatorial Africa made him a living symbol of his own philosophy of reverence for life. [CT1098.S45R5] 92 AC 68
1. Schweitzer, Albert, 1875-1965. I. Title.

ROBACK, Abraham Aaron, 922.443
1890-
In Albert Schweitzer's realms, a symposium. Cambridge, Mass., Sci-Art Publishers [1962] 441p. illus. 24cm. [CT1098.S45R58] 61-18922
1. Schweitzer, Albert, 1875- I. Title.

SCHWEITZER, Albert, 1875- 208.1
Albert Schweitzer: an anthology. Enlarged ed., ed. by Charles R. Joy. [Gloucester, Mass., Peter Smith, 1961, c.1947] 355p. (Beacon Press bk. rebound in cloth) Bibl. 3.75
I. Joy, Charles Rhind, 1885- ed. II. Title.

SCHWEITZER, Albert, 1875- 208.1
Albert Schweitzer; an anthology, ed. by Charles R. Joy. Presentation ed. Boston, Beacon Press, 1947. xxviii, 323 p. 24 cm. "Bibliography of books by Dr. Schweitzer": p. [xi]-xiii. [B3329.S52E5 1947] 47-11732
I. Joy, Charles Rhind, 1885- ed. II. Title.

SCHWEITZER, Albert, 1875- 208.1
Albert Schweitzer, an anthology ed. by Charles R. Joy. New York, Harper [c1947] xxviii, 323 p. 22 cm. "Bibliography of books by Dr. Schweitzer": p. [xi]-xiii. [B3329.S52E5 1947a] 47-12409
I. Joy, Charles Rhind, 1885- ed. II. Title.

SCHWEITZER, Albert, 1875- 248.4
The light within us. New York, Philosophical Library [1959] 58p. 20cm. [B3329.S53V63] 59-1813
I. Title.

SCHWEITZER, 266'.025'0924 B
Albert, 1875-1965.
Albert Schweitzer: reverence for life; the inspiring words of a great humanitarian. With a forword [sic] by Norman Cousins. Selected by Peter Seymour. Illustrated by Walter Scott. [Kansas City, Mo., Hallmark Cards, inc., c1971] 62 p. illus. 20 cm. (Hallmark editions) [CT1098.S45A27] 71-147796 ISBN 0-87529-203-8 2.50
I. Title: Reverence for life.

SCHWEITZER, Albert, 1875- 248.4
1965.
The light within us. Westport, Conn., Greenwood Press [1971, c1959] 58 p. 23 cm. Translation of Vom Licht in uns. Bibliography: p. 58. [B3329.S53V63 1971] 75-139151 ISBN 0-8371-5767-6
I. Title.

SCHWEITZER, 266'.025'0924 B
Albert, 1875-1965.
On the edge of the primeval forest & More form the primeval forest : experiences and observations of a doctor in equatorial Africa / by Albert Schweitzer. New York : AMS Press, [1976] p. cm. Translation by C. T. Campion of the author's Zwischen Wasser und Urwald, and of Mitteilungen aus Lambarene. Reprint of the 1948 ed. published by Macmillan, New York. [BV3625.G3S36 1976] 75-41244 ISBN 0-404-14598-1 : 18.50
1. Schweitzer, Albert, 1875-1965. 2. Missions—Gabon. 3. Missions, Medical—Gabon. 4. Lambarene, Gabon. 5. Missionaries, Medical—Gabon—Biography. 6. Missionaries, Medical—Switzerland—Biography. I. Schweitzer, Albert, 1875-1965. Mitteilungen aus Lambarene. 1976. II. Title.

SEAVER, George. 922.443
Albert Schweitzer: Christian revolutionary, by George Seaver. New York and London, Harper & brothers [1946] 3 p. l., 130 p. 20 cm. [Full name: George Fenn Seaver] Bibliography: p. 125-127. [CT1098.S45S3 1946] 46-8094
1. Schweitzer, Albert, 1875- I. Title.

SEAVER, George, 1890- 922.443
Albert Schweitzer, the man and his mind. Rev. ed. New York, Harper [1956, c1955] ix, 370p. illus., ports. 24cm. [CT1098.S45S35 1956] 56-2431
1. Schweitzer, Albert, 1875- I. Title.

SEAVER, George, 1890- 922.443
Albert Schweitzer, the man and his mind; with 30 illus. from photos. New York, Harper [1947] xiii, 346 p. plates, ports. 25 cm. Full name: George Fenn Seaver. [CT1098.S45S35 1947a] 47-11620
1. Schweitzer, Albert, 1875- I. Title.

SEAVER, George, 1890- 920.043
Albert Schweitzer, a vindication; being a reply to The challenge of Schweitzer, by John Middleton Murry. Boston, Bencon Press, 1951. 120p. 20cm. [CT1098.S45S] A54
1. Schweitzer, Albert, 1875- 2. Murry, John Middleton, 1889- The challenge of Schweitzer. I. Title.

SEAVER, George, 1890- 922.443
Albert Schweitzer, Christian revolutionary. 2d ed., rev. and enl. New York, Harper [1955] 128p. 21cm. [CT1098.S45S3] 55-11897
1. Schweitzer, Albert, 1853- I. Title.

SEAVER, George, 1890- 922.443
Albert Schweitzer, the man and his mind. Rev. ed. New York, Harper [1956, c1955] ix, 370p. illus., ports. 24cm. [CT1098.S45S35 1956] 56-2431
1. Schweitzer, Albert, 1875- I. Title.

SIMON, Charlie May Hogue, 922.443
1897-
All men are brothers; a portrait of Albert Schweitzer. Photos. by Erica Anderson. [1st ed.] New York, Dutton, 1956. 192 p. illus. 21 cm. [CT1098.S45S44] 56-8305
1. Schweitzer, Albert, 1875-1965. I. Title.

TO Dr. Albert 922.443
Schweitzer; a festchrift commemorating his 80th birthday from a few of his friends. Evanston, Ill., 1955. 178p. 22cm. Edited by H. A. Jack. [CT1098.S45T6] 55-2440
1. Schweitzer, Albert, 1875- I. Jack, Homer Alexander, ed.
Contents omitted.

Schweitzer, Albert, 1875-1965—Juvenile literature.

ATWOOD, Ann. 113
For all that lives / by Ann Atwood and Erica Anderson ; with the words of Albert Schweitzer. New York : Scribner, [1975] [32] p. : col. ill. ; 21 x 27 cm. The meaning of life and man's alienation from himself and his natural environment is examined in brief selections, illustrated with photographs, from the works of Albert Schweitzer. [B3329.S54A86] 74-7809 ISBN 0-684-14001-2 lib. bdg. : 6.95
1. Schweitzer, Albert, 1875-1965—Juvenile literature. 2. [Schweitzer, Albert, 1875-1965.] 3. Life—Juvenile literature. 4. [Life.] I. Anderson, Erica, joint author. II. Schweitzer, Albert, 1875-1965. III. Title.

JOHNSON, Spencer. 266'.025'0924 B
The value of dedication : the story of Albert Schweitzer / by Spencer Johnson. 1st ed. La Jolla, Calif. : Value Communications, c1979. p. cm. (ValueTales) Presents a biography of Albert Schweitzer who based his philosophy on what he called "reverence for life" and dedicated his life to serving humanity. [CT1018.S45J63] 92 79-21805 ISBN 0-916392-44-9 : 5.95
1. Schweitzer, Albert, 1875-1965—Juvenile literature. 2. [Schweitzer, Albert, 1875-1965.] 3. Missionaries, Medical—Gabon—Biography—Juvenile literature. 4. Theologians—Europe—Biography—Juvenile literature. 5. Musicians—Europe—Biography—Juvenile literature. 6. Altruism—Juvenile literature. 7. [Missionaries.] 8. [Theologians.] 9. [Musicians.] 0. [Altruism.] I. Title.

MONTGOMERY, 266'.025'0924 B
Elizabeth Rider.
Albert Schweitzer, great humanitarian. Illustrated by William Hutchinson. Champaign, Ill., Garrard Pub. Co. [1971] 144 p. illus., ports. 22 cm. ([A People in the arts and sciences book]) A biography of the musician, minister, and teacher who gave up a comfortable teaching career to become a missionary doctor in the African jungle. [CT1098.S45M63] 92 70-132035 ISBN 0-8116-4510-X 2.59
1. Schweitzer, Albert, 1875-1965—Juvenile literature. 2. [Schweitzer, Albert, 1875-1965.] 3. [Physicians.] I. Hutchinson, William M., illus. II. Title.

Schweitzer, Albert, 1875-1965—Theology.

ICE, Jackson Lee. 201'.1
Schweitzer: prophet of radical theology. Philadelphia, Westminster Press [1971] 208 p. 21 cm. Includes bibliographical references. [BX4827.S35I3] 74-141991 ISBN 0-664-20906-8 7.50
1. Schweitzer, Albert, 1875-1965—Theology. I. Title. II. Title: Prophet of radical theology.

SCHWEITZER, Albert, 1875- 232
1965.
The theology of Albert Schweitzer for Christian inquirers, by E. N. Mozley. With an epilogue by Albert Schweitzer. Westport, Conn., Greenwood Press [1974] vii, 108 p. 20 cm. Reprint of the 1950 ed. published by A. and C. Black, London. [BR85.S295 1974] 73-16630 ISBN 0-8371-7204-7 7.75
1. Schweitzer, Albert, 1875-1965—Theology. 2. Jesus Christ—Messiahship. 3. Eschatology. I. Mozley, Edward Newman, 1875-1950. II. Title.

Schwenckfeld, Casper, 1490?-1561.

SCHULTZ, Selina Gerhard, 922.443
1880-
Caspar Schwenckfeld von Ossig (1489-1561) spiritual interpreter of Christianity, apostle of the middle way, pioneer in modern religious thought, by Selina Gerhard Schultz... Norristown, Pa., The Board of publication of the Schwenckfelder church, 1946. xx p., 1 l. 453 p. front. (port.) 24 cm. Bibliography: p. 415-418. [BX9749.S36] 47-1563
1. Schwenckfeld, Casper, 1490?-1561. I. Title.

Schwenkfelder church—Catechisms and creeds.

SCHULTZ, Christopher, 238.99
1718-1789.
Short questions concerning the Christian doctrine of faith according to the testimony of the Sacred scriptures, answered and confirmed. For the purpose of instructing youth in the first principles of religion. By the Rev. Christopher

Schultz, senior. Translated from the original German by Prof. I. Daniel Rupp ... Skippackville, Pa., Printed by J. M. Schuenemann, 1863. xii, 140 p. 16 cm. Translation of the author's Kurze fragen liber die christliche glaubenslehre, 1855, originally published (1763) under title: Catechismus, oder Anfanglicher unterricht christlicher glaubens-lehre. [BX9749.S32] 35-32561
1. Schwenkfelder church—Catechisms and creeds. I. Rupp, Israel Daniel, 1803-1878, tr. II. Title.

SCHWENKFELDER church. 264.099
Liturgy and ritual.
Book of worship for church and home, with orders of service, prayers, and other aids to devotion, prepared by the Committee of ministers of the General conference of the Schwenkfelder church. Pennsburg, Pa., The Board of publication of the Schwenkfelder church [c1928] 200 p. 17 cm. [BX9749.A4P4 1928] 29-2791
I. Title.

Schwenkfelder Church—Hymns—History and criticism.

SEIPT, Allen Anders. 783.9'52
Schwenkfelder hymnology and the sources of the first Schwenkfelder hymn-book printed in America. Philadelphia, Americana Germanica Press, 1909. [New York, AMS Press, 1971] 112 p. illus. 22 cm. (Americana Germanica [7]) Originally presented as the author's thesis, University of Pennsylvania, 1906. Contents.Contents.—Introduction.—Descriptive bibliography (p. 17-36)—The Schwenkfelder hymn-writers of the 16th and 17th centuries.—Hymns used by the Schwenkfelders before 1762.—Caspar Weiss: the originator of the Schwenkfelder hymn-book.—George Weiss: writer and compiler of hymns.—Balthaser Hoffmann, Christopher Hoffmann, and Hans Christoph Huebner.—Christopher Schultz and the printed hymn-book.—Bibliography (p. 111-112) [BV481.S3S52 1971] 77-134414 ISBN 0-404-09908-4 6.50
1. Schwenkfelder Church—Hymns—History and criticism. 2. Hymns, German—Bio-bibliography. I. Title. II. Series: Americana Germanica; monographs devoted to the comparative study of the literary, linguistic, and other cultural relations of Germany and America [7]

Schwenkfelder Church—Prayer-books and devotions.

SCHWENCKFELD, Caspar, 242.8
1490?-1561.
Passional and prayer book. In modern translation by John Joseph Stoudt. [1st ed.] Pennsburg, Pa., Schwenkfelder Library, 1961. 139p. illus. 23cm. 'First appeared in Nurnberg in 1539 with the title, Deutsch Passional vnsers Herren Jesu Christi, mit schonen trostilchen Gebetlein.' [BV262.S313] 61-18289
1. Schwenkfelder Church—Prayer-books and devotions. I. Title.

Schwenkfelders—History—Sources.

JOHN, Martin, 1624-1707. 289.9
The tumultuous years : Schwenkfelder chronicles, 1580-1750 : the reports of Martin John, Jr. and Balthazar Hoffmann / translated by L. Allen Viehmeyer. 1st ed. Pennsburg, Pa. : Schwenkfelder Library, c1980. v, 157 p. ; 23 cm. [BX9749.J64 1980] 79-92386 ISBN 0-935980-00-8 : 3.00
1. Schwenkfelders—History—Sources. I. Hoffmann, Balthazar, 1687-1775, joint author. II. Title.
Publisher's address 1 Seminary St., Pennsburg, PA 18073. Publisher's address 1 Seminary, St., Pennsburg, PA 18073.

Schwerdtfeger, Johann Samuel William, 1734-1803.

SCHWERDTFEGER, Hazel Mae 922.471
Memoirs of Reverend J. Samuel Schwerdtfeger, 'the Saint of St. Lawrence Seaway,' first pastor of Upper Canada's first Protestant church, U. E. Loyalist and Lutheran patriarch of America. Carlton [dist. Comet, c.]1961. 84p. illus. (Reflection bk.) 61-16227 2.50
1. Schwerdtfeger, Johann Samuel William, 1734-1803. I. Title.

Science.

HUEBNER, Charlotte K 244
The science of human equation [1st ed.] Glendale, Calif., Lincoln Printers & Publishers, [1954] 172p. 21cm. [BR126.H8] 54-42457
I. Title.

MCBRIDE, Cora Emma, Mrs. 220.
1869-
The science of Christian economy; the everlasting gospel, by Cora Emma McBride and Thomas Garth McBride ... New York, Cincinnati [etc.] The Abingdon press [c1920] 429 p. 20 cm. $2.50. [BS670.M3] 20-22525
I. McBride, Thomas Garth, joint author. II. Title.

MATHEWS, Shailer, 1863- 215
Contributions of science to religion, by Shailer Mathews...with the cooperation of William E. Ritter, Robert A. Milikan...[and others] New York, [etc.] D. Appleton and company, 1924. vii p., 1 l., 427 p. illus., plates, diagrs. 21 cm. [BL240.M37] 24-28230
1. Science. 2. Religion and science—1900- I. Title.

MATHEWS, Shailer, 1863- 215
Contributions of science to religion, by Shailer Mathews...with the cooperation of William E. Ritter, Robert A. Milikan...[and others] New York [etc.] D. Appleton and company, 1927. xi, 427 p. illus., plates, diagrs. 21 cm. [BL240.M37 1927] 27-13021
1. Science. 2. Religion and science—1900- I. Title.

REED, Lucas Albert.
The scriptural foundations of science, by L. A. Reed ... with many illustrations by the author. Battle Creek, Mich., Review and herald pub. co., 1901. 272 p. incl. illus., pl. 16°. 1-25524
I. Title.

RICE, William North, 1845- 270
The poet of science, and other addresses, by William North Rice ... New York, Cincinnati, The Abingdon press [c1919] 225 p. 19 1/2 cm. [BR85.R5] 19-15945
I. Title.
Contents omitted.

STEVENS, Samuel Eugene, 1839-
Science and superstition [by] Samuel Eugene Stevens ... New York, Truth seeker company, 1913. 4 p. l., [11]-119 p. 20 cm. 14-3759 1.25
I. Title.

*THOMAS, Owen C. 261.5
Science challenges faith. New York, Seabury [1967] 80p. illus. 21cm. (Senior-high-sch. unit. Study units on contemp. concerns.) Prepd. under the auspices of the Dept. of Christian Educ. of the Episcopal Church. .95 pap.,
I. Title.

Science—Addresses, essays, lectures.

BEHR, Herman, ed. 133.9
... The new science: lectures by Henry Ward Beecher, Henry James, Harriet Beecher Stowe, Hugh Latimer, William T. Stead, Luther Burbank, and others; with a foreword, edited and published by Herman Behr. New York, H. Behr; London, K. Paul, Trench, Trubner & co., ltd. [c1930] xii, 311 p. 22 1/2 cm. (His Transcendental series. v. 2) Spiritualistic messages. [BF1290.B4 vol. 2] 30-23056
I. Beecher, Henry Ward, 1813-1887. II. Title.

HUXLEY, Thomas Henry, 1825- 215
1895.
Essays upon some controverted questions. Freeport, N.Y., Books for Libraries Press [1973] p. (Essay index reprint series) Reprint of the 1892 ed. Contents.Contents.—Prologue.—The rise and progress of palaeontology.—The interpreters of Genesis and the interpreters of nature.—Mr. Gladstone and Genesis.—The evolution of theology: an anthropological study.—Science and morals.—Scientific and pseudo-scientific realism.—Science and pseudo-science.—An Episcopal trilogy.—Agnosticism.—The value of witness to the miraculous.—Agnosticism: a rejoinder.—Agnosticism and Christianity.—The lights of the church and the light of science.—The keepers of the herd of swine.—Illustrations of Mr. Gladstone's controversial methods.—Hasisadra's adventure. [Q171.H916 1973] 73-1231 ISBN 0-518-10048-0
1. Science—Addresses, essays, lectures. 2. Religion and science—1860-1899—Addresses, essays, lectures. I. Title.

HUXLEY, Thomas Henry, 1825- 215
1895.
Science and Hebrew tradition; essays. New York, Greenwood Press [1968] xvi, 372 p. 23 cm. (His Collected essays, v. 4) "Originally published in 1896." Contents.Contents.—On the method of Zadig (1880).—The rise and progress of palaeontology (1881).—Lectures on evolution (New York, 1876).—The interpreters of Genesis and the interpreters of nature (1885).—Mr. Gladstone and Genesis (1886).—The lights of the church and the light of science (1890).—Hasisadra's adventure (1891).—The evolution of theology: an anthropological study (1886) [Q171.H902 vol. 4] 71-29961
1. Science—Addresses, essays, lectures. 2. Bible and science—Addresses, essays, lectures. 3. Evolution—Addresses, essays, lectures. 4. Paleontology—Addresses, essays, lectures. I. Title.

HUXLEY, Thomas Henry, 1825- 215
1895.
Science and Hebrew tradition; essays by Thomas H. Huxley. New York, D. Appleton and company, 1897. 1 p. l., [v]-xvi, 372 p. 19 cm. "Authorized edition." [Q171.H948] [504] 32-24466
1. Science—Addresses, essays, lectures. 2. Bible and science. 3. Evolution. 4. Paleontology. I. Title.
Contents omitted.

MATHEWS, Shailer, 1863-1941. 215
Contributions of science to religion, by Shailer Mathews, with the cooperation of William E. Ritter [and others] Freeport, N.Y., Books for Libraries Press [1970, c1924] vii, 427 p. illus. 23 cm. (Essay index reprint series) [BL240.M37 1970] 79-117822
1. Science—Addresses, essays, lectures. 2. Religion and science—1926-1945—Addresses, essays, lectures. I. Ritter, William Emerson, 1856-1944. II. Title.

SIMPSON, George, 1908-
Science as morality; an essay toward unity. Yellow Springs, Ohio, American Humanist Association [1953] 60p. 23cm. (Humanist pamphlet, 1) A55
1. Science—Addresses, essays, lectures. I. Title.

Science and religion.

BEERS, Forrest William.
Light and shadow; or, Christianity and the current religious "sciences." Rev. ed. Cincinnati, O., M. W. Knapp, 1899. 137 p. 12°. (Full salvation quarterly, v. 5, no. 2) 99-2069
I. Title.

COLVILLE, William J.
The people's handbook of spiritual science. W. J. Colville's private course of lessons for the use of students. Boston, Banner of light pub co., 1902. 92 p. 20 cm. Subjects entries: Mental healing. 2-7289
I. Title.

GALYON, Carrie Barbour. 220
The science of religion, based upon the works and words of Jesus the Christ, by Carrie Barbour Galyon ... New York, The Bloomfield press [c1922] 2 p. l., [7]-513 p. 17 1/2 cm. [BR125.G2] 22-16061
I. Title.

HAND, James Edward, ed.
Ideals of science & faith; essays by various authors, ed. by the Rev. J. E. Hand... London, G. Allen; New York, Longmans, Green, & co., 1904. xix, 332, [1] p. 19 1/2 cm. 5-2580
I. Title.
Contents omitted.

HARRIS, John, 1802-1856. 213
The pre-Adamite earth: contributions to theological science. By John Harris ... 4th thousand. Rev. and enl. Boston, Gould and Lincoln, 1851. 1 p. l., [5]-300 p. 20 cm. [BL225.H4 1851] 7-6266
I. Title.

HARRIS, John, 1802-1856. 215
The pre-Adamite earth: a contribution to theological science. By John Harris ... 6th ed., rev. and enl. Boston, Gould and Lincoln; New York, Sheldon and company; [etc., etc.] 1870. 1 p. l., [5]-300 p. 20 cm. [BL240.H3] 17-17488
I. Title.

HARRIS, John, 1802-1856.
The pre-Adamite earth: contributions to theological science. By John Harris ... 5th thousand. Rev. and Enl. Boston, Gould and Lincoln, 1854. 1 p. l., [5]-300 p. 20 cm. G S
I. Title.

LEWIS, Arthur Morrow. 215
The struggle between science and superstition, by Arthur M. Lewis. Chicago, C. H. Kerr & company, 1916. 188 p. 17 cm. [BL245.L4] 17-17639
1. Science and religion. 2. Persecution. I. Title.

MASCALL, Exic Lionel, 1905-
Christian theology and natural science: some questions on their relations. New York, Ronald Press [1956] 328p. (The Bampton lectures, 1956)
I. Title.

MATHER, Kirtley Fletcher. 215
Christian fundamentals in the light of modern science [by] Kirtley F. Mather... [Granville, O., Times press, c1924] 3 p. l., 85, [1] p. 15 1/2 cm. Alternate pages blank for "Notes." "A list of recent books recommended for study": p. 85. "An outline prepared in 1924 for a group of Denison university students meeting on Sunday mornings in the Baptist church at Granville, Ohio." [BL240.M35] 24-7741
I. Title.

MORROW, Ethel Belle. 261.5
Scientific views of religion. New York, Philosophical Library [1957] 348p. 22cm. [BR126.M62] 57-13974
I. Title.

PRICE, George McCready, 1870- 215
Science and religion in a nutshell, by George McCready Price ... Washington, D. C. [etc.] Review & herald publishing association [c1923] 61 p. 20 cm. [BL240.P76] 23-8932
I. Title.

RICE, William North, 1845-
Christian faith in an age of science, by William North Rice ... 2d ed. New York, A. C. Armstrong and son, 1904. xi, 425 p. illus. 20 1/2 cm. Contents.pt. I. History of scientific discoveries which have affected religious beliefs.--pt. II. Status of certain doctrines of Christianity in an age of science.--pt. III. General status of Christian evidences. 13-22651
I. Title.

RODGER, James George, 1852- 215
Passages from the scientist's bible, translated by James George Rodger. Washington, D.C., University union international, inc. [c1931] 4 p. l., 3-202 p. illus. 21 cm. [BS534.R55] 32-22252
I. Title.

SCIENTISTS who believe; 215
ten interviews with Christian men of science. Elgin, Ill., David C. Cook Pub. Co. [1964, c.1963] 63p. 22cm. price unreported. pap.,

SIMMONS, Daniel A.
The science of religion, fundamental faiths expressed in modern terms, by Daniel A. Simmons... New York, Chicago [etc.] Fleming H. Revell company [c1916] 224 p. 19 1/2 cm. $1.00. 17-1169
I. Title.

SMITH, Orlando Jay, 1842-1908.
Balance the fundamental verity, by Orlando J. Smith, offering a key to the fundamental scientific interpretations of

the system of nature, a definition of natural religion, and a consequent agreement between science and religion. With an appendix containing critical reviews by scientific and religious writers, and a reply by the author to his critics. Boston and New York, Houghton, Mifflin and company, 1904. xi, 286 p., 1 l. 20 1/2 cm. 4-27153
I. Title.

WAGGETT, Philip Napier, 1862-
The scientific temper in religion, and other addresses; by the Rev. P. N. Waggett ... London, New York [etc.] Longmans, Green and co., 1905. xii p., 1 l., 286 p. 19 cm. W6-116
I. Title.
Contents omitted.

WHITE, Edward Arthur, 1907- 215
Science and religion in American thought; the impact of naturalism. Stanford, Stanford University Press, 1952. viii, 117 p. 24 cm. (Stanford University publications. University series. History, economics, and political science,v. 8) [BL245.W63] AS36.L54 vol. 8 52-5982
I. Title.

Science and religion—1945—

SHIDELER, Emerson W 215
Believing and knowing: the meaning of truth in Biblical religion and in science [by] Emerson W. Shideler. [1st ed.] Ames, Iowa State University Press, 1966. xvii, 196 p. 24 cm. Bibliography: p. 185-188. [BL240.2.S56] 66-14588
1. Science and religion—1945- I. Title.

Science and the humanities.

DICTIONARY of scientific illustrations and symbols, moral truths mirrored in scientific facts ... By a barrister of the honorable society of the Inner Temple. New York, W. B. Ketcham [c1894] 420 p. 21 cm. [PN6338.S4D6] 13-18404

SNOW, Charles Percy, baron Snow, 1905-
The two cultures: and a second look. [2d ed.] [New York] New American Library [1964] 92 p. 20 cm. (Mentor book MP557 "An expanded version of [the author's] The two cultures and the scientific revolution." 66-53449
1. Science and the humanities. I. Title.

Science—History

WALSH, James Joseph, 1865- 215
The popes and science; the history of the papal relations to science during the middle ages and down to our own time, by James J. Walsh ... Knights of Columbus edition (30,000) New York, Fordham university press, 1911. 3 p. l., [v]-xii, 431 p. 19 1/2 cm. [BX961.S4W3 1911] 42-2612
1. Science—Hist. 2. Popes. 3. Religion and science—History of controversy. I. Title.

WHITE, Andrew Dickson, 1832- 213 1918.
The warfare of science. By Andrew Dickson White ... New York, D. Appleton and company, 1876. 151 p. 19 1/2 cm. "In its earlier abridged form ... given as a Phi beta kappa oration at Brown university and ... published in the Popular science monthly."--Pref. [BL245.W6 1876a] 15-3387
1. Science—Hist. 2. Religion and science—History of controversy. I. Title.

WOOD, E[zra] M[organ]
Beginnings of faith and science, by E. M. Wood ... Pittsburg, Pa., J. Horner book company, ltd. [1903] 221 p.20 cm. 4-2590
I. Title.

Science—Miscellanea.

KIPPER, Herman Brunswick, 215 1882-
Christianity and the gamut of evolution; the final goal: immortal life, by H. B. Kipper. Boston, Christopher Pub. House [1967] 254 p. 21 cm. [Q173.K57] 67-23753
1. Science—Miscellanea. 2. Evolution. 3. Religion and science—1946- I. Title.

Science—Philosophy.

AYRES, Clarence Edwin, 1891- 215
Science: the false messiah & Holier than thou; the way of the righteous [by] Clarence E. Ayres. [1st ed.] Clifton [N.J.] A. M. Kelley [1973] xii, 240 p. 22 cm. (Reprints of economic classics) Reprints of the 1927 and 1929 editions, both published by Bobbs-Merrill Co., Indianapolis, with a new introd. [B67.A79] 71-130660 ISBN 0-678-00774-8
1. Science—Philosophy. 2. Inventions. 3. Religion and science—1926-1945. 4. Ethics. 5. Social ethics. I. Ayres, Clarence Edwin, 1891- Holier than thou. 1973. II. Title. III. Title: Holier than thou.

Scientists, American.

HEFLEY, James C. 248.8'8
Adventurers with God; scientists who are Christians, by James C. Hefley. [1st ed.] Grand Rapids, Zondervan Pub. House [1967] 124 p. ports. 21 cm. [Q141.H4] 67-11619
1. Scientists, American. 2. Religion and science—1946- I. Title.

Scientists, British.

RAISTRICK, Arthur. 289.6'42
Quakers in science and industry; being an account of the Quaker contributions to science and industry during the 17th and 18th centuries. New York, Kelley, 1968. 361 p. illus., geneal. tables, ports. 23 cm. Reprint of the 1950 edition with a new introd. [BX7676.R3 1968] 68-18641
1. Friends, Society of. Gt. Brit. 2. Friends, Society of—Biography. 3. Scientists, British. 4. Great Britain—Industries—History. I. Title.

Scientology.

BRADDESON, Walter. 131'.35
Scientology for the millions. Los Angeles, Sherbourne Press [1969] 154 p. 21 cm. (For the millions series, FM 30) Bibliography: p. 154. [BP605.S2B7] 70-83568 2.50
1. Scientology. 2. Dianetics. I. Title.

BROWN, Henry S. 211
The bible of the religion of science, by H.S. Brown... Milwaukee, Wis., The author, 1882. viii, 405, iii p. front. (port.) 20 cm. [BL2775.B7] 38-34598
I. Title.

GARRISON, Omar V. 299
The hidden story of scientology / Omar V. Garrison. Secaucus, N.J. : Citadel Press, 1974. 232 p. ; 22 cm. Includes bibliographical references. [BP605.S2G37] 74-80818 ISBN 0-8065-0440-4 : 8.50
1. Scientology. I. Title.

GARRISON, Omar V. 323.44'2'0973
Playing dirty : the secret war against beliefs / Omar V. Garrison. 1st ed. Los Angeles : Ralston-Pilot, c1980. 265 p. : ill. 23 cm. Includes index. [BP605.S2G38] 19 80-142084 ISBN 0-931116-04-X : 10.50
1. Scientology. 2. Religious liberty—United States. I. Title.

HUBBARD, La Fayette 133'.35 Ronald, 1911-
Mission into time [by] L. Ron Hubbard. Los Angeles [American Saint Hill Organization, 1973] ix, 106 p. illus. 22 cm. (His A Scientology book) [BP605.S2H82 1973] 74-151712 ISBN 0-88404-023-2 6.00
1. Hubbard, La Fayette Ronald, 1911- 2. Scientology. I. Title.

HUBBARD, La Fayette 131'.35 B Ronald, 1911-
Mission into time [by] L. Ron Hubbard. Los Angeles [American Saint Hill Organization, 1973] ix, 106 p. illus. 22 cm. (His A Scientology book) [BP605.S2H82 1973] 74-151712 ISBN 0-88404-023-2 6.00
1. Hubbard, La Fayette Ronald, 1911- 2. Scientology. I. Title.

HUBBARD, La Fayette Ronald, 254 1911-
The organization executive course : an encyclopedia of scientology policy / by L. Ron Hubbard. Los Angeles : American Saint Hill Organization, 1974. 8 v. : ill. ; 32 cm. Vols. numbered 0-7. Includes index. [BP605.S2H826] 74-195055 ISBN 0-88404-033-X
1. Scientology. I. Title.

HUBBARD, La Fayette Ronald, 294 1911-
The Phoenix lectures / by L. Ron Hubbard. 3d ed. Los Angeles : American Saint Hill Organization, 1974, c1969. x, 320 p. ; 21 cm. "Lecture series given by L. Ron Hubbard to the professional course, Phoenix, Arizona, in July 1954, compiled into book form by the editorial staff of the Publications Organization World Wide." [BP605.S2H83 1974] 74-195931 ISBN 0-88404-006-2 : 7.00
1. Scientology. I. Publications Organization World Wide. II. Title.

HUBBARD, La Fayette Ronald, 299 1911-
Scientology 0-8 : the book of basics / by L. Ron Hubbard. 1st American ed. Los Angeles : American St. Hill Organization, c1970. 152 p. ; 21 cm. [BP605.S2H835 1970] 75-322012
1. Scientology. I. Title.

HUBBARD, La Fayette Ronald, 299 1911-
The volunteer minister's handbook / by L. Ron Hubbard ; [photography by L. Ron Hubbard]. Los Angeles : Church of Scientology of California, c1976. lxxi, 674 p. : ill. ; 29 cm. "A Dianetics publication." Includes index. Bibliography: p. 562-564. [BP605.S2H837 1976] 76-27819 ISBN 0-88404-039-9
1. Scientology. I. Title.

HUBBARD, La Fayette 131.3'5 Ronald, 1911-
When in doubt, communicate ... Quotations from the works of L. Ron Hubbard. Compiled by Ruth Minshull and Edward M. Lefson. Ann Arbor, Mich., Scientology Ann Arbor [1969] 166 p. col. illus. 19 cm. [BP605.S2H84] 73-11921 4.00
1. Scientology. I. Title.

KAUFMAN, Robert. 131'.35
Inside scientology; how I joined scientology and became superhuman. [New York] Olympia Press [1972] xvi, 279 p. 24 cm. [BP605.S2K38 1972] 73-189412 ISBN 0-7004-0110-5 6.95
1. Scientology. I. Title.

MALKO, George. 131.3'5
Scientology: the now religion. New York, Delacorte Press [1970] xv, 205 p. 22 cm. [BP605.S2M3] 73-108660 5.95
1. Scientology. I. Title.

PRESS view the FBI raid 323.44'2'0973 : a collection of photographs and press covering the FBI raid of July 8, 1977 on the Church of Scientology. [Los Angeles : Church of Scientology of California, [1977 or 1978] 31 p. : ill. ; 28 cm. [BP605.S2P73] 78-102289 ISBN 0-915598-17-5 pbk. : 2.00
1. United States. Federal Bureau of Investigation. 2. Scientology. 3. Religious liberty—United States. 4. Church and state in the United States. I. Church of Scientology of California, Los Angeles.

SCIENTOLOGY: a world religion emerges in the space age. 294 [Hollywood, Calif.] Church of Scientology Information Service, Dept. of Archives [1974] xvi, 109, 63 p. illus. 32 cm. (Church of Scientology Information Service. Dept. of Archives. Archival series, 1) [BP605.S2S3] 74-171028 10.00
1. Scientology. I. Church of Scientology Information Service. Dept. of Archives. II. Series: Church of Scientology Information Service. Dept. of Archives. Archival series — Church of Scientology Information Service, Dept. of Archives, 1.

SUCCESS with scientology. 131'.35 [Hollywood, Calif.] : Church of Scientology Information Service, Dept. of Archives, c1976. 106 p. : ill. ; 23 cm. (Archival series - Church of Scientology Information Service, Department of Archives ; 2) Testimonials. [BP605.S2S9] 76-5564 ISBN 0-915598-01-9 : 3.95
1. Scientology. I. Series: Church of Scientology Information Service. Dept. of Archives. Archival series — Church of Scientogy Information Service, Dept. of Archives ; 2.

WALLIS, Roy. 131'.35
The road to total freedom : a sociological analysis of scientology / Roy Wallis. New York : Columbia University Press, 1976,i.e.1977 p. cm. Includes index. Bibliography: p. [BP605.S2W34 1976] 76-27273 ISBN 0-231-04200-0 : 12.00
1. Scientology. I. Title.

WALLIS, Roy. 301.5'8
The road to total freedom : a sociological analysis of Scientology / [by] Roy Wallis. London : Heinemann Educational, 1976. xiv, 282 p. : 1 ill. ; 25 cm. Includes index. Bibliography: p. [270]-279. [BP605.S2W34 1976b] 77-358879 ISBN 0-435-82916-5 : £6.50
1. Scientology. I. Title.

WASHINGTON, D. C. Founding 265'.5 Church of Scientology.
Ceremonies of the Founding Church of Scientology. New ed. East Grinstead (Sx.), Hubbard College of Scientology, 1966. 79 p. 20 1/2 cm. 12/6 (B 67-2805) [BP605.S2A45 1966] 67-89459
1. Scientology. 2. Marriage service. I. Hubbard College of Scientology. II. Title.

Scientology—Congresses.

INTERNATIONAL Conference for 299 World Peace and Social Reform, Anaheim, Calif., 1976.
The International Conference for World Peace and Social Reform & Human Rights Prayer Day, 1976 : [proceedings]. [Washington] : Church of Scientology Information Service, Dept. of Archives, c1977. 208 p. : ill. ; 23 cm. (Archival series - Church of Scientology Information Service, Dept. of Archives ; 3) [BP605.S2I57 1976] 77-71240 ISBN 0-915598-14-0 : 6.50
1. Scientology—Congresses. I. Series: Church of Scientology Information Service. Dept. of Archives. Archival series — Church of Scientology Information Service, Dept. of Archives ; 3.

Scientology—Dictionaries.

HUBBARD, La Fayette 131'.35 Ronald, 1911-
Dianetics and scientology technical dictionary / by L. Ron Hubbard. Los Angeles : Church of Scientology of California, Publications Organization, 1975. x, 577 p. : ill. ; 24 cm. "A Dianetics publication." [BP605.S2H795 1975] 75-327422 ISBN 0-88404-037-2
1. Scientology—Dictionaries. 2. Dianetics—Dictionaries. I. Title.

Scotch in Franconia.

DILWORTH, Mark. 271'.1'04333
The Scots in Franconia : a century of monastic life / Mark Dilworth. Totowa, N.J. : Rowman and Littlefield, 1974. 301 p. : ill. ; 23 cm. Includes index. Bibliography: p. 282-289. [BX2618.S3117D54 1974b] 74-195058 ISBN 0-87471-453-2 : 13.50
1. Sankt Jakob (Monastery), Wurzburg. 2. Scotch in Franconia. I. Title.

Scotch-Irish in North Carolina.

HURLEY, James Franklin, 922.573 1870-
The prophet of Zion-Parnassus, Samuel Eusebius McCrorkle, by James F. Hurley and Julia Goode Eagan. Richmond, Va., Pub. for the authors by Presbyterian committee of publication 1935. 121 p. incl. col. front. 22 cm. Bibliography: p. 121. [BX9225.M19H8] 36-3984
1. McCorkle, Samuel Eusebius, 1746-1811. 2. Scotch-Irish in North Carolina. I. Eagan, Julia Goode, joint author. II. Presbyterian church in the U. S. Committee of publication. III. Title.

Scotland—Church history.

BURLEIGH, John H. S. 274.1
A church history of Scotland. London, New York, Oxford University Press, 1960[ ] 456p. illus. (maps) Bibl.: p.[423]-424 and bibl. notes 60-50629 6.75
1. Scotland—Church history. I. Title.

CAIRNS, William Thomas, d.1944. 208
The religion of Dr. Johnson, and other essays. Freeport, N.Y., Books for Libraries Press [1969, c1946] xiii, 137 p. 23 cm. (Essay index reprint series) Contents.Contents.—The religion of Doctor Johnson.—John Newton: a vindication.—The constituents of a good hymn.—Jupiter Carlyle and the Scottish moderates.—A reformation diarist and his times. Bibliographical footnotes. [BR783.C3 1969] 71-93324
1. Johnson, Samuel, 1709-1784—Religion and ethics. 2. Scotland—Church history. I. Title.

CAIRNS, William Thomas, d.1944. 204
... *The religion of Dr. Johnson,* and other essays. London, New York [etc.] G. Cumberlege, Oxford university press, 1946. xiii, 137, [1] p. 19 cm. At head of title: The Rev. William T. Cairns, D.D. [BR783.C3] A 46
1. Johnson, Samuel, 1709-1784. 2. Scotland—Church history. I. Title.
Contents omitted.

DONALDSON, Gordon. 274.1
Scotland: church and nation through sixteen centuries. New York Barnes & Noble [1974, c1972] 128 p. 23 cm. Bibliography p 124-125. [BR782.D57] ISBN 0-06-491738-X 5.00
1. Scotland—Church history. I. Title.
L.C. card number for original edition: 60-4701.

DONALDSON, Mary Ethel Muir, 1876- 274.1
"Till Scotland melts in flame"; talks on Scottish church history for young people and others. With commendation by the Primus of the Scottish Episcopal Church. London, Faith Press. New York, Morehouse-Gorham Co. [1949] xii, 132 p. 19 cm. [BR782.D62] 49-26374
1. Scotland—Church history. 2. Episcopal Church in Scotland—Hist. I. Title.

FREE Presbyterian Church of Scotland. Synod.
History of the Free Presbyterian Church of Scotland (1893-1933) compiled by a committee appointed by the Synod of the Free Presbyterian Church. Inverness, Free Presbyterian Church of Scotland, 1965. [2], ix, 314 p. 21 cm. [BX9095.F7A43 1965] 68-113544 10/6
1. Free Presbyterian Church of Scotland—History. 2. Scotland—Church history. I. Title.

HAY, Malcolm Vivian, 1881- 282.
A chain of error in Scottish history, by M. V. Hay ... London, New York [etc.] Longmans, Green and co. ltd., 1927. xx, 243 p. 22 1/2 cm. "The object of this book is to show ... the mentality and methods of English and Scottish historians generally in their treatment of a particular section of ecclesiastical history."--Pref. [BR784.H3] 27-25403
1. Scotland—Church history. I. Title.

HENDERSON, George David, 1888- 274.1
Religious life in seventeenth century Scotland, by G. D. Henderson ... Cambridge [Eng.] The University press, 1937. 4 p. l., 311 p. 22 1/2 cm. "The book is largely based upon articles which have made their appearance in historical and theological journals."--Pref. "Notes & references": p. 239-306. [BR785.H45] 38-6574
1. Scotland—Church history. 2. Religious thought—Scotland. 3. Religious thought—17th cent. I. Title.

MITCHELL, Anthony, bp. 1868-1917.
...*Biographical studies in Scottish church history,* by Anthony Mitchell...delivered in St. Paul's church, Chicago, Illinois, May 7 to 14, 1914. Milwaukee, The Young churchman company; [etc., etc.] 1914. vi p., 1 l., [2], 301, [1] p. front., plates, ports. 19 1/2 cm. (Half-title: The Hale lectures, Western theological seminary, Chicago, Ill. Series of 1913-14) Series title also at head of t.-p. [BR789.M5] 15-1014
1. Scotland—Church history. 2. Scotland—Biog. I. Title.
Contents omitted.

RALEIGH, Thomas, Sir 1850-1920.
Annals of the church in Scotland, by Sir Thomas Raleigh ... together with his own autobiographical notes and some reminiscences by Sir Harry R. Reichel. London, New York [etc.] H. Milford, Oxford university press, 1921. li, 344 p. 22 cm. [BR782.R3] 22-16186
1. Scotland—Church history. I. Title.

SPOTTISWOOD, John, Abp. of St. Andrews, 1565-1639. 274.1
The history of the Church of Scotland. New York, AMS Press [1973] 3 v. 24 cm. Reprint of the 1847-51 ed. printed for the Spottiswoode Society, Edinburgh, which was issued as no. 93 of Bannatyne Club Publications. With biographical sketches and notes by M. Russell. [BR785.S682] 76-176004 ISBN 0-404-52840-6 70.00
1. Scotland—Church history. I. Title. II. Series: Bannatyne Club, Edinburgh. Publications no. 93.

Scotland—Church history—Bibliography.

MACGREGOR, Malcolm Blair. 016.27411
The sources and literature of Scottish church history / by Malcolm B. Macgregor. Merrick, N.Y. : Richwood Pub. Co., [1976] p. cm. Reprint of the 1934 ed. published by J. McCallum, Glasgow. Includes indexes. [Z7778.S3M2 1976] [BR782] 76-1125 ISBN 0-915172-10-0 : 20.00
1. Scotland—Church history—Bibliography. 2. Church history—Bibliography. 3. Scotland—Bio-bibliography. I. Title.

Scotland—Church history—Dictionaries.

TOWILL, Edwin Sprott. 274.11
People and places in the story of the Scottish Church / [by] Edwin Sprott Towill ; illustrated by Colin Gibson. Edinburgh : St. Andrew Press, 1976. xix, 99 p. : ill., ports. ; 24 cm. [BR781.T68] 77-367785 ISBN 0-7152-0322-3 : £3.25. pbk.
1. Scotland—Church history—Dictionaries. 2. Christian biography—Scotland. I. Title.

Scotland Neck, N. C. Trinity Church.

SMITH, Stuart Hall. 283.756
The history of Trinity Parish, Scotland Neck [and] Edgecombe Parish, Halifax County [by] Stuart Hall Smith [and] Claiborne T. Smith, Jr. Scotland Neck, N. C., 1955. 115p. illus. 24cm. [BX5980.S4T7] 55-25504
1. Scotland Neck, N. C. Trinity Church. 2. Edgecomb Parish, Halifax Co., N. C. 3. Smith, Claiborne T. I. Title.

Scotland—Religion.

HIGHET, John 274.1
The Scottish churches; a review of their state 400 years after the Reformation. [dist. New York, Humantites Pr., 1961, c.1960] 224p. 61-2868 6.00
1. Scotland—Religion. 2. Scotland—Church history. I. Title.

Scotland—Social conditions.

MECHIE, Stewart. 309.1'411
The Church and Scottish social development, 1780-1870 / Stewart Mechie. Westport, Conn. : Greenwood Press, 1975, c1960. xi, 181 p. ; 22 cm. Reprint of the ed. published by Oxford University Press, London, New York, which was issued as the Cunningham lectures, 1957. Includes bibliographical references and index. [HN398.S3M4 1975] 75-3740 ISBN 0-8371-8060-0
1. Church of Scotland. 2. Scotland—Social conditions. I. Title. II. Series: Cunningham lectures ; 1957.

MECHIE, Stewart. 941
The church and Scottish social development, 1780-1870. London, New York, Oxford University Press, 1960. 181p. 23cm. (The Cunningham lectures, 1957) [HN398.S3M4] 60-50239
1. Scotland—Soc. condit. 2. Church of Scotland. I. Title.

Scott, George Robert White, 1842-1902.

[SCOTT, Mary Elizabeth (Dow)] Mrs. comp. 920.
In memoriam: Rev. George Robert White Scott, PH. D., D. D. Boston, Priv. print.; [Cambridge, Mass., The Riverside press] 1905. v, 239, [1] p. front. (port.) 25 cm. [BX7260.S33S3] 5-6919
1. Scott, George Robert White, 1842-1902. I. Title.

Scott, Latayne Colvett, 1952-

SCOTT, Latayne Colvett, 1952- 230'.9'33
The Mormon mirage : a former Mormon tells why she left the church / Latayne Colvett Scott. Grand Rapids : Zondervan Pub. House, c1979. xi, 276 p. ; 24 cm. Includes indexes. Bibliography: p. 257-261. [BX8645.S35] 79-17717 ISBN 0-310-38910-0 10.95
1. Scott, Latayne Colvett, 1952- 2. Mormons and Mormonism—Doctrinal and controversial works—Church of Christ authors. I. Title.

Scott, Levi, bp., 1802-1882.

MITCHELL, James, 1818-1903. 922.773
The life and times of Levi Scott, D.D., one of the bishops of the Methodist Episcopal church. By James Mitchell, D.D. With a preface by Rev. D. P. Kidder... New York, Phillips & Hunt; Cincinnati, Cranston & Stowe, 1885. 272 p. front. (port.) 19 cm. [BX8495.S36M5] 36-37410
1. Scott, Levi, bp., 1802-1882. I. Title.

Scott, Thomas, 1747-1821.

SCOTT, John, 1777-1834. 922.
The life of the Rev. Thomas Scott, D. D., rector of Aston Sandford, Bucks: including a narrative drawn up by himself, and copious extracts of his letters. By John Scott ... Boston, S. T. Armstrong and Crocker & Brewster; New York, J. P. Haven, 1822. xii, [13]-454 p. front. (port.) 19 cm. [BX5199.S3S3 1822] 39-3984
1. Scott, Thomas, 1747-1821. I. Title.

SCOTT, John, 1777-1834. 922.
The life of the Rev. Thomas Scott, D. D., rector of Aston Sandford, Bucks: including a narrative drawn up by himself, and copious extracts of his letters. By John Scott ... New-York, White, Gallaher & white, 1828. xii, [13]-418 p. 18 cm. [BX5199.S3S3 1828] 39-824
1. Scott, Thomas, 1747-1821. I. Title.

SCOTT, John] 1777-1834. 922.
Memoir of the Rev. Thomas Scott, rector of Aston Sandford, Bucks; abridged from his Life comp. by his son. Augusta, Me., P. A. Brinsmade, 1830. 236 p. 25 cm. L. C. copy imperfect: p. 9-12 wanting: p. 23-236 mutilated. [BX5199.S3S32] 49-30031
1. Scott, Thomas, 1747-1821. I. Title.

SCOTT, Thomas, 1747-1821. 922.
The force of truth: an authentic narrative. By Thomas Scott ... From the last London edition ... Philadelphia, Printed and published by G. M. & W. Snider, 1827. viii, [9]-141 p. 15 cm. [BX5199.S3A3 1827] 12-18354
I. Title.

SCOTT, Thomas, 1747-1821. 922.342
The force of truth: an authentic narrative. By Thomas Scott ... New York, R. Carter & brothers, 1857. 133 p. 16 cm. (Lettered on cover: Carter's cabinet library. 4) [BX5199.S3A3 1857] 33-8062
I. Title.

Scott, Walter, 1796-1861.

BAXTER, William, 1820-1880. 922.673
Life of Elder Walter Scott: with sketches of his fellow laborers, William Hayden, Adamson Bentley, John Henry, and others. By William Baxter. Cincinnati, Bosworth, Chase & Hall, 1874. x, 11-450 p. front. (port.) 20 cm. [BX7343.B3B3] 36-32757
1. Scott, Walter, 1796-1861. 2. Hayden, William, 1799-1863. 3. Bentley, Adamson, 1785-1864. 4. Henry, John, 1797-1844. I. Title.

NETH, John Watson. 230'.0924
Walter Scott speaks; a handbook of doctrine. Milligan College, Tenn., Emmanuel School of Religion, 1967. 156 p. 20 cm. Revision of author's thesis, Butler University. Bibliography:p. 146-147. [BX7343.S3N4 1967] 67-25396
1. Scott, Walter, 1796-1861. I. Title.

SCOTT, Walter, Sir bart., 1771-1832.
The beauties of Sir Walter Scott, and Thomas Moore, esquire; selected from their works; with historical and explanatory notes. By B. F. French ... 10th ed.--enl. Philadelphia, 1828. ix p., 1 l., 204 p. front. 15 cm. "Beauties of Moore": p. [167]-204. [PR5303.F7] 28-17236
I. Moore, Thomas, 1779-1852. II. French, Benjamin Franklin, 1799-1877, comp. III. Title.

STEVENSON, Dwight Eshelman, 1906- 922.673
Walter Scott; voice of the golden oracle, a biography by Dwight E. Stevenson. St. Louis, Mo., Christian board of publication [1946] 240 p. front. (port.) 20 1/2 cm. Bibliographical references included in "Notes" (p. 225-230) Bibliography: p. 231-233. [BX7343.S3S77] 46-22985
1. Scott, Walter, 1796-1861. I. Title.

Scott, William Anderson, 1813-1885.

DRURY, Clifford Merrill, 1897- 285'.10924 (B)
William Anderson Scott, "no ordinary man." Glendale, Calif., A. H. Clark Co., 1967. 352 p. illus., ports. 25 cm. Bibliography: p. [344]-345. [BX9225.S34D7] 67-22431
1. Scott, William Anderson, 1813-1885. I. Title.

SMYLIE, James. 285.
Brief history of the trial of the Rev. William A. Scott, D.D., from its commencement before the late Presbytery of New Orleans, in July, 1845, to its "termination" by the General assembly, in May, 1847. With important documents and grave disclosures never before published. By James Smylie ... New Orleans, The author, 1847. vi, 74 p., 1 l. 23 1/2 cm. [BX9193.S35S5] 44-36663
1. Scott, William Anderson, 1813-1885. I. Title.

Scottish confession of faith, 1560.

BARTH, Karl, 1886-1968. 238'.5'2
The knowledge of God and the service of God according to the teaching of the Reformation, recalling the Scottish confession of 1560 / by Karl Barth ; translated by J. L. M. Haire and Ian Henderson. 1st AMS ed. New York : AMS Press, 1979. xxix, 255 p. ; 23 cm. Reprint of the 1939 ed. published by Scribner, New York, which was issued as Gifford lectures, 1937-1938. Includes index. [BX9183.B37 1979] 77-27187 ISBN 0-404-60495-1 : 24.00
1. Reformed Church—Doctrinal and controversial works—Reformed authors. 2. Scottish confession of faith, 1560. 3. Theology, Doctrinal. I. Title. II. Series: Gifford lectures ; 1937-1938.

Scovel, Myra.

SCOVEL, Myra. 266'.5'7320924
The Chinese ginger jars [by] Myra Scovel with Nelle Keys Bell. [1st ed.] New York, Harper [1962] 189p. 22cm. Autobiographical. [BV3427.S38A3] 62-7299
I. Title.

SCOVEL, Myra. 285'.1'0922 B
In clover / Myra Scovel. 1st ed. Philadelphia : Westminster Press, c1980. 120 p. ; 21 cm. [BX9225.S355A34] 79-24882 ISBN 0-664-21366-9 : 8.95
1. Scovel, Myra. 2. Scovel, Frederick Gilman. 3. Presbyterians—United States—Biography. 4. Missionaries—Asia—Biography. 5. Retirement—United States—Biography. I. Title.

Scranton (Diocese)

[COMERFORD, Thomas J] 1857- 282. 1924, ed.
Souvenir of dual jubilee; consecration of the Rt. Rev. M. J. Hoban, D. D. (1896-1921), erection of the Scranton diocese (1868-1918). Scranton, Pa., International textbook press, 1922. 5 p. l., 5-210 p. col. front., plates, ports. 23 cm. Foreword signed: The Historical committee, Rev. T. J. Comerford, Rev. J. J. McCabe, Rev. D. J. Connor. [BX1417.S4C6] 22-15910
1. Hoban, Michael John, bp., 1853-1926. 2. Scranton (Diocese) I. McCabe, John Joseph, 1867-1937, joint ed. II. Connor, Daniel Joseph, 1881-1927, joint ed. III. Title.

Scranton (Diocese)—History.

GALLAGHER, John P., 1924- 282.748
A century of history; the Diocese of Scranton, 1868-1968, by John P. Gallagher. Foreword by J. Carroll McCormick. [Scranton] Diocese of Scranton [1968] xiv, 615 p. illus., map (on lining paper), ports. 23 cm. Bibliographical references included in "Notes" (p. 463-524) [BX1417.S4G3] 68-56284 9.50
1. Scranton (Diocese)—History. I. Title.

Screens (Church decoration)

BOND, Francis, d. 1918. 729.
Screens and galleries in English churches, by Francis Bond ... illustrated by 152 photographs and measured drawings. London, New York, and Toronto, H. Frowde, 1908. xii, 192 p. incl. front., illus. 23 1/2 cm. (Church art in England. 1] Bibliography: p. [ix]-xii. [NA5080.B7] 9-3348
1. Screens (Church decoration) 2. Church architecture—England. I. Title.

VALLANCE, Aymer, 1862- 729.960942
English church screens; being great roods, screenwork & rood-lofts of parish churches in England & Wales, by Aymer Vallance. New York, C. Scribner's sons; London, B. T. Batsford, ltd., 1936. xii, 103, [1] p. col. front., illus., plates (part col., 1 double) 26 1/2 cm. "Printed in Great Britain." [NA5080.V3] [247.2] 37-1661
1. Screens (Church decoration) 2. Church architecture—Gt. Brit. 3. Church architecture—Details. I. Title.

VALLANCE, Aymer, 1862- 729.962 1943.
Greater English church screens, being great roods, screen-work & rood- lofts in cathedral, monastic & collegiate churches in England & Wales. London, New York, B. T. Batsford [1947] viii, 184 p. illus. 27 cm. "A supplement and sequel to ... English church screens."--Dust jacket. Full name: William Howard Aymer Vallance. Bibliographical footnotes. [NA5080.V32] [[247.2]] 48-3331
1. Screens (Church decoration) 2. Church architecture—Gt. Brit. 3. Church architecture—Details. I. Title.

Screven, William, 1629?-1713.

BAKER, Robert Andrew 286.1320924
The first Southern Baptists. Nashville, Broadman [c.1966] 80p. 21cm. (Broadman hist. monograph) Bibl. [BX6495.S4B3] 66-10663 1.25 pap.,
1. Screven, William, 1629?-1713. 2. Charleston, S. C. First Baptist Church. I. Title.

BAKER, Robert 286.1320924 (B) Andrew.
The first Southern Baptists [by] Robert A. Baker. Nashville, Broadman Press [c1966] 80 p. 21 cm. (A Broadman historical monograph) Bibliographical references included in "Notes" (p. 69-80) [BX6495.S4B3] 66-10663
1. Screven, William, 1629?-1713. 2. Charleston, S.C. First Baptist Church. I. Title.

Scripps, John, 1785-1865.

RANSFORD, Charles Orrin. 922.773
John Scripps. Methodist preacher, newspaperman. Shelbina, Mo., 1960. 97p. illus. 23cm. Includes bibliography. [BX8495.S38R3] 60-27432
1. Scripps, John, 1785-1865. I. Title.

Scruples.

ABATA, Russell M. 248'.4
Helps for the scrupulous / Russell M. Abata. Liguori, Mo. : Liguori Publications, 1976. 127 p. ; 18 cm. [BX1759.5.S4A2] 76-21430 ISBN 0-89243-061-3 pbk. : 1.75
1. Scruples. I. Title.

O'FLAHERTY, V. M. 241.1
How to cure scruples [by] V. M. O'Flaherty. Milwaukee, Bruce [1966] x, 108p. 17cm. Bibl. [BX1759.5.S4033] 66-25043 2.75
1. Scruples. I. Title.

Scudder, Ida Sophia, 1870-

WILSON, Dorothy Clarke. 926.1
Dr. Ida; the story of Dr. Ida Scudder of Vellore. [1st ed.] New York, McGraw-Hill [1959] 358 p. illus. 21 cm. [BV3269.S356W5] 59-14469
1. Scudder, Ida Sophia, 1870- 2. Missions, Medical—India. I. Title.

Sculpture.

VAN ZELLER, Hubert, 1905- 731.882
Approach to Christian sculpture. New York, Sheed & Ward [1959] 191 p. illus. 21 cm. Secular name: Claude Van Zeller. [NB1910.V3] 59-12088
1. Sculpture. 2. Christian art and symbolism. I. Title. II. Series.

Sculpture—Bourges.

BAYARD, Tania. 726'.591
Bourges Cathedral : the west portals / Tania Bayard. New York : Garland, 1976. vii, 437 p. : ill. ; 21 cm. (Outstanding dissertations in the fine arts) Originally presented as the author's thesis, Columbia, 1968. Bibliography: p. 431-437. [NB551.B7B38 1976] 75-23780 ISBN 0-8240-1977-6 lib.bdg. : 30.00
1. Bourges. Saint-Etienne (Cathedral) 2. Sculpture—Bourges. 3. Sculpture, Gothic—Bourges. 4. Facades—Bourges. 5. Doorways—Bourges. I. Title. II. Series.

Sculpture, Buddhist—Exhibitions.

BEGLEY, Wayne E. 732'.4
Indian Buddhist sculpture in American collections. [Catalog text by Wayne E. Begley. Louisville, Ky., J.B. Speed Art Museum, 1968] [60] p. illus., maps. 26 cm. Cover title. Catalog of an exhibition held at J.B. Speed Art Museum Feb. 27 through Mar. 21, 1968. Errata slip inserted. Bibliography: p. [54] [NB1002.B43] 72-194295
1. Sculpture, Buddhist—Exhibitions. 2. Sculpture, Buddhist—India. 3. Sculpture, Indic—United States. I. Speed Art Museum, Louisville, Ky. II. Title.

Sculpture, Buddhist—Nara, Japan (City)

KOBAYASHI, Takeshi, 1903- 732'.7 1969.
Nara Buddhist art, Todai-ji / by Takeshi Kobayashi ; translated and adapted by Richard L. Gage. 1st English ed. New York : Weatherhill, 1975. 157 p. : ill. (some col.) ; 24 cm. (Heibonsha survey of Japanese art ; v. 5) Translation of Todai-ji no Daibutsu. [NB1057.N36K6213] 74-22034 ISBN 0-8348-1021-2 : 12.50
1. Todaiji, Nara, Japan. 2. Sculpture, Buddhist—Nara, Japan (City) 3. Sculpture—Nara, Japan (City) I. Title. II. Series.

Sculpture, Buddhist—Wu-t'ai hsien, China.

RHIE, Marylin M. 732'.4
The Fo-kuang ssu : literary evidences and Buddhist images / Marylin M. Rhie. New York : Garland Pub., 1977. xi, 274 p. : ill. ; 21 cm. (Outstanding dissertations in the fine arts) Reprint of the author's thesis, University of Chicago, 1970. "Translation of Tun-huang MS (Stein) 397": p. 47-64. Bibliography: p. 183-194. [BQ6345.W842F67 1977] 76-23690 ISBN 0-8240-2721-3 lib.bdg. : 32.50
1. Fo kuang ssu, Wu-t'ai hsien, China—History. 2. Tun-huang manuscripts. Ms. 397. 3. Sculpture, Buddhist—Wu-t'ai hsien, China. 4. Sculpture—Wu-t'ai hsien, China. I. Tun-huang manuscripts. Ms. 397. English. 1977. II. Title. III. Series.

Sculpture, Hindu.

HARLE, James C. 732'.4
Gupta sculpture : Indian sculpture of the fourth to the sixth centuries A.D. / J. C. Harle. Oxford [Eng.] : Clarendon Press, 1974. xii, 57 p., [40] leaves of plates : ill. ; 29 cm. Bibliography: p. [32]. [NB1002.H33] 75-306296 ISBN 0-19-817322-9 : 19.25
1. Gupta dynasty. 2. Sculpture, Hindu. I. Title.
Distributed by Oxford University Press New York.

Sculpture—History.

DEBIDOUR, Victor 731.8'8'209 Henry.
Christian sculpture. [1st ed.] Translated from the French by Robert J. Cunningham. Additional material by Eleanor A. Anderson. New York, Hawthorn Books [1968] 188, [2] p. illus. 21 cm. (The Twentieth century encyclopedia of Catholicism, v. 122. Section 12: Catholicism and the arts) Translation of Breve histoire de la sculpture chretienne. Bibliography: p. [191]. Bibliographical footnotes. [N7830.D3313] 67-14867
1. Sculpture—History. 2. Christian art and symbolism. I. Title. II. Series: The Twentieth century encyclopedia of Catholicism, v. 122

Sculpture, India.

BACHHOFER, Ludwig, 1894- 732'.4
Early Indian sculpture. New York, Hacker Art Books, 1972. 2 v. in 1. 161 plates. 32 cm. Reprint of the 1929 ed. Bibliography: p. 125-128. [NB1002.B3 1972] 79-143338 ISBN 0-87817-058-8 50.00
1. Sculpture, Indic. 2. Sculpture, Buddhist—India. I. Title.

LANNOY, Richard. 732'.4
The eye of love : in the temple sculpture of India / Richard Lannoy ; with drawings by Harry Baines. New York : Grove Press : distributed by Random House, 1977, c1976 160 p. : ill. ; 24 cm. Bibliography: p. [159]-160. [NB1002.L34] 76-54403 ISBN 0-8021-0137-2 : 12.50
1. Sculpture, Indic. 2. Erotica. 3. Temples—India. I. Title.

LIPPE, Aschwin. 732'.4
The Freer Indian sculptures. Washington, Smithsonian Institution, 1970. xv, 54 p. map, 55 plates (part col.) 31 cm. (Freer Gallery of Art. Oriental studies no. 8) Bibliography: p. 47-49. [NB1002.L56] 71-609901
1. Sculpture, Indic. 2. Sculpture, Hindu. 3. Sculpture, Buddhist—India. I. Freer Gallery of Art, Washington, D.C. II. Title. III. Series: Freer Gallery of Art, Washington, D.C. Oriental studies, no. 8

SAHAI, Bhagwant, 1929- 732'.4
Iconography of minor Hindu and Buddhist deities / Bhagwant Sahai. New Delhi : Abhinav Publications, 1975. xiii, 295 p., [14] leaves of plates : ill. ; 25 cm. Running title: Iconography of some important minor Hindu and Buddhist deities. "The present work ... embodies in the main the thesis approved for the degree of Ph.D. by the University of Patna in 1965." Includes index. Bibliography: p. [263]-274. [NB1002.S24] 75-904218 ISBN 0-88386-610-2 : 24.00
1. Sculpture, Indic. 2. Gods, Hindu, in art. 3. Gods, Buddhist, in art. I. Title. II. Title: Iconography of some important minor Hindu and Buddhist deities.
Distributed by South Asia Books.

Sculpture, India Exhibitions.

LERNER, Martin. 732'.4
Images of divinity; sculpture from India, Nepal, Thailand, and Cambodia. Selections from the Norton Simon, Inc. Museum of Art and the Norton Simon Foundation. Introd. and catalogue by Martin Lerner. Photographs by Lee Boltin. Foreword by Thomas Hoving. Statement by Norton Simon. [New York] Metropolitan Museum of Art [1974] p. cm. Catalog of an exhibition held at the Metropolitan Museum of Art. [NB1002.L47] 74-989 ISBN 0-87099-088-8
1. Sculpture, Indic—Exhibitions. 2. Sculpture, Nepali—Exhibitions. 3. Sculpture, Thai—Exhibitions. 4. Sculpture, Khmer—Exhibitions. 5. Gods in art. I. Norton Simon, Inc. Museum of Art. II. Norton Simon Foundation. III. New York (City). Metropolitan Museum of Art. IV. Title.

Sculpture, Jaina.

BHATTACHARYA, Brindavan 732'.4 Chandra, 1893-
The Jaina iconography / B. C. Bhattacharya ; foreword by B. N. Sharma. 2d rev. ed. Delhi : Motilal Banarsidass, 1974. xi, 171 p., [27] leaves of plates : ill. ; 23 cm. Includes quotations in Sanskrit and index. Bibliography: p. [145]-164. [NB1002.B47 1974] 75-900652 21.00
1. Sculpture, Jaina. 2. Gods in art. I. Title.
Distributed by Verry

Sculpture, Medieval.

SHERIDAN, Ronald. 731'.88'9
Gargoyles and grotesques : paganism in the medieval church / Ronald Sheridan and Anne Ross. Boston : New York Graphic Society, 1975. 127 p. : ill. ; 29 cm. Includes index. Bibliography: p. 125. [NB170.S47 1975b] 74-21494 ISBN 0-8212-0644-3 : 14.95
1. Sculpture, Medieval. 2. Paganism in art. 3. Church decoration and ornament. I. Ross, Anne, Ph.D., joint author. II. Title.

Sculpture, Romanesque—Lincoln, Eng.

ZARNECKI, George. 726'.59
Romanesque sculpture at Lincoln Cathedral. Lincoln, Friends of Lincoln Cathedral, 1968. 24 p. 36 plates, illus. 22 cm. (Lincoln Minster pamphlets. Second series no. 2) Bibliographical references included in "Notes" (p. 22-24) [NB471.L5Z3] 79-458153 7/6
1. Lincoln Cathedral. 2. Sculpture, Romanesque—Lincoln, Eng. I. Friends of Lincoln Cathedral. II. Title. III. Series.

Sea in the Bible.

AMSON, Peter 225.855146 Frederick, 1889-
Christ and the sailor; a study of the maritime incidents in the New Testament. Foreword by Thomas D. Roberts. Fresno, Calif., Acad. Lib. [1963] 198p. 20cm. Bibl. 1.50 pap.,
1. Sea in the Bible. 2. Fishing in the Bible. 3. Galilee, Sea of. 4. Apostles. 5. Bible—Concordances, English. I. Title.

ANSON, Peter 225.855146 Frederick, 1889-
Christ and the sailor; a study of the maritime incidents in the New Testament. With a foreword by Thomas D. Roberts. Fresno, Calif., Academy Library Guild [1956?] 198p. 20cm. [BS2545] 56-13886
1. Sea in the Bible. 2. Fishing in the Bible. 3. Galilee, Sea of. 4. Apostles. 5. Bible—Concordances. English. I. Title.

Seaboard, N.C. Methodist Church.

OUR church-then and now; a history of Seaboard Methodist Church, 1880-1958 ... Richmond, Va., Whittet and Shepperson [1959?] x, 155p. illus. 24cm.
1. Seaboard, N.C. Methodist Church. I. Seaboard, N.C. Methodist Church. Committee on Church History.

Seabury, Samuel, 1801-1872.

JOHNSON, Samuel Roosevelt, 1802-1873. 922.373
A discourse delivered ... at the Church of the Annunciation, city of New York, on the 25th day of June, A. D., 1873, in memory of Samuel Seabury, D. D., presbyter of the diocese of New York, professor of Biblical learning and interpretation of Scripture in the General theological seminary. By the Rev. Samuel Roosevelt Johnson ... [New York? 1873?] 2 p. l., iii, [3]-71 p., 1 l. illus. 23 cm. [BX5995.S3J6] 35-29962
1. Seabury, Samuel, 1801-1872. I. Title.

Seabury, Samuel, bp., 1729-1796.

BEARDSLEY, Eben Edwards, 1808-1891. 922.373
Life and correspondence of the Right Reverend Samuel Seabury, D.D., first bishop of Connecticut, and of the Episcopal church in the United States of America. By E. Edwards Beardsley ... Boston, Houghton, Mifflin and company, 1881. xvii, 497 p. front. (port.) 22 1/2 cm. [BX5995.83B4] 35-23992
1. Seabury, Samuel, bp., 1729-1796. I. Title.

SEABURY, Samuel, bp., 1729-1796.
Discourses on several important subjects, by the late Right Rev. Samuel Seabury ... Published from manuscripts prepared by the author for the press. New-York, Printed and sold by T. & J. Swords, no. 99 Pearl-street, 1798. vii, 279 p. 21 cm. [BX5987.S4D49] A 32
I. Title.
Contents omitted.

SEABURY, Samuel, bp., 1729-1796.
Discourses on several important subjects, by the late Right Rev. Samuel Seabury ... Published from manuscripts prepared by the author for the press. New-York, Printed and sold by T. & J. Swords, no. 99 Pearl-street, 1798. vii, 279 p. 21 cm. [BX5987.S4D49] A 32
I. Title.
Contents omitted.

SEABURY, Samuel, bp., 1729-1796. 252.
Discourses on several subjects. By Samuel Seabury ... New York, Printed by T. and J. Swords, for J. Rivington, bookseller, no. 1, Queen-street. 1793. 2 v. 21 cm. [BX5937.S4D5] 25-1463
I. Title.

SEABURY, Samuel, bp., 1729-1796. 252.
Discourses on several subjects. By Samuel Seabury ... New York, Printed by T. and J. Swords, for J. Rivington, bookseller, no. 1, Queen-street. 1793. 2 v. 21 cm. [BX5937.S4D5] 25-1463
I. Title.

SEABURY, William Jones, 1837-
Memoir of Bishop Seabury, by William Jones Seabury ... New York, E. S. Gorham; [etc., etc.] 1908. vii, 453 p. incl. front. (port.) 21 cm. 9-6964
1. Seabury, Samuel, bp., 1729-1796. I. Title.

SHEA, George, 1826-1895. 922.
Memoir concerning the Seabury commemoration held at St. Paul's cathedral, London, the fourteenth day of November, A.D. 1884. Printed chiefly from a manuscript monograph introductory to a unique volume in the possession of George Shea, the pages of which are inset with all the original correspondence and other proof of that historical event. Boston and New York, Houghton, Mifflin and company, 1893. 98 p. front. (port.) fold. tab. 22 1/2 cm. "Documents relating to the Episcopal succession and the consecration of Samuel Seabury": p. [83]-98. [BX5995.S3S5] 22-10313
1. Seabury, Samuel, bp., 1729-1796. I. Title.

STEINER, Bruce E. 283'.092'4 B
Samuel Seabury, 1729-1796; a study in the High Church tradition [by bruce E. Steiner] [Athens] Ohio University Press [1972, c1971] xiii, 508 p. illus. 22 cm. Bibliography: p. 464-482. [BX5995.S3S73] 78-181686 ISBN 0-8214-0098-3 13.50
1. Seabury, Samuel, Bp., 1729-1796.

THOMS, Herbert, 1885- 922.373
Samuel Seabury; priest and physician, Bishop of Connecticut. Hamden, Conn., Shoe String, 1963[c.1962] 166p. illus. 22cm. 63-12263 4.95
1. Seabury, Samuel, Bp., 1729-1796. I. Title.

Seabury, Warren Bartlett, 1877-1907.

[SEABURY, Joseph Bartlett] 1846-1923. 922.
The vision of a short life; a memorial of Warren Bartlett Seabury, one of the founders of the Yale mission college in China ... by his father. Cambridge, Printed at the Riverside press, 1909. xii p., 1 l., 192 p. front., plates, ports. 21 cm. [BV3427.S4S4] 25-23364
1. Seabury, Warren Bartlett, 1877-1907. 2. Missions—China. I. Title.

Seals (Numismatics)

KING, Edwin James, Sir, 1877-1952. 255'.79
The seals of the Order to St. John of Jerusalem / by E. J. King. New York : AMS Press, 1980. p. cm. Reprint of the 1932 ed. published by Methuen, London. Includes index. [CD5547.K5 1980] 78-63355 ISBN 0-404-16248-7 : 24.50
1. Knights of Malta. 2. Seals (Numismatics) I. Title.

Sealy, Gayle Burch.

SEALY, Shirley. 289.3'3 B
Forever after / Shirley Sealy. Salt Lake City : Deseret Book Co., 1979. 137 p., [1] leaf of plates : port. ; 24 cm. [BX8695.S32S42] 79-17933 ISBN 0-87747-779-5 : 5.95
1. Sealy, Gayle Burch. 2. Sealy, Devro. 3. Sealy, Shirley. 4. Mormons and Mormonism in Utah—Biography. 5. Toxemia of pregnancy—Biography. I. Title.

Seamen.

MOTHERS' correspondence club, Indianapolis.
Mothers' correspondence club. [Program] [Indianapolis, 19 v. 15 1/2 cm. The object of the club is to mother orphan navy and army boys, and provide Christian home influence. [BV2665.M6] CA 19
1. Seamen. 2. Soldiers. I. Title.

Seamen—Hymns.

AMERICAN seamen's friend society.
Seaman's devotional assistant, and mariners' hymns; prepared under direction of the American seamen's friend society ... New York, The Society, 1838. v. [1], 7-512 p. 12 cm. The compilation is largely the work of Joshua Leavitt, general agent of the society. cf. Pref. [BV463.A5 1888] 41-31274
1. Seamen—Hymns. 2. Seamen—Religious life. I. Leavitt, Joshua, 1794-1873, comp. II. Title.

AMERICAN seamen's friend society.
Seamen's hymns and devotional assistant; prepared under the direction of the American seamen's friend society. New York, The Society, 1846. 443 p. 12 cm. [BV463.A5 1846] 41-31275
1. Seamen—Hymns. 2. Seamen—Religious life. I. Title.

STOWE, Phineas, comp. 783.
Ocean melodies and seamen's companion; a collection of hymns and music for the use of bethels, chaplains of the Navy, and private devotion of mariners. 12th ed. Boston, 1866. 208 p. 15 cm. [M2117.S912O3 1866] 49-56439
1. Seamen—Hymns. I. Title.

Seamen—Missions and charities.

AMERICAN seamen's friend society.
The acts of the apostles of the sea; an eighty years' record of the work of the American seamen's friend society ... [New York? 01909] 64 p. illus. 23 cm. Introductory note signed: George McPherson Hunter, secretary. [HV3064.A68] 22-5982
1. Seamen—Missions and charities. I. Hunter, George McPherson, comp. II. Title.

Seamen—Prayer-books and devotions—English.

AMERICAN seamen's friend society. 242
Seamen's manual of worship ... 2d ed. New York, The American seamen's friend society, 1929. 51 p. 17 cm. Foreword signed: George Sidney Webster, secretary. Hymns with music: p. 25 50. [BV199.S5A62 1929] 29-8399
I. Webster, George Sidney, 1853- II. Title.

PARKER, Joseph F 264.1
Prayers at sea. Richmond, Press of Whittet and Shepperson, 1956[i. e. 1957] 280p. 17cm. [BV273.P3 1957] 57-43690
1. Seamen—Prayer-books and devotions—English. I. Title.

PARKER, Joseph F 264.1
Prayers at sea. Richmond, Press of Whittet and Shepperson, 1956. 192p. 17cm. [BV273.P3] 56-11170
1. Seamen— Prayer-books and devotions—English. I. Title.

Seamen—Religious life.

BULLEN, Frank Thomas, 1857-1915.
With Christ at sea; a personal record of religious experiences on board ship for fifteen years. By Frank T. Bullen ... New York, Frederick A. Stokes company [1900] 3 p. l. [iii]-iv p., 1 l. 325 p. 19 cm. [BV4591.B8] 1-29165
1. Seamen—Religious life. I. Title.

DAVIS, John K. comp.
The cabin boy's locker. Compiled chiefly from the volumes of the Sailor's magazine. By J. K. Davis ... New York, Printed by R. Craighead, 1853. x, [11]-190 p. 15 1/2 cm. Prose and verse. [BV4590.D3] 43-34012
1. Seamen—Religious life. I. The Sailors' magazine and seamen's friend. II. Title.

LORRAIN, Alfred M. 252
The square-rigged cruiser; or, Lorrain's sea-sermons ... by Alfred M. Lorrain ... Cincinnati, Printed at the Methodist book concern, for the author, 1851. 252 p. 17 cm. [BV4316.S3L6] 44-30270
1. Seamen—Religious life. 2. Sermons, American. I. Title.

Seances.

*KENNEDY, Edith Ann 133.91
God and I through seance. New York, Vantage [1966] 119p. 21cm. 2.75 bds.,
1. Seances. 2. Spiritualism. I. Title.

Searle, Verna.

SEARLE, Verna. 280'.4 B
Reach for tomorrow / by Verna Searle. Plainfield, N.J. : Haven Books, 1981, c1980. xiv, 128 p. ; 21 cm. Bibliography: p. 127-128. [BR1725.S425A36] 19 80-82694 ISBN 0-88270-449-4 pbk. : 4.95
1. Searle, Verna. 2. Christian biography—United States. 3. Divorcees—United States—Biography. I. Title.

Sears, Mrs. Angeline (Brooks) 1817-1848.

HAMLINE, Melinda, Mrs. 922.773
Memoirs of Mrs. Angeline B. Sears, with extracts from her correspondence. By Mrs. Melinda Hamline ... Cincinnati, Swormstedt and Power, for the Methodist Episcopal church, 1850. 294 p. front. (port.) 16 cm. [BX8495.S4H3] 36-87399
1. Sears, Mrs. Angeline (Brooks) 1817-1848. I. Title.

Season.

HITCHCOCK, Edward, 1793-1864. 215
Religious lectures on peculiar phenomena in the four seasons ... delivered to the students in Amherst college, in 1845, 1847, 1848 and 1849. By Edward Hitchcock ... 2d ed. Amherst, J. S. & C. Adams, 1851. 144 p. col. front. 19 cm. [BL262.H5] 31-1159
1. Season. 2. Natural theology. I. Title.
Contents omitted.

Seasons.

GANNETT, William Channing, 1840-1923. 252.
A year of miracle. A poem in four sermons. By W. C. Gannett. Boston, G. H. Ellis, 1882. 106 p. 15 cm. Contents.Treasures of the snow.--Resurrection.--Flowers.--The harvest-secret. [BX9843.G43Y4] 24-25235
1. Seasons. I. Title.

HITCHCOCK, Edward, 1793-1864. 215
Religious lectures on peculiar phenomena in the four seasons ... delivered to the students in Amherst college, in 1845, 1847, 1848 and 1849. By Edward Hitchcock ... Amherst, J. S. & C. Adams, 1850. vi p., 1 l., [9]-143 p. col. front., plates (1 col.) 18 1/2 cm. [BL262.H5 1850] 39-825
1. Seasons. 2. Natural theology. I. Title.
Contents omitted.

HITCHCOCK, Edward, 1793-1864. 215
Religious lectures on peculiar phenomena in the four seasons ... delivered to the students in Amherst college, in 1845, 1847, 1848, and 1849. By Edward Hitchcock ... 3d ed. Boston, Phillips, Sampson, and company, 1853. 144 p. front., plates. 19 1/2 cm. [BL262.H5 1853] 41-30621
1. Seasons. 2. Natural theology. I. Title.
Contents omitted.

Seaton, Elizabeth Ann, 1774-1821.

DAUGHTERS of St. Paul. 271.91024 B
Mother Seton : wife, mother, educator, foundress, saint : profile by the Daughters of St. Paul, based on "Elizabeth Seton" by Msgr. Joseph Bardi. Spiritual gems of Mother Seton. Boston : St. Paul Editions, 1975. 140 p. : ill. ; 22 cm. [BX4705.S57D3 1975] 75-6861 3.95 pbk. : 2.95
1. Seaton, Elizabeth Ann, 1774-1821. I. Bardi, Giuseppe, Mons. Elisabetta Anna Seton. II. Seton, Elizabeth Ann, 1774-1821. Spiritual gems. 1975. III. Title.

Seattle. University Unitarian Church.

HARTWICH, Ethelyn Miller.
The first fifty years; a history of University Unitarian Church. [Seattle, University Printing Co., 1962?] 1 v. (unpaged) 65-37661
1. Seattle. University Unitarian Church. I. Title.

Sebastian, Saint.

ROBERTO, Brother, 1927- 922.244
The soldier died twice; a story of St. Sebastian. Illus. by Elaine Shears. Notre Dame, Ind., Dujarie Press [1955] 94p. illus. 24cm. [BR1720.S3R6] 55-33456
1. Sebastian, Saint. I. Title.

Secker, Thomas, apb. of Canterbury, 1693-1768.

PORTEUS, Beilby, bp. of London, 1731-1808. 922.
A review of the life and character of Archbishop Secker, By Beilby Porteus ... New-York: Re-printed from the London edition, by Hugh Gaine, at the Bible and

crown in Hanover-square, 1773. 2 p. l., iii, [1], ixviii p. front. (port.) 20 cm. [BX5199.S4P7] 21-13288
1. Secker, Thomas, apb. of Canterbury, 1693-1768. I. Title.

Second advent.

ABRAM, Victor P. 232.6
The restoration of all things. Amherst, N. H., Chestnut Hill Rd. Kingdom Pr., [c.1962] 149p. 21cm. 62-18059 2.00
1. Sandford, Frank W., 1862-1948. 2. Second Advent. I. Title.

ABRAM, Victor P 232.6
The restoration of all things. Amherst, N. H., Kingdom Press [1962] 149p. 21cm. 'The first eleven chapters ... appeared as successive monthly instalments in the Standard during 1951 and 1952.' [BV3785.S18A65] 62-18059
1. Stanford, Frank W., 1862-1948. 2. Second Advent. I. Title.

ALLEN, Gordon E 1923- 232.6
The second coming of Jesus, with an exposition of the book of Revelation. Goldsboro, N. C., Carolina Print. Co. [1960] 147p. 22cm. [BT886.A4] 60-16977
1. Second Advent. 2. Bible. N. T. Revelation—Commentaries. I. Title.

ANDERSON, Robert, Sir, 1841-1918. 236'.3
Forgotten truths / by Sir Robert Anderson. [2d ed.] Grand Rapids, Mich. : Kregel Publications, c1980. xiv, 150 p. ; 20 cm. Reprint of the 1914 ed. published by J. Nisbet, London. "Sir Robert Anderson library." Includes bibliographical references and index. [BT885.A53 1980] 80-17526 ISBN 0-8254-2130-6 : 3.95 (pbk.)
1. Jews—Election, Doctrine of. 2. Second Advent. I. Title.

ANDERSON, Roy Allan. 236
Abandon earth : last call / Roy Allan Anderson. Mountain View, Calif. ; Oshawa, Ont. : Pacific Press, c1982. 78 p. ; 18 cm. [BT886.A52] 19 82-2091 ISBN 0-8163-0476-9 pbk. : 2.95
1. Second Advent. 2. Eschatology. I. Title.

BAILEY, Alice Anne (LaTrobe-Bateman) 1880-1949.
The reappearance of the Christ. New York, Lucis Pub. Co. [1960] 208 p. 24 cm. 68-32382
1. Second advent. 2. Jesus Christ—Theosophical interpretations. I. Title.

BAKER, Alonzo L.
The hope of the world, by Alonzo L. Baker ... Mountain View, Calif., Omaha, Neb. [etc.] Pacific press publishing association [c1925] 3p.1., 9-390 p. incl. front., illus. 23 cm. Illustrated lining-papers. [BT835.B15] 25-10706
1. Second advent. I. Title.

BARKER, Harold P 232.6
Coming twice. New York, Loizeaux Bros. [19--] 159p. 19cm. (Treasury library, no.25) [BT885.B24] 56-26551
1. Second Advent. I. Title.

BERKHOF, Louis, 1873- 232.6
The second coming of Christ. Grand Rapids, W. B. Eerdmans Pub. Co., 1953. 102p. 23cm. [BT885.B42] 53-9734
1. Second Advent. I. Title.

BERKOUWER, Gerrit Cornelis, 1903- 232'.6
The return of Christ, by G. C. Berkouwer. Grand Rapids, Eerdmans [1972] 477 p. 23 cm. (His Studies in dogmatics) Translation of De wederkomst van Christus. Includes bibliographical references. [BT886.B4513] 72-178664 ISBN 0-8028-3393-4 9.95
1. Second Advent. 2. Eschatology. I. Title.

BIBLE. English. Selections. 1933. 232.6
Scriptural prophecies concerning the coming of Christ Jesus and the fulfillment, arranged from the Bible by Maude A. Rucker ... Keytesville, Mo., The Courier publishing company [c1933] 83 (i. e. 92) p. 22 cm. Pages with half-title and blank pages not included in the pagination. [BT885.R8] 34-662
1. Second advent. I. Rucker, Maude (Applegate) Mrs. II. Title.

BIEDERWOLF, William Edward, 1867- 232.
The millennium Bible, Being a help to the study of the Holy Scriptures in their testimony to the second coming of Our Lord and Saviour Jesus Christ, by William Edward Biederwolf ... Chicago, Ill., The W. P. Blessing company [c1924] 728 p. 23 cm. [BT885.B49] 24-20784
1. Second advent. 2. Bible—Criticism, interpretation, etc. I. Title.

BIEDERWOLF, William Edward, 1867-1939. 220.8'232'6
The millennium Bible, being a help to the study of the Holy Scriptures in their testimony to the second coming of our Lord and Saviour Jesus Christ. Grand Rapids, Baker Book House [1966] 728 p. 24 cm. Reprint of the 1924 ed. [BT885.B49 1966] 64-8345
1. Bible—Criticism, interpretation, etc. 2. Second Advent. I. Title.

BLACKINTON, Dora J. Mrs. 220
God speaks from the sky in open vision; a message to the churches based upon the parable of the ten virgins referring to the second coming of Christ, by Dora J. Blackinton. [Los Angeles, West coast pub. co.] 1927. 127 p. 22 cm. On cover: God speaks from the sky in three heaven-set scenes: an angel face appears in a cloud. [BR125.B53] 28-17683
I. Title.

BLACKSTONE, William E., 1841- 232.
Jesus is coming, By W. E. B. ... (Revised ed.) Chicago, New York [etc.] Fleming H. Revel company [c1908] 252 p. 29 1/2 cm. [BT885.B5 1908] 9-133
1. Second advent. I. Title.

BLACKSTONE, William E., 1841- 232.
Jesus is coming, by W. E. B. ... (Presentation edition) ... Chicago, New York, Fleming H. Revell company; [etc., etc., 1917] 3 p. l., 5-262 p. illus. 19 1/2 cm. [BT885.B5 1917] 18-15936
1. Second advent. I. Title.

BLACKSTONE, William E., 1841- 232.6
Jesus is coming, by W. E. B. ... New York, Chicago [etc.] Fleming H. Revell company [c1932] 252 p. diagrs. 19 1/2 cm. [BT885.B5 1932] 32-32898
1. Second advent. I. Title.

BLODGETT, Ralph H., 1940- 232'.6
Rapture! : Is it for real? / Ralph Blodgett. Mountain View, Calif. : Pacific Press Pub. Association, c1975. 64 p. : graphs ; 19 cm. Includes index. [BT886.B53] 75-27618
1. Second Advent. I. Title.

BOLLMAN, Calvin Porter, 1853- 232.
Heralds of the King, Our Lord's great prophecy of His second advent; a verse-by-verse study of the twenty-fourth chapter of Matthew, by Calvin P. Bollman ... Washington, D.C., New York, N.Y. [etc.] Review and Herald publishing association [c1920] 128 p. incl. front., illus. 19 1/2 cm. Text on 3d and 4th pages of cover. [BT885.B6] 20-18181
I. Title.

[BOUDINOT, Elias] 1740-1821. 232.
The second advent, or coming of the Messiah in glory, shown to be a Scripture doctrine, and taught by divine revelation, from the beginning of the world. By an American layman... Trenton, (N.J.) Published by D. Fenton & S. Hutchinson... 1815. xix, 573 p. 23 cm. [BT885.B75] 6-31234
1. Second advent I. Title.

*BOYER, A. Leslie 232
Christ is coming. New York, Vantage [c.1965] 48p. 21cm. 2.50 bds.,
I. Title.

BRIDWELL, Charles William, 1872- 236
The second coming of Christ; a discussion of this truth and related subjects which vitally concern our time. By Rev. Chas. W. Bridwell ... Denver, Col., The Pentecostal union [1915] 2 p. l., [3]-294 p. front. (port.) 20 cm. [BT885.B8] 15-19419
1. Second advent. 2. Millennium. I. Title.

BROOKES, James Hall, 1830-1897. 230
Present truth: being the testimony of the Holy Ghost on the second coming of the Lord, the divinity of Christ, and the personality of the Holy Ghost, with an introduction on the study of the Word. [By] James H. Brookes ... Prefatory remarks by Geo. C. Needham [and others] ... evangelists. Springfield, Ill., E.A. Wilson, 1877. 2 p. l., 236 p. 16 cm. [BT85.B7] 40-21301
1. Jesus Christ—Person and offices. 2. Second advent. 3. Holy Ghost. I. Title.

BROUGHTON, Leonard Gaston, 1864- 232.
The second coming of Christ, by Len. G. Broughton ... New York, Chicago [etc.] Fleming H. Revell company [c1907] 156 p. 20 cm. [BT885.B88 1907] 7-12677
1. Second advent. I. Title.

BROWN, Arthur Isaac, 1897- 232.6
I will come again. Findlay, Ohio, Fundamental Truth Publishers [1947] 115 p. 21 cm. [BT885.B887] 48-15934
1. Second Advent. I. Title.

BROWN, Charles Ewing, 1883- 232.
The hope of His coming, by Chas. E. Brown... Anderson, Ind., Gospel trumpet company [c1927] vii, 9-276 p. 19 cm. [BT885.B89] 27-14551
1. Second advent. 2. Millennium. I. Title.

BROWNVILLE, Charles Gordon, 1898- 232.6
The romance of the future, by C. Gordon Brownville ... New York [etc.] Fleming H. Revell company [c1938] 156 p. 19 1/2 cm. "The second coming of Christ in its various relationships."--Foreword. [BT885.B895] 38-10802
1. Second advent. 2. Millennium. I. Title.

CARDEY, Elmer L. 232.6
The countdown of history. Grand Rapids, Mich., Baker Bk. [c.]1962. 198p. 23cm. 62-20455 2.95
1. Second Advent. I. Title.

CARPENTER, Ellsworth, 1886- 232.6
Coming to earth! (Very very soon) "The mighty God, the everlasting Father, the Prince of peace." Based on Bible prophecies ... By ellsworth Carpenter ... Prohibition Park, S. I., N. Y., Newer-knowledge publishers [c1940] 212 p. incl. illus., plates. diagrs., charts. 21 cm. [BX6154.C35] 40-12497
1. Second advent. 2. End of the world. 3. Seventh-day Adventists—Doctrinal and controversial works. I. Title.

CARROLL, Benajah Harvey, 1843-1914. 232.6
The day of the Lord, by B. H. Carroll ... compiled by J. W. Crowder ... edited by J. B. Cranfill ... Nashville, Tenn., Broadman press [c 1936] 221 p. 20 cm. [BT885.C34] 36-37499
1. Second advent. 2. Judgement-day. 3. Baptists—Sermons. 4. Sermons, American. I. Crowder, Joseph Wade, 1873- comp. II. Cranfill, James Britton, 1858- ed. III. Title.

CLARK, Raymond. 296
"Things to come", the second coming of Christ, the coming kingdom of God and events connected therewith, by Raymond Clark... [Plainfield, N.J., c1927] 74, [4] p. 19 1/2 cm. [BT875.C6] 27-18399
1. Second advent. 2. Millennium. I. Title.

†CRIBB, C. C. 236'.3
The coming kingdom / C. C. Cribb. Raleigh : Manhattan, ltd., c1977. 154 p. ; 18 cm. Selections from the author's From now till eternity. [BT886.C68] 77-70213 1.75
1. Bible—Prophecies. 2. Second Advent. 3. Millennium. I. Title.
Publisher's address: P. O. Box 18601, Raleigh, NC 27609

CRISWELL, Wallie A. 232'.6
Welcome back, Jesus! / W. A. Criswell. Nashville : Broadman Press, c1976. 189 p. ; 21 cm. [BT886.C7] 76-27482 ISBN 0-8054-1939-X : 5.95
1. Second Advent. I. Title.

DAVID, Ira E. 232.
Christ our coming King, by Ira E. David, PH. D., with an introdiction by Rev. David J. Fant, jr. Harrisburg, Pa., New York, N. Y., Christian alliance publishing company [c1928] 116 p. 18 cm. (On cover: The Alliance colportage series) [BT885.D17] 28-13859
1. Second advent. I. Title.

DAVIES, Caleb.
The United States in relation to the Messiah's return. Cleveland, Ohio, Knox pub. co., 1898. 1 p. l., 61 p. 12 degree. 98-139
I. Title.

DE HAAN, Martin Ralph, 1891-1964. 236'.3
The second coming of Jesus / by M. R. De Haan. Grand Rapids : Zondervan Pub. House, [1978] c1944. p. cm. [BT885.D35 1978] 78-14020 ISBN 0-310-23460-3 : 4.95
1. Second Advent. I. Title.

DOUGLASS, Herbert E. 236'.3
The end : unique voice of Adventists about the return of Jesus / Herbert E. Douglass ; [cover photo, Morton Beebe]. Mountain View, Calif. : Pacific Press Pub. Association, c1979. 192 p. ; 22 cm. (Dimension ; 139) Includes bibliographical references and indexes. [BT886.D68] 79-88435 pbk. : 4.95
1. Seventh-Day Adventists—Doctrinal and controversial works—Seventh-Day Adventist authors. 2. Second Advent. 3. Millennialism. I. Title.

DOUGLASS, Herbert E. 232'.6
Parable of the hurricane / by Herbert E. Douglass. Mountain View, Calif. : Pacific Press Pub. Association, c1980. 32 p. ; 14 cm. [BT886.D69] 80-10712 ISBN 0-8163-0356-8 pbk. : .75
1. Second Advent. 2. Mississippi—Hurricane, 1969—Miscellanea. 3. Louisiana—Hurricane, 1969—Miscellanea. 4. Dominica—Hurricane, 1979—Miscellanea. I. Title.
Distributed by the Greater New York Bookstore, 12 W. 40th St., New York, NY

DOUTY, Norman Franklin, 1899- 232.6
Has Christ's return two stages? [1st ed.] New York, Pageant Press [c1956] 127p. 21cm. Includes bibliography. [BT885.D67] 56-12598
1. Second Advent. I. Title.

DUFFIELD, John Thomas, 1823-1901. 232.
A discourse delivered at the opening of the Synod of New Jersey in the First Presbyterian church of Elizabeth, N. J., October 16, 1866, by the moderator, the Rev. John T. Duffield, D. D. With notes and an appendix. Published by request. Philadelphia, J. S. Claxton, 1866. 64 p. 20 cm. Cover-title: That blessed hope. Prof. Duffield's discourse on the second advent. A defence of the doctrine of the Westminister confession. Second thousand. Philadelphia, J. S. Claxton, 1867. [BT885.D87] 21-17150
1. Second advent. I. Title. II. Title: That blessed hope.

DUNHAM, Truman Richard, 1899- 232.6
The great tribulation, by Rev. T. Richard Dunham ... with foreword by William L. Pettingill ... Hoytville, O., Fundamental truth store [c1933] 77 p. front. (port.) 19 cm. [BT885.D88] 33-6353
1. Second advent. I. Title. II. Title: Tribulation, The great.

*EARLE, Ralph. 232.6
What the Bible says about the second coming. Grand Rapids, Mich., Baker Book House [1973, c1970] 90 p, 18 cm. (Baker book house direction books) Previous editions have title: Behold, I come. Bibliography: p. 89-90 [BT886] ISBN 0-8010-3307-1 0.95 (pbk.)
1. Second Advent. I. Title.

EASTEP, Durward Belmont, 1900- 282.6
Bringing back the King ... A simple study of the second coming of Christ, by D. B. Eastep ... with introduction by H. A. Ironside ... Covington, Ky., Kentucky Bible depot [c1934] 64 p. diagr. 19 cm. Advertising matter: p. 62-64. "Some good books on prophecy": p. 60-61. [BT885.E2] 34-41263

1. Second advent. 2. Bible—Prophecies. I. Title.

ECKMAN, George Peck, 1860- 1920. 232.
When Christ comes again, by George P. Eckman. New York, Cincinnati, The Abingdon press [c1917] 287 p. 19 1/2 cm. [BT885.E3] 17-12376 1.25
1. Second advent. I. Title.

EDDLEMAN, H. Leo, comp. 232.6082
The second coming. Nashville, Broadman [1964, c.1963] 112p. 21cm. 64-10814 2.75 bds.,
1. Second Advent. I. Title.

EHLE, Charles Edwin 1878- 232.6
The Scripture's reply to arguments against "the second coming of Christ," by Charles E. Ehle ... Findlay, O., Fundamental truth publishers [c1934] 64 p. 18 cm. [BT885.E45] 35-403
1. Second advent. I. Title.

FITCH, Charles, 1804-1843. 236
Letter to Rev. J. Litch, on the second coming of Christ, with the sentiments of Cotton Mather on the same subject, approved by Thomas Prince ... By Charles Fitch ... Boston, J. V. Himes, 1841. iv, [5]-71, [1] p. 16 cm. [BT885.F5] 26-24368
1. Second advent. I. Litch, J. II. Title.

FRASER, Neil McCormick. 232'.6
The gladness of His return; a closer look at the second coming [by] Neil M. Fraser. [1st ed.] Neptune, N.J., Loizeaux Brothers [1967] 127 p. 20 cm. Final vol. in the author's trilogy; the 1st of which is The grandeur of Golgotha; and the 2d of which is The glory of His rising. [BT886.F7] 66-25721
1. Second Advent. I. Title.

FROST, Henry Weston, 1858- 232.6
The second coming of Christ; a review of the teaching of Scripture concerning the return of Christ ... by Henry W. Frost ... Grand Rapids, Mich., Wm. B. Eerdmans publishing company, 1934. 251 p. 20 cm. [BT885.F68] 34-14512
1. Second advent. I. Title.

GAEBELEIN, Arno Clemens, 1861- 232.6
The hope of the ages; the Messianic hope in revelation, in history and in realization, by Arno Clemens, Gaebelein ... New York, N. Y., Publication office "Our hope." London, Pickering & Inglis; [etc., etc., c1938] 3 p. l., [3]-187 p. 21 cm. [BT885.G23] 38-36248
1. Second advent. 2. Jesus Christ—Messiahship. I. Title.

GAEBELEIN, Arno Clemens, 1861- 236
The return of the Lord; what the New Testament teaches about the second coming of Christ. An examination of the leading passages in the New Testament dealing with His return. By Arno Clemens Gaebelein ... New York, N. Y., Publication office "Our hope" [c1925] 125 p. 19 cm. [BT885.G25] 25-22593
1. Second advent. 2. Bible. N. T.—Ciritcism, interpretation, etc. I. Title.

GORDON, Samuel Dickey, 1859- 232.
Quiet talks about Our Lord's return, by S. D. Gordon ... New York, Chicago [etc.] Fleming H. Revell company [c1912] 206 p. 19 cm. [BT885.G65] 14-2357
1. Second advent. I. Title.

GRAY, James Martin, 1851- 1935. 232.
Prophecy and the Lord's return; a collection of popular articles and addresses, by James M. Gray ... New York, Chicago [etc.] Fleming H. Revell company [1917] 119 p. 19 1/2 cm. Reprinted in part from various sources. [BT885.G7] 17-31761
1. Second advent. I. Title.

GRIFFITH, Roland Edward. 232.6
The gospel of the second coming [by] Roland Edward Griffith. Oakland, Calif., The Advocate press, c1946. 136 p. illus. 19 1/2 cm. [BT885.G53] 46-16145
1. Second advent. I. Title.

GROMACKI, Robert Glenn. 236
Are these the last days? Old Tappan, N.J., Revell Co. [1969, c1970] 190 p. 21 cm. [BS647.2.G76] 73-96250 4.50

1. Bible—Prophecies. 2. Second Advent. I. Title.

HALDEMAN, Isaac Massey, 1845- 232.
The coming of Christ, both pre-millennial and imminent, by I. M. Haldeman... New York, N.Y., C. C. Cook [c1906] 3 p. l., 325 p. 20 cm. [BT885.H2] 6-20181
1. Second advent. I. Title.

HAMILTON, Floyd Eugene, 1890- 236.3
The basis of millennial faith, by the Reverend Floyd E. Hamilton... Grand Rapids, Mich., Wm. B. Eerdmans publishing company, 1942. 100 p. 20 cm. Bibliographical references included in "Notes" (p. 147-149) [BT885.H265] 42-21025
1. Second advent. 2. Millennium. I. Title.

HARRISON, William K. 232.6
Hope triumphant: studies on the rapture of the church, 153p. 22cm. [BT886.H3] 66-9661 2.95
1. Second Advent. I. Title.

HAYNES, Carlyle Boynton, 1882- 232.6
Our Lord's return, by Carlyle B. Haynes. Rev. and reillustrated. Nashville, Southern Pub. Association [1964] 125 p. illus., map. 21 cm. (A Summit book) [BT885.H29 1964] 63-21241
1. Second Advent. I. Title.

HAYNES, Carlyle Boynton, 1882- 232.
Our Lord's return; an earnest review of the Scriptural evidences which establish the great Christian doctrine of the second coming of Christ, together with a close study of the prophecies relating to this glorious event and the early fulfilment of these prophecies. By Carlyle B. Haynes ... Mountain View, Calif., Brookfield, ill. [ect.] Pacific press publishing association, 1918. 128 p. incl. front., illus. 19 1/2 cm. [BT885.H29 1918a] 26-5863
1. Second advent. I. Title.

HAYNES, Carlyle Boynton, 1882- 232.6
The return of Jesus ... by Carlyle B. Haynes. Takoma Park, Washington, D.C., Review and herald publishing association [1943] 2 p. l., 7-350 p. incl. front., illus., diagrs. 20 1/2 cm. [BT885.H3 1943] 43-12016
1. Second advent. 2. Seventh-day Adventists—Doctrinal and controversial works. I. Title.

HAYNES, Carlyle Boynton, 1882- 232.
Twelve great signs of the return of Jesus; an exposition of the Bible predictions relating to "the time of the end"' with special reference to the evidences demonstrating the imminence of the second coming of Our Lord, and an explanation of the fulfilment of these divine prophecies in present-day developments, and the conditions which now prevail in the world and in the church, by Carlyle B. Haynes ... Takoma Park, Washington, D.C., Peekskill, N.Y. [etc.] Review and herald publishing association [c1925] 128 p. incl. front. illus. 19 1/2 cm. [BT885.H35] 25-6645
1. Second advent. I. Title.

HEAGLE, David, 1836-1922. 232.
That blessed hope; the second coming of Christ considered with special reference to post-millennial and pre-millennial discussions, also an appendix treating of related topics, by David Heagle ... Philadelphia, New York [etc.] American Baptist publication society [c1907] 176 p. 20cm. "Recent views and literature concerning the advent": p. 168-172. [BT885.H4] 7-28624
1. Second advent. 2. Millenium. I. Title.

HIS glorious appearing; 232.6
an exposition of Matthew twenty-four. Rev. and illustrated ... 43d ed.-350th thousand. Washington, D.C., Review and herald publishing assn., 1904. 119 p. front., illus. 21 cm. [BT885.H6 1904] 32-30707
1. Second advent. 2. Bible. N.T. Matthew XXIV—Commentaries. I. Review and herald publishing association.

HOLLEY, Joseph Winthrop, 1874- 232.6
Regnum montis; Scriptural and historical evidence that the destiny of the South is interwoven with the second coming of Christ. New York, William-Frederick Press, 1954. 112p. illus. 23cm. [BT885.H714] 54-8116
1. Second Advent. 2. Negroes. I. Title.

HOLLEY, Joseph Winthrop, 1874- 232.6
Regnum montis and its contemporary; heralding the second coming of Christ in the decade, 1995-2005, and the end of the world of things material. New York, William-Frederick Press, 1958. 141p. 23cm. [BT885.H713] 57-12740
1. Second Advent. I. Title.

HOLLISTER, Horace Edward. 232.6
"I will come again"--Jesus; the five successive phases of the Advent. A fresh analysis of the Old and New Testament prophetic writings concerning the second coming of Christ the Messiah. Chicago, Society for Bible Re-search, 1950. 319 p. 23 cm. [BT885.H715] 51-20325
1. Second Advent. I. Title.

HOLT, Basil Fenelon, 1902- 232.6
What time is it! The second coming of Christ and the signs of the times, by Basil F. Holt...with introduction by William E. Biederwolf... Cincinnati, O., The Standard publishing company [c1936] 239 p. 19 1/2 cm. "Many of the chapters...were originally in the form of addresses delivered to congregations in Indiana."--Author's foreword. Bibliography: p.235-239. [BT885.H72] 37-1933
1. Second advent. I. Title.

HOWELL, Albert Thomas. 232.6
The glorious appearing, by Rev. Albert Thomas Howell ... New York, N.Y., The Hobson book press, 1946. xiii, 94 p. incl. front. (diagr.) 21 1/2 cm. Addresses. [BT885.H86] 46-22135
1. Second advent. I. Title.

HUGHES, Archibald, 1905- 232.6
A new heaven and a new earth; an introductory study of the coming of the Lord Jesus Christ and the eternal inheritance. Foreword by C. H. Nash. Philadelphia, Presbyterian and Reformed Pub. Co., 1958. 233p. 22cm. Includes bibliography. [BT885.H864] 58-13254
1. Second Advent. I. Title.

HUTCHINSON, Samuel. 232.6
A Scriptural exhibition of the mighty conquest, and glorious triumph of Jesus Christ, over sin, death, and hell; and His exaltation, His second coming, the day of judgment, and the capacity, equality, and success of His reign; and the ultimate triumph of His ransomed. By Rev. Samuel Hutchinson ... Norway, Me., Printed at the Observer office, by A. Barton, 1828. 144 p. 18 cm. [BT885.H88] 37-37979
1. Second advent. I. Title.

INGRAM, John Calvin. 232.6
"The coming of Christ", by John Calvin Ingram. [Ashland, Kan. Printed by the Clark county clipper, c1932] 100 p. 23 cm. On cover: The dawn of a new era. [ET885.I 5] 32-14310
1. Second advent. I. Title.

INTERNATIONAL Congress on Prophecy, 1st, New York, 1952. 232.6
Hastening the day of God; prophetic messages from the International Congress on Prophecy, in Calvary Baptist Church, New York City, November 9-16, 1952. Compiled and edited by John W. Bradbury. Wheaton, Ill., Van Kampen Press [1953] 262p. 22cm. [BT885.I55 1952a] 53-10677
1. Second Advent. I. Bradbury, John W., ed. II. Title.

INTERNATIONAL Congress on Prophecy. 2d, New York, 1955. 232.6
Understanding the times; prophetic messages delivered at the 2nd International Congress on Prophecy, New York City. Editors: William Culbertson, Herman B. Centz. Grand Rapids, Zondervan Pub. House [1956] 290p. 22cm. 'Produced for American Association for Jewish Evangelism, Winona Lake, Indiana.' [BT885.I55 1955] 57-20452

1. Second Advent. I. Culbertson, William, ed. II. Centz, Herman B., ed. III. Title.

ISENBURG, Merle. 232.
"The second coming of Our Lord Jesus Christ and the events associated therewith"; a series of sermons on the second coming of Our Lord Jesus Christ, by Rev. Merle Isemburg ... preached in the church Sunday evenings in the spring and the summer of 1926. [Sidney, N.Y., c1927] 159 p. incl., port. 20 cm. [BT885.I7] 27-21747
1. Second advent. I. Title.

KATTERJOHN, Arthur D. 230'.6
The tribulation people / by Arthur D. Katterjohn, with Mark Fackler. Carol Stream, Ill. : Creation House, c1975. 137 p. ; 21 cm. Bibliography: p. 135-137. [BT886.K34] 75-24586 ISBN 0-88419-115-X : 3.50
1. Second Advent. 2. Rapture (Christian eschatology) 3. Tribulation (Christian eschatology) I. Fackler, Mark, joint author. II. Title.

[KEEFER, Glen Elgin] 1889- 296
Definite signs of this age closing, by "a business man" ... Westport, Conn. and Antwerp, O., G. E. Keefer, c1925. 63 p. incl. tab. port., diagr. 19 cm. "First edition, August 1924; third edition, August 1925." [BT875.K35] 25-22471
1. Second advent. 2. Bible—Prophecies. I. Title.

[KING, Thomas Benton] 1838- 236.
John Counsellor's evolution; or, A real experience of the second coming. St. Louis, Mo., The John Counsellor publishing co., 1903. 447 p. 23 1/2 cm. [BR126.K5] 3-13942
I. Title.

KRIKORIAN, Meshach Paul, 1890- 232'.6
The Apocalypse of Jesus Christ; an interpretation of Our Saviour's second advent "with power and great glory", by M. P. Krikorian. Philadelphia, Dorrance [1973] 171 p. illus. 22 cm. [BT886.K73] 73-84493 ISBN 0-8059-1906-6 5.00
1. Second Advent. I. Title.

LADD, George Eldon, 1911- 232.6
The blessed hope. Grand Rapids, Eerdmans, 1956. 167p. 23cm. [BT885.L23] 56-10166
1. Second Advent. I. Title.

LADD, George Eldon, 1911- 232.6
Jesus Christ and history. Chicago, Inter-Varsity Press [1963] vii, 62 p. 21 cm. (IVP series in contemporary Christian thought, 5) Bibliography: p. 60-62. [BT886.L3] 63-8556
1. Second Advent. I. Title.

LITCH, Josiah. 232.6
Christ yet to come: a review of Dr. I. P. Warren's "Parousia of Christ." By Rev. Josiah Litch ... with an introduction by Rev. A. J. Gordon ... Boston, American millennial association, 1880. xii, [13]-192 p. 20 cm. [BT885.W32] 37-15931
1. Warren, Israel Perkins, 1814-1892. The parousia. 2. Second advent. I. American millennial association. II. Title.

LORD, Willis, 1809-1888. 232.6
The blessed hope: or, The glorious coming of the Lord ... By Willis Lord, D. D. Chicago, W. G. Holmes, 1877. 4 p. l., 176 p. 20 cm. [BT885.L85] 33-37783
1. Second advent. I. Title. II. Title: The glorious coming of the Lord.

LUND, Gerald N. 232'.6
The coming of the Lord [by] Gerald N. Lund. Salt Lake City, Utah, Bookcraft, 1971. xii, 241 p. 24 cm. Includes bibliographical references. [BT886.L85] 79-175135
1. Second Advent. I. Title.

MCBIRNIE, William S. 236
50 progressive messages from Armageddon to new earth, by William S. McBirnie... Norfolk, Va., McBirnie Publications association [19 v. 18 1/2 cm. "Second edition, January, 1944." [BT885.M28] 44-6842
1. Second advent. 2. Millennium. I. Title.

MCCONKIE, Bruce R. 236'.3
The millennial Messiah : the second

coming of the Son of Man / Bruce R. McConkie. Salt Lake City, Utah : Deseret Book Co., c1982. xxiii, 726 p. ; 24 cm. Includes index. [BT886.M42 1982] 19 81-19599 ISBN 0-87747-896-1 : 15.95
1. Mormon Church—Doctrinal and controversial works. 2. Second Advent. I. Title.

MCCOWN, Chester Charlton, 1877- 232.
The promise of His coming; a historical interpretation and revolution [i.e. revaluation] of the idea of the second advent, by Chester Charlton McCown... New York, The Macmillan company, 1921. xvi, 256 p. 19 1/2 cm. [BT885.M313] 22-206
1. Second advent. I. Title.

MCKEE, Bill. 232'.6
Orbit of ashes; Jesus is coming! Wheaton, Ill., Tyndale House Publishers [1972] 142 p. 18 cm. [BT886.M33] 72-75965 ISBN 0-8423-4750-X 1.25
1. Second Advent. I. Title.

MCPHERSON, Aimee Semple, 1890- 236
The second coming of Christ. Is He coming? How is He coming? When is He coming? For whom is He coming? [By] Aimee Semple McPherson. Los Angeles [c1921] 120 p. port. 16 1/2 x 13 cm. [BT885.M37] 43-40688
1. Second advent. I. Title.

MANFORD, Erasmus. 230.
An oral debate on the coming of the Son of man, endless punishment, and universal salvation. Held in Milton, Ind., Oct. 26, 27, and 28, 1847. Between Erasmus Manford...and Benjamin Franklin... Indianapolis, Indiana state journal steam-press, 1848. 2 p. l., 368 p. 18 1/2 cm. [BX9946.M4] 2-14072
1. Second advent. 2. Future punishment. 3. Universalism—Addresses, essays, lectures. I. Franklin, Benjamin, 1819-1898. II. Title.

MARANATHA bells; 232.6
the blessed hope in prose and poetry ... New York city, A. C. Gaebelein, inc. [c1935] 126 p. 21 cm. Edited by A. C. Gaebelein. cf. Pref. [BT885.M383] 36-2380
1. Second advent. I. Gaebelein, Arno Clemens, 1861- ed.

MARSH, Elmer G. 232.
Simple A B Z's of the second coming, by E. G. Marsh ... Cincinnati, O., Revivalist press [c1929] 68 p. 20 cm. [BT885.M384] 30-5072
1. Second advent. I. Title.

MAXWELL, Arthur Stanley, 1896- 232.6
The coming King; ten great signs of Christ's return. Mountain View, Calif., Pacific Press Pub. Association [1953] 127p. illus. 20cm. [BT885.M395] 53-8825
1. Second Advent. I. Title.

MAXWELL, Arthur Stanley, 1896- 232'.6
Man the world needs most, by Arthur S. Maxwell. Mountain View, Calif., Pacific Press Pub. Association [1970] 96 p. illus., ports. 18 cm. [BT886.M38] 79-117952
1. Second Advent. I. Title.

MILLER, William, 1782-1849. 236
Evidence from Scripture and history of the second coming of Christ, about the year 1813; exhibited in a course of lectures. By William Miller. Troy, N.Y., E. Gates, 1838. viii, [9]-280 p. 19 cm. [BT885.M52] 44-39166
1. Second advent. I. Title.

MOFFETT, Jonas William, 1858- 232.
The second coming of Christ; the great tribulation, battle of Armageddon, restoration of Israel, the millennium, when and where, and signs of His coming, from a lawyer's standpoint, J. W. Moffett. Abilene, Tex. [c1925] 75 p. 20 1/2 cm. [BT885.M53] 25-16506
1. Second advent. I. Title.

MORGAN, George Campbell, 1863- 232.
Sunrise. "Behold, he cometh!" An introduction to a study of the second advent, by G. Campbell Morgan, D.D. New York, Chicago [etc.] Fleming H. Revell company [c1912] 95 p. 18 1/2 cm. "The chapters in this book were preached as sermons." [BT885.M57] 12-6050
1. Second advent. I. Title.

MORRISON, Henry Clay, 1857- 232.
The second coming of Christ. By Rev. H. C. Morrison ... Louisville, Ky., The Pentecostal publishing company [c1914] 120 p. 19 1/2 cm. [BT885.M65] 14-5438
1. Second advent. I. Title.

MUNHALL, Leander Whitcomb, 1843-1934. 232.6
The Lord's return. [8th ed.] Grand Rapids, Kregel Publications [1962] 224 p. 20 cm. [BT886.M8 1962] 62-13175
1. Second Advent. I. Title.

NICHOL, Francis David, 1897- 232.6
Behold, He cometh; a discussion of the solemn truth of the unexpectedness of Christ's coming a warning against the temptations and dangers that confront the church today, and an appeal to make ready to meet God face to face, by Francis D. Nichol. Takoma Park, Washington, D.C., Review and herald publishing association [c1938] 252 p. 20 1/2 cm. [BX6154.N52] 38-12724
1. Second advent. 2. Seventh-day Adventists—Doctrinal and controversial works. I. Title.

NICHOL, Francis David, 1897- 232.6
Signs of Christ's coming, current events fulfillingBible prophecy, by Francis D. Nichol... Takoma Park, Washington, D.C., South Bend, Ind. [etc.] Review and herald publishing association [c1931] 96 p. front., illus. 19 1/2 cm. [BT885.N5] 31-3386
1. Second advent. I. Title.

ODLE, Joe T. 236'.3
The coming of the King [by] Joe T. Odle. Nashville, Tenn., Broadman Press [1974] 128 p. 18 cm. [BT886.O29] 73-91612 ISBN 0-8054-1926-8 1.95 (pbk.)
1. Second Advent. I. Title.

ODLE, Joe T. 232'.6
Is Christ coming soon? [By] Joe T. Odle. Nashville, Broadman Press [1971] xvii, 127 p. 20 cm. (A Broadman inner circle book) [BT886.O3] 74-151622 ISBN 0-8054-8112-5
1. Second Advent. I. Title.

ORCHARD, Richard E. 232'.6
Look who's coming / Richard E. Orchard. Springfield, Mo. : Gospel Pub. House, c1975. 123 p. ; 18 cm. (Radiant books) [BT886.O7] 74-33870 ISBN 0-88243-541-8 pbk. : 1.25
1. Second Advent. I. Title.

PACHE, Rene. 232.6
The return of Jesus Christ; translated by William Sanford LaSor, from a text somewhat abridged by the author. Chicago, Moody Press [1955] 448p. 22cm. [BT885.P15] 55-43714
1. Second Advent. I. Title.

PANKHURST, Christabel. 232.
The Lord cometh! the world crisis explained, by Christabel Pankhurst. New York, The Book stall [c1923] 115 p. 19 1/2 cm. [BT885.P18] 29-8824
1. Second advent. 2. Bible—Prophecies. I. Title.

PANKHURST, Christabel. 232.
Seeing the future, by Christabel Pankhurst... New York and London, Harper & brothers, 1929. vi p., 1 l., 328 p. 19 1/2 cm. A companion volume to the author's The world's unrest.--Publisher's announcement. "First edition." [BT885.P2] 29-2495
1. Second advent. 2. Bible—Prophecies. I. Title.

PARKER, Elsie G (Hill) Mrs. 1882- 232.6
King Jesus is coming (a treatise on the two-fold second coming of Christ.) By Rev. Elsie G. Parker. Berkeley, Calif., Rev. Elsie G. Parker [c1936] 1 p. l., v-vii, 9-188 p. 23 cm. [BT885.P28] 36-17926
1. Second advent. I. Title.

PAYNE, John Barton, 1922- 232.6
The imminent appearing of Christ. Grand Rapids, Mich., Eerdmans [c.1962] 191p. Bibl. 61-10865 3.75
1. Second Advent. I. Title.

PIERSON, Arthur Tappan, 1837-1911. 232.
The second coming of Our Lord, by Rev. Arthur T. Pierson, D.D. Philadelphia, H. Altemus [c1896] 50 p. 18 cm. [BT885.P43] 12-37597
1. Second advent. I. Title.

PIERSON, Robert H. 232'.6
What's just ahead / by Robert H. Pierson. Nashville : Southern Pub. Association, c1978. p. cm. [BT886.P53] 78-14219 ISBN 0-8127-0187-9 pbk. : 0.75
1. Second Advent. 2. End of the world. I. Title.

PROPHETIC Bible conference, Chicago, 1914. 236
The coming and kingdom of Christ; a stenographic report of the Prophetic Bible conference hele at the Moody Bible institute of Chicago, February 24-27, 1914; including a list of some exponents of premillennialism. Chicago, The Bible institute colportage association [c1914] 252 p. 1 illus. 22 cm. [BT885.P85] 14-10257
1. Second advent. I. Title.

RAND, Howard B., 1889- 232.6
The hour cometh! Merrimac, Mass., 01860, Destiny Pubs. [c.1966] vii, 0p. 280p. illus. 21cm. Bibl. [BT886.R3] 66-16453 3.75
1. Second Advent. I. Title.

RAND, Howard B 1889- 232.6
The hour cometh! By Howard B. Rand. Merrimac, Mass., Destiny Publishers [1966] vii, 280 p. illus. 21 cm. Bibliographical notes. [BT886.R3] 66-16453
1. Second Advent. I. Title.

REESE, Alexander, 1881-1969. 232'.6
The approaching advent of Christ / by Alexander Reese. Grand Rapids : Grand Rapids International Publications, 1975. 328 p. ; 23 cm. Reprint of the 1937 ed. published by Marshall, Morgan & Scott, London; with a new pref. Includes bibliographical references and indexes. [BT885.R3 1975] 73-85374 ISBN 0-8254-3610-9 : 5.95
1. Bible—Prophecies. 2. Second Advent. I. Title.

RIGGLE, Herbert McClellan, 1872- 232.6
Jesus is coming again, by H. M. Riggle ... Anderson, Ind., Gospel trumpet company, [1943] viii, 9-156 p. 19 1/2 cm. [Christian life library series, ed. by H. L. Phillips] [BT885.R52] 43-44453
1. Second advent. 2. Millennium. I. Title.

RIMMER, Harry, 1890- 232.6
... The coming King, by Harry Rimmer ... Grand Rapids, Mich., Wm. B. Eerdmans publishing company, 1941. 3 p. l., 9-90 p. 20 cm. (His Shadows of things to come, 4) [BT885.R6] 41-12389
1. Second advent. I. Title.

ROBINSON, John Arthur Thomas, Bp., 1919- 232.6
Jesus and His coming; the emergence of a doctrine. New York, Abingdon Press [1958, c1957] 192p. 23cm. (William Belden Noble lectures, Harvard University, 1955) [BT885.R724] 58-997
1. Second Advent. I. Title.

ROBINSON, John Arthur Thomas, Bp., 1919- 232.6
Jesus and His coming; the emergence of a doctrine. New York, Abingdon Press [1958, c1957] 192 p. 23 cm. (William Belden Noble lectures, Harvard University, 1955) [BT885.R724] 58-997
1. Second Advent. I. Title.

ROBINSON, John Arthur Thomas, Bp., 1919- 232'.6
Jesus and His coming / John A. T. Robinson. [2d ed.] Philadelphia : Westminster Press, c1979. 192 p. ; 22 cm. Includes bibliographical references and indexes. [BT886.R55 1979] 79-14078 ISBN 0-664-24278-2 pbk. : 6.95
1. Second Advent. I. Title.

RUSKIN, Edward V 232.6
The hill of stoning; studies in the predictions about the early return of Jesus, their fulfillment, and related subjects. [1st ed.] New York, Vantage Press [1956] 263p. 21cm. [BT885.R83] 55-11650
1. Second Advent. I. Title.

SHELDON, Henry Clay, 1845-1928. 232.
Studies in recent adventism, by Henry C. Sheldon ... New York, Cincinnati, The Abingdon press [c1915] 160 p. 17 1/2 cm. [BT885.S34] 15-18896
1. Second advent. I. Title.

SHEPPARD, William John Limmer, 1861- 232.
The Lord's coming and the world's end, by W. J. L. Sheppard ... London, Society for promoting Christian knowledge; New York, The Macmillan company, 1918. 96 p. 18 1/2 cm. [BT885.S35] 19-18153
I. Title.

SHULER, John Lewis, 1887- 296
Is the end near? By John L. Shuler... Nashville, Tenn., Atlanta, Ga. [etc.] Southern publishing association [c1928] 128 p. incl. front., illus. 19 1/2 cm. [BT875.S53] 29-17172
1. Second advent. 2. Bible—Prophecies. I. Title.

SILVER, Jesse Forest. 236
The Lord's return, seen in history and in Scripture as premillennial and imminent, by Jesse Forest Silver; with an introduction by Bishop Wilson T. Hogue ... New York, Chicago [etc.] Fleming H. Revell company [1914] 311 p. 19 1/2 cm. "Works cited": p. 13-15. [BT885.S4] 14-5440
1. Second advent. I. Title.

SILVER, Jesse Forest.
The Lord's return, seen in history and in Scripture as pre-millennial and imminent, by Jesse Forest Silver; with an introduction by Bishop Wilson T. Hogue ... New York, Chicago [etc.] Fleming H. Revell company [c1914] 311 p. 19 1/2 cm. $1.00 14-5440
I. Title.

*SPURGEON, C.H. 1834-1892. 232.6
12 sermons on the second coming of Christ / C. H. Spurgeon Grand Rapids : Baker Book House, 1976. 143p. ; 20 cm. (His Library) [BT885] ISBN 0-8010-8066-5 pbk. : 1.95.
1. Second advent. 2. Advent sermons. I. Title.

STANTON, Gerald B 1918- 232.6
Kept from the hour; a systematic study of the rapture in Bible prophecy. Grand Rapids, Zondervan Pub. House, 1956. 820p. 22cm. [BT885.S77] 57-15551
1. Second Advent. I. Title. II. Title: Rapture in Bible prophecy.

STEVENS, Jesse Columbus. 323.6
The end draws near; or, The certainty of Christ's second coming, by Jesse C. Stevens. Takoma Park, Washington, D. C., Review and herald publishing assn. [c1938] 96 p. incl. front., illus., plates. 20 cm. [BX6154.S8] 38-11594
1. Second advent. 2. End of the world. 3. Seventh-day Adventists—Doctrinal and controversial works. I. Title.

*SWAFFORD, Z. W. 232.6
He will come [simple studies of the second coming of Jesus Christ] Little Rock, Ark., Baptist Pubns. [c.1964] 71p. 21cm. .75 pap.,
I. Title.

TAYLOR, George Floyd, 1881- 232.
The rainbow, by Rev. G. F. Taylor ... Franklin Springs, Ga., Publishing [!] house of the Pentecostal holiness church [c1924] 223 p. 18 1/2 cm. [BT885.T18] 24-22020
1. Second advent. I. Title.

TORREY, Reuben Archer, 1856-1928 232'.6
The return of the Lord Jesus, by R. A. Torrey. Grand Rapids, Baker Bk. [1966] 144p. 20cm. Collation of Scripture passages on the second coming of Christ for individual study [BT865] 67-2890 2.50
1. Second Advent. 2. Millennium. I. Title.

TRUMBULL, Charles Gallaudet, 1872- 232.6
Prophecy's light on today, by Charles G.

Trumbull ... introduction by Howard A. Kelly ... New York [etc.] Fleming H. Revell company [c1987] 191 p. 19 1/2 cm. [BT885.T7] 38-1022
1. Second advent. 2. End of the world. I. Title.

TYNG, Stephen Higginson, 1839-1898. 232.6
He will come; or, Meditations upon the return of the Lord Jesus Christ to reign over the earth, by Stephen H. Tyng, jr. ... with an introduction by Stephen H. Tyng ... New York, Nucklow & Simon, 1877. 212 p. 18 cm. [BT885.T9 1877] 31-11230
1. Second advent. I. Title.

TYNG, Stephen Higginson, 1839-1898. 232.6
He will come; or, Meditations upon the return of the Lord Jesus Christ, to reign over the earth, by Stephen H. Tyng, jr. ... with an introduction by Stephen H. Tyng ... [2d ed.] New York, Mucklow & Simon, 1877. 212 p. 18 cm. [BT885.T9 1877a] 31-11231
1. Second advent. I. Title.

URMY, William Smith.
Christ came again; the paromia of Christ a past event; the kingdom of Christ a present fact, with a emminant emohatology ... by William S. Urmy, D.D. New York, Eaton & Mains; Cincinnati, Curts & Jennings [c1900] 394 p. 19 cm. [BT835.U75] 0-1887
1. Second advent. 2. Emohatology. I. Title.

VANDEMAN, George E. 232'.6
The day the cat jumped / by George E. Vandeman. Mountain View, Calif. : Pacific Press Pub. Association, c1978. 93 p. ; 19 cm. [BT886.V36] 77-91116 pbk. : 0.75
1. Second Advent. I. Title.

VINES, Jerry. 232'.6
"I shall return" - Jesus / Jerry Vines. Wheaton, Ill. : Victor Books, c1977. 128 p. ; 18 cm. [BT886.V56] 76-55631 ISBN 0-88207-702-3 pbk. : 1.75
1. Second Advent. 2. Eschatology. I. Title.

VOS, Geerhardus, 1862- 232.
The teaching of Jesus concerning the kingdom of God and the church, by Geerhardus Vos ... New York, American tract society [1903] vi, 208 p. 19 cm. (Half-title: The teachings of Jesus, ed. by J. H. Kerr ...) [BS2415.T4V7] 4-57
1. Jesus Christ—Kingdom. 2. Secons advent. I. Title.

WALVOORD, John F 232.6
The return of the Lord. Findlay, Ohio, Dunham Pub. Co. [c1955] 160 p. 20 cm. [BT885.W24] 58-30303
1. Second Advent. I. Title.

WATSON, George Douglas, 1845-1924. 236
Steps to the throne. By George D. Watson ... Louisville, Ky., Pickett publishing co., 1898. 168 p. 18 cm. [BT885.W35] 98-966
1. Second advent. I. Title.

WHITE, James Edson. 236
The coming King... By James Edson White. Nashville, Tenn., Ft. Worth, Tex. [etc.] Southern publishing association [c1907] 2 p. l., iii-vi, 7-318 p. illus. (part col.) 20 cm. "Contributions on special subjects treated in this book from the pens of J. O. Corliss, M. E. Kellogg, and G. C. Tenney." [BT885.W5 1907] 7-8501
1. Second advent. I. Title.

WHITE, James Edson.
The coming King ... By James Edson White. Nashville, Tenn., Southern publishing association, 1904. 2 p. l., vii-xii, 13-321 p. incl. front., illus., plates. 20 cm. [BT885.W5 1904] 4-32683
1. Second advent. I. Title.

WIGHT, Francis Asa, 1854- 236
Communism and fascism destroyed at Christ's second coming, by Francis Asa Wight ... Harrisburg, Pa., The Evangelical press [c1937] 72 p. 18 cm. [BT885.W62] 39-582
1. Second advent. 2. End of the world. I. Title.

WILKERSON, David R. 232'.6
Jesus Christ solid rock; the return of Christ [by] David Wilkerson, with Kathryn Kuhlman [and others] Grand Rapids, Zondervan Pub. House [1973] 117 p. illus. 18 cm. "Zondervan books." [BT886.W53] 73-159523 0.95
1. Second Advent. I. Title.

WILSON, George Washington, 1853- 236
The sign of The coming; or, Premillennialism, unscriptural and unreasonable, by George W. Wilson ... With an introduction by Rev. W. X. Ninde ... Boston, The Christian witness company, 1899. 3 p. l., 5-366 p. front. (port.) 18 1/2 cm. [BT885.W7] 99-1918
1. Second advent. 2. Millennium. I. Title.

WOOD, Leon James. 232.6
Is the rapture next? An answer to the question: Will the church escape the tribulation? Grand Rapids, Zondervan Pub. House [1956] 120 p. 20 cm. [BT885.W82] 56-41993
1. Second Advent. I. Title.

WOODS, John Purvis. 232.6
The final invasion of God. Boston, W. A. Wilde Co. [1951] 87 p. 20 cm. [BT885.W85] 51-13848
1. Second Advent. I. Title.

WUEST, Kenneth Samuel, 1893- 220.15
Prophetic light in the present darkness. [1st ed.] Grand Rapids W. B. Eerdmans Pub. Co., 1955. 135p. 20cm. (His Word studies in the Greek New Testament, 15) [BT885.W8] 55-22579
1. Second Advent. I. Title.

ZEOLI, Anthony. 232.6
The second coming of Christ, by Anthony Zeoli... Norristown, Pa., F. Weber [c1929] 72 p. 19 cm. [BT885.Z4] 39-28336
1. Second advent. I. Title.

Second Advent—Addresses, essays, lectures.

HALDEMAN, Isaac Massey, 1845- 232.
Why I preached the second coming, by I. M. Haldeman... New York, Chicago [etc.] Fleming H. Revell company [c1919] 2 p. l., 7-160 p. 19 1/2 cm. [BT885.H265] 19-18655
I. Title.

HALDEMAN, Isaac Massey, 1845- 232.
Why I preached the second coming, by I. M. Haldeman... New York, Chicago [etc.] Fleming H. Revell company [c1919] 2 p. l., 7-160 p. 19 1/2 cm. [BT885.H265] 19-18655
I. Title.

HOLDEN, John Stuart. 232.
Will the Christ return? Addresses on the second coming of our Lord, by J. Stuart Holden ... New York, Chicago [etc.] Fleming H. Revell company [c1918] 88 p. 19 cm. [BT885.H7] 18-13652
I. Title.

HOLDEN, John Stuart. 232.
Will the Christ return? Addresses on the second coming of our Lord, by J. Stuart Holden ... New York, Chicago [etc.] Fleming H. Revell company [c1918] 88 p. 19 cm. [BT885.H7] 18-13652
I. Title.

LINDSEY, Hal. 232'.6
When is Jesus coming again / by Hal Lindsey and others. Carol Stream, Ill. : Creation House, c1974. 96 p. : ports. ; 18 cm. (New leaf library) Bibliography: p. 83-96. [BT886.L56] 75-3613 ISBN 0-88419-110-9 : 1.45
1. Second Advent—Addresses, essays, lectures. 2. Tribulation (Christian eschatology)—Addresses, essays, lectures. 3. Rapture (Christian eschatology)—Addresses, essays, lectures. I. Title.

Second Advent—Biblical teaching.

PENTECOST, J. Dwight. 236
Will man survive? : The Bible looks at man's future / by J. Dwight Pentecost. Zondervan books ed. Grand Rapids, Mich. : Zondervan Pub. House, 1980, c1971. 208 p. ; 21 cm. Reprint of the ed. published by Moody Press, Chicago. [BT886.P46 1980] 79-27422 ISBN 0-310-30931-X pbk. : 4.95
1. Second Advent—Biblical teaching. 2. Eschatology—Biblical teaching. I. Title.

Second Advent—Early works to 1800—Addresses, essays, lectures.

APOCALYPTIC spirituality : 236
treatises and letters of Lactantius, Adso of Montier-en-Der, Joachim of Fiore, the Franciscan spirituals, Savonarola / translation and introd. by Bernard McGinn ; pref. by Marjorie Reeves. New York : Paulist Press, 1980, c1979 xviii, 334 p. ; 23 cm. (The Classics of Western spirituality) Includes indexes. Bibliography: p. 311-316. [BT885.A65] 79-90834 ISBN 0-8091-0305-2 : 11.95 ISBN 0-8091-2242-1 pbk. : 7.95
1. Second Advent—Early works to 1800—Addresses, essays, lectures. 2. Antichrist—Early works to 1800—Addresses, essays, lectures. 3. Apocalyptic literature—Early works to 1800—Addresses, essays, lectures. I. McGinn, Bernard, 1937- II. Series: Classics of Western spirituality.

Second Advent—Juvenile literature.

THAYNE, Mirla Greenwood. 811'.5'4
When He comes again. Illus. by Adell Reese Palmer. Salt Lake City, Deseret Book Co., 1968. [77] p. col. illus. 29 cm. "When He comes again, words and music by Mirla Greenwood Thayne": p. [76-77] [BT886.T49] 68-56386
1. Jesus Christ—Biography—Juvenile literature. 2. Second Advent—Juvenile literature. I. Palmer, Adell Reese, illus. II. Title.

Second advent—Sermons.

BOWDEN, William Sheldon. 232.6
The dawn of day; or, Hope for tomorrow, by Rev. William Sheldon Bowden ... New York, N.Y., The Hobson book press, 1946. 6 p. l., 151 p. 21 cm. [BT885.B78] 46-20668
1. Second advent—Sermons. I. Title.

FORD, William Herschel, 1900- 232.6
Seven simple sermons on the second coming, by W. Herschel Ford ... Introduction by William W. Ayer ... Grand Rapids, Mich., Zondervan publishing house [1945] 104 p. 20 cm. [BT885.F63] 45-7958
1. Second advent—Sermons. I. Title.

HALDEMAN, Isaac Massey, 1845-1933 232.6
Ten sermons on the second coming of Our Lord Jesus Christ, preached in the First Baptist church, New York City, from October 15 to December 17, 1916, by the pastor, I. M. Haldeman. Grand Rapids, Mich., Baker Bk., 1963. 748p. 21cm. 4.95
1. Second advent—Sermons. 2. Baptists—Sermons. 3. Sermons, American. I. Title.

MOORE, H. L., Bp. 232'.6
The promise of His coming, by H. L. Moore. Cleveland, Tenn., Bethel Book Publishers [1965] 98 p. 20 cm. [BT886.M63] 225.9 78-207517
1. Church of God of Prophecy—Sermons. 2. Second Advent—Sermons. 3. Sermons, American. I. Title.

ROBERSON, Lee. 232.6
Some golden daybreak sermons on the second coming of Christ. Wheaton, Ill., Sword of the Lord Publishers [1957] 116p. 21cm. Includes some golden daybreak, hymn with music, by Carl Blackmore. [BT885.R72] 57-41655
1. Second Advent—Sermons. 2. Baptists—Sermons. 3. Sermons, American. I. Title.

SPURGEON, Charles Haddon, 1834-1892 252.3
Sermons on the second coming of Christ. Selected, ed. by Chas. T. Cook. Grand Rapids, Mich., Zondervan [c.1962] 256p. 23cm. (Lib. of Spurgeon's sermons v.18) A62 2.95
1. Second Advent—Sermons. I. Title.

SPURGEON, Charles Haddon, 1834-1892. 232.6
Spurgeon's sermons on the second coming, condensed and edited by David Otis Fuller ... Grand Rapids, Mich., Zondervan publishing house [1943] 3 p. l., 5-147 p. 20 cm. [BT885.S75] 43-10020
1. Second advent—Sermons. 2. Baptists—Sermons. 3. Sermons, English. I. Fuller, David Otis, 1903- ed. II. Title.

WHITE, John Wesley. 232'.6
Re-entry; striking parallels between today's news events and Christ's second coming. Foreword by Billy Graham. Grand Rapids, Mich., Zondervan Pub. House [1970] 164 p. 21 cm. "A series of six sermons given on three Sundays of January 1969 in the Peoples Church, Toronto." [BT886.W48] 75-112868 3.95
1. Second Advent—Sermons. 2. Sermons, English—Canada. I. Title.

Second Presbyterian Church, Staunton, Va.

SECOND Presbyterian Church, Staunton, Va. 285'.1755'911
A history of the Second Presbyterian Church, Staunton, Virginia, 1875-1975. Staunton, Va. : The Church, c1975. 76 p. : ill. ; 24 cm. Includes index. [BX9211.S8S4 1975] 75-332489
1. Second Presbyterian Church, Staunton, Va. 2. Staunton, Va.—Biography. I. Title.

Second sight.

MACKENZIE, Andrew. 133.8'6
Riddle of the future; a modern study of precognition; with a preface by Robert H. Thouless. New York, Taplinger, [1975 c1974] 172 p. 22 cm. Includes index. Bibliography: p. 164-168. [BF1325.M14] 75-8199 ISBN 0-8008-6795-5 8.50.
1. Second sight. I. Title.

MACKENZIE, Andrew. 133.8'6
Riddle of the future : a modern study of precognition / by Andrew Mackenzie ; with a preface by Robert H. Thaless. New York : New American Library 1978,c1974. 162p. ; 18 cm. (A Signet Book.) Includes index. Bibliography p.154-158. [BF1325.M14] ISBN 0-451-08096-3 pbk. : 1.75
1. Second sight. I. Title.
L.C. card no. for Taplinger ed. 75-8199.

MACRAE, Norman, ed. 133.3'2
Highland second-sight, with prophecies of Coinneach Odhar and the Seer of Petty ... Introductory study by Wm. Morrison. Edited by Norman Macrae. [Norwood, Pa.] Norwood Editions, 1972. 202 p. 24 cm. Reprint of the 1908 ed. Contents.Contents.—Morrison, Wm. Highland second-sight.—Martin's account of the second-sight.—Frazer of Tiree on the second-sight.—Some incidents from Theophilus Insulanus.—Aubrey's account.—Pepys' correspondence on the second-sight.—Boswell and Johnson's accounts.—A remarkable instance of second-sight.—Some modern instances.—Prophecies: Dr. Kennedy's instances.—The Petty seer.—The Brahan seer. [BF1325.M17 1972] 72-7291
1. Second sight. 2. Prophecies (Occult sciences) I. Title.

†MACRAE, Norman, ed. 133.3'2
Highland second-sight : with prophecies of Coinneach Odhar and the Seer of Petty and numerous other examples from the writings of Aubrey, Martin, Theophilus Insulanus, the Rev. John Fraser, Dean of Argyle and the Isles, Rev. Dr. Kennedy of Dingwall, and others / edited by Norman Macrae ; introductory study by Wm. Morrison. Folcroft, Pa. : Folcroft Library Editions, 1977. p. cm. Reprint of the 1908 ed. published by G. Souter, Dingwall, Scot. [BF1325.M17 1977] 77-19117 ISBN 0-8414-2305-9 lib. bdg. : 20.00
1. Second sight. 2. Prophecies (Occult sciences) I. Title.

OSBORN, Arthur Walter, 1891- 133.8'6
The future is now; the significance of precognition, by Arthur W. Osborn. Wheaton, Ill., Theosophical Pub. House [1967, c1961] 254 p. 20 cm. (A Quest book) [BF1325.O7] 67-5395
1. Second sight. 2. Dreams. I. Title.

OSBORN, Arthur Walter, 1891- 133.8
The future is now; the significance of

precognition. New Hyde Park, N.Y., University Books [1962, c1961] 254 p. 24 cm. [BF1325.O7 1962] 61-9321
1. Second sight. 2. Dreams. I. Title.

SPENCE, Lewis, 1874- 133.322
Second sight, its history and origins. London, New York, Rider [1951] 190 p. 24 cm. Full name: James Lewis Thomas Chalmers Spence. [BF1325.S6] 52-18155
1. Second sight. I. Title.

Secoya Indians—Missions.

STEVEN, Hugh. 266'.0092'4 B
Never touch a tiger / by Hugh Steven. Nashville : T. Nelson, c1980. 156 p. ; 20 cm. [F3722.1.S43J637] 80-18225 ISBN 0-8407-5737-9 pbk. : 4.95
1. Johnson, Mary, 1927- 2. Wycliffe Bible Translators. 3. Secoya Indians—Missions. 4. Indians of Mexico—Missions. 5. Missionaries—Mexico—Biography. 6. Missionaries—Ecuador—Biography. 7. Indians of South America—Ecuador—Missions. I. Title.

Secrecy in rabbinical literature.

WEWERS, Gerd A. 301.15
Geheimnis und Geheimhaltung im rabbinischen Judentum / von Gerd A. Wewers. Berlin ; New York : de Gruyter, 1975. xiv, 394 p. ; 23 cm. (Religionsgeschichtliche Versuche und Vorarbeiten ; Bd. 35) Originally presented as the author's thesis, Gottingen, 1974. Bibliography: p. 385-394. [BL25.R37 Bd. 35] [BM496.5] 296.1'08 75-513774 ISBN 3-11-005858-8 : DM68.00
1. Secrecy in rabbinical literature. I. Title. II. Series.

Secret Gospel according to Mark.

SMITH, Morton, 1915- 229'.8
Clement of Alexandria and a secret Gospel of Mark. Cambridge, Mass., Harvard University Press, 1973. x, 452 p. illus. 25 cm. English, Greek, or Latin. Bibliography: p. 423-444. [BS2860.S42S53] 72-148938 ISBN 0-674-13490-7
1. Clemens, Titus Flavius, Alexandrinus. 2. Secret Gospel according to Mark. I. Title.

SMITH, Morton, 1915- 229'.8
The Secret Gospel; the discovery and interpretation of the Secret Gospel according to Mark. [1st ed.] New York, Harper & Row [1973] ix, 148 p. illus. 22 cm. [BS2860.S42S55 1973] 72-11363 ISBN 0-06-067411-3 5.95
1. Secret Gospel according to Mark. I. Title.

Secret Gospel according to Mark—Congresses.

FULLER, Reginald Horace. 226'.3'06
Longer Mark : forgery, interpolation, or old tradition? / Reginald Horace Fuller ; W. Wuellner, editor. Berkeley, Calif. : Center for Hermeneutical Studies, 1975. p. cm. (Protocol of the eighteenth colloquy) Bibliography: p. [BS2585.2.F84] 76-12558 ISBN 0-89242-017-0 : 2.00
1. Bible. N.T. Mark—Criticism, interpretation, etc.—Congresses. 2. Secret Gospel according to Mark—Congresses. I. Title. II. Series: Center for Hermeneutical Studies. Protocol series of the colloquies ; 18.

Secret societies.

CHRISTIAN convention, Aurora, Ill., 1867.
Minutes of the Christian convention, held at Aurora, Illinois, Oct. 31st and Nov. 1, 1867. Containing the proceedings & resolutions of the Convention [respecting freemasonry] ...2d. ed., rev. Chicago, E. A. Cook, 1868. 3 p. l., [5]-108 p. 18 cm. [HS186.C55] 9-18406
1. Secret societies. 2. Freemasons. I. Title.

INQUIRE Within.
Light-bearers of darkness, by Inquire Within [pseud.] Houston, Trumpet Press [1963] 207 p. 22 cm. 68-48110
1. Secret societies. 2. Occult sciences. I. Title.

PHELPS, John Wolcott, 1813-1885.
Secret societies, ancient and modern. An outline of their rise, progress, andcharacter with respect to the Christian religion and republican government. Ed. by Gen'l J. W. Phelps ... Chicago, Ill., E. A. Cook & co., 1873. xii, [13]-240 p. 19 cm. [HS191.P53] 9-9747
1. Secret societies. I. Title.

Secret societies—Africa, West.

COLE, J Augustus.
A revelation of the secret orders of Western Africa. Including an explanation of the beliefs and customs of African heathenism. By J. Augustus Cole... Dayton, O., United brethren publishing house, 1886. 99 p. 19 cm. [HS319.C65] 9-11127
1. Secret societies—Africa, West. 2. Africa—Religion. I. Title.

Secret societies— United States

ACKER, Julius William. 284.177
Strange altars; a scriptural appraisal of the lodge. Saint Louis, Concordia Pub. House [1959] 94p. 19cm. Includes bibliography. [HS164.A3] 59-2478
1. Secret societies— U. S. I. Title.

Sects.

ALGERMISSEN, Konrad, 1889- 280
Christian sects. Tr. from German by J. R. Foster. New York, Hawthorn [c.1962] 128p. 21cm. (Twentieth cent. encyclopedia of Catholicism, v.139. Sect. 14: Outside the church) Bibl. 62-12932 3.50 bds.,
1. Sects. I. Title.

ALGERMISSEN, Konrad 1889- 280
Christian seets, Translat*d from the German by J. R. Foster, [1st ed.] New York, Hawthron Books [1962] 128p. 24cmcm. (The Twentieth century encyclopedia of Catholicism, v. 139. Section 11: Outside the church) Translation of Das Sektenwesen der Gegenwart. Includes bibliography. [BR157.A473] 62-12932
1. Sects. I. Title.

ANSON, Peter Frederick, 1889- 280
Bishops at large, by Peter F. Anson. With an introd. by Henry St. John. New York, October House [1965, c1964] 593 p. illus., ports. 23 cm. Bibliography: p. 545-572. [BR157.A56] 65-11510
1. Sects. I. Title.

[BRANAGAN, Thomas, b.1774. 280
A concise view, of the principal religious denominations, in the United States of America, comprehending a general account of their doctrines, ceremonies, and modes of worship ... With notes political and philosophical; adapted to the capacities and principles of the youth as well as the adults of the American republic. Philadelphia: Printed by John Cline, Fourth near Arch street, 1811. viii, [9]-324 p. front. 15 cm. Signed at end. [BR157.B7] 6-30309
1. Sects. 2. Sects—U. S. 3. Religions. 4. Toleration. I. Title.

BURRELL, Maurice Claude. 289
Whom then can we believe? / by J. Stafford Wright and Maurice C. Burrell. Chicago : Moody Press, 1976. p. cm. London ed., with authors' names in reverse order, published in 1973 under title: Some modern faiths. Includes bibliographical references. [BR157.B84 1976] 75-34304 ISBN 0-8024-9502-8 : 0.95
1. Sects. I. Wright, John Stafford, joint author. II. Title.

EVANS, Christopher Riche. 133'.06
Cults of unreason [by] Christopher Evans. [1st American ed.] New York, Farrar, Straus and Giroux [1974, c1973] 257 p. 22 cm. [BF1999.E83 1974] 73-87694 ISBN 0-374-13324-7 7.95
1. Sects. I. Title.

EVANS, Christopher Riche 133.06
Cults of unreason [by] Dr. Christopher Evans. [New York, Dell, 1975, c1974] 252 p. 20 cm. (A Delta book) [BF1999.E83 1975] 2.75 (pbk.)
1. Sects. I. Title.
L.C. card number for original ed.: 73-87694

HALL, Angus. 200'.9
Strange cults / by Angus Hall. Garden City, N.Y. : Doubleday, 1976. 144 p. : ill. ; 27 cm. (A New library of the supernatural) [BP603.H34] 76-5344 ISBN 0-385-11324-2 : 8.95
1. Sects. I. Title. II. Series.

[HARDY, Henry] 280
Nazareth against Nice, or, An impartial review of the existing church, their creeds and principles, from the standpoint of the written word of God. By Iconoclast [psued.]... Washington, D.C. [T. McGill & co., printers] 1887. 212 p., 1 l. 24 cm. [BR157.H25] 32-15466
1. Sects. 2. Trinity. 3. Reformation. I. Title.

HARPER, Marvin Henry, 1901- 294
Gurus, swamis, and avataras: spiritual masters and their American disciples. Philadelphia, Westminster Press [1972] 271 p. 22 cm. Bibliography: p. [251]-266. [BP603.H37] 76-175547 ISBN 0-664-20927-0 7.50
1. Sects. 2. Religions. I. Title.

HAYWARD, John, 1781-1862. 280
The book of religions; comprising the veiws, creeds, sentiments, or opinions, of all the principal religious sects in the world, particularly of all Christian denominations in Europe and America, to which are added church and missionary statistics, together with biographical sketches. By John Hayward ... Boston, J. Hayward, 1842. 432 p. 20 cm. [BR157.H3 1842] 24-9306
1. Sects. 2. Religions. 3. Christian biography. I. Title.

HAYWARD, John, 1781-1862. 280
The book of religions; comprising the views, creeds, sentiments, or opinions, of all the principal religious sects in the world, particularly of all Christian denominations in Europe and America, to which are added church and missionary statistics, together with biographical sketches. By John Hayward ... [3d. ed.] Boston, J. Hayward, 1843. 432 p. 19 cm. [BR157.H3 1843] 24-9307
1. Sects. 2. Religions. 3. Christian biography. I. Title.

HAYWARD, John, 1781-1862. 280
The book of religions; comprising the views, creeds, sentiments, or opinions, of all the principal religious sects in the world, particularly of all Christian denominations in Europe and America; to which are added, church and missionary statistics, together with biographical sketches. By John Hayward ... Boston, Sanborn, Carter, Bazin and company, 1857. 432 p. 19 1/2 cm. [BR157.H3 1857] 33-33638
1. Sects. 2. Religions. 3. Christian biography. I. Title.

HAYWARD, John, 1781-1862. 280
The book of religions; comprising the views, creeds, sentiments, or opinions, of all the principal religious sects in the world particularly of all Christian denominations in Europe and America: to which are added church and missionary statistics, together with biographical sketches. By John Hayward ... Boston, Sanborn, Bazin and Ellsworth, 1858. 432 p. 19 1/2 cm. [BR157.H3 1858] 24-11622
1. Sects. 2. Religions. 3. Christian biography. I. Title.

HAYWARD, John, 1781-1862. 280.973
The religious creeds and statistics of every Christian denomination in the United States and British provinces. With some account of the religious sentiments of the Jews, American Indians, Deists, Mahometans, &c., alphabeticayly arranged. By John Hayward. Boston, J. Hayward, 1836. 156 p. 18 1/2 cm. [BR515.H4] 33-38337
1. Sects. 2. Sects—U.S. 3. Church statistics—U.S. I. Title.

HEATH, Carl, 1869- 273
Social and religious heretics in five centuries. With a new introd. for the Garland ed. by Sylvia Strauss. New York, Garland Pub., 1972. 12, 158 p. 22 cm. (The Garland library of war and peace) Reprint of the 1936 ed. [BR157.H4 1972] 78-147622 ISBN 0-8240-0397-7
1. Sects. 2. Heresies and heretics. I. Title. II. Series.

HOWELLS, Rulon S. 280.973
A compilation of Christian beliefs, by Rulon S. Howells. Salt Lake City, Utah, The Deseret book company, 1932. 164 p. fold. tab. 20 cm. Lettered on cover: Do men believe what their church prescribes? Bibliography: p. 12-14 [BR157.H6] 32-16414
1. Sects. 2. Sects—U.S. I. Title. II. Title: Christian beliefs.

HOWELLS, Rulon Stanley, 1902- 280
His many mansions; a compilation of Christian beliefs, by Rulon S. Howells. With a comparative chart of ten Christian denominations on twenty-three important doctrinal questions. Illustrated with diagrams of the intricate and interesting organizations of the leading Christian churches which have been condensed into an authoritative and understandable form. New York, World Pub. [1972, c1967] 225 p. illus. 22 cm. Includes bibliographical references. [BR157.H62 1972] 76-159843 5.95
1. Sects. 2. Sects—United States. 3. Creeds—Comparative studies. I. Title.

HOWELLS, Rulon Stanley, 1902- 280
His many mansions; a compilation of Christian beliefs, illustrated with diagrams of the intricate and interesting organizations of the leading Christian churches which have here been condensed for the first time into an authoritative and understandable form. By Rulon S. Howells. New York, The Greystone press, 1940. vi p., 2 l., 7-252 p. fold. tab. (in pocket) diagrs. 20 1/2 cm. "Special references": p. 246-247. [BR157.H62] 40-32058
1. Sects. 2. Sects—U.S. 3. Creeds—Comparative studies. I. Title. II. Title: Christian beliefs.

IRVINE, William C., comp. 280
Heresies exposed; a brief critical examination in the light of the Holy Scriptures of some of the prevailing heresies and false teachings of today. New York, Loizeaux Bros. [1953] 225p. 20cm. First ed. published in 1917 under title: Timely warnings. [BR157.I7 1953] 54-36212
1. Sects. 2. Heresies and heretics. I. Title.

KELLETT, Arnold. 203
Isms and ologies; a guide to unorthodox and non -- Christian beliefs. New York, Philosophical Library [1965] 156 p. 19 cm. Bibliography: p. 149-156. [(BR157)] 65-28943
1. Sects. I. Title.

KRULL, Vigilius Herman, 1874- 280
Christian denominations, by Rev. Vigilius H. Krull, c. p.p. s. 13th ed. (thirty-five thousand) Cleveland, O., Columbus, O., J. W. Winterich [c1925] 240 p. 19 cm. [BR157.K7 1925] 25-13080
1. Sects. 2. Catholic church—Doctrinal and controversial works—Catholic authors. I. Title.

KRULL, Vigilius Herman, 1874- 280
Christian denominations, by Rev. Vigilius H. Krull ... 14th ed. Chicago, Ill., M. A. Donohue & co., [c1936] x, 248 p. 19 cm. [BR157.K7 1936] 36-11488
1. Sects. 2. Catholic church—Doctrinal and controversial works—Catholic authors. I. Title.

KRULL, Vigilius Herman, 1874- 280
Christian denominations; or, A brief exposition of the history and the teachings of Christian denominations found in English-speaking countries. By Father Vigilius H. Krull ... Collegeville, Ind., St. Joseph's printing office, 1911. 2 p. l., 7-224, [7] p. 19 cm. [BR157.K7] 11-27927
1. Sects. I. Title.

LEHRBURGER, Egon, 1904- 280
Strange sects and cults: a study of their origins and influence [by] Egon Larsen. New York, Hart Pub. Co. [1972, c1971] 245 p. 21 cm. Bibliography: p. 231-232. [BR157.L44 1972] 79-189636 ISBN 0-8055-1044-3 5.95

1. Sects. I. Title.

LYON, William Henry, 1846- 1915. 280
A study of the Christian sects, with an introductory chapter on the Jews, by William H. Lyon ... 13th ed., rev. and enl. by John Malick. Boston, The Beacon press, inc., 1926. vii, 257 p. 19 1/2 cm. "References": p. 235-252. [BR157.L8 1926] 26-6193
1. Sects. 2. Jews. I. Malick, John, ed. II. Title.

LYON, William Henry, 1846- 1915. 280
A study of the sects. By William H. Lyon ... Boston, Unitarian Sunday-school society, 1891. v p., 1 l., 190 p. 18 1/2 cm. Contains "References". [BR157.L8 1891] 26-6192
1. Sects. 2. Jews. I. Title.

LYON, William Henry, 1846- 1915. 280
A study of the sects. By William H. Lyon ... 6th ed. With an index. Boston, Unitarian Sunday-school society, 1895. v p., 1 l., 207 p. 18 1/2 cm. Includes "References". [BR157.L8 1895] 32-34054
1. Sects. 2. Jews. I. Title.

MANWELL, Reginald Dickinson, 1897- 280
The church across the street; an introduction to the ways and beliefs of fifteen different faiths, by Reginald D. Manwell, Sophia Lyon Fahs. Rev. ed. Boston, Beacon [1963, c.1962] 318p. illus. 22cm. Bibl. 62-13635 3.95
1. Sects. I. Fahs, Sophia Blanche (Lyon) 1876- joint author. II. Title.

MANWELL, Reginald Dickinson, 1897- 280
The church across the street, by Reginald D. Manwell and Sophia Lyon Fahs. Boston, The Beacon press, 1946. xiii, 258 p. col. illus. (incl. ports.) 24 cm. Errata slip mounted on lining-paper. Bibliography: p. 257-258. [BR157.M33] 47-1165
1. Sects. I. Fahs, Sophia Blanche (Lyon) 1876- joint author. II. Title.

MANWELL, Reginald Dickinson, 1897- 280
The church across the street, by Reginald D. Manwell and Sophia Lyon Fahs. Boston, Beacon Press, 1947. xiii, 258 p. illus., ports. 24 cm. Bibliography: p. 257-258. [BR157.M33 1947] 47-4121
1. Sects. I. Fahs, Sophia Blanche (Lyon) 1876- joint author. II. Title.

MOLLAND, Einar 280
Christendom; the Christian churches, their doctrines, constitutional forms, and ways of worship. [Translated from the Norwegian] New York, Philosophical Library [1959] xiv, 418p. 23cm. (16p.bibl.) 59-65285 10.00
1. Sects. I. Title.

MURRAY, Robert Henry, 1874- 1947. 270
Group movements throughout the ages. Freeport, N.Y., Books for Libraries Press [1972] 377 p. illus. 23 cm. (Essay index reprint series) Reprint of the 1935 ed. Contents.Contents.—The Montanists; or, The priest versus the prophet.—The Franciscans; or, The realisation of the ideal.—The Friends of God; or, The quest of the ideal under difficulties.—Port Royal; or, The group in miniature.—The Methodists; with a reference to the Evangelicals.—The Oxford group movement; with a reference to the Tractarians. Includes bibliographies. [BV4487.O9M87 1972] 72-301 ISBN 0-8369-2810-5
1. Oxford Group. 2. Sects. 3. Revivals—History. I. Title.

PETTEE, Julia, 1872-
List of churches; official forms of the names for denominational bodies with brief descriptive and historical notes. Chicago, American Library Assn., 1948. 569-653 p. 28 cm. "Reprinted from Julia Pettee's List of theological subject headings and corporate church names based upon the headings in the catalogue of the Union Theological Seminary, New York City, copyrighted 1947." A 48
1. Sects. 2. Sects—U.S. I. New York. Union Theological Seminary. Library. II. Title.

PHELAN, Macum, 1874- 280
Handbook of all denominations, containing an account of their origin and history: a statement of their faith and usages; together with the latest statistics on their activities, location, and strength, nineteen fifteen, prepared by M. Phelan. Nashville, Tenn., Dallas, Tex. [etc.] Publishing house of the M. E. church, South, Smith & Lamar, agents, 1915. 191 p. 20 cm. [BR157.P5] 15-24927 0.75
1. Sects. I. Title.

PHELAN, Macum, 1874- 280
Handbook of all denominations. Rev. ed., nineteen twenty-four, prepared by M. Phelan. 3d ed. Nashville, Tenn., Cokesbury press, 1924. viii, 186 p. 20 cm. [BR157.P5 1924] 24-29781
1. Sects. I. Title.

PHELAN, Macum, 1874- 280
Handbook of all denominations, compiled by M. Phelan 4th ed. Nashville, Tenn., Cokesbury press, 1927. viii, 215 p. 20 cm. [BR157.P5 1927] 27-8575
1. Sects. I. Title.

PHELAN, Macum, 1874- 280
Handbook of all denominations. compiled by M. Phelan. 5th ed. Nashville, Tenn., Cokesbury press, 1929. viii, 231 p. 19 1/2 cm. [BR157.P5 1929] 29-8854
1. Sects. I. Title.

PHELAN, Macum, 1874- 280.973
New handbook of all denominations; rewritten and completely revised, compiled by M. Phelan. 6th ed. Nashville, Tenn., Cokesbury press, 1930. 314 p. 19 cm. [BR157.P5 1930] 30-29294
1. Sects. I. Title.

PHELAN, Macum, 1874- 280.973
New handbook of all denominations, compiled by M. Phelan. 7th revision. Nashville, Tenn., Cokesbury press [c1933] 327 p. 20 cm. Bibliography: p. 323-327. [BR157.P5 1933] 33-4366
1. Sects. I. Title.

THE Pitts-street chapel lectures. 280
Delivered in Boston by clergymen of six different denominations, during the winter of 1858... Boston, J. P. Jewett and company; Cleveland, O., H. P. B. Jewett, 1858. vi, 7-366 p. 20 1/2 cm. [BR157.P65 1858] 38-20545
1. Sects.
Contents omitted.

[PUTNAM, Ellen Tryphosa Harrington] 280
Where in the city? Boston, Roberts brothers, 1868. ix, 349 p. 18 cm. Narrative of a young man's experience in search of the true church. [BR157.P8 1868] 45-42984
1. Sects. I. Title.

[PUTNAM, Ellen Tryphosa Harrington] 280
Where is the city? 2d ed. Boston, Roberts brothers, 1868. ix, 349 p. 18 cm. Narrative of a young man's experience in search of true church. [BR157.P8 1868a] 45-43042
1. Sects. I. Title.

RHODES, Arnold Black, ed. 280
The church faces the isms [by] the members of the faculty of the Louisville Presbyterian Theological Seminary, Louisville, Kentucky. Assoc. eds.: Frank H. Caldwell, L. C. Rudolph. Nashville, Abingdon [1964, c.1958] 304p. 23cm. (Apex bks., R4) Bibl. 2.25 pap.,
1. Sects. I. Louisville Preyterian Theological Seminary (1901-) II. Title.

RHODES, Arnold Black, ed. 280
The church faces the isms [by] the members of the faculty of the Louisville Presbyterian Theological Seminary, Louisville, Kentucky. Arnold Black Rhodes, editor. Associate editors: Frank H. Caldwell and L.C. Rudolph. New York, Abingdon Press [1958] 304p. 24cm. Includes bibliographies. [BR157.R48] 58-5392
1. Sects. I. Louisville Presbyterian Theological Seminary (1901-) II. Title.

ROBERTSON, Irvine 289
What the cults believe. Chicago, Moody [c.1966] 128p. 22cm. Bibl. [BR157.R58] 66-16223 2.95
1. Sects. I. Title.

ROUTH, Eugene Coke, 1874- 280
Who are they? Shawnee, Printed by O[klahoma] B[aptist] U[niversity] Press [1951] 71 p. 18 cm. [BR157.R6] 51-3097
1. Sects. 2. Baptists — Doctrinal and controversial works. I. Title.

SANDERS, John Oswald, 1902- 280
Cults and isms ancient and modern. [8th] rev., enl. [ed.] Grand Rapids, Mich., Zondervan [1963, c.1948] 167p. 21cm. Firt ed. pub. in 1948 under title: Heresies ancient and modern. Bibl. 63-17746 2.50
1. Sects. I. Title.

SOME modern religions,
by J. Oswald Sanders [and] J. Stafford Wright. [1st ed.] Chicago, Inter-varsity press [1956] 61p. 19cm. (Foundations for faith)
1. Sects. I. Sanders, J Oswald. II. Wright, John Stafford, joint author. III. Inter-varsity Christian Fellowship of the United States of America. IV. Series.

SPERRY, Willard Learoyd, 1882- ed.
Religion and our divided denominations; one of a series of volumes on religion in the post-war world, edited by Dean Willard L. Sperry. By Williard L. Sperry, John LaFarge, S.J., John T. McNeil [and others] ... Cambridge, Harvard university press, 1945. ix, 115 p. 19 cm. (Half-title: Religion in the post-war world, ed. by W. L. Sperry. Vol. I) A 45
1. Sects. 2. U.S.—Religion. I. Title.
Contents omitted

SPERRY, Willard Learoyd, 1882-1954, ed. 280
Religion and our divided denominations. By Willard L. Sperry [and others] Freeport, N.Y., Books for Libraries Press [1971, c1945] ix, 115 p. 23 cm. (Essay index reprint series) "Originally published as v. 1. of [the editor's] Religion in the post-war world." Contents.Contents.—Our present disunity, by W. L. Sperry.—Roman Catholicism, by J. LaFarge.—Protestantism, by J. T. McNeill.—Judaism, by L. Finkelstein.—Humanism, by A. MacLeish. Includes bibliographical references. [BR516.S76 1971] 74-128315 ISBN 0-8369-2201-8
1. Sects. 2. U.S.—Religion—1901-1945. I. Title.

STUBER, Stanley Irvin, 1903- 280
How we got our denominations; a primer on church history. [Rev. ed.] New York, Association Press [1959] 254 p. 20 cm. Includes bibliography. [BR157.S77 1959] 59-12104
1. Sects. 2. Church history. I. Title.

STUBER, Stanley Irving, 1903- 280
Denominations -- how we got them. New York, Association Press [1958] 127 p. 16 cm. (An Association Press reflection book) "Condensed and revised from How we got our denominations." Includes bibliography. [BR157.S775] 58-6474
1. Sects. 2. Church history. I. Title.

STUBER, Stanley Irving, 1903- 270
How we got our denominations; a primer on church history, by Stanley I. Stuber, [Rev. ed.] New York, Association Press [1965] 254 p. 20 cm. Bibliography: p. 251-254. [BR157.S77] 65-23134
1. Sects. 2. Church history. I. Title.

STUBER, Stanley Irving, 1903- 280
How we got our denominations, a primer on church history. New York, Association Press, 1948. 224 p. 20 cm. [BR157.S77 1948] 48-7141
1. Sects. 2. Church history. I. Title.

STUBER, Stanley Irving, 1903- 280
How we got our denominations; an outline of church history, by Stanley I. Stuber. New York, Association press, 1927. xiv, 225 p. 19 1/2 cm. "Reference list": p. 219-221. [BR157.S77] 27-11602
1. Sects. 2. Church history. I. Title.

SUMMERBELL, Martyn, 1847- 280
Our friends in other folds; an excursion in amity, by Martyn Summerbell ... Boston, The Christopher publishing house [c1929] 133 p. 21 cm. [BR157.S9] 29-21684
1. Sects. I. Title.

TANIS, Edward J 280
What the sects teach; Jehovah's Witnesses, Seventh- Day Adventists, Christian Science [and] Spiritism. Grand Rapids, Baker Book House, 1958. 89 p. 22 cm. [BR157.T2] 59-184
1. Sects. I. Title.

TWELVE modern apostles and their creeds, 280'.0922
by Gilbert K. Chesterton [and others] With an introd. by William Ralph Inge. Freeport, N.Y., Books for Libraries Press [1968] 209 p. 22 cm. (Essay index reprint series) Reprint of 1926 ed. Contents.Contents.—The future of Christianity, by W. R. Inge.—Why I am a Catholic, by G. K. Chesterton.—Why I am an Episcopalian, by C. L. Slattery.—Why I am a Presbyterian, by H. S. Coffin.—Why I am a Lutheran, by N. Soderblom.—Why I am a Baptist, by E. Y. Mullins.—Why I am a Quaker, by R. M. Jones.—Why I am a Methodist, by F. M. North.—Why I am a Congregationalist, by C. E. Jefferson.—Why I am a Unitarian, by S. M. Crothers.—Why I am a Mormon, by R. Smoot.—Why I am a Christian Scientist, by C. Smith.—Why I am an unbeliever, by C. Van Doren. [BR157.T8 1968] 68-16982
1. Sects. I. Chesterton, Gilbert Keith, 1874-1936. II. Inge, William Ralph, 1860-1954. III. Title: Modern apostles and their creeds.

TWELVE modern apostles and their creeds, 280
by Gilbert K. Chesterton, Bishop Charles L. Slattery, Dr. Henry Sloane Coffin, and others, with an introduction by the Rt. Rev. William Ralph Inge. New York, Duffield and company, 1926. 5 p. l., 3-209 p. 21 cm. [BR157.T8] 26-24172
1. Sects. I. Chesterton, Gilbert Keith, 1874-1936. II. Inge, William Ralph, 1860- III. Title: Modern apostles and their creeds.
Contents omitted.

VAN BAALEN, Jay Karel, 1890- 280
Christianity versus the cults. Grand Rapids, Eerdmans [1958] 136 p. 22 cm. [BR157.V3] 58-9530
1. Sects. I. Title.

VIGEVENO, H. S. 291
The listener, by H. S. Vigeveno. Glendale, Calif., G/L Regal Books [1971] 153 p. 18 cm. [BR157.V5] 73-123872 ISBN 0-8307-0084-6 0.95
1. Sects. 2. Religions. 3. Atheism. I. Title.

WESTIN, Gunnar, 1890- 280
The free church through the ages. Translated from the Swedish by Virgil A. Olson. Nashville, Broadman Press [1958] 380 p. 22 cm. [BR157.W352] 58-8926
1. Sects. I. Title.

WILSON, Bryan R. 301.5'8
Religious sects; a sociological study [by] Bryan Wilson. New York, McGraw-Hill [1970] 256 p. illus., maps, ports. 19 cm. (World university library) Bibliography: p. 245-251. [BR157.W54 1970] 68-13141 2.45
1. Sects. I. Title.

WYATT, Clair L. 289.3'73
" ... some that trouble you ..."; subcultures in Mormonism [by] Clair L. Wyatt. Salt Lake City, Bookcraft [1974] x, 92 p. 24 cm. Includes bibliographical references. [BX8635.5.W9] 74-75167 ISBN 0-88494-209-0 2.95
1. Church of Jesus Christ of Latter-Day Saints—Apologetic works. 2. Sects. I. Title.

WYRICK, Herbert McNultie, 1893- 289
Seven religious isms; an historical and Scriptural review, by Herbert M. Wyrick ... Grand Rapids, Mich., Zondervan publishing house [c1940] 99 p. 19 1/2 cm. [BR157.W85] 40-35709
1. Sects. I. Title.

Sects—Addresses, essays, lectures.

SECTARIANISM : 301.18'31
analyses of religious and non-religious sects / edited by Roy Wallis. New York : Wiley, 1975. 212 p. ; 23 cm. (Contemporary issues series ; 10) "A Halsted Press book."

Includes bibliographical references. [BP603.S4 1975] 75-9715 ISBN 0-470-91910-8 : 13.95
1. Sects—Addresses, essays, lectures. I. Wallis, Roy.

Sects—Australia.

VAN SOMMERS, Tess 280.0994
Religions in Australia; the Pix series extended to 41 beliefs. Adelaide, Rigby [San Francisco, Tri-Ocean, c.1966] 248p. illus. 25cm. Articles orig. pub. in Pix. [BR1480.V3] 65-19137 6.45 bds.,
1. Sects—Australia. I. Title.

Sects—Burundi.

HOHENSEE, Donald, 1939- 280'.0967'572
Church growth in Burundi / by Donald Hohensee. South Pasadena, Calif. : William Carey Library, c1977. vi, 153 p. : ill. ; 22 cm. Includes index. Bibliography: p. [145]-151. [BR1443.B86H64] 76-54342 ISBN 0-87808-316-2 pbk. : 4.95
1. Sects—Burundi. 2. Church growth—Burundi. I. Title.

Sects—Controversial literature.

BREESE, Dave W. 289
Know the marks of cults / Dave Breese. Wheaton, Ill. : Victor Books, [1975] 128 p. ; 18 cm. (An Input book) [BR157.B73] 75-21907 ISBN 0-88207-704-X pbk. : 1.50
1. Sects—Controversial literature. I. Title.

FILLMORE, Lowell. 289.9
Things to be remembered. Lee's Summit, Mo., Unity School of Christianity, 1952. 186p. 17cm. [BX9890.U5F547] 55-44649
1. Unity School of Christianity—Doctrinal and controversial works. II. Title.

PATRICK, Ted. 200'.1'9 B
Let our children go! / By Ted Patrick, with Tom Dulack. 1st ed. New York : Dutton, 1976. 285 p. : ill. ; 22 cm. "Thomas Congdon books." [BP603.P37 1976] 75-45298 ISBN 0-525-14450-1 : 7.95
1. Patrick, Ted. 2. Sects—Controversial literature. 3. Youth—Religious life. I. Dulack, Tom, 1935- joint author. II. Title.

PATRICK, Ted. 200'.1'9
Let our children go! / by Ted Patrick, with Tom Dulack. New York : Ballantine Books, 1977c1976. vii, 176p. : ill. ; 18 cm. [BP603.P37 1976] ISBN 0-345-25663-8 pbk. : 1.95
1. Patrick, Ted. 2. Sects-Controversial literature. 3. Youth-Religious life. I. Dulack, Tom., joint author. II. Title.
L.C. card no. for 1976 E.P. Dutton ed.: 75-45298.

Sects—England.

SELBIE, William Boothby, 1862- 274.
English sects, a history of noncomformity, by W. B. Selbie ... New York, H. Holt and company. London, Williams and Norgate [1912] v, 7-256 p. 17 1/2 cm. (Half-title: Home university library of modern knowledge, no. 46) Bibliography: p. 252-268. [BR755.S4] 12-15245
1. Sects—England. I. Title.

SELBIE, William Boothby, 1862-
English sects, a history of nonconformity, by W. B. Selbie... New York, H. Holt and company; [etc., etc., 1912] v, 7-256 p. 17 1/2 cm. (Half-title: Home university library of modern knowledge, no. 46) Bibliography: p. 252-253. 12-15245
I. Title.

Sects—France.

CHARLTON, Donald Geoffrey 209.44
Secular religions in France, 1815-1870. New York, Pub. for the Univ. of Hull v)by Oxford [c.1963] 249p. 23cm. (Univ. of Hull pubns.) Bibl. 63-5127 5.60
1. Sects—France. 2. France—Religion. 3. Philosophy, French. I. Title.

CHARLTON, Donald Geoffrey. 209.44
Secular religions in France, 1815-1870. London, New York, Published for the University of Hull by the Oxford University Press, 1963. 249 p. 23 cm. (University of Hull publications) [BR843.C48 1963] 63-5127
1. Sects — France. 2. France — Religion. 3. Philosophy, French. I. Title.

Sects—Great Britain

BENSON, Robert Hugh, 1871-1914. 274.2
Non-Catholic denominations, by the Rev. Robert Hugh Benson, M. A. New impression. London, New York [etc.] Longmans, Green and co., 1915. xv, 217 p. 20 cm. (Half-title: The Westminster library, a series of manuals for Catholic priests and student, ed. by the Right Rev. Mgr. Bernard Ward ... and the Rev. Herbert Thurston ...) [BR744.B4] 41-21844
1. Sects—Gt. Brit. 2. Catholic church—Doctrinal and controversial works—Catholic authors. I. Title.

Sects—History—Sources.

DURNBAUGH, Donald F., comp. 280'.4
Every need supplied : mutual aid and Christian community in the free churches, 1525-1675 / edited by Donald F. Durnbaugh. Philadelphia : Temple University Press, 1974. xiv, 258 p. : ill. ; 23 cm. (Documents in free church history) Includes documents translated from German and Dutch. Includes indexes. Bibliography: p. [235]-242. [BR157.D86] 73-94279 ISBN 0-87722-031-X : 15.00
1. Sects—History—Sources. 2. Church charities—History—Sources. I. Title. II. Series.

Sects—Ireland.

CARTY, Xavier. 274.15
The churches in Ireland; facts about: Church of Ireland, Presbyterians, Methodists, Jews, Society of Friends. [Dublin] Catholic Truth Society of Ireland [1968] 35 p. 18 cm. "These articles were first published in the Redemptorist record ... [Jan.-July 1966]" [BR793.C37] 70-281664
1. Sects—Ireland. I. Catholic Truth Society of Ireland. II. Title.

Sects—Japan.

OFFNER, Clark B. 299.56
Modern Japanese religions, with special emphasis upon their doctrines of healing [by] Clark B. Offner [and] Henry van Straelen. Leiden, E. J. Brill; New York, Twayne, 1963. 296 p. illus., ports. 21 cm. Bibliography: p. [283]-290. [BL2202.O3] 62-22211
1. Sects — Japan. 2. Japan — Religion. I. Straelen, Henricus van, 1903- joint author. II. Title.

OFFNER, Clark B. 299.56
Modern Japanese religlons, with special emphasis upon their doctrines of healing [by] Clark B. Offner, Henry van Straelen. Leiden, E. J. Brill; New York, Twayne, 1963. 296p. illus., ports. 21cm. Bibl. 62-22211 8.00
1. Sects—Japan. 2. Japan—Religion. I. Straelen, Henricus van, 1903- joint author. II. Title.

THOMSEN, Harry. 299.56
The new religions of Japan. [1st ed.] Rutland, Vt., C. E. Tuttle Co. [1963] 269 p. illus. 22 cm. Bibliography: p. 259-264. [BL2202.T5] 63-8715
1. Sects — Japan. 2. Japan — Religion. I. Title.

THOMSEN, Harry. 299'.56
The new religions of Japan / Harry Thomsen. Westport, Conn. : Greenwood Press, 1978, c1963. 269 p., [8] leaves of plates : ill. ; 23 cm. Reprint of the ed. published by C. E. Tuttle, Rutland, Vt. Includes index. Bibliography: p. 259-264. [BL2202.T5 1978] 77-13846 ISBN 0-8371-9878-X lib.bdg. : 19.75
1. Sects—Japan. 2. Japan—Religion. I. Title.

Sects, Medieval.

LEFF, Gordon. 273/.09/02
Heresy in the later Middle Ages: the relation of heterodoxy to dissent, c. 1250-c. 1450. Manchester, Manchester Univ. Pr.; New York, Barnes & Noble [1967] 2v. 25cm. Bibl. [BT1315.2.L4 1967] 67-113563 15.00 set,
1. Sects, Medieval. 2. Theology, Doctrinal—Hist.—Middle Ages. 3. Heresies and heretics. I. Title.

RUNCIMAN, Sir Steven, 1903-
The medieval Manichee, a study in Christian dualist heresy. Cambridge, University Press, 1960. x, 212 p. 23 cm. "First edition 1947; reprinted 1960." 63-57418
1. Sects, Medieval. 2. Manichaeism. 3. Dualism. I. Title.

RUNCIMAN, Steven, 1903- 273.2
The medieval Manichee, a study of the Christian dualist heresy. Cambridge [Eng.] Univ. Press, 1947. x, 212 p. 22 cm. Full name: James Cochran Stevenson Runciman. Bibliography: p. 180-199. [BR253.R8] 47-30740
1. Sects, Medieval. 2. Manichaesim. 3. Dualism. I. Title.

RUNCIMAN, Steven James Cochran Stevenson Runciman 1903- 273.2
The medieval Manichee; a study of the Christian dualist heresy. New York, Viking [1961] 212p. (Compass bk. C86) Bibl. 1.45 pap.,
1. Sects, Medieval. I. Title.

TURBERVILLE, Arthur Stanley, 1888-1945 270.5
Mediaeval heresy & the Inquisition. Hamden [Conn.] Archon [dist. Shoe String, 1964] vi, 264p. 22cm. Bibl. 64-11061 6.00
1. Sects, Medieval. 2. Heresy. 3. Inquisition. I. Title.

WAKEFIELD, Walter Leggett, comp. 273'.09'021
Heresies of the high Middle Ages. Selected sources translated and annotated by Walter L. Wakefield and Austin P. Evans. New York, Columbia University Press, 1969. xiv, 865 p. 24 cm. (Records of civilization: sources and studies, no. 81) Includes bibliographical references. [BT1315.2.W32] 68-28402 22.50
1. Sects, Medieval. I. Evans, Austin Patterson, joint comp. II. Title. III. Series.

Sects—North America.

PIEPKORN, Arthur Carl, 1907-1973. 200'.973
Profiles in belief : the religious bodies of the United States and Canada / by Arthur Carl Piepkorn. 1st ed. New York : Harper & Row, c1977- v. ; 24 cm. Contents.Contents.—v. 1. Roman Catholic, Old Catholic, Eastern Orthodox. Includes bibliographies and index. [BR510.P53 1977] 76-9971 ISBN 0-06-066580-7 : 15.95
1. Sects—North America. I. Title.

Sects—Nyasaland.

WISHLADE, R. L. 280.096897
Sectarianism in southern Nyasaland. New York, Pub. for the Intl. African Inst. by Oxford [c.]1965. 162p. illus., map. 23cm. Bibl. [BR1443.N9W5] 65-5669 5.20
1. Sects—Nyasaland. 2. Nyasaland—Church history. I. International African Institute. II. Title.

WISHLADE, R L 280.096897
Sectarianism in southern Nyassland [by] R. L. Wishlade. London, New York, Published for the International African Institute by the Oxford University Press, 1965. 162 p. illus., map. 28 cm. Bibliography: p. 157-159. [BR1443.N9W5] 65-5669
1. Sects — Nyassaland. 2. Nyassland — Church history. I. International African Institute. II. Title.

Sects—Religion.

BACKMAN, Milton Vaughn. 280'.0973
Christian churches of America : origins and beliefs / Milton V. Backman, Jr. Provo, Utah : Brigham Young University Press, [1976] xvii, 230 p. : ill. ; 23 cm. Includes index. Bibliography: p. 215-219. [BR516.5.B33] 75-30772 ISBN 0-8425-0028-6 : 11.95 ISBN 0-8425-0029-4 pbk. : 7.95
1. Sects—Religion. 2. United States—Religion. I. Title.

Sects—Russia.

CONYBEARE, Frederick Cornwallis, 1856-1924 281.947
Russian dissenters. New York, Russell & Russell, 1962 [c.1921] 370p. (Harvard theological studies, 10) Bibl. 61-13779 7.50
1. Sects—Russia. 2. Dissenters—Russia. I. Title.

CONYBEARE, Frederick Cornwallis, 1856-1924.
... Russian dissenters, by Frederick C. Conybeare ... Cambridge, Harvard university press; [etc., etc.] 1921. x, 370 p. 23 1/2 cm. (Harvard theological studies. x) "List of Russian periodicals cited": p. [vii] [BX599.C6] 21-16144
1. Sects, Russian. 2. Dissenters—Russia. I. Title.

Sects—Southern States.

HARRELL, David Edwin. 261.8'34'5196073
White sects and Black men in the recent South. Foreword by Edwin S. Gaustad. Nashville, Vanderbilt University Press, 1971. xix, 161 p. 21 cm. Bibliography: p. 135-152. [BR535.H37] 72-157742 ISBN 0-8265-1171-6 6.50
1. Sects—Southern States. 2. Church and race problems—Southern States. I. Title.

Sects—United States

BACH, Marcus. 289
They have found a faith, by Marcus Bach. Indianapolis, New York, The Bobbs-Merrill company [1946] 300 p. 22 cm. "First edition." [BR516.B27] 46-7535
1. Sects—U.S. I. Title.

BACH, Marcus, 1906- 289
They have found a faith. Freeport, N.Y., Books for Libraries Press [1971, c1946] 300 p. 23 cm. (Essay index reprint series) [BR516.5.B3 1971] 74-134049 ISBN 0-8369-2481-9
1. Sects—United States. I. Title.

BEAM, Maurice. 291.9
Cults of America. [New York, Macfadden-Bartell Corp., 1964] 127 p. 18 cm. [BR516.5B4] 64-5760
1. Sects — U.S. I. "A Macfadden original." II. Title.

BELCHER, Joseph, 1794-1859. 277.3
The religious denominations in the United States; their history, doctrine, government and statistics. With a preliminary sketch of Judaism, paganism and Mohammedanism. By Joseph Belcher ... Embellished with nearly two hundred engravings. Philadelphia, J. E. Potter, 1854. xii, 13-1024 p. incl. illus., plates, ports. front. 25 cm. [BR515.B5] 33-38332
1. Sects—U.S. 2. Sects. 3. Religions. I. Title.

BESTIC, Alan. 269'.2'0973
Praise the Lord and pass the contribution. New York, Taplinger Pub. Co. [1971] xii, 259 p. 22 cm. [BR516.2.B47 1971b] 77-155804 ISBN 0-8008-6460-3 6.50
1. Sects—U.S. 2. Evangelists—U.S. 3. Church finance—U.S. I. Title.

BISHOP, Charles Cager, 1898- 280.973
Churches, 253,762; their doctrines, history, government. Wellington? Tex., '1951. 84 p. 23 cm. [BR516.B5 1951] 51-4621
1. Sects—U. S. 2. U. S.—Religion. I. Title.

BODENSIECK, Julius, 1894- 280.973
Isms new and old, by Julius Bodensieck. Columbus, O., The Book concern [1938?] 111 p. 20 cm. "Books...consulted": p. 4-5. [BR516.B6] 40-9540
1. Sects—U.S. I. Title.
Contents omitted.

BRADEN, Charles Samuel, 1887- 280.973
These also believe; a study of modern American cults & minority religious movements. New York, Macmillan Co., 1949. xv. 491 p. 22 cm. [BR516.B697] 49-8917
1. Sects—U. S. I. Title.
Contents omitted.

BRADEN, Charles Samuel, 1887- ed. 277.3
Varieties of American religion; the goal of religion as interpreted by representative exponents of seventeen distinctive types of religious thought. Edited by Charles Samuel Braden. Freeport, N.Y., Books for Libraries Press [1971, c1936] viii, 294 p. 23 cm. (Essay index reprint series) Contents.Contents.—Fundamentalism, by W. B. Riley.—Orthodox protestantism, by W. H. Foulkes.—Liberal protestantism, by E. F. Tittle.—Radical protestantism, by E. S. Ames.—Sacramentarianism, by G. C. Stewart.—Barthianism, by E. G. Homrighausen.—Roman Catholicism, by F. J. Sheen.—Mormonism, by J. A. Widtsoe.—Unity, by C. Fillmore.—Christian Science, by A. F. Gilmore.—Ethical culture, by H. J. Bridges.—Humanism, by J. H. Dietrich.—Spiritualism, by M. A. Barwise.—Theosophy, by A. P. Warrington.—Orthodox Judaism, by L. Jung.—National Judaism, by S. Goldman.—Reform Judaism, by F. A. Levy. Includes bibliographical references. [BR516.5.B7 1971] 76-156616 ISBN 0-8369-2307-3
1. Sects—U.S. 2. U.S.—Religion—1901-1945. I. Title.

BRADEN, Charles Samuel, 1887- ed. 277.3
Varieties of American religion; the goal of religion as interpreted by representative exponents of seventeen distinctive types of religious thoughts. edited by Charles Samuel Braden ... Chicago, New York, Willett, Clark & company, 1936. viii p., 1 l., 294 p. 21 cm. [BR516.B7] 36-16482
1. Sects—U. S. 2. U. S.—Religion. I. Title.
Contents omitted.

BROWN, Charles Ewing, 1883- 277.3
Modern religious faiths, by Charles Ewing Brown... Anderson, Ind., Gospel trumpet co. [c1941] v p., 1 l., 9-199 p. 19 cm. [BR516.B73] 41-22554
1. Sects—U.S. 2. U.S.—Religion. I. Title.

CHRISTIANITY today. 261.2
The challenge of the cults; a Christianity today symposium, by Harold Lindsell [and others] Grand Rapids, Zondervan Pub. House [1961] 80p. 21cm. 'Most of the articles ... first appeared in the Dec. 19, 1960 issue of Christianity today.' Includes bibliography. [BR516.5.C45] 61-42475
1. Sects—U. S. I. Lindsell, Harold, 1913- II. Title.

CHRISTIANITY today. Symposium 289
The challenge of the cults; a Christianity Today symposium, by Harold Lindsell [others] Grand Rapids, Zondervan [c.1961] 80p. Bibl. 61-42475 1.00 pap.,
1. Sects—U. S. I. Lindsell, Harold, 1913-

CLARK, Elmer Talmage, 1886- 280.973
The small sects in America. Rev. ed. [Gloucester, Mass., P. Smith 1964, c.1937, 1949] 256p. 22cm. (Abingdon bk. rebound) Bibl. 3.25
1. Sects—U.S. 2. U.S.—Religion. I. Title.

CLARK, Elmer Talmage, 1886-
The small sects in America. Rev. ed. New York, Abingdon Press [1957? c1949] 256 p. 22 cm. (Apex books) Includes bibliography 68-32270
1. Sects—U.S. 2. U.S.—Religion. I. Title.

CLARK, Elmer Talmage, 1886- 280.973
The small sects in America. Rev. ed. New York, Abingdon-Cokesbury Press [1949] 256 p. 24 cm. Bibliography: p. 236-240. [BR516.C57 1949] 49-10200
1. Sects—U. S. 2. U. S.—Religion. I. Title.

CLARK, Elmer Talmage, 1886- 280.973
The small sects in America, by Elmer T. Clark. Nashville, Cokesbury press [c1937] 311 p. 20 1/2 cm. Bibliography: p. 289-306. [BR516.C37] 37-35144
1. Sects—U.S. 2. U.S.—Religion. I. Title.

CONFRONTING the cults, 280
by Gordon R. Lewis [Philadelphia, Presbyterian & Reformed Pub. Co.] 1966. 198p. 22cm. Bibl. [BR516.5.L4] 66-26791 1926- 2.95
1. Sects—U.S.

FERM, Vergilius Ture Anselm, 1896- ed. 280
The American church of the Protestant heritage. New York, Philosophical Library [1953] 481p. 21cm. Includes bibliographies. [BR516.F45] 53-7607
1. Sects—U. S. 2. Protestant churches—U. S. I. Title.
Contents omitted.

FERM, Vergilius Ture Anselm, 1896- ed. 280'.4'0973
The American church of the Protestant heritage. Westport, Conn., Greenwood Press [1972, c1953] 481 p. chart. 22 cm. Contents.Contents.—The Moravian Church, by J. R. Weinlick.—The Lutheran Church in America, by V. Ferm.—The Mennonites, by J. C. Wenger.—The Presbyterian Church in America, by C. M. Drury.—The Protestant Episcopal Church in the United States of America, by W. H. Stowe.—The Reformed Church in America, by M. J. Hoffman.—Unitarianism, by E. T. Buehrer.—The Congregational Christian churches, by M. M. Deems.—Baptist churches in America, by R. G. Torbet.—The United Presbyterian Church in America, by W. E. McCulloch.—The Society of Friends in America (Quakers) by W. E. Berry.—The Evangelical Mission Covenant Church and the free churches of Swedish background, by K. A. Olsson.—The Church of the Brethren, by D. W. Bittinger.—The Evangelical and Reformed Church, by D. Dunn.—Methodism, by E. T. Clark.—The Universalist Church of America, by R. Cummins.—The Evangelical United Brethren Church, by P. H. Eller.—Seventh-Day Adventists, by L. E. Froom.—Disciples of Christ, by R. E. Osborn.—Churches of Christ, by E. West.—The Church of God (Anderson, Indiana) by C. E. Brown. Includes bibliographies. [BR516.5.F47 1972] 76-138228 ISBN 0-8371-5585-1
1. Sects—United States. 2. Protestant churches—United States. I. Title.

GORRIE, Peter Douglass, 1813-1884. 280.973
The churches and sects of the United States; containing a brief account of the origin, history, doctrines, church government, mode of worship, usages, and statistics of each religious denomination, so far as known. By Rev. P. Douglass Gorrie. New York, L. Colby, 1850. 1 p. l., [v]-xii, [13]-240 p. 20 cm. [BR515.G6] 33-38336
1. Sects—U. S. I. Title.

HARDON, John A 284
The Protestant churches of America. Westminster, Md., Newman Press, 1956. 365p. 22cm. [BR516.H25] 56-13249
1. Sects—U. S. 2. Protestant churches—U. S. 3. U. S.—Religion. I. Title.

HARDON, John A. 284.0973
The Protestant churches of America. [Rev. ed.] Westminster, Md., Newman Press, 1958. 365 p. 21 cm. [BR516.5.H3 1958] 62-51063
1. Sects—United States. 2. Protestant churches—United States. 3. United States—Religion—1945- I. Title.

HARDON, John A. 280'.4'0973
The Protestant churches of America [by] John A. Hardon. Rev. ed. Garden City, N.Y., Image Books [1969] 439 p. 19 cm. Includes bibliographical references. [BR516.5.H3 1969] 69-12858 1.45
1. Sects—U.S. 2. Protestant churches—U.S. 3. U.S.—Religion—1945- I. Title.

HEDLEY, George Percy, 1899- 280
The Christian heritage in America, by George Hedley. New York, The Macmillan company, 1946. x p., 1 l., 177 p. 19 1/2 cm. "First printing." [BR516.H4] 46-5546
1. Sects—U.S. I. Title.

HOEKEMA, Anthony A., 1913- 289.0973
The four major cults: Christian Science, Jehovah's Witnesses, Mormonism, Seventh-Day Adventism. Grand Rapids, Eerdmans [1963] xiv, 447 p. 24 cm. Bibliography: p. 417-435. [BR516.5.H6] 63-17783
1. Sects—U.S. 2. Christian Science. 3. Jehovah's Witnesses. 4. Mormons and Mormonism. 5. Seventh-Day Adventists. I. Title.

JOHNSON, Ashley Sidney, 1857-1925. 280
The great controversy; a Biblical and historical search after the true basis of Christian union [by] Ashley S. Johnson ... Knoxville, Tenn., Printed for the author by Ashley S. B. Newman & co. [191-!] 294 p. 20 cm. [BR516.J57] 40-1655
1. Sects—U. S. 2. Disciples of Christ—Doctrinal and controversial works. I. Title.

JOHNSON, Ashley Sidney, 1857-1925. 280
The great controversy, by Ashley S. Johnson. Revised and brought to 1939 by M. D. Baumer ... Cincinnati, O., F. L. Rowe [c1939] 2 p. l., [7]-287 p. 20 cm. [BR516.J57 1939] 39-16398
1. Sects—U. S. 2. Disciples of Christ—Doctrinal and controversial work. I. Baumer, Michael Dan, 1867- ed. II. Title.

JONES, Kenneth, 1920- 277.3
Strange new faiths. Anderson, Ind., Gospel Trumpet Co. [1954] 127p. 20cm. [BR516.J76] 54-31765
1. Sects—U. S. I. Title.

JUDAH, J. Stillson. 280'.0973
The history and philosophy of the metaphysical movements in America, by J. Stillson Judah. Philadelphia, Westminster Press [1967] 317 p. 24 cm. Bibliographical footnotes. [BR516.J8] 67-11672
1. Sects—United States. I. Title.

KERR, High Thomson, 1909- 284
What divides Protestants today. New York, Association Press [1958] 127p. 16cm. (An Association Press reflection book) Includes bibliography. [BR516.5.K4] 58-11532
1. Sects—U. S. 2. Protestant churches—U. S. I. Title.

LANDIS, Benson Young, 1897- 280.973
Religion in the United States [by] Benson Y. Landis. New York, Barnes & Noble [1965] viii, 120 p. 22 cm. (Everyday handbooks) [BR516.5.L3] 65-14270
1. Sects—U.S. I. Title.

LEWIS, Gordon Russell, 1926- 280
Confronting the cults, by Gordon R. Lewis. Philadelphia, Presbyterian and Reformed Pub. Co., 1966. 198 p. 22 cm. Includes bibliographical references. [BR516.5.L4] 66-26791
1. Sects—United States. I. Title.

LOOK. 280.973
A guide to the religions of America; the famous Look magazine series on religion, plus facts, figures, tables, charts, articles, and comprehensive reference material on churches and religious groups in the United States. Edited by Leo Rosten. [New York] Simon and Schuster, 1955. xiii, 282 p. 23 cm. "Contains the complete series of articles on religion published in Look from 1952-1955." [BR516.L77] 55-7133
1. Sects—United States. I. Rosten, Leo Calvin, 1908- ed. II. Title: Religions of America.

LOOK 280.973
Religions in America; a completely revised and up-to-date guide to churches and religious groups in the United States. The famous Look magazine series on religion, plus facts, figures, tables, charts, articles, and comprehensive reference material. Ed. by Leo Rosten. New York, S. & S., 1963 [c.1952-1963] 414p. 21cm. (Essandess) 5.95; 1.95 pap.,
1. Sects—U.S. 2. U.S.—Religion. I. Rosten, Leo Calvin, 1908- ed. II. Title. III. Title: Religions of America.

MARTIN, Walter Ralston, 1928- 280
The Christian and the cults; answering the cultist from the Bible. Grand Rapids, Division of Cult Apologetics, Zondervan Pub. House [1956] 152p. 21cm. (The Modern cult library series) Includes bibliography. [BR516.M25] 57-17619
1. Sects—U. S. 2. Religions. I. Title.

MARTIN, Walter Ralston, 1928- 291.9
The kingdom of the cults; an analysis of the major cult systems in the present Christian era. Grand Rapids, Mich., Zondervan [c.1965] 443p. 25cm. Bibl. [BR516.5.M283] 64-22840 5.95
1. Sects—U.S. I. Title.

MARTIN, Walter Ralston, 1928- 280'.0973
The kingdom of the cults; an analysis of the major cult systems in the present Christian era, by Walter R. Martin. [Rev. ed.] Minneapolis, Bethany Fellowship [1968] 443 p. 23 cm. Bibliography: p. 435-440. [BR516.5.M283 1968] 70-192
1. Sects—U.S. I. Title.

MARTIN, Walter Ralston, 1928- 289.9
The rise of the cults. Grand Rapids, Division of Cult Apologetics, Zondervan Pub. House [1955] 117p. 20cm. [BR516.M28] 56-1128
1. Sects—U. S. 2. Religions. I. Title.

MARTIN, Walter Ralston, 1928-
The rise of the cults. Grand Rapids, Division of Cult Apologetics, Zondervan Pub. House [1957] 117p. 20cm. 'Second printing (Revised and enlarged)--1957
1. Sects—U. S. 2. Religions. I. Title.

MARTIN, Walter Ralston, 1928- 289
Rise of the cults / Walter Martin. Rev. and enl. Santa Ana, Calif. : Vision House, c1977, 1978 printing. 133 p. ; 21 cm. Includes index. Bibliography: p. [127]-129. [BL2530.U6M37 1977] 77-86536 ISBN 0-88449-070-X pbk. : 2.98
1. Sects—United States. 2. Religions. I. Title.

MATHISON, Richard R. 209.73
Faiths, cults, and sects of America: from atheism to Zen. Indianapolis, Bobbs-Merrill [c.1960] 384p. 22cm. 60-13589 5.00 bds.,
1. Sects—U. S. 2. U. S.—Religion. I. Title.

MATHISON, Richard R 209.73
Faiths, cults, and sects of America: from atheism to Zen. [1st ed.] Indianapolis, Bobbs-Merrill [1960] 384p. 22cm. [BR516.5.M29] 60-13589
1. Sects—U. S. 2. U. S.—Religion. I. Title.

MATHISON, Richard R. 209.73
God is a millionaire [Bobbs, dist. New York, Macfadden, 1962, c.1960] 384p. 21cm. (Charter bks. 106) Orig. pub. under title: Faiths, cults and sects of America. Bibl. 1.85 pap.,
1. Sects—U.S. 2. U.S.—Religion. I. Title.

MAYER, Fred Emanuel, 1892- 280.973
American churches, beliefs and practices, by F. E. Mayer ... St. Louis, Mo., Concordia publishing house, 1946. xiii, 102 p. 19 cm. (Concordia teacher training series) "Suggested bibliography": p. 100-102. [BR516.M36] 46-18835
1. Sects—U.S. 2. Creeds—Comparative studies. I. Title.

MAYER, Frederick Emanuel, 1892- 280.973
American churches, beliefs practices, by F. E. Mayer ... St. Louis, Mo., Concordia publishing house, 1946. xiii, 102p. 19cm. (Concordia teacher training series) 'Suggested bibliography': p.100-102. [BR516.M36] 46-18835
1. Sects—U. S. 2. Creeds—Comparative studies. I. Title.

MAYER, Frederick Emanuel, 1892- 280
The religious bodies of America. St. Louis, Concordia Pub. House [1954] 587p. 26cm. Includes bibliography. [BR516.M37] 54-2818
1. Sects—U. S. 2. Creeds— Comparative studies. 3. Lutheran Church—Doctrinal and controversial works. I. Title.

MAYER, Frederick Emanuel, 1892-1954. 280
The religious bodies of America. 2d ed. Saint Louis, Concordia Pub. House, 1956. xiii, 591p. 25cm. Includes bibliographies. [BR516.M37 1956] 56-4924
1. Sects—U. S. 2. Creeds—Comparative

studies. 3. Lutheran Church—Doctrinal and controversial works. I. Title.

MAYER, Frederick Emanuel, 1892-1954. 280
The religious bodies of America. 3d ed. Saint Louis, Concordia Pub. House, 1958. xiii, 591p. 25cm. Includes bibliographies. [BR516.5.M3 1958] 58-4617
1. Sects—U. S. 2. Creeds—Comparative studies. 3. Lutheran Church—Doctrinal and controversial works. I. Title.

MAYER, Frederick Emanuel, 1892-1954. 280
The religious bodies of America. 4th ed., rev. by Arthur Carl Piepkorn. Saint Louis, Concordia Pub. House, 1961. xiii, 598p. 25cm. Includes bibliographies. [BR516.5.M3 1961] 61-15535
1. Sects—U. S. 2. Creeds—Comparative studies. 3. Lutheran Church—Doctrinal and controversial works. I. Piepkorn, Arthur Carl, 1907- II. Title.

MEAD, Frank Spencer, 1898- 280.973
Handbook of denominations in the United States. Rev. and enl. ed. New York, Abingdon Press [c1956] 255p. 24cm. Bibliography: p. 229-237. [BR516.M38 1956] 55-10270
1. Sects—U. S. 2. U. S.—Religion. I. Title.

MEAD, Frank Spencer, 1898- 280.973
Handbook of denominations in the United States. 2d rev. ed. New York, Abingdon Press [1961] 272p. 24cm. Bibliography: p. 249-257. [BR516.5.M38 1961] 61-8412
1. Sects—U. S. 2. U. S.—Religion. I. Title.

MEAD, Frank Spencer, 1898- 200'.973
Handbook of denominations in the United States / Frank S. Mead. New 6th ed. Nashville : Abingdon Press, [1975] 320 p. ; 23 cm. Includes index. Bibliography: p. 291-305. [BR516.5.M38 1975] 75-2363 ISBN 0-687-16569-5 : 5.95
1. Sects—United States. I. Title.

MEAD, Frank Spencer, 1898- 280.0973
Handbook of denominations in the United States [by] Frank S. Mead. New 4th ed. New York, Abingdon Press [1965] 271 p. 24 cm. Bibliography: p. 246-256. [BR516.5.M38 1965] 65-21980
1. Sects—United States. I. Title. II. Title: Denominations in the United States.

MEAD, Frank Spencer, 1898- 280'.0973
Handbook of denominations in the United States [by] Frank S. Mead. New 5th ed. Nashville, Abingdon Press [1970] 265 p. 24 cm. Bibliography: p. 235-245. [BR516.5.M38 1970] 70-109675 3.95
1. Sects—U.S. I. Title. II. Title: Denominations in the United States.

MEAD, Frank Spencer, 1898- 280.973
Handbook of denominations in the United States. New York, Abingdon-Cokesbury Press [1951] 207 p. 24 cm. [BR516.M38] 51-11298
1. Sects—U.S. 2. U.S.—Religion. I. Title.

MUNRO, William Fraser, 1894- 280.97
A brief dictionary of the denominations. Nashville, Tidings, 1908 Grand Ave. [1964] 64p. 19cm. [BR516.5.M8] 64-25536 .60
1. Sects—U. S. I. Title.

NEEDLEMAN, Jacob. 290
The new religions. [1st ed.] Garden City, N.Y., Doubleday, 1970. xii, 245 p. 22 cm. Includes bibliographical references. [BL2520.N4] 71-121951 5.95
1. Sects—United States. 2. Religions. I. Title.

ORRMONT, Arthur. 289
Love cults & faith healers. New York, Ballantine Books [1961] 192p. 18cm. (Ballantine books, F456K) Includes bibliography. [BR516.5.O75] 61-2029
1. Sects—U. S. I. Title.

PFEFFER, Leo, 1910- 280
Creeds in competition: a creative force in American culture. [New York] Harper [1958] 176p. 22cm. [BR516.5.P43] 58-10373
1. Sects—U. S. 2. Church and state in the U. S. I. Title.

POOVEY, William Arthur, 1913- 280.973
Your neighbor's faith; a Lutheran looks at other churches. Minneapolis, Augsburg Pub. House [1961] 139p. illus. 20cm. 'Reprint of articles that appeared in One magazine from May 1959 to November 1960.' [BR516.5.P6] 61-6998
1. Sects—U. S. 2. Lutheran Church—Doctrinal and controversial works. I. Title.

PREECE, Harold. 280.973
... Dew on Jordan. New York, E. P. Dutton & company, inc. [1946] 221 p. 21 cm. At head of title: By Harold Preece & Celia Kraft. "First edition." [BR516.P7] 46-3270
1. Sects—U.S. I. Kraft, Celia, joint author. II. Title.

RELIGIOUS denominations in the United States, their past history, present condition, and doctrines, accurately set forth in fifty-three ... articles written by eminent clerical and lay authors ... together with complete and well-digested statistics. To which is added a historical summary of religious denominations in England and Scotland. 280'.0973 New York : AMS Press, 1975. 656, 208 p., [24] leaves of plates : ill. ; 24 cm. (Communal societies in America) The first section is a revision of He pasa ekklesia, compiled by I. D. Rupp and published in 1844. The second section (which has special t.p.: History of religious denominations in England and Scotland) is apparently an abridgment of Cyclopaedia of religious denominations, published in 1853 by J. J. Griffin, London. Reprint of the 1861 ed. published by C. Desilver, Philadelphia. [BR516.5.R46 1975] 72-2943 ISBN 0-404-10709-5 : 67.50
1. Sects—United States. 2. Church statistics—United States. 3. Sects—Great Britain. I. Rupp, Israel Daniel, 1803-1878, ed. He pasa ekklesia. II. Desilver, Charles, firm, Philadelphia. III. Cyclopaedia of religious denominations. IV. Title: History of religious denominations in England and Scotland.

THE rise of the cults.
Grand Rapids, Division of Cult Apologetics, Zondervan Pub. House [1957] 117p. 20cm. 'Second printing (Revised and enlarged)--1957'
1. Sects—U. S. 2. Religions. I. Martin, Walter Ralston, 1928-

ROBERTS, Waldemar 280.973
Jesus Christ, Light of the World: Protestant and Orthooox Center, New York World's Fair, 1964-1965. New York, Nelson [c.1964] 96p. illus. (1 col.) facsims., plan, ports. 26cm. 64-17739 1.95 bds.,
1. Sects—U.S. I. Title.

ROBERTS, Waldemar. 280.973
Jesus Christ, Light of the World: Protestant and Orthodox Center, New York World's Fair, 1964-1965. New York, T. Nelson [1964] 96 p. illus. (1 col.) facsims., plan, ports. 26 cm. [BR516.R6] 64-17739
1. Sects — U.S. I. Title.

ROSTEN, Leo Calvin, 1908- comp. 280'.0973
Religions of America : ferment and faith in an age of crisis : a new guide and almanac / edited with extensive comments and essays, by Leo Rosten. New York : Simon and Schuster, [1975] 672 p. ; 22 cm. Expanded version of the work first published in 1955 under title: A guide to the religions of America; and in 1963 under title: Religions in America. Includes bibliographical references and index. [BR516.5.R67 1975] 74-11703 ISBN 0-671-21970-7 : 12.95 ISBN 0-671-21971-5 pbk. : 5.95 pbk.
1. Sects—United States. 2. United States—Religion. I. Title.

ROWLEY, Peter. 290'.973
New gods in America; an informal investigation into the new religions of American youth today. New York, D. McKay Co. [1971] xv, 208 p. illus., ports. 21 cm. Bibliography: p. 205-208. [BL80.2.R66] 72-165087 5.95
1. Sects—U.S. 2. Youth—Religious life. 3. Religions. I. Title.

RUPP, Israel Daniel, 1803-1878, ed. 200'.973
He pasa ekklesia; an original history of the religious denominations at present existing in the United States, containing authentic accounts of their rise, progress, statistics and doctrines. Written expressly for the work by eminent theological professors, ministers, and lay-members of the respective denominations. Freeport, N.Y., Books for Libraries Press [1973] p. Reprint of the 1844 ed. [BR516.5.R86 1973] 72-12769 ISBN 0-8369-7149-3
1. Sects—United States. I. Title.

[RUPP, Israel Daniel] 1803-1878, ed. 280.973
The religious denominations in the United States; their past history, present condition, and doctrines, accurately set forth in fifty carefully-prepared articles, written by eminent clerical and lay authors connected with the respective persuasions. Together with complete and well-digested statistics. To which is added, A historical summary of religious denominations in England and Scotland ... Philadelphia, C. Desilver, 1859. 621, 208 p. ports. 25 cm. The main part of the work was first published in Philadelphia, 1844, under title: He pasa ekkiesta. "A historical summary of religious denominations in England and Scotland" (208 p. at end) is an abridgement of a work published in Glasgow, 1853, under title: The cyclopaedia of religious denominations. [BR515.R9 1859] 35-35223
1. Sects—U. S. 2. Sects. 3. Church statistics—U. S. 4. Sects—Gt. Brit. I. Title.

SHEEDER, Franklin I 280
The story of the denominations; a course for older young peopleand adults. Teacher's ed. Boston, Pilgrim Press [1953] 65, 92p. illus. 21cm. (Pilgrim series) [BR516.S47 1953] 53-33411
1. Sects—U. S. I. Title.

SMALL, Charles Herbert, 1861- 280
Corner-stones of faith; or, The origin and characteristics of the Christian denominations of the United States, by Rev. Charles H. Small...with corroborative statements from eminent divines of the leading denominations; introduction by Rev. John Henry Barrows... New York, E. B. Treat & company, 1898. 268, [271]-306, 309-407, 411-420, 428-469 p. incl. front., illus. (incl. ports.) 21 cm. Includes bibliographies. [BR157.S6] C-277
1. Sects—U.S. I. Title.

SMITH, Hannah Whitall, 1832-1911. 280'.0973
Religious fanaticism : extracts from the papers of Hannah Whitall Smith / edited with an introd. by Ray Strachey, consisting of an account of the author of these papers, and of the times in which she lived, together with a description of the curious religious sects and communities of America during the early and middle years of the nineteenth century. New York : AMS Press, 1976. p. cm. (Communal societies in America) Reprint of the 1928 ed. published by Faber & Gwyer, London. Includes index. [BR516.5.S55 1976] 72-8252 ISBN 0-404-11005-3 : 16.50
1. Smith, Hannah Whitall, 1832-1911. 2. Sects—United States. 3. Fanaticism. I. Title.

SPENCE, Hartzell, 1908- 209.73
The story of America's religions. Published in cooperation with the editors of Look magazine. New York, Holt, Rinehart and Winston [1960, c.1957-1960] ix, 86p. illus., col. plates, 35cm. 60-12319 14.95; regular ed. (no illus.) 4.00
1. Sects—U. S. 2. U. S.—Religion. I. Title. II. Title: America's religions.

SPENCE, Hartzell, 1908- 209.73
The story of America's religions. Nashville, Abingdon [1962, c.1957-1960] 258p. 21cm. (Apex Bks. K 3) 1.50 pap.,
1. Sects—U.S. 2. U.S.—Religion. I. Title. II. Title: America's religions.

SPENCE, Hartzell, 1908- 209.73
The story of America's religions. Published in co-operation with the editors of Look magazine. [1st ed] New York, Holt, Rinehart and Winston [1960] 86 p. illus. 35 cm. Deluxe ed. with illustrations. [BR516.5S7 1960] 60-12319
1. Sects — U.S. 2. U.S. — Religion. I. Title.

STARKES, M. Thomas. 280'.0973
Confronting popular cults [by] M. Thomas Starkes. Nashville, Broadman Press [1972] 122 p. 19 cm. Includes bibliographical references. [BR516.5.S74] 72-79177 ISBN 0-8054-1805-9
1. Sects—United States. I. Title.

TAPPERT, Theodore Gerhardt, 1904- 280.973
Our neighbors' churches. [Philadelphia] Muhlenberg Press [1954] 96p. illus. 18cm. (Faith and action series) [BR516.T35] 54-4810
1. Sects—U. S. I. Title.

TOWNS, Elmer L. 280'.07'73
Is the day of the denomination dead? By Elmer L. Towns. Nashville, T. Nelson [1973] 160 p. illus. 21 cm. Includes bibliographical references. [BR516.5.T68] 73-6993 ISBN 0-8407-5052-8 5.95
1. Sects—United States. 2. United States—Religion. 3. Independent churches—United States. I. Title.

TYLER, Alice (Felt) 1892- 277.3
Freedom's ferment; phases of American social history from the Colonial period to the outbreak of the Civil War. [Gloucester, Mass., P. Smith, 1963, c.1944] 608p. 21cm. (Harper torchbks., TB1074 Acad. lib. rebound) Bibl. 4.75
1. Sects—U.S. 2. U.S.—Hist.—1815-1861. 3. U.S.—Soc. life & cust. I. Title.

TYLER, Alice Felt, 1892- 277.3
Freedom's ferment; phases of American social history from the colonial period to the outbreak of the Civil War. New York, Harper & Row [1962, c.1944] 608p. illus. 21cm. (Harper Torchbk., Acad. Lib. TB/1074) Bibl. 2.75 pap.,
1. Sects—U.S. 2. U.S.—Hist.—1815-1861. 3. U.S.—Soc life & cust. I. Title.

TYLER, Alice (Felt) 1892- 309.1'73
Freedom's ferment; phases of American social history to 1860. Freeport, N.Y., Books for Libraries Press [1970, c1944] x, 608 p. illus., plans, ports. 24 cm. (Essay index reprint series) Bibliography: p. 551-589. [BR516.5.T9 1970] 78-128324 ISBN 8-369-18983-
1. Sects—U.S. 2. U.S.—History—1815-1861. 3. U.S.—Social life and customs—1783-1865. I. Title.

VAN BAALEN, Jan Karel, 1890- 280.973
The chaos of cults; a study in present-day isms. 2d rev. and enl. ed. Grand Rapids, Mich., Eerdmans, 1956. 409 p. 23 cm. [BR516.V3] 56-58880
1. Sects — U.S. 2. U.S. — Religion. I. Title.

VAN BAALEN, Jan Karel, 1890- 280.973
The chaos of cults; a study in present-day isms. 3d rev. and enl. ed. Grand Rapids, Eerdmans [1960] 444 p. 23 cm. Includes bibliography. [BR516.5.V3] 00-50834
1. Sects — U.S. 2. U.S. — Religion. I. Title.

VAN BAALEN, Jan Karel, 1890- 280.973
The chaos of cults; a study in present-day isms. 6th ed., rev. and enl. Grand Rapids, Mich., Eerdmans, 1947 [c1938] 280 p. 20 cm. Bibliography: p. 272-280. [[BR516.V]] A 51
1. Sects—U.S. 2. U.S.—Religion. I. Title.

VAN BAALEN, Jan Karel, 1890- 280.973
The chaos of cults; a study in present-day "isms", by Jan Karel Van Baalen Grand Rapids, Mich., Wm. B. Eerdmans publishing company [c1938] 5 p. l., 7-227 p. 21 cm. "These chapters are the author's response to requests for another edition of his 'Our birthright and the mess of meat' (1929). The entire work ... has been recast and largely rewritten."--Pref. "Selected bibliography": p. 211-227. [BR516.V3] 39-11391
1. Sects—U.S. 2. U.S.—Religion. I. Title.

VAN BAALEN, Jan Karel, 1890- 289
The gist of the cults; Christianity versus false religion, by the Rev. J. K. Van Baalen ... Grand Rapids, Mich., Wm. B. Eerdmans publishing company, 1944. 64 p. 19 cm. [BR516.V32] 44-47145
1. Sects—U.S. I. Title.

WARSHAW, Thayer S., 1915- 220.6
A compact guide to Bible-based beliefs / Thayer S. Warshaw. Nashville : Abingdon, [1981] c1978. [48] p. ; 22 cm. Includes index. [BS538.7.W37 1981] 19 80-19820 ISBN 0-687-09254-X pbk. : 1.50
1. Bible—Influence—United States. 2. Sects—United States. I. Title. II. Title: Bible-based beliefs.

WEBER, Julius A. comp. 290
Religions and philosophies in the United States of America, compiled by Julius A. Weber. Los Angeles, Calif., Wetzel publishing co., inc. [c1931] 333 p. 19 1/2 cm. [BR525.W35] 31-10188
1. Sects—U.S. 2. U.S.—Religion. I. Title.

WEIGEL, Gustav, 1906- 277
Churches in North America: an introduction. New York, Schocken [c.1961, 1965] 152p. 21cm. (SB95) [BR516.5.W4] 1.75 pap.,
1. Sects—U. S. 2. Protestant churches—U.S. I. Title.

WEIGEL, Gustave, 1906- 277
Churches in North America: an introduction. Baltimore, Helicon Press [1961] 152 p. 23 cm. [BR516.5.W4] 61-17627
1. Sects—U.S. 2. Protestant churches—U.S. I. Title.

WHALEN, William Joseph 280
Faiths for the few; a study of minority religions. Milwaukee. Bruce [c.1963] x, 201p. 22cm. Bibl. 63-19634 3.75
1. Sects—U. S. I. Title.

WHALEN, William Joseph. 291'.0973
Minority religions in America [by] William J. Whalen. Staten Island, N.Y., Alba House [1972] Includes bibliographies. [BR516.5.W438] 79-38979 ISBN 0-8189-0239-6
1. Sects—U.S. I. Title.

WHALEN, William Joseph 280.0973
Separated brethren; a survey of non-Catholic denominations in the United States [by] William J. Whalen. 2d rev. ed. Milwaukee, Bruce [1966] x, 288p. illus. 22cm. Bibl. [BR516.5.W44 1966] 66-15845 1.95 pap.,
1. Sects—U. S. I. Title.

WHALEN, William Joseph 280.973
Separated brethren; a survey of non-Catholic Christian denominations in the United States. Rev. ed. Milwaukee, Bruce Pub. Co. [c.1961] 284p. illus. Bibl. 61-8014 1.95 pap.,
1. Sects—U. S. I. Title.

WHALEN, William Joseph. 280
Separated brethren; a survey of non-Catholic Christian denominations in the United States. Milwaukee, Bruce Pub. Co. [1958] 284 p. illus. 23 cm. Includes bibliography. [BR516.W44] 57-13118
1. Sects — U.S. I. Title.

WHALEN, William Joseph. 280'.0973
Separated brethren; a survey of Protestant, Anglican, Orthodox, Old Catholic, and other denominations in the United States, by William J. Whalen. Rev. and enl. Huntington, Ind., Our Sunday visitor [1972] 302 p. 21 cm. Bibliography: p. 293-294. [BR516.5.W44 1972] 70-177998
1. Sects—U.S. I. Title.

YEARBOOK of American 270.05873
churches; information on all faiths in the U.S.A. Thirty-third issue; ed. for 1965. Ed. by Benson Y. Landis. New York, Natl. Council of the Churches of Christ [c.1965] 314p. 23cm. annual. 16-5726 7.50; 6.25 pap.,
1. Sects—U.S. I. Landis, Benson Y., ed.

YEARBOOK of American 202
churches; information on all faiths in the U.S.A. 29th issue, 1961. Ed. by Benson Y. Landis. New York 27,475 Riverside Drive. Office of Publication and Distribution. National Council of the Churches of Christ in the U.S.A., [c.1960] 314p. Title varies 16-5726 5.95 bds.,
1. Sects—U. S. I. Federal Council of the Churches of Christ in America.

Sects—United States—Addresses, essays, lectures.

DENOMINATIONALISM / 280'.0973
edited by Russell E. Richey. Nashville : Abingdon, c1977. 288 p. ; 22 cm. [BR516.5.D45] 76-49103 ISBN 0-687-10469-6 : 15.95 ISBN 0-687-10470-X pbk. : 6.95
1. Sects—United States—Addresses, essays, lectures. I. Richey, Russell E.

DENOMINATIONALISM / 280'.0973
edited by Russell E. Richey. Nashville : Abingdon, c1977. 288 p. ; 22 cm. [BR516.5.D45] 76-49103 ISBN 0-687-10469-6 : 15.95 ISBN 0-687-10470-X pbk. : 6.95
1. Sects—United States—Addresses, essays, lectures. I. Richey, Russell E.

Sects—United States—Dictionaries.

MELTON, J. Gordon. 200'.973
The encyclopedia of American religions / J. Gordon Melton. Wilmington, N.C. : McGrath Pub. Co., c1978. 2 v. ; 27 cm. "A Consortium book." Includes bibliographical references and index. [BL2530.U6M443] 78-78210 ISBN 0-8434-0643-7 : 87.50 (set)
1. Sects—United States—Dictionaries. 2. Cults—United States—Dictionaries. I. Title.

SHULMAN, Albert M. 291'.0973
The religious heritage of America / by Albert M. Shulman. 1st ed. San Diego : A.S. Barnes ; London : Tantivy Press, c1981. p. cm. Includes index. [BL2530.U6S5] 19 81-3594 ISBN 0-498-02162-9 : 22.50
1. Sects—United States—Dictionaries. 2. United States—Religion—Dictionaries. I. Title.

Sects—United States—Directories.

ECUMENISM Research 280'.025'73
Agency.
The state of the churches in the U.S.A., 1973, as shown in their own official yearbooks : a study resource / by Ecumenism Research Agency. Sun City, Ariz. : The Agency, [1973] 24 p. ; 23 cm. [BR516.5.E28 1973] 75-311308
1. Sects—United States—Directories. 2. United States—Religion—1945- I. Title.

Secular institutes

HALEY, Joseph Edmund, ed. 271
Apostolic sanctity in the world; a symposium on total dedication in the world and secular institutes. [Notre Dame, Ind., University of Notre Dame Press, 1957. xiv, 210p. 24cm. 'Presented as a proceedings of ... various conferences held from 1952-1956. Selected papers from these meetings, reports on the various groups existing in the United States and Canada, the basic church documents regarding secular institutes, and an exhaustive bibliography [p. 197-210] have been integrated into a whole.' [BX808.H3] 57-7491
1. Secular institutes. I. Title.

PERRIN, Joseph Marie, 267.182
1905-
Secular institutes; consecration to God and life in the world. Translated by Lancelot C. Sheppard. New York, P. J. Kenedy [1961] 122p. 19cm. Translation of Conscration Diel et presence au monde. Includes bibliography. [BX818.A1P413] 61-8785
1. Secular institutes I. Title.

REIDY, Gabriel. 267.182
Secular institutes. [1st ed.] New York, Hawthorn Books [1962] 124p. 21cm. (The Twentieth century encyclopedia of Catholicism, v.87. Section 8: The organization of the church) Includes bibliographies. [BX818.A1R4] 62-12930
1. Secular institutes. I. Title.

Secularism.

AUBREY, Edwin Ewart, 1896- 211
Secularism a myth; an examination of the current attack on secularism. [1st ed.] New York, Harper [1954] 191p. 22cm. (The Ayer lectures for 1953) [BL2750.A8] 54-6900
1. Secularism. I. Title.

BLAIKIE, Robert J. 231
'Secular Christianity' and God who acts, by Robert J. Blaikie. [1st U.S. ed.] Grand Rapids, Mich., Eerdmans [1970] 256 p. 22 cm. Includes bibliographical references. [BS543.B53 1970] 72-129849 2.95
1. Bible—Theology. 2. Secularism. I. Title.

BLAMIRES, Harry. 211.6
The Christian mind. New York, Seabury Press, 1963. 181 p. 22 cm. [BR121.1.B5] 63-15452
1. Secularism. 2. Christianity — 20th cent. I. Title.

BONHAM, John Milton. 211
Secularism; its progress and its morals, by John M. Bonham ... New York, London, G. P. Putnam's sons, 1894. iv, 396 p. 19 1/2 cm. [BL2775.B62] 33-16409
1. Secularism. 2. Rationalism. I. Title.

CHILDRESS, James F., comp. 211'.6
Secularization and the Protestant prospect. Edited, with an introd. by James F. Childress and David B. Harned. Philadelphia, Westminister Press [1970] 220 p. 19 cm. Includes bibliographical references. [BL2747.8.C47] 77-98118 3.50
1. Secularism. 2. Secularization (Theology) I. Harned, David Baily, joint comp. II. Title.

ELLUL, Jacques. 211'.6
The new demons / Jacques Ellul ; translated by C. Edward Hopkin. New York : Seabury Press, [1975] viii, 228 p. ; 22 cm. "A Crossroad book." Translation of Les nouveaux possedes. Includes bibliographical references. [BL2747.8.E4313] 75-6969 ISBN 0-8164-0266-3 : 9.95
1. Secularism. 2. Christianity—20th century. 3. Mythology. I. Title.

GLASNER, Peter E. 301.5'8
The sociology of secularisation : a critique of a concept / Peter E. Glasner. London ; Boston : Routledge & K. Paul, 1977. viii, 137 p. ; 22 cm. (International library of sociology) Includes index. Bibliography: p. 123-134. [BL2747.8.G445] 77-368411 ISBN 0-7100-8455-2 : 11.00
1. Secularism. 2. Sociology—Methodology. I. Title.

HARING, Bernhard, 1912- 234'.2
Faith and morality in the secular age, by Bernard Haring. [1st ed.] Garden City, N.Y., Doubleday, 1973. 237 p. 22 cm. [BL2747.8.H33] 73-79876 ISBN 0-385-03837-2 6.95
1. Secularism. 2. Religion and culture. 3. Faith. 4. Prayer. I. Title.

HEWITT, Emily C. 211'.6
Models of secularization in contemporary sociological theory [by] Emily C. Hewitt, Lawrence H. Mamiya [and] Michael C. Mason. [New York, Auburn Theological Seminary] 1972. i, 44 p. 28 cm. (Auburn Studies in Education, publication #1) Bibliography: p. 43-44. [BL2747.8.H47] 72-184966 1.00
1. Secularism. 2. Religion and sociology. I. Mamiya, Lawrence H., joint author. II. Mason, Michael C., joint author. III. Title. IV. Series.

HOLYOAKE, George Jacob, 1817-
1906.
English secularism; a confession of belief, by George Jacob Holyoake... Chicago, The Open court publishing company, 1896. xii p., 1 l., 146 p. front. (port.) 20 cm. Orginally appeared as a series of articles in the "Open court" cf. Pref. [BL2775.H63] 3-7081
1. Secularism. I. Title.

HOWARD, Thomas. 200'.1
Chance or the dance? / Thomas Howard. Wheaton, Ill. : H. Shaw, [1979] c1969. 157 p. ; 21 cm. Previously published under title: an antique drum. [BL2747.8.H68 1979] 79-15004 ISBN 0-87788-032-8 pbk. : 3.95
1. Secularism. I. Title.

KALLEN, Horace Meyer, 1882- 211
Secularism is the will of God; an essay in the social philosophy of democracy and religion. New York, Twayne Publishers [c1954] 233p. 23cm. [BL2775.K315] 55-14050
1. Secularism. 2. Religious liberty. 3. U. S.—Religion. I. Title.

LOEN, Arnoldus Ewout, 211'.6
1896-
Secularization; science without God? [By] Arnold E. Loen. Translated by Margaret Kohl. Philadelphia, Westminster Press [1967] 213 p. 23 cm. [BL2747.8.L613 1967a] 67-21794
1. Secularism. I. Title.

MCCLENDON, Gene. 211
Secularism and salvation. [1st ed.] New York, Vantage Press [1958, c1957] 76p. 21cm. [BL2775.M225] 58-14528
1. Secularism. I. Title.

MARTIN, David A. 211'.6
The religious and the secular; studies in secularization [by] David Martin. New York, Schocken Books [1969] xi, 164 p. 23 cm. Bibliography: p. 157-161. [BL2747.8.M35] 69-17729 5.00
1. Secularism. I. Title.

MARTY, Martin E., 1928- 261
The modern schism; three paths to the secular [by] Martin E. Marty. [1st U.S. ed.] New York, Harper & Row [1969] 191 p. 22 cm. Includes bibliographical references. [BL2747.8.M37 1969] 74-85042 5.95
1. Secularism. I. Title.

MILLER, Samuel Howard, 211.6
1900-
The dilemma of modern belief. [1st ed.] New York, Harper & Row [1963] 113 p. 22 cm. (The Lyman Beecher lectures, Yale Divinity School) [BL2747.8.M5] 63-11893
1. Secularism. 2. Christianity — 20th cent. — Addresses, essays, lectures. I. Title.

NATIONAL Catholic alumni 211
federation.
Man and modern secularism; essays on the conflict of the two cultures. New York, National Catholic alumni federation, 1940. 4 p. l., 157 p., 1 l. 23 cm. Papers originally delivered at the 1939 convention of the National Catholic alumni federation. cf. Editor's note. Contents.--Religion in the making of America.--Secularism and the unmaking of America.--Religion in the remaking of America.--The Catholic answer.--The return to American higher Catholic education of the formal teaching of theology as a science. [BX1753.N3] 41-13246
1. Secularism. 2. Catholic church—Apologetic works. 3. U. S.—Religion. 4. Church and education in the U. S. 5. Theology—Study and teaching—Catholic church. I. Title.

NEWBIGIN, James Edward 211.6
Lesslie, Bp.
Honest religion for secular man, by Lesslie Newbigin. Philadelphia, Westminster Press [1966] 159 p. 19 cm. (Adventures in faith) Based on the Firth lectures, University of Nottingham, 1964. [BL2747.8.N4] 66-16552
1. Secularism. I. Title.

SZCZESNY, Gerhard 211
The future of unbelief. Tr. from German by Edward B. Garside. New York, Braziller, 1961 [c.1958, 1961] 221 p. 60-11665 4.00
1. Secularism. I. Title.

VAHANIAN, Gabriel, 1927- 211.6
The death of God; the culture of our post-Christian era. New York, Braziller [1966, c.1957-1961] xxxiii, 253p. 21cm. Bibl. [BL2759.V3] 1.95 pap.,
1. Secularism. 2. Civilization, Modern. I. Title.

VAHANIAN, Gabriel, 1927- 211.6
The death of God; the culture of our post-Christian era. New York, G. Braziller, 1961. 253 p. 21 cm. Includes bibliography. [BL2759.V3] 61-9962
1. Secularism. 2. Civilization, Modern. I. Title.

VON HILDEBRAND, Dietrich, 1889- 282'.09'04
Trojan horse in the city of God. Chicago, Franciscan Herald Press [1967] xiii, 233 p. 21 cm. Bibliographical references included in "Notes" (p. 227-233) [BX1755.V6] 67-22202
1. Catholic Church—Doctrinal and controversial works. 2. Secularism. I. Title.

Secularism—Addresses, essays, lectures.

CHRISTIAN hope and the secular. 211'.6 Edited by Daniel F. Martensen. Minneapolis, Augsburg Pub. House [1969] ix, 115 p. 22 cm. (Christian hope series) Contents.Contents.—Dialogical theology: an introductory essay, by D. F. Martensen.—A Biblical view of the secular, by V. R. Gold.—The dialectic of the secular, by W. H. Capps.—Eastern Orthodoxy and the secular, by D. F. Martensen.—Marxism and the secular; by R. L. Moellering.—Church worship and the secular, by R. Johnson. Includes bibliographical references. [BL2747.8.C49] 73-84811 2.50
1. Secularism—Addresses, essays, lectures. 2. Theology—20th century—Addresses, essays, lectures. I. Martensen, Daniel F., ed.

THE Secular mind : 211'.6 transformations of faith in modern Europe / edited by W. Warren Wagar. New York : Holmes & Meier, 1982. p. cm. Includes index. Bibliography: p. [BL2747.8.S33] 19 81-20019 ISBN 0-8419-0766-8 : 24.50
1. Secularism—Addresses, essays, lectures. I. Wagar, W. Warren.
Contents omitted.

Secularism—Controversial literature.

HARKNESS, Georgia Elma, 1891- 211
The modern rival of Christian faith; an analysis of secularism. New York, Abingdon-Cokesbury Press [1952] 223 p. 23 cm. [BT1210.H335] 52-7073
1. Secularism—Controversial literature. 2. Apologetics—20th cent. I. Title.

HARKNESS, Georgia Elma, 1891-1974. 239'.09'04
The modern rival of Christian faith : an analysis of secularism / Georgia Harkness. Westport, Conn. : Greenwood Press, 1978, c1952. 223 p. ; 22 cm. Reprint of the ed. published by Abingdon Press, New York. Includes index. [BT1211.H37 1978] 77-27000 ISBN 0-313-20174-9 lib.bdg. : 16.25
1. Secularism—Controversial literature. 2. Apologetics—20th century. I. Title.

HONG, Howard, 1912- 239
This world and the church; studies in secularism. Minneapolis, Augsburg Pub. House [1955] 143p. 22cm. 'Lectures delivered at the 1952 mid-wint convocation, Luther Theological Seminary, St. Faul, Minnesota'. [BT1210.H56] 55-7121
1. Secularism—Controversial literature. 2. Apologetics—20th cent. I. Title.

HONG, Howard Vincent, 1912- 239
This world and the church; studies in secularism. Minneapolis, Augsburg Pub. House [1955] 143 p. 22 cm. "Lectures delivered at the 1952 mid-winter convocation, Luther Theological Seminary, St. Paul. Minnesota." [BT1210.H56] 55-7121
1. Secularism—Controversial literature. 2. Apologetics—20th cent. I. Title.

MOLLEGEN, Albert T. 239
Christianity and modern man the crisis of secularism. Indianapolis, Bobbs-Merrill [c.1961] 160p. 61-7895 3.50
1. Secularism—Controversial literature. 2. Apologetics—20th cent. I. Title.

Secularism—Europe.

CHADWICK, Owen. 190
The secularization of the European mind in the nineteenth century : the Grifford lectures in the University of Edinburgh for 1973-4 / Owen Chadwick. Cambridge [Eng.] ; New York : Cambridge University Press, 1975. 286 p. ; 22 cm. (Gifford lectures ; 1973-74) Includes bibliographical references and index. [BL2765.E85C48] 75-16870 ISBN 0-521-20892-0 : 18.95
1. Secularism—Europe. 2. Europe—Intellectual life. I. Title. II. Series.

Secularism—History—Addresses, essays, lectures.

SACRALIZATION and secularization. 211'.6 Edited by Roger Aubert. New York, Paulist Press [1969] viii, 182 p. 24 cm. (Concilium: theology in the age of renewal. Church history, v. 47) Includes articles translated from several languages by various persons. Bibliographical footnotes. [BL2747.8.S23] 76-96949 4.50
1. Secularism—History—Addresses, essays, lectures. I. Aubert, Roger, ed. II. Series: Concilium (New York) v. 47

Secularism—India.

THOMAS, Madathilparampil M. 211'.6
The secular ideologies of India and the secular meaning of Christ / M. M. Thomas. Bangalore : Published for The Christian Institute for the Study of Religion and Society by The Christian Literature Society, Madras, 1976. viii, 207 p. ; 22 cm. (Confessing the faith in India series ; no. 12) Includes bibliographical references and index. [BL2765.I5T46] 76-904071 Rs14.00
1. Secularism—India. 2. Christianity—India. I. Title. II. Series.

Secularism—United States.

MAYERS, Ronald B. 211
Religious ministry in a transcendentless culture / Ronald B. Mayers. Washington, D.C. : University Press of America, c1980. vii, 154 p. ; 22 cm. Includes index. Bibliography: p. 141-152. [BL2747.8.M39] 19 79-3424 ISBN 0-8191-0889-8 pbk. : 8.95
1. Secularism—United States. 2. Philosophy, Modern—20th century. I. Title.

ST. Francis College, Loretto, Pa.
The Third Order Secular. Loretto, Pa., Saint Francis Jamor Seminary, 1956. 199 p. illus., ports. 24 cm. (Its Mariale, 1956) 64-43956
I. Title.

Secularization (Theology)

BILDSTEIN, Walter J. 201'.1
Radical response / Walter J. Bildstein. 2d ed. Hicksville, N.Y. : Exposition Press, [1974] xvi, 144 p. ; 21 cm. (An Exposition-testament book) First ed. published in 1972 under title: Secularization: the theology of John A. T. Robinson, a radical response. Bibliography: p. [131]-144. [BX5199.R722B54 1974] 74-186984 ISBN 0-682-47931-4 : 6.50
1. Robinson, John Arthur Thomas, Bp., 1919- 2. Secularization (Theology) I. Title.

CHERESO, James C. 261
Here & now; the sacred secular, by James C. Chereso. Dayton, Ohio, G. A. Pflaum, 1969. 128 p. illus. 18 cm. (Witness book, C14) (Christian identity series.) Includes bibliographical references. [BT83.7.C44] 79-97045 0.95
1. Secularization (Theology) 2. Secularism. I. Title.

DEAN, Thomas, 1938- 261.2
Post-theistic thinking : the Marxist-Christian dialogue in radical perspective / Thomas Dean Philadelphia : Temple University Press, [1975] xvi, 300 p. ; 23 cm. Includes index. Bibliography: p. 283-287. [BT83.7.D4] 74-83202 ISBN 0-87722-037-9 : 12.95
1. Marx, Karl, 1818-1883. 2. Secularization (Theology) 3. Communism and Christianity. I. Title.

FENN, Richard K. 301.5'8
Toward a theory of secularization / by Richard K. Fenn. [Storrs, Conn.] : Society for the Scientific Study of Religion, c1978. xxii, 91 p. ; 23 cm. (Monograph series - Society for the Scientific Study of Religion, ; no. 1) Includes index. Bibliography: p. 83-87. [BT83.7.F46] 78-61587 ISBN 0-932566-00-6 : 4.50
1. Secularization (Theology) I. Title. II. Series: Society for the Scientific Study of Religion. Monograph series — Society for the Scientific Study of Religion ; no. 1.

KEE, Alistair, 1937- 231
The way of transcendence: Christian faith without belief in God. Harmondsworth, Penguin, 1971. xxix, 241 p. 19 cm. (Pelican books A1309) Includes bibliographical references. [BT83.7.K4] 70-28820 ISBN 0-14-021309-0 £0.35
1. Secularization (Theology) 2. God—History of doctrines. I. Title.

LYNCH, William F., 1908- 261
Christ and Prometheus; a new image of the secular [by] William F. Lynch. [Notre Dame, Ind.] University of Notre Dame Press [1970] 153 p. 23 cm. Includes bibliographical references. [BT83.7.L9] 70-122046 5.95
1. Secularization (Theology) I. Title.

MARTIN, David, 1929- 301.5'8
A general theory of secularization / David Martin. New York : Harper & Row, c1978. ix, 353 p. ; 23 cm. Includes index. Bibliography: p. [309]-341. [BT83.7.M37 1978b] 78-3130 ISBN 0-06-136179-8 : 23.50.
1. Secularization (Theology) I. Title.

RICHARD, Robert L 230
Secularization theology [by] Robert L. Richard. [New York] Herder and Herder [1967] x, 190 p. 21 cm. [BT83.7.R5] 67-25882
1. Secularization (Theology) 2. Theology, Doctrinal—Hist.—20th cent. I. Title.

RICHARD, Robert L 230
Secularization theology [by] Robert L. Richard. London, Burns & Oates; [New York] Herder and Herder, 1967 [i. e. 1968.] 192 p. 21 cm. 30/- (SBN 223 29847 5) [BT83.7.R5 1968] 68-90879
1. Secularization (Theology) 2. Theology, Doctrinal—Hist.—20th cent. I. Title.

RICHARD, Robert L. 230
Secularization theology [by] Robert L. Richard. [New York] Herder and Herder [1967] x, 190 p. 21 cm. [BT83.7.R5] 67-25882
1. Secularization (Theology) 2. Theology, Doctrinal—History—20th century. I. Title.

SMITH, Harry E. 261
Secularization and the university, by Harry E. Smith. Foreword by Harvey Cox. Richmond, Va., John Knox Press [1968] 172 p. 21 cm. Bibliographical references included in "Notes" (p. [161]-172) [BT83.7.S6] 68-25015 2.95
1. Secularization (Theology) 2. Universities and colleges—Religion. I. Title.

THILS, Gustave, 1909- 200
A "non-religious" Christianity? [Translated by John A. Otto.] Staten Island, N.Y., Alba House [1970] xii, 168 p. 22 cm. Translation of Christianisme sans religion? Includes bibliographical references. [BT83.7.T4813] 78-129171 4.95
1. Secularization (Theology) I. Title.

TODRANK, Gustave Herman, 1924- 262.7
The secular search for a new Christ, by Gustave H. Todrank. Philadelphia, Westminster Press [1969] 174 p. 21 cm. Bibliographical references included in "Notes" (p. 171-174) [BT83.7.T6] 73-76992 2.65
1. Secularization (Theology) 2. Salvation. I. Title.

Secularization (Theology)—Addresses, essays, lectures.

NOTRE Dame Colloquium, University of Notre Dame, 1967. 230
The spirit and power of Christian secularity Albert Schlitzer, editor. Contributors: Bernard Cooke [and others] Notre Dame [Ind.] University of Notre Dame Press [1969] xi, 216 p. 24 cm. Bibliographical footnotes. [BT83.7.N6 1967] 75-75154 10.00
1. Secularization (Theology)—Addresses, essays, lectures. 2. Secularism—Addresses, essays, lectures. I. Schlitzer, Albert L., 1902- ed. II. Cooke, Bernard J. III. Title.

Secularization (Theology)—History of doctrines—20th century.

AUSMUS, Harry J., 1937- 209'.03
The polite escape : on the myth of secularization / Harry J. Ausmus. Athens : Ohio University Press, c1982. xii, 189 p. ; 24 cm. Includes index. Bibliography: p. 179-184. [BT83.7.A95 1982] 19 81-16924 ISBN 0-8214-0650-7 : 23.95
1. Secularization (Theology)—History of doctrines—20th century. 2. Nihilism (Philosophy)—History—20th century. I. Title.

Securities, Tax-exempt—United States.

TAX exempt financing : 343.7305'23 tax planning / Henry S. Klaiman, chairman. New York, N.Y. (810 7th Ave., New York 10019) : Practising Law Institute, c1982. 1048 p. ; 22 cm. (Tax law and estate planning series) "Prepared for distribution at the tax exempt financing-tax planning program, March-April 1982." "J4-3504." [KF6383.Z9T38 1982] 347.303523 19 82-80120 : 25.00
1. Securities, Tax-exempt—United States. 2. Industrial development bonds—Taxation—Law and legislation—United States. 3. Mortgage bonds, Tax-exempt—Law and legislation—United States. I. Klaiman, Henry S., 1940- II. Title. III. Series. IV. Tax law and practice course handbook series ; no. 167

Security (Psychology)

CAMPBELL, Elizabeth W. 268.61
Security for young children, the foundation for spiritual values; a booklet for teachers and parents who live with three-year-old children in home, church, and school. Boston, Pilgrim Press [1952] 99 p. illus. 23 cm. [HQ784.S43C3] 268.432 52-10166
1. Security (Psychology) 2. Child study. I. Title.

Seder.

FREDMAN, Ruth Gruber, 1934- 296.4'37
The Passover Seder : afikoman in exile / Ruth Gruber Fredman. Philadelphia : University of Pennsylvania Press, 1980. p. cm. (Symbol and culture) Includes index. Bibliography: p. [BM695.P35F73] 19 80-52810 ISBN 0-8122-7788-0 : 18.00
1. Jews. Liturgy and ritual. Hagadah—Criticism, interpretation, etc. 2. Seder. I. Title. II. Series.

JEWS. Liturgy and ritual. Hagadah. 296
The Seder service for Passover eve in the home, arranged by Mrs. Philip Cowen. A completely revised English translation, with new notes, music and illustrations. 3d ed. ... New York, P. Cowen. 5665-1905. 1 p. l., v-xv, 12-142 p. illus. 19 cm. Preface signed: L. G. C. Hebrew and English. Contains music. [BM675.P4C6 1905] 5-11915
I. Cowen, Lillie (Cohen) "Mrs. Philip Cowen", 1850- II. Title.

Seder Eliyahyu.

KADUSHIN, Max, 1895- 296
The theology of Seder Eliahu; a study in organic thinking, by Rabbi Max Kadushin ... New York, Bloch publishing company, 1932- v. 24 cm. [BM517.S4K3] 33-4602
1. Seder Eliyahyu. 2. Jews—Religion. I. Title.

Sedgwick, Catharine Maria, 1780-1867.

BEACH, Seth Curtis, 1837-1932. 920.
Daughters of the Puritans; a group of brief biographies, by Seth Curtis Beach. Boston, American Unitarian association, 1905. 4 p. l., 286 p. 20 cm. [CT3260.B4] 5-36484
1. Sedgwick, Catharine Maria, 1780-1867. 2. Ware, Mrs. Mary Lovell (Pickard) 1798-1849. 3. Child, Mrs. Lydia Maria (Francis) 1802-1880. 4. Dix, Dorothea Lynde, 1802-1887. 5. Ossoll, Sarah Margaret (Fuller) marchesa. 6. Stowe, Mrs. Harriet Elizabeth

(Beecher) 1811-1866. 7. Alcott, Louisa May 1832-1888. 8. 1810-1850. I. Title.

Sedgwick co., Kan.—Social conditions

LANDIS, Benson Young, 1897- 261.
... *Sedgwick county, Kansas;* a church and community survey, by Benson Y. Landis ... New York, George H. Doran company [c1922] x p., 1 l., 13-83 p. illus (incl. map) fold. tab., diagrs. 23 cm. (Committee on social and religious surveys) [BR555.K3S4] 22-8734
1. Sedgwick co., Kan.—Soc. condit. 2. Churches—Kansas—Sedgwick co. I. Title.

Seel, David John, 1925-

SEEL, David John, 1925- 266'.025'0924
Challenge and crisis in missionary medicine / by David J. Seel. Pasadena, Calif. : William Carey Library, [1979] p. cm. Includes bibliographical references. [R722.32.S4A33] 79-16015 ISBN 0-87808-172-0 pbk. : 3.95
1. Seel, David John, 1925- 2. Missionaries, Medical—Korea—Biography. 3. Missions, Medical. I. Title.

Seeley, Sir John Robert, 1834-1895. Ecce homo.

[PARKER, Joseph] 1830-1902. 232
Ecce Deus; essays on the life and doctrine of Jesus Christ. With controversial notes on "Ecce Homo". Boston, Roberts brothers, 1867. 1 p. l., [5]-8, 11-363 p. 18 cm. [BT201.P25] 16-1210
1. Seeley, Sir John Robert, 1834-1895. Ecce homo. 2. Jesus Christ—Divinity. I. Title.

[PARKER, Joseph] 1830-1902. 232
Ecce Deus, essays on the life and doctrine of Jesus Christ. With controversial notes on "Ecce Homo." Boston, Roberts brothers, 1868. 1 p. l., [5]-8, 11-373 p. 18 cm. "A new edition, revised and enlarged." [BT201.P25 1868] 35-24706
1. Seeley, Sir John Robert, 1834-1895. Ecce Homo. 2. Jesus Christ—Divinity. I. Title.

Seelos, Franz Xaver, 1819-1867.

CURLEY, Michael Joseph, 1900- 282'.0924 B
Cheerful ascetic: the life of Francis Xavier Seelos, C.SS.R., by Michael J. Curley. New Orleans, Redemptorist Fathers, 1969. ix, 436 p. illus., ports. 24 cm. Bibliography: p. [405]-420. [BX4705.S517C85] 76-12639
1. Seelos, Franz Xaver, 1819-1867. I. Title.

Sefer ha-Razim.

NIGGEMEYER, Jens-Heinrich. 133.4'3
Beschworungsformeln aus dem "Buch der Geheimnisse" (Sefar ha-razim) : zur Topologie der magischen Rede / Jens-Heinrich Niggemeyer. Hildesheim ; New York; Olms, 1975. 274 p., [1] leaf of plates : 1 ill. ; 21 cm. (Judaistische Texte und Studien ; Bd. 3) The appendix contains 36 texts translated from the Hebrew. Includes indexes. Bibliography: p. 248-256. [BM525.A3719N53] 76-452157 ISBN 3-487-05648-8
1. Sefer ha-Razim. 2. Cabala. 3. Incantations, Hebrew. 4. Magic, Jewish. I. Title. II. Series.

Sefer Yezirah.

SUARES, Carlo. 296.1'6
The Sepher Yetsira, including the original astrology according to the Qabala and its zodiac / Carlo Suares ; translated from the French by Micheline & Vincent Stuart. Boulder, Colo. : Shambhala ; New York : distributed in the U.S. by Random House, 1976. 173 p. ; 22 cm. [BM525.A419S913] 76-14206 ISBN 0-87773-093-8 : 5.95
1. Sefer Yezirah. 2. Cabala. 3. Astrology. I. Title: The Sepher Yetsira ...

UNDERSTANDING Jewish mysticism : a source reader : the Merkabah tradition and the Zoharic tradition / [edited] by David R. Blumenthal. New York : Ktav Pub. House, 1978. p. cm. (The Library of Judaic learning ; v. 2) Includes index. Bibliography: p. [BM526.U5] 78-6544 ISBN 0-87068-334-9 : 10.00 pbk. : 5.95 296.1'6
1. Sefer Yezirah. 2. Hekhalot. 3. Cabala—History. 4. Mysticism—Judaism. I. Blumenthal, David R.

Seghers, Charles Jean, abp. 1839-1886.

BAETS, Maurice de, 1863-1931 922.271
The Apostle of Alaska; life of the Most Reverend Charles John Seghers. A translation of Maurice de Baets' "Vie de monseigneur Seghers," by Sister Mary Mildred, S.S.A. With a foreword by the Most Reverend John C. Cody ... Paterson, N.J., St. Anthony guild press, 1943. xi, [1], 292 p. incl. front. (port.) illus. (incl. cost of arms) 22 1/2 cm. Bibliographical foot-notes. [BX4705.S52B23] 43-22884
1. Seghers, Charles Jean, abp. 1839-1886. 2. Catholic church—Missions. I. Mary Mildred, sister, 1875- II. Title.

Seghers, Charles Jean, Abp., 1839-1886—Juvenile literature.

BETZ, Eva (Kelly) 1897- 92
Apostle of the ice and snow; a life of Bishop Charles Seghers, by Eva K. Betz. Valatie, N.Y., Holy Cross Press [1964?] 126 p. illus. 23 cm. [BX4705.S52B4] 64-8535
1. Seghers, Charles Jean, Abp., 1839-1886 — Juvenile litereature. I. Title.

BOSCO, Antoinette 922.271
Charles John Seghers, pioneer in Alaska; illustrated by Matthew Kalmenoff. New York, P. J. Kenedy [c.1960] 190p. 22cm. (American background books, 16) (Bibl. notes:p.185-186) 60-14643 2.50
1. Seghers, Charles Jean, Abp., 1839-1886—Juvenile literature. I. Title.

BOSCO, Antoinette, 1928- 922.271
Charles John Seghers, pioneer in Alaska; illustrated by Matthew Kalmenoff. New York, P. J. Kenedy [1960] 190p. illus. 22cm. (American background books, 16) [BX4705.S52B6] 60-14643
1. Seghers, Charles Jean, Abp., 1839-1886—Juvenile literature. I. Title.

Sego, James, 1927-

SEGO, James, 1927- 783.8'092'4 B
Sego / by James Sego, with Robert Paul Lamb. Plainfield, N.J. : Logos International, c1977. xii, 156 p., [3] leaves of plates : ill. ; 21 cm. [ML420.S45A3] 77-83855 ISBN 0-88270-247-5 pbk. : 2.95
1. Sego, James, 1927- 2. Gospel musicians—United States—Biography. I. Lamb, Robert Paul, joint author.

Segregation in education.

O'NEILL, Joseph Eugene, 1910- ed. 261.83
A Catholic case against segregation. Foreword by Richard Cardinal Cushing; New York, Macmillan, 1961. xiv, 155 p. 22 cm. Bibliographical footnotes. [LB3062.O5] 61-16759
1. Segregation in education. 2. Church and social problems—Catholic Church. I. Title.

Segregation—Religious aspects.

CHURCHILL, Rhona. 261.83
White man's God. Pref. by Joost de Blank. New York, Morrow, 1962. 205 p. illus. 22 cm. [BR1450.C5 1962a] 62-15759
1. Segregation—Religious aspects. 2. Africa, South—Race question. I. Title.

HORNE, George, 1895- 261.83
The twentieth-century cross; a book for every thinking, patriotic, Christian American in our time. [1st ed.] New York, Greenwich Book Publishers [1960- v. 21cm. [BT734.3.H6] 60-10772
1. Segregation—Religious aspects. 2. U.S.—Race question. I. Title.

INGRAM, Tolbert Robert, 1913- ed. 261.83
Essays on segregation. Boston, St. Thomas Press, 1960. v, 106p. 19cm. [BT734.3.I5] 60-13820
1. Segregation—Religious aspects. I. Title.

INGRAM, Tolbert Robert, 1913- ed. 261.83
Essays on segregation, edited by T. Robert Ingram. [Rev. ed.] Houston [Tex., St. Thomas Press, 1960 [i.e. 1963] iv, 108 p. 19 cm. [BT734.3.I 5] 66-3174
1. Segregation — Religious aspects. I. Title.

MCGOWAN, Herman Craig. 220.8301451
God's garden of segregation. [1st ed.] New York, Vantage Press [1961] 94p. illus. 21cm. [BT734.3.M24] 61-3448
1. Segregation—Religious aspects. I. Title.

MASTON, Thomas Bufford, 1897- 261.83
Segregation and desegregation: a Christian approach. New York, Macmillan, 1959. 178p. 22cm. Includes bibliography. [BT734.3.M3] 59-8224
1. Segregation— Religious aspects. I. Title.

RAMSEY, Paul. 261.83
Christian ethics and the sit-in. New York, Association Press [1961] 128p. 20cm. [BT734.3.R3] 61-8182
1. Segregation—Religious aspects. 2. Negroes—Segregation. I. Title.

RAMSEY, Paul [Robert Paul Ramsey] 261.83
Christian ethics and the sit-in. New York, AssociationPress [c.1961] 128p. Bibl. 61-8182 2.50 bds.,
1. Segregation—Religious aspects. 2. Negroes—Segregation. I. Title.

SELLERS, James Earl. 261.83
The South and Christian ethics. New York, Association Press [1962] 190 p. 20 cm. [E185.61.S48] 62-16877
1. Segregation—Religious aspects. 2. Negroes—Segregation. I. Title.

TILSON, Charles Everett. 220.832341
Segregation and the Bible. New York, Abingdon Press [1958] 176 p. 21 cm. Includes bibliography. [BT734.3.T5] 58-7437
1. Segregation—Religious aspects. I. Title.

Seguin, Edward, 1812-1880. Mentally handicapped children—Education.

TALBOT, Mabel E. 371.92
Edouard Seguin: a study of educational approach to the treatment ofmentally defective children. New York, Bur. of Pubns., Teachers Coll. [1965, c.1964] xiii, 150p. illus. 21cm. (TC ser. in special educ.) Bibl. [LC4602.T3] 64-23753 2.75 pap.,
1. Seguin, Edward, 1812-1880. Mentally handicapped children—Education. I. Title.

Seguin, Tex.—Biography.

ST. James Catholic Church, Seguin, Tex. 282'.764'34
The centennial story, 1873-1973. Seguin, Tex. : St. James Catholic Church, [1973?] 64 p. : ill. ; 28 cm. Cover title. [BX4603.S63S347 1970z] 75-331288
1. St. James Catholic Church, Seguin, Tex. 2. Seguin, Tex.—Biography. I. Title.

Seguin, Tex. First Methodist Church.

WEINERT, Willie Mae. 287.6764
Methodism in Seguin, 1841-1951. [Seguin, Tex.] First Methodist Church of Seguin, 1951. 67p. illus. 23cm. [BX8481.S45W4] 56-26549
1. Seguin, Tex. First Methodist Church. 2. Methodist Church in Texas. I. Title.

Segundo, Juan Luis.

HENNELLY, Alfred T. 230'.2'0924
Theologies in conflict : the challenge of Juan Luis Segundo / Alfred T. Hennelly. Maryknoll, N.Y. : Orbis Books, c1979. xxiii, 200 p. ; 24 cm. Includes bibliographies. [BT83.57.S449H46] 79-11760 ISBN 0-88344-287-6 pbk. : 8.95
1. Segundo, Juan Luis. 2. Liberation theology. I. Title.

TAMBASCO, Anthony J. 2411'.042
The Bible for ethics : Juan Luis Segundo and first-world ethics / Anthony J. Tambasco. Lanham, MD : University Press of America, [1981] p. cm. Bibliography: p. [BX4705.S523T35] 19 80-6253 ISBN 0-8191-1556-8 lib. bdg. : 19.25 ISBN 0-8191-1557-6 (pbk.) : 10.50
1. Segundo, Juan Luis. 2. Bible—Criticism, interpretation, etc.—History—20th century. 3. Ethics in the Bible—History. I. Title.

Segur, Louis Gasion Adrien de, bp., 1820-1881.

THE blind friend of the poor; reminiscences of the life and works of Mgr. de Segur, by one of his spiritual children. Translated from the French by Miss Mary McMahon. New York. Cincinnati [etc.] Benziger brothers. 1883. 139 p. 16 cm. Dedications signed: G.V. [BX470.S525B52] 37-29681 922.244
1. Segur, Louis Gasion Adrien de, bp., 1820-1881. I. Gustave. II. McMahon, Mary, tr.

Segye Kidokkyo T'ongil Sillyong Hyophoe.

BROMLEY, David G. 301.5'8
Moonies in America : cult, church, and crusade / David G. Bromley and Anson D. Shupe, Jr. Beverly Hills : Sage Publications, c1979. 269 p. ; 23 cm. (Sage library of social research ; v. 92) Includes index. Bibliography: p. 257-263. [BX9750.S4B76] 79-16456 ISBN 0-8039-1060-6 : 15.00 ISBN 0-8039-1061-4 pbk. : 7.95
1. Segye Kidokkyo T'ongil Sillyong Hyophoe. 2. Moon, Sun Myung. 3. Holy Spirit Association for the Unification of World Christianity. I. Shupe, Anson D., joint author. II. Title.

SONTAG, Frederick. 289.9 B
Sun Myung Moon and the Unification Church / Frederick Sontag. Nashville, Tenn. : Abingdon Press, c1977. 224 p. : ill. ; 23 cm. Bibliography: p. 217-224. [BX9750.S4S66] 77-9075 ISBN 0-687-40622-6 : 8.95
1. Segye Kidokkyo T'ongil Sillyong Hyophoe. 2. Moon, Sun Myung. I. Title.

STREIKER, Lowell D. 200'.973
The cults are coming! / Lowell D. Streiker. Nashville : Abingdon, c1978. 127 p. : ill. ; 20 cm. Includes bibliographical references. [BL2530.U6S84] 78-1588 pbk. : 3.95
1. Segye Kidokkyo T'ongil Sillyong Hyophoe. 2. Krishna—Cult—United States. 3. Cults—United States. 4. Children of God (Movement) I. Title.

THE Unification Church ; as others see us / [edited by W. Farley Jones] . [Washington] : Holy Spirit Association for the Unification of World Christianity, 1974. vii, 156 p. : ill. ; 28 cm. Letters received by the Holy Spirit Association for the Unification of World Christianity. [BP605.S25U53] 74-17902 289.9
1. Segye Kidokkyo T'ongil Sillyong Hyophoe. 2. Moon, Sun Myung. I. Jones, William Farley, 1943- comp. II. Segye Kidokkyo T'ongil Sillyong Hyophoe. III. Title: As others see us.

Segye Kidokkyo T'ongil Sillyong Hyophoe—Doctrinal and controversial works.

KIM, Young Oon. 230
Unification theology & Christian thought / Young Oon Kim. 1st ed. New York : Golden Gate Pub. Co., 1975. xi, 302 p. ; 21 cm. Includes bibliographies and index. [BT75.2.K53] 74-32590
1. Segye Kidokkyo T'ongil Sillyong Hyophoe—Doctrinal and controversial works. 2. Theology, Doctrinal. 3. Theology, Doctrinal—History. I. Title.

YAMAMOTO, J. Isamu. 289.9
The puppet master : an inquiry into Sun Myung Moon and the Unification Church

/ J. Isamu Yamamoto. Downers Grove, Ill. : InterVarsity Press, c1977. 136 p. ; 21 cm. Includes bibliographical references. [BX9750.S4Y36] 76-55622 ISBN 0-87784-740-1 pbk. : 3.95
1. Segye Kidokkyo T'ongil Sillyong Hyophoe—Doctrinal and controversial works. 2. Moon, Sun Myung.

Segye Kidokkyo T'ongil Sillyong Hyophoe—Sermons.

MOON, Sun Myung. 230
The new future of Christianity / Sun Myung Moon. Washington : Unification Church International, 1974. vii, 144 p., [1] fold. leaf of plates : ill. ; 20 cm. Translation of 2 speeches delivered at the Waldorf Astoria, and Madison Square Garden, New York on Sept. 17 and 18, 1974 respectively. Contents.Contents.—God's new way of life.—The new future of Christianity. [BX9750.S4M66] 74-24931
1. Segye Kidokkyo T'ongil Sillyong Hyophoe—Sermons. 2. Sermons, Korean—Translations into English. 3. Sermons, English—Translations from Korean. I. Title.

Segye Kidokkyo T'ongil Sillyong Hyophoe—Addresses, essays, lectures.

EXPLORING Unification 230'.9'9
theology / edited by M. Darrol Bryant and Susan Hodges. 2d ed. Barrytown, N.Y. : Unification Theological Seminary ; New York : distributed by Rose of Sharon Press, c1978. viii, 168 p. ; 23 cm. (Conference series - Unification Theological Seminary ; no. 1) "[Outgrowth] of a series of conversations at the Unification Theological Seminary in Barrytown, New York, during February and April of 1977." [BX9750.S4E95 1978b] 78-63274 ISBN 0-932894-00-3 pbk. : 6.95
1. Segye Kidokkyo T'ongil Sillyong Hyophoe—Addresses, essays, lectures. 2. Moon, Sun Myung—Addresses, essays, lectures. I. Bryant, M. Darrol. II. Hodges, Susan. III. Series: Unification Theological Seminary. Conference series — Unification Theological Seminary ; no. 1..

Segye Kidokkyo T'ongil Sillyong Hyophoe—Doctrinal and controversial works—Congresses.

EVANGELICAL-UNIFICATION 230'.99
dialogue / edited by Richard Quebedeaux, Rodney Sawatsky. 1st ed. Barrytown, N.Y. : Unification Theological Seminary ; New York : distributed by the Rose of Sharon Press, c1979. 374 p. ; 23 cm. (Conference series - Unification Theological Seminary ; no. 3) Transcription of a dialogue held in June and October, 1978 at Unification Theological Seminary, Barrytown, N.Y. [BX9750.S4E92] 79-89421 ISBN 0-932894-02-X pbk. : 6.95
1. Segye Kidokkyo T'ongil Sillyong Hyophoe—Doctrinal and controversial works—Congresses. 2. Evangelicalism—Congresses. I. Quebedeaux, Richard. II. Sawatsky, Rodney. III. Series: Unification Theological Seminary. Conference series — Unification Theological Seminary ; no. 3.

Sekhem-khet, King of Egypt.

GHUNAIM, Muhammad Zakariya. 932
The lost pyramid. New York, Rinehart [1956] 175p. illus. 22cm. [DT73.S3G5] 913.32 56-11024
1. Sekhem-khet, King of Egypt. 2. Sakkara—Antiq. 3. Pyramids. I. Title.

Selden, Eric L.

SELDEN, Eric L. 231
The God of the present age / by Eric L. Selden. [Independence, Mo.] : Herald Pub. House, c1981. 170 p. ; 20 cm. [BT102.S44] 19 80-26149 ISBN 0-8309-0305-4 : 8.50
1. Selden, Eric L. 2. God. I. Title.

Self.

EASTCOTT, Michal J. 299'.934
I, the story of the self / Michal Eastcott. 1st Quest ed. Wheaton, Ill. : Theosophical Pub. House, c1980. 201 p. : ill. ; 21 cm. (A Quest book) Includes index. Bibliography: p. [193]-195. [BF697.E46] 80-51552 ISBN 0-8356-0541-8 (pbk.) : 5.50
1. Self. 2. Theosophy. I. Title.

SCHUYLER, Henry Clement, 1876- 128
Life's final goal; charting a course by the light of reason, by Henry C. Schuyler ... Philadelphia, Pa., The Peter Reilly company; London, B. Herder [c1939] x, 365 p. 23 cm. [BD431.S285] 40-4913
1. Self. 2. Religion—Philosophy. I. Title.

SYMONDS, Percival Mallon, 1893- 153.72
The ego and the self. New York, Appleton-Century-Crofts [1951] ix, 229 p. 21 cm. (The Century psychology series) Bibliography: p. 193-220. [BR175.S9] 51-9302
1. Self. I. Title.

Self-actualization (Psychology)

ABATA, Russell M. 248.4'82
How to develop a better self-image / Russell M. Abata. Liguori, Mo. : Liguori Publications, c1980. 96 p. ; 18 cm. [BF637.S4A33] 79-91440 ISBN 0-89243-119-9 pbk. : 2.25
1. Self-actualization (Psychology) 2. Self-perception. 3. Christian life—1960- I. Title.

HUMPHRIES, Jackie. 248.4
All the things you aren't ... yet ... / Jackie Humphries. Waco, Tex. : Word Books, c1980. 165 p. ; 22 cm. Includes bibliographical references. [BF637.S4H85] 77-92468 ISBN 0-8499-2891-5 pbk. : 5.95
1. Self-actualization (Psychology) 2. Emotions. 3. Christian life—1960- I. Title.

Self-control.

PARAMANANDA, swami, 1883- 179.9
Self-mastery, by Swami Paramananda ... 4th ed. rev. and enl. Boston, Mass., The Vedanta centre [c1923] 84 p. 19 cm. (His Practical series, no. 2) "Reprinted from the Vedanta monthly 'The message of the East'." [R132.V3P375 1923] 33-34189
1. Self-control. I. Title.

Self-control—Moral and religious aspects.

COOK, E. Wake.
Betterment, individual, social, and industrial; or, Highest efficiency through the golden rules of right nutrition; welfare work; and the higher industrial developments, by E. Wake Cook. New York, F.A. Stokes company [1906] xii, 349 p. 19 1/2 cm. 6-40953
I. Title.

STOOP, David A. 248.4
Self talk / David Stoop. Old Tappan, N.J. : F.H. Revell, c1982. p. cm. [BV4647.S39S76] 19 81-12136 ISBN 0-8007-5074-8 : 5.95
1. Self-control—Moral and religious aspects. I. Title.

Self identity.

NOREM, Harian.
Me, my self and God; teacher's guide. Minneapolis, Augsburg Publishing House [1965] [Minneapolis? 1965?] 80 p. 28 cm. 30 p. illus. 28 cm. A senior high course of the American Lutheran Church Curriculum. Student's book. Art work by Paul Snyder. 67-49049
1. Self identity. 2. Personality — Religious interpretation. I. Title.

Self-incrimination (Jewish law)

KIRSCHENBAUM, Aaron. 296.1'8
Self-incrimination in Jewish law. Introd. by Arthur J. Goldberg. New York, Burning Bush Press [1970] xii, 212 p. 22 cm. Bibliography: p. 192-204. [LAW] 70-82311 6.95
1. Self-incrimination (Jewish law) I. Title.

Self-love (Theology)

ALLEN, Charles Livingston, 1913- 248.4
The secret of abundant living / Charles L. Allen. Old Tappan, N.J. : Revell, c1980. 157 p. ; 22 cm. [BV4639.A384] 80-17524 ISBN 0-8007-1123-8 : 6.95
1. Self-love (Theology) 2. Self-acceptance. 3. Christian life—Methodist authors. I. Title.

DEFERRARI, Teresa Mary 241
The problem of charity for self; a study of the doctrine and its presentation to college students. [Boston] St. Paul Eds. [dist. Daughters of St. Paul, c.1962] 205p. 22cm. 62-20471 3.50; 2.50 pap.,
1. Self-love (Theology) I. Title.

SCHULLER, Robert Harold. 248.4
Self-esteem, the new reformation / Robert H. Schuller. Waco, Tex. : Word Books, c1982. 177 p. : ill. ; 23 cm. Includes bibliographical references. [BV4639.S3458 1982] 19 82-8356 ISBN 0-8499-0299-1 : 8.95
1. Self-love (Theology) 2. Pastoral psychology. I. Title.

Self-love (Theology)—History of doctrines—Early church, ca. 30-600.

O'DONOVAN, Oliver. 241'.4
The problem of self-love in St. Augustine / Oliver O'Donovan. New Haven : Yale University Press, c1980. p. cm. Includes indexes. Bibliography: p. [BV4639.O38] 80-5397 ISBN 0-300-02468-1 : 14.00
1. Augustinius, Aurelius, Saint, Bp. of Hippo—Ethics. 2. Self-love (Theology)—History of doctrines—Early church, ca. 30-600. 3. Christian ethics—Early church, ca. 30-600. I. Title.

Self (Philosophy)

DEUTSCH, Eliot. 126
Personhood, creativity, and freedom / Eliot Deutsch. Honolulu : University Press of Hawaii, c1982. 157 p. ; 22 cm. Includes bibliographical references and index. [BD450.D457 1982] 19 82-4891 ISBN 0-8248-0800-2 : 20.00
1. Self (Philosophy) 2. Consciousness. 3. Causation. 4. Time. 5. Free will and determinism. 6. Ethics. I. Title.

LEE, Jung Young. 232.9'54
Patterns of inner process : the rediscovery of Jesus' teachings in the I ching and Preston Harold / Jung Young Lee. 1st ed. Secaucus, N.J. : Citadel Press, c1976. p. cm. Includes bibliographical references. [PL2464.Z6L38] 76-8858 ISBN 0-8065-0528-1 pbk. : 5.95
1. Jesus Christ—Teachings. 2. Harold, Preston. 3. I ching. 4. Self (Philosophy) I. Title.

Self-realization.

BARING, Margery Louise, 1908- 133
The greater freedom; the heritage of the innate self ... [by] Margery Louise Baring. Reno, Nev., Printed by Silver state press, c1943. 2 p. l., 7-195 p. 18 1/2 x 14 cm. Book 1 of a trilogy: books 2 and 3 have titles "Ours for discovery, a guide to the inner journey" and "Good news, an eleventh hour dispatch," respectively. [BF1999.B376] 44-20284
I. Title.

BILLION, Anna, 1932- 131'.32
Kundalini, secret of the ancient yogis / Anna Billion. West Nyack, NY : Parker Pub. Co., c1979. 239 p. : ill. ; 24 cm. [BP605.S4B54] 78-12684 ISBN 0-13-516781-7 : 9.95
1. Self-realization. 2. Yoga. I. Title.

CYGON, Joseph R 1887-- 234
Journey towards self-realization; an interpretation of the Christian Gospels in relation to certain psychological and metaphysical aspects of soul regeneration. San Gabriel, Calif., Willing Pub. Co. [1955] 267p. 21cm. Includes bibliography. [BJ1470.C9] 55-28235
1. Self-realization. 2. Bible. N. T. Gospels—Criticism, interpretation, etc. I. Title.

DUNNAM, Maxie D. 254
The manipulator and the church [by] Maxie D. Dunnam, Gary J. Herbertson [and] Everett L. Shostrom. Nashville, Abingdon Press [1968] 176 p. illus. 21 cm. Includes bibliographical references. [BV652.2.D8] 68-27627 3.50
1. Self-realization. 2. Church renewal. 3. Church group work. I. Herbertson, Gary J., joint author. II. Shostrom, Everett L., 1921- joint author. III. Title.

HANNUM, John A. 248
Living goals for everyone; achieving insight through self-development. New York, Exposition [c.1963] 78p. 21cm. 3.00
I. Title.

ISHERWOOD, Margaret. 200
Searching for meaning; a religion of inner growth for agnostics and believers. Philadelphia, Macrae Smith Co. [1971, c1970] 175 p. illus. 24 cm. [BJ1470.I83 1971] 73-150681 ISBN 0-8255-4700-8 5.95
1. Self-realization. 2. Religion. I. Title.

NOONAN, Richard H., 1916- 248'.4
52 weeks to a great new life [by] Richard H. Noonan. West Nyack, N.Y., Parker Pub. Co. [1973] 274 p. 24 cm. [BJ1470.N66] 73-12033 ISBN 0-13-314872-6 6.95
1. Self-realization. I. Title.

PREMANANDA, Swami, 1903- 179.9
The blessdness of the inner life. Washington, Self-Revelation Church [c1957] 213p. illus. 21cm. [BJ1470.P68] 58-44329
1. Self-realization. I. Title.

*SUBRAMUNIYA, Master. 294.548
The self god, by Master Subramuniya. San Francisco, Calif., Comstock house, [1973, c1972] 70 p., 14 cm. "A Western Mystic's insight into Self-Realization." Previously published in 1959 by Wailua University of Contemplative Arts and in 1971 by Gilmore and Co. [BL1228] 2.00 (pbk.)
1. Self-realization. 2. Satisfaction. I. Title.

*THORNE, Milton 252.076
Everbody is a somebody. New York, Carlton [1966] 63p. 21cm. (Reflection bk.) 2.00
I. Title.

*THORNE, Milton 252.076
Everbody is a somebody. New York, Carlton [1966] 63p. 21cm. (Reflection bk.) 2.00
I. Title.

TOURNIER, Paul. 248.4
The adventure of living. Translated by Edwin Hudson. [1st ed.] New York, Harper & Row [1965] 250 p. 22 cm. Bibliographical footnotes. [BJ1470.T613] 65-20459
1. Self-realization. I. Title.

YUKTESWAR, Swami, 1855-1936. 294.5'44
The holy science. Kaivalya darsanam. 7th ed. Los Angeles, Self-Realization Fellowship, 1972 [c1949] xxiv, 77 p. illus. 19 cm. [BP605.S4Y8 1972] 77-88199 ISBN 0-87612-051-6 2.50
1. Self-realization. I. Title.

Self-Realization Fellowship—Biography.

KRIYANANDA, Swami. 181'.45'0924 B
The path : autobiography of a Western yogi / by Swami Kriyananda (Donald Walters) ; with a preface by John W. White. Nevada City, Calif. : Ananda Publications, 1977. xviii, 640 p. : ill. ; 22 cm. Includes index. [BP605.S43K744] 77-7287 ISBN 0-916124-11-8 : 15.00
1. Kriyananda, Swami. 2. Self-Realization Fellowship—Biography. I. Title.

Self-realization fellowship—Hymns.

YOGANANDA, paramhansa, 1893- 783.
Cosmic chants, spiritualized songs. [2d ed.] Los Angeles, Self-Realization Pub. House, 1943 [c1938] 60 p. 26 cm. Unacc. melodies. [M2131.S25Y6] 51-46295
1. Self-realization fellowship—Hymns. 2. Hymns, English. I. Title.

YOGANANDA, Paramahansa, 1893-1952 783.5
Cosmic chants. Words and music of 60 spiritualized songs. [5th ed.] Los Angeles, Self-Realization, 1963 [c.1938-1963] 84p. photo., col. illus. 27cm. Unacc. melodies. 63-4544 2.50; plastic bdg.
1. Self-Realization Fellowship—Hymns. 2. Hymns, English. I. Title.

Self-realization—Societies, etc.

HENDERSON, C. William. 291.4
Awakening : ways to psychospiritual growth / C. William Henderson. Englewood Cliffs, N.J. : Prentice-Hall, [1975] xi, 244 p. ; 21 cm. (A Spectrum book) (Transpersonal books) [BP603.H46] 75-11596 ISBN 0-13-055467-7 : 8.95 ISBN 0-13-055459-6 pbk. : 3.95
1. Self-realization—Societies, etc. 2. Sects. 3. Religions. I. Title.

Selling—Personnel management.

STAUNTON, J. Donald. 658.4'071245
Increasing the effectiveness of the field sales force / J. Donald Staunton. Brattleboro, VT : CBI Pub. Co., 1982. p. cm. Bibliography: p. [HF5439.5.S723 1982] 19 82-20589 ISBN 0-8436-0876-5 : 59.95
1. Selling—Personnel management. 2. Sales personnel, Training of. I. Title.

Selma, Calif. St Joseph's Catholic Church.

HALLMAN, Lillian C.
The harvest is great; a semi-centennial history of the Catholic community of Selma, California, by Lillian C. Hallman. Selma, Calif., St. Joseph Church, 1963. 92 p. illus., ports. 28 cm. 67-41597
1. Selma, Calif. St Joseph's Catholic Church. I. Title.

Selwyn, George Augustus, bp. of Lichfield, 1809-1878.

CREIGHTON, Louise (von Glehn) Mrs. 1850- 922.
G. A. Selwyn, D. D., bishop of New Zealand and Lichfield, by Louise Creighton ... With 2 maps. London, New York [etc.] Longmans, Green and co., 1923. xi, [1], 180 p incl. front., map. 19 cm. [BX5199.S45C7] 23-7940
1. Selwyn, George Augustus, bp. of Lichfield, 1809-1878. I. Title.

TUCKER, Henry William, 1830-
Memoir of the life and episcopate of George Augustus Selwyn, D.D. bishop of New Zealand, 1841-1869, bishop of Lichfield, 1867-1878. By the Rev. H. W. Tucker ... New York, Pott, Young, and co., 1879. 2 v. fronts. (ports) illus., maps, facism. 23 cm. 15-18993
I. Title.

Semantics (Philosophy)

CHRISTIAN, William A 201
Meaning and truth in religion. Princeton, N.J., Princeton University Press, 1964. ix, 273 p. 23 cm. Bibliographical footnotes. [BL65.L2C5] 64-12180
1. Semantics (Philosophy) 2. Religion and language. I. Title.

PETERSON, Thomas D. 251'.00141
Wittgenstein for preaching : a model for communication / Thomas D. Peterson. Lanham, Md. : University Press of America, c1980. xiv, 180 p. : ill. ; 22 cm. Bibliography: p. 179-180. [B3376.W564P39] 19 80-5802 ISBN 0-8191-1342-5 : 17.00 ISBN 0-8191-1343-3 (pbk.) : 8.75
1. Wittgenstein, Ludwig, 1889-1951. 2. Semantics (Philosophy) 3. Communication (Theology) 4. Communication—Methodology. I. Title.

SHERWOOD, John C 149.9
Discourse of reason; a brief handbook of semantics and logic. New York, Harper [1960] 112 p. 21 cm. Includes bibliography. [BS40.S5] 60-9136
1. Semantics (Philosophy) 2. Logic. I. Title.

Semi-Pelagianism.

PROSPER, Tiro, Aguitanus, Saint 281.1
Defense of St. Augustine. Tr. [from Latin] annotated by P. DeLetter Westminster, Md., Newman [c.]1963. v, 248p. 23cm. (Ancient Christian writers; works of the Fathers in tr., no. 32) Bibl. 62-21490 3.75
1. Augustinus, Aurelius, Saint Bp. of Hippo Bp. of Hippo. 2. Semi-Pelagianism. I. Letter, Prudentius de, ed. and tr. II. Title. III. Series.

Seminarians.

DUBAY, Thomas. 271
The seminary rule: an explanation of the purposes behind it and how best to carry it out. With a foreword by Joseph Francis Rummel. Westminster, Md., Newman Press, 1954. 140p. 23cm. [BX903.D8] 54-5896
1. Seminarians. I. Title.

LOUISVILLE, Ky. Southern Baptist theological seminary.
Catalogue of the Southern Baptist theological seminary. Louisville, Kentucky. Louisville, Seminary press, v. plates. 23 cm. ca 11
I. Title.

MARCETTEAU, Benjamin Felix, 1877- 264.02
The major seminarian. Paterson, N.J., St. Anthony Guild Press, 1948. xii, 491 p. 18 cm. [BX903.M29] 49-7260
1. Seminarians. 2. Catholic Church—Prayer-books and devotions—English. I. Title.

MARCETTEAU, Benjamin Felix, 1877- 264.02
The young seminarian, by B. F. Marcetteau ... Paterson, N.J., St. Anthony guild press, 1943. xv, 536 p. 15 cm. [BX903.M3] 43-17965
1. Seminarians. I. Title.

MINOR Seminary Conference, Catholic University of America.
Minor seminary conference on a continuing study of outcomes; the proceedings of the annual minor seminary conference, conducted at the Catholic University of America, May 11-13, 1962. Edited by Cornelius M. Cuyler. Washington, Catholic University of America Press [1963] vi, 95 p. 22 cm. 66-31439
1. Seminarians. 2. Prediction of scholastic success. I. Cuyler, Cornelius M., ed. II. Title.

MINOR Seminary Conference. 12th, Catholic University America, 1961. 207
Minor Seminary Conference on outcomes the proceedings of the twelfth Minor Seminary Conference, conducted at the Catholic University of America, May 12, 13, and 14, 1961. Ed. by Cornelius M. Cuyler. Washington, D.C., Catholic Univ. of Amer. Pr. [c.]1961. v, 90p. 61-66767 1.50 pap.,
1. Seminarians. 2. Prediction of scholastic success. I. Cuyler, Cornelius M., ed. II. Title.

MYERS, Rawley. 271
This is the seminary. Milwaukee, Bruce Pub. Co. [1953] 123p. 21cm. [BX903.M43] 53-2191
1. Seminarians. I. Title.

MYERS, Rawley.
This is the seminary. Milwaukee, Bruce [1963] 91 p. 18 cm. First published in 1951. 67-22847
1. Seminarians. 2. Priesthood. I. Title.

NEW York. Union theological seminary. 016.
Announcement of courses of study. New York, 18 v. 23 1/2 cm. annual. 18 - 1901/02 have title: The courses of study in the Union theological seminary. [BV4070.U621] CA 7
I. Title.

PHILADELPHIA theological seminary of Saint Charles Borromeo. 207.748
St. Charles seminary, Overbrook, a history of the Theological seminary of Saint Charles Borromeo, Overbrook, Philadelphia, Pennsylvania, 1832-1943, with a chronological record of ordinations from the establishment of the diocese to the present, and with Pictures of the secular clergy of the Archdiocese of Philadelphia, 1943. Foreword by His Excellency the Most Rev. Hugh L. Lamb ... [Philadelphia, Jefferies & Manz, c1943] ix, 401 p. incl. illus. (coat of arms) ports. plates, ports. 24 cm. Bibliography: p. 373-374. [BX915.P46A4] 44-4189
I. Title.

ST. Vincent college, Beatty, Pa.
Catalogue of the officers, faculty, and students of St. Vincent college and seminary. [Beatty v. plates. 22 1/2 cm. [LD4837.S53] CA 10
I. Title.

SCHECHTER, Solomon, 1847-
Seminary addresses, and other papers, by S. Schechter ... Cincinnati, Ark publishing co., 1915. xiv p., 1 l., 253 p. front. (port.) 21 1/2 cm. $1.25 15-17793
I. Title.

SCHULTZ, Charles Henry, 1856- 251
Sacred eloquence; a guide book for seminarians, by Charles H. Schultz ... Baltimore, Md., John Murphy company [c1926] viii, 269 p. 21 cm. [BV4211.S3] 26-12510
I. Title.

THE seminarian.
New York, The General theological seminary, 18 v. plates, ports. 24 cm. 99-2740
I. New York. General theological seminary of the Protestant Episcopal church in the U.S.

WERSELL, Thomas W., ed. 922.473
Why I am at the seminary; forty-one true stories by theological students. Rock Island, Ill., Augustana [c.1962] 160p. 21cm. 62-21691 1.75 pap.,
1. Seminarians. I. Title.

Seminarians—Meditations.

DANAGHER, Edward F 248.8
Son, give me your heart. Milwaukee, Bruce Pub. Co. [1964] viii, 149 p. 17 cm. [BX2182.2.D3] 63-23266
1. Seminarians — Meditations. I. Title.

PRINDEVILLE, Carlton A., 1894- 242
Meditations for seminarians, by Rev. Carlton A. Prindeville. St. Louis, Mo., and London, B. Herder book co., 1946. vii p., 1 l., 408 p. 22 cm. [BX2182.P7] 47-353
1. Seminarians—Meditations. I. Title.

YOUNG, Valentine 242.2
Daily meditations for seminarians. Chicago, Franciscan Herald Press [c.1960] 337p. front. 60-11993 1.75 pap.,
1. Seminarians—Meditations. I. Title.

Seminarians—Psychology.

HERR, Vincent V. 155.2
The personality of seminarians; a study guide and reference work [by] Vincent V. Herr. Staten Island, N.Y., Alba House [1969, i.e. 1970] xiv, 157 p. 22 cm. Bibliography: p. [151]-153. [BX903.H45] 72-94698 ISBN 8-18-901683- 4.95
1. Seminarians—Psychology. I. Title.

Seminarians—Religious life.

ALEXANDRIA, Va. Protestant Episcopal Theological Seminary in Virginia. 207.755
Alumni directory, Virginia Theological Seminary. [Alexandria?] v. 21cm. Issues for 1958-'published as a supplement to the Seminary journal.' [BV4070.A417] 58-27119
I. Title.

ALLEGHENY, Pa. Western theological seminary of the Presbyterian church. 285
Alumni re-union of the Western theological seminary, held April 16-18, 1872. Pittsburgh, W.G. Johnston & co., printers, 1872. 80 p. 21 cm. E 14
I. Title.

AMERICAN Association of Theological Schools. Task Force on Spiritual Development. 207'.11
Voyage, vision, venture; a report [by the] Task Force on Spiritual Development, David E. Babin [and others] Dayton, Ohio, American Association of Theological Schools, 1972. 45 p. 23 cm. [BV4011.6.A45] 72-190320
1. Seminarians—Religious life. 2. Spiritual life. I. Babin, David E. II. Title.

ANDOVER theological seminary. Alumni association.
Andover theological seminary. Necrology ... Boston, v. 23 1/2 cm. 1-22028
I. Title.

ANGRISANI, Giuseppe, Bp., 1894- 248
It is you I beckon; a book of spiritual inspiration for seminarians, based on the exhotation Menti nostrae of Pope Pius XII. Translated by Joseph A. McMullin. New York, Benziger Bros. [1957] 337p. 20cm. [BX903.A5] 57-31394
1. Seminarians—Religious life. I. Title.

DE HUECK, Catherine, 1900- 250
Dear Seminarian. Milwaukee, Bruce [1950] 87 p. 19 cm. [BX903.D4] 51-2185
1. Seminarians—Religious life. I. Title.

DREW university, Madision, N.J Theological seminary. 207.74974
Alumni record of Drew theological seminary, 1867-1905. Compiled by the biographical secretary of the Alumni association. Madison, N.J., S. G. Ayres, 1906. 615 p. 21 cm. Preface signed: S. G. Ayres. [BV4070.D74] 6-26517
I. Ayres, Samuel Gardiner, 1865- comp. II. Title.

DREW university, Madison, N.J. Theological seminary. 207.74974
... *Alumni record,* 1869-1895. New York, W. B. Ketcham [1895] 306 p. 20 1/2 cm. "Prefatory note" signed S. G. Ayres. [BV4070.D74 1895] 1-24303
I. Ayres, Samuel Gardiner, 1865- II. Title.

DREW university, Madison, N.J. Theological seminary. 207.74974
Alumni record of Drew theological seminary, Madision, New Jersey, 1867-1925, edited by William Pearson Tolley ... [Madison, N.J.] The Seminary, 1926. xv, 676 p. 23 1/2 cm. [BV4070.D74 1925] 27-8218
I. Tolley, William Pearson, 1900- ed. II. Title.

FARRELL, Melvin 248.83
First steps to the priesthood, an explanation of the Christian life for minor seminarians. Milwaukee, Bruce Pub. Co. [c.1960] 206 p. 60-15478 3.95
1. Seminarians—Religious life. I. Title.

FARRELL, Melvin L 248.89
First steps to the priesthood, an explanation of the Christian life for minor seminarians [by] Melvin Farrell. Milwaukee, Bruce Pub. Co. [1960] viii, 206 p. 23 cm. [BX903.F3] 60-15478
1. Seminarians — Religious life. I. Title.

GOEBEL, Edmund J. 248
Pax Christi; letters to a young seminarist [by] Rev. Edmund J. Goebel ... New York, Milwaukee, Wis. [etc.] The Bruce publishing compnay [c1929] 6 p. l., [3]-208 p. 19 cm. [BX2385.G6] 29-12700
I. Title.

GOEBEL, Edmund Joseph, 1896- 248
Pax Christi, letters to a young seminarist [by] Rev. Edmund J. Goebel ... New York, Milwaukee, Wis. [etc.] The Bruce publishing company [c1929] 6 p. l., [3]-203 p. 19 cm. [BX2385.G6] 29-12700
1. Seminarists—Religious life. I. Title.

NASH, Robert. 242
The seminarian at his prie-dieu. Westminster, Md., Newman Press, 1951. 312 p. 23 cm. [BX903.N3] 52-6323
1. Seminarians — Religious life. I. Title.

NEW York. Union theological seminary. 016.
Alumni catalogue of the Union theological seminary in the city of New York, 1836-1926, compiled by Rev. Charles Ripley Gillett ... New York, 1926. xiv, 635 p. 24 cm. [BV4070.U64 1926] 27-2192

I. Gillett, Charles Ripley, 1855- ed. II. Title.

NEW York. Union theological seminary. 207.7471
Alumni catalogue of the Union theological seminary in the city of New York, 1836-1936. New York, 1937. ix, 551 p. 23 1/2 cm. "Corrections" slip inserted between p. [ii] and [iii] [BV4070.U64 1936] 37-22667
I. Title.

ROMB, Anselm William, 1929- 248.892
As one who serves, by Anselm W. Romb. Milwaukee, Bruce Pub. Co. [1966] viii. 134 p. 21 cm. [BX903.R6] 66-24256
1. Seminarians — Religious life. I. Title.

RUNG, Albert.
The seminarian, his character and work, by Rev. Albert Rung ... New York, P. J. Kenedy & sons [1916] 182 p. 18 cm. "First impression, October, 1916. Second impression, November, 1916." [BX900.R8] 17-7041 0.75
I. Title.

WALSH, James Edward, bp., 1891- 266.2
Maryknoll spiritual directory, compiled by James E. Walsh ... titular bishop of Sata. New York, Field afar press [1947] ix, 277 p. 21 1/2 cm. [BV2300.C35W3] 47-25330
1. Catholic foreign mission society of America. 2. Seminarians—Religious life. I. Title.

Seminarians—Statistics.

COLUMBIA theological seminary, Columbia, S. C.
Annual catalogue of the officers and students. Columbia, S. C. v. plates. 24 cm. ca 10
I. Title.

CROZER theological seminary (upland) Hester, Pa. 016.
... *Annual catalog.* Philadelphia [etc.] v. plates, port. 23 cm. At head of title: Bulletin of the Crozer theological seminary ... [BV4070.C82] CA 10
I. Title.

HARTFORD theological seminary, Hartford, Conn.
Annual register. Hartford, Conn., 18 plates. 18-23 cm. At head of title, 18 Hartford seminary publications, no. [new ser.] Title varies, 18 Catalogue. 18 Annual register. ca 7
I. Title.

LANCASTER, Pa. Theological seminary of the Reformed church in the United States.
Annual catalogue. [Lancaster, v. pl. 23 cm. ca 10
I. Title.

LONSWAY, Francis A. 207'.11'2
Ministers for tomorrow; a longitudinal study of Catholic seminarians in theology, by Francis A. Lonsway. Washington, Center for Applied Research in the Apostolate, 1972. ix, 119 p. illus. 29 cm. (CARA information service) Bibliography: p. 117-119. [BX905.L65] 72-181297
1. Seminarians—Statistics. 2. Theology—Study and teaching—United States—Statistics. I. Title.

MOUNT Holyoke college.
Annual catalogues of the teachers and pupils of the Mount Holyoke female seminary ... Pub. for the Memorandum society. Northampton, Mass [etc.] 18 v. 23 cm. [LD7092.48] 7-12056
I. Title.

PITTSBURGH. Western theological seminary. 016.
Annual catalogue. Pittsburgh, 18 v. in illus., plates. 22 1/2-23 1/2 cm. 1850/51, 1853/54, 1856/57, 1857/60, 1860/63 have title "Triennial catalogue ..." and contain lists of alumni. [BV4070.W52] 8-858
I. Title.

Seminarians—United States.

GEORGE, Denise. 207'.33
How to be a seminary student and survive / Denise George. Nashville, Tenn. : Broadman Press, c1981. 119 p. ; 21 cm. Includes bibliographical references. [BV4030.G46] 19 80-65845 ISBN 0-8054-6930-3 pbk. : 3.95
1. Seminarians—United States. I. Title.

LOUISVILLE, Ky. Southern Baptist Theological Seminary.
Graduate theses of Southern Baptist Theological Seminary, 1894-1962. [Louisville, Ky.] 1962. v, A-64, B-66 p. 67-81220
I. Title.

LOUISVILLE, Ky. Southern Baptist Theological Seminary.
Graduate theses of Southern Baptist Theological Seminary, 1894-1962. [Louisville, Ky.] 1962. v, A-64, B-66 p. 67-81220
I. Title.

Seminary extension—Addresses, essays, lectures.

DISCIPLING through theological education by extension : a fresh approach to theological education in the 1980s / edited by Vergil Gerber. Chicago : Moody Press, c1980. 191 p. ; 22 cm. Includes bibliographical references. [BV4164.D57] 19 80-19327 ISBN 0-8024-2218-7 : 4.95 207'.15
1. Seminary extension—Addresses, essays, lectures. 2. Theology—Study and teaching—Addresses, essays, lectures. I. Gerber, Vergil.

Seminary extension—Collected works.

KINSLER, F. Ross. 207'.11
The extension movement in theological education : a call to the renewal of the ministry / by F. Ross Kinsler. South Pasadena, Calif. : William Carey Library, [1978] xv, 288 p. : ill. ; 22 cm. Bibliography: p. 283-288. [BV4164.K56] 78-5992 ISBN 0-87808-734-6 pbk. : 6.95
1. Seminary extension—Collected works. I. Title.

Seminary extension—Directories.

WELD, Wayne. 207'.8
The world directory of theological education by extension [by] Wayne C. Weld. South Pasadena, Calif., William Carey Library [1973] xiii, 374 p. 23 cm. Bibliography: p. 359-374. [BV4164.W44] 73-8894 ISBN 0-87808-134-8 5.95 (pbk.)
1. Seminary extension—Directories. I. Title. II. Title: Theological education by extension.

Seminary extension—Latin America.

MULHOLLAND, Kenneth B. 207'.7283
Adventures in training the ministry : a Honduran case study in theological education by extension / by Kenneth Mulholland ; with foreword by F. Ross Kinsler. [Nutley, N.J.] : Presbyterian and Reformed Pub. Co., 1976. xvi, 219 p. : diagrs. ; 21 cm. (Studies in the world church and missions) "Grew out of an S.T.M. thesis presented to the faculty of the Lancaster Theological Seminary in 1971 ..." Bibliography: p. 209-219. [BV4140.L3M84] 76-5151 5.95
1. Seminary extension—Latin America. 2. Seminary extension—Honduras—Case studies. 3. Theology—Study and teaching—Latin America. I. Title. II. Series.

Seminary extension—Philippine Islands.

HILL, David Leslie, 1932- 207'.599
Designing a theological education by extension program; a Philippine case study [by] D. Leslie Hill. South Pasadena, Calif., William Carey Library [1974] x, 197 p. illus. 23 cm. Bibliography: p. 193-197. [BV4164.H54] 73-12788 ISBN 0-87808-312-X 3.95 (pbk.)
1. Seminary extension—Philippine Islands. I. Title.

HILL, David Leslie, 1932- 207'.599
Designing a theological education by extension program; a Philippine case study [by] D. Leslie Hill. South Pasadena, Calif., William Carey Library [1973] p. Bibliography: p. [BV4164.H54] 73-12788 ISBN 0-87808-312-X
1. Seminary extension—Philippine Islands. I. Title.

Semite philosophy-History.

ORIENTAL club of Philadelphia. 297
Thirty years of oriental studies, issued in commemoration of thirty years of activity of the Oriental club of Philadelphia; ed. by Roland G. Kent, secretary of the club. Philadelphia, 1918. 84 p. 23 cm. On cover: 1888-1918. Bibliography: p. 10. [PJ2.O84] 19-3543
1. Semite philology—Hist. 2. Aryan philology—Hist. I. Kent, Roland Grubb, 1877- ed. II. Peters, John Punnett, 1852-1921. III. Rogers, Robert William 1804-1930. IV. Jastrow, Morris, 1861-1921. V. Hopkins, Edward Washburn, 1857-1932. VI. Title. VII. Title: Oriental studies, Thirty years of.
Contents omitted.

Semites — Religion.

RINGGREN, Helmer, 1917- 299.9
Religions of the ancient Near East. Translated by John Sturdy. Philadelphia, Westminster Press [1973] vi, 197 p. 22 cm. Translation of Framre Orientens religioner i gammal tid. Bibliography: p. [191]-193. [BL1600.R513 1973] 72-8587 ISBN 0-664-20953-X 7.50
1. Semites—Religion. I. Title.

SMITH, William Robertson, 1846-1894. 299'.2
Lectures on the religion of the Semites; the fundamental institutions. With an introd. and additional notes by Stanley A. Cook. Prologomenon by James Muilenberg. 3d ed. [New York] Ktav Pub. House, 1969. 27, ix-lxiv, 718 p. 23 cm. (The Library of Biblical studies) Reprint of the 1927 ed. Includes bibliographical references. [BL1600.S6 1969] 69-11428
1. Semites—Religion. 2. Cultus, Semitic. I. Title. II. Series.

SMITH, William Robertson, 1846-1894. 292.2
The religion of the Semites; the fundamental institutions. New York, Meridian Books, 1956. xiv, 507 p. 21 cm. (The Meridian library, ML4) First published in 1889 as the first series of the author's "Lectures on the religion of the Semites" (Burnett lectures, Aberdeen University, 1888-89) Bibliographical footnotes. [BL1600.S6 1956] 56-11577
1. Semites — Religion. 2. Sacrifice. 3. Cultus, Semitic. I. Title.

SMITH, William Robertson, 1846-1894. 299'.2
The religion of the Semites; the fundamental institutions. [1st Schocken paperback ed.] New York, Schocken Books [1972] xiv, 507 p. 21 cm. Reprint of the 1894 ed. published under title: Lectures on the religion of the Semites. Includes bibliographical references. [BL1600.S6 1972] 76-179483 ISBN 0-8052-0346-X 3.95
1. Semites—Religion. 2. Cultus, Semitic. I. Title.

Semitic philology—Addresses, essays, lectures.

BIBLICAL and Near Eastern studies : festschrift in honor of William Sanford LaSor / edited by Gary A. Tuttle. Grand Rapids : Eerdmans, 1978, c1977. p. cm. Includes indexes. "The bibliography of William Sanford LaSor": p. [BS540.B4457] 77-10797 16.50 220.6
1. LaSor, William Sanford—Addresses, essays, lectures. 2. LaSor, William Sanford—Bibliography. 3. Bible—Criticism, interpretation, etc.—Addresses, essays, lectures. 4. Semitic philology—Addresses, essays, lectures. I. La Sor, William Sanford. II. Tuttle, Gary A.
Contents omitted

Semitic race—Religion.

CURTISS, Samuel Ives, 1814-1904.
Primitive Semitic religion today: a record of researches, discoveries and studies in Syria, Palestine and the Sinaitic peninsula, by Samuel Ives Curtiss ... Chicago, New York [etc.] Fleming H. Revell company, 1902. 288 p. illus., plates. 22 cm. "Altars and sacrifices in the primitive art of Babylonia" by the Rev. W. Hayes Ward: p. 266-277. [BL1600.C8] 2-14007
1. Semitic race—Religion. 2. Cultus, Semitic. 3. Folk-lore, Semitic. 4. Syria—Antiq. 5. Palestine—Antiq. 6. Petra, Arabia. 7. Assyro-Babylonian religion. I. Ward, William Hayes, 1835-1916. II. Title.

Sempangi, F. Kefa.

SEMPANGI, F. Kefa. 289.9 B
A distant grief / F. Kefa Sempangi, with Barbara R. Thompson. Glendale, Calif. : GL Regal Books, c1979. 192 p. ; 21 cm. Includes bibliographical references. [BX9375.R438S45] 79-50394 ISBN 0-8307-0684-4 (pbk.) : 3.95
1. Sempangi, F. Kefa. 2. Redeemed Church of Uganda—Clergy—Biography. 3. Clergy—Uganda—Biography. I. Thompson, Barbara R., joint author. II. Title.

Sen, Keshab Chandra, 1838-1884.

MULLER, Friedrich Max, 1823-1900. 294.5'562'0924 B
Keshub Chunder Sen / F. Max Mueller ; edited by Nanda Mookerjee. Calcutta : S. Gupta, 1976. ii, xvii, 117 p. ; 23 cm. Includes bibliographical references. [BL1265.S4M84 1976] 76-904243 Rs10.00 ($2.00 U.S.)
1. Sen, Keshab Chandra, 1838-1884. 2. Brahma-samaj—Biography. I. Mookerjee, Nanda. II. Title.

Seneca Indians—Religion and mythology.

MCELWAIN, Thomas. 299'.78
Mythological tales and the Allegany Seneca : a study of the socio-religious context of traditional oral phenomena in an Iroquois community / by Thomas McElwain. Stockholm : Almqvists & Wiksell International, [1978] 118 p. ; 25 cm. (Stockholm studies in comparative religion ; 17) Extra t.p. with thesis statement inserted. Includes texts in Seneca. Thesis—University of Stockholm. Includes indexes. Bibliography: p. 114-116. [E99.S3M25] 80-451173 ISBN 91-22-00181-6 pbk. : 17.75
1. Seneca Indians—Religion and mythology. 2. Indians of North America—New York (State)—Religion and mythology. I. Title. II. Series.
Distributed by Humanities Press, Atlantic Highlands, NJ 07716

Seneca Indians—Rites and ceremonies.

CHAFE, Wallace L. 299.7
Seneca thanksgiving rituals. Washington, U.S. Govt. Print. Off., 1961. iii, 302 p. 24 cm. ([U.S.] Bureau of American Ethnology Bulletin 183) Includes music. Bibliography: p. 300. "Recorded versions of the thanksgiving rituals": p. 301-302. [E51.U6 no. 183] 62-60358
1. Seneca Indians—Rites and ceremonies. 2. Seneca language—Texts. I. Series.

Seneca language—Glossaries, vocabularies, etc.

[WRIGHT, Asher] 1803-1875. 245.
Go 'wana gwa'ih sat'hah yon de'yas dah'gwah ... A spelling-book in the Seneca language: with English definitions. Buffalo-Creek Reservation, Mission press, 1842. 112 p. 19 cm. [PM2296.Z5W8] 13-11251
1. Seneca language—Glossaries, vocabularies, etc. I. Title.

Seneca language—Texts.

BIBLE. N. T. Gospels. Seneca. 1874. Wright. 226
Ho i'wiyos'dos hah neh cha ga'o hee dus,

gee ih' niga'ya dos'ha gee, neh nan'do wah'gaah he'ni a'di wa'noh daah. The four Gospels in the Seneca language. New York, American Bible society, 1874. 445 p. 18 cm. "Translated by Asher Wright."-- Brit. and for Bible soc., Hist. cat., no. 8079. [BS345.S37 Gospels 1874] 36-5012
1. Seneca language—Texts. I. Bible. Seneca. N. T. Gospels.1874. Wright. II. Wright, Asher, 1803-1875, tr. III. American Bible society. IV. Title.

[WRIGHT, Asher] 1803-1875, ed. 245.
Gaa nah shoh neh de o waah'sao'nyoh gwah Na'wenni'yuh. Honont'gah deh hodi'yado'nyoh. New-York, American tract society, 1852. 232 p. 16 cm. Seneca hymn book. [PM2296.Z71 1852] 7-9882
1. Seneca language—Texts. 2. Hymns, Seneca. I. American tract society. II. Title.

[WRIGHT, Asher, 1803-1875, ed. 245.97
Gaa nah shoh neh deo waah'sao'nyoh'gwah na'wenni'yuk. Honont'gahdeh hodi'yado'nyoh. New York, American tract society [1860] 352, [62] p. 15 1/2 cm. Seneca hymn book. "Songs of Zion" (in English, with music): [62] p. at end. [PM2296.Z71 1860] [497] 33-11269
1. Seneca language—Texts. 2. Hymns, Seneca. I. American tract society. II. Title.

Seneca, Lucius Annaeus.

GUMMERE, Ricahrd Mott, 1883-
Seneca the philosopher, and his modern message, by Richard Mott Gummere ... Boston, Mass., Marshall Jones company [c1922] xvi, 150 p. 19 cm. (Half-title: Our debt to Greece and Rome, editors, G. D. Hadzsits ... D. M. Robinson ...) Bibliography: p. 145. [PA6675.G8] 22-14144
1. Seneca, Lucius Annaeus. 2. Literature, Comparative—Latin and modern. 3. Literature, Comparative—Modern and Latin. I. Title.

Senses and sensation.

BOLOGNE, Charles Damian, 1911- 242
My friends, the senses; translated by Jane Howes. Foreword by Gerald Vann. New York, P. J. Kenedy [1953] 206p. 21cm. [BF233.B642] 53-11511
1. Senses and sensation. I. Title.

CONFREY, Burton, 1898- 377
Sensory training for Catholic schools [by] Burton Confrey ... Manchester, N. H., Magnificat press, 1938. 386 p. front. illus. plates 23 cm. Includes bibliographies [LB1057.C6] [370.15993] 38-9317
1. Senses and sensation. 2. Catholic church—Education. 3. Psychology. Physiological. 4. Education of children. I. Title.

[JOHNSON, Charles Alfred] 236.
The seven senses in man and through out the nature of the almighty infinite in the created and uncreated. Minneapolis Minn., 1907. 128 p. 18 cm. Signed: Charles Alfred Johnson. [BR126.J5] 7-23294
I. Title.

Senter, Ruth Hollinger, 1944-

SENTER, Ruth Hollinger, 1944- 248.8'43
The seasons of friendship : a search for intimacy / Ruth Senter. Grand Rapids, Mich. : Zondervan Pub. House, c1982. 156 p. ; 23 cm. [BV4527.S36 1982] 19 82-8565 ISBN 0-310-38830-9 : 7.95
1. Senter, Ruth Hollinger, 1944- 2. Women—Religious life. 3. Christian biography—United States. 4. Friendship. I. Title.

Separate Baptists—History.

COLONIAL Baptists and southern revivals. 286'.175
New York : Arno Press, 1980. ix, 166 p., p. 156-242, [1] leaf of plates : ill. ; 23 cm. (The Baptist tradition) Reprint of Baptist foundations in the South, by William L. Lumpkin, published in 1961 by Broadman Press, Nashville, and of Elder John Leland, Jeffersonian itinerant, by L. H. Butterfield, published in 1952 in v. 62 of the Proceedings of the American Antiquarian Society, Worcester, Mass. Bibliography: p. 163-166. [BX6389.63.C64 1980] 79-52585 ISBN 0-405-12452-X : 22.00
1. Leland, John, 1754-1841. 2. Separate Baptists—History. 3. Baptists—Southern States—History. 4. Separate Baptists—Clergy—Biography. 5. Clergy—Virginia—Biography. 6. Virginia—Biography. I. Lumpkin, William Latane. Baptist foundations in the South. 1980. II. Butterfield, Lyman Henry. Elder John Leland, Jeffersonian itinerant. 1980. III. Series: Baptist tradition.

LUMPKIN, William Latane. 286
Baptist foundations in the South; tracing through the Separates the influence of the Great Awakening, 1754-1787. Nashville, Broadman Press [1961] 166 p. 21 cm. [BX6389.63.L8] 61-12413
1. Separate Baptists—History. 2. Baptists—Southern States—History. I. Title.

Sephardim.

POOL, David de Sola. 1885- 915.693
The World of the Sephardim. [Articles based on lectures by] David de Sola Pool, Raphael Patai [and] Abraham Lopes Cardozo. New York, Herzl Press, 1960. 71 p. illus. 17 cm. (Herzl Institute pamphlet no. 15) [DS112.W67] 60-1413
1. Sephardim. 2. Jews — Soc. life & cust. I. Title.

WORLD of the Sephardim. 915.693
[Articles based on lectures by] David de Sola Pool, Raphael Patai [and] Abraham Lopes Cardozo. New York, Herzl Press, c.1960. 71p. illus., diagrs. 17cm. (Herzl Institute pamphlet no. 15) 60-1413 .50 pap.,
1. Sephardim. 2. Jews—Soc. life & cust. I. Pool, David de Sola.

ZIMMELS, Hirsch Jakob. 296
Ashkenazim and Sephardim: their relations, differences, and problems as reflected in the rabbinical reponsa. With a forword by Israel Brodie. London, Oxford University Press, 1958. xiv, 347 p. illus. 23 cm. (Jews' College publications, new ser., no. 2) Bibliographical footnotes. [BM182.Z5] 58-4526
1. Sephardim. 2. Jews—Rites and ceremonies. 3. Responsa. I. Title. II. Series: London, Jews' College. Publication, new ser., no. 2

Sephardim—California—Los Angeles.

STERN, Stephen. 305.8'924'079494
The Sephardic Jewish community of Los Angeles / Stephen Stern. New York : Arno Press, 1980, c1977. 417 p. : ill. ; 24 cm. (Folklore of the world) Originally presented as the author's thesis, Indiana University, 1977. Bibliography: p. 408-417. [BM225.L6S73 1980] 80-734 ISBN 0-405-13324-3 : 35.00
1. Jews—California—Los Angeles—Social life and customs. 2. Sephardim—California—Los Angeles. 3. Judaism—California—Los Angeles. 4. Los Angeles (Calif.)—Religious life and customs. I. Title.

Sephardim—New York (N.Y.)—History—20th century.

ANGEL, Marc. 974.7'1004924
La America : the Sephardic experience in the United States / Marc D. Angel. 1st ed. Philadelphia : Jewish Publication Society of America, 1982. p. cm. Bibliography: p. Includes index. [F128.9.J5A53] 19 81-20923 ISBN 0-8276-0205-7 : 15.95
1. Gadol, Moise S. 2. Amerikah. 3. Sephardim—New York (N.Y.)—History—20th century. 4. Sephardim—New York (N.Y.)—Biography. 5. New York (N.Y.)—Ethnic relations. I. Title.

Sephardim—U.S.—Biography.

BIRMINGHAM, Stephen. 920.073
The grandees; America's Sephardic elite. [1st ed.] New York, Harper & Row [1971] xiii, 368 p. illus., fold. geneal. table, ports. 25 cm. Bibliography: p. 355-357. [E184.J5B552 1971] 70-95942 10.00
1. Sephardim—U.S.—Biography. 2. Jews in the United States—Biography. I. Title.

Sepulchral monuments.

BANZER, Joseph, & co. 726.
Designs for monuments, by Joseph Banzer & co. New York, Printed by Korff bro's & co. [1877] 1 p. l., 64 pl. (partly double) 16 x 27 1/2 cm. [NB1857.B2] CA 11
1. Sepulchral monuments. I. Title.

BELDEN, Franklin Edson.
Temples of peace; or, The endowed community mausoleum vs. earth-burial and cremation, showing the temporary and unsanitary character of the cemetery, the harshness of sanitary incineration, the kindness and permanence of the sanitary community mausoleum endowed; written by Franklin Edson Belden ... Seattle, Wash., The author, 1916. 64 p. incl. front., illus. 26 cm. [GT3320.B4] 16-15354
1. Sepulchral monuments. 2. Burial. I. Title.

BLISS, Harry Augustus, 1867- comp. 726.
Memorial markers and headstones, comp. by Harry A. Bliss... Buffalo, N.Y., 1920. [89] p. illus. 23 1/2 cm. Title vignette (portrait). [NB1857.B5] 20-22834
1. Sepulchral monuments. I. Title.

CATERSON, Robert. 726.
... General monumental work; mausoleums, vasults mountments, etc. Woodlawn, New York city. [New York, c1905] 161 p. illus. 23 x 18 cm. [NB1857.C35] 5-20740
1. Sepuichral monuments. I. Title.

[CRITCHFIELD, A]
The Reporter's illustrated monumental draughtsman. The only work ever published devoted exclusively to monumental designing. A complete treatise on object, profile, elevation, plan and perspective drawing in its application to monumental work. Chicago, Nichols & company, c1895. [126] p. illus. 14 x 28 cm. Illustrations called plate no. 1-64. [NB1851.C9] ca 11
1. Sepulchral monuments. I. Title.

DAY, Ernest Hermitage, 1866-
... Monuments and memorials, by the Rev. E. Hermitage Day ... With forty-one illustrations. London & Oxford, Mowbray; Milwaukee, Young churchman co. [1915] xxiii, 200 p. incl. front., plates. front., 40 pl. 15 cm. (The arts of the church) A 21
1. Sepulchral monuments. 2. Sepulchral monuments—Gt. Brit. I. Title.

NATIONAL Sculpture Society, New York
Enduring memory, in stone, in metal, in beauty. [New York, 1946?] [52] p. illus., plates. 35 cm. A49
1. Sepulchral monuments. 2. Sculpture. I. Title.

PALLISER, Palliser & co., firm, architects. 726.
Palliser's memorials and headstones, together with the orders of architecture and a large number of miscellaneous designs and details of every description, making a most valuable and complete book for designers, cutters, carvers and the general public. By Palliser, Palliser & co. ... New York, J. S. Ogilvie publishing co., 1891. 140 p. incl. illus., 94 pl. on 48 l. 35 cm. [NB1857.P2] 11-32347
1. Sepulchral monuments. 2. Epitaphs. 3. Architecture—Designs and plans. I. Title.

WILSON, Henry (Marble dealer) 726.
Portfolio of monumental designs, by Henry Wilson. St. Louis, Mo., St. Louis, J. McKittrick & co., 1874. 1 p. l., 50 pl. 16 1/2 x 30 cm. Title within ornamental border. [NB1857.W7] CA 11
1. Sepulchral monuments. I. Title.

Sepulchral monuments—Catalogs.

COOK & Watkins. 726.
[Catalogue] Cook & Watkins, importers and manufacturers of granite, marble and statuary ... Boston, Mass. [Boston, Cook & Watkins, c1896- v. front., plates. 36 cm. Cover-title of v. 1: Original monumental designs. At head of title of no. 4: Cook & Watkins' no. 4 design book. [NB1857.C7] 1-15296
1. Sepulchral monuments—Catalogs. I. Title.

MEMORIAL craftsman's guide 726.8
... Iron Mountain, Mich., Memorial craftman's guide [c1934- v. illus. 21 cm. [NB1857.M4] ca 35
1. Sepulchral monuments—Catalogs.

Sepulchral monuments—England.

GARDNER, Arthur.
Alabaster tombs of the pre-reformation period in England, by Arthur Gardner ... Cambridge [Eng.] The University press, 1940. xix, 218 p. incl. illus., plates, tables. front. 25 1/2 cm. A revision and expansion of an article in the Archaeological journal for 1923. cf. Introd. Bibliographical foot-notes. Bibliography included in "Introduction" (p. xv-xix) A 41
1. Sepulchral monuments—England. 2. Sculpture, Medieval. 3. Alabaster. I. Title.

Sepulchral monuments—Europe.

CURL, James Stevens, 1937- 726'.8'094
A celebration of death : an introduction to some of the buildings, monuments, and settings of funerary architecture in the Western European tradition / James Stevens Curl. 1st U.S. ed. New York : Scribner, 1980. xxiv, 404 p. : ill. ; 26 cm. Includes index. Bibliography: p. 378-390. [GT3242.C87 1980b] 19 79-93075 ISBN 0-684-16613-5 : 35.00
1. Sepulchral monuments—Europe. 2. Tombs—Europe. 3. Cemeteries—Europe. 4. Fureral rites and ceremonies—Europe. I. Title.

Sepulchral monuments—Greece.

GARDNER, Percy, 1846-1937.
Sculptured tombs of Hellas, by Percy Gardner ... London, Macmillan and co., ltd. New York, The Macmillan co., 1896. xix, 259, [1] p. illus., XXX pl. (incl. front.) 20 cm. [NB1370.G2] 11-13924
1. Sepulchral monuments—Greece. 2. Sculpture, Greek. 3. Funeral rites and ceremonies—Greece. I. Title.

Sepulchral monuments—New England.

FORBES, Harriette (Merrifield) Mrs. 1856-
Gravestones of early New England and the men who made them, 1653-1800, by Harriette Merrifield Forbes, with illustrations from photographs by the author. Boston, Houghton Mifflin company, 1927. 5 p. l., 141 p. front., plates. 27 cm. "Seven hundred and eighty copies of this first edition, of which seven hundred and fifty are for sale, were printed at the Riverside press, Cambridge, Massachusetts, in November, 1927 This is number 778." [NB1855.F6] [F3F69] 27-28096
1. Sepulchral monuments—New England. 2. Boston—Sepulchral monuments. 3. Stone-cutters. I. Title.

Sequences (Liturgy)

BANNISTER, Henry Marriott, 1854-1919 783.2'3'54
Anglo-French sequelae. Ed. from the papers of the late Henry Marriott Bannister by Anselm Hughes. Nashdom Abbey, Alainsong Mediaeval Music Sdo., 1934. [Farnbordugh, England, Gregg Pr., 1966] 142p. music. 23cm. Facsim ed. p. [18]-19. Liturgical list of the earlier English sequences: p. [129]-135. [M2.P6B35 1934a] 67-2911 14.00
1. Sequences (Liturgy) I. Hughes, Anselm, 1889- ed. II. Plainsong and Mediaeval Music Society. III. Title.
Available from Gregg Pr., in Ridgewood, N. J.

Serafim, Saint, 1759-1833.

DE BEAUSOBRE, Iulia. 922.147
Flame in the snow, a Russian legend, by Iulia de Beausobre ... London, Constable [1945] 168 p. front. (port.) plates. 19 cm. "First published 1945." [BX395.S37D4] 45-10789
1. Serafim, Saint, 1759-1833. I. Title.

JONES, Franklin, comp. 248'.9'19
The spiritual instructions of Saint Seraphim of Sarov. Edited and with an introd. by Franklin Jones (Bubba Free John). Los Angeles, Dawn Horse Press [1973] xi, 83 p. 21 cm. [BX597.S37J57] 73-89308 ISBN 0-913922-05-6 1.95 (pbk.)
1. Serafim, Saint, 1759-1833. I. Motovilov, Nikolai Aleksandrovich. II. Dobbie-Bateman, A. F. The life and spiritual instructions of St. Seraphim of Sarov. 1973. III. Serafim, Saint, 1759-1833. A conversation of St. Seraphim of Sarov with Nicholas Motovilov concerning the aim of a Christian life. 1973. IV. Title.
Contents omitted.

JONES, Franklin, comp. 248'.9'19
The spiritual instructions of Saint Seraphim of Sarov. Edited and with an introd. by Franklin Jones (Bubba Free John). Los Angeles, Dawn Horse Press [1973] xi, 83 p. 21 cm. Contents.Contents.—The life and spiritual instructions of St. Seraphim of Sarov, by A. F. Dobbie-Bateman.—A conversation of St. Seraphim of Sarov with Nicholas Motovilov concerning the aim of a Christian life.—The spiritual technique of St. Seraphim and the Adept-Saints of the Eastern Christian Church. [BX597.S37J57] 73-89308 ISBN 0-913922-05-6 1.95
1. Serafim, Saint, 1759-1833. I. Motovilov, Nikolai Aleksandrovich. II. Dobbie-Bateman, A. F. The life and spiritual instructions of St. Seraphim of Sarov. 1973. III. Serafim, Saint, 1759-1833. A conversation of St. Seraphim of Sarov with Nicholas Motovilov concerning the aim of a Christian life. 1973. IV. Title.

ZANDER, Valentine. 281.9'092'4 B
St. Seraphim of Sarov / Valentine Zander ; translated by Sister Gabriel Anne ; introd. by Boris Bobrinskoy. Crestwood, N.Y. : St. Vladimir's Seminary Press, 1975. p. cm. German translation has title: Seraphim von Sarow. Bibliography: p. [BX597.S37Z33 1975] 75-42136 ISBN 0-913836-28-1 : 4.95
1. Serafim, Saint, 1759-1833. I. Title.

Sergeant, John, 1710-1749.

HOPKINS, Samuel, 266'.5'87441
1693-1755.
Historical memoirs relating to the Housatonic Indians. Boston, S. Kneeland, 1753. New York, W. Abbatt, 1911. [New York, Johnson Reprint Corp., 1972] 198 p. facsims. 24 cm. Reprint of the 1911 ed., which was issued as Extra number 17 of The Magazine of history with notes and queries. [E99.S8H7 1972] 72-2288 9.00
1. Sergeant, John, 1710-1749. 2. Stockbridge Indians—Missions. I. Title. II. Series: The Magazine of history with notes and queries. Extra numbers, 17.

Sergii Radonezhskii, Saint, 1314?-1392.

KOVALEVSKY, Pierre. 281.9'3 B
Saint Sergius and Russian spirituality / by Pierre Kovalevsky ; translation by W. Elias Jones. Crestwood, N.Y. : St. Vladimir's Seminary Press, 1976. p. cm. Translation of Saint Serge et la spiritualite russe. Includes index. Bibliography: p. [BX597.S45K6913] 76-13018 ISBN 0-913836-24-9 : 5.50
1. Sergii Radonezhskii, Saint, 1314?-1392. 2. Russia—Religious life and customs. I. Title.

ZERNOV, Nicolas. 922.147
St. Sergius--builder of Russia, by Nicolas Zernov, D. PHIL., with the life, acts and miracles of the holy abbot Sergius of Radonezh, translated from the Russian by Adaline Delafeld. Published for the Fellowship of St. Alban and St. Sergius. London, Society for promoting Christian knowledge; New York, The Macmillan company [1939] xi, 155, [1] p. plates. 19 cm. [BX395.S4Z4] 40-9397
1. Sergil Radonezhskil, Saint, 1314?-1392. I. "Delafeld, Adeline, 1831- tr. II. Fellowship of St. Alban and St. Sergius. III. Society for promoting Christian knowledge, London. IV. Title.

Sermon, English Translation from German-Middle H igh German.

TAULER, Johannes 252.6
1300(ca.)-1361.
Signposts to perfection; a selection from the sermons of Johann Tauler. Selected, edited, and translated by Elizabeth Strakosch. St. Louis, Herder [1958] 140 p. 19 cm. [BV5080.T25 1958] 59-900
1. Sermons, German — Middle High German — Translations into English. 2. Sermons, English — Translations from German — Middle High German. I. Title.

TAULER, Johannes, 252.02
1300(ca.)-1361.
Spiritual conferences. Translated and edited by Eric Colledge and Sister M. Jane. St. Louis, Herder [1961] 283 p. 21 cm. (Cross and crown series of spirituality, no. 20) "Translation of selected sermons compiled from Die Predigten Taulers, published ... 1910, in the series: Deutsche Texte des Mittelaiters, vol. xi." [BV5080.T257] 61-15363
1. Sermons, German — Middle High German — Translations into English. 2. Sermons, English — Translations from German — Middle High German. I. Title.

Sermon on the Mount.

ADAMS, Frank Durward. 226.
Did Jesus mean it? A series of eight great life-lessons based upon four fundamental sayings of Jesus as recorded in the Sermon on the Mount, by Frank Durward Adams, D.D. [Boston, The Universalist publishing house, c1923] 208 p. 18 1/2 cm. [BT380.A5] 23-4887
I. Title.

ALLEN, Charles Livingstone, 242
1913-
The Sermon on the Mount [by] Charles L. Allen. Westwood, N.J., Revell [1966] 187 p. 21 cm. [BT380.A63] 66-21902
1. Sermon on the Mount. I. Title.

ALLEN, Erastus D. 226.
The spirit of Christ's sermon on the Mount, by E. D. Allen ... [St. Louis, 1921]. 2 p. l, 3-56 p. 17 cm. [BT380.A6] 24-16981
1. Sermon on the Mount. I. Title.

ANDREWS, Charles Freer, 226.2
1871-1940
The Sermon on the Mount. Foreword by Rabindranath Tagore, introd. note by Agatha Harrison. New York, Collier [1962] 157p. 18cm. (AS341V) .95 pap.,
1. Sermon on the Mount. I. Ravindranatha Thakura, Sir, 1861-1941. II. Title.

ARNOLD, Eberhard, 226'.2'206
1883-1935.
Salt and light; talks and writings on the Sermon on the Mount. [Ed. & tr. from German by the Society of Brothers] Rifton, N. Y., Plough 1967. xxxi, 309p. 20cm. [BT380.A7] 67-18009
1. Sermon on the Mount. I. Bruderhof Communities. II. Title.

ARNOLD, Eberhard, 1883- 226'.9'06
1935.
Salt and light : talks and writings on the Sermon on the Mount / by Eberhard Arnold ; [edited and translated from the German by the Hutterian Society of Brothers]. 2d ed. Rifton, N.Y. : Plough Pub. House, 1977. xxvii, 309 p. ; 18 cm. [BT380.A7 1977] 77-1204 ISBN 0-87486-170-5 pbk. : 3.00
1. Sermon on the Mount. I. Title.

ATKINS, Gaius Glenn, 1868- 226.2
From the hillside. Boston, Pilgrim Press [1948] vii, 119 p. 20 cm. [BT380.A8] 48-3895
1. Sermon on the Mount. I. Title.

AUGUSTINUS, Aurelius, 226.2
Saint, Bp. of Hippo.
Commentary on the Lord's Sermon on the Mount, with seventeenth related sermons. Tr. by Denis J. Kavanagh. Washington, D.C., Catholic Univ. of America Pr. [1963, c.1951] vi, 382p. 22cm. (Writings of Saint Augustine, v.3; The Fathers of the church, a new translation, v.11) 63-18826 5.00
1. Sermon on the Mount. 2. Sermons, Latin—Translations into English. 3. Sermons, English—Translations from Latin. I. Kavanagh, Denis Joseph, 1886- tr. II. Title. III. Series.

AUGUSTINUS, Aurelius, 226.2
Saint, Bp. of Hippo.
Commentary on the Lord's Sermon on the Mount, with seventeen related sermons; translated by Denis J. Kavanagh. New York, Fathers of the Church, inc., 1951. vi, 382 p. 22 cm. (Writings of Saint Augustine, v. 3) The Fathers of the Church, a new translation, v. 11. Translation of De Sermone Domini in Monte, and other sermons. [BR60.F3A8 vol. 3] 52-1735
1. Sermon on the Mount. 2. Sermons, Latin—Translations into English. 3. Sermons, English—Translations from Latin. I. Title.

AUGUSTINUS, Aurelius, 226.2
Saint, Bp. of Hippo.
Commentary on the Lord's Sermon on the Mount, with seventeen related sermons. Translated by Denis J. Kavanaugh. Washington, Catholic University of America Press [1963, c195a] vi. 382 p. 22 cm. (Writings of Saint Augustine., v. 3) The fathers of the church, a new translation, v. 11. Translation of De Sermone Domini in Monte, and other sermons. [BR60.F3A8] 63-18826
1. Sermon on the mount. 2. Sermons, Latin — Translations in English. 3. Sermons, English — Translations from Latin. I. Kavanagh, Denis Joseph, 1886- II. Title. III. Series: The Fathers of the church, a new translation, v. 11

AUGUSTINUS, Aurelius, Saint,
Bp. of Hippo.
The Lord's Sermon on the mount. Translated by J. J. Jepson. With an introd. and notes by the editors. Westminster, Md., Newman Press, 1956. 227 p. (Ancient Christian writers, 5) 68-48103
I. Jepson, John James, 1882- II. Title. III. Series.

AUGUSTINUS, Aurelius, 226.2
Saint, Bp. of Hippo.
The Lord's Sermon on the mount, tr. by John J. Jepson, with an introd. and notes by the editors. Westminster, Md., Newman Press, 1948. 227 p. 23 cm. (Ancient Christian writers; the works of the Fathers in translation, no. 5) Translation of De Sermone Domini in monte. Bibliographical references included in "Notes" (p. [175]-209) [BR60.A35 no. 5] 48-7809
1. Sermon on the Mount. I. Jepson, John James, 1882- tr. II. Title. III. Series.

AUGUSTINUS, Aurelius, 226'.9'066
Saint, Bp. of Hippo.
The preaching of Augustine; "Our Lord's Sermon on the mount". Edited and with an introd. by Jaroslav Pelikan. Translated by Francine Cardman. Philadelphia, Fortress Press [1973] xxi, 186 p. 18 cm. (The Preacher's paperback library, 13) Translation of De Sermone Domini in monte. Includes bibliographical references. [BT380.A8513] 72-87061 ISBN 0-8006-4012-8 3.75 (pbk.)
1. Sermon on the Mount. I. Cardman, Francine, tr. II. Title.

BACON, Benjamin Wisner, 226.
1860-1932.
The Sermon on the Mount, its literary structure and didactic purpose; a lecture delivered at Wellesley college May 20, 1901 and subsequently revised and enlarged with the addition of three appendices, adapted to exhibit by analytical and synthetic criticism the nauture and interconnection of the greater discourse of Jesus by BenjaminW. Bacon ... New York, The Macmillan company; London, Macmillan & co., ltd., 1902. xiii, 262 p. 17 cm. [BT380.B3] 211887
1. Sermon on the Mount. I. Title.

BAKER, Abijah Richardson, 1805-
1876.
A question book on the topics in Christ's Sermon on the Mount. For churches, Sabbath schools, and families. Vol. iii. for adults. By Rev. A. R. Baker ... Boston, Graves & Young, 1863. 108 p. 15 cm. A32
1. Sermon on the Mount. 2. Bible. N. T. Matthew v-vii—Ctechisms, question-books. I. Title.

BATES, Walter Gurney. 226.2
Our Lord's great sermon, with an introduction, The Kingdom of heaven, by Walter Gurney Bates. New York, N.Y., The Hobson book press, 1945. viii p., 1 l., 147 p. incl. front. (port.) 21 1/2 cm. Reproduced from type-written copy. [BT380.B35] 46-772
1. Sermon on the Mount. I. Title.

BIBLE. N. T. English. 225.52
Selections. 1899.
The sermon on the Mount and other extracts from the New Testament; a verbatim translation from the Greek, with notes on the mystical or arcane sense by J. M. Pryse. New York, E. B. Page & co., 1899. 2 p. l., 80 p. 18 cm. [BS2261.P7] 99-2878
1. Sermon on the Mount. I. Pryse, James Morgan, 1859- ed. & tr. II. Bible. English. Selections. N. T. 1899. III. Title.

BIBLE N. T. Matthew V-VII. 226.2
English. 1957. Bowman-Tapp
The Gospel from the Mount; a new translation and interpretation of Matthew, chs, 5 to 7, by John Wick Bowman and Roland W. Tapp. Philadelphia, Westminster Press [1957] 189p. 21cm. [BT380.B67] 57-9708
1. Sermon on the Mount. I. bowman, John Wick, 1894- ed. and tr. II. Tapp, oland W., ed. and t-. III. Title.

BIBLE N. T. Matthew V-VII. 226.2
English. Paraphrases. 1954. Scher
The Master-speech: the Sermon in the Mount; a nonsectarian interpretation of Matthew 5-7, with questions and answers for study, by Andrew R. Scher. [1st ed.] New York, Exposition Press [1954] 60p. 21cm. [BT380.S33] 54-5753
1. Sermon on the Mount. I. Scher, Andrew R. II. Title.

BIBLE. N. T. Matthew. v-vii.
English. 1908.
The Sermon on the Mount, from the translation authorized by King James, A. D. 1611; together with the revised version of A. D. 1901. New York, Duffield & company, 1908. [54] p. 19 cm. Ornamental borders. 8-6990
I. Title.

BIBLE. N.T. Matthew 23-VIII 226.2
1. English. 1955. Authorized.
The Sermon on the Mount. Introd. by Norman Vincent Peale. Wood engravings by John De Pol. [1st ed.] Cleveland, World Pub. Co. [1955] 50p. illus. 21cm. [BT380.A3 1955] 55-8255
1. Sermon on the Mount. I. Title.

BOARDMAN, George Dana, 226.2
1828-1903.
Studies in the mountain instruction. By George Dana Boardman ... New York, D. Appleton and company, 1881. 360 p. 19 1/2 cm. "Lectures, nine of which were delivered in Association hall, Philadelphia ...during the autumn of 1880." [BT380.B6] 32-18160
1. Sermon on the Mount. 2. Bible. N.T. Matthew v-vii—Criticism, interpretation, etc. 3. Jesus Christ—Teachings. I. Title.

BOICE, James 226'.9'07
Montgomery, 1938-
The Sermon on the Mount; an exposition. Grand Rapids, Zondervan Pub. House [1972] 328 p. 23 cm. Includes bibliographical references. [BT380.2.B56] 72-83882 5.95
1. Sermon on the Mount.

BONHAM, Tal D., 1934- 226'.2'066
The demands of discipleship; the relevance of the Sermon on the Mount, by Tal D. Bonham. [1st ed.] Pine Bluff, Ark., Discipleship Bk. Co. [1967] 178p. 23cm. Bibl. [BT380.2.B6] 67 28446 3.95
1. Sermon on the Mount. I. Title.
The author is Southern Baptist. Publisher's address: 2604 W. 40th St., Pine Bluff, Ark. 71601.

BONHOEFFER, Dietrich, 1906- 226.2
1945.
The cost of disciship, tr. by R. H. Fuller;

foreword by the Bishop of Chichester and memoir of the author by B. Leibholz, with a pref. by Reinhold Niebuhr. New York, Macmillan Co., 1949 [c1948] 198 p. port. 20 cm. Translation of Nachfolge. [BT380.B66 1949] 49-8038
1. Sermon on the Mount. I. Fuller, Reginald Horace, tr. II. Title.

BONHOEFFER, Dietrich, 1906-1945 226.2
The cost of discipleship. [Tr. from German] Rev., unabridged [6th] ed. containing material not previously tr. New York, Macmillan [1963, c.1959] 352p. 18cm. (MP131) Bibl. 1.45 pap.,
1. Sermon on the Mount. I. Title.

BONHOEFFER, Dietrich, 1906-1945.
The cost of discipleship. [Translated from the German by R. H. Fuller, with some revision by Irmgard Booth] Rev. [i.e. 2d] & unabridged ed. containing material not previously translated. New York, Macmillan [1963] 352 p. 18 cm. (Macmillan paperbacks) Translation oc Nachfolge. 68-79193
1. Sermon on the Mount. I. Title.

BONHOEFFER, Dietrich, 1906-1945. 226.2
The cost of discipleship. [Translated from the German by R. H. Fuller, with some revision by Irmgard Booth] Rev. [i.e. 2d] & unabridged ed. containing material not previously translated. New York, Macmillan [1959] 285 p. 23 cm. Translation of Nachfolge. [BT380.B66 1959] 60-677
1. Sermon on the Mount. I. Title.

BRISCOE, D. Stuart. 248'.4
Now for something totally different : a study of the sermon on the Mount / Stuart Briscoe. Waco, Tex. : Word Books, c1978. 178 p. ; 23 cm. [BT380.2.B74] 77-92474 ISBN 0-8499-0018-2 : 6.95
1. Sermon on the mount. 2. Christian life—1960- I. Title.

BROWNE, John R. 1876- 226.2
The great sermon, by John R. Browne. Boston, Mass., The Stratford company (c1935) 3 p. 1., ll p., 1 l., 74 p. 18 1/2 cm. [BT380.B75] 35-12061
1. Sermon on the Mount. 2. New thought. I. Title.

CARSON, D. A. 226'.9'07
The Sermon on the mount : an evangelical exposition of Matthew 5-7 / D. A. Carson. Grand Rapids, Mich. : Baker Book House, c1978. 157 p. ; 23 cm. Includes bibliographical references. [BT380.2.C33] 77-93260 ISBN 0-8010-2423-4 : 6.95
1. Sermon on the mount. 2. Bible. N.T. Matthew V-VII—Commentaries. I. Sermon on the mount. II. Title.

CHAMBERS, Oswald.
Studies in the Sermon on the Mount, by Oswald Chambers ... Cincinnati, O., God's revivalist press [c1915] 122 p. 20 cm. 15-26794 0.50
I. Title.

CHAPPELL, Clovis Gillham, 1882- 226.2
The Sermon on the Mount, by Clovis G. Chappell ... Nashville, Tenn., Cokesbury press, 1930. 227 p. 19 cm. Sermons. [BT380.C55] 30-11390
1. Sermon on the Mount. I. Title.

COHON, Beryl David, 1898- 226.2
Jacob's well; some Jewish sources and parallels to the Sermon on the Mount. New York, Bookman Associates [1956] 112p. 23cm. [BT380.C57] 56-4459
1. Sermon on the Mount. I. Title.

COHON, Beryl David, 1898- 226.2
Jacob's well; some Jewish sources and parallels to the Sermon on the Mount. New York, Bookman Associates [1956] 112p. 23cm. [BT380.C57] 56-4459
1. Sermon on the Mount. I. Title.

CONNICK, C. Milo 226.2
Build on the rock; you and the Sermon on the Mount. [Westwood, N.J.] Revell [c.1960] 191p. Includes bibliography. 22cm. 60-5503 2.95
1. Sermon on the Mount. I. Title.

DAILY, Starr, pseud. 226.206
The magnificent love; a gospel of divine love based on the Sermon on the Mount. Westwood, N.J., Revell [1964] 144 p. 20 cm. 64-16604
1. Sermon on the Mount. 2. Love (Theology) I. Title.

DAVIES, William David, 1911- 226.2
The Sermon on the Mount, by W. D. Davies. Cambridge [Eng.] University Press, 1966. 163 p. 19 cm. [BT380.2.D35] 66-17057
1. Sermon on the Mount. I. Title.

DAVIES, William David, 1911- 226.2
The setting of the Sermon on the Mount. [New York] Cambridge [c.]1964. xiii, 546p. 24cm. Bibl. 64-630 12.50
1. Sermon on the Mount. I. Title.

DAVIES, William David, 1911- 201
The setting of the Sermon on the Mount. Cambridge [Eng.] University Press, 1964. xiii, 546 p. 24 cm. Bibliography: p. 481-504. [BT380.D37] 64-630
1. Sermon on the Mount. I. Title.

DIBELIUS, Martin, 1883- 226.2
The Sermon on the Mount, by Martin Dibelius. New York, C. Scribner's sons, 1940. vi p., 2 l., 147, [1] p. 20 cm. "The John C. Shaffer lectures at the Divinity school of Yale university [1937]"--Foreword. [BT380.D5] 40-34444
1. Sermon on the Mount. I. Title.

DRIVER, John, 1924- 226'.906
Kingdom citizens / John Driver ; introd. by John H. Yoder. Scottdale, Pa. : Herald Press, 1980. 156 p. ; 21 cm. [BT380.2.D72] 80-16171 ISBN 0-8361-1935-5 (pbk.) : 6.95
1. Sermon on the mount. 2. Christian life—Mennonite authors. 3. Christian life—Biblical teaching. I. Title.

EDDLEMAN, H Leo. 226.2
Teachings of Jesus in Matthew 5-7. Nashville, Convention Press [1955] 146p. 20cm. [BT380.E3] 56-21488
1. Sermon on the Mount. I. Title.

FINDLAY, James Alexander. 226.
The realism of Jesus, a paraphrase and exposition of the Sermon on the Mount, by J. Alexander Findlay ... New York, George H. Doran company [1924] viii p., 1 l., 11-182 p. 19 1/2 cm. [BT380.F5] 25-2674
1. Sermon on the Mount. I. Title.

FISHER, Fred L. 226'.9'06
The Sermon on the mount / Fred L. Fisher. Nashville : Broadman Press, c1976. 154 p. ; 22 cm. Includes bibliographical references. [BT380.2.F545] 75-8373 ISBN 0-8054-1355-3 bds. : 5.95
1. Sermon on the mount.

FOX, Emmet. 226.2
The Sermon on the Mount; a general introduction to scientific Christianity in the form of a spiritual key to Matthew v, vi, and vii. [By] Emmet Fox. New York, Church of the healing Christ [c1934] viii, 156 p. 20 cm. [BT380.F6] 34-20736
1. Sermon on the Mount. 2. Bible. N. T. Matthew v.-vii-Criticism. interpretation, etc. I. Title.

FOX, Emmet. 226.2
The Sermon on the Mount; a general introduction to scientific Christianity in the form of a spiritual key to Matthew v, vi and vii, by Emmet Fox. New York and London, Harper & brothers, 1935. x p., 1 l., 154 p. 20 cm. "Second edition." [BT380.F6 1935] 35-17928
1. Sermon on the Mount. 2. Bible. N. T. Matthew v-vii—Criticism, interpretation, etc. I. Title.

FOX, Emmet. 226.2
The Sermon on the Mount; a general introduction to scientific Christianity in the form of a spiritual key to Matthew v, vi, and vii, by Emmet Fox. New York and London, Harper & brothers [1938] x p., 1 l., 153, [1] p. 20 cm. "Eleventh edition." [BT380.F6 1938 a] 39-3205
1. Sermon on the Mount. 2. Bible. N. T. Matthew v-vii—Criticism, interpretation, etc. I. Title.

FOX, Emmet. 226.2
The Sermon on the Mount; a general introduction to scientific Christianity in the form of a spiritual key to Matthew v, vi and vii, by Emmet Fox. New York and London, Harper & brothers [c1938] x p., 1 l., 153 p. 20 cm. "Seventeenth edition." [BT380.F6 1938 g] 42-81819
1. Sermon on the Mount. 2. Bible. N. T. Matthew v-vii—Criticism, interpretation, etc. I. Title.

FRIEDLANDER, Gerald, 1871-
The Jewish sources of the Sermon on the Mount, by Gerald Friedlander ... London, G. Routledge & sons, limited; New York, The Bloch publishing company, 1911. xxx, 301 p. 19 cm. A 15
1. Sermon on the Mount. I. Title.

FRIEDLANDER, Gerald, 1871-1923. 226'.2
The Jewish sources of the Sermon on the Mount. New York, Ktav Pub. House, 1969. lviii, 301 p. 24 cm. (The Library of Biblical studies) Reprint of the 1911 ed., with a new "Prolegomenon, by Solomon Zeitlin." Includes bibliographical references. [BT380.F67 1969] 67-11897
1. Sermon on the Mount. I. Title. II. Series.

FROST, Bede, father, 1877- 226.2
Founded upon a rock, an introduction to the Sermon on the Mount, by Bede Frost. New York, The Macmillan company [1935] 207 p. 19 cm. "Printed in Great Britain." [Sevular name: Albert Ernest Frost] [BT380.F7] 38-30023
1. Sermon on the Mount. 2. Christianity—20th cent. I. Title.

GENUNG, George Frederick, 1850- 226.
The Magna charta of the kingdom of God; plain studies in Our Lord's Sermon on the Mount. By George F. Genung, D. D. Philadelphia. American Baptist publication society, 1900. vi p., 1 l., 164 p. 19 cm. [BT380.G4] 0-3193
1. Sermon on the Mount. I. Title.

GESNER, Herbert Mortimer.
The life worth living; or, The religion of Christ; a systematic and popular exposition of the greatest religious document the world has ever seen, commonly known as the Sermon on the Mount, by Herbert Mortimer Gesner ... Boston, R. G. Badger; [etc., etc., c1915] 2 p. l., 3-359 p. 20 cm. (Lettered on cover: Library of religious thought) 15-7259 1.25
I. Title.

GUELICH, Robert A. 226'.906
The Sermon on the mount : a foundation for understanding / Robert A. Guelich. Waco, Tex. : Word Books, c1982. 451 p. ; 24 cm. Includes indexes. Bibliography: p. 423-431. [BT380.2.G83 1982] 19 81-52521 ISBN 0-8499-0110-3 : 17.50
1. Sermon on the mount. I. Sermon on the mount. English. 1982. II. Title.

HAYES, Doremus Almy, 1863- 226.
The heights of Christian living; a study of the Sermon on the Mount, by Doremus A. Hayes ... New York, Cincinnati [etc.] The Abingdon press [c1929] 312 p. 19 1/2 cm. "A brief bibliography": p. 309-312 [BT380.H3] 29-20531
1. Sermon on the Mount. I. Title.

HENDRIKSEN, William. 226.2
The Sermon on the Mount, by Wm. Hendriksen ... Grand Rapids, Mich., Wm. B. Eerdmans publishing co., 1934. 256 p. 20 cm. Bibliography at end of each chapter. [BT380.H37] 35-10726
1. Sermon on the Mount. I. Title.

HERR, Johannes. 226.
The illustrating mirror; or A funndamental illustration of christ's Sermon on the Mount. For all lovers of the truth to examine their faith and to promote their observance of the doctrines of our Lord and Savior Jesus Christ. Translated from the German. Lancaster, Pa., E. Barr, 1858. 360 p. 16 cm. [BT380.H413] 52-47295
1. Sermon on the Mount. I. Title.

HILL, Daniel Harvey, 1821-1889. 226.2
A consideration of the Sermon on the Mount. By Major D. H. Hill ... Philadelphia, W. S. & A. Martien, 1858. 3 p. l., [5]-282 p. 18 1/2 cm. [BT380.H5] 31-33821
1. Sermon on the Mount. I. Title.

HUNTER, Archibald Macbride. 226.2
A pattern for life; an exposition of the Sermon on the Mount. Philadelphia, Westminster Press [1953] 124p. 20cm. 'First published in Great Britain in 1953 ... under the title: Design for life.' [BT380.H85 1953a] 53-11817
1. Sermon on the Mount. I. Title.

HUNTER, Archibald Macbride. 226.2
A pattern for life; an exposition of the Sermon on the Mount: its making,its exegesis, and its meaning, by Archibald M. Hunter. Rev. ed. Philadelphia, Westminister Press [1965] 127 p. 19 cm. First published in London in 1953 under title: Design for life. [BT380.2.H85] 66-11517
1. Sermon on the Mount. I. Title.

JENKINS, Isaac C. 226.
... *The Sermon on the Mount,* an interpretation, by I. C. Jenkins. Nashville, Tenn., Cokesbury press, 1925. 116 p. 19 cm. (Cokesbury devotional series) [BT380.J4] 25-15689
1. Sermon on the Mount. I. Title.

JONES, Eli Stanley, 1884- 282.9
The Christ of the Mount; a working philosophy of life [by] E. Stanley Jones. New York, Cincinnati [etc.] The Abingdon press [c1931] 332 p. 20 cm. [BT380.J6 1931] 31-30537
1. Sermon on the Mount. I. Title.

JONES, Eli Stanley, 1884- 232.9
The Christ of the Mount; a working philosophy of life [by] E. Stanley Jones. New York, Cincinnati [etc.] The Abingdon press [1931] 332 p. 20 cm. "First edition printed October, 1931; second printing, October, 1931; third printing, October, 1931." [BT380.J6 1931 c] 31-12479
1. Sermon on the Mount. I. Title.

JORDAN, Clarence. 226'.2
Sermon on the Mount. [Rev. ed.] Valley Forge [Pa.], Judson Press [1970, c1952] 126 p. 20 cm. (A Koinonia publication) [BT380.2.J67 1970] 78-17614 1.95
1. Sermon on the Mount. I. Title.

KING, Henry Churchill, 1858-1934. 232.
The way of life, a revised and enlarged reprint of those portions of the author's Ethics of Jesus, dealing with the Sermon on the Mount, with a special discussion of war and the teaching of Jesus, by Henry Churchill King ... New York, The Macmillan company, 1918. 4 p. l., 129 p. 17 1/2 cm. [BS2415.K5] 18-17460
1. Jesus Christ—Teachings. 2. Sermon on the Mount. I. Title.

KISSINGER, Warren S., 1922- 226'.9'06
The Sermon on the Mount : a history of interpretation and bibliography / by Warren S. Kissinger. Metuchen, N.J. : Scarecrow Press, 1975. xiii, 296 p. ; 22 cm. (ATLA bibliography series ; no. 3) Includes indexes. Part II was developed and greatly expanded from the bibliography and books of the late W. Harold Row. [BT380.2.K5 1975] 75-29031 ISBN 0-8108-0843-9 : 12.50
1. Sermon on the Mount. 2. Sermon on the mount—Bibliography. 3. Beatitudes—Bibliography. I. Title. II. Series: American Theological Library Association. ATLA bibliography series ; no. 3.

LAMSA, George Mamishisho, 1893- 226.2
The kingdom on earth, by George M. Lamsa. Lee's Summit, Mo., Unity Books [distributed by Hawthorn Books, New York] 1966. 192 p. 20 cm. [BT380.2.L3] 66-25237
1. Sermon on the Mount. I. Title.

LIGON, Ernest M., 1897- 201
The psychology of Christian personality. New York, Macmillan, 1961 [c.1935] 393p. (Macmillan paper. back, 76) Bibl. 1.95 pap.,
1. Sermon on the Mount. 2. Personality. 3. Psychology, Religious. I. Title. II. Title: Christian personality

LIGON, Ernest Mayfield, 1897- 201
The psychology of Christian personality, by Ernest M. Ligon ... New York, The Macmillan company, 1935. x p., 2 l., 393 p. 22 cm. "Interpretation of the teachings

of the Sermon on the Mount in terms of psychology."--Pref. Bibliography: p. 373-378. [BT380.L5] 35-22951
1. Sermon on the Mount. 2. Personality. 3. Psychology, Religious. I. Title. II. Title: Christian personality.

LINDSAY, Alexander Dunlop, 1870- 226.2
The moral teaching of Jesus; an examination of the Sermon on the Mount, by A. D. Lindsay ... New York and London, Harper & brothers, 1937. v, 7-185, [1] p. 20 cm. "Six addresses ... given in Balliol college chapel."--Introd. "First edition." [BT380.L53 1937 a] 38-465
1. Sermon on the Mount. 2. Jesus Christ—Ethics. I. Title.

LINDSAY, Alexander Dunlop Lindsay, baron, 1879- 226.2
The moral teaching of Jesus; an examination of the Sermon on the Mount, by A. D. Lindsay ... New York and London, Harper & brothers, 1937. v, 7-185, [1] p. 20 cm. "Six addresses ... given in Bailiol college chapel."--Introd. "First edition" [BT380.L53 1937a] 38-465
1. Jesus Christ—Ethics. 2. Sermon on the Mount. I. Title.

LONG, James, 1949- 248'.48
Life, Jesus-style : scaling the sermon on the mount / by James Long. Wheaton, Ill. : Victor Books, c1978. 160 p. : ill. ; 18 cm. (SonPower youth publication) [BT380.2.L6] 78-58692 ISBN 0-88207-575-6 : 1.95
1. Sermon on the mount. 2. Christian life—1960- I. Title.

MCAFEE, Cleland Boyd, 1866-
Studies in the Sermon on the Mount, by Cleland Boyd McAfee ... New York, Chicago [etc.] Fleming H. Revell company [c1910] 208 p. 19 1/2 cm. $1.00. 10-27039
I. Title.

MCARTHUR, Harvey K. 226.2
Understanding the Sermon on the Mount. New York, Harper [c.1960] 192p. 22cm. Bibl.: p.181-186 60-11783 3.50 half cloth,
1. Sermon on the Mount. I. Title.

MCARTHUR, Harvey K. 226'.9'06
Understanding the Sermon on the mount / by Harvey K. McArthur. Westport, Conn. : Greenwood Press, 1978, c1960. p. cm. Reprint of the ed. published by Harper, New York. Includes indexes. Bibliography: p. [BT380.2.M3 1978] 78-16404 ISBN 0-313-20569-8 lib.bdg. : 15.25
1. Sermon on the mount. I. Title.

MANN, Gerald. 248.4
Why does Jesus make me nervous? : Taking the Sermon on the Mount seriously / Gerald Mann. Waco, Tex. : Word Books, c1980. 164 p. ; 21 cm. Includes bibliographical references. [BT380.2.M34] 19 80-51445 ISBN 0-8499-2926-1 (pbk.) : 5.95
1. Sermon on the mount. I. Title.

MARRIOTT, Horace. 226.
The Sermon on the Mount, by the Rev. Horace Marriott ... with a preface by the Lady Margaret professor of divinity at Oxford ... London, Society for promoting Christian knowledge; New York and Toronto, The Macmillan co., 1925. xii, 274 p. 22 cm. [BT380.M35] 25-19510
1. Sermon on the Mount. I. Title.

MAURO, Philip. 220.
The gospel of the kingdom, with an examination of modern dispensationalism, by Philip Mauro ... Boston, Hamilton brothers [c1928] 258 p. 20 cm. [BS511.M4] 29-6548
I. Title.

MEIER, Henry Albert. 226.
The Sermon on the Mount, interpreted by Henry Albert Meier ... Cleveland, O., Central publishing house [c1924] 1 p. l., v-viii, 165 p. 20 cm. [BT380.M4] 25-2159
1. Sermon on the Mount. I. Title.

METZLER, Burton. 226'.2'066
Light from a hillside; the message of the Sermon on the Mount. Elgin, Ill., Brethren Press [1968] 140 p. 21 cm. [BT380.2.M4] 68-1648
1. Sermon on the Mount. I. Title.

MILITZ, Annie (Rix) Mrs. 226.
The Sermon on the Mount; an interpretation, by Annie Rix Militz. Rev. ed. [New York] The Absolute press [1904] vii, [2], ix-x, 136 p. 16 1/2 cm. Title within colored ornamental border. [BT380.M5] 4-35054
1. Sermon on the Mount. I. Title.

MILLER, John W., 1926- 226'.2
The Christian way; a guide to the Christian life based on the Sermon on the Mount, by John W. Miller. Scottdale, Pa., Herald Press [1969] 136 p. 18 cm. Bibliography: p. 136. [BT380.2.M5] 78-76622
1. Sermon on the Mount. I. Title.

MILLER, Robert Henry. 226.2
The life portrayed in the Sermon on the Mount, by Robert Henry Miller ... Boston, W. A. Wilde company [c1934] 215 p. col. front. 19 1/2 cm. [BT380.M54] 35-1679
1. Sermon on the Mount. 2. Bible. N.T. Matthew V-VII—Commentaries. 3. Christian life. I. Title.

MORGAN, Edward J 1906- 226.2
No thought for tomorrow. Grand Rapids, Eerdmans [1961] 123p. 23cm. [BT380.2.M65] 60-53087
1. Sermon on the Mount. I. Title.

MYRES, William V 226.2
Design for happiness. Nashville, Broadman Press [1961] 124p. 21cm. Includes bibliography. [BT380.2.M9] 61-12416
1. Sermon on the Mount. I. Title.

OVERBURY, Emily Ethel. Mrs. 220
From beyond the veil; or, Sermons delivered from the mount of undersdtanding, by Emily Ethel Overbury. Monrovia, Calif., Emily E. Overbury [c1929] 2 p. l., [7]-141, [1] p., 1 l. 20 cm. [BR125.O83] 29-23912
I. Title.

PARK, John Edgar.
The wonder of His gracious words; an exposition of the Sermon on the Mount, by John Edgar Park. Boston, New York [etc.] The Pilgrim press [c1909] vii, 201 p. 20 cm. 9-31250 1.00
I. Title.

PENTECOST, J. Dwight. 226'.9'07
Design for living : the Sermon on the mount / by J. Dwight Pentecost. Chicago : Moody Press, [1975] 208 p. ; 22 cm. [BT382.P44] 75-12818 ISBN 0-8024-2128-8 : 5.95
1. Sermon on the mount. I. Title.

PENTECOST, J. Dwight. 226'.907
The Sermon on the mount : contemporary insights for a Christian lifestyle / J. Dwight Pentecost ; cover design by Bill Taylor Collins. 2d ed. Portland, Or. : Multnomah Press, c1980. 224 p. ; 22 cm. First ed. published in 1975 under title: Design for living. Includes indexes. [BT380.2.P37 1980] 80-13167 ISBN 0-930014-40-5 pbk. : 5.95
1. Sermon on the mount. I. Title.

PINK, Arthur Walkington, 1886-1952. 226.2
An exposition of the Sermon on the Mount. Grand Rapids, Baker Book House, 1959 [c1953] 422p. 23cm. [BT380.P5 1959] 59-8344
1. Sermon on the Mount. I. Title.

PINK, Arthur Walkington, 1886-1952 226.2
An exposition of the Sermon on the Mount. [1st ed.] Swengel, Pa., Bible Truth Depot, 1950. 442 p. 22 cm. [BT380.P5] 51-3606
1. Sermon on the Mount. I. Title.

PRABHAVANANDA, Swami, 1893- 226.206
The Sermon on the Mount according to Vedanta. Hollywood, Calif., Vedanta [c.1964] 110p. 19cm. [BT304.94.P68] 64-8660 2.50 bds.,
1. Sermon on the Mount. 2. Jesus Christ—Hindu interpretations. I. Title.

RIGA, Peter J. 232.95'4
Be sons of your father [by] Peter J. Riga. [Staten Island, N.Y., Alba House, 1969] xv, 126 p. 20 cm. [BT380.2.R5] 75-77648 3.95
1. Sermon on the Mount. I. Title.

SANDERS, John Oswald, 1902- 226'.9'077
Real discipleship; a devotional exposition of the Sermon on the Mount [by] J. Oswald Sanders. Grand Rapids, Zondervan Pub. House [1973, c1972] 160 p. 18 cm. London ed. published under title: The world's greatest sermon. Includes bibliographies. [BT380.2.S26 1972] 73-2653 1.25 (pbk.)
1. Sermon on the Mount. I. Title.

SAVAGE, Henry Edwin.
The gospel of the kingdom: or, The Sermon on the Mount, considered in the light of contemporary Jewish thought and ideals, by H. E. Savage ... London, New York [etc.] Longmans, Green, and co., 1910. xviii, 274 p. 23 cm. Contents.I. The kingdom of God.--II. The Sermon on the Mount.--III. The Beatitudes.--IV. Influence on the world.--V. The interpretation of the law.--VI. The works of righteousness.--VII. Undistracted service.--VIII. The church in the world.--IX. True discipleship.--X. The sermon in St. Luke's Gospel.--Index. 11-25956
I. Title.

SERMON on the Mount. English. 226.9'05203
The Sermon on the Mount, being the fifth, sixth & seventh chapters of the Gospel according to St. Matthew in the King James version of the Holy Bible. Chicago, Monastery Hill Bindery, 1968. [21] p. 1 col. illus. 27 cm. Limited ed. issued with season's greetings by Hertzberg-New Method, inc., to commemorate their 100 years of service, 1868-1968, especially that of the Monastery Hill Bindery which was founded in 1868. [BT380.A3 1968] 76-289196

THE sermon on the Mount (sermons) and the Magnificat; edited by Jaroslav Pelikan. Saint Louis, Concordia pub. house [1956] xxi, 383p. 24cm. (His Works, v. 21) The Sermon on the Mount, translated by Jaroslav Pelikan; The Magnificat, by A. T. W. Steinhaeuser.
1. Sermon on the Mount. 2. Magnificat. I. Luther, Martin, 1483-1546. II. Pelikan, Jaroslav, 1923- ed.

SHEARER, John Bunyan, 1832-1919. 226.2
The Sermon on the Mount; a study, by J. B. Shearer ... Richmond, Va., Presbyterian committee of publication [c1906] 146 p. 20 1/2 cm. [BT380.S5] 6-36466
1. Sermon on the Mount. I. Title.

SHEPARD, Thomas Griffin. 1848-
... The Sermon on the Mount; a sacred cantata for soli, chorus and piano (or organ) text selected from the Gospel according to St. Matthew. Vocal score ... New York, G. Schirmer, 1901. 3 p. l., 44 p. 26 1/2 cm. 2-16729
I. Title.

SHINN, Roger Lincoln 226.2
Sermon on the Mount. Philadelphia, United Church [c.1959, 1962] 112p. 19cm. (Pilgrim bk.) 62-19785 1.45 pap.,
1. Sermon on the Mount. I. Title.

SPURGEON, Charles Haddon, 1834-1892.
Sermons on the Sermon on the Mount. Condensed and edited by Al Bryant. Grand Rapids, Mich. Zondervan Publishing House [1956] 153 p.
1. Sermon on the Mount. 2. Sermons, English. I. -Bryant, Al, 1926- ed. II. Title.

STAFFORD, Geoffrey Wardle. 226.
The Sermon on the Mount, the charter of Christianity, by Geoffrey Wardle Stafford. New York, Cincinnati, The Abingdon press [c1927] 248 p. 19 cm. [BT380.S67] 27-18909
1. Sermon on the Mount. I. Title.

STOTT, John R. W. 226'.9'077
Christian counter-culture : the message of the Sermon on the Mount / John R. W. Stott. Downers Grove, Ill. : InterVarsity Press, 1978. 222 p. ; 21 cm. (The Bible speaks today) Includes bibliographical references. [BT380.2.S86 1978] 77-27687 ISBN 0-87784-660-X : 3.95
1. Sermon on the mount. I. Title.

STRANG, Lewis Clinton, 1869-1935. 226.2
The Master and the modern spirit, by Lewis C. Strang ... New York, Roland publishing company, 1925. x. 274 p. 24 cm. "The Master and the modern spirit' uses the Sermon on the Mount as a sort of backbone or connecting link on which to hang its speculations and opinions."--p. ix. [BT380.S7] 25-21154
1. Sermon on the Mount. I. Title.

THOMAS, Leslie Grier, 1895-
The Sermon on the Mount; a series of studies in the moral and religious teaching of Jesus. Nashville, Tennessee, Gospel Advocate, 1958. x, 203 p.
1. Sermon on the Mount. I. Title.

THOMPSON, Ernest Trice, 1894- 226.2
The Sermon on the Mount and its meaning for today. [Rev. ed.] Richmond, va., John Knox [1961, c.1946, 1961] 128p. (Aletheia paperbacks) Bibl. 61-3735 1.45 pap.,
1. Sermon on the Mount. I. Title.

THOMPSON, Ernest Trice, 1894- 226.2
The Sermon on the Mount and its meaning for today. [Rev. ed.] Richmond, John Knox Press [1953, c1946] 154 p. 21 cm. [BT380.T46 1953] 53-11761
1. Sermon on the Mount.

THOMPSON, Ernest Trice, 1894- 226.2
The Sermon on the Mount and its meaning for today, by Ernest Trice Thompson. Richmond, Va., John Knox press [1946] 5 p. l., 13-162 p. 21 1/2 cm. Bibliographical references included in "Notes" and "Acknowledgments" (p. 159-162) [BT380.T46] 46-8357
1. Sermon on the Mount. I. Title.

THURNEYSEN, Eduard, 1888- 226.206
The Sermon on the Mount. Tr. [from German] by William Childs Robinson, Sr., with James M. Robinson. Richmond, Va., Knox [c.1964]. 82p. 19cm. (Chime paperbacks) Bibl. 64-12625 1.00 pap.,
1. Sermon on the Mount. 2. Bible. N. T. Matthew v-vii—Criticism, interpretation, etc. I. Title.

TREASURE, Geoff. 248'.4
Living right side up / Geoff Treasure ; [ill., Jake Sutton]. American ed. Wheaton, Ill. : Victor Books, c1977. 158 p. : ill. ; 18 cm. (An Input book) Originally published under title: Living out a revolution. [BT380.2.T75 1977] 76-48574 ISBN 0-88207-746-5 pbk. : 1.95
1. Sermon on the mount. 2. Christian life—1960- I. Title.

VIGEVENO, H. S. 226'.2
Climbing up the mountain, children, by H. S. Vigeveno. Glendale, Calif., G/L Regal Books [1968] 184 p. 18 cm. [BT380.2.V5] 68-18058
1. Sermon on the Mount. I. Title.

WARD, James Edward. 226.2
The Master on the Mount, by James Edward Ward ... Toronto, New York [etc.] Longmans, Green and company [1943] vi, 137 p. 21 cm. "First printing: February, 1943." [BT380.W25] 43-13071
1. Sermon on the Mount. I. Title.

WEAKLEY, Clare. 226'.9'06
Happiness unlimited : John Wesley's commentary on the Sermon on the Mount / edited and adapted by Clare G. Weakley, Jr. Plainfield, NJ : Logos International, c1979. xiv, 297 p. ; 21 cm. Includes bibliographical references. [BS2575.2.W39] 79-84844 ISBN 0-88270-368-4 pbk. : 3.95
1. Sermon on the mount. 2. Happiness. 3. Salvation. I. Wesley, John, 1703-1791. Sermons on several occasions. II. Title.

WEST, Edward N. 226.2
God's image in us; a meditation on Christ's teachings in His Sermon on the Mount. [1st ed.] Cleveland, World Pub. Co. [1960] 181 p. 21 cm. [BT380.2.W45] 60-5809
1. Sermon on the Mount. I. Title.

WHITE, Ellen Gould (Harmon) 1827-1915. 226.2
Thoughts from the Mount of Blessing. Mountain View, Calif., Pacific Press Pub.

Association [c1956] 172 p. 18 cm. [BT380.W45 1956] 56-7169
1. Sermon on the Mount. I. Title.

WHITE, Ellen Gould (Harmon) 226.2
1827-1915.
Thoughts from the Mount of Blessing. Mountain View, Calif., Pacific Press Pub. Assn. [1948] 159 p. illus. (part col.) 22 cm. [BT380.W45 1948] 48-10178
1. Sermon on the Mount. I. Title.

WOELLNER, Fredric Philip, 226.2
1890-
The highlands of the mind; a psychological analysis of the Sermon on the Mount, by Fredric P. Wellner ... Pasadena, Calif., Sunday morning press, 1930. 291 p. front. 20 1/2 cm. [BT380.W6] 30-19847
1. Sermon on the Mount. I. Title.

Sermon on the Mount—Addresses, essays, lectures.

WRIGHT, William Burnet, 226.
1838-1924.
Master and men; or, The Sermon on the Mountain practiced on the plain, by William Burnet Wright ... Boston and New York, Houghton, Mifflin and company, 1894. 240 p., 1 l. 18 1/2 cm. [BT380.W7] 45-29019
1. Sermon on the Mount—Addresses, essays, lectures. I. Title.

Sermon on the Mount — Juvenile literature.

ALLSTROM, Elizabeth C. 226
Truly, I say to you. Woodcuts by Mel Silverman. Nashville, Abingdon [c.1966] 62p. illus. (pt. col.) 25cm. [BT380.2.A65] 66-10565 3.00
1. Sermon on the Mount — Juvenile literature. I. Silverman, Mel, illus. II. Title.

ALLSTROM, Elizabeth C j226
Truly, I say to you, by Elizabeth Allstrom. Woodcuts by Mel Silverman. New York, Abingdon Press [1966] 62 p. illus. (part col.) 25 cm. [BT380.2.A65] 66-10565
1. Sermon on the Mount — Juvenile literature. I. Silverman, Mel, illus. II. Title.

Sermon on the Mount —Meditations.

KEPLER, Thomas Samuel, 226.2
1897-
Jesus' design for living. Nashville, Abingdon Press [c1955] 127p. 20cm. [BT380.K4] 55-5045
1. Sermon onthe Mount—Meditations. I. Title.

MEYER, Frederick 226.2
Brotherton, 1847-1929.
The Sermon on the Mount; the directory of the devout life. Grand Rapids, Baker Book House, 1959. 191p. 21cm. [BT380.M46 1959] 60-2245
1. Sermon on the Mount —Meditations. 2. Christian life. I. Title.

PENNINGTON, Chester A. 242
The Word among us [by] Chester A. Pennington. Philadelphia, United Church Press [1973] 125 p. front. 24 cm. "A Pilgrim Press book." Poems. [BT380.2.P36] 73-8503 ISBN 0-8298-0259-2 4.95
1. Sermon on the Mount—Meditations. 2. Lord's prayer—Meditations. I. Title.

Sermon on the Mount—Sermons.

CHRYSOSTOMUS, Joannes, 226'.2'066
Saint, Patriarch of Constantinople, d.407.
The preaching of Chrysostom; Homilies on the Sermon on the mount. Edited with an introd. by Jaroslav Pelikan. Philadelphia, Fortress Press [1967] ix, 230 p. 18 cm. (The Preacher's paperback library) Part of a larger work, Homilies on the Gospel of Saint Matthew, Homiliae in Matthaeum. Bibliographical footnotes. [BR65.C45H63 1967] 67-13057
1. Sermon on the Mount—Sermons. 2. Sermons, Greek—Translations into English. 3. Sermons, English—Translations from Greek. I. Pelikan, Jaroslav Jan, 1923- ed. II. Title.

CROWE, Charles M 226.2
Sermons from the Mount. Nashville, Abingdon Press [1954] 159p. 21cm. [BT380.C7] 54-5941
1. Sermon on the Mount—Sermons. 2. Methodist Church—Sermons. 3. Sermons, American. I. Title.

FITZGERALD, Ernest A. 226'.2
There's no other way [by] Ernest A. Fitzgerald. Nashville, Abingdon Press [1970]. 144 p. 20 cm. [BT380.2.F55] 75-124753 3.50
1. Sermon on the Mount—Sermons. 2. Methodist Church—Sermons. 3. Sermons, American. I. Title.

HARGROVE, Hubbard Hoyt, 226.206
1895-
At the master's feet; expository sermons on the Sermon on the Mount. Grand Rapids, Mich., Baker Bk. 1963 [c.1944] 211p. 21cm. (Evangelical pulpit lib.) 63-12028 2.95
1. Sermon on the Mount—Sermons. 2. Baptists—Sermons. 3. Sermons, English. I. Title.

HARGROVE, Hubbard Hoyt, 1895- 226
At the Master's feet, a series of expository sermons from the Sermon on the Mount, by H. H. Hargrove ... Nashville, Tenn., Broadman press [1944] 211 p. 19 1/2 cm. [BT380.H26] 44-8924
1. Sermon on the Mount—Sermons. 2. Bible, N.T. Matthew V-VII—Sermons. I. Title.

KAISER, Paul, 1852-
Blessed are ye. A series of sermons on the Beatitudes of the Sermon on the mount. By Dr. theol. Paul Kaiser ... Tr. by B. Lederer ... Burlington, Ia., The German literary board, 1906. 140 p. 20 cm. 6-27789
I. Lederer, Bruno, tr. II. Title.

KAISER, Paul, 1852-
The law in the light of the gospel. A series of sermons on the precepts of Christ concerning the law in the Sermon on the Mount. By Dr. Theol. Paul Kaiser ... Tr. from the German. Burlington, Ia., The German literary board, 1909. 146 p. 20 cm. 9-18363
I. Title.

LLOYD-JONES, David Martyn 226.2
Studies in the Sermon on the Mount. [v.1] Grand Rapids, Eerdmans [1959] 320p. v. 23cm. 60-34 4.50
1. Sermon on the Mount—Sermons. I. Title.

LLOYD-JONES, David Martyn 226.2
Studies in the Sermon on the Mount. v.2. Grand Rapids, Mich., Eerdmans [1961] 337p. 60-34 4.50
1. Sermon on the Mount—Sermons. I. Title.

LLOYD-JONES, David Martyn. 226.2
Studies in the Sermon on the Mount. 1st ed. Grand Rapids, Eerdmans [1959-60] 2v. 23cm. [BT380.L56] 60-34
1. Sermon on the Mount—Sermons. I. Title.

MCAFEE, Cleland Boyd, 1866- 226.2
Studies in the Sermon on the Mount, by Cleland Boyd McAfee ... New York, Chicago [etc.] Fleming H. Revell company [1910] 208 p. 19 1/2 cm. [BT380.M3] 10-27039
1. Sermon on the Mount—Sermons. 2. Presbyterian church—Sermons. 3. Sermons, American. I. Title.

PLOTZKE, Urban Werner, 226.206
1907-
God's own Magna charta. [Tr. from German by J. Holland Smith] Westminster, Md., Newman [1964, c.1963] 198p. 19cm. 64-1943 4.25
1. Sermon on the Mount—Sermons. 2. Beatitudes—Sermons. I. Title.

THIELICKE, Helmut, 1908- 226.2
Life can begin again; sermons on the Sermon on the Mount. Tr. [from German] by John W. Doberstein. Philadelphia, Fortress [c.1963] 215p. 22cm. 63-12535 3.75
1. Sermon on the Mount—Sermons. 2. Lutheran Church—Sermons. 3. Sermons. English—Translations from German. 4. Sermons, German—Translations into English. I. Title.

Sermon stories.

SADLER, Alfred J. 253
Story-sermons for juniors, by Alfred J. Sadler; with an introduction by Calvin W. Laufer. New York, Cincinnati, The Abingdon press [c1923] 224 p. 19 1/2 cm. [BV4315.S3] 23-18112
I. Title.

*SCHOFIELD, Joseph A. Jr. 243
Favorite object talks, by Joseph A. Schofield. Grand Rapids, Mich, Baker Book House [1973, c1951] 144 p. 20 cm. (Object Lesson series) [BV4307.S7] ISBN 0-8010-8017-7 1.50 (pbk.)
1. Sermon stories. I. Title.

VERSTEEG, Robert John 252
The secret life of the Good Samaritan, and other stories. [Nashville, Abingdon, c.1963] 96p. 20cm. 63-7482 2.00 bds.,
1. Sermon stories. I. Title.

VERSTEEG, Robert John. 252
The secret life of the Good Samaritan, and other stories. [New York, Abingdon Press, 1963] 96 p. 20 cm. [BV4307.S7V4] 63-7482
1. Sermon stories. I. Title.

VICKLAND, William, comp. 240.8
The little brown church of the air; sermon stories, compiled and arranged by William Vickland ... Chicago, The Reilly & Lee co., [c1931] 188 p. 19 1/2 cm. [BV4301.V5] 31-5641
I. Title. II. Title: Sermon stories.
Contents omitted.

Sermons

ABBOT, Abiel, 1770-1828.
Sermons, by the late Rev. Abiel Abbot...With a memoir of his life, by S. Everett. Boston, Wait, Greene & co., 1831. ixx, [71]-72, 297 p. 21 cm. "Publications of Dr. Abbot": p. [71]-72. 5-9382
I. Everett, S. II. Title.

ABERNETHY, Arthur Talmage, 243
1872-
Twenty-five best sermons, by Arthur Talmage Abernethy, PH. D.; with an introduction by Congressman William D. Upshaw. Cincinnati, O., The Standard publishing company [c1920] 367 p. 19 1/2 cm. [BV3797.A35] 21-542
I. Title.

ALBERTSON, Charles Carroll,
1865-
Chapel talks; a collection of sermons to college students, by Charles Carroll Albertson ... New York, Chicago [etc.] Fleming H. Revell company [c1916] 192 p. 19 1/2 cm. $1.00 16-21231
I. Title.

ALBERTSON, Charles Carroll,
1865-
College sermons [by] Charles Carroll Albertson ... Philadelphia, The Westminster press, 1909. 194 p. front. (port.) 19 1/2 cm. $0.75 9-31978
I. Title.

ALBRECHT, Joseph H. 252.7
The Gospel in our day; collected sermons. New York, Vantage [1962, c.1961] 96p. 2.50 bds.,
I. Title.

ALLEN-MICHAEL. 299
To the youth of the world / channeled through Allen-Michael. Berkeley, Calif. : Starmast Publications, c1973. iv, 350 p., [8] leaves of plates : ill. ; 21 cm. (The Everlasting gospel) Cover title: From the universe ... to the youth of the world. [BP610.A413] 74-186417 2.95
I. Title.

ALLISON, George William. 243
Out of the ashes, and other sermons, by George William Allison ... Nashville, Tenn., Cokesbury press, 1928. 189 p. 19 1/2 cm. [BX9178.A4708] 28-1726
I. Title.

... The American pulpit;
sermons by ministers of verious denominations, 1916 ed. Brooklyn, N. Y. [The Brooklyn daily eagle] 1916. 64 p. 29 cm. (The Eagle library, vol. xxxi, no. 5, serial no. 196) On cover: Sermons ... delivered during the year 1915. Contains advertising matter. 16-24731
I. Brooklyn daily eagle.

ARGOW, Wendelin Waldemar 242
Wieland, 1891-
Beyond, by W. Waldemar W. Argow ... Cedar Rapids, Ia., Corn publishing company, 1931. 130 p. 19 cm. "The contents of this volume appeared originally on the weekly calendars of the Peoples church, Cedar Rapids, Iowa, and the May memorial church, Syracuse."--Foreword. [BR125.A68 1931] 33-37361
I. Title.

ASTERIUS, bp. of Amasia, 265.
ca.375-405.
Ancient sermons for modern times, by Asterius, bishop of Amasia, circa 375-405, a. d., put into English from the Greek, by Galusha Anderson ... and Edgar Johnson Goodspeed ... New York, Boston [etc.] The Pilgrim press [1904] 157 p. 17 cm. [BR65.A43] 4-14156
I. Anderson, Galusha, 1832-1918, tr. II. Goodspeed, Edgar Johnson, 1871- tr. III. Title.

AYCOCK, Dell. Mrs. 016.
Object sermons, by Dell Aycock ... Kansas City, Mo., Nazarene publishing house [c1927] 86 p. front. (port.) 20 cm. [BV1535.A8] 27-16448
I. Title.

BAILEY, George W
Sermons of George W. Bailey. Edited by J. D. Thomas. Abilene, Texas, Biblical research press, 1961. 272p. port. 23cm. (Great preachers of today, v.2)
I. Title. II. Series.

BAILEY, John Barton. 252
Onward to Christ, and other sermons, by John Barton Bailey ... Ray, Ariz., 1928. 2 p. l., vii-xi, 118 p. 20 cm. [BX833.B2506] 28-24978
I. Title.

BAIRD, P. J., ed. 242
From out of the West, messages from Western pulpits. Stockton, Calif., Lantern Pr., 1962. 156p. illus. 21cm. 3.50
I. Title.

BAIRD, Paul Jesse, ed
From out of the West: messages from western pulpits. Stockton, Calif., Lantern Press, 1962. 156 p. illus. 21 cm. Bibliographical references included in "Footnotes": (p. 156) NUC63
I. Title.

BAKER, William H
Plain pointed practical preaching. Old-fashioned Bible Chautaugua Sermons. New York, Greenwich Book Pub., 1956. 312 p. NUC66
1. Sermons. I. Title.

BANKS, Louis Albert, 1855- 287
Hidden wells of comfort; being v. 1 of Banks' sermons, by Rev. Louis Albert Banks ... Cleveland, O., The Banks publishing company; [etc., etc., 1900] 1 p. l., 298, [3] p. 23 cm. [BX8333.B3H55] 1-29633
I. Title.

BANKS, Louis Albert, 1855-
John and his friends; a series of revival sermons. New York and London, Funk & Wagnalls co., 1899. viii, 299 p. 12° Jul
I. Title.

BANKS, Louis Albert, 1855- 287
The new ten commandments, and other sermons, by Louis Albert Banks ... New York, Chicago [etc.] Fleming H. Revell company [c1922] 186 p. 19 cm. [BX8333.B3N4] 23-615
I. Title.

BANKS, Louis Albert, 1855- 287
The sinner and his friends; a volume of evangelistic sermons, by Rev. Louis Albert Banks ... New York and London, Funk & Wagnalls company, 1907. iv, 339 p. 20 cm. [BX8333.B3S5] 7-23975
I. Title.
Contents omitted

BARLASS, William, d. 1817. 243
Sermons on practical subjects. By William Barlass ... With the correspondence between the author the Rev. John Newton

... never before published. And a biographical sketch of the author prefixed, by Peter Wilson ... New York; Published by James Eastburn & co. literary rooms, corner of Broadway and Pine-street. Abrham Paul, printer, 1818. 2 p. l., [7]-607 p. 23 1/2 cm. [BX9178.B345S4] 2-4362
I. Newton, John, 1725-1807. II. Title.

BARNES, George Owen, 1827-
Beraysheeth, or, In the beginning, by George O. Barnes, evangelist; ed. by Mary B. Craig ... Dayton, O., J. J. Scruby [c1910] 1 p. l., [5]-142 p., 1 l. 19 cm. 10-16970 1.00.
I. Craig, Mrs. Mary Brown, 1863- ed. II. Title.

BARTON, Levi Elder, 1870- 252.
Three dimensions of love, and other sermons [by] L. E. Barton ... Boston, R. G. Badger [c1929] 106 p. 21 cm. [BX6333.B37T5] 29-10520
I. Title.

BASCOM, Henry Bidleman. bp., 287
1796-1850.
Sermons from the pulpit. By H. B. Bascom ... 1st series. Louisville. Ky., Printed by Morton & Griswold for the author and company. 1850. 378 p. front. (port.) 20 cm. [BX8333.B394S4 1850] 8-864
I. Title.

BASCOM, John, 1827-1911.
Sermons and addresses, by John Bascom ... New York and London, G. P. Putnam's sons, 1913. iii, 356 p. 21 cm. 13-10610 1.25
I. Title.
Contents omitted.

BASHFORD, James Whitford, 287
bp., 1849-1919.
The demand for Christ, addresses and sermons, by James W. Bashford ... New York, Cincinnati, The Methodist book concern [c1920] 238 p. 19 cm. [BX8333.B4D4] 20-8353
I. Title.

BELLAMY, Joseph, 1719-1790. 252.
The law, our school-master; a sermon preached at Litchfield June 8, 1756, before the Association of Litchfield County. By Joseph Bellamy ... Published with great enlargements ... New-Haven, Printed by J. Parker, and company [1762] 1 p. l., 77, [1] p. 19 cm. Head-piece. [BX7233.B58L3] 21-18449
I. Title.

BENNETT, Robinson Potter Dunn,
1869-
What I tell my junior congregation; a serie of object sermons preached to the junior congregation of Summit Presbyterian church, Germantown, Pa., by the pastor, Robinson P. D. Bennett ... with an introduction by Alexander Henry ... Philadelphia, The Westminster press, 1912. 173 p. 19 cm. 12-10628 1.00
I. Title.

BEST sermons; 252.0082
v.8. 1962. Protestant Ed. Ed. by G. Paul Butler. Foreword by Bishop Gerald Kennedy. Princeton, N.J., Van Nostrand [c.1962] 328p. 24cm. 44-51581 5.95
1. Sermons. I. Butler, George Paul, 1900- ed.

BEST sermons; 252.0082
v.9. 1964. Protestant ed. Princeton, N.J., Van Nostrand [c.1964] 321p. 24cm. irregular. Ed.: 1964--G. P. Butler. 44-51581 5.95 bds.,
1. Sermons. I. Butler, George Paul, 1900- ed.

BEST sermons 252.0082
x- 1966-1968 New York Trident Pr. v. 22-25cm. irregular. Ed.: 1944- G. P. Butler Vols. for 1959-68 called "Protestant edition" [BV4241.B38] 7.95
1. Sermons. I. Butler, George Paul, 1900- ed.

BEST sermons. 1944- 252.0082
Chicago, New York, Ziff-Davis publishing company [1944- v. 24 cm. Editor: 1944- G. P. Butler. [BV4241.B38] 44-51581
1. Sermons. I. Butler, George Paul, 1900- ed.

BIEDERWOLF, William Edward, 243
1867-
When the song of the Lord began and other sermons, by William Edward Biederwolf ... Chicago, The Bible institute colportage ass'n [c1928] 126 p. 19 cm. [BX9178.B48W4] 28-18407
I. Title.

BIEDERWOLF, William 252.051
Edward, 1867-1939.
What of the night? Grand Rapids, W. B. Eerdmans Pub. Co., 1947. 94 p. 20 cm. (Home devotional library) [BX9178.B48W35] 47-25331
1. Sermons. 2. Presbyterian church—Sermons. 3. Sermons, American. I. Title.

BIRDSALL, Ralph, 1871-
Sermons in summer, delivered in Christ church, Cooperstown, by Rev. Ralph Birdsall ... Cooperstown, N. Y., The Arthur H. Crist co. [c18142] 235 p. 20 cm. 12-28370 1.00
I. Title.

BISSELL, Shelton. 261
Unofficial Christianity, by Shelton Bissell, B.D. Boston, R. G. Badger [c1918] 3 p. l., 9-98 p. 19 cm. (Lettered on cover: Library of religious thought) $1.00 "These little sermons were preached by the author in the First Congregational church of Boise, Idaho, during the late winter of 1916-1917."--Foreword. [BR123.B5] 18-4362
I. Title.

BLACK, F. G. 243
Lectures and sermons embracing the sovereignty, holiness, wisdom and benevolence of God; the moral agency of man considered as subject to and capable of moral government, all reconciled with the endless punishment of the finally impenitent, the filial relationship of the believer to God, the final state of the righteous, and the world by the gospel converted to God. By Rev. F. G. Black ... Cincinnati, H. S. & J. Applegate, & co., 1851. vi, [7]-240 p. 18 1/2 cm. [BX9178.B55L4] 30-2134
I. Title.

BLACK, Warren Columbus, 1843-
1915.
God's estimate of man, and other sermons, together with an autobiographical sketch, by the late Rev. W. E. Black ... with an introduction by Rev. H. M. DuBose D. D. pub. by his son, Rev. M. M. Black. Nashville, Tenn., Dallas, Tex. etc. Publishing house of the M. E. church, Smith & Lamar, agents. 1915 204 p. front. (port.) 19 1/2 cm. 16-2260 0.75
I. Title.

BLACKWOOD, Andrew 252.04
Watterson, 1882- comp.
The Protestant pulpit, an anthology of master sermons from the Reformation to our own day. Nashville, Abingdon [1966, c.1947] 318p. 23cm. (Apex bk., W2) [BV4241.B5] 47-12188 1.95 pap.,
1. Sermons. I. Title.

BLACKWOOD, Andrew 252.04
Watterson, 1882- comp.
The Protestant pulpit, an anthology of master sermons from the Reformation to our own day. Nashville, Abingdon-Cokesbury Press [1947] 318 p. 24 cm. [BV4241.B5] 47-12188
1. Sermons. I. Title.

BLAIR, Hugh, 1718-1800.
Sermons, by Hugh Blair ... 2nd complete American ed. ... Philadelphia Hickman & Hazzard, 1822. 2 v. front. (port.) 22 1/2 cm. 4-24598
I. Title.

BLESSING, William Lester, 1900-
Fountain of youth. Denver, House of Prayer for All People-[c1958] 123 p. NUC65
1. Sermons. I. Title.

BOLTON, Horace Wilbert 1839.
Victory assured; sermons preached by H. W. Bolton, D. D. Camden, N. J. Press of L. F. Bonaker & son, 1906. 157 p. front. (port.) 19 1/2 cm. 6-22899
I. Title.

BOOK, William Henry. 252
Sermons for the people, by William Henry Book ... Cincinnati, The Standard publishing company [c1918] 203 p. 20 cm. [BX7327.B7S4] 19-1194
I. Title.

BOOTH, Evangeline Cory, 1865- 243
Toward a better world, by Evangeline Booth. Garden City, N.Y., Doubleday, Doran & company, inc., 1928. 4 p. l., 244 p. front. (port.) 20 cm. Sermons. [BX9727.B6T6] 28-30526
I. Title.

BORDEN, Eli Monroe, 1874.
Jacob's ladder, a book of sermons preached by E.M. Borden, at Neosho, Missouri, in October, 1913. Stenographically reported. Also a few written extracts. Ed. by T.B. Clark. Little Rock, Ark., Christian pilot publishing co., [c1914] 352 p. front., ports. 20cm. $1.25 14-15193
I. Clark, t.b., ed. II. Title.

BOSSAERT, M.
Short sermons on Gospel texts, by Rev. M. Bessaert. New York, J. F. Wagner [c1916] iv, 147 p. 21 1/2 cm. $1.00. 16-10697
I. Title.

BOWEN, Nathaniel. 1779-1839.
Sermons on Christian doctrines and duties. by the Right Rev. Nathaniel Bowen ... Charleston [S.C.] A. E. Miller, 1842. 2 v. 24 cm. 5-9381
I. Title.

BOWES, George Seaton.
Information and illustration. Helps gathered from facts, figures, anecdotes, books etc. for sermons, lectures, and addresses. By the Rev. G. S. Bowes ... New York, R. Carter and bros., 1884. viii, 416 p. 19 cm. 16-1215
I. Title.

BOWES, George Seaton.
Information and illustration. Helps gathered from facts, figures, anecdotes, books etc. for sermons, lectures, and addresses. By the Rev. G. S. Bowes ... New York, R. Carter and bros., 1884. viii, 416 p. 19 cm. 16-1215
I. Title.

BRADLEY, Charles, 1789- 252.03
1871.
Practical and parochial sermons. By the Rev. Charles Bradley ... New York, D. Appleton & company; [etc., etc.] 1849 288, [5]-232 p. 24 cm. [BX5133.B7P7] 30-14937
I. Title. II. Title: Sermons, Practical and parochial.

BRANCH, James Orson.
Sermons, by Rev. James Orson Branch, D. D. Oxford, Ga., J. Magath, 1909. 3 p. l., [9]-323 p. 20 cm. 9-30150 1.25
I. Title.

BRANDT, John Lincoln, 1860-
Soul saving; revival sermons, by John L. Brandt ... St. Louis, Mo., The Christian publishing co. [c1907] 332 p. front. (port.) 20 cm. 8-788
I. Title.

BRATCHER, Samuel Robert, 252
1886-
Advertising Jesus, and other sermons, by S. R. Bratcher. Nashville, Tenn., Cokesbury press, 1931. 288 p. 19 cm. [BV4253.B7] 31-3670
I. Title.

BRINEY, John Benton, 1839- 252
Sermons and addresses, by J. B. Briney ... Cincinnati, The Standard publishing company [c1922] 430 p. 19 1/2 cm. [BX7327.B75S4] 22-22908
I. Title.

BROADDUS, Andrew, 1770-1848. 208.
The sermons and other writings of the Rev. Andrew Broaddus. With a memoir of his life, by J.B. Jeter, D.D. Edited by A. Broaddus. New York, L. Colby; Richmond, Va., Virginia Baptist S.S. and publishing society, 1852. xiv, 557 p. front. (port.) 19 cm. [BX6217.B86a] A 31
I. Jeter, Jeremiah Bell, 1802-1880. II. Broaddus, Andrew, 1818-1900. III. Title.

BROADUS, John Albert, 1827- 252.
1895.
Sermons and addresses. By John A. Broadus ... 2d ed. 4th thousand. Baltimore, H.M. Wharton and company, 1887. ix, 445 p. front. (port.) 19 1/2 cm. [BX6333.B67S4 1887] 23-14326
I. Title.

BRODIE, James Fairbairn, 240
1854-1910.
Tent and home, and other sermons, by the Reverend James Fairbairn Brodie, D.D.; with an introduction by Professor John Wright Buckham ... A memorial volume. Boston, New York [etc.] The Pilgrim press [c1912] xi, 187 p. 2 port. (incl. front.) 19 cm. $1.25. 12-25466
I. Title.

BROOKE, Stopford Augustus, 221
1832-1916.
The Old Testament and modern life, by Stopford A. Brooke. New York, Dodd, Mead and company, 1896. 352 p. 19 1/2 cm. Twenty sermons preached 1883-1894. "A word of criticism": p. 7-19. [BS1171.B7] 4-4026
I. Title.

BROOKS, Frank Lester, 1860-.
Prevailing prayer. Sermons preached in the Grace Methodist Episcopal church, Taunton, Mass., by the Rev. Frank L. Brooks ... [Hyannis, Mass., Printed by F. B. & F. P. Goss, c1909] 56 p. front. (port.) 19 cm. 9-16466
I. Title.

BROOKS, Phillips, bp., 1835- 252
1893.
Sermons. Sixth series. By the Rt. Rev. Phillips Brooks ... New York, E. P. Dutton and company, 1901. v, 362 p. 20 cm. 4-14245
1. Sermons. I. Title.

BROOKS,Phillips, bp., 1835=1893.
[sermons] New York, E. P. Dutton & company, 1910. Contents.1st ser. The purpose and use of comfort, and other sermons.--2d ser. The candel of the Lord, and other sermons.--3d ser. Sermons preached in English churches, and other sermons.--4th ser. Vistions and tasks, ant other sermons.--5th ser. The light of the world, and other sermons.-- 6th ser. The battle of life, and other sermons--7th ser. Sermons for the principal festivals and fasts of the church year, ed. by Rev. John Cotton Brooks--8th ser. New starts in life, andother sermons.--9th ser. The law of growth, and other sermons.--10th ser. Seeking life, and other sermons. A11
1. Sermons. I. Brooks, John Cotton, 1810-1907, ed. II. Title.

BUCHANAN, James Craig.
The imperishable heart, and other pulpit addresses, by James Craig Buchanan, M. D. Boston, The Gorham press; [etc., etc.] c1917] 259 p. 20 cm. (Lettered on cover: Library of religios thoughts) 17-6230 1.25
I. Title.

BURKE, Thomas F. 248
Reconstruction virtues, an Advent course of sermons, proposing Christian remedies for present chaotic social conditions drawn from the store room of the mother of civilization, the Catholic church. By Thomas F. Burke, c. s. p. New York, The Paulist press, 1920. 5 p. l., 66 p. 19 cm. [BX1756.B85 1920] 20-10776
I. Title.

BUSBY, Horace W. 243
Practical sermons of persuasive power... a series of...gospel sermons delivered at different places throughout the brotherhood. By Horace W. Busby... Brownwood, Tex., Way of truth publishing co., 1929- v. port. 23 cm. [BV3797.B78] 29-10307
I. Title.

BUSHNELL, Horace, 1802-1876.
The spirit in man; sermons and selections by Horace Bushnell ... Centenary ed. New York, C. Scribner's sons, 1903. xi, 473 p. 20 1/2 cm. Bibliography, by Henry Barrett Learned: p. 445-473. 3-10700
I. Title.

BUSHNELL, John Edward, 1858- 243
Summit views and other sermons, by John Edward Bushnell ... New York, Chicago [etc.] Fleming H. Revell company [c1919] 190 p. 19 cm. [BX9178.B85S8] 20-2353
I. Title.

BUTTNER, Heinrich.
Golgotha; passion week sermons, by P. Heinrich Buttner. Tr. from the German. Burlington, Ia., The German literary board 1905. 2 p. l., [7]-107 p. 20 cm. 5-8414
I. Title.

BUTTNER, Heinrich.
Golgotha; passion week sermons, by P. Heinrich Buttner. Tr. from the German. Burlington, Ia., The German literary board 1905. 2 p. l., [7]-107 p. 20 cm. 5-8414
I. Title.

BUTTNER, Heinrich.
Golgotha; passion-tide sermons, by Pastor Heinrich Buettner; tr. from the German. 2d rev. ed. Burlington, Ia., The German literary board, 1912. 4 p. l., 7-122 p. 21 cm. With this is bound the author's He is risen ... 12-5170 0.85
I. Title.

BUTTNER, Heinrich.
Golgotha; passion-tide sermons, by Pastor Heinrich Buettner; tr. from the German. 2d rev. ed. Burlington, Ia., The German literary board, 1912. 4 p. l., 7-122 p. 21 cm. With this is bound the author's He is risen ... 12-5170 0.85
I. Title.

CALDWELL, Erskine, 1903-
The sure hand of God. [New York] New American Library [1958] 142 p. 18 cm. (Signet books) 68-33577
I. Title.

CALLAN, Charles Jerome, father, 1877- 282
A parochial course of doctrinal instructions for all Sundays and holydays of the year based on the teachings of the Catechism of the Council of Trent and harmonized with the Gospels and Epistles of the Sundays and feasts, prepared and arranged by the Rev. Charles J. Callan, o. r., and the Rev. John A. McHugh, o. p. ... with and introduction by the Most Rev. Patrick J. Hayes ... New York, Joseph F. Wagner (inc.); [etc., etc., c1921]) v. 21 cm. Dogmatic series, v. 1- "References" at end of each chapter. "General references": vol. i. p. [499]-508. Vols. 1- [Secular name: Charles Louis Callan] [BX1751.C2 1921] 21-2530
I. McHugh, John Ambrose, father, 1880- joint author. II. Title.

CALVARY 's cross, 252'.63
by Dwight L. Moody . . . and others. Grand Rapids, Baker Bk. [1966] 97p. 20cm. (Minister's handbk. ser.) [BV4241.C3] 67-2873 1.95 bds.,
1. Sermons. I. Moody, Dwight Lyman, 1837-1899.
Contents omitted.

CAMERON, William A. 252.
The gift of God, and other sermons, by Rev. W. A. Cameron ... New York, George H. Doran company [c1925] viii p., 2 l., [13]-230 p. 19 1/2 cm. [BX6333.C35G3] 26-3143
I. Title.

CAMPBELL, Reginald John, 1867- 252.
Sermons addressed to individuals, by Reginald J. Campbell... New York, A. C. Armstrong & son, 1905. viii, 328 p. 20 cm. [BX7233.C33S4] 5-2408
I. Title.

CAMPBELL, Reginald John, 1867- 252.
The song of ages; sermons by Reginald J. Campbell... New York, A. C. Armstrong & sons, 1905. 3 p. l., [3]-308 p. front. (port.) 20 cm. [BX7233.C33S6] 5-40809
I. Title.

CAMPBELL, Reginald John, 1867-
Thursday mornings at the City Temple, by the Rev. R. J. Campbell... New York, The Macmillan company, 1908. xi, 308 p. 19 1/2 cm. Printed in Great Britain. Twenty sermons, with a few exceptions, preached at the Thursday midday service in the City Temple during the last twelve months. cf. Pref., dated May 19, 1908. 9-35041
I. Title.

CARPENTER, Charles Knapp.
When the wild crab-apple puts forth blossoms; nature sermons preached in the First Methodist Episcopal church, Aurora, Ill., by the Reverend Charles Knapp Carpenter ... Cincinnati, Jennings and Graham; New York, Eaton and Mains [c1911] 293, [1] p. incl. front., illus., plates. 20 cm. 11-22012 1.25
I. Title.
Contents omitted.

CASTLE, Nicholas, 1837-
The witness of the spirit, by Bishop N. Castle ... Dayton, O., United brethren publishing house, 1902. iii, 5-84 p. 17 cm. (Doctrinal series) 2-21590
I. Title.

CECIL, Lord Martin, 1909- 248
Being where you are. New Canaan, Conn., Keats Pub. [1974] 204 p. 18 cm. (A Pivot original) [BP605.E4C42] 73-93652 1.50 (pbk.).
I. Title.

CHAMBRE, Albert St. John.
Sermons on the Apostles' creed. New York, T. Whittaker [1898] vii, 162 p. 12 degree. Aug
I. Title.

CHAPMAN, J. Wilbur, 1859-
Chapman's pocket sermons no. 1- By Rev. J. Wilbur Chapman, D. D. New York, Chicago [etc.] Fleming H. Revell company [c1910- v. 16 cm. 11-566
I. Title.

CHAPMAN, James Archer, 1885- 252
Launching out into the deep, and other sermons, by J. A. Chapman ... Nashville, Tenn., Cokesbury press, 1925. 107 p. 18 cm. [BV4253.C5] 26-8211 1.00
I. Title.

CHAPMAN, Michael Andrew. 248
The epistle of Christ; short sermons for the Sundays of the year on texts taken from the epistles, by the Reverend Michael Andrew Chapman ... St. Louis and London, B. Herder book co., 1927. vii, 264 p. 20 cm. [BX1756.C5 1927] 27-17438
I. Title.

CHAPMAN, Michael Andrew. 248
The faith of the gospel: brief sermons for the Sundays of the year, by the Reverend Michael Andrew Chapman ... St. Louis, Mo., and London, B. Herder book co., 1926. viii, 249 p. 20 cm. [BX1756.C5 1926] 26-23087
I. Title.

CHAPPELL, Ashley. 287
Sermons on great tragedies of the Bible, by Rev. Ashley Chappell ... with a preface by Bishop Sam R. Hay. New York, George H. Doran company [c1924] ix p. 1 l., 13-136 p. 20 cm. [BX8333.C4S4] 24-25199
I. Title.

*CHAPPELL, Clovis G. 252.6
Chappell's special day sermons / Clovis G. Chappell. Grand Rapids : Baker Book House, 1976c1964. 204p. ; 20 cm. [BV4254] ISBN 0-8010-2383-1 : 2.95
1. Sermons. I. Title.

*CHAPPELL, Clovis G. 252
The sermon on the Mount by Clovis G. Chappell Grand Rapids, Baker Book [1975] 227 p. 20 cm. (Clovis G. Chappell Library) [BV4253] ISBN 0-8010-2363-7 2.95 (pbk.)
1. Sermons. I. Title.

*CHAPPELL, Clovis G. 252
Sermons from the miracles [by] Clovis G. Chappell Grand Rapids Baker Book [1975 c1965] 224 p. 20 cm. (Clovis G. Chappell Library) [BV4253] ISBN 0-8010-2362-9 2.95 (pbk.)
1. Sermons. I. Title.

CHAPPELL, Clovis Gillham. 262.
Sermons on New Testament characters, by Rev. Clovis G. Chappell ... New York, George H. Doran company [c1924] 189 p. 20 cm. [BS2430.C4] 24-23310 1.60
I. Title.

CHAPPELL, Clovis Gillham, 1882- 220
Sermons on Biblical characters, by Rev. Clovis G. Chappell, D. D. New York, George H. Doran company [c1922] 194 p. 20 cm. [BS571.C45] 22-19973
I. Title.

CHEEVER, Samuel, 1639-1724. 252
Gods sovereign government among the nations asserted in a sermon preached before His Excellency the Governour, the Honourable Council, and Representatives of the province of the Massachusetts-Bay in New-England, on May 28. 1712. being the day for election of Her Majesties council for that province. By Samuel Cheever ... Boston: Printed by B. Green: Sold at the Booksellers Shops, 1712. 1 p. l., 53 p. 14 cm. [BV4260.M5 1712] 24-9338
I. Massachusetts. Colony, Council, 1712. II. Title.

CHEEVER, Samuel, 1639-1724. 252
Gods sovereign government among the nations asserted in a sermon preached before His Excellency the Governour, the Honourable Council, and Representatives of the province of the Massachusetts-Bay in New-England, on May 28. 1712. being the day for election of Her Majesties council for that province. By Samuel Cheever ... Boston: Printed by B. Green: Sold at the Booksellers Shops, 1712. 1 p. l., 53 p. 14 cm. [BV4260.M5 1712] 24-9338
I. Massachusetts. Colony, Council, 1712. II. Title.

CHRISTY, George H.
Sunday morning talks prepared for Bible class no. 20 of the Presbyterian congregation of Sewickley, Pennsylvania, by George H. Christy. New York, The Knickerbocker press, 1912. viii p., 1 l., 289 p. front. (port.) 20 1/2 cm. 12-21982
I. Title.

COBIA, Daniel, 1811-1837.
Sermons by the Rev. Daniel Cobia ... With an introduction, and a sermon on the occasion of his death, by William W. Spear ... Charleston [S.C.] J. P. Beile, 1838. xi, 542 p. 24 cm. 16-24746
I. Spear, William W. Ministerial devotedness ... II. Title.

CONDIT, Jonathan Bailey, 1808-1876. 252
Christians, fellow-helpers to the truth. A sermon delivered in Bath, June 26, 1844, before the Maine missionary society, at its thirty-seventh anniversary, by Rev. J. B. Condit ... Portland, Thurston, Ilsley & co., printers, 1844. 52 p. 22 cm. "Report of the trustees of the Maine missionary society, at their thirty-seventh annual meeting, in Bath, June 26, 1844": p, [23]-52. [B V2360. M3 A4 1844] 26-22138
I. Congregational conference and missionary society of Maine. II. Title.

CONWELL, Russell Herman, 1843-1925. 252.
Sermons for the great days of the years, by Rev. Russell H. Conwell ... New York, Geroge H. Doran company [c1922] vi, 9-226 p. 19 1/2 cm. [BX6333.C6S4] 22-14828 1.50
I. Title.

COOK, Silas Arthur, 1875-
The quest of truth; lecture-sermons, being a study of various fields of Christian truth [by] S. Arthur Cook ... Cincinnati, Jennings and Graham; New York, Eaton and Mains [c1912] 306 p. 19 1/2 cm. $1.25 Bibliography at end of each chapter. 12-20216
I. Title.

COOK, Silas Arthur, 1875-
The quest of truth; lecture-sermons, being a study of various fields of Christian truth [by] S. Arthur Cook ... Cincinnati, Jennings and Graham; New York, Eaton and Mains [c1912] 306 p. 19 1/2 cm. $1.25 Bibliography at end of each chapter. 12-20216
I. Title.

COOMBS, James Vincent, 1849-
The Christ of the church, sermons, lectures and illustrations, by J. V. Coombs ... Cincinnati, The Standard publishing company [c1916] 244 p. 20 cm. 16-5057
I. Title.

COSSUM, William Henry, 1863-
Mountain peaks of prophecy and sacred history, by W. H. Cossum, m. a. Chicago, The Evangel publishing house [c1911] 2 p. l., 7-195 p. maps. 20 cm. 11-5345 0.65
I. Title.

COTTAM, Joseph Almond, 1881-
Some fundamental gospel truths in modern light; a book for present day use, by the Rev. Joseph A. Cottam ... Being a number of sermons, talks, and articles, on subjects of interest to preachers, teachers, and Christian believers. New York, Broadway publishing company 19129 2 p. l., ii, 110 p. front (port) 20 cm. 12-27875 0.75
I. Title.

COX, Frank 251.027
Select sermon materials. Grand Rapids, Mich., Baker Bk. [c.]1963. 93p. 22cm. (Sermon lib.) 1.00 pap.,
I. Title.

CULPEPPER, Burke. 243
Put God first, by Rev. Burke Culpepper, D. D.; a series of evangelistic sermons delivered through the South and West. Louisville, Ky., Pentecostal publishing company [c1925] 168 p. 20 cm. [BV3797.C85] 25-25764
I. Title.

CULPEPPER, Burke. 243
Put God first, by Rev. Burke Culpepper, D. D.; a series of evangelistic sermons delivered through the South and West. Louisville, Ky., Pentecostal publishing company [c1925] 168 p. 20 cm. [BV3797.C85] 25-25764
I. Title.

CUMMING, John, 1807-1881. 220
Voices of the night. By the Rev. John Cumming ... Boston, J. P. Jewett and company; Cleveland, O., Jewett, Proctor, and Worthington, 1854. viii, 277 p. 19 cm. "Most of these Voices, in somewhat different forms, were uttered from the pulpit."--Pref. [BR125.C865] 15-618
I. Title.

*CUNNINGHAM, Charles B. 227.8
Simple studies in Timothy, Titus, and Philemon. Grand Rapids, Mich., Baker Bk. [c.]1964. 108p. 22cm. (Dollar sermon lib.) 1.00 pap.,
I. Title.

DALLMANN, William i. e. Charles Frederick William, 1862-
The ten commandments explained in sermonic lectures ... 2d ed., rev. Pittsburg, Pa., American Lutheran pub. board, 1900. 335 p. 12 degree. 1-29462
I. Title.

DARGAN, Edwin Charles, 1852- 252.
The hope of glory, and other sermons, by Edwin Charles Dargan ... New York, Chicago [etc.] Fleming H. Revell company [c1919] 153 p. 20 cm. [BX6333.D3H6] 19-18543
I. Title.

DARLINGTON, Elliot Christopher Bearns, 1895- 252.
Summer sermons, preached in the Church of the heavenly rest and Chapel of the beloved disciple, New York city, by Rev. Elliott C. B. Darlington, LL. B. New York, Chicago [etc.] Fleming H. Revell company [c1929] 63 p. front. (port.) 20 cm. [BX5937.D3A3] 29-24203
I. Title.

DAWLEY, William Wallace, 1850-
Tonic thoughts from the sermons of Dr. W. W. Dawley. Syracuse, N. Y., Farther lights society [c1915] [78] p. front. (mounted port.) 19 cm. 16-1098 0.50
I. Title.

DAWSON, William James 1854-
The reproach of Christ, and other sermons, by W. J. Dawson ... with an introduction by Newell Dwight Hillis. New York, London [etc.] F. H. Revell company [1903] 281 p. 21 cm. 3-21026
I. Title.

DEWHURST, Frederick Eli, 1855-1906. 252.
The investment of truth, and other sermons, by Frederic E. Dewhurst ... with an introduction by Albion W. Small. Chicago, The University of Chicago press, 1907. xv, 274 p. front. (port.) 20 cm. [BX7233.D5 I 6] 7-23074
I. Title.

DHIRANANDA, swami. 204
Glimpses of light; a collection of excerpts from sermons on oriental and accidental

philosophies and religions, by Swami Dhirananda ... [Los Angeles, Aetna printing co., c1929] 7 p. l., 17-146, [1] p. 21 cm. [BL27.D4] 29-17517
I. Title.

DICKENS, John Lunsford, 1853-
Sermons, practical devotional, by Rev. J. L. Dickens ... Galv[eston] Oscar Springer print, 1916. 158 p. illus. (port.) 18 cm. 16-5721 0.75
I. Title.

DICKINSON, Jonathan, 1688-1747. 243
The witness of the Spirit. A sermon preached at Newark in New-Jersey, May 7th, 1740, wherein is distinctly shewn, in what way and manner the spirit himself beareth witness to the adoption of the children of God. On occasion of a wonderful progress of converting grace in those parts. By Jonathan Dickinson ... Boston: N. E. Printed and sold by S. Kneeland and T. Green, in Queen-Street, over against the Prison, 1740. 1 p. l., 28 p. 20 cm. [BX9178.D5W5] 22-21135
I. Title.

DODSON, Ralph H. 252.076
The ten commandments, and other sermons, by Ralph H. Dodson ... [Bernie, Mo., Bernie news print] c1930. 59 p. illus. (port.) 15 cm. [BX8333.D58T4] 30-20362
I. Title.

DOWLING, George Thomas.
Saturday night sermons, by Rev. Geo. Thos. Dowling ... New York, T. Whittaker [1904] viii, 131 p. front. 19 1/2 cm. 4-31295
I. Title.

DUDDEN, Frederick Homes, 1874- 283.
The dead and the living and other sermons, by F. Homes Dudden... London, New York [etc.] Longmans, Green and co., 1920. vii, 120 p. 19 1/2 cm. [BX5133.D8D4] 20-18238 1.75.
I. Title.

DUNCAN, Walter Wofford T 1869- 280
Our Protestant heritage; three sermons by W. Wofford T. Duncan, at Emory Methodist Episcopal church, Pittsburgh, Pennsylvania. New York, Cincinnati, The Methodist book concern [c1922] 130 p. 19 cm. [BX4810.D8] 22-18823
I. Title.

ECKMAN, George Peck, 1860-
Passion week sermons, by George P. Eckman, D.D. Cincinnati, Jennings and Graham; New York, Eaton and Mains [c1909] 262 p. 19 cm. On back of cover: Christian festivals. 9-29182 1.00
I. Title.

ECKMAN, George Peck, 1860-1920. 252.
The young man with a program, and other sermons to young men, by George P. Eckman... Cincinnati, Jennings and Graham; New York, Eaton and Mains [c1905] 142 p. front. (port) 19 cm. (Half-itile: The Methodist pulpit. [2d series] [BV4310.E3] 5-32518
I. Title.

EELLS, Edward.
The gospel for both worlds; ten sermons preached in our Father's house (Memorial church) Worcester, by Edward Eells ... Boston, Sherman, French & company, 1911. 3 p. l., 133 p. 10 cm. $0.60. 11-21882
I. Title.

ELLIOTT, Walter, 1842-
Parish sermons on moral and spiritual subjects for all Sundays and feasts of obligation, by Rev. Walter Elliott... New York, The Paulist press, 1913. xiii, 457 p. 24 cm. 13-25355 1.50
I. Title.

ELLMORE, Alfred.
Sermons, reminiscences, both pleasant and sad; and silver chimes, by Alfred Ellmore. Austin, Tex., Firm foundation publishing house, 1914. 220 p. front. (port.) 19 1/2 cm. 15-8999 1.00
I. Title.

ELLMORE, Alfred.
Sermons and sayings, by Alfred Ellmore and others; missionary. Cincinnati, O., F. L. Rowe, 1918. 242 p. 1 l., front. (port.) 20 cm. [BX6777.E5S4] 18-10690
I. Title.

ENGSTROM, Theodore Wilhelm, 1916- ed. 252.0082
Great sermons from master preachers of all ages. First series. Grand Rapids, Zondervan Pub. House [1951] 180 p. illus. 20 cm. [BV4241.E673] 51-11553
1. Sermons. I. Title.

FAIRBAIRN, Andrew Martin, 1838-1912. 252.
Christ in the centuries, and other sermons, by A. M. Fairbairn ... New York, E. P. Dutton & co. [1893] viii, 223, [1] p. front. (port.) 19 cm. (Half-title: Preachers of the age) Bibliography: [1] p. at end. [BX7233.F27C5] 2-24003
I. Title.

FAITH and immortality;
selected sermons, New York [etc.] Vantage Press [1959] 81p.
I. Kemp, Richard A

FAITH and immortality;
selected sermons, New York [etc.] Vantage Press [1959] 81p.
I. Kemp, Richard A

FANT, Clyde E., comp. 252'.008
20 centuries of great preaching; an encyclopedia of preaching [by Clyde E Fant, Jr. and William M. Pinson Jr. Donald E. Hammer, research associate. Waco, Tex., Word Books [1971] 13 v. illus. 24 cm. Includes bibliographies. [BV4241.F34] 78-156697
1. Sermons. 2. Preaching—History. I. Pinson, William M., joint comp. II. Title.

FARRAR, Frederic William, 1831-1903.
"In the days of thy youth." Sermons on practical subjects, preached at Marlborough college, from 1871-1876. By F. W. Farrar ... 3d ed. New York, E. P. Dutton and company, 1877. xv, 398 p. 19 cm. 16-3274
I. Title.

FARRAR, Frederic William, 1831-1903. 283.
The silence, and the Voices of God, with other sermons. By Frederic W. Farrar ... New York, E. P. Dutton & company, 1877. ix, 11-238 p. 19 cm. [BX5133.F3S5] 16-9636
I. Title.

FISH, Henry Clay, 1820-1877. 252
History and repository of pulpit eloquence, (deceased divines) containing the masterpieces of Bossuet, Bourdaloue...etc., etc., with discourses from Chrysostom, Basil...and others among the "fathers", and from Wickliffe, Luther...etc., of the "reformers". Also sixty other celebrated sermons...historical sketches of preaching...and biographical and critical notices...By Rev. Henry C. Fish... New York, M. W. Dodd, 1856. 2 v. front. (8 port.) 24 cm. [BV4241.F5] 22-21896
1. Sermons. 2. Preaching—Hist. I. Title.

FISH, Henry Clay, 1820-1877. 252
Pulpit eloquence of the nineteenth century; being supplementary to the History and repository of pulpit eloquence, deceased divines; and containing discourses of eminent living ministers in Europe and America, with sketches biographical and descriptive, by Rev. Henry C. Fish. With a supplement, carrying down the work to 1874, and including discourses by Beech, Adams, Parker, Talmadge, and many others. With an introductory essay by Edwards A. Park New York, Dodd & Mead [c1874] xi, [2], 14-919 p. front., ports. 23 1/2 cm. [BV4241.F52 1874] 22-21895
1. Sermons. I. Park, Edwards Amasa, 1808-1900. II. Title.

FISK, Pliny, 1792-1825. 279.
Sermons of Rev. Messrs. Fisk & Parsons, just before their departure on the Palestine mission. Boston [S. T. Armstrong] 1819. 52 p. 24 cm. Cover title. Contains 2 sermons, each with special t.-p.: The dereliction and restoration of the Jews ... by Levi Parsons. Boston, 1819 and The Holy Land, an interesting field of missionary enterprise ... by Pliny Fisk. Boston, 1819. [BV3200.F5] 49-36496
I. Parsons, Levi, 1792-1822. II. Title.

FISKE, George Walter, 1872- 252.5
In a college chapel; occasional chapel talks at Oberlin college, by George Walter Fiske. New York and London, Harper & brothers, 1932. x p., 2 l., 126 p. 18 1/2 cm. "First edition." [BV4310.F45] 32-9865
I. Oberlin college. II. Title. III. Title: Chapel talks at Oberlin college.

FORMAN, Raymond Lalor. 287
Rough-hewed, and other sermons, by Raymond Lalor Forman. New York, Cincinnati, The Abingdon press [c1927] 211 p. 19 1/2 cm. [BX8333.F58R6] 27-18916
I. Title.

FORMAN, Raymond Lalor. 287
Rough-hewed, and other sermons, by Raymond Lalor Forman. New York, Cincinnati, The Abingdon press [c1927] 211 p. 19 1/2 cm. [BX8333.F58R6] 27-18916
I. Title.

FOSTER, L[orenzo] R.
My first sermons ... v. no. 1. Scranton, Pa., 1899. pl. port. 8 degree. 99-5637
I. Title.

FOSTER, Rupert Clinton, 1888- 252
The everlasting gospel, by Rupert Clinton Foster ... Cincinnati, O., The Standard publishing company [c1929] 316 p. 20 cm. A collection of sermons and essay on a wide variety of themes. [BX7327.F6E8] 29-11733
I. Title.

FOSTER, Rupert Clinton, 1888- 252
The everlasting gospel, by Rupert Clinton Foster ... Cincinnati, O., The Standard publishing company [c1929] 316 p. 20 cm. A collection of sermons and essay on a wide variety of themes. [BX7327.F6E8] 29-11733
I. Title.

FRANCIS, James Allan, 1854-1928. 252.
Christ is all and other sermons, by James Allan Francis ... Philadelphia, Boston [etc.] The Judson press [c1928] 6 p. l., 3-159 p. front. (port.) 20 cm. [BX6333.F7C5] 28-20153
I. Title.

FRANCIS, James Allan, 1864- 252.
The real Jesus, and other sermons, by James Allan Francis ... Philadelphia, Boston [etc.] The Judson press [c1926] 5 p. l., 3-131 p. front. (port.) 20 cm. [BX6333.F7R4] 27-2983
I. Title.

FREEMAN, James Edward, bp., 1866- 252.
The Christ of the byways, and other little newspaper sermons, by the Right Reverend James E. Freeman ... New York, Chicago [etc.] Fleming H. Revell company [c1928] 191 p. 20 cm. [BX5937.F7C5] 28-19802
I. Title. II. Title: Little newspaper sermons.

FREEMAN, James Edward, 1866- 252.
Everyday religion; little "Tribune" sermons, by James E. Freeman ... New York, Chicago [etc.] Fleming H. Revell company [c1920] 3 p. l., 5-219 front. (port.) 20 cm. [BX5937.F7E8] 21-3688
I. Title. II. Title: Little "Tribune" sermons.

FREEMAN, James Edward, 1866- 252.
Everyday religion; little "Tribune" sermons, by James E. Freeman ... New York, Chicago [etc.] Fleming H. Revell company [c1920] 3 p. l., 5-219 front. (port.) 20 cm. [BX5937.F7E8] 21-3688
I. Title. II. Title: Little "Tribune" sermons.

FROST, S. E., 1899- ed. 252.0082
The world's great sermons, edited by S. E. Frost, jr. ... Garden City, N.Y., Halcyon house [1943] xiii p., 1 l., 395 p. 22 cm. Each sermon preceded by a biographical sketch of the author. "First edition." [BV4241.F76] 43-17477
1. Sermons. I. Title.

FROST, S. S. Jr. ed. 252
The world's great sermons, edited by S. E. Frost, jr. Garden City, N. Y., Garden City Books, 1960 [c.1943] xiii, 395p. 22cm. Each sermon preceded by a biographical sketch of the author. 2.95 bds.,
1. Sermons. I. Title.

GANNETT, William Channing, 1840-1923. 252.
A year of miracle. A poem in four sermons. By W. C. Gannett. Boston, G. H. Ellis, 1888. 106 p. 15 cm. [BX9843.G43Y4 1888] 24-10089
I. Title.

GARNER, Lloyd W.
Could it be you? "T.V." sermons. Foreword by Dr. C.C. Warren. New York, Exposition Press [c1961] 107 p. 21 cm. 64-25899
I. Title.

GARR, A. G. 243
Gems from the pulpit; choice sermons on salvation, healing, Holy Spirit, and second coming of Our Lord Jesus Christ. By Evangelist A. G. Garr. Los Angeles, Calif., F. A. Sharp [c1927] 191 p. front., plates, ports. 19 1/2 cm. [BV3797.G3] 27-15638
I. Title.

GEIERMANN, Peter. 282.
The eucharistic Emmanuel; sermons for the forty hours' devotion, by the Rev. Peter Geiermann ... St. Louis, Mo. and London, B. Herder book co., 1927. v, 151 p. 20 cm. [BX2215.G4] 27-16457
I. Title.

GEIERMANN, Peter. 282.
The eucharistic Emmanuel; sermons for the forty hours' devotion, by the Rev. Peter Geiermann ... St. Louis, Mo. and London, B. Herder book co., 1927. v, 151 p. 20 cm. [BX2215.G4] 27-16457
I. Title.

GESTA Romanorum. English. 879
Gesta Romanorum; or, Entertaining moral stories, invented by the monks as a fireside recreation, and commonly applied in their discourses from the pulpit, whence the most celebrated of our own poets and others, from the earliest times, have extracted their plots. Translated from the Latin, with preliminary observations and copious notes, by Charles Swan. Rev. and corr. by Wynnard Hooper. [New York] Dover Publications [1959] lxxvi, 425 p. 21 cm. "An unabridged and unaltered republication of the Bohn library edition of 1876." [PA8323.E5S9 1959] 59-4176
I. Swan, Charles, tr. II. Hooper, Wynnard, ed.

GIFFORD, Orrin Philip, 1847- 252.
The shadow of the rock, and other sermons, by Orin Philip Gifford ... New York, Chicago [etc.] Fleming H. Revell company [c1927] 137 p. 20 cm. [BX6333.G5S5] 27-20140
I. Title.

GOLLADAY, Robert Emory.
Sermons on the catechism ... by Robert Emory Golladay ... Pub. for the author. [Columbus, O.] Lutheran book concern, 1915 v. front. (port.) 20 cm. 15-25971
I. Title.

GOULD, George H[enry] 1827-1899.
In what life consists and other sermons, by Rev. George H. Gould, D. D. Boston, Chicago, The Pilgrim press [1903] 1 p. l., 386 p. front. (port.) 25 cm. 3-14971
I. Title.

GRAHAM, William.
The fruits of the devotion to the Sacred Heart; a course of sermons for the first Fridays of the year, by Rev. William Graham. New York, J. F. Wagner [1909] 119 p. 20 cm. 10-4252 0.75
I. Title.

GREAT sermons of the world.
Grand Rapids, Mich., Baker Book House [1958] 454p. 22cm. 'A reprint with deletions of the edition printed in 1926.'
1. Sermons. I. Macartney, Calrence Edward Noble, 1879-1957, comp. ed.

GUNN, John R. 252
One hundred more three-minute sermons, by Rev. John R. Gunn ... Garden City, N. Y., Doubleday, Doran & company, inc., 1929. xi, 136 p. 20 cm. [BV4253.G82] 20-3152
I. Title.

GUNN, John R. 252
One hundred three-minute sermons, by Rev. John R. Gunn ... New York, George H. Doran company [c1927] xi, 15-162 p. 20 cm. [BV4253.G8] 27-11511
I. Title.

GWILYM, David Vaughan. 252.
The vision that transforms and other sermons, by Rev. David Vaughan Gwilym... New York, Continental publishing co., 1900. 59 p. 19 cm. [BX5937.B885V5] 0-2523
I. Title.

HAAS, John Augustus William, 1862- 252.
In the light of faith; baccalaureate sermons and educational addresses, by John A. W. Haas... Philadelphia, Pa., The United Lutheran publication house [c1922] ix p., 1 l., 13-287 p. 19 1/2 cm. [BX8066.H316] 22-15587
I. Title.

HALDEMAN, Isaac Massey, 1845-
Is the coming of Christ before or after the millennium? By I. M. Haldeman...preached Sunday evening, October 29, 1916... New York, N.Y., C. C. Cook [c1917] 75 p. 20 cm. Sermon number three of series. 17-9579 0.25
I. Title.

HALDEMAN, Isaac Massey, 1845-
This hour not the hour of the Prince of peace, by I. M. Haldeman, D.D., preached in the Brooklyn Baptist temple before the New York state convention, October 27, 1915... New York, C. C. Cook [c1916] 56 p. 20 cm. 16-2255 0.20
I. Title.

HALL, Frank Oliver, 1860-
Soul and body; a book of sermons preached in the Church of the divine paternity, New York city, by Frank Oliver Hall, D.D. Boston, Mass., Universalist publishing house, 1909. 218 p. 18 cm. $1.00 9-30149
I. Title.

HALL, James Hamilton.
The exodus from death. Sermons "concerning those who have fallen asleep." By Rev. James Hamilton Hall... Nashville, Tenn., Press of Marshall & Bruce co., 1903. 252 p. 20 cm. 3-17288
I. Title.

HAM, John W. 243
Reaping for Christ; illustrative evangelistic sermons, by John W. & Ham ... with an introduction by Curtis Lee Laws ... New York, Chicago [etc.] Fleming H. Revell company [c1928] 160 p. 19 1/2 cm. [BV3797.H34] 28-12569
I. Title.

HANSON, Miles. 252.
The hills of God, by Miles Hanson... Boston, Mass., New York [etc.] The Beacon press, inc. [c1923] 252 p. front. (port.) pl. 21 cm. Sermons. [BX9843.H43H5] 23-17572
I. Title.

HARRIS, William Shuler. 244
Sermons by the devil, fully related by Rev. W. S. Harris ... illustrated by Paul Krafft and others. Harrisburg, Pa., The Minter company [1904] 1 p. l., 304 p. incl. illus., plates. 22 cm. [BV4515.] 4-13645
I. Title.

HARVEY, Edwin Lawrence, 1865-
Sermons on Bible characters, by Rev. Edwin L. Harvey. Waukesha, Wis., Metropolitan church association [c1909] xii, 242 p. incl. front. (port.) 19 cm. 10-388 0.50
I. Title.

HAYES, Everis Anson, 1855-
Sermons by a layman, by Everis A. Hayes. Boston, The Christopher publishing house [c1927] 158 p. 21 cm. [B4125.H458] 27-18403
I. Title.

HECHEL, P.
Short sermons on Catholic doctrine; a plain and practical exposition of the faith in a series of brief discourses for the ecclesiastical year, by the Rev. P. Hebel ... New York, J. F. Wagner [c1912- v. 21 cm. 13-2123
I. Title.

HEDGE, Frederic Henry, 1805-1890. 252.
Sermons, by Frederic Henry Hedge ... Boston, Roberts brothers, 1891. c.vi, 341 p. 20 cm. [BX9843.H5S4] 24-9313
I. Title.

HEDGE, Frederic Henry, 1805-1890. 252.
Sermons, by Frederic Henry Hedge ... Boston, American Unitarian association, 1902. vi, 341 p. 19 cm. [BX9843.H5S43] 24-9311
I. Title.

HENSON, Poindexter Smith, 1831-1914.
The four faces, and other sermons, by P. S. Henson ... Philadelphia, Boston [etc.] The Griffith & Rowland press [c1911] 5 p. l., 3-256 p. front. (port.) 20 1/2 cm. 11-29369 1.00
I. Title.

HEPWORTH, George Hughes, 1833-1902. 243
We shall live again; the third series of sermons which have appeared in the Neb York Sunday herald, by George H. Hepworth ... New York, E. P. Dutton & company, 1903. vii, 271 p. 19 1/2 cm. [BX9178.H4H43] 3-5961
I. Title.

HERE they stand : 252'.06'147
biblical sermons from Eastern Europe / compiled and edited by Lewis A. Drummond. London : Marshall, Morgan and Scott, 1976. v, 186 p. : maps ; 22 cm. [BX6333.A1H47] 77-373921 ISBN 0-551-05539-1 : £2.95
1. Sermons. 2. Baptists—Sermons. I. Drummond, Lewis A.

HERE they stand : 252'.06'147
Biblical sermons from Eastern Europe / compiled and edited by Lewis A. Drummond. Valley Forge, Pa. : Judson Press, 1978, c1976. 186 p. : maps ; 21 cm. [BX6333.A1H47 1978] 77-92876 ISBN 0-8170-0790-3 : pbk. : 4.95
1. Sermons. 2. Baptists—Sermons. I. Drummond, Lewis A.

HINSON, Walter Benwell, 1862- 252.
A grain of wheat, and other sermons, by Walter Benwell Hinson ... Chicago, The Bible institute colportage ass'n [c1922] 3 p. l., 5-141 p. 20 cm. [BX6333.H5G7] 23-211
I. Title.

HINSON, Walter Benwell, 1862- 232.
Jesus the carpenter, by Walter Benwell Hinson ... Portland, Or., Carlson printing company [1926] 4 p. l., [5]-143 p. 20 cm. [BT201.H55 1926] 26-21363
I. Title.

HINSON, Walter Benwell, 1862-
Jesus the carpenter; sermons, by Walter Benwell Hinson ... Portland, Or., Press of Brockmann brothers [c1914] 1 p. l., 125 p. front. (port.) 18 1/2 cm. 15-6762
I. Title.

HINSON, Walter Benwell, 1862- 252.
The real Lord's prayer; sermons by Walter Benwell Hinson ... Portland, Or., Press of Brockmann printing & stationery co. [c1922] 2 p. l., 3-208 p. 19 1/2 cm. [BV234.H5] 23-2932
I. Title.

HODGES, George, 1856-
The battles of peace, by George Hodges ... New rev. ed. New York, The Macmillan company, 1914. 3 p. l., 273 p. 20 cm. A 14
1. Sermons. I. Title.

HODGES, George, 1856-
The year of grace, by George Hodges ... New York, T. Whittaker [c1906] v, 306 p. 19 cm. "Sermons, most of which were preached in the chapel of Stanford university --Dedication. 6-46334
I. Title.

HOGAN, Thaddeus.
Sermons, doctrinal and moral, by Rt. Rev. Thaddeus Hogan, R.M. New York, P. J. Kenedy & sons [c1915] 320 p. front. (port.) 23 cm. 16-563 1.50
I. Title.

HOLLAND, Henry Scott, 1847-1918. 283.
Facts of the faith; being a collection of sermons not hitherto published in book form, by Henry Scott Holland ... Edited with a preface by Christopher Cheshire ... London, New York [etc.] Longmans, Green and co., 1919. xv, [1], 294 p., 1 l. 20 cm. "Nearly all the sermons in this volume were preached in S. Paul's cathedral, and were subsequently reported in the 'Church times' and the 'Christian world pulpit.'" [BX5133.H6F3] 20-5986
I. Cheshire, Christopher, ed. II. Title.

HOLLAND, Henry Scott, 1847-1918. 283.
Facts of the faith; being a collection of sermons not hitherto published in book form, by Henry Scott Holland ... Edited with a preface by Christopher Cheshire ... London, New York [etc.] Longmans, Green and co., 1919. xv, [1], 294 p., 1 l. 20 cm. "Nearly all the sermons in this volume were preached in S. Paul's cathedral, and were subsequently reported in the 'Church times' and the 'Christian world pulpit.'" [BX5133.H6F3] 20-5986
I. Cheshire, Christopher, ed. II. Title.

HOLT, Basil. 252.
Visions from the Vaal; sermons and addresses, by Basis Holt... Cincinnati, O., The Standard publishing company [c1929] 204 p. 20 cm. "Delivered from the platform of the Central church of Christ, Johannesburg."--Arthor's pref. [BX7327.H6V5] 29-16972
I. Title.

HORN, Edward Traill, 1850-
Summer sermons, by Edward T. Horn. Reading, Pa., Pilger publishing house, 1908. 199 p. 20 cm. 8-16956
I. Title.

HOUGH, Lynn Harold, 1877- 287
The imperial voice, and other sermons and addresses, by Lynn Harold Hough... New York, The Macmillan company, 1924. ix p. 1 l., 146 p. 19 1/2 cm. [BX8333.H615] 24-8799
I. Title.

HOUGH, Lynn Harold, 1877- 287
The imperial voice, and other sermons and addresses, by Lynn Harold Hough... New York, The Macmillan company, 1924. ix p. 1 l., 146 p. 19 1/2 cm. [BX8333.H615] 24-8799
I. Title.

HOUGH, Lynn Harold, 1877- 287
Imperishable dreams, by Lynn Harold Hough. New York, Cincinnati [etc.] The Abingdon press [c1929] 254 p. 19 1/2 cm. A collection of sermons. [BX8333.H6I52] 29-11898
I. Title.

HOUGH, Lynn Harold, 1877- 287
Imperishable dreams, by Lynn Harold Hough. New York, Cincinnati [etc.] The Abingdon press [c1929] 254 p. 19 1/2 cm. A collection of sermons. [BX8333.H6I52] 29-11898
I. Title.

*HOVEY, Bryon P. 252.6
Holy day sermons. New York, Exposition [c.1964] 106p. 21cm. 3.00
I. Title.

*HOVEY, Bryon P. 252.6
Holy day sermons. New York, Exposition [c.1964] 106p. 21cm. 3.00
I. Title.

HOWARD, Henry, 1859- 287
The peril of power and other sermons, by the Rev. Henry Howard ... New York, George H. Doran company [c1925] v. p., 1 l., 9-258 p. 19 1/2 cm. $2.00. [BX8333.H7P4] 25-7294
I. Title.

HUMPHREY, Jerry Miles, 1872- 242
Impressive talks, by J. M. Humphrey ... Lima, O., True gospel grain publishing company, 1918. 223 p. 20 cm. $1.50 [BV4832.H85] 18-11167
I. Title.

HUMPHREY, Jerry Miles, 1872- 174.
Railroad sermons from railroad stories, by J. M. Humphrey ... Chicago, Ill., Messenger publishing company, 1917. 84 p. 18 cm. $0.25 [BV4596.R3H8] 18-20643
I. Title.

HUMPHREY, Jerry Miles, 1872-
Sermons that never die, by J. M. Humphrey ... Chicago, Christian witness co. [c1913] 174 p. 19 1/2 cm. $0.75 13-2469
I. Title.

HUMPHREY, Jerry Miles, 1872- 243
X-ray sermons, by J. M. Humphrey... Omaha, Neb., "Anywhere" evangelistic workers' publishing house [c1924] 247 p. 19 1/2 cm. [BV3797.H8] 24-8383
I. Title.

HURLBUT, Jesse Lyman, 1843-1930, ed. 252
Sunday half hours with great preachers. The greatest sermons by the greatest preachers of the Christian faith in all ages. A sermon for every Sunday in the year, edited by Rev. Jesse Lyman Hurlbut ... [n. p., pref. 1907] xvi, 17-681 p. incl. front. ports. 24 cm. [BV4241.H8 1907a] 38-7107
1. Sermons. 2. Clergy. I. Title.

HUTCHINSON, Aaron, 1722-1800. 252.
A reply to the Remarks of the Rev. Mr. John Tucker, pastor of the First church in Newbury, on a sermon preached at Newbury-Port, April 23. 1767 intitled Valour for the truth. By Aaron Hutchinson ... Boston, New-England: Printed and Sold by Thomas & John Fleet, in Cornhill; Sold also by Bulkeley Emerson in Newbury-Port, and Abijah Bond, in Concord, 1768. 54, [1] p. 20 cm. [BX7233.H82V3] 24-21546
I. Tucker, John, 1719-1792. Remarks on a sermon of the Rev. Aaron Hutchinson ... entitled: Valour for the truth. 1767. II. Title.

HUXLEY, Thomas Henry, 1825-1895.
Lectures & lay sermons, by Thomas Huxley. London, J. M. Dent & sons, ltd.; New York, E. P. Dutton & co. [1910] xvii, 294 p. illus. 18 cm. (Half-title: Everyman's library, ed., by Ernest Rhys. Sicence) Title within ornamental border. Introduction by Sir Oliver Lodge. Bibliography: p. xvi. A 11
I. Title.

INGERSOLL, Robert Green, 1833-1899.
A thanksgiving sermon, by Robert G. Ingersoll. Also a Tribute to Henry Ward Beecher ... New York, C. P. Farrell, 1897. 1 p. l., 78 p. 21 cm. 12-34561
I. Title.

IVINS, William Mills, 1851-1915.
The soul of the people; a New year's sermon, by William M. Ivins. New York, The Century co., 1906. 1 p. l., 68, [1] p. 19 cm. Title within ornamental border. [BV4282.I 8] 6-13698
I. Title.

JEFFERSON, Charles Edward, 1860- 252.
Forefathers' day sermons, by Rev. Charles E. Jefferson ... Boston, Chicago, The Pilgrim press [c1917] 4 p. l., 290 p. 20 cm. [BX7233.J4F7] 17-24675
I. Title.

JEFFERSON, Charles Edward, 1860-1937. 252.
Nature sermons, by Charles E. Jefferson ... New York, Chicago [etc.] Fleming Revell company [c1925] 175 p. 20 cm. [BX7233.J4N3] 25-9817
I. Title.

JELLET, Henry, 1821-1901.
Sermons on special and festival occasions, by Henry Jellett ... with an introduction by J. H. Bernard ... With portrait. London, New York, Bombay and Calcutta, Longmans, Green, and co., 1907. xix, 198 p. front. (port.) 20 cm. 8-15138
I. Bernard, John Henry, 1860- II. Title.

JETT, Curtis, 1875- 922
From prison to pulpit. Life of Curtis Jett. Louisville, Ky., Pentecostal publishing co. [c1919] 79 p. front. (port.) 19 cm. [BV4935.J4A4] 19-2788
I. Title.

JEZREEL, James Jershom, 1840-1885.
Extracts from the flying roll. Being a series of sermons compiled for the Gentile churches of all sects and denominations, and addressed to the lost tribes of the house of Israel. By James J. Jezreel. Vol. i. Jerusalem, 1st of 1st month, 1881. [New York, C. F. Bloom, printer, c1881] 2 p. l., vi, xxix, [1], 206, 267, 249 p. 22 cm. Three sermons, each originally issued in 7 parts, 1879-1881. No more published? [Original name: James White] ca 18
I. Title.

JOHNSON, Samuel, 1822-1882.
Lectures, essays, and sermons, by Samuel Johnson ... With a memoir by Samuel Longfellow ... Boston, New York, Houghton, Mifflin and company, 1883. 2 p. l., 466 p. front. (port.) 21 cm. "List of Mr. Johnson's printed works": p. 465-466. Contents.--Memoir.--Lectures, essays, and sermons: Florence. The Alps of the ideal and the Switzerland of the Swiss. Symbolism of the sea. Fulfillment of functions. Equal opportunity for woman. Labor parties and labor reform. The law of the blessed life. Gain in loss. The search of God. Fate. Living by faith. "The duty of delight." Transcendentalism.--Appendix. A 40
I. Longfellow, Samuel, 1819-1892. II. Title.

JOHNSON, William Bishop, 1858-
The scourging of a race, and other sermons and addresses, by W. Bishop Johnson ... Washington, Beresford, printer, 1904. viii, 228 p. front. (port.) 20 cm. 4-26231
I. Title.

JONES, Arthur Gray, 1868-1929. 243
Temple builders, and other sermons, by Arthur Gray Jones ... New York, Chicago [etc.] Fleming H. Revell company [c1929] 192 p. 20 cm. [BX9178.J57T4] 29-18757
I. Title.

*JONES,J.D. 252
The gospel of grace / by J.D.Jones Grand Rapids : Baker Book house, 1976. vii, 282, [1]p. ; 20 cm. (Minister's paperback library) [BV 253] ISBN 0-8010-5067-7 pbk. : 3.95
1. Sermons. I. Title.

JONES, J Sparhawk, 1841-
The invisible things, and other sermons, by J. Sparhawk Jones ... New York [etc.] Longmans, Green, and co., 1907. 3 p. l., 232 p. 20 cm. 7-9535
I. Title.

JONES, J Sparhawk, 1841-
Saved by hope, by J. Sparhawk Jones ... Philadelphia, The Westminster press, 1911. 206 p. 20 cm. Contents.A letter of counsel.--God's hope.--Our brother.--Micah and his Levite.--The power of conscience.--Peter's question.--The thunders of Horeb.--The way.--The pool of Bethesda.--The inspiration of the Almighty.--Religion--a prophet.--The sight of the soul.--From man to God.--A New Year sermon.--Life immortal. 11-12247 1.00
I. Title.

JORDAN, Gerald Ray, 1896- 252.076
What is yours! and other sermons, by G. Ray Jordan ... introduction by Bishop Edwin D. Mouzon ... New York, Chicago [etc.] Fleming H. Revell company [c1930] 156 p. 20 cm. [BX8333.J65W5] 30-9420
I. Title.

KANAMORI, Paul M. 243
The three hour sermon on God, sin and salvation, by Paul Kanamori ... with foreword by Robert E. Speer. New York, Chicago [etc.] Fleming H. Revell company [c1920] 140 p. 20 cm. [BV3797.K3] 20-12828
I. Title.

KELLEMS, Jesse R.
Glorying in the cross, and other sermons, by Jesse R. Kellems ... with introduction by George L. Lobdell ... St. Louis, Mo., Christian board of publication [c1914] 141 p. front. (port.) 20 cm. 15-20656 1.00
I. Title.

KELLY, Thomas L.
Some plain sermons, by Rev. Thomas L. Kelly ... St. Louis, Mo. [etc.] B. Herder, 1911. 4 p. l., 319 p. 20 cm. 11-14111 1.25
I. Title.

KERR, Hugh Thomson, 1871- 243
The highway of life, and other sermons, by Hugh T. Kerr... New York, Chicago [etc.] Fleming H. Revell company [c1917] 186 p. 19 1/2 cm. [BX9178.K4H5] 18-27
I. Title.

KINGMAN, Henry, 1863-1921.
A way of honor, and other college sermons, by Henry Kingman, D.D. New York, Chicago [etc.] Fleming H. Revell company [c1911] 4 p. l., 11-210 p. 21 cm. $1.00 "The following addresses were ... delivered in the Congregational church of Claremont, California." 12-277
I. Title.

KINGSLEY, Charles, 1819-1875.
The eternal goodness, and other sermons, by Charles Kingsley. New York, Boston, T. Y. Crowell & company [1895?] 152 p. front. (port.) 17 1/2 cm. 6-24773
I. Title.
Contents omitted.

KINGSLEY, Charles, 1819-1875.
The eternal goodness, and other sermons, by Charles Kingsley. New York, Boston, T. Y. Crowell & company [1895?] 152 p. front. (port.) 17 1/2 cm. 6-24773
I. Title.
Contents omitted.

KINGSLEY, Charles, 1819-1875. 252
The good news of God; sermons, by Charles Kingsley. London, Macmillan and co., limited; New York, The Macmillan company, 1898. 3 p. l., 324 p. 19 1/2 cm. First edition, 1859. [BX5133.K5G6] 4-10415
I. Title.

KINGSLEY, Charles, 1819-1875. 252
The good news of God; sermons, by Charles Kingsley. London, Macmillan and co., limited; New York, The Macmillan company, 1898. 3 p. l., 324 p. 19 1/2 cm. First edition, 1859. [BX5133.K5G6] 4-10415
I. Title.

KINGSLEY, Charles, 1819-1875. 283.
Sermons on national subjects. By Charles Kingsley. London and New York, Macmillan and co., 1890. vii, 494 p. 19 1/2 cm. First published, 1852-54. [BX5133.K5S45] 4-22457
I. Title.

KINGSLEY, Charles, 1819-1875. 283.
Village sermons and Town and country sermons, by Charles Kingsley. [New ed.] London and New York, Macmillan and co., 1890. ix p., 1 l., 452 p. 19 1/2 cm. "The two volumes of sermons contained in this book were originally published separately." [BX5133.K5V5] 4-22455
I. Title. II. Title: Town and country sermons.

KINGSLEY, Charles, 1819-1875.
Westminster sermons, with a preface, by Charles Kingsley. London and New York, Macmillan and co., 1890. 1 p. l., xxx, 312 p. 19 1/2 cm. First published, 1874. 4-19341
I. Title.

KLEISER, Grenville, 1868- comp. 252
The world's great sermons, comp. by Grenville Kleiser ... with assistance from many of the foremost living preachers and other theologians; introduction by Lewis O. Brastow ... New York and London, Funk & Wagnalls company [c1908] 10 v. 16 cm. [BV4241.K6] 8-33883
1. Sermons. I. Title.

KNUDSEN, Carl. 252.058
Renewed by the spirit; sermons on spiritual discoveries, by Carl Knudsen ... New York, Chicago [etc.] Fleming H. Revell company [c1930] 2 p. l., 7-178 p. 20 cm. [BX7233.K8R4] 30-32306
I. Title.

KOLATCH, Alfred J., 1916-
Sermons and sermon snacks. New York, J. David [c1963] 213 p. 23 cm. 67-47397
I. Title.

KUEGELE, Frederick.
Country sermons on free texts. v. i. 2d ed., rev. and enl. By Rev. F. Kuegele ... Crimora, Va., Augusta publishing company, 1902. v. 21 cm. 2-23422
I. Title.

LAW, Marion. 252.
Visions, and other sermons, by the Rev. Marion Law ... Milwaukee, Wis., Morehouse publishing co. [c1924] xii, 218 p., 1 l. front. 19 cm. [BX5937.L2V5] 24-5748
I. Title.

LAW, Samuel Warren. 252.
Sermons. By Samuel Warren Law ... New York, J. A. Gray, printer, 1857. 234 p. 19 cm. [BX8333.L3S4] 18-13720
I. Title.

LEE, Chauncey, 1763-1842.
Sermons on the distinguishing doctrines and duties of experimental religion, and especially designed for revivals. By Chauncey Lee ... Middletown (Conn.) Printed by E. & H. Clark, 1824. xii, [13]-479 p. 17 1/2 cm. 15-20498
I. Title.

LEE, John Francis, 1870- 251
Building the sermon, by J. Francis Lee ... Atlanta, Ga., A. B. Caldwell publishing co., 1921. 94 p. 18 1/2 cm. [BV4211.L4] 22-3564
I. Title.

LEE, Umphrey. 287
Jesus, the pioneer, and other sermons, by Umphrey Lee, with an introduction by President Charles C. Seleeman. Nashville, Tenn., Cokesbury press, 1925. vii, 115 p. 19 1/2 cm. [BX8333.L4J4] 25-23434
I. Title.

LIDDON, Henry Parry, 1829-1890. 221
Sermons on Old Testament subjects, by H. P. Liddon ... 4th impression. London, New York and Bombay, Longmans, Green, and co., 1898 xii, 379 p. 20 cm. [BS1171.L5 1898] 2-21451
I. Title.

LITTELL, Franklin Hamlin, ed. 252
Sermons to intellectuals from three continents [by] William Sloane Coffin, Jr. [others] New York, Macmillan [1963] 160p. 22cm. 63-10003 3.95
1. Sermons. I. Title.

LITTLEFAIR, Duncan Elliot, 1912-
The nature of God; sermon series. Grand Rapids, Mich., Fountain Street Baptist Church, 1964. 1 v. (various pagings) 20 cm. Eight sermons, each with its own pagination. 65-27114
I. Title.

LITTLEFAIR, Duncan Elliot, 1912-
The nature of God; sermon series. Grand Rapids, Mich., Fountain Street Baptist Church, 1964. 1 v. (various pagings) 20 cm. Eight sermons, each with its own pagination. 65-27114
I. Title.

*LOCKYER, Herbert. 1886- 251.01
Triple truths of Scripture; unique expositions of Scriptural Trilogies. Grand Rapids, Mich., Baker Book House [1973] 3 v., 21 cm. (The Lockyer Bible preacher's library). [BV4379] ISBN 0-8010-5529-6 1.95 ea. (pbk.)
1. Sermons. I. Title.

*LOCKYER, Herbert. 1886- 251.01
Twin truths of Scripture: a unique study of the pairing of Biblical themes. Grand Rapids, Mich, Baker Book House [1973] 2 v., 21 cm. (The Lockyer Bible preacher's library) [BV4379] ISBN 0-8010-5529-6 1.95 ea. (pbk.)
1. Sermons. I. Title.

LOGAN, John, 1748-1788. 243
Sermons and expository lectures. By the late Rev. John Logan ... with an introduction, by Rev. D. D. Whedon, D. D., ed. by "The Minister's library association." 6th ed. New York, D. Appleton and company, 1855. 188 p. 24 cm. [BX9178.L7S4] 18-4912
I. Whedon, Daniel Denison, 1808-1885. II. Minister's library association, ed. III. Title.

LONG, Simon Peter, 1860- 252.
The crime against Christ and a sermon to the Sunday evening club of Chicago; six sermons delivered in the Chicago loop in Holy week and Easter Sunday evening in 1921, by the Rev. Simon Peter Long ... Neil Saterlee, reporter. Burlington, Ia., The Lutheran literary board, 1923. 85 p. 20 cm. [BX8066.L6C7] 23-6910
I. Saterlee, Neil. II. Title.

LONG, Simon Peter, 1860-
The eternal epistle; sermons on the epistles for the church year, by Rev. S. P. Long ... Miss Florence May Welty, reporter ... Columbus, O., The F. J. Heer printing co., 1908. 893 p. front. (port.) 24 cm. 9-848
I. Welty, Florence May. II. Title.

LONG, Simon Peter, 1860-
The eternal epistle; sermons on the epistles for the church year, by Rev. S. P. Long ... Miss Florence May Welty, reporter ... Columbus, O., The F. J. Heer printing co., 1908. 893 p. front. (port.) 24 cm. 9-848
I. Welty, Florence May. II. Title.

LOWE, Arnold Hilmar. 243
Adventuring with Christ; sermons from a metropolitan pulpit, by Arnold Hilmar Lowe ... New York, Chicago [etc.] Fleming H. Revell company [c1929] 181 p. 20 cm. [BX9178.L73A2] 29-29229
I. Title.

LUCAS, Abner H 1862-
The call of to-day; sermons preached in the First Methodist Episcopal church, Montclair, N. J., by Abner H. Lucas ... Cincinnati, Jennings and Graham; New York, Eaton and Main [c1905] 152 p. front. (port.) 19 cm. (Half-title: The Methodist pulpit [2d series]) 5-33899
I. Title.

MACARTHUR, Robert Stuart, 1841-
The Christic reign, and other sermons, by Robert Stuart MacArthur ... Philadelphia, New York [etc.] American Baptist publication society [1908] 273 p. 21 cm. 8-18559
I. Title.

MACARTHUR, Robert Stuart, 1841-1923. 252.
The question of the centuries. Some sermons on personal relationship of the disciple to the kingdom of heaven. By Robert Stuart MacArthur ... Cleveland, O., F. M. Barton, c1905. 94 p. incl. front. (port.) 19 1/2 cm. [BX6333.M33Q4] 6-4
I. Title.

MACARTHUR, Robert Stuart, 1841-1923. 252.
The question of the centuries. Some sermons on personal relationship of the disciple to the kingdom of heaven. By Robert Stuart MacArthur ... Cleveland, O., F. M. Barton, c1905. 94 p. incl. front. (port.) 19 1/2 cm. [BX6333.M33Q4] 6-4
I. Title.

MACARTNEY, Clarence Edward Noble, 1879- comp. 252
Great sermons of the world, compiled and edited by Rev. Clarence Edward Macartney, D.D. Boston, Mass., The Stratford company, 1926. 4 p. l., 3-586 p. 21 1/2 cm. [BV4241.M2] 26-17845
1. Sermons. I. Title.

MCCONNELL, Francis J., 1871-
Christian focus; a series of college sermons, by Francis J. McConnell... Cincinnati, Jennings & Graham; New York, Eaton & Mains [c1911] 229 p. 19 1/2 cm. $1.00 "These sermons were delivered in Appleton chapel. Harvard university, during a two years' service as a member of the Board of preachers of the university. 11-21879
I. Title.

MCDANIEL, George White, 1875- 252.
Seeing the best; sermons and addresses, by George W. McDaniel ... New York, George H. Doran company [c1923] 167 p. 19 1/2 cm. [BX6333.M35S4] 23-7121
I. Title.
Contents omitted.

MCDONOUGH, Michael Vincent, 1863-
One year with God; sixty sermons and meditations for pulpit and pious reading, by Rev. Michael V. McDonough... Boston,

Mass., Angel guardian press, 1915. 4 p. l., 256 p. 24 cm. $1.00 15-19854
I. Title.

MACEWEN, William, 1734-1762. 270
Select essays, doctrinal & practical, on a variety of the most important and interesting subjects in divinity. Together with a sermon, on the great matter and end of gospel preaching. By the Rev. William M'Ewen... 1st American from the 6th London ed. Salem, N.Y., Pub. by J. Stevenson, jr., at the Salem book-store, J. P. Reynolds, printer, 1814. 274 p. 17 cm. 11-2599
I. Title.

MACGOWAN, Robert.
What is religion, and other sermons, by Robert MacGowan ... Lancaster, Pa., Wickersham press, 1916. 63 p., 1 l. 21 cm. 16-10458 0.50
I. Title.

MCKEEHAN, Hobart D. ed. 252
Great modern sermons, edited by Hobart D. McKeehan... New York, Chicago [etc.] Fleming H. Revell company [c1923] 212 p. 19 1/2 cm. [BV4241.M3] 23-10804
1. Sermons. I. Title.

MCKEEHAN, Hobart Deitrich. 252.
The patrimony of life, and other sermons by Hobart D. McKeehan... introduction by Joseph Fort Newton... New York, Chicago [etc.] Fleming H. Revell company [c1925] 137 p. 19 1/2 cm. [BX9577.M3P3] 25-20608
I. Title.

MCPHEETERS, Julian C. 287
Sons of God, by Julian C. McPheeters... Upland, Ind., Taylor university press [c1929] 211 p. 19 1/2 cm. "A series of sermons delivered ... at the University Methodist Episcopal church, South, Tucson, Arizona, during the year 1928."--Foreword. [BX8333.M32586] 30-954
I. Title.

MCREYNOLDS, Albert B. 252.066
Soul-winning and stewardship sermons, by A. B. McReynolds... 2d ed., enl. and rev. St. Louis, Mo., Christian board of publication, 1931. 259 p. front. (port.) 19 1/2 cm. [BX7327.M3M3 1931] 31-7531
I. Title. II. Title: Stewardship sermons.

MALONE, Thomas H.
The ideal persistent, [by] Rev. T. H. Malone, addresses delivered during 1915-1916. Denver, Col. [Press of the Smith-Brooks company, c1916] 149 p. 21 cm. 16-10890
I. Title.
Contents omitted.

MALONE, Thomas H.
The ideal persistent, [by] Rev. T. H. Malone, addresses delivered during 1915-1916. Denver, Col. [Press of the Smith-Brooks company, c1916] 149 p. 21 cm. 16-10890
I. Title.
Contents omitted.

MANTLE, John Gregory, 1852- 287
The counterfeit Christ, and other sermons, by J. Gregory Mantle ... New York, Chicago [etc.] Fleming H. Revell company [c1920] 203 p. front. (port.) 19 1/2 cm. [BX8333.M35C6] 21-3504
I. Title.

MARJORIBANKS, Thomas.
... The sevenfold I am, by the Rev. Thomas Marjoribanks ... New York, C. Scribner's sons, 1913. vii, [1], 146 p., 1 l., 19 cm. (The short course series; ed. by Rev. John Adams ...) A 13
1. Jesus Christ—Words. 2. Sermons. I. Title.

MASHECK, Charles L. 248
You and others ed. by Philip R. Hoh. Illus. by Noel G. Miles, Jr. Philadelphia, Lutheran Church Pr. 1966. 103 p. (LCA sunday sch. ser) pap. 1.00 teacher's ed. pap. 1.25
I. Title.

MATHER, Increase, 1639-1723.
Soul-saving gospel truths; delivered in several sermons, wherein is shewed; I. The unreasonableness of those excuses which men make for their delaying to come to the Lord Jesus Chri[st] for salvation. II. That for men to despair of th[e] forgiveness of their sins because the[y] have been great, is a great evil. III. That every man in thw world [is] going into eternity. By Increase Mather... Philadelphia; Printed by B. Franklin, 1743 [1744] 167 p. 13 1/2 x 7 1/2 cm. At end: Boston, printed 1701. Philadelphia, reprinted, 1744. T.-p. mutilated; p. 35-38 wanting. 6-1771
I. Title.

MAURICE, Frederick Denison, 283.
1805-1872.
Sermons preached in country churches, by Frederick Denison Maurice. London, Macmillan and co., limited; New York, The Macmillan company, 1903. viii, 362 p. 19 1/2 cm. "First edition, 1873; second edition, 1880; reprinted, 1903." [BX5133.M3S4] 3-22954
I. Title.

MAURICE, Frederick Denison, 283.
1805-1872.
The spirit of love and other sermons, by Frederick Denison Maurice. New York, Boston, T. Y. Crowell & company [c1895] 149 p. front. (port.) 17 cm. [BX5133.M3S6] 30-1760
I. Title.

MELTZER, Bernard. 811'.54
Bernard Meltzer's Guidance for living / Bernard Meltzer. New York : Dial Press, c1982. p. cm. [PS3563.E4495G8] 19 82-5158 ISBN 0-385-27657-5 : 12.95
I. [Guidance for living] II. Title.

MITCHELL, Charles Bayard, 1857-
The noblest quest, and other sermons preached in the First Methodist Episcopal church, Cleveland, O., by Charles Bayard Mitchell... Cincinnati, Jennings and Graham; New York, Eaton and Mains [c1905] 163 p. front. (port.) 19 cm. (Half-title: The Methodist pulpit. [Second series]) 5-25628
I. Title.

MITCHELL, David C. 243
The nonsense of neutrality, and other sermons from a city pulpit, by D. C. Mitchell... Glasgow, New York [etc.] Thomson & Cowan, 1925. 189 p. 19 cm. [BX9178.M59N6] 25-19919
I. Title.

MITCHELL, David C. 243
The nonsense of neutrality, and other sermons from a city pulpit, by D. C. Mitchell... Glasgow, New York [etc.] Thomson & Cowan, 1925. 189 p. 19 cm. [BX9178.M59N6] 25-19919
I. Title.

MOFFETT, Robert.
Seeking the old paths, and other sermons; with an introduction by E. V. Zollars, and a biographical sketch by J. R. Gaff. Cleveland, O., The author [1899] xii, 303 p. port. 12°. 0-14
I. Title.

MOODY, Dwight Lyman, 1837- 252'.63
1899.
Calvary's cross, by Dwight L. Moody ... and others. Grand Rapids, Baker Book House [1966] 97 p. 20 cm. (Minister's handbook series) [BV4241.C3] 67-2873
1. Sermons. I. Title.

MOODY, Dwight Lyman, 1837-1899.
"Thou fool!" and eleven other sermons never before published, by the late Dwight L. Moody ... New York, The Christian herald [c1911] vi, 215 p. 18 cm. 11-22089 0.50
I. Title.

MOODY, Dwight Lyman, 1837-1899.
"What is Christ to me?" and other sermons ... New York, Street & Smith [1900] 214 p. 12 degree (Alliance library. no. 9) 0-1845
I. Title.

MOODY, Dwight Lyman, 1837-1899.
"What is Christ to me?" and other sermons ... New York, Street & Smith [1900] 214 p. 12 degree (Alliance library. no. 9) 0-1845
I. Title.

MOODY, Samuel, 1676-1747.
The debtors monitor, directory & comforter: or, The way to get & keep out of debt. In three sermons. By Samuel Moodey M. A., pastor of the church at York, N. E. Boston: Printed by B. Green, for Samuel Gerrish at his shop at the north side of the Town-house, 1715. 1 p. l., ii, 99 p. 13 cm. 4-20300
I. Title.

MORGAN, William Sacheus, 1865-
Nuggets of gold, by William S. Morgan. Albany, N.Y., Press of the Marshman-Beebe co., 1909. 2 p. l., 3-56 p. 17 1/2 cm. "This course of sermons was delivered at the First Unitarian church, Albany, N.Y., during the season of 1908-9." 10-9736
I. Title.

MORGAN, William Sacheus, 1865-
Nuggets of gold, by William S. Morgan. Albany, N.Y., Press of the Marshman-Beebe co., 1909. 2 p. l., 3-56 p. 17 1/2 cm. "This course of sermons was delivered at the First Unitarian church, Albany, N.Y., during the season of 1908-9." 10-9736
I. Title.

MORRILL, G[ulian] L[ansing]
1857-
The moralist [by] G. L. Morrill. Minneapolis, Harrison & Smith co., 1904. 64 p. 19 1/2 cm. "'The moralist' is a collection of 'people's pulpit' sermons. One appears every week in the Minneapolis journal." 5-2935
I. Title.

MORRIS, E. C., 1855-
Sermons, addresses and reminiscences and important correspondence, with a picture gallery of eminent ministers and scholars. By E. C. Morris, D.D. Introduction by R. H. Boyd, D.D. Nashville, Tenn., National Baptist publishing board, 1901. 1 p. l., 7-322 p. front., illus. (ports.) 23 cm. Cover-title: Reflections from the public services of E. C. Morris, D.D. 5-17084
I. Title.

MORRISON, George Herbert.
The weaving of glory; Sunday evening addresses from a city pulpit by the Rev. G. H. Morrison ... London, New York [etc.] Hodder and Stoughton [n.d.] xii, 355 p. 19 1/2 cm. Printed in Great Britain by T. and A. Constable ... at the University press, Edinburgh. A 21
I. Title.

MORRISON, Henry Clay, 1857- 287
The Christ of the Gospels, by Henry Clay Morrison ... New York, Chicago [etc.] Fleming H. Revell company [c1926] 103 p. 19 1/2 cm. [BX8333.M6C5] 27-5047
I. Title.

MORRISON, Henry Clay, 1857- 287
Sermons for the times, by Rev. H. C. Morrison, D.D. Louisville, Ky., Pentecostal publishing company [c1921] 133 p. 19 1/2 cm. [BX8333.M6S4] 21-13509
I. Title.

MOZLEY, James Bowling, 1813- 283.
1878.
Sermons, parochial and occasional, by J. B. Mozley ... New ed. London and New York, Longmans, Green, and co., 1895. xi, 355 p. 20 cm. [BX5133.M8S35 1895] 15-22828
I. Title.

MOZLEY, James Bowling, 1813- 283.
1878.
Sermons preached before the University of Oxford and on various occasions, by J. B. Mozley ... 2d ed. New York, E. P. Dutton and company, 1876. xiii, 304 p. 19 cm. [BX5133.M8S4] 17-24393
1. Sermons. I. Title.

MOZLEY, James Bowling, 1813- 283.
1878.
Sermons preached before the University of Oxford and on various occasions, by J. B. Mozley ... 10th impression. London, New York [etc.] Longmans, Green, and co., 1906. xiii, 304 p. 20 cm. [BX5133.M8S4 1906] 15-16163
I. Title.

MULLINS, Edgar Young, 1860-
The life in Christ, by Edgar Young Mullins ... New York, Chicago [etc.] Fleming H. Revell company [c1917] 239 p. 20 cm. 17-11448 1.25
1. Sermons. I. Title.

MUNSEY, William Elbert, 1833- 287
1877.
Sermons and lectures. By William Elbert Munsey ... edited by John C. Keener ... Nashville, Tenn., Dallas, Tex. [etc.] Publishing house of the M. E. church, South, Smith & Lamar, agents, 1920-24. 2 v. 19 cm. (v. 2: 20 cm.) First published in 1878-86. Vol. 1, 15th thousand. Vol. 2 has imprint: Nashville, Tenn., Cokesbury press, 1924. [BX8333.M82S4 1920] 24-25656
I. Keener, John Christian, 1819-1906, ed. II. Title.

MUNSEY, William Elbert, 1833- 287
1877.
Sermons and lectures ... by William Elbert Munsey, D. D., edited by John C. Keener ... Nashville, Tenn., Cokesbury press, 1924. 2 v. 20 cm. First published in 1878-86. [BX8333.M82S4 1924] 24-29662
I. Keener, John Christian, 1819-1906, ed. II. Title.

MURRAY, W[illiam] L[emuel]
S[howell] 1848-
Sermons to young people in St. Paul's M. E. church, by W. L. S. Murray ... stenographically reported by Prof. J. E. Fuller ... [Wilmington, Del, Press of Charles H. Gray] 1903. 64 p. 18 cm. Portrait of author of t.-p. 3-31451
I. Title.

THE New Jersey preacher:
or, Sermons on plain & practical subjects. By some of the ministers of the Gospel, residing in the state of New Jersey. Vol. 1 ... Trenton, D. Fenton; New-Brunswick, Charles D. Green & co., L. Deare, printer, 1813. 464 p. 22 cm. Ed. by George S. Woodhull and Isaac V. Brown. No more published? 12-3136
I. Woodhull, George Spafford, 1773-1834, ed. II. Brown, Isaac Van Arsdale

NEWELL, James Reginald. 248
Short sermons for the Sundays of the year, by Rev. J. R. Newell ... New York, Joseph F. Wagner, inc.; [etc., etc., c1919] 3 p. l., 167 p. 21 1/2 cm. [BX1756.N4 1919] 20-3802
I. Title.

NEWTON, Joseph Fort, 1876-
An ambassador, City temple sermons, by Joseph Fort Newton ... New York, Chicago [etc.] Fleming H. Revell company [c1916] 2 p. l., 7-226 p. 19 1/2 cm. 17-293
I. Title.

NEWTON, Joseph Fort, 1876- 230.
The truth and the life and other sermons, by Joseph Fort Newton ... New York, George H. Doran company [c1926] viii p., 2 l., 13-340 p. 19 1/2 cm. [BX9943.N4T7] 26-10714
I. Title.

NICHOLS, Gideon Parsons, 1837-
The preciousness of God's thoughts; sermons and addresses, by G. Parsons Nichols, D.D.; with a memoir. New York, Chicago [etc.] F. H. Revell company [c1909] 233 p. front. (port.) 20 cm. $1.25 1909; A 25989; Fleming H. Revell. 9-32487
I. Title.

NOBLE, Franklin.
Sermons in illustration, by Franklin Noble, D. D. New York, E. B. Treat & company, 1907. 248 p. 21 cm. The greater part of these sermon sketches have been printed in the Treasury magazine. cf. Pref. 7-37986
I. Title.

O'HARA, John, 1905-
Stories of venial sin, from Pipe night. New York, Avon Book Co. [1947] 129 p. 20 cm. (Avon modern short story monthly, 39) Full name: John Henry O'Hara. 47-11730
I. Title.

O'NEILE, Charles E. 248
Convincing the world ... Sermons for the Sundays, by Charles E. O'Neile ... Part i Advent to Pentecost, part ii Pentecost to Advent. New York, N. Y., The Society for the propagation of the faith [c1927] 3 p. l., [ix]-xi p., 1 l., 527 p. 20 cm. [BX1756.O5 1927] 27-18638
I. Title. II. Title: Sermons for the Sundays.

O'NEILE, Charles E. 248
Giving testimony ... sermons for the

holydays and for other occasions, by Charles E. O'Neile ... New York, N. Y., The Society for the propagation of the faith [1927] vii, 544 p. 20 cm. [BX1756.O5G5] 27-23518
I. Title.

ORCHARD, William Edwin, 1877- 252.
The finality of Christ, and other sermons, by Rev. W. E. Orchard ... New York, George H. Doran company [c1922] 191 p. 20 cm. [BX7233.O7F5] 23-7130 1.35
I. Title.

ORCHARD, William Edwin, 1877- 252.
The finality of Christ, and other sermons, by Rev. W. E. Orchard ... New York, George H. Doran company [c1922] 191 p. 20 cm. [BX7233.O7F5] 23-7130 1.35
I. Title.

PALMER, Albert Wentworth, 1879- 252.
The new Christian epic; sermons in the modern spirit... by Albert W. Palmer... Boston, Chicago, The Pilgrim press [c1927] 195 p. 18 cm. [BX7233.P27N4] 28-3694
I. Title.

PARDINGTON, G P.
The still small voice; quiet hour talks, by Rev. G. P. Pardington, PH. D. New York, Alliance press company [1902] 244 p. 19 cm. 3-864
I. Title.

PARKER, Theodore, 1810-1860. 204
Lessons from the world of matter and the world of man, by Theodore Parker; edited with a preface, by Rufus Leighton. Boston, American Unitarian association [1908] 5 p. l., 419 p. 21 cm. [His Works. Centenary ed. v. 5] "The selections have been made from the sermons of ten years, extending from 1849 to 1859."--Editor's pref. [BX9815.P3 1907 vol. 5] A 12
I. Leighton, Rufus, jr., ed. II. Title.
Contents omitted.

PATTISON, Thomas Harwood, 1838-1904.
The south wind, and other sermons, by T. Harwood Pattison ... Philadelphia, American Baptist publication society, 1905. viii, [2], 11-288 p. front. (port.) 20 cm. 5-10068
I. Title.

PAULSON, Stephen M.
Short sermons for daily life, by Stephen M. Paulson. Williamsport, Pa., Grit publishing co., 1907. [51] p. port. 24 cm. 7-33566
I. Title.

PENDLETON, William Frederick, bp., 1845- 226.
The ten blessings; a series of twelve sermons, by Bishop W. F. Pendleton. Bryn Athyn, Pa., Academy book room, 1922. 159 p. 18 cm. [BT382.P4] 24-23323
I. Title.

PEPPERT, F.
Short sermons on the Gospels, by Rev. F. Peppert. New York, J. F. Wagner [c1914] iv, 225 p. 22 cm. 15-1485 1.00
I. Title.

PERIN, George Landor, 1854- 230.
The sunny side of life; sermons preached in the Everyday church, Boston, by Rev. George L. Perin, D. D. Boston, Every-day church publishing company [1900] 4 p. l., 386 p. front. (port.) 20 cm. [BX9943.P4S8] 1-29781
1. Sermons. I. Title.

PERKINS, George William, 1804-1856.
Sermons, by George W. Perkins. With a Memoir. New-York, A. D. F. Randolph, 1859. 44, 331 p. incl. front. (port.) 20 cm. 15-16176
I. Title.

PETERS, Madison Clinton, 1859-
Sermons that won the masses, by Madison C. Peters ... Philadelphia, New York [etc.] The Griffith & Rowland press [1908] 192 p. 19 cm. 8-30283
I. Title.

PETRY, Ray C., 1903- ed. 252
No uncertain sound; sermons that shaped the pulpit tradition. Phildelphia, Westminster Press [1948] xiii, 331 p. 24 cm. Bibliography: p. [309]-325. [BV4241.P4] 48-4009
1. Sermons. 2. Preaching—Hist. I. Title.

PFATTEICHER, Ernst Philip Henry, 1874- 232.
Sermons on the Gospels, Advent to Trinity, by Ernst P. Pfatteicher ... Philadelphia, General council publication house [c1918] x, 11-317 p. 21 cm. [BX8066.P5S4] 18-23697
I. Title.

PIERCE, Charles C[ampbell]
The hunger of the heart for faith, and other sermons delivered at the Cathedral open-air services, Washington, D.C. by the Rev. Charles C. Pierce ... with an introduction by the Bishop of Washington. Milwaukee, The Young churchman co., 1906. xii, 225 p. front. (port.) 20 cm. 6-6896
I. Title.

PIERCE, Charles C[ampbell]
The hunger of the heart for faith, and other sermons delivered at the Cathedral open-air services, Washington, D.C. by the Rev. Charles C. Pierce ... with an introduction by the Bishop of Washington. Milwaukee, The Young churchman co., 1906. xii, 225 p. front. (port.) 20 cm. 6-6896
I. Title.

POLING, Daniel Alfred, 1884- ed. 252.0082
A treasury of great sermons, selected by Daniel A. Poling, with biographical notes and comments. New York, Greenberg [1944] ix, 198 p. 21 cm. [BV4241.P53] 44-51172
1. Sermons. I. Title.

POLING, Daniel Alfred, 1884- 252.
What men need most, and other sermons, by Rev. Daniel A. Poling ... New York, George H. Doran company [c1923] x p., 1 l., 13-232 p. 20 cm. [BX9527.P6] 23-16410 1.60
I. Title.

POTTER, Henry Codman, bp., 1834-1908. 252.
Sermons of the city, by Henry C. Potter ... New York, E. P. Dutton & company, 1881. x, 338 p. 20 cm. [BX5937.P7S4] 12-37806
I. Title.

POTTS, James Henry, 1848-
The upward leading; pulpit talks under various auspices, by James Henry Potts. Cincinnati, Jennings and Graham; New York, Eaton and Mains [1905] 131 p. front. (port.) 19 cm. (Half-title: The Methodist pulpit [2d series]) 5-3719
I. Title.

PROVIDENCE preacher;
a series of sermons and other instructions, in monthly numbers ... [Ed.] by Thomas Williams. v. 1; March 1859-Feb. 1860. Providence, Pierce & Berry, printers, 1859-[60] 312 (i. e. 288) pp. 23 cm. Paging irregular: pp. 193-288 incorrectly numbered [217]-312. 1-27733

PURVES, George Tybout, 1852-1901. 252
Faith and life; sermons by George Tybout Purves ... with an introductory note by Benjamin B. Warfield ... Philadelphia, Presbyterian board of publication and Sabbath-school work, 1902. xxx, 377 p. 21 cm. [BX9178.P8F3] 2-14464
I. Title.

PURVES, George Tybout, 1852-1901. 252
Faith and life; sermons by George Tybout Purves ... with an introductory note by Benjamin B. Warfield ... Philadelphia, Presbyterian board of publication and Sabbath-school work, 1902. xxx, 377 p. 21 cm. [BX9178.P8F3] 2-14464
I. Title.

PURVIS, Samuel Warrington, 1867-
The God of the lucky, and other sermons [by] Rev. Samuel W. Purvis, D. D. ... As reprinted from the Evening bulletin, Philadelphia. Philadelphia, National publishing company, 1926. 384 p. front. (port.) 20 cm. A 26
I. Title.

RALEIGH, Albert Sidney.
Scientifica hermetica; an introduction to the science of alchemy; the text of the hermetic sermons on "An introduction to the gnosis of the nature of things" and the sacred sermons, together with the esoteric commentary, giving in full, the esoteric key to these two great sermons. The official interpretation of the Hermetic brotherhood of Atlantis, by Dr. A. S. Raleigh (Hach Mactzin El Dorado Can.) ... San Francisco, Calif., Hermetic publishing co.; Chicago, Sterling publishing co., 1916. 4 p. l., 3-113 p. 24 cm. 16-13340 10.00
I. Hermes Trismegistus. II. Title.

RALEIGH, Albert Sidney.
The shepherd of men; an official commentary on the sermon of Hermes Trismegistos, by Dr. A. S. Raleigh (Hach Mactzin El Dorado Can.) ... San Francisco, Calif., Hermetic publishing company; Chicago, Sterling publishing company, 1916. 3 p. l., [5]-145 p. 24 cm. 16-13339 2.00
I. Hermes Trismegistus. II. Title.
Contents omitted.

RALEIGH, Albert Sidney.
Woman and super-woman; a trumpet call to the woman of the present generation to come out of the shell and create the humanity of the future, and through the mothering of the new types, bring forth the coming race, by Dr. A. S. Raleigh (Hach Mactzin El Dorado Can.) ... San Francisco, Cal., Hermetic publishing company; Chicago, Sterling publishing company, 1916. 121 p. 24 cm. 16-13342 1.50
I. Title.

RANSOME, Harry.
A Lent with St. John; a thought for every day in Lent from the first epistle of St. John, by Harry Ransome ... Milwaukee, The Young churchman company, 1912. x, 152 p. 19 cm. 12-3383 0.30
I. Title.

REED, Lewis Thurston, 1870- 252.
When God was near; sermons preached in the Flatbush Congregational church, Brooklyn, N.Y., by Lewis Thurston Reed ... New York, Chicago [etc.] Fleming H. Revell company [c1917] 160 p. 19 1/2 cm. [BX7233.R4W5] 18-25
I. Title.

REESE, T. O. 243
The unpardonable sin, and other sermons, by Evangelist T. O. Reese ... Louisville, Ky., Pentecostal publishing company [c1926] 228 p. front. (port.) 19 1/2 cm. [BV3797.R4] 26-13438
I. Title.

RICE, Merton Stacher, 1872- 230
The expected church; twelve sermons by M. S. Rice ... New York, Cincinnati, The Abingdon press [c1923] 216 p. 19 1/2 cm. [BV600.R45] 23-11357
I. Title.

RITCHIE, Arthur.
Twetny-four sermons from St. Ignatus' pulpit, by the Rev. Arthur Ritchie ... Milwaukee, The Young churchman co., 1903. 298 p. 21 cm. 3-32165
I. Title.

ROBERTSON, Frederick William, 1816-1853.
Sermons ... by Frederick W. Robertson. London, J. M. Dent & co.; New York, E. P. Dutton & co. [1906-09] 3 v. 18 cm. (Half-title: Everyman's library, ed. by Ernest Rhys. Theology & philosophy) Title within ornamental border; illustrated end-papers. "First edition, February 1906; reprinted, May 1906; May 1907; December 1907; April 1909." "F. W. Robertson's sermons with a commendation by Canon Barnett newly arranged in three volumes." Contents.--v. 1. Sermons on religion & life.--v. 2. Sermons on Christian doctrine.--v. 3. Sermons on Bible subjects. Bibliography: v. 1, p. [12]; v. 2, p. 8; v. 3, p. 8. A 11
I. Title.

ROSS, John Elliot, 1884- 238.
Five minute sermons; short talks on life's problems, by Rev. J. Elliot Ross ... St. Louis, Mo., and London, B. Herder book co., 1925. 5 p. l., 314 p. 20 cm. [BX1756.R6 1925] 25-5347
I. Title.

ROSS, John Elliot, 1884- 238.
Five minute sermons; short talks on life's problems, by Rev. J. Elliot Ross ... St. Louis, Mo., and London, B. Herder book co., 1925. 5 p. l., 314 p. 20 cm. [BX1756.R6 1925] 25-5347
I. Title.

ROSS, John Elliot, 1884- 238.
Five minute sermons; short talks on life's problems. Second series. By Rev. J. Elliot Ross ... St. Louis, Mo. and London, B. Herder book co., 1928. 5 p. l., 3-313 p. 20 cm. [BX1756.R62] 29-590
I. Title.

ROSS, John Elliot, 1884- 238.
Five minute sermons; short talks on life's problems. Second series. By Rev. J. Elliot Ross ... St. Louis, Mo. and London, B. Herder book co., 1928. 5 p. l., 3-313 p. 20 cm. [BX1756.R62] 29-590
I. Title.

ROYDEN, Agnes Maude, 1876- 252
The friendship of God, by A. Maude Royden ... New York & London, G. P. Putnam's sons, 1924. ix, 138 p. 20 cm. Sermons. [BR125.R76 1924 a] 24-6670 1.25
I. Title.

RUTLEDGE, George Perry, 1869-
Pushing the world along; a series of sermons, by George P. Rutledge. Cincinnati, The Standard publishing company [c1915] 172 p. 19 1/2 cm. 16-2869
I. Title.

RUTLEDGE, George Perry, 1869-
Pushing the world along; a series of sermons, by George P. Rutledge. Cincinnati, The Standard publishing company [c1915] 172 p. 19 1/2 cm. 16-2869
I. Title.

SADLER, William Alan, ed. 252.0082
Master sermons through the ages. New York, Harper [c.1963] 228p. 22cm. 63-7608 3.95
1. Sermons. I. Title.

SADLER, William Alan, ed. 252.0082
Master sermons through the ages. [1st ed.] New York, Harper & Row [1963] 228 p. 22 cm. [BV4241.S2] 63-7608
1. Sermons. I. Title.

SCHNEIDER, Jacob U comp.
Sermons for the home circle; sixty-five gospel messages by Evangelical pastors, compiled by Rev. Jacob U. Schneider, PH. D. St. Louis, Mo., Chicago, Ill., Eden publishing house [c1923] 432 p. 24 cm. [BX7927.S3S4] 23-16412
I. Title.

SCHUYLER, Hamilton.
The intellectual crisis confronting Christianity; four sermons preached in Trinity church, Trenton, N. J., on the Sundays in November, 1911, by the rector, the Rev. Hamilton Schuyler. New York, E. S. Gorham, 1911. 80 p. 20 cm. 12-1226
I. Title.

SCHUYLER, Hamilton.
The intellectual crisis confronting Christianity; four sermons preached in Trinity church, Trenton, N. J., on the Sundays in November, 1911, by the rector, the Rev. Hamilton Schuyler. New York, E. S. Gorham, 1911. 80 p. 20 cm. 12-1226
I. Title.

SCOTT, Robert, 1860- ed. 252
Modern sermons by world scholars, edited by Robert Scott and William C. Stiles ... introduction by Newell Dwight Hillis ... New York and London, Funk & Wagnalls company [c1909] 10 v. 16 cm. Contents.--i. Abbot to Bosworth--ii. Bowman to Coa.--iii. Crafer to Fitchett--iv. Foster to Hyde.--v. Hoyt to Loofs.--vi. Mackistosh to Moore.--vii. Moorshead to Porter.--viii. Radford to Selble.--ix. Shakan to Thomas--x. Thwing to Wemer. General index. [BV4241.S3] 9-32484
1. Sermons. I. Stiles, William Curtis, 1851-1911, joint ed. II. Title.

SEEHUUS, Knut, 1859- comp.
The old paths. Sermons on the second

gospel series according to the Church of Norway. By pastors and professors of the Norwegian Evangelical Lutheran church of America. Collected and ed. by Knut Seehuus... Decorah, Ia., Lutheran publishing house, 1914. 436 p. 1 l., [2] p. 23 1/2 cm. $1.50 "Published by order of the clerical conference of the Synod of the Norwegian Evangelical Lutheran church of America."--Foreword. 14-18758
I. Title.

SEISS, Joseph A[ugustus] 1823-
Recent sermons. By Joseph A. Seiss... Philadelphia, Board of publication of the General council, 1904. 325 p. front. (port.) 21 cm. 4-31289
I. Title.

SELL, Henry Thorne, 1854- 252
Five-minute sermons in objects, for young folks, by Henry T. Sell... New York, Chicago [etc.] Fleming H. Revell company [c1924] 152 p. 19 1/2 cm. [BV4315.S4 1924] 24-17963
I. Title. II. Title: Sermons in objects.

SELL, Henry Thorne, 1854- 252
Five-minute sermons in objects, for young folks, by Henry T. Sell... New York, Chicago [etc.] Fleming H. Revell company [c1924] 152 p. 19 1/2 cm. [BV4315.S4 1924] 24-17963
I. Title. II. Title: Sermons in objects.

SELL, Henry Thorne, 1854- 252
Five minute sermons in stories for young folks, by Henry T. Sell... New York, Chicago [etc.] Fleming H. Revell company [c1923] 159 p. 19 1/2 cm. [BV4315.S4] 23-6197
I. Title.

SELL, Henry Thorne, 1854- 252
Five minute sermons in stories for young folks, by Henry T. Sell... New York, Chicago [etc.] Fleming H. Revell company [c1923] 159 p. 19 1/2 cm. [BV4315.S4] 23-6197
I. Title.

SELWYN, George Augustus, 283.
bp. of Lichfield, 1809-1878
Sermons preached chiefly in the church of St. John the Baptist, New Windsor, by George Augustus, lord bishop of New Zealand; late curate of the parish. Eton, Printed for private circulation, by E. P. Williams, 1842. 4 p. l., [vii]-x p., 1 l., 235, [1] p. 17 cm. [BX5133.S4S4] 21-12051
I. Title.

A series of sermons on the distinctive principles of the great historic church movements, by the representative pastors of Grand Rapids, Michigan. [Grand Rapids, Mich., James Bayne company, 1900?] 140 p. ports. 19 1/1 cm. A 13
1. Sermons. I. Fulton, John Milton. II. Arthur, Frederick Prentiss, 1859- III. Bradley, Dan Freeman, 1857- IV. Bergmann, Rabbi. V. Lewis, Edward George. VI. McCormick, John Newton, bp., 1863- VII. Cooley, George Eliot. VIII. Randall, John Herman, 1872-
Contents omitted.

SERMONS in the making.
Dallas, American Guild Press [c1956] 180p. 20cm.
1. Sermons. I. Melton, William Walter, 1879-

**SERVANT of peace.* 248.8'3
New York, Harcourt [1967] (Roots of faith, bk. 3) JHS 2.40 pap.,

SHANNON, Frederick F., 1877.
The soul's atlas and other sermons, by Rev. Frederick F. Shannon ... New York, Chicago [etc.] Fleming H. Revell company [c1911] 3 p. l., 9-226 p. 19 1/2 cm. $1.00. 11-26769
I. Title.

SHANNON, Frederick Franklin, 252
1877-
The economic Eden, and other sermons, by Frederick F. Shannon ... New York, Chicago [etc.] Fleming H. Revell company [c1921] 192 p. 19 1/2 cm. [BV4253.S52] 21-21898
I. Title.

SHANNON, Frederick Franklin, 252.
1877-
God's faith in man, and other sermons, by Frederick F. Shannon ... New York, Chicago [etc.] Fleming H. Revell company [c1919] 186 p. 19 1/2 cm. [BX9527.S5G6] 19-18656
I. Title.

SHANNON, Frederick Franklin, 252
1877-
The infinite artist, and other sermons, by Frederick F. Shannon ... New York, The Macmillan company, 1921. 5 p. l., 129 p. 19 1/2 cm. [BV4253.S55] 21-17828
I. Title.

SHANNON, Frederick Franklin, 252
1877-
The infinite artist, and other sermons, by Frederick F. Shannon ... New York, The Macmillan company, 1921. 5 p. l., 129 p. 19 1/2 cm. [BV4253.S55] 21-17828
I. Title.

SHANNON, Frederick Franklin, 252
1877-
Sermons for days we observe, by Frederick F. Shannon ... New York, George H. Doran company [c1922] 192 p. 19 1/2 cm. $1.50. [BV4253.S58] 22-20067
I. Title.

SHERRICK, Marvin Manam, 1868-
Topical sermon notes, by Marvin M. Sherrick, A.M. [Elgin, Ill., Brethren publishing house, c1916] 93 p. 16 cm. $0.50 16-15068
I. Title.

SHIPMAN, Jacob S.
Sermons by the Rev. Jacob S. Shipman ... New York, E. P. Dutton & company, 1902. v, 177 p. front. (port.) 20 cm. 3-606
I. Title.

SIKES, Stutely David, 1880- 243
God used sermons, by Evangelist S. David Sikes ... Fort Wayne, Ind., The Glad tidings publishing company [c1928] 163 p. 1 mounted illus., port. 20 1/2 cm. [BV3797.S5] 28-11220
I. Title.

SIMEON, Charles, 1759-1836.
Expository outlines on the whole Bible. Grand Rapids, Zondervan Publishing House, 1956- v. Formerly published as "Horae homileticae" Contents.v.5.Psalm 1 through Psalm 72.
1. Sermons. 2. Bible — Commentaries I. Title.

SIMMONS, George Frederick, 252.
1814-1855.
Six sermons. By George F. Simmons. Boston and Cambridge, J. Monroe and company, 1856. 134 p. 18 1/2 cm. [BX9843.S55S5] 24-10090
I. Title.

SKELLY, Andrew M. 248
Sermons and addresses, by the Rev. A. M. Skelly, O.P. St. Louis, Mo. and London, B. Herder book co., 1929. viii, 361 p. 19 1/2 cm. [BX1756.S5] 29-7702
I. Title.

SLEDD, Robert Newton.
True heroism; and other sermons... Richmond, Va., The B. F. Johnson pub. co., 1899. 389 p. pl., port. 8° Sep
I. Title.

SLOSSON, Edwin Emery, 1865- 220
1929.
Sermons of a chemist, by Edwin E. Slosson... New York, Harcourt, Brace and company [c1925] vii, 319 p. 19 1/2 cm. [BR125.S544] 25-21786
I. Title.

SMITH, Herbert Booth. 243
The new earth, and other sermons, by Herbert Booth Smith... New York, Chicago [etc.] Fleming H. Revell company [c1920] 224 p. 19 cm. [BX9178.S55N4] 20-12141
I. Title.

SMITH, James Henry Oliver, 252
1857-
What think ye of Christ? and other sermons, by J. H. O. Smith. Pentecostal ed. Cincinnati, O., The Standard publishing company [c1927] 298 p. 19 1/2 cm. [BX7327.S6W5 1927] 27-18284
I. Title.

SMITH, Robert Elmer, 1868- 287
Midweek messages, by Robert Elmer Smith; introduction by William O. Shepard... New York, Cincinnati, The Abingdon press [c1925] 192 p. 17 1/2 cm. [BX8333.S573M5] 25-19058
I. Title.

SMITH, Robert Elmer, 1868- 287
Midweek messages, by Robert Elmer Smith; introduction by William O. Shepard... New York, Cincinnati, The Abingdon press [c1925] 192 p. 17 1/2 cm. [BX8333.S573M5] 25-19058
I. Title.

SMITH, Rodney, 1860- 243
Gipsy Smith's best sermons, as delivered in Brooklyn, and published in book form by arrangement with the Brooklyn daily eagle... Neu York, J. S. Ogilvie publishing company, c1907. 255 p. front. (port.) 19 1/2 cm. (On cover: Railroad edition, no. 46) [BV3797.S56] 7-16359
I. Title.

SMITH, Rodney, 1860- 243
Real religion; revival sermons delivered during his twentieth visit to America, by Gipsy Smith... New York, George H. Doran company [c1922] 170 p. 19 1/2 cm. $1.35. [BV3797.S57] 22-23138
I. Title.

SMITH, Roy Lemon, 1887- 252.
Spare tires and other essays, by Roy L. Smith ... with introduction by Edwin Markham ... New York, Chicago [etc.] Fleming H. Revell company [c1927] 156 p. 20 cm. [BX8333.S575S6] 27-23317
I. Title.

SNAPE, John, 1870- 252
Remember Jesus Christ, and other sermons, by John Snape ... New York, R. R. Smith, inc., 1930. x, 174 p. 20 cm. [BX6333.S56R4] 30-9982
I. Title.

SNAPE, John, 1870- 252.
Soul-trapping, and other sermons. by John Snape, D. D. Philadelphia, Boston [etc.] The Judson press [c1927] 6 p. l., 3-150 p. 20 cm. [BX6333.S56S6] 27-10330
I. Title.

SOUL-STIRRING sermons;
a collection of sermons on a variety of subjects vital to the spiritual welfare of the human family ... Anderson, Ind., Gospel trumpet company [c1915] 448 p. 18 1/2 cm. $1.00. 15-21953

SPEARMAN, Henry Kuhns, 1875- 252.
1928.
Soul magnets; twelve sermons from New Testament texts, by Rev. Henry Kuhns Spearman ... compiled as a memorial by Mrs. Elizabeth F. Spearman. [Philadelphia, Printed by The A. M. E. book concern] 1929. xvii, 18-116 p. port. 19 cm. [BX8472.S7] 29-24850
I. Spearman, Mrs. Elizabeth Frances (Morris) ed. II. Title.

*SPEARS, Gene, Jr. 252
Seventy feet nearer the stars: sermons to help build your church. New York, Vantage [c.1964] 112p. 21cm. 2.50 bds.,
I. Title.

SPURGEON, Charles Haddon, 252.
1834-1892.
Sermons of the Rev. C. H. Spurgeon, of London. 3d series. New York, Sheldon, Blakeman & company; Boston, Gould & Lincoln; [etc., etc.] 1857. x, [11]-448 p. front. 20 cm. [BX6333.S6S4 1857] 27-3789
I. Title.

STANFORD, John, 1751-1834. 200
The goodness of God in the conversion of youth: a sermon on the death of Charles I. S. Hazzard, son of the late Alderman Hazzard, who died of the late epidemic, aged 18 years. In which are introduced, an account of his very early enjoyment of the grace of God, and the exercise of his mind to the period of his death. Transcribed from the diary written with his own hand. By John Stanford ... New-York: Printed by T. & J. Swords, no. 99 Pearl-street, 1799. 2 p. l., [7]-60 p. 16 cm. [BR1725.H3S8] 45-27209
I. Hazzard, Charles I. S., 1780-1798. II. Title.

STEWART, James Alexander, 1910-
God's new thing.Lectures and sermons on revival. West Asheville, The Trumpet [n.d.] 71 p. 22 cm. (Revival series no. 6)
I. Title.

STIDGER, William Le Roy, 287
1886-
Building sermons with symphonic themes, by William L. Stidger, D.D. New York, George H. Doran company [c1926] 273 p. 19 1/2 cm. [BX8333.S75B8] 26-10870
I. Title.

STIDGER, William Le Roy, 251
1886-
There are sermons in books, by William L. Stidger ... with an introduction by Bishop Edwin Holt Hughes. New York, George H. Doran company [c1922] xxii p., 1 l., 25-232 p. 19 1/2 cm. [BV4235.B6S7] 22-15313
I. Title.

STIDGER, William Le Roy, 251
1886-
There are sermons in books, by William L. Stidger ... with an introduction by Bishop Edwin Holt Hughes. New York, George H. Doran company [c1922] xxii p., 1 l., 25-232 p. 19 1/2 cm. [BV4235.B6S7] 22-15313
I. Title.

STIDGER, William Le Roy, 251
1886-
There are sermons in books, by William L. Stidger ... with an introduction by Bishop Edwin Holt Hughes. New York, George H. Doran company [c1922] xxii p., 1 l., 25-232 p. 19 1/2 cm. [BV4235.B6S7] 22-15313
I. Title.

STILLPASS, Leo Joseph.
Faith for the space age; three sermons... [Johnstown, Pa., 1959] 1 v. 28 cm. Alternate pages blank.
I. Title.

STIMSON, Henry Albert, 1842-
The new things of God; sermons, by Henry A. Stimson ... New York; Chicago [etc.] F. H. Revell company [c1908] 280 p. 21 cm. 8-28071
I. Title.

STIMSON, Henry Albert, 1842-
The new things of God; sermons, by Henry A. Stimson ... New York; Chicago [etc.] F. H. Revell company [c1908] 280 p. 21 cm. 8-28071
I. Title.

STONE, Henry Morgan.
The witness of the heart, and other sermons, by the Rev. Henry Morgan Stone. New York [etc.] Longmans, Green and co., 1909. 7 p. l., [3]-203 p. front. (port.) 2 pl. 20 cm. $1.25 9-9477
I. Title.

STONE, John Timothy, 1868- 243
Places of quiet strength, and other sermons, by John Timothy Stone ... New York, George H. Doran company [c1923] xi p., 1 l., 11-250 p. 19 1/2 cm. (Half-title: Fourth church pulpit: First series) [BX9178.S8P5] 23-10325
I. Title.

STRICKLER, Givens Brown, 1840-
Sermons, by Rev. G. B. Strickler ... New York, Chicago [etc.] Fleming H. Revell company [c1910] 273 p. 20 1/2 cm. $1.00 10-4248
I. Title.

[STRONG, Sydney Dix] 1860- 252.
A Seattle pulpit, January 1-Easter Sunday, 1919. [Seattle, 1919] cover-title, [130] p. 15 1/2 x 8 1/2 cm. Various pagings. Sermons delivered by Sydney Strong in Queen Anne Congregational church, Seattle. [BX7233.S85S45] 21-6473
I. Title.

[STRONG, Sydney Dix] 1860- 252.
A Seattle pulpit, New Year's day to Easter, 1918. [Seattle, 1918] cover-title, [122] p. 15 1/2 x 8 1/2 cm. Various pagings. Contains sermons delivered by Sydney Strong in Queen Anne Congregational church, Seattle; opinions on immortality, by a number of college presidents and citizens of Seattle (15, [1] p.); and "Hymns of democracy" (7, [1] p.) [BX7233.S85S42] 18-13717
I. Title.

[STRONG, Sydney Dix] 1860- 252. *A Seattle pulpit,* September-December, 1918 ... [Seattle, 1919?] cover-title, [96] p. 15 1/2 x 9 cm. Various pagings. Sermons delivered by Sydney Strong in Queen Anne Congregational church, Seattle. [BX7233.S85S44] 21-6474
I. Title.

STUART, George Rutledge, 1857- 287
The snare of the fowler, and other sermons new and old, by George R. Stuart; being a revised and enlarged edition of "Sermons by George R. Stuart". Nashville, Tenn., Cokesbury press, 1924. 234 p. front. (port.) 19 1/2 cm. [BX8333.S77S4 1924] 24-13483
I. Title.

SUMMERBELL, Martyn, 1847-
Faith for the college man; college sermons, by Martyn Summerbell ... Dayton, O., Press of the Christian publishing association, 1915. 237 p. port. 19 1/2 cm. $1.00. 15-19852
I. Title.

SWANN, George Betts.
Sermons, by George Swann ... Owensboro, Ky., Progress printing company, incorporated [c1916] v. 20 cm. 16-24556
I. Title.

SWEENY, Nelson D.
Sermons for the sign-boards; or, Lessons from everyday life, a series of addresses, by Nelson D. Sweeny. Cincinnati, Printed for the author by Jennings and Graham [c1913] 246 p. incl. front., plates. ports. 20 cm. $1.00 13-26728
I. Title.

SWEETSER, Edwin Chapin, 1847- 230.
The image of God, and other sermons, by Edwin C. Sweetser ... New York, Chicago [etc.] Fleming H. Revell company [c1923] 236 p. 19 1/2 cm. [BX9943.S8 I 6] 23-10932
I. Title.

SWEETSER, Edwin Chapin, 1847- 230.
The image of God, and other sermons, by Edwin C. Sweetser ... New York, Chicago [etc.] Fleming H. Revell company [c1923] 236 p. 19 1/2 cm. [BX9943.S8 I 6] 23-10932
I. Title.

TALMAGE, Thomas De Witt, 1832-1902. 243
500 selected sermons, by T. De Witt Talmage New York, The Christian herald, 1900. 20 v. front. (port.) 21 1/2 cm. For contents, see advertisement at end of each volume. A comprehensive general index to the entire work, at end of v. 20. [BX9178.T3F5] 0-3287
I. Title.

TAYLOR, William Mackergo, 1829-1895. 252
Contrary winds and other sermons, by Wm. M. Taylor ... 3d thousand. New York, A. C. Armstrong & son, 1899. 372 p. 21 1/2 cm. [BX9178.T33C6] 29-29162
I. Title.

THOBURN, Wilbur W[ilson]
In terms of life; sermons and talks to college students. [Palo Alto, Cal.] Stanford university, 1899. 242 p., 1 l. port. 12°. Sep
I. Title.

TILTON, Howard W[inslow]
Lay sermons. New York, Doubleday & McClure co. 1899. 5 p. l., 173 p. 12 ° Dec
I. Title.

TILTON, Howard W[inslow]
Lay sermons. [Council Bluffs, Ia., New nonpareil co., 1899] 127 p. 16° Feb
I. Title.

TONNE, Arthur J., Rt. Rev. Msgr. 252.62
Lent and the laws of the church; seven sermons plus--one for Good Friday, one for Easter. [Emporia, Kan., Didde Printing Co., 1962, c.1961] 64p., 1.50, pap., plastic binding
I. Title.

TORREY, Reuben Archer, 1856- 243
Soul-winning sermons God has used in saving myriads of sinners all around the globe, presented in the order in which they were delivered. by R. A. Torrey... New York, Chicago [etc.] Fleming H. Revell company [c1925] 485 p. 23 cm. [BV3797.T575] 25-9230
I. Title.

TREASURY of the world's great sermons / compiled by Warren W. Wiersbe. Grand Rapids : Kregel Publications, c1977. x, 662 p. ; 26 cm. Based on The world's great sermons, compiled by G. Kleiser, and Modern sermons by world scholars, edited by R. Scott and W. C. Stiles. Includes indexes. [BV4241.T73] 77-72366 ISBN 0-8254-4011-4 : 12.95 252'.008
1. Sermons. I. Wiersbe, Warren W. II. Kleiser, Grenville, 1868-1953, comp. The world's great sermons. III. Scott, Robert, 1860- ed. Modern sermons by world scholars.

TUCKWELL, William, 1829-
Nuggets from the Bible mine, extracted by the Rev. W. Tuckwell ... London, New York [etc.] Hodder and Stoughton [1913] viii, 274 p. 20 1/2 cm. Collection of thirty-two sermons. 13-12485
I. Title.

TUCKWELL, William, 1829-
Nuggets from the Bible mine, extracted by the Rev. W. Tuckwell ... London, New York [etc.] Hodder and Stoughton [1913] viii, 274 p. 20 1/2 cm. Collection of thirty-two sermons. 13-12485
I. Title.

THE Twentieth century pulpit / edited by James W. Cox. Nashville : Abingdon, c1978. 301 p. ; 22 cm. [BV4241.T93] 77-21997 ISBN 0-687-42715-0 pbk. : 8.95 252
1. Sermons. I. Cox, James William, 1923-

UBER, Thomas Barclay, 1880- 252.
Soul-winning sermons, by T. B. Uber ... Princeton, Ill., Record printing & publishing co., c1923. 105 p. incl. front. (port.) 18 1/2 cm. [BX8066.U3S6] 23-7112
I. Title.

UTLEY, Uldine Mabelle. 243
Five petals, by Uldine Mabelle Utley ... [Philadelphia, Printed by MacCalla & co., inc.] c1926. 71 p. 19 1/2 cm. Portrait mounted on cover. "Uldine Mabelle Utley's first sermons; five messages the Holy Spirit gave her in her eleventh, twelfth, thirteenth and fourteenth years." [BV3797.U8] 27-1736
I. Title.

UTLEY, Uldine Mabelle. 243
Five petals, by Uldine Mabelle Utley ... [Philadelphia, Printed by MacCalla & co., inc.] c1926. 71 p. 19 1/2 cm. Portrait mounted on cover. "Uldine Mabelle Utley's first sermons; five messages the Holy Spirit gave her in her eleventh, twelfth, thirteenth and fourteenth years." [BV3797.U8] 27-1736
I. Title.

THE vaccine of faith. [Sermons and discourses] New York Jonathan David [1957] 174p. 22cm.
I. Roodman, Solomon.

VALENTINE, Milton, 1825-1906.
Christian trugh and life. Sermons. Philadelphia, Lutheran pub. soc. [1898] 358 p. port. 8° 98-1097
I. Title.

VAN BUREN, James Heartt, bp., 1850-
Sermons that have helped, by the Rt. Rev. James H. Van Buren, D.D., biship of Porto Rico ... New York, E. P. Dutton & co., 1908. 3 p. l., 215 p. 20 cm. $1.25 8-30600
I. Title.

VANCE, James Isaac, 1862- 252
God's open: sermons that take us out-of-doors, by James I. Vance ... New York, Chicago [etc.] Fleming H. Revell company [c1924] 204 p. front. 19 1/2 cm. [BX9178.V2G6] 24-13488
I. Title.

VAN DYKE, Henry, 1852-
Straight sermons to young men and other human beings, preached before the universities of Yale, Harvard and Princeton, by Henry Van Dyke... New York, C. Scribner's sons, 1893. xiii p., 1 l., 233 p. 18 1/2 cm. 13-25808
I. Title.
Contents omitted.

VAN WYK, William P. 251.027
My sermon notes for special days. Grand Rapids, Mich., Baker Bk. [c.]1962. 79p. 22cm. 1.00 pap.,
I. Title.

VAUGHAN, John Stephen, bp., 1853- 248
Sermons for all the Sundays, and for the chief feasts throughout the year, by the Right Reverend John S. Vaughan ... with an introduction by the Most Reverend John J. Glennon ... New York, Joseph F. Wagner (inc.); [etc., etc., 1920] 2 v. 23 cm. [BX1756.V3 1920] 20-8598
I. Title.

VAUGHN, Clement Read, 1827-
Sermons: apologetic, doctrinal and miscellaneous. By Rev. C. R. Vaughan ... Richmond, Va., The Presbyterian committee of publication [1902] 363 p. 21 cm. 2-23925
I. Title.

VOORSANGER, Jacob, 1852-1908.
Sermons and addresses, by Jacob Voorsanger .. with an introduction by Martin A. Meyer ... ed. by Otto Irving Wise. New York, Bloch publishing company, 1913. x, 378 p. front. (port.) 21 cm. $2.00. 13-15965
I. Wise, Otto Irving, ed. II. Title.

WALKER, Robert, 1716-1783. 243
Sermons on practical subjects, by Robert Walker... 3d ed. Philadelphia, Printed by R. Aitken & son, in Market street, 1790. iv, 295 p. 15 1/2 cm. [BX9178.W3S4 1790] 22-20245
I. Title.

WALKER, William Bruce 252
What think ye of Christ, and other evangelistic sermons. Grands Rapids, Mich., Baker Bk. [c.]1962. 69p. 22cm. 1.00 pap.,
I. Title.

WALLACE, Wilfrid, 1838-1896.
Sermons for the Christian year, by the late Dom Wilfrid Wallace... with a preface by Dom Bede Camm... St. Louis, Mo., and Freiburg (Baden) B. Herder, 1910. 3 v. 20 cm. $4.00 Contents.v. 1. Advent to Quinquagesima.--v. 2. First Sunday in Lent to Whit Sunday.--v. 3. Trinity Sunday to the 24th Sunday after Pentecost. 10-13184
I. Camm, Bede, 1864- ed. II. Title.

WALSH, Michael L., d.1913.
Sermons and addresses, by Rev. Michael L. Walsh. New York, G. A. Scheyer [c1914] 3 p. l., 9-335 p. 19 cm. $2.00 15-1235
I. Title.

WATKINSON, William Lonsdale, 1838-1925.
The supreme conquest, and other sermons preached in America, by W. L. Watkinson ... New York, Chicago [etc.] F. H. Revell company [c1907] 244 p. 21 cm. 7-21542
I. Title.

WATSON, Richard, 1781-1833. 252.
Sermons and sketches of sermons. By the Rev. Richard Watson. New York, Lane & Scott, 1851. 2 v. 23 cm. [BX8333.W4S4] 25-25456
I. Title.

WEIGLE, Charles Frederick, 1870- 243
The victorious life, and other sermons, by Charles F. Weigle ... Chicago, Ill., Meyer & brother, c1919. 140 p. front. (port.) 17 1/2 cm. [BV3797.W4] 19-10070
I. Title.

WHELAN, John A. 252
Sermons, by Rev. John A. Whelan ... New York, Cincinnati [etc.] Benziger brothers, 1924. 294 p. 20 1/2 cm. [BX1756.W5S4] 25-1101
I. Title.

WHITEFIELD, George, 1714-1770. 248
Fifteen sermons preached on various important subjects, by George Whitefield ... Carefully corrected and revised according to the best London edition. To which is prefixed, A sermon, on the character, preaching, &c. of the Rev. Mr. Whitefield, by Joseph Smith ... New-York, Printed by Hugh Gaine, 1794. iv, [5]-324 p. 15 1/2 cm. [BX9178.W5F5] A32
1. Sermons. 2. Whitefield, George, 1714-1770. I. Smith, Josiah, 1704-1781. II. Title.

WHITEFIELD, George, 1714-1770.
Sermons on various subjects. ... By George Whitefield ... Philadelphia, Printed and sold by B. Franklin, in Market street, v. 13 cm. 10-10992
I. Title.

WHITELAW, Thomas, 1840-
Jehovah-Jesus, by Rev. Thomas Whitelaw ... New York, C. Scribner's sons, 1913. iii, [4], 143, [1] p. 19 cm. (The short course series; ed. by Rev. John Adams ...) A 13
1. Sermons. 2. Jesus Christ. 3. God. I. Title.

WHITESELL, Faris Daniel, 1895- comp. 252
Great expository sermons, compiled by Faris D. Whitesell. Westwood, N.J., F. H. Revell Co.[1964] 190 p. 21 cm. [BV4241.W5] 64-20188
1. Sermons. I. Title.

WILLIAMS, Robert S.
Sermons and addresses, by Robert S. Williams ... Jackson, Tenn., H. Bullock, 1902. 265 p. front., (port.) 20 cm. 2-16094
I. Title.

WILLIAMS, Thomas, 1779-1876. 252.
Sermons on important subjects. By Thomas Williams, a minister of the gospel. Hartford: Printed by Peter B. Gleason, 1810. iv, [5]-231 p. 19 cm. [BX7233.W47S4] 24-15964
I. Title.

WILLIAMSON, Isaac Dowd 1807-1876.
Sermons for the times and the people. By Rev. I. D. Williamson, D.D. Boston, Universalist publishing house, 1883. 252 p. 18 cm. "Originally published in the year 1849."--Pref. 5-20077
I. Title.

WILSON, Lewis Gilbert, 1858- 252.
One hundred one-minute sermons, by Lewis Gilbert Wilson; a book of religious suggestion and practical efficiency in the life of the church, for private reading, or newspaper publicity ... Boston, Mass., New York [etc.] The Beacon press [c1923] 3 p., l., 103 p. 19 1/2 cm. [BX9843.W75O6] 23-7847
I. Title.

WILSON, Lewis Gilbert, 1858- 252.
The uplifted hands and other sermons, by Lewis Gilbert Wilson ... [Hopedale, Mass.] The Women's alliance of the Hopedale memorial church [192-?] 2 p. l., 136 p. front. (port.) 2 pl. 18 1/2 cm. [BX9843.W75U6] 24-13110
I. Title.
Contents omitted.

WILSON, Louis C., ed.
Twentieth century sermons and addresses; being a series of practical and doctrinal discourses by some of our representative men and women ... Ed. by Louis C. Wilson ... with an introduction by J. A. Lord ... Cincinnati, O., The Standard publishing company, 1902. xii p., 1 l., 434 p. incl. front., illus., pl., port. 20 1/2 cm. 2-28805
I. Title.

WILSON, William. 252
The blessedness of a nation whose God is Jehovah: a sermon. By William Wilson ... Pittsburgh, Printed by W. Allinder, 1840. 55, [1] p. 21 cm. [BR115.P7W5] 24-19497
I. Title.

WISE, William Herman. 287
Then the Lord, by W. H. Wise ... [Chicago, c1928] 185 p. front. (port.) 19 cm. Sermons. [BX8333.W55T5] 28-22471
I. Title.

WOMEN, Parley Paul
The coming creed, by Parley Paul Womer ... Boston, Sherman, French & company, 1911. 5 p. l., 88 p. 19 1/2 cm. $0.80 [1910; A 278713] 11-724
I. Title.

THE wondrous cross, and other sermons, by David James Burrell ... New York, W. B. Ketcham [c1898] 2 p. l., 3-151 p. 19 1/2 cm. 98-983

WOODHULL, George H. 252. *Three minute sermons,* by George H. Woodhull. Boston, R. G. Badger [c1920] 2 p. l., 7-81 p. 19 1/2 cm. (Lettered on cover: Library of religious thought) [BX7233.W6T5] 20-9306
I. Title.

WORKMAN, George Coulson. *The servant of Jehovah;* or, The passion-prophecy of Scripture analysed and elucidated, by George Coulson Workman ... London, New York [etc.] Longmans, Green, and co., 1907. xxvi, 250 p. 19 1/2 cm. A 21
I. Title.

WORLD'S Christian citizenship conference. 2d, Portland, Or., 1913. *Second World's Christian citizenship conference,* Portland, Oregon, June 29-July 6, 1913. Official report. Pittsburgh, Pa., The National reform association [1913] 303 p. illus. (ports) 26 cm. "The Conference was projected and managed by the National reform association."--p. 5. 16-24035
I. National reform association. II. Title.

WRIGHT, Abiel Holmes, 1840-1920. 208. *Story, song and sermon,* with an autobiographical sketch, by Rev. Abiel Holmes Wright ... Portland, Me., The Lakeside press, 1911. 271 p. incl. front. (port.) pl. 21 cm. $1.25. [BX7117.W7] 11-29100
I. Title.

YEISER, John Green, 1845-1911. 252. *Texts and talks by the late Rev. John G. Yeiser,* compiled and edited by his daughter, Idabelle Yeiser. [Philadelphia, A. M. E. book concern c1928] 2 p. l., 7-84 p. 16 cm. [BX8472.Y4] 28-21658
I. Yeiser, Idabelle, ed. II. Title.

ZOLLIKOFER, Georg Joachim, 1730-1788. *Sermons on the dignity of man, and the value of the objects principally relating to human happiness.* From the German of the late Rev. George Joachim Zollikofer, minister of the reformed congregation at Leipsick. By the Reverend William Tooke, F.R.S. In two volumes. First American edition. Worcester [Mass.] Printed by Thomas & Sturtevant for Isaiah Thomas, jun., 1807. 2 v. 22 cm. A 33
I. Tooke, William, 1744-1820, tr. II. Title.

Sermons—Addresses, essays, lectures, etc.

ANDREWS, Matthew T 1865- 252 *Growing a soul,* by Matthew T. Andrews, D.D. Philadelphia, Boston [etc.] The Judson press [c1926] 6 p. l., 143 p. 20 cm. Sermons and addresses. [BV4253.A5] 26-14015
I. Title.

DICKINSON, James Taylor, 1861- 252. *The preceding God,* by Rev. James Taylor Dickinson, D. D. Philadelphia, Pa., The Judson press [1921] 6 p. l., 3-217 p. 20 cm. Contents.Sermons.--Addresses.--Tributes and appreciation.--Letters from abroad. [BX6333.D5P7] 21-4339
I. Title.

LUCCOCK, Halford Edward, 1885- 287 *The haunted house,* and other sermons, by Halford E. Luccock. New York, Cincinnati, The Abingdon press [c1923] 248 p. 19 cm. [BX8333.L8H3] 23-17702
I. Title.

MUNGER, Theodore Thornton, 1830-1910. *The freedom of faith,* by Theodore T. Munger ... Boston and New York, Houghton, Mifflin and company [189-?] vi, 397 p. 20 cm. Seventeen sermons, preceded by an essay on "The new theology." 4-19457
I. Title.

[MURRAY, James] 1732-1782. 252 *Sermons to ministers of state.* By the author of, Sermons to asses. Dedicated to Lord North, prime minister of England, for the use of the religions, political, and philosophical rationalists, in Europe and America. Philadelphia: Printed and sold by Robert Bell, in Third street, 1783. 79 p. 19 cm. Dedication signed: James Murray, New-Castle, upon Tyne, October 19th, 1781. Ten "Sermons", followed (p. [76]-79) by the "laughable composition, which hath been handed about in manuscript at Philadelphia" ... "reported to be written by the Rev. J. W-th-sp-n, D. D., one of the members of the American Congress: The humble confession, declaration, recantation and apology of Benjamin Towne, printer in Philadelphia." [BX5202.M85 1783] [AC901.D8 vol. 15] 9-29955
I. Witherspoon, John, 1723-1794. II. Title.

PEABODY, Francis Greenwood, 1847- 252 *Afternoons in the College chapel:* short addresses to young men on personal religion, by Francis Greenwood Peabody ... Boston & New York, Houghton, Mifflin & company, 1898. vi p., 1 l., 213, [1] p. 19 cm. Addresses delivered in College chapel, Harvard university. [BV4310.P45] 98-1873
I. Title.

ROWE, Frederick Louis, 1866- comp. *Pioneer sermons and addresses* ... comp. by F. L. Rowe assisted by M. A. C. Cincinnati, O., F. L. Rowe, 1908. 295 p. 20 cm. 8-15130
I. Title.

*SPURGEON, C. H. 252 *Twelve sermons on conversion,* [by] C. H. Spurgeon. Grand Rapids, Baker Book House, [1974] 147 p. 20 cm. [BV4222] ISBN 0-8010-8027-4. 1.95 (pbk.)
1. Sermons—Addresses, essays, lectures, etc. I. Title.

*SPURGEON, C. H. 252 *Twelve sermons on repentance,* [by] C. H. Spurgeon. Grand Rapids, Baker Book House, [1974] 131 p. 20 cm. [BV4222] ISBN 0-8010-8028-2 1.95 (pbk.)
1. Sermons—Addresses, essays, lectures, etc. I. Title.

*SPURGEON, C. H. 252 *Twelve sermons on various subjects* [by] C. H. Spurgeon. Grand Rapids, Baker Book House, [1974] 125 p. 20 cm. [BV4222] ISBN 0-8010-8029-0 1.95 (pbk.)
1. Sermons—Addresses, essays, lectures, etc. I. Title.

STIDGER, William Le Roy, 1886- *Standing room only,* by Rev. William L. Stidger ... With an introduction by Bishop Theodore S. Henderson. New York, George H. Doran company [c1921] xx p., 1 l., 23-170 p. incl. front., illus., plates. 19 1/2 cm. $2.00 [BV662.S7] 21-14937
I. Title.

Sermons—Aids, analyses, outlines, etc.

BACHMAN, Albert John, 1887- 251 *Sermon outlines:* a collection of one hundred and fifty original outlines of sermons, by A. J. Bachman. Nashville, Tenn., McQuiddy printing company, 1921. 316 p. 15 x 8 cm. Most of the leaves printed on one side only. [BV4223.B25] 22-3486
I. Title.

*BOLICK, James H. 251.027 *Sermon outlines for revival preaching.* Grand Rapids, Mich., Baker Bk. [c.1964] 105p. 22cm. (1.00 sermon lib.) 1.00 pap.,
I. Title.

BUTLER, Burris 251.027 *Doctrinal sermon outlines.* Cincinnati, Standard [c.1962] 64p. 22cm. (Sermon outline ser.) 1.00 pap.,
I. Title.

COMPTON, W. H., comp. 251.027 *Sermon outlines from God's word.* [Westwood, N.J.] Revell [c.1961] 64p. (Revell's sermon outline ser.) 61-9246 1.00 pap.,
I. Title.

CRAWFORD, Cecil Clement, 1893- 226. ... *Sermon outlines on Acts,* by C. C. Crawford. Cincinnati, The Standard publishing company [c1919] 284 p. 20 cm. [BS2625.C75] 20-2350
I. Title.

ELY, Simpson, 1849- *Sermons, essays and outlines,* by Simpson Ely; comp. by his son Marcellus R. Ely. Cincinnati, O., Standard publishing company [c1910] vi, 201 p. front. (port.) 20 cm. 10-18388 1.00
I. Ely, Marcellus Randall, 1872- comp. II. Title.

EVANS, William, 1870- *How to prepare sermons and gospel addresses,* by William Evans ... Chicago, The Bible institute colportage association [c1913] 178 p. 20 cm. 13-2507 1.00
I. Title.

HILLS, Oscar Armstrong, 1837- 251 *Familiar talks on sermon building,* by Rev. Oscar A.Hills... New York, Chicago [etc.] Fleming H. Revell company [c1918] 96 p. 19 1/2 cm. [BV4211.H4] 19-244
I. Title.

LESETRE, Henri, 1848- *Sermon plans for all the Sundays of the year,* with a chapter on how and what to preach, from the French of Abbe H. Lesetre. New York, J. F. Wagner [c1912] xx, 100 p. 21 cm. $1.00 13-688
I. Title.

TURNBULL, Ralph G *The Christian faces his world.* Grand Rapids, Mich., Baker book house, 1964. 99 p. (Bible Companion series for lesson and sermon preparation) 68-23504
1. Sermons—Aids, analyses, outlines, etc. I. Title.

Sermons, American.

ABBOTT, Lyman, 1835-1922. 252.058 *Signs of promise,* Sermons preached in Plymouth pulpit, Brooklyn, 1887-9. By Lyman Abbott. Printed from stenographic reports. New York, Fords, Howard & Hulbert, 1889. 301 p. 20 cm. [BX7233.A15S5] 33-1566
1. Sermons, American. I. Title.

AHRENDT, Vivian. 252 *A call to prayer,* by Vivian Ahrendt. Anderson, Ind., The Warner press [c1937] iii, 5-159 p. 19 cm. [BV4241.A3] 37-17377
1. Sermons, American. I. Title.

ALLEN, R. Earl 252.061 *Bible paradoxes.* [Westwood, N. J.] Revell [c.1963] 128p 21cm. 63-17107 2.50 bds.,
1. Sermons, American. 2. Southern Baptist Convention—Sermons. I. Title.

ALLEN, R. Earl. 252.061 *Bible paradoxes.* [Westwood, N.J.] Revell [1963] 128 p. 21 cm. [BX6333.A3B5] 63-17107
1. Sermons. America. 2. Southern Baptist Convention — Sermons. I. Title.

THE American preacher; 252 or, A collection of sermons from some of the most eminent preachers, now living in the United States, of different demoninations in the christian church. Elizabeth-Town, N. J., Printed by S. Kollock for the editors, 1791-93. 4 v. 21 cm. Pref. signed: David Austin. L. C. set Incomplete: v. 4 wanting. [BV4241.A512] 49-39705
1. Sermons, American. I. Austin, David, 1760-1831.

THE American pulpit 252.0082 *series ...* Book 1- New York, Nashville, Abingdon-Cokesbury press [1945- v. 17 cm. [BV4241.A65] 45-14985
1. Sermons, American.

AMES, Edward Scribner, 1870- 252.066 *Letters to God and the devil,* by Edward Scribner Ames ... New York and London, Harper & brothers, 1933. viii p., 1 l., 113 p. 20 cm. "First edition." [BX7327.A5L4] 33-27382
1. Sermons, American. I. Title.

AMICK, Fred A 252 *Hearing for eternity.* Rosemead, Calif., Old Paths Book Club, 1954- v. illus. 21cm. [BV4301.A6] 54-40237
1. Sermons, American. 2. Sermons, American. I. Title.

ANDERSON, John Wesley, 1855- 920. *From the plains to the pulpit,* by J. W. Anderson. Houston, Tex., State printing company, 1907. 214 p. front. (port.) plates. 19 cm. [BX6495.A6A2] 7-89012
I. Title.

ANDERSON, Lynn, 1936- 252'.06'63 *Steps to life* / by Lynn Anderson. Abilene, Tex. : Biblical Research Press, c1977. vi, 201 p. ; 23 cm. (The 20th century sermons series ; v. 10) Includes bibliographical references. [BX7077.Z6A857] 77-20518 ISBN 0-89112-310-5 : 5.95
1. Churches of Christ—Sermons. 2. Sermons, American. I. Title.

ANDERSON, Norman G 252 *Power for tomorrow.* Minneapolis, T. S. Denison [1961] 223p. 22cm. [BV4301.A65] 61-16790
1. Sermons, American. I. Title.

ANDERSON, Norman G. 252.04'1 *The priceless ingredient* [by] Norman G. Anderson. Old Tappan, N.J., F. H. Revell Co. [1971] 124 p. 21 cm. Short sermons based on the author's television program, Power for tomorrow. [BX8066.A53P75] 79-139609 ISBN 0-8007-0427-4 3.50
1. Lutheran Church—Sermons. 2. Sermons, American. I. Power for tomorrow. II. Title.

ANDERSON, William Franklin, bp., 1860- 287 *The compulsion of love;* sermons preached at Ossining-on-Hudson, N. Y., in the Highland avenue Methodist Episcopal church, by Rev. William F. Anderson ... Cincinnati, Jennings and Pye; New York, Eaton and Mains [c1904] 163 p. front. (port.) 19 cm. (Half-title: The Methodist pulpit) [BX8333.A6C6] 4-9467
1. Sermons, American. I. Title.

ANDERSON, William Madison, 1889-1935. 252.051 *The faith that satisfies;* sermons. New York, Loizeaux Bros. [1948] vi. 247 p. port. 20 cm. [BX9178.A55F3] 48-28128 resbyterian Church--Sermons.
1. Sermons, American. I. Title.

APOSTOLON, Billy. *Hands full of honey.* Grand Rapids, Mich., Baker book house, 1964. 83 p. (Apostolon's Pulpit Masters' Sermons) NUC67
1. Sermons, American. I. Title.

*APOSTOLON, Billy 252.3 *The preaching of the cross.* Grand Rapids, Mich. Baker Bk. [c.]1963. 82p. 22cm. (Apostolon's pulpit master's sermons) 1.00 pap.,
I. Title.

APOSTOLON, Billy. *The preaching of the cross.* Grand Rapids, Mich. Baker book house, 1963. 82 p. (Apostolon's Pulpit Master's Sermons) NUC67
1. Sermons, American. I. Title.

APPLETON, Nathaniel, 1693-1784. 252.058 *The clearest and surest marks of our being so led by the Spirit of God,* as to demonstrate that we are the children of God. Set forth in several discourses from Romans VIII, XIV. Part of which was delivered at the Thursday-lecture in Boston, January 13, 1742,3. By Nathanael Appleton, M.A. pastor of the First church in Cambridge ... Boston, Printed by Green, Bushell, and Allen for D. Henchman in Cornhill. 1748. 1 p. l., vii, [1], 215 p. 14 1/2 cm. Signatures: 1 leaf. Edges trimmed when rebound: p. 215 mutilated. [BX7233.A6C6] 9-22525
1. Sermons, American. I. Title.

ARMSTRONG, Housen Parr. *Living in the currents of God.* St. Louis, Bethany press [1962] 112 p. 21 cm. NUC63
1. Sermons, American. I. Title.

ARMSTRONG, James Francis, 1750-1816. 252'.05'2
Light to my path : sermons / by James F. Armstrong ; edited by Marian B. McLeod. Trenton : First Presbyterian Church, c1976. 68 p. : ill. ; 22 cm. [BX9178.A67L53] 77-366763
1. Presbyterian Church—Sermons. 2. Sermons, American. I. Title.

ASH, Anthony Lee. 252'.06'6
The word of faith. Abilene, Tex., Biblical Research Press [1973] v, 218 p. 23 cm. (The 20th century sermon series, v. 8) [BX7327.A75W6] 73-89757 4.95
1. Disciples of Christ—Sermons. 2. Sermons, American. I. Title.

BAILEY, Barry, 1926- 252'.07
Living with your feelings / Barry Bailey. Nashville : Abingdon, c1980. 78 p. : ill. ; 21 cm. [BX8333.B24L58] 79-27889 ISBN 0-687-22380-6 : 5.95
1. Methodist Church—Sermons. 2. Sermons, American. I. Title.

BAILEY, Barry, 1926- 248.4'876
With best wishes / Barry Bailey. Nashville : Abingdon, c1982. 95 p. ; 21 cm. [BX8333.B24W57] 19 81-20632 ISBN 0-687-45842-0 pbk. : 6.95
1. Methodist Church—Sermons. 2. Sermons, American. I. Title.

BAILEY, James H., 1934- 232.9'5
The miracles of Jesus for today / James H. Bailey. Nashville : Abingdon, c1977. 127 p. ; 19 cm. [BT366.B33] 76-51202 ISBN 0-687-27070-7 pbk. : 3.95
1. Jesus Christ—Miracles—Sermons. 2. Methodist Church—Sermons. 3. Sermons, American. I. Title.

BAIRD, Jesse H. 222.12
God's law of life; thirteen sermons, by Jesse H. Baird, D. D. Caldwell, Id., The Caxton printers, ltd., 1931. 2 p. l., 134 p. 20 cm. [BX9178.B3294G6] 31-13256
1. Sermons, American. I. Title.

BAKER, Harold Edwin, 1896- 252
Sparks from the anvil of truth, by Rev. H. E. Baker ... [East Liverpool, O., 1944] 175 p. front. (2 port.) 19 1/2 cm. [BV4253.B3] 44-24730
1. Sermons, American. I. Title.

BAMBERG, Ad Hubert.
Popular sermons on the catechism, from the German of Rev. A. Hubert Bamberg, ed. by Rev. Herbert Thurston ... New York, Cincinnati [etc.] Benziger brothers, 1914- v. 20 1/2 cm. 14-18579
I. Thurston, Herbert, 1856- ed. II. Title.

BANCROFT, William Henry.
The anthem angelic, and other sermons, by Rev. William Henry Bancroft ... Philadelphia, Printed by G. W. Jacobs & co. [c1905] 4 p. l., 331 p. front. (port.) 19 1/2 cm. Sermons delivered to the congregation of Buckingham Presbyterian church, of Berlin, Md. cf. Foreword. 5-15705
I. Title.

BANKS, Louis Albert, 1855- 287
The King's stewards, by Rev. Louis Albert Banks, D.D. New York, American tract society [c1902] iv, [5]-315 p. front. (port.) 21 cm. A collection of sermons. [BX8333.B3K5] 2-17251
1. Sermons, American. I. Title.

BANKS, Louis Albert, 1855- 287
A year's prayer-meeting talks, by Rev. Louis Albert Banks ... New York and London, Funk & Wagnalls company, 1899. viii, 289 p. 19 cm. [BX8333.B3Y4] 99-5575
1. Sermons, American. I. Title. II. Title: Prayer-meeting talks.

BARNEY, Kenneth D. 236
Preparing for the storm / Kenneth D. Barney. Springfield, Mo. : Gospel Pub. House, [1975] 96 p. ; 18 cm. (Radiant books) [BV4253.B35] 74-21021 pbk. : 1.25
1. Sermons, American. I. Title.

BARNHOUSE, Donald Grey, 1895-1960. 226'.6'07
Acts, an expositional commentary / Donald Grey Barnhouse, with Herbert Henry Ehrenstein. Grand Rapids : Zondervan Pub. House, c1979. 233 p. ; 23 cm. [BS2625.4.B32 1979] 79-16213 ISBN 0-310-20510-7 : 9.95
1. Presbyterian Church—Sermons. 2. Bible. N.T. Acts—Sermons. 3. Sermons, American. I. Ehrenstein, Herbert Henry, joint author. II. Title.

BARNHOUSE, Donald Grey, 1895-1960. 227'.81'07
Thessalonians—an expositional commentary / Donald Grey Barnhouse. Grand Rapids : Zondervan Pub. House, c1977. 111 p. ; 21 cm. [BS2725.B37 1977] 77-1507 5.95
1. Presbyterian Church—Sermons. 2. Bible. N.T. Thessalonians—Sermons. 3. Sermons, American. I. Title.

BEAN, George M 1918- 252.5
The armor of God; sermons preached to the Class of 1957. New York, Morehouse-Gorham, 1957. 125p. 16cm. [BV4316.S7B39] 57-10616
1. Sermons, American. 2. U. S. Military Academy, West Point. I. Title.

BEAN, George M 1918- 252.550974731
Be filled with gladness; sermons preached to the Class of 1959 by their chaplain. [West Point? N. Y.] 1959. 110p. 16cm. [BV4316.S7B395] 59-43545
1. Sermons, American. 2. U. S. Military Academy, West Point. I. Title.

BEAN, George M 1918- 252.5
Be not conformed to this world; sermons preached to the Class of 1955 by their chaplain. New York, Morehouse-Gorham Co., 1955. 117p. 16cm. [BV4316.S7B4] 55-37389
1. Sermons, American. 2. U. S. Military Academy, West Point. I. Title.

BEAN, George M 1918- 252
No other gods; sermons preached to the Class of 1956 by their chaplain. New York, Morehouse-Gorham Co., 1956. 117p. 16cm. [BV4316.S7B43] 56-10120
1. Sermons. American. 2. U. S. Military Academy, West Point. I. Title.

BEAN, George M 1918- 252.5
The power of His might; sermons preached to the Class of 1958 by their chaplain. [West Point? N. Y.] 1958. 93p. 16cm. [BV4316.S7B44] 58-2435
1. Sermons, American. 2. U. S. Military Academy, West Point. I. Title.

BECKELHYMER, Hunter, comp. 252.06'6
The vital pulpit of the Christian church; a series of sermons by representative men among the Disciples of Christ. With introd. and a brief biographical sketch of each contributor. St. Louis Bethany Press [1969] 287 p. ports. 24 cm. [BX7327.A1B37] 69-17883
1. Disciples of Christ—Sermons. 2. Sermons, American. I. Title.

BEECHER, Henry Ward, 1813-1887. 252.
Sermons, by Henry Ward Beecher, Plymouth church, Brooklyn. Selected from published and unpublished discourses, and revised by their author ... New York, Harper & brothers, 1869. 2 v, front. (port.) 22 1/2 cm. [BX7233.B4S45 1869] 15-28256
I. Title.

BEECHER, Lyman, 1775-1863. 252
Lyman Beecher and the reform of society: four sermons, 1804-1828. New York, Arno Press, 1972. 107 p. 23 cm. (Religion in America, series II) Contents.—The practicality of suppressing vice by means of societies instituted for that purpose.—A reformation of morals practicable and indispensable.—The remedy for duelling.—Six sermons on the nature, occasions, signs, evils, and remedy of intemperance. [BV4253.B4] 71-38437 ISBN 0-405-04058-X
1. Sermons, American. I. Title.

BELLAMY, Joseph, 1719-1790. 252.3
Sermons upon the following subjects, viz. The divinity of Jesus Christ. The millenium. The wisdom of God, in the permission of sin. By Joseph Bellamy, A. M., minister of the gospel at Bethlem ... Boston: Printed and sold by Edes and Gill; and by S. Kneeland, in Queen-street, M.DCC,LViii. vi, 209, [2] p. 16 x 10 cm. [BX7233.B57S4] [230.4] 5-19181
1. Sermons,American. 2. Jesus Christ—Divinity. 3. Millennium. 4. Sin. I. Title.

BENTON, Harry, 1873- 252.
Rural sermons; inspiring sermons illuminated by the things of nature well known to all farmers, by Harry Benton ... Eugene, Ore, Eugene Bible university press, 1926. 288 p. pl. 20 cm. [BV4316.F3B4] 27-1375
I. Title.

BEST sermons ... 252
1924- New York, Harcourt, Brace and company [c1924]- v. 21 cm. Editor: 1924- J. F. Newton. [BV4241.B4] 24-23319
1. Sermons, American. I. Newton, Joseph, 1876- ed.

BEST sermons ... 252.0058
Edited with introduction and biographical notes by Joseph Fort Newton ... v. [1]-4; 1924-[27] New York, Harcourt, Brace and company [1924-27] 4 v. 21 cm. No more published. [BV4241.B4] 24-23319
1. Sermons, American. I. Newton, Joseph Fort, 1876- ed.

BININGER, Clem E. 232.96'35
The seven last words of Christ, by Clem E. Bininger. Grand Rapids, Baker Book House [1969] 109 p. 21 cm. [BT456.B55] 71-98138 2.95
1. Jesus Christ—Seven last words—Sermons. 2. Presbyterian Church—Sermons. 3. Sermons, American. I. Title.

BIRD, John L. 227'.91
Faith that works; a study guide on the Book of James, by John L. Bird. Grand Rapids, Zondervan Pub. House [1968, c1965] 94 p. 21 cm. "Addresses ... delivered ... at Duke Street Baptist Church, Richmond, Surrey." [BS2785.4.B5] 68-22174
1. Bible. N.T. James—Sermons. 2. Sermons, American. 3. Baptists—Sermons. I. Title.

BISHOP, John, 1908- 232.9'01
Seeing Jesus today; a portrait of Jesus the man. Valley Forge [Pa.] Judson Press [1973, c1969] 158 p. 20 cm. [BT306.3.B56 1973] 72-6302 ISBN 0-8170-0575-7 pap 2.50
1. Jesus Christ—Biography—Sermons. 2. Methodist Church—Sermons. 3. Sermons, American. I. Title.

BJORGE, James R. 252'.041
The love road to Calvary : sermons for Lent and Easter on I Corinthians 13 / James R. Bjorge. Minneapolis : Augsburg Pub. House, c1982. 92 p. ; 20 cm. [BS2675.4.B47] 19 81-52268 ISBN 0-8066-1900-7 pbk. : 3.95
1. Lutheran Church—Sermons. 2. Bible. N.T. Corinthians, 1st XIII—Sermons. 3. Sermons, American. I. Title.

BLACK, V. P., 1918- 252
We persuade men, by V. P. Black. Abilene, Tex., Biblical Research Press [1969] iv, 226 p. 23 cm. (The 20th century sermons series, v. 2) [BV4253.B47] 72-87861
1. Sermons, American. I. Title.

BLACKBURN, William Maxwell, 1828-1898, ed. 285.
The Kirkpatrick memorial; or, Biographical sketches of father and son, and a selection from the sermons of the Rev. Jacob Kirkpatrick, jr., the sketches by the Rev. George Hale, D.D. Edited by the Rev. Wm. M. Blackburn. Philadelphia, Westcott & Thompson, 1867. 312 p. 2 port. (incl. front.) 20 cm. [BX9225.K6B6] 3-31337
1. Kirkpatrick, Jacob, 1785-1866. 2. Kirkpatrick, Jacob, 1828-1859. 3. Sermons, American. I. Kirkpatrick, Jacob, 1828-1859. II. Hale, George, 1812-1888. III. Title.

BLAIR, Charles E. 252
The silent thousands suddenly speak! [By] Charles E. Blair. Foreword by J. Sidlow Baxter. Grand Rapids, Zondervan Pub. House [1968] 149 p. 23 cm. [BV4253.B5] 68-22833
1. Sermons, American. I. Title.

BLOOD, William Morris, 1867- comp.
The humiliation of Christ; five sermons preached by five bishops of the Methodist Episcopal church presiding at as many annual conferences of the Southwest Kansas conference. By William M. Blood, Henry W. Cummings ... Pub. for the Southwest Kansas annual conference. Cincinnati, The Methodist book concern [c1913] 122 p. ports. 19 1/2 cm. $0.50. 13-4444
I. Cummings, Henry W., joint comp. II. Title.
Contents omitted.

BORDERS, William Holmes, 1905- 252.061
Men must live as brothers. [Twenty sermons which were first preached in the Wheat Street Baptist Church, Atlanta[Atlanta, 1947?] 243 p. 23 cm. [BX6452.B57] 48-2479
1. Sermons, Americans. 2. Baptists — Sermons I. Title.

BOREHAM, Frank William, 1871. 248
A bunch of everlasting; or, Texts that made history, a volume of sermons, by F. W. Boreham ... New York, Cincinnati, The Abingdon press [c1920] 256 p. 19 1/2cm. [BR1702.B6] 20-8882
I. Title.

BOSLEY, Harold Augustus, 1907- 252'.07
Men who build churches; interpretations of the life of Paul [by] Harold A. Bosley. Nashville, Abingdon Press [1972] 158 p. 19 cm. [BS2506.B65] 72-701 ISBN 0-687-24801-9
1. Paul, Saint, apostle—Sermons. 2. Methodist Church—Sermons. 3. Sermons, American. I. Title.

BOWIE, Walter Russell, 1882- 252.03
When Christ passes by, by Walter Russell Bowie; with an introduction by Joseph Fort Newton. New York and London, Harper & brothers, 1932. x, 134 p. 20 cm. "First edition." [BX5937.B6W5] 33-114
1. Sermons, American. I. Title.

BOYCE, Edward H. 252
With Christ in the mount; mountain experiences in the life of Christ. [Sermons] New York, Exposition Press [1951] 128 p. 23 cm. [BV4253.B64] 51-5040
1. Sermons. American. I. Title.

*BOYER, Frank J. 252.5
Sermon outlines for special occasions. Grand Rapids, Mich., Baker Bk. [1967] 114p. 21cm. (Preaching helps ser.) 1.50 pap.,
1. Sermons, American. 2. Presbyterian Church—Sermons. I. Title.

BRAATEN, Carl E., 1929- 252'.04'1
The whole counsel of God, by Carl E. Braaten. Philadelphia, Fortress Press [1974] x, 166 p. 23 cm. Sermons. [BX8066.B65W47] 73-88345 ISBN 0-8006-1064-4 5.95
1. Lutheran Church—Sermons. 2. Sermons, American. I. Title.

BRADY, James Boyd, 1845-1912. 287
Selected souvenir sermons delivered in People's temple, Boston, Mass. By Rev. James Boyd Brady ... and furnished for publication as a parting memento by request of the people. Boston, B. J. Stetson & co., printers, 1899. 3 p. l., 456 p. front. (port.) plates. 23 cm. The plates are printed on both sides. [BX8333.B62S4] 99-3330
1. Sermons, American. I. Title.

BRENT, Charles Henry, bp., 1862-
Prisoners of hope, and other sermons, by the Rt. Rev. Charles H. Brent ... New York [etc.] Longmans Green, and co., 1915. x, 279 p. 19 1/2 cm. 15-8047 1.50
I. Title.

BRISCOE, D. Stuart. 252
What works when life doesn't / Stuart Briscoe. Wheaton, Ill. : Victor Books, c1976. 143 p. ; 21 cm. [BS1430.4.B677] 75-26443 ISBN 0-88207-725-2 pbk. : 1.95
1. Bible. O.T. Psalms—Sermons. 2. Sermons, American. I. Title.

BRISTOL, Frank Milton, bp., 1851- 287
The religious instinct of man, by Rev. Frank M. Bristol ... Cincinnati, Jennings and Pye; New York, Eaton and Mains [c1904] 157 p. front. (port.) 19 cm. (Half-

title: The Methodist pulpit) [BX8333.B74R4] 4-3357
1. Sermons, American. I. Title.

BRITE Divinity School. 252'.00973
The word we preach; sermons in honor of Dean Elmer D. Henson, by faculty and trustees of Brite Divinity School, Texas Christian University. Edited by Hunter Beckelhymer. [Fort Worth, Texas Christian University Press, c1970] xi, 149 p. port. 24 cm. Contents.Contents.—A tribute, by J. M. Moudy.—Our Father, who art in heaven, by W. O. Harrison.—This Jesus whom you crucified, by H. Beckelhymer.—The meaning of Easter, by M. J. Suggs.—The family of God, by J. W. Stewart.—What matters is faith, by W. D. Hall.—The full blessing of Christ's gospel, by A. T. DeGroot.—The citadel of hope, by G. Routt.—Under new management, by N. J. Robison.—The marks of a Christian, by W. R. Baird.—Making your life count, by R. A. Olsen.—Between God and Caesar, by H. L. Lunger.—The problem of grief, by C. H. Sanders.—Go placidly amid the noise and haste, by G. T. Walker.—Christianity—A spectator sport? By G. A. Shelton.—On the way, by R. A. Hoehn.—A people for the future, by G. L. Smith.—A ministry without hocus-pocus, by W. R. Naff.—The ministry of compassion, by C. F. Kemp.—Violent physicians, by M. D. Bryant.—Treasure in earthen vessels, by W. E. Tucker. Includes bibliographical references. [BV4241.B627] 79-143563
1. Sermons, American. I. Henson, Elmer D., 1901- II. Beckelhymer, Hunter, ed. III. Title.

BRONG, Rosco, 1908- 252.06
For His name's sake; a simple score of short sermons fitting first truths to last days. [1st ed.] New York, Greenwich Book Publishers [c1963] 82 p. 21 cm. [BX6333.B685F6] 63-22175
1. Sermons, American. 2. Baptists — Sermons. I. Title.

BROOKS, Phillips bp., 1835-1893. 252.
Seeking life, and other sermons, by the Rt. Rev. Phillips Brooks ... 10th series. New York, E. P . Dutton and company, 1904. vii, 374 p. 20 cm. "With this volume the publication of the sermons of Bishop Brooks closes" --Pref. [BX5845.B7S5] 4-22843
1. Sermons, American. I. Title.

BROOKS, Phillips, Bp., 1835-1893. 252.03'73
Selected sermons, edited and with an introd. by William Scarlett. Freeport, N.Y., Books for Libraries Press [1971, c1949] 377 p. port. 23 cm. (Essay index reprint series) [BX5937.B83S39 1971] 79-142610 ISBN 0-8369-2146-1
1. Protestant Episcopal Church in the U.S.A.—Sermons. 2. Sermons, American.

BROOKS, Phillips, Bp., 1835-1893. 252.
Sermons New York, Dutton, 1878. 371 p. 20 cm. Protestant Episcopal Church in the U. S. A.--Sermons. [BX5937.B83S4 1878] 52-49613
1. Sermons, American. I. Title.

BROOKS, Phillips, bp., 1835-1893. 252.03
Sermons, by the Rt. Rev. Phillips Brooks, D.D. First series. 26th thousand. New York, E. P. Dutton and company, 1902. vii, 371 p. 19 1/2 cm. [BX5845.B7S4] 4-10411
1. Sermons, American. I. Title.

BROOKS, Phillips, bp., 1835-1893. 252.03
Twenty sermons, by the Rt. Rev. Phillips Brooks, D.D. Fourth series. New York, E. P. Dutton & company, 1903. viii, 369 p. 19 1/2 cm. [BX5845B7S44 1903] 4-10413
1. Sermons, American. I. Title.

BROWN, Howard Nicholson, 1849-
Freedom and truth, and other sermons in King's chapel, with a brief historical sketch, by Howard N. Brown, D.D. Boston, W. B. Clarke co., 1916. iv p., 1 l., 337 p. front. 20 1/2 cm. 17-2493
I. Title.

BROWN, Hugh Stowell, 1823-1886. 252.
Lectures for the people. By the Rev. Hugh Stowell Brown... First series, with a biographical introduction, by Dr. Shelton Mackenzie. [Authorized edition] Philadelphia, G.G. Evans, 1860. 414 p. front. (port.) 19 cm. [BX6333.B735L4 1860] 1-101
1. Sermons, American. I. Mackenzie, Robert Shelton, 1809-1880. II. Title.

BROWNSON, William. 252
Do you believe? : Contemporary insight on the question of faith / William Brownson. Grand Rapids, Mich. : Zondervan Pub. House, c1975. 217 p. ; 18 cm. [BS2615.4.B76] 74-25324 1.95
1. Bible. N.T. John—Sermons. 2. Sermons, American. I. Title.

BRUEGGEMANN, Walter. 252'.05'834
Living toward a vision : Biblical reflections on shalom / by Walter Grueggemann. Philadelphia : United Church Press, c1976. p. cm. (A Shalom resource) Includes bibliographical references. [BX9886.Z6B78] 76-22172 ISBN 0-8298-0322-X pbk. : 4.95
1. United Church of Christ—Sermons. 2. Sermons, American. I. Title.

BRUNER, Benjamin Harrison, 1888- 252
Toward the sunrising [by] B. H. Bruner. Nashville, Tenn., Cokesbury press [c1935] 279 [1] p. 22 1/2 cm. Sermons. [BV4253.B75] 35-8491
1. Sermons, American. I. Title.

BUCKMINISTER, Harold Chase, 1927-1955.
To help other men; a selection from the sermons of Harold C. Buckminster, 1960. Pinehurst, N.C. E. W. Buckminster, 1960. xxix, 129 p. illus., ports. 24 cm. 63-7318
1. Sermons, American. I. Title.

BUECHNER, Frederick, 1926- 252.051
The magnificent defeat. New York, Seabury [c.1966] 144p. 22cm. [BX9178.B75M3] 66-12638 3.50
1. Sermons, American. 2. Presbyterian Church—Sermons. I. Title.

BURGHARDT, Walter J. 252'.02
Tell the next generation : homilies and near homilies / Walter J. Burghardt. New York ; Paulist Press, c1980. x, 225 p. : ill. ; 23 cm. Includes bibliographical references. [BX1756.B828T44] 79-91895 ISBN 0-8091-2252-9 pbk. : 6.95
1. Catholic Church—Sermons. 2. Sermons, American. I. Title.

BURKE, John James, 1857- 248
The armor of light; short sermons on the Epistles for every Sunday in the year, by the Rev. J. J. Burke ... St. Louis, Mo., and London, B. Herder book co., 1925. ix, 224 p. 19 cm. [BX1756.B83 1925] 25-19508
I. Title.

BURKS, John James, 1857-1936. 248
The great problem; a sermon for every Sunday and feast day in the year, by Rev. J. J. Burke ... St. Louis, Mo., Freiburg (Baden) B. Herder; [etc., etc.] 1909. 3 p. l., 316 p. 20 cm. [BX1756.B83G7] 9-17340
1. Sermons, American. I. Title.

BURRELL, David James, 1844-1926.
The cloister book, for shut-in worshipers and pastorless congregations, by David James Burrell ... New York city, American tract society; [c1909] 4 p. l., [7]-340 p. front. (port.) 19 cm. [X9185.B8 1909] 9-29569
1. Sermons, American. I. Title.

BURRELL, David James, 1844-1926. 252
"For Christ's crown," and other sermons. By David James Burrell ... New York, W. B. Ketcham [1896] 370 p. 19 1/2 cm. [BX9178.B8F6] 45-50417
1. Sermons, American. I. Title.

BURRELL, David James, 1844-1926. 252
The golden passional, and other sermons by David James Burrell ... New York, W. B. Ketcham [1897] 2 p. l. [3]-338 p. 19 1/2 cm. [BX9178.B8G6] 45-50420
1. Sermons, American. I. Title.

BURRELL, David James, 1844-1926. 252
The gospel of gladness. By David James Burrell, D.D. New York, American tract society [1892] 318 p. 19 cm. [BX9178.B8G62] 45-50418
1. Sermons, American. I. American tract society. II. Title.

BURRELL, David James, 1844-1926. 252
"The morning cometh." Talks for the times. By Rev. David James Burrell, D.D. New York, American tract society [1893] 320 p. 19 cm. [BX9178.B8M6] 45-50419
1. Sermons, American. 2. American tract society. I. Title.

BURRELL, David James, 1844-1926. 252
The spirit of the age, and other sermons. By David James Burrell ... New York, W. B. Ketcham [1895] 381 p. 19 1/2 cm. [BX9178.B8S6] 45-50421
1. Sermons, American. I. Title.

BURRELL, David James, 1844-1926. 243
The unaccountable man, by David James Burrell ... New York, Chicago [etc.] Fleming H. Revell company [c1900] 3 p. l., 9-310 p. 20 cm. [BX9178.B8U6] 0-6365
1. Sermons, American. I. Title.

BUSHNELL, Horace, 1802-1876. 252.
Sermons for the new life. By Horace Bushnell. 7th ed. New York, C. Scribner, 1864. vi p., 1 l., [9]-456 p. 19 1/2 cm. [BX7233.B8S4 1864] 1-146
1. Sermons, American. I. Title. II. Title: New life, Sermons for the.

BUSHNELL, Horace, 1902-1876. 252.
Sermons for the new life, by Horace Bushnell. Rev. ed. New York, Scribner, Armstrong & co., 1876. 2 p. l., [iii]-vi, [9]-456 p. 19 1/2 cm. [BX7233.B8S4 1876] 1-147
1. Sermons, American. I. Title. II. Title: New life, Sermons for the.

CAMPBELL, Ernest T. 261.8
Locked in a room with open doors [by] Ernest T. Campbell. Waco, Tex., Word Books [1974] 180 p. 23 cm. Includes bibliographical references. [BX9178.C26L6] 73-91554 5.95
1. Presbyterian Church—Sermons. 2. Sermons, American. I. Title.

CARCICH, Theodore. 252'.07'3
Carcich at 7:30 : sermons preached at camp meetings / by Theodore Carcich. Nashville : Southern Pub. Association, [1975] 95 p. ; 21 cm. [BX6123.C36] 74-30869 ISBN 0-8127-0091-0
1. Seventh-Day Adventists—Sermons. 2. Sermons, American. I. Title.

CARCICH, Theodore. 252'.06'73
So what's there to live for? Nashville, Southern Pub. Association [1972] 63 p. 19 cm. [BX6123.C37] 72-88858 ISBN 0-8127-0064-3 Pap. 0.50
1. Seventh-Day Adventists—Sermons. 2. Sermons, American. I. Title.

CHAMBERS, Moses Leonard, 1880- 252
The man who can whip his luck, by Rev. M. L. Chambers. [Somerset, Ky., The Commonwealth, print, 1926?] cover-title, 52, [2] p. 18 cm. Includes poems. [BV4253.C45] 43-19213
1. Sermons, American. I. Title.

CHANDLER, Daniel Ross, 1937- 280 B
The official, authorized biography of the Reverend Dr. Preston Bradley. [1st ed.] New York, Exposition Press [1971] 115, [2] p. 21 cm. (An Exposition-testament book) Bibliography: p. [117] [BR1725.B68C48] 78-166186 ISBN 0-682-47333-2 4.50
1. Bradley, Preston, 1888- 2. Sermons, American. I. Title.

CHAPIN, Edwin Hubbell, 1814-1880. 252'.09'1
Humanity in the city. New York, Arno Press, 1974 [c1854] 252 p. port. 23 cm. (Metropolitan America) Reprint of the ed. published by De Witt & Davenport, New York. [BX9943.C5H85 1974] 73-11901 ISBN 0-405-05389-4 12.00
1. Universalist Church—Sermons. 2. Sermons, American. I. Title. II. Series.

CHAPPELL, Clovis Gillham, 1882- 225.92'2
Men that count, by Clovis G. Chappell. Grand Rapids, Baker Book House [1967] 164 p. 20 cm. (Ministers paperback library) Reprint of the 1929 ed. Sermons. Contents.Contents.—Needless poverty: James.—Worry and its cure: Paul.—All things new: Paul.—A great believer: Paul.—At the cross: Paul.—A successful service: Peter.—Kept: Peter.—A pilgrim's progress: the man born blind.—The glory of the ordinary: Andrew.—A fighter: Zacchaeus.—A woman's revenge: John the Baptist.—A beautiful vocation: Onesiphorus.—Making life count: author of Hebrews.—A wholehearted saint: Caleb.—Mr. Sorrowful: Jabez.—The spoiled dream: Jeremiah. [BS571.5.C46 1967] 67-18173
1. Bible—Biography. 2. Sermons, American. I. Title.

CHAPPELL, Wallace D. 252'.07'6
All for Jesus! / Wallace D. Chappell. Nashville : Broadman Press, [1975] 95 p. ; 20 cm. [BX8333.C522A44] 74-27926 ISBN 0-8054-5231-1 : 3.50
1. Methodist Church—Sermons. 2. Sermons, American. I. Title.

CHAPPELL, Wallace D. 252.07
His continued witness. Nashville, Abingdon [c.1964] 140p. 20cm. 64-16146 2.50 bds.,
1. Sermons, American. 2. Methodist Church—Sermons. I. Title.

CHAPPELL, Wallace D 252.07
Receiving God's fullness. New York, Abingdon Press [1960] 126p. 20cm. [BX8333.C522R4] 60-9196
1. Sermons, American. 2. Methodist Church—Sermons. I. Title.

CHAPPELL, Wallace D. 232.9'7
When Jesus rose [by] Wallace D. Chappell. Nashville, Broadman Press [1972] 127 p. 21 cm. [BT485.C5] 72-90034 ISBN 0-8054-2218-8 3.95
1. Jesus Christ—Resurrection—Sermons. 2. Methodist Church—Sermons. 3. Sermons, American. I. Title.

CHAPPELL, Wallace D. 252.07
Who Jesus says you are. Nashville, Abingdon [c.1962] 96p. 62-7225 2.00 bds.,
1. Sermons, American. 2. Methodist Church—Sermons. I. Title.

CHERINGTON, Fletcher B. 252.
Siftings; exerpts from sermons preached in Plymouth Congregational church, San Francisco, California, by Rev. F. B. Cherington, D.D. San Francisco [F. H. Abbott] 1900. 64 p. incl. port. 19 1/2 x 10 1/2 cm. "No. 45. Issued by the Young People's society of Christian endeavor of Plymouth Congregational church, San Francisco, Cal." [BX7233.C5785] 1-30031
1. Sermons, American. 2. Christian life. I. Title.

CLAP, Mathaniel, 1669-1745.
The Lord's voice, crying to his people; in some extraordinary dispensations considered in a sermon, upon Micah vi. 9. Preached 27d. i m. 1715. Occasioned by the terrible tragedies of a man barbarously murdering his wife and her sister, and then burning his house, March 22, 1715. Together with some account about the poor man written for the benefit of the living. By Nathaniel. Clap, M.A. preacher of the gospel at N. Port, R. Island. Boston; Printed by G. Green, sold at the booksellers shops, 1715. 1 p. l. 137. [1] p. 18 cm. Imperfect: p. 73-74, 79-80, 99-102, 133-[138] wanting. "Some of the last words of several dying persons: a discourse on Luke, xxiii, 39043. The last sermon heard by the poor man. Preached April 10, 1715. Boston, 1715": p. 73- 137. [BX7253.C592L5] 2-18534
I. Title.

CLAUSEN, Robert Howard, comp. 252'.04'1
The cross and the cries of human need; messages for Lent and every season. The meaning of the cross for human problems portrayed in six selections from the plays of Arthur Miller, John Osborne, Edward Albee, Frank D. Gilroy, Eugene Ionesco. Minneapolis, Augsburg Pub. House [1973] 127 p. 20 cm. [BX8066.C5C76] 72-90255 ISBN 0-8066-1301-7 2.95
1. Lutheran Church—Sermons. 2. Sermons,

American. 3. Christianity and literature. I. Title.
Contents Omitted.

CLEVELAND, Earl E. 242
Free at last [by] E. E. Cleveland. Washington, Review and Herald Pub. Association [1970] 447 p. col. illus., col. ports. 26 cm. [BX6123.C55] 70-97596
1. Seventh-Day Adventists—Sermons. 2. Sermons, American. I. Title.

CLEVELAND, Edward Earl. 261.8'34'5196073
Living soul; "we shall overcome" [by] E. E. Cleveland. Nashville, Southern Pub. Association [1974] 219 p. illus. 21 cm. [BX6123.C56] 73-91286 ISBN 0-8127-0078-3 1.95 (pbk.).
1. Seventh-Day Adventists—Sermons. 2. Sermons, American. 3. United States—Race question. I. Title.

COBURN, John B. 248'.48'3
The hope of glory : exploring the mystery of Christ in you / John B. Coburn. New York : Seabury Press, c1976. p. cm. "A Crossroad book." [BX5937.C63H66] 75-37751 ISBN 0-8164-1208-1 : 7.95. ISBN 0-8164-2117-X pbk. : 3.95
1. Protestant Episcopal Church in the U.S.A.—Sermons. 2. Sermons, American. I. Title.

COCKING, George, 1862- 922.773
From the mines to the pulpit; or, Success hammered out of the rock. Cincinnati, Printed for the author by Jennings & Pye [c1901] 177 p. port. 19 cm. [BX495.C58A3] 3-8352
I. Title.

COFFEY, John W. 252
Grace in the wilderness, by John W. Coffey, Jr. [Nashville, T. Nelson, 1974] p. cm. "Nelson giant print inspirational." [BV4253.C63] 74-18292 ISBN 0-8407-5579-1 3.50 (pbk.)
1. Sermons, American. 2. Sight-saving books. I. Title.

COFFIN, William Sloane. 252'.051
The courage to love / William Sloane Coffin. 1st ed. San Francisco : Harper & Row, c1982. 100 p. ; 22 cm. Contents.Contents. Introduction — The courage to love — The limits of life — Thorns in the flesh — Being called — Homosexuality — Abortion — The promised time — The arms race — The soviets — Beating burn-out. Includes bibliographical references and index. [BX9426.C63C68 1982] 19 81-48386 ISBN 0-06-061508-7 : 9.95
1. Reformed Church—Sermons. 2. Sermons, American. I. Title.

COLMAN, Benjamin, 1673-1747.
Sermons preached at the lecture in Boston, from Luke xi. 21, 22. Shewing i. That the soul of man is a noble palace which the great God built for Himself. ii. That it is now become as a garison or strong hold, which Satan keeps against God. iii. That there is a wretched peace and cursed quiet. which the carnal heart lies in under Satans tyranny. iv. That the victorious Saviour rescues whom He pleases, and will rescue all His chosen, from Satans power and tyranny. To which is added. A discourse from Psalm cxxii. i. ... By Benjamin Colman, a pastor of a church in Boston. Boston, Printed by B. Green. for S. Gerrish & D. Henchman, sold at their shops, 1717. 1 p. l., 163, [1] p. 15 cm. "A discourse of the pleasure of religious worship, in our publick assemblies. From Psalm cxxii. i":p. [131]-163. has separate t.-p. A 33
1. Sermons, America. I. Title.

CONKLING, Wallace Edmonds. 252.03
True values [by] Wallace Edmonds Conkling ... Milwaukee, Morehouse publishing co.; London, A. R. Mowbray & co., ltd. [c1931] viii p., 2 l., [3]-54 p. 18 cm. "Addresses in Saint Luke's church, Germantown, Philadelphia, during Lent, 1930."--Foreword. [BX5937.C663T7] 31-5980
1. Sermons, American. 2. Good and evil. 3. Free will and determinism. I. Title.

CONWELL, Russell Herman, 1843- 252.
Borrowed axes, and other sermons, by Russell H. Conwell ... Philadelphia, Boston [etc.] The Judson press [c1923] 4 p. l., 112 p. front. (port.) 20 cm. [BX6333.C6B6] 24-3491
I. Title.

CORDLEY, Richard, 1829-1904.
Sermons [by] Richard Cordley, D. D., for thirty-eight years pastor of Plymouth church, Lawrence, Kansas. Pub. by the church, 1912. Boston, New York [etc.] The Pilgrim press, 1912. xiv, 122 p. 20 cm. 12-7796 1.00
I. Title.

CRAVNER, William Charles.
The daystar at midnight. New York, Vantage Press [c1962] 91 p. port. 21 cm. 63-10802
1. Sermons, American. I. Title.

CRAWFORD, Percy B ed. 252.0082
Echoes of Pinebrook, a series of timely messages, edited and compiled by Rev. Percy B. Crawford. Philadelphia, Penna., The Young people's church of thed air [c1941] 86 p. 20 cm. [BV4241.C77] 42-778
1. Sermons, American. I. Young people's church of the air. II. Title.

CRAWFORD, Percy Bartimus, ed. 252.0082
Echoes of Pinebrook, a series of timely messages, edited and compiled by Rev. Percy B. Crawford. Philadelphia, Penna., The Young people's church of the air [c1941] 88 p. 20 cm. [BV4241.C77] 42-778
1. Sermons, American. I. Young people's church of the air. II. Title.

CRAWFORD, Percy Bartimus. 252
Whither goest thou? A series of radio messages preached on 250 stations over the Mutual network by Percy B. Crawford ... East Stroudsburg, Pa., The Pinebrook book club [1946] 138 p. 19 1/2 cm. A revision of the author's Salvation full and free. cf. Copyright application. [BV4241.C78 1946] 47-15018
1. Sermons, American. I. Title.

CRISWELL, Wallie A. 224'.5
Expository sermons on the book of Daniel, by W. A. Criswell. Grand Rapids, Mich., Zondervan Pub. Co. [1968-72] 4 v. 22 cm. Contents.Contents.—v. 1. Introductory materials and discussion.—v. 2. Daniel I-III.—v. 3. Daniel IV-VI.—v. 4. Daniel VII-XII. [BS1555.4.C7] 68-27468
1. Bible. O.T. Daniel—Sermons. 2. Sermons, American. 3. Baptists—Sermons. I. Title.

CRISWELL, Wallie A. 227'.92'06
Expository sermons on the Epistles of Peter / W. A. Criswell. Grand Rapids : Zondervan Pub. House, c1976. p. cm. [BS2795.4.C74] 76-26486 5.95
1. Baptists—Sermons. 2. Bible. N.T. Peter—Sermons. 3. Sermons, American. I. Title.

CROWLEY, Dale. 252
Fifty radio sermons; evangelist Dale Crowley's golden anniversary book. Washington, National Bible Knowledge Association [1972] xii, 221 p. 22 cm. [BV4253.C77] 72-89559 5.00
1. Sermons, American. I. Title.

[CUDNEY, Isaiah] 1847- 252.099
The city of New Jerusalem. [Los Angeles, Wolfer printing company, c1932] 1 p. l., 5-921 p. front., plates (1 col.) ports. 23 cm. [BX9998.C8] 32-17068
1. Sermons, American. I. Title.
Contents omitted.

CULBERTSON, William. 252
The faith once delivered; keynote messages from Moody Founder's Week. Chicago, Moody Press [1972] 192 p. 22 cm. Addresses delivered annually, 1953-1971. [BV4253.C84] 72-181584 ISBN 0-8024-2520-8 4.95
1. Sermons, American. I. Moody Bible Institute of Chicago. II. Title.

CUSHMAN, Robert, d.1625. 252.058
Self-love, by Robert Cushman, 1621. "The first sermon preached in New England, and the oldest extant of any delivered in America". Chelsea, Mass., H. H. Tucker [c1895] 58 p., 1 l. 19 cm. "Appendix. Containing some account of the life and character of Mr. Robert Cushman, from the time of his being settled with the Rev. John Robinson, in the city of Leyden, Holland in the year 1609, to the time of his arrival in America" (by John Davis): p. [55]-58. [BX7233.C82 1895] 35-30451
1. Sermons, American. 2. New England—Hist.—Colonial period. I. Davis, John, 1761-1847. II. Title.

CUSTIS, W. Keith. 252'.05'1
Into a new age and other sermons / W. Keith Custis. [Upper Marlboro? Md.] : Custis, c1975. 200 p. ; 24 cm. Includes bibliographical references. [BX9178.C85I57] 75-29693
1. Presbyterian Church—Sermons. 2. Sermons, American. I. Title.

DARGAN, Edwin Charles, 1852- 252.
The changeless Christ, and other sermons, by Edwin Charles Dargan ... New York, Chicago [etc.] Fleming H. Revell company [c1918] 1 p. l., 5-194 p. 20 cm. [BX6333.D3C5] 18-11173
I. Title.

DASKAM, Max F ed. 252.0082
Sermons from an ecumenical pulpit. Boston, Starr King Press [1956] 254p. 22cm. [BV4241.D28] 56-10078
1. Sermons, American. I. Title.

DAVIES, Samuel, 1724-1761. 252.051
Sermons on important subjects, by the late reverend and pious Samuel Davies ... To which are prefixed, memoirs and character of the author: and two sermons on occasion of his death, by the Rev. Drs. Gibbons and Finley ... Boston: Printed and published by Lincoln & Edmunds, no. 53, Cornhill. 1811. 3 v. 22 cm. Edited by Thomas Gibbons. Vol. 1. "2d American ed., containing 19 sermons never before published in America". [BX9178.D35S4 1811] 33-15311
1. Sermons, American. 2. Presbyterian church—Sermons. I. Gibbons, Thomas, 1720-1785, ed. II. Finley, Samuel, 1715-1766. III. Title.

DAVIES, Samuel, 1724-1761. 252.051
Sermons on important subjects. By The Reverend Samuel Davies ... With an essay on the life and times of the author, by Albert Barnes. Stereotyped ed., containing all the author's sermons ever published ... 4th ed. New York and Pittsburg, R. Carter, 1845. 3 v. 20 cm. Edited by Thomas Gibbons. [BX9178.D35S4 1845] 33-16408
1. Sermons, American. 2. Presbyterian church—Sermons. I. Gibbons, Thomas, 1720-1785, ed. II. Barnes, Albert, 1798-1870. III. Title.

DAVIES, Samuel, 1724-1761. 252.051
Substance of sermons, by Samuel Davies ... Given in his own words ... By the compiler of the Sailor's companion Designed for gratutituous circulation. New York, M. W. Dodd, 1851. 394 p. 20 cm. "Extracts from a sermon preached at Nassau hall, Princeton, May 23, 1761. Occassioned by the death of the Rev. Samuel Davies ... By Samuel Finley": p. [385]-394. [BX9178.D35S42 1851] 33-16428
1. Sermons, American. 2. Presbyterian church—Sermons. I. Finley, Samuel, 1715-1766. II. Title.

DEANE, Samuel, 1733-1814.
Four sermons to young men, from Titus ii. 6. Preached at Falmouth, by Samuel Deane, A. M., junior pastor of the First church of Christ in that place. Salem: Printed and sold by Samuel and Ebenezer Hall, 1774. vi p., 1 l., 104 p. 21 cm. A 35
1. Sermons, American. I. Title.

DE HAAN, Martin Ralph, 1891- 252
The chemistry of the blood and other stirring messages, by M. R. De Haan ... Grand Rapids, Mich., Zondervan publishing house [1943] 183 p. diagr. 20 cm. "Sermons ... first preached over the coast-to-coast network of the Mutual broadcasting system ... First published in the form of small booklets, but by popular demand ... bound in one volume."--Foreword. [BV4301.D38] 43-15115
1. Sermons, American. I. Title.

DE HAAN, Martin Ralph, 1891- 252
Signs of the times, and other prophetic messages. Grand Rapids, Zondervan Pub. House [1951] 182 p. 20 cm. [BV4301.D382] 51-11552
1. Sermons, American. I. Title.

DE HAAN, Martin Ralph, 1891- 252
The tabernacle, the house of blood. Grand Rapids, Zondervan Pub. House [1955] 185p. illus. 20cm. [BV4301.D385] 55-14895
1. Sermons, American. I. Title.

DENNIS, Fred E. 252
Fifty short sermons, by Fred E. Dennis ... 1st ed. Grand Rapids, Mich., Wm. B. Eerdmans publishing company, 1942- v. front. (port.) 20 cm. [BV4253.D4] 42-23497
1. Sermons, American. I. Title.

DICKEY, Douglas A
Sermons for sidetracked saints; 11 lifechanging sermons, by Douglas A. Dickey. [Foreword by Dean E. Walker] Cincinnati, Standard Pub. [c1965] 112 p. Bibliographical footnotes. 68-98184
1. Sermons, American. 2. Disciples of Christ—Sermons. I. Walker, Dean Everest, 1898- II. Title.

DIXON, Robert L.
Saving faith and other sermons. Nashville, Gospel-Advocate Co., 1963. 166 p. illus., ports. Includes "The life of H. A. Dixon" and "Mrs. H. A. Dixon" by G. K. Wallace. 65-43998
1. Sermons, American. 2. Churches of Christ-Sermons. I. Wallace, Gervias Knox, 1903- II. Title.

DONDERS, Joseph G. 252'.6
Jesus, the way : reflections on the Gospel of Luke / Joseph G. Donders. Maryknoll, N.Y. : Orbis Books, c1979. viii, 307 p. ; 21 cm. Includes index. [BS2595.4.D66] 79-4167 ISBN 0-88344-240-X pbk. : 7.95
1. Jesus Christ—Person and offices—Sermons. 2. Catholic Church—Sermons. 3. Bible. N.T. Luke—Sermons. 4. Sermons, American. 5. Church year sermons. I. Title.

DORCHESTER, Mass. Second church. 285.
Sermon and addresses commemorative of the twenty-fifth anniversary of the ordination of Rev. James H. Means as pastor of the Second church, Dorchester, July 13th and 14th, 1873. Boston, Congregational publishing society, 1873. 72 p. 24 cm. [BX7255.B7D7 1873] 27-489
I. Means, James Howard, 1823-1894. II. Title.

DOUGLAS, George William, 1850-1926. 252.03
Sermons preached in St. John's church, Washington, D.C., By George William Douglas, S.T.D. New York, A. D. F. Randolph and company, inc. [1893] viii, 294 p. 20 1/2 cm. [BX5937.D7S4] 33-9893
1. Sermons, American. I. Title.

DOUGLAS, Lloyd Cassel, 1877-1951. 252
The living faith [by] Lloyd C. Douglas, from his selected sermons. Boston, Houghton Mifflin, 1955. 344 p. 22 cm. [BV4253.D68] 55-6127
1. Sermons, American. I. Title.

DOUGLASS, Herbert E., comp. 252'.06'7
If I had one sermon to preach. Edited by Herbert E. Douglass. Washington, Review and Herald Pub. Association [1972] 190 p. ports. 21 cm. (Review and Herald sermon library series) (Discovery paperbacks) Contents.Contents.—Alexander, W. Mingled motives.—Bradford, C. E. Rich man, poor man, Christian.—Brooks, C. D. A hope called blessed.—Bush, F. F. The church called Christian.—Dower, N. R. That I may win Christ.—Fearing, A. The song of Moses and the lamb.—Hackett, W. J. How man finds freedom.—Hegstad, R. R. An offbeat subject.—Lesher, W. R. Two ways with people.—Loveless, W. A. Burn your labeling machine.—Osborn, J. W. The magnificent decision.—Pease, N. F. The answered question.—Pierson, R. H. Hope and help for you!—Spangler, J. R. Is the Cross out of date?—Venden, L. Two lost boys.—Vitrano, S. P. Keeping the great commandment.—Wood, K. H. The leukemia of noncommitment. Includes bibliographical references. [BX6123.D68] 72-78420

1. Seventh-Day Adventists—Sermons. 2. Sermons, American. I. Title.

DURKEE, James Stanley, 1866- 252. Friendly chats of the Friendly hour, by J. Stanley Durkee ... Atlanta, The Harrison company [c1929] ix, 238 p. 20 cm. Talks from the "Friendly hour" programs, broadcast by the National broadcasting company. [BX7233.D77F7] 30-3790
I. Title. II. Title: The Friendly hour, Friendly chats of.

EARLE, Absalom Backas. 922
Work of an evangelist. Review of fifty years. By Rev. A. B. Earle... Boston, J. H. Earle, 1881. 66 p. 15 cm. "Fifieth anniversary sermon [delivered in Tremont temple, Boston, Mass., Nov. 14, 1880]": p. 35-66. [BV3785.E3A3] 37-33214
1. Sermons, American. I. Title.

EDWARDS, Jonathan, 1703-1758. 204
Selected sermons of Jonathan Edwards, edited with introduction and notes, by H. Norman Gardiner ... New York, The Macmillan company. London, Macmillan & co., ltd., 1904. xxix, 181 p. front, (port.) pl., facsim. 14 1/2 cm. [Macmillan's pocket American and English classics] [BX7117.E33G3] 4-16197
I. Gardiner, Harry Norman, 1855-1927, ed. II. Title.

ELDERSVELD, Peter H. 252.05731
Nothing but the Gospel; radio messages presented by Peter H. Eldersveld. Collected by the Radio Committee of the Christian Reformed Church. Grand Rapids, W. B. Eerdmans Pub. Co. [1966] xix, 162 p. port. 23 cm. [BX6827.E4N6] 66-30327
1. Christian Reformed Church—Sermons. 2. Sermons, American. I. Christian Reformed Church. Radio committee. II. Title.

THE 11 o'clock news & other 252
experimental sermons / edited by John Killinger. Nashville : Abingdon Press, [1975] 156 p. : ill. ; 23 cm. [BV4241.E55] 75-16357 ISBN 0-687-11639-2 : 6.95
1. Sermons, American. I. Killinger, John.

ELLIOTT, Stephen, bp., 252.08
1806-1866.
Sermons by the Right Reverend Stephen Elliott...with a memoir by Thomas M. Hanckel, esq. New York, Pott and Amery, 1867. xxxv, 594 p. front. (mounted port.) 23 cm. [BX5987.E55S4] 33-1377
1. Sermons, American. I. Hanckel, Thomas M. II. Title.

ELMORE, Carl Hopkins, 252.05
1878-
The inexhaustible Christ, by Carl Hopkins Elmore. New York and London, Harper & brothers, 1935. vii, 130 p. 19cm. Sermons. "First edition." [BX9178.E516] 35-2670
1. Sermons, American. 2. Presbyterian church—Sermons. I. Title.

ELY, Samuel.
Two sermons, preached at Somers, March 18, 1770, when the church and people were under peculiar trials. By Samuel Ely, preacher of the gospel in Somers ... Hartford [Conn.]: Printed by Ebenezer Watson, 1771. iv, [5]-62 p. 19cm. A33
1. Sermons, American. I. Title.

ENGELBERT, E. F. 252.6
A still small voice. Grand Rapids, Mich., Eerdmans [1965, c.1964] 216p. 21cm. [BX8066.E57S7] 64-8906 3.50 bds.,
1. Sermons, American. 2. Lutheran Church—Sermons. I. Title.

ENGSTROM, Theodore W., ed. 252
Great sermons by great American preachers, compiled and edited by Theodore W. Engstrom ... Grand Rapids, Mich., Zondervan publishing house [1943] 3 p. l., 9-234 p. 20 cm. [BV4241.E67] 43-15279
1. Sermons, American. I. Title.

ENGSTROM, Theodore W ed. 252
Victorious and fruitful living, and other sermons, a compilation of sermons written by leading teachers, preachers and evangelists in the Holiness movement. C. W. Butler, H. C. Morrison, J. C. McPheeters [and others]... Compiled and edited by Theodore W. Engstrom... Grand Rapids, Mich., Zondervan publishing house [1942] 116 p. 19 1/2 cm. [BV4241.E68] 42-18410
1. Sermons, American. I. Butler, Charles, William 1873- II. Title.

ENGSTROM, Theodore Wilhelm, 252
1916- ed.
Great sermons by great American preachers. Grand Rapids, Mich., Zondervan Pub. House [1943] 234 p. 20 cm. [BV4241.E67] 43-15279
1. Sermons, American. I. Title.

ENGSTROM, Theodore Wilhelm, 252
1916- ed.
Victorious and fruitful living, and other sermons; a compilation of sermons written by leading teachers, preachers and evangelists in the Holiness movement. C. W. Butler, H. C. Morrison, J. C. McPheeters [and others] Grand Rapids, Mich., Zondervan Pub. House [1942] 116 p. 20 cm. [BV4241.E68] 42-18410
1. Sermons, American. I. Butler, Charles William, 1873- II. Title.

THE Episcopal series of 252.03
the Protestant hour Radio program)
The word on the air. Edited by Girault M. Jones. Foreword by Henry I. Loutit. New York, Seabury Press, 1964. 157 p. 21 cm. "Twenty -- six sermons preached on The Episcopal hour during the past decade." [BX5937.A1E6] 64-14889
1. Sermons. American. 2. Protestant Episcopal Church in the U.S.A. — Sermons. I. Jones, Girault M., Bp., ed. II. Title.

EPISCOPAL series of the 252.03
Protestant hour (The) (Radio program)
The word on the air. Ed. by Girault M. Jones. Foreword by Henry I. Louttit. New York, Seabury [c.]1964. 157p. 21cm. Twenty-six sermons preached on TheEpiscopal hour during the past decade. 64-14889 1.95 pap.,
1. Sermons, American. 2. Protestant Episcopal Church in the U.S.A.—Sermons. I. Jones, Girault M., Bp., ed.

FAGERBURG, Frank Bentamin, 252.06
1898-
Here for a purpose. Valley Forge, Pa., Judson [c.1963] 95p. 20cm. 63-19833 1.75 pap.,
1. Sermons, American. 2. Baptist Church—Sermons. I. Title.

FAIRBANKS, Edward Taylor, 252.
1836-1919.
The wrought brim: twelve discourses given in the South church, St. Johnsbury, Vermont, by Edward Taylor Fairbanks, twenty-eight years pastor, 1874-1902. Published by W. W. Husband. St. Johnsbury, Vt., Press of the Caledonian company, 1902. 4 p. l., 195, [1] p. front. (port.) pl. 25 cm. "Second edition of 200 volumes." This copy not numbered. Each plate accompanied by guard sheet with descriptive letterpress. [BX7233.F3W7] 2-30389
1. Sermons, American. I. Title.

FERGUSON, Charles Wright, 252
1901-
Great themes of the Christian faith, as presented by G. Campbell Morgan [and others] Arr. by Charles W. Ferguson. Freeport, N.Y., Books for Libraries Press [1969, c1930] viii, 204 p. 23 cm. (Essay index reprint series) [BV4241.F4 1969] 68-58788
1. Sermons, American. I. Morgan, George Campbell, 1863-1945. II. Title.

FERGUSON, Charles Wright, 252
1901 comp.
Great themes of the Christian faith, as presented by G. Campbell Morgan, George A. Buttrick...[and others] arranged by Charles W. Ferguson. New York, R. R. Smith, inc., 1930. viii p., 2 l., 3-204 p. 20 1/2 cm. [BV4241.F4] 30-32857
1. Sermons, American. I. Morgan, George Campbell, 1863- II. Buttrick, George Arthur 1892- III. Title.

FERRE, Nels Fredrick 252
Solomon, 1908-
The extreme center [by] Nels F. S. Ferre. Waco, Tex., Word Books [1973] 184 p. 23 cm. Includes bibliographical references. [BV4253.F428] 73-84581 5.95
1. Sermons, American. I. Title.

FERRE, Nels Fredrick Solomon, 252
1908-
God's new age, a book of sermons. New York, Harper [c.1956-1962] 160p. 62-7285 3.00 bds.,
1. Sermons, American. I. Title.

FERRIS, Theodore 252'.0373
Parker, 1908-
This is the day : selected sermons / Theodore Parker Ferris. 2d ed. Dublin, N.H. : Yankee, c1980. 368 p. : port. ; 23 cm. [BX5937.F42T5 1980] 19 76-39640 ISBN 0-911658-16-5 (pbk.) : 10.00
1. Protestant Episcopal Church in the U.S.A.—Sermons. 2. Sermons, American. I. Title.

FERRISS, Walter, 1768-1806.
Five sermons on the following subjects. viz I. The love of God to his creatures. II. The Christian's evidence of his having passed from death into life. iii. The finite nature of things unseen. iv. God's love to Zion. V. The Lamb of God which taketh away the sin of the world. By The late Rev. Walter Feriss... To which is subjoined a festival sermon by Brother Hosea Ballou, delivered at Chester (Vt.) June 24. A. L. 5806. Randolph (pver.) Printed by Sereno Wright. 1807. 104 p. 23 cm. A 33
1. Sermons, American. I. Ballou, Hosea, 1771-1852. II. Title.

FINNEY, Charles 227'.106
Grandison, 1792-1875.
Principles of victory / Charles G. Finney ; Louis Gifford Parkhurst, Jr., compiler and editor. Minneapolis, Minn. : Bethany House, c1981. p. cm. Bibliography: p. [BS2665.4.F56 1981] 19 81-15464 ISBN 0-87123-471-8 pbk. : 4.95
1. Bible. N.T. Romans—Sermons. 2. Sermons, American. I. Parkhurst, Louis Gifford, 1946- II. Title.

FISHER, Fred C 1884- 252
The kingdom of light. Lakeland, Fla., Alliance Publishers [1948] 237 p. 20 cm. [BV4253.F45] 49-15906
1. Sermons. American. I. Title.

FISHER, Wallace E. 252'.62
Because God cares : messages for Lent and Easter / Wallace E. Fisher. Minneapolis : Augsburg Pub. House, c1980. 112 p. ; 20 cm. [BX8066.F52B4] 19 80-67791 ISBN 0-8066-1852-3 pbk. : 4.75
1. Lutheran Church—Sermons. 2. Sermons, American. I. Title.

FISHER, Wilfred, 1914-- 243
Winning men to Christ. Under auspices of the Kentucky Mountain Holiness Association. [Vancleve? Ky., 1954] 100p. 20cm. [BV4253.F46] 54-37270
1. Sermons, American. I. Title.

FOLJAMBE, Samuel W. 252
The hand of God in American history. A sermon delivered before the executive and legislative departments of the government of Massachusetts, at the annual election, Wednesday,January 5, 1876. By Rev. S. W. Foljambe. Boston, Wright & Potter, state printers, 1876. 58 p. 21 1/2 cm. No. 8 in a volume lettered: Massachusetts election sermons, 18 Printed by order of the Massachusetts House of representatives. [BV4260.M4] 40-19181
I. Title.

FOOT, Joseph Ives, 1796- 252.051
1840.
Sermons of Rev. Joseph I. Foot ... with a brief biographical sketch, by Rev. George Foot. Philadelphia, Hooker & Agnew; New York, Gould, Newman & Saxton, 1841. iv, 5-600 p. 24 1/2 cm. [BX9178.F63S4] 33-15304
1. Sermons, American. I. Foot, George, 1800?-1867. II. Title.

FORBES, Robert, 1844-
The changeless Christ, and other sermons, by Rev. Robert Forbes, D.D. Cincinnati, Jennings and Graham; New York, Eaton and Mains [1905] 116 p. front. (port.) 19 cm. (Half-title: The Methodist pulpit [2d series]) 5-7892
I. Title.

FOSDICK, Harry Emerson, 252.061
1878-
A great time to be alive; sermons on Christianity in wartime, by Harry Emerson Fosdick. New York and London, Harper & brothers [1944] vi p., 2 l., 235 p. 20 cm. "First edition." [BX6333.F57G7] 44-9198
1. Sermons, American. 2. World war, 1939—-Addresses, sermons, etc. I. Title.

FOSDICK, Harry Emerson, 252.061
1878-
The hope of the world; twenty-five sermons on Christianity today, by Harry Emerson Fosdick. New York and London, Harper & brothers, 1933. vii p., 1 l., 240 p. 20 cm. "First edition." [BX6333.F57H6] 33-27365
1. Sermons, American. I. Title.

FOSDICK, Harry Emerson, 252.061
1878-
Living under tension; sermons on Christianity today, by Harry Emerson Fosdick. New York and London, Harper & brothers [c1941] ix, 253 p. 20 cm. "First edition." [BX6333.F57L5] 41-21164
1. Sermons, American. I. Title.

FOSDICK, Harry Emerson, 252.061
1878-
On being fit to live with, sermons on post-war Christianity, by Harry Emerson Fosdick. New York and London, Harper & brothers [1946] ix, [2], 219 p. 19 1/2 cm. "First edition." [BX6333.F58O5] 46-11853
1. Sermons, American. I. Title.

FOSDICK, Harry Emerson, 252.061
1878-
The secret of victorious living. New York, Harper [c.1934-1966] 208p. 21cm. (Chapelbks., 19 H) [BX6333.F57S4] 34-39191 1.45 pap.,
1. Sermons, American. I. Title.

FOSDICK, Harry Emerson, 1878-
The secret of victorious living. New York, Harper & Row [c1966] 208 p. 21 cm. (Harper Chapel Books, CB19H) 68-90734
1. Sermons, American. I. Title.

FOSDICK, Harry Emerson, 252.061
1878-
The secret of victorious living: sermons on Christianity today, by Harry Emerson Fosdick. New York and London, Harper & brothers, 1934. vii, [1] p., 1 l., 246 p. 20 cm. "First edition." [BX6333.F57S4] 34-39191
1. Sermons American. I. Title.

FOSDICK, Harry Emerson, 252.06'1
1878-1969.
A great time to be alive; sermons on Christianity in wartime. Freeport, N.Y., Books for Libraries Press [1972, c1944] vi, 235 p. 23 cm. (Essay index reprint series) [BX6333.F57G7 1972] 78-167341 ISBN 0-8369-2688-9
1. Sermons, American. 2. World War, 1939-1945—Addresses, sermons, etc. I. Title.

FOSDICK, Harry Emerson, 252.061
1878-1969.
What is vital in religion; sermons on contemporary Christian problems. [1st ed.] New York, Harper [1955] 238 p. 22 cm. [BX6333.F57W5] 55-8522
1. Sermons, American. I. Title.

FOSTER, Rupert Clinton, 1888-
The everlasting gospel. Murfreesboro, Tenn., Dehoff publications [1961] 316 p. 20 cm. "Sermons and essays." 63-16797
1. Sermons, American. I. Title.

FOSTER, Rupert Clinton, 1888-
The everlasting gospel. Murfreesboro, Tenn., Dehoff publications [1961] 316 p. 20 cm. "Sermons and essays." 63-16797
1. Sermons, American. I. Title.

FOXCROFT, Thomas, 1697-1769. 252.
The blessings of a soul in health and prospering to be supremely wish'd for. A sermon deliver'd (in part) at a family-meeting in private; Boston, Mar. 3. 1741, 2. By Thomas Foxcroft ... Boston: Printed and sold by S. Kneeland and T. Green. in Queenstreet over against the prison, 1742. 2 p. l., 52 p. 19 cm. Caption: The best wish, a soul in health & prospering. (Half-title: Mr. Foxcroft's sermon upon soul-prosperily and health) [BX7233.F72B4] 6-12823
1. Sermons, American. I. Title.

FRANZMANN, Martin H 252.6
Ha! Ha! among the trumpets, by Martin H. Franzmann. Saint Louis, Concordia

Pub. House [1966] [BX8066.F67H3] 66-15516
1. Sermons, American. I. Title.

FRATERNAL camp-meeting 252.07
sermons, preached by ministers of the various branches of Methodism at the Round lake campmeeting. New York, July, 1874. With an account of the fraternal meeting. Phonographically reported by S. M. Stiles and J. G. Patterson. With an introduction by Bishop Peck. New York Nelson & Phillips; Cincinnati, Hitchcock & Walden, 1875. 498 p. incl. front. 19 cm. [BX8333.A1F7] 33-3412
1. Sermons American. I. Title: Round lake camp-meeting of the Methodist Episcopal church. Fraternal meeting, 1st, 1874. II. Title: Camp-meeting sermons.

FROTHINGHAM, Octavius Brooks, 1822-1895.
The radical pulpit, comprising discourses by O. B. Frothingham and Prof. Felix Adler. New York, D. M. Bennett [n.d.] 1 v. (various pagings) 68-66060
1. Sermons—American. I. Title.

FRY, Evan, 1902-1959. 252'.09'33
Evan Fry : illustrations from radio sermons / edited and compiled by Norman D. Ruoff. [Independence, Mo.] : Herald House, c1975. 160 p. ; 21 cm. Compiled from the author's radio sermons delivered under the title: Hear ye Him. [BX8676.F67 1975] 74-84763 ISBN 0-8309-0131-0 : 6.50
1. Reorganized Church of Jesus Christ of Latter-Day Saints—Sermons. 2. Sermons, American. I. Title: Illustrations from radio sermons.

FULLAM, Everett L. 252'.033
Facets of the faith / Everett L. Fullam. Lincoln, Va. : Chosen Books, c1982. 133 p. ; 21 cm. "Prepared ... as talks for the Episcopal Series of the Protestant Hour produced by the Episcopal Radio-TV Foundation, Atlanta, Georgia"—Pref. [BX5937.F79F33 1982] 19 82-4482 ISBN 0-912376-81-3 pbk. : 4.95
1. Episcopal Church Sermons. 2. Sermons, American. I. Title.
Publisher's address: Lincoln, VA 22078

GADDIS, Maxwell Pierson, 1811- ed. 287
The Ohio conference offering: or. Sermons and sketches of sermons. on familiar and practical subjects, from the living and the dead. In two parts. Edited by Rev. Maxwell P. Gaddis ... Cincinnati. Printed at the Methodist book concern for the editor. 1851. 429 p. front. (port.) 19 cm. [BX8333.A1G3] 6-14385
1. Sermons. American. I. Title.

GARRISON, R. Benjamin. 252'.07
Are you the Christ? And other questions asked about Jesus / R. Benjamin Garrison. Nashville : Abingdon, c1978. 96 p. ; 20 cm. Includes bibliographical references and index. [BX8333.G29A73] 77-11904 ISBN 0-687-01720-3 pbk. : 3.50
1. Methodist Church—Sermons. 2. Sermons, American. I. Title.

GIFFORD, Orrin Phillip, 1847- 252.
Honest debtors; sermons and addresses, by Orrin Philip Gifford, D. D. Philadelphia, Boston [etc.] The Judson press [c1922] 5 p. l., 3-248 p. front. (port.) 20 cm. [BX6333.G5H6] 22-22643
1. Sermons, American. I. Title.

GILKEY, Charles Whitney, 1882- 252.061
Perspectives, by Charles W. Gikey ... with an introduction by Robert R. Wicks ... New York and London, Harper & brothers, 1933. x, 118 p. 20 cm. "First edition." [BX6333.G54P4] 33-7697
1. Sermons, American. I. Title.

GILLINGHAM, E. Leonard, 1931- 252'.076
Dealing with conflict / E. Leonard Gillingham. Nashville : Abingdon, c1982. 143 p. ; 22 cm. [BX8333.G48D4 1982] 19 81-20662 ISBN 0-687-10329-0 : 7.95
1. Methodist Church—Sermons. 2. Sermons, American. I. Title. II. Title: Conflict.

GILMORE, J. Herbert. 261.8'34'51
When love prevails; a pastor speaks to a church in crisis [by] J. Herbert Gilmore. Grand Rapids, Eerdmans [1971] 141 p. 23 cm. "Sermons were preached in the First Baptist Church in Birmingham, Alabama." [BT734.2.G53] 70-162039 3.95
1. Sermons, American. 2. Baptists—Sermons. 3. Church and race problems—Sermons. I. Title.

GLASGOW, Samuel McPheeters, 1883- 248
My tomorrow's self, by Samuel McPheeters Glasgow ... New York, R. R. Smith, inc., 1931. 5 p. l., 3-152 p. 20 cm. Sermons. [BX9178.G53M8] 31-11078
1. Sermons, American. I. Title.

GLENNIE, Alexander. 252
Sermons preached on plantations. Freeport, N.Y., Books for Libraries Press, 1971. viii, 161 p. 23 cm. (Black heritage library collection) Reprint of the 1844 ed. published under title: Sermons preached on plantations to congregations of Negroes. [BV4316.S6G45 1971] 75-161260 ISBN 0-8369-8819-1
1. Sermons, American. I. Title. II. Series.

GOODELL, Charles Le Roy, 1854- 252.07
Radiant reveries, by Charles L. Goodell ... New York [etc.] Fleming H. Revell company [c1932] 3 p. l., 5-154 p. 20 cm. "These sermons were delivered during suceeding Sundays from May 1st. 1932. over the lines of the National broadcasting company."--Foreword. [BX8333.G6R3] 32-32277
1. Sermons, American. I. Title.

GOODELL, Charles LeRoy, 1854- 248
Life reveries, by Charles L. Goodell ... New York, Chicago [etc.] Fleming H. Revell company [c1930] 175 p. 20 cm. "These sermons, which were delivered from June 1st to October 12th, were broadcast over WJZ and associated stations by the National broadcasting company."--Foreword. [BV4253.G57] 31-1608
1. Sermons, American. I. Title.

GOODELL, Charles LeRoy, 1854- 248
Soul reveries, by Charles Goodell ... New York, Chicago [etc.] Fleming H. Revell company [c1931* 180 p. front. (port.) 20 cm. "Sermons delivered ... over the air by the courtesy of the National broadcasting company and associated stations."--Foreword. [BX8333.G6S6] 32-3757
1. Sermons, American. I. Title.

GOSSELINK, Marion Gerard. 252.05'732
The things eternal; sermons of a Dutch dominie. Grand Rapids, Baker Book House, 1967. 85 p. 22 cm. [BX9527.G57T49] 67-28326
1. Reformed Church in America—Sermons. 2. Sermons, American. I. Title.

GOWAN, Donald E. 251
Reclaiming the Old Testament for the Christian pulpit / Donald E. Gowan. Atlanta : John Knox Press, c1980. vi, 163 p. ; 24 cm. Includes bibliographical references and index. [BS1191.5.G68] 79-87743 ISBN 0-8042-0166-8 : 12.50
1. Presbyterian Church—Sermons. 2. Bible. O.T.—Homiletical use. 3. Bible. O.T.—Sermons. 4. Sermons, American. I. Title.

GRAF, Arthur E. 252'.6
Joybells of life; Advent to Easter sermons, includes a Lenten series on favorite hymns, by Arthur E. Graf. Giddings, Tex., Faith Publications [1973] 216 p. 20 cm. [BX8066.G7J69] 73-84707
1. Lutheran Church—Sermons. 2. Sermons, American. 3. Hymns, English—History and criticism. I. Title.

GRAFT, Arthur E
Bought with a price; lenten and stewardship sermons, as well as sermons for various occasions. Springfield, Ill., Faith Publications [1961] 140 p. front. (port.) 20 cm. 64-69756
I. Title.

GRAY, James M 1851- 252.08
The teaching and preaching that counts; expository messages from the Old and the New Testaments, doctrinal, historical, devotional and prophetic, by James M. Gray ... New York [etc.] Fleming H. Revell company [c1934] 153 p. 20 cm. [BX6077.G7T4] 35-244
1. Sermons, American. I. Title.

GREGG, David, 1846-1919. 243
Things of Northfield, and other things that should be in every church, by Rev. David Gregg ... New York, E. B. Treat & company, 1899. 5 p. l., [3]-143 p. front. 19 cm. [BX9178.G7T5] 99-439
1. Sermons, American. I. Title.

GULLIXSON, Thaddeus Frank, 1882- 252.04'1
Down into the arena, and other sermons, by T. F. Gullixson. Minneapolis, Augsburg Pub. House [1968] v, 175 p. 21 cm. [BX8066.G8D6] 68-25800 3.95
1. Lutheran Church—Sermons. 2. Sermons, American. I. Title.

GUNN, John R. 252
A lamp unto my feet, by Rev. John R. Gunn ... New York, R. Long & R. R. Smith, inc., 1932. xii, 177 p. 20 cm. [BV4253.G78] 248 32-4880
1. Sermons, American. I. Title.

GUNN, John R. 226
Snapshots from the Gospels, by John R. Gunn. New York [etc.] Fleming H. Revell company [c1933] 171 p. 20 cm. [BV4253.G84] 252 33-15371
1. Sermons, American. I. Title.

GUNSAULUS, Frank Wakeley, 1856-1921. 252.
Paths to the city of God, by Frank W. Gunsaulus. New York, Chicago [etc.] Fleming H. Revell company [c1906] 3 p. l., 9-311 p. 20 cm. [BX7233.G8P35] 6-41778
1. Sermons, American. I. Title.

HAGEN, John Francis, 1890- 252
Hearts at attention, by John Francis Hagen... New York [etc.] Fleming H. Revell company [c1935] 111 p. 21 cm. Chapel talks at the New York military academy, Cornwall, N.Y. [BV4310.H25] 35-5802
1. Sermons, American. I. New York military academy, Cornwall, N.Y. II. Title.

HAGG, G Erik. 252.041
Sermons for special days. Rock Island, Ill., Augustana Press [1962] 160p. 20cm. [BX8066.H37S4] 62-12912
1. Sermons, American. 2. Lutheran Church—Sermons. I. Title.

HALLOCK, Gerard Benjamin Fleet, 1856- comp. 366.08
Fraternal sermons and addresses, by outstanding ministers of various denominations, and presented to many fraternal orders and their friends on special occasions. There is included also a cyclopedia of illustrations, of testimonies, of quotable poetry and of historical facts, together with prayers for different observances, a series of appropriate texts and themes, scripture and prayers for corner-stone laying, and a collection of brief but suggestive outlines of sermons and addresses. Compiled and edited by Rev. G. B. F. Hallock... New York, R. R. Smith, inc., 1931. xvi, 259 p. 19 1/2 cm. [BV4241.H25] 31-6057
1. Sermons. American. 2. Prayers. 3. Secret societies. 4. Homiletical illustrations. I. Title.

HALLOCK, Gerard Benjamin Fleet, 1856- comp. 252
One hundred choice sermons for children; story sermons, drama sermons, object sermons, sermons for special days and occasions and for the entire church year, by over thirty different ministers most gifted in addressing children and young people, compiled and edited by Rev. G. B. F. Hallock ... New York, George H. Doran company [c1924] xv, 19-290 p. 23 1/2 cm. [BV4315.H27] 24-4981
1. Sermons, American. 2. Children's sermons. I. Title.

HALLOCK, Gerard Benjamin Fleet, 1856- comp. 252
Three hundred five-minute sermons for children, a cyclopedia of choice and practical present-day sermons to children; story sermons, object sermons, drama sermons, lessons from nature, art, science, fables, legends and folk-lore, missionary talks and sermons, with especially ample inclusion of those appropriate to the special days and occasions of the church and secular year, compiled and edited by Rev. G. B. F. Hallock, D.D. Garden City, N.Y.; Doubleday, Doran & company, inc., 1928. xviii p., 1 l. 362 p. 22 cm. [BV4315.H275] 28-30164
1. Sermons, American. 2. Children's sermons. I. Title.

HALLOCK, Robert Crawford, 1857- 251
Dramatized sermons, the new homiletic, by Robert C. Hallock ... New York, George H. Doran company [c1924] viii p., 1 l. 11-281 p. 19 1/2 cm. $1.50 [BV4235.D7H3] 24-13489
I. Title.

HAMILTON, James Wallace, 1900- 252
Ride the wild horses! The Christian use of our untamed impulses. Westwood, N. J., Revell [1952] 160 p. 22 cm. [BV4253.H33] 52-8205
1. Sermons, American. I. Title.

HAMILTON, James Wallace, 1900- 261
The thunder of bare feet. [Westwood, N.J.] Revell [1964] 100 p. 21 cm. (Sermons on Christian social concerns) [BV4253.H34] 64-12200
1. Sermons, American. I. Title.

HAMILTON, James Wallace, 1900-1968. 252
Still the trumpet sounds. Old Tappan, N.Y., Revell [1970] 191 p. 21 cm. [BV4253.H335] 77-112461 4.50
1. Sermons, American. I. Title.

HAMILTON, James Wallace, 1900-1968. 252
What about tomorrow? Old Tappan, N.J., Revell [1972] 187 p. port. 21 cm. [BV4253.H342] 74-177396 ISBN 0-8007-0491-6 4.95
1. Sermons, American. I. Title.

HAMILTON, James Wallace, 1900-1968. 252
Where now is thy God? [By] J. Wallace Hamilton. Old Tappan, N.J., F. H. Revell Co. [1969] 128 p. 21 cm. [BV4253.H343] 69-12837 3.50
1. Sermons, American. I. Title.

HARDEMAN, N. B. 252
Hardeman's tabernacle sermons, a series of twenty-two sermons delivered in the Ryman auditorium, Nashville, Tenn., March 28-April 16, 1922, by N. B. Hardeman ... Nashville, Tenn., McQuiddy printing company, 1922. 287 p. ports. 23 cm. [BX7327.H3H3] 22-16237
I. Title.

HARRELL, Costen Jordan, 1885- 252.07
Christian affirmations. New York, Abingdon Press [1961] 126p. 20cm. [BX333H235C45] 61-11036
1. Sermons, American. 2. Methodist Church—Sermons. I. Title.

HARRINGTON, Donald Szantho. 232.903
As we remember Him. Boston, Beacon Press [1965] xi, 111 p. 24 cm. [BT306.3.H3] 65-20785
1. Jesus Christ — Biog. — Sermons. 2. Sermons, American. 3. Unitarian churches — Sermons. I. Title.

HARRIS, Thomas Lake, 1823-1906. 252
Truth and life in Jesus. Sermons, by the Rev. Thomas L. Harris ... Preached in the Mechanics' institution, David street, Machester, October, November, and December, 1859 ... New York, New church publishing association, 1860. vi, [2], 199 p. 17 cm. [BN9998.H4 1860] 31-4033
1. Sermons, American. I. Title.

HARRISVILLE, Roy A. 252.04'1
Pick up your trumpet [by] Roy A. Harrisville. Minneapolis, Augsburg Pub. House [1970] 135 p. 20 cm. [BX8066.H46P5] 70-101110 2.50
1. Lutheran Church—Sermons. 2. Sermons, American. I. Title.

HAVNER, Vance, 1901- 248.486
Why not just be Christians? Westwood, N. J., F. H. Revell Co. [1964] 128 p. 20 cm. [BX6333.H345W5] 64-20183

1. Sermons, American. 2. Christian life. 3. Baptists — Sermons. I. Title.

HECHT, Abraham B
Spiritual horizons. New York, G. M. T. publishers [1964] ix, 143 p. 24 cm. 65-2233
1. Sermons, American. I. Title.

HECKART, Robert H 252.099
Behold sPilgrim Holiness Church-- Sermons. [BX8795.P456H4] 60-17848
1. Sermons, American. I. Title.

HENRY, Carl Ferdinand Howard, 243
1913-
The evangelical pulpit, comp. by Carl F.H. Henry and Rutherford L. Decker. Grand Rapids, W.B. Eerdmans Pub. Co., 1948- v. 21 cm. [BV4241.H45] 48-2869
1. Sermons, American. I. Decker, Rutherford Losey, joint comp. II. Title.

HENRY, Carl Ferdinand Howard, 252
1913-
New strides of faith, by Carl F. H. Henry. Chicago, Moody Press [1972] 140 p. 22 cm. (Moody evangelical focus) Bibliography: p. 139-140. [BV4253.H46] 72-77956 ISBN 0-8024-5917-X 2.25
1. Sermons, American. I. Title.

HEPWORTH, George Hughes, 252.
1833-1902.
Herald sermons. Second series. By George H. Hepuorth ... New York, E. P. Dutton & company, 1897. iv, 232 p. 19 cm. [BX7233.H37H42] 3-1874
I. Title.

HIBBS, Ben, 1901- comp. 252
White House sermons. Edited by Ben Hibbs. Introduction by Richard Nixon. [1st ed.] New York, Harper & Row [1972] xii, 216 p. 22 cm. [BV4241.H5] 70-184407 ISBN 0-06-063897-4 5.95
1. Sermons, American. I. Title.

HILL, Harry Granison, 252.066
1874-
Rational religion, by Harry Granison Hill ... Cincinnati, O., The Caxton press, 1931. xviii p., 1 l., 321 p. front. (port.) 20 1/2 cm. "Radio sermons given in the temple of the air and broadcast over WLW during the winter of 1930-1931." [BV4301.H5] 31-11929
1. Sermons, American. 2. New thought. I. Title.

HILL, Luther Leonidas, 1823- 287
1893.
Sermons, addresses and papers of Rev. Luther Leonidas Hill, published for private circulation by his children, Montgomery, Alabama, 1919. New York, The Fleming H. Revell press, 1919. 2 p. l., 3-314 p. front., plates, ports. 19 1/2 cm. [BX8333.H55S] 19-18657
I. Title.

HINES, John Elbridge, 231'.7
Bp., 1910-
Thy kingdom come, by John E. Hines. [1st ed.] New York, Morehouse-Barlow, 1967. 123 p. 21 cm. [BX5937.H5T5] 67-12971
1. Protestant Episcopal Church in the U.S.A.—Sermons. 2. Sermons, American. 3. Kingdom of God—Sermons. I. Title.

HOBART, Nehemiah, 1648-1712. 252.
The absence of the Comforter described and lamented, in a discourse on Lam. I. 16. By the Reverend M. Nehemiah Hobart, late pastor of the church of Christ at Newton. [Quotations] New-London: Printed & sold by Timothy Green, 1717. 1 p. l., x, 316 p. 15 1/2 cm. Signature: A-U, X4. "To the reader" signed: Eliphalet Adams. Signatures: A-U, X. "To the reader: signed: Eliphalet Adams. [BX7233.H565A3] 31-13897
1. Sermons, American. I. Adams, Eliphalet, 1677-1753. II. Title.

HOEKSEMA, Herman. 227'.106
God's eternal good pleasure / Herman Hoeksema ; edited and partially rev. by Homer C. Hoeksema. Grand Rapids, Mich. : Reformed Free Pub. Association : distributed by Kregel Publications, [c1979] 371 p. ; 23 cm. [BS2665.4.H63] 79-65565 ISBN 0-916206-19-X : 9.95
1. Protestant Reformed Churches of America—Sermons. 2. Bible. N.T. Romans IX-XI—Sermons. 3. Sermons, American. I. Hoeksema, Homer C. II. Title.

HOLLAND, John W. 248
Life's pay checks; sermonettes for everyday life, by John W. Holland ... New York, Chicago [etc.] Fleming H. Revell company [c1930] 127 p. 19 1/2 cm. [BX8333.H57L5] 31-1509
1. Sermons, American. I. Title.

HOLMES, John Haynes, 1879- 252.08
The sensible man's view of religion, by John Haynes Holmes; with an introduction by Stephen S . Wise. New York and London, Harper & brothers, 1933. ix p., 1 l., 126 p. 20 cm. "First edition." [BX9843.H72S4] 33-17920
1. Sermons, American. I. Title.

HOPKINS, Samuel, 1721-1803.
Sin, thro' divine interposition, an advantage--to the universe; and yet, this no excuse for sin, or encouragement to it. Illustrated and proved: and God's wisdom and holiness in the permission of sin; and that His will herein is the same with His revealed will: shewn and confirmed. In three sermons, from Rom. III. 5, 6, 7, 8. By Samuel Hopkins, A.M., a minister of the gospel at Sheffield... Boston, Printed and sold by Daniel and John Kneeland, opposite to the prison in Queen-street, 1759. 1 p. l., iii. 66 p. 21 cm. A34
1. Sermons, American. I. Title.

HORNE, Hugh R. 230.6
Light on great Bible themes. Grand Rapids, Mich., Eerdmans [c.1964] 103p. 23cm. 63-20682 2.50
1. Sermons, American. 2. Baptists— Sermons. I. Title.

HORTON, Wade H. 252'.09'9
Evangel sermons / Wade H. Horton. Cleveland, Tenn. : Pathway Press, c1977. 127 p. ; 21 cm. Sermons printed in the Church of God evangel, 1974-1976. [BX7034.Z6H673] 76-57860 ISBN 0-87148-287-8 : 2.50
1. Church of God (Cleveland, Tenn.)— Sermons. 2. Sermons, American. I. Title.

HOUGH, Lynn Harold, 1877- 252.07
The university of experience, by Lynn Harold Hough; with an introduction by Reinhold Niebuhr. New York and London, Harper & brothers, 1932. ix, 122 p. 20 cm. "First edition." [BX8333.H6U8] 33-1428
1. Sermons, American. I. Title.

HOVIS, William Forney. 252.07
Poetic sermons, by William Forney Hovis ... New York [etc.] Fleming H. Revell company [c1932] 149 p. 19 1/2 cm. Prose and verse. [BX8333.H68P6] 32-24818
1. Sermons, American. I. Title.

HOW can these be?
Grand Rapids? Zondervan Publishing House, 1961. 87p.
1. Sermons, American. 2. Sermons, Baptist. I. Lewis, Bill H

HOWARD, Henry, 1859- 252.05
The defeat of fear, and other studies, by Henry Howard ... New York, Chicago [etc.] Fleming H. Revell company [c1931] 217 p. 19 1/2 cm. [BX9178.H6D4] 31-25651
1. Sermons, American. I. Title.
Contents omitted.

HUDNUT, Robert K. 252'.05'1
An active man and the Christ, by Robert K. Hudnut. Philadelphia, Fortress Press [1972] xiv, 114 p. 18 cm. Includes bibliographical references. [BX9178.H7A25] 72-75650 ISBN 0-8006-0119-X 2.50
1. Presbyterian Church—Sermons. 2. Sermons, American. I. Title.

HUTCHENS, Paul. 252
When God says 'No,' and other radio address by Paul Hutchens, Grand Rapids, Mich., Wm. B. Eerdmans publishing co., 1943. 72 p. 20 cm. [BV4301.H8] 43-5070
1. Sermons, American. I. Title.

HUTTENLOCKER, Keith. 252
Alive; steps to personal renewal. Anderson, Ind., Warner Press [1970] 111 p. port. 19 cm. [BV4253.H84] 75-102374
1. Sermons, American. I. Title.

IRONSIDE, Henry Allan, 1876- 252
"Charge that to my account" and other gospel messages, by H. A. Ironside ... Chicago, The Bible institute colportage association [c1931] 3 p. l., 5-122 p., 1 l. 19 cm. [BV3797.I7] 31-34424
1. Sermons, American. I. Title.

IRONSIDE, Henry Allan, 1876- 252
Divine priorities, and other messages, by H. A. Ironside... New York [etc.] Fleming H. Revell company [1945] 104 p. 19 1/2 cm. [BV4253.I7] 45-3139
1. Sermons, American. I. Title.

IVINS, Dan. 220.9'2
God's people in transition / Dan Ivins. Nashville, Tenn. : Broadman Press, c1981. 153 p. ; 20 cm. [BS571.5.I93 1981] 19 80-65971 ISBN 0-8054-6932-X pbk. : 6.95
1. Bible—Biography—Sermons. 2. Sermons, American. 3. Baptists—Sermons. I. Title.

JENKINS, Burris Atkins, 252.066
1869-
My job-preaching; samples for preachers and laymen, by Burris Jenkins. Nashville, Tenn., Cokesbury press [c1932] 220 p. 19 cm. [BX7327.J4M8] 32-25306
1. Sermons, American. I. Title.

JOHNSON, Merle 252'.07'674
Allison.
Ancient fires for modern man, by Merle Allison Johnson "Pastor X." Nashville, Tidings [1973] 87 p. 19 cm. [BX8333.J58A6] 72-95672 1.25 (pbk.)
1. Methodist Church—Sermons. 2. Sermons, American. I. Title.

JONES, Edgar De Witt, 252.066
1876-
Blundering into paradise, by Edgar DeWitt Jones; with an introduction by Gaius Glenn Atkins. New York and London, Harper & brothers, 1932. x, 126 p. 20 cm. "First edition." [BX7327.J8B6] 33-1760
1. Sermons, American. I. Title.

JONES, Samuel Porter, 1847- 243
1906.
Sam Jones' sermons. Chicago, Rhodes & McClure, 1896. 2 v. fronts., illus. (ports.) 21 cm. Paged continuously. [BV3797.J85S4 1896] 37-39619
1. American sermons. 2. Methodist church—Sermons. 3. Sermons American. I. Title.

KANE, John Henry, 1901- 252
Bible chats, by John H. Kane. Anderson, Ind., The Warner press [c1942] 2 p. l., vii-viii, [2], ix-x, 11-150 p. illus. (ports.) 19 1/2 cm. [BV4301.K3] 43-6960
1. Sermons, American. I. Title.

KELLER, Edward L. comp. 252
Great sermons by young preachers, compiled by Edward L. Keller ... New York, R. R. Smith, inc., 1931. xii, 244 p. 20 cm. [BV4241.K4] 31-11799
1. Sermons, American. I. Title.

KELLER, Edward Levi, 1884- 252
comp.
Great sermons by young preachers, compiled by Edward L. Keller ... New York, R. R. Smith, inc., 1931. xii, 244 p. 19 1/2 cm. [BV4241.K4] 31-11799
1. Sermons, American. I. Title.

KEMPER, Frederick W. 232.9'6
The trials of Jesus : meditations and sermons for Lent and Easter / Frederick W. Kemper. St. Louis : Concordia Pub. House, c1977. 95 p. ; 21 cm. [BT431.K45] 76-40444 ISBN 0-570-03743-3 : 3.95
1. Jesus Christ—Passion—Sermons. 2. Lutheran Church—Sermons. 3. Sermons, American. I. Title.

KEMPTON, A[rthur] C 1870-1900.
Pilgrim sermons, by A. C. Kempton. Chicago, New York [etc.] F. H. Revell company, c1903. 248 p., 1 l. front. (port.) 19 cm. 4-3356
I. Title.

KERNAHAN, Arthur Earl, 1888- 252
comp.
Great sermons for growing disciples, compiled by A. Earl Kernahan ... New York [etc.] Fleming H. Revell company [c1934] 160 p. 19 1/2 cm. [BV4241.K44] 35-500
1. Sermons, American. I. Title.

KERR, Hugh Thomson, 1871- 252.051
Old things new, by Hugh Thomson Kerr... New York, Chicago [etc.] Fleming H. Revell company [c1931] 192 p. 19 1/2 cm. Sermons. [BX9178.K4O6] 31-14633
1. Sermons, American. I. Title.

KERSHNER, Howard Eldred, 248.42
1891-
Diamonds, persimmons, and stars. New York, Bkmailer. [1964] 163p. 22cm. 64-18966 3.00
1. Sermons, American. I. Title.

KETCHAM, Robert Thomas, 252.06
1889-
Sermons [2v.] Des Plaines, Ill., Regular Baptist Pr. 188 Oakton Blvd. [c.1966] 2v. (176; 176p.) 20cm. Contents.v.1. The death hymn of Christ, and other sermons.--v.2. Why was Christ a carpenter, and other sermons. [BX6333.K45S4] 66-15924 2.95 ea., sBaptists--Sermons.
1. Sermons, American. 2. Sermons, American. I. Title.

KILLINGER, John, comp. 252
Experimental preaching. Edited by John Killinger. Nashville, Abingdon Press [1973] 175 p. 21 cm. [BV4241.K48] 72-8419 ISBN 0-687-12423-9 3.95
1. Sermons, American. 2. Preaching. I. Title.
Contents omitted.

KILLINGER, John 252
The thickness of glory. Nashville, Abingdon [c.1964, 1965] 158p. 20cm. [BV4253.K5] 65-10811 2.75 bds.,
1. Sermons, American. I. Title.

KILLINGER, John. 252
The thickness of glory. New York, Abingdon Press [1965] 158 p. 20 cm. [BV4253.K5 1965] 65-10811
1. Sermons, American. I. Title.

KINARD, J. Spencer, 252'.09'33
1940-
The worth of a smile : spoken words for daily living / by J. Spencer Kinard. Englewood Cliffs, N.J. : Prentice-Hall, c1976. 217 p. ; 21 cm. Essays delivered by the author on the Mormon Tabernacle Choir's weekly program, Music and the spoken word. Includes bibliographical references and index. [BX8639.K56W67] 75-42298 ISBN 0-13-969139-1 : 5.95
1. Church of Jesus Christ of Latter-Day Saints—Sermons. 2. Sermons, American. I. Title.

KIRBY, Wallace H. 252'.076
The ordinary becomes extraordinary / Wallace H. Kirby ; photographs by Burnie Batchelor. Raleigh, N.C. (228 W. Edenton St., Raleigh, 27603) : Edenton Street United Methodist Church, c1980. 164 p., [8] p. of plates : col. ill. ; 24 cm. [BX8333.K54O73] 19 80-69653 12.50
1. Methodist Church—Sermons. 2. Sermons, American. I. Title.

KLEISER, Grenville, 1868- 252
comp.
Vital sermons; model addresses for study, compiled by Grenville Kleiser; for the exclusive use of Grenville Kleiser's mail course students. New York and London, Funk & Wagnalls company [c1935] viii, 292 p. 21 cm. On cover: Public speaking. [BV4241.K58] 35-8617
1. Sermons, American. 2. Preaching. I. Title.

KRONER, Richard, 1884- 252
The new dimension of the soul; chapel addresses. Foreword by Henry Pitney Van Dusen. Edited by John E. Skinner. Philadelphia, Fortress Press [1964, c1963] xi, 147 p. 18 cm. [BV4316.T5K7] 63-19549
1. Sermons, American. 2. Theological seminaries — Sermons. I. Title.

KRUMBINE, Miles Henry, 252.041
1891-
Little evils that lay waste life, by Miles H. Krumbine ... with an introduction by Lynn Harold Hough. New York and London, Harper & brothers, 1933. xi, 128 p. 20 cm. "First edition." [BX8066.K65L5] 33-13474
1. Sermons, American. I. Title.

KUEGELE, Frederick, 1846- 252.041
1916.
Country sermons ... By F. Kuegele ... Baltimore, Md., 1895-1901. 4 v. 21-21 cm. Title varies slightly. Vols. 3 and 4 have imprint: Crimora, Va., Augusta publishing

company. Contents.--i-ii. On free texts.--iii-iv. Gospel sermons. [BX8066.K75C6 1895] 1-12838
1. Sermons American 2. Lutheran church—Sermons. I. Title.

KYKER, Rex P., 1921- 252'.0663
Sermons for today / by Rex P. Kyker. Abilene, Tex. : Biblical Research Press, c1980- v. ; 22 cm. [BX7077.Z6K94] 19 80-50106 ISBN 0-89112-401-2 (v. 1) : 9.95
1. Churches of Christ—Sermons. 2. Sermons, American. I. Title.

LACY, Donald Charles, 1933- 252'.07'6
Gems from James / by Donald Charles Lacy. Philadelphia : Dorrance, [1974] 61 p. ; 22 cm. [BS2785.4.L32] 74-78302 ISBN 0-8059-2024-2 : 4.95
1. Methodist Church—Sermons. 2. Bible. N.T. James—Sermons. 3. Sermons, American. I. Title.

LANGDON, Addison L 1844-
A book of Sunday sermons. Meditations of twenty years, by Addison L. Langdon, "The evangelist" ... Selected ... Quincy, Ill., The Empire publishing company, 1896. 144 p. illus. (port.) 24 cm. [PS2199.L65B6] 27-25721
I. Title.

LARRISON, C. Owen. 287
The pearly gates; or, Open portals to the better land. By Rev. C. Owen Larrison ... [Central City, Nebr.] The author, 1899. 102 p. incl. front. (port.) 20 cm. [BX8333.L25P4] 99-3583
1. Sermons, American. I. Title.

LARSEN, Paul E. 223'.7'06
Wise up & live! Wisdom from Proverbs [by] Paul E. Larsen. Glendale, Calif., G/L Regal Books [1974] 239 p. 18 cm. "A Bible commentary for laymen." Includes bibliographical references. [BS1465.4.L37] 73-86222 ISBN 0-8307-0219-9 1.25 (pbk.).
1. Bible. O.T. Proverbs—Sermons. 2. Sermons, American. I. Title.

LARSON, Bruce. 252'.051
Believe and belong / Bruce Larson. Old Tappan, N.J. : Power Books, c1982. 155 p. ; 21 cm. [BX9178.L36B44] 19 81-23508 ISBN 0-8007-1288-9 : 6.95
1. Presbyterian Church—Sermons. 2. Sermons, American. I. Title.

LAURIN, Roy Leonard, 1898- 252
What the Bible says ... by Roy L. Laurin; series no. 1- [Los Angeles, c1941- v. illus. 19 cm. "The ... messages were ... given ... to the radio audience of The family Bible' ... over station KHJ, Los Angeles."--Pref., v. 1. [BV4301.L38] 41-9446
1. Sermons, American. I. Title.

LAW, Marion. 252.
Horizons, and other sermons, by the Rev. Marion Law ... Milwaukee, Wis., Morehouse publishing co. [c1928] ix p., 1 l., 253, [1] p. 19 cm. [BX5937.L2H6] 28-13129
I. Title.

LAW, Marion, 1869-1930. 237.2
Beyond the veil, and other sermons, by the late Rev. Marion Law ... Milwaukee, Wis., Morehouse publishing co. [c1931] xii p., 1 l., 290 p. 20 cm. [BX5937.L2B4] 31-7156
1. Sermons, American. 2. Immortality. I. Title.

THE Laymen's hour (Radio program) 252.06131
Four-minute talks for laymen [by] Gene E. Bartlett [and others] Valley Forge [Pa.] Judson Press [1966] 128 p. 22 cm. "52 talks which were broadcast on The Laymen's hour." Bibliographical footnotes. [BX6333.A1L26] 66-12538
1. Sermons, American. 2. Baptists — Sermons. I. Bartlett, Gene E. II. Title.

LAYMEN'S hour (The) 252.06131
(Radio program) Four-minute talks for laymen [by] Gene E. Bartlett [others] Valley Forge[Pa.] Judson Pr. [1966] 128p. 22cm. 52 talks which were broadcast on the layman's hour. Bibl. [BX6333.A1L26] 66-12538 1.95 pap.,
1. Sermons, American. 2. Baptists—Sermons. I. Bartlett, Gene E.

LEACH, William Herman, 1888- comp. 252
Prize sermons, Church management contest, compiled by William H. Leach; board of judges, Gaius Glenn Atkins, Charles W. Ferguson, William Peter King, William H. Leach [and] J. W. G. Ward. Nashville, Cokesbury press [c1934] 222 p. 19 cm. The leading seventeen sermons of the 1934 Church management sermon contest, including the winning sermon "The margin of goodness" by W. O. Carrington. cf. Foreword. "The men who wrote these sermons": p. 213-222. [BV4241.L4] 35-1041
1. Sermons, American. I. Carrington, Williiam Orlando, 1878-The margin of goodness. II. Church management. III. Title.

LEAVELL, Landrum P. 252'.6
Sermons for celebrating / Landrum P. Leavell. Nashville : Broadman Press, c1978. 138 p. ; 20 cm. [BX6333.L3948S47] 77-90220 ISBN 0-8054-2231-5 pbk. : 2.75
1. Sermons, American. 2. Baptists—Sermons. I. Title.

*LEE, Luther, 1800-1889. 252.07173
Five sermons and a tract, edited with and introduction by Donald W. Dayton. Chicago, Holrad House, 1975. 135 p. 23 cm. [BV4211] 3.00 (pbk.)
1. Sermons, American. 2. Wesleyan Methodist Church of America. I. Title.
Publisher's address: 5104 N. Christiana Ave. 60625.

LEE, Robert Greene, 1886- 252'.06'1
Latest of Lee [by] Robert G. Lee. Jefferson City, Mo., Le Roi Publishers [1973] 123 p. 22 cm. Sermons. [BX6333.L3953L37] 72-94717 4.95
1. Sermons, American. 2. Baptists—Sermons. I. Title.

LEE, Robert Greene, 1886-
The place called heaven. Orlando, Christ for the World publishers [c1959] 58 p. 63-50602
1. Sermons, American. 2. Sermons, Baptist. I. Title.

LEESTMA, Harold F. 252
Listen to the wind : how to live your faith / Harold F. Leestma. Waco, Tex. : Word Books, [1974] 100 p. ; 21 cm. Consists of previously delivered messages. [BV4253.L33] 74-82659 pbk. : 2.95
1. Sermons, American. I. Title.

LEMONS, Frank W., 1901- 252.09'9
Perennial Pentecost [by] Frank W. Lemons. [1st ed.] Cleveland, Tenn., Pathway Press [1971] 126 p. 16 cm. [BX7020.Z6L45] 74-167943
1. Church of God—Sermons. 2. Sermons, American. I. Title.

LETCHFORD, Peter. 242'.722
Help! I don't know how to pray. Amen / by Peter Letchford. 1st ed. Nashville : Impact Books, c1976. 146 p. ; 21 cm. [BV230.L435] 76-29332 4.95
1. Lord's prayer—Sermons. 2. Sermons, American. I. Title.

LINTNER, Robert Caspar, 1892- 252
Clouds for chariots, by Robert Caspar Linter. New York [etc.] Fleming H. Revell company [c1940] 3 p. l., 9-121 p. 20 cm. [BV4253.L5] 40-9272
1. Sermons, American. I. Title.

LITTLE, Charles Joseph, 1840-1911. 252.
The angel in the flame; sermons preached at Evanston, Ill., in the First Methodist Episcopal church, by Charles J. Little ... Cincinnati, Jennings and Pye; New York, Eaton and Mains [1904] 143 p. front. (port.) 19 cm. (Half-title: The Methodist pulpit) [BX8333.L5A6] 4-5001
I. Title.

LOCKYER, Herbert. 241
"V" for victory; sermons on the Christian's victories, by Herbert Lockyer ... Grand Rapids, Mich., Zondervan publishing house [c1941] 3 p. l., 11-99 p. 20 cm. [BV4253L63] 42-3777
1. Sermons, American. I. Title.

LORD, Eleazer, 1788-1871. 922.573
Memoir of the Rev. Joseph Stibbs Christmas. By E. Lord. New York, J. P. Haven and J. Leavitt, 1831. vii, [13]-213 p. 20 cm. Sermons by Mr. Christmas: p. 115-213. [BX9225.C53L6] 36-21119
1. Christmas, Joseph Stibbs, 1808-1830. 2. Sermons, American. I. Title.

LORING, Israel, 1682-1772.
The service of the Lord must be chosen presently and without delay. A sermon preach'd at Concord, Dec. 29. 1737 at the request of two religious societies of young men there. And now publish'd at the desire of many who heard it. To which, two more are added, and both preach'd at Concord. Shewing, i. That persons may be very confident, that they are real Christians, when they are utterly destitute of saving grace. ii. That men should pray for spiritual light, that they may behold the wonderous truths which are treasured up in God's word. By Israel Loring, M. A., pastor of a church in Sudbury. Boston, Printed by S. Kneeland and T. Green, for J. Edwards, at his shop in Cornhill, 1738. 1 p. l., 138 p. 13 x 7 cm. "Books printed for, and sold by J. Edwards, at his shop in Cornhill": 3 p. at end. The titles of the two additional sermond are, "False hopes discovered," and "spiritual light to be prayed for." 3-3881
I. Title.

LUCCOCK, Robert Edward, 1915- 252.6
The power of His name; a book of sermons. [1st ed.] New York, Harper [1960] 159p. 22cm. [BV4253.L824] 60-8138
1. Sermons, American. I. Title.

MACARTHUR, Robert Stuart, 1841-
Advent, Christmas, New Year, Easter, and other sermons, by Robert Stuart MacArthur ... Philadelphia, New York [etc.] American Baptist publication society [1908] 285 p. 20 cm. 8-7590
I. Title.

MACARTNEY, Clarence Edward Noble, 1879- 220.92
The greatest men of the Bible, by Clareermons. [BS571.M225] 41-17712
1. Sermons, American. I. Title.

MACARTNEY, Clarence Edward Noble, 1879-1957. 252.05
Along life's highway. Compiled and edited by Harry E. Farra. Grand Rapids, Mich., Baker Book House [1969] 103 p. 21 cm. ([The New minister's handbook series]) [BX9178.M172A63] 75-97726 2.95
1. Presbyterian Church—Sermons. 2. Sermons, American. I. Title.

MCCRACKEN, Robert James. 252
Questions people ask. New York, Harper [1951] 188 p. 21 cm. [BV4253.M27] 51-8607
1. Sermons, American. I. Title.

MCGAUGHEY, C. E., 1905- 252.6'63
The hope of the world, by C. E. McGaughey. Abilene, Tex., Biblical Research Press [1971] v, 198 p. 23 cm. (The 20th century sermons series, v. 6) On spine: 20th century sermons. [BX7077.Z6M24] 74-180791 4.50
1. Churches of Christ—Sermons. 2. Sermons, American. I. Title.

MCGEE, J Vernon. 252
The fruit of the sycamore tree, and other sermons. Wheaton, Ill., Van Kampen Press [1952] 81 p. 20 cm. [BV4253.M37] 52-1202
1. Sermons, American. I. Title.

MCGEE, John Vernon, 1904- 252
The fruit of the sycamore tree, and other sermons. Wheaton, Ill., Van Kampen Press [1952] 81p. 20cm. [BV4253.M37] 52-1202
1. Sermons, American. I. Title.

MCKEE, Elmore McNeill, 1896- ed.
Preaching in the new era, edited by Elmore McNeill McKee... Garden City, N.Y., Doubleday, Doran & company, inc., 1929. xviii, 270 p. 21 cm. [BC4241.M26] 29-10524
1. Sermons, American. I. Title.

MCKEE, Elmore McNeill, 1896- ed. 252.5
What can students believe? Sermons by Harry Emerson Fosdick, James Rowland Angell, Ernest Fremont Tittle [and others] ...Arranged by Elmore McNeill McKee... New York, R. R. Smith, inc., 1931. vi p., 2 l., 3-138 p. 19 1/2 cm. "Ten sermons preached in the Yale chapel."--Pref. [BV4241.M263] 31-6410
1. Sermons, American. I. Fosdick, Harry Emerson, 1878- II. Yale university. III. Title.

MACKENZIE, Robert, 1845-1925. 243
The loom of Providence, by Robert Mackenzie, D.D. New York, Chicago [etc.] Fleming H. Revell company [c1904] 3 p. l., 5-253 p. 21 cm. (Half-title: The international pulpit) [BX9178.M2453L6] 4-22963
1. Sermons, American. I. Title.

*MC KENZIE, E. C. comp. 251.02
2700 quotes for sermons and addresses comp. by E. C. McKenzie. Grand Rapids, Baker Book House [1974] 140 p. 22 cm. [BV4223] ISBN 0-8010-5948-8 1.95 (pbk.)
1. Sermons, American. 2. Quotations. I. Title.

MCKIM, Randolph Harrison, 1842-1920. 252.
The gospel in the Christian year and in Christian experience; practical sermons for the people, Advent to Trinity, by Randolph H. McKim... New York, London [etc.] Longmans, Green, and co., 1902. xii, 343 p. 19 1/2 cm. [BX5937.M2756G6] 2-25771
1. Sermons, American. I. Title.

MCLELLAN, Hugh. 252
Hugh McLellan's sermons... St. Louis, Mo., The Bethany press, 1928. 151 p. 20 cm. [BX7327.M28A4] 29-944
I. Title.

MACLENNAN, David Alexander, 1903- 252.05'1
Sermons from Thanksgiving to Easter [by] David A. MacLennan. Valley Forge [Pa.] Judson Press [1968] 156 p. 23 cm. [BX9178.M1786S4] 68-13607 3.95
1. Presbyterian Church—Sermons. 2. Sermons, American. I. Title.

MACLENNAN, David Alexander, 1903- 252.6
Sermons of faith and hope [by] David A. MacLennan. Valley Forge [Pa.] Judson Press [1971] 144 p. 23 cm. Includes bibliographical references. [BX9178.M265S4] 73-144083 ISBN 0-8170-0509-9 4.95
1. Presbyterian Church—Sermons. 2. Sermons, American. I. Title.

MACMULLEN, Wallace, 1860- 287
The Captain of our faith, by Rev. Wallace MacMullen... Cincinnati, Jennings and Graham; New York, Eaton & Mains [c1904] 4 p. l., 7-139 p. front. (port.) 19 cm. (Half-title: The Methodist pulpit) [BX8333.M3C3] 4-19454
1. Sermons, American. I. Title.

MAFFITT, John Newland, 1794-1850. 287
Pulpit sketches. By Rev. John Newland Maffit...First series. Louisville, Ky., W. H. Johnston, 1839. xi, [13]-178 p. 18 1/2 cm. [BX8333.M33P8] 9-3810
1. Sermons, American. I. Title.

MAIER, Walter Arthur, 1893- 252.041
The Lutheran hour; winged words to modern America, broadcast in the coast to coast radio crusade for Christ, by Walter A. Maier ... St. Louis, Mo., Concordia publishing house, 1931. xii, 324 p. 20 cm. [BX8066.M25L3] 32-1315
1. Sermons, American. 2. Lutheran church—Sermons. I. Title.

MALLOUGH, Don. 252.09'9
Crowded detours. Grand Rapids, Mich., Baker Book House [1970] 111 p. 21 cm. [BX6198.A7M3] 72-115636 2.95
1. Assemblies of God, General Council—Sermons. 2. Sermons, American. I. Title.

MALLOUGH, Don 252.099
If I were God. Grand Rapids, Baker Bk. [c.1966] 109p. 21cm. [BV4253.M377] 67-2290 1.95
1. Sermons, American. I. Title.

MANN, Leonard W. 252'.07'6
The best of the good news / edited by Leonard W. Mann. Nashville : Tidings, [1974] v, 98 p. ; 19 cm. [BX8333.A1M3] 74-80894 pbk. : 1.50
1. Methodist Church—Sermons. 2. Sermons, American. I. Title.

MARSHALL, Peter, 1902- 252'.05'1 1949.
Mr. Jones, meet the Master; sermons and prayers of Peter Marshall. Boston, G. K. Hall, 1973 [c1950] 330 p. 25 cm. Large print ed. Includes bibliographical references. [BX9178.M363M5 1973] 73-9911 ISBN 0-8161-6132-1 9.95 (lib. bdg.)
1. Presbyterian Church—Sermons. 2. Sermons, American. 3. Prayers. I. Title.

MARSTEN, Francis Edward, 252.051 1851-1915.
The freedom of Christ and other lectures, by Francis E. Marsten ... Boston, D. Lothrop company [c1891] 4 p. l., [11]-328 p. 19 cm. [BX9178.M3652F7] 32-13527
1. Sermons, American. I. Title.

MAULDIN, Kenneth, 1918- 252'.05'1
Table talk with Jesus / Kenneth Mauldin. Nashville : Abingdon Press, [1979] p. cm. [BS2595.4.M38] 78-13750 ISBN 0-687-40820-2 : 3.75
1. Presbyterian Church—Sermons. 2. Bible. N.T. Luke—Sermons. 3. Sermons, American. I. Title.

MEAD, Frank Spencer, 252.0082 1898- ed.
The pulpit in the South; sermons of today. New York, Revell [1950] 220 p. 21 cm. [BV4241.M4] 50-11379
1. Sermons, American. I. Title.

MEAD, Sidney Earl, 1904- 252
Love and learning / Sidney E. Mead ; introd. by Martin E. Marty ; edited by Mary Lou Doyle. Chico, CA : New Horizons Press, 1978. p. cm. Bibliography: p. [BV4253.M43] 78-14207 ISBN 0-914914-13-8 : 10.00. ISBN 0-914914-12-X pbk. : 5.00
1. Sermons, American. I. Doyle, Mary Lou. II. Title.

MEEKS, Rufus Polk.
At the feet of Jesus; or, Twenty-five sermons concerning the Saviour ... With a life-sketch of the author, and of his father. Cincinnati, The Standard pub. co. [1899] vi, 345 p. port. 8 degrees. Oct
I. Title.

MEEKS, Rufus Polk, 1849- 232
At the feet of Jesus; or, Twenty-five sermons concerning the Saviour, by R. P. Meeks. With a life-sketch of the author, and of his father ... Cincinnati, The Standard publishing company [1899] vi, 345 p. front., ports. 23 1/2 cm. "Life-sketch of the author" (p. 1-17) signed: Mollie L. Meeks. "General John H. Meeks" (p. 18-31) signed: T. B. L. [i.e. Theophilus Brown Larimore] [BT201.M35] 99-4676
1. Jesus Christ—Person and offices. 2. Meeks, John Henderson, 1814. 3. Sermons, American. I. Meeks, Mollie (Larimore) 1852- II. Larimore, Theophilus Brown, 1843-1929. III. Title.

MELEAR, James Melville. 287
Hopes that perish, and other sermons. By James M. Mellear ... Knoxville, Tenn., Ogdon bros. & co., printers, 1899. 3 p. l., 128 p. front. (port.) 20 cm. [BX8333.M4H6] 99-1323
1. Sermons, Americans. I. Title.

MERCER, Robert Hampton. 252.03
The soul's anchorage. Boston, Christopher Publ. House [1964] 209 p. 21 cm. [BX5937.M523S6] 64-15616
1. Sermons, American. 2. Protestant Episcopal Church in the U.S.A. — Sermons. I. Title.

MERRITT, George W. 252'.06'63
Truth for today : [five-minute radio sermons] / by George W. Merritt ; illustrated by Merlyn Jones. Nashville : Gospel Advocate Co., c1976. x, 187 p. : ill. ; 20 cm. [BX7327.M584T78] 76-18471 ISBN 0-89225-203-0
1. Christian Church (Disciples of Christ)—Sermons. 2. Sermons, American. I. Title.

MILLER, Charles Edward, 252.02 1929-
Announcing the good news; homilies on the "A" cycle of readings for Sundays and holy days [by] Charles E. Miller, Oscar J. Miller, and Michael M. Roebert. Staten Island, N.Y., Alba House [1971] xii, 196 p. 21 cm. [BX1756.A2M55] 74-169144 ISBN 0-8189-0215-9 3.95
1. Catholic Church—Sermons. 2. Sermons, American. I. Miller, Oscar J., 1913- II. Roebert, Michael M. III. Title.

MILLER, Charles Edward, 252'.02 1929-
Breaking the bread; homilies on the "B" cycle of readings for Sundays and holy days [by] Charles E. Miller, Oscar J. Miller [and] Michael M. Roebert. Staten Island, N.Y., Alba House [1972] xi, 214 p. 21 cm. [BX1756.A2M56] 72-6155 ISBN 0-8189-0254-X 3.95
1. Catholic Church—Sermons. 2. Sermons, American. I. Miller, Oscar J., 1913- II. Roebert, Michael M. III. Title.

MILLER, Charles Edward, 252'.6 1929-
Opening the treasures : a book of daily homily-meditations / Charles E. Miller. New York, N.Y. : Alba House, c1982. xv, 555 p. ; 21 cm. [BX1756.M554O63] 19 81-19095 ISBN 0-8189-0424-0 : 12.95
1. Catholic Church—Sermons. 2. Sermons, American. I. Catholic Church. Lectionary for Mass (U.S.). Sundays and feasts. II. Title.

MILLIS, William Alfred, 252. 1868-
Half hours with college students, by William Alfred Millis ... Boston, Mass., The Stratford company, 1926. 4 p. l., 200 p. 19 cm. Sermons. [BV4310.M55] 26-4588
I. Title.

MONDAY club.
Sermons on the International Sunday-school lessons for 1876-19 [1st]- series. Boston, Chicago, The Pilgrim press, 1876-19 v. 20 cm. Imprint varies. [BV1560.M6] 0-6941
1. Sermons, American. I. Title. II. Title: International Sunday-school lessons.

MOODY, Dwight Lyman, 1837- 243 1899.
Moody's great sermons; twenty-four discourses, by Dwight L. Moody ... Complete biography of the famous revivalist. Entirely new ed. Chicago, Laird & Lee [1899] 2 p. l., iii-x, 347 p. 2 port. (incl. front.) 20 cm. [BV3797.M7G85] 0-924
1. Sermons, American. I. Title.

MOODY, Dwight Lyman, 1837- 252 1899
Moody's latest sermons. Authorized ed. Grand Rapids, Mich., Baker Bk. [1965] 126p. facsim. 20cm. [BV3797.M7L3] 65-20555 1.95 bds.,
1. Sermons, American. 2. Evangelistic sermons. I. Title.

MOODY, Dwight Lyman, 1837- 252 1899.
Moody's latest sermons. Authorized edition, printed from verbatim reports. Chicago, New York [etc.] Fleming H. Revell company, 1900. 2 p. l., 9-126 p. 19 cm. [BV3797.M7L3 1900 a] 37-7784
1. Sermons, American. I. Title.

MOORE, Arthur James, Bp., 252.07 1888-
Fight on! Fear not! [Sermons] Nashville, Abingdon [c.1962] 144p. 21cm. 62-19133 2.50
1. Sermons, American. 2. Methodist Church—Sermons. I. Title.

MOORE, Harmon D ed. 252.6
And our defense is sure; sermons and addresses from the Pentagon Protestant pulpit. Edited by Harmon D. Moore, Ernest A. Ham [and] Clarence E. Hobgood. New York, Abingdon Press [1964] 191 p. 23 cm. "The Pentagon Protestant pulpit is the outgrowth of occasional weekday noon-hour services conducted by chaplains in the concourse of the Pentagon ... The pulpit now operates under a committee of chaplains of the Army, Navy, and Air Force." [BV4241.M58] 64-14618
1. Sermons, American. I. Title. II. Title: Pentagon Protestant pulpit.

MORGAN, Geraldine, 1927- 248'.2 B
Shadows in the sunshine. Philadelphia, Dorrance [1973] 92 p. 22 cm. [BX7020.Z8M58] 73-77629 ISBN 0-8059-1858-2 4.00
1. Morgan, Geraldine, 1927- 2. Church of God—Sermons. 3. Sermons, American. I. Title.

MORRIS, Ebenezer Joseph, 252 1845-
Sermons to my friends, by E. J. Morris ... Boston, Mass., The Stratford company [c1930] 3 p. l., 162 p. 19 cm. [BV4253.M6] 31-30542
1. Sermons, American. I. Title.

MOTTER, Alton M ed. 252.0082
Sunday evening sermons; fifteen selected addresses delivered before the noted Chicago Sunday Evening Club. Introd. by Harry Emerson Fosdick. [1st ed.] New York, Harper [1952] 191 p. 20 cm. [BV4241.M73] 52-11443
1. Sermons, American. I. Title.

MURRAY, Alfred Lefurgy, 1900- 252 ed.
The young minister's pulpit; a series of sermons by young ministers, edited by Alfred L. Murray ... Grand Rapids, Mich., Zondervan publishing house [c1936] 120 p. 20 cm. [BV42411.M8] 36-23905
1. Sermons, American. I. Title.

MURRAY, John, 1742-1793.
The last solemn scene. A sermon, preached at the church in Black-street, Boston, May 22, 1768. By the Rev. John Murray, A. M. late pastor of the Presbyterian church in this town ... Newburyport [Mass.]: Re-printed and sold by G. J. Osborne. mdccxciii. 1793. 69 p. 20 cm. A 33
1. Sermons, American. I. Title.

MURRAY, John, 1742-1793. 252
The origin of evil, traced in a sermon preached at the Presbyterian church in Newbury-port, May 23d. 1784, and published at the unwearied importunity of some of the hearers. By John Murray, A. M. pastor of said church ... Newburyport [Mass.]: Printed and sold by John Mycall, mdcclxxxv. 100 p. 20 cm.
1. Sermons, American. I. Title.

MURRAY, William Henry 252.058 Harrison, 1840-1904.
Music-hall sermons. By William H. H. Murray ... Second series. Boston, J. R. Osgood and company, 1873. iv, 207 p. 19 cm. [BX7233.M85M72] 33-7461
1. Sermons, American. I. Title.

MY dear people; occasional sermons after old Capuchin fashion. New York, J. F. Wagner [1957] xii, 275p. 24cm.
1. Sermons, American. 2. Occasional sermons. I. Buessing, Venantius.

NADAL, Bernard Harrison, 252.07 1812-1870.
The new life dawning, and other discourses, of Bernard H. Nadal ... Edited, with a memoirs, by Rev. Henry A. Buttz, M. A., and an introduction by Bishop R. S. Foster ... New York, Nelson & Phillips; Cincinnati, Hitchcock & Walden, 1873. 421 p. front. (port.) 20 cm. [BX833.N34N4] 33-8318
1. Sermons, American. I. Buttz, Henry Anson, 1835-1920, ed. II. Title.

NADER, Sam 1919- ed. 252.0082
Sermons for the new age. New York, Morehouse-Gorham Co., 1948. xi, 209 p. 21 cm. [BV4241.N3] 48-9568
1. Sermons, American. I. Title.

NEASE, Floyd William, 252.099 1893-1930.
Symphonies of praise, by Rev. Floyd William Nease ... introduction by the Rev. Roy T. Williams ... Kansas City, Mo., Nazarene publishing house [c1931] 192 p. front. (port.) 20 cm. Sermons. [BX8699.N3N4] 31-22131
1. Sermons, American. I. Title.

NEIL, Samuel Graham. 252.06
Victorious Christianity, by Samuel Graham Neil ... New York, Chicago [etc.] Fleming H. Revell company [c1931] 192 p. front. (port.) 20 cm. "Addresses which embody ... practical suggestions regarding the church--its ministry, and methods."--Pref. [BX6333.N4V5] 31-19978
1. Sermons, American. I. Title.

NEWTON, Joseph Fort, 252.091 1876-
The angel in the soul, by Joseph Fort Newton, with an introduction by Howard Chandler Robbins... New York and London, Harper & brothers, 1932. 6 p. l., 122 p. 20 cm. "First edition." [BX9943.N4A63] 32-29526
1. Sermons, American. I. Title.

NEWTON, Joseph Fort, 1876- 242 1950.
Everyday religious living. New York, Abingdon-Cokesbury Press [1951] 256 p. 16 cm. [BV4253.N42] 51-14229
1. Sermons, American. I. Title.

NEWTON, Richard, 1813- 252.03 1887.
The heath in the wilderness, or, Sermons to the people, by the late Rev. Richard Newton, D.D., to which is added the story of his life and ministry, by W. W. N. New York, R. Carter and brothers, 1888. lix, 13-374 p. front. (port.) 19 cm. [BX5937.N4H4] 33-8315
1. Sermons, American. I. Newton, William Wilberforce, 1843-1914. II. Title.

NICHOLS, Gus, 1892- 252.0663
Sermons of Gus Nichols. Edited by J. D. Thomas. [1st ed.] Abilene, Tex., Biblical Research Press [1966] viii, 275 p. port. 23 cm. (Great preachers of today, 9) [BX7077.Z6A35 vol. 9] 66-9306
1. Churches of Christ—Sermons. 2. Sermons, American. I. Title. II. Series.

NICHOLS, Roy C., 1918- 252'.076
Footsteps in the sea / Roy C. Nichols. Nashville : Abingdon, c1980. 126 p. ; 21 cm. [BX8333.N48F66] 79-26826 ISBN 0-687-13270-3 : 5.95
1. Methodist Church—Sermons. 2. Sermons, American. I. Title.

NICHOLS, Samuel, 1787- 252.08 1880.
Sermons, by The Rev. Samuel Nichols ... Edited by Rev. Sylvester Clarke ... New York, Ivison, Blakeman, Taylor, & co., 1882. 2 p. l., vi, [7]-396 p. front. (port.) 20 cm. [BX5937.N5S4] 33-5393
1. Sermons, American. I. Clarke, Sylvester, 1833-1904, ed. II. Title.

NIEBUHR, Reinhold, 1892-1971. 252
Justice and mercy. Edited by Ursula M. Niebuhr. [1st ed.] New York, Harper & Row [1974] x, 139 p. 21 cm. Includes bibliographical references. [BV4253.N5 1974] 73-18704 ISBN 0-06-066171-2 5.95
1. Sermons, American. 2. Prayers. I. Title.

NIXON, William G 1865-1926. 252.
W. G. Nixon's sermons. Memorial ed. University Park, Ia., John Fletcher college press [c1928 3 p. l., 5-149 p. port. 20 cm. [BX8333.N5W5] 28-20786
I. Title.

NORDEN, Rudolph F 208
The voice of the prophets; sixteen timely pulpit meditations based on texts from the sixteen Old Testament prophets. Saint Louis, Concordia Pub. House [1963] xi, 161 p. 23 cm. [BX8066.N6V6] 63-20177
1. Sermons, American. 2. Lutheran Church — Sermons. I. Title.

NORTON, Jacob, 1764-1858. 922.573
A valedictory discourse, delivered before the First religious society in Weymouth, in two parts. On the morning and afternoon of Lord's day, July 4, 1824. By Jacob Norton. Published by request ... Boston, N. Balch, jr., printer, 1824. 52 p. 24 cm. [BX7260.N57A35] 37-16730
1. Sermons, American. I. Title.

OAKMAN, Arthur A. 252'.09'33
Arthur A. Oakman : themes from his radio sermons / edited by Stephen Gregson. Independence, Mo. : Herald Pub. House, 1978. 199 p. ; 20 cm. [BX8676.O29A77] 78-7712 ISBN 0-8309-0216-3 : 6.50
1. Reorganized Church of Jesus Christ of Latter-Day Saints—Sermons. 2. Sermons, American. I. Gregson, Stephen.

OGILVIE, Lloyd John. 252'.051
The bush is still burning : the Christ who

makes things happen in our deepest needs / Lloyd John Ogilvie. Waco, Tex. : Word Books, c1980. 257 p. ; 23 cm. [BX9178.O43B87] 19 79-55924 ISBN 0-8499-0128-6 : 8.95
1. Presbyterian Church—Sermons. 2. Sermons, American. I. Title.

OGILVIE, Lloyd John. 252'.05'1
Drumbeat of love : the unlimited power of the Spirit as revealed in the Book of Acts / Lloyd John Ogilvie. Waco, Tex. : Word Books, c1976. 291 p. ; 23 cm. Includes bibliographical references. [BS2625.4.O36] 76-19535 ISBN 0-87680-483-0 : 7.95
1. Presbyterian Church—Sermons. 2. Bible. N.T. Acts—Sermons. 3. Sermons, American. I. Title.

OGILVIE, Lloyd John. 227'.8106
Life as it was meant to be / Lloyd John Ogilvie. Ventura, Calif. : Regal Books, c1980. 157 p. ; 24 cm. [BS2725.4.O34] 19 80-50541 ISBN 0-8307-0740-9 : 8.95
1. Presbyterian Church—Sermons. 2. Bible. N.T. Thessalonians—Sermons. 3. Sermons, American. I. Title.
Publisher's address: 2300 Knoll Dr., Ventura, CA 93003

OLYPHANT, Vernon Murray, 252.051 1860-1893.
Christ our life; sermons by V. M. Olyphant. New York, A. D. F. Randolph & company [1893] vi p., 1 l., [9]-191 p. 19 cm. [BX9178.O47C5] 33-8321
1. Sermons, American. I. Title.

PARKER, Theodore, 1810-1860. 204
Sermons of religion, by Theodore Parker; ed. with a preface by Samuel A. Eliot. Boston, American Unitarian association [c1908] 2 p. l., vii-xi p., 1 l., 346 p. 21 cm. [His Works. Centenary ed. v. 3] [BX9815.P3 1907 vol. 3] [BX9843.P3S4 1908] 252. 9-850 1.00
I. Eliot, Samuel Atkins, 1862- ed. II. Title.

PATTEN, Bebe. 252
Give me back my soul. [1st ed.] Oakland, Calif., Patten Foundation, 1972. 190 p. 22 cm. Sermons preached in Christian Cathedral, Oakland, Calif., 1962-72, and first published in the Trumpet call. [BV4253.P27] 73-158771 4.95
1. Sermons, American. I. Title.

PATTERSON, W. Morgan, ed. 252.061
Professor in the pulpit; sermons preached in Alumni Memorial Chapel by the faculty of the Southern Baptist Theological Seminary, comp., ed. by W. Morgan Patterson, Raymond Bryan Brown. Nashville, Tenn., Broadman Press [c.1963] vi, 150 p. 21 cm. Bibl. 63-19073 2.25, pap.
1. Sermons, American. 2. Southern Baptist Convention—Sermons. I. Brown, Raymond Bryan, joint ed. II. Louisville, Ky. Southern Baptist Theological Seminary. III. Title.

PAYNE, Daniel 252.07'83 Alexander, Bp., 1811-1893.
Sermons and addresses, 1853-1891. Edited, with an introd. by Charles Killian. New York, Arno Press, 1972. 1 v. (various pagings) ports. 24 cm. (Religion in America, series II) [BX8449.P3A5 1972] 70-38458 ISBN 0-405-04079-2
1. Methodist Church—Sermons. 2. Sermons, American. I. Title.

PEARCE, William, bp., 252.07 1862-
Our incarnate Lord, by Bishop William Pearce. Chicago, Ill., Light and life press [1931] 114 p. 19 cm. Sermons. [BX8333.P46O8] 31-23782
1. Sermons, American. I. Title.

PEELOR, Harry N. 252.07
Angel with a slingshot. Nashville, Abingdon [1962, c.1961] 127p. 23cm. 62-16811 2.50
1. Sermons, American. 2. Methodist Church—Sermons. I. Title.

PENTECOST, J. Dwight. 252
Man's problems—God's answers, by J. Dwight Pentecost. Chicago, Moody Press [1971] 192 p. 22 cm. [BV4253.P38] 72-155685 3.95
1. Sermons, American. I. Title.

PHILIPS, T Roland., 252.05
God hath spoken. Grand Rapids, Eerdmans [1959] 181p. illus. 23cm. [BX9178.P54G6] 59-12935
1. Sermons, American. 2. Presbyterian Church—Sermons. I. Title.

PHILLIPS, Harold Cooke, 252.061 1892-
Seeing the invisible, by Harold Cooke Phillips; with an introduction by Harry Emerson Fosdick. New York and London, Harper & brothers, 1932. xii, 122 p. 20 cm. "First edition." [BX6333.P54S4] 32-30289
1. Sermons, American. I. Title.

PIPPIN, Frank Johnson, 1906- 252
The roads we travel. St. Louis, Bethany Press [1966] 128 p. 21 cm. Includes bibliographical references. [BV4241.P52] 66-14599
1. Sermons, American. I. Title.

PITKIN, John Budd, 1802- 252.08 1835.
Sermons, by Rev. J. B. Pitkin...With a memoir of the author, by Rev. S. G. Bulfinch. Boston, D. Reed, 1837. 352 p. front. (port.) 19 1/2 cm. [BX9843.P7645S4] 31-3540
1. Sermons, American. I. Bulfinch, Stephen Greenleaf, 1809-1870. II. Title.

PLAIN sermons by practical preachers, original sermons on the Gospels or Epistles of all the Sundays and the principal feasts, ... New York, J. F. Wagner c1916 2 v. 21 1/2 cm. $3.00 16-8829

PONTIUS, Myron Lee. 252.066
The resurrection of the unknown soldier [by] Myron Lee Pontius. Nashville, Tenn., Cokesbury press [c1935] 104 p. 21 cm. [BX7327.P55R4] 35-38143
1. Disciples of Christ—Sermons. 2. Sermons, American. I. Title.

PORTER, Rue. 243
"Musings"; gospel sermons that reach the heart, by Rue Porter ... Wichita, Kan., Christian worker pub. co. [1940] 3 p. l., 215 p. port. 22 cm. [BV4253.P6] 41-10227
1. Sermons, American. I. Title.

POTTER, Thomas. 252.07
The evangelical economy developed; in a series of discourses on the facts, institutions, appliances, effects, and final results of the Christian system; a Rev. Thomas Potter ... Zapesville, O., Printed by E. C. Church, 1848. 356 p. 22 cm. [BX8333.P68E8] 32-34069
1. Sermons, American. I. Title.

PREUS, David W. 269
Go with the gospel / David W. Preus. Minneapolis : Augsburg Pub. House, c1977. 112 p. ; 20 cm. [BV2074.P73] 76-27075 ISBN 0-8066-1560-5 pbk. : 2.95
1. Great Commission (Bible)—Sermons. 2. Lutheran Church—Sermons. 3. Sermons, American. 4. Evangelistic work. I. Title.

PRINCE, Thomas, 1687-1758. 252.
A sermon delivered by Thomas Prince, M. A. on Wensday, October 1, 1718, at his ordination to the pastoral charge of the South church in Boston, N. E. In conjunction with the Reverend Mr. Joseph Sewall. Together with the charge, by the Reverend Increase Mather, D. D. and a copy of what was said at giving the right hand of fellowship: by the Reverend Cotton Mather, D. D. To which is added, a Discourse of the validity of the ordination by the hands of presbyters, previous to Mr. Sewall's on September 16, 1713. By the late Reverend and learned Mr. Ebenezer Pemberton, pastor of the same church. Boston: Printed by J. Franklin for S. Gerrish, and sold at his shop near the Old meeting house, 1718. 4 p. l., 76 p., 1 l., [2], 15 p. 18 cm. [Miscellaneous pamphlets. v. 216, no. 2] Signatures: A-K4, L2, A-B4, C2 (C1-2 wanting) The Discourse has special t.-p. and separate paging. Imperfect: p. 13-15 of the Discourse wanting. [AC901.M5 vol. 216] 31-11210
1. Sermons, American. 2. Ordination. I. Mather, Increase, 1639-1723. II. Mather, Cotton, 1663-1728. III. Title.

PROUDFIT, Alexander Moncrief, 252 1770-1843.
The ruin and recovery of man. A series of discourses on the distinguishing doctrines of Christianity. By Alexander Proudfit ... Salem, (N. Y.) Printed by Dodd & Rumsey, 1806. 412 p. 18 x 11 cm. Binder's title: Proudfit's sermons. [BX9178.P75B8] 32-33661
1. Sermons, American. I. Title.

PULLEY, Frank Easton, 1906- 252.5
Blessed are the peacemakers; sermons preached to the Class of 1953 by their chaplain. New York, Morehouse-Gorham Co., 1953. 128p. 16cm. [BV4316.S7P78] 53-2293
1. Sermons, American. 2. U. S. Military Academy, West Point. I. Title.

PULLEY, Frank Easton, 1906- 252.5
Cadet chapel sermons; sermons preached to the Class of 1949 by theirchaplain. New York, Morehouse-Gorham Co., 1949. 111 p. 16 cm. [BV4316.S7P79] 49-4886
1. Sermons, American. 2. U. S. Military Academy, West Point. I. Title.

PULLEY, Frank Easton, 1906- 252.5
Christ, thy Captain; sermons preached to the Class of 1952 by their chaplain. New York, Morehouse-Gorham Co., 1952. 135 p. 16 cm. [BV4316.S7P792] 52-4012
1. U.S. Military Academy, West Point. 2. Sermons, American. I. Title.

PULLEY, Frank Easton, 1906- 252.5
Help from the hills; sermons preached to the Class of 1951 by their chaplain. New York, Morehouse-Gorham Co., 1951. 127 p. 16 cm. [BV4316.S7P793] 51-4938
1. U.S. Military Academy, West Point. 2. Sermons, American. I. Title.

PULLEY, Frank Easton, 1906- 252
Soldiers of the cross; sermons preached to the Class of 1950 by their chaplain. New York, Morehouse-Gorham Co., 1950. 108 p. 16 cm. Bibliography: p. 107-108. [BV4316.S7P796] 50-8439
1. U.S. Military Academy, West Point. 2. Sermons, American. I. Title.

PULLEY, Frank Easton, 1906- 252
Thine is the kingdom; sermons preached to the Class of 1954 by their chaplain. New York, Morehouse-Gorham Co., 1954. 120p. 16cm. [BV4316.S7P797] 54-2882
1. Sermon, American. 2. U. S. Military Academy, West Point. I. Title.

PULPIT digest. 252.0082
The best from Pulpit digest. Great Neck, N.Y., Pulpit Digest Pub. Co. [1951] 319 p. 21 cm. [BV4241.P763] 51-2778
1. Sermons, American. I. Title.

PURVIS, Cleo. 252
Christ and the common man. Louisville, Ky., Herald Press [1956] 114p. illus. 20cm. [BV4253.P8] 56-42691
1. Sermons, American. I. Title.

PURVIS, Samuel Warrington, 252.07 1867-
Life's four windows, and other sermons, by Samuel W. Purvis ... Philadelphia, National publishing company [c1931] 6 p. l., 338, [2] p. front. (port.) 20 cm. [BX8333.P74L5] 31-25986
1. Sermons, American. I. Title.

PUTNAM, Roy C., 1928- 252'.7
Those he came to save / Roy C. Putnam. Nashville : Abingdon, c1978. 142 p. ; 19 cm. [BX8333.P78T48] 77-13764 ISBN 0-687-41862-3 pbk. : 4.95
1. Methodist Church—Sermons. 2. Sermons, American. I. Title.

RADER, Paul, 1879- 243
God's blessed man; soul stirring sermons, by Paul Rader ... New York, George H. Doran company [c1922] viii p., 1 l., 11-196 p. front. (port.) 20 cm. [BV3797.R24] 23-1224 1.50
I. Title.

RATIFF, Dale Hedrick, 1928- 252
The challenge of Christ; a book of sermons. [1st ed.] New York, Exposition Press [1955] 77p. 21cm. [BV4253.R37] 55-9410
1. Sermons, American. I. Title.

READ, David Haxton 252'.05'242 Carswell.
Curious Christians [by] David H. C. Read. Nashville, Abingdon Press [1973] 144 p. 19 cm. [BX9178.R367C87 1973] 72-5201 ISBN 0-687-10101-8 pap. 1.95
1. Presbyterian Church—Sermons. 2. Sermons, American. I. Title.

READ, David Haxton 252'.05 Carswell.
An expanding faith, by David H. C. Read. Grand Rapids, Eerdmans [1973] 116 p. 18 cm. (An Eerdmans evangelical paperback) [BX9178.R367E96] 73-7620 ISBN 0-8028-1539-1 1.95 (pbk.)
1. Presbyterian Church—Sermons. 2. Sermons, American. I. Title.

READ, David Haxton 252.05'131 Carswell.
The presence of Christ; sermons [by] David H. C. Read. [Denville, N.J.] Pannonia Press, 1968. 91 p. 21 cm. [BX9178.R367P7] 68-31878
1. Presbyterian Church—Sermons. 2. Sermons, American. I. Title.

READ, David Haxton 252.05 Carswell.
Religion without wrappings, by David H. C. Read. Grand Rapids, Mich., Eerdmans [1970] 216 p. 21 cm. [BX9178.R367R4] 79-127626 4.95
1. Presbyterian Church—Sermons. 2. Sermons, American. I. Title.

READ, David Haxton 252.05 Carswell.
Sons of Anak; the gospel and the modern giants, sermons. New York, Scribner [1964] 208 p. 21 cm. [BX9178.R367S6] 64-12835
1. Sermons, American. 2. Presbyterian Church—Sermons. I. Title. II. Title: The gospel and the modern giants.

READ, David Haxton 253'.2 Carswell.
Unfinished Easter: sermons on the ministry / David H. C. Read. 1st ed. San Francisco : Harper & Row, c1978. 132 p. ; 20 cm. (Harper's ministers paperback library ; RD 263) [BX9178.R367U53 1978] 77-20454 ISBN 0-06-066812-1 pbk. : 4.95
1. Presbyterian Church—Sermons. 2. Sermons, American. I. Title.

REDPATH, Alan. 252.06
The Bible speaks to our times. Westwood, N.J., Revell [1968] 124 p. 21 cm. [BV4253.R38] 68-11370
1. Sermons, American. 2. Sermons, English. I. Title.

REDPATH, Alan. 224'.1
Faith for the times; studies in the prophecy of Isaiah, chapters 40 to 66. Old Tappan, N.J., Revell [1972- v. 21 cm. Contents.Contents.—pt. 1. The promise of deliverance. [BS1520.R4] 72-4621 ISBN 0-8007-0550-5 3.95
1. Bible. O.T. Isaiah XL-LXVI—Sermons. 2. Sermons, American. I. Title.

REDPATH, Alan. 224'.1 s
The fruit of deliverance : studies in the prophecy of Isaiah, chapters 55 to 66 / Alan Redpath. Old Tappan, N.J. : Revell, c1976. 93 p. ; 21 cm. (His Faith for the times ; pt. 3) [BS1520.R4 pt. 3] [BS1520.5] 224'.1 75-42352 ISBN 0-8007-0779-6 : 3.95
1. Bible. O.T. Isaiah LV-LXVI—Sermons. 2. Sermons, American. I. Title.

REDPATH, Alan. 224'.1 s
The Plan of deliverance; studies in the prophecy of Isaiah, chapters 49 to 54. Old Tappan, N.J., Revell [1974] 127 p. 21 cm. (His Faith for the times, pt. 2) [BS1520.R4 pt. 2] [BS1520] 224'.1 74-4033 ISBN 0-8007-0657-9 3.95
1. Bible. O.T. Isaiah XLIX-LIV—Sermons. 2. Sermons, American. I. Title. II. Series.

REDPATH, Alan. 224'.1 s
The promise of deliverance; studies in the prophecy of Isaiah, chapters 40 to 66. Old Tappan, N.J., Revell [1972] 160 p. 21 cm. (His Faith for the times, pt. 1) [BS1520.R4 pt. 1] [BS1520] 224'.1 74-160894 ISBN 0-8007-0550-5 3.95
1. Bible. O.T. Isaiah XL-LXVI—Sermons. 2. Sermons, American. I. Title. II. Series.

REES, Seth Cook. 200
Burning coals. Advanced chapters out of "Fire from heaven" ... By Seth C. Rees ... Cincinnati, O., M. W. Knapp, c1898. 84 p. 19 cm. (On cover: Pentecostal holiness library. v. 1, no. 11) [BX8795.P25A43] 98-1646

1. Sermons, American I. Title.

REESE, Curtis Williford, 1887- ed. 252
Humanist sermons, edited by Curtis W. Reese ... Chicago, London, The Open court publishing company, 1927. xviii, 262 p., 1 l. 22 1/2 cm. [BX9834.A1R4] 28-5411
1. Sermons, American. 2. Unitarianism. 3. Humanism—20th cent. I. Title.

REORGANIZED Church of Jesus Christ of Latter-Day Saints. Council of Twelve Apostles. 252'.093'3
Twelve sermons. Independence, Mo., Herald Pub. House, 1972] 151 p. 18 cm. [BX8676.A2] 76-182436 ISBN 0-8309-0069-1 3.00
1. Reorganized Church of Latter-Day Saints—Sermons. 2. Sermons, American. I. Title.

REYNOLDS, Louis Bernard, 1917- 252'.06'73
Great texts from Romans, by Louis B. Reynolds. Nashville, Tenn., Southern Pub. Association [1972] 94 p. 18 cm. [BS2665.4.R48] 72-75378
1. Seventh-Day Adventists—Sermons. 2. Bible. N.T. Romans—Sermons. 3. Sermons, American. I. Title.

RILEY, William Bell, 1861- 252.061
At sunset; or, After 80, by W. B. Riley ... Butler, Ind., The Higley press [c1943] 159 p. 20 cm. "Sermons ... prepared and preached since my 80th birthday."--Foreword. [BX6333.R5A8] 44-20279
1. Baptists—Sermons. 2. Sermons, American. I. Title.

RILEY, William Bell, 1861- 252.061
Ten burning questions, by William B. Riley ... New York, Chicago [etc.] Fleming H. Revell company [c1932] 200 p. 20 cm. [BX6333.R5T4] 32-15725
1. Sermons, American. 2. Sociology, Christian. I. Title.

THE Riverside preachers : 252
Fosdick/McCracken/Campbell/Coffin / Paul H. Sherry, editor. New York : Pilgrim Press, c1978. 176 p. : ports. ; 21 cm. [BV4241.R54] 78-11812 ISBN 0-8298-0360-2 pbk. : 5.95
1. Fosdick, Harry Emerson, 1878-1969. 2. Sermons, American. I. Fosdick, Harry Emerson, 1878-1969. II. Sherry, Paul H., 1933-

ROBBINS, Chandler, 1738-1799. 252.
A sermon. Preached before His Excellency Jonh [!] Hancock, esq., governor; His Honor Samuel Adams ... the honourable the Council, and the honourable the Senate and House of representatives, of the commonwealth of Massachusetts, May 25, 1791. Being the day of general election. by Chandler Robbins ... Boston, Massachusetts: Printed by Thomas Adams, Printer to the honourable the General court, 1791. 51 p. 23 cm. Half-title: Mr. Robbin's election sermon, May 25, 1791. [BV4260.M5 1791] 7-28578
I. Title.

ROBBINS, Howard Chandler, 1876- 252.
Cathedral sermons, by Howard Chandler Robbins, preached in the Cathedral of St. John the Divine. New York and London, Harper & brothers, 1927. 10 p. l., 261 p. 20 cm. [BX5937.R56C3] 27-20938
I. Title.

ROBBINS, Robert. 252.058
Divine sovereignty in the salvation, and damnation of sinners vindicated: in a discourse, delivered at West Chester, in Colchester. By Robert Robbins ... Norwich [Conn.] Printed by Ebenezer Bushnell, M,DCC,XCII. 67 p. 20 cm. Half-title: Mr. Robbin's Discourse on Romans ix. 18. [BX7233.R48D5] 4-8880
1. Sermons. American. 2. Predestination. I. Title.

ROBERTS, Arthur O. 252.096
Move over, Elijah; sermons in poetry and prose, by Arthur O. Roberts. Newberg, Or., Barclay Press [1967] vii, 161 p. 23 cm. [BX7733.R6] 67-24903
1. Friends, Society of—Sermons. 2. Sermons, American. I. Title.

ROGERS, William Hubert, ed. 252.061
The word we preach; sermons by representative men in the Baptist ministry, edited by W. H. Rogers... Philadelphia, Boston [etc.] The Judson press [c1931] 5 p. l., 3-287 p. diagr. 20 1/2 cm. "Sermons by representative ministers of the Northern Baptist convention."--Note of explanation. [BX6333.A1R6] 31-17186
1. Sermons, American. I. Northern Baptist convention. II. Title.

ROLSTON, Holmes, 1900- 227'.92'07
The Apostle Peter speaks to us today / Holmes Rolston. Atlanta : John Knox Press, c1977. 99 p.; 21 cm. [BS2795.4.R64] 76-44974 ISBN 0-8042-0201-X pbk. : 2.95
1. Presbyterian Church—Sermons. 2. Bible. N.T. 1 Peter—Sermons. 3. Sermons, American. I. Title.

ROMEYN, John Brodhead, 1777-1825.
A sermon, delivered at the opening of the general assembly of the Presbyterian church in the United States of America, May, 1811. By John B. Romeyn ... New-York, Published by Whiting & Watson, 1811. 50 p. 21 cm. A 32
1. Sermons, American. I. Title.

ROSE, Stephen C. 252'.05'1
Sermons not preached in the White House, by Stephen C. Rose. Introductory essay by Reinhold Niebuhr. New York, R. W. Baron Pub. Co., 1970. 155 p. 21 cm. "A Cambria Press book." [BX9178.R67S47] 70-108974 4.95
1. Presbyterian Church—Sermons. 2. Sermons, American. I. Title.

RUSSELL, William D., 1938- comp. 252.09'3'3
The word became flesh; sermons on New Testament texts, edited by William D. Russell. [Independence, Mo.] Herald Pub. House [1967] 284 p. 21 cm. Bibliographical footnotes. [BX8676.R8] 67-26969
1. Reorganized Church of Jesus Christ of Latter-Day Saints—Sermons. 2. Sermons, American. I. Title.

SACRIFICE / 291.3'4
edited by M.F.C. Bourdillon, Meyer Fortes. London : Published by Academic Press for the Royal Anthropological Institute of Great Britain and Ireland, 1980. xix, 147 p. ; 24 cm. "Based on the proceedings of a Conference on Sacrifice held at Cumberland Lodge, Windsor, England from February 23rd to 25th, 1979." Includes index. Contents.Contents.—On understanding sacrifice / J.H.M. Beattie — Sacrifice in the Old Testament / J.W. Rogerson — Sacrifice in the New Testament and Christian theology / S.W. Sykes — Ritual in performance and interpretation / Suzanne Campbell-Jones — A commensal relationship with God / Audrey Hayley — Postscript, a place for sacrifice in modern Christianity? / S. Barrington-Ward and M.F.C. Bourdillon. Bibliography: p. [137]-143. [BL570.S24] 19 80-40424 ISBN 0-12-119040-4 : 21.00
1. Sacrifice—Congresses. I. Bourdillon, M. F. C. II. Fortes, Meyer. III. Conference on Sacrifice Cumberland Lodge) (1979 :

SANDERS, James A., 1927- 252'.05'1
God has a story too : sermons in context / James A. Sanders. Philadelphia : Fortress Press, c1979. xi, 145 p. ; 22 cm. Includes bibliographical references and index. [BX9178.S28G62] 77-15244 ISBN 0-8006-1353-8 pbk. : 5.75
1. Presbyterian Church—Sermons. 2. Bible—Hermeneities. 3. Sermons, American. 4. Preaching.

SAUNDERS, Landon B. 252
The power of receiving / by Landon B. Saunders. Abilene, Tex. : Biblical Research Press, c1979. v, 183 p. ; 23 cm. (The 20th century sermons series ; v. 12) [BV4253.S33] 79-50142 ISBN 0-89112-312-1 : 7.95
1. Sermons, American. I. Title.

SAVILLE, Henry Martyn, 1868- 252.03
A score of sermons, simple, short, serial, and single, by The Reverend Henry Martyn Saville ... Milwaukee, Morehouse publishing co.; London, A. R. Mowbray & co., ltd. [c1931] iv p., 1 l., 211, [1] p. 19 cm. [BX5937.S3S4] 31-23948
1. Sermons, American. I. Title.

SCHAEFFER, Francis August. 252
No little people; sixteen sermons for the twentieth century [by] Francis A. Schaeffer. Downers Grove, Ill., InterVarsity Press [1974] 271 p. 21 cm. [BV4253.S34] 74-78675 ISBN 0-87784-765-7 3.50
1. Sermons, American. I. Title.

SCHREIBER, Vernon R. 252'.61
My redeemer lives : messages from the Book of Job for Lent and Easter / Vernon R. Schreiber. Minneapolis, : Augsburg Pub. House, [1974] 79 p. ; 20 cm. [BS1415.4.S37] 74-14170 ISBN 0-8066-1453-6 pbk. : 2.50
1. Lutheran Church—Sermons. 2. Bible. O.T. Job—Sermons. 3. Sermons, American. I. Title.

SCOTT, John, 1820- 252.07
Pulpit echoes: or, Brief miscellaneous discourses. By John Scott, D. D. Cincinnati, C. A. Scott; Pittsburgh, Methodist board of publication, 1873. 312 p. 20 cm. [BX8333.S38P8] 33-8319
1. Sermons, American. I. Title.

SCOTT, William Anderson, 1813-1885. 222'.2'0924
Wedge of gold : [the folly and fall of Achan] : a careful look at the sin of covetousness / W. A. Scott. Swengel, Pa. : Reiner Publications, [1974?] 162 p. ; 19 cm. Discourses delivered in the Calvary Church, San Francisco. Reprint of the 1855 ed. [BX9178.S4W4 1974] 74-187954 2.95
1. Presbyterian Church—Sermons. 2. Sermons, American. 3. Achan (Biblical character) I. Title.

SEABURY, Samuel, bp., 1729-1796. 252.
Discourses on several subjects. By Samuel Seabury ... Hudson: Published by William E. Norman. 1815. 2 v. front. (port.) 22 cm. [BX5937.S4D5 1815] 32-35149
1. Sermons, American. I. Title.

SEARLE, Robert Wyckoff, ed. 252.00822
Contemporary religious thinking; seventeen sermons on the church's responsibilities in the period just ahead, edited by the Rev. Robert Wyckoff Searle ... and the Rev. Frederick A. Bowers ... New York, Falcon press [c1933] xii, 212 p. 23 cm. [BV4241.S37] 33-14848
1. Sermons, American. I. Bowers, Frederick A., 1863- joint ed. II. Title.

SERMONS by the sea. 252.0082
New York, Cincinnati [etc.] The Abingdon press [c1938] 120 p. 19 1/2 cm. "These ten sermons ... were preached in the ... auditorium at Ocean Grove, New Jersey, during the 1938 season."--Foreword. [BV4241.S416] 38-24879
1. Sermons, American.

SERMONS for days of 252'.05'9
fast, prayer, and humiliation and execution sermons : facsimile introductions [i.e. reproductions] / selected and introduced by Ronald A. Bosco. Delmar, N.Y. : Scholars' Facsimiles & Reprints, 1978. xcv, 451 p. ; 23 cm. (The Puritan sermon in America, 1630-1750 ; 1) (The Sermon in America, 1620-1800) Title on spine: Humiliation & execution sermons. Bibliography: p. lxxxv-xcii. [BV4241.P83 vol. 1] 78-14769 ISBN 0-8201-1320-4 (set) : 170.00
1. Sermons, American. I. Bosco, Ronald A. II. Title: Humiliation & execution sermons. III. Series: Puritan sermon in America, 1630-1750 ; 1. IV. Series: Sermon in America, 1620-1800.

SERMONS in American 261
history; selected issues in the American pulpit, 1630-1967. Prepared under the auspices of the Speech Communication Association. DeWitte Holland, editor. Hubert Vance Taylor and Jess Yoder, assistant editors. [Nashville, Abingdon Press, 1971] 542 p. 25 cm. [BV4241.S4186] 76-148072 ISBN 0-687-37794-3 11.95
1. Sermons, American. I. Holland, DeWitte Talmadge, 1923- ed. II. Speech Communication Association.

SERMONS preached at the 252'.02
Church of St. Paul the Apostle, New York, during the year 1863 ; with an introd. by Joseph F. Gower. New York : Arno Press, 1978 [c1863] 377 p. ; 21 cm. (The American Catholic tradition) Reprint of the 1864 ed. published by D. & J. Sadlier Co., New York; with a new introd. by J. Gower. Includes bibliographical references. [BX1756.A2S45 1978] 77-11309 ISBN 0-405-10851-6 : 24.00
1. Catholic Church—Sermons. 2. Sermons, American. I. Church of St. Paul the Apostle, New York. II. Title. III. Series.

SHAMBLIN, J. Kenneth. 252.06
Life comes as choice [by] J. Kenneth Shamblin. Nashville, Abingdon Press [1967] 175 p. 21 cm. [BX8333.S45L5] 67-11018
1. Methodist Church—Sermons. 2. Sermons, American. I. Title.

SHANNON, Frederick Franklin, 1877- 287
The breath in the winds, and other sermons, by Frederick F. Shannon ... New York, Chicago [etc.] Fleming H. Revell company [c1918] 173 p. 19 1/2 cm. [BX8333.S5B8] 19-2926
I. Title.

SHANNON, Frederick Franklin, 1877- 252.076
Christ eternal, by Frederick F. Shannon ... New York [etc.] Fleming H. Revell company [c1934] 153 p. 19 1/2 cm. [BV4253.S506] 34-38547
1. Sermons, American. I. Title.

SHANNON, Frederick Franklin, 1877- 252.076
The Christ of God; sermons on the poet eternal, by Frederick F. Shannon ... New York, London [etc.] Fleming H. Revell company [1946] 3 p. l., 9-128 p. 19 1/2 cm. [BV4253.S5065] 47-538
1. Sermons, American. I. Title.

SHANNON, Frederick Franklin, 1877- 252.076
The Christian God and other addresses, by Frederick F. Shannon ... New York [etc.] Fleming H. Revell company [c1937] 152 p. 19 1/2 cm. [BV4253.S507] 37-32409
1. Sermons, American. I. Title.

SHANNON, Frederick Franklin, 1877- 252
The country faith, by Frederick F. Shannon ... New York, The Macmillan company, 1922. 4 p. l., 135 p. 19 1/2 cm. [BV4253.S51] 22-18942
1. Sermons, American. I. Title.

SHANNON, Frederick Franklin, 1877- 252
The soul's atlas and other sermons, by the Rev. Frederick F. Shannon ... New York, Chicago [etc.] Fleming H. Revell company [c1911] 3 p. l., 9-226 p. 19 1/2 cm. [BV4253.S6] 11-26769
1. Sermons, American. I. Title.

SHANNON, Frederick Franklin, 1877- 252.076
The universe within, by Frederick F. Shannon ... with an appreciation by Gaius Glenn Atkins ... New York [etc.] Fleming H. Revell company [c1931] 186 p. 19 1/2 cm. "A new volume of Shannon's sermons."--p. 7. [BV4253.S625] 31-33780
1. Sermons, American. I. Title.

SHEDD, William Greenough Thayer, 1820-1894. 252'.05'1
Sermons to the natural man / William G. T. Shedd. Edinburgh ; Carlisle, Pa. : Banner of Truth Trust, 1978. [2], xi, 422 p. ; 23 cm. Reprint of the 1st ed. published in 1871 by Scribner, New York. Includes bibliographical references. [BX9178.S45S4 1977] 78-312986 ISBN 0-85151-260-7 : 8.95
1. Presbyterian Church—Sermons. 2. Sermons, American. I. Title.

SHEETS, Herchel H. 226'.06
Enemy versions of the Gospel; the Gospel according to Jesus' enemies, by Herchel H.

Sheets. [Nashville] Upper Room [1973] 72 p. 20 cm. [BT306.3.S53] 73-80050 1.00
1. Jesus Christ—Biography—Sermons. 2. Methodist Church—Sermons. 3. Sermons, American. I. Title.

SHEPPARD, John Augustine, 1849-1925. 248
Plain practical sermons, by Rt. Rev. Mgr. John A. Sheppard, V.G. 2d ed. New York, Christian press association publishing company, 1904. 3 p. l., 5-465 p. 19 1/2 cm. [BX1756.S4P6 1904] 4-12978
1. Sermons, American. I. Title.

SHERMAN, Cecil E. 252'.06'1
Modern myths [by] Cecil E. Sherman. Nashville, Broadman Press [1973] 122 p. 20 cm. [BX6333.S48M62] 72-94401 ISBN 0-8054-5216-8 1.50 (pbk)
1. Sermons, American. 2. Baptists—Sermons. I. Title.

SHIPLER, Guy Emery, 1881- ed. 252
Sermons of goodwill; the Churchman's first series on brotherhood and goodwill. New York, Association Press, 1948. 239 p. 22 cm. "Each sermon ... was broadcast ... over Station WOR, New York." [BV4241.S49] 48-9505
1. Sermons, American. I. The Churchman. II. Title.

SHOEMAKER, Samuel Moor, 1893- 252.03
Confident faith, by Samuel M. Shoemaker, jr. ... New York [etc.] Fleming H. Revell company [c1932] 190 p. 19 1/2 cm. "Sermons which ... have, for the most part, been preached during the past few months in Calvary church, New York."--Foreword. [BX5937.S45C6] 32-12499
1. Sermons, American. 2. Protestant Episcopal church in the U.S.A.—Sermons. I. New York. Calvary church (Protestant Episcopal) II. Title.

SHOEMAKER, Samuel Moor, 1893- 232.963
If I be lifted up; thoughts about the cross, by Samual M. Shoemaker, jr. ... New York, Chicago [etc.] Fleming H. Revell company [c1931] 179 p. 19 1/2 cm. [BT453.S5] 31-8059
1. Jesus Christ—Crucifixion. 2. Sermons, American. I. Title.

SHOEMAKER, Samuel Moor, 1893- 252.
Religion that works; sermons of practical Christian life, by S. M. Shoemaker, jr. ... with an introduction by Albert Parker Fitch ... New York, Chicago [etc.] Fleming H. Revell company [c1928] 128 p. 19 1/2 cm. [BX5967.S45R4] 28-15515
1. Sermons, American. I. Title.

SILL, Sterling W. 248'.48'933
The laws of success / Sterling W. Sill. Salt Lake City : Deseret Book Co., 1975. 219 p. : port. ; 24 cm. Includes index. [BX8639.S5L38] 75-18818 ISBN 0-87747-556-3
1. Church of Jesus Christ of Latter-Day Saints—Sermons. 2. Sermons, American. I. Title.

SILL, Sterling W. 252'.09'3
Principles, promises, and powers [by] Sterling W. Sill. Salt Lake City, Utah, Deseret Book Co., 1973. xiii, 308 p. 24 cm. [BX8639.S5P7] 73-87714 ISBN 0-87747-506-7 3.95
1. Church of Jesus Christ of Latter-Day Saints—Sermons. 2. Sermons, American. I. Title.

SILL, Sterling W. 252'.0933
The upward reach / by Sterling W. Sill. Bountiful, Utah : Horizon Publishers, c1980. 407 p. : port. ; 24 cm. Reprint. Originally published: Salt Lake City : Bookcraft, 1962. Includes index. [BX8639.S5U6 1980] 19 80-83863 ISBN 0-88290-167-2 : 9.95
1. Mormon Church—Sermons. 2. Sermons, American. I. Title.

SIMMONS, Billy. 227'.91'077
A functioning faith; expositions on the Epistle of James. Waco, Tex., Word Books [1967] 144 p. 22 cm. Bibliographical footnotes. [BS2785.4.S5] 67-26936
1. Bible N.T. James—Sermons. 2. Sermons, American. 3. Baptists—Sermons. I. Title.

SIMMONS, William James. 252
One great fellowship. [1st ed.] Nashville, Marshall & Bruce [1967] xi, 158 p. 20 cm. Sermons originally delivered over Station WSM-TV, Nashville, Tenn., on the Community worship program. Bibliographical footnotes. [BV4301.S5] 67-31551
1. Sermons, American. I. Title.

SKEELE, Amos, 1833-1915. 252.
The salt of the earth, and other sermons. by Amos Skeele, S.T.D.: ed., with a sketch of his life, by Francis Leseure Palmer. Milwaukee, Morehouse publishing co., 1921. 6 p. l., [3]-223 p. front. (port.) plates. 20 cm. [BX5937.S5S3] 21-2329
I. Palmer, Francis Leseure, 1863- ed. II. Title.

SKINNER, Clarence Russell, 1881- ed. 204
A free pulpit in action, edited by Clarence R. Skinner. New York, The Macmillan company, 1931. vi p., 1 l., 328 p. 21 cm. Sermons delivered at the Boston Community church. [BX9999.B6C6] 31-2571
1. Sermons, American. I. Boston. Community church. II. Title.

SKINNER, Clarence Russell, 1881-1949, ed. 252
A free pulpit in action. Edited by Clarence R. Skinner. Freeport, N.Y., Books for Libraries Press [1971] vi, 328 p. 23 cm. (Essay index reprint series) Reprint of the 1931 ed. Sermons delivered at the Boston Community Church. [BV4241.S545 1971] 71-156718 ISBN 0-8369-2333-2
1. Sermons, American. I. Boston. Community Church. II. Title.

SLAATTE, Howard Alexander. 252'.07
Discovering your real self : sermons of existential relevance / Howard A. Slaatte. Landam, MD : University Press of America, [1980] p. cm. [BX8333.S566D57] 19 80-8289 ISBN 0-8191-1178-3 (pbk.) : 7.50 ISBN 0-8191-1177-5 : 15.75
1. Methodist CHurch—Sermons. 2. Sermons, American. I. Title.

SLEETH, Ronald Eugene. 252.07'6
Splinters in the quick [by] Ronald E. Sleeth. Waco, Tex., Word Books [1971] 144 p. 23 cm. Sermons. Includes bibliographical references. [BX8333.S5726S65] 78-144359 3.95
1. Sermons, American. 2. Methodist Church—Sermons. I. Title.

SMITH, Bailey E. 248.4
Real Christianity / Bailey E. Smith. Nashville, Tenn. : Broadman Press, 1980, c1979. 185 p. ; 22 cm. [BS262.4.S62] 79-50335 ISBN 0-8054-5168-4 : 5.95
1. Baptists—Sermons. 2. Bible. N.T. Acts—Sermons. 3. Sermons, American. I. Title.

SMITH, Franklin Campbell. 252
The shield of faith and other sermons, by the Reverend Franklin Campbell Smith. Grand Rapids, Mich., Wm. B. Eerdmans publishing co., 1941. 187 p. 20 cm. [BV4253.S73] 41-6832
1. Sermons, American. I. Title.

SMITH, Jonathan Ritchie, 1852- 243
The wall and The gates, and other sermons, by J. Ritchie Smith ... Philadelphia, The Westminster press, 1919. 278 p. front. (port.) 19 cm. [BX9178.S6W3] 19-16631
I. Title.

SMITH, Roy Lemon, 1887- 252.07
Barbed arrows, by Roy L. Smith ... New York, R. R. Smith, inc., 1931. x p., 1 l., 171 p. 20 cm. Sermons. [BX8333.S575B3] 31-28908
1. Sermons, American. I. Title.

SMITH, William, 1727-1803. 252.
The works of William Smith, D. D., late provost of the College and academy of Philadelphia ... Philadelphia: Published by Hugh Maxwell and William Fry, no. 25, North Second street, 1803. 2 v. front. (port.) 22 cm. [BX5937.S585W6] 36-25396
1. Sermons, American. I. Title.

SMUCKER, Donovan Ebersole, 1915- comp. 252.'.008
Rockefeller chapel sermons of recent years, compiled by Donovan E. Smucker. Chicago, University of Chicago Press [1967] xx, 226 p. 23 cm. [BV4241.S57] 66-30215
1. Sermons, American. I. Chicago. University. Rockefeller Memorial Chapel. II. Title.

SNETHEN, Nicholas, 1769-1845. 252.077
Sermons of the late Nicholas Snethen, minister ... in the Methodist Protestant church. Written by himself, in the sixty-ninth year of his age. Edited by Worthington Garrettson Snethen ... 2d ed. Washington, D. C., U. Ward, 1846. xviii, [19]-480 p. 20 cm. [BX8333.S577S4 1846 a] 32-12694
1. Sermons, American. I. Snethen, Worthington Garrettson, ed. II. Title.

SOCKMAN, Ralph Washington, 1889- 252.07
The Unemployed Carpenter, by Ralph W. Sockman; with an introduction by Henry Sloane Coffin. New York and London, Harper & brothers, 1933. viii, 119 p. 20 cm. "first edition." [BX8333.S58S82] 33-10569
1. Sermons, American. I. Title.

SPEER, Gordon C ed. 248
Talks to youth [by] Preston Bradley [and others] New York, Abingdon-Cokesbury Press [1949] 127 p. 20 cm. [BV4310.S5] 49-10132
1. Sermons, American. 2. Youth—Religious life. I. Title.

SPEIGHT, Harold Edwin Balme, 1887- ed. 252
Week-day sermons in King's chapel; sermons preached to week-day congregations in King's chapel, Boston, by Peter Ainslie; Bishop William F. Anderson; Dean Charles R. Brown ... [and others] edited with a foreword, by Harold E. B. Speight. New York, The Macmillan company, 1925. 184 p. 19 1/2 cm. [BV4241.S64] 25-20417
I. Ainslie, Peter, 1867- II. King's chapel, Boston. III. Title.

*SPURGEON, C. H. 252
Christ's glorious achievements by C. H. Spurgeon Grand Rapids Baker Book. [1975] 128 p. 20 cm. [BV42.53] ISBN 0-8010-8042-8 1.95 (pbk.)
1. Sermons, American. I. Title.

STEDMAN, Ray C. 226'.6
Birth of the body : [Acts 1-12] / Ray C. Stedman ; [foreword by Hal Lindsey]. Santa Ana, Calif. : Vision House, c1974. 200 p. ; 21 cm. [BS2625.4.S73] 74-82549 ISBN 0-88449-019-X. ISBN 0-88449-013-0 pbk. : 2.95
1. Bible. N.T. Acts I-XII—Sermons. 2. Sermons, American. I. Title.

STEDMAN, Ray C. 227'.207
Expository studies in 1 Corinthians : the deep things of God / Ray C. Stedman. Waco, Tex. : Word Books, c1981. 342 p. ; 21 cm. (A Discovery Bible study book) [BS2675.4.S8] 19 81-51005 ISBN 0-8499-2937-7 (pbk.) : 7.95
1. Bible. N.T. Corinthians, 1st—Sermons. 2. Sermons, American. I. Title. II. Title: Expository studies in First Corinthians. III. Series.

STEDMAN, Ray C. 227'.9406
Expository studies in 1 John : life by the Son / Ray C. Stedman. Waco, Tex. : Word Books, c1980. 381 p. ; 21 cm. (A Discovery Bible study book) [BS2805.4.S75] 19 80-51449 ISBN 0-8499-2918-0 (pbk.) : 8.95
1. Bible. N.T. 1 John—Sermons. 2. Sermons, American. I. Title.

STEDMAN, Ray C. 227'.1'077
From guilt to glory / Ray C. Stedman. Waco, Tex. : Word Books, c1978- v. ; 21 cm. Includes bibliographical references. [BS2665.4.S73] 77-92460 ISBN 0-8499-0077-8 : 6.95
1. Bible. N.T. Romans—Sermons. 2. Sermons, American. I. Title.

STEDMAN, Ray C. 252'.00973
Growth of the body : [Acts 13-20] / Ray C. Stedman. Santa Ana, Calif. : Vision House Publishers, c1976. 202 p. ; 21 cm. [BS2625.4.S74] 76-47845 ISBN 0-88449-059-9 : 2.95
1. Bible. N.T. Acts XIII-XX—Sermons. 2. Sermons, American. I. Title.

STEDMAN, Ray C. 227'.5'07
Riches in Christ / Ray C. Stedman. Waco, Tex. : Word Books, c1976. 215 p. ; 21 cm. (Discovery books) [BS2695.4.S73] 76-2860 ISBN 0-87680-462-8 : 5.95
1. Bible. N.T. Ephesians I-III—Sermons. 2. Sermons, American. I. Title.

STEELE, Daniel, 1824-1914.
Half-hours with St. John's epistles. Boston and Chicago, Christian witness co., 1901. xxviii, 261 p. front. (port.) 12 degree. 1-31133
I. Title.

STEIMLE, Edmund A. 252.04'1
Disturbed by joy; sermons, by Edmund A. Steimle. Philadelphia, Fortress Press [1967] ix, 182 p. 18 cm. [BX8066.S716D5] 67-13059
1. Lutheran Church—Sermons. 2. Sermons, American. I. Title.

STEIMLE, Edmund A. 252'.04'1
From death to birth: sermons, by Edmund A. Steimle. Philadelphia, Fortress Press [1973] ix, 128, [3] p. 22 cm. Bibliography; p. [131] [BX8066.S716F7] 73-79327 ISBN 0-8006-1037-7 3.25
1. Lutheran Church—Sermons. 2. Sermons, American. I. Title.

STEVENS, William Bacon, bp., 1815-1887. 254
The building of a diocese. A discourse delivered at the centennial celebration of the founding of the diocese of Pennsylvania, May 24, 1884, in Christ church, Philadelphia. By the Rt. Rev. Wm. Bacon Stevens ... Philadelphia, McCalla & Stavely, printers, 1884. 49 p. front., pl. 24 cm. [BX5918.P4S7] 23-2515
I. Title.

STEVENSON, Dwight Eshelman, 1906- 252
Faith takes a name. [1st ed.] New York, Harper [c1954] 189p. 22cm. [BV4253.S77] 53-10979
1. Sermons, American. 2. Christiana—Name. I. Title.

STEWART, Alexander Doig. 252.03
The shock of revelation [by] Alexander Stewart. New York, Seabury Press [1967] vii, 152 p. 22 cm. Based on a series of television appearances.—Cf. dust jacket. Bibliographical references included in "Notes" (p. 149-152) [BX5937.S842S5] 67-11469
1. Protestant Episcopal Church in the U.S.A.—Sermons. 2. Sermons, American. I. Title.

SUMMERFIELD, John, 1798-1825. 252.076
Sermons and sketches of sermons. By the Rev. John Summerfield, A. M., late a preacher in connexion with the Methodist Episcopal church. With an introduction by the Rev. Thomas E. Bond, M.D. ... New-York, Harper & brothers, 1842. xx, [9]-437 p. 22 1/2 cm. [BX8333.S8S4] 32-12692
1. Sermons, American. I. Bond, Thomas Emerson, 1813-1872. II. Title.

SUMMERFIELD, John, 1798-1825. 252.076
Sermons and sketches of sermons. By the Rev. John Summerfield, A.M., late a preacher in connection with the Methodist Episcopal church. With an introduction by the Rev. Thomas E. Bond, M.D. ... New York, Harper & brothers, 1845. 3 p. l., [v]-xx, [9]-437 p. 24 cm. [BX8333.S8S4 1845] 33-1578
1. Sermons, American. I. Bond, Thomas Emerson, 1813-1872. II. Title.

SUMMERS, Thomas Osmond, 1812-1882, ed. 252.07
Sermons by Southern Methodist preachers. Edited by T. O. Summers ... Nashville, Tenn., Southern Methodist publishing house, 1881. 407 p. front., ports. 19 1/2 cm. [BX8333.A1S8] 32-12091
1. Sermons, American. I. Title.

SWEETING, George, 1924- 252
The city; a matter of conscience, and other messages. Chicago, Moody Press [1972]

128 p. 22 cm. [BV4253.S83] 72-77947 ISBN 0-8024-1565-2 2.95
1. Sermons, American. I. Title.

SWEETING, George, 1924- 252
Special sermons on major Bible doctrines / by George Sweeting. Chicago : Moody Press, c1981. p. cm. [BV4253.S834] 19 81-14150 ISBN 0-8024-8209-0 : 3.95
1. Sermons, American. I. Title.

SWEETING, George, 1924- 261
Special sermons on special issues / by George Sweeting. Chicago : Moody Press, c1981. 127 p. ; 22 cm. Includes bibliographical references. [BV4253.S835] 19 80-26754 ISBN 0-8024-8207-4 pbk. : 2.95
1. Sermons, American. I. Title.

SWIFT, Polemus Hamilton, 1855-
Magnetism of the cross; sermons preached in Wesley Methodist Episcopal church, Chicago, by Polemus Hamilton Swift... Cincinnati, Jennings and Graham; New York, Eaton and Mains [1904] 133 p. front. (port.) 19 cm. (Half-title: the Methodist pulpit) [BX8833.S85M3] 4-22840
I. Title.

SWING, David, 1830-1894. 252.051
David Swing's sermons... Chicago, W. B. Keen, Cooke & co., 1874. 144 p. front. 24 cm. Portrait on t.-p. [BV4253.S85S4] 31-915
1. Sermons, American. I. Title.

TAPPAN, David, 1752-1803.
The character and best exercises of unregenerate sinners set in a scriptural light, in a discourse delivered by David Tappan, A.M., pastor of the Third church in Newbury. Published at the desire of many who heard it. Newburyport [Mass.]: Printed and sold by John Mycall, 1782. 60 p. 20 1/2 cm. A 35
1. Sermons, American. I. Title.

TENNENT, Gilbert, 1703-1764. 243
Discourses, on several important subjects. By Gilbert Tennent, A.M., minister of the gospel in Philadelphia. Philadelphia: Printed by W. Bradford at the Bible in Second-street. MDCCXLV. 3 p. l., iii-vi, [7]-358 p., 1 l. 15 cm. Each part has special t.-p. Signatures: 2 leaves (t.-p. and contents) A-Z4, Aa-Yy4. [BX9178.T35D5] 6-25452
1. Sermons, American. 2. Justification. I. Title.
Contents omitted.

THOMAS, D. Reginald. 252.05131
To know God's way [by] D. Reginald Thomas. Westwood, N.J., Revell [1966] 154 p. 21 cm. [BX9178.T37T6] 66-21895
1. Presbyterian Church—Sermons. 2. Sermons, American. 3. Christian life—Presbyterian authors. I. Title.

THOMAS, James David, 252'.06'6
1910- comp.
Spiritual power. Edited by J. D. Thomas. Abilene, Tex., Biblical Research Press [1972] viii, 338 p. 23 cm. At head of title: Great single sermons. [BX7327.A1T43] 74-170920
1. Disciples of Christ—Sermons. 2. Sermons, American. I. Title. II. Title: Great single sermons.

THOMPSON, John Rhey.
Burden bearing, and other sermons, by John Rhey Thompson. New York, Eaton & Mains; Cincinnati, Jennings & Graham [1905] 261 p. front. (port.) 19 cm. "The sermons in this book were preached extemporaneously at Grace Methodist Episcopal church, Brooklyn, during the years 1883-84." 5-10067
I. Title.

THURSTON, Eli, 1808-1869. 266.
A sermon, delivered at Bath, June 27, 1849, before the Maine missionary society, at its forty-second anniversary. By Eli Thurston... Portland, Printed at the Mirror office, 1849. 52 p. 23 cm. "Forty second annual report of the trustees of the Maine missionary society at their annual meeting in Bath, June 27, 1849": p. 21-52. [BV2360.M3A4] 26-22126
I. Congregational conference and missionary society of Maine. II. Title.

TILLICH, Paul, 1886- 252
The eternal now. New York, Scribners [1965, c.1956-1963] 185p. 21cm. (SL114) [BV4253.T575] 1.25 pap.,
1. Sermons, American. I. Title.

TILLICH, Paul, 1886- 252.041
The shaking of the foundations [sermons] New York, C. Scribner's Sons, 1948. 186 p. 20 cm. Full name: Paul Johannes Oskar Tillich. [BV4253.T6] 48-7226
1. Sermons, American. I. Title.

TILLICH, Paul, 1886-1965.
The shaking of the foundations [sermons] New York, C. Scribner's Sons [1965, c1948] 186 p. 20 cm. 68-61471
1. Sermons, American. I. Title.

TILLICH, Paul [Johannes 252.041
Oskar]
The new being. New York, Scribner [c.1955] 179p. 21cm. Companion vol. to the author's The shaking of the foundations. (Scribner library SL20) 1.25 pap.,
1. Sermons, American. I. Title.

TILLICH, Paul [Johannes 252.041
Oskar]
The shaking of the foundations. New York, Scribner [c.1948] 186p. 21cm. (Scribner Library, SL 30) 1.25 pap.,
1. Sermons, American. I. Title.

TILLICH, Paul Johannes Oskar, 252
1886-
The eternal now. New York, Scribners [c.1963] 185p. 21cm. 63-17938 2.95
1. Sermons, American. I. Title.

TITTLE, Ernest Fremont, 252.07
1885-
A world that cannot be shaken, by Ernest Fremont Tittle; with an introduction by Halford E. Luccock. New York and London, Harper & brothers, 1933. x, 137 p. 20 cm. "First edition." [BX8333.T5W3] 33-17922
1. Sermons, American. I. Title.

TO God be the glory; 252
sermons in honor of George Arthur Buttrick. Edited by Theodore A. Gill. Nashville, Abingdon Press [1973] 159 p. 24 cm. Contents.Contents.—Stewart, J. S. To God be the glory!—Robinson, J. A. T. Evil and the God of love.—Read, D. H. C. News from another network.—Ferris, T. P. On leaving home.—Little, G. One thing I do.—Marney, C. Our present higher good.—Steere, D. V. The ultimate underpinning.—Bennett, J. C. The radicalism of Jesus.—Lehmann, P. Which way is left?—Terrien, S. A time to speak.—Williams, G. H. Creatures of a Creator, members of a body, subjects of a kingdom.—Abbey, M. R. Christ's liberating mandate.—Harrelson, W. Resisting and welcoming the new.—Winn, A. C. The plaines and simplest thing in the world.—Buechner, F. Air for two voices.—Buttrick, D. G. The commandment will not change.—Campbell, E. T. Every battle isn't Armageddon.—Farley, E. Boundedness: the provincialist capture of the church of our Lord and Savior Jesus Christ. [BV4241.T63] 73-8690 ISBN 0-687-42233-7 5.50
1. Buttrick, George Arthur, 1892- 2. Sermons, American. I. Buttrick, George Arthur, 1892- II. Gill, Theodore Alexander, 1920- ed.
Contents omitted.

TODD, Galbraith Hall 232.96
Culture and the cross. Grand Rapids, Mich., Baker Book House, [c.]1959. 111p. 21cm. 59-15535 2.00
1. Sermons, American. I. Title.

TRUEBLOOD, David Elton, 1900- 252
The yoke of Christ, and other sermons. [1st ed.] New York, Harper [1958] 192 p. 22 cm. [BV4253.T7] 58-10364
1. Sermons, American. I. Title.

TRUETT, George Washington, 252.
1867-
A quest for souls, comprising all the sermons preached and prayers offered in a series of gospel meetings held in Fort Worth, Texas, June 11-24, 1917, by George W. Truett ... compiled and edited by J. B. Cranfill, LL.D. (Stenographically reported by J. A.) Dallas, Tex., Texas Baptist book house [c1917] vii, 379 p. 20 cm. "Stenographically reported by Mr. J. A. Lord."--Foreword. [BX6333.T8Q5] 18-101
1. Sermons, American. I. Cranfill, James Britton, 1858- II. Title.

TRUETT, George 252.061
Washington, 1867-
We would see Jesus, and other sermons, by George W. Truett ... compiled and edited by J. B. Cranfill, LL.D. New York, Chicago [etc.] Fleming H. Revell company [c1915] 224 p. 19 1/2 cm. [BX6333.T8W4] 16-1650
1. Sermons, American. I. Cranfill, James Britton, 1858- ed. II. Title.

*TRUETT, George Washington, 252
1867-1944.
"Follow thou Me." Grand Rapids, Mich., Baker Book House [1973, c.1959] 241 p. 20 cm. (Minister's paperback library) First published in 1932. [BV4253] ISBN 0-8010-8791-0 pap., 2.95
1. Sermons, American. I. Title.

TUCKER, Julius Lafayette, 252
1895-
God in the shadows, by J. L. Tucker. Nashville, Southern Pub. Association [1972] 63 p. 19 cm. (Better living series) [BV4253.T77] 72-88859 ISBN 0-8127-0067-8
1. Sermons, American. I. Title.

TULLIS, Don D., 1878- 252
God's garage. Philadelphia, Dorrance [1948] 190 p. 20 cm. [BV4253.T8] 48-0305
1. Sermons, American. I. Title.

TUTTLE, Alexander 252.07
Harrison, 1844-
The living word, by Rev. A. H. Tuttle, D.D. Cincinnati, Jennings and Pye; New York, Eaton and Mains [1904] 150 p. front. (port.) 19 cm. (Half-title: The Methodist pulpit) [BX8333.T8L5] 4-1614
1. Sermons, American. I. Title.

URBANO, Paul. 232.9'63
The marks of the nails. St. Paul, Minn., Yellow Bird Division, Economic Information, inc. [1973] vii, 111 p. 22 cm. Includes bibliographical references. [BX5937.U7M37] 73-90039 ISBN 0-913514-04-7 3.50
1. Protestant Episcopal Church in the U.S.A.—Sermons. 2. Jesus Christ—Seven last words—Sermons. 3. Sermons, American. I. Title.

VAN BUSKIRK, Lawrence, 1775-
1797.
Six sermons, preached by the late Mr. Lawrence V. Buskirk, B.A., candidate for the holy ministry ... New-York, Printed and sold, by T. Kirk, 112, Chatham-street, 1797. viii, 123 p. 16 1/2 cm. "Preface" signed: John C. Kunze, D.D. A 35
1. Sermons, American. I. Kunze, Johann Christoph, 1744-1807. II. Title.

VANCE, James Isaac, 1862- 252.051
Sermons in argot, by James I. Vance ... New York, R. R. Smith, inc., 1931. vi p., 2 l., 3-180 p. 19 1/2 cm. [BX9178.V2S4] 31-11714
1. Sermons, American. I. Title.

VANDENBERG, William Ernest 242
1916-
Devotions for church groups, by William E. Vanden Berg. Grand Rapids, Baker Book House [1966] 126 p. 20 cm. [BX9527.V3] 67-2210
1. Reformed Church in America—Sermons. 2. Sermons, American. I. Title.

VIRGINIA Council of Churches. 252
Watchers of the springs; a collection of rural life sermons and addresses. Richmond [1950] ix, 132 p. 23 cm. [BV4241.V5] 51-18848
1. Sermons, American. 2. Rural churches. I. Title. II. Title: Rural life sermons.

WAGONER, Walter D. 252'.05834
Mortgages on paradise / Walter D. Wagoner. Nashville : Abingdon, c1981. 125 p. ; 20 cm. [BX9886.Z6W335] 19 80-20138 ISBN 0-687-27220-3 pbk. : 4.95
1. United Church of Christ—Sermons. 2. Sermons, America. I. Title.

WALKER, Granville T. 242
Go placidly amid the noise and haste; meditations on the "desiderata," by Granville T. Walker. Fort Worth, Texas Christian University Press, 1973. 103 p. 23 cm. (Texas Christian University monographs in religion, no. 2) Includes bibliographical references. [BX7327.W28G6] 73-78070 3.50
1. Disciples of Christ—Sermons. 2. Sermons, American. I. Title. II. Series: Texas Christian Univeristy, Fort Worth. Monographs in religion, no. 2.

WALKER, Granville T. 252'.06'3
Go placidly amid the noise and haste : meditations on the "Desiderata" / by Granville T. Walker. St. Louis : Bethany Press, c1975. 102 p. ; 22 cm. Includes bibliographical references. [BX7327.W28G6 1975] 75-37546 ISBN 0-8272-1217-8 pbk. : 3.95
1. Christian Church (Disciples of Christ)—Sermons. 2. Sermons, American. I. Title.

WALL, Zeno, 1882- 252.061
Heartening messages, by Zeno Wall ... Nashville, Tenn., Broadman press [c1944] xiii, 179 p. 19 1/2 cm. [BX6333.W23H4] 45-2004
1. Baptists—Sermons. 2. Sermons, American. I. Title.

WALLACE, Foy Esco, 1896- 252
The certified gospel, by Foy E. Wallace, jr. Port Arthur, Tex., O. C. Lambert & son [c1937] 6 p. l., 110 p. incl. ports. 20 1/2 cm. "Sermons...preached...in Port Arthur, Texas, from October 26 to November 10, 1937 and...printed daily in the Port Arthur news."--Introd. [BV4253.W33] 38-8536
1. Sermons, American. I. Title.

WALLIS, Charles 252.0082
Langworthy, 1921- ed.
Notable sermons from Protestant pulpits. New York, Abingdon Press [1958] 206 p. 23 cm. [BV4241.W3] 58-9526
1. Sermons, American. I. Title.

WALSH, John Tomline. 252
A book of sermons, practical and controversial, by Jno. Tomline Walsh ... Cincinnati, O., R. W. Carroll & co.; New Berne, N.C., J. T. Walsh, 1870. vi, 346 p. 23 cm. "The sixth sermon is ... by J. Randolph Tucker ... the eighteenth sermon, by Bro. Geo. Plannenburg."--Pref. [BX7327.W3B6] 37-10874
1. Sermons, American. I. Tucker, John Randolph, 1822-1897 II. Plattenburg, George. III. Title.

WALTER, Nehemiah, 1663-1750. 232
A discourse concerning the wonderfulness of Christ. Delivered in several sermons. By Nehemiah Walter ... Boston in New-England: Printed by B. Green, for Eleazer Phillips, at his shop at the lower end of King street. 1713. 1 p. l., vi, [6], 240 p. 15 cm. [BT200.W25] 45-45756
1. Jesus Christ—Person and offices—Early works to 1800. 2. Sermons, American. I. Title.

WALTHER, Carl Ferdinand 252'.04'1
Wilhelm, 1811-1887.
The word of His Grace : occasional and festival sermons / by C. F. W. Walther ; translated and edited by the Evangelical Lutheran Synod Translation Committee. Lake Mills, Iowa : Graphic Pub. Co., 1978. viii, 260 p. (p. 260 blank) ; 24 cm. [BX8066.W3W67 1978] 78-70539 ISBN 0-89279-014-8 : 9.95
1. Lutheran Church—Sermons. 2. Sermons, American. I. Title.
Available From Bethny College Book Store, 734 Marsh St., Mankado., MA 56001

WALTHOUR, John Buckman, 252.5
1904-
Our hearts beat high, ten of the sermons preached to the West Point class of 1947 by their chaplain, John B. Walthour. New York, The Macmillan company, 1947. 7 p. l., 111 p. 16 cm. Illustrated lining-papers. [BV4316.S7W28] 47-5317
1. Sermons, American. 2. U.S. Military academy, West Point. I. Title.

WALTHOUR, John Buckman, 252.5
1904-
With eyes up; ten of the sermons preached to the West Point class of 1946 by their chaplain, John B. Walthour. New York, The Macmillan company, 1946. 7 p. l., 3-102 p. 16 cm. Illustrated lining-papers. [BV4316.S7W3] 46-4845

1. Sermons, American. 2. U.S. Military academy, West Point. I. Title.

WARD, Alfred George, 1881- 922.
The whirlwind prophet, and other sermons by A. G. Ward. Springfield, Mo., Gospel publishing house [1927] 4 p. l., 11-128 p. 19 cm. (On cover: Pulpit and pew; full gospel series) [BX8795.P25W3] 44-27416
1. Sermons, American. I. Title.

WARFIELD, Benjamin Breckinridge, 1851-1921. 252'.05
Faith and life / Benjamin B. Warfield. Edinburgh ; Carlisle, Pa. : Banner of Truth Trust, 1974. viii, 458 p. ; 19 cm. First published 1916. [BX9178.W33F3 1974] 75-320416 ISBN 0-85151-188-0 : £0.90
1. Presbyterian Church—Sermons. 2. Sermons, American. I. Title.

WARNER, D. J. Benson, 1868- 922
Brief sketch of life from childhood to fifty years; proverbial Scriptural references, Bible reading and Scriptural text references. Sermons ... by Evangelist J. Benson Warner ... [New Orleans, Rentschler printing company] 1918. 64 p. front. (port.) 19 cm. [BV3785.W3A3] 19-1517
I. Title.

WATT, John A. 252
The old, old story from the Old Testament; a series of addresses by John Watt. New York, Loizeaux Bros. [1954?] 192 p. 19 cm. [BS1151.5.W37] 75-304078
1. Bible. O.T.—Sermons. 2. Sermons, American. I. Title.

WAYLAND, Francis, 1796-1865. 252.061
Occasional discourses, including several never before published. By Francis Wayland... Boston, J. Loring, 1833. 376 p. 19 1/2 cm. [BX6333.W3O4] 32-34569
1. Sermons, American. I. Title.

WAYLAND, Francis, 1796-1865. 252.061
Sermons to the churches. By Francis Wayland. New York, Sheldon, Blakeman, & company; Boston, Gould & Lincoln; [etc., etc.] 1858. viii, [9]-281 p. 19 1/2 cm. [BX6333.W3S4] 33-8322
1. Sermons, American. I. Title.

WAYLAND, Francis, 1796-1865. 252.5
University sermons. Sermons delivered in the chapel of Brown university. By Francis Wayland, president of the university. Boston, Gould, Kendall, and Lincoln, 1849. viii, 328 p. 20 cm. [BV4310.W37] 33-8310
1. Sermons, American. I. Title.

WAYS of the Christian life, sermons by the sea, second series. New York, Cincinnati [etc.] The Abingdon press [c1939] 141 p. 19 1/2 cm. [BV4241.S416 2d ser.] 39-23179 252.0082
1. Sermons, American. I. Title: Sermons by the sea, second series.

WEBB, Lance. 252'.07
God's surprises / Lance Webb. Nashville : Abingdon, c1976. 175 p. ; 20 cm. Includes bibliographical references. [BX8333.W4164G6] 75-44495 ISBN 0-687-15447-2 : 6.95
1. Methodist Church—Sermons. 2. Sermons, American. I. Title.

WEBBER, Edward Frederick. 232
The man every one ought to know, by Dr. E. F. Webber ... [Oklahoma City] c1942. 312 p. incl. pl., 2 port. 22 1/2 cm. [BV4301.W4] 42-21912
1. Sermons, American. I. Title.

WELCH, Reuben. 252
When you run out of fantastic ... persevere / Reuben Welch. [Nashville] : Impact Books, c1976. 147 p. ; 22 cm. [BS2775.4.W44] 76-20999 ISBN 0-914850-42-3 : 4.95
1. Bible. N.T. Hebrews—Sermons. 2. Sermons, American. I. Title.

WELSH, Wiley A 252.066
Villains on white horses; sermons on passages from Paul, by W. A. Welsh. Saint Louis, Bethany Press [1964] 155 p. 23 cm. [BX7327.W38V5] 64-25219
1. Sermons, American. 2. Disciples of Christ — Sermons. I. Title.

WELSHIMER, Pearl Howard, 1873- 252
Welshimer's sermons, by P. H. Welshimer. Cincinnati, O., The Standard publishing company [c1927] 252 p. 19 1/2 cm. [BX7327.W4W4] 28-3557
I. Title.

*WESBERRY, James P. 252
When hell trembles and other sermons for revival [by] James P. Wesberry Grand Rapids, Baker Book House [1974] 118 p. 20 cm. [BV3797] ISBN 0-8010-9558-1 3.95
1. Sermons, American. I. Title.

WESTON, Sidney Adams, 1877- ed. 252
Sermons I have preached to young people, edited by Sidney A. Weston ... Boston, Chicago, The Pilgrim press [c1931] 4 p. l., 3-170 p. 20 1/2 cm. [BV4310.W4] 31-31475
1. Sermons, American. I. Title.

WHEN you need a special sermon series. St. Louis, MO : Concordia Pub. House, c1981. 103 p. ; 23 cm. By Paul L. Maier and others. [BX8066.A1W52] 19 81-476 ISBN 0-570-03836-7 : 5.95 252'.04133
1. Lutheran Church—Sermons. 2. Sermons, American.

WHITE, Willie W
The greatest work in the world; a new study on the fundamentals. Questions by Don De Welt. Joplin, Mo., College Press [c1961] 255 p. 23 cm. (Bible study textbook series) 67-31250
1. Sermons, American. 2. Disciples of Christ — Sermons. I. Title. II. Series.

WHITING, Thomas A. 248.4
Be good to yourself / Thomas A. Whiting. Nashville : Abingdon, c1981. 128 p. ; 22 cm. "Material for sermons to be broadcast on ... the Protestant Hour beginning in July 1981." Includes bibliographical references. [BX8333.W425B4] 19 80-27304 ISBN 0-687-02800-0 : 6.95
1. Methodist Church—Sermons. 2. Sermons, American. I. Protestant hour (Radio program) II. Title.

WILKE, Richard B., 1930- 242'.722
Our Father / Richard B. Wilke. Nashville : Abingdon, c1978. 95 p. ; 18 cm. [BV233.W53] 77-17112 ISBN 0-687-29544-0 : 4.95
1. Methodist Church—Sermons. 2. Lords's prayer—Sermons. 3. Sermons, American. I. Lords prayer. English. 1977. II. Title.

WILLIAMS, David Forest, 1846-1931. 252.076
Sermons, by the late Rev. D. Forest Williams... Oak Hill, O., Mrs. D. F. Williams [c1932] 189 p. incl. front. (port.) 19 cm. Edited by Mrs. D. F. Williams. cf. Foreword. [BX8333.W45S4] 32-22226
1. Sermons, American. I. Williams, Catherine Jane, "Mrs. D. Forest Williams," ed. II. Title.

WILLIAMS, Gershom Mott, bp., 1857-
Human questions and divine answers; short sermons expressly written for lay readers in the American church, by Gershom Mott Williams... Milwaukee, The Young churchman company, 1913. x, 299 p. 19 1/2 cm. 13-5407
I. Title.

WILLIAMS, Granville Mercer, 1889- 252'.03'3
Joy in the Lord [by] Granville M. Williams. Wakefield, Mass., Parameter Press [1972] 123 p. 24 cm. "Retreat addresses given at various times to the Sisters of the Society of St. Margaret." [BX5937.W475J69] 71-189764 ISBN 0-88203-001-9 2.00
1. Protestant Episcopal Church in the U.S.A.—Sermons. 2. Sermons, American. I. Title.

WILLIAMS, Joseph W 1883- 252.4
Songs in the night. [1st ed.] New York, Pageant Press [1952] 245 p. 21 cm. [BV4253.W44] 52-4914
1. Sermons, American. I. Title.

WILLIAMS, Smallwood Edmond, 1907- 252.09'9
Significant sermons. Washington, Bible Way Church [1970] 164 p. 20 cm. [BX6510.B676W54] 77-117015 3.50
1. Bible Way Churches of Our Lord Jesus Christ World Wide—Sermons. 2. Sermons, American. I. Title.

WIRT, Sherwood Eliot, comp. 252'.00973
Great preaching; evangelical messages by contemporary Christians. Edited by Sherwood Eliot Wirt and Viola Blake. Waco, Tex., Word Books [1970] 173 p. 23 cm. Contents.Contents.—When Christ becomes real, by M. S. Augsburger.—From Galilee to Manhattan, by D. H. C. Read.—God's universe, by G. B. Wilson.—"I am ...," by T. Rees.—The rending of the veil, by M. L. Loane.—The Holy Spirit in action, by O. C. J. Hoffmann.—Made, marred, mended, by B. Graham.—The third he, by H. J. Ockenga.—Repent, by J. E. Haggai.—This business of being converted, by R. G. Turnbull.—You can be sure, by D. J. Kennedy.—Touched by Jesus, by O. Roberts.—The burning heart, by H. O. Jones.—The Christian extra, by P. S. Rees.—Living in high gear, by P. M. Nagano.—Redeeming the time, by S. F. Olford.—Christian responsibility to a changing world, by R. B. Munger.—The source of our life, by E. L. R. Elson.—The wasteland and the springs, by G. Kennedy.—A living hope, by L. Ford.—The crown of life, by W. Fitch.—Coming! By W. A. Criswell. [BV4241.W57] 76-134253 4.50
1. Sermons, American. I. Blake, Viola, 1921- joint comp. II. Title.

WISE, Jeremiah, d.1756.
Rulers the ministers of God for the good of their people. A sermon preached before His Excellency William Burnet, esq.; the honourable the lieu. governour, the Council and Representatives of the province of the Massachusetts-Bay in New-England, May 28, 1729, being the day for the election of His Majesty's Council. By Jeremiah Wise, M.A. pastor to a church of Christ in Berwick ... Boston: Printed by T. Fleet, printer to the honourable House of representatives. Sold by T. Hancock, at the Bible and three crowns near the town dock, 1729. 54, [1] p. 19 1/2 cm. 3-7704
I. Title.

WRIGHT, Bruce Simpson, 1879- 252.07
Chancel windows [by] Bruce S. Wright. Nashville, Cokesbury press [c1933] 152 p. 1 l. 19 cm. [BX8333.W7C45] 33-6347
1. Sermons, American. I. Title.

WRIGHT, John Joseph, Cardinal, 1909- 232.9'635
Words in pain : meditations on the last words of Jesus / John Cardinal Wright. Rev. ed. Notre Dame, Ind. : Ave Maria Press, 1978. 79 p. : ill. ; 19 cm. [BT456.W7 1978] 77-20727 ISBN 0-87793-144-5 pbk. : 2.95
1. Jesus Christ—Seven last words—Sermons. 2. Catholic Church—Sermons. 3. Sermons, American. I. Title.

WYNN, Daniel Webster, 1919- 252.07
Timeless issues [by] Daniel W. Wynn. New York, Philosophical Library [1967] x, 144 p. 22 cm. [BX8472.W9] 66-20219
1. Methodist Church—Sermons. 2. Sermons, American. I. Title.

YOHN, David Waite. 225.6'6
The Christian reader's guide to the New Testament. Grand Rapids, Mich., Eerdmans [1973] 200 p. 22 cm. [BS2341.3.Y64] 73-76532 ISBN 0-8028-1505-7 3.45
1. Bible. N.T.—Sermons. 2. Sermons, American. I. Title.

YORKE, Peter Christopher, 1864-1925. 252.02
Sermons, by Rev. P. C. Yorke... San Francisco, The Text book publishing company, 1931. 2 v. front. (ports.) 19 cm. Preface signed: Ralph Hunt. [BX1756.Y6S4] 31-19561
1. Sermons, American. I. Hunt, Ralph, ed. II. Title.

YOUNG, Robert T., 1935- 252'.07'6
A sprig of hope : sermons of encouragement & expectation / Robert T. Young. Nashville : Abingdon, c1980. 144 p. ; 20 cm. [BX8333.Y63S68] 79-20946 ISBN 0-687-39260-8 pbk. : 4.95
1. Methodist Church—Sermons. 2. Sermons, American. I. Title.

ZELLER, Harry K. 242
Free to be, free to give. Elgin, Ill., Brethren Press [1974] 156 p. port. 21 cm. [BX7827.Z4F7] 74-5487 ISBN 0-87178-295-2 4.95
1. Church of the Brethren—Sermons. 2. Sermons, American. 3. Meditations. I. Title.

Sermons, American—Afro-American authors.

GOD'S trombones;
seven negro sermons in verse. Drawings by Aaron Douglas, lettering by C. B. Falls. New York, The Viking Press, 1959. 56p. 23cm.
I. Johnson, James Weldon, 1871-1938. II. Title: Negro sermons in verse.

PREACHING the gospel / Henry J. Young, editor ; with contributions by William Holmes Borders ... [et al.]. Philadelphia : Fortress Press, c1976. vi, 89 p. ; 22 cm. [BV4241.5.P73] 75-36449 ISBN 0-8006-1223-X pbk. : 2.95 252'.00973
1. Sermons, American—Afro-American authors. I. Young, Henry J. II. Borders, William Holmes, 1905-

Sermons, American—Collected works.

CYCLOPEDIA of sermons ... Five volumes complete in one. Grand Rapids, Kregel, 1956. vii, 667p.
I. Burns, Jabez, 1805-1876.

THE Puritan sermon in America, 1630-1750. Delmar, N.Y. : Scholars' Facsimiles & Reprints, 1978-1979. v. ; 23 cm. (The Sermon in America, 1620-1800) Contents.Contents.—1. Bosco, R. A. Sermons for days of fast, prayer, and humiliation and execution sermons. Includes bibliographies. [BV4241.P83] 79-9593 ISBN 0-8201-1320-4 (v. 1) : 170.00 252
1. Sermons, American—Collected works. 2. Preaching—New England—History—Collected works. 3. Puritans—New England—Collected works. I. Series: Sermon in America, 1620-1800.

STEIMLE, Edmund A., ed. 252.041
Renewal in the pulpit; sermons, by younger preachers. Edited and with an introd. by Edmund A. Steimle. Philadelphia, Fortress Press [1966] xvii, 190 p. 17 cm. (The Preacher's paperback library, v. 7) [BX8066.A1S73] 66-19980
1. Lutheran Church—Sermons—Collections. 2. Sermons, American—Collections. I. Title.

WALKER, Carl C., 1893- 243
Walker's gospel sermons, by Evangelist Carl C. Walker ... with introduction by J. H. Foresman ... Joplin, Mo., Walker's gospel messenger [c1924] 8 p., 1 l., 9-238 p. 2 port.(incl. front.) 20 cm. [BV3797.W3] 24-30978
I. Title.

WRIGHT, Lawrence, 1862-
Eighteen sermons on great themes; a strong, concise presentation of the great fundamental truths of the gospel and of Christian living, by Evangelist Lawrence Wright ... Des Moines, Ia., The Christian union, 1909. viii, [9]-274 p. incl. front. (port.) 20 1/2 cm. 9-10155
I. Title.

Sermons, American — Jewish authors.

ADLER, Morris. 296.4'2
The voice still speaks; message of the Torah for contemporary man. Compiled by Jacob Chinitz. Foreword by Louis Finkelstein. New York, Bloch Pub. Co. [1969] xviii, 436 p. 25 cm. Transcriptions of sermons. [BM740.2.A3] 68-57433 10.00
1. Sermons, American—Jewish authors. 2. Sermons, Jewish—U.S. I. Title.

BAKER, Julius L. 296.4'2
Pri Yehudah, by Julius L. Baker. Columbus, Ohio, Printed by Pfeifer Print. Co. [1967] viii, 219 p. 24 cm. Text in English. [BM740.2.B27] 67-7523

1. Sermons, American—Jewish authors. 2. Sermons, Jewish—United States. I. Title.

BERZON, Bernard L. 296.4'2
Sermons the year 'round : ninety sermons covering all sidrot, holidays, and special occasions / by Bernard L. Berzon. Middle Village, N.Y. : Jonathan David Publishers, c1978. Viii, 337 p. ; 22 cm. [BS1225.4.B47] 78-15088 ISBN 0-8246-0239-0 : 14.95
1. Bible. O.T. Pentateuch—Sermons. 2. Sermons, American—Jewish authors. 3. Sermons, Jewish—United States. I. Title.

BLANK, Sheldon H. 221.6
Prophetic thought : essays and lectures / Sheldon H. Blank. Cincinnati : Hebrew Union College Press, c1977. x, 167 p. ; 26 cm. (Jewish perspectives ; v. 2) "Bibliography of the writings of Sheldon H. Blank": p. 159-167. [BS1171.2.B55] 77-5898 ISBN 0-87820-501-2 : 12.50
1. Bible. O.T.—Criticism, interpretation, etc.—Addresses, essays, lectures. 2. Sermons, American—Jewish authors. 3. Sermons, Jewish—United States. I. Title. II. Series.
Publisher's address : 3101 Clifton Ave., Cincinati, Ohio 45220

CAHN, Judah. 296.4'2
View from the pulpit / by Judah Cahn. New York, N.Y. : Ktav Pub. House, 1982. x, 159 p. ; 24 cm. [BM740.2.C33 1982] 19 81-23673 ISBN 0-87068-765-4 : 12.50
1. Sermons, American—Jewish authors. 2. Sermons, Jewish—United States. I. Title.

CHIEL, Samuel. 296.4'2
The gift of life / by Samuel Chiel. New York : Ktav Pub. House, 1979. xi, 171 p. ; 24 cm. [BM740.2.C44] 19 80-117466 12.50
1. Sermons, American—Jewish authors. 2. Sermons, Jewish—United States. I. Title.

COHEN, Seymour J. 296.4'2
A time to speak, by Seymour J. Cohen. New York, J. David [1968] 314 p. 24 cm. Sermons. [BM740.2.C62] 68-19957
1. Sermons, American—Jewish authors. 2. Sermons, Jewish—United States. I. Title.

COHON, Beryl David, 1898- 296.4'2
Shielding the flame; a personal and spiritual inventory of a liberal rabbi, by Beryl D. Cohon. New York, Bloch Pub. Co. [1972] ix, 118 p. 22 cm. [BM740.2.C64] 72-4801 ISBN 0-8197-0293-5 4.95
1. Sermons, American—Jewish authors. 2. Sermons, Jewish—United States. I. Title.

COHON, Beryl David, 1898- 296.4'2
1976.
Come, let us reason together : sermons presented in days of crisis / by Beryl D. Cohon ; foreword by Abram L. Sachar. New York : Bloch Pub. Co., c1977. xii, 75 p. ; 22 cm. [BM740.2.C58 1977] 76-24330 ISBN 0-8197-0397-4 : 5.95
1. Sermons, American—Jewish authors. 2. Sermons, Jewish—United States. I. Title.

DONIN, Hayim 296.42
Beyond thyself: a collection of sermons. New York, Bloch [c.1965] vii, 131p. 21cm. [BM740.2.D6] 65-19611 3.75
1. Sermons, American—Jewish authors. 2. Sermons, Jewish—U.S. I. Title.

DONIN, Hayim.
Beyond thyself: a collection of sermons. New York, Bloch Pub. Co. [1965] vii, 131 p. 21 cm.
1. Sermons, American — Jewish authors. 2. Sermons, Jewish — U.S. I. Title.

DONIN, Hayim. 296.42
Beyond thyself: a collection of sermons. New York, Bloch Pub. Co. [1965] vii, 131 p. 21 cm. [BM740.2.D6] 65-19611
1. Sermons, American — Jewish authors. 2. Sermons, Jewish — U.S. I. Title.

ELKINS, Dov Peretz. 296.8'346
A tradition reborn; sermons and essays on liberal Judaism. Foreword by Robert Gordis. South Brunswick, A. S. Barnes [1973] 292 p. 22 cm. [BM740.2.E43 1973] 73-2772 ISBN 0-498-01381-2
1. Sermons, American—Jewish authors. 2. Sermons, Jewish—United States. I. Title.

FREEHOF, Solomon Bennett, 296.4'2
1892-
J. Leonard Levy, prophetic voice, by Solomon B. Freehof and Vigdor W. Kavaler. [Pittsburgh, Rodef Shalom Congregation, 1970] xv, 233 p. port. 24 cm. Includes selected lectures by J. L. Levy. [BM740.F674] 75-263848
1. Sermons, American—Jewish authors. 2. Sermons, Jewish—U.S. I. Kavaler, Vigdor W., joint author. II. Levy, Joseph Leonard, 1865-1917.

FREEHOF, Solomon Bennett, 296.4'2
1892-
Preaching the Bible; sermons for Sabbaths and high holy days [by] Solomon B. Freehof. New York, Ktav Pub. House [1974] p. [BM740.2.F64] 74-889 ISBN 0-87068-244-X 12.50
1. Sermons, American—Jewish authors. 2. Sermons, Jewish—United States. 3. High Holy Day sermons. I. Title.

FREEHOF, Solomon Bennett, 296.3
1892-
Spoken and heard; sermons and addresses, by Solomon B. Freehof. [Pittsburgh, Rodef Shalom Congregation, 1972] ix, 264 p. 24 cm. "Bibliography from Essays in honor of Solomon B. Freehof, by T. Wiener and L. Freehof: p. [229]-264. [BM740.2.F65] 73-161280
1. Freehof, Solomon Bennett, 1892-—Bibliography. 2. Sermons, American—Jewish authors. 3. Sermons, Jewish—United States. I. Title.

GITTELSOHN, Roland 296.4'2
Bertram, 1910-
Fire in my bones; essays on Judaism in a time of crisis [by] Roland B. Gittelsohn. New York, Bloch Pub. Co. [1969] xvi, 284 p. 22 cm. Includes bibliographical references. [BM740.2.G53] 78-93295 5.95
1. Sermons, American—Jewish authors. 2. Sermons, Jewish—U.S. I. Title.

GORDON, Solomon. 296.42
Voice of the heart. New York, Bloch Pub. Co. [1965] 147 p. 23 cm. [BM740.2G64] 64-66010
1. Sermons, American — Jewish authors. 2. Sermons, Jewish — u.s. I. Title.

HIRSCH, David 296.8'346'0924 B
Einhorn.
Rabbi Emil G. Hirsch, the reform advocate. Chicago, Whitehall Co. [1968] ii, 191 p. 24 cm. [BM755.H47H5] 68-24717
1. Hirsch, Emil Gustav, 1851-1923. 2. Jesus Christ—Crucifixion. 3. Sermons, American—Jewish authors. 4. Sermons, Jewish—U.S

KOLATCH, Alfred J., 296.4'2'08
1916-
Sermons for the sixties, by Alfred J. Kolatch. Introd. by Ben Zion Bokser. New York, J. David [c1965] 193 p. 24 cm. [BM740.2.K63] 65-26588
1. Sermons, American—Jewish authors. 2. Sermons, Jewish—U.S. I. Title.

LANDAU, Sol, 1920- 296'.0924
Bridging two worlds; Rabbi Ezekiel Landau (1888-1965): his written and spoken legacy. Foreword by Helene Landau. New York, J. David [1968] xii, 123 p. group port. 23 cm. Bibliography: p. 122-123. [BM755.L32L3] 68-19961
1. Landau, Ezekiel, 1888-1965. 2. Sermons, American—Jewish authors. 3. Sermons, Jewish—United States. I. Title.

LEVINTHAL, Israel Herbert, 296
1888-
A new world is born; sermons and addresses, by Israel Herbert Levinthal... New York and London, Funk & Wagnalls company, 1943. xiii, 305 p. 20 1/2 cm. Bibliographical foot-notes. [BM740.L475] 43-7771
1. Sermons, American—Jewish authors. I. Title.

LOOKSTEIN, Joseph Hyman, 296.4'2
1902-
Yesterday's faith for tomorrow / by Joseph H. Lookstein. New York : Ktav Pub. House, 1979. xvi, 189 p. ; 24 cm. Includes bibliographical references. [BM740.2.L63] 79-117233 12.15
1. Sermons, American—Jewish authors. 2. Sermons, Jewish—United States. I. Title.

MOWSHOWITZ, Israel. 296.4
Fires to warm us / by Israel Mowshowitz. New York : Ktav Pub. House, c1978. xi, 234 p. ; 24 cm. [BM740.2.M67] 79-115357 10.00
1. Sermons, American—Jewish authors. 2. Sermons, Jewish—United States. I. Title.

MOWSHOWITZ, Israel. 296.4'2
To serve in faithfulness / by Israel Mowshowitz. New York : Ktav Pub. House, [1975] xiii, 249 p. ; 24 cm. [BM740.2.M68] 74-32465 ISBN 0-87068-271-7 : 10.00
1. Sermons, American—Jewish authors. 2. Sermons, Jewish—United States. I. Title.

RUDIN, Jacob Philip. 296.4'2
Very truly yours; a creative harvest of forty years in the pulpit. Introd. by Roland B. Gittelsohn. New York, Bloch Pub. Co. [1971] xiv, 299 p. 22 cm. [BM740.2.R8] 76-163016 ISBN 0-8197-0279-X 6.50
1. Sermons, American—Jewish authors. 2. Sermons, Jewish—U.S. I. Title.

SILVERMAN, Hillel E., 296.4'2
1924-
From heart to heart / by Hillel E. Silverman. New York : Ktav Pub. House, 1979. xi, 219 p. ; 24 cm. [BM740.2.S49] 19 80-117851 10.00
1. Sermons, American—Jewish authors. 2. Sermons, Jewish—United States. I. Title.

STEINBACH, Alexander Alan, 296.42
1894-
Through storms we grow, and other sermons, lectures, and essays. Introd. by Robert Gordis. New York, Bloch Pub. Co. [1964] x, 260 p. 24 cm. [BM735.S7] 64-24231
1. Sermons, American—Jewish authors. 2. Sermons, Jewish. I. Title.

STEINBERG, Milton, 1903- 296.3'08
1950.
A believing Jew; the selected writings of Milton Steinberg. Freeport, N.Y., Books for Libraries Press [1971, c1951] 318 p. 23 cm. (Essay index reprint series) Contents.Contents.—God and the world's end.—The social crisis and the retreat of God.—A protest against a new cult.—The future of Judaism in America.—A specimen Jew.—American Jewry's coming of age.—Indignation - a lost Jewish virtue.—The right not to be a Jew.—Commentary magazine.—The test of time.—When I think of Seraye.—Latter day miracles: Israel.—Our persistent failures.—A pity for the living.—The depth of Evil.—From the mountaintops.—Telling oneself the truth.—On being the victim of injustice.—The Sabbath of Sabbaths.—The fear of life.—Remember us unto life.—If man is God.—To hold with open arms. [BM740.S754 1971] 76-152215 ISBN 0-8369-2256-5
1. Sermons, American—Jewish authors. 2. Sermons, Jewish—U.S. 3. Judaism—U.S.—Addresses, essays, lectures. I. Title.

WANEFSKY, Joseph. 222'.1'06
From the shadow of insight. New York, Philosophical Library [1974] 149 p. 22 cm. [BS1225.4.W28] 73-82166 ISBN 0-8022-2128-9 6.00
1. Bible. O.T. Pentateuch—Sermons. 2. Sermons, American—Jewish authors. 3. Sermons, Jewish—United States. I. Title.

Sermons, American—Negro authors.

OUTSTANDING Black sermons / 252
J. Alfred Smith, Sr., editor. Valley Forge, Pa. : Judson Press, [1976] 96 p. ; 22 cm. Contents.Contents.—Belk, L. S. The eyes of the Lord.—Blanford, C. The church and its mission.—Booth, L. V. The master dreamer.—Clark, E. M. How a people make history.—Gregory, H. C. The shepherd.—Jones, O. C. The preacher's dilemma.—Matthews, J. V. When, from our exile ....—Moyd, O. P. Membership or movement?—Shaw, W. J. A day of trouble.—Smith, J. A. The future of the Black church.—Stewart, J. H. The cost of citizenship.—Thomas, R. C. The gateway to life.—Wright, H. S. Rules for the road. Includes bibliographical references. [BV4241.5.O9] 76-2084 ISBN 0-8170-0664-8 pbk. : 2.95
1. Sermons, American—Negro authors. I. Smith, James Alfred.
Contents omitted.

PHILPOT, William M., comp. 252
Best Black sermons. Editor: William M. Philpot. Valley Forge [Pa.] Judson Press [1972] 96 p. 22 cm. Contents.Contents.—Introduction, by G. C. Taylor.—Three dimensions of a complete life, by M. L. King, Jr.—Handicapped lives, by W. H. Borders, Sr.—The God who takes off chariot wheels, by D. E. King.—What man lives by, B. E. Mays.—The hot winds of change, by S. B. McKinney.—Going from disgrace to dignity, by O. Moss, Jr.—A strange song in a strange land, by D. T. Shannon.—Time is winding Up! By K. M. Smith.—What is your name? By H. H. Watts.—The relevancy of the Black church to the new generation, by H. L. Williams.—Black theology, by G. S. Wilmore, Jr.—Suggested tools for the preacher, by W. B. Hoard (p. 95-96) [BV4241.5.P48] 72-75358 ISBN 0-8170-0533-1 1.95
1. Sermons, American—Negro authors. I. Title.

Sermons, American. Presbyterian church—Sermons.

DAVIES, Samuel, 1724- 252.051
1761.
Sermons on important subjects, by the Reverend Samuel Davies ... With an essay on the life and times of the author, by Albert Barnes. Stereotype ed., containing all the author's sermons ever published ... New-York, Dayton and Saxton, 841. 3 v. 20 cm. Edited by Thomas Gibbons. [BX9178.D35S4 1841] 33-16407
1. Sermons, American. Presbyterian church—Sermons. I. Gibbons, Thomas, 1720-1785, ed. II. Barnes, Albert, 1798-1870. III. Title.

PRINCETON theological seminary.
The sermon delivered at the inauguration of the Rev. Archibald Alexander, D. D., as professor of didactic and polemic theology, in the Theological seminary of the Presbyterian church in the United States of America [by Samuel Miller] To which are added, the professor and students [by Philip Milledoler] New-York, Whiting and Watson, 1812. 122 p. 23 cm. A 19
I. Alexander, Archibald, 1772-1851. II. Miller, Samuel, 1769-1850. III. Milledoler, Philip, 1775-1852. IV. Title.

Sermons, American (Selections, extracts, etc.)

ASSOCIATION Press, New 252.0082
York.
Words to change lives; a kaleidoscopic view of contemporary religious expression. New York [c1957] 128p. 16cm. (An Association Press reflection book) [BV4241.A76] 57-5494
1. Sermons, American (Selections: Extracts, etc.) I. Title.

BEECHER, Henry Ward, 1813- 204
1887.
Life thoughts, gathered from the extemporaneous discourses of Henry Ward Beecher. By one of his congregation. Boston, Phillips, Sampson and company, 1858. 299 p. 19 cm. Preface signed: Edna Dean Proctor. [BX7117.B4L5] 26-22113
1. Sermons, American (Selections, extracts, etc.) I. Proctor, Edna Dean, 1829-1923, ed. II. Title.

BEECHER, Henry Ward, 1813- 204
1887.
Life thoughts, gathered from the extemporaneous discourses of Henry Ward Beecher. By one of his congregation. 10th thousand. Boston, Phillips, Sampson and company, 1858. xviii, 299 p. 20 cm. Preface signed: Edna Dean Proctor. [BX7117.B4L5 1856 a] 26-22116
1. Sermons, American (Selections: Extracts, etc.) I. Proctor, Edna Dean, 1829-1923, ed. II. Title.

BEECHER, Henry Ward, 1813- 252.
1887.
Metaphors, similes and other characteristic sayings of Henry Ward Beecher. Compiled from discourses reported by T.J. Ellinwood, with introduction by Homer B. Sprague, Ph.D. New York, A.J. Graham & co., 1895. 217 p. front. (port.) 18 cm. [BX7233.B4M4] 40-25729
1. Sermons, American (Selections:

Extracts, etc.) I. Ellinwood, Truman Jeremiah, 1830-1921, comp. II. Title.

BEECHER, Henry Ward, 1813- 1887. 208.
Proverbs from Plymouth pulpit; selected from the writings and sayings of Henry Ward Beecher, by William Drysdale. Revised in part by Mr. Beecher, and under revision by him at the time of his death. New York, D. Appleton and company, 1887. 230 p. 19 cm. [BX7117.B4P7] 44-29706
1. Sermons, American (Selections: Extracts, etc.) I. Drysdale, William, 1852-1901, comp. II. Title.

BEECHER, Henry Ward, 1813-1887.
Sermon briefs, by Henry Ward Beecher; transcribed from the author's manuscript notes of unpublished discourses, and ed., by John R. Howard and Truman J. Ellinwood. Boston, New York [etc.] The Pilgrim press [c1905] 263 p. facsims. 21 cm. 5-37779
I. Howard, John Raymond, 1837- ed. II. Ellinwood, Truman Jeremiah, 1830- joint ed. III. Title.

ECKLEY, Joseph, 1750-1811.
A sermon delivered at the installation of the Rev. Horace Holley, to the pastoral care of the church and society in Hollis street, Boston. March 8, 1809. By Joseph Eckley... Boston, Printed by J. Belcher, State street, 1809. 53 p. 23 cm. [BN7233.E26S4] 6-24654
I. Title.

FREEMAN, James Edward, bp., 1866- 252.
Voices of assurance, by the Rt. Rev. James E. Freeman ... Milwaukee, Morehouse publishing co.; London, A. R. Mowbray & co. [c1928] x p., 1 l., 71, [1] p. front. (port.) 18 cm. (Half-title: Washington cathedral series) "Brief synopses of sermons preached in the Washington cathedral."--Pref. [BX5937.F7V6] 28-21077
I. Title. II. Series.

JOHNSTON, Robert, 1871- 1935. 208.1
The soul's struggle, by Robert Johnston ... New York [etc.] Fleming H. Revell company [c1938] 186 p. front. (port.) 20 cm. Edited by Elsie Metcalf. [BX5937.J413S6] 38-30217
1. Sermons, American (Selections: Exracts, etc.) I. Metcalf, Elsie, 1881- ed. II. Title.

MACARTNEY, Clarence Edward Noble, 1879- 251
Macartney's illustrations; illustrations from the sermons of Clarence Edward Macartney ... New York, Nashville, Abingdon-Cokesbury press [1945] 421 p. 22 cm. [BX9178.M17214] 45-6822
1. Sermons, American (Selections: Extracts, etc.) I. Title.

Sermons, American (U.S.)

CHAPMAN, J. Wilbur, 1859- 1918. 243
Awakening sermons, by J. Wilbur Chapman, D. D., compiled and edited by Edgar Whitaker Work, D. D. New York, Chicago [etc.] Fleming H. Revell company [c1928] 186 p. illus. 20 cm. [BV3797.C49] 28-21662
I. Work, Edgar Whitaker, 1862- ed. II. Title.

CLAUSEN, Bernard Chancellor, 1892- 220
The door that has no key; sermons for true Americans, by Bernard C. Clausen ... Philadelphia, Boston [etc.] The Judson press [1925] 5 p. l., 111 p. 19 1/2 cm. [BR125.C56] 25-5625
I. Title.

COOPER, William A. 252.078
The awakening; sermons and sermonettes on special occasions. New York, Expostion [c.1963] 120p. 21cm. 3.00
I. Title.

DAVENPORT, William Edwards, 1862-
Poetical sermons including the ballad of Plymouth church, by William E. Davenport. New York [etc.] G. P. Putnam's sons, 1897. v, 278 p. 18 cm. [PS1513.D7 1897] 24-23753
I. Title.

EYRE, Richard M. FIC
The awakening / Richard M. Eyre. Salt Lake City, Utah : Bookcraft, c1981. 190 p. ; 23 cm. [PS3555.Y68A9] 813'.54 19 81-67309 ISBN 0-88494-430-1 : 6.95
I. Title.

FRASER, Abelk McIver, 1856- 285.
Doctor Fraser and his sermons, ed. by Rev. William E. Hudson ... New York, Chicago [etc.] Fleming H. Revell company [c1920] 159 p. front. (port.) plates. 20 cm. [BX9225.F7A4] 21-3505
I. Hudson, William E., ed. II. Title.

MANDERSON, Rita, 1916- 248.2'4
The awakening. [Baltimore, Printed by Reese Press, 1968] 213 p. ports. 22 cm. [BV4935.M28A3] 68-6922
I. Title.

MORGAN, John Vyrnwy, 1860- ed. 252
The Cambro-American pulpit, by Rev. Vyrnwy Morgan. New York and London, Funk & Wagnalls company, 1898. xviii, 595 p. front., ports. 20 cm. "Biographical sketches": p. 578-595. [BV4241.M6] 99-294
1. Sermons, American (U.S.) 2. Welsh in the U.S. I. Title.

WILLIAMS, Thomas, 1779-1876. 252.
Sermons on important subjects. By Thomas Williams, a minister of the gospel. Hartford: Printed by Peter B. Gleason, 1810. iv, [5]-231 p. 19 cm. [BX7233.W47S4] 24-15964
I. Title.

Sermons, American—Women authors.

WOMEN and the world, 252'.00973
sermons / edited by Helen Gray Crotwell. Philadelphia : Fortress Press, c1977. p. cm. [BV4241.W65] 77-78627 ISBN 0-8006-1318-X pbk. : 4.25
1. Sermons, American—Women authors. I. Crotwell, Helen Gray, 1925-

Sermons, Americans Preaching.

*RILEY, Miles O'Brian. 251.077
To whom it may concern, introd by Merla Zellerbach. 1st ed. [Los Altos,Calif., Practical Press, 1975] x,110p. 21cm. [BV4235] 75-13134 5.00(pbk.)
1. Sermons,American .sPreaching. I. Title.
Pub. address: P.o.Box 960,94022.

Sermons, Anglo- Saxon.

AELFRIC, Abbot of Eynsham. 252'.00924
Homilies of AElfric: a supplementary collection, being twenty-one full homilies of his middle and later career for the most part no previously edited with some shorter pieces mainly passages added to the second and third series; edited from all the known manuscripts with introduction, notes, Latin sources and a glossary by John C. Pope. London, New York [etc.] Oxford U. P. for the Early English Text Society, 1967- v. fronts., plates (facsims.). 22 1/2 cm. Includes bibliographical references. [PR1119.A2 no. 259, etc.] (v.1 67-90497
1. Sermons, Anglo- Saxon. I. (Early English Text Society. [Publications. Original series] no. 259) v. 1: II. Pope, John Collins, 1904- ed. III. Title.

Sermons, Australian.

SHILTON, Lance R 242.3
The Word made flesh. Grand Rapids, Zondervan Pub. House [1963] 120 p. 21 cm. [BV4253.S65] 63-1183
1. Sermons, Australian. I. Title.

WALKER, Alan. 252
God is where you are. Grand Rapids, Eerdmans [1962] 128 p. 20 cm. (Preaching for today) [BV4253.W32] 62-5296
1. Sermons, Australian. I. Title.

Sermons, British.

BROOKS, Phillips bp 1835-1893..
Sermons preached in English chruches, by the Rt. Rev. Phillips Brooks, D.D. New York, E. P. Dutton & co., 1901. viii, 311 p. 19 1/2 cm. First published 1883. [BX5845B7S47 1901] 4-10412
I. Title.

BROOKS, Phillips, bp., 1835-1893. 252.03
Sermons preached in English churches, by the Rt. Rev. Phillips Brooks, D.D. New York, E. P. Dutton & co., 1901. viii 311 p. 19 1/2 cm. First published 1883. [BX5845.B7S6 1901] 4-5615
I. Title.

LEWIS, Alexander i. e. Ora Alexander, 1864-
Sermons preached in England, by Rev. Alexander Lewis... introduction by Rev. J. Morgan Gibbon... New York, Chicago [etc.] F. H. Revell company [c1906] 233 p. incl. front. (port.) plates. 20 cm. 6-45134
I. Title.

REDPATH, Alan. 224'.1
Faith for the times/deliverance / by Alan Redpath. Old Tappan, N.J. : Revell, 1977. p. cm. Originally published 1972-76 in 3 v. with collective title Faith for the times: studies in the prophecy of Isaiah, chapters 40 to 66. [BS1520.R4 1977] 77-22980 ISBN 0-8007-0855-5 : 3.95
1. Bible. O.T. Isaiah XL-LXVI—Sermons. 2. Sermons, British. I. Title.

SPURGEON, Charles Haddon, 1834-1892. 252.
Sermons of the Rev. C. H. Spurgeon, of London. 3d series. New York, Sheldon, Blakeman & company; Boston, Gould & Lincoln; [etc., etc.] 1857. x, [11]-448 p. front. 20 cm. [BX6333.S6S4 1857] 27-3789
I. Title.

Sermons, Canadian.

YOUNG, W. Harold, ed. 252
Great Canadian preaching, edited with introduction and biographical notes by W. Harold Young... New York, George H. Doran company [c1925] xiv p., 1 l., 17-297 p. 19 1/2 cm. [BV4241.Y6] 26-2578
1. Sermons, Canadian. I. Title.

Sermons — Composition and delivery.

ANDERSON, George Smith
Sermon science, or, The law of discourse. Containing the essential principles of Scripture exposition and of sermon construction ("Sermon builder" revised) ... Atlanta, Ga., The Foote & Davies co., 1900. 213 p. illus. 12 cm. Nov
I. Title.

BENSON, Robert Hugh, 1871- 1914. 248
Sermon notes, by the late Monsignor Robert Hugh Benson, ed. by the Rev. C. C. Martindale ... New York, London [etc.] Longmans, Green, and co., 1917. 2 v. front. (facsim.) 19 cm. Printed in Great Britain. Contents.--1st ser. Anglican.--2 ser. Catholic. [BX1756.B4 1917] 17-29756
I. Martindale, Cyril Charlie, 1879- ed. II. Title.

BOTELER, Mattie M.
Sermon notes from the ministry of Jesus; suggestive outlines for preachers and teachers, by Mattie M. Boteler... Cincinnati, O., The Standard publishing company, [c1915] 269 p. 19 1/2 cm. 15-26793
I. Title.

LEABEL, Pius A
St. Vincent Strambi's guide to sacred eloquence. From the Italian of St. Vincent Mary Strambi, passionist and afterward Bishop of Macerata and Tolentino. St. Meinrad, Ind., Abbey Press, 1962. ix, 138 p. 19 cm. 65-70534
1. Strambi, St. Vincent Mary, 1745- Guide to sacred eloquence. 2. Sermons — Composition and delivery. I. Title. II. Title: Guide to sacred eloquence.

ST. Vincent Strambi's guide to sacred eloquence. From the Italian of St. Vincent Mary Strambi, passionist and afterward Bishop of Macerata and Tolentino. St. Meinrad, Ind., Abbey Press, 1962. ix, 138 p. 19 cm. 65-70534
1. Strambi, St. Vincent Mary, 1745- Guide to sacred eloquence. 2. Sermons — Composition and delivery. I. Title: Guide to sacred eloquence.

Sermons, Coptic.

BUDGE, Ernest Alfred Thompson Wallis, Sir, 1857-1934, ed. 230'.1'7 s
Coptic homilies in the dialect of Upper Egypt / edited from the papyrus codex Oriental 5001 in the British Museum by E. A. Wallis Budge. New York : AMS Press, 1977. lv, 424 p., 5 leaves of plates : ill. ; 23 cm. (His Coptic texts ; v. 1) Reprint of the 1910 ed. published by the British Museum, London. Includes bibliographical references. [PJ2197.B8 1977 vol. 1] [BV4249.C6] 252'.01'7 77-3585 ISBN 0-404-11317-6 : 45.00
1. Sermons, Coptic. 2. Coptic language—Texts. I. Title.

Sermons, English.

ARNOLD, Thomas, 1795-1842. 252
Sermons preached in the chapel of Rugby school, with an address before confirmation. By Thomas Arnold... 1st American ed. New York; D. Appleton & co.; Philadelphia, G. S. Appleton, 1846. viii, 9-284 p. 18 cm. [BX5133.A7S4 1846] 31-934
1. Sermons, English. I. Title.

ARNOT, William, 1808-1875. 252
Roots and fruits of the Christian life; or, Illustrations of faith and obedience. By the Rev. William Arnot ... London, New York [etc.] T. Nelson and sons, 1860. 2 p. l., [9]-430 p. 19 1/2 cm. [BV4253.A7] 33-7478
1. Sermons, English. I. Title.

ATKINS, Gaius Glenn, 1868- ed. 252.00822
Master sermons of the nineteenth century, edited by Gaius Glenn Atkins. Chicago, New York, Willett, Clark & company, 1940. xii, 243 p. 21 cm. [BV4241.A8] 40-10855
1. Sermons, English. I. Title.
Contents omitted.

AVIGDOR, Isaac C
Ten for two. Sermons for all holidays of the year. New York, J. David [c1960] 319p. 23cm.
1. Sermons -English. I. Title.

BAILLIE, John, 1886-1960 248.485
Christian devotion, addresses. New York, Scribners [c.1962] 119p. 20cm. Bibl. 62-17723 2.50
1. Sermons, English. 2. Christian life—Presbyterian authors. I. Title.

BAILLIE, John, 1886-1960. 248.485
Christian devotion; addresses. London, Oxford University Press, 1962. 88 p. 20 cm. [BV4501.2.B3] 63-2947
1. Sermons, English. 2. Christian life—Presbyterian authors. I. Title.

BAILLIE, John, 1886-1960. 248.485
Christian devotion, addresses. New York, Scribner [1962] 119p. 20cm. Includes bibliographies. [BV4501.2.B3] 62-17723
1. Sermons, English. 2. Christian life—Presbyterian authors. I. Title.

BARTLETT, Genus E comp. 252.
Voices from templed hills; selected sermons, compiled by G. E. Bartlett, editor. Parkersburg, W. Va., The Baptist banner publishing co. [c1927] 4 p. l., 13-237 p. front. (ports.) 20 cm. [BX6333.A1B3] 28-3442
1. Sermons. English. I. Title.

BAUERLE, Richard E., 1928- 224.5'2
I, the prophet : dramatic monologs for today from twelve Old Testament prophets / by Richard Bauerle. St. Louis, Mo. : Concordia Pub. House, c1981. p. cm. [BS1505.4.B38] 19 81-3140 ISBN 0-570-03835-9 pbk. : 5.95
1. Lutheran Church—Sermons. 2. Bible. O.T. Prophets—Sermons. 3. Sermons, English. 4. Christian drama, American. 5. Monologues. I. Title.

BELLHOUSE, Geoffrey Turner.
Immortal longings. New York, Philosophical Library [1951] 128 p. 19 cm. A 52
1. Sermons, English. I. Title.

BETHANY college sermons, 252
by the younger graduates. Cincinnati, O., The Standard publishing company [c1930] 190 p. 20 cm. "Editor's note" signed: E. W. Thornton. [BX7327.A1B4] 30-3989
1. Sermons, English. I. Thornton, Edwin William, 1863- ed. II. Bethany college. Bethany, W. Va.

BRITISH preachers. 252
[v. 1- 1925- London & New York, G. P. Putnam's sons, ltd. [1925]- v. 19 1/2 cm. Editor: 1925- Sir James Marchant. [BV4241.B63] 25-16006
1. Sermons, English. I. Marchant, Sir James, 1867- ed.

BROOKE, Stopford Augustus, 1832-1916. 252.
Christ in modern life: sermons preached in St. James's chapel, York street, St. James's square, London, by the Rev. Stopford A. Brooke ... New York, D. Appleton and company, 1877. viii, 408 p. 20 1/2 cm. [BX9843.B79C7 1877] 25-23358
1. Sermons, English. I. Title.

BROOKE, Stopford Augustus, 1832-1916. 252.
Faith and freedon. By Stopford A. Brooke. Boston, G. H. Ellis, 1881. xxiii, 342 p. 20 cm. [BX9843.B79F3] 9-5840
1. Sermons, English. I. Title.

BROOKE, Stopford Augustus, 1832-1916
Sermons preached in St. James's chapel, York street, London. By the Rev. Stopford A. Brooke, M. A., Honorary Chaplain in ordinary to the Queen. Boston, Fields, Osgood, & co., 1869. viii, 323 p. 20 cm. A34
1. Sermons, English. I. Brooke, Stopford Augustus, 1832-1916 II. Title.

BROWN, Bertha B. Mrs. 922
The life and sermons of Ray York, known as the boy evangelist; being a sketch of his early life, an account of his conversion, his call to the ministry, his first sermon, and his subsequent ministerial life, with a few sermons and sermon outlines. Compiled by Mrs. Bertha B. Brown, 1st ed. Kansas City, Mo., Chas. E. Brown printing co., 1898. 229 p. front., ports. 20 cm. [BV3785.Y6B7] 37-37090
1. York, Ray Earl, 1882- 2. Sermons, English. I. Title.

BURDER, George, 1752-1832.
Village sermons; or, Sixty-five plain and short discourses on the principal doctrines of the Gospel, intended for the use of families, Sunday-schools, or companies assembled for religious instruction in country villages. By George Burder...Woodward's third corrected edition. Philadelphia, Printed for and by William W. Woodward, no. 52, Second, the corner of Chestnut-street, 1808. 2 v. 18 cm. A 32
1. Sermons, English. I. Title.

CARPENTER, Nathanael. 222'.4406
Achitophel / Nathanael Carpenter. Amsterdam : Theatrum Orbis Terrarum ; Norwood, N.J. : W. J. Johnson, 1979. 64 p. ; 22 cm. (The English experience, its record in early printed books published in facsimile ; no. 914) Photoreprint of the 1629 ed. printed for M.S., London. STC 4669. [BS1325.C35 1979] 19 79-84094 ISBN 90-221-0914-3 : 9.00
1. Church of England—Sermons. 2. Bible. O.T. 2 Samuel, XVII, 23—Sermons. 3. Sermons, English. I. Title. II. Series: English experience, its record in early printed books published in facsimile ; no. 914.

CARPENTER, Spencer Cecil, 1877- 252.03
The house of pilgrimage, sermons preached in the Temple church, by S. C. Carpenter ... New York, The Macmillan company [1932] vi, 206 p. 20 cm. "First published in 1932." "Printed in Great britain." [BX5133.C35H6] 32-32899
1. Sermons, English. I. Title.

CHURCH of England. 252.03
Homilies.
Certaine sermons or Homilies, appointed to be read in churches, in the time of Queen Elizabeth I, 1547-1571. 2 vols. in 1. Gainesville, Fla., Scholars' Facsimiles & Reprints, 1968. xii, 323 p. 23 cm. "A facsimile reproduction of the edition of 1623 with an introduction by Mary Ellen Rickey and Thomas B. Stroup." [BX5133.A1A3 1623a] 68-17016 ISBN 0-8201-1008-6
1. Church of England—Sermons. 2. Sermons, English. I. Title.

CHURCH, Richard William, 1815-1890.
Human life and its conditions; sermons preached before the University of Oxford in 1876-1878, with three ordination sermons, by R. W. Church ... London and New York, Macmillan and co., 1894. ix, 194 p. 19 1/2 cm. A 14
I. Title.

CLARKE, Samuel, 1675-1729. 230'.3
The works, 1738 / Samuel Clarke. New York : Garland Pub., 1976. p.cm. (British philosophers and theologians of the 17th & 18th centuries ; no. 12) Reprint of the 1738 ed. printed for J. and P. Knapton, London, under title: The works of Samuel Clarke. Contents.Contents.—v. 1. Sermons on several subjects.—v. 2. Sermons on several subjects. Eighteen sermons on several occasions. Sixteen sermons on the being and attributes of God, the obligations of natural religion, and the truth and certainty of the Christian revelation.—v. 3. A paraphrase on the four Evangelists. Three practical essays on baptism, confirmation, and repentance. An exposition of the church catechism. A letter to Mr. Dodwell concerning the immortality of the soul. Reflections on Amyntor.—v. 4. The scripture doctrine of the Trinity. Several tracts relating to the subject of the Trinity. A collection of papers which passed between the late learned M. Leibnitz and Dr. Clarke. A letter to Benjamin Hoadly. [BX5037.C5 1976] 75-11207 ISBN 0-8240-1762-5 : 25.00 per vol.
1. Church of England—Sermons. 2. Church of England—Doctrinal and controversial works—Collected works. 3. Clarke, Samuel, 1675-1729. 4. Bible. N.T. Gospels—Paraphrases, English. 5. Sermons, English. 6. Trinity—Early works to 1800—Collected works. I. Title. II. Series.

CONIARIS, Anthony M. 252'.01'9
Gems from the Sunday gospels in the Orthodox Church : talks based on the yearly cycle of Sunday Gospel lessons / by Anthony M. Coniaris. Minneapolis : Light and Life Pub. Co., [1975- v. ; 21 cm. Contents.Contents.—v. 1. January through June. [BX330.C62] 74-81199 ISBN pbk. : 3.95
1. Orthodox Eastern Church—Sermons. 2. Sermons, English. I. Title.

CRISWELL, Wallie A. 252'.6'1
With a Bible in my hand / W. A. Criswell. Nashville, Tenn. : Broadman Press, c1978. 192 p. ; 22 cm. [BX6333.C77W57] 78-69708 6.95
1. Baptists—Sermons. 2. Sermons, English. I. Title.

CROWE, Charles M ed. 252
Great southern preaching; vital Christianity as interpreted by the sermons of some of the leading contemporary exponents of the gospel message in the southern states, edited by Charles M. Crowe, with an invocation by Joseph Fort Newton. New York, The Macmillan company, 1926. xiii, 280 p. 20 cm. With brief notices of the authors. [BV4241.C8] 26-18022
1. Sermons, English. I. Title.

DONDERS, Joseph G. 252'.02
Jesus, the stranger : reflections on the Gospels / Joseph G. Donders. Maryknoll, N.Y. : Orbis Books, c1978. viii, 290 p.; 21 cm. [BX1756.D634J47] 77-21783 ISBN 0-88344-234-5 : 8.95 ISBN 0-88344-235-3 pbk. : 4.95
1. Catholic Church—Sermons. 2. Sermons, English. I. Title.

DONNE, John, 1572-1631. 252.03'42
Donne's Prebend sermons. Edited, with an introd. and commentary, by Janel M. Mueller. Cambridge, Mass., Harvard University Press, 1971. xi, 361 p. 25 cm. First published in LXXX sermons preached by that learned and reverend divine, John Donne, Dr in Divinitie, London, 1640. Includes bibliographical references. [BX5133.D61M8] 77-143229 ISBN 0-674-21485-4 10.00
1. Church of England—Sermons. 2. Sermons, English. 3. Preaching—History—England. I. Mueller, Janel M., 1938- ed. II. Title: Prebend sermons.

DRASTIC discipleship, 252.4
and other expository sermons, by Raymond W. McLaughlin, others. Grand Rapids, Mich., Baker Bk. [c.]1963. 116p. 20cm. (Evangelical pulpit lib.) 63-21470 2.95 bds.,
1. Sermons, English. I. McLaughlin, Raymond W.

DRASTIC discipleship, and other expository sermons, by Raymond W. McLaughlin and others. Grand Rapids, Baker Book House, 1963. 116 p. 20 cm. (Evangelical pulpit library)
1. Sermons, English.

DYER, William, d.1696.
The believer's golden chain; embracing the substance of some dissertations on Christ's famous titles. A view of Zion's glory, and Christ's voice to London. By William Dyer ... With A guide to prayer; being the substance of some essays on the spirit and gift of prayer. By Isaac Watts, D.D. Compiled and published by S. S. Henderson. Wheeling, Va., Printed by J. B. Wolff, 1849. x, [11]-599, [1] p. 18 1/2 cm. [BX5201.D8 1849] 43-32303
1. Sermons, English. 2. Prayer. I. Watts, Isaac, 1674-1748. A guide to prayer. II. Henderson, S. S., comp. III. Title. IV. Title: Christ's famous titles.

DYER, William, d.1696.
Christ's famous titles, and The believer's golden chain, handled in divers sermons; together with his Cabinet of jewels; or, A glimpse of Sion's glory. By William Dyer ... Printed at Newburyport: by Blunt and March, State-street --1796. vi, [7]-312 p. 12 cm. Published also under title: The believer's golden chain. [BX5201.D8 1796] 43-81954
1. Sermons, English. I. Title. II. Title: The believer's golden chain.

THE English pulpit; 252
collection of sermons by the most eminent living divines of England... New York, R. Carter & brothers, 1849. 400 p. 23 1/2 cm. [BV4241.E65] 33-28665
1. Sermons, English.

THE English sermon : 252'.03
an anthology. Cheadle : Carcanet Press, 1976. 3 v. ; 22 cm. Contents.Contents.—v. 1. 1550-1650.—v. 2. 1650-1750.—v. 3. 1750-1850. Includes bibliographies. [BX5133.A1E53] 76-375017 ISBN 0-85635-093-1 (v. 1) : 17.95
1. Church of England—Sermons. 2. Sermons, English.

FABER, Frederick William, 1814-1863. 252'.02
Spiritual conferences / by Frederick William Faber. New ed. Rockford, Ill. : Tan Books and Publishers, 1978. 345 p. ; 21 cm. "Originally published in 1957 by the Peter Reilly Co. Philadelphia." [BX1756.F28S64 1978] 78-66304 ISBN 0-89555-079-2 : 7.00
1. Catholic Church—Sermons. 2. Sermons, English. I. Title.

FARRAR, Frederic William, 1831-1903.
Eternal hope; five sermons preached in Westminster abbey, November and December, 1877, by the Rev. Frederic W. Farrar ... With a new preface. London, Macmillan and co., limited; New York, The Macmillan company, 1904. ixviii, [1], 227 p. 20 cm. A 34
1. Sermons, English. I. Title.

FARRER, Austin Marsden. 252'.03'08
The brink of mystery / Austin Farrer ; edited by Charles C. Conti ; foreword by J. L. Houlden. London : SPCK, 1976. x, 171 p. ; 23 cm. [BX5133.F33B74] 76-373635 ISBN 0-281-02896-6 : £3.95
1. Church of England—Sermons. 2. Sermons, English. I. Conti, Charles C. II. Title.

FARRER, Austin Marsden. 252'.03
The end of man. Grand Rapids, W. B. Eerdmans [1974, c1973] p. cm. Sermons. [BX5133.F33E52 1974] 74-3061 ISBN 0-8028-1579-0 3.45 (pbk.).
1. Church of England—Sermons. 2. Sermons, English. I. Title.

FERRE, Gustave A comp. 252
The Upper Room Chapel talks. Nashville, The Upper room [1957] 128p. 19cm. [BV4241.F44] 57-13007
1. Sermons, English. I. The Upper room. II. Title.

FINE, William M., ed. 252
That day with God. Edited by William M. Fine. Foreword by Richard Cardinal Cushing. [1st ed.] New York, McGraw-Hill [1965] xiv, 213 p. 24 cm. Principally excerpts from sermons. [E842.9.F5] 64-66265
1. Kennedy, John Fitzgerald, Pres. U.S., 1917-1963—Funeral and memorial services. 2. Sermons, English. I. Title.

FLEETWOOD, William, bp. of Ely, 1656-1723.
The works of the Right Reverend William Fleetwood, D. D., sometime bishop of Ely. A new ed. ... Oxford, University press, 1854. 3 v. 23 cm. Contents.v. 1. Sermons. v. 2. Sermons and charges. v. 3. Chronicon preciosum, and miscellaneous pieces. 12-32245
I. Title.

FOLKMAN, Jerome D., 1907-
"Rights and Responsibilities," and other High Holiday sermons. By J. D. Folkman and S. A. Arnold. Columbus, Temple Israel, 1965. 51 p. 19 cm. (Pulpit Publications, no. 17.) Cover title. 67-83227
1. Sermons — English. I. Arnold, Steven Anchory. II. Title. III. Series.

FORDYCE, James, 1720-1796. 378.
Sermons to young women ... By James Fordyce ... Third American from twelfth London edition. Philadelphia, M. Carey; [etc., etc.] 1809. 2 v. in. 1. 18 cm. [BV4313.F6] [BV4313.F6 1809] 378. A 34
1. Sermons, English. 2. Woman. I. Title.

FOSTER, John, 1770-1843. 252.061
Miscellaneous essays on Christian morals; experimental and practical. Originally delivered as lectures in the Broadmead chapel, Bristol, England. By John Foster ... New-York, D. Appleton & co.; Philadelphia, G. S. Appleton, 1844. vi. p., 1 l., [9]-252 p. 16 cm. Preface signed: J. E. Ryland. [BX6333.F6M5] 33-35977
1. Sermons, English. I. Ryland, Jonathan Edwards, 1798-1866, ed. II. Title.

FULLER, Andrew, 1754-1815. 248
God's approbation of our labours necessary to the hope of success. A sermon delivered at the annual meeting of the Bedford union, May 6, 1801. By Andrew Fuller. Published by request. New-York: Printed by Issac Collins and son, for C. Davis, no. 167, Water-street, 1802. vii, 51 p. 15 cm. [With his The backslider ... New-York, 1802] [BX6217.F83] 33-39243
1. Sermons, English. I. Title.

GATES, A. Avery, 1887- comp. 252
Boston preachers; pulpit addresses by ministers of Boston and its vicinity, compiled by Rev. A. Avery Gates... New York, Chicago [etc.] Fleming H. Revell company [1927] 387 p. 19 1/2 cm. [BV4241.G3] 27-20939
1. Sermons, English. I. Title.

GLANVILL, Joseph, 1636-1680. 252'.03
Some discourses, sermons, and remains : 1681 / Joseph Glanvill. New York : Garland Pub., 1979. 422, 25 p. ; 23 cm. (British philosophers and theologians of the 17th & 18th centuries) Reprint of the 1681 ed. printed for H. Mortlock and J. Collins, London. [BX5133.G53S65 1979] 75-11221 ISBN 0-8240-1775-7 : 33.00
1. Church of England—Sermons. 2. Sermons, English. I. Title. II. Series.

GLASSE, James D. 252'.0834
The art of spiritual snakehandling, and other sermons / James D. Glasse. Nashville : Abingdon, c1978. 112 p. ; 19

cm. [BX9886.Z6G562] 78-12342 ISBN 0-687-01890-0 pbk. : 3.95
1. United Church of Christ—Sermons. 2. Sermons, English. I. Title.

GUNTHER, Peter F comp. 252
Great sermons by great preachers. Chicago, Moody Press [1960] 159p. 19cm. (Moody pocket books, 56) [BV4241.G84] 60-50743
1. Sermons, English. I. Title.

HALLOCK, Gerard Benjamin Fleet, 1856- comp. 252
One hundred best sermons for special days and occasions, with accompanying cyclopedia of choice illustrations ... compiled and edited by Rev. G. B. F. Hallock ... New York, George H. Doran company [c1923] xiv p., 1 l. 552 p. 23 1/2 cm. [BV4241.H3] 23-8306
1. Sermons. English. 2. Homiletical illustrations. I. Title.

HALLOCK, Gerard Benjamin Fleet, 1856- comp. 252
One hundred best sermons for special days and occasions, with accompanying cyclopedia of choice illustrations ... compiled and edited by Rev. G. B. F. Hallock ... Garden City, N.Y., Doubleday, Doran & company, inc., 1929. 2 p. l. vii-xiv p., 1 l. 529 p. 21 cm. [BV4241.H3 1929] 29-12640
1. Sermons. English. 2. Homiletical illustrations. I. Title.

HENRY, Philip, 1631-1696. 232
Christ all in all; or, What Christ is made to believers. With a brief memoir of the author. Swengel, Pa., Reiner Publications, 1970. xi, 380 p. 20 cm. Reprint of the 1691 ed. [BT200.H45 1970] 70-261961 3.95
1. Jesus Christ—Person and offices—Sermons. 2. Church of England—Sermons. 3. Sermons, English. I. Title.

HOUSE, Erwin, ed. 252
The homilist: a series of sermons for preachers and laymen. Original and selected. By Erwin House, A.M. New York, Carlton & Porter, 1860. 496 p. 19 cm. [BV4241.H6] 33-22244
1. Sermons, English. I. Title.

HOWSON, George William Saul, 1860-1919. 252.
Sermons by a lay headmaster, preached at Gresham's school, 1900-1918, by G. W. S. Howson, M.A. With 2 illustrations. London, New York [etc.] Longmans, Green and co., 1920. viii, 147 p. front. (port.) pl. 19 1/2 cm. [BV4310.H7] 20-18239
I. Title.

HURLBUT, Jesse Lyman, 1843- ed. 252
Great sermons by great preachers' the greatest preachers of the the Christian faith in all ages; a sermon for every Sunday in the year, edited by Rev. Jesse Lyman Hurlbut ... Philadelphia, Chicago, etc., The John C. Winston company [c1927] 2 p. l., vii-xvi, 17-658 p. front., ports. 22 cm. "Originally published in 1871, under the same title and with the same plan, ably wrought out by the Rev. M. Laird Simons ... nearly half of the sermons in this volume are different from those in the earlier editor."--Pref. [BV4241.H77] 28-28175
1. Sermons, English. 2. Clergy. I. Title.

HURLBUT, Jesse Lyman, 1843- ed. 252
Sunday half hours with great preachers. The greatest sermons by the greatest preachers of the Christian faith in all ages. A sermon for every Sunday in the year. Ed. by Rev. Jesse Lyman Hurlbut ... Chicago, Philadelphia [etc.] The J. C. Winston co. [c1907] xvi, 17-681 p. incl. front. ports. 22 cm. [BV4241.H8] 7-40516
1. Sermons, English. 2. Clergy. I. Title.

IF I could preach just once 252
[by] Bertrand Russell [and others] Freeport, N.Y., Books for Libraries Press [1971, c1929] 255 p. 23 cm. (Essay index reprint series) Contents.Contents.—The power of the word, by J. Drinkwater.—The pagan in the heart, by L. Lewisohn.—The unknown future, by P. Gibbs.—Lucifer; or, The root of evil, by G. K. Chesterton.—There came one running, by H. N. MacCracken.—How to become a Christian, by H. Cecil.—For all bishops and other clergy, by S. Kaye-Smith.—The importance of style, by H. S. Canby.—Behind the veil of death, by A. C. Doyle.—The three voices of nature, by J. A. Thomson.—Morals and health, by T. Horder.—On the evils due to fear, by B. Russell.—The road to redemption, by J. Collins. [BV4241.I5 1971] 73-167364 ISBN 0-8369-2457-6
1. Sermons, English. I. Russell, Bertrand Russell, Hon., 3d Earl, 1872-1970.

IF I could preach just once 252
[by] Hon. Bertrand Russell, Dr. Joseph Collins, John Drinkwater [and others] ... New York and London, Harper & brothers, 1929. 4 p. l., 3-255, [1] p. 23 cm. Contents.--The power of the word, by J. Drinkwater.--The pagan in the heart, by L. Lewisohn.--The unknown future, by P. Gibbs.--Lucifer; or, The root of evil, by G. K. Chesterton.--There came one running, by H. N. MacCracken.--How to become a Christian, by H. Cecil.--For all bishops and other clergy, by Sheila Kaye-Smith.--The importance of style, by H. S. Canby.--Behind the veil of death, by A. C. Doyle.--The three voices of nature, by J. A. Thomson.--Morais and health, by T. Horder.--On the evils due to fear, by B. Russell.--The road to redemption, by J. Collins. [BV4241.I 5] 29-16571
1. Sermons, English. I. Russell, Bertrand Russell, 3d earl, 1872-

INGLIS, Ervine P 252.058
What Christianity has to say. Webster Groves, Mo., Woman's Association of the First Congregational Church (United Church of Christ) [1962] 55p. illus. 23cm. [BX7233.I5W5] 62-20099
1. Sermons, English. 2. Congregational churches—Sermons. I. Title.

JAGGAR, Thomas Augustus, bp., 1839-1912. 252.
The man of the ages, and other recent sermons, by the Rt. Rev. Thomas A. Jaggar ... New York, J. Pott & co., 1898. 4 p. l., 3-413 p. 20 cm. [BX5937.J3M3] C-59
1. Sermons, English. I. Title.

JAY, William, 1769-1853.
Sermons, by William Jay. With an appendix, containing A sermon preached before the Bedford union:--and an essay on marriage. [Second American from the second London edition] ... From Sidney's press, Printed for I. Cooke and co. New Haven, 1814. 478 p., 1 l., vi, 22, 32 p. 22 cm. A sermon preached before the Bedford union, and An essay on marriage, each have also special t.-p. A 32
1. Sermons, English. I. Title. II. Title: A sermon preached before the Bedford union. III. Title: Marriage, An essay on.

JAY, William, 1769-1853. 252
Sixty-two sermons. Grand Rapids, Baker Book House, 1955. 454p. 21cm. [Co-operative reprint library] First published in 1879 under title: Sunday evening sermons and Thursday evening lectures. [BX5201] 55-8791
1. Sermons, English. I. Title.

JOHN Paul II, Pope, 1920- 252'.02
Africa, apostolic pilgrimage / John Paul II ; compiled and indexed by the Daughters of St. Paul. Boston, Ma. : Daughters of St. Paul, c1980. 427 p. : ill. ; 19 cm. "Reprinted with permission from L'Osservatore Romano, English edition." Cmpiled and indexed by the Daughters of St. Paul. Includes index. [BX1756.J64A38] 19 80-21712 ISBN 0-8198-0708-7 : 8.95 ISBN 0-8198-0709-5 (pbk.) : 7.95
1. Catholic Church—Sermons. 2. John Paul II, Pope, 1920- 3. Sermons, English. 4. Popes—Voyages and travels—Africa. I. Daughters of St. Paul. II. Title.

JOHN Paul II, Pope, 1920- 252'.02
Far East journey of peace and brotherhood / by Pope John Paul II ; compiled and indexed by the Daughters of St. Paul. Boston : St. Paul Editions, c1981. p. cm. "Reprinted ... from L'Osservatore romano, English edition"—Verso of t.p. Includes index. [BX1756.J64F37] 19 81-8877 ISBN 0-8198-2603-0 : 8.00 ISBN 0-8198-2604-9 pbk. : 7.00
1. Catholic Church—Doctrinal and controversial works—Catholic authors—Addresses, essays, lectures. 2. Catholic Church—Sermons. 3. Sermons, English. I. Daughters of St. Paul. II. Title.
Publisher's address: 50 St. Paul's Ave., Boston, MA 02130

JOHN Paul II, Pope, 1920- 252'.55
The whole truth about man : John Paul II to university faculties and students / edited with an introduction by James V. Schall, S.J. ; indexed by the Daughters of St. Paul. Boston, Mass. : St. Paul Editions, c1981. 354 p. ; 19 cm. "Reprinted ... from L'Osservatore Romano, English edition"—T.p. verso. Includes index. Bibliography: p. [347] [BX1756.J64W46] 19 81-5689 ISBN 0-8198-8201-1 : 7.95 ISBN 0-8198-8202-X pbk. : 6.95
1. Catholic Church—Sermons. 2. Catholic Church—Doctrinal and controversial works—Catholic authors—Addresses, essays, lectures. 3. Sermons, English. I. Schall, James V. II. Title.
Publisher's address: 50 St. Paul's Ave., Boston, MA 02130

JONES, John Daniel, 1865- 252.058
Morning and evening, by the Rev. J. D. Jones ... New York and London, Harper & brothers, 1935. 319 p. 20 cm. "First edition." [BX7233.J6M6 1935] 35-3555
1. Sermons, English. 2. Congregational churches—Sermons. I. Title.

JONES, John Daniel, 1865- 252.058
Richmond Hill sermons, by the Rev. J. D. Jones ... New York and London, Harper & brothers [c1933] 285 p. 20 cm. "First edition." [BX7233.J6R5 1933] 33-5853
1. Sermons, English. I. Title.

KAUFMAN, Edmund George. 252.097
Living creatively [by] Edmund G. Kaufman. Newton, Kan., Faith and Life Press [1966] 169 p. 20 cm. Bibliographical footnotes. [BX8127.K3L5] 66-20385
1. Sermons, English. 2. Mennonites — Sermons. I. Title.

KEMP, Charles F 1912 ed. 251
Life-situation preaching. St. Louis, Bethany Press [1956] 224p. 23cm. [BV4241.K42] 56-10170
1. Sermons, English. I. Title.

KENDALL, R. T. 252
Jonah : an exposition : sermons preached at Westminster Chapel, London / R. T. Kendall. Grand Rapids : Zondervan Pub. House, 1979, c1978. 268 p. ; 21 cm. [BS1605.4.K46 1979] 79-1370 ISBN 0-310-38311-0 pbk. : 5.95
1. Bible. O.T. Jonah—Sermons. 2. Sermons, English. I. Title.

KINGSLEY, Charles, 1819-1875. 283.
The water of life, and other sermons, by Charles Kingsley. London and New York, Macmillan and co., 1890. viii, 242 p. 19 1/2 cm. On verso of t.-p.: New edition. [BX5133.K5W3] 4-22454
1. Sermons, English. I. Title.

KRATZIG, Henry H. comp. 252.
The voice of Norfolk; radio messages from the city's foremost preachers; compiled by Henry H. Kratzig ... introduction by Ira S. D. Knight ... New York, Chicago [etc.] Fleming H. Revell company [c1929] xiii, 153, [1] p. 20 cm. [BV4301.K7] 29-24207
1. Sermons, English. I. Title. II. Title: Radio messages.

KRUMBINE, Miles Henry, 1891- ed. 252.
American Lutheran preaching; twenty-five sermons by ministers of the United Lutheran church; edited, with an introduction, by Miles H. Krumbine ... New York and London, Harper & brothers, 1928. xvii, 301 p. 22 cm. [BX8066.A1K7] 28-23315
1. Sermons, English. I. Title.
Contents omitted.

LATIMER, Hugh, Bp. of Worcester, 1485?-1555. 252.03
Selected sermons of Hugh Latimer. Edited by Allan G. Chester. Charlottesville, Published for the Folger Shakespeare Library [Washington, by] University of Virginia Press [1968] xxxiv, 209 p. 23 cm. (Folger documents of Tudor and Stuart civilization) Contents.Contents.—A chronological table.—Introduction.—Convocation sermon. —Sermon on the plowers.—First sermon before Edward VI.—Second sermon before Edward VI.—Sixth sermon before Edward VI.—Seventh sermon before Edward VI.—Last sermon before Edward VI.—First sermon on the Lord's Prayer.—Sermon for Christmas Day.—Sermon for St. Stephen's Day. [BX5133.L3S4] 68-14091
1. Church of England—Sermons. 2. Sermons, English. I. Chester, Allan Griffith, 1900- ed. II. Title. III. Series.

LATIMER, Hugh, Bp. of Worcester, 1485?-1555. 252'.03
Sermons. New York, AMS Press [1971] xvii, 379 p. 19 cm. Reprint of the 1906 ed., which was issued as no. 40 of Everyman's library: theology and philosophy. [BX5133.L3 1971] 76-172301 ISBN 0-404-03886-7 15.00
1. Church of England—Sermons. 2. Sermons, English.

LATIMER, Hugh, bp. of Worcester, 1485!-1555.
Sermons by Hugh Latimer, sometime bishop of Worcester. London, J. M. Dent & co.; New York, E. P. Dutton & co., [1906] xix, 379 p. 18 cm. (Half-title: Everyman's library, ed. by Ernest Rhys. Theology & philosophy. [no. 40]) Illustrated lining-papers. "First edition. Feb. 1906; reprinted, Apr, 1906." Introduction by Canon Beeching. Bibliography: p. xvii. A 11
I. Beeching, Henry Charles, 1859-1919, ed. II. Title.

LLOYD-JONES, David Martyn 252
Romans : an exposition of chapter 8:5-17, the sons of God / D. M. Lloyd-Jones. Grand Rapids : Zondervan, 1975, c1974. xi, 438 p. ; 23 cm. "Sermons ... preached in Westminster Chapel between March 1960 and April 1961." Includes text of Romans VIII, 5-17. Includes bibliographical references. [BS2665.4.L585 1975] 75-321704 8.95
1. Bible. N.T. Romans VIII, 5-17—Sermons. 2. Sermons, English. I. Bible. N.T. Romans VIII, 5-17. English. 1975. II. Title.

†LLOYD-JONES, David Martyn. 227'.1'06
Romans : an exposition of chapter 8:17-39 : the final perseverance of the saints / D. M. Lloyd-Jones. Grand Rapids : Zondervan Pub. House, 1976. xii, 457 p. ; 23 cm. Sermons delivered on Friday nights in Westminster Chapel, May 1961-May 1962. Includes text of Romans VIII, 17-39. [BS2665.4.L59] 76-2574 ISBN 0-310-33573-6 pbk. : 1.95
1. Bible. N.T. Romans VIII, 17-39—Sermons. 2. Sermons, English. I. Bible. N.T. Romans VIII, 17-39. English. 1976. II. Title.

LLOYD-JONES, David Martyn. 227'.1
Romans; an exposition of chapters 3.20-4.25, atonement and justification [by] D. M. Lloyd-Jones. [Grand Rapids, Mich.] Zondervan Pub. House [1971, c1970] xiii, 250 p. 23 cm. "Sermons ... apart from the first ... delivered during the Friday nights of the period, February to October, 1957 [at Westminster Chapel, London]" [BS2665.4.L57 1971] 72-25015 5.95
1. Bible. N.T. Romans III, 20-IV, 25—Sermons. 2. Sermons, English. I. Title.

LLOYD-JONES, David. Martyn. 227'.5'077
The Christian soldier : an exposition of Ephesians 6:10 to 20 / [by] D. M. Lloyd-Jones. Edinburgh ; Carlisle, Pa. : Banner of Truth Trust, 1978. 363 p. ; 23 cm. [BS2695.4.L5] 78-312186 ISBN 0-85151-258-5 : Write for information
1. Bible. N.T. Ephesians VI, 10-20—Sermons. 2. Sermons, English. I. Title.

LLOYD-JONES, David Martyn. 227'.5'077
God's ultimate purpose : an exposition of Ephesians 1, 1 to 23 / [by] D. M. Lloyd-Jones. Edinburgh ; Carlisle, Pa. : Banner of Truth Trust, 1978. 447 p. ; 23 cm. [BS2695.4.L537] 79-317121 ISBN 0-85151-272-0 : 9.95
1. Bible. N.T. Ephesians I—Sermons. 2. Sermons, English. I. Title.

LLOYD-JONES, David Martyn. 227'.5
God's way of reconciliation (studies in Ephesians, chapter 2) [by] D. Martyn Lloyd-Jones. Grand Rapids, Baker Book

House [1972] vii, 380 p. 22 cm. [BS2695.4.L54] 73-160675 ISBN 0-8010-5519-9 7.95
1. Bible. N. T. Ephesians II—Sermons. 2. Sermons, English. I. Title.

LLOYD-JONES, David Martyn. 248.485842
Spiritual depression; its causes and cure [by] D. Martyn Lloyd-Jones. Grand Rapids, Eerdmans [1965] 300 p. 23 cm. Sermons. [BX7233.L57S6] 65-18094
1. Sermons, English. 2. Congregational churches — Sermons. I. Title.

LLOYD-JONES, David Martyn. 227'.1
Romans; an exposition of chapter 6, the new man [by] D. M. Lloyd-Jones. Grand Rapids, Mich., Zondervan Pub. House [1973, c1972] xii, 313 p. 23 cm. Sermons delivered on Friday nights in Westminister Chapel, Oct. 1958-Apr. 1959. [BS2665.4.L58 1973] 74-161756 6.95
1. Bible. N.T. Romans VI—Sermons. 2. Sermons, English. I. Title.

LOCKYER, Herbert. 252
Fairest of all, and other sermons, by Dr. Herbert Lockyer. Grand Rapids, Mich., W. B. Eerdmans publishing co. [c1936] 157 p. 20 cm. [BV4253.L6] 37-12795
1. Sermons, English. I. Title.

MCALPIN, Edwin Augustus, 1874- ed. 252
Prize sermons, edited by Rev. Edwin A. McAlpin ... chairman, Rev. C. Wallace Petty ... Rev. Hugh T. Kerr ... [and] Rev. J. Newton Davies ... New York, The Macmillan company, 1932. xiii, 309 p. 20 1/2 cm. [BV4241.M15] 33-21
1. Sermons, English. I. Petty, Carl Wallace, 1884-1932, joint ed. II. Kerr, Hugh Thomson, 1871- joint ed. III. Davies, John Newton, 1881- joint ed. IV. Title.

MCCORMICK, William Patrick Alyn, 1877- 252.03
Christ's message to us today. Broadcast from St. Martin-in-the-Fields by the Rev. W. P. G. McCormick. London, New York [etc.] Longmans, Green and co, 1931. vii, 63, [1] p. 19 1/2 cm. [BX5133.M12C5] 31-20099
1. Sermons, English. 2. Christianity—Addresses, essays, lectures. I. Title.
Contents omitted.

MACDONALD, George, 1824-1905. 252'.05'8
Creation in Christ / George Macdonald ; edited by Rolland Hein from the three v. of Unspoken sermons. Wheaton, Ill. : H. Shaw Publishers, 1976. 342 p. ; 21 cm. (Wheaton literary series) A condensation of the author's Epea aptera. Unspoken sermons, 1st-3d ser., originally published, 1867-1889. [BV4253.M322 1976] 76-11282 ISBN 0-87788-860-4 : 4.95
1. Sermons, English. I. Title.

MCKEEHAN, Hobart Deitrich, 1897- ed. 252
Anglo-American preaching, edited and with an introduction by Hobart D. McKeehan... New York and London, Harper & brothers, 1928. xiii, 216 p. 19 1/2 cm. [BV4241.M27] 28-11114
1. Sermons, English. I. Title.
Contents omitted.

MACKENZIE, Lachlan, 1754-1819. 252'.05'2
The happy man : the abiding witness of Lachlan Mackenzie. Edinburgh ; Carlisle, Pa. : The Banner of Truth Trust, 1979. 249 p., [2] leaves of plates : ill. ; 23 cm. [BX9178.M245H36 1979] 79-320576 ISBN 0-85151-282-8 : 7.95
1. Presbyterian Church—Sermons. 2. Presbyterian Church—Doctrinal and controversial works—Presbyterian authors—Miscellanea. 3. Sermons, English. I. Title.

MACKINTOSH, Hugh Ross, 1870= 252.052
The highway of God, by H. R. Mackintosh... New York, C. Scribner's sons [1932] 3 p. l., ix-x, 253, [1] p. 21 1/2 cm. (Half-title: "The scholar as preacher" (Fifth series)) Printed in Great Britain. Sermons. [BX9178.M246H5] 32-20737
1. Sermons, English. I. Title.

MCLAUGHLIN, Raymond W. 251
Drastic discipleship, and other expository sermons, by Raymond W. McLaughlin and others. Grand Rapids, Baker Book House, 1963. 116 p. 20 cm. (Evangelical pulpit library) [BV4241.D7] 63-21470
1. Sermons, English. I. Title.

MACLAURIN, John, 1693-1754. 243
Sermons and essays: by the late Rev. Mr. John McLaurin ... Published from the author's manuscripts, by John Gillies ... To which is prefixed, some account of the life and character of the author. Philadelphia, Published by W. W. Woodward, no. 52, corner of Second and Chesnut streets. W. McCulloch, printer, 1811. xx p., 2 l., [25]-384 p. 18 x 10 1/2 cm. [BX9178.M25S4] 20-15448
1. Sermons, English. I. Gillies, John, 1712-1796, ed. II. Title.

MACPHERSON, Ian, 1912- comp. 252'.008
More sermons I should like to have preached, edited by Ian Macpherson. Westwood, N.J., F. H. Revell Co. [1967] 178 p. 20 cm. Contents.Contents.—What is vital in life, by G. T. Bellhouse.—The perfect worker, by G. N. M. Collins.—The sin of prayerlessness, by G. B. Duncan.—The wind of the spirit, by R. A. Finlayson.—The unshaken kingdom, by D. MacLeod.—The psalm of the two ways, by G. C. Morgan.—The proof of greatness, by K. E. Roach.—How to be saved, by W. E. Sangster.—Sin and forgiveness, by A. Ross.—The power of His Resurrection, by J. S. Stewart.—His greatest hour, by D. P. Thomson.—I have kept the faith, by J. K. Thomson.—Blast-off, by J. H. Withers.—Our unrestricted God, by A. S. Wood.—Treasure in earthen vessels, by G. Kennedy.—On being finely aware and richly responsible, by R. J. McCracken.—Let's celebrate! By D. A. MacLennan.—On explaining everything, by D. H. C. Read.—Shepherd, guide, and host, by W. G. Scroggie.—The water of the well at Bethlehem, by G. S. Wakefield. [BV4241.M329 1967] 67-9264
1. Sermons, English. I. Title.

MACPHERSON, Ian, 1912- ed. 252.0082
Sermons I should like to have preached [Westwood, N.J.] Revell [1965, c.1964] 131p. 20cm. [BV4241.M33] 65-3846 2.95 bds.,
1. Sermons, English. I. Title.

MARCHANT, James, Sir, 1867- ed. 252
If I had only one sermon to preach. English series. Sermons by twenty English ministers, edited, with a preface, by Sir James Marchant ... New York and London, Harper & brothers, 1928. viii, [9]-307 p. 21 cm. [BV4241.M35 1928 a] 28-21999
1. Sermons, English. I. Title.
Contents omitted.

MARSH, Frederick Edward, 1858-1919. 252
Night scenes of the Bible, by F. E. Marsh. Grand Rapids, Baker Book House [1967, c1904] 131 p. 20 cm. [BV4253.M4] 67-18185
1. Sermons, English. I. Title.

MARSH, Frederick Edward, 1858-1919. 252
Night scenes of the Bible, by F. E. Marsh. Grand Rapids, Baker Book House [1967, c1904] 131 p. 20 cm. [BV4253.M4 1967] 67-18185
1. Sermons, English. I. Title.

MARTINEAU, James, 1805-1900.
Hours of thought on sacred things. By James Martineau ... Boston, Roberts borthers, 1876. vii, 344 p. 18 cm. A 34
1. Sermons, English I. Title.

MATHER, Thomas Bradley, 1893- comp. 252
Voices of living prophets; a symposium of present-day preaching, compiled by Thomas Bradley Mather... Nashville, Cokesbury press [c1933] 299, [1] p. 22 1/2 cm. [BV4241.M37] 33-4179
1. Sermons, English. I. Title.

MATLOCK, Charles Rubein, 1888- ed. 252.053
The Cumberland Presbyterian pulpit; nineteen dynamic sermons by nineteen Cumberland Presbyterian ministers, compiled and edited by Charles R. Matlock... Nashville, Tenn., Cumberland Presbyterina pub. house, 1930. ix, 211 p. 21 cm. [BX9178.A1M3] 30-10029
1. Sermons, English. I. Title.

M'CHEYNE, Robert Murray, 1813-1843. 252.052
The sermons of the Rev. Robert Murray M'Cheyne ... New York and Pittsburgh, R. Carter, 1847. vii, [9]-518 p. front. (port.) 23 1/2 cm. [BX9178.M177S4] 33-1577
1. Sermons, English. I. Title.

MONTEFIORE, Hugh, comp. 252'.008
For God's sake; sermons from Great St. Mary's. [1st American ed.] Philadelphia, Fortress Press [1969, c1968] 287 p. 18 cm. First published in 1968 under title: Sermons from Great St. Mary's. [BV4241.M57 1969] 71-84544
1. Sermons, English. I. Cambridge, Eng. St. Mary the Great (Church) II. Title.

MORRIS, Colin M. 230'.7
Bugles in the afternoon / Colin Morris. Philadelphia : Westminster Press, [1979], c1977. 117 p. ; 19 cm. [BX8333.M584B83 1979] 78-23273 ISBN 0-664-24260-X pbk. : 4.95
1. Methodist Church—Sermons. 2. Sermons, English. 3. Christianity—20th century—Addresses, essays, lectures. I. Title.

MORRIS, Colin M. 261
The hammer of the Lord; signs of hope [by] Colin Morris. Nashville, Abingdon Press [1974, c1973] 160 p. 20 cm. Includes bibliographical references. [BX8333.M584H35 1974] 73-12234 ISBN 0-687-16547-4 4.75
1. Methodist Church—Sermons. 2. Sermons, English. I. Title.

MORRIS, Colin M. 252'.07'1
Mankind my church [by] Colin Morris. Nashville, Abingdon Press [1972, c1971] 160 p. 22 cm. Includes bibliographical references. [BX8333.M584M35 1972] 78-185547 ISBN 0-687-23137-X 2.45
1. Methodist Church—Sermons. 2. Sermons, English. I. Title.

MORRISON, Charles Clayton, 1874- ed. 252
The American pulpit; a volume of sermons by twenty-five of the foremost living American preachers, chosen by a poll of all the Protestant ministers in the United States, nearly twenty-five thousand of whom cast their votes, edited by Charles Clayton Morrison ... New York, The Macmillan company, 1925. 384 p. 19 1/2 cm. [BV4241.M7] 25-25763
1. Sermons, English. I. Title.

MORRISON, Henry Clay, 1857-
Commencement sermons delivered in Asbury college chapel, 1913, 1914, 1915. By H. C. Morrison ... Louisville, Ky., Pentecostal publishing company, c1915. 72 p. front. (port.) 22 cm. 15-19303
I. Title.
Contents omitted.

MOTTER, Alton M ed. 252.0082
Great preaching today; a collection of 25 sermons delivered at the Chicago Sunday Evening Club. [1st ed.] New York, Harper [c1955] 255p. 22cm. [BV4241.M72] 54-12330
1. Sermons, English. I. Title.

MOULE, Handley Carr Glyn, bp. of Durham, 1841-1920. 252.
The old gospel for the new age, and other sermons, by Prof. H. C. G. Moule. Chicago [etc.] Fleming H. Revell company [c1901] 239 p. 19 cm. "Professor Moule, by W. Robertson Nicoll": p. 5-10. [BX5133.M68] A 41
1. Sermons, English. I. Nicoll, William Robertson, Sir 1851-1920 II. Title.

MURRY, John Middleton, 1889-1957. 252
Not as the scribes; lay sermons. Edited with an introd. by Alec R. Vidler. [New York, Horizon Press] [1960] 255p. Bibl. footnotes. 60-14654 3.75
1. Sermons, English. I. Title.

NABERS, Charles Haddon, ed. 243
The Southern Presbyterian pulpit; pulpit addresses by ministers of the Presbyterian church in the United States, edited by Charles Haddon Nabers ... with introduction by Charles L. Goodell ... New York, Chicago [etc.] Fleming H. Revell company [c1928] 296 p. 20 cm. With brief notices of the authors. [BX9178.A1N3] 28-19893
1. Sermons, English. I. Title.

NEWMAN, John Henry, cardinal, 1801-1890.
Discourses addressed to mixed congregations, by John Henry cardinal Newman. New impression. London, New York [etc.] Longmans, Green, and co., 1902. viii, 376 p. 19 cm. (On cover: The works of Cardinal Newman) A 33
1. Sermons, English. 2. Catholic church—Sermons. I. Title.

NEWMAN, John Henry, cardinal, 1801-1890. 252.02
Favorite Newman sermons, selected from the works of John Henry cardinal Newman by Daniel M. O'Connell ... Milwaukee, The Bruce publishing company [c1932] xiv, p., 1 l., 413, [1] p. 20 1/2 cm. [BX1756.N5 1932] 32-9012
1. Sermons, English. 2. Catholic church—Sermons. I. O'Connell, Daniel M., ed. II. Title.

NEWMAN, John Henry, cardinal, 1801-1890. 283.
Fifteen sermons preached before the University of Oxford, between A.D. 1826 and 1843, by John Henry Newman ... New impression. London, New York [etc.] Longmans, Green, and co., 1900. xxiii, 351, [1] p. 19 cm. (On cover: The works of Cardinal Newman) On cover: Oxford university sermons. [[BX5133.N4F]] A 33
1. Sermons, English. I. Title. II. Title: Oxford university sermons.

NEWMAN, John Henry, Cardinal, 1801-1890. 252.03
Newman against the liberals : 25 classic sermons / by John Henry Newman ; selected with a pref. by Michael Davis. New Rochelle, N.Y. : Arlington House, c1978. 400 p. ; 20 cm. Selections from the author's Parochial and plain sermons. [BX5133.N4P32 1978] 77-14444 ISBN 0-87000-394-1 : 11.95
1. Church of England—Sermons. 2. Sermons, English. I. Title.

NEWMAN, John Henry, cardinal, 1801-1890. 283.
Parochial and plain sermons, by John Henry Newman ... New impression. London, New York [etc.] Longmans, Green, and co., 1900-02. 8 v. 19 cm. (On cover: The works of Cardinal Newman) Preface signed: W. J. Copeland. Vols. 1, 3, 5-8, 1901; v. 2, 1902; v. 4, 1900. "The first six volumes are reprinted from the six volumes of 'Parochial sermons'; the seventh and eighth formed the fifth volume of 'Plain sermons ...'," --Pref. [[BX5133.N4P]] A 33
1. Sermons, English. I. Copeland, William John, 1804-1855, ed. II. Title.

NEWMAN, John Henry, Cardinal, 1801-1890. 252.03
The preaching of John Henry Newman. Edited and with an introd. by W. D. White. Philadelphia, Fortress Press [1969] x, 227 p. 18 cm. (The Preacher's paperback library, 10) Bibliographical footnotes. [BX5133.N4P7 1969] 77-84540 2.45
1. Church of England—Sermons. 2. Sermons, English. I. White, W. D., ed. II. Title.

NEWMAN, John Henry, Cardinal, 1801-1890. 252.03'08
Sermons bearing on subjects of the day. Westminster, Md., Christian Classics, 1968. xxi, 424 p. 21 cm. Bibliographical footnotes. [BX5133.N4S4 1968] 68-24084
1. Church of England—Sermons. 2. Sermons, English. I. Title.

NEWMAN, John Henry, cardinal, 1801-1890.
Sermons preached on various occasions, by John Henry, cardinal Newman. New impression. London, New York [etc.] Longmans, Green, and co., 1900. xi, 337 p., 1 l. 19 cm. (On cover: The works of Cardinal Newman) A 33
1. Sermons, English. 2. Catholic church—Sermons. I. Title.

NORTH, Frederick J. ed. 232.
Easter sermons by representative preachers, edited by Frederick J.North ... New York, George H. Doran company [1926] 188, [1] p. 20 cm. [BV4259.N6] 26-13757
1. Sermons, English. I. Title.

NORWOOD, Frederick William. 252.
Moods of the soul, by the Rev. F. W. Norwood ... New York, George H. Doran company [1923] 214 p. 19 1/2 cm. Printed in Great Britain. Sermons. [BX7233.N67M6] 24-6980
I. Title.

OGDEN, Uzal, 1744-1822. 252.
Four sermons, on important subjects; delivered in Saint George's and Saint Paul's chapels, in the city of New York By the Reverend Uzal Ogden. Elizabeth-town: Printed by Shepar [BX5937.O5F6] 6-25430
I. Title.

PALEY, William, 1743-1805.
Sermons on several subjects by the late Rev. William Paley, D.D., subdean of Lincoln, prebendary of St. Paul's and rector of Bishop Wearmouth. Philadelphia: Printed for Hopkins and Early, no. 170, Market-street. Fry and Kammerer, printers, 1808. xv, [17]-384 p. 22 cm. A 34
1. Sermons, English. 2. Church of England—Sermons. I. Title.

PHILLIPS university sermons, 252.
by the younger graduates. Cincinnati, O., The Standard publishing company [c1929] 201 p. 20 cm. "Editor's note" signed: E. W. Thornton. [BX7327.A1P45] 29-24649
1. Sermons, English. I. Thornton, Edwin William, 1863- ed. II. Phillips university, Enid, Okl.

PIERCE, Ralph Milton, ed. 252
Preachers and preaching in Detroit, edited with introduction and life-sketches, by Ralph Milton Pierce ... New York, Chicago [etc.] Fleming H. Revell company [c1926] 283 p. 21 cm. [BV4241.P5] 26-8841
1. Sermons, English. 2. Clergy—Michigan—Detroit. I. Title.

POLLOCK, Bertram, bp. of 283.42
Norwich, 1863-
The church and English life; sermons by the the Right Reverend Bertram Pollock ... London, New York [etc.] Longmans, Green and co., 1832. xviii, 158 p. 20 cm. Reprinted in part from various periodicals. [BX5133.P6C5] 32-4413
1. Sermons, English. 2. Church of England. I. Title.

PORTEUS, Beilby, bp. of London, 1731-1808.
Sermons on several subjects. By the Right Reverend Beilby Porteus ... First American from the ninth London edition. Hartford: Printed for Oliver D. Cooke, by Lincoln & Gleason. 1806. cviii, 445 p. 22 cm. A 33
1. Sermons, English. I. Title.

POUND, James Presley, ed. 252
Voices of the age, edited by J. Presley Pound; with an introduction by Peter Ainslie. New York and London, Harper & brothers, 1929. xiv, 222 p., 1 l. 21 cm. [BV4241.P55] 29-15355
1. Sermons, English. I. Title.

ROBERTSON, Frederick 252.03
William, 1816-1853.
Christian progress by oblivion of the past, and other sermons. By the Rev. Frederick W. Robertson. New York, Boston, T. Y. Crowell & company [18-] 2 p. l., 146 p. front. (port.) 18 cm. [BX5133.R6C5] 31-2098
1. Sermons, English. I. Title.

ROBERTSON, Frederick William, 1816-1853.
"The human race" and other sermons. Preached at Cheltenham, Oxford, and Brighton. By the late Rev. Frederick W. Robertson. New York, Harper & bros., 1881. viii, 236 p. 20 cm. A 34
1. Sermons, English. I. Title.

ROBERTSON, Frederick William, 1816-1853.
Sermons on religion & life, by Frederick W. Robertson. London, J. M. Dent & co.; New York, E. P. Dutton & co. [1907] 332 p. 18 cm. (Half-title: Everyman's library, ed. by Ernest Rhys. Theology & philosophy [no. 37]) Illustrated end-papers. "First edition. Feb. 1906. Reprinted May 1906 and May 1907." "With a commendation by Canon Barnett." Bibliography: p. [12] A 10
1. Sermons, English. I. Title.

ROWLAND, Joseph Medley, 252.
1880- comp.
The Southern Methodist pulpit, compiled by J. M. Rowland ... Nashville, Tenn., Cokesbury press, 1927. 196 p. 20 cm. [BX8333.A1R6] 27-19798
1. Sermons, English. I. Title.

RUSSELL, Robert, of 252
Wadhurst, Sussex.
Seven sermons: viz. i. Of the unpardonable sin against the Holy Ghost; or, The sin unto death. ii. The saint's duty and exercise: in two parts. Being an exhortation to, and directions for prayer. iii. The acdepted time and day of salvation. iv. The end of time, and beginning of eternity. v. Joshua's resolution to serve the Lord. vi. The way to heaven made plain. vii. The future state of man, or, A treatise of the resurrection.--A funeral sermon. By Robert Russell ... 52d ed. Philadelphia: Printed and sold by W. Dunlap, at the Newest-printing-office, the south side of the Jersey-market, mdcclxvi. iii, [1], 5-172 p. 14 cm. [BV4253.R8 1766] 11-22223
1. Sermons, English. I. Title.

RUSSELL, Robert, 252
ofWadhurst,Sussex.
Seven sermons, viz. i. Of the unpardonable sin against the Holy Ghost: or, The sin unto death. ii. The saint's duty and exercise: in two parts, being an exhortation to, and direction for prayer. iii. The accepted time and day of salvation. iv. The end of time, and beginning of eternity. v. Joshua's resolution to serve the Lo[rd] vi. The way to heaven made plain. vii. The future state of man; or, A [trea]tise on the resurrection. By Robert Russell ... Wilmington, Del. Printed by James Wilson, for Mathew Carey. Philadelphia, 1806. 144 p. 15 cm. L. C. copy imperfect: t.-p. and p. [3]-4 multilated; p. 5-8 wanting. [BV4253.R8 1806] 42-26336
1. Sermons, English. I. Title.

RUSSELL, Robert, of 252
Wadhurst, Sussex.
Seven sermons on different important subject; --viz.--Of the unpardonable sin against the Holy Ghost; or, The sin unto death. The saint's duty and exercise; in two parts. Being an exhortation to, and directions for prayer. The accepted time, and day of salvation. The end of time, and beginning of eternity. Joshua's resolution to serve the Lord. The way to heaven made plain. The future state of man; or, A treatise of the resurrection. New-Haven; Printed for John Tiebout, bookseller, no. 246, Water street, New York, 1802. 138 p. 14 cm. [BV4253.R8 1802] 42-34898
1. Sermons, English. I. Title.

SAMPSON, Ashley, ed. 252.
Famous English sermons, edited, with an introduction, by Ashley Sampson. London, New York [etc.] T. Nelson & sons ltd. [1940] xvi, [17]-383, [1] p. 19 cm. "First published, 1940." [BV4241.S25]
1. Sermons, English. I. Title.

SEITZ, Josiah Augustus, 1837-
1922.
The colloquy; conversations about the order of things and final good, held in the Chapel of the blessed St. John...Summarized in verse, by Josiah Augustus Seitz... New York, G. P. Putnam's sons, 1897. iv p., 1 l., 236 p. 22 cm. [PS2799.S4] 30-13016
I. Title.

SELECTED English 252.00822
sermons; sixteenth to nineteenth centuries, with an introduction by the Rt. Rev. Hensley Henson... London, Oxford university press, H. Milford [1939] xvi, 412 p. 15 1/2 cm. (Half-title: The world's classics, 464) "First published in 'The world's classics' in 1939." Contents.The plough, by Hugh Latimer.--Death's duel, by John Donne.--Constant prayer, by John Hales.--The city of peace, by Thomas Adams.--The marriage ring, by Jeremy Taylor.--Of submission to the divine will, by Isaac Barrow,--Christianity mysterious, and the wisdom of God in making it so, by Robert South.--Upon the ignorance of man, by Joseph Butler.--The restlessness of human ambition, by Thomas Chalmers.--The invisible world, by J. H. Newman.--The powers of love, by James Martineau.--The reversal of human judgement, by J. B. Mozley.--The restoration of the erring, by F. W. Robertson.--Religion in common life, by John Caird.--The ethics of forgiveness by W. C. Magee.--Influences of the Holy Spirit, by H. P. Liddon.--The Trinity, by R. W. Dale. [BV4241.S413] 39-17575
1. Sermons, English. I. Henson, Herbert Hensley, bp. of Durham. 1863-

SERMON classics by great 252
preachers / compiled by Peter F. Gunther. Rev. ed. Chicago : Moody Press, c1982. 160 p. ; 22 cm. Rev. ed. of: Great sermons by great preachers. [1960] Contents.Contents.—The fire sermon / Dwight Lyman Moody — Sinners in the hands of an angry God / Jonathan Edwards — The most wonderful sentence ever written / Reuben Archer Torrey — God's love to fallen man / John Wesley — Repentance / George Whitefield — Fury not in God / Thomas Chalmers — Accidents, not punishments / Charles Haddon Spurgeon — A living stone / Handley C.G..Moule. [BV4241.S414 1982] 19 81-16899 ISBN 0-8024-3328-6 : 4.95
1. Sermons, English. I. Gunther, Peter F.

SERMONS of power, 252
Pentecost series; sermons by Edwin Du Bose Mouzon, William E. Barton, M. Ashby Jones [and others] ... Nashville, Tenn., Cokesbury press, 1930. 163 p. 19 cm. Contents.--Foreword, by W. P. King.--The meaning of Pentecost, by E. D. Mouzon.--The birthday of the church, by W. E. Barton.--The work of the Holy Spirit, by T. F. Gallor.--The test of translation, by M. A. Jones. --The earnest of our inheritance, by M. S. Rice.--When the Spirit is come, by W. E. Snyder.--Calvary and Pentecost, by S. P. Spreng.--The power of the Christian life, by R. H. Stover.--The fire from heaven, by J. I. Vance. [BV4241.S42] 30-9424
1. Sermons, English. I. Mouzon Edwin DuBose,

SHANNON, Frederick Franklin, 252
1877-
The unfathomable Christ, and other sermons, by Frederick F. Shannon ... New York, Chicago [etc.] Fleming H. Revell company [c1926] 3 p. l., 9-194 p. 19 1/2 cm. [BV4253.S62] 26-14442
I. Title.

SIMPSON, Hubert Louis, 252.052
1880-
The nameless longing, by Hubert L. Simpson. New York, Harper & brothers, 1931. 2 p. l., vii-xi, 305 p. 19 1/2 cm. Sermons. [BX9178.S5215N3] 31-9017
1. Sermons, English. I. Title.

SIMPSON, Hubert Louis, 232.958
1880-
Testament of love [by] Hubert L. Simpson ... New York, Chicago etc., The Abingdon press [1935] 125 p. 20 1/2 cm. "Lenten addresses on the Seven words from the cross."--p. [5] [BT455.S49] 35-13957
1. Jesus Christ—Seven last words. 2. Sermons, English. I. Title.

SMALRIDGE, George, bp. of 252.03
Bristol, 1663-1719.
Sixty sermons preached upon several occasions, by George Smalridge... A new ed. ... Oxford, The University press, 1852. 2 v. 22 cm. [BX5133.S546S5] 33-8314
1. Sermons, English. I. Title.

SMITH, Roy Lemon, 1887- comp. 252
The Minneapolis pulpit; a collection of sermons, by fifteen representative preachers, compiled by Roy L. Smith ... New York, Chicago [etc.] Fleming H. Revell company [c1929] 187 p. 20 cm. With brief notices of the authors. [BV4241.S55] 30-541
1. Sermons, English. I. Title.

SOARES, Theodore Gerald, 252
1869- ed.
University of Chicago sermons, by members of the university faculties, ed. by Theodore Gerald Soares ... Chicago, Ill., The University of Chicago press [c1915] xii, 348 p. 21 cm. [BV4241.S6] 15-8998
1. Sermons, English. I. Chicago. University. II. Title.

*SPURGEON, Charles H. 252.'55
1834-1892.
12 sermons to young people / Charles H. Spurgeon. Grand Rapids : Baker Book House, 1976. 143p. ; 20 cm. (His Library) Formerly printed under the title "Twelve sermons to young men" [BV 4310] ISBN 0-8010-8065-7 pbk. : 1.95.
1. Sermons, English. 2. Young adults. I. Title.

STAMM, Frederick K. comp. 252.
The Reformed church pulpit, by Frederick K. Stamm; introduction by the Rev. Joseph Fort Newton ... New York, The Macmillan company, 1928. xiii 329 p. 19 1/2 cm. [BX9577.A1S7] 28-2250
1. Sermons, English. I. Title.

STELZLE, Charles, 1869- comp. 252
If I had only one sermon to preach; sermons by twenty-one ministers, edited with an introduction, by Dr. Charles Stelzle. New York and London, Harper & brothers, 1927. xiii p., 1 l., 319 p. 22 cm. [BV4241.S7] 27-24113
1. Sermons, English. I. Title.

STEWARDSON, Langdon Cheeves,
1850-
College sermons, by Langdon Cheves Stewardson ... New York [etc.] Longmans, Green, and co., 1913. x, 332 p. 21 cm. 13-6913 1.50
I. Title.

*STEWART, James Stuart, 252'.05
1896-
The gates of new life [by] James S. Stewart. Grand Rapids, Mich., Baker Book House [1972] x, 251 p. 20 cm. (James S. Stewart library) First published in Edinburgh as part of the Scholar as preacher series. [BV4241] ISBN 0-8010-7974-8 pap., 2.95
1. Sermons, English. I. Title.

SUDDARDS, William, b.1805, 252
comp.
The British pulpit: consisting of discourses by the most eminent living divines, in England, Scotland, and Ireland: accompanied with pulpit sketches: to which are added, Scriptural illustrations; and selections on the office duties and responsibilities of the Christian ministry. By the Rev. W. Suddards ... 7th ed. ... New York and Pittsburg, R. Carter, 1845. 2 v. fronts (ports.) 22 1/2 cm. [BV4241.S8 1845] 19-12771
1. Sermons, English. I. Title.

SYLVESTER, J. Walter, 1868-
Guides to the higher life; selections from the sermons and other writings of Rev. J. Walter Sylvester...selected and ed. by Annie T. Keyser... [Albany? N.Y.] 1903. 131 p. 17 cm. 3-29857
I. Title.

TAYLOR, Charles Forbes.
The life story and sermons of the English boy preacher, Charles Forbes Taylor, the boy Moody and Sankey. Buffalo, N.Y., Baker, Jones & company, 1913. 182 p. front., port. 21 cm. $1.00. Sermons found in this book were preached in the Delaware avenue Baptist church, Buffalo, N.Y. cf. Introd. 13-25598
I. Title.

TEMPLE, William, abp. of 252.03
York, 1881-
Christian faith and life; being eight addresses delivered in the University church at Oxford, February 8th-15th, 1931, by William Temple, archbishop of York. New York, The Macmillan company, 1931. 139 p. 19 1/2 cm. [BX5133.T4C4 1931 a] 31-19287
1. Sermons, English. I. Title.

THIS great company : 252
sermons by outstanding preachers of the Christian tradition / selected and edited by David Poling ; foreword by Keith Miller. New Canaan, Conn. : Keats Pub., c1976. xiv, 200 p., [1] leaf of plates : ill. ; 23 cm. Bibliography: p. 200. [BV4241.T47] 74-75977 ISBN 0-87983-123-5 : 4.95
1. Sermons, English. I. Poling, David, 1928-

THORNTON, Edwin William, 1863-ed. 252.
Special sermons for special occasions, ed. by E. W. Thornton. Cincinnati, O., The Standard publishing company [c1921] 338 p. 19 1/2 cm. [BX7327.T5S7] 22-1385
1. Sermons, English. I. Title.

TIBBITTS, George Franklin, 1864- ed. 252
The pilgrim's guide; 52 lighthouses along the ocean of life ... edited by George F. Tibbitss ... Park-of-the-Palms, Keystone Heights, Fla. [etc.] The Gospel volunteers of the world (incorporated) [1946] xviii, 600 p., 1 l. plates, ports. 20 1/2 cm. [BV4241.T5] 47-16597
1. Sermons, English. I. Title.

TONNE, Arthur, 1904-
Five-minute parish talks. [Emporia, Kan., Didde, 1962] 60 p. 23 cm. 63-78236
1. Sermons, English. I. Title.

TURNBULL, Ralph G. ed. 252.008
If I had only one sermon to preach, ed. by Ralph G. Turnbull. Grand Rapids, Baker Bk. [1966] 151p. 21cm. [BV4241.T83] 66-18304 2.95
1. Sermons, English. I. Title.

VENN, John, 1759-1813. 252.03
Sermons, by the Rev. John Venn ... 1st American, from the 3d London ed. Boston, R. P. & C. Williams, 1821-22 [v. 1, 22] 3 v. in. 2 22 cm. Vol. 1 and part of vol. II (sermons 1-12, with t.p. dated 1821) are paged continuously to form the 1st vol. of the present set. The remaining sermons of vol. II (with separate t.p. dated 1822) and vol. III, paged continuously, form the 2d vol. [BX5133.V4S4 1821] 33-16430
1. Sermons, English. 2. Church of England—Sermons. I. Title.

WATTS, Isaac, 1674-1748.
Nine sermons, preached in the years 1718-19, by the late Isaac Watts, D.D. Now first published from mss. in the family of a contemporary [!] friend. With a preface, by John Pye Smith ... New-York, Eastburn, Kirk, & co.; [etc., etc.] 1813. xi p., 1 l., [15]-251 p. 17 1/2 cm. [BX5201.W3N5] A 35
1. Sermons, English. I. Title.

WATTS, Isaac, 1674-1748.
Sermons on various subjects, divine and moral; with a sacred hymn suited to each subject. Designed for the use of Christian families, as well as for the hours of devout retirement. By I. Watts ... The 7th ed. Boston, Printed and sold by Rogers and Fowle, 1746. 2 v. in 1. 20 cm. Paged continuously. [BX5201.W3S4] A 30
1. Sermons, English. I. Title.

WELSBY, Paul A., comp. 261.8
Sermons and society: an Anglican anthology; edited by Paul A. Welsby. Harmondsworth, Penguin, 1970. 364 p. 19 cm. (Pelican books, A1173) Bibliography: p. 360-[362] [BX5133.A1W4] 79-22020 ISBN 0-14-021173-X 10/-
1. Church of England—Sermons. 2. Sermons, English. 3. Great Britain—Social conditions—Collections. I. Title.

WESLEY, John, 1703-1791. 287
Sermons, on several occasions. By the late Rev. John Wesley ... Hudson [N.Y.]: Printed and published by William E. Norman, 1810. viii, [9]-332 p. 19 1/2 cm. [BX8333.W418S4] 38-33097
1. Sermons, English. 2. Methodist church—Sermons. I. Title.

WHAT we preach; 252.
sermons by representative men in the Baptist ministry. Philadelphia, Boston [etc.] The Judson press [c1929] 5 p. l., 3-275 p. 20 cm. [BX6333.A1W5] 29-9662
1. Sermons, English.

WHICHCOTE, Benjamin, 1609-1683. 252'.03
Select sermons of Benjamin Whichcote. A facsim. reproduction / with an introd. by John Andrew Bernstein. Delmar, N.Y. : Scholars' Facsimiles & Reprints, 1977. xii, xl, 307 p. ; 23 cm. Photoreprint of the 1742 ed., edited by W. Wishart and printed by T. W. and T. Ruddimans for G. Hamilton and J. Balfour, Edinburgh, under title: Select sermons of Dr. Whichcot; originally selected and introduced by the third earl of Shaftesbury. Bibliography: pt. 1, p. xi-xii. [BX5133.W5264S3 1977] 77-16025 ISBN 0-8201-1306-9 : 30.00
1. Church of England—Sermons. 2. Sermons, English. I. Title.

WILSON, John, D.D. 252
The polar star, and centre of comfort, by John Wilson, D.D. Containing several very admirable sermons, together with the beautiful works of William M'Ewen, D.D., with a paraphrase on the book of Job, and also a select private family physician, which no doubt, will be the means of saving many lives in the course of the present age. With beautiful moral history. And also heavenly sermons and hymns for children; in short, the calculation is to suit from the learned philosopher to the child. Published by James Sharan ... New-York: Printed by John Low, ... MDCCCXVI. 1 p.l., [v]-vi, [7]-301 p. 17 cm. "The choice of a rural life: a poem. By Wm. Fairfield, esq.": p. 223-248. [BV4253.W47] 37-35236
1. Sermons, English. 2. Medicine, Popular. 3. Country life—Poetry. I. McEwen, William, 1734-1762. II. Fairfield, William. III. Sharan, James, comp. IV. Title.

WRIGHT, Ronald Selby, 1908- 252'.55
Take up God's armour : talks to schools and colleges. London, Oxford U.P., 1967. xii, 212 p. 19 cm. Includes bibliographical references [BX9178.W73T3] 67-101002
1. Church of Scotland—Sermons. 2. Sermons, English. I. Title.

ZINZENDORF, Nicolaus Ludwig, Graf von, 1700-1760. 252'.04'6
Nine public lectures on important subjects in religion, preached in Fetter Lane Chapel in London in the year 1746. Translated & edited by George W. Forell. Iowa City, University of Iowa Press, 1973. xxxii, 138 p. 24 cm. Bibliography: p. [105]-138. [BX8577.Z5N56] 72-93784 ISBN 0-87745-036-6
1. Moravian Church—Sermons. 2. Sermons, English. I. Title.

Sermons, English—16th century.

FOXE, John, 1516-1587. 252'.03
The English sermons of John Foxe / facsimile reproduction with an introd. by Warren W. Wooden. Delmar, N.Y. : Scholars' Facsimiles & Reprints, 1978. xxii, [364] p. ; 23 cm. Photoreprint ed. of 2 works, the 1st published in 1570 by J. Daye, London; the 2d published in 1578 by C. Barker, London. Contents.Contents.—A sermon of Christ crucified.—A sermon preached at the christening of a certaine Jew. [BX5133.F74S47 1978] 77-29100 ISBN 0-8201-1267-4 : 35.00
1. Church of England—Sermons. 2. Sermons, English—16th century. I. Foxe, John, 1516-1587. A sermon of Christ crucified. 1978. II. Foxe, John, 1516-1587. A sermon preached at the christening of a certaine Jew. 1978. III. Title.
Contents omitted.

Sermons, English—18th century—History and criticism.

GRAY, James, 1923- 252'.03
Johnson's sermons: a study. Oxford, Clarendon Press, 1972. xv, 263 p., iv leaves. ports. 23 cm. Bibliography: p. [245]-255. [PR3534.G7] 73-158318 ISBN 0-19-812033-8
1. Johnson, Samuel, 1709-1784. 2. Sermons, English—18th century—History and criticism. I. Title.
Distributed by Oxford University Press N.Y. 13.75.

Sermons, English—Australia.

WALKER, Alan, 1911- 252'.07
God, the disturber. Waco, Tex., Word Books [1973] 136 p. 23 cm. [BX8333.W224G6] 73-76967 3.95
1. Methodist Church—Sermons. 2. Sermons, English—Australia. I. Title.

Sermons—English—Baptist—Collections.

*SPURGEON, Charles Haddon, 1834-1892 252.06
Lectures to my students [by] C. H. Spurgeon. Grand Rapids, Mich., Zondervan [1972] 443 p. 23 cm. This is a new ed. containing Selected Lectures from Series 1, 2 and 3, 1954. [BX63333.] 6.95
1. Sermons—English—Baptist—Collections. I. Title.

Sermons, English—Canada.

ARCHIBALD, Frank E. 252'.07'92
An essential greatness, by Frank E. Archibald. Windsor, N.S., Lancelot Press [1968] 164 p. 21 cm. [BX9882.A8 1968] 72-180379 2.50
1. United Church of Canada—Sermons. 2. Apostles' Creed. 3. Sermons, English—Canada. I. Title.

BREWING, Willard E., 1881- 252
Faith for these times, by Willard Brewing ... Toronto, New York, Collins [1945] v, 159 p. 21 1/2 cm. "First Edition." [BX9882.B7] 45-18655
1. United church of Canada—Sermons. 2. Sermons, English—Canada. I. Title.

FERRY, John G comp. 252'.00971
Outstanding sermons from Canadian pulpits, edited by John G. Ferry. Vancouver, Evergreen Press, c1966. x, 149 p. ports. 23 cm. unpriced (C 67-4250) [BV4241.F46] 68-75081
1. Sermons, English—Canada. I. Title.

GRIFFITH, Arthur Leonard, 1920- 252'.07'92
Ephesians : a positive affirmation : the Ephesian letter today / Leonard Griffith. Waco, Tex. : Word Books, [1975] 173 p. ; 23 cm. Includes bibliographical references. [BS2695.4.G74] 75-3638 5.95
1. United Church of Canada—Sermons. 2. Bible. N.T. Ephesians—Sermons. 3. Sermons, English—Canada. I. Title.

JOHNSTON, Minton C. 248.42
24 hours to live. Nashville, Abingdon [c.1963] 112p. 20cm. 63-14594 2.25 bds.,
1. Sermons, English—Canada. 2. Baptist Church—Sermons. I. Title.

JOHNSTON, Minton C. 248.42
24 hours to live New York, Abingdon Press [1963] 112 p. 20 cm. Messages broadcast on the Canadian Broadcasting Corporation network. [BX6333.J66T9] 63-14594
1. Sermons, English — Canada. 2. Baptist Church — Sermons. I. Title.

JOHNSTON, Minton C. 248.081
Washing elephants, and other paths to God. Nashville, Abingdon [c.1965] 127p. 19cm. [BX6333.J66W3] 65-14821 2.25 bds.,
1. Sermons, English—Canada. 2. Baptists—Sermons. I. Title.

JOHNSTON, Minton C. 248.081
Washing elephants, and other paths to God [by] Minton C. Johnston. New York, Abingdon Press [1965] 127 p. 19 cm. [BX6333.J66W3] 65-14821
1. Sermons, English — Canada. 2. Baptists — Sermons. I. Title.

YOUNG, William Harold, ed. 252
Great Canadian preaching, edited, with introduction and biographical notes, by W. Harold Young ... New York, George H. Doran company [1925] xiv p., 1 l., 17-297 p. 19 1/2 cm. [BV4241.Y6] 26-2578
1. Sermons, English—Canada. I. Title.

Sermons, English—Collections.

BRONG, Rosco, D. D. 252.06
Love builds up: a simple score of short sermons addressed to saints and sinners. Lexington, Ky., 657 St. Anthony Dr., Amen Bk. Loft, c.1963. 80p. 23cm. 3.00; 1.00 pap.,
I. Title.

*SPURGEON, Charles Haddon, 1834-1892. 252'.008
Charles H. Spurgeon. Introd. by Andrew W. Blackwood. Grand Rapids, Baker Book House [1972, c.1949] 256 p. 19 cm. (Great pulpit masters) [BV4241] pap., 2.95
1. Sermons, English—Collections. I. Title.

Sermons, English—History and criticism

CHRISMAN, Lewis Herbert, 1883- 250.
The message of the American pulpit, by Lewis H. Chrisman ... New York, R.R. Smith, Inc, 1930. vii p., 2 l., 255 p. 19 1/2 cm. [BV4208.U6C5] 30-3334
1. Sermons, English—Hist. & crit. 2. Preaching. I. Title. II. Title: The American pulpit, The message of.

Sermons, English—Ireland.

[BERNARD, John Henry, abp. of Dublin] 1860-
Peplographia dvblinensis: memorial discourses preached in the chapel of Trinity college, Dublin, 1895-1902 ... London Macmillan and co. limited; New York, The Macmillan company, 1902. viii. 219 p. 20 cm. Preface signed: J. H. Bernard. [LF904.A3B4] 16-21169
I. Title.

HAMELL, Patrick J., ed. 252.6082
Sermons for Sundays & feasts, by 68 Irish priests and prelates. Dublin, Browne & Nolan [dist. Mystic, Conn., Lawrence Verry, 1964] xii, 522p. 22cm. Bibl. 64-9585 6.00
1. Sermons, English—Ireland. 2. Catholic Church—Sermons. I. Title.

HAMELL, Patrick J., ed. 252.6
Sunday and feast homilies, by 62 Irish priests. Ed. by Patrick J. Hamell. Dublin, Browne & Nolan [dist. Mystic, Conn., Verry,1965] 128p. 23cm. [BX1756.A2] 65-7960 3.50 bds.,
1. Sermons, English—Ireland. 2. Catholic Church—Sermons. 3. Church year—Sermons. I. Title.

Sermons, English—Middle English, 1100-1500.

BELFOUR, Algernon Okey, ed.
Twelfth-century homilies in ms. Bodley 343. London, New York, Published for the Early English Text Society by the Oxford University Press [1962- v. facsim. 23 cm. (Early English Text Society. Original series, no. 137) Series: Early English Text Society, London. Publications, no. 137) Contents.pt. 1. Text and translation. NUC64
1. Sermons, English — Middle English (110-1500) I. Title. II. Series.

GRISDALE, D. M. ed. 252.02
Three Middle English sermons from the Worcester chapter manuscript F.10, edited by D. M. Grisdale, M. A. Kendal, Printed by T. Wilson for members of the School of English language in the University of Leed, 1939. xxx, 111 p. 23 cm. (Half-title: Leeds School of English language. Texts and monographs, no. v) "The first sermon has title: Hugonis Lgat in Passione Domini. "Select glossary": p. 104-111. [BV4241.A2G7] 40-82976
1. Sermons, English—Middle English (1100-1500) 2. English language—Middle English (1100-1500)—Texts. I. Legat, Hugo, fl. 1401-1427. II. Worcester cathedral. Library. Mass, (F. 10) III. Title.

MORRIS, Richard, 1833-1894, ed. 252'.0242
Old English homilies and homiletic treatises (Sawles warde, and Pe wohunge of Ure Lauerd: Ureisuns of Ure Louerd and of Ure Lefdi, &c.) of the twelfth and thirteenth centuries. Edited from mss. in the British Museum, Lambeth, and Bodleian Libraries, with introd., translation, and notes, by Richard Morris. New York, Greenwood Press [1969] lxiii, 330 p. 23 cm. (Early English Text Society. [Publications] O. S. 29 & 34) Reprint of the 1868 ed. [PR1119.A2 no. 29, 34 1969] 69-19533
1. Sermons, English—Middle English, 1100-1500. I. Title. II. Series: Early English Text Society. Publications. Original series, no. 29, 34

WIMBLEDON, R. 252.02
Wimbledon's sermon: Redde rationem villicationis tue; a Middle English sermon of the fourteenth century. Edited by Ione Kemp Knight. Pittsburgh, Duquesne University Press [1967] vii, 147 p. 27 cm. (Duquesne studies. Philological series, 9) "The text is ... based on Corpus Christi MS. 357." First published under title: A sermon no lesse fruteful than famous. Bibliographical footnotes. [BX890.W48 1967] 66-29692
1. Sermons, English—Middle English, 1100-1500. I. Knight, Ione Kemp, ed. II. Title. III. Title: Redde rationem villicationis tue. IV. Series.

Sermons, English—Scotland.

CANDLISH, Robert Smith, 1806-1873. 222'.11'06
Genesis / by Robert S. Candlish. Grand Rapids : Kregel Publications, 1979. p. cm. First published under title: Contributions towards the exposition of the Book of Genesis. Reprint of the new ed., carefully rev., published in 1868 by A. and C. Black, Edinburgh, under title: The Book of Genesis expounded in a series of discourses. [BS1235.C32 1979] 79-14084 ISBN 0-8254-2315-5 : 14.95
1. Bible. O.T. Genesis—Sermons. 2. Sermons, English—Scotland. I. Title.

DUNCAN, John, 1796-1870. 252.05'2'41
Pulpit and communion table; edited by David Brown. [New ed.] Inverness, Free Presbyterian Publications, 1969. [8], 243 p. 23 cm. [BX9178.D754P8] 72-497581 ISBN 0-902506-01-3 12/6
1. Free Church of Scotland—Sermons. 2. Sermons, English—Scotland. 3. Lord's Supper—Meditations. I. Brown, David, 1803-1897, ed. II. Title.

HUNTER, Archibald Macbride 225.6
Teaching and preaching the New Testament. Philadelphia, Westminster [c.1963] 191p. 23cm. Bibl. 63-12596 3.75
1. Forsyth, Peter Taylor, 1848-1921. 2. Sermons, English—Scotland. 3. Bible. N. T.—Addresses, essays, lectures. I. Title.

HUNTER, Archibald Macbridge. 225.6
Teaching and preaching the New Testament. Philadelphia. Westminister Press [1963] 191 p. 23 cm. Bibliographical references included in footnotes. [BS2395.H8] 63-12596
1. Sermons, English — Scotland. 2. Bible.N. T. — Addresses, essays, lectures. 3. Forsyth, Peter Taylor, 1848-1921. I. Title.

MORRISON, George Herbert, 1866-1928.
The ever open door, by George H. Morrison, D.D. New York, R. R. Smith, inc., 1930. 286 p., 1 l. 19 1/2 cm. 36-2668
1. Sermons, English—Scotland. I. Title.

MORRISON, George Herbert, 1866-1928. 252.052
Morning sermons, by George H. Morrison ... New York [etc.] Fleming H. Revell company [c1932] 251 p. 20 cm. Preface signed: Christine Morrison. [BX9178.M6M6] 32-12712
1. Sermons, English—Scotland. I. Morrison, Christine Marie (Auchinvole) "Mrs. George H. Morrison," ed. II. Title.

SMITH, Andre. 252
How beautiful : a series of short sermons / Andre Smith. Aberdeen : University Press, 1971. 84 p. ; 19 cm. [BV4253.S725] 75-314125 £0.35
1. Sermons, English—Scotland. I. Title.

STEWART, James Stuart, 1896- 252'.05'1
King for ever / James S. Stewart. Nashville, Tenn. : Abingdon Press, [1975] 160 p. ; 23 cm. [BX9178.S7917K5] 75-313215 ISBN 0-687-20883-1 : 5.95
1. Presbyterian Church—Sermons. 2. Sermons, English—Scotland. I. Title.

STEWART, James Stuart, 1896- 252'.05'2
River of life, by James S. Stewart. Nashville, Abingdon Press [1972] 160 p. 23 cm. [BX9178.S7917R58] 72-2031 ISBN 0-687-36480-9 3.50
1. Presbyterian Church—Sermons. 2. Sermons, English—Scotland. I. Title.

STEWART, James Stuart, 1896- 252.05'2
The wind of the spirit [by] James S. Stewart. Nashville, Abingdon Press [1969, c1968] 191 p. 23 cm. [BX9178.S7917W5 1969] 69-18447 3.95
1. Presbyterian Church—Sermons. 2. Sermons, English—Scotland. I. Title.

Sermons, English (Selections: Extracts, etc.)

CLARK, John Brittan, 1864- 244
Guide-posts along the way, extracts from sermons, by Rev. John Brittan Clark... [Washington, D.C., 1926. 2 p. l., 9-94 p. front. (port.) pl. 16 1/2 cm. [BX8915.C65] 27-1158
I. Title.

LORD, Fred Townley, 1893- 252.061
The faith that sings. [Essays] Nashville, Broadman Press [1951] 119 p. 20 cm. [BX6333.L57F3] 51-11400
1. Sermons, English (Selections: Extracts, etc.) I. Title.

Sermons, English Translations from French.

BOURDALOUE, Louis, 1632-1704. 248
Bourdalou at Versaile, 1670, from the French by Alicia Du Pont de Nemours. New York, Brentano's, 1919. 173 p. front. 21 cm. Half-title: Two sermons before His Majesty the King Louis XIV. [BX1756.B82F4] 19-16115
I. Du Pont de Nemours, Alicia, tr. II. Title.

VINET, Alexandre Rodolphe, 1797-1847. 252.
Gospel studies. By Alexander Vinet ... With an introduction by Robert Baird ... New York, M. W. Dodd, 1849. viii, 373 p. 19 cm. [BV4254.F7V54 1849a] 45-52865
1. Sermons, French—Translations into English. 2. Sermons, English—Translations from French. I. Title.

Sermons, English—Translations from German.

ADLER, Elisabeth, ed. 252.4
Here for a reason; Christian voices in a Communist state. [Tr. by Leslie Seiffert] New York, Macmillan [1964] 136p. 21cm. 64-17716 2.95
1. Sermons, German—Translations into English. 2. Sermons, English—Translations from German. 3. Germany (Democratic Republic, 1949-)—Religion. I. Title. II. Title: Christian voices in a Communist state.

EBELING, Gerhard, 1912- 242'.722
On prayer : the Lord's Prayer in today's world / by Gerhard Ebeling ; [translated by James W. Leitch]. Philadelphia : Fortess Press, 1978, c1966. 111 p. ; 18 cm. Translation of Vom Gebet. [BV230.E2313 1978] 78-5079 ISBN 0-8006-1336-8 pbk. : 2.95
1. Lord's prayer—Sermons. 2. Sermons, English—Translations from German. 3. Sermons, German—Translations into English. I. Title.

JOHN Paul II, Pope, 1920- 230'.2
Germany-pilgrimage of unity and peace / John Paul II ; compiled and indexed by the Daughters of St. Paul. Boston, MA : St. Paul Editions, c1981. 285 p. : ill. ; 19 cm. Speeches previously published in L'Osservatore romano, English ed. Includes index. [BX891.J646] 19 81-2126 ISBN 0-8198-3013-5 : 6.00 ISBN 0-8198-3014-3 pbk. : 5.00
1. Catholic Church—Addresses, essays, lectures. 2. Catholic Church—Sermons. 3. Sermons, English—Translations from German. 4. Sermons, German—Translations into English. I. Daughters of St. Paul. II. Title.
Publisher's address: 50 St. Paul's Ave., Boston, MA 02130

KOBERLE, Adolf, 1898- 252.04'1
The invitation of God. Translated by Roy Barlag. Saint Louis, Concordia Pub. House [1968] 238 p. 22 cm. Sermons preached 1950-1957 at the university church in Tubingen, Germany. Translation of Die Einladung Gottes. [BX8066.K583E53] 68-12893
1. Lutheran Church—Sermons. 2. Sermons, English—Translations from German. 3. Sermons, German—Translations into English. I. Title.

LUTHER, Martin, 1483-1546.
A selection of the most celebrated sermons of Martin Luther... Never before published in the United States. To which is prefixed a biographical history of his life. Philadelphia, C. Desilver, 1856. 204 p. front. (port.) 20 cm. [With Calvin, Jean. A selection of the most celebrated sermons of John Calvin...Philadelphia, 1856] [BR332.S5 1856] 4-21339
1. Sermons, English—Translations from German. 2. Sermons, German—Translations into English. 3. Lutheran church—Sermons. I. Title.

MOLTMANN, Jurgen. 252'.04'1
The gospel of liberation. Translated by H. Wayne Pipkin. Waco, Tex., Word Books [1973] 136 p. 23 cm. [BX8066.M6G67] 73-77952 5.95
1. Lutheran Church—Sermons. 2. Sermons, German—Translations into English. 3. Sermons, English—Translations from German. I. Title.

RAHNER, Karl, 1904- 252.02
Biblical homilies. [Translated by Desmond Forristal and Richard Strachan. New York] Herder and Herder [1966] 191 p. 21 cm. Delivered in the university church, Innsbruck, 1953-1958. [BX1756.R25B53] 66-24386
1. Catholic Church—Sermons. 2. Sermons, German—Translations into English. 3. Sermons, English—Translations from German. I. Title.

SCHWEITZER, Albert, 1875-1965. 252'.04
Reverence for life / Albert Schweitzer ; translated by Reginald H. Fuller. New York : Irvington, [1979] c1969. p. cm. Translation of Strassburger Predigten. Reprint of the 1st ed. published by Harper & Row, New York. [BV4254.G3S3213 1979] 79-19338 ISBN 0-89197-920-4 : 8.95
1. Sermons, English—Translations from German. 2. Sermons, German—Translations into English. I. Title.

SCHWEIZER, Eduard, 1913- 252
God's inescapable nearness. Translated and edited by James W. Cox. Waco, Tex., Word Books [1971] 124 p. 23 cm. Includes bibliographical references. [BV4254.G3S34] 77-134938 3.95
1. Sermons, German—Translation into English. 2. Sermons, English—Translations from German. I. Title.

SERMONS.
Edited and translated by John W. Doberstein. Philadelphia, Muhlenberg press [1959- v. 24cm. (His Works, v. 51-)
1. Sermons, German—Translations into English. lish. I. Luther, Martin, 1483-1546. II. Doberstein, John W., ed.

THIELICKE, Helmut, 1908- 230.4'1'0924
How modern should theology be? Translated by H. George Anderson. Philadelphia, Fortress Press [1969] v, 90 p. 20 cm. Translation of Wie modern darf die Theologie sein? [BX8066.T46W513] 69-14620 2.50
1. Lutheran Church—Sermons. 2. Sermons, German—Translations into English. 3. Sermons, English—Translations from German. I. Title.

THIELICKE, Helmut, 1908- 226'.806
The waiting Father / Helmut Thielicke ; translated with an introduction by John W. Doberstein. San Francisco : Harper & Row, [1981], c1959. 192 p. ; 21 cm. Translation of: Das Bilderbuch Gottes. [BT375.2.T5 1981] 19 75-12284 ISBN 0-06-067991-3 : 5.05
1. Jesus Christ—Parables—Sermons. 2. Lutheran Church—Sermons. 3. Sermons, German—Translations into English. 4. Sermons, English—Translations from German. I. [Bilderbuch Gottes.] English II. Title.

THOLUCK, August, 1799-1877. 232.96
Light from the cross; with a biographical introd. by J. C. Macaulay. Chcago, Moody Press, 1952. 293 p. 23 cm. (The Wycliffe series of Christian classics) "Translator's preface" signed: R. L. B. [i. e. Robert Christopher Lundin Brown] Full name: Friedrich August Gottreu Tholuck. [BT430.T4] 52-2780
1. Jesus Christ — Passion — Sermons. 2. Sermons, English — Translations from German. 3. Sermons, German — Translations into English. I. Title.

WALTHER, C. F. W. 1811-1887. (Carl Ferdinand Wilhelm), 252'.041322
Selected sermons / Henry J. Eggold, translator. St. Louis : Concordia Pub. House, c1981. 192 p. : ill. ; 24 cm. (Selected writings of C.F.W. Walther) (Series: Walther, C. F. W. (Carl Ferdinand Wilhelm), 1811-1887. Selections. English. 1981.) Bibliography: p. 192. [BX8066.W3S47213] 19 81-3097 ISBN 0-570-08276-5 : 12.95
1. Lutheran Church—Sermons. 2. Sermons, English—Translations from German. 3. Sermons, German—Translations into English. I. [Sermons.] English. Selections II. Title. III. Series.

Sermons, English—Translations from Greek.

CHRYSOSTOMUS, Joannes, Saint, Patriarch of Constantinople, d. 407. 225.92
In praise of Saint Paul. Tr. [from Greek] by Thomas Halton. [Boston] St. Paul Eds. [dist. Daughters of St. Paul, c.1963] 123p. 20cm. 63-14467 2.00; 1.00 pap.,
1. Paul, Saint, Apostle—Sermons. 2. Sermons, Greek—Translations into English. 3. Sermons, English—Translations from Greek. I. Halton, Thomas, tr. II. Title.

MELITO, Saint, Bp. of Sardis, 2dcent. 232
On Pascha and fragments / Melito of Sardis ; texts and translations edited by Stuart George Hall. Oxford : Clarendon Press, 1979. xlix, 99 p. ; 21 cm. (Oxford early Christian texts) Parallel texts in English and Greek. Includes bibliographical references and index. [BT430.M413] 79-308762 ISBN 0-19-826811-4 : 19.95
1. Jesus Christ—Passion—Sermons. 2. Sermons, English—Translations from Greek. 3. Sermons, Greek. 4. Theology—Early church, ca. 30-600. I. Hall, Stuart George. II. Title. III. Series.

Sermons, English Translations from Jewish.

STERN, Harry Joshua, 1897-
Entrusted with spiritual leadership; a collection of addresses. New York, Bloch, 1961. 120 p. 24 cm.
1. Sermons, Jewish, in English. 2. Sermons, American. I. Title.

Sermons, English Translations from Korean.

MOON, Sun Myung. 230
The new future of Christianity / Sun Myung Moon. Washington : Unification Church International, 1974. vii, 144 p., [1] fold. leaf of plates : ill. ; 20 cm. Translation of 2 speeches delivered at the Waldorf Astoria, and Madison Square Garden, New York on Sept. 17 and 18, 1974 respectively. Contents.Contents.—God's new way of life.—The new future of Christianity. [BX9750.S4M66] 74-24931
1. Segye Kidokkyo T'ongil Sillyong Hyophoe—Sermons. 2. Sermons, Korean—Translations into English. 3. Sermons, English—Translations from Korean. I. Title.

Sermons, English—Translations from Latin.

BERNARD de Clairvaux, Saint, 1091?-1153. 230'.2 s
On the Songs of Songs. Translated by Kilian Walsh. Introd. by M. Corneille Halfants. Spencer, Mass., Cistercian Publications, 1971- v. 23 cm. (The

works of Bernard of Clairvaux, v. 2,) (Cistercian Fathers series, no. 4,) [BX890.B5 1970 vol. 2, etc.] [BS1485] 223'.9'07 73-168262 ISBN 0-87907-104-4 (v. 1) 7.95 (v. 1)
1. Bible. O.T. Song of Solomon—Sermons. 2. Sermons, Latin—Translations into English. 3. Sermons, English—Translations from Latin. I. Title. II. Series: Bernard de Clairvaux, Saint, 1091?-1153. Works. English. 1970, v. 2 [etc.]

BERNARD de Clairvaux, Saint, 1091?-1153. 252'.02
Sermons on conversion / Bernard of Clairvaux ; translated with an introd. by Marie-Bernard Said. Kalamazoo, Mich. : Cistercian Publications, 1981. 282 p. : map ; 23 cm. (The Cistercian Fathers series ; no. 25) "The translations herein presented have been made from the critical edition of Jean Leclercq and H.M. Rochais, Sancti Bernardi opera, volume IV, published at Rome in 1966 by Editiones Cistercienses." Includes indexes. Contents.Contents. On conversion, a sermon to clerics.—Lenten sermons on the psalm He who dwells. Bibliography: p. 263. [BX1756.B42S5 1981] 19 80-25325 ISBN 0-87907-125-7 (v. 1) : 26.95 pbk. : 7.00
1. Catholic Church—Sermons. 2. Sermons, English—Translations from Latin. 3. Sermons, Latin—Translations into English. I. Said, Marie Bernard. II. Title.

BONAVENTURA, Saint, Cardinal, 1221-1274. 252'.02
Rooted in faith: homilies to a contemporary world. Translation and introductory essay by Marigwen Schumacher. Foreword by Peter Damian Fehlner. Chicago, Franciscan Herald Press [1974] xxxii, 133 p. illus. 21 cm. [BX1756.B58S413] 73-19533 ISBN 0-8199-0465-1 5.95
1. Catholic Church—Sermons. 2. Sermons, Latin—Translations into English. 3. Sermons, English—Translations from Latin. I. Title.
Contents omitted.

BRENNAN, Richard, 1833?-1893. 922.21
A popular life of our Holy Father, Pope Pius the Ninth drawn from the most reliable authorities. By Rev. Richard Brennan ... 6th ed. New York, Cincinnati, and St. Louis, Benziger brothers, 1877. xii [7]-282 p. incl. front., illus. (incl. ports.) 21 cm. [BX1373.B7 1877 f] 39-32767
1. Pius IX, pope, 1792-1878. I. Title.

CAESARIUS, Saint, Bp. of Arles, 470?-543. 281.4
Sermons; translated by Mary Magdeleine Mueller. New York, Fathers of the Church, inc., 1956- v. 22cm. (The Fathers of the church, a new translation, v. 31) Bibliography: v. 1, p. xxvi-xxvii. [BR60.F3C3] 56-3628
1. Sermons, Latin—Translation into English. 2. Sermons, English—Translations from Latin. I. Title. II. Series.

HIERONYMUS, Saint. 223.206
The homilies of Saint Jerome. Translated by Marie Liguori Ewald. Washington, Catholic University of America Press [1964-66] 2 v. 22 cm. (The Fathers of the church, a new translation, v. 48, 57) Contents.—v. 1. 1-59 on the Psalms.—v. 2. Homilies 60-96. Bibliography: v. 1, p. xxxi. [BR60.F3H5] 64-13360
1. Bible. O.T. Psalms—Sermons. 2. Sermons, Latin—Translations into English. 3. Sermons, English—Translations from Latin. I. Ewald, Marie Liguori, 1905- tr. II. Title. III. Series: The Fathers of the church, a new translation, v. 48, [etc.]

MAGNIFICAT : 232.91
homilies in praise of the Blessed Virgin Mary / by Bernard of Clairvaux and Amadeus of Lausanne ; translated by Marie-Bernard Said and Grace Perigo ; introd. by Guntram Bischoff. Kalamazoo, Mich. : Cistercian Publications Inc., 1979. p. cm. (Cistercian Fathers series ; no. 18) "A translation from the Latin of Sermones in laudibus Beatae Virginis Matris, by Bernard of Clairvaux (1090-1153), and Homiliae octo Amedei Episcopi Lausannensis de laudibus Beatae Mariae, of Amadeus of Lausanne (1110-1159)." Includes index. [BT608.A1M33] 78-6249 ISBN 0-87907-118-4 : 15.95
1. Mary, Virgin—Sermons. 2. Sermons, English—Translations from Latin. 3. Sermons, Latin—Translations into English. I. Bernard de Clairvaux, Saint, 1091?-1153. II. Amadeus, Saint, Bp. of Lausanne, 1110 (ca.)-1159.

PETRUS CHRYSOLOGUS, Saint, Bp. of Ravenna. 252
Saint Peter Chrysologus: selected sermons, and Saint Valerian: homilies. Translated by George E. Ganss. Washington, Catholic University of America Press [1965, c1953] viii, 454 p. 22 cm. (The Fathers of the Church, a new transiation. v. 17) Bibliography: p. 24. Bibliographical footnotes. [BR60.F3P473] 65-27500
1. Sermons, Latin—Translations into English. 2. Sermons, English—Translations from Latin. I. Valerianus Saint, Bp. of Cintez. II. Title. III. Series.

Sermons, English—Translations from Norwegian.

HELLENBROEK, Abraham, 1658-1731.
A sermon by Abraham Hellenbroek ... From Canticles chap. 11. ver. 15. Take us the foxes, the little foxes that spoil the vines; for our vines have tender grapes. Being one of that Rev. author's printed discourses on the Song of Solomon. Published at Rotterdam, anno 1717. Tr. from the Dutch. Boston: N.E., Printed and sold by S. Kneeland and T. Green, 1742. 1 p. l., 31 p. 17 1/2 cm. 17-1299
I. Title.

KOREN, Vilhelm, 1826-1910. 252'.04'1
Truth unchanged, unchanging : selected sermons, addresses, and doctrinal articles / by Ulrik Vilhelm Koren ; translated and edited by the Evangelical Lutheran Synod Translation Committee. Lake Mills, Iowa : Graphic Pub. Co., 1978. iv, 251 p. : port. ; 24 cm. [BX8066.K633T78 1978] 78-70540 ISBN 0-89279-016-4 : 9.95
1. Lutheran Church—Sermons. 2. Sermons, English—Translations from Norwegian. 3. Sermons, Norwegian—Translations into English. 4. Theology, Lutheran—Addresses, essays, lectures. I. Evangelical Lutheran Synod. Translation Committee. II. Title.

Sermons, English Translations from Polish.

JOHN Paul II, Pope, 1920- 252'.02
Pilgrim to Poland / John Paul II. Boston : Daughters of St. Paul, c1979. p. cm. [BX1756.J64P54] 79-21177 pbk. : 2.00
1. Catholic Church—Sermons. 2. Sermons, Polish—Translations into English. 3. Sermons, English—Translations from Polish. I. Title.

Sermons, English—Translations from Portuguese.

JOHN Paul II, Pope, 1920- 252'.02
Brazil : journey in the light of the Eucharist / John Paul II ; compiled and indexed by the Daughters of St. Paul. [Boston] : St. Paul Editions, c1980. 400 p., [8] leaves of plates : ill. (some col.) ; 19 cm. "Reprinted ... from L'Osservatore Romano, English edition." Includes index. [BX1756.J64B7] 19 80-24395 ISBN 0-8198-1102-5 : 8.00 ISBN 0-8198-1103-3 pbk. : 7.00
1. Catholic Church—Sermons. 2. Sermons, English—Translations from Portuguese. 3. Sermons, Portuguese—Translations into English. I. Daughters of St. Paul. II. Title.

Sermons, English—Translations from Spanish.

ESCRIVA de Balaguer, Jose Maria, 1902- 252'.02
Christ is passing by : homilies / Josemaria Escriva de Balaguer. Chicago : Scepter Press, [1974] 276 p., [18] leaves of plates : ill. ; 22 cm. Translation of Es Cristo que pasa. Includes bibliographical references and indexes. [BX1756.E77E813] 74-78783
1. Catholic Church—Sermons. 2. Sermons, English—Translations from Spanish. 3. Sermons, Spanish—Translations into English. I. Title.

JOHN Paul II, Pope, 1920- 252'.02
Puebla-a pilgrimage of faith / by Pope John Paul II. Boston : St. Paul Editions, c1979. p. cm. Addresses and homilies. [BX1756.J64P83] 79-21600 ISBN 0-8198-0629-3 pbk. : 2.00
1. Catholic Church—Sermons. 2. Sermons, Spanish—Translations into English. 3. Sermons, English—Translations from Spanish. I. Title.

ROMERO, Oscar A. 1917-1980. (Oscar Arnulfo) 252'.02
A martyr's message of hope : six homilies / by Oscar Romero. Kansas City, Mo. : Celebration Books, c1981. xii, 180 p. ; 18 cm. Original Spanish homilies, as delivered by Archbishop Romero, on cassettes under title: Un mensaje esperanzado de un martir. Contents.Contents. The Holy Spirit — An assassination that speaks to us of resurrection — Christ—true shepherd — The poor — The church — In death is our life. [BX1756.R56M4613] 19 80-84886 ISBN 0-934134-09-X pbk. : 5.95
1. Catholic Church—Sermons. 2. Sermons, English—Translations from Spanish. 3. Sermons, Spanish—Translations into English. I. [Mensaje esperanzado de un martir.] English II. Title.
Publisher's address: 115 E. Armor, Box 281, Kansas City, MO 64141

Sermons, English—Translations from Welsh.

EVANS, Christmas, 1766-1838. 252.061
Sermons of Christmas Evans. A new translation from the Welsh. With a memoir and portraiture of the author, by Rev. Joseph Cross. Richmond, Sold by J. Early, 1850. 304 p. pl. 23 1/2 cm. Added t.-p. (with portrait of author) has title: Life and works ... [BX6333.E8S45 1850] 33-29269
1. Sermons, English—Translations from Welsh. 2. Sermons, Welsh—Translations into English. I. Cross, Joseph, 1813-1898, tr. II. Title.

EVANS, Christmas, 1766-1838. 252.061
Sermons of Christmas Evans, a new translation from the Welch, with a memoir and portraiture of the author. By Rev. Joseph Cross. Chicago, Church & Goodman, 1867. 394 p. front. 23 1/2 cm. Added t.-p. (with portrait of author) has title: Life and sermons ... [BX6333.E8S45 1867] 33-29269
1. Sermons, English—Translations from Welsh. 2. Sermons, Welsh—Translations into English. I. Cross, Joseph, 1813-1898, tr. II. Title.

Sermons, Episcopalian.

CRAVNER, William Charles 252.03
The faith magnificent. New York, Vantage Press [c.1961] 93p. front. port. 2.95 bds.,
1. Sermons, Episcopalian. I. Title.

Sermons for Children.

BOWIE, Walter Russell, 1882- 252
Sunny windows, and other sermons for children, by Walter Russell Bowie ... New York, Chicago [etc.] Fleming H. Revell company [c1921] 190 p. 20 cm. [BV4315.B65] 21-3695
I. Title.

CHAMBERS, Samuel David. 252
"If I were you": story sermons from the alphabet for boys and girls, by S. D. Chambers, M. A. New York, Chicago [etc.] Fleming H. Revell company [c1919] 4 p., l., 7-155 p. 20 cm. [BV4315.C45] 19-18624
I. Title.

CHIDLEY, Howard James, 1878- 252
Story sermons for children, by Rev. Howard J. Chidley... New York, George H. Doran company [c1920] 2 p. l., vii-xi, 15-164 p. 19 1/2 cm. [BV4315.C55] 20-5984
I. Title.

CLEVELAND, Edmund Janes, 1878-
Philus, the stable boy of Bethlehem; and other children's story- sermons for Christmas and other days and seasons of the Christian year. by Edmund J. Cleveland, with foreword by the Rt. Rev. Charles L. Slattery, D.D., illustrated by Paul Martin. New York and London, Harper & brothers, 1927. xv, 132 p. front., plates. 19 1/2 cm. [PZ7.C599Ph] 27-19779
I. Title.

CONZAD, Simeon Earl. 252
Story talks for boys and girls, by Simeon E. Conzad. New York, Round table press, inc., 1935. ix p., 1 l., 13-220 p. 20 cm. [BV4315.C65] 35-18253
I. Title.

DICKERT, Thomas Wilson, 1869- 252
Sermons for juniors in the Sunday school, congregation, and home circle, by Thomas Wilson Dickert ... with an introduction by Paul Seibert Leinbach ... New York, Chicago [etc.] Fleming H. Revell company [c1923] 3 p. l., 3-203 p. 20 cm. [BV4315.D5] 23-10869
I. Title.

FRENCH, Howard Dean. 244
The lost cricket and other stories for children [by] Howard Dean French. New York, Cincinnati [etc.] The Abingdon press [c1930] 203 p. 20 cm. [BV4315.F7] 30-12043
I. Title.

HALLOCK, Robert Crawford, 1857- 252
Behind the Big hill; a year os six-minute sermons for children, by Robert C. Hallock and G. B. F. Hallock. New York, R. R. Smith, inc., 1930. xii, 232 p. 19 1/2 cm. [BV4315.H277] 30-10033
I. Hallock, Gerard Benjamin Fleet, 1856- joint author. II. Title.

HANSEN, Andrew, 1882- 252
Wandering stars; ten-minute sermons for the junior congregation, by Rev. Andrew Hansen. New York, Holder & Stoughton, George H. Doran company [c1916] 5 p. l., 9-163 p. 20 1/2 cm. $1.00 [BV4315.H28] 16-21251
I. Title.

HENRY, Edwin Arthur, 1866- 252
Little foxes; stories for boys and girls, by E. A. Henry ... introduction by Charles W. Gordon ... (Ralph Connor) New York, Chicago [etc.] Fleming H. Revell company [c1922] 160 p. front. 19 1/2 cm. [BV4315.H4] 23-988
I. Title.

HUTCHISON, Stuart Nye. 252
For the children's hour, more five-minute sermons, by Stuart Nye Hutchison New York, Chicago [etc.] Flemming H. Revell company [c1918] 192 p. 20 cm. [BV4315.H9] 19-789
I. Title.

HUTCHISON, Stuart Nye.
The soul of a child, five-minute sermons to children, by Stuart Nye Hutchison ... New York, Chicago [etc.] Fleming H. Revell company [c1916] 191 p. 20 cm. Reprinted in part from the Presbyterian of the South. 16-8477 1.00
I. Title.

JEFFERSON, Charles Edward, 1860-
My Father's business; a series of sermons to children, by Charles Edward Jefferson ... New York, T. Y. Crowell & co. [1909] 5 p. l., 3-266 p., 1 l. front., plates. 21 cm. 9-25794 1.25
I. Title.

JOHNSON, Samuel Lawrence. 252'.53
Captain Ducky & other children's sermons / S. Lawrence Johnson. Nashville : Abingdon, c1976. 125 p. ; 19 cm. Thirty-eight stories with a moral, including such titles as "Growing Up," "Too Much Is Too Much," and "Do You Chicken?" [BV4315.J627] 76-4913 ISBN 0-687-04630-0 : 3.95
I. Title.

LAMBERTSON, Floyd Wesley, 1891- 252
The unguarded gate; a series of sermons for children, leading to decision day and covering the school year, by Floyd W. Lambertson. New York, Cincinnati, The Abingdon press [c1926] 190 p. illus. 20 cm. [BV4315.L25] 26-17500
I. Title.

LUND, T. Fenwick. 252
A boy for sale, and twenty-five other children sermons, by T. Fenwick Lund. Supplement no. 8 of the Pastor's ideal sermon book (Quick service for busy pastor's series) compiled and edited by St. John Halstead. Clinton, Ind., Pastor's ideal book co. [c1924] 119 p. 19 1/2 cm. [BV4315.L7] 24-16338
I. Halstead, St. John comp.-Pastor's ideal sermon book. II. Title.

PATTON, Carl Safford, 1866- 244
Two minutes stories, as told by Carl S. Patton to boys and girls who listened and came back for more. Chicago, New York, Willett, Clark & Colby, 1930. 4 p. l., 131 p. 19 cm. [BV4315.P35] 30-11584
I. Title.

REUTER, Frederick.
Short sermons for the children's mass, by Rev. Frederick Reuter. New York, J. F. Wagner [c1914] 4 p. l., 189 p. 21 1/2 cm. $1.00. 15-534
I. Title.

REUTER, Frederick A.
Anecdote-sermonettes for children's mass, by Rev. Frederick A. Reuter ... Baltimore, Md., John Murphy company [c1918] 97 p. 19 1/2 cm. $0.75. [BX2370.R5] 18-7411
I. Title.

ROBERTS, George, 1880- 253
88 children's sermons for all occasions, by George Roberts... New York, Chicago [etc.] Fleming H. Revell company [c1929] 189 p. 20 cm. [BV4315.R55] 29-14035
I. Title. II. Title: Children's sermons.

ROSS, A[bel] Hastings, 1831-
Sermons for children. By A. Hastings Ross ... Boston and Chicago, Congregational Sunday-school and publishing society [c1887] x, 323 p. 20 cm. 3-22863
I. Title.

SELL, Henry Thorne, 1854- 252
...Sermons in action for young folks, by Henry T. Sell... New York, Chicago [etc.] Fleming H. Revell company [c1926] 160 p. 19 1/2 cm. (Five-minute series) [BV4315.S45] 26-9173
I. Title.

SIEGART, William Raymond, 252.041 1897-
He started from nowhere, and other stories, by W. R. Siegart. Philadelphia, Pa., The United Lutheran publication house [c1940] 189 p. illus. 20 cm. [BV4315.S54] 41-1082
I. Title.

SPEAK unto the children of Israel. Sermons for every sabbath and festival of the year of Jewish children. New York, Bloch [1958;] 164p. 22cm.
1. Sermons for Children. I. Newman, J

STALL, Sylvanus, 1847-1915. 252
Five minute object sermons to children, through eye-gate and ear-gate into the city of child-soul, by Sylvanus Stall ... [New rev. ed.] 13th thousand. Philadelphia [etc.] The Vir publishing company [c1907] 256 p. front. (port.) 18 1/2 cm. [BV4315.S65 1907] 7-33565
I. Title.

STALL, Sylvanus, 1847-1915. 252
Five minute object sermons to children, through eye-gate and ear-gate into the city of child-soul, by Sylvanus Stall ... [New rev. ed.] 13th thousand. Philadelphia [etc.] The Vir publishing company [c1907] 256 p. front. (port.) 18 1/2 cm. [BV4315.S65 1907] 7-33565
I. Title.

STANLEY, Arthur Penrhyn, 1815-1881.
Sermons for children, including The Beatitudes and The faithful servant; preached in Westminster abbey by Arthur Penrhyn Stanley ... New York, C. Scribner's sons, 1900. 4 p. l., 157 p. 16 1/2 cm. 4-10416
I. Title.

*THOMPSON, Orin D. 252.53
Even if I'm bad? sermons for children. Illus. by William R. Johnson. Minneapolis, Augsburg [c.1966] 80p. illus. 22cm. 1.75 pap.,
I. Title.

*THOMPSON, Orin D. 252.53
Even if I'm bad? sermons for children. Illus. by William R. Johnson. Minneapolis, Augsburg [c.1966] 80p. illus. 22cm. 1.75 pap.,
I. Title.

WELLS, Amos Russel, 1862-
Three years with the children; one hundred and fifty-six children's sermons for pastors, illustrations for primary Sunday-school teachers, and object lessons and blackboard talks for superintendents of junior societies. New York, Chicago [etc.] F. H. Revell co. [1900] 282 p. 12°. 0-6730
I. Title.

Sermons for children—Lutheran Church.

*CROSS, Luther S. 252.53
Story sermons for children. Grand Rapids, Mich., Baker Bk. [1966] 102p. illus. 20cm. 1.50 pap.,
1. Sermons for children—Lutheran Church. I. Title.

Sermons, German.

FAHLING, Adam. 252.041
German gospel sermons with English outlines, by Adam Fahling ... St. Louis, Mo., Concordia publishing house, 1928. viii, 428 p. 24 cm. [BX8066.F3G4] 30-33492
1. Sermons, German. 2. Sermons—Outlines. I. Title.

RAD, Gerhard von, 1901-1971. 251
Biblical interpretations in preaching / Gerhard von Rad ; translated by John E. Steely. Nashville : Abingdon, c1977. 125 p. ; 21 cm. Translation of Predigt-Meditationen. [BX8066.R22P7413] 76-43248 ISBN 0-687-03444-2 : 5.95
1. Lutheran Church—Sermons. 2. Bible—Homiletical use. 3. Sermons, German. I. Title.

SCHWEITZER, Albert, 252.04'143 1875-1965.
Reverence for life. Translated by Reginald H. Fuller. [1st ed.] New York, Harper & Row [1969] 153 p. 22 cm. Translation of Strassburger Predigten. [BV4244.S3613] 71-85052 4.95
1. Sermons, German. I. Title.

THIELICKE, Helmut, 252'.04'1 1908-
How to believe again. Translated by H. George Anderson. Philadelphia, Fortress Press [1972] 220 p. 22 cm. Translation of Und wenn Gott wäre. [BX8066.T46U5313] 72-75656 ISBN 0-8006-0123-8 3.95
1. Lutheran Church—Sermons. 2. Sermons, German. I. Title.

Sermons, Jewish.

ADLER, Rudolph J.
A tree of life. [n.p., 1962] 131 p. 23 cm. Cover reads: Sermons and essays for American Jewry. NUC63
I. Title.

BERGER, Julius. 296
The weekly sermon; sermons on the portion of the week and for the holydays and festivals, by Julius Berger ... New York, Bloch publishing company, 1931. viii, 296 p. 20 cm. [BM740.B35] 31-5533
1. Sermons, Jewish. I. Title.

BERZON, Bernard L 296.42
Good beginnings; [sermons] New York, J. David [1962] 2 1p. 23cm. [BM740.2.B4] 62-13695
1. Sermons, Jewish. I. Title.

BOSNIAK, Jacob, 1887- 296
Interpreting Jewish life; sermons and addresses by Jacob Bosniak ... with a foreword by Professor Louis Finkelstein ... New York, Bloch publishing co., 1944. xviii, 155 p. 21 1/2 cm. Bibliographical foot-notes. [BM740.B6] 44-25988
1. Sermons, Jewish. 2. Sermons, American—Jewish authors. I. Title.

FELDMAN, Abraham J., 1893- 296
God's fools; sixteen discourses by Rabbi Abraham J. Feldman ... Delivered before Reform congregation Keneseth Israel, Philadelphia, Pa., 1923-1924. [New York, Bloch publishing company, 1924?] 4 p. l., 3-208 p. 23 cm. At head of discourses: Series XXXXII no. 1-[14] [BM740.F4] 31-1145
1. Sermons, Jewish. 2. Jews—Civilization. 3. Jews in the U.S. I. Title.

FELDMAN, Abraham Jehiel, 296 1893-
"Hills to climb"; eight discourses, by Rabbi Abraham J. Feldman ... Harford, Conn., Beth Israel pulpit, 1931. 128 p. 18 1/2 cm. "Published volumes by Rabbi Abraham J. Feldman": p. 127-128. [BM740.F45] 252 31-22329
1. Sermons, Jewish. I. Title.

GLAZER, Simon, 1878- 296
Book of sermons for all occasions by Rabbi Simon Glazer. New York, The Star Hebrew book co. [c1930] 256 p. 21 cm. [BM740.G6] 31-94
1. Sermons, Jewish. I. Title.

GOLDMAN, Moses, 1866- 296
Jewish ideals and interpretations, by Moses Goldman ... [New York, Printed by General linotypers, c1931] 111, [1] p. port. 21 cm. "A collection of pulpit lectures and sermons."--Introd. [BM740.G65] 31-23431
1. Sermons, Jewish. I. Title.

HALPERN, Abraham E., 1891- 296.42 1962
A son of faith; from the sermons of Abraham E. Halpern, 1891-1962. Ed. by Bernard S. Raskas. New York, Bloch [c.1962] 320p. illus. 24cm. 62-20630 5.00
1. Sermons, Jewish. I. Title.

HARRISON, Leon, 1866-1928. 296
The religion of a modern liberal; the selected sermons of thirty-five years in the Jewish ministry, by Leon Harrison ... edited, with an introduction, by Abram Leon Sachar; foreword by Stephen S. Wise ... New York, Bloch publishing co., 1931. xvii p., 1 l., 282 p. front. (port.) 20 cm. [BM740.H28] 31-3085
1. Sermons, Jewish. I. Sachar, Abram Leon, 1899- ed. II. Title.

KAHN, Robert I
Judaism and the space age and other sermons. Houston, Texas, Temple Emanuel [1962?] 52 p. 64-48738
1. Sermons, Jewish. I. Title.

KELLNER, Abraham A
With perfect faith, sermons for the sixties ... St. Louis, Mo., H. F. Epstein Hebrew Academy, 1962. 176 p. 64-53392
1. Sermons, Jewish. I. Title.

LEVI, Harry, 1875- 296
A rabbi speaks, by Rabbi Harry Levi ... Boston, The Chapple publishing co., ltd., 1930. x, 213 p. 19 1/2 cm. Sermons. [BM740.L47] 31-11797
1. Sermons, Jewish I. Title.

MASLIANSKY, Zebi Hirsch, 296 1856-
Sermons, by Reverend Zevi Hirsch Masliansky, translated by Edward Herbert; revised and edited by Rabbi Abraham J. Feldman. New York, Hebrew publishing company, 1926. 4 p. l., vii-x, 345 p. front. (port.) 23 cm. [BM740.M3 1926] 27-5434
I. Herbert, Edward, 1865- tr. II. Feldman, Abraham J., 1893- ed. III. Title.

PESIKTA de-Rab Kahana. 296.4'2 English
Pesikta de-Rab Kahana / R. Kahana's compilation of discourses for Sabbaths and festal days ; translated from Hebrew and Aramaic by William G. (Gershon Zev) Braude and Israel J. Kapstein. 1st ed. Philadelphia : Jewish Publication Society of America, [1975] lvii, 593 p. ; 24 cm. Includes bibliographical references and indexes. [BM517.P34E53] 74-6563 ISBN 0-8276-0051-8 : 15.00
1. Bible. O.T.—Sermons. 2. Sermons, Jewish. I. Kahana. II. Braude, William Gordon, 1907- III. Kapstein, Israel James, 1904-

Sermons, Jewish— Africa, South.

RABINOWITZ, Louis Isaac, 296.42 1906-
Sabbath light; sermons on the Sabbath evening service. Johannesburg, Fieldhill Pub. Co.; selling agents: Bloch Pub. Co., New York, 1958. 1v. 23cm. Includes 'Evening service for Sabbath' (Hebrew and English) [BM740.R2876] 59-29225
1. Sermons, Jewish—Africa, South. 2. Sermons, English—Africa, South. I. Title.

RABINOWITZ, Louis Isaac, 296.42 1906-
Sparks from the anvil: sermons for Sabbaths, holy days and festivals. New York, Bloch Pub. Co., 1955. 347p. 22cm. [BM740.R288] 55-7543
1. Sermons, Jewish— Africa, South. 2. Sermons, English—Jewish authors. I. Title.

Sermons, Jewish—Canada.

ROSENBERG, Stuart E 296.43
Man is free; sermons and addresses. New York, Bloch Pub. Co., 1957. 155p. 22cm. [BM740.R668] 57-13232
1. Sermons, Jewish—Canada. 2. Sermons, English—Jewish authors—Canada. I. Title.

ROSENBERG STUART E. 296.4
A time to speak of man, faith, and society. New York, Bloch Pub. Co. [c.]1960. v, 181p. 22cm. 60-15795 3.50
1. Sermons, Jewish—Canada. 2. Sermons, English—Jewish authors—Canada. I. Title.

Sermons, Jewish—Israel.

HEAR, oh Israel;
sermons... delivered on various Sabbaths... on the festivals and on special occasions. New York, P. Feldheim, 1958. viii, 359p. 23cm.
I. Rosenblatt, Samuel, 1902-

RABINOWITZ, Louis 222'.1'06 Isaac, 1906-
Torah and flora / L. I. Rabinowitz. New York : Sanhedrin Press, c1977. p. cm. Includes index. [BS1225.4.R3] 76-58906 ISBN 0-88482-917-0 : 9.95
1. Bible. O.T. Pentateuch—Sermons. 2. Bible—Natural history. 3. Sermons, Jewish—Israel. 4. Sermons, English—Israel—Jewish authors. I. Title.

Sermons, Jewish—United States

BARON, Joseph Louis, 1894- 296
In quest of integrity and other discourses, by Rabbi Joseph L. Baron PH. D., delivered at Temple Emanu-El B'ne Jeshurun, Milwaukee, Wisconsin. Chicago, Ill., The Argus book shop, inc., 1936. 57. [1] p. 23 cm. [BM740.B3] 36-7514
1. Sermons, Jewish—U. S. 2. Sermons, American—Jewish authors. I. Title.

BERZON, Bernard L. ed. 296
Manual of holiday and occasional sermons, published under the auspices of the Rabbinical council of America. Rabbi Bernard L. Berzon, editor-in-chief; associate editors: Rabbi Emanuel Marcus, Rabbi Akiba Predmesky. New York, Rabinical council press, 1943. 208 p. 21 1/2 cm. Bibliographical foot-notes. [BM740.B46] 44-48752
1. Sermons, Jewish—U.S. 2. Sermons, American—Jewish authors. I. Marcus, Emanuel, joint ed. II. Predmesky, Akiba, joint ed. III. Rabinical council of America. IV. Title.

BEST Jewish sermons 296.42
[of 5723-5724] New York, Jonathan David [c.1964] 211p. 22cm. Ed.: S. I. Teplitz. 58-3698 5.95
1. Sermons, Jewish—U.S. 2. Sermons, American—Jewish authors. I. Teplitz, Saul I., ed.

BEST Jewish sermons. 296.42
New York, Jonathan David Co. v. 22cm. Editor: S. I. Teplitz. [BM740.B48] 58-3698
1. Sermons, Jewish —U.S. 2. Sermons, American—Jewish authors. I. Teplits, Saul I., ed.

BEST Jewish sermons of 296.42
5721-5722. Ed. by Rabbi Saul I. Teplitz. New York, Jonathan David [c.1962] 238p. 21cm. 58-3698 5.95
1. Sermons, Jewish—U.S. 2. Sermons, American—Jewish authors. I. Teplitz, Saul I., ed.

BURSTEIN, Abraham, 1893- ed. 296
New York, Bloch publishing company 1932 xiii, 309 p. 20 cm. [BM735.B8] [[222.1]] 32-5884
1. Sermons Jewish—U.S. 2. Sermons American—Jewish authors. 3. Bible. O. T.Pentateuch—Sermons. 4. Bible—Sermons—O.T.Pentateuch. I. Title.

COHEN, Beryl David, 1898- 296.42
My King and my God, intimate talks on the devotions of life. New York, Bloch Pub. Co. [1963] 239 p. 21 cm. [BM740.2.C6] 63-12428
1. Sermons, Jewish — U.S. 2. Sermons, American — Jewish authors. I. Title.

COHON, Beryl David, 1898- 296.42
From generation to generation; with a pref. by Samuel S. Cohon. Boston, B. Humphries ['1951] 133 p. 21 cm. [BM740.C63] 52-8905
1. Sermons, Jewish—U. S. 2. Sermons, American—Jewish authors. I. Title.

COHON, Beryl David, 1898- 296.42
Out of the heart; intimate talks from a Jewish pulpit on the personal issues of life. [1st ed.] New York, Vantage Press [c1957] 120p. 21cm. [BM740.C64] 57-11258
1. Sermons, Jewish—U. S. 2. Sermons, American—Jewish authors. I. Title.

EPSTEIN, Harry Hyman, 1903- 296
Judaism and progress; sermons and addresses, by Rabbi Harry H. Epstein; with a preface by the Rev. Dr. Leo Jung... New York, Bloch publishing co., 1935. xiv, 287 p. 20 cm. [BM740.E63] 35-4139
1. Sermons, Jewish—U.S. 2. Sermons, American—Jewish authors. I. Title.

EPSTEIN, Reuben. 296
The blueprint of creation, by Reuben Epstein ... New York, N.Y., Rachmann publishing company, 5703-1943. 176 p. 22 cm. [BM740.E64] 43-15538
1. Sermons, Jewish—U.S. 2. Sermons, American—Jewish authors. I. Title.

FELDMAN, Abraham Jehiel, 1893- 296
The faith of a liberal Jew, by Rabbi Abraham J. Feldman. Hartford, Conn., Beth Israel pulpit, 1931. 96 p. 18 1/2 cm. "Four sermons."--Foreword. [BM740.F38] 31-35702
1. Sermons, Jewish—U.S. 2. Sermons, American—Jewish authors. I. Title.

FELDMAN, Abraham Jehiel, 1893- 296
Sources of Jewish inspiration, by Rabbi Abraham J. Feldman ... Harford, 1934. 209, [3] p. 19 cm. "Published volumes by Rabbi Abraham J. Feldman": p. [211]-[212] [BM740.F48] 34-22202
1. Sermons, Jewish—U.S. 2. Sermons, American—Jewish authors. I. Title.

FRIEDMAN, Theodore. 296.7
Judgment and destiny; sermons for the modern Jew. New York, J. David [1965] 203 p. 23 cm. [BM740.2.F7] 63-17361
1. Sermons, Jewish — U.S. 2. Sermons, American — Jewish authors. I. Title.

GERSTEIN, Israel. 296
Reveille or taps? Sermons, essays and addresses, by Rabbi Israel Gerstein: foreword by Prof. Meyer Waxman. New York, Bloch publishing company, 1943. xiv p., 1 l., 258 p. 24 cm. [BM740.G4] 43-15824
1. Sermons, Jewish—U.S. 2. Sermons, American—Jewish authors. I. Title.

GOLDFARB, Solomon David 296.42
Torah for our time; sermons and studies based on Biblical texts for Sabbaths and holidays. New York, Bloch [1965] 183p. 24cm. [BM740.2.G57] 65-27337 4.95
1. Sermons, Jewish—U.S. 2. Sermons, American—Jewish authors. 3. Sermons, Jewish—U.S. 4. Sermons, Jewish—U.S. 5. Sermons, Americans—Jewish authors I. Title.

GOLDMAN, Moses B 1896- 296
Jewish ideals and interpretations, by Moses Goldman ... [New York, Printer by General linotypers, c1931] iii, [1] p. port. 21 cm. "A collection of pulpit lectures and sermons."--Introd. [BM74.G65] 31-23431
1. Sermons, Jewish—U. S. 2. Sermons, American—Jewish authors. I. Title.

GREENBERG, Sidney, 1917- 296.42
Adding life to our years. With a foreword by Morris Adler. New York, J. David [1959] 205p. 23cm. [BM740.2.G7] 59-10539
1. Sermons, Jewish—U. S. 2. Sermons, American —Jewish authors. I. Title.

GREENBERG, Sidney, 1917- 296.42
Finding ourselves; sermons on the art of living. New York, J. David [c.1964] xii, 258p. 22cm. [BM740.2.-G72] 64-19751
1. Sermons, Jewish—U.S. 2. Sermons, American—Jewish authors. I. Title.

GUTHEIM, James Koppel, 1817-1886. 296
The temple pulpit; a selection of sermons and addresses delivered on special occassions, by Rev. James K. Gutheim ... New York, Jewish times, 1872. viii, 175 p. 20 cm. [BM740.G8] 16-1211
1. Sermons, Jewish—U. S. 2. Sermons, America—Jewish authors. I. Title.

HAMMER, Louis. 296
A word in season...Sermons and occasional addresses, by Rabbi Louis Hammer. Brooklyn, Judaica publishing co., 1944. xiii, 17-172 p. 20 1/2 cm. [BM740.H27] 44-36365
1. Sermons, Jewish—U.S. 2. Sermons, American—Jewish authors. I. Title.

HELLER, Abraham Mayer, 1896- 296
Jewish survival; sermons and addresses by Abraham Mayer Heller ... New York, Behrman's Jewish book house, 1939. xiv, 271 p. 22 1/2 cm. [BM740.H35] 40-2059
1. Sermons, Jewish—U.S. 2. Sermons, American—Jewish authors. I. Title.

HERSHMAN, Abraham Moses, 1880- 296.42
Israel's fate and faith. Detroit, Congregation Shaarey Zedek, 1952. 352 p. 25 cm. [BM740.H37] 52-29314
1. Sermons. Jewish—U. S. 2. Sermons, American—Jewish authors. 3. Judaism—Addresses, essays, lectures. I. Title.

HERSHMAN, Abraham Moses, 1880- 296.42
Religion of the age and of the ages. New York, Bloch Pub. Co., 1953. 134p. 24cm. [BM740.H372] 53-10660
1. Sermons, Jewish—U. S. 2. Sermons, Jewish—American authors. I. Title.

HYAMSON, Moses, 1863- 296
Sabbath and festival addresses, by Rev. Dr. M. Hyamson ... New York, Bloch publishing company, 1936. viii p., 1 l., 205 p. 22 cm. [BM740.H92] 36-9302
1. Sermons, Jewish—U. S. 2. Sermons, American—Jewish authors. I. Title.

JUNG, Leo, 1892- 296
Crumbs and character; sermons, addresses, and essays by Leo Jung ... New York, N.Y., The Night and day press, 5702-1942. 2 p. l., ii p., 2 l., 3-315 p., 3 l. 24 1/2 cm. [BM740.J8] 42-21027
1. Sermons, Jewish—U.S. 2. Sermons, American-Jewish authors. 3. Jews—Religion—Addresses, essays, lectures. I. Title.

JUNG, Leo, 1892- 296.42
Harvest: sermons, addresses, studies. New York, P. Feldheim, 1956. 324p. 24cm. [BM740.J83] 57-23159
1. Sermons, Jewish—U. S. 2. Sermons, Amerioan—Jewish authors. 3. Judaism—Addresses, essays, lectures. I. Title.

JUNG, Leo, 1892- 296.42
Harvest: sermons, addresses, studies. New York, P. Feldheilm, 1956. 324p. 24cm. [BM740.J83] 57-23159
1. Sermons, Jewish—U. S. 2. Sermons, American—Jewish authors. 3. Judaism—Addresses, essays, lectures. I. Title.

KAHAN, Aaron. 296
Oaks and acorns; addresses to youth and their elders based on Pentateuchal portions, by Captain Aaron Kahan, chaplain, U.S.A. ... New York, Bloch publishing co., 1945. xvii, [1],197 p. 22 cm. [BM740.K25] 45-6437
1. Sermons, Jewish—U.S. 2. Sermons, American—Jewish authors. I. Title.

KAHANE, Charles Ph. 296
The echo of tradition; a collection of sermons for Jewish holidays and other occasions, by Charles Ph. Kahane ... New York city, Pardes publishing house, inc., 1935. 88 p. 22 cm. [BM740.K26] 38-7720
1. Sermons, Jewish—U. S. 2. Sermons, American—Jewish authors. I. Title.

KANOTOPSKY, Harold B 296.42
Rays of Jewish splendor; selected sermons. [Brooklyn] Young Israel of Eastern Parkway [1956] 92p. 23cm. [BM740.K273] 56-23995
1. Sermons, Jewish—U. S. 2. Sermons, American —Jewish authors. I. Title.

KELLNER, Abraham A 296.42
My pulpit; sermons of times and seasons. [Long Branch, N. J.,] 1951. 207p. 23cm. [BM740.K39] 53-20373
1. Sermons, Jewish—U. S. 2. Sermons, American—Jewish authors. I. Title.

KELLNER, Abraham A. 296
A rabbi's faith; sermons of hope and courage, by Abraham A. Kellner ... Albany, N.Y., Earle printing corporation, 1945. xiv, 225 p. 23 1/2 cm. [BM740.K4] 46-20914
1. Sermons, Jewish—U.S. I. Title.

KOHLER, Kaufmann, 1843-1926. 296
A living faith; selected sermons and the addresses from the literary remains of Dr. Kaufmann Kohler; ed. by Samuel S. Cohoa. Cincinnati, Hebrew Union College Press, 1948 [i.e. 1949] vii, 312 p. 24 cm. [BM740.K57] 49-1582
1. Sermons, Jewish—U.S. 2. Sermons, American—Jewish authors. I. Title.

KRAUSKOPF, Joseph, 1858-
Prejudice, its genesis and exodus by Joseph Krauskopf ... New York, Bloch publishing co., 1909. iv, 92 p. 19 cm. "These papers were first delivered from the pulpit of reform congregation Keneseth Israel, Philadelphia, at the weekly Sunday services, in the spring of 1908." 9-2255
I. Title.

LEVI, Gerson Baruch, 1878- 296
The thanksgiving of the spirit and other sermons, by Gerson B. Levi. Chicago, The Argus book shop, 1938. 5 p. l., 7-169, [1] p. 23 1/2 cm. [BM740.L46] 38-16564
1. Sermons, Jewish—U.S. 2. Sermons, American—Jewish authors. I. Title.

LEVINTHAL, Israel Herbert, 1888- 296.38081
Judaism speaks to the modern world. London, New York, Abelard-Schuman [1963] 191 p. 23 cm. (Ram's horn books) [BM740.2.L4] 63-18670
1. Sermons, Jewish—U.S. 2. Sermons, American—Jewish authors. I. Title.

LOOKSTEIN, Joseph Hyman, 1902- 296.4'2
Faith and destiny of man; traditional Judaism in a new light, by Joseph H. Lookstein. New York, Bloch Pub. Co. [1967] x, 174 p. 24 cm. Bibliographical footnotes. [BM740.2.L6] 67-22918
1. Sermons, Jewish—United States. 2. Sermons, American—Jewish authors. I. Title.

MARK, Julius, 1898- 296.42
Reaching for the moon, and other addresses. New York, Farrar, Straus and Cudahy [1959] 177p. 22cm. [BM740.2.M3] 59-9171
1. Sermons, Jewish—U. S. 2. Sermons, American— Jewish authors. I. Title.

MASLIANSKY, Zebi Hirsch, 1856-1943. 296.42
Sermons. Translated by Edward Herbert. With a biographical sketch by Sulamith Schwartz Nardi. Rev. and edited by Abraham J. Feldman. New York, Hebrew Pub. Co. [1960] 345p. illus. 21cm. [BM740.M3 1960] 61-191
1. Sermons, Jewish— U. S. 2. Sermons, Yiddish—Translations into English. 3. Sermons, English— Translations from Yiddish. I. Title.

NAROT, Joseph R. 296.42
For whom the rabbi speaks; a collection of sermons and articles, by Joseph R. Narot. [1st ed.] Miami, Fla., Rostrum Bks. [1966] 134p. 22cm. [BM740.2.N3] 66-6312 1.65 pap.,
1. Sermons, Jewish—U.S. 2. Sermons, American—Jewish authors. I. Title.
Temple Israel of Greater Miami, 173 NE 19th, Miami, Fla. 33132

PILCHIK, Ely Emanuel. 296.42
Jeshurun sermons. New York, Bloch Pub. Co., 1957. 261p. 21cm. [BM740.P56] 57-8136
1. Sermons, Jewish—U. S. 2. Sermons, American —Jewish authors. I. Title.

PILCHIK, Ely Emanuel. 296.42
Jeshurun sermons New York, Bloch Pub. Co., 1957. 261p. 21cm. [BM740.P56] 5m-8136
1. Sermons, Jewish—U. S. 2. ermons, American—Jewish authors. I. Title.

RACKOVSKY, Isaiah. 296
Words and thoughts; thirteen radio addresses by Isaiah Rackovsky ... [Omaha] The U.O.C. Radio committee [1943] 72 p. 23 cm. [BM740.R32] 43-15542
1. Sermons, Jewish—U.S. 2. Sermons, American—Jewish authors. I. Omaha. United orthodox congregations. Radio committee. II. Title.

REICHERT, Irving Frederick, 1895- 296.42
Judaism & the American Jew; selected sermons & addresses. San Francisco, Grabhorn Press, 1953. 245p. 29cm. [BM740.R385] 54-591
1. Sermons, Jewish—U. S. 2. Sermons, American—Jewish authors. I. Title.

REICHMAN, Jacob. 296
The voice of Jacob; legend comment, sermons and lectures, by Rabbi Jacob Reichman. New York, Pardes publishing house, inc., 1940. 256 p. incl. port. 22 cm. [RM740.R4] 40-10995
1. Sermons, Jewish—U.S. 2. Sermons, American—Jewish authors. 3. Talmud—Legends. I. Title.

RICHMOND, Harry R 1890- 296.43
God on trial. [Sermons] New York, B. Wheelwright Co., 1955. 156p. 21cm. [BM740.R47] 55-6261
1. Sermons, Jewish—U. S. 2. Sermons, American— Jewish authors. I. Title.

ROODMAN, Solomon. 296.42
The suburbs of the Almighty; sermons and discourses. New York, J. David [c1962] 235 p. 23 cm. [BM740.2.R6] 62-15963
1. Sermons, Jewish — U.S. 2. Sermons, American — Jewish authors. I. Title.

ROSENBLATT, Samuel, 1902- 296
Our heritage, by Samuel Rosenblatt ... New York, Bloch publishing company, 1940. x, 256 p. 24 cm. "Notes": p. [243]-253. [BM740.R67] 40-12491
1. Sermons, Jewish—U. S. 2. Sermons, American—Jewish authors. I. Title.

SALIT, Norman, 1896-1960 296.42
The worlds of Norman Salit; sermons, papers, addresses. Posthumously chosen, ed. by Abraham Burstein. New York, Bloch [1966] 315p. port. 24cm. [BM740.2.S25] 66-8697 5.50
1. Sermons, Jewish—U.S. 2. Sermons, American—Jewish authors. I. Burstein, Abraham, 1893- ed. II. Title.

SCHICK, Joseph, 1891- 296
Joseph's harvest, by Rabbi Dr. Joseph Schick... New York, 1933. 96 p. 20 1/2 cm. [BM740.S36] 35-2799
1. Sermons, Jewish—U.S. 2. Sermons, American—Jewish authors. I. Title.

SILVERSTEIN, Baruch. 296.4'2
A Jew in love. New York, J. David [c1966] x, 188 p. 22 cm. [BM740.2.S5] 66-17799
1. Sermons, Jewish—U. S. 2. Sermons, American—Jewish authors. I. Title.

SINGER, Joseph I 6.422
Margin for triumph; timeless answers to timely questions. New York, Bloch Pub. Co., 1958. 270 p. 23 cm. [BM740.S673] 58-3426
1. Sermons, Jewish — U.S. 2. Sermons, American — Jewish authors. I. Title.

SITSKIN, Leon. 296
Judaism as a religion; a series of holiday sermans, by Rabbi Leon Sitskin. New York, Bloch publishing company, 1937. 6 p. l., 3-156 p. 20 cm. [BM740.S83] 8-2112
1. Sermons, Jewish—U.S. 2. Sermons, American—Jewish authors. I. Title.

STEINBERG, Milton, 1903- *296.42
1950.
From the sermons of Rabbi Milton Steinberg. Edited by Bernard Mandelbaum. New York, Bloch, 1954- v. 24 cm. Contents.--[1] High holydays and major festivals.--[2] Only human--the eternal alibi; the weekly Sidrah and general themes. [BM740.2.S7] 54-12316
1. Sermons, Jewish—U.S. 2. Sermons, American—Jewish authors. I. Mandelbaum, Bernard, 1922- ed. II. Title. III. Title: Only human—The eternal alibi.

TOMORROW'S religion;
sermons and studies distributed by Rabbi Jacob Joseph School and Mesifta. New York, Gertz Bros. [1957?] 143p.
1. Sermons, Jewish—U. S. 2. Judaism—Addresses, essays & lectures. I. Kellner, Abraham A

WEINSTEIN, Jacob Joseph, 296.42
1902
The place of understanding; comments on the portions of the week and the holiday cycle. New York, Bloch Pub. Co., 1959. 181 p. 22 cm. [BM740.W38] 59-6855
1. Sermons, Jewish — U.S. 2. Bible. O.T. Pentateuch — Sermons. 3. Festival-day sermons — Jewish authors. 4. Sermons, American — Jewish authors. I. Title.

WEISFELD, Israel Harold, ed. 296
The message of Israel, edited and compiled by Israel H. Weisfeld ... twenty-four religious essays and sermons by outstanding orthodox, conservative and reform rabbis; with an introduction by Dr. Meyer Waxman ... New York, Bloch publishing co., 1936. 4 p. l., viii p., 1 l., xxxvii, 285 p. 22 cm. [BM735.W4] 36-31524
1. Sermons, Jewish—U.S. 2. Sermons, American—Jewish authors. 3. Festivals—Jews. I. Title.

WEISFELD, Israel Harold. 296
My son, by Israel H. Weisfeld ... Fifty-four chapters on character-molding and ideals for youth, based on the fifty-four sidrot of the Pentateuch. Foreword by Dr. Louis L. Mann ... New York, Bloch publishing co., 1941. xix, 306 p. 21 cm. [BM740.W4] 42-1591
1. Sermons, Jewish—U.S. 2. Sermons, American—Jewish authors. I. Title.

WHAT does God mean to you?
and other sermons. New York, Bloch Publishing Company, 1959. 59p.
1. Sermons. Jewish—U. S. 2. Sermons, American—Jewish authors. I. Newman, Louis Israel, 1893-

WOLSEY, Louis, 1877- 296
Sermons and addresses. Philadelphia, Congregation Rodeph Shalom, 1950. vi, 79 p. port. 24 cm. [BM740.W64] 50-35067
1. Sermons, Jewish — U.S. 2. Sermons, American — Jewish authors. I. Title.

Sermons, Latin.

JOANNES De Rupella 232.91
ca.1190-1245.
Eleven Marian sermons [by] John de La Rochelle. Edited by Kilian F. Lynch. St. Bonaventure, N.Y., Franciscan Institute, 1961. xxiv, 103 p. 24 cm. (Franciscan Institute publications. Text series, no. 12) Includes bibliographical references. [BT608.J6] 73-253541
1. Mary, Virgin—Sermons. 2. Catholic Church—Sermons. 3. Sermons, Latin. I. Lynch, Kilian F., ed. II. Title. III. Series: St. Bonaventure University, St. Bonaventure, N.Y. Franciscan Institute. Text series, no. 12

Sermons—Outlines.

†AHO, Gerhard. 251'.02
The lively skeleton : thematic approaches and outlines / Gerhard Aho. St. Louis : Concordia Pub. House, c1977. 47 p. ; 23 cm. (The Preacher's workshop series ; book 4) Bibliography: p. 46-47. [BV4223.A36] 77-10721 ISBN 0-570-07403-7 pbk. : 1.95
1. Sermons—Outlines. 2. Preaching. I. Title. II. Series.

ANDERSON, T M 251
Searching the Scriptures. Kansas City, Mo., Beacon Hill Press [1948] 140 p. 20 cm. [BV4223.A5] 48-3390
1. Sermons—Outlines. I. Title.

ANDREWS, R L
Sermon outlines on Old Testament characters, by R. L. Andrews. Athens, Ala., C. E. I. Pub. Co. [c1964] 80 p. NUC65
1. Sermons — Outlines. 2. Bible. O. T. — Biography. I. Title.

*APOSTOLON, Billy. 251'.02
Choice sermon outlines. Grand Rapids, Mich., Baker Book House [1973, c.1972] 55 p. 22 cm. (Dollar sermon library) ISBN 0-8010-0046-7 1.00 (pbk.)
1. Sermons—Outlines. I. Title.

*APOSTOLON, Billy, comp. 251.02
Heart-touching sermon outlines. Grand Rapids, Mich., Baker Book House, [1974] 61 p. 22 cm. [BV4223] ISBN 0-8010-0078-5 1.00 (pbk.)
1. Sermons—Outlines. I. Title.

APOSTOLON, Billy 252.6
These days we remember. Grand Rapids, Mich., Baker Bk. [c.]1962. 103p. 22cm. 1.00 pap.,
1. Sermons—Outlines. I. Title.

*APPELMAN, Hyman. 251.02
Appelman's sermon outlines & illustrations. Grand Rapids, Baker Book House [1974 c1944] 121 p. 20 cm. Title on spine: Sermon outlines & illustrations. [BX1756.Q5] ISBN 0-8010-0072-6 1.95 (pbk.)
1. Sermons—Outlines. I. Title. II. Title: Sermon outlines & illustrations.

APPELMAN, Hyman, 1902- 251
Appelman's Sermon outlines and illustrations, by Hyman J. Appelman ... Grand Rapids, Mich., Zondervan publishing house [c1944] 129 p. 20 cm. [Full name: Hyman Jedidiah Appelman] [BV4223.A6] 45-16394
1. Sermons—Outlines. I. Title.

APPELMAN, Hyman, 1902- 251
Pointed sermon outlines and illustrations. Grand Rapids, Zondervan Pub. House [1953] 118p. 21cm. [BV4223.A63] 53-1944
1. Sermons—Outlines. 2. Homiletical illustrations. I. Title. II. Title: Sermon outlines and illustrations.

APPELMAN, Hyman Jedidiah, 251
1902-
Pointed sermon outlines and illustrations. Grand Rapids, Zondervan Pub. House [1953] 118 p. 21 cm. [BV4223.A63] 53-1244
1. Sermons — Outlines. 2. Homiletical illustrations. I. Title. II. Title: Sermon outlines and illustrations.

AUSTIN, William R. 251.02
The Zondervan pastor's annual, 1966. Grand Rapids, Mich., Zondervan [c.1965] 383p. 21cm. [BX6333.A1A8] 65-19507 3.95
1. Sermons—Outlines. 2. Baptists—Sermons—Outlines. I. Title.

AUSTIN, William R. 251.02
The Zondervan pastor's manual for 1967. Grand Rapids, Mich., Zondervan [1966] 383p. 21cm. [BX6333.A1A8] 65-19507 3.95 bds.,
1. Sermons—Outlines. 2. Baptists—Sermons—Outlines. I. Title. II. Title: Pastor's manual.

BAILEY, Augustus Caesar. 251
Pearls of the deep, by the Rev. A. C. Bailey ... [Gary, Ind., Bolar printing co., 1928] 180 p. 19 cm. [BV4223.B27] 29-4334
1. Sermons—Outlines. I. Title.

BETOWSKI, Edward Maximilian. 251
Turning to God; sermon notes on conversion, by Rev. Edward M. Betowski ... New York, P. J. Kenedy & sons [c1933] xviii, 372, [4] p. 22 cm. Alternate pages and [4] pages at end are blank for "Notes on conversion." Bibliography: p. 290. [BX1756.A1B4] 34-562
1. Sermons—Outlines. 2. Catholic church—Sermons. 3. Homiletical illustrations. 4. Conversion. I. Title.

*BOLICK, James H. 251'.02
Sermon outlines for saints and sinners. Grand Rapids, Mich., Baker Book House [1973] 64 p. 22 cm. (Dollar sermon library) ISBN 0-8010-0596-5 1.00 (pbk.)
1. Sermons—Outlines. I. Title.

BONELL, Harold C. 251'.02
Sparks of the kindling [by] Harold C. Bonell. Valley Forge [Pa.] Judson Press [1968] 128 p. 23 cm. [BV4223.B6] 68-22754 3.95
1. Sermons—Outlines. 2. Meditations. I. Title.

BROOKS, George, Rev., of 251'.02
Johnstone.
201 sermon outlines. Grand Rapids, Baker Book House [1966] 110 p. 20 cm. (Minister's handbook series) Selections from the author's Five hundred plans of sermons, 1863. [BV4223.B68] 67-2597
1. Sermons — Outlines. I. Title. II. Title: Sermon outlines.

BROWN, Jeff D. 251.027
Sermon outlines on the Old Testament. Grand Rapids, Mich., Baker [c.]1962. 111p. 22cm. 1.00 pap.,
1. Sermons—Outlines. I. Title.

BROWNLOW, Leroy, 1914- 251
Seed for the sower, three hundred suggestive sermons. Fort Worth Tex. [1948] 200 p. 20 cm. [BV4223.B72] 48-3823
1. Sermons—Outlines. I. Title.

BROWNLOW, Leroy, 1914- 251
Sermons you can preach. Fort Worth, Tex., Brownlow Publications [1958] 143p. illus. 21cm. [BV4223.B73] 58-19106
1. Sermons—Outlines. I. Title.

BRYANT, Al, 1926- comp. and ed.
Sermon outlines: installations, dedications, weddings and other occasions. Grand Rapids, Zondervan [c1957] 56 p. (Loose-leaf sermon outline series) 63-7259
1. Sermons — Outlines. I. Title.

BRYANT, Al, 1926- comp. and ed.
Sermon outlines for use by laymen. Grand Rapids, Zondervan [c1957] 63 p. (Loose-leaf sermon outline series) 63-7260
1. Sermons — Outlines. I. Title.

BRYANT, Al, 1926- ed. 251
Sermon outlines for worship and devotional services. Grand Rapids, Zondervan Pub. House [1954] 122p. 20cm. [BV4223.B76] 55-249
1. Sermons—Outlines. I. Title.

BRYANT, Al, 1926- comp. and ed.
Sermon outlines on prayer. Grand Rapids, Zondervan [c1956] 64 p. (Loose-leaf sermon outline series) 63-7261
1. Sermons — Outlines. 2. Prayer. I. Title.

BRYANT, Al, 1926- comp.
Sermon outlines on the home (including sermons addressed to parents and children) Grand Rapids, Zondervan [c1957] 62 p. (Loose-leaf sermon outline library) 63-7262
1. Sermons — Outlines. I. Title.

BULL, Paul Bertie, 1864- 251
A preacher's note-book; outline sermons and illustrations for every Sunday and holy day in the church's year, by Paul B. Bull ... New York, The Macmillan company [1938] xxiv p., 1 l., 27-589 p. 20 cm. "Made in Great Britain." "First published, 1938." [BV4223.B77] 39-1563
1. Sermons—Outlines. 2. Church year sermons. 3. Church of England—Sermons. I. Title.

BURNS, Jabez, 1805-1876. 251.027
500 sketches and skeletons of sermons; includes nearly one hundred on types and metaphors Grand Rapids, Kregel publications, 1963. viii, 638 p. 24 cm. "Five volumes complete in one." [BV4223.B82] 63-11463
1. Sermons — Outlines I. Title.

BURNS, Jabez, 1805-1876. 252.002
300 sermon sketches on Old and New Testament texts Grand Rapids, Kregel Publications, 1961. 394 p. 24 cm. "Originally published in a volume entitled The pulpit encyclopedia." [BV4223.B85] 61-14902
1. Sermons — Outlines. I. Title.

BURNS, Jabez, 1805-1876. 251'.02
200 Scriptural sermon outlines. [1st American ed. Grand Rapids, Kregel Publications [1969] 424 p. 21 cm. (His Sermon outline series) First published in 1875 under title: Two hundred sketches and outlines of sermons. [BV4223.B86 1969] 75-92502 4.95
1. Sermons—Outlines. I. Title.

BUTLER, Burris, 1909--
Christian living sermon outlines. Cincinnati, Standard Pub. Co. [c1962] 64 p. (Sermon outline series) Cover title: Sermon outlines on Christian living. 64-63853
1. Sermon — Outlines. I. Title. II. Series.

CALLAWAY, Timothy Walton, 251
1874-
1,000 threefold Scriptural outlines ... by T. W. Callaway ... Grand Rapids, Mich., Zondervan publishing house [c1943] 4 p. l., 7-148 p. 20 cm. [BV4223.C38] 44-1046
1. Sermons—Outlines. I. Title.

CHANDLER, Ward B 251.027
Chandler's choice series sermon outlines. Grand Rapids, Baker Book House, 1958. 161p. 20cm. [BV4223.C48] 58-8383
1. Sermons—Outlines. I. Title. II. Title: Choice series sermon outlines.

CHAPMAN, James Blaine, 1884- 251
Chapman's Choice outlines and illustrations, by James B. Chapman, D.D. Grand Rapids, Mich., Zondervan publishing house [1947] 103 p. 20 cm. [BV4223.C5] 47-23420
1. Sermons—Outlines. 2. Homiletical illustrations. I. Title. II. Title: Choice outlines and illustrations.

CHAPMAN, Michael Andrew. 248
The prayer of faith; brief sermon outlines for the Sundays of the year, on the orations or collects of the mass, by the Reverend Michael Andrew Chapman ... St. Louis, Mo., and London, B. Herder book co., 1928. ix, 311 p. 19 cm. [BX1756.C5P7] 28-21998
I. Title.

CLEMENS, E. Bryan. 251.027
Sermon outlines you can preach. Natick, Mass., W.A. Wilde [1963] 79p. 22cm. 63-22171 1.25 pap.,
1. Sermons—Outlines. I. Title.

COCKBURN, Harold Andrew. 251
The touch of the Master's hand, and other sermon outlines. Introd. by John Sutherland Bonnell. New York, F. H. Revell Co. [1949] 128 p. 21 cm. [BV4223.C58] 49-8922
1. Sermons—Outlines. I. Title.

*COMPTON, W. H. 251
Salvation sermon outlines, comp. by W. H. Compton. Grand Rapids, Baker Book House [1973, c.1961] 62 p. 22 cm. (Dollar sermon library) [BV4223] ISBN 0-8010-2349-1 1.00 (pbk.)
1. Sermons—Outlines. 2. Preaching. I. Title.

*COMPTON, W. H. 251'.02
Vital sermon outlines. Grand Rapids, Baker Book House [1972] 66 p. 22 cm. (Dollar sermon library) [BV4223] ISBN 0-8010-2340-8 pap., 1.00
1. Sermons—Outlines. I. Title.

CONNELL, Francis Jeremiah, 251
1888-
Sunday sermon outlines. Foreword by Patrick A. O'Boyle. New York, F. Pustet Co., 1955. 324p. 24cm. [BX1756.A1C6] 55-43368
1. Sermons—Outlines. I. Title.

CONWAY, Marion H., comp. 251
Sermon suggestions; or, Pulpit points. Grand Rapids, Mich., Baker Bk. 1965] c.1957] 91p. 21cm. ((1.00 sermon lib.) [BV4223.C59] 1.00 pap.,
1. Sermons—Outlines. I. Title.

COOKSEY, Nicias Ballard, 251
1846-
Bible talk outlines, two hundred alphabetically arranged by Rev. N. B. Cooksey... Olney, Ill., Cooksey publishing company [1916] 77 p. 19 cm. [BV4223.C6] 16-19098
1. Sermons—Outlines. I. Title.

*COTTRELL, Ralph
Sermon outlines through the Bible. Grand

Rapids, Mich., Baker Bk. [1967] 90p. 21cm. ((1.00 sermon lib.) [251'.02] 1.00 pap.,
1. Sermons—Outlines. I. Title.

COX, Frank Lucius, 1895- 252
Moses' last birthday, and other sermons. Nashville, Gospel Advocate Co., 1956. 136p. 22cm. [BV4223.C65] 57-31388
1. Sermons—Outlines. I. Title.

CRABTREE, T. T. 251.02
The Zondervan pastor's annual, 1968. Grand Rapids, Zondervan [1967] v. 21cm. [BX6333.A1A8] 65-19507 3.95
1. Sermons—Outlines. 2. Baptists—Sermons Outlines. I. Title.

CRAWFORD, Cecil Clement, 1893- 232.96
Sermon outlines on the cross of Christ; especially designed for pre-Easter devotional and evangelistic campaigns, by C. C. Crawford ... Nashville, Tenn., McQuiddy printing company [c1933] 172 p. 19 cm. Bibliography: p. 170-172. [BT430.C58] 34-4035
1. Jesus Christ—Passion—Sermons. 2. Sermons—Outlines. I. Title.

CRAWFORD, Cecil Clement, 1893- 252.
Sermon outlines, volume one: The restoration plea. By C. C. Crawford ... St. Louis, Mo., Restoration publishing company [1927] 324 p. 19 cm. No more published. [BX7327.C7S4] 27-17842
1. Sermons—Outlines. I. Title.

CRAWFORD, Isaiah Wadsworth. 251
Helps for the busy minister; sermons, sketches, outlines, texts and subjects, by I. W. Crawford ... Louisville, Ky., I. W. Crawford company [c1925] 144 p. front. (port.) 20 cm. Blank pages for "Memoranda" (141-144) [BV4223.C8] 26-2314
1. Sermons—Outlines. I. Title.

DAVIS, Ozora Stearns, 1866- 251
Preaching on church and community occasions, by Ozora S. Davis. Chicago, Ill., The University of Chicago press [1928] viii, 223 p. 20 cm. (Half-title: The University of Chicago publications in religious education ... Handbooks of ethics and religion) [BV4223.D3] 28-31134
1. Sermons—Outlines. I. Title.

DEDRICHS, Wilhelm, 1885- 248
Sermon thoughts for Sundays and holy days, by the Rev. William Dedrichs; adapted from the German by the Rev. Charles Cannon ... St. Louis, Mo. and London, B. Herder book co., 1929. ix, 152 p. 19 cm. [BX1756.D43P7] 29-22239
1. Sermons—Outlines. I. Cannon, Charles, 1873- tr. II. Title.

DORAN'S minister's manual; 251
a study and pulpit guide for the calendar year, 1926- New York, George H. Doran company, 1926- v. 23 cm. Editor: 1926- G. B. F. Hallock. [BV4223.D55] 25-21658
1. Sermons—Outlines. 2. Homiletical illustrations. I. Hallock, Gerard Benjamin Fleet, 1856- ed. II. Title: Minister's manual.

DOWNIE, Hugh Kerr, 1883- 251
Practical sermon outlines. Grand Rapids, Zondervan Pub. House [1947] [3] l., 5-118 p. 20 cm. [BV4223.D63] 47-26844
1. Sermons—Outlines. I. Title.

EDWARDS, Francis Henry, 1897- 252.093
Missionary sermon studies, by F. Henry Edwards. Independence, Mo., Herald publishing house [c1940] 320 p. 23 cm. Includes blank pages for notes. [BX8639.E3M5] 40-10371
1. Sermons—Outlines. 2. Mormons and Mormonism—Sermons. I. Title.

ELLIS, J., comp. 251.02
The seed basket; 300 sermon outlines and suggestions, compiled by J. Ellis. Grand Rapids, Baker Book House [1966] 90 p. 22 cm. [BV4223.E62] 66-31709
1. Sermons—Outlines. I. Title.

*ELLIS, J. comp. 252.02
Sermons in a nutshell; outlines for sermons and addresses, comp., arranged by J. Ellis. Grand Rapids, Mich., Baker Bk. [1968] 66p. 22cm. ($1.00 sermon lib.) 1.00 pap.,
1. Sermons—Outlines. I. Title.

ENGSTROM, Theodore W., ed. 251
Sermon outlines and illustrations, compiled and edited by Theodore W. Engstrom ... Grand Rapids, Mich., Zondervan publishing house [1942] 3 p. l., 5-168 p. 20 cm. [BV4223.E65] 43-1285
1. Sermons—Outlines. 2. Homiletical illustrations I. Title.

ENGSTROM, Theodore W., 1916- 251
Golden nuggets ... compiled, condensed and edited by Theodore W. Engstrom ... Grand Rapids, Mich., Zondervan publishing house [1944] v. 20 cm. [BV4223.E63] 45-3387
1. Sermons—Outlines. 2. Homiletical illustrations. I. Title.

ENGSTROM, Theodore Wilhelm, 1916- ed. 251
Golden nuggets, vol. 4: The Gospels. Grand Rapids, Mich., Zondervan Pub. House [1944] 277 p. 20 cm. Later pub. as v. 4 of the author's Treasury of Gospel gems; no other vols. pub. under this title. [BV4223.E63] 45-3387
1. Sermons—Outlines. 2. Homiletical illustrations. I. Title.

ENGSTROM, Theodore Wilhelm, 1916- ed. 251
188 heart-reaching sermon outlines. Grand Rapids, Zondervan [1950] 112 p. 20 cm. [BV4223.E64] 50-11976
1. Sermons—Outlines. I. Title.

ENGSTROM, Theodore Wilhelm, 1916- ed. 251
Sermon outlines and illustrations. Grand Rapids, Mich., Zondervan Pub. House [1942] 168 p. 20 cm. [BV4223.E65] 43-1285
1. Sermons—Outlines. 2. Homiletical illustrations. I. Title.

ENGSTROM, Theodore Wilhelm, 1916- ed. 251
Treasury of Gospel gems. Grand Rapids, Zondervan Pub. House [19 v. 20 cm. Contents.v. 5, Acts through II Thessalonians. [BV4223.E66] 48-20039
1. Sermons—Outlines. 2. Homiletical illustrations. I. Title.

THE Expositor's ministers annual ... a companion volume for a yearly subscription to the Expositor, the minister's magazine; 324 original sermons, arranged in 52 chapters for 52 weeks in the calendar year; 52 Sunday service outlines, thought stimulators and suggestion; 1 chapter of 12 original communion sermons ... 1929- Cleveland, F. M. Barton company, inc. [c1928- v. 23 cm. Editor: 1929- J. M. Ramsey. Title varies: 1984- The Minister's annual. [BV4200.E8] 28-27968
1. Sermons—Outlines. 2. Homiletical illustrations. I. Ramsey, Joseph McCray, ed. II. Title: Ministers annual.

FALLIS, William J., comp. 251.027
Broadman sermon outlines. Nashville, Broadman Press [c.1960] 64p. 21cm. 60-9531 1.00 pap.,
1. Sermons—Outlines. I. Title.

FOOTE, Ulysses Grant, 1870- 251
106 sermon outlines [by] Rev. U. G. Foote, D. D. Louisville, Ky., Pentecostal publishing company [c1927] 219 p. 19 1/2 cm. [BV4223.F6] 27-9592
1. Sermons—Outlines. I. Title.

FREDA, Weston Harry, 1889- 251
The minister's minute messages; a unique loose-leaf note book, by W. Harry Freda, D. D.; not a substitute for thinking but a mine of suggestions for original thought ... Cleveland, O. [c1932] cover-title, 108 numb. l. 21 cm. Printed on one side of leaf only. "52 analyzed outlines for sermons, 52 human interest illustrations, 52 suggestive topics and texts, 52 pointed paragraphs." Extra unnumbered blank leaves for "Notes" interspersed. [BV4223.F7] 32-19048
1. Sermons—Outlines. 2. Homiletical illustrations. I. Title.

GEIERMANN, Peter. 248
Outline sermons for Sundays and feast days, in accordance with the spirit of "The liturgical year" of Dom Gueranger ... by the Rev. Peter Geiermann ... St. Louis, Mo. and London, B. Herder book co., 1929. x, 173 p. 19 cm. [BX1756.A1G4] 29-12789
1. Sermons—Outlines. I. Title.

GIRARDEY, Ferrol, 1839-
The word of God preached to children. A course of sketches for sermons, on the creed, the means of grace, and the commandments, by the Rev. Ferrol Girardey, C. SS. R. New York, J. F. Wagner [c1913] vi, 378 p. 22 cm. 14-4591 1.50
I. Title.

GOUDGE, Henry Leighton, 1866- 252
Christian teaching and the Christian year, subjects for sermons for two years, by H. L. Goudge ... New ed., rev. and enl. London and Oxford, A. R. Mowbray & co., limited: New York and Milwaukee, Morehouse publishing co., 1937. 51, [1] p. 19 cm. "A short bibliography": p. 49-51. [BV30.G63 1937] 38-30372
1. Sermons—Outlines. 2. Church year sermons. I. Title. II. Title: Subjects for sermons for two years.

GREENWAY, Alfred L 251.027
Sermon plans and story illustrations. Grand Rapids, Baker Book House, 1959. 96p. 21cm. (Minister's handbook series) [BV4223.G65] 60-1141
1. Sermons—Outlines. I. Title.

*HALLOCK, E. F. 251.02
Bible-centered Sermon Starters, by E. F. Hallock. Grand Rapids, Mich., Baker Book House, [1974] 63 p. 22 cm. [BV4223] ISBN 0-8010-4112-0 1.00 (pbk.)
1. Sermons—Outlines. I. Title.

HALLOCK, Gerard Benjamin Fleet, 1856- ed. 251
Cyclopedia of sermon outlines for special days and occasions; a comprehensive collection of suggestive material for the outstanding days and seasons of the entire church year, also for fraternities, etc., compiled and edited by Rev. G. B. F. Hallock ... New York, George H. Doran company [c1925] xv, p., 1 l. 19-325 p. 22 cm. [BV4223.H16] 25-21579
1. Sermons—Outlines. 2. Homiletical illustrations. I. Title.

HALLOCK, Gerard Benjamin Fleet, 1856- 252.002
Five hundred sermon themes. Westwood, N. J., Revell [1952] 448 p. 21 cm. [BV4223.H18] 52-11091
1. Sermons—Outlines. I. Title.

HALLOCK, Gerard Benjamin Fleet, 1856- 252.002
The practical use cyclopedia of sermon suggestion, clues to great sermons from neglected texts; 300 outline sketches of striking and unusual texts and themes appropriate to both year-round presentation and for special days and occasions: 650 suggestive topics and texts for the church and civic year: also a treasury of 2,000 vital themes for vital preaching appropriate for general use, written and compiled by Rev. G. B. F. Hallock ... [New York] Harper & brothers [1942] xxiv- 281 p. 22 cm. [BV4223.H22] 42-12185
1. Sermons—Outlines. I. Title.

HALSTEAD, St. John, comp. 251
Pastor's ideal sermon book, containing sermon outlines by eminent pastors, comp. and ed. by St. John Halstead ... Evansville, Ind., Printed by Keller-Crescent co. [c1920] 3 p. l. [5]-162 p. 19 cm. [BV4223.H25] 20-22529
I. Title.

HANNAM, Thomas. 251
The pulpit assistant; containing more than three hundred outlines or skeletons of sermons, chiefly extracted from various authors: with an essay on the composition of a sermon, by the Rev. Thomas Hannam... From the 5th London ed., revised, corrected, and enlarged by the Rev. James Anderson. Pochester, D. Hoyt, 1842. xxiv, 750 p. 24 cm. [BV4223.H27 1842] 33-8867
1. Sermons—Outlines. I. Anderson, James of Chelmsford, ed. II. Title.

[HARRIS, W] Prebyterian minister. 251.027
Miracles and parables of the Old Testament; homiletic outlines. by a London minister. Grand Rapids, Baker Book House, 1959. 427p. 23cm. First published in 1878 under title: Outlines of sermons on the miracles and parables of the Old Testament. [BV4223.H32 1959] 59-8345
1. Sermons—Outlines. 2. Miracles. 3. Parables. I. A London minister. II. Title.

HAYDEN, Edwin V. 251'.02
Preaching through the Bible / by Edwin V. Hayden. Joplin, Mo. : College Press Pub. Co., 1981. xxiii, 533 p. ; 22 cm. (The Bible study textbook series) Includes index. [BS491.5.H38 1981] 19 81-82987 ISBN 0-89900-145-9 pbk. : 8.95
1. Bible—Sermons—Outlines, syllabi, etc. 2. Sermons—Outlines. I. Title. II. Series.

*HAYDEN, Eric. 251.02
Complete Sermon outlines. Grand Rapids, Mich., Baker Book House, [1974]. 62 p. 22 cm. [BV4223] ISBN 0-8010-4113-9. 1.00 (pbk.)
1. Sermons—Outlines. I. Title.

HENRY, Matthew, 1662-1714. 251
Sermon outlines, a choice collection of thirty-five model sermons; selected and edited by Sheldon B. Quincer. [1st ed.] Grand Rapids, W. B. Eerdmans Pub. Co., 1955. 148p. 23cm. (The World's great sermons in outline) [BV4223.H36] 55-1079
1. Sermons—Outlines. I. Title. II. Series.

HESLOP, William Greene, 1886- 251
Seed thoughts; outlines of sermons, sermon illustrations, points for preachers, seeds for sowers, truth for teachers, supplied for soul-winners [by] W. G. Heslop ... Grand Rapids, Mich., Zondervan publishing house [1943] 4 p. l., 11-121 p. 20 cm. [BV4223.H4] 43-10017
1. Sermons—Outlines. 2. Homiletical illustrations. I. Title.

HICKS, Bun E. 228
Simplified sermon outlines of Revelation and prophetical subjects, by Bun E. Hicks ... [Cleveland, Tenn.] c1931. 1 v. 21 cm. Cover-title; loose-leaf. [BV4223.H5] 31-35703
1. Sermons—Outlines. I. Title.

HOLDCRAFT, Paul Ellsworth, 1891- 251
440 more snappy sermon starters New York, Abingdon Press [1954] 127p. 20cm. [BV4223.H6] 54-4102
1. Sermons—Outlines. I. Title.

*HORNBERGER, J. C. 251.02
Sketches of revival sermons, original and selected. Grand Rapids, Mich., Baker Bk. [1967 69p. 22cm. ((1.00 sermon lib.) 1.00 pap.,
1. Sermons—Outlines. I. Title.

*HORRELL, B. C. 251.02
Fifty sermon outlines on conversion. Grand Rapids, Mich., Baker Bk. [c.1966] 70p. 22cm. 1.00 pap.,
I. Title.

*HORRELL, B. C. 251.02
Fifty sermon outlines on forgiveness. Grand Rapids, Mich., Baker Bk. [1966] 70p. 22cm. ((1.00 sermon lib.) 1.00 pap.,
I. Title.

*HORRELL, Benjamin. 251'.02
150 topical sermon outlines on Christ. Grand Rapids, Mich., Baker Book House [1973] 54 p. 22 cm. (Dollar sermon library) ISBN 0-8010-4065-5 1.00 (pbk.)
1. Sermons—Outlines. I. Title.

*HORRELL, Benjamin C. 251.02
150 topical sermon outlines on Romans, [by] Benjamin C. Horrell. Grand Rapids, Baker Book House [1974] 58 p. 22 cm. (Dollar sermon library) [BV4223] ISBN 0-8010-4101-5 1.00 (pbk.)
1. Sermons—Outlines. I. Title.

HUMPHREY, Jerry Miles, 1872- 251
50 ready-cut sermons, by Evangelist J. M. Humphrey... Chicago, Ill., Christian witness co. [c1925] 243 p. 20 cm. [BV4223.H8] 26-2315
1. Sermons—Outlines. I. Title.

*INGLIS, Charles. 251'.02
Dynamic sermon outlines. Grand Rapids, Mich., Baker Book House [1973] 61 p. 22 cm. (Dollar sermon Library) [BV4223] ISBN 0-8010-5028-6 1.00 (pbk.)
1. Sermons—Outlines. I. Title.

JASPER, K G 251
Living helps for preacher and people. New York, Comet Press Books, 1958. 79p. 21cm. (A Relections book) [BV4223.J3] 58-4083
1. Sermons—Outlines. 2. Homilectieal illustrations. I. Title.

JERNIGAN, John C. 251
Sermon outlines with helps, for ministers and Christian workers. By Jno. C. Jernigan. [Cleveland, Tenn., c1929] 4 p. l., 400 p. port. 22 cm. [BV4223.J4] 29-15354
1. Sermons—Outlines. I. Title.

*JOHNSON, Carl G. 251.'02
Preaching truths for perilous times / Carl G. Johnson. Grand Rapids : Baker Book House, 1976. 93p. ; 20 cm. [BV4223] ISBN 0-8010-5062-6 pbk. : 1.95
1. Sermons-Outlines. 2. Preaching. I. Title.

KERR, David W 251.027
Sermon outlines on great Bible texts. [Westwood, N. J.] Revell [1959] 64p. 21cm. (Revell's sermon outline series) [BV4223.K4] 59-8729
1. Sermons—Outlines. I. Title.

KRUTZKY, Paul Gustave, 1874- 251
comp.
Themes for vital preaching; a book of references and suggestions for the gospel ministry, containing outlines, lessons and selected texts for the Sundays and festivals of the church year, compiled and edited by Rev. Paul Krutzky and Rev. Carl Betz ... Garden City, N. Y., Doubleday, Doran & company, inc., 1929. xix p., 2 l., 3-245 p. 20 cm. [BV4223.K7] 29-3987
1. Sermons—Outlines. I. Betz, Carl Frederick William, 1877- joint comp. II. Title.

KURFEES, Marshall Clement, 251
1856-1931.
Outlines of sermons and inspirational talks. Lufkin, Tex., 1953. 62p. 24 cm. [BV4223.K82] 53-19469
1. Sermons—Outlines. I. Title.

KURFEES, Marshall Clement, 251
1856-1931.
The sermon outlines of M. C. Kurfees, compiled and published by B. C. Goodpasture ... Atlanta, Ga., B. C. Goodpasture, 1936- v. 21 cm. Photolithographed. [BV4223.K8] 36-8091
1. Sermons—Outlines. I. Goodpasture, Benjamin Cordell, 1895- comp. II. Title.

LAMBERT, Aloysius Albert, 251
1842-1909.
Pulpit sketches, by Rev. A. A. Lambert, missionary. Volume I. Chicago, The Henneberry company [1907] viii, 7-324 p. 20 1/2 cm. No more published? [BV4228.L3] 7-15457
1. Sermons—Outlines. I. Title.

LAPPIN, Samuel Strahl, 1870- 251
Lappin's sermon outlines, by S. S. Lappin ... Cincinnati, O., The Standard publishing company [c1925] 224 p. 20 cm. [BV4223.L33] 25-4418
I. Title.

LEACH, William Herman, 1888- 252
ed.
Sermon hearts, by William H. Leach ... Nashville, Cokesbury press [c1931] 320 p. 20 cm. "The author places within this volume the condensed outlines of one hundred and fifty great sermons by many preachers." [BV4223.L38] 31-17544
1. Sermons—Outlines. I. Title.

LEACH, William Herman, 1888- 252
comp.
Sermon hearts from the Gospels, compiled by William H. Leach ... Condensed outlines of one hundred and fifty published sermons on the Gospels by contemporary preachers of note. Nashville, Tenn., Cokesbury press [c1934] 328 p. 20 cm. "Sources of material": p. 315-321. [BV4223.L38 1934] 34-24996
1. Sermons—Outlines. I. Title.

LEACH, William Herman, 1888- 252
comp.
Sermon hearts from the Psalms, compiled by William H. Leach; condensed outlines of one hundred and fifty published sermons on the Psalms by preachers of distinction. Nashville, Cokesbury press [c1936] 319 p. 20 cm. [BV4223.L382] 36-5072
1. Sermons—Outlines. I. Title.

*LENSKI, R. C. H. 251
Preaching on John; sermon outlines, sermons, homiletical hints. Grand Rapids, Baker Book House [1973] 194 p. 20 cm. First published in 1933 under title: Saint John. [BV4223] 2.95 (pbk.)
1. Sermons—Outlines. I. Title.

LEWIS, Marvin. 251
Information and inspiration; sermon themes and poems and readings, by Evangelist Marvin Lewis. Grand Rapids, Mich., Zondervan publishing house [1942] 56 p. 19 1/2 cm. [BV4223.L47] 42-17008
1. Sermons—Outlines. I. Title.

LOGSDON, S Franklin. 251
Original sermon outlines, plus hints and helps on how to make sermon outlines. Grand Rapids, Zondervan Pub. House [1954] 128p. 20cm. [BV4223.L6] 54-34229
1. Sermons— Outlines. 2. Preaching. I. Title.

*LYNN, Thomas. 251
150 biographical illustrations, by Thomas Lynn with Jimmy Law. Grand Rapids, Baker Book House, [1975 c1973] 96 p. 20 cm. [BV4223] 1.95 (pbk.)
1. Sermons—Outlines. 2. Homiletical illustrations. I. Law, Jimmy. joint author II. Title.

MCCLUNG, Fred W 1909- 251
God's picture gallery. Fayetteville, Ark. [1953] 172p. illus. 22cm. [BV4223.M2] 53-26459
1. Sermons—Outlines. I. Title.

MCDERMOTT, Andrew W., 251.027
comp.
Sermon outlines from great preachers. [Westwood, N. J.] Revell [1959] 64p. 21cm. (Revell's sermon outline series) [BV4223.M16] 59-8731
1. Sermons—Outlines. I. Title.

MCGINTY, Claudius Lamar 251.027
Sermon outlines for holy living. [Westwood, N. J.] Revell [c.1960] 64p. 21cm. (Revell's sermon outline series) 60-8462 1.00 pap.,
1. Sermons—Outlines. I. Title.

MCGINTY, Claudius Lamar, 251
1885-
Sermon outlines. [Westwood, N. J.] Revell [1957- v. 19cm. [BV4223.M17] 57-6853
1. Sermons—Outlines. I. Title.

*MACLAREN, Alexander 251.02
Sermon outlines on the Psalms, by Alexander Maclaren [others] Grand Rapids. Mich., Baker Bk. [1966] 142p. 20cm. (Preaching helps ser.) Reprinted from the orig. ed. pub. by Hodder & Stoughton, London, in 1900. 1.50 pap.,
1. Sermons—Outlines. I. Title.

MCLAREN, Alexander, 1826- 251
1910.
Sermon outlines; a choice collection of thirty-five mode sermons, selected and edited by Sheldon B. Quincer. Grand Rapids, Eerdmans, 1954. 151p. 23cm. (The World's great sermons in outline) [BV4223.M2] 54-6232
1. Sermons—Outlines. I. Title.

MACLENNAN, David Alexander, 251
1903-
Resources for sermon preparation. Philadelphia, Westminster Press [1957] 239p. 21cm. [BV4223.M22] 57-9604
1. Sermons—Outlines. I. Title.

*MACPHERSON, Ian. 251.02
Bible sermon outlines / Ian Macpherson. Grand Rapids : Baker Book House, 1976c1966. 191p. ; 20 cm. Includes index. [BV4223] ISBN 0-8010-5993-3 pbk. : 2.95
1. Sermon-Outlines. I. Title.

*MACPHERSON, Ian. 251.02
Live sermon outlines. Grand Rapids, Baker Book House [1974] 64 p. 22 cm. (Dollar sermon library) [BV4223] ISBN 0-8010-5956-9 1.00 (pbk.)
1. Sermons—Outlines. I. Title.

MACPHERSON, Ian, real 251.027
name: John Cook Macpherson.
Sermon outlines from sermon masters. Nashville, Abingdon Press [c.1960] 224p. 20cm. 60-5474 2.50 bds.,
1. Sermons—Outlines. I. Title.

MACPHERSON, Ian, 1912- 251.02
Bible sermon outlines. Nashville, Abingdon [c.1966] 191p. 23cm. Bibl. [BV4223.M23] 66-12926 3.95
1. Sermons—Outlines. 2. Bible—Sermons—Outlines. I. Title.

MACPHERSON, Ian, 1912- 251'.02
Kindlings; outlines and sermon starters. Old Tappan, N.J., Revell [1969] 159 p. 21 cm. [BV4223.M235] 72-77481 3.95
1. Sermons—Outlines. I. Title.

MACPHERSON, Ian, 1912- 251.027
Sermon outlines from sermon masters. New York, Abingdon Press [1960-62] 2v. 20cm. Contents.[1] New Testament.--[2] Old Testament. [BV4223.M24] 60-5474
1. Sermons— Outlines. I. Title.

MACPHERSON, Ian [John 251.027
Cook Macpherson] 1912-
Sermon outlines from sermon masters--Old Testament. Nashville, Abingdon [c.1962] 240p. 20cm. 60-5474 3.00
1. Sermons—Outlines. I. Title.

MARK, Harry Clayton, 251.027
1906-
Patterns for preaching; the art of sermon making. Grand Rapids, Zondervan Pub. House [1959] 183p. 23cm. [BV4223.M28] 59-39706
1. Sermons—Outlines. 2. Preaching. I. Title.

*MEES, Otto. 251.02
Outlines for funeral sermons; and other helps. Grand Rapids, Baker Book House [1974] 320 p. 20 cm. (Minister's handbook series) [BV4223] ISBN 0-8010-5946-1 2.95 (pbk.)
1. Sermons—outlines. I. Title.

MIDDLETON, John 252.02
Stanislaus.
Living for God, by Rev. John S. Middleton ... New York, P. J. Kenedy & sons [c1934] xvii, [1], 333 p. 22 1/2 cm. [BX1756.M55L5] 35-243
1. Sermons—Outlines. 2. Church year sermons. 3. Catholic church—Sermons. 4. Sermons, American. I. Title.

MILLER, Milburn H 251
Ideas for sermons and talks. Anderson, Ind., Warner Press [1957] 149p. 19cm. [BV4223.M48] 57-3912
1. Sermons— Outlines. I. Title.

THE ministers manual; 251.058
a study and pulpit guide. 1926- New York, Harper. v. 21-23 cm. annual. Title varies: 1926-46, Doran's ministers manual (cover title, 1947: The Doran's ministers manual) Editor: 1926- G. B. F. Hallock (with M. K. W. Heicher, 1942- Vols. 1-5 were pub. by Doubleday, Doran [etc.] [BV4223.M5] 25-21658
1. Sermons—Outlines. 2. Homiletical illustrations. I. Hallock, Gerald Benjamin Fleet, 1856- ed.

MINISTERS manual (The) 251.058
(Doran's) Comp., ed. by M.K.W. Heicher. 41st annual issue. New York, Harper [c.1965] xviii, 357p. 22cm. Title varies. annual. 25-21658 3.95 bds.,
1. Sermons—Outlines. 2. Homelectical illustrations. I. Heicher, M.K.W., ed. II. Title: Doran's minister's manual.

MINISTERS manual (The) 251.058
(Doran's Comp., ed. by M. K. W. Heicher. 42nd annual issue. New York, Harper [c.1966] xii, 372p. 21cm. Title varies. annual. 25-21658 3.95 bds.,
1. Sermons—Outlines. 2. Homiletical illustrations. I. Heicher, M. K. W., ed. II. Title: Doran's minister's manual.

MINISTERS manual (The): 251.027
a study and pulpit guide for the calendar year 1961. 36th annual issue, compiled and edited by Rev. M. K. W. Heicher. New York, Harper [c.1960] xii, 388p. 21cm. Title varies: 1926-46, Doran's ministers manual (cover title, 1947: The Doran's ministers manual) 25-21658 3.50 half cloth,
1. Sermons—Outlines. 2. Homiletical illustrations. I. Heicher, M. K. W., ed.

MINISTERS manual (The); 251.058
a study and pulpit guide. 1968- New York, Harper. v. 21cm. annual. Title varies. Ed.: 1968- Vols. 1-5 were pub. by Doubleday, Doran [etc.] [BV4223.M5] 25-21658 3.95 bds.,
1. Sermons—Outlines. 2. Homiletical illustrations. I. Heicher, M.K.W. ed.

MINISTERS' research 251'.02
service. William F. Kerr, general editor. Wheaton, Ill., Tyndale House Publishers [1970] 854 p. 26 cm. Includes bibliographies. [BV4223.M53] 76-103985
1. Sermons—Outlines. 2. Pastoral theology. I. Kerr, William F., ed.

MOORE, Hight C 1871- 251
Nuggets from golden texts. Nashville, Broadman Press [1953] 112p. 20cm. [BV4223.M56] 53-12023
1. Sermons—Outlines. I. Title.

MOORE, Walter Lane, 1905- 251.027
Outlines for preaching [by] Walter L. Moore. Nashville, Broadman Press [1965] 80 p. 21 cm. [BV4223.M58] 65-15602
1. Sermons — Outlines. I. Title.

MORGAN, George Campbell, 251
1863-
Searchlights from the Word; being 1188 sermon-suggestions, one from every chapter in the Bible, by G. Campbell Morgan, D.D. New York, Chicago [etc.] Fleming H. Revell company [c1926] 421 p. 23 cm. [BV4223.M6] 26-14553
1. Sermons—Outlines. I. Title.

NICOLL, William Robertson, 251
Sir 1851-1923, ed.
300 sermon outlines on the New Testament. Grand Rapids, Baker Book House, 1956. 279p. 21cm. [BV4223.N53 1956] 56-7588
1. Sermons—Outlines. I. Title.

101 select sermon outlines by 251
Vaughan, Exell, Spurgeon, Robinson, and others. Grand Rapids, Baker Book House, 1953. 95p. 21cm. (Minister's handbook series) [BV4223.O5] 54-16109
1. Sermans—Outlines.

PARKER, Joseph, 1830-1902. 251
Sermon outlines; a choice collection of thirty-five model sermons. Selected and edited by Sheldon B. Quincer. Grand Rapids, Eerdmans [1958] 150p. 23cm. (The World's great sermons in outline, v. 4) [BV4223.P34] 58-7570
1. Sermons—Outlines. I. Title.

*PENTZ, Croft M. 251.02
Expository outlines on the gospel of John, [by] Croft M. Pentz. Grand Rapids, Baker Book House [1974] 53 p. 22 cm. (Dollar sermon library) [BV4223] ISBN 0-8010-6960-2 1.00 (pbk.)
1. Sermons—Outlines. I. Title.

*PENTZ, Croft M. 251.02
52 simple sermon outlines. Grand Rapids, Baker Bk. [1968] 82p. 22cm. (Dollar sermon lib.) 1.00 pap.,
1. Sermons—Outlines. I. Title.

*PENTZ, Croft M. 251.02
48 simple sermon outlines. Grand Rapids, Mich., Baker Bk [c.]1965. 82p. 22cm. 1.00 pap.,
I. Title.

PENTZ, Croft M. 251.027
175 simple sermon outlines. Grand Rapids, Mich., Baker Bk. [c.]1963. 87p. 22cm. (Sermon lib.) 1.00 pap.,
I. Title.

PENTZ, Croft M., comp. 248.4
1001 sentence sermons, for every need--for church bulletin boards, bulletins, newspapers, etc. Grand Rapids, Mich., Zondervan [c.1962] 61p. 21cm. 1.00 pap.,
I. Title.

*PENTZ, Croft M. 251.02
Sermon outlines from the psalms, [by] Croft M. Pentz. Grand Rapids, Mich., Baker Book House, [1974] 63 p. 22 cm. [BV4223] ISBN 0-8010-6974-2 1.00 (pbk.)
1. Sermons—Outlines. I. Title.

PERKINS, Benjamin J. 252.
The flaming sword. Consists of sketches and skeletons of sermons by Rev. Benjamin J. Perkins. Memphis, Tenn.

[Howe institute press, c1917] 346 p. 20 cm. [BX6333.P4F5] 18-666
I. Title.

PERKINS, Benjamin J. 252.
The flaming sword. Consists of sketches and skeletons of sermons by Rev. Benjamin J. Perkins. Memphis, Tenn. [Howe institute press, c1917] 346 p. 20 cm. [BX6333.P4F5] 18-666
I. Title.

PERREN, Christopher, 1839- 243
ed.
Outline sermons and plans for evangelistic work, by eminent pastors and evangelists, edited by Rev. C. Perren ... Chicago, New York [etc.] Fleming H. Revell company [c1903] 473 p. 20 cm. [BV3797.P4] 3-29856
1. Sermons—Outlines. 2. Evangelistic work. 3. Homiletical illustrations. I. Title.

PIERSON, Robert H. 251.02
What shall I speak about? 250 suggestions and helps in preparing talks and sermons for many occasions. Nashville, Southern Pub. [c.1966] 255p. 22cm. [BV4223.P53] 66-3991 4.95
1. Sermons—Outlines. I. Title.

PIERSON, Robert H 251.02
What shall I speak about? 250 suggestions and helps in preparing talks and sermons for many occasions, by Robert H. Pierson. Nashville, Southern Pub. Association [1966] 255 p. 22 cm. [BV4223.P53] 66-3991
1. Sermons—Outlines. I. Title.

PRIDEAUX, Sherburne Povah 251.02
Tregelles, 1880-
More outline sermons on general subjects. London, A. R. Mowbray; New York, Morehouse-Gorham Co. [1952] 96p. 19cm. [BV4223.P7] 57-17917
1. Sermons— Outlines. I. Title.

PULPIT themes; 251
one hundred outlines of sermons, by Matthew Henry, Christmas Evans, Andrew Fuller, and others. Grand Rapids, Baker Book House, 1954. 227p. 20cm. [Co-operative reprint library] 'A reprint of Pulpit themes and Preacher's assistant, part II.' [BV4223.P84] 54-11088
1. Sermons—Outlines. I. Henry, Matthew, 1662-1714.

RAPKING, Aaron Henry, 1886- 251
ed.
The town and country pulpit; suggestions for worship by and for town and country pastors, edited by Aaron H. Rapking. New York, Board of missions and church extension, the Methodist church, 1943. 206 p. 22 1/2 cm. [BV4223.R3] 43-12771
1. Sermons—Outlines. 2. Homiletical illustrations. I. Methodist church (United States) Board of missions and church extension. II. Title.

SCHROEDER, George W 251
You can speak for God; 130 devotional talk outlines for laymen. Nashville, Broadman Press [1958] 132p. 22cm. [BV4223.S35] 58-5415
1. Sermons—Outlines. I. Title.

SELF, William L. 251'.02
The Saturday night special : [sermons] / William L. Self. Waco, Tex. : Word Books, c1977. 135 p. ; 23 cm. [BV4223.S42] 77-75469 ISBN 0-8499-0013-1 : 5.95
1. Sermons—Outlines. I. Title.

SERMON outlines, 251
by Charles Simon and others. Grand Rapids, Baker Book House, 1954. 2v. in 1. 24cm. 'Formerly publishec as Theological sketchbook; or, Skeletons of sermons.' [BV4223.S43] 54-3031
1. Sermons—Outlines. I. Simeon, Charles, 1759-1836.

SERMON seeds; 251
[outlines from the writings of Alexander Maclaren, and others. Grand Rapids, Baker Book House, 1956. 95p. 21cm. (Minister's handbook series, v. 10) [BV4223.S45] 56-10682
1. Sermons—Outlines. I. McLaren, Alexander, 1826-1910.

SHERRICK, Marvin Manam, 251'.02
1868-
Topical sermon notes, by Marvin M. Sherrick. Grand Rapids, Baker Bk. [1967] 76p. 22cm. [BV4233] 67-6258 1.00 pap.,
1. Sermons—Outlines. I. Title.

SMALL, John Bryan, bp., 252.07
1845-
Practical and exegetical pulpiteer. Synopses of discourses delivered by Rev. John B. Small...with an introduction by Rev. Wm. H. Goler... York, Pa., P. Anstadt & sons, 1895. viii, [9]-312 p. 21 cm. [BX8472.S6] 33-8320
1. Sermons—Outlines. I. Title.

SMITTY, William H. 251'.02
300 sermon outlines from the Old Testament / William H. Smitty. Nashville, Tenn. : Broadman Press, c1982. 118 p. ; 21 cm. [BS1151.5.S64] 19 81-67996 ISBN 0-8054-2242-0 pbk. : 3.95
1. Bible. O.T.—Sermons. 2. Sermons—Outlines. 3. Baptists—Sermons. 4. Sermons, American. I. Title. II. Title: Three hundred sermon outlines from the Old Testament.

SPURGEON, Charles Haddon, 251
1834-1892.
C. H. Spurgeon's Sermon notes, Genesis to Revelation; 193 sermon outlines, edited and condensed by David Otis Fuller. Four volumes in one. Grand Rapids, Mich., Zondervan publishing house [c1941] 334 p. incl. front. (facsim.) 20 cm. [BV4223.S6] 42-777
1. Sermons—Outlines. I. Fuller, David Otis, 1908- ed. II. Title.

SPURGEON, Charles Haddon, 251
1834-1892.
Choice sermon notes. Grand Rapids, Zondervan Pub. House [1952] 215 p. illus. 20 cm. [BV4223.S58] 52-34664
1. Sermons — Outlines. I. Title.

SPURGEON, Charles Haddon, 251
1834-1892.
My sermon notes; a selection from outlines of discourses delivered at the Metropolitan Tabernacle, with anecdotes and illus. [Westwood, N.J., Revell [1956.] 1067 p. 21 cm. [[BV4223]] 56-9829
1. Sermons-Outlines. I. Title.

*SPURGEON, Charles 251'.02
Haddon, 1834-1892.
Stimulating sermon outlines, by Charles H. Spurgeon and others. Grand Rapids, Mich., Baker Book House [1973, c.1972] 61 p. 22 cm. (Dollar sermon library) ISBN 0-8010-7962-4 1.00 (pbk.)
1. Sermons—Outlines. I. Title.

STAUFFER, Joshua, 1891- 251
"Give ye them to eat"; or, Sermon outlines. Berne, Ind., Light and Hope Publications [c1951] 192 p. 20 cm. [BV4223.S76] 52-20938
1. Sermons — Outlines. I. Title.

STRONG, Charles O., comp. 251.027
Selected sermon outlines. Grand Rapids, Mich., Zondervan [c.1963] 119p. 21cm. 2.50 bds.,
I. Title.

*TAYLOR, Richard S. 251'.02
Timely sermon outlines; compiled by Richard S. Taylor. Grand Rapids, Mich., Baker Book House [1973] 64 p. 22 cm. (Dollar sermon library) ISBN 0-8010-8789-9 1.00 (pbk.)
1. Sermons—Outlines. I. Title.

THOMAS, Leslie Grier, 1895- 251
God amid the shadows, a collection of Bible subjects homiletically treated, by Leslie G. Thomas ... Chattanooga, Tenn., L. G. Thomas, 1944. 197 p. 17 1/2 cm. Bibliography: p. 194-197. [BV4223.T5] 44-47552
1. Sermons—Outlines. I. Title.

THOMAS, Leslie Grier, 1895- 251
ed.
One hundred sermons; a collection of Bible subjects homiletically treated, edited by Leslie G. Thomas. Nashville, Tenn., Gospel advocate company [c1940] 281, [1] p. 18 1/2 cm. Bibliography: p. [279]-281. "General reference works": p. [282] [BX7094.C95T52] 40-11096
1. Sermons—Outlines. 2. Churches of Christ—Sermons. I. Title.

THOMAS, William Henry 251
Griffith, 1861-1924.
Sermon outlines, exegetical and expository, by W. H. Griffith Thomas, D.D. Grand Rapids, Mich., Wm. B. Eerdmans publishing company, 1947. 4 p. l., 11-135 p. 20 cm. [BV4223.T53] 47-1930
1. Sermons—Outlines. I. Title.

TIDWELL, Josiah Blake, 1870- 251
1946.
Selected sermon outlines, by J. B. Tidwell ... Grand Rapids, Mich., Zondervan publishing house [1947] 4 p. l., 11-120 p. 20 cm. [BV4223.T55] 47-23500
1. Sermons—Outlines. I. Title.

TONNE, Arthur, Rt. Rev. 251.027
Msgr.
Stories for sermons; 513 stories on God, with complete index and cross index; v.14 [Emporia, Kans., Didde, c.1963 161p. 23cm. 2.50 pap.,
I. Title.

*TORREY, Reuben Archer, 251'.02
1856-1928
Suggestive sermon outlines, ed. by R. A. Torrey. Grand Rapids, Baker Bk. [1968] 77p. 22cm. ($1.00 sermon lib.) 1.00 pap.,
1. Sermons—Outlines. I. Title.

TURNBULL, Ralph G 251.027
Sermon substance. Grand Rapids, Baker Book House, 1958. 224 p. 23 cm. [BV4223.T85] 58-59824
1. Sermons — Outlines. I. Title.

TURNBULL, Ralph G. 251.02
Spokesmen for God (Isaiah, Jeremiah) by Ralph G. Turnbull. Grand Rapids, Baker Bk. [1966] 88p. 22cm. (Bible companion ser. for lesson and sermon preparation) [BV4223.T87] 66-9309 1.00 pap.,
1. Sermons—Outlines. I. Title.

TURNBULL, Ralph G. 251.02
Spokesmen for God (Isaiah, Jeremiah) by Ralph G. Turnbull. Grand Rapids, Baker Book House [1966] 88 p. 22 cm. (His Bible companion series for lesson and sermon preparation) [BV4223.T87] 66-9309
1. Sermons—Outlines. I. Title.

VAN WYK, William P., 1874- 226.8
1943.
My sermon notes on parables and metaphors, by Rev. William P. Van Wyke. Grand Rapids, Mich., Baker book house, 1947. 110 p. 20 cm. [BT375.V3] 47-20025
1. Jesus Christ—Parables—Sermons. 2. Sermons—Outlines. I. Title.

VAN WYK, William Peter, 220.92
1874-1943.
My sermon notes on Biblical characters. Grand Rapids, Baker Book House, 1948. 153 p. 21 cm. [BV4223.V29] 48-8455
1. Sermons—Outlines. 2. Bible—Biog. I. Title.

VAN WYK, William Peter, 221.92
1874-1943.
My sermon notes on Old Testament characters. Grand Rapids, Baker Book House, 1948. 144 p. 20 cm. [BV4223.V3] 48-7116
1. Sermons—Outlines. 2. Bible—Biog. I. Title.

VAN WYK, William Peter, 226.8
1874-1943.
My sermon notes on parables and metaphors. Grand Rapids, Baker Book House, 1947. 110 p. 20 cm. [BT375.V3] 47-20025
1. Jesus Christ—Parables—Sermons. 2. Sermons—Outlines. I. Title.

WAKEHAM, Richard King, 1848- 248
Sketches for sermons, chiefly on the Gospels, for the Sundays and holydays of the year; by Rev. R. K. Wakeham ... New York J. F. Wagner 1903 229 p. 20 1/2 cm. Interleaved. [BX1756.W3S5] 3-32167
1. Sermons—Outlines. I. Title.

WEBB, Aquilla. 251
Cyclopedia of sermon outlines by Rev. Aquilla Webb ... with introduction by Rev. Charles L. Goodell, D. D. New York, George H. Doran company [c1923] xvi p., 1 l., 19-336 p. 22 cm. [BV4223.W4] 23-17192
I. Title.

WEBB, Aquilla. 251
Cyclopedia of sermon outlines by Rev. Aquilla Webb ... with introduction by Rev. Charles L. Goodell, D. D. New York, George H. Doran company [c1923] xvi p., 1 l., 19-336 p. 22 cm. [BV4223.W4] 23-17192
I. Title.

WEBER, Gerard P., 1918- 251.02
Love one another; sermon outlines for Sundays and holydays, by Gerard Weber, James Killgallon. Foreword by Albert Meyer. Staten Island, N.Y., Alba [c.1965] 175p. 22cm. [BV4223.W43] 65-17978 3.95
1. Sermons—Outlines. 2. Love (Theology)—Sermons. I. Killgallon, James, 1914- joint author. II. Title.

WEBER, Gerard P 1918- 251.02
Love one another; sermon outlines for Sundays and holydays. by Gerard Weber and James Killgallon. Foreword by Albert Meyer. Staten Island, N.Y., Alba House [1965] 175 p. 22 cm. [BV4223.W43] 65-17978
1. Sermons — Outlines. 2. Love (Theology) — Sermons. I. Killgallon, James, 1914- joint author. II. Title.

WELSHIMER, Pearl Howard, 1873-
1957.
Sermon outlines. Soul winning!Church building! By P. H. Welshimer. Compiled by Mildred Welshimer Phillips. Cincinnati, Standard Pub. [196-] 64 p. port. Includes "Preaching with purpose" by Edwin V. Hayden. 68-39777
1. Sermons-Outlines. I. Phillips, Mildred Welshimer, comp. II. Hayden, Edwin V., 1913- Preaching with purpose. III. Title.

WHITE, Reginald E. O. 251.02
Sermon suggestions in outline. Grand Rapids, Mich., Eerdmans [1966, c.1965] 75p. 22cm. Contents.Ser. 1 January-June [BV4223.W437] 65-25194 145 pap.,
1. Sermons—Outines. I. Title.

WHITE, Richard C., 1872- 251
The sermons of R. C. White; illustrations by Miss Theresa Hargett. Murfreesboro, Tenn., G. W. De Hoff [1945] 113 p. front. (port.) diagrs. 20 cm. [BV4223.W44] 46-14716
1. Sermons—Outlines. I. Title.

WHITEFIELD, George, 1714- 251
1770.
Sermon outlines; a choice collection of thirty-five model sermons. Selected and edited by Sheldon B. Quincer. Grand Rapids, Erdmans, 1956. 150p. 23cm. (The World's great sermons in outline) [BV4223.W444] 56-13871
1. Sermons—Outlines. I. Title.

WHITESELL, Faris Daniel, 251.027
1895-
Expository sermon outlines: Old and New Testament. [Westwood, N.J.] Revell [1959] 64 p. 21 cm. (Revell's sermon outline series) [BV4223.W446] 59-8728
1. Sermons — Outlines. I. Title.

WHITESELL, Faris Daniel, 208
1895-
Sermon outlines on favorite Bible chapters. [Westwood, N.J.] Revell [1962] 64 p. 21 cm. (Revell's sermon outline series) [BV4223.W4462] 62-10740
1. Sermons — Outlines. I. Title.

WILLIAMS, Ernest Swing, 251'.02
1885-
My sermon notes; the Gospels and Acts, by E. S. Williams. Springfield, Mo., Gospel Pub. House [1967] 224 p. (p. 213-224, blank for "Notes") 23 cm. [BV4223.W447] 67-27320
1. Sermons—Outlines. I. Title.

WILLIAMS, Jerome Oscar, 1885- 251
Heart sermons in outline. Nashville, Broadman Press [1949] 144 p. 20 cm. [BV4223.W448] 49-9207
1. Sermons—Outlines. I. Title.

WILLIAMS, Jerome Oscar, 1885- 251
Seed for sermons, by Jerome O. Williams ... Nashville, Tenn., Broadman press [1945] 6 p. l., 135 p. 20 cm. [BV4223.W45] 46-12277
1. Sermons—Outlines. I. Title.

WILLIAMS, Jerome Oscar, 1885- 251.027
Sermons in outline. Nashville, Broadman Press [1960, c.1943] 210p. (Broadman Starbooks) 1.50 pap.,
1. Sermons—Outlines. I. Title.

WILLIAMS, Jerome Oscar, 1885- 251
Sermons in outline, by Jerome O. Williams ... Nashville, Tenn., Broadman press [1943] 210 p. 19 1/2 cm. [BV4223.W46] 43-4202
1. Sermons—Outlines. I. Title.

THE Zondervan pastor's annual for 1969. 251'.02 Grand Rapids. Zondervan. v. 21cm. [BX6333.A1A8] 65-19507 3.95 bds.,
1. Sermons—Outlines. 2. Baptists—Sermons—Outlines.

Sermons, Scottish.

BLACK, Hugh, 1868- 243
... Listening to God, by Hugh Black ... New York, Chicago [etc.] Fleming H. Revell company [c1906] 310 p. 20 1/2 cm. At head of title: Edinburgh sermons. [BX9178.B62L5] 6-42404
I. Title. II. Title: Edinburgh sermons.

BLAIR, Hugh, 1718-1800. 243
Sermons, by Hugh Blair, D.C., one of the ministers of the High church, and professer of rhetoric and belles letters in the University of Edinburgh. To which is prefixed, that admired tract on the internal evidence of the Christian religion. By Soame Jenyns ... London, Printed: Baltimore: Reprinted, for the Rev. M. L. Weems, by Samuel and John Adams, bookprinters, in Market-street, between South and Gay-streets. MDCCXCII-MDCCXCIII. 2 v. 21 cm. Vol. 1, 16th edition: v. 2, 13th edition, 1793. Imprint varies slightly. [BX9178.B] A 32
I. Jenyns, Soame, 1704-1787. II. Title.

MCNEILL, John, 1854
Rev. John McNeill's ("The Scotch Spurgeon.") popular sermons. Delivered during the World's fair in Chicago, and in his Regent Square church, London England ...Ed. by J. B. McClure. Chicago, Rhodes & McClure pub. co., 1898. 2 p. l., 13-373 p. illus. pl., port.12° Feb
I. Title.

SIMPSON, Hubert Louis, 1880- ed. 243
Twenty sermons by famous Scotch preachers, edited by Hulbert [!] L. Simpson and D. P. Thomson, with a foreword by Rev. Principal D. S. Cairns ... New York, George H. Doran company [1924] 237 p. 19 1/2 cm. Printed in Great Britain. Glasgow edition (Thomson & Cowan) published under title: "United free church sermons", which appears as half-title and running title in the present edition. [BX9178.A1S5] 25-19060
1. Sermons, Scottish. I. Thomson, David Patrick, joint ed. II. Title. III. Title: United free church sermons.

Sermons—Study and teaching.

*FOUSHEE, Clyde. 264.6
Animated object talks. Grand Rapids, Mich., Baker Book House [1973, c1956] 159 p, 20 cm. (Object lesson series.) [BV4531.2] ISBN 0-8010-3459-0 1.50 (pbk.)
1. Sermons—Study and teaching. I. Title.

RICE, Clarence Edgar.
Illustrations for sermons; or, Helps to effective preaching with a chapter on the source and use of illustrations, by Clarence Edgar Rice. New York and London, G. P. Putnam's sons, 1903. xiii, 211 p. 19 1/2 cm. 3-22545
I. Title.

WARD, James Thomas, 1820-1897. 252.
Sermons to my students. By Rev. James Thomas Ward... Baltimore, Md., Press of Wm. J. C. Dulany company, 1898. xv, 330 p. front. (port.) 20 cm. "Sixteen sermons...delivered to the classes graduating from Western Maryland college in the years 1871-1886, inclusive."--Introd. Biographical introduction by Rev. James William Reese. Includes lists of graduating classes, Western Maryland college, 1871-1896. [BV4310.W2] 23-14327
I. Westminister, Md. Western Maryland college. II. Title.

Sermons — Texts for sermons.

BIBLE. English. Selections. 1942. Authorized. 251
Scripture texts for special days and occasions; helps for holy days and holidays, by Wm. C. Steenland ... Grand Rapids, Mich., Zondervan publishing house [1942] 95 p. 19 1/2 cm. [BV4223.S77] 42-19456
1. Sermons—Texts for sermons. I. Steenland, William C., ed. II. Title.

DUBOIS, Marcel.
Reflexions sur les messes dominicales. Montreal, Filles de Saint Paul, Apostolat des Editions [1964] 249 p. 20 cm. 66-72434
1. Sermons — Texts for sermons. 2. Mass — Sermons. 3. Church year — Meditations. I. Title.

DUBOIS, Marcel.
Reflexions sur les messes dominicales. Montreal, Filles de Saint Paul, Apostolat des Editions [1964] 249 p. 20 cm. 66-72434
1. Sermons — Texts for sermons. 2. Mass — Sermons. 3. Church year — Meditations. I. Title.

*FREY, Lash 251.02
Crusade for souls, and other sermon outlines, by Lash Frey, William Willis. Grand Rapids, Mich., Baker Bk. [c.]1965. 91p. 23cm. ((1.00 sermon lib.) 1.00 pap.,
1. Sermons—Text for sermons. I. Willis, William, joint author. II. Title.

GOULOOZE, William, 1903-1955. 251
1500 themes for series preaching. Grand Rapids, Baker Book House, 1956. 156p. 20cm. [BV4223.G6] 56-7576
1. Sermons—Texts for sermons. I. Title.

HOVEY, Byron P. 252.4
Living in the eye of a hurricane: sermons for every day. New York, Exposition [c.1962] 56p. 21cm. 2.75
I. Title.

*JOHNSON, Carl G. 251.02
Scriptural sermon outlines. Grand Rapids, Mich., Baker Bk. [c.]1965. 112p. 22cm. (1.00 sermon lib.) 1.00 pap.
1. Sermons—Texts for sermons. I. Title.

JONES, Edgar De Witt, 1876- 252
When Jesus wrote on the ground; studies, expositions and meditations in the life of the spirit, by Edgar De Witt Jones ... with an appreciation by Dr. Charles Clayton Morrison ... New York, George H. Doran company [c1922] 3 p. l., x, [2], 13-234 p. 20 cm. [BX7327.J8W45] 22-19972 1.50
I. Title.

NESPER, Paul William, 1891- 251
Biblical texts. [2d ed.] Columbus, Ohio, Wartburg Press [1952] 442p. 20cm. First published in 1923 under title: Biblical texts for special occassions. [BV4223.N35 1952] 54-28198
1. Sermons—Texts for sermons. 2. Lectionaries —Hist. & crit. I. Title.

Sermons—Yearbooks.

REVELL'S minister's annual. 264.0081 1966 Westwood, N.J., Revell [c.1965] 363p. 21cm. Ed.: 1966- D. A. MacLennan [BV4241.R44] 64-20182 3.95 bds.,
1. Sermons—Yearbooks. I. MacLennan, David Alexander, 1903- ed. II. Title: Minister's annual.

REVELL'S minister's annual. 264.0081 1967 Westwood N. J., Revell [c.1966] 380p. 21cm. Ed.: 1967- D.A. MacLennan [BV4241.R44] 64-20182 3.95 bds.,
1. Sermons—Yearbooks. I. MacLennan, David Alexander, 1903-ed. II. Title: Minister's annual.

REVELL'S minister's annual, 1965. 264.0081 Westwood, N.J., Revell [c.1964] 383p. 21cm. Ed.: 1965- D. A. MacLennan. 64-20182 3.95 bds.,
1. Sermons—Yearbooks. I. MacLennan, David Alexander, 1903- ed. II. Title: Minister's annual.

Serpent-worship.

HAMBLY, Wilfrid Dyson, 1886- 291.2124
Serpent worship in Africa, by Wilfrid D. Hambly ... 8 plates in photogravure and 1 map ... Chicago, 1931. 85 p. front. (fold map) VIII pl. 24 1/2 cm. (Field museum of natural history ... Publication 289. Anthropological series. vol. XXI, no. 1) Bibliography: p. 77-81. [GN2.F4 vol. 21, no. 1] 31-33982
1. Serpent-worship. I. Title.

HOWEY, M. Oldfield. 291.3'7
The encircled serpent; a study of serpent symbolism in all countries and ages, by M. Oldfield Howey. London, Rider. Detroit, Gale Research Co., 1975. p. cm. Reprint of the 1926 ed. Includes bibliographies. [BL441.H6 1975] 74-19166 ISBN 0-8103-4133-6 20.00
1. Serpent worship. 2. Symbolism. I. Title.

Serpents (in religion, folk-lore, etc.)

LA BARRE, Weston, 1911- 289.9
They shall take up serpents; psychology of the southern snake-handling cult. New York, Schocken Books [1969] ix, 208 p. illus. 21 cm. Reprint of the 1962 ed., with a new introd. by the author. Bibliographical references included in "Notes" (p. 183-198) [BL441.L3 1969] 71-91547 2.45
1. Serpents (in religion, folk-lore, etc.) 2. Serpent worship—Southern States. 3. Psychology, Religious. I. Title.

LA Barre, Weston, 1911- 291.212
They shall take up serpents; psychology of the southern snake-handling cult. Minneapolis, University of Minnesota Press [1962] 208 p. illus. 23 cm. Includes bibliography. [BL441.L3 1962] 61-18819
1. Barefoot, Beauregard. 2. Serpents (in religion, folk-lore, etc.) 3. Serpent-worship. I. Title.

Serpents (in religion, Folk-lore, etc.)—Addresses, essays, lectures.

BUCHLER, Ira R. 291.2'12
The Rainbow Serpent : a chromatic piece / ed., Ira R. Buchler, Kenneth Maddock. The Hague : Mouton, 1978. x, 227 p. : with ill. ; 24 cm. (World Anthropology) "Distributed in the USA and Canada by Aldine, Chicago." Papers prepared by Ira R. Buchler, Kenneth Maddock and Charles P. Mountford for the 9th International Congress of Anthropological and Ethnological Sciences held in Chicago, 1973. Includes bibliographies and indexes. [BL441.B82] 79-307301 ISBN 0-202-90090-8 : 33.00
1. Serpents (in religion, Folk-lore, etc.)—Addresses, essays, lectures. 2. Mythology, Australian (Aboriginal)—Addresses, essays, lectures. I. Maddock, Kenneth, 1927- joint author. II. Mountford, Charles Pearcy, 1890-1977, joint author. III. International Congress of Anthropological and Ethnological Sciences, 9th, Chicago, 1973. IV. Title. V. Series.

Serpents in the Bible.

JOINES, Karen Randolph, 1938- 221.6'4
Serpent symbolism in the Old Testament: a linguistic, archaeological, and literary study. Haddonfield, N.J., Haddonfield House [1974] vii, 127 p. 21 cm. Includes bibliographical references. [BS1199.S37J64] 74-11359 ISBN 0-88366-005-9 25.00
1. Serpents in the Bible. 2. Serpents (in religion, folk-lore, etc.) I. Title.

Serra, Junipero, 1713-1784.

AINSWORTH, Katherine, 1908- 282'.0924 B
In the shade of the juniper tree; a life of Fray Junipero Serra [by] Katherine Ainsworth and Edward M. Ainsworth. With a pref. by Salvador Garcia. [1st ed.] Garden City, N.Y., Doubleday, 1970. xii, 199 p. 22 cm. Bibliography: p. [189]-190. [F864.S417] 76-98541 5.95
1. Serra, Junipero, 1713-1784. I. Ainsworth, Edward Maddin, 1902-1968, joint author. II. Title.

BOLTON, Ivy May, 1879- 922.2
Father Junipero Serra; illustrated by Robert Burns. New York, Messner 1952 160 p. illus. 22 cm. Bibliography: p. 156-157. [F864.S418] 52-9144
1. Serra, Junipero, 1713-1784.

BOWDEN, Dina Moore. 271',3'024 B
Junipero Serra in his native isle (1713-1749) / text, Dina Moore Bowden ; photos., Stefan Laszlo ; drawings, Xam. Palma [Majorca] : s.n., 1976. 170 p. : ill. ; 30 cm. Includes bibliographical references. [F864.S44B68] 77-372391 ISBN 8-440-01725-1
1. Serra, Junipero, 1713-1784. 2. Majorca—Church history. 3. Franciscans—Balearic Islands—Majorca—Biography. I. Laszlo, Stefan. II. Title.

CULLEN, Thomas Francis, 1877- 922.2
The spirit of Serra, by the Reverend Thomas F. Cullen; with an introduction by the Most Rev. Francis P. Keough ... New York, N. Y., Spiritual book associates [c1935] 202 p. front., plates, ports., facsim. 21 cm. "Published by the Franciscan missionaries of Mary ... North Providence, R. I."--p. [2] [F864.S43] 35-21228
1. Serra, Junipero, 1713-1784. 2. Missions—California. 3. Franciscans in California. I. Title.

ENGLEBERT, Omer, 1893- 922.2
The last of the conquistadors, Junipero Serra, 1713-1784. Translated from the French by Katherine Woods. [1st ed.] New York, Harcourt, Brace [1956] 368 p. illus. 25 cm. Includes bibliography. [F864.S442] 56-7917
1. Serra, Junipero, 1713-1784. I. Title.

ENGLEBERT, Omer, 1893- 282'.092'4 B
The last of the conquistadors, Junipero Serra, 1713-1784. Translated from the French by Katherine Woods. Westport, Conn., Greenwood Press [1974, c1956] ix, 368 p. illus. 23 cm. Reprint of the ed. published by Harcourt, Brace, New York. Bibliography: p. 355-359. [F864.S442 1974] 74-5924 ISBN 0-8371-7523-2
1. Serra, Junipero, 1713-1784. I. Title.

HABIG, Marion Alphonse, 1901- 922.246
Man of greatness; Father Junipero Serra, by Marion A. Habig and Francis Borgia Steck. Chicago, Franciscan Herald Press [1964] 172 p. illus., ports. 21 cm. Bibliography: p. 171-172. [F864.S464] 64-14251
1. Serra, Junipero, 1713-1784 I. Steck, Francis Borgia, 1884- joint author. II. Title.

KING, Kenneth Moffat. 922.2
Mission to paradise: the story of Junipero Serra and the missions of California. Chicago, Franciscan Herald Press [c1956] 190p. illus: 23cm. Includes bibliography. [F864] 57-3010
1. Serra, Junipero, 1713-1784. 2. Missions—California. I. Title.

LOTH, John H. 266.2794
Catholicism on the march, the California missions. New York, Vantage [c.1961] 93p. illus. Bibl. 61-66083 2.75 bds.,
1. Serra, Junipero, 1713-1784. 2. Missions—California. 3. Franciscans in California. 4. Indians of North America—California. I. Title.

PIRUS, Betty L. 266'.2'0924 B
Before I sleep / Betty L. Pirus. 1st ed. New York : Vantage Press, c1977. 206 p. ; 21 cm. Bibliography: p. 203-206. [F864.S535] 77-151737 ISBN 0-533-02580-X : 6.95
1. Serra, Junipero, 1713-1784. 2. Missions—California—History. 3. California—History—To 1846. 4. Franciscans—California—History. 5. Franciscans—California—Biography. I. Title.

SERRA, Junipero, 1713-1784. 266'.2
A letter of Junipero Serra to the reverend

father prencher Fray Fermin Francisco de Lasuen; a bicentennial discovery. Translated and edited by Francis J. Weber. Boston, D. R. Godine, 1970. [15] p. 23 cm. "Five hundred copies ... Copy number 369." Includes bibliographical references. [F864.S39713 1970] 71-107215
1. Serra, Junipero, 1713-1784. 2. Lasuen, Fermin Francisco de, 1736-1803. I. Lasuen, Fermin Francisco de, 1736-1803. II. Title.

SULLIVAN, Marion F. 282'.0924 B
Westward the bells [by] Marion F. Sullivan. [Staten Island, N.Y., Alba House, 1971] xvi, 220 p. illus. 22 cm. Bibliography: p. 211-215. [F864.S5425] 75-169139 ISBN 0-8189-0218-3 6.95
1. Serra, Junipero, 1713-1784. 2. Indians of North America—California—Missions. I. Title.

Serra, Junipero, 1713-1784—Juvenile literature.

MARTINI, Teri. 922.2
Sandals on the golden highway; a life of Junipero Serra. Illus. by Nino Carbe. Paterson, N. J., St. Anthony Guild Press [1959] 139p. illus. 24cm. [F864.S475] 59-13344
1. Serra, Junipero, 1713-1784—Juvenile literature. I. Title.

MARTINI, Teri. 922.2
Sandals on the golden highway; a life of Junipero Serra. Illus. by Nino Carbe. Paterson, N. J., St. Anthony Guild Press [1959] 139p. illus. 24cm. [F864.S475] 59-13344
1. Serra, Junipero, 1713-1784—Juvenile literature. I. Title.

REPPLIER, Agnes, 1855-1950 922.2
Junipero Serra, pioneer colonist of California, [by] Agnes Repplier. New York, All Saints Pr. [1962, c.1933] 184p. 17cm. (As.236) .50 pap.,
1. Serra, Junipero, Father, 1713-1784. 2. Missions—California. 3. Franciscans in California. 4. California—Hist.—To 1846. I. Title.

REPPLIER, Agnes, 1855-1950. 922.2
Junipero Serra, pioneer colonist of California [by] Agnes Repplier. Garden City, N. Y., Doubleday, Doran & co., inc., 1933. vi p. 2 l., 312 p. 22 cm. Maps on lining-papers; illustrated t.-p. "First edition." [F864.S54] 33-32578
1. Serra, Junipero, Father, 1713-1984. 2. Missions—California. 3. Franciscans in California. 4. California—Hist.—To 1846. I. Title.

REPPLIER, Agnes, 1858- 922.2
Junipero Serra, pioneer colonist of California [by] Agnes Repplier. Garden City, N.Y., Doubleday, Doran & co., inc., 1933. vi p., 2 l., 312 p. 21 1/2 cm. Maps on lining-papers: illustrated t.-p. "First edition." [F864.S54] 33-32578
1. Serra, Junipero, fray, 1713-1784. 2. Missions—California. 3. Franciscans in California. 4. California—hist.—To 1846. I. Title.

WOODGATE, Mildred 282.0924
Violet, 1904-
Junipera Serra, apostle of California, 1713-1784 by M. V. Woodgate. Westminster, Md., Newman [1966] 162p. illus. 27cm. Bibl. [F8.64.S546] 66-8807 3.95
1. Serra, Juniper, 1713-1784. I. Title.

Servant of Jehovah.

ASTON, Frederick Alfred. 224'.1
The challenge of the ages; new light on Isaiah 53. 21st ed., rev. Scarsdale, N.Y., Research Press, 1970 [c1963] 24 p. 24 cm. Includes bibliographical references. [BS1520.A87 1970] 74-99176
1. Bible. O.T. Isaiah LIII—Criticism, interpretation, etc. 2. Servant of Jehovah. I. Bible. O.T. Isaiah LIII. English. 1970. II. Title.

JEREMIAS, Joachim, 1900-
The servant of God [by] W. Zimmerli [and] J. Jeremias. Rev. ed. Naperville, Ill., A. R. Allenson, 1965. 126 p. 22 cm. (Studies in Biblical theology, no. 20) English translation of the article from Kittel's Theologisches Worterbuch zum NT. Includes bibliography. 67-75658
1. Servant of Jehovah. I. Jeremias, Jachim, 1900- II. Title. III. Series.

NORTH, Christopher Richard, 224.1
1888-
The suffering servant in Deutero-Isaiah; an historical and critical study. London, Oxford University Press, 1948. vii, 247 p. 23 cm. Errats slip inserted. Bibliography: p. [223]-235. [BS1515.N6] 50-2157
1. Servant of Jehovah. 2. Bible. O. T. Isaiah XL-LXVI—Criticism, interpretation, etc. I. Title.

NORTH, Christopher Richard, 224.1
1888-
The suffering servant in Deutero-Isaih : 2d ed. London, Oxford University Press, 1956. xi, 264p. 23cm. Bibliography: p. [240]-253. [BS1515.N6 1956] 56-59025
1. Servant of Jehovah. 2. Bible. O. T. Isaiah XL-LXVI—Criticism, interpretation, etc. I. Title.

NORTH, Christopher Richard, 224.1
1888-
The suffering servant in Deutero-Isainh; an historical and critical study. 2d ed. London, Oxford University Press, 1956. xi, 264p. 23cm. Bibliography: p. [240]-253. [BS1515.N6 1956] 56-59025
1. Servant of Jehovah. 2. Bible. D.T. Isaiah XI-LXVI—Criticism. interpretation, etc. I. Title.

SLABAUGH, Warren W 1879-1954. 232
The role of the Servant. Elgin, Ill., Brethren Pub. House [1954] 160p. 20cm. [BT205.S62] 54-43033
1. Servant of Jehovah. I. Title.

ZIMMERLI, Walther, 1907- 232.1
The servant of God [by] W. Zimmerli [and] J. Jeremias. Naperville, Ill., A. R. Allenson [1957] 120p. 22cm. (Studies in Biblical theology, no. 20) 'This English translation of the article from Kittel's Theologisches Worterbuch zum NT was drafted by Harold Knight and afterwards completed by the editorial staff of the publisher, with help both from Professor Jeremias and his assistants in Gottingen. First published in ... (Stuttgart 1952)' Bibliography: p. 105-107. [BT235.Z5] 57-21804
1. Servant of Jehovah. I. Jeremias, Joachim, 1900- II. Title. III. Series.

Servant of Jehovah—Addresses, essays, lectures.

LA SOR, William 221.8'95694
Sanford.
Israel : a Biblical view / by William Sanford La Sor. Grand Rapids, Mich. : Eerdmans, c1976. 108 p. ; 18 cm. [BS1199.S4L3] 75-46520 pbk. : 2.45
1. Bible—History of Biblical events—Addresses, essays, lectures. 2. Bible. O.T. Prophets—Criticism, interpretation, etc.—Addresses, essays, lectures. 3. Servant of Jehovah—Addresses, essays, lectures. 4. Church—Biblical teaching—Addresses, essays, lectures. I. Title.

Servants of Charity.

DAUGHTERS of Saint Mary 922.245
of Providence.
The pilgrim of love; a short popular sketch of the life of the servant of God, Father Aloysius Guanella, founder of the Servants of Charity and of the Daughters of Saint Mary of Divine Providence. [Chicago, 1952] 117p. illus. 22cm. [BX4705.G626D3] 53-18199
1. Guanella, Luigi, 1842-1915. 2. Servants of Charity. I. Title.

Servants of Relief for Incurable Cancer.

MARY Joseph, Sister, O.P. 271.972
Out of many hearts. Hawthorne, N.Y., Servants of Relief for Incurable Cancer [1965] 309p. illus., ports. 22cm. [BX4446.8.Z8M3] 65-3823 price unreported
1. Lathrop, Rose (Hawthorne) 1851-1926. 2. Servants of Relief for Incurable Cancer. I. Title.

Servetus, Michael, 1509 or 11-1553.

BAINTON, Roland H. 922.8146
Hunted heretic; the life and death of Michael Servetus, 1511-1553. With a new foreword by the author. Boston, Beacon Press [c.1953, 1960] xiv, 270p. illus. 21cm. (Beacon ser. in liberal religion, no. 2) 1.75 pap.,
1. Servetus, Michael, 1509 or 11-1553. I. Title.

BAINTON, Roland Herbert, 922.8146
1894-
Hunted heretic; the life and death of Michael Servetus, 1511-1553. Boston, Beacon Press [1953] 270 p. illus. 22 cm. [BX9869.S4B3] 53-10320
1. Servetus, Michael, 1509 or 11-1553. I. Title.

BAINTON, Ronald Herbert, 922.8146
1894-
Nunted heretic the life and death of Michael Servetus, 1511-1553. With a new foreword by the author. Boston, Beacon Press [1960] 270p. illus. 21cm. (Beacon series in liberal religion, LR2) Includes bibliography. [BX9869.S4B3 1960] 60-16079
1. Servetus, Michael, 1509 or 11-1553. I. Title.

FULTON, John Farquhar, 922.8146
1899-
Michael Servetus, humanist and martyr; with a bibliography of his works and census of known copies, by Madeline E. Stanton. New York, H. Reichner, 1953 [c1954] 98p. port., map, facsims. 23cm. (Historical Library, Yale Medical Library, and Dept. of the History of Medicine, Yale University. Publication no. 22) 'Selected source materials':p.98-95. [BX9869.S4F8] 54-14685
1. Servetus, Michael, 1509 or 11-1553. I. Stanton, Madeline Earle II. Title. III. Series: Yale University. School of mEdicine. Dept. of the History of Medicine. Publication no. 22

ODHNER, Carl Theophilus, 922.
1863-
Michael Servetus, his life and teachings, by Carl Theophilus Odhner ... Philadelphia, Press of J. B. Lippincott company, 1910. v. 94, [2] p. 2 port. (incl. front.) 19 1/2 cm. [BX9869.S4O3] 11-2096
1. Servetus, Michael, 1509 or 11-1553. I. Title.

Service books (Music)—Catholic Church.

FISKE, William O comp.
The offertorium: a complete collection of music for the Sunday and holy day services of the Catholic church... by William O. Fiske. Boston, O. Ditson [1872] 247 p. 22 x 28 cm. [M2012.F4904] 68-125021
1. Service books (Music)—Catholic Church. I. Title.

Service, Christian,

BOYD, Nelson.
What makes service Christian? New York, Friendship Press [1967] 63 p. 15 cm. (Questions for Christians, no. 10) 68-88499
1. Service, Christian, I. Title. II. Series.

GILBERT, Richard Henry, 1855- 248
The spirit of service, by Richard H Gilbert, D. D. Boston, The Gorham press, 1918. 2 p. l., 3-119 p. 20 cm. (Lettered on cover: Library of religious thought) [BV4501.G5] 18-18978 1.00
I. Title.

HOUTZ, Alfred, 1844-
The Master's call to service, by Rev. A. Houtz... Philadelphia, Reformed church publication board, 1910. 135 p. 20 cm. $0.60 10-11862
I. Title.

LAWRENCE, John Benjamin, 1873-
Power for service, by Rev. J. Benj. Lawrence, introduction by Rev. B. H. Carroll ... New Orleans, La., C. O. Chalmers, 1909. xiv, 261 p. 19 cm. 9-16147
I. Title.

LILYERS, Jean 268.7
Sing of Christmas, a Christmas service for church school. Rock Island, Ill., Augustana Press [c.1960] 16p. illus., diagrs. 21cm. .10 pap.,
I. Title.

*PAETKAU, Walter 258
Start where you are: a guide to local Christian service. Drawings by Esther Groves. Newton, Kan., Faith & Life [1966, c.1965] 73p. illus. 21cm. 1.00 pap.,
I. Title.

PRESCOTT, Edmund E.
The new midweek service, by Edmund E. Prescott. Nashville, Tenn., Cokesbury press, 1929. 119 p. 20 cm. Bibliography: p. 119. [BX8336.P7] 29-2964
I. Title.

PURVES, George Tybout, 1852-
1901.
Joy in service. Forgetting, and pressing onward. Until the day day dawn. [By] Rev. George T. Purves ... The teacher and pastor. [By] Prest. F. L. Patton ... New York, American tract society [1901] 96 p. front. (port.) 20 cm. 2-753
I. Patton, Francis Landey, 1843-1932. II. Title.

[REID, William Thomas] 1843-
comp.
Belmont school chapel service. [Boston, Stanhope press, F. H. Gilson company, c1905] 3 p. l., 171 p. 21 cm. 5-29969
I. Title.

Service industries—Management.

FITZSIMMONS, James A. 658.5
Service operations management / James A. Fitzsimmons, Robert S. Sullivan. New York : McGraw-Hill, c1982. xiv, 449 p. : ill. ; 25 cm. (McGraw-Hill series in quantitative methods for management) Includes bibliographies and index. [HD9980.5.F55] 19 81-13680 ISBN 0-07-021215-5 : 25.00
1. Service industries—Management. 2. Operations research. I. Sullivan, Robert S. II. Title. III. Series.

JOSEPH, William. 658
Professional service management / William Joseph. New York : McGraw-Hill, c1983. p. cm. Includes index. [HD9980.5.J67] 19 82-6563 ISBN 0-07-039267-6 : 24.95
1. Service industries—Management. I. Title.

Service (Theology)

JEWS. Liturgy and ritual. 296.4'3
High Holy Day prayers.
A contemporary High Holiday service for teenagers and ... [by] Sidney Greenberg and S. Allan Sugarman. Hartford, Conn., Prayer Book Press [1970] 1 v. (loose-leaf) illus. 30 cm. On cover: Mahazor le-Rosh ha-shanah ule-Yom ha-ki-purim (romanized form) Hebrew and English. [BM666.G658] 74-123891 ISBN 8-7677-0405-
I. Greenberg, Sidney, 1917- II. Sugarman, S. Allan. III. Jews. Liturgy and ritual. High Holy Day prayers. English. IV. Jews. Liturgy and ritual. Children's services. V. Title.

SCHULTEJANN, Marie. 361.7'5
Ministry of service : a manual for social involvement / by Marie Schultejann. New York : Paulist Press, c1976. 113 p. ; 19 cm. Bibliography: p. 102-113. [BT738.4.S34] 76-16901 ISBN 0-8091-1967-6 pbk. : 1.95
1. Service (Theology) 2. Social service. I. Title.

SWINDOLL, Charles R. 248.4
Improving your serve : the art of unselfish living / Charles R. Swindoll. Waco, Tex. : Word Books, c1981. 219 p. ; 23 cm. Includes bibliographical references. [BT738.4.S94] 19 80-54553 ISBN 0-8499-0267-3 : 8.95
1. Service (Theology) I. Title.

WASHBURN, Henry 261.8'3'0922
Bradford, 1869-1962.
The religious motive in philanthropy: studies in biography. Freeport, N.Y., Books for Libraries Press [1970, c1931] 172 p. 23 cm. (Essay index reprint series)

Contents.Contents.—Introduction.—Samuel Barnett.—Vincent de Paul.—Francis of Assisi.—Jesus of Nazareth. [BT738.4.W36 1970] 72-105047 ISBN 8-369-16344-
1. Service (Theology) 2. Christian biography. I. Title.

Service (Theology)—Case studies.

AFFLECK, Afton Grant. 248'.48'933
Love is the gift / Afton Grant Affleck. Salt Lake City : Bookcraft, c1977. x, 149 p. ; 24 cm. [BT738.4.A35] 77-75305 ISBN 0-88494-316-X pbk. : 3.95
1. Service (Theology)—Case studies. 2. Christian life—Mormon authors—Case studies. I. Title.

Service (Theology)—Study and teaching.

BELL, Arthur Donald. 268'.8'6
In Christian love [by] A. Donald Bell. Nashville, Convention Press [1968] x, 128 p. illus. 19 cm. "Church study course [of the Sunday School Board of the Southern Baptist Convention] This book is number 0474 in category 4, section for adults and young people." Includes bibliographical references. [BX6225.B48] 68-11671
1. Service (Theology)—Study and teaching. 2. Religious education—Text-books for adults—Baptist. 3. Religious education—Text-books for young people—Baptist. I. Southern Baptist Convention. Sunday School Board. II. Title.

MEIBURG, Albert L. 268'.61
Called to minister [by] Albert L. Meiburg. Nashville, Convention Press [1968] ix, 111 p. 19 cm. "Church study course [of the Sunday School Board of the Southern Baptist Convention] This book is number 0411 in category 4, section for adults and young people." Includes bibliographical references. [BX6225.M42] 68-11670
1. Service (Theology)—Study and teaching. 2. Religious education—Text-books for adults—Baptist. 3. Religious education—Text-books for young people—Baptist. I. Southern Baptist Convention. Sunday School Board. II. Title.

Services, responsive.

READINGS for the celebration of life; selections for the use of free congregations. Boston, Meeting House Press, 1957. 164p. 22cm.
1. Services, responsive. I. Patton, Kenneth Leo, 1911-

Servites—History

VOSBURGH, Joseph Mary, 1892- 271.79
The vine of seven branches; a history of the Order of Servants of Mary, 1233-1955. Chicago, Stabat Mater Press [1955] 221p. 21cm. [BX4040.S5V6] 57-20295
1. Servites—Hist. I. Title.

Seton, Elizabeth Ann, Mother, 1774-1821.

BOYLE, Mary Electa, sister. 271.97
Mother Seton's Sisters of charity in western Pennsylvania [by] Sister Mary Electa Boyle. [Greensburg, Pa.] 1946. 1 p. l., x, 251 p. front., plates, ports., facsims. 23 1/2 cm. Bibliographical foot-notes. [BX4470.G65B6] 46-19981
1. Seton, Elizabeth Ann, mother, 1774-1821. 2. Sisters of charity of Mother Seton, Greensburg, Pa. I. Title.

BURTON, Katherine (Kurz) Mrs. 1890- 922.273
It is dear persuasion; the life of Elizabeth Ann Seton, by Katherine Burton... London, New York [etc.] Longmans, Green and co., 1940. xi, 304 p. 21 1/2 cm. "First edition." Bibliography: p. 303-304. [BX4705.S57B8 1940] 40-27305
1. Seton, Elizabeth Ann, mother, 1774-1821. 2. Sisters of charity of St. Vincent de Paul. I. Title.

CUSHING, Richard James, Cardinal, 1895- 922.273
Blessed Mother Seton. [Boston] St. Paul Eds. [dist. Daughters of St. Paul, c.1963] 96, [61]p. illus. 22cm. 63-16333 3.00; 2.00 pap.,
1. Seton, Elizabeth Ann, 1774-1821. I. Seton, Elizabeth Ann, 1774-1821. II. Title.

CUSHING, Richard James, Cardinal, 1895- 922.273
Blessed Mother Seton. [Boston] St. Paul Editions [1963] 96, [61] p. illus. 22 cm. "Spiritual gems, written by Blessed Elizabeth Ann Seton": p. [55]-[97] "Pictorial biography of Blessed Mother Seton": p. [99]-[155] [BX4700.S4C8] 63-16333
1. Seton, Elizabeth Ann, 1774-1821. I. Seton, Elizabeth Ann, 1774-1821. II. Title.

DIRVIN, Joseph I. 922.273
Mrs. Seton, foundress of the American Sisters of Charity. New York, Farrar [c.1962] 498p. illus. 22cm. Bibl. 62-10503 6.95 bds.,
1. Seton, Elizabeth Ann, 1774-1821. 2. Sisters of Charity of St. Vincent de Paul. I. Title.

DIRVIN, Joseph I. 922.273
Mrs. Seton. Foreword by Francis Cardinal Spellman. Preface by Amleto Cardinal Cicognani [New York] Avon [1964, c.1962] 544p. 19cm. (N109) .95 pap.,
1. Seton, Elizabeth Ann; 1774-1821. 2. Sisters of Charity of St. Vincent de Paul. I. Title.

DIRVIN, Joseph I. 271'.91'024 B
Mrs. Seton, foundress of the American Sisters of Charity / Joseph I. Dirvin. New canonization ed. New York : Farrar, Straus and Giroux, 1975. xix, 498 p., [8] leaves of plates : ill. ; 21 cm. Includes index. Bibliography: p. [465]-469. [BX4705.S57D5 1975] 75-321767 ISBN 0-374-51255-8 : 4.95
1. Seton, Elizabeth Ann, 1774-1821. 2. Sisters of Charity of St. Vincent de Paul. I. Title.

DIRVIN, Joseph I. 922.273
Mrs. Seton, foundress of the American Sisters of Charity. New York, Farrar, Straus and Giroux, 1962 498 p. illus. 22 cm. Includes bibliography. [BX4705.S57D5] 62-10503
1. Seton, Elizabeth Ann, 1774-1821. 2. Sisters of Charity of St. Vincent de Paul.

ELIZABETH Seton's two Bibles, her notes and markings / compiled and edited by Ellin M. Kelly. Huntington, Ind. : Our Sunday Visitor, c1977. 184 p. : ill. ; 21 cm. Includes bibliographical references and indexes. [BX4700.S4E43] 77-80539 ISBN 0-87973-741-7 pbk. : 3.95 271'.91'024 B
1. Seton, Elizabeth Ann, Saint, 1774-1821. 2. Bible—Influence. 3. Christian saints—United States—Biography. I. Seton, Elizabeth Ann, Saint, 1774-1821. II. Kelly, Ellin M. III. Bible. English. Douai. Selections. 1805.

*FEENEY, Leonard, 1897- 282'092'4 B
Elizabeth Seton: an American woman Huntington, In., Our Sunday Visitor [1975] 304 p. frontis. 18 cm. [BX4705.S] 75-21599 ISBN 0-87973-861-8 3.50 (pbk.)
1. Seton, Elizabeth Ann, 1774-1821. I. Title.

FEENEY, Leonard, 1897- 922.273
Elizabeth Seton, an American woman, her story by Leonard Feeney, S.J. New York, America press, 1938. 3 p. l., 272 p. front., ports. 19 1/2 cm. [BX4705.S57F4] 38-25911
1. Seton, Elizabeth Ann, mother, 1774-1821. 2. Sisters of charity of St. Vincent de Paul. I. Title.

FEENEY, Leonard, 1897- 282'.092'4 B
Mother Seton : Saint Elizabeth of New York (1774-1821) / Leonard Feeney. Rev. ed. Cambridge [Mass.] : Ravengate Press, [1975] p. cm. [BX4705.S57F4 1975] 75-23224 ISBN 0-911218-06-8 pbk. : 2.95
1. Seton, Elizabeth Ann, 1774-1821. I. Title.

FEENEY, Leonard, 1897- 922.273
Mother Seton, an American woman. New York, Dodd, Mead, 1947. vi 212 p. ports. 21 cm. Previously pub. under title: Elizabeth Seton, an American woman. [BX4705.S57F4 1947] 47-11485
1. Seton, Elizabeth Ann, Mother, 1774-1821. 2. Sisters of Charity of St. Vincent de Paul. I. Title.

FULLER, Margaret Mary, 1883- 922.273
Mother Seton's favorite devotions, by a sister of charity, Mt. St. Vincent-on-Hudson, New York city. New York, P. J. Kenedy & sons, 1940. 2 p. l., 48 p. front. (port.) 15 cm. [Name in religion: Mary, sister] [BX4705.S857F8] 41-3524
1. Seton, Elizabeth Ann, mother, 1774-1821. I. Title.

GLASS, Fides, sister, 1889- 922.273
The Seton ballad, a true story in verse and pictures of Mother Elizabeth Seton, by Sister M. Fides Glass ... Greensburg, Pa. [Mother Seton guild, Seton Hill unit, 1941] vii, 61 p. col. front., illus. 28 cm. [Secular name: Regina Marie Glass] [BX4705.S57G6] 45-86
1. Seton, Elizabeth Ann, mother, 1774-1821. I. Title.

HOARE, Mary Regis, sister. 922.273
Virgin soil; Mother Seton from a different point of view, by Sister Mary Regis Hoare... Boston, The Christopher publishing house [1942] xii, [2], 15-176 p. incl. general. tables, diagr. plates, 2 port. (incl. front.) 20 cm. Bibliography: p. 104-106. [BX4705.S57H6] 42-16426
1. Seton, Elizabeth Ann, mother, 1774-1821. I. Title.

KELLY, Ellin M. 271'.91'024 B
Numerous choirs : a chronicle of Elizabeth Bayley Seton and her spiritual daughters / compiled and edited by Ellin M. Kelly. Evansville, Ind. : Mater Dei Provincialate, c1981- v. <1 > : ill. ; 23 cm. Contents.Contents.—v. 1. The Seton years, 1774-1821. Includes bibliographical references and index. [BX4700.S4K44] 19 81-80304 ISBN 0-9605784-0-4 (vol. 1) : 15.00
1. Seton, Elizabeth Ann, Saint, 1774-1821. 2. Daughters of Charity of St. Vincent de Paul. Emmitsburg Province. I. Title.
Publisher's address: 9400 New Harmony Rd., Evansville, IN 47712

LAVERTY, Rose Maria. 922.273
Loom of many threads; the English and French influences on the character of Elizabeth Ann Bayley Seton. New York, Paulist Press [c1958] 258p. illus. 22cm. Includes bibliography. [BX4705.S57L3] 59-7577
1. Seton, Elizabeth Ann, 1774-1821. I. Title.

[MCCANN, Mary Agnes, sister] 1851- 922.273
Mother Seton, foundress of the Sisters of charity. Mount St. Joseph-on-the-Ohio, Sisters of charity, 1909. 3 p. l., 5-74 p., 1 l. front., plates, ports. 21 1/2 cm. [BX4705.S57M2] 10-2991
1. Seton, Elizabeth Ann, mother, 1774-1821. 2. Sisters of charity of St. Vincent de Paul. I. Title.

MELVILLE, Annabelle (McConnell) 1910- 922.273
Elizabeth Bayley Seton, 1774-1821. New York, Scribner [c1960] 411p. illus. 22cm. Includes bibliography. [BX4705.S57M4 1960] 61-3468
1. Seton, Elizabeth Ann, 1774-1821. 2. Sisters of Charity of St. Vincent de Paul. I. Title.

MELVILLE, Annabelle McConnell, 1910- 271'.91'024 B
Elizabeth Bayley Seton, 1774-1821 / by Annabelle M. Melville. New York : Scribner, [1976] c1951. xix, 411 p., [4] leaves of plates : ill. ; 22 cm. "Hudson River editions." Includes index. Bibliography: p. 383-391. [BX4700.S4M44 1976] 76-8053 ISBN 0-684-14735-1 lib.bdg. : 12.50
1. Seton, Elizabeth Ann, Saint, 1774-1821. 2. Christian saints—United States—Biography.

MELVILLE, Annabelle (McConnell) 1910- 922.273
Elizabeth Bayley Seton, 1774-1821 New York, Scribner, 1951. xvii, 411 p. illus. ports. 22 cm. Bibliography: p. 383-391. [BX4705.S57M4] 51-14503
1. Seton, Elizabeth Ann, Mother, 1774-1821. 2. Sisters of Charity of St. Vincent de Paul. I. Title.

POWER-WATERS, Alma (Shelley), 1896- 922.273
Mother Seton First American-born saint Revised edition. New York : Pocket Books [1976 c1957] viii, 182 p. : 18 cm. (Archway Paperback) Originally published under the title: Mother Seton and the Sisters of Charity. [BX4705.S57P67] ISBN 0-671-29785-6 pbk. : 1.25
1. Seton, Elizabeth Ann, 1774-1821 2. Sisters of Charity of St. Vincent de Paul. I. Title.
L.C. card no. for 1957 Vision Books edition: 57-7699.

POWER-WATERS, Alma (Shelley) 1896- 922.273
Mother Seton and the Sisters of Charity. Illustrated by John Lawn. New York, Vision Books [1957] 190p. illus. 22cm. (Vision books, 24) [BX4705.S57P67] 57-7699
1. Seton, Elizabeth Ann, 1774-1821. 2. Sisters of Charity of St. Vincent de Paul. I. Title.

SADLIER, Agnes, 1860- 922
Elizabeth Seton, foundress of the American Sisters of charity, her life and work, by Agnes Sadlier ... New York, D. and J. Sadlier & co. [1905] 2 p. l., [iii]-iv p., 1 l., 289 p. front., plates, ports. 18 1/2 cm. [BX4705.S57S3] 5-16606
1. Seton, Mother Elizabeth Ann, 1774-1821. I. Title.

SADLIER, Agnes, 1860- 922
Elizabeth Seton, foundress of the American Sisters of charity, her life and work, by Agnes Sadlier ... New York, D. and J. Sadlier & co. [1905] 2 p. l., [iii]-iv p., 1 l., 289 p. front., plates, ports. 18 1/2 cm. [BX4705.S57S3] 5-16606
1. Seton, Mother Elizabeth Ann, 1774-1821. I. Title.

WHITE, Charles Ignatius, 1807-1877. 922
Life of Mrs. Eliza A. Seton, foundress and first superior of the Sisters or daughters of charity in the United States of America; with copious extracts from her writings, and an historical sketch of the sisterhood from its foundation to the time of her death. By Charles I. White, D.D., to which is added an appendix containing a summary of the history of the Sisters of charity to the year 1879 ... 3d ed. Baltimore, Kelly, Piet and company, 1879. 504 p. front. (port.) plates. 19 1/2 cm. [BX4705.S57W5 1879] 12-40223
1. Seton, Mother Elizabeth Ann, 1774-1821. 2. Sisters of charity of St. Vincent de Paul. I. Title.

WHITE, Charles Ignatius, 1807-1877. 922
Life of Mrs. Eliza A. Seton, foundress and first superior of the Sisters or daughters of charity in the United States of America; with copious extracts from her writings, and an historical sketch of the sisterhood from its foundation to the time of her death. By Charles I. White, D.D., to which is added an appendix containing a summary of the history of the Sisters of charity to the year 1879 ... 3d ed. Baltimore, Kelly, Piet and company, 1879. 504 p. front. (port.) plates. 19 1/2 cm. [BX4705.S57W5 1879] 12-40223
1. Seton, Mother Elizabeth Ann, 1774-1821. 2. Sisters of charity of St. Vincent de Paul. I. Title.

WHITE, Charles Ignatius, 1807-1878. 922.273
Life of Mrs. Eliza A. Seton, foundress and first superior of the Sisters or daughters of charity in the United States of America; with copious extracts from her writings, and an historical sketch of the sisterhood from its foundation to the present time. By Rev. Charles L. White ... New-York, E. Dunigan and brother, 1853. 3 p. l., [3]-581 p. front. (port.) 19 cm. [BX4705.S57W5 1853] 37-18477
1. Seton, Elizabeth Ann, mother, 1774-1821. 2. Sisters of charity of St. Vincent de Paul. I. Title.

WHITE, Charles Ignatius, 1807-1878. 922.273
Life of Mrs. Eliza A. Seton, foundress and first superior of the Sisters or Daughters of charity in the United States of America; with copious extracts from her writings, and an historical sketch of the sisterhood from its foundation to the time of her death. By Charles I. White, D.D. 2d rev. ed. Baltimore, J. Murphy & co; London, C. Dolman, 1856. 462 p. front. (port.) 20 cm. [BX4705.S57W5 1856] 37-18478
1. Seton, Elizabeth Ann, mother, 1774-1821. 2. Sisters of charity of St. Vincent de Paul. I. Title.

WHITE, Charles Ignatius, 1807-1878. 922.273
Mother Seton, mother of many daughters; revised and edited by the Sisters of Charity of Mount St. Vincent-on-Hudson, New York. Foreword by Amleto Giovanni Cicognani, introd. by Salvator M. Burgio. New York, Doubleday, 1949. xx, 300 p. 21 cm. First published in 1853 under title: Life of Mrs. Eliza A. Seton. [BX4705.S57W5 1949] 49-11731
1. Seton, Elizabeth Ann, Mother, 1774-1821. 2. Sisters of Charity of St. Vincent de Paul. I. Title.

Seton, Elizabeth Ann, Mother, 1774-1821-Juvenile literature.

†HINDMAN, Jane F. 271'.91'024 B
Elizabeth Ann Seton, mother, teacher, saint for our time / by Jane F. Hindman. New York : Arena Lettres, c1976. vii, 82, [1] p. ; 18 cm. Bibliography: p. [83] A brief biography of the Catholic convert who founded a religious order and the first parochial school in the United States. She was proclaimed a saint in 1975. [BX4700.S4H56] 92 76-15327 pbk. : 1.50
1. Seton, Elizabeth Ann, Saint, 1774-1821—Juvenile literature. 2. [Seton, Elizabeth Ann, Saint, 1774-1821.] 3. Christian saints—United States—Biography—Juvenile literature. 4. [Saints.] I. Title.

POWER-WATERS, Alma (Shelley) 1896- 920
Mother Seton and the Sisters of Charity. Condensed for very young readers from the original Vision book. Illus. by W. T. Mars. New York, Guild [dist. Golden c.1957, 1963] 76p. illus. (pt. col.) 24cm. (Jr. Vision bk.) 63-22935 2.50 bds.,
1. Seton, Elizabeth Ann, 1774-1821—Juvenile literature. 2. Sisters of Charity of St. Vincent de Paul—Juvenile literature. I. Title.

POWER-WATERS, Alma (Shelley) 1896- 92
Mother Seton and the Sisters of Charity, by Alma Power-Waters. Condensed for very young readers from the original Vision book. Illustrated by W.T. Mars. New York, Guild Press [1963] 76 p. illus. (part col.) 24 cm. (A Junior Vision book) [BX4700.S4P6] 63-22935
1. Seton, Elizabeth Ann, 1774-1821—Juvenile literature. 2. Sisters of Charity of St. Vincent de Paul—Juvenile literature. I. Title.

ROBERTO, Brother, 1927- 922.273
Please bring the children; a story of Mother Elizabeth Seton. Illus. by Carolyn Lee Jagodits. Notre Dame, Ind., Dujarie Press [1959] 94p. illus. 24cm. [BX4705.S57R6] 59-3312
1. Seton, Elizabeth Ann, 1774-1821—Juvenile literature. I. Title.

Settle, Glenn Tom.

[TOWNSEND, Leroy Clifford] 1900- 784.756
"Thunder an' lightnin' britches", the astounding truth about "Wings over Jordan" by Ommo Aummen [pseud.] St. Petersburg, Fla., Blue peninsula sanctuary [1942] [74] p. front., pl., ports. 18 1/2 cm. The story of the "Wings over Jordan" choir and its originator, Reverend Glenn T. Settle. [ML3556.T69T4] 43-2210
1. Settle, Glenn Tom. 2. "Wings over Jordan" (Choir) I. St. Petersburg, Fla. Blue peninsula sanctuary. II. Title.

Seung Sahn.

SEUNG Sahn. 294.3'927'08
Dropping ashes on the Buddha : the teaching of Zen master Seung Sahn / compiled and edited by Stephen Mitchell. 1st Evergreen ed. New York : Grove Press : distributed by Random House, 1976. xii, 232 p. ; 21 cm. (An Evergreen book) [BQ9266.S48] 75-37236 ISBN 0-8021-4015-7 : 4.95
1. Seung Sahn. 2. Zen Buddhism—Addresses, essays, lectures. I. Title.

Seven churches.

STRAUSS, Lehman. 226'.806
Prophetic mysteries revealed : the prophetic significance of the Parables of Matthew 13 and the Letters of Revelation 2-3 / by Lehman Strauss. 1st ed. Neptune, N.J. : Loizeau Brothers, 1980. 255 p. ; 20 cm. Includes index. Bibliography: p. 243-245. [BT375.2.S75] 19 80-17540 ISBN 0-87213-832-1 : 7.25
1. Jesus Christ—Parables. 2. Bible. N.T. Matthew XIII—Prophecies. 3. Bible. N.T. Revelation II-III—Prophecies. 4. Seven churches. I. Title.

WARD, Harold B. 275.61
The seven golden candlesticks, by Harold B. Ward. New York, Carlton Press [1972] 123 p. 21 cm. (A Hearthstone book) [BR185.W37] 72-172300 3.75
1. The seven churches. I. Title.

The seven churches—Sermons.

JONES, George Curtis, 1911- 261.1
Candles in the city [by] G. Curtis Jones. Waco, Tex., Word Books [1973?] 92, [1] p. 22 cm. Bibliography: p. [93] [BS2825.4.J66] 72-96356 3.50
1. Disciples of Christ—Sermons. 2. The seven churches—Sermons. 3. Sermons, American. 4. City churches. I. Title.

RICHARDS, Edward H. 228'.06
The Revelation letters : expository sermons on the Seven Churches / by E. H. Richards. Nashville, Tenn. : Eric Publishers, c1975. x, 188 p. ; 23 cm. Bibliography: p. 187-188. [BS2825.4.R5] 75-330251 5.95
1. The seven churches—Sermons. 2. Baptists—Sermons. 3. Sermons, American. I. Title.

Seven gods of fortune.

CHIBA, Reiko 291.211
The seven lucky gods of Japan. Rutland, Vt., Tuttle [1965, c.1966] 42p. (on double leaves) illus. 17cm. [BL2211.S36C5] 65-25467 2.95
1. Seven gods of fortune. I. Title.

Seven (The number)

ROYSE, Pleasant E.
The great importance of the Sabbatic number seven as connected with the characters, actions and events of the Bible. By Rev. P. E. Royse ... With an epitomy [!] of the annotations, and a brief outline of the seven ages of the great Christian church. To which is added an instructive appendix for the interpretation of events of the Bible, with emblems, types, and antitypes, in wonderful periods of seven. By Arthur Ferris, B. D. [Helena, Mont., Williams, Thurber & co.] 1890. 149 p., 1 l., 83 p. 23 cm. Lettered on cover: The mystic number seven; a pastoral poem. Appendix has separate paging and special t.-p.: The trumpet. Computation of time by chronological topics, showing that the coming of the Messiah is at hand. By Arthur Ferris. Fargo, N. D., The Fargo stationery and publish'g co., 1889. [PS2736.R33G8 1890] 30-7580
1. Seven (The number) 2. Second advent. I. Bible—History of Biblical events—Poetry. II. Ferris, Arthur. III. Title. IV. Title: Sabbatic number seven. V. Title: The trumpet.

Seventh-day Adventists.

ANDROSS, Matilda (Erickson) Mrs. 1880-
Story of the advent message, prepared for the Young people's missionary volunteer department of the General conference of Seventh-day Aventists, by Matilda Erickson Andross. Washington, D.C., South Bend, Ind. [etc.] Review and herald publishing association [c1926] 352 p. incl. front., illus. 20 cm. [BX6115.A7] 26-5711
1. Seventh-day Adventists. I. Seventy-day Adventists. General conference. II. Title.

ASOCIACION General de la Iglesia Adventista del Septimo Dia. 286.7
Manual de la iglesia. Mountain View, Calif., Publicaciones Interamericanas, Pacific Pr. [c.]1963. 317p. 17cm. 3.00
I. Title.

BAKER, Alonzo Lafayette, 1894- 286.7
Belief and work of Seventh-day Adventists, by Alonzo L. Baker. Mountain View, Calif., Brookfield, Ill. [etc.] Pacific press publishing association, c1942. 93 p. incl. front., illus. 19 cm. [BX6154.B3] 44-3762
1. Seventh-day Adventists. I. Title.

BATES, Joseph, 1792-1872. 922.673
The early life and later experience and labors of Elder Joseph Bates, ed. by Elder James White. Battle Creek, Mich., press of the Seventh-day Adventist publishing association, 1877. xvi, 17-320 p. front. (port.) 1 illus. 18 cm. "The body of the work is reprint of the Autobiography ..."--Editor's pref. [BX6193.B3.A3 1877] 36-25156
1. Seventh-day Adventists. I. White, James, 1821-1881, ed. II. Title.

BATES, Joseph, 1792-1872. 922.
The early life and later experience and labors of Elder Joseph Bates, ed. by Elder James White. Battle Creek, Mich., Steam press of the Seventh-day adventist publishing asociation, 1878. 820 p. front. (port.) 19 cm. "The body of this work is a reprint of the Autobiography."--Editor's pref. [BX6196.B3A3] 22-578
1. Seventh-day Adventists. I. White, James, 1821-1881, ed. II. Title.

BATES, Joseph, 1792-1872. 922.
The early life and later experience and labors of Elder Joseph Bates, ed. by Elder James White. Battle Creek, Mich, Steam press of the Seventh-day adventist publishing association, 1878. 820 p. front. (port.) 19 cm. "The body of this work is a reprint of the Autobiography,"--Editor's pref. [BX6196.B3A3] 22-578
1. Seventh-day adventists. I. White, James, 1821-1881, ed. II. Title.

CAMPBELL, George A 286.7
Mary Kennedy's victory. Mountain View, Calif., Pacific Press Pub. Association [1953] 95p. illus. 19cm. [BX6154.C25 1953] 53-11217
1. Seventh-Day Adventists. I. Title.

CAMPBELL, George A. 286.7
Mary Kennedy's victory, a composite story, by G. A. Campbell. Mountain View, Calif., Omaha, Neb. [etc.] Pacific press publishing association [c1931] 92 p. 19 1/2 cm. [BX6154.C25] 31-23316
1. Seventh-day Adventists. I. Title.

CANRIGHT, Dudley M 1840?-
The Lord's day, from neither Catholics nor pagans; an answer to Seventh-day adventism on this subject, by Rev. D.M. Canright... New York, Chicago etc. Fleming H. Revell company c1915 1 p. l., 13-260 p. front. (port.) 19 1/2 cm. p $1.00 16-1704
I. Title. II. Title: An answer to Seventh-day adventism.

DAMSTEEGT, P. Gerard. 286.7'3
Foundations of the Seventh-Day Adventist message and mission / by P. Gerard Damsteegt. Grand Rapids : Eerdmans, c1977. xv, 348 p. : ill. ; 23 cm. Includes indexes. Bibliography: p. 314-334. [BX6121.D35] 76-56799 7.95
1. Seventh-Day Adventists. I. Title.

DANIELLS, Arthur Grosvenor, 1858-1935. 286.7
The abiding gift of prophecy, by Arthur Grosvenor Daniells. Mountain View, Calif., Omaha, Neb. [etc.] Pacific press publishing association [c1936] 378 p. front. (port.) 21 cm. [BX6154.D29] 36-7156
1. Seventh-day Adventists. 2. Bible—Prophecies. I. Title. II. Title: Prophecy, The abiding gift of.

DOWARD, Jan S. 242'.6'3
Catch the bright dawn : the redemption story Genesis to Revelation / Jan Doward ; [editor, Bobbie Jane Van Dolson]. Washington : Review and Herald Pub. Association, c1978. 378 p. ; 21 cm. "This book is published in collaboration with the Youth Department as an enrichment of the Morning watch devotional plan." Offers devotional passages to be read day by day. [BV4850.D68] 78-5081 pbk. : 4.50
1. Seventh-Day Adventists.. 2. Youth—Prayer-books and devotions—English. 3. Devotional calendars—Seventh-Day Adventists—Juvenile literature. 4. [Prayer books and devotions.] I. Van Dolson, Bobbie Jane. II. Title.

DUFFIE, Malcolm B.
"Those tent meetings": a rhyming recital, founded on actual facts and every-day experiences. By M. B. Duffie ... Battle Creek, Mich., 1889. 88 p. incl. illus., plates. 17 x 14 cm. [PS1555.D3] 26-23653
1. Seventh-day Adventists. I. Title.

A Guide to better living; 286.7
ways to health and happiness. Nashville, Southern Pub. Assn., c1949. 101 p. illus.(part col.) 30 cm. [BX6154.G8] 49-1384
1. Seventh-Day Adventists.

HANLEY, May Carr. Mrs. 286.7
Pastor La Rue, the pioneer, by May Carr Hanley and Ruth Wheeler.. Takoma Park, Washington, D. C., Peekskill, N. Y. [etc.] Review and herald publishing association [c1937] 190 p. incl. front., illus. plates, ports., facsim. 21 cm. [BX6193.L3H3] 37-25294
1. La Rue, Abram, 1822-1903. 2. Seventh-day Adventists. I. Wheeler, Mrs. Ruth (Carr) 1899- joint author. II. Title.

HOUTEFF, Victor T. 286.7
...The shepherd's rod, the 144,000 of Revelation 7--call for reformation, by V. T. Houteff... Los Angeles, Calif., Universal publishing association [c1931- v. diagrs. (1 fold.) 19 1/2 cm. [BX6154.H6] 31-5041
1. Seventh-day Adventists. I. Title.

HOWELL, Emma Elizabeth, 1895- 286.7
The great Advent movement, by Emma E. Howell ... Takoma Park, Washington, D.C., Peekskill, N.Y. [etc.] Review and herald publishing assn. [c1935] 239 p. incl. front., illus. 19 1/2 cm. "Issued by the Young people's department of missionary volunteers, General conference of Seventh-day Adventists." Bibliography: p. 6. [BX6153.H6] 35-15285
1. Seventh-day Adventists. I. Seventh-day Adventists. General conference. II. Title.

HOWELL, Emma Elizabeth, 1895- 286.7
The great Advent movement, by Emma E. Howell ... Takoma Park, Washington, D.C., Review and herald publishing assn. [1941] 251 p. incl. front., illus. 19 1/2 cm. "Issued by the Young people's department of missionary volunteers, General conference of Seventh-day Adventists." "Revised, 1941." Includes bibliographical notes. [BX6153.H6 1941] 41-23858
1. Seventh-day Adventists. I. Seventh-day Adventists. General conference. II. Title.

KNOCHE, Vikki. 248.4'8673
Keith and the cactus patch / Vikki Knoche. Mountain View, CA : Pacific Press, [1981] p. cm. A young boy eventually learns the consequences of not obeying his mother and promptly preparing for the Sabbath. [BX6154.K6] 19 81-1084 ISBN 0-8163-0426-2 pbk. : 1.75
1. [Seventh-Day Adventists.] 2. Sabbath—Juvenile literature. 3. Children—Religious life—Juvenile literature. 4. [Sabbath.] 5. [Christian life.] I. Title.
Distributed by the Greater New York Bookstore, 12 W. 40th St., New York, NY

LANE, Sands Harvey. 286.
Our paradise home; the earth made new and the restoration of all things, by S. H. Lane ... Battle Creek, Mich., Review and

herald publishing company [c1903] 128 p. incl. front., illus. 21 cm. [BX6154.L3] 3-20211
I. Title.

[LONGACRE, Charles S] 286.
Freedom, civil and religious; the American conception of liberty for press, pulpit, and public, as guaranteed in the federal constitution. Issued by the Religious liberty association, Washington, D. C. Washington, D. C., New York, N. Y. [etc.] Review and herald publishing association [c1920] 128 p. incl. front., illus. 20 cm. [BX6154.L4] 21-7636
1. Seventh-day Adventists. 2. Religious liberty. 3. Sunday legislation—U. S. I. Religious liberty association, Washington, D. C. II. Title.

LOUGHBOROUGH, John Norton, 286'.7
1832-1924.
The great Second Advent movement, its rise and progress. New York, Arno Press, 1972. 480 p. illus. 23 cm. (Religion in America, series II) Reprint of the 1905 ed. [BX6121.L6 1972] 71-38453 ISBN 0-405-04073-3
1. Seventh-Day Adventists. 2. Adventists. I. Title.

*MAXWELL, Arthur S. 286'.73
Your friends the Adventists. Mountain View, Calif., Pacific Pr. Pub. [1968] 95p. illus. 18cm. .30 pap.
1. Seventh-Day Adventists. I. Title.

MAXWELL, Arthur Stanley, 230.6'73
1896-
Good news for you, by Arthur S. Maxwell. Washington, Review and Herald Pub. Association [1966] 256 p. col. illus. 21 cm. [BX6154.M29] 66-25273
1. Seventh-Day Adventists. I. Title.

MAXWELL, Arthur Stanley, 286.7
1896-
Your friends, the Adventists. Mountain View, Calif., Pacific Press Pub. Association [1960] 95p. illus. 29cm. [BX6154.M35] 61-679
1. Seventh-Day Adventists. I. Title.

MILLER, George Frazier. 286.7
Adventism answered (the Sabbath question) Part first: Passing of the law and the introduction of grace. Part second: Some phases of the gospel liberty. By George Frazier Miller ... Brooklyn, N.Y., Guide printing and publishing company, 1905. 214 p. 20 1/2 cm. [BX6124.M46] 6-5699
1. Seventh-day Adventists. I. Title.

MITCHELL, David, 1914- 286.7
Seventh-Day Adventists, faith in action. [1st ed.] New York, ,vantage Press [1958] 334p. illus. 21cm. [BX6154.M5] 58-10668
1. Seventh-Day Adventists. I. Title. II. Title: Faith in action.

MORRILL, Madge (Haines) Mrs. 244
Finding the light, by Madge Haines Morrill ... Takoma Park, Washington, D.C., Review and herald publishing association [c1939] 154 p. incl. front. 20 1/,cm. Tail-pieces. [Full name: Mrs. Madge Arty (Haines) Morrill] [BX6154.M63] 244 39-23877
1. Seventh-day Adventists. I. Title.

NICHOL, Francis David, 230.67
1897-
Answers to objections: an examination of the major objections raised against the teachings of Seventh-day Adventists, by Francis D. Nichol. Takoma Park, Washington, D.C., Peekskill, N.Y. [etc.] Review and herald publishing assn. [c1932] 1 p. i., 5-254 p. 20 cm. [BX6145.N5] [286.7] 32-15420
1. Seventh-day Adventists. I. Title.

OLSEN, Mahlon Ellsworth, 286.
1873-
A history of the origin and progress of Seventh-day Adventists, by M. Ellsworth Olsen ... Washington, D. C., South Bend, Ind. [etc.] Review and herald publishing association [c1925] 768 p. incl. front., illus., ports., facsims., diagrs. 23 cm. "A partial bibliography": p. 746. [BX6153.O6] 25-18282
1. Seventh-day Adventists. I. Title.

OLSEN, Mahlon Ellsworth, 286'.73
1873-1952.
A history of the origin and progress of Seventh-Day Adventists. Washington, Review and Herald Pub. Association. [New York, AMS Press, 1972] 768 p. illus. 22 cm. Reprint of the 1925 ed. Bibliography: p. 746. [BX6153.O6 1972] 76-134375 ISBN 0-404-08423-0 30.00
1. Seventh-Day Adventists. I. Title.

OSWALD, Helen K. 922.673
That book in the attic [6th ed.] Mountain View, Calif., Pac.Pr.Pub. [1964, c.1939] 112p. 22cm. (Destiny bk., D-101) 63-22374 1.50 pap.,
1. Seventh-day Adventists. I. Title.

OSWALD, Helen K. Mrs. 922.673
That book in the attic; the true story of a girl who passed through the fires of affliction and presecution that she might obey God and His word. By HelenK. Oswald. Mountain View, Calif., Omaha, Neb. [etc.] Pacific press publishing association [c1939] 160 p. 21 cm. [BX6193.O7A3] 39-11394
1. Seventh-day Adventists. I. Title.

OUR changing world, 230.63
whither bound? Authors, Alonzo L. Baker, Frederick Lee, Roy F. Cottrell [and others] ... Mountain View, Calif., Omaha, Neb. [etc.] Pacific press publishing association [c1933] 142 p. incl. plates. 20 cm. [BX6154.O85] 33-8765
1. Seventh-day Adventists. I. Baker, Alonzo Lafayette, 1894.

PUTNAM, C E. 263.
Legalism and the seventh-day question: can Sinai law and grace co-exist? By C. E. Putnam ... Chicago, The Bible institute colportage ass'n [c1920] 96 p. 17 cm. [BV125.P8] 20-17891
I. Title.

ROBINSON, Dores Eugene. 286.7
The story of our health message; the origin, character, and development of health education in the Seventh-Day Adventist Church. Nashville, Southern Pub. Association [1955] 431p. 18cm. (Christian home library) [BR115.H4R62 1955] 55-3318
1. Seventh-Day Adventists. 2. Hygiene. 3. Medicine and religion. I. Title. II. Title: Our health message.

ROBINSON, Dores Eugene. 286.7
The story of our health message; the origin, character, and development of health education in the Seventh-day Adventist church, by Dores Eugene Robinson ... Nashville, Tenn., Southern publishing association [c1943] 364 p. incl. front., illus. (incl. ports., facsim.) 20 1/2 cm. (Ministerial reading course selection for 1944, Ministerial association of Seventh-day Adventists) [BR115.H4R62] 44-648
1. Seventh-day Adventists. 2. Hygiene. 3. Medicine and religion. I. Title. II. Title: Our health message.

SANDEL, Irene V. 286.
The Good Shepherd calleth His sheep, by Irene V. Sandel ... Los Angeles, Cal., Gem publishing company [c1926] 158 p. incl. front. 19 1/2 cm. [BX6154.S3] 26-8562
1. Seventh-day Adventists. I. Title.

SEVENTH-DAY Adventists. 286'.73
General Conference. Bureau of Public Relations.
Seventh-Day Adventist fact book; a reference notebook. Nashville, Southern Pub. Association [1967] 94 p. 19 cm. Pages 87-90 blank for "Local directory"; p. 91-94 blank for "Memo." [BX6154.S395] 67-19918
1. Seventh-Day Adventists. I. Title.

SEVENTH-DAY Adventists. 286.7
General conference. Dept. of education.
Lessons in denominational history, prepared by a special committee for introductory use in the secondary schools of the church. Washington, D.C., Dept. of education, General conference of Seventh-day Adventists [c1942] 336 p. diagr. 23 1/2 cm. "References" at end of each chapter. [BX6153.A55] 43-6424
1. Seventh-day Adventists. I. Title.

SEVENTH-DAY Adventists 268.867
General Conference Sabbath School Dept.
Sabbath school manual; official handbook for Sabbath school officers and teachers. Nashville, Southern Pub. Association [1956] 167 p. illus. 18 cm. [BX6113.S47] 56-27806
I. Seventh-Day Adventists. General Conference. Sabbath School Dept. II. Title.

SPAYD, Lucian Wilson, 1854- 286.
The two covenants and the Sabbath, embracing an exposition of the two Bible testaments; a review of the "Two covenants", by Eld. Uriah Smith of the Seventh day Adventists; and of the Seventh day Adventist teaching in general. By Eld. L. W. Spayd. Owosso, Mich., The Owosso press publishing company, 1898. 224 p. 19 cm. [BX6154.S7] 96-191
1. Seventh-day Adventists. 2. Adventists. 3. Sunday. I. Title.

SPICER, William Ambrose, 286.
1866-
Certainties of the Advent movement, by W. A. Spicer ... Takoma Park, Washington, D.C., South Bend, Ind., Review and herald publishing association [c1929] 3 p. l., 11-283 p. 21 cm. [BX6154.S78] 29-19217
1. Seventh-day Adventists. 2. Bible—Prophecies. I. Title. II. Title: Advent movement.

SPICER, William Ambrose, 286.7
1866-
The spirit of prophecy in the Advent movement; a gift that builds up ... by William A. Spicer. Takoma Park, Washington, D.C., Peekskill, N.Y. [etc.] Review and herald. publishing association [c1937] 128 p. incl. front., illus., ports. 19 1/2 cm. [BX6154.S75] 37-20732
1. Seventh-day Adventists. I. Title.

[STEVENS, J Adams] 266.
The layman's missionary movement; its development and leadership, prepared for the Home missionary department. Mountain View, Calif., Kansas City, Mo. [etc.] Pacific press publishing association [c1922] 3 p. l., 9-128 p. front., illus. (incl. ports.) 19 cm. Prefatory note signed: J. Adams Stevens. [BV2766.A5S7] 22-2608
1. Seventh-day Adventists. I. Title.

WHITE, Ellen Gould (Harmon) 232
Mrs., 1827-1915.
... Sketches from the life of Christ and the experience of the Christian church. By Mrs. E. G. White, 2d ed. Battle Creek, Mich., Review and herald; Oakland, Cal., Pacific press, 1882. vi, 7-154 p. 17 1/2 cm. (Spiritual gifts. v. 1) [BT301.W435] 33-37489
1. Jesus Christ—Miscellanea. 2. Seventh-day Adventists. I. Title.

WHITE, James, 1821-1881. 922.
Life sketches. Ancestry, early life, Christian experience, and extensive labors of Elder James White, and his wife Mrs. Ellen G. White. Battle Creek, Mich., Press of the Seventh-day adventist publishing association, 1880. viii, [9]-416 p. illus., 2 port. (incl. front.) 18 1/2 cm. Written in part by Ellen G. White. [BX6193.W54A3] 12-40240
1. Seventh-day Adventists. I. White, Ellen G. (Harmon) "Mrs. James White," 1827-1915, joint author. II. Title.

WILCOX, Francis McLellan. 286.7
Seventh-day Adventists in time of war, by Francis McLellan Wilcox ... Takoma Park, Washington, D.C., Peekskill, N.Y. [etc.] Review and herald publishing assn. [c1936] 407 p. incl. front. (port.) 23 1/2 cm. Maps on lining-papers. [BX6154.W555] 36-11249
1. Seventh-day Adventists. 2. European war, 1914-1918—War work—Seventh-day Adventists. 3. Evil, Non-resistance to. 4. Military service, Compulsory. I. Title.

Seventh-day Adventists — Addresses, essays, lectures.

NYMAN, Aaron.
Astounding errors; the prophetic message of the Seventh-day adventists and the chronoly of Pastor C. T. Russell in the light of history and Bible knowledge, by Aaron Nyman. [Chicago, Nya Vecko-Posten, c1914] 419 p. front. (port.) charts. 20 cm. 4-20392 1.00
I. Title.

NYMAN, Aaron.
Astounding errors; the prophetic message of the Seventh-day adventists and the chronology of Pastor C. T. Russell in the light of history and Bible knowledge, by Aaron Nyman. [Chicago, Nya Vecko-Posten, c1914] 419 p. front. (port.) charts. 20 cm. 4-20392 1.00
I. Title.

OLIPHANT, Bill, ed. 286.7
Seventh-Day Adventists today: a report in depth. Homer Norris, art. Contributors: Dorothy Aitken [and others] Nashville, Southern Pub. Association [1966] 159 p. illus., ports. 28 cm. [BX6154.O4] 66-5923
1. Seventh-day Adventists — Addresses, essays, lectures. I. Aitken, Dorothy Lockwood. II. Title.

SIGNS of the times. 286.7
The living witness; significant articles from the Signs of the times, 1874 -- 1959. Edited by Richard Lewis. Mountain View, Calif., Pacific Press Pub. Association [1959] 264 p. 23 cm. [BX6111.S5] 59-12526
1. Seventy-day Adventists — Addresses, essays, lectures. I. Title.

Seventh-Day Adventists — Anti-Seventh-Day Adventist polemic.

FRANKE, Elmer Ellsworth, 1861-
1946.
The "2300 days" and the sanctuary, a clear exposition of Seventh-day Adventism answering the question: did the judgment begin in 1844? Is [New York, 1964] 54 p. 65-48402
1. Seventh-Day Adventists — Anti-Seventh-Day Adventist polemic. I. Title.

FRANKE, Elmer Ellsworth, 1861-
1946.
The "2300 days" and the sanctuary, a clear exposition of Seventy-day Adventism answering the question: did the judgment egin in 1844? Is forgiveness of sins conditional or absolute? Was the Atonement finished on the cross? What happened in 1844? [New York, 1964] 54 p. 65-48402
1. Seventh-Day Adventists — Anti-Seventh-Day Adventist polemic. I. Title.

Seventh-Day Adventists—Biography.

ALLEN, Sydney. 917.93'52'03
Directional signals; memories of a Seventh-day Adventist boyhood in the West. Nashville, Southern Pub. Association [1970] 190 p. 21 cm. [BX6193.A4A3] 74-123335
I. Title.

COVINGTON, Ava Marie, 1905- 922.6
They also served; stories of pioneer women of the Advent movement, by Ava M. Covington. Takoma Park, Washington, D.C., Review and Herald publishing assa. [c1940] 191 p. illus. (ports.) 20 cm. [BX6191.C6] 40-33657
1. Seventh-day Adventists—Biog. I. Title.
Contents omitted.

DICK, Everett Newfon, 922.673
1898-
Founders of the message, by Everett Dick ... Takoma Park, Washington, D. C., Review and herald publishing association [c1938] 333 p. 19 cm. [BX6191.D5] 38-34589
1. Seventh-day Adventists—Biog. I. Title.
Contents omitted.

GOD'S hand in my life 248'.9'673
I compiled by Lawrence T. Geraty. Nashville : Southern Pub. Association, [1977] p. cm. [BX6191.G63] 77-12585 ISBN 0-8127-0151-8 pbk. : 4.95
1. Seventh-Day Adventists—Biography. 2. Christian life—Seventh-Day Adventist authors. I. Geraty, Lawrence T.

OCHS, Daniel A., 286'.7'0922 B
1890-
The past and the presidents : biographies of the General Conference presidents / by Daniel A. Ochs and Grace Lillian Ochs. Nashville : Southern Pub. Association,

[1974] 231 p. : ports. ; 21 cm. [BX6191.O26] 73-92699 ISBN 0-8127-0084-8 pbk. : 4.95
1. Seventh-Day Adventists—Biography. I. Ochs, Grace Lillian, joint author. II. Title.

WALL, Frank E., 1894-1972. 286'.7'0922 B
Uncertain journey : Adventist workers with a Mennonite heritage / Frank E. Wall and Ava C. Wall. Washington : Review and Herald Pub. Association, [1974] 160 p. ; 21 cm. Bibliography: p. 159-160. [BX6189.A1W34 1974] 74-196956 3.50
1. Seventh-Day Adventists—Biography. 2. Converts, Seventh-Day Adventist. 3. Mennonites—History. I. Wall, Ava C., joint author. II. Title.

WHY I joined ... 286'.7'0922 B
moving stories of changed lives, as told to Herbert E. Douglass. [Editor: Thomas A. Davis] Washington, Review and Herald Pub. Association [1974] 63 p. ports. 19 cm. [BX6191.W45] 74-78174
1. Seventh-Day Adventists—Biography. I. Douglass, Herbert E.

Seventh-Day Adventists—British Columbia.

COOPER, Charles S. 286.7711
Wilderness parish. Mountain View, Calif., Pacific Press [c.1961] 136p. illus. 61-10881 4.00
1. Seventh-Day Adventists—British Columbia. I. Title.

Seventh-Day Adventists—California.

MCCUMBER, Harold Oliver, 1895- 286'.7794
The Advent message in the Golden West, by Harold O. McCumber. Rev. Mountain View, Calif., Pacific Press Pub. Association [1968] 184 p. illus., map, ports. 22 cm. (Dimension, 106) First ed. published in 1946 under title: Pioneering the message in the Golden West. [BX6153.M2 1968] 68-5957
1. Seventh-Day Adventists—California. I. Title.

Seventh-Day Adventists—Canada.

COFFEY, Cecil Reeves, 1925- 286'.771
Seventh-Day Adventists in Canada, by Cecil Coffey. Nashville, Southern Pub. Association [1968] 79 p. illus. (part col.), col. map. 28 cm. [BX6154.C57] 68-2260
1. Seventh-Day Adventists—Canada. I. Title.

Seventh-Day Adventists — Collected works.

WHITE, Ellen Gould (Harmon) 1827-1915. 286.7
Selected messages from the writings of Ellen G. White; significant and ever-timely counsels gathered from periodical articles, manuscript statements, and certain valuable pamphlets and tracts long out of print. Washington, Review and Herald Pub. Association [1958] 2 v. 18 cm. (Christian home library) [BX6111.W515] 58-2733
1. Seventh-Day Adventists — Collected works. 2. Theology — Collected works — 19th cent. I. Title.

Seventh-Day Adventists—Controversial works.

†PAXTON, Geoffrey J. 286'.73
The shaking of Adventism / Geoffrey J. Paxton. Wilmington, Del. : Zenith Publishers, c1977. 172 p. ; 24 cm. Based on the author's thesis. University of Queensland, Australia. Includes index. Bibliography: p. 159-169. [BX6154.P35] 77-88139 ISBN 0-930802-01-2 : 6.95
1. Seventh-Day Adventists—Controversial works. I. Title.

Seventh-Day Adventists—Dictionaries.

SEVENTH-DAY Adventist Bible student's sourcebook. 286.7
Ed. by Don F. Neufeld, Julia Neuffer. Washington, D.C., 6856 Eastern Ave., N.W., Review and Herald Pub. Assn., 1962. 1189p. 25cm. (Commentary reference ser., v.3) Successor to the Source book for Bible students pub. in 1919. 62-9139 13.75
1. Seventh-Day Adventists—Dictionaries. 2. Theology—Dictionaries. I. Neufeld, Don F., ed. II. Neuffer, Julia, ed. III. Source book for Bible students. IV. Title: Bible student's source book.

SEVENTH-DAY Adventist 286.73
encyclopedia; v.10 Washington, Review & Herald 1966. xviii, 1452p. maps. 25cm. (Commentary ref. ser. v.10) [BX6154.S39] 66-17322 14.75
1. Seventh-Day Adventists—Dictionaries.

SEVENTH-DAY Adventist 286'.73
encyclopedia. Rev. ed. Washington : Review and Herald Pub. Association, 1976. xx, 1640 p. : map ; 25 cm. (Commentary reference series ; v. 10) [BX6154.S39 1976] 75-43265
1. Seventh-Day Adventists—Dictionaries.

Seventh-Day Adventists—Doctrinal and controversial works.

ABBOTT, George Knapp, 1880- 286.7
The witness of science to the testimonies of the spirit of prophecy; studies in the testimonies and science given at Pacific Union College. [Sanitarium, Calif.] 1947. 236 p. illus. 24 cm. Includes bibliographies. [BX6154.A56] 48-95
1. White, Ellen Gould (Harmon) 1827-1915. 2. Seventh-Day Adventists—Doctrinal and controversial works. 3. Medicine and religion. I. Title.

ABBOTT, George Knapp, 1880- 286.7
The witness of science to the testimonies of the spirit of prophecy. Rev. ed. Mountain View, Calif., Pacific Press Pub. Assn. [1948] 365 p. 23 cm. [BX6154.A56 1948] 49-2401
1. White, Ellen Gould (Harmon) 1827-1915. 2. Seventh-Day Adventists—Doctrinal and controversial works. 3. Medicine and religion. I. Title.

ANDERSON, Roy Allan. 230.6'73
A better world. Nashville, Southern Pub. Association [1968] 206 p. 21 cm. (His God's eternal plan, v. 3) [BX6154.A565] 68-18210
1. Seventh-Day Adventists—Doctrinal and controversial works. I. Title.

ANDERSON, Roy Allan 230'.073
Faith that conquers fear. Nashville, Southern Pub. [1967] 171p. 21cm. (His God's eternal plan, v. 1) [BX6154.A567] 67-25226 2.50 pap.,
1. Seventh-Day Adventists— Doctrinal and controversial works. I. Title.

ANDERSON, Roy Allan. 230.6'73
Love finds a way. Nashville, Southern Pub. Association [1967] 184 p. 21 cm. (His God's eternal plan, v. 2) [BX6154.A5672] 67-23319
1. Seventh-Day Adventists—Doctrinal and controversial works. I. Title.

ANDREASEN, Milian Lauritz, 1876- 230.67
The faith of Jesus. Washington, Review and Herald Pub. Association [1949] 574 p. 18 cm. (Christian home library) First published in 1939 under title: The faith of Jesus and the commandments of God. [BX6154.A57 1949] 50-1849
1. Seventh-Day Adventists—Doctrinal and controversial works. I. Title.

ANDREASEN, Milian Lauritz, 1876- 230.67
The faith of Jesus and the commandments of God, by M. L. Andreasen ... Takoma Park, Washington, D.C., Review and herald publishing association [c1939] 571 p. 21 cm. (Ministerial reading course selection for 1940, Ministerial association of the Seventh-day Adventists) [BX6154.A57] 39-31165
1. Seventh-day Adventists—Doctrinal and controversial works. I. Title.

ANDREASEN, Milian Lauritz, 1876- 230.67
A faith to live by, by M. L. Andreasen ... Takoma Park, Washington, D. C., Review and herald publishing association, 1943. 256 p. 21 cm. [BX6154.A58] 43-11026
1. Seventh-day Adventists—Doctrinal and controversial works. 2. Young men—Religious life. I. Title.

ANDREASEN, Milian Lauritz, 1876- 230.67
The sanctuary service, by M. L. Andreasen ... Takoma Park, Washington, D.C., Peekskill, N.Y. etc. Review and herald publishing assn. [c1937] 2 p. l., 7-311 p. 20 1/2 cm. "Published for the 1938 Ministerial reading course of Seventh-day Adventists."--Verse of 1st prelim. leaf. [BX6154.A6] 37-20989
1. Seventh-day Adventists—Doctrinal and controversial works. I. Title.

ANDREASEN, Milian Lauritz, 1876- 230.67
The sanctuary service, 2d ed. rev. Washington, Review and Herald Pub. Assn. [1947] 413 p. 18 cm. (Christian home library) [BX6154.A6 1947] 47-24763
1. Seventh-Day Adventists—Doctrinal and controversial works. I. Title.

ANDREASEN, Milian Lauritz, 1876- 230.67
What can a man believe? Mountain View, Calif., Pacific Press Pub. Association [1951] vii, 211 p. 18 cm. [BX6154.A63] 51-5268
1. Seventh-Day Adventists—Doctrinal and controversial works. I. Title.

BEACH, Walter Raymond. 248.4867
Dimensions in salvation. Washington, Review and Herald Pub. Association [1963] 329 p. col. illus. 18 cm. Bibliography: p. 319-320 [BX6154.B1] 63-17765
1. Seventh Day Adventists — Doctrinal and controversial works. 2. Christian life. I. Title.

BIBLE readings for the home; 230.67
a study of 200 vital Scripture topics in question and answer form, contributed by a large number of Bible scholars. Rev., newly illus. Nashville, Southern Pub. Assn., 1963. 568p. illus. (pt. col.) 27cm. Bibl. 63-12806 apply
1. Seventh-Day Adventists—Doctrinal and controversial works.

BIBLE readings for the home;
a study of 200 vital Scripture topics in question-and-answer form. Rev. Washington, D.C., Review and Herald Publishing Association, 1958. 768 p. illus. 18 cm. NUC63
1. Seventh-day Adventists—Doctrinal and controversial works.

BIBLE readings for the home; 230.67
a study of 200 vital Scripture topics in question-and-answer form, contributed by a large number of Bible scholars. Completely rev. and newly illustrated. Washington, Review and Herald Pub. Association, 1949. 768 p. illus. 23 cm. [BX6154.B55 1949] 52-3240
1. Seventh-Day Adventists—Doctrinal and controversial works.

BIBLE readings for the home; 230.67
a topical study in question-and-answer form contributed by a large number of Bible students. More than three hundred beautiful illustrations. Takoma park, Washington, D. C., Review and herald publishing asociation, 1942. 702. [706-794 p. inl. front. illus., diagrs. 23 cm. Illustrated lining-papers. Four blank pages following p. 702 for family register. [BX6154.B55] 230.67 42-5028 42-5028
1. Seventh-day Adventists-Doctrinal and controversal works.

BIBLE readings for the home; 230.67
a topical study in question-and-answer form contributed by a large number of Bible students. More than three hundred beautiful illustrations. Takoma park, Washington, D. C., Review and herald publishing asociation, 1942. 702. [706-794 p. inl. front. illus., diagrs. 23 cm. Illustrated lining-papers. Four blank pages following p. 702 for family register. [BX6154.B55] 230.67 42-5028 42-5028
1. Seventh-day Adventists-Doctrinal and controversal works.

BIETZ, Arthur Leo 230.67
Exploring God's answers. Mountain View, Calif., Pacific Press Pub. Association [c.1960] 182p. diagr. 23cm. 60-11199 3.95
1. Seventh-Day Adventists—Doctrinal and controversial works. I. Title.

BIRD, Herbert S. 230.67
Theology of Seventh-Day Adventism. Grand Rapids, Mich., Eerdmans [c.1961] 137p. Bibl. 61-10858 3.00
1. Seventh-Day Adventists—Doctrinal and controversial works. I. Title.

BRADFORD, Charles E. 251
Preaching to the times : the preaching ministry in the Seventh-day Adventist Church / Charles E. Bradford. Washington : Review and Herald Pub. Association, [1975] 144 p. ; 21 cm. (Discovery paperbacks) Bibliography: p. 143-144. [BV4211.2.B672] 75-318950 3.25
1. Seventh-Day Adventists—Doctrinal and controversial works. 2. Preaching. I. Title.

BRANSON, William H. 286.7
Reply to Canright; the truth about Seventh-day Adventists, by William H. Branson ... Takoma Park, Washington, D. C., Peekskill, N. Y. [etc.] Review and herald publishing association [c1933] 319 p. 1 illus. 20 cm. [BX6154.C32B7] 33-21264
1. Canright, Dudley Marvin, 1840-1919. 2. White, Mrs. Ellen Gould (Harmon) 1827-1915. 3. Seventh-day Adventists—Doctrinal and controversial works. 4. Sabbath. 5. Commandments, Ten. I. Title.

BRANSON, William Henry, 1887- 230.67
Drama of the ages. Nashville, Southern Pub. Association [1953] 544p. 18cm. (Christian home library) [B6154.B7 1953] 53-24295
1. Seventh-Day Adventists— Doctrinal and controversial works. I. Title.

BRANSON, William Henry, 1887- 230.67
Drama of the ages. Nashville, Southern Pub. Association, 1950. 584 p. illus. 23 cm. [BX6154.B7] 50-13648
1. Seventh-Day Adventists—Doctrinal and controversial works. I. Title.

BRANSON, William Henry, 1887- 286.7
Reply to Canright; the truth about Seventh-day Adventist, by Willam H. Branson ... Takoma Park, Washington, D. C., Peekskill, N. Y. [etc.] Review and herald publishing association [c1933] 319 p.1 illus. 20 cm. [BX6154.C32B7] 33-21264
1. Seventh-day Adventist—Doctrinal and controversial works. 2. Sabbath. 3. Commandments, Ten. I. Canrih, Dudley Marvin, 1840-1919. II. White, Ellen Gould (Harmon) 1827-1915. III. Title.

BUNCH, Taylor Grant. 230.67
The everlasting gospel versus Babylon the great [by] Taylor G. Bunch. [Loma Linda, Calif.] c1934. cover-title, 2 p. l., 239 p. 27 cm. "This course ... has been prepared ... for ... the students of the College of medical evangelists."--Introd. remarks. [BX6155.B8] 34-16381
1. Seventh-day Adventists—Doctrinal and controversial works. I. Title.

BUNCH, Taylor Grant. 228
The seven epistles of Christ. Washington, Review and Herald Pub. Assn. [1947] 254 p., [1] l. 20 cm. Bibliography: leaf at end. [BS2825.B838] 47-26505
1. Seventh-day Adventists—Doctrinal and controversial works. 2. Bible. N.T. Revelation I-III—Criticism, interpretation, etc. I. Title.

BURMAN, Charles Augustus. 230.67
Academic course Bible doctrines, by C. A. Burman ... (Rev. ed.) Berrien Springs, Mich., Printed for the General conference department of education, The College press, 1935. 213, [6] p. 20 cm. Blank pages for "Notes" ([6] at end) [BX6155.B83 1935] 36-7510
1. Seventh day Adventists—Doctrinal and controversial works. I. Title.

CAMPBELL, George A 230.67
How many ways to heaven? Why so many denominations? Mountain View, Calif., Pacific Press Pub. Association [1953] 86p. illus. 19cm. (Stories that win series) [BX6154.C23] 53-6428
1. Seventh-Day Adventists—Doctrinal and controversial works. 2. Sects. I. Title.

CANRIGHT, Dudley Marvin, 1840-1919. 230.67
Seventh-day Adventism refuted, in a nutshell. Grand Rapids, Mich. Baker Bk., 1962. 83p. 19cm. A reprint of a series of ten tracts. . . published . . . in 1889. 62-6808 .75 pap.,
1. Seventh-Day Adventists—Doctrinal and controversial works. I. Title.

CHAIJ, Fernando. 236
Preparation for the final crisis; a compilation of passages from the Bible and the spirit of prophecy, with comments by Fernando Chaij. With an appendix by M. E. Loewen. [1st ed.] Mountain View, Calif., Pacific Press Pub. Association [1966] 189 p. illus. 22 cm. Includes quotations from the writings of Ellen G. White. [BX6154.C42] 66-29118
1. Seventh-Day Adventists—Doctrinal and controversial works. I. White, Ellen Gould (Harmon) 1827-1915. II. Title.

CHRISTIAN, Lewis Harrison. 236
Facing the crisis in the light of Bible prophecy, by L. H. Christian... Takoma Park, Washington, D.C., Peekskill, N.Y. [etc.] Review and herald publishing association [c1937] 320 p. incl. front., illus. 20 1/2 cm. [BX6154.C45] 38-1719
1. Seventh-day Adventists—Doctrinal and controversial works. 2. End of the world. I. Title.

CLEVELAND, Earl E. 230.6'73
Mine eyes have seen [by] E. E. Cleveland. Washington, Review and Herald Pub. Association [1968] 126 p. 20 cm. [BX6154.C55] 68-18742
1. Seventh-Day Adventists—Doctrinal and controversial works. I. Title.

CLEVELAND, Edward Earl. 230'.67
The gates shall not / by E. E. Cleveland. Nashville, TN : Review and Herald Pub. Association, c1981. 92 p. ; 21 cm. [BX6154.C54] 19 80-27033 ISBN 0-8127-0325-1 : Price unreported
1. Seventh-Day Adventists—Doctrinal and controversial works. I. Title.

[CONRADI, Ludwig Richard] 1856-1939. 286.7
The founders of the Seventh day Adventist denomination ... [Plainfield, N.J., Printed for the author by the American Sabbath tract society, 1939] 79 p. 1 illus. 19 1/2 cm. Portrait on t.-p. On cover: By L. Richard Conradi. A translation, re-cast and enlarged by the author, of the Lebensbeschrelbung von prediger O. R. L. Grozier. "Index of authorities": p. 75-79. [BX6124.C63] 41-24702
1. Seventh-day Adventists—Doctrinal and controversial works. I. American Sabbath tract society. II. Title.

DELAFIELD, D. A. 241'.6'74
What's in your clothes closet? / D. A. Delafield. Washington : Review and Herald Pub. Association, c1974. 94 p. ; 21 cm. Includes bibliographical references. [BX6154.D38] 74-78482 2.50
1. Seventh-Day Adventists—Doctrinal and controversial works. 2. Clothing and dress—Moral and religious aspects. I. Title.

DOUTY, Norman Franklin, 1899- 286.7
Another look at Seventh-Day Adventism, with special reference, Questions on doctrine. Grand Rapids, Mich., Baker Bk., 1962. 224p. 23cm. Bibl. 62-17678 3.50
1. Seventh-day Adventists—Doctrinal and controversial works. I. Title.

*DOWARD, Jan S. 286.7
Battleground, by Jan S. Doward. [Rev. ed.] Nashville, Southern Pub. [c.1968] 95p. 21cm. Orig. pub. in 1954 under title Out of the Storm. 1.50 pap.,
1. Seventh-Day Adventists—Doctrinal and controversial works. I. Title.

*EDWARDS, Josephine Cunnington 286.7
Reuben's portion. Illus. by Joseph W. Malmede. Nashville Southern Pub. Assn. [1967, c.1957] 208p. illus. 21cm. (Summit bk.) 1.50 pap.,
1. Seventh-Day Adventists—Doctrinal and controversial works. I. Title.

EDWARDS, Walter Oscar, 1880- 230.67
Great fundamentals of the Bible, by Walter O. Edwards. Mountain View, Calif., Omaha, Neb. [etc.] Pacific press publishing association [c1938] 192 p. col. front., illus. (incl. facsim.) diagrs. 24 1/2 cm. (On cover: Home guide, vol. iii) [AG105.H724 vol. 3] (080) 38-23571
1. Seventh-day Adventists—Doctrinal and controversial works. I. Title.

EMMERSON, Elson Henry, 1888- 230.67
Bible doctrine study outline for a six hour college course, with suggestive adaptations for a four hour course, by Elson H. Emmerson. Angwin, Calif., Bible department, Paicifc union college, 1935. 1 p. l., a-g, 168 numb. l. 27 1/2 cm. Mimeopgraphed. [BX6155.E6 1935] 39-32263
1. Seventh-day Adventists—Doctrinal and controversial works. I. Title.

EMMERSON, Elson Henry, 1888- 230.67
Bible doctrines study outline for a six hour college course, with suggestive adaptations for a four hour course, by Elson H. Emmerson... Revised. Angwin, Calif., Pacific union college press, 1939. ix, 230 p. diagrs. 23 1/2 cm. [BX6155.F6 1939] 39-32264
1. Seventh-day Adventists—Doctrinal and controversial works. I. Title.

EMMERSON, W. L. 230.67
The Bible speaks; scripture readings systematically arranged for home and class study, answering nearly one thousand questions. Addit. notes gathered, prepd. by Francis A. Soper. Abridged. Mountain View, Calif., Pacific Pr. Pub. [1967,c.1949] 250p. illus. 19cm. [BX6154.E55] .95 pap.,
1. Seventh-Day Adventists—Doctrinal and controversial works. 2. Bible—Examinations, questions, etc. I. Title.

EMMERSON, W L 230.67
The Bible speaks, containing one hundred forty-one readings systematically arranged for home and class study and answering nearly three thousand questions. Additional notes gathered and prepared by Francis A. Soper. Mountain View, Calif., Pacific Press Pub. Assn. [1949] 704 p. illus. 23 cm. [BX6154.E55] 49-2546
1. Seventh-Day Adventists—Doctrinal and controversial works. 2. Bible—Examinations, questions, etc. I. Title.

ENGELKEMIER, Joe. 922.673
Ready to answer. Illus. by Alan Forquer. Washington, Review and Herald Pub. Association [1965] 158 p. illus. 22 cm. Bibliographical footnotes. [BX6154.E6] 65-18676
1. Seventh-Day Adventists—Doctrinal and controversial works. I. Title.

*FAGEL, William A. 286.7
Trois heures a vivre [Mountain View, Calif., Pacific Pr. Pub., 1968] 63p. 18cm. (Eds. Inter-Americaines) French language ed. of Three hours to live, tr. by Louise Wyns. .30 pap.,
1. Seventh Day Adventists—Doctrinal and Controversial works. I. Title.

FLECK, Alcyon Ruth 922.6728
A brand from the burning; a true story of the life of a Roman Catholic priest and of his conversion to the Seventh-Day Adventist Church where he is now a minister. Mountain View Calif., Pacific Press Pub. Association [c.1960] 183p. 23cm. 60-8299 4.50
1. Seventh-Day Adventists— Doctrinal and controversial works. 2. Catholic Church—Doctrinal and controversial works—Protestant authors, I. Title.

FRAZEE, Willmonte Doniphan, 1906- 234
Ransom and reunion through the sanctuary / W. D. Frazee. Nashville : Southern Pub. Association, c1977. 124 p. ; 20 cm. [BX6154.F67] 77-76135 ISBN 0-8127-0138-0 pbk. : 3.95
1. Seventh-Day Adventists—Doctrinal and controversial works. 2. Sanctuary doctrine (Seventh-Day Adventists) I. Title.

FRAZEE, Willmonte Doniphan, 1906- 234
Ransom and reunion through the sanctuary / W. D. Frazee. Nashville : Southern Pub. Association, c1977. 124 p. ; 20 cm. [BX6154.F67] 77-76135 ISBN 0-8127-0138-0 pbk. : 3.95
1. Seventh-Day Adventists—Doctrinal and controversial works. 2. Sanctuary doctrine (Seventh-Day Adventists) I. Title.

FREIWIRTH, Paul K., 1927- 286'.73 B
Why I left the Seventh-Day Adventists, by Paul K. Freiwirth. [1st ed.] New York, Vantage Press [1970] 120 p. 21 cm. Bibliography: p. 107-120. [BX6154.F68] 72-194741 3.50
1. Seventh-Day Adventists—Doctrinal and controversial works. I. Title.

GILBERT, Fred Carnes, 1867- 230.67
Messiah in His sanctuary; a series of Bible studies on the sanctuary and its services, in both type and anti-type, with particular application to the church following the Advent movement of the years 1834-1844, by F. C. Gilbert ... Takoma Park, Washington, D. C., South Bend, Ind. [etc.] Review and herald publishing association [c1937] 248 p. incl. front. (port.) illus. 24 cm. Bibliography: p. 241. [BX6154.G5] 37-12675
1. Seventh-day Adventists—Doctrinal and controversial works. 2. Typology (Theology) 3. Atonement. I. Title. II. Title: Sanctuary, Messiah in His.

HARDE,. Frederick E J 230.67
Giants of faith. Washington, Review and Herald Pub. Association [1961] 100p. 22cm. [BX6154.H3] 61-11981
1. Seventh-Day Adventists—Doctrinal and controversial works. I. Title.

HETZELL, M. Carol. 230'.6'73
Gelebter Glaube = Foi vecue = Faith alive / M. Carol Hetzell. Hamburg : Saatkorn-Verlag, c1975. 163 p. : ill. (some col.) ; 30 cm. [BX6154.H4] 75-516307
1. Seventh-Day Adventists—Doctrinal and controversial works. 2. Seventh-Day Adventists—Pictorial works. I. Title. II. Title: Foi vecue. III. Title: Faith alive.

HOEHN, Edward, 1893- 230.67
God's plan for your life. Mountain View, Calif., Pacific Press Pub. Association [1953] 135p. 20cm. [BX6154.H54] 53-8824
1. Seventh-Day Adventists—Doctrinal and controversial works. I. Title.

HOEN, Reu Everett, 1888- 922.673
The Creator and His workshop. Mountain View, Calif., Pacific Press Pub. Association [1951] ix, 176 p. 21 cm. [BX6154.H56] 51-4690
1. Seventh-Day Adventists—Doctrinal and controversial works. I. Title.

KNIGHT, Henry. 230.63
One God, one country, one church. [1st ed.] New York, VantagePress [1956] 116p. 21cm. [BX6154.K58] 55-11663
1. Seventh-Day Adventists —Doctrinal and controversial works. I. Title.

KUBO, Sakae, 1926- 232'.6
God meets man : a theology of the Sabbath and the Second Advent / Sakae Kubo. Nashville : Southern Pub. Association, c1978. 160 p. ; 21 cm. Bibliography: p. 157-160. [BV125.K8] 78-6616 ISBN 0-8127-0171-2 : write for information.
1. Seventh-Day Adventists—Doctrinal and controversial works. 2. Sabbath. 3. Second Advent. I. Title.

LEE, Leonard C. 230.67
I found the way. Cover and illus. by James Converse. Mountain View, Calif., Pacific Press Pub. Association [c.1961] 122p. 61-10878 .50 pap.,
1. Seventh-Day Adventists—Doctrinal and controversial works. I. Title.

*LIBBY, Raymond H. 286.7
Quoi! Plus de Dieu? Et autres messages bibliques. [Mountain View, Calif., Pacific Pr. Pub., 1968] 65p. 18cm. (Eds. Inter-Americaines) French language tr. of What! No God? tr. by Danielle Volf-Ducret. .30 pap.,
1. Seventh Day Adventist—Doctrinal and controversial works. I. Title.

*LIBBY, Raymond H. 286.7
Quoi! Plus de Dieu? Et autres messages bibliques. [Mountain View, Calif., Pacific Pr. Pub., 1968] 65p. 18cm. (Eds. Inter-Americaines) French language tr. of What! No God? tr. by Danielle Volf-Ducret. .30 pap.,
1. Seventh Day Adventist—Doctrinal and controversial works. I. Title.

LIBBY, Raymond H. 230'.6'73
What! No God? And other brief Bible messages, by Raymond H. Libby. Mountain View, Calif., Pacific Press Pub. Association [1967] 76 p. front. 19 cm. [BX6154.L47] 66-29535
1. Seventh-Day Adventists—Doctrinal and controversial works. 2. Theology—Miscellanea. I. Title.

LICKEY, Arthur E 230.67
Fundamentals of the everlasting gospel. May be used for instructing those desiring baptism and membership in the Seventh-Day Adventist Church. Takoma Park, Washington, D. C., Review and Herald Pub. Assn., c1947. 64 p. illus. (part col.) ports. 24 cm. [BX6154.L5] 48-4977
1. Seventh-Day Adventists—Doctrinal and controversial works. I. Title.

LICKEY, Arthur E. 230.67
God speaks to modern man. Washington, D.C., Review & Herald, 1963[c.1952, 1963] 448p. col. illus. 27cm. 63-3624 15.75
1. Seventh-Day Adventists—Doctrinal and controversial works. I. Title.

LICKEY, Arthur E. 230.67
Highways to truth; God speaks to modern man. Washington, Review and Herald Pub. Association [1952] 544 p. illus. 22 cm. [BX6154.L52] 52-33808
1. Seventh-Day Adventists—Doctrinal and controversial works. I. Title.

LORENZ, Felix A. 230'.6'73
The only hope / by Felix A. Lorenz. Nashville, Tenn. : Southern Pub. Association, c1976. 112 p. ; 21 cm. [BX6154.L66] 75-43059 ISBN 0-8127-0108-9
1. Seventh-Day Adventists—Doctrinal and controversial works. I. Title.

LOWE, Harry William. 289.9
Radio Church of God; how its teachings differ from these of Seventh-day Adventists, by Harry W. Lowe. Mountain View, Calif., Pacific Press Pub. Association [1970] 143 p. 19 cm. Includes bibliographical references. [BR1725.A77L68] 77-101250
1. Armstrong, Herbert W. 2. Radio Church of God. 3. Seventh-Day Adventists—Doctrinal and controversial works.

MCMILLAN, J. A. 230.67
Days of destiny. Washington, Review and Herald Pub. Association [1949] 192 p. illus. 23 cm. [BX6154.M2] 50-309
1. Seventh-Day Adventists—Doctrinal and controversial works. I. Title.

MARSH, Frank Lewis. 230.67
Fundamental biology, by Frank Lewis Marsh ... Lincoln, Neb., The author, 1941. 2 p. l., iv, 128 (i. e. 129) numb. l. diagr. 28 x 21 cm. Reproduced from type-written copy. Includes extra numbered leaf 63a. "First impression." "Written specifically for Seventh-day Adventists."--Introd. "Scientific papers by the author": leaf 123. "Literature cited": leaves 124-128. [BX6154.M23] 41-27766
1. Seventh-day Adventists—Doctrinal and controversial works. 2. Religion and science—1900- I. Title.

MARTIN, Walter Ralston, 1928- 230.67
The truth about Seventh-Day Adventism Grand Rapids, Zondervan Pub. House [1960] 248p. 23cm. Includes bibliography. [BX6154.M27] 60-10154
1. Seventh-Day Adventists—Doctrinal and controversial works. I. Title.

*MAXWELL, Arthur S. 230.673
Bible made plain. Mountain View, Calif., Pacific Pr. Pub. [1968] 128p. illus., 18cm. T.p. and text in Russian. .50 pap.,
1. Seventh-Day Adventists—Doctrinal and controversial works. I. Title.

MAXWELL, Arthur S. 286.7
C'est la fin! [Mountain View, Calif., Pacific Pr. Pub., [1968] 94p. 18cm. (Eds. Inter-Americaines) French language ed. of This is the end! tr. by Louise Wyns. .30 pap.,

1. Seventh Day Adventists—Doctrinal and controversial works. I. Title.

MAXWELL, Arthur Stanley, 1896- 230.67
Your Bible and you; priceless treasures in the Holy Scriptures. Washington, Review and Hearld Pub. Association [1959] 480p. illus. 26cm. [BX6154.M33] 59-4846
1. Seventh-Day Adventists—Doctrinal and controversial works. I. Title.

MITTLEIDER, Kenneth J. 286'.73
Your church and you, by Kenneth J. Mittleider. Nashville, Southern Pub. Association [1972] 61 p. 21 cm. [BX6154.M53] 72-81260
1. Seventh-Day Adventists—Doctrinal and controversial works. I. Title.

NICHOL, Francis David, 1897- 230.67
The answer to modern religious thinking; a discussion of current religious trends in their relation to the distinctive teachings of Seventh-day Adventists, by Francis D. Nichol. a Takoma Park, Washington, D.C., Peekskill, N.Y. [etc.] Review and herald publishing assn. [c1936] 318 p. 23 1/2 cm. Bibliography: p. 315-318. [BX6145.N48] 36-31252
1. Seventh-day Adventists—Doctrinal and controversial works. 2. Christianity—Apologetic works—20th cent. I. Title.

NICHOL, Francis David, 1897- 230.67
Answers to objections; an examination of the major objections raised against the teachings of Seventh-Day Adventists. Foreword by W. H. Branson. Rev. and greatly enl. Washington, Review and Herald Pub. Association [1952] 895 p. 24 cm. [BX6154.N5] 52-43231
1. Seventh-Day Adventists — Doctrinal and controversial works. I. Title.

NICHOL, Francis David, 1897- 922.673
Ellen G. White and her critics; an answer to the major charges that critics have brought against Mrs. Ellen G. White. Foreword by J. L. McElhany. Takoma Park, Washington, D.C., Review and Herald Pub. Association [1951] 703 p. 23 cm. Bibliography: p. 679-703. [BX6193.W5N5] 51-2779
1. White, Ellen Gould (Harmon) 1827-1915. 2. Seventh-Day Adventists — Doctrinal and controversial works. I. Title.

NICHOL, Francis David, 1897- 230.67
Let's live our beliefs; a discussion of Seventh-Day Adventist beliefs in terms of their practical relation to everyday living. Takoma Park, Washington, D.C., Review and Herald Pub. Assn. [1947] 192 p. 21 cm. [BX6154.N54] 47-6305
1. Seventh-Day Adventists—Doctrinal and controversial works. I. Title.

NICHOL, Francis David, 1897- 286.7
Reasons for our faith; a discussion of questions vital to the proper understanding and effective presentation of certain Seventh-Day Adventist teachings. Washington, Review and Herald Pub. Assn. [1947] 444 p. 24 cm. [BX6154.N58] 48-12090
1. Seventh-day Adventists—Doctrinal and controversial works. I. Title.

NIES, Richard, 1928- 234
Security of salvation / by Richard Nies. Nashville : Southern Pub. Association, c1978. p. cm. Includes bibliographical references. [BT751.2.N53] 78-17523 pbk. : 0.95
1. Seventh-Day Adventists—Doctrinal and controversial works. 2. Salvation. I. Title.

NIGHTINGALE, Reuben H. 269'.2
Crossing Jordan at flood tide / [R. H. Nightingale]. Mountain View, Calif. : Pacific Press Pub. Association, [1975] 155 p. ; 19 cm. [BV3790.N48] 75-16541 pbk. : 2.95
1. Seventh-Day Adventists—Doctrinal and controversial works. 2. Evangelistic work. I. Title.

OCHS, William Benjamin. 23067
Living faith. Washington, Review and Herald [1954] 192p. 21cm. [BX6154.O3] 54-27846

1. Seventh-Day Adventists—Doctrinal and controversial works. I. Title.

PADDOCK, Charles Lee, 1891- 248
Highways to happiness. Washington, Review and Herald Pub. Association [1950] 384 p. illus. (part col.) 22 cm. [BX6154.P25] 50-13911
1. Seventh-Day-Adventists — Doctrinal and controversial works. I. Title.

PEASE, Norval F. 234'.2
The faith that saves [by] Norval F. Pease. [Washington, Review and Herald Pub. Association, c1969] 64 p. 18 cm. Cover title. [BT772.P38] 76-128408
1. Seventh-Day Adventists—Doctrinal and controversial works. 2. Faith. I. Title.

PEREZ MARCIO, Braulio 286.7
Libertad del temor [por] Braulio Perez Marcio, Hector Pereyra Suarez, Fernando Chaij. Mexico, Ediciones Interamericanas [dist. Mountain View, Calif., Pacific Pr., c.1964] 510p. illus. (pt. col.) 23cm. Bibl. 64-4099 9.25
1. Seventh-Day Adventists—Doctrinal and controversial works. I. Pereyra Suarez, Hector. II. Chaij, Fernando. III. Title.

PETERSON, Frank Loris. 230.67
The hope of the race. Rev. Nashville, Southern Pub. Assn. [1946] 333 p. illus., ports. 21 cm. [BX6154.P45 1946] 49-4204
1. Seventh-Day Adventists—Doctrinal and controversial works. 2. Seventh-Day Aventists, Negro. I. Title.

PETERSON, Frank Loris. 230.67
The hope of the race, by Frank Loris Peterson. Nashville, Tenn., Southern publishing association [c1934] 333 p. incl. front., illus., ports., diagrs. col. pl. 21 cm. [BX6154.P45] 35-1032
1. Seventh-day Adventists—Doctrinal and controversial works. 2. Negroes—Religion. I. Title.

PIERSON, Robert H. 248'.48'673
Beloved leaders : inspirational essays on Seventh-Day Adventist Christian leadership / written as personal message to the leaders of the Seventh-Day Adventist Church—both denominational workers and lay leaders by Robert H. Pierson. Mountain View, Calif. : Pacific Press Pub. Association, c1978. 142 p. ; 22 cm. Includes bibliographical references. [BX6154.P49] 77-91404 pbk. : 3.95
1. Seventh-Day Adventists—Doctrinal and controversial works. 2. Christian life—Seventh-Day Adventist authors. I. Title.

PIERSON, Robert H. 230'.6'73
We still believe / Robert H. Pierson. Washington : Review and Herald Pub. Association, [1975] 254 p. ; 22 cm. [BX6154.P5] 75-312405 6.95
1. Seventh-Day Adventists—Doctrinal and controversial works. 2. Christian life—Seventh-Day Adventist authors. I. Title.

PRICE, Ernest Bruce, 1932- 289.9
God's channel of truth, is it the Watchtower? By E. B. Price. Mountain View, Calif., Pacific Press Pub. Association [c1967] 112 p. illus. 19 cm. [BX6154.P68] 67-308895
1. Seventh-Day Adventists—Doctrinal and controversial works. 2. Jehovah's Witnesses—Doctrinal and controversial works. I. Title.

PRICE, George McCready, 1870- 230.67
If You were the creator; a reasonable credo for modern man, by George McCready Price ... Mountain View, Calif., Portland, Or. [etc.] Pacific press publishing association [1942] 3 p. l., 5-170 p. 20 1/2 cm. [BX6154.P7] 42-20880
1. Seventh-day Adventists—Doctrinal and controversial works. I. Title.

PRICE, George McCready, 1870- 228'.06'6
The time of the end. Nashville, Southern Pub. Association [1967] 171 p. 22 cm. [BS2825.2.P74] 67-31686
1. Seventh-Day Adventists—Doctrinal and controversial works. 2. Bible. N.T. Revelation, XIII-XVII—Criticism, interpretation, etc. I. Title.

READ, Walter E 1883- 230.67
The Bible, the spirit of prophecy, and the church. Washington, Review and Herald Pub. Association [1952] 192p. 20cm. [BX6154.R33] 52-68266
1. Seventh-Day Adventists—Doctrinal and controversial works. 2. Bible— Evidences, authority, etc. 3. Prophets. 4. Church. I. Title.

REBOK, Denton Edward, 1897- 230.63
Believe His prophets. Washington, Review and Herald Pub. Association [1956] 320p. 18cm. (Christian home library) [BX6154.R338] 56-38678
1. Seventh-Day Adventists—Doctrinal and controversial works. I. Title.

REBOK, Denton Edward, 1897- 230.67
God and I are partners. Washington, Review and Herald Pub. Association [1951] 126 p. illus. 16 cm. (Little giant pocket series) [BX6154.R34] 51-27688
1. Seventh-Day Adventists — Doctrinal and controversial works. I. Title.

REYNOLDS, Louis Bernard, 1917- 230.67
The dawn of a brighter day; light through the darkness ahead, by Louis B. Reynolds ... Nashville, Tenn., The Southern publishing association [1945] 96 p. incl. front., illus. (incl. ports.) 19 1/2 cm. [BX6154.R4] 45-20162
1. Seventh-day Adventists—Doctrinal and controversial works. 2. Seventh-day Adventists, Negro. I. Title.

RICHARDS, Harold Marshall Sylvester, 1894- 230.67
What Jesus said. Nashville, Southern Pub. Association [1957] 576p. illus. 18cm. [BX6154.R45] 57-28028
1. Seventh-Day Adventists—Doctrinal and controversial works. I. Title.

RICHARDS, Harold Marshall Sylvester, 1894- 230.67
Why I am a Seventh-Day Adventist [by] H. M. S. Richards. Washington, Review and Herald Pub. Association [1965] 128 p. illus., ports. 21 cm. [BX6154.R47] 66-3284
1. Seventh-Day Adventists — Doctrinal and controversial works. I. Title.

RITCHIE, Cyril J. 286.7
While it is day. Mountain View, Calif., Pacific Press Pub. Association [1951] xii, 179 p. 20 cm. [BX6154.R5] 51-21257
1. Seventh-Day Adventists — Doctrinal and controversial works. 2. Second Advent. I. Title.

ROBERTSON, John J. 234'.1
Tongues : what you should know about glossolalia / by John J. Robertson. Mountain View, Calif. : Pacific Press Pub. Association, c1977. 58 p. ; 19 cm. [BS2545.G63R62] 76-6618 pbk. : 0.75
1. Seventh-Day Adventists—Doctrinal and controversial works. 2. Glossolalia—Biblical teaching. I. Title.

SCHWARTZ, Gary. 301.5'8'0973
Sect ideologies and social status. Chicago, University of Chicago Press [1970] x, 260 p. 23 cm. Includes bibliographical references. [BT738.S369 1970] 72-120598 ISBN 0-226-74216-4
1. Seventh-Day Adventists—Doctrinal and controversial works. 2. Sociology, Christian—United States. 3. Pentecostal churches—Doctrinal and controversial works. I. Title.

SETON, Bernard E., 1913- 230'.673
These truths shall triumph : studies in Christian doctrines / Bernard E. Seton. Washington, D.C. : Review and Herald Pub. Association, [1981] p. cm. [BX6154.S37] 19 81-8495 ISBN 0-8280-0099-9 : 5.50
1. Seventh-Day Adventists—Doctrinal and controversial works. I. Title.

SEVENTH-DAY Adventists. General conference. 230.67
Belief and work of Seventh-day Adventists. Century of progress ed. Published for the General conference of Seventh-day Adventists. Washington, D.C. Mountain View, Calif., Omaha [etc.] Pacific press publishing association [c1934] 2 p. l., 3-96 p. incl. front., illus. 19 1/2 cm. [BX6154.A5 1934] 34-37656
1. Seventh-day Adventists—Doctrinal and controversial works. I. Title.

SEVENTH-DAY Adventists. Evangelistic council. 253
Report of Evangelistic council and Ministerial association meetings, General conference, San Francisco, May 22 to June 5, 1941 ... Takoma Park, Washington, D.C., Review and herald publishing association [1941] 285 p. incl. forms. 20 cm. (Ministerial reading course selection for 1942, Ministerial association of Seventh-day Adventists) [BX6154.A45] 42-9993
1. Seventh-day Adventists—Doctrinal and controversial works. 2. Evangelistic work. I. Seventh-day Adventists. Ministerial association. II. Title.

SEVENTH-DAY Adventists answer questions on doctrine; 230.67 an explanation of certain major aspects of Seventh-Day Adventist belief, prepared by a representative group of Seventh-Day Adventist leaders, Bible teachers, and editors. Washington, Review and Herald Pub. Association [1957] 720 p. 21 cm. Includes bibliography. [BX6154.S4] 57-4838
1. Seventh-Day Adventists — Doctrinal and controversial works. 2. Questions and answers — Theology. I. Title: Questions on doctrine.

SEVENTH-DAY Adventists. General Conference. 230.67
Our firm foundation; a report of the Seventh-Day Adventist Bible conference held September 1-13, 1952, in the Sligo Seventh-Day Adventist Church, Takoma Park, Maryland. Washington, Review and Herald Pub. Association [1953] 2v. 22cm. Bibliographical footnotes. Bibliography: v. 1, p. 714-716. [BX6154.A45 1952] 53-21443
1. Seventh-Day Adventists—Doctrinal and controversial works. I. Title.

SEVENTH-DAY Adventists. General Conference. Dept. of Education. 230.67
Principles of life from the Word of God; a systematic study of the major doctrines of the Bible. Mountain View, Calif., Pacific Press Pub. Association, for the Dept. of Education, General Conference of Seventh-Day Adventists [1952] 508p. illus. 24cm. [BX6155.S44] 52-14728
1. Seventh-Day Adventists—Doctrinal and controversial works. 2. Theology, Doctrinal—Popular works. I. Title.

SHELDON, Jean, 1956- 248'.5
Sharing Jesus : what witnessing is really all about / by Jean Sheldon. Mountain View, Calif. : Pacific Press Pub. Association, c1981. 144 p. ; 18 cm. Includes bibliographical references. [BV4520.S45] 79-27841 ISBN 0-8163-0350-9 pbk. : 4.95
1. Seventh-Day Adventists—Doctrinal and controversial works. 2. Witness bearing (Christianity) I. Title.
Distributed by the Greater New York Bookstore, 12 W. 40th St., New York, NY

SHULER, John Lewis, 1887- 230.67
Helps to Bible study, by J. L. Shuler... Takoma Park, Washington, D.C. [etc.] Review and herald publishing assn. [c1934] 63 p. 17 1/2 cm. [BX6154.S56] [220] 34-20734
1. Seventh-day Adventists—Doctrinal and controversial works. I. Title.

SHULER, John Lewis, 1887- 230'.6'73
The search for truth / J. L. Shuler. Washington : Review and Herald Pub. Association, 1980. 141 p. : 19 cm. [BX6154.S562] 79-19715 pbk. : .50
1. Seventh-Day Adventists—Doctrinal and controversial works. I. Title.

[SPICER, William Ambrose] 1866- 230.07
Beacon lights of prophecy ... Takoma Park, Washington, D.C., Peekskill, N.Y. [etc.] Review and herald pub. assn. [c1935] 2 p. l., 3-415 p. col. front., illus. (incl. ports., maps) col. plates. 21 cm. "By W. A. Spicer."--1st prelim. leaf. [BX6154.S65] 35-3984
1. Seventh day Adventists—Doctrinal and controversial works. 2. Bible—Prophecies. 3. End of the world. I. Title.

SPICER, William Ambrose, 1866- 230.67
Signs of Christ's coming, foretold in Matthew 24, by William A. Spicer ...

Takoma Park, Washington, D.C., Review and herald publishing association [c1941] 96 p. incl. front., illus. 19 1/2 cm. [BX6154.S75] 41-12016
1. Seventh-day Adventists—Doctrinal and controversial works. 2. Second advent. I. Title.

SYME, Eric. 322'.1
A history of SDA church-state relations in the United States. Mountain View, Calif., Pacific Press Pub. Association [1973] 167 p. 22 cm. (Dimension 117) Includes bibliographical references. [BX6154.S93] 73-91831
1. Seventh-Day Adventists—Doctrinal and controversial works. 2. Church and state in the United States. I. Title.

TAYLOR, Clifton L 230.67
Outline studies from the Testimonies. 5th ed., rev. Washington, Review and Herald Pub. Association [1955] 480p. 18cm. (Christian home library) [BX6111.W625T3 1955] 56-17895
1. Seventh-Day Adventists—Doctrinal and controversial works. 2. White, Ellen Gould (Harmon) 1827-1915. I. Title.

VANDEMAN, George. 231'.7
Tying down the sun / George Vandeman. Mountain View, Calif. : Pacific Press Pub. Association, c1978. 96 p. : ill. ; 18 cm. [BS651.V28] 78-61749 pbk. : 0.85
1. Seventh-Day Adventists—Doctrinal and controversial works. 2. Creation—Biblical teaching. 3. Evolution and Christianity. I. Title.

VANDEMAN, George E. 263.2
A day to remember. Mountain View, Calif., Pacific Pr. Pub. [c.1965] 103p. 19cm. [BX6154.V25] 65-24345 .30 pap.,
1. Seventh-Day Adventists—Doctrinal and controversial works. I. Title.

VANDEMAN, George E. 286.73
Destination life. Mountain View, Calif., Pacific Pr. Pub. [c.1966] 92p. 18cm. [BX6154.V254] 66-21954 .30 pap.,
1. Seventh-Day Adventists—Doctrinal and controversial works. I. Title.

VANDEMAN, George E. 230.67
Planet rebellion. Nashville, Southern Pub. Association [1960] 448 p. illus. 18 cm. Includes bibliography. [BX6154.V26] 60-2151
1. Seventh-Day Adventists — Doctrinal and controversial works. I. Title.

*VANDEMAN, George E. 286.7
Un jour memorable [Mountain View, Calif., Pacific Pr. Pub., 1968] 93p. 18cm. (Eds. Inter-Americaines) French language ed. of A day to remember, tr. by Danielle Volf-Ducret. .30 pap.,
1. Seventh Day Adventists—Doctrinal and controversial works. I. Title.

VAN DOLSON, Leo R. 261.8'32'1
Healthy, happy, holy / Leo R. Van Dolson, J. Robert Spangler. Washington : Review and Herald Pub. Association, [1975] 208 p. ; 23 cm. Bibliography: p. 206-208. [BX6154.V24] 74-21006 3.50
1. Seventh-Day Adventists—Doctrinal and controversial works. 2. Medicine and religion. 3. Evangelistic work. 4. Missions, Medical. I. Spangler, J. Robert, joint author. II. Title.

WAGNER, Harry L. 230.67
Out of darkness, by Harry L. Wagner. New York city, Stuyvesant press corp. [1946] iii-xvi, [17]-358 p. 21 cm. [BX6144.W3] 46-18968
1. Seventh-day Adventists—Doctrinal and controversial works. I. Title.

*WALDO, Charlotte E. 286.7
It's a great life. Nashville, Southern Pub. Assn. [1967, c.1959] 182p. 20cm. (Summit bk.) 1.50 pap.,
1. Seventh-Day Adventists—Doctrinal and Controversial works. I. Title.

WALKER, Allen. 230.67
Last-day delusions. Nashville, Southern Pub. Association [1957] 128p. 18cm. [BX6154.W298] 57-40146
1. Seventh-Day Adventists—Doctrinal and controversial works. I. Title.

WALKER, Allen. 230.67
Last-day delusions. Nashville, Southern Pub. Association [1956] 128 p. 18 cm. [BX6154.W298] 57-40146
1. Seventh Day Adventists. — Doctrinal and controversial works. I. Title.

WALKER, Allen. 263.2
The law and the Sabbath. Nashville, Southern Pub. Association [1953] 240p. 21cm. [BX6154.W3] 54-17875
1. Seventh-Day Adventists—Doctrinal and controversial works. 2. Sabbath. I. Title.

WEARNER, Alonzo Joseph, 230.67
1892-
Fundamentals of Bible doctrine; sixty studies in the basic facts of the everlasting gospel arranged for Seventh-day Adventist schools of nursing, by Alonzo J. Wearner. Angwin, Calif., Pacific union college press [c1931] 349 p. diagrs. 23 1/2 cm. [BX6154.W4] 220.7 31-30735
1. Seventh-day Adventists—Doctrinal and controversial works. I. Title. II. Title: Bible doctrine, Fundamentals of.

WEARNER, Alonzo Joseph, 230.67
1892-
Fundamentals of Bible doctrine; sixty studies in the basic facts of the everlasting gospel arranged for classes in advanced Bible doctrines, by Alonzo J. Wearner ... 2d ed. Takoma Park, Washington, D.C., South Bend, Ind. [etc.] Review and herald publishing assn. [c1935] 421 p. diagrs. 20 cm. [BX6154.W4 1935] [220.7] 35-499
1. Seventh-day Adventists—Doctrinal and controversial works. I. Title. II. Title: Bible doctrine, Fundamentals of.

WEEKS, Howard B. 269'.2
Adventist evangelism in the twentieth century [by] Howard B. Weeks. Washington, Review & Herald Pub. Association [1969] 320 p. illus., facsims., ports. 24 cm. Includes bibliographies. [BX6154.W43] 68-25111
1. Seventh-day Adventists—Doctrinal and controversial works. 2. Evangelistic work. I. Title.

*WHITE, Elena G. de. 286.7
Mensajes selectos de los ecritos de Elena G. de White; v.1. Mountain View, Calif., Pacific Pr. [1967] 520p. 18cm. Titulo de este libro en ingles: Selected messages. 3.75
1. Seventh-day Adventists—Doctrinal and controversial works. I. Title.

WHITE, Ellen Gould (Harmon) 286.7
1827-1915.
Early writings of Ellen G. White. Washington, D.C., Review and herald publishing association [1945] 9 p., 1 l., 11-127 p., 1 l., 133-316 p. 17 1/2 cm. (On cover: Christian home library) "Fourth American edition."--Pref. [BX6111.W5 1945] 45-5282
1. Seventh-day Adventists—Doctrinal and controversial works. I. Experience and views. II. Spiritual gifts. III. Title.
Contents omitted.

WHITE, Ellen Gould (Harmon) 289
1827-1915.
Early writings of Mrs. White. Experience and views, and Spiritual gifts, volume one. By Mrs. E. G. White. 2d ed. Battle Creek, Mich., Review and herald; Oakland, Cal., Pacific press, 1882. [268] p. 18 cm. Each work paged separately. Includes Supplement to Experience and views. [BX6111.W5 1882] 44-29718
1. Seventh-day Adventists—Doctrinal and controversial works. I. Title. II. Title: Spiritual gifts III. Title: Experience and views

WHITE, Ellen Gould (Harmon) 289
1827-1915.
Early writings of Mrs. White. Experience and views, and Spiritual gifts, volume one. By Mrs. E. G. White. 5th ed. Battle Creek, Mich., Review and herald; Oakland, Cal., Pacific press, 1893. [268] p. 19 1/2 cm. Each work paged separately. Includes Supplement to Experience and views. [BX6111.W5 1893] 44-29717
1. Seventh-day Adventists—Doctrinal and controversial works. I. Title. II. Title: Experience and views. III. Title: Spiritual gifts.

WHITE, Ellen Gould 286.7
(Harmon), 1827-1915
The great controversy between Christ and Satan. New York, Pyramid [1967,c.1950] 576p. 18cm. Pub. 1870-78, under title: The spirit of prophecy. (N-1719) [BX6111.W57 1950] .95 pap.,
1. Seventh-Day Adventists—Doctrinal and controversial works. I. Title.

WHITE, Ellen Gould (Harmon) 286.7
1827-1915.
The great controversy between Christ and Satan; the conflict of the ages in the Christian dispensation. Mountain View, Calif., Pacific Press Pub. Association [c1950] xiii, 709 p. illus. (part col.) ports. 23 cm. Published, 1870-78, under title: The spirit of prophecy. Bibliography: p. 681-683. [BX6111.W57] 51-21254
1. Seventy-Day Adventists—Doctrinal and controversial works. I. Title.

WHITE, Ellen Gould (Harmon) 286.7
Mrs., 1827-1915.
The great controversy between Christ and Satan, the conflict of the ages in the Christian dispensation, by Ellen G. White ... Mountain View, Calif., Portland, Ore. [etc.] Pacific press publishing assocation [c1927] 802 p. front., illus. (incl. ports.) 22 1/2 cm. Published, 1870-1878, under title: The spirit of prophecy. [BX6111.W57 1927] 27-10061
1. Seventh-day Adventists—Doctrinal and controversial works. I. Title.

WHITE, Ellen Gould (Harmon) 286.7
Mrs., 1827-1915.
The great controversy between Christ and Satan during the Christian dispensation. By Mrs. E. G. White ... 11th ed. Rev. and enl. Sixty-second thousand. Oakland, Cal., New York [etc.] Pacific press publishing company, 1888. 5 p. l., v-xv, [1], 17-704 p. front., 1 illus., plates, ports., diagr. 23 cm. Published, 1870-78, under title: The spirit of prophecy. [BX6111.W57 1888] 37-7025
1. Seventh-day Adventists—Doctrinal and controversial works. I. Title.

WHITE, Ellen Gould (Harmon)
1827-1915.
The great controversy between Christ and Satan; the conflict of the ages in the Christian dispensation. Mountain View, Calif., Pacific Press Pub. Association [1958, c1911] 719 p. 22 cm. (Conflict of the ages series) Published in 1884 as v. 4 of The spirit of prophecy. Bibliography included in notes. 63-72029
1. Seventh-Day Adventists — Doctrinal and controversial works. I. Title.

WHITE, Ellen Gould (Harmon) 286.7
1827-1915
[He epikeimene pale] Mountain View, Calif., Pacific Pr. Pub. [c.1964] 144p. illus. 20cm. Selections in Greek from the author's The great controversy between Christ and Satan pub. 1870-78, under the title: The spirit of prophecy. Pub. in English in 1936 under the title: Impending conflict. [BX6111.W5715] 65-362 1.00 pap.,
1. Seventh-Day Adventists—Doctrinal and controversial works. I. Title.

WHITE, Ellen Gould (Harmon) 286.7
1827-1915
Premiers ecrits. Mountain View, Calif., Pac. Pr. Pub. [1963, c.1962] 328p. 18cm. (Pubns. inter-americaines) 62-21828 3.50
1. Seventh-day Adventists—Doctrinal and controversial works. I. Title.

WHITE, Ellen Gould 230.67
(Harmon) Mrs., 1827-1915.
Selections from the Testimonies, by Ellen G. White ... selected from "Testimonies for the church" ... Nashville, Tenn., Southern publishing association [c1936] 3 v. 20 cm. Includes advertising matter. [BX6111.W62] 37-15588
1. Seventh-day Adventists—Doctrinal and controversial works. I. Title.

WHITE, Ellen Gould 230.63
(Harmon) 1827-1915.
Spiritual gifts. Facsimile reproduction. Washington, Review and Herald Pub. Association [1944, c1945] 4 v. in 2. 15 cm. Each volume has reproduction of original t.p. [BX6111.W58] 50-19571
1. Seventh-Day Adventists—Doctrinal and controversial works. I. Title.
Contents omitted.

WHITE, Ellen Gould 230.67
(Harmon) 1827-1915.
The story of patriarchs and prophets; the conflict of the ages illustrated in the lives of holy men of old. Washington, Review and Herald Pub. Association, 1958. 832 p. illus. 23 cm. [BX6111.W599 1958] 58-1760
1. Seventh-Day Adventists — Doctrinal and controversial works. 2. Patriarchs (Bible) 3. Prophets. I. Title.

WHITE, Ellen Gould 230.67
(Harmon) 1827-1915.
The story of patriarchs and prophets; the conflict of the ages illustrated in the lives of holy men of old. Mountain View, Calif., Pacific Press Pub. Assn. [1947?] 793 p. illus. 22 cm. (Her Conflict of the ages series, v. 1) Cover title: Patriarchs and prophets. [BX6111.W53 1947] 48-10176
1. Seventh-Day Adventists—Doctrinal and controversial works. 2. Patriarchs (Bible) 3. Prophets. I. Title.

WHITE, Ellen Gould (Harmon) 251
Mrs., 1827-1915.
The story of patriarchs and prophets; the conflict of the ages illustrated in the lives of holy men of old, by Ellen G. White ... Washington, D.C., South Bend, Ind. [etc.] Review and herald publishing association, 1922. 790, [9] p. incl. front., illus. 22 1/2 cm. [BX6111.W53 1922] 22-23589
1. Seventh-day Adventists—Doctrinal and controversial works. 2. Patriarchs (Bible) 3. Prophets. I. Title.

WHITE, Ellen Gould 230.67
(Harmon) 1827-1915.
The story of redemption, a concise presentation of the conflict of the ages drawn from the earlier writings of Ellen G. White. Washington, Review and Herald Pub. Assn. [1947] 445 p. 18 cm. (Christian home library) [BX6111.W5982] 47-7769
1. Seventh-Day Adventists—Doctrinal and controversial works. I. Title.

WHITE, Ellen Gould 230.67
(Harmon) 1827-1915.
Testimony treasures; counsels for the church as selected from the Testimonies. Mountain View, Calif., Pacific Press Pub. Association [1949] 3 v. 18 cm. (Christian home library) "These three volumes ... constitute an integral part of the Introductory spirit of prophecy library." [BX6111.W622] 50-366
1. Seventh-Day Adventists—Doctrinal and controversial works. I. Title. II. Series.

WHITE, Ellen Gould (Harmon) 286.7
1827-1915.
The triumph of God's love; the story of the vindication of the character of God and the salvation of mankind. Nashville, Southern Pub. Association [1957] 429p. illus. 26cm. Published, 1870-78, under title: The spirit of prophecy. [BX6111.W57 1957] 57-3640
1. Seventh-Day Adventists—Doctrinal and controversial works. I. Title.

WHITE, Julius Gilbert. 230.67
The Christian's experience in the conquest of sin, by Julius Gilbert White ... Madison College, Tenn., The author [1942] 6 p. l., 287 p. port., diagrs. 23 1/2 cm. [BX6154.W46] 42-24854
1. Seventh-day Adventists—Doctrinal and controversial works. I. Title.

WHITE, Julius Gilbert. 230.67
The Christian's experience in the conquest of sin, by Julius Gilbert White. Asheville, N.C., The author, distributed by Health and character education institute [1945] 6 p. l., 300 p. port., diagrs. 23 1/2 cm. [BX6154.W46 1945] 45-9243
1. Seventh-day Adventists—Doctrinal and controversial works. I. Title.

WILCOX, Francis McLellan. 230.67
The coming crisis, by Francis McLellan Wilcox ... A brief review of several Bible prophecies culminating in the last-day crisis; also a compilation of significant statements from the writings of Mrs. Ellen G. White relative to this crisis ... 2d ed., rev. and enl. Takoma Park, Washington, D.C., Review and herald publishing association [1947] 160 p. 20 cm. [BX6154.W55 1947] 47-19742
1. Seventh-day Adventists—Doctrinal and controversial works. 2. Second advent. I. White, Ellen Gould (Harmon) 1827-1915. II. Title.

WILCOX, Francis McLellan. 286.7
The early and latter rain; a heart-to-heart discussion of a vital and all-important experience for the church as a whole and for each individual member. By Francis McLellan Wilcox... Takoma Park, Washington, D.C., Review and herald publishing assn. [c1938] 3 p. l., [9]-187 p. illus. 20 cm. [BX6154.W553] 38-10066
1. Seventh-day Adventists—Doctrinal and controversial works. 2. End of the world. I. Title.

WILCOX, Llewellyn A. 236
Now is the time, by Llewellyn A. Wilcox. Rev. ed. Escondido, Calif., Outdoor Pictures [1966] 279 p. 22 cm. [BX6154.W556 1966] 66-19548
1. Seventh-Day Adventists—Doctrinal and controversial works. 2. Eschatology. I. Title.

WILCOX, Milton Charles, 286. 1853-1935.
Questions and answers. No. 1, gathered from the Question corner department of the Signs of the times, by Milton C. Wilcox... Mountain View, Cal., Pacific press publishing association [191-?] viii, 9-255 p. 18 1/2 cm. Published in 1938 under title: Questions answered. No more published? [BX6154.W57] 39-800
1. Seventh-day Adventists—Doctrinal and controversial works. I. Title.

WILCOX, Milton Charles, 230.67 1853-1935.
Questions answered, gathered from the Question corner department of the "Signs of the times", by Milton C. Wilcox... Mountain View, Cal., Omaha, Neb. [etc.] Pacific press publishing association [c1938] 245 p. 21 cm. [BX6154.W57] 38-6563
1. Seventh-day Adventists—Doctrinal and controversial works. I. Title.

YOUR Bible and you;
priceless treasures in the Holy Scriptures. Mountain View, Pacific Press Publ. [1959] 480p. illus. 26cm.
1. Seventh-Day Adventists—Doctrinal and controversial works. I. Maxwell, Arthur Stanley, 1896-

Seventh-Day Adventists—Doctrinal and controversial works—Addresses, essays, lectures.

THE Channel : 220.6
communication for Biblical, theological, and related studies. Washington : [General Conference of Seventh-Day Adventists], 1976. 56 p. ; 28 cm. Contents.Contents.—Abstracts : Ford, D. A rhetorical study of certain Pauline addresses. Maxwell, D. M. The significance of the Parousia in the theology of Paul. Butler, J. Adventism and the American experience. Ford, D. The abomination of eschatology in Biblical eschatology.—Papers: Baldwin, D. D. SDA presuppositions to Bibliocal studies, a call for presupposition research. Johnsson, W. G. SDA presuppositions to Biblical studies. Edwards, R. D. Tithing in the Middle Ages. Includes bibliographical references. [BS540.C52] 77-356447
1. Seventh-Day Adventists—Doctrinal and controversial works—Address, essays, lectures. 2. Bible—Criticism, interpretation, etc.—Addresses, essays, lectures. I. Seventh-Day Adventists. General Conference.

REVIVAL and 230'.6'73
reformation [by] Robert H. Pierson [and others] Washington, Review and Herald Pub. Association [1974] 156 p. 22 cm. Speeches presented at the 1973 Annual Council of the Seventh-day Adventists. [BX6154.R39] 74-77806 4.95
1. Seventh-Day Adventists—Doctrinal and controversial works—Addresses, essays, lectures. I. Pierson, Robert H.

Seventh-Day Adventists—Doctrinal and controversial works—Adventist authors—Miscellanea.

FORD, Desmond. 230'.6'73
Answers on the way : scriptural answers to your questions / by Desmond Ford. Mountain View, Calif. : Pacific Press Pub. Association, c1977. 155 p. ; 22 cm. (Dimension ; 121) Includes bibliographical references. [BX6154.F57] 76-17704 pbk. : 3.95
1. Seventh-Day Adventists—Doctrinal and controversial works—Adventist authors—Miscellanea. I. Title.

Seventh-Day Adventists—Doctrinal and Controversial works—Juvenile literature.

*SPARKS, Enid 286.7
Dana's date with trouble, and other true stories. Illus. by Vance Locke. Nashville, Southern Pub. Assn. [1967, c.1960] 204p. illus. 21cm. (Summit bk.) 1.50 pap.,
1. Seventh-Day Adventists—Doctrinal and Controversial works—Juvenile literature. I. Title.

Seventh-Day Adventists—Doctrinal and controversial works—Seventh-Day Adventist authors.

DOUGLASS, Herbert E. 236'.3
The end : unique voice of Adventists about the return of Jesus / Herbert E. Douglass ; [cover photo, Morton Beebe]. Mountain View, Calif. : Pacific Press Pub. Association, c1979. 192 p. ; 22 cm. (Dimension ; 139) Includes bibliographical references and indexes. [BT886.D68] 79-88435 pbk. : 4.95
1. Seventh-Day Adventists—Doctrinal and controversial works—Seventh-Day Adventist authors. 2. Second Advent. 3. Millennialism. I. Title.

JEWETT, Dick. 262'.001
Let's fan the flame : an eleventh-hour challenge for Seventh-Day Adventists to finish their task / Dick Jewett ; [cover ill. Jack Pardue]. Washington : Review and Herald Pub. Association, c1979. 142 p. ; 20 cm. [BX6151.J48] 79-12033 pbk. : 5.95
1. Seventh-Day Adventists—Doctrinal and controversial works—Seventh-Day Adventist authors—Addresses, essays, lectures. 2. Church renewal—Addresses, essays, lectures. I. Title.

KEOUGH, G. Arthur, 1909- 230'.67
Our church today : what it is and can be / G. Arthur Keough. Nashville, TN : Review and Herald Pub. Assoc., c1980. 124 p. ; 21 cm. Includes bibliographical references. [BV600.2.K42] 19 80-19816 ISBN 0-8127-0300-6 pbk. : 4.95
1. Seventh-Day Adventists—Doctrinal and controversial works—Seventh-Day Adventist authors. 2. Church. I. Title.

OUR real roots : 213
scientific support for creationism / compiled by Leo R. Van Dolson from articles appearing in the Science and religion section of Ministry magazine. Washington : Review and Herald Pub. Association, c1979. 189 p. : ill. ; 21 cm. Includes bibliographical references. [BS651.O93] 78-21688 7.95
1. Seventy-Day Adventists—Doctrinal and controversial works—Seventh-Day Adventist authors—Addresses, essays, lectures. 2. Creation—Addresses, essays, lectures. I. Van Dolson, Leo R. II. The Ministry for world evangelism.
Publisher's address: Takoma Park, Washington, D.C. 20012.

Seventh-Day Adventists—Education.

BARGER, R. Curtis. 268'.433
Tomorrow in your hand; a guide for the Christian leader and teacher of earliteens and youth [by] R. Curtis Barger. Washington, Review and Herald Pub. Association [1966] 176 p. illus. 22 cm. Bibliography: p. 175-176. [BV1485.B3] 66-28651
1. Seventh-Day Adventists—Education. 2. Christian education of young people. I. Title.

BARTLETT, W T. 268
Sabbath school ideals, by W. T. Bartlett. Nashville, Tenn., Southern publishing association [c1940] 144 p. 20 cm. [BX6113.B3] 40-29732
1. Seventh-day Adventists—Education. 2. Religious education. I. Title.

CADWALLADER, Edward 377.863 Miles, 1896-
A history of Seventh-Day Adventist education. Rev. ed. [Lincoln? Neb.] c1956. 218 l. 29cm. [LC586.A3C3 1956] 57-17618
1. Seventh-Day Adventists—Education. I. Title.

CADWALLADER, Edward 377.867 Miles, 1896-
A history of Seventh-Day Adventist education. 3d ed. [Lincoln? Neb.] c1958. 314p. 28cm. [LC586.A3C3 1958] 59-18893
1. Seventh-Day Adventists—Education. I. Title.

CADWALLADER, Edward 377.863 Miles, 1896-
A history of Seventh-Day Adventist education. [Lincoln? Neb.] c1954. 54 l. 29cm. [LC586.A3C3] 55-20550
1. Seventh-Day Adventists—Education. I. Title.

HOWELL, Emma Elizabeth, 268.334 1895-
So you're the secretary of the Sabbath school, by Emma E. Howell. Mountain View, Calif., Brookfield, Ill. [etc.] Pacific press publishing association [c1941] 128 p. 1 illus. 20 cm. [BX6113.H6] 41-6970
1. Seventh-day Adventists—Education. I. Title.

LOWE, Harry William. 253
Evangelism in the Sabbath school. Washington, Review and Herald Pub. Assn. [1948] 192 p. 21 cm. [BX6113.L6] 49-14540
1. Seventh-Day Adventists—Education. 2. Evangelistic work. I. Title.

MOORE, Mary Hunter. 268.6
A workman not ashamed, by Mary Hunter Moore ... Nashville, Tenn., Southern publishing association [c1941] 111 p. incl. front., illus. 19 1/2 cm. [BX6113.M6] 43-19225
1. Seventh-day Adventists—Education. 2. Religious education—Teaching methods. I. Title.

NASH, Gerald R. 268.867
Evangelism through the Sabbath school. Washington, D.C., Review & Herald [1964] 192p. 22cm. 64-17652 price unreported
1. Seventh-Day Adventists—Education. 2. Evangelistic work. I. Title.

NASH, Gerald R 268.8673
Planning better Sabbath schools, by Gerald R. Nash. Washington, Review and Herald Pub. Association [1965] 190 p. 22 cm. [BX6113.N316] 65-18672
1. Seventh-Day Adventists — Education. 2. Religious education. I. Title.

OGLE, Mary S 1905- 268.863
You and your Sabbath school. Washington, Review and Herald, 1949. 189 p. 20 cm. [BX6113.O4] 50-55678
1. Seventh-Day Adventists—Education. 2. Religious education. I. Title.

SEVENTH-DAY Adventists. 268.4 General Conference. Sabbath School Dept.
Teaching teachers to teach; especially prepared for teachers of the primary, junior, earliteen, and youth divisions of our Sabbath schools, by the General Conference, Sabbath School Department. Rev. ed. Nashville, Southern Pub. Association [c1964] 406 p. illus. 22 cm. [BV1534.S42 1964] 63-21240
1. Seventh-Day Adventists—Education. 2. Religious education—Teaching methods. I. Title.

SEVENTH-DAY 268'.8'673 Adventists. General Conference. Sabbath School Dept.
The Sabbath school manual : for Sabbath school officers and teachers / prepared by the Sabbath School Dept. of the General Conference of Seventh-day Adventists. Nashville : Southern Pub. Association, c1979. 96 p. ; 22 cm. Includes index. Bibliography: p. 89-93. [BX6113.S47 1979] 79-501 ISBN 0-8127-0228-X pbk. : 2.95
1. Seventh-Day Adventists—Education. I. Title.

TENNEY, John Ellis, 1861- 878.
A manual for the use of church and mission schools of the southern union conference of Seventh-day adventists, by J. E. Tenney. [Nashville, Tenn., Ft. Worth, Tex, etc.] Southern publishing association, 1907. 2 p. l., [3]-70 p. 19 1/2 cm. [LC586.A3T4] 7-38894
1. Seventh-day adventists—Education. I. Title.

WHITE, Ellen Gould 377'.8'673 (Harmon) 1827-1915.
Counsels on education, as presented in the nine volumes of Testimonies for the church, by Ellen G. White. Mountain View, Calif., Pacific Press Pub. Association [1968] 264 p. 18 cm. "Souvenir edition." [LC586.A3W52 1968] 68-6054
1. Seventh-Day Adventists—Education. I. Title.

WHITE, Ellen Gould 268.867 (Harmon) Mrs., 1827-1915.
Counsels on Sabbath school work; a compilation from the writings of Ellen G. White. Washington, D.C., Review and herald publishing assn. [c1938] 192 p. 16 1/2 cm. [BX6111.W48] 39-3541
1. Seventh-day Adventists—Education. 2. Religious education. I. Title.

WILL, Stanley S. 268'.8'673
Teach : a guide to effective Sabbath school teaching / by Stanley S. Will ; ill. by Jim Padgett. Rev. ed. Nashville : Southern Pub. Association, c1974. 220 p. : ill. ; 21 cm. Bibliography: p. 219-220. [BX6155.W54 1974] 74-18927 ISBN 0-8127-0087-2 pbk. : 2.95
1. Seventh-Day Adventists—Education. 2. Christian education—Teaching methods. I. Title.

Seventh-Day Adventists—Education—United States.

HILDE, Reuben. 377'.8673
Showdown : can Seventh-Day Adventist education pass the test? / Reuben Hilde. Washington : Review and Herald Pub. Association, 1980. p. cm. [LC586.S48H54] 79-28511 6.50
1. Seventh-Day Adventists—Education—United States. 2. Education—United States—Philosophy. I. Title.

[Seventh-Day Adventists—Fiction.]

LANTRY, Kimber J., 1953- JUV
Uncle Uriah and Tad / by Kimber J. Lantry. Mountain View, Calif. : Pacific Press Pub. Association, c1981. 80 p. : ill. ; 22 cm. (Trailblazer for Jesus) In 1902 when a young Adventist boy becomes an apprentice at a religious publishing house in Battle Creek, Michigan, he is troubled by the publishing of non-Adventist books. [PZ7.L294Un 1981] [Fic] 19 80-11479 ISBN 0-8163-0361-4 pbk. : 4.95
1. [Seventh-Day Adventists—Fiction.] 2. [Apprentices—Fiction.] 3. [Printing—Fiction.] 4. [Christian life—Fiction.] I. Title.

Seventh-day Adventists. General conference.

MCKIBBIN, Alma Estelle 221 (Baker) Mrs., 1871-
...Last of Old Testament times, stories from Israel [by] Mrs. Alma E. McKibbin: published for the Department of education of the General conference of Seventh-day Adventists. (Rev. 1926) Mountain View, Calif., Portland, Or. [etc.] Pacific press publishing association [c1926] xi, [1], 220 p. illus. (incl. maps) 20 cm. [Bible lessons series] At head of title: Bible lessons for the fifth grade. [BS1194.M3 1926] 26-15084
I. Seventh-day Adventists. General conference. II. Title.

PECK, Sarah Elizabeth. 230.
... God's great plan; for use in the seventh and eighth grades of school years beginning with an even number, when the work is alternated ... [By] Sarah E. Peck. Pub. for the Department of education of the General conference of Seventh-day Adventists. Mountain View, Calif., Portland, Or. [etc.] Pacific press publishing association, 1922. xi, [1], 506 p. illus. 20 cm. (Bible lessons [series]) [BX6155.P4] 22-21494
1. Seventh-day Adventists. General conference. I. Title.

ROCKWELL, Esther (Francis) 222. Mrs., 1887-
... When the world was young, the story of Genesis [by] Esther Francis-Rockwell; pub. for the Department of education on the General conference of Seventh-day adventists. Mountain View, Calif., Portland, Or. [etc.] Pacific press publishing association, 1924. xiii, [1], 319 p. incl. illus., map. 20 cm. [Bible lessons series] At head of title: Bible lessons for the third grade. [Full name: Mrs. Mary Esther (Francis) Rockwell] [BS1239.R6] 24-23628
1. Seventh-day Adventists. General conference. II. Title.

WHITE, Ellen Gould (Harmon) 215 Mrs., 1827-1915.
Principles of true science; or, Creation in the light of revelation; a compilation from the Bible and the Spirit of prophecy of the plainly factual and sublimely spiritual truths of creation and their application to human life. From the writings of Mrs. Ellen G. White. (Recommended by the Department of education of the General conference of Seventh-day Adventists) Takoma Park, D.C., Washington college press, 1929. 720 p. 18 1/2 cm. Previously published as two books under titles: Science in the Bible, and Principles of true science. This edition is also revised and enlarged. cf. Foreword signed: Marion E. Cady. [BX6111.W597 1929] 29-15062
I. Cady, Marion Ernest, 1865- ed. II. Seventh-day Adventists. General conference. III. Title.

Seventh-Day Adventists. General Conference. Young People's Missionary Volunteer Department

BOND, Charles Lester, 267.6267 1888-
The master comrade manual; a study and service guide for master comrades, and superintendents of the Junior society of missionary volunteers, prepared for the Young people's department of missionary volunteers of the General conference of Seventh-day Adventists, by C. Lester Bond. Takoma Park, Washington, D.C. Review and herald publishing association, [c1938] 255 p. illus. 19 cm. [BV2495.A67B6] 39-5315
1. Seventh-day Adventists. Young people's missionary volunteer department. I. Title.

KRUM, Nathaniel. 266.67
The MV story. Washington, Review and Herald Pub. Association [1963] 252 p. illus. 22 cm. [BX6153.K7] 63-17761
1. Seventh-day Adventists. General Conference. Young People's Missionary Volunteer Dept. I. Title.

WHITE, Ellen Gould (Harmon) 171.1 Mrs., 1827-1915.
Messages to young people, by Ellen G. White ... (Compiled by Missionary volunteer department, General conference of Seventh-day Adventists) ... Nashville, Tenn., Atlanta, Ga.[etc.] Southern publishing association [c1930] 1 p. l., 7-499 p. front. 18 1/2 cm. [BX6111.W596] 30-13243
I. Seventh-day Adventists. General conference. II. Title.

Seventh-day Adventists—Government.

CRISLER, Clarence Creager, 286.7 1877-1936.
Organization; its character, purpose, place, and development in the Seventh-day Adventist church, by C. C. Crisler. Takoma Park, Washington, D. C., Review and herald publishing association, 1938. 265 p. 20 cm. [BX6154.C7] 38-23351
1. Seventh-day Adventists—Government. I. Title.

MONTGOMERY, Oliver. 286.7
Principles of church organization and administration, by Oliver Montgomery ... Takoma Park, Washington, D.C., Review and herald publishing association [1942] 296 p. 20 cm. (Ministerial reading course selection for 1943, Ministerial association of Seventh-day Adventists) Bibliographical foot-notes. [BX6154.M62] 42-52148
1. Seventh-day Adventists—Government. I. Title.

Seventh Day Adventists—Government—Juvenile literature.

WOOD, Miriam. 262'.5'673
Joey finds out how his church works / Miriam Wood. Washington : Review and Herald Pub. Association, c1979. 93 p. : ill. ; 22 cm. [BX6159.W66] 79-10882 pbk. : 3.95
1. Seventh Day Adventists—Government—Juvenile literature. I. Title.

Seventh-day Adventists—Great Britain

HAGSTOTZ, Gideon David, 286.742 1896-
The Seventh-day Adventists in the British isles, 1878-1933, by Gideon David Hagstotz, PH. D. Lincoln, Neb., Union college press [c1936] vi, 9-231 p. 22 1/2 cm. Issued also as thesis (PH. D.) University of Missouri. Bibliography: p. 223-226. [BX6158.H3 1936a] 37-562
1. Seventh-day Adventists—Gt. Brit. I. Title.

Seventh-Day Adventists—History

CHRISTIAN, Lewis Harrison. 286.7
The fruitage of spiritual gifts, the influence and guidance of Ellen G. White in the Advent movement. Washington, Review and Herald Pub. Assn. [1947] 446 p. port. 22 cm. [BX6153.C48] 48-685
1. White, Ellen Gould]Bermon:, 1827-1915. 2. Seventh-Day Adventists—Hist. I. Title.

CHRISTIAN, Lewis 286.773 Harrison.
Sons of the north, and their share in the Advent movement, by Lewis Harrison Christian. Mountain View, Calif., Portland, Or. [etc.] Pacific press publishing association [1942] 2 p. l., [3]-249, [1] p. illus. (incl. ports.) 20 cm. [BX6143.C45] 42-22958
1. Seventh-day Adventists—Hist. 2. Scandinavians in the U.S. I. Title.

HERNDON, Booton. 286.7
The seventh day; the story of the Seventh-Day Adventists. [1st ed.] New York, McGraw- Hill [1960] 267p. 21cm. [BX6153.H4] 60-14998
1. Seventh-Day Adventists—Hist. I. Title.

HERNDON, Booton. 286'.73
The Seventh Day : the story of the Seventh-Day Adventists / by Booton Herndon. Westport, Conn. : Greenwood Press, 1979, c1960. 267 p. ; 23 cm. Reprint of the ed. published by McGraw-Hill, New York. [BX6153.H4 1979] 78-11705 ISBN 0-313-21054-3 : 20.75
1. Seventh-Day Adventists—History. I. Title.

NICHOL, Francis David, 922.673 1897-
The midnight cry, a defense of William Miller and the Millerites, by Francis D. Nichol ... Takoma Park, Washington, D.C., Review and Herald publishing association [1944] 560p. front plates ports facsims 23 / cm (Ministerial reading course selection for 1945, Ministerial association of Seventh-day Adventists) Bibliography: p. 519-548. [BX6193.M5N5] 44-41821
1. Miller, William, 1782-1849. 2. Seventh-day Adventists—Hist. I. Title.

OLSON, A. V. 1884-1963. 286.7'3 (Albert Victor),
Thirteen crisis years, 1888-1901 : from the Minneapolis meeting to the reorganization of the General Conference A.V. Olson. Rev. ed. Washington, D.C. : Review and Herald Pub. Association, c1981. 335 p. ; 22 cm. Rev. ed. of: Through crisis to victory, 1888-1901. 1966. Includes bibliographical references. [BX6153.O63 1981] 19 82-150391 : 12.95
1. Seventh-Day Adventists—History. I. Title.

OLSON, Albert Victor, 286.73 1884-1963
Through crisis to victory, 1888-1901; from the Minneapolis meeting to the reorganization of the General Conference, by A. V. Olson. Washington. D. C., Review & Herald [1966] 320p. 22cm. Bibl. [BX6153.O63] 66-20839 4.95
1. Seventh-Day Adventists—Hist. I. Title.

SEVENTH-DAY Adventists 286.709 General Conference Dept of Education
The story of our church. Mountain View, Calif., Pacific Press Pub. Association [c1956] 580 p. illus. 24 cm. [BX6153.A57] 56-13326
1. Seventh-Day Adventists — Hist. I. Title.

SPALDING, Arthur 286.709 Whitefield, 1877-
Captains of the host ... a history of Seventh-Day Adventists ... Washington, Review and Herald Pub. Association [1949] v. illus., ports., maps. 21 cm. Vol. 2 has title: Christ's last legion. [BX6153.S615] 49-2497
1. Seventh-Day Adventists—Hist. I. Title. II. Title: Christ's last legion.

SPALDING, Arthur 286.709 Whitefield, 1877-
Footprints of the pioneers. Washington, Review and Herald Pub. Assn., c1947. 224 p. illus., ports., maps (on lining-papers) 23 cm. [BX6153.S62] 48-12172
1. Seventh-day Adventists—Hist. I. Title.

SPICER, William Ambrose, 286.7 1866-
After one hundred years, 1844-1944; how the work of Seventh-day Adventists has spread to the ends of the earth, by William A. Spicer. Takoma Park, Washington, D.C., Printed by the Review and hearld publishing assocaition, 1944. 96 p. incl. front., illus. (incl. ports.) 18 1/2 cm. [BX6153.S64] 44-7341
1. Seveth-day Adventists—Hist. I. Title.

SPICER, William Ambrose, 286.7 1866-
Pioneer days of the Advent movement, with notes on pioneer workers and early experiences, by William A. Spicer ... Illustrated by Pauline Whitson. Washington, D.C., Review and herald publishing association [c1941] 256 p. illus. (incl. ports.) 20 cm. [BX6158.S65] 42-848
1. Seventh-day Adventists—Hist. I. Title.

Seventh-Day Adventists—History—Sources.

WINDOWS : 289'.73 selected readings in Seventh-Day Adventist church history, 1844-1922 / compiled by Emmett K. Vande Vere. Nashville : Southern Pub. Association, c1975. 319 p. ; 22 cm. Includes bibliographies and index. [BX6153.W56] 75-27641 ISBN 0-8127-0104-6
1. Seventh-Day Adventists—History—Sources. I. Vande Vere, Emmett K.

Seventh—Day Adventists History Sources Microform catalogs.

THE Millerites and 016.286'7 *early Adventists :* an index to the microfilm collection of rare books and manuscripts / edited by Jean Hoornstra. Ann Arbor, Mich. : University Microfilms International, 1978. v, 64 p. ; 28 cm. Guide to the microfilm collection held by University Microfilms International. [Z7845.A35M34] [BX6115] 78-20434 ISBN 0-8357-0340-1 : 15.00
1. Sevent-Day Adventists—History—Sources—Microform catalogs. 2. University Microfilms International—Catalogs. 3. Adventists—History—Sources—Microform catalogs. 4. Books on microfilm—Catalogs. 5. Manuscripts on microfilm—Catalogs. I. Hoornstra, Jean. II. University Microfilms International.

Seventh day Adventists—History—Study and teaching.

EDWARDS, Harry Elmo, 1892- 286.7
Guide and test sheets for denominational history, by Harry E. Edwards ... and Mary E. Lamson ... 3d ed. Berrien Springs, Mich., The College press [c1935] xi, 82, [2], 32 p. 23 1/2 cm. Part ii has special half title and separate paging. Blank pages for "Notes" (2 following p. 82) "Key to abbreviations": p. xi. Contents.--pt. i. Guide sheets.--pt. ii. Test sheets. [BX6155.E35 1935] 35-6470
1. Seventh day Adventists—Hist.—Study and teaching. I. Title.

Seventh-day Adventists—Hymns.

SEVENTH-DAY Adventists. 783.
The Seventh-day Adventist hymn and tune book, for use in divine worship. Published by the General conference. Battle Creek, Mich., Review & herald publishing house. Oakland, Cal., Pacific press, 1886. vi, 7-640 p. 21 cm. "F. E. Belden and Edwin Barnes ... musical editors."--Pref. [M2131.S3S4 1886] 45-42030
1. Seventh-day Adventists—Hymns. 2. Hymns, English. I. Belden, Franklin Edson, ed. II. Barnes, Edwin, joint ed. III. Title.

SEVENTH-DAY Adventists. 783.9 General conference committee.
The church hymnal; official hymnal of the Seventh-day Adventist church. Takoma Park, Washington, D.C., Review and herald publishing association [c1941] 1 p. l., 5-640 p. 22 1/2 cm. With music. Preface signed: General conference committee. [M2131.S3C5] 41-7405
1. Seventh-day Adventists—Hymns. 2. Hymns, English. I. Title.

Seventh-day Adventists in Europe.

CHRISTIAN, Lewis Harrison. 286.74
Pioneers and builders of the Advent cause in Europe by Lewis Harrison Christian... Mountain View, Calif., Omaha, Neb. [etc.] Pacific press publishing association [c1937] 164 p. incl. front., illus. 20 1/2 cm. [BX6153.C5] 37-10285
1. Seventh-day Adventists in Europe. I. Title.

Seventh-Day Adventists. Liturgy and ritual.

PEASE, Norval F. 264.06'73
And worship him, by Norval F. Pease. Nashville, Southern Pub. Association [1967] 95 p. 22 cm. Bibliography: p. 95. [BX6154.P37] 67-3208
1. Seventh-Day Adventists. Liturgy and ritual. I. Title.

Seventh-Day Adventists—Missions.

AITKEN, Dorothy 266.6 (j) Lockwood.
My love, the Amazon, By Dorothy Aitken. Illus. by Jim Padgett. Nashville, Southern Pub. Association [1968] 128 p. illus. 21 cm. [BV2851.A586] 68-24020
1. Seventh-Day Adventists—Missions. 2. Missions—Amazon Valley. 3. Amazon River—Description and travel. I. Title.

AITKEN, James J. 266.6'73
White wings, green jungle; the story of the Fernando Stahl, the first Seventh-Day Adventist missionary plane in South America, by James and Dorothy Aitken. Mountain View, Calif., Pacific Pr. Pub. [c.1966] 96p. illus., ports. 22cm. (Destiny bk., D-112) [PBV2495.A94] 66-28099 1.50 pap.,
1. Seventh-Day Adventists—Missions. 2. Aeronautics in missionary work. 3. Missions—South America. I. Aitken, Dorothy Lockwood, joint author. II. Title.

ALLEN, Sydney. 266.6'7599'1
One week with a modern missionary. Washington, Review and Herald Pub. Association [1970] 96 p. illus., ports., map. 22 cm. [BV3380.A45] 76-106498
1. Seventh-Day Adventists—Missions. 2. Missions—Luzon. I. Title.

AMUNDSEN, Wesley. 266.67
The trail of the seventy, by Wesley Amundsen. Takoma Park, Washington, D. C., Review and herald publishing association [1942] 126 p. 20 cm. Cover-title: On the trail of the seventy. [BV2495.A77] 42-13194
1. Seventh-day Adventists—Missions. I. Title. II. Title: On the trail of the seventy.

ANDROSS, Matilda (Erickson) 28674 Mrs. 1880-
Sunshine and shadow in southern Europe, by Matilda Erickson Andross. Takoma Park, Washington, D.C., Review and herald publishing assn. [c1939] [BV2495.A8] 39-17797
1. Seventh-day Adventists—Missions. 2. Europe, Southern—Descr. & trav. I. Title.

BAERG, John. 266.6'781
Brazil; where the action is. Washington, Review and Herald Pub. Association [1969] 160 p. 22 cm. [BV2853.B6B27] 70-84991
1. Seventh-Day Adventists—Missions. 2. Missions—Brazil. 3. Missionary stories. I. Title.

CASON, Mabel (Earp) 266.6'7'0924
1892-
Steering by the star. Nashville, Southern Pub. Association [1968] 134 p. 22 cm. [BV3460.C35] 68-56069
1. Seventh-Day Adventists—Missions. 2. Missions—Korea. I. Title.

CHRISTENSEN, Otto 266'.6'75177
H., 1898-
Mission Mongolia; the untold story [by] Otto H. Christensen. Washington, Review and Herald Pub. Association [1974] 123 p. illus. 21 cm. [BV3420.M7C48] 74-182317 3.50
1. Seventh-Day Adventists—Missions. 2. Christensen, Otto H., 1898- 3. Missions—Mongolia (Inner Mongolia) I. Title.

COTT, Elizabeth (Buhler) 266.6'78
Jewels from green hell; stories of the Davis Indians of British Guiana [by] Betty Buhler Cott. Washington, Review and Herald Pub. Association [1969] 256 p. illus., map, ports. 22 cm. [BV2087.C68] 71-81309
1. Seventh-Day Adventists—Missions. 2. Missionary stories. 3. Missions—South America. I. Title.

DOWN, Goldie M. 260.6'7'0922
If I have twelve sons, by Goldie Down. Nashville, Southern Pub. [1968] 95p. 22cm. [BV2495.D68] 68-55391 3.75
1. Seventh-Day Adventists—Missions. 2. Converts, Seventh-Day Adventist. I. Title.

MCFADDEN, Elizabeth Spalding juv
Some rain must fall. Mountain View, Calif., Pacific Pr. Pub. [c.1965] 89p. 22cm. (Destiny bk., D-104) [BV2087.M28] 65-16848 1.50 pap.,
1. Seventh-Day Adventists—Missions. I. Title.

MOSAIC of adventure : 266'.6'73
a scrapbook of student missionary experiences and documents / by Donna June Evans. Nashville : Southern Pub. Association, c1976. 96 p. ; 23 cm. [BV2495.M67] 76-3876 ISBN 0-8127-0112-7
1. Seventh-Day Adventists—Missions. 2. College students in missionary work. I. Evans, Donna June, 1949-

†RANKIN, Molly K. 266'.7'3
I heard singing / by Molly K. Rankin. Mountain View, Calif. : Pacific Press Pub. Association, c1976. 125 p. ; 22 cm. (A Destiny book ; D151) [BV3680.N5R36] 74-27533 pbk. : 3.50
1. Seventh-Day Adventists—Missions. 2. Missions—New Guinea. I. Title.

SCHWARTZ, Frederick J., 266'.673
comp.
Thailand and the Seventh-Day Adventist medical and missionary work, by Frederick J. Schwartz. Berrien Springs, Mich., Andrews University, 1972. 195 p. illus. 28 cm. "A collection of most of the news releases of the 'Far Eastern Division outlook' as well as articles ... from 'The review and herald'." [BV3315.S37] 72-83283
1. Seventh-Day Adventists—Missions. 2. Missions—Thailand. 3. Missions, Medical—Thailand. I. Title.

SEVENTH-DAY Adventists. Mission board.
Outline of mission fields, entered by Seventh-day Adventists ... 5th ed., 1927. Takoma Park, Washington D.C., Mission board of Seventh-day Adventists [1927] 224 p. 18 cm. [BV2495.A15 1927] 45-31259
1. Seventh-day Adventists—Missions. I. Title.

STIRLING, Betty. 301.15'4
Attitudes of Seventh-Day Adventist college students toward missions; a report of research conducted by Betty Stirling with the assistance of Gordon Butler, Anees Haddad, and Jack Lawson. Loma Linda, Calif., Loma Linda University, Graduate School [1969] 124 p. 26 cm. (Loma Linda University. Dept. of Sociology and Anthropology. Occasional papers, no. 1) Running title: Attitudes toward missions. [BV2495.S8] 73-10723
1. Seventh-Day Adventists—Missions. 2. College students—Religious life—Statistics. I. Title. II. Title: Attitudes toward missions. III. Series.

WANGERIN, Theodora 266.6'7'0924
Scharffenberg.
God sent me to Korea. Cover photo by Robert Sheldon. Washington, Review and Herald Pub. Association [1968] 128 p. 22 cm. [BV3462.W3A3] 68-22281
1. Seventh-Day Adventists—Missions. 2. Missions—Korea. I. Title.

WESTPHAL, Barbara 266.6'7'0924 B
(Osborne)
John, the intrepid, missionary on three continents, by Barbara Westphal. Washington, Review and Herald Pub. Association [1968] 188 p. 22 cm. [BV2831.W43] 68-22280
1. Seventh-Day Adventists—Missions. 2. Missions—Latin America. I. Title.

WESTPHAL, Barbara 266.678
(Osborne)
These Fords still run. Mountain View, Calif., Pacific Press Pub. Association [1962] 136 p. illus. 23 cm. [BV2831.W45] 62-13527
1. Ford, Orley. 2. Ford, Lillian Gertrude (Shafer) 1894- 3. Seventh-Day Adventists — Missions. 4. Missions — Spanish America. I. Title.

WOOD, Miriam. 266.6'7955
All my dusty babies; one week's visit in New Guinea, November 30-December 7, 1970. Washington, Review & Herald Pub. Co. Assn. [1972] 174 p. illus. 22 cm. [BV3680.N5W66] 79-190580 Pap. 2.95
1. Seventh Day Adventists—Missions. 2. Missions—New Guinea. I. Title.

WOODWARD, H. G. 275.48
... *Kerala, the gem of India,* by H. G. Woodward. Mountain View, Calif.; Omaha, Neb. [etc.] Pacific press publishing association [c1936] 3 p. l., 5-160 p. incl. front. plates. 19 1/2 cm. [BV3280.M25W6] [266.67] 36-19432
1. Seventh-day Adventists—Missions. 2. Missions—Madras (Presidency) I. Title.

Seventh-Day Adventists—Missions—South America—Juvenile literature.

WESTPHAL, Barbara 266'.673 B
Osborne.
Gaucho land boy : the Westphals in South America / by Barbara Westphal. Mountain View, Calif. : Pacific Press Pub. Association, c1982. p. cm. (Trailblazer) Memoirs of the family of the first Adventist minister to South America, before the turn of the century. [BV2851.W47] 19 81-14079 ISBN 0-8163-0454-8 pbk. : 5.95
1. Seventh-Day Adventists—Missions—South America—Juvenile literature. 2. [Westfall family.] 3. [Seventh-Day Adventists—Missions—South America.] 4. Missions—South America—Juvenile literature. 5. Westfall family—Juvenile literature. I. Title.

Seventh-Day Adventists Newfoundland.

MATTHEWS, Ray A. 286.7'718
Gospel anchors aweigh! : Adventist beginnings in Newfoundland / Ray A. Matthews ; [cover ill., Dale Rusch]. Mountain View, Calif. : Pacific Press Pub. Association, c1980. 109 p. : ill. ; 22 cm. (A Destiny book ; D-178) [BX6153.M28] 79-87732 pbk. : 4.95
1. Seventh-DayAdventists—Newfoundland. I. Title.

Seventh-Day Adventists—Pictorial works.

UTT, Richard H. 286'.73
The builders; a photo story of Seventh-Day Adventists at work around the world, by Richard H. Utt. Mountain View, Calif., Pacific Press Pub. Association [1970] 128 p. illus. (part col.), ports. 26 cm. [BX6154.U69] 74-125991
1. Seventh-Day Adventists—Pictorial works. I. Title.

Seventh Day Adventists—Pictures, illustrations, etc.

UTT, Richard H 286.7
A century of miracles. Mountain View, Calif., Pacific Press Pub. Association [1963] 190 p. illus. 28 cm. [BX6154.U7] 63-16042
1. Seventh Day Adventists — Pictures, illustrations, etc. I. Title.

UTT, Richard H 286'.73
A century of miracles, by Richard H. Utt. Mountain View, Calif., Pacific Press Pub. Association [c1966] 160 p. illus. (part col.), ports. (part col.) 27 cm. [BX6154.U7] 66-15534
1. Seventh-Day Adventists — Pictures, illustrations, etc. I. Title.

Seventh-Day Adventists—Publishing.

HETZELL, M. Carol. 655.5'94
The undaunted; the story of the publishing work of Seventh-Day Adventists, by M. Carol Hetzell. Mountain View, Calif., Pacific Press Pub. Association [1967] 181 p. illus., ports. 23 cm. Bibliography: p. 179-181. [BX6153.H43] 66-30804
1. Seventh-Day Adventists — Publishing. I. Title.

Seventh-day Adventists—Sermons.

BELLAH, Charles Greeley, 252.067
1873-
The King's highway. Washington, Review and Herald Pub. Association [1953] 279p. 21cm. [BX6123.B43] 53-36892
1. Seventh-Day Adventists—Sermons. 2. Sermons, American. I. Title.

BIETZ, Arthur Lee. 222.16
Guideposts to happiness, by Arthur Leo Bietz ... Berkeley, Calif., Printed at Superior press [1943] 209 p. incl. port. 20 1/2 cm. [BX6123.B5] 43-9846
1. Seventh-day Adventists—Sermons. 2. Sermons, American. I. Title.

CARCICH, Theodore. 252'.07'3
Carcich at 7:30 : sermons preached at camp meetings / by Theodore Carcich. Nashville : Southern Pub. Association, [1975] 95 p. ; 21 cm. [BX6123.C36] 74-30869 ISBN 0-8127-0091-0
1. Seventh-Day Adventists—Sermons. 2. Sermons, American. I. Title.

CARCICH, Theodore. 252'.06'73
So what's there to live for? Nashville, Southern Pub. Association [1972] 63 p. 19 cm. [BX6123.C37] 72-88858 ISBN 0-8127-0064-3 Pap. 0.50
1. Seventh-Day Adventists—Sermons. 2. Sermons, American. I. Title.

CLEVELAND, Earl E. 242
Free at last [by] E. E. Cleveland. Washington, Review and Herald Pub. Association [1970] 447 p. col. illus., col. ports. 26 cm. [BX6123.C55] 70-97596
1. Seventh-Day Adventists—Sermons. 2. Sermons, American. I. Title.

CLEVELAND, 261.8'34'5196073
Edward Earl.
Living soul; "we shall overcome" [by] E. E. Cleveland. Nashville, Southern Pub. Association [1974] 219 p. illus. 21 cm. [BX6123.C56] 73-91286 ISBN 0-8127-0078-3 1.95 (pbk.).
1. Seventh-Day Adventists—Sermons. 2. Sermons, American. 3. United States—Race question. I. Title.

DOUGLASS, Herbert E., 252'.06'7
comp.
If I had one sermon to preach. Edited by Herbert E. Douglass. Washington, Review and Herald Pub. Association [1972] 190 p. ports. 21 cm. (Review and Herald sermon library series) (Discovery paperbacks) Contents.Contents.—Alexander, W. Mingled motives.—Bradford, C. E. Rich man, poor man, Christian.—Brooks, C. D. A hope called blessed.—Bush, F. F. The church called Christian.—Dower, N. R. That I may win Christ.—Fearing, A. The song of Moses and the lamb.—Hackett, W. J. How man finds freedom.—Hegstad, R. R. An offbeat subject.—Lesher, W. R. Two ways with people.—Loveless, W. A. Burn your labeling machine.—Osborn, J. W. The magnificent decision.—Pease, N. F. The answered question.—Pierson, R. H. Hope and help for you!—Spangler, J. R. Is the Cross out of date?—Venden, L. Two lost boys.—Vitrano, S. P. Keeping the great commandment.—Wood, K. H. The leukemia of noncommitment. Includes bibliographical references. [BX6123.D68] 72-78420
1. Seventh-Day Adventists—Sermons. 2. Sermons, American. I. Title.

MACE, Joseph Willis, 252.067
1872-1936.
Ablaze for God; devotional talks by J. W. Mace. Takoma Park, Washington, D.C., Review and herald publishing association [c1938] 262 p. 18 cm. [BX6123.M3] 38-14041
1. Seventh-day Adventists—Sermons. 2. Sermons—American. I. Title.

REYNOLDS, Louis 252'.06'73
Bernard, 1917-
Great texts from Romans, by Louis B. Reynolds. Nashville, Tenn., Southern Pub. Association [1972] 94 p. 18 cm. [BS2665.4.R48] 72-75378
1. Seventh-Day Adventists—Sermons. 2. Bible. N.T. Romans—Sermons. 3. Sermons, American. I. Title.

RICHARDS, Harold Marshall 252.067
Sylvester, 1894-
Day after tomorrow, and other sermons. Washington, Review and Herald Pub. Association [1956] 188p. 21cm. [BX6123.R48] 56-35989
1. Seventh-Day Adventists— Sermons. 2. Sermons, American. I. Title.

RICHARDS, Harold Marshall 252.067
Sylvester, 1894-
New radio lectures, by H. M. S. Richards. Glendale, Calif., Glendale academy press [c1935] 165 p. 21 1/2 cm. [BX6123.R5] 35-9194
1. Seventh-day Adventists—Sermons. 2. Sermons, American. I. Title.

RICHARDS, Harold Marshall 252.067
Sylvester, 1894-
Radio sermons. Washington, Review and Herald Pub. Assoication [1952] 253 p. 22 cm. [BX6123.R52] 52-32721
1. Seventh-Day Adventists — Sermons. 2. Sermons, American. I. Title.

SHULER, John Lewis, 1887- 236'.3
Power for a finished work : preparing the way and making ready a people for the Lord / by J. L. Shuler. Mountain View, Calif. : Pacific Press Pub. Association, c1978. 64 p. ; 19 cm. [BT823.S54] 78-53212 price unreported
1. Seventh-Day Adventists—Sermons. 2. Eschatology—Sermons. 3. Sermons, American. I. Title.

Seventh-Day Adventists — Sources.

THE Spirit of prophecy treasure chest; an Advent source collection of materials relating to the gift of prophecy in the remnant church and the life and ministry of Ellen G. White. The textbook for Prophetic guidance in the Advent movement, a Seventh-day Adventist correspondence course. Washington, Printed by the Review and Herald Pub. Assn., for Prophetic Guidance School of the Voice of Prophecy, 1960. 192 p. illus., ports. 25 cm.
1. White, Ellen Gould (Harmon) 1827-1915. 2. Seventh-Day Adventists — Sources.

Seventh-Day Adventists—Southern States.

HANSEN, Louis A. 286'.775
From so small a dream, by Louis A. Hansen. Nashville, Southern Pub. Association [1968] 288 p. 21 cm. [BX6153.H33] 68-29501
1. Seventh-Day Adventists—Southern States. I. Title.

Seventh-Day Adventists—United States—Biography.

NOT by bread alone : 286.7'3 B
ten stories of people who turned the dial and discovered through "It is written" that "Man shall not live by bread alone but by every word that proceeds out of the mouth of God" ... / compiled by Nellie Vandeman. Mountain View, Calif. : Pacific Press Pub. Association, c1981. 64 p. ; 18 cm. [BX6191.N67] 19 81-11316 ISBN 0-8163-0452-1 pbk. : .95
1. Seventh-Day Adventists—United States—Biography. 2. "It is written" (Television program) I. Vandeman, Nellie.

Seventh-Day Adventists—United States—Biography—Addresses, essays, lectures.

MY unforgettable parents 286'.73
: how they bent the twig / compiled by Kay Kuzma. Mountain View, Calif. : Pacific Press Pub. Association, c1978. 176 p. ; 18 cm. (A Redwood paperback ; 109) [BX6191.M9] 77-93134 pbk. : 2.50
1. Seventh-Day Adventists—United States—Biography—Addresses, essays, lectures. 2. Christian education of children—Addresses, essays, lectures. I. Kuzma, Kay.

Seventh-Day Adventists—United States—History.

WOOD, Miriam. 269'.2
Those happy golden years : the way we were during the heyday of evangelism / Miriam Wood. Washington : Review and Herald Pub. Association, 1980. p. cm. [BX6153.W66] 79-22844 pbk. : 5.95 5.95
1. Seventh-Day Adventists—United States—History. 2. Evangelistic work—United States—History. I. Title.

Seventh-Day Adventists—Zaire.

PIERSON, Robert H. 266'.6'767518
Angels over Elisabethville : a true story of God's providence in time of war / by Robert H. Pierson. Mountain View, Calif. : Pacific Press Pub. Association, c1975. 88 p. : ill. ; 22 cm. (A Destiny book ; D-150) [DT665.E4P53] 74-28684 ISBN pbk. : 2.95
1. Seventh-Day Adventists—Zaire. 2. Pierson, Robert H. 3. Lubumbashi—History. I. Title.

Seventh-day Baptists.

BURDICK, William Lewis, comp.
A manual of Seventh day Baptist church procedure: compiled by William Lewis Burdick and Corliss Fitz Randolph. Plainfield, Published for the Seventh day Baptist General conference, by the American Sabbath tract society, 1923. 98 p. 19 1/2 cm. [BX6398.B7] 23-11135
1. Seventh-day Baptists. I. Randolph, Corliss Fitz, 1863- joint comp. II. Seventh-day Baptists. General conference. III. Title.

BURDICK, William Lewis, comp.
A manual of Seventh day Baptist church procedure (revised) compiled and edited by William Lewis Burdick ... and Corliss Fitz Randolph ... Plainfield, N.J., Published for the Seventh day Baptist general conference by the American Sabbath tract society, 1926. 120 p. fold. pl. 20 cm. [BX6398.B7 1926] 27-9577
1. Seventh-day Baptists. I. Randolph, Corliss Fitz, 1863- joint comp. II. Seventh-day Baptists. General conference. III. Title.

DAVIS, Samuel Davis, 922.673
1824-1907.
Autobiography of Rev. Samuel D. Davis, edited by Corliss Fitz Randolph. Plainfield, N. J., American Sabbath tract society (Seventh day Baptist) 1942. v, 98 p. front. (port.) 22 cm. Cover-title: Rev. Samuel D. Davis, 1824-1907; an autobiographical sketch. "223 copies were printed." [BX6399.D38A3] 42-17012
I. Randolph, Corliss Fitz, 1863- ed. II. American Sabbath tract society. III. Title.

RANDOLPH, Corliss Fitz, 1863-
A history of Seventh day Baptists in West Virginia including the Woodbridgetown and Salemville churches in Pennsylvania and the Shrewsbury church in New Jersey; by Corliss Fitz Randolph ... Plainfield, N. J., Printed for the author by the American Sabbath tract society, 1905. xxiv p., 2 l., 504 p. front., illus., plates, ports., double maps, facsims. 24 cm. "Authorities": p. [xi]-xiv. [BX6394.W4R3] 6-1283
1. Seventh-day Baptists. 2. Seventh-day Baptists—West Virginia. I. Title.

SEVENTH-DAY Baptists. General conference.
Seventh day Baptists in Europe and America; a series of historical papers written in commemoration of the one hundredth anniversary of the organization of the Seventh day Baptist General conference: celebrated at Ashaway, Rhode Island, August 20-25, 1902. Plainfield, N.J., Printed for the Seventh day Baptist General conference by the American Sabbath tract society, 1910. 2 v. fronts., illus., plates, ports., facsims. 23 cm. $5.00. Paged continuously. [BX6393.A5 1910] 10-19198
1. Seventh-day Baptists. I. Title.

Seventh-day Baptists—Doctrinal and controversial works.

LEWIS, Abram Herbert, 1836- 230.
1908.
A Seventh-day Baptist hand-book. By A. H. Lewis... Alfred Centre, N.Y., American Sabbath tract society, 1887. 3 p. l., [3]-60, [4] p. 17 1/2 cm. [BX6397.L4] 41-24301
1. Seventh-day Baptists—Doctrinal and controversial works. I. American Sabbath tract society. II. Title.

SEVENTH-DAY Baptists. 230.67
Seventh day Baptist beliefs. Plainfield, N.J., The American Sabbath tract society [c1941] ix, [1] p., 1 l., 99 p. 18 cm. Prepared by a committee appointed by the General conference held in Shiloh, New Jersey, in 1937 to prepare a teacher's manual including Scripture references, as a supplement to the Statement of belief of Seventh day Baptists. cf. p. vi-ix. [BX6397.A35] 42-1942
1. Seventh-day Baptists—Doctrinal and controversial works. I. American Sabbath tract society. II. Title.

Seventh-Day Baptists—History—Addresses, essays, lectures.

SEVENTH Day Baptists in 286'.3'09
Europe and America / Seventh Day Baptist General Conference. New York : Arno Press, 1980, c1910. 2 v. (xxv, 1500 p.) [178] leaves of plates : ill. ; 24 cm. (The Baptist tradition) Reprint of the ed. printed for the Seventh Day Baptist General Conference by the American Sabbath Tract Society, Plainfield, N.J. Includes bibliographies and index. [BX6393.S48 1980] 79-52605 ISBN 0-405-12470-8 : 14.00
1. Seventh-Day Baptists—History—Addresses, essays, lectures. I. Seventh-Day Baptists. General Conference. II. Series: Baptists tradition.

Seventh-day Baptists in Pennsylvania—History.

ZERFASS, Samuel Grant, 286.3
1866-
Souvenir book of the Ephrata Cloister : complete history from its settlement in 1728 to the present time : included is the organization of Ephrata Borough and other information of Ephrata connected with the cloister / by S. G. Zerfass. New York : AMS Press, 1975. 84 p., [1] leaves of plates : ill. ; 23 cm. (Communal societies in America) Reprint of the 1921 ed. published by J. G. Zook, Lititz, Pa. [F159.E6Z58 1975] 72-2960 ISBN 0-404-10724-9 : 12.50
1. Seventh-day Baptists in Pennsylvania—History. 2. Ephrata Community—History. 3. Ephrata, Pa.—History. I. Title.

Seventh-day Baptists—Rhode Island.

WESTERLY, R.I. 286.37459
Pawcatuck Seventh day Baptist church.
The first hundred years; Pawcatuck Seventh day Baptist church, Westerly, Rhode Island, 1840-1940. Westerly, R.I., The Utter company, 1940. 331 p. incl. front., 1 illus., pl. plates, ports. 23 1/2 cm. G. B. Utter, chairman, Publication committee. cf. p. [6] [BX6395.W4] 41-13425
1. Seventh-day Baptists—Rhode Island. I. Utter, George Benjamin, 1881- II. Title.

Severinus, Saint, d. 482.

EUGIPPIUS. 281.1'080
Evgippii Vita Sancti Severini. Recensvit en commentario critico instrvxit Pivs Knoell. Vindobonae, apvd C. Geroldi filivm, 1886; New York, Johnson Reprint, 1968. 3 p. 1., xiii, [2], 102p. 1 I. 23cm. (Added t.-p.: Corpys scriptorvm ecclesiasticorvm latinorvm . . . vol. 8 [Pars II] Evgippii Opera, pars II) [BR60.C6 vol. 9] AC 34 15.00 pap.,
1. Severinus, Saint, d. 482. I. Knoll, Pius. ed. II. Title.

EUGIPPIUS 281.40924
Leben des heiligen Severin. Ubersetzt von Carl Rodenberg. 3.,neubearb. Aufl. Leipzig, Verlag der Dykschen Buchhandlung [1884] . New York, Johnson Reprint [1965] 88p. 19cm. (Die Geschichtschreiber der deutschen Vorzeit. 2. Gesamtausg., Bd. 4) Tr. from T. Mommsen's ed. pub. in the Scriptores rerum Germanicarum in 1898 [BR1720.S4 E85 1965] 66-3872 Price unreported
1. Severinus, Saint, d. 482. I. Rodenberg, Carl, 1854-1926, ed. and tr. II. Title.

EUGIPPIUS 281.40924
The life of Saint Severin. Tr. by Ludwig Bieler with Ludmilla Krestan. Washington, Catholic Univ. of Amer. [c.1965] x, 139p. map. 22cm. (Fathers of the church, a new tr. v. 55) Bibl. [BR60.F3E853] 65-12908 4.40
1. Severinus, Saint, d. 482. I. Bieler, Ludwig, tr. II. Title. III. Series.

EUGIPPUS. 922.
The life of Saint Severinus, by Eugippius; tr. into English for the first time, with notes, by George W. Robinson ... Cambridge, Harvard university press; [etc., etc.] 1914. 141 p. fron. (map) 21 cm. (Half-title: Harvard translations) "A list of editions and translations of the Life": p. 117-121. [BR1720.S4R6] 15-1806 1.50
1. Severinus, Saint, d. 482. I. Robinson, George Washington, 1872- tr. II. Title.

Severus, Sulpicius.

ANDEL, G. K. van. 231'.7
The Christian concept of history in the chronicle of Sulpicius Severus / G. K. van Andel. Amsterdam : Adolf M. Hakkert, 1976. 195 p. ; 22 cm. Includes indexes. Bibliography: p. 169-176. [BR115.H5A47] 77-364625 ISBN 9-02-560722-5
1. Severus, Sulpicius. 2. History (Theology)—History of doctrines. I. Title.

Sewall, Jotham, 1760-1850.

SEWALL, Jotham. 922.
A memoir of Rev. Jotham Sewall, of Chesterville, Maine. By his son, Rev. Jotham Sewall. Boston, Tappan & Whittemore; Bangor, E. F. Duren, 1853. viii, [9]-407, [1] p. front. (port.) 19 1/2 cm. [BX7260.S4S4] 1-2920
1. Sewall, Jotham, 1760-1850. I. Title.

Sewel, Willem, 1653-1720.

HULL, William Isaac, 922.86492
1868-
Willem Sewel of Amsterdam, 1653-1720, the first Quaker historian of Quakerism, by William I. Hull ... [Swarthmore Pa., Swarthmore college] 1933. xii p., 1 l., 225 p. front., pl., facsims. 24 cm. (Half title: Swarthmore college monographs on Quaker history, [no. 1]) "A chronological list of Willem Sewel's published writings and translations": p. 207-211; "A list of Judith Zinspenning Sewel's published writings": p. 212-213. [BX7795.S465H8] 34-11042
1. Sewel, Willem, 1653-1720. 2. Friends, Society of—Hist. I. Title.

Sewickley, Pa. Presbyterian Church.

ROBB, Mary Cooper. 285.174885
The Presbyterian Church of Sewickley, Pennsylvania, 1838-1963. Prepared under the auspices of the church's General Committee on its 125th anniversary. [Sewickley? 1963] 104 p. illus. 22 cm. [BX9211.S6R6] 63-13781
1. Sewickley, Pa. Presbyterian Church. I. Title.

Sex.

BRIFFAULT, Robert, 1876-. 176
Sin and sex. New York, The Maculay company, 1931. 253 p. 21 cm. [Full name: Robert Stephen Briffault] [HQ61.B7] 31-7449
1. Sex. 2. Sex and religion. 3. Ethics—Hist. 4. Christian ethics. I. Title.

BRIFFAULT, Robert, 261.8'34'1
1876-1948.
Sin and sex / Robert Briffault. New York : AMS Press, 1976. 253 p. ; 19 cm. Reprint of the 1931 ed. published by Macaulay Co., New York. [HQ61.B7 1976] 72-9623 ISBN 0-404-57418-1 : 12.50
1. Sex. 2. Sex and religion. 3. Ethics—History. 4. Christian ethics. I. Title.

HOWARD, William Lee, 1860- 176
1918.
Start your child right, confidential advice to parents and teachers, by William Lee Howard, M.D. New York, Chicago [etc.] Fleming H. Revell company [c1910] 135 p. 19 1/2 cm. [HQ56.H8] 10-20925 0.75
1. Sex. I. Title.

HULME, William Edward, 248.8
1920-
God, sex, & youth. Englewood Cliffs, N. J., Prentice-Hall [1959] 179p. 21cm. [BV4780.S4H8] 59-7807
1. Sex. I. Title.

LOWERY, Daniel L 222.1606
Life and live; the commandments for teenagers. Glen Rock, N.J., Paulist Press (1964) 224 p. 18 cm. (Deus books) [HQ35.L6] 64-14154
1. Sex. 2. Adolescence. I. Title.

LOWERY, Daniel L. 222.1606
Life and love; the commandments for teenagers. Glen Rock, N.J., Paulist Pr. [c.1964] 224p. 18cm. (Deus bks.) 64-14154 .95 pap.,
1. Sex. 2. Adolescence. I. Title.

ORAISON, Marc 241
Learning to love; frank advice for young Catholics. Tr. [from French] by Andre Humbert [1st Eng. lang. ed.] New York, Hawthorn [c.1965] 143p. illus. 21cm. Bibl. [HQ35.O73] 65-12400 3.95
1. Sex. 2. Adolescence. I. Title.

PAZ, Octavio, 1914- 128
Conjunctions and disjunctions. Translated from the Spanish by Helen R. Lane. New York, Viking Press [1974] 148 p. illus. 22 cm. "A Richard Seaver book" Includes bibliographical references. [HQ21.P2813] 72-9732 ISBN 0-670-23717-5 7.95
1. Sex. 2. Sex and religion. I. Title.

PIPER, Otto, 1891- 176
The Christian interpretation of sex, by Otto A. Piper... New York, C. Scribner's sons, 1941. xv, 234 p. 21 cm. "A bibliographical guide to further study": p. [213]-219. [BV4780.S4P5] 41-14065
1. Sex. 2. Sexual ethics. 3. Marriage. I. Title.

PITTENGER, William Norman, 177
1905-
The Christian view of sexual behavior; a reaction to the Kinsey report. Greenwich, Conn., Seabury Press, 1954. 71p. 20cm. [BT708.P54] [BT708.P54] 176 54-8587 54-8587
1. Kinsey, Alfred Charles, 1894- 2. Sex. 3. Sexual ethics. I. Title.

REYNOLDS, Jim, 1942- 261.8'34'1
Secrets of Eden : God and human sexuality / Jim Reynolds. Austin, Tex. : Sweet Pub. Co., [1975] 191 p. ; 18 cm. Includes bibliographies. [HQ31.R444] 74-25859 ISBN 0-8344-0087-1 pbk. : 1.95
1. Sex. 2. Sexual ethics. 3. Marriage. I. Title.

RHYMES, Douglas A. 261.83
No new morality; Christian personal values and sexual morality. Indianapolis, Bobbs [c.1964] 155p. 22cm. Bibl. 64-24646 3.50 bds.,
1. Sex. I. Title.

RHYMES, Douglas A 261.83
No new morality; Christian personal values and sexual morality [by] Douglas Rhymes. Indianapolis, Bobbs-Merrill [1964] 155 p. 22 cm. Bibliography: p. 151-155. [HQ1051.R45] 64-24646
1. Sex. I. Title.

SCHOTT, Walter Edgar. 211
The immaculate deception. Or cosmic sex without dogma, by Walter Edgar Schott. [Sausalito, Calif., Priv. print. by Ethel M. Schott, c1925] [277] p. 24 cm. [BL2775.S355] 25-3758
I. Title. II. Title: Cosmic sex without dogma

STEINHARDT, Irving David. 176
Ten sex talks to boys (10 years and older) by Irving David Steinhardt ... with twelve illustrations. Philadelphia & London, J. B. Lippincott company [c1914] 2 p. l., 3-187 p. illus., pl. 19 cm. "The originals of these lectures ... were published in the medical magazine 'pediatrics' after the author had delivered them before ... the Hebrew educational society, of Brooklyn, N. Y., before the New era club and the Emanu-El brotherhood of New York city, and several other clubs."--Pref. [HQ41.S87] 14-11775
1. Sex. 2. Boys. I. Title.

TALMEY, Bernard S. 176
Genesis; a manual for the instruction of children in matters sexual, for the use of parents, teachers, physicians and ministers, by B. S. Talmey ... with nineteen cuts, forty-seven drawings, in the text. New York, The Practitioners' publishing co. [c1910] x, [9]-194 p. illus. 30 cm. Bibliography: p. 177-181. [HQ56.T2] 10-15793
1. Sex. I. Title.

TAPP, Sidney Calhoun, 1870- 176
What every man and woman should know about the Bible, by Sidney C. Tapp ... Kansas City, Mo., The author [c1917] 303 p. illus. (incl. port.) 19 cm. [HQ61.T3] 17-20850
1. Sex. I. Title.

VON HILDEBRAND, Dietrich, 1889- 233
Man and woman. Chicago, Franciscan Herald Press [1966] 103 p. 21 cm. [BT708.V6] 65-25840
1. Sex. 2. Love (Theology) I. Title.

WILLIAMS, Milan Bertrand. 176
Sex problems as related to health and disease, morality and religion, heredity and environment, both in the individual and society at large, by Evangelist M. B. Williams...New and rev. ed. 7th ed. New York, Chicago [etc.] Fleming H. Revell company [c1910] 251 p. 19 1/2 cm. $1.00. [HQ31.W73] 10-6073
1. Sex. I. Title.

WYRTZEN, Jack, 1913-
Sex and the Bible. Introd. by Charles J. Woodbridge. [Grand Rapids, Mich., Zondervan Pub. House [c1958] 63 p. 20 cm.
1. Sex. 2. Hygiene, Sexual. I. Title.

Sex and Judaism.

FELDMAN, David Michael, 1929- 296.3'87'83426
Birth control in Jewish law : marital relations, contraception, and abortion as set forth in the classic texts of Jewish law / by David M. Feldman. Westport, Conn. : Greenwood Press, 1980, c1968. xiii, 322 p. ; 24 cm. Reprint of the ed. published by New York University Press, New York. Includes index. Bibliography: p. 305-314. [BM720.S4F44 1980] 79-16712 ISBN 0-313-21297-X lib. bdg. : 25.00
1. Sex and Judaism. 2. Birth control (Jewish law) 3. Abortion (Jewish law) I. Title.

GORDIS, Robert, 1908- 296.3'87'8341
Love & sex : a modern Jewish perspective / Robert Gordis. 1st ed. New York : Farrar Straus Giroux, 1978. xii, 290 p. ; 22 cm. Includes indexes. Bibliography: p. 279-282. [BM720.S4G67 1978] 77-20192 ISBN 0-374-19252-9: 8.95
1. Sex and Judaism. 2. Sexual ethics. 3. Marriage, Mixed. I. Title.

Sex and law.

DALY, Cahal B. 241
Morals, law, and life, by Cahal B. Daly. Chicago, Scepter [1966] 228p. 19cm. Bibl. 66-21148 2.95; .95 pap.,
1. Williams, Glanville Llewelyn, 1911- The sanctity of life and the criminal law. 2. Sex and law. I. Title.

Sex and religion.

BAILEY, Derrick Sherwin, 1910- 233
Sexual relation in Christian thought. New York, Harper [1959] 312p. 22cm. London ed. (Longmans) has title: The man-woman relation in Christian thought. [BT708.B3 1959a] 59-10326
1. Sex and religion. I. Title.

BAYNE, John Sloane, 1875- 220.86126
Back to Eden, the secret of the Temple, by John S. Bayne ... Philadelphia, The David McKay co., [1932.] 220 p. incl. front. pt., plan. 22 1/2 cm. Printed in Great Britain. [BS680.S5B3] 41-35214
1. Sex and religion. I. Title.

BIANCHI, Eugene C. 261.8'34'1
From machismo to mutuality : essays on sexism and woman-man liberation / by Eugene C. Bianchi and Rosemary R. Ruether. New York : Paulist Press, c1976. v, 142 p. ; 22 cm. Includes bibliographical references. [HQ61.B53] 75-25443 ISBN 0-8091-0202-1 : 5.95
1. Sex and religion. 2. Sexual ethics. 3. Sex discrimination. I. Ruether, Rosemary Radford, joint author. II. Title.

BLENKINSOPP, Joseph, 1927- 241
Sexuality and the Christian tradition. Dayton, Ohio, Pflaum Press, 1969. xi, 127 p. 21 cm. (Themes for today) Bibliographical footnotes. [HQ63.B5] 79-93011 2.95
1. Sex and religion. 2. Sex (Theology) I. Title.

COHEN, Chapman, 1868- 291.1'7834'1
Religion & sex : studies in the pathology of religious development / by Chapman Cohen. New York : AMS Press, 1975. xiii, 286 p. ; 18 cm. Reprint of the 1919 ed. published by T. N. Foulis, London, in series: The Open mind library. Includes bibliographical references and index. [BL65.S4C63 1975] 72-9631 ISBN 0-404-57430-0 : 14.50
1. Sex and religion. I. Title.

COLE, William Graham, 1917-
Sex in Christianity and psychoanalysis. New York, Oxford University Press, 1966. xvi, 329 p. 20 cm. (A Galaxy book. GB 168) Issued also in microfilm form as thesis, Columbia University, under title: Interpretations of sex in Christianity and psychoanalysis. Bibliographical footnotes. 68-109682
1. Freud, Sigmund, 1856-1939. 2. Sex and religion. 3. Sexual ethics. 4. Sex (Psychology) 5. Psychoanalysis. I. Title.

DEMANT, Vigo Auguste, 1893- 261.83
Christian sex ethics; an introduction, by V. A. Demant. [1st ed.] New York, Harper & Row [1963] 127 p. 20 cm. "Notes and references": p. 123-127. [HQ63.D4 1963a] 64-15481
1. Sex and religion. 2. Sexual ethics. I. Title.

GAMBLE, Eliza Burt Mrs. 291.
The god-idea of the ancients; or, Sex in religion, by Eliza Burt Gamble ... New York [etc.] G. P. Putnam's sons, 1897. vii, 339 p. 23 1/2 cm. [BL460.G3] 21-902
I. Title. II. Title: Sex in religion.

GENNE, Elizabeth 261.83
Christians and the crisis in sex morality; the church looks at the facts about sex and marriage today, by Elizabeth and William Genne. New York, Association [c.1962] 123p. 16cm. (Association Pr. reflection bk.) 62-9379 .50 pap.,
1. Sex and religion. 2. Sexual ethics. I. Gennee, William H., joint author. II. Title.

GOLDBERG, Ben Zion, 1895- 291
The sacred fire; the story of sex in religion. Introd. by Charles Francis Potter. New York, Grove [1962, c.1930, 1958] 288p. illus. 18cm. (Black cat bk., BC-23) Bibl. .75 pap.,
1. Sex and religion. I. Title.

GOLDBERG, Ben Zion, 1895-
The sacred fire; the story of sex in religion, with an introduction by Charles Francis Potter. New York, Grove Press [1962] 288 p. illus. (Black cat book, 23) 63-12845
1. Sex and religion. I. Title.

GOLDBERG, Ben Zion, 1895- 200.
The sacred fire; the story of sex in religion, by B. Z. Goldberg ... New York, H. Liveright, 1930. xv, 386 p. illus., diagr. 23 cm. Bibliography: p. [369]-376. [BL65.S4G6] 30-5610
1. Sex and religion. I. Title.

GOLDBERG, Ben Zion, 1895- 200.016126
The sacred fire; the story of sex in religion, by B. Z. Goldberg ... Garden City, N. Y., Garden City publishing company, inc. [1933?] xv, 386 p. illus., diagr. 22 cm. Bibliograph: p. 371-376. [BL65.S4G6 1933] 201 33-29668
1. Sex and religion. I. Title.

GOLDBERG, Ben Zion, 1895- 200
Sex in religion [by] B. Z. Goldberg. New York, Liveright [1970, c1930] xv, 386 p. illus. 21 cm. Originally published under title: The sacred fire. Bibliography: p. 371-376. [BL65.S4G6 1970] 78-131281 2.95
1. Sex and religion. I. Title.

GREET, Kenneth G. 261.83
The mutual society; aspects of the relationship of men and women. London, Epworth Pr. [dist. Mystic, Conn., Verry, 1964, c.1962] 170p. 19cm. (Beckly soc. service lect., 1962) Bibl. 64-5177 2.50 bds.,
1. Sex and religion. I. Title. II. Series.

GREGG, Richard Bartlett, 1885-
Spirit through body. Boston, University Press of Cambridge, 1956. 53p. 23cm. A57
1. Sex and religion. 2. Sexual ethics. I. Title.

GREGG, Richard Bartlett, 1885-
Spirit through body. Boston, University Press of Cambridge, 1956. 53p. 23cm. A57
1. Sex and religion. 2. Sexual ethics. I. Title.

HAUGHTON, Rosemary.
The holiness of sex. St. Meinrad, Ind., Abbey Press Publications [1965] 96 p. 17 cm. (Marriage paperback library) 67-39742
1. Sex and religion. I. Title.

HODGSON, Leonard, 1889- 241.5
Sex and Christian freedom, an enquiry. New York, Seabury Press [1967] 127 p. 22 cm. Bibliographical footnotes. [HQ63.H577 1967b] 67-21832
1. Sex and religion. 2. Sexual ethics. I. Title.

HOWARD, Clifford, 1868- 261.8'34'1
Sex and religion : a study of their relationship and its bearing upon civilization / by Clifford Howard. New York : AMS Press, 1975. xi, 201 p. ; 19 cm. Reprint of the 1925 ed. published by Williams and Norgate, London. [HQ63.H6 1975] 72-9654 ISBN 0-404-57463-7 : 16.00
1. Sex and religion.

LUTHERAN Church--Missouri Synod. Family Life Committee. 261.83
Sex and the church; a sociological, historical, and theological investigation of sex attitudes. Oscar E. Feucht. ed. [others] St. Louis. Concordia Pub. House [c.1961] xiv, 277p. illus. (Marriage and family research series, v.5) Bibl. 60-5351 3.50
1. Sex and religion. 2. Sexual ethics. I. Feucht, Oscar E., ed. II. Title. III. Series.

OCHS, Carol. 231
The myth behind the sex of God : toward a new consciousness—transcending matriarchy and patriarchy / Carol Ochs. Boston : Beacon Press, c1977. xiii, 177 p. ; 21 cm. Includes index. Bibliography: p. 155-169. [BL65.S4O25 1977] 76-48519 ISBN 0-8070-1112-6 : 9.95
1. Sex and religion. 2. Sex (Theology) I. Title.

PASTORAL psychology. 261.8
Sex and religion today, edited by Simon Doniger. New York, Association Press [1953] 238p. 20cm. (Pastoral psychology series) 'Articles ... selected ... from the pages of ... Pastoral psychology.'--Dust jacket. [BL65.S4P3] 53-11816
1. Sex and religion. 2. Psychology, Pastoral. I. Doniger, Simon, ed. II. Title.

PATAI, Raphael, 1910- 220.830142
Sex and family in the Bible and the Middle East. [1st ed.] Garden City, N. Y., Doubleday. 1959. 282p. 22cm. Includes bibliography. [BS680.S5P3] 59-8268
1. Sex and religion. 2. Near East—Soc. life & cust. I. Title.

SABRAMES, Demosthenes S. 201'.1
The satanizing of woman; religion versus sexuality [by] Demosthenes Savramis. Translated from the German by Martin Ebon. [1st ed. in the U.S.A.] Garden City, N.Y., Doubleday, 1974. ix, 226 p. 22 cm.. Translation of Religion und Sexualitat. Includes bibliographical references. [BL65.S4S2313] 72-96232 ISBN 0-385-04485-2 6.95
1. Sex and religion. I. Title.

**THE secrets of our sexuality :* role liberation for the Christian / edited by Gary R. Collins. Waco, Tex. : Word Books, c1976. 185p. ; 22 cm. (Continental congress on the family) [AQ61] 76-2865 ISBN 0-87680-847-X pbk. : 3.95 261.8'34'17
1. Sex and religion. I. Collins, Gary R. comp.

SEX and family in the Bible and the Middle East. Garden City, N. Y., Doubleday [1959] 272p. 18cm. (Dolphin Books, C40) Includes bibliography.
1. Sex and religion. 2. Near East —Soc. life & cust. I. Patai, Raphael, 1910-

SHARP, Watson. 261.8'34'1
The Catholic & the Jewish approach to sex & their relative influence upon the cultural character of our society / Watson Sharp. [1st ed.]. [Albuquerque, N.M.] : American Classical College Press, [1977] 17 leaves ; 28 cm. Cover title. [HQ63.S45] 77-24674 ISBN 0-89266-012-0 : 37.75
1. Sex and religion. I. Title: The Catholic & the Jewish approach to sex & their relative influence ...

TAPP, Sidney C., 1870-
Sexology of the Bible; the fall and redemption of man a matter of sex, by Sidney C. Tapp ... Kansas City, Mo., The Burton publishing company [c1913] 181 p. incl. front. (port.) 18 1/2 cm. 13-25356
I. Title.

TAPP, Sidney Calhoun, 1870-
Sexology of the Bible; the fall and redemption of man a matter of sex. By Sidney C. Tapp ... Kansas City, Mo., 2d and rev. ed., Pub. by the author, under auspices of the Sidney C. Tapp international Biblical society [c1915] 179 p. incl. port. 18 1/2 cm. 15-14676
I. Title.

UNITED Church of Christ. 261.8'34'17
Human sexuality : a preliminary study / the United Church of Christ. New York : United Church Press, c1977. 258 p. ; 21 cm. Bibliography: p. 255-258. [HQ61.U54 1977] 77-25398 ISBN 0-8298-0341-6 pbk. : 5.95
1. Sex and religion. 2. Sex in the Bible. 3. Sexual ethics. 4. Sex instruction. I. Title.

VALENTE, Michael F. 261.8'34'1
Sex: the radical view of a Catholic theologian, by Michael F. Valente. New York, Bruce Pub. Co. [1970] 158 p. 21 cm. Includes bibliographical references. [HQ63.V32] 79-132466 2.95
1. Sex and religion. 2. Sexual ethics. 3. Sex (Theology) I. Title.

VALENTINI, Norberto. 261.8'34'17
Sex and the confessional [by] Norberto Valentini [and] Clara Di Meglio. Translated by Melton S. Davis. New York, Stein and Day [1974] 213 p. 25 cm. Translation of Il sesso in confessionale. [HQ63.V3413] 73-91861 ISBN 0-8128-1681-1 6.95
1. Sex and religion. 2. Sexual ethics. 3. Confession. I. Di Meglio, Clara, joint author. II. Title.

WEIR, James, 1856-1906. 176
The psychical correlation of religious emotion and sexual desire. By James Weir, jr., M.D. 2d ed. Louisville, Ky., Courier-journal job printing co., 1897. 4 p. l., [11]-338 p. 18 1/2 cm. A third, revised and enlarged edition, in which, however, some chapters of the present edition are omitted, was published under title: Religion and lust; or, The psychical correlation [etc.] Chicago, 1905. [HQ61.W4 1897a] 9-9347
1. Sex and religion. I. Title.

WEIR, James, 1856-1906. 176
Religion and lust; or, The psychical correlation of religious emotion and sexual desire, by James Weir, jr. ... 3d ed., rev. and enl., with additional notes. Chicago, Chicago medical book co., 1905. 233 p. 21 cm. Bibliography: p. [231]-233. Published also under title: The psychical correlation of religious emotion and sexual desire ... 2d ed. [HQ61.W4 1905] 5-21026
1. Sex and religion. I. Title.

WILKIN, Vincent. 233
The image of God in sex. New York, Sheed & Ward, 1955. 88p. illus. 20cm. [BT708.W5] 55-14070
1. Sex and religion. I. Title.

Sex and religion—Addresses, essays, lectures.

HUMAN sexuality in our 261.8'34'1
time : what the church teaches / edited by George A. Kelly. [Boston] : St. Paul Editions, c1979. 212 p. ; 22 cm. Lectures given by the faculty of the Institute for Advanced Studies in Catholic Doctrine at St. John's University during the spring of 1978. Includes bibliographical references and index. [HQ63.H8] 79-15114
1. Catholic Church—Doctrinal and controversial works—Addresses, essays, lectures. 2. Sex and religion—Addresses, essays, lectures. 3. Sexual ethics—Addresses, essays, lectures. I. Kelly, George Anthony, 1916- II. St. John's University, New York. Institute for Advanced Studies in Catholic Doctrine.

Sex and religion—History.

PHAYER, J. Michael. 261.8'34'1
Sexual liberation and religion in nineteenth century Europe / J. Michael Phayer. London : Croom Helm ; Totowa, N.J. : Rowman and Littlefield, c1977. 176 p. : ill. ; 23 cm. Includes index. Bibliography: p. 165-173. [HQ63.P47] 76-30351 ISBN 0-87471-947-X : 16.50
1. Sex and religion—History. 2. Germany—Christianity. 3. France—Christianity. I. Title.

PHIPPS, William E., 1930- 261.8'3
The sexuality of Jesus: theological and literary perspectives [by] William E. Phipps. [1st ed.] New York, Harper & Row [1973] 172 p. 21 cm. Includes bibliographical references. [BL65.S4P5] 72-78067 ISBN 0-06-066561-0 5.95
1. Jesus Christ—Biography. 2. Sex and religion—History. I. Title.

Sex—Biblical teaching.

SUMRALL, Lester Frank, 241'.66
1913-
60 things God said about sex / by Lester Sumrall. Nashville : T. Nelson Publishers, c1981. ix, 151 p. ; 21 cm. Includes bibliographical references. [BS680.S5S93] 19 80-39699 ISBN 0-8407-5756-5 pbk. : 3.95
1. Sex—Biblical teaching. 2. Sexual ethics. I. Title.

Sex—Cause and determination.

ABBOUD, Michael Ben, 612.606
1898-
Love, life, and truth. Boston, Christopher Pub. House [1951] 60 p. 21 cm. [BS680.S5A18] 51-9513
1. Sex—Cause and determination. I. Title.

ABBOUD, Michael Ben, 612.606
1898-
The secret of sexes, revealed and controlled. From the Bible. By Michael Ben Abboud. [Hazleton, Pa., 1947] 3 p. l., 58 p., 3 l. port. 21 cm. [BS680.S5A2] 47-20833
1. Sex—Cause and determination. I. Title.

Sex customs—History—Addresses, essays, lectures.

BULLOUGH, Vern L. 261.8'357
Sexual practices & the medieval church / Vern L. Bullough & James Brundage. Buffalo, N.Y. : Prometheus Books, 1982. xii, 289 p. ; 24 cm. Includes index. Bibliography: p. 225-226. [HQ14.B84 1982] 19 80-85227 ISBN 0-87975-141-X : 18.95 ISBN 0-87975-151-7 pbk. : 9.95
1. Sex customs—History—Addresses, essays, lectures. 2. Sex (Theology)—History of doctrines—Middle Ages—600-1500—Addresses, essays, lectures. I. Brundage, James A. II. Title. III. Title: Sexual practices and the medieval church.

Sex discrimination against women—Addresses, essays, lectures.

RUETHER, Rosemary 261.8'34'1
Radford.
New woman/new earth : sexist ideologies and human liberation / Rosemary Radford Ruether. New York : Seabury Press, [1975] p. cm. "A Crossroad book." Includes index. Bibliography: p. [HQ1154.R83] 75-17649 ISBN 0-8164-1205-7 : 8.95
1. Sex discrimination against women—Addresses, essays, lectures. 2. Women in Christianity—Addresses, essays, lectures. 3. Race discrimination—Addresses, essays, lectures. 4. Sex role—Addresses, essays, lectures. I. Title.

TYRRELL, F. G.
Brimstone bargains in the marriage market; or, The traffic in sex; stories and studies of the exaggeration and perversion of sex and the degradation of woman growing out of her economic dependence; an appeal for justice and freedom, by Rev. F. G. Tyrrell, D.D. St. Louis, Puritan publishing co., 1904. xvi, [3], 20-424 p. incl. front., illus. 23 1/2 cm. 4-7824
I. Title.

Sex in marriage.

HAMILTON, Kenneth. 261.8'34'1
To be a man, to be a woman / Kenneth & Alice Hamilton. Nashville : Abingdon Press, 1975, c1972. 159 p. : ill. ; 22 cm. [HQ734.H2588 1975] 75-306287 ISBN 0-687-42149-7 pbk. : 2.95
1. Sex in marriage. 2. Conduct of life. I. Hamilton, Alice, joint author. II. Title.

MILES, Herbert 261.8'34'18
Jackson, 1907-
Sexual happiness in marriage : a Christian interpretation of sexual adjustment in marriage / Herbert J. Miles ; ill. by R. Earl Cleveland. Rev. ed. Grand Rapids : Zondervan Pub. House, c1976. p. cm. Bibliography: p. [HQ31.M63 1976] 76-29620 pbk. : 1.75
1. Sex in marriage. I. Title.

Sex in the Bible.

DUBARLE, Andre 220.8'30141
Marie, 1910-
Love and fruitfulness in the Bible, by A. M. Dubarle. Translated by Religious Book Consultants. De Pere, Wis., St. Norbert Abbey Press, 1968. 82, [1] p. 20 cm. Translation of Amour et fecondite dans la Bible. Bibliography: p. [83] [BS680.S5D813] 68-58124 ISBN 0-8316-1028-X 2.95
1. Sex in the Bible. 2. Marriage—Biblical teaching. I. Title.

HEFLEY, James C. 220.8'176
Sex, sense, and nonsense; what the Bible does and doesn't say about sex [by] James C. Hefley. Elgin, Ill., D. C. Cook Pub. Co. [1971] 96 p. 19 cm. Bibliography: p. 95-96. [BS680.S5H4] 71-147213 0.95
1. Sex in the Bible. I. Title.

HORNER, Thomas 220.8'30141'7
Marland, 1927-
Sex in the Bible [by] Tom Horner. Rutland, Vt., C. E. Tuttle Co. [1974] 188 p. 20 cm. [BS680.S5H6] 73-87676 ISBN 0-8048-1124-5 7.50
1. Sex in the Bible.

K*UIJF, T. C. de 220.830141
The Bible on sexuality Tr. by F. Vander Heijden. DePere, Wis., St. Norbert Abbey Pr. [c.]1966 103 p. 17 cm [BS680S5K713] 66-16989 pap., .95
1. sex in the bible. I. Title.

KRUIJF, Th C de. 220.830141
The Bible on sexuality, by T. C. De Kruijf. Translated by F. Vander Heijden. DePere, Wis., St. Norbert Abbey Press, 1966. 103 p. 17 cm. [BS680.S5K713] 66-16989
1. Sex in the Bible. I. Title.

SCORER, Charles Gordon 220.8176
The Bible and sex ethics today [by] C. G. Scorer. [1st ed. London, Tyndale P., 1966.] 124p. 20cm. (A Tyndale paperback) [BS680.S5S35] 66-72628 1.50 pap.,
1. Sex in the Bible. I. Title.
Available from Inter-Varsity, Chicago.

Sex Information and Education Council of the U.S.—Controversial literature.

CHAMBERS, Claire. 211'.6
The SIECUS circle: a humanist revolution/ by Claire Chambers Belmont, Mass. : Western Islands, c1977. xvi, 506 p. ; 21 cm. Includes bibliographical references and index. [BL2747.6.C47] 75-41650 ISBN 0-88279-119-2 pbk. : 6.95
1. Sex Information and Education Council of the U.S.—Controversial literature. 2. Humanism—Controversial literature. 3. Secularism—United States—Controversial literature. I. Title.

Sex instruction.

BELGUM, David Rudolph, 261.8'3
1922-
The church and sex education, by David Belgum. Wilbur G. Volker, editor. Philadelphia, Lutheran Church Press [c1967] 128 p. 21 cm. (Consult series, no. 3) Includes bibliographical references. [HQ56.B325] 68-2696
1. Sex instruction. I. Title.

DILLON, Valerie (Vance)
A Christian guide to your child's sex life [by] Valerie Vance Dillon and Walter J. Imbiorski. [Chicago, Delaney Publications, 1966] 120 p. illus. 22 cm. 67-82714
1. Sex instruction. I. Title.

FOERSTER, Friedrich Wilhelm, 176
1869-
Marriage and the sex-problem, by Dr. F. W. Foerester... translated by Meyrick Booth...with a foreword by Right Reverend Monsignor Fulton J. Sheen. New York, Frederick A. Stokes company, 1936. xxv, 228 p. 19 1/2 cm. "A translation of the third edition of Sexualethik und sexual padagogik --Translators's foreword. [HQ31.F67] 36-20981
1. Sex instruction. 2. Marriage. 3. Sexual ethics I. Title.

GILLET, Martin Stanislas, 176
abp., 1875-
Innocence and ignorance, by M. S. Gillet, O. P. Translated, with foreword, by J. Elliot Ross ... New York, The Devin-Adair company [1917] xxiv, 19 p. front. 20 cm. [Secular name: Stanislas Gillet] [HQ56.G5] 17-25869
1. Sex instruction. 2. Christian ethics—Catholic authors. I. Ross, John Elliot, 1884- tr. II. Title.

GILLET, Martin Stanislas, 176
pere, 1875-
Innocence and ignorance, by M. S. Gillet, O. P. Translated, with foreword, by J. Elliot Ross ... New York, The Devin-Adair company [1917] xxiv, 190 p. front. 20 cm. [Secular name: Stanislas Gillet] [HQ56.G5] 17-25869
1. Sex instruction. 2. Christian ethics—Catholic authors. I. Ross, John Elliot, 1884- tr. II. Title.

HENNRICH, Kilian J. 176
Watchful elders; a word to parents and educators about educating children to purity [by] Rev. Kilian J. Hennrich ... Milwaukee, Wis., New York [etc.] The Bruce publishing company [c1929] 60 p. 19 1/2 cm. "The contents of this booklet are based on two publications issued by the Catholic school organization in Duesseldorf, both by unknown authors." --p. 5. [HQ56.H45] 29-12780
1. Sex instruction. I. Title.

KELLY, Audrey, 1924-
A Catholic parent's guide to sex education. Pref. by Alphonse H. Clemens. Greenwich, Conn. Fawcett Publications [1964] 160 p. 21 cm (Crest book, d685) 66-84986
1. Sex instruction. 2. Sex and religion. I. Title. II. Series.

KIRSCH, Felix Marie, 1884- 176.1
Sex education and training in chastity, by Rev. Felix M. Kirsch ... with a foreword by the Most Rev. John. T. McNicholas ... New York, Cincinnati [etc.] Benziger brothers, 1930. 3 p. l., v-xxxix, 540 p. 17 cm. "A large section of the present book was presented to the Faculty of philosophy of the Catholic university, in partial fulfillment of the requirements for the degree of doctor of philosophy."--p. xxxvii. Bibliography: p. 503-526. [HQ56.K48] 612.6 30-32731
1. Sex instruction. 2. Chastity. I. Title.

KIRSCH, Felix Marie, 1884- 176.1
Training in chastity; a problem in Catholic character education, by Felix M. Kirsch ... New York, Cincinnati [etc.] Benziger brothers, 1930. xxviii, 373, [1] p. 23 cm. Thesis (PH. D.)--Catholic university of America, 1930. Vita. Bibliography: p. 351-373. [HQ56.K5 1930] 612.6 30-21073
1. Sex instruction. 2. Catholic church—Education. 3. Chastity. 4. Moral education. I. Title.

MEYER, Fulgence, father, 176
1876-1938.
Safeguards of chastity; a frank, yet reverent instruction on the intimate matters of personal life for young men, by Rev. Fulgence Meyer ... Cincinnati, O., St. Francis book shop, 1929. vi p., 2 l., 84 p., 1 l. front. 17 cm. [Secular name: Alphonse Meyer] [HQ41.M4] 29-6430
1. Sex instruction. I. Title.

O'REILLY, Sean, 1922- 261.8'34
In the image of God; a guide to sex education for parents. Middleburg, Va., Notre Dame Institute Press [1974] iv, 53 p. 22 cm. Bibliography: p. 53. [HQ57.2.O73] 74-76101 1.85 (pbk.)
1. Sex instruction. 2. Sex and religion. I. Title.

. . . Report of the Consultation of Christian Educators on sex education . . . Cincinnati, Nov. 13-15, 1958. [New York? 1959?] 1 v. (various pagings) illus. 28cm. Includes bibliographies.
1. Sex instruction. I. National Council of the Churches of Christ in the United States of America. Division of Christian Education. II. Consultation of Christian Educators on Sex Education, Cincinnati, 1958.

SHANNON, Thomas Washington, 176
1866-
Science of life and sex purity; invaluable knowledge of God's sacred laws of sex nature and heredity; vital information for all married and marriageable men and women; comprehensive guide to parents and teachers, for the instruction of children in sex purity; facts to help parents safeguard the morals of their children against ignorant or vicious associates ... by Prof. Thomas W. Shannon ... embracing a department on prenatal culture, infant care, children's diseases and remedies ... Marietta, O., The S. A. Mullikin company [c1917] 477 p. front., illus., plates. 20 cm. $1.95. [HQ56.S53] 17-17730
1. Sex instruction. 2. Sexual ethics. 3. Infants—Care and hygiene. I. Title.

TALMEY, Bernard Simon, 1862- 1926 176
Genesis; a manual for the instruction of children in matters sexual, for the use of parents, teachers, physicians and ministers, by B. S. Talmey ... with nineteen cuts, forty-seven drawings, in the text. New York, The Practitioners' publishing co. [c1910] x, [9]-194 p. illus. 20 cm. Bibliography: p. 177-181. [HQ56.T2] 10-15793
1. Sex instruction. I. Title.

TEASLEY, Daniel Otis, 1876- 176
Where do they come from? A book for children, explaining in simple, modest words the mystery of the origin of life and the sacredness of procreation, by D. O. Teasley ... Anderson, Ind., Gospel trumpet company [c1917] 96 p. incl. front., illus. 18 1/2 cm. [HQ56.T4] 17-27759 0.50.
1. Sex instruction. I. Title.

Sex instruction for youth.

DRAKEFORD, John W. 261.8'34'175
Made for each other [by] John W. Drakeford. Nashville, Broadman Press [1973] 152 p. 21 cm. Includes bibliographical references. [HQ35.D67] 72-90039 ISBN 0-8054-5608-2 4.95
1. Sex instruction for youth. 2. Sexual ethics. I. Title.

Sex (Psychology)

HAICH, Elisabeth. 294.5'4
Sexual energy and yoga / by Elisabeth Haich ; translated by D. Q. Stephenson. 1st American ed. New York : ASI Publishers, 1975, c1972. 158 p., [6] leaves of plates : ill. ; 21 cm. Translation of Sexuelle Kraft und Yoga. [BF692.H313 1975] 74-83158 ISBN 0-88231-009-7 pbk. : 5.00
1. Sex (Psychology) 2. Yoga, Hatha. I. Title.

Sex—Religious aspects—Christianity—Juvenile literature.

CHRISTENSON, Larry, 1928- 649'.65
The wonderful way that babies are made / Larry Christenson ; illustrated by Dwight Walles. Minneapolis, Minn. : Bethany House Publishers, c1982. p. cm. Presents in poetry and from a Christian viewpoint how God created the living things upon the earth so they could reproduce their own kind—including people. [BT708.C45 1982] 19 82-12813 ISBN 0-87123-627-3 : 7.95
1. Sex—Religious aspects—Christianity—Juvenile literature. 2. Sex instruction for children. 3. [Sex—Religious aspects—Christianity.] 4. [Sex instruction for children.] I. Walles, Dwight, ill. II. Title.

Sex (Theology)

AQUINAS Institute of Philosophy and Theology. Institute of Spiritual Theology 241
Sex, love, & the life of the spirit. Augustine Rock, ed. Chicago, Priory Pr. [c.1966] xii, 236p. 23cm. (Its Special lects., v.1, 1965) Bibl. [BT708.A7] 66-17485 5.00
1. Sex (Theology) I. Rock, Augustine, ed. II. Title. III. Series.

BURBRIDGE, Branse. 248'.4
The sex thing: you, love, and God. Wheaton, Ill., H. Shaw Publishers [1973, c1972] 124 p. illus. 18 cm. [BT708.B87 1973] 72-94100 ISBN 0-87788-763-2 1.25 (pbk.)
1. Sex (Theology) I. Title.

CALLAHAN, Sidney Cornelia. 241
Beyond birth control; the Christian experience of sex. New York, Sheed and Ward [1968] 248 p. 21 cm. Includes bibliographical references. [BT708.C3] 68-13848
1. Sex (Theology) 2. Marriage. I. Title.

DEJONG, Peter, 1945- 261.8'34'1
Husband & wife : the sexes in Scripture and society / Peter DeJong, Donald R. Wilson. Grand Rapids : Zondervan Pub. House, c1979. 224 p. ; 21 cm. Includes bibliographical references and indexes. [BT708.D44] 78-11989 ISBN 0-310-37760-9 : 6.95
1. Sex (Theology) 2. Marriage. 3. Sex role. I. Wilson, Donald Reid, 1931- joint author. II. Title.

FOX, Robert Joseph, 1927- 241'.6'6
Charity, morality, sex, and young people / Robert J. Fox. Huntington, Ind. : Our Sunday Visitor, inc., [1975] 173 p. ; 18 cm. [BT708.F69] 74-21889 ISBN 0-87973-763-8 pbk. : 1.95
1. Sex (Theology) 2. Youth—Conduct of life. I. Title.

GREEN, Ernest L. 261.8'34'1
Male and female created He them / by Ernest L. Green. Grand Rapids : Kregel Publications, c1977. 86 p. ; 19 cm. [BT708.G68] 77-79188 ISBN 0-8254-2717-7 pbk. : 1.95
1. Sex (Theology) 2. Marriage. I. Title.

*HICKEY, Marilyn. 241.'6'65
In the shadow of Gomer. Harrison, Ark. : New Leaf Press [1976]c1975. 82p. ; 21 cm. [BT708] 75-32006 ISBN 0-89221-009-5 pbk. : 2.50
1. Sex (Theology) 2. Prostitution. I. Title.

HOLLIS, Harry. 261.8'34'1
Thank God for sex : a Christian model for sexual understanding and behavior / Harry Hollis, Jr. Nashville : Broadman Press, [1975] 167 p. ; 21 cm. Includes bibliographical references. [BT708.H63] 75-3730 ISBN 0-8054-6114-0 : 4.95
1. Sex (Theology) I. Title.

JEWETT, Paul King. 220.8'30141'2
Man as male and female : a study in sexual relationships from a theological point of view / by Paul K. Jewett. Grand Rapids : Eerdmans, [1975] 200 p. ; 21 cm. Includes indexes. Bibliography: p. 189-190. [BT708.J48] 74-32471 ISBN 0-8028-1597-9
1. Sex (Theology) 2. Woman (Theology)—Biblical teaching. I. Title.

JOHN Paul II, Pope, 1920- 241'.66
Love and responsibility / Karol Wojtyla (Pope John Paul II) ; translated by H.T. Willetts. Rev. ed. New York : Farrar, Straus, Giroux, 1981. 319 p. ; 21 cm. Translation of: Milosc i odpowiedzialnosc. Includes bibliographical references and index. [BT708.J6313 1981] 19 81-2261 ISBN 0-374-19247-2 : 11.95
1. Sex (Theology) 2. Sexual ethics. I. [Milosc i odpowiedzialnosc.] English II. Title.

JOHN Paul II, Pope, 1920- 241'.66
Love and responsibility / Karol Wojtyla (Pope John Paul II) ; translated by H.T. Willetts. Rev. ed. New York : Farrar, Straus, Giroux, 1981. p. cm. Translation of: Milosc i odpowiedzialnosc. Includes bibliographical references and index. [BT708.J6313 1981] 19 81-2261 ISBN 0-374-19247-2 : 15.00
1. Sex (Theology) 2. Sexual ethics. I. [Milosc i odpowiedzialnosc.] English II. Title.

KUBO, Sakae, 1926- 241'.66
Theology and ethics of sex / by Sakae Kubo. Nashville, Tenn. : Southern Pub. Assoc., c1980. p. cm. Includes bibliographical references. [BT708.K8] 80-17299 ISBN 0-8127-0294-8 pbk. : 4.50
1. Sex (Theology) 2. Sexual ethics. I. Title.

LAHAYE, Tim F. 301.41'8
The act of marriage : the beauty of sexual love / by Tim and Beverly LaHaye. Grand Rapids : Zondervan Pub. House, c1976. 294 p. : ill. ; 21 cm. Bibliography: p. 292-294. [BT708.L42] 75-37742 6.95 pbk. : 3.95
1. Sex (Theology) 2. Marriage. I. LaHaye, Beverly, joint author. II. Title.

MACE, David Robert. 261.8'3
The Christian response to the sexual revolution [by] David R. Mace. Nashville, Abingdon Press [1970] 142 p. 19 cm. Bibliography: p. 137-142. [BT708.M3] 76-124748
1. Sex (Theology) I. Title.

MAY, William E., 1928- 241'.66
Sex, marriage, and chastity : reflections of a Catholic layman, spouse, and parent / by William E. May. Chicago, Ill. : Franciscan Herald Press, 1981. xi, 170 p. ; 21 cm. Includes bibliographical references and index. [BT708.M39 1981] 19 81-4701 ISBN 0-8199-0821-5 : 9.50
1. Sex (Theology) 2. Marriage. 3. Chastity. I. Title.

MICKLEY, Richard R. 261.8'34'1
Christian sexuality : a reflection on being Christian and sexual / by Richard R. Mickley ; illustrated by Shelagh. 2d ed. rev., with study guide. Los Angeles : Universal Fellowship Press, c1976. 186 p. : ill. ; 22 cm. "A chi-rho book." Includes bibliographical references. [BT708.M5 1976] 77-670034 3.95
1. Sex (Theology) 2. Sexual ethics. I. Title.

NELSON, James Bruce. 261.8'34'1
Embodiment : an approach to sexuality and Christian theology / James B. Nelson. Minneapolis : Augsburg Pub. House, c1978. 303 p. ; 22 cm. Includes bibliographical references and indexes. [BT708.N44] 78-55589 ISBN 0-8066-1655-5 : 8.95
1. Sex (Theology) 2. Sexual ethics. I. Title.

*O'BRIEN, William J. FIC
Sex and salvation. Port Washington, N.Y., Ashley Books [1973] 180 p. 22 cm. 73-76540 6.95
I. Title.
Publisher's address: Box 768, Port Washington, NY 11050.

PITTENGER, William Norman, 1905- 241
Making sexuality human [by] W. Norman Pittenger. Philadelphia, Pilgrim Press [1970] 96 p. 22 cm. [BT708.P56] 79-126862 3.95
1. Sex (Theology) I. Title.

PURYEAR, Herbert B. 299'.93
Sex and the spiritual path : based on the Edgar Cayce readings / by Herbert B. Puryear. Virginia Beach, Va. : A.R.E. Press, c1980. xiii, 225 p. ; 22 cm. [BX9999.V5P87] 19 81-107746 ISBN 0-87604-129-2 (pbk.) : 5.95
1. Association for Research and Enlightenment. 2. Cayce, Edgar, 1877-1945. Edgar Cayce readings. 3. Sex (Theology) I. Cayce, Edgar, 1877-1945. Edgar Cayce readings. II. Title.
Publisher's address P. O. Box 595, Virginia Beach, VA 23451.

ROBISON, James, 1943- 241'.66
Sex is not love / James Robison. Rev. ed. Wheaton, Ill. : Tyndale House Publishers, c1979. 80 p. ; 18 cm. (Life's answer series) [BT708.R56 1979] 19 79-89531 ISBN 0-8423-5877-3 pbk. : 1.95
1. Sex (Theology) I. Title.

SAPP, Stephen. 261.8'34'1
Sexuality, the Bible, and science / by Stephen Sapp. Philadelphia : Fortress Press, c1977. xi, 140 p. ; 24 cm. Bibliography: p. 136-140. [BT708.S25] 76-62617 ISBN 0-8006-0503-9 : 8.25
1. Sex (Theology) 2. Sex in the Bible. 3. Sex differences. I. Title.

SMALL, Dwight Hervey. 241'.6'6
Christian: celebrate your sexuality; a fresh, positive approach to understanding and fulfilling sexuality. Old Tappan, N.J., Revell [1974] 221 p. 21 cm. Includes bibliographical references. [BT708.S6] 74-11161 ISBN 0-8007-0661-7 5.95
1. Sex (Theology) I. Title.

STAFFORD, Tim. 301.41
A love story / Tim Stafford. Grand Rapids : Zondervan Pub. House, c1977. 160 p. ; 21 cm. Questions and answers about sex from a Christian point of view. [BT708.S7] 77-2136 ISBN 0-310-32970-1 : 5.95 ISBN 0-310-32971-X pbk. : 2.95
1. Sex (Theology) 2. [Sex (Theology)] I. Title.

TAPP, Sidney Calhoun, 1870- 176
Sex, the key to the Bible, by Sidney C. Tapp ... Kansas City, Mo., The author [c1918] 1 p. l., 5-172 p., 1 l. incl. plates, ports. 18 1/2 cm. [HQ61.T25] 18-10603
I. Title.

TOMCZAK, Larry, 1949- 241'.6'6
Straightforward / by Larry Tomczak. Plainfield, N.J. : Logos International, c1978. xiii, 123 p. : ill. ; 21 cm. [BT708.T65] 78-59856 ISBN 0-88270-311-0 pbk. : 2.95
1. Sex (Theology) 2. Youth—Religious life. 3. Marriage—Catholic Church. I. Title.

TRITON, A. N. 248'.4
Living & loving [by] A. N. Triton. Downers Grove, Ill., Inter-Varsity Press [1973, c1972] 95 p. 18 cm. [BT708.T74 1973] 73-75894 ISBN 0-87784-548-4 1.25 (pbk.)
1. Sex (Theology) I. Title.

UNSWORTH, Richard P. 261.8'34'12
Dignity & exploitation : Christian reflections on images of sex in the 1970s : a study document prepared at the request of and approved by the Advisory Council on Church and Society, the United Presbyterian Church in the U.S.A. / Richard P. Unsworth. New York : [Advisory Council on Church and Society of the United Presbyterian Church in the U.S.A. : available from Presbyterian Distribution Service, 1974] 49 p. ; 22 cm. Bibliography: p. 43-48. [BT708.U57] 74-190628 pbk. : 1.00
1. Sex (Theology) I. United Presbyterian Church in the U.S.A. Advisory Council on Church and Society. II. Title.

WESSLER, Martin F. 241
Christian view of sex education; a manual for church leaders, by Martin F. Wessler. St. Louis, Concordia Pub House [1967] 87 p. 23 cm. (Concordia sex education series, book 6) Bibliography: p. 79-83. "Films, filmstrips, slides, and tapes": p. 83-85. [BT708.W4] 67-24875
1. Sex(Theology) 2. Sex instruction. I. Title.

Sex (Theology)—Addresses, essays, lectures.

DIMENSIONS of human sexuality / edited by Dennis Doherty. 1st ed. Garden City, N.Y. : Doubleday, 1979. p. cm. Includes bibliographical references and index. [BT708.D55] 79-7046 ISBN 0-385-15040-7 : 8.95 241
1. Sex (Theology)—Addresses, essays, lectures. I. Doherty, Dennis.

FITTI, Charles J. 241'.6'6
Between God and man / Charles J. Fitti. New York : Philosophical Library, c1978. 49 p. : ill. ; 21 cm. [BT708.F57] 78-50527 ISBN 0-8022-2225-0 : 6.75
1. Sex (Theology)—Addresses, essays, lectures. 2. Sexual ethics—Addresses, essays, lectures. 3. Religion and science—1946- —Addresses, essays, lectures. I. Title.

MALE and female : 261.8'34'1
Christian approaches to sexuality / edited by Ruth Tiffany Barnhouse, and Urban T. Holmes, III ; with a foreword by John Maury Allin. New York : Seabury Press, c1976. xiii, 274 p. ; 23 cm. "A Crossroad book." Bibliography: p. 271-274. [BT708.M34] 75-42380 ISBN 0-8164-2118-8 : 4.95
1. Sex (Theology)—Addresses, essays, lectures. 2. Sex—Addresses, essays, lectures. 3. Marriage—Addresses, essays, lectures. 4. Women—Addresses, essays, lectures. 5. Homosexuality—Addresses, essays, lectures. I. Barnhouse, Ruth Tiffany, 1923- II. Holmes, Urban Tigner, 1930-

RELIGION & sexuality : 241'.66
Judaic-Christian viewpoints in the USA / edited by John M. Holland. San Francisco, CA : Association of Sexologists, c1981. v, 69 p. ; 22 cm. (Monograph / Association of Sexologists ; #1) Series statement on cover: T.A.O.S. sexology monograph ; #1. Contents.Contents.—Introduction / John M. Holland — Jewish views of sexuality / Allen Bennett — Roman Catholic views of sexuality / James H. Schulte —Protestant views of sexuality / Letha Scanzoni — Toward a theology of human sexuality / James B. Nelson — Afterword / William Simon. Includes bibliographical references. [BT708.R44] 19 81-66867 ISBN 0-939902-00-1 pbk. : 5.95
1. Sex (Theology)—Addresses, essays, lectures. 2. Sex and Judaism—Addresses, essays, lectures. I. Holland, John M. II. Association of Sexologists. III. Title: Religion and sexuality.
Distributed by Multi-Media Resource Ctr.,

1525 Franklin St., San Francisco, CA 94109

Sex (Theology)—Biblical teaching.

DILLOW, Joseph C. 223'.9'06
Solomon on sex / Joseph C. Dillow. New York : T. Nelson, c1977. 196 p. ; 24 cm. Includes bibliographical references. [BS1485.3.D55] 77-1049 ISBN 0-8407-5117-6 : 6.95
1. Bible. O.T. Song of Solomon—Commentaries. 2. Sex (Theology)—Biblical teaching. I. Title.

GOLLWITZER, Helmut. 241'.6'6
Song of love : a Biblical understanding of sex / Helmut Gollwitzer ; translated by Keith Crim. Philadelphia : Fortress Press, c1979. 79 p. ; 20 cm. Translation of Das hohe Lied der Liebe. Includes bibliographical references. [BS680.S5G5813] 78-14667 ISBN 0-8006-1360-0 : 3.95
1. Bible. O.T. Song of Solomon—Theology. 2. Sex (Theology)—Biblical teaching. I. Title.

Sex (Theology)—Biblical teaching—Addresses, essays, lectures.

THE Liberating word : 220.6
a guide to nonsexist interpretation of the Bible / edited by Letty M. Russell, in cooperation with the Task Force on Sexism in the Bible, Division of Education and Ministry, National Council of the Churches of Christ in the U.S.A. Philadelphia : Westminster Press, c1976. p. cm. Bibliography: p. [BS680.S5L5] 76-18689 ISBN 0-664-24751-2 pbk. : 3.95
1. Bible—Criticism, interpretation, etc.—Addresses, essays, lectures. 2. Sex (Theology)—Biblical teaching—Addresses, essays, lectures. 3. Woman (Theology)—Biblical teaching—Addresses, essays, lectures. I. Russell, Letty M. II. National Council of the Churches of Christ in the United States of America. Task Force on Sexism in the Bible.

Sex (Theology)—History of doctrines.

KERN, Louis J., 1943- 261.8'357
An ordered love : sex roles and sexuality in Victorian Utopias : the Shakers, the Mormons, and the Oneida Community / by Louis J. Kern. Chapel Hill : University of North Carolina Press, c1981. p. cm. Includes index. Bibliography: p. [BT708.K47] 80-10763 ISBN 0-8078-1443-1 : 24.00 ISBN 0-8078-4074-2 pbk. : 12.50
1. Oneida Community—History. 2. Sex (Theology)—History of doctrines. 3. Sex customs—United States—History—19th century. 4. Sex role. 5. Shakers—United States—History. 6. Mormons and mormonism in the United States—History. I. Title.

PHIPPS, William E., 1930- 261.8'3
Was Jesus married? The distortion of sexuality in the Christian tradition [by] William E. Phipps. [1st ed.] New York, Harper & Row [1970] vii, 239 p. 22 cm. [BT708.P47 1970] 74-126282 5.95
1. Jesus Christ. 2. Paul, Saint, apostle. 3. Sex (Theology)—History of doctrines. I. Title.

Sexism in Christian education.

SAWICKI, Marianne. 268'.6
Faith & sexism : guidelines for religious education / Marianne Sawicki. New York : Seabury Press, 1979. p. cm. "A Crossroad book." [BV1464.S28] 79-5176 ISBN 0-8164-0105-5 pbk. : 3.95
1. Sexism in Christian education. 2. Christian education and language. 3. Christian education—Text-books—Catholic. 4. Sex (Theology) I. Title.

Sexism in liturgical language.

WATKINS, Keith. 264
Faithful and fair : transcending sexist language in worship / Keith Watkins. Nashville : Abingdon, c1981. 128 p. ; 20 cm. Includes bibliographical references. [BV178.W37] 19 80-39698 ISBN 0-687-12707-6 pbk. : 4.95
1. Sexism in liturgical language. I. Title.

Sexism in religion.

BRAXTON, Bernard. 291.1'7834'12
Sex and religion in oppression : a view on the sexual exploitation of women under paganism, Hinduism, Mohammedianism [sic], and Christianity / by Bernard Braxton. Washington : Verta Press, c1978. vi, 220 p. ; 23 cm. Includes index. Bibliography: p. 211-216. [BL458.B7] 78-64512 ISBN 0-930876-05-9 : 8.95 ISBN 0-930876-06-7 pbk. : 3.95
1. Sexism in religion. I. Title.

Sexism—Moral and religious aspects.

PAPA, Mary Bader. 305.4'2
Christian feminism : completing the subtotal woman / Mary Bader Papa. Chicago, Ill. : Fides/Claretian, c1981. xiii, 186 p. ; 20 cm. [HQ1154.P32] 19 81-5368 ISBN 0-8190-0644-0 : 6.95
1. Sexism—Moral and religious aspects. 2. Feminism—Moral and religious aspects. 3. Women's rights—Biblical teaching. 4. Women in Christianity. 5. Women in church work. 6. Women (Theology) I. Title.

Sextons—Juvenile literature.

MCCAW, Mabel 647 (j)
(Niedermeyer)
A friend at church. Art by Mary Richards Gibson. St. Louis, Bethany Press, 1968. 1 v. (unpaged) col. illus. 21 cm. [BV705.M3] 68-26110
1. Sextons—Juvenile literature. I. Gibson, Mary Richards, illus. II. Title.

Sexual deviation—United States.

RATLIFF, Dale 261.8'34'158
Hedrick, 1928-
Minor sexual deviance : diagnosis and pastoral treatment / Dale H. Ratliff. Dubuque, Iowa : Kendall/Hunt Pub. Co., c1976. ix, 54 p. ; 23 cm. Bibliography: p. 51-54. [HQ72.U53R37] 76-29284 ISBN 0-8403-1605-4 : 3.50
1. Sexual deviation—United States. 2. Pastoral counseling. I. Title.

Sexual disorders.

MAZAT, Alberta, 1919- 613.9'6
That Friday in Eden / by Alberta Nazat. Mountain View, CA : Pacific Press Pub. Association, 1981. p. cm. [RC556.M39] 19 80-25391 ISBN 0-8163-0401-7 pbk. : 3.95
1. Sexual disorders. 2. Marriage. 3. Sex (Theology) I. Title.
Distributed by the Greater New York Bookstore, 12 W. 40th St., New York, NY

Sexual ethics.

BABBAGE, Stuart Barton. 176
Christianity and sex. Chicago, Inter-varsity Press [1963] 59 p. 21 cm. (IVP series in contemporary Christian thought, 4) Includes bibliography. [HQ63.B2] 63-8554
1. Sexual ethics. 2. Sex and religion. I. Title.

BLACKWELL, Elizabeth, 241'.6'6
1821-1910.
Essays in medical sociology. New York, Arno Press, 1972. 2 v. in 1. 22 cm. (Medicine & society in America) Reprint of the 1902 ed. Includes bibliographical references. [HQ32.B55 1972] 73-180555 ISBN 0-405-03935-2
1. Sexual ethics. 2. Prostitution. 3. Social medicine. I. Title. II. Series.

BOROWITZ, Eugene B. 296.3'85
Choosing a sex ethic; a Jewish inquiry [by] Eugene B. Borowitz. [New York] Published by Schocken Books for B'nai B'rith Hillel Foundations [1969] ix, 182 p. 21 cm. (Hillel library series) Bibliography: p. 175-182. [HQ32.B65] 73-79123 5.00
1. Sexual ethics. 2. Ethics, Jewish. I. B'nai B'rith Hillel Foundations. II. Title. III. Series.

BRASEFIELD, Nell R. 616.95
Commandment seven, by Nell R. Brasefield ... Boston, Mass., The Christopher publishing house [c1931] 2 p. l., 81 p. illus. 19 cm. [HQ31.B77 1931a] 176 35-31102
1. Sexual ethics. 2. Venereal diseases. I. Title.

BRASEFIELD, Nell R. 616.95
Commandment seven, by Nell R. Brasefield ... [Lebanon, Pa., Dale print shop, c1931] 1 p. l., 81 p. illus. 19 cm. [HQ31.B77] 176 31-5656
1. Sexual ethics. 2. Venereal diseases. I. Title.

BRAV, Stanley Rosenbaum, 176
1908-
Since Eve; a Bible-inspired sex ethic for today. [1st ed.] New York, Pageant Press [1959] 204p. 24cm. [HQ31.B773] 59-8653
1. Sexual ethics. 2. Bible—Ethics. I. Title.

BROWN, S. Spencer N. 176
Understanding love and sex, by S. Spencer N. Brown. [Waco, Tex., Printed by Texian Press, 1967] viii, 198 p. 24 cm. Bibliography: p. 195-198. [HQ31.B92] 67-17535
1. Sexual ethics. I. Title.

CABOT, Richard Clarke, 1868- 176
1939.
Christianity and sex, by Richard C. Cabot, M.D. New York, The Macmillan company, 1937. vii, 78 p. 20 cm. [HQ31.C2] 37-25776
1. Sexual ethics. 2. Sex and religion. I. Title.

CATHOLIC Church. 241.6'6
Congregatio pro Doctrina Fidei.
Declaration on certain questions concerning sexual ethics / Sacred Congregation for the Doctrine of the Faith ; [translated from the Latin]. London : Catholic Truth Society, [1976] 21 p. ; 19 cm. "Do 486." Includes bibliographical references. [HQ32.C39 1976] 76-368339 ISBN 0-85183-159-1 : £0.15
1. Catholic Church. Congregatio pro Doctrina Fide. 2. Sexual ethics. 3. Christian ethics. I. Title.

CONFERENCE on Christian 261
politics, economics and citizenship. Commission on the relation of the sexes.
The relation of the sexes; being the report presented to the Conference on Christian politics, economics and citizenship at Birmingham, April 5-12, 1924. London, New York [etc.] Published for the conference committee by Longmans, Green and co., 1924. xii, 219, [1] p. 18 1/2 cm. (Half-title: C.O.P.E.C. commission reports. vol. Iv) "Third impression, November 1924." W. F. Lofthouse, chairman. [HN30.C6 vol. IV] 25-6845
1. Sexual ethics. 2. Marriage. I. Title.

CONVERSATIONS on love 261.8'34'18
and sex in marriage [by] Jim and June Cicero, Ivan and Joyce Fahs. Waco, Tex., Word Books [1972] 138 p. 22 cm. [HQ31.C755] 72-84157 3.50
1. Sexual ethics. 2. Sex in marriage. I. Cicero, Jim.

CONVERSATIONS on love 261.8'34'18
and sex in marriage [by] Jim and June Cicero, Ivan and Joyce Fahs. Waco, Tex., Word Books [1972] 138 p. 22 cm. [HQ31.C755] 72-84157 3.50
1. Sexual ethics. 2. Sex in marriage. I. Cicero, Jim.

COOKE, Nicholas Francis, 176
1829-1885.
Satan in society, by Nicholas Francis Cooke ... With an introduction by Caroline E. Corbin ... together with a biographical sketch of the author, by Eliza Allen Starr ... Chicago, C. F. Vent company, 1889. 426 p. front. (port.) 20 cm. [HQ31.C77 1889] 9-6224
1. Sexual ethics. I. Starr, Eliza Allen, 1824-1901. II. Title.

DEDEK, John F., 1929- 241.6'6
Contemporary sexual morality, by John F. Dedek. New York, Sheed and Ward [1971] x, 170 p. 20 cm. Bibliography: p. 163-170. [HQ32.D43] 79-152319 ISBN 0-8362-1159-6 5.95
1. Sexual ethics. I. Title.

DERSTINE, Clayton F. 176
The path to noble manhood ... a book for parents, men and boys on sex life. Right knowledge, right proportion, right time, By C. F. Derstine ... Grand Rapids, Mich., Zondervan publishing house [1944] 92 p. 20 cm. [HQ31.D43] 44-11857
1. Sexual ethics. I. Title.

DOLAN, Albert Harold. 222.12
A modern messenger of purity; sermons concerning the sixth commandment, delivered at the Eastern shrine of the Little Flower, by the Reverend Albert H. Dolan ... Chicago, Ill., The Carmelite press, 1932. 3 p. l., 9-188 p. 19 cm. First printing. [BV4695.D6] 33-6352
1. Therese, Saint, 1873-1897. 2. Sexual ethics. 3. Catholic church—Discipline. 4. Catholic church—Sermons. 5. Sermons, American. I. Title. II. Title: Commandment, The sixth.

DUVALL, Evelyn Ruth (Millis), 176
1906-
Why wait till marriage? Special Catholic ed. New York, Association [1968,c.1965] 128p. 18cm. Bibl. [HQ31.D983] .75 pap.,
1. Sexual ethics. I. Title.

DUVALL, Evelyn Ruth (Millis) 176
1906-
Why wait till marriage? By Evelyn Millis Duvall. Special Catholic ed. New York, Association Press [1965] 128 p. 23 cm. Bibliography: p. 119-125. [HQ31.D983 1965a] 65-27834
1. Sexual ethics. I. Title.

EPSTEIN, Louis M. 1887- 176
Sex laws and customs in Judaism. New York, Bloch Pub. Co., 1948. x, 251 p. 23 cm. "Companion to an earlier work, Marriage laws in the Bible and the Talmud." Bibliography: p. [235-]-246. [BM720.S4E6] 48-8415
1. Sexual ethics. 2. Ethics, Jewish. I. Title.

EPSTEIN, Louis M., 1887- 296.3'85
1949.
Sex laws and customs in Judaism. Introd. by Ari Kiev. New York, Ktav Pub. House [1968, c1967] xxii, 251 p. 24 cm. "Companion to an earlier work: Marriage laws in the Bible and the Talmud." Bibliography: p. [235]-246. [BM720.S4E6 1968] 67-22751
1. Sexual ethics. 2. Ethics, Jewish. I. Title.

FLINT, Joseph Frederick, 176
1850-
In Potiphar's house; or, The young man in peril. By Rev. J.F. Flint. With an introduction by H.S. Pomeroy... New York, J.B. Alden, 1890. 178 p. 19 1/2 cm. [HQ36.F62] 9-10104
1. Sexual ethics. I. Title.

*FRANKL, George. 241.66
The failure of the sexual revolution. London, Kahn & Averill [1975 c1974] 190 p. 22 cm. Includes index. Bibliography: p. 186-190. [HQ31] ISBN 0-900707-35-6
1. Sexual ethics. I. Title.
Distributed by Humanities Press for 6.95.

GARDNER, Augustus Kinsley, 176
1821-1876.
Conjugal sins against the laws of life and health and their effects upon the father, mother and child. By Augustus K. Gardner ... New York, J. S. Redfield, 1870. 240 p. 19 cm. [HQ31.G24] 9-9902
1. Sexual ethics. 2. Hygiene, Sexual. I. Title.

GARDNER, Augustus Kinsley, 176
1821-1876.
Conjugal sins against the laws of life and health, and their effects upon the father, mother and child. By Augustus K. Gardner ... New York, J. S. Redfield. 1870. 240 p. 19 cm. On cover: Fifth edition. [HQ31.G24 1870 e] 37-17699
1. Sexual ethics. 2. Hygiene, Sexual. I. Title.

GARDNER, Augustus Kinsley, 176
1821-1876.
Conjugal sins against the laws of life and health and their effects upon the father, mother and child. By Augustus K. Gardner ... Twentieth thousand. Rev. ed., with a new preface. New York, G. J. Moulton, 1874. 3 p. l., [5]-240 p. 19 1/2 cm. [HQ31.G25] 9-9903
1. Sexual ethics. 2. Hygiene, Sexual. I. Title.

GATTERER, Michael, 1862- 176
Educating to purity; thoughts on sexual teaching and education proposed to clergymen, parents and other educators, by Dr. Michael Gatterer ... and Dr. Francis Krus ... authorized translation from the 3d German ed., adpated and supplemented with an extensive appendix by Rev. C. Van der Donckt ... Ratisbon, New York [etc.] F. Pustet & co., 1912. 318 p. 19 1/2 cm. [HQ56.G3] 12-18523
1. Sexual ethics. 2. Sex instruction. I. Krus, Frang, 1871- joint author. II. Van der Donekt, Cyril, 1865- III. Title.

GEIS, Rudolph. 176
Principles of Catholic sex morality, by Dr. Rudolph Geis ... translated and edited by Charles Bruehl, PH. D.; with a preface by Dominic Pruemmer ... New York, J. F. Wagner, inc.; London, B. Herder [c 1930] xix, 105 p. 18 cm. Bibliography: p. 104-105. [HQ63.G37] 31-1805
1. Sexual ethics. 2. Catholic church—Discipline. I. Bruehl, Charles Paul, 1876- ed. and tr. II. Title. III. Title: Catholic sex morality. translation of Katholische sexualethik.

GINDER, Richard. 261.8'34'17
Binding with briars : sex and sin in the Catholic Church / Richard Ginder. Englewood Cliffs, N.J. : Prentice-Hall, [1975] ix, 251 p. ; 24 cm. Includes index. Bibliography: p. 237-244. [HQ59.G56] 75-11610 ISBN 0-13-076299-7
1. Catholic Church—Doctrinal and controversial works—Catholic authors. 2. Sexual ethics. 3. Sex and religion. I. Title.

GRAY, Arthur Herbert, 1868- 176
Men, women, and God; a discussion of sex questions from the Christian point of view, by the Rev. A. Herbert Gray ... New York, George H. Doran company [1923] xviii, 199, [1] p. 20 cm. Fourth edition. [HQ31.G75 1923] 24-17024
1. Sexual ethics. I. Title.

GRAY, Arthur Herbert, 1868- 176
Men, women, and God; a discussion of sex questions from the Christian point of view. Rev. ed. By the Rev. A. Herbert Gray ... New York and London, Harper & brothers, 1938. xx p., 1 l., 149 p. 20 cm. "Revised edition." [HQ31.G75 1938] 39-446
1. Sexual ethics. I. Title.

GRIFFIN, Graeme Maxwell, 1932- 261.8'3
Towards a Christian approach to sex, by Graeme M. Griffin. Melbourne [Presbyterian Board of Christian Education] 1969. 54 p. 22 cm. Includes bibliographical references. [HQ32.G63] 70-526114 1.25
1. Sexual ethics. 2. Sex and religion. I. Presbyterian Church of Australia. Board of Christian Education. II. Title.

GRIMM, Robert 261.8
Love and sexuality. Tr. [from French] foreword. by David R. Mace. New York, Association [c.1964] 127p. 20cm. 64-19746 3.50
1. Sexual ethics. 2. Sex and religion. I. Title.

GUINDON, Andre, 1933- 241'.6'6
The sexual language : an essay in moral theology / Andre Guindon. [Toronto] : University of Ottawa Press, 1976. x, 476 p. ; 21 cm. Bibliography: p. [441]-476. [HQ31.G943] 77-371039 ISBN 0-7766-0050-8
1. Sexual ethics. 2. Christian ethics. I. Title.

HALL, George F evangelist. 176
Plain points on personal purity; or, Startling sins of the sterner sex. A book for men only. By Evangelist Geo. F. Hall... Chicago, Columbian book company, 1892. 317 p. front. (port.) 19 1/2 cm. [HQ36.H17] 9-9889
1. Sexual ethics. 2. Social ethics. I. Title.

HALL, Winfield Scott, 1861- 176
From youth into manhood [by] Winfield S. Hall ... introduction by George J. Fisher ... New York, Young men's Christian association press, 1909. 106 p. illus. 18 cm. [HQ41.H3] 9-25276
1. Sexual ethics. 2. Sex instruction. I. Title.

HALL, Winfield Scott, 1861- 176
From youth into manhood [by] Winfield S. Hall ... introduction by George J. Fisher ... 13th ed. New York, Association press, 1919. 106 p. illus. 17 1/2 cm. [HQ41.H3 1919] 19-19476
1. Sexual ethics. 2. Sex instruction. I. Title.

HALL, Winfield Scott, 1861- 176
... Instead of "wild oats", a little book for the youth of eighteen and over, by Winfield Scott Hall ... with a foreword by Edward Bok ... New York, Chicago [etc.] Fleming H. Revell company [c1919] 62 p. 17 cm. (The Edward Bok books of self-knowledge for young people and parents ... no. 3) [HQ36.H2] 12-8400
1. Sexual ethics. I. Title.

HIS guide to sex, 261.8'34'1
singleness & marriage / C. Stephen Board & others. Downers Grove, Ill. : InterVarsity Press, [1974] 130 p. ; 18 cm. [HQ31.H57] 74-83476 pbk. : 1.95
1. Sexual ethics. 2. Marriage. I. Board, Stephen. II. His.
Contents omitted.

HORTON, M. B. Mrs. 176
The divine law of birth, "Every wise woman buildeth her house;" "All her household are clothed with scarlet." By Mrs. M. B. Horton. Boston, T. H. Carter & sons, 1867. 68 p. 17 cm. [HQ46.H82] 9-10101
1. Sexual ethics. I. Title.

HUMAN sexuality : 261.8'34'1
new directions in American Catholic thought : a study / commissioned by the Catholic Theological Society of America ; Anthony Kosnik, chairperson ... [et al.]. New York : Paulist Press, c1977. xvi, 322 p. ; 24 cm. Includes index. Bibliography: p. 275-291. [HQ32.H822] 77-74586 ISBN 0-8091-0223-4 : 8.50
1. Sexual ethics. 2. Sex (Theology) I. Kosnik, Anthony. II. Catholic Theological Society of America.

HUMAN sexuality : 261.8'34.'1
new directions in American Catholic thought / a study commissioned by the Catholic Theological Society of America, Anthony Kosnik, chairperson....b[et al. b] Garden City New York : Doubleday & Co., Inc., 1979, c1977 350 p ; 18 cm. Includes index. Bibliography: p. 301-318 [HQ32H822] ISBN 0-385-15041-5 pbk. : 3.95
1. Sex ual ethics 2. Sex (Theology) I. Kosnik, Anthony. II. Catholic Theological Society of America.
L.C. card no for 1977 Paulist Press ed.: 77-74586

IGERET ha-kodesh. English and Hebrew. 296.7'4
The holy letter : a study in medieval Jewish sexual morality, ascribed to Nahmanides / translated and with an introduction by Seymour J. Cohen. New York : Ktav Pub. House, 1976. 155 p. : 22 cm. Added t.p.: Igeret ha-kodesh ha-meyuhas la-Ramban. Includes bibliographical references. [BM720.S4I3313] 76-44550 ISBN 0-87068-490-6 : 7.50
1. Sexual ethics. 2. Ethics, Jewish. I. Cohen, Seymour J. II. Moses ben Nahman, ca. 1195-ca. 1270. Igeret ha-kodesh. III. Title. IV. Title: Igeret ha-kodesh ha-meyuhas la-Ramban.

KEANE, Philip S. 261.8'34'17
Sexual morality : a Catholic perspective / by Philip S. Keane. New York : Paulist Press, 1977. viii, 236 p. ; 23 cm. Includes bibliographical references and index. [HQ32.K39] 77-83536 ISBN 0-8091-2070-4 pbk. : 5.95 ISBN 0-8091-0230-7 : 10.00
1. Sexual ethics. 2. Christian ethics—Catholic authors. I. Title.

KING, Elisha Alonzo, 1870- 176
Clean and strong; a book for young men, by E. A. King and F. B. Meyer ... Boston and Chicago, United society of Christian endeavor [c1909] 136 p. 18 1/2 cm. [HQ36.K5] 9-30891
1. Sexual ethics. I. Meyer, Frederick Brotherton, 1847- joint author. II. Title.

KING, Elisha Alonzo, 1870- 176
Clean and strong; a book for young men, by E. A. King and F. B. Meyer ... Boston and Chicago, United society of Christian endeavor [c1917] 198 p. 16 x 9 cm. On cover: War edition. [HQ36.K5 1917] 18-3472
1. Sexual ethics. 2. Hygiene, Sexual. I. Meyer, Frederick Brotherton, 1847- II. Title.

LOWRY, Oscar, 1872- 176
A virtuous woman; sex life in relation to the Christian life, by Rev. Oscar Lowry ... Grand Rapids, Mich., Zondervan publishing house [c1938] 160 p. 20 cm. [HQ31.L86] 38-38769
1. Sexual ethics. 2. Woman—Social and moral questions. I. Title.

LOWRY, Oscar, 1873- 176
The way of a man with a maid; sexology for men and boys, by Oscar Lowry ... Grand Rapids, Mich., Zondervan publishing house [c1940] 160 p. 20 cm. A companion volume to the author's "A virtuous woman". cf. Introd. [HQ36.L75] 40-13995
1. Sexual ethics. I. Title.

LUDER, William Fay, 1910- 241
A new approach to sex. Boston, Farnsworth Books, [1966] xx, 103 p. front. 18 cm. [HQ31.L8754] 66-1876
1. Sexual ethics. I. Title.

[MCCALLEN Robert Seth] 176
"Palaces of sin"; or, "The devil in society" ... a history of "society's sins" that appall the civilized world ... By Col. Dick Maple [pseud.] ... St. Louis, Mo., National book concern [1902] 333 p. incl. front. (port.) plates. 21 1/2 cm. [HQ31.M135] 2-19901
1. Sexual ethics. 2. Social ethics. I. Title.

MACE, David Robert. 176
Does sex morality matter? By David R. Mace ... London, New York [etc.] Rich & Cowan [1943] 157 p. 18 cm. (On cover: The 'Needs of to-day' series) Bibliographical foot-notes. [HQ31.M183] 44-14408
1. Sexual ethics. I. Title.

MCGLOIN, Joseph T 176
Yeara a little! or, Why did God come up with two sexes? Illustrated by Don Baumgart. Milwaukee, Bruce Pub. Co. [1961] 134p. illus. 21cm. (His Love--. and live, book 2) [HQ31.M184] 61-17981
1. Sexual ethics. 2. Christian ethics—Catholic authors. I. Title.

MCGLOIN, Joseph T. 176
Yearn a little! or, Why did God come up with two sexes? Illus. by Don Baumgart. Milwaukee, Bruce [c.1961] 134p. illus. (His Love--and live, bk., 2) 61-17981 1.35 pap.,
1. Sexual ethics. 2. Christian ethics—Catholic author. I. Title.

MCGOEY, John H. 261.8'34'1
Dare I love? / John H. McGoey. Huntington, Ind. : Our Sunday Visitor, 1974, c1971. ix, 131 p. : ill. ; 20 cm. [HQ31.M1844] 74-16464 ISBN 0-87973-762-X pbk. : 2.75
1. Sexual ethics. 2. Love. I. Title.

MAY, William E., 1928- 261.8'34'1
On understanding Human sexuality / by William E. May and John F. Harvey. Chicago : Franciscan Herald Press, c1977. 79 p. ; 18 cm. (Synthesis series) A critical analysis of Human sexuality. Includes bibliographical references. [HQ32.M383] 77-14377 ISBN 0-8199-0720-0 pbk. : 1.95
1. Sexual ethics. 2. Sex and religion. 3. Sexual deviation. I. Harvey, John Francis, 1918- joint author. II. Human sexuality. III. Title.

NORTHCOTE, Hugh. 261.8'34'17
Christianity and sex problems. 2d ed. rev. and enl. Philadelphia, F. A. Davis Co., 1916. [New York, AMS Press, 1974] xvi, 478 p. 23 cm. Includes bibliographical references. [HQ31.N87 1974] 72-9668 ISBN 0-404-57486-6
1. Sexual ethics. I. Title.

PIPER, Otto A 1891- 176
The Biblical view of sex and marriage. New York, Scribner [1960] 239p. 22cm. Includes bibliography. [HQ31.P64] 60-14021
1. Sexual ethics. 2. Marriage. I. Title.

PLATT, Smith H. 176
Princely manhood. A private treatise: for adults only, on the procreative instinct, as related to moral and Christian life. By Rev. S. H. Platt ... Bridgeport, Conn., S. Harrison & co., 1873. 115 p. 13 1/2 cm. [HQ31.P7] 9-10113
1. Sexual ethics. I. Title.

PLATT, Smith H. 176
Queenly womanhood. A private treatise: for females only, on the sexual instinct, as related to moral and Christian life. [A complement to "Princely manhood" for males only.] By Rev. S. H. Platt ... Brooklyn, N.Y., S. Harrison & co., 1875. 167 p. 16 cm. [HQ31.P72] 9-10112
1. Sexual ethics. I. Title.

RINZEMA, J. 241'.6'6
The sexual revolution; challenge and response, by J. Rinzema. Translated by Lewis B. Smedes. Grand Rapids, Eerdmans [1974] 107 p. 20 cm. Includes bibliographical references. [HQ31.R6213] 73-14712 ISBN 0-8028-1545-6 2.45 (pbk.)
1. Sexual ethics. I. Title.

ROY, Rustum, 1924- 241
Honest sex [by] Rustum and Della Roy. [New York] New American Library [1968] 209 p. illus. 21 cm. Bibliography: p. 187-199. [HQ31.R86] 68-18258
1. Sexual ethics. I. Roy, Della, joint author. II. Title.

SAVORY, George Washington, 1856- 176
"Hell upon earth" made heaven; or, The marriage secrets of a Chicago contractor, as told to Rev. George W. Savory. 3d ed. Claremont, Cal., The Order of the orange blossom [c1907] 158 p. 17 cm. [HQ31.S28] 7-32571
1. Sexual ethics. I. Title.

SMEDES, Lewis B. 261.8'34'1
Sex for Christians : the limits and liberties of sexual living / by Lewis B. Smedes. Grand Rapids : Eerdmans, c1976. 250 p. ; 18 cm. [HQ32.S55] 76-791 ISBN 0-8028-1618-5 pbk. : 2.95
1. Sexual ethics. 2. Sex in marriage. 3. Christian ethics. I. Title.

STEINMETZ, Urban G. 261.8'34'1
The sexual Christian [by] Urban G. Steinmetz. St. Meinrad, Ind., Abbey Press, 1972. ix, 98 p. 21 cm. (A Priority edition) [HQ63.S73] 72-85374 1.50
1. Sexual ethics. 2. Sex and religion. I. Title.

TREVETT, Reginald Frederick 176
The church and sex. New York, Hawthorn Books [1960] 126p. (bibl.) 21cm. (The Twentieth century encyclopedia of Catholicism. v.103. Section 9: The church and the modern world) 60-8782 2.95 half cloth,
1. Sexual ethics. I. Title.

TREVETT, Reginald Frederick, 1904- 176
The church and sex. [1st ed.] New York, Hawthorn Books [1960] 126 p. 21 cm. (The Twentieth century encyclopedia of Catholicism, v. 103. Section 9: The church and the modern world) Includes bibliography. [HQ31.T748] 60-8782
1. Sexual ethics. I. Title.

WEATHERHEAD, Leslie Dixon, 1893- 176
The mastery of sex through psychology and religion, by Leslie D. Weatherhead ... assisted by Dr. Marion Greaves ... with forewords by the Rev. A. Herbert Gray ... and J. R. Rees ... and an epilogue by Principal W. F. Lofthouse ... New York, The Macmillan company, 1939. xxv, 246 p. 19 1/2 cm. [HQ31.W45 1932] 32-3863
1. Sexual ethics. 2. Sex introduction. I. Graves, Marion, joint. II. Title.

WHITE, John, 1924(Mar.5)- 261.8'34'15
Eros defiled : the Christian & sexual sin / John White. Downers Grove, Ill. : Inter-Varsity Press, c1977. 169, [3] p. ; 21 cm. Includes bibliographical references. [HQ31.W5] 76-39711 ISBN 0-87784-781-9 pbk. : 3.95
1. Sexual ethics. 2. Sexual deviation. I. Title.

WIER, Frank E
Sex and the whole person; a Christian view. Teacher's book. New York,

Abingdon Press [c1962] 64 p. 23 cm. Bibliography: p. 63-64. 67-24104
1. Sexual ethics. 2. Sex and religion. 3. Sex instruction. I. Title.

WOOD, Frederic C. 241
Sex and the new morality, by Frederic C. Wood, Jr. New York, Association Press [1968] 157 p. 21 cm. Bibliographical references included in "Notes" (p. 151-157) [HQ31.W797] 68-17779 2.25
1. Sexual ethics. 2. Situation ethics. I. Title.

Sexual ethics—Addresses, essays, lectures.

SEXUAL ethics and Christian 176
responsibility; some divergent views. Edited by John Charles Wynn. New York, Association Press [1970] 224 p. 21 cm. Includes bibliographical references. [HQ32.S4] 76-93431 6.95
1. Sexual ethics—Addresses, essays, lectures. I. Wynn, John Charles, ed.

TAYLOR, Michael J., 241'.6'6
comp.
Sex: thoughts for contemporary Christians. Edited by Michael J. Taylor. Garden City, N.Y., Doubleday, 1973 [c.1972] 240 p. 18 cm. (Image Book, D324) Bibliography: p. [237]-240. [HQ32.T36] 70-171400 ISBN 0-385-03893-3 1.45 (pbk.)
1. Sexual ethics—Addresses, essays, lectures. I. Title.

Sexual ethics for youth.

KALT, William J 176
Man and woman [by] William J. Kalt and Ronald J. Wilkins. Chicago, Regnery [1967] v, 90 p. illus. 23 cm. (To live is Christ. Discussion booklet 1) Chicago, Regnery [1967] vii, L88 p. 23 cm. (To live is Christ. Discussion leader manual 1) Bibliography: p. L79-L82. HQ35.K32 Manual Bibliography: p. 89-90. [HQ35.K32] 67-29304
1. Sexual ethics for youth. I. Wilkins, Ronald J., joint author. II. Title.

STEINKE, Peter L. 241
Right, wrong, or what? By Peter L. Steinke. St. Louis, Concordia Pub. House [1970] 85, [1] p. illus. 21 cm. (Perspective, 10) Bibliography: p. 85-[86] A compilation of the opinions of young people between the ages of fifteen and twenty on sexual ethics. [HQ35.S83] 73-114729
1. Sexual ethics for youth. 2. [Sexual ethics.] I. Title.

*TAYLOR, Gerald J., M.D. 241.5
Adolescent freedom and responsibility: a guide to sexual maturity. New York, Exposition [c.1965] 68p. illus. 21cm. (Exposition-banner bk.) 3.50
I. Title.

WYRTZEN, Jack, 1913- 176
Sex is not sinful? A Biblical view of the sex revolution. Grand Rapids, Zondervan Pub. House [1970] 64 p. 21 cm. (A Zondervan paperback) Bibliography: p. 64. Explains the position of the Scriptures on sexual morality. [HQ35.W9] 79-81063 0.95
1. Sexual ethics for youth. 2. [Sexual ethics for youth.] 3. [Christian life.] I. Title.

Sexual ethics—History

SEX in history. *177
New York, Distributed by the Vanguard Press [c1954] 336p. 22cm. (A Thames and Hudson book) [HQ12.T3 1954] 176 54-6991
1. Sexual ethics—Hist. 2. Sex and religion. 3. Moral conditions. I. Taylor, Gordon Rattray.

TAYLOR, Gordon Rattray 176
Sex in history. New York, Ballantine Books [c.1954] 320p. 19cm. (S367K) .75 pap.,
1. Sexual ethics—Hist. 2. Sex and religion. 3. Moral conditions. I. Title.

TAYLOR, Gordon Rattray. 176
Sex in history [by] G. Rattray Taylor. New York, Harper [1973] 336 p. 21 cm. (Torchbooks, TB1743) First published in 1954 in London by Thames & Hudson. Includes bibliography. [HQ12.T3] ISBN 0-06-131743-8 3.45 (pbk.)
1. Sexual ethics—History. 2. Sex and religion. 3. Moral conditions. I. Title.
L.C. card no. for the 1954 ed.: 54-23129.

Sexual ethics—Juvenile literature.

BROWN, S. Spencer N. 241
Christian answers to teenage sex questions, by S. Spencer N. Brown. [1st ed.] Atlanta, Hallux [1970] vi, 198 p. 24 cm. (A Genesis Press book) Bibliography: p. 195-198. Answers from a Christian viewpoint the questions teenagers ask about sex and love. [HQ63.B74] 79-123355 ISBN 0-87667-061-3 4.95
1. Sexual ethics—Juvenile literature. 2. Sex and religion—Juvenile literature. 3. [Sexual ethics.] 4. [Sex and religion.] I. Title.

Seybert, John, bp., 1791-1860.

SPRENG, Samuel Peter, 922.773
1853-
The life and labors of John Seybert, first bishop of the Evangelical association. By Rev. S. P. Spreng ... Cleveland, O., Published for the Evangelical association by Lauer & Mattill, 1888. 3 p. l., 11-439 p. front. (port.) 21 cm. [BX7543.S4S6] 36-33223
1. Seybert, John, bp., 1791-1860. I. Title.

Seymour, Conn. Methodist Episcopal church.

SHARPE, William Carvosso, 287.
1839-1924.
Annals of the Methodist Episcopal church, of Seymour, Conn., by W. C. Sharpe ... Seymour, Conn., Record print, 1885. 144 p. front., pl., ports. 20 1/2 cm. "Edition of 1896" stamped at foot of t.-p. [BX8481.S5S5] 11-33713
1. Seymour, Conn. Methodist Episcopal church. I. Title.

Sha'rani, 'Abd al-Wahhab ibn Ahmad, 1493 (ca.)-1565 or 6.

WINTER, Michael. 297'.4'0924
Society and religion in early Ottoman Egypt : studies in the writings of 'Abd al-Wahhab al-Sharani / Michael Winter. New Brunswick [N.J.] : Transaction Books, c1982. x, 345 p. ; 24 cm. (Studies in Islamic culture and history) Includes index. Bibliography: p. 318-326. [BP80.S5W57 1982] 19 81-3042 ISBN 0-87855-351-7 : 39.95
1. Sha'rani, 'Abd al-Wahhab ibn Ahmad, 1493 (ca.)-1565 or 6. 2. Sufism—Egypt. I. Title. II. Series.
Publisher's address Bldg. 4051, Rutgers-State Univ. New Burnswick, NJ 08903.

Shabbethai Zebi, 1626-1676.

EVELYN, John, 1620- 296.6'1 B
1706.
The history of Sabatai Sevi, the suppos'd Messiah of the Jews (1669). Introd. by Christopher W. Grose. Los Angeles, William Andrews Clark Memorial Library, University of California, 1968. viii, [10], 41-111 p. 22 cm. (Augustan Reprint Society. Publication no. 131) Contains a reproduction of the author's note, "To the reader" and "The history of Sabatai Sevi, the pretended Messiah of the Jews, in the year of our Lord, 1666. The third impostor" from his "The history of the three late famous impostors, viz. Padre Ottomano, Mahomed Bei, and Sabatai Sevi ... published in 1669. "Reproduced from a copy in the William Andrews Clark Memorial Library." [BM755.S45E92 1968] 68-66889
1. Shabbethai Zebi, 1626-1676. I. Title. II. Series.

[KATZENSTEIN, Julius] 922.96
1890-
The Messiah of Ismir, Sabbatai Zevi, by Joseph Kastein [pseud.] translated by Huntley Paterson. New York, The Viking press, 1931. 4 p. l., 3-346 p. front., plates, ports. 22 cm. Bibliography: p. 341-343. [BM755.S45K3] 31-24862
1. Shabthai Tsebi, 1626-1676. I. Paterson, Huntley, tr. II. Title. III. Title: Translation of Sabbatai Zewi, der messias von Ismir.

SCHOLEM, Gershom 296.6'1 B
Gerhard, 1897-
Sabbatai Sevi; the mystical Messiah, 1626-1676. [Translated by R. J. Zwi Werblowsky. Princeton, N.J.] Princeton University Press [1973] xxvii, 1000 p. illus. 24 cm. (Bollingen series, 93) Rev. and augm. translation of Shabtai Tsevi veha-tenu'ah ha-shabta'it bi-yeme hayav. Bibliography: p. [931]-956. [BM199.S3S3713 1973] 75-166389 ISBN 0-691-09916-2 25.00
1. Shabbethai Zebi, 1626-1676. 2. Sabbathaians. I. Title. II. Series.

Shabthai Tsebi, 1626-1676—Drama.

ASCH, Shalom, 1880- 892.472
Sabbatai Zevi; a tragedy in three acts and six scenes with a prologue and an epilogue, by Sholom Ash; authorized translation from the Russian version by Florence Whyte and George Rapall Noyes. Philadelphia, The Jewish publication society of America, 1930. 131 p. front. 19 cm. 30-10043
1. Shabthai Tsebi, 1626-1676—Drama. I. Whyte, Florence, tr. II. Noyes, George Rapall, 1873- joint tr. III. Title.

Shackford, John Walter, 1878-

BROWN, Elmore. 268'.3'0924
The struggle for trained teachers; the story of John W. Shackford's early efforts to provide trained teachers in the church. [Nashville? 1966] xii, 87 p. illus., port. 21 cm. Without thesis statement. Thesis (M.A.)—Boston University School of Theology. Bibliographical footnotes. [BX8495.S48B7] 67-2036
1. Shackford, John Walter, 1878- I. Title.

Shah, Idries, Sayed, 1924- — Addresses, essays, lectures.

SUFI studies: East and 297'.4
West; a symposium in honor of Idries Shah's services to Sufi studies by twenty-four contributors marking the 700th anniversary of the death of Jalaluddin Rumi (A.D. 1207-1273) Edited by L. F. Rushbrook Williams. [1st ed.] New York, Dutton [1973] xxxvi, 260 p. 22 cm. Includes bibliographical references. [BP80.S483S9] 73-178387 ISBN 0-525-21195-0 10.00
1. Shah, Idries, Sayed, 1924- —Addresses, essays, lectures. 2. Sufism—Addresses, essays, lectures. I. Shah, Idries, Sayed, 1924- II. Jalal al-Din Rumi, Mawlana, 1207-1273. III. Williams, Laurence Frederic Rushbrook, 1890- ed.

Shahn, Ben, 1896-

BIBLE. O.T. Ecclesiastes. j223
English. 1965.Authorized.
Ecclesiastes; or, The preacher. In the King James translation of the Bible. With drawings by Ben Shahn, engraved in wood by Stefan Martin. Calligraphy by David Soshensky. New York, Spiral Press, 1965. 1 v. (unpaged) illus. 34 cm. 285 numbered copies. No. for copyright. [BS1473] 67-578
1. Shahn, Ben, 1896- illus. I. Title. II. Title: The preacher.

Shahrines.

GILLETT, Henry Martin, 232.931
1902-
Famous shrines of Our Lady. With a foreword by the Apostolic Delegate of England. Westminster, Md., Newman Press, 19 v. plates. 20cm. Bibliography: v.2, p. 277-284. [BT650.G52] 54-14504
1. Shahrines. 2. Mary, Virgin— Oultus. I. Title.

Shakarian, Demos, 1913-

SHAKARIAN, Demos, 1913- 289.9 B
The happiest people on earth : the long-awaited personal story of Demos Shakarian / as told to John and Elizabeth Sherrill. Old Tappan, N.J. : Chosen Books : distributed by F. H. Revell Co., c1975. 187 p. ; 22 cm. [BX8764.Z8S474] 75-33902 ISBN 0-912376-14-7 : 6.95
1. Shakarian, Demos, 1913- 2. Full Gospel Business Men's Fellowship International. I. Sherrill, John. II. Sherrill, Elizabeth. III. Title.

Shakers.

ANDREWS, Edward Deming, 289.8
1894-
The Shaker order of Christmas, by Edward and Faith Andrews. New York, Oxford University Press, 1954. unpaged. illus. 16cm. [BX9781.A5] 54-12701
1. Shakers. 2. Christmas. I. Andrews, Faith, joint author. II. Title.

ANDREWS, Edward Deming, 289.8
1894-1964.
Fruits of the Shaker tree of life : memoirs of fifty years of collecting and research / Edward Deming Andrews, Faith Andrews. Stockbridge, Mass. : Berkshire Traveller Press, c1975. 222 p. : ill. ; 28 cm. [BX9771.A64 1975] 75-33901 ISBN 0-912944-31-5 : 17.50. ISBN 0-912944-32-3 pbk. : 8.95
1. Shakers. I. Andrews, Faith, joint author. II. Title.

ANDREWS, Edward Deming, 335'.9'73
1894-1964.
Work and worship: the economic order of the Shakers [by] Edward Deming Andrews and Faith Andrews. Greenwich, Conn., New York Graphic Society [1974] 224 p. illus. 26 cm. Bibliography: p. 219-222. [BX9771.A65 1974] 73-89949 ISBN 0-8212-0593-5 10.95
1. Shakers. I. Andrews, Faith, joint author. II. Title.

AVERY, Giles Bushnell, 1815- 289.
1890.
Sketches of "Shakers and Shakerism." Synopsis of theology of United society of believers in Christ's second appearing. By Giles B. Avery. Albany, Weed, Parson's & company, printers, 1884. cover-title, 50, [2] p. incl. illus., pl. 18 1/2 cm. [BX9771.A9] 44-27080
1. Shakers. I. Title.

BATES, Paulina. 289.8
The divine book of holy and eternal wisdom, revealing the word of God: out of whose mouth goeth a sharp sword ... Written by Paulina Bates ... Including other illustrations and testimonies. Arranged and prepared for the press at New Lebanon, N.Y. ... Published by the United society called "Shakers". Printed at Canterbury, N. H., 1849. 2 v. in 1. 22 cm. Paged continuously. Preface signed: Seth Y. Wells, Calvin Green, editors. [BX9771.B3] 32-103
1. Shakers. I. Wells, Seth Youngs, ed. II. Green, Calvin, joint ed. III. Title.

BLINN, Henry Clay, 1824-1905.
The manifestation of spiritualism among the Shakers, 1837-1847... By Henry C. Blinn. East Canterbury, N.H. 1899. 1 p. l., 101 p. 17 1/2 cm. Cover-title: Spiritualism among the Shakers. [BX9778.S7B6] 27-
1. Shakers. 2. Spiritualism. I. Title. II. Title: Spiritualism among the Shakers.

BROWN, Thomas, b.1766. 289.8
An account of the people called Shakers: their faith, doctrines, and practice, exemplified in the life, conversations, and experience of the author during the time he belonged to the society. To which is affixed A history of their rise and progress to the present day. By Thomas Brown. Troy, Printed by Parker and Bliss. Sold at the Troy bookstore; by Websters and Skinners, Albany, and by S. Wood, New-York ... 1812. xii, [13]-372 p. 18 cm. [BX9771.B8] 31-1148
1. Shakers. I. Title.

BROWN, Thomas, b.1766. 289.8
An account of the people called Shakers : their faith, doctrines, and practice, exemplified in the life, conversations, and experience of the author during the time he belonged to the society : to which is affixed a history of their rise and progress to the present day / by Thomas Brown. New York : AMS Press, [1977] p. cm. (Communal societies in America) Reprint of the 1812 ed. published by Parker and

Bliss, Troy. [BX9771.B8 1977] 77-17584 ISBN 0-404-08459-1 : 14.50
1. Brown, Thomas, b. 1766. 2. Shakers. 3. Shakers—New York (State)—Biography. 4. New York (State)—Biography. I. Title.

BROWN, Thomas, b.1766. 289.8
An account of the people called Shakers: their faith, doctrines, and practice, exemplified in the life, conversations, and experience of the author during the time he belonged to the society. To which is affixed a history of their rise and progress to the present day. Troy, Printed by Parker and Bliss, 1812 [New York, AMS Press, 1972] 372 p. 22 cm. [BX9771.B8 1972] 70-134415 ISBN 0-404-08459-1 14.50
1. Shakers. I. Title.

CHAPMAN, Eunice (Hawley) Mrs. 289.8
An account of the conduct of the Shakers, in the case of Eunice Chapman & her children, written by herself. Also, a refutation of the Shakers' remonstrance to the proceedings of the Legislature of New-York, in 1817, by Thomas Brown. To which are added, the deposition of Mary Dyer, who petitioned the Legislature of the state of New-Hampshire, for relief in a similar case. Also, depositions of others who have heen members of the Shaker society. Also, the proceedings of the Legislature of the state of New-York, in the case of Eunice Chapman. Lebanon, O., Printed by Van Vleet & Camron, 1818. "Shaker tenets. The religious [!] sentiments of the Shakers ... disclosed in a poem": p. 101-105. [BX9773C47] 31-31306
1. Shakers. I. Brown, Thomas, fl. 1812. II. Dyer, Mary (Marshall) Mrs. III. New York (State) Legislature. IV. Title.

CONDITION of society; 289.8
and its only hope, in obeying the everlasting gospel, as how developing among believers in Christ's second appearing ... Union Village, O., Printed and pub. at the "Day-star" office, 1847. 120 p. 15 cm. "Made up of selections from the "Day-star."-Pref. [B X9771. C6] 5-1916
1. Shakers. I. Day-star, Union Village, o.

DESROCHE, Henri. 289.8'0973
The American Shakers; from neo-Christianity to presocialism. Translated from the French and edited by John K. Savacool. Amherst, University of Massachusetts Press, 1971. 357 p. illus., maps. 25 cm. Translation of Les Shakers americains d'un neo-christianisme a un pre-socialisme? Includes bibliographical references. [BX9766.D413] 78-123537 9.50
1. Shakers. I. Title.

DOW, Edward French. 289.8
A portrait of the Millennial church of Shakers, by Edward F. Dow. Orono, Me., Printed at the University press, 1931. 52 p. 22 1/2 cm. (On cover: University of Maine studies. Second series, no. 19) The Maine bulletin, vol. xxxiv, no. 1. Bibliography: p. 46-47. [BX9772.D6] 31-27743
1. Shakers. I. Title. II. Title: The Millennial church of Shakers.

DUNLAVY, John, 1769-1826. 230'.9'8
The manifesto. [1st AMS ed.] New York, AMS Press [1972] vi, 520 p. 22 cm. Reprint of the 1818 ed. [BX9771.D9 1972] 74-134416 ISBN 0-404-08460-5 21.00
1. Stone, Barton Warren, 1772-1844. 2. Shakers. I. Title.

DUNLAVY, John, 1769-1826. 289.
The manifesto, or A declaration of the doctrines and practice of the church of Christ. By John Dunlavy ... Pleasant Hill, Ky. P. Bertrand, printer, 1818. vi, 520 p. 22 cm. "The substance of a letter to Barton W. Stone": p. [439]-520. [BX9771.D9 1818] 24-12276
1. Shakers. I. Stone, Barton Warren, 1772-1844. II. Title.

DUNLAVY, John, 1769-1826. 289.
The manifesto, or A declaration of the doctrine and practice of the church of Christ. By John Dunlavy ... Printed at Pleasant-Hill, Ky., mdcccxviii. New York, Reprinted by E. O. Jenkins, 1847. viii, 486 p. 24 cm. "The substance of a letter to Barton W. Stone": p. [411]-486. [BX9771.D9] 31-54
1. Stone, Barton Warren, 1773-1844. 2. Shakers. I. Title.

DUNLAVY, John, 1769-1826. 289.8
The nature and character of the true church of Christ proved by plain evidences, and showing whereby it may be known and distinguished from all others. Being extracts from the writings of John Dunlavy ... New York, Printed by G. W. Wood, 1847. 93 p. 20 cm. "Extracts ... from a work entitled 'The manifesto, or A delcaration of the doctrines and practice of the church of Christ'." [BX9771.D935] 34-13016
1. Shakers. I. Title.

DUNLAVY, John, 1769-1826. 230.98
Plain evidences, by which the nature and character of the true church of Christ may be known and distinguished from all others. Taken from a work entitled "The manifesto, or, A declaration of the doctrines and practice of the church of Christ"; published at Pleasant Hill, Kentucky, 1818. By John Dunlavy ... Albany, Printed by Hoffman and White, 1834. 120 p. 19 cm. "Extracts from a letter addressed to Barton W. Stone, by John Dunlavy": p. [105]-119. [BX9771.D93 1934a] 33-17071
1. Stone, Barton Warren, 1772-1844. 2. Shakers. I. Title.

DYER, Joseph. 289.8
A compendious narrative, elucidating the character, disposition and conduct of Mary Dyer, from the time of her marriage, in 1799, till she left the society called Shakers, in 1815. With a few remarks upon certain charges which she has since published against that society. Together with sundry depositions. By her husband, Joseph Dyer. To which is annexed, a remonstrance against the testimony and application of the said Mary, for legislative interference. Concord [N.H.], Printed by Isaac Hill, for the author, 1819. iv, [5]-88 p. 19 cm. [BX9773.M4D9] 34-24956
1. Marshall, Mary, b. 1789. 2. Shakers. I. Title.

EADS, Harvey L. b.1807. 289.8
Shaker sermons; scripto-rational. Containing the substance of Shaker theology. Together with replies and criticisms logically and clearly set forth. By H. L. Eads... Shakers, N.Y., The Shaker manifesto, 1879. 3 p. l., 222 p. front. (port.) 23 1/2 cm. [BX9771.E25] 31-2741
1. Shakers. 2. Sermons, American. I. Title.

EADS, Harvey L. b.1807. 252
Shaker sermons; scripto-rational. Containing the substance of Shaker theology. Together with replies logically and clearly set forth. By H. L. Eads... 3d ed., rev. and enl. South Union, Ky., 1884. iv, 287 p. front. (port.) 23 1/2 cm. [BX9771.E25 1884a] 31-1143
1. Shakers. 2. Sermons, American. I. Title.

EADS, Harvey L. b.1807. 289.
Shaker sermons; scripto-rational. Containing the substance of Shaker theology. Together with replies and criticisms logically and clearly set forth. By H. L. Eads... 4th ed., rev. and enl. South Union, Ky., 1887. vi, 320 p. front. (port.) 24 cm. [BX9771.E25] 6-25444
1. Shakers. I. Title.

EADS, Harvey L. b.1807. 289.8
Shaker sermons; scripto-rational. Containing the substance of Shaker theology. Together with replies and criticisms logically and clearly set forth. By H. L. Eads... 5th ed., rev. and enl. South Union, Ky., 1889. vi, 366 p. front. (port.) 23 1/2 cm. [BX9771.E25 1889] 31-1139
1. Shakers. 2. Sermons, American. I. Title.

ELKINS, Hervey. 289.8
Fifteen years in the senior order of Shakers: a narration of facts concerning that singular people. Hanover [N.H.] Dartmouth Press, 1853. [New York, AMS Press, 1973] 136 p. 23 cm. [BX9771.E4 1973] 72-2984 ISBN 0-404-10746-X 7.50
1. Shakers. I. Title.

ELKINS, Hervey. 289.8
Fifteen years in the senior order of Shakers: a narration of facts, concerning that singular people. By Hervey Elkins... Hanover [N.H.] Dartmouth press, 1853. 136 p. 23 cm. "Lines by Charlotte Cushman, suggested by a visit to the Shaker settlement, near Albany, N.Y.": p. [5]-6; "Ans er to lines by Charlotte Cushman [by a Shaker girl]": p. [7]-8. [BX9771.E4] 32-2742
1. Shakers. I. Cushman, Charlotte Saunders, 1816-1876. II. Title.

EVANS, Frederick William, 1808-1893. 289.
Ann Lee (the founder of the Shakers), a biography, with memoirs of William Lee, James Whittaker, J. Hocknell, J. Meacham, and Lucy Wright; also a compendium of the origin, history, principles, rules, and regulations, government and doctrines of the United society of believers in Christ's second appearing. By F. W. Evans, 4th ed. ... London, J. Burns; Mount Lebanon, New York, F. W. Evans [1869?] x, [11]-187 p. 17 cm. [BX9771.E85 1869] 24-16998
1. Lee, Ann, 1736-1784. 2. Lee, William, 1749-1784. 3. Whittaker, James, 1751-1787. 4. Hocknell, John, 1723?-1799. 5. Meacham, Joseph, 1742-1786. 6. Wright, Lucy, 1760-1821. 7. Shakers. 8. Shakers—Biog. I. Title. II. Title: "With the exception of title-page and pp. 185-187 it is printed from the same plates as his 'Shaker compendium' ..." cf. MacLean's Bibl. of Shaker lit., p. 25.

[EVANS, Frederick William] 1808-1893. 289.8'092'4 B
Autobiography of a Shaker, and Revelation of the Apocalypse. With an appendix. New and enl. ed., with port. Philadelphia, Porcupine Press, 1972. xvi, 271 p. port. 22 cm. (The American Utopian adventure) Reprint of the 1888 ed. [BX9793.E8A3 1972] 79-187481 ISBN 0-87991-002-X
1. Evans, Frederick William, 1808-1893. 2. Bible. N.T. Revelation—Prophecies. 3. Shakers. I. Title. II. Title: Revelation of the Apocalypse.

EVANS, Frederick William, 1808-1893. 289.8
Autobiography of a Shaker, and Revelation of the Apocalypse. With an appendix ... Mt. Lebanon, N.Y., F. W. Evans, 1869. 162 p. 21 cm. [BX9793.E8A3 1869] 24-19496
1. Shakers. 2. Bible, N.T. Revelation—Prophecies. 3. Bible—Prophecies—N.T. Revelation. I. Title.

[EVANS, Frederick William] 1808-1893. 289.8
Autobiography of a Shaker, and Revelation of the Apocalypse, With an appendix ... New York, American news company [1869] 162 p. 21 cm. [BX9793.E8A3 1869a] 31-11669
1. Shakers. 2. Bible. N.T. Revelation—Prophecies. 3. Bible—Prophecies—N.T. Revelation. I. Title.

[EVANS, Frederick William] 1808-1893. 922.
Autobiography of a Shaker, and Revelation of the Apocalypse. With an appendix, New and enlarged ed., with portrait ... Glasgow, United publishing company; New York, American news co., 1888. xvi, 271, [1] p. front. (port.) 19 1/2 cm. [BX9793.E8A3 1888] 24-16999
1. Evans, Frederick William, 1808-1893. 2. Shakers. I. Title.

EVANS, Frederick William, 1808-1893. 289.8'0973
Shaker communism; or, Tests of divine inspiration. The second Christian or gentile Pentecostal Church, as exemplified by seventy communities of Shakers in America. London, J. Burns, 1871. [New York, AMS Press, 1974] vii, 120 p. 19 cm. (Communal societies in America) Published in New Lebanon, N.Y., in 1853 under title: Tests of divine inspiration. [BX9771.E9 1974] 72-2987 ISBN 0-404-10749-4
1. Shakers. I. Title.

EVANS, Frederick William, 1808-1893. 289.8
Shakers : compendium of the origin, history, principles, rules and regulations, government, and doctrines of the United Society of Believers in Christ's Second Appearing ... / by F. W. Evans. 4th ed. New York : AMS Press, 1975. 190 p. ; 19 cm. (Communal societies in America) Reprint of the 1867 ed. published in New Lebanon, N.Y. Bibliography: p. [188]-190. [BX9771.E85 1975] 72-2985 ISBN 0-404-10747-8
1. Shakers. 2. Shakers—Biography. 3. Lee, Ann, 1736-1784. 4. Lee, William, 1740-1784. 5. Whittaker, James, 1751-1787. 6. Hocknell, John, 1723?-1799. 7. Meacham, Joseph, 1742-1796. 8. Wright, Lucy, 1760-1821. I. Title: Compendium of the origin, history, principles, rules and regulations, government, and doctrines of the United Society of Believers in Christ's Second Appearing.

EVANS, Frederick William, 1808-1893. 289.
Shakers, Compendium of the origin, history, principles, rules and regulations, government, and doctrines of the United society of believers in Christ's second appearing. With biographies of Ann Lee, William Lee, Jas. Whittaker, J. Hocknell, J. Meacham, and Lucy Wright. By F. W. Evans ... New York, D. Appleton and company, 1859. x; [11]-189 p. 18 cm. [BX9771.E85 1859] 24-19739
1. Lee, Ann, 1736-1784. 2. Lee, William, 1740-1784. 3. Whittaker, James, 1751-1787. 4. Hocknell, John, 1723?-1799. 5. Meacham, Joseph, 1742-1796. 6. Wright, Lucy, 1760-1821. 7. Shakers. 8. Shakers—Biog. I. Title.

EVANS, Frederick William, 1808-1893. 289.
Shakers. Compendium of the origin, history, principles, rules and regulations, government, and doctrines of the United society of believers in Christ's second appearing. With biographies of Ann Lee, William Lee, Jas. Whittaker, J. Hocknell, J. Meacham, and Lucy Wright. By F. W. Evans ... New Lebanon, N.Y. [Albany, C. Van Benthuysen & sons, printers] 1867. x, [11]-192 p. 17 1/2 cm. Fourth edition. [BX9771.E85 1867] 25-23582
1. Lee, Ann, 1736-1784. 2. Lee, William, 1740-1784. 3. Whittaker, James, 1751-1787, 4. Hocknell, John, 1723?-1799. 5. Meacham, Joseph, 1742-1796. 6. Wright, Lucy, 1760-1821. 7. Shakers. 8. Shakers—Biog. I. Title.

EVANS, Frederick William, 1808-1893. 289.8
Shakers; compendium of the origin, history, principles, rules and regulations, government, and doctrines of the United Society of Believers in Christ's Second Appearing. With biographies of Ann Lee, William Lee, Jas. Whittaker, J. Hocknell, J. Meacham, and Lucy Wright. New York, B. Franklin [1972] 184 p. 19 cm. (Burt Franklin research and source work series. Philosophy & religious history monographs, 101) [BX9771.E85 1972] 72-75873 ISBN 0-8337-4091-1
1. Shakers. 2. Shakers—Biography.

EVANS, Frederick William, 1808-1893. 289.
Tests of divine inspiration; or, The rudimental principles by which true and false revelation, in all eras of the world, can be unerringly discriminated ... By F. W. Evans. New Lebanon [N.Y.] United society called Shakers, 1853. v, [7]-127 p. 19 1/2 cm. Published in London, 1871, under title: Shaker communism. [BX9771.E9] 25-23581
1. Shakers. I. Title.

GIBSON, Marywebb. 289.8769
Shakerism in Kentucky, founded in America by Ann Lee, by Marywebb Gibson. Cynthiana, Ky., The Hobson press [1942] ix p., 1 l., 141 p. incl. front. pl., facsim. 23 cm. Reproduced from type-written copy. "First printing, May, 1942." [BX9771.G5] 42-24398
1. Shakers. 2. Pleasanthill, Ky. I. Title.

GREENE, Nancy Lewis. 289.8
Ye olde Shaker bells, by Nacy Lewis Greene ... Lexington, Ky. [Transyvania printing co.] c1930. 83 p. front., plates. 23 cm. Contains records of the Shaker colony at Pleasanthill, Ky., from January 1856 to April 1865, and a story with a Shaker background. [BX9768.P6G7] 30-19366
1. Shakers. 2. Pleasanthill, Ky. 3. U. S.—Hist.—Civil war—Personal narratives. I. Title.

HOLLISTER, Alonzo Giles. 238.98
Pearly gate of the true life and doctrine for believers in Christ... 2d ed., imporved and enl. By A. G. Hollister and C. Green. Mount Lebanon,N.Y., 1896. iv, 255 p. 17 cm. Lettered on cover: Pearly gate Bible lessons, Part 1. "The following is...Scripture teaching in harmony with Shaker principles

and practice."-- Pref. No more published? [BX9774.H6 1896] 31-2728
1. Shakers. 2. Bible—Catechisms, question-books. I. Green, Calvin, joint author. II. Title.

HUTTON, Daniel Mac-Hir. 289.8
Old Shaketown and the Shakers; a brief history of the rise of the United society of believers in Christ's second coming, the establishment of the Pleasant Hill colony, their beliefs, customs and pathetic end. By Daniel Mac-Hir Hutton ... Harrodsburg, Ky., Harrodsburg Herald press, 1936. 67 p. illus. (incl. ports., plan, music) 23 cm. [BX9772.H8] 37-18429
1. Shakers. 2. Pleasanthill, Ky. I. Title.

IN memoriam:
Elder Henry C. Blinn, 1824-1905. Concord, N. H. Rumford printing co., 1905. 131 p. front. (port.) 20 cm. "Autobiographical notes": p. 3-40. 11-21811
1. Blinn, Henry Clay, 1824-1905. 2. Shakers.

LAMSON, David Rich, 1806-1886. 289.8
Two years' experience among the Shakers. New York, AMS Press [1972] 212 p. illus. 22 cm. Reprint of the 1848 ed. [BX9773.L3 1972] 71-134418 ISBN 0-404-08477-X 8.50
1. Shakers. I. Title.

LAMSON, David Rich, 1806-1886. 289.
Two years' experience among the Shakers; being a description of the manners and customs of that people, the nature and policy of their government, their marvellous intercourse with the spiritual world, the object and uses of confession, their inquisition, in short, a condensed view of Shakerism as it is. By David R. Lamson ... West Boylston, The author, 1848. 212 p. incl. front., illus. 18 cm. [BX9773.L3] 1-1945
1. Shakers. I. Title.

LEONARD, William (of Harvard, Mass.) 289.
A discourse on the order and propriety of divine inspiration and revelation ... Also, A discourse on the second appearing of Christ, in and through the order of the female. And a discourse on the propriety and necessity of a united inheritance in all things, in order to support a true Christian community. By Wm. Leonard ... Harvard, The United Society, 1853. iv, [5]-88 p. 19 1/2 cm. [BX9771.L4] 5-1554
1. Shakers. I. Title.

[MACE, Aurelia Gay] 1835-1910. 289.
The aletheia; spirit of truth. A series of letters in which the principles of the united society known as Shakers are set forth, and illustrated. By Aurelia [pseud.]... Farmington, Me., Press of Knowlton, McLeary & co., 1899. xiv p., 1 l., [17]-135 p. incl. front. plates, ports. 23 1/2 cm. Comprises a series of letters, published in the Messenger, Bangor, Me., 1883-1884, with communications and short articles from the Shaker manifesto. cf. Introd. "Appendix. Shaker church covenant, or constitution": p. [119]-135. [BX9771.M18 1899] 99-2672
1. Shakers. I. Title.

MACE, Aurelia Gay, 1835-1910. 289.
The aletheia; spirit of truth. A series of letters in which the principles of the United society known as Shakers are set forth and illustrated. By Aurelia G. Mace... 2d ed. Farmington, Me., Press of the Knowlton & McLeary co., 1907. 3 p. l., [ix]-xiv p., 1 l., [17]-146 p. front., plates, ports. 24 cm. Half-title: Aurelia's book. First edition, 1899, published under the pseudonym Aurelia. [BX9771.M3 1907] 7-41105
1. Shakers. I. Title.

MACE, Aurelia Gay, 1835-1910. 289.8
The aletheia: spirit of truth; a series of letters in which the principles of the United Society known as Shakers are set forth and illustrated. 2d ed. Farmington, Me., Press of the Knowlton & McLeary Co., 1907. [New York, AMS Press, 1974] 146 p. illus. 19 cm. (Communal societies in America) [BX9771.M18 1974] 72-2989 ISBN 0-404-10751-6 12.50
1. Shakers. I. Title.

MACE, Fayette. 289.
Familiar dialogues on Shakerism; in which the principles of the United society are illustrated and defended. By Fayette Mace... Portland, C. Day and co., printers, 1837. 120 p. 18 cm. [BX9771.M2] 24-13126
1. Shakers. I. Title. II. Title: Shakerism.

MACE, Fayette. 289.8
Familiar dialogues on Shakerism; in which the principles of the United society are illustrated and defended. By Fayette Mace... Portland, C. Day and co., printers, 1838. 120 p. 19 cm. [BX9771.M2 1836] 31-31297
1. Shakers. I. Title. II. Title: Shakerism.

MACLEAN, John Patterson, 1848- 289.
Shakers of Ohio; fugitive papers concerning the Shakers of Ohio, with unpublished manuscripts, by J. P. MacLean ... Columbus, O., The F. J. Heer printing co., 1907. 415 p. illus., plates, ports., plans. 23 1/2 cm. [BX9767.O3M3] 8-795
1. Shakers. I. Title.

MCNEMAR, Richard, 1770-1839. 289.8'09769
The Kentucky revival; or, A short history of the late extraordinary outpouring of the spirit of God in the western states of America, agreeably to Scripture promises and prophecies concerning the latter day, with a brief account of the entrance and progress of what the world call Shakerism among the subjects of the late revival in Ohio and Kentucky. Presented to the true Zion traveler as a memorial of the wilderness journey. New York, E. O. Jenkins, 1846. [New York, AMS Press, 1974] 156 p. 19 cm. (Communal societies in America) "Observations on church government, by the Presbytery of Springfield" (p. [133]-156) has special t.p. [BX9767.K4M3 1974] 72-2990 ISBN 0-404-10752-4 9.00
1. Shakers. 2. Revivals—Kentucky. 3. Church polity. I. Springfield (Ohio). Presbytery. Observations on church government. 1974. II. Title.

MCNEMAR, Richard, 1770-1839. 289.
The Kentucky revival, or, A short history of the late extraordinary out- pouring of the spirit of God in the western states of America, agreeably to Scripture-promises, and prophecies concerning the latter day: with a brief account of the entrance and progress of what the world call Shakerism, among the subjects of the late revival in Ohio and Kentucky. Presented to the true Zion-traveller, as a memorial of the wilderness journey. By Richard M'Nemar... Cincinnati, From the press of John W. Browne, office of Liberty Hall, 1807. vii, [9]-119, [1] p. 18 1/2 cm. First edition. With this is bound: Shakers, Springfield (Ohio) presbytery. Observations on church government--Cincinnati, 1807. [BX9767.K4M3 1807] 24-19719
1. Shakers. I. Title.

MCNEMAR, Richard, 1770-1839. 289.
The Kentucky revival, or, A short history of the late extraordinary outpouring of the spirit of God, in the western states of America, agreeably to Scripture promises, and prophecies concerning the latter day: with a brief account of the entrance and progress of what the world call Shakerism, among the subjects of the late revival in Ohio and Kentucky. Presented to the true Zion-traveller, as a memorial of the wilderness journey. By Richard M'Nemar... Cincinnati, Printed; Albany, Reprinted by E. and E. Hosford, 1808. viii, [9]-119 p. 17 cm. With this is bound: Shakers. Springfield, (Ohio) presbytery. Observations on church government...Cincinnati, Printed: Albany,Re- printed. 1808. [BX9767.K4M3 1808] 24-16577
1. Shakers. I. Title.

MCNEMAR, Richard, 1770-1839. 289.
The Kentucky revival; or, A short history of the late extraordinary outpouring of the spirit of God, in the western states of America, agreeably to Scripture promises and prophecies, concerning the latter day: with a brief account of the entrance and progress of what the world call Shakerims, among the subjects of the late revival in Ohio and Kentucky. Presented to the true Zion-traveller as a memorial of the wilderness journey. By Richard M'Nemar ... Pittsfield, Re-printed by Phinehas Allen, 1808. 148 p. 17 cm. With this is bound: Shakers. Springfield (Ohio) presbytery. Observations on church government...Pittsfield, 1808. [BX9767.K4M3 1808 a] 24-19721
1. Shakers. I. Title.

MCNEMAR, Richard, 1770-1839. 289.
The Kentucky revival, or A short history of the late extraordinary out- pouring of the spirit of God, in the Western states of America agreeably to Scripture promises and prophecies concerning the latter day, with a brief account of the entrance and progress of what the world call Shakerism, among the subjects of the later revival in Ohio and Kentucky. Presented to the true Zion-traveller, as a memorial of the wilderness journey. By Richard McNemar... Cincinnati. Printed, 1807. Albany, Re-printed, 1808 Union village, 1837. 2 p. l., [9]-119 p. 17 1/2 cm. "Third edition." Imperfect: All after p. 86 wanting. [BX9767.K4M3 1837] 24-19717
1. Shakers. I. Title.

MCNEMAR, Richard, 1770-1839. 289.
The Kentucky revival; or, A short history of the late extraordinary outpouring of the spirit of God in the western states of America, agreeably to Scripture promises and prophecies concerning the latter day; with a brief account of the entrance and progress of what the world call Shakerism among the subjects of the late revival in Ohio and Kentucky. Presented to the true Zion-traveler as a memorial of the wilderness journey. By Richard McNemar... New York, Preprinted by E. O. Jenkins, 1846- 156 p. 10 cm. First edition published 1807. "Observations on church government, by the presbytery of Springfield" (p. [133]-156) has special t.-p. [BX9767.K4M3 1846] 24-19718
1. Shakers. 2. Revivals—Kentucky. I. Shakers. Springfield (Ohio) Presbytery. II. Title.

[MCNEMAR, Richard, 1770-1839, comp. 289.8
The other side of the question. In three parts. I. An explanation of the proceedings of Eunice Chapman and the Legislature, against the United society ... in the state of New York. II. A refutation of the false statements of Mary Dyer against the said society, in the state of New-Hampshire. III. An account of the proceedings of Abram Van Vleet, esq., and his associates, against the said United society at Union Village, Ohio. Comprising a general vindication of the character of Mother and the elders against the attacks of public slander--the edicts of prejudiced party--and the misguided zeal of lawless mobs. Published by order of the United society at Union Village, Ohio... Ciccinnati: Looker, Reynolds & co. printers, 1819. 164 p.18 cm. "Compiled by Eleazer Wright--pseud. of Richard McNemar--Calvin Morrell, Matthew Houston, Samuel Sering."--J. P. MacLean, A bibliography of Shaker literature, 1905. [BX9766.M25] 31-33809
1. Shakers. 2. Chapman, Mrs. Eunice (Hawley) 3. Dyer, Mrs. Amry (Marshall) 4. Van Vleet, Abram. I. Morrell, Calvin joint comp. II. Houston, Matthew, 1764-1848, joint comp. III. Sering, Samuel, joint comp. IV. Title.

[MCNEMAR, Richard] 1770-1839. 289.8
A review of the most important events relating to the rise and progress of the United society of believers in the West; with sundry other documents connected with the history of the society. Collected from various journals, by E. Wright [psued.]... Union Village, O., [Union press] 1831. 2 p. l., 3-34, [33]-34, [35]-56, 43-54, 24 p. 13 cm. Pages 41-56 incorrectly numbered: a correct signature inserted at end. "Epistle dedicatory of the Union press" (1st prelim. leaf) dated: Watervilet, May 1, 1832. With this is bound the author's A little selection of choice poetry... by E.W. (C.S.)...Watervilet, O., 1835. [BX9766.M3] 31-31302
1. Shakers. I. Title.

MARSHALL, Mary, b.1780. 289.8
A portraiture of Shakerism. New York, AMS Press [1972] xvi, 446 p. 22 cm. Reprint of the 1822 ed. [BX9773.M3A3 1972] 70-134420 ISBN 0-404-08461-3 17.50
1. Lee, Ann, 1736-1784. 2. Shakers. I. Title.

MARSHALL, Mary, b.1780. 289.8
A portraiture of Shakerism, exhibiting a general view of their character and conduct, from the first appearance of Ann Lee in New-England, down to the present time. And certified by many respectable authorities. Drawn up by Mary M. Dyer ... [Concord, N. H.] Printed for the author, 1822. xvi, [17]-446 p. 18 cm. [BX9773.M4A3 1822] 34-17902
1. Lee, Ann, 1736-1784. 2. Shakers. I. Title.

MARSHALL, Mary, b.1780. 289.
Reply to the Shakers' statements, called a "Review of the Portraiture of Shakerism," with an account of sickness and death of Betsy Dyer; a sketch of the journey of the author: and testimonies from several persons. By Mary M. Dyer, author of the "Portraiture of Shakerism" ... Concord [N. H.] Printed for the author, 1824. 112 p. 19 cm. [BX9773.M4S6] 3-4868
1. Shakers. I. Title.

MARSHALL, Mary, b.1780. 289.8
The rise and progress of the serpent from the garden of Eden, to the present day: with a disclosure of Shakerism, exhibiting a general view of their real character and conduct-- from the first appearance of Ann Lee. Also, the life and sufferings of the author, who was Mary M. Dyer, but now is Mary Marshall. Concord, N. H., Printed for the author, 1847. iv, [2], [7]-268 p. front. (port.) 19 cm. [BX9773.M4A3 1847] 34-24957
1. Lee, Ann, 1736-1784. 2. Shakers. I. Title.

[MENDON, Dan] 289.8
Lo here and lo there! or, The grave of the heart ... New York, Printed for the author, 1846. vi, [7]-92 p. 1 illus. 23 cm. "Advertisement" (p. [iii]-vi) signed: Dan Mendon, Baltimore, Md. A pamphlet against the Shakers. [BX9773.M44] 32-2716
1. Shakers. I. Title. II. Title: The grave of the heart.

MILLER, Amy Bess Williams. 289.8
Shaker herbs : a history and a compendium / Amy Bess Miller. 1st ed. New York : C. N. Potter : distributed by Crown Publishers, c1976. xiv, 272 p. : ill. ; 26 cm. Includes index. Bibliography: p. 260-263. [BX9785.M4M54 1976] 76-40485 ISBN 0-517-52494-5 : 12.95
1. Shakers. 2. Herbs—Therapeutic use. 3. Botany, Medical. I. Title.

PHILLIPPI, Joseph Martin, 1869- 289.
Shakerism; or, The romance of a religion, by J. M. Phillippi ... Dayton, O., The Otterbein press, 1912. 133 p. plates. 20 cm. [BX9765.P5] 17-18374
1. Shakers. I. Title.

*PIKE, Kermit, comp. 230.98
A guide to Shaker manuscripts in the Library of the Western Reserve Historical Society. With an inventory of its Shaker photographs. Cleveland, Western Reserve Historical Society, 1974. xiii, 159 p. 28 cm. [BX9771] 74-84640 7.50 (pbk.)
1. Shakers. I. Title.
Available from the Society's Publication department 10825 E. Boulevard Cleveland, Ohio 44106

REPORT of the examination of the Shakers of Canterbury and Enfield, before the New-Hampshire legislature, at the November session, 1818, including the testimony at length; several extracts from Shaker publications; the bill which passed the House of representatives: the proceedings in the Pillow case; together with the letter of James W. Spinney. From notes taken at the examination. Concord, N.H., Printed by E. B. Tripp, 1849. 100 p. 22 cm. Cover-title: Shaker examination before the New-Hampshire legislature, November session, 1848. [BX9767.N4R4] 32-2718 289.8
1. Shakers. 2. Pillow, William H. I.

Spinney, James W. II. Title: Shaker examination before the New-Hampshire legislature. November session, 1848.

SEARS, Clara Endicott, 1863- comp. 245.
Gleanings from old Shaker journals, compiled by Clara Endicott Sears ... Boston and New York, Houghton Mifflin company, 1916. xiii,298p., 1. front., illus, (incl. facsims, music)plates, parts, 20 cm. [BX9766.S4] 16-22423
1. Shakers. I. Title.

SHAKER Museum, Old Chatham. 289.8'09747'39
The Shaker Museum, Old Chatham, N.Y. [Old Chatham, Shaker Museum Foundation, 1968] [47] p. illus. 24 cm. Cover title. Text by J. S. Williams and R. W. Meader. [BX9772.S5] 68-30329
1. Shakers. I. Williams, John Stanton, 1901- II. Meader, Robert W.

SHAKERS. 289.8
The constitution of the United Societies, of Believers (called Shakers). New York : AMS Press, 1976. p. cm. (Communal societies in America) Reprint of the 1833 ed. published in Watervliet, Ohio. [BX9776.S48 1976] 72-2992 ISBN 0-404-10754-0
1. Shakers. I. Title.

SHAKERS. 289.8
The constitution of the United societies of believers (called Shakers) containing sundny [!] covenants and articles of agreement [!], definitive of the legal grounds of the institution... Watervliet, (Ohio) 1833. [138] p. 18 cm. Various pagings. Compiled by Richard McNemar. cf. J. P. MacLean, A bibliography of Shaker literature, 1905. Includes (besides the covenants of 1810, 1812, 1814, 1818, 1829, 1830): A revision and confirmation of the social compact of the United society called Shakers, at Pleasant Hill, Kentucky...Harrodsburg, Ky., Printed by Randall and Jones, 1830 (with special t.-p.) Circular epistle (signed: From the ministry and elders. New-Lebanon, September 1, 1829) General rules of the United society, and summary articles of mutual agreement and release: ratified and confirmed. by the society at Watervliet, Montgomery county, Ohio January, 1833. An improved edition of the church covenant, or constitution of the United Societies, called Shakers established principles and regulations of the United society of believers called Shakers. Printed at Albany, in the year 1830; and now reprinted with sundry improvements suggested by the author...Watervliet, O., 1882 (with special t.-p.) [BX9776.A3 1833] 33-34680
I. McNemar, Richard, 1770-1839, comp. II. Title.

SHAKERS. 289.8
A summary view of the Millenial church, or United society of believers, commonly called Shakers. Comprising the rise, progress and practical order of the society. Together with the general principles of their faith and testimony...2d ed., rev. and improved. Republished by the United society, with the approbation of the ministry. Albany, Printed by C. Van Benthuysen, 1848. vii, [1], 384 p. 19 1/2 cm. Preface signed: Calvin Green, Seth Y. Wells. [BX9771.A3 1848] 31-2737
1. Shakers. I. Green, Calvin, ed. II. Wells, Seth Youngs, ed. III. Title.

SHAKERS. 289.8
A summary view of the Millennial church, or United society of believers, (commonly called Shakers.) comprising the rise, progress and practical order of all the society; together with the general principles of their faith and testimony. Published by order of the ministry, in union with the church... Albany, Printed by Packard & Van Benthuysen, 1823. xvi, 320 p. 19 cm. Preface signed: Calvin Green, Seth Y. Wells. [BX9771.A3 1823] 24-30647
1. Shakers. I. Green, Calvin, ed. II. Wells, Seth Youngs, ed. III. Title.

SHAKERS. 289.8
A summary view of the Millennial Church, or United Society of Believers, commonly called Shakers. Comprising the rise, progress, and practical order of the society. Together with the general principles of their faith and testimony. 2d ed., rev. and improved. Republished by the society with the approbation of the ministry. Albany, Printed by C. Van Benthuysen, 1848. [New York, AMS Press, 1973] vii, 384 p. 23 cm. Pref. signed: Calvin Green, Seth Y. Wells. Includes bibliographical references. [BX9771.A3 1973] 72-2993 ISBN 0-404-10755-9 20.00
1. Shakers. I. Green, Calvin. II. Wells, Seth Youngs. III. Title.

SHAKERS. 922.8842
Testimonies of the life, character, revelations and doctrines of our ever blessed Mother Ann Lee, and the elders with her; through whom the word of eternal life was opened in this day of Christ's second appearing; collected from living witnesses, by order of the ministry, in union with the church... Hancock: Printed by J. Tallcott & J. Deming, junrs., 1816. xl, 405, [1] p. 18 cm. "[Collected] by Rufus Bishop, in 1812, and revised by Seth Y. Wells...'Sometimes called "The secret book of the elders."--MacLean, J. P. A bibliography of Shaker literature, 1905. [BX9793.L4A4 1816] 31-2080
1. Lee, Ann, 1736-1784. 2. Lee, William, 1740-1784. 3. Whittaker, James, 1751-1787. 4. Shakers. I. Bishop, Rufus. II. Wells, Seth Youngs. III. Title. IV. Title: The secret book of the elders.

SPRIGG, June. 289.8
By Shaker hands / June Sprigg. 1st ed. New York : Knopf, 1975. xi, 212, vii p. : ill. ; 31 cm. Includes index. Bibliography: p. [209]-212. [BX9771.S67 1975] 75-8214 ISBN 0-394-49144-0 : 15.00
1. Shakers. I. Title.

WHITE, Anna, 1831-1910. 289.8
Shakerism; its meaning and message, by Anna White and Leila S. Taylor. New York, AMS Press [1972] 417 p. illus. 22 cm. Reprint of the 1904 ed. [BX9771.W5 1972] 73-134421 ISBN 0-404-08462-1 21.00
1. Shakers. I. Taylor, Leila Sarah, joint author. II. Title.

WHITE, Anna, 1831-1910. 289.
Shakerism, its meaning and message; embracing an historical account, statement of belief and spiritual experience of the church from its rise to the present day. By Anna White and Leila S. Taylor ... Columbus, O., Press of F. J. Heer [c1904] 417 p. front., plates, ports. 20 cm. [BX9771.W5] 5-3724
1. Shakers. I. Taylor, Leila Sarah, joint author. II. Title.

WHITWORTH, John McKelvie. 301.34
God's blueprints : a sociological study of three utopian sects / John McKelvie Whitworth ; foreword by David Martin. London ; Boston : Routledge and K. Paul, 1975. xiii, 258 p. ; 24 cm. Includes index. Bibliography: p. 249-255. [BX9771.W535] 75-313022 ISBN 0-7100-8002-6 : 23.00
1. Shakers. 2. Oneida Community. 3. Bruderhof Communities. I. Title.

WOODS, John, b.1780.
Shakerism unmasked; or, A narrative, shewing the entrance of the Shakers into the western country, their strategems and devices, discipline and economy; together with what may seem necessary to exhibit the true state of that people. By John Woods ... Paris, K[y.] Printed at the office of the Western observer, 1826. 84 p. 17 1/2 cm. 3-18336
I. Title.

[YOUNGS, Benjamin Seth] b.1773? 289.
The testimony of Christ's second appearing containing a general statement of all things pertaining to the faith and practice of the chruch of God in this latter-day; published in union. By order of the ministry... Lebanon, State of Ohio From the Press of John M'Clean Office of the Western star 1803. 600, [2] p., 1 l., 19 cm. Preface signed by David Darrow, John Meacham and Benjamin S. Youngs, of whom the two first named "signed their names not as authors, but as counsellors, and as sanctioning the work". cf. Notes, p. xiv, 4th ed. [BX9771.Y7 1908] 3-4866
1. Shakers. I. Title.

[YOUNGS, Benjamin Seth] b.1773? 289.
The testimony of Christ's second appearing; containing a general statement of all things pertaining to the faith and practice of the church of God in this latter-day. Published by order of the ministry, in union with the church... 2d ed., corrected and imporved. Albany: Printed by E. and E. Hosford...State-street, 1810. xxxvii, 620, [2] p. 18 cm. [BX9771.Y7 1810] 3-12117
1. Shakers. I. Title.

[YOUNGS, Benjamin Seth,] b.1773? 289.
The testimony of Christ's second appearing; containing a general statement of all things pertaining to the faith and practice of the church of God in this latter day. Published by order of the ministry, in union with the church... 3d ed., corrected and improved. Union Village, O., B. Fisher and A. Burnett, printers, 1823. xxv, [1], 573, [3] p. 19 1/2 cm. [BX9771.Y7 1923] 3-12118
1. Shakers. I. Title.

[YOUNGS, Benjamin Seth], b.1773? 289.
Testimony of Christ's second appearing, exemplified by the principles and practice of the true church of Christ. History of the progressive work of God, extending from the creation of man to the "harvest"-- comprising the four great dispensations now consummating in the millennial church...Anti-Christ's kingdom, or churches, contrasted with the church of Christ's first and second appearing, the kingdom of the God of heaven... 4th ed. [Albany, N.Y., Published by the United society, called Shakers [Van Benthuysen, printer, 1856] xxix, 631, [1] p. 23 cm. Preface to 1st edition signed by David Darrow, John Meacham and Benjamin S. Youngs, of whom the two first-named "signed their names not as authors, but as counsellors, and as sanctioning the work". Preface to 4th edition signed by Benjamin S. Youngs and Calvin Green. [BX9771.Y7 1856] 3-11405
1. Shakers. I. Title.

Shakers. — Addresses, essays, lectures.

EADS, H. L.
Shaker sermons; scripto-rational. Containing the substance of Shaker theology. Together with replies and criticisms logically and clearly set forth. By H. L. Eads... New ed., rev. and enl. Shakers, N.Y., The Shaker manifesto, 1884. iv p., 1 l., 271 p. front. (port.) 23 1/2 cm. 6-25443
I. Title.

SHAKER Historical Society 289.873
Selected papers. Cleveland, 1957. 111 p. 24 cm. [BX9759.S5] 57-13233
1. Shakers. — Addresses, essays, lectures. 2. Warrensville, O. — Hist. I. Title.
Shakerism for today, by M.C. Andorn. -- Shaker medicines, by H.D. Piercy. -- Early Warrensville: The forest primeval, 1807-1817, by C.B. Piercy.

Shakers—Bibliography

ERIE Co., N.Y. Buffalo and Erie County Public Library. 016.2898
Shaker literature in the rare book room of the Buffalo and Erie County Public Library. A bibliography compiled by Esther C. Winter and rev. by Joanna S. Ellett. Buffalo, 1967. 43 p. 23 cm. First ed., 1940, has title: Shaker literature in the Grosvenor Library. [Z7845.S5E7 1967] 76-6215 2.00
1. Shakers—Bibliography. I. Winter, Esther Caroline, 1910- II. Ellett, Joanna S., ed. III. Title.

MACLEAN, John Patterson, 1848- 016.
A bibliography of Shaker literature, with an introductory study of the writings and publications pertaining to Ohio believers. By J. P. MacLean. Columbus, O., Pub. for the author by F. J. Heer, 1905. 71 p. front. (2 port.) 23 cm. [Z7845.S5M2] 5-8719
1. Shakers—Bibl. I. Title.

MACLEAN, John Patterson, 1848-1939. 016.2898
A bibliography of Shaker literature, with an introductory study of the writings and publications pertaining to Ohio believers. New York, B. Franklin [1971] 71 p. 23 cm. (Burt Franklin bibliography & reference series, 422. Essays in literature and criticism, 138) Reprint of the 1905 ed. [Z7845.S5M2 1971] 72-156118 ISBN 0-8337-2173-9
1. Shakers—Bibliography.

NEW York. Public library. 016.
List of works in the New York public library relating to Shakers. [New York, 1904] 10 p. 26 cm. Caption title. Reprinted from its Bulletin, November, 1904. [Z7845.S5N6] 5-41869
1. Shakers—Bibl. I. Title.

Shakers—Bibliography—Catalogs.

EMMA B. King Library. 016.2898
Catalog of the Emma B. King Library of the Shaker Museum. Compiled under the direction of Robert F. W. Meader. Old Chatham, N.Y., 1970. 62 p. illus., facsims. 25 cm. [Z7845.S5E54] 70-21542
1. Shakers—Bibliography—Catalogs. I. Meader, Robert F. W. II. Title.

WESTERN Reserve Historical Society, Cleveland. 016.2898
The Shaker collection of the Western Reserve Historical Society : a reel list of the manuscripts and a short title list of the printed materials contained in the microform collection. Glen Rock, N.J. : Microfilming Corp. of America, 1977. ix, 77 p. ; 28 cm. [Z7845.S5W47 1977] [BX9771] 77-156035 ISBN 0-667-00522-6 : 4400.00
1. Western Reserve Historical Society, Cleveland. 2. Shakers—Bibliography—Catalogs. 3. Microfilms—Catalogs. I. Title.

Shakers—Collected works.

JACKSON, Rebecca, 1795-1871. 298'.8
Gifts of power : the writings of Rebecca Jackson, black visionary, Shaker eldress / edited, with an introduction, by Jean McMahon Humez. Amherst : University of Massachusetts Press, 1981. p. cm. Bibliography: p. [BX9771.J3 1981] 19 81-4684 ISBN 0-87023-299-1 : 20.00
1. Shakers—Collected works. 2. Theology—Collected works—19th century. I. Humez, Jean McMahon, 1944- II. Title.

MORSE, Flo. 289'.8'0973
The Shakers and the world's people / by Flo Morse. New York : Dodd, Mead, c1980. p. cm. Includes index. Bibliography: p. [BX9759.M67] 79-27271 ISBN 0-396-07809-5 : 15.00
1. Shakers—Collected works. I. Title.

Shakers—Harvard, Mass.

SEARS, Clara Endicott, 1863- comp. 289.8'09744'3
Gleanings from old Shaker journals / compiled by Clara Endicott Sears. Westport, Conn. : Hyperion Press, 1975, c1916. p. cm. (The Radical tradition in America) Reprint of the ed. published by Houghton Mifflin, Boston. [BX9768.H3S4 1975] 75-344 ISBN 0-88355-247-7 : 26.00
1. Shakers—Harvard, Mass. 2. Harvard, Mass.—History. I. Title.

Shakers—History

ANDREWS, Edward Deming, 1894- 289.8
The people called Shakers; a search for the perfect society. New enl. ed. [Gloucester, Mass., P. Smith, 1964, c.1963] xvi, 351p. illus., facsims. 22cm. (Dover bk., T1081 rebound) Bibl. 4.00
1. Shakers—Hist. I. Title.

ANDREWS, Edward Deming, 1894- 289.8
The people called Shakers; a search for the perfect society. New enl. ed. New York, Dover Publications [1963] xvi, 351 p. illus., facsims. 22 cm. "T1081." Bibliography: p. 293-297. [BX9765.A6 1963] 63-17896
1. Shakers — Hist. I. Title.

ANDREWS, Edward Deming, 1894-1964. 289.8
The people called Shakers; a search for the perfect society. New York, Oxford University Press, 1953. xvi, 309 p. illus. 24 cm. Bibliography: p. 293-297. [BX9765.A6] 53-9181
1. Shakers—History. I. Title.

MELCHER, Marguerite (Fellows) 289.8
The Shaker adventure. [Gloucester, Mass., P. Smith, 1965, c.1941] ix, 319p. (Princeton bk. rebound) Bibl. (Princeton bk. rebound) Bibl. [BX9765.M4] 5.00
1. Shakers—Hist. I. Title.

MELCHER, Marguerite (Fellows) 289.8
The Shaker adventure. Cleveland, Chio Western Reserve University Press 1960[c.1941, 1957] ix, 319p. 22cm. (bibl. note: p. 294-301) 41-51750 3.00 pap.,
1. Shakers—Hist. I. Title.

MELCHER, Marguerite (Fellows) Mrs. 289.8
The Shaker adventure, by Marguerite Fellows Melcher. Princeton, Princeton university press; London, H. Milford, Oxford university press. 1941. ix, 319 p. 24 cm. Illustration on t.-p.; head-pieces. "Sources": p. 294-301. [BX9765.M4] 41-51750
1. Shakers—Hist. I. Title.

Shakers—Hymns.

ANDREWS, Edward Deming, 1894- 783.2898
The gift to be simple; songs, dances and rituals of the American Shakers. New York, Dover [1962, c.1940] 167p. illus. xi, 170p. (T22) Bibl. 1.50 pap.,
1. Shakers—Hymns. 2. Shakers—Music. 3. Shakers. 4. Hymns, English. I. Title.

[BLINN, Henry Clay, 1824-1905, comp. 783.9
A sacred repository of anthems and hymns, for devotional worship and praise... Canterbury, N.H. 1852. xiii, 222. [1] p. 20 1/2 cm. Preface signed: H. C. B. [i.e. Henry Clay Blinn] "Compiled by Marcia Hastings and Henry C. Blinn."--MacLean, J. P. Music is alphabetic notation, employing the letters a to g. A bibliography of Shaker literature. 1905. [M2131.S4B5] 31-35628
1. Shakers—Hymns. 2. Hymns, English. I. Hastings, Marcia, joint comp. II. Title.

[MCNEMAR, Richard, 1770-1839. 245.298
A little selection of choice poetry new and old, doctrinal and devotional. Submitted to the patronage of the pious, by E. W. (C.S.)... Waterviliet, O., 1835. 55 p. 14 cm. (With McNemar, Richard. A review of the most important events relating to the rise and progress of the United society of believers... Union Village, O., 1831. Imperfect: p. 21-55 wanting. cf. J. P. MacLean, A bibliography of Shaker literature, 1905, p. 18. [BX9766.M3] 31-31303
1. Shakers—Hymns. 2. Hymns, English. I. Title.

[MCNEMAR, Richard, 1770-1839, comp. 245.
A selection of hymns and poems; for the use of believers. Collected from sundry authors, by Philos Harmonise [pseud.] Watetvliet [i.e. Watervliet] O., 1833. 1 p. l., [4]-180, [4] p.18 cm. [BV442.M3] 27-17490
1. Shakers—Hymns. 2. Hymns, English. I. Title.

NORTH family of Mt. Lebanon, N.Y.
Original Shaker music, published by the North family. Of Mt. Lebanon, Col. co., N.Y. ... New York, W. A. Pond & company, 1893. 271 p. 21 cm. Hymns, compiled by Daniel Offord, Lucy Bowers, and Martha J. Anderson. cf. MacLean, J. P. A bibliography of Shaker literature, 1905, p. 80. [M2181.S4N6] 46-34491
1. Shakers—Hymns. 2. Hymns, English. I. Offord, Daniel, 1843-1911? comp. II. Bowers, Lucy, joint comp. III. Anderson, Martha J., joint comp. IV. Title.

SHAKERS. 783.9
A colleciton of hymns and anthems adapted to public worship Published by the Shakers... East Canterbury, N.H., 1892. 1 p. l., iv, 144 p. 23 1/2 cm. Preface signed: H. C. B., [i.e. Henry Clay Blinn?] [M2131.S4B6] 31-4464
1. Shakers—Hymns. 2. Hymns, English. I. Blinn, Henry Clay, 1824-1905. II. Title.

SHAKERS. 245.298
A collection of millenial hymns, adapted to the present order of the church... Canterbury, N.H., Printed in the United society, 1847. 200 p. 14 cm. Without music. [BV442.A3 1847] 31-33808
1. Shakers—Hymns. 2. Hymns, English. I. Title.

SHAKERS. 264'.2
A collection of millennial hymns adapted to the present order of the church. New York : AMS Press, 1975. 200 p. ; 19 cm. (Communal societies in America) Reprint of the 1847 ed. printed in the United Society, Canterbury, N.H. Includes index. [BV442.S55 1975] 72-2991 ISBN 0-404-10753-2 : 10.50
1. Shakers—Hymns. 2. Hymns, English. I. Title.

SHAKERS. 245.298
[Hymns] [Canterbury? N.H., 1842?] 176, 4, [16] p. 14 cm. Collection of hymns and poems without t.-p., preceded by the tunes, in manuscript, of 122 hymns (31 p.) Music with staff notation, employing the letters a-g. The hymns are designated by title instead of number; the first is "The conquest"; the last, "Good employment". 31-35627
1. Shakers—Hymns. 2. Hymns, English. I. Title.

[WELLS, Seth Youngs], comp. 245.
Millennial praises ... Containing a collection of gospel hymns, adapted to the day of Christ's second appearing. Composed for the use of His people. Hancock, Printed by Josiah Tallcott. 1812. viii, 288, [4] p. 18 cm. In four parts. [BV442.W4 1812] 24-19713
1. Shakers—Hymns. 2. Hymns, English. I. Title.

[WELLS, Seth Youngs], comp. 245.
Millennial praises, containing a collection of gospel hymns, in four parts; adapted to the day of Christ's second appearing. Composed for the use of His people. Hancock, Printed by Josiah Tallcott, junior. 1813. viii, 288, [4] p. 18 cm. [BV442.W4 1813] 24-19712
1. Shakers—Hymns. 2. Hymns, English. I. Title.

Shakers—Hymns—History and criticism.

PATTERSON, Daniel Watkins. 783'.026'98
The Shaker spiritual / by Daniel W. Patterson. Princeton, N.J. : Princeton University Press, c1978. p. cm. "Checklist of additional manuscripts cited": Includes index. "Checklist of Shaker song manuscripts": [ML3178.S5P4] [M2131.S4] 77-85557 ISBN 0-691-09124-2 : 65.00
1. Shakers—Hymns—History and criticism. 2. Shakers—Hymns. 3. Hymns, English. I. Title.

THOMASON, Jean Healan. 090
Shaker manuscript hymnals from South Union, Kentucky. With comment on the musical notation by Fann R. Herndon. Introd. by Julia Neal. Bowling Green, Kentucky Folklore Society, c1967. v, 56 p. facsims., music. 22 cm. (Kentucky folklore series no. 3) Discussion of 15 manuscript hymnals in the library of Western Kentucky University. [ML3178.S5T5] 78-3026 1.00
1. Shakers—Hymns—History and criticism. 2. Musical notation. I. Kentucky Library. II. Herndon, Fann R. III. Title. IV. Series.

Shakers—Industries.

ANDREWS, Edward Deming, 1894- 289.8
... The community industries of the Shakers, by Edward D. Andrews ... Albany, The University of the state of New York, 1932. 322 p. illus. (incl. port.) 19 cm. (New York state museum. Handbook 15) Imprint date on cover: 1933. "Selected bibliography": p. 294-300. "Manuscripts in the Andrews collection": p. 301-307. [BX9784.A6] 33-28028
1. Shakers—Indus. I. Title.

ANDREWS, Edward Deming, 1894-1964. 289.8
The community industries of the Shakers. Philadelphia, Porcupine Press, [1972 i.e.1973] 322 p. illus. 22 cm. (The American utopian adventure) Reprint of the 1932 ed., issued as Handbook 15 of the New York State Museum. Bibliography: p. 294-307. [BX9784.A6 1972] 77-187478 ISBN 0-87991-010-0 13.50
1. Shakers—Industries. I. Title. II. Series: New York (State). State Museum, Albany. Handbook, 15.

ANDREWS, Edward Deming, 1894-1964. 289.8
The community industries of the Shakers. Introd. by Cynthia Elyce Rubin. [Charlestown, Mass.] Emporium Publications [1971?, c1932] 322 p. illus. 20 cm. Original ed. issued as New York State Museum handbook 15. Bibliography: p. 294-307. [BX9784.A6 1932a] 72-88941 ISBN 0-88278-005-0 3.95
1. Shakers—Industries. I. Title. II. Series: New York (State). State Museum, Albany. Handbook 15.

Shakers Juvenile literature.

YOLEN, Jane H. 289.8
Simple gifts : the story of the Shakers / by Jane Yolen ; illustrated by Betty Fraser. New York : Viking Press, [1976] p. cm. Includes index. Bibliography: p. Traces the rise and decline of the Shakers who immigrated to the United States from England in 1774, settling throughout New England. [BX9771.Y67] 76-14420 ISBN 0-670-64584-2 : 6.95
1. Shakers Juvenile literature. 2. [Shakers.] I. Fraser, Betty. II. Title.

Shakers—Kentucky—History.

NEAL, Julia. 289.8'09769
The Kentucky Shakers / Julia Neal. [Lexington] : University Press of Kentucky, c1977. 97, [1] p., [4] leaves of plates : ill. ; 22 cm. (The Kentucky Bicentennial bookshelf) Bibliography: p. 95-[98] [BX9767.K4N42] 76-46029 ISBN 0-8131-0236-7 : 4.95
1. Shakers—Kentucky—History. I. Title. II. Series.

Shakers—Music.

ANDREWS, Edward Deming, 1894- 783.2898
The gift to be simple; songs, dances and rituals of the American Shakers, by Edward D. Andrews. New York, J. J. Augustin [1940] xi, 170 p. front., plates, facsims. (incl. music) diagrs. 23 cm. Some of the songs with music (unaccompanied melodies) "Selected References": p. 160-163. [M2131.S4A5] [BV442.A5] 40-30330
1. Shakers—Music. 2. Shakers—Hymns. 3. Shakers. 4. Hymns. English. I. Title.

[EVANS, Frederick William] 1808-1893, comp. 783.
Shaker music, Inspirational hymns and melodies illustrative of the resurrection life and testimony of the Shakers ... Albany, Weed, Parsons and company, 1875. 1 p. l., 67 p., 1 l. 19 1/2 x 23 cm. [M2131.S4E7] 2-24601
I. Title.

Shakers—Music—History and criticism.

COOK, Harold E., 1904-1968. 783'.026'98
Shaker music; a manifestation of American folk culture. Lewisburg [Pa.] Bucknell University Press [1973] 312 p. illus. 25 cm. Bibliography: p. 296-302. [ML3178.S5C6] 71-161507 ISBN 0-8387-7953-0 15.00
1. Shakers—Music—History and criticism. 2. Shakers—Hymns—History and criticism. I. Title.

Shakers — North Union, Ohio.

PIERCE, Caroline Behlen, 1886- 289.8771
The Valley of God's Pleasure; a saga of the North Union Shaker community, [1st ed.] New York, Stratford House, 1951. 247 p. illus. 24 cm. [BX9768.N7P5] 51-13140
1. Shakers — North Union, Ohio. I. Title.

Shakers—Ohio.

MACLEAN, John Patterson, 1848-1939. 289.8'09771
Shakers of Ohio : fugitive papers concerning the Shakers of Ohio, with unpublished manuscripts / by J. P. MacLean. Philadelphia : Porcupine Press, 1975. 415 p., [7] leaves of plates : ill. ; 22 cm. (The American utopian adventure : Series two) Reprint of the 1907 ed. published by F. J. Heer Print. Co., Columbus, Ohio. Includes bibliographical references. [BX9767.O3M3 1975] 74-32001 ISBN 0-87991-020-8 lib.bdg. : 17.50
1. Shakers—Ohio. I. Title.

Shakers—Pictorial works.

THOMAS, Samuel W., 1938- comp. 289.8'09769'485
The simple spirit; a pictorial study of the Shaker community at Pleasant Hill, Kentucky [compiled by] Samuel W. Thomas [and] James C. Thomas. [Harrodsburg, Ky.] Pleasant Hill Press, 1973. 128 p. illus. 25 cm. Part of illustrative matter in pocket. [BX9768.P6T47] 73-83223
1. Shakers—Pictorial works. 2. Pleasanthill, Ky.—Pictorial works. I. Thomas, James Cheston, 1939- joint comp. II. Title.

Shakers—Relations—Disciples of Christ.

KIRKPATRICK, Jerald L
The effect of the Shaker conversions on the Christian Church in Kentucky and Ohio, 1805-1811. Fort Worth Tex., 1967. iii, 60, [2] l. Typescript (carbon copy) Bibliography: leaves 56-60.SDisciples of Christ--Relations--Shakers. 68-98102
1. Shakers—Relations—Disciples of Christ. I. Title.

Shakers—South Union, Ky.

NEAL, Julia. 289.8'09769
By their fruits : the story of Shakerism in South Union, Kentucky / by Julia Neal. Philadelphia : Porcupine Press, 1975, c1947. 279 p., [4] leaves of plates : ill. ; 22 cm. (The American utopian adventure : series two) Reprint of the ed. published by the University of North Carolina Press, Chapel Hill. Includes index. Bibliography: p. 271-273. [BX9768.S8N4 1975] 74-26579 ISBN 0-87991-003-8
1. Shakers—South Union, Ky. I. Title.

NEAL, Julia. 289.8769
By their fruits; the story of Shakerism in South Union, Kentucky. Chapel Hill, Univ. of North Carolina Press, 1947. 279 p. illus., ports., map (on lining-papers) 24 cm. Bibliography: p. 271-273. [BX9768.S8N4] 47-31003
1. Shakers—South Union, Ky. I. Title.

Shakers—United States.

ROBINSON, Charles Edson, 1836-1925. 289.8'0973
A concise history of the United Society of Believers called Shakers / by Charles Edson Robinson. Westport, Conn. : Hyperion Press, 1975, c1893. p. cm. (The Radical tradition in America) Reprint of the ed. printed at East Canterbury, N.H. [BX9766.R6 1975] 75-342 ISBN 0-88355-245-0 : 13.50
1. Shakers—United States. I. Title.

ROBINSON, Charles Edson, 1836-1925. 298.8
The Shakers and their homes : a concise history of the United Society of Believers called Shakers Charles Edson Robinson. Canterbury, N.H. : Shaker Village. ,1976. ix, 134p. : ill. ; 23 cm. [BX9765] 76-2209

ISBN 0-912274-62-X 10.00 ISBN 0-912274-58-1 pbk. : 3.95
1. Shakers-United States I. Title.

Shakers—United States—Juvenile literature.

FABER, Doris, 1924- 289.8'0973
The perfect life: the Shakers in America. New York, Farrar, Straus and Giroux [1974] vii, 215 p. illus. 21 cm. Bibliography: p. 207-208. Traces the history of the Shakers in America, from their founding in England to their few surviving colonies in New England. [BX9766.F3] 73-90968 ISBN 0-374-35819-2 6.95
1. Shakers—United States—Juvenile literature. 2. [Shakers.] I. Title.

Shakers—United States—Pictorial works.

THE Shaker image / 289.8'0974
Elmer R. Pearson, picture editor ; [text by] Julia Neal ... ; with a pref. by Walter Muir Whitehill ; and captions by Amy Bess Miller and John H. Ott. Boston : New York Graphic Society, 1974. 190 p. : ill. ; 29 cm. "The Shakers as they saw themselves and as others saw them [by] Julia Neal": p. 23-60. Published in collaboration with the Shaker Community, Inc., Hancock, Mass. Bibliography: p. 189-190. [BX9766.S5] 73-89954 ISBN 0-8212-0539-0 : 17.50
1. Shakers—United States—Pictorial works. I. Pearson, Elmer R. II. Neal, Julia. III. Shaker Community, inc.

Shakers—Watervliet, N.Y.—Exhibitions.

FILLEY, Dorothy M. 289.8'09747'42
Recapturing Wisdom's Valley : the Watervliet Shaker heritage, 1775-1975 / by Dorothy M. Filley ; edited by Mary L. Richmond. Colonie, N.Y. : Town of Colonie, c1975. p. cm. Published on the occasion of an exhibition celebrating the bicentennial of Shaker settlement. [BX9768.W2F53] 75-27133 ISBN 0-89062-010-5
1. Shakers—Watervliet, N.Y.—Exhibitions. 2. Watervliet, N.Y.—History—Exhibitions. I. Title.

Shakespeare, William, 1564-1616.

COX, Roger L. 809.9'33
Between earth and heaven; Shakespeare, Dostoevsky, and the meaning of Christian tragedy, by Roger L. Cox. [1st ed.] New York, Holt, Rinehart and Winston [1969] xix, 252 p. 22 cm. Bibliography: p. 249-252. [PN49.C65] 76-80348 ISBN 0-308-18427- 5.95
1. Shakespeare, William, 1564-1616. 2. Dostoevskii, Fedor Mikhailovich, 1821-1881. 3. Christianity in literature. 4. Tragic, The I. Title.

ELLIOTT, George Roy, 1883-1963. 822.3'3
Dramatic providence in Macbeth; a study of Shakespeare's tragic theme of humanity and grace. With a supplementary essay on King Lear. Westport, Conn., Greenwood Press [1970, c1960] xvi, 252 p. 23 cm. [PR2823.E4 1970] 70-90501
1. Shakespeare, William, 1564-1616. Macbeth. 2. Shakespeare, William, 1564-1616. King Lear. 3. Christianity in literature. I. Title.

KING, Walter N. 822.3'3
Hamlet's search for meaning / Walter N. King. Athens : University of Georgia Press, c1982. xii, 180 p. ; 24 cm. Includes bibliographical references and index. [PR2807.K48 1982] 19 81-12979 ISBN 0-8203-0597-9 : 17.50
1. Shakespeare, William, 1564-1616. Hamlet. 2. Shakespeare, William, 1564-1616—Religion and ethics. 3. Christianity in literature. 4. Psychoanalysis and literature. I. Title.

Shakespeare, William, 1564-1616—Histories.

MROZ, Mary Bonaventure, Sister, 1906- 822.3'3
Divine vengeance; a study in the philosophical backgrounds of the revenge motif as it appears in Shakespeare's chronicle history plays. New York, Haskell House Publishers, 1971. x, 168 p. 22 cm. Thesis—Catholic University of America. Reprint of the 1941 ed. Bibliography: p. 142-158. [PR2982.M7 1971] 77-120130 ISBN 0-8383-1091-5
1. Shakespeare, William, 1564-1616—Histories. 2. Revenge in literature. I. Title.

Shakespeare, William, 1564-1616—Dramatic production.

DOEBLER, John. 822.3'3
Shakespeare's speaking pictures : studies in iconic imagery / John Doebler. 1st ed. Albuquerque : University of New Mexico Press, c1974 [i.e.1975] xiv, 236 p., [16] leaves of plates : 35 ill. ; 25 cm. Includes index. Bibliography: p. 216-229. [PR2997.A53D6] 74-83386 ISBN 0-8263-0349-8 : 12.50
1. Shakespeare, William, 1564-1616—Dramatic production. 2. Shakespeare, William, 1564-1616—Allegory and symbolism. 3. Shakespeare, William, 1564-1616—Knowledge—Art. 4. Christian art and symbolism. 5. Icons in literature. I. Title.

Shakespeare, William, 1564-1616—Knowledge—Bible.

REES, James, 1802-1885. 822.3'3
Shakespeare and the Bible, to which is added prayers on the stage, proper and improper; Shakespeare's use of the sacred name of Deity; the stage viewed from a scriptural and moral point; the old mysteries and moralities, the precursors of the English stage. Philadelphia, Claxton, Remsen & Haffelfinger, 1876. [Folcroft, Pa.] Folcroft Library Editions, 1973. [PR3012.R4 1973] 72-14367 ISBN 0-8414-1348-7
1. Shakespeare, William, 1564-1616—Knowledge—Bible. 2. Theater—Moral and religious aspects. I. Title.

Shakespeare, William, 1564-1616—Knowledge—Occult sciences.

ANDERSON, Nancy E. 133.5
Astrology according to Shakespeare : antique astrology revised / Nancy E. Anderson, Ashland, Or. : Aquarius Press, 1974. vi, 129 p. : ill. ; 18 cm. Bibliography: p. 127-129. [PR3053.A5 1974] 74-79035 2.95
1. Shakespeare, William, 1564-1616—Knowledge—Occult sciences. 2. Astrology. I. Title.

SPALDING, Thomas Alfred, 1850- 133.4'2'0942
Elizabethan demonology; an essay in illustration of the belief in the existence of devils, and the powers possessed by them, as it was generally held during the period of the Reformation, and the times immediately succeeding; with special reference to Shakspere and his works. [Folcroft, Pa.] Folcroft Press [1970] xii, 151 p. 22 cm. Reprint of the 1880 ed. Includes bibliographical references. [BF1517.G7S7 1970] 72-194074
1. Shakespeare, William, 1564-1616—Knowledge—Occult sciences. 2. Demonology. 3. Devil in literature. I. Title.

SPALDING, Thomas Alfred, 1850- 133.4'2'0942
Elizabethan demonology : an essay ... / by Thomas Alfred Spalding. Norwood, Pa. : Norwood Editions, 1975. xii, 151 p. ; 24 cm. Reprint of the 1880 ed. published by Chatto and Windus, London. Includes bibliographical references. [BF1517.G7S7 1975] 75-33925 ISBN 0-88305-943-6 : 25.00
1. Shakespeare, William, 1564-1616—Knowledge—Occult sciences. 2. Demonology. 3. Demonology in literature. I. Title.

Shakespeare, William, 1564-1616—Religion and ethics.

ACKERMANN, Carl. 822.3'3
The Bible in Shakespeare / by Carl Ackermann. Norwood, Pa. : Norwood Editions, 1975. 124 p. ; 23 cm. Reprint of the ed. published by Lutheran Book Concern, Columbus, Ohio. [PR3012.A3 1975] 75-28045 ISBN 0-88305-011-0 : 12.50
1. Shakespeare, William, 1564-1616—Religion and ethics. 2. Bible in literature. I. Title.

ACKERMANN, Carl. 822.3'3
The Bible in Shakespeare. [Folcroft, Pa.] Folcroft Library Editions, 1971. 124 p. 24 cm. "Limited to 150 copies." Reprint. [PR3012.A3 1971] 72-194896
1. Shakespeare, William, 1564-1616—Religion and ethics. 2. Bible in literature. I. Title.

BROWN, James Buchan, 1832-1904. 822.3'3
Bible truths with Shakspearian parallels, by J. B. Selkirk (pseud.). 6th ed. London, Whittaker, 1886. [New York, AMS Press, 1975] xii, 115 p. 18 cm. [PR3012.B7 1975] 74-19106 ISBN 0-404-01136-5 10.00
1. Shakespeare, William, 1564-1616—Religion and ethics. 2. Bible in literature. I. Title.

BULLOCK, Charles, 1829-1911. 822.3'3
Shakspeare's debt to the Bible / by Charles Bullock. With memorial ill. Norwood, Pa. : Norwood Editions, 1975. p. cm. Reprint of the 1879 ed. published by "Hand and Heart" Pub. Offices, London. [PR3012.B78 1975] 75-28245 ISBN 0-88305-866-9 lib. bdg. : 10.00
1. Shakespeare, William, 1564-1616—Religion and ethics. 2. Bible in literature. I. Title.

EATON, Thomas Ray. 822.3'3
Shakespeare and the Bible: showing how much the great dramatist was indebted to Holy Writ for his profound knowledge of human nature, by T. R. Eaton. London, J. Blackwood. [New York, AMS Press, 1972] 226 p. front. 19 cm. Reprint of the 1860 ed. [PR3012.E3 1972] 77-144601 ISBN 0-404-02237-5
1. Shakespeare, William, 1564-1616—Religion and ethics. 2. Bible in literature. I. Title.

FITCH, Robert Elliot, 1902- 822.3'3
Shakespeare: the perspective of value, by Robert E. Fitch. Philadelphia, Westminster Press [1969] 304 p. 21 cm. "Notes and references": p. [249]-290. [PR3011.F5] 73-78481 3.50
1. Shakespeare, William, 1564-1616—Religion and ethics. 2. Religion and literature. I. Title.

FRYE, Roland Mushat. 822.33
Shakespeare and Christian doctrine. Princeton, N.J., Princeton University Press, 1963. ix, 314 p. 23 cm. Bibliography: p. 295-303. [PR3011.F7] 63-9990
1. Shakespeare, William, 1564-1616—Religion and ethics. 2. Religion and literature. I. Title.

MENDL, Robert William Sigismund, 1892- 822.33
Revelation in Shakespeare; a study of the supernatural, religious and spiritual elements in his art. London, J. Calder [dist. New York, Humanities, 1965, c.1964] 223p. 22cm. Bibl. [PR3011.M45] 65-5764 6.00
1. Shakespeare, William, 1564-1616—Religion and ethics. 2. Religion in literature. I. Title.

MILWARD, Peter. 822.3'3
Shakespeare's religious background. Bloomington, Indiana University Press [1973] 312 p. 23 cm. Bibliography: p. [307]-312. [PR3011.M5 1973b] 73-77854 ISBN 0-253-35200-2 12.50
1. Shakespeare, William, 1564-1616—Religion and ethics. 2. Great Britain—Church history—16th century. I. Title.

MUTSCHMANN, Heinrich, 1885- 822.3'3
Shakespeare and Catholicism, by H. Mutschmann and K. Wentersdorf. New York, AMS Press [1969, c1952] xvii, 446 p. geneal. tables. 23 cm. Bibliography: p. 416-429. [PR3011.M8 1969] 71-105107
1. Shakespeare, William, 1564-1616—Religion and ethics. 2. Shakespeare, William, 1564-1616—Biography. 3. Great Britain—Church history—16th century. I. Wentersdorf, Karl, joint author.

NOBLE, Richmond Samuel Howe, d.1940. 822.3'3
Shakespeare's Biblical knowledge and use of the Book of common prayer, as exemplified in the plays of the first folio. New York, Octagon Books, 1970. xi, 303 p. 23 cm. [PR3012.N6 1970] 78-111329
1. Shakespeare, William, 1564-1616—Religion and ethics. 2. Shakespeare, William, 1564-1616—Criticism, Textual. 3. Church of England. Book of common prayer. 4. Bible in literature. I. Title.

REES, James, 1802-1885. 822.3'3
Shakespeare and the Bible, to which is added prayers on the stage, proper and improper; Shakespeare's use of the sacred name of Deity; the stage viewed from a scriptural and moral point; the old mysteries and moralities—the precursors of the English stage. Philadelphia, Claxton, Remsen & Haffelfinger, 1876. [New York, AMS Press, 1972] 188 p. illus. 19 cm. [PR3012.R4 1972] 70-174307 ISBN 0-404-05235-5
1. Shakespeare, William, 1564-1616—Religion and ethics. 2. Theater—Moral and religious aspects. 3. Bible and literature. I. Title.

VYVYAN, John. 822.33
Shakespeare and the rose of love; a study of the early plays in relation to the medieval philosophy of love. New York, Barnes & Noble, 1960. 200 p. 23 cm. [PR3069.L6V9] 60-4340

1. Shakespeare, William, 1564-1616—Religion and ethics. 2. Love in literature. 3. Philosophy, Medieval. I. Title.

Shakespeare, William, 1564-1616—Tragedies.

COURSEN, Herbert R. 822.3'3
Christian ritual and the world of Shakespeare's tragedies / Herbert R. Coursen, Jr. Lewisburg [Pa.] : Bucknell University Press, [1975] p. cm. Includes index. Bibliography: p. [PR2983.C69] 74-201 ISBN 0-8387-1518-4 : 18.00
1. Shakespeare, William, 1564-1616—Tragedies. 2. Shakespeare, William, 1564-1616—Religion and ethics. 3. Christianity in literature. I. Title.

CREETH, Edmund. 822.3'3
Mankynde in Shakespeare / Edmund Creeth. Athens : University of Georgia Press, c1976. 192 p. ; 24 cm. Includes index. Bibliography: p. 186-187. [PR2983.C74] 74-15204 ISBN 0-8203-0373-9 : 8.50
1. Shakespeare, William, 1564-1616—Tragedies. 2. Moralities, English—History and criticism. 3. Mankind (Fictitious character) I. Title.

HUNTER, Robert Grams. 822.3'3
Shakespeare and the mystery of God's judgments / Robert G. Hunter. Athens : University of Georgia Press, c1976. 208 p. ; 24 cm. Includes bibliographical references and index. [PR2983.H8] 75-11449 ISBN 0-8203-0388-7 : 8.50
1. Shakespeare, William, 1564-1616—Tragedies. 2. Shakespeare, William, 1564-1616—Religion and ethics. 3. Christianity in literature. I. Title.

Shakespeare, William. Macbeth.

ELLIOTT, George Roy 822.33
Dramatic providence in Macbeth; a study of Shakespeare's tragic theme of humanity and grace, with a supplementary essay on King Lear [2nd ed.] Princeton, N.J., Princeton University Press, 1960 [c.1958, 1960] xvi, 252p. 23cm. 60-14792 5.00
1. Shakespeare, William. Macbeth. 2. Shakespeare, William. King Lear. 3. Christianity in literature. I. Title.

Shaktism.

KESHAVADAS, Swami, 1934- 294.5'514
Cosmic Shakti Kundalini (the universal mother) : a devotional approach / Sadguru Sant Keshavadas. Washington : Temple of Cosmic Religion, c1976. 112 p. : ill. ; 22 cm. [BL1245.S4K47] 76-11347 3.50
1. Shaktism. 2. Kundalini. I. Title.

PAYNE, Ernest 294.5'514
Alexander, 1902-
The Saktas : an introductory and comparative study / Ernest A. Payne. New York : Garland Pub., 1979. 153 p., [3] leaves of plates : ill. ; 19 cm. (Reprint of the 1933 ed. published by Y.M.C.A. Pub. House, Calcutta, in series: The religious life of India.) (Oriental religions ; 8) Includes index. Bibliography: p. [141]-147. [BL1245.S4P3 1979] 78-74270 ISBN 0-8240-3905-X : 20.00
1. Shaktism. I. Title. II. Series. III. Series: Religious life of India.

PUSHPENDRA Kumar, 1936- 294.5'514
Sakti cult in ancient India, with special reference to the Puranic literature / Pushpendra Kumar. Varanasi : Bhartiya Pub. House, 1974 [i.e.,1975] xviii, 317 p., [4] leaves of plates : ill. ; 23 cm. Essentially a revision of the author's thesis, University of Delhi, 1967, with title: Sakti cult in the Puranas. Includes index. Bibliography: p. [279]-290. [BL1245.S4P85] 74-904146 16.00
1. Shaktism. I. Title.
Distributed by South Asia Books.

REYMOND, Lizelle. 294.5'42
Shakti; a spiritual experience. Introd. by Shri Anirvan. [1st ed.] New York, Knopf; [distributed by Random House] 1974. viii, 51 p. illus. 19 cm. "A Far West Press book." [BL1245.S4R43 1974] 74-7725 ISBN 0-394-49339-7
1. Shaktism. I. Title.

WOODROFFE, John 294.3'4'211
George, Sir, 1865-1936.
Hymns to the goddess. [Madras] Ganesh; distributed by Vedanta Press, Holywood, Calif., 1973. xii, 335 p. 23 cm. Includes bibliographical references. [BL1245.S4W58 1973] 74-152777 ISBN 0-87481-306-9 6.00
1. Shaktism. 2. Hymns, Sanskrit. 3. Sanskrit poetry—Translations into English. 4. English poetry—Translations from Sanskrit. I. Title.

WOODROFFE, John George, 294.5'514
Sir, 1865-1936.
Shakti and Shakta / by Arthur Avalon (Sir John Woodroffe). New York : Dover Publications, 1978. xx, 732 p. ; 22 cm. Reprint of the 6th ed. published by 1965 by Ganesh, Madras under title: Sakti and sakta. [BL1245.S4W6 1978] 77-93380 ISBN 0-486-23645-5 : 7.95
1. Shaktism. I. Title.

Shaktism—History.

BHATTACHARYYA, Narendra 294.5'514
Nath.
History of the Sakta religion / by Narendra Nath Bhattacharyya ; edited by Mrs. Nirmal Jain. New Delhi : Munshiram Manoharlal Publishers, 1974, 1973. xiii, 188 p. ; 23 cm. Includes index. Bibliography: p. [167]-171. [BL1245.S4B49] 75-900273 12.00
1. Shaktism—History. I. Title.
Distributed by South Asia Books, Columbia, Miss.

Shalem Institute for Spiritual Formation.

EDWARDS, Tilden. 248.4
Spiritual friend / Tilden H. Edwards. New York : Paulist Press, c1980. viii, 264 p. ; 23 cm. Bibliography: p. 261-264. [BV5053.E38] 19 79-91408 ISBN 0-8091-2288-X (pbk.) : 7.95
1. Shalem Institute for Spiritual Formation. 2. Spiritual direction. I. Title.

Shamanism.

*BLACKER, Carmen. 297.56
The catalpa bow; a study of shamanistic practices in Japan. London, George Allen and Unwin [1975] 376 p. ill. 22 cm. Includes index. Bibliography: p. 350-359. [BL2370.55] ISBN 0-04-398004-X.
1. Shamanism. 2. Japan—Religion. I. Title.
Distributed by Rowman and Littlefield for 18.50.

[CH'UN, Yuan] 895.1'1'1
ca.343-ca.277B.C.
The nine songs; a study of shamanism in ancient China [edited by] Arthur Waley. [San Francisco] City Lights Books [1973] 64 p. illus. 21 cm. Includes bibliographical references. [BL1825.C45 1973] 73-84228 ISBN 0-87286-075-2 2.50 (pbk.)
1. Shamanism. 2. China—Religion. 3. Chinese poetry—Translations into English. 4. English poetry—Translations from Chinese. I. Waley, Arthur, ed. II. Title.

ELIADE, Mircea. 1907- 291.62
Shamanism: archaic techniques of ecstasy. Tr. from French by Willard R. Trask [Rev., enl. New York, Bollingen Found.; dist.] Pantheon [c.1964] xxii, 610p. 25cm. (Bollingen ser., 76) Bibl. 63-10339 6.00
1. Shamanism. I. Title. II. Series.

ELIADE, Mircea, 1907- 291.6'2
Shamanism: archaic techniques of ecstasy. Translated from the French by Willard R. Trask. [Princeton, N.J.] Princeton University Press [1972, c1964] xxiii, 610 p. 22 cm. (Princeton/Bollingen paperbacks) (Bollingen series, 76) Translation of Le chamanisme et les techniques archaiques de l'extase. Bibliography: p. 518-569. [BL2370.S5E413 1972] 74-171056 ISBN 0-691-09827-1 ISBN 0-691-01779-4 (pbk.) 3.95
1. Shamanism. I. Title. II. Series.

PARK, Willard Z. 970.62
... Shamanism in western North America; a study in cultural relationships, by Willard Z. Park ... Evanston and Chicago, Northwestern university, 1938. viii, 166 p. 24 cm. (Northwestern university. Studies in the social sciences. no. 2) "The present study has developed from a dissertation presented for the degree of doctor of philosophy at Yale university. That manuscript has been extensively revised with the inclusion of new and valuable comparative data."--Pref. Bibliography: p. 159-163. [E98.R3P23] [299.7] 38-14755
1. Shamanism. 2. Indians of North America—Religion and mythology. 3. Indians of North America—The West. 4. Palute Indians—Religion and mythology. I. Title.

Shamanism—Addresses, essays, lectures.

HALIFAX, Joan. 291.6'2
Shamanic voices : a survey of visionary narratives / Joan Halifax. 1st ed. New York : Dutton, c1979. xi, 268 p. [8] leaves of plates : ill. ; 21 cm. Includes bibliographical references. [BL2370.S5H34 1979] 78-17126 pbk. : 6.95
1. Shamanism—Addresses, essays, lectures. I. Title.

Shamanism—Korea—Case studies.

HARVEY, Youngsook Kim.
Six Korean women : the socialization of shamans / Youngsook Kim Harvey. St. Paul : West Pub. Co., c1979. p. cm. (Monograph - The American Ethnological Society ; 65) Includes index. Bibliography: p. [BL2370.S5H36] 78-27500 ISBN 0-8299-0243-0 : 10.95
1. Shamanism—Korea—Case studies. 2. Women—Korea—Biography. I. Title. II. Series: American Ethnological Society. Monographs ; 65.

Shamanism—Mexico.

DRURY, Nevill, 1947- 291.6'2
Don Juan, Mescalito, and modern magic : the mythology of inner space / Nevill Drury. London ; Boston : Routledge & Kegan Paul, 1978. x, 229 p. : ill. ; 22 cm. Includes index. Bibliography: p. 222-225. [BL2370.S5D78] 77-30326 ISBN 0-7100-8582-6 pbk. : 6.75
1. Castaneda, Carlos. 2. Juan, Don, 1891- 3. Shamanism—Mexico. 4. Magic. 5. Hallucinogenic drugs and religious experience. I. Title.

Shamanism—Peru.

SHARON, Douglas. 299'.8
Wizard of the four winds : a shaman's story / Douglas Sharon. New York : Free Press, c1978. p. cm. Includes bibliographical references and index. [BL2370.S5S53 1978] 78-3204 ISBN 0-02-928580-1 : 13.95
1. Tuno, 1930- 2. Shamanism—Peru. I. Title.

Shamokin, Pa. Trinity Lutheran church.

MARTIN, Richard Byers, 284.174831
1909-
History of Trinity Lutheran church, Shamokin, Pennsylvania, 1840-1940, by Richard Byers Martin. Philadelphia, The United Lutheran publication house, 1940. 85 p. front., pl., ports. 19 cm. Bibliography: p. 82-85. [BX8076.S5T7] 40-10263
1. Shamokin, Pa. Trinity Lutheran church. I. Title.

Shango.

BASCOM, William Russell, 299'.6
1912-
Shango in the New World, by William Bascom. Austin, African and Afro-American Research Institute, University of Texas at Austin [1972] 23 p. illus. 23 cm. (University of Texas at Austin. African and Afro-American Research Institute. Occasional publication 4) "Originally presented at the XXXIX Congreso Internacional de Americanistas in Lima in August 1970 and was delivered as a lecture at the University of Texas at Austin in March 1972." Bibliography: p. 21-23. [BL2532.S5B37] 72-195339
1. Shango. I. Title. II. Series: Texas. University at Austin. African and Afro-American Research Institute. Occasional publication 4.

SIMPSON, George Eaton, 1904-
The Shango cult in Trinidad. [1. ed.] Rio Piedras? Institute of Caribbean Studies, University of Puerto Rico, 1965. 140 p. illus. 24 cm. (Caribbean monograph series, no. 2) Bibliography: p. 131-136. 67-14258
I. Title.

Shannon, Jones B.

CASE studies in the campus 253
ministry; an occasional paper. [Editor: Clement W. Welsh. Cambridge, Mass.] Church Society for College Work [1968] 62 p. 28 cm. Cover title. "This collection of essays ... [presented] to Jones B. Shannon." [BV1610.C34] 75-303368
1. Shannon, Jones B. 2. Church work with students—Addresses, essays, lectures. 3. Chaplains, University and college—Addresses, essays, lectures. I. Shannon, Jones B. II. Welsh, Clement, 1913- ed. III. Church Society for College Work.

Shao Yung, 1011-1077.

LIU, Da. 133.3'3
I ching numerology : based on Shao Yung's classic Plum blossom numerology / Da Liu. 1st ed. San Francisco : Harper & Row, c1979. xiii, 145 p. : ill. ; 21 cm. Includes bibliographical references. [BF1623.P9L58 1979] 77-20459 ISBN 0-06-061668-7 : 4.95
1. Shao Yung, 1011-1077. I ching mei hua shu. 2. Symbolism of numbers. I. Shao Yung, 1011-1077. I ching mei hua shu. II. Title.

Shapira, Moses Wilheim, 1830?-1884.

ALLEGRO, John Marco, 222.15044
1923-
The Shapira affair. [1st ed.] Garden City, N.Y., Doubleday, 1965. 139 p. illus., facsims., map, ports. 22 cm. [BS1272.5.S5A55] 65-10640
1. Shapira, Moses Wilheim, 1830?-1884. 2. Bible. Manuscripts, Hebrew. O. T. Deuteronomy. I. Title.

Shapiro, Karl Jay.

WOLK, Daniel S
The Judaism of Karl Shapiro: A search for identity. Cincinnati, 1964. iii, 70 p. 28 cm. Rabbinical thesis--Hebrew Union College--Jewish Institute of Religion, Cincinnati. Typewritten. 68-54350
1. Shapiro, Karl Jay. I. Title.

Shapra Indians—Missions.

TARIRI, Shapra chief. 278.5
My story; from jungle killer to Christian missionary, as told to Ethel Emily Wallis.

[1st ed.] New York, Harper & Row [1965] 126 p. illus. (part col.) map, ports. 25 cm. (Harper jungle missionary classics) [F3430.1.S47T3] 65-15394
1. Shapra Indians—Missions. 2. Missions—Peru. 3. Wycliffe Bible Translators. I. Wallis, Ethel Emily. II. Title. III. Title: From jungle killer to Christian missionary.

Shared time (Religious education)

CONFERENCE ON SHARED TIME, University of Rhode Island, 1965.
Proceedings. Edited by W. Chris Heisler. [Sponsored by the Rhode Island Education Association. Providence? 1965] 91 p.
1. Shared time (Religious education) I. Heisler, W. Chris, ed. II. Rhode Island Education Association. III. Title.

Sharian, Bedros, 1892?

*SHARIAN, Bedros M. 1892?- B
I love America; Missionary address and my experiences here and there, [by] Bedros M. Sharian Sr. 1st. ed. New York, Vantage [1974] 64 p. 22 cm. [BV4501.2] 248 ISBN 0-533-01044-6 3.95
1. Sharian, Bedros, 1892? 2. Christian life. I. Title.

Sharing.

ROORBACH, Harriet A. 248.4 (j)
I learn about sharing, by Harriet A. Roorbach. Nashville, Abingdon Press [1968] 31 p. illus. (part col.) 21 cm. [BV772.R64] 68-10706
1. Sharing. 2. Christian giving—Juvenile literature. I. Kurek, Sarah, illus. II. Title.

Sharp, John Kean, 1892-

SHARP, John Kean, 1892- 282'.092'4 B
An old priest remembers, 1892-1978 / John K. Sharp. 2d enl. ed. Hicksville, N.Y. : Exposition Press, c1978. 216 p. ; 24 cm. [BX4705.S5847A35 1978] 78-69764 ISBN 0-682-49183-7 : 10.00
1. Sharp, John Kean, 1892- 2. Catholic Church—Clergy—Biography. 3. Clergy—United States—Biography.

Sharp, Martha Thompson, 1830-1847.

HELM, James Isbell, 1811-1880. 922.573
Memoir of Martha Thompson Sharp, by her pastor, Rev. Jas. I. Helm ... Philadelphia, Daniels & Smith, 1849. 198 p. front. 14 1/2 cm. [BR1725.S45H4] 38-7136
1. Sharp, Martha Thompson, 1830-1847. I. Title.

Shavu'oth (Feast of Weeks)—Addresses, essays, lectures.

THE Shavuot anthology 296.4'38 / Philip Goodman. 1st ed. Philadelphia : The Jewish Publication Society of America, 1975, c1974 xxv, 369 p. : ill. ; 24 cm. "Music for Shavuot, compiled and edited by Paul Kavon": p. [323]-337. Bibliography: p. 353-369. [BM695.S5S5] 74-25802 ISBN 0-8276-0057-7 : 7.95
1. Shavu'oth (Feast of Weeks)—Addresses, essays, lectures. 2. Shavu'oth (Feast of Weeks)—Literary collections. I. Goodman, Philip, 1911-

Shaw, Bernard, 1856-1950—Religion and ethics.

SHAW, George Bernard, 1856-1950.
Back to Methuselah; a metabiological pentateuch. Baltimore, Penguin Books [1961, c1949] 314 p. 18 cm. (Penguin books, 200) 66-670291
I. Title.

SMITH, Warren Sylvester, 1912- 822'.912
Bishop of Everywhere : Bernard Shaw and the Life Force / Warren Sylvester Smith. University Park : Pennsylvania State University Press, c1982. 191 p. ; 24 cm. Includes index. Bibliography: p. 181-183. [PR5368.R4S55 1982] 19 81-17700 ISBN 0-271-00306-5 : 15.95
1. Shaw, Bernard, 1856-1950—Religion and ethics. I. Title.

Shaw, Elijah, 1793-1851.

BROWN, Letitia J (Shaw) Mrs., 1829-1887. 922.
Memoir of Elder Elijah Shaw. By his daughter. With an introduction by Elder D. Millard... Boston and Philadelphia, L.J. Shaw, 1852. 2 p. l., 377 p. front. (port.) 20 cm. [BX6793.S4B8] 26-10910
1. Shaw, Elijah, 1793-1851. I. Title.

Shaw, Knowles, 1834-1878.

BAXTER, William, 1820-1880. 922.673
Life of Knowles Shaw, the singing evangelist. By William Baxter. Cincinnati, O., Oskaloosa, Ia., Central book concern, 1879. vi, [7]-237 p. front. (port.) 19 cm. [BX7343.B5B3] 36-32762
1. Shaw, Knowles, 1834-1878. I. Title.

Shaw, Mrs. Ellen Prestage (Havergal) 1823-1886.

HAVERGAL, Maria Vernon Graham, 1821-1887. 922.342
Outlines of a gentle life. A memorial sketch of Ellen P. Shaw. Edited by her sister, Maria V. G. Havergal ... New York, A. D. F. Randolph & co., 1887. 3 p. l., 183, [1] p. 19 1/2 cm. [BX5199.S485H3] 31-12635
1. Shaw, Mrs. Ellen Prestage (Havergal) 1823-1886. I. Title.

Shaw, Russell B.

KOOB, C. Albert. 377'.8'273
S.O.S. for Catholic schools; a strategy for future service to Church and nation [by] C. Albert Koob and Russell Shaw. [1st ed.] New York, Holt, Rinehart and Winston [1970] 150 p. 22 cm. [LC501.K637] 78-102147 4.95
1. Catholic Church in the United States—Education. 2. Shaw, Russell B., joint author. I. Title.

Shaw, William Hudson, 1859-1944.

ROYDEN, Agnes Maude, 1876- 922.342
A threefold cord. New York, Macmillan Co., 1948. 125 p. illus. 21 cm. [BX5199.S487R6 1948] 48-8626
1. Shaw, William Hudson, 1859-1944. 2. Shaw, Effle, d. 1944. I. Title.

Shawnee language—Texts.

BIBLE. N. T. Gospels. Shawnee. 1929. 226.
The four Gospels of Our Lord Jesus Christ, in Shawnee Indian language [by] Thos. W. Alford. [Xenia, O., W. A. Galloway, c1929] 200 p. 24 cm. Title from cover. The Gospel of Matthew has special t.-p. in English and Shawnee: The Gospel of Our Lord and Saviour Jesus Christ according to Matthew, translated into the Shawnee Indian language by Thomas W. Alford, or Ganwrpinhsikv, being the version set forth A. D. 1611, conpared with the most ancient authorities and revised A. D. 1881 ... "The Shawnee alphabet": p. 199-200. [BS345.S47 Gospels 1929] 30-3223
1. Shawnee language—Texts. I. Alford, Thomas Wildcat, tr. II. Title.

Shea, John Dawson Gilmary, 1824-1892.

GUILDAY, Peter Keenan, 1884-
John Gilmary Shea, father of American Catholic history, 1824-1892, by Peter Guilday ... New York, The United States Catholic historical society, 1926. 171 p. front., plates, ports., facsims. 23 cm. "Reprinted from Records and studies, July, 1926." "Bibliography of Shea's works": p. 155-171. A29
1. Shea, John Dawson Gilmary, 1824-1892. I. Title.

Shealy, Terence J., 1863-1922.

TREACY, Gerald C., ed. 922.
Father Shealy--a tribute, edited by Gerald C. Treacy, S.J. Mount Manresa, Fort Wadsworth, N.Y. [c1927] viii, 134 p. pl., ports. 20 cm. [BX4705.S585T7] 28-17049
1. Shealy, Terence J., 1863-1922. I. Title.

TREACY, Gerald Carr, 1883- ed. 922
Father Shealy-- A tribute, edited by Gerald C. Treacy, S.J. Mount Manresa, Fort Wadsworth, N.Y. [c1927] vii, 134 p. pl., ports. 20 cm. [BX4705.S585T7] 28-17049
1. Shealy, Terence J., 1863-1922. I. Title.

Shedd, William Ambrose, 1865-1918.

SHEDD, Mary Lewis, Mrs. 982
The measure of a man; the life of William Ambrose Shedd, missionary to Persia, by Mary Lewis Shedd, with an introduction by Robert E. Speer ... New York, George H. Doran company [c1922] xxi p., 1 l., 25-280 p. front. (port.) plates, maps. 19 1/2 cm. $2.00 [BV3217.S5S5] 22-23123
1. Shedd, William Ambrose, 1865-1918. 2. Missions—Persia. I. Title.

Sheed, Francis Joseph, 1897-

SHEED, Francis Joseph, 1897- 282'.092'4 B
The church and I [by] Frank Sheed. [1st ed.] Garden City, N.Y., Doubleday, 1974. 383 p. 22 cm. [BX4705.S587A33] 73-83670 ISBN 0-385-08440-4 7.95
1. Sheed, Francis Joseph, 1897- 2. Catholic Church—Doctrinal and controversial works—Catholic authors. I. Title.

Sheehan, Michael John, 1858-1925.

CONNELL, Francis Jeremiah 1888- 922.273
Reverend Michael J. Sheehan, C. SS. R.: a modern apostle, 1858-1925, by the Rev. Francis J. Connell ... [Boston? The Mission church press, 1926] v11, 67 p. front., plates, ports. 18 1/2 cm. [BX4705.S588C6] 33-32110
1. Sheehan, Michael John, 1858-1925. I. Title.

Sheehan, Patrick Augustine, 1852-1913.

BOYLE, Francis.
Canon Sheehan; a sketch of his life and works, by Rev. Francis Boyle, c. c. New York, P. J. Kenedy and sons, 1927. viii, 95 p. 19 cm. Printed in Great Britain. [BX4765.S6B6] 27-27983
1. Sheehan, Patrick Augustine, 1852-1913. I. Title.

HEUSER, Herman Joseph, 1851-1933. 922.
Canon Sheehan of Doneraile; the story of an Irish parish priest as told chiefly by himself in books, personal memoirs and letters, by Herman J. Heuser ... New York [etc.] Longmans, Green and co., 1917. xix, 405 p., 1 l. front., 1 illus., plates. ports., facsim. 24 cm. "The emigrant's return," with music: p. [356] "Canon Sheehan's works": 1 leaf at end. [BX4705.S6H5] 17-30758
1. Sheehan, Patrick Augustine, 1852-1913. I. Title.

Sheen, Fulton John, Bp., 1895-1979.

CONNIFF, James C G 922.273
The Bishop Sheen story. Greenwich, Conn., Fawcett Publications, c1953. 32p. illus. 29cm. [BX4705.S612C6] 53-4243
1. Sheen, Fulton John, Bp., I. Title.

NOONAN, Daniel P. 282'.0924
Missionary with a mike: the Bishop Sheen story, by D. P. Noonan. [1st ed.] New York, Pageant Press [1968] 213 p. 21 cm. [BX4705.S612N6] 68-17834
1. Sheen, Fulton John, Bp., 1895- I. Title.

NOONAN, Daniel P. 282'.0924 [B]
The passion of Fulton Sheen, by D. P. Noonan. New York, Pyramid Books [1975, c1972] 156 p. illus. 18 cm. [BX4705.S612N63] 70-173885 ISBN 0-515-03658-7 1.25 (pbk.)
1. Sheen, Fulton John, Bp., 1895- I. Title.

SHEEN, Fulton J. 1895-1979. (Fulton John), 282'.092'4 B
Treasure in clay : the autobiography of Fulton J. Sheen. Complete and unabridged. Garden City, N.Y. : Image Books, 1982. xviii, 366 p. : ill. ; 23 cm. [BX4705.S612A37 1982] 19 81-43271 ISBN 0-385-17709-7 : 8.95
1. Sheen, Fulton J. (Fulton John), 1895-1979. 2. Catholic Church—Bishops—Biography. 3. Bishops—United States—Biography. I. Title.

SHEEN, Fulton John, Bp., 1895- 248
The choice; the sacred or profane life. [New York, Dell, 1963, c.1954-1957] 240p. illus. 17cm. (Life is worth living ser.; Chapel Bk. 1270) .50 pap.,
I. Title.

SHEEN, Fulton John, 1895- 230
The divine romance, by Fulton J. Sheen ... Rev. ed. New York, London, The Century co. [c1930] 4 p. l., vii-viii p., 2 l., 3-142 p. 19 1/2 cm. [BX1754.S56 1930] 30-33552
I. Title.

SHEEN, Fulton John, 1895- 230
The divine romance, by Fulton J. Sheen ... Rev. ed. New York, London, The Century co. [c1930] 4 p. l., vii-viii p., 2 l., 3-142 p. 19 1/2 cm. [BX1754.S56 1930] 30-33552
I. Title.

*SHEEN, Fulton John, Bp 1895- 201
The Fulton J. Sheen treasury. New York, Popular Lib. [1967] 512p. 18cm. (Eagle bks., 125-5 1.25 pap.,
I. Title.
Contents omitted.

SHEEN, Fulton John, Bp., 1895- 248
Life is worth living. Illus. by Dik Browne. Garden City, N. Y., Garden City Books [1955, c1953] 180p. 22cm. Transcribed from tape recordings of the author's television talks.sCatholic Church--Addresses, essays, lectures. [BX890.S533] 55-3406
I. Life is worth living (Television program) II. Title.

SHEEN, Fulton, John, Bp., 1895- 248
Science, psychiatry and religion. [New York, Dell, 1962, c.1954-1957] 190p. 16cm. (7858) From the Life is worth living television ser. .50 pap.,
I. Title.

SHEEN, Fulton John, 1895- 282'.092'4 B
Treasure in clay : the autobiography of Fulton J. Sheen. Garden City, N.Y. : Doubleday, 1980. p. cm. [BX4705.S612A37] 19 80-1051 ISBN 0-385-15985-4 : 14.95
1. Sheen, Fulton John, 1895- 2. Catholic Church—Bishops—Biography. 3. Bishops—United States—Biography. I. Title.

Sheetz, Ann Kindig.

SHEETZ, Ann Kindig. 248'.2 B
Born again, but still wet behind the ears / Ann Kindig Sheets. 1st ed. Chappaqua, N.Y. : Christian Herald Books, c1979. 160 p. ; 21 cm. [BR1725.S454A33] 78-64839 ISBN 0-915684-43-8 : 6.95
1. Sheetz, Ann Kindig. 2. Christian biography—United States. 3. Christian life—1960- I. Title.

Sheffey, Robert Sayers, 1820-1902.

STORY of the life of Robert Sayers Sheffey, a courier of the long trail - God's gentleman -a man of prayer and unshaken faith. [Bluefield, Va., 195-?] 173p. ports. 23cm.
1. Sheffey, Robert Sayers, 1820-1902. 2. Mehodism. I. Barbery, Willard Sanders.

Sheffield, Mrs. Sarah Wilder (Sexton) 1823-1864.

IN memory of a beloved wife and mother. February 26, 1864. 922 [n. p.,

1864!] 126 p. front. (port.) 21 cm. A memorial of Sarah Sheffeld. "The addresses of Rev. Mr. Gaston, delivered at the funeral service in Sauerties, Fev. 28th": p. [71]-91. "The address of Rev. Dr. Prentiss, delivered at the funeral service in the Mercer street church, New York, March 1": p. [98]-107. [BR1725.S455 I 6] 35-24693
1. Sheffield, Mrs. Sarah Wilder (Sexton) 1823-1864. I. Gaston, John, 1825-1901. II. Prentiss, Geroge Lewis, 1816-1903.

Sheikh, Bilquis.

SHEIKH, Bilquis. 248'.246'0924 B
I dared to call him Father / Bilquis Sheikh, with Richard Schneider. [Lincoln, Va.] : Chosen Books ; Waco, Tex. : distributed by Word Books, c1978. 173 p. ; 23 cm. [BV2626.4.S53A33] 77-15603 ISBN 0-912376-22-8 : 7.95
1. Sheikh, Bilquis. 2. Converts from Islam—Biography. I. Schneider, Richard, 1922- II. Title.

Sheil, Bernard James, Bp.

TREAT, Roger L 922.273
Bishop Sheil and the CYO. New York, Messner [1951] 211 p. illus. 22 cm. [BX4705.S613T7] 51-14642
1. Sheil, Bernard James, Bp. 2. Catholic Youth Organization of the Archdiocese of Chicago. I. Title.

Shelbyville, Tenn. First Presbyterian Church—History.

COGSWELL, Robert E
Written on many hearts; the history of the First Presbyterian Church, Shelbyville, Bedford County, Tennessee, 1815-1965. Nashville, Tenn. Parthenon Press [n.d.] 279 p. 24 cm. 68-27603
1. Shelbyville, Tenn. First Presbyterian Church—History. I. Shelbyville, Tenn. First Presbyterian Church. II. Title.

Shelbyville, Tex. First Methodist Church.

CLOUSE, Joe V
The history of First Methodist Church, Shelbyville, Texas, established 1825. [Shelbyville, Tex., 1946] 49 p. 25 cm. Bibliographical footnotes. 64-40107
1. Shelbyville, Tex. First Methodist Church. I. Title.

Sheldon, Charles Monroe, 1857-1946.

CLARK, Glenn, 1882- 922.573
The man who walked in His steps ... St. Paul [1946] 60, [2] p. port. 19 cm. "Writings of Glenn Clark": p. [61]-[62] [BX7260.S5C5] 47-22128
1. Sheldon, Charles Monroe, 1857-1946. I. Title.

HENRICHS, Henry Frederick, 1876- ed. 922.573
In His steps today, by Charles M. Sheldon. St. Charles of Topeka, by Charles W. Helsley. Obsequies. Ed., comp. and designed by Henry F. Henrichs. Memorial ed. Litchfield, Ill., Sunshine Press [1948] 96 p. illus. ports. 21 cm. Cover title: St. Charles of Topeka. [BX7260.S5H4] 49-13304
1. Sheldon, Charles Monroe, 1857-1946. I. Sheldon, Charles Monroe, 1857-1946. In His steps today. II. Helsley, Charles Warren, 1893- III. Title. IV. Title: St. Charles of Topeka.

SHELDON, Charles Monroe, 1857- 208.1
Dr. Sheldon's scrap book. New York, Christian herald association, 1942. x p., 1 l., 13-224 p. front. (port.) 28 x 21 1/2 cm. [BR85.S445] 42-14978
I. Christian herald association, New York. II. Title.

SHELDON, Charles Monroe, 1857-
The first Christian daily paper, and other sketches ... to which is added a sketch of the Rev. Dr. Sheldon's life and work. New York, Street & Smith [1900] 192 p. 12°. (Alliance library, no. 11) 0-2750
I. Title.

SHELDON, Charles Monroe, 1857-
The first Christian daily paper, and other sketches ... to which is added a sketch of the Rev. Dr. Sheldon's life and work. New York, Street & Smith [1900] 192 p. 12°. (Alliance library, no. 11) 0-2750
I. Title.

SHELDON, Charles Monroe, 1857- 242
Life's treasure book, past, present, and future, by Charles M. Sheldon ... [Elgin, Ill., c1929] 1 p. l., 5-112 p. 19 1/2 cm. Part of pages blank. [BV4832.S435] 30-10034
I. Title.

Sheldon, Gilbert, Abp. of Canterbury, 1508-1677.

SYKES, Norman, 1897- 274.2
From Sheldon to Secker; aspects of English church history, 1660-1768. Cambridge [Eng.] University Press, 1959. 237 p. 22 cm. (The Ford lectures, 1958) Includes bibliography. [BR756.S96 1959] 59-2371
1. Sheldon, Gilbert, Abp. of Canterbury, 1508-1677. 2. Secker, Thomas of Canterbury, Abp. 1693-1768. 3. Gt. Brit. — Church history — 17th cent. 4. Gt. Brit. — Church history — 18th cent. I. Title.

Sheldon, Henry Clay, 1845-1928.

ROSSER, George Elijah. 922.773
A new era in philosophical theology; a set forth in the works of Rev. Henry Clay Sheldon, D. D., by George E. Rosser ... Macon, Ga., The J. W. Burke company [c1934] xiv p., 1 l., 479 p. 24 cm. Bibliograpy: p. [473]-479. [BX8495.S535R6] 34-19839
1. Sheldon, Henry Clay, 1845-1928. I. Title.

Sheldon, Mrs. Amelia (Sheldon)

AMELIA Sheldon; 922
as a daughter, sister, wife and mother. Written for the Massachusetts Sabbath school society, and approved by the Committee of publication. Boston, Massachusetts, Sabbath school society, 1851. 54 p. incl front. 15 cm. Signed: H.E.H. Attributed to Eliza A. Warner. [BR1725.S46A5] 38-7122
1. Sheldon, Mrs. Amelia (Sheldon) I. H.H.E. II. H.E.H. III. Warner, Eliza A., supposed author. IV. Massachusetts Sabbath school society. Committee of publication.

Sheldon, William, 1830-1902.

SHELDON, Lucy. 286.
The life and labors of William Sheldon, written and compiled by his daughter, Lucy Sheldon ... Mendota, Ill., Western advent Christian publication association, 1902. 304 p. front., pl., ports. 20 cm. "A model preacher" [poem by Jennie Sheldon Bowden]: p. 7-9. [BX6193.S5S5] 3-31
1. Sheldon, William, 1830-1902. I. Title.

[SHELDON, William] d.1871.
The millennium: the good time coming. With a history of experiments on the odic force. By the author of Millennial institutions, The seventh vial. and The theological mystery. Springfield, Mass., S. Bowles & company, printers, 1862. 196 p. fold. plan. 21 cm. Appendix contains extracts from the Journal of man, etc. 6-17190
I. Title.

Shelton, Albert Leroy, 1875-1922.

SHELTON, Flora Beal, Mrs. 922.
Shelton of Tibet, by Flora Beal Shelton; with an introduction by J. C. Ogden and The afterglow, by Edgar Dewitt Jones ... New York, George H. Doran company [c1923] xv p., 2 l., 21-319 p. front., plates, ports. 20 cm. [BV3427.S5S5] 23-11207
1. Shelton, Albert Leroy, 1875-1922. 2. Missions—Tibet. I. Title.

Shelton, Albert Leroy, 1875-1922—Drama.

HUNLEY, John Bunyan, 1881- 266
Shelton and the crimson trail; a missionary drama, by J. B. Hunley... Cincinnati, O., Powell and White [c1924] 40 p. 19 cm. "In this drama the writer has endeavored to put into concrete from some of the great achievements and experiences of Dr. Shelton's life."--Foreword. [BV2086.H8] 25-1265
1. Shelton, Albert Leroy, 1875-1922—Drama. I. Title.

Shelton, Elwood, 1926-1975.

SHELTON, Barbara. 248'.86'0924
Woody / Barbara Shelton, with Bob Terrell. Chappaqua, N.Y. : Christian Herald Books, 1979. p. cm. [RC406.A24S53] 79-50949 ISBN 0-915684-52-7 pbk. : 4.95
1. Shelton, Elwood, 1926-1975. 2. Amyotrophic lateral sclerosis—Biography. 3. Christian life—1960- I. Terrell, Bob, joint author. II. Title.

Shelton, Joe Ann.

O'BRIEN, Bonnie Ball. 269'.2'0924 B
So great the journey : an inspirational profile of Joe Ann Shelton / Bonnie Ball O'Brien. Nashville, Tenn. : Broadman Press, c1980. 169 p. : ill. ; 22 cm. [BR1725.S462O27] 19 79-52332 ISBN 0-8054-5593-0 : 5.95
1. Shelton, Joe Ann. 2. Christian biography—United States. 3. Singers—United States—Biograpy. I. Title.

Shema' (Jewish prayer)—Juvenile literature.

KLAPERMAN, Libby M 296.43
Jeremy and Judy say the Sh'ma. Story by Libby M. Klaperman. Pictures by Patricia Villemain. New York, Behrman House [cu956] unpaged. illus. 21cm. (The Play-and-learn library) [BM670.S15K56] 57-1654
1. Shema' (Jewish prayer)—Juvenile literature. I. Title.

Shepard, Cyrus, 1798-1840.

MUDGE, Zachariah Atwell, 1813-1888. 922.773
The missionary teacher; a memoir of Cyrus Shepard, embracing a brief sketch of the early history of the Oregon mission. By Rev. Z. A. Mudge. Edited by D. P. Kidder. New-York, Lane & Tippett, for the Sunday-school union of the Methodist Episcopal church, 1848. 221 p. incl. front., illus. 16 cm. [BX8495.S54M8] 36-37408
1. Shepard, Cyrus, 1798-1840. 2. Indians of North America—Missions. 3. Missions—Oregon. 4. Methodist Episcopal church—Missions. I. Kidder, Daniel Parish, 1815-1891, ed. II. Sunday school union of the Methodist Episcopal church. III. Title.

Shepard, Fred Douglas, 1855-1915.

RIGGS, Alice Claudia (Shepard) Mrs. 1885-
Shepard of Aintab, by Alice Shepard Riggs. New York, Interchurch press [c1920] xx, 200 p. front., plates, ports. 20 cm. Map on front lining-papers. [BV3177.S5R5] 20-13710
1. Shepard, Fred Douglas, 1855-1915. I. Title.

Shepherd, Massey Hamilton, 1913- — Addresses, essays, lectures.

WORSHIP points the way : 264
a celebration of the life and work of Massey Hamilton Shepherd, Jr. / edited by Malcolm C. Burson. New York, N.Y. : Seabury Press, 1981. p. cm. Contents.Contents.—Johnson, S. E. Massey Shepherd and the Episcopal Church.—Hardy, E. R. Some liturgical and monastic memories.—Coburn, J. B. The prayers of Massey Shepherd as Chaplain to the House of Deputies.—Garrett, S. M. Prayer book presence in colonial America.—Porter, H. B. Toward an unofficial histor of Episcopal worship.—Holmes, U. T. Education for liturgy.—White, J. F. Towards a liturgical strategy.—Stevick, D. B. Towards a phenomenology of praise.—Empereur, J. L. Liturgy and spirituality.—Willebrands, J. C. Latinity and Catholic unity.—Edwards, O. C., Jr. Extreme asceticism in early Syriac Christianity.—Donnelly, D. Augustine of Hippo, psychologist-Saint.—Petersen, W. H. Clio in church. "A bibliography of the works of Massey Hamilton Shepherd, Jr.": p. [BV176.W67] 19 80-25249 ISBN 0-8164-0482-8 : 15.95
1. Shepherd, Massey Hamilton, 1913- — Addresses, essays, lectures. 2. Liturgics—Addresses, essays, lectures. I. Shepherd, Massey Hamilton, 1913- II. Burson, Malcolm C.

Sheppard, Hugh Richard Lawrie, 1880-1987.

NORTHCOTT, Reginald James. 922.342
Dick Sheppard and St. Martin's, by R. J. Northcott, with introduction by Pat McCormick ... London, New York [etc.] Longmans, Green and co. [1937] xvii, 109 p. front., 2 port. 19 cm. "First published, 1937; second impression, December, 1937." [BX5199.S5315N6 1937 a] 38-15980
1. Sheppard, Hugh Richard Lawrie, 1880-1987. 2. Westminster, Eng. Gt. Martin-in-the-Fields (Parish) I. McCormick, William Patrick Glyn, 1877- II. Title.

SHEPPARD, Hugh Richard Lawrie, 1880- 225
The impatience of a parson, a plea for the recovery of vital Christianity, by H. R. L. Sheppard ... with an introduction by Professor E. D. Soper ... Garden City, N.Y., Doubleday, Doran & company, inc., 1928. xviii, 227 p. 19 1/2 cm. [BR121.S487] 28-6313
I. Title.

Sheraton, William M.

SHERATON, William M. 248'.4
It's faster to heaven in a 747, by William m. Sheraton. Its faster to heaven in a seven forty-seven New York, Sheed and Ward [1973] vii, 167 p. 21 cm. [TL540.S458A33] 73-5258 ISBN 0-8362-0526-X 5.95
1. Sheraton, William M. I. Title.

Sherlock, Thomas, Bp. of London, 1678-1761.

CARPENTER, Edward. 922.342
Published for the Church historicalo society for promoting Christian knowledge. 1678-1791, bishop of Banger 1728; of Salsbury 1734; of London 1748. By Edward CarpSociety for promoting Christian knowledge. New York, The Macmillan company, 1936. xiii, 335, [1] p. incl. front. (port.) 22 cm. Bibliography: p. 327-330. [BX5199.S532C3] 38-1232
1. Sherlock, Thomas, bp. of London, 1678-1761. I. Church historical society. II. Society for promoting Christian knowledge, London. III. Title.

CARPENTER, Edward Frederick, 1910- 922.342
Thomas Sherlock, 1678-1761, Bishop of Bangor 1728 of Salisbury 1734; of London 1748. London, Society for Promoting Christian Knowledge.; New York, Macmillan Co., 1936. xiii, 335 p. port. 22 cm. Bibliography: p. 327-330. [BX5199.S532C3] 38-1232
1. Sherlock, Thomas, Bp. of London, 1678-1761. I. Title.

Sherman, John, 1772-1828. One God in one person only ... 1805.

DOW, Daniel, 1772-1849.
Familiar letters, to the Rev. John Sherman, once pastor of a church in Mansfield, in particular reference to his late anti-trinitarian treatise. By Daniel Dow ... 2d ed. Worcester: Printed by Thomas & Sturtevant, 1806. 51 p. 23 cm. (Miscellaneous pamphlets. v. 884 [no. 7]) 25-24088
1. Sherman, John, 1772-1828. One God in

one person only ... 1805. 2. Trinity. I. Title.

DOW, Daniel, 1772-1849. 231
Familiar letters, to the Rev. John Sherman, once pastor of a church in Mansfield; in particular reference to his late anti-trinitarian treatise. By Daniel Dow ... Hartford: Printed by Lincoln & Gleason, 1806. 51 p. 23 cm. [BT110.D6] 25-22614
1. Sherman, John, 1772-1828. One God in one person only ... 1805. 2. Trinity. I. Title.

Sheron, Carole, 1944-

SHERON, Carole, 1944- 286.7'3 B
The rise & fall of superwoman : the story of a woman who found herself and her God / Carole Sheron. Nashville, Tenn. : Southern Pub. Association, c1980. 93 p. ; 17 cm. (Orion) [BX6193.S53A37] 79-26704 ISBN 0-8127-0270-0 pnk. : 2.50
1. Sheron, Carole, 1944- 2. Seventh-Day Adventists—United States—Biography. 3. Amphetamine abuse—United States—Biography. I. Title.

Sherrill, Helen Hardwicke.

SHERRILL, John L. 241'.6424
Mother's song / John Sherrill. Lincoln, Va. : Chosen Books, c1982. 134 p. ; 23 cm. [R726.S53 1982] 19 82-9527 ISBN 0-912376-80-5 lib. bdg. : 7.95
1. Sherrill, Helen Hardwicke. 2. Terminal care—Moral and ethical aspects. 3. Right to die—Religious aspects—Christianity. 4. Pneumonia—Patients—United States—Biography. I. Title.
Publisher's address: Lincoln, VA 22078.

Sherwood, Adiel, 1791-1879.

[SHERWOOD, Julia L.] 920.
Memoir of Adiel Sherwood, D.D. Written by his daughter. Assisted by Rev. S. Boykin. Philadelphia, Grant & Faires, 1884. 416 p. front. (port.) 20 1/2 cm. Preface signed: Julia L. Sherwood. [BX6495.S47S5] 27-21723
1. Sherwood, Adiel, 1791-1879. I. Boykin, Samuel, 1829-1899, joint author. II. Title.

Sherwood, Bill.

SHERWOOD, Bill. 248'.48'3
Let's begin again / by Father Sherwood as told to Jamie Buckingham. Plainfield, N. J. : Logos International, c1975. xiv, 126 p. ; 21 cm. [BX5995.S3454A34] 74-33671 ISBN 0-88270-117-7 : 5.95 ISBN 0-88270-118-5 pbk. : 3.50
1. Sherwood, Bill. 2. Sherwood, Erma. I. Buckingham, Jamie. II. Title.

Sherwood, Mrs. Mary Martha (Butt) 1775-1851.

THE life of Mrs. Sherwood
... Abridged for the Presbyterian board of publication. Phrladelphia, Presbyterian board of publication [c1857] 157 p. front. (port.) 18 cm. Preface signed: J. H. Material selected from "The life of Mrs. Sherwood," edited by Sophia Kelly. [PR5449.S4Z5 1857] 21-3204
1. Sherwood, Mrs. Mary Martha (Butt) 1775-1851. I. Presbyterian church in the U. S. A. Board of publication. II. Kelly, Sophia (Sherwood) Streeten, Mrs. b. 1815. III. H., J. IV. J. H.

SHERWOOD, Mary Martha (Butt) 221.
Mrs., 1775-1851.
Scripture prints, with explanations in the form of familiar dialogues; by Mrs. Sherwood. New York, Pendleton and Hill, 1832. iv, 254 p. front., plates. 17 cm. [BS551.S45] 21-1065
I. Title.

Sherwood, Tenn. Epiphany Mission.

JONES, George William, 283.768
1888-1952.
Candles in the dark boreen; writings. [Sherwood? Tenn., 1954] 321p. illus. 24cm. [BX5980.S5J6] 55-57973
1. Sherwood, Tenn. Epiphany Mission. I. Title.

Shetler, States G. (Samuel Grant), 1871-1942.

SHETLER, Sanford Grant, 289.7'3 B
1912-
Preacher of the people : a biography of S.G. Shetler (1871-1942), bishop, evangelist, pastor, teacher / Sanford G. Shetler ; introduction by J.C. Wenger. Scottdale, Pa. : Herald Press, 1982. 286 p. : ill. ; 22 cm. Bibliography: p. 284-286. [BX8143.S53S53] 19 81-13387 ISBN 0-8361-1247-4 : 16.95 ISBN 0-8361-1248-2 (pbk.) : 13.95
1. Shetler, S. G. (Samuel Grant), 1871-1942. 2. Mennonites—Bishops—Biography. 3. Bishops—United States—Biography. I. Title.

Shi Kwei-piao, 1844-1925.

HUNT, William Remfry. 275.
A Chinese story-teller; or, The changed story, by Wm. Remfry Hunt...with foreword by W. P. Bentley... St. Louis, Mo., Christian publishing company [c1903] 167 p. front., plates. (incl. port.) 20 cm. [BV3415.H85] 3-22523
1. Shi, Kuel-piao, 1845-1925. 2. Missions—China. I. Title.

OSGOOD, Elliott Irving, 922.
1871-1940.
Shi, the story-teller; the life and work of Shi Kweipiao, Chinese story-teller and pastor. By Elliott I. Osgood ... Cincinnati, O., Powell & White [1926] 228 p. front., plates, ports. 20 cm. [BV3427.S55O8] 26-22398
1. Shi Kwei-piao, 1844-1925. 2. Missions—China. I. Title.

Shields, Thomas Todhunter, 1873-1955.

TARR, Leslie K. 286'.0924 B
Shields of Canada; T. T. Shields, 1873-1955, by Leslie K. Tarr. Grand Rapids, Baker Book House [1967] 218 p. illus., facsim., ports. 23 cm. [BX6495.S49T3] 67-29222
1. Shields, Thomas Todhunter, 1873-1955. I. Title.

TARR, Leslie K 286'.0924 (B)
Shields of Canada; T. T. Shields, 1873-1955, by Leslie K. Tarr. Grand Rapids, Baker Book House [1967] 218 p. illus., facsim., ports. 23 cm. [BX6495.S49T3] 67-29222
1. Shields, Thomas Todhunter, 1873-1955. I. Title.

Shiites.

*FAIZ I, A.Q. 297'.82
The prince of martyrs : a brief account of the Im am Husayn / by Abu l-Q asim Faiz i. Oxford : George Ronald, [1978] c1977. 68p. ; 20 cm. Label mounted on t.p.: Distributed in the U.S by Bah a i Pub. Trust, Wilmette, Ill. Includes bibliographical references. [BP193.13] ISBN 0-85398-073-X pbk. : 2.95
1. al-Husayn ibn Ali, d. 680. 2. Shiites. I. Title.

HOLLISTER, John Norman 297.82
The Shi'a of India. London, Luzac [dist. Mystic, Conn., Verry, 1965] xiv, 440p. illus. 25cm. (Luzac's oriental religious ser. v.8) Bibl. [BP195.S5H6] 54-32595 12.50
1. Shiites. 2. Mohammedans in India. I. Title. II. Series.

AL-TABATABA'I, 297'.82
Muhammad Husayn, 1903or4
Shi'ite Islam, by 'Allamah Sayyid Muhammad Husayn Tabataba'i. Translated from the Persian and edited with an introd. and notes by Seyyed Hossein Nasr. [1st ed.] Albany, State University of New York Press, 1975. xiv, 253 p. 24 cm. (Persian studies series, no. 5) Translation of Shi'ah dar Islam. Bibliography: p. 239-244. [BP193.5.T3213] 74-8289 ISBN 0-87395-272-3 ISBN 0-87395-273-1 (microfiche)
1. Shiites. I. Title.

Shiites—History.

JAFRI, Syed Husain 297'.82'09021
M.
Origins and early development of Shi'a Islam / S. Husain M. Jafri. London ; New York : Longman, 1978. p. cm. Includes index. Bibliography: p. [BP192.4.J33] 78-40611 ISBN 0-582-78080-2 : 23.50
1. Shiites—History. I. Title.

Shiites—Iran.

FISCHER, Michael M. J., 301.5'8
1946-
Iran : from religious dispute to revolution / Michael M. J. Fischer. Cambridge, Mass. : Harvard University Press, 1980. xiv, 314 p. : ill. ; 24 cm. (Harvard studies in cultural anthropology ; 3) Includes index. Bibliography: p. 293-303. [BP192.7.I68F57] 79-24330 ISBN 0-674-66315-2 : 17.50
1. Shiites—Iran. 2. Islam and politics—Iran. 3. Iran—Politics and government—1941-1979. 4. Iran—Religious life and customs. I. Title. II. Series.

Shiites—Iran—History.

BAYAT, Mangol. 297'.1977'0955
Mysticism and dissent : socioreligious thought in Qajar Iran / Mangol Bayat. 1st ed. Syracuse, N.Y. : Syracuse University Press, 1982. xvii, 228 p. ; 24 cm. Includes index. Bibliography: p. 213-222. [BP192.7.I68B39 1982] 19 82-5498 ISBN 0-8156-2260-0 : 25.00
1. Shiites—Iran—History. 2. Islam and politics—Iran. 3. Iran—Religion. 4. Iran—History—Qajar dynasty, 1779-1925. I. Title.

Shin (Sect)

SUZUKI, Daisetz Teitaro, 294.3'92
1870-1966.
Shin Buddhism. [1st ed.] New York, Harper & Row [1970] 93 p. 22 cm. [BL1442.S5S9 1970] 71-86908 3.95
1. Shin (Sect) I. Title.

Shin (Sect)—Doctrines.

BLOOM, Alfred. 294.3'42
Tannisho : a resource for modern livivng / by Alfred Bloom. Honolulu : Buddhist Study Center, 1981. 102 p. ; 23 cm. Includes bibliographical references. [BQ8749.S554T35326] 19 80-39523 ISBN 0-938474-00-6 pbk. : 4.95
1. Shinran, 1173-1263. Tannisho. 2. Shin (Sect)—Doctrines. I. Title.
Publisher's address : Office of Buddhist Education, 1727 Pali Hwy., Honolulu, HI 96813.

YAMAMOTO, Kosho 294.392
The other-power; the final answer arrived at in Shin Buddhism Oyama, Japan Karinbunko [Austin. Tex., Perkins Oriental, c.1965] viii, 146p. front. 19cm. Bibl. [BL1442.S5Y3] 66-3014 3.00
1. Shin (Sect)—Doctrines. I. Title.

Shingon (Sect)

KIYOTA, Minoru, 1923- 294.3'92
Shingon Buddhism : theory and practice / by Minoru Kiyota. Los Angeles : Buddhist Books International, [1978] p. cm. Bibliography: p. [BQ8965.4.K59] 77-27894 ISBN 0-914910-09-4 : 8.95. ISBN 0-914910-10-8 pbk. : 6.95
1. Shingon (Sect) I. Title.

RAMBACH, Pierre, 294.3'925'0952
1925-
The secret message of tantric Buddhism / Pierre Rambach ; [translated from the French by Barbara Bray]. New York : Rizzoli International Publications, 1979. 169 p. : ill. (some col.) ; 35 cm. Translation of Le Bouddha secret. Includes index. Bibliography: p. 165. [BQ8965.4.R3513] 78-58701 ISBN 0-8478-0192-6 : 15.00
1. Shingon (Sect) 2. Tantric Buddhism—Japan. I. Title.

Shingon (Sect)—Collected works.

KUKAI, 774-835. 294.3'9
Kukai: major works. Translated, with an account of his life and a study of his thought, by Yoshito S. Hakeda. New York, Columbia University Press, 1972. xiv, 303 p. 23 cm. (Records of civilization: sources and studies, no. 87) (UNESCO collection of representative works: Japanese series) "Prepared for the Columbia College program of translations from the oriental classics." Bibliography: p. [281]-287. [BQ8999.K8313 1972] 72-3124 ISBN 0-231-03627-2 12.50
1. Shingon (Sect)—Collected works. I. Hakeda, Yoshito S., tr. II. Title. III. Series. IV. Series: Records of civilization: sources and records, no. 87.

Shinran, 1173-1263.

BLOOM, Alfred. 294.364
Shinran's gospel of pure grace. Tucson, Published for the Association for Asian Studies by the University of Arizona Press, 1965. xiv, 97 p. 24 cm. (Association for Asian Studies. Monographs and papers, no. 20) Bibliography: p. 89-93. [BL1442.S53B55] 64-8757
1. Shinran, 1173-1263. I. Association for Asian Studies. II. Title. III. Series.

BLOOM, Alfred. 294.3'42
Tannisho : a resource for modern livivng / by Alfred Bloom. Honolulu : Buddhist Study Center, 1981. 102 p. ; 23 cm. Includes bibliographical references. [BQ8749.S554T35326] 19 80-39523 ISBN 0-938474-00-6 pbk. : 4.95
1. Shinran, 1173-1263. Tannisho. 2. Shin (Sect)—Doctrines. I. Title.
Publisher's address : Office of Buddhist Education, 1727 Pali Hwy., Honolulu, HI 96813.

KIKUMURA, Norihiko. 294.3'63 B
Shinran: his life and thought. Los Angeles, Nembutsu Press [1972] 192 p. 23 cm. Translation of Shinran. [BQ8749.S557K513] 70-172538 4.95
1. Shinran, 1173-1263.

Shinto.

ASTON, William George, 299'.561
1841-1911.
Shinto : the way of the gods / by W. G. Aston. New York : Krishna Press, 1974. ii, 390 p. : ill. ; 23 cm. Originally published in 1905 by Longmans, Green, London, New York. Includes bibliographical references and index. [BL2220.A8 1974] 72-98090 ISBN 0-87968-076-8 : 34.95.
1. Shinto.

ASTON, William George, 1841- 290.
1911.
Shinto. (the way of the gods). by W. G. Aston ... London, New York [etc.] Longmans, Green, and co., 1905. 3 p. l., ii, 390 p. illus. 22 cm. [BL2220.A8] W6-204
1. Shinto. I. Title.

BALLOU, Robert Oleson, 299.56
1892-
Shinto, the unconquered enemy; Japan's doctrine of racial superiority and world conquest, with selections from Japanese texts, by Robert O. Ballou. New York, The Viking press, 1945. xi, 239 p. 21 cm. "Annotated bibliography": p. 217-226. [BL2220.B3] 45-9650
1. Shinto. 2. Japan—Pol. & govt. 3. Japan—Nationality. I. Title.

HERBERT, Jean, 1897- 299'.561
Shinto; at the fountain-head of Japan. With a pref. by Yukitada Sasaki. New York, Stein and Day [1967] 622 p. illus., geneal. table, map. 25 cm. Translation of Aux sources du Japon. Bibliography: p. 533-560. [BL2220.H413 1967] 66-24531
1. Shinto. I. Title.

HOLTOM, Daniel Clarence, 299.56
1884-
Modern Japan and Shinto nationalism; a study of present-day trends in Japanese religions. Rev. ed. New York, Paragon 1963[c.1943, 1947] 226p. 24cm. (Haskell lects. in comparative religion) Bibl. 63-22615 7.50
1. Shinto. 2. Japan—Religion. 3. Nationalism and religion—Japan. I. Title.

HOLTOM, Daniel Clarence, 1884- 299.56
Modern Japan and Shinto nationalism; a study of presentday trends in Japanese religions, by D. C. Holtom. Chicago, Ill., The University of Chicago press [1943] ix, 173 p. 22 1/2 cm. (Half-title: The Haskell lectures in comparative religion) Bibliography at end of each chapter. [BL2220.H56] 43-1539
1. Shinto. 2. Japan—Religion. 3. Japan—Nationality. 4. Nationalism and religion—Japan. I. Title.

HOLTOM, Daniel Clarence, 1884- 299.56
Modern Japan and Shinto nationalism; a study of present-day trends in Japanese religions. Rev. ed. Chicago, Univ. of Chicago Press [1947] ix, 226 p. 23 cm. (The Haskell lectures in comparative religion) Includes bibliographies. [BL2220.H56 1947] 47-31095
1. Shinto. 2. Japan—Religion. 3. Japan—Nationality. 4. Nationalism and religion—Japan. I. Title. II. Title: Haskell lectures in comparative religion, Univ. of Chicago.

HOLTOM, Daniel Clarence, 1884- 299.561
The national faith of Japan; a study in modern Shinto. New York, Paragon [c.] 1965. xiii, 329p. illus., facsims., general. table, plan, port. 24cm. An unaltered and unabridged reprint of the work first pub. in London 1938. Bibl. [BL2220.H58] 65-26102 10.00
1. Shinto. I. Title.

HOLTOM, Daniel Clarence, 1884- 299.561
The national faith of Japan; a study in modern Shinto, by D. C. Holtom. New York, Paragon Book Reprint Corp., 1965. xiii, 329 p. illus., facsims., geneal. table, plan, port. 24 cm. "An unaltered and unabridged reprint of the work first published in London 1938." Bibliographical footnotes. [BL2220.H58] 65-26102
1. Shinto. I. Title.

KATO, Genchi, 1873-1965. 299'.561
A study of Shinto; the religion of the Japanese nation. New York, Barnes & Noble [1971] ix, 250 p. 23 cm. Reprint of the 1926 ed., with a pref. Bibliography: p. [217]-230. [BL2220.K35 1971] 75-29406 ISBN 0-389-04070-3
1. Shinto. I. Title.

MASON, Joseph Warren Teets, 1879- 290.56
The meaning of Shinto; the primaeval foundation of creative spirit in modern Japan, by J. W. T. Mason ... New York, E. P. Dutton & co., inc. [c1935] 252 p. 20 cm. "First edition." [BL2220.M3] 35-5956
1. Shinto. I. Title.

MASON, Joseph Warren Teets, 1879-1941 299'.561
The meaning of Shinto; the primaeval foundation of creative spirit in modern Japan. Port Washington, N. Y., Kennikat [1967. c.1935] 252p. 22cm. Bibl. [BL2220.M3 1967] 67-27624 7.00
1. Shinto. I. Title.

ONO, Motonori, 1904- 299.56
Shinto, the Kami Way, by Sokyo Ono in collaboration with William P. Woodard. Sketches by Sadao Sakamoto. [Tokyo, Rutland, Vt.] Bridgeway Press [1961, c1962] 118 p. illus. 22 cm. "First published in 1960 ... under the title: The Kami Way; an introduction to Shrine Shinto." [BL2220.O5 1962] 61-14033
1. Shinto, I. Title: The Kami Way.

PICKEN, Stuart D. B. 299'.561
Shinto, Japan's spiritual roots / Stuart D.B. Picken ; introd. by Edwin O. Reischauer. 1st ed. Tokyo ; New York : Kodansha International Ltd. ; New York, N.Y. : distributed in the U.S. by Kodansha International/USA through Harper & Row, 1980. 80 p. : col. ill. ; 31 cm. [BL2220.P5 1980] 79-91520 ISBN 0-87011-410-7 : 17.50
1. Shinto. 2. Japan—Civilization—Shinto influences. I. Title.

ROSS, Floyd Hiatt. 299.56
Shinto, the way of Japan. Boston, Beacon Press [1965] xvii, 187 p. illus. 24 cm. Bibliography: p. 175-176. [BL2220.R6] 65-13533
1. Shinto. I. Title.

TERRY, Milton Spenser, 1840-
The Shinto cult; a Christian study of the ancient religion of Japan, by Milton S. Terry ... Cincinnati, Jennings and Graham; New York, Eaton and Mains [c1910] 98 p. 17 1/2 cm. "Select bibliography": p. 97-98. 10-14956 0.30.
I. Title.

TERRY, Milton Spenser, 1840-1914. 299.
The Shinto cult; a Christian study of the ancient religion of Japan, by Milton S. Terry ... Cincinnati, Jennings and Graham; New York, Eaton and Mains [1910] 96 p. 17 1/2 cm. "Select bibliography": p. 97-98. [BL2220.T4] 10-14956
1. Shinto. I. Title.

WHEELER, Post, 1869- 299.56
The sacred scriptures of the Japanese, with all authoritative variants, chronologically arranged, setting forth the narrative of the creation of the cosmos, the divine descent of the sky-ancestor of the imperial house and the lineage of the earthly emperors, to whom the Sun-Deity has given the rule of the world unto ages eternal. New York, H. Schuman [1952] xivi, 562 p. 24 cm. Translations of the Kojiki and the Nihongi, supplemented and amplified by translation of a number of lesser works, collated and combined in a connected narrative. "Sources": p. [xviii]-xxvii. [BL2220.W45] 52-14316
1. Shinte. 2. Mythology. Japanese. 3. Japan—Kings and rulers. I. Yasuinaro. d. 723. Kojiki. II. Nihongi. III. Title.

Shinto shrines—Ise, Japan.

WATANABE, Yasutada, 1922- 726'.1'9561095218
Shinto art: Ise and Izumo shrines. Translated by Robert Ricketts. [1st English ed.] New York, Weatherhill/Heibonsha [1974] 190 p. illus. (part col.) 24 cm. (The Heibonsha survey of Japanese art, v. 3) Translation of Ise to Izumo. [NA6057.I79W3713] 73-88471 ISBN 0-8348-1018-2 10.00
1. Shinto shrines—Ise, Japan. 2. Shinto shrines—Izumo, Japan. I. Title. II. Series.

Shipton, Ursula.

HARRISON, William Henry, Spiritualist. 133.3'2'0924
Mother Shipton investigated : the result of critical examination in the British Museum Library of the literature relating to the Yorkshire sibyl / by William H. Harrison. Folcroft, Pa. : Folcroft Library Editions, 1977. p. cm. Reprint of the 1881 ed. published by W. H. Harrison, London. [BF1815.S5H37 1977] 77-3412 ISBN 0-8414-4911-2 lib. bdg. : 10.00
1. Shipton, Ursula. 2. Prophets—England—Yorkshire—Biography. 3. Yorkshire, Eng.—Biography. I. Title.

Shirkutu.

DOUGHERTY, Raymond Philip, 1877-1933. 299'.21
The shirkutu of Babylonian deities. New York : AMS Press, 1980. p. cm. Reprint of the 1923 ed. published by Yale University Press, New Haven, which was issued as v. 5-2 of Yale oriental series, Researches. Includes index. [BL1625.S38D68 1980] 19 78-63548 ISBN 0-404-60295-9 : 25.00
1. Shirkutu. 2. Babylonia—Religious life and customs. 3. Assyro-Babylonian language—Texts. I. Title. II. Series: Yale oriental series : Researches ; v. 5-2.

Shirley, James, 1596-1666.

RADTKE, Stephen John.
James Shirley: his Catholic philosophy of life ... by Rev. Stephen J. Radtke ... Washington, D. C., The Catholic university of America, 1929. ix, 113 p. front. (port.) 24 cm. Thesis (PH. D.)--Catholic university of America, 1929. Bibliography: p. 101-107. [PR3146.R3 1929] 29-18328
1. Shirley, James, 1596-1666. I. Title.

Shivaji, Raja, 1627-1680.

VERMA, Virendra. 954.02'5'0924
Shivaji, a captain of war with a mission / by Virendra Verma. Poona : Youth Education Publications : distributors, Youth Book Agencies, 1976. iii, 93, [1] p., [3] leaves of plates : maps ; 22 cm. Bibliography: p. [94] [DS461.9.S5V44] 76-905100 Rs14.00 ($2.00 U.S.)
1. Shivaji, Raja, 1627-1680. 2. India—Kings and rulers—Biography. 3. India—History, Military. I. Title.

Shneor Zalman ben Baruch, 1747-1812.

GLITZENSTEIN, Abraham Chanoch, 1929- 296.0924
The arrest and liberation of Rabbi Shneur Zalman of Liadi; the history of yud-teth Kislev: the universally famous Chassidic festival of the 19th day of Kislev commemorating the liberation of Rabpi Shneur Zalman of Liadi, as compiled and edited from the writings and traditions of the leaders and followers of Chabad-Chassidism, by A. C. Glitzenstein. Translated and adapted into English by Jacob Immanuel Schochet. Brooklyn, Kehot Publication Society, 1964. 125 p. facsim., port. 24 cm. On spine: The history of yud-teth Kislev. Translation of Hag ha-geulah Bibliography: p. 115-116. "Published works of Rabbi Shneur Zalman of Ladi": p. 120-125. [BM755.S525G53] 65-28161
1. Shneor Zalman ben Baruch, 1747-1812. I. Title. II. Title: The history of yud-teth Kislev.

Shockley, Norman.

SHOCKLEY, Norman. 242
Back from the edge / Norman Shockley ; [ill. by Frances Welch Taylor]. Nashville, Tenn. : Upper Room, c1980. 91 p. : ill. ; 19 cm. [BV4832.2S5218] 79-56163 ISBN 0-8358-0392-9 pbk. : 3.75
1. Shockley, Norman. 2. Meditations. I. Title.

Shoemaker, Samuel Moor, 1893-1963.

HARRIS, Irving D. 283'.092'4 B
The breeze of the spirit : Sam Shoemaker and the story of Faith at work / Irving Harris. New York : Seabury Press, 1978. p. cm. "A Crossroad book." [BX5995.S347H37] 78-18237 ISBN 0-8164-0399-6 : 8.95
1. Shoemaker, Samuel Moor, 1893-1963. 2. Protestant Episcopal Church in the U.S.A.—Clergy—Biography. 3. Clergy—United States—Biography. 4. Faith at work. I. Title.

Shoghi, effendi.

BACH, Marcus, 1906- 922.97
Shoghi Effendi; an appreciation. New York, Hawthorn Books [1958] unpaged. 24cm. [BP395.S5B2] 58-10095
1. Shoghi, effendi. I. Title.

Shooting Creek-Murphy Parish.

BARKER, Esther T. 287'.632'0922 B
Shooting Creek was our parish / by Esther T. Barker. Chicago : Adams Press ; Maryville, TN : may be ordered from Barker, c1977. 209 p. : ill. ; 22 cm. [BX6081.S53B37] 77-353941 3.95
1. Shooting Creek-Murphy Parish. 2. Barker, Paul A. 3. Barker, Esther T. I. Title.

Shorrosh, Anis.

HEFLEY, James C. 248'.246'094 B
The liberated Palestinian : the Anis Shorrosh story / James and Marti Hefley. Wheaton, Ill. : Victor Books, c1975. 172 p. : ill. ; 21 cm. [BV3785.S46H43] 75-36003 ISBN 0-88207-652-3 pbk. : 2.95
1. Shorrosh, Anis. I. Hefley, Marti, joint author. II. Title.

Short stories.

BRUNINI, John Gilland, 1899- ed.
Stories of our century by Catholic authors, edited by John Gillard Brunini and Francis X. Connolly. Rev. ed. New York, Doubleday [1959] 317 p. 18 cm. (Doubleday Image Books D 23) 63-7220
1. Short stories. 2. Catholic literature. I. Connolly, Francis Xavier, 1909- joint ed. II. Title.

HOYT, Wayland, 1838-1910.
For shine and shade; short essays in practical religion. Philadelphia, Amer. Baptist pub. society [1899] 204 p. 12 °. 99-935
I. Title.

SMITH, Almiron, 1841-1919. 922.773
A blind man's stories; short, true stories for young and old, saint and sinner; amusing, touching, and terrible incidents; wonderful answers to prayer, etc. By the Rev. Almiron Smith...Volumes 1 and 2 combined... [Syracuse, N.Y., A. Smith, c1910] 80 p. incl. ports. 18 cm. Paged continuously. [BV3785.S55A28] 37-36767
I. Title.

Shovu'oth (Feast of Weeks)—Juvenile literature.

CEDARBAUM, Sophia N. 296.4
Shovuos, the birthday of the Torah. Pictures by Clare and John Ross. [New York] Union of Amer. Hebrew Congregations [c.1961] 30p. col. illus. 61-9697 .59 bds.,
1. Shovu'oth (Feast of Weeks)—Juvenile literature. I. Title.

Showalter, Carol.

SHOWALTER, Carol. 248'.2 B
3D / Carol Showalter. Orleans, Mass. : Rock Harbor Press, 1978, c1977. 144 p. ; 22 cm. [BX9225.S43A35] 77-90947 5.95
1. Showalter, Carol. 2. Diet, Discipline, and Discipleship, inc. 3. Presbyterians—United States—Biography. 4. Reducing—Moral and religious aspects. I. Title.

Shreveport, La. Highland Baptist Church.

CAYLOR, John, 1894-
History of Highland Baptist Church, Shreveport, Louisiana, 1916-1966, by John Caylor and Marian Thurmond. [Shreveport, La., Highland Baptist Church, 1966] vi, 73 p. illus., ports. 23 cm. 68-92156
1. Shreveport, La. Highland Baptist Church. 2. Baptists—Shreveport, La. I. Thurmond, Marian Smith, joint author. II. Title.

Shrines.

ARADI, Zsolt. 232.931
Shrines to Our Lady around the world. New York, Farrar, Straus and Young [1954] 213 p. illus. 27 cm. [BX2320.A7] 54-10580
1. Shrines. I. Title.

DORCY, Mary Jean, 1914- 232.931
Shrines of Our Lady. Illustrated by Johannes Troyer. New York, Sheed & Ward [1956] 160p. illus. 21cm. [BT650.D6] 56-9531
1. Shrines. I. Title.

JAMES, Edwin Oliver, 1886- 291.35
From cave to cathedral; temples and shrines of prehistoric, classical, and early Christian times [by] E. O. James. New York, F. A. Praeger [1965] 404 p. 200 illus., plans. 24 cm. Bibliography: p. [381]-388. [BL580.J3] 65-10910
1. Shrines. I. Title.

WALSH, William James, 1844- ed.
The apparitions and shrines of heaven's bright Queen in legend, poetry and history, from the earliest ages to the present time; compiled from approved Catholic publications by William J. Walsh, with introduction by Monsignor Bernard O'Reilly ... New York, New Orleans,

Carey-Stafford company [c1906] 4 v. fronts. (v. 1-2, ports.) plates. 22 1/2 cm. [BT650.W2 1906] 7-5072
1. Mary, Virgin—Legends. 2. Shrines. I. Title.

Shrines—Europe.

CARTWRIGHT, John K. 271.73
The Catholic shrines of Europe; with photos. by Alfred Wagg. Foreword by Martin J. O'Connor. New York, McGraw-Hill [1955] 212 p. illus. 26 cm. [BX2320.C37] 54-11259
1. Shrines—Europe. I. Title.

Shrines—Fatima, Portugal.

RYAN, Finbar Patrick, abp., 1882-
Our Lady of Fatima, by Monsignor Finbar Ryan...With a foreword by His Grace Most Reverend John Pius Dowling... St. Louis, Mo., B. Herder book company, 1939. 186 p., 2 l. front., plates, phot., map. 18 1/2 cm. Printed in Ireland. "Some books about Fatima": p. 182-185. A 40
1. Mary, Virgin—Apparitions and miracles (Modern) 2. Fatima, Nossa Senhora da. 3. Shrines—Fatima, Portugal. I. Title.

Shrines—Mexico.

PROUTY, Amy 232.9317
Mexican shrines; a pearl for the Lovely Lady. Philadelphia, Dorrance [c.1960] 28p. illus. 60-53142 2.75
1. Shrines—Mexico. I. Title.

Shrines—Palestine.

THE Catholic digest. 231.73
Marian shrines in the Holyland. St. Paul [1959] 64p. illus. 21cm. (Shrines of the world) [BX2320.C39] 60-23455
1. Shrines—Palestine. I. Title.

ZANDER, Walter. 263'.042'5694
Israel and the holy places of Christendom. New York, Praeger [1971] viii, 248 p. 23 cm. Includes bibliographical references. [DS119.6.Z3] 74-154352 8.50
1. Shrines—Palestine. 2. Israel—Foreign relations. I. Title.

Shrines—United States.

MURPHY, Walter Thomas, 1915- 246'.9'0973
Famous American churches and shrines. Walter T. Murphy, editor. Catholic ed. Bloomfield Hills, Mich., Walmur Pub. Co. [1968] 119 p. illus. 18 cm. [BX4600.M85] 68-28363 4.95
1. Shrines—United States. 2. Churches—United States. I. Title.

THORNTON, Francis Beauchesne, 1898- 282.7
Catholic shrines in the United States and Canada. New York, W. Funk [1954] xii, 340p. illus., maps. 24cm. [BX2320.T4] 53-10386
1. Shrines—U. S. 2. Shrines— Canada. I. Title.

WOODS, Ralph Louis, 1904- 282.7
Pilgrim places in North America; a guide to Catholic shrines, by Ralph L. and Henry F. Woods; with a preface by Michael Williams. New York, Toronto, Longmans, Green and co., 1939. xxv, 194 p. front., plates. 18 1/2 cm. Maps on lining-papers. "First edition." [BX2320.W6] 39-14087
1. Shrines—U.S. 2. Shrines—Canada. I. Woods, Henry Fitzwilliam, 1872- joint author. II. Title.

Shuck, Mrs. Henrietta (Hall) 1817-1844.

DUNAWAY, Thomas Sanford, 1872-1932. 922.651
Pioneering for Jesus; the story of Henrietta Hall Shuck, by Thomas S. Dunaway, D. D. Nashville, Tenn., Sunday school board of the Southern Baptist convention [1930] 160 p. incl front., illus. (incl. ports.) 20 cm. Pages 158-160 blank. [BV3427.S57D8] 32-9274
1. Shuck, Mrs. Henrietta (Hall) 1817-1844. 2. Missions—China. I. Title.

Shulhan 'arukh.

SPECTOR, Ivar, 1898- 296
The ethics of the Shulhan 'aruk, by Dr. Itzehak Spector ... Tacoma, Wash., Uraitha publishing co., 1930. xii p., 1 l., [15]-88 p. 20 1/2 cm. "A doctor's dissertation ... for the PH.D. degree at the University of Chicago, June, 1928."--p. lll. Bibliography: p. 87-88. [BM520.S55S6] 30-7648
1. Shulhan 'arukh. 2. Ethics, Jewish. I. Title.

SPECTOR, Ivar, 1898- 296
The ethics of the Shulhan 'aruk, by Ivar Spector ... 3d ed. Seattle, Uraitha publishing co., 1935. xii p., 1 l., [15]-88 p. 20 1/2 cm. Issued also as thesis (PH.D.) University of Chicago. Bibliography: p. 87-88. [BM520.S55S6 1935] 35-20281
1. Shulhan 'arukh. 2. Ethics, Jewish. I. Title.

Shumaker, Ida Cora, 1873-1946.

MOW, Anetta Cordula, 1899- 922.654
Miss Ida; the story of Ida Shumaker, compiled by Anetta C. Mow. Elgin, Ill., Brethren publishing house [1947] 80 p. incl. plates, ports. port. 20 cm. [BV3269.S43M6] 47-1889
1. Shumaker, Ida Cora, 1873-1946. I. Title.

Shyne, Cornelius A., 1861-1943.

KANE, William Terence, 1880- 922.273
Cornelius Shyne, S.J., by W. Kane, S.J. Chicago, Cudahy library, Loyola university, 1945. 3 p. l., 333 p. front. (port.) 19 1/2 cm. [BX4705.S615K3] 45-16482
1. Shyne, Cornelius A., 1861-1943. I. Loyola university, Chicago. Elizabeth M. Cudahy memorial library. II. Title.

Sia—Sermons.

FARRAR, Frederick William, 1831-1903. 233.2
Saintly workers: or The conquest of sin, by C6 New York, Chicago [etc.] Fleming H. Revell company [1897] 147 p. 17 cm. [BT715.F2] 40-24805
1. Sia—Sermons. 2. Church of England—Sermons. 3. Sermons, English. I. Title.

Siade, Madeleine.

GANDHI, Mohandas Karamchand, 1869-1948. 923.254
Gandhi's letters to a disciple. With an introd. by John Haynes Holmes. [1st American ed.] New York, Harper [1950] 234 p. 22 cm. Indian ed. (Navajivan) published in 1949 under title: Bapu's letters to Mira. [BT33.G3A45 1950] 50-8532
1. Siade, Madeleine. I. Title.

Siam—History

MCFARLAND, Bertha Blount. 926.1
Our garden was so fair; the story of a mission in Thailand, by Bertha Blount McFarland. Philadelphia, The Blakiston company, distributed by Fleming H. Revell company, New York and London [c1943] 141 p. front. (port.) 19 cm. [BV3317.M34M3] 44-3298
1. McFarland, George Bradley, 1866-1942. 2. Siam—Hist. I. Title.

Sibthorp, Richard Waldo, 1792-1879.

SYKES, Christopher, 1907- 922.242
Two studies in virtue. [1st American ed.] New York, Knopf, 1953. 256p. illus. 22cm. [BX4705.S62S9 1953a] 53-6864
1. Sibthorp, Richard Waldo, 1792-1879. 2. Catholic Church in England. 3. Zionism—Hist. I. Title.

Sibyls.

ALEXANDER, Paul Julius, 1910- 133.3'248
The oracle of Baalbek; the Tiburtine Sibyl in Greek dress, by Paul J. Alexander. Washington, Dumbarton Oaks Center for Byzantine Studies; [distributed by J. J. Augustin, Locust Valley, N.Y.] 1967. xii, 151 p. illus. 24 cm. (Dumbarton Oaks studies, 10) Includes the Greek text and an English translation. The Greek text (p. 9-22) is edited on the basis of the Latin versions and the Greek MSS. preserved in codices Athos 1527 (Karakallou 14), Vaticanus Graecus 1120, and Atheniensis Bibliothecae Nationalis 2725 (—Suppl. 725) Includes bibliographical references. [BF1768.A4] 75-27113
1. Sibyls. I. Title. II. Title: The Tiburtine Sibyl in Greek dress. III. Series.

BEVAN, Edwyn Robert, 1870-1943. 231'.74
Sibyls and seers : a survey of some ancient theories of revelation and inspiration / by Edwyn Bevan. Folcroft, Pa. : Folcroft Library Editions, 1976. p. cm. Reprint of the 1928 ed. published by G. Allen & Unwin, London. Includes bibliographical references and index. [BL96.B4 1976] 76-30583 ISBN 0-8414-1750-4 lib. bdg. : 25.00
1. Sibyls. 2. Prophets. 3. Revelation. 4. Inspiration. I. Title.

Sicily—Religion.

ZUNTZ, Gunther, 1902- 292'.08
Persephone: three essays on religion and thought in Magna Graecia. Oxford, Clarendon Press, 1971. xiii, 427 p., 31 plates; illus., plans. 25 cm. Bibliography: p. 414-417. [BL793.S5Z85] 72-300059 ISBN 0-19-814286-2 £9.00
1. Empodocles. Katharmoi. 2. Sicily—Religion. 3. Persephone. 4. Greece—Religion. I. Title.

Sick.

[BAKER, Harriette Newell (Woods) Mrs.] 1815-1893. 248
The sick man's friend; by the author of William's return;--The twin brothers, &c. Philadelphia, Tract and book society of the Evangelical Lutheran congregation of St. John's church [18-] 1 p. l., 30 p. 21 cm. "A serious address to the young": p. [20]-30. [BV4585.B3] 34-14167
1. Sick. I. Title.

CROKE, John Joseph. 265.8
Happiness for patients, by John Joseph Croke; illustrations by Carle Michel Boog. New York, Hospital publishing co. [c1933] 109, [1] p., 1 l. front., illus. 21 cm. "First edition." [BX2170.S5C7] 33-16990
1. Sick. 2. Consolation. 3. Catholic church—Prayer-books and devotions. I. Title.

CROKE, John Joseph, 1894-1939. 265.8
Happiness for patients, by Rev. John Joseph Croke ... 3d ed. New York, N.Y., Catholic book publishing co. [1947] 4 p. l., 7-111, [1] p. incl. front., illus. 20 1/2 cm. [BX2170.S5C7 1947] 47-23499
1. Sick. 2. Sick—Prayer-books and devotions—English. 3. Consolation. 4. Catholic church—Prayer-books and devotions—English. I. Title.

DEEMS, Charles Force, 1820-1893. comp. 244
Sunshine for dark hours. A book for invalids, compiled by Charles F. Deems ... New York, W. B. Ketcham; Edinburg, J. Gemmell 1889. 96 p. 19 cm. Poetry and prose. [BV4585.D4] 37-13881
1. Sick. I. Title.

DICKS, Russell Leslie, 1906- 242
Your self and health; a book of inspirational readings, by Russell L. Dicks ... New York London, Harper & brothers, 1939. 4 p. l., 58 p. 19 cm. On cover: Parables of health, selections from prose and poetry, and Scriptural passages to strengthen mind and body. "First edition." [BV4585.D52 1939] 41-76
1. Sick. I. Title.

GARESCHE, Edward Francis, 1876- 264.
The patient's book; thoughts of cheer, consolation, encouragement and information for the sick, especially in hospitals. By Edward F. Garesche ... Milwaukee, Wis., The Catholic hospital association, 1925. viii, 151 p. 14 cm. [BX2170.S5G3] 25-15536
1. Sick. I. Title.

GARESCHE, Edward Francis, 1876- 264.
The patient's guide; thoughts of cheer, consolation, encouragement and information for the sick, especially in hospitals. By Edward F. Garesche ... Milwaukee, Wis., The Hospital publishing company, 1925. viii, 149 p. 14 cm. A revised edition of the author's "The patient's book". [BX2170.S5G33] 26-270
1. Sick. I. Title.

GARESCHE, Edward Francis, 1876- 242
Your stay in the hospital; thoughts of information, cheer, consolation and encouragement for the sick, especially in hospitals. New York, Vista Maria Press [1951] 112 p. 19 cm. Published in 1925 under title: The patlent's book. [BX2170.S5G3 1951] 51-28823
1. Sick. 2. Sick—Prayer-books and devotions—English. 3. Catholic Church—Prayer-books and devotions—English. I. Title.

KIERKEGAARD, Soren Aabye, 1813-1855. 233.2
The sickness unto death, by S. Kierkegaard, translated, with an introduction, by Walter Lowrie. Princeton, Princeton university press, 1941. xix, 231 p. 19 cm. [BT715.K52] 42-895
1. Sick. I. Lowrie, Walter, 1868- tr. II. Title.

LETTERS from a sick room 248
... Written for the Massachusetts Sabbath school society, and revised by the Committee of publication. Boston, Massachusetts Sabbath school society, 1845. xii, [13]-132 p. incl. front. 16 1/2 cm. [BV4585.L5] 35-32294
1. Sick. I. Massachusetts Sabbath school society. Committee of publication.

MILLER, Donald Ferdinand, 1903- 248
Blessings in illness, by Rev. Donald F. Miller, C. AS. R. St. Paul, Minn., Catechetical guild, 1944. 96 p. 17 cm [BX2373.S5M5] 44-47143
1. Sick. I. Title.

STOTT, Roscoe Gilmore, 1880- 243
Dear shut-in; information and inspiration for the valiant who march the road to recovery, by Roscoe Gilmore Stott, with symbolic drawings by Charles Logan Smith II ... Cynthiana, Ky., The Hobson book press, 1944. 2 p. l., vii-viii p., 1 l., 120 p. illus. 21 1/2 cm. Reproduced from type-written copy. [BV4585.S8] 44-28896
1. Sick. I. Title.

ZEPP, J. Albert, comp. 242
The shut-in cause, Published for the purpose of bringing well people closer to God's dear, suffering ones, and to bring us all closer to our Maker. Compiled by J. Albert Zepp... [Melrose, Md.] 1899. [100,) p. ports. 15 1/2 x 13 1/2 cm. [BV4585.Z4] 99-3722
1. Sick. I. Title.

Sick children—Prayer-books and devotions.

SLADEN, Kathleen 242.4
While you're sick, Illus. by Mary Alice Bahler. Richmond, Va., Knox [1966, c.1965] 63p. illus. 21cm. First pub. in 1965 in Ontario, Canada under title: When we are sick. [BV4910.5.S55] 66-13306 1.95 bds.,
1. Sick children—Prayer-books and devotions. I. Title.

Sick—Prayer-books and devotions.

BANKS, Alfred John Gayner, 1886- comp. 258
The Great Physician; a manual of devotion for those who care for the sick, selected

and arranged by A. J. Gayner Banks ... and W. Sinclair Bowen ... New York, The Macmillan company [1927] xvi, 196 p. 19 cm. Printed in Great Britain. [BV4335.B3] 27-27933
I. Bowen, William Sinclair, 1867- joint comp. II. Title.

BARCLAY, William. lecturer in the University of Glasgow. 242.4
Prayers for help and healing. [1st U.S. ed.] New York, Harper [1968] 124p. 18cm. [BV270.B3 1968] 68-29568 3.50
1. Sick—Prayer-books and devotions. I. Title.

BARCLAY, William, lecturer in the University of Glasgow. 242.4
Prayers for help and healing. New York, Harper & Row [1975, c1968] 124 p. 18 cm. [BV270.B3] 68-29568 ISBN 0-06-060481-6 1.75 (pbk.)
1. Sick—Prayer-books and devotions. I. Title.

BRENNEMAN, Helen Good 242.4
My comforters; a book of daily inspiration for those who are ill. Scottdale, Pa., Herald Pr. [c.1966] 80p. illus., port. 27cm. [BV4910.B74] 66-13156 1.50 pap.,
1. Sick—Prayer-books and devotions. I. Title.

DOERFFIER, Alfred, jr. 242
The yoke made easy, by Alfred Doerffier ... St. Louis, Mo., Concordia publishing house, 1935. vi, 119 p. 20 cm. "Meditations and prayers for the sick, convalescents, and invalids."--p. ii. [BV4585.D6] 35-6285
1. Sick—Prayer-books and devotions. I. Title.

KARSTORP, Lennart. 242'.4
May I have a word with you, Lord? : Prayers when you are ill / Lennart Karstorp. 1st American ed. Cleveland : Collins, 1978. 61 p. ; 19 cm. (A Fount book) Translation of Far jag tala med dig, Herre? [BV270.K3513 1978] 78-69704 ISBN 0-529-05497-3 pbk. : 2.95
1. Sick—Prayer-books and devotions. I. Title.

KELLETT, Arnold, ed. 242.4
Prayers for patients; a collection of prayers for those who are ill or in need. Westwood, N. J., F. H. Revell Co. [c1964] 111 p. 17 cm. "Notes on sources and authors": p. 100-111. [BV270.K4] 66-4555
1. Sick — Prayer-books and devotions. I. Title.

KOHN, Harold E. 242.4
Wide horizons; a book of faith for the sick, by Harold E. Kohn. Nashville, Tidings [1970?] 42 p. illus. 22 x 9 cm. [BV4910.K64] 70-128172
1. Sick—Prayer-books and devotions. I. Title.

MAY, Edward C. 242.4
I was sick and You visited me; a book of prayers, by Edward C. May. Minneapolis, Augsburg Pub. House [1968] 127 p. 21 cm. [BV270.M33] 68-13425
1. Sick—Prayer-books and devotions. I. Title.

Sick—Prayer-books and devotions—English.

BERRIAN, William, 1787-1862, comp. 242
Devotions for the sick room, and for times of trouble, compiled from ancient liturgies and the writings of holy men. From the first London edition, with alterations and additions, by the Rev. William Berrian ... New York, Stanford & Swords, 1847. 2 p. l., [7]-113, 104 p. 20 cm. "Prayer for the sick and afflicted. By William Berrian": 104 p. at end. [BV4585.B4 1847] 35-32586
1. Sick—Prayer-books and devotions—English. I. Title. II. Title: Prayers for the sick and afflicted.

BIBLE. English. Selections. 1905. Authorized. 220.52
The Bible for the sick; a compilation by Henry King Hannah ... New York, T. Whittaker [1905] ix, 238 p. 19 cm. [BS391.H33] 5-42039
1. Sick—Prayer-books and devotions—English. I. Hannah, Henry King, 1865?-1920, comp. II. Title.

BICKERSTETH, Edward Henry, bp. of Exeter, 1825-1906. 248
Water from the well-spring, for the Sabbath hours of afficted believers; being a complete course of morning and evening meditations for every Sunday in the year, by Edward Henry Bickersteth ... New York, R. Carter & brothers, 1856. 1 p. l., [v]-x, [11]-254 p. 18 cm. [BV4585.B5] 35-33515
1. Sick—Prayer-books and devotions—English. I. Title.

BILT, F. C. van de. 242'.4
Light and twilight : thoughts and prayers for the sick / by F. C. van de Bilt and T. J. Moorman ; translated from the Dutch by David Smith. Chicago, Ill. : Franciscan Herald Press, 1981, 1980. p. cm. Translation of Licht en duister. [BV270.B4813] 19 80-19556 ISBN 0-8199-0805-3 : 5.50
1. Sick—Prayer-books and devotions—English. I. Moorman, T. J., joint author. II. Title.

BRACHER, Marjory Louise 242.4
The anchor of hope; meditations for the seriously ill. Philadelphia, Fortress [c.1964] 63p. 15cm. Alternate pages blank. 64-18149 1.25 bds.,
1. Sick—Prayer-books and devotions—English. I. Title.

CAMPION, Albert E comp. 242.4
Prayers for Christian healing. New York, Morehouse-Gorham [1958] 96p. 18cm. [BV270.C2] 58-11445
1. Sick—Prayer-books and devotions—English. I. Title.

COLE, Jonathan. 242
Meditations for the sick. By Jonathan Cole. Boston, J. Munroe and company, 1837. vii, [5]-119 p. 16 cm. [BV4585.C6] 35-28545
1. Sick—Prayer-books and devotions—English. 2. Meditations. I. Title.

CRANFORD, Mary Poole. 242
From my window; to shut-ins all over the world. New York, Pageant Press [1953] 146p. illus. 21cm. Essays. [BV4585.C7] 53-12317
1. Sick—Prayer-books and devotions—English. I. Title.

CRUMPLER, Frank H. 242'.4
God is near; bedside companion of inspiration and strength [by] Frank H. Crumpler. Old Tappan, N.J., F. H. Revell [1973] 63 p. 19 cm. [BV4910.C78] 73-1707 ISBN 0-8007-0589-0 2.50
1. Sick—Prayer-books and devotions—English. I. Title.

DEVOTIONAL aids for the chamber of sickness. Prepared for the Presbyterian board of publication. Philadelphia, Presbyterian board of publication [1846] 176 p. 11 cm. [BV4585.D47 1846] 35-32301 242
1. Sick—Prayer-books and devotions—English. I. Presbyterian church in the U. S. A. Board of publication.

DICKS, Russell Leslie, 1906- 265.8
Comfort ye my people, a manual of the pastoral ministry [by] Russell L. Dicks, B.D. New York, The Macmillan company, 1947. ix p., 1 l., 136 p. 16 1/2 cm. "First printing." [BV270.D5] 47-1161
1. Sick—Prayer-books and devotions—English. I. Title.

DICKS, Russell Leslie, 1906- 242
Meditations for the sick, by Russell L. Dicks, with a foreword by Richard C. Cabot. Chicago, New York, Willett, Clark & company, 1937. x p., 1 l., 113 p. 20 cm. "Notes": p. 113. [BV4585.D5] 38-9497
1. Sick—Prayer-books and devotions—English. I. Title.

DICKS, Russell Leslie, 1906- 242
... Thy health shall spring forth; readings in religion and health. New York, The Macmillan company, 1945. vii p., 1 l., 61 p. 19 1/2 cm. At head of title: Russell L. Dicks. "First printing." Bibliographical references included in "Notes" (p. 61) [BV4585.D515] 45-8953
1. Sick—Prayer-books and devotions—English. I. Title.

DOBERSTEIN, John W comp. 248
On wings of healing, prayers and readings for the sick and shut-in, compiled by John W. Doberstein, designed & illustrated by W. P. Schoonmaker. Philadelphia, The Muhlenberg press [1942] 6 p. l., 15-104 p. illus. (part col.) 29 x 23 cm. [BV4585.D58] 42-12940
1. Sick—Prayer-books and devotions—English. I. Title.

DOERFFLER, Alfred, 1884- 242'.4
The burden made light / Alfred Doerffler. St. Louis : Concordia Pub. House, [1975] p. cm. [BV4910.D6] 74-34213 ISBN 0-570-03026-9 pbk. : 3.95
1. Sick—Prayer-books and devotions—English. I. Title.

DOERFFLER, Alfred, 1884- 242'.4
The yoke made easy / Alfred Doerffler. St. Louis : Concordia Pub. House, [1975] p. cm. Large print ed. [BV4910.D63 1975] 75-2344 ISBN 0-570-03027-7 pbk. : 3.95
1. Sick—Prayer-books and devotions—English. 2. Meditations. 3. Sight-saving books. I. Title.

DONNE, John, 1572-1631. 242'.4
We lie down in hope : selections from John Donne's meditations on sickness / John J. Pollock, editor. Elgin, Ill. : D. C. Cook Pub. Co., c1977. 93 p. : ill. ; 22 cm. Selections from John Donne's Devotions upon emergent occasions. [BV270.D62 1977] 77-78505 ISBN 0-89191-095-6 pbk. : 3.95
1. Sick—Prayer-books and devotions—English. I. Pollock, John J. II. Title.

FORD, Josephine Massyngberde. 248'.86
The hospital prayer book / J. Massyngberde Ford. New York : Paulist Press, [1975] vi, 106 p. ; 18 cm. [BV4910.F65] 74-30984 ISBN 0-8091-1838-6 pbk. : 1.65
1. Sick—Prayer-books and devotions—English. I. Title.

GOEBEL, Edmund Joseph, 1896- 265.8
Saints to help the sick and the dying, with appropriate prayers and reflections, by Edmund J. Goebel ... New York, Cincinnati [etc.] Benziger brothers, 1937. x, 129 p. illus., pl. 18 cm. [BX2170.S5G6] 38-16
1. Sick—Prayer-books and devotions—English. 2. Patron saints. I. Title.

GRANTHAM, Rudolph E. 242'.4
The healing relationship, by Rudolph E. Grantham. [Nashville] The Upper Room [1972] 79 p. 18 cm. [BV4910.G7] 72-81154 1.00
1. Sick—Prayer-books and devotions—English. I. Title.

KREBS, Joseph Alois, 1827-1907. 265.8
Devotions and prayers for the sick-room. With an appendix containing prayers and devotional exercises for the use of religious sick-nurses. From the original of Rev. Jos. Aloysius Krebs ... New York, Cincinnati [etc.] Benziger brothers, 1900. 247 p. 17 cm. [BX2170.S5K7] 0-509
1. Sick—Prayer-books and devotions—English. 2. Catholic church—Prayer-books and devotions—English. I. Title.

KUYPER, Abraham, 1837-1920. 242
In the shadow of death; meditations for the sick-room and at the death-bed, by Abraham Kuyper ... translated from the Dutch by John Hendrik De Vries ... Grand Rapids, Mich., Wm. B. Eerdmans publ. co. [c1929] ix p., 2 l., 317 p. 20 cm. [BV4585.K82] 38-6570
1. Sick—Prayer-books and devotions—English. 2. Consolation. I. De Vries, John Hendrik, 1859 tr. II. Title.

LAUTERBACH, William August, 1903- 242'.4
Look down from above : prayers at the sickbed / William A. Lauterbach. St. Louis : Concordia Pub. House, c1977. 32 p. ; 16 cm. [BV270.L35] 77-5897 ISBN 0-570-03051-X pbk. : 0.95
1. Sick—Prayer-books and devotions—English. I. Title.

LEBUFFE, Francis Peter, 1885- 264.02
Prayers for the dying ... by Francis P. LeBuffe, S. J. New York, The America press [c1935] 64 p. front. 15 cm. ("Let us pray" series, v) [BX2170.D9L4] 40-4931
1. Sick—Prayer-books and devotions—English. 2. Consolation. 3. Catholic church—Prayer-books and devotions—English. I. Title.

LILES, Lester R comp. 242.4
Streams of healing; a book of comfort. [Westwood, N. J.] Revell [1958] 160p. 21cm. [BV4910.L5] 58-11019
1. Sick—Prayer-books and devotions—English. I. Title.

LYONS, James W. 242'.802
Steps into light : a prayerbook of Christian belief / James W. Lyons. Notre Dame, Ind. : Ave Maria Press, c1978. 62 p., [1] leaf of plates : ill. ; 21 cm. [BX2130.L93] 78-50791 ISBN 0-87793-149-6 pbk. : 1.75
1. Catholic Church—Prayer-books and devotions—English. 2. Catholic Church—Doctrinal and controversial works, Popular. 3. Sick—Prayer-books and devotions—English. I. Title.

MARSHALL, Thomas Chalmers, 1868- comp. 264.1
Immateria medica; a collection of prayers for the use of the sick and those who minister to the sick. By Rev. Thomas C. Marshall ... Boston, Mass., The Stratford company [c1934] 2 p. l., 3-58 p. 16 cm. [BV270.M3] 34-37472
1. Sick—Prayer-books and devotions—English. I. Title.

MAYFIELD, L. H. 242.4
Behind the clouds--light; meditations for the sick and distressed. Nashville, Tenn., Abingdon [c.1965] 63p. illus. 20cm. [BV4910.M3] 65-938 1.50 bds.,
1. Sick—Prayer-books and devotions—English. I. Title.

MORAL, Herbert Renard, 1901- 242.4
How to have better health through prayer. Noroton, Conn., Life-Study Fellowship [1955] 190p. 21cm. [BV4585.M6] 55-58701
1. Sick—Prayer-books and devotions—English. I. Title.

NOEL, Baptist Wriothesley, 1798-1873. 242
Meditations in sickness and old age. By Baptist W. Noel ... Philadelphia, H. Perkins; Boston, Perkins & Marvin, 1838. viii, [13]-148 p. 16 cm. [BV4585.N6] 35-33491
1. Sick—Prayer-books and devotions—English. I. Title.

PERREYVE, Henri, 1831-1865. 242
La journee des malades. Daily life of the sick; or, Consolation in the hour of suffering. By M.I'Abe Henri Perregve. With an introduction by Rev. L. Petetot...Translated from the French. Philadelphia, P. F. Cunningham & son, 1875. 288 p. 19 cm. [BV4585.P4] 35-32290
1. Sick—Prayer-books and devotions—English. I. Title. II. Title: Daily life of the sick.

PORTER, Rose, 1845-1906. 242
Gain by loss; or, The garment of praise, by Rose Porter ... Boston, D. Lothrop company [1891] 76 p. 15 cm. [BV4585.P65] 35-33489
1. Sick—Prayer-books and devotions—English. I. Title.

PORTER, Rose, 1845-1906. FIC
In the shadow of His hand: thoughts for lonely hours. By Rose Porter ... New York, A. D. F. Randolph & company [1882] 6 p. l., 11-105 p. 19 cm. [PV4585.P6] 242 35-33490
1. Sick—Prayer-books and devotions—English. I. Title.

POWER, P. B. 242'.4
A book of comfort for those in sickness / P. B. Power. Edinburgh ; Carlisle, Pa. : Banner of Truth Trust, 1974. 100 p. ; 19 cm. [BV4910.P68] 75-322816 ISBN 0-85151-203-8 : £0.40
1. Sick—Prayer-books and devotions—English. 2. Consolation. I. Title.

PROTESTANT Episcopal church 242
in the U.S.A. Forward movement committee.
Hope and courage, a handbook of messages, devotions and Scripture for the use of the sick and those who minister to them. Cincinnati, O., The Forward movement [1944] 95 p. 19 cm. "Copyright by Gilbert Prower Symons." Text on p. [2] and [3] of cover. "Some books on health and healing": p. 92-93. [BV4585.P7] 44-33127
1. Sick—Prayer-books and devotions—English. I. Symons, Gilbert Prower, 1879- II. Title.

ROBERTSON, John M. 248'.86
Here I am, God, where are you? : Prayers & promises for hospital patients / John M. Robertson. Wheaton, Ill, : Tyndale House Publishers, c1976. [63] p. : ill. ; 18 cm. [BV270.R63] 75-21652 ISBN 0-8423-1416-4 pbk. : 1.45
1. Sick—Prayer-books and devotions—English. I. Title.

SCHULTZ, Harold Peters. 242.4
Strength and power, a book for the sick. Philadelphia, Christian Education Press [1956] 90p. 20cm. Poems and prose. [BV4910.S35] 56-8237
1. Sick—Prayer-books and devotions—English. I. Title.

SCHULTZ, Harold Peters. 242.4
Strength and power, a book for the sick. Philadelphia, Christian Education Press [1956] 90p. 20cm. Poems and prose. [BV4910.S35] 56-8237
1. Sick—Prayers-books and devotions—English. I. Title.

TIRY, Clara Mary, 1894- 265.8
Comfort for the sick, 3d rev. ed. Milwaukee, Apostolate of Suffering, 1947. xvi, 390 p. 20 cm. Full name: Clara Mary Anne Tiry. [BX2170.S5T48 1947] 48-12270
1. Sick—Prayer-books and devotions—English. I. Title.

TIRY, Clara Mary, 1894- 242
Happy hours with Christ; reflections for the sick, by Clara M. Tiry, with a foreword by the Most Reverend Moses E. Kiley ... Milwaukee, The Bruce publishing company [c1940] xviii p., 1 l., 187 p. 19 1/2 cm. "The chapters gathered...here...appeared originally as first-page articles in 'Our Good Samaritan'."--Pref. [BX2170.S5T5] 41-870
1. Sick—Prayer-books and devotions—English. I. Title.

TOPPING, Lella Lyon. 242
The burden of ill-health, how to bear it, by Leila Lyon Topping... New York, E. P. Dutton & company, 1894. 63 p. 14 1/2 cm. [BV4585.T6] 35-33488
1. Sick—Prayer-books and devotions—English. I. Title.

*VAN Dalfsen, Patricia. 242.4
Good morning, Lord: devotions for shut-ins. Grand Rapids : Baker Book House, 1976. 48, [5]p. ; 19 cm. (The good morning Lord series) [BV4910] ISBN 0-8010-9264-7 : 2.45.
1. Sick-Prayer-books and devotions-English 2. Suffering. I. Title.

VANDENBERGH, C. W. 242'.4
Sunbursts for the spirit / C. W. Vandenbergh ; [art work by Donald Perry]. Special ed. Washington Crossing, Pa. : Pine Row Publications, c1979. 54 p. : ill. ; 22 cm. [BV270.V37] 79-90313 ISBN 0-935238-02-6 pbk. : pbk. : 3.25
1. Sick—Prayer-books and devotions—English. 2. Aged—Prayer-books and devotions—English. 3. Consolation. I. Title.

WARD, William B 242.4
The Divine Physician; devotions for the sick. [2d ed.] Richmond, John Knox Press [1957] [68] p. 18 cm. [BV4910.W3 1957] 57-4113
1. Sick — Prayer-books and devotions — English. I. Title.

WARD, William B 242.4
The Divine Physician; devotions for the sick. Richmond, John Knox Press [1953] unpaged. 16cm. [BV4585.W28] 53-11762
1. Sick—Prayer-books and devotions—English. I. Title.

WARD, William B 242.4
The Divine Physician; devotions for the sick. [2d ed.] Richmond. John Knox Press [1957] [68]p. 18cm. [BV4910.W3 1957] 57-4113
1. Sick—Prayer-books and devotions—English. I. Title.

[WARE, John Fothergill 242
Waterhouse] 1818-1881.
The silent pastor; or, Consolations for the sick ... Boston, J. Munroe and company, 1848. iv, 136 p., 1 l. 16 1/2 cm. Preface signed: J. F. W. W. [i.e. John Fothergill Waterhouse Ware] [BV4585.W3] 35-32296
1. Sick—Prayer-books and devotions—English. I. Title.

WISLoFF, Fredrik, 1904- 242'.4
On our Father's knee; devotions for times of illness. Minneapolis, Augsburg Pub. House [1973, c1966] 137 p. 15 cm. Translation of Pa var Herres fang. [BV4910.W5613] 72-90264 ISBN 0-8066-1309-2 1.95 (pbk.)
1. Sick—Prayer-books and devotions—English. 2. Consolation. I. Title.

Sick—Psychology.

PARKER, Paul E. 248'.86
What's a nice person like you doing sick? / Paul E. Parker, with David Enlow. Carol Stream, Ill. : Creation House, [1974] 80 p. : ill. ; 20 cm. (New leaf library) [RC49.P35] 74-82838 ISBN 0-88419-082-X pbk. : 1.45
1. Sick—Psychology. 2. Medicine and religion. I. Enlow, David R., joint author. II. Title.

Sick—Religious life.

BITTNER, Vernon J. 248'.86
Make your illness count / Vernon J. Bittner. Minneapolis : Augsburg Pub. House, c1976. 126 p. ; 20 cm. [BV4910.B5] 76-3862 ISBN 0-8066-1532-X pbk. : 3.50
1. Sick—Religious life. I. Title.

BITTNER, Vernon J. 248'.86
You can help with your healing : a guide for recovering wholeness in body, mind, and spirit / Vernon J. Bittner. Minneapolis : Augsburg Pub. House, c1979. 143 p. ; 20 cm. [BV4910.B525] 78-66946 ISBN 0-8066-1698-9 pbk. : 3.95
1. Sick—Religious life. I. Title.

BOWMAN, Leonard. 248'.86
The importance of being sick : a Christian reflection / by Leonard Bowman. [Wilmington, N.C.] : Consortium, c1976. 218 p. ; 23 cm. [BV4910.B68] 76-19774 ISBN 0-8434-0604-6 : 12.00
1. Sick—Religious life. I. Title.

Sidonius Apollinaris, Saint, 431 or 2-ca. 487.

STEVENS, Courtenay 270.2'092'4 B
Edward.
Sidonius Apollinaris and his age / by C. E. Stevens. Westport, Conn. : Greenwood Press, 1979, c1933. xiv, 224 p., [2] leaves of plates : ill. ; 22 cm. Reprint of the ed. published by the Clarendon Press, Oxford. Includes index. Bibliography: p. [213]-220. [BR1720.S5S73 1979] 78-21112 ISBN 0-313-20850-6 lib. bdg. : 22.50
1. Sidonius Apollinaris, Saint, 431 or 2-ca. 487. 2. Christian saints—France—Biography. I. Title.

Siedliska, Maria Franciszka, Mother, 1842-1902.

BURTON, Katherine (Kurz), 922.273
1890-
Where there is love; the life of Mother Mary Frances Siedliska of Jesus the Good Shepherd. New York, Kenedy [1951] 200 p. illus. 21 cm. [BX4705.S624B8] 51-14256
1. Siedliska, Maria Franciszka, Mother, 1842-1902. I. Title.

Siegburg, Ger. St. Michael (Benedictine abbey)

WISPLINGHOFF, Erich. 271'.1'04333
Die Benediktinerabtei Siegburg / im Auftr. d. Max-Planck-Inst. f. Geschichte bearb. von Erich Wisplinghoff. Berlin ; New York : de Gruyter, 1975. ix, 263 p. ; 25 cm. (His Das Erzbistum Koln ; 2) (Die Bistumer der Kirchenprovinz Koln) (Germania sacra ; n. F., 9) (Series: Wisplinghoff, Erich. Das Erzbistum Koln ; 2.) Includes index. Bibliography: p. 2-5. [BX1534.A1G53 n.F. 9, pt. 2] [BX2618.S5] 75-512994 ISBN 3-11-005752-2 : DM110.00
1. Siegburg, Ger. St. Michael (Benedictine abbey) I. Title. II. Series.

Siegfried.

MADELEY, Dora Ford.
The heroic life and exploits of Siegfried, the dragonslayer; an old story of the north, retold by Dora Ford Madeley, with twelve illustrations by Stephen Reid. New York, T. Y. Crowell & company [1910] vii, 166 p., 1 l. col. front., col. pl. 20 cm. A 10
1. Siegfried. 2. Mythology, Norse. I. Title.

Sifra di-tseni 'uta

ROSENBERG, Roy A., 1930- 296.1'6
comp.
The anatomy of God: the Book of concealment, the Great holy assembly and the Lesser holy assembly of the Zohar, with the Assembly of the tabernacle. Translation, introd., and annotations by Roy A. Rosenberg. New York, Ktav Pub. House, 1973. vii, 196 p. 24 cm. Bibliography: p. 189. [BM525.A6A27] 72-14428 ISBN 0-87068-220-2 8.50
1. Sifra di-tseni 'uta 2. Idra raba. 3. Idra zuta. 4. Idra de-mashkena. 5. Cabala. I. Title.

Sight-saving books.

BIBLE. N.T. English. 225.5'2
1967. Jerusalem Bible.
The New Testament of the Jerusalem Bible / general editor, Alexander Jones. Large-type reader's ed. Garden City, N.Y. : Doubleday, [1975] c1967. 1112 p. ; 24 cm. [BS2095.J4 1975] 75-329095 ISBN 0-385-04868-8 : 12.95
1. Sight-saving books. I. Jones, Alexander, 1906- II. Title.

BURGESS, Alan. 266'.023'0924 B
Daylight must come : the story of a courageous woman doctor in the Congo / Alan Burgess. Boston : G. K. Hall, 1975, c1974. 520 p. ; 25 cm. Originally published under title: Hostage. Large print ed. [BV3625.C63R633 1975b] 75-6727 ISBN 0-8161-6281-6 lib.bdg.: 12.95
1. Roseveare, Helen. 2. Sight-saving books. I. Title.

DOERFFLER, Alfred, 223'.2'06
1884-
The mind at ease / Alfred Doerffler. St. Louis, Mo. : Concordia Pub. House, [1976] c1957. p. cm. Large print ed. [BS1430.4.D63 1976] 75-43869 ISBN 0-570-03040-4 pbk. : 3.95
1. Bible. O.T. Psalms—Meditations. 2. Sight-saving books. I. Title.

JESUS : 232.9'01
the four Gospels, Matthew, Mark, Luke, and John, combined in one narrative and rendered in modern English. Boston : G. K. Hall, 1975, c1973. xxviii, 351 p. : map ; 25 cm. Large print ed. Includes index. [BT299.2.J47 1975] 75-5681 ISBN 0-8161-6275-1 lib.bdg. : 9.95
1. Jesus Christ—Biography—Sources, Biblical. 2. Sight-saving books.

ROBINSON, Haddon W. 242
Psalm twenty-three : a devotional / by Haddon W. Robinson. Large print ed. Chicago : Moody Press, 1976, c1968. 127 p. : ill. ; 21 cm. [BS1450.23d.R6 1976] 76-21233 2.95
1. Bible. O.T. Psalms XXIII—Meditations. 2. Sight-saving books.

ROGERS, Dale Evans. 248'.4
Where He leads / Dale Evans Rogers. Boston : G. K. Hall, 1975, c1974. p. cm. Large print ed. [BR1725.R63A327 1975] 75-20039 ISBN 0-8161-6321-9 lib.bdg. : 8.95
1. Rogers, Dale Evans. 2. Sight-saving books. I. Title.

ROGERS, Dale Evans. 784'.092'4 B
The woman at the well. Boston, G. K. Hall, 1973 [c1970] 304 p. 25 cm. Large print ed. [BR1725.R63A33 1973] 73-9912 ISBN 0-8161-6135-6 8.95 (lib. bdg.)
1. Rogers, Dale Evans. 2. Sight-saving books. I. Title.

SANDERS, John Oswald, 1902- 232
Consider Him / by J. Oswald Sanders. Chicago : Moody Press, c1976. p. cm. Large print ed. [BT306.4.S24 1976] 76-15012 ISBN 0-8024-1613-6 pbk. : 2.95
1. Jesus Christ—Meditations. 2. Sight-saving books. I. Title.

STEARN, Jess. 133.8'092'4 B
A prophet in his own country; the story of the young Edgar Cayce. Boston, G. K. Hall, 1974. 575 p. 25 cm. Large print ed. [BF1027.C3S72 1974b] 74-14982 ISBN 0-8161-6239-5
1. Cayce, Edgar, 1877-1945. 2. Sight-saving books. I. Title.

STROBER, Gerald S. 269'.2'0924 B
Graham : a day in Billy's life / Gerald S. Strober. Boston : G. K. Hall, 1977, c1976. 294 p. ; 24 cm. Large print ed. [BV3782.G69S87 1977] 77-598 ISBN 0-8161-6468-1 : 10.95
1. Graham, William Franklin, 1918- 2. Sight-saving books.

TEN BOOM, Corrie. 269'.2'0924 B
Tramp for the Lord / by Corrie ten Boom, with Jamie Buckingham. Boston : G. K. Hall, 1974. xx, 305 p. 25 cm. Large print ed. [BR1725.T35A37 1974b] 74-20672 ISBN 0-8161-6259-X
1. Ten Boom, Corrie. 2. Sight-saving books. I. Buckingham, Jamie, joint author. II. Title.

Sign of Jonah.

EDWARDS, Richard Alan. 232.9
The sign of Jonah in the theology of the Evangelists and Q. London, S.C.M. Press, 1971. xi, 122 p. 22 cm. (Studies in Biblical theology. 2d series, 18) Bibliography: p.[111]-117. [BS2555.2.E33 1971b] 72-189247 ISBN 0-334-01499-9
1. Bible. N.T. Gospels—Criticism, interpretation, etc. 2. Sign of Jonah. 3. Q document (Biblical criticism) I. Title. II. Series.
Available from Allenson, 9.95, ISBN 0-8401-4068-1, pap. 7.45, ISBN 0-8401-3068-6

EDWARDS, Richard Alan. 232.96
The sign of Jonah in the theology of the Evangelists and Q. Naperville, Ill., A. R. Allenson [1971?] viii, 122 p. 22 cm. (Studies in Biblical theology, 2d ser., 18) Bibliography: p. [111]-117. [BS2555.2.E33] 74-153931 ISBN 0-8401-3068-6
1. Bible. N.T. Gospels—Criticism, interpretation, etc. 2. Sign of Jonah. I. Title. II. Series.

Signs and symbols.

DILLISTONE, Frederick 246
William, 1903-
Christianity and symbolism. Philadelphia, Westminster Press [1955] 320p. 22cm. [BL600.D5] 55-8598
1. Signs and symbols. 2. Symbolism. 3. Sacraments. I. Title.

MAUCK, Earle L.
Ten thousand coincidences; signs of the cross ... by Earle A. Mauck. [Baltimore] 1937- v. 23 1/2 cm. [CT275.M464553A3] 37-21818
I. Title. II. Title: Coincidences, Ten thousand.

Sihler, Wilhelm, 1801-1885.

SPITZ, Lewis 284'.1'0924 B
William, 1922-
Life in two worlds; biography of William Sihler, by Lewis W. Spitz. Saint Louis, Concordia Pub. House [1968] 199 p. 21 cm. Bibliographical references included in "Notes" (p. 178-191) [BX8080.S38S6] 68-13364
1. Sihler, Wilhelm, 1801-1885. I. Title.

Sikh devotional literature.

YOGIJI, Harbhajan Singh Khalsa. 294.6'4'3
The teachings of Yogi Bhajan / Siri Singh Sahib Bhai Sahib Harbhajan Singh Khalsa Yogiji. New York : Hawthorn Books, c1977. ix, 193 p. ; 21 cm. [BL2018.42.Y63 1977] 76-56526 ISBN 0-8015-7461-7 pbk. : 5.95
1. Sikh devotional literature. I. Title.

Sikh gurus—Biography.

ENGLE, Jon, 1948- 294.6'61'0922 B
Servants of God : lives of the Ten Sikh Gurus / by Jon Engle ; illustrated by Jonas Gerard. Franklin, N.H. : Sant Bani Ashram, 1980. 192 p., [1] leaf of plates : ports. ; 21 cm. Bibliography: p. 189-192. [BL2017.8.E53] 19 79-63457 ISBN 0-89142-035-5 pbk. : 6.00
1. Sikh gurus—Biography. I. Title.
Publishers Address: Sant Bani Ashram, Franklin, NH 03235

GUPTA, Hari Ram. 294.6'6'10922 B
History of Sikh gurus. New Delhi, U. C. Kapur [1973] xiv, 320 p. maps. 22 cm. Includes bibliographical references. [BL2017.8.G87] 73-906123
1. Sikh gurus—Biography. 2. Sikhism—History. I. Title.
Distributed by South Asia Books; 8.50

JOHAR, Surinder Singh. 294.6'61
Guru Tegh Bahadur : a biography / Surinder Singh Johar. New Delhi : Abhinav Publications, 1976 262 p., [1] leaf of plates : ill. ; 22 cm. Includes index. Bibliography: p. 245-249. [BL2017.9.T4J64] 75-908901 11.50
1. Tegh Bahadur, 9th guru of the Sikhs, 1621-1675. 2. Sikh gurus—Biography. I. Title.
Distributed by South Asia Books Columbia, Mo.

Sikh gurus—Biography—Addresses, Essays, lectures.

GERU Tegh Bahadur : 294.6'61 B
background and the supreme sacrifice : a collection of research articles / edited by Gurbachan Singh Talib. Patiala : Punjabi University, 1976. xvi, 250 p. ; 25 cm. (Guru Tegh Bahadur's martyrdom tercentenary memorial series) Includes bibliographical references. [BL2017.9.T4G86] 77-900595 Rs30.00
1. Tegh Bahadur, 9th guru of the Sikhs, 1621-1675—Addresses, essays, lectures. 2. Sikh gurus—Biography—Addresses, Essays, lectures. 3. Sikhism—Addresses essays, lectures. I. Talib, Gurbachan Singh, 1911- II. Series: Guru Tegh Bahadara tiji shahidi shatabadi prakashana lari.

Sikh shrines.

JOHAR, Surinder Singh. 294.6'3'5
The Sikh gurus and their shrines / Surinder Singh Johar. Delhi : Vivek Pub. Co., 1976. viii, 328, p., [8] leaves of plates : ill. ; 23 cm. Includes index. Bibliography: p. [309]-313. [BL2018.36.A1J63] 76-905134 Rs65.00
1. Sikh shrines. 2. Sikhism. I. Title.

Sikhism.

ADI-GRANTH, English 294.553
Sri Guru-Granth Sahib. English version. Tr. annotated by Gopal Singh. New York, Taplinger [1965, c.1962] 4v. 29cm. [BL2017.4] 65-22279 80.00 set,
I. Singh, Gopal, 1917- ed. and tr. II. Title.

ARCHER, John Clark, 1881-1957. 294.6'172
The Sikhs in relation to Hindus, Moslems, Christians, and Ahmadiyyas; a study in comparative religion. New York, Russell & Russell [1971, c1946] xi, 353 p. illus. 23 cm. Includes bibliographical references. [BL2018.15.A72 1971] 76-139895
1. Sikhism. 2. India—Religion. I. Title.

COLE, William Owen. 294.6
The Sikhs : their religious beliefs and practices / W. Owen Cole and Piara Singh Sambhi. London ; Boston : Routledge & K. Paul, 1978. xxvii, 210 p., [4] leaves of plates : ill. ; 23 cm. (Library of beliefs and practices) Includes index. Bibliography: p. 196-204. [BL2018.C65] 78-315607 ISBN 0-7100-8842-6 : 16.50 ISBN 0-7100-8843-4 pbk. : 8.50
1. Sikhism. I. Sambhi, Piara Singh, joint author. II. Title. III. Series.

MACAULIFFE, Max Arthur, 1842-1913 294.553
The Sikh religion, its gurus. sacred writings, and authors Delhi, S. Chand [1963] 6v. in 3 (various p.) illus. 23cm. Includes tr. of the Adi-Granth. The rags of the Granth Sahib (vol. 5. p. [333]-351) are unaccompanied melodies. [BL2018.M313 1963] SA 66 set of 3v., 21.00
1. Sikhism. 2. India—Religion. I. Adi-Granth. II. Title.

MCLEOD, W. H. 294.5'53'0924 B
Guru Nanak and the Sikh religion [by] W. H. McLeod. Oxford, Clarendon P., 1968. xii, 259 p. 24 cm. Bibliography: p. 233-240. [BL2017.9.N3M27] 74-373992 50/-
1. Nanak, 1st guru of the Sikhs, 1469-1538. 2. Sikhism. I. Title.

PHILOSOPHY of Sikhism. 294.5'53
[2d ed.] Delhi, Sterling Pubs., 1966. 316p. 23cm. Bibl. [BL2018.S534 1966] [PL480:I-E7866] SA67 7.50
1. Sikhism. 2. Philosophy, Sikh. I. Singh, Sher, Gyani
American distributor: Verry, Mystic, Conn.

Sikhism—Addresses, essays, lectures.

MCLEOD W H 294.6
The evolution of the Sikh community : five essays / W. H. McLeod. Delhi : Oxford University Press, 1975[i.e.1976] viii, 118 p. ; 22 cm. Includes index. Bibliography: p. [111]-114. [BL2018.M317] 76-900871 8.00
1. Sikhism—Addresses, essays, lectures. I. Title.
Distributed by Oxford, New York.

Sikhism—History

SINGH, Harbans, 1907- 294.55309
The heritage of the Sikh. New York, Asia Pub. [dist. Taplinger, 1965, c.1964] 219p. 25cm. [BL2017.6.S52] 65-16114 13.00
1. Sikhism—Hist. I. Title.

Sikhs.

ADI-GRANTH. 294.553
Selections from the sacred writings of the Sikhs. Translated by Trilochan Singh [and others] Revised by George S. Fraser. Introd. by S. Radhakrishnan. Foreword by Arnold Toynbee. New York, Macmillan, 1960. 288 p. 23 cm. (UNESCO collection of representative works: Indian series) "Might be described as an authorized English version of some of the sacred hymns of the Sikh scriptures." Contents.Contents.—Selections from the Adi Guru Granth.—Selections from the Dasm Granth. [BL2020.S5A54 1960] 60-4217
I. Daswen Padshah ka Granth. II. Singh, Trilochan, tr. III. Title. IV. Series.

ARCHER, John Clark, 1881-
The Sikhs in relation to Hindus, Moslems, Christians, and Ahmadiyyas. A study in comparative religion, by John Clark Archer. [Princeton university press, 1946. xi, 353 p. plates. 23 cm. Bibliographical foot-notes. A 46
1. Sikhs. 2. India—Religion. I. Title.

ARJUN, 5th guru of the Sikhs, 1563-1606. 294.553
The psalm of peace; an English translation of Guru Arjun's Sukhmani, by Teja Singh. With a foreword by Nicholas Roerich. [Bombay, New York] Indian Branch, Oxford University Press [1950] xvii, 122 p. 19 cm. "Sukhmanl ... [is included] in the Holy Granth." [BL2020.S5A723] 52-4900
1. Sikhs. I. Singh, Teja. tr. II. Title.

CUNNINGHAM, Joseph Davey, 1812-1851. 299
A history of the Sikhs, from the origin of the nation to the battles of the Sutlej. by Joseph Davey Cunningham ... ed by H. L. O. Garrett ... New and rev. ed. with two maps. London, New York [etc.] H. Milford, Oxford university press, 1918. iii, 429 p. front., fold. map. fold. geneal tab. 20 cm. "Biographical note on the Cunningham family": p. [xiv]-xvi. Bibliography: p. [xviii]-xix. [DS485.P2C9 1918] 19-14932
1. Sikhs. I. Garrett, Herbert Leonard Offley, 1881- ed. II. Title.

MACAULIFFE, Max Arthur, 1842-1913, tr. 294.
The Sikh religion, its gurus, sacred writings and authors, by Max Arthur Macauliffe ... Oxford, Clarendon press, 1909. 6 v. front. (ports.) plates. 22 cm. Translations of the Granth Sahib, or sacred book of the Sikhs, interspersed in the lives of the gurus, with historical and critical introduction. [BL2020.S5M3] 10-9301
1. Sikhs. I. Adi-Granth. II. Title.

TEJA SINGH. 294.553
Sikhism, its ideals and institutions, by Teja Singh ... London, New York [etc.] Longmans, Green & co., ltd., 1938. vi p., 1 l., 146 p. 19 cm. "A collection of essays ... on the different essential features of Sikhism."--Pref. [BL2020.S5T4] 39-13501
1. Sikhs. I. Title.

THIND, Bhagat Singh, 1892- 294.553
Divine wisdom ... by Bhagat Singh Thind ... Salt Lake City [c1925] v. front. (port., v. 2) plates. 20 1/2 cm. [BL2020.S5T48] 25-18401
1. Sikhs. I. Title.

THIND, Bhagat Singh, 1892- 294.553
Radiant road to reality; tested science of religion, by Dr. Bhagat Singh Thind. New York, 1939. xx p., 1 l., 221 p. front., ports. 18 1/2 cm. [BL2020.S5T5] 39-30786
1. Sikhs. I. Title.

Sikhs—Addresses, essays, lectures.

MCLEOD, W. H. 294.6'0954'552
The evolution of the Sikh community : five essays / W. H. McLeod. Oxford : Clarendon Press, 1976. viii, 119 p. ; 23 cm. Includes index. Bibliography: p. [111]-114. [DS432.S5M25] 76-369262 ISBN 0-19-826529-8 : 8.75
1. Sikhs—Addresses, essays, lectures. 2. Sikhism—Addresses, essays, lectures. I. Title.
Distributed by Oxford University Press N.Y. N.Y.

Sikhs in India—Biography—Juvenile literature.

SCOTTI, Juliet. 294.6'8'30924 B
Kirpal Singh : the story of a saint / compiled and adapted for children by Juliet Scotti and Ricki Linksman ; ill. by Valerie Tarrant. 1st ed. [Bowling Green, Va.] : Sawan Kirpal Publications, 1977. xi, 92, [2] p. : ill. ; 28 cm. (Children's series ; no. 1) Bibliography: p. [94] Relates episodes from the life of Kirpal Singh, a spiritual leader who became president of the World Fellowship of Religions. [BL2017.9.S53S35] 92 77-79840 ISBN 0-918224-05-5 pbk. : 3.95
1. Kirpal Singh, 1894-1974—Juvenile literature. 2. [Kirpal Singh, 1894-1974.] 3. Sikhs in India—Biography—Juvenile literature. 4. [Sikhs] I. Linksman, Ricki, 1952- joint author. II. Tarrant, Valerie, 1951- III. Title.

Siksika Indians—Religion and mythology.

MCCRACKEN, Harold, 1894- 299'.7
A heritage of the Blackfeet [by] Harold McCracken and Paul Dyck. [Cody, Wyo., Buffalo Bill Historical Center, 1972] 22 p. illus. 26 cm. ([Buffalo Bill Historical Center] Educational series, no. 1) Cover title. Contents.Contents.—A Blackfoot sacred ceremony, preserved, by H. McCracken.—The Thunder Medicine Pipe of the Blackfeet people, by P. Dyck.—Boy Chief's Thunder Medicine Pipe, by P. Dyck. [E99.S54M27] 72-80570
1. Siksika Indians—Religion and mythology. 2. Siksika Indians—Rites and ceremonies. 3. [Siksika Indians—Religion and mythology.] 4. [Siksika Indians—Rites and ceremonies.] I. Dyck, Paul, 1917- II. Title. III. Series.

WISSLER, Clark, 1870-1947. 299'.7
Mythology of the Blackfoot Indians / by Clark Wissler and D. C. Duvall. New York : AMS Press, 1976 163 p. ; 23 cm. Reprint of the 1909 ed. published by order of the Trustees of the American Museum of Natural History, New York, which was issued as v. 2, pt. 1 of the Museum's Anthropological papers. Includes bibliographical references. [E99.S54W525 1975] 74-9019 ISBN 0-404-11916-6 : 11.50
1. Siksika Indians—Religion and mythology. 2. Indians of North America—Great Plains—Religion and mythology. I. Duvall, D. C., joint author. II. Title. III. Series: American Museum of Natural History, New York. Anthropological papers ; v. 2, pt. 1.

Silberman, Lou H.—Addresses, essays, lectures.

THE Divine helmsman : 296.3'11
studies on God's control of human events, presented to Lou H. Silberman / edited by James L. Crenshaw and Samuel Sandmel. New York : KTAV Pub. House, c1980. xviii, 273 p. : port. ; 24 cm. Contents.Contents.—A Bibliography of Lou Silberman's writings.—Crenshaw, J. L. The birth of skepticism in ancient Israel.—Harrelson, W. Ezra among the wicked in 2 Esdras 10.—Keck, L. E. The law and "the law of sin and death" (Rom 8:1-4).—Meyer, P. W. Romans10:4 and the end of the law.—Sandmel S. Some comments on providence in Philo.—Knight, D. A. Jeremiah and the dimensions of the moral life.—Berg, S. B. After the exile.—Talbert, C. H. Prophecies of future greatness.—Greenberg, M. The vision of Jerusalem in Ezekiel 8-11.—Patte, D. Charting the way of the helmsman on the high seas.—Fackenheim, E. L. New hearts and the old covenant.Hauer, C., Jr. When history stops.—Samuelson, N. Causation and choice in the philosophy of Ibn Daud.—Mills, L. O. The self as helmsman. Includes bibliographical references and index. [BM645.P7D58] 19 79-29644 ISBN 0-87068-700-X : 20.00
1. Silberman, Lou H.—Addresses, essays, lectures. 2. Bible—Criticism and interpretation, etc.—Addresses, essays, lectures. 3. Providence and government of God (Judaism)—Addresses, essays, lectures. I. Silberman, Lou H. II. Crenshaw, James L. III. Sandmel, Samuel.

Silence.

OATES, Wayne Edward, 1917- 248'.3
Nurturing silence in a noisy heart / Wayne E. Oates. 1st ed. Garden City, N.Y. : Doubleday, 1979. 134 p. ; 22 cm. "A Doubleday-Galilee original." Includes index. Bibliography: p. [127]-132. [BJ1499.S5O2] 78-20089 ISBN 0-385-14787-2 : 7.95
1. Silence. I. Title.

PARAMANANDA, swami, 1883- 179
Creative power of silence, by Swami Paramananda ... Boston, Mass., The Vedanta centre; La Crescenta, Calif., Ananda Ashrama [c1923] 82 p. 19 cm. (His Practical series, no. 5) "Reprinted from the Vedanta monthly 'The message of the East'." [B132.V3P288] 34-5845
1. Silence. I. Title.

WATHEN, Ambrose G., 1931- 255'.1'06
Silence; the meaning of silence in the rule of St. Benedict [by] Ambrose G. Wathen. Washington, Cistercian Publications, 1973. xviii, 240 p. illus. 23 cm. (Cistercian studies series, no. 22) Originally presented as the author's thesis, St. Paul University, Ottawa. Bibliography: p. 235-240. [BX3004.Z5W37 1973] 74-188556 ISBN 0-87907-822-7
1. Benedictus, Saint, Abbot of Monte Cassino. Regula. 2. Silence. I. Title. II. Series.

Sill, Sterling W.

SILL, Sterling W. 289.3'3 B
The nine lives of Sterling W. Sill : an autobiography. Bountiful, Utah : Horizon Publishers, c1979. 286 p. ; 24 cm. Includes

index. [BX8695.S38A36] 80-111657 ISBN 0-88290-118-4 : 6.50
1. Sill, Sterling W. 2. Mormons and Mormonism in the United States—Biography. 3. Insurance—United States—Agents—Biography. I. Title.

Silva, Antonio Jose da, 1705-1739.

KOHUT, George Alexander, 1874-1933. 296.
Jewish martyrs of the inquisition in South America. By George Alexander Kohut ... Baltimore, The Friedenwald company, 1895. 2 p. l., 87 p. 24 cm. "Reprinted from the Publications of the American Jewish historical society, no. 4, 1895." Includes sketch of Antonio Jose da Silva (p. 35-50) and extracts from various authorities (p. 59-81) "Bibliography of works relating to Antonio Jose da Silva": p. 81-84. [F2239.J5K7] 3-20928
1. Silva, Antonio Jose da, 1705-1739. 2. Jews in South America. 3. Inquisition. South America. 4. Maranos in South America. I. Title.

Silvan, Matteo.

SILVAN, Matteo. 282'.092'4 B
Lazarus, come out! : the story of my life / Matthew Silvan ; [translated from the original Italian edition, Quella "violenza" di Dio ... storia della mia vita by Vera Giannini]. New York : New City Press, c1981. 224 p. ; 21 cm. [BX4705.S6325A3413] 19 80-82599 ISBN 0-911782-36-2 (pbk.) : 5.95
1. Silvan, Matteo. 2. Catholics—Italy—Biography. I. [Quella violenza di Dio.] English II. Title.
Publisher's address: 206 Skillman Ave., Brooklyn, NY 11211

Silver, Abba Hillel, 1893-

SILVER, Daniel Jeremy, ed. 296.082
In the time of harvest, essays in honor of Abba Hillel Silver on the occasion of his 70th birthday. Board of eds.: Solomon B. Freehof [others] New York Macmillan [1963] viii, 459p. port. 26cm. Bibl. 62-21613 10.00
1. Silver, Abba Hillel, 1893- 2. Judaism—Addresses, essays, lectures. 3. Jews—Hist.—Addresses, essays, lectures. I. Title.

Simeon, Charles, 1759-1836.

HOPKINS, Hugh Alexander Evan. 283'.092'4 B
Charles Simeon of Cambridge / Hugh Evan Hopkins. [Grand Rapids, Mich.] : W. B. Eerdmans Pub. Co., 1977. 236 p. : ill. (on lining paper) ; 25 cm. Includes bibliographical references and index. [BX5199.S55H66 1977] 77-153375 ISBN 0-8028-3498-1 : 7.95
1. Simeon, Charles, 1759-1836. 2. Church of England—Clergy—Biography. 3. Clergy—England—Cambridge—Biography. 4. Cambridge, Eng.—Biography. I. Title.

SIMEON, Charles, 1759-1836. 922.
A faithful servant; the life and labors of the Rev. Charles Simeon. Selected from the larger work of Rev. William Carus. By Rt. Rev. William Meade, D.D. New York, Depository of Protestant Episcopal society for promotion of evangelical knowledge, 1853. xi, [13]-114 p. 19 1/2 cm. Contains selections from the author's writings and correspondence. [BX5995.S36A33] 35-37792
I. Carus, William, 1804-1891, ed. II. Meade, William, bp., 1789-1862, comp. III. Title.

SIMEON, Charles, 1759-1836. 922.342
Memoirs of the life of the Rev. Charles Simeon... With a selection from his writings and correspondence. Edited by the Rev. William Carus...The American edition, edited by the Right Rev. Chas. P. McIlvaine... New York, Pittsburgh, R. Carter 1847. xxvii, 491 p. front. (port.) 23 1/2 cm. "Recollections of the Rev. Charles Simeon. By the Right Rev. Daniel Wilson": p. [484] [BX5199.S55A3 1847] 33-24798
I. Carus, William, 1804-1891, ed. II. McIlvaine, Charles Pettit, bp., 1799-1873, ed. III. Wilson, Daniel, bp., 1778-1838. IV. Title.

SIMEON, Charles, 1759-1836. 922.342
*Memoirs of the life of the Rev. Charles Simeon ...*with a selection from his writings and correspondence. Edited by the Rev. William Carus...The American edition, edited by the Right Rev. Chas. P. McIlvaine... New York, R. Carter & brothers, 1852. xxvii, 491 p. front. (port.) 23 cm. "Recollections of the Rev. Charles Simeon. By the Right Rev. Daniel Wilson": p. [484]-491. [BX5199.S55A3 1852] 33-24799
I. Carus, William, 1804-1891, ed. II. McIlvaine, Charles Pettit, bp., 1799-1873, ed. III. Wilson, Daniel, bp., 1778-1858. IV. Title.

SMYTH, Charles Hugh Egerton, 1903- 922.342
Simeon & church order; a study of the origins of the evangelical revival in Cambridge in th eighteenth century ... by Charles Smyth ... Cambridge [Eng.] The University press, 1940. xx, 315, [1] p. front., plates, ports. 22 cm. (The Birkbeck lectures for 1937-8) "Select bibliography": p. xix-xx. [BX5199.S55S5] 41-10795
1. Simeon, Charles, 1759-1836. 2. Evangelical revival. 3. Evangelicalism—Church of England. 4. Church of England—Government. I. Title.

Simhat Torah — Juvenile literature.

SIMON, Norma. 296.439
Simhat Torah. Illus. by Ayala Gordon. [New York] United Synagogue Commission on Jewish Education, c1960. unpaged. illus. 25 cm. [BM695.S6S5] 60-3736
1. Simhat Torah — Juvenile literature. I. Title.

Simma, Maria, 1915-

SIMMA, Maria, 1915- 248'.2
My personal experiences with the poor souls / Maria Simma. Chicago : Franciscan Herald Press, [1978] p. cm. Translation of Meine Erlebnisse mit Armen Seelen. [BX4705.S6355A313] 78-16270 ISBN 0-8199-0744-8 : 7.95
1. Simma, Maria, 1915- 2. Purgatory. 3. Spiritualism. I. Title.

Simmons, James B., d. 1905.

MACARTHUR, Robert Stuart, 1841-
A foundation builder; sketches in the life of Rev. James B. Simmons, D.D., comp. by Robert Stuart MacArthur ... pub. under the direction of the trustees of Simmons college, Abilene, Texas ... New York, Chicago [etc.] Fleming H. Revell company [c1911] 141 p. front., illus., plates, ports. 19 1/2 cm. $1.00 11-27168
I. Simmons, James B., d. 1905. II. Title.

MACARTHUR, Robert Stuart, 1841-1923. 922.
A foundation builder; sketches in the life of Rev. James B. Simmons, D.D., compiled by Robert Stuart MacArthur ... published under the direction of the trustees of Simmons college, Abilene, Texas ... New York, Chicago [etc.] Fleming H. Revell company [1911] 141 p. front., illus., plates, ports. 19 1/2 cm. [BX6495.S5M3] 11-27168
1. Simmons, James B., d. 1905. I. Title.

Simms, Florence, 1873-1923.

ROBERTS, Richard, 1874- 922
Florence Simms; a biography, by Richard Roberts. New York, The Woman's press, 1926. 292 p. front. (port.) 19 cm. [BV1370.S5R6] 26-20263
1. Simms, Florence, 1873-1923. I. Title.

Simon Stock, Saint, 1165?-1265.

CARMELITES. Third Order. 2d National Conference, Chicago and Englewood, N. J., 1949 271.73
Take this scapular! Commemorating the seventh centenary of the brown scapular given to St. Simon Stock, prior general of the Carmelites, on July16, 1251. [Conferences given April 23, 24, 30, and May 1, 1949] by Carmelite fathers and tertiaries. Chicago, Carmelite Third Order Press, 1949. 270 p. illus. 19 cm. Biblioigraphy: p. 266-270. [BX2310.S3C3 1949] 50-28633
1. Simon Stock, Saint, 1165?-1265. 2. Mary, Virgin. 3. Scapulars. I. Title.

ERNEST, Brother, 1897- 922.242
Our Lady comes to Newenham; a story of St. Simon Stock and the scapular. Illus. by Mary Barnet. Notre Dame, Ind., Dujarie Press [1951] 87 p. illus. 24 cm. [BX4700.S53E7] 52-16006
1. Simon Stock, Saint, 1165?-1265. 2. Carmelites. I. Title.

MAGENNIS, Peter Elias, father, 1868- 922.
The life of St. Simon Stock, by the Most Rev. P. E. Magennis... New York City, The Carmelite press [192-?] 3 p. l., 9-79 p. incl. front. (port.) 18 cm. [BX4700.S53M3] 42-30172
1. Simon Stock, Saint, 1165?-1265. I. Title.

Simony.

WEBER, Nicholas Aloysius, 1876-
A history of simony in the Christian church, from the beginning to the death of Charlemagne (814) ... by the Reverend N. A. Weber ... Baltimore, J. H. Furst company, 1909. xi, 254, 17 p. 20 cm. Thesis (D.TH.)--Catholic university of America, Washington, D.C., 1909. Bibliography: p. 243-248. [BV779.W4] 9-12887
1. Simony. I. Title.

Simplicity.

COOPER, John Charles. 248.4
The joy of the plain life / John Charles Cooper. Nashville, TN : Impact Books, c1981. 159 p. ; 21 cm. Bibliography: p. 155-159. [BJ1496.C67] 19 81-47070 ISBN 0-914850-62-8 pbk. : 5.95
1. Simplicity. 2. Christian life—1960- I. Title.
Publisher's address: P.O.Box 1094 San Luis Obispo, CA 93406

ELLER, Vernard. 248'.4
The simple life; the Christian stance toward possessions, as taught by Jesus, interpreted by Kierkegaard. Grand Rapids, Mich., W. B. Eerdmans Pub. Co. [1973] 122 p. 21 cm. Includes bibliographical references. [BJ1496.E36] 73-6589 ISBN 0-8028-1537-5 2.25
1. Jesus Christ—Teachings. 2. Kierkegaard, Soren Aabye, 1813-1855. 3. Simplicity. I. Title.

FINNERTY, Adam, 1944- 261.8
No more plastic Jesus : global justice and Christian lifestyle / Adam Finnerty. Maryknoll, N.Y. : Orbis Books, 1977c1976 p. cm. Bibliography: p. Discusses the seriousness of the worldwide dilemma of hunger, depletion of natural resources, and pollution and suggests ways to "reclaim the planet", particularly ways that the church as an institution can help and also ways responsive adults in adopting a simple, truly Christian lifestyle can contribute to global change. [BJ1496.F5] 76-13174 ISBN 0-88344-340-6 : 8.95 ISBN 0-88344-341-4 pbk. : 3.95
1. Simplicity. 2. Church and social problems. 3. Civilization, Modern—1950- 4. [Human ecology.] 5. [Environmental policy.] 6. [Church and social problems.] 7. [Conduct of life.] 8. [Civilization, Modern—1950-] I. Title.

FINNERTY, Adam Daniel, 1944- 261.8
No more plastic Jesus : global justice and christian lifestyles / Adam Finnerty. New York : Dutton, 1978, c1977. 223p. ; 21 cm. (A Dutton paperback) [BJ1496.5] ISBN 0-525-47496-X pbk. : 3.95
1. Simplicity. 2. Church and social problems. 3. Civilization, Modern — 1950- I. Title.
L.C. card no. for 1977 Orbis Books ed.: 76-13174.

FOSTER, Richard J. 234'.1
Freedom of simplicity / Richard J. Foster. 1st ed. San Francisco : Harper & Row, c1981. viii, 200 p. ; 22 cm. Includes bibliographical references and indexes. [BJ1496.F67 1981] 19 80-8351 ISBN 0-06-062832-4 : 9.95
1. Simplicity. I. Title.

GISH, Arthur G. 261.8
Beyond the rat race [by] Arthur G. Gish. Scottdale, Pa., Herald Press [1973] 192 p. 18 cm. Sequel to The New Left and Christian radicalism. Bibliography: p. 183-189. [BJ1496.G57] 73-9336 ISBN 0-8361-1724-7 1.45 (pbk.)
1. Simplicity. I. Title.

GISH, Arthur G. 261.8
Beyond the rat race [by] Arthur G. Gish. Scottdale, Pa., Herald Press [1973] 192 p. 18 cm. Sequel to The New Left and Christian radicalism. Bibliography: p. 183-189. [BJ1496.G57] 73-9336 ISBN 0-8361-1724-7 1.45
1. Simplicity. I. Title.

LEGTERS, Leonard L. 248
The simplicity of the spirit-filled life, by L. L. Legters ... Philadelphia, Penna., Christian life literature fund [c1930] 69 p. 19 cm. [BV4501.L42] 30-20258
I. Title.

PECK, George Terhune, 1916- 248'.48'96
Simplicity; a rich Quaker's view, by George Peck. [Wallingford, Pa., Pendle Hill, 1973] 32 p. 20 cm. (Pendle Hill pamphlet, 189) [BJ1496.P4] 72-97851 ISBN 0-87574-189-4 0.70
1. Simplicity.

SMITH-DURLAND, Eugenia, 1935- 248'.4
Voluntary simplicity : study-action guide / prepared for Alternatives by Eugenia Smith-Durland. [Bloomington, Ind. : Alternatives, 1978] iii, 95 p. : ill. ; 22 cm. Cover title. Includes bibliographical references. [BJ1496.S63] 78-60408 ISBN 0-914966-05-7 pbk. : 3.00
1. Simplicity. 2. Holidays. I. Alternatives (Corporation) II. Title.

ZIEGLER, Edward Krusen, 1903- 248'.48'65
Simple living / Edward K. Ziegler. Elgin, Ill. : Brethren Press, 1974. 127 p. ; 18 cm. Bibliography: p. 124-127. [BJ1496.Z53] 74-8716 ISBN 0-87178-791-1 : 1.25
1. Simplicity. I. Title.

Simplicity—Addresses, essays, lectures.

LIVING more simply : 241'.4
Biblical principles & practical models / edited by Ronald J. Sider. Downers Grove, Ill. : Inter-Varsity Press, c1980. 206 p. ; 21 cm. Includes bibliographical references. [BJ1496.L58] 79-3634 ISBN 0-87784-808-4 pbk. : 4.95 4.95
1. Simplicity—Addresses, essays, lectures. I. Sider, Ronald J.

Simplicity—Religious aspects.

MATTISON, Judith N. 242
Help me adapt, Lord : discovering new blessings while learning to live with less / Judith Mattison. Minneapolis : Augsburg Pub. House, c1981. 96 p. : ill. ; 20 cm. [BJ1496.M37] 19 80-67797 ISBN 0-8066-1859-0 pbk. : 4.50
1. Simplicity—Religious aspects. 2. Christian life—1960- I. Title.

ROBBINS, Howard Chandler, 1876- 270
Simplicity toward Christ, by Howard Chandler Robbins ... New York, C. Scribner's sons, 1927. viii p., 1 l., 230 p. 20 cm. [BR125.R629] 27-22724
I. Title.

Simplicity—Religious aspects—Christianity.

GIBSON, William E. 248.4
A covenant group for lifestyle assessment : revised participant's manual / by William E. Gibson and the Eco-Justice Task Force. New York : United Presbyterian Program Agency, 1981. vi, 121 p. : ill. ; 28 cm. [BV4647.S48G54 1981] 19 82-118775 4.00 (pbk.)

1. Simplicity—Religious aspects—Christianity. 2. Christian life—1960- 3. Church group work. I. Center for Religion, Ethics, and Social Policy (U.S.). Eco-Justice Task Force. II. Title.

Simpson, Albert Benjamin, 1843-1919.

SIMPSON, Albert B., 1844-
We would see Jesus, by Rev. A. B. Simpson. New York, The Alliance press company [c1910] [64] p. 18 cm. $0.25 11-19552
I. Title.

SIMPSON, Albert B., 1844-
When the Comforter came, by Rev. A. B. Simpson. New York, The Alliance press company [c1911] [128] p. 19 cm. $0.60 11-19547
I. Title.

SIMPSON, Albert B., 1844- 230
1919.
The four-fold Gospel, by Rev. A. B. Simpson, D.D., with an introduction by Rev. Fredric H. Senft ... New York, N.Y., Christian alliance publishing company [c1925] 128 p. 18 cm. (On cover: The Alliance colportage series) [BT77.S55] 25-18130
I. Title.

THOMPSON, Albert Edward, 285.
1870-
The life of A. B. Simpson ... by A. E. Thompson, M.A., with special chapters by Paul Rader, James M. Gray, D.D., J. Gregory Mantle, D.D., R. H. Glover, M.D., Kenneth Mackenzie, F. H. Senft, B.A., W. M. Turnbull, D.D. ... Brooklyn, N.Y., The Christian alliance publishing company [c1920] 2 p. l., ix-xiv p., 1 l., 300 p. front., ports. 20 1/2 cm. "Official authorized edition." [BX9225.S45T5] 26-9940
1. Simpson, Albert Benjamin, 1844-1919. 2. Christian and missionary alliance. I. Title.

TOZER, Aiden Wilson, 1897- 922.89
Wingspread; Albert B. Simpson, a study in spiritual altitude, By A. W. Tozer. Centenary ed. Harrisburg, Pa., Christian publications incorporated, 1943. 143 p. front. (port.) 19 1/2 cm. [BX6700.C3S57] 43-16802
1. Simpson, Albert Benjamin, 1843-1919. I. Title.

Simpson, John, 1793-1860.

SIMPSON, John Thomas, 1870- 929.2
ed.
History of the Reverend John Simpson. [Red Bank? N.J.] 1956. 139 p. illus. 29 cm. [BX8495.S548S5] 61-33013
1. Simpson, John, 1793-1860. 2. Simpson family. I. Title.

Simpson, Matthew, bp., 1811-1864.

CLARK, Robert Donald, 922.773
1910-
The life of Matthew Simpson. New York, Macmillan, 1956. xi, 344 p. 22 cm. Bibliographical references included in "Notes" (p. 307-333) [BX8495.S55C55] 56-13618
1. Simpson, Matthew, Bp., 1811-1884.

CROOKS, George Richard, 922.773
1822-1897.
The life of Bishop Matthew Simpson, of the Methodist Episcopal church, by George R. Crooks ... New York, Harper & brothers, 1890. xii p., 1 l., 542 p. front., illus., plates, ports., facsims. (1 double) 23 cm. [BX8495.S55C7] 33-37373
I. Simpson, Matthew, bp., 1811-1884. II. Title.

WILSON, Clarence True, 1872- 922.
Matthew Simpson, patriot, preacher, prophet, by Clarence True Wilson. New York, Cincinnati [etc.] The Methodist book concern [c1929] 133 p. front. (port.) 16 1/2 cm. [BX8495.S95W5] 29-20527
1. Simpson, Matthew, bp., 1811-1864. I. Title.

Simpson, William Sparrow, 1828-1897.

SIMPSON, William John 922.342
Sparrow, 1859-
Memoir of the Rev. W. Sparrow Simpson, D.D., rector of St. Vedast and sub-dean of St. Paul's cathedral; compiled and edited by W. J. Sparrow Simpson ... London, New York [etc.] Longmans Green and co., 1899. 4 p. l., 203, [1] p. front. (port.) plates. 19 1/2 cm. "Appendix of literary work": p. [193]-200. [BX5199.S547A3] 2-545
1. Simpson, William Sparrow, 1828-1897. I. Title.

Sims, Walter Hines, comp.

QUINN, Eugene F 245'.2
A hymnal concordance. Compiled by Eugene F. Quinn. Louisville, Ky., Personalized Printing [1966] 1 v. (unpaged) 22 cm. [BV380.Q5] 68-1083
1. Sims, W. Hines, comp. The Baptist hymnal. 2. Hymns, English—Indexes. I. Title.

Sin.

ANDROS, Thomas, 1759-1845. 233.2
An essay in which the doctrine of a positive divine efficiency exciting the will of men to sin, as held by some modern writers, is candidly discussed, and shown to be 1. Unphilosophical. 2. Inconsistent with the plain and obvious sense of the Holy Scriptures, and of course a departure from the simplicity of the gospel; and 3. A novel doctrine, utterly repugnant to the faith of the Christian church in all past ages. By Thomas Andros ... Boston: Printed for Samuel T. Armstrong, by Crocker & Brewster, no. 50, Cornhill, July, 1820. xii, 13-132 p. 17 1/2 cm. [B5715.A2] 40-24801
1. Sin. I. Title.

BARBOUR, Clifford Edward. 233
Sin and the new psychology [by] Clifford E. Barbour ... New York [etc.] The Abingdon press [c1930] 260 p. 19 1/2 cm. [BT715.B3] 20-28858
1. Sin 2. Psychology, Religious. 3. Psychoanalysis. I. Title.

BERKOUWER, Gerrit 233'.2
Cornelis, 1903-
Sin, by G. C. Berkouwer. [Translated by Philip C. Holtrop] Grand Rapids, Eerdmans [1971] 599 p. 23 cm. (His Studies in dogmatics) Translation of De Zonde, originally published in 2 v. Includes bibliographical references. [BT715.B4513] 73-27796 9.95
1. Sin.

BICKNELL, Edward John, 1882- 233.
The Christian idea of sin and original sin in the light of modern knowledge; being the Pringle-Stuart lectures for 1921 delivered at Keble college, Oxford, by E. J. Bicknell ... London, New York [etc.] Longmans, Green, and co., 1922. x, 129 p. 19 cm. (Pringle-Stuart lectures for 1921) [BT715.B6] 22-24832
1. Sin. 2. Psychology. I. Title.

BRUNKEN, Juergen.
The seven human mountains; or, The personification of sin. Copyrighted ... by Juergen Brunken. [Cordell, Okl., Printed by J. Brunken] c1916. 96 p. 23 cm. 16-17885
I. Title. II. Title: The personification of sin.

*BUSCH, Fred W. 233
The case against original sin; Minerva presents a diploma to Eve. New York, Pageant [c.1964] 124p. 22cm. 2.75
I. Title.

CAIE, Norman Macleod. 283.
The seven deadly sins, by Rev. Norman Macleod Caie ... New York, George H. Doran company [c1923] 96 p. 20 cm. [BV4625.C3] 23-4576 1.00
I. Title.

CARRADINE, Beverly.
The old man. By Rev. B. Carradine ... Ouisville, Ky., Pentecostal pub. co. [c1896] 270 p. incl. front. (port.) 19 cm. On "whether or not there is a principle or

CULPEPPER, John B.
Sin, by Rev. J. B. Culpepper. Louisville, Ky., Pentecostal publishing[company [c1914] 91 p. 19 cm. 14-11779 0.25
I. Title.

CHERBONNIER, Edmond La 233.2
Beaume, 1918-
Hardness of heart; a contemporary interpretation of the doctrine of sin. [1st ed.] Garden City, N. Y., Doubleday, 1955. 188p. 22cm. (Christian faith series) [BT701.C47] 55-5500
1. Sin. I. Title.

CLARK, Peter, 1693-1768. 233.
The Scripture-doctrine of original sin, stated and defended. In a summer-morning's conversation, between a minister and a neighbour. Con- taining remarks on a late anonymous pamphlet entitle, "A winter-evening's conversation, upon the doctrine of original sin, between a minister and three of his neighbours, accidentally met", &c. With an appendix, in reply to a supplement in the New-Haven edition to that pamphlet. By Peter Clark...Recommended in a preface by several ministers... Boston, Printed and sold by S. Kneeland, opposite to the Probate office in Queen-street, 1758. 2 p. l., 132, 24 p. 18 cm. Imperfect: p. 23-24 wanting. [BT720.W4C6 1758] 22-12667
1. Sip. 2. Webster, Samuel, 1719-1796. A winter-evening's conversation. I. Title.

CLARKE, Andral Wellington, 210
1896-
What is the unpardonable sin? By A. Wellington Clarke, TH.B. Boston, Mass., Meador publishing company [c1929] 64 p. 19 1/2 cm. [BT721.C6] 30-9736
1. Sin. I. Title.

COOK, E.W. 233.
The origin of sin, and its relations to God and the universe, by Rev. E.W. Cook ... New York and London, Funk & Wagnalls company, 1899. xvii, 19-387 p. 19 1/2 cm. [BT715.C75] 99-1103
1. Sin. 2. Future punishment. I. Title.

DEWEESE, Henry Harrison
Coercion and perversion; or, Primeval degenerates, by H. H. De Weese ... Columbus, O., 1904. 90 p. 20 cm. 5-2409
I. Title.

DICKSON, Mathes Daniel. 233.2
The way of the transgressor, by Rev. Mathes Daniel Dickson ... New York, N.Y., The Hobson book press, 1946. 3 p. l., ix-xvii, [1], 323 p. incl. front., 1 illus. 22 cm. [BV4625.D5] 46-20760
1. Sin. I. Title.

DOGGETT, Marshall 233.2
Wellington, 1855-
The tragedy of sin, by Rev. M. W. Doggett ... Kingsport. Tenn., Southern publishers, inc. [c1935] ix, 175 p. 20 cm. [BT715.D6] 35-1825
1. Sin. 2. Eschatology. I. Title.

ECK, Herbert Vincent Shortgrave.
Sin, by the Rev. H. V. S. Eck... London, New York [etc.] Longmans, Green & co., 1907. xii, 241 p. 19 1/2 cm. (Half-title: The Oxford library of practical theology...) A21
1. Sin. I. Title.

EDWARDS, Jonathan, 1703- 233.
1758.
The great Christian doctrine of original sin defended; evidences of it's truth produced, and arguments to the contrary answered. Containing, in particular, A reply to the objections and arguings of Dr. John Taylor, in his book, intitled, "The Scripture-doctrine of original sin proposed to free and candid examination", &c. By the late Reverend and learned Jonathan Edwards ... Boston, New-England: Printed and Sold by S. Kneeland, opposite to the Probate-office in Queen-street, 1758. 1 p. l., xviii, 386, [7] p. 22 cm. [BT720.E2 1758] 28-7115
1. Sin. 2. Taylor, John, 1694-1761. The Scripture doctrine of original sin. I. Title. II. Title: With this is bound his Remarks on the Essays, on the principles of morality, and natural religion. In a letter to a minister of the Church of Scotland ... Edinburgh, 1756.

FAGAN, Sean. 241'.3
Has sin changed? / Sean Fagan. Garden City, N.Y. : Image Books, 1979, c1977. 216 p. ; 18 cm. [BT715.F16 1979] 79-7492 ISBN 0-385-15501-8 pbk. : 2.95
1. Sin. I. Title.

FARRELL, Walter, 1902-1951 233.2
Sin. New York, Sheed and Ward [1960] 94p. (Canterbury books) 'From [the author's] A companion to the Summan, vol. II.' 60-51669 .75 pap.,
1. Sin. I. Title.

FITCH, Eleazar Thompson, 233.
1791-1871.
An inquiry into the nature of sin; in which the views advanced in "Two discourses on the nature of sin," are pursued; and vindicated from objections, stated in the Christian advocate. By Eleazar T. Fitch. New-Haven, A. H. Maltby, 1827. 95 p. 21 cm. [BT715.F55] 35-33929
1. Sin. I. Title.

[FLETCHER, John William] 283.
1729-1785.
An appeal to matter of fact and common sense; or, A rational demonstration of man's corrupt and lost estate ... New York, Printed by Kirk & Robinson, for the Methodist society, and sold by E. Cooper, and J. Wilson, at the Book room, 1804 236 p. 17 1/2 cm. By John William Fletcher. cf. Diet. nat. biog., v. 19. p. 313. [BV4625.F6] [(BT720.F)] 233. A32
1. Sin. I. Title.

FOSTER, Randolph Sinks bp. 239
1820-1903
... *Sin.* by Randolph S. Foster ... New York, Eaton & Mains; Cincinnati, Curts & Jennings, 1899. 4 p. l. [3]-308 p. 23 cm. (Studies in theology. vi) [BT15.F7 vol. 6] 99-3535
1. Sin. I. Title.

GEHMAN, Henry E. 233.
Sin and evil, their origin, meaning, cause, remedy, doom, by Henry E. Gehman ... Harrisburg, Pa., The Evangelical press, 1928. 55 p. 18 cm. [BT715.G4] 28-3813
1. Sin. 2. Evil. I. Title.

GROSS, Joseph B d.1891. 233.
Sins reconsidered and illustrated. By Rev. J. B. Gross ... Philadelphia, J. B. Lippincott & co., 1882. 136 p. 19 cm. [BT715.G8] 233 ISBN 40-24807
1. Sin. I. Title.

HALL, Noel. 283.23
The seven root sins, by Noel Hall ... London, New York [etc.] Oxford university press, 1936. 3 p. l., 58 p. 19 cm. "Printed in India." These studies first appeared in the National Christian council review. ef. 2d prelim. leaf. [BV4625.H3] 37-5201
1. Sin. I. Title.

HARING, Bernhard, 1912- 233'.22
Sin in the secular age [by] Bernard Haring. [1st ed.] Garden City, N.J., Doubleday, 1974. 215 p. 22 cm. Includes bibliographical references. [BT715.H25] 73-10539 ISBN 0-385-09017-X 5.95
1. Sin. I. Title.

HEMINGER, Carl 233.14
The sin of Adam and Eye. New York, Vantage Press [c.1960] 141p. 22cm. 3.00 bds.,
I. Title.

HUNOLT, Franz, 1691-1746. 233.2
The bad Christian; or, Sermons on the seven deadly sins, and the different sins against God and our neighbor which flow therefrom. In seventy-six sermons, adapted to all the Sundays and holy days of the year. With a full index of all the sermons,

and an alphabetical index of the principal subjects treated, and copious marginal notes. By the Rev. Father Francis Hunolt...Translated from the original German edition of Cologne, 1740. By the Rev. J. Allen... New York, Cincinnati [ect.] Benziger brothers, 1888. 2 v. 23 cm. (Half-title: Hunolt's sermons, vol. iii-iv) [BX1756.H8 vol. 3-4] (252.02) 37-19946
1. Sin. 2. Catholic church—Sermons. 3. Sermons, English—Translations from German. 4. Sermons, German—Translations into English. I. Allen, J., tr. II. Title.

HYDE, William DeWitt, 1858-1917. 233.
Sin and its forgiveness, by William DeWitt Hyde ... Boston and New York, Houghton Mifflin company, 1909. vii, [1] p., 1 l., [1] p., 1 l. 18 cm. (Half-title: Modern religious problems, ed. by A. W. Vernon) [BT715.H8] 9-29362
1. Sin. 2. Forgiveness of sin. I. Title.

*JANSSENS, Paul Mary, Sr. 233'.2
Things go better with peace. [by] Paul Mary Janssens [and] Pauletta Overbeck. Notre Dame, Ind. Fides Publishers [1973] 122 p. 20 cm. [BT715.] ISBN 0-8190-0480-4. 1.50 (pbk.)
1. Sin. I. Overbeck, Pauletta, Sr. II. Title.

KERANS, Patrick. 261.8
Sinful social structures. New York, Paulist Press [1974] vi, 113 p. 18 cm. (Topics in moral argument) Includes bibliographical references. [BT738.K39] 74-76716 ISBN 0-8091-1830-0 1.45 (pbk.).
1. Sin. 2. Social ethics. I. Title.

KIERKEGAARD, Soren Aabye, 1813-1855. 248'.3
The sickness unto death : a Christian psychological exposition for upbuilding and awakening / by Soren Kierkegaard ; edited and translated with introd. and notes by Howard V. Hong and Edna H. Hong. Princeton, N.Y. : Princeton University Press, c1980. p. cm. Includes index. Bibliography: p. [BT715.K5313] 79-3218 ISBN 0-691-07247-7 : 16.50
1. Sin. 2. Despair. I. Hong, Howard Vincent, 1912- II. Hong, Edna Hatlestad, 1913- III. Title.

KRUMM, John McGill, 1913- 233.2
The art of being a sinner [by] John M. Krumm. New York, Seabury Press [c1967] 128 p. 22 cm. Bibliographical references included in "Notes" (p. 125-128) [BT715.K7] 67-10844
1. Sin. 2. Salvation — Popular works. I. Title.

KUIPER, Henry J ed. 234
Sermons on sin and grace, Lord's days: i-vii ... by ministers in the Reformed and Christian Reformed churches. Edited by Henry J. Kuiper ... Grand Rapids, Mich., Zondervan publishing house [c1936] 112 p. 20 cm. (Half-title: Sermons on the catechism, vol. i) "The Heidelberg catechism ... has been chosen as the guide for these sermons."-Foreword. [BX9426.A1K8 vol. 1] [BT715.K8] 238.41 36-30053
1. Sin. 2. Grace (Theology) 3. Reformed church—Sermons. 4. Sermons, American. I. Title.

LE QUEUX, William, 1864-
The sign of the seven sins. Philadelphia, J. B. Lippincott oc., 1901 [1900] 281 p. 12° Dec
I. Title.

*LEONARD, B. G. 241
Except . . . for fornication. New York, Carlton [c.1966] 61p. 21cm. (Reflection bk.) 2.00
I. Title.

LITTLEFAIR, Duncan E., 1912- 233'.2
Sin comes of age / by Duncan E. Littlefair. Philadelphia : Westminster Press, [1975] 191 p. ; 22 cm. Includes bibliographical references and index. [BV4625.L54] 75-23277 ISBN 0-664-20807-X : 6.50
1. Sin. 2. Good and evil. 3. Sins. 4. Salvation. I. Title.

LOCKYER, Herbert. 241.3
The sins of saints; scriptural unfolding of victorious living, by Herbert G. Lockyer. Neptune, N.J., Loizeaux Bros. [1970] 255 p. 20 cm. [BV4625.L57] 75-108378 3.50
1. Sins. 2. Christian life—1960- I. Title.

[MCCALLEN, Robert Seth]
"The devil in robes"; or, The sin of priests. The gory hand of Catholicism stayed ... Homes of Cuba, Puerto Rico and the Philippine Island united ... Introductory by ... J. S. Carr ... St. Louis, Mo., Columbia book concern, 1899. 472 p. illus. 8 cm. Published anonymously. 0-1958
I. Title.

MCCLAIN, Dayton E 241
The sin of omission. Philadelphia, Dorrance [1959] 78p. 20cm. [BV4625.M3] 59-5749
1. Sin. I. Title.

MCDONOUGH, Michael Vincent, 1863-
The chief sources of sin; seven discourses on pride covetousness, lust, anger, gluttony, envy, sloth, by Rev. M. V. McDonough. Baltimore, Md., New York, Metropolitan press, John Murphy company [c1910] 114 p. 19 1/2 cm. $0.75 10-8422
I. Title.

MCGOWAN, Francis Xavier, 1854-1903. 233.
Two series of lenten sermons on I. Sin and its remedies II. The seven deadly sins, by Rev. Francis X. McGowan ... New York & Cincinnati, F. Pustet & co., 1902. 3 p. l., 224 p. 19 1/2 cm. [BT715.M14 1902] 2-15872
1. Sin. 2. Christian ethics—Catholic authors. 3. Lenten sermons. I. Title.

MACKAY, William Mackintosh. 233.
The disease and remedy of sin, by the Rev. W. Mackintosh Mackay... New York, George H. Doran company [1919] xii, 308 p. 23 cm. [BT715.M15] 20-10742
1. Sin. 2. Psychology, Pathological. I. Title.

MACKINTOSH, Robert, 1858- 233.
Christianity and sin, by Robert Mackintosh, D. D. New York, C. Scribner's sons, 1914. vii, 231 p. 19 cm. (On verso of half-title: Studies in theology) Bibliography: p. 219-224. [BT715.M2] 14-30728
1. Sin. I. Title.

MAHONEY, Edward J. 233.
Sin and repentance, by the Rev. E. J. Mahoney ... introduction by Thomas M. Schwertner ... New York, The Macmillan company, 1928. ix, 95 p. 17 cm. (Half title: The treasury of the faith series: 26) [BT715.M27 1928 a] 28-27962
1. Sin. 2. Repentance. I. Title.

MALY, Eugene H. 233'.2
Sin; Biblical perspectives, by Eugene H. Maly. Dayton, Ohio, Pflaum/Standard [1973] viii, 110 p. 21 cm. Includes bibliographical references. [BT715.M277] 73-79518 ISBN 0-8278-0006-1 1.95 (pbk.)
1. Sin.

MANNING, Henry Edward, cardinal, 1808-1892. 233.2
Sin and its consequences. By His Eminence Henry Edward Manning ... 3d ed. New York, Montreal, D. & J. Sadlier & company [1876?] vi p., 1 l., 9-264 p. 19 cm. [BT715.M28] 39-34110
1. Sin. 2. Christian ethics—Catholic authors. I. Title.

MARSH, Charles E. 233.
The origin of sin: or, The true system of the universe. By C. E. Marsh. Lawn Ridge, Ill., 1898. 55 p. 19 cm. [BT715.M3] 99-1321
1. Sin. I. Title.

MARTIN, William Benjamin James. 241.3
Little foxes that spoil the vines [by] W. B. J. Martin. Nashville, Abingdon Press [1968] 127 p. 20 cm. [BV4625.M34] 68-17448
1. Sins. I. Title.

MAY, William F. 241.3
A catalogue of author sins; a contemporary examination of christian conscience, by William F. May [1st ed.] New York, Holt [1967] ix, 208p. 22cm. Bibl. [BV4625.M38] 66-13494 4.95
1. Sins. I. Title.

MENNINGER, Karl, 1893- 233'.2
Whatever became of sin? New York, Hawthorn Books [1973] viii, 242 p. 25 cm. Includes bibliographical references. [BV4625.M46] 72-7776 7.95
1. Sin. I. Title.

MILLER, C. W. 233.2
The conflict of centuries. By C. W. Miller... Nashville, Tenn., Southern Methodist publishing house, 1883. 308 p. 19 cm. [BT715.M6] 40-25491
1. Sin. 2. Regeneration (Theology) I. Title.

NELSON, Levi, 1779-1855. 233.
A letter to the theological professors at New Haven, concerning their supposition that God may not have been able to prevent sin in a moral system; with an appendix. Also, a few thoughts on the origin of sin. By Levi Nelson ... Norwich [Conn.] J. G. Cooley, 1848. 87 p. 23 cm. [BT715.N4] 41-33062
1. Taylor, Nathaniel William, 1786-1858. 2. Sin. 3. Providence and government of God. I. Title.

NILES, Samuel, 1743-1814. 233.2
Remarks on a sermon preached before the Plymouth association of ministers in the third Congregational society in Milldeborough, Sept. 26, 1810, by John Reed, D. D., pastor of the 1st church and congregation in Bridgewater. By Samuel Niles A. M., pastor of the 1st church and congregation in Abington ... Boston; Printed and sold by Lincoln & Edmands, no. 53 Cornhill, 1813. 62 p. 24 cm. [BX7233.R397S43] 35-32286
1. Reed, John, 1751-1831. A sermon preached before the Plymouth association of ministers. 2. Sin. 3. Free will and determinism. 4. Congregational churches—Sermons. I. Title.

NOTES on sins and their remedies, together with The Christian's mirror, by a group of priests. With a foreword by the Rev. Canon K. E. Kirk ... London, The Faith press, ltd.; Milwaukee, The Morehouse publishing co. [1835] xiii, 121 p. 18 1/2 cm. Pages [114]-[115] numbered cxiv-cxv. "First published, January, 1935." By M. F. G. Donovan and others. cf. Brit. mus. Catalogue. Accessions, June, 1935. "Suggested books": p. cxiv. [BV4611.N6] 36-19966 248
1. Sin. 2. Christian ethics—Anglican communion. 3. Imitatio Christl. I. Donovan, Marcus.

ODEGARD, Holtan Peter, 1923- 261.7
Sin and science; Reinhold Niebuhr as political theologian. Yellow Springs, Ohio. Antioh Press [1956] 245p. 22cm. Bibliography:p. [221]-234. [BX4827.N5O3] 56-8247
1. Niebuhr, Reinhold, 1892- 2. Sin. 3. Christianity and politics. I. Title.

ORCHARD, William Edwin, 1877-
Modern theories of sin, by W. E. Orchard, D.D. (Thesis approved for the degree of Doctor of divinity in the university of London) Second impression. Boston, The Pilgrim press; London, J. Clarke & co., 1910. 3 p. l., 161, [1] p. 21 1/2 cm. A 11
1. Sin. I. Title.

ORR, James, 1844-1913.
Sin as a problem of today, by James Orr ... New York & London, Hodder & Stoughton [1910] viii, 324 p. 21 cm. A 11
1. Sin. I. Title.

PALMER, O. R. 240
Deliverance from the penalty and power of sin, by O. R. Palmer. Chicago, The Bible institute colportage association [c1912] 3 p. l., 3-119 p. 17 cm. 12-16913
I. Title.

PARKER, Theodore, 1810-1860. 177
Sins and safeguards of society, by Theodore Parker; ed. with notes by Samuel B. Stewart. Boston, American Unitarian association [1909] 6 p. l., 388 p. 21 cm. (His Works. Centenary ed., v. 9) "The sermons collected in this volume are concerned with certain phases of public morals and public education."--Editor's pref. [BX9815.P3

1907] A12
I. Stewart, Samuel Barrett, 1839-1927, ed. II. Title.

PASTORAL treatment of sin, by P. Delhaye [and others. Translation from the French by Charles Schaldenbrand, Firmin O'Sullivan and Eugene Desmarchelier] New York, Desclee [1968] 319 p. 22 cm. Bibliographical footnotes. [BT715.P3713 1968] 68-25350 7.50 233'.2
1. Sin. I. Delhaye, Philippe.

PECK, George Clarke, 1865-1927.
Old sins in new clothes, by George Clarke Peck. New York, Eaton & Mains; Cincinnati, Jennings & Pye [1904] 317 p. 18 cm. 4-7339
I. Title.
Contents omitted.

PECKHAM, Le Roy Bliss, 1858- 233
Sin, original and actual; the plain people's plaint, by T. K. E. ... Boston, R. G. Badger; [etc., etc., c1915] xiii, 121 p. 18 cm. "Editor's signed: W. G. Sette. In verse. On cover: By a true night-errant. [HN78.P4] 15-15734 1.00
I. Sette, W. G., ed. II. Title. III. Title: The plain peoples plaint.

PEEBLES, Isaac Lockhart. 233.
Sin; the occurrence of the word "sin" in the English and Greek Bibles; its origin, meaning, nature, kinds, and results, by Isaac Lockhart Peebles ... Nashville, Tenn., Dallas, Tex. [etc.] Publishing house of the M. E. church, South, Smith & Lamar, agents, 1918. 57 p. front. (port.) 19 cm. [BT715.P4] 18-17501
I. Title.

POTTEBAUM, Gerard A. 233.14
They disobeyed. Illus. by Robert Strobridge. Dayton, Ohio; 38 W. 5th St., Geo. A. Pflaum, c.1963. unpaged. col. illus. 18cm. (Little people's paperbacks, LPP3) .35 pap.,
I. Title.

REGNIER, Jerome, 1918- 233.2
What is sin? Translated from the French by Una Morrissy. Westminster, Md., Newman Press [1961* 125p. 18cm. Translation of La sens du peche. [BT715.R413] 61-66766
1. Sin. I. Title.

RICE, John R., 1895- 233.2
When a Christian sins. Wheaton, Ill., Sword of the Lord Publishers [1954] 134p. 21cm. [BT715.R47] 55-16793
1. Sin. I. Title.

RICoUR, Paul. 233'.2
The symbolism of evil. Translated from the French by Emerson Buchanan. [1st ed.] New York, Harper & Row [1967] xv, 357 p. 22 cm. (Religious perspectives, v. 17) [BT715.R48] 67-11506
1. Sin. 2. Good and evil. I. Title. II. Series.

RIGA, Peter J 262'.8
Sin and penance; insights into the mystery of salvation. Milwaukee, Bruce Pub. Co. [1962] 187 p. 23 cm. [BX2265.2.R5] 62-19191
1. Sin. 2. Penance. I. Title.

RILEY, William Bell, 1861-1947. 241
God's seven abominations, by W. B. Riley and Robert G. Lee. Wheaton, Ill., Van Kampen Press [c1954] 80p. 20cm. [BV4625.R5] 55-14164
1. Sin. I. Lee, Robert Greene, 1886- II. Title.

RONDET, Henri, 1898- 233.2
The theology of sin. Translated by Royce W. Hughes. Notre Dame, Ind., Fides Publishers Association [1960] 131p. 20cm. (Themes of theology) Translation of Notes sur la theologie du peche. Includes bibliography. [BT715.R613] 60-15437
1. Sin. I. Title.

ROSENTHAL, George David, 1881-1938. 248
Sins of the saints. [Rev. ed.] New York, Morehouse-Gorham Co., 1958. 164p. 19cm. [BV4625.R6 1958] 58-13713
1. Sins. 2. Christian ethics—Anglican authors. I. Title.

SCHOONENBERG, Peter, 1911- 233.2
Man and sin; a theological view [by] Piet Schoonenberg. Tr. by Joseph Donceel. Chicago, Regnery [1968.c.1965] ix, 205p. 17cm. (71L-730) Tr. of De macht der zonde. Bibl. [BT715.S333] 65-23519 1.75 pap.,
1. Sin. I. Title.

SCHOONENBERG, Peter, 1911- 233.2
Man and sin; a theological view [by] Piet Schoonenberg. Translated by Joseph Donceel. [Notre Dame, Ind.,] University of Notre Dame Press, 1965. ix, 205 p. 21 cm. Translation of De macht der zonde. Bibliographical footnotes. [BT715.S333] 65-23519
1. Sin. I. Title.

SELLE, Robert L. 1865-
Sin; its origin, purpose, power, result, and cure. By Rev. Robert L. Selle... Louisville, Ky., Penticostal publishing company [c1913] 60 p. front. (port.) 19 1/2 cm. $0.50 13-22684
I. Title.

SHEEN, Fulton John, 1895- 232.958
Victory over vice, by Rt. Rev. Fulton J. Sheen ... New York, P. J. Kenedy & sons [c1939] 6 p. l., 107 p. 16 1/2 cm. [BT455.S46] 39-10749
1. Jesus Christ—Seven last words. 2. Sin. 3. Catholic church—Sermons. 4. Sermons, American. I. Title.

SHEPARD, William Edward. 233.
Sin, the tell-tale; or, Be sure your sin will find you out, by W. E. Shepard ... Cincinnati, O., God's revivalist press [c1917] 365 p. front. (port.) 19 1/2 cm. $1.00. [BT720.S5] 17-19830
I. Title.

[SIMONDS, William] 1822- 233.2
1859.
The sinner's friend, or The disease of sin, its consequences, and the remedy ... By the author of the "Pleasant way." Written for the Massachusetts Sabbath school society, and revised by the Committee of publication. Boston, Massachusetts Sabbath school scoiety, 1845. vi, [2], [9]-360 p. 16 cm. [BT715.S65] 40-24810
1. Sin. I. Massachusetts Sabbath school society. Committee of publication. II. Title.

SIN 233.2082
[by] Marc Oraison [others] Tr. by Bernard Murchland, Raymond Meyerpeter. Introd. by Bernard Murchland. New York, Macmillan, 1962 [c.1959-1962] 177p. 22cm. 61-15162 4.50
1. Sin. 2. Sin—Psychology. I. Oraison, Marc. II. Murchland, Bernard, ed. and tr.

SIN and its consequences. 233.
Boston, American Unitarian association, 1854. vi p., 1 l., [9]-62 p. 16 cm. [BT715.S6] 44-12887
1. Sin. I. Channing, William Ellery, 1780-1842. II. Dewey, Orville, 1794-1882. III. American Unitarian association.
Contents omitted.

SIN and salvation.
Napierville, Ill., SCM Book Club [1956] 128p. 18cm.
1. Sin. 2. Salvation. I. Newbigin, James Edward Lesslie, Bp.

SINS of the day, 233.2
[1st ed.] London, New York, Longmans, Green [1959] 75 p. 18 cm. [BV4625.S5] 59-8177
1. Sins.

SMALLEY, John, 1734-1820. 252.
The consistency of the sinner's inability to comply with the gospel; with his inexcusable guilt in not complying with it, illustrated and confirmed: in two discourses, on John VIth, 44th. By John Smalley, A.M. pastor of a church in Farmington. Hartford: Printed by Green & Watson, near the Great Bridge, 1769. 71 p. 18 cm. [BX7233.S6C6] 24-19490
I. Title.

SQUIER, Miles Powell, 1792- 233.2
1866.
The problem solved; or, Sin not of God. By Miles P. Squier ... New York, M. W. Dodd, 1855. xiii, [15]-255 p. 19 cm. [BT715.S7] 37-13901
1. Sin. 2. Providence and government of God. I. Title. II. Title: Sin not of God.

STONE, Stewart, 1854-195. 283.
The seven capital sins; outlines for instructions, by the Rev. Stewart Stone ... with foreword by William Walter Webb ... Milwaukee, Morehouse publishing co.; London, A. R. Mowbray & co. [c1926] xi, 56 p. 19 cm. [BV4625.S8] 26-18646
I. Title.

STROUP, Ner Wallace, 1870-
The face of sin, viewed historically and doctrinally, by Rev. N. Wallace Stroup. Cincinnati, Jennings and Graham; New York, Eaton and Mains [c1908] 312 p. 19 cm. 8-29856
I. Title.

SUE, Eugene, 1804-1857.
Avarice--Anger. Two of the seven cardinal sins. Illustrated with etchings by Adrian Marcel. By Eugene Sue. Boston, F. A. Niccolls & co. [1899] viii p., 2 l., 13-346 p. incl. front. 3 pl. 23 cm. (Half-title: The seven cardinal sins. Avarice) Edition de luxe, limited to 1000 copies; this copy not numbered. Anger (p. 175-346) has half-title: The seven cardinal sins. Anger. [Name originally: Marie Joseph Sue] [PQ2446.S62 1899 vol. 4] 0-702
I. Title. II. Title: Anger.

SUE, Eugene, 1804-1857.
Pride--one of the seven cardinal sins. Illustrated with etchings by Adrian Marcel. By Eugene Sue. Boston, F. A. Niccols & co. [1899] 2 v. 8 pl. (incl. fronts.) 23 cm. (Half-title: The seven cardinal sins. Pride) Edition de luxe, limited to 1000 copies; this copy not numbered. [Name originally: Marie Joseph Sue] [PQ2446.S62 1899 vol. 1-2] 99-5006
I. Title.

SUE, Eugene, 1804-1857.
Luxury--Gluttony. Two of the seven cardinal sins. Illustrated with etchings by Adrian Marcel. By Eugene Sue. Boston, F. A. Niccolls & co. [c1889] 4 p. l., 13-352 [1] p. 5 pl. (incl. front.) 23 cm. (Half-title: The seven cardinal sins. Luxury) Edition de luxe; no. 159 of an edition limited to 1000 copies. Gluttony (p. 219-[353]) has half-title: The seven cardinal sins. Gluttony. Doctor Gasterini. [Name originally: Marie Joseph Sue] [PQ2446.S62 1899 vol. 5] 0-703
I. Title.

TALBERT, Daniel H.
The pleasures of sin, by Daniel H. Talbert. Indianapolis, Ind., The author, 1910. 128 p. front. (port) 20 cm. $1.00 10-6163
I. Title.

TAYLOR, Richard Shelley, 233.2
1912-
A right conception of sin; its importance to right thinking and right living, by Richard S. Taylor ... Kansas City, Mo., Nazarene publishing house, 1939. 121 p. 19 1/2 cm. [BT715.T27] 40-1846
1. Sin. 2. Atonement. I. Title.

TENNANT, Frederick, Robert,
1866-
The concept of sin, F. R. Tennant ... Cambridge, University press, 1912. 3 p. l., 281 [1] p. 19 cm. A 13
1. Sin. I. Title.

TENNANT, Frederick Robert, 233.
1866-
The origin and propagation of sin; being the Hulsean lectures delivered before the University of Cambridge in 1901-2, by F. R. Tennant ... Cambridge, University press, 1902. xv, 231 p. 20 cm. [BT715.T2] 3-4666
1. Sin. I. Hulsean lectures 1901-2. II. Title.

THELEN, Mary Frances, 1911- 233.2
Man as sinner in contemporary American realistic theology [by] Mary Frances Thelen ... New York, King's crown press, 1946. xii, 223 p. 23 cm. Issued also as thesis (PH.D.) Columbia university, 1946. Bibliography: p. [208]-217. [BT715.T47 1946a] A 47
1. Sin. 2. Sin—History of doctrines. 3. Man (Theology) 4. Theology, Doctrinal—Hist.—U.S. I. Niebuhr, Reinhold, 1892- II. Title.

THOMPSON, Otis, 1776-1859. 233.
Review of the Rev. Thomas Andros's Essay on the doctrine of divine efficiency. Providence, Printed by Miller & Hutchens, 1821. 146 p. 21 cm. [BT715.A23T5] 52-56431
1. Andros, Thomas, 1759-1845. An essay in which the doctrine of a positive divine efficiency exciting the will of men to sin ... is candidly discussed. 2. Sin. I. Title.

[WEBSTER, Samuel] 1719- 283.
1796.
The winter evening conversation vindicated; against the remarks of the Rev. Mr. Peter Clark of Danvers. In a piece intitled, A summer morning's conversation, &c., herein the principal arguments of said piece, from Scripture, reason and antiquity, are considered, and shown to be of no validity, by the author of The winter evening conversation ... Boston, Printed and sold by Edes and Gill, at their printing office next to the prison in Queen-street [1758?] 116 p. 20 1/2 cm. [BT720.W4C62] 23-5880
1. Webster, Samuel, 1719-1796. A winter evening's conversation. 2. Clark, Peter, 1693-1768. A summer morning's conversation. 3. Sin. I. Title.

WESLEY, John, 1703-1791.
The doctrine of the original sin, according to Scripture reason, and experience, in answer to Dr. Taylor, by the Rev. John Wesley. New York, J. Soule and T. Mason, 1817. 377, [3] p. 18 cm. A34
1. Sin. I. Taylor, John, 1694-1761. II. Title.

WHEELER, Francis L. 233.2
God, man, and sin by the Rev. Francis L. Wheeler London, New York [etc.] Skeffington & son, ltd. [1945] 62 p. 19 cm. (Half-title: New world outlook series) [BT715.W65] 46-920
1. Sin. 2. Salvation. I. Title.

WINES, Abijah, 1766-1833.
An inquiry into the nature of the sinner's inability to make a new heart, or to become holy. Containing some remarks on the Hon. Nathaniel Niles' "Letter to a friend," By Abijah Wines ... Windsor [Vt.] Published by P. Merrifield & co., 1812. 169 p. 16 cm. "Thomas M. Pomroy, printer." The last page is the inside of the back cover; front cover wanting. A32
1. Sin. 2. Niles, Nathaniel, 1741-1828. A letter to a friend ... concerning the doctrine ... that impenitent sinners have natural power to make themselves new hearts. I. Title.

WOOD, Nathan Robinson, 1874- 231.
The witness of sin, a theodicy, by Rev. Nathan Robinson Wood ... New York, Chicago [etc.] Fleming H. Revell company [c1905] 151 p. 20 cm. [BT160.W8] 5-39497
I. Title.

WOODS, Leonard, 1774-1854. 233.14
An essay on native depravity. By Leonard Woods ... Boston, W. Peirce, 1835. 1 p. l., [v]-vi p., 1 l., [9]-230 p. 19 cm. [BT720.W8] 33-28504
1. Sin. I. Title.

WORCESTER, Noah, 1758-1837. 233.2
Last thoughts, on important subjects, in three parts. I. Man's liability to sin. Ii. Supplemental illustrations. iii. Man's capacity to obey. By Noah Worcester ... Cambridge [Mass.] Brown, Shattuck, and co., 1833. iv, [iii]-iv, 323, [1] p. 18 1/2 cm. [BT715.W8] 40-24812
1. Sin. I. Title.

ZARTMAN, Rufus Calvin. 233.2
The unpardonable sin, by Rufus Calvin Zartman... Philadelphia, Pa., The Heidelberg press [c1932] 136 p. 21 1/2 cm. [BT715.Z25] 32-25303
1. Sin. 2. Sermons, American. I. Title.

Sin—Addresses, essays, lectures.

PITTENGER, William Norman, 233'.2
1905-
Cosmic love and human wrong : the reconception of meaning of sin, in the light of process thinking / by Norman Pittenger. New York : Paulist Press, c1978. v, 102 p. ; 20 cm. "The chapters ... were originally delivered as lectures at Texas Christian University, Fort Worth, Texas, in 1971." [BT715.P57] 77-99301 ISBN 0-8091-2093-3 pbk. : 4.95
1. Sin—Addresses, essays, lectures. 2. Process theology—Addresses, essays, lectures. I. Title.

SUE, Eugene, 1804-1857.
Envy. One of the seven cardinal sins. Illustrated with etchings by Adrian Marcel. By Eugene Sue. Boston, F. A. Niccolls & co. [1900] 4 p. l., 13-331 p. 5 pl. (incl. front.) 23 cm. (Half-title: The seven cardinal sins. Envy) Edition de luxe, limited to 1000 copies; this copy not numbered. [Name originally: Marie Joseph Sue] [PQ2446.S62 1899 vol 3] 0-1665
I. Title.

SWEETEN, Howard W. 233.
Must we sin? by Howard W. Sweeten, evangelist; a treatise of the sin question from the standpoint of reason and revelation. Introduction by Rev. L. L. Pickett ... Louisville, Ky., Pentecostal publishing company [c1919] 184 p. 20 cm. [BT715.S9] 19-16629
I. Title.

TAYLOR, Michael J., 233'.2'08
comp.
The mystery of sin and forgiveness. Michael J. Taylor, editor. Contributors:

Paul Anciaux [and others] Staten Island, N.Y., Alba House [1971] xiv, 285 p. 21 cm. Contents.Contents.—Introduction, by M. J. Taylor.—The mystery of sin: The sense of sin in the modern world, by R. O'Connell. Missing the mark, by B. Vawter. Towards a Biblical catechesis of the Decalogue, by P. Tremblay. Sin and community in the New Testament, by J. Murphy-O'Connor. The reality of sin; a theological and pastoral critique, by K. F. O'Shea.—The mystery of forgiveness: The sacrament of penance; an historical outline, by M.-B. Carra de Vaux Saint-Cyr. The ecclesial dimension of penance, by P. Anciaux. Confession: psychology is not enough, by L. Monden. Confession as a means of self-improvement, by J. F. Filella. Communal penance; a liturgical commentary and catechesis, by G.-M. Nissim.—Mystery of original sin: New thinking on original sin, by J. P. Mackey. Evolution and original sin, by P. Smulders. Original sin and man's situation, by P. Schoonenberg. A catechesis on original sin, by M. van Caster. Bibliography: p. [279]-281. [BT715.T25] 70-140284 ISBN 0-8189-0198-5 3.95
1. Sin—Addresses, essays, lectures. 2. Forgiveness of sin—Addresses, essays, lectures. 3. Sin, Original—Addresses, essays, lectures.

*WEDGE, Florence 241.3
Envious? Who, me? Pulaski, Wis., Franciscan Pubs. [1967] 60p. 19cm. .25 pap.,
I. Title.

Sin—Biblical teaching.

[EASTON, Peter Zaccheus] 233.2
1846-1915.
The Scripture doctrine in reference to the seat of sin in the regenerate man ... New York, A. D. F. Randolph & co. [1872] 125 p. 17 cm. Introduction signed: Peter Z. Easton. [BT715.E2] 40-24804
1. Sin—Biblical teaching. I. Title.

GELIN, Albert 220.82332
Sin in the Bible. Old Testament [by] Albert Gelin. New Testament [by] Albert Descamps. Tr. by Charles Schaldenbrand. New York, Desclee [1965] 140p. 22cm. Orig. appeared in French as part of Theologie du peche.' Bibl. [BT715.G47] 65-15629 3.75
1. Sin—Biblical teaching. I. Descamps, Albert. II. Title.

MILLER, Patrick D. 231.7
Sin and judgment in the prophets : a stylistic and theological analysis / Patrick D. Miller, Jr. Chico, Calif. : Scholars Press, c1982. 143 p. ; 23 cm. (Society of Biblical Literature monograph series ; no. 27) Bibliography: p. [141]-143. [BS1199.S54M54 1982] 19 81-8950 ISBN 0-89130-514-9 : 19.50 ISBN 0-89130-515-7 pbk. : 16.00
1. Bible. O.T. Prophets—Criticism, interpretation, etc. 2. Sin—Biblical teaching. 3. Judgment of God—Biblical teaching. I. Title. II. Series.

Sin—Biblical teaching—Addresses, essays, lectures.

SIN, salvation, and the 234
spirit : commemorating the fiftieth year of the Liturgical Press / general editor, Daniel Durken. Collegeville, Minn. : Liturgical Press, c1979. p. cm. [BS680.S57S56] 79-20371 ISBN 0-8146-1078-1 : 10.50 ISBN 0-8146-1079-X pbk. : 8.50
1. Liturgical Press—Addresses, essays, lectures. 2. Sin—Biblical teaching—Addresses, essays, lectures. 3. Salvation—Biblical teaching—Addresses, essays, lectures. 4. Holy Spirit—Biblical teaching—Addresses, essays, lectures. I. Durken, Daniel. II. Liturgical Press.

WIGGLESWORTH, Edward, 1693- 233.
1765.
An enquiry into the truth of the imputation of the guilt of Adam's first sin to his posterity. Being the substance of several private lectures in Harvard college, on the third article in the sixth chapter of the Westminster confession of faith. By Edward Wigglesworth ... Boston: Printed by J. Draper, for D. Henchman over against the Brick-Meeting-House in Cornhil. 1738. 4 p. l., 90 p. 20 cm. Half-title: Dr. Wigglesworth's lectures on the imputation of Adam's first sin to his posterity. [BT710.W5] 24-8252
I. Title.

Sin—History of doctrines.

HOFMANN, Hans, 1923- 230.41
The theology of Reinhold Niebuhr. Translated by Louise Pettibone Smith. New York, Scribner, 1956. 269p. 22cm. [BX4827.N5H63] 56-5663
1. Niebuhr, Reinhold, 1892- 2. Sin—History of doctrines. I. Title.

HOFMANN, Hans F., 1923- 230.41
The theology of Reinhold Niebuhr Translated by Louise Pettibone Smith. New York Scribner 1956. 269 p. 22 cm. [BX4827.N5H63] 56-5663
1. Niebuhr, Reinhold, 1892- 2. Sin — History of doctrines. I. Title.

PALACHOVSKY, V. 233.2
Sin in the Orthodox Church, by V. Palachovsky. And in the Protestant churches, by C. Vogel. [Tr. from French by Charles Schaldenbrand] New York, Desclee [1966] 106p. 22cm. 66-11142 3.50
1. Sin—History of doctrines. 2. Orthodox Eastern Church—Relations—Protestant Churches. 3. Protestant churches—Relations— Relations—Orthodox Estern Church. I. Vogel, Cyrille. II. Title.

Sin in literature.

PAOLINI, Shirley J. 851'.1
Confessions of sin and love in the Middle Ages : Dante's Commedia and St. Augustine's Confessions / Shirley J. Paolini. Washington, D.C. : University Press of America, c1982. p. cm. Includes index. Bibliography: p. [PQ4419.D4P36] 19 81-40724 ISBN 0-8191-2240-8 : 22.50 ISBN 0-8191-2241-6 (pbk.) : 11.25
1. Dante Alighieri, 1265-1321. Divina commedia. 2. Augustine, Saint, Bishop of Hippo. Confessiones. 3. Sin in literature. 4. Love in literature. 5. Confession in literature. I. Title.

Sin, Mortal.

BLOOMFIELD, Morton 233.21
Wilfred, 1913-
The seven deadly sins; an introduction to the history of a religious concept, with special reference to medieval English literature. [East Lansing] Michigan State College Press, 1952. xiv, 482 p. front. 24 cm. ([Michigan. State College of Agriculture and Applied Science, East Lansing] Studies in language and literature) Bibliography: p. [257]-306. [BV4625.B55] 52-4902
1. Sin, Mortal. 2. Anglo-Saxon literature—Hist. & crit. 3. English literature—Early English (1100-1500)—Hist. & crit. I. Title. II. Series.

GRAHAM, William. 233.02
Non serviam; a Lenten course of seven sermons on the subject of mortal sin, by the Rev. W. Graham. New York, J. F. Wagner [1904] 2 p. l., 58 p. 21 cm. [BT715.G75] 41-32808
1. Sin, Mortal. 2. Catholic church—Sermons. 3. Sermons, American. I. Title.

WEBB, Lance 233.2
Conquering the seven deadly sins. Nashville, Abingdon [1965, c.1955] 224p. 21cm. (Apex bks., V5) [BV4625.W42] 55-6768 1.25 pap.,
1. Sin, Mortal. I. Title.

WEBB, Lance. 233.2
Conquering the seven deadly sins. New York, Abingdon Press [1955] 224p. 23cm. [BV4625.W42] 55-6768
1. Sin, Mortal. I. Title.

Sin, Original.

AUGUSTINUS, 230'.09'015 s
Aurelius, Saint, Bp. of Hippo.
Against Julian. Translated by Matthew A. Schumacher. Washington, Catholic University of America Press [1974, c1957] p. cm. (Writings of Saint Augustine, v. 16) Reprint of the ed. published by Fathers of the Church, inc., New York, which was issued as v. 35 of the Fathers of the church, a new translation. Bibliography: p. [BR60.F3A82 vol. 16] [BR65.A65] 233'.14 74-10838 ISBN 0-8132-0035-0
1. Sin, Original. 2. Apologetics—Early church, ca. 30-600. I. Title. II. Series: The Fathers of the church, a new translation, v. 35.

AUGUSTINUS, 230'.09'015 s
Aurelius, Saint, Bp. of Hippo.
Against Julian. Translated by Matthew A. Schumacher. New York, Fathers of the Church, inc., 1957. xx, 407 p. 22 cm. (Writings of Saint Augustine, v. 16) (The Fathers of the church, a new translation, v. 35.) Bibliography: p. xix-xx. [BR60.F3A8 vol. 16] [BR65.A65] 233'.14 74-168247
1. Sin, Original. 2. Apologetics—Early church, ca. 30-600. I. Title. II. Series.

BOARDMAN, Henry Augustus, 233.14
1808-1880.
The Scripture doctrine of original sin explained and enforced: in two discourses. By H. A. Boardman... Philadelphia, W. S. Martien, 1839. 1 p. l., [vii]-ix p., 1 l., [13]-124 p. 20 cm. [BT720.B6] 40-24813
1. Sin, Original. 2. Presbyterian church—Sermons. 3. Sermons, American. I. Title.

BRUMER, William T 233.14
Children of the Devil; a fresh investigation of the fall of man and original sin, by William T. Bruner. New York, Philosophical Library [1966] xix, 311 p. 21 cm. Bibliography: p. 298-299. [BT720.B78] 65-21756
1. Sin, Original. 2. Fall of man. I. Title.

BRUNER, William T. 233.14
Childern of the Devil; a fresh investigation of the fall of man and original sin. New York, Philosophical [c.1966] xix, 311p. 21cm. Bibl. [BT720.B78] 65-21756 5.95
1. Sin, Original. 2. Fall of man. I. Title.

BUSCH, Fred W
The case against original sin; Minerva presents a diploma to Eve. New York, Pageant Press [1964] 124 p. 21 cm. 66-6886
1. Sin, Original. I. Title.

CLARK, Peter, 1694-1768. 233
A defence of the principles of the "Summer-morning's conversation concerning the doctrine of original sin." Against the exceptions of the author of the "Winter evening's conversation vindicated." Wherein the said doctrine is further illustrated and confirmed, by valid Scripture, reason, and antiquity. Concluded with an expostulatory address. By Peter Clark, A.M. Boston: Printed and sold by Edes and Gill in Queen-street, 1760. 160, [3] p. 22 1/2 cm. [BT720.W4C625] 45-49528
1. Clark, Peter, 1694-1768. A summer morning's conversation. 2. Webster, Samuel, 1719-1796. The winter evening's conversation vindicated. 3. Sin, Original. I. Title.

CLARK, Peter, 1694-1768. 233
The Scripture-doctrine of original sin, stated and defended. In a summer-morning's conversation, between a minister and a neighbour. Containing remarks on a late anonymous pamphlet, entitled, "A winter-evening's conversation, upon the doctrine of original sin, between a minister and three of his neighbours, accidentally met," &c. With an appendix, in reply to a supplement in the New-Haven edition of that pamphlet. By Peter Clark ... Recommended in a preface by several ministers ... Boston: Printed and sold by S. Kneeland, opposite to the Probate office in Queen-street, 1758. 2 p. l., 132, 24 p. 18 cm. [BT720.W4C6 1758] 22-12667
1. Webster, Samuel, 1719-1895. A winter evening's conversation upon the doctrine of original sin. 2. Sin, Original. I. Title.

CONN, Reuben R. 233.14
The human moral problems; an inquiry into some of the dark points connected with the human necessities for a supernatural Saviour, by R.R. Conn. New York, A. C. Armstrong and son, 1889. 69 p. 19 cm. [BT715.C7] 40-24802
1. Sin, Original. I. Title.

DE ROSA, Peter. 233'.14
Christ and original sin. Milwaukee, Bruce Pub. Co. [1967] xi, 138 p. 22 cm. (Impact books) Bibliographical footnotes. [BT720.D45] 67-19791
1. Jesus Christ—Person and offices. 2. Sin, Original. I. Title.

EDWARDS, Jonathan, 1703- 233.
1758.
The great Christina doctrine of original sin defended, evidences of its truth produced, and arguments to the contrary answered; containing in particular a reply to the objections and arguings of Dr. John Taylor in his book intitled "The Scripture doctrine of original sin proposed to free and candid examination," & c. 4th ed. Boston, Printed; London, Reprinted by R. Noble for j. Murgatroyd, 1789. xxviii, 436 p. 23 cm. [BT720.E2 1789] 50-44478
1. Sin, Original. 2. Taylor, John, 1694-1761. The Scripture doctrine of original sin. I. Title.

EDWARDS, Jonathan, 1703- 285'.8 s
1758.
Original sin. Edited by Clyde A. Holbrook. New Haven, Yale University, 1970. xi, 448 p. 24 cm. (His Works, v. 3) Includes bibliographical references. [BX7117.E3 1957 vol. 3] [BT720] 233'.14 72-179794 ISBN 0-300-01198-9
1. Sin, Original. I. Holbrook, Clyde A., ed.

[FLETCHER, John William] 233.14
1729-1785.
An appeal to matter of fact and common sense. Or, A rational demonstration of man's corrupt and lost estate ... New York, Published by John Wilson and Daniel Hitt, for the Methodist connection in the Unites States; 1810. xi, [13]-236 p. 16 cm. "Author's letter" (p. [iii]) signed: J. Fletchere. [BT720.F6 1810] 40-25493
1. Sin, Original. I. Title.

[FLETCHER, John William] 233.14
1729-1785.
An appeal to matter of fact and common sense; or, A rational demonstration of man's corrupt and lost estate ... New York, Pub. by J. Emory and B. Waugh for the Methodist Episcopal church, 1830. 165 p. 18 cm. Author's letter (p. [3]) signed: J. Fletchere. [BT720.F6 1830] 40-23739
1. Sin, Original. I. Title.

[FLETCHER, John William] 233.14
1729-1793
An appeal to matter of fact and common sense. Or, A rational demonstration of man's corrupt and lost estate ... Bristol [Eng.]: printed, Philadelphia re-printed by Melchoir Steiner, in Race-street, near Third-street. M.DCC.LXXXII. xi, 13-271 p. 17 cm. Author's letter (p. iii) signed: J. Fletcher. [BT720.F6 1783] 40-23738
1. Sin, Original. I. Title.

HAAG, Herbert, 1915- 233'.14
Is original sin in Scripture? Translated by Dorothy Thompson. With an introd. by Bruce Vawter. New York, Sheed and Ward [1969] 127 p. 21 cm. Translation of Biblische Schopfungslehre und kirchliche Erbsundenlehre. Bibliographical references included in "Notes" (p. 109-127) [BT710.H1313] 69-16995 3.95
1. Sin, Original. 2. Fall of man. I. Title.

HOPKINS, Daniel C. 233.22
tHe law of sin and death: or, The true theory of human depravity. Something novel on an old topic. By Rev. D. C. Hopkins. New York, Pub. for the author, by M. W. Dodd, 1858. vi, [7]-66 p. 19 cm. [BT720.H65] 40-23740
1. Sin, Original. 2. Fall of man. I. Title.

KIERKEGAARD, Soren Aabye, 216
1813-1855.
The concept of dread. Translated with introd. and notes by Walter Lowrie. [2d ed.] Princeton, Princeton University Press, 1957. xiii, 154p. 23cm. Bibliographical references included in 'Notes' (p. [147]-152) [BT720.K52 1957] 57-13241
1. Sin, Original. 2. Psychology, Religious. 3. Fear. I. Title.

KIERKEGAARD, Soren Aabye, 233'.14
1813-1855.
The concept of anxiety : a simple psychologically orienting deliberation on the dogmatic issue of hereditary sin / by Soren Kierkegaard ; edited and translated

with. introd. and notes by Reidar Thomte, in collaboration with Albert B. Anderson. Princeton, N.J. : Princeton University Press, c1980. p. cm. Translation of Begrebet Angest. Includes index. Bibliography: p. [BT720.K52 1980] 79-3217 ISBN 0-691-07244-2 : 18.50
1. Sin, Original. 2. Psychology, Religious. 3. Anxiety. I. Thomte, Reidar. II. Anderson, Albert, 1928- III. Title.

LANDIS, Robert Wharton, 1809-1883. 233.22
The doctrine of original sin, as received and taught by the churches of the reformation, stated and defended, and the error of Dr. Hodge in claiming that this doctrine recognizes the gratuitous imputation of sin, pointed out and refuted. By Robert W. Landis ... Richmond, Va., Whittet & Shepperson, 1884. xviii, 541 p. 24 cm. [BT720.L2] 40-23741
1. Hodge, Charles, 1797-1878. 2. Sin, Original. I. Title.

MURRAY, John, 1898- 233.14
The imputation of Adam's sin. Grand Rapids, Eerdmans [1959] 95p. 20cm. Includes bibliography. [BT720.M78] 59-10078
1. Sin, Original. I. Title.

NILES, Samuel, 1674-1762. 283.
The true Scripture doctrine of original sin stated and defended. In the way of remarks on a late piece, intitled, "The Scripture-doctrine of original sin proposed to free and candid examination. By John Taylor. The second edition." To which is premised a brief discourse on the decrees of God, in general, and on the election of grace, in particular. Being, the substance of many meditations, in the course of a long life, and now published as his Boston, N. E. Printed and sold by S. Kneeland, opposite to the probate-office in Queen-street. 1757. 3 p. l., 320 p. 18 1/2 cm. [BT720.T33N5 1757] 45-48582
1. Taylor, John, 1624-1761. The Scripture doctrine of original sin. 2. Sin, Original. I. Title.

PINK, Arthur Walkington, 1886-1952. 233'.2
Gleanings from the Scriptures; man's total depravity. Chicago, Moody Press [1970, c1969] 347 p. 24 cm. [BT720.P53] 73-80942 5.95
1. Sin, Original. 2. Man (Theology) I. Title.

ROSA, Peter de.
Christ and original sin, by... Milwaukee, Bruce, 1967. xi, 138 p. 23 cm. 68-66232
1. Sin, Original. 2. Incarnation. I. Title.

SPRING, Gardiner, 1785-1873. 230
A dissertation on native depravity. By Gardiner Spring ... New-York, J. Leavitt, 1833. 93 p. 23 cm. [BT720.S63] 43-42182
1. Sin, Original. I. Title. II. Title: Native depravity.

TROOSTER, Stephanus Gerardus Maria, 1915- 233'.14
Evolution and the doctrine of original sin, by S. Trooster. Translated by John A. Ter Haar. Glen Rock, N.J., Newman Press [1968] v, 138 p. 21 cm. Translation of Evolutie in de erfzondeleer. Bibliographical footnotes. [BT720.T713] 68-24814 4.95
1. Sin, Original. I. Title.

YARNOLD, Edward. 233'.14
The theology of original sin. Notre Dame, Ind., Fides Publishers [1971] 95 p. 18 cm. (Theology today, no. 28) Bibliography: p. 92-93. [BT720.Y37] 72-185902 ISBN 0-85342-278-8
1. Sin, Original. I. Title.

Sin, Original—Biblical teaching.

DUBARLE, A. M. 233.14
The Biblical doctrine of original sin. Tr. [from French] by E. M. Stewart. New York, Herder & Herder [1965, c.1964] 245p. 21cm. Bibl. [BT720.D7813] 64-20437 4.95 bds.,
1. Sin, Original—Biblical teaching. I. Title.

DUBARLE, Andre Marie, 1910- 233.14
The Biblical doctrine of original sin [by] A. M. Dubarle. Translated by E. M. Stewart. New York, Herder and Herder [1965, c1964] 245 p. 21 cm. Translation of Le peche originel dans l'Ecriture. Bibliographical footnotes. [BT720.D7813] 64-20437
1. Sin, Original — Biblical teaching. I. Title.

KEYSER, Leander Sylvester, 1856- 233.
Man's first disobedience, an interpretation and defense of the Biblical narrative of the fall of man, by Leander S. Keyser ... New York, The Macmillan company, 1924. 84 p. 19 1/2 cm. [BT710.K4] 24-21948
I. Title.

Sin, Original—History of doctrines.

HUTCHINSON, George P. 233'.14
The problem of original sin in American Presbyterian theology, by George P. Hutchinson. [Nutley, N.J.] Presbyterian and Reformed Pub. Co., 1972. x, 119 p. 23 cm. (An International library of philosophy and theology: Biblical and theological studies) Bibliography: p. 117-119. [BT720.H87] 77-190463 2.95
1. Sin, Original—History of doctrines. 2. Theology, Presbyterian—United States. I. Title. II. Series: International library of philosophy and theology: Biblical and theological studies series.

NYMEYER, Frederick, 1897-
Origin of damnation and sin is not by inheritance but is cosmological. [South Holland, Ill.] Libertarian Press [c1967] xviii, 202 p. 68-61007
1. Sin, Original—Hist. of doctrines. I. Title.

RONDET, Henri, 1898- 233'.14
Original sin: the patristic and theological background. Translated from the French by Cajetan Finegan. Staten Island, N.Y., Alba House [1972] 282 p. 22 cm. Translation of Le peche originel dans la tradition patristique et theologique. Includes bibliographical references. [BT720.R6413] 72-1792 ISBN 0-8189-0249-3 4.95
1. Sin, Original—History of doctrines. I. Title.

SMITH, Hilrie Shelton, 1893- 233.14
Changing conceptions of original sin; a study in American theology since 1750. New York, Scribner, 1955. 242p. 22cm. [BT720.S5] 55-9682
1. Sin, Original—History of doctrines. 2. Theology, Doctrinal—Hist.—U. S. I. Title.

VANDERVELDE, George. 233'.14
Original sin : two major trends in contemporary Roman Catholic reinterpretation / George Vandervelde. Washington, D.C. : University Press of America, c1981. 350 p. ; 24 cm. Reprint. Originally published: Amsterdam : Rodopi, 1975. Bibliography: p. 335-350. [BT720.V3 1981] 19 81-40000 ISBN 0-8191-1849-4 : 24.00 ISBN 0-8191-1850-8 (pbk.) : 13.25
1. Sin, Original—History of doctrines. 2. Theology, Catholic—History—20th century. I. Title.

Sin, Original—Miscellanea.

CHANCE, Roger James Ferguson, Sir, 1893- 230
Apple and Eve / [by] Roger Chance. London : Villiers Publications, 1976. 91 p. ; 23 cm. [BT720.C38] 77-359988 ISBN 0-900777-08-7 : £3.00
1. Jesus Christ—Person and offices—Miscellanea. 2. Sin, Original—Miscellanea. I. Title.

Sin—Sermons.

FINNEY, Charles Grandison, 1792-1875. 233.208
The guilt of sin; evangelistic messages. Grand Rapids, Kregel Publications [1965] 124 p. 20 cm. (The Charles G. Finney memorial library: Evangelistic sermon series) "Selected from Sermons on the way of salvation." [BV3797.F53] 65-258453
1. Sin — Sermons. 2. Evangelistic sermons. 3. Sermons, American. I. Title.

HARRELL, Costen Jordan, 1885- 233.2
The way of the transgressor, a book of sermons concerning sin, by Costen J. Harrell. New York, Nashville, Abingdon-Cokesbury press [1942] 178 p. 20 cm. [BT715.H3] 42-4877
1. Sin—Sermons. 2. Methodist church—Sermons. 3. Sermons, American. I. Title.

ROBERSON, Lee. 233.2
5 ancient sins. Wheaton, Ill., Sword of the Lord Publishers [1954] 74p. 21cm. [BV4625.R58] 55-16567
1. Sin—Sermons. 2. Baptists—Sermons. 3. Sermons, American. I. Title.

SHELDON, David Newton, 1807-1889. 233.2
Sin and redemption: a series of sermons, to which is added an oration on moral freedom. By D. N. Sheldon ... New York, Sheldon, Lamport & Blakeman; Boston, Gould & Lincoln; [etc., etc.] 1856. xiv, [15]-332 p. 19 cm. [BT715.S47] 40-37143
1. Sin—Sermons. 2. Redemption—Sermons. 3. Baptists—Sermons. 4. Sermons, American. I. Title.

Sin, Unpardonable.

CRISPIN, Thomas. 233.22
Sin against the Holy Ghost and exposition of religious frauds. By Thomas Crispin ... Detroit, Mich., 1881. 1 p. l., 79, [1] p. 20 cm. [BT721.C8] 40-24814
1. Sin, Unpardonable. I. Title.

WILSON, James Patriot, 1769-1830. 233.22
A free conversation on the unpardonable sin: wherein the blasphemy against the Holy Spirit, the final apostasy, and the sin unto death, are shown to have been originally distinct. By James P. Wilson. Philadelphia, Towar, J. & D. M. Hogan; Pittsburgh, Hogan & co., 1830. 171 p., 1 l. 17 1/2 cm. [BT715.W7] 40-24811
1. Sin, Unpardonable. I. Title.

Sinai. Saint Catharine (Basilian monastery)

FORSYTH, George H. 726'.7'09531
The Monastery of Saint Catherine at Mount Sinai: the church and fortress of Justinian. Plates. By George H. Forsyth and Kurt Weitzmann, with Ihor Sevcenko and Fred Anderegg. Ann Arbor, University of Michigan Press [1973] 20 p., 198 p. of illus. (part col.) 36 cm. [NA6084.S5F67] 68-29257 ISBN 0-472-33000-4 37.50 45.00 (after Dec. 31, 1973)
1. Sinai. Saint Catharine (Basilian monastery) I. Weitzmann, Kurt, 1904- II. Title. III. Title: The church and fortress of Justinian.

WEITZMANN, Kurt, 1904- 755'.2
The Monastery of Saint Catherine at Mount Sinai, the icons / photos. by John Galey. Princeton, N.J. : Princeton University Press, [1975- p. cm. Includes index. Contents.Contents.—1. Weitzmann, K. From the sixth to the tenth century. [N8189.E32S558] 75-3482 ISBN 0-691-03543-1 : 75.00
1. Sinai. Saint Catharine (Basilian monastery) 2. Icons, Byzantine—Sinai—Catalogs. 3. Icons—Sinai—Catalogs. I. Galey, John. II. Title.

Sinclair, David Ainslie, 1850-1902.

BEST, Nolan Rice, 1871- 922
Two Y men; David A. Sinclair, secretary, Edwin L. Shuey, layman; partners in the service of the Young men's Christian association and other good works, by Nolan Rice Best ... New York, Association press, 1925. vi p., 1 l., 132 p. front. (2 port.) 20 cm. [BV1085.S5B4] 25-9320
1. Sinclair, David Ainslie, 1850-1902. 2. Shuey, Edwin Longstreet, 1857-1924. I. Title.

Sinclair, Max.

SINCLAIR, Max. 280'.4'0924 B
Halfway to heaven / Max Sinclair. Minneapolis, Minn. : Bethany House, c1982. 188 p. ; 21 cm. [BR1725.S468A34 1982] 19 82-9587 ISBN 0-87123-258-8 (pbk.) : 3.95
1. Sinclair, Max. 2. Christian biography—England. 3. Physically handicapped—England—Biography. 4. Christian life—1960- 5. Suffering—Religious aspects—Christianity. I. Title.

[Singers.]

DUNHAM, Montrew. 783.7 B
Mahalia Jackson : young gospel singer / by Montrew Dunham ; illustrated by Robert Doremus. Indianapolis : Bobbs-Merrill, [1974] 200 p. : col. ill. ; 20 cm. (Childhood of famous Americans) Bibliography: p. 198. A biography of the gospel singer who in her desire to sing only for God rose to world fame. [ML3930.J2D8] 92 74-260
1. Jackson, Mahalia, 1911-1972—Juvenile literature. 2. [Jackson, Mahalia, 1911-1972.] 3. [Singers.] 4. [Negroes—Biography.] I. Doremus, Robert, ill. II. Title.

MCDEARMON, Kay. 783.7 B
Mahalia, gospel singer / Kay McDearmon ; illustrated by Nevin and Phyllis Washington. New York : Dodd, Mead, c1976. 45 p. : ill. ; 24 cm. A brief biography of the renowned gospel singer who hoped, through her art, to break down some of the barriers between black and white people. [ML3930.J2M2] 92 75-33882 ISBN 0-396-07280-1 : 4.50
1. Jackson, Mahalia, 1911-1972—Juvenile literature. 2. [Jackson, Mahalia, 1911-1972.] 3. [Singers.] I. Washington, Nevin. II. Washington, Phyllis. III. Title.

[Singers, American.]

CORNELL, Jean Gay. 783.7 B
Mahalia Jackson: queen of gospel song. Illustrated by Victor Mays. Champaign, Ill., Garrard Pub. Co. [1974] 96 p. illus. (part col.) 24 cm. (Americans all) A biography of the renowned gospel singer who wanted more than anything else to "sing for the Lord." [ML3930.J2C67] 92 73-14713 ISBN 0-8116-4581-9 4.25
1. Jackson, Mahalia, 1911-1972—Juvenile literature. 2. [Jackson, Mahalia, 1911-1972.] 3. [Singers, American.] 4. [Negro musicians.] I. Mays, Victor, 1927- II. Title.

JACKSON, Jesse. 783'.7 B
Make a joyful noise unto the Lord! the life of Mahalia Jackson, queen of gospel singers. Boston, G. K. Hall, 1974. 207 p. 24 cm. Large print ed. A biography of the famous black gospel singer who hoped, through her art, to break down some of the barriers between black and white people. [ML3930.J2J2 1974b] 92 74-18252 ISBN 0-8161-6254-9
1. Jackson, Mahalia, 1911-1972—Juvenile literature. 2. [Jackson, Mahalia, 1911-1972.] 3. [Singers, American.] 4. [Sight-saving books.] I. Title.

[Singers—United States.]

JACKSON, Jesse. 783'.7 B
Make a joyful noise unto the Lord! The life of Mahalia Jackson, queen of gospel singers. Illustrated with photos. New York, T. Y. Crowell [1974] 160 p. illus. 21 cm. (Women of America) Bibliography: p. [vii]-viii. A biography of the famous black gospel singer who hoped, through her art, to break down some of the barriers between black and white people. [ML3930.J2J2] 92 72-7549 ISBN 0-690-43344-1 4.50
1. Jackson, Mahalia, 1911-1972—Juvenile literature. 2. [Jackson, Mahalia, 1911-1972.] 3. [Singers—United States.] I. Title.

Singers—United States—Biography.

DEKORTE, Juliann. 783.7'092'4 B
Finally home / by Juliann DeKorte. Old Tappan, N.J. : F. H. Revell Co., c1978. 128 p., [9] leaves of plates : ill. ; 22 cm. At head of title: Ethel Waters. [ML420.W24D4] 78-5697 ISBN 0-8007-0934-9 : 5.95
1. Waters, Ethel, 1900-1977. 2. Singers—United States—Biography. I. Title.

WATERS, Ethel, 1900-1977. 783.7'092'4 B
His eye is on the sparrow : an autobiography / by Ethel Waters with Charles Samuels. Westport, Conn. : Greenwood Press, 1978, c1951. p. cm.

Reprint of the ed. published by Doubleday, Garden City, N.Y. [ML420.W24A3 1978] 77-27496 lib.bdg. : 17.50
1. Waters, Ethel, 1900- 2. Singers—United States—Biography. I. Samuels, Charles. II. Title.

Singh, Bakht.

SMITH, Daniel, 1915?- 922.342
Bakht Singh of India, a prophet of God. Foreword by H. Enoch. Introd. by Robert V. Finlay. Washington, International Students Press [1959] 87 p. illus., ports. 22 cm. [BV3269.S5S6] 67-4582
1. Singh, Bakht. 2. Evangelistic work — India. 3. Missions — India. I. Title.

Singh, Kirpat.

ARNSBY-JONES, George. 294.553 (B)
The harvest is rich; the mission of Kirpal Singh. [1st ed.] New York, Pageant Press [1965] 179 p. port. 21 cm. [BL2017.9.S53A7] 64-66433
1. Singh, Kirpat. I. Title.

Singh, Sawan, 1858-1948.

KIRPAL Singh, 1894-1974. 294.6'61
Godman / Kirpal Singh. [3d ed.]. Bowling Green, Va. : Sawan Kirpal Publications, 1979. xv, 185, [3] p. : ports ; 21 cm. Bibliography: p. [187]-[188] [BL2017.9.S56K57 1979] 19 78-68503 ISBN 0-918224-07-1 pbk. : 2.50
1. Singh, Sawan, 1858-1948. I. Title.
Publisher's address: Box 24 Bowling Green, VA 22427

Singh, Sundar, 1889-

LYNCH-WATSON, Janet. 266'.023'0924 B
The saffron robe : a life of Sadhu Sundar Singh / by Janet Lynch-Watson. Grand Rapids, Mich. : Zondervan Pub. House, 1976, c1975. 157 p. ; 18 cm. Reprint of the ed. published by Hodder and Stoughton, London, in series: Hodder Christian paperbacks. [BV5095.S5L9 1976] 76-44813 pbk. : 1.75
1. Singh, Sundar, 1889- 2. Christian biography—India. I. Title.

Single people.

EVENING, Margaret. 261.8'34'1
Who walk alone : a consideration of the single life / Margaret Evening. Downers Grove, Ill. : InterVarsity Press, 1974. 222 p. ; 22 cm. Bibliography: p. 221-222. [HQ800.E85 1974b] 75-24160 ISBN 0-87784-767-3 : 3.95
1. Single people. 2. Single people—Sexual behavior. I. Title.

Single people—Conduct of life.

LUM, Ada. 261.8'3'1
Single & human / Ada Lum. Downers Grove, Ill. : InterVarsity Press, c1976. 81 p. ; 18 cm. Includes bibliographical references. [HQ800.L84] 75-44625 ISBN 0-87784-361-9 : 1.95
1. Single people—Conduct of life. 2. Single people—Religious life. I. Title.

Single people in the Bible.

HARBOUR, Brian L. 220.9'2 B
Famous singles of the Bible / Brian L. Harbour. Nashville, Tenn. : Broadman Press, c1980. 140 p. ; 19 cm. Includes bibliographical references. [BS579.S55H37] 19 79-56309 ISBN 0-8054-5640-6 pbk. : 3.50
1. Bible—Biography. 2. Single people in the Bible. I. Title.

Single people—Prayer-books and devotions—English.

JEPSON, Sarah Anne. 248'.84
Devotions for the single set, by Sarah Jepson. [1st ed.] Carol Stream, Ill., Creation House [1972] 114 p. 22 cm. [BV4596.S5J467] 70-182855
1. Single people—Prayer-books and devotions—English. I. Title.

STENERSON, Ruth. 242'.64
Bible readings for singles / Ruth Stenerson. Minneapolis, Minn. : Augsburg Pub. House, c1980. 110 p. ; 18 cm. [BV4596.S5S83] 19 80-65543 ISBN 0-8066-1788-8 pbk. : 2.95
1. Single people—Prayer-books and devotions—English. I. Title.

Single people—Religious life.

FIX, Janet. 248'.84
For singles only / Janet Fix, with Zola Levitt. Old Tappan, N.J. : Revell, c1978. p. cm. [BV4596.S5F58] 78-9754 ISBN 0-8007-0946-2 pbk. : 3.95
1. Single people—Religious life. I. Levitt, Zola, joint author. II. Title.

HADIDIAN, Allen, 1950- 248.8'4
A single thought / by Allen Hadidian. Chicago : Moody Press, c1981. 117 p. ; 22 cm. Includes bibliographical references. [BV4596.S5H32] 19 81-38347 ISBN 0-8024-0878-8 pbk. : 3.95
1. Single people—Religious life. 2. Single people in the Bible. I. Title.

HENSLEY, John Clark, 1912- 248'.4
Coping with being single again / J. Clark Hensley. Nashville : Broadman Press, c1978. 136 p. ; 21 cm. Bibliography: p. 124-126. [BV4596.S5H46] 78-52623 ISBN 0-8054-5420-9 : 4.95
1. Single people—Religious life. 2. Divorcees—Religious life. 3. Widows—Religious life. 4. Widowers—Religious life. I. Title.

JEPSON, Sarah Anne. 248.8'4
For the love of singles [by] Sarah Jepson. [1st ed.] Carol Stream, Ill., Creation House [1970] 96 p. 22 cm. [BV4596.S5J47] 72-131443 2.95
1. Single people—Religious life. I. Title.

JEPSON, Sarah Anne. 248'.84
Solo = formerly titled For the love of singles / Sarah Jepson. Carol Stream, Ill. : Creation House, c1978. 96 p. ; 18 cm. [BV4596.S5J47 1978] 78-107492 ISBN 0-88419-134-6 pbk. : 1.95
1. Single people—Religious life. I. Title. II. Title: For the love of singles.

MCALLASTER, Elva Arline, 1922- 248'.4
Free to be single / Elva McAllaster. 1st ed. Chappaqua, N.Y. : Christian Herald Books, c1979. 279 p. ; 23 cm. Includes bibliographical references. [BV4596.S5M32] 78-64838 ISBN 0-915684-45-4 : 7.95
1. McAllaster, Elva Arline, 1922- 2. Single people—Religious life. I. Title.

SROKA, Barbara. 248'.4
One is a whole number / Barbara Sroka. Wheaton, Ill. : Victor Books, c1978. 132 p. ; 21 cm. (The Family concern series) [BV4596.S5S76] 78-52782 ISBN 0-88207-631-0 pbk. : 2.95
1. Single people—Religious life. 2. Single people—Conduct of life. I. Title. II. Series.

TOWNS, James E. 248'.84
One is not a lonely number / by James E. Towns. Dallas : Crescendo Publications, c1977. 125 p. ; 18 cm. Includes bibliographies. [BV4596.S5T68] 77-80924 ISBN 0-89038-040-6 pbk. : 1.95
1. Single people—Religious life. I. Title.

UNGER, Dominic J 248.8
The mystery of love for the single. Chicago, Franciscan Herald Press [1958] 192 p. 21 cm. [BX2350.9.U5] 58-10453
1. Single people — Religious life. I. Title.

VETTER, Bob. 248'.4
Jesus was a single adult / Bob & June Vetter. Elgin, Ill. : D.C. Cook Pub. Co., c1978. 160 p. : ill. ; 21 cm. [BV4596.S5V47] 77-88655 ISBN 0-89191-109-X pbk. : 3.95
1. Single people—Religious life. I. Vetter, June, joint author. II. Title.

Single women.

CLARK, Carol. 248'.48'93
A singular life; perspectives for the single woman. Salt Lake City, Deseret Book Co., 1974. 60 p. 24 cm. [HQ800.C58] 74-81406 ISBN 0-87747-531-8 3.50
1. Single women. 2. Mormons and Mormonism. 3. Women—Religious life. I. Title.

OTTENSEN, Carol Clark. 248'.48'93
A singular life; perspectives for the single woman [by] Carol Clark. Salt Lake City, Deseret Book Co., 1974. 60 p. 24 cm. [HQ800.O82] 74-81406 ISBN 0-87747-531-8 3.50
1. Single women. 2. Mormons and Mormonism. 3. Women—Religious life. I. Title.

Single women—Conduct of life.

MCGINNIS, Marilyn 248'.4
Single; the woman's view. Old Tappan, N.J., Revell [1974] 159 p. illus. 21 cm. [BJ1610.M29] 74-9837 ISBN 0-8007-0678-1 4.95
1. Single women—Conduct of life. 2. Single women—Religious life. I. Title.

PAYNE, Dorothy. 248.8'43
Women without men; creative living for singles, divorcees and widows. Philadelphia, Pilgrim Press [1969] x, 150 p. 22 cm. Includes bibliographical references. Bibliography: p. 141-150. [BJ1610.P28] 71-94758 4.95
1. Single women—Conduct of life. I. Title.

Single women—Religious life.

ANDREWS, Gini. 248'.843
Your half of the apple; God & the single girl. Foreword by Francis Schaeffer. Grand Rapids, Zondervan Pub. House [1972] 159 p. 22 cm. [BV4596.S5A5] 72-189574 3.95
1. Single women—Religious life. I. Title.

SANDS, Audrey Lee. 266
Single and satisfied. Wheaton, Ill., Tyndale House Publishers [1971] 136 p. 18 cm. [BV4596.S5S25] 70-123295 ISBN 0-8423-5890-0
1. Single women—Religious life. I. Title.

Sinking Spring, Pa. St. John's Reformed Dutch church.

KERSHNER, William J. -1852- 277
Record St. John's Reformed church, Sinking Spring, Pennsylvania, 1883-1913. [By] Rev. W. J. Kershner... [n.p., 1913?] 2 p. l., 58 p. 23 1/2 cm. [BX9531.S6K4 1913] 20-16841
1. Sinking Spring, Pa. St. John's Reformed Dutch church. I. Title.

KERSHNER, William Jacob, 1852-1926. 277
Record St. John's Reformed church, Sinking Spring, Pennsylvania, 1883- 1913. [By] Rev. W. J. Kershner ... [n. p., 1913?] 2 p. l., 58 p. 23 1/2 cm. [BX9531.S6J66] 20-16841
1. Sinking Spring, Pa. St. John's Reformed Dutch church. I. Title.

Sioux Falls, S.D.—Biography.

TINGLEY, Ralph. 286'.1783'371
Mission in Sioux Falls : the First Baptist Church, 1875-1975 / Ralph & Kathleen Tingley. Sioux Falls, S.D. : First Baptist Church, c1975. 222 p. : ill. ; 24 cm. Includes bibliographical references. [BX6480.S73F577] 75-29740
1. First Baptist Church, Sioux Falls, S.D. 2. Sioux Falls, S.D.—Biography. I. Tingley, Kathleen, joint author. II. Title.

Sipe, Onjya, 1951-

SIPE, Onjya, 1951- 248'.2'0924 B
Devil's dropout : Manson follower turns to Christ / by Onjya Sipe, with Robert L. McGrath. Milford, Mich. : Mott Media, c1976. 204 p. ; 21 cm. [BV4935.S56A33] 76-17648 ISBN 0-915134-16-0 : 5.95. ISBN 0-915134-17-9 pbk. : 2.95
1. Sipe, Onjya, 1951- 2. Conversion. I. McGrath, Robert L., joint author. II. Title.

A sister of St. Dominic.

CATERINA da Siena, Saint, 1347-1380. 242
Thoughts from the writings of St. Catherine of Siena, comp. by a sister of St. Dominic ... [Des Plaines, Ill., Printing dept. of St. Mary's training school [1922] 1 p. l., 5-112 p., 1 l. 13 cm. Lettered on cover: For each day of the year. [BX2179.C3E5 1922] 22-23731
1. A sister of St. Dominic. I. Title.

Sister of the Third Order Regular of St. Francis of the Congregation of Our Lad

MARY Florence, Sister, O. S. F. 922.273
Our mother; a portrait of Venerable Mother Mary Adelaide, foundress of the Sisters of St. Francis of the Congregation of Our Lady of Lourdes, whose motherhouse is in Sylvania, Ohio. with a foreword by Karl J. Alter. [Sylvania'] 1959. 55p. illus. 23cm. [BX4520.3.Z8M25] 60-44
1. Mary Adelaide, Mother, 1874- 2. Sisters of the Third Order Reguiar of St. Francis of the Congregation of Our Lady of Lourdes, Sylvania, Ohio. I. Title.

Sisterhood of St. Mary.

DIX, Morgan, 1827-1908. 922.373
Harriet Starr Cannon, first mother superior of the Sisterhood of St. Mary. A brief memoir by Morgan Dix ... New York, London and Bombay, Longmans, Green, and co., 1896. 3 p. l., 149 p. pl., 2 port. (incl. front.) coat of arms. 19 cm. [BX5995.C23D5] 37-11167
1. Sisterhood of St. Mary, inc. I. Canon, Harriet Starr, 1823-1896. II. Title.

MARY Hilary, Sister. 271.98
Ten decades of praise; the story of the Community of Saint Mary during its first century, 1865-1965. Racine, Wis., DeKoven Found. for Church Work [dist. Sisters of St. Mary, Box 311, c.1965] 226, [8]p. illus., map. ports. 22cm. Bibl. [BX5973.S47M3] 65-4002 4.00
1. Sistenhood of St. Mary. I. Title.

MARY Hilary, Sister. 271.98
Ten decades of praise; the story of the Community of Saint Mary during its first century, 1865-1965. Racine, Wis., DeKoven Found. [1967, c.1965] 226, [8]p. illus., maps, ports. 21cm. Bibl. [BX5973.S47M3] 65-4002 1.65 pap.,
1. Sisterhood of St. Mary. I. Title.

PROTESTANT Episcopal church in the U. S. A. Liturgy and ritual. Diurnal. Benedictine. 264.
The day office of the monastic breviary. Translated into English and adapted to the kalendar and missal of the American church. Peekskill, N. Y., Printed for the community of St. Mary, St. Mary's convent, 1918. xx, 316, 96 p. 18 cm. [BX5947.B8A323 1918] 264 ISBN 19-16093 Revised
1. Sisterhood of St. Mary, inc. I. Title.

Sisterhoods.

BARRY, Joseph Gayle Hurd, 1858-
From a convent tower, by J. G. H. Barry, D. D. New York, E. S. Gorham, 1919. 186 p. 19 cm. [BX5973.S5B3] 19-16114
I. Title.

BENNETT, A H.
Through an Anglican sisterhood to Rome, by A. H. Bennett, with a preface by Sr. Scholastica M. Ewart ... London, New York, Longmans, Green and co., 1914. xi, [1] 203 p. front., 8 pl. 20 cm. A14
1. Sisterhoods. I. Title.

CODE, Joseph Bernard, 1899- 922.
Great American foundresses, by the Rev. Joseph B. Code ... New York, The Macmillan company, 1929. xviii p. 2 l., 512 p. ports. 22 1/2 cm. [Bx4225.C6] 30-810
1. Sisterhoods. 2. Catholic church—Biog. 3. Woman—Biog. 4. U.S.—Biog. I. Title.

CODE, Joseph Bernard, 1899- 922.273
The veil is lifted, by Rev. Joseph B. Code ... Milwaukee, The Bruce publishing company [c1932] xix, [1], 161 p. incl. front., ports. 19 cm. "The material of this book has been taken from the author's 'great American foundresses.'"--Pref. "Supplementary reading" at the end of each chapter. [BX4225.C63] 32-7804
1. Sisterhoods. 2. Catholic hcurch—Biog. 3. Woman—Biog. 4. U.S.—Biog. I. Title.

DEHEY, Elinor Tong. Mrs. 271.9
Religious orders of women in the United States: Catholic; accounts of their origin, works and most important institutions, interwoven with histories of many famous foundresses, by Elinor Tong Dehey: with an introduction by the Right Reverend Joseph Schrembs ... Rev. ed. [Hammond, Ind., W. B. Conkey company, c1930] xxxi, 908 p. incl. front., illus. (incl. ports.) 24 cm. [BX4220.U6D4 1930] 30-22058
1. Sisterhoods. 2. Convents and nunneries—U. S. I. Title.

EHL, Anton. 271.9
The spiritual direction of sisters; a manuel for priests and superiors, adapted from the second German edition of Rev. A. Ehl by Rev. Felix M. Kirsch ... New York, Cincinnati [etc.] Benzinger brothers, 1931. xix, 483 p. 17 cm. Bibliography: p. 465-475. [BX2413.E5 1931] 31-15432
1. Sisterhoods. 2. Convents and nunneries. 3. Monasticism and religious orders. 4. Canon law. I. Kirsch, Felix Marie, 1884- ed. and tr. II. Title.

MARY Jeremy, Sister, 1907- 922.273
All the days of my life. [1st ed.] Indianapolis, Bobbs-Merrill [1959] 191 p. 22 cm. [BX4705.M4217A3] 59-14295
I. Title.

NATIONAL federation of temple sisterhoods.
Proceedings of the National federation of temple sisterhoods; first general convention, Cincinnati, January 21-23, 1913, first biennial meeting, Chicago, January 19-21, 1915. [Cincinnati? 1915] 6 p. l., 15-92 p. 26 cm. "Membership list": p. 81-85. 15-14852
I. Title.

POTTER, Henry Codman, bp., 1834-1908.
Sisterhoods and deaconesses at home and abroad, by the Rev. Henry C. Potter ... New-York, E. P. Dutton & company, 1873. 358 p. 18 cm. 12-38002
I. Title.

SISTERHOOD of the holy nativity.
Rules and constitutions of the Sisters of the holy nativity. [Cambridge, Mass., The Riverside press] 1889. x, 145 p. 15 cm. [BX5973.S5A3] 45-29754
I. Title.

SISTERS of Saints Cyril and Methodius. 271.979
Adveniat regnum tuum. Sisters of SS. Cyril and Methodius, Danville, Pennsylvania, 1909-1959. [Danville 1959] 80 p. illus. 32 cm. "Golden jubilee program [Sept. 7, 1959]" inserted. [BX4491.8.A42] 60-23459
I. Title.

SISTERS of the Third order regular of St. Francis, Oldenburg, Ind. 271.
Historical sketch of the Convent and Academy of the Sisters of St. Francis in Oldenburg, Indiana, and of the work of their community in the United States ... Oldenburg, Ind., The Community, 1901. 4 p. l., 11-289 p. plates, ports. 20 1/2 cm. On cover: Souvenir of the golden jubilee [of the] Sisters of St. Francis, Oldenburg, Ind. [BX4515.S35A5] 45-46464
I. Title.

SISTERS of the Third order regular of St. Francis, Oldenburg, Ind. 271.
Historical sketch of the Convent and Academy of the Sisters of St. Francis in Oldenburg, Indiana, and of the work of their community in the United States ... Oldenburg, Ind., The Community, 1901. 4 p. l., 11-289 p. plates, ports. 20 1/2 cm. On cover: Souvenir of the golden jubilee [of the] Sisters of St. Francis, Oldenburg, Ind. [BX4515.S35A5] 45-46464
I. Title.

STEPHEN, Caroline Emelia. 261
The service of the poor; being an inquiry into the reasons for and against the establishment of religious sisterhoods for charitable purposes. By Caroline Emelia Stephen. London & New York, Macmillan & co., 1871. vi p., 1 l., 342 p., 1 l. 20 cm. [HV530.S8] 9-23180
1. Sisterhoods. I. Title.

Sisters adorera of the precious blood.

LIFE of Mother Catherine 921.
Aurelia of the Precious Blood, foundress of the Institute of the precious blood, 1833-1905, by a member of the institute; introduction by Rev. A. M. Skelly, O. P. St. Louis, Mo. and London, B. Herder book co., 1929. xxii, 205 p. front., pl., ports. 23 cm. [BX4705.C345L5] 29-16326
1. Catherine Aurelie du Precieux Sang, Mother, 1833-1905. 2. Sisters adorera of the precious blood.

Sisters Marianites of Holy Cross — History

SISTERS Marianites of Holy Cross. Louisiana Province. 271.979
Marianite centennial in Louisiana, 1848-1948. New Orleans, Marianites of Holy Cross [1948] 330 p. illus. 23 cm. [BX4448.5.A44] 60-23552
1. Sisters Marianites of Holy Cross — Hist. I. Title.

Sisters of bon secours of Paris.

HAYES, James M. 271.940973
The Bon secours sisters in the United States [by] James M. Hayes; with an introduction by Archbishop Curley ... Washington, D.C., National capital press, 1931. 285 p. front., plates, ports. 20 cm. [BX4445.S3H3] 32-2481
1. Sisters of bon secours of Paris. I. Title.

WILLIAMS, Thomas David, 1872- 922.273
The life of Mother St. Urban of the Congregation of the sisters of bon secours of Paris, by Rev. Thomas David Williams ... Baltimore, Md., John Murphy company, 1936. 336 p. front. (port.) 20 cm. [BX4705.S185W5] 36-87914
1. St. Urban, mother, 1857-1933 2. Sisters of bon secours of Paris. I. Title.

Sisters of charity.

FARRELL, Mary Xavier, sister, 1849- 922.273
Happy memories of a Sister of charity, by Sister M. Xavier Farrell, with illustrations by Sister M. Fides Glass. St. Louis, Mo., and London, B. Herder book co., 1941. 3 p. l., v-vii, 190 p. incl. plates. 2 port. (incl. front.) 21 cm. [Secular name: Roselia Farrell] [BX4705.F26A4] 42-2191
I. Title.

HEROINES of charity: 271.9
containing the Sisters of Vincennes, Jeanne Biscot, Mdlle, Le Gras, Madame de Miramion, Mrs. Seton, the Little sisters of the poor, etc., etc., with a preface, by Aubrey De Vere. esq. New York, Boston [etc.] D. & J. Sadlier & co. [186-?] 2 p. l., [ix]-xxxi, 260 p. front. (port.) 20 cm. [BX4225.H4] 34-12476
1. Sisters of charity. I. De Vere, Aubrey Thomas, 1814-1902.

HEROINES of charity: 922.2
containing the Sisters of Vincennes, Jeanne Biscot, Mlle. Le Gras, Madame de Miramion. Mrs. Seton, the Little sisters of the poor, etc., etc., with a preface by Aubrey De Vere, esq. New York, Montreal, D. & J. Sadlier & co. [1863?] 2 p. l., [ix]-xxxi, 260 p. front. (port.) 18 cm. [BX4225.H4 1863] 37-15498
1. Sisters of charity. I. De Vere, Aubrey Thomas, 1814-1902.

JAMESON, Anna Brownell (Murphy) Mrs. 1794-1860.
Sisters of charity, Catholic and Protestant. And the communion of labor. By Mrs. Jameson. Boston, Ticknor and Fields, 1857. 302 p. 19 cm. "The second edition." [BX4452.J3 1857] A 34
1. Sisters of charity. 2. Nurses and nursing. 3. Women in charitable work. I. Title.

MCCANN, Mary Agnes, Sister, 1851-
Little blossoms of love, kindness, and obedience, scattered during a lifetime in honor of Our Immaculate Mother by Sister Mary Agnes McCann ... v. 1- Mount St. Joseph-on-the-Ohio, Sisters of charity, 1910- v. front., plates. 21 cm. 10-25868
I. Title.

SISTERS of charity of Nazareth, Nazareth, Ky.
Manual of the Sisters of charity; a collection of prayers, compiled for the use of the Society of Sisters of charity in the diocese of Louisville, Ky. Baltimore, New York, J. Murphy company [c1908] 435 p. 14 1/2 cm. 8-20165
I. Title.

SOEUR Eugenie. 922.244
The life and letters of a Sister of charity. By the author of "A sketch of the life of S. Paula". Baltimore, J. Murphy & co., 1873. xi, 13-237 p. front. (port.) 16 cm. Preface, sour, 1836-1868. Preface signed: A.M.D. Selections from Meditations etc., By Soeur Eugenie--1836-1868 [BX4705.E75S6] 37-16307

Sisters of Charity—Addresses, essays, lectures.

JAMESON, Anna Brownell Murphy, 1794-1860. 271'.9'1
Sisters of charity, Catholic and Protestant and The communion of labor / by Mrs. Jameson. Westport, Conn. : Hyperion Press, 1976. p. cm. (Pioneers of the woman's movement ; 8) Reprint of the 1857 ed. published by Ticknor and Fields, Boston. [BX4237.J35 1976] 75-15087 ISBN 0-88355-268-X : 19.75
1. Sisters of Charity—Addresses, essays, lectures. 2. Women in charitable work—Addresses, essays, lectures. 3. Nursing—Moral and religious aspects—Addresses, essays, lectures. I. Jameson, Anna Brownell Murphy, 1794-1860. The communion of labor. 1976. II. Title.

Sisters of charity, Irish.

THE life and work of Mary 922
Aikenhead, foundress of the Congregation of Irish sisters of charity, 1787-1858, by a member of the Congregation, with a preface by Father John Sullivan ... London, New York [etc.] Longmans, Green and co., 1924. ix p., 1 l., 476 p. front., plates, ports., facsim. 22 cm. [BX4705.A4L5] 24-12844
1. Aikenhead, Mary, 1787-1858. 2. Sisters of charity, Irish.

MEDITATIONS for the annual retreat; for the use of the Sisters of charity. 2d ed. Baltimore and New York, J. Murphy & co., 1898. 362 p. 16 degree. 98-765

THE teaching of Mary 922.
Aikenhead, selections from "The life and work" by a member of her Congregation, with some extracts from the letters of Fr. Robert St. Leger, S.J. London, New York [etc.] Longmans, Green and co., 1925. viii, 156 p. 17 cm. $1.00. [BX4705.A4L52 1925] 25-9655
1. Aikenhead, Mary, 1787-1858. 2. Sisters of charity, Irish.

Sisters of charity of Cincinnati, Ohio.

MCCANN, Mary Agnes, sister, 1851- 271.
The history of Mother Seton's daughters, the Sisters of charity of Cincinnati, Ohio ... by Sister Mary Agnes McCann ... New York [etc.] Longmans, Green and co., 1917- v. fronts., plates, ports., facsims. 24 1/2 cm. Bibliography: v. 1, p. [xxi]-xxvii. [BX4470.C5M3] 17-3157
1. Sisters of charity of Cincinnati, Ohio. 2. Seton, Mother Elizabeth Ann, 1774-1821. I. Title.

Sisters of Charity of Leavenworth (Kansas)

GILMORE, Julia, Sister. 922.273
Come north! The life-story of Mother Xavier Ross, foundress of the Sisters of Charity of Leavenworth. Illus. by Patricia De Buck. New York, McMullen Books, 1951. 310 p. illus. 21 cm. [BX4705.R7252G5] 52-6153
1. Ross, Xavier, Mother, 1813-1895. 2. Sisters of Charity of Leavenworth (Kansas) I. Title.

Sisters of charity of Mother Seton, Greensburg, Pa.

BOYLE, Mary Electa, sister. 271.97
Mother Seton's Sisters of charity in western Pennsylvania [by] Sister Mary Electa Boyle. [Greensburg, Pa.] 1946. 1 p. l., x, 251 p. front., plates, ports., facsims. 23 1/2 cm. Bibliographical foot-notes. [BX4470.G65B6] 46-19981
1. Seton, Elizabeth Ann, mother, 1774-1821. 2. Sisters of charity of Mother Seton, Greensburg, Pa. I. Title.

Sisters of charity of Nazareth, Nazareth, Ky.

FOX, Columba, sister. 922.
... The life of the Right Reverend John Baptist Mary David (1761-1841) bishop of Bardstown and founder of the Sisters of charity of Nazareth, by Sister Columba Fox ... with an introduction by Paul L. Blakely ... New York, The United States Catholic historical society, 1925. 4 p. l., 240, [3] p. plates, ports., facsims. 24 cm. (United States Catholic historical society. Monograph series ix) Bibliography: p. 193-195. [BX4705.D28F6] [E184.C3U6] 325. 26-1286
1. David, John Baptist Maria, bp., 1761-1841. 2. Sisters of charity of Nazareth, Nazxareth, Ky. I. Title.

MCGILL, Anna Blanche. 271.
The Sisters of charity of Nazareth, Kentucky, by Anna Blanche McGill ... New York, The Encyclopedia press [c1917] xvi, 436 p. front., plates, ports., facsims. 22 cm. Bibliography: p. xv-xvi. [BX4470.N3M3] 17-16334
1. Sisters of charity of Nazareth, Nazareth, Ky. I. Title.

Sisters of charity of Providence.

BURTON, Katherine (Kurz) 1890- 922.271
The table of the King; the story of Mother Gamelin, foundress of the Sisters of Charity of Providence. New York, McMullen Books [1952] 244p. illus. 21cm. [BX4705.G22B8] 53-1399
1. Camelin, Emelie Eugenie (Tavernier) 1800-1851. 2. Sisters of Charity of Providence. I. Title.

MARY James, sister, 1872-1937. 271.97
Providence, a sketch of the Sisters of charity of Providence in the Northwest, 1856-1931, by Sister Mary James, with a foreword by His Excellency Rt. Rev. Edward J. O'Dea ... [Portland, Or., Kilham stationery & printing co., c1931] ix p., 2 l., 88 p. 1 illus., plates (1 double) ports. 19 cm. [Secular name: Mary Padden] [BX4470.P7M3] 43-19224
1. Sisters of charity of Providence. I. Title.

SCHOFFEN, Elizabeth, 1861- 271.
"The demands of Rome," by Elizabeth Schoffen (Sister Lucretia); her own story of thirty-one years as a sister of charity in the order of the Sisters of charity of Providence of the Roman Catholic church. Portland, Or., The author [c1917] 223 p. incl. front., plates, ports., facsims. 20 cm. [BX4216.S5A3] 17-10882 0.50
I. Title.

SCHOFFEN, Elizabeth, 1861- 271.
"The demands of Rome," by Elizabeth Schoffen (Sister Lucretia) 2d ed. Her own story of thirty-one years as a sister of charity in the order of the Sisters of charity of Providence of the Roman Catholic church. Portland, Or., The author [c1920] 223 p. incl. front., plates, ports.,

facsims. 18 cm. [BX4216.S5A3 1920] 20-2840
I. Title.

Sisters of Charity of St. Augustine.

GAVIN, Donald Phillip, 1911- 271.97
In all things charity; history of the Sisters of Charity of St. Augustine, Cleveland, Ohio, 1851-1954. Milwaukee, Bruce Press [1955] 164 p. illus. 23 cm. (Catholic life publications) [BX4470.C54G3] 56-59131
1. Sisters of Charity of St. Augustine. I. Title.

Sisters of Charity of Saint Elizabeth, Convent Station, N. J.

MCENIRY, Blanche Marie, Sister, 1906- 922.273
Woman of decision; the life of Mother Mary Xavier Mehegan, foundress of the Sisters of Charity of Saint Elizabeth, Convent, New Jersey. New York, McMullen Books [1953] 232p. illus. 21cm. [BX4705.M484M3] 53-8121
1. Mehegan, Mary Xavier, Mother, 1825-1915. 2. Sisters of Charity of Saint Elizabeth, Convent Station, N. J. I. Title.

SHARKEY, Mary Agnes, 1866- 271.9109749
The New Jersey Sisters of charity ... by Sister Mary Agnes Sharkey ... New York, Longmans, Green and co., 1933. 3 v. fronts., plates, ports., fold. map, facsims. 24 1/2 cm. Contents.I-II. Mother Mary Xavier Mehegan, the story of seventy-five years, 1859-1933.--III. Our missions, 1859-1933. [BX4470.C6S5] 33-32247
1. Mehegan, Mary Xavier, mother, 1825-1915. 2. Sisters of charity of Saint Elizabeth. Covent Station, N.J. 3. Convent Station, N.J. College of Sant Elizabeth. I. Title.

Sisters of Charity of St. Vincent de Paul.

BURTON, Katherine (Kurz) Mrs. 1890- 922.273
It is dear persuasion; the life of Elizabeth Ann Seton, by Katherine Burton... London, New York [etc.] Longmans, Green and co., 1940. xi, 304 p. 21 1/2 cm. "First edition." Bibliography: p. 303-304. [BX4705.S57B8 1940] 40-27305
1. Seton, Elizabeth Ann, mother, 1774-1821. 2. Sisters of charity of St. Vincent de Paul. I. Title.

LIFE of Mademoiselle Le Gras (Louise de Marillac), foundress of the Sisters of charity. Preceded by letters of Mgr. Mermillod ... and of Very Rev. A. Fiat ... Translated from the French by a Sister of charity. New York, Cincinnati [etc.] Benziger brothers, 1884. 366 p., 1 l. 20 cm. [BX4700.L5H5] 34-23708 922.244
1. Le Gras, Louise (de Marillac) Saint, 1591-1660. 2. Sisters of charity of St. Vincent de Paul. 3. Sisters of charity. I. Sister of charity, tr.

MELVILLE, Annabelle (McConnell) 1910- 922.273
Elizabeth Bayley Seton, 1774-1821. New York, Scribner [c1960] 411p. illus. 22cm. Includes bibliography. [BX4705.S57M4 1960] 61-3468
1. Seton, Elizabeth Ann, 1774-1821. 2. Sisters of Charity of St. Vincent de Paul. I. Title.

MELVILLE, Annabelle (McConnell) 1910- 922.273
Elizabeth Bayley Seton, 1774-1821 New York, Scribner, 1951. xvii, 411 p. illus. ports. 22 cm. Bibliography: p. 383-391. [BX4705.S57M4] 51-14503
1. Seton, Elizabeth Ann, Mother, 1774-1821. 2. Sisters of Charity of St. Vincent de Paul. I. Title.

POWER-WATERS, Alma (Shelley), 1896- 922.273
Mother Seton First American-born saint Revised edition. New York : Pocket Books [1976 c1957] viii, 182 p. : 18 cm. (Archway Paperback) Originally published under the title: Mother Seton and the Sisters of Charity. [BX4705.S57P67] ISBN 0-671-29785-6 pbk. : 1.25
1. Seton, Elizabeth Ann, 1774-1821 2. Sisters of Charity of St. Vincent de Paul. I. Title.
L.C. card no. for 1957 Vision Books edition: 57-7699.

SETON, Elizabeth Ann, mother, 1774-1821. 922.273
The soul of Elizabeth Seton; a spiritual autobiography culled from Mother Seton's writings and memoirs, by a Daughter of charity of St. Vincent de Paul, Saint Joseph's college, Emmitsburg, Maryland. New York, Cincinnati [etc.] Benziger brothers, 1936. 98 p. front., plates, facsim. 17 cm. [BX4705.S57A3] 37-10141
1. Sisters of charity of St. Vincent de Paul. I. A daughter of charity of St. Vincent de Paul, Saint Joseph's college, Emmitsburg, Md. II. Title.

VINCENT Saint, 1576?-1660. 271.91
The conferences of St. Vincent de Paul to the Sisters of Charity. Translated from the French by Joseph Leonard. Westminster, Md., Newman Press, 1952. 4 v. 22 cm. [BX4462.V513] 52-3073
1. Sisters of Charity of St. Vincent de Paul. 2. Spiritual life — Catholic authors. I. Title.

VINCENT de Paul, Saint, 1581-1660. 271.91
The conferences of St. Vincent de Paul to the Sisters of Charity. Translated from the French by Joseph Leonard. Westminster, Md., Newman Press 1952. 4 v. 22 cm. Translation of Conferences spirituelles pour l'explication des regles des Soeurs de charite. [BX4462.V513] 52-3073
1. Sisters of Charity of St. Vincent de Paul. 2. Spiritual life — Catholic authors. I. Title.

Sisters of Charity of St. Vincent de Paul—Juvenile literature.

POWER-WATERS, Alma (Shelley) 1896- 92
Mother Seton and the Sisters of Charity, by Alma Power-Waters. Condensed for very young readers from the original Vision book. Illustrated by W.T. Mars. New York, Guild Press [1963] 76 p. illus. (part col.) 24 cm. (A Junior Vision book) [BX4700.S4P6] 63-22935
1. Seton, Elizabeth Ann, 1774-1821—Juvenile literature. 2. Sisters of Charity of St. Vincent de Paul—Juvenile literature. I. Title.

Sisters of Charity of St. Vincent de Paul of New York—History

WALSH, Marie de Lourdes. 271.91
The Sisters of Charity of New York, 1809-1959. Foreword by Francis Cardinal Spellman. New York, Fordham University Press [1960] 3 v. illus. 24 cm. Includes bibliography. [BX4463.6.N5W3] 60-10735
1. Sisters of Charity of St. Vincent de Paul of New York — Hist. I. Title.

WALSH, Marie de Lourdes 271.91
The Sisters of Charity of New York, 1809-1959 [3v.] Foreword by Francis Cardinal Spellman. New York, Fordham University [c.1960] 3v. various p. illus. Bibl. 60-10735 15.00
1. Sisters of Charity of St. Vincent de Paul of New York—Hist. I. Title.

Sisters of Charity of the Blessed Virgin Mary, Dubuque, Iowa.

COOGAN, Jane. 271'.91
The price of our heritage : history of the Sisters of Charity of the Blessed Virgin Mary / M. Jane Coogan. Dubuque, Iowa : Mount Carmel Press, 1975- v. : ill. ; 23 cm. Includes index. Contents.Contents.—v. 1. 1831-1869. Bibliography: v. 1, p. 471-490. [BX4467.C66] 75-318954 4.00 (v. 1)
1. Sisters of Charity of the Blessed Virgin Mary, Dubuque, Iowa. I. Title.

SISTERS of charity of the Blessed Virgin Mary, Dubuque, Ia. 271.
In the early days, pages from the annals of the Sisters of charity of the Blessed Virgin Mary, St. Joseph's convent, Mount Carmel, Dubuque, Iowa, 1833-1887 ... St. Louis, Mo. [etc.] B. Herder, 1912. 1 p. l., viii, 367 p. front., plates, ports. 24 cm. [BX4470.D8A5] 12-494
I. Title.

Sisters of charity of the Incarnate word, San Antonio.

FINCK, Mary Helena, sister, 1886- 271.97
The congregation of the Sisters of charity of the Incarnate word of San Antonio, Texas. A brief account of its origin and its work. By Sister Mary Helena Finck... Washington, D.C., The Catholic university of America, 1925. vii, 282 p. 23 1/2 cm. Thesis (PH.D)--Catholic university of America, 1925. [Secular name: Laura Cecilia Finck] Bibliography: p. 219-222. [EX4470.S3F5 1925] 25-11445
1. Sisters of charity of the Incarnate word, San Antonio. I. Title.

Sisters of divine providence.

FOUCAULT, Alphonse Gabriel, bp., 1843-1929. 922.2
The Venerable Jean-Martin Moye, apostolic missionary: founder of the Sisters of providence in Lorraine: and the Christian virgins in China; translated from the French of the Most Reverend A. G. Foucault ... by the Sisters of divine providence of Kentucky; foreword to the English translation by Reverend Peter Gilday ... Melbourne, Ky., Sisters of divine providence of Kentucky [c1932] xii, 108 p., 1 l. incl. front. (mounted port.) plates. 19 cm. [BX4705.M74F6] 33-6354
1. Moye, Jean Martin, 1730-1793. 2. Sisters of divine providence. 3. Christian virgins. I. Sisters of divine providence. Kentucky, tr. II. Title.

Sisters of Divine Providence of San Antonio, Texas—History

CALLAHAN, Mary Geneosa, 1901- 271.97
The history of the Sisters of Divine Providence, San Antonio, Texas. Milwaukee, Bruce Press [1955] 304p. illus. 24cm. (Catholic life publications) [BX4475.S43C3] 56-3366
1. Sisters of Divine Providence of San Antonio, Texas—Hist. I. Title.

Sisters of Loretto at the Foot of the Cross.

GRAVES, William Whites, 1871- 922.273
Life and times of Mother Bridget Hayden, by W. W. Graves ... St. Paul Kan., Journal press, 1938. 324 p. illus. (incl. ports.) 21 cm. (Graves historical series, no. 8) [BX4705.H34G7] 38-36497
1. Hayden, Bridget, mother, 1814-1890. 2. Sisters of Loretto at the foot of the cross. 3. Osage Indians—Missions. I. Title.

MINOGUE, Anna Catherine, 1874-
Loretto; annals of the century, by Anna C. Minogue...with an introduction by The Most Rev. John J. Glennon... New York, The American press, 1912. xii, 252 p., 1 l. front., plates, ports., facsims. 23 1/2 cm. [BX4475.S3M5] 12-9630
1. Sisters of Lorette at the foot of the cross. I. Title.

OWENS, Lilliana, 1898-
The Florissant heroines. [Florissant? Mo., 1960] 45p. illus. 20cm. 'Basically chapter three of . . . [the author's] doctoral dissertation. The history of the Sisters of Loretto in the trans-Mississippi West.' Includes bibliography. [BX4476.O9] 62-27242
1. Sisters of Loretto at the Foot of the Cross. I. Title.

OWENS, Lilliana, 1898-
Loretto in Missouri, by M. Lilliana Owens. Foreword by Joseph Cardinal Ritter. St. Louis, Herder [c1965] xiv, 254 p. illus. 21 cm. Bibliography: p. 219-229. [BX4476.Z6M55] 64-66156
1. Sisters of Loretto at the Foot of the Cross. I. Title.

OWENS, Lilliana, 1898-
Loretto in Missouri; foreword by Joseph Cardinal Ritter. St. Louis, B. Herder Book Co. [c1965] 254 p. plates, port. O. 65-75287
1. Sisters of Loretto at the Foot of the Corss. I. Title.

Sisters of mercy.

BAUMAN, Mary Beata. 922.2415
A way of mercy; Catherine McAuley's contribution to nursing, [1st ed.] New York, Vantage Press [1958] 182p. illus. 21m)0cm. [RT37.M18B3] 58-10650
1. McAuley, Mary Catherine, 1778-1841. 2. Sisters of Mercy. I. Title.

COATELY, Mary Josephine, Sister. 271.92
The Sisters of mercy; historical sketches, 1831-1931, by Sister Mary Josephine Gately. New York, The Macmillian company, 1931. xix p., 3 l., 3-503 p. front., ports. 22 1/2 cm. 4 p. l., 113 p. 19 1/2 cm. Supplementary manual to the Sisters of mercy, historical sketches, 1831-1931. New York The Macmillan company, 1931. [BX4482.G3 Supply.] 31-9504
1. Sisters of mercy. I. Title.

MANCHESTER, N.H. Mount St. Mary's convent. 922.273
Reverend Mother M. Xavier Warde, foundress of the Order of mercy in the United States; the story of her life, with brief sketches of her foundations, by the Sisters of mercy, Mount St. Mary's, Manchester, New Hampshire; preface by the Rt. Rev. Denis M. Bradley, D.D. Boston, Marlier and company, limited, 1902. xv, [1] 287 p. front., plates, ports. 19 cm. [BX4705.W32M3] 2-30097
1. Warde, Mary Francis Xavier, mother, 1810?-1884. 2. Sisters of mercy. I. Title.

MARY of the angels sister, 1897- 922.273
One life in Christ; the life-story of Mother Catherine McAuley, by Sister Mary of the Angels, R.S.M. Illustrated by Lyof Treguebouff. New York, P. J. Kenedy & sons [c1940] 141 p. front. (port.) plates. 19 1/2 cm. Each of the four chapters accompanied by illustrated half-title, with quotation, not included in paging. [BX4705.M13M3] 40-11392
1. McAuley, Mary Catherine, mother, 1787-1841. 2. Sisters of mercy. 3. [Secular name: Marie Christine Simon] I. Title.

MERCEDES, Sister, 1846- comp. 264.
The mercy manual containing the little office of the Blessed Virgin Mary, the office of the dead and prayers used by the Sisters of mercy, compiled by "Mercedes" from approved sources. Rev. 1925. Pittsburgh, Pa., Sold at Convent of mercy [c1925] 1 p. l., 513, [1] p. front. 14 cm. [Secular name: Mary Antonio Gallagher] [BX2060.M5M4 1925] 25-24298
I. Title.

MERCEDES, Sister, 1846- comp. 264.
The mercy manual, containing the Little office of the Blessed Virgin Mary, the Office of the dead and prayers used by the Sisters of mercy, compiled by "Mercedes" from approved sources. Rev. 1928. Pittsburgh, Pa., Sold at Convent of mercy [c1928] 1 p. l., 514 p. front., plates. 14 cm. [Secular name: Mary Antonio Gallagher] [BX2060.M5M4 1928] 28-7643
I. Title.

MERCEDES, sister, originally Mary Antonio Gallagher, 1846-
The mercy manual, containing little office B. V. M. and for the dead; and prayers used daily by the Sisters of mercy. Comp. by "Mercedes" from approved sources, for the special use of the Sisters of mercy of the Pittsburg diocese. Beatty, Pa., St. Xavier's convent print, 1903. 3 p. l., 324 p. front., plates. 16 x 12 cm. 4-5000
I. Title.

MERCEDES, Sister, originally Mary Antonio Gallagher, 1846-
The mercy manual, containing the little office of the Blessed Virgin Mary and the office for the dead, tr. by Rev. Jas. L. Meagher, D. D., and prayers used by the Sisters of mercy, comp. by "Mercedes," from a approved sources. New York, Christian press association publishing

company [c1911] 1 p. l., 464 p. front., plates. 14 cm. 11-10048 1.00
I. Meagher, James Luke, tr. II. Title.

MERCEDES, Sister, 1846- comp.
The mercy manual, containing the little office of the Blessed Virginia Mary, and the office for the dead, and prayers used by the Sisters of mercy, comp. by "Mercedes" from approved sources. Rev. 1918. Pittsburgh, Pa., James McMillin printing company [c1918] 1 p. l., 439 p. front. 14 cm. [Suclar name: Mary Antonio Gallagher] 19-4982
I. Title.

MERCEDES, Sister, 1846- comp. 264.
The mercy manual containing the little office of the Blessed Virgin Mary. The office of the dead, and prayers used by the Sisters of mercy, comp. by "Mercedes" from approved sources. Rev. 1922. Pittsburgh, Pa., James McMillin printing company [c1922] 1 p. l., 512 p. front. 13 cm. [Secular name: Mary Antonio Gallaghers] [BX2060.M5M4 1922] 22-13471
I. Title.

MILEY, Mary Hilda, Sister, 1881- 922.273
The ideals of Mother McCauley and their influence; foundress, educator, social welfare worker, by Sister Mary Hilda Miley ... New York, P. J. Kenedy & sons [c1931] 68 p. 2 port. (incl. front.) 19 1/2 cm. [Secular name: Gertrude Ann Miley] [BX4705.M13M5] 31-18165
1. McAuley, Mother Mary Catherine, 1787-1841. 2. Sisters of mercy. I. Title.

MILEY, Mary Hilda, Sister, 1881- 922.273
A poem of beauty; the artistic soul of Mother Catherine McAuley, foundress of the Sisters of Mercy, by Sister Mary Hilda Miley ... with a foreword by Reverend Leonard Feeney, S.J. New York, P. J. Kenedy & sons [1942] x p., 2 l., 3-66 p. front. (port.) 18 cm. [Secular name: Gertrude Ann Miley] [BX4705.M13M52] 42-13444
1. McAuley, Mary Catherine, mother, 1787-1841. 2. Sisters of mercy. I. Title.

O'CONNOR, Mary Edwardine, 1898- 922.273
Into Thy hands. St. Meinrad, Ind., Printed by the Abbey Press [1957] 105p. 19cm. Includes bibliography. [BX4705.M13O3] 57-45927
1. McAuley, Mary Catherine, 1787-1841. 2. Sisters of Mercy. I. Title.

RAYMOND MARIE, Sister. 922.273
Courageous Catherine; Mother Mary Catherine the first Sister of Mercy. Illustrated by Sister Mary. Milwaukee, Bruce Pub. Co. [1958] 152p. illus. 22cm. (Catholic treasury books) [BX4705.M13R3] 58-122
1. McAuley, Mary Catherine, 1778-1841. 2. Sisters of Mercy. I. Title.

SISTERS of mercy, Pittsburgh. 271.
Memoirs of the Pittsburgh Sisters of mercy, comp. from various sources, 1843-1917. New York, The Devin-Adair company [c1918] xii, 467, [1] p. front., plates, ports. 21 cm. $3.00 [BX4484.P6S5] 18-4938
I. Title.

THERESE MARIE, sister. 922.273
For mercy's sake; the story of Mother Catherine McAuley, foundress of the Sisters of mercy, by Sister Therese Marie, R.S.M.; illustrations by Virginia Nelson. New York, The Declan X. McMullen company, 1947. 3 p. l., 90 p. illus. 24 cm. [BX4705.M13T5] 47-19572
1. McAuley, Mary Catherine, mother, 1787-1841. 2. Sisters of mercy. I. Title.

Sisters of mercy. Buffalo.

FITZGERALD, Mary Innocentia, sister. 271.92
A historical sketch of the Sisters of mercy in the diocese of Buffalo, 1857-1942, by Sister Mary Innocentia Fitzgerald ... with a foreword by His Excellency, the Most Reverend John A. Duffy ... Buffalo, N.Y., Mount Mercy academy, 1942. xviii, [2], 132 p. front. (port.) plates, map, diagrs. 20 cm. "Principal sources": p. 121-122. [BX4484.B9F5] 43-4803
1. Sisters of mercy. Buffalo. 2. Mount Mercy academy, Buffalo. I. Title.

Sisters of Mercy. Cedar Rapids, Iowa.

HOLLAND, Mary Ildephonse, Sister, 1884- 271.97
Lengthened shadows, a history of the Sisters of Mercy, Cedar Rapids, Iowa. New York, Bookman Associates, 1952. 337 p. illus. 24 cm. [BX4484.C4H6] 52-4509
1. Sisters of Mercy. Cedar Rapids, Iowa. I. Title.

Sisters of mercy. Chicago.

[O'BRIEN, Gabriel, mother, 1844-1908. 271.
Reminiscences of seventy years (1846-1916) Sister of mercy, Saint Xavier's, Chicago. Chicago, Ill., The Fred J. Ringley co., 1916. 6 p. l., viii, 325 p., 1 l. incl. 1 illus., pl. front., plates, ports. 23 cm. By Mother Gabriel O'Brien. [BX4484.C4502] 43-32301
1. Sisters of mercy. Chicago. I. Title.

Sisters of mercy—Drama.

SISTERS of mercy, Chicago. 791.6
The pageant-masque of mercy ... composed by the Sisters of mercy province of Chicago. [Chicago] 1931. 1 p. l., 56 p. 1 illus., diagr. 23 cm. "1831. A presentation of the origin and development of the Sisters of mercy through one hundred years. 1931." [BX4482.A3] 32-2683
1. Sisters of mercy—Drama. 2. Pageants. I. Title.

Sisters of Mercy. England—Juvenile literature.

GARNETT, Emmeline, 1924- 271.92
Florence Nightingale's nuns. Illus. by Anne Marie Jauss. New York, Vision Books [dist. Farrar, Straus & Cudahy, c.1961] 185p. (Vision books, 49) 61-5896 1.95
1. Sisters of Mercy. England—Juvenile literature. 2. Nightingale, Florence, 1820-1910—Juvenile literature. 3. Crimean War, 1853-1856—Hospitals, charities, etc.—Juvenile literature. I. Title.

Sisters of mercy. Harrisburg, Pa.

MCENTEE, Mary Veronica, sister, 1871- 271.920974818
The Sisters of mercy of Harrisburg, 1869-1939, by Sister Mary Veronica McEntee...with an introduction by Right Reverend Monsignor M. M. Hassett...foreword by the Most Reverend George L. Leech... Philadelphia, The Dolphin press, 1939. xviii, 416 p. front., plates, ports. 23 1/2 cm. "Necrology": p. 387-405. [Secular name: Rose McEntee] [BX4484.H3M3] 39-16210
1. Sisters of mercy. Harrisburg, Pa. I. Title.

Sisters of mercy—History

[CARROLL, Mary Teresa Austin] mother, d.1909. 1
Leaves from the annals of the Sisters of mercy ... By a member of the Order of mercy ... New York, The Catholic publication society co., 1881- v. 19 1/2 cm. [Secular name: Margaret Ann Carroll] Contents.I. Ireland: containing sketches of the convents established by the holy foundress.--II. Sketches of the order in England, at the Crimea, in Scotland, Australia, and New Zealand. [BX4482.C3] 45-51716
1. Sisters of mercy—Hist. I. Title.

Sisters of mercy, Kansas City, Mo., ed.

MARIN, Michel Ange, 1697-1767.
The fervent novice, from the French of Rev. Father Marin, of the Order of Minims. 1st American ed., edited by the Sisters of mercy, St. Agnes' academy, Kansas City, Mo. Chicago, Ill., D. B. Hansen & sons [c1914] 1 p. l., [5]-363 p. 20 cm. 14-11782 1.00
1. Sisters of mercy, Kansas City, Mo., ed. I. Title.

Sisters of mercy. Maryland.

COSTELLO, Mary Loretto. Sister 271.92
The Sisters of mercy of Maryland, 1855-1930, by Sister Mary Loretto Costello ... with an introduction by the Right Reverend Thomas J. Shahan ... St. Louis, Mo., and London, B. Herder book co., 1931. xvi, 249 p. front., plates, ports. 24 cm. [BX4483.U6C6] 31-4087
1. Sisters of mercy. Maryland. I. Title.

Sisters of mercy. Mississippi.

BERNARD, Mary Mother 1856- 271.9209762
The story of the Sisters of mercy in Mississippi 1860-1930, by a member of the community, Mother M. Bernard. New York, P. J. Kenedy & sons, 1931. xviii p., 1 l., 281 p. front., plates, ports. 23 cm. [Secular name: Margaret McGuire] [BX4483.U6B4] 31-11586
1. Sisters of mercy. Mississippi. I. Title.

Sisters of mercy. Nebraska.

CROGHAN, Mary Edmund, sister. 271.92
.-. *Sisters of mercy of Nebraska, 1864-1910,* by Sister Mary Edmund Croghan ... Washington, D.C., The Catholic university of America press, 1942. vii, 158 p. 23 cm. Thesis (PH.D.)--Catholic university of America, 1942. Bibliography: p. 151-155. [BX4483.U6C7] A 42
1. Sisters of mercy. Nebraska. 2. Catholic church in Nebraska. I. Title.

Sisters of Mercy. Pittsburgh.

MCHALE, M. Jerome. 271'.92'074811
On the wing : the story of the Pittsburgh Sisters of Mercy, 1834-1968 / Sister M. Jerome McHale. New York : Seabury Press, 1980. p. cm. "A Crossroad book." Includes index. Bibliography: p. [BX4483.5.P59M32] 19 80-19428 ISBN 0-8164-0466-6 : 15.00
1. Sisters of Mercy. Pittsburgh. I. Title.

Sisters of Mercy. Providence.

O'CONNOR, Mary Loretto, Sister, 1911- 271.92
Mercy marks the century. Providence, Sisters of Mercy [1951] 161 p. illus., ports. 28 cm. Bibliography: p. 147. [BX4484.P703] 51-28812
1. Sisters of Mercy. Providence. I. Title.

Sisters of mercy.Rochester, N.Y.

[MARY Antonia, sister] 1889- 271.920974789
Mercy, by a Sister of mercy. Rochester, N.Y., George P. Burns press, inc. [c1932] 3 p. l., 11-59 p. pl., ports. 19 1/2 cm. [BX4484.R6M3] 32-16949
1. Sisters of mercy.Rochester, N.Y. 2. Catholic church—Biog. 3. Woman—Biog. I. Title.

Sisters of Mercy. Sacramento, Calif. (Diocese)

MORGAN, Mary Evangelist. 271.920979454
Mercy, generation to generation; history of the first century of the Sisters of Mercy, Diocese of Sacramento, California. Foreword by Joseph T. McGucken. San Francisco, Fearon Publishers [c1957] 278p. illus. 22cm. [BX4484.S14M6] 57-9844
1. Sisters of Mercy. Sacramento, Calif. (Diocese) I. Title.

Sisters of Mercy. St. Louis.

SMITH, Mary Constance. 271.
A sheaf of golden years, 1856-1906, by Mary Constance Smith. New York, Cincinnati [etc.] Benziger brothers, 1906. 191 p. front. (port.) plates. 19 1/2 cm. "The following pages record the life and labors of a little community of Sisters of mercy who came to St. Louis in 1856."--Pref. "Poems written on different occasions by Sisters of Mercy, St. Louis, Mo.": p. [107]-170. [BX4484.S2S6] 6-21924
1. Sisters of Mercy. St. Louis. I. Title.

Sisters of Mercy. Scranton.

PAYE, Anne. 271'.992'00974837
Heritage of faith : century of Mercy in the Diocese of Scranton, 1874-1975 / Anne Paye. Dallas, Pa. : Mercy Information Center, c1976. ix, 76 p., [8] leaf of plates : ill. ; 22 cm. "First appeared as a year-long series of articles in the diocesan newspaper, 'The Catholic light'." [BX4483.6.S38P39] 77-372818
1. Sisters of Mercy. Scranton. I. Title.

Sisters of Mercy, Tennessee—History.

FOX, Mary Loyola. 271'.92'09768
A return of love; the story of the Sisters of Mercy in Tennessee, 1866-1966. [Milwaukee?] Bruce Pub. Co. [1967] xii, 188 p. illus., ports. 22 cm. Bibliography: p. 179. [BX4483.6.T4F6] 67-28892
1. Sisters of Mercy, Tennessee—History. I. Title.

Sisters of mercy. United States

BURTON, Katherine (Kurz) 1890- 271.92
His mercy endureth forever, by Katherine Burton, with a foreword by Francis cardinal Spellman, archbishop of New York. Tarrytown, N.Y., Sisters of mercy, 1946. vii p., 1 l., 273 p. 21 cm. [BX4483.U6B8] 46-17705
1. Sisters of mercy. U.S. I. Title.

BURTON, Katherine (Kurz) 1890- 271.92
So surely anchored. New York, P. J. Kenedy [1949, c1948] 260 p. illus., ports. 21 cm. [BX4483.U6B816] 49-1727
1. Sisters of Mercy.U. S. I. Title.

HERRON, Mary Eulalia. Sister. 271.
The Sisters of mercy in the United States, 1843-1928, by Sister Mary Eulalia Herron ... with an introduction by the Reverend Francis E. Tourscher ... New York, The Macmillan company, 1929. xvii p., 1 l., 434 p. front. (port.) 23 cm. [BX4483.U6H4] 29-6876
1. Sisters of mercy. U. S. I. Title.

Sisters of Mercy. United States.—History.

SABOURIN, Justine. 271'.92'073
The amalgamation : a history of the union of the Religious Sisters of Mercy of the United States of America / Justine Sabourin. Saint Meinrad, Ind. : Abbey Press, c1976. p. cm. Includes index. Bibliography: p. [BX4482.2.S2] 75-19927 ISBN 0-87029-059-2 : 12.95
1. Sisters of Mercy. United States.—History. I. Title.

Sisters of Notre Dame de Namur.

THE American foundations of the Sisters of Notre Dame de Namur, 271. compiled from the annals of their convents by a member of the congregation. Philadelphia, The Dolphin press, 1928. xxiii, 690 p. incl. illus., plates. front. (port.) 23 cm. [BX4485.e5A7] 26-25068
1. Sisters of Notre Dame de Namur.

THE life of Mere St. Joseph 922 (Marie Louise Francoise Blin de Bourdon) co-foundress and second superior general of the Institute of Sisters of Notre Dame of Namur, by a member of the same institute ... London, New York [etc.] Longmans, Green and co., 1923. x, 285, [1] p. front., plates, ports. 23 cm. "Based ... on the French edition published in 1920."--Note, p. v. [BX4705.B55L5] 23-18952 5.00
1. Blin de Bourdon, Marie Louise Francoise, in religion Mother St.

Joseph, 1756-1838. 2. Sisters of Notre Dame de Namur.

LIFE of the Reverend 922.2493
Mother Julia, foundress and first superior of the Sisters of Notre Dame, of Namur. Translated from the French. With the history of the order in the United States. New York, The Catholic publication society; Boston, P. Donahue; [etc., etc.] 1871. xi p., 1 l., [15]-351 p. incl. front. (port.) 19 cm. [BX4705.B5L5] 37-8037
1. Billiart, Julie, 1751-1816. 2. Sisters of Notre Dame de Namur. I. Catholic publication society, New York.

MCMANAMA, Mary Fidelis, 1886- 922.2493
Treasure in a field; the life of Venerable Mother St. Joseph, cofoundress of the Sisters of Notre Dame de Namur, nee Viscountess Marie Louise Francoise Blin de Bourdon, heiress of the Barony de Gezaincourt. Milwaukee, Bruce Pub. Co. [1960] 215p. illus. 22cm. [BX4485.3.Z8S25] 60-15480
1. Saint Joseph, Mother, 1756-1838. 2. Sisters of Notre Dame de Namur. I. Title.

MCNAMEE, Mary Dominica. 271.979
Willamette interlude. Palo Alto, Calif., Pacific Books [1959] 302 p. illus. 23 cm. Includes bibliography. [BX4485.3.M33] 59-9810
1. Sisters of Notre Dame de Namur. I. Title.

[QUINLAN, Sara-Alice Katharyne] 1872- 271.97
In harvest fields by sunset shores; the work of the Sisters of Notre Dame on the Pacific coast, by a member of the congregation. Diamond jubilee ed., 1851-1926. San Francisco, Gilmartin company, 1926. xii p., 1 l., 317 p., 1 l., xxiii, [5] p. plates, ports. 23 cm. "Epilogue: Address of Most Rev. Archbishop Edward J. Hanna, D. D., at the Diamond jubilee celebration, June 8, 1926, Belmont, California.": p. [313]-317. Appendix (p. [1]-[xxiv] at end) includes verses. [Name in religion: Anthony, Sister] [BX4485.S5Q5] 32-2709
1. Sisters of Notre Dame de Namur. 2. Catholic church in Pacific states—Education. I. Hanna, Edward Joseph, abp., 1860 II. Title.

Sisters of Notre Dame de Namur—Missions.

AIMEE, Julie, Sister 266.252
With dedicated hearts. Foreword by Sister Eleanor Joseph. Sisters of Notre Dame de Namur [dist. New York, Fordham, c.] 1963. 261p. illus. 24cm. 63-14409 4.95
1. Sisters of Notre Dame de Namur—Missions. 2. Missions—Japan. I. Title.

Sisters of Notre Dame—History

MARY Vincentia, Sister, S. N. D. 271.97
Their quiet tread; growth and spirit of the Congregation of the Sisters of Notre Dame through its first one hundred years, 1850-1950. Milwaukee, Bruce Press [1955] 555p. illus. 23cm. [BX4485.S49M3] 56-3367
1. Sisters of Notre Dame—Hist. I. Title.

Sisters of Our Lady of charity of the Good Shepherd.

BOARDMAN, Anne (Cawley) 922.244
Good Shepherd's fold; a biography of St. Mary Euphrasia Pelletier, R. G. S., foundress of the Congregation of Our Lady of Charity of the Good Shepherd of Angers. [1st ed.] New York, Harper [c1955] 292p. illus. 22cm. [BX4700.P38B6] 54-12327
1. Pelletler, Arie de Sainte Euphrasie, Saint, 1796-1868. 2. Sisters of Our Lady of Charity of the Good Shepherd. I. Title.

MARY of Saint Teresita sister, 1902- 271.97
The social work of the Sisters of the Good Shepherd; an explanation of the origin, spirit and social work, together with an analyzation of a few cases. By Sister Mary of St. Teresita ... Cleveland, O., Cadillac press [c1938] 4 p. l., 235, [11] p. incl. front., illus., pl., port. 23 1/2 cm. [Secular name: Catherine Mary O'Connor] Bibliography: p. [6]-[7] at end. [BX4485.S55M3] 40-31475
1. Sisters of Our Lady of charity of the Good Shepherd. I. Title.

Sisters of Our Lady of charity of the refuge.

ORY, Joseph Marie. 271.
The origin of the Order of Our Lady of charity, or its history from its foundation until the revolution, translated from the French of Father Joseph Mary Ory ... by one of the religious of Our Lady of charity of Buffalo, N. Y. Buffalo, N. Y., Le Couteulx leader press, 1918. 2 p. l., iii-vi, 674 p. front., illus. (incl. ports.) 24 cm. [BX4485.S6O72] 18-23244
1. Eudes, Jean, Saint, 1601-1680. 2. Sisters of Our Lady of charity of the refuge. I. Immaculate Heart, sister, 1874- tr. II. Title.

Sisters of Providence, Saint Mary-of-the-Woods, Ind.

GUERIN, Theodore, mother, 1798-1856. 922.273
Journals and letters of Mother Theodore Guerin, foundress of the Sisters of Providence of Saint Mary of-the-Woods, Indiana; edited with notes by Sister Mary Theodosia Mug; foreword by His Excellency, the Most Reveerned Joseph E. Ritter ... Saint Mary-of-the-Woods, Ind., Providence press [c1937] xxviii p., 2 l., 452 p. front., plates, ports., facsim. 24 cm. [Secular name: Anne Therese Guerin] [BX4705.G65A4] 37-6400
1. Sisters of Providence, Saint Mary-of-the-Wood, Ind. I. Mug, Mary Theodore, sister, 1860- ed. II. Title.

MUG, Mary Theodosia, sister, 1860- 973.776
Lest we forget; the Sisters of Providence of St. Mary-of-the-Woods in civil war service, by Sister Mary Theodosia Mug. St. Mary-of-the-Woods, Ind., Providence press [c1931] 79 p. plates, ports. 19 cm. [Secular name: Helen Mary Mug] [BX4485.S87M8] 31-33307
1. Sisters of Providence, Saint Mary-of-the-Woods, Ind. 2. U. S.—Hist.—Civil war—Hospitals, charities, etc. I. Title.

Sisters of Providence, Saint Mary-of-the-Woods, Ind.—History

BROWN, Mary Borromeo, Sister, 1879- 271.97
The history of the Sisters of Providence of Saint Mary-of-the-Woods; with an introd. by Paul C. Schulte. New York, Benziger Bros., 1949- v. illus., ports., maps. 24 cm. Secular name: Mary Alma Agnes brown. Contents.V. 1. 1806-1856. Includes bibliographies. [BX4485.S87B7] 49-5512
1. Sisters of Providence, Saint Mary-of-the-Woods, Ind.—Hist. I. Title.

Sisters of St. Agnes, Fond du Lac.

NABER, Vera 271.979
With all devotedness; chronicles of the Sisters of St. Agnes, Fond du Lac, Wisconsin. New York, Kenedy [c.1959] vi, 312p. illus. 22cm. 60-5904 3.95
1. Sisters of St. Agnes, Fond du Lac. I. Salvation II. Title.

Sisters of Saint Ann.

MARIE Jean de Pathmos, Sister. 271.979
A history of the Sisters of Saint Anne. Translated from the French by Sister Marie Anne Eva. [1st American ed.] New York, Vantage Press [1962- c1961- v. illus. 21 cm. Contents.Contents.—v. 1. 1850-1900. Includes bibliography. [BX4486.4.M3] 61-14779
1. Sisters of Saint Ann. 2. Marie Anne, Mother, 1809-1890. I. Marie Anne Eva, Sister, tr.

Sisters of St. Casimir.

BURTON, Katherine (Kurz) 1890- 271.979
Lily and sword and crown; the history of the congregation of the Sisters of St. Casimir, Chicago, Illinois, 1907-1957. Milwaukee, Bruce Press [1958] 178p. illus. 23cm. (Catholic life publications) [BX4486.5.B85] 59-4019
1. Sisters of St. Casimir. I. Title.

MACIULIONIS, Joseph R. father. 922.273
Sister Helen, the Lithuanian flower, by Joseph R. Maciulionis, M.I.C. New York, J. F. Wagner, inc.; London, B. Herder [c1944] xii, [2], 210 p. front., plates, ports. 21 cm. [BX4705.H453M3] 45-5799
1. Helen, sister, 1895-1919. 2. Sisters of St. Casimir. I. Title.

Sisters of St. Francis of Penance and Christian Charity.

MARY Paul, Sister, O. S. F. 922.2492
The chose Catherine. [1st ed.] New York, Pageant Press [1959, c1958] 186p. illus. 21cm. [BX4705.D18M27] 58-59576
1. Daeman, Magdalena, 1787-1858. 2. Sisters of St. Francis of Penance and Christian Charity. I. Title.

MASON, Mary Liguori, sister, 1863- 922.2492
Mother Magdalen Daemen and her congregation. Sisters of St. Francis of penance and Christian charity. The achievements of a century, 1835-1935, by Sister M. Liguori Mason ... with a foreword by Very Rev. Thomas Plassman ... [Buffalo, Rauch & Stoeckl printing co., 1935] 5 p. l., [9]-430, [10] p. col. front., plates, ports. 20 1/2 cm. [Secular name: Emily Mary Mason] Bibliography: p. [424] [BX4705.D18M3] 38-30035
1. Daemen, Magdalena, mother, 1787-1858. 2. Sisters of St. Francis of penance and Christian charity. I. Title.

Sisters of St. Joseph.

MEDAILLE, Jean Pierre, 1610-1669. 271.976
The spiritual legacy of John Peter Medaille, S. J.; an intercongregational publication of the Sisters of St. Joseph. [Paterson? N. J.] 1959. 95p. 22cm. 'Members of only ten of the twenty-one congregations which stemmed from the original foundation of the Sisters of St. Joseph at Carondelet constituted the 'working committee.' [BX4488.M4] 60-17893
1. Sisters of St. Joseph. I. Sisters of St. Joseph of Carondelet. II. Title.

MOTHER Saint John 922.244
Fontbonne, foundress of the congregation of the Sisters of Saint Joseph of Lyons; this translation is adapted from the original French edition by a Sister of Saint Joseph ... New York, P. J. Kenedy & sons [c1936] xv, 403 p. front. (port.) plates. 24 1/2 cm. [BX4705.F62S5] 37-2213
1. Fontbonne, Jeanne, 1759-1843. 2. Sisters of St. Joseph. I. Mary Leonilla, sister, 1885- tr. II. Title: Translation of Simple et grande: Mere Saint-Jean Fontbonne.

SISTERS of Saint Joseph 271.976
Return to the fountainhead; addresses at the tercentenary celebration of the Sisters of St. Joseph, Le Puy, France, July 17, 18, 19. 20, 1950. by His Eminence, Cardinal Gerlier, and other French churchmen. En amont, in an English edition by the Sisters of St. Joseph of Carondelet, Fontbonne College, St. Louis. Translators and editors: Sister Mary Berchmans Fournier [and others] St. Louis, Sisters of St. Joseph of Carondelet, 1952. 143p. illus. 21cm. Includes bibliography. [BX4487.S5E53] 53-19922
1. Sisters of St. Joseph. 2. Sisters of St. Joseph of Carondelet. I. Title.

Sisters of St. Joseph, Brentwood, N.Y.

MEANY, Mary Ignatius 271.976
By railway or rainbow; a history of the Sisters of St. Joseph of Brentwood. Brentwood, N.Y., Pine Pr., 1964. xii, 336p. illus., map (on lining papers) ports. 24cm. Bibl. 63-23383 price unreported
1. Sisters of St. Joseph, Brentwood, N.Y. I. Title.

Sisters of St. Joseph, Buffalo.

IMMACULATA, Sister, 1913- 271.976
Like a swarm of bees: Sisters of Saint Joseph of Buffalo. Designs by Sister M. Dorothy. Buffalo, Mount Saint Joseph [1957] 213p. 22cm. Includes bibliography. [BX4490.B8 I5] 58-20660
1. Sisters of St. Joseph, Buffalo. I. Title.

Sisters of St. Joseph, Nazareth, Mich.

MCCARTHY, Mary Barbara, sister, 1886- 271.976
A covenant with stones ... by Sister Mary Barbara, S.S.J.; historical reminiscences on the fiftieth anniversary: 1889-1939 of the foundation of the Congregation of the Sisters of Saint Joseph in Michigan. Nazareth, Mich., The Sisters of Saint Joseph, 1939. xii, 132 p. illus. 27 cm. Music: p. 125. [BX4490.N3M3] 39-15560
1. Sisters of St. Joseph, Nazareth, Mich. I. Title.

Sisters of Saint Joseph of Carondelet.

SAVAGE, Mary Lucide, Sister, 1865-
The congregation of Saint Joseph of Carondelet; a brief account of its work in the United States (1650-1922) by Sister Mary Lucida Savage ... with an introduction by Most Reverend John Joseph Glennon ... St. Louis, Mo., and London, B. Herder book co., 1923. xviii, 334 p. front., plates. ports. 23 1/2 cm. Bibliography: p. 310-318. [BX4503.U6S3] 23-17837
1. Sisters of Saint Joseph of Carondelet. I. Title.

SISTERS of St. Joseph of 271.976
Carondelet, by Sister Dolorita Marie Dougherty [others] foreword by Joseph Cardinal Ritter. St. Louis. B. Herder. 1966. x, 509p. illus. map ports. 24cm. Bibl. [BX4489.6.C3S5] 66-17097 7.00
1. Sisters of St. Joseph of Carondelet. I. Dougherty, Dolorita Marie, 1909-

Sisters of St. Joseph of Carondelet. Province of St. Paul.

HURLEY, Helen Angela, Sister. 271.97
On good ground; the story of the Sisters of St. Joseph in St. Paul. Minneapolis, University of Minnesota Press [1951] xiii, 312 p. illus., ports., map. 23 cm. "Bibliographical notes": p. 289-301. [BX4490.S3H8] 51-14167
1. Sisters of St. Joseph of Carondelet. Province of St. Paul. I. Title.

Sisters of St. Joseph of Carondelet. Rochester, N.Y.

A Sister of St. Joseph. 271.976
Sisters of Saint Joseph of Rochester, by a Sister of Saint Joseph. [Rochester? N.Y.] 1950. vii, 163 p. illus., port. 20 cm. Bibliography: p. 159-160. [BX4490.R6S5] 50-12942
1. Sisters of St. Joseph of Carondelet. Rochester, N.Y. I. Sisters of St. Joseph of Carondelet. Rochester, N.Y. II. Sisters of St. Joseph of Carondelet. Rochester, N.Y. III. Title.

Sisters of Saint Joseph of Carondelet. Troy province.

HISTORY of the 271.97609747
Sisters of Saint Joseph of Carondelet in the Troy province; with an introduction by the Right Reverend Thomas P. Phelan ... Troy, N.Y. [Albany, The Argus press] 1936. 5 p. l., 3-404 p., 1 l. incl. illus., plates. port. 24 cm. Maps on lining-papers. [BX4489.U6H5] 36-37503
1. Sisters of Saint Joseph of Carondelet. Troy province.

Sisters of St. Joseph of Cluny.

MARTINDALE, Cyril Charlie, 1879- 922.244
The life of Mere Anne-Marie Javouhey. London, New York, Longmans, Green

[1953] 140p. illus. 19cm. [BX4705.J38M3] 54-1646
1. Javouhey, Anne Marie, Mother, 1779-1851. 2. Sisters of St. Joseph of Cluny. I. Title.

Sisters of St. Joseph of Newark.

MCCAFFREY, Patrick 271.9760974932
Romaeus, 1887-
From dusk to dawn; a history of the Sisters of Saint Joseph of Newark, New Jersey, by the Reverend P. R. McCaffrey ... New York, Cincinnati [etc.] Benziger brothers, 1932. xi, 300, [1] p. front., plates, ports. 24 cm. [BX4502.M3] 32-9467
1. Sisters of St. Joseph of Newark. I. Title.

MCDERMOTT, Rosarii. 922.242
The undivided heart; the life of Mother Evangelista, first Mother General of the Sisters of St. Joseph of Newark. With a foreword by Thomas A. Boland. [Newark, N. J., Sisters of St. Joseph of Newark [1961] 236p. illus. 21cm. Includes bibliography. [BX4705.G1115M3] 61-41336
1. Gaffney, Evangelista, 1855-1920. 2. Sisters of St. Joseph of Newark. I. Title.

Sisters of St. Joseph, Philadelphia.

MARIA HESTKA, Sister, 271.976
1883-
Sisters of St. Joseph of Philadelphia: a century of growth and development, 1847-1947. Westminster, Md., Newman Press, 1950. xii, 380 p. illus., ports. 22 cm. Secular name: Mary Elizabeth Logue. Bibliography: p. [297]-318. "Translations of Mother St. John Fourrier": p. 359. [BX4490.P5M3] 50-8164
1. Sisters of St. Joseph, Philadelphia. I. Title.

Sisters of St. Louis.

MARY Pauline, Sister 271.979
God wills it; centenary story of the Sisters of St. Louis. With a pref. by Rev. Dr. O'Callaghan. Fresno, Calif., Academy Guild Press [1960] x, 320p. illus. 23cm. (bibl. footnotes) 60-9247 6.00
1. Sisters of St. Louis. I. Title.

Sisters of St. Mary, St. Louis.

A history of the Sisters of 271.
St. Mary of St. Louis, Mo., comp. from original sources by a sister of St. Mary on the occasion of the golden jubilee celebration of the foundation of the community, 1872-1922. [St. Louis, A. B. Dewes printing and stationery co., c1922] 192, [4] p. incl. illus., pl., ports. 26 cm. [BX4510.S55H5] 23-1856
1. Sisters of St. Mary, St. Louis. I. A sister of St. Mary.

Sisters of the Good Shepherd, Philadelphia.

[NORRIS, M. St. Anthony]
Sister, 1859-
The annals of the Good Shepherd, Philadelphia, 1850-1925, by a memberof the order. Philadelphia, Convent of the Good Shepherd, 1925. 3 p. l., [5]-271 p. front., pl., ports. 19 cm. [BX4475.S4N6] 26-5012
1. Sisters of the Good Shepherd, Philadelphia. I. Title.

Sisters of the holy cross.

BETZ, Eva (Kelly) 1897- 922.273
Stout hearts and gentle hands; the life of Mother Angela, of the Sisters of the Holy Cross [by] Eva K. Betz. Valatie, N.Y., Holy Cross Press, 1964. 106 p. 23 cm. [BX4496.Z8B4] 64-8534
1. Gillespie, Angela, 1824-1887. 2. Sisters of the Holy Cross. I. Title.

ELEANORE, Mary, Sister 271.97
1890-
On the King's highway; a history of the Sisters of the holy cross of St. Mary of the immaculate conception, Notre Dame, Indiana, by Sister M. Eleanore... New York, London, D. Appleton and company, 1931. xi p., 3 l., 3-447 p. front., plates, ports. 22 1/2 cm. [BX4485.S85E6] 31-19563
1. Sisters of the holy cross. I. Title.

MCALLISTER, Anna 922.273
(Shannon) 1888-
Flame in the wilderness; life and letters of Mother Angela Gillespie, C.S.C., 1824-1887, American foundress of the Sisters of the holy cross, by Anna Shannon McAllister, with a foreword by the Most Reverend John T. McNicholas ... [Paterson, N.J., St. Anthony guild press] 1944. xiv p., 1 l., 358 p. front. (port.) plates. 21 cm. (Centenary chronicles of the Sisters of the holy cross. Vol. VI) Bibliographical foot-notes. [BX4705.G52M3] 45-722
1. Gillespie, Angela, mother, 1824-1887. 2. Sisters of the holy cross. I. Title.

Sisters of the holy cross—Biography

SISTERS of the holy 922.273
cross.
Pioneers and builders ... [Hammond, Ind., Printed by W. B. Conkey company, c1941] x p., 1 l., 215 p. ports. 21 cm. (Centenary chronicles of the Sisters of the holy cross, Saint Mary's of the immaculate conception, Notre Dame, Holy Cross, Indiana, 1841-1941. [vol. iii]) [BX4510.S5A47] 41-6911
1. Sisters of the holy cross—Biog. I. Title.

SISTERS of the holy cross. 271.97
Superior generals ... Paterson, N.J., Saint Anthony guild press [c1941] vi, 177 p. front., ports. 21 cm. (Centenary chronicles of the Sisters of the holy cross, Saint Mary's of the immaculate conception, Notre Dame, Holy Cross, Ind. vol. II) [BX4510.S5A5] 41-4194
1. Sisters of the holy cross—Biog. I. Title. Contents omitted.

Sisters of the Holy Family of Nazareth.

CEGIELKA, Francis A. 271.97
"Nazareth" spirituality [by] Francis A. Cegielka. Authorized translation from Polish by Sister M. Theophame and Mother M. Laurence. Milwaukee, Bruce Pub. Co. [1966] viii, 175 p. 22 cm. [BX4497.Z7C413] 66-5051
1. Sisters of the Holy Family of Nazareth. I. Title.

DECHANTAL, Sister. 271'.97
Out of Nazareth; a centenary of the Sisters of the Holy Family of Nazareth in the service of the Church [by] M. DeChantal. Foreword by John Cardinal Krol. [1st ed.] New York, Exposition Press [1974] xii, 375 p. 24 cm. (An Exposition-testament book) Bibliography: p. 359-363. [BX4497.D4] 74-174483 ISBN 0-682-47820-2 17.50
1. Sisters of the Holy Family of Nazareth. I. Title.

Sisters of the Holy Family of Nazareth—Bibliography.

MENZENSKA, Mary 016.255'97
Jane.
Guide to Nazareth literature, 1873-1973 : works by and about the Congregation of the Sisters of the Holy Family of Nazareth / compiled by Mary Jane Menzenska. 1st ed. Philadelphia : Sisters of the Holy Family of Nazareth, 1975. xvii, 263 p. ; 26 cm. Includes index. Bibliography: p. 247-249. [Z7840.S55M45] [BX4497] 73-85752
1. Sisters of the Holy Family of Nazareth—Bibliography. I. Sisters of the Holy Family of Nazareth. II. Title.

Sisters of the Holy Family of San Francisco.

KAVANAGH, Dennis John, 1877- 271.
The Holy family sisters of San Francisco; a sketch of their first fifty years, 1872-1922, by Rev. D. J. Kavanagh, S. J.; with foreword by His Grace, the Most Reverend Edward J. Hanna ... San Francisco, Cal., Gilmartin co., 1922. 4 p. l., 328 p. front., plates. ports. 23 cm. [BX4510.S6K3] 23-4886
1. Sisters of the Holy family of San Francisco. I. Title.

TERESITA, Sister.
Mother Dolores, the story of the foundress of the Sisters of the Holy Family. San Francisco, Sisters of the Holy Family [1956?] 238-246 p. port. 23 cm. "Reprinted from Review for religious, September, 1956." 67-26671
1. Armer, Dolores, Mother, 1851-1905. 2. Sisters of the Holy Family of San Francisco. I. Title.

Sisters of the Holy Names of Jesus and Mary.

EULALIA TERESA, Sister, 922.271
1898-
So short a day; the life of Mother Marie-Rose, foundress of the Congregation of the Sisters of the Holy Names of Jesus and Mary, 1811-1849. New York, McMullen Books [c1954] 281p. illus. 21cm. [BX4705.M395E8] 55-14158
1. Marie Rose, Mother, 1811-1849. 2. Sisters of the Holy Names of Jesus and Mary. I. Title.

WITH wings as doves, 922.271
by Sister Mary Eustolia, M.A. Oakland, Calif., College of the Holy names, 1942. xiv, 177, [1] p. incl. front. 21 cm. A translation, by Sister Mary Eustolia, from "Notices biographiques des Soeurs des saints noms de Jesus et de Marie, de 1846 a 1866" (Montreal, 1900) of the lives of the sisters who were admitted to the Congregation by Mother Rose personally, supplemented by a reprint of Sister Eustolia's translated resume of the "Life of the mother foundress." cf. Foreword. [BX4510.S7W5] 42-23112
1. Sisters of the holy names of Jesus and Mary. I. Mary Eustolia, sister, tr. II. Oakland, Calif. College of the Holy names.

Sisters of the Infant Jesus.

BURNS, Katherine. 271.97
Symbolized by a shrine; the story of the Nursing Sisters of the Sick Poor. [Brooklyn? 1955] 271p. 22cm. [BX4510.S84B8] 56-4692
1. Sisters of the Infant Jesus. I. Title.

Sisters of the Order of St. Dominic, Adrian, Mich.

ELLEN VINCENT, sister, 791.6
1916-
Heritage; a choric pageant relating the history of the Sisters of Saint Dominic of Adrian, Michigan, in commemoration of their golden jubilee, 1892-1942 [by] Sister Ellen Vincent, O.P. [Adrian, Sisters of Saint Dominic, c1942] [23] p. 22 1/2 cm. [Secular name: Helen Marie McClain] [PS3509.L474H4] 43-7330
1. Sisters of the Order of St. Dominic, Adrian, Mich. I. Title.

Sisters of the Order of St. Dominic, Brooklyn.

CRAWFORD, Eugene 271.9720974721
Joseph, 1900-
The daughters of Dominic on Long Island, the Brooklyn Sisters of Saint Dominic, the history of the American congregation of the holy cross, Sisters of the Third order of Saint Dominic of the Diocese of Brooklyn, by Reverend Thomas E. Molloy ... New York, Cincinnati [etc.] Benziger brothers, 1938. xxi, [1], 389 p. front., plates, ports., diagr. 23 cm. "Critical notes": p. 357-367: Bibliography: p. 372-376. [BX4344.B7C7] 38-14463
1. Sisters of the Order of St. Dominic, Brooklyn. I. Title.

CRAWFORD, Eugene 271.9720974721
Joseph, 1900-
The Daughters of Dominic on Long Island, the Brooklyn Sisters of Saint Dominic the history of the American Congregation of the Holy Cross, Sisters of the Third Order of Saint Dominic of the Diocese of Brooklyn. With a foreword by Thomas E. Molloy. New York, Benziger Bros, 1938-53. 2v. illus., ports. 24cm. Bibliography: v.1. p.372-376; v.2,p. 291-312. [BX4344.B7C7] 38-14463
1. Sisters of the Order of St. Dominic, Brooklyn. I. Title.

Sisters of the Order of St. Dominic, New York.

BOARDMAN, Anne Cawley. 922.273
Such love is seldom; a biography of Mother Mary Walsh, O. P. [1st ed.] New York, Harper [1950] xiii, 236 p. illus., ports. 22 cm. [BX4705.W2575B6] 50-10800
1. Walsh, Mary, Mother, 1850-1922. 2. Sisters of the Order of St. Dominic, New York. I. Title.

Sisters of the Order of St. Dominic, Sinsinawa, Wis.

MCCARTY, Mary Eva, 271.972
Sister.
The Sinsinawa Dominicans; outlines of twentieth century development, 1901-1949. Dubuque, Iowa, Printed by the Hoermann Press [1952] 591p. illus. 24cm. [BX4510.S93M2] 53-17039
1. Sisters of the Order of St. Dominic, Sinsinawa, Wis. I. Title.

O'CONNOR, Mary Paschala, 271.9
Sister, 1882-
Five decades; history of the Congregation of the Most Holy Rosary, Sinsinawa, Wisconsin, 1849-1899. Sinsinawa, Wis., Sinsinawa Press, 1954. 370p. illus. 24cm. [BX4510.S93O25] 54-37083
1. Sisters of the Order of St. Dominic, Sinsinawa, Wis. I. Title.

SYNON, Mary. 922.273
Mother Emily of Sinsinawa, American pioneer. Milwaukee, Bruce Pub. Co. [c1955] 279p. illus. 23cm. [BX4705.P6595S9] 55-1260
1. Power, Emily, Mother, 1844-1909. 2. Sisters of the Order of St. Dominic. Sinsinawa, Wis. I. Title.

Sisters of the Poor of St. Francis.

GOSSENS, Bruno. 922.243
The Venerable servant of God, Mother Frances Schervier, foundress of the congregation of the Sisters of the poor of St. Francis; from the German of Bruno Gossens ... by Ferdinand B. Gruen ... New York, P. J. Kenedy & sons [c1935] 64 p. illus. 16 cm. [BX4705.S51G62] 35-7508
1. Schervier, Franziska, 1819-1876. 2. Sisters of the poor of St. Francis. I. Gruen, Ferdinand Bernard, 1882- tr. II. Title. III. Title: Translation of Die gottselige mutter Franziska Schervier.

JEILER, Ignatius, 1823- 922.243
1904.
The Venerable Mother Frances Schervier, foundress of the congregation of the Sisters of the poor of St. Francis. A sketch of her life and character. By the Very Rev. Ignatius Jeiler ... Authorized translation. By Rev. Bonaventure Hammer, O. S. F. With a preface by the Rt. Rev. C. M. Maes ... St. Louis, Mo., B. Herder, 1895. xxvi, 492, [3] p. front. (port.) 20 cm. [BX4705.S51J4] 37-18476
1. Schervier, Franziska, 1819-1876. 2. Sisters of the poor of St. Francis. I. Hammer, Bonaventure, 1842-1917, tr. II. Title.

MAYNARD, Theodore, 1890- 922.243
Through my gift: the life of Frances Schervier. New York, P. J. Kenedy [1951] 318 p. port. 21 cm. "Bibliographical note": p. 315-318. [BX4705.S51M3] 51-11216
1. Schervier, Franziska, 2. Sisters of the Poor of St. Francis. I. Title.

Sisters of the Precious Blood.

NOT with silver or gold; 271.97
a history of the Sisters of the congregation of the Precious Blood, Salem Heights, Dayton, Ohio, 1834-1944, by a Sister of the Precious Blood. Dayton, O., Sisters of the Precious Blood, 1945. xii, 464 p. front., plates, ports., coat of arms. 23 1/2 cm. "A general survey of sources": p. 416-417. Bibliographical references included in "notes on the text" (p. 418-444) [BX4510.S985N6] 45-22159

1. Sisters of the Precious Blood. I. A Sister of the Precious Blood.

Sisters of the Presentation of the Blessed Virgin Mary—Prayer-books and devotions—English.

SISTERS of the 264.02
Presentation of the Blessed Virgin Mary, Fitchburgh, Mass.
Manual of prayers for the Sisters of the Presentation of the Blessed Virgin Mary. New York, P. J. Kenedy [1953] 161p. illus. 15cm. [BX2060.P7A3] 55-28628
1. Sisters of the Presentation of the Blessed Virgin Mary—Prayer-books and devotions—English. I. Title.

Sisters of the Third order of St. Francis, Glen Riddle, Pa.

MARY Barnaba, Sister, 271.973
1875-
A diamond crown for Christ the King, a story of the first Franciscan foundation in our country, 1855-1930, by Sister Mary Barnaba ... Glen Riddle, Pa., The Sisters of St. Francis, Convent of Our Lady of Angels, 1930. xiv p., 2 l., 3-309 p. front., plates, ports, 24 1/2 cm. [Secular name: Bessie Boyd Castor] [BX4364.G55M3] 30-13891
1. Sisters of the Third order of St. Francis, Glen Riddle, Pa. I. Title.

Sisters of the Third Order of St. Francis of Assisi.

HANOUSEK, Mary Eunice, 271.973
Sister.
A new Assisi; the first hundred years of the Sisters of St. Francis of Assisi, Milwaukee, Wisconsin, 1849-1949. Milwaukee, Bruce Pub. Co. [1948] xiv, 231 p. illus., ports. 25 cm. "Notes and references": p. 212-226. [BX4515.S24H3] 48-3313
1. Sisters of the Third Order of St. Francis of Assisi. I. Title.

Sisters of the Third order of Saint Francis of penance and of charity, Tiffin, O.

[WALLENHORST, Mary 271.97
Euphrasia, sister] 1906-
Sisters of the Third order of Saint Francis of penance and of charity, Tiffin, Ohio, 1869-1942, by a member of the community. [Paterson, N.J., St. Anthony guild press, 1942] xiv, 126 p. incl. front., illus. (incl. ports.) 22 1/2 cm. [Secular name: Valeta Agnes Wallenhorst] "References": p. 125-126. [BX4515.S25W3] 42-50013
1. Sisters of the Third order of Saint Francis of penance and of charity, Tiffin, O. I. Title.

Sisters of the Third order of St. Francis of the Holy family.

GOLDEN, Mary Cortona, 271.
Sister, 1883-1926.
The Sisters of St. Francis of the Holy family, Jesus, Mary, and Joseph, by Sister Mary Cortona Gloden St. Louis, Mo., and London, B. Herder book co., 1928. xxi, 278 p. front., plates. ports. 23 cm. Bibliography: p. xvii. [BX4510.S45G5] 28-31144
1. Sisters of the Third order of St. Francis of the Holy family. I. Title.

MOUSEL, Eunice, Sister, 271.97
1896-
They have taken root : the Sisters of the Third Order of St. Francis of the Holy Family. New York, Bookman Associates [1954] 384p. illus. 24cm. [BX4515.S3M6] 54-13447
1. Sisters of the Third Order of St. Francis of the Holy Family. I. Title.

Sisters of the Third Order of St. Francis of the Immaculate Virgin Mary, Mother of God.

AS a living oak
biography of Mother Baptista Etzel, third Mother Superior of the Sisters of St. Francis, Pittsburgh, Pa. Milwaukee, Bruce [c1956] vi, 133p. plates 22cm. (Catholic life publications)
1. Etzel, Baptista, Mother, d. 1925. 2. Sisters of the Third Order of St. Francis of the Immaculate Virgin Mary, Mother of God. I. Aronth, Mary Aurelia, 1881-

Sisters of the Third Order of St. Francis of the Perpetual Adoration.

LUDWIG, Mileta, Sister. 271.973
A chapter of Franciscan history; the Sisters of the Third Order of Saint Francis of Perpetual Adoration, 1849-1949. New York, Bookman Associates [1950] 455 p. illus. ports. map. 24 cm. Bibliographical footnotes. "Author's commentary as sources and procedures". p.[443]-446. [BX4515.S33L83] 50-10952
1. Sisters of the Third Order of St. Francis of the Perpetual Adoration. I. Title.

Sisters of the Third order of St. Francis of the perpetual adoration, La Crosse, Wis.

[LUDOVICKA, Mary] Mother, 271.
1844-
Our community; the origin and the development through seventy years of the congregation of the Sisters of the Third order of St. Francis of the perpetual adoration, La Crosse, Wisconsin, 1849-1919, by a member of the community. La Crosse, Wis., St. Rose convent, 1920. 8 p. l., 287 p. front., plates, ports., facism. 24 cm. [Secular name: Louisa Keller] [BX4364.L14L8] 21-1079
1. Sisters of the Third order of St. Francis of the perpetual adoration, La Crosse, Wis. I. Title.

Sisters of the Third order of St. Francis, Pittsburgh.

POPP, Clarissa, sister, 271.973
1862-
History of the Sisters of St. Francis of the diocese of Pittsburgh, Pennsylvania, 1868-1938; by Sister M. Clarissa Popp. Mt. Alvernia, Millvale, Pa., Sisters of St. Francis, 1939. xiv p., 1 l., 308 p. illus. (incl. ports.) 24 cm. [Secular name: Annie E. Popp] [BX4364.P5P6] 40-1721
1. Sisters of the Third order of St. Francis, Pittsburgh. I. Title.

Sisters of the Third Order Regular of St. Francis of Allegany, New York.

BURTON, Katherine (Kurz) 271.973
1890-
Cry jubilee! Allegany, N. Y., Sisters of St. Francis of the Third Order Regular [1960] 227p. illus. 22cm. [BX4520.2.B8] 60-51670
1. Sisters of the Third Order Regular of St. Francis of Allegany, New York. I. Title.

Sisters of the Third Order Regular of St. Francis, Oldenburg, ind.

CLARISON, Mother, 1865- 271.973
With the Poverello; history of the Sisters of Saint Francis, Oldenburg, Indiana, by Mother M. Clarissa and Sister Mary Olivia. New York, P. J. Kenedy [1948] xii, 333 p. port. 21 cm. Secular name: Mary Dillhoff. [BX4515.S35C5] 48-11162
1. Sisters of the Third Order Regular of St. Francis, Oldenburg, ind. I. Mary Olivia, Sister, 1909- joint author. II. Title.

Sisters of the Visitation—Prayer-books and devotions—English.

SISTERS of the Visitation. 264.02
Baltimore.
The Visitation manual: a collection of prayers and instructions compiled according to the Spiritual directory and spirit of Saint Francis de Sales, founder of the Religious Order of the Visitation of Holy Mary. [Rev. ed.] New York, G. Grady Press, 1955. 508p. 16cm. [BX2060.V5A5 1955] 56-150
1. Sisters of the Visitation—Prayer-books and devotions—English. I. Title.

SISTERS of the visitation of
Holy Mary, Brooklyn, N.Y.
Jubilee gems of the Visitation order; comp. and tr. from approved sources and dedicated to their pupils by the Sisters of the visitation of Holy Mary, Brooklyn, New York, 1855-1905. New York, Christian press association publishing company, 1905. 365 p. 19 cm. 5-10415
I. Title.

Sisters servants of the immaculate heart of Mary.

MARIA Alma, sister, 1887- 271.97
Sisters, servants of the immaculate heart of Mary, with life and letters of our founder, Reverend Louis Florent Gillet; introduction by His Eminence Cardinal Dougherty; by Sister Maria Alma ... Philadelphia, Pa., The Dolphin press, 1934. xviii, 347 p. front., plates, ports., map, facsims. 24 cm. [Secular name: Marie E. Joan Ryan] [BX4515.S8M3] 34-9047
1. Sisters, servants of the immaculate heart of Mary. 2. Gillet, Louis Florent, 1813-1892. I. Title.

A retrospect, three score years and ten, Sisters, servants of the immaculate heart of Mary, by a member of the congregation, St. Mary's college and academy, Monroe, Michigan, November, 1915. New York, Cincinnati [etc.] Benziger brothers, 1916. 190 p. front., plates, ports. 21 1/2 cm. $1.00. 16-13987
1. Sisters servants of the immaculate heart of Mary.

THE sisters of the I.H.M.; 271.
the story of the founding of the congregation of the Sisters, servants of the immaculate heart of Mary and their work in the Scranton diocese, by a member of the Scranton community. New York, P. J. Kenedy & sons, 1921. xv, 503 p. front., plates, ports. 24 cm. [BX4515.S8S5] 22-936
1. Sisters, servants of the immaculate heart of Mary. I. A member of the Scranton community.

SISTERS, servants of the 271.97
immucalate heart of Mary.
... Rules and constitutions of the Sisters, servants of the immaculate heart of Mary. New York, Printed by the Catholic publication society co. [19--] 80 p. 17 1/2 cm. At head of title: J. M. J. A. T. [BX4515.S8A5] 37-24317
I. Catholic church, Liturgy and ritual. Sisters, servants of the immaculate heortof Mary. II. Title.

Sisters, Servants of the Immaculate Heart of Mary—History

MARIA Alma, Sister, 1887- 271'.979

Sisters, Servants of the Immaculate Heart of Mary, 1845-1967, by Mother Maria Alma. Introd. by John Cardinal Krol. Lancaster, Pa., Dolphin Press, 1967. xiv, 463 p. illus., ports. 24 cm. Bibliographical footnotes. [BX4522.M3] 67-8841
1. Sisters, Servants of the Immaculate Heart of Mary—History.

ROSALITA, Sister, ed. 271.97
Achievement of a century; the motherhouse and missions, congregation of the Sisters, Servants of the Immaculate Heart of Mary Monroe, Michigan, 1845-1945. [Detroit? c1948] xiii, 299 p. illus. 24 cm. [BX4515.S8R59] 49-2138
1. Sisters, Servants of the Immaculate Heart of Mary—Hist. I. Title.

ROSALITA, Sister. 271.97
No greater service; the history of the Congregation of the Sisters, Servants of the Immaculate Heart of Mary, Monroe, Michigan, 1845-1945. With a foreword by Edward Cardinal Mooney. Detroit, 1948. xx, 863 p. illus., ports., facsims. 24 cm. Bibliography: p. [813]-833. [BX4515.S8R6] 49-1233
1. Sisters, Servants of the Immaculate Heart of Mary—Hist. I. Title.

Sitenhop, Yente (Glaser)

BUKSBAZEN, Lydia 922.96
(Sitenhof) 1908-
They looked for a city. Philadelphia, Friends of Israel Missionary and Relief Society [1955] 216p. illus. 20cm. [BV2622.S5B8] 56-17705
1. Sitenhop, Yente (Glaser) 2. Sitenhof, Benjamin. I. Title.

Sites, Nathan, 1830-1895.

SITES, Sarah (Moore) Mrs., 922.
1838-1912.
Nathan Sites; an epic of the East, by S. Moore Sites; with introduction by Bishop William Fraser McDowell ... New York, Chicago [etc.] Fleming H. Revell company [c1912] 256 p. front., plates (part col.) ports. 21 1/2 cm. [BV3427.S58S5] 13-6553
1. Sites, Nathan, 1830-1895. 2. Missions—China. I. Title.

Situation ethics.

BARR, O. Sydney. 241
The Christian new morality; a Biblical study of situation ethics [by] O. Sydney Barr. New York, Oxford University Press, 1969. x, 118 p. 22 cm. Bibliography: p. 117-118. [BJ1251.B344] 69-17758 4.00
1. Situation ethics. I. Title.

COX, Harvey Gallagher, comp. 241
The situation ethics debate, edited with an introd. by Harvey Cox. Philadelphia, Westminster Press [1968] 285 p. 19 cm. Bibliography: p. [273]-285. [BJ1251.F55C6] 68-11991
1. Fletcher, Joseph Francis, 1905- Situation ethics. 2. Situation ethics. I. Title.

PIKE, James Albert, Bp., 241
1913-1969.
You & the new morality; 74 cases [by] James A. Pike. New York, Harper & Row [1967] viii, 147 p. 21 cm. Includes bibliographical references. [BJ1251.P53] 67-14935
1. Situation ethics. 2. Christian ethics—Anglican authors. I. Title.

Siva (Hindu deity)

O'FLAHERTY, Wendy 294.5'2'11
Doniger.
Asceticism and eroticism in the mythology of Siva. London, New York, Oxford University Press, 1973. xii, 386 p. illus. 24 cm. Bibliography: p. [326]-340. [BL1218.O34] 73-180569 ISBN 0-19-713573-0 £8.00
1. Siva (Hindu deity) 2. Mythology, Hindu. I. Title.

O'FLAHERTY, Wendy 294.5'211
Doniger
Siva, the erotic ascetic / Wendy Doniger O'Flaherty. New York : Oxford University Press, 1981, c1973. xi, 386 p., [4] leaves of plates : ill. ; 20 cm. Reprint of the ed. published by Oxford University Press, London and New York, under title: Asceticism and eroticism in the mythology of Siva. Includes indexes. Bibliography: p. [326]-340. [BL1218.O34 1981] 19 81-127 ISBN 0-19-520250-3 (pbk.) : 8.95
1. Siva (Hindu deity) 2. Mythology, Hindu. I. [Asceticism and eroticism in the mythology of Siva] II. Title.

SIDDHANTASHASTREE, 294.5'513
Rabindra Kumar, 1918-
Saivism through the ages / by Rabindra Kumar Siddhantashastree. New Delhi : Munshiram Manoharlal Publishers, c1974, 1975. viii, 188 p. ; 23 cm. Includes index. Bibliography: p. [171]-173. [BL1218.S5 1975] 75-902111 9.00
1. Siva (Hindu deity) 2. Sivaism. I. Title.
Distributed by South Asia Books, Columbia, Mo.

Siva (Hindu deity)—Art.

KRAMRISCH, Stella, 704.9'48945211
1898-
The presence of Siva / Stella Kramrisch ; photography by Praful C. Patel. Princeton, N.J. : Princeton University Press, c1981. x, 514 p., 32 leaves of plates : ill. ; 24 cm. Includes index. Bibliography: p. [489]-509.

[NB1007.S67K7] 19 80-8558 ISBN 0-691-03130-4 : 37.50 ISBN 0-691-10119-1 (lim. pbk. ed.) : 16.50
1. Siva (Hindu deity)—Art. 2. Sculpture, Hindu—India—Elephanta Island. 3. Cave temples—India—Elephanta Island. 4. Sculpture, Hindu—India—Ellora. 5. Cave temples—India—Ellora. I. Title.

Sivaism.

GOPALA, Chetti, D. 230.
New light upon Indian philosophy; or, Swedenborg and Saiva siddhanta, by D. Gopaul Chetty ... With a foreword by L. B. de Beaumont, D. SC. London and Toronto, J. M. Dent & sons, ltd. New York, E. P. Dutton & co., 1923. xxxvi, 218 p., 1 l. front. (port.) 19 cm. [BX8711.G6] 25-7414
1. Swedenborg, Emmanuel, 1688-1772. 2. Sivaism. 3. India—Religion. 4. Philosophy, Hindu. I. Title.

LALLA, 14thcent.
The word of Lalla the prophetess; being the sayings of Lal Ded or Lal Diddi of Kashmir (Granny Lal) known also as Laleshwari, Lalla Yogishwari & Lalishri, between 1300 & 1400 A. D. Done into English verse from the Lallavakyani or Lal-waskhi and annotated by Sir Richard Carnac Temple, bt. ... Cambridge [eng.] The University press, 1924. xiii p., 1 l., 292 p. 23 cm. [PK2225.L3E5 1924] 25-7234
1. Sivaism. 2. India—Religion. I. Temple, Richard Cranac, Sir, bart, 1850- ed. and tr. II. Title.

SHULMAN, David Dean, 294.5'513
1949-
Tamil temple myths : sacrifice and divine marriage in the South Indian Saiva tradition / David Dean Shulman. Princeton, N.J. : Princeton University Press, c1980. xvi, 471 p. : ill. ; 24 cm. Includes indexes. Bibliography: p. [427]-455. [BL1245.S5S53] 79-17051 ISBN 0-691-06415-6 : 30.00
1. Sivaism. 2. Mythology, Tamil. 3. Temples, Hindu—India—South India. 4. Sacred marriage (Mythology) 5. Sacrifice (Hinduism) I. Title.

SIVARAMAN, K. 181'.4
Saivism in philosophical perspective; a study of the formative concepts, problems, and methods of Saiva Siddhanta [by] K. Sivaraman. [1st ed.] Delhi, Motilal Banarsidass [1973] xiv, v, 687 p. 24 cm. Bibliography: p. [646]-656. [BL1245.S5S58] 73-91126
1. Sivaism. 2. Saiva Siddhanta philosophy. I. Title.
Distributed by Verry, Mystic Conn. for 22.50; ISBN: 0-8426-0538-x.

TAIMNI, I. K., 1898- 294.5'513
The ultimate reality and realization : Siva-sutra, with text in Sanskrit, transliteration in roman, translation in English, and commentary / by I. K. Taimni. 1st ed. Madras ; Wheaton, Ill. : Theosophical Pub. House, 1976. xiv, 215 p. ; 22 cm. [BL1146.V326S527] 76-903636 Rs21.00
1. Vasugupta. Sivasutra. 2. Sivaism. I. Vasugupta. II. Title.

Skaggs, Fred R.

SKAGGS, Fred R. 248'.48'61
Colors of the mind / by Fred R. Skaggs, William L. Trimyer. Richmond, Va. : Skipworth Press, c1978. 179 p. ; 21 cm. Includes bibliographical references. [BV4501.2.S474] 78-55597 ISBN 0-931804-01-9 : 3.95
1. Skaggs, Fred R. 2. Trimyer, William L. 3. Christian life—1960- I. Trimyer, William L., joint author. II. Title.

Skarga, Plotr, 1536-1612.

BOLEK, Francis, 1886- 922.2438
The life of Father Skarga, by Rev. Francis Bolek, M.A. Buffalo, N.Y., The Riverside press of Buffalo, inc. [1943] 67, [1] p. incl. front. (port.) illus. 24 cm. Bibliography: p. 65-[68] [BX4705.S666B6] 43-16722
1. Skarga, Plotr, 1536-1612. I. Title.

Skattebol, Olaf, 1847-1930.

SKATTEBoL, Olaf, 284'.1'0924 B
1847-1930.
Translation of extracts of biographical notes, memories from childhood, youth, etc. / written by Olaf Skattebol ; [translated by Enevold F. Schroder]. Oslo : Enevold F. Schroder, 1976] 25 leaves ; 30 cm. Cover title. [BX8080.S396A3513] 76-381853
1. Skattebol, Olaf, 1847-1930. 2. Lutheran Church—Clergy—Biography. 3. Clergy—Norway—Biography. I. Title.

Skau, Annie Margareth, 1911-

GLEASON, Gene. 266.0250924 B
Joy to my heart. [1st ed.] New York, McGraw-Hill [1966] 215 p. 22 cm. [BV3427.S59G6] 65-28591
1. Skau, Annie Margareth, 1911- 2. Missions—China. I. Title.

Skepticism.

ELLIS, John, b.1815.
Skepticism and divine revelation. By John Ellis ... New York, The author, 1882. iv, 260 p. 18 1/2 cm. 16-25021
I. Title.

[FELLOWS, John] 1759-1844. 211
The character and doctrines of Jesus Christ. From the author's manuscript. To which is added, Reasons for scepticism, in revealed religion. By John Hollis. Also, The history of the man after God's own heart. New York-- Printed for J. Fellows.-- 1796-. 2 p. l., 113 p. front. 17 cm. No. 1 in a volume of three pieces lettered: Doctrines of Christ. Signa- tures: [A]3, B-K6, L4 (last leaf blank) "The character and doctrines of Jesus Christ" is by John Fellows. cf. Dexter, Yale biog. and annals, 4th ser., p. 267. The third piece is slightly abridged from "The life of David; or, The history of the man after God's own heart." attributed to Peter Annet and ascribed also to Archibald Campbell and to others. cf. B.M.; Dict. nat. biog.; Halkett & Laing. Imperfect: p. 25-26 and 101-104 wanting. [BL2773.F4] 31-4598
1. Skepticism. 2. Jesus Christ. 3. David, king of Israel. I. Hollis, John, 1757-1824. Sober and serious reasons for scepticism. II. Annet, Peter, 1693-1769. III. Title. IV. Title: The history of the man after God's own heart.

POST, Truman Marcellus, 1810- 211
1886.
The skeptical era in modern history; or, The infidelity of the eighteenth century, the product of spiritual despotism, By T. M. Post. New York, C. Scribner, 1856. xii, [9]-264 p. 18 cm. [BL2758.P6] 39-430
1. Skepticism. 2. Eighteenth century. I. Title.

RUMKE, Henricus Cornelius, 239
1893-
The psychology of unbelief; character and temperament in relation to unbelief. Tr. from the Dutch by M. H. C. Willems. New York, Sheed [1962] 80p. 18cm. (Canterbury Bks.) .75 pap.,
1. Skepticism. 2. Character. 3. Apologetics—20th cent. I. Title.

SHEPARD, William Edward.
Wrested Scriptures made plain, or, Help for holiness skeptics. Louisville, Ky., Pentecostal herald press, 1900. 174 p. 12°. 0-6556
I. Title.

STRATHMANN, Ernest 211.7'092'4
Albert, 1906-
Sir Walter Ralegh; a study in Elizabethan skepticism, by Ernest A. Strathmann. New York, Octagon Books, 1973 [c1951] ix, 292 p. 23 cm. Reprint of the ed. published by Columbia University Press, New York. Includes bibliographical references. [DA86.22.R2S86 1973] 73-8897 ISBN 0-374-97640-6 11.50
1. Raleigh, Walter, Sir, 1552?-1618. 2. Skepticism.

TRUMBULL, Henry Clay, 1830-1903.
How to deal with doubts and doubters; actual experiences with troubled souls, by H. Clay Trumbull ... Rev. ed. New York, Young men's Christian association press, 1907. xvii, 131 p. 18 cm. 7-24831
I. Title.

Skepticism—Controversial literature.

AUGUSTINUS, Aurelius, 189.2
Saint, Bp. of Hippo.
Against the Academics; translated and annotated by John J. O'Meara. Westminster, Md., Newman Press, 1950 [i. e. 1951] vi, 213 p. 23 cm. (Ancient Christian writers; the works of the Fathers in translation, no. 12) Bibliographical references included in "Notes" (p. [153]-199) [BR60.A35 no. 12] 51-2548
1. Skepticism—Controversial literature. I. O'Meara, John Joseph. ed. and tr. II. Title. III. Series.

BROWNSON, Orestes Augustus, 239.7
1803-1876.
Charles Elwood: or, The infidel converted. By O. A. Brownson. Boston, C. C. Little and J. Brown, 1840. xi, 262 p. 18 cm. "I am willing the public should take the book as an account ... of my own former unbelief and present belief."--Pref. [BT1210.B75] 35-36626
1. Skepticiam—Controversial literature. 2. Christianity—Apologetic works—19th cent. I. Title.

HALL, Robert, 1764-1831. 289
Modern infidelity considered with respect to its influence on society; in a sermon, preached at the Baptist meeting, Cambridge. By Robert Hall ... First American, from the third English edition. Charlestown [Mass.]; Printed and sold by Samuel Etheridge. Sold also by the booksellers in Boston, 1801. vi, [7]-55 p. 20 cm. [BT1210.H3 1801] 36-3155
1. Skepticism—Controversial literature. 2. Baptists—Sermons. I. Title.

MEADOWCROFT, Ralph Sadler. 239
Postlude to skepticism. Louisville, Ky., Cloister Press [1947] 288 p. 20 cm. (Cloister vital books) [BT1210.M4] 48-2140
1. Skepticism—Controversial literature. 2. Apologetics—20th cent. I. Title.

NELSON, David, 1793-1844. 239.7
The cause and cure of infedility; including a notice of the author's unbelief and the means of his rescue. By Rev. David Nelson, M. D. 2d stereotype ed., cor. by the author. New York, American tract society [186-?] 399 p. 20 cm. [BT1210.N4] 38-19306
1. Skepticism—Controversial literature. 2. Apologetics—19th cent. I. American tract society. II. Title.

NELSON, David, 1793-1844. 239.7
The cause and cure of infidelity; including a notice of the author's unbelief and the means of his rescue. By Rev. David Nelson, M. D. 2d stereotyped ed., cor. by the author. New York, American tract society [185-?] 399 p. front. (port.) 20 cm. [BT1210.N4] 17-19450
1. Skepticism—Controversial literature. 2. Apologetics—19th cent. I. Title.

NEWTON, Richard Heber, 1840- 239.
1914.
Philistinism; plain words concerning certain forms of modern scepticism, by R. Heber Newton ... New York & London, G. P. Putnam's sons, 1885. ix p., 1 l., 332 p. 17 1/2 cm. [BT1210.N45] 47-35828
1. Skepticism—Controversial literature. 2. Apologetics—19th cent. I. Title.

SOPER, David Wesley, 1910- 239.7
Epistle to the skeptics. New York, Association Press [c1956] 109 p. 21 cm. [BT1210.S67] 56-6444
1. Skepticism — Controversial literature. 2. Apologetics — 20th cent. I. Title.

WALKER, James Barr, 922.8173
1805-1887.
Philosophy of skepticism and ultraism, wherein the opinions of Rev. Theodore Parker, and other writers are shown to be inconsistent with sound reason and the Christian religion. By James B. Walker... New York, Derby & Jackson; Cincinnati, Rickey, Mallory & Webb; [etc., etc.] 1857. ix, [11]-286 p. 19 1/2 cm. [BX9869.P3W3] 38-3770
1. Parker, Theodore, 1810-1860. 2. Skepticism—Controversial literature. 3. Apologetics—19th cent. I. Title.

Skepticism—History

BAUMER, Franklin Le Van. 149.7309
Religion and the rise of scepticism. [1st ed.] New York, Harcourt, Brace [1960] 308p. 21cm. Includes bibliography. [BL2747.8.B35] 60-10918
1. Skepticism—Hist. I. Title.

Skepticism—History—17th century.

TALMOR, Sascha. 192
Glanvill : the uses and abuses of scepticism / by Sascha Talmor. 1st ed. Oxford ; New York : Pergamon Press, c1981. xv, 102 p., [1] leaf of plates : port. ; 22 cm. Includes index. Bibliography: p. 96-99. [B1201.G54T34 1981] 19 81-196927 ISBN 0-08-027407-2 : 20.00 20.00
1. Glanvill, Joseph, 1636-1680. 2. Skepticism—History—17th century. I. Title.

Skiles, William West, 1807-1862.

COOPER, Susan Fenimore, 922.
1813-1894, ed.
William West Skiles: a sketch of missionary life at Valle Crucis in western North Carolina, 1842-1862 ... edited by Susan Fenimore Cooper ... New York, J. Pott & co., 1890. 141 p. 19 cm. [BX5995.S39C6] 4-24212
1. Skiles, William West, 1807-1862. I. Title.

Skin—Diseases.

CAMPBELL, George Gordon, 616
1863-
Common diseases of the skin, with notes on diagnosis and treatment, by G. Gordon Campbell ... New York, The Macmillan company, 1920. viii, 229 p. illus. 23 cm. [BL71.C3] 20-3572
1. Skin—Diseases. I. Title.

WOLFF, Bernard. 616
Practical dermatology; a condensed manual of diseases of the skin; designed for the use of students and practitioners of medicine, by Bernard Wolff ... Chicago, Cleverland, press, 1906. 3 p. l., [9]-278 p. illus. 27 cm. [BL71.W8] 6-36196
1. Skin—Diseases. I. Title.

Skinner, Harry—Juvenile literature.

DOWN, Goldie M. 266'.673 B
You never can tell when you may meet a leopard / Goldie M. Down. Washington : Review and Herald Pub. Association, 1980. p. cm. A biography of a Seventh-day Adventist missionary who began his work in India in 1915 at the age of 21. [BV3271.S54D68] 92 19 80-24401 ISBN 0-8280-0026-3 : 4.95
1. Skinner, Harry—Juvenile literature. 2. [Skinner, Harry.] 3. Missionaries—Burma—Biography—Juvenile literature. 4. Missionaries—Australia—Biography—Juvenile literature. 5. Religious literature—Publication and distribution—India—Biography—Juvenile literature. 6. [Missionaries.] I. Title.

Skoptsi.

JOSEPHSON, Emanuel Mann, 281.9
1895-
The unheeded teachings of Jesus; or, Christ rejected; the strangest story never told. Illustrated by Andre Michaillot. New York, Chedney Press [c1959] 96p. illus. 19cm. ('Blacked-out' history series) Includes bibliography. [BX9798.S47J6] 59-15870
1. Skoptsi. I. Title.

Skrefarud, Lars Olsen, 1840-1910.

RONNING, Nils Nilsen, 1870- 922
Lars O. Skrefsrud, an apostle to the Santals, by N. N. Ronning. Minneapolis, Minn., The Santal mission in America [c1940] 2 p. l., 7-93 p. plates, ports., map. 20 1/2 cm. [BV3269.S6R6] 40-11927

1. Skrefarud, Lars Olsen, 1840-1910. 2. Missions—Santals. I. Title.

Skripnikova, Aida Mikhailovna, 1942—

AIDA of Leningrad: 272 B
the story of Aida Skripnikova; edited by Xenia Howard-Johnston and Michael Bourdeaux. [Reading, Eng.] Gateway Outreach [1972] [8], 121 p. port. 23 cm. [BX6495.S52A75 1972] 73-160416 ISBN 0-901644-09-9 £1.50
1. Skripnikova, Aida Mikhailovna, 1942- 2. Persecution—Russia. I. Howard-Johnston, Xenia, ed. II. Bourdeaux, Michael, ed.

THE Evidence that convicted 272 B
Aida Skripnikova [edited] by [Xenia Howard-Johnson and] Michael Bourdeaux. Elgin, Il[l.] D. C. Cook [1973, c1972] 154 p. 18 cm. First published under title: Aida of Leningrad. [BX6495.S52A75 1973] 73-78712 ISBN 0-912692-22-7 1.25 (pbk.)
1. Skripnikova, Aida Mikhailovna, 1942- 2. Persecution—Russia. I. Howard-Johnson, Xenia, ed. II. Bourdeaux, Michael, ed.

Sky-gods.

JAMES, Edwin Oliver, 291.212
1886-
The worship of the Sky-god; a comparative study in Semitic and Indo-European religion. [London] Univ. of London, Athlone Pr. [dist. New York, Oxford, c.] 1963. vi, 175p. 23cm. (Jordan lects. in comparative religion, 6) Bibl. 63-6471 4.00
1. Sky-gods. I. Title. II. Series.

Slander.

FERGUSON, Richard, fl.1814. 248
The fiery-flying serpent slender, and the brazen serpent charity, delineated; or A saint and a slanderer as oppostie fo the Ancient of days and the Genius of darkness; being a selection from vocabularies, digests of law, and approved authors upon divinity both French and English, to restrain slander and promote charity. By Richard Ferguson, minister of the gospel in the M. E. C... Whinchester, Va. Printed by Jonathan Foster, for the publisher. 1814. 252 p. 16 cm. [BV4627.S6F4] 34-41702
1. Slander. 2. Charity. I. Title.

SLANDER and its victims;
with sketches on Death, the Resurrection, and the Judgment. By S. A. W. of Virginia. Baltimore, 1859. 1 p. l., viii, [3]-86 p. 19 cm. 8-36472
I. W., S. A.

Slattery, Charles Lewis, bp., 1867-1930.

ROBBINS, Howard Chandler, 922.373
1876-
Charles Lewis Slattery, by Howard Chandler Robbins. New York and London, Harper & brothers, 1931. xii p., 1 l., 341 p. front., illus. (facsims.) plates., ports. 22 cm. "First edition." Bibliography: p. 330-332. [BX5995.S4R6] 31-29287
1. Slattery, Charles Lewis, bp., 1867-1930. I. Title.

SLATTERY, Charles Lewis, 283.
bp., 1867-
Following Christ, by Charles Lewis Slattery... New ed., enl. Boston and New York, Houghton Mifflin company, 1929. 3 p.l., 189, [1] p. 19 cm. [BX5930.S5 1929] 29-9762
I. Title.

SLATTERY, Charles Lewis, 283.
bp., 1867-
Following Christ, by Charles Lewis Slattery... New ed., enl. Boston and New York, Houghton Mifflin company, 1929. 3 p.l., 189, [1] p. 19 cm. [BX5930.S5 1929] 29-9762
I. Title.

SLATTERY, Charles Lewis. 283.
bp., 1867-1930.
Following Christ, by Charles Lewis Slattery... Boston and New York, Houghton Mifflin company, 1928. 3 p. l., 166, [1] p. 19 cm. [BX5930.S5] 28-7055
I. Title.

SLATTERY, Charles Lewis, 283.
bp., 1867-1930.
Following Christ, by Charles Lewis Slattery... Boston and New York, Houghton Mifflin company, 1928. 3 p. l., 166, [1] p. 19 cm. [BX5930.S5] 28-7055
I. Title.

Slaugh family (George Alfred Slaugh, 1868-1945)

JACOBSON, Gladys (Slaugh) comp.
Legacy; the story of George Alfred Slaugh and Rachel Maria Goodrich, their children and their children's children. Salt Lake City, 1964. 287 p. illus., geneal. tables. 29 cm. 68-49888
1. Slaugh family (George Alfred Slaugh, 1868-1945) 2. Mormons and Mormonism—Geneal. I. Title.

Slaughtering and slaughter-houses—Jews.

BERMAN, Jeremiah J 1902- 296
Shehitah; a study in the cultural and social life of the Jewish people [by] Jeremiah J. Berman, D. H. L. New York, Bloch publishing company, 1941. 7 p. l., 514 p. plates, port., facsims. 24 cm. [BM720.S6B4] 41-15579
1. Slaughtering and slaughter-houses—Jews. I. Title.

BERMAN, Jeremiah Joseph, 296
1902-
Shehitah; a study in the cultural and social life of the Jewish people. New York, Bloch Pub. Co., 1941. 514 p. plates. port., facsims. 24 cm. [BM720.S6B4] 41-15579
1. Slaughtering and slaughter-houses—Jews. I. Title.

Slaughtering and slaughter-houses—Jews—Addresses, essays, lectures.

LEWIN, Isaac, 1906- 296.6'7
Unto the mountains : essays / by Isaac Lewin. New York : Hebrew Pub. Co., 1975. 127 p. : ill. ; 24 cm. Includes bibliographical references. [BM21.A4L5] 75-15208 5.95
1. Agudas Israel. 2. Lewin, Aron, 1879-1941. 3. Slaughtering and slaughter-houses—Jews—Addresses, essays, lectures. I. Title.
Contents omitted.

Slavery.

CLARKE, Richard Frederick, 922.
1839-1900.
Cardinal Lavigerie and the African slave trade, edited by Richard F. Clarke ... London, and New York, Longmans, Green, and co., 1889. viii p., 2 l, 379 p. 23 cm. [BX4705.L4C5] 922 ISBN 33-24787
I. Title.

HENDRICKSON, Ford, 1875-
The "black convent" slave, the climax of nunnery exposures; awful disclosures, the "Uncle Tom's cabin" of Rome's "convent slavery," by Ford Hendrickson ... Toledo, O., Protestant missionary publishing company, 1914. 131 p. illus., port. 17 1/2 cm. $0.25 14-18574
I. Title.

WELD, Theodore 221.8'30145'22
Dwight, 1803-1895.
The Bible against slavery; or, An inquiry into the genius of the Mosaic system, and the teachings of the Old Testament on the subject of human rights. Pittsburgh, United Presbyterian Board of Publication, 1864. Detroit, Negro History Press, 1970. vii, 154 p. 22 cm. [HT915.W4 1970] 74-92447
1. Slavery. 2. Slavery in the United States—Controversial literature—1864. I. Title.

Slavery and the church.

BIRNEY, James Gillespie, 261.8'3
1792-1857.
The American churches: the bulwarks of American slavery. New York, Arno Press, 1969. 44 p. 23 cm. (The Anti-slavery crusade in America) Reprint of the 1842 ed. [E449.B617 1969] 79-82174
1. Slavery and the church. I. Title. II. Series.

SCHERER, Lester 261.8'34'4930973
B., 1931-
Slavery and the churches in early America, 1619-1819 / by Lester B. Scherer Grand Rapids : Eerdmans, [1975] 163 p. ; 23 cm. Includes bibliographical references and index. [HT913.S33] 75-5817 ISBN 0-8028-1580-4 : 7.95
1. Slavery and the Church. 2. Slavery in the United States—History. I. Title.

Slavery and the church—Catholic Church.

CARAVAGLIOS, 261.8'34'4930973
Maria Genoino.
The American Catholic Church and the Negro problem in the XVIII-XIX centuries / Maria Genoino Caravaglios ; edited by Ernest L. Unterkoefler. Charleston, S.C. : Caravaglios, [1974] xv, 375 p. : facsims. ; 25 cm. Includes index. Bibliography: p. [353]-368. [HT917.C3C37] 74-195927
1. Slavery and the church—Catholic Church. 2. Slavery in the United States. I. Title.

MILLER, Richard Roscoe. 326.973
Slavery and Catholicism. Durham, N. C., North State Publishers [1957] 259p. illus. 22cm. [E441.M65] 57-8157
1. Slavery and the church—Catholic Church. 2. Slavery in the U. S. I. Title.

Slavery and the church—Congregational Church.

WHIPPLE, Charles King, 177'.5
1808-1900.
Relation of the American Board of Commissioners for Foreign Missions to slavery. New York, Negro Universities Press [1969] 247 p. 23 cm. On spine: Foreign mission to slavery. Reprint of the 1861 ed. [E449.A523 1969] 70-75560
1. American Board of Commissioners for Foreign Missions. 2. Slavery and the church—Congregational Church. 3. Slavery in the United States—Controversial literature—1861. I. Title. II. Title: Foreign mission to slavery.

Slavery and the church—Friends.

DRAKE, Thomas Edward, 326.973
1907-
Quakers and slavery in America. New Haven, Yale University Press, 1950. viii, 245 p. 24 cm. (Yale historical publications. Miscellany 51) "Bibliographical note": p. [201]-236. [E441.D75] 50-12921
1. Slavery and the church—Friends. 2. Society of Friends 3. Slavery in the U. S.—Anti-slavery Movements. I. Title. II. Series.

DRAKE, Thomas Edward, 326.973
1907-
Quakers and slavery in America. Gloucester, Mass., P.Smith, 1965[c.1950] viii, 245p. 21cm. Bibl. [E441.D75] 65-3504 4.75
1. Slavery and the church—Friends, Society of. 2. Slavery in the U.S.—Anti-slavery movements. I. Title.

Slavery and the church—Friends, Society of—History—Sources.

THE Quaker origins of 261.8'345'6
antislavery / edited with an introd. by J. William Frost. Norwood, Pa. : Norwood Editions, 1980. p. cm. [E441.Q34] 79-27345 ISBN 0-8482-3961-X lib. bdg. : 25.00
1. Friends, Society of—History—Sources. 2. Slavery and the church—Friends, Society of—History—Sources. 3. Slavery in the United States—Anti-slavery movements—Sources. I. Frost, Jerry William.

Slavery and the church—Methodist Episcopal Church.

HARRIS, William 261.8'34'493
Logan, Bp., 1817-1887.
The constitutional powers of the General Conference, with a special application to the subject of slaveholding. Freeport, N.Y., Books for Libraries Press, 1971. 156 p. 23 cm. (The Black heritage library collection) Reprint of the 1860 ed. Includes bibliographical references. [HT917.M4H37 1971] 74-146265 ISBN 0-8369-8740-3
1. Methodist Episcopal Church. General Conference, 1856. 2. Slavery and the church—Methodist Episcopal Church. I. Title. II. Series.

MATHEWS, Donald G. 261.8
Slavery and Methodism; a chapter in American morality, 1780-1845, by Donald G. Mathews. Princeton, N.J., Princeton University Press, 1965. xi, 329 p. 21 cm. Bibliography: p. 305-324. [E449.M428] 65-17148
1. Slavery and the church—Methodist Episcopal Church. I. Title.

MATHEWS, Donald G. 287'.673
Slavery and Methodism : a chapter in American morality, 1780-1845 / by Donald G. Mathews. Wesport, Conn. : Greenwood Press, 1978, c1965. xi, 329 p. ; 23 cm. Reprint of the ed. published by Princeton University Press, Princeton, N.J. Includes index. Bibliography: p. 305-324. [E449.M428 1978] 78-13249 ISBN 0-313-21045-4 lib. bdg. :22.50
1. Methodist Episcopal Church—History. 2. Slavery and the church—Methodist Episcopal Church. 3. Slavery in the United States—Anti-slavery movements. I. Title.

MATLACK, Lucius C. 287'.6'73
The history of American slavery and Methodism from 1780 to 1849, and History of the Wesleyan Methodist Connection of America. Freeport, N.Y., Books for Libraries Press, 1971. 2 pts. (368, 15 p.) in 1. 23 cm. (The Black heritage library collection) Reprint of the 1849 ed. [E441.M43 1971] 77-138342 ISBN 0-8369-8734-9
1. Wesleyan Methodist Connection (or Church) of America. 2. Slavery and the church—Methodist Episcopal Church. I. Title. II. Title: History of the Wesleyan Methodist Connection of America. III. Series.

MATTISON, Hiram, 261.8'34'493
1811-1868.
The impending crisis of 1860; or, The present connection of the Methodist Episcopal Church with slavery. Freeport, N.Y., Books for Libraries Press, 1971. 136 p. 23 cm. (The Black heritage library collection) Reprint of the 1858 ed. Includes bibliographical references. [HT917.M4M35 1971] 75-149870 ISBN 0-8369-8750-0
1. Slavery and the church—Methodist Episcopal Church. I. Title. II. Series.

NORWOOD, John Nelson, 287'.673
1879-
The schism in the Methodist Episcopal Church, 1844 : a study of slavery and ecclesiastical politics / by John Nelson Norwood Philadelphia : Porcupine Press, 1976. 225 p. : map (on lining papers) ; 22 cm. (Perspectives in American history ; no. 33) Originally presented as the author's thesis, Cornell University. Reprint of the 1923 ed. published by Alfred University, Alfred, N.Y., which was issued as v. 1. of Alfred University studies. Includes index. Bibliography: p. [195]-217. [BX8237.N6 1976] 76-10284 ISBN 0-87991-357-6 lib.bdg. : 12.50
1. Methodist Episcopal Church—History. 2. Methodist Episcopal Church, South—History. 3. Slavery and the church—Methodist Episcopal Church. I. Title. II. Series: Perspectives in American history (Philadelphia) ; no.33. III. Series: Alfred University studies ; v. 1.

SCOTT, Orange, 1800-1847. 261.8'3
The grounds of seccession from the M. E. Church. New York, Arno Press, 1969. 229 p. 23 cm. (The Anti-slavery crusade in America) Reprint of the 1848 ed. [E449.S3 1969] 71-82219
1. Methodist Episcopal Church—Doctrinal and controversial works. 2. Slavery and the

church—Methodist Episcopal Church. I. Title. II. Series.

SWANEY, Charles Baumer, 1888- 261.8'3
Episcopal Methodism and slavery, with sidelights on ecclesiastical politics. New York, Negro Universities Press [1969] 356 p. 23 cm. Reprint of the 1926 ed. Bibliography: p. 341-351. [E449.S96 1969] 69-16562
1. Slavery and the church—Methodist Episcopal Church. I. Title.

Slavery and the church—Presbyterian church.

PRESBYTERIAN church in the U. S. Executive committee of publication. 285.
The distinctive principles of the Presbyterian church in the United States, commonly called the Southern Presbyterian church, as set forth in the formal declarations, and illustrated by extracts from proceedings of the General assembly, from 1861-70. To which is added, extracts from the proceedings of the O. S. Assembly, from 1861-67; and of the N. S. Assembly, from 1861-66. 3d ed. Richmond, Presbyterian committee of publication [c1873?] 4 x, 5-135 p. 19 cm. [BX8965.A5 1870] 24-25252
1. Slavery and the church—Presbyterian church. I. Title.

Slavery and the church—Protestant Episcopal church.

WILBERFORCE, Samuel, successively bp. of Oxford and of Winchester, 1805-1873. 261
A reproof of the American church. By the Bishop of Oxford. Extracted from a "History of the Protestant Episcopal church in America", by Samuel Wilberforce, A.M. With an introduction by An American churchman. New York, W. Harned, 1846. 59 p. 21 cm. [E449.W66] 11-12557
1. Slavery and the church—Protestant Episcopal church. 2. Slavery in the U.S.—Controversial literature—1846. I. Title.

Slavery in Barbados.

BENNETT, J Harry. 326.972981
Bondsmen and bishops; slavery and apprenticeship on the Codrington Plantations of Barbados, 1710-1838. Berkeley, University of California Press, 1958. ix, 176p. tables. 24cm. (University of California publications in history, v. 62) Bibliographical references included in 'Notes' (p.145-166) [E173.C15 vol. 62] A 59
1. Slavery in Barbados. 2. Society for the Propagation of the Gospel in Foreign Parts. London. 3. Church of England—Missions. 4. Codrington College, Barbados. I. Title. II. Series: California. University. University of California publications in history, v. 62

Slavery in the Bible.

BARTCHY, S. Scott. 227'.2
[Mallon chresai (romanized form)] first-century slavery and the interpretation of 1 Corinthians 7:21, by S. Scott Bartchy. [Missoula, Mont.] Published by Society of Biblical Literature for the Seminar on Paul, 1973. ix, 199 p. 22 cm. (SBL dissertation series, 11) Originally presented as the author's thesis, Harvard. Bibliography: p. 185-199. [BS2675.2.B33 1973] 73-83723 ISBN 0-88414-022-9
1. Bible. N.T. 1 Corinthians VII, 21—Criticism, interpretation, etc. 2. Slavery in the Bible. 3. Slavery—History. I. Title. II. Title: First-century slavery and the interpretation of 1 Corinthians 7:21. III. Series: Society of Biblical Literature. Dissertation series, 11.

Slavery in the United States.

GRAVELY, William, 1939- 287'.632'0924 B
Gilbert Haven, Methodist abolitionist; a study in race, religion, and reform, 1850-1880. Edited by the Commission on Archives and History of the United Methodist Church. Nashville, Abingdon Press [1973] 272 p. illus. 24 cm. Bibliography: p. 258-263. [BX8495.H28G7] 72-14179 ISBN 0-687-14702-6 8.95
1. Haven, Gilbert, Bp., 1821-1880. 2. Slavery in the United States. 3. Church and race problems—United States. I. United Methodist Church (United States). Commission on Archives and History.

TILMON, Levin, 1807-1863. 922.773
A brief miscellaneous narrative of the more early part of the life of L. Tilmon, pastor of a colored Methodist Congregational church in the city of New York. Written by himself. Jersey City, W. W. & L. A. Pratt, printers, 1858. 1 p. l., 97 p. 17 cm. Verso of p. 59 unnumbered and blank. [BX8473.T5A3] 37-12163
1. Slavery in the U.S. I. Title.

Slavery in the United States—Anti-slavery movements.

RICE, Madeleine (Hooke) 1903- 326.973
American Catholic opinion in the slavery controversy. Gloucester, Mass., P. Smith [1965, c.1944] 177p. 21cm. (Studies in hist., econs. and public law, no. 508) Bibl. Title. (Series: Studies in history, economics, and public law (Gloucester, mass.) no. 508) [E441.R5] 65-1399 3.50
1. Slavery in the U.S.—Anti-slavery movements. 2. Slavery and the church—Catholic Church. 3. Catholics in the U.S. I. Title. II. Series.

STANGE, Douglas C. 261.8'34'4930973
Patterns of antislavery among American Unitarians, 1831-1860 / Douglas C. Stange. Rutherford, N.J. : Fairleigh Dickinson University Press, c1977. p. cm. A revision of the author's thesis, Harvard University. Includes index. Bibliography: p. [E449.S898] 75-18245 ISBN 0-8386-1797-2 : 15.00
1. Slavery in the United States—Anti-slavery movements. 2. Slavery and the church—Unitarian churches. 3. Abolitionists—United States. I. Title.

Slavery in the United States—Controversial literature.

WOOLMAN, John, 1720-1772. 289.6'0924 B
The journal and major essays of John Woolman. Edited by Phillips P. Moulton. New York, Oxford University Press, 1971. xviii, 336 p. 24 cm. (A Library of Protestant thought) Contents.Contents.—The journal of John Woolman.—Major essays of John Woolman: Introduction to the essays. Some considerations on the keeping of Negroes. Considerations on keeping Negroes, part second. A plea for the poor. Bibliography: p. 315-318. [BX7795.W7A3 1971b] 71-171970 10.50
1. Slavery in the United States—Controversial literature. 2. Poor. I. Title. II. Series.

Slavery in the United States—Controversial literature—1729.

SANDIFORD, Ralph, 1693-1733. 261.8
A brief examination of the practice of the times. New York, Arno Press, 1969. 74 p. 23 cm. (The Anti-slavery crusade in America) Reprint of the 1729 ed. [E446,S36 1969] 70-82221
1. Slavery in the United States—Controversial literature—1729. I. Title. II. Series.

Slavery in the United States—Controversial literature—1737.

LAY, Benjamin, 1677-1759. 261.8'3
All slave-keepers that keep the innocent in bondage. New York, Arno Press, 1969. 271 p. 23 cm. (The Anti-slavery crusade in America) Reprint of the 1737 ed. [E446.L4 1969] 72-82203
1. Slavery in the United States—Controversial literature—1737. 2. Slavery and the church—Friends, Society of. I. Title. II. Series.

Slavery in the United States—Controversial literature—1753-1770.

WOOLMAN, John, 1720-1772. 289.6'08
The works of John Woolman. New York, Garrett Press, 1970. xiii, xiv, 436 p. 22 cm. Reprint of the 1774 ed., with a new foreword by William A. Beardslee. [BX7617.W6 1970] 75-93672
1. Friends, Society of—Collected works. 2. Slavery in the United States—Controversial literature—1753-1770. I. Title.

WOOLMAN, John, 1720-1772. 289.6'08
The works of John Woolman. With a new foreword by William A. Beardslee. New York, MSS Information Corp. [1972] p. "Reprint of the first edition published ... in 1774." [BX7617.W6 1972] 72-8107 ISBN 0-8422-8135-5
1. Friends, Society of—Collected works. 2. Slavery in the United States—Controversial literature—1753-1770.

Slavery in the United States—Controversial literature—1816.

CHRISTIE, John W. 261.8'3
George Bourne and The Book and slavery irreconcilable, by John W. Christie and Dwight L. Dumond. Wilmington, Historical Society of Delaware [1969] xi, 206 p. 24 cm. (Presbyterian Historical Society. [Publications], v. 9) "A chronological list of the publications of George Bourne": p. 99-101. [E446.B77C45] 75-12112 5.00
1. Bourne, George, 1780-1845. 2. Slavery in the United States—Controversial literature—1816. I. Dumond, Dwight Lowell, 1895- joint author. II. Delaware Historical Society. III. Bourne, George, 1780-1845. The Book and slavery irreconcilable. 1969. IV. Title. V. Series.

Slavery in the United States—Controversial literature—1820.

WRIGHT, John, (of Washington) 326.
A refutation of the sophisms, gross misrepresentations, and erroneous quotations contained in "An American's" "Letter to the Edinburgh reviewers"; or, Slavery inimical to the character of the great Father of all, unsupported by divine revelation, a violation of natural justice, and hostile to the fundamental principles of American indendence. By John Wright ... Washington, D.C. Printed for the author, 1820. viii, [9]-52 p. 22 1/2 cm. Copy 2. [Miscellaneous pamphlets, v. 1017, no. 4] Copy 3. [Slavery pamphlets, v. 28, no. 13] [E446.W95] [AC901.M5 vol. 1017] 252. 10-32261
1. Slavery in the U.S.—Controversial literature—1820. 2. Letter to the Edinburgh reviewers. I. Title.

Slavery in the United States—Controversial literature—1835.

SUNDERLAND, La Roy, 1802-1885. 220.8'30145'22
The testimony of God against slavery, or A collection of passages from the Bible, which show the sin of holding property in man; with notes. Boston, Webster & Southard, 1835. St. Clair Shores, Mich., Scholarly Press, 1970. 104 p. 21 cm. [E449.S958 1970] 73-92444
1. Slavery in the United States—Controversial literature—1835. I. Title.

Slavery in the United States—Controversial literature—1836.

GRIMKE, Angelina Emily, 1805-1879. 261.8
Appeal to the Christian women of the South. New York, Arno Press, 1969. [illegible] p. 22 cm. (The Anti-slavery crusade in America) Reprint of the 1836 ed. On spine: To Christian women of the South. [E449.G863 1969] 77-82195
1. Slavery in the United States—Controversial literature—1836. I. Title. II. Title: To Christian women of the South. III. Series.

Slavery in the United States—Controversial literature—1843.

FOSTER, Stephen Symonds, 1809-1881. 261.8'3
The brotherhood of thieves. New York, Arno Press, 1969. 75 p. 23 cm. (The Anti-slavery crusade in America) Reprint of the 1886 ed. [E449.F765 1969] 79-82190
1. Slavery in the United States—Controversial literature—1843. 2. Slavery and the church. I. Title. II. Series.

Slavery in the United States—Controversial literature—1844.

ENGLAND, John, Bp., 1786-1842. 261.8'3
Letters of the late Bishop England to the Hon. John Forsyth, on the subject of domestic slavery: to which are prefixed copies, in Latin and English, of the Pope's apostolic letter, concerning the African slave trade, with some introductory remarks, etc. New York, Negro Universities Press [1969] xi, 156 p. 23 cm. Reprint of the 1844 ed. [E449.E58 1969] 74-97400
1. Slavery in the United States—Controversial literature—1844. 2. Slavery—Justification. I. Forsyth, John, 1780-1841.

Slavery in the United States—Controversial literature—1846.

BARNES, Albert, 1798-1870. 261.8'3
An inquiry into the scriptural views of slavery. New York, Negro Universities Press [1969] 384 p. 23 cm. On spine: Scriptural views of slavery. Reprint of the 1857 ed. Bibliographical footnotes. [E449.B262 1969] 68-58048
1. Slavery in the United States—Controversial literature—1846. 2. Slavery in the Bible. I. Title. II. Title: Scriptural views of slavery.

BARNES, Albert, 1798-1870. 261.8'3
An inquiry into the scriptural views of slavery. Philadelphia, Parry & McMillan, 1855. Detroit, Negro History Press [1969] 384 p. 22 cm. Title on spine: Scriptural views of slavery. Bibliographical footnotes. [E449.B262 1969b] 75-92415
1. Slavery in the United States—Controversial literature—1846. 2. Slavery in the Bible. I. Title. II. Title: Scriptural views of slavery.

Slavery in the United States—Controversial literature—1853.

HOSMER, William. 261.8'34'493
Slavery and the church. New York, Negro Universities Press [1969] 200 p. 22 cm. [E449.H823 1969] 70-82465 ISBN 0-8371-1646-5
1. Slavery in the United States—Controversial literature—1853. 2. Slavery and the church. I. Title.

HOSMER, William. 261.83'4'493
Slavery and the church. Freeport, N.Y., Books for Libraries Press, 1970 [c1853] 200 p. 23 cm. (The Black heritage library collection) [E449.H823 1970] 78-133156 ISBN 0-8369-8711-X
1. Slavery in the United States—Controversial literature—1853. 2. Slavery and the church. I. Title. II. Series.

Slavery in the United States—Controversial literature—1855.

LEE, Luther, 1800-1889. 241
Slavery examined in the light of the Bible. Syracuse, N.Y., Wesleyan Methodist Book Room, 1855; Detroit, Negro History Press [1969] 185 p. 22 cm. [E449.L47 1969] 76-92434
1. Slavery in the United States—Controversial literature—1855. I. Title.

Slavery in the United States—Controversial literature—1856.

HOW, Samuel Blanchard, 1790-1868. 261.83'4'493
Slaveholding not sinful. Slavery, the

punishment of man's sin, its remedy, the gospel of Christ. Freeport, N.Y., Books for Libraries Press, 1971 [c1855] 136 p. 23 cm. (The Black heritage library collection) "An argument before the General Synod of the Reformed Protestant Dutch Church, October, 1855." Includes bibliographical references. [E449.H842 1971] 70-152922 ISBN 0-8369-8766-7
1. Slavery in the United States—Controversial literature—1856. 2. Slavery—Justification. I. Reformed Church in America. General Synod. II. Title. III. Series.

Slavery in the United States—Controversial literature—1857.

BARNES, Albert, 1798-1870. 261.8'3
The church and slavery. New York, Negro Universities Press [1969] 204 p. 23 cm. Reprint of the 1857 ed. Includes bibliographical references. [E449.B26 1969b] 71-98714 ISBN 0-8371-2771-8
1. Slavery in the United States—Controversial literature—1857. 2. Slavery and the church. 3. Slavery and the church—Presbyterian Church. I. Title.

BARNES, Albert, 1798-1870. 261.8'3
The church and slavery. With an appendix. Philadelphia, Parry & McMillan, 1857. Detroit, Negro History Press [1969?] 204 p. 22 cm. [E449.B26 1969] 79-92416
1. Slavery in the United States—Controversial literature—1857. 2. Slavery and the church. 3. Slavery and the church—Presbyterian Church. I. Title.

CHEEVER, George Barrell, 1807-1890. 261.8
God against slavery. New York, Arno Press, 1969. 272 p. 23 cm. (The Anti-slavery crusade in America) Reprint of the 1857 ed. [E449.C49 1969c] 79-82182
1. Slavery in the United States—Controversial literature—1857. I. Title. II. Series.

CHEEVER, George Barrell, 1807-1890. 261.8
God against slavery, and the freedom and duty of the pulpit to rebuke it, as a sin against God. New York, Negro Universities Press [1969] 272 p. 24 cm. Reprint of the 1857 ed. [E449.C49 1969b] 70-97360
1. Slavery in the United States—Controversial literature—1857. I. Title.

CHEEVER, George Barrell, 1807-1890. 261.8
God against slavery: and the freedom and duty of the pulpit to rebuke it, as a sin against God. Miami, Fla., Mnemosyne Pub. Inc., 1969. viii, 272 p. 23 cm. Reprint of the 1857 ed. [E449.C49 1969] 76-78995
1. Slavery in the United States—Controversial literature—1857. I. Title.

ROSS, Frederick Augustus, 1796-1883. 261.8'3
Slavery ordained of God. New York, Negro Universities Press [1969] 186 p. 18 cm. Reprint of the 1857 ed. [E449.R82 1969] 69-16570
1. Slavery in the United States—Controversial literature—1857. 2. Slavery—Justification. 3. Slavery and the church—Presbyterian Church. I. Title.

ROSS, Frederick Augustus, 1796-1883. 261.8'3
Slavery ordained of God. New York, Haskell House Publishers, 1970. 186 p. 23 cm. Reprint of the 1857 ed. [E449.R82 1970] 70-95445
1. Slavery in the United States—Controversial literature—1857. 2. Slavery—Justification. 3. Slavery and the church—Presbyterian Church. I. Title.

ROSS, Frederick Augustus, 1796-1883. 261.8'3
Slavery ordained of God. Miami, Fla., Mnemosyne Pub. Co. [1969] 186 p. 23 cm. Reprint of the 1857 ed. [E449.R82 1969b] 74-83876
1. Slavery in the United States—Controversial literature—1857. 2. Slavery—Justification. 3. Slavery and the church—Presbyterian Church. I. Title.

SLOANE, James Renwick Wilson, 1823-1886. 922.573
Life and work of J. R. W. Sloane, D.D.; professor of theology in the Reformed Presbyterian seminary at Allegheny City, Penn. 1868-1886 and pastor of the Third Reformed Presbyterian church, New York, 1856-1868. Edited by his son. New York, A. C. Armstrong and son, 1888. 2 p. l., 3-440 p. front. (port.) 22 1/2 cm. [BX9225.S47A3] 36-22113
1. Slavery in the U.S.—Controversial literature—1857. 2. Presbyterian church—Sermons. 3. Sermons, American. I. Sloane, William Milligan, 1850-1928, ed. II. Title.

Slavery in the United States—Controversial literature—1860.

CHEEVER, George Barrell, 1807-1890. 241
The guilt of slavery and the crime of slaveholding, demonstrated from the Hebrew and Greek scriptures. New York, Negro Universities Press [1969] viii, 472 p. 23 cm. Reprint of the 1860 ed. Bibliographical footnotes. [E449.C512 1969] 69-16586
1. Bible—Criticism, interpretation, etc. 2. Slavery in the United States—Controversial literature—1860. I. Title.

Slavery in the United States—Controversial literature—1864.

GOODWIN, Daniel Raynes, 1811-1890. 261.8'3
Southern slavery in its present aspects: containing a reply to a late work of the Bishop of Vermont on slavery. New York, Negro Universities Press [1969] 343 p. 23 cm. Reprint of the 1864 ed. Includes bibliographical references. [E449.H793G6 1969] 78-97452
1. Hopkins, John Henry, Bp., 1792-1868. A scriptural, ecclesiastical and historical view. 2. Slavery in the United States—Controversial literature—1864. I. Title.

Slavery in the United States—History.

CHRISTY, David, b.1802- 261.8'3
Pulpit politics; or, Ecclesiastical legislation on slavery, in its disturbing influences on the American Union. New York, Negro Universities Press [1969] 624 p. port. 23 cm. Reprint of the 1862 ed. Bibliographical footnotes. [E449.C5573 1969] 77-77197
1. Slavery in the United States—History. 2. Slavery and the church. I. Title.

WEEKS, Stephen Beauregard, 1865-1918. 289.6'75
Southern Quakers and slavery; a study in institutional history. New York, Bergman Publishers [1968] xiv, 400 p. map. 24 cm. (Johns Hopkins University studies in historical and political science, extra volume 15) Reprint of the 1896 ed. Bibliography: p. [345]-362. [H31.J62 vol. 15, 1968] 66-28477
1. Friends, Society of—History. 2. Slavery in the United States—History. I. Title. II. Series: Johns Hopkins University. Studies in historical and political science. Extra volumes, 15.

Slavery in the United States—North Carolina.

MCKIEVER, Charles Fitzgerald. 261.8
Slavery and the emigration of North Carolina Friends. Murfreesboro, N.C., Johnson Pub. Co. [1970] viii, 88 p. 21 cm. Bibliography: p. [81]-88. [BX7648.N8M3] 79-18192
1. Friends, Society of. North Carolina. 2. Slavery in the United States—North Carolina. I. Title.

Slavery in the United States—Personal narratives.

DAVIS, Noah, 1803or4- 286'.1'0924 B
A narrative of the life of Rev. Noah Davis, a colored man, written by himself. [Philadelphia, Rhistoric Publications, 1969] 86 p. illus., port. 21 cm. (Afro-American history series) (Rhistoric publications, no. 213.) Cover title. Reprint of the 1859 ed., with "Noah Davis and the Narrative of restraint; a bibliographical note, by Maxwell Whiteman" added. [E444.D37 1969] 74-77050
1. Davis, Noah, 1803 or 4- 2. Slavery in the United States—Personal narratives. 3. Freedmen in Maryland. I. Title.

Slaves of the Immaculate Heart of Mary—Biography.

CONNER, Robert, 1950- 282'.092'4 B
Walled in / Robert Connor. New York : New American Library, c1979. 308 p. ; 18 cm. (A Signet book) [BX4795.S52C663] 79-110500 ISBN 0-451-08662-7 : 2.25
1. Connor, Robert, 1950- 2. Slaves of the Immaculate Heart of Mary—Biography. I. Title.

Slavs—Church history.

SPINKA, Matthew, 1890- 274.96
... A history of Christianity in the Balkans; a study in the spread of Byzantine culture among the Slavs, by Matthew Spinka ... Chicago, Ill., The American society of church history [c1933] 3 p. l., 202 p. 24 1/2 cm. (Studies in church history, v. 1) "Selected bibliography": p. 189-191. [BR737.S6S6] 33-15775
1. Slavs—Church history. 2. Orthodox Eastern church—Hist. I. Title. II. Title: Christianity in the Balkans.

VLASTO, A. P. 301.29'174'91804
The entry of the Slavs into Christendom; an introduction to the medieval history of the Slavs [by] A. P. Vlasto. Cambridge [Eng.] University Press, 1970. xii, 435 p. fold. map. 24 cm. Bibliography: p. 407-422. [BR253.V57] 70-98699 6/10/- ($19.50)
1. Slavs—Church history. I. Title.

Slavs in the United States.

EDWARDS, Charles Eugene. 266'.5'132
The coming of the Slav. Philadelphia, Westminster Press, 1921. [San Francisco, R and E Research Associates, 1972] 148 p. map. 22 cm. Bibliography: p. 117. [BV2788.S68E4 1972] 71-165782 ISBN 0-88247-158-9 8.00
1. Presbyterian Church in the U.S.A.—Missions. 2. Slavs in the United States. I. Title.

Slavs, Southern—Church history.

SPINKA, Matthew, 1890- 209'.496
A history of Christianity in the Balkans; a study in the spread of Byzantine culture among the Slavs. [Hamden, Conn.] Archon Books, 1968 [c1933] 202 p. 23 cm. Bibliography: p. 189-191. [BR737.S6S6 1968] 68-20379
1. Orthodox Eastern Church—History. 2. Slavs, Southern—Church history. I. Title. II. Title: Christianity in the Balkans.

Slessor, Mary Mitchell, 1848-1915.

BUCHAN, James, 1916- 266'.52'0924 B
The expendable Mary Slessor / James Buchan. New York : Seabury Press, 1981, c1980. xii, 253 p. : ill. ; 23 cm. Includes bibliographical references and index. [BV3625.N6S588 1981] 19 81-1799 ISBN 0-8164-2320-2 pbk. : 7.95
1. Slessor, Mary Mitchell, 1848-1915. 2. Missionaries—Nigeria—Biography. 3. Missionaries—Great Britain—Biography. I. Title.

CHRISTIAN, Carol, 1923- 266'.5'2'0924 B
God and one redhead: Mary Slessor of Calabar, by Carol Christian and Gladys Plummer. Grand Rapids, Mich., Zondervan Pub. House [1971, c1970] 190 p. illus. 21 cm. Bibliography: p. [185]-186. [BV3625.N6S59 1971] 75-156246 1.95
1. Slessor, Mary Mitchell, 1848-1915. 2. Missions—Calabar, Nigeria. I. Plummer, Gladys, 1891- joint author. II. Title.

EVANS, Alec Richard.
Mary Slessor; the white queen of Calabar, by A.R. Evans. Rev. by Ruth I. Johnson. Chicago, Moody Press [c1966] 63 p. 20 cm. 68-31089
1. Slessor, Mary Mitchell, 1848-1915. 2. Missions—Calabar, Old. 3. Church of Scotland—Missions. I. Johnson, Ruth I. II. Title.

LIVINGSTONE, William Pringle. 922.
Mary Slessor of Calabar, pioneer missionary, by W. P. Livingstone ... 4th ed. London, New York [etc.] Hodder and Stoughton, 1916. vi, 347 p. front., plates. port. 23 cm. [BV3625.N5L] A 16
1. Slessor, Mary Mitchell, 1848-1915. 2. Missions—Calabar, Old. I. Title.

LIVINGSTONE, William Pringle. 922.
Mary Slessor of Calabar, pioneer missionary, by W. P. Livingstone ... 6th ed. London, New York [etc.] Hodder and Stoughton, 1916. xi, 347 p. front. (port.) plates, maps. 23 cm. [BV3625.N5L5] 16-22663
1. Slessor, Mary Mitchell, 1848-1915. 2. Missions—Calabar, Old. I. Title.

LIVINGSTONE, William Pringle. 922.
The story of Mary Slessor for young people. The white queen of Okoyong; a true story of adventure, heroism and faith, by W. P. Livingstone ... New York, George H. Doran company [c1917] xii p. 1 l., 208 p. illus. 20 cm. [BV3625.N5L6] 17-4476 1.00
1. Slessor, Mary Mitchell, 1848-1915. I. Title. II. Title: The white queen of Okoyong.

MILLER, Basil William, 1897- 922.566
Mary Slessor, missionary heroine. Grand Rapids,Mich., Zondervan [1965, c.1946] 132p. 21cm. [BV625.N6S64] 46-17815 1.00 pap.,
1. Slessor, Mary Mitchell, 1848-1915. I. Title.

MILLER, Basil William, 1897- 922.566
Mary Slessor, white queen of Calabar, by Basil Miller. Grand Rapids, Mich., Zondervan publishing house [1946] 139 p. 20 cm. [BV3625.N6S64] 46-17815
1. Slessor, Mary Mitchell, 1848-1915. I. Title.

ROBINSON, Virgil E. 266'.52'0924 B
Mighty Mary; the story of Mary Slessor [by] Virgil E. Robinson. Washington, Review and Herald Pub. Association [1972] 127 p. illus. 22 cm. (Penguin series) [BV3625.N6S647] 79-172787
1. Slessor, Mary Mitchell, 1848-1915. I. Title.

SYME, Ronald, 1910- 266.54669
Nigerian pioneer; the story of Mary Slessor. Illustrated by Jacqueline Tomes. New York, Morrow, 1964. 189 p. illus. 21 cm. Bibliography: p. 13-14. [BV3625.N6S65] 64-15170
1. Slessor, Mary Mitchell, 1848-1915. 2. [Slessor, Mary Mitchell, 1848-1915.] 3. Missions—Calabar, Nigeria. 4. [Missionaries.] I. Title.

YOUNG-O'BRIEN, Albert Hayward, 1898- 922.566
She had a magic; the story of Mary Slessor, by Brian O'Brien [pseud.] [1st ed.] New York, Dutton, 1959 [c1958] 281 p. illus. 21 cm. [BV3625.N6S66] 59-5779
1. Slessor, Mary Mitchell, 1848-1915. I. Title.

Slipyi, Osyp, Cardinal,

DRAGAN, Antin.
Our Ukrainian Cardinal. Design and layout by Bohdan Tytla. Jersey City, Ukrainian National Association and Svoboda Press [1966] [88] p. illus., ports. (part. col.) facsims. 68-27655
1. Slipyi, Osyp, Cardinal, 2. Ukraine—Church history—Sources. I. Ukrainian National Association. II. Title.

Sloan, Archibald, d. 1851.

BOARDMAN, Henry Augustus, 1808-1880. 174.4
The Bible in the counting-house; a course of lectures to merchants. By H. A. Boardman, D.D. Philadelphia, Lippincott, Grambo & co., 1853. 2 p. l., vii-xii, 13-420 p. 18 1/2 cm. "A discourse occasioned by the death of Mr. Archibald Sloan ... October 9th, 1851": p. 387-420. [BV4596.B8B6 1853] 37-18196
1. Sloan, Archibald, d. 1851. 2. Business ethics. 3. Christian ethics—Addresses, essays, lectures. 4. Sermons, American. I. Title.

BOARDMAN, Henry Augustus, 1808-1880. 174.4
The Bible in the counting-house; a course of lectures to merchants. By H.A. Boardman, D.D. 5th ed. Philadelphia, Lippincott, Grambo & co., 1854. 2 p. l., vii-xii, 13-420 p. 19 1/2 cm. "A discourse occasioned by the death of Mr. Archibald Sloan ... October 9th, 1851": p. 387-420. [BV4596.B8B6 1854] 37-16275
1. Sloan, Archibald, d. 1851. 2. Business ethics. 3. Christian ethics—Addresses, essays, lectures. 4. Sermons, American. I. Title.

Slovak Evangelical Lutheran Synod of the United States of America—History

DOLAK, George. 284.173
A history of the Slovak Evangelical Lutheran Church in the United States of America, 1902-1927. Saint Louis, Mo., Concordia Pub. House [c1955] 207p. illus. 24cm. [BX8060.S55D6] 55-11458
1. Slovak Evangelical Lutheran Synod of the United States of America—Hist. I. Title.

Slow learning children—Programmed instruction.

KROTH, Jerome A. 371.92'6
A programmed primer in learning disabilities, by Jerome A. Kroth. Springfield, Ill., Thomas [1971] x, 283 p. illus., forms. 24 cm. Bibliography: p. 283. [LC4661.K74] 73-24901
1. Slow learning children—Programmed instruction. I. Title.

Sluyter, Richard, 1787-1843.

CURRIE, Robert Ormiston.
A memoir of the Rev. Richard Sluyter ... By R. Ormiston Currie. With an introduction, by the Rev. Philip Milledoler ... New York, J. Moffet, 1846. xv, [17]-132 p. front. (port.) 16 cm. 9-14885
1. Sluyter, Richard, 1787-1843. I. Milledoler, Philip, 1775-1852. II. Title.

Small churches.

DUDLEY, Carl S., 1932- 254
Making the small church effective / Carl S. Dudley. Nashville : Abingdon, c1978. 192 p. ; ill. ; 22 cm. Includes bibliographies and index. [BV637.8.D83] 78-2221 ISBN 0-687-23044-6 : 4.95
1. Small churches. I. Title.

MADSEN, Paul O. 254
The small church—valid, vital, victorious / by Paul O. Madsen. Valley Forge, Pa. : Judson Press, [1975] 126 p. ; 22 cm. [BV637.8.M32] 74-22519 ISBN 0-8170-0669-9 pbk. : 3.95
1. Small churches. I. Title.

RAY, David R., 1942- 254
Small churches are the right size / David R. Ray. New York : Pilgrim Press, c1982. xix, 206 p. ; 21 cm. Bibliography: p. 203-206. [BV637.8.R39 1982] 19 82-11256 ISBN 0-8298-0620-2 (pbk.) : 7.95
1. Small churches. I. Title.

SURREY, Peter J. 1928- (Peter John), 254'.24
The small town church / Peter J. Surrey. Nashville : Abingdon, c1981. 128 p. ; 21 cm. (Creative leadership series) Bibliography: p. 128. [BV637.8.S93] 19 81-622 ISBN 0-687-38720-5 pbk. : 4.95
1. Small churches. 2. Rural churches. I. Title. II. Series.

Small churches—Addresses, essays, lectures.

SMALL churches are beautiful / edited by Jackson W. Carroll. 1st ed. New York : Harper & Row, c1977. p. cm. Includes bibliographical references. [BV637.8.S62 1977] 76-62948 ISBN 0-06-061319-X : 7.95 261
1. Small churches—Addresses, essays, lectures. I. Carroll, Jackson W.

Small churches—Miscellanea.

JOHNSON, Merle Allison. 253
How to be happy in the non-electric church / Merle Allison Johnson ; illustrated with line drawings by Charles Fox. Nashville : Abingdon, c1979. 112 p. : ill. ; 23 cm. [BV637.8.J63] 78-26463 ISBN 0-687-17706-5 : 6.95
1. Small churches—Miscellanea. 2. Clergy—Office. 3. Pastoral theology. I. Title.

Smarius, Corrnelius Francis, 1823-1870. Points of controversary.

[STOTESBURY, Charles C] 282
The Roman Catholic not the one only true religion, not an infallible church, being remarks upon Points of controversy, a series of lectures by C. F. Smarius, missionary of the Society of Jesus. [Philadelphia] 1868. 188 p. 17 cm. [Bx1751.S614S8] 48-42520
1. Smarius, Corrnelius Francis, 1823-1870. Points of controversary. 2. Catholic Church—Doctrinal and controversial works—Protestant authors. I. Title.

Smelt, Caroline Elizabeth, 1800-1817.

WADDEL, Moses, 1770-1840. 920.7
Memoirs of Miss Caroline E. Smelt. By Moses Waddel ... Philadelphia, H. Perkins; Boston, Perkins, Marvin, and co., 1835. 158 p. 16 cm. [BR1725.S47W3 1835] 38-8154
1. Smelt, Caroline Elizabeth, 1800-1817. I. Title.

Smet, Eugenie Marie Josephe, 1825-1871.

BAZIN, Marie Rene, 1883-
She who lived her name, Mary of Providence, foundress of the Society of the Helpers of the Holy Souls. Westminster Md., Newman Press [1948] 209 p. 23 cm. Name in religion: Marie de Saint Justin, Sister. A 50
1. Smet, Eugenie Marie Josephe, 1825-1871. 2. Helpers of the Holy Souls. I. Title.

BUEHRIE, Marie Cecilia. 1887- 922.244
I am on fire: Blessed Mary of Providence, foundress of the Helpers of the Holy Souls, 1825-1871. Milwaukee, Bruce Press [1963] 264 p. illus. 23 cm. (Catholic life publications) [BX4367.Z8S4] 63-4805
1. Smet, Eugenie Marie Josephe, 1825-1871. 2. Helpers of the Holy Souls. I. Title.

Smet, Pierre Jean de, 1801-1873.

HOPKINS, J G E 922.278
Black robe peacemaker, Pierre de Smet. Illustrated by W. N. Wilson. New York, P. J. Kenedy [1958] 188p. illus. 22cm. (American background books [8]) [F591.S632] 58-11453
1. Smet, Pierre Jean de, 1801-1873. 2. Indians of North America—Missions. I. Title.

LAVEILLE, E. 922
The life of Father de Smet, S. J. (1801-1873) by E. Laveille, S. J., authorized translation by Marian Lindsay, introduction by Charles Coppens ... New York, P. J. Kenedy & sons, 1915. xxii p., 1 l., 400 p. front., plates, ports., fold. map (in pocket) 22 cm "Principal authorities consulted": p. [391] [F591.S635] 16-2173
1. Smet, Pierre Jean de, 1801-1873. 2. Indians of North America—Missions. I. Lindsay, Marian, tr. II. Title.

MAGARET, Helene, 1906- 922.278
Father DeSmet, pioneer priest of the Rockies, by Helene Magaret. New York, Toronto, Farrar & Rinehart, inc. [1940] 5 p. l., 3-371 p. front. (port.) 22 cm. Thesis (PH.D.)--University of Iowa, 1940. Without thesis note. Map on lining-papers. [F591.S64] 40-29581
1. Smet, Pierre Jean de, 1801-1873. 2. Indians of North America—Missions. I. Title.

MARGARET, Helene, 1906- 922.278
Father De Smet, pioneer priest of the Rockies. Milwaukee, Bruce Pub. Co. [1940] 856 p. port., map (on lining-papers) 21 cm. Issued also as thesis, Univ. of Iowa. [F591.S64 1940a] 48-9451
1. Smet, l'lere Jean de, 1801-1873. 2. Indians of North America—Missions. I. Title.

MARGARET, Helene, 1906- 922.278
Father DeSmet, pioneer priest of the Rockies, by Helene Margaret. New York, Toronto, Farrar & Rinehart, inc. [c1940] 5 p. l., 3-371 p. front. (port.) 22 cm. Map on lining-papers. [F591.S64] 40-29581
1. Smet, Pierre Jean de, 1801-1873. 2. Indians of North America—Missions. I. Title.

SANDBERG, Harold William, 1902- 922.278
Black-robed Samson; the story of Peter de Smet, S.J., the apostle of the Indians. Illustrated by Paul A. Grout. [St. Meinrad, Ind., 1952] 75 p. illus. 22 cm. "A Grail publication." [F591.S644] 52-12081
1. Smet, Pierre Jean de, 1801-1873. I. Title.

SMET, Pierre Jean de, 1801-1873. 266'.2'0924 B
Oregon missions and travels over the Rocky Mountains in 1845-46 / Pierre-Jean De Smet. Fairfield, Wash. : Ye Galleon Press, 1978, c1977. p. cm. Reprint of the 1847 ed. published by E. Dunigan, New York; with new foreword. Includes index. Bibliography: p. [E78.O6S637 1978] 78-11056 ISBN 0-87770-132-6 : 14.95
1. Smet, Pierre Jean de, 1801-1873. 2. Indians of North America—Oregon—Missions. 3. Oregon—Description and travel. 4. Missions—Oregon. 5. Rocky Mountains. 6. Northwestern States—Description and travel. I. Title.

TERRELL, John Upton, 1900- 922.278
Black robe; the life of Pierre-Jean de Smet, missionary, explorer & pioneer. Garden City, N.Y., Doubleday [c.]1964. 381p. maps (on lining-papers) 22cm. 64-19231 4.95
1. Smet, Pierre Jean de, 1801-1873. I. Title.

TERRELL, John Upton, 1900- 922.278
Black robe; the life of Pierre-Jean de Smet, missionary, explorer & pioneer. [1st ed.] Garden City, N.Y., Doubleday, 1964. 381 p. maps (on lining papers) 22 cm. [F591.S647] 64-19231
1. Smet, Pierre Jean de, 1801-1873. I. Title.

Smet, Pierre Jean de, 1801-1873—Juvenile literature.

HOPKINS, Joseph G E 922.278
Black robe peacemaker, Pierre de Smet. Illustrated by W. N. Wilson. New York, P.J. Kenedy [1958] 188 p. illus. 22 cm. (American background books [8]) [F591.S632] 58-11453
1. Smet, Pierre Jean de, 1801-1873 — Juvenile literature. 2. Indians of North America — Missions — Juvenile literature. I. Title.

PITRONE, Jean Maddern 266.20924
The Great Black Robe. Illus. by Peggy Worthington Best. [Boston] St. Paul Ed. [dist. Daughters of St. Paul, c.1965] 121, [2]p. col. illus. 22cm. Bibl. [F591.S643] 65-17554 1.50 pap.,
1. Smet, Pierre Jean de, 1801-1873—Juvenile literature. 2. Indians of North America—Missions Juvenile literature. I. Title.

PITRONE, Jean Maddern. 266.20924
The Great Black Robe. Illustrated by Peggy Worthington Best. Boston, St. Paul Editions, [1965] 121, [2] p. col. illus. 22 cm. Bibliography: p. [123] [F591.S643] 65-17554
1. Smet, Pierre Jean de, 1801-1873—Juvenile literature. 2. Indians of North America—Missions—Juvenile literature. I. Title.

Smith, Alfred Emanuel, 1873-1944.

MOORE, Edmund Arthur, 1903- 329.01
A Catholic runs for President; the campaign of 1928. New York, Ronald Press Co. [1956] 220p. illus. 21cm. Includes bibliography. [E796.M6] 56-10167
1. Smith, Alfred Emanuel, 1873-1944. 2. Presidents—U. S.—Election—1928. 3. Catholic Church in the U.S. 4. Church and state in the U.S I. Title.

MOORE, Edmund Arthur, 1903- 329.3'023
A Catholic runs for President; the campaign of 1928, by Edmund A. Moore. Gloucester, Mass., P. Smith, 1968 [c1956] xv, 220 p. illus., facsims., ports. 21 cm. Includes bibliographies. [E796.M6 1968] 68-5894
1. Smith, Alfred Emanuel, 1873-1944. 2. Presidents—United States—Election—1928. 3. Catholic Church in the United States. 4. Church and state in the United States. I. Title.

Smith, Angie Frank, 1889-1962.

SPELLMAN, Norman W., 1928- 287'.6'0924
Growing a soul : the story of A. Frank Smith / Norman W. Spellman. Dallas : SMU Press, c1979. xiii, 513 p., [8] leaves of plates ; ill. ; 24 cm. Includes bibliographical references and index. [BX8495.S574S63] 78-20876 ISBN 0-87074-171-3 : 15.00
1. Smith, Angie Frank, 1889-1962. 2. Methodist Church—Bishops—Biography. 3. Bishops—Texas—Biography. 4. Texas—Biography. I. Title.

Smith, Caleb, 1723-1762.

SMITH, Caleb, 1723-1762.
A brief account of the life of the late Rev. Caleb Smith, A.M., minister of the gospel, at Newark mountains; who died October 22, 1762. Chiefly [!] extracted from his diary, and other private papers... Woodbridge, in New-Jersey; Printed by James Parker, 1763. 2 p. l., 60 p. 20 1/2 cm. A 32
1. Smith, Caleb, 1723-1762. I. Title.

Smith, Catherine, joint comp.

SMITH, Edward W. comp. 220
The Bible directory; 5000 facts from Holy writ; the rare, the curious, the sublime, the instructive, the interesting. Compiled and published by E. W. Smith and Catherine Smith. Rochester, N.Y. [Burnett printing co., c1906] 167 p. 17 x 13 1/2 cm. [BS417.S5 1906] 7-13926
1. Smith, Catherine, joint comp. I. Title.

Smith, Charles Merrill.

SMITH, Charles Merrill. 287'.6'0924 B
Different drums : how a father and son bridged generations with love and understanding / by Charles Merrill Smith ; with a foreword and an afterword by Terrence Lore Smith. 1st ed. New York : Saturday Review Press, [1975] 166 p. ; 22 cm. [BX8495.S575A33 1975] 75-15539 7.95
1. Smith, Charles Merrill. 2. Conflict of generations. I. Smith, Terrence Lore. II. Title.

Smith, Chuck, 1927-

SMITH, Chuck, 1927- 289.9
The reproducers; new life for thousands [by] Chuck Smith with Hugh Steven. Glendale, Calif., G/L Regal Books [1972] 146 p. illus. 20 cm. [BV4447.S58] 72-77115 ISBN 0-8307-0159-1 1.95
1. Smith, Chuck, 1927- 2. Costa Mesa, Calif. Calvary Chapel. 3. Church work with youth—Costa Mesa, Calif. I. Steven, Hugh. II. Title.

Smith, Daisy, 1891-1972.

HOPE Evangeline. 266'.0092'4 B
Daisy : the fascinating story of Daisy Smith, wife of Dr. Oswald J. Smith, missionary, statesman, and founder of the Peoples Church, Toronto / Hope Evangeline. Grand Rapids : Baker Book House, c1978. xiii, 247 p., [8] leaves of plates : ill. ; 21 cm. [BX9225.S477H66] 78-103025 ISBN 0-8010-3328-4 : 6.95
1. Smith, Daisy, 1891-1972. 2. Toronto. Peoples Church. 3. Smith, Oswald J. 4. Presbyterians—Canada—Biography. I. Title.

Smith, David H., 1921-

SMITH, David H., 1921- 286'.1'0924 B
Remember the good times / David H. Smith. Nashville, Tenn. : Broadman Press, c1978. 128 p. : ill. ; 20 cm. [BX6495.S538A37] 78-66817 ISBN 0-8054-5704-6 pbk. : 2.95
1. Smith, David H., 1921- 2. Baptists—United States—Biography. I. Title.

Smith, Delbert Deane, 1922-

SMITH, Mildred Nelson. 230'.93'3
The Master's touch; true stories of a seventy's ministry. [Independence, Mo., Herald Pub. House, 1973] 272 p. 21 cm. [BX8678.S55S64] 73-75883 ISBN 0-8309-0091-8 5.95
1. Smith, Delbert Deane, 1922- 2. Reorganized Church of Jesus Christ of Latter Day Saints—Doctrinal and controversial works. I. Title.

Smith, Elias, 1769-1846.

MCMASTER, Gilbert, 1778-1854. 922.
An essay, in defence of some fundamental doctrines of Christianity; including a review of the writings of Elias Smith, by Gilbert McMaster... Schenectady [N.Y.] Printed by Riggs and Stevens, 1815. iv, 120 p. 22 1/2 cm. [BT1480.M3] A 32
1. Smith, Elias, 1769-1846. 2. Socinianism. 3. Christianity. I. Title.

SMITH, Elias, 1679-1846. 922.673
The life, conversion, preaching, travels and sufferings of Elias Smith. Written by himself ... Vo. I. Boston, Ms., Sold by the author, at no. 140, Hanover st. [B. True, printer] 1840. xii, [13]-372 p. front. (port.) 15 1/2 cm. No more published. [BX6793.S6A3 1840] 36-32451
I. Title.

SMITH, Elias, 1769-1846. 922.673
The life, conversion, preaching, travels, and sufferings of Elias Smith. Written by himself ... Portsmouth, N.H., Printed by Beck & Foster; sold by the author, no. 2, Ladd-street, and James F. Shores, no. 1, Market-street; by the Christian preachers in the United States; and the booksellers, 1816. xii, [13]-406 p. front. (port.) 18 cm. [BX6793.S6A3 1816] 36-32452
I. Title.

SMITH, Elias, 1769-1846. 286'.63 B
The life, conversion, preaching, travels, and sufferings of Elias Smith / Elias Smith. New York : Arno Press, 1980. 406, [1] leaf of plates : port. ; 22 cm. (The Baptist tradition) Reprint of the 1816 ed. printed by Beck & Foster, Portsmouth, N.H. [BX6793.S6A3 1980] 79-52606 ISBN 0-405-12471-6 : 30.00
1. Smith, Elias, 1769-1846. 2. General Convention of the Christian Church—United States—Biography. I. Title.

Smith, Elizabeth King.

LEXINGTON, Ky. Christ church. 283.769
Christ church, 1796-1946, a brief history of its one hundred and fifty years in the service of Christ. Lexington, Ky., 1946. ix p., 1 l. 106 p. front., 1 illus., plates, ports, facsims. 27 1/2 cm. "Co-authors: Elizabeth King Smith, Mary Le Grand Didlake." Bibliography: p. 107-108. [BX5980.L45C5] 47-19573
1. Smith, Elizabeth King. I. Didlake, Mary Le Grand. II. Title.

Smith, Eunice Winchester, 1821-1840.

SESSIONS, Alexander Joseph, 1809-1892. 922
The religious experience of Eunice Winchester Smith: who died July 6, 1840, aged 19 years. By Alexander J. Sessions ... Salem [Mass.] Ives and Pease, printers, 1840. 70 p., 1 l. 12 cm. "The contents of the following pages were comprised, mainly, in a discourse, that was delivered upon the Sabbath subsequent to the death of Miss Smith."--p. [3] [BR1725.S5S4] 38-4795
1. Smith, Eunice Winchester, 1821-1840. I. Title.

Smith family.

SMITH, Jesse Nathaniel, 1834-1906. 922.8373
Journal of Jesse N. Smith, compiled and edited by Nephi Jensen. [Salt Lake City, Stevens & Wallis, inc., c1940] 136 p. incl. front., ports. (1 double) 19 1/2 cm. [BX8695.S55A35] 40-33662
1. Smith family. 2. Mormons and Mormonism. I. Jensen, Nephi, 1876- ed. II. Title.

Smith, Frederick Madison, 1874-1946.

HUNT, Larry E. 289.3'3 B
F.M. Smith : Saint as reformer, 1874-1946 / by Larry E. Hunt. Independence, Mo. : Herald Pub. House, c1982. 2 v. (488 p.) ; 20 cm. Originally presented as the author's thesis (doctoral—Missouri-Columbia, 1978) Bibliography: p. 476-488 (v. 2) [BX8695.S73H86 1982] 19 81-7213 ISBN 0-8309-0320-8 : 11.00
1. Smith, Frederick Madison, 1874-1946. 2. Mormons—United States—Biography. I. Title.

SMITH, Ruth Lyman (Cobb) Mrs. 922.
Concerning the prophet Frederick Madison Smith, by his wife Ruth Lyman Smith. Rev. ed. Kansas City, Mo., Burton publishing company [c1924] 4 p. l., 13-148, [1] p. front., ports. 19 cm. [BX8695.S73S6] 25-14307
1. Smith, Frederick Madison, 1874- I. Title.

Smith, Fredrick W.

SMITH, Fredrick W. 248'.2'0924 B
Journal of a fast / Fredrick W. Smith. New York : Schocken Books, 1976, c1972. 216 p. ; 21 cm. Includes bibliographical references. [BV5055.S6 1976] 75-36493 ISBN 0-8052-3609-0 : 7.95
1. Smith, Fredrick W. 2. Fasting. I. Title.

Smith, George Williamson, 1836-

BROWN, William Montgomery, bp., 1855-
The level plan for church union, by William Montgomery Brown...with an introduction on "The origin and development of the historic episcopate," by the Rev. George Williamson Smith...and with an appendix on "The chief barrier to Christian unity" by "Anglican presbyter" [pseud.] New York, T. Whittaker, 1910. 2 p. l., [ix]-xxviii, (4], [3]-524 p. front. 19 1/2 cm. "Authorities": p. 523-524. 10-22936 1.50
1. Smith, George Williamson, 1836- 2. Whatham, Arthur E. I. Title.

Smith, Hannah Whitall, 1832-1911.

SMITH, Hannah Whitall, 1832-1911. 280'.0973
Religious fanaticism : extracts from the papers of Hannah Whitall Smith / edited with an introd. by Ray Strachey, consisting of an account of the author of these papers, and of the times in which she lived, together with a description of the curious religious sects and communities of America during the early and middle years of the nineteenth century. New York : AMS Press, 1976. p. cm. (Communal societies in America) Reprint of the 1928 ed. published by Faber & Gwyer, London. Includes index. [BR516.5.S55 1976] 72-8252 ISBN 0-404-11005-3 : 16.50
1. Smith, Hannah Whitall, 1832-1911. 2. Sects—United States. 3. Fanaticism. I. Title.

SMITH, Hannah (Whitall) Mrs., 1832-1911.
The unselfishness of God and how I discovered it; a spiritual autobiography, by H. W. S. (Mrs. Pearsall Smith) New York, Chicago [etc.] F. H. Revell company [1903] 312 p. 20 1/2 cm. [BR1785.S53A3] 3-23850
I. Title.

Smith, Helene.

FLOURNOY, Theodore, 1854-1920 133.9
From India to the planet Mars, a study of a case of somnambulism with glossolalia. Introd. by C. T. K. Chari. New Hyde Park, N. Y., University Bks. [c.1963] 457p. illus. 22cm. 63-16228 10.00
1. Smith, Helene. 2. Spiritualism. 3. Somnamnulism. 4. Glossolalia. I. Title.

Smith, Henry Boynton, 1815-1877.

STEARNS, Lewis French, 1847-1892. 922.
... Henry Boynton Smith, by Lewis F. Stearns ... Boston and New York, Houghton Mifflin and company, 1892. vi, 368 p. 19 cm. (American religious leaders) [BX9225.S5S8] 12-38940
1. Smith, Henry Boynton, 1815-1877. I. Title.

Smith, Henry Preserved, 1874-1927.

WARFIELD, Benjamin Breckinridge, 1851-1921 220.13
Limited inspiration. Grand Rapids, Mich., Baker Bk. [1962] 54p. 23cm. (Intl. lib. of philosophy and theology; Biblical and theological studies) Appeared orig. in the January 1894 issue of the Presbyterian and Reformed review, under the title: Professor Henry Preserved Smith on inspiration. 61-11747 1.25 pap.,
1. Smith, Henry Preserved, 1874-1927. 2. Bible—Inspiration—History of doctrines. I. Title.

Smith, Hershel.

SMITH, Hershel. 248'.2 B
The devil and Mr. Smith [by] Hershel Smith, with Dave Hunt. Old Tappan, N.J., F. H. Revell Co. [1974] 192 p. 21 cm. Autobiographical. [BV4935.S63A33] 74-3043 ISBN 0-8007-0662-5 2.95
1. Smith, Hershel. 2. Satanism. 3. Conversion. I. Hunt, Dave, joint author. II. Title.

Smith, Hezekiah, 1737-1805.

GUILD, Reuben Aldridge, 1822-1899. 923.673
Chaplain Smith and the Baptists; or, Life, journals, letters, and addresses of the Rev. Hezekiah Smith, D. D., of Haverhill, Massachusetts. 1737-1805. By Reuben Aldridge Guild ... Philadelphia, American Baptist publication society [1885] 429 p. 20 cm. [BX6495.S54G8] 36-24354
1. Smith, Hezekiah, 1737-1805. I. American Baptist publication society. II. Title.

Smith, Hilrie Shelton, 1893-

HENRY, Stuart Clark, ed. 277.3
A miscellany of American Christianity; essays in honor of H. Shelton Smith. Durham, N.C., Duke [c.]1963. viii, 390p. port. 24cm. Bibl. 63-14288 10.00
1. Smith, Hilrie Shelton, 1893- 2. U.S.—Religion—Addresses, essays, lectures. 3. Theology, Doctrinal—Hist.—U.S. I. Title. Contents omitted.

Smith, Hyrum, 1800-1844.

CORBETT, Pearson Harris, 1900- 922.8373
Hyrum Smith, patriarch. Salt Lake City, Deseret [c.1963] 472p. illus. 24cm. Bibl. 63-1781 3.95
1. Smith, Hyrum, 1800-1844. I. Title.

Smith, John, 1722-1771. The doctrine of Christianity, as held by the people called Quakers, vindicated.

TENNENT, Gilbert, 1703-1764.
The late association for defence farther encouraged: or, Defensive war defended; and its consistency with true Christianity represented. In a reply to some exceptions against war, in a late composure, intituled, The doctrine of Christianity, as held by the people called Quakers, vindicated. By Gilbert Tennent, A.M. ... Philadelphia: Printed and Sold by B. Franklin and D. Hall. MDCCXLVIII. iv, 183 p. 18 1/2 cm. [E198.T3] 4-20246
1. Smith, John, 1722-1771. The doctrine of Christianity, as held by the people called Quakers, vindicated. 2. U.S.—Hist.—King George's war. 1744-1748—Addresses, sermons, etc. I. Title.

Smith, John, 1794-1831.

TREFFRY, Richard. 922.742
Memoirs of the life, character, and labours of the Rev. John Smith, late of Sheffield. By Richard Treffry, jun. ... 1st American ed. New-York, B. Waugh and T. Mason, for the Methodist Episcopal church, 1833. 328 p. 13 1/2 cm. Imperfect: much mutilated. [BX8359.S6T7] 33-28647
1. Smith, John, 1794-1831. I. Title.

Smith, John, d. 1612.

DEXTER, Henry Martyn, 1821-1890. 922.642
The true story of John Smyth, the Se-Baptist, as told by himself and his contemporaries; with an inquiry whether dipping were a new mode of baptism in England, in or about 1641; and some consideration of the historical value of certain extracts from the alleged "ancient records" of the Baptist church of Epworth. Crowie, and Butterwick (Eng.), lately published and claimed to suggest important modifications of the history of the 17th century. With collections toward a bibliography of the first two generations of the Baptist controversy. By Henry Martyn Dexter. Boston, Lee and Shepard, 1881. viii, 166 p. 27 cm. Title vignette: tall-plaza. Bibliography: p. 37-128. [BX6495.S58D4] 36-94885
1. Smith, John, d. 1612. 2. Baptists—Hist. I. Title.

Smith, Joseph, 1805-1844.

ANDERSON, Richard Lloyd. 289.3'092'4 B
Joseph Smith's New England heritage; influences of grandfathers Solomon Mack and Asael Smith. Salt Lake City, Desert Book Co., 1971. xix, 230 p. illus. 24 cm. Bibliography: p. [225]-227. [BX8695.S6A68] 74-186263 ISBN 0-87747-460-5 4.95
1. Smith, Joseph, 1805-1844. 2. Smith family. I. Title.

ANDRUS, Hyrum Leslie, 1924- 230.9'3'0924
Foundations of the millennial kingdom of Christ [by] Hyrum L. Andrus. Salt Lake City, Bookcraft, 1968- v. 24 cm. Contents.Contents.—v. 1. God, man, and the universe.—v. 2. Principles of

perfection.—v. 3. Doctrines of the kingdom. Bibliographical footnotes. [BX8635.2.A5] 68-56891 5.95 (v. 1)
1. Smith, Joseph, 1805-1844. 2. Mormons and Mormonism—Doctrinal and controversial works. I. Title.

ANDRUS, Hyrum Leslie, 922.8373
1924-
Joseph Smith, the man and the seer. Salt Lake City, Deseret Book Co., [1960] 144p. illus. 24cm. Includes bibliography. [BX8695.S6A72] 60-42656
1. Smith, Joseph. 1805-1844. I. Title.

ANDRUS, Hyrum Leslie, 1924- 289.3
Joseph Smith and world government. Salt Lake City, Deseret Book Co. 1958. 127p. illus. 20cm. [BX8695.S6A7] 58-2284
1. Smith, Joseph, 1805-1844. I. Title.

ANDRUS, Hyrum Leslie, 922.8373
1924-
Joseph Smith, the man and the seer. Salt Lake City, Deseret Book Co. [c.1960] 144p. illus. (part col.) 60-42656 2.50
1. Smith, Joseph, 1805-1844. I. Title.

ARBAUGH, George 280.3
Bartholomew, 1905-
Revelation in Mormonism, its character and changing forms, by George Bartholomew Arbaugh. Chicago, Ill., The University of Chicago press [1932] x p., 1 l., 252 p. illus. (incl. facsim.) diagr. 23 1/2 cm. Thesis (PH.D.)--University of Iowa, 1931. Without thesis note. Bibliography: p. 235-241. [BX8643.R4A7 1931] 33-3811
1. Smith, Joseph, 1805-1844. 2. Mormons and Mormonism. 3. Book of Mormon. I. Title.

BACKMAN, Milton 289.3'0924
Vaughn.
Joseph Smith's first vision; the first vision in its historical context [by] Milton V. Backman, Jr. Salt Lake City, Bookcraft, 1971. xiv, 209 p. illus., maps, ports. 24 cm. Bibliography: p. [193]-204. [BX8695.S6B3] 72-149592
1. Smith, Joseph, 1805-1844. 2. Visions. 3. New York (State)—Religion. I. Title.

BACKMAN, Milton 289.3'092'4 B
Vaughn.
Joseph Smith's first vision : confirming evidences and contemporary accounts / Milton V. Backman, Jr. 2nd ed., rev. and enl. Salt Lake City, Utah : Bookcraft, c1980. xiv, 227 p. : ill., ports., maps ; 24 cm. Includes index. Bibliography: p. [211]-222. [BX8695.S6B3 1980] 19 80-65981 ISBN 0-88494-399-2 : 6.95
1. Smith, Joseph, 1805-1844. 2. Mormons—United States—Biography. 3. Visions. 4. New York (State)—Church history. I. Title.

BEARDSLEY, Harry Markle, 922.8373
1893-
Joseph Smith and his Mormon empier, by Harry M. Beardsley ... Boston and New York, Houghton Mifflin company, 1931. xii p., 2 l., 3-421 p. front., plates, ports. 22 1/2 cm. Bibliography: p. [405]-412. [BX8695.S6B4] 31-33418
1. Smith, Joseph, 1805-1844. 2. Mormons and Mormonism. I. Title.

BENNETT, John C. 289.
The history of the saints; or, An expose of Joe Smith and Mormonism. By John C. Bennett. 3d ed. Boston, Leland & Whiting; New York, Bradbury, Soden, & co.; [etc., etc.] 1842. 1 p. l., ii, [3]-344 p. incl. plates, plan. 2 port. (incl. front.) 18 cm. Cover-title: Mormonism exposed. [BX8645.B45 1842b] 35-32577
1. Smith, Joseph, 1805-1844. 2. Mormons and Mormonism. 3. Mormons and Mormnism in Illinois, I. Title. II. Title: Mormonism exposed.

BLAIR, William W. 289.
Joseph the seer; his prophetic mission vindicated, and the divine origin of the Book of Mormon defended and maintained; being a reply by Elder William W. Blair ... to Elder William Sheldon ... Plano, Ill., Printed and published by the Board of publication of the Reorganized church of Jesus Christ of Latter day saints, 1877. iv, [5]-200 p., 17 1/2 cm. [BX8627.B5] 23-18670
1. Smith, Joseph, 1805-1844. 2. Sheldon, William, 1830-1902. Mormonism examined ... 3. Book of Mormon. I. Title.

BLAKE, Reed. 289.3'092'4 B
24 hours to martyrdom Salt Lake City, Bookcraft [1973] xiii, 157 p. illus. 19 cm. Bibliography: p. [151]-157. [BX8695.S6B5] 73-77238
1. Smith, Joseph, 1805-1844. I. Title.

BOOK of Mormon.
The Book of Mormon; an account written by the hand of Mormon upon plates taken from the plates of Nephi. By Joseph Smith, Junior. Palmyra, N. Y. Printed by E. B. Grandin for the author. 1830 588 p. 20 cm. [BX8623 1830] 49-34953
1. Smith, Joseph, 1850-1844. I. Title.

BOOK of Mormon. Spanish 289.3
Libro de Mormon. Traducido de las laminas originales al ingles por Jose Smith, hijo. [Traducido del ingles al espanol por Carlos R. Hield] Independence, Mo., Junta de Publicaciones, Iglesia Reorganizada de Jesucristo de los Santos de los Ultimos Dias [dist. Herald House] [c.]1960. 839p. 19cm. 60-3097 3.50; 2.00 pap.,
1. Smith, Joseph, 1805-1844. I. Title.

BRODIE, Fawn (McKay) 289.3'0924 B
1915-
No man knows my history; the life of Joseph Smith, the Mormon prophet, by Fawn M. Brodie. 2d ed., rev. and enl. New York, Knopf, 1971. xiii, 499, xx p. illus., map, ports. 22 cm. Bibliography: p. 490-499. [BX8695.S6B7 1971] 71-136333 ISBN 0-394-46967-4 10.00
1. Smith, Joseph, 1805-1844. I. Title.

BRODIE, Fawn (McKay) 922.8373
1915-
No man knows my history; the life of Joseph Smith, the Mormon prophet, by Fawn M. Brodie. New York, A. A. Knopf, 1945. ix p., 4 l., 476, xix, [1] p. front., plates, ports., fold. map, facsims. 22 cm. On cover: AAK fellowship biography. "First edition." Bibliography: p. 466-476. [BX8695.S6B7] 45-9481
1. Smith, Joseph, 1805-1844. I. Title.

CANNON, George Quayle, 922.8373
1827-1901.
The life of Joseph Smith, the prophet. By George Q. Cannon. Salt Lake City, Utah, Juvenile instructor office, 1888. xxvii p., 1 l, [21]-512 p. 2 port (incl. front) 23 1/2 cm. [BX8695.S6C3] 36-30780
1. Smith, Joseph, 1805-1844. I. Title.

CHASE, Daryl, 1901- 922.8373
Joseph the prophet, as he lives in the hearts of his people, by Daryl Chase ... Salt Lake City, Utah, Deseret book company, 1944. 4 p. l., [7]-179 p. 20 1/2 cm. Bibliographical references included in "Notes" (p. [173]-179) [BX8695.S6C5] 44-47519
1. Smith, Joseph, 1805-1844. I. Title.

CHEVILLE, Roy 289.3'092'2 B
Arthur, 1897-
Joseph and Emma Smith, companions for seventeen and a half years, 1827-1844 / by Roy A. Cheville. Independence, Mo. : Herald Pub. House, c1977. 206 p. ; 21 cm. [BX8695.S6C53] 76-44549 ISBN 0-8309-0174-4 : 8.00
1. Smith, Joseph, 1805-1844. 2. Smith, Emma Hale. 3. Mormons and Mormonism—Biography. I. Title.

CLARK, George Edward, 922.8373
1887-
I cry Joseph; fifty-four evidences of the divine calling of Joseph Smith. [Portland? Or., c1952] 151p. 22cm. [BX8695.S6C58] 53-28235
1. Smith, Joseph, 1805-1844. I. Title.

COWAN, Richard O., 1934- 289.3
Doctrine and covenants : our modern scripture / by Richard O. Cowan. Rev. ed. Provo, Utah : Brigham Young University, [1978] p. cm. Includes index. Bibliography: p. [BX8628.C69 1978] 78-19190 ISBN 0-8425-1316-7 pbk. : 5.95
1. Smith, Joseph, 1805-1844. Doctrine and covenants. 2. Mormons and Mormonism—Doctrinal and controversial works. I. Title.

COWAN, Richard O., 1934- 289.3
The Doctrine and covenants, our modern scripture [by] Richard O. Cowan. 2d ed. rev. Provo, Utah, Brigham Young University Press [1969] xix, 151 p. illus. 28 cm. Bibliography: p. 145-146. [BS8628.C69 1969] 76-243194
1. Smith, Joseph, 1805-1844. Doctrine and covenants. 2. Mormons and Mormonism—Doctrinal and controversial works. I. Title.

CROWE, W L. 289.
The Mormon Waterloo, being a condensed and classified array of testimony and arguments against the false prophet, Joseph Smith, his works, and his church system and doctrines, based upon standard history, science, the Bible, and Smith against himself, by Elder W. L. Crowe ... [St. Paul, Neb., 1902?] 160 p. 20 cm. [BX8645.C85] 22-10331
1. Smith, Joseph, 1805-1844. 2. Mormons and Mormonism. I. Title.

CROWTHER, Duane S 922.8373
The prophecies of Joseph Smith. Salt Lake City, Bookcraft, 1963. 413 p. illus., ports., maps. 24 cm. [BX8695.S6C7] 64-3499
1. Smith, Joseph, 1805-1844. I. Title.

CURTIS, Thomas Arnold, 289.3'2
1953-
The pearl of great price comprehensive concordance, by Thomas A. Curtis and Jeffery Hill. Salt Lake City, Hawkes Publications [1973] 190 p. 21 cm. [BX8629.P5C87] 73-78980 2.95
1. Smith, Joseph, 1805-1844. The pearl of great price—Concordances. I. Hill, Jeffery, joint author. II. Smith, Joseph, 1805-1844. The pearl of great price. III. Title.

CURTIS, Thomas Arnold, 289.3'2
1953-
The pearl of great price comprehensive concordance, by Thomas A. Curtis and Jeffery Hill. Salt Lake City, Hawkes Publications [1973] 190 p. 21 cm. [BX8629.P5C87] 73-78980 2.95
1. Smith, Joseph, 1805-1844. The pearl of great price—Concordances. I. Hill, Jeffery, joint author. II. Smith, Joseph, 1805-1844. The pearl of great price. III. Title.

DOXEY, Roy Watkins, 230'.9'33
1908- ed.
Latter-day prophets and the Doctrine and covenants / compiled by Roy W. Doxey. Salt Lake City : Deseret Book Co., 1978. 4 v. ; 21 cm. Includes indexes. Bibliography: v. 4, p. 505-508. [BX8628.D69 1978] 78-17475 15.95
1. Smith, Joseph, 1805-1844. Doctrine and covenants. 2. Mormons and Mormonism—Doctrinal and controversial works. I. Smith, Joseph, 1805-1844. Doctrine and covenants. II. Title.

ETZENHOUSER, Rudolph, 289.3'22
1856-
From Palmyra, New York, 1830, to Independence, Missouri, 1894. Independence, Mo., Ensign Pub. House, 1894. [New York, AMS Press, 1971] 444 p. 22 cm. The Book unsealed, rev. and enl., which was first published in 1892, forms part one of this work. [BX8627.E78 1971] 73-134393 ISBN 0-404-08435-4 17.50
1. Smith, Joseph, 1805-1844. 2. Book of Mormon. 3. Mormons and Mormonism—Doctrinal and controversial works. I. Title.

EVANS, John Henry, 1872- 922.8373
Joseph Smith, an American prophet, by John Henry Evans. New York, The Macmillan company, 1933. xi p., 2 l., 3-447 p. front., plates, ports., facsim. 24 cm. Bibliography: p. 435-437. [BX8695.S6E85] 33-8271
1. Smith, Joseph, 1805-1844. 2. Mormons and Mormonism. I. Title.

[FITCH, T Mrs.]
A brief history of the Church of Jesus Christ of Latterday saints, from the birth of the prophet Joseph Smith to the present time. By the author of the "Life of Brigham Young" ... Salt Lake City, G. Q. Cannon & sons co. 1893. viii, [9]-173 p. 19 cm. A11
1. Smith, Joseph, 1805-1844. 2. Mormons and Mormonism. I. Title.

GIBBONS, Francis 289.3'092'4 B
M., 1921-
Joseph Smith, martyr, prophet of God / Francis M. Gibbons. Salt Lake City : Deseret Book Co., 1977. ix, 377 p. ; 23 cm. Includes index. Bibliography: p. 366-368. [BX8695.S6G52] 77-2019 ISBN 0-87747-637-3 : 6.95
1. Smith, Joseph, 1805-1844. 2. Mormons and Mormonism in the United States—Biography. 3. Mormons and Mormonism—History. I. Title.

GREGG, Thomas. 289.
The prophet of Palmyra; Mornonism reviewed and examined in the life, character, and career of its founder, from "Cumorah hill" to Carthage jail and the desert, together with a complete history of the Mormon era in Illinois, and an exhaustive investigation of the "Spalding manuscript" theory of the origin of the Book of Mormon, by Thomas Gregg. New York, J. B. Alden, 1890. xiv p., 1 l., 552 p. incl. front., plates, ports. 20 cm. [BX8645.G8] 19-7125
1. Smith, Joseph, 1805-1844. 2. Mormons and Mormonism in Illinois. 3. Spalding, Solomon, 1761-1816. I. Title.

HARRISON, G T 1901- 922.8373
Mormons are peculiar people. New York, Vantage Press [1954] 180p. 23cm. [BX8695.S6H3] 54-10241
1. Smith, Joseph, 1805-1844. I. Title.

HARTSHORN, Leon R. 289.3'0924 B
Joseph Smith: prophet of the restoration, by Leon R. Hartshorn. Salt Lake City, Deseret Book Co., 1970. 124 p. 24 cm. Includes bibliographic references. [BX8695.S6H32] 71-130321 ISBN 0-87747-372-2 3.95
1. Smith, Joseph, 1805-1844.

HILL, Donna. 289.3'092'4 B
Joseph Smith, the first Mormon / by Donna Hill. 1st ed. Garden City, N.Y. : Doubleday, 1977. xviii, 527 p., [8] leaves of plates : ill. ; 25 cm. Includes index. Bibliography: p. [495]-513. [BX8695.S6H54] 73-15345 ISBN 0-385-00804-X : 12.50
1. Smith, Joseph, 1805-1844. 2. Mormons and Mormonism—Biography. I. Title.

HILTON, Lynn M. 289.3'2
A concordance of the Pearl of great price [by] Lynn M. Hilton. Provo, Utah, Brigham Young University Press [1968] iv, 91 p. 28 cm. [BX8629.P6H5 1968] 68-3571
1. Smith, Joseph, 1805-1844. Pearl of great price—Concordances. I. Title.

HULLINGER, Robert N. 289.3'22
Mormon answer to skepticism : Why Joseph Smith wrote the book of Mormon / by Robert N. Hullinger. St. Louis, Mo. : Clayton Pub. House, c1980. xiv, 201 p. : ill. ; 23 cm. Includes index. Bibliography: p. [181]-188. [BX8627.H78] 19 79-54055 ISBN 0-915644-18-5 (pbk.) : 14.95
1. Smith, Joseph, 1805-1844. 2. Book of Mormon. 3. Mormons and Mormonism—Doctrinal and controversial works—Lutheran authors. I. Title.

JACKSON, Ronald 289.3'092'4 B
Vern.
The seer, Joseph Smith, his education from the Most High / by Ronald Vern Jackson. 3d ed., expanded and bound. Salt Lake City : Hawkes Pub. Inc., c1977. 248 p. : ill. ; 23 cm. Includes bibliographical references. [BX8695.S6J25 1977] 77-77303 ISBN 0-89036-088-X : 3.95
1. Smith, Joseph, 1805-1844. 2. Mormons and Mormonism in the United States—Biography. I. Title.
Publisher's address 3775 S. 500W. Box 15711, Salt Lake City, UT 84115

LUDLOW, Daniel H. 289.3'2
A companion to your study of the Doctrine and covenants / Daniel H. Ludlow. Salt Lake City : Deseret Book Co., 1978. 2 v. ; 24 cm. Vol. 2: Appendixes. [BX8628.L77] 78-64752 ISBN 0-87747-722-1(v.1) : 16.95
1. Smith, Joseph, 1805-1844. Doctrine and covenants. I. Title.

[MAYHEW, Henry] 1812-1887. 280.
History of the Mormons; or, Latter-day saints. With memoirs of the life and death of Joseph Smith, the "American Mahomet." Auburn [N.Y.] Derby and Miller, 1852. vii p., 1 l., [17]-399 p. incl. plates. front. 20 cm. First published in London in 1851, under title: The Mormons: or Latter-day saints. Edited by Charles Mackay. [BX8611.M3 1852] 39-17850
1. Smith, Joseph, 1805-1844. 2. Mormons and Mormonism. I. Mackay, Charles, 1814-1889, ed. II. Title.

[MAYHEW, Henry] 1812-1887. 280.
...History of the Mormons: or Latter-day saints. With memoirs of the life and death of Joseph Smith, the "American Mahomet". Auburn [N.Y.] Derby and Miller, 1853. vii p., 1 l., [17]-399 p. incl. plates. front. 20 cm. At head of title: Second thousand. First published in London in 1851, under title: The Mormons: or Latter-day saints. Edited by Charles Mackay. [BX8611.M3 1853] 5-28796
1. Smith, Joseph, 1805-1844. 2. Mormons and Mormonism. I. Mackay, Charles, 1814-1889, ed. II. Title.

[MAYHEW, Henry] 1812-1887. 280.
...History of the Mormons: or, Latter-day saints. With memoirs of the life and death of Joseph Smith, the "American Mahomet." Auburn and Buffalo, Miller, Orton & Mulligan, 1854. vii, [1], [17]-399 p. incl. plates. front. 19 1/2 cm. At head of title: Third thousand. First published in London in 1851, under title: The Mormons: or Latter-day saints. Edited by Charles Mackay. [BX8611.M3 1854] 35-34755
1. Smith, Joseph, 1805-1844. 2. Mormons and Mormonism. I. Mackay, Charles, 1814-1889, ed. II. Title.

MAYHEW, Henry, 1812-1887. 289.3'09
The Mormons; or Latter-day Saints: a contemporary history. New York, AMS Press [1971] 326 p. illus. 22 cm. Reprint of the 1852 ed. [BX8611.M3 1971] 71-134398 ISBN 0-404-08440-0 12.50
1. Smith, Joseph, 1805-1844. 2. Mormons and Mormonism. I. Title.

[MAYHEW, Henry] 1812-1887. 280.
The religious, social, and polictical history of the Mormons, or Latter-day saints, from their origin to the present time; containing full statements of their doctrines, government and condition, and memoirs of their founder, Joseph Smith. Edited, with important additions, by Samuel M. Smucker ... New York, Hurst & company [c1881) viii, [7]-466 p. incl. front., plates. 20 cm. First published in London in 1851, under title: The Mormons: or Latter-day saints. [BX8611.M3 1881] 28-25245
1. Smith, Joseph, 1805-1844. 2. Mormons and Mormonism. I. Schmucker, Samuel Moshelm, 1823-1863, ed. II. Title.

[MAYHEW, Henry] 1812-1887. 280.
The religious, social, and political history of the Mormons, or Latter-day saints, from their origin to the present time; containing full statements of their doctrines, government and condition, and memoirs of their founder, Joseph Smith, Edited, with important additions, by Samuel M. Smucker... New York and Auburn, Miller, Orton & Mulligan, 1856. viii, [17]-460 p. incl. plates. 18 cm. First published in London in 1851, under title: The Mormons: or Latter-day saints. [BX8611.M3 1856] 28-25244
1. Smith, Joseph 1805-1844. 2. Mormons and Mormonism. I. Schmucker, Samuel Moshelm, 1823-1863, ed. II. Title.

[MAYHEW, Henry] 1812-1887. 280.
The religious, social, and political history of the Mormons, or Latter-day saints, from their origin to the present time; containing full statements of their doctrines, government and condition, and memoirs of their founder, Joseph Smith. Edited, with important additions, by Samuel M. Smucker... New York, C. M. Saxton, 1858. viii, [17]-460 p. incl. plates. col. front. 20 cm. First published in London in 1851, under title The Mormons: or Latter-day saints. [BX8611.M3 1858] 36-3416
1. Smith, Joseph, 1805-1844. 2. Mormons and Mormonism. I. Schmucker, Samuel Moshelm, 1823-1863, ed. II. Title.

MORRIS, Nephi Lowell. 922.
Prophecies of Joseph Smith and their fulfillment, by Nephi Lowell Morris. Salt Lake City, Deseret book company, 1920. vi, [2], 198 p. illus. (incl. facsims.) 19 cm. [BX8695.S6M6] 20-22060
1. Smith, Joseph, 1805-1844. 2. Mormons and Mormonism. I. Title.

MORRIS, Nephi Lowell. 922.
Prophecies of Joseph Smith and their fulfillment, by Nephi Lowell Morris. Salt Lake City, Deseret book company, 1926. xiii, [1], 329 p. illus. (incl. facsims.) port. 19 1/2 cm. [BX8695.S6M6 1926] 26-21779
1. Smith, Joseph, 1805-1844. 2. Mormons and Mormonism. I. Title.

NEELEY, Deta Petersen. 922.8373
A child's story of the prophet Joseph Smith, by Deta Petersen Neeley and Nathan Glen Neeley. Salt Lake City, Deserat News Press, 1958. 164p. illus. 20cm. [BX8695.S6N4] 59-21394
1. Smith, Joseph, 1805-1844 I. Neeley, Nathan Glen, joint author. II. Title.

NIBLEY, Hugh, 1910- 289.3
The myth makers. Salt Lake City, Bookcraft [1961] 293p. 24cm. Includes bibliography. [BX8635.5.N5] 61-59773
1. Smith, Joseph, 1805-1844. 2. Mormons and Mormonism—Apologetic works. I. Title.

NIBLEY, Preston. 922.8373
Joseph Smith, the prophet, by Preston Nibley ... Salt Lake City, Utah, Deseret news press, 1944. 2 p. l., 572 p. front., ports. 24 cm. [BX8695.S6N5] 44-9390
1. Smith, Joseph, 1805-1844. I. Title.

PARRY, Edwin Francis, 1860- comp. 922.8373
Stories about Joseph Smith, the prophet; a collection of incidents related by friends who knew him ... Compiled by Edwin F. Parry. Salt Lake City, Utah, The Deseret news press, 1934. 192 p. illus. 16 cm. "A companion volume to 'Joseph Smith's teachings'." [BX8695.S6P3] 35-2674
1. Smith, Joseph, 1805-1844. 2. Mormons and Mormonism. I. Title.

PEARL of Great Price Symposium, Brigham Young University, 1975. 230'.9'33
Pearl of Great Price Symposium : a centennial presentation, November 22, 1975 / sponsored by the Department of Ancient Scripture. 1st ed. Provo, Utah : Brigham Young University, 1976. iii leaves, 103 p. ; 28 cm. Includes bibliographical references. [BX8629.P5P4 1975] 76-370968 pbk. : 2.00
1. Smith, Joseph, 1805-1844. The pearl of great price—Congresses. 2. Mormons and Mormonism—Doctrinal and controversial works—Congresses. I. Brigham Young University, Provo, Utah. Dept. of Ancient Scripture.

PETERSEN, LaMar, 1910- 289.3'092'4 B
Hearts made glad : the charges of intemperance against Joseph Smith the Mormon prophet / LaMar Petersen ; drawings by Linda Marion. [Salt Lake City : Petersen], c1975. iv, 258 p. : ill. ; 23 cm. Includes index. Bibliography: p. 245-253. [BX8695.S6P39] 75-21678
1. Smith, Joseph, 1805-1844. 2. Temperance. I. Title.

PETERSEN, Mark E. 289.3'22
Those gold plates! / Mark E. Petersen. Salt Lake City : Bookcraft, c1979. 125 p. : ill. ; 24 cm. Includes index. [BX8627.P45] 79-63402 ISBN 0-88494-364-X pbk. : 3.95
1. Smith, Joseph, 1805-1844. 2. Book of Mormon—Antiquities. I. Title.

RILEY, Isaac Woodbridge, 1869-1933. 922.
The founder of Mormonism: a psychological study of Joseph Smith, jr., by I. Woodbridge Riley ... with an introductory preface by Prof. George Trumbull Ladd. New York, Dodd, Mead & company, 1902. xix, 446 p. facsim. 20 cm. Bibliography: p. 427-446. [BX8695.S6R5] 2-16103
1. Smith, Joseph, 1805-1844. 2. Mormons and Mormonism. I. Title.

SEIBEL, George, 1872- 289.
The Mormon saints; the story of Joseph Smith, his golden bible, and the church he founded, by George Seibel. Pittsburgh, The Lessing company, 1919. 103 p. 17 cm. [BX8635.S4] 19-15408
1. Smith, Joseph, 1805-1844. 2. Mormons and Mormonism. I. Title.

SMITH, Henry Allen, 1907- 922.8373
The day they martyred the prophet, a historical narrative. Salt Lake City, Bookcraft [c1963] 279 p. illus., port. 24 cm. [BX8695.S6S57] 64-3694
1. Smith, Joseph, 1805-1844.. 2. Smith, Hyrum, 1800-1844. I. Title.

SMITH, Joseph, 1805-1844.
A brief history of Joseph Smith, the prophet, by himself. Salt Lake City, Utah, Deseret Sunday school union, 1910. 1 p. l., [5]-63 p. 17 cm. $0.25 "Closing years of Joseph Smith, the prophet, by Edward H. Anderson": p. 51-63. 11-3979
I. Anderson, Edward H. II. Title.

SMITH, Joseph, 1805-1844. 289.3
Joseph Smith, prophet-statesman; readings in American political thought. Edited, with introductions, by G. Homer Durham ... [Salt Lake City] The Bookcraft company, 1944. xiv, 225 p. pl., 3 port. (incl. front.) on 2 l., plan. 22 1/2 cm. "First edition." Bibliographical foot-notes. [BX8695.S6A45] 44-51866
I. Durham, George Homer, 1911- ed. II. Title.

SMITH, Joseph, 1805-1944.
Teachings of the prophet Joseph Smith taken from the sermons and writings as they are found in the documentary history and other publications of the Church and written or published in the days of the Prophet's ministry, selected and arranged by . . . Joseph Fielding Smith, and his assistants. Salt Lake City, Deseret, 1965 [c1938] 410 p. 24 cm. 66-82320
I. Title.

SMITH, Joseph Alexander, 1850- 261
Sinless anger; a presentation of the Bible view of anger, and The pastoral gift as revealed in the Scriptures, by Joseph A. Smith ... Kingswood, Ky., J. A. Smith [c1922] 52 p. incl. port. 19 1/2 cm. [BR123.S6] CA 23
I. Title. II. Title: The pastoral gift.

SMITH, Joseph Fielding, 1876- 289.309
Church history and modern revelation, covering the first period: Joseph Smith, the prophet. Alphabetical index and digest of the above study course, by Andrew K. Smith. [Salt Lake City] Council of the Twelve Apostles of the Church of Jesus Christ of Latter-Day Saints [1953] 2v. 24cm. [BX8611.S66] 54-22110
1. Smith, Joseph, 1805-1844. 2. Mormons and Mormonism— Hist. I. Title.

SMITH, Lucy (Mack) Mrs., b.1776. 922.
Biographical sketches of Joseph Smith the prophet and his progenitors for many generations, by Lucy Smith... Lamoni, Ia., The Reorganized church of Jesus Christ of latter day saints, 1908. 1 p. l., iv, 371 p. 20 cm. [BX8695.S6S6] 22-14659
1. Smith, Joseph, 1805-1844. 2. Smith family. 3. Mack family. I. Title.

SMITH, Lucy (Mack) 1776-1855. 922.8373
History of Joseph Smith, by his mother, Lucy Mack Smith. With notes and comments by Preston Nibley. Salt Lake City, Bookcraft, 1958. 355 p. illus. 24 cm. "Originally entitled The history of Mother Smith, by Herself," and first published in 1843. [BX8695.S6S63 1958] 61-21185
1. Smith, Joseph, 1805-1844. I. Title.

SMITH, Lucy (Mack) 1776-1855. 922.8373
History of Joseph Smith, by his mother, Lucy Mack Smith. With notes and comments by Preston Nibley. Salt Lake City, Bookcraft, 1958. 355 p. illus. 24 cm. "Originally entitled The history of Mother Smith, by Herself," and first published in 1843. [BX8695.S6S63 1958] 61-21185
1. Smith, Joseph, 1805-1844. I. Title.

SMITH, Mildred Nelson. 613.2
The Word of Wisdom : a principle with promise / by Mildred Nelson Smith. Independence, Mo. : Herald Pub. House, c1977. p. cm. Bibliography: p. [BX8643.D5S57] 76-46311 ISBN 0-8309-0175-2 : 12.00
1. Smith, Joseph, 1805-1844. 2. Nutrition. 3. Hygiene. 4. Mormons and Mormonism. I. Title.

STEWART, John J
Joseph Smith, the Mormon prophet, by John J. Stewart. Salt Lake City, Mercury Pub. Co. [c1966] 257 p. illus. 68-6683
1. Smith, Joseph, 1805-1844. 2. Mormons and mormonism. I. Title.

STEWART, John J 922.8373
Joseph Smith, democracy's unknown prophet. Salt Lake City, Merenry Pub. Co. [1960] 119 p. illus. 16 cm. [BX8695.S6S8] 60-34862
1. Smith, Joseph, 1805-1844. I. Title. II. Title: Democracy's unknown prophet.

TANNER, Jerald.
Changes in Joseph Smith's History, by Jerald & Sandra Tanner. Salt Lake City, Modern Microfilm Co. [1965] 88 p. illus. 29 cm. Loose-leaf. 66-63301
1. Smith, Joseph, 1805-1844. 2. Mormons and Mormonism. I. Tanner, Sandra, joint author. II. Title.

TERRY, Keith. 289.3
From the dust of decades; a saga of the papyri and mummies [by] Keith Terry and Walter Whipple. Salt Lake City, Bookcraft, 1968. 118 p. illus., facsims. 24 cm. Includes bibliographical references. [BX8622.T44] 68-29490
1. Smith, Joseph, 1805-1844. 2. Mormons and Mormonism—History—Sources. I. Whipple, Walter, joint author. II. Title.

TODD, Jay M. 289.3'2
The saga of the Book of Abraham [by] Jay M. Todd. Salt Lake City, Deseret Book Co., 1969. ix, 404 p. illus., facsims., maps, ports. 24 cm. [BX8629.P6T6] 71-82121 4.95
1. Smith, Joseph, 1805-1844. The pearl of great price. Book of Abraham. I. Title. II. Title: Book of Abraham.

TULLIDGE, Edward Wheelock. 922.8373
Life of Joseph the prophet. By Edward W. Tullidge. Plano, Ill., Published by the Board of publication of the Reorganized church of Jesus Christ of latter day saints, 1880. xii, 827 p. 4 port (incl. front.) 22 cm. [BX8695.S6T8] 36-31811
1. Smith, Joseph, 1805-1844. 2. Mormons and Mormonism. I. Reorganized church of Jesus Christ of latter-day saints. Board of publication. II. Title.

WIDTSOE, John Andreas, 1872- 922.S373
Joseph Smith; seeker after truth, prophet of God. Salt Lake City, Deseret News Press, 1951. x, 385 p. illus., ports. 24 cm. "A chrouology featuring political highlights in the career of Joseph Smith . . . by Dr. G. Homer Durham": p. [361]-370. bibliography: p. [371]-375. [BXS695.S6W52] 52-31355
1. Smith, Joseph, 1805-1844. I. Title.

WIDTSOE, John Andreas, 1872- 922.
Joseph Smith as scientist; a contribution to Mormon philosophy, by John A. Widtsoe ... Salt Lake City, Utah, The General board, Young men's mutual improvement associations, 1908. 1 p. l., 173 p. 23 1/2 cm. [BX8695.S6W5] 8-20997
1. Smith, Joseph, 1805-1844. I. Title.

WIDTSOE, John Andreas, 1872-1952. 215
Joseph Smith as scientist; a contribution to Mormon philosophy. Salt Lake City, Bookcraft [c1964] 162 p. 24 cm. Bibliographical footnotes. [BX8695.S6W5] 65-1772
1. Smith, Joseph, 1805-1844. I. Title.

WOOD, Wilford C ed. 289.322
Joseph Smith begins his work. Salt Lake City? 1958- v. illus., ports., map, facsims. 24 cm. Contents.-- v. 1. Book of Mormon. [BX8621.W6] 58-2314
1. Smith, Joseph, 1805-1844. 2. Mormons and Mormonism. I. Title.

THE Words of Joseph Smith : the contemporary accounts of the Nauvoo discourses of the Prophet Joseph / compiled and edited by Andrew F. Ehat and Lyndon W. Cook ; with a foreword by Truman G. Madsen. Provo, Utah : Religious Studies Center, Brigham Young University ; Salt Lake City, Utah : Distributed by Bookcraft, c1980. xxv, 447 p. ; 24 cm. (Religious studies monograph series ; v. 6) Includes indexes. [BX8695.S6W67] 19 80-70806 ISBN 0-88494-419-0 : 10.95 289.3'092'4

1. Smith, Joseph, 1805-1844. 2. Mormon Church—Doctrinal and controversial works. 3. Mormons—United States—Biography. I. Ehat, Andrew F. II. Cook, Lyndon W. III. Series.

[WYL, W.] 289.
... Joseph Smith, the prophet, his family and his friends. A study based on facts and documents. With fourteen illustrations. Salt Lake City, Tribune printing and publishing company, 1886. 4 p. l., [5]-320 p. illus. 17 cm. (Added t.-p.: Mormon portraits, or The truth about the Mormon leaders from 1830 to 1886 ... by Dr. W. Wyl. [v. 1]) [BX8645.W9] 5-28265
1. Smith, Joseph, 1805-1844. 2. Mormons and Mormonism. I. Title.

[WYMETAL, Wilhelm von Ritter 1838-1896. 289.
Joseph Smith the prophet, his family and his friends, A study based on facts and documents. Salt Lake City, Tribune Print. and Pub. Co., 1886. 320 p. illus. 17 cm. (His Mormon portraits; or, The truth about the Mormon leaders from 1830 to 1886. [v. 1]) [BX8645.W9] 5-28265
1. Smith, Joseph, 1805-1844. 2. Mormons and Mormonism. I. Title.

Smith, Joseph, 1805-1844—Chronology.

CONKLING, J. Christopher, 1949- 289.3'092'4 B
A Joseph Smith chronology / J. Christopher Conking ; prepared for BEI Productions, inc. Salt Lake City : Deseret Book Company, 1979. ix, 276 p. : map ; 25 cm. Includes index. Bibliography: p. 253-266. [BX8695.S6C64] 79-896 ISBN 0-87747-734-5 : 7.95
1. Smith, Joseph, 1805-1844—Chronology. 2. Mormons and Mormonism in the United States—Biography. I. BEI Productions. II. Title.

Smith, Joseph, 1805-1844—Collected works.

ANDRUS, Hyrum Leslie, 1924- comp. 289.3'092'4 B
They knew the prophet. Compiled by Hyrum L. Andrus and Helen Mae Andrus. Salt Lake City, Bookcraft [1974] xii, 207 p. 24 cm. [BX8695.S6A73] 74-75538 ISBN 0-88494-210-4
1. Smith, Joseph, 1805-1844—Collected works. I. Andrus, Helen Mae, joint comp. II. Title.

Smith, Joseph, 1805-1844. Doctrine and covenants.

BERRETT, William Edwin. 230.93
Teachings of the Doctrine and covenants. Salt Lake City, Deseret Book Co., 1956. 289p. 24cm. Bibliographical footnotes. [BX8628.B4] 57-640
1. Smith, Joseph, 1805-1844. Doctrine and covenants. I. Title.

BLUTH, John V., comp. 230.93
Concordance to The doctrine and covenants, compiled by John V. Bluth. Salt Lake City, Utah, The Deseret book company, 1945. 3 p. l., 501 p. 23 1/2 cm. "First edition 1945." [BX8628.B56] 46-16246
1. Smith, Joseph, 1805-1855. The doctrine and covenants. I. Title.

THE Doctrine and covenants speaks, by Roy W. Doxey. Salt Lake City, Deseret Book Co. [1964- v. 24 cm. Bibliography: v. 1, p. [563]-564. [BX8628.D685] 64-57862 289.3
1. Smith, Joseph, 1805-1844. Doctrine and covenants.

DOXEY, Roy Watkins, 1908- 230.93
The Doctrine and convenants and the future. [Salt Lake City] Desert Book Co., 1954. 96p. 20cm. [BX8628.D68] 54-38486
1. Smith, Joseph, 1805-1844. Doctrine and covenants. 2. Eachatology. I. Title.

DOXEY, Roy Watkins, 1908- 289.3
The Doctrine and covenants speaks, by Roy W. Doxey. Salt Lake City, Deseret Book Co. [1964- v. 24 cm. Bibliography: v. 1, p. [563]-564. [BX8628.D685] 64-57862
1. Smith, Joseph, 1805-1844. Doctrine and covenants. I. Title.

DOXEY, Roy Watkins, 1908- ed. 289.3
The Latter-day prophets and the Doctrine and covenants. Salt Lake City, Deseret Book Co., 1963-65. 4 v. 24 cm. [BX8628.D69] 64-2097
1. Smith, Joseph, 1805-1844. Doctrine and covenants. I. Smith, Joseph, 1805-1844. Doctrine and covenants. II. Title.

EDWARDS, Francis Henry, 1897- 230.93
... A commentary on the Doctrine and covenants (sections 1 to 131) by F. Henry Edwards; a brief historical treatment of each section, stating the conditions under which it was given, its import for the time it was given, and its application to the problems and needs of the church today. Independence, Mo., Herald publishing house, 1946. 447, [1] p. 20 1/2 cm. (The Priesthood library) "First edition, August 1938. Revised edition, September 1946." [BX8628.E3] 47-16470
1. Smith, Joseph, 1805-1844. Doctrine and covenants. 2. Reorganized church of Jesus Christ of latter-day saints. Book of doctrine and covenants. I. Title.

LOUTENSOCK, Sarah. 289.3
The plan of salvation; a Christian's defense of the economic system of Jesus Christ. Boston, Forum Pub. Co. [1963] 504 p. illus. 24 cm. [BX8628.L6] 63-599
1. Smith, Joseph, 1805-1844; The doctrine and covenants of the Church of Jesus Christ of Latter-Day Saints. 2. Mormons and Mormonism — Doctrinal and controversial works. I. Title.

LUNDWALL, Nels Benjamin, 1884- comp. 289.3
The vision; or, The degrees of glory (Doc. and cov. section 76) being a compilation of rare and invaluable writings by authorities of the Church of Jesus Christ of Latter-Day Saints, as well as quotations from eminent historians, philosophers, Catholic fathers and Protestant leaders on the doctrine of salvation for the living and the dead. Salt Lake City [1939?] 148 p. 24 cm. [BX8628.L8 1939] 47-39686
1. Smith, Joseph, 1805-1844. Doctrine and covenants. 2. Mormons and Mormonism—Doctrinal and controversial works. I. Title.

LUNDWALL, Nels Benjamin, 1884- comp. 289.3
The vision; or, The drgrees of glory (Doc. and cov. section 76) being a compilation of rare and invaluable writings by authorities of the Church of Jesus Christ of latter-day saint, as well as quotations from eniment historians, philosophers, Catholic fathers and Protestant leaders on the doctrine of salvation for the living and the dead. N. B. Lundwall, compiler and publisher. Salt Lake City, Utah [1942] 5 p. l., 167 p. 23 1/2 cm. Illustrated half-title in color. "Third edition." [BX8628.L8 1942] 44-25096
1. Smith, Joseph, 1805-1844. Doctrine and covenants. 2. Mormons and Mormonism—Doctrinal and controversial works. I. Title.

SMITH, Joseph, 1805-1844.
Joseph Smith's teachings; a classified arrangement of the doctrinal sermons and writings of the great Latter-day prophet, comp. by Edwin F. Parry, from the authorized "History of the Church of Jesus Christ of Latter-day saints." Salt Lake City, Utah, The Deseret news, 1912. 192 p. 16 cm. $0.75 12-7887
I. Parry, Edwin F., comp. II. Title.

SPERRY, Sidney Branton, 1895- 238.93
Doctrine and covenants compendium. Salt Lake City, Bookcraft 1960. 779 p. 24 cm. Includes bibliography. [BX8628.S7] 60-52227
1. Smith, Joseph, 1805-1844. Doctrine and covenants. I. Title.

Smith, Joseph, 1805-1844. Doctrine and covenants—Concordances.

STARKS, Arthur E 1911- 230.93
A complete concordance to the doctrine and covenants. Independence, Mo., Herald Pub. House, 1951. 212 p. 23 cm. [BX8628.S8] 51-4179
1. Smith, Joseph, 1805-1844. Doctrine and convenants — Concordances. I. Title.

WIDTSOE, John Andreas, 1872- 230.
A concordance to the book of Doctrine and covenants of the Church of Jesus Christ of latter-day saints. By Elder John A. Widtsoe. Salt Lake City, Utah, The Deseret Sunday school union, 1906. 2 p. l., [iii]-iv, 205 p. 17 1/2 cm. [BX8628.W5] 6-26082
1. Smith, Joseph, 1805-1844. Doctrine and covenants—Concordances. I. Title.

Smith, Joseph, 1805-1844—Family.

MCGAVIN, Elmer Cecil. 922.8373
The family of Joseph Smith. Salt Lake City, Bkcraft [c.1963] 296p. 24cm. 63-4148 3.25
1. Smith, Joseph, 1805-1844—Family I. Title.

SMITH, Lucy (Mack) 1776-1855. 289.3'0922 B
Biographical sketches of Joseph Smith, the prophet. New York, Arno Press, 1969. 282 p. 23 cm. (Religion in America) Reprint of the 1908 ed. [BX8695.S6S6 1969] 73-83439
1. Smith, Joseph, 1805-1844—Family. 2. Mack family. I. Title.

Smith, Joseph, 1805-1844—Juvenile literature.

PETERSEN, Emma Marr. 289.3'092'4 B
The Prophet's story for young people. Salt Lake City, Bookcraft, 1973. v, 121 p. illus. 24 cm. [BX8695.S6P38] 73-90804
1. Smith, Joseph, 1805-1844—Juvenile literature. I. Title.

Smith, Joseph, 1805-1844. Pearl of great price.

CLARK, James Ratcliffe, 1910- 289.3
The story of the Pearl of great price. [1st ed.] Salt Lake City, Bookcraft [1955] 253p. illus. 24cm. [BX8629.P6C55] 56-16603
1. Smith, Joseph, 1805-1844. Pearl of great price. I. Title. II. Title: Pearl of great price.

HUNTER, Milton Reed, 1902- ed. 289.3
Pearl of great price commentary; a selection from the revelations, translations and narrations of Joseph Smith. 1st ed. Salt Lake City, Stevens & Wallis, 1948. xii, 264 p. illus. 24 cm. [BX8629.P52 1948] 49-222
1. Smith, Joseph, 1805-1844. Pearl of great price. 2. Mormons and Mormonism—Doctrinal and controversial works. I. Title.

NEELEY, Deta Petersen. 289.3
A child's story of the Pearl of great price. Salt Lake City, Printed by the Deseret News Press, 1954. 143p. illus. 20cm. [BX8629.P58N4] 54-42578
1. Smith, Joseph, 1805-1844. Pearl of great price. I. Title.

STEWART, Ora (Pate) 1910- 289.3
We believe a simplified treatment of the Articles of faith. [1st ed.] Salt Lake City, Bookcraft [1954] 112p. 16cm. [BX8629.P6S8] 55-23528
1. Smith, Joseph, 1805-1844. The pearl of great price. I. Title.

ZIEGLER, Wesley Moody, 1911- 289.3
An analysis of the Articles of faith. [Pasadena, Calif., 1949] 236, vii p. 24 cm. [BX8629.P6Z5] 49-6859
1. Smith, Joseph. 1805-1844. The pearl of great price. 2. Mormons and Mormonism—Doctrinal and controversial works. I. Title.

Smith, Joseph, 1805-1844. Pearl of great price—Concordances.

HILTON, Lynn M 289.32
A concordance of the Pearl of great price. [Provo, Utah] Brigham Young University, Extension Publications] c1961. iv, 91p. 28cm. [BX8629.P6H5] 61-59897
1. Smith, Joseph, 1805-1844. Pearl of great price—Concordances. I. Title.

Smith, Joseph Fielding, 1876-

HESLOP, J. M. 289.3'3'0924 B
Joseph Fielding Smith; a prophet among the people [by] J. M. Heslop and Dell R. Van Orden. Salt Lake City, Deseret Book Co., 1971. xi, 171 p. ports. 24 cm. [BX8695.S63H48] 77-175121 ISBN 0-87747-454-0 3.95
1. Smith, Joseph Fielding, 1876- I. Van Orden, Dell R., joint author.

MCCONKIE, Joseph F. 289.3'3 B
True and faithful; the life story of Joseph Fielding Smith [by] Joseph F. McConkie. Salt Lake City, Utah, Bookcraft, 1971. 102 p. illus. 24 cm. Includes bibliographical references. [BX8695.S64M25] 76-175137
1. Smith, Joseph Fielding, 1876- I. Title.

SMITH, Joseph Fielding, 1876- comp. 922.8373
Life of Joseph F. Smith, sixth president of the Church of Jesus Christ of latter-day saints ... compiled by Joseph Fielding Smith ... [Salt Lake City] The Deseret news press, 1938. 490 p. front., ports., facsim. 23 1/2 cm. [BX8695.S6S57] 39-3104
1. Smith, Joseph Fielding, 1838-1918. 2. Smith, Hyrum, 1800-1844. 3. Mormons and Mormonism. I. Title.

SMITH, Joseph Fielding, 1913- 289.3'3 B
The life of Joseph Fielding Smith, tenth President of the Church of Jesus Christ of the Latter-day Saints [by] Joseph Fielding Smith, Jr. and John J. Stewart. Salt Lake City, Deseret Book Co., 1972. xvi, 404 p. illus. 24 cm. Bibliography: p. [389]-392. [BX8695.S64S6] 72-90344 ISBN 0-87747-484-2 4.95
1. Smith, Joseph Fielding, 1876- I. Stewart, John J., joint author. II. Title.

Smith, Joseph H.

ROSE, Delbert R. 287.673
A theology of Christian experience; interpreting the historic Wesleyan message. Minneapolis, Bethany [c.1965] 314p. ports. 22cm. Bibl. [BX6.N42R6] 65-20789 4.95
1. Smith, Joseph H. 2. National Holiness Association. I. Title.

ROSE, Delbert R 287.673
A theology of Christian experience; interpreting the historic Wesleyan message, by Delbert R. Rose. [2d ed.] Minneapolis, Bethany Fellowship [1965] 314 p. ports. 22 cm. Revision of thesis, State University of Iowa. Bibliography: p. 307-314. [BX6.N42R6] 65-20789
1. Smith, Joseph H. 2. National Holiness Association. I. Title.

ROSE, Delbert R. 230'.6
Vital holiness : a theology of Christian experience : interpreting the historic Wesleyan message / Delbert R. Rose. 3d ed. Minneapolis : Bethany Fellowship, c1975. 322 p. ; 22 cm. Originally presented as the author's thesis, State University of Iowa; rev. 1st-2d ed. published under title: A theology of Christian experience. Includes index. Bibliography: p. 311-318. [BX8495.S583R67 1975] 75-328165 ISBN 0-87123-539-0 pbk. : 3.95
1. Smith, Joseph H. 2. National Holiness Association. I. Title.

Smith, Josiah, 1704-1781. Humane impositions proved unscriptural.

FISHER, Hugh, d.1734. 252.
A preservative from damnable errors, in the unction of the Holy One. A sermon preach'd, at the opening of a presbytery, at Charlestown in S. Carolina; some time before the Reverend Mr. Joseph Smith's sermon (which is publish'd against it, with the title, of Humane impositions prov'd unscriptual &c.) and now published, (with the advice of some reverend ministers adhering to the Westminster confession) to vindicate the truths contained in it, from Mr. Smith's mis-representations, and exceptions. Together with a postscript containing some remarks, upon Mr. Smith's preface, and sermon. By Hugh Fisher ... [Boston] Printed in the year, MDCCXXX. 1 p., l., 84 p. 17 1/2 cm. [BX7233.F5272P7] 44-48291
1. Smith, Josiah, 1704-1781. Humane

impositions proved unscriptural. 2. Congregational churches—Sermons. I. Title.

Smith, Malcolm, 1938-

†SMITH, Malcolm, 1938- 269'.2'0924 B
Follow me! : The apprenticing of disciples / Malcolm Smith. Plainfield, N.J. : Logos International, c1976. 168 p. ; 22 cm. [BR1725.S54A33] 76-41065 5.95. pbk. : 5.95
1. Smith, Malcolm, 1938- 2. Clergy—New Jersey—Biography. 3. Christian life—1960- I. Title.

SMITH, Malcolm, 1938- 248'.3
How I learned to meditate / Malcolm Smith. Plainfield, N.J. : Logos International, c1977. viii, 127 p. ; 21 cm. [BX8762.Z8S637] 77-18482 ISBN 0-88270-253-X pbk. : 2.95
1. Smith, Malcolm, 1938- 2. Pentecostals—Clergy—Biography. 3. Clergy—United States—Biography. 4. Clergy—England—Biography. 5. Meditation. I. Title.

Smith, Mary Ettie V. (Coray)

GREEN, Nelson Winch. 289.3'3'0924 B
Mormonism: its rise, progress, and present condition. Embracing the narrative of Mrs. Mary Ettie V. Smith, of her residence and experience of fifteen years with the Mormons; containing a full and authentic account of their social condition—their religious doctrines, and political government ... By N. W. Green. Hartford, Belknap & Bliss, 1870. [New York, AMS Press, 1972] 472 p. illus. 22 cm. [BX8695.S7G74 1972] 79-134401 ISBN 0-404-08445-1 19.50
1. Smith, Mary Ettie V. (Coray) 2. Mormons and Mormonism. I. Title.

Smith, Matthew Hale, 1810-1879.

BROWNE, Lewis Crebasa. 230.
Review of the life and writings of M. Hale Smith; with a vindication of the moral tendency of Universalism, and the moral character of Universalists. By L. C. Browne. Boston, A. Tompkins, 1847. 360 p. 19 1/2 cm. [BX9947.S7B7] 28-1485
1. Smith, Matthew Hale, 1810-1879. 2. Universalism. I. Title.

Smith, Michelle.

SMITH, Michelle. 133.4'22'0926
Michelle remembers / by Michelle Smith and Lawrence Pazder. New York : Congdon & Lattes : distributed by St. Martin's Press, c1980. p. cm. [BF1548.S65 1980] 80-67862 ISBN 0-312-92531-X (St. Martin's) : 12.95
1. Smith, Michelle. 2. Satanism—Case studies. I. Pazder, Lawrence, joint author. II. Title.

Smith, Mrs. Amanda (Berry) 1837-1915.

TAYLOR, Marshall William, 1846-1887. 922.7666
The life, travels, labors, and helpers of Mrs. Amanda Smith, the famous Negro missionary evangelist. By Rev. Marshall W. Taylor ... With an introduction by Rev. J. Krehbiel ... Cincinnati, Printed by Cranston & Stowe for the author, 1886. 63 p. front. (port.) 17 1/2 cm. [BV3785.S56T3] 37-36766
1. Smith, Mrs. Amanda (Berry) 1837-1915. I. Title.

Smith, Mrs. Eliza Roxey (Snow) 1804-1887.

THE life and labors of Eliza 922.
R. Snow Smith; with a full account of her funeral services. Salt Lake City, Utah, The juvenile instructor office, 1888. 37. 24 p. 18 cm. "Doctrines of the Church o Jesus Christ of Latter-day saints ... by Elder John Morgan": 24 p. at end. [BX8695.S5L5] 20-23356
1. Smith, Mrs. Eliza Roxey (Snow) 1804-1887. I. Church of Jesus Christ of latter-day saints. II. Morgan, John.

Smith, Mrs. Mary Ettie V. (Coray) b. 1829.

GREEN, Nelson Winch. 922.
Fifteen years among the Mormons: being the narrative of Mrs. Mary Ettie V. Smith, late of Great Salt Lake City: a sister of one of the Mormon high priests ... By Nelson Winch Green. New York, H. Dayton; Indianapolis, Ind., Asher & company, 1859. xvi, 17-408 p. 19 cm. [BX8695.S7G7] 22-19204
1. Smith, Mrs. Mary Ettie V. (Coray) 2. Mormons and Mormonism. I. Title.

GREEN, Nelson Winch. 922.
Fifteen years amont the Mormons; being the narrative of Mrs. Mary Ettie V. Smith, late of Great Salt Lake City: a sister of one of the Mormon high priests, she having been personally acquainted with most of the Mormon leaders, and long in the confidence of the "Prophet", Brigham Young. By Nelson Winch Green. New York, C. Scribner, 1858. xvi, 17-388 p. front. (port.) 19 cm. Mrs. Smith's narrative is in the first person, but the authorship is claimed by Green in the Introduction. [BX8695.S7G] A 24
1. Smith, Mrs. Mary Ettie V. (Coray) b. 1829. 2. Mormons and Mormonism. I. Title.

Smith, Mrs. Sarah Lanman (Huntington) 1802-1836.

HOOKER, Edward William, 1794-1875. 275.
Memoir of Mrs. Sarah L. Huntington Smith, late of the American mission in Syria. By Edward W. Hooker, D.D. 3d ed. New York, American tract society [1846] 396 p. front. (port.) 19 1/2 cm. [BV3202.S5H6 1846] 22-6803
1. Smith, Mrs. Sarah Lanman (Huntington) 1802-1836. 2. Missions—Syria. I. Title.

HOOKER, Edward William, 1794-1875.
Memoir of Mrs. Sarah L. Huntington Smith, late of the American mission in Syria. By Edward E. Hooker, D.D. 3d ed. Boston, T. R. Marvin, 1846. 396 p. front. (port.) 19 cm. [BV8202.S5H6 1846a] 22-6804
1. Smith, Mrs. Sarah Lanman (Huntington) 1802-1836. 2. Missions—Syria. I. Title.

HOOKER, Edward William, 1794-1875. 275.
Memoir of Mrs. Sarah Lanman Smith, late of the mission in Syria... By Edward W. Hooker. Boston, Perkins & Marvin; Philadelphia, H. Perkins, 1839. 407 p. front. (port.) 20 cm. [BV3202.S5H6 1839] 22-19210
1. Smith, Mrs. Sarah Lanman (Huntington) 1802-1836. 2. Missions—Syria. I. Title.

Smith, Nancy Anne.

SMITH, Nancy Anne. 248'.2'0924 B
Winter past / Nancy Anne Smith. Downers Grove, Ill. : InterVarsity Press, c1977. 119 p. ; 21 cm. [BR1725.S548A35] 77-6036 ISBN 0-87784-723-1 pbk. : 2.95
1. Smith, Nancy Anne. 2. Christian biography—United States. 3. Mental illness—United States—Biography. I. Title.

Smith, Normand, 1800-1833.

HAWES, Joel, 1789-1867. 922
Memoir of Normand Smith; or, The Christian serving God in his business. By Rev. Joel Hawes, D.D. New-York, The American tract society [1839?] 72 p. 15 cm. "Memoir of Nathaniel Ripley Cobb": p. 70-72. [BR1725.S55H3] 33-17755
1. Smith, Normand, 1800-1833. 2. Cobb, Nathaniel Ripley, 1798-1834. I. American tract society. II. Title.

HAWES, Joel, 1789-1867. 922
Memoir of Normand Smith, jun., or, The Christian serving God in his business. By Rev. Joel Hawes, D. D. Hartford, Spalding & Storrs, 1839. iv, [9]-77 p. 10 cm. [BR1725.S55H3 1839 a] 38-3184
1. Smith, Normand, 1800-1833. I. Title.

Smith, Robert A., 1819-1862.

FITZGERALD, Oscar Penn, bp., 1829-1911. 923.473
Robert A. Smith. By Bishop O. P. Fitzgerald... Nashville, Tenn., Barbee & Smith, agents, 1896. cover-title, p. 109-139. 15 1/2 cm. (...Eminent Methodists, no. 5) [BX8491.E6 no.5] [[922.7]] 37-33230
1. Smith, Robert A., 1819-1862. I. Title.

Smith, Rodney, 1860-1947.

BAYLISS, Edward Ebenezer, 1843- comp. 922
The Gipsy Smith missions in America; a volume commerative of his sixth evangelistic campaign in the United States, 1906-1907, by Edward E. Bayliss ... [and others]. Boston, Mass., The Interdenominational publishing company, 1907. 158 p. front., ports. 20 1/2 cm. [BV3785.86123] 7-6164
1. Smith, Rodney, 1800- I. Title.

LAZELL, David. 269'.2'0924[B]
Gipsy Smith: from the forest I came. Chicago, Moody [1973, c.1970] 256 p. illus., ports. 18 cm. First published in London under title: From the forest I came: the story of Gipsy Rodney Smith. [BV3785] ISBN 0-8024-2959-9 pap., 0.95
1. Smith, Rodney, 1860-1947. I. Title. II. Title: From the forest I came.
L.C. card no. for the London edition: 74-516965.

SMITH, Rodney, 1860- 922
Forty years an evangelist, by Gipsy Smith... New York, Goerge H. Doran company [c1923] vi p., 1 l., 9-259 p. front. (port.) 20 cm. [BV3785.S6A5] 23-12857
I. Title.

SMITH, Rodney, 1860- 922
Gipsy Smith; his life and work, by himself; introductions by G. Campbell Morgan and Alexander McLaren, D.D. New York, Chicago [etc.] Fleming H. Revell company, 1902. 4 p. l., [5]-330 p. front., plates, ports. 21 1/2 cm. [BV3785.S6A4 1902] 2-11748
1. Smith, Rodney, 1860- I. Title.

Smith, Ronald Gregor.

GOD, secularization, and history; essays in memory of Ronald Gregor Smith. Edited by Eugene Thomas Long. [1st ed.] Columbia, University of South Carolina Press [1974] xii, 161 p. 22 cm. [BR50.G545] 73-15712 ISBN 0-87249-293-1 7.95 201'.1
1. Smith, Ronald Gregor. 2. Smith, Ronald Gregor—Bibliography. 3. Theology. I. Smith, Ronald Gregor. II. Long, Eugene Thomas, ed.
Contents omitted.

Smith, St. Clair W., 1844-1909.

WILSON, Ealon V. 286'.63 B
The colorful and eventful life of St. Clair W. Smith, nineteenth century trail-blazer, western frontier missionary, Christian college founder-president, preacher and educator, by Ealon V. Wilson. With accounts of ancestors, contemporaries and descendants across the land, from Kentucky and Tennessee to Texas, New Mexico, California, etc. [Limited 1st ed.] Memphis, 1967. 46 p. illus. 21 cm. [BX6793.S63W55] 74-166166
1. Smith, St. Clair W., 1844-1909. 2. Smith family. I. Title.

Smith, Stephen Rensselaer, 1788-1850.

SAWYER, Thomas Jefferson, 1804-1899. 922.
Memoir of Rev. Stephen R. Smith. By Thomas J. Sawyer. Boston, A. Tompkins, 1852. x, [13]-423 p. front. (port.) 19 1/2 cm. [BX9969.S6S3] 5-6452
1. Smith, Stephen Rensselaer, 1788-1850. I. Title.

Smith, Susy.

SMITH, Susy. 248'.246'0924 B
The conversion of a psychic / by Susy Smith. 1st ed. Garden City, N.Y. : Doubleday, 1978. 127, [2] p. ; 22 cm. Bibliography: p. [129]. [BV4935.S65A33] 76-50790 ISBN 0-385-12638-7 : 5.95
1. Smith, Susy. 2. Converts—Arizona—Tucson—Biography. 3. Pentecostals—Arizona—Tucson—Biography. 4. Tucson, Ariz.—Biography. I. Title.

Smith, Sydney, 1771-1845.

BULLETT, Gerald William, 1894-1958. 824.7 B
Sydney Smith : a biography & a selection. Westport, Conn., Greenwood Press [1971] 316 p. port. 23 cm. Reprint of the 1951 ed. [BX5199.S73B84 1971] 77-138578 ISBN 0-8371-5777-3
1. Smith, Sydney, 1771-1845.

REID, Stuart Johnson, 1848-1927. 922
A sketch of the life and times of the Rev. Sydney Smith ... based on family documents and the recollections of personal friends, by stuart J. Reid. New York, Harper & brothers, 1885. xx, 409 p. incl. front. (port.) illus. fold. facsim. 22 cm. [PR5458.R4] A 22
1. Smith, Sydney, 1771-1845. I. Title.

SMITH, Sydney, 1771-1845. 922
A memoir of the Reverend Sydney Smith. By his daughter, Lady Holland. With a selection from his letters, ed. by Mrs. Austin ... New York, Harper & brothers, 1855. 2 v. 19 cm. Vol. 2: letters. [PR5458.A3 1855 a] 15-22587
1. Smith, Sydney, 1771-1845. I. Holland, Saba (Smith) Holland, lady, d. 1866. II. Austin, Mrs. Sarah (Taylor) 1793-1867, ed. III. Title.

SMITH, Sydney, 1771-1845. 214.72
The works of the Rev. Sydney Smith ... New York, E. G. Taylor. 1846. 333 p. 24 cm. Article originally published in the "Edingburg review," speeches, letters, etc. [PR5455.A2 1846] 33-31338
I. Title.

SMITH, Sydney, 1771-1845.
The works of the Rev. Sydney Smith ... Philadelphia, Carey and Hart, 1844. 3 v. 20 cm. (On cover: Modern British essayists) "Articles originally published in the 'Edinburgh review'." [PR5455.A2 1844] 8-13242
I. Title.

SMITH, Sydney, 1771-1845.
The works of the Rev. Sydney Smith. Three volumes, completee in one. Philadelphia, Carey and Hart, 1848. 2 p. l., 3-480 p. front. (port.) 25 cm. (Added t.-p.: The modern British essayists. vol. iii) On cover: British essayists. Chiefly articles from the Edinburgh review. [PR5455.A2 1848] 41-31540
I. Title.

SMITH, Sydney, 1771-1845.
The works of the Rev. Sydney Smith ... Boston, Phillips, Sampson, and company, 1856. 480 p. front. (port.) 25 cm. (Lettered on cover: The modern British essayists) "Articles oroginally published in the Edingburgh review": p. 9-364. [PR5455.A2 1856] 15-19162
I. Title.

Smith, Thelma, 1904-

OGLE, Mary S., 1905- 266.6'7'0924 B
In spite of danger; the story of Thelma Smith in China [by] Mary S. Ogle. Washington, Review and Herald Pub. Association [1969] 159 p. map (on lining papers) 22 cm. [BV3427.S63O35] 74-84995
1. Smith, Thelma, 1904- 2. Seventh-Day Adventists—Missions. 3. Missions—China. I. Title.

Smith, Thomas Mather, 1796-1864.

[PERRY, William Stevens, bp.] 1832-1898. 922.
A memorial of the Rev. Thomas Mather Smith, D. D., late Milnor professor of systematic divinity in the Theological seminary of the diocese of Ohio, and sometime president of Kenyon college. By

W. S. P. [Cambridge, Printed by H. O. Houghton and co.] 1866. 1 p. l., 68 p. 22 cm. [BX5995.S48P4] 9-24559
1. Smith, Thomas Mather, 1796-1864. I. Title.

Smith, Uriah, 1832-1903.

DURAND, Eugene F. 286.7'3 B
Yours in the blessed hope, Uriah Smith / Eugene F. Durand. Washington, D.C. : Review and Herald Pub. Association, c1980. 320 p. : ill. ; 21 cm. "Books by Uriah Smith": p. 320. [BX6193.S63D87] 80-11675 9.95
1. Smith, Uriah, 1832-1903. 2. Seventh-Day Adventists—Clergy—Biography. 3. Clergy—United States—Biography. I. Title.

Smith, Wesley E.

SMITH, Wesley E. 248'.2 B
Gateway to power, by Wesley E. Smith. [Monroeville, Pa.] Whitaker Books [1973] 144 p. 18 cm. [BR1725.S5517A33] 73-81104 ISBN 0-88368-043-2 1.25 (pbk.)
1. Smith, Wesley E. I. Title.
Publisher's address: 607 Laurel Dr. Monroeville, Pa. 15146.

Smith, Wilbur Moorehead, 1894- — Addresses, essays, lectures.

EVANGELICAL roots : 269'.2
a tribute to Wilbur Smith / edited by Kenneth S. Kantzer. Nashville : T. Nelson, c1978. 250 p. ; 21 cm. Includes bibliographical references. [BR1640.E86] 77-17963 7.95
1. Smith, Wilbur Moorehead, 1894- — Addresses, essays, lectures. 2. Bible—Criticism, interpretation, etc.—Addresses, essays, lectures. 3. Evangelicalism—Addresses, essays, lectures. I. Smith, Wilbur Moorehead, 1894- II. Kantzer, Kenneth S.

SMITH, Wilbur Moorehead, 1894- 285'.131'0924 B
Before I forget, by Wilbur M. Smith. Chicago, Moody Press [1971] 304 p. 24 cm. Autobiographical. [BR1725.S552A3] 79-155684 5.95
I. Title.

Smith, William Austin, 1872-1922.

SLATTERY, Charles Lewis, bp., 1867- 922.
William Austin Smith; a sketch, by Charles Lewis Slattery, illustrated by nine essays of Dr. Smith. New York, E. P. Dutton & company [c1925] ix p., 1 l., 244 p. front., plates, port. 20 cm. [BX5995.S5S5] 25-4938
1. Smith, William Austin, 1872-1922. I. Title.

Smith, William Benjamin, 1850-1934. Der vorchristilche Jesus.

CAMPBELL, William A. 282
The corner stone of Christianity; an introduction to the symbolic criticism of W. B. Smith, by W. A. Campbell. La Salle, Ill., The Open court pupblishing company, 1938. 63 p. 18 cm. Printed in Jamaica. [BT205.S72C3] 40-14961
1. Smith, William Benjamin, 1850-1934. Der vorchristilche Jesus. 2. Jesus chrits—Historicity. 3. Christianity-Origin I. Title. II. Title: Symbolic criticism of W. B. Smith, An introduction to the

Smith, William Robertson, 1846-1894.

BEIDELMAN, Thomas O. 200'.92'4 B
W. Robertson Smith and the sociological study of religion / T. O. Beidelman ; with a foreword by E. E. Evans-Pritchard. Chicago : University of Chicago Press, 1975. xiv, 92 p. ; 23 cm. Bibliography: p. 69-92. [BX9225.S55B46] 74-7568 ISBN 0-226-04158-1 : 8.95 pbk. : 1.95
1. Smith, William Robertson, 1846-1894. 2. Religion and sociology—History. I. Title.

RAVEN, Charles Earle, 1885- 922.541
Centenary of the birth on 8th November 1846 of the Reverend Professor W. Robertson Smith, the University of Aberdeen, 8th November 1946. Aberdeen, University Press, 1951. 17 p. port. 25 cm. (Aberdeen University studies, no. 128) Comprises orations by C. E. Raven and S. A. Cook. Bibliographical footnotes. [BX9225.S55R3] 51-4743
1. Smith, William Robertson, 1846-1894. I. Cook, Stanley Arthur, 1873-1949. II. Title. III. Series.

Smithburg, Md Trinity Evangelical Lutheran church.

HESSE, Ferdinand, 1866- 284.1752
History of the Smithburg charge composed on Trinity, Smithburgh, Md., Mt. Moriah, Foxville, Md., St. Paul's Greensburg, Md. ... by Rev. Fredinand Hesse ... [Hagerstown, Md. Hagerstown bookbinding and printing co.] 1912. 3 p. l., [9]-125 p., 1 illus. (incl. ports.) 22 cm. [BX8076.S6T7] 33-37510
1. Smithburg, Md Trinity Evangelical Lutheran church. 2. Foxville, Md. Moriah Evangelical Lutheran church. 3. St. Paul's Evangeliscal Lutheran church. Washington co., Md. I. Title. II. Title: Smithsburg charge.

Smithtown Branch, N.Y. First Presbyterian Church of Smithtown.

MEHALICK, J. Richard. 285'.1747'25
Church and community, 1675-1975 : the story of the First Presbyterian Church of Smithtown, New York / J. Richard Mehalick. 1st ed. Hicksville, N.Y. : Exposition Press, c1976. 151 p. : ill. ; 24 cm. Bibliography: p. 149-150. [BX9211.S67F575] 76-355016
1. Smithtown Branch, N.Y. First Presbyterian Church of Smithtown. I. Title.

Smuller, Henry W., 1808-1881.

[SMULLER, Adelaide M] 922.89
A golden sunset. Sketches and meditations. New York, A. D. F. Randolph and co. [1889] 75 p. 19 cm. "In memoriam. Rev. Henry W. Smuller." [BX7093.S6S6] 37-18195
1. Smuller, Henry W., 1808-1881. I. Title.

Smyth, Clement, bp., 1810-1865.

[HENRY, Mary Gertrude, sister] 1857- 922.273
The life of the Most Reverend Clement Smyth, d. d., o. c. s. c., second bishop of Dubuque, 1858-1865; compiled by a Sister of the visitation, h. M.; preface by Most Reverend Mathias Clement Lenihan ... Peosta, Ia., New Melleray abbey [c1937] 1 p. l., 5-259 p. front., plates, ports. 19 cm. Written by Sister Mary Gertrude Henry. cf. Pref. [Secular name: Ann Louise Henry. [BX4705.S663H4] 37-25749
1. Smyth, Clement, bp., 1810-1865. 2. Catholic church in Iowa. I. Title.

Smyth, Egbert Coffin, 1829-1904.

SMYTH, Egbert Coffin, 1829-1904, defendant.
The Andover hersy. In the matter of the complaint against Egbert C. Smyth and others, professors of the Theological Institution in Phillips Academy, Andover. Professor Smyth's argument, together with the statements of Professors Tucker, Harris, Hincks, and Churchill. Boston, Cupples, Upham, 1887 [Cleveland, Ohio, Bell & Howell, 1965] 130 p. 21 cm. NUC66
1. Smyth, Egbert Coffin, 1829-1904. 2. Congregational Churches — Government. I. Andover Theological Seminary. II. Title.

Smyth, John Paterson, d. 1932. How we got our Bible.

WINNINGTON-INGRAM, Arthur Foley, bp. of London, 1858- 221
Old Testament difficulties, by the Right Rev. A. F. Winnington-Ingram ... (Being a collection of papers written for working men.) Published under the direction of the Tract committee. 23d thousand. London, Society for promoting Christian knowledge; New York, E. S. Gorham; [etc., etc.] 1907. 64 p. 17 cm. "The first two papers are practically an analysis of Mr. Paterson Smyth's book, 'How we got our Bible'."-- p. [2] [BS1115.W5] 40-36813
1. Smyth, John Paterson, d. 1932. How we got our Bible. 2. Bible. O. T.—Criticism, interpretation, etc. 3. Bible, English—Versions. 4. Bible—Criticism, interpretation, etc.—O. T. I. Society for promoting Christian knowledge, London. Tract committee. II. Title.

Snake cults (Holiness churches)

CARDEN, Karen W. 289.9
The persecuted prophets / Karen W. Carden and Robert W. Pelton. South Brunswick : A. S. Barnes, [1975] p. cm. [BX7990.H6C28 1975] 74-10322 ISBN 0-498-01511-4 : 9.95
1. Snake cults (Holiness churches) 2. Holiness churches—Appalachian Mountains, Southern. I. Pelton, Robert W., 1934- joint author. II. Title.

HOLLIDAY, Robert Kelvin, 1933- 289.9
Tests of faith. Oak Ill, W. Va, Fayette Tribune, 1966. 104p. illus., ports. 23cm. Bibl. [BX7990.H6H59] 66-25996 5.00
1. Snake cults (Holiness churches) 2. Holiness churches I. Title.

PELTON, Robert W., 1934- 289.9
Snake handlers: God-fearers? Or, fanatics? [By] Robert W. Pelton and Karen W. Carden. Nashville, T. Nelson [1974] 110, [49] p. illus. 21 cm. [BX7990.H6P38] 74-3046 2.95 (pbk)
1. Snake cults (Holiness churches) I. Carden, Karen W., joint author. II. Title.

Snake-dance.

FEWKES, Jesse Walter, 1850-1930. 299'.7
The snake ceremonials at Walpi / by J. Walter Fewkes. New York : AMS Press, [1977] vi, 126 p., [3] leaves of plates : ill. ; 23 cm. (Series: Fewkes, Jesse Walter, 1850-1930, ed. A journal of American ethnology and archaeology ; v. 4.) At head of title: Hemenway Southwestern Archaeological Expedition. Reprint of the 1894 ed. published by Houghton Mifflin, Boston, which was issued as vol. 4 of A journal of American ethnology and archaeology. Bibliography: p. 124-126. [E99.H7F39 1977] 76-17497 ISBN 0-404-58044-0 : 17.50
1. Snake-dance. 2. Hopi Indians—Religion and mythology. 3. Indians of North America—Arizona—Religion and mythology. 4. Walpi, Ariz.—Social life and customs. I. Hemenway Southwestern Archaeological Expedition, 1886-1894. II. Title. III. Series.

Snethen, Nicholas,

FEEMAN, Harlan Luther, 1873- 922.773
Francis Asbury's silver trumpet; Nicholas Snethen: nonpartisan church statesman and preacher of the Gospel, 1769-1845. Illustrated by Will Cairns. [Nashville, 1950] 155 p. illus., port. 22 cm. Bibliography: p. 147-149. [BX8495.S635F4] 51-795
1. Snethen, Nicholas, I. Title.

Snoddy, Elmer Ellsworth, 1863-1936.

FORTUNE, Alonzo Willard, 1873- 922.
Thinking things through with E. E. Snoddy, by Alonzo W. Fortune. A College of the Bible seventy-fifth anniversary volume. St. Louis, The Bethany press [c1940] 199 p. 20 cm. "References" and "Unpublished papers and addresses": p. 198; "Published articles": p. 199. [BX7343.S6F6] 922 ISBN 40-10035
1. Snoddy, Elmer Ellsworth, 1863-1936. I. Title.

Snow, Erastus, 1818-1888.

LARSON, Andrew Karl. 289.3'0924 B
Erastus Snow; the life of a missionary and pioneer for the early Mormon Church. Salt Lake City, University of Utah Press [1971] 814 p. illus., facsims., ports. 27 cm. (University of Utah publications in the American West, v. 5) Bibliography: p. [775]-787. [BX8695.S747L37] 75-634390 ISBN 0-87480-031-5
1. Snow, Erastus, 1818-1888. I. Series: Utah. University. Publications in the American West, v. 5.

Snow, Harriet Eliza, 1821-1838.

LOOMIS, D W. Mrs. 922
A memoir of Harriet Eliza Snow. By Mrs. D. W. Loomis ... Written for the Massachusetts Sabbath school society, and revised by the Committee of publication. Boston, Massachusetts Sabbath school society, 1840. viii, [9]-288 p. 16 cm. [BR1725.S63L6] 38-7478
1. Snow, Harriet Eliza, 1821-1838. I. Massachusetts Sabbath school society. Committee of publication. II. Title.

Snow, Jimmy.

SNOW, Jimmy. 269'.2'0924 B
I cannot go back / Jimmy Snow, with Jim and Marti Hefley ; [introd. by Johnny Cash]. Plainfield, N.J. : Logos International, c1977. 157 p., [8] leaves of plates : ill. ; 21 cm. [BV3785.S62A34] 76-566691 ISBN 0-88270-193-2 : 5.95 ISBN 0-88270-194-0 pbk. : 2.95
1. Snow, Jimmy. 2. Evangelists—Tennessee—Nashville—Biography. 3. Assemblies of god, general council—Clergy—Biography. 4. Nashville—Biography. I. Hefley, James C., joint author. II. Hefley, Marti, joint author. III. Title.

Snow, Joseph, 1715-1803.

WILSON, Arthur Edward. 277.45
Weybosset Bridge in Providence Plantations, 1700-1790, being an account of a quest for liberty, with portraits of many saints and sinners, and a special study of the Rev'd Joseph Snow, Jun'r. Boston, Pilgrim Press [1947] xi, 275 p. map (on lining-papers) 22 cm. Bibliography: p. 261-267. [BR555.R4W5] 47-12123
1. Snow, Joseph, 1715-1803. 2. Rhode Island—Church history. I. Title.

Snow, Lorenzo, 1814-1901.

ROMNEY, Thomas Cottam, 1876- 922.83
The life of Lorenzo Snow, fifth president of the Church of Jesus Christ of Latter-Day Saints. [Salt Lake City, S. U. P. Memorial Foundation, 1955] 485p. illus. 23cm. [BX8695.S75R6] 57-44586
1. Snow, Lorenzo, 1814-1901. I. Title.

SMITH, Eliza Roxey (Snow) Mrs., 1804-1887. 922.
Biography and family record of Lorenzo Snow, one of the twelve apostles of the Church of Jesus Christ of latter-day saints. Written and compiled by his sister, Eliza R. Snow Smith ... Salt Lake City, Utah, Deseret news company, printers, 1884. xvi, 581 p. 2 port. (incl. front.) 23 1/2 cm. "Genealogies": p. 488-495. [BX8695.S75S6] 24-718
1. Snow, Lorenzo, 1814-1901. 2. Snow family (Oliver Snow, 1775-1845) 3. Church of Jesus Christ of latter-day saints. I. Title.

Snow, Lorenzo. 1814-1901—Juvenile literature.

NEELEY, Deta Petersen. 289.3'0924 B
A child's story of the prophet Lorenzo Snow, by Deta Peterson [i.e. Petersen] Neeley, Nathan Glen Neeley, and Melba Jensen Friday. Salt Lake City, Deseret Book Co., 1968. 100 p. 20 cm. A biography of a convert to the Church of Jesus Christ of Latter-day Saints who served his Church as a missionary, as a state prisoner, and eventually as its President. [BX8695.S75N4] 92 70-4178 2.25
1. Snow, Lorenzo. 1814-1901—Juvenile literature. 2. [Snow, Lorenzo, 1814-1901.]

I. Neeley, Nathan Glen, joint author. II. Priday, Melba Jensen, joint author. III. Title.

Snow, Michael.

SNOW, Michael. 261.8'73
Christian pacifism : fruit of the narrow way / Michael Snow. Richmond, Ind. : Friends United Press, c1981. xiii, 96 p. : ill. ; 22 cm. Includes bibliographical references. [BT736.4.S65] 19 81-69724 ISBN 0-913408-67-0 (pbk.) : 6.95
1. Snow, Michael. 2. Peace (Theology) I. Title.

Snowden, John Baptist, 1801-1885.

SNOWDEN, John Baptist, 1801-1885. 287'.632'0924 B
From whence cometh, 1767-1977 / by John Baptist Snowden, Thomas Baptist Snowden, and Houston D. Snowden ; [photos. reproduced by David Barrash]. 1st ed. New York : Vantage Press, c1980. 138 p. : ill. ; 22 cm. [BX8495.S642A37] 78-66056 ISBN 0-533-04135-X : 6.95
1. Snowden, John Baptist, 1801-1885. 2. Methodist Church—Clergy—Biography. 3. Snowden family. 4. Clergy—United States—Biography. I. Snowden, Thomas Baptist. II. Snowden, Houston D. III. Title.

Soccino, Fausto, 1539-1604.

CORY, David Munroe. 922.81
Faustus Socinus, by David Munroe Cory, PH. D. Boston, Mass, The Becon press, inc., 1932. ix p., 1 l., 155 p. front. (port.) plates. map. 22 cm. Bibliography: p. 153-155. [BT1480.C6] 33-585
1. Soccino, Fausto, 1539-1604. I. Title.

Social action—Case studies.

HADDEN, Jeffrey K. 261.8'3
Gideon's gang: a case study of the church in social action [by] Jeffrey K. Hadden and Charles F. Longino, Jr, with the assistance of Myer S. Reed, Jr. Philadelphia, United Church Press [1974] 245 p. 22 cm. "A Pilgrim Press book." Includes bibliographical references. [BX9886.Z7D3944] 74-6156 ISBN 0-8298-0275-4 6.95
1. Congregation for Reconciliation, Dayton, Ohio. 2. Congregation for Reconciliation, Cincinnati. 3. Social action—Case studies. I. Longino, Charles F., 1938- joint author. II. Title.

Social case work.

MCKENNEY, Charles R 261
Moral problems in social work. Milwaukee, Bruce [1951] 131 p. 22 cm. (Science and culture series) [HV43.M25] 51-8471
1. Social case work. 2. Christian ethics—Catholic authors. I. Title.

Social conditions.

NASH, Henry Sylvester, 1854-1912. 261
Genesis of the social conscience; the relation between the establishment of Christianity in Europe and the social question, by H. S. Nash ... New York, The Macmillan company; London, Macmillan & co., ltd., 1897. viii, 309 p. 20 cm. "Notes": p. 305. [HN31.N2] 8-31808
1. Social conditions. 2. Sociology, Christian—Hist. 3. Social ethics—Hist. I. Title.

TENNEY, Edward Payson, 1835-1916. 261
Contrasts in social progress, by Edward Payson Tenney ... Rev. ed. Concord, N.H., The Rumford press, 1910. xvi, 421 p. 22 1/2 cm. Bibliography: p. [411]-417. [HN35.T4 1910] 10-11863
1. Social conditions. 2. Religions. I. Title.

Social conflict.

BROWN, Harold O. J., 1933- 261.8'3
Christianity and the class struggle [by] Harold O. J. Brown. New Rochelle, N.Y., Arlington House [1970] 221 p. 21 cm. Includes bibliographical references. [HM136.B74] 73-101958 7.00
1. Social conflict. 2. Apologetics—20th century. I. Title.

Social ethics.

BARRY, Vincent E. 170
Applying ethics : a text with readings / Vincent Barry. Belmont, Calif. : Wadsworth, c1982. xiv, 402 p. ; 23 cm. Previously published as: Personal and social ethics. 1978. Includes bibliographies and index. [HM216.B18 1982] 19 81-3058 ISBN 0-534-01000-8 pbk. : 14.95
1. Social ethics. 2. United States—Moral conditions. I. Title.

COLEMAN, James Melville. 301
Social ethics; an introduction to the nature and ethics of the state [by] James Melville Coleman ... New York, The Baker & Taylor co. [1903] 357 p. 19 1/2 cm. [BV630.C6 1903] 3-5948
I. Title.

COLEMAN, James Melville. 301
Social ethics, an introduction to the nature and ethics of the state [by] James Melville Coleman ... New York, Chicago [etc.] Fleming H. Revell company [c1922] 7 p. l., 13-357 p. 19 1/2 cm. [BV630.C6 1922] 22-14141 1.25.
I. Title.

CONNELL, Francis Jeremiah, 1888- 261
Morals in politics and professions, a guide for Catholics in public life. Westminster, Md., Newman Bookshop, 1946. vi, 187 p. 23 cm. Bibliographical references included in "Notes" at end of each chapter. [HM216.C66] 47-5279
1. Social ethics. 2. Professional ethics. 3. Church and social problems—Catholic Church. I. Title.

GIBBS, John C. 303.3'72
Social intelligence : measuring the development of sociomoral reflection / John C. Gibbs, Keith F. Widaman, in collaboration with Anne Colby ; with a foreword by Lawrence Kohlberg. Englewood Cliffs, N.J. : Prentice-Hall, c1982. xiv, 271 p. ; 29 cm. Includes index. Bibliography: p. [185]-189. [HM216.G453 1982] 19 82-3824 ISBN 0-13-815910-6 : 24.95
1. Social ethics. 2. Reasoning (Psychology)—Testing. I. Widaman, Keith F. II. Colby, Anne. III. Title.

PAGE, Kirby, 1890- 261
Living triumphantly, by Kirby Page. New York, Farrar & Rinehart, incorporated [c1934] 5 p. l., 308 p. 22 1/2 cm. "An anthology of 100 daily readings": p. 108-304. [HM216.P32] 34-41427
1. Social ethics. 2. Christian ethics. 3. Sociology, Christian. I. Title.

RYRIE, Charles Caldwell, 1925- 170
What you should know about social responsibility / by Charles C. Ryrie. Chicago : Moody Press, c1982. 117 p. ; 21 cm. (Current christian issues) [HM216.R95 1982] 19 81-16804 ISBN 0-8024-9417-X pbk. : 3.50
1. Social ethics. 2. Christian ethics. 3. Social problems. I. Title. II. Series.

SLEEPER, Charles Freeman. 220.8'17
Black power and Christian responsibility; some Biblical foundations for social ethics [by] C. Freeman Sleeper. Nashville, Abingdon Press [1968, c1969] 221 p. 23 cm. Bibliography: p. 205-217. [BS680.E84S5] 69-12769 4.50
1. Bible—Ethics. 2. Social ethics. 3. Negroes—History—1964- I. Title.

STIVERS, Richard. 302.5
Evil in modern myth and ritual / Richard Stivers. Athens, Ga. : University of Georgia Press, c1982. 189 p. ; 23 cm. Includes index. Bibliography: p. 178-185. [HM216.S765 1982] 19 81-21907 16.00
1. Social ethics. 2. Deviant behavior. 3. Good and evil. I. Title.

YODER, John Howard. 232
The politics of Jesus; vicit Agnus noster [by] John H. Yoder. Grand Rapids, Mich., Eerdmans [1972] 260 p. 21 cm. Includes bibliographical references. [BT202.Y63] 72-77188 ISBN 0-8028-1485-9 3.45
1. Jesus Christ—Person and offices. 2. Social ethics. 3. Pacifism. I. Title.

Social ethics—Addresses, essays, lectures.

COLEMAN, James Melville. 301
Social ethics, an introduction to the nature and ethics of the state [by] James Melville Coleman ... New York, Chicago [etc.] Fleming H. Revell company [c1916] 7 p. l., 13-357 p. 19 1/2 cm. First published 1903. [BV630.C6 1916] 16-21410 1.00.
I. Title.

THE Social message of the gospels. 241
Edited by Franz Bockle. New York, Paulist Press [1968] viii, 180 p. 24 cm. (Councilium: theology in the age of renewal. Moral theology, v. 35) Includes articles translated from several languages by various persons. Contents.Contents.—Preface, by F. Bockle.—Articles: Empirical social study and ethics, by W. Korff. What does a non-Christian expect of the church in matters of social morality, by R. Garaudy. Social cybernetics as a permanent function of the church, by C. Wagner. World trade and international cooperation for development, by A. Ferrer. How can the church provide guidelines in social ethics? by P. Herder-Dorneich. Races and minorities: a matter of conscience by J. Musulin. The modern sexual revolution, by G. Struck. Prudence and moral change, by F. Furger.—Bibliographical survey: Strength and weakness of the declaration on the Jews, by J.-P. Lichtenberg.—Documentation Concilium: Peace through revolution, by Concilium General Secretariat and H. Gross-Mayr. Bibliographical footnotes. [HM216.S56] 68-31249
1. Social ethics—Addresses, essays, lectures. I. Bockle, Franz, ed. II. Series: Concilium (New York) v. 35

Social Gospel.

HANDY, Robert T. ed. 261
The Social Gospel in America, 1870-1920. New York, Oxford [c.1966.] xii, 399p. 24cm. (Lib. of Protestant thought) Bi2l*Contents omitted. [BT738.H29] 66-14977 7.00
1. Social Gospel. 2. Sociology, Christian—Hist. Series) I. Title.
Contents omitted.

HANDY, Robert T ed. 261
The Social Gospel in America, 1870-1920, edited by Robert T. Handy. New York, Oxford University Press, 1966. xii, 399 p. 24 cm. (A Library of Protestant thought) Contents.Contents.--Gladden.--Ely.--Rauschenbusch. Bibliography: p. 391-393. [BT38.H29] 66-14977
1. Social Gospel. 2. Sociology, Christian—Hist. I. Title. II. Series.

JOHNSON, Frederick Ernest, 1884- 265.
The social gospel and personal religion; are they in conflict. By F. Ernest Johnson ... prepared for the Educational committee of the Commission on the church and social service. New York, Association press, 1922. 1 p. l., 49 p. 19 cm. [BR115.S6J6] 22-24592
I. Title.

KNUDTEN, Richard D. 285'.8'0924 B
The systematic thought of Washington Gladden, by Richard D. Knudten. New York, Humanities Press, 1968. ix, 301 p. geneal. table. 24 cm. Bibliography: p. 265-294. [BX7260.G45K58] 68-27098 6.50
1. Gladden, Washington, 1836-1918. 2. Social gospel. I. Title.

WHITE, Donald Cedric, 1939- 261'.0973
The social gospel : religion and reform in changing America / Ronald C. White, Jr. and C. Howard Hopkins ; with an essay by John C. Bennett. Philadelphia : Temple University Press, 1976. xix, 306 p. : ill. ; 22 cm. Includes bibliographical references and index. [BT738.W45] 75-34745 ISBN 0-87722-083-2 : 15.00 ISBN 0-87722-084-0 pbk. :
1. Social gospel. 2. Sociology, Christian—United States. I. Hopkins, Charles Howard, 1905- joint author. II. Title.

Social gospel—Addresses, essays, lectures.

BOASE, Paul H., comp. 261.8'08
The rhetoric of Christian socialism [by] Paul H. Boase. New York, Random House [1969] ix, 173 p. 21 cm. (A Random house study in speech, SSP9) (Issues and spokesmen series.) Contents.Contents.—Infidel attack on property, by J. Cook.—Labor's view of the situation, by R. H. Newton.—The church and the gospel of push, by W. D. P. Bliss.—Christianity versus socialism, by L. Abbott.—The coming brotherhood, by F. Willard.—The problem of the city, by J. Strong.—The opportunity of the church, by G. D. Herron.—The new apostolate, by W. Rauschenbusch.—The new evangel, by W. Gladden.—My account with the unknown soldier, by H. E. Fosdick.—The Koinonia story, by C. Jordan.—A knock at midnight, by M. L. King. Includes bibliographical references. [BT738.B57] 69-14470 1.95
1. Social gospel—Addresses, essays, lectures. I. Title.

Social gospel—History.

FISHBURN, Janet Forsythe, 1937- 261'.0973
The fatherhood of God and the Victorian family : the Social Gospel in America / Janet Forsythe Fishburn. Philadelphia : Fortress Press, [1982] c1981. p. cm. Includes index. Bibliography: p. [BX6495.R3F57 1982] 19 81-43090 ISBN 0-8006-0671-X : 19.95
1. Rauschenbusch, Walter, 1861-1918. 2. Social gospel—History. 3. United States—Church history—19th century. 4. United States—Church history—20th century. I. Title.

Social gospel—History—19th century.

HOPKINS, Charles Howard, 1905-
The rise of the social gospel in American Protestantism, 1865-1915. New York : AMS Press, [1982, c1940] x, 352 p. ; 23 cm. Reprint. Originally published: New Haven : Yale University Press, 1940. (Yale studies in religious education ; 14) Includes bibliographical references and index. [BT738.H666 1982] 75-41141 ISBN 0-404-14771-2 : 30.00
1. Social gospel—History—19th century. 2. Social gospel—History—20th century. 3. Theology, Doctrinal—United States—History—19th century. 4. Theology, Doctrinal—United States—History—20th century. 5. United States—Church history—19th century. 6. United States—Church history—20th century. I. Title.

Social gospel—Sermons.

HERRON, George Davis, 1862-1925. 252.05'8
Social meanings of religious experiences. With a new introd. by Timothy L. Smith. New York, Johnson Reprint Corp., 1969 [c1896] xxvi, 237 p. 18 cm. (Series in American studies) Bibliography: p. xxv-xxvi. [BT738.H46 1969] 74-79658
1. Social gospel—Sermons. 2. Congregational churches—Sermons. 3. Sermons, American. I. Title. II. Series.

Social Gospel. sociology, Christian—Hist. series.

HANDY, Robert T. ed 261
The Social Gospel in america, 1870-1920. New York, oxford [c.1966]. xii, 399 24 cm (lib. of Protestant thought) Contents.Gladden Ely.—Rauchenbusch Bibl. [BT738.H29] 66-14977
1. Social Gospel. sociology, Christian—Hist. series. I. Title. II. Series.

Social history—1960-

CAUTHEN Wilfred Kenneth. 261.8
The ethics of enjoyment : the Christian's pursuit of happiness / by Kenneth Cauthen. Atlanta : John Knox Press, c1975. 124 p. ; 21 cm. Includes

bibliographical references. [HN18.C32] 75-13466 ISBN 0-8042-0815-8
1. Social history—1960- 2. Social ethics. 3. Church and social problems. 4. Technology and ethics. I. Title.

Social history—20th century.

MCCLELLAND, William Grigor. 261.8
And a new earth : making tomorrow's society better than today's / by W. Grigor McClelland. London : Friends Home Service Committee, 1976. [7], 91 p. ; 19 cm. (Swarthmore lecture ; 1976) Includes bibliographical references. [HN18.M214] 76-382485 ISBN 0-85245-122-9 : £0.90
1. Social history—20th century. 2. Friends. I. Title.

Social justice.

CONSULTA 261.8'3'098
Latinoamericana de Iglesia y Sociedad. 2d, El Tabo, Chile, 1966.
Social justice and the Latin churches. Translated by Jorge Lara-Braud. Richmond, Va., John Knox Press [1969] 137 p. 21 cm. "[Edited] summary of the discussions and reports presented at the second Latin American Conference on Church and Society." Sponsored by Church and Society in Latin America. Translation of America hoy. [HN39.L3C613 1966c] 72-79313 ISBN 0-8042-1505-7 2.95
1. Social justice. 2. Church and social problems—Latin America. 3. Protestant churches—Latin America. I. Iglesia y Sociedad en America Latina. II. Title.

Social problems.

AMES, John Quincy. 267.
Social adjustment through the Young men's Christian associations, by J. Quincy Ames ... Chicago, Ill., Young men's Christian association college [c1927] cover-title, 75 p. 23 cm. (Monograph no. v of "The changing Young men's Christian association" series) [BV1100.A78] 27-18306
1. Social problems. 2. Young men's Christian associations. I. Title.

CARLYLE, Thomas, 1795-1881. 309.
Past and present, by Thomas Carlyle: with an introduction by Julia Patton ... New York, The Macmillan company, 1927. xxi p. 1 l., 341 p. incl. front. 19 cm. (The modern readers' series) [HN388.C33 1927] 27-7284
1. Social problems. 2. Gt. Brit.—Soc. condit. I. Patton, Julia, 1873- ed. II. Title. III. Series.

CARPENTER, Edward, 1844- 824.
England's ideal, and other papers on social subjects, by Edward Carpenter. London, S. Sonnenschein & co., lim.; New York, C. Scribner's sons, 1902. 3 p. l., 177 p. 20 cm. [Social science series. 9] "First ed., June, 1887 ... Fourth ed., September, 1902." [HN389.C3] 6-14784
1. Social problems. 2. Gt. Brit.—Soc. condit. I. Title.
Contents omitted.

CHOU, Po-chin, 1891- 261.8
Commonism, a plan for implementing the Christian answer to A communism, by Pik Kum Chau. With forewords by Hollington K. Tong and John W. Bailey, and a biographical sketch of the author by Charles R. Shepherd. [1st ed.] New York, Exposition Press [1957] 256p. illus. 21cm. [HN18.C3884] 57-10656
1. Social problems. I. Title.

DE COURCY, Arthur George. 216
Completer light: a gospel of Americanism; or, Science of the proposition that all men are created equal ... written by Arthur George De Courcy. New York city, Modern facts publishing co. [c1923- v. 21 cm. [HN64.D373] 24-2257
1. Social problems. I. Title.

DENNIS, James Shepard, 1842- 261
1914.
Social evils of the non-Christian world, by the Rev. James S. Dennis ... New York, Student volunteer movement for foreign mission [c1898] 172 p. front. (port.) plates 19 cm. "This text-book ... contains a portion of volume i, of 'Christian mission and social progress', by ... James S. Dennis,"--Explanatory note. [HN32.D4 1898] 34-34308
1. Social problems. 2. Missions, Foreign. 3. Manners and customs. I. Title.

DENNIS, James Shepard, 1842- 261
1914.
Social evils of the non-Christian world, by the Rev. James S. Dennis ... New York, Student volunteer movement for foreign missions, 1899. 172 p. front., plates (incl. ports.) 19 cm. (On cover: Student volunteer series) "This text-book ... contains a reprint of a portion of volume i, of 'Christian mission and social progress', by ... james S. Dennis."--p. 5. [HN32.D4] 98-2252
1. Social problems. 2. Missions, Foreign. 3. Manners and customs. I. Title.

EDE, William Moore.
The attitude of the church to some of the social problems of town life, by the Rev. W. Moore Ede ... With a preface by the Right Rev. the Lord Bishop of Durham. Cambridge, The University press, 1896. xiii p., 1 l., 131 p. 19 1/2 cm. Half-title: The Hulsean lectures for 1895. Contents.--Prefatory note.--I. The function of the church in the work of social reform.--II. The problem of the unemployed and the duty of the church.--III. The omes of the people.--IV. The attitude of the church towards the vices of our towns. [JS3081.1896.E3] 8-17311
1. Social problems. 2. Sociology, Christian. 3. Labor and laboring classes. I. Hulsean lectures, 1895-1986. II. Title.

ELY, Richard Theodore, 1854- 261
Social aspects of Christianity, and other essays, by Richard T. Ely ... New York, T. Y. Crowell & company [c1889] x p., 1 l., 132 p. 19 1/2 cm. Reprinted in part from various periodicals. Contents.--Social aspects of Christianity.--The church and the world.--Philanthropy.-- Ethics and economics. [HN31.E5 1889] 10-13456
1. Social problems. 2. Sociology, Christian I. Title.

ELY, Richard Theodore, 1854- 261
Social aspects of Christianity, and other essays. By Richard T. Ely ... New and enl. ed. (9th thousand) New York, Boston, T. Y. Crowell & company, [1895?] x p., 1 l., 161 p. 19 1/2cm. Reprinted in part from various periodicals. Contents.Social aspects of Christianity.--The church and the world.--Philanthropy.-- Ethics and economics.--The social crisis and the church's opportunity. [HN31.E5 1895] 10-13457
1. Social problems. 2. Sociology, Christian. I. Title.

GAUDREAU, Marie Agnes of 261
Rome, sister, 1905-
... The social thought of French Canada as reflected in the Semaine sociale, by Sister Marie Agnes of Rome Gaudreau ... Washington, D.C., The Catholic university of America press, 1946. xii, 266 p. 23 cm. (The Catholic university of America. [Studies in sociology] Vol. 18) Thesis (PH.D.)--Catholic university of America, 1945. "Selected bibliography": p. 253-260. [HN39.C2G36] A 46
1. Social problems. 2. Church and social problems—Catholic church. 3. Semaine sociale du Canada. I. Title.

HEYER, Robert, comp. 261.8'3
Discovery in the press [compiled by] Robert Heyer [and] Tom Sheehan. Paramus, N.J., Paulist Press [1969] 132 p. illus. 21 cm. (Discovery series) [BV4531.2.H483] 71-79921 1.95
1. Social problems. 2. Youth—Religious life. I. Sheehan, Tom, joint comp. II. Title.

KAVANAUGH, John, 1912- ed. 261.8
The Quaker approach to contemporary problems. Edited by John Kavanaugh. Westport, Conn., Greenwood Press [1970, c1953] xi, 243 p. 23 cm. Contents.Contents.—Introduction, by J. Whitney.—Peace and war, by H. J. Cadbury.—Relief and reconstruction, by R. C. Wilson.—Economic life, by K. E. Boulding.—Business and industry, by D. R. Yarnall.—Education, by H. H. Brinton.—Race relations, by I. D. Reid.—Civil liberties, by H. A. Freeman.—Crime and punishment, by C. Bok.—Prisons and prisoners, by H. Van Etten.—Science, by K. Lonsdale.—Health and healing, by H. E. Collier.—Present secular philosophies, by D. E. Trueblood.—Quakers and the Russians, by E. Jackson.—Epilogue, by C. E. Pickett. [HN18.K3 1970] 70-110047
1. Social problems. 2. Church and social problems—Friends, Society of. I. Title.

LAND, Philip S *301
Democratic living [by] Philip S. Land, John L. Thomas, and Mortimer H. Gavin. Experimental ed. Chicago, Loyola University Press [1952- v. illus. 24cm. Vol. 2 by W. A. Nolan, A. S. Foley, and P. S. Aland. [HN37.C3L32] 301.153 52-3816
1. Social problems. 2. Church and social problems—Catholic Church. I. Title.

LAND, Philip S. 301.46
Democratic living [by] Philip S. Land, John L. Thomas, and Mortimer H. Gavin. Experimental ed. Chicago, Loyola University Press [1952] 435 p. illus. 24 cm. [HN37.C3L32] 301.153 52-3816
1. Social problems. 2. Church and social problems—Catholic Church. I. Title.

LEDLIE, John Andrew, 1898- 261
Ventures in Christian living; a discussion course in social and economic questions, by John A. Ledlie; with program projects for further study. New York, Association press, 1932. 62 p. 17 cm. "Sources of quotations used in this volume": p. 62 [BR115.S6L38] 32-31855
1. Social problems. 2. Girls—Societies and clubs. 3. Boys—Societies and clubs. I. Title.

MCCABE, Joseph, 1867- 824.
The tyranny of shams, by Joseph McCabe ... New York, Dodd, Mead and company, 1916. xv, 296 p. 19 1/2 cm. "Printed in Great Britain." "This book is a frank criticism of most of the dominant ideas and institutions of our time."--Pref. [HN389.M15] 16-22762
1. Social problems. 2. Gt. Brit.—Soc. condit. 3. Moral conditions. I. Title. II. Title: Shams, The tyranny of.

NIEBUHR, Reinhold, 1892- 261.8
Love and justice; selections from the shorter writings of Reinhold Niebuhr. Ed. by D. B. Robertson. [Magnolia, Mass., P. Smith. 1967.c. 1957] 309p. 20cm. (Meridian bk. rebound) [HN18.N5] 4.00
1. Social problem. I. Title.

NIEBUHR, Reinhold, 1892- 261.8
Love and justice; selections from the shorter writings of Reinhold Niebuhr. Edited by D. B. Robertson. Philadelphia, Westminster Press [1957] 309p. 24cm. [HN18.N5] 57-9745
1. Social problems. I. Title.

NIEBUHR, Reinhold, 1892- 261.8
Love and Justice; selections from the shorter writings of Reinhold Niebuhr. Edited by D. B. Robertson. Philadelphia. Westminster Press [1957] 309p. 24cm. [HN18.N5] 57-9745
1. Social problems. I. Title.

PARKER, Theodore, 1810-1860. 204
Social classes in a republic, by Theodore Parker; ed. with notes by Samuel A. Eliot. Boston, American Unitarian association [n. d.] 5 p. l., 346 p. 21 cm. [His Works. Centenary ed. v. 19] "The sermons and essays collected in this volume deal with the application of Parker's religious principles to certain practical problems of social organization."--Editor's pref. [BX9815.P3 1907 vol. 10] A 12
1. Social problems. I. Eliot, Samuel Atkins, 1862- ed. II. Title.
Contents omitted.

PASMA, Henry K. 171.
Things a nation lives by, by Henry K. Pasma ... Richmond, Va., Pub. for the author by Presbyterian committee of publication [c1924] 179 p. 19 cm. [BR115.S6P3] 24-23074
1. Social problems. I. Title.

PROTESTANT Episcopal church in
the U. S. A. Joint commission on social service.
Triennial report submitted to the General convention by the Joint commission on social service of the Protestant Episcopal church. New York, Church missions house [1919]- v. 23 cm. [BX5978.A2] 20-10837
1. Social problems. 2. U. S.—Soc. condit. I. Title.

RYAN, John Augustine, 1869- 322
The church and socialism, and other essays, by John A. Ryan... Washington, The University press, 1919. vii, 251 p. 19 1/2 cm. (Half-title: The social justice books) Reprinted from various periodicals. Contents.The church and socialism.--Principles and proposals of social reform.--A living wage.--The legal minimum wage.--Moral aspects of the labor union.--The church and the workingman.--The moral aspects of speculation.--False and true conceptions of welfare.--Birth control.--Woman suffrage.--Social service as a profession. [HN37.C3R8] 20-221
1. Social problems. 2. Sociology, Christian. 3. Socialism and Catholic church. I. Title.

SEARS, Charles Hatch, 1870- 261
The redemption of the city, by Charles Hatch ... introduction by Edward Judson, D. D. Philadelphia, Boston [etc.] The Griffith & Rowland press [1911] xvi, 248 p. front., illus., plates, map, fold. tab. 20 cm. "Notes of references" at end of each chapter. Bibliography: p. 241-246. [BV2775.S45] 12-57
1. Social problems. 2. Cities and towns. 3. Sociology, Christian. 4. City churches. I. Title.

Social problems—Miscellanea.

SHELDON, Charles Monroe, 248
1857-
In His steps to-day. What would Jesus do in solving the problems of present political, economic and social life? By Charles M. Sheldon ... New York, Chicago [etc.] Fleming H. Revell company [c1921] 192 p. 19 1/2 cm. [BS2417.S7S5] 21-14652
I. Title.

SLATTERY, Margaret. 246
He took it upon himself, by Margaret Slattery. Boston, New York [etc.] The Pilgrim press [c1914] 62 p. incl. front., port., plates. 18 1/2 cm. The illustrations are mounted. Ornamental borders. [BJ1474.S5] 14-19174 0.60
1. Social problems—Miscellanea. 2. Altruism. I. Title.

[STEWART, John] 1749-1822. 309.
The moral state of nations, or Travels over the most interesting parts of the globe, to discover the source of moral motion; communicated to lead mankind through the conviction of the senses to intellectual existence, and an enlightened state of nature ... In the year of man's retrospective knowledge, by astronomical calculation 5000. [Year of the common era, 1790] Granville, Middletown, N.J., Reprinted by G. H. Evans, 1837. 5 p. l., [3]-126, 122 p. front., illus. 19 cm. "The revelation of nature: wherein the source of moral motion is disclosed ... [By John Stewart. Granville, Middletown, N. J.] 1835": 122 p. at end. [HN388.S75 1837] 8-36329
1. Social problems—Miscellanea. 2. Gt. Brit.—Soc. condit. I. Title.

Social psychiatry.

WESTBERG, Granger E 253.5
Community psychiatry and the clergyman, by Granger E. Westberg and Edgar Draper. Springfield, Ill., C. C. Thomas [1966] xxi, 110 p. 24 cm. [BV4012.W428] 66-14277
1. Social psychiatry. 2. Pastoral counseling. 3. Psychiatry and religion. I. Draper, Edgar, 1926- joint author. II. Title.

Social reformers—Great Britain.

MARTIN, Hugh, 1890- 261.8'3'0922
ed.
Christian social reformers of the nineteenth century, by James Adderley [and others] Freeport, N.Y., Books for Libraries Press [1970] vi, 242 p. illus., ports. 23 cm. (Essay index reprint series) Reprint of the 1927 ed. Contents.Contents.—Introduction: The Christian social movement in the nineteenth century, by W. Temple.—John Howard, by S. K. Ruck.—William Wilberforce, by R. Coupland.—Anthony Ashley Cooper, by C. Smith.—Charles

Dickens, by A. J. Carlyle.—Florence Nightingale, by M. Scharlieb.—John Malcolm Ludlow, by C. E. Raven.—William Morris, by H. Martin.—George Cadbury, by H. G. Wood.—Henry Scott Holland, by J. Adderley.—James Keir Hardie, by A. F. Brockway. [HN385.M3 1970] 70-107725
1. Social reformers—Gt. Brit. 2. Sociology, Christian. I. Adderley, James Granville, 1861-1942. II. Title.

SCHENK, Wilhelm. 309.1'41'062
The concern for social justice in the Puritan Revolution / by W. Schenk. Westport, Conn. : Greenwood Press, 1975. xi, 180 p. : ill. ; 22 cm. Reprint of the 1948 ed. published by Longmans, Green, London, New York. Includes bibliographical references. [HN388.S3 1975] 74-29794 ISBN 0-8371-8003-1 : 11.75
1. Social reformers—Great Britain. 2. Great Britain—Social conditions. 3. Great Britain—History—Puritan Revolution, 1642-1660. I. Title.

Social sciences.

HILLER, Margaret, 1891- 267.5573
Public affairs, size 16, by Margaret Hiller... New York, N.Y., The Womans press [c1939] 3 pt. in 13 v. diagr., for 21 1/2 cm. "Part one is especially for adults concerned with the younger girls' program of the Y. W. C. A. Part two is for club program committees and advisers; it contains general suggestions about public affairs in a club program, and gives devices for discovering or stimulating interest along these lines. Parts one and two are printed together and are basic for Girl reserve leaders. The program units of part three are printed separately." Includes bibliographies. [BV1393.G5H5] 40-11769
1. Social sciences. 2. Young women's Christian associations. I. Title.

Social sciences—Research—Moral and religious aspects.

REYNOLDS, Paul Davidson. 300'.72
Ethics and social science research / Paul Davidson Reynolds. Englewood Cliffs, N.J. : Prentice-Hall, c1982. xiv, 191 p. ; 23 cm. (Prentice-Hall methods and theories in the social sciences series) Includes indexes. Bibliography: p. 170-181. [H62.R469] 19 81-15893 ISBN 0-13-290965-0 pbk. : 9.95
1. Social sciences—Research—Moral and religious aspects. I. Title. II. Series.

Social sciences—Research—Moral and religious aspects—Addresses, essays, lectures.

ETHICAL issues in 174'.9301
social science research / edited by Tom L. Beauchamp ... [et al.]. Baltimore : Johns Hopkins University Press, c1982. xii, 436 p. ; 24 cm. Includes index. Bibliography: p. 417-422. [H62.E76 1982] 19 81-12419 ISBN 0-8018-2655-1 : 25.00 ISBN 0-8018-2656-X pbk. : 8.95
1. Social sciences—Research—Moral and religious aspects—Addresses, essays, lectures. I. Beauchamp, Tom L.

Social sciences—Study and teaching.

CATHOLIC University of America. O) workshop on the Social Sciences in Catholic College Programs, 1953.
The social sciences in Catholic college programs; the procedings of the Workshop on the Social Sciencex s in Catholic College Programs, conducted at the Catholic University of America, june 12 to 23, 1953. Edited by Roy J. Deferari. Washington, Catholic University of America Press, 1954. v, 180p. illus. 23cm. Includes bibliographies. A54
1. Social siience—Study and teaching. 2. Catholic Church— Education. I. Defezari, Roy Joseph, 1890- ed. II. Title.

Social service.

BRACKETT, Jeffrey Richardson, 250 1860-
Social service through the parish, by Jeffrey R. Brackett ... New York, The National council, Department of Christian social service, 1923. 4 p. l., 148, [1] p. 19 cm. [BV4400.B7] 23-8703
1. Social service. 2. Church work. I. Title.

CAMARA, Helder, 1909- 248'.48'2
The desert is fertile. Translated by Dinah Livingstone. Maryknoll, N.Y., Orbis Books, 1974. vi, 61 p. illus. 21 cm. [HV40.C3313] 73-89315 ISBN 0-88344-078-4 3.95
1. Social service. 2. Social problems. 3. Church and social problems. I. Title.

EDWARDS, Richard Henry.
Volunteer social service by college men, by Richard Henry Edwards ... New York [etc.] Association press [c1914] 63 p. 14 1/2 cm. On cover: Student Young men's Christian association. 14-22329
I. Title.

FELTON, Ralph Almon, 1882- 250
Serving the neighborhood, by Ralph A. Felton. New York city, Pub. jointly by Council of women for home missions and Interchurch world movement of North America [c1920] 3 p. l., 153 p. illus. 19 1/2 cm. [BV4400.F4] 20-12978
1. Social service. 2. Church work. I. Title.

MACFARLAND, Charles Stedman, 248 1866-
Spiritual culture and social service, by Charles S. Macfarland... New York, Chicago [etc.] Fleming H. Revell company [c1912] 222 p. 19 1/2 cm. [BV4501.M25] 13-4373
I. Title.

NIEBUHR, Reinhold, 1892- 261
The contribution of religion to social work, by Reinhold Niebuhr ... New York, Pub. for the New York school of social work by Columbiauniversity press, 1932. x, 108 p., 1 l. 20 cm. (Half-title: The Forbes lectures of the New York school of socialwork) New York school of social work publications. Bibliography: p. [97] [BV4400.N5] 33-297
1. Social service. 2. Sociology, Christian—Addresses, essays, lectures. 3. Religion and sociology. I. Title.

NIEBUHR, Reinhold, 1892- 361.7'5 1971.
The contribution of religion to social work. New York, AMS Press [1971, c1932] x, 103 p. 19 cm. (The Forbes lectures of the New York School of Social Work) Bibliography: p. [95]-[97] [BV4400.N5 1971] 74-172444 ISBN 0-404-04708-4
1. Social service. 2. Sociology, Christian—Addresses, essays, lectures. 3. Religion and sociology. I. Title. II. Series.

SANDERSON, Ross Warren, 1884- 261
The church serves the changing city, by Ross W. Sanderson for the Dept. of the Urban Church, with the co-operation of the Committee on Field Research, National Council of Churches. [1st ed.] New York, Harper [1955] 252p. illus. 22cm. [BV4400.S35] 55-6788
1. Social service. 2. Church work. 3. City churches. I. Title.

SCHAEFFER, William Christ, 265. 1851-
The greater task; studies in social service ... by William C. Schaeffer ... New York, Chicago [etc.] Fleming H. Revell company [c1919] 174 p. 19 1/2 cm. $1.25 [BR115.S6S3] 19-5353
I. Title.

WHITE, Ellen Gould (Harmon) 258 1827-1915.
Welfare ministry; instruction in Christian neighborhood service. Washington, Review and Herald Pub. Assn. [1952] 349 p. 18 cm. (Christian home library) [BV4400.W45] 52-1493
1. Social service. 2. Church work. 3. Seventh-Day Adventists—Charities. I. Title.

WISHART, Alfred Wesley.
The social mission of the church, by Alfred Wesley Wishart ... Pub. for the Social service commission of the Northern Baptist convention, Shailer Mathews ... chairman of the Editorial committee. Philadelphia, Boston [etc.] American Baptist publication society [1910] 55 p. 20 cm. (On cover: Social service series) 10-9434 0.20
I. Title.

Social service—Moral and religious aspects.

ETHICAL issues in 174'.9362
social work / edited by Shankar A. Yelaja. Springfield, Ill. : Thomas, c1982. xiv, 451 p. : ill. ; 24 cm. Includes bibliographies and index. [HV41.E83 1982] 19 81-14460 ISBN 0-398-04620-4 : 44.75 ISBN 0-398-04621-2 pbk : 35.50
1. Social service—Moral and religious aspects. I. Yelaja, Shankar A.

Social settlements—Bibliography

BIBLIOGRAPHY of college, 016.
social, university and church settlements. Comp. by Caroline Williamson Montgomery ... for the College settlements association. 5th ed., rev. and enl. Chicago [Blakely press] 1905. 147 p. 23 cm. First and 2d editions (1893, 1895) compiled by M. Katherine Jones; 3d by J. P. Gavit. A select bibliography, with a directory giving address, short historical and descriptive sketches and list of references. [Z7164.S665B 1905] 7-4828
1. Social settlements—Bibl. I. Montgomery, Caroline (Williamson) Mrs. 1865- II. College settlements association.

Social surveys.

CARROLL, Charles Eden, 1877- 264
...The community survey in relation to church effciency; a guide for workers in the city, town, and country church, by Charles E. Carroll: with an introduction by Bishop Francis J. McConnell. New York. Cincinnati. The Abingdon press [c1915] xiv, 128 p. front., diagrs. 21 cm. (Constructive church series) The author's doctoral dissertation University of Denver, 1914, but not published as a thesis. Bibliography: p. 119-122. [BV652.C3] 15-27771
1. Social surveys. 2. Church work. I. Title. II. Series.

PRESBYTERIAN church in the 277.72 United States of America, Board of home missions. Dept. of church and country life.
A rural survey in Indiana, made by the Department of church and country life of the Board of home missions of the Presbyterian church in the U. S. A. ... made in cooperation with the Interdenominational council of the churches of Indiana. [New York, Redfield brothers, inc., 1911?] 93 p. incl. illus. (incl. maps) tables, diagrs. 23 cm. "The field work of this investigation was done by Mrs. Ralph A. Felton and Mr. Clarence A. Neff." [BR555.I 6P7] 13-695
1. Social surveys. 2. Rural churches—Indiana. I. Interdenominational council of the churches of Indiana. II. Felton Ralph Almon, 1882- III. Neff, Clarence Alvin, 1885- IV. Title.

PRESBYTERIAN church in the 261. U. S. A. Board of home missions. Dept. of church and country life.
Ohio rural life survey. "Northwestern Ohio" ... Presbyterian Department of church and country life. New York [1913?] 70 p. illus. (incl. map) diagrs. 23 cm. "Contributors, Robert B. Wilson, Clarence A. Neff; Arthur O. Stockbridge, historian." [BR555.O3P7] Agr
1. Social surveys. 2. Ohio—Social conditions. I. Title.

PRESBYTERIAN church in the 261. U. S. A. Board of home missions. Dept. of church and country life.
Ohio rural life survey. "Southeastern Ohio" .. Presbyterian Department of church and country life. New York [1913?] 64 p. illus. (incl. map) diagrs. 23 cm. [BR555.O3P8] Agr
1. Social surveys. 2. Ohio—Social conditions. I. Title.

STOTTS, Herbert Edward, *254 1916-
The church inventory handbook. Denver, Wesley Press [1952] 235 p. illus. 24 cm. [BV652.S77] 52-27459
1. Social surveys. 2. Church work. I. Title.

Social surveys—Columbia River Valley.

FREDERICK, Arthur L, 1894- 277.97
The Columbia basin project area and its churches; a report to the Department of Church Planning and Strategy of the Washington and Northern Idaho Council of Churches and Christian Education, Seattle, Washington, September 3 and 4, 1950, by Arthur L. Frederick and Ross W. Sanderson. [Seattle] Washington State Council of Churches, '1950. 63 p., 64-65 (i. e. 66), 3 l. maps. 28 cm. "State of Washington highway map, Department of Highways, State of Washington, 1950": fold. col. map inserted. Bibliography: p. 63. [BR555.W3F7] 50-12911
1. Social surveys—Columbia River Valley. 2. Churches—Location. I. Sanderson, Ross Warren, 1884- joint author. II. Washington and Northern Idaho Council of Churches and Christian Education. III. Title.

FREDERICK, Arthur Lester, 277.97 1894-
The Columbia basin project area and its churches; a report to the Department of Church Planning and Strategy of the Washington and Northern Idaho Council of Churches and Christian Education, Seattle, Washington, September 3 and 4, 1950, by Arthur L. Frederick and Ross W. Sanderson. [Seattle] Washington State Council of Churches, c1950. 63p. 64-65 (i. e. 66), 3 1. maps. 28cm. 'State of Washington highway map, Department of Highways, State of Washington, 1950': fold. col. map inserted. --The Columbia basin and its churches. Supplement. [Seattle] Bibliography: p. 63. [BR555.W3F7] 50-12911
1. Social surveys—Columbia River Valley. 2. Churches—Location. I. Sanderson, Ross Warren, 1884- joint author. II. Washington and Northern Idaho Council of Churches and Christian Education. III. Title.

Social surveys—Louisville, Ky.

DOUGLASS, Harlan Paul, 277.69 1871- comp.
Interdenominational survey of metropolitan Louisville, Kentucky, January 1944. [Louisville? 1944] vi, 57 p. maps. 28 cm. "Sponsored by the Louisville Council of Churches and the Louisville Ministerial Association in cooperation with the Home Missions Council of North America." [BR560.L8D6] 51-45962
1. Social surveys—Louisville, Ky. 2. Louisville, Ky.—Churches. I. Title.

Social work with delinquents and criminals—New York (City)

MARIE Lucita, Sister. 259
Manhattan mission. [1st ed.] Garden City, N.Y., Doubleday, 1967. 192 p. 22 cm. [BV2657.M35A3] 67-10393
1. Social work with delinquents and criminals—New York (City) 2. Church work with juvenile delinquents. 3. Evangelistic work—New York (City) I. Title.

Socialism.

BINYON, Gilbert Clives.
The Christian faith and the social revolution, by the Rev. Gilbert Clive Binyon ... London, Society for promoting Christian knowledge: New York, Macmillan, 1921. vi p., 1 l., 88 p. 19 cm. A 21
1. Socialism. 2. Socialism, Christian. I. Title.

RYAN, John Augustine, 1869-
Alleged socialism of the church fathers, by Rev. John A. Ryan... St. Louis, Mo. [etc.] B. Herder, 1913. 3 p. l., 81 p. 19 cm. [HX26.R8] 13-24334
1. Socialism. I. Title.

VAUGHAN, Bernard, 1847-1922.
Socialism from the Christian standpoint: ten conferences, by Father Bernard Vaughan ... New York, The Macmillan company, 1912. 3 p. l., 3-389 p. front. (port.) 19 cm. (On cover: The Macmillan standard library) A 17
1. Socialism. 2. Socialism and Catholic church. I. Title.

Socialism—Addresses, essays, lectures.

FABIAN essays in socialism, by G. Bernard Shaw, Sidney Webb, William Clarke, Sydney Olivier, Annie Besant, Graham Wallas and Hubert Bland: ed. by G. Bernard Shaw, with a new preface for this edition by Mrs. Shaw. Boston, The Ball publishing co., 1909. xivi p., 1 l., 218 p. 20 cm. [BX246.F2 1909] 9-35445
1. Socialism—Addresses, essays, lectures. 2. Socialism in Gt. Brit. I. Shaw, George Bernard, 1856- ed. II. Passfield, Sidney James Webb, 1859- III. Clarke, William, m. a. Cambridge. IV. Olivier, Sydney Haldane Olivier, baron, 1859- V. Besant, Annie (Wood) Mrs. 1847- VI. Wallas, Graham, 1858- VII. Bland, Hubert, 1856-1914. VIII. Fabian society, London.
Contents omitted.

Socialism and Catholic church.

DE LEON, Daniel, 1852-1914. 235
Abolition of ,poverty; socialist versus ultramontane economics and politics, by Daniel De Leon. New York city, New York labor news co., [19--] 2 p. l., 63 p. 19 cm. On cover: Socialist labor party. A series of nineteen editorials originally published in the Daily people under title: Father Gassonians. [HX536.D33] 40-25291
1. Gasson, Thomas Ignatius, 1859-1930 2. Socialism and Catholic church. I. Title. II. Title: Socialist versus ultramontane economics and politics.

DONOSO Cortes, Jaun, marques de Valdegamas, 1809-1853. 261
An essay on Catholicism, authority and order considered in their fundamental principles / by Juan Donoso Cortes. Westport, Conn. : Hyperion Press, 1979. p. cm. Translation of Ensayo sobre el catolicismo, el liberalismo y el socialismo. Reprint of the 1925 ed. published by J. F. Wagner, New York, in series: My bookcase series. [BX1753.D6 1979] 78-59018 ISBN 0-88355-692-8 : 26.50
1. Socialism and Catholic Church. 2. Catholic Church—Doctrinal and controversial works—Catholic authors. 3. Sociology, Christian (Catholic) I. Title. II. Title: Catholicism, authority and order.

DONOSO CORTES, Juan, marquis de Valdegamas, 1809-1853. 282
Essay on Catholicism, liberalism and Socialism considered in their fundamental principles, By Don Juan Donoso Cortes, marques of Valdegamas.From the original Spanish. To which is prefixed a sketch of the life and works of the author, from the Italian of G. E. de Castro. Translated by Madeleine Vinton Goddard. Philadelphia, J. B. Lippincott & co., 1862. xvi, 17-335 p. 19 cm. [BX1753.D6] 35-34422
1. Socialism and Catholic church. 2. Sociology, Christian—Catholic authors. 3. Catholic church—Doctrinal and controversial works—Catholic authors. I. Castro G. E. de. II. Dabigren, Madelene (Vinton) Mrs. 1835-1898, tr. III. Title. IV. Title: Catholicism, liberalism and socialism.

MORGAN, Thomas Brynmor, 1886- 261
Faith is a weapon. New York, Putnam [1952] 278 p. 22 cm. [BX1397.M6] 52-5279
1. Socialism and Catholic Church. 2. Communism and religion. 3. Catholic Church — Relations (diplomatic) I. Title.

Socialism and Catholic Church—Addresses, essays, lectures.

CHRISTIANITY and socialism 261.7
/ edited by Johann -Baptist Metz and Jean-Pierre Jossua. New York : Seabury Press, 1978. viii, 133 p. ; 23 cm. (Concilium : religion in the seventies ; 105) "A Crossroad book." Includes bibliographical references. [BX1396.3.C47] 77-90100 ISBN 0-8164-2148-X pbk. : 4.95
1. Socialism and Catholic Church—Addresses, essays, lectures. I. Metz, Johannes Baptist, 1928- II. Jossua, Jean Pierre. III. Series: Concilium (New York) ; 105.

Socialism and Catholic Church—Canada.

BAUM, Gregory, 1923- 261.7
Catholics and Canadian socialism : political thoughts in the thirties and forties / Gregory Baum. New York : Paulist Press, c1980. 240 p. ; 23 cm. Includes index. Bibliography: p. 235-236. [BX1396.3.B38 1980.] 19 81-124707 ISBN 0-8091-2357-6 (pbk.) : 9.95
1. Socialism and Catholic Church—Canada. I. Title.

Socialism and religion.

HOWARD, Irving E. 261.85
The Christian alternative to socialism [by] Irvin E. Howard. Introd. by Howard E. Kershner. Arlington, Va., Better Bks., 1966 [i.e.1967] xiii, 153p. ports. 21cm. [HX536.H78] 66-29719 2.50 pap.,
1. Socialism and religion. I. Title.

Socialism and religion—History—Addresses, essays, lectures.

KARL Barth and radical politics 230'.4'0924
/ edited and translated by George Hunsinger. Philadelphia : Westminster Press, c1976. 236 p. ; 20 cm. Contents.Contents.—Hunsinger, G. Introduction.—Barth, K. Jesus Christ and the movement for social justice (1911).—Marquardt, F.-W. Socialism in the theology of Karl Barth.—Gollwitzer, H. Kingdom of God and socialism in the theology of Karl Barth.—Diem, H. Karl Barth as socialist: controversy over a new attempt to understand him.—Schellong, D. On reading Karl Barth from the left.—Bettis, J. Political theology and social ethics.—Hunsinger, G. Conclusion: toward a radical Barth. Includes bibliographical references. [BX4827.B3K34] 76-976 ISBN 0-664-24797-0 : 6.00
1. Barth, Karl, 1886-1968—Addresses, essays, lectures. 2. Socialism and religion—History—Addresses, essays, lectures. I. Hunsinger, George.
Contents omitted.

Socialism—Christian.

ADDERLEY, James Granville, 1861-
Old seed on new ground, by James Adderley...with twelve cartoons by Low. London and New York, G.P. Putnam's sons, 1920. 191 p. illus. 22 cm. A21
1. Socialism, Christian. I. Title.

COFER, David Brooks.
Saint-Simonism in the radicalism of Thomas Carlyle. [Austin, Tex.] Printed by Von Boeckmann-Jones [c1931; New York, Haskell House, 196-] 68 p. 23 cm. Cover-title. Reprint? Bibliography: p. 67-68. 68-104023
1. Carlyle, Thomas, 1795-1881. 2. Saint-Simon, Claude Henri, comte de, 1760-1825. 3. Socialism—Christian. 4. Social problems in literature. I. Title. II. Title: The radicalism of Thomas Carlyle.

HENDRICKS, Robert J. 335'.973
Bethel and Aurora [by Robert J. Hendricks; an experiment in communism as practical Christianity, with some account of past and present ventures in collective living. New York, Press of the Pioneers, 1933. [New York, AMS Press, 1971] xv, 324 p. illus. 22 cm. [HX656.B4H4 1971] 75-134380 ISBN 0-404-08428-1 14.00
1. Socialism, Christian. 2. Bethel, Mo. 3. Aurora, Or. I. Title.

[ONEIDA Community] 335'.9'74764
Mutual criticism / introd. by Murray Levine and Barbara Benedict Bunker. Syracuse, N.Y. : Syracuse University Press, 1975. xxx, 96 p. ; 21 cm. "May most likely be attributed to John Humphrey Noyes." Reprint of the 1876 ed. published by the Office of the American Socialist, Oneida, N.Y. Bibliography: p. xxix-xxx. [HX656.O5O54 1975] 75-6236 ISBN 0-8156-2169-8 : 8.50 ISBN 0-8156-2170-1 pbk. 4.75
1. Oneida Community. 2. Socialism, Christian. I. Noyes, John Humphrey, 1811-1886. II. Levine, Murray, 1928- III. Bunker, Barbara Benedict. IV. Title.

PELLEY, William Dudley, 1885- 335.7
No more hunger; an exposition of Christian democracy ... by William Dudley Pelley ... Asheville, N. C., The Foundation for Christian economics [c1933- v. illus. 19 cm. [BR115.S6P35] 34-5308
1. Socialism, Christian. I. Title.

ROBERTS, William Nesbit. 261
The answer; or, The kingdom [by] William Nesbit Roberts. Boston, R. G. Badger [c1931] 3 p. l., ix-xviii p., 1 l., 9-172 p. 20 cm. "The decision ... which will enable us ... to administer the wealth of the world on a Christian and scientific basis."--Introd. [BR115.S6R65] 31-21206
1. Socialism, Christian. 2. Sociology, Christian. 3. Kingdom of God. 4. Jews—Political and social conditions. I. Title.

STUMME, John R., 1942- 230'.092'4
Socialism in theological perspective : a study of Paul Tillich, 1918-1933 / by John R. Stumme. Missoula, Mont. : Scholars Press, [1978] p. cm. (AAR dissertation series ; 21 ISSN 0145-272Xs) Originally presented as the author's thesis, Union Theological Seminary. Vita. Bibliography: p. [BX4827.T53S78 1978] 78-3675 ISBN 0-89130-232-8 : 7.50
1. Tillich, Paul, 1886-1965. 2. Socialism, Christian. I. Title. II. Series: American Academy of Religion. Dissertation series — American Academy of Religion ; 21.

Socialism, Christian—Addresses, essays, lectures.

LEWIS, John, 1889- ed. 261.8'5
Christianity and the social revolution. Edited by John Lewis, Karl Polanyi [and] Donald K. Kitchin. Freeport, N.Y., Books for Libraries Press [1972] 526 p. 23 cm. Reprint of the 1935 ed. Includes bibliographical references. [HX51.L53 1972] 79-37892 ISBN 0-8369-6729-1
1. Socialism, Christian—Addresses, essays, lectures. 2. Communism—Addresses, essays, lectures. 3. Communism and religion—Addresses, essays, lectures. I. Polanyi, Karl, 1886-1964, joint ed. II. Kitchin, Donald K., joint ed. III. Title.

Socialism, Christian—Catholic authors.

DAWSON, Christopher Henry, 1889- 261
Beyond politics, by Christopher Dawson. New York, Sheed & Ward, 1939. 4 p. l., 3-136 p. 20 cm. "Printed in Great Britain." [BR115.P7D33] 39-8501
1. Socialism, Christian—Catholic authors. 2. Church and state. I. Title.

Socialism—Congresses.

CAPITALISM and socialism 261.8'5
: a theological inquiry : proceedings of a conference held July 9-14, 1978 in Airlie, Virginia / edited by Michael Novak. Washington : American Enterprise Institute for Public Policy Research, [1979] p. cm. Bibliography: p. [HX13.C36 1978] 79-14220 ISBN 0-8447-2153-0 : 10.75
1. Socialism—Congresses. 2. Capitalism—Congresses. 3. Theology—Congresses. I. Novak, Michael.

Socially handicapped children—Education.

AMERICAN Institutes for Research in the Behavioral Sciences. 371.9'6
Preschool program in compensatory education. [Washington] U.S. Office of Education [1969- v. 26 cm. "It works, 1." "Series of successful compensatory education programs." Includes various editions of some volumes. [LC4051.A43] 73-601219
1. Socially handicapped children—Education. 2. Education, Preschool. I. Title. II. Title: It works, 1.

Socially handicapped children Education Brooklyn New York.

LORRANCE, Arleen, 1939- 371.9'67'0974723
The Love Project / by Arleen Lorrance. Rev. ed. San Diego, Calif. : LP Publications, 1978. p. cm. [LC4093.B76L67 1978] 78-15162 ISBN 0-916192-14-8 pbk. : 3.50
1. Socially handicapped children—Education—New York (State)—Brooklyn. 2. Child psychology. 3. Social choice. I. Title.

Socially handicapped children—Education—Congresses.

NATIONAL Conference on Educational Objectives for the Culturally Disadvantaged, Hot Springs, Ark., 1967. 371.9'6
Education for the culturally disadvantaged; proceedings. [Little Rock, Ark.] South Central Region Educational Laboratory [1967 or 8] 116 p. 23 cm. "Prepared under contract number OEC-4-7-062100-3074 with the United States Office of Education." [LC4055.N3 1967] 68-57294
1. Socially handicapped children—Education—Congresses. I. South Central Region Educational Laboratory. II. Title.

Socially handicapped children—Education—United States.

EDUCATING the children of the poor. 371.9'6
Prepared for the ASCD Elementary Education Council, by Alexander Frazier, editor [and others] Washington, Association for Supervision and Curriculum Development [1968] xi, 41 p. 23 cm. Bibliography: p. 39-41. [LC4091.E34] 68-31162 2.00
1. Socially handicapped children—Education—United States. 2. Education, Urban. I. Frazier, Alexander, ed. II. Association for Supervision and Curriculum Development. Elementary Education Council.

Socially handicapped children—Education—Washington, D.C.

HOBSON, Julius W. 371.9'67
The damned children; a layman's guide to forcing change in public education, by Julius W. Hobson. Photos. by George de Vincent. [Washington, Washington Institute for Quality Education, 1970] 39 p. illus., group port. 21 x 26 cm. [LC4092.D6H6] 74-188621 1.50
1. Socially handicapped children—Education—Washington, D.C. I. Title.

Socially handicapped—Education—United States.

WELLS, Reese. 371.9'67'0973
How to administer programs for disadvantaged adults, by Reese Wells [and] Curtis Ulmer. Englewood Cliffs, N.J., Prentice-Hall [1972] 56 p. illus. 28 cm. (Prentice-Hall adult education series) [LC4823.W4] 73-37372 ISBN 0-13-402057-X Pap. $3.95
1. Socially handicapped—Education—United States. I. Ulmer, Curtis, joint author. II. Title.

Societas Sacerdotalis Sanctae Crucis.

THIERRY, Jean Jacques. 255'.095
Opus Dei : a close-up / Jean-Jacques Thierry ; translated by Gilda Roberts. New York : Cortland Press, c1975. 197 p. : 23 cm. Bibliography: p. [195]-197. [BX809.S49T4713] 75-325600 pbk. : 5.95
1. Societas Sacerdotalis Sanctae Crucis. I. Title.
Publisher's address: 505 Fifth Ave., N.Y., N.Y. 10017.

Society for promoting Christian knowledge, London.

ALLEN, William Osborne Bird. 267'.18'342
Two hundred years: the history of the Society for Promoting Christian Knowledge, 1698-1898, by W. O. B. Allen and Edmund McClure. New York, B. Franklin [1970] vi, 551 p. 22 cm. (Burt Franklin research & source works series, 622. History, economics and social science, 212) Reprint of the 1898 ed. [BX5013.S6A8 1970] 76-135171 ISBN 0-8337-0044-8
1. Society for Promoting Christian

Knowledge, London. I. McClure, Edmund, d. 1922, joint author. II. Title.

CLARKE, William Kemp 266.3
Lowther, 1879-
Eighteenth century piety, by W. K. Lowther Clarke. London, Society for promoting Christian knowledge. New York, The Macmillan company [1944] viii, 160 p. plates, ports. 22 cm. "First published 1944." "Contribute[s] to the history of the S.P.C.K., first by summarising the books published by the society in the eighteenth century; secondly by telling the story of ... Henry Newman, secretary from 1708 to 1743."--Pref. Bibliographical foot-notes. [BX5013.S6C59] 45-1688
1. Society for promoting Christian knowledge, London. 2. Newman, Henry, 1670-1743. I. Title.

CLARKE, William Kemp 274.
Lowther, 1879-
A short history of S.P.C.K., by W. K. Lowther Clarke ... London, Society for promoting Christian knowledge; New York, The Macmillan company, 1919. viii p., 1 l., [11]-106 p. 18 cm. [BX5013.S6C6] 19-15955
1. Society for promoting Christian knowledge, London. I. Title.

PISTIS, Sophia 273.
Pistis sophia, literally translated from the Coptic by George Horner; with an introduction by F. Legge, F.S.A. London, Society for promoting Christian knowledge; New York and Toronto, The Macmillan co., 1924. xlviii, 205 p., 1 l. 25 1/2 cm. The introduction includes bibliographical references. [BT1390.P5 1924] 25-16746
I. Horner, George William, 1849?- tr. II. Legge, Francis. III. Title.

SWETE, Henry Barclay, 1835- 236
1917.
The life of the world to come; six addresses given by the late Henry Barclay Swete... 4th thousand. London, Society for promoting Christian knowledge; New York, tHe Macmillan company, 1917. xi, 114 p., 1 l., front. (port.) 19 cm. [BT901.S8] 18-14211
I. Title.

Society for promoting Christian knowledge. London. Tract committee.

GARDENER, Alice, 1854-1927. 281.
... Synesius of Cyrene, philosopher and bishop. By Alice Gardner ... Pub. under the direction of the Tract committee. London. Society for promoting Christian knowledge; New York. E. & J. B. Young & co., 1886. xii, 179, [1] p. 17 cm. (The Fathers for English readers) [BR1705.F4S8] 20-17700
1. Synesius, Cyrenneus, bp. of Ptolemais. 2. Society for promoting Christian knowledge. London. Tract committee. I. Title.

Society for promoting Christian knowledge. Tract committee.

FOWLER, Montague, 1858-
Some notable archbishops of Canterbury. By the Rev. Montague Fowler ... Pub. under the direction of the Tract comittee. London [etc.] Society for promoting Christian knowledge; New York, E. & J. B. Young and co., 1895. 222 p. col. front., col. ports. 22 cm. 10-13327
1. Society for promoting Christian knowledge. Tract committee. I. Title.

Society for Propagation of the Gospel in New England.

KELLAWAY, William. 266'.5'90974
The New England Company, 1649-1776 : missionary society to the American Indians / William Kellaway. Westport, Conn. : Greenwood Press, 1975, c1961. 303 p. : map ; 22 cm. Reprint of the ed. published by Longmans, London. Includes index. "List of manuscript sources": p. 284-287. [E98.M6K28 1975] 74-33895 ISBN 0-8371-7995-5
1. Society for Propagation of the Gospel in New England. 2. Indians of North America—Missions. I. Title.

Society for Psychical Research, London.

MACKENZIE, Andrew. 133
The unexplained; some strange cases in psychical research. With an introd. by H. H. Price. London, New York, Abelard-Schuman [1970] xvii, 180 p. 22 cm. [BF1411.M17 1970] 68-14570 5.95
1. Society for Psychical Research, London. 2. Occult sciences. 3. Psychical research. I. Title.

Society for Psychical Research, London. Library.

SOCIETY for Psychical 016.1338
Research, London. Library.
Catalogue of the Library of the Society for Psychical Research, London, England. Boston : G. K. Hall, 1976. v, 341 p. ; 37 cm. [Z6878.P8S6 1976] [BF1031] 76-358758 ISBN 0-8161-0008-X lib.bdg. : 49.00
1. Society for Psychical Research, London. Library. 2. Psychical research—Bibliography—Catalogs. 3. Occult sciences—Bibliography—Catalogs. I. Title.

Society for the Propagation of the Faith.

BURTON, Katherine (Kurz) 922.244
1890-
Difficult star; the life of Pauline Jaricot, by Katherine Burton ... New York, London [etc.] Longmans, Green and co., 1947. x, 239 p. front. (port.) pl. 21 cm. Bibliography: p. 231. [BX4705.J37B8] 47-3702
1. Jaricot, Pauline Marie, 1790-1862. 2. Society for the propagation of the faith. I. Title.

HICKEY, Edward John, 1893- 266'.2
The Society for the Propagation of the Faith: its foundation, organization, and success (1822-1922). [New York, AMS Press, 1974] x, 195 p. 23 cm. Reprint of the author's thesis, Catholic University of America, 1922, which was issued as v. 3 of the Catholic University of America. Studies in American church history. Includes bibliographical references. [BV2155.S7H5 1974] 73-3557 ISBN 0-404-57753-9 8.50
1. Society for the Propagation of the Faith. 2. Catholic Church—Missions. I. Series: Catholic University of America. Studies in American church history, v. 3.

WINDEATT, Mary Fabyan, 922.244
1910-
Pennies for Palline; the story of Marie Pauline Jaricot, foundress of the Society for the Propagation of the Faith. Illustrated by Paul A. Grout. [St. Meinrad, Ind., 1952] 245p. illus. 22cm. 'A Grail publication.' [BX4705.J37W5] 52-14492
1. Jarieot, Paciline Marie, 1799-1862. 2. Society for the Propagation of the ,faith. I. Title.

Society for the propagation of the gospel in foreign parts.

MAYHEW, Jonathan, 1720- 277.3
1766.
A defence of the Observations on the charter and conduct of the Society for the propagation of the gospel in foreign parts against an anonymous pamphlet, falsly [!] intitled, A candid examination of Dr. Mayhew's Observations, &c. and also against the Letter to a friend annexed thereto, said to contain a short vindication of said society. By one of its members. By Jonathan Mayhew, D.D., pastor of the West church in Boston... Boston, Printed and sold by R. S. Draper, in Newbury-street; Edes and Gill, in Queen-street; and T. & J. Fleet, in Cornhill, 1763. 144 p. 20 1/2 cm. [With Caner, Henry. A candid examination of Dr. Mayhew's Observations on the charter and conduct of the Society. Boston, 1763] [BV2763.S8M32] 266.3 34-16739
1. Caner, Henry, 1700-1792. A candid examination. 2. Society for the propagation of the gospel in foreign parts. I. Title.

Society for the Propagation of the Gospel in Foreign Parts, London.

[CANER, Henry] 1700-1792. 277.3
A candid examination of Dr. Mayhew's Observations on the charter and conduct of the Society for the propagation of the gospel in foreign parts. Interspers'd with a few brief reflections upon some other of the doctor's writings. To which is added, A letter to a friend, containing a short vindication of the said society, against the mistakes and misrepresentations of the doctor in his observations on the conduct of that society. By one of its members. Boston, New England, Printed, and sold by Thomas and John Fleet, in Cornhill; and Green & Ruslell (!) and Edes & Gill, in Queenstreet, 1763. 2 p., l, 93 p. 20 1/2 cm. With this is bound: Mayhew, Jonathan. A defense of the Observations on the charter and conduct of the Society for the propagation of the gospel. Boston, 1763. Pages 57-64 wrongly numbered, 49-56. Attributed to Henry Caner, p.p. to Samuel Johnson, D.D. and to Timothy Cutler, D.D. cf. Alden Bradford, Memoirs of the life and writings of Rev. Jonathan Mayhew, D.D., 1838, p. 279-180. "A short vindication of the society, etc ... By one of its members in a letter to a friend" (p. 81-93) is by Samuel Johnson, d.d. [BV2763.S8M32] 266.3 A17
1. Mayhew, Jonathan, 1720-1706. Observations on the charter and conduct of the Society for the propagation of the gospel. 2. Society for the propagation of the gospel in foreign parts, London. I. Johnson, Samuel, 1696-1772. II. Cutler, Timothy, 1683-1705. III. Title.

HUMPHREYS, David, 1689- 266.3'7
1740.
An historical account of the incorporated Society for the Propagation of the Gospel in Foreign Parts. New York, Arno Press, 1969. xxxi, 356 p. 2 fold. maps. 23 cm. (Religion in America) Reprint of the 1730 ed. [BV2500.A6H9 1969] 75-83426
1. Society for the Propagation of the Gospel in Foreign Parts, London. 2. Missions—North America. I. Title.

KLINGBERG, Frank 266.3'747
Joseph, 1883-
Anglican humanitarianism in colonial New York, by Frank J. Klingberg. Freeport, N.Y., Books for Libraries Press [1971] x, 295 p. 24 cm. Reprint of the 1940 ed. Contents.Contents.—Leading ideas in the annual S.P.G. sermons, particularly with reference to native peoples.—The noble savage as seen by the S.P.G. missionary.—Sir William Johnson and the S.P.G.—The S.P.G. program for Negroes in colonial New York.—Three notable annual S.P.G. sermons: A plea for humanitarianism for the Negro in the institution of slavery, February 16, 1710-11, by W. Fleetwood. An argument for the Christianization of whites, Negroes, and Indians as sound imperial policy, February 20, 1740-41, by T. Secker. A statement of British manifest destiny, involving aborigines protection and ultimate Negro freedom, February 21, 1766, by W. Warburton.—A select bibliography (p. [251]-265) [BV2500.A6K55 1971] 71-164612 ISBN 0-8369-5896-9
1. Society for the Propagation of the Gospel in Foreign Parts, London. 2. Church of England—Sermons. 3. Missions—New York (State) 4. Indians of North America—Missions. 5. Negroes—New York (State) 6. Missions—Sermons. 7. Sermons, English. I. Title.

KLINGBERG, Frank Joseph, 266.3
1883-
Anglican humanitarianism in colonial New York, by Frank J. Klingberg ... Philadelphia, The Church historical society [c1940] x p., 2 l., [3]-295 p. 24 cm. ([Church historical society, Philadelphia] Publication no. 11) [BV2500.A6K55] 40-33059
1. Society for the propagation of the gospel in foreign parts, London. 2. Missions—New York (State) 3. Indians of North America—Missions. 4. Negroes—New York (State) 5. Missions—Sermons. 6. Church of England—Sermons. 7. Sermons, English. I. Title.
Contents omitted.

MAYHEW, Jonathan, 1720- 266.3
1766.
Observations on the charter and conduct of the Society for the Propagation of the Gospel in Foreign Parts. New York, Arno Press, 1972. 176 p. 23 cm. (Religion in America, series II) Reprint of the 1763 ed. [BV2763.S8M3 1972] 72-38456 ISBN 0-405-04077-6
1. Society for the Propagation of the Gospel in Foreign Parts, London. 2. Apthorp, East, 1732 or 3-1816. Considerations on the institution and conduct of the Society for the Propagation of the Gospel. 3. Church of England in New England. I. Title.

MAYHEW, Jonathan, 1720-1766. 277.
Observations on the charter and conduct of the Society for the propagation of the gospel in foreign parts; designed to show their non-conformity to each other. With remarks on the mistakes of East Apthorp, M.A., missionary at Cambridge, in quoting, and representing, the sense of said charter, &c. As also various incidental reflections relative to the Church of England, and the state of religion in North-America, particularly in New-England. By Jonathan Mayhew, D.D., pastor of the West-church in Boston... Boston, New-England: Printed by Richard and Samuel Draper, in Newbury-street, Edes and Gill, in Queen-street, and Thomas and John Fleet at the Heart and crown in Cornhill, M,DCC,LXIII. 176 p. 23 cm. With this is bound the author's: A defence of the Observations on the charter and conduct of the Society for the propagation of the gospel in foreign parts, against an anonymous pamphlet falsly [!] intitled, A candid examination of Dr. Mayhew's Observation, &c., and also against The letter to a friend annexed thereto, said to contain a short vindication of said society. By One of its members...Boston, 1763. 144 p. Copy 2. With this is bound: [Secker, Thomas] An answer to Dr. Mayhew's Observations on the charter and conduct of the Society for the propagation of the gospel in foreign parts. London, printed; Boston reprinted, 1764. 59 p.; and the author's Remarks on an anonymous tract, entitled An answer to Dr. Mayhew's Observations ... Being a second defence of the said Observations ... Boston, 1764. 86 p., 1 l. [BV2763.S8M3] 4-22445
1. Society for the propagation of the gospel in foreign parts, London. 2. Apthorp, East, 1732 or 3-1816. Considerations on the institution and conduct of the Society for the Propagation of the gospel. 3. Church of England in New England. I. Title.

Society of African Missions.

BANE, Martin J 266.266
Heroes of the hinterlands; the Bresillac story. With a foreword by Francis Cardinal Spellman. New York, Shamrock Guild [c1959] 112p. illus. 23cm. [BV2300.S5B3] 59-14652
1. Marion-Bresillac, Melchior Marie Joseph de, Bp., 1813-1859. 2. Society of African Missions. I. Title.

Society of Catholic Medical Missionaries.

BURTON, Katherine (Kurz) 266.2
1890-
According to the pattern; the story of Dr. Agnes McLaren and the Society of Catholic medical missionaries, by Katherine Burton. New York, Toronto, Longmans, Green and co., inc., 1946. 3 p. l., 3-252 p. 21 cm. "First edition." Bibliography: p. 243-244. [BV2300.S53B8] 46-989
1. McLaren, Agnes, 1837-1913. 2. Dengel, Anna, 1892- 3. Society of Catholic medical missionaries. I. Title.

LONG, Richard F. 266.2
Nowhere a stranger, by Richard F. Long. [1st ed.] New York, Vantage Press [1968] 132 p. illus. 22 cm. [BV2300.S53L6] 68-3916
1. Society of Catholic Medical Missionaries. I. Title.

SOCIETY of Catholic Medical 266.2
Missionaries.
If it matters ... [Philadelphia, Medical

Mission Sisters, c1967] 210 p. illus. (part col.), maps. 28 cm. [R722.S55] 76-9032
1. Title.

Society of Friends—India—History.

SYKES, Marjorie. 289.6'54
Quakers in India : a forgotten century / Marjorie Sykes. London ; Boston : Allen & Unwin, 1980. x, 178 p. ; 22 cm. Includes index. Bibliography: p. [155] [BX7716.I4S94] 19 80-40223 ISBN 0-04-275003-2 (pbk.) : 12.95 (U.S.)
1. Society of Friends—India—History. 2. Society of Friends—Missions—India. 3. Missions—India. 4. India—Church history. I. Title.

Society of Frinds—Missions—Jordan—R am All ah.

JONES, Christina H. 289.6'5694
Friends in Palestine / by Christina H. Jones. Richmond, Ind. : Friends United Press, c1981. vii, 202 p., [8] p. of plates : ill., ports. ; 21 cm. [BV3210.J6J66] 19 81-65764 ISBN 0-913408-62-X (pbk.) : 8.95
1. Friends Boys School (R am All ah, Jordan)—History. 2. Friends Girls School (R am All ah, Jordan)—History. 3. Society of Frinds—Missions—Jordan—R am All ah. 4. Missions—Jordan—R am All ah. I. Title.
Publisher's Address: 101 Quaker Hill Drive, Richmond, IN 47374

Society of life.

MOTT, Francis John, 1901- 289.9
Christ the seed, by Francis J. Mott. Boston, A. A. Beauchamp, 1939. xv, [1], 406 p. diagrs. (1 double) 22 1/2 cm. [BX9798.S55M58] 40-2801
1. Society of life. 2. Religions (Proposed, universal, etc.) I. Title.

MOTT, Francis John, 1901- 289.9
Consciousness creative, an outline of the science, religion, and philosophy of universal integration, by Francis J. Mott. Boston, A. A. Beauchamp, 1937. ix p., 2 l., 3-395 p. diagrs. (1 fold.) 22 1/2 cm. [BX9798.S55M6] 38-877
1. Society of life. 2. Religions (Proposed, universal, etc.) I. Title.

MOTT, Francis John, 1901- 289.9
The Society of life; covenant, by-laws and form of communion of the parent centre, together with a simple introduction to the religion and philosophy of integration as illustrated by the covenant-organism, by Francis J. Mott. 3d ed. Boston, A. A. Beauchamp, 1937. xxii, 54 p. 20 cm. [BX9798.S55M63 1937] 38-1228
1. Society of life. I. Title.

MOTT, Francis John, 1901- 289.9
Vision and organization; periodicity in social structures, by Francis J. Mott. Boston and London, A. A. Beauchamp, 1938. xi, 242 p. fold. pl. 22 1/2 cm. Bibliography: p. [227] [BX9798.S55M65] 38-18152
1. Society of life. 2. Religions (Proposed, universal, etc.) I. Title. II. Title: Periodicity in social structures.

Society of paradiseism.

ULRAM, Richard, 1874- 133
The emissary: the key heaven. Final eternal facts of God in actuality versus satanic-inspired falsehood (religion) by Richard Ulram Jersey City, N.J., Society of paradiseism [c1940] vi, 378 p. 25 cm. [BF1999.U4] [159.961] 40-14999
1. Society of paradiseism. I. Title.

Society of St. John the Evangelist.

BENSON, Richard Meux, 1824-1915. 271.83
The religious vocation, by Richard Meux Benson ... edited on behalf of the Society by the Rev. H. P. Bull ... with an introduction by the Rev. Lucius Cary ... London and Oxford, A. R. Mowbray & co., limited; New York, Morehouse-Gorham co. [1939] 315, [1] p. 21 cm. "First published in 1939." [BX5184.B4] 39-24414
1. Society of St. John the Evangelist. Rule. 2. Vocation (in religious orders, congregations, etc.) I. Bull, Henry Power, ed. II. Title.

SMITH, Robert Cheney, 1911-
The Cowley Fathers in America; the early years. [n.p., 1958] 75 p. illus. 22 cm.
1. Society of St. John the Evangelist. I. Title.

Society of St. Paul.

BOZARTH, Rene. 271'.8
The single eye; lectures on the life of the Society of St. Paul, a religious order within the Episcopal Church. 2d ed. Gresham, Or., St. Paul's Press [1968] 220 p. 22 cm. [BX5971.S6B6 1968] 70-1287
1. Society of St. Paul. I. Title.

Society of St. Vincent de Paul.

MURPHY, Charles Kavanagh.
The spirit of the Society of St. Vincent de Paul, by Charles K. Murphy ... Preface by the Most Rev. Finbar Ryan ... Dublin and Cork, Cork university press, Educational company of Ireland; London, New York [etc.] Longmans Green and co., 1940. 3 p. l., ix-xiv p., 1 l. 208, [1] p. 19 cm. "First published 1940." Bibliographical foot-notes. A 40
1. Society of St. Vincent de Paul. I. Title.

Society of St. Vincent de Paul. Milwaukee (Archidocese)

SCHIMBERG, Albert Paul. 1885- 360.621
Humble harvest; the Society of St. Vincent de Paul in the Milwaukee Archidocese, 1849-1949. Milwaukee, Bruce Pub. Co. [1949] ix, 179 p. illus., ports. 23 cm. [BX809.S7M5] 49-6783
1. Society of St. Vincent de Paul. Milwaukee (Archidocese) I. Title.

Society of St. Vincent de Paul. United States

MCCOLGAN, Daniel T. 360.621
A century of charity; the first one hundred years of the Society of St. Vincent de Paul in the United States. Milwaukee, Bruce [1951] 2 v. illus. ports. 24 cm. Includes bibliographies. [BX809.S7A3] 52-133
1. Society of St. Vincent de Paul. U. S. I. Title.

SOCIETY of St. Vincent de Paul. U. S. Metropolitan central council of New York. 267.
Report. New York, 18-19 v. 22-26 cm. Issues for 18-1915 published by the council under its earlier name: Superior council of New York. [BX809.S7N6] 48-36483
I. Title.

Society of the Divine Word—Addresses, essays, lectures.

THE Word in the world : Divine Word missionaries '76 Black apostolate / [editor, John Boberg, editorial assistants, Patricia Ritter, Terry Steib ; illustrations, Art Haase]. Techny, Ill. : Society of the Divine Word, [1976?] 208 p. : ill. ; 29 cm. [BX1407.N4W65] 77-352490 266'.2'73
1. Society of the Divine Word—Addresses, essays, lectures. 2. Afro-American Catholics—Addresses, essays, lectures. I. Boberg, John T. II. Ritter, Patricia. III. Steib, Terry. IV. Society of the Divine Word.

Society of the Divine Word—Missions.

SOCIETY of the Divine Word. 266'.2
The Word in the world : Divine Word missionaries, 1875-1975 / [edited by Divine Word missionaries ; sketches by Ron Berger ; photos. by Steve Dunwell]. Techny, Ill. : The Society, [1975] 191 p., [1] fold. leaf of plates : ill. (some col.) ; 29 cm. [BV2300.S6S6 1975] 75-311879
1. Society of the Divine Word—Missions. I. Title.

Society of the helpers of the holy souls.

DUNNE, Peter M 1889- 922.
Mother Mary of St. Bernard of the Society of the helpers of the holy souls, by Peter M. Dunne, s. j. New York, P. J. Kenedy & sons, 1929. viii, 145 p. front. (port.) plates. 20 cm. [BX4705.M37D8] 29-15941
1. Marie de St. Bernard, Me, 1850-1913. 2. Society of the helpers of the holy souls. I. Title.

Society of the Holy Child Jesus.

BISGOOD, Marie Therese, 1891- 922.273
Cornelia Connelly; a study in fidelity. With an introd. by James Walsh. Westminster, Md., Newman Press [1963] xiii, 326 p. illus., ports. 22 cm. "Sources": p. 318-319. Bibliographical footnotes. [BX4705.C77B58] 63-25041
1. Connelly, Cornelia Augusta (Peacock) 1809-1879. 2. Society of the Holy Child Jesus. I. Title.

THE life of Cornelia Connelly, 1809-1879, foundress of the Society of the Holy Child Jesus, by a member of the society; with a preface by Cardinal Gasquet ... London, New York [etc.] Longmans, Green and co., 1922. xvi, 486 p. front., illus. (incl. facsim.) plates, ports. 23 cm. [BX4705.C77L5] 22-10878 922
1. Connelly, Mrs. Cornelia Augusta (Peacock) 1809-1879. 2. Society of the Holy Child Jesus.

THE life of Cornelia Connelly, 1809-1879, foundress of the Society of the Holy Child Jesus, by a religious of the society; with a preface by Cardinal Gasquet ... With portrait, 2nd ed., abridged and rev. New York, London [etc.] Longmans, Green and co., 1924. xvi, 260 p. front. (port.) 20 cm. Printed in Great Britain. [BX4705.C77L5 1924] 25-6443 922
1. Connelly, Mrs. Cornelia Augusta (Peacock) 1809-1879. 2. Society of the holy Child Jesus.

MARY Eleanor, Mother, 1903- 271.979
His by choice; the Sisters of the Holy Child Jesus. With a pref. by Fulton J. Sheen. Photos. by Thomas C. Walsh. Milwaukee, Bruce Press [c1960] 115p. illus. 22cm. (Catholic life publications) [BX4527.M35] 61-3446
1. Society of the Holy Child Jesus. I. Title.

SOCIETY of the Holy Child Jesus. American Province. 271.97
Annals of the Society of the Holy Child Jesus, American Province, 1862-1882 [by] Mother M Mildred. Colldale, Pa., Bailey Print Co. [1950] 113 p. 23 cm. [BX4515.S83A7 1862/1882] 52-17587
I. Title.

Society of the Precious Blood—History.

ST. Charles Seminary, Carthagena, Ohio.
Centenary celebration: St. Charles Seminary, Motherhouse, and major seminary of the American Province, 1861-1961. [Carthagena, Ohio] Society of the Precious Blood [1961] 95 p. illus., ports. 24 cm.
1. Society of the Precious Blood—History. I. Title.

Society of the Sacred Heart.

MONAHAN, Maud. 922.
Life and letters of Janet Erskine Stuart, superior general of the Society of the sacred heart, 1857-1914, by Maud Monahan, with an introduction by His Eminence Cardinal Bourne ... London, New York [etc.] Longmans, Green and co., 1922. xii p., 1 l., 524 p. front., plates, ports., facsim. 23 cm. [BX4705.S85M6] 22-20451
1. Society of the sacred heart. I. Stuart, Janet Erskine, 1857-1914. II. Title.

MONAHAN, Maud. 922.
Saint Madeleine Sophie, foundress of the Society of the sacred heart, 1779 to 1865, by Maud Monahan; with a preface by His Eminence Cardinal Bourne ... 2d impression. London, New York [etc.] Longmans, Green and co., 1925. x p., 1 l., 105 p. front. (port.) 19 cm. [BX4700.M2M6 1925] 25-11722
1. Madeleine Sophie, Saint, 1779-1865. 2. Society of the Sacred heart. I. Title.

O'LEARY, M. 377.82
Education with a tradition; an account of the educational work of the Society of the Sacred heart, by M. O'Leary ... with a preface by Professor F. A. Cavenagh, M. A. New York, Longmans, Green & company, 1936. xxiii, 340 p. front., plates, port. 22 cm. "Frontispiece accompanied by guard sheet with descriptive letterpress. "This book was submitted as a thesis for the P.H. D. degrees of the University of London."--Pref. Bibliography: p. 318-329. [BX4436.O4 1936 a] 37-7835
1. Society of the Sacred heart. 2. Catholic church—Education. I. Title.

O'LEARY, Mary Florence Margaret. 377.82
Education with a tradition; an account of the educational work of the Society of the Sacred heart, by Mary O'Leary ... with a preface by Professor F. A. Cavenagh, M.A. New York, Longmans, Green & company, 1936. xxiii, 340 p. front., plates, port. 22 cm. Frontispiece accompanied by guard sheet with descriptive letterpress. "Submitted as a thesis for the Ph.D. degree of the University of London."--Pref. Bibliography: p. 318-329. [BX4436.O4 1936a] 37-7835
1. Society of the Sacred heart. 2. Catholic church—Education. I. Title.

REPPLIER, Agnes, 1858- ed.
For remembrance a little record of loyalty and fidelity made with much love by the children of Eden. Edited, at their request, by Agnes Repplier ... Philadelphia, Patterson & White co., 1901. 94 p. front., plates, ports. 22 cm. Souvenir of the celebration of the 100th anniversary of the foundation of the Society of the Sacred heart, commemorated at Eden hall, Torresdale, Pa., Nov. 21, 1900. Printed for private circulation only. [BX4438.T7R4] 1-31049
1. Society of the Sacred Heart. I. Title.

Society of the Sacred Heart—History.

WILLIAMS, Margaret Anne, 1902- 271'.93
The Society of the Sacred Heart ; history of a spirit 1800-1975 / [by] Margaret Williams. London : Darton Longman and Todd, 1978. 406 p. ; 22 cm. Includes index. Bibliography: p. [385]-390. [BX4436.2.W54 1978] 78-318957 ISBN 0-232-51395-3 : 11.50
1. Society of the Sacred Heart—History. I. Title.
Distributed by Christian Classics, 205 Willis St., Westminster, MD 21157

Society of the sisters of the holy names of Jesus and Mary.

[MARY Alicia, sister] 1873- 922.273
The Rose of Jesus and Mary; a life of the foundress of the Sisters of the holy names of Jesus and Mary, by one of her spiritual daughters. Portland, Or., Printed by the Metropolitan press, 1934. 109 p. front. (port.) 14 1/2 cm. [Secular name: Julia E. Allehoff] [BX4706.M395M8] 35-497
1. Marie Rose, mere, 1811-1840. 2. Society of the sisters of the holy names of Jesus and Mary. I. Title.

Society, Primitive.

SMITH, Gordon Hedderly, 1902- 291
The missionary and primitive man; an introduction to the study of his mental characteristics and his religion. Chicago, Van Kampen Press [1947] 216 p. illus., map. 21 cm. Bibliography: p. 205-212. [GN400.S6] 48-1045
1. Society, Primitive. 2. Savages. I. Title.

Socinianism.

HARE, Edward, 1774-1818. 230.8
The principal doctrines of Christianity

defended against the errors of Socinianism: being an answer to the Rev. John Grundy's lectures. By Edward Hare. New York, Pub. by B. Waugh and T. Mason, for the Methodist Episcopal church, 1835. 396 p. 18 cm. Published, Manchester, 1814, under title: A preservative against the errors of Socinianism. [BX9847.H3] 35-28550
1. Grundy, John, 1782-1843. 2. Socinianism. I. Title.

HARE, Edward, 1774-1818. 230.8
The principal doctrines of Christianity defended against the errors of Socinianism: being an answer to the Rev. John Grundy's lectures. By Edward Hare. New-York, Pub. by T. Mason and G. Lane, for the Methodist Episcopal church, 1837. 396 p. 18 cm. Published, Manchester, 1814, under title: A preservative against the errors of Socinianism. [BX9847.H3 1837] 35-29984
1. Grundy, John, 1782-1843. 2. Socinianism. I. Title.

KOT, Stanislaw, 1885- 288
Socinianism in Poland; the social and political ideas of the Polish Antitrinitarians in the sixteenth and seventeenth centuries. Translated from the Polish by Earl Morse Wilbur. Boston,Starr King Press [1957] xxvii, 226p. 22cm. Translation of Idelogja polityczna 1 spoleczna Braci Polskich zwanych Arjanaml. Bibliographical footnotes. [BT1480.K63] 57-12746
1. Socinianism. I. Title.

MCMASTER, Gilbert, 1778-1854. 922.
An essay, in defence of some fundamental doctrines of Christianity; including a review of the writings of Elias Smith, by Gilbert McMaster... Schenectady [N.Y.] Printed by Riggs and Stevens, 1815. iv, 120 p. 22 1/2 cm. [BT1480.M3] A 32
1. Smith, Elias, 1769-1846. 2. Socinianism. 3. Christianity. I. Title.

WILBUR, Earl Morse, 1866- 288.09
A history of Unitarianism; Socianism and its antecedents, by Earl Morse Wilbur, D.D. Cambridge, Mass., Harvard university press, 1945. xiii, 617 p. 22 cm. Bibliographical foot-notes. [BT1480.W5] A 45
1. Socianism. I. Title.

Sociology.

BRANFORD, Victor, 1864- 309.
Interpretations and forecasts: a study of survivals and tendencies in contemporary society. By Victor Branford ... New York and London, M. Kennerley, 1914. 6 p. l., 411, [3], cdxv-cdxxiv p. 22 1/2 cm. [Full name: Victor Verasis Branford] [HN389.B82 1914a] 44-16986
1. Sociology. 2. Gt. Brit—Soc. condit. I. Title.

CATHOLIC university of America. Commission on American citizenship. 261
Better men for the better times. Washington, D.C., The Commission on American citizenship, The Catholic university of America [c1943] 7 p. l., 125 p. 23 1/2 cm. "First printing, December, 1943" [HM51.C34] 44-3274
1. Sociology. 2. Sociology, Christian—Catholic authors. I. Title.

CLIFF, John, 1833
The science of man, by Captain John Cliff. Chicago, Marshall-Jackson company, 1907. 70 p. 21 cm. Contents.Introductory.--The decalogue.--The science of man.--The transform- ation of man. The standard of man.--Advanced culture by sentineal. Advanced sociology--Natural theology.--Friendship and friend. 7-6163
I. Title.

KIDD, Benjamin, 1858-1916. 301
Social evolution, by Benjamin Kidd. New ed. with a new preface. New York and London, Macmillan and co., 1895. ix, 374 p. 19 1/2 cm. [BM101.K5 1895] 37-6983
1. Sociology. 2. Civilization. I. Title.

PATTON, Cornelius Howard, 1860- 261
God's world, by Cornelius Howard Patton ... New York, R. R. Smith, inc., 1931. xiii, 297 p. 20 cm. "Suggested reading" at end of each chapter. [HN31.P3] 31-24026
1. Sociology. 2. Sociology, Christian. 3. Race problems. 4. World politics. 5. Progress. 6. Geography, Economic. I. Title. Contents omitted.

Sociology, Biblical.

BELO, Fernando, 1933- 226'.306
A materialist reading of the Gospel of Mark / Fernande Belo ; translated from the French by Matthew J. O'Connell. Maryknoll, N.Y. : Orbis Books, [1981] p. cm. Translation of Lecture materialiste de l'evangile de Marc. Bibliography: p. [BS2585.5.B4413] 19 80-24756 ISBN 0-88344-323-6 pbk. : 12.95
1. Bible. N.T. Mark—Commentaries. 2. Sociology, Biblical. 3. Marxian economics. I. Title.

THE Bible almanac / 220.3
edited by James I. Packer, Merrill C. Tenney, William White, Jr. Nashville : T. Nelson, c1980. 765 p., [12] leaves of plates : ill. ; 24 cm. Includes bibliographical references and index. [BS635.2.B48] 79-23475 ISBN 0-8407-5162-1 : 14.95
1. Bible—History of contemporary events, etc. 2. Sociology, Biblical. I. Packer, James Innell. II. Tenney, Merrill Chapin, 1904- III. White, William, 1934-

THE Bible and our social responsibility. Teacher's ed. Guidance material, by Marvin E. Smith and Harold L. Lunger. St. Louis, Bethany Press [c1958] 127p. 20cm. (A Bethany Bible course)
1. Sociology, Biblical. I. Lunger, Harold L

CONE, Orello, 1835-1905. 225.
Rich and poor in the New Testament: a study of the primitive Christian doctrine of earthly possession, by Orello Cone ... New York, The Macmillan company. London ... A. & C. Black, 1902. Viii. 245 p. 21 cm. [BS2545.S5C6] 2-26524
1. Sociology, Biblical. I. Title.

DIERKS, Hartwig, 1890- 221.83
The social teachings of Moses and of representative prophets ... by Hartwig Dierks ... St. Louis, Mo., Concordia publishing house, 1940. vi, 159 p. 19 cm. Thesis (TH. D.)--Kansas City Baptist theological seminary, 1939. On cover: Social teachings of the Old Testament. Bibliography: p. 159. [BS1199.S6D5 1939] 40-7575
1. Sociology, Biblical. I. Title. II. Title: Social teachings of the Old Testament.

ELLIOTT, John Hall. 227'.9206
A home for the homeless : a sociological exegesis of 1 Peter, its situation and strategy / John H. Elliott. Philadelphia : Fortress Press, c1981. p. cm. Includes bibliographical references and indexes. [BS2795.2.E42] 19 80-28855 ISBN 0-8006-0659-0 : 24.95
1. Bible. N.T. 1 Peter—Criticism, interpretation, etc. 2. Sociology, Biblical. I. Title.

FISKE, George Walter, 1872- 232.9
A study of Jesus' own religion, by George Walter Fiske ... New York, The Macmillan company, 1932. xvi, 360 p. 20 cm. "A companion volume to the author's ... The recovery of worship."-- Introd., p. viii. "Selected bibliography": p. 349-351. [BS2415.F53 1932] 32-32006
1. Jesus Christ—Teachings. 2. Sociology, Biblical. I. Title.

GIORDANI, Igino, 1894- 261.8'3
The social message of Jesus / Igino Giordani ; translated by Alba I. Zizzamia. Boston : St. Paul Editions, c1977. xi, 406 p. ; 18 cm. Reprint of the 1943 ed. published by St. Anthony Guild Press, Paterson, N.J. Includes index. Bibliography: p. 383-394. [BS2417.S7G52 1977] 77-4489 4.50 pbk. : 3.50
1. Jesus Christ—Teachings. 2. Sociology, Biblical. I. Title.
Publisher's address : St. Paul's Catholic Book and Film Center, 172 Tremont St., Boston, MA

GOTTWALD, Norman Karol, 1926- 301.5'8
The tribes of Yahweh : a sociology of the religion of liberated Israel, 1250-1050 B.C. / Norman K. Gottwald. Maryknoll, N.Y. : Orbis Books, c1979. p. cm. Includes bibliographical references and indexes. [BS1199.S6G67] 78-24333 ISBN 0-88344-498-4 : 29.95 pbk. : 19.95
1. Jews—History—1200-953 B.C. 2. Bible. O.T.—Theology. 3. Sociology, Biblical. 4. Twelve tribes of Israel. I. Title.

JACOBSON, David, 1909- 220.83
The social background of the Old Testament. by David Jacobson, PH. D. Cincinnati, Hebrew union college press, 1942. xi, 327 p. 21 cm. [Hebrew union college Alumni publication series vol. ii] "This study was offered as the scientific dissertation for [the degree of doctor of philosophy at Cambridge university] ... It has, however, for publication been carefully revised and considerably expanded from its original form."--Foreword. Bibliography: p. 313-323. [BS670.J3] 42-17890
1. Sociology, Biblical. I. Title.

KEEBLE, Samuel Edward, 1853- ed.
The social teaching of the Bible, edited by Samuel E. Keeble ... for the Wesleyan Methodist union for social service. New York, Eaton & Mains; Cincinnati, Jennings & Graham [1909] xii, 283, [1] p. 19 cm. Bibliographies at the end of most of the chapters. Printed in England. W 10
1. Sociology, Biblical. I. Bedale, Charles Lees, 1879-1919. II. Wesleyan Methodist union for social service. III. Title.
Contents omitted.

KENT, Charles Foster, 1867-1925. 220.
The social teachings of the prophets and Jesus, by Charles Foster Kent ... New York, C. Scribner's sons, 1917. xiii, 364 p. 20 cm. "Selected bibliography": p. 343-347. [BS670.K4] 17-12971
1. Sociology, Biblical. I. Title.

KLEMME, Huber F 220.83
The Bible and our common life. Philadelphia, Christian Education Press [1953] 123p. 21cm. [BS670.K55] 53-9921
1. Sociology, Biblical. I. Title.

MCCONNELL, Franz Marshall, 1862- 220.8331
The rights and obligations of labor according to the Bible, by F. M. McConnell... Dallas, Tex., Storm publishing company [c1937] vii, 65 p. 20 cm. [BS671.M3] 37-12274
1. Sociology, Biblical. 2. Labor and laboring classes. I. Title.

MATHEWS, Shailer, 1863- 248
Jesus on social institutions, by Shailer Mathews... New York, The Macmillan company, 1928. 158 p. 19 1/2 cm. "This little book...replaces my Social teaching of Jesus, although I have not hesitated to use some portions of this older work."--Pref. [BS2417.S7M3] 28-24974
1. Sociology, Biblical. 2. Jesus Christ—Teachings. I. Title.

MATHEWS, Shailer, 1863- 261
The Social teaching of Jesus; an essay in Christian sociology, by Shailer Mathews... New York, The Macmillan company; London, Macmillan and co., ltd. 1897. vi p., 1 l., 235 p. 19 cm. "Appeared originally as a series of essays in the American journal of sociology."--Prefatory note. [HN31.M42] 4-11773
1. Sociology, Biblical. I. Title.

MATHEWS, Shailer, 1863-1941. 261.8
Jesus on social institutions, by Shailer Mathews. Edited, and with an introd., by Kenneth Cauthen. Philadelphia, Fortress Press [1971] lxxiii, 166 p. 19 cm. (Lives of Jesus series) Reprint of the 1928 ed., with a new introd. Based on the author's Social teaching of Jesus. Includes bibliographical references. [BS2417.S7M3 1971] 72-139346 5.95
1. Jesus Christ—Teachings. 2. Sociology, Biblical. I. Title.

MONTGOMERY, John Harold. 248
... *The social message of Jesus,* by John H. Montgomery ... introduction by Shailer Mathews. New York, Cincinnati, The Abingdon press [1923] 173 p. 21 cm. (The Abingdon religious education texts, D. G. Downey, general editor. College series, G. H. Betts, editor) Bibliography: p. 172-173. "Suggested readings" at end of each chapter. [BS2417.S7 M6] 23-17492
1. Jesus Christ—Teachings. 2. Sociology, Biblical. I. Title.

MOUZON, Edwin Du Bose, bp., 1869- 248
The program of Jesus, by Edwin Du Bose Mouzon ... New York, George H. Doran company [c1925] x p., 2 l., [15]-255 p. 20 cm. (Half-title: The Cole lectures for 1925. delivered before Vanderbilt university) [BS2417.S7M7] 26-10483
1. Jesus Christ—Teachings. 2. Sociology, Biblical. I. Title.

ROLSTON, Holmes, 1900- 225.83
The social message of the apostle Paul... by Holmes Rolston... Richmond, Va., John Knox press [1942] 250 p. 19 1/2 cm. (The James Sprunt lectures, 1942) "Delivered at Union theological seminary in Virginia, February 1-7, 1942."--p. [6] Bibliographical references included in "Acknowledgments" (p. [8-10]) [BS2655.S6R6] 42-18314
1. Sociology, Biblical. 2. Bible. N.T. Epistles of Paul—Theology. 3. Bible—Theology—N.T. Epistles of Paul. I. Title.

SCHUMACHER, Henry, 1883- 225.8301
Social message of the New Testament, by H. Schumacher ... Milwaukee, The Bruce publishing company [c1937] xviii, 228 p. 22 cm. (Half-title: Religion and culture series, J. Husslein ... general editor) "Footnotes": p. 217-221. [BS2545.S5S4] 37-9464
1. Sociology, Biblical. 2. Sociology, Christian—Catholic authors. I. Title.

SCOTT, Ernest Findlay, 1868- 225.8301
Man and society in the New Testament, by Ernest F. Scott, D. D. New York, C. Scribner's sons, 1946. viii p., 2 l., 299 p. 21 cm. [BS670.S4] 46-5934
1. Sociology, Biblical. 2. Bible, N.T.—Theology. I. Title.

STEVENS, Rene 220.83
The Bible and today's headlines. New York, Greenwich [1962, c.1961] 56p. 22cm. 61-17973 2.50
1. Sociology, Biblical. I. Title.

STEVENS, Rene. 220.83
The Bible and today's headlines. [1st ed.] New York, Greenwich Book Publishers [c1961] 56 p. 22 cm. [BS670.S7] 61-17973
1. Sociology, Biblical. I. Title.

VOLLMER, Philip, 1860-1929. 232.9
New testament sociology for higher institutions of learning, brotherhoods and advanced Bible classes, by Philip Vollmer ... New York, Chicago [etc.] Fleming H. Revell company [1923] 319 p. 19 cm. "Classified selected bibliography": p. 20-24; "Parallel readings" at the beginning of most of the chapters. [BS2545.85V6] [225.8301] 23-11366
1. Sociology, Biblical. 2. Sociiology, Christian. 3. Jesus Christ—Teachings. I. Title.

Sociology, Biblical—Study and teaching.

SINGER, Richard E 221.8301
If the prophets were alive today; Ruth and Jerry find some answers. New York, Bookman Associates [1957] 191p. illus. 23cm. [BS670.S5] 57-2151
1. Sociology, Biblical—Study and teaching. I. Title.

Sociology, Buddhist—Asia, Southeastern.

SWEARER, Donald K., 1934- 294.3'37
Buddhism and society in southeast Asia / Donald K. Swearer. [Chambersburg, Pa.] : Anima Books, 1981. p. cm. Bibliography: p. [BQ410.S93] 19 81-8048 ISBN 0-89012-023-4 (pbk.) : 3.00
1. Sociology, Buddhist—Asia, Southeastern. 2. Buddhism—Asia, Southeastern. 3. Buddhism—Asia, Southeastern—Audio-visual aids—Catalogs. I. Title.

Sociology, Buddhist—United States.

KASHIMA, Tetsuden. 294.3'0973
Buddhism in America : by Tetsuden Kashima. Tetsuden Kashima. Westport, Conn. : Greenwood Press, 1977. xvii, 272 p., [1] leaf of plates : ill. ; 22 cm. (Contributions in sociology ; no. 26) Includes index. Bibliography: p. 257-264. [BQ8712.9.U6K37] 76-57837 ISBN 0-8371-9534-9 lib.bdg. : 17.50
1. Buddhist Churches of America. 2. Sociology, Buddhist—United States. 3. Japanese in the United States. I. Title.

Sociology, Christain—Study and teaching.

HEISEY, Paul Harold, 1886- 261.07
Studies in social problems, by Paul Harold Heisey and Amos John Traver; prepared under the auspices of the Parish and church school board of the United Lutheran church in America. Philadelphia, Pa., The United Lutheran publication house [c1938] 3, xvi, 5-86 p. illus. 18 cm. On cover: Leader's edition. "Reference books for further reading": p. xii-xvi. [BR115.S6H38] 38-31239
1. Sociology, Christain—Study and teaching. I. Traver, Amos John, 1889- joint author. II. United Lutheran church in America. Parish and church school board. III. Title.

HEISEY, Paul Harold, 1886- 261.07
Studies in social problems, by Paul Harold Heisey and Amos John Traver; prepared under the auspices of the Parish and church school board of the United Lutheran church in America. Philadelphia, Pa., The United Lutheran publication house [c1938] 86 p. illus. 18 cm. On cover: Student's edition. [BR115.S6H37] 38-30367
1. Sociology, Christain—Study and teaching. I. Traver, Amos John, 1889- joint author. II. United Lutheran church in America. Parish and church school board. III. Title.

Sociology, Christian.

ABBOTT, Lyman, 1835-1922. 261.8
Christianity and social problems. With a new introd. by Timothy L. Smith. New York, Johnson Reprint Corp., 1970. xxi, v, 370 p. 19 cm. (Series in American studies) Reprint of the 1896 ed. Includes bibliographical references. [BT738.A2 1970] 70-110386
1. Sociology, Christian. I. Title.

ABBOTT, Lyman, 1835-1922. 261
Christianity and social problems, by Lyman Abbott. Boston and New York, Houghton, Mifflin and company, 1896. v p., 1 l., 370 p. 18 1/2 cm. [BR115.S6A3] 4-3768
1. Sociology, Christian. I. Title.

AINSLIE, Peter, 1867-1934. 265.
Some experiments in living, by Peter Ainslie. New York, Association press, 1933. 6 p. l., 190 p. 19 1/2 cm. [BR115.S6A4] 33-10933
1. Sociology, Christian. I. Title.

[ALLIBONE, Samuel Austin] 265.
1816-1889.
A review, by a layman of a work entitled, "New themes for the Protestant clergy: creeds without charity, theology without humanity, and Protestantism without Christianity.". . Philadelphia, Lippincott, Grambo, and co., 1852. 2 p. l., [13]-139 p. 19 cm. [BR115.86A6] 35-37793
1. Colwell, Stephen, 1800-1871. New themes for the Protestant clergy 2. Sociology, Christian. 3. Charity. I. Title.

AMERICAN Unitarian 261
association. Dept. of social and public service.
Social service series. Bulletin. Boston, American Unitarian association [19 v. 19 cm. [HN37.U5A6] 14-10638
1. Sociology, Christian. 2. Social problems. I. Title.

ANDREEN, Paul Harold, 1891- 261
The clash, by Paul H. Andreen. Minneapolis, Augsburg publishing house, 1938. 3 p. l., 152 p. 20 1/2 cm. "Acknowledgments": p. [149]-152. [BR115.S6A65] 38-7999
1. Sociology, Christian. I. Title.

BAAB, Otto Justice. 232.8
Jesus Christ our Lord [by] Otto Justice Baab. New York, Cincinnati [etc.] The Abingdon press [c1937] 209 p. 20 cm. "A program looking to the Fundamental reorganization of human society and of human nature."--Pref. [BT215.B2] 37-6351
1. Jesus Christ—Divinity. 2. Sociology, Christian. I. Title.

BABSON, Roger Ward, 1875- 261
New tasks for old churches, studies of the industrial community as the new frontier of the church, by Roger W. Babson ... New York, Chicago [etc.] Fleming H. Revell company [c1922] 190 p. illus., fold. diagr. 19 cm. [BV625.B3] 22-26066
1. Sociology, Christian. I. Title.

BABSON, Roger Ward, 1875- 265.
Religion and business, by Roger W. Babson ... New York, The Macmillan company, 1920. 5 p. l., 3-221 p. illus. (incl. map) pl. 19 cm. [BR115.E2B3] 20-20966
1. Sociology, Christian. 2. Churches—U. S. I. Title. II. Title: Business, Religion and.

BABSON, Roger Ward, 1875- 261
Religion and business, by Roger W. Babson ... New York, The Macmillan company, 1922. 5 p. l., 3-221 p. illus. (map) tables. 20 cm. [BR115.E3B3 1922] 41-318245
1. Sociology, Christian. I. Title. II. Title: Business, Religion and.

BAKER, Richard Terrill. 261
The seed and the soil, by Richard Terrill Baker. New York, Friendship press [c1941] ix p., 2 l., [3]-180 p. 20 cm. "Reading list": p. [177]-180. [BR115.S6B27] 41-8452
1. Sociology, Christian. I. Title.

BALCH, William Monroe.
Christianity and the labor movement, by William Monroe Balch ... Boston, Sherman, French & company, 1912. 4 p. l., 196 p. 20 cm. [HD6336.B2] w 13-21182 ISBN 12-21182
1. Sociology, Christian. 2. Labor and laboring classes. I. Title.

BARKER, John Marshall, 1849- 261
The social gospel and the new era, by John Marshall Barker ... New York, The Macmillan company, 1919. ix, [1], 232 p. 19 1/2 cm. Bibliography at end of chapters. [HN31.B15] 19-15521
1. Sociology, Christian. I. Title.

BARNES, Charles Wesley, 1857- 261
Social messages, The new sanctification, by Charles W. Barnes. New York, Cincinnati, The Methodist book concern [c1915] 100 p. ports. 18 1/2 cm. $0.50. [HN31.B17] 15-7308
1. Sociology, Christian. I. Title.
Contents omitted.

BARTLETT, Robert Merrill, 301
1898-
Builders of a new world [by] Robert Merrill Bartlett ... New York, Friendship press [c1933] 5 p. l., 3-166 p. 20 cm. [HN31.B175] 261 33-16563
1. Sociology, Christian. 2. World politics. 3. Missions, Foreign. I. Title.

BATTEN, Samuel Zane, 1859- 261
Building a community, by Samuel Zane Batten ... Philadelphia, Boston [etc] The Judson press [c1922] 167 p. 19 cm. (Half-title: Judson training manuals for the school of the church, ed. by W. E. Raffety, H. E. Tralle, W. E. Chalmers) "References" at end of each chapter. [HN31.B18] 22-25567
1. Sociology, Christian. I. Title.

BATTEN, Samuel Zane, 1859- 261
The new world order, by Samuel Zane Batten ... Philadelphia, Boston [etc.] American Baptist publication society [c1919] 6 p. l., 3-175 p. 18 cm. "References" at end of each chapter. [HN31.B19] 19-4577
1. Sociology, Christian. 2. Reconstruction (1914- I. Title.
Contents omitted.

BATTEN, Samuel Zane, 1859- 261
The new world order, by Samuel Zane Batten ... Philadelphia, Boston [etc.] American Baptist publication society [c1919] 6 p. l., 3-175 p. 18 cm. "References" at end of each chapter. [HN31.B19] 19-4577
1. Sociology, Christian. 2. Reconstruction (1914- I. Title.
Contents omitted.

BATTEN, Samuel Zane, 1859- 261
1925.
The social task of Christianity; a summons to the new crusade, by Samuel Zane Batten ... New York, Chicago [etc.] Flemming H. Revell company [c1911] 234 p. 21 cm. Bibliography at end of each chapter. [HN31.B2] 11-26657
1. Sociology, Christian. I. Title.

BAUM, Gregory, 1923- 301.5'8
The church as institution / edited by Gregory Baum and Andrew Greeley. New York : Herder and Herder, 1974. 160 p. ; 23 cm. (Concilium ; 91) On cover: The New concilium: religion in the seventies. Includes bibliographical references. [BT738.B3] 73-6430 ISBN 0-8164-2575-2 : 3.95
1. Sociology, Christian. I. Greeley, Andrew M., 1928- joint author. II. Title. III. Series: Concilium (New York) ; 91.

BAUM, Gregory, 1923- 261.8
Religion and alienation : a theological reading of sociology / Gregory Baum. New York : Paulist Press, c1975. v, 296 p. ; 23 cm. Includes bibliographies and index. [BT738.B32] 75-28652 ISBN 0-8091-0205-6 : 10.95 ISBN 0-8091-1917-X pbk. : 6.95
1. Sociology, Christian. 2. Alienation (Theology) I. Title.

BEACH, Waldo. 261'.0973
Christian community and American society. Philadelphia, Westminster Press [1969] 190 p. 21 cm. Includes bibliographical references. [BT738.B33] 69-14196 6.00
1. Sociology, Christian. 2. U.S.—Social history—1945- I. Title.

BEATON, David, 1848- 301
Selfhood and serivce; the relation of Christian personality to wealth and social redemption, by David Beaton. Chicago, New York [etc.] Fleming H. Revell company, 1898. 220 p., 1 l. 19 1/2 cm. [BR115.S6B433] 45-53901
1. Sociology, Christian. I. Title.

BELL, Bernard Iddings, 1886- 261
Right and wrong after the war; an elementary consideration of Christian morals in the light of modern social problems, by Bernard Iddings Bell ... Boston and New York, Houghton Mifflin company, 1918. viii p., 2 l., 186, [2] p. 19 cm. [HN31.B4] 18-12013
1. Sociology, Christian. 2. Social problems. 3. European war, 1914-1918—Influence and results. I. Title.

BELL, William Melvin, bp., 261
1860-
The social message of Our Lord, by William Melvin Bell ... Dayton, O., The Otterbein press [c1909] 6 p. l., 181 p. front. (port.) 20 cm. [HN31.B5] 9-20930
1. Sociology, Christian. I. Title.

BENEDICT, Ivan Howland. 261
The great problem, by Ivan Howland Benedict, M. A. Boston, Sherman, French & company, 1911. 4 p. l., 190 p. 21 cm. [HN31.B55] 11-28868 1.00
1. Sociology, Christian. I. Title.
Contents omitted.

BENNETT, John Coleman, 1902- 261
Social salvation; a religious approach to the problems of social change, by John C. Bennett. New York, London, C. Scribner's sons; 1935. xv,, 222 p. 20 cm. [HN31.B56] 35-7655
1. Sociology Christian. I. Title.

BERLE, Adolf Augustus, 1866- 261
Christianity and the social range, by Adolph A. Berle ... New York, McBride, Nast & company, 1914. 6 p. l., 3-389 p. 21 cm. "Several of the closing chapters have appeared in the Bibliotheen sacrs."--Pref. [HN31.B57] 14-18385
1. Sociology, Christian. 2. Social problems. I. Title.
Contents omitted.

BIGELOW, Herbert Seely, 1870- 261
The religion of revolution [by] Herbert S. Bigelow ... Cincinnati, O., D. Kiefer, 1916. 4 p. l., [7]-113 p. front. (port.) pl. 20 cm. [HN31.B64] 17-11723
1. Sociology, Christian. 2. Social problems. I. Title.

BIRCH, Bruce C. 261.8
The predicament of the prosperous / Bruce C. Birch and Larry L. Rasmussen. 1st ed. Philadelphia : Westminster Press, c1978. p. cm. (Biblical perspectives on current issues) Includes index. Bibliography: p. [BT738.B52] 78-18412 ISBN 0-664-24211-1 : 4.95
1. Sociology, Christian. 2. Wealth—Biblical teaching. 3. Human ecology—Moral and religious aspects. 4. Christian ethics. 5. Christianity and economics. I. Rasmussen, Larry L., joint author. II. Title. III. Series.

BLAND, Salem Goldworth, 261'.8
1859-1950.
The new Christianity; or, The religion of the new age. Introd. by Richard Allen. [Toronto, Buffalo] University of Toronto Press [1973] xxvi, 89 p. 22 cm. (The Social history of Canada) "The original edition of the work appeared in 1920." Includes bibliographical references. [BT738.B54 1973] 73-95815 ISBN 0-8020-1954-4 2.50 (pbk.)
1. Sociology, Christian. 2. Church and social problems. I. Title. II. Series.

BODEIN, Vernon Parker. 922.673
The development of the social thought of Walter Rauschenbusch, by Vernon Parker Bodein ... [New York, 1937] 1 p. l., p. 420-431. 24 cm. "Part of a dissertatión entitled 'The relation of the social gospel of Walter Rauschenbusch to religious education' presented to Yale university for the degree of doctor of philosophy [1936]" "Reprinted...from Religion in life, summer issue, 1937." [BX6495.R3B6 1937] 38-8544
1. Rausechenbusch, Walter, 1861-1918. 2. Sociology, Christian. I. Title.

BODEIN, Vernon Parker.
The social gospel of Walter Rauschenbusch and its relation to religious education, by Vernon Parker Bodein. New Haven, Yale university press; London, H.Milford, Oxford university press, 1944. ix p., 1 l., 168, [2] p. 23 1/2 cm. (Half-title: Yale studies in religious education. XVI) Originally the author's thesis (PH.D.) Yale university, 1936; rewritten for this publication. cf. Pref. "The publication of this volume has been aided by the Samuel B. Sneath memorial publication fund." Bibliography: p. [158]-168. A 44
1. Rauschenbusch, Walter, 1861-1918. 2. Sociology, Christian. 3. Religious education. I. Yale university. Samuel B. Sneath memorial publication fund. II. Title.

BOOTH, Henry Kendall, 1876- 261
The Great Galilean returns: a survey of the eclipse and rediscovery of Jesus' gospel of the kingdom, by Henry Kendall Booth. New York, C. Scribner's sons; London, C. Scribner's sons, ltd., 1936. xvi p. 1 l., 218 p. 19 1/2 cm. "A brief list of recommended books": p. 213. [BR115.S6B55] 36-15231
1. Sociology, Christian. 2. Sociology, Christian—Hist. 3. Kingdom of God. I. Title.

BRADFORD, Amory Howe, 1846- 261
1911.
My brother, by Amory H. Bradford ... Boston, New York [etc.] The Pilgrim press [c1910] 1 p. l., v-vii, 282 p. 21 cm. [HN31.B7] 10-28482 1.25
1. Sociology, Christian. I. Title.
Contents omitted.

BROWN, Charles Reynolds, 265.
1862-
The social message of the modern pulpit, by Charles Reynolds Brown... New York, C. Scribner's sons, 1906. ix p., 1 l., 293 p. 20 cm. Delivered at Yale university as the Lyman Beecher lectures for the year 1905-06. cf. Pref. [BR115.S6B7] 6-32406
1. Sociology, Christian. I. Title.

BROWN, William Adams, 1865- 261
Christianity and industry; addresses given to a group of industrial secretaries of the Young women's Christian association, by William Adams Brown... New York, The Womans press, 1919. 58 p. 17 1/2 cm. [HN31.B72] 19-16052
1. Sociology, Christian. I. Title.

BULL, Paul Bertie, 1864- 265.
The economics of the kingdom of God, by Paul B. Bull, C. R. New York, The Macmillan company, 1927. 223, [1] p. 20 cm. Printed in Great Britain. "Some books referred to": p. [224] [BR115.S6B8] 28-28010
1. Sociology, Christian. I. Title.

CAMPBELL, Reginald John, 1867- 261
Christianity and the social order, by R. J. Campbell... New York, The Macmillan company, 1907. xiii, 284 p. 20 cm. [HN31.C2] 7--41762
1. Sociology, Christian. 2. Socialism. I. Title.

CASSERLEY, Julian Victor Langmead, 1909-
Morals and man in the social sciences. London, New York, Longmans, Green [1951] ix, 230 p. 20 cm. A 52
1. Sociology, Christian. 2. Social sciences. I. Title.

CASTLE, Edgar Bradshaw, 1897-
Building the new age, by E. B. Castle ... London, New York [etc.] Rich & Cowan [1945] 156 p. 18 cm. [Needs of to-day series, ed. by W. E. Boardman. 26] Bibliographical foot-notes. A 46
1. Sociology, Christian. I. Title.

CHADWICK, William Edward, 1858- 920.
Social relationships in the light of Christianity (The Hulsean lectures for 1909-1910) by W. Edward Chadwick ... London, New York [etc.] Longmans, Green, and co., 1910. xxi, [1], 344 p. 20 cm. [HN31.C4] 10-15122
1. Sociology, Christian. 2. Social problems. I. Hulsean lectures, 1909-1910. II. Title.

CHADWICK, William Edward, 1858- 920.
Social relationships in the light of Christianity (The Hulsean lectures for 1909-1910) by W. Edward Chadwick ... London, New York [etc.] Longmans, Green, and co., 1910. xxi, [1], 344 p. 20 cm. [HN31.C4] 10-15122
1. Sociology, Christian. 2. Social problems. I. Hulsean lectures, 1909-1910. II. Title.

CHAFFEE, Edmund Bigelow, 1887- 261
The Prostestant churches and the industrial crisis, by Edmund B. Chaffee ... with a foreword by Henry Sloane Coffin. New York, The Macmillan company, 1933. xii p., 2 l., 243 p. 21 cm. [HN39.U6C3] 33-27399
1. Sociology, Christian. 2. Church and labor. 3. Prostestant churches—U. S. I. Title.

CHRISTIAN bases of world order ... by Henry A. Wallace [and others] ... New York, Nashville, Abingdon-Cokesbury press [1943] 255 p. 20 1/2 cm. (The Merrick lectures for 1943) These lectures were a part of the Conference on Christian bases of world order held at Ohio Wesleyan university, Mary 8-12, 1943. cf. Pref. [BR115.S6C49] 43-51138 261
1. Sociology, Christian. 2. Christianity—20th cent. 3. Social problems. I. Wallace, Henry Agard, 1888-
Contents omitted.

CHRISTIAN faith and the common life, by Nils Ehrenstrom, M.F. Dibelius, William Temple [and others] ... Chicago, New York, Willett, Clark & company, 1938. xii, 195 p. 20 1/2 cm. (Half-title: The official Oxford conference books, vol. iv) Contents.Introduction, by Nils Ehrenstrom.--The message of the New Testament [BR115.S6C54] 38-27612 261.082
1. Sociology, Christian. 2. Christian life. 3. Natural law. I. Ehrenstrom, Nils. II. World conference on church, community and state, Oxford, 1937.

THE Christian message for the world today; a joint statement of the world wide mission of the Christian church. New York, Round table press, inc., 1934. 2 p. l., 7-203 p. 19 1/2 cm. A. L. Warnshuls, chairman of the group responsible for the book. [BV2030.C5] 34-3922 266.082
1. Sociology, Christian. 2. Missions, Foreign. I. Warnshuls, Abbe Livingston, 1877-

CHRISTIANITY and social order. [Harmondsworth, Middlesex; Baltimore] Penguin Books [1956] 120p. (Pelican books, A 345) 'First published ... 1942; reprinted ... 1956.'
1. Sociology, Christian. I. Temple, William, Abp. of canterbury, 1881-1944.

CHURCH and Society Study Conference, Chicago, 1961. 261.1
Christian responsibility to society, a Biblical-theological statement. Newton, Kan., Faith and Life Press [1963] 18 p. 23 cm. (Church and society series, no. 2) "Published for the Board of Christian Service of the General Conference Mennonite Church." [BT738.C5] 63-3226
1. Sociology, Christian. I. General Conference Mennonite Church. Board of Christian Service. II. Title.

CLEMENT, Marcel. 261.7
Christ and revolution. Translated from the French by Alice von Hildebrand, with Marilyn Teichert. New Rochelle, N.Y., Arlington House [1974] 123 p. 21 cm. Translation of Le Christ et la revolution. Includes bibliographical references. [BT738.C5513] 74-3060 ISBN 0-87000-233-3 6.95
1. Sociology, Christian. 2. Socialism. I. Title.

COE, George Albert, 1862- 261
What is religion doing to our consciences! By George A. Coe. New York, C. Scribner's sons, 1943. ix p., 1 l., 120 p. 19 1/2 cm. [BR115.S6C58] 43-6711
1. Sociology, Christian. 2. Christianity—20th cent. 3. Christian ethics. I. Title.

COFFIN, Henry Sloane, 1877- 261
... In a day of social rebuilding; lectures on the ministry of the church, by Henry Sloane Coffin ... New Haven, Yale university press [etc.] 1918. 5 p. l., 212 p., 1 l., 20 1/2 cm. (The forty-fourth series of the Lyman Beecher lectureship on preaching in Yale university) [HN31.C55] 18-9504
1. Sociology, Christian. I. Title.

COFFIN, Henry Sloane, 1877- 261
A more Christian industrial order ... by Henry Sloane Coffin ... New York, The Macmillan company, 1920. 3 p. l., 86 p. 19 1/2 cm. [HN31.C57] 20-6208
1. Sociology, Christian. I. Title.

COLLINGS, Lewis Edward. 261
The Christian contract, by Lewis Edward Collings. [New York, Libman's law printery, [c1915] cover-title, 2 p. l., [3]-60 p. 23 cm. [HN31.C6] 15-2858
1. Sociology, Christian. I. Title.
Contents omitted.

COLWELL, Stephen, 1800-1871. 261.8
New themes for the Protestant clergy. New York, Arno Press, 1969. xv, 383 p. 23 cm. (Religion in America) Reprint of the 1851 ed. Includes bibliographical references. [BT38.C65] 71-83417
1. Sociology, Christian. 2. Charity. 3. Protestantism. I. Title.

[COLWELL, Stephen] 1800-1871. 261
New themes for the Protestant clergy; creeds without charity, theology without humanity, and Protestantism without christianity: with notes by the editor on the literature of charity, population, pauperism, political economy, and Protestant. Phildelphia, Lippincott, Grambo & co. 1851. 1 p l., v-xv, 5-382 p. 20 cm. Contain biblographies. [BR115.S6C6] 36-4358
1. Sociology, Christian. 2. Charity. 3. Protestantism. I. Title.

COMMITTEE in the ear and the religious outlook. 261
The church and industrial reconstruction. The Committee on the war and the religious outlook. New York, Association press, 1920. viii, 296 p. 22 cm. "Selected bibliography": p. 237-286 [HN31.C62] 20-15930
1. Sociology, Christian. 2. Labor and laboring classes-1914- 3. Reconstruction (1914-) I. Title.

COMMITTEE on the war and the religious outlook. 261
The church and industrial reconstruction, the Committee on the war and the religious outlook. New York, Association press, 1921. viii, 290 p. 19 cm. "Selected bibliography": p. 273-286. [HN31.C62 1921] 26-10197
1. Sociology, Christian. 2. Labor and laboring classes—1914— 3. Reconstruction (1914-1939) I. Title.

COMMONS, John Rogers, 1862- 304
Social reform and the church, by John R. Commons ... With an introduction by Prof. Richard T. Ely. New York, T. Y. Crowell & company [1894] x, 176 p. 17 cm. [HN31.G63] 4-3769
1. Sociology, Christian. I. Title.

CONANT, Judson E. 261
The growing menace of the "social gospel," by J. E. Conant ... Chicago, The Bible institute colportage ass'n [c1937] 72 p. 18 1/2 cm. [BR115.S6C63] 43-19988
1. Sociology, Christian. 2. Christianity—20th cent. I. Bible institute colportage association, Chicago. II. Title.

CONFERENCE on Christian politics, economics and citizenship. Commission on the social function of the church. 301.58
The social function of the church; being the report presented to the Conference on Christian politics, economics and citizenship at Birmingham, April 5-12, 1924. London, New York [etc.] Published for the conference committee by Longmans, Green and col. 1924. xii, 265, [1] p. 18 1/2 cm. (Half-title: C.O.P.E.C. commission reports. vol. XI) "Third impression, November 1924." The Rt. Rev. the Lord Bishop of Lichfield (Dr. Kempthorne) chairman. Bibliographies; p. 230-234. [H N30. C6 vol. xi b] 25-9584
1. Sociology, Christian 2. Christianity. 3. Missions. I. Title.

CONSTANT, Alphonse Louis, 1810-1875. 232.993
The last incarnation. Gospel legends of the nineteenth century. By A. Constant. Translated by Francis Geo. Shaw. Boston, W. D. Ticknor & co., 1848. 93 p. 18 1/2 cm. [BT309.C7 1848] 35-30466
1. Jesus Christ—Fiction. 2. Sociology, Christian. I. Shaw, Francis George, 1809-1882, tr. II. Title.

CONSTANT, Alphonse Louis, 1810-1875. 232.993
The last incarnation. Gospel legends of the nineteenth century. By A. Constant. Translated by Francis Geo. Shaw. New York, W. H. Graham, 1848. 93 p. 18 cm. [BT309.C7 1848 a] 35-37075
1. Jesus Christ—Fiction. 2. Sociology, Christian. I. Shaw, Francis George, 1809-1882, tr. II. Title.

CONSTANT, Alphonse Louis, 1810-1875. 232.993
The last incarnation. Springfield, Ill., C. Kohlman [c1878] cover-title, 60 p. 23 cm. Translated by F. G. Shaw. [BT309.C7 1878] 35-32349
1. Jesus Christ—Fiction. 2. Sociology, Christian. I. Shaw, Francis George, 1809-1882, tr. II. Title.

CONSTANT, Alphonse Louis, 1810-1875. 232.99
The last incarnation, translated from the French of A. Constant. Boston, The Gorham press; Toronto, The Copp Clark co., limited [c1914] 6 p. l., 9-171 p. 19 1/2 cm. "Third American edition." Preface signed: Charles H. Kohlman. "The phraseology of the first English edition [translated by F. G. Shaw] has been substantially retained."--Pref. [BT309.C7 1914] 30-83468
1. Jesus Christ—Fiction. 2. Sociology, Christian. I. Shaw, Francis George, 1809-1882, tr. II. Kohlman, Charles H. III. Title.

COUGHLIN, Charles E. 261
Father Coughlin, selected discourses. [Philadelphia, Educational guild, c1932] cover-title, vi, [7]-62 p. 21 cm. [HN37.C3C6] 32-19176
1. Sociology, Christian. I. Educational guild. II. Title.
Contents omitted.

COVERT, William Chalmers, 1864- 261
Facing our day [by] William Chalmers Covert. New York, Cincinnati [etc.] The Abingdon press [c1934] 132 p. 20 cm. Bibliography: p. 176-188. [BR479.C6] 34-3920
1. Sociology, Christian. I. Title.

CRAFTS, Wilbur Fisk, 1850-1922. 261
Familiar talks on that boy and girl of yours; sociology from viewpoint of the family, by Wilbur F. Crafts ... introduced by Rev Robert Watson, D. D. New York, The Baker & Taylor co.[c1922] 432 p. illus. 20 cm. [HN31.C7] 22-25565
1. Sociology, Christian. I. Title. II. Title: That boy and girl of yours. Familiar talks on.

CRAIG, Archibald Gordon, 1873- 248
Two masters. The teaching of Jesus considered as a contribution to sociology, by Archibald Gordon Craig. Jersey City, N. J., A Craig [1931] 1 p. l., [5]-89 p. 18 cm. [BS2417.S7C7] 232 38-14602
1. Jesus Christ—Teachings. 2. Sociology, Christian. I. Title.

CRIPPS, Richard Stafford, Sir, 1889- 261
Towards Christian democracy, by Stafford Cripps. New York, Philosophical library [1946] 4 p. l., 101 p. 22 1/2 cm. First published in London in 1945. [BR115.S6C77 1946] 47-170
1. Sociology, Christian. 2. Christianity—20th cent. I. Title.

CRIPPS, Richard Stafford, Sir, 1889-1952. 261
Towards Christian democracy. Westport, Conn., Greenwood Press [1970, c1945] 90 p. 23 cm. [BT738.C73 1970] 76-100226
1. Sociology, Christian. 2. Christianity—20th century. I. Title.

CUNNINGHAM, William, 1849-1919. 265.
Christianity and politics, by William Cunningham ... Boston, and New York, Houghton Mifflin company, 1915. x, [1] 270, [2] p. 21 cm. Lowell lectures delivered in the autumn of 1914, revised for publication. cf. Pref. Appendix: The attitude of the church towards war: p. 249-[263] [BR115.P7C8] 15-2766
1. Sociology, Christian. 2. Church and state. 3. Church and state in Great Britain. 4. War. I. Title. II. Title: Lowell institute lectures, 1914.

DAIM, Wilfried. 261.7
Christianity, Judaism, and revolution. Translated by Peter Tirner. New York, Ungar [1973] ix, 181 p. 22 cm. Translation of Christentum und Revolution. [BT738.D313] 73-163148 ISBN 0-8044-5266-0 7.50
1. Sociology, Christian. 2. Revolution (Theology) I. Title.

DAVIS, Jerome, 1891- ed. 265.
Christianity and social adventuring, edited and with an introduction by Jerome Davis. New York & London, The Century co. [c1927] xii, 373 p. 21 cm. [BR115.S6D3] 27-23321 2.50
1. Sociology, Christian. I. Title.

DAWSON, Joseph Martin, 1879- 261
Christ and social change, by Joseph Martin Dawson ... Philadelphia, Boston [etc.] The Judson press [1937] 6 p. l., 3-222 p. 20 cm. "Published, September 1937." [BR115.S6D33] 37-29119
1. Sociology, Christian. I. Title.

DEANE, Herbert Andrew, 1921- 261.8
The political and social ideas of St. Augustine. NewYork, Columbia [1966, c.1963] 356p. 21cm. (Columbia paperback, 69) [BR65.A9D4] 63-9809 2.45 pap.,
1. Augustinus. Aurelius. Saint, Bp. of Hippo—Sociology. 2. Sociology, Christian. I. Title.

DEANE, Herbert Andrew, 1921- 261.8
The political and social ideas of St. Augustine. New York, Columbia University Press, 1963. 356 p. 28 cm. [BR65.A9D4] 63-9809
1. Augustinus, Aurelius, Saint, Bp. of

Hippo — Sociology. 2. Sociology, Christian. I. Title.

DEMANT, Vigo Auguste, 1893- 261
God, man and society; an introduction to Christian sociology, by V. A. Demant ... with foreword by Julian D. Hamlin ... Milwaukee, Wis., Morehouse publishing co. [1934] xii p., 2 l., [3]-288, [1] p. 19 cm. "First American edition." [BR115.S6D35] 34-19313
1. Sociology, Christian. I. Title.

DICKINSON, Charles Henry, 1857- 265.
The religion of the social passion, by Charles Henry Dickinson ... Chicago, The Christian century press, 1923. 4 p. l., 11-248 p. 20 cm. [BR115.S6D45] 24-8052
1. Sociology, Christian. 2. Humanism—20th cent. I. Title. II. Title: Social passion, The religion of the.

DIFFENDORFER, Ralph Eugene, 1879- 261
The church and the community, by Ralph E. Diffendorfer ... New York city, Council of women for home missions and Interchurch world movement of North America [c1920] xii, 177 p. illus. (incl. plan) diagrs. 20 cm. Bibliography: p. 175-177. [HN31.D5] 20-8654
1. Sociology, Christian. I. Title.

DOUDS, William S. 231.7
"Thy kingdom come ... Why now now?" or, "The kingdom of God," by William S. Douds. Introduction by E. Stanley Jones. [Greenville, Pa., The Beaver press, 1942] x p., 1 l., 287, [3] p. diagr. 20 cm. "Second printing, 1942." [BT94.D6 1942] 43-18217
1. Sociology, Christian. 2. Kingdom of God. I. Title.

EARP, Edwin Lee, 1867- 261
The rural church serving the community, by Edwin L. Earp ... New York, Cincinnati, The Abingdon press [c1918] 144 p. 19 1/2 cm. Bibliography: p. 141-142. [BV638.E3] 18-16973
1. Sociology, Christian. 2. Farm life. 3. Rural churches. I. Title.

EARP, Edwin Lee, 1867- 261
Social aspects of religious institutions, by Edwin L. Earp ... New York, Eaton & Mains; Cincinnati, Jennings & Graham [c1908] xii, 152 p. 19 1/2 cm. Bibliography: p. 140-150. [HN31.E15] 8-2648
1. Sociology, Christian. I. Title.

EARP, Edwin Lee, 1867- 261
The social engineer, by Edwin L. Earp ... New York, Eaton & Mains; Cincinnati, Jennings & Graham [c1911] xxiii, 326 p. 20 1/2 cm. [HN31.E3] 11-10649
1. Sociology, Christian. 2. Social problems. I. Title.

[EASTMAN, Fred, 1886- 261
Fear God in your own village, by Richard Morse [pseud.] New York, H. Holt and company, 1918. 4 p. l., 212 p. 19 1/2 cm. [BV638.E35] 18-6438
1. Sociology, Christian. I. Title.

EDDY, George Sherwood, 1871- 265.
Religion and social justice, by Sherwood Eddy. New York, George H. Doran company [c1927] vi p., 1 l., 9-219 p. 20 cm. Bibliographical foot-notes. [BR115.S6E15] 28-716
1. Sociology, Christian. 2. U.S.—Soc. condit. 3. Social problems. I. Title.

EDDY, George Sherwood, 1871-
...Religion and social justice, by Sherwood Eddy. New York, George H. Doran company [c1927] 96 p. 19 1/2 cm. (Christianity and industry. no. 12) "This special edition has been made for wide distribution. A library edition is also printed in 215 pages." A28
1. Sociology, Christian. 2. U. S.—conditions. 3. Social problems. I. Title.

EDDY, George Sherwood, 1871- 261
Revolutionary Christianity, by Sherwood Eddy. Chicago, New York, Willett, Clark & company, 1939. x, 229 p. 20 1/2 cm. "Notes" at end of each chapter. [BR115.S6E17] 39-27588
1. Sociology, Christian. I. Title.

ELIOT, Thomas Stearns 261.83
Christianity and culture: The idea of a Christian society and Notes toward the definition of culture. New York, Harcourt, Brace [1960, c.1940, 1949] 202p. 21cm. (A Harvest book, HB32) 60-1931 1.95 pap.,
1. Sociology, Christian. 2. Culture. I. Title.

ELLWOOD, Charles Abram, 1873- 265.
Christianity and social science; a challenge to the church by Charles A. Ellwood ... New York, The Macmillan company, 1923. x, 220 p. 20 cm. "A sequel to The reconstruction of religion."--Pref. "Suggested readings" at end of each chapter. [BR115.S6E3] 23-12637
1. Sociology, Christian. I. Title.

ELLWOOD, Charles Abram, 1873- 265.
The reconstruction of religion; a sociological view, by Charles A. Ellwood ... New York, The Macmillan company, 1922. xv, p., 1 l., 323 p. 20 1/2 cm. [BR115.S6E85] 22-7867
1. Sociology, Christian. I. Title.

ELLWOOD, Charles Abram, 1873- 261
The reconstruction of religion; a sociological view, by Charles A. Ellwood ... New York, The Macmillan company, 1923. xv, [2], 337 p. 20 cm. "A selected list of books in English suggested for collateral reading": p. 319-324. [BR115.S6E35 1923] 41-31825
1. Sociology, Christian. I. Title.

ELLWOOD, Charles Abram, 1873- 261
The world's need of Christ, by Charles A. Ellwood ... with a foreword by Samuel McCrea Cavert ... New York, Nashville, Abingdon-Cokesbury press [c1940] 237 p. 20 1/2 cm. "Suggestions for further reading": p. 233-234. [BR115.S6E37] 40-27866
1. Sociology, Christian. I. Title.

FELTON, Ralph Almon, 1882- F35
... Adventures in service; a study of the rural and small town Epworth league and its community, by Ralph A. Felton ... New York, Cincinnati [etc.] The Methodist book concern [c1928] 96 p. 19 1/2 cm. (Christian comradeship series, W. E. J. Gratz, editor) "Approved by the Committee on curriculum of the Board of education of the Methodist Episcopal church." On cover: Adventures in service in villages and the open country. [HN31] ISBN 28-18295
1. Sociology, Christian. 2. Country life—U.S. 3. Social service. 4. Epworth league. I. Title.

FERGUSON, Charles, 1863- 261
The religion of democracy; a memorandum of modern principles, by Charles Ferguson. New York and London, Funk & Wagnalls company, 1900. iv p. 1 l., 7-170 p. 19 1/2 cm. Another edition (San Francisco, D. P. Elder) has title: The religion of democracy; a manual of devotion. [HN31.F4 1900 a] 1-29482
1. Sociology, Christian. 2. Social problems. 3. Democracy. I. Title.

FERRE, Nels Fredrick Solomon, 1908- 261
Christianity and society. [1st ed.] New York, Harper [1950] viii, 280 p. 22 cm. (His Reason and the Christian faith, v. 8) Bibliographical footnotes. [BR115.S6F44] 50-6197
1. Sociology, Christian. I. Title.

FERRE, Nels Fredrick Solomon, 1908- 261
Christianity and society, by Nels F. S. Ferre. Freeport, N.Y., Books for Libraries Press [1970, c1950] viii, 280 p. 23 cm. (Essay index reprint series) "Originally published as volume III of [the author's] Reason and the Christian faith series." Includes bibliographical references. [BT738.F47 1970] 78-117791
1. Sociology, Christian. I. Title.

FISCHER, Emil Eisenhardt, 1882- 261
Social problems; the Christian solution [by] E.E. Fischer ... Philadelphia, Pa., The United Lutheran publication house [c1927] 187 p. 19 1/2cm. Bibliography: p. 183-187. [HN31.F46] 28-1271
1. Sociology, Christian. I. Title.

FORBES, Elmer Severance, ed. 261
Social ideals of a free church, ed. by Elmer Severance Forbes. Boston, American Unitarian association, 1913. 3 p. l., 139 p. 19 cm. "This volume contains a number of the papers and addresses delivered at a conference held in Boston under the auspices of the Department of social and public service of the American Unitarian association."-- Introd. [HN31.F6] 14-30275
1. Sociology, Christian. I. American Unitarian association. Dept. of social and public service. II. Title.

[FRASER, Alexander N] 1880- 261
The social gospel and the Bible; a business man turns to his Bible to learn the truth concerning the social gospel ... Pittsburgh, Pa., Printed for free distribution by the author, 1939. 84 p. 15 cm. On cover: By Alexander Fraser. [BR115.S6F67] 42-28773
1. Sociology, Christian. I. Title.

FREMANTLE, William Henry, 1831-1916. 265.
Christian ordinances and social progress; being the William Belden Noble lectures for 1900, by the Hon. and Very Rev. William Henry Fremantle ... Boston and New York, Houghton, Mifflin and company, 1901. xvi p., 1 l., 278 p., 1 l. 20 cm. [BR115.S6F7] 1-31619
1. Sociology, Christian. 2. Church polity. I. Title.

FRIESEN, Gerhard, 1886-
The significance of the principle of self-sacrifice for a Christian social order. Newton,Kansas, Howard Schrag Mimeograph Service, 1961. 112 p. front. 21 cm. Includes bibliography.
1. Sociology, Christian. 2. Christian — societies. I. Title.

FRIESEN, Gerhard, 1886-
The significance of the principle of self-sacrifice for a Christian social order. Newton,Kansas, Howard Schrag Mimeograph Service, 1961. 112 p. front. 21 cm. Includes bibliography. 64-27080
1. Sociology, Christian. 2. Christian — societies. I. Title. II. Title: Christian social order.

GARDNER, Charles Spurgeon, 1859- 261
The ethics of Jesus and social progress, by Charles S. Gardner ... New York, George H. Doran company, Hodder & Stoughton [c1914] 361 p. 19 1/2 cm. Bibliography: p. 357-361. [HN31.G2] 14-6852
1. Jesus Christ—Ethics. 2. Sociology, Christian. 3. Christian ethics. I. Title.

GARVIE, Alfred Ernest, 1861- 261
Can Christ save society? [By] A. E. Garvie ... New York, Cincinnati [etc.] The Abingdon press [c1933] 244 p. 18 1/2 cm. [BR115.S6G3 1933a] 33-37666
1. Sociology, Christian. I. Title.

GILBERT, Charles Kendall, 1878-
The social opportunity of the churchman, by Charles K. Gilbert ... and Charles N. Lathrop ... New York, Presiding bishop and council [1922] 2 p. l., 107 p. 19 cm. First published 1921. A 23
1. Sociology, Christian. I. Lathrop, Charles Mewton, 1871- joint author. II. Title.

GILBREATH, Joseph Earl. 261
Individual worth in a social crisis, by J. Earl Gilbreath ... introduction by Norman E. Richardson. New York [etc.] Fleming H. Revell company [c1938] 128 p. 19 1/2 cm. [BR115.S6G47] 39-2570
1. Sociology, Christian. I. Title.

GILL, Eric, 1882-1940.
Christianity and the machine age, by Eric Gill. London, The Sheldon press; New York, The Macmillan company [1940] vii, [1], 72 p. 19 cm. (Half-title: The Christian news-letter books, no. 6) [Full name: Arthur Eric Rowton Peter Joseph Gill] A 42
1. Sociology, Christian. I. Title.

GLADDEN, Washington, 1836-1918. 261.8'3
Applied Christianity : moral aspects of social questions / Washington Gladden. New York : Arno Press, 1976 [c1886] 320 p. ; 21 cm. (Social problems and social policy—the American experience) Reprint of the ed. published by Houghton, Mifflin, Boston. [HN31.G54 1976] 75-17224 ISBN 0-405-07494-8 : 18.00
1. Sociology, Christian. I. Title. II. Series.

GLADDEN, Washington, 1836-1918. 261
Applied Christianity; moral aspects of social questions, by Washington Gladden. Boston and New York, Houghton, Mifflin and company, 1886. 2 p. l., 320 p. 18 cm. [HN31.G54] 8-36961
1. Sociology, Christian. I. Title.

GLADDEN, Washington, 1836-1918. 261
Applied Christianity: moral aspects of social questions, by Washington Gladden. Boston and New York, Houghton, Mifflin and company [190-?] 2 p. l., 320 p. 18 cm. [HN31.G56] 4-5617
1. Sociology, Christian. I. Title.

GLADDEN, Washington, 1836-1918. 261.8'3
Social salvation / Washington Gladden. Reprint ed. with a new introd. Hicksville, N.Y. : Regina Press, 1975, c1902. 5, v, 240 p. ; 23 cm. Reprint of the ed. published by Houghton Mifflin, Boston, which was issued as the 1902 Lyman Beecher lecture. Contents.Contents.—Religion and the social question.—The care of the poor.—The state and the unemployed.—Our brothers in bonds.—Social vices.—Public education.—The redemption of the city. Bibliography: p. [237]-240. [HN31.G65 1975] 74-78270 ISBN 0-88271-008-7
1. Sociology, Christian. 2. Social ethics. I. Title. II. Series: Lyman Beecher lectures ; 1902.

GLADWIN, John W. 261.8
God's people in God's world : Biblical motives for social involvement / John Gladwin's. Downers Grove, Ill. : InterVarsity Press, c1979, 1980 printing. 191 p. : 21 cm. [BT738.G527] 19 80-7726 ISBN 0-87784-607-3 (pbk.) : 5.95
1. Sociology, Christian. 2. Christianity and politics. I. Title.

GLOCK, Charles Y. 261
To comfort and to challenge: a dilemma of the contemporary church, by Charles Y. Glock, Benjamin B. Ringer [and] Earl R. Babbie. Berkeley, University of California Press, 1967. 268 p. 24 cm. Based on research done in 1952 by the Bureau of Applied Social Research of Columbia University for the Dept. of Christian Social Relations of the National Council of the Protestant Episcopal Church. Bibliographical footnotes. [BT738.G54] 67-15560
1. Sociology, Christian. 2. U.S. — Religion. I. Ringer, Benjamin Ber4ard, 1920- joint author. II. Babbie, Earl R., Joint author. III. Columbia University. Bureau of Applied Social Research. IV. Protestant Episcopal Church in the U.S.A. National Council. Dept. of Christian Social Relations. V. Title.

GORE, Charles, bp. of Oxford, 1853-1932. 265.
Christ and society ... by Charles Gore ... New York, C. Scribner's sons, 1928. 7 p. l., 218 p. 21 cm. (Halley Stewart lectures, 1927) [BR115.S6G6 1928a] 28-21925
1. Jesus Christ—Social teachings. 2. Sociology, Christian. I. Title.

GRAY, Arthur Herbert, 1868- 261
The one way of hope, an appeal to men and women in the twenties, by A. Herbert Gray. New York Cincinnati [etc.] The Abingdon press, 1937. ix, 11-167, [1] p. 19 cm. "Made in Great Britain." [HN31.G78] 38-5163
1. Sociology, Christian. 2. Christianity—20th cent. I. Title.

GREEVER, Walton Harlowe, 1870- 261
Human relationships and the church, by W. H. Greever ... New York [etc.] Fleming H. Revell company [c1939] 96 p. 20 cm. [BR115.S6G7] 39-32150
1. Sociology, Christian. I. Title.

GROUNDS, Vernon C. 261.8'3
Evangelicalism and social responsibility, by Vernon C. Grounds. Scottdale, Pa., Herald Press [1969] 39 p. 20 cm. (Focal pamphlet no. 16) "This paper was read at the Evangelicals in Social Action Peace Witness Seminar held at Eastern Mennonite College, Harrisonburg, Virginia, November 30, 1967." Bibliographical

references included in "Footnotes" (p. 39) [BT738.G75] 79-4724 0.50 (pbk)
1. Sociology, Christian. 2. Evangelicalism. I. Title.

GUSTAFSON, James M. 241
The church as moral decision-maker [by] James M. Gustafson. Philadelphia, Pilgrim Press [1970] 163 p. 22 cm. Includes bibliographical references. [BT738.G85] 74-124454 5.95
1. Sociology, Christian. 2. Church. 3. Christian ethics. I. Title.

GUTIERREZ, Gustavo, 1928- 201'.1
A theology of liberation: history, politics, and salvation. Translated and edited by Sister Caridad Inda and John Eagleson. Maryknoll, N.Y., Orbis Books, 1973. xi, 323 p. 22 cm. Includes bibliographical references. [BT738.G8613] 72-85790 4.95
1. Sociology, Christian. 2. Theology—20th century. 3. Christianity—Latin America. I. Title.

HAHN, Herman J. 1888- 335.7
"He stirreth up the people", the social implications of the teachings of Jesus, by Herman J. Hahn. Buffalo, N.Y., Salem evangelical brotherhood [c1931] 217 p. front., (port) illus. 19 cm. "Collection of....radio sermons."--Foreword. [HN31.H25] 31-16155
1. Sociology, Christian. I. Title.

HALL, Thomas Cuming, 1858- 261
Social solutions in the light of Christian ethics, by Thomas C. Hall ... New York, Eaton & Mains; Cincinnati, Jennings & Graham c1910. 2 p. l., 3-390 p. 20 1/2 cm. $1.50 "Selected bibliography": p. 369-384. [HN31.H3] 10-3642
1. Sociology, Christian. I. Title.

HALL, Volton, 1854- 220
Things as they are, by Bolton Hall...with an introduction by G. D. Herron. Boston, Small, Maynard & company, 1899. xvii, 292 p. 17 1/2 cm. [BR125.H8] 99-4920
1. Sociology, Christian. I. Title.

HARLAN, Rolvix, 1876- 261
Brotherhood & civilisation, by Rolvix Harlan ... delivered in Liverpool, September 19, 1921. London, New York [etc.] Hodder and Stoughton ltd. [1921] 159, [1] p. 19 cm. (The John Clifford lecture for 1921) [HN31.H33] 23-10922
1. Sociology, Christian. I. Title.

HARRIS, Samuel Smith, bp., 1841-1888. 200
... The relation of Christianity to civil society, by Samuel Smith Harris ... Delivered in the church of the Holy Trinity, Philadelphia, in advent, 1882. New York, T. Whittaker, 1883. 222 p. 19 1/2 cm. (The Bohlen lectures, 1882) [BR115.S6H35] 43-1035
1. Sociology, Christian. I. Title.

HENDERSON, Charles Richmond, 1848-1915. 261
Social duties from the Christian point of view; a textbook for the study of social problems, by Charles Richmond Henderson ... Chicago, The University of Chicago press, 1909. xiii, 332 p. 19 1/2 cm. (Half title: Constructive Bible studies, ed. by E. De W. Burton. [Advanced and supplemetary series]) Series title also on t.p. "References to literature" at end of chapters. [HN31.H4] 9-8935
1. Sociology, Christian. I. Title.

HENRY, Carl Ferdinand Howard, 1913- 261
Aspects of Christian social ethics [by] Carl F. H. Henry. Grand Rapids, W. B. Eerdmans Pub. Co. [1964] 190 p. 22 cm. (The Payton lectures, 1963) Bibliographical footnotes. [BT38.H4] 63-20686
1. Sociology, Christian. I. Title. II. Series.

HERRON, George Davis, 1862-1925. 261
The Christian society. With a new introd. by Milton Cantor. New York, Johnson Reprint Corp., 1969. xxix, 158 p. 18 cm. (Series in American studies) Reprint of the 1894 ed. Bibliography: p. xxviii-xxix. [BT738.H45 1969] 78-79659
1. Sociology, Christian. 2. Social gospel. I. Title. II. Series.

HERRON, George Davis, 1862-1925. 261
The Christian society, by George D. Herron ... Chicago New York [etc.] F. H. Revell company, 1894. 158 p. 19 cm. "Excepting the fourth, the following chapters were ... a course of lectures to the students of Michigan university ... The fourth chapter was spoken to the Congregational club of Minnesota."--Pref. [HN31.H54] A 13
1. Sociology, Christian. I. Title.
Contents omitted.

HERRON, George Davis, 1862-1925. 261
The Christian state; a political vision of Christ. A course of six lectures delivered in churches in various American cities. By George D. Herron ... New York, Boston, T. Y. Crowell & co. [c1895] 216 p. 17 cm. [HN31.H48] 18-21986
1. Sociology, Christian. I. Title.

HERRON, George Davis, 1862-1925. 261
The new redemption. A call to the church to reconstruct society according to the gospel of Christ. By George D. Herron ... New York, Boston, T. Y. Crowell & company [c1893] 176 p. 18 cm. [HN31.H5] 9-3807
1. Sociology, Christian. I. Title.

HIGH, Stanley, 1895- 261
... Today's youth and tomorrow's world. New York, Friendship press [c1933] 4 p. l., 3-186 p. 20 cm. [HN31.H55] 33-17428
1. Sociology, Christian. 2. Youth. I. Title.

HOBSON, John Atkinson, 1858- 261
God and mammon; the relations of religion and economics, by J. A. Hobson. New York, The Macmillan company [1931] vi, 58 p. 19 1/2 cm. "Printed in Great Britain." Published also as no. 13 of the Forum series. [BR115.E3H6] 32-88
1. Sociology, Christian. 2. Social ethics. I. Title.

HODGKIN, Henry Theodore, 1877- 261
Personality and progress, by Henry T. Hodgkin ... Garden City, N.Y., Doubleday, Doran & company, inc., 1929. 178 p. 19 cm. Printed in Great Britain. [HN31.H6] 29-12603
1. Sociology, Christian. I. Title.

HODGKIN, Henry Theodore, 1877-1933 265.
... The Christian revolution; an essay on the method of social progre s by Henry T. Hodgkin ... New York, George H. Doran company [1923] 316 p. 19 1/2 cm. (Half-title: Christian revolution series, no. 17) [BR115.S6H6] 23-6999
1. Sociology, Christian. 2. Movement towards a Christian international. I. Title.

HOLT, Arthur Erastus. 265.
Christian fellowship and modern industry, by Arthur E. Holt. Boston, Chicago, The Pilgrim press [c1923] 2 p. l., 55 p. diagr. 20 cm. (Discussion outlines for fellowship courses) [BR115.S6H7] 23-12638
1. Sociology, Christian. 2. Industry. I. Title.

HOLT, Arthur Erastus. 250
Social work in the churches; a study in the practice of fellowship, by Arthur E. Holt. Prepared for the Educational committee of the Commission on the church and social service of the Federal council of the churches of Christ in America. Boston, Chicago, The Pilgrim press [c1922] 5 p. l., [3]-131 p. 21 1/2 cm. "Directory of social service agencies": p. [129]-131. [BV4400.H6] 22-18109
1. Sociology, Christian. 2. Church work. I. Federal council of the churches of Christ in America. Educational committee. II. Title.

HOWERTON, James Robert, 1861- 261
The church and social reforms, by James R. Howerton ... with an introduction by Rev. J. Preston Searle ... New York, Chicago [etc.] Fleming H. Revell company [c1913] 127 p. 19 1/2 cm. $0.75 "This little book is the outcome of lectures delivered by the writer." [HN31.H7] 13-12617
1. Sociology, Christian. I. Title.

HOWERTON, James Robert, 1861- 261
The church and social reforms, by James R. Howerton ... with an introduction by Rev. J. Preston Searle ... New York, Chicago [etc.] Fleming H. Revell company [c1913] 127 p. 20 cm. "This little book is the outcome of lectures delivered by the writer." [HN31.H7] 13-12617 0.75
1. Sociology, Christian. I. Title.

HUNTING, Harold Bruce, 1879- 261
Your world and how to live in it; pupil's work book (grades nine and ten) [by] Harold B. Hunting. With drawings by Janice Newton. New York, Cincinnati [etc.] The Abingdon press [c1938] 123 p. illus. 19 cm. (Half-title: The Abingdon religious education texts; John W. Langdale, general editor. Guides to Christian living; Paul H. Vieth, editor) [HN31.H78] A 41
1. Sociology, Christian. 2. Religious education—Text-books for children. I. Title.

HUNTING, Harold Bruce, 1879- 261
Your world and how to live in it: teacher's guide and general resource book [by] Harold B. Hunting. New York, Cincinnati [etc.] The Abingdon press [c1938] 146 p. 20 cm. (Half-title: The Abingdon religious education texts; J. W. Langsdale, general editor. Guides to Christian living; P. H. Vieth, editor) "For further reading" at end of most of the chapters. [HN31.H79] 38-13661
1. Sociology, Christian. I. Title.

HUTCHINS, Grace, 1885- 265.
Jesus Christ and the world today, by Grace Hutchins and Anna Rochester. New York, George H. Doran company [c1922] 149 p. 20 cm. Bibliography in "Suggestions for study groups": p. 145-149. [BR115.S6H8] 22-14834
1. Sociology, Christian. I. Rochester, Anna, 1880- joint author. II. Title.

HUTCHINSON, Paul, 1890- 261
The ordeal of western religion, by Paul Hutchinson. Boston and New York, Houghton Mifflin company, 1933. xiv p., 1 l., 139 p. 20 cm. [BR115.S6H83] 33-24463
1. Sociology, Christian. 2. Christianity. I. Title.

HUTCHINSON, Paul, 1890- 261
... World revolution and religion [by] Paul Hutchinson. New York, Cincinnati [etc.] The Abingdon press [c1931] 201 p. 21 cm. (The Abingdon religious education monographs, J. W. Langdale, general editor) "A reading list": p. 199-201. [BR115.S6H85] 31-8066
1. Sociology, Christian. 2. Revolutions. 3. Religion. I. Title.

INGE, William Ralph, 1830- 261
The social teaching of the church [by] W. R. Inge ... New York, Cincinnati [etc.] The Abingdon press [c1930] iii p. 20 cm. [The Beckly social service lecture] [BR115.S6 I 5 1930 a] 30-24939
1. Sociology, Christian. I. Title.

JENKINS, James Harvey, 1847- 204
Free land and fire from the altar; or, The four great earthly powers, the laws, logic, sentiments and physical works of men overtaken by the scorching truth and light of divine revelation. Written by J. H. Jenkins ... Thomasville, Ga., Davis & Cox, printers, 1902. 4 p. l., 108 p. 18 1/2 cm. Pages 105-108 duplicated. [BR126.J36] 3-16398
1. Sociology, Christian. I. Title.

JOHNSON, Frederick Ernest, 1884- 261
The church and society, [by] F. Ernest Johnson. New York, Cincinnati [etc.] The Abingdon press [c1935] 224 p. 20 cm. [HN31.J6] 35-2822
1. Sociology, Christian. I. Title.

JOHNSON, Frederick Ernest, 1884- 261
The social gospel re-examined, by F. Ernest Johnson. New York and London, Harper & brothers, [c1940] 6 p. l., 261 p. 20 cm. (Rauchenbusch lectures, Colgate-Rochester divinity schools, Rochester, New York) "First edition." [BR115.S6J615] 40-34183
1. Sociology, Christian. 2. Theology, Doctrinal—Addresses, essays lectures. I. Title.

KELLEY, Dean M. 261
Why conservative churches are growing; a study in sociology of religion [by] Dean M. Kelley. [1st ed.] New York, Harper & Row [1972] xiii, 184 p. illus. 22 cm. Includes bibliographical references. [BT738.K38] 77-175156 6.95
1. Sociology, Christian. 2. Church growth. I. Title.

KELLEY, Dean M. 261
Why conservative churches are growing : a study in sociology of religion / Dean M. Kelley. New and updated ed. New York : Harper & Row, c1977. p. cm. Includes bibliographical references and index. [BT738.K38 1977] 77-20337 ISBN 0-06-064301-3 pbk. : 3.95
1. Sociology, Christian. 2. Church growth. I. Title.

KELLEY, James Prentice, 1849- 261
The economics of Christianity [by] James P. Kelley. Boston, Chicago, The Pilgrim press [c1931] xii, 247 p. 20 cm. [BR115.E3K35] 31-8699
1. Sociology, Christian. 2. Christian ethics. 3. Christian life. I. Title.

KING, Henry Churchill, 1858-1934. 261
The moral and religious challenge of our times the guiding principle in human development, reverence for personality, by Henry Churchill King ... New York, The Macmillan company, 1911. xviii p., 1 l., 393 p. 20 cm. [HN31.K5] 11-31945
1. Sociology, Christian. I. Title.

KING, William Peter, 1871- ed. 261
Social progress and Christian ideals, edited by William P. King. Nashville, Cokesbury press [c1931] 360 p. 21 1/2 cm. Bibliography: p. 355-360. [HN31.K55] 31-30952
1. Sociology, Christian. I. Myers, James, 1882- II. Taylor, Alva Wilmot, 1871- III. Jenson, Howard Elkenberry, 1889- IV. Title.
Contents omitted.

KRETZMANN, Paul Edward, 1883- 261
The Christian woman as a social worker; forty analyzed lessons for class discussion or private study, by P. E. Kretzmann ... [Berne, Ind., Economy printing concern, inc., c1929] 131 p. 19 cm. [HN31.K7] 29-12925
1. Sociology, Christian. 2. Social problems. I. Title.

KUHN, Clyde Leslie 1877- 261
Scientific social theology, by Rev. Clyde L. Kuhn ... Grand Rapids, Mich., Wm. B. Eerdmans publishing company, 1936. 6 p. l., 15-311 p. 20 cm. [HN31.K8] 37-9658
1. Sociology, Christian. I. Title.

LAMBETH conference, 1930. 283.42
... Encyclical letter from the bishops, with resolutions and reports. London, Society for promoting Christian knowledge; New York, The Macmillan company [1930] 2 p. l., 5, 5A-5H, 6-200 p. 23 cm. At head of title: The Lambeth conference, 1930. [BX5021.I6 1930] 31-29079
1. Sociology, Christian. I. Title.

LANDIS, Benson Young, 1897- ed. 261
Religion and the good society, an introduction to social teachings of Judaism, Catholicism and Protestantism, edited by Benson Y.Landis ... New York, N.Y., The National conference of Christians and Jews, 1942. 94 p. 21 1/2 cm. Contents.Introduction, by E. R. Clinchy.--Interpretations of social ideals: 1. Judaism, by D. de S. Pool. 2. Catholicism, by R. A. McGowan. 3. Protestantism, by B. Y. Landis.--A comparison of social ideals.--Significant recent declarations on social reconstruction.--A discussion syllabus.--Source materials (p. 85-94) [HN35.L25] 43-8415
1. Sociology, Christian. 2. Sociology, Jewish. I. National conference of Christians & Jews. II. Title.

LANDIS, Benson Young, 1897- ed. 261
Religion and the good society; an introduction to social teachings of Judaism, Catholicism and Protestantism, edited by Benson Y. Landis ... New York, N.Y., The National conference of Christians and

Jews, 1943. 110 p. 21 1/2 cm. "First printing, 1942. Third printing, revised, 1943." Bibliography: p. 96-110. [BR115.S6L28 1943] 43-6590
1. Sociology, Christian. 2. Social problems. 3. Reconstruction (1939-) I. National conference of Christians & Jews. II. Title.

LANGDALE, John William, 1874- 261
Citizenship and moral reform, by John W. Langdale. New York, Cincinnati, The Abingdon press [c1931] 157 p. 20 cm. [HN31.L3] 21-7258
1. Sociology, Christian. 2. Social problems. 3. Citizenship. I. Title.

LESTER, Muriel, 1883- 261
Dare you face facts? By Muriel Lester ... New York, London, Harper & brothers [c1940] x p., 2 l., 125 p. 19 1/2 cm. "First edition." [BR115.S6L46 1940] 40-9542
1. Sociology, Christian. I. Title.

LINGLE, Walter Lee, 1868- 220
...The Bible and social problems / by Walter L. Lingle. . . New York,Chicago [etc.] Fleming H. Revell company [c1929] 192p. 191 2cm. (The James Sprant lectures, 1929. Union theological seminary, Richmond, Va.) [BS670.L6544] 29-8816
1. Sociology, Christian. I. Title.

LIPSCOMB, Andrew Adgate, 1816-1890. 301
The social spirit of Christianity, presented in the form of essays. By Rev. A. A. Lipscomb. Philadelphia, H. D. Moore [1846] viii, [9]-140 p. 22 cm. [HN31.L6] 19-2140
1. Sociology, Christian. I. Title.

LLOYD, Roger Bradshaigh. 261
The beloved community, by Roger Lloyd ... New York, The Macmillan company, 1937. 183 p. 22 cm. "Manufactured in Great Britain." [BR115.S6L53] 38-9161
1. Sociology, Christian. 2. Church. I. Title.

LLOYD, Roger Bradshaigh. 261
Revolutionary religion: Christianity, fascism and communism by Roger Lloyd ... New York and London, Harper & brothers [c1938] 190 p. 20 cm. "First edition." [BR115.P7L55 1938 a] 38-8538
1. Sociology, Christian. 2. Fascims. 3. Communism. I. Title.

LONG, Robert W., 1935- ed. 260
Renewing the congregation, edited by Robert W. Long. Minneapolis, Augsburg Pub. House [1966] ix, 213 p. illus. 22 cm. Bibliography: p. 209-213. [BV625.L6] 66-22567
1. Sociology, Christian. 2. Pastoral theology. I. Title.

LORIMER, George Claude, 1838-1904. 261
Christianity and the social state, by George C. Lorimer ... Philadelphia, A. F. Rowland [c1898] xix p., 1 l., 488 p. front. (port) 21 cm. [HN31.L7] 98-1238
1. Sociology, Christian. I. Title.

LUCCOCK, Halford Edward, 1885- 261
Christian faith and economic change [by] Halford E. Luccock ... New York, Cincinnati [etc.] The Abingdon press [c1936] 208 p. 20 cm. [BR115.S6L75] 36-8631
1. Sociology, Christian. I. Title.

LUNGER, Harold L
Being Christian in our time. St. Louis, Christian Board of Publication [c1963] 2 v. (Christian discipleship series, III, parts 1-2) Contents.Contents. -- v. 1. Basic course III, parts 1 and 2. -- v. 2. Guidebook.
1. Sociology, Christian. I. Title. II. Series.

LUNGER, Harold L
Being Christian in our time. St. Louis, Christian Board of Publication [c1963] 2 v. (Christian discipleship series, III, parts 1-2) Contents.Contents. -- v. 1. Basic course III, parts 1 and 2. -- v. 2. Guidebook. 65-28589
1. Sociology, Christian. 2. Christian ethics. I. Title. II. Series.

LYON, David, 1948- 261
Christians & sociology : the challenge of sociology, a Christian response / David Lyon. Downers Grove, Ill. : InterVarsity Press, [1976] c1975. 89, [4] p. ; 18 cm. Bibliography: p. [93] [BT738.L93 1976] 76-21458 ISBN 0-87784-578-6 pbk. : 1.95
1. Sociology, Christian. I. Title.

MCCONNELL, Francis John, bp., 1871- 265.
... Christian citizenship; an elective course for young people. By Francis J. McConnell... New York, Cincinnati, The Methodist book concern [c1922] 93 p. 19 cm. (Studies in Christian living) "Approved by the Committee on curriculum of the Board of Sunday schools of the Methodist Episcopal church." [BR115.S6M2] 22-22704
1. Sociology, Christian. I. Title.

MCCONNELL, Francis John, bp., 1871- 261
... The Christian ideal and social control, by Francis J. McConnell... Chicago, Ill., The University of Chicago press [1932] xiii, 174, [1] p. 20 cm. (The Barrows lectures, 1930-31) [BR115.S6M25] 32-24419
1. Sociology, Christian. I. Title.

MCCONNELL, Francis John, bp., 1871- 261
Human needs and world Christianity, by Francis John McConnell. New York, Friendship press [c1929] vi p., 1 l., 259 p. 1 l. 19 1/2 cm. [HN31.M17] 29-11661
1. Sociology, Christian. 2. Social problems. I. Title.

MCDOWELL, John, 1870- 261
The fellowship of toil; messages on industrial relationships, by John McDowell...introduction by Cleland B. McAfee... New York, Chicago [etc.] Fleming H. Revell company [c1930] 8 p. l., 5-150 p. 19 1/2 cm. [HN31.M18] 31-1479
1. Sociology, Christian. 2. Church and labor. I. Title.

MACFARLAND, Charles Stedman, 1866- ed. 261
The Christian ministry and the social order; lectures delivered in the Course in pastoral functions at Yale divinity school, 1908-1909; ed. by Charles S. Macfarland. New Haven, Conn. Yale university press; [etc., etc.] 1909. vi p., 2 l. 3-303 p. 21 1/2 cm. [HN31.M2] 9-15877
1. Sociology, Christian. I. Yale university. Divinity school. II. Title.
Contents omitted.

MACFARLAND, Charles Stedman, 1866- 265.
Christian service and the modern world, by Charles S. Macfarland. New York [etc.] Fleming H. Revell company [c1915] 140 p. 19 1/2 cm. $0.75 [BR115.S6M3] 16-1649
1. Sociology, Christian. I. Title.

MACFARLAND, Charles Stedman, 1866- 261
The Great Physician and His healing ministry, by Charles S. Macfarland. New York, Cicago [etc.] Fleming H. Revell company [c1915] 2 p. l., 15-82 p. 18 1/2 cm. "A selection from [the author's] "Christian service and the modern world." [BR115.S6M315] 40-19043
1. Sociology, Christian. 2. Hygiene. I. Title.

MACINTOSH, Douglas Clyde, 1877- 261
... Social religion, by Douglas Clyde Macintosh ... New York, C. Scribner's sons; London, C. Scribner's ons, ltd., 1939. xv, 336 p. 21 cm. (His Religion today and tomorrow). [BR115.S6M32] 39-17218
1. Sociology, Christian. 2. Kingdom of God. I. Title.

MACMURRAY, John, 1891- 261
Creative society; a study of the relation of Christianity to communism, by John Macmurray; foreword by Sherwood Eddy. New York, Association press, 1936. 168 p. 21 cm. [HX536.M32 1936] 36-27287
1. Sociology, Christian. 2. Christianity—20th cent. 3. Communism. I. Title.

MALVERN conference, Malvern college, Malvern, Eng., 1941. 261
Malvern, 1941: the life of the church and the order of society; being the proceedings of the Archibishop of York's Conference. London, New York [etc.] Longmans, Green and co. [1941] xv, 235 p. 22 1/2 cm. "First published 1941." [BR115.S6M335] 43-10021
1. Sociology, Christian. I. Title.

MARTIN, David A. 230
The breaking of the image : a sociology of Christian theory and practice / David Martin. New York : St. Martin's Press, 1980, c1979. p. cm. [BT738.M333 1980] 79-23108 ISBN 0-312-09522-8 : 22.50
1. Sociology, Christian. 2. Symbolism. 3. Secularization (Theology). 4. Social change. I. Title.

MATHEWS, Shailer, 1863- 261
The individual and the social gospel, by Shailer Mathews...pub. jointly by the Missionary education movement and Laymen's missionary movement. New York, Missionary education movement of the United States and Canada, 1914. 3 p. l., 84 p. 17 1/2 cm. [HN31.M27] 14-18412
1. Sociology, Christian. I. Title.
Contents omitted.

MATHEWS, Shailer, 1863- 261
The individual and the social gospel, by Shailer Mathews...pub. jointly by the Missionary education movement and Laymen's missionary movement. New York, Missionary education movement of the United States and Canada, 1914. 3 p. l., 84 p. 17 1/2 cm. [HN31.M27] 14-18412
1. Sociology, Christian. I. Title.
Contents omitted.

MATHEWS, Shailer, 1863- 261
The social gospel, by Shailer Mathews.. Philadelphia, Boston [etc.] The Griffith & Rowland press [1910] 168 p. 19 cm. "Books suggested for supplementary reading": p. 167-168. [HN31.M3] 10-3643
1. Sociology, Christian. I. Title.

MEHL, Roger. 301.5'8
The sociology of Protestantism. Translated by James H. Farley. Philadelphia, Westminster Press [1970] xii, 324 p. 24 cm. Translation of Traite de sociologie du protestantisme. Bibliography: p. [319]-320. [BX4811.M4313 1970] 70-104041 10.00
1. Sociology, Christian. 2. Protestantism. I. Title.

MEN and religion forward movement.
Social service message. Men and religion movement; a survey of social perils and how the church can more effectively combat them. New York [etc.] Association press, 1913. 3 p. l., 183 p. 20 cm. Bibliography: p. 179-183. E 13
1. Sociology, Christian. 2. Social problems. I. Title.

MESS, Henry Adolphus. 265.
Studies in the Christian gospel for society, by H. A. Mess ... New York, George H. Doran company [1924] vii, 9-248 p. 20 cm. Printed in Great Britain. [BR115.S6M4] 25-9422
1. Sociology, Christian. I. Title.

METHODIST Episcopal church. Study conference on the significance of Jesus Christ in the modern world, Ohio Wesleyan university, 1931. 287.6063
The significance of Jesus Christ in the modern world; Ohio Wesleyan university, Delaware, Ohio, June 24-July 3, 1931 ... the reports of the fourteen commissions on this theme as revised by the Study conference ... [New York, Cincinnati, etc.] The Methodist book concern [c1931] 14 v. fold. diagrs. 23 cm. In case; title from cover. roup iii. The Christian approach to the modern world: Commission 1. The church, a Christian fellowship.--2. Christian education.--3. Evangelist.--4. Missionary motivation. Contents.Group i. The effects of modern world trends on human life: Commission 1. Modern business and industry.--2. Race consciousness and nationalism.--3. Thechanging standards of the family.--4. The secularization of life.--5. The penetration of modern trends among all races, with an accompanying growing interdependence of nations and peoples. Group ii. The Christian message for the modern world: Commission 1. The Christian conception of personality.--2. The Christian conception of God.--Jesus Christ, the dynamic of life.--4. The validity and value of the Christian experience.--5. Christian ethics and society. Bibliography at end of most of the volumes. [BX8381.A55] 32-1553
1. Sociology, Christian. 2. Social problems. I. Title. II. Title: Jesus Christ in the modern world, The significance of.

MOBERG, David O. 261.83
The church as a social institution; the sociology of American religion. Englewood Cliffs, N. J., Prentice-Hall, 1962. 569 p. 24 cm. (Prentice-Hall sociology series) Includes bibliography. [BV625.M6] 62-10140
1. Sociology, Christian. 2. Religion and sociology. 3. U.S.—Religion. I. Title.

MONTGOMERY, Harry Earl. 261
Christ's social remedies, by Harry Earl Montgomery ... New York and London, G. P. Putnam's sons, 1911. iii p., 1 l., 433 p. 20 cm. [HN31.M7] 11-3382 1.50
1. Sociology, Christian. I. Title.
Contents omitted.

MORRISON, Charles Clayton, 1874- 261
The social gospel and the Christian cultus, by Charles Clayton Morrison. New York and London, Harper & brothers, 1933. xii, 259 p. 20 cm. [Rauschenbusch lectures, Colgate-Rochester divinity school, Rochester, N.Y.) "First edition." [HN31.M74] 33-13992
1. Sociology, Christian. I. Title.

MORSE, Richard. 261
Fear God in your own village, by Richard Morse. New York, H. Holt and company, 1918. 4 p. l., 212 p. 19 1/2cm. [BV638.M7] 18-6438
1. Sociology, Christian. I. Title.

MYERS, James, 1882- 265.
Religion lends a hand; studies of churches in social action, by James Myers ... New York and London, Harper & brothers, 1929. xi p., 1 l., 167 p. front. 20 cm. Bibliography: p. 153-158. [BR115.S6M9] 29-20893
1. Sociology, Christian. I. Title.

NATIONAL conference of Methodist students. 1st, Louisville, Ky., 1924. 287.
Through the eyes of youth: industry--race--war--public opinion--the church. National conference of Methodist students, Louisville, Kentucky, April 18-20, 1924. New York, Cincinnati, The Abingdon press [1924] 193 p. 18 cm. Foreword signed: Halford E. Luccock. [BX8207.N3 1924] 25-7594
1. Sociology, Christian. I. Luccock, Halford Edward, 1885- ed. II. Title.

NEARING, Scott, 1883- 301
Social religion; an interpretation of Christianity in terms of modern life, by Scott Nearing ... From an address delivered before the Friends' general conference, Ocean Grove, New Jersey, July 7, 1910. New York, The Macmillan company, 1913. xvi p., 2 l., 227 p. 20 cm. [HN31.N4] 13-1915
1. Sociology, Christian. 2. Social problems. I. Title.

NELSON, Ralph Waldo, 1888- 232.9
The experimental logic of Jesus, by Ralph Waldo Nelson. New York [etc.] Fleming H. Revell company [c1936] 452 p. front. 21 cm. [BS2415.N4] 36-20419
1. Jesus Christ—Teachings. 2. Sociology, Christian. 3. Logic. I. Title.

NICOLL, William Robertson, Sir, 1851-
The Christian attitude towards democracy, by Sir W. Robertson Nicoll ... Reprinted from the British weekly London, New York [etc.] Hodder and Stoughton [n.d.] 5 p. l., [3]-76 p. 16 cm. A 13
1. Sociology, Christian. 2. Church work. I. Title.
Contents omitted.

NIEBUHR, Heimut Richard, 1894- 280
The social sources of denominationalism [Gloucester. Mass., Peter Smith, 1963, c.1929] 304p. 18cm. (Meridian living age bk., LA11 rebound) Bibl. 3.50
1. Sociology, Christian. 2. Sects. I. Title.

NIEBUHR, Helmut Richard, 1894- 280
The social sources of denominationalism.

Hamden, Conn., Shoe String Press [1954, c1929] 304p. 23cm. Bibliography: p.285-295. [BR115.S8N] A55
1. Sociology, Christian. 2. Sects. I. Title.

NIEBUHR, Helmut Richard, 1894- 200
The social sources of denominationalism, by H. Richard Niebuhr ... New York, H. Holt and company [c1929] viii p., 2 l., 3-304 p. 22 cm. "Notes": p. 285-295. [BR115.S6N5] 29-25156
1. Sociology, Christian. 2. Sects. I. Title.

NIEBUHR, Helmut Richard, 1894-1962. 280
The social sources of denominationalism. New York, Meridian Books, 1957. 304 p. 18 cm. (Living age books, LA11) [BR115] 57-6685
1. Sociology, Christian. 2. Sects. I. Title.

NIXON, Justin Wroe, 1886- 261
The moral crisis in Christianity, by Justin Wroe Nixon. New York and London, Harper & brothers, 1931. xi, 197 p. 20 cm. [Rauschenbusch lectures, Colgate-Rochester divinity school, Rochester, N. Y.] "First edition." [BR115.S6N56] 31-33781
1. Sociology, Christian. 2. Christianity. I. Title.

NORTH, Gary. 261.1
Unconditional surrender : God's program for victory / Gary North. Tyler, TX : Geneva Press, c1981. ix, 265 p. : forms ; 24 cm. Includes indexes. Bibliography: p. 239-248. [BT738.N64] 19 81-150589 ISBN 0-939404-00-1 : 9.95
1. Sociology, Christian. I. Title.

OLDHAM, Joseph Houldsworth, 1874- 261
Real life is meeting, by J. H. Oldham, with chapters by H. A. Hodges and Philip Mairet. London, The Sheldon press; New York, The Macmillan company [1942] 3 p. l., 80 p. 18 1/2 cm. (Half-title: The Christian news-letter books. General editor: A. R. Vidler ... No. 14) "First published 1942." "Papers ... [which] have appeared during the past year as supplements to the Christian news-letter."--Introd. [BR115.S6037] 43-14265
1. Sociology, Christian. 2. Christianity—20th cent. I. Hodges, Herbert Arthur, 1905- II. Mairet, Philippe, 1886- III. Title.

OLDHAM, Joseph Houldsworth, 1874-
The resurrection of Christendom, by J. H. Oldham. London, The Sheldon press; New York, The Macmillan company [1940] vii, [1], 70 p., 1 l. 19 cm. (Half-title: The Christian news-letter books. General editor: A. R. Vidler. no. 1) A 41
1. Sociology, Christian. I. Title.

*O'NEILL, David P. 261.1
Christian behavior; does it matter what you do, or only what you are? Dayton, Ohio, Pflaum [1973] 95 p. illus. 16 cm. (Christian experience series: Witness Book 19) [BR115] ISBN 0-8278-2126-3 0.95 (pbk.)
1. Sociology, Christian. 2. Christianity—20th century. I. Title.

OPPEN, Dietrich von. 261.8'3
The age of the person; society in the twentieth century. Translated by Frank Clarke. Foreword by James Luther Adams. Philadelphia, Fortress Press [1969] xii, 211 p. 23 cm. Translation of Das personale Zeitalter. Bibliographical footnotes. [BT738.O613] 71-84536 5.50
1. Sociology, Christian. I. Title.

OSBORNE, William Frederick.
The faith of a layman; studies in the recoil from a professional religion, by William Frederick Osborune ... London, New York [etc.] Cassell & co., ltd., 1910. viii, 238 p. 19 cm. "What I have really done has been to make Prof. Rauschenbusch's stimulatingbook a point of departure for the registering of my own judgment on some of the causes that have led ... to the ... importance of the Church in contemporary society."--Pref. A 10
1. Sociology, Christian. I. Title.

OSTHATHIOS, Geevarghese, Metropolitan, 1918- 261.8'345
Theology of a classless society / by Geevarghese Mar Osthathios. U.S. ed. Maryknoll, N.Y. : Orbis Books, 1980, c1979. 159 p. ; 21 cm. Includes bibliographical references and index. [BT738.O77 1980] 79-27013 ISBN 0-88344-500-X pbk. : 8.95
1. Sociology, Christian. 2. Social classes—Moral and religious aspects. I. Title.

OXNAM, Garfield Bromley, 1891- 261
The ethical ideals of Jesus in a changing world, by G. Bromley Oxnam ... New York, Nashville, Abingdon-Cokesbury press [c1941] 135 p. 19 1/2 cm. "Lectures ... delivered to the students of Florida southern college."--Pref. [BR115.S6O9] 41-14176
1. Jesus Christ—Ethics. 2. Sociology, Christian. I. Title.

PAGE, Kirby, 1890- 261
Living courageously, by Kirby Page. New York, Farrar & Rinehart, incorporated [c1936] 5 p. l., 3-319 p. 21 1/2 cm. "Ten cycles of readings for 100 days": p. [113]-314. [HN31.P13] 36-33941
1. Sociology, Christian. 2. Cooperation—U.S. 3. Christian ethics. I. Title.

PAGE, Kirby, 1890- 248
Religious resources for personal living and social action, by Kirby Page ... An exploration with an anthology of verse and prose. New York, Toronto, Farrar & Rinehart incorporated [c1939] 4 p. l., 600 p. incl. facsim. 22 1/2 cm. Includes music. [BR115.S6P255] 39-27005
1. Sociology, Christian. 2. Liturgies. I. Title.

PALMER, Parker J. 261
The church, the university, and urban society: focus on the church [by] Parker J. Palmer [and] Elden Jacobson. [New York, Dept. of Higher Education, National Council of Churches, 1971] viii, 37 p. 28 cm. "Paper number 2 in a series of seven reports produced for the project on church, university, and urban society of the Department of Higher Education, National Council of Churches." [BT738.P28] 73-29861 0.50
1. Sociology, Christian. 2. Urban churches. 3. Religious and ecclesiastical institutions. I. Jacobson, Elden, joint author. II. National Council of the Churches of Christ in the United States of America. Dept. of Higher Education. III. Title.

PARSONS, Edward Smith, 1863- 920.
The social message of Jesus; a course of twelve lessons, Edward S. Parsons ... [2d ed.] New York, National board of the Young womens Christian associations of the United States of America [c1912] 115, [5] p. 19 cm. Part of pages blank for "Notes" [HN31.P15] 13-856 0.40
1. Sociology, Christian. I. Title.

PARTNERSHIP,
the study of an idea. Chicago, S. C. M. Book Club [1956] 127p. 18cm. (The Merrick lectures, 1955)
1. Sociology, Christian. I. Warren, Max Alexander Cunningham, 1904-

PATTEN, Simon Nelson, 1852-1922. 301.5'8
The social basis of religion. With an introd. for the Garland ed. by Michael Hudson. New York, Garland Pub., 1974 [c1911] 13, xviii, 247 p. 22 cm. (The Neglected American economists) Reprint of the ed. published by Macmillan, New York, in series: American social progress series. Includes bibliographical references. [BT738.P34 1974] 74-10846 ISBN 0-8240-1028-0
1. Sociology, Christian. I. Title. II. Series. III. Series: American social progress series.

PATTEN, Simon Nelson, 1852-1922. 301
... The social basis of religion, by Simon N. Patten ... New York, The Macmillan company, 1911. xviii, 247 p. 20 cm. (American social progress series) [HN31.P2] 11-5215
1. Sociology, Christian. 2. History—Philosophy. I. Title.

PEABODY, Francis Greenwood, 1847-1936. 248
Jesus Christ and the social question; an examination of the teaching of Jesus in its relation to some of the problems of modern social life, by Francis Greenwood Peabody ... New York, The Macmillan company; London, Macmillan & co., ltd., 1900. vii, 374 p. 20 cm. [BS2417.S7P4] 1-29227
1. Jesus Christ—Teachings. 2. Sociology, Christian. 3. Sociology, Biblical. I. Title.

PEABODY, Francis Greenwood, 1847-1936. 248
Jesus Christ and the social question; an examination of the teaching of Jesus in its relation to some of the problems of modern social life. By Francis Greenwood Peabody ... New York, The Macmillan company; London, Macmillan & co., ltd., 1915. 3 p. l., 374 p. 19 cm. (Half-title: The Macmillan standard library) [BS2417.S7P] A 15
1. Jesus Christ—Teachings. 2. Sociology, Christian. 3. Sociology, Biblical. I. Title.

PLANTZ, Samuel, 1859-1924 261
The church and the social problem; a study in applied Christianity, by Samuel Plantz ... Cincinnati, Jennings and Graham; New York, Eaton and Mains [c1906] 256 p. 20 1/2 cm. [HN31.P6] 6-30015
1. Sociology, Christian. I. Title.

PLOWRIGHT, Bernard Clifford. 261
Rebel religion; Christ, community and church, by B. C. Plowright ... introduction by John MacMurray ... New York Round table press, inc., 1937. 195 p. 20 1/2cm. [BR115.S6P6 1937] 37-18994
1. Sociology, Christian. 2. Kingdom of God. 3. Communism. 4. Fascism. I. Title.

POTTER, Henry Codman, bp., 1834-1908. 261
... Man: men: and their Master: delivered at Gambier, Ohio. November, 1901. by Henry C. Potter. New York, E. S. Gorham [1902] 158 p. 20 cm. (Half-title: The Bedell lectures) Series title also at head of t.-p. [HN31.P7] 7-9616
1. Sociology, Christian. I. Title.

POTTER, Henry Codman, 1834-1908. 261
The modern man and his fellow man; being the William L. Bull lectures for the year 1902, by Henry Codman Potter ... Philadelphia, Printed for the committee by G. W. Jacobs & co. [1903] 1 p. l., 173 p. 20 cm. Lectures delivered to the students of the Philadelphia divinity school, in the church of the Holy Trinity. Philadelphia, January 21st, 23d, 28th, and 30th, 1902, afterwards at Yale university and published with two additional lectures by the same author, in the volume of Yale lectures entilted "The citizen in his relation to the industrial situation". Contents.--The situation.--The working man.--The capitalist.--The consumer. [HN31.P7] 3-12529
1. Sociology, Christian. I. Title.

PRALL, William, 1853- 261
Civic Christianity, by William Prall ... New-York, T. Whittaker, 1895. vii, 209 p. 19 cm. Sermons ... some of them have appeared in full or in part in the churchman, in the Detorit free press, and in other journals.--p. v. [HN31.P75] 18-21985
1. Sociology, Christian. I. Title.

QUICK, Oliver Chase, 1885-
Christianity and justice, by O. C. Quick ... London, The Sheldon press; New York, The Macmillan company [1940] v, 73, [1] p. 19 cm. (Half-title: The Christian news-letter books, no. 5. General editor: A. R. Vidler) A 42
1. Jesus Christ—Teachings. 2. Sociology, Christian. 3. Justice. I. Title.

QUINNEY, Richard. 261
Providence, the reconstruction of social and moral order / Richard Quinney. New York : Longman, c1980. x, 118 p. : ill. ; 25 cm. (Professional book series) Includes bibliographical references and index. [BT738.Q56] 79-20423 ISBN 0-582-28143-1 lib. bdg. : 14.95
1. Sociology, Christian. 2. Socialism, Christian. I. Title.

RASCHKE, Carl A. 261.8
The bursting of new wineskins : reflections on religion and culture at the end of affluence / by Carl A. Raschke. Pittsburgh : Pickwick Press, 1978. ix, 228 p. ; 22 cm. (Pittsburgh theological monograph series ; 24) [BT738.R32] 78-16604 ISBN 0-915138-34-4 pbk. : 7.50
1. Sociology, Christian. 2. Wealth—Moral and religious aspects. 3. Liberalism (Religion)—United States. I. Title. II. Series.

RAUSCHENBUSCH, Walter, 1861-1918. 261
Christianity and the social crisis. Edited by Robert D. Cross. New York, Harper & Row [1964] xxv, 429 p. 21 cm. (American perspectives) Harper torchbooks. The University library, TB3059. Bibliographical footnotes. [BT738.R34 1964] 64-57260
1. Sociology, Christian. I. Title.

RAUSCHENBUSCH, Walter, 1861-1918. 261
Christianity and the social crisis, by Walter Rauschenbusch ... New York, The Macmillan company; London, Macmillan & co., ltd., 1907. xv, 429 p. 21 cm. [BR115.S6R35 1907] 7-13925
1. Sociology, Christian. I. Title.

RAUSCHENBUSCH, Walter, 1861-1918. 261
Christianity and the social crisis, by Walter Rauschenbusch ... New York, The Macmillan company; London, Macmillan & co., ltd., 1920. xv, 429 p. 20 cm. [BR115.S6R35 1920] 22-16514
1. Sociology, Christian. I. Title.

RAUSCHENBUSCH, Walter, 1861-1918. 200
Christianizing the social order, by Walter Rauschenbusch ... New York, The Macmillan company, 1912. xii p., 1 l., 493 p. 20 cm. [BR115.S6R36] 12-26399
1. Sociology, Christian. I. Title.

RAUSCHENBUSCH, Walter, 1861-1918. 208.1
A gospel for the social awakening; selections from the writings of Walter Rauschenbusch, compiled by Benjamin E. Mays, with an introd. by C. Howard Hopkins. New York, Association Press, 1950. 187 p. 20 cm. (A Haddam House book) Bibliography: p. [6] [BR115.S6R38] 51-1462
1. Sociology, Christian. I. Title.

RAUSCHENBUSCH, Walter, 1861-1918. *261.8
A Rauschenbusch reader; the kingdom of God and the social gospel. Compiled by Benson Y. Landis; with an interpretation of the life and work of Walter Rauschenbush by Harry Emerson Fosdick. [1st ed.] New York, Harper [1957] 167 p. 22 cm. [BR115.S6R39] 57-7351
1. Sociology, Christian. I. Landis, Benson Young, 1897- comp. II. Title.

RAUSCHENBUSCH, Walter, 1861-1918. 261
The righteousness of the kingdom, edited and introduced by Max L. Stackhouse. Nashville, Abingdon Press [1968] 320 p. 24 cm. Bibliography: p. 289-312. [BT738.R345] 68-17441
1. Sociology, Christian. 2. Kingdom of God. I. Title.

RAUSCHENBUSCH, Walter, 1861-1918. 261
The social principles of Jesus / by Walter Rauschenbusch ; written under the direction of Sub-committee on College Courses, Sunday School Council of Evangelical Denominations and Committee on Voluntary Study, Council of North American Student Movements. Folcroft, Pa. : Folcroft Library Editions, 1976. 198 p. ; 26 cm. Reprint of the 1916 ed. published by Association Press, New York, which was issued as 4th year, pt. 1 of College voluntary study courses. [BS2417.S7R3 1976] 76-50566 ISBN 0-8414-7308-0 lib. bdg. : 15.00
1. Jesus Christ—Teachings. 2. Sociology, Christian. 3. Christian ethics. I. Title. II. Series: College voluntary study courses ; 4th year, pt. 1.

RAUSCHENBUSCH, Walter, 1861-1918. 232.
... The social principles of Jesus, by Walter Rauschenbusch ... written under the direction of Sub-committee on college courses, Sunday school council of evangelical denominations and Committed on voluntary study, council of North American student movements. New York [etc.] Association press, 1916. 5 p. l., 198

p. 17 cm. (College voluntary study course, fourth year--pt. i) [BS2417.S7R3] 16-18568
1. Sociology, Christian. 2. Christian ethics. I. Title.

RAUSCHENBUSCH, Walter, 1861- 1918. 261
A theology for the social gospel. Nashville, Abingdon Press [1961, c.1917] 279p. 21cm. (Apex books, E7) 61-40 1.75 pap.,
1. Sociology. Christian. 2. Theology, Doctrinal. I. Title.

RAUSCHENBUSCH, Walter, 1861- 1918. 200
A theology for the social gospel, by Walter Rauschenbusch ... New York, The Macmillan company, 1917. 5 p. l., 279 p. 20 cm. "Four lectures on the Nathaniel W. Taylor foundation before the annual convocation of the Yale school of religion ... presented in elaborated form." [BR115.S6R4] 17-31090
1. Sociology, Christian. 2. Theology, Doctrinal. I. Title.

RAUSCHENBUSCH, Walter, 1861- 1918. 261
A theology for the social gospel, by Walter Rauschenbusch ... New York, The Macmillan company, 1922. 5 p. l., 279 p. 20 cm. "Four lectures on the Nathaniel W. Taylor foundation before the annual convocation of the Yale school of religion ... presented in elaborated form."--Foreword. [BR115.S6R4 1922] 41-31826
1. Sociology, Christian. 2. Theology, Doctrinal. I. Title.

RECKITT, Maurice Benington, 1888- 261
Faith and society; a study of the structure, outlook and opportunity of the Christian social movement in Great Britain and the United States of America, by Maurice B. Reckitt ... London, New York [etc.] Longman's, Green and co., 1932. 3 p. l., ix-xii, 467, [1] p. 23 cm. "Appended note, by V. A. Demant, on the prospects of Christian sociology in Amrica": p. 227-231. "Organizations composing the Christian social movement": p. 465-467. [BR115.S6R5] 32-29659
1. Sociology, Christian. 2. Civilization, Christian. I. Demant, Vigo Auguste. II. Title. III. Title: Christian social movement in Great Britain and the United States.

RECKITT, Maurice Bennington, 1888- 261.8
Militant here in earth; considerations on the prophetic function of the church in the twentieth centrry. London, New York, Longmans, Green [1958] 160p. 19cm. [BR115.S6R523] 58-14551
1. Sociology, Christian. 2. Civilization, Modern. I. Title.

REDEKOP, Calvin Wall, 1925- 260
The free church and seductive culture, by Calvin Redekop. Diagrams by Ivan Moon. Scottdale, Pa., Herald Press [1970] 189 p. port. 20 cm. Includes bibliographical references. [BT738.R39] 78-114844
1. Sociology, Christian. 2. Dissenters, Religious. I. Title.

REUMANN, John Henry Paul. 261
Righteousness and society, ecumenical dialog in a revolutionary age, by John Reumann and William Lazareth. Philadelphia, Fortress Press [1967] xi, 242 p. 18 cm. Bibliographical footnotes. [BT738.R5] 68-12326
1. Sociology, Christian. I. Lazareth, William Henry, 1928- II. Title.

REUMANN, John Henry Paul. 261
Righteousness and society, ecumenical dialog in a revolutionary age, by John Reumann and William Lazareth. Philadelphia, Fortress Press [1967] xi, 242 p. 18 cm. Bibliographical footnotes. [BT738.R5] 68-12326
1. Sociology, Christian. I. Lazareth, William Henry, 1928- II. Title.

ROBINSON, Clarence Cromwell, 1878- 261
Christian teaching on social and economic questions confronting older boys and young men, by Clarence C. Robinson... New York [etc.] Association press, 1914. x, 102 p. 17 1/2 cm. [Boy life series] "References for the different studies": p. 3-7. [HN31.R7] 14-15038
1. Sociology, Christian. I. Title.

ROHDE, John Martin, 1852- 261
God and government; or, Christ our king in civic and social righteousness, by J. Martin Rohde...introduction by Hon. A. C. Matthews... New York, Eaton & Mains; Cincinnati, Jennings & Graham [1904] 301 p. 19 1/2 cm. [HN31.R73] 4-22861
1. Sociology, Christian. I. Title.
Contents, omitted.

ROSE, Tom. 261.8
After our present trials—the coming victory : proposals on how to overcome the troubles that plague us / by Tom Rose and Robert Metcalf. Memphis, Tenn. (P.O. Box 11110, Memphis, Tenn. 38111) : Christian Studies Center, c1980. xi, 192 p. ; 21 cm. (Coronation series ; 5) Spine title: The comingvictory. Includes indexes. Bibliography: p. 163-183. [BT738.R66] 19 80-68679 6.95 (pbk.)
1. Sociology, Christian. 2. United States—Moral conditions. I. Metcalf, Robert M. II. Title. III. Title: The coming victory.

SCHROEDER, W. Widick. 261
Cognitive structures and religious research; essays in sociology and theology, by W. Widick Schroeder. East Lansing, Michigan State University Press, 1970. xiii, 211 p. 25 cm. Includes bibliographical references. [BT738.S36494] 76-136266 ISBN 0-87013-150-8 7.50
1. Sociology, Christian. I. Title.

SCOTT, Robert Balgarnie Young, 1899- ed. 261.04
Towards the Christian revolution; R. B. Y. Scott and Gregory Vlastos, editors. Chicago, New York, Willett, Clark & company, 1936. viii p., 2 l., 254 p. 21 cm. "Acknowledgments": p. 253-254. [BR115.S6S42] 281.04 37-27241
1. Sociology, Christian. 2. Kingdom of God. I. Vlastos, Gregory, joint ed. II. Title.
Contents omitted.

SCUDDER, Vida Dutton, 1861- 301
The church and the hour, reflections of a socialist churchwoman, by Vida D. Scudder, A. M. New York, E. P. Dutton & co. [c1917] vii p., 1 l., 133 p. 19 cm. Reprinted from various periodicals. [HN31.S4] 17-10459 1.00
1. Sociology, Christian. I. Title.

SHAFER, Luman Jay, 1887- 172.4
The Christian alternative to world chaos, by Luman J. Shafer. New York, Round table press, inc., 1940. xi p., 1 l., 208 p. 20 cm. [BR115.P4S5] 40-4293
1. Sociology, Christian. 2. Peace. I. Title.

SHRIGLEY, Eugene Wilford, 1895- 261
Our community and the Christian ideal [by] Eugene Wilford Shrigley. New York, Cincinnati, [etc.] The Abingdon press [c1936] 93 p. 17 cm. Bibliography: p. 93. [BR115.S6S45] 36-25827
1. Sociology, Christian. I. Title.

SINGER, Anna M. 922.673
Walter Rauschenbusch and his contribution to social Christianity, by Anna M. Singer, A.M. Boston, R. G. Badger [c1926] xi, 13-136 p. 21 1/2 cm. "Sources": p. 133. Bibliography of Walter Bauschenbusch's publications: p. 135-136. [BX6495.R3S5] 26-9623
1. Rauschenbusch, Walter, 1861-1918. 2. Socialogy, Christian. I. Title.

SLOAN, William Niccolls, 1849- 261
Social regeneration the work of Christianity, by the Rev. W. N. Sloan, PH. D. Philadelphia, The Westminster press, 1902. xiii, 142 p. 19 cm. [HN31.S6] 2-16115
1. Sociology, Christian. I. Title.

SMITH, John Owen. 261.8
Give the whole gospel a chance / John Owen Smith. Nashville : Tidings, [1974?] x, 101 p. ; 19 cm. Includes bibliographical references. [BT738.S565] 74-27908
1. Sociology, Christian. 2. Church and social problems. I. Title.

SMITH, Samuel George, 1852- 1915. 301
Democracy and the church, by Samuel George Smith ... New York and London, D. Appleton and company, 1912. xv, 356, [1] p. 20 cm. Bibliography: p. 353-346. [HN31.S64] 12-25773
1. Sociology, Christian. I. Title.

SMYTHE, Lewis Strong Casey. 261
The Christian in today's world : inner city to world community / Lewis Smythe. 1st ed. Hicksville, N.Y. : Exposition Press, [1974] 174 p. ; 21 cm. Includes bibliographical references. [BT738.S59] 75-300670 ISBN 0-682-48055-X : 6.50
1. Sociology, Christian. 2. Church and social problems. I. Title.

THE Social application of religion ... Cincinnati, Jennings and Graham; New York, Eaton and Mains [c1908] 139 p. 21 cm. (The Merrick lectures for 1907-8) Contents.Contents.--i. The spirit of social unrest, by C. Steizle.--ii. Woman's conscience and social amelioration, by Jane Addams.--iii. Some ethical aspects of the labor movement, by C. P. Nelli.--iv. Industry and religion: their common ground and interdependence, by G. taylor.--v. Christianity and the social situation, By G. P. Eckman. [HN31.S7] 9-35064 301
1. Sociology, Christian. I. Steizle, Charles, 1869- II. Addams, Jane, 1860-1935. III. Neill, Charles Patrick, 1865- IV. Taylor, Graham, 1851- V. Eckman, George Peck, 1860-

THE social sources of denominationalism. Cleveland, World Publishing Co. [1962] 304p. (Meridian Books) A Living age book, LA 11.
1. Sociology—Christian. 2. Sects. I. Niebuhr, Helmut Richard, 1894-

STACKHOUSE, Max L. 261.1
Ethics and the urban ethos; an essay in social theory and theological reconstruction [by] Max L. Stackhouse. Boston, Beacon Press [1972] 220 p. 21 cm. Includes bibliographical references. [BT738.S695 1972] 77-179155 ISBN 0-8070-1136-3 7.95
1. Sociology, Christian. 2. Sociology, Urban. I. Title.

STAMP, Josiah Charles Stamp, baron, 1880- 261
Christianity and economics, by Sir Josiah Stamp ... introduction by Rufus M. Jones ... New York, The Macmillan company, 1938. x p., 2 l., 194 p. 20 1/2 cm. [Great issues of life series] "Published November, 1936. First printing." [HB72.S654] 38-34330
1. Sociology, Christian. 2. Sociology, Christian—Hist. I. Title.

STEAD, Francis Herbert, 1857- 1928. 270
The story of social Christianity, by Francis Herbert Stead ... New York, George H. Doran company; London, J. Clarke & co., limited [1924] 2 v. 20 cm. ("The living church" series) Printed in Great Britain. [BR115.S6S66] 25-3086
1. Sociology, Christian. 2. Church history. I. Title.

STRONG, Josiah, 1847-1916. 261
The new era; or, The coming kingdom, by Rev. Josiah Strong ... New York, The Baker & Taylor co. [c1893] 1 p. l., v-xx, 374 p. 20 1/2 cm. [HN31.S87] 12-39169
1. Sociology, Christian. I. Title.

STRONG, Josiah, 1847-1916. 265.
The next great awakening, by Josiah Strong ... New York, The Baker & Taylor company, 1902. 2 p. l., 3-233 p. 18 1/2 cm. [BR115.S6S7 1902] 2-9162
1. Sociology, Christian. I. Title.
Contents omitted.

STRONG, Josiah, 1847-1916. 265.
The next great awakening, by Josiah Strong ... (8th thousand.) New York, The Baker & Taylor company [c1905] xxxiii, 13-233 p. 19 cm. [BR115.S6S7 1905] 5-33503
1. Sociology, Christian. I. Title.
Contents omitted.

STUCKENBERG, John Henry Wilburn, 1835-1903. 261
Christian sociology. By J. H. W. Stuckenberg ... New York, I. K. Funk & co., 1880. v, ii, 379 p. 19 1/2 cm. [HN31.S9] 12-39120
1. Sociology, Christian. I. Title.

STUCKENBERG, John Henry Wilburn, 1835-1903. 261
Christian sociology. By J. H. W. Stuckenberg ... New York, I. K. Funk & co., 1880. v, ii, 379 p. 19 1/2 cm. [HN31.S9] 12-39120
1. Sociology, Christian. I. Title.

STUCKENBERG, John Henry Wilburn, 1835-1903. 261
Christian sociology. By J. H. W. Stuckenberg ... New York, Funk & Wagnalls, 1890. v, ii, 375 p. 19 1/2 cm. [HN31.S9 1890] 36-16741
1. Sociology, Christian. I. Title.

SWIFT, Albert. 261
First principles of Christian citizenship, by the Rev. Albert Swift, with an introduction by the Rev. G. Campbell Morgan, D.D. New York, Chicago [etc.] Fleming H. Revell company [1908] 2 p. l., 7-151, [1] p. diagr. 19 cm. Printed in Great Britain. [HN31.S93] 13-25069
1. Sociology, Christian. I. Title. II. Title: Christian citizenship, First principles of.

SWIFT, Arthur Lessner, 1891- 261
New frontiers of religion, the church in a changing community [by Arthur L. Swift, jr. ... New York, The Macmillan company, 1938. xii, 171 p. 21 cm. "First printing." [BV625.S97] 38-13097
1. Sociology, Christian. 2. Religion and sociology. 3. Church. I. Title.

TAYLOR, Alva Wilmot, 1871- 261
Christianity and industry in America, by Alva W. Taylor ... New York, Friendship press [c1933] xi, 212 p. 19 1/2 cm. "A selected reading list": p. [200]-204. [HN39.U6T3] 33-20851
1. Sociology, Christian. 2. Labor and laboring classes—U.S.—1914- I. Title.

TAYLOR, Graham, 1851- 261
Religion in social action, by Graham Taylor, with an introduction by Jane Addams. New York, Dodd, Mead and company, 1913. xxxv p., 1 l., 279 p. 19 1/2 cm. "References": p. 259-279. [HN31.T3] 13-25668
1. Sociology, Christian. I. Title.

TEMPLE, William, abp. of Canterbury, 1881- 261
Christianity and social order, by William Temple ... New York, Penguin books, inc. [1942] 93 p. 18 cm. On cover: A Penguin special. "First published August, 1942." [BR115.S6T4] 42-22742
1. Sociology, Christian. I. Title.

TEMPLE, William Abp. of Canterbury, 1881-1944.
Christianity and social order. [Harmondsworth, Middlesex; Baltimore] Penguin Books [1966] 120 p. (Pelican books, A345) "First published... 1942; reprinted... 1956."
1. Sociology, Christian. I. Title.

TEMPLE, William, Abp. of Canterbury, 1881-1944. 261
Christianity and social order / William Temple ; foreword by Edward Heath ; introd. by Ronald H. Preston. London : Shepheard-Walwyn, 1976. 119 p. ; 20 cm. Reprint of the 1942 ed. published by Penguin Books, Harmondsworth; with new foreword and introd. Includes bibliographical references. [BT738.T36 1976] 76-377418 ISBN 0-281-02898-2 : £2.95. ISBN 0-281-02897-4 pbk.
1. Sociology, Christian. I. Title.

TEMPLE, William, Abp. of Canterbury, 1881-1944. 261.8
Christianity and social order / William Temple ; introduction by Ronald H. Preston. New York : Seabury Press, 1977, c1976. 119 p. ; 22 cm. "A Crossroad book." Includes bibliographical references. [BT738.T36 1977] 77-23138 ISBN 0-8164-0348-1 : 6.95
1. Sociology, Christian. I. Title.

THOMPSON, Kenneth A. 262'.03'42
Bureaucracy and Church reform: the organizational response of the Church of England to social change 1800-1965, by Kenneth A. Thompson. Oxford, Clarendon P., 1970. xxiii, 264 p. 23 cm. Bibliography: p. [244]-253. [BX5150.T47] 70-457735 55/-
1. Church of England—Government. 2. Sociology, Christian. I. Title.

THOMPSON, Robert Ellis, 1844-1924. 261
De civitate Dei. The divine order of human society; being the L. P. Stone lectures for 1891, delivered in Princeton theological seminary, by Prof. Robert Ellis Thompson... Philadelphia, J. D. Wattles, 1891. vi, 274 p. 19 cm. [HN31.T45] 36-13089
1. Sociology, Christian. I. Title. II. Title: The divine order of human society.

THUNG, Mady A. 301.5'8
The precarious organisation : sociological explorations of the Church's mission and structure / Mady A. Thung. The Hague : Mouton, [1976] xiv, 348 p. ; 24 cm. (Religion and society ; 5) Includes index. Bibliography: p. [326]-342. [BT738.T525] 76-483997 ISBN 9-02-797652-X : 15.00
1. Sociology, Christian. 2. Mission of the church. I. Title. II. Series: Religion and society (The Hague) ; 5.
Distributed by Humanities

TIPLADY, Thomas, 1882- 301
Social Christianity in the new era, by Thomas Tiplady ... New York, Chicago [etc.] Fleming H. Revell company [c1919] 3 p. l., 5-190 p. 19 1/2 cm. [HN31.T5] 19-27523
1. Sociology, Christian. 2. Social problems. I. Title.

TIPPY, Worth Marion, 1867- ed. 301
The socialized church; addresses before the first national conference of the social workers of Methodism, St. Louis, November 17-19, 1908; ed. by the secretary, Worth M. Tippy, D.D., for the Methodist federation for social service. New York, Eaton & Mains; Cincinnati, Jennings & Graham [c1909] 288 p. 18 1/2 cm. [HN31.T6] 9-21269
1. Sociology, Christian. I. Methodist federation for social service. II. Title.

TITTLE, Ernest Fremont, 1885- 261
Christians in an unchristian society [by] Ernest Fremont Title... New York, Association press [c1939] vii, 62 p. 19 1/2 cm. (Hasen books on religion) [BR115.S6T52] 39-15291
1. Sociology, Christian. 2. Kingdom of God. I. Title.

TOWARDS a new world.
Translated and condensed from the Italian. London, Staten Island, N. Y., St. Paul Publications [1958] xvi, 276p. illus. 22cm. Translation of Per un mondo nuovo.
1. Sociology, Christian. 2. Civilization, Christian. I. Lombardi, Riccardo.

TRAWICK, Arcadius McSwain, 1869- 261
The city church and its social mission; a series of studies in the social extension of the city church [by] A. M. Trawick ... New York [etc.] Association press, 1913. viii, 166 p. 19 cm. Bibliography: p. 161-166. [HN31.T7] 13-15192
1. Sociology, Christian. 2. City churches. I. Title.

TRIBE, Reginald Herman. 261
The Christian social tradition, by Reginald Tribe ... London, Society for promoting Christian knowledge; New York, The Macmillan company [1935] ix, 11-293 p. 19 cm. "First published, 1935." "Books recommended for further reading": p. 286-287. [HN31.T73 1935] 36-10651
1. Sociology, Christian. I. Society for promoting Christian knowledge, London. II. Title.

TRIMBLE, Malcome Calvis. *261.8
Our awakening social conscience; the emerging kingdom of God. [1st ed.] New York, Vantage Press [1958] 158 p. 21 cm. [BT738.T7] 58-10676
1. Sociology, Christian. 2. Kingdom of God. I. Title.

THE universal church and the world of nations, 261.082 by Marquess of Lothian, Sir Alfred Zimmern, O. H. von der Gablentz [and others]... Chicago, New York, Willett, Clark & company, 1938. xii, 315 p. 20 cm. (Half-title: The official Oxford conference books, vol. VII) [BR115.P7U5] 38-27613
1. Sociology, Christian. 2. International law and relations. 3. War and religion. 4. Peace. 5. Nationalism and nationality. I. Lothian, Philip Henry Kerr, 11th marquis of, 1882- II. World conference on church, community and state, Oxford, 1937.
Contents omitted.

VAN LOAN, Anna Fitz Gerald. 301
The power to right our wrongs; evidence from events that Christian principles are best aiding humanity, by Anna Fitz Gerald Van Loan. New York, Chicago [etc.] Fleming H. Revell company [c1915] 231 p. 19 1/2 cm. $1.00 [HN31.V3] 15-3778
1. Sociology, Christian. I. Title.

VEDDER, Henry Clay, 1853-1935. 265.
The gospel of Jesus and the problems of democracy, by Henry C. Vedder ... New York, The Macmillan company, 1914. ix p., 2 l., 410 p. 20 cm. Bibliography: p. 377-388. [BR115.S6V4] 14-15717
1. Sociology, Christian. 2. Social problems. I. Title.

WALLACE, Henry Agard, 1888- 304
Paths to plenty, by Henry A. Wallace... Washington, D.C., National home library foundation, 1938. x, 150 p. 16 cm. (Earl foundation lectures) [HN31.W23] 39-19733
1. Sociology, Christian. 2. Capitalism. 3. Democracy. 4. U.S.—Economic policy. I. Title.
Contents omitted.

WALLACE, Henry Agard, 1888- 304
The price of freedom, by Henry A. Wallace; foreword by David Cushman Coyle. Washington, D.C., National home library foundation, 1940. xvi, 106 p. 16 cm. (On cover: General welfare series) Earl foundation lectures. First published, 1938, under title: Paths to plenty. [HN31.W23 1940] 41-2626
1. Sociology, Christian. 2. Capitalism. 3. Democracy. I. Title.
Contents omitted.

WALLACE, Henry Agard, 1888- 261
Statesmanship and religion, by Henry A. Wallace... New York, Round table press, inc., 1934. 139 p. front. 20 cm. [BR115.S6W27] 34-27126
1. Sociology, Christian. 2. U.S.—Economic policy. I. Title.

WALTER, J. A. 261
Sacred cows : exploring contemporary idolatry / J. A. Walter. Grand Rapids, Mich. : Zondervan Pub. House, 1980, c1979. 217 p. ; 21 cm. Reprint of the ed. published by Paternoster Press, Exeter, Devon, Eng., under title: A long way from home. Includes bibliographical references and index. [BT738.W333 1980] 80-13419 ISBN 0-310-42421-6 pbk. : 5.95
1. Sociology, Christian. 2. Civilization, Modern—1950- I. Title.

WAMBLE, Irving W 248
Who is my neighbor? New York, Vantage Press [1952] 124 p. 23 cm. [BR115.S6W286] 52-6959
1. Sociology, Christian. I. Title.

WARD, Harry Frederick, 1873- 261
...Christianizing community life, by Harry F. Ward...and Richard Henry Edwards...written from outline prepared by Sub-committee on college courses, Sunday school council of evangelical denominations adn Committee on voluntary study, Council of North American student movements. New York [etc.] Association press, 1917. 4 p. l., 176 p. 17 cm. (College voluntary study courses, fourth year--part II) [HN31.W25] 17-9480
1. Sociology, Christian. I. Edwards, Richard Henry, 1877- joint author. II. Sunday school council of evangelical denominations. Sub-committee on college courses. III. Council of North American student movements. Committee on voluntary study. IV. Title.

WARD, Harry Frederick, 1873- ed. 261
Social creed of the churches, ed. by Harry F. Ward. New York, Eaton & Maine; Cincinnati, Jennings & Graham [c1912] 2 p. l., 3-185 p. 19 cm. "This volume is authorized by the Commission on the church and social service of the Federal council of the churches of Christ in America." References at end of each chapter. [HN31.W4] 12-9982
1. Sociology, Christian. I. Title.

WARD, Harry Frederick, 1873- ed. 261
The social creed of the churches, by Harry F. Ward... New York, Eaton & Mains; Cincinnati, Jennings & Graham [c1914] 196 p. 19 cm. "The declaration of principles, which has come to be popularly known as 'The social creed of the churches', was adopted in its present form at the quadrennial meeting of the Federal council of the churches of Christ in America at Chicago, December, 1912." "References": p. 15. "Best books" at end of each chapter. [HN31.W4 1914] 14-7273
1. Sociology, Christian. I. Title.

WARD, Harry Frederick, 1873- ed. 261
Social ministry; an introduction to the study and practice of social service, ed. for the Methodist federation for social service by the editorial secretary, Harry F. Ward. New York, Eaton & Mains; Cincinnati, Jennings & Graham [c1910] 1 p. l., v-viii, 318 p. 18 1/2 cm. $1.00 Bibliography at end of each chapter. [HN31.W3] 10-22974
1. Sociology, Christian. 2. Social problems. I. Title.

WARREN, Max Alexander Cunningham, 1904-
Partnership, the study of an idea. Chicago, S.C.M. Book Club [1956] 127 p. 18 cm. (The Merrick lectures, 1955)
1. Sociology, Christian. I. Title.

WASHBURN, Henry Bradford, 1869- 920.02
The religious motive in philanthropy; studies in biography, by Henry Bradford Washburn ... Philadelphia, University of Pennsylvania press; London, H. Milford, Oxford university press, 1931. xix, 172 p. 21 cm. (Half-title: The George Dana Boardman lectureship in Christian ethics) [HN31.W43] 31-24926
1. Barnett, Samuel Augustus, 1844-1913. 2. Vincent de Paul, Saint, 1576?-1660. 3. Francesco d'Assisi, Saint, 1182-1226. 4. Jesus Christ. 5. Sociology, Christian. I. Title.
Contents omitted.

WATSON, David, (minister) 301
Social advance, its meaning, method, and goal, by the Rev. David Watson. London, New York [etc.] Hodder and Stoughton [1911] xxi p., 1 l., 336 p. 20 1/2 cm. "Chapters II, III, and V. of this book were delivered in Edinburgh university as the Gunning lectures of 1910-11."--Pref. [HN31.W44] 13-13248
1. Sociology, Christian. 2. Social problems. I. Title.

WEBBER, Robert. 261
The secular saint : a case for evangelical social responsibility / by Robert E. Webber. Grand Rapids, Mich. : Zondervan Pub. House, c1979. p. cm. Includes bibliographical references and index. [BT738.W344] 79-12181 ISBN 0-310-36640-2 : 7.95
1. Sociology, Christian. 2. Christianity and culture. I. Title.

WENTZ, Frederick K. 261
Set free for others [by] Frederick K. Wentz. Drawings by Edith Aberle. New York, Friendship Press [1969] 157 p. illus. 19 cm. Bibliography: p. 156-157. [BT738.W42] 68-59133 ISBN 3-7709-0115- 1.50
1. Sociology, Christian. 2. Church and the world. I. Title.

WILLIAMS, Charles David bp. 1860-1923 261
The Christian ministry and social problems, by Charles D. Williams... New York, The Macmillan company, 1917. 6 p. l., 3-133 p. 18 cm. (Half-title: Church principles for lay people) [BS670.W5] 17-18971
1. Sociology, Christian. I. Title.

WILLIS, Hugh Evander, 1875- 301
The law of social justice; principles of the law of the kingdom of heaven (right living) the law of Jesus from a lawyer's viewpoint, by Hugh Evander Willis ... New York, Association press, 1918. 6 p. l., 3-182, p. 19 1/2 cm. [HN31.W6] 18-19389
1. Sociology, Christian. I. Title.

WILMORE, Gayraud S. 261.83
The secular relevance of the church. Philadelphia, Westminster [c.1962] 89p. 19cm. (Christian perspectices on soc. problems) 62-14177 1.25 pap.,
1. Sociology, Christian. I. Title.

WILSON, Grace Hannah, 1888- 267'.5'973
The religious and educational philosophy of the Young Women's Christian Association; a historical study of the changing religious and social emphases of the association as they relate to changes in its educational philosophy and to observable trends in current religious thought, educational philosophy, and social situations, by Grace H. Wilson. New York, Bureau of Publications, Teachers College, Columbia University, 1933. [New York, AMS Press, 1972, ie 1973] 156 p. 22 cm. Reprint of the 1933 ed., issued in series: Teachers College, Columbia University. Contributions to education, no. 554. Originally presented as the author's thesis, Columbia. Bibliography: p. 149-156. [BV1350.W73 1972] 70-177632 ISBN 0-404-55554-3 10.00
1. Young Women's Christian Associations. United States. 2. Sociology, Christian. 3. United States—Social conditions. I. Title. II. Series: Columbia University. Teachers College. Contributions to education, no. 554.

WIRT, Sherwood Eliot. 261
The social conscience of the evangelical. [1st ed.] New York, Harper & Row [1968] xiii, 177 p. 22 cm. Includes bibliographical references. [BT738.W53] 68-11736
1. Sociology, Christian. 2. Evangelicalism. I. Title.

WORLD'S Young women's Christian association. 261
The Christian basis of a new society, a study outline ... based on the contributions of an international group of correspondents, and also on official oecumenical documents ... Compiled by Rose Terlin, rapporteur of the World's Y.W.C.A. study on the Christian basis of a new society. Geneva, Switzerland, Washington, D.C., World's Young women's Christian association [1942?] 80 p. 23 cm. "Printed in U.S.A." "Suggested readings": p. 79-80. [HN31.W73] 43-17874
1. Sociology, Christian. I. Terlin, Rose R. II. Title.

ZAHNISER, Charles Reed. 920.
Social Christianity; the gospel for an age of social strain, by Charles Reed Zahniser, PH.D. Nashville, Tenn., The Advance publishing co., 1911. 173 p. 19 1/2 cm. $0.75. [HN31.Z3] 11-1168
1. Sociology, Christian. I. Title.

Sociology, Christian—Addresses, essays, lectures.

BAUM, Gregory, 1923- 261
The social imperative / by Gregory Baum. New York : Paulist Press, c1979. v, 254 p. ; 21 cm. (An Exploration book) Includes bibliographical references. [BT738.B322] 78-70824 ISBN 0-8091-2187-5 pbk. : 6.95
1. Sociology, Christian—Addresses, essays, lectures. I. Title.

BENNETT, John Coleman, 1902- ed. 261
Christian social ethics in a changing world; an ecumenical theological inquiry. New York, Association [c.1966] 381p. 21cm. Working papers prepd. under the sponsorship of the Dept. on Church and Society, World Council of Churches, for the 1966 world conf. Bibl. [BT738.B4] 66-10118 5.50
1. Sociology, Christian—Addresses, essays, lectures. I. World Council of Churches. Division of Studies. Dept. on Church and Society. II. World Conference on Church and Society, Geneva, 1966. III. Title.

BROWN, Charles Reynolds, 1862- 265.
...Social rebuilders [by] Charles Reynolds Brown... New York, Cincinnati, The Abingdon press [c1921] 188 p. 19 cm. (The Mendenhall lectures, seventh series, delivered at De Pauw university) [BR115.S6B72] 21-18517
1. Sociology, Christian—Addresses, essays, lectures. I. Title.

THE Church amid revolution; 261
a selection of the essays prepared for the World Council of Churches Geneva Conference on Church and Society. Edited by Harvey G. Cox. New York, Association Press [1967] 256 p. 21 cm. [BT738.C52] 67-21140
1. Sociology, Christian—Addresses, essays, lectures. I. Cox, Harvey Gallagher, ed. II. World Conference on Church and Society, Geneva, 1966.

CHURCH conference of social work. 261
Religion functioning socially. Studies presented at meetings of the Church conference of social work, Atlantic City, 1936, Indianapolis, 1937. Leland Foster Wood, editor. [New York] Social service department, Federal council of the churches of Christ in America, 1938. [96] p. 21 1/2 cm. [BR115.86C56] 39-15556
1. Sociology, Christian—Addresses, essays, lectures. I. Wood, Leland Foster, 1885- ed. II. Title.

COX, Harvey Gallagher, ed. 261
The Church amid revolution; a selection of the essays prepared for the World Council of Churches Geneva Conference on Church and Society. Edited by Harvey G. Cox. New York, Association Press [1967] 256 p. 21 cm. [BT738.C52] 67-21140
1. Sociology Christian—Addresses, essays, lectures. I. World Conference on Church and Society, Geneva, 1966. II. Title.

GINGERICH, Melvin, 1902- 261.8'3
The Christian and revolution. Scottdale, Pa., Herald Press [1968] 229 p. 20 cm. (The Conrad Grebel lectures, 1967) Bibliography: p. [209]-224. [BT738.G5] 68-12028 4.50
1. Sociology, Christian—Addresses, essays, lectures. I. Title. II. Series.

GRIFFITHS, Brian, comp. 261.8'73
Is revolution change? edited by Brian Griffiths. London, Inter-Varsity Press, 1972. 111 p. 18 cm. (I.V.P. Pocketbook) Contents.Contents.—The law and order issue, by B. Griffiths.--Reform or revolution? by F. Catherwood.—The way of Christ, by A. Kreider.—Revolution and revelation, by R. Padilla.—The social impact of the Gospel, by S. Escobar.—Conclusion: the Christian way. Includes bibliographical references. [BT738.G73] 72-176215 ISBN 0-85110-355-3
1. Sociology, Christian—Addresses, essays, lectures. 2. Revolutions—Addresses, essays, lectures. 3. Church and social problems—Addresses, essays, lectures. I. Title.
Available from Inter-Varsiy, Pap 1.25, ISBN 0-87784-545-X

HODGES, George, 1856-1919. 301
Faith and social service; eight lectures delivered before the Lowell institute, by George Hodges ... New York, T. Whittaker, 1896. 4 p. l., 7-270 p. 19 1/2 cm. [BR115.S6H55] 4-3774
1. Sociology, Christian—Addresses, essays, lectures. I. Title.

HOLT, Arthur Erastus, 1876- 261
This nation under God, [by] Arthur E. Holt... Chicago, New York, Willett, Clark & company, 1939. 7 p. l., 295 p. 20 1/2 cm. [Rauschenbusch lectures. Colgate-Rochester divinity school, Rochester, New York] Notes at end of each of the chapters. [BR115.S6H72] 39-29496
1. Sociology, Christian—Addresses, essays, lectures. 2. Democracy. I. Title.

LEONARD, Adna Wright, bp., 1874- 261.04
Decisive days in social and religious progress [by] Adna Wright Leonard ... New York, Cincinnati [etc.] The Abingdon press [c1935] 155 p. 19 1/2 cm. A revision of the series of lectures delivered during the summer of 1934 at Chautauqua, N.Y. cf. Pref. "References": p. 155. [BR115.S6L45] 35-6980
1. Sociology, Christian—Addresses, essays, lectures. 2. Evangelistic work. I. Title.

MCCONNELL, Francis John, bp., 1871- 261
Christianity and coercion [by] Francis John McConnell... Nashville, Cokesbury press [c1933] 128 p. 22 cm. (The Fondron lectures, 1933) [BR115.S6M252] 33-34799
1. Sociology, Christian—Addresses, essays, lectures. 2. Church and state. 3. Authority (Religion) I. Title.

QUEST for reality: 261.8'3
Christianity and the counter culture [by] Carl F. H. Henry and others. Downers Grove, Ill., InterVarsity Press [1973] 161 p. 21 cm. Papers presented at a conference sponsored by the Institute for Advanced Christian Studies, held in Chicago, Oct., 1971. Includes bibliographical references. [BR115.W6Q47] 73-75892 ISBN 0-87784-761-4 2.95
1. Sociology, Christian—Addresses, essays, lectures. 2. Civilization, Secular—Addresses, essays, lectures. I. Henry, Carl F. H. II. Institute for Advanced Christian Studies. III. Title: Counter culture.

READ, Ralph Harlow, 1903- ed. 261
The younger churchmen look at the church, edited by Ralph H. Read ... with an introduction by Kirby Page. New York, The Macmillan company, 1935. xvi, 345 p. 21 cm. "Reference books": p. 335-336. [BV600.R4] 35-6029
1. Sociology, Christian—Addresses, essays, lectures. 2. Church. 3. Socialism, Christian. I. Title.

A Reader in sociology : 261.8
Christian perspectives / Charles P. De Santo, Calvin Redekop, William L. Smith-Hinds, editors. Scottdale, Pa. : Herald Press, 1980. 736 p. : ports ; 21 cm. Includes bibliographies and indexes. [BT738.R38] 79-22381 ISBN 0-8361-1221-0 : 12.95
1. Sociology, Christian—Addresses, essays, lectures. 2. Sociology—Addresses, essays, lectures. I. De Santo, Charles. II. Redekop, Calvin Wall, 1925- III. Smith-Hinds, William L., 1938-

RELIGION and public affairs, in honor of Bishop Francis John McConnell ... edited by Harris Franklin Rall. New York, The Macmillan company, 1937. xii, 240 p. 20 1/2 cm. 261
Contents.Francis John McConnell, by H. F. Rall.--The struggle of labor, by Heber Blankenhorn.--Civil liberties, by Roger Baldwin--Social security, by Abraham Epstein.--International relations, by S. G. Inman.--East and west, by Sarvapalli Radhakrishnan.--The world of ideas, by E. S. Brightman.--The public mind, by G. A. Coe.--Social change, by H. F. Rall. [HN30.R4] 38-259
1. McConnell, Francis John, bp., 1871- 2. Sociology, Christian—Addresses, essays, lectures. I. Rall, Harris Franklin, 1870- ed.

ROBERTSON, D. B., ed. 261
Voluntary associations, a study of groups in free societies; essays in honor of James Luther Adams. Ed. by D. B. Robertson. Richmond, Knox [1966] 448p. port. 24cm. [BT738.R6] 66-21648 9.75
1. Sociology, Christian—Addresses, essays, lectures. 2. Church— Addresses, essays, lectures. 3. Associations, institutions, etc. I. Adms, James Luther, 1901- II. Title.
Contents omitted.

ROBERTSON, D. B. ed. 261
Voluntary associations, a study of groups in free societies: essays in honor of James Luther Adams. Edited by D. B. Robertson. Richmond, John Knox Press [1966] 448 p. port. 24 cm. Contents.The nature of voluntary associations, by K. Hertz. -- Associational thought in early Calvinism, by F. S. Carney. -- The religious background of the idea of a loyal opposition, by G. H. Williams. -- The meaning of "church" in Anabatism and Roman Catholicism: past and present, by M. Novak. -- Hobbe's theory of associations in the seventeenth-century milieu, by D. H. Robertson. -- The voluntary principle in religion and religious freedom in America, by R. T. Handy. -- The political theory of voluntary association in early nineteenty-century German liberal thought, by G. G. Iggers. -- Rauschenbusch's view of the church as a dynamic voluntary association, by D. E. Smucker. -- A note on creative freedom and the state in the social philosophy of Nicolas Berdyaev, by D. E. Sturm -- Missionary societies and the development of other forms of associations in India, by R. W. Taylor. -- The communaute de travail: experimentation in Integral association, by V. H. Fletcher. -- "The politics of mass society": significance for the churches, by W. A. Pitcher. -- A new pattern of community, by F. H. Littell. -- The crisis of the congregation: a debate, by G. Fackre. -- The voluntary church: a moral appraisal, by J. M. Gustafason. -- SANE as a voluntary organization, by H. A. Jack. -- James Luther Adams: a biographical and intellectual sketch, by M. L. Stackhouse. -- Voluntary associations as a key to history, by J. D. Hunt. -- A bibliography of the writings of James Luther Adams, by R. B. Potter. [BT738.R6] 66-21648
1. Sociology, Christian — Addresses, essays, lectures. 2. Church — Addresses, essays, lectures. 3. Associations, institutions, etc. I. Adams, James Luther, 1901- II. Title.

SMITH, Roy Lemon, 1887- 261
Building a new world, by Roy L. Smith ... Los Angeles, First M. E. church [c1937] 116 p. 20 cm. (First church pulpit. Booklet no. 29) [HN31.S637] 37-4435
1. Sociology, Christian—Addresses, essays, lectures. I. Title.

SOCIOLOGY and theology, 261.8
alliance and conflict / edited by David Martin, John Orme Mills, W. S. F. Pickering ; with an introd. by John Orme Mills. New York : St. Martin's Press, c1980. 204 p. ; 23 cm. Includes indexes. Bibliography: p. [190]-198. [BT738.S62 1980] 79-27012 ISBN 0-312-74007-7 : 17.95
1. Sociology, Christian—Addresses, essays, lectures. I. Martin, David, 1929- II. Mills, John Orme. III. Pickering, W. S. F.

TILLICH, Paul, 1886-1965. 261.8'08
Political expectation. [1st ed.] New York, Harper & Row [1971] xx, 187 p. 22 cm. Contents.Contents.—Introduction, by J. L. Adams.—Christianity and modern society.—Protestantism as a critical and creative principle.—Religious socialism.—Basic principles of religious socialism.—Christianity and Marxism.—The state as expectation and demand.—Shadow and substance: a theory of power.—The political meaning of Utopia. [BT738.T54 1971] 78-124700 5.95
1. Sociology, Christian—Addresses, essays, lectures. 2. Socialism, Christian—Addresses, essays, lectures. 3. Political science—Addresses, essays, lectures. I. Title.

TILLICH, Paul, 1886-1965. 261.8
Political expectation / Paul Tillich. Macon, GA : Mercer University Press, 1981, c1971. p. cm. (ROSE ; no. 1) Reprint. Originally published: 1st ed. New York : Harper & Row, 1971. Includes index. [BT738.T54 1981] 19 81-11253 ISBN 0-86554-021-7 : 13.95
1. Sociology, Christian—Addresses, essays, lectures. 2. Socialism, Christian—Addresses, essays, lectures. 3. Political science—Addresses, essays, lectures. I. Title. II. Series.
Contents deleted.

TITTLE, Ernest Fremont, 1885- 261
Jesus after nineteen centuries [by] Ernest Fremont Tittle. New York, Cincinnati [etc.] The Abingdon press [c1932] 217 p. 21 1/2 cm. "These lectures were delivered on the Lyman Beecher foundation at Yale university." [BR115.S6T53] 33-298
1. Sociology, Christian—Addresses, essays, lectures. 2. Social problems—Addresses, essays, lectures. I. Title.

TITTLE, Ernest Fremont, 1885- 204
A way to life, by Ernest Fremont Tittle. New York, H. Holt and company [c1935] xii, 183 p. 19 1/2 cm. "The substance of this book was presented in a series of lectures on the Ayer foundation at Colgate-Rochester divinity school in April, 1935."--Pref. [BR85.T55] 35-21555
1. Sociology, Christian—Addresses, essays, lectures. I. Title.

TOWARD a discipline of social 177
ethics: essays in honor of Walter George Muelder. Paul Deats, Jr., editor. Boston, Boston University Press, 1972. viii, 328 p. port. 25 cm. Contents.Contents.—Walter G. Muelder: an appreciation of his life, thought, and ministry, by C. E. Lincoln and P. Deats, Jr.—The tasks and methods of social ethics: The quest for a social ethic, by P. Deats, Jr. The relevance of historical understanding, by J. M. Gustafson. The struggle for political consciousness, by A. F. Geyer. The logic of moral argument, by R. B. Potter, Jr.—Ethics, power, and strategy: Toward a Christian understanding of power, by T. S. Sample. The disciplines of power: the necessity and limits of coercion, by J. D. Stamey. The dilemma of Christian social strategy, by J. P. Wogaman. The demand for economic justice: southern Africa and the Portuguese colonies, by F. Houtart.—The church and social responsibility: Political participation—a Christian view, by G. McGovern. The social gospel and race relations: a case study of a social movement, by P. N. Williams. Institutions, unity, and mission, by J. K. Matthews. Public and private dimensions of ethical responsibility, by L. H. DeWolf.—Communitarian Christian ethics: a personal statement and a response, by W. G. Muelder.—A bibliography of the writings of Walter G. Muelder (p. 321-328) [BT738.T68] 70-189020 10.00
1. Muelder, Walter George, 1907-—Bibliography. 2. Sociology, Christian—Addresses, essays, lectures. 3. Social ethics—Addresses, essays, lectures. I. Deats, Paul, ed. II. Muelder, Walter George, 1907-

USHER-WILSON, R.N. 261
The Church must modernize men [by] R. N. Usher-Wilson. Grand Rapids, Eerdmans [1967] 32 p. 21 cm. Bibliographical footnotes. [BT738.U72] 68-1864
1. Sociology, Christian—Addresses, essays, lectures. I. Title.

VRIES, Egbert de, 1901- ed. 261
Man in community; Christian concern for the human in changing society. New York, Association [c.1966] 382p. 21cm. Working papers prepd. under the sponsorship of the Dept. on Church and Society, World Council of Churches, for the 1966 world conf. Bibl. [BT738.V7] 66-11797 5.50
1. Sociology, Christian—Addresses, essays, lectures. I. World Council of Churches. Division of Studies. Dept. on Church and Society. II. World Conference on Church Society, Geneva, 1966. III. Title.

VRIES, Egbert de, ed. 261
Man in community; Christian concern for the human in changing society. New York, Association Press [1966] 382 p. 21 cm. Working papers prepared under the sponsorship of the Dept. on Church and Society, World Council of Churches, for the 1966 world conference. Bibliographical footnotes. [BT738.V7] 66-11797
1. Sociology, Christian—Addresses, essays, lectures. I. World Council of Churches. Division of Studies. Dept. on Church and Society. II. World Conference on Church Society, Geneva, 1966. III. Title.

Sociology, Christian—Adventist authors.

BAKER, Alonzo Lafayette, 1894- 335
Is the world going red? Is capitalism doomed? Will socialism prevail? Is communism or fascism just around the corner? When will the working classes get justice and security? By Alonzo L. Baker ... Mountain View, Calif., Omaha, Neb. [etc.] Pacific press publishing association [c1935] 96 p. illus. (incl. ports., map) 20 cm. [HN37.A35B3] 35-6062
1. Sociology, Christian—Adventist authors. 2. Socialism. 3. U. S.—Econ. condit.—1918- I. Title.

Sociology, Christian—Anglican authors.

BELL, Bernard Iddings, 1886- 261
A Catholic looks at his world; an approach to Christian sociology, by Bernard Iddings Bell ... New York Milwaukee, Morehouse publishing co., 1936. 130 p. 19 cm. (Half-title: The layman's library) [BR115.S6B44] 36-5246
1. Sociology, Christian—Anglican authors. I. Title.

ELIOT, Thomas Stearns, 1888- 261
The idea of a Christian society [by] T.S. Eliot. New York, Harcourt, Brace and company [c1940] vii, 104 p. 22 cm. "Three lectures...with some revision and

division..delivered in March 1939 at...Corpus Christi college, Cambridge, on the Boutwood foundation."--Pref. "First American edition." Bibliographical references in "Notes" (p. 67-90) [HN37.A6E45 1940] 40-3912
1. Sociology, Christian—Anglican authors. I. Title.

RECKETT, Maurice Benington, 1888- 261
A Christian sociology for to-day: an abridged edition of Faith and society, by Maurice B. Reckitt ... London, New York [etc.] Longmans, Green and co., 1934. xi, 286 p. 22 cm. [BR115.S6R52 1934] 35-5088
1. Sociology, Christian—Anglican authors. 2. Civilization, Christian. I. Title.

WESTCOTT, Brooke Foss, bp. of Durham, 1825-1901. 265.
Social aspects of Christianity, by Brooke Foss Westcott ... London and Cambridge and New York, Macmillan and co., 1887. xx, 202 p. 19 cm. "Sermons ... preached (with two exceptions) during my residence at Westminister in August and December, 1886."--Pref. [BR115.S6W4 1887] 38-38942
1. Sociology, Christian—Anglican authors. 2. Church of England—Sermons. 3. Sermons, English. I. Title.
Contents omitted.

Sociology, Christian—Australia.

MOL, J. J. 261'.0994
Christianity in chains; a sociologist's interpretation of the churches' dilemma in a secular world [by] Hans Mol. [Melbourne] Nelson [1969] vii, 120 p. 22 cm. (Nelson's Australasian paperbacks) Bibliography: p. 110-115. [BT738.M55] 72-493507 2.95
1. Sociology, Christian—Australia. 2. Christianity—20th century. I. Title.

Sociology, Christian—Case studies.

LAYNE, Norman R. 301.5'8
Ascension at the cross roads: a case study of a church caught in the turbulence of rapid social change, by Norman R. Layne, Jr. and Jack O. Balswick. Athens, Institute of Community and Area Development, University of Georgia, 1973. vii, 72 p. 29 cm. Bibliography: p. 55-56. [BX8076.S28E924] 73-622076 2.00
1. Evangelical Lutheran Church of the Ascension, Savannah, Ga. 2. Sociology, Christian—Case studies. I. Balswick, Jack O., joint author. II. Title.

Sociology, Christian (Catholic)

ABELL, Aaron Ignatius, 1903- 1965, comp. 261
American Catholic thought on social questions. Indianapolis, Bobbs-Merrill [1968] lv, 571 p. 21 cm. (The American heritage series, 58) Bibliography: p. xliii-liv. [BX1753.A6] 66-30548
1. Sociology, Christian (Catholic) I. Title.

ALBERIONE, Giacomo Giuseppe, 1884- 233
Fundamentals of Christian sociology. [Boston] St. Paul Eds. [dist. Daughters of St. Paul, c.1962] 183p. 22cm. 61-17985 2.50; 1.50 pap.,
1. Sociology, Christian (Catholic) I. Title.

†ALBERIONE, Giacomo Giusseppe, 1884-1971. 261.8
Design for a just society = (originally entitled Fundamentals of Christian sociology) / by James Alberione ; updated by the Daughters of St. Paul. [Boston] : St. Paul Editions, c1976. 247 p. : ill. ; 23 cm. Includes index. Bibliography: p. 223-224. [BT738.A4 1976] 76-975 4.00 pbk. : 3.00
1. Sociology, Christian (Catholic) I. Daughters of St. Paul. II. Title.

CALVEZ, Jean Yves, 1927- 261.85
The church and social justice; the social teaching of the popes from Leo XIII to Pius XII, 1878-1958, by Jean-Yves Calvez, Jacques Perrin. [Tr. by J. R. Kirwan] Chicago, Regnery Co. [1962] 466p. 23cm. 62-52204 7.50
1. Sociology, Christian (Catholic) I. Perrin, Jacques, 1901- joint author. II. Title.

CHENU, Marie Dominique, 1895- 261.85
The theology of work; an exploration. Tr. by Lilian Soiron. Chicago, Regnery [1966, c.1963] vii, 114p. 18cm. (Logos, 51L-708) Bibl. [BX1753.C4213] 66-3744 1.25 pap.,
1. Sociology, Christian (Catholic) 2. Christianity and economics. 3. Work (Theology) I. Title.

CHRISTIAN social conscience (The), v.4, by a group of laymen [Tr. from French] NotreDame, Ind., Fides [1966, c.1965] 112p. 21cm. (St. Severin ser. for adult Christians, v.4; Fides paper back textbks., PBT-20) [BT738.M613] 66-3247 1.75 pap., 261
1. Sociology, Christian (Catholic)

COLLA, Rienzo, ed.
Preti-operai al Concilio. Vicenza, La Locusta [1965] 60 p. 68-32291
1. Sociology, Christian (Catholic) 2. Priest workers. I. Title.

DE BENEDICTIS, Matthew M., 1914- 189'.4
The social thought of Saint Bonaventure; a study in social philosophy, by Matthew M. De Benedictis. Westport, Conn., Greenwood Press [1972, c1946] xv, 276 p. 22 cm. Original ed. issued as v. 93 of the Catholic University of America philosophical series. Originally presented as the author's thesis, Catholic University of America, 1946. Bibliography: p. 267-271. [B765.B74D4 1972] 73-138108 ISBN 0-8371-5684-X
1. Bonaventura, Saint, Cardinal, 1221-1274. 2. Sociology, Christian (Catholic) 3. Social ethics. I. Title. II. Series: Catholic University of America. Philosophical studies, v. 93.

DIRKSEN, Cletus Francis, 1907- 261
Catholic social principles. St. Louis, Herder [c.1961] 247p. Bibl. 61-17788 4.00
1. Sociology, Christian (Catholic) 2. Individuality. 3. Liberty. I. Title.

DOMENACH, Jean Marie, comp. 282.44
The Catholic avant-garde; French Catholicism since World War II [compiled by] Jean-Marie Domenach and Robert de Montvalon. [1st ed. Translated from the French by Brigid Elson and others] New York, Holt, Rinehart and Winston [1967] x, 245 p. 22 cm. Bibliographical references included in "Notes" (p. 241-245) [BX1530.2.D613] 67-10093
1. Catholic Church in France. 2. Sociology, Christian (Catholic) I. Montvalon, Robert de, joint comp. II. Title.

DONOSO Cortes, Jaun, marques de Valdegamas, 1809-1853. 261
An essay on Catholicism, authority and order considered in their fundamental principles / by Juan Donoso Cortes. Westport, Conn. : Hypérion Press, 1979. p. cm. Translation of Ensayo sobre el catolicismo, el liberalismo y el socialismo. Reprint of the 1925 ed. published by J. F. Wagner, New York, in series: My bookcase series. [BX1753.D6 1979] 78-59018 ISBN 0-88355-692-8 : 26.50
1. Socialism and Catholic Church. 2. Catholic Church—Doctrinal and controversial works—Catholic authors. 3. Sociology, Christian (Catholic) I. Title. II. Title: Catholicism, authority and order.

FANFANI, Amintore 261
Catechism of Catholic social teaching. Translated [From the Italian] by Henry J. Yannone. Westminster, Med., Newman Press [c.]1960. xxvii, 208p. 22cm. Bibl.: p.xiii-xvi 60-10719 2.95
1. Sociology, Christian (Catholic) 2. Church and state—Catholic Church. I. Title.

GREELEY, Andrew M., 1928- 261.8
No bigger than necessary : an alternative to socialism, capitalism, and anarchism / Andrew M. Greeley. New York : New American Library, 1977. 181 p. ; 21 cm. "A Meridian book." Includes bibliographical references and index. [BT738.G67] 77-77502 ISBN 0-452-00471-3 pbk. : 3.95
1. Sociology, Christian (Catholic) 2. Christianity and economics. I. Title.

GUERRY, Emile Maurice, Abp., 1891- 261.83
The social doctrine of the Catholic Church. Tr. by Miriam Hederman. New York, Alba House [dist. St. Paul, 1962] 287p. 21cm. Bibl. 62-13995 4.95
1. Sociology, Christian (Catholic) I. Title.

GUERRY, Emile Maurice, Abp.,1891- 261.83
The social doctrine of the Catholic Church. Translated by Miriam Hederman. New York, Alba House [c1961] 287 p. 21 cm. Translation of La doctrine sociale de l'Eglise. Includes bibliography. [BT738.G813] 62-13995
1. Sociology, Christian (Catholic) I. Title.

GUERRY, Emile Maurice, Abp.,1891-
The social teaching of the church. Translation by Miriam Hederman London, New York, St. Paul Publications [1961] 225 p. 23 cm. Translation of La doctrine sociale de l'eglise. "Mater et magistra' [on recent developments of the social question in the light of Christian teachings] encyclical letter of Pope John XXIII." Bibliography: p. [169]. 63-56994
1. Sociology, Christian (Catholic) 2. Church and social problems — Catholic Church. I. Catholic Church. Pope, 1958- (Joannes XXIII) Mater et magistra (15 May 1961) English. II. Title.

HAIPT, Maria Carl Mother 261.8
Social aspects of the Christian faith contained in Mater et magistra and Pacem in terris. Glen Rock, N.J., Paulist [c.1965] 95p. 18cm. (Deus bks.) At head of title: Study guide. Bibl. [BT738.H28] 65-14764 .75 pap.,
1. Sociology, Christian (Catholic) 2. Catholic Church. Pope, 1958-1963 (Joannes XXIII) Mater et magistra (15 May 1961) 3. Catholic Church. Pope, 1958-1963 (Joannes XXIII) Pacem in terris (11 Apr. 1963). I. Title.

HOFFNER, Joseph, Bp. 261
Fundamentals of Christian sociology. Translated by Geoffrey Stevens. Westminster, Md. Newman Press [1965] 196 p. 22 cm. Translation of Christliche Gesellschaftslehre. [BT738.H613 1965] 65-26782
1. Sociology, Christian (Catholic) I. Title.

KELLY, George Anthony, 1916- 261
Who should run the Catholic Church? : Social scientists, theologians, or bishops? / George A. Kelly. Huntington, IN : Our Sunday Visitor, inc., c1976. 224 p. ; 22 cm. Includes bibliographical references and index. [BX1751.2.K37] 76-3291 ISBN 0-87973-755-7 : 8.95
1. Catholic Church—Doctrinal and controversial works—Catholic authors. 2. Sociology, Christian (Catholic) I. Title.

LAURENTIN, Rene. 261.8'3
Liberation, development, and salvation. Translated by Charles Underhill Quinn. Maryknoll, N.Y., Orbis Books [1972] xvii, 238 p. 24 cm. Translation of Developpement et salut. Bibliography: p. 235-238. [BT738.L3513] 72-156970 5.95
1. Sociology, Christian (Catholic) 2. Church and underdeveloped areas. I. Title.

LEPP, Ignace, 1909- 261.83
The Christian failure. Tr. by Elizabeth Strakosch. Westminster, Md., Newman [c.] 1962] 192p. illus. 19cm. 62-51062 3.50
1. Sociology, Christian (Catholic) 2. Catholic Church—Relations. I. Title.

LINK, Mark J. 261
Man in the modern world; perspectives, problems, profiles [by] Mark J. Link. Chicago, Loyola University Press [1967] x, 256 p. illus. 24 cm. [BT738.L5] 67-3706
1. Sociology, Christian (Catholic) 2. Religious education—Text-books for young people—Catholic Church. I. Title.

LOMBARDI, Riccardo. 261
Towards a new world. Translated and condensed from the Italian. New York, Philosophical Library [1958] 276p. illus. 22cm. [BX1753.L633] 58-4833
1. Sociology, Christian (Catholic) 2. Civilization, Christian. I. Title.

MCKENZIE, Leon. 261.7
Designs for progress; an introduction to Catholic social doctrine. [Boston] St. Paul Eds. [1968] 126, [3] p. 22cm. Bibl. [BX1753.M234] 67-31069 2.00; 1.00 pap.,
1. Sociology, Christian (Catholic) I. Title.

MORRISS, Frank. 261.8
The Catholic as citizen : the church's social teaching : order, justice, freedom, peace / by Frank Morriss. Chicago : Franciscan Herald Press, c1979. xv, 126 p. ; 19 cm. [BT738.M63] 19 79-233112 ISBN 0-8199-0775-8 : 6.95
1. Sociology, Christian (Catholic) 2. Social ethics. I. Title.

NEWMAN, John Henry, Cardinal, 262.2
The Christian in society; a theological investigation. Helicon [dist. New York, Taplinger, c.1962] 208p. 22cm. 62-17433 4.50 bds.,
1. Sociology, Christian (Catholic) I. Title.

O'CONNOR, Daniel A. 261.8
Catholic social doctrine. Westminster, Md., Newman Press, 1956. 204p. 23cm. [BX1753.O27] 55-10551
1. Pius XII, Pope, 1876- 2. Sociology, Christian (Catholic) I. Title.

SHEED, Francis Joseph, 1897- 261.8
Society and sanity. London, New York, Sheed and Ward [1953] 225p. 22cm. [BX1753.S49 1953] 53-3135
1. Sociology, Christian (Catholic) I. Title.

STALEY, Ronald 261
Catholic principles of social justice; including the entire text of the encyclical: Pacem in terris. Foreword by Sister Patricia Marie. Los Angeles, Lawrence [c.1964] xiv, 98p. maps, ports. 22cm. Bibl. 64-59864 1.00 pap.,
1. Sociology, Christian (Catholic) I. Catholic Church. Pope, 1958-1963 (Joannes XXIII) Pacem in terris (11 Apr. 1963) II. Title.

STALEY, Ronald. 261
Catholic principles of social justice: including the entire text of the encyclical: Pacem in terris. Foreword by Sister Patricia Marie. Los Angeles, Lawrence Pub. Co. [1964] xiv, 98 p. maps, ports. 22 cm. Bibliography: p. 98. [BT738.S7] 64-5986
1. Sociology, Christian (Catholic) I. Catholic Church. Pope, 1958-1963 (Joannes XXIII) Pacem in Terris (11 Apr. 1963) II. Title.

WALGRAVE, Jan Henricus, 1911- 261.01
Person and society; a Christian view, by John H. Walgrave. Pittsburgh, Duquesne University Press [1965] 182 p. 23 mcm. (Duquesne studies. Theological series, 5) "The original edition of this book was published in Dutch as the introduction to a four volume set entitled Welfare, well-being and happiness. It was translated by Walter van de Putte." Bibliographical footnotes. [BT738.W29] 65-22936
1. Sociology, Christian (Catholic) I. Title.

WALSH, Marion Michael. 260
A new Christendom : how we will build it / by Marion Michael Walsh. Omaha : Help of Christians Publications, c1976. 124 p. ; 22 cm. Includes index. Bibliography: p. 110-113. [BX1753.W27] 75-39175 2.00
1. Sociology, Christian (Catholic) 2. Civilization, Christian. I. Title.

WELTY, Eberhard 261
A handbook of Christian social ethics, v.1. [Translated from the German by Gregor Kirstein, rev. and adapted by John Fitzsimons. New York] Herder and Herder [1960] xvi. [395]p. 22cm. Contents.v. 1. Man in society. Bibl.: p. 359-368 59-14749 6.95
1. Sociology, Christian (Catholic) I. Title. II. Title: Christian social ethics.

WICKER, Brian, 1929- 261
Culture and liturgy. New York, Sheed [1964, c.1963] xii, 212p. 20cm. Bibl. 64-13571 3.50
1. Sociology, Christian (Catholic) I. Title.

Sociology, Christian (Catholic)—Addresses, essays, lectures.

ABOVE every name : 261.1
the lordship of Christ and social systems /

edited by Thomas E. Clarke. Ramsey, N.J. : Paulist Press, c1980. 308 p. ; 21 cm. (Woodstock studies ; 5) Includes bibliographical references. [BX1753.A28] 19 80-82082 ISBN 0-8091-2338-X (pbk.) : 7.95
1. Sociology, Christian (Catholic)—Addresses, essays, lectures. 2. Church and social problems—Catholic Church—Addresses, essays, lectures. I. Clarke, Thomas E. II. Series.

KROL, John Joseph, 1910- 261
To insure peace acknowledge God / by John Cardinal Krol. Boston : St. Paul Editions, c1978. p. cm. [BX1753.K76] 78-12341 5.50 pbk. : 3.95
1. Sociology, Christian (Catholic)—Addresses, essays, lectures. I. Title.
Publisher's address: St. Paul Catholic Film and Book Center, Tremont St., Boston, MA

Sociology, Christian—Catholic authors.

BRAUER, Theodor, 1880- 301
Economy and society; a discussion of the relations between economic and social developments, by Dr. Theodore Brauer ... St. Paul, Minn., Wanderer printing company, 1940. 73 p. 20 cm. [HN37.C3B66] 41-1109
1. Sociology, Christian—Catholic authores. 2. Economics. I. Title.

BREHMER, Robert George, jr. 261
Social doctrines of the Catholic church, by Robert G. Brehmer, jr. ... with a preface by Reverend James M. Gillis ... New York, G. P. Putnam's sons, 1936. x, 11-141 p. 21 cm. Bibliography: p. 139-141. [HN37.C3B68] 37-1349
1. Sociology, Christian—Catholic authors. I. Title.

BRUEHL, Charles Paul, 1876- 261
The Pope's plan for social reconstruction; a commentary on the social encyclicals of Pius xi, by Charles P. Bruehl ... New York, The Devin-adair co. [c1939] xii, 356 p. 22 cm. Bibliography: p. 349-353. [HN37.C38687] 39-27779
1. Pius xi, pope, 1857-1939. 2. Sociology, Christian—Catholic authors. I. Title.

COLLEGEVILLE, Minn. St. John's abbey. 301
The social problem ... Compiled and published by St. John's abbey ... Collegeville, Minn. [c1936- v. 23 cm. "Sponsored by Minnesota branch. Catholic central verein of America, Young people's social guild, archdiocese of St. Paul, Minnesota, Catholic action program, diocese of St. Cloud, Minnesota." "Readings" at end of each chapter. [HN37.C3C54] 38-3298
1. Sociology, Christian—Catholic authors. I. Title.

COUGHLIN, Charles Edward, 1891- 304
Why leave our own? 13 addresses on Christainity and Americanism, by Rev. Chas. E. Coughlin ... broadcast over a national network, January 8-April 2, 1939. [Detroit, The Inland press, c1939. 2 p. l., 7-176 p. 19 cm. [HN37.C3C65] 39-17785
1. Sociology, Christian—Catholic authors. 2. U. S.—Pol. & govt.—1933- I. Title.

DE LA BEDOYERE, Michael, 1900- 204
No dreamers weak; a study of Christian realism as against visionary utopianism in avoiding another great war and making a real peace. Milwaukee, Bruce Pub. Co. [1945] 168 p. 20 cm. [BX1395] A 48
1. Sociology, Christian—Catholic authors. 2. Christianity—20th cent. I. Title. II. Title: Christian realism as against visionary utopianism.

ENGLISH, Michael Ignatius, 1907- 261
Rebuilding the social order [by] Michael I. English, S.J., and William L. Wade, S.J. Chicago, Ill., Loyola university press, 1939. vii, [1] 104 p. 22 cm. Includes bibliographies. [BX1753.E6 1939 a] 39-34137
1. Sociology. Christian—Catholic authors. 2. Sociology, Christian—Study and teaching. I. Wade, William Ligon, 1906- joint author. II. Title.

ENGLISH, Michael Ignatius, 1907- 261
Rebuilding the social order [by] Michael I. English, S.J., and William L. Wade, S.J. St. Louis, Chicago [etc.] John S. Swift co., inc. [c1939] vii, 108 p. 21 1/2 cm. Planographed. Includes bibliographies. [BX1753.E6] 39-10824
1. Sociology, Christian—Catholic authors. 2. Sociology, Christian—Study and teaching. I. Wade, William Ligon, 1906- joint author. II. Title.

EUSTACE, Cecil John, 1903- 261.7
Catholicism, communism and dictatorship; a short study of the problems confronting Catholics under totalitarian forms of government, by C. J. Eustace ... with a preface by Rev. J. A. Keating, S.J. New York, Chicago [etc.] Benziger brothers, 1938. v, 7-10, [2], 11-149 p. 19 cm. Bibliography: p, 142-143. [BX1397.E8] 38-12098
1. Sociology, Christian—Catholic authors. 2. Communism. 3. Fascism. I. Title.

FIVE great encyclicals; 261
labor, education, marriage, reconstructing the social order, atheistic communism ... with discussion club outlines by Rev. Gerald C. Treacy, S. J. New York, The Paulist press [c1939] 4 p. l., 215, [1] p. 20 cm. [BX860.A42] 39-17567
1. Sociology, Christian—Catholic authors. I. Catholic church. Pope, 1878-1903 (Leo xiii) II. Catholic church. Pope, 1922-1939 (Pius xi) III. Treacy, Gerald Carr, 1883- ed. IV. Catholic church. Pope.
Contents omitted.

FURFEY, Paul Hanly, 1896- 261
Fire on the earth, by Paul Hanly Furfey New York, The Macmillan company, 1936. ix, p., 2 l., 159 p. 21 cm. [HN37.C3F8] 36-17679
1. Sociology, Christian—Catholic authors. 2. Catholic church—Apologetic works. I. Title.
Contents omitted.

FURFEY, Paul Hanly, 1896- 261
Three theories of society, by Paul Hanly Furfey ... New York, The Macmillan company, 1937. xii, 251 p. 21 cm. "First printing." [HN37.C8F83] 37-39053
1. Sociology, Christian—Catholic authors. I. Title.

GLENN, Paul Joseph, 1893- 261
Sociology: a class manual in the philosophy of human society, by Paul J. Glenn ... St. Louis, Mo., and London, B. Herder book co., 1935. x, 400 p. 20 cm. [HN37.C3G5] 34-40285
1. Sociology, Christian—Catholic authors. I. Title.

HUGHES, Philip, 1895- ed. 261
The popes' new order; a systematic summary of the social encyclicals and addresses, from Leo XIII to Pius XII, by Philip Hughes ... New York, The Macmillan co., 1944. viii p., 1 l., 331 p. 20 1/2 cm. [BX1753.H] A 44
1. Sociology, Christian—Catholic authors. I. Catholic church. Pope. II. Title.

JERROLD, Douglas, 1893- 261
The future of freedom, notes on Christianity and politics, by Douglas Jerrold. New York, Sheed & Ward, 1938. ix, 306 p. 21 cm. "Printed in Great Britain." [Full name: Douglas Francis Jerrold] [BX1397.J4] 38-19624
1. Sociology, Christian—Catholic authors. 2. Christianity—20th cent. 3. Civilization, Christian. 4. World politics. I. Title.

LUGAN, Alphonse, 1869-1931. 265.
Social principles of the gospel, by Alphonse Lugan; translated from the French by T. Lawrason Riggs, with a preface by John A. Ryan. New York, The Macmillan company, 1928. xii, 262 p. 19 1/2 cm. "The present volume represents the first two parts (Lee grandes directives sociales) of the Abbe Lugan's monumental work on The social teachings of Jesus."--Translator's note. [Full name: Alphonse Marie Lugan] [BR115.S6L8] 28-22472
1. Sociology, Christian—Catholic authors. I. Riggs, Thomas Lawrason, 1888- tr. II. Title.

MCNABB, Vincent Joseph, 1868- 261
Old principles and the new order, by Vincent McNabb, O.P. New York, Sheed & Ward, 1942. xvi, 246 p. 19 1/2 cm. [HN37.C3M413] 43-459
1. Sociology, Christian—Catholic authors. 2. Economics. 3. Land. 4. Cities and towns. I. Title.

MAGNER, James Aloysius, 1901- 261.7
For God and democracy, by James A. Magner. New York, The Macmillan company, 1940. 4 p. l., 3-158 p. 21 cm. "First printing." [BX1790.M28 1940] 40-33349
1. Sociology, Christian—Catholic authors. 2. Church and state—Catholic church. 3. Attitude (Psychology) I. Title.
Contents omitted.

MILLER, John Bleecker, 1856-1922. 261
Leo XIII and modern civilization, by J. Bleecker Miller... New York, The Eskdale press [c1897] 3 p. l., [5]-189 p. 19 1/2 cm. [HN31.M6] 8-31809
1. Sociology, Christian—Catholic authors. 2. Catholic church. Pope, 1878-1903 (Leo XIII) Rerum novarum (15 May 1931) 3. Catholic church. I. Title.

THE modern social and economic order; 261
a symposium specially written for Our Sunday visitor. Huntington, Ind., Our Sunday visitor press [c1939] 8 p. l., 372, [12] p. 20 cm. "First edition, 20,000 copies, February 1, 1939." [HN37.C3M6] 39-15544
1. Sociology, Christian—Catholic authors. 2. Communism.

MUELLER, Franz, 1900- 261
Heinrich Pesch and his theory of Christian solidarism, by Franz H. Mueller ... St. Paul, Minn., The College of St. Thomas [1941] 50 p. 19 1/2 cm. (Aquin papers: no. 7) [Full name: Franz Hermann Joseph Mueller] Bibliographical references included in "Notes" (p. 47-50) [HN37.C3M8] 43-6931
1. Pesch, Heinrich, 1854-1926. 2. Sociology, Christian—Catholic authors. 3. Economics. I. St. Paul. College of St. Thomas. II. Title.

MUNTSCH, Albert, 1873- 252.02
Social thought and action; a series of social sermons, by the Rev. Albert Muntsch ... St. Louis, Mo., and London, B. Herder book co., 1934. x, 234 p. 20 cm. [BX1753.M93] 34-8168
1. Sociology, Christian—Catholic authors. 2. Catholic church—Sermons. 3. Sermons, American. I. Title.

O'BRIEN, Mary Consilia, sister, 1903- 261
Christian social principles, by Sister Mary Consilia O'Brien...with an introduction by Rt. Rev. Msgr. Fulton J. Sheen ... New York, P. J. Kenedy & sons [c1941] xvi, 621 p. 21 cm. [Secular name: Helen Cecilia O'Brien] Includes bibliographies. [HN37.c3O23] 41-15240
1. Sociology, Christian—Catholic authors. I. Title.

O'BRIEN, Mary Consilia, sister, 1903- 261
Christian social principles, by Sister Mary Consilia O'Brien ... with an introduction by Rt. Rev. Msgr. Fulton J. Sheen ... New York, P. J. Kenedy & sons [c1941] xvi, 621 p. 21 cm. [Secular name: Helen Cecilia O'Brien] Includes bibliographies. [HN37.C3O23] 41-15240
1. Sociology, Christian—Catholic authors. I. Title.

THE Pope and the people; 261
select letters and addresses on social questions, by His Holiness Pope Leo xiii. Edited by the Rev. W. H. Eyre, S. J. London and Leamington, Art and book company; New York [etc.] Benziger brothers, 1895. x p., 1 l., 266 p. 19 cm. [HN37.C3A3 1895] 37-37490
1. Sociology, Christian—Catholic authors. I. Eyre, William H., ed. II. Catholic church. Pope, 1878-1903 (Leo xiii)
Contents omitted.

PRINCE, John Francis Theodore, 1906- 261
Creative revolution [by] J. F. T. Prince. Milwaukee, The Bruce publishing company [c1937] xiii p., 1 l., 106 p., 1 l. 23 cm. (Half-title: Science and culture series; Joseph Husslein ... general editor) [HN37.C3P7] 37-306984
1. Sociology, Christian—Catholic authors. I. Title.

RACE: nation: person; 261
social aspects of the race problem, a symposium by Joseph T. Delos [and others] ... With a preface by His Excellency Bishop Joseph W. [.] Corrigan ... New York, Barnes & Noble, inc., 1944. xi, 436 p. 23 1/2 cm. "The Catholic university of America undertook, in connection with its Semicentennial celebration, the arduous task of assembling this symposium--of soliciting, collecting and translating the various monographs."--Pref. Edited by Bishop Joseph M. Corrigan and G. Barry O'Toole. cf. Editor's pref. [HN37.C3R3] 44-2962
1. Sociology, Christian—Catholic authors. 2. Race problems. 3. Totalitarianism. I. Corrigan, Joseph Moran, bp., 1879-1942, ed. II. O'Toole, George Barry, 1886- joint ed. III. Catholic university of America.
Contents omitted.

RACE: nation: person; 261
social aspects of the race problem, a symposium by Joseph T. Delos [and others] ... With a preface by His Excellency Bishop Joseph W. [.] Corrigan ... New York, Barnes & Noble, inc., 1944. xi, 436 p. 23 1/2 cm. "The Catholic university of America undertook, in connection with its Semicentennial celebration, the arduous task of assembling this symposium--of soliciting, collecting and translating the various monographs."--Pref. Edited by Bishop Joseph M. Corrigan and G. Barry O'Toole. cf. Editor's pref. [HN37.C3R3] 44-2962
1. Sociology, Christian—Catholic authors. 2. Race problems. 3. Totalitarianism. I. Corrigan, Joseph Moran, bp., 1879-1942, ed. II. O'Toole, George Barry, 1886- joint ed. III. Catholic university of America.
Contents omitted.

ROSS, Eva Jeany. 301
Rudiments of sociology, by E. J. Ross ... Rev. ed. New York, Milwaukee [etc.] The Bruce publishing company [c1939] xv, 303 p. illus., diagrs. 21 cm. (Half-title: Science and culture texts; Joseph Husslein ... general editor) "Seventh printing." "Recommended readings and questions": p. 255-294. [HN37.C3R69 1930] 39-22858
1. Sociology, Christian—Catholic authors. I. Title.

SCHWER, Wilhelm, 1876- 301
Catholic social theory, by Wilhelm Schwer ... translated by Bartholomew Landheer ... with a preface by Dr. Franz Mueller ... St. Louis, Mo., and London, B. Herder book co., 1940. xv, 360 p. 21 cm. (Half-title: Social studies. College series, ed. by Franz Mueller ...) Bibliography: p. 326.341. [HN37.C3S36] 40-10645
1. Sociology, Christian—Catholic authors. I. Landheer, Bartholomew, 1904- tr. II. Title.

SLATER, Thomas, 1855-1928. 261
Questions of moral theology, by Rev. Thomas Slater... New York, Cincinnati [etc.] Benziger brothers, 1915. 4 p. l., 15-426 p. 23 cm. Reprinted from the Irish ecclesiastical record, the Irish theological quarterly, and the American ecclesiastical review. cf. pref. [HN37.C3S6] 15-9218
1. Sociology, Christian—Catholic authors. 2. Christian ethics—Catholic authors. I. Title.
Contents omitted.

SMITH, Reginald Anthony Lendon. 261
The Catholic church and social order, by R. A. L. Smith ... London, New York [etc.] Longmans, Green and co. [1943] 162 p. 19 cm. "First published 1943." Bibliographical foot-notes. [BX1753.S57] A 44
1. Sociology, Christian—Catholic authors. I. Title.

SOCIAL wellsprings ... 261
selected, arranged, and annotated by Joseph Husslein ... Milwaukee, The Bruce publishing company [c1940-42] 2 v. 24 cm. Contents.i. Fourteen epochal documents, by Pope Leo xiii.--ii. Eighteen encyclicals of social reconstruction by Pope Pius xi. Includes bibliographies. [HN37.C3A3 1940] 41-1099

1. Sociology, Christian—Catholic authors. I. Catholic church, Pope, 1922-1939 (Pius xi) II. Husslein, Joseph Caspar, 1873- comp. III. Catholic church. Pope, 1878-1903 (Leo xiii)

THORNING, Joseph Francis, 1896- 261
Builders of the social order, by the Reverend Joseph F. Thorning... Ozone Park, N.Y., Catholic literary guild, 1941. xv, 183 p. 21 cm. [Full name: Joseph Francis Xavier Thorning] [HN37.C3T45] 41-11895
1. Sociology, Christian—Catholic authors. I. Title.

WARD, Louis B. 922.273
Father Charles E. Coughlin; an authorized biography, by Louis B. Ward... Detroit, Mich., Tower publications, incorporated [c1933] xv, 352 p. front. (port.) illus. (facsims.) plates, plan. 25 cm. Maps on lining-papers. [BX4705.C7795W3] 33-31101
1. Coughlin, Charles Edward, 1891- 2. Sociology, Christian—Catholic authors. 3. U.S.—Economic conditions—1918- 4. Catholic church—Sermons. 5. Sermons, American. I. Title.

WELSH, Mary Gonzaga, sister. 377.82
... The social philosophy of Christian education [by] Sister Mary Gonzaga Welsh ... Washington, D.C., The Catholic education press [1936] xi, 98 p. 23 cm. (The Catholic university of America. Educational research monographs, T. G. Foran, editor. vol. IX ... no. 2) Issued also as thesis (PH.D.) Catholic university of America. Bibliography: p. 91-98. [LC485.W4 1936a] 37-18423
1. Sociology, Christian—Catholic authors. 2. Catholic church—Education. 3. Religious education. I. Title.

WILLIGAN, Walter Luke. 251
Social order by Walter L. Willigan ... [and] John J. O'Connor ... New York, London [etc.] Longmans, Green and co., 1941. xii p. 1 l., 703 p. illus. (map) diagrs. 21 cm. "First edition." Bibliography at end of each chapter. p. 355-376. [HM66.W54 1941] 41-5431
1. Sociology, Christian—Catholic authors. I. O'Connor, John Joseph, 1904- joint author. II. Title.

WILLIGAN, Walter Luke. 301
Sociology, by Walter L. Willigan ... [and] John J. O'Connor ... New York, London [etc.] Longmans, Green and co., 1940. xi, 387 p. diagrs. 21 cm. "First edition." Bibliography at end of some of the chapters; "Critical essay on authorities": p. 355-376. [HN37C3W5] 40-13512
1. Sociology, Christian—Catholic authors. I. O'Connor, John Joseph, 1904- joint author. II. Title.

Sociology, Christian (Catholic)—History.

ELIAS, John L., 1933- 301.24
Conscientization and deschooling : Freire's and Illich's proposals for reshaping society / by John L. Elias. Philadelphia : Westminster Press, c1976. p. cm. Bibliography: p. [BT738.E39] 76-20618 ISBN 0-664-20787-1 : 12.95
1. Illich, Ivan D. 2. Freire, Paulo, 1921- 3. Sociology, Christian (Catholic)—History. 4. Social change. 5. Education—Philosophy. I. Title.

Sociology, Christian (Catholic)—History of doctrines—20th century.

CURRAN, Charles E. 261.8'0973
American Catholic social ethics : twentieth-century approaches / Charles E. Curran. Notre Dame : University of Notre Dame Press, c1982. p. cm. Includes index. [BX1753.C86] 19 82-4829 ISBN 0-268-00603-2 : 18.95
1. Catholic Church—United States—History—20th century. 2. Sociology, Christian (Catholic)—History of doctrines—20th century. 3. Christian ethics—History of doctrines—20th century. 4. Social ethics—History—20th century. I. Title.

SCHALL, James V. 261.8
The social thought of John Paul II / by James V. Schall. Chicago, Ill. : Franciscan Herald Press, [1981] p. cm. Bibliography: p. [BX1753.S32] 19 81-12497 ISBN 0-8199-0838-X : 6.95
1. John Paul II, Pope, 1920- —Political and social views. 2. Sociology, Christian (Catholic)—History of doctrines—20th century. I. Title.

Sociology, Christian (Catholic)—Papal documents.

SOCIAL justice / 261
[compiled by] Vincent P. Mainelli. Wilmington, N.C. : Consortium Books, 1978. xxvi, 496 p. ; 24 cm. (Official Catholic teachings) Includes bibliographical references and index. [BX1753.S625] 78-53833 ISBN 0-8434-0712-3 : 15.95. ISBN 0-8434-0718-2 pbk. : 8.95
1. Catholic Church—Doctrinal and controversial works—Catholic authors—Papal documents. 2. Sociology, Christian (Catholic)—Papal documents. I. Mainelli, Vincent P. II. Series.

Sociology, Christian (Catholic)—Statistics.

KOTRE, John N. 282.73
The view from the border; a social-psychological study of current Catholicism [by] John N. Kotre. Chicago, Aldine [1971] x, 268 p. illus., forms. 22 cm. (Aldine treatises in social psychology) Bibliography: p. 261-264. [BT738.K68] 73-131044 ISBN 0-202-25040-7
1. Sociology, Christian (Catholic)—Statistics. 2. Christianity—Psychology—Statistics. I. Title.

Sociology, Christian (Catholic)—Study and teaching.

GREMILLION, Joseph B. 261
Continuing Christ in the modern world; teaching Christian social concepts in the light of Vatican Council II, by Joseph Gremillion. Dayton, Ohio, Paflaum [1967] 189p. illus, map. 17cm. Bibl. [BX1753.G7] 67-28059 1.00 pap.,
1. Sociology, Christian (Catholic)—Study and teaching. I. Title.

KALT, William J. 261
The community of the free [by] William J. Kalt and Ronald J. Wilkins. Chicago, Regnery [1968] ii, 121 p. illus. 23 cm. (To live is Christ. Discussion booklet 6) Bibliographical footnotes. [BT38.K3] 68-55751
1. Sociology, Christian (Catholic)—Study and teaching. I. Wilkins, Ronald J., joint author. II. Title.

Sociology, Christian—Congresses.

CONFERENCE on Christian politics, economics and citizenship.
The proceedings of C.O.P.E.C.; being a report of the meetings of the Conference on Christian politics, economics and citizenship ... London, New York [etc.] Published for the conference committee by Longmans, Green and co., 1924- v. 19 1/2 cm. [HN383.C6] 24-16313
1. Sociology, Christian—Congresses. I. Title.

CONFERENCE on Christian politics, economics and citizenship. Regional conference, Sheffield, 1924.
The fourfold challenge of to-day, being a record of the proceedings of the Sheffield regional C O P E C conference, October 15th, 16th and 17th, 1924, edited for the Sheffield C O P E C continuation committee, by Henry Cecil ... With introduction by the Right Rev. the Lord Bishop of Manchester ... London, New York [etc.] Longmans, Green and co., 1925. 199 p. 19 cm. Effects slip inserted. [HN383.C7S5] 25-12651 1.00.
1. Socology, Christian—Congresses. I. Cecil, Henry, 1879- ed. II. Title.

Sociology, Christian—Connecticut Valley.

LUCAS, Paul R. 277.44'2
Valley of discord : church and society along the Connecticut River, 1636-1725 / Paul R. Lucas. Hanover, N.H. : University Press of New England, 1976. xiv, 275 p. ; 25 cm. Includes index. Bibliography: p. 207-214. [BR520.L8] 75-22520 ISBN 0-87451-121-6 : 12.00
1. Sociology, Christian—Connecticut Valley. 2. Connecticut Valley—Church history. I. Title.

Sociology, Christian—Early church.

CASE, Shirley Jackson, 1872- 270.1
The social triumph of the ancient church, by Shirley Jackson Case. New York and London, Harper & brothers, 1933. 6 p. l., 3-250 p. 20 cm. "The chapters of this book were delivered, in a somewhat abbreviated form, as the Rauschenbusch memorial lectures at Colgate-Rochester divinity school during Alumni week, April 18-21, 1933."--Pref. "first edition. [BR163.C3] 33-21604
1. Sociology, Christian—Early church. I. Title.

CASE, Shirley Jackson, 1872-1947. 301.5'8
The social origins of Christianity. New York, Cooper Square Publishers, 1975. vii, 263 p. 22 cm. Reprint of the 1923 ed. published by the University of Chicago Press, Chicago. Bibliography: p. 255-258. [BR166.C37 1975] 74-84544 ISBN 0-8154-0501-4 8.00 (lib. bdg.).
1. Sociology, Christian—Early church. I. Title.

CASE, Shirley Jackson, 1872-1947. 301.5'8
The social triumph of the ancient church. Freeport, N.Y., Books for Libraries Press [1971] 250 p. 23 cm. Reprint of the 1933 ed. "Delivered, in a somewhat abbreviated form, as the Rauschenbusch memorial lectures at Colgate-Rochester Divinity School ... April 18-21, 1933." Includes bibliographical references. [BR163.C3 1971] 76-164596 ISBN 0-8369-5880-2
1. Sociology, Christian—Early church. I. Title.

GIORDANI, Igino, 1894- 281.2
The social message of the early church fathers [by] Igino Giordani, translated from the Italian by Alba I. Zizzamia ... Paterson, N.J., St. Anthony guild press, 1944. x p., 1 l., 356 p. 23 1/2 cm. "The present volume is the third in a history of early Christian social thought."--Translator's note. Bibliographical foot-notes. Bibliography: p. 335-345. [BR165.G52] 45-2002
1. Sociology, Christian—Early church. 2. Fathers of the church. I. Zizzamia, Alba Isabel, 1910-tr. II. Title.

MCKERROW, James Clark, 1888- 261
Religion and history, by James Clark McKerrow, M.B. London, New York [etc.] Longmans, Green and co., 1934. 2 p. l., vii-ix p., 2 l., 192, [1] p. 20 1/2 cm. [BR165.M216] 35-11445
1. Sociology, Christian—Early church. 2. Gnosticism. I. Title.
Contents omitted.

Sociology, Christian—Early church, ca. 30-600.

ADAMS, Jeremy duQuesnay. 260
The populus of Augustine and Jerome; a study in the patristic sense of community. New Haven, Yale University Press, 1971. viii, 278 p. 23 cm. Bibliography: p. 252-266. [BR166.A3] 70-140521 ISBN 0-300-01402-3 12.50
1. Augustinus, Aurelius, Saint, Bp. of Hippo—Sociology. 2. Hieronymus, Saint. 3. Sociology, Christian—Early church, ca. 30-600. 4. Populus (The Latin word) I. Title.

GAGER, John G. 270.1
Kingdom and community : the social world of early Christianity / John G. Gager. Englewood Cliffs, N.J. : Prentice-Hall, [1975] xiii, 158 p. ; 24 cm. (Prentice-Hall studies in religion series) Includes bibliographical references and index. [BR166.G33] 74-28199 ISBN 0-13-516211-4 : 6.95
1. Sociology, Christian—Early church, ca. 30-600. I. Title.

GIORDANI, Igino, 1894- 261.8
The social message of the early church fathers / Igino Giordani ; translated by Alba I. Zizzamia. Boston : St. Paul Editions, c1977. x, 356 p. ; 19 cm. Translation of Il messaggio sociale dei primi padri della chiesa. Reprint of the 1944 ed. published by St. Anthony Guild Press, Paterson, N.J. Includes index. Bibliography: p. 335-345. [BR166.G5613 1977] 77-4935 4.50 pbk. : 3.50
1. Sociology, Christian—Early church, ca. 30-600. 2. Fathers of the church. I. Title.

THEISSEN, Gerd. 261.8
Sociology of early Palestinian Christianity / Gerd Theissen ; translated by John Bowden. 1st American ed. Philadelphia : Fortress Press, 1978. viii, 131 p. ; 22 cm. Translation of Soziologie der Jesusbewegung. Includes bibliographical references and indexes. [BR166.T4713 1978] 77-15248 ISBN 0-8006-1330-9 pbk. : 4.50
1. Sociology, Christian—Early church, ca. 30-600. I. Title.

ZEHNLE, Richard F. 270.1
The making of the Christian church. Notre Dame, Ind., Fides Publishers [1969] xii, 168 p. 20 cm. Includes bibliographical footnotes. [BR165.Z38] 70-95638 ISBN 0-8190-0517-7 2.50
1. Sociology, Christian—Early church, ca. 30-600. I. Title.

Sociology, Christian—Early church, ca. 30-600—Addresses, essays, lectures.

GRANT, Robert McQueen, 1917- 261.1
Early Christianity and society : seven studies / Robert M. Grant. New York : Harper & Row, [1977] p. cm. Includes index. Bibliography: p. [BR166.G7] 77-7844 ISBN 0-06-063411-1 : 10.95
1. Sociology, Christian—Early church, ca. 30-600—Addresses, essays, lectures. I. Title.

MALHERBE, Abraham J. 261.8
Social aspects of early Christianity / Abraham J. Malherbe. Baton Rouge : Louisiana State University Press, c1977. xii, 98 p. ; 23 cm. (Rockwell lectures) Delivered at Rice University, April 1975. Includes bibliographical references and index. [BR166.M34] 77-3876 ISBN 0-8071-0261-X : 7.95
1. Sociology, Christian—Early church, ca. 30-600—Addresses, essays, lectures. I. Title. II. Series.

THEISSEN, Gerd. 306'.6
The social setting of Pauline Christianity : essays on Corinth / by Gerd Theissen ; edited and translated and with an introduction by John H. Schutz. Philadelphia : Fortress Press, c1982. p. cm. Translation of: Studien zur Soziologie des Urchristentums. Bibliography: p. [BS2675.2.T4313] 19 81-43087 ISBN 0-8006-0669-8 : 19.95
1. Bible. N.T. Corinthians—Criticism, interpretation, etc.—Addresses, essays, lectures. 2. Sociology, Christian—Early church, ca. 30-600—Addresses, essays, lectures. I. [Studien zur Soziologie des Urchristentums.] English II. Title.

Sociology, Christian—England.

COX, Jeffrey. 283'.42165
The English churches in a secular society : Lambeth, 1870-1930 / Jeffrey Cox. New York ; Oxford : Oxford University Press, 1982. p. cm. Includes index. Bibliography: p. [BX5101.C64] 19 82-2157 ISBN 0-19-503019-2 : 29.95
1. Church of England—History. 2. Church of England—England—Lambeth (London)—History. 3. Sociology, Christian—England. 4. England—Church history. 5. Sociology, Christian—England—Lambeth (London) 6. Lambeth (London, England)—Church history. 7. London (England)—Church history. I. Title.

Sociology, Christian—England—History.

COWLING, Maurice. 261.8
Religion and public doctrine in modern England / Maurice Cowling. Cambridge [Eng.] ; New York : Cambridge University Press, 1980- v. <1> ; 23 cm. (Cambridge studies in the history and theory of politics) Includes index. Bibliography: v. 1, p. 469. [BR759.C67] 19 80-40614 ISBN 0-521-23289-9 (v. 1) : 49.50
1. Sociology, Christian—England—History. 2. Conservatism—England—History. I. Title.

NORMAN, Edward R. 261
Church and society in England 1770-1970 : a historical study / by e.R. Norman Oxford : Clarendon Press, 1976. 507 p. ; 24 cm. Includes index. Bibliography: p. [475]-494. [BR744.N67] 76-377182 ISBN 0-19-826435-6 : 25.50
1. Sociology, Christian—England—History. I. Title.
Distributed by Oxford University Press, NY

Sociology, Christian—England—Parts of Lindsey.

OBELKEVICH, James. 301.5'8
Religion and rural society : South Lindsey, 1825-1875 / James Obelkevich. Oxford [Eng.] : Clarendon Press, 1976. xiii, 353 p. : maps ; 23 cm. Includes index. Bibliography: p. [337]-346. [BR765.P37O23] 77-350970 ISBN 0-19-822426-5 : 25.25
1. Sociology, Christian—England—Parts of Lindsey. 2. Parts of Lindsey, Eng.—Religious life and customs. I. Title.
Distributed by Oxford University Press NY NY

Sociology, Christian—Fiction.

SHELDON, Charles Monroe, 1857-
In His steps; "What would Jesus do?" by Charles M. Sheldon ... Rev. ed. Chicago, Advance publishing co., 1899. 2 p. l., 284 p. 19 1/2 cm. [PS2809.S55 I 5 1899 a] 99-3675
1. Sociology, Christian—Fiction. I. Title.

SHELDON, Charles Monroe, 1857-
In His steps. What would Jesus do? By Charles M. Sheldon ... [Elgin, Ill.; Chicago, D. C. Cook publishing company] c1899. 96 p. illus. 21 1/2 x 17 cm. Caption title. [PS2809.S55 I 5 1899] 0-187
1. Sociology, Christian—Fiction. I. Title.

Sociology, Christian—France.

SCHWARTZ, Christina, 282.44
sister, 1907-
... Catholic church working through its individual members in any age and nation. makes a positve social contribution as seen in France, 1815-1870 ... by Sister M. Christina Schwartz ... Washington, D. C., The Catholic university of America press, 1939. x, 193 p. maps. 23 cm. Thesis (PH. D.)--Catholic university of America. [Secular name: Elizabeth C. Schwartz] Bibliography: p. 95-108. [BX1530.S4] 40-1915
1. Sociology, Christian—France. 2. Sociology, Christian—Catholic authors. 3. Catholic church in France—Charities. I. Title.

Sociology, Christian—Great Britain

ARMITAGE, John James 261.0942
Richard.
To Christian England, by John Armitage. London, New York [etc.] Longmans, Green and co. [1942] vi, 105 p. 19 cm. "First published 1942." [HN39.G7A8] 42-24293
1. Sociology, Christian—Gt. Brit. I. Title.

LITTLE, David. 261'.0942
Religion, order, and law; a study in pre-Revolutionary England. [1st ed.] New York, Harper & Row [1969] v, 269 p. 21 cm. (Harper torchbooks. The Library of religion and culture, TB1418.) Includes bibliographical references. [BR757.L66] 70-84041 2.95
1. Weber, Max, 1864-1920. Dieprotestantische Ethik und der Geist des Kapitalismus. 2. Church of England—Doctrinal and controversial works. 3. Sociology, Christian—Gt. Brit. 4. Religion and law. 5. Puritans. I. Title.

MACARTHUR, Kathleen 922.742
Walker.
The economic ethics of John Wesley [by] Kathleen Walker MacArthur. New York, Cincinnati [etc.] The Abingdon press [c1936] 166 p. 19 1/2 cm. Bibliography: p. 155-166. [BX8495.W5M23] 37-7821
1. Wesley, John, 1763-1791. 2. Sociology, Christian—Gt. Brit. 3. Sociology, Christian—Methodist authors. I. Title.

PRINGLE, John Christian, 258
1872-
Social work of the London churches; being some account of the Metropolitan visiting and relief association, 1843-1937. Prepared under the direction of the Executive committee of the association and in co-operation with the London association of voluntary school care committee workers, by J. C. Pringle ... London, Oxford university press, H. Milford, 1937. xv, 291 p. 19 cm. Bibliography: p. 275-282. [BX5110.L7P7] 38-22486
1. Sociology, Christian—Gt. Brit. 2. Social service. 3. Metropolitan visiting and relief association, London. I. London association of voluntary school care committee workers. II. Title.

Sociology, Christian—History.

HOPKINS, Charles Howard, 261
1905-
The rise of the social gospel in American Protestantism: 1865-1915, by Charles Howard Hopkins. New Haven, Yale [1967,c.1940] xiv. 352p. 21cm. (Half-title: Yale Studies in religious educ. xiv) Presented for the degree of Ph.D at Yale [1937] Pub. under the joint sponsorship of the Samuel B. Smeath memorial pubns. fund of the Yale divinity sch. and the Rauschenbusch memorial lectship. found. of the Colgate-Rochester divinity sch. [HN39.U6H6 1967] 41-1101 8.50; 2.45 pap.,
1. Sociology, Christian—Hist. 2. Theology, Doctrinal—Hist.—U. S. I. Title. II. Title: The social gospel in American Protestantism.

HOPKINS, Charles Howard, 261
1905-
The rise of the social gospel in American Protestantism, 1865-1915, by Charles Howard Hopkins. New Haven, Yale university press; London, H. Milford, Oxford university press, 1940. xii, 352 p., 1 l. 28 1/2 cm. (Half-title: Yale studies in religious education. XIV) "Presented for the degree of doctor of philosophy at Yale university [1837]" "Published under the joint sponsorship of the Samuel B. Sneath memorial publication fund of the Yale university divinity school and the Rauschenbusch memorial lectureship foundation of the Colgate-Rochester divinty school." [HN39.U6H6 1940 a] 41-1101
1. Sociology, Christian—Hist. 2. Theology, Doctrinal—Hist.—U.S. I. Title. II. Title: The social gospel in American Protestantism.

HYMA, Albert, 1893- 261
Christianity, capitalism and communism, a historical analysis, by Albert Hyma ... Ann Arbor, Mich., G. Wahr, 1937. 3 p. l., 303 p. 24 cm. Label mounted over imprint: Published by the author. Errata slip mounted on verso of p. 303. [HN31.H88] 38-2000
1. Sociology, Christian—Hist. 2. Capitalism. 3. Communism. I. Title.

MACMURRAY, John, 1891- 261
The clue to history, by John Macmurray... New York and London, Harper & brothers, 1939. 2 p. l., vii-xi, [1], 242, [1] p. 21 1/2 cm. "First edition." [BR125.M3395 1939] 39-13838
1. Sociology, Christian—Hist. 2. Christianity and other religions—Judaism. 3. Jewish question. 4. Fascism. 5. Communism. I. Title.
Contents omitted.

MCNEILL, John Thomas, 1885- 261
Christian hope for world society, by John T. McNeill... Chicago, New York, Willett, Clark & company, 1937. vii p., 1 l., 278 pl 20 1/2 cm. "Bibliography of modern works": p. 299-278. [HN31.M22] 38-10176
1. Sociology, Christian—Hist. I. Title.

SPENCER, Malcolm, 1877- ed. 265.
Social discipline in the Christian community, past, present and future, edited by Rev. Malcolm Spencer ... London, New York [etc.] Longmans, Green and co. ltd., 1926. viii, 117, [1] p. 19 cm. [BR115.S6S62] 26-12608
1. Sociology, Christian—Hist. I. Title.
Contents omitted.

TROELTSCH, Ernest, 1865-1923. 261
The social teaching of the Christian churches [2.v.] by Ernst Troeltsch.Translated [from the German] by Olive Wyon, with an introduction by H. Richard Niebuhr. New York, Harper [c.1960] 2v. 1019p. 21cm. (Harper Torchbooks, The Cloister library, TB-71; TB-72) Paged continuosly. Bibl. notes. pap., v.1, 2.25; v.2, 2.45
1. Sociology, Christian—Hist. 2. Church history. I. Wyon, Olive, tr. II. Title.

TROELTSCH, Ernst, 1865-1923. 261
... The social teaching of the Christian churches, by Ernst Troeltsch. Translated by Olive Wyon, with an introductory note by Charles Gore ... New York, The Macmillan company, 1931. 2 v. 24 cm. (Halley Stewart publications, I) Paged continuously. "Printed in Great Britain." "First published in English in 1931." Notes include bibliographical material. [HN31.T75] 32-946
1. Sociology, Christian—Hist. 2. Church history. I. Wyon, Olive, tr. II. Title.

VISSER 'T HOOFT, Willem Adolph,
1900-
The background of the social gospel in America. St. Louis, Bethany Press [1963] 187 p. 22 cm. (Abbott books) Originally published in Haarlem, Netherlands, in 1928. 63-73732
1. Sociology, Christian—History. 2. Theology, Doctrinal—History—U.S. I. Title. II. Title: Social gospel in America.

WAGNER, Donald Owen, 261.0942
1897-
The Church of England and social reform since 1854, by Donald D. Wagner, PH. D New York, Columbia university press; London, P. S. King & son, ltd., 1930. 341 p. 23 cm. (Half-title: Studies in history, economics and public law, ed. by the Faculty of political science of Columbia university, no. 325) Published also as thesis (PH. D.) Columbia university. Bibliography: p. 328-336. [H31.C7 no. 325] [HN39.G7W3 1930a] (306.2) 30-27974
1. Sociology, Christian—Hist. 2. Church of England—Hist. 3. Socialism in Great Britain. 4. Church and state in Great Britain. I. Title.

Sociology, Christian—History—20th century.

MCCANN, Dennis. 261.8
Christian realism and liberation theology : practical theologies in conflict / Dennis McCann. Maryknoll, N.Y. : Orbis Books, c1981. vi, 250 p. ; 24 cm. Includes index. Bibliography: p. 241-244. [BT738.M25] 19 80-23163 ISBN 0-88344-086-5 pbk. : 9.95
1. Niebuhr, Reinhold, 1892-1971. 2. Sociology, Christian—History—20th century. 3. Christian ethics—History—20th century. 4. Social ethics—History—20th century. 5. Liberation theology. I. Title.

Sociology, Christian (Lutheran)

CARLSON, Edgar Magnus, 261.8
1908-
The church and the public conscience. Philadelphia, Muhlenberg Press [c1956] 104p. 20cm. [BR115.S6C27] 55-11782
1. Sociology, Christian (Lutheran) I. Title.

CARLSON, Edgar Magnus, 261.8
1908-
The church and the public conscience / Edgar M. Carlson. Westport, Conn. : Greenwood Press, 1981, c1956. p. cm. Reprint of the ed. published by Muhlenberg Press, Philadelphia. [BT738.C357 1981] 19 79-8710 ISBN 0-313-20813-1 lib. bdg. : 17.50
1. Sociology, Christian (Lutheran) I. Title.

FORELL, George Walfgang 270.6
Faith active in love; an investigation of the principles underlying Luther's social ethics. Minneapolis, Augsburg Pub. House [1960, c.1954] 198p. port. 20cm. Bibliography: p.190-198 2.00 pap.,
1. Luther, Martin, 1483-1546. 2. Sociology, Christian (Lutheran) 3. Social ethics. I. Title.

FORELL, George Wolfgang. 270.6
Faith active in love; an investigation of principles underlying Luther's social ethics. [1st ed.] New York, American Press [1954] 198p. port. 21cm. Bibliography: p. 190-198. [BR333.F58] 54-10896
1. Luther, Martin, 1483-1546. 2. Sociology, Christian (Lutheran) 3. Social ethics. I. Title.

Sociology, Christian—Lutheran authors.

PFATTEICHER, Ernst Philip 261.04
Henry, 1874-
Christian social science ... by E. P. Pfatteicher; with forewords by Rees Edgar Tulloss and T. A. Kantonen. New York, Falcon press [c1933] vii, 191 p. 21 cm. (Kessler foundation lectures ... Hamma divinity school) [BR115.S6P4] 33-9130
1. Sociology, Christian—Lutheran authors. 2. Church work. I. Title.

REHWINKEL, Alfred Martin, 261
1887-
The world today; a challenge to the Christian church, by Alfred M. Rehwinkel ... St. Louis, Mo., Concordia publishing house, 1940. 107 p. 18 1/2 cm. [BR115.S6R54] 41-2053
1. Sociology, Christian—Lutheran authors. I. Title.

Sociology, Christian—Manitoba—Steinbach.

HARDER, Leland, 1926- 277.127'4
Steinbach and its churches. Elkhart, Ind., Work of the Church Dept., Mennonite Biblical Seminary, 1970. vi, 109 p. illus., maps. 28 cm. [BR580.S7H3] 73-263850
1. Sociology, Christian—Manitoba—Steinbach. 2. Steinbach, Manitoba—Church history. I. Title.

Sociology, Christian—Massachusetts—Holyoke.

UNDERWOOD, Kenneth 261.8'3
Wilson.
Protestant and Catholic: religious and social interaction in an industrial community. Westport, Conn., Greenwood Press [1973, c1957] xxi, 484 p. illus. 22 cm. Bibliography: p. 409-417. [BR560.H7U5 1973] 72-9051 ISBN 0-8371-6567-9 18.25
1. Catholic Church—Relations—Protestant churches. 2. Sociology, Christian—Massachusetts—Holyoke. 3. Protestant churches—Relations—Catholic Church. I. Title.

Sociology, Christian (Methodist)

HARKNESS, Georgia Elma, 1891- 261
The Methodist Church in social thought and action. Ed. by the Bd. of Soc. & Econ. Relations of the Methodist Church. Nashville, Abingdon [c.1964] 172p. 23cm. 64-16150 1.50 pap.,
1. Sociology, Christian (Methodist) I. Methodist Church (United States) Board of Social and Economic Relations. II. Title.

HARKNESS, Georgia Elma, 1891- 261
The methodist Church in social thought and action. Edited by the Board of Social and Economic Relations of the Methodist Church. New York, Abingdon Press [1964] 172 p. 23 cm. [BT738.H3] 64-16150
1. Sociology, Christian (Methodist) I. Methodist Church (United States) Board of Social and Economic Relations. II. Title.

SCHILLING, Sylvester Paul 261.83
Methodism and society in theological perspective. Edited by the Board of Social

and Economic Relations of the Methodist Church. Nashville, Abingdon Press [c.1960] 318p. 24cm. (Methodism and society, v. 3) Bibl.: p.309-311. tables. 60-11221 5.00
1. Sociology, Christian (Methodist). I. Methodist Church (United States) Board of Social and Economic Relations. II. Title. III. Series.

SCHILLING, Sylvester Paul, 1904- 261.83
Methodism and society in theological perspective. Edited by the Board of Social and Economic Relations of the Methodist Church. New York, Abingdon Press [1960] 318p. tables. 24cm. (Methodism and society, v.3) Bibliography: p.300-311. [BT738.S36] 60-11221
1. Sociology, Christian (Methodist) I. Methodist Church (United States) Board of Social and Economic Relations. II. Title. III. Series.

Sociology, Christian—Methodist authors.

HUGHES, Hugh Price, 1847-1902. 252.07
Social Christianity; sermons delivered in St. Jame's hall, London, by Hugh Price Hughes, M.A. New York, Funk and Wagnalls, 1895. xix, 281 p. 21 cm. [BR115.S6H76] 37-9766
1. Sociology, Christian—Methodist authors. 2. Methodism—Sermons. 3. Sermons, English. I. Title.

JONES, Eli Stanley, 1884- 261
Christ's alternative to communism [by] E. Stanley Jones. New York, Cincinnati [etc.] The Abingdon press [c1935] 302 p. 19 cm. [HN37.M4J6] 35-5050
1. Sociology, Christian—Methodist authors. 2. Kingdom of God. 3. Communism. I. Title.

WILLIAMS, Horace W. 1895- 258
Social action and world service, by Horace W. Williams. Nashville, New York [etc.] The Methodist publishing house [1942] 87 p. illus. 19 1/2 cm. "Issued by the Department of Christian education of adults ... Nashville, Tennessee, the Division of the local church, the Board of education, the Methodist church." Bibliography: p. 80-84. "Resource materials for workers with adults": p. 85-87. [BR115.S6W46] 43-4969
1. Sociology, Christian—Methodist authors. 2. Methodist church (United States)—Missions. I. Methodist church (United States) Board of education. Dept. of Christian education of adults. II. Title.

Sociology, Christian-Papal teaching.

CATHOLIC Church. Pope (Joannes XXIII), 1958-1963(JoannesXXIII)Materet istra(15May1961)English. Mater Et Magistra (15 May 1961) English
Mater et magistra; encyclical letter of Pope John XXIII on Christianity and social progress. Translation by H. E. Winstone. Washington, The pope Speaks Magazine [1962] 51 p. 20 cm. Reprinted from The Pope speaks, v. 7, no. 4, p. 295-342. 65-13548
1. Sociology, Christian-Papal teaching. I. Title.

Sociology, Christian—Quaker authors.

BRINTON, Howard Haines, 1884- 289.6
...*Divine-human society*... by Howard H. Brinton ... Philadelphia, The Book committee of the religious Society of Friends of Philadelphia and vicinity [1938] 107 p. 19 1/2 cm. (William Penn lecture, 1938) "Delivered at Race street meeting house, Philadelphia." "A sequel to the Swarthmore lecture entitled Creative Worship."--Pref. [BX7731.B76] 30-22725
1. Sociology, Christian—Quaker authors. I. Friends, Society of. Philadelphia Yearly meeting. Book committee. II. Title.

Sociology, Christian—Russia.

LANE, Christel. 301.5'8
Christian religion in the Soviet Union : a sociological study / by Christel Lane. Albany : State University of New York Press, 1977. p. cm. Includes index. Bibliography: p. [BR933.L36] 77-801 ISBN 0-87395-327-4 : 25.00
1. Sociology, Christian—Russia. 2. Sects—Russia. I. Title.

Sociology, Christian—Scotland—Aberdeen.

MACLAREN, A. Allan. 301.5'8'094125
Religion and social class; the disruption years in Aberdeen [by] A. Allan MacLaren. London, Boston, Routledge & K. Paul [1974] xii, 268 p. 22 cm. (The Scottish series) Includes bibliographical references. [BR788.A23M32] 73-91034 ISBN 0-7100-7789-0 15.50
1. Sociology, Christian—Scotland—Aberdeen. 2. Aberdeen, Scot.—Church history. I. Title.

Sociology, Christian—Study and teaching.

BANDAS, Rudolph George, 1896- 261
Modern problems in the light of Christian principles; a manual for classes, study clubs, and open forums of college and university students, prepared under the direction of Rudolph G. Bandas ... Chicago, Ill., Loyola university press, 1937. v. 19 1/2 cm. "Published under the auspices of the Confraternity of Christian doctrine of the Archdiocese of St. Paul." Bibliography at end of most of the chapters. [HN37.C3B3] 38-11
1. Sociology, Christian—Study and teaching. 2. Sociology, Christian—Catholic authors. I. Title.

BAXTER, Edna M. 1895- 266.61
Living and working in our country (a unit in weekday religious education for Christian citizenship series for grades five and six) [by] Edna M. Baxter. New York, Cincinnati [etc.] Printed for the International committee on co-operative publication of weekday church school curriculum by the Methodist book concern [c1938] 199 p. illus. (map) 22 cm. Music: p. 185-189. Bibliography: p. 191-199. [BV1583.B35] [331] 39-2315
1. Sociology, Christian—Study and teaching. 2. Week-day church schools—Teachers' manuals. I. Title.

CABOT, Ella (Lyman) Mrs. 1866- 268.61
Teacher's manual for Our part in the world, by Ella Lyman Cabot ... Rev. ed. Boston, Mass., The Beacon press, inc., 1933. xxvii, 104 p. 21 cm. (Half-title: The new Beacon course of graded lessons, W. I. Lawrence, Florence Buck, editors) "Note to the revised edition" signed: Waltstill Hastings Sharp, editor. Includes bibliographies. [BX9821.C3 1932 Manual] 33-28777
1. Sociology, Christian—Study and teaching. 2. Citizenship—Study and teaching. 3. Ethics—Study and teaching. I. Sharp Waltstill Hasting, ed. II. Title.

CABOT, Ella (Lyman) Mrs. 1866-1934. 268.61
Our part in the world, by Ella Lyman Cabot ... Boston, Mass., The Beacon press [c1918] xvi, 187 p. 21 cm. (Half-title: The new Beacon course of graded lessons) [BX9821.C3 1918] 18-17917
1. Sociology, Christian—Study and teaching. 2. Citizenship—Study and teaching. 3. Ethics—Study and teaching. I. Title.

CHEVERTON, Cecil Frank, 1889- 261
The Bible and social living ... [by] C. F. Cheverton. St. Louis, Mo., Christian board of publication [c1940-41] 4 v. illus. 19 cm. "This study is ... based upon an outline produced in cooperation with the Young people's section of the Curriculum committee of the United Christian missionary society."--Foreword. v. 1. Contents.[v. 1.] In the home and in the community.--[v. 1.] In government and in the church.--[v. 3.] In our work.--[v. 4.] Bible spokesmen for God. [BR115.S6C47] 40-32974
1. Sociology, Christian—Study and teaching. I. United Christian missionary society. Dept. of religious education. Curriculum committee. II. Title.

CONFREY, Burton, 1898- 261
Social studies; a textbook in social science for Catholic high schools, by Burton Confrey ... With readings referred to in text. New York, Cincinnati [etc.] Benziger brothers, 1934. xxiv p., 1 l., 652 p. 1 l., 112 p. illus. (incl. ports.) 21 cm. On cover: Teacher's manual edition. "Teacher's manual" has special t.p. and separate pagination (112 pages at end) [H N37. C3 C56 1934] 34-1613
1. Sociology, Christian—Study and teaching. 2. Sociology, Christian—Catholic authors. 3. Social sciences. I. Title.

GRIFFITHS, Louise Benckenstein Mrs. 261
... *Living together in today's world,* by Louise Benckenstein Griffiths. New York, Friendship press [c1941] viii, 120 p. illus. 19 cm. At head of title: A course for junior high school groups. Includes music. [BR115.S6G73] 41-26525
1. Sociology, Christian—Study and teaching. I. Title.

HERRING, Hubert Clinton, 1889- 261
The church and social relations; a text for discussion groups and church school classes, by Hubert C. Herring ... and Benson Y. Landis ... Boston, Chicago, The Pilgrim press [c1926] x, 159 p. 17 cm. "Preliminary edition ... issued for experimental use by discussion groups and church school classes."--Mounted slip. Advertising matter: p. 156-157. Bibliography at end of most of the chapters. [BV625.H4] 27-3332
1. Sociology, Christian—study and teaching. I. Landis, Benson Young, 1897- joint author. II. Title.

JOHNSON, Frederick Ernest, 1884- 265.
... *Christian ideals in industry,* by F. Ernest Johnson and Arthur E. Holt ... New York, Cincinnati, The Methodist book concern [c1924] 136 p. 19 cm. (Life and services, series, ed. by H. H. Meyer) "Approved, by the Committee on curriculum of the Sunday Schools of the Methodist Episcopal church." [BR115.E3J6] 24-7123
1. Sociology, Christian—Study and teaching. 2. Labor and Laboring classes. I. Holt, Arthur Erastus, joint author. II. Title.

JONES, Mary Alice, 1898- 248
... *Young America makes friends,* by Mary Alice Jones, with stories by Rebecca Caudill. New York, Friendship press [c1933] 3 p. l., 122 p. 20 cm. At head of title: A course for juniors. "Reference list" at end of each unit. [BV457.J6] 268.62 33-12917
1. Sociology, Christian—Study and teaching. 2. Missions—Study and teaching. I. Caudill, Rebecca. II. Title.

O'BRIEN, Mary Consilia, sister, 1903- 261
Catholic sociology, presented to Catholic students and based on the encyclicals of Leo XIII and Pius XI [by] Sister Mary Consilia O'Brien... New York, P. J. Kenedy & sons [c1939] xviii, 364 p., 1 l. 21 cm. On cover: For upper grades and study clubs. "For the teacher and mature readers": p. 363-364. [Secular name; Helen Cecilia O'Brien] [HN37.C3O2] 39-21698
1. Leo XIII, pope, 1810-1903. 2. Pius XI, pope, 1857-1939. 3. Sociology, Christian—Study and teaching. 4. Sociology, Christian—Catholic authors. I. Title.

STOCK, Harry Thomas. 261.07
Social issues for young pleple [by] Harry Thomas Stock ... Boston, Mass., International society of Christian endeavor [c1933] viii, 92 p. 19 cm. "Written at the request of the Educational council of the International society [of Christian endeavor]"--Foreword. [HN31.S83] 33-20233
1. Sociology, Christian—Study and teaching. I. International society of Christian endeavor. II. Title.

THE Story of research in sociology of religion: Garrett Theological Seminary, 1929-1972, including the Bureau of Social and Religious Research, established 1941. 261.1'07'2 Evanston, Ill., Garrett Theological Seminary [1972] 53 p. 23 cm. [BT738.S76] 72-186163 1.25
1. Garrett Theological Seminary. 2. Sociology, Christian—Study and teaching. I. Garrett Theological Seminary. II. Garrett Theological Seminary. Bureau of Social and Religious Research.

WAGNER, Oscar Walter, 1903- 241.07
Levels of brotherhood; a coursebook for adults. Philadelphia, United Church [1964] 60p. illus. 21cm. Bibl. 64-14504 .75
1. Sociology, Christian—Study and teaching. 2. Brotherliness—Study and teaching. 3. Brotherliness—Study and teaching. I. Title.

WEBB, Charles Thomas, 1889- 261
The kingdom within; the relation of personal character to the problems of the world without, by Charles T. Webb ... New York, The Macmillan company, 1934. xix, 230 p. 20 1/2 cm. (A church school series, ed. by J. W. Suter, jr.) "Notes": p. [221]-229; "Books of reference": p. 230. [BR115.S6W34] 34-19019
1. Sociology, Christian—Study and teaching. 2. Utopias. 3. Character. I. Title.

WHITE, Lillian, 1896- 268.61
Boys and girls living as neighbors, a guide for teachers, including source materials and teaching procedures [by] Lillian White. New York, Cincinnati [etc.] The Abingdon press [c1938] 196 p. 20 cm. (Half-title: The Abingdon religious education texts, J. W. Langdale, general editor; Guides to Christian living, P.H. Vieth, editor) Bibliography at end of most of the chapters. [BV1475.W46] (261) 38-30370
1. Sociology, Christian—Study and teaching. I. Title.

WHITE, Lillian, 1896- 268.61
Boys and girls living as neighbors, pupil's work book [by]Lillian White. New York, Cincinnati [etc.] The Abingdon press [c1938] 136 p. illus., diagrs. 18 1/2 cm. (Half-title: The Abingdon religious education texts, J. W. Langdale, general editor: Guides to Christian living P. H. Vieth, editor) [BV1475.W45] (261) 38-30371
1. Sociology, Christian—Study and teaching. I. Title.

YOUNGER, George D 261
The Bible calls for action. Philadelphia, Judson Press [1959] 107 p. 19 cm. [TB738.Y6] 59-8732
1. Sociology, Christian — Study and teaching. I. Title.

YOUNGER, George D. 261
The Bible calls for action / George D. Younger. Valley Forge, PA : Judson Press, c1978. 93 p. ; 22 cm. Includes bibliographical references. [BT738.Y6 1978] 78-2686 ISBN 0-8170-0795-4 : pbk. : 3.95
1. Sociology, Christian—Study and teaching. I. Title.

Sociology, Christian—Texas—Dallas Co.—Case studies.

KING, Morton Brandon, 1913- 261.8'3
Measuring religious dimensions; studies of congregational involvement [by] Morton B. King [and] Richard A. Hunt. Dallas, Southern Methodist University [1972] 136 p. 23 cm. (Studies in social science, no. 1) Bibliography: p. 64-68. [BR555.T4K56] 72-195903
1. Sociology, Christian—Texas—Dallas Co.—Case studies. 2. Dallas Co., Tex.—Religious life and customs—Case studies. I. Hunt, Richard A., 1931- joint author. II. Title. III. Series: Studies in social science (Dallas) no. 1.

Sociology, Christian—U.S.

CAMPBELL, Thomas Charles, 1929- 261.8
The fragmented layman; an empirical study of lay attitudes, by Thomas C. Campbell and Yoshio Fukuyama. Philadelphia, Pilgrim Press [1970] xvi, 252 p. 24 cm. (Studies in religion and society) Includes bibliographical references. [BT738.C34] 79-125960 ISBN 0-8298-0182-0 12.00
1. Sociology, Christian—U.S. 2. Laity—

United Church of Christ. I. Fukuyama, Yoshio, 1921- joint author. II. Title. III. Series: Studies in religion and society series

HAMMOND, Phillip E. 306'.6
The role of ideology in church participation / Phillip Everett Hammond. New York : Arno Press, 1980. ca. 400 p. ; 24 cm. (Dissertations on sociology) Originally presented as the author's thesis, Columbia University, 1960. Includes bibliography. [BR517.H35 1980] 79-9003 ISBN 0-405-12972-6 lib. bdg. : 24.00
1. Sociology, Christian—United States. 2. Church membership. 3. Ideology. I. Title. II. Series.

SCHWARTZ, Gary. 301.5'8'0973
Sect ideologies and social status. Chicago, University of Chicago Press [1970] x, 260 p. 23 cm. Includes bibliographical references. [BT738.S369 1970] 72-120598 ISBN 0-226-74216-4
1. Seventh-Day Adventists—Doctrinal and controversial works. 2. Sociology, Christian—United States. 3. Pentecostal churches—Doctrinal and controversial works. I. Title.

Sociology, Christian—United States—Addresses, essays, lectures.

AMERICAN denominational 306'.6
organization : a sociological view / [compiled by] Ross P. Scherer. Pasadena, CA : William Carey Library, c1980. viii, 378 p. ; 22 cm. Includes bibliographical references and index. [BR516.5.A43] 80-13859 ISBN 0-87808-173-9 pbk. : 14.95
1. Sociology, Christian—United States—Addresses, essays, lectures. 2. Christian sects—United States—Addresses, essays, lectures. 3. United States—Religion—1960-—Addresses, essays, lectures. I. Scherer, Ross P., 1922-
Publisher's address 1705 N. Sierra Bonita Ave., P. O. Box 128 C, Pasadena, CA 91104.

Sociology, Christian—Universalist authors.

LALONE, Emerson Hugh. 261
And thy neighbor as thyself; a story of Universalist social action. [By] Emerson Hugh Lalone ... Boston, Mass., The Universalist publishing house, 1939. 3 p. l., 126 p. 21 cm. "References": p. 99-100. [HN37.U6L3] 40-9228
1. Sociology, Christian—Universalist authors. 2. Universalist church—U. S. I. Title.

Sociology—History

WILLIAMS, Melvin J 261
Catholic social thought; its approach to contemporary problems. With a foreword by Paul Hanly Furfey. New York, Ronald Press Co. [1950] xv. 567 p. 24 cm. Bibliography: p. 495-530. [HM19.W5] 50-7775
1. Sociology—Hist. 2. Sociology, Christian—Catholic authors. I. Title.

Sociology, Islamic.

QUTB, Sayyid, 1903- 309.1'176'7
1966.
Social justice in Islam [by] Sayed Kotb. Translated from the Arabic by John B. Hardie. New York, Octagon Books, 1970 [c1953] ix, 298 p. 22 cm. (American Council of Learned Societies. Near Eastern Translation Program [Publication] no. 1) Translation of al-'Adalah al-ijtima'iyah fi al-Islam (romanized form) Bibliography: p. 282. [HN40.M6Q683 1970] 75-96205
1. Sociology, Islamic. I. Title. II. Series: American Council of Learned Societies Devoted to Humanistic Studies. Near Eastern Translation Program. Publication no. 1

TURNER, Bryan S. 301.5'8'0917671
Weber and Islam : a critical study / [by] Bryan S. Turner. London ; Boston : Routledge & Kegan Paul, 1974. ix, 212 p. ; 23 cm. (International library of sociology) Includes bibliographical references and index. [BP173.25.W4T87] 74-77201 ISBN 0-7100-7848-X : 13.50
1. Weber, Max, 1864-1920. 2. Sociology, Islamic. I. Title.

Sociology, Islamic—Addresses, essays, lectures.

SHARI'ATI, 'Ali. 297'.197'8
On the sociology of Islam : lectures / by Ali Shari'ati ; translated from the Persian by Hamid Algar. Berkeley : Mizan Press, c1979. 125 p. ; 21 cm. Bibliography: p. 34-37. [BP173.25.S52] 79-83552 ISBN 0-933782-00-4 : 3.95
1. Sociology, Islamic—Addresses, essays, lectures. 2. Man (Islam)—Addresses, essays, lectures. I. Title.

Sociology, Jewish.

CRONBACH, Abraham, 1882- 296
The Bible and our social outlook, by Abraham Cronbach ... Cincinnati, Union of American Hebrew congregations, 1941. x, 383 p. illus. 21 cm. Includes bibliographies. [HN40.J5C7] 42-50519
1. Sociology, Jewish. I. Union of American Hebrew congregations. II. Title.

ELIAS, Joseph. 296
Social order, the Jewish view. New York, 1947. 76 p. 17 cm. (Jewish pocket books, 3) [HN40.J5E4] 47-28451
1. Sociology, Jewish. I. Title.

INFIELD, Henrick F. ed.
Essays in Jewish sociology, labour and cooperation in memory of Dr. Noah Barou, 1889-1955. London, New York, T. Yoseloff [in conjunction with the world Jewish congress, 1962] xiii, 167 p. 23 cm. 63-30486
1. Barou, Noah, 1899-1955. 2. Sociology — Jews. 3. Sociology. 4. Labor — Jews. 5. Labor. I. Title.

KERTZER, Morris Norman, 361.7
1910- ed.
The rabbi and the Jewish social worker. [Edited by Morris N. Kertzer] New York, Commission on Synagogue Relations, Federation of Jewish Philanthorpies [1964?] vii, 192 p. 23 cm. Includes bibliographies. [BM729.S7K4] 64-4906
1. Sociology, Jewish. 2. Social service. I. Title.

KUTZIK, Alfred J 296.38
Social work and Jewish values: basic areas of consonance and conflict. Washington, Public Affairs Press [1959] 01p. 24cm. [BM729.S7K8] 59-10230
1. Sociology, Jewish. 2. Social service. I. Title.

VORSPAN, Albert. 301.452
Justice and Judaism; the work of social action [by] Albert Vorspan and Eugene J. Lipman. Illustrated by Russell Roman. New York, Union of American Hebrew Congregations [1956] 271p. illus. 24cm. [HN40.J5V6] [HN40.J5V6] 296 56-3849 56-3849
1. Sociology, Jewish. I. Lipman, Eugene J., joint author. II. Title.

VORSPAN, Albert.
Justice and Judaism; the work of social action [by] Albert Vorspan and Eugene J. Lipman. Illustrated by Russel Roman. [Rev., 4th ed.] New York, Union of American Hebrew Congregations [1959] 271 p. illus. Includes bibliographies.
1. Sociology, Jewish. I. I. Lipman, Eugene J., joint author. II. Title.

Sociology, Mohammedan.

LEVY, Reuben.
The social structure of Islam, being the second edition of The sociology of Islam. Cambridge, [Eng.] University Press, 1957. vii, 536p. 22cm. Bibliography: p.506-521. A57
1. Sociology, Mohammedan. I. Title.

LEVY, Reuben.
The social structure of Islam, being the second edition of The sociology of Islam. Cambridge [Eng.] University Press, 1957. vii, 536p. 22cm. Bibliography: p. 506-521. A 57
1. Sociology, Mohammedan. I. Title.

QUTB, Sayyid, 1903- 915.6
Social justice in Islam [by] Sayed Kotb; translated from the Arabic by John B. Hardie. Washington, American Council of Learned Societies, 1953. viii, 298 p. 22 cm. (American Council of Learned Societies [Devoted to Humanistic Studies] Near Eastern Translation Program. [Publication] no. 1) Bibiliography: p. 282. [HN40.M6Q683] 53-2971
1. Sociology, Mohammedan. I. Title. II. Series.

WATT, William Montgomery. 915.6
Islam and the integration of society. [Evanston, Ill.] Northwestern University Press, 1961. ix, 293 p. 23 cm. Bibliographical footnotes. [HN40.M6W3 1961] 61-12986
1. Sociology. Mohammedan. I. Title.

Sociology, Rural.

BURT, Roy E. 266.0714
A young people's course on Christianity and the rural life of the world, by Roy E. Burt... New York, Missionary education movement of the United States and Canada [c1931] 2 p. l., 73 p. 18 1/2 cm. Includes bibliographies. [BV2090.B8] 32-32274
1. Sociology, Rural. 2. Religious education. I. Title.

GRIFFETH, Ross John. 230.8328354
The Bible and rural life, by Ross John Griffeth. Cincinnati, O., The Standard publishing company [c1937] 117, [8] p. illus. 19 cm. Blank pages for "Notes" (8 at end) [BS670.G7] 37-20873
1. Sociology, Rural. 2. Sociology, Biblical. I. Title.

Socrates.

MUZZEY, David Saville, 1870- 922
Spiritual heroes: a study of some of the world's prophets, by David Saville Muzzey ... New York, Doubleday, Page & company, 1902. xi, 305 p. 20 cm. [BL72.M8] 2-13784
1. Socrates. 2. Jesus Christ. 3. Aurelius Antoninus. Marcus, emperor of Rome, 121-180. 4. Paul, Saint, Apostle. 5. Augustinus Aurelius, Saint. bp. of Hippo. 6. Muhammad, the prophet. 7. Luther, Martin, 1483-1546. 8. Prophets. 9. Jeremiah, the prophet. 0. Buddha and Buddhism. I. Title.
Contents omitted.

PLATO.
Plato's Apology, Crito and Phaedo of Socrates. Literally translated by Henry Cary ... With an introduction by Edward Brooks, jr. Philadelphia, D. McKay [c1897] xi, 13-774 p. 16 cm. ()Pocket literal translations of the classics] [PA3617.P7P6] 12-37853
I. Cary, Henry, 1804-1870, tr. II. Brooks, Edward, 1868?- tr. III. Title.

PLATO.
Plato's Apology of Socrates and Crito and a part of the Phaedo by Rev. C. L. Kitchel... Text ed. New York, Cincinnati [etc.] American book company [c1898] 1 p. l., 41-110 p. 18 cm. [PA4290.A3 1898 a] 12-37798
I. Kitchel, Cornelius Ladd, 1841-1929, ed. II. Title.

PLATO.
Plato's Euthyphro, with introduction and notes by William Arthur Heidel ... New York, Cincinnati [etc.] American book company [1902] 115 p. 19 cm. (Greek series for colleges and schools) 2-18348
I. Heidel, William Arthur, 1868- ed. II. Title.

PLATO.
Socrates and the soul of man; incorporating Plato's Phaedo, translated by Desmond Stewart, with an introd. by E. A. Havelock. Boston, Beacon Press, 1951. 104p. 20cm. A53
I. Stewart, Desmond, tr. II. Title.

Sodality of St. Peter Claver for the African missions.

BIELAK, Stanislawa 922.2438
Kostka, siostra, 1885-
The servant of God, Mary Theresa Countess Ledochowska, foundress of the Sodality of Saint Peter Claver, by Valeria Bielak. 2d ed., rev. and amplified by the author. Saint Paul, Minn., The Sodality of St. Peter Claver [c1944] xxii, 226 p. front., plates, ports. 19 1/2 cm. [Secular name: Waleria Bielak] [BX4705.L445B52 1944] 44-12886
1. Ledochowska, Maria Teresa Halka, hrabina, 1863-1922. 2. Sodality of St. Peter Claver for the African missions. I. Title.

Sodality of the Blessed Virgin Mary.

CHILDREN of Mary. New 267.442
York archdiocesan union.
Manual of the Archdiocesan union of sodalities of the Blessed Virgin Mary New York. New York, Cincinnati [etc.] Benziger brothers. 1937. 5 p. l., [5]-104 p. illus. (incl. port.) pl. 14 1/2 cm. By W. J. B. Daly. [BX2055.C42N4 1937] 37-6823
I. Daly, William J. B. II. Title.

MANUAL of the sodalities 264.02
of the Blessed Virgin Mary and of the Sacred heart of Jesus. Boston, Duffy, Cashman & co. [c1884] 72, 3-24 p. 14 1/2 cm. Compiled by William Byrne. [BX2055.V5 1884] 38-19162
I. Catholic church. Liturgy and ritual. English. II. Sodality of the Blessed Virgin Mary. III. Archconfraternity of the Sacred heart of Jesus. IV. Byrne, William, 1836-1912, comp.

MANUAL of the sodalities 264.02
of the Blessed Virgin Mary and of the Sacred heart of Jesus. Boston, T. B. Noonan & co., 1881. 72, 3-24 p. 14 cm. Compiled by William Byrne. [BX2055.V5 1881a] 38-19161
I. Catholic church. Liturgy and ritual. English. II. Sodality of the Blessed Virgin Mary. III. Archconfraternity of the Sacred heart of Jesus. IV. Byrne, William, 1836-1912, comp.

MARY Florence, sister, 267.182
1911-
The sodality movement in the United States, 1926-1936, by Sister Mary Florence, S.L. (Bernice Wolff ...) St. Louis, Mo., The Queen's work. [c1939] 214 p. incl. pl., maps. 21 cm. [Secular name: Bernice Louise Wolff] Bibliography: p. 211-214 [BX800.V6M3] 40-326
1. Sodality of the Blessed Virgin Mary. I. Title.

MULLAN, Elder, 1865-1925. 267.
Sodality of Our Lady; hints and helps for those in charge, by Father Elder Mullan ... New York, P. J. Kenedy and sons; London, R. & T. Washbourne, ltd. [c1907] xv, 242 p. 19 cm. [Full name: Alexius Joseph Elder Mullan] [BX809.V6M8] 7-23632
1. Sodality of the Blessed Virgin Mary. I. Title.

OPITZ, Heinrich, 1859-1910. 267.
Sodality of our Lady; under the banner of Mary, by Father Henry Opitz, S. J.; translated by a sodalist of our Lady, edited by Father Elder Mullan, S. J. New York, P. J. Kenedy & sons [c1908] 206 p. 16 cm. [BX809.V6O6] 9-3895
1. Sodality of the blessed Virgin Mary. I. Mullan, Elder, 1865-1925, ed. II. Title.

SODALITY of the Blessed 264.02
Virgin Mary.
The book of the junior sodalists of Our Lady; a manual for the Sodality of Our Lady and St. Aloysius, the Sodality of Our Lady and the holy angels and all junior sodalities in schools and elsewhere, compiled and arranged by Father Elder Mullan, S. J. New York, P. J Kenedy & sons [1916] 2 p. l., [xi]-xii p., 2 l., [3]-461 p. 14 cm. [BX2055.V3 1916 a] 16-15118
I. Catholic church, Liturgy and ritual. English. II. Mullan, Elder, 1865-1925, comp. III. Title.

SODALITY of the Blessed 264.02
Virgin Mary.
Campion college sodality manual for the use of members of the sodalities of Our

Lady ... Prairie du Chien, Wis., Campion college, 1916. 368 p. incl. front., illus. 13 cm. [BX2055.V5 1916] 16-017
1. Catholic church. Liturgy and ritual. English. II. Campion college of the Sacred heart, Prairie du Chien, Wis. III. Title.

SODALITY of the Blessed Virgin Mary. 264.02
Manual of the Sodality of the Blessed Virgin Mary, compiled from the best manuals ... New York & Cincinnati, F. Pustet & co. [1892] iv p., 1 l., 7-208 p. front. 13 cm. Compiled by John Harpes, S. J. [BX2055.V5 1892] 38-19160
I. Catholic church. Liturgy and ritual. English. II. Harpes, John, 1852-1918, comp. III. Title.

SODALITY of the Blessed Virgin Mary. 264.02
Manual of the Sodality of the Blessed Virgin Mary, with offices, prayers, devotions and hymns for the use of sodalities. Compiled from authentic sources ... New York, Apostleship of prayer [c1897] ix, [1], 316 p. 15 cm. [BX2055.V5 1897] 38-19159
I. Catholic church. Liturgy and ritual. English. II. Title.

SODALITY of the Blessed Virgin Mary. 264.02
Manual of the Sodality of the Blessed Virgin Mary. Compiled and revised by Rev. Paul Griffith. Baltimore, Md., New York, John Murphy company [1902] 90, [2] p. 13 cm. [BX2055.V5 1902] 38-20494
I. Catholic church. Liturgy and ritual. English. II. Griffith, Paul, 1846-1919, comp. III. Title.

SODALITY of the Blessed Virgin Mary. 264.02
Manual of the Sodality of the Blessed Virgin Mary, edited by the Rev. James J. Duffy. Philadelphia, P. Reilly, 1918. 4 p. l., 133 p. 14 cm. [BX2055.V5 1918] 18-20040
I. Catholic church. Liturgy and ritual. English. II. Duffy, James Joseph, 1873- ed. III. Title.

SODALITY of the Blessed Virgin Mary. 264.02
Manual of the Sodality of the Blessed Virgin Mary. 12th, rev. ed. Philadelphia, H. L. Kilner & co. [c1907] 134 p. 13 cm. [BX2055.V5 1907] 7-3089
I. Catholic church. Liturgy and ritual. English. II. Title.

[SODALITY of the Blessed Virgin Mary] 264.02
The new sodality manual, written, reivsed, and edited by Daniel A. Lord, S.J. ... St. Louis, Mo., The Queen's work [1945] 331, [3] p. 21 cm. "First printing, May 1945." "Included ... are some portions of the old Sodality manual by Edward F. Garesche, S.J." [BX2055.V5 1945] 45-18412
I. Catholic church. Liturgy and ritual. English. II. Lord, Daniel Aloysius, 1888- III. Garesche, Edward Francis, 1876- IV. Title.

Sodality of the Blessed Virgin Mary-Meditations and prayerbooks.

A manual of mental prayers,
one for every day of the year. Compiled by Theologians Sodality Academy, St. Mary's College, St. Mary's, Kansas. St. Louis, The Queen's Work [c1958] 573p. 15cm.
1. Sodality of the Blessed Virgin Mary-Meditations and prayerbooks. 2. Meditations. I. Mental prayer: challenge to the lay apostle. II. St. Mary'w College St. Marys, Kan.

[SODALITY of the Blessed Virgin Mary] 264.02
New sodality prayer book, compiled from approved sources, and methodically arranged, by a priest of the diocese of Fort Wayne. New York and Cincinnati, F. Pustet & co. [c1886] 363 p. front. 12 cm. Compiled by John F. Lang. [BX2055.V5 1886 a] 33-19152
I. Catholic church. Liturgy and ritual. English. II. Lang, John Francis, 1848-1929, comp. III. Title.

Soderblom, Nathan, Abp., 1866-1931.

CURTIS, Charles J. 284'.10924
Soderblom, ecumenical pioneer, by Charles J. Curtis. Minneapolis, Augsburg Pub. House [1967] viii, 149 p. illus., ports. 22 cm. Includes bibliographies. [BX8080.S6C8] 67-11719
1. Soderblom, Nathan, Abp., 1866-1931. I. Title.

Soergel, Mary.

SOERGEL, Mary. 248'.2
Sing a gentle breeze : a story of a disintegrating family seeking wholeness / Mary Soergel. Wheaton, Ill. : Tyndale House Publishers, 1977. 266 p. ; 21 cm. [BR1725.S65A37] 76-47301 ISBN 0-8423-5889-7 : 4.95
1. Soergel, Mary. 2. Christian biography—Wisconsin. I. Title.

Sofia. Natsionalna khudozhestvena galeriia.

SOFIA. Natsionalna khudozhestvena galeriia. Branch for Medieval Bulgarian Pictorial Art. 704.948'2
Old Bulgarian art / K. Paskaleva ; [translator, Marguerite Alexieva]. [Sofia] : Sofia Press, 1976. 57 p. : chiefly col. ill. ; 20 x 22 cm. On cover: National Art Gallery. Plan of gallery: [1] leaf inserted. [N8189.B8S63 1976] 77-458444
1. Sofia. Natsionalna khudozhestvena galeriia. 2. Icons, Bulgarian—Catalogs. 3. Icons—Bulgaria—Sofia—Catalogs. I. Paskaleva, Kostadinka Georgieva. II. Title.

Soga, Mina, 1893-

SEABURY, Ruth Isabel. 922
Daughter of Africa, by Ruth Isabel Seabury ... Boston, Chicago, The Pilgrim press [1945] 1 p. l., vii, 144 p. front. (port.) 171 /2 cm. Biographical sketch of Mina Soga. "Planned by the Missionary education movement of the United States and Canada as a part of its interdenominational program of foreign mission literature." "A selected reading list": p. 143-144. [BV3557.S6S4] 45-9075
1. Soga, Mina, 1893- I. Missionary education movement of the United States and Canada. II. Title.

Soka Gakkai.

BRANNEN, Noah S. 294.3'9
Soka Gakkai; Japan's militant Buddhists, by Noah S. Brannen. With photos. by Hideo Fujimori. Richmond, John Knox Press [1968] 181 p. illus. ports. 21 cm. Bibliographical references included in "Notes and acknowledgments" (p. [171]-177) "A selected bibliography of works in English": p. [179]-181. [BL1442.S6B7] 68-25017 5.50
1. Soka Gakkai.

DATOR, James Allen. 294.3'65
Soka Gakkai, builders of the third civilization: American and Japanese members. Seattle, University of Washington Press [1969] xiii, 171 p. 23 cm. Bibliography: p. 151-171. [BL1442.S6D3] 68-8509 7.95
1. Soka Gakkai.

MURATA, Kiyoaki, 1922- 294.3'65
Japan's new Buddhism; an objective account of Soka Gakkai, by Kiyoaki Murata. Foreword by Daisaku Ikeda. [1st ed.] New York, Walker/Weatherhill [i.e. J. Weatherhill; distributed by Walker, 1969] xii, 194 p. illus., ports. 24 cm. Bibliography: p. 183-186. [BL1442.S6M87] 74-83640 5.95
1. Soka Gakkai. I. Title.

Soka Gakkai—Doctrines.

WILLIAMS, George M. 294.3'9
NSA seminar report, 1968-71. Compiled and edited from lectures delivered by George M. Williams. Santa Monica, Calif., World Tribune Press, 1972. iii, 120 p. illus. 23 cm. [BL1442.S6W54] 72-75438
1. Soka Gakkai—Doctrines. 2. Soka Gakkai—United States. I. Nichiren Shoshu Academy. II. Title.

WILLIAMS, George M. 294.3'92
NSA seminars : an introduction to true Buddhism / by George M. Williams. Santa Monica, Calif. : World Tribune Press, 1974. 101 p. : ill. ; 22 cm. [BQ8418.5.W54] 74-77643
1. Soka Gakkai—Doctrines. 2. Nichiren Shoshu Academy. I. Title.

Soka Gakkai—Doctrines—Addresses, essays, lectures.

IKEDA, Daisaku. 294.3'4
Guidance memo / Daisaku Ikeda ; translated by George M. Williams. Santa Monica, Calif. : World Tribune Press, [1975] 288 p. ; 19 cm. Includes index. [BQ8418.7.I3816] 75-13664 ISBN 0-915678-00-4
1. Soka Gakkai—Doctrines—Addresses, essays, lectures. I. Title.

Soka Gakkai—Prayer-books and devotion—English.

THE Lotus Sutra : 294.3'8
its history and practice today. Santa Monica, Calif. : World Tribune Press, c1977. 78 p. : ill., [1] leaf of plates ; 18 cm. [BQ2057.L67] 77-152891
1. Soka Gakkai—Prayer-books and devotion—English. 2. Saddharmapundarika—Criticism, interpretation, etc.

Sokolova, Irina.

HARTFIELD, Hermann, 1942- 286'.13 B
Irina, a love stronger than terror / Hermann Hartfield ; [translated by Henry Wagner]. Chappaqua, N.Y. : Christian Herald Books, 1981. 316 p. ; 21 cm. Translation of: Irina oder die Enkel der Revolution. [BX6493.H3513] 19 81-65724 ISBN 0-915684-90-X pbk. : 6.95
1. Sokolova, Irina. 2. Nikitin, Alexander. 3. Baptists—Soviet Union—Biography. 4. Persecution—Soviet Union—History—20th century. 5. Soviet Union—Church history—1917- I. [Irina oder die Enkel der Revolution.] English II. Title.

Sokolow, Nahum, 1859-1936.

KLING, Simcha. 920.5
Nachum Sokolow, servant of his people. New York, Herzl Press [1960] 205p. 22cm. [DS151.S6K55] 60-50588
1. Sokolow, Nahum. 1859-1936. I. Title.

KLING, Smicha 920.5
Nachum Sokolow, servant of his people. New York, Herzl Press [c.1960] 205p. 22cm. 60-50588 3.50
1. Sokolow, Nahum, 1859-1936. I. Title.

Solano, Francisco, Saint, 1549-1610.

[DEYMANN, Clementine, father] 1844-1896. 922.
Life of St. Francis Solanus, apostle of Peru. By a priest of the Order of St Francis ... New York, Cincinnati [etc.] Benziger brothers [1888] 1 p. l., 11 p., 1 l., 132 p. front. 18 cm. [Seculer name: John Henry Daymans] [BX4700.S6D4] 39-18062
1. Solano, Francisco, Saint, 1549-1610. I. Title.

GREENE, Genard, 1921- 922.285
Above the wind's roar; a story of Saint Francis Solano. Illus. by Brother Bernard Howard. Notre Dame, Ind., Dujarie Press [1953] 95p. illus. 24cm. [BX4700.S6G7] 53-2905
1. Solano, Francisco, Saint, 1549-1610. I. Title.

ROYER, Fanchon, 1902- 922.285
St. Francis Solanus, apostle to America. Paterson, N. J., St. Anthony Guild Press, 1955. 207p. illus. 23cm. Includes bibliography. [BX4700.S6R6] 55-14671
1. Soland, Francisco, Saint, 1549-1610. I. Title.

WINDEATT, Mary Fabyan, 1910- 922.285
Song in the south, the story of Saint Francis Solano, apostle of Argentina and Peru, by Mary Fabyan Windeatt, illustrated by Gedge Harmon. New York, Sheed & Ward, 1946. 4 p. l., 191 p. illus. 22 cm. [BX4700.S6W53] 47-15516
1. Solano, Francisco, Saint, 1549-1610. I. Title.

Soldiers—Hymns.

THE soldier's hymn-book:
for camp worship. 63d thousand. [Richmond] Soldiers' tract association, M. E. church, South [Chas. H. Wynne, printer] 1864. 64 p. 12 cm. 15-9194
1. Soldiers' tract association, Methodist Episcopal church, South.

YOUNG men's Christian associations. International committee. Army and navy dept. 783.9
The service song book, prepared for the men of the army and navy by the Army and navy department of the National board of the Young men's Christian associations ... edited by Clarence A. Barbour. New York, Association press [c1941] 252 p. 18 cm. With music. "Special services": p. 195-221. "Scripture reading": p. 223-241. [M2198.Y4B25 1941] 43-2556
1. Soldiers—Hymns. 2. Hymns, English. 3. Songs, English. I. Barbour, Clarence Augustus, 1867-1937, ed. II. Title.

YOUNG men's Christian associations, New York.
The soldier's hymn book... [New York] The New York Young men's Christian association [1861] 62 p. 11 cm. Without music. [BV463.Y6] 40-37718
1. Soldiers—Hymns. 2. Hymns, English. I. Title.

Soldiers—Prayer-books and devotions—English.

DRUKKER, Raymond B., 1897- 242
At ease! By Raymond B. Drukker ... Grand Rapids, Mich., Wm. B. Eerdmans publishing co., 1942. 89 p. 18 1/2 cm. "Inspirational readings."--Pref. [BV4588.D7] 43-848
1. Soldiers—Prayer-books and devotions—English. I. Title.

A handy companion, dedicated to our soldiers and sailors, and to the honor and glory of the cross and flag, by a Vincentian father ... Philadelphia, H. L. Kilner & co. [c1917] 105 p. 12 cm. [BX2110.A3] 17-31683 264.
I. Murphy, Andrew C., 1868- comp. II. Catholic church. Liturgy and ritual.

JEWS. Liturgy and ritual. 296
Prayer book; abridged for Jews in the armed forces of the United States ... New York city, National Jewish welfare board [c1943] 1 p. l., viii, [1], 331 p.; 1 p. l., 45, [4] p. 12 1/2 cm. "Revised edition." Hebrew and English on opposite pages. [BM667.S6A5 1943] 43-13665
1. Soldiers—Prayer-books and devotions—English. I. Jewish welfare board. II. Title.

[KOKKINAKIS, A. T.] 264.019
Greek Orthodox prayer book, for the use of soldiers and sailors of the United States of America. [n.p.] The Greek Orthodox archdiocese of North and South America, 1944. 1 p. l., [1], 78, 78 p. 14 cm. Greek and English text on opposite pages, numbered in duplicate. Added t.-p. in Greek. "Compiled and prepared by Archimandrite A. T. Kokkinakis and the Rev. T. P. Theodorides." "Second edition." [BX376.E5K6] 45-5055
1. Soldiers—Prayer-books and devotions—English. 2. Orthodox Eastern church—Prayer-books and devotions—English. 3. Soldiers—Prayer-books and devotions—Greek. 4. Orthodox Eastern church—Prayer-books and devotions—Greek. I. Theodorides, Theodore Polychronios, 1900- II. North and South America (Archdiocese, Orthodox) III. Title.

LELEN, Joseph Mary, 1873- 264.02
Soldiers and sailors manual, edited by Rev. J.M. Lelen, PH.D. A companion and spiritual guide for U.S. armed forces ... [New York, Catholic book pub. co., 1941] 224, [3] p. front., 1 illus. 11 cm. Three blank pages at end for "Notes." [BX2373.S7L4] 41-11609
1. Soldiers—Prayer-books and devotions—

English. 2. Catholic church—Prayer-books and devotions—English. I. Title.

MACDUFF, John Ross, 1818-1895. 248
The soldier's text-book; or, Confidence in time of war. By J. R. Macduff ... Boston, American tract society [186-?] 48, 16 p. 13 1/2 cm. "Hymns": 16 p. at end. [BV4588.M25] 6-30299
1. Soldiers—Prayer-books and devotions—English. I. American tract society. II. Title.

[MYGATT, Gerald] 1887- comp. 264.1
Soldiers' and sailors' prayer book. A non-sectarian collection of the finest prayers of the Protestant, Catholic and Jewish faiths, for the men and women of the United States army, the United States navy, the United States Marine corps, the United States Coast guard, the United States maritime service ... [New York, A. A. Knopf, 1944] 126, [2] p. 15 1/2 x 12 cm. "Compiled by Gerald Mygatt ... and Chaplain (Lieutenant Colonel) Henry Darlington." "First edition." [BV273.M9] 44-3297
1. Soldiers—Prayer-books and devotions—English. I. Darlington, Henry, 1880- joint comp. II. Title.

POLING, Daniel Alfred, 1884- ed. 264.1
The Armed Forces prayer book. [1st ed.] New York, Prentice-Hall [1951] ix, 116 p. 16 cm. [BV273.P6] 51-10358
1. Soldiers — Prayer-books and devotions — English. I. Title.

PRESBYTERIAN church in the U.S.A. Committee on camps and church activities. 264
A prayer book for the armed forces and others in the national service. [Philadelphia] The Committee on camps and church activities of the Wartime service commission of the Presbyterian church in the U.S.A. [1943] 94 p., 1 l. 14 cm. [BV273.P73] 43-17808
1. Soldiers—Prayer-books and devotions—English. I. Title.

PROTESTANT Episcopal church in the U. S. A. Army and navy commission. 264.03
A prayer book for soldiers and sailors. New York, Pub. for the Army and Navy commission of the Protestant Episcopal church by the Church pension fund, 1941. 2 p. l., 91 p. 14 cm. Text on lining-paper. "Second edition, October 1941." [BV273.P75] 42-5726
1. Soldiers—Prayer-books and devotions—English. I. Title.

SHEEN, Fulton John, 1895- 264.1
The armor of God; reflections and prayers for wartime, by Rt. Rev. Msgr. Fulton J. Sheen. New York, P. J. Kenedy & sons [1943] 192 p. incl. front., illus. 11 1/2 cm. [BX2170.S6545] 43-13672
1. Soldiers—Prayer-books and devotions—English. 2. Catholic church—Prayer books and devotions—English. I. Title.

SIZOO, Joseph Richard, 1884- 242
On guard, by Joseph R. Sizoo ... New York, The Macmillan company, 1941. [223] p. 16 1/2 cm. "First printing." [BV4588.S45] 41-22506
1. Soldiers—Prayer-books and devotions—English. 2. Calendars. I. Title.

SMITH, James, of Cheltenham, Eng. 248
Christ alone: a book for all. By the Rev. James Smith... Boston, American tract society [186-?] 64 p. 13 1/2 cm. [BV4588.S54] 6-29183
1. Soldiers—Prayer-books and devotions—English. I. Title.

SMITH, James, of Cheltenham, Eng. 248
Important questions. By the Rev. James Smith... Boston, American tract society [186-?] 64 p. 13 1/2 cm. [BV4588.S565] 6-29184
1. Soldiers—Prayer-books and devotions—English. I. Title.

SMITH, James, of Cheltenham, Eng. 248
The morning sacrifice; or, A help to devotion. By the Rev. James Smith ... Boston, American tract society [186-?] 64 p. 13 1/2 cm. [BV4588.S57] 6-29179
1. Soldiers—Prayer-books and devotions—English. I. Title.

YLVISAKER, Nils Martin, 1882- 264
Service prayer book, with Bible readings, hymns and orders of worship. Dedicated to the army, navy, Marine and Air corps of the United States, Compiled and edited by N. M. Ylvisaker ... [Minneapolis, Augsburg publishing house] 1940. 5 p. l., 219 p. front. 12 cm. [BV273.Y4] 41-1739
1. Soldiers—Prayer-books and devotions—English. I. Title.

Soldiers—Prayer-books and devotions—Hebrew.

JEWISH welfare board. 296
Ministering to the Jews in the armed forces of the United States; prayers for the sick, military funeral service and memorial service. New York, N.Y., Jewish welfare board [c1942] iv, 60 p. 13 1/2 cm. Prepared by Aryeh Lev. cf. Foreword. [BM667.S6J4] 45-29871
1. Soldiers—Prayer-books and devotions—Hebrew. 2. Soldiers—Prayer-books and devotions—English. I. Lev, Aryeh. II. Title.

JEWS. Liturgy and ritual. Daily prayers. 296.4
Prayer book for Jewish personnel in the Armed Forces of the United States. [New York? 1958] 470p. 13cm. 'Prepared by the Commission on Jewish Chaplaincy of the National Jewish Welfare Board.' Hebrew and English. [BM667.S6A6] 58-11572
1. Soldiers—Prayer-books and devotions—Hebrew. I. National Jewish Welfare board II. Title.

NATIONAL Jewish welfare board. 296
Ministering to the Jews in the armed forces of the United States; prayers for the sick, military funeral service and memorial service. New York, N. Y., Jewish welfare board [c1942] iv, 60 p. 14 cm. Prepared by Aryeh Lev. of. Foreword. [BM667.S6N3] 45-29871
1. Soldiers—Prayer-books and devotions—Hebrew. 2. Soldiers—Prayer-books and devotions—English. I. Lev, Aryeh. II. Title.

Soldiers — Religious life.

BERGHERM, William H 248.8
No greater glory. Illustrated by Howard Larkin. Mountain View, Calif., Pacific Press Pub. Association [1959] 104p. illus. 20cm. [BV4588.B45] 59-13495
1. Soldiers—Religious life. 2. Seventh-Day Adventists. I. Title.

BORSI, Giosue, 1888-1915. 248
A soldier's confidences with God; spiritual colloquies of Giosue Borsi; authorized translation by Rev. Pasquale Maltese; appreciation and foreword by Arthur Bennington. New York, P. J. Kenedy & sons, 1918. xxii, 362 p. front. (port.) 17 cm. [BV4588.B65] 18-15268
I. Maltese, Pasquale, tr. II. Title.

BRASTED, Alva Jennings, 1876- 248
For victorious living [by] Alva J. Brasted. Written for men in the U.S. army, navy, and Marine corps. Boston, Mass., World's Christian endeavor union [1942] viii p., 1 l., 11-157 p. 15 cm. [BV4588.B7] 43-1284
1. Soldiers—Religious life. I. World's Christian endeavor union. II. Title.

BRASTED, Alva Jennings, 1876- 259
Service to service men, by Alva J. Brasted. Minneapolis, Minn., Augsburg publishing house [c1941] 63 p. 28 cm. [BV4457.B7] 41-12643
1. Soldiers—Religious life. 2. U.S.—Army—Chaplains. I. Title.

COMBS, Louis K. 248.8
So ... you're in the service, by Louis K. Combs, Jr. Glendale, Calif., G/L Regal [1968] 164p. illus. 18cm. [BV4588.C59] 68-25808 .95 pap.,
1. Soldiers—Religious life. I. Title.

FISKE, George Walter, 1872- 248
Finding the comrade God; the essentials of a soldierly faith [by] G. Walter Fiske ... New York, Association press, 1918. xii, 236 p. 17 cm. [BV4501.F5] 18-22821
I. Title.

FISKE, George Walter, 1872- 248
Finding the comrade God; the essentials of a soldierly faith [by] G. Walter Fiske ... New York, Association press, 1918. xii, 236 p. 17 cm. [BV4501.F5] 18-22821
I. Title.

FITZGERALD, Lawrence P 248
Military service and you. Philadelphia JudsonPress 1956 96p. illus. 19cm. Includes bibliography. [BV4588.F57] 57-17599
1. Soldiers— Religious life. 2. Military service, Compulsory—U. S. I. Title.

GARDNER, John, 1868- 248
Letters to "Bill" on faith and prayer, by John Gardner, D.D. New York, London [etc.] Fleming H. Revell comany [1943] 91 p. 16 1/2 cm. [BV4588.G32] 43-12556
1. Soldiers—Religious life. I. Title.

JONES, William Hubert, 1923- 248
Guide to Greetings! For teachers and leaders of preinduction discussion groups. Washington, National Catholic Community Service [1953] 128p. 22cm. [BV4457.J65] 54-27853
1. Soldiers—Religious life. 2. Discussions. I. O'Donnell, Thomas J. Greetings! II. Title. III. Title: Greetings. IV. Title: Pre-induction discussion groups.

LAMB, David Smith. 248
Till we meet again, by David S. Lamb. Cleveland, O., Steven publishers [1944] xxx, 174 p. incl. front. (port.) illus. 15 1/2 cm. [BV4588.L3] 44-13846
1. Soldiers—Religious life. 2. Soldiers—Prayer-books and devotions—English. I. Title.

LAMB, David Smith. 248
Till we meet again, by David S. Lamb. Cleveland, O., Steven publishers [1945] xv, 174 p. incl. front. (port.) illus. 15 1/2 cm. [BV4588.L3 1945] 45-4938
1. Soldiers—Religious life. 2. Soldiers—Prayer-books and devotions—English. I. Title.

NYGAARD, Norman Eugene, ed. 242
Strength for service to God and country; daily devotional messages for men in the services, edited by Chaplain Norman E. Nygaard. New York, Nashville, Abingdon-Cokesbury press [1942] [381] p. 13 x 10 1/2 cm. Text on lining-papers. [BV4588.N9] 43-13070
1. Soldiers—Religious life. I. Title.

[ROBERTS, David Ellsworth] 1863- comp. 248
Sayings & songs for soldiers & sailors ... New York, National war work council of Young men's Christian associations [1918] 62 p. col. front., 1 illus. 13 cm. "Eighth edition." Contains music. "Compiled by David E. Roberts and Rev. De Witt M. Benham." [BV4588.R6 1918 a] 21-14455
1. Soldiers—Religious life. 2. Soldiers—Hymns. 3. Hymns, English. I. Benham, De Witt Miles, joint comp. II. Title.

THE soldier's pocket-book. 248
Philadelphia, Presbyterian board of publication [c1861] 64 p. 12 cm. Includes prayers, hymns and "Scripture selections". [BV4588.S75] 40-18270
1. Soldiers—Religious life. I. Presbyterian church in the U. S. A. (Old school) Board of publication.

SPINK, James F. 248
Service men's guide; or, Helps heavenward, by James F. Spink ... New York, Loizeaux brothers [1943] 96 p. illus. (part col., incl. ports.) 13 1/2 cm. [BV4588.S83] 43-8664
1. Soldiers—Religious life. 2. World war, 1939—Religious aspects. I. Title.

THINK on these things; 242
sources of courage, hope, and faith for those serving their country. Boston, The Beacon press, 1941. 5 p. l., 77, [9] p. 15 1/2 cm. Foreword signed: Frederick M. Eliot. Nine blank pages at end for "Notes." Prose and verse. [BV4588.T5] 41-9447
1. Soldiers—Religious life. I. Eliot, Frederick May.

WARD, Arthur Sterling, ed. 242
Strength for service to God and country; daily devotional messages for those in the services. Rev. ed., edited by Arthur Sterling Ward. New York, Abingdon-Cokesbury Press [1950] 1 v. (unpaged) 14 cm. "Based on the World War II edition edited by Norman E. Nygaard." [BV4588.S87 1950] 51-9195
1. Soldiers — Religious life. I. Title.

WRIGHT, Ronald Selby, 1908- ed. 248
Soldiers also asked ... edited by Ronald Selby Wright ... London, New York [etc.] Oxford university press, 1943. x, 149, [1] p. 16 1/2 x 13 cm. [Full name:Ronald William Vernon Selby Wright] [BV4588.W7] 44-4707
1. Soldiers—Religious life. I. Title.

Solitude.

CAILLIET, Emile, 1894- 248
Alone at high noon; reflections on the solitary life. Grand Rapids, Zondervan Pub. House [1971] 94 p. 21 cm. (A Zondervan "reflections" book) [BJ1499.S6C3] 74-133356 2.95
1. Solitude. I. Title.

CASHEN, Richard Anthony. 248.4'7
Solitude in the thought of Thomas Merton / by Richard Anthony Cashen. Kalamazoo, Mich. : Cistercian Publications, 1981. vii, 201 p. ; 23 cm. (Cistercian studies series ; no. 40) Bibliography: p. 181-201. [BX4705.M542C37] 19 80-19876 ISBN 0-87907-840-5 : 15.50 ISBN 0-87907-940-1 pbk. : 7.50
1. Merton, Thomas, 1915-1968. 2. Solitude. 3. Loneliness. I. Title. II. Series.

MEIKLE, James, 1730-1799.
Solitude sweetened; or, Miscellaneous meditations, on various religious subjects, written in distant parts of the world. By James Meikle ... First Kentucky edition, from the fourth American edition. Paris, Ky., Printed and published by John Lyle, 1816. xii, [13]-312 p. 18 cm. A 31
I. Title.

Solitude—Addresses, essays, lectures.

DUNNE, John S., 1929- 248
The reasons of the heart : a journey into solitude and back again into the human circle / John S. Dunne. New York : Macmillan, c1978. xiii, 172 p. ; 22 cm.. Includes bibliographical references and index. [BJ1499.S6D86] 77-16082 6.95
1. Solitude—Addresses, essays, lectures. 2. God—Addresses, essays, lectures. 3. Life—Addresses, essays, lectures. I. Title.

Solomon ben Isaac, called Rash, 1040-1105.

AMERICAN academy for Jewish research. 206
Rashi anniversary volume. New York, [Philadelphia, Press of the Jewish publication society] 1941. 248 p. 23 1/2 cm. (Its Texts and studies, vol. 1) "Essays on Rabbi Solomon ben Isaac of Troyes, France, the 900th anniversary of whose birth was celebrated by world Jewry last year... edited by Professor H.L. Ginaberg."--Editorial statement. Bibliographical foot-notes. [DS101.A343 vol. 1] [296.082] 42-1717
1. Solomon ben Isaac, called RaShi, 1040-1100. I. Ginsberg, Harold Louis, ed. II. Jewish publication society of America. III. Title.
Contents omitted.

BURSTEIN,Abraham, 1893- 922.96
The boy called Rashi, by Abraham Burstein; illustrated by Stanley Maxwell. New York, Behrman's Jewish book houses, 1940. 6 p. l., 116 p. illus. 20 cm. [BM755.S6B8] 40-12492
1. Solomon ben Issac, called RaShi, 1040-1105. I. Title.

HAILPERIN, Herman, 1899- 222.107
Rashi and the Christian scholars. [Pittsburgh] University of Pittsburgh Press [1963] xvii, 379 p. 24 cm. Bibliographical references included in "Notes" (p. 267-358) [BS1161.S58H3] 62-7929
1. Solomon ben Isaac, called RaSHI, 1040-

1105. 2. Nicolas de Lyre, d. 1349. 3. Bible — Criticism, interpretation, etc. — Hist. I. Title.

LIBER, Maurice. 922.
Rashi, by Maurice Liber; tr. from the French by Adele Szold. [Philadelphia] The Jewish publication society of America, 1906. 3 p. l., [3]-278 p. incl. geneal. tab. front, (map) plates. 19 1/2 cm. Bibliography: p. [229]-239. [BM755.S6L5] 6-14778
1. Solomon ben Isaac, called RaShi, 1040-1105. I. Szold, Adele, tr. II. Jewish publication society of America. III. Title.

LIBER, Maurice, 1884- 296.6'1 B
Rashi. Translated from the French by Adele Szold. New York, Hermon Press, [1970] 278 p. illus., geneal. table, map. 24 cm. Reprint of the 1906 ed. Includes bibliographical references. [BM755.S6L5 1970] 70-136767 7.50
1. Solomon ben Isaac, called RaSHI, 1040-1105. I. Title.

Solomon, Brother, 1745-1792.

BATTERSBY, William John. 922.244
Brother Solomon, martyr of the French Revolution. New York, Macmillan [1960] vi, 181 p. plates, port., facsim. 23 cm. [BX4705.S669B] A63
1. Solomon, Brother, 1745-1792. 2. France — Hist. — Revolution. 3. France — Church history. I. Title.

Solomon, king of Israel.

BARTLETT, Willard. 211
King Solomon's goat, by Willard Bartlett ... [1st ed.] Boston, Everett print [c1918] 1 p. l., 142 p. 18 cm. [BL2775.B35] 19-19378
I. Title.

THE "Beloved of the Lord." 221.92
a sketch of the life of Solomon, the last king of Israel. Written for the American Sunday-school union, and revised by the Committee of publication. Philadelphia, American Sunday-school union [1845] 204 p. incl. front., illus., plates, plans. 16 cm. Added t.-p. (illustrated): A sketch of the life of Solomon, the last king of Israel. [BS580.S6B4] 37-10033
1. Solomon, king of Israel. I. American Sunday-school union.

BIBLE. O. T. Proverbs. English. 1929.
Teachings of Solomon, presented by Alfred Walls. Philadelphia, Chicago [etc.] The John C. Winston company [c1929] viii, 127 p. 19 cm. [BS1463.W] 29-23769
I. Walls, Alfred, ed. II. Title.

CONWAY, Moncure Daniel, 1832-1907. 221.9'24 B
Solomon and Solomonic literature. New York, Haskell House, 1973. viii, 248 p. 23 cm. [BS580.S6C6 1973] 72-2032 ISBN 0-8383-1478-3 10.95
1. Solomon, King of Israel. 2. Hebrew literature—History and criticism. I. Title.

ELKIN, Benjamin. 398.22
The wisest man in the world; a legend of ancient Israel, retold by Benjamin Elkin. Pictures by Anita Lobel. New York, Parents' Magazine Press [1968] [46] p. col. illus. 26 cm. While visiting King Solomon, the Queen of Sheba tests his wisdom with increasingly difficult problems. [BS580.S6E4] AC 68
1. [Solomon, King of Israel.] I. Lobel, Anita, illus. II. Title.

FARRAR, Frederic William, 1831-1903. 221.92
... *Solomon,* his life and times, by Rev. F. W. Farrar ... New York, Chicago [etc.] Fleming H. Revell company [189-?] viii, 217 p. 20 cm. (Men of the Bible) [BS580.S6F3] 37-10889
1. Solomon, king of Israel. I. Title.

FLEG, Edmond, 1874- 221.92
The life of Solomon, by Edmond Fleg ... translated from the French by Viola Gerard Garvin. New York, E. P. Dutton & co., inc. [c1930] 239 p. 21 1/2 cm. [BS580.S6F5] 30-6074
1. Solomon, king of Israel. I. Garvin, Viola Gerard, tr. II. Title.

FREEHOF, Lillian B (Simon) 1906- 221.92
Stories of King Solomon; illustrated by Seymour R. Kaplan. Philadelphia, Jewish Publication Society of America [c1955] 175p. illus. 28cm. [BS580.S6F7] 55-8423
1. Solomon, King of Israel. I. Title.

GAUBERT, Henri, 1895- 221.9'24 B
Solomon the magnificent. Translated by Lancelot Sheppard and A. Manson. New York, Hastings House [1970] xix, 191 p. illus. 20 cm. (The Bible in history, v. 5) "A Giniger book." Bibliography: p. 187-188. [BS580.S6G313 1970] 69-15815 ISBN 0-8038-6685-2 5.95
1. Solomon, King of Israel. I. Title. II. Series.

GOODMAN, John.
Long-lost chronicles of Solomon, and poems, by John Goodman ... Cleveland, O., J. B. Savage, printer, 1884. 58 p. 23 cm. [PS1753.G7L6] 28-4741
1. Solomon, king of Israel. I. Title.

HALLOCK, Mary Angeline (Ray) Lathrop, Mrs. b.1810. 221.92
The child's history of King Solomon. By Mrs. M. A. Hallock ... New York, The American tract society [c1869] 128 p. incl. front., illus. 15 1/2 x 13 cm. [BX580.S6H3 1869] 32-18652
1. Solomon, king of Israel. I. American tract society. II. Title.

HILDE, Reuben. 222'.530924
The king was no fool / Reuben Hilde. Washington, D.C. : Review and Herald Pub. Association, [1980] p. cm. [BS580.S6H54] 80-12916 pbk. : 4.50
1. Solomon, King of Israel. 2. Bible. O.T. Proverbs—Criticism, interpretation, etc. I. Title.

SMITH, Daniel, 1806-1852. 221.92
The life of Solomon, king of Israel; by Rev. Daniel Smith... Revised by the editors. New York, Published by G. Lane, for the Sunday school union of the Methodist Episcopal church, 1840. 168 p. incl. front., illus. 13 1/2 cm. (On cover: S[unday] s[chool] & y[ouths] library. 239) [BS580.S6S6] 37-10028
1. Solomon, king of Israel. I. Sunday school union of the Methodist Episcopal church. II. Title.

WILSON, Clifford A. 221.92'4
A greater than Solomon is here, by Clifford Wilson. [Melbourne, Australian Institute of Archaeology in association with Word of Truth Productions, 1968] 40 p. 21 cm. (A Word of truth production) [BS580.S6W53] 78-467107 unpriced
1. Solomon, King of Israel. 2. Jesus Christ—Person and offices. I. Australian Institute of Archaeology. II. Title.

Solomon, King of Israel—Drama.

KESSELRING, Joseph, 1902-1967. 812'.5'2
Mother of that wisdom; a historical play in two acts. [1st ed.] New York, Exposition Press [1973] ix, 253 p. 21 cm. (An Exposition-banner book) [PS3521.E775M6 1973] 73-173398 ISBN 0-682-47673-0 5.50
1. Solomon, King of Israel—Drama. I. Title.

Solomon, king of Israel—Fiction.

SAPHIRE, Saul, 1893-
King Solomon; historical romance by Saul Saphire ... [New York] 1931. 1 p. l., 512 p. front. (port.) 23 1/2 cm. 31-22429
1. Solomon, king of Israel—Fiction. I. Title (transliterated): Shlomoh ha-Melckh. II. Title.

Solomon, King of Israel—Juvenile literature.

KELLNER, Esther. 221.9
Solomon the Wise. Garden City, N. Y. [N. Doubleday, 1961] 64p. illus. 21cm. (Know your Bible program) [BS580.S6K4] 61-3964
1. Solomon, King of Israel—Juvenile literature. I. Title.

WILLS, Garry, 1934- j221.9
Solomon the Wise. Garden City, N. Y. [N. Doubleday, 1961] 64 p. illus. 21 cm. (The Catholic know-your-Bible program) [BS580.S6W5] 61-3966
1. Solomon, King of Israel — Juvenile literature. I. Title.

Solomon, King of Israel—Legends—History and criticism.

PRITCHARD, James Bennett, 1909- 221.9'22
Solomon and Sheba, edited by James B. Pritchard. New York, Praeger [1974] p. cm. [BS580.S6P74] 72-79551 ISBN 0-275-46540-3 15.00
1. Solomon, King of Israel—Legends—History and criticism. 2. Sheba, Queen of—Legends—History and criticism. I. Title.

PRITCHARD, James Bennett, 1909- 221.9'22
Solomon & Sheba / James B. Pritchard, ed. ; [contributors] Gus W. van Beek ... [et al.]. London : Phaidon, 1974. 160 p., [48] p. of plates : ill., facsims., maps, plans ; 26 cm. Distributed in the U.S.A. by Praeger, New York. Includes index. Bibliography: p. 152-158. [BS580.S6P74 1974b] 74-196853 ISBN 0-7148-1613-2 : 17.50
1. Solomon, King of Israel—Legends—History and criticism. 2. Sheba, Queen of—Legends—History and criticism. I. Van Beek, Gus Willard, 1922- II. Title.

Solomon's temple.

BUNYAN, John, 1628-1688. 252.
Solomon's temple spiritualiz'd or, Gospel-light fetch'd out of the temple at Jerusalem; to let us more easily into the glory of New-Testament truths. By John Bunyan. A new edition... Philadelphia, Printed and Sold by Stewart & Cochran, No. 34, south Second-street, 1792. viii, (t9] -168 p. 14 cm. [BR75.B86 1792] 26-12116
I. Title.

BUNYAN, John, 1628-1688. 252.
Solomon's temple spiritualized; or, Gospel-light brought out of the temple at Jerusalem, to let us more easily into the glory of New-Testament truths. By John Bunyan. The first Albany edition... Printed and sold in Albany, By Charles T. & George Webster, no. 46, State-street, Corner of Middle-lane, m,dcc,xc. xiv, [15]-192 p. 14 cm. [BR75.B86 1790] 2-9879
I. Title.

BUNYAN, John, 1628-1688. 252.
Solomon's temple spiritualized; or, Gospel-light fetched out of the temple at Jerusalem, to let us more easily into the glory of New-Testament truths. By John Bunyan ... Hartford; Printed by John Babcock, 1802. vi, [7]-144 p. 15 1/2 cm. [BR75.B86 1802] 26-12117
I. Title.

SCHMIDT, Emanuel, 1868-
Solomon's temple in the light of other Oriental temples, by Emanuel Schmidt, PH. D. Chicago, The University of Chicago press, 1902. 65, [4] p., 1 l. incl. diagr., plan. 25 cm. Vita. Bibliography: p. 64-65. 2-15200
1. Solomon's temple. 2. Temples, Oriental. I. Title.

Solov'ev, Vladimir Sergeevich, 1853-1900.

STREMOOUKHOFF, D. 230
Vladimir Soloviev and his messianic work / D. Stremooukhoff ; translated from the French by Elizabeth Meyendorff ; edited by Phillip Guilbeau and Heather Elise MacGregor. Belmont, Mass. : Nordland Pub. Co., 1980, c1979. 394 p. ; 22 cm. Translation of Vladimir Soloviev et son oeuvre messianique. Includes index. Bibliography: p. 383-388. [B4267.S813] 19 78-78264 ISBN 0-913124-36-2 pbk. : 37.50
1. Solov'ev, Vladimir Sergeevich, 1853-1900. I. Guilbeau, Phillip. II. MacGregor, Heather Elise. III. Title.

Soltau, Henrietta Eliza, 1843-1934.

CABLE, Mildred. 922
A woman who laughed: Henrietta Soltau, who laughed at impossibilities and cried: "It shall be done". By Mildred Cable and Francesca French. London, Philadelphia [etc.] The China inland mission, 1934. vii p., 1 l., 11-240 p. front., plates, ports. 19 cm. "First edition June, 1934 ... reprinted September, 1934 ... reprinted November, 1934 ..." [BR1725.S66C3 1934 b] 35-6036
1. Soltau, Henrietta Eliza, 1843-1934. I. French, Francesca L., joint author. II. Title.

CABLE, Mildred. 922
A woman who laughed: Henrietta Soltau, who laughed at impossibilities and cried: "It shall be done". By Mildred Cable and Francesca French. London, Philadelphia [etc.] The China inland mission, 1934. vii p., 1 l., 11-240 p. front., plates, ports. 19 cm. "First edition June, 1934 ... reprinted September, 1934 ... reprinted November, 1934 ..." [Full name: Alice Mildred Cable] [BR1725.S66C3] 35-6036
1. Soltau, Henrietta Eliza, 1843-1934. I. French, Francesca Law, joint author. II. Title.

Soma.

WASSON, Robert Gordon, 1898- 294.5'2'12
Soma and the fly-agaric; Mr. Wasson's rejoinder to Professor Brough. Cambridge, Mass., Botanical Museum of Harvard University, 1972. 57 p. illus. 25 cm. (Ethno-mycological studies, no. 2) Bibliography: p. 50-51. [BL1215.S6W36] 73-159656 3.00
1. Brough, John, 1917- 2. Soma. 3. Amanita muscaria. 4. Mushrooms (in religion, folk-lore, etc.) I. Title. II. Series.

WASSON, Robert Gordon, 1898- 294.5'21'2
Soma: divine mushroom of immortality, by R. Gordon Wasson. [New York] Harcourt Brace Jovanovich [1971] xiii, 380 p. illus., maps, col. plates. 26 cm. (Ethno-mycological studies, no. 1) Reprint of the 1968 ed. Includes bibliographical references. [BL1215.S6W37 1971] 74-25987 15.00
1. Soma. 2. Mushrooms (in religion, folk-lore, etc.) I. Title. II. Series.

Somerset. Eng.—Church history.

ARCHBOLD, William Arthur Jobson, 1865-
...The Somerset religious houses. By W.A.J. Archbold...Prince Consort dissertation, 1890. Cambridge [Eng.] University press, 1892. xii, 407 p. fold. map. 19 1/2 cm. (Cambridge historical essays. no. vi "250 copies printed of which 200 only are for sale." "Chief authorities consulted": p. [ix]-x. (Name originally: William Arthur Jobson] [BX2504.85A7] 2-22067
1. Somerset. Eng.—Church history. 2. Reformation—England. 3. Monasteries—England. I. Prince Consort dissertation. 1800. II. Title.

CHRISTIANITY in Somerset / 274.23'8
edited by Robert W. Dunning. [Bridgwater] : Somerset County Council, 1976. xii, 132 p. : ill., maps, music, plans, ports. ; 21 x 22 cm. Includes index. Bibliography: p. 126-127. [BR763.S5C48] 76-379389 ISBN 0-9503615-2-6 : £1.60
1. Somerset, Eng.—Church history. I. Dunning, Robert William, 1916-

ROBINSON, Joseph Armitage, 1858-
Somerset historical essays, by J. Armitage Robinson ... London, Pub. for the British academy, by H. Milford, Oxford university press, 1921. vii, [1], 159, [1] p. 26 cm. Half-title: The British academy. [BR763.S5R6] 22-19558
1. Somerset, Eng.—Church history. I. British academy, London. II. Title.
Contents omitted.

Son of God—History of doctrines.

BROOKS, Keith Leroy, 1888- 226.
The Son of God; a verse by verse commentary of John's Gospel, to be written by yourself with the aid of the

Bible, suggested by Keith L. Brooks. Los Angeles, Cal, Bible institute of Los Angeles [c1923] 109, [3] p. 23 cm. Blank pages for "Notes" (3 at end) [BS2615.B7] ca23
I. Title.

CLYMER, Reuben Swinburne, 1878-
The Son of God; the mystical teachings of the masters, or the Christic interpretation, giving a short sketch of the early life of Jesus and of His training by the Essenean order, and interpretation of some of his teachings, in harmony with the fundamental principles of the Temple of illumination, known as the "Christic interpretation"... by R. Swinburne clymer. Allentown, Pa., The Philosophical publishing co. [c1913] 94, 53 p. front., pl. 21 cm. "Authorized text-book of the Temple of illumination." "Announcement, Soul science and success, the Christic interpretation and mystic Christianity, as taught by the Temple of illuminati...the philosophy of immortality," and "A catalog of books on soul science, the Christic interpretation and mystic Christianity": 53 p. at end. 13-24171 0.50
I. Title.

CLYMER, Reuben Swinburne, 1878-
The Son of God; the mystical teachings of the masters, giving a short sketch of the early life of Jesus and of His training by the Essenean order, and an interpretation of some of His teachings, in harmony with the fundamental principles of the Temple of illumination, known as the "Christic interpretation"... by R. Swinburne Clymer. Allentown, Pa., The Philosophical publishing co. [c1916] 2 p. l., [7]-107, 28, 24 p. front., pl. 20 1/2 cm. "Announcement, Soul science and success, the Christic interpretation and mystic Christianity authorized by Temple of illuminati... the philosophy of immortality," and "A catalog of Rosicrucian and soul science and success books": 28, 24 p. at end. 17-863 0.50
I. Title.

HENGEL, Martin. 232
The Son of God : the origin of Christology and the history of Jewish-Hellenistic religion / Martin Hengel ; [translated by John Bowden from the German]. 1st American ed. Philadelphia : Fortress Press, 1976. xii, 100 p. ; 22 cm. Translation of Der Sohn Gottes. Includes bibliographical references and indexes. [BT198.H4613 1976] 75-37151 ISBN 0-8006-1227-2 pbk. : 3.75
1. Son of God—History of doctrines. 2. Jesus Christ—History of doctrines—Early church, ca. 30-600. I. Title.

Son of Man.

ABBOTT, Edwin Abbott, 1838-1926.
"The Son of man"; or, Contributions to the study of the thoughts of Jesus, by Edwin A. Abbott... Cambridge, University press, 1910. iii, 372 p. [2] p. 22 1/2 cm. (Diatessarica, part viii) A 11
I. Title.

BORSCH, Frederick Houk. 232'.1
The Christian and Gnostic Son of Man. Naperville, Ill., A. R. Allenson [1970] 130 p. 22 cm. (Studies in Biblical theology, 2d ser., 14) Includes bibliographical references. [BT232.B58] 77-131585
1. Son of Man. I. Title. II. Series.

BORSCH, Frederick Houk. 232'.1
The Son of Man in myth and history. Philadelphia, Westminster Press [1967] 431 p. 23 cm. (The New Testament library) Revision of the author's thesis, University of Birmingham. Bibliographical footnotes. [BT232.B6 1967] 67-25329
1. Son of Man. I. Title.

HAMERTON-KELLY, R. G. 225.8'232
Pre-existence, wisdom, and the Son of Man; a study of the idea of pre-existence in the New Testament, by R. G. Hamerton-Kelly. Cambridge [Eng.] University Press, 1973. xii, 310 p. 23 cm. (Society for New Testament Studies. Monograph series, 21) Bibliography: p. 281-294. [BS2545.P684H35] 72-78890 ISBN 0-521-08629-9 23.50
1. Son of Man. 2. Pre-existence—Biblical teaching. I. Title. II. Series: Studiorum Novi Testamenti Societas. Monograph series, 21.
Distributed by Cambridge University Press N.Y.

HIGGINS, Angus John Brockhurst 232.904
Jesus and the Son of Man, by A. J. B. Higgins. Philadelphia, Fortress [1965, c.1964] 223p. 23cm. Bibl. [BT232.H5] 65-21083 4.25
1. Son of Man. I. Title.

MCDOWELL, Edward Allison, 1898- 232.1
Jesus and His cross. Nashville, Broadman Press [195-, c1944] 216p. 20cm. First published in 1944 under title: Son of Man and Suffering Servant. [BT205.M17] 58-42578
1. Son of Man. 2. Servant of Jehovah. 3. Jesus Christ—Person and offices. I. Title.

MCDOWELL, Edward Allison, 1898- 232.1
Son of Man and Suffering Servant, a historical and exegetical study of synoptic narratives revealing the consciousness of Jesus concerning His person and mission, by Edward A. McDowell ... [Nashville, Broadman press, 1944] 216 p. 20 1/2 cm. Bibliographical foot-notes. [BT205.M17] 44-8643
1. Jesus Christ—Person and offices. 2. Son of man. 3. Servant of Jehovah. I. Title.

MOLONEY, Francis J. 226'.5'06
The Johannine Son of Man / Francis J. Moloney. Roma : LAS, 1976. xv, 265 p. ; 24 cm. (Biblioteca di scienze religiose ; 14) Originally presented as the author's thesis, Oxford, 1975. Includes indexes. Bibliography: p. [221]-240. [BT232.M64 1976] 77-368906
1. Bible. N.T. John—Criticism, interpretation, etc. 2. Son of Man. I. Title.

TODT, Heinz Eduard. 232.1
The Son of Man in the synoptic tradition [by] H. D. Todt. [Translated by Dorothea M. Barton] Philadelphia, Westminster Press [1965] 366 p. 23 cm. (The New Testament library) Bibliography: p. [353]-357. [BT232.T613] 65-22392
1. Son of Man. 2. Bible. N. T. Gospels — Criticism, Interpretation, etc. I. Title.

Son of Man—Biblical teaching.

GANDIER, Alfred, 1861- 232.
The Son of man coming in His kingdom; a study of the apocalyptic element in the teaching of Jesus, by Alfred Gandier ... New York, George H. Doran company [c1922] x p., 1 l., 15-154 p. 19 1/2 cm. $1.25. [BT885.G3] 22-14600
I. Title.

HIGGINS, Angus John Brockhurst. 232
The Son of Man in the teaching of Jesus / A. J. B. Higgins. Cambridge [Eng.] ; New York : Cambridge University Press, 1980. p. cm. (Monograph series - Society for New Testament Studies ; 39) Includes index. Bibliography: p. [BT232.H53] 79-42824 ISBN 0-521-22363-6 : 17.95
1. Bible. N.T. Gospels—Criticism, interpretation, etc. 2. Son of Man—Biblical teaching. I. Title. II. Series: Studiorum Novi Testamenti Societas. Monograph series ; 39.

Son, Yang-won.

AN, Yong-jun. 275.19 B
The triumph of Pastor Son; from Korea ... a true story of faith under persecution [by] Yong Choon Ahn with Phyllis Thompson. Downers Grove, Ill., InterVarsity Press [1974, c1973] 96 p. 18 cm. [BX9225.S62A83 1974] 73-93140 ISBN 0-87784-555-7 1.50 (pbk.)
1. Son, Yang-won. I. Thompson, Phyllis, joint author. II. Title.

Sona Mona Singh.

PARKHURST, Lucia A. 922.
Sona Mona Singh; missionary stories for children, by Lucia A. Parkhurst. New York, Cincinnati, The Abingdon press [c1927] 47 p. incl. front., plates, port. 19 cm. [BV3269.S65P3] 27-14222
1. Sona Mona Singh. 2. Missions—Inda. I. Title.

Songs.

BARNES, Camilus Milo 1862-
Sweet harmonies; a new song book of gospel songs for use in revivals and all religious gatherings, Sunday-schools, etc. Composed and selected by C. M. Barnes ... Eureka Springs, Ark., C. M. Barnes, 1903. 1 p. l., [1], 10, [346] p. front. (port.) 20 1/2 cm. Original copyright, 1896. 3-14228
I. Title.

BOTTOME, Francis, 1823-1894.
Songs from the parsonage [by] Francis Bottome. New York, A. D. F. Randolph and company [c1894] xi p., 1 l., [15]-166 p. incl. front. (port.) 17 1/2 cm. Dedication signed: Margaret Bottome; biographical sketch (p. [15]-24) signed: W. M. B. [i. e. William McDonald Bottome?] [PS1112.B23S6 1894] 20-17133
I. Title.

BURN, John Henry, 1858-
The churchman's treasury of song, gathered from the Christian poetry of all ages, by John Henry Burn ... New York, E. P. Dutton and company, 1907. xx, 427, [1] p. 17 1/2 cm. Printed in Edinburgh. 8-35516
I. Title.

BURN, John Henry, 1858-
The churchman's treasury of song, gathered from the Christian poetry of all ages, by John Henry Burn ... New York, E. P. Dutton and company, 1907. xx, 427, [1] p. 17 1/2 cm. Printed in Edinburgh. 8-35516
I. Title.

DAVIS, Grace Weiser. Mrs.
Favorite gospel songs: a hymn and tune book adapted to evangelistic meetings, prayer meetings, Sabbath schools, Epworth leagues ... Ed. by Mrs. Grace Weiser Davis, Rev. Elisha A. Hoffman. Ira Orwig Hoffman, music editor. Chicago, Hope pub. co. [1901] 192 pp. 20 cm. On cover: New and enl. ed. 2-4169
I. Title.

GRANGER, Lucy Nichols. 28-7920
Songs by the way. By Lucy Nichols Granger ... Ann Arbor [Mich.] Register publishing house, 1886. iv, [5]-104 p. 14 cm. [PS1759.G7]
I. Title.

*GROOMER, Vera MacKinnon 268.432
Illustrating Sabbath songs for tiny tots--cradle roll. Mountain View Calif. Pacific Pr. Pub. [1967] 119p. illus. 28cm. 3.25, pap., wire bdg.
I. Title.

HACKLEMAN, William E M comp. 783.8
Excell's male quartets and choruses, suitable for special music in church services, gospel meetings, Sunday school, Christian endeavor, etc., edited and compiled by W. E. M. Hackleman [and] Edwin O. Excell... Chicago, Ill., E. O. Excell company, c1925. [128] p. 20 cm. [M2063.4.B3] 32-10567
I. Excell, Edwin Othello, 1890- joint comp. II. Title. III. Title: Male quartets and choruses. IV. Title: Quartets and choruses.

HACKLEMAN, William E M comp. 783.8
Excell's male quartets and choruses, suitable for special music in church services, gospel meetings, Sunday school, Christian endeavor, etc., edited and compiled by W. E. M. Hackleman [and] Edwin O. Excell... Chicago, Ill., E. O. Excell company, c1925. [128] p. 20 cm. [M2063.4.B3] 32-10567
I. Excell, Edwin Othello, 1890- joint comp. II. Title. III. Title: Male quartets and choruses. IV. Title: Quartets and choruses.

HOOD, John J., ed.
Songs of love and praise, no. 6; for use in meetings for Christian worship or work. Philadelphia & Chicago, J. J. Hood, 1900. 223 p. incl. front. (port.) 12 °. Jul
I. Sweney, Lizzie E., joint ed. II. Title.

*JOHNSON, Gary 783.0242.
Son songs for christian folk. Minneapolis Bethany Fellowship [1975] 18p. ill. music 21 cm. Includes index. Contents.Contents:Vol.2. [M2070.] ISBN 0-87123-509-9. 1.50(pbk.)
1. Songs. I. Title.

JUSTUS, Emory W.
Grace divine, a book of songs for all churches of all faiths; new and original words to old and familiar tunes ... by Emory W. Justus ... Jefferson City, Mo., E. W. Justus [c1917] 57 p. 14 cm. 17-8914
I. Title.

KIRKPATRICK, W[illia]m J comp.
Songs of praise and victory by Wm. J. Kirkpatrick and Dr. H. L. Gilmour assisted by Rev. Chas. A. Tushingham. Philadelphia, Pepper pub. co. [c1899] 76 pp., 2 l. 12 degree. Cover-title. 1-310
I. Title.

LANGLEY, Charles K.
Bethel chimes; a collection of new songs for the Sabbath school, church, and home. By Chas. K. Langley and R. H. Randall. Chicago, Ill., R. H. Randall, 1891 144 p. 22 cm. 3-6034
I. Title.

LAZARUS, Emma, 1849-1887.
Songs of a Semite; The dance to death, and other poems. By Emma Lazarus ... New York, Office of "The American Hebrew," 1882. 4 p. l., [5]-80 p. 34 cm. "The dance to death; a historical tragedy in five acts," with special t.-p.: 2 p. l., [5]-48 p. [PS2233.S6 1882] 13-20282
I. Title. II. Title: The dance to death.

LORENZ, Edmund Simon, and others
Songs for work and workship, for use in Sunday schools, young people's societies ... etc. Dayton, O., Lorenz & co., 1900. 224 p. 8 degrees. May
I. Title.

MCLEOD, Malcolm James, 1867- 242
"Songs in the night," by Malcolm James McLeod... New York, Chicago [etc.] Fleming H. Revell company [c1919] 192 p. 19 1/2 cm. $1.25. "These addresses set forth the comfort of God's presence in circumstances of difficulty and sorrow." [BV4900.M3] 19-11795
I. Title.

MILLER, Joaquin, 1841-1913.
Songs of the soul, by Joaquin Miller ... San Francisco, The Whitaker & Ray company, 1896. 5 p. l., 9-162 p., 1 l. 20 cm. [Real name: Cincinnatus Hiner Miller] [PS2397.S57 1896] 24-18218
I. Title.

MUNHALL, Leander Whitcomb, comp. 783.
Songs of worship and grace. For use in devotional and evangelistic services. By L. W. Munhall ... New York, Eaton and Mains; Cincinnati, Jennings and Pye [c1900] [68] p. 18 cm. [M2198.M966S5] Mus
I. Title.

O'CONOR, John Francis Xavier, 1852-
Songs of the soul, by J. F. X. O'Conor... [New York, John Lane co., 1917] 3 p. l., 3-104 p., 1 l. illus. 21 cm. p. 102-104, advertising matter. [PS2486.O53S6] 17-16194
I. Title.

O'CONOR, John Francis Xavier, 1852-
Songs of the soul, by J. F. X. O'Conor ... [New York, John Lane co., 1917] 3 p. l., 3-104 p., 1 l. illus. 21 cm. p. 102-104, advertising matter. [PS2486.O53S6] 17-16194
I. Title.

OSLIN, S J.
Eureka carols; an excellent and varied collection of sacred songs, solos, duets, quartets, for use in Sunday schools, gospel meetings, revival services, and all religious gatherings, written and comp. by Rev. S. J. Oslin, G. L. Lindsey, and G. L. Young, with J. H. Smith, W. J. Sides, W. J. Smith, J. T. Key, H. A. Key and J. D. McAllister, as associate authors. Containing the rudiments of music by H. N. Lincoln. Dallas, Tex. [etc.] Songland co. [c1901] 16, [17-128] pp. 21 cm. 2-4164
I. Title.

OSLIN, S J.
Eureka carols; an excellent and varied collection of sacred songs, solos, duets, quartets, for use in Sunday schools, gospel meetings, revival services, and all religious gatherings, written and comp. by Rev. S. J. Oslin, G. L. Lindsey, and G. L. Young, with J. H. Smith, W. J. Sides, W. J. Smith, J. T. Key, H. A. Key and J. D. McAllister, as associate authors. Containing the rudiments of music by H. N. Lincoln. Dallas, Tex. [etc.] Songland co. [c1901] 16, [17-128] pp. 21 cm. 2-4164
I. Title.

PATTERSON, Rachel Elizabeth, b.1820. 245.2
Songs in affliction: a collection of miscellaneous poems, written during seasons of protracted illness. By Lizzie Patterson. 2d ed., enl. Baltimore, Printed by Sherwood & co., 1853. viii, [9]-80 p. 19 cm. [PS2524.P53 1853] [811.39] 32-22802
I. Title.

PERRIN, Daniel A. 1839-
New songs; sacred, patriotic, sentimental, comp. for the young peoples societies, the church, Sunday schools and home, by the Rev. D. A. Perrin ... Normal, Ill., D. A. Perrin & co. [c1910] [73] p. 21 cm. [With his Ave Maria: or, The Mother of Jesus in verse ... Normal, Ill. [c1910]] 11-1947
I. Title.

PHELPS, Sylvanus Dryden, 1816-1895.
Songs for all seasons, a scriptural and poetical calendar for holidays, birthdays, and all days, by Rev. S. Dryden Phelps, D. D. ... New York, Boston [etc.] Silver, Burdett & company, 1891. xiv, 406 p. front. (port.) 19 cm. [PS2558.P53] 24-18680
I. Title.

PIERCE, Charles Clark, comp.
Songs of heaven from many hearts, comp. by Rev. Charles Clark Pierce, D.D. Los Angeles, Cal., The Neuner company, 1915. 62 p., 1 l. group of ports. 24 1/2 cm. $1.00 15-10686
I. Title.

[ROBERTS, David Ellsworth] 1863- comp. 248
Sayings & songs for soldiers & sailors ... Baltimore, Md., Maryland tract society [c1917] 1 p. l., 60 p. col. front., 1 illus. 19 cm. "Compiled by David E. Roberts and Rev. DeWitt M. Benham." Contains music. "Sixth edition, for Pennsylvania soldiers and sailors." On cover: Presented by Forty-third street Presbyterian church sunday school, Pittsburgh, Pa. [BV4588.R6 1917 e] 32-18640
I. Benham, DeWitt M., joint comp. II. Title.

[ROBERTS, David Ellsworth] 1863- comp. 248
Sayings & songs for soldiers & sailors ... Baltimore, Md., Maryland tract society [c1917] 1 p. l., 60 p. col. front., 1 illus. 19 cm. "Compiled by David E. Roberts and Rev. DeWitt M. Benham." Contains music. "Sixth edition, for Pennsylvania soldiers and sailors." On cover: Presented by Forty-third street Presbyterian church sunday school, Pittsburgh, Pa. [BV4588.R6 1917 e] 32-18640
I. Benham, DeWitt M., joint comp. II. Title.

[ROBERTS, David Ellsworth] 1863- comp. 248
Sayings & songs for soldiers & sailors ... Baltimore, Md., Maryland tract society [c1918] 62 p. col. front., 1 illus. 13 cm. "Compiled by David E. Roberts and Rev. DeWitt M. Benham." Contains music. "Seventh edition." [BV4588.R6 1918] 32-18641
I. Benham, DeWitt M., joint comp. II. Title.

SANKEY, Ira David 1840- ed.
Junior Christian endeavor songs, comp. by Ira D. Sankey, John Willis Baer and William Shaw. Boston, United society of Christian endeavor [c1893] cover-title, 127 p. 23 1/2 cm. Without music. 4-329274
I. Baer, John Willis, 1861- joint ed. II. Shaw, William, joint ed. III. Title.

SHELTON, Don Odell, 1867- 220
Better than gold, by Don O. Shelton ... New York, The National Bible institute, 1926. 4 p. l., 227 p. 18 1/2 cm. [BR125.S4485] 27-5314
I. Title.

WHITEHILL, Michel, ed. 783
Everybody's favorite sacred songs ... Michel Whitehill, editor. New York, Amsco music publishing co., inc. [c1940] cover-title, 102 p. 30 1/2 x 23 cm. ("Everybody's favorite series", no. 36) Words in English; some in other languages also. Piano or organ accompaniment. [M2110.W66E8] 40-343762
I. Title. II. Title: Sacred songs.

WINKWORTH, Catherine, 1827-1878, tr. 245.
Songs for the household. Sacred poetry; mostly translated from the German by Catherine Winkworth. New York, R. Worthington, 1882. xxiii, [1], 258 p. front., pl. 19 cm. Half-title: Lyra Germanica: hymns for the Sundays and chief festivals of the Christian year. "Hymns ... selected from Chevalier Bunsen's 'Versuch eines allgemeinen gesang und gebetbuchs, published in 1833. From the large number there given ... little more than one hundred have been chosen."--Pref. Reprint of the first series only of the translator's "Lyra Germanica". [BV355.G3W7] 11-29171
I. Bunsen, Christian Karl Josias, freiherr von, 1791-1860. II. Title. III. Title: Lyra Germanica.

WOODWORTH, Samuel, 1785-1842.
Melodies, duets, trios, songs, and ballads, pastoral, amatory, sentimental, patriotic, religious, and miscellaneous. Together with metrical epistles, tales and recitations. By Samuel Woodworth. 3d ed., comprising many late productions never before published. New-York, Pub. for the author, by Elliot & Palmer, 1831. 3 p. l., [5]-288 p. front., plates. 15 1/2 cm. Added t.-p., engraved, with vignette. Includes The bucket (p. 12-13) Without music; tunes indicated by title. [PS3355.M4 1831] 20-14410
I. Title.

Songs, English.

FITZGERALD, James Newbury, bp., 1837-1906, ed.
Ocean Grove Christian songs. Editors: Bishop J. N. FitzGerald... Rev. Chas. H. Yatman...Tali Esen Morgan...Pub. for the Ocean Grove association, New Jesery, Ocean Grove New York, T. E. Morgan, c1902. [128] p. 21 cm. 3-3954
I. Title.

GENERAL church of the New Jerusalem. 783.9
A song book for social gatherings in the General church of the New Jerusalem. Rev. ed., 1930. Bryn Athyn, Pa., Academy book room, 1916 [i. e. 1930] 1 p. l., 149 p. 21 cm. Lettered on cover: Social song book. [M2131.S8H83] 31-3143
1. Songs, English. 2. Bryn Athyn, Pa. Academy of the New church—Songs and music. 3. Students' songs. 4. Hymns, English. I. Title. II. Title: Social song book.

Songs in the Night (Radio program)

*WIERSBE, Warren W. 248'.48'76
Songs in the night; devotional messages from the worldwide radio program. Grand Rapids, Mich., Baker Book House [1973] 144 p. illus. (inside covers) 22 cm. [BV4501] ISBN 0-8010-9535-2 1.95 (pbk.)
1. Songs in the Night (Radio program) 2. Christian life—Methodist authors—Addresses, essays, lectures. I. Moody Memorial Church, Chicago. Radio Program. II. Title.

[Songs, Jewish.]

DAUGHERTY, Leonard.
Beautiful songs of Zion; a collection of new and old songs suited to all kinds of religious work and worship. Cincinnati, Standard pub. co., 1900. [191] p. 8 degree. 0-4422
I. Title.

JEWS. Liturgy and ritual. 296.4'37
One little goat : a Passover song / adapted and illustrated by Marilyn Hirsh. New York : Holiday House, c1979. [32] p. : col. ill. ; 22 x 24 cm. Translation of Had gadya. After a little goat is eaten by a cat, trouble cumulates until the Holy One puts things right. The song is sung at the end of the seder on Passover. [BM670.H28H57] 78-24354 ISBN 0-8234-0345-9 Reinforced : 6.95
1. [Songs, Jewish.] 2. [Passover.] I. Hirsh, Marilyn. II. [Had gadya. English] III. Title.

Songs of praise.

DEARMER, Percy, 1867-1936. 783.9
Songs of praise discussed; a handbook to the best-known hymns and to others recently introduced, compiled by Percy Dearmer, with notes on the music by Archibald Jacob. London, Oxford university press, H. Milford, 1933. xxxii, 559, [1] p. illus. (music) 22 cm. [ML3186.D28] 33-27462
1. Songs of praise. 2. Hymns, English—Hist. & crit. I. Jacob, Archibald. II. Title.

Sons of temperance of North America.

DE WITT, William Radcliffe, 1792-1867. 178.
A discussion on the order of the Sons of temperance, between Rev. W. R. De Witt ... and Rev. W Easton ... together with a letter from Rev. W. Easton, in reply to Rev. H. Harbaugh, on the same secret order ... Philadelphia, T. R. Simpson, 1847. viii, [9]-278 p. 20 cm. [HV5287.S75D5] 10-4521
1. Sons of temperance of North America. 2. Secret societies. I. Easton, William, joint author. II. Title.

Sorabji Kharsedji Langrana, 1823-1894.

"THEREFORE"; 922.
an impression of Sorabji Kharsedji Langrana and his wife Franscina ... [London, New York, etc.] Oxford university press, H. Milford, 1924. 86, [2] p. front., plates, ports., fold. map. 22 1/2 x 18 cm. [BV3269.S7T4] 25-16285
1. Sorabji Kharsedji Langrana, 1823-1894. 2. Sorabju, Franscina Santya, 1833 or 34-1910.

Soren, Francisco Fulgencio, 1869-1933.

BRATCHER, Lewis Malen, 1888- 922.681
Francisco Fulgencio Soren, Christ's interpreter to many lands. by L. M. Bratcher. Nashville, Tenn., Broadman press [c1938] 224 p. plates, ports. 22 cm. [BV2853.B6B72] 38-14467
1. Soren, Francisco Fulgencio, 1869-1933. 2. Missions—Brazil. 3. Southern Baptist convention—Missions. I. Title.

Sorokin, Pitirim Alexandrovich, 1889-1968.

MATTER, Joseph Allen, 1901- 171'.8
Love, altruism, and world crisis: the challenge of Pitirim Sorokin. Chicago, Nelson-Hall [1974] xvi, 313 p. 23 cm. Bibliography: p. 285-301. [BJ1474.M49] 73-84209 ISBN 0-88229-114-9 9.95
1. Sorokin, Pitirim Aleksandrovich, 1889-1968. 2. Altruism. 3. Love. I. Title.

MATTER, Joseph Allen, 1901- 171'.8
Love, altruism, and world crisis : the challenge of Pitirim Sorokin / Joseph Allen Matter. Totowa, N.J. : Littlefield, Adams, 1975, c1974. xvi, 313 p. ; 21 cm. (A Littlefield, Adams quality paperback ; no. 311) Reprint of the ed. published by Nelson-Hall, Chicago. Includes index. Bibliography: p. 285-301. [BJ1474.M49 1975] 75-11740 ISBN 0-8226-0311-X pbk. : 3.95
1. Sorokin, Pitirim Alekandrovich, 1889-1968. 2. Altruism. 3. Love. I. Title.

Sorrows of the Blessed Virgin Mary, Devotion to.

DOHERTY, Edward Joseph, 1890- 232.931
Splendor of sorrow; for sinners only, by Eddie Doherty. New York, Sheed & Ward, 1943. 4 p. l., 79 p. 19 1/2 cm. [BX2161.5.S6D6] 43-15463
1. Sorrows of the Blessed Virgin Mary, Devotion to. I. Title.

FABER, Frederick William, 1814-1863. 232.931
The foot of the cross; or, The sorrows of Mary. New ed. Philadelphia, P. Reilly Co. [1956] 406p. 24cm. [BX2161.5.S6F2 1956] 57-2960
1. Sorrows of the Blessed Virgin Mary, Devotion to. I. Title.

MORRIS, Hilary. 232.931
Our Lady of Sorrows, a book of meditations. Westminister, Md., Newman Bookshop, 1946. 101 p. 20 cm. [BX2161.5.S6M6] 47-7790
1. Sorrows of the Blessed Virgin Mary, Devotion to. I. Title.

RAYMOND, Father, 1903- 232.931
God, a woman, and the way. Illustrated by John Andrews. Milwaukee, Bruce Pub. Co. [1955] 169p. illus. 23cm. [BX2161.5.S6R3] 55-7112
1. Sorrows of the Blessed Virgin Mary, Devotion to. I. Title.

VANN, Gerald, 1906- 232.931
The seven swords; with eight reproductions from the paintings of El Greco. [New York] Sheed and Ward, 1953. 82p. illus. 23cm. [BX2161.5.S6V3 1953] 53-5195
1. Sorrows of the Blessed Virgin Mary, Devotion to. I. Title.

Soto (Sect)

KENNETT, Jiyu, 1924- 294.3'927
Selling water by the river: a manual of Zen training. New York, Vintage Books [1972] xxv, 317 p. 21 cm. [BL1442.S65K45 1972b] 72-1063 ISBN 0-394-71804-6 2.45
1. Soto (Sect) I. Title.

Soto (Sect)—Addresses, essays, lectures.

TIMELESS spring : 294.3'927
a Soto Zen anthology / edited and translated by Thomas Cleary. 1st ed. Tokyo ; New York : Weatherhill, c1980. 176 p. ; 21 cm. "A Wheelwright Press book." [BQ9416.T55] 79-26677 ISBN 0-8348-0148-5 pbk. : 7.95
1. Soto (Sect)—Addresses, essays, lectures. 2. Priests, Zen—Japan—Biography. I. Cleary, Thomas F., 1949-

Sotoshu.

KENNETT, Jiyu, 1924- 294.3'927
Selling water by the river: a manual of Zen training. New York, Pantheon Books [1972] xxv, 317 p. 25 cm. Includes bibliographical references. [BQ9415.4.K45] 70-38836 ISBN 0-394-46743-4 10.00
1. Sotoshu. I. Title.

KENNETT, Jiyu, 1924- 294.3'927
Zen is eternal life / Jiyu Kennett. Emeryville, Calif. : Dharma Pub., c1976. xxxi, 452 p. : ill. ; 20 cm. First published in 1972 under title: Selling water by the river. Includes index. [BQ9415.4.K45 1976] 76-9387 ISBN 0-913546-37-2 : 12.95 ISBN 0-913546-38-0 pbk. : 5.95
1. Sotoshu. I. Title.

Sotoshu—Collected works.

YOKOI, Yuho, 1918- 294.3'927
Zen Master Dogen : an introduction with selected writings / by Yuho Yokoi, with the assistance of Daizen Victoria ; and with a foreword by Minoru Kiyota. 1st ed. New York : Weatherhill, 1976. 217 p. ; 23 cm. [BQ9449.D652Y63] 75-33200 ISBN 0-8348-0112-4 : 10.00 pbk. : 4.50
1. Dogen, 1200-1253. 2. Sotoshu—Collected works. I. Victoria, Daizen, 1939- joint author. II. Dogen, 1200-1253. Selected works. 1976. III. Title.

Sotoshu—Sermons.

DESHIMARU, Taisen. 294.3'4
The voice of the valley : Zen teachings / by Taisen Deshimaru ; edited by Philippe Coupey. Indianapolis : Bobbs-Merrill, c1979. p. cm. Includes index. [BQ9435.D47V64] 78-11207 ISBN 0-672-52520-8 : 10.95. ISBN 0-672-52586-0 pbk. : 7.95
1. Sotoshu—Sermons. 2. Buddhist sermons, English. I. Coupey, Philippe. II. Title.

Sotto il Monte, Italy.

SULLIVAN, Kay. 248.29
Journey of love; a pilgrimage to Pope John's birthplace. Photos. by Daniel M. Madden. Book design by Edward R. Wade. With a foreword by Richard Cardinal Cushing. New York, Appleton-Century [1966] 121 p. illus., map, ports. 27 cm. [BX1378.2.S8 1966] 66-22238
1. Joannes XXIII, Pope, 1881-1963. 2. Sotto il Monte, Italy. I. Title.

Soubirous. Bernadette, Saint, 1844-1879.

BLANTON, Margaret (Gray) 922.244
Mrs.
Bernadette of Lourdes, by Margaret Gray Blanton. London, New York [etc.] Longmans, Green and co., 1939. xi, 285 p. 2 port. (incl. front.) plates 21 1/2 cm. "Printed in the United States of America." "First edition." [BX4760.S65B5] 40-27025
1. Soubirous, Bernadette, Saint, 1844-1879. I. Title.

BLANTON, Margaret (Gray) 922.244
The miracle of Bernadette. Englewood Cliffs, N. J., Prentice-Hall [1958] 288p. illus. 22cm. First ed. published in 1939 under title: Bernadette of Lourdes. Includes bibliography. [BX4700.S65B5 1958] 58-7144
1. Soubirous, Bernadette, Saint, 1844-1879. I. Title.

CLARKE, Richard Frederick, 231.
1839-1900.
Lourdes, its inhabitants, its pilgrims, and its miracles. With an account of the apparitions at the grotto and a sketch of Bernadette's subsequent history. By Richard F. Clarke, S.J. New York, Cincinnati, [etc.] Benziger brothers, 1888. 224 p. incl. plates. front. 17 1/2 cm. [BT653.C55] 12-31408
1. Soubirous Bernadette, Saint, 1844-1879. 2. Lourdes. I. Title.

CRISTIANI, Leon, 1879- 922.22
Saint Bernadette. [Translated by Patrick O'Shaughnessy] Staten Island, N.Y. Alba House [1965] 181 p. 20 cm. [BX4700.S65C73] 65-15727
1. 1. Soubrious, Bernadette, Saint, 1844-1879. I. Title.

DAUGHTERS of St. Paul. 92
Light in the grotto; the life of St. Bernadette, written and illustrated by the Daughters of St. Paul. [Boston] St. Paul Editions [1967] 94 p. illus. 22 cm. (Their Encounter books) A biography of the young French maid whose quiet insistence on the reality of her vision in the grotto at Lourdes brought the establishment of a famous Catholic shrine. [BX4700.S65D35] AC 67
1. Soubirous, Bernadette, Saint, 1844-1879. I. Title.

ERNEST, Brother, 1897- 231.73
Our Lady comes to Lourdes. Illus. by Laurie McCawley. Notre Dame, Ind., Dujarie Press [1951] 93 p. illus. 24 cm. [BT653.E7] 51-6548
1. Soubirous, Bernadette, Saint, 1844-1879. 2. Lourdes. I. Title.

ESTRADE, Jean Baptiste.
My witness, Bernadette; the authentic sourcebook of the apparitions at Lourdes by an eyewitness. Translated from the French by J. H. Le Breton Girdlestone. With a pref. by Robert Hugh Benson. Springfield, Ill., Templegate [1951, '1946] xix, 221 p. 19 cm. A52
1. Soubirous. Bernadette, Saint, 1844-1879. 2. Lourdes. 3. Mary, Virgin—Apparitions and miracies. I. Title.

KEYES, Frances Parkinson 922.244
(Wheeler) Mrs. 1885-
Bernadette, maid of Lourdes, by Frances Parkinson Keyes. [New York, J. Messner, inc.] 1940. 153 p. front., plates, ports., facsim. 22 cm. Illustrated lining-papers. Also published with the addition of a foreword and an "Author's note", under title: The sublime shepherdess, the life of Saint Bernadette of Lourdes. Bibliography: p. 157-158. [BX4700.S65K4 1940a] 40-89278
1. Soubirous, Bernadette, Saint, 1844-1879. I. Title.

KEYES, Frances Parkinson 922.244
(Wheeler) 1885-
Bernadette of Lourdes, shepherdess, Sister, and Saint, [Rev. version, with new material added. New York] J. Messner [1953] 152p. illus. 22cm. 'Originally issued under the title The sublime shepherdess.' [BX4700.S65K4 1953] 53-1047
1. Soubirous, Bernadette, Saint, 1844-1879. I. Title.

KEYES, Frances Parkinson 922.244
(Wheeler) Mrs. 1885-
The sublime shepherdess; the life of Saint Bernadette of Lourdes, by Frances Parkinson Keyes. [New York] J. Messner, inc., 1940. 182 p. front., plates, ports., facsim. 21 1/2 cm. Illustrated lining-papers. Bibliography: p. 181-182. [BX4700.S65K4] 40-27397
1. Soubirous, Bernadette, Saint, 1844-1879. I. Title.

KUHN, Anna, 1900- 922.244
A Queen's command, by Anna Kuhn, drawings by Frank Marasco. Milwaukee, The Bruce publishing company [c1940] 3 p. l., 138 p. illus. 21 cm. [Full name: Mary Frances Anna Kuhn] [BX4700.S65K8] 40-34301
1. Soubirous Bernodette Saint 1844-1879. I. Title.

THE Lily of Mary: 921.
Bernadette of Lourdes, the Venerable Sister Mary Bernard, nun of the congregation of the Sisters of charity of Nevers, France; a short life of Bernadette of Lourdes, by the author of La confidente de l'immaculee (entitled in English Bernadette of Lourdes) New York city, The Bureau of the Immaculate conception [1918] 90 p. front., plates, ports. 18 cm. [BX4705.S7L5] 18-13256 0.30
1. Soubirous, Bernadette, in religion Sister Marie Bernard, 1844-1879.

MCREAVY, Lawrence Leslie. 922.244
"Bernadette", child of Mary, by Fr. L. L. McReavy... St. Louis, B. Herder book co. [1933] 198 [2] p. col. front. (port.) 19 cm. Printed in Great Britain. Bibliography: p. [200] [BX4705.S7M3] 33-36384
1. Soubirous, Bernadette, Saint, 1844-1879. I. Title.

MATT, Leonard von 922.244
Bernadette of Lourdes [by] Leonard von Matt, Francis Trochu. [Tr. from German] New York, Universe [c.1963] 47p. 80 illus. (incl. ports., facsims.) 18cm. (Orbis bks., 4) Summary of St. Bernadette: a pictorial biography, by Leonard von Matt and Francis Trochu. 63-18345 1.75 pap.,
1. Soubirous, Bernadette, Saint. 1844-1879. 2. Lourdes—Descr.—Views. I. Trochu, Francis, 1877- II. Title.

MATT, Leonard von. 922.244
St. Bernadette; a pictorial biography, by Leonard von Matt and Francis Trochu. Translated from the French by Herbert Rees. Chicago, H. Regnery Co. [1957] 91p. illus. 25cm. [BX4700.S65M35] 57-2781
1. Soubirous, Bernadette, Saint, 1844-1879. 2. Lourdes— Descr.—Views. I. Trochu, Francis, 1877- joint author. II. Title.

NOWAK, Andrew Thomas 231.73
Francis.
American ambassadors to Lourdes; the story of St. Bernadette and of G. I. visitors to the Shrine in 1945-1946. [1st ed.] New York, Exposition Press [1955] 514p. 21cm. [BT653.N68] 54-12477
1. Soubirous, Bernadette, Saint, 1844-1879. 2. Lourdes. I. Title.

PAULI, Hertha Ernestine, 922.244
1909-
Bernadette, Our Lady's little servant. Illustrated by Georges Vaux. New York, Vision Books [1956] 187p. illus. 22cm. (Vision books, 5) [BX4700.S65P3] 56-5200
1. Soubirous, Bernadette, Saint, 1844-1879. I. Title.

PETITOT, Hyacinthe, 1870- 922.244
1934.
Saint Bernadette, by Henri Petitot. Translated from the French. Chicago, H. Regnery Co., 1955. 130p. 18cm. (Angelus books) Translation of Histoire exacte de la vie interieure et rellgieuse de ste. Bernadette. [BX4700.S65P413] 55-4767
1. Soubirous, Bernadette, Saint, 1844-1879. I. Title.

PETITOT, Hyacinthe, 1870- 922.244
1934.
The true story of Saint Bernadette. Translated by a Benedictine of Stanbrook Abbey. Westminster, Md., Newman Press [1950] viii, 195 p. 22 cm. Translation of Histoire exacte de la vie interieure et religieuse de ste Bernadette. [BX4700.S65P414] 51-3572
1. Soubirous, Bernadette, Saint, 1844-1879. I. Title.

PRUVOST, S. 231.
The wonders of Massabielle at Lourdes, apparitions, miracles, pilgrimages; a narrative in thirty-two parts adapted to May or October devotions, by the Rev. S. Pruvost, translated from the French by Rev. Joseph A. Fredette, foreword by the Rt. Rev. Joseph H. McMahon, with thirty illustrations. Boston, Matthew F. Sheehan company, 1925. 9 p. l., [3]-206 p. front., plates, ports. 20 cm. "Our Lady of Lourdes" [with music]: p. 187-189. [BT653.P7] 25-23078
1. Soubirous, Bernadette, Saint, 1844-1879. 2. Lourdes. 3. Miracles. I. Fredette, Joseph A., tr. II. Title.

ST. Bernadette; a pictorial biography, by Leonard von Matt and Francis Trochu. Translated from the French by Herbert Rees. London, New York, Longmans, Green [1957] 91p. illus.
1. Soubirous, Bernadette, Saint, 1844-1879. 2. Lourdes—Descr.—Views. I. Matt, Leonard von. II. Trochu, Francis, 1877- joint author.

SAINT-PIERRE, Michel de, 922.244
1916-
Bernadette and Lourdes. Translated from the French by Edward Fitzgerald. Garden City, N. Y., Image Books [1955, c1954] 266p. 18cm. (A Doubleday image book, D16) [BX4700] 55-805
1. Soubirous, Bernadette, Saint, 1844-1879. 2. Lourdes. I. Title.

SHARKEY, Donald C. 1912-- 231.73
After Bernadette; the story of modern Lourdes [by] Don Sharkey. Milwaukee, The Bruce publishing company [1945] 166 p. incl. front. (map) plates, ports. 20 1/2 cm. "The literature of Lourdes": p. 158-166. [BT653.S52] 45-7127
1. Soubirous, Bernadette, Saint, 1844-1879. 2. Lourdes. I. Title.

TROCHU, Francis, 1877- 922.244
Saint Bernadette Soubirous, 1844-1879. Translated and adapted by John Joyce. London, New York, Longmans, Green [1958, c1957] 400 p. illus. 23 cm. Includes bibliography. [BX4700.S65T683] 58-2886
1. Soubirous, Bernadette, Saint, 1844-1879 I. Title.

TROCHU, Francis, 1877- 922.244
Saint Bernadette Soubirous, 1844-1879. Translated and adapted by John Joyce. [New York] Pantheon [1958, c1957] 400 p. illus. 22 cm. [BX4700.S65T683] 58-14803
1. Soubirous, Bernadette, Saint, 1844-1879. I. Title.

TROUNCER, Margaret 922.244
(Lahey) 1906-
Saint Bernadette, the child and the nun. New York, Sheed and Ward [1958] 248 p. 22 cm. Includes bibliography. [BX4700.S65T7] 58-5881
1. Soubirous, Bernadette, Saint, 1844-1879. Full name: Margaret Duncan (Lahey) Trouncer. I. Title.

Soubirous, Bernadette, Saint, 1844-1879—Juvenile literature.

ROBERTO Brother 1927- 92
The girl and the grotto; a story of Saint Bernadette. Illus. by Carolyn Lee Jagodits. Notre Dame, Ind., Dujarie Pr. [c.1966] 94p. illus. 24cm. [BX4700.S65R53] 66-12689 2.25 bds.,
1. Soubirous, Bernadette, Saint, 1844-1879—Juvenile literature. I. Title.

STAFFORD, Ann, pseud. 92
The young Bernadette. Illus. by Denise Brown. New York, Roy [1966, c.1965] 144p. illus. 21cm. [BX4700.S65S7 1965] 66-13351 3.25 bds.,
1. Soubirous, Bernadette, Saint, 1844-1879—Juvenile literature. I. Title.

Soul.

ALEXANDER, grand duke of 289.9
Russia, 1866-1933.
The religion of love, by Alexander, grand duke of Russia; translated by Jean S. Proctor. New York, London, The Century co. c1929 xx p., 2 l., 3-310 p. 19 1/2 cm. [BL390.A55] 29-9636
1. Soul. 2. Spiritual life. I. Religions (Proposed, universal, etc.) II. Proctor, Jean S., tr. III. Title.

ALEXANDER, James Bradun, 1831-
The soul and its bearings; showing the material quality of the soul, and the mechanical nature of its functions, and of the business relations it sustains with the environment on one side, and the rest of the corporal organism on the other. By James B. Alexander ... Minneapolis, Minn. [Press of Pioneer printing co.] 1909. xi, 337 p. 20 cm. [BD553.A3] 9-7146
1. Soul. I. Title.

ALGER, William Rounseville, 128
1822-1905.
The destiny of the soul. A critical history of the doctrine of a future life. By William Rounseville Alger. 14th ed., with a new supplementary chapter ... Boston, Roberts brothers, 1889. 8 p. l., v-xii, 8-883 p. 28 cm. [BD421.A38] E 16
1. Soul. 2. Future life. 3. Immortality. I. Title.

ALLEN, Eula.
You are forever. Virginia Beach, Va., A.R.E. Press, c1966. 88 l. illus. 27 cm. Interpretation from the psychic readings of Edgar Cayce. The 3d book of the author's trilogy. NUC68
1. Soul. 2. Immortality. I. Cayce, Edgar, 1877-1945. II. Title.

ATKINS, Gaius Glenn, 1868- 252.
Craftsmen of the soul, and other addresses by Gaius Glenn Atkins ... New York, Chicago [etc.] Fleming H. Revell company [c1925] 203 p. 20 cm. [BX7233.A8C7] 25-20733
I. Title.

AUGUSTINUS, Aurelius, 281.4
Saint bp. of Hippo.
Concerning the teacher (De magistro) and On the immortality of the soul (De immortalitate aminae) by St. Aurelius Augustine, bishop of Hippo ... translated from the Latin with the addition of a preface by George G. Leckie ... New York, London, D. Appleton-Century company, incorporated [c1938] xxxviii, 88 p. 20 cm. (Half-title: Appleton-Century philosophy source-books; S. P. Lamprecht, editor) "Reader's bibliography": p. 87-88. [BR65.A67E6 1938] 38-4045
I. Leckie, George Gaines, tr. II. Title. III. Title: On the immortality of the soul.

AUGUSTINUS, Aurelius, Saint,
Bp, of Hippo.
Concerning the teacher (De magistro) and On the immortality of the soul (De immortalitate animae). Translated from the Latin with the addition of a preface by George C. Leckie. New York, Appleton-Century-Crofts [1960? c1938] xxxviii, 88 p. 21 cm. (Appleton-Century philosophy source-books) "Reader's bibliography": p. 87-88. NUC65
I. Leckie, George Gaines, tr. II. Title. III. Title: On the immortality of the soul.

AUGUSTINUS, Aurelius, Saint, bp. of Hippo. 233.5
... De quantitate animae; The measure of the soul; Latin text, with Anglishtranslation and notes by Francis E. Tourscher ... Philadelphia, The Peter Reilly company; London, B. Herder, 1933. xi, 230 p. diagrs. 17 cm. At head of title: Saint Augustine. [BT740.A78] 33-19231
1. Soul. I. Tourscher, Francis Edward, 1870- tr. II. Title. III. Title: The measure of the soul.

AUGUSTINUS, Aurelius, Saint, Bp. of Hippo. 233.5
The greatness of the soul [and] The teacher; translated and annotated by Joseph M. Colleran. Westminster, Md., Newman Press, 1950. 255 p. 22 cm. (Ancient Christian writers. The works of the Fathers in translation, no. 9) Bibliographical references included in "Notes" (p. [187]-239) [BR60.A35 no. 9] 50-6436
1. Soul. 2. Knowledge, Theory of (Religion) 3. Signs and symbols. 4. Inner light. I. Title. II. Title: The teacher. III. Series.

AVICENNA, 980?-1037. 181.947
Avicenna's de anima (Arabic text), being the psychological part of Kitab al-Shifa: Edited by F. Rahman. London. New York, Oxford University Press, 1959. x, 298p. 22cm. (University of Durham publications) [B751.K5 1959] 59-2127
1. Soul. I. Rahman. F., ed. II. Title. III. Series: Durham, Eng. University. Publications

BALTZER, Frederick. 220
Soul rhapsodies, by Frederick Baltzer. Pittsburgh, Pa., 1927. 157, [2] p. 19 1/2 cm. Essays. [BR125.B362] 28-3453
I. Title.

BLUND, Iohannes, d.1248. 128
Tractatus de anima; edited by D. A. Callus and R. W. Hunt. London, Published for the British Academy by Oxford U.P., 1970. xxiv, 127 p. 26 cm. (Auctores Britannici Medii Aevi, 2) Latin text with English introd. and notes. [B765.B663T7 1970] 74-20964 ISBN 0-19-725635-X £5/-/-
1. Aristoteles. De anima. 2. Avicenna, 980-1037. 3. Soul. I. Callus, Daniel Angelo Philip, ed. II. Hunt, Richard William, 1908- ed. III. British Academy, London (Founded 1901) IV. Title. V. Series.

BOARDMAN, George Dana, 1828-1903. 233.5
The two bodies, by George Dana Boardman ... [Oberlin? O., 1903] 1 p. l., 487-494 p. 23 cm. "Reprint from Bibliotheca sacra, July, 1908." [BT748.B6] 41-80187
1. Soul. 2. Resurrection. I. Title.

BOOTH, Maud Ballington (Charlesworth) Mrs., 1865.
The curse of septic soul-treatment, by Maud Ballington Booth. New York, Chicago, F. H. Revell company [c1892] 60 p. 19cm. 12-30829
I. Title.

BOOTH, Maud Ballington (Charlesworth) Mrs., 1865.
The curse of septic soul-treatment, by Maud Ballington Booth. New York, Chicago, F. H. Revell company [c1892] 60 p. 19cm. 12-30829
I. Title.

BRADFORD, Amory Howe, 1846-1911. 128
The ascent of the soul, by Amory H. Bradford ... New York, The Outlook company, 1902. xi, 319 p. 21 cm. [BD421.B7] 2-27521
1. Soul. I. Title.

BRONSON, George Cathcart.
Soul immortal a subjective impression [poems] by George Cathcart Bronson. [Chicago, G. Setton-Thompson. 1902] 170 p. 19 1/2 cm. 2-15998
I. Title.

BRUNSON, Grace Myra (Pitchford) "Mrs. J. R. Brunson," 1878- 244
Soul winner's journey to the heavenly land, by Mrs. J. R. Brunson. [Scottsville, Ky., The Citizen-times] c1922. cover-title, 117, [3] p. 20 cm. [BV4515.B75] 22-16528
I. Title.

BUSH, George, 1796-1859. 233.5
The soul; or, An inquiry into Scriptural psychology, as developed by the use of the terms, soul, spirit, life, etc., viewed in its bearings on the doctrine of the resurrection. By George Bush... New York, J. S. Redfield, 1845. 141 p. 19 1/2 cm. [BT741.B8] 35-37818
1. Soul. 2. Resurrection. I. Title.

CANNAN, Gilbert, 1884- 218
The release of the soul, by Gilbert Cannan ... New York, Boni and Liveright [1920]. 5 p. l; 166 p. diagrs. 20 cm. [BD431.C25] 20-8452
1. Soul. 2. Life. I. Title.

CANRIGHT, Dudley M 1840?- 218
A history of the doctrine of the soul, among all races and peoples, ancient and modern, including theologians, philosophers, scientists, and untutored aboriginees; carefully brought down to the present time. By Eld. D.M. Canright... 2d ed., rev. Battle Creek, Mich., Seventh-day Adventist publishing association, 1882. x, [11]-186 p. 19 1/2 cm. [BL290.C3 1882] 31-1163
1. Soul. 2. Immortality. 3. Intermediate state. I. Title.

CARPENTER, Hugh Smith, 1824-1899. 233.5
Here and beyond; or, The new man, the true man. By Hugh Smith Carpenter. New York, Mason brothers, 1859. xvi, [17]-845 p. 19 cm. [BT741.C2] 40-37145
1. Soul. 2. Regeneration (Theology) I. Title.

CARUS, Paul, 1852- 128
Whence and whither; an inquiry into the nature of the soul, its origin and its destiny, by Dr. Paul Carus ... Chicago, Open court publishing company, 1900. viii, 188 p. 20 cm. [BD421.C32] A 14
1. Soul. I. Title.

CASTLEBERRY, John Jackson, 1877- 252
The soul of religion, and other addresses, by John J. Castleberry ... introduction by Edgar De Witt Jones ... New York, Chicago [etc.] Fleming H. Revell company [c1926] 192 p. 20 cm. [BX7327.C35S6] 26-19468
I. Title.

CAUGHEY, James, 1810?-1891. 922
Glimpses of life in soul-saving; or, Selections from the journal and other writings of the Rev. James Caughey. With an introduction by Rev. Daniel Wise, d. d. New York, W. C. Palmer, jr., 1868. xiv, [15]-477 p. 21 cm. [BV3785.C3A25] 37-36529
I. Title.

[CLARK, Susie Champney] 1856-
The open door of the soul, By Deborah Morrison [pseud.] Boston, Mass., The C. M. Clark publishing company, 1908. 4 p. l., 132 p. 19 1/2 cm. 9-589
I. Title.

CLYMER, Reuben Swinburne, 1878-
Christisis. Higher soul culture. Prepared for the use of our teachers in the great work... By R. Swinburne Clymer. Allentown, Pa., Philosophical publishing co. [c1911] 1 p. l., 5-192 p. 23 1/2 cm. Alternating pages blank. 12-964 10.00
I. Title.

CLYMER, Reuben Swinburne, 1878- 133
Christisis; a course of study in higher soul culture as a means to awaken the mind to the truth, the way and the life; then directing the faculties of the awakened mind to bring about soul consciousness, better known as Christification. By Rev. Dr. R. Swinburne Clymer ... Quakertown, Pa., The Philosophical publishing co. [1945] 1 p. l., [vii]-x, [11]-234 p. front. 23 1/2 cm. (On cover: Rosicrucian series) Alternate pages blank. "The first edition [1911] ... was followed by a very special deluxe edition in 1917 ... The present edition is a revision of the 1911 edition."--Introductory remarks. [BF1999.C62 1945] 46-12491
I. Title.

CLYMER, Reuben Swinburne, 1878- 133
The science of the soul; the art and science of building an illuminated and immortal soul; the method for the attainment of soul or cosmic consciousness and oneness with God; the spiritual ethics for the new age, by Rev. Dr. R. Swinburne Clymer ... Quakertown, Pa., The Philosophical publishing co. [1944] 1 p. l., [v]-xv, 287 p. 24 1/2 cm. [BF1999.C662 1944] 44-1044
I. Title.

CLYMER, Reuben Swinburne, 1878- 232
Soul consciousness is the way to Christhood; the mystical interpretation of the teachings of the illuminati, by R. Swinburne Clymer. (Authorized ed.) Quakertown, Pa., The Philosophical publishing company [1925] 1 p. l., [5]-173 p. 23 1/2 cm. [BF1999.C6633] 26-24169
I. Title.

[CLYMER, Reuben Swinburne] 1878- 128
Soul science and immortality. The art of building a soul. The secret of the coming Christ. Authorized text book of the Church of illumination. Allentown, Pa., The Philosophical publishing co. [c1911] 1 p. l., 7-200 p. 23 1/2 cm. [BF1999.C665] 11-6486
1. Soul. 2. Reincarnation. I. Title.

COCHRAN, Wesley, 1814-1888. 233.5
The life of human souls. By Rev. Wesley Cochran ... Philadelphia, Perkinpine & Higgins [1868] 224 p. 17 cm. [BT741.C65] 40-25494
1. Soul. I. Title.

COFFIN, Joseph Herschel, 1880- 128
The soul comes back, by Joseph Herschel Coffin ... New York, The Macmillan company, 1929. 207 p. diagrs. 20 1/2 cm. [BT741.C67] 29-7516
1. Soul. 2. Personality. I. Title.

COLLINS, Elijah Thomas. 128
The soul: its origin and relation to the body; to the world; and to immortality. By E. T. Collins ... Cincinnati, Jennings & Pye; New York, Eaton & Mains [c1901] 335 p. 21 cm. [BT741.C7] 1-10337
1. Soul. I. Title.

COLTON, Ann Ree. 133
The soul and the ethic. [1st ed.] Glendale, Calif., Arc Pub. Co. [c1965] viii, 262 p. 22 cm. [BF1999.C6886] 67-31989
1. Soul. I. Title.

COOK, Martha. 922
The soul's awakening, by Martha Cook... Lansing, Mich., Pub. for the author by Salvation union press, c1944. 118 p. port. 21 1/2 cm. [BV3785.C56A3] 44-31670
I. Title.

COWGILL, George W. 128
A study of the soul, by G. W. Cowgill Boston, The Christopher publishing house [c1929] 123 p., 1 l. 21 cm. "Reference books": 1 l. at end. [BT741.C78] 29-8636
1. Soul. I. Title.

CRAWSHAW, William Henry, 1861-1940. 128
The indispensable soul, by William H. Crawshaw. New York, The Macmillan company, 1931. 4 p. l., 3-315 p. 20 cm. [BT741.C783] 31-33777
1. Soul. 2. Relativity. 3. Inutiion. I. Title.

CUSTARD, Harry Lewis, 1893-1966. 128'.3
Seeing life whole; a philosophy of the human soul, whose indwelling spirit seeks to guide its life, as its inherent powers unfold through body, mind, and intellect, striving to create a balanced personality, by Harry Lewis Custard and Edith May Custard. Arlington, Va., Unity of Knowledge Publications [1967] 206 p. illus. 28 cm. [BD421.C8] 67-23373
1. Soul. 2. Mind and body. I. Custard, Edith May (Best) 1900- joint author. II. Title.

DILLOW, Ida Souers Mrs.
Life within life; or, Soul development. By Mrs. Ida Souers Dillow. Cleveland, O., 1906. xii, 179 p. 19 cm. 6-30481
I. Title.

DIXON, Joseph Lawrence, 1896- 128'.1
The community of the mind, by Joseph L. Dixon. New York, Philosophical Library [1967, c1966] 166 p. 22 cm. [BD421.D5] 66-26964
1. Soul. 2. Thought and thinking. I. Title.

DONALDSON, Oscar Fielding, 1872- 233.5
The soul and its life; or, Thinking of life clearly, by Oscar F. Donaldson. Boston, The Christopher publishing house [1944] 1 p. l., vii-xi, 13-196 p. 19 cm. [BT745.D6] 44-24163
1. Soul. I. Title.

DONCEEL, Joseph F 1906- 128
Philosophical anthropology, by J. F. Donceel. New York, Sheed and Ward [1967] xii, 496 p. illus. 22 cm. First and 2d ed. published under title: Philosophical psychology. Includes bibliographies. [BD421.D6 1967] 67-13769
1. Soul. 2. Philosophical anthropology. I. Title.

DOREE, Nadage.
Is your soul progressing? By Nadage Doree ... New York, The American news company, 1908. 2 p. l., iii-xvi, 17-281 p. front. (port.) 20 cm. p. 207-281, advertising matter. 8-14678
I. Title.

DROLLINGER, Emma Ruder, Mrs., 1865- 133
The new Messiah and the journey of the soul, by E. Ruder Drollinger. Los Angeles, Cal., J. F. Rowny press, 1920. viii, 9-239 p. front. (port.) 19 1/2 cm. Lettered on cover: Vol. II. [BF1999.D83] 21-4892
I. Title.

DUDLEY, Louise, 1884-
The Egyptian elements in the legend of the body and soul ... Baltimore, J. H. Furst company, 1911. xi, 182 p. 23 cm. Thesis (PH. D.)--Bryn Mawr college. gVita. Bibliography: p. ix-xi. 12-764
I. Title.

EARLE, William, 1919- 212
Mystical reason / William Earle. South Bend, Ind. : Regnery/Gateway, c1980. p. cm. [BD423.E2] 79-92079 ISBN 0-89526-677-6 pbk. : 6.95
1. Soul. 2. God. 3. Identity. 4. Reason. 5. Phenomenology. I. Title.

EMERY, Susan L. 1846- 242
The inner life of the soul; short spiritual messages for the ecclesiastical year, by S. L. Emery. New York, London [etc.] Longmans, Green, and co., 1903. xiv, 269 p. 20 cm. [BX2182.E5] 4-1631
I. Title.

EMERY, Susan L. 1846- 242
The inner life of the soul; short spiritual messages for the ecclesiastical year, by S. L. Emery. New York, London [etc.] Longmans, Green, and co., 1903. xiv, 269 p. 20 cm. [BX2182.E5] 4-1631
I. Title.

ESTES, Hiram Cushman, 1823-1901. 283.5
The Christian doctrine of the soul. An essay. By H. C. Estes ... Boston, Noyes, Holmes and company, 1873. 4 p. l., [5]-163 p. 17 1/2 cm. [BT741.E7] 40-25495
1. Soul. I. Title.

FERRIS, George Hooper, 1867-1917. 220
The soul's Christmas, by Rev. George H. Ferris... Philadelphia, Boston [etc.] The Griffith and Rowland press [c1917] 4 p. l., 3-69 p. 18 1/2 cm. [BR125.F4] 17-31676
I. Title.

FLAGG, William Joseph, 1818-1898. 181.4
Yoga; or, Transformation; a comparative statement of the various religious dogmas concerning the soul and its destiny, and of Akkadian, Hindu, Taoist, Egyption, Hebrew, Greek, Christian, Mohammedan, Japanese and other magic, by William J. Flagg... New York, J. W. Bouton. London, G. Redway, 1898. vii, 376 p. 25 cm. [BL290.F5] (128) 30-34024
1. Soul. 2. Yoga. I. Title.

*FORSYTH, P. T. 264.1
The soul of prayer. Grand Rapids. Mich.

Eerdmans [1965] 92p. 20cm. First pub. in 1916. 1.45 pap.,
I. Title.

FREW, Duncan J. 218
The discovery of the soul and the law of its development; philosophical, biological, ethical, historical, by Duncan J. Frew. Salt Lake City, Utah, F. T. Darvill, 1923. 131 p. illus., diagrs. 24 cm. [BL290.F7] 23-10406
1. Soul. I. Title.

GALLAUDET, Thomas Hopkins, 1787-1851. 233.
The child's book on the soul ... By Rev. T. H. Gallaudet ... With questions, adapted to the use of Sunday schools and of infant schools. Hartford, Cook and co., 1831. 2 v. plates. 14 cm. Vol. 1: 2d ed., inproved. [BT743.G2 1831] 40-23743
1. Soul. I. Title.

GALLAUDET, Thomas Hopkins, 1787-1851. 233.5
The child's book on the soul. Two parts in one. By Rev. T. H. Gallaudet ... New York, American tract society [1836] 2 p. l., [3]-155 p. front., plates. 15 cm. Added t.-p., engraved, [BT743.G2 1836a] 31-13884
1. Soul. I. Title.

GALLAUDET, Thomas Hopkins, 1787-1851. 233.
The child's book on the soul. Two parts in one ... By Rev. T. H. Gallaudet ... 5th ed., with questions. Hartford, Belknap & Hamersley, 1636. 2 v. in l. plates. 14 cm. Cover dated 1837. [BT743.G2 1836b] 40-23744
1. Soul. I. Title.

[GARRETSON, James Edmund] 1828-1895. 128
Two thousand years after; or, A talk in a cemetery. By John Darby [pseud.]... Philadelphia, Claxton, Remsen & Haffelfinger, 1876. xii, 13-106 p. 18 cm. Contents.--General argument.--The soul.--Who, and what is man? [BT741.G2] 11-22232
1. Soul. I. Title.

GILES, Chauncey, 1813-1893. 128
Lectures on the nature of spirit, and of man as a spiritual being. By Chauncey Giles ... New York, General convention of the New Jerusalem in the United States of America, 1867. 206 p. 20 cm. [BD421.G4] 11-22001
1. Soul. 2. Future life. I. Title.

GREEN, Harrison.
The soul and spirit of man ... Lawrence, Mass., J. Ward, jr., 1899. 155 p. port. 8 degree. 99-2245
I. Title.

[GROU, Jean Nicolas]5 1731-1803. 242
The hidden life of the soul, from the French, by the author of "A Dominican artist," "Life of Madame Louise de France," etc. ... Philadelphia, J. B. Lippincott and co., 1871. xvi, 256 p. 18 cm. [BV4833.G7] 5-1562
I. Title.

HALL, Alexander Wilford, 1819-1902. 128
The immortality of the soul philosophically demonstrated. By A. Wilford Hall...With a synopsis of the opinions of ancient and modern philosophers on the subject of the immortality of the soul. Compiled by Rev. E. h. Vaughan ... Together with an essay on dreams, tokens of the grandeur of the soul. By Joseph Addison... New York, Peabody, Macey & co., 1882. 1 p. l., [5]-50 p. 19 cm. [BD421.H2] 11-22000
1. Soul. 2. Dreams. I. Vaughan, E. H. II. Addison, Joseph, 1672-1719. III. Title.

HALLIDAY, Samuel Byram, 1812-1897. 922.573
Winning souls: sketches and incidents during forty years of pastoral work. By Rev. S. B. Halliday. New York, J. B. Ford and company, 1873. viii, [9]-165 p. 19 1/2 cm. [BX7260.H14A3] 36-2820
I. Title.

HALLIDAY, Samuel Byram, 1812-1897. 922.573
Winning souls: sketches and incidents during forty years of pastoral work. By Rev. S. B. Halliday. New York, J. B. Ford and company, 1873. viii, [9]-165 p. 19 1/2 cm. [BX7260.H14A3] 36-2820
I. Title.

HASKIN, Dorothy C. 253.7
Soul-winning, the Christian's business. Grand Rapids, Mich., Baker Book House [c.]1959. 53p. 22cm. .75 pap.,
I. Title.

HILL, Lysander, 1834-
Cosmic law; the immortality of the soul and the existence of God, by Hon. Lysander Hill. 2d ed. Chicago, Sterling publishing company, 1916. 3 p. l., v-xiv, 9-317 p. front. (port.) illus. 20 cm. Pub. 1909 under title: The two great questions. 16-6551
I. Title.

HOLMES, Edmond Gore Alexander, 1850- 128
The problem of the soul. A tract for teachers; being an attempt to determine what limits, if any, there are to the transforming influence of education, by Edmond Holmes. New York, E. P. Dutton & co. [1918] 3 p. l., 9-115, [1] p. 19 cm. [BD421.H73] E18
1. Soul. 2. Education. I. Title.

HUSE, Raymond Howard, 1880-
The soul of a child, by Raymond H. Huse ... Cincinnati, Jennings and Graham; New York, Eaton and Mains [c1914] 168 p. 19 cm. 14-8212 0.75
I. Title.

IVES, Charles Linnaeus, 1831-1879. 233.5
The Bible doctrine of the soul; or, Man's nature and destiny, as revealed. by Charles L. Ives ... Philadelphia, Claxton, Remsen & Haffelfinger, 1878. 1 p. l., x, 11-334 p. 20 cm. New edition, entirely rewritten, of a work first published in 1873. cf. Introd. [BT741.I 8 1878] 35-38383
1. Soul. I. Title.

JOHNSON, Aubrey Rodway 221.019
The vitality of the individual in the thought of ancient Israel [2d ed.] Cardiff, Univ. of Wales Pr. [dist. Mystic, Conn., Verry, 1965] xi, 154p. 23cm. Bibl. [BS1199.P9J6] 65-29536 4.00
1. Soul. 2. Bible. O.T. — Psychology. I. Title.

JONES, Rufus Matthew, 1863- 233.5
The testimony of the soul, by Rufus M. Jones ... New York, The Macmillan company, 1936. vi p., 1 l., 215 p. 21 cm. "This volume constitutes the Ayer lectures for 1936."--Pref. [BT741.J65] 36-8632
1. Soul. 2. Mysticism. I. Title.

KELLOGG, John Harvey, 1852- 233.5
Harmony of science and the Bible on the nature of the soul and the doctrine of the ressurection. By J. H. Kellogg ... Battle Creek, Mich., Review and herald publishing association, 1879. viii, [9]-224 p. 18 cm. [BT741.K3] 40-25496
1. Soul. 2. Resurrection. I. Title.

KEMP, Joseph W.
The soul-winner and soul-winning, by the Rev. Joseph W. Kemp ... New York, George H. Doran company [c1916] 91 p. 20 cm. 16-14819 0.60
I. Title.

KIRKLAND, Henry Burnham. 811.5
The soul of the city, and other verse, by Henry Burnham Kirkland, with illustrations by T. de Postels. New York, The Springfield press [c1931] 1 p. l., 7-170 p. front., plates. 19 cm. [PS3521.I699S6 1931] 245.2 31-8795
I. Title.

LAFARGUE, Paul, 1842-1911. 218
The origin and evolution of the idea of the soul, by Paul Lafargue; tr. by Charles H. Kerr. Chicago, C. H. Kerr & company, co-operative [1922] 127 p. 17 cm. [BL290.L3] 22-23802
1. Soul. I. Kerr, Charles H., 1860- tr. II. Title.

LAIRD, John, 1887-1946. 128'.1
The idea of the soul. Freeport, N.Y., Books for Libraries Press [1970] viii, 192 p. 23 cm. Reprint of the 1924 ed. Bibliography: p. 189-191. [BT741.L15 1970] 76-107811
1. Soul. 2. Personality. I. Title.

LAMBERT, J R 128
What is man? His nature and destiny. The spirit, or soul; is it immortal? Does it survive in death of the body in a conscious state? The views of mortal soulist examined and refuted ... By Elder J. R. Lambert ... Lamoni, Ia., Printed at the Patriot office [c1891] 1 p. l., iii p., 1 l., [5]-249 p. 17 cm. [BT741.L2] 3-4374
1. Soul. 2. Immortality. 3. Future life. I. Title.

LARKIN, Edgar Lucien, 1847- 128
The matchless altar of the soul, symbolized as a shining cube of diamond, one cubit in dimensions, and set within the Holy of holies in all grand esoteric temples of antiquity, by Edgar Lucien Larkin ... Los Angeles, Cal., E. L. Larkin, 1916. ix, 306 p. front. (port.) plates. 21 cm. [BD421.L45] 17-2356 1.50
1. Soul. I. Title.

LODGE, David, 1935- FIC
Souls and bodies / David Lodge. New York : Morrow, 1982, c1980. 243 p. ; 22 cm. Previously published as: How far can you go? : London : M. Secker & Warburg, 1980. [PR6062.O36H6 1982] 823'.914 19 81-14026 ISBN 0-688-00933-6 : 12.50
I. Title.

MACKENZIE, J. N. Landseer. 218
The universal medium; a new interpretation of the soul, by J. N. Landseer Mackenzie... London, A. H. Stockwell; New York city, D. V. Nichols [1922] xvii, 139 p. 19 cm. [BL290.M3] 23-2934
1. Soul. I. Title.

MEAD, Charles Marsh, 1836-1911. 233.5
The soul here and hereafter; a Biblical study. By Charles M. Mead ... Boston, The Congregational publishing society [1879] xv, 462 p. 18 1/2 cm. [BT741.M4] 40-25497
1. Soul. 2. Future life. I. Congregational publishing society. II. Title.

MEIKLE, James, 1730-1799. 242
The select remains of Mr. James Meikle. Late surgeon in Cornwath; or, Extracts from manuscripts found among his papers: entitled, i. The monthly memorial; or, A periodical interview with the king of terrors. ii. A secret survey into the state of the soul. iii. The house of mourning; or, Poems on melancholy subjects. iv. The tomb. Pittsburgh; Published by R. Patterson & Lambdin. Butler & Lambdin, printers. 1819. 1 p. l., [v]-ix, [10]-299 p. 19 cm. [BV4831.M42] 39-2999
I. Title.

MILLS, James Porter, 1847- 128
Mind's silent partner, the high counselor within, by James Porter Mills, M.D. New York, E. J. Clode, 1922. xiv, 306 p. front. (port.) 20 1/2 cm. [BF1999.M69] 22-7676
1. Soul. 2. Spiritual life. 3. Mind and body. I. Title.

MILTON, William Hammond, 1868-
The cure of souls; or, Christ's treatment of the individual, by Wm. H. Milton ... New York, T. Whittaker, inc. [c1908] x, 227 p. 19 1/2cm. $1.00. 8-31017
I. Title.

MOOSE, A H. 233.5
Of men and souls; a scientific treatise exposing so-called Christian religious cults, supposedly based upon the Bible, but in truth thoroughly anti-Biblical and condemned by the latter. It proves incontestably that the Scriptures were wrongly translated in many instances, in the first place, and are further falsified by modern prophets of Baal to corroborate their base preachments, thus reducing the Bible to a 'testament' of paganism. By A. H. Moose. New York, N. Y., The Rainbow, 1938. 126, [1] p. 20 cm. [BT743.M6] 38-22650
1. Soul. 2. Immortality. 3. Bible—Criticism, interpretation, etc. I. Title.

MOZUMDAR, Akhar Kumar. 220
Christ on the road of today; a romance of soul, by A. K. Mozumdar ... Los Angeles, Messianic publishing co., 1927. 3 p. l., 5-203 p. 20 cm. [BR125.M773] 28-5683
I. Title.

*NEIDERER, Rodney P. 248.42
For when tomorrow comes; on man's quest for his immortal soul. New York, Exposition [c.1964] 63p. 21cm. (EP 42087) 2.50
I. Title.

NORRIS, Zoe Anderson.
The color of his soul, by Zoe Anderson Norris. New York & London, Funk & Wagnalls co., 1902. 3 p. l., 220 pp. 19 x 10 cm. 2-3925
I. Title.

NORRIS, Zoe Anderson.
The color of his soul, by Zoe Anderson Norris. New York, R. F. Fenno & company, 1903. 3 p. l., 220 p. 19 x 11 cm. 3-14990
I. Title.

NORTH, Robert Grady, 1916- 233
Teilhard and the creation of the soul. Introd. by Karl Rahner. Milwaukee, Bruce [1967] xiv, 317p. 23cm. (St. Louis Univ. (Saint Marys) theol. studies. 5) Index of Teilhard writings: p. 308-317. Bibl. [B2430.T374N6] 67-15250 7.95
1. Teilhard de Chardin, Pierre. 2. Soul. I. Title. II. Series.

OLFORD, Stephen F. 243
The secret of soul-winning. Chicago, Moody [c.1963] 124p. 20cm. 2.50
I. Title.

OLIVER, [Harold Purcell] 1856-
The science of the spirit, soul and body; a page from [the occult side of life, by Doctor Oliver ... Philadelphia, G. F. Lasher, printer [1904] 338 p. front., plates, ports. 21 cm. 4-26234
I. Title.

ON selfhood and Godhood;
the Gifford lectures, delivered at the University of St. Andrews during sessions 1953-54 and 1954--55, revised and expanded. London, Allen & Unwin. New York, Macmillan (N. Y.) [1957] xxxvi, 436p. 23cm. (Saint Andrews university. Gifford lectures. 1953/55) Muirhead library of philosophy.
1. Soul. 2. Religion—Philosophy. I. Campbell, Charles Arthur, 1897- II. Series.

OSBORN, Lucy Reed (Drake) Mrs. 1844-
Light on soul winning, by Mrs. Lucy D. Osborn ... New York, Chicago [etc.] Fleming H. Revell company [c1911] 160 p. front. (port.) 20 cm. 11-10949 0.75
I. Title.

PALUMBO, Anthony, 1879- 133
The mirror of your soul; life's epitomology is non plus ultra. By Anthony Palumbo, Colombo... Boston, Meador publishing company, 1935. 70 p. 20 cm. [BF1999.P25] [(159.961)] 42-8035
I. Title.

PARKER, Franklin Ellsworth, 1861-
Christian wisdom; a key to lessons in earth life, by Franklin E. Parker ... Cambridge, Mass., The University press [c1916] xiii, 273 p. 20 cm. 17-1619
I. Title.

PARKER, Franklin Ellsworth, 1861-
Christian wisdom; a key to lessons in earth life from a soul understanding [by] Franklin E. Parker. Boston, Chapman & Grimes [c1936] 3 p. l., iv, [2], 7-547 p. 1 illus. 24 cm. 36-7990
I. Title.

*PATTON, Walter S. 233.5
Soul surgery. New York, Vantage [c.1964] 47p. 21cm. 2.00 bds.,
I. Title.

PECK, Joseph E. 128
Soul problems, with other papers. By Joseph E. Peck ... New York, C. P. Somerby, 1875. 63 p. 19 cm. [BD421.P3] 11-21998
1. Soul. 2. Church and state in the U. S. I. Title.
Contents omitted.

PEURSEN, C. A. van 128.1
Body, soul, spirit: a survey of the body-mind problem. Eng. ed. tr. from Dutch by Hubert H. Hoskins, additional matter by

the author. New York, Oxford [c.]1966 vii, 213p. 20cm. [BD422.D8P43] 66-70782 4.80
1. Soul. 2. Mind and body. 3. Philosophical anthropology. I. Title.

PEURSEN, C A van. 128.1
Body, soul, spirit: a survey of the body-mind problem, [by] C.A. Van Peursen. English edition translated from the Dutch by Hubert H. Hoskins with additional matter bythe author. London, Oxford U.P.,1966. vii, 213 p. 19 1 2 cm. 30/- (B66-6595) Originally published as Lichaam, ziel, greest. Utrecht, Erven J. Bijieveld, 1956. [BD422.D8P43] 66-70782
1. Soul. 2. Mind and body. 3. Philosophical anthropology. I. Title.

PHILIPSON, Clifford Andrew, 1900- 128
The reality of the soul, by Clifford A. Philipson. Newark, N. J., The author [c1934] 90 p. front. (port.) 19 cm. [BF1999.P545] 34-36605
I. Title.

POULSON, Omer Bruce, 1881
Soul winning in the Sunday-school, by Rev. O. B. Poulson. Harrisburg, Pa., Publishing house of the United evangelical church [c1911] 116 p. 18 cm. 12-23687 0.30
I. Title.

POWELL, Mac, 1871- 218
The soul, what it is, its essence, its origin, its development, its immortality, its destiny ... by Mac Powell. Beevill, Tex., Picayune print [c1923] 6 p. l., 53 p. 25 cm. [BL290.P6] 23-12626
1. Soul. I. Title.

REANY, William, 1887- 233.5
The creation of the human soul; a clear and concise exposition from psychological, theological, and historical aspects, by Rev. William Reany, D. D. New York, Cincinnati [etc.] Benziger brothers, 1932. 237 p. 23 cm. Errata slip inserted at end. Printed in Great Britain. Bibliography: p. 214-232. [BT741.R25] 83-28389
1. Soul. I. Title.

REYES, Benito F. 128'.1
Scientific evidence of the existence of the soul, by Benito F. Reyes. [Rev. ed.] Wheaton, Ill., Theosophical Pub. House [1970] xx, 259 p. 23 cm. Bibliography: p. [244]-251. [BL290.R45 1970] 70-122432
1. Soul. I. Title.

RICE, Elaine B. 131.
Soul growth; a book of spiritual revelation-- teaching the natural growth of the human soul. By Elaine B. Rice. Minneapolis, Minn., Adviser publishing company, 1928. 3 p. l., 9-91, [1] p. 19 cm. [BF639.R347] 29-9442
I. Title.

RICHARDSON, Merrick Abner, 1841-
The personality of the soul, by M. A. Richardson... Chicago, The author, 1905. 1 p. l., 5-202 p. 20 1/2 cm. 5-15575
I. Title.
Contents omitted.

ROBINSON, James William. 243
Soul crises, our relation to the great war, by James William Robinson. Boston, The Gorham press, 1918. 291 p. 19 1/2 cm. (Lettered on cover: Library of religious thought) $1.25 [BX9178.R6S6] 18-10692
I. Title.

ROOT, [Jean Christie] "Mrs. J. H. Root."
A soul's meditations; comp. and arranged by Mrs. J. H. Root. [New York, Bonnell, Silver & co.] 1900. 189 p. 16 degrees. 1-22090
I. Title.

SARAYDARIAN, H. 291.4'2
The hidden glory of the inner man / by H. Saraydarian. Agoura, Calif. : Aquarian Educational Group, c1968, 1975 printing. 95 p. ; 27 cm. "1st revised impression." Original ed. has title: Magnet of life. Includes bibliographical references. [BF1999.S336 1975] 74-33110
1. Soul. I. Title.

SAXTON, N. S. 233.5
The light of life; or, The true idea of soul ... By N. S. Saxton ... New York, The author, 1865. 87 p. 18 1/2 cm. [BT741.S2] 40-37147
1. Soul. 2. Mind and body. I. Title. II. Title: The true idea of soul.

[SCOFIELD, Anna (Bishop) Mrs. 1835-
Insights and heresies, pertaining to the evolution of the soul, by Ammyeetis (Persian) [pseud.] Boston, The Christopher press, 1913. 3 p. l., iv, 7-180 p. 19 cm. 13-25475 1.00
I. Title.

[SCOFIELD, Anna (Bishop) mrs.] 1835-
Insights and heresies pertaining to the evolution of the soul, by Ammyeetis (Persian) [pseud.] 2d ed., 1916. Boston, Christopher publishing house [c1916] 3 p. l., iv, 7-180 p. 19 cm. 17-164 0.50
I. Title.

SIMMONS, James P. 128
War in heaven. A disquisition, Biblical and rational, concerning angels, devils, and men, and the creation, fall, and redemption of the human soul... By James P. Simmons ... Cincinnati, R. Clarke & co., printers, 1871. x, [9]-314 p. 23 1/2 cm. [BT741.S5] 44-35226
1. Soul. I. Title.

SMITH, Phineas A. 233.
Every body's book. The Bible view of the soul; personality of God; the devil, his origin, personality power and doom; also, and exposition of the spiritual rapping. By Phineas A. Smith Rochester, N.Y., Smith & Clough, printers, 1850. 96 p. 13 1/2 cm. [BT743.S55] 44-50288
1. God. 2. Soul. 3. Spiritualism. I. Title.

SNYDER, Gerrit.
The soul-winner's Gospel; the saving doctrines of the Gospel of John, interpreted and applied in personal work with resultant conversions, by Gerrit Snyder, with introduction by Andrew C. Zenos, D. D. Kansas City, Mo., Publishing house of the Pentecostal church of the Nazarene [c1914] 141 p. 20 cm. 15-1649 0.50
I. Title.

SOUL-WINNING;
the Christian's business. Grand Rapids, Baker Book House, 1959. 53p.
I. Haskin, Dorothy (Clark) 1905-

SPICER, Tobias, b.1788. 128
Spirit life, and its relations. By Rev. T. Spicer ... Albany, Munsell & Rowland, 1859. 216 p. 19 1/2 cm. [BD421.S7] 11-21997
1. Soul. I. Title.

STANTON, Stephen Berrien.
Soul and circumstance, by Stepen Berrien Stanton ... New York, C. Scribner's sons, 1910. vi, 310 p. 19 cm. $1.00. 10-24313
I. Title.

STEPHENS, Charles Asbury, 1845- 128
Pluri-cellular man. Whence and what is the intellect, or "soul"? What becomes of the soul? Is it possible to save the soul? From the biological standpoint. By C. A. Stephens ... Norway Lake, Me., The Laboratory company, 1892. 114 p. 20 cm. [BD421.S8] 12-22118
1. Soul. 2. Life. I. Title.

STEVEN, George.
The psychology of the Christian soul. By George Steven ... 4th ed. London, New York [etc.] Hodder and Stoughton [1911] vii, 304 p. 20 cm. (The Cunningham lectures for 1911) A 13
1. Soul. I. Title.

STORRS, Richard Salter, 1821-1900.
... The constitution of the human soul. Six lectures delivered at the Brooklyn institute, Brooklyn, N.Y., by Richard S. Storrs, jr., D.D. New York, R. Carter & brothers, 1857. xiv, [15]-338 p. 23 1/2 cm. (Half-title: Graham lectures ... v. 1) Series title also at head of t.-p. 18-12131
1. Soul. I. Title.

STRASSER, Stephen, 1905- 128
The soul in metaphysical and empirical psychology. (translated by Henry J. Koren) Pittsburgh, Duquesne University, 1957. 275 p. 27 cm. (Duquesne studies. Philosophical series, 7) [BD422.D8S813] 58-26
1. Soul. 2. Self. 3. Physchology. I. Title.

SWEDENBORG, Emanuel, 1688-1772. 230.94
Posthumous tracts, now first translated from the Latin of Emanuel Swedenborg ... by James John Garth Wilkinson ... London, W. Newbery; Boston, U.S., O. Clapp, 1847. 5 p. l., [3]-149 p. 22 1/2 cm. [With his Outlines of a philosophical argument of the infinite ... London, 1847] Binder's title: Swedenborg [Works] vol. 6. [BX8711.A2 1719 vol. 6] [BX8712.P7 1847] (230.94) 36-29686
1. Soul. 2. Mind and body. I. Wilkinson, James John Garth, 1812-1899, tr. II. Title.
Contents omitted.

SWEDENBORG, Emanuel, 1688-1772.
The soul, or Rational psychology, by Emanuel Swedenborg; tr. and ed. by Frank Sewall, A.M., from the Latin edition of Dr. J. F. Immanuel Tafel, Tubingen, 1849. New York, New Church board of publication, 1887. 2 p. l., [iii]-xxvi, [3]-388 p. 24 1/2 cm. Added t.-p.: [Title-page of the Latin edition] Eman. Swedenborgii ... Regnum animale anatomice, physice et philosophice perlustratum: cujus pars septima de anima agit; e chirographo ejus in Bibliotheca regiae acedemiae bolmiensis asservato nunc primum edidit dr. Jo. Fr. Im. Tafel ... Tubingae, 1849. [BF110.S8] 18-12133
1. Soul. 2. Psychology. I. Sewall, Frank, 1837-1915, tr. II. Tafel, Johann Friedrich Immanuel, 1796-1863. III. Title. IV. Title: Rational psychology.

SYME, David, 1827-1908. 128
The soul; a study and an argument, by David Syme... London, Macmillan and co., limited; New York, The Macmillan company, 1903. xxxi, 234 p. 20 cm. [BT741.S9] 3-15245
1. Soul. 2. Psychology. I. Title.
Contents omitted.

TARA, 1921- 128'.1
The evolution of the soul. [1st ed.] Milwaukee, Wis., Universal Creative Research Institute [1970] 248 p. 23 cm. Includes bibliographies. [BD421.T35] 77-103413 10.00
1. Soul. I. Title.

THOMAS Aquinas Saint, 1225?-1274. 233.5
The soul; a translation of St. Thomas Aquinas' De anima, by John Patrick Rowan. St. Louis, B. Herder Book Co., 1949. viii, 291 p. 22 cm. [BT740.T48] 50-776
1. Soul. I. Rowan, John Patrick, tr. II. Title.

THOMAS, Franklin A. 128
Soul science; the proof of life after death, by Franklin A. Thomas ... Boston, Machine composition co., 1920. 287 p. 19 1/2 cm. [BF1999.T5] 70-3269
1. Soul. 2. Spiritualism. I. Title.

THOMAS, George Finger. 233.5
Spirit and its freedom, by George F. Thomas. Chapel Hill, The University of North Carolina, 1939. xii p., 2 l., 149 p. 21 cm. (Half-title: The John Calvin McNair lectures) [BT741.T5] 39-15292
1. Soul. 2. Social ethics. I. Title.

THOMPSON, George B., 1862-
Soul winning, by George B. Thompson ... Washington, D.C. [etc.] Review & herald publishing assn. [c1916] 192 p. 18 1/2 cm. $0.75 17-9256
I. Title.

[TRUEB, Carl Theodul] 1872-
Let the new nation arise; a treatise on the subject of purification and the gathering of the purified, by Carl Theodul [pseud.] ... Denver, Col., The Balance publishing company; [etc., etc.] 1908. 157 p. 20 cm. 9-4916
I. Title.

UNDERHILL, Evelyn, 1875-1941.
Concerning the inner life; with the house of the soul. London, Methuen, New York, Dutton [1956] 149 p. 20 cm.
I. Title.

VONIER, Anscar, 1875-1938. 233.5
The human soul and its relations with other spirits, by Dom Anscar Vonier ... 3d ed., ... London, St. Louis, Mo., B. Herder. 1925. xi.391. [1] p. 19 cm. "Printed in Germany." [BT741.V6 1925] 35-20823
1. Soul I. Title.

WARD, Alfred George, 1881- 220
Soul-food for hungry saints, by A. G. Ward. Springfield, Mo., The Gospel publishing house [c1925] 2 p. l., 7-141 p. 19 cm. (Pulpit and pew, full gospel series) [BR125.W295] 25-27560
I. Title.

WEBB, William Walter, 1857-
The cure of souls; a manual for the clergy, based chiefly upon English and oriental authorities, by William Walter Webb ... with commendatory preface by Isaac Lea Nicholson ... 2d ed. Milwaukee, The Young churchman co.; [etc., etc.] 1910. xxxii, 248 p. 20 cm. 10-8177
I. Title.

[WETZEL, Elizabeth (Saylor)] Mrs., 1868- 233.5
Everlasting-Gospel; science of soul, the early and latter rain. Philadelphia, Pa., Soul scientist [c1939] xxxix p., 1 l., 291 p. 21 cm. [BT743.W4] 39-17799
1. Soul. I. Title. II. Title: Soul, Science of.

WETZEL, Elizabeth (Saylor) 1868- 233.5
Showers of blessing. Philadelphia, Soul Scientist [1952] 300 p. 21 cm. [BT743.W42] 52-4213
1. Soul. I. Title.

WILSON, Floyd Baker, 1845-
The discovery of the soul, out of mysticism, light and progress, by Floyd B. Wilson ... New York, R. F. Fenno & company [c1908] 4 p. l., 11-247 p. 20 cm. 8-6093
I. Title.

WILSON, Floyd Baker, 1845-
The discovery of the soul, out of mysticism, light and progress, by Floyd B. Wilson ... New York, R. F. Fenno & company [c1908] 4 p. l., 11-247 p. 20 cm. 8-6093
I. Title.

WOELFKIN, Cornelius, 1859-1928. 252.
Chambers of the soul, by Rev. Cornelius Woelfkin. Boston and Chicago, United society of Christian endeavor [c1901] 120 p. 17 cm. "The following addresses were delivered at the Quiet hour services in the Cincinnati convention of the Young people's society of Christian endeavor."--Pref. [BV4310.W57] 2-1802
I. Title.
Contents omitted.

WUNDER, Clinton, 1892- 256
"Crowds of souls" for the church and the kingdom, by Clinton Wunder ... with introduction by Clarence A. Barbour ... New York, Chicago [etc.] Fleming H. Revell company [c1926] 3 p. l., 5-183 p. front, illus., pl. 19 1/2 cm. [BV652.W8] 26-11258
I. Title.

ZURCHER, Jean R. 128'.1
The nature and destiny of man; essay on the problem of the union of the soul and the body in relation to the Christian views of man, by J. R. Zurcher. Translated by Mabel R. Bartlett. New York, Philosophical Library [1969] xx, 186 p. 22 cm. Translation of L'homme, sa nature et sa destinee. Bibliography: p. 173-183. [BD450.Z813] 69-14360 6.00
1. Soul. 2. Philosophical anthropology. I. Title.

Soul—Addresses, essays, lectures.

BUCK, Jirah Dewey, 1838-1916.
The soul and sex in education, morals, religion, and adolescence; scientific psychology for parents and teachers, with a chapter on love, marriage, celibacy, and divorce, by Jirah D. Buck ... Cincinnati, Stewart & Kidd company, 1912. xxiii, 175 p. front. 22 cm. 12-21973 1.25.
I. Title.

HEATH, Frank Stowe.
Soul laws in sexual, social, spiritual life ... 2d ed., rev. Cincinnati, M. W. Knapp, 1899. 125 p. 12° (Pentecostal holiness library, v. 2, no. 10) Apr
1. Title.

MCGINN, Bernard, 1937- comp. 233'.5
Three treatises on man; a Cistercian anthropology. Edited by Bernard McGinn. [Spencer, Mass.] Cistercian Publications; [distributed by] Consortium Press, Washington, 1974 [c1972] p. cm. (Cistercian Fathers series, no. 24) Contents.Contents.—McGinn, B. Introduction.—William of St. thierry. The nature of the body and soul. Translated by B. Clark.—The letter of Isaac of Stella on the soul. Translated by B. McGinn.—Treatise on the spirit and the soul. Translated by E. Leiva and St. Benedicta Ward. Includes bibliographical references. [BT743.M25] 74-8679 ISBN 0-87907-024-2 10.95
1. Soul—Addresses, essays, lectures. 2. Man (Theology)—Addresses, essays, lectures. I. Guillaume de Saint-Thierry, 1085 (ca.)-1148. De natura corporis et animae. English. 1974. II. Isaac of Stella, d. 1169. Epistola de anima. English. 1974. III. Alcherus, of Clairvaux, 12th cent. De anima et spiritu. English. 1974. IV. Title. V. Title: Treatise on the spirit and the soul.

*RICE, John R. 250
Why our churches do not win souls. Murfreesboro, Tenn., Sword of the Lord, Box 1099 [c.1966] 178p. 21cm. 2.50
I. Title.

Soul—Collected works.

ARTHUR, Eric, comp. 242
They are not dead! Thoughts concerning the immortality of the soul chosen from the writings of notable authors, by Eric Arthur and Mrs. Wilbraham Ward. New York, Dodd, Mead and company [1919] 127, [1] p. front. 14 1/2 cm. Printed in Great Britain. [BV4900.A7] 21-18467
I. Ward, Mrs. Wilbraham, joint comp. II. Title.

KENNY, Anthony John Patrick. 128'.1
The anatomy of the soul; historical essays in the philosophy of mind [by] Anthony Kenny. New York, Barnes & Noble [1973] ix, 146, [1] p. 23 cm. Bibliography: p. [147] [BD421.K46 1973b] 74-161932 ISBN 0-06-493638-4 8.50
1. Soul—Collected works. 2. Mind and body—Collected works. I. Title.

SOUL Delight (The); 242
this is a collection of shared thoughts born of the inspiration that is the calm possession of those who know a daily, an hourly walk and talk with the One Great Eternal Spirit of the universe. By Anonymous. Boston, Christopher Pub. House [c.1961] 91p. 2.50 bds.,

Soul—History of doctrines.

BURNS, Norman T. 233'.5'09
Christian mortalism from Tyndale to Milton [by] Norman T. Burns. Cambridge, Harvard University Press, 1972. 222 p. 24 cm. A revision of the author's thesis, University of Michigan. Bibliography: p. [203]-213. [BT741.2.B87 1972] 72-75406 ISBN 0-674-12875-3 10.00
1. Soul—History of doctrines. 2. Immortality—History of doctrines. I. Title.

Soul (Judaism)

HIRSCH, W. 296.3'2
Rabbinic psychology; beliefs about the soul in Rabbinic literature of the Talmudic period, by W. Hirsch. New York, Arno Press, 1973. 291 p. port. 23 cm. (The Jewish people: history, religion, literature) Reprint of the 1947 ed. published by E. Goldston, London. Originally presented as the author's thesis, University of London. Bibliography: p. 281-286. [BM645.S6H5 1973] 73-2208 ISBN 0-405-05272-3 16.00
1. Soul (Judaism) 2. Immortality (Judaism) 3. Sin (Judaism) I. Title. II. Series.

Soul—Juvenile literature.

HEIDE, Florence Parry. 233'.5
Changes / written by Florence Parry Heide. St. Louis : Concordia Pub. House, c1978. p. cm. As the body changes, the soul grows strong in the spirit of God. [BT791.2.H43] 77-13912 ISBN 0-570-07788-5 : 2.95
1. Soul—Juvenile literature. 2. Body, Human—Juvenile literature. 3. [Soul.] 4. [Body, Human.] I. Title.

Soule, Henry Birdsall, 1815-1852.

SOULE, Caroline Augusta (White) Mrs., 1824-1903. 922.8173
Memoir of Rev. H. B. Soule. By Caroline A. Soule ... New York, H. Lyon; Auburn [N.Y.] M. W. Fish, 1852. v. p., 1 l., [9]-396 p. front. (port.) 20 cm. Selections from H. B. Soule's writings: p. 173-396. [BX9969.S7S6] 37-8739
1. Soule, Henry Birdsall, 1815-1852. 2. Universalist church—Sermons. 3. Sermons, American. I. Title.

Soule, Joshua, bp., 1781-1867.

DU BOSE, Horace Mellard, bp., 1858- 922.
... Life of Joshua Soule, by Horace M. Du Bose ... Nashville, Tenn., Dallas, Tex., Publishing house of the M. E. church, South, Smith & Lamar, agents, 1911. 285 p. front. (port.) 19 1/2 cm. (Methodist founders' series, ed. by Bishop W. A. Candler) [BX8495.S7D8] 11-12709
1. Soule, Joshua, bp., 1781-1867. I. Title.

South Africa General Mission.

SHANK, Ezra Abram, 1902- 922
Fervent in spirit; the biography of Arthur J. Bowen. Chicago, Moody Press [1954] 192p. illus. 22cm. [BV3557.B6S5] 54-4911
1. Bowen, Arthur John, 1871- 2. South Africa General Mission. I. Title.

South Africa—Race relations.

DE GRUCHY, John W. 261.8'34'51968
The church struggle in South Africa / by John W. De Gruchy. Grand Rapids : W. B. Eerdmans Pub. Co., c1979. xv, 267 p. : map ; 21 cm. Includes bibliographical references and index. [DT763.D397] 78-26761 ISBN 0-8028-1786-6 : 7.95
1. South Africa—Race relations. 2. Church and race relations—South Africa. 3. South Africa—Church history. I. Title.

REGEHR, Ernie. 261.8'34'510968
Perceptions of apartheid : the churches and political change in South Africa / Ernie Rehehr. Scottsdale, Pa. : Herald Press, c1979. 309 p. : map ; 23 cm. Includes bibliographical references and index. [DT763.R387 1979] 79-9172 7.95
1. South Africa—Race relations. 2. Church and race relations—South Africa. 3. South Africa—Church history. I. Title.

South America.

GRUBB, Kenneth G. 278
South America, the land of the future, by Kenneth G. Grubb; with four illustrations & a map. London, New York [etc.] World dominion press, 1931. iv, 5-71 p. 4 pl., map. 19 cm. [F2208.G88] 31-9618
1. South America. 2. Missions—South America. I. Title.

GRUBB, Kenneth George. 278
South America, the land of the future, by Kenneth G. Grubb; with four illustrations & a map. London, New York [etc.] World dominion press, 1931. iv, 5-71 p. 4 pl., map. 19 cm. [F2206.G88] 31-9618
1. South America. 2. Missions—South America. I. Title.

STUNTZ, Homer Clyde, bp., 1858-1924. 278
South American neighbors, by Homer C. Stuntz. New York, Cincinnati, The Methodist book concern [1916] x, 211 p. front., plates, ports., fold. map. 19 cm. "Edited under the direction of the Missionary education movement of the United States and Canada." Bibliography: p. 207-211. [BV2851.S9 1916a] [266] 33-32848
1. South America. 2. Missions—South America. I. Missionary education movement of the United States and Canada. II. Title.

STUNTZ, Homer Clyde, bp., 1858-1924. 278
South American neighbors, by Homer C. Stuntz. New York, Missionary education movement of the United States and Canada, 1916. x, 212 p. front., plates, ports., fold. map. 19 1/2 cm. "Edited under the direction of the Missionary education movement of the United States and Canada." Bibliography: p. 208-212. [BV2851.S9] 16-14106
1. South America. I. Title.

South America—Religion.

MACKAY, John Alexander, 1889- 278
The other Spanish Christ; a study in the spiritual history of Spain and South America, by John A. Mackay... New York, The Macmillan company, 1933. xv, 288 p. incl. front. (map) 22 1/2 cm. [BR660.M3 1933] 33-2306
1. South America—Religion. 2. Catholic church in South America. 3. Catholic church in Spain. 4. Missions—South America. I. Title.

South Asia—Religion—Addresses, essays, lectures.

RELIGION and social 301.5'8'0954
conflict in South Asia / edited by Bardwell L. Smith. Leiden : Brill, 1976. 117 p. ; 25 cm. (International studies in sociology and social anthropology, v. 22) Includes bibliographical references and index. [BL1055.R43] 76-371071 ISBN 9-00-404510-4 : fl 42.00
1. South Asia—Religion—Addresses, essays, lectures. 2. Religion and sociology—Addresses, essays, lectures. I. Smith, Bardwell L., 1925-

South Asia—Religious life and customs.

CONFERENCE on Religion in South Asia, University of California, Berkeley, 1961. 209.54
Religion in South Asia; [papers] Edited by Edward B. Harper. Seattle, University of Washington Press, 1964. 199 p. illus. 26 cm. Previously published in a special supplementary issue of the Journal of Asian Studies. Includes bibliographies. [BL1055.C6 1961aa] 64-23197
1. South Asia—Religious life and customs. I. Harper, Edward B., ed. II. California. University. III. Title.

South Boston. St. Peter's Church.

KUCAS, Antanas, 1900- 282.74461
Sv. Petro lietuviu parapija South Bostone. The history of St. Peter's Lituanian parish, South Boston. Adapted from the Lithuanian text by Albert J. Contons. Boston, 1956. 303 p. illus., ports. 23 cm. Lithuanian and English. "Auksiniam parapijos jubillejui pamineti, 1904-1954." Bibliography: p. 299. [BX4603.B7S53] 64-40740
1. South Boston. St. Peter's Church. I. Title.

South Carolina—Church history.

BOLTON, S. Charles. 283'.757
Southern Anglicanism : the Church of England in colonial South Carolina / S. Charles Bolton. Westport, Conn. : Greenwood Press, 1982. xiv, 220 p. ; 22 cm. (Contributions to the study of religion,) ISSN 0196-7053 ; no. 5) Includes index. Bibliography: p. [205]-211. [BX5881.B64 1982] 19 81-6669 ISBN 0-313-23090-0 lib. bdg. : 29.95
1. Church of England—South Carolina. 2. Church of England—Southern States. 3. South Carolina—Church history. 4. Southern States—Church history. I. Title. II. Series.

South Carolina—History—Colonial period, ca. 1600-1775.

DALCHO, Frederick, 1770?-1836. 283'.757
An historical account of the Protestant Episcopal Church in South-Carolina. New York, Arno Press, 1972. vii, 613 p. 23 cm. (Religion in America, series II) Reprint of the 1820 ed. [BX5917.S6D2 1972] 71-38445 ISBN 0-405-04064-4
1. Protestant Episcopal Church in the U.S.A.—South Carolina. 2. South Carolina—History—Colonial period, ca. 1600-1775. I. Title.

South Congregational Church, Middletown, Conn.

ABERNETHY, William Beaven, 1939- 264'.05'8
A new look for Sunday morning / William Beaven Abernethy. Nashville : Abingdon, [1975] 176 p. ; 20 cm. Includes bibliographical references. [BX7255.M63S682] 74-34387 ISBN 0-687-27805-8 pbk. : 4.50
1. South Congregational Church, Middletown, Conn. 2. Public worship—Case studies. 3. Religious education—Case studies. I. Title.

South Dakota—Church history.

PARKER, Donald Dean, 1899- 277.83
Early churches and towns in South Dakota. [Brookings? S. D., 1964?] 132 p. map. 18 x 22 cm. Bibliography: p. 132. [BR555.S62P29] 66-64965
1. South Dakota—Church history. 2. Cities and towns—South Dakota. I. Title.

PARKER, Donald Dean, 1899- 277.83
Founding the church in South Dakota. [Brookings, S.D., pref. 1962] 116, [27] p. map. 18 x 22 cm. Bibliography: p. [133] [BR555.S62P3] 62-64111
1. South Dakota—Church history. I. Title.

SNEVE, Virginia Driving Hawk. 283'.783
That they may have life : the Episcopal Church in South Dakota, 1859-1976 / Virginia Driving Hawk Sneve. New York : Seabury Press, c1977. xiv, 224 p. : ill. ; 23 cm. Includes index. Bibliography: p. 218-220. [BX5917.5.S8S65] 76-55342 ISBN 0-8164-2141-2 : 5.95
1. Protestant Episcopal Church in the U.S.A.—South Dakota. 2. South Dakota—Church history. I. Title.

South, Robert, 1634-1716.

SOUTH, Robert, 1634-1716. 283.
Sermons preached upon several occasions, by Robert South ... A new ed. ... Oxford, University press, 1842. 5 v. 22 cm. The present edition of Dr. South's sermons consists of three parts. The first three volumes correspond with the first six volumes of the old editions. The last two volumes contain posthumous discourses. The appendix to the fifth volume contains three sermons published by Edmund Curil, with the Life of the author, 1717. The Life is prefixed to the first volume of the present edition. cf. Advertisement, vol. I. [BX5133.S6S4 1842] 24-11626
1. South, Robert, 1634-1716. I. Title.

Southern Baptist Convention.

COOPER, Owen. 248'.48'6132
The future is before us. Nashville, Broadman Press [1973] 120 p. 21 cm. [BX6207.S68C66] 72-96155 ISBN 0-8054-5533-7 3.95
1. Southern Baptist Convention. 2. Christian life—Baptist authors. I. Title.

COTHEN, Grady C. 269'.2
Unto all the world : bold mission / Grady C. Cothen ; introd. by Albert McClellan. Nashville : Broadman, c1979. 130 p. ; 19 cm. [BX6207.S68C67] 79-50341 ISBN 0-8054-5508-6 pbk. : 2.25
1. Southern Baptist Convention. 2. Evangelistic work. 3. Missions. I. Title. II. Title: Bold mission.

CROSS, Irvie Keil, 1917- 286.1769
The truth about conventionism. Little

Rock, Ark., Printed by Seminary Press [1955] 80 p. illus. 24 cm. [BX6207.A4084] 55-42019
1. Southern Baptist Convention. 2. United Baptists. Kentucky. Cumberland River Association. I. Title.

CROSS, Irvie Keil, 1917- 286.1769
The truth about conventionism; the Southern Baptist Convention, a new denomination. 2d ed., rev. and enl. Little Rock, Ark., Printed by Seminary Press [1956] 93 p. illus. 23 cm. [BX6207.A4084 1956] 56-38686
1. Southern Baptist Convention. 2. United Baptists. Kentucky. Cumberland River Association. I. Title.

DOBBINS, Gaines Stanley, 260
1886-
Working together in a spiritual democracy; B. A. U. study course, by Gaines S. Dobbins ... Nashville, Tenn., The Sunday school board of the Southern Baptist convention [c1935] 128 p. 19 cm. "Books for further reading and reference" at end of each chapter. [BX6205.B115D6] 36-7299
1. Southern Baptist convention. 2. Baptist adult union. I. Southern Baptist convention. Sunday school board. II. Title.

THE dreamer cometh.
Atlanta, Home Mission Board, Southern Baptist Convention [1960] 104p. 22cm. (Southern Baptist Convention. Home Mission studies. 1961 graded series)
1. Rice, Luther, 1783-1836. 2. Southern Baptist Convention. I. Carleton, William A II. Series.

EIGHMY, John Lee. 261.8'3
Churches in cultural captivity; a history of the social attitudes of Southern Baptists. With an introd. and epilogue by Samuel S. Hill, Jr. [1st ed.] Knoxville, University of Tennessee Press [1972] xvii, 249 p. 24 cm. Bibliography: p. 211-240. [HN39.U6E38] 70-111047 ISBN 0-87049-115-6 11.50
1. Southern Baptist Convention. 2. Church and social problems—Baptists. 3. Southern States—Social conditions. I. Title.

GARRETT, James Leo. 286'.132
Are Southern Baptists "Evangelicals"? / by James Leo Garrett, Jr., E. Glenn Hinson, James E. Tull. Macon, Ga. : Mercer University Press, c1982. p. cm. Includes index. Bibliography: p. [BX6462.7.G37 1982] 19 82-18870 ISBN 0-86554-033-0 : 14.95
1. Southern Baptist Convention. 2. Evangelicalism—United States. I. Hinson, E. Glenn. II. Tull, James E. III. Title.

A history of the Ozark division mountain mission schools of the home mission board Southern Baptist Convention. Russellville, Ark. [Hugh Dudley Morton] 1958. 56p. front.
I. Morton, Hugh Dudley, 1880-

ISOM, Dudley R. 267.246
Baptist brotherhood manual [by] Dudley R. Isom. Nashville, Tenn., The Sunday school board of the Southern Baptism convention [c1935] 91 p. illus. (facsims.) diagr. 19 1/2 cm. [BX6205.B117I7] 36-947
1. Southern Baptist convention. 2. Baptist brotherhood of the South. I. Title.

JOHNSON, Walter Nathan, 286.
1875-
Spinal adjustment in Southern Baptist life, by Walt N. Johnson ... Mars Hill, N.C., The Mars Hill press [1931] 63 p. 19 1/2 cm. [BX6241.J6] 44-36676
1. Southern Baptist convention. I. Title.

KELSEY, George D. 286'.132
Social ethics among Southern Baptists, 1917-1969, by George D. Kelsey. Metuchen, N.J., Scarecrow Press, 1973 [c1972] ix, 274 p. 22 cm. (ATLA monograph series, no. 2) A revision of the author's thesis, Yale. [BX6207.A48K44 1972] 72-6332 ISBN 0-8108-0538-3 7.50
1. Southern Baptist Convention. 2. Church and social problems—Baptists. 3. Social ethics. I. Title. II. Series: American Theological Library Association. ATLA monograph series, no. 2.

LAWRENCE, John Benjamin, 286.175
1873-
Co-operating Southern Baptists. Atlanta, Home Mission Board, Southern Baptist Convention [1949] 114 p. 20 cm. [BX6241.L3] 49-2672
1. Southern Baptist Convention. I. Title.

LUNSFORD, William, 1859- 254
comp.
Veterans of the cross, by William Lunsford... Dallas, Tex., Baptist standard publishing co., 1921. 210 p. front., ports. 19 1/2 cm. Articles and addresses by various contributors, published by authority of the Relief and annuity board, Southern Baptist convention. [BX6345.L8] 21-9623
I. Southern Baptist convention. Relief and annuity board. II. Title.

MCCLELLAN, Albert. 286'.132
Meet Southern Baptists / Albert McClellan. Nashville : Broadman Press, c1978. 82 p. : ill. ; 28 cm. Cover title. Bibliography: p. 82. [BX6207.S68M33] 78-52960 ISBN 0-8054-6534-0 pbk. : 2.95
1. Southern Baptist Convention. 2. Baptists—History. I. Title.

MCDANIEL, George White, 1875- 286
The people called Baptists, by George W. McDaniel. Nashville, Tenn., The Sunday school board of the Southern Baptist convention [c1919] 172 p. 20 1/2 cm. [BX6331.M2] 19-13063
I. Title.

MASTERS, Victor Irvine, 1867- 261
C Atlanta, Ga., Publicity department of the Home mission board of the Southern Baptist convention [c1916] 223 p. 20 cm. Bibliography: p. 215-216. [BV638.M3] 16-23599
I. Southern Baptist convention. II. Title. III. Title: Country church in the South

MULLINS, Edgar Young, 1860- 230
Christianity at the cross roads, by E. Y. Mullins ... Nashville, Tenn, Sunday school board of the Southern Baptist convention [c1924] vii p., 1 l., 11-289 p. 20 cm. [BT78.M9 1924 a] 25-12178
I. Title.

POTTER, C. Burtt. 241'.04'6132
Baptists: the passionate people [by] C. Burtt Potter, Jr. Nashville, Broadman Press [1973] 128 p. 21 cm. Includes bibliographical references. [BX6207.A48P67] 72-94400 ISBN 0-8054-8802-2 1.50 (pbk.)
1. Southern Baptist Convention. I. Title.

SCARBOROUGH, Lee Rutland, 286.175
1870-
Marvels of divine leadership; or, The story of the Southern Baptist 75 million campaign, by L. R. Scarborough ... Nashville, Tenn., Sunday school board Southern Baptist convention [c1920] 245 p. illus. (ports.) 23 1/2 cm. [BX6241.S3] 34-40551
1. Southern Baptist convention. I. Title. II. Title: The story of the Southern Baptist 75 million campaign.

SHURDEN, Walter B. 230'.6'132
Not a silent people; controversies that have shaped Southern Baptists [by] Walter B. Shurden. Nashville, Broadman Press [1972] 128 p. 21 cm. (A Broadman inner circle book) "Most of the following chapters were first published in the Student in a somewhat revised form during 1970-1971." Includes bibliographical references. [BX6331.2.S53] 79-178066 ISBN 0-8054-8801-4
1. Southern Baptist Convention. 2. Baptists—Doctrinal and controversial works. I. Title.

SOUTHERN Baptist Convention.
Sunday School Board. Baptist Training Union Dept.
Training Union program materials, 1962; descriptions and classification by themes. [Nashville, Baptist Sunday School Baord, 1962] 85 p. 63-67704
I. Title.

SPAIN, Rufus B. 261.8'3
At ease in Zion; social history of Southern Baptists, 1865-1900 [by] Rufus B. Spain. Nashville, Vanderbilt University Press [1967] xiii, 247 p. 24 cm. Bibliography: p. 222-228. [HN39.U6S6] 66-10367
1. Southern Baptist Convention. 2. Church and social problems—Baptists. I. Title.

VAN NESS, Isaac J., 1860- ed.
Training in church membership; for use as text book in study courses either with the individual, with the church B.Y.P.U., or as supplemental studies in the church Sunday school. I. J. Van Ness, D.D., editorial secretary ... Nashville, Tenn., Sunday school board Southern Baptist convention [c1908] 128 p. 17 1/2 cm. "The book is published under the general instruction of the Southern Baptist convention"--Note. 8-27126
1. Southern Baptist convention. I. Title.

WALLACE, Oates Charles Symonds,
1856-
What Baptists believe; the New Hampshire confession, an exposition ... [by] O. C. S. Wallace... Nashville, Tenn., Sunday school board, Southern Baptist convention [c1913] 208 p. 18 cm. $0.50 14-1490
I. Title.

Southern Baptist Convention. Annuity Board.

BAKER, Robert Andrew. 658.32'5
The thirteenth check; the jubilee history of the Annuity Board of the Southern Baptist Convention, 1918-68 [by] Robert A. Baker. Nashville, Broadman Press [1968] vi, 248 p. illus., ports. 22 cm. Contents.Contents.—The pioneer: William Lunsford (1918-27)—The salesman: Thomas J. Watts (1927-47)—The conserver: Walter R. Alexander (1947-54)—The executive: R. Alton Reed (1955-) [BX6345.5.B3] 72-2893 2.85
1. Southern Baptist Convention. Annuity Board. 2. Southern Baptist Convention—Clergy—Salaries, pensions, etc. I. Title.

Southern Baptist Convention. Baptist Brotherhood Commission.

BROWN, Archie E 267.2461
A million men for Christ; the history of the Baptist Brotherhood. Nashville, Convention Press [1956] 179p. 21cm. [BX6207.A40834] 56-10337
1. Southern Baptist Convention. Baptist Brotherhood Commission. I. Title.

SCHROEDER, George W 267.2461
The brotherhood guidebook, a guide for organizing and operating a brotherhood. Nashville, Broadman Press [1950] 152 p. 21 cm. [BX6205.S6S3] 50-12073
1. Southern Baptist Convention. Baptist Brotherhood Commission. I. Title.

SCHROEDER, George W 267.2461
The church brotherhood guidebook; a guide for organizing and operating a church brotherhood. [Rev. Nashville, Broadman Press, 1960] 192 p. illus. 20 cm. First published in 1950 under title: The brotherhood guidebook. [BX6205.B117S3] 60-9894
1. Southern Baptist Convention. Baptist Brotherhood Commission. I. Title.

Southern Baptist Convention—Biography.

ROUTH, Porter, 286'.132'0922 B
1911-
Chosen for leadership : sketches of 39 presidents of the Southern Baptist Convention / Porter Routh. Nashville : Broadman Press, c1976. 110 p. : ports. ; 19 cm. Published in 1953 under title: Meet the presidents. [BX6493.R68 1976] 76-14632 ISBN 0-8054-6529-4 pbk. : 2.50
1. Southern Baptist Convention—Biography. 2. Baptists—Biography. I. Title.

ROUTH, Porter, 1911- 922.673
Meet the presidents. Nashville, Broadman Press [1953] 98p. illus. 16cm. [BX6241.R68] 53-9909
1. Southern Baptist Convention—Biog. I. Title.

Southern Baptist Convention—Charities.

ALEXANDER, Walter Richardson, 258
1889-
Doing likewise, three vital Southern Baptist ministries. Nashville, Sunday School Board of the Southern Baptist Convention [1947] 146 p. 20 cm. "A suggested bibliography": p. 143. [BX6347.A4] 47-12395
1. Southern Baptist Convention—Charities. I. Title.

Southern Baptist Convention—Clergy—Anecdotes, facetiae, satire, etc.

IF I had my ministry to live over, I would .... / compiled by Rick Ingle. 253
Nashville : Broadman Press, c1977. 131 p. ; 20 cm. [BV660.2.I53] 77-78154 ISBN 0-8054-2704-X pbk. : 2.50
1. Southern Baptist Convention—Clergy—Anecdotes, facetiae, satire, etc. 2. Clergy—Office—Anecdotes, facetiae, satire, etc. 3. Pastoral theology—Anecdotes, facetiae, satire, etc. 4. Clergy—United States—Anecdotes, facetiae, satire, etc. I. Ingle, Rick.

Southern Baptist convention—Clergy—Salaries, pensions, etc.

GARDNER, Ruth Carver. 254
Christ's gift to the churches [by] Ruth Carver Gardner. Nashville, Tenn., Broadman press [c1936] 120 p. 19 1/2 cm. "Addendum: The relief and annuity board of the Southern Baptist convention; eighteen years of service and growth 1918-1936, by Thomas J. Watts, D.D., executive secretary": p. 113-120. [BX6345.5.G3] 36-7507
1. Southern Baptist convention—Clergy—Salaries, pensions, etc. 2. Southern Baptist conventions. Relief and annuity board. I. Watts, Thomas Joseph, 1874- II. Title.

WATTS, James Washington, 1896-
Living of the gospel, by J. Wash Watts ... Nashville, Broadman press [c1939] 150 p. front., illus. (maps) 2 port. (incl. front.) 19 1/2 cm. [BX6345.5.W3] 39-16661
1. Southern Baptist convention—Clergy—Salaries, pensions, etc. 2. Southern Baptist convention. Relief and annuity board. I. Title.

Southern Baptist Convention—Congresses.

FUTURISTIC Conference, 230'.6'132
Ridgecrest, N.C., 1977.
Proceedings of major presentations : Futuristic Conference / sponsored by the Sunday School Board of the Southern Baptist Convention, March 21-25, 1977, Ridgecrest, North Carolina. Nashville : The Board, c1977. v, 140 leaves : ill. ; 29 cm. Includes bibliographical references. [CB161.F795 1977] 77-155217
1. Southern Baptist Convention—Congresses. 2. Twentieth century—Forecasts—Congresses. 3. Baptists—Southern States—Congresses. I. Southern Baptist Convention. Sunday School Board.

Southern Baptist convention—Education.

JOHNSON, Charles D 377.86175
Higher education of Southern Baptists; an institutional history, 1826-1954. Waco, Tex., Baylor University Press [1956, c1955] xviii, 465p. ports. 23cm. Bibliography: p. [447]-[449] [LC562.J6] 56-3091
1. Southern Baptist Convention—Education. 2. Universities and colleges—Southern States. I. Title.

MAGRUDER, Edith Clysdale. 377.861
A historical study of the educational agencies of the Southern Baptist Convention, 1845-1945. New York, Bureau of Publications, Teachers College, Columbia University, 1951. xi, 161 p. 24 cm. (Columbia University. Teachers College. Contributions to education, no. 974) Bibliography: p. 139-152. [LC561.M3] 51-10968
1. Southern Baptist Convention—Education. I. Title. II. Series.

PRICE, John Milburn, 922.673
1884- ed.
Baptist leaders in religious education, compiled and edited by J. M. Price ... Nashville, Tenn., Broadman press [1943] 174 p. 23 cm. [BX6223.P7] 43-11611
1. Southern Baptist convention—Education. 2. Southern Baptist

convention—Biog. 3. Religous education—Biog. I. Title.

PRICE, John Milburn, 1884- 268.86
A program of religious education, by J. M. Price ... L. L. Carpenter ... [and] A. E. Tibbs ... New York [etc.] Fleming H. Revell company [c1937] 288 p. 21 cm. "A selected bibliography for class use" at the end of each part. [BX6219.P7] 37-5194
1. Southern Baptist convention—Education. 2. Religious education. 3. Baptists—Education. I. Carpenter, Levy Leonidas, 1891- II. Tibbs, Albert Elias, 1901- III. Title.

SOUTHERN Baptist 377'.8'6132
Convention. Education Commission.
Baptist education study task. Nashville [196 - v. 29 cm. Cover title. Contents.Contents.—2. The history of Southern Baptist higher education, by Leon McBeth. Bibliography: v. 2, p. 49-51. [LC561.S623] 67-30407
1. Southern Baptist Convention—Education. I. McBeth, Leon. II. Title.

Southern Baptist Convention—Education—History.

BRIGHAM, Judith, 268'.8'6132
1915-
A historical study of the educational agencies of the Southern Baptist Convention, 1845-1945. New York, Bureau of Publications, Teachers College, Columbia University, 1951. [New York, AMS Press, 1972, i.e. 1973] xi, 161 p. 22 cm. Reprint of the 1951 ed., issued in series: Teachers College, Columbia University. Contributions to education, no. 974. Originally presented as the author's thesis, Columbia. Bibliography: p. 139-152. [LC561.S63B7 1972] 77-177047 ISBN 0-404-55974-3 10.00
1. Southern Baptist Convention—Education—History. I. Title. II. Series: Columbia University. Teachers College. Contributions to education, no. 974.

Southern Baptist Convention—Government.

BAPTIST ecclesiology. 262'.06'1
New York : Arno Press, 1980. 115, 80 p. ; 23 cm. (The Baptist tradition) Reprint of 2 works, the 1st originally published as the author's thesis, University of Chicago, 1906; the second, published by the author, Seminary Hill, Tex., 1934. Contents.Contents.—Allison, W. H. Baptist councils in America—Barnes, W. W. The Southern Baptist Convention. Includes bibliographies. [BX6340.B36 1980] 79-52582 ISBN 0-405-12449-X : 18.00
1. Southern Baptist Convention—Government. 2. Baptists—United States—Government. I. Allison, William Henry, 1870-1941. Baptist councils in America. 1980. II. Barnes, William Wright, 1883- The Southern Baptist Convention. 1980. III. Series: Baptist tradition.

BARNES, William 286.106375
Wright, 1883-
The Southern Baptist convention; a study in the development of ecclesiology, William Wright Barnes ... Seminary Hill, Tex., The author [1934] 4 p. l., 80 p. 22 cm. Bibliography: p. 80. [BX6241.B35]
1. Southern Baptist convention—Government. I. Title.

CROUCH, Austin. 286.175
How Southern Baptists do their work. Nashville, Broadman Press ['1951] 99 p. 20 cm. [BX6241.C7] 52-21508
1. Southern Baptist Convention—Government. I. Title.

Southern Baptist Convention-Handbooks, manuals, et c.

SOUTHERN Baptist Convention.
Executive Committee.
The Southern Baptist Convention organization manual. 1st ed. Nashville, Tenn., 1964. 1 v. (various pagings) 28 cm. 66-57702
1. Southern Baptish Convention—Handbooks, manuals, etc. I. Title.

Southern Baptist Convention—History.

BAKER, Robert Andrew. 286'.132'09
The Southern Baptist Convention and its people, 1607-1972 [by] Robert A. Baker. Nashville, Tenn., Broadman Press [1974] 477 p. 24 cm. Bibliography: p. 465-469. [BX6207.S68B34] 73-91614 ISBN 0-8054-6516-2 11.95
1. Southern Baptist Convention—History. I. Title.

BARNES, William Wright, 286.175
1883-
The Southern Baptist Convention, 1845-1953. Nashville, Broadman Press [1954] x, 330 p. 24 cm. Bibliography: p. 314-323. [BX6207.A4083] 53-13534
1. Southern Baptist Convention—Hist. I. Title.

BURTON, Joe 286'.132'0924 B
Wright, 1907-1976.
Road to recovery : Southern Baptist renewal following the Civil War, as seen especially in the work of I. T. Tichenor / Joe W. Burton. Nashville : Broadman Press, c1977. 168 p. ; 20 cm. Bibliography: p. 166-168. [BX6207.S68B87] 76-24062 ISBN 0-8054-6530-8 bds. : 6.95
1. Southern Baptist Convention—History. 2. Tichenor, Isaac Taylor, 1825-1902. 3. Baptists—Clergy—Biography. 4. Clergy—Georgia—Atlanta—Biography. 5. Atlanta—Biography. I. Title.

MCBETH, Leon. 261.8'34'12
Women in Baptist life / Leon McBeth. Nashville : Broadman Press, c1979. 190 p. ; 20 cm. Bibliography: p. 188-190. [BX6207.S68M32] 78-54245 ISBN 0-8054-6925-7 : 5.95
1. Southern Baptist Convention—History. 2. Women, Baptist—United States. I. Title.

TULL, James E. 286'.132'09
A history of Southern Baptist Landmarkism in the light of historical Baptist ecclesiology / James E. Tull. New York : Arno Press, 1980, c1960. xi, 709 p. ; 24 cm. (The Baptist tradition) Originally presented as the author's thesis, Columbia, 1960. Bibliography: p. [693]-709. [BX6207.S68T84 1980] 79-52578 ISBN 0-405-12446-5 : 52.00
1. Southern Baptist Convention—History. 2. Landmarkism. I. Title. II. Series: Baptist tradition.

VALENTINE, Foy. 261.8'34'51042
A historical study of Southern Baptists and race relations, 1917-1947 / Foy D. Valentine. New York : Arno Press, 1980. 258 p. ; 24 cm. (The Baptist tradition) Originally presented as the author's thesis, Southwestern Baptist Theological Seminary, 1949. Bibliography: [235]-258. [BX6207.S68V34 1980] 79-52579 ISBN 0-405-12447-3 : 20.00
1. Southern Baptist Convention—History. 2. Church and race relations—Southern States—Case studies. 3. Southern States—Church history. I. Title. II. Series: Baptist tradition.

WAMBLE, G. Hugh, 1923- 286.173
Through trial to triumph. Nashville, Convention Press [1958] 142 p. 19 cm. Includes bibliography. [BX6207.A4089] 58-2884
1. Southern Baptist Convention — Hist. I. Title.

Southern Baptist Convention—History—20th century.

THOMPSON, James J., 286'.132
1944-
Tried as by fire : Southern Baptists and the religious controversies of the 1920s / James J. Thompson, Jr. Macon, GA : Mercer University Press, c1982. xv, 224 p. ; 24 cm. Revision of thesis (Ph.D.)—University of Virginia, 1971. Includes indexes. Bibliography: p. [217]-219. [BX6207.S68T47 1982] 19 82-8056 ISBN 0-86554-032-2 : 13.95
1. Southern Baptist Convention—History—20th century. 2. Theology, Baptist—History—20th century. I. Title.

Southern Baptist Convention—History—Anecdotes, facetiae, satire, etc.

HERRING, Reuben. 286'.173
The Baptist almanac and repository of indispensable knowledge : being a compendium of events both amazing and amusing of that great host known far and wide as Baptists ... / Reuben Herring. Nashville : Broadman Press, c1976. 159 p. : ill. ; 24 cm. Includes index. Bibliography: p. 153-155. [BX6235.H47] 75-35397 ISBN 0-8054-6521-9 pbk. : 5.95
1. Southern Baptist Convention—History—Anecdotes, facetiae, satire, etc. 2. Baptists—United States—History—Anecdotes, facetiae, satire, etc. I. Title.

Southern Baptist Convention. Home Mission Board.

GRUVER, Kate Ellen, ed.
Apogee. Atlanta, Home Mission Board, Southern Baptist Convention [1963] 103 p. illus. 19 cm. (Southern Baptist Convention. Home Mission Board. Home Mission studies. 1964 graded series) [Supplement] Teacher's guide [by] Dorothy Pryor. [Atlanta, Home Mission Board, Southern Baptist Convention, 1963] 26 p. illus. 28 cm. 65-39738
1. Southern Baptist Convention. Home Mission Board. 2. Southern Baptist Convention — Missions. 3. Missions, Home. I. Title. II. Series.

LAWRENCE, John Benjamin, 266.6
1873-
History of the Home Mission Board. Nashville, Broadman Press [1958] 170p. 21cm. Includes bibliography. [BV2766.B5L32] 58-8922
1. Southern Baptist Convention. Home Mission Board. I. Title.

RUTLEDGE, Arthur B. 266.6'173
Mission to America; a century and a quarter of Southern Baptist home missions [by] Arthur B. Rutledge. Nashville, Broadman Press [1969] xiv, 271 p. illus., ports. 22 cm. Includes bibliographical references. [BV2766.B5R84] 78-84499 5.95
1. Southern Baptist Convention. Home Mission Board. 2. Southern Baptist Convention—Missions. 3. Missions, Home. I. Title.

Southern Baptist Convention—Missions.

BISHOP, Ivyloy. 266.61
Appointment for Andy [by] Ivyloy and Amelia Bishop. Nashville, Convention Press [1959] 104p. illus. 19cm. (1959 Foreign Mission graded series, intermediate) A Publication of the Foreign Mission Board, Richmond, Virginia. [BV2520.B57] 59-9678
1. Southern Baptist Convention—Missions. I. Bishop, Amelia, joint author. II. Title.

CARVER, Saxon Rowe.
James Robb, pioneer. Illustrated by William Moyers. Atlanta, Home Mission Board, Southern Baptist Convention [1963] 75 p. illus. 20 cm. (Southern Baptist Convention. Home Mission Board. Home Mission studies. 1964 graded series) [Supplement] Teacher's guide [by] Margaret Sharp. [Atlanta, Home Mission Board, Southern Baptist Convention, 1963] 27 p. illus. 28 cm. 65-7967
1. Robb, James Henry. 2. Southern Baptist Convention — Missions. 3. Missions, Home — Juvenile literature. I. Title. II. Series.

CAUTHEN, Baker James. 266.6'132
Advance: a history of Southern Baptist foreign missions [by] Baker J. Cauthen, and others. Nashville, Broadman Press [1970] 329 p. illus., ports. 22 cm. Bibliography: p. 319-323. [BV2520.C26] 71-117307 4.95
1. Southern Baptist Convention—Missions. 2. Southern Baptist Convention. Foreign Mission Board. I. Title.

CAUTHEN, Baker James. 266.61
By all means, by Baker James Cauthen, and others. Nashville, Convention Press [1959] 148p. illus. 19cm. (1959 Foreign Mission graded series) [BV2520.C27] 59-9679
1. Southern Baptist Convention—Missions. 2. Missions, Foreign. I. Title.

CAYLOR, John, 1894- 266.61
A path of light, by John Caylor and others. Atlanta, Home Mission Board, Southern Baptist Convention [1950] 118 p. 21 cm. [BV2520.C3] 50-12910
1. Southern Baptist Convention—Missions. I. Title.
Contents Omitted.

CLARK, Willie Thorburn, 922.6
1868-
Handmaidens of the King to foreign lands, by W. Thorburn Clark... Richmond, Va., Educational dept., Foreign mission board, Southern Baptist convention [c1932] 179 p. ports. 19 1/2 cm. [BV2520.C55] 32-14311
1. Southern Baptist convention—Missions. 2. Baptists—Missions. 3. Missionaries. 4. Woman—Biog. I. Southern Baptist convention. Foreign mission board. II. Title.

CLARK, Willie Thorburn, 266.61
1868-
Outriders for the King, by W. Thorburn Clark. Richmond, Va., Educational dept., Foreign mission board, Southern Baptist convention [c1931] 153 p. ports. 20 cm. Bibliography included in foreword. [BV2520.C6] 31-15537
1. Southern Baptist convention—Missions. 2. Baptists—Missions. 3. Missionaries. I. Southern Baptist convention. Foreign mission board. II. Title.

COLEMAN, Inabelle Graves. 266.61
The march of missions. Nashville, Sunday School Board of the Southern Baptist Convention [1945] 139 p. 19 cm. A textbook used in the Baptist Training Union study course. [BV2520.C623] 48-40943
1. Southern Baptist Convention—Missions. 2. Missions—Study and teaching. I. Baptist, Traning Union. II. Title.

CRISWELL, W A. 266.6
Passport to the world, by W. A. Criswell and Duke K. McCall. Nashville, Broadman Press ['1951] 139 p. 21 cm. [BV2520.C7] 52-6218
1. Southern Baptist Convention—Missions. 2. Flights around the world. I. Title.

CRISWELL, Wallie A 266.6
Passport to the world, by W. A. Criswell and Duke K. McCall. Nashville, Broadman Press [1951] 139 p. 21 cm. [BV2520.C7] 52-6218
1. Southern Baptist Convention—Missions. 2. Flights around the world. I. McCall, Duke K., joint author. II. Title.

DECKER, Florence Frazer 266.61
(Roston) Mrs. 1893-
World airways for the King, by Florence Boston Decker. Nashville, Tenn., Broadman press [c1941] 156 p. front., illus. (maps.) plates, ports. 19 cm. Bibliography: p. 156. [BV2520.D4] 41-11604
1. Southern Baptist convention—Missions. 2. Baptists—Missions. I. Title.

GILL, Everett, 1869- 274
Europe and the gospel, by Everett Gill ... Richmond, Va., Educational dept., Foreign mission board, Southern Baptist convention [c1931] 1 p. l., 5-174 p. plates. 20 cm. [BV2855.G5] 266.61 31-23313
1. Southern Baptist convention—Missions. 2. Missions—Europe. 3. Europe—Religion. 4. Baptists—Europe. I. Southern Baptist convention. Foreign mission board. II. Title.

HECK, Fannie E. S.
In royal service, the mission work of southern Baptist women, by Fannie E. S. Heck ... Richmond, Va., Educational department, foreign mission boards, Southern Baptist convention, 1913. 380 p. front., plates, ports. 19 1/2 cm. $0.50 Bibliography: p. 370. 13-26461
I. Title.

HULLUM, Everett, 1942- 266'.022
And a cast of thousands : the human touch in special mission ministries / written by Everett Hullum and Celeste Loucks ; photographed by Jim Wright. Atlanta : Home Mission Board, Southern Baptist Convention, c1978. 189 p. : ill. ; 29 cm. [BV2520.H8] 78-103577 6.95

1. Southern Baptist Convention—Missions. 2. Missions, Home. I. Loucks, Celeste, 1947- joint author. II. Wright, Jim. III. Title.

IT'S your turn.
Atlanta, Home Mission Board, Southern Bapist Convention [1956] Atlanta, Home Mission Board, Southern Baptist Convention [1956] 84p. illus. 21cm. 24p. ports. 21cm. (1957 graded series of home mission studies. Mission field: U.S.A.)
1. Southern Baptist Convention—Missions. 2. Missions, Home—Literature. I. Eubanks, Margaret Kime. II. Title: —Junior source book by John Caylor and Primary teaching helps by Margaret Kime Eubanks and Elsie Rives.

LACKEY, Margaret McRae. 277.
From strength to strength. by Margaret McRae Lackey. Atlanta, Ga., The Home mission board of the Southern Baptist convention [c1923] 2 p. l., [7]-139 p. front., illus., plates, ports. 19 cm. [BV2766.B5L3] 23-11353
1. Southern Baptist convention—Missions. I. Title.

LACKEY, Margaret McRae. 275.
"Laborers together", a study of Southern Baptist missions in China, by Margaret McRae Lackey ... New York, Chicago [etc.] Fleming H. Revell company [c1921] 126 p. front., illus. (maps) plates, ports. 20 cm. [BV3415.L25] 21-12369
I. Title.

LAWRENCE, John Benjamin, 266. 1873-
Home missions in the new world, by J. B. Lawrence. Atlanta, Ga., Home mission board, Southern Baptist convention [1943] 128 p. front. (map) plates, ports., diagrs. 19 1/2 cm. Bibliography: p. 128. [BV2766.B5L33] 44-1052
1. Southern Baptist convention—Missions. 2. Baptists—Southern states. 3. Missions, Home. I. Southern Baptist convention. Home mission board. II. Title.

LAWRENCE, Una Roberts Mrs. 266.61
The keys of the kingdom, by Una Roberts Lawrence. Atlanta, Ga., The Home mission board, Southern Baptist convention [c1934] 128 p. 20 cm. [BV2766.B5L34] 34-5492
1. Southern Baptist convention—Missions. 2. Missions, Home. 3. Missions—Study and teaching. I. Title.

LEAVELL, Roland Quinche, 277.5 1891-
Christianity our citadel, by Roland Q. Leavell... Atlanta, Ga., Home mission board, Southern Baptist convention [1943] 2 p. l., [7]-95 p. 19 1/2 cm. [BV2766.B5L4] [266.6] 44-14430
1. Southern Baptist convention—Missions. 2. Missions—Southern states. 3. Missions, Home. I. Southern Baptist convention. Home missions board. II. Title.

LEDBETTER, Edith Limer.
The gracious adventurers. Atlanta, Home Mission Board, Southern Baptist Convention [1963] 92 p. 20 cm. 17 p. illus. 28 cm. (Southern Baptist Convention. Home Mission Board. Home Mission studies 1964 graded series) [Supplement] Teacher's guide [by] Marjorie Rowden. [Atlanta, Home Mission Board, Southern Baptist Convention, 1963] 65-25809
1. Southern Baptist Convention — Missions. 2. Missions, Home. I. Title. II. Series.

LOUCKS, Celeste, 1947- 266'.6'132
American montage : the human touch in language missions / written by Celeste Loucks ; photographed by Everett Hullum. Atlanta : Home Mission Board, Southern Baptist Convention, c1976. p. cm. (Human touch photo-text series ; 3) [BV2766.B5L68] 76-41911 6.95
1. Southern Baptist Convention—Missions. 2. Missions, Home. 3. Missions—United States. I. Hullum, Everett, 1942- II. Southern Baptist Convention. Home Mission Board. III. Title. IV. Series.

NEW friends for Freddy;
photos. [by] L. O. Griffith. [Atlanta, Home Mission Board, Southern Boptist Convention, 1956?] 1v. (unpaged) illus. 20x27cm.
1. Southern Baptist Convention—Missions. 2. Missions, Home—Juvenile literature. I. Berge, Louise.

QUARLES, James Cowardin, 278 1883-
Christ in the silver lands [by] James C. Quarles. Richmond, Va., Foreign mission board, Southern Baptist convention, 1935. x, 141 p. plates, 5 port. on 1 pl., double map. 19 cm. Title vignette. "Second edition." "Reading list": p. 125-126. [BV2851.Q8 1935 a] 266.61 37-3815
1. Southern Baptist convention—Missions. 2. Missions—South America. I. Southern Baptist convention. Foreign mission board. II. Title.

RAY, T. Bronson, 1868- 266.61 1934.
Southern Baptists in the great adventure [by] T. B. Ray, D. D.; introduction by W. O. Carver. Nashville, Tenn., The Sunday school board of the Southern Baptist convention [c1934] 201 p. 19 cm. [BV2520.R32] 34-40867
1. Southern Baptist convention—Missions. 2. Baptists—Missions. 3. Missions. Foreign. I. Carver, William Owen, 1868- ed. II. Title.

REDFORD, Courts. 266.061
Spiritual frontiers in home missions. Atlanta, Home Mission Board, Southern Baptist Convention [1948] 104 p. 19 cm. (Graded series on frontiers) [BV2766.B5R4] 48-15763
1. Southern Baptist Convention—Missions. 2. Missions—U. S. 3. Missions, Home. I. Title. II. Series.

SAWGRASS missionary.
Atlanta, Home Mission Board, Southern Baptist Coventiom [1960] 73p. illus. 22cm. (1961 graded series of home mission studies: Our Baptist heritage in missions)
1. Southern Baptist Convention—Missions. 2. Missions, Home—Juvenile literature. I. Provence, Elizabeth. II. Series: Southern Baptist Convention. Home Mission Board. Home mission studies. 1961 graded series

SMITH, Bertha. 266'.6'32
Our lost world / Bertha Smith ; foreword by Vance Havner. Nashville, Tenn. : Broadman Press, c1981. 158 p. ; 20 cm. [BV2520.S59] 19 80-68537 ISBN 0-8054-6324-0 pbk. : 3.95
1. Southern Baptist Convention—Missions. 2. Missions. 3. Baptists—Missions. I. Title.

SOUTHERN Baptist 266.61 Convention. Foreign Mission Board.
Light for the whole world; a symposium [by] the Board's secretaries] M. Theron Ranking [and others] Nashville, Braodman Press [1948] 124 p. diagrs. 19 cm. (Foreign Missions study series) [BV2520.S64] 48-9600
1. Southern Baptist Convention—Missions. I. Ranking, Milladge Theron, II. Title.

SOUTHERN Baptist 266.61 convention. Sunday school board.
Witnessing at home and around the world; a study of Southern Baptist missions for 1937. Nashville, Tenn., The Sunday school board of the Southern Baptist convention [c1937] 1 p. l., 2, 116, [1] p. 23 cm. In two parts. Each part has special t.-p. Includes bibliographies. [BV2520.A8S65] 38-5487
1. Southern Baptist convention—Missions. 2. Baptists—Missions. I. Southern Baptist convention. Home mission board. II. Southern Baptist convention. Foreign mission board. III. Lawrence, John Benjamin, 1873- ed. IV. Burton, Joe, 1907- joint ed. V. Coleman, Inabelle Graves, comp. VI. Title.
Contents omitted.

STEEPLES against the sky.
Atlanta, Home Mission Board, Southern Baptist Convention [1961] 108p. 20cm. (1962 graded series of home mission studies: New churches for out time)
1. Southern Baptist Convention—Missions. 2. Missions, Home. I. Ledbetter, Edith Limer. II. Series: Southern Baptist Convention. Home Mission Board. Home Mission studies. 1962 graded series

STEWART, Willie Jean. 266.61
By clipper plane and stratoliner, by Willie Jean Stewart. Nashville, Tenn., Broadman press [c1941] 140 p. incl. front., illus. 19 cm. "Reading list": p. 117-119. [BV2520.S75] 41-10226
1. Southern Baptist convention—Missions. I. Title.

THE trail of itchin' feet,
by Hazel and Sam Mayo. Atlanta, Home Mission Board, Southern Baptist Convention [1956] Atlanta, Home Mission Board, Southern Baptist Convention [1956] 94p. 21cm. 24p. port. 21cm.
1. Southern Baptist Convention—Missions. 2. Missions, Home. 3. Migrant labor, U. S. I. Mayo, Hazel. II. Mayo Sam, joint author. III. Caylor, John, 1894- IV. Title: —Intermediate source book by John Cayler and Teaching helps by Louise Carter Fallis.

THE trail of itchin' feet,
by Hazel and Sam Mayo. Atlanta, Home Mission Board, Southern Baptist Convention [1956] 94p. 21cm. -- Intermediate source book by John Caylor and Teaching helps by Louise Carter Fallis, Atlanta, Home Mission Board, Southern Baptist Convention [1956] 24p. port. 21cm.
1. Southern Baptist Convention—Missions. 2. Missions, Home. 3. Migrant labor, U. S. I. Mayo, Hazel. II. Mayo, Sam, joint author. III. Caylor, John, 1894-

TWENTIETH century pioneers.
Atlanta, Home Mission Board, Southern Baptist Convention [1956] Atlanta, Home Mission Board, Southern Baptist Convention [1956] 91p. 20cm. 23p. port. 20cm. (1957 graded series of home mission studies. Mission field: U.S.A.)
1. Southern Baptist Convention-Missions. 2. Missions, Home. 3. Southern Baptist Convention. Home Mission Board. I. Howard, W F II. Title: —Young people. Source book by John Caylor and Teaching helps by Amelia Morton Bishop.

VICTORS in the land.
Atlanta, Home Mission Board, Southern Baptist Convention [1961?] 88p. 20cm. (1962 graded series of home mission studies: New churches for our time)
1. Southern Baptist Convention—Missions. 2. Missions, Home. I. Hopkins, Lila. II. Series: Southern Baptist Convention. Home Mission Board. Home Mission studies. 1962 graded series

WAYS of witnessing.
Atlanta, Home Mission Board, Southern Baptist Convention [1958] 119p. illus. 21cm. (Southern Baptist Convention. Home Mission Board. Home mission studies. 1959 graded series)
1. Southern Baptist Convention—Missions. 2. Missions, Home. I. Caylor, John, 1894- II. Series.

WEBB, Leland. 266'.6'132
How in this world : a consideration of strategy in the foreign missions outreach of Southern Baptists / Leland Webb. Nashville, Tenn. : Convention Press, [1974] viii, 119 p. : ill. ; 21 cm. (Foreign mission graded series, 1974) [BV2520.W4] 75-319215
1. Southern Baptist Convention—Missions. I. Title.

WRIGHT, Mary Emily. 266.
The missionary work of the Southern Baptist convention, by Mary Emily Wright; with introduction by Lansing Burrows, D.D. Philadelphia, American Baptist publication society [1902] xix, 412 p. 20 cm. "List of authorities consulted": p. [404] [BV2520.W7] 2-13238
1. Southern Baptist convention—Missions. I. Title.

Southern Baptist Convention—Missions—Addresses, essays, lectures.

EDUCATING for Christian 266'.6132 *missions* : supporting Christian missions through education / Arthur L. Walker, Jr., editor. Nashville, Tenn. : Broadman Press, c1981. 179 p. ; 21 cm. Includes bibliographical references. [BV2520.E38] 19 80-68751 ISBN 0-8054-6934-6 pbk. : 5.95
1. Southern Baptist Convention—Missions—Addresses, essays, lectures. 2. Christian education—Addresses, essays, lectures. 3. Missions—Addresses, essays, lectures. I. Walker, Arthur L. 1926- (Arthur Lonzo),

Southern Baptist convention — Missions — Brazil.

JOHNSON, Leslie Leonidas, 1883-
It happened in Brazil; a narration personal experiences over a space of nearly thirty-nine years, by a missionary of the Foreign mission board of the Southern Baptist convention. [Oklahoma City, Printed by the Messenger press, 1960] 96 p. ports. 22 cm. 64-52300
1. Southern Baptist convention — Missions — Brazil. 2. Brazil — Missions. 3. Baptist — Missions — Brazil. I. Title.

Southern Baptist Convention—Missions—Study and teaching.

CHRISTIAN, Mary, 266.6'1676'1 1899-
Uganda safari. Nashville, Convention Press [1971] 96 p. illus., ports. (p. 89-96 blank for notes) 20 cm. (Foreign mission graded series) [BV3625.U3C5] 74-142065
1. Southern Baptist Convention—Missions—Study and teaching. 2. Missions—Uganda—Study and teaching. I. Title.

Southern Baptist Convention—Relations—Catholic Church—Congresses.

BAPTIST-CATHOLIC 286'.173 Regional Conference, Daytona Beach, Fla., 1971.
Issues and answers; [speeches] Sponsored by Home Mission Board, Dept. of Interfaith Witness and Bishreps' Committee for Ecumenical and Interreligious Affairs for National Conference of Catholic Bishops. [Prepared by the Dept. of Interfaith Witness, Home Mission Board of the Southern Baptist Convention. Atlanta, Ga., 1971] 114 l. 28 cm. Cover title. [BX6329.R6B35 1971] 75-24067
1. Southern Baptist Convention—Relations—Catholic Church—Congresses. 2. Catholic Church—Relations—Southern Baptist Convention—Congresses. I. Southern Baptist Convention. Dept. of Interfaith Witness. II. Catholic Church. National Conference of Catholic Bishops. Bishops' Committee for Ecumenical and Interreligious Affairs. III. Title.

Southern Baptist Convention. Sunday School Board.

BAKER, Robert Andrew. 268.86132
The story of the Sunday School Board [by] Robert A. Baker. Nashville, Convention Press [1966] vi, 254 p. illus., ports. 22 cm. Includes bibliographical references. [BX6222.A48B3] 66-12886
1. Southern Baptist Convention Sunday School Board I. Title.

BURROUGHS, Prince 268.861 Emanuel, 1871-
Fifty fruitful years, 1891-1941, the story of the Sunday school board of the Southern Baptist convention, by P. E. Burroughs ... Nashville, The Broadman press, [c1941] xiv p., 1 l., 333 p. plates, ports. (1 fold.) map, facsims. 23 cm. [BX6222.A48B8] 41-20130
1. Southern Baptist convention. Sunday school board. I. Title.

FROST, James Marion, 1849-
The memorial supper of Our Lord, a plea for organic church life ... [by] J. M. Frost ... Nashville, Tenn., Sunday school board, Southern Baptist convention [c1908] 282 p. front., plates. 20 cm. "Issued under the Eva Carvey publishing fund. Given by B. E. Garvey, New Liberty. Ky., January, 1899. Fifth book." 8-5267
I. Title.

SHURDEN, Walter B. 268.1
The Sunday School Board : ninety years of service / Walter B. Shurden. Nashville, Tenn. : Broadman Press, c1981. 96 p. : ill., ports. ; 28 cm. Includes bibliographical references. [BX6222.S683S58] 19 80-68749 ISBN 0-8054-6558-8 pbk. : 3.50
1. Southern Baptist Convention. Sunday School Board. I. Title.

Southern Baptist Convention. Sunday School Board—History.

BURTON, Joe Wright, 1907-1976. 268'.8'61768
Road to Nashville / Joe W. Burton. Nashville : Broadman Press, 1978,c1977. 138 p. ; 20 cm. Bibliography: p. 137-138. [BX6207.S68B86 1977] 78-102284 ISBN 0-8054-6532-4 : 6.95
1. Southern Baptist Convention. Sunday School Board—History. I. Title.

Southern Baptist convention. Woman's missionary union.

BUCY, Wilma Geneva. 266.61
The new why and how of Woman's missionary union, by Wilma Geneva Bucy. Nashville, Tenn., The Sunday school board of the Southern Baptist convention [c1934] 118 p. diagr. 19 cm. [BV2520.B77] 34-37471
1. Southern Baptist convention. Woman's missionary union. I. Title.

BUCY, Wilma Geneva. 266.
Woman's missionary union at work, auxiliary to Southern Baptist convention ... [by] Wilma Geneva Bucy. Nashville, Tenn., The Sunday school board of the Southern Baptist convention [1944] 166 p. 18 1/2 cm. A revision of the author's Why and how of Woman's missionary union. cf. Pref. [BV2520.B77 1944] 44-26828
1. Southern Baptist convention. Woman's missionary union. I. Southern Baptist convention. Sunday school board. II. Title.

COLEMAN, Inabelle Graves. 266.61
For this cause, by Inabelle Graves Coleman ... Nashville, Tenn., Broadman press [c1938] 119 p. 18 1/2 cm. Bibliography: p. 119. [BV2520.C62] 38-32169
1. Southern Baptist convention. Woman's missionary union. 2. Southern Baptist convertion—Missions. 3. Missions, Foreign. I. Title.

COX, Ethlene (Boone) Mrs. 1890- 266.6175
Following in His train [by] Ethlene Boone Cox. Nashville, Broadman press [c1938] 7, [1] p., 2 l., 11-217 p. plates, ports., facsim. 21 cm. "History of Woman's missionary union."--Foreword. [Full name: Mrs. Willie Ethlene (Boone) Cox] "List of references": p. 211. [BV2520.C63] 38-13649
1. Southern Baptist convention. Woman's missionary union. I. Title.

CRAWLEY, Sadie Tiller. 266.6
World awareness. Nashville, Convention Press [1963] 134 p. 19 cm. Includes bibliography. [BV2520.C67] 63-11174
1. Southern Baptist Convention. Women's Missionary Union. 2. Missions—Theory. I. Title.

HUNT, Alma. 266.61
History of Woman's Missionary Union. Nashville, Convention Press [1964] xi, 209 p. 22 cm. Bibliography: p. 199-201. [BV2520.A74H8] 64-19978
1. Southern Baptist Convention. Women's Missionary Union. I. Title.

HUNT, Alma. 266'.6'1
History of Woman's Missionary Union / Alma Hunt. Rev. ed. Nashville : Convention Press, c1976. xiii, 241 p. : ports. ; 21 cm. "Chapters 11-12, Catherine B. Allen." "This is a course in the subject area Missions of the Church study course." Includes bibliographical references and index. [BV2520.A2S6833 1976] 77-359418
1. Southern Baptist Convention. Woman's Missionary Union. I. Title.

JAMES, Minnie (Kennedy) "Mrs. W. C. James," 1874- 922.673
Fannie E. S. Heck; a study of the hidden springs in a rarely useful and victorious life [by] Mrs. W. C. James. Nashville, Broadman press [c1939] xxii, 192 p. plates, ports., facsim. 20 cm. "For parallel reading": p. 192. [BX6495.H4J3] 40-1072
1. Heck, Fannie Exile Scudder, 1862-1915. 2. Southern Baptist convention. Woman's missionary union. I. Title.

LANE, Myrie (Anderson) Mrs. 1907- 266.61
Five times ten, a child's story of Woman's missionary union, by Myrle Anderson Lane. Nashville, Broadman press [c1938] 64 p. incl. front., illus., plates, ports. 23 cm. [Full name: Mrs. Mayme Myrle (Anderson) Lane] [BV2520.A74L3] 39-6776
1. Southern Baptist convention. Woman's missionary union. I. Title.

NEEL, Isa-Beall (Williams) "Mrs. W. J. Neel." 266.61
His story in Georgia W. M. U. history ... by Mrs. W. J. Neel ... [Atlanta] Woman's missionary union auxiliary to the Georgia Baptist convention, 1939. xi, [3], 181 p. illus., plates, ports. 19 cm. "Books" and "Leaflets": p. 173. [BV2520.N4] 39-31171
1. Southern Baptist convention. Woman's missionary union. I. Title.

THOMAS, Lonnie (Benson) Mrs., 1899- 266.61
To be continued, a conversational history of Woman's missionary union, by Lonnie Benson Thomas. Nashville, Tenn., Broadman press [c1938] 66 p. pl., ports. 20 cm. [Full name: Mrs. Lonnie Elizabeth (Benson) Thomas] [BV2520.A74T5] 38-17070
1. Southern Baptist convention. Woman's missionary union. I. Title.

USSERY, Annie (Wright) 922.673
The story of Kathleen Mallory. Nashville, Broadman Press [c1956] 199p. illus. 22cm. [BX6495.M29U8] 57-6324
1. Mallory, Kathleen Moore, 1879-1954. 2. Southern Baptist Convewtion. Woman's Missionary Union. I. Title.

Southern Bible institute, Milligan, Tenn.

TYNDALL, John William, 1877- 220
Bible course for Southern Bible institute ... By John W. Tyndall ... Charlotte, N.C., Southern printing co., c1922. 4 v. 22 1/2 cm. [BS605.T9] 23-2156
1. Southern Bible institute, Milligan, Tenn. I. Title.

Southern Methodist University—Football—History.

POUNCEY, Temple. 796.332'63'097642812
Mustang mania : Southern Methodist University / by Temple Pouncey. Huntsville, Ala : Strode Publishers, c1981. 311 p. : ill., ports. ; 24 cm. [GV958.S69P68] 19 80-53025 ISBN 0-87397-176-0 : 9.95
1. Southern Methodist University—Football—History. I. Title.

Southern States—Church history.

BAILEY, Kenneth Kyle, 1923- 284.0975
Southern white Protestantism in the twentieth century [by] Kenneth K. Bailey. [1st ed.] New York, Harper & Row [1964] x, 180 p. 22 cm. "A bibliographical essay": p. 169-172. [BR535.B3] 64-19493
1. Southern States—Church history. 2. Protestantism—Southern States. I. Title.

BAILEY, Kenneth Kyle, 1923- 280'.4'0975
Southern white Protestantism in the twentieth century [by] Kenneth K. Bailey. Gloucester, Mass., P. Smith, 1968 [c1964] ix, 180 p. 21 cm. Includes bibliographical references. [BR535.B3 1968] 68-3689
1. Southern States—Church history. 2. Protestantism—Southern States. I. Title.

Southern States—Civilization—20th century.

GAILLARD, Frye, 1946- 975'.043
Race, rock & religion : profiles from a southern journalist / Frye Gaillard. Charlotte, NC : East Woods Press, 1982. 189 p. : ports. ; 24 cm. [F216.2.G34 1982] 19 82-11325 ISBN 0-914788-59-0 : 12.95
1. Southern States—Civilization—20th century. 2. Southern States—Popular culture. 3. Southern States—Biography. I. Title. II. Title: Race, rock, and religion.

Southern States—History—1865-

BAILEY, Hugh C. 283'.0924 B
Edgar Gardner Murphy, gentle progressive, by Hugh C. Bailey. Coral Gables, Fla., University of Miami Press [1968] xii, 274 p. illus., ports. 21 cm. Bibliography: p. [247]-258. [BX5995.M85B3] 68-29705 8.50
1. Murphy, Edgar Gardner, 1869-1913. 2. Southern States—History—1865- I. Title.

Southern States—Race relations.

PETERSON, Thomas Virgil, 1943- 261.8'34'4930975
Ham and Japheth : the mythic world of whites in the antebellum South / by Thomas Virgil Peterson ; with a foreword by William A. Clebsch. Metuchen, N.J. : Scarecrow Press, 1978. xiii, 181 p. ; 23 cm. (ATLA monograph series ; no. 12) Based on the author's thesis, Stanford, 1975. Includes index. Bibliography: p. [159]-175. [BS580.H27P47] 78-15716 ISBN 0-8108-1162-6 lib. bdg. : 9.00
1. Ham (Biblical character) 2. Japheth (Biblical character) 3. Southern States—Race relations. 4. Southern States—Religious life and customs. 5. Slavery in the United States. I. Title. II. Series: American Theological Library Association. ATLA monograph series ; no. 12.

Southern States—Religion.

BROOKS, Lee Marshall. 323.352
Urban communities of the South, by Lee M. Brooks ... with the assistance of Sara E. Smith ... and Evelyn C. Brooks, for the Committee on religious education re-study of the Presbyterian church in the United States. Chapel Hill, Institute for research in social science, 1946. 2 p. l., ii, 112 numb. l. fold. map. 27 1/2 x 21 1/2 cm. [BR535.B67] 46-27417
I. Title.

CALDWELL, Erskine, 1903- 277.5
Deep South; memory and observation. New York, Weybright and Talley [1968] 257 p. 24 cm. "Part 1 of Deep South was first published in England under the title In the shadow of the steeple." [BR535.C29] 68-12867
1. Caldwell, Erskine, 1903- 2. Southern States—Religion. 3. Protestant churches—Southern States. I. Title. II. Title: In the shadow of the steeple.

DOROUGH, C. Dwight, 1912- 269'.2'0975
The Bible belt mystique, by C. Dwight Dorough. Philadelphia, Westminster Press [1974] 217 p. 22 cm. Includes bibliographical references. [BR535.D67] 74-11395 ISBN 0-664-20709-X
1. Southern States—Religion. I. Title.

Southern States—Religion—Addresses, essays, lectures.

HILL, Samuel S. 277.5
Religion and the solid South [by] Samuel S. Hill, Jr. with Edgar T. Thompson [and others] Nashville, Abingdon Press [1972] 208 p. maps. 22 cm. (An Abingdon original paperback) Includes bibliographical references. [BR535.H49] 72-175282 ISBN 0-687-36003-X
1. Southern States—Religion—Addresses, essays, lectures. I. Title.

Southern States—Social conditions.

FARISH, Hunter Dickinson, 1897-1945. 261.8'3'0975
The circuit rider dismounts; a social history of Southern Methodism, 1865-1900. New York, Da Capo Press, 1969 [c1938] 400 p. ports. 24 cm. (The American scene: comments and commentators) (A Da Capo Press reprint series.) (A Da Capo Press reprint edition.) Thesis—Harvard University, 1936. Bibliography: p. [371]-378. [BX8237.F3 1969] 77-87534
1. Methodist Episcopal Church, South—History. 2. Southern States—Social conditions. I. Title.

Southside Baptist Church, St. Petersburg, Fla.—History.

GRAVES, James F. 286'.1759'63
Three churches : one spirit / James F. Graves, Delos L. Sharpton, Lewis C. Lampley. Nashville : Broadman Press, c1978. 159 p. : ill. ; 19 cm. [BX6480.S29S663] 77-81205 ISBN 0-8054-6309-7 pbk. : 2.95
1. Southside Baptist Church, St. Petersburg, Fla.—History. 2. First Baptist Church, St. Petersburg, Fla.—History. 3. Tabernacle Baptist Church, St. Petersburg, Fla.—History. 4. Southside Tabernacle Baptist Church, St. Petersburg, Fla.—History. I. Sharpton, Delos L., joint author. II. Lampley, Lewis C., joint author. III. Title.

Southwell, Robert, 1561?-1595.

MOSELEY, Daisy Haywood. 928.2
Blessed Robert Southwell. New York, Sheed & Ward [1957] 182p. 21cm. [BX4705.S688M6] 57-10188
1. Southwell, Robert, 1561?-1595. I. Title.

Southwest, Old—Religion.

POSEY, Walter Brownlow, 1900- 277.6
Religious strife on the Southern frontier. [Baton Rouge] Louisiana State University Press, 1965. xviii, 112 p. 21 cm. (The Walter Lynwood Fleming lectures in Southern history) [BR535.P6] 65-16509
1. Southwest, Old—Religion. 2. Sects—Southwest, Old. I. Title. II. Series. III. Series: Louisiana. State University and Agricultural and Mechanical College. Walter Lynwood Fleming lectures in Southern history

Southwick Congregational Church.

SOUTHWICK Congregational Church. Church History Committee. 285'.87'4426
Southwick Congregational Church history, 1773-1973. [Southwick, Mass., 1973] 68 p. illus. 19 cm. Cover title. Bibliography: p. 66. [BX7255.S73S687 1973] 73-175211
1. Southwick Congregational Church. I. Title.

Sower, Christopher, 1693?-1758.

LONGENECKER, Steve, 1951- 974.8'02'0922 B
The Christopher Sauers : courageous printers who defended religious freedom in early America / Steve Longenecker. Elgin, Ill. : Brethren Press, 1981. p. cm. Includes index. Bibliography: p. [BX7841.L63] 19 81-10075 ISBN 0-87178-141-7 pbk. : 7.95
1. Sower, Christopher, 1693?-1758. 2. Sower, Christopher, 1721-1784. 3. Church of the Brethren—Pennsylvania—Biography. 4. Sowers family. 5. Printers—Pennsylvania—Biography. 6. Pennsylvania—Biography. I. Title.

The sower (Parable)

EGBERT, John Paul, 1849?-1927. 226.8
Some lessons from the parable of the sower, the parable of growth, and the law of the harvest, by J. P. Egbert. Buffalo, Ulbrich & Kingsley, 1886. 3 p. l., 209 p. 18 1/2 cm. On cover: Sewing, growth and reaping. [BT378.S7E3] 35-29033
1. The sower (Parable) I. Title. II. Title: Sowing, growth and reaping.

STENNETT, Samuel, 1728-1795. 226.
Discourses on the parable of the sower. By Samuel Stennett ... 1st American, from the London ed. of 1786. Bridgeton, N. J., J. Davis & J. Bright, 1823. 331 p. front. (port.) 18 cm. "Brief memoirs of the late Rev. Samuel Stennett, D. D.": p. [5]-18. [BT378.S7S8 1823] 23-14328
1. The sower (Parable) I. Title.

The sower (Parable)—Sermons.

HALL, John, 1806-1894. 226.8
The sower and the seed, by John Hall, D.D. Philadelphia, Presbyterian board of

publication [1856] 127 p. 14 1/2 cm. [BT378.S7H3] 35-30439
1. The sower (Parable)—Sermons. 2. Presbyterian church—Sermons. I. Presbyterian church in the U.S.A. Board of publication. II. Title.

Sozialdemokratische Partei Deutschlands.

NIEWYK, Donald L., 1940- 329.9'43
Socialist, anti-Semite, and Jew; German social democracy confronts the problem of anti-Semitism, 1918-1933 [by] Donald L. Niewyk. Baton Rouge, Louisiana State University Press [1971] x, 254 p. 23 cm. Bibliography: p. 223-242. [JN3970.S6N5] 79-137123 ISBN 0-8071-0531-7 8.95
1. Sozialdemokratische Partei Deutschlands. 2. Antisemitism—Germany. I. Title.

Space and time.

EFROS, Israel Isaac, 1890-
... The problem of space in Jeuish mediaeval philosophy, by Israel Isaac Efros ... New York, Columbia university press, 1917. 5 p. l., 125 p. 1 l. diagrs. 24 1/2 cm. (Columbia university oriental studies. vol. xi) Thesis (PH. D.)--Columbia university, 1916. Vita. [B757.58E3] 19-4883
1. Space and time. 2. Philosophy, Jewish. 3. Philosophy, Medieval. I. Title.

EFROS, Israel Isaac, 1890-
... The problem of space in Jewish mediaeval philosophy, by Israel Isaac Efron ... New York, Columbia university press, 1917. 5 p. l., 125 p. diagrs. 24 1/2 cm. (Columbia university Oriental studies, vol. xi) Issued also as the author's thesis, Columbia university. [B757.S8E32] 19-13415
1. Space and time. 2. Philosophy, Jewish. 3. Philosophy, Medieval. I. Title. II. Title: Space in Jewish mediaeval philosophy.

LIDDELL, Anna Forbes.
Alexander's Space, time and deity, a critical consideration [by] Anna Forbes Liddell ... Chapel Hill, N. C., The Department of philosophy [1925?] 70 p. 24 cm. (University of North Carolina studies in philosophy, no. 2) [BD632.A42] 26-27059
1. Alexander, Samuel, 1859- Space, time, and deity. 2. Space and time. 3. God. I. Title.

OCKHAM, William, d.ca.1849, supposed author.
... The Tractatus de successivis, attributed to William Ockham, edited with a study on the life and works of Ockham by Philotheus Boehmer, O.F.M. St. Bonaventure, N..Y., The Franciscan institute, St. Bonaventure college, 1944. xi, p., 1 l., 122 p. 22 1/2 cm. (Franciscan institute publications, no. 1) The text is based on four known manuscripts of the work. cf. p. 27. "A bibliography on Ockham": p. 16-23. [BD632.O3] 44-6639
1. Space and time. 2. Motion. I. Bohner, Philotheus, pater, ed. II. Title.

PENDLETON, Charles Rittenhouse. 289.4
Space and extense in the spiritual world. Bryn Althyn, Pa., 1962. 66 p. 23 cm. [BX8711.P4] 63-36811
1. Swedenborg, Emanuel, 1688-1772. 2. Space and time. I. Title.

ROBB, Alfred Arthur, 1873-
A theory of time and space, by Alfred A. Robb ... Cambridge, University press, 1914. vi, 373 p. diagrs. 25 cm. A 15
1. Space and time. 2. Relativity (Physics) I. Title.

WALTER, Johnston Estep, 1843-
Nature and cognition of space and time, by Rev. Johnston Estep Walter ... West Newton, Pa., Johnston and Penney [c1914] 186 p. 20 cm. $1.35 [BD632.W3] 14-2362
1. Space and time. I. Title.

Space theology.

DOLPHIN, Lambert. 215'.2
Lord of time and space. Westchester, Ill., Good News Publishers [1974] 79 p. 18 cm. (One evening book) Includes bibliographical references. [BL254.D64] 73-92178 0.95 (pbk.)
1. Space theology. 2. Time (Theology) 3. Religion and science—1946- I. Title.

STEVENS, Clifford J. 215
Astrotheology for the cosmic adventure [by] Clifford J. Stevens. Techny, Ill., Divine Word Publications [1969] 87 p. illus. 18 cm. Includes bibliographical references. [BL254.S7] 75-94093 1.95
1. Space theology. I. Title.

TORRANCE, Thomas Forsyth, 1913- 232.9'7
Space, time, and resurrection / by Thomas F. Torrance. Grand Rapids : Eerdmans, [1977] p. cm. Includes bibliographical references and index. [BT481.T67] 76-19069 ISBN 0-8028-3488-4 pbk. : 4.95
1. Jesus Christ—Resurrection. 2. Jesus Christ—Ascension. 3. Space theology. I. Title.

TORRANCE, Thomas Forsyth, 1913- 232.5
Space, time and resurrection / [by] Thomas F. Torrance. Edinburgh : Handsel Press, 1976. xiii, 196 p. ; 23 cm. Includes bibliographical references and index. [BT481.T67 1976b] 77-367706 ISBN 0-905312-007-3 : £5.00
1. Jesus Christ—Resurrection. 2. Jesus Christ—Ascension. 3. Space theology. I. Title.

Spaeth, Adolph i.e. Phillip Friedrich Adolph Theodor, 1839-1910.

SPAETH, Harriett Reynolds (Krauth) "Mrs. Adolph Spaeth." 922.
Life of Adolph Spaeth, D.D., LL. D. ... told in his own reminiscences, his letters and the recollections of his family and friends, ed. by his wife. Philadelphia, General council publication house, 1916. viii p., 2 l., 439 p. front., 1 illus. (music) plates, ports. 20 1/2 cm. $2.00. "Dr. Spaeth's publications": p. 411-424. [BX8080.S7S7] 17-24305
1. Spaeth, Adolph i.e. Phillip Friedrich Adolph Theodor, 1839-1910. I. Title.

Spain—Biography.

PEERS, Edgar Allison. 920.046
St. John of the Cross, and other lectures and addresses, 1920-1945. Freeport, N.Y., Books for Libraries Press [1970] 231 p. 23 cm. (Biography index reprint series) Reprint of the 1946 ed. Contents.Contents.—St. John of the Cross ... the Rede lecture for 1932.—Some centenary lectures: Ramon Lull: doctor illuminate. Columbus, America, and the future. Juan Luis Vives and England. Lope de Vega: two portraits. A forgotten mystic: Fra Josep of Montserrat.—Aspects of the Catalan Renaissance: Beginnings of the Renaissance: Aribau, Cabanyes. Rubio i Ors and the Jocs Florals. Jacinto Verdaguer. Joan Maragall.—Modern Spain: Angel Ganivet. The real Blasco Ibanez. Francesc Macia. Antonio Machado. Alfonso XIII and Spain's future. Includes bibliographical references. [DP58.P35 1970] 70-136650 ISBN 0-8369-8045-X
1. Juan de la Cruz, Saint, 1542-1591. 2. Spain—Biography. 3. Spanish literature—History and criticism. I. Title.

PULGAR, Fernando del, 1436?-1492. 946'.0092
Claros varones de Castilla [by] Fernando del Pulgar; a critical edition, with introduction and notes by Robert Brian Tate. Oxford, Clarendon Press, 1971. lxviii, 118 p. 23 cm. Text in Spanish; introd. and notes in English. Bibliography: p. [108]-114. [DP58.P8 1971] 248'.22'0924 78-575284 ISBN 0-19-815702-9 £2.90
1. Spain—Biography. I. Tate, Robert Brian, ed. II. Title.

Spain—Church history.

LEA, Henry Charles, 1825-1900. 274.6
Chapters from the religions history of Spain connected with the Inquisition. New York, Burt Franklin [1967] 522 p. 23 cm. (Burt Franklin research & source work series, 245) Selected essays [in] history and social science, 31. Title on spine: Religious history of Spain. Reprint of the 1890 ed. English with Spanish appendix. Bibliographical footnotes. [BX1735.L4] 68-56760
1. Spain—Church history. 2. Inquisition. Spain—Hist. 3. Liberty of the press. I. Title. II. Title: Religious history of Spain.
Contents Ommitted

LEA, Henry Charles, 1825-1900. 274.6
Chapters from the religious history of Spain connected with the Inquisition. New York, Burt Franklin [1967] 522 p. 23 cm. (Burt Franklin research & source work series, 245) (Selected essays [in] history and social science, 31.) Title on spine: Religious history of Spain. Reprint of the 1890 ed. English with Spanish appendix. Contents.Contents.—Censorship of the press.—Mystics and illuminati.—Endemoniadas.—El Santo Nino de la Guardia.—Brianda de Bardaxi.—Appendix of documents. Bibliographical footnotes. [BX1735.L4 1967] 68-56760
1. Inquisition. Spain—History. 2. Spain—Church history. 3. Liberty of the press. I. Title. II. Title: Religious history of Spain.

LEA, Henry Charles, 1825-1909. 272.
Chapters from the religious history of Spain connected with the Inquisition ... By Henry Charles Lea, LL. D. Philadelphia, Lea brothers & co., 1890. 1 p. l., [v]-xii p., 1 l., [15]-522 p. 21 cm. Bibliographical foot-notes. [BX1735.L4] 12-36165
1. Spain—Church history. 2. Inquisition. Spain—Hist. 3. Liberty of the press. I. Title.
Contents omitted.

LINEHAN, Peter. 282.46
The Spanish church and the Papacy in the thirteenth century. Cambridge [Eng.] University Press, 1971. xvii, 389 p. 23 cm. (Cambridge studies in medieval life and thought, third series, no. 4) Bibliography: p. 335-365. [BR1024.L55] 75-154505 ISBN 0-521-08039-8
1. Spain—Church history. 2. Papacy—History. I. Title. II. Series.

Spain—Court and courtiers.

COLLIER, William Miller, 1867-
At the court of His Catholic Majesty, by William Miller Collier ... with illustrations from photographs. Chicago, A. C. McClurg & co., 1912. xvi, 330 p. front., plates, ports. 22 cm. [DP240.C6] 12-10652
1. Alfonso xiii, king of Spain, 1886-1941. 2. Victoria Eugenia, queen consort of Alfonso xiii, king of Spain, 1887- 3. Spain—Court and courtiers. I. Title.

Spain—Description and travel

BORROW, George Henry, 1803-1881.
The Bible in Spain; or, The journeys, adventures, and imprisonments of an Englishman in an attempt to circulate the Scriptures in the peninsula, by George Borrow; with the notes and glossary of Ulick Ralph Burk, M.A. New York, G.P. Putnam's sons; [etc., etc.] 1908. xxv, 838 p. front., plates., fold. map, 20 1/2 cm. [PR415.F05 vol. 1] 12-16161
1. Spain—Descr. & trav. I. Burke, Ulick Ralph, 1845-1895. II. Title.

Spain-Description and travel-Views.

MATT, Leonard von. 922.246
St. Ignatius of Loyola: a pictorial biography. by Leonard von Matt and Hugo Rahner. Translated from the German by John Murray. Chicago, H. Regnery Co. [1956] vi, 106p. 226plates, maps. 25cm. [BX4700.L7M42] 56-14083
1. Loyola. Ignacio de. Saint 1491-1566. 2. Spain—Deser. & trav.—Views. 3. Italy—Descr. & trav.— Views. I. Rahner, Hugo, 1900- joint author. II. Title.

Spain-History-20th century

*PRESTON, Paul. ed. 946.082
Spain in crisis : the evolution and decline of the Franco regime / Editor, Paul Preston. New York : Barnes & Noble Books, 1976. 341p. ; 23 cm. Includes bibliographical references and index. [BP257] 75-41577 ISBN 0-06-495711-X : 15.00.
1. Franco Bahamonde, Francisco, 1892-1975. 2. Spain-History-20th century 3. Spain-politics and government. I. Title.

Spain—Religious life and customs.

CHRISTIAN, William A., 1944- 282'.46
Local religion in sixteenth-century Spain / William A. Christian, Jr. Princeton, N.J. : Princeton University Press, c1981. viii, 283 p. : ill. ; 23 cm. Includes bibliographical references and index. [BX1584.C49] 19 80-7513 ISBN 0-691-05306-5 : 17.50
1. Catholic Church in Spain—History. 2. Spain—Religious life and customs. I. Title.

SPAIN. Constitution. 264
Constitution of the Spanish monarchy. Promulgated at Cadiz on the 19th of March, 1812. Philadelphia, Printed by G. Palmer. 1814. 1 p. l., vii, [3]-58 p. 21 cm. [JN8161.A5 1814] [AC901.M5 vol. 857] [AC901.M5 vol. 959.] 264 9-34031
I. Title.

Spalding, Arthur Whitefield, 1877-1954.

MCFADDEN, Elizabeth Spalding. 286'.73 B
A fire in my bones : a biography of Arthur Whitefield Spalding / by Elisabeth Spalding McFadden and Ronald W. Spalding ; [cover art by Fred Irvin]. Mountain View, Calif. : Pacific Press Pub. Association, c1979. 144 p. : port. ; 22 cm. Includes bibliographical references. [BX6193.S67M32] 78-71387 pbk. : 3.95
1. Spalding, Arthur Whitefield, 1877-1954. 2. Seventh-Day Adventists—United States—Biography. I. Spalding, Ronald W., joint author. II. Title.

Spalding, Catherine, 1790-1850.

SPILLANE, James Maria. 271'.91'0924
Kentucky spring. St. Meinrad, Ind., Abbey Press [1968] 293 p. 18 cm. Bibliography: p. 291-293. [BX4705.S715S65] 68-29322
1. Spalding, Catherine, 1790-1850. 2. Sisters of Charity of Nazareth, Nazareth, Ky. I. Title.

Spalding, Franklin Spencer, bp., 1865-1914.

MELISH, John Howard, 1875- 922.
Franklin Spencer Spalding, man and bishop, by John Howard Melish. New York, The Macmillan company, 1917. vii, 297 p. front. (port.) 23 cm. [BX5995.S7M5] 17-14393
1. Spalding, Franklin Spencer, bp., 1865-1914. I. Title.

Spalding, John, d. 1795.

SPALDING, John, d.1795. 922.
Some account of the convincement, and religious progress, of John Spalding, late of Reading. With his Reasons for leaving the national established mode of worship. New-York, Printed and sold by Samuel Wood, no. 362, Pearl-street, 1808. 132 p. 14 1/2 cm. [BX7795.S7A3] [BX7795.S] 922. A32
1. Spalding, John, d. 1795. 2. Friends, Society of. I. Title.

Spalding, John Lancaster, Abp., 1840-1916.

COSGROVE, John J. 922.273
Most Reverend John Lancaster Spalding, first bishop of Peoria. Mendota, Ill., Wayside Press, Wayside Publishing Division, 1501W. Washington Rd. c.1960. 160p. illus. 27cm. 60-51068 4.50
1. Spalding, John Lancaster, Abp., 1840-1916. I. Title.

ELLIS, John Tracy, 1905- 922.273
John Lancaster Spalding, first bishop of Peoria, American educator. Milwaukee, Bruce [1962, c.1961] 106p. illus. 19cm. (Gabriel Richard lect.) 62-12433 2.75

1. Spalding, John Lancaster, Abp., 1840-1916. I. Title.

SWEENEY, David Francis 282.0924
The life of John Lancaster Spalding, First Bishop of Peoria, 1840-1916. [New York] Herder & Herder [1966, c.1965] 384p. port. 22cm. (Makers of Amer. Catholicism, v.1) Bibl. [BX4705.S7S39] 65-13480 7.50
1. Spalding, John Lancaster, Abp., 1840-1916. I. Title.

Spalding, Martin John, Abp., 1810-1872.

SPALDING, John Lancaster, abp., 1840-1916. 922.
The life of the Most Rev. M. J. Spalding, D.D., archbishop of Baltimore, By J. L. Spalding... New York, The Catholic publication society; Baltimore, J. Murphy & co., 1873. vi, [7]-468 p. front. (port.) 23 1/2 cm. [BX4705.S73S6] 12-38886
1. Spalding, Martin John, abp., 1810-1872. I. Title.

SPALDING, Martin John, abp., 1810-1872. 204
Miscellanea; comprising reviews, lectures, and essays, on historical, theological, and miscellaneous subjects. By M. J. Spalding... Louisville, Ky., Webb, Gill & Levering, 1855. 15, [xvi]-lxi p., 1 l., 17-639 p. 24 cm. [BX890.S63] 22-10340
I. Title.

SPALDING, Thomas W. 282'.092'4 B
Martin John Spalding: American churchman [by] Thomas W. Spalding. Washington, Catholic University of America Press [1973] xi, 373 p. 23 cm. Bibliography: p. 353-364. [BX4705.S73S64] 74-171040 12.00
1. Spalding, Martin John, Abp., 1810-1872.

Spanish America.

TRULL, George Harvey. 278
Talks on Latin America, by George H. Trull ... New York city, Sunday school department, Board of foreign missions of the Presbyterian church in the U.S.A. [c1916] 110 p. fold. map. 18 1/2 cm. $0.25 "Bibliography on Latin America": p. 109-110. [BV2830.T8] 16-22843
1. Spanish America. 2. Missions—Spanish America. 3. Presbyterian church in the U.S.A.—Missions. I. Title.

Spanish America—Religion.

RYCROFT, William Stanley. 278
Religion and faith in Latin America. With a foreword by Alberto Rembao. Philadelphia, Westminster Press [1958] 208p. 21cm. Includes bibliography. [BR600.R82] 58-5838
1. Spanish America—Religion. 2. Protestant churches—Spanish America. I. Title.

Spanish Americans in the United States

CLARK, Elmer Talmage, 1886- 277.2
Latin America, U.S.A., by Elmer T. Clark ... and Harry C. Spencer ... New York, Joint division of education and cultivation, Board of missions and church extension, the Methodist church [1942] 1 p. l., 5-62 p. 19 cm. [BV2788.S7C55] [226.7] 42-22745
1. Spanish Americans in the U.S. 2. Missions—U.S. I. Spencer, Harry Chadwick, 1905- joint author. II. Methodist church (United States) Board of missions and church extension. Joint division of education and cultivation. III. Title.
Contents omitted.

Spanish literature—Bibliography.

BOEHMER, Eduard, 1827-1906. 016.2746
Bibliotheca Wiffeniana. Spanish reformers of two centuries from 1520; their lives and writings, according to the late Benjamin B. Wiffen's plan and with the use of his materials. New York, B. Franklin [1971?] 3 v. 24 cm. (Burt Franklin bibliographical and reference series no. 32) On spine: Spanish reformers of two centuries. Reprint of the 1874-1904 ed. [Z7830.B672] 72-184809
1. Bible—Versions, Spanish. 2. Spanish literature—Bibliography. 3. Reformation—Spain—Bibliography. I. Wiffen, Benjamin Barron, 1794-1867. II. Title. III. Title: Spanish reformers of two centuries.

Spanish literature—Translation into English—Bibliography

ADAMS, Agatha Boyd. 371.
Contemporary Spanish literature in English translation, by Agatha Boyd Adams, and Nicholson B. Adams; an outline for individual and group study. Chapel Hill, The University of North Carolina press, 1929. 50 p. 23 cm. (North Carolina. University. University extension division) University of North Carolina extension bulletin, vol. VIII no. 9) Bibliography: p. [43]-45. [LC6301.N43] [Z2694.T7A2] 016. 29-16043
1. Spanish literature—Translation into English—Bibl. 2. English literature—Translations from Spanish—Bibl. 3. Spanish literature—20th cent.—Bibl. 4. Spain—Bibl. I. Adams, Nicholson, Barney, 1895- joint author. II. Title.

Spanish missions of California.

CRUMP, Spencer. 266'.2'794
California's Spanish missions : their yesterdays and todays / by Spencer Crump ; with ill. from historical archives, supplemented by modern photos. 1st ed. Corona del Mar, Calif. : Trans-Anglo Books, [1975] 95 p. : ill. ; 29 cm. Includes index. Bibliography: p. 8-9. [F864.C93] 73-88320 ISBN 0-87046-028-5 : 6.95
1. Spanish missions of California. 2. Indians of North America—California—Missions. 3. California—History—To 1846. I. Title.

CRUMP, Spencer 266.2794
California's Spanish missions yesterday and today. [Los Angeles, Trans-Anglc, c.1964] 64p. illus. (pt. col.) maps. 21cm. (Great Amer. hist. ser. Tab. bk.) Cover title. 64-23504 1.00 pap.,
1. Spanish missions of California. I. Title.

FORBES, Harrie Rebecca Piper (Smith) "Mrs. A. S. C. Forbes."
California missions and landmarks and how to get there; a practical guide, together with a historical sketch of the missions and landmarks, the Pious Fund and El camino real; with methods of transportation and accommodations, fares, rates and distances from San Francisco and Los Angeles to each point issued by Mrs. Armitage S. C. Forbes ... Los Angeles Official guide, 1903. 104 p. illus. incl. ports., maps) 17 1/2 cm. Advertising matter: p. 89-104. [F870.M6F6] 3-13905
1. Spanish missions of California. I. Title.

JAMES, George Wharton, 1858-1923. 271'.0'3109794
The old Franciscan missions of California. Boston, Milford House [1973] xvi, 287 p. illus. 22 cm. A condensation of the author's In and out of the old missions of California. Reprint of the 1913 ed. published by Little, Brown, Boston. [F864.J23 1973] 73-4860 ISBN 0-87821-116-0 25.00 (lib. bdg.)
1. Spanish missions of California. 2. Franciscans in California. I. Title.

JAMES, George Wharton, 1858-1923. 266'.2'794
The old Franciscan missions of California / by George Wharton James. Boston : Longwood Press, 1977. xvi, 287 p., [31] leaves of plates : ill. ; 22 cm. Reprint of the 1913 ed. published by Little, Brown, Boston. [F864.J23 1977] 77-91532 ISBN 0-89341-321-6 lib.bdg. : 25.00
1. Franciscans—California. 2. Spanish missions of California. I. Title.

KOCHER, Paul H. 266'.2'794
California's old missions : the story of the founding of the 21 Franciscan missions in Spanish Alta California, 1769-1823 / by Paul H. Kocher. Chicago : Franciscan Herald Press, c1976. xi, 177 p. : ill. ; 21 cm. At head of title: A Bicentennial book. Includes index. Bibliography: p. 169-171. [F864.K62] 76-2699 ISBN 0-8199-0601-8 : 6.95
1. Franciscans—Missions. 2. Spanish missions of California. 3. Franciscans in California. 4. Missions—California. 5. California—History—To 1846. I. Title.

POWERS, Laura Bride.
Historic tales of the old missions for boys and girls ... [By] Laura Bridge Powers ... San Francisco, W. N. Brunt [c1902] 4 p. l., [11]-155 p. incl. front., plates. 19 cm. A 20
1. Spanish missions of California. I. Title.

SULLIVAN, Ella C., 1864- 271.309794
The story of the old Spanish missions of the Southwest, by Ella C. Sullivan ... and Alfred E. Logie ... Chicago, New York, Lyons and Carnahan [c1939] 3 p. l., 213, [3] p. front., illus. 19 1/2 cm. [F870.M6S95 1939] 39-32989
1. Spanish missions of California. 2. Franciscans in California. 3. Spanish missions of the U.S. I. Logie, Alfred Ernest, 1871- joint author. II. Title. III. Title: Spanish missions of the southwest.

SULLIVAN, Ella C., 1864-
The story of the old Spanish missions of the Southwest, by Ella C. Sullivan ... and Alfred E. Logie ... Chicago, New York, Lyons and Carnahan [c1927] v, 217 p. front., illus. 19 1/2 cm. [E870.M6S95] 28-4341
1. Spanish missions of California. 2. Franciscans in California. 3. Spanish missions of the U.S. I. Logie, Alfred Ernest, 1871- joint author. II. Title. III. Title: Spanish missions of the Southwest.

TRUESDELL, Amelia Woodward, Mrs. 1839-1912.
A California pilgrimage. By one of the pilgrims, Amelia Woodward Truesdell. 2d ed. San Francisco, S. Carson & co., 1884. 125 p. front. 19 x 16 cm. In verse. A 22
1. Spanish missions of California. I. Title.

Spanish missions of New Mexico.

PARSONS, Francis B. 266'.2'79
Early 17th century missions of the Southwest : with historical introduction / by Francis B. Parsons; book design and drawings by Harold A. Wolfinbarger, Jr. Tucson, Ariz. : D. S. King, c1975. viii, 111 p. : ill. ; 23 cm. Includes index. Bibliography: p. 106-107. [F799.P35] 74-32368 ISBN 0-912762-21-7. ISBN 0-912762-20-9 pbk.
1. Spanish missions of New Mexico. 2. Spanish missions of Arizona. 3. Franciscans—Missions. 4. New Mexico—History—To 1848. 5. Arizona—History—To 1912. I. Title.

Spanish missions of Texas.

BROOKS, Charles Mattoon, jr. 976.4
Texas missions; their romance and architecture [by] Charles Mattoon Brooks, jr. Dallas, Tex., Dealey and Lowe, 1936. 8 p. l., 3-154 p., 1 l., [9] p. plates, plans. 25 1/2cm. Maps on lining-papers. Bibliography: p. 153-154. [F395.M6B76] [NA5230.T4B7] 37-8125
1. Spanish missions of Texas. I. Title.

Sparks, Jared, 1789-1866.

CHANNING, William Ellery, 1780-1842. 252.
Unitarian Christianity, a discourse on some of the distinguishing opinions of Unitarians, delivered at Baltimore, May 5, 1819 [by] William Ellery Channing. Centenary ed. Boston. Mass., American Unitarian association [1919] 1 p. l., 5-81 p. 19 cm. Introduction signed: E. M. W. [BX9843.C5S55 1919] 21-17181
1. Sparks, Jared, 1789-1866. 2. Unitarianism. I. W., E. M., ed. II. E. M. W., ed. III. Title.

Sparks, Jared, 1789-1866. Letters on the ministry ritual and doctrines of the Protestant Episcopal church.

REVIEW of the Rev. Jared Sparks' letters on the Protestant Episcopal church, in reply to the Rev. Dr. Wyatt's sermon ... Baltimore: Published by N. G. Maxwell, no. 148 Market street. 1820. John D. Toy, printer. 60 p. 23 1/2 cm. "From the 'Christian disciple', published at Boston." [BX5936.R4] 2-20756 262
1. Sparks, Jared, 1789-1866. Letters on the ministry ritual and doctrines of the Protestant Episcopal church.

Sparrow, William, 1801-1874.

WALKER, Cornelius, 1819-1907. 922.373
The life and correspondence of Rev. William Sparrow ... by Rev. Cornelius Walker ... Philadelphia, J. Hammond, 1876. viii, 17-433 p. front. (port.) 24 cm. [BX5995.S73W3] 31-9299
1. Sparrow, William, 1801-1874. I. Title.

Spaugh, Herbert, 1896-

HARDING, Barbara. 284'.6'0924 B
The boy, the man, and the Bishop; a biography of the Everyday Counselor, Bishop Herbert Spaugh. [Charlotte, N.C., Barnhardt Brothers, 1970] 178 p. illus., ports. 22 cm. [BX8593.S63H3] 79-20294
1. Spaugh, Herbert, 1896- I. Title.

Spaulding, Solomon, 1761-1816.

DICKINSON, Ellen E. Mrs. 289.
New light on Mormonism, by Mrs. Ellen E. Dickinson, with introduction by Thurlow Weed. New York, Funk & Wagnalls, 1885. 4 p., 2 l., [11]-272 p. 20 cm. Includes a discussion of the relationship of the "Book of Mormon" to Spaulding's Manuscript found". [BX8645.D5] 11-21984
1. Spaulding, Solomon, 1761-1816. 2. Mormons and Mormonism—Doctrinal and controversial works. 3. Book of Mormon. I. Title.

[SCHROEDER, Theodore Albert] 1864- 289.
The origin of the Book of Mormon, re-examined in its relation to Spaulding's "Manuscript found" ... [Salt Lake City, Utah, 1901] cover-title, 56 p. 22 cm. [BX8627.S72O7] 1-23599
1. Spaulding, Solomon, 1761-1816. 2. Book of Mormon. I. Title.

Species, Origin of.

CLARK, Harold Willard, 1891- 213
Genes and Genesis, by Harold W. Clark... Mountain View, Calif., Portland, Or.[etc.] Pacific press publishing assn. [1940] 3 p. l., 5-155 p. 20 cm. (Ministerial reading course selection for 1941, Ministerial association of Seventh-day Adventists) [BS51.C55] 41-517
1. Species, Origin of. 2. Bible and science. 3. Genetics. 4. Evolution. 5. Creation. I. Title.

The Speer Family.

BECKER, Paula. 783.7
Let the song go on; fifty years of gospel singing with the Speer family. Nashville, Tenn., Impact Books [1971] 175 p. ports. 22 cm. [ML421.S67B4] 75-159560 3.95
1. The Speer Family. 2. Gospel music—United States—History and criticism. I. Title.

Speer, Kathleen.

SPEER, Alfred W. 133.9'1'0924 B
There is no death / by Alfred W. Speer. London ; New York : Regency Press, 1977. 119 p., [2] p. of plates : 2 ill., port. ; 23 cm. Cover title: After life's sunset, there is no death. [BF1311.F8S64] 78-317493 6.00
1. Speer, Kathleen. 2. Future life. 3. Spiritualism. I. Title. II. Title: After life's sunset, there is no death.

Speer, Robert Elliott, 1867-1947.

GUILD, Roy Bergen, 1872- ed. 230
... The church-after the war--what? [By] Robert E. Speer, Cary B. Wilmer [and]

George W. Coleman, introduction by Fred B. Smith, Roy B. Guild, editor. New York, Association press, 1919. v. 89 p. 20 cm. At head of title: Published for the Commission on interchurch federations of the Federal council of the churches of Christ in America. Contents.--The work of the church today, by R. E. Speer--The church of the future, by C. B. Wilmer.--Moving toward the light, by G. W. Coleman.- Declarations of the Atlantic City conference. [BV600.G8] 19-8016
1. Speer, Robert Elliott, 1867- 2. Wilmer, Cary Breckinridge, 1859- 3. Coleman, George William, 1867- 4. Federal council of churches of Christ im America. Commission on inter-church federation. I. Title.

SPEER, Robert Elliott, 1867- 230
The new opportunity of the church, by Robert E. Speer. New York, The Macmillan company, 1919. 4 p. l., 111 p. 16 1/2 cm. [BV600.S6] 19-7660
I. Title.

SPEER, Robert Elliott, 1867- 220
Seeking the mind of Christ, by Robert E. Speer. New York, Chicago [etc.] Fleming H. Revell company [c1926] 187 p. 19 1/2 cm. [BR125.S745] 26-21878
I. Title.

SPEER, Robert Elliott, 1867- 922
... Some great leaders in the world movement, by Robert E. Speer. New York, Chicago [etc.] Fleming H. Revell company [c1911] 295 p. 20 cm. (The Cole lectures for 1911 delivered before Vanderbilt university) $1.25 [BR1703.S7] 11-28679
I. Title.
Contents omitted.

SPEER, Robert Elliott, 1867- 230.4
Some living issues, by Robert E. Speer. New York, Chicago [etc.] Fleming H. Revell company [c1930] 280 p. 20 1/2 cm. [BR125.S746] 30-13739
I. Title.

WHEELER, William Reginald, 1889- 922.573
A man sent from God; a biography of Robert E. Speer. Introd. by John A. Mackay. [Westwood, N. J., Revell [1956] 333p. illus. 22cm. [BX9225.S643W45] 56-5242
1. Speer, Robert Elliott, 1867-1947. I. Title.

Spelling reform—Texts.

BIBLE. N. T. Mark. English. 1882. Authorized. 421.4
The Gospel by Mark, according to the Authorized version in phonetic spelling, by C. W. K. For a first reading book ... New York, Funk & Wagnalls, 1882. 1 p. l., 118, [9] p. 15 x 12 cm. On cover: Mark's gospel phonetic. "Alfabet for the lerner" laid in. [PE1152.B67 Mark 1882] [226.3] 40-18551
1. Spelling reform—Texts. I. Knudsen, Carl W., 1818-1894, ed. II. Bible. English. N. T. Mark. 1882. Authorized. III. Title.

Spellman, Anne Corey, 1877-

WESTERN, Helen, 1908- 922
Fifty years of service, a challenge to womanhood; an appreciation of Anne C. Spellman, missionary, president of the Missionary workers, inc., by Helen Western ... [Detroit, Embassy press, 1946] 128 p. front., plates (incl. music) ports. 20 cm. "First printing." [BV2657.S7W4] 46-18293
1. Spellman, Anne Corey, 1877- I. Title.

Spellman, Francis Joseph, Cardinal, 1889-1967.

GANNON, Robert Ignatius, 1893-
The Cardinal Spellman story. New York, Pocket Books [1963] x, 579 p. 18 cm. (Permabook edition. M7510) Bibliographical references included in "Notes" (p. 547-556) 64-24854
1. Spellman, Francis Joseph, Cardinal, 1889- I. Title. II. Series.

GANNON, Robert Ignatius, 1893- 922.273
The Cardinal Spellman story. [1st ed.] Garden City, N. Y., Doubleday, 1962. 477 p. illus. 24 cm. Includes bibliography. [BX4705.S74G3] 62-8395
1. Spellman, Francis Joseph, Cardinal, 1889-

IN memoriam: 262'.135'0924
Francis Cardinal Spellman, Archbishop of New York. [New York] Society of the Friendly Sons of Saint Patrick in the City of New York, 1968. 59 p. ports. (part col.) 25 cm. [BX4705.S74I5] 70-268394
1. Spellman, Francis Joseph, Cardinal, 1889-1967. I. Society of the Friendly Sons of St. Patrick in the City of New York.

STEIBEL, Warren. 262.1350924
Cardinal Spellman, the man. With an introd. by Francis Cardinal Spellman. [1st ed.] New York, Appleton-Century [1966] 121 p. illus., ports. 27 cm. Adapted from the ABC-Television documentary of Cardinal Spellman: the man. [BX4705.S74S7] 66-27903
1. Spellman, Francis Joseph, Cardinal, 1889- I. American Broadcasting Company. II. Title.

Spence, William H., 1875-1936.

SPENCE, Hartzell, 1908- 922.773
One foot in heaven, the life of a practical person, by Hartzell Spence; illustrated by Donald McKay. New York, London, Whittlesey house, McGraw-Hill book company, inc. [c1940] 4 p. l., 3-298 p. illus., port. 22 cm. Illustrated t.-p. [BX8495.S72S7] 40-33661
1. Spence, William H., 1875-1936. I. McKay, Donald, illus. II. Title.

Spencer, Herbert, 1820-1903.

[DODGE, Mary Abigail] 1833-1896.
The insuppressible book. A controversy between Herbert Spencer and Frederic Harrison. From the "Nineteenth century" and "Pall Mall gazette", with comments by Gail Hamilton [pseud.] Boston, S. E. Cassino and company, 1885. 3 p. l., 278 p. 19 cm. A 28
I. Title.
Contents omitted.

[DODGE, Mary Abigail] 1833-1896.
The insuppressible book. A controversy between Herbert Spencer and Frederic Harrison. From the "Nineteenth century" and "Pall Mall gazette", with comments by Gail Hamilton [pseud.] Boston, S. E. Cassino and company, 1885. 3 p. l., 278 p. 19 cm. A 28
I. Title.
Contents omitted.

GREENE, William Batchelder, 1819-1878. 133
The blazing star; with an appendix treating of the Jewish kabbala. Also, a tract on the philosophy of Mr. Herbert Spencer, and one on New-England transcendentalism. By William B. Greene. Boston, A. Williams and co., 1872. 180 p. illus. 20 cm. [BF1611.G74] 11-14365
1. Spencer, Herbert, 1820-1903. 2. Cabala. 3. Transcendentalism. I. Title.

LUCAS, George Joseph, 1852-
... Agnosticism and religion; being an examination of Spencer's religion of the unknowable preceded by a history of agnosticism ... by Rev. George J. Lucas ... Baltimore, J. Murphy & co., 1895. 153 p. 25 cm. Thesis (D. THEOL.)--Catholic university of America. [B1658.U5L8] 17-2302
1. Spencer, Herbert, 1820-1903. 2. Agnosticism. I. Title.

LUCAS, George Joseph, 1852-
... Agnosticism and religion: being an examination of Spencer's religion of The unknowable, preceded by a history of agnosticism ... by Rev. George J. Lucas ... Baltimore, J. Murphy & co., 1895. 136, [1] p. 25 cm. Thesis (D. TH.)--Catholic university of America. [B1658.U5L79] 20-8482
1. Spencer, Herbert, 1820-1903. 2. Agnosticism. I. Title.

SPENCER, Herbert, 1820-1903.
First principles of a new system of philosophy. By Herbert Spencer ... New York, D. Appleton and company, 1865. vii, 508 p. 19 cm. [B1658.F4 1865] 15-24188
I. Title.

SPENCER, Herbert, 1820-1903.
First principles of a new system of philosophy. By Herbert Spencer ... New York, D. Appleton and company, 1865. vii, 508 p. 19 cm. [B1658.F4 1865] 15-24188
I. Title.

SPENCER, Herbert, 1820-1903.
Illustrations of universal progress; a series of discussions. By Herbert Spencer ... With a notice of Spencer's "New system of philosophy." New York, D. Appleton and company, 1880. 1 p. ll, [v]-xxiv p., 1 l., 439 p. 20 cm. 8-13234
I. Title.
Contents omitted.

Spencer, Ivan, 1888-1970.

MELOON, Marion. 289.9 B
Ivan Spencer, willow in the wind / by Marion Meloon. Plainfield, N.J. : Logos International, c1974. xv, 234 p., [4] leaves of plates : ill. ; 21 cm. Errata slip inserted. [BX8764.Z8S75] 74-82565 ISBN 0-88270-091-X : 5.95 ISBN 0-88270-092-8 pbk. : 2.95.
1. Spencer, Ivan, 1888-1970. 2. Elim Bible Institute.

Spencer, Thomas, 1791-1811.

RAFFLES,s Thomas, 1788-1863. 922.542
Memoirs of the life and ministry of the late Rev. Thomas Spencer, of Liverpool: with an appendix, containing a selection from his papers, &c. and additional papers. Together with a poem on his death, by James Montgomery. By Thomas Raffles ... To which is added Reflections on mortality, by the Rev. Charles Buck. Hartford: Published by Everard Peck. Sheldon & Goodwin. Printers, 1815. iv, [5] -360 p. front. (port.) 18 cm. Second American edition, 1814. [BX7260.S7R3 1815 a] 33-15578
1. Spencer, Thomas, 1791-1811. I. Montgomery, James, 1771-1854. II. Buck. Charles, 1771-1815. III. Title.

RAFFLES, Thomas, 1788-1863. 922.542
Memoirs of the life and ministry of the late Rev. Thomas Spencer, of Liverpool; with an appendix, containing a selection from his papers, &c., By Thomas Raffles ... 2d American ed. Boston, Published by Charles Williams, and Samuel T. Armstrong, 1814. S. T. Armstrong, printer. vi, [7]-311 p. front. (port.) 18 cm. [BX7260.S7R3 1814 b] 40-25731
1. Spencer, Thomas, 1791-1811. I. Title.

RAFFLES, Thomas, 1788-1863. 922.542
Memoirs of the life and ministry of the late Rev. Thomas Spencer, of Liverpool: with an appendix, containing a selection from his papers, &c., by Thomas Raffles ... 2d American ed. Hartford, Published by George Sheldon, & co., 1814. vi, [7]-311 p. 19 cm. [BX7260.S7R3 1814 a] 33-35150
1. Spencer, Thomas, 1791-1811. I. Title.

Spener, Phillipp Jacob, 1635-1705.

RICHARD, Marie E. 922.443
Philip Jacob Spener and his work. By Marie E. Richard ... Philadelphia, Lutheran publication society, 1897. 154 p. 15 1/2 cm. (Lettered on cover: Lutheran handbook series) "Augustus Hermann Francke and his work" (with special t.-p.): p. [91]-154. [BX4983.S6R5] 3-22073
1. Spener, Phillipp Jacob, 1635-1705. 2. Francke, August Hermann, 1663-1727. I. Title.

Spengler, Lazarus, 1479-1534.

GRIMM, Harold John, 1901- 270.6'092'4 B
Lazarus Spengler : a lay leader of the Reformation / by Harold J. Grimm. Columbus : Ohio State University Press, [1978] p. cm. Includes index. Bibliography: p. [BR350.S67G74] 78-13508 ISBN 0-8142-0290-X : 15.00
1. Spengler, Lazarus, 1479-1534. 2. Reformation—Germany, West—Nuremberg—Biography. 3. Nuremberg—Biography.

Spengler, Oswald, 1880-1936. Der Untergang des Abendiandes.

INFELD, Harry. 296
Israel in The decline of the West, by Harry Infeld. New York, Bloch publishing company, 1940. xi, 257 p. 21 cm. "A scientific interpretation of Israel's fate in the light of Spengler's conception of history as expounded in the Untergang des Abendiandes."--Introd. [DS113.I 5] 40-4804
1. Spengler, Oswald, 1880-1936. Der untergang des Abendiandes. 2. Jews—Civilization. I. Title.

INFELD, Herman Zvi, 1899- 296
Israel in The decline of the West, by Harry Infeld. New York, Block Pub. Co., 1940. xi, 257 p. 21 cm. "A scientific interpretation of Israel's fate in the light of Spengier's conception of history as expounded in the Untergang des Abendlandes." [DS113.I 5] 40-4804
1. Spengler, Oswald, 1880-1936. Der Untergang des Abendiandes. 2. Jews — Civilization. I. Title.

Spenser, Edmund—Dictionaries, indexes, etc.

NELSON, William, 1908-
The poetry of Edmund Spenser; a study. New York, Columbia University Press [1965] 350 p. 20 cm. (Columbia paperbacks. 65) 67-44970
I. Title.

POETICAL works,
edited with critical notes by J. C. Smith and E. de Selincourt. With an introduction by E. de Selincourt, and a glossary. London. New York, Oxford university press [1957] lxvii, 736p. illus., facsims. 19cm. (Oxford standard authors) Reprint of 1912 ed.
I. Spenser, Edmund, 1552?-1599. II. Smith, James Cruickshaks, 1867-1946. ed. III. DeSelincourt, Ernest, 1870-1943, ed

SPENSER, Edmund, 1552?-1599.
Poetical works, edited with critical notes by J. C. Smith and E. de Selincourt. With an introduction by E. do Selincourt, and a glossary. London, New York, Oxford university press [1957] lxvii, 736 p. illus., facsims. 19 cm. [Oxford standard authors] Reprint of 1912 ed.
I. Smith, James Cruickshanks, 1867-1946, ed. II. De Selincourt, Ernest, 1870-1943, ed. III. Title. IV. Series.

WHITMAN, Charles Huntington, 1873-1937.
A subject-index to the poems of Edmund Spenser, by Charles Huntington Whitman...pub. under the auspices of the Connecticut academy of arts and sciences. New Haven, Yale university press; [etc., etc.] 1918. xi, 261 p. 24 cm. [PR2362.W5] 19-15595
1. Spenser, Edmund—Dictionaries, indexes, etc. I. Title.

Speyr, Adrienne von.

BALTHASAR, Hans Urs von, 1905- 282'.092'4 B
First glance at Adrienne von Speyr / Hans Urs von Balthasar ; translated by Antje Lawry & Sr. Sergia Englund. San Francisco : Ignatius Press, c1981. 249 p. ; 21 cm. Translation of: Erster Blick auf Adrienne von Speyr. [BX4705.S75B313] 19 81-167170 ISBN 0-89870-003-5 pbk. : 6.95
1. Speyr, Adrienne von. I. [Erster Blick auf Adrienne von Speyr.] English II. Title.
Publisher's address: 1100 Sloat Blvd., San Francisco, CA 94132

Spike, Robert Warren.

SPIKE, Paul, 1947- 323.4'092'4 B
Photographs of my father. [1st ed.] New York, Knopf; [distributed by Random House] 1973. 259 p. illus. 22 cm. Autobiographical. [BX7260.S72A33 1973] 72-11042 ISBN 0-394-47334-5 6.95
1. Spike, Robert Warren. 2. Spike, Paul, 1947- I. Title.

Spilman, Bernard Washington, 1871-

GREEN, Charles Sylvester, 1900- 922.673
B. W. Spilman, the Sunday school man. Nashville, Broadman Press [1953] 154p. illus. 21cm. [BV1518.S6G7] 53-32887
1. Spilman, Bernard Washington, 1871- I. Title.

Spinola, Carlo, 1564-1622.

BROECKAERT, Joseph, 1807-1880. 922.252
Life of the Blessed Charles Spinola of the Society of Jesus: with a sketch of the other Japanese martyrs, beatified on the 7th of July, 1867. By Joseph Broeckaert, S.J. New York, J.G. Shea, 1869. 250 p. front. (port.) illus. (plan) pl. 19cm. Translated from the French by John Dawson Gilmary Shea. [BX4705.S76B7] 37-36761
1. Spinola, Carlo, 1564-1622. 2. Jesuits in Japan. I. Shea, John Dawson Gilmary, 1824-1892, tr. II. Title.

Spinola. Christoph Rojas de, Bp., 1626-1995.

MILLER, Samuel Jefferson Thomas, 1919- 280.1
Cristobal Rojas y Spinola, cameralist and irenicist, 1626-1695 [by] Samuel J. T. Miller and John P. Spielman, Jr. Philadelphia, American Philosophical Society, 1962. 108p. 30cm. (Transactions of the American Philosophical Society, new ser., v. 52, pt. 5) Bibliography: p. 101-105. [Q11.P6 n.s., vol. 52, pt. 5] 62-21092
1. Spinola. Christoph Rojas de, Bp., 1626-1995. 2. Christian union—Hist. I. Spielman, John Philip, 1930- II. Title. III. Series: American Philosophical Society, Transactions, new ser., v. 52, pt. 5

Spinoza, Benedictus de, 1632-1677.

BROWNE, Lewis, 1897- 921.3
Blessed Spinoza; a biography of the philosopher, by Lewis Browne ... New York, The Macmillan company, 1932. xiii p., 1 l, 3-334 p. front., plates, ports., facsims. 22 cm. "Selected bibliography": p. 321-323. [B3997.B75] 32-26514
1. Spinoza, Benedictus de, 1632-1677. I. Title.

HAMPSHIRE, Stuart, 1914-
Spinoza. Harmondsworth, Middlesex, Penguin Books [1951] 234 p. 18 cm. (The Pelican philosophy series, 1) Pelican books, A 253. Bibliographical preface: p. 9-[10] A52
1. Spinoza, Benedictus de, 1632-1677. I. Title.

HAMPSHIRE, Stuart, 1914-
Spinoza, [Reprinted with revisions. Harmondsworth, Middlesex] Penguin Books [1962] 237 p. 18 cm. (Pelican books, A253) Bibliographical preface: p. 9-[10] 64-17523
1. Spinoza, Benedictus de, 1632-1677. I. Title. II. Series.

KAYSER, Rudolf, 1889 921.8492
Spinoza, portrait of a spiritual hero, by Rudolf Kayser, with an introduction by Albert Einstein. Translated by Amy Allen and Maxim Newmark. New York, Philosophical library [c1946] xix p., 1 l., 326 p. front. (port.) 22 cm. Bibliography: p. 323-326. [B3997.K33] 47-1566
1. Spinoza, Benedictus de, 1632-1677. I. Allen, Amy, tr. II. Newmark, Maxim, joint tr. III. Title.

MARK, Thomas Carson, 1941- 111.8'3
Spinoza's theory of truth. New York, Columbia University Press, 1972. viii, 137 p. front. 21 cm. Bibliography: p. [129]-132. [B3999.T7M3] 72-3721 ISBN 0-231-03621-3 7.00
1. Spinoza, Benedictus de, 1632-1677. 2. Truth. I. Title.

ROTH, Leon. 198.
Spinoza, Descartes & Maimonides, by Leon Roth ... Oxford, The Clarendon press, 1924. 4 p. l., [7]-148 p. 20 cm. [B3998.R6] 24-18520
1. Spinoza, Benedictus de, 1632-1677. 2. Descartes, Rene, 1596-1650. 3. Moses ben Maimon, 1135-1204. I. [Full name: Hyman Leon Roth] II. Title.

SPINOZA, Benedictus de, 1632-1677.
Imporovement of the understanding, Ethics, and Correspondence of Benedict de Spinoza, translated from the Latin by R. H. M. Elwes, with an introduction by Frank Sewall, A.M. New York & London, M. W. Dunne [1901] xxxiii, 427 p. col. front. 24 cm. (Added t.-p.: Universal classics library) On spine: Autograph edition. [B3958.E53 1901 a] 44-36724
I. Elwes, Robert Harvey Monro, 1853- tr. II. Title.

SPINOZA, Benedictus de, 1632-1677. 171
Improvement of the understanding, Ethics and Correspondence of Benedict de Spinoza; tr. from the Latin by R. H. M. Elwes, with an introduction by Frank Sewall, A.M. Washington [D.C.] & London, M. W. Dunne [c1901] xxxiii, 427 p. col. front. 24 cm. (Added t.-p.: Universal classics library) Autograph edition de luxe. Title inclosed in colored ornamental borders. [B3955.E4] [PN6013.U5] 1-13726
I. Elwes, Robert Harvey Monro, tr. II. Title.

SPINOZA institute of America, inc., New York. 921.3
Baruch Spinoza; addresses and messages delivered and read at the College of the city of New York, on the occasion of the tercentenary of Spinoza, November 23rd, 1932. New York, Spinoza institute of America, inc., 1933. 77 p. front. (port.) 24 cm. "Addresses and messages ... prepared for the Spinoza tercentenary celebration held by the Spinoza institute of America."--Introd. note. [B3951.S6] 33-9782
1. Spinoza, Benedictus de, 1632-1677. I. New York. College of the city of New York. II. Title.

WATON, Harry. 181.3
The kabbalah and Spinoza's philosophy as a basis for an idea of universal history, by Harry Waton ... New York, Spinoza institute of America, inc., 1931- v. illus. 24 cm. [BM525.W35] 31-11187
1. Spinoza, Benedictus de, 1632-1677. 2. Cabala. 3. History—Philosophy. I. Spinoza institute of America, inc., New York. II. Title.

WOLFSON, Abraham. 921.3
Spinoza; a life of reason, by Abraham Wolfson. New York, Modern classics, [c1932] viii p., 2 l., 3-347 p. incl. pl., facsims, front., plates, ports. 24 cm. Bibliography: p. [329]-334. [B3997.W75] 32-34668
1. Spinoza, Benedictine de, 1632-1677. I. Title.

Spinoza, Benedictus de, 1632-1677—Bibliography

*OKO, Adolph S., comp. 016.19909492
The Spinoza bibliography. Boston, G. K. Hall, 1964. 700p. 26cm. Pub. under the auspices of the Columbia Univ. Libs. 40.00
1. Spinoza, Benedictus de, 1632-1677—Bibl. I. Columbia University. Libraries. II. Title.

Spinoza, Benedictus de, 1632-1677—Portraits.

MILLNER, Simon L. 921.8492
The face of Benedictus Spinoza, by Simon L. Millner. [New York, Machmadim art editions, inc., 1946] 2 p. l. 51 p., 3 l. plates, ports. 26 x 20 1/2 cm. [B3997.M5] 46-13044
1. Spinoza, Benedictus de, 1632-1677—Portraits. I. Title.

Spinoza, Benedictus de, 1632-1677. Tractatus theologico-politicus.

STRAUSS, Leo. 210
Spinoza's critique of religion. [Translated by E. M. Sinclair] New York, Schocken Books [1965] 351 p. 24 cm. Bibliographical references included in "Notes" (p. [271]-304) [B3985.Z7S73] 65-10948
1. Spinoza, Benedictus de, 1632-1677. Tractatus theologico-politicus. I. Title.

Spinsters.

"SINGLE blessedness": 176.2
or, Single ladies and gentlemen, against the slander of the pulpit, the press, and the lecture-room ... New York, C. S. Francis & co.; Boston, Crosby, Nichols & co., 1852. xxiv, 297 p. 19 1/2 cm. [HQ800.S5] 37-35037
1. Spinsters. 2. Bachelors.

Spira, Francesco, d. 1548.

BACON, Nathaniel, 1593-1660.
A relation of the fearful estate of Francis Spira, after he turned apostate from the Protestant church to popery. In the year, 1548. Compiled by Nath. Bacon, esq; Boston: Printed and sold by Fowle and Draper, at their office opposite the Founder's-arms, Marlborough-street. M.DCC.LXII. vi, 7-36 p. 16 cm. [BV4936.B3 1762] 45-25377
1. Spira, Francesco, d. 1548. I. Title.

[BACON, Nathaniel] 1593-1660. 922
A relation of the fearful state of Francis Spira, after he turned apostate from the Protestant to the Romish church. To which is added, some account of the miserable lives and deaths of John Child & George Edwards: and a short notice of Julian the Apostate, and of the celebrated Origen. Corrected and revised. With notes to the whole, by the Rev. W. C. Brownlee, A.M. Philadelphia: Printed and sold by Andrew Hogan, no. 2. Hinckle's court, Race, near Sixth street. Sold also by D. Hogan, 249, Market st. 1814. x, [11]-153 p. 15 cm. [BR1703.B18 1814] 45-25366
1. Spira, Francesco, d. 1548. 2. Child, John, 1638?-1684. 3. Edwards, George, 1661-1704. 4. Julianus, Apostata, emperor of Rome, 331-363. 5. Origenes. I. Brownlee, William Craig, 1784-1860 II. Title.

Spirals (in religion, folk-lore etc.)

PURCE, Jill. 291
The mystic spiral : journey of the soul / Jill Purce. New York : Thames and Hudson, 1980, c1974. 128 p. : ill. (some col.) ; 28 cm. (Art and imagination) [BL325.S7P87 1980] 19 79-67664 ISBN 0-500-81005-2 (pbk.) : 8.95
1. Spirals (in religion, folk-lore etc.) I. Title.
Distributed by W. W. Norton, New York, NY

Spirit—Biblical teaching.

BIBLE. English. 220.5'205
Catholic Biblical Association of America. Selections. 1973.
The Spirit Bible. Compiled by Eugene S. Geissler. Notre Dame, Ind., Ave Maria Press [1973] 272 p. 17 cm. [BS192.3.A1 1973.N67] 73-88004 ISBN 0-87793-062-7 2.25 (pbk.)
1. Spirit—Biblical teaching. 2. Holy Spirit—Biblical teaching. I. Geissler, Eugene S., comp. II. Title.

KNOWLES, Ellin J. (Troy), "Mrs. J. H. Knowles," 1835-
Spirit and life; selections from Bible readings. Boston, New York [etc.] Silver, Burdett & co., 1899. xiv p., 1 l., 287 p. port. 12 degrees. 99-1244
I. Title.

*SMITH, Sandra 133.93
Return: the Gospel of Spirits, assembled by Sandra and Dorothy Smith. New York, Vantage [c.1966] 68p. 21cm. 2.75 bds.,
I. Title.

Spirit phone calls.

ROGO, D. Scott. 133.9
Phone calls from the dead / D. Scott Rogo and Raymond Bayless. Englewood Cliffs, N.J. : Prentice-Hall, c1979. viii, 172 p. : ill. ; 24 cm. Includes index. Bibliography: p. 165-168. [BF1382.R63] 78-23746 ISBN 0-13-664334-5 : 8.95
1. Spirit phone calls. I. Bayless, Raymond, joint author. II. Title.

Spirit possession.

BOURGUIGNON, Erika, 1924- 133.4'7
Possession / Erika Bourguignon. San Francisco : Chandler & Sharp Publishers, c1976. p. cm. (Chandler & Sharp series in cross-cultural themes) Includes index. Filmography: p. [BL482.B68] 76-524 ISBN 0-88316-549-X pbk. : 2.50
1. Spirit possession. 2. Trance. 3. Voodooism. I. Title.

WALKER, Sheila S. 133.4'26
Ceremonial spirit possession in Africa and Afro-America; forms, meanings, and functional significance for individuals and social groups. Leiden, Brill, 1972 [1973] xii, 179 p. 25 cm. (Dissertationes ad historiam religionum pertinentes, v.4) Bibliography: p. [175]-179. [BL482.W34] 73-168738
1. Spirit possession. I. Title. II. Series. III. Supplementa ad Numen, Altera series
Available from Humanities Press, New York, for 19.95.

Spirit possession—Addresses, essays, lectures.

SPIRIT possession in the Nepal Himalayas / edited by John T. Hitchcock & Rex L. Jones ; translation of French articles by Harriet Leva Beegun. New Delhi : Vikas Pub. House, c1976. xxviii, p. : ill., map ; 25 cm. Bibliography: p. 390-401. [BL482.S64] 76-902895 Rs95.00 299'.1'495
1. Spirit possession—Addresses, essays, lectures. 2. Shamanism—Nepal—Addresses, essays, lectures. I. Hitchcock, John Thayer, 1917- II. Jones, Rex L.

SPIRIT possession in the Nepal Himalayas / edited by John T. Hitchcock and Rex L. Jones ; translations of French articles by Harriet Leva Beegun. Warminster : Aris & Phillips ; Beaverton, Or. : distributed by International Scholarly Book Services, c1976. xxviii, 401 p. : ill. (some col.) ; 23 cm. Essays. Errata slip inserted. Bibliography: p. 390-401. [BL482.S68] 76-381845 ISBN 0-85668-029-X : 27.50 pbk. : 14.50 299'.1495
1. Spirit possession—Addresses, essays, lectures. 2. Nepal—Religion—Addresses, essays, lectures. I. Jones, Rex L.

Spirit possession—Case studies.

CASE studies in spirit possession / edited by Vincent Crapanzano, Vivian Garrison. New York : Wiley, c1977. xvi, 457 p. ; 24 cm. (Contemporary religious movements) "A Wiley-Interscience publication." Includes bibliographies and index. [BL482.C37] 76-26653 ISBN 0-471-18460-8 : 21.50 133.4'26
1. Spirit possession—Case studies. I. Crapanzano, Vincent, 1939- II. Garrison, Vivian, 1933-

Spirit writings.

AGERSKOV, Johanne. 133.9'3
Questions and answers : first and second supplement to Toward the light / [Johanne Agerskov]. Copenhagen ; New York : Toward the Light Pub. House, 1979. 115, 125 p. ; 22 cm. Translation of Sporgsmal og svar. Includes bibliographical references. [BF1308.D4A33213 1979] 79-9594 ISBN 8-7878-7152-1 pbk. : 4.25
1. Spirit writings. I. Title.

AGERSKOV, Johanne. 133.9'3
Toward the light : a message to mankind from the transcendental world / [Johanne Agerskov]. Copenhagen ; New York : Toward the Light Pub. House, 1979. xii, 348 p. ; 23 cm. Translation of Vandrer

mod Lyset. [BF1308.D4A3413 1979] 79-9599 ISBN 8-7878-7150-5 : 8.50
1. Jesus Christ—Spiritualistic interpretations. 2. Spirit writings. I. Title.

†ALBRITTON, Clarice. 133.9'3
Beyond the lighthouse / by Clarice Albritton. Marina del Rey, Calif. : DeVorss, c1977. xii, 144 p. : ill. ; 22 cm. [BF1301.A29] 77-83447 ISBN 0-87516-243-6 pbk. : 4.25
1. Spirit writings. I. Title.

ANDREWS, Sheila. 133
In the beginning was the world / [by] Sheila Andrews. London ; New York : Regency Press, 1974. 158 p. ; 22 cm. [BF1301.A57] 75-308146 ISBN 0-7212-0343-4 : £1.80
1. Spirit writings. I. Title.

BANDER, Peter. 133.9'3
Voices from the tapes; recordings from the other world. New York, Drake Publishers [1973] 167 p. illus. 23 cm. [BF1380.B36] 73-181609 6.95
1. Spirit writings. 2. Phonotapes in psychical research. I. Title.

BAUGHMAN, Grace A. 133.9'3
Life after death, by Grace Baughman and Harold Baughman. [Sacramento, Calif.] Celestial Press [1972] iii, 247 p. 19 cm. (A Wisdom book) Cover title. [BF1301.B372] 78-162877
1. Spirit writings. I. Baughman, Harold A., joint author. II. Title.

BAYNE, Netta. 133.9'3
The Aquarius Wayfarer. London, New York, Regency Press, 1973. 88 p. 19 cm. [BF1301.B374] 74-177051 ISBN 0-7212-0304-3 £0.90
1. Spirit writings. I. Title.

BERRY, John Raymond. 133.9
The golden thread. A series of communications from a consciousness known as John; received by members of his family and transcribed to this published form for all to share and ponder. Edited by John Raymond Berry. New York, Philosophical Library [1970] xv, 128 p. 22 cm. "This is the second volume of the life and writings of John. The first volume was published in 1962 under the title Golden leaves." [BF1301.B45] 77-124515 4.95
1. Spirit writings. I. Dye, John Thomas, 1923-1945. II. Title.

BIRDSONG, Robert E. 133.9'3
Mission to mankind : a cosmic autobiography / by Robert E. Birdsong. 1st ed. Eureka, Calif. : Sirius Books, [1975] 122 p. : ill. ; 22 cm. Based on recorded conversations with the late Peg Birdsong. [BF1301.B-47] 74-18195 ISBN 0-917108-12-4 : 6.35 ISBN 0-917108-08-6 pbk. : 3.50
1. Birdsong, Robert E. 2. Birdsong, Peg. 3. Spirit writings. I. Birdsong, Peg. II. Title.

BISHIP, Neal. 133.9'3
Everywhere the light : the story of Zittelle / Neal Biship. 1st ed. Port Washington, N.Y. : Ashley Books, c1979. 225 p. ; 23 cm. [BF1301.B48 1979] 78-14861 ISBN 0-87949-137-X : 9.95
1. Brigance, Zittelle Biship, 1897-1974. 2. Biship, Neal. 3. Spirit writings. I. Title.

BOSS, Judy. 133.8'0924 B
In silence they return : a message of spiritual assurance / by Judy Boss. Saint Paul, Minn. : Llewellyn Publications, 1972. 216 p. : ill. ; 21 cm. [BF1283.B617A35] 76-351834 ISBN 0-87542-080-X
1. Boss, Judy. 2. Spirit writings. I. Title.

BROWN, Rosemary. 133.9
Unfinished symphonies; voices from the beyond. Foreword by the Bishop of Southwark. New York, W. Morrow, 1971. 190 p. front. 22 cm. [BF1315.B76 1971] 78-151911 5.95
1. Spirit writings. 2. Composers.

CAHAGNET, Louis Alphonse, 133.9'3 1809-1885.
The celestial telegraph : or, Secrets of the life to come revealed through magnetism / Louis Alphonse Cahagnet. New York : Arno Press, 1976. p. cm. (The Occult) Reprint of the 1850 ed. published by G. Pierce, London. [BF1291.C29 1976] 75-36832 ISBN 0-405-07944-3 : 14.00
1. Spirit writings. I. Title. II. Series: The Occult (New York, 1976-)

CHURCHILL, Winston, Sir, 133.9'3 1874-1965 (Spirit)
Churchill returns / by Robert R. Leichtman. Columbus, Ohio : Ariel Press, c1981. 96 p. ; 18 cm. (From heaven to earth) [BF1311.C58C45 1981] 19 81-66847 ISBN 0-89804-065-5 (pbk.) : 3.00
1. Spirit writings. I. Leichtman, Robert R. II. Title. III. Series.
Publisher's address: 2582 Shrewsbury Rd., Columbus, OH 43221

COBLENTZ, Flora. 133.9'3
For all who seek. San Jose, Calif., Redwood Press [1973] xxiii, 184 p. 24 cm. [BF1301.C57] 73-75413 5.95
1. Spirit writings. I. Title.

[CROWLEY, Aleister] 1875- 133.9'3 1947.
The book of the law <technically called Liber al vel legis sub figura CCXX as delivered by XCIII = 418 to DCLXVI> An Ixii sol in Aries March 21, 1973 e.v. [Oceanside, Calif., Thelema Publications, 1973] 52 p. 17 cm. Originally published in 1909 in v. 1 of Equinox. [BF1301.C753 1973] 72-96601 ISBN 0-913576-01-8
1. Spirit writings. I. Title.

CROWLEY, Aleister, 1875- 133.9'3 1947.
The equinox of the gods : the official organ of the A..A.. / [Aleister Crowley]. New York : Gordon Press, 1974. v, 137 p. : ill. ; 24 cm. Originally published in 1936 as v. 3, no. 3 of the Equinox. Cf. John Symonds. The great beast. 1951, p. 307. Includes the author's The book of the law (p. [13]-38) and bibliographical references. [BF1301.C76 1974] 73-21404 ISBN 0-87968-157-8 lib.bdg. : 34.95
1. Spirit writings. I. Crowley, Aleister, 1875-1947. The book of the law. 1974. II. Title.

CROWLEY, Aleister, 1875- 133.9'3 1947.
The law is for all : an extended commentary written by Aleister Crowley on The book of the law / edited and with an introd. by Israel Regardie. St. Paul : Llewellyn Publications, 1975. p. cm. [BF1301.C7533C76] 75-14027 12.95
1. Crowley, Aleister, 1875-1947. The book of the law. 2. Spirit writings. I. Crowley, Aleister, 1875-1947. The book of the law. II. Title.

CUMMINS, Geraldine 133.93 Dorothy, 1890-
Swan on a black sea; a study in automatic writing: the Cummins-Willett scripts. Transmitted by Geraldine Cummins. Edited by Signe Toksvig. With a foreword by C. D. Broad. [Rev. ed.] New York, S. Weiser [1970] lxii, 168 p. facsims. 23 cm. "These scripts ... purport to be communications from the surviving spirit of Mrs. Charles Tennant." [BF1301.C87 1970b] 77-22959 6.50
1. Spirit writings. I. Toksvig, Signe, 1891- ed. II. Coombe Tennant, Winifred Margaret (Pearce-Serocold) 1874-1956. III. Title.

DEWEY, Mark. 133.9
A man from space speaks: Amano. Transcribed by Mark Dewey. [Houston? Tex.] c1966. 38 l. 28 cm. Cover title. [BF1311.M4D48] 71-20347
1. Spirit writings. I. Amano. II. Title.

DOUCE, P. M. 133.9'3
Incredible alliance : transmissions from T. S. Eliot through the mediumship of P. M. Douce / P. M. Douce ; with a foreword by Harry K. Panjwani. Philadelphia : Dorrance, [1975] xii, 135 p. : ill. ; 22 cm. [BF1311.E47D68] 74-27761 ISBN 0-8059-2110-9 : 5.95
1. Eliot, Thomas Stearns, 1888-1965. 2. Spirit writings. I. Eliot, Thomas Stearns, 1888-1965. II. Title.

DOUCE, P. M. 133.9'3
Incredible alliance : transmissions from T. S. Eliot through the mediumship of P. M. Douce / P. M. Douce ; with a foreword by Harry K. Panjwani. Philadelphia : Dorrance, [1975] xii, 135 p. : ill. ; 22 cm. [BF1311.E47D68] 74-27761 ISBN 0-8059-2110-9 : 5.95
1. Eliot, Thomas Stearns, 1888-1965. 2. Spirit writings. I. Eliot, Thomas Stearns, 1888-1965. II. Title.

HOLMES, Jesse Herman, 133.9'3 (Spirit) 1864-1942
As we see it from here / Jesse Herman Holmes and the Holmes research team. Franklin, N.C. : Metascience Corp., Publications Division, c1980. 142 p. : ill., port. ; 24 cm. (Life's energy fields ; v. 4) Includes index. [BF1311.H65H64] 19 81-110996 ISBN 0-935436-03-0 : 9.75
1. Spirit writings. I. Title. II. Series.
Publisher's address: Box 747, Franklin, NC 28734

JESUS Christ (Spirit) 133.9'3
Talks with Christ and his teachers : through the psychic gift of Elwood Babbitt / [edited] by Charles H. Hapgood. Turners Falls, Mass. (2001 Center, Turners Falls) : Threshold Books, c1981. xxii, 235 p. ; 22 cm. Includes index. [BF1311.J5J47] 19 81-52841 11.95
1. Jesus Christ (Spirit) 2. Spirit writings. I. Babbitt, Elwood, 1922- II. Hapgood, Charles H. III. Title.

JOHNSON, Lilian D. 133.9'3
Spray from an inland sea, by Lilian D. Johnson. Boston, Branden Press [1974] 126 p. 23 cm. [BF1301.J58] 73-83344 ISBN 0-8283-1527-2 6.95
1. Spirit writings. 2. Future life. I. Title.

JOHNSTON, Jean Hope. 133.9'3
For sceptics also: a collection of writings from philosophers of the East and West received through the mediumship of Jean Hope Johnston. London, New York, Regency Press, 1971. 182 p. 20 cm. [BF1290.J63] 72-171301 ISBN 0-7212-0135-0 £1.20
1. Spirit writings. I. Title.

KING, Frederick Walter, 133.9'013 1906-
Say not goodbye, by F. W. King. London, New York, Regency Press, 1971. 132 p. 23 cm. [BF1301.K52] 74-889314 ISBN 0-7212-0126-1 £1.20
1. Spirit writings. I. Title.

LITVAG, Irving. 133.9'3'0924 B
Singer in the shadows; the strange story of Patience Worth. New York, Macmillan [1972] xiii, 293 p. 21 cm. Includes bibliographical references. [BF1301.W865L58] 70-165570 7.95
1. Worth, Patience. 2. Spirit writings. I. Title.

MESSAGES from Maitreya 299'.93 *the Christ.* London ; Los Angeles : Tara Press, c1980- v. ; 22 cm. Contents.Contents.—v. 1. One hundred messages. [BF1301.G86] 19 80-52483 ISBN 0-936604-01-8 (pbk. : v. 1) : 5.00 (U.S.)
1. Spirit writings. 2. Maitreya (Buddhist deity)
Publisher's address 6867 Iris Circle, Los Angeles, CA 10068.

MONTGOMERY, Ruth Schick, 133.9'3 1912-
Companions along the way / Ruth Montgomery. New York : Coward, McCann & Geoghegan, [1974] 256 p. ; 22 cm. [BF1290.M66 1974] 74-79680 ISBN 0-698-10619-9 : 6.95
1. Jesus Christ—Spiritualistic interpretations. 2. Spirit writings. I. Title.

MONTGOMERY, Ruth Schick, 133.9'3 1912-
Companions along the way / Ruth Montgomery. Boston : G. K. Hall, 1975, c1974. xxxvii, 412 p. ; 25 cm. Large print ed. [BF1290.M66 1975] 75-4988 ISBN 0-8161-6277-8 lib.bdg. : 11.95
1. Jesus Christ—Spiritualistic interpretations. 2. Spirit writings. 3. Sight-saving books. I. Title.

MOON, Margaret. 133.9'3
Wedge : the extraordinary communications of an earthbound spirit / received in automatic writing by Margaret and Maurine Moon ; with commentary by Maurine Moon. 1st ed. St. Paul : Llewellyn Publications, 1975. 113 p., [4] leaves of plates : ill. ; 21 cm. [BF1301.M68] 75-309094 ISBN 0-87542-497-X pbk. : 3.95
1. Spirit writings. I. Moon, Maurine, joint author. II. Wedge, Jude. III. Title.

MOSES, William Stainton, 133.9'3 1840-1892.
Spirit teachings / William Stainton Moses. New York : Arno Press, 1976. p. cm. (The Occult) Reprint of the 1924 ed. published by London Spiritualist Alliance. [BF1301.M755 1976] 75-36910 ISBN 0-405-07968-0 : 18.00
1. Spirit writings. I. Title. II. Series: The Occult (New York, 1976-)

NADA-YOLANDA, 1925- 133.9'3
Angels and man. Channeled by the spiritual hierarchy through Nada-Yolanda. [1st ed.] Miami, Published for the Hierarchal Board and the University of Life by Mark-Age [1974] 138 p. 24 cm. [BF1301.N23] 73-90881 ISBN 0-912322-03-9 6.00
1. Spirit writings. I. Title.

NADA-YOLANDA, 1925- 133.9
Evolution of man, channeled by the spiritual Hierarchy through Nada-Yolanda. [1st ed.] Miami, Fla., Published for the Hierarchal Board by Mark Age [1971] 160 p. 24 cm. [BF1301.N24] 71-147256 ISBN 0-912322-02-0 6.00
1. Spirit writings. I. Title.

NADA-YOLANDA, 1925- 133.9
Mark Age period and program, channeled by the spiritual hierarchy through Nada-Yolanda. [1st ed.] Miami, Fla., Published for the Hierarchal Board by Mark-Age [1970] 350 p. 24 cm. [BF1290.N33] 79-121117 10.00
1. Spirit writings. I. Title.

NADA-YOLANDA, 1925- 133.9'3
Visitors from other planets, channeled by the spiritual hierarchy through Nada-Yolanda. [1st ed.] Miami, Fla., Published for the Hierarchal Board and the University of Life by Mark-Age [1974] 334 p. 24 cm. [BF1301.N247 1974] 73-90880 ISBN 0-912322-04-7 10.00
1. Spirit writings. I. Title.

NORMAN, Ruth, 1900- 133.9'3
Have you lived on other worlds before? : An emissary for thirty two worlds speaks to earth / by Ruth Norman. 1st ed. El Cajon, Calif. : Unarius Educational Foundation, c1980- v. : ill. ; 22 cm. [BF1301.N67] 19 80-121108 ISBN 0-932642-59-4 : pbk. : 6.95 ISBN 0-932642-60-8 pbk. (vol. 2) : 5.95
1. Spirit writings. I. Title.
Publisher's address: P. O. Box 1042, El Cajon, CA 92022

NORMAN, Ruth, 1900- 133.9'3
"32 earth worlds of the Intergalactic Confederation speak!! (to planet Earth) [Transmitted by Ruth E. Norman, Vaughn Spaegel and Thomas Miller. 1st ed. El Cajon, Calif., Unarius—Science of Life, 1974. 3 v. (1394 p.) illus. 22 cm. (Their Tesla speaks series, v. 4) Cover title: 32 Intergalactic Confederation planets speak. Spine title: Tesla speaks. [BF1290.N67] 74-180409
1. Spirit writings. I. Spaegel, Vaughn, joint author. II. Miller, Thomas, 1946- joint author. III. Title. IV. Title: 32 Intergalactic Confederation planets speak. V. Series.

1000 keys to the truth 133.9'3 : spiritual guidelines for Latter Days & Second Coming. 1st ed. Miami, Fla. : School of Education of Life, Mark-Age, c1976. 155 p. ; 22 cm. Includes index. [BF1301.O64 1976] 76-363286 ISBN 0-912322-51-9 : 5.00
1. Spirit writings.

OSCOTT, Francesco 133.9'3 Luciano.
The secret of the sphinx by Pharaoh Amigdar, assisted by ... others / [reported by] F. L. Oscott ; translated from the Italian by Gavin Gibbons. Sudbury : Spearman, 1977. xi, 173 p., [12] p. of plates : ill., facsims., maps, plans ; 23 cm. Translation of Amigdar, il segreto della sfinge. Spine title: Amigdar, the secret of the sphinx. [BF1311.E43O7213] 77-367644 ISBN 0-85435-083-7 : £3.95
1. Spirit writings. 2. Sphinxes—Miscellanea. 3. Egypt—Civilization—Miscellanea. I. Title. II. Title: Amigdar, the secret of the sphinx.

PARK, S E. Mrs. 135.
Instructive communications from spirit life. Written through the mediumship of Mrs. S.

E. Park, by the instrumentality of her spirit husband, who departed this life in 1863. Boston, New York, W. White and company, 1869. 222 p. 2 port. (incl. front.) 20 cm. [BF1291.P25] 11-4753
I. Title.

PARK, S E. Mrs. 135.
Instructive communications from spirit life. Written through the mediumship of Mrs. S. E. Park, by the instrumentality of her spirit husband, who departed this life in 1863. Boston, New York, W. White and company, 1869. 222 p. 2 port. (incl. front.) 20 cm. [BF1291.P25] 11-4753
I. Title.

PEEBLES, Edwin. 133.9'3
Hidden truths. Bloomington, Ill. [1974] x, 347 p. 24 cm. [BF1290.P4] 73-86026
1. Spirit writings. I. Title.

PROPHET, Elizabeth Clare. 299
The chela and the path / El Morya ; dictated to the messenger Elizabeth Clare Prophet. Colorado Springs : Summit University Press, c1976. 128 p., [1] leaf of plates : ill. ; 21 cm. "A Summit Lighthouse publication." [BP605.G68P76] 76-7634 ISBN 0-916766-12-8 : 2.95
1. Great White Brotherhood. 2. Spirit writings. I. el Morya. II. Title.

PROPHET, Elizabeth Clare. 299
Cosmic consciousness : the putting on of the garment of the Lord / Lanello ; dictated to the messenger Elizabeth Clare Prophet. Colorado Springs : Summit University Press, c1976- v. : ill. ; 22 cm. "A Summit Lighthouse publication." Originally published in the periodical Pearls of wisdom. [BF1301.P83] 74-24023 ISBN 0-916766-17-9 : 2.95 (v. 1)
1. Spirit writings. I. Prophet, Mark. II. Title.

PROPHET, Elizabeth Clare. 133.9
The greater way of freedom : dictations of the ascended masters given to the messenger Elizabeth Clare Prophet. Colorado Springs, Colo. : Summit University Press, c1976. 81 p., [1] leaf of plates : ill. ; 21 cm. "A Summit Lighthouse publication." Includes bibliographical references. [BF1301.P84] 76-7636 ISBN 0-916766-14-4 : 2.95
1. Spirit writings. I. Title.

PROPHET, Mark. 230
My soul doth magnify the Lord! Revelations of Mary the mother of Jesus to the messengers Mark and Elizabeth Prophet. Sons and Daughters of Dominion ed. Colorado Springs [Colo.] Summit Lighthouse [1974- v. col. illus. 23 cm. (Their The golden word of Mary series, book 1-) [BF1311.M42P76] 73-83759
1. Mary, Virgin—Miscellanea. 2. Spirit writings. I. Prophet, Elizabeth, joint author. II. Title.

PROPHET, Mark. 248
Studies in alchemy / by Saint Germain. Colorado : Summit Lighthouse, c1974. 92 p., [1] leaf of plates : col. ports ; 21 cm. (Alchemy series ; v. 1) "The instruction set forth ... was given to Mark L. Prophet by the Ascended Master Saint Germain." [BF1311.S25P76] 75-321272
1. Spirit writings. I. Saint-Germain, comte de, d. 1784? II. Title.

RIVAIL, Hippolyte Leon Denizard, 1803-1869. 133.9
Spiritualist philosophy : the spirits' book / Hippolyte Leon Denizard Rivail (Allan Kardec, pseud.). New York : Arno Press, 1976. p. cm. (The Occult) Translation of Le livre des esprits. Reprint of the 1893 ed. published in London. [BF1290.R5413 1976] 75-36918 ISBN 0-405-07973-7 : 24.00
1. Spirit writings. I. Title. II. Series: The Occult (New York, 1976-)

ROBERTS, Jane. 133.9
Seth speaks; the eternal validity of the soul. Notes by Robert F. Butts New York, Bantam Books [1974, c1972] xxi, 486 p. illus. 18 cm. [BF1301.R595] 1.95 (pbk.)
1. Spirit writings. 2. Spiritualism. 3. Reincarnation. I. Seth. II. Title.
L.C. card number for original ed.: 78-38925.

ROBERTS, Jane, 1929- 133.9'3
The afterdeath journal of an American philosopher / Jane Roberts. Englewood Cliffs, N.J. : Prentice-Hall, c1978. p. cm. Includes index. [BF1311.J25R62] 78-4040 ISBN 0-13-018515-9 : 8.95
1. Spirit writings. I. James, William, 1842-1910. II. Title.

ROBERTS, Jane, 1929- 133.9'3
The individual and the nature of mass events : a Seth book / by Jane Roberts ; notes by Robert F. Butts. Englewood Cliffs, N.J. : Prentice-Hall, c1981. 304 p. ; 24 cm. Includes index. [BF1301.R59] 19 80-22600 ISBN 0-13-457259-9 : 11.95
1. Spirit writings. I. Seth. II. Title.

ROBERTS, Jane, 1929- 133.9'3
The nature of personal reality: a Seth book. Notes by Robert F. Butts. Englewood Cliffs, N.J., Prentice-Hall [1974] xxiv, 510 p. 23 cm. [BF1301.R593] 74-7356 ISBN 0-13-610576-9 3.95 (pbk.)
1. Spirit writings. I. Seth. II. Title.

ROBERTS, Jane, 1929- 133.9
Seth speaks; the eternal validity of the soul. Notes by Robert F. Butts. Englewood Cliffs, N.J., Prentice-Hall [1972] xxiv, 505 p. 24 cm. [BF1301.R595] 78-38925 ISBN 0-13-807206-X 7.95
1. Spirit writings. 2. Spiritualism. 3. Reincarnation. I. Seth. II. Title.

ROBERTS, Jane, 1929- 133.9
The "unknown" reality : a Seth book / Jane Roberts ; notes and introd. by Robert F. Butts. Englewood Cliffs, N.J. : Prentice-Hall, c1977- v. ; 24 cm. Includes index. [BF1031.R596 1977] 77-1092 ISBN 0-13-938704-8 : 8.95
1. Spirit writings. I. Seth. II. Title.

SEASON of changes : 133.9'3
ways of response : a psychic interpretation of the coming changes in, on, and about the earth and the corresponding transformations within man; based on passages selected from the readings of the Associations of the Light Morning. Virginia Beach, Va. : Heritage Publications, [1974] vi, 290 p. ; 23 cm. Includes bibliographical references. [BF1301.S33] 74-188817 3.95
1. Spirit writings. I. Associations of Light Morning.

SMITH, Susy. 133.9'3
The book of James [1974] Susy Smith. New York : Putnam, [1974] 212 p. ; 22 cm. Bibliography: p. 211-212. [BF1311.J25S55] 74-79667 ISBN 0-399-11392-4 : 6.95
1. Spirit writings. I. James, William, 1842-1910. II. Title.

STANFORD, Ray. 232.91'6
Fatima prophecy; days of darkness, promise of light. [Austin, Tex.] Association for the Understanding of Man [1972] 194 p. illus. 23 cm. Bibliography: p. [187]-188. [BF1311.M42S7] 72-86078 6.95
1. Mary, Virgin—Apparitions and miracles (Modern) 2. Spirit writings. I. Title.

STANFORD, Ray. 133.9'3
The spirit unto the churches : an understanding of man's existence in the body through knowledge of the seven glandular centers : from the psychic readings of Ray Stanford. Rev. ed. Austin, Tex. : Association for the Understanding of Man, c1977. xi, 212 p. : ill. ; 28 cm. [BF1301.S644 1977] 75-24921 ISBN 0-915908-06-9 : 8.50
1. Spirit writings. 2. Endocrine glands—Miscellanea. I. Title.

SULLIVAN, Eileen. 133.9'3
Arthur Ford speaks from beyond / by Eileen Sullivan. Chicago : J. P. O'Hara, c1975. 186 p. ; 23 cm. [BF1301.S885 1975] 74-25385 ISBN 0-87955-317-0 : 6.95
1. Spirit writings. I. Ford, Arthur A. II. Title.

SULLIVAN, Eileen. 133.9'3
Arthur Ford speaks from beyond. Greenwich, Conn. : Fawcett, 1976c1975. 207p. ; 18 cm. (A Fawcett Crest Book) [BF130a.S885] pbk. : 1.50
1. Spirit writings. I. Title.
L.C. card no of 1975 J.P. O'Hara edition:74-25385.

SWAIN, Jasper. 133.9'013
From my world to yours : a young man's account of the afterlife / by Jasper Swain ; edited by Noel Langley. New York : Walker, 1977. 101 p. ; 22 cm. Psychic conversations with the author's dead son, Mike Swain. "First published under a pseudonym in a privately-printed edition." [BF1301.S892 1977] 76-52573 ISBN 0-8027-0573-1 : 5.95
1. Swain, Jasper. 2. Swain, Mike. 3. Spirit writings. I. Swain, Mike. II. Title.

SWANSON, Mildred Burris. 133.9'1
God bless U, daughter, by Mildred Burris Swanson, Mark Twain. [Independence, Mo., Midwest Soc. of Psychic Res. [1968] vii. 169p. 23cm. [BF1301.S95] 68-2840 4.95
1. Spirit wirtings. I. Clemens, Samuel Langhorne, 1835-1910. II. Title.
Publisher's address: 2500 S. Norwood, Independence, Mo. 64052.

TOWLER, Flora, 1896- 133.9
The angel of death. London, New York, Regency Press, 1972. 160, [2] p. 2 illus. 23 cm. [BF1290.T68] 72-197699 ISBN 0-7212-0236-5 £1.80
1. Spirit writings. I. Title.

TRUTZSCHLER von Falkenstein, Ingeborg, Baroness. 133.9'3
The book of rings / by Ingeborg Baroness Trutzschler von Falkenstein, Kenneth John Westward. London ; New York : Regency Press, 1977. 105 p. ; 23 cm. [BF1301.T724] 78-317492 £2.40 $6.00 (U.S.)
1. Spirit writings. I. Westward, Kenneth John, joint author. II. Title.

TURNER, Kenneth Weston, comp. 133.9'3
Meditations from the great American Indians. Edited and arranged by Kenneth Weston Turner. Lakewood, Colo., New Thought Science Center of Light and Truth, c1970. 56 l. illus. 28 cm. In verse. [BF1290.T87] 73-154222
1. Spirit writings. I. Title.

TWEDDELL, Margaret Flavell. 133.9'3
Witness from beyond : new cosmic concepts on death and survival received from the late A. D. Mattson, S.T.D., through the clairvoyant, Margaret Flavell Tweddell / transcribed and edited by Ruth Mattson Taylor. New York : Hawthorn Books, c1975. xii, 152 p. ; 22 cm. Bibliography: p. 150-152. [BF1301.T74 1975] 75-5033 ISBN 0-8015-8776-X : 6.95
1. Spirit writings. I. Mattson, Alvin Daniel, 1895-1970. II. Taylor, Ruth Mattson. III. Title.

TZANGAS, George J. 230
Have you talked to Him? / By John Christian [i.e. G. J. Tzangas]. Akron, Ohio : J. Christian, [1974] 66 leaves ; 23 cm. [BF1301.T95] 74-84034
1. Spirit writings. 2. Theology—Miscellanea. I. Title.

WALKER, Jeanne, 1924- 133.9'013'0924 B
Always, Karen / by Jeanne Walker ; foreword by George Daisley. New York : Hawthorn Books, [1975] 137 p., [4] leaves of plates : ill. ; 22 cm. Bibliography: p. 137. [BF1301.W14 1975] 74-20288 ISBN 0-8015-2840-2 : 6.95
1. Walker, Karen, 1949-1970. 2. Spirit writings. I. Walker, Karen, 1949-1970. II. Title.

WALKINS, Susan M., 1945- 133.9'3
Conversations with Seth / Susan M. Watkins ; introd. by Jane Roberts. Englewood-Cliffs, N.J. : Prentice-Hall, c1980. p. cm. Includes index. [BF1301.W226] 80-17760 ISBN 0-13-172007-4 : 10.95
1. Spirit writings. 2. Spiritualism. 3. Reincarnation. I. Seth. II. Roberts, Jane, 1929- III. Title.

WHITE, Stewart Edward, 1873-1946. 133.9'3
The Betty book : excursions into the world of other-consciousness made by Betty between 1919 and 1936 / now recorded by Stewart Edward White. New York : Dutton, 1977, c1937. 302 p. ; 19 cm. [BF1301.W5954 1977] 76-46780 ISBN 0-525-47447-1 pbk. : 3.50
1. Spirit writings. I. White, Elizabeth Calvert Grant, 1881-1939. II. Title.

WICKLAND, Carl August, 1861- 133.9
30 years among the dead / Carl A. Wickland. San Bernardino, Calif. : Borgo Press, 1980. p. cm. Reprint of the 1974 ed. published by Newcastle Pub. Co., Van Nuys, Calif., in series: A Newcastle occult book. [BF1301.W597 1980] 19 80-19669 ISBN 0-87877-325-8 : 12.95
1. Spirit writings. I. Title.

WOJCIK, Stanley L. 133.1'22
Ghosts are everywhere / by Stanley L. Wojcik ; illustrated by Alice Kupper, photographer, Glenn Tompkins, artist. South Amboy, N.J. : Amboy Press, c1977. 290 p. : ill. ; 22 cm. [BF1290.W6] 77-88348 pbk. : 4.95
1. Spirit writings. 2. Ghosts. I. Title.
Publisher's address: P.O. Box 343 South Amboy, NJ 08879

WOODCOX, Benjamin Franklin. 133.
Fragments of spiritual knowledge pertaining to the spiritual world; fragments of spiritual knowledge, clairvoyantly and clairaudiently received and transplanted to paper by Benjamin F. Woodcox ... Battle Creek, Mich., Woodcox & Fanner [c1923] 80 p. 19 1/2 cm. $1.35. Bound with this: His Spiritual evolution ... Battle Creek, Mich. [c1921] [BF1301.W85] 23-5496
I. Title.

YARBO, Chelsa Quinn, 1942- 133.9'3
Messages from Michael / Chelsea Quinn Yarbo. New York : Playboy Press, 1980, c1979. 284p. ; 18cm (A Playboy paperback [BF1301.Y37] ISBN 0-872-16766-6 pbk. : 2.50
1. Spirit writings. 2. Soul — Miscellanea I. Lansing, Jessica. II. Michael, (spirit) III. Title.
LC card no. for 1979 Playboy Press hardcover ed. : 79-13717

YARBRO, Chelsea Quinn, 1942- 133.9'3
Messages from Michael on the nature of the evolution of the human soul / Chelsea Quinn Yarbro. 1st ed. Chicago : Playboy Press ; New York : trade distribution by Simon and Schuster, c1979. xiv, 303 p. ; 22 cm. The communications from Michael received by Jessica Lansing. [BF1301.Y37] 79-13717 ISBN 0-87223-526-2 : 8.95
1. Spirit writings. 2. Soul—Miscellanea. I. Lansing, Jessica. II. Michael (Spirit) III. Title.

†ZENOR, Richard. 133.9'3
Agasha, master of wisdom : his philosophy and teachings / by William Eisen ; foreword by James Crenshaw ; teachings received through the instrumentality of Richard Zenor. 1st ed. Marina del Rey, Ca. : DeVorss, c1977. 352 p., [1] leaf of plates : ports. ; 24 cm. Includes bibliographical references. [BF1290.Z45] 77-85423 ISBN 0-87516-241-X : 10.95
1. Spirit writings. I. Eisen, William. II. Title.

ZENOR, Richard. 133.9'3
The Agashan discourses : the Agashan teachers speak on the who, what, where, when, and why of life on the earth plane / compiled and edited by William Eisen ; teachings received through the instrumentality of Richard Zenor. 1st ed. Marina Del Rey, CA : DeVorss, c1978. 368 p., [1] leaf of plates : ill. ; 24 cm. [BF1290.Z46] 77-85424 ISBN 0-87516-242-8 : 11.95
1. Spirit writings. I. Eisen, William. II. Title.

Spirit writings—Congresses.

THE Great White Brotherhood in the culture history and religion of America : teachings of the ascended masters given to Elizabeth Clare Prophet. 299
Colorado Springs : Summit University Press, c1976. xi, 347 p., [5] leaves of plates : ill. ; 23 cm. Record of a four-day conference for spiritual freedom, held at Mount Shasta, 1975. "A Summit Lighthouse publication." Includes bibliographical references. [BP605.G68G74] 76-7635 ISBN 0-916766-16-0 pbk. : 5.95
1. Great White Brotherhood—Congresses. 2. Spirit writings—Congresses. I. Prophet, Elizabeth Clare.

Spirits.

BERG, Joseph Frederick, 1812-1871. 235
Abaddon, and Mahanaim; or, Daemons and guardian angels. By Joseph F. Berg ... Philadelphia, Higgins & Perkinpine, 1856. 272 p. 19 cm. [BT961.B4] 33-33138
1. Spirits. I. Title. II. Title: Daemons and guardian angles.

BERKHOF, H 235
Christ and the powers. Translated from the Dutch by John Howard Yoder. Scottdale, Pa., Herald Press [1962] 62p. 20cm. [BT962.B413] 62-13713
1. Spirits. 2. Bible. N. T.—Theology. I. Title.

CAYLEY, Edward Hamilton.
The late Dr. Sedgwick and the spirit medium (based upon facts) a ... narrative revealing in story a comprehensive ... outline of spirit philosophy, and the methods employed by mediums to foist it upon a credulous public ... Dayton, O., United brethren pub. house, 1900. 100 p. 16 cm. Jul
I. Title.

GARESCHE, Edward Francis, 1876- 235
Communion with the spirit world, a book for Catholics and non-Catholics, by Edward F. Garesche ... New York, The Macmillan company, 1925. 159 p. 20 cm. [BT961.G3] 25-18793
I. Title.

JUNG-STILLING, Johann Heinrich, 1740-1817.
Scenes in the world of spirits, of Henry Stilling ... Translated from the third original edition ... New-Market: Printed by Ambrose Henkel & co. [1815?] xiv, 282 p., 1 l. 18 cm. Translator's preface signed: G. S. [i. e. Gottlieb Shober] Salem, N. Carolina, Nov. 1, 1814. [PT2370.J7S32] 4-35687
I. Shoeber, Gottlieb, 1756-1838, tr. II. Title.

LAW, Bimala Churn, 1892- 294.3
The Buddhist conception of spirits. 2d ed., rev. and enl. London, Luzac [dist. Mystic, Conn., Verry, 1965] xi, 114p. 21cm. (Law's res. ser., pub. no.3) First ed., 1923. [BL1475.S65L3] 40-14176 2.50
1. Spirits. 2. Buddha and Buddhism. I. Title.

SCHLIER, Heinrich, 1900- 225.6
Principalities and powers in the New Testament. [New York] Herder & Herder [c.1961] 88p. (Quaestiones disputatae, 3) 61-9373 1.95 pap.,
1. Spirits. 2. Bible. N.T.—Theology. I. Title.

[TONNA, Charlotte Elizabeth (Browne) Mrs.] 1790-1846. 235
"Principalities and powers in heavenly places." By Charlotte Elizabeth [pseud.] With an introduction, by the Rev. Edward Bickerstoth. New-York, J. S. Taylor & co., 1842. xii, [13]-298 p. 19 1/2 cm. [BT961.T6] 38-4786
1. Spirits. I. Title.

VAN ZELLER, Dom Hubert 248
Famine of spirit. Springfield, Ill., Templegate [1964] 194p. 18cm. 3.50
I. Title.

WHATELY, Richard, abp. of Dublin, 1787-1863. 235
A view of the Scripture revelations respecting good and evil angels. By Richard Whately... 2d ed. Philadelphia, Lindsay & Blakiston, 1856. x, 11-174 p. 19 cm. [BT961.W5] A 25
1. Spirits. I. Title. II. Title: Angels, Good and evil.

WOOD, E[zra] M[organ]
Schools for spirits, By E. M. Wood ... Pittsburgh, Pa., J. Horner book company, limited [1903] 3 p. l., 9-173 p. 19 cm. 3-13479
I. Title.
Contents omitted.

Spirits. Bible. N.T. — Theology.

BERKHOF, Hendrikus. 235
Christ and the powers. Translated from the Dutch by John Howard Yoder. Scottdale, Pa., Herald Press [1962] 62 p. 20 cm. [BT962.B413] 62-13713
1. Spirits. Bible. N.T. — Theology. I. Title.

Spiritual direction.

BARRY, William A. 248.4
The practice of spiritual direction / William A. Barry and William J. Connolly. New York : Seabury Press, 1982. xii, 211 p. ; 21 cm. Bibliography: p. [210]-211. [BX2350.7.B35 1982] 19 81-14566 ISBN 0-8164-2357-1 pbk. : 11.95
1. Spiritual direction. I. Connolly, William J. II. Title.

BLEIDORN, Eugene F. 253.5
Help me, Father; a technique of spiritual direction. Milwaukee, Bruce Pub. Co. [c.1960] 134p. Bibl. 60-15476 3.00
1. Spiritual direction. I. Title.

BORDERS, M. Edward. 237.
A better country. (3d ed.] By Rev. M. Edward Borders ... Chicago, Ill., The Christian witness company [c1918] 102 p. front, (port.) 19 1/2cm. [BT846.B6 1918] 19-1659
I. Title.

CATHOLIC University of America. Workshop on Spiritual Formation and Guidance-Counseling in the CCD Program, 1961. 253.5082
Spiritual formation and guidance-counseling in the CCD program; the proceedings of the Workshop on Spiritual Formation and Guidance-Counseling in the CCD Program, conducted at the Catholic Univ. of America, June 16 to June 27, 1961. Ed. by Joseph B. Collins. Washington, D.C., Catholic Univ. [c.] 1962. ix, 248 p. 22 cm. Bibl. 62-4669 2.50, pap.
1. Spiritual direction. 2. Pastoral counseling. 3. Catholic Church—Education. 4. Confraternity of Christian Doctrine. I. Collins, Joseph Burns, 1897- ed. II. Title.

EDWARDS, Tilden. 248.4
Spiritual friend / Tilden H. Edwards. New York : Paulist Press, c1980. viii, 264 p. ; 23 cm. Bibliography: p. 261-264. [BV5053.E38] 19 79-91408 ISBN 0-8091-2288-X (pbk.) : 7.95
1. Shalem Institute for Spiritual Formation. 2. Spiritual direction. I. Title.

FRIENDS, Society of. Philadelphia Yearly meeting. 289.
Christian advices; published by the Yearly meeting of Friends, held in Philadelphia. Philadelphia, Kimber & Conrad, 1808. 2 p. l., 112 p. 15 cm. [BX7607.P4] 3-23770
I. Title.

JENTGES, Damian. 248.4
Search for sanctity. Fresno, Calif., Academy Guild Press [c.1959] 203p. illus. (ports.) 22cm. 59-10452 3.95
1. Spiritual direction. I. Title.

JONES, Alan W., 1940- 253.5
Exploring spiritual direction : an essay on Christian friendship / Alan Jones. New York : Seabury Press, 1982. 135 p. ; 22 cm. Includes bibliographical references. [BV5053.J63 1982] 19 81-18420 ISBN 0-8164-0506-9 : 12.95
1. Spiritual direction. I. Title.

KELLY, Gerald A 271
Guidance for religious. Westminster, Md., Newman Press, 1956. 321p. 22cm. [BX2438.K4] 56-11420
1. Spiritual direction. 2. Monastic and religious life. I. Title.

*KRIYANANDA, Swami. 294.5
Letters to truth seekers. [by] Swami Kriyananda. Nevada City, Calif., Ananda Publications, [1973] 104 p., 21 cm. [BX382] 1.50 (pbk.)
1. Spiritual direction. 2. Address, essays, lectures. I. Title.

LAPLACE, Jean, S.J. 241'.1
Preparing for spiritual direction. Translated by John C. Guinness. Chicago, Franciscan Herald Press [1975] 192 p. 22 cm. Translation of La direction de conscience. Reprint of the 1967 ed. published by Herder & Herder, New York, under title: The direction of conscience. [BX2350.7.L3213 1975] 74-17135 ISBN 0-8199-0550-X 6.95
1. Spiritual direction. I. Title.

LEECH, Kenneth. 248.3
Soul friend : the practice of Christian spirituality / Kenneth Leech ; introd. by Henri J. M. Nouwen. 1st American ed. San Francisco : Harper & Row, c1980. p. cm. Includes index. Bibliography: p. [BV5053.L43 1980] 79-2994 ISBN 0-06-065225-X : 8.95
1. Spiritual direction. I. Title.

MOORE, David 248.484
Spirtual prescriptions for health, happiness and abundance. New York, Speller [c.1966] p. 92 18 cm pap. 1.00
I. Title.

PARENTE, Pascal P 1890- 248.482
Spiritual direction. Rev. ed. New York, St. Paul Publications [1961] 158p. 21cm. Includes bibliography. [BX2350.7.P3 1961] 61-13713
1. Spiritual direction. I. Title.

PICHON, Almire, 1843-1919. 248.482
Seeds of the Kingdom; notes from conferences, spiritual directions, meditations. Edited and translated by Lyle Terhune. Westminster, Md., Newman Press, 1961. 271p. 23cm. [BX2350.7.P53] 60-10734
1. Spiritual direction. 2. Meditations. I. Title.

ROLDAN, Alejandro, 1910- 234'.8
Personality types and holiness, by Alexander Roldan. Tr. by Gregory McCaskey. Staten Island, N.Y., Alba [1968] 384p. illus. 22cm. (Mental health ser. [8]) Tr. of Introduction a la ascetica diferencial. Bibl. [BX2350.7.R613] 67-16844 6.50
1. Spiritual direction. 2. Perfection (Catholic) 3. Personality. 4. Psychology, Religious. I. Title.

STEINER, Rudolf, 1861-
The spiritual guidance of man and of mankind, by Dr. Rudolf Steiner; ed. by H. Collison. The authorized English translation. [Bethlehem, Pa., Printed by the Times publishing co., c1915] 100 p. 20 cm. 16-6646 0.50
I. Collison, Harry, ed. II. Title.

VANDERWALL, Francis W. 248.4'82
Spiritual direction : an invitation to abundant life / by Francis W. Vanderwall ; with a foreword by Henri J.M. Nouwen. New York : Paulist Press, c1981. xi, 99 p. ; 21 cm. [BX2350.7.V36 1981] 19 81-83185 ISBN 0-8091-2399-1 (pbk.) : 3.95
1. Spiritual direction. I. Title.

Spiritual direction—Addresses, essays, lectures.

ABBA : 248.4
guides to wholeness and holiness, East and West : papers from a symposium / sponsored by the Institute of Cistercian Studies at the Abbey of New Clairvaux, Vina, California, June 1978 ; edited by John R. Sommerfeldt. Kalamazoo, Mich. : Cistercian Publications, 1982. p. cm. (Cistercian studies series ; no. 38) [BX2438.A22] 19 81-1800 ISBN 0-87907-838-3 : 22.95
1. Spiritual direction—Addresses, essays, lectures. 2. Spiritual direction—Comparative studies—Addresses, essays, lectures. I. Sommerfeldt, John R. II. Institute of Cistercian Studies (Vina, Calif.) III. Title. IV. Series.

Spiritual direction—History—Addresses, essays, lectures.

SPIRITUAL direction / 248.4
John Sullivan, editor. Washington, D.C. : ICS Publications, 1980. ix, 230 p. ; 21 cm. (Carmelite studies) Includes bibliographical references. [BX2438.S64] 19 80-26654 ISBN 0-9600876-8-0 pbk. : 6.95
1. Teresa, Saint, 1515-1582—Addresses, essays, lectures. 2. Juan de la Cruz, Saint, 1542-1591—Addresses, essays, lectures. 3. Therese, Saint, 1873-1897—Addresses, essays, lectures. 4. Spiritual direction—History—Addresses, essays, lectures. 5. Carmelites—Spiritual life—Addresses, essays, lectures. I. Sullivan, John, 1942- II. Series.

Spiritual directors.

GABRIELE di Santa Maria Maddelena, Father. 262.14
The spiritual director, according to the principles of St. John of the Cross. Translated by a Benedictine of Stanbrook Abbey. Westminster, Md., Newman Press [1952?] 131p. 22cm. [BX1912.G15] 52-14617
1. Juan de la Cruz, Saint, 1542-1591. 2. Spiritual directors. I. Title.

SIMONEAUX, Henry J 271
Spiritual guidance and the varieties of character. [1st ed.] New York, Pageant Press [1956] 248p. 24cm. [BX903.S5] 56-11344
1. Spiritual directors. 2. Seminarians—Religious life. I. Title.

Spiritual exercises.

ALBERIONE, Giacomo Giuseppe, 1884-1971. 242
Meditation notes on Paul the Apostle, model of the spiritual life. [Translated by Aloysius Milella. Boston] St. Paul Editions [1972] 100 p. facsims. 20 cm. [BS2506.A4 1972] 72-83471 2.00
1. Paul, Saint, apostle—Meditations. 2. Spiritual exercises. I. Title.

BROU, Alexandre, 1862- 242
The Ignatian way to God; translated from the French of Alexandre Brou by William J. Young. Milwaukee, Bruce Pub. Co. [1952] 156 p. 22 cm. Translation of La spiritualite de Saint Ignace. Includes bibliography. [BX2179.L8B743] 52-2739
1. Loyola, Ignacio de, Saint, 1491-1556. 2. Spiritual exercises. 3. Spiritual life—Catholic authors. I. Title.

CHILSON, Richard. 242
The way to Christianity : in search of spiritual growth / by Richard Chilson. Minneapolis, Minn. : Winston Press, c1979. 343 p. ; 24 cm. [BX2182.2.C52] 19 79-64652 ISBN 0-03-053426-7 pbk. : 6.95
1. Spiritual exercises. I. Title.

CORBISHLEY, Thomas, tr. 242
The spiritual exercises of Saint Ignatius. A new translation by Thomas Corbishley. New York, P. J. Kenedy [1963] 124 p. 18 cm. [The Silver treasury series] [BX2179.L7E5 1963] 63-12296
1. Spiritual exercises I. Title.

DE MELLO, Anthony, 1931- 248.3
Sadhana, a way to God : Christian exercises in Eastern form / Anthony de Mello. 5th ed. St. Louis : Institute of Jesuit Sources ; Anand, India : Gujarat Sahitya Prakash Anand Press, 1978, 1979 printing. xi, 134 p. ; 22 cm. (Study aids on Jesuit topics ; no. 9) [BX2182.2.D39 1978] 19 78-70521 ISBN 0-912422-38-6 : 4.50 ISBN 0-912422-46-7 (pbk) : 3.00
1. Spiritual exercises. I. Title. II. Series.

DEVEREUX, Christina Anne, 1898- 242
Come and see; meditations for an eight day retreat, according to the "Spiritual exercises of St. Ignatius." Milwaukee, Bruce [1951] 119 p. 20 cm. [BX2182.D4] 51-8682
1. Loyola. Ignacio de, Saint, 1491-1556. Exercitia spiritualla. 2. Spiritual exercises. I. Title.

FLEMING, David L., 1934- 242
A contemporary reading of The spiritual exercises : a companion to St. Ignatius' text / David L. Fleming. Experimental ed. St. Louis : Institute of Jesuit Sources, 1976. xv, 91 p. ; 23 cm. (Study aids on Jesuit topics ; no. 2) [BX2179.L8F56] 76-2125 ISBN 0-912422-11-4 : 2.00
1. Loyola, Ignacio de, Saint, 1491-1556. Exercitia spiritualia. 2. Spiritual exercises. I. Loyola, Ignacio de, Saint, 1491-1556. Exercitia spiritualia. II. Title. III. Series.

FLEMING, David L., 1934- 242
A contemporary reading of The spiritual exercises : a companion to St. Ignatius' text / David L. Fleming. 2d ed., rev. St. Louis : Institute of Jesuit Sources, 1980, c1978. xiii, 98 p. ; 23 cm. (Study aids on

Jesuit topics ; no. 2) Includes index. [BX2179.L8F56 1980] 19 80-81812 ISBN 0-912422-47-5 (pbk.) : 3.00 ISBN 0-912422-48-3 (sewn pbk.) : 4.00
1. Loyola, Ignacio de, Saint, 1491-1556. Exercitia spiritualia. 2. Spiritual exercises. I. Loyola, Ignacio de, Saint, 1491-1556. Exercitia spiritualia. II. Title. III. Series.

JONES, William McKendrey. 242
A guide to living power / by William M. Jones. Atlanta : John Knox Press, [1975] 120 p. ; 21 cm. [BV4509.5.J66] 74-19969 ISBN 0-8042-1105-1 : 3.95
1. Spiritual exercises. 2. Mental discipline. I. Title.

LOYOLA, Ignacio de, Saint, 1491- 242
The spiritual exercises of St. Ignatius : a literal translation and a contemporary reading / David L. Fleming. St. Louis : Institute of Jesuit Sources, 1978. xxiv, 244 p. ; 24 cm. (Study aids on Jesuit topics ; no. 7) Translation of Exercitia spiritualia. Edition for 1976 by D. L. Fleming published under title: A contemporary reading of The spiritual exercises. Includes index. [BX2179.L7E5 1978] 77-93429 ISBN 0-912422-32-7 : 12.00. ISBN 0-912422-28-9 pbk. : 7.00. ISBN 0-912422-31-9 Smyth sewn pbk. : 8.00
1. Spiritual exercises. I. Fleming, David L., 1934- II. Fleming, David L., 1934- A contemporary reading of The spiritual excercises. III. Title. IV. Series.

LOYOLA, Ignacio de, Saint, 1491-1556 242
The spiritual exercises of St. Ignatius. Tr. by Anthony Mottola. Introd. by Robert W. Gleason. Garden City, N.Y., Doubleday [c.1964] 200p. 18cm. (Image bk. org. D170) 64-12784 .85 pap.,
1. Spiritual exercises. I. Mottola, Anthony, tr. II. Title.

LOYOLA, Ignacio de, Saint, 1491-1556. 242
The spiritual exercises of St. Ignatius. A new translation based on studies in the language of the autograph, by Louis J. Puhl. Westminster, Md., Newman Press, 1951. xiii, 216 p. 20 cm. [BX2179.L7E5 1951] 51-10438
1. Spiritual exercises. I. Title.

LOYOLA, Ignacio de, Saint, 1491-1556. 242
The spiritual exercises of Saint Ignatius. A new translation by Thomas Corbishley. New York, P. J. Kenedy [1963] 124 p. 18 cm. [The Silver treasury series] [BX2179.L7E5 1963] 63-12296
1. Spiritual exercises I. Corbishley, Thomas, tr. II. Title.

LOYOLA, Ignacio de, Saint, 1491-1556. 242
The spiritual exercises of St. Ignatius. Translated by Anthony Mottola. Introd. by Robert W. Gleason. [1st ed.] Garden City, N.Y., Image Books [1964] 200 p. 18 cm. (An Image book original) "D 170." [BX2179.L7E5 1964] 64-12784
1. Spiritual exercises. I. Mottola, Anthony, tr. II. Title.

MCQUADE, James J 242.64
How to give the spiritual exercises of St. Ignatius to lay apostles. Chicago, Loyola University Press, 1962. 94p. 24cm. [BX2179.L8M32] 61-18210
1. Loyola, Ignacio de, Saint, 1491-1556. Exercitia spiritualia. 2. Spiritual exercises. I. Title.

MARGERIE, Bertrand de. 242'.1
Theological retreat : with some Ignatian spiritual exercises / Bertrand de Margerie ; translated by A. Owen. Chicago : Franciscan Herald Press, c1976. xxix, 333 p. ; 24 cm. Includes indexes. Bibliography: p. 309-311. [BX2179.L8M33] 76-50929 ISBN 0-8199-0656-5 : 10.95
1. Loyola, Ignacio de, Saint, 1491-1556. Exercitia spiritualia. 2. Spiritual exercises. I. Title.

NOTES on the spiritual exercises. [Maryland] Woodstock College Press, 1956. 336p.
I. Rahner, Hugo, 1900-

POTTER, Mary, Mother, 1847-1913. 232.931
To Jesus through Mary; spiritual exercises for consecrating one's self to Mary. New York, Catholic Book Pub. Co. [1952] 256p. illus. 16cm. Previous ed. published under title: Spiritual exercises of Mary. [BX2182.P67 1952] 53-606
1. Spiritual exercises. I. Title.

PROGOFF, Ira. 158'.12
The practice of process meditation : the Intensive Journal way to spiritual experience / by Ira Progoff. New York, N.Y. : Dialogue House Library, c1980. 343 p. ; 25 cm. [BL624.P76] 19 80-68847 ISBN 0-87941-008-6 : 12.95
1. Spiritual exercises. 2. Meditation. 3. Mantras. I. Title.
Publisher's address: 80 E. 11th New York, NY 10013

RAHNER, Karl, 1904- 242
Spiritual exercises. Translated by Kenneth Baker. [New York] Herder and Herder [1965] 287 p. 22 cm. Translation of Betrachtungen zum ignatianischen Exerzitienbuch. [BX2179.L8R33] 65-21949
1. Loyola, Ignacio de, Saint, 1491-1556. Exercitia spiritualia. 2. Spiritual exercises. 3. Retreats.

SHEEHAN, John F. X. 242
On becoming whole in Christ : an interpretation of the spiritual exercises / John F. X. Sheehan. Chicago : Loyola University Press, c1978. 124 p. ; 21 cm. Reprint of the ed. published by Dimension Books, Denville, N.J. [BX2179.L7S47 1978] 78-9936 ISBN 0-8294-0278-0 pbk. : 2.95
1. Loyola, Ignacio de, Saint, 1491-1556. Exercitia spiritualia. 2. Spiritual exercises. I. Title.

SPIRITUAL exercises to serve for the annual retreat of a Carmelite, 242 by the ecclesiastical superior of a Carmelite convent, tr. from the French by a religious of the Carmel of New Orleans. New Orleans, La., Monastery of discalced Carmelite, 1919. 271 p. 22 1/2 cm. [BX2188.C3S7] 20-8881

STANLEY, David Michael, 1914- 242
A modern scriptural approach to the Spiritual exercises [by] David M. Stanley. Chicago, Institute of Jesuit Sources, 1967. xvi, 358 p. 24 cm. Bibliography: p. 331-334. [BX2179.L8S7] 67-25219
1. Loyola, Ignacio de, Saint, 1491-1556. Exercitia spiritualia. 2. Spiritual exercises. 3. Mediations. 4. Retreats. I. Title.

VILLACASTIN, Tomas de, 1570-1649. 230'.2 s
A manuall of devout meditations, 1618 / Tomas de Villacastin. Ilkley : Scolar Press, 1976. 558 p. ; 20 cm. (English Recusant Literature, 1558-1640 ; v. 326) (Series: Rogers, David Morrison, comp. English recusant literature, 1558-1640 ; v. 326.) Original Spanish title: Manual de consideraciones y ejercicios espirituales. "Allison and Rogers 848; STC 16877." Includes original t.p.: A manuall of devout meditations and exercises, instructing how to pray mentally, drawne for the most part, out of the spiritual exercises of B. F. Ignatius ... Includes index. [BX1750.A1E5 vol. 326] [BX2186] 242 77-371652 ISBN 0-85967-342-1
1. Spiritual exercises. I. Loyola, Ignacio de, Saint, 1491-1556. Exercitia spiritualia. II. Series.

Spiritual healing.

BARTOW, Donald W. 248.8'6
The adventures of healing : how to use New Testament practices and receive New Testament results / Donald W. Bartow. Canton, Ohio : Life Enrichment Publishers, 1981. p. cm. [BT732.5.B36] 19 80-84933 ISBN 0-938736-02-7 (pbk.) : 5.95
1. Spiritual healing. I. Title.

DEVANANDAM, Rajamma, 1910- 289.9 B
I serve the God of miracles / by Rajamma Devanandam. Jasper, Ark. (P.O. Box 447, Jasper 72641) : End-Time Handmaidens, c1980. 95 p., [17] p. of plates : ill. ; 21 cm. [BT732.5.D48] 19 81-119151 3.50 (pbk.)
1. Devanandam, Rajamma, 1910- 2. Spiritual healing. I. Title.

DIORIO, Ralph A., 1930- 234'.13
Called to heal / Ralph A. DiOrio. 1st ed. Garden City, N.Y. : Doubleday, 1982. p. cm. [BT732.5.D56 1982] 19 82-45354 ISBN 0-385-18226-0 : 12.95
1. DiOrio, Ralph A., 1930- 2. Spiritual healing. I. Title.

FARICY, Robert L., 1926- 248.3'2
Praying for inner healing / Robert Faricy. New York : Paulist Press, c1979. vii, 86 p. ; 21 cm. Includes bibliographical references. [BT732.5.F37 1979] 79-92857 ISBN 0-8091-2250-2 (pbk.) : 2.95
1. Spiritual healing. 2. Prayer. I. Title.

LAWRENCE, Roy, 1931- 253
Christian healing rediscovered / Roy Lawrence. Rev. ed. Downers Grove, Ill. : InterVarsity Press, c1980. p. cm. "A combined edition of Christian healing rediscovered (1976) and Invitation to healing (1979)." [BT732.5.L33 1980] 80-7470 ISBN 0-87784-621-9 pbk. : 3.95
1. Lawrence, Roy, 1931- 2. Spiritual healing. I. Lawrence, Roy, 1931- Invitation to healing. II. Title.

PETERSON, John H. 234'.13
Healing touch / John H. Peterson. Wilton, Conn. : Morehouse-Barlow, c1981. 102 p. ; 19 cm. Includes bibliographies. [BT732.5.P45 1981] 19 81-81629 ISBN 0-8192-1291-1 pbk. : 4.95
1. Spiritual healing. I. Title.

REIDT, Wilford H. 234'.13
Jesus, God's way of healing and power to promote health : featuring the miracle ministry of Dr. John G. Lake / by Wilford H. Reidt. Tulsa, Okla. : Harrison House, c1981. 171 p. ; 21 cm. [BT732.5.R44] 19 81-184397 ISBN 0-89274-197-X (pbk.) : 4.95
1. Lake, John G. 2. Spiritual healing. I. Title.

SHILOH, Ailon. 615.8'52
Faith healing : the religious experience as a therapeutic process / by Ailon Shiloh. Springfield, Ill. : Thomas, c1981. xiv, 110 p. ; 24 cm. Includes index. Bibliography: p. 101-108. [BT732.5.S52] 19 81-8993 ISBN 0-398-04509-7 : 16.75
1. Spiritual healing. I. Title.

THOMPSON, Carroll J., 1912- 615.8'52
The miracle of holistic healing / by Carroll J. Thompson. Port Washington, N.Y. : Ashley Books, 1982. p. cm. [BT732.5.T48] 19 81-17589 ISBN 0-87949-203-1 : 12.95
1. Thompson, Carroll J., 1912- 2. Spiritual healing. 3. Holistic medicine. 4. Healers—Illinois—Biography. 5. Illinois—Biography. I. Title.

WAGNER, James K. 234'.13
Blessed to be a blessing / James K. Wagner. Nashville, Tenn. : Upper Room, c1980. 143 p. ; 22 cm. Bibliography: p. 132-143. [BT732.5.W33] 19 80-52615 ISBN 0-8358-0410-0 pbk. : 4.50
1. Spiritual healing. I. Title.

Spiritual healing and spiritualism—Addresses, essays, lectures.

FIVE great healers speak here 615.8'52 / compiled by Nancy and Esmond Gardner. Wheaton, IL. : Theosophical Pub. House, 1982. xxii, 138 p. : ports. ; 21 cm. "A Quest book." Includes bibliographical references. [BF1275.F3F58 1982] 19 82-50164 ISBN 0-8356-0567-1 (pbk.) : 6.25
1. Spiritual healing and spiritualism—Addresses, essays, lectures. 2. Mental healing—Addresses, essays, lectures. 3. Healers—Biography. I. Gardner, Nancy, 1909- II. Gardner, Esmond, 1901-

Spiritual life.

ADLER, Felix, 1851- 170
The essentials of spirituality, by Felix Adler. New York, J. Pott & co., 1905. 2 p. l., 92 p. 19 cm. [BJ1581.A25] 5-32520
1. Spiritual life. I. Title.

ADLER, Felix, 1851-1933. 170
Incompatibility in marriage, by Felix Adler. New York, London, D. Appleton and company, 1930. 4 p. l., 104 [1] p. 19 1/2 cm. [BJ1581.A26] 30-6393
1. Spiritual life. 2. Ethics. 3. Marriage. I. Title.

ADLER, Felix, 1851-1933. 218
The reconstruction of the spiritual ideal; Hibbert lectures, delivered in Manchester college, Oxford, May, 1923, by Felix Adler. New York, London, D. Appleton and company, 1924. 3 p. l., 218 p. 19 1/2 cm. [BL25.H5 1928] [BD431.A42] 294. 24-4875
1. Spiritual life. I. Title.

ALLEN, Mark, 1946- 294.3'444
Tantra for the West : a guide to personal freedom / Marcus Allen ; [cover photo by Dean Campbell, cover art by Linda Cook, artwork by Rebecca Donicht]. Berkeley, Calif. : Whatever Pub., c1980. p. cm. Bibliography: p. [BL624.A45] 80-316 ISBN 0-931432-07-3 : 10.95 ISBN 0-931432-06-5 pbk. : 5.95
1. Spiritual life. 2. Religious life (Tantric Buddhism) I. Title.

AMAR Jyoti, Swami. 294.5'43
Retreat into eternity : an Upanishad-book of aphorisms / Swami Amar Jyoti. Boulder, Colo. : Truth Consciousness, c1981. 128 p. : ill. (some col.) ; 22 x 28 cm. Includes index. [BL624.A47] 19 80-54236 ISBN 0-933572-03-4 pbk. : 10.95
1. Spiritual life. I. Title.
Publisher's address: Gold Hill, Salina Star rte., Boulder, CO 80302

AMAR Jyoti, Swami. 291.4
Spirit of Himalaya : the story of a truth seeker / Swami Amar Jyoti. Tucson, Ariz. : Truth Consciousness, c1979. 123 p., [8] leaves of plates : 8 col. ill. ; 23 cm. [BL624.A48] 78-73995 ISBN 0-933572-00-X : 7.95
1. Spiritual life. I. Title.

AMICK, Lon Gilbert, 1920- 248
The divine journey; a guide to spiritual understanding, by Lon Amick. Illustrated by Arthur Kraft. Philadelphia, Dorrance [1968] 78 p. illus. 21 cm. [BV4501.2.A45] 68-14765
1. Spiritual life. I. Title.

ANANDAMURTI. 294
Baba's grace; discourses of Shrii Shrii Anandamurti. [Los Altos Hills, Calif., Ananda Marga Publications, 1973] 197 p. illus. 19 cm. [BP610.A513] 74-75331 ISBN 0-88476-001-4 2.95
1. Spiritual life. I. Title.

ANANDAMURTI. 294
The great universe; discourses on society. [Los Altos Hills, Calif., Ananda Marga Publications, c1973] 271 p. illus. 19 cm. [BP610.A514] 74-75332 ISBN 0-88476-002-2 3.25
I. Title.

ANDREW, Father, 1869-1946. 248
Love's fulfilment; an anthology from the writings of Father Andrew. Edited by Kathleen E. Burne. With an introd. by Bishop Lumsden Barkway. London, A. R. Mowbray; New York, Morehouse-Gorham Co. [1957] 192p. 21cm. [BV4501.A66] 57-14180
1. Spiritual life. I. Title.

ANDREWS, Charles Freer, 1871- 248
Christ in the silence [by] C. F. Andrews. New York, Cincinnati [etc.] The Abingdon press [c1933] 299 p. 19 1/2 cm. "Books that may help the reader"; p. 298-299. [BV4501.A67 1933 a] 33-33096
1. Spiritual life. I. Title.

ARNOLD, Eberhard, 1883-1935. 248 s
The experience of God and his peace : a guide into the heart and soul of the Bible / by Eberhard Arnold. Rifton, N.Y. : Plough Pub. House, 1975. x p., p. 189-315 ; 20 cm. (His Inner land ; v. 3) Translation of chapters 6-7 of Innenland. [BV4495.A7413 vol. 3] [BV4503] 248 75-9720 ISBN 0-87486-155-1 : 4.50
1. Spiritual life. 2. God. I. Title.

ARNOLD, Eberhard, 1883-1935. 248 s
The Living Word / by Eberhard Arnold. Rifton, N.Y. : Plough Pub. House, c1975. xv p., p. 441-576 ; 19 cm. (His Inner land ; v. 5) "Translated from the 1936 ed. of Innenland. Includes index. [BV4495.A7413 vol. 5] [BV4503] 248'.42 75-33241 ISBN 0-87486-157-8
1. Spiritual life. I. Title.

ARNOLD, Eberhard, 1883- 248 s
1935.
The struggle of the conscience / by Eberhard Arnold. Rifton, N.Y. : Plough Pub. House, 1975. (His Inner land ; v. 2) Translation of chapters 4-5 of Innenland. [BV4495.A7413 vol. 2] [BV4503] 248 75-1335 ISBN 0-87486-154-3 : 4.25
1. Spiritual life. I. Title.

ARNSBY-JONES, George 299
The pilgrimage of James : an odyssey of inner space / by George Arnsby Jones. 1st ed. Pensacola, Fl. : Rookfield Press, 1977c1976 110 p. ; 22 cm. Imprint from label mounted on t.p. [BL624.A76] 76-27107 ISBN 0-917610-01-6 pbk. : 2.95
1. Spiritual life. I. Title.

AUGUSTINUS, Aurelius, Saint, 242
Bp. of Hippo. Spurious and doubtful works.
Little book of contemplation; edited and rev. into modern English by Joseph Whittkofski. New York, Morehouse-Gorham, 1950. 101 p. 16 cm. With facsimile reproduction of the t. p. of the edition of 1577: S.Avgvstines Manuell, or litle booke of the Contemplation of Christ. or of Gods worde ... At London, Printed by Iohn Daye ... 1577. [BX2179.A8E5 1950] 50-10895
1. Spiritual life. I. Title.

BAKER, Nelson Alloway, 1856-
Pneu-ho-mology; a discourse on the spiritual and physical nature of man, by Dr. N. A. Baker. Pub. by the author. [Minneapolis, Printed by Heywood mfg. co.] 1912. 4 p. l., [3]-290 p. front. (port.) 19 cm. 12-2562
I. Title.

BARING, Margery Louise, 1908- 133
Ours for discovery, a guide to the inner journey, [by] Margery Louise Baring ... Reno, Nev., Silver state press [c1944] 2 p. l., 7-215 p. 18 1/2 x 14 cm. Book 2 of a trilogy; books 1 and 3 have titles The greater freedom; the heritage of the innate self and Good news, an eleventh hour dispatch, respectively. [BF1999.B3763] 44-25094
I. Title.

BARRY, Freedom 233
I do; spiritual awakening through individual endeavor. New York, Vantage [c.1963] 61p. 21 cm. 3.00 bds.,
I. Title.

BARTLETT, Alden Eugene, 1873- 248
The joy maker; a guide to happiness, by A. Eugene Bartlett, D.D. New York, Chicago [etc.] Fleming R. Revell company [c1918] 188 p. 20 cm. [BV4501.B3] 18-13650
I. Title.

BEET, Joseph Agar, 1840-1924. 248
The new life in Christ; a study in personal religion, by Joseph Agar Beet, D.D. Nashville, Tenn., Dallas, Tex., [etc.] Lamour & Barton [1922] xv, 347 p. 19 cm. "This volume is a necessary sequel to an earlier one entitled Through Christ to God." [BV4501.B418] 33-36481
1. Spiritual life. 2. Theology, Doctrinal. I. Title.

BIEDERWOLF, William Edward, 248
1867-
The growing Christian; or, The development of the spiritual life, by Rev. William Edward Biederwolf ... Chicago, Ill., Winona Lake, Ind., The Winona publishing company [1903] 121 p. 17 cm. [BV4501.B53] 3-28139
I. Title.

*BOGARD, David. 133.9
Valleys & vistas; after losing life's partner. Grand Rapids, Baker Book House, [1974] 94 p. illus. 21 cm. [BV4011.6] ISBN 0-8010-0625-2 3.95
1. Spiritual life. I. Title.

BOLTON, Margaret, mother 244
1873-
The spiritual way by Mother Bolton... Yonkers-on-Hudson, New York, World book company, 1929- v. illus. (part col.)18 1/2 cm. Contains music. [BX980.B6] 30-7736
I. Title.

BOLTON, Margaret mother 228.2
1873-
The spiritual way; manual, by Mother Bolton ... Yonkers-on-Hudson, N. Y., World book company, 1930. viii, 183 p. illus. 18 1/2 cm. [BX980.B6] 30-21310
I. Title.

[BONA, Giovanni] cardinal, 230.
1609-1674.
A treatise of spiritual life, leading man by an easy and clear method from the commencement of conversion to the very summit of sanctity. Translated from the Latin of Mgr. Charles Joseph Morozzo ... by Rev. D. A. Donovan ... Poplar Bluff, Mo., The author, 1893. x [11]-513 p. 19 1/2 cm. Commonly attributed to Carlo Giuseppe Morozzo since its first publication in 1674. The authorship of Giovanni Bona is affirmed by Marco Vattasso in his edition of Bona's Hortus caelestium deliciarum (Roma, 1918) p. xxxix. [BV5080.B83C82 1893] 47-34758
I. Morozzo, Carlo Giuseppe, bp., 1645-1729, supposed author. II. Donovan, Daniel A., tr. III. Title.

BOYD, Thomas Parker. 243
The principia of the spiritual life, by Thomas Parker Boyd ... San Francisco, Calf., California press, 1934. 3 p. l., iii, 222 p. 18 cm. [BV4501.B693] 35-2673
1. Spiritual life. I. Title.

BRADFORD, Amory Howe, 1846- 220
1911.
The inward light, by Amory H. Bradford ... New York, T. Y. Crowell & co., [1905] ix, p., 2 l., 3-359 p. 20 cm. [BR125.B716] 5-33905
1. Spiritual life. 2. Immanence of God. I. Title.
Contents omitted.

BRETT, Jesse, 1858- 242
The way of vision; an aspect of spiritual life, by the Rev. Jesse Brett ... London, New York, [etc.] Longmans, Green, and co., 1923. viii, 117 p. front. 19 cm. Published in 1922. [BV4832.B745] 22-24830 1.75
I. Title.

BRIGHTMAN, Edgar Sheffield, 248
1884-
The spiritual life [by] Edgar Sheffield Brightman. New York, Nashville, Abingdon-Cokesbury press [1942] 218 p. 20 1/2 cm. (The Cole lectures. Vanderbilt university) The substance of the Cole lectures of 1942. cf. Pref. [BV4501.B735] 42-21863
1. Spiritual life. I. Title.

BROWN, Charles Ewing, 1883- 248
Adventures in the spiritual life, by Charles E. Brown ... Anderson, Ind., The Warner press [1946] ix, 10-212 p. 19 1/2 cm. [BV4501.B737] 46-1966
1. Spiritual life. I. Title.

BRUNTON, Paul. 248
A hermit in the Himalayas, by Paul Brunton. New York, E. P. Dutton & co., inc., 1937. 4 p. l., [5]-322 p. front. 21 cm. "First edition." [BV4501.B7562] 37-4072
1. Spriralthough life. I. Title.

BRUNTON, Paul. 248
The secret path; a technique of spiritual self-discovery for the modern world, by Paull Brunton ... New York, E. P. Dutton & co., inc. [c1935] 222 p. 20 cm. "First edition." [BV4501.B7565] 35-10460
1. Spiritual life. I. Title.

BRUNTON, Paul, 1898- 248
The secret path; a technique of spiritual self-discovery for the modern world. New York, Dutton, 1958 [c1935] 128p. 19cm. (A Dutton everyman paperback, D29) [BL624] 58-59641
1. Spiritual life. I. Title.

BUBBA Free John. 294.5'44
Breath and name : the initiation and foundation practices of free spiritual life / Bubba Free John. 1st ed. San Francisco : Dawn Horse Press, 1977. 275 p. : ports. ; 22 cm. Bibliography: p. [266]-275. [BP610.B812] 77-72993 ISBN 0-913922-29-3 : 5.95
1. Spiritual life. I. Title.

BUBBA Free John. 299
The enlightenment of the whole body : a rational and new prophetic revelation of the truth of religion, esoteric spirituality, and the divine destiny of man / by Bubba Free John. 1st ed. Middletown, Calif. : Dawn Horse Press, 1978. 600 p., [1] leaf of plates : ill. ; 23 cm. Includes index. Bibliography: p. 588-594. [BP610.B813] 77-94504 ISBN 0-913922-35-8 : 8.95
1. Spiritual life. I. Title.

BUBBA Free John. 294.5'6'1
The paradox of instruction : an introduction to the esoteric spiritual teaching of Bubba Free John / by Bubba Free John. 1st ed. Honolulu : The Dawn Horse Press, 1977. xv, 89 p. : ports. ; 22 cm. Bibliography: p. 79-86. [BP610.B816] 77-71191 ISBN 0-913922-27-7 : 3.50
1. Spiritual life. I. Title.

BUBBA Free John. 294.5'6'1
The paradox of instruction : an introduction to the esoteric spiritual teaching of Bubba Free John / by Bubba Free John. 2d ed., rev. and expanded. San Francisco : Dawn Horse Press, 1977. 326 p. : ill. ; 23 cm. (Vision Mound Ceremony publications) Includes bibliographical references. [BP610.B816 1977b] 77-81836 ISBN 0-913922-28-5 : 5.95
1. Spiritual life. I. Title.

BUBBA Free John. 299
The way of divine communion : the foundation practices of the Free Communion Church / by Bubba Free John ; edited and with an introd. by the staff of Vision Mound Seminary. 1st ed. San Francisco : Dawn Horse Press, 1976. v, 45 p. : ill. ; 22 cm. [BP610.B818] 76-25712 ISBN 0-913922-26-9 : 2.00
1. Spiritual life. I. Title.

BUCHANAN, Uriel.
Spiritual life, by Uriel Buchanan ... New York, R. F. Fenno company, 1913. 110 p. 19 cm. 13-11000 0.50
I. Title.

BUNTING, John Summerfield. 248
The secret of a quiet mind, the building of the life within, by the Reb. John S. Bunting ... New York, Chicago [etc.] Fleming H. Revell company [c1929] 127 p. 19 1/2 cm. [BV4501.B783] 29-2493
1. Spiritual life. I. Title.

BUTTERWORTH, Eric. 248.4'8'99
Unity of all life. [1st ed.] New York, Harper & Row [1969] 209 p. 22 cm. Bibliographical references included in "Notes" (p. 205-209) [BX9890.U5B82] 75-85053 5.95
1. Unity School of Christianity. 2. Spiritual life. I. Title.

CAILLIET, Emile, 1894- 248
Journey into light. Grand Rapids, Zondervan Pub. House [1968] 117 p. 23 cm. [BV4501.2.C23] 68-12954
1. Spiritual life. I. Title.

CASTEEL, John Laurence, 1903- 259
ed.
Spiritual renewal through personal groups; edited with an introd. and an interpretation. New York, Association Press [1957] 220 p. 21 cm. [BV4501.C3454] 57-11602
1. Spiritual life. 2. Church group work. I. Title.

CASWELL, Edwin Whittier, 242
1844-1923.
Meditations for the quiet hour, by Rev. Edwin Whittier Caswell; with a preface by Arthur B. Sanford, D. D. Boston, R. G. Badger [c1924] 271 p. front. (port.) 20 cm. [BV4832.C35] 24-13961
I. Title.

CATE, Harold Webster. 171.1
Truth, do you know me? By Harold Webster Cate. [Antrim, N. H.] H. W. Cate, c1930. 70 p., 1 l. 17 cm. [BV4510.C35] 30-17798
1. Spiritual life. 2. Christian life. I. Title.

CHAMBERS, Arthur.
Problems of the spiritual, by the Reverend Arthur Chambers ... Philadelphia, G. W. Jacobs & co. [1907] 7 p. l., 241 p. 20 cm. 8-12822
I. Title.

CHAMBERS, Arthur, d.1918. 133.
Thoughts of the spiritual, by the Reverend Arthur Chambers ... Philadelphia, G. W. Jacobs & co. [c1905] 1 p. l., [5]-241 p. 20 cm. [BF1261.C46] 5-8084
1. Spiritual life. I. Title.
Contents omitted.

CHAPMAN, J Wilbur, 1859-1918.
The spiritual life of the Sunday school. Boston and Chicago, United society of Christian endeavor [1899] 62 p. 16 degrees. 99-3746
I. Title.

CHINMOY. 181'.45
Arise! Awake! Thoughts of a Yogi. New York, F. Fell [1972] 1 v. (unpaged) illus. 22 cm. [BL624.C46 1972] 76-175425 ISBN 0-8119-0207-2 5.95
1. Spiritual life. 2. Devotional calendars. I. Title.

CHRISTENSEN, Bernhard 248
Marinus, 1901-
Fire upon the earth, by Bernhard Christensen. Minneapolis, Lutheran free church publishing company, 1941. 256 p. 20 1/2 cm. [BV4501.C49] 43-14476
1. Spiritual life. I. Title.

CLARK, Fred. 248
Spiritual treasure in earthen vessels, by Fred Clark... Dallas, Tex., Mathis, Van Nort & company [1939] 4 p. l., 134 p. 26 cm. [BV4501.C62] 40-4829
1. Spiritual life. I. Title.

CLAYDON, Graham. 248.3
Time with God / Graham Claydon. Grand Rapids, MI : Zondervan, [1982] c1979. p. cm. Originally published: Leicester, England : Inter-Varsity Press, 1979. Bibliography: p. [BV4501.2.C557 1979] 19 82-7033 ISBN 0-310-45202-3 : 1.95
1. Spiritual life. 2. Prayer. I. Title.

COE, Edward Benton, 1842- 220
1914.
Life indeed, by Edward B. Coe ... New York, Chicago [etc.] Fleming H. Revell company [c1899] 267 p. 18 1/2 cm. Religious essays. [BR125.C623] 99-3055
1. Spiritual life. I. Title.

COE, Frances. 248.4
Insearch—discovering the real you / Frances Coe and Ivan Coe. 1st ed. Smithtown, N.Y. : Exposition Press, c1981. xi, 92 p. ; 22 cm. (An Exposition-testament book) [BV4501.2.C625] 19 80-70889 ISBN 0-682-49713-4 : 6.50
1. Spiritual life. I. Coe, Ivan. II. Title.

CONKLIN, Robert, 1921- 248
Reach for the sun : a story / by Robert Conklin ; ill. and calligraphy by Robert Bowman. New York : Simon and Schuster, c1978. [57] p. : ill. ; 22 cm. [BL624.C66] 77-20338 ISBN 0-671-24936-3 : 6.95
1. Spiritual life. I. Title.

CORLESS, Roger. 248.4
The art of Christian alchemy : transfiguring the ordinary through holistic meditation / Roger Corless. New York : Paulist Press, c1981. 118 p. ; 21 cm. Bibliography: p. 105-118. [BL624.C666] 19 81-80872 ISBN 0-8091-2388-6 (pbk.) : 4.95
1. Spiritual life. I. Title.

CRONK, Walter. 291.4
Explore your own inner space / Walter Cronk. Marina del Rey, Calif. : DeVorss, c1979. 194 p., [1] leaf of plates : ill. ; 21 cm. [BL624.C76] 79-53568 ISBN 0-87516-376-9 pbk. : 6.50
1. Spiritual life. 2. Physical research. I. Title.

DADA, 1917- 291.4'4
Beyond the mind : conversations on the deeper significance of living / by Dada. San Francisco : Dada, 1978. viii, 134 p. : ill. ; 23 cm. [BL624.D25] 77-85723 ISBN 0-930608-01-1 pbk. : 3.95
1. Spiritual life. 2. Conduct of life. I. Title.

DAVIS, Roy Eugene. 294.5'4
Darshan: the vision of light. Lakemont, Ga., CSA Press [1971] 206 p. illus. 23 cm. [BF1997.D38A3] 72-185617 ISBN 0-87707-075-X 5.95
1. Spiritual life. I. Title.

DAVIS, Roy Eugene. 248'.4
With God we can! / Roy Eugene Davis. Lakemont, Ga. : CSA Press, c1978. 248 p.

: port. ; 22 cm. [BL624.D32] 78-51817 ISBN 0-87707-211-6 : 4.95
1. Spiritual life. I. Title.

DEAL, William S. 248.42
Problems of the spirit-filled life. Kansas City, Mo., Beacon Hill Pr. [1961] 158p. Bibl. 61-5092 2.00
1. Spiritual life. I. Title.

DELP, Paul S 248.42
The Journey of the human spirit; the story of man's quest for fulfillment. Foreword by Glenn Randall Phillips. [1st ed.] New York, Exposition Press [1962] 104 p. 21 cm. (An Exposition-Testament book) [BV4501.2.D44] 62-21055
1. Spiritual life. I. Title.

DENT, Phyllis.
The growth of the spiritual life, by Phyllis Dent, M.B.E. London, New York, etc., Rich & Cowan [1944] 128 p. 18 cm. (On cover: The 'Needs of to-day' series, 25) "First published 1944." 44-5925
1. Spiritual life. I. Title.

DICKMAN, R. Thomas. 234
In God we should trust / by R. Thomas Dickman. Roslyn Heights, N.Y. : Libra Publishers, c1977. 122 p. ; 21 cm. Includes bibliographical references. [BV4501.2.D495] 78-307279 6.95
1. Spiritual life. 2. Justice. 3. Grace (Theology) I. Title.

DICKSON, James Jacobs, 1880-1956.
The Bible of pure spiritualism, for world purist temples of pure spiritualism religion and for individual followers of all tongues. A 20th century direct revelation. [San Francisco, Calif., 1962] 100 p. illus. 18 x 22 cm. Two ports. tipped in. "Heard, written down, compiled and printed by Daisy Gibson Buettner." Rev. James J. Dickson was the medium. 64-36090
I. Title.

DOHERTY, Catherine de Hueck, 1900- 248.4
Molchanie : the silence of God / Catherine de Hueck Doherty. New York : Crossroad, 1982. 100 p. ; 22 cm. [BV4501.2.D596 1982] 19 81-17281 ISBN 0-8245-0407-0 : 7.95
1. Spiritual life. 2. Silence. I. Title.

DOUGALL, Lily, 1858-1923. 265.
The Christian doctrine of health; a handbook on the relation of bodily to spiritual and moral health, by Lily Dougall ... New York, The Macmillan company, 1923. x p., 1 l., 181 p. 19 1/2 cm. [BR115.H4D6] 23-12636
I. Title.

DRAKE, Frederick William. 922
Masters of the spiritual life, by F. pw. Drake... London, New York [etc.] Longmans, Green and co., 1916. viii p., 1 l., 160 p. front. 19 1/2 cm. [BR1703.D7] 19-4639
I. Title.

DRESSER, Horatio Willis, 1866-
The philosophy of the spirit; a study of the spiritual nature of man and the presence of God, with a supplementary essay on the logic of Hegel, by Horatio W. Dresser... New York and London, G.P. Putnam's sons, 1908. xiv p., 1 l., 543 p. 22 1/2 cm. [BD555.D7] 8-16563
1. Hegel, Georg Wilhelm Friedrich, 1770-1831. 2. Spiritual life. 3. Philosophy and religion. I. Title.

DRESSER, Horatio Willis, 1866- 131
The power of silence; an interpretation of life in its relation to health and happiness, by Horatio W. Dresser... Boston, G. H. Ellis, 1895. 219 p. 20 cm. [BF639.D7] 10-22014
1. Spiritual life. 2. New thought. I. Title.

DRESSER, Horatio Willis, 1866- 131
The power of silence; an interpretation of life in its relation to health and happiness, by Horatio W. Dresser...15th impression. New York & London, G. P. Putnam's sons, 1903. 219 p. 19 cm. "The substance of a course of lectures delivered in Boston, during the winter of 1893-94, and not originally intended for publication."-Pref. to 10th ed. [BF639.D7 1903] 17-31594
1. Spiritual life. 2. New thought. I. Title. II. Title: Silence, The power of.

DRESSER, Horatio Willis, 1866- 131
The power of silence; a study of the values and ideals of the inner life, by Horatio W. Dresser... 2d ed., rev. and enl. New York and London, G. P. Putnam's sons, 1904. 3 p l., [v]-356 p. 19 1/2 cm. (Half-title: The Inner life series) [BF639.D7 1904] 4-30179
1. Spiritual life. 2. New thought. I. Title.

EDWARDS, Ethel. 291.4'2
Psychedelics and inner space. Cincinnati, Psyche Press [1969] 253 p. 22 cm. Bibliographical footnotes. [BL624.E35] 70-6653
1. Spiritual life. 2. Hallucinogenic drugs and religious experience. I. Title.

ELLIS, Mary Leith.
Growing in faith and knowledge. Illustrated by Beatrice Darwin. Richmond, The CLC Press [1967] 96 p. illus. 21 cm. (The Covenant Life Curriculum) Teaching units. Richmond, The CLC Press [1967] 88 p. (The Covenant Life Curriculum) 68-44481
I. Title.

ERB, Fannie Stienbrecher, Mrs. 248
Gold tried in the fire, by Mrs. Fannie Erb... [Hubbard, Or., c1936] 397 p. 19 1/2 cm. [BV4501.E65] 36-1890
1. Spiritual life. 2. Suffering. I. Title.

ERNST, John. 291.4'4
Sadhana in our daily lives : a handbook for the awakening of the spiritual self / as written by John Ernst and Frederick Daniel. Oak View, Calif. : Valley Lights Publications, c1981. 302 p. in various pagings ; 23 cm. [BL624.E76] 19 81-51360 ISBN 0-960648-20-8 (pbk.) : 9.95
1. Spiritual life. 2. Meditations. I. Title.
Publisher's address : P. O. Box 355, Oak View, CA 93022.

EVERETT, Walter Goodnow, 1860- 248
The life of the spirit in contemporary civilization ... by Walter Goodnow Everett ... New York, H. Holt and company [c1935] 3 p. l., 3-78 p. 16 cm. (The Foorster lecture, 1983-34, at the University of California) [BV4501.E88] 35-5923
1. Spiritual life. I. Title.

FABER, Frederick William, 1814-1863.
Growth in holiness; or, The progress of the spiritual life. With a pref. by Ronald Chapman. Westminster, Md., Newman press [1960] xix, 372 p. 20 cm. (The Orchard books) "First published 1854. Orchard books edition March 1960. Reprinted July 1960." 63-15011
I. Title. II. Series.

FARMER, Harvey. 248
Waiting upon God, by Harvey Farmer ... Chicago, The Bible institute colportage ass'n. [c1933] 31 p. 19 cm. [BV4510.F3] 33-24060
1. Spiritual life. I. Title.

*FEDOTOV, G. P., comp. 281.947
A treasury of Russian spirituality [Gloucester, Mass., P. Smith, 1965] xviii, 501p. (Harper torchbk., Acad. lib. rebound) Bibl. 5.00
I. Title.

*FEDOTOV, G. P., comp. 281.947
A treasury of Russian spirituality. New York, Harper [1965] xviii, 501p. illus. 21cm. (Harper torchbk.; Cathedral lib., TB303) Bibl. 2.95 pap.,
I. Title.

FENELON, Francois de Salignac de La Mothe-, abp., 1651-1715. 248
Christian perfection, by Francois de Salignac de La Mothe Fenelon, edited and prefaced by Charles F. Whiston, translated by Mildred Whitney Stillman. New York and London, Harper & brothers [1947] xiii, 208 p. front. (port.) 19 1/2 cm. "Translation of Fenelon's instructions et avis sur divers points de la morale et de la perfection chretienne ... made from the Lefevre, Paris, 1858 edition ... and checked ... with the Lebel, Paris, 1823 edition."--Introd. "First edition." [BV4502.F43] 47-2077
1. Spiritual life. I. Whiston, Charles F. 1900- ed. II. Stillman, Mildred (Whitney) 1890- tr. III. Title.

FERRANTI, Philip, 1945- 248'.86
Overcoming our obsessions : a spiritual odyssey / by Philip Ferranti. Palm Springs, Calif. : ETC Publications, c1979. p. cm. [BV4501.2.F453] 78-31663 ISBN 0-88280-069-8 : 10.00
1. Spiritual life. 2. Obsessive-compulsive neuroses. I. Title.

FERRE, Nels Fredrick Solomon, 1908- 248
Strengthening the spiritual life. [1st ed.] New York, Harper [1951] 63 p. 20 cm. [BV4501.F38] 51-10175
1. Spiritual life. I. Title.

FERRIS, George Hooper. 170
Elements of spirituality; or, The spiritual man, by Rev. George Hooper Ferris... Philadelphia, The Griffith & Rowland press, 1912. 77 p. 19 1/2 cm. [BJ1581.F4] 13-792 0.50
1. Spiritual life. I. Title.

FERRUCCI, Piero. 158'1
What we may be : techniques for psychological and spiritual growth / Piero Ferrucci ; foreword by Laura Huxley. 1st ed. Los Angeles : J.P. Tarcher ; Boston : Distributed by Houghton Mifflin Co., c1981. p. cm. Includes index. Bibliography: p. [BL624.F47] 19 81-51107 ISBN 0-87477-192-7 : 11.95
1. Spiritual life. I. Title.

FOSTER, Constance J. 248
Launching your spiritual power in the space age. Foreword by Norman Vincent Peale [New York] C. & R Anthony, 300 Park Ave. S. [1965, c.1964] 148p. 22cm. (Master pubn.) [BV4501.2.F64] 65-3489 3.00 bds.,sChristian life.
I. Title.

FOULKS, Frances Warder. 248
Steps in spiritual unfoldment. by Frances W. Foulks ... Holyoke, Mass., The Elizabeth Towne co., inc.; London, L. N. Fowler & company [c1929] x, 11-249 p. 17 cm. [BV4501.F68] 29-3312
I. Title.

FRANCK, Frederick, 1909- 291.4'4
Pilgrimage to now/here. With 19 drawings by the author. [Maryknoll, N.Y., Orbis Books, 1974] 156 p. illus. 24 cm. [BL624.F72] 73-78933 ISBN 0-88344-386-4 6.95
1. Franck, Frederick, 1909- 2. Spiritual life. I. Title.
Pbk. 3.95; ISBN 0-88344-387-2.

FRANCOIS de Sales Saint,bp. of Geneva 1567-1622
A selection from the spiritual letters of es. Francis de Sales ... Translated by H. L. Sidney Lear ... London, New York [etc.] Longmans, Green, and co., 1907. viii, 248 p. 11 cm. Letters 136, 138, 142, and 158 have been omitted in this edition. W8-57
I. Lear, Henrietta Louisa (Farrer) Mrs. tr. II. Title.

FRANCUCH, Peter Daniel, 1934- 299'.93
Fundamentals of human spirituality / by Peter Daniel Francuch. Santa Barbara, Calif. : Spiritual Advisory Press, 1982. p. cm. [BL624.F73] 19 81-16660 ISBN 0-939386-01-1 : 25.00
1. Spiritual life. I. Title.
Publishers address: P. O. Box 6344, Santa Barbara, CA 93111.

*FURLONG, Monica. 113.8
The End of our exploring. New York, Coward, McCann & Geoghegan, [1974, c1973]. 192 p. 23 cm. [BV4485] 73-92110 ISBN 0-698-10587-7. 6.95.
1. Spiritual life. I. Title.

GABLE, J. W.
Spiritual counsel and encouragement, by Rev. J. W. Gable ... This bookk is especially designed to reach the common class of people, and is adapted to the average reader ... Harrisburg, Pa., Central printing & publishing house, 1907. 99 p. incl. front. (port.) 20 cm. 7-25242
I. Title.

GAMMON, Roland. 291.4
Nirvana now / Roland Gammon. New York, N.Y. : World Authors, c1980. xv, 536 p. ; 24 cm. [BL624.G34] 19 79-57483 ISBN 0-89975-003-6 : 14.95
1. Gammon, Roland. 2. Spiritual life. I. Title.
Distributed by Hippocrene Books, Inc., 171 Madison Ave., New York, NY 10016

GARESCHE, Edward Francis, 1876- 248
The paths of goodness, some helpful thoughts on spiritual progress, by Rev. Edward F. Garesche, S.J. New York, Cincinnati [etc.] Benziger brothers, 1920. 164 p. front. 18 cm. [BX2350.G23] 20-22020
I. Title.

GAWRYN, Marvin, 1951- 291.4'48
Reaching high : the psychology of spiritual living / Marvin Gawryn. 1st ed. Berkeley, Calif. : Spiritual Renaissance Press, c1980. xii, 165 p. ; 22 cm. [BL624.G37] 19 80-24306 ISBN 0-938380-00-1 : 11.95 ISBN 0-938380-01-X pbk. : 7.95
1. Spiritual life. 2. Psychology, Religious. I. Title.
Distributed by Bookpeople, 2940 Seventh St., Berkeley, CA 94710

GEIERMANN, Peter.
The narrow way; a brief, clear, systematical exposition of the spiritual life for the laity, and a practical guidebook to Christian perfection for all of good will, by Rev. Peter Geiermann ... introduction by Very Rev. Thomas P. Brown ... New York, Cincinnati [etc.] Benziger brothers, 1914. xxi, 11-340 p. 18 cm. 14-10040 0.60
I. Title.

GOD'S light as it came to me. 248
Boston, Roberts brothers. 1895. 128 p. 18 cm. [BV4501.G5755] 32-33250
1. Spiritual life.

GOLDSMITH, Joel S., 1892-1964. 248'.4
Living between two worlds. Edited by Lorraine Sinkler. [1st ed.] New York, Harper & Row [1974] xii, 128 p. 20 cm. [BL624.G64 1974] 73-18679 ISBN 0-06-063191-0 4.95
1. Spiritual life. I. Title.

GOLDSMITH, Joel S., 1892-1964. 248'.4
Living between two worlds. Edited by Lorraine Sinkler. Boston, G. K. Hall, 1974. 227 p. 25 cm. Large print ed. [BL624.G64 1974b] 74-18246 ISBN 0-8161-6255-7
1. Spiritual life. 2. Sight-saving books. I. Title.

*GORDON, Prentiss M. 248.2
The high cost of living, [by] Prentiss M. Gordon. New York, Vantage Press, [1974]. 106 p. 21 cm. [BV4520] ISBN 0-533-00912-X. 4.50
1. Spiritual life. 2. Religious experience. I. Title.

GRAHAM, Aelred, 1907- 200
Contemplative Christianity : an approach to the realities of religion / Aelred Graham. New York : Seabury Press, [1975] c1974. x, 131 p. ; 22 cm. "A Crossroad book." Includes index. [BV4501.2.G724 1975] 74-26989 ISBN 0-8164-0269-8 : 6.95
1. Spiritual life. 2. Christianity—20th century. 3. Christianity and other religions. I. Title.

GREENE, Gwendolen Maud (Parry) Mrs. 1878- 248
The prophet child, by Gwendolen Plunket Greene. New York, E. P. Dutton & co., inc. [c1937] vii, 165 p. front. 19 1/2 cm. "First edition." [BV4501.G687] 37-3615
1. Spiritual life. 2. Children. I. Title.

GREENE, Gwendolen Maud (Parry) Mrs. 1878- 927.8
Two witnesses; a personal recollection of Hubert Parry and Friedrich von Hugel, by Gwendolen Greene. London and Toronto, J. M. Dent and sons, ltd.; New York, E. P. Dutton & co., inc. [1930] v. [1], 199 p. 2 port. (incl. front.) 20 cm. [BX4668.G7] 31-15891
1. Parry, Sir Charles Hubert Hastings, bart., 1848-1918. 2. Hugel, Friedrich, freiherr von, 1852-1925. 3. Spiritual life. I. Title.

GRITTER, George. 248
The quest for holiness; or, The development of spiritual life. [1st ed.] Grand Rapids, W. B. Eerdmans Pub. Co., 1955. 78p. 23cm. Includes bibliography. [BV4501.G778] 55-1149
1. Spiritual life. I. Title. II. Title: The development of spiritual.

GROU, Jean Nicolas, 1731-1803. 248
Manual for interior souls. Newly edited and introduced by Donal O'Sullivan. New ed. Westminster, Md., Newman Press [1955] 273p. 20cm. [BV4833.G7 1955] 56-902
1. Spiritual life. I. Title.

GURU Bawa, Shaikh Muhaiyaddeen. 294
The divine luminous wisdom that dispels the darkness; God-man, man-God, by M. R. Shaikh Muhaiyaddeen Guru Bawa. Philadelphia, Delaware Valley Printers [1972] viii, 276 p. illus. 22 cm. [BL624.G87] 72-188357
1. Spiritual life. I. Title.

GURU Bawa, Shaikh Muhaiyaddeen. 294.54
Truth & light: brief explanations [by] M. R. Guru Bawa [narrators Lee Hixon, Will Noffke]. Philadelphia Guru Bawa Fellowship of Philadelphia 1974. 144 p. illus. 18 cm. Radio interviews with Guru Bawa. [BL624.G884] 74-76219 ISBN 0-914390-03-1 4.95
1. Spiritual life. I. Hixon, Lex. II. Noffke, Will. III. Title.
Pbk. 1.95; ISBN 0-914390-04-X.

GURUBAWA, Shaikh Muhaiyaddeen. 297'.4
Songs of God's grace [by] M. R. Guru Bawa. [Translators: Ajwad Macan-Markar and others] Philadelphia, Guru Bawa Fellowship of Philadelphia [1973] vi, 154 p. illus. 21 cm. [BL624.G8813] 73-91016 1.95 (pbk.)
1. Spiritual life. I. Macan-Markar, Ajwad, tr. II. Title.
Publisher's address: 5820 Overbrook Avenue, Phildelphia, Penn 15210

GUTH, William Westley, 1871-
Spiritual values, By William W. Guth ... Cincinnati, Jennings and Graham; New York, Eaton and Mains [c1912] 205 p. 20 cm. 12-20214 1.00
I. Title.

GUTHRIE, Kenneth Sylvan.
Of the presence of God; being a practical method for beginning an interior life, by Rev. Kenneth Sylvan Guthrie ... Medford, Mass., The Prophet publishing house [1904] 4 p. l., 106 (i. e. 104) p. 20 cm. 4-25391
I. Title.

GUTHRIE, William Norman, 1868- comp. 264.
Offices of mystical religion, projecting congregationally the inner disciplines of the life toward God. In occasional use at St. Mark's-in-the-Bouwerie, Manhattan; compiled and edited by William Norman Guthrie. New York, London, The Century co. [c1927] xxxi, 416 p. 20 cm. [BX5947.B8G8] 27-20139 2.50
I. Title.

HARPER, Michael. 231'.3
Walk in the Spirit. Plainfield, N.J., Logos International [1970, c1968] 96 p. 18 cm. Bibliography: p. 95-96. [BV4501.2.H354 1970] 78-135047 ISBN 0-340-02994-3 0.95
1. Spiritual life. 2. Holy Spirit. I. Title.

HARRIS, Obadiah Silas. 291.4'4
The new consciousness / Obadiah Silas Harris. Midland, Mich. : Pendell Pub. Co., 1977. vii, 147 p. ; 24 cm. Includes bibliographical references. [BL624.H33] 76-57918 6.95
1. Spiritual life. 2. Consciousness. I. Title.

HERFORD, Brooke, 1830-1903.
The small end of great problems, by Brooke Herford ... New York, London [etc.] Longmans, Green, and co., 1902. 3 p. l., 303 p. front. (port.) 20 cm. 2-12312
1. Spiritual life. I. Title.
Contents omitted.

HERMAN, Nicolas, 1611-1691. 248
The spiritual maxims of Brother Lawrence, together with The character, by the chronicler of the "Conversations" and Gathered throughs ... Newly translated into English. Philadelphia, The Griffith and Rowland press [1907] 57 [1] p. 18 cm. "The 'Character' is a sketch of Brother Lawrence ... The author is the charonicler of the 'Conversations', probably in Beaufort, grand vicar to m. de Chalons, Cardinal de Noailles."--Pref. signed: H. C. [Name in religion: Laurent de la Resurrection] [BX2349.H4] A 34
1. Spiritual life. I. Title.

HESCHEL, Abraham Joshua, 1907-1972. 296.7'4
A passion for truth. New York, Farrar, Straus and Giroux [1973] xv, 336 p. 22 cm. [BM723.H47 1973] 72-94721 ISBN 0-374-22992-9 8.95
1. Menahem Mendel, of Kock, 1788-1859. 2. Kierkegaard, Soren Aabye, 1813-1855. 3. Israel ben Eliezer, Ba'al Shem Tob, called BeSHT, 1700 (ca.)-1760. 4. Spiritual life. 5. Hasidism. I. Title.

HINKLEY, Frederic Allen. 252.
Afterglow [by] Frederic A. Hinckley. Boston, Press of G. H. Ellis, 1892. 81 p. 15 cm. [BX9843.H64A4] 3-6050
1. Spiritual life. I. Title.
Contents omitted.

HOCKER, Clarence. 204
The greatest object in the universe; studies concerning the greatest object of life, and how to attain it. By Clarence Hocker ... [San Diego, Calif., The City printing company, c1929] 102, [2] p. 20 cm. [BR125.H6565] 30-16456
I. Title.

HOPE, Ludvig, 1871-1954. 248.4841
Spirit and power. Translated by Iver Olson. Minneapolis, Hauge Lutheran Innermission Federation, 1959. 197p. 24cm. [BV4501.H53448] 60-25225
1. Spiritual life. 2. Holy spirit. I. Title.

HUGHSON, Shirley Carter, 1867-1949. 248.4
To tell the godly man; selections from the writings of Shirley Carter Hughson. Arr. and edited by William Joseph Barnds. [1st ed.] West Park, N. Y., Holy Cross Press [1958] 181p. 21cm. [BV4501.2.H8] 58-14162
1. Spiritual life. I. Title.

HUMPHREY, Jerry Miles, 1872-
Spiritual lessons from every-day life, by J. M. Humphrey ... Lima, O., True gospel grain publishing company, 1914. 210 p. 20 cm. $1.00 14-6838
I. Title.

HUNTER, Allan Armstrong, 1893- 248
Secretly armed, by Allan A. Hunter. New York and London, Harper & brothers, [c1941] x p., 1 l., 159 p. 19 cm. "First edition." [BV4501.H875 1941] 41-10228
1. Spiritual life. I. Title.

HUNTER, John Edward, 1909- 248.42
Let us go on to maturity, by John E. Hunter. [1st ed.] Grand Rapids, Zondervan [1967] 136p. 21cm. [BV4501.2.H847] 67-17226 2.95
1. Spiritual life. I. Title.

IKIN, Alice Graham, 1895- 242
Bay windows into eternity; glimpses into unseen. Foreword by J. B. Phillips. New York, Macmillan, 1961. 117 p. 20 cm. [BV4501.2.I4 1961] 61-13308
1. Spiritual life. I. Title.

IN silence with God.
Translation from the 4th German edition by Elizabethe Corathiel--Noonan. Chicago, Regnery, 1956. 157p. 22cm.
1. Spiritual life. 2. Meditations. I. Baur, Benedikt, 1877-

IN silence with God.
Translation from the 4th German edition by Elizabethe Corathiel-Noonan. Chicago, Regnery, 1956. 157p. 22cm.
1. Spiritual life. 2. Meditations. I. Baur, Benedikt, 1877-

JAE Jah Noh. 291.4'2
Do you see what I see : a message from a mystic / by Jae Jah Noh. Wheaton, Ill. : Theosophical Pub. House, 1977. 159 p. ; 21 cm. (A Quest book) [BL624.J33] 77-5255 ISBN 0-8356-0499-3 pbk. : 3.95
1. Spiritual life. 2. Mysticism. I. Title.

JOCELYN, Beredene. 299
Citizens of the cosmos : the key to life's unfolding from conception through death to rebirth / Beredene Jocelyn. New York : Continuum, 1981. p. cm. Includes index. [BL624.J63] 19 81-5537 ISBN 0-8264-0052-3 : 14.95
1. Spiritual life. 2. Life cycle, Human—Miscellanea. 3. Reincarnation. I. Title.

JOHN, Bubba Free. 299'.93
Scientific proof of the existence of God will soon be announced by the White House! : prophetic wisdom about the myths and idols of mass culture and popular religious cultism, the new priesthood of scientific and political materialism, and the secrets of enlightenment hidden in the body of man / by Da Free John. 1st ed. Middletown, Calif. : Dawn Horse Press, 1980. 431 p. : port. ; 23 cm. Includes indexes. [BL624.J636] 19 80-81175 ISBN 0-913922-48-X pbk. : 12.95 12.95
1. Spiritual life. 2. Religion. I. Title.
Distributed by Publisher's service, Box 3914, San Rafael, CA 94902

JOHNSON, Elias Henry, 1841-1906. 248
The highest life; a story of shortcomings and a goal, including a friendly analysis of the Koswick movement, by E. H. Johnson ... New York, A. C. Armstrong and son, 1901. ix p., 2 l., [3]-183 p. 20 cm. [BV4501.J55] 1-31454
1. Spiritual life. 2. Keswick movement. I. Title.

JOHNSON, Raynor Carey. 248.4
The spiritual path, by Raynor C. Johnson. [1st ed.] New York, Harper & Row [1971] viii, 216 p. 22 cm. Bibliography: p. 213-216. [BL624.J64 1971] 70-160634 6.95
1. Spiritual life. I. Title.

JOHNSTONE, Robert. 291.4
The lost world : does it exist? / by Robert Johnstone. Gerrards Cross : Smythe ; Atlantic Highlands, N.J. : distributed by Humanities Press, 1978. [8], 152 p. : ill. ; 23 cm. Includes bibliographical references and index. [BL624.J645] 79-306285 ISBN 0-901072-75-3 : 10.00
1. Spiritual life. I. Title.

JONES, Franklin. 294.5'44
The method of the Siddhas. [1st ed.] Los Angeles, Dawn Horse Press [1973] xvii, 364 p. illus., ports. 22 cm. [BL624.J67] 73-85299 ISBN 0-913922-01-3 3.95
1. Spiritual life. I. Title.

JONES, Rufus Matthew, 1863- 248
New eyes for invisibles, by Rufus M. Jones ... New York, The Macmillan company, 1943. ix, p., 1 l., 185 p. 19 1/2 cm. [BV4501.J586] 43-3684
1. Spiritual life. I. Title.

JONES, Rufus Matthew, 1863- 248
The radiant life, by Rufus M. Jones ... New York, The Macmillan company, 1944. viii p., 1 l., 154 p. 19 1/2 cm. A companion volume to the author's New eyes for invisibles. cf. Pref. "First printing." Bibliographical foot-notes. [BV4501.J588] 44-4541
1. Spiritual life. I. Title.

JONES, Rufus Matthew, 1863- 248
Spiritual energies in daily life, by Rufus M. Jones ... New York, The Macmillan company, 1922. xx, 179 p. 20 cm. [BV4501.J59] 22-18687
1. Spiritual life. I. Title.

JONES, Rufus Matthew, 1863- 248
Spiritual energies in daily life, by Rufus M. Jones ... New and rev. ed. New York, The Macmillan company, 1936. xx, 196 p. 20 cm. [BV4501.J59 1936] 36-7291
1. Spiritual life. I. Title.

JONES, Rufus Matthew, 1863-1948. 208.1
Rufus Jones speaks to our time, an anthology; edited by Harry Emerson Fosdick. New York, Macmillan, 1951. xvii, 289 p. port. 25 cm. "Books written by Rufus Jones": p. 287-289. "Books edited by Rufus Jones": p. 289. [BX7617.J6] 51-13983
1. Friends, Society of—Collected works. 2. Spiritual life. 3. Mysticism. I. Title.

JONES, W. Paul. 248.4
The province beyond the river / W. Paul Jones. New York : Paulist Press, c1981. x, 150 p. ; 22 cm. [BV4501.2.J66] 19 81-80045 ISBN 0-8091-2363-0 (pbk.) : 5.95
1. Jones, W. Paul. 2. Spiritual life. I. Title.

JORDAN, Gerald Ray, 1896- 248
Beyond despair; when religion becomes real. New York, Macmillan, 1955. 166p. 21cm. [BV4501.J66] 55-14241
1. Spiritual life. I. Title.

KAMEI, Marlene. 234
Stone lantern essays : services for the collapse of the living room capet / by Marlene Kamei ; [graphics by Janet Cannon]. 1st ed. Taos, N.M. : Plumbers Ink Press, 1980. iii, 60 p. : ill. ; 17 cm. [BL624.K33] 79-91969 ISBN 0-935684-02-6 pbk. : 3.50
1. Spiritual life. 2. Spiritual exercises. I. Title.

KELSEY, Morton T. 248.4
Adventure inward : Christian growth through personal journal writing / Morton T. Kelsey. Minneapolis, Minn. : Augsburg Pub. House, c1980. 216 p. : ill. ; 20 cm. Bibliography: p. 211-216. [BV4509.5.K35] 19 80-65551 ISBN 0-8066-1796-9 pbk. : 7.95
1. Spiritual life. 2. Diaries. I. Title.

KESHAVADAS, Swami, 1934- 294.5'4
Sadguru speaks : spiritual disciplines and mystical teachings / Sant Keshavadas. Washington : Temple of Cosmic Religion, c1975. 95 p. : ports ; 23 cm. [BL624.K47] 76-354610 3.50
1. Spiritual life. I. Title.

KESKAR, Vishwanath 181.4
Pillars of life, by Shri Vishwanath Keskar; with foreword by J. G. Phelps Stokes. New York, 1931. 130, [1] p. illus. 19 cm. Lectures. [B133.K5P5] [248] 31-9785
1. Spiritual life. I. Title.

KIERKEGAARD, Soren Aabye, 1813-1855 248
Edifying discourses [2v.] Tr. from Danish by David F. Swenson, Lillian Marvin Swenson. Minneapolis, Augsburg [c.1943-1962] 2v. (239;253p.) 22cm. 62-53676 1.75 pap., ea.,
1. Spiritual life. I. Title.

KIERKEGAARD, Soren Aabye, 1813-1855. 248
Edifying discourses, by Soren Kierkegaard ... translated from the Danish by David F. Swenson and Lillian Marvin Swenson. Minneapolis, Minn., Augsburg publishing house [1943- v. 22 cm. [BV4505.K44] 43-15536
1. Spiritual life. I. Swenson, David Ferdinand, 1876-1940, tr. II. Swenson, Lillian B. (Marvin) joint tr. III. Title.

KIERKEGAARD, Soren Aabye, 1813-1855. 248
The gospel of our sufferings; Christian discoures, being the third part of Edifying discourses in a different vein. published in 1847 at Copenhagen. Tr. from Danish by A. S. Aldworth. W. S. Ferrie. Grand Rapids, Mich., Eerdmans [1964] 150p. 20cm. 64-22016 1.45 pap.,
1. Spiritual life. 2. Affliction. I. Title.

KIERKEGAARD, Soren Aabye. 1813-1855. 248
Purity of heart is to will one thing; spiritual preparation for the office of confession; tr. from the Danish with an introductory essay by Douglas V. Steere. [Rev. Ed.] New York, Harper [1948] 220 p. 20 cm. "Included in ... [the author's] Edifying addresses ... (Ophyggellge taler)" [BV4505.K46 1948] 48-9399
1. Spiritual life. I. Steere, Douglas Van, 1901- II. Title.

KIERKEGAARD, Soren Aabye, 1813-1855 248
Purity of heart is to will one thing; spiritual preparation fro the feast of confession, by Soren Kierkegaard; translated from the Danish with an introductory essay by Douglas V. Steere ... New York and London, Harper & brothers, 1938. xxviii p., 1 l., 207 p. 19 1/2 cm. "Purity of heart is to will one

thing ... was included in ... Edifying addresses ... (Opbyggelige taler)"--Translator's introd. "First edition." "Notes": p. 206-207. [BV4505.K46] 38-23159
1. Spiritual life. I. Steere, Douglas Van, tr. II. Title.

KIERKEGAARD, Soren Aabye, 1813-1855 248
Works of love; some Christian reflections in the form of discourses. Tr. by Howard and Edna Hong. Preface by R. Gregor Smith [Gloucester, Mass., P. Smith, 1965, c.1962] 378p. 21cm. (Harper torchbk., TB122. Cloister lib. rebound) Bibl. [BV4505] 3.85
1. Spiritual life. I. Title.

KIERKEGAARD, Soren Aabye, 1813-1855 248
Works of love; some Christian reflections in the form of discourses. Tr. by Howard and Edna Hong. Pref. by R. Gregor Smith. New York, Harper [1964, c.1962] 378p. 21cm. (Harper torchbks., TB122. Cloister lib.) Bibl. 64-7445 1.85 pap.,
1. Spiritual life. I. Title.

KIERKEGAARD, Soren Aabye, 1813-1855. 248
Works of love; some Christian reflections in the form of discourses. Translated by Howard and Edna Hong. New York, Harper [1962] 383 p. 22 cm. [BV4505.K42 1962] 62-7293
1. Spiritual life. I. Title.

KIERKEGAARD, Soren Aabye, 1813-1855. 248
Works of love, by Soren Kierkegaard, translated from the Danish by David F. Swenson and Lillian Marvin Swenson. With an introduction by Douglas V. Steere. Princeton, N.J., Princeton university press, 1946. xiv, 317 p. 24 cm. Bibliographical references included in "Notes" (p. [311]-317) [BV4505.K42] A 46
1. Spiritual life. I. Swenson, David Ferdinand, 1876-1940, tr. II. Swenson, Lillian Bessie (Marvin) joint tr. III. Title.

KIERKEGAARD, Sooren Aabye, 1813-1855. 248
Edifying discourses, a selection. Edited with an introd. by Paul L. Holmer. Translated by David F. and Lillian Marvin Swenson. New York, Harper [1958] 265 p. 21 cm. (Harper torchbooks, TB32) Contents.Contents.—The expectation of faith.—Every good and perfect thing is from above.—Love shall cover a multitude of sins.—The Lord gave and the Lord hath taken away, blessed by the name of the Lord.—Remember now thy Creator in the days of thy youth.—The expectation of an eternal happiness.—Man's need of God constitutes his highest perfection.—Love conquers all.—The narrowness is the way.—The glory of our common humanity.—The unchangeableness of God. [BV4505.K46 1958] 58-7107
1. Spiritual life. I. Title.

KIERKEGAARD, Soren Aabye, 1813-1855. 248.4
Works of love. Translated from the Danish by David F. Swenson and Lillian Marvin Swenson. With an introd. by Douglas V. Steere. Port Washington, Kennikat Press [1972, c1946] xiv, 317 p. 23 cm. Translation of Kjerlighedens gjerninger. Includes bibliographical references. [BV4505.K42 1972] 70-153224 ISBN 0-8046-1534-9
1. Spiritual life. I. Title.

KIKLIN, Joseph Louis J 1868-1926. 242
Our tryst with Him ... by the Very Reverned Msgr. J. L. J. Kirlin ... New York, The Macmillan company, 1925. 3 p. l., 9-192 p. 20 cm. [BX2182.K5] 25-3468
I. Title.

KIRKLAND, Bryant M. 248.4
Growing in Christian faith. Nashville, Tidings [c1963] 71 p. 19 cm. [BV4501.2.K52] 63-22407
1. Spiritual life. I. Title.

KLUG, Ronald, 1939- 248.4'6
How to keep a spiritual journal / by Ronald Klug. Nashville : T. Nelson Publishers, c1982. 142 p. ; 21 cm. Bibliography: p. 131-136. [BV4509.5.K56 1982] 19 82-14383 ISBN 0-8407-5815-4 : 4.95
1. Spiritual life. 2. Diaries—Authorship. 3. Christian literature—Authorship. 4. Christian literature—Publication and distribution. I. Title.

KNORR, Lester. 291.2
The way to God / Lester Knorr. Virginia Beach, Va. : Donning Co., c1980. p. cm. (A Unilaw library book) [BL624.K595] 19 80-21268 ISBN 0-89865-042-9 (pbk.) : 4.95
1. Spiritual life.

KOOPMAN, Leroy. 248'.4
Beauty care for the eyes / by Leroy Koopman. Grand Rapids : Zondervan Pub. House, c1975. p. cm. [BV4501.2.K63] 75-21124 pbk. : 1.50
1. Spiritual life. I. Title.

KOOPMAN, Leroy. 248'.4
Beauty care for the hands / LeRoy Koopman. Grand Rapids : Zondervan Pub. House, c1977. 93 p. ; 18 cm. Includes index. [BV4501.2.K64] 77-3709 ISBN 0-310-26832-X pbk. : 1.50
1. Spiritual life. I. Title.

LACHAPELLE, Dolores. 291.4
Earth wisdom / Dolores LaChapelle ; photos. by Steven J. Meyers, drawings by Randy LaChapelle. 1st ed. Los Angeles : Guild of Tutors Press, c1978. 183 p. : ill. ; 28 cm. (New natural philosophy series) Includes index. Bibliography: p. 173-179. [BL624.L32] 77-93140 ISBN 0-89615-003-8 : 9.95
1. Spiritual life. 2. Nature—Religious interpretations. I. Title. II. Series.

LAMM, William Robert, 1899- 922.242
The spiritual legacy of Newman [by] William R. Lamm ... Milwaukee, The Bruce publishing company [c1934] xxii, 234 p. front. (port.) 21 cm. (Half-title: Religion and culture series, J. Husslein ... general editor) Bibliography: p. 232-234. [BX4705.N5L25] 34-34756
1. Spiritual life. I. Newman, John Henry, cardinal 1801-1890. II. Title.

LINDSAY, John, 1923- 211
Man's spiritual quest; a survey of man's search for ultimate truth, meaning, and security in the universe which is his home, his school, his house of worship. [1st ed.] New York, Greenwich Book Publishers, 1957. 76p. 21cm. [BL2780.L63] 57-9792
I. Title.

LOGAN, Kathrine R. 170
Your thoughts and you, by Kathrine R. Logan ... New York, George H. Doran company [c1927] xii p., 2 l., 17-188 p. 20 cm. Blank pages for "Preserving the best." (178-188) [BJ1581.L565] 27-11600
1. Spiritual life. I. Title.

LOVASIK, Lawrence George, 1913-
Stepping stones to sanctity; practical hints for religious and lay people, by ... New York, Macmillian, 1956. 151 p. 21 cm. 68-72469
1. Spiritual life. I. Title.

LUDWIG, David J. 248.4
In good spirits / David J. Ludwig. Minneapolis : Augsburg Pub. House, c1982. 144 p. ; 20 cm. [BV4501.2.L83 1982] 19 82-70944 ISBN 0-8066-1919-8 pbk. : 5.50
1. Spiritual life. 2. Interpersonal relations. I. Title.

MCCALLA, George Washington 1849-
The gift that abides (I John ii:27) A setting forth of some truths disclosed by "the anointing" which have special bearing upon the deeper phases of religious life and light, by G. W. McCalla. Philadelphia, G. W. McCalla, 1905. 4 p. l., 5-124 p. 18 cm. 5-21450
I. Title.

MCGHIE, Anna E. 242
The miracle hand around the world, by Anna E. McGhie. Ft. Valley, Ga., Printed for the author, Anna E. McGhie [1942] 3 p. l., 5-190 p. front., plates, ports. 20 cm. [BV4501.M262] 42-21359
1. Spiritual life. I. Title.

MACNEIL, John, Presbyterian evangelist of Australia. 248
The spirit-filled life, by the Rev. John MacNeil ... Introduction by Rev. Andrew Murray ... New York, Chicago [etc.] Fleming H. Revell company [1896] 1 p. l., 126 p. 19 1/2 cm. [BV4501.M335 1896] 45-52686
1. Spiritual life. I. Title.

MACQUARRIE, John. 248'.4
Paths in spirituality. [1st U.S. ed.] New York, Harper & Row [1972] 134 p. 22 cm. Includes bibliographical references. [BV4501.2.M32 1972] 70-183765 ISBN 0-06-065366-3 4.95
1. Spiritual life. I. Title.

MANU. 294.5
The laws of Manu, translated, with extracts from seven commentaries, by G. Buhler. Oxford, The Clarendon press, 1886. cxxxviii p., 1 l., 620 p. 22 1/2 cm. (Added t.-p.: The sacred books of the East ... vol. xxv) [BL1010.S3 vol. 25] [(290.3)] 32-34310
I. Buhler, Georg, 1837-1898, ed. and tr. II. Title.

MARECHAL, Paul. 248.4
Dancing madly backwards : a journey into God / Paul Marechal ; foreword by Morton Kelsey. New York : Crossroad, 1982. xiv, 104 p. ; 21 cm. Includes bibliographical references. [BV4501.2.M339 1982] 19 81-17285 ISBN 0-8245-0408-9 (pbk.) : 5.95
1. Spiritual life. I. Title.

MARITAIN, Jacques, 1882- 248
Prayer and intelligence, being La vie d'oraison of Jacques and Raissa Maritain, translated by Algar Thorold. New York, Sheed & Ward, 1943. 3 p. l., v-xi, 56 p. 16 cm. [BV4502.M3 1943] 44-2787
1. Spiritual life. 2. Prayer. I. Maritain, Raissa, Joint author. II. Thorold, Algar Labouchere, 1866-1936, tr. III. Title.

MARSH, F. E. 1858-1919. (Frederick Edward), 248.4
Living God's way / by F.E. Marsh. Grand Rapids, MI : Kregel Publications, 1981, c1958. 229 p. ; 19 cm. Reprint. Originally published: The spiritual life. Des Moines, Iowa : Boone Pub. Co., 1958. [BV4501.2.M3634 1981] 19 80-8073 ISBN 0-8254-3233-2 (pbk.) : 4.95
1. Spiritual life. I. [Spiritual life] II. Title.

MARTIN, John Fount, 1839-
Two in one: the story of two blended lives exemplifying and illustrating the meaning and final perfected state of human existence. By J. Fount Martin ... Fresno, Cal., Franklin printing house, 1907. 282 p. incl. front. (port.) 18 cm. 7-33559
I. Title.

MARX, Michael, ed.
Protestants and Catholics on the spiritual life. Collegeville, Minn., Liturgical Press [1965] viii, 106 p. 23 cm. Reprinted from Worship magazine, December, 1965. 68-5348
1. Spiritual life. I. Title.

MASSON, Thomas Lansing, 1866- 248
...Within; a guide to the spiritual life, by Thomas L. Masson... New York, Holston house, Sears publishing company [c1931] xviii p., 1 l., 21-325 p. 19 1/2 cm. Bibliography: p. 311-316. [BV4501.M38] 31-24866
1. Spiritual life. 2. Spirituality. I. Title.

MAST, Isaac Newton, 1844-1914. 233.5
The relation which must exist between Christ manifested in spiritual life and the souls of his worshippers in their existence wholly spiritual. A study of soul-powers superintellectual. Final writings of I. N. Mast. Ottumwa, Ia. [c1931] 1 p. l., [5]-367 p. 20 1/2 cm. [BR126.M3] 31-9787
I. Title.

MATA, Daya. 294.5'4
Only love = formerly Qualities of a devotee / by Daya Mata. Los Angeles : Self-Realization Fellowship, 1976. xvi, 277 p., [12] leaves of plates : ill. ; 20 cm. [BP605.S36M37 1976] 75-44633 ISBN 0-87612-215-2 : 6.50
1. Spiritual life. I. Title. II. Title: Qualities of a devotee.

MAY, Gerald G. 269
Pilgrimage home : the conduct of contemplative practice in groups / Gerald G. May. New York : Paulist Press, c1979. viii, 184 p. ; 23 cm. Includes bibliographical references. [BV4501.2.M42] 78-61720 ISBN 0-8091-2143-3 pbk. : 8.95
1. Spiritual life. 2. Prayer groups. I. Title.

*MAYNARD, Aurora 248
The inner guidance. New York, Vantage [c.1965] 116p. 21cm. 2.75 bds.,
I. Title.

*MAYNARD, Aurora 248
The inner guidance. New York, Vantage [c.1965] 116p. 21cm. 2.75 bds.,
I. Title.

MERSHON, Stephen Lyon, 1859- 248
Celestical phones; or Voice from the invisible, by S. L. Mershon. Rahway, N. J., The Mershon company [1900] 63 p. 19 cm. [BV4501.M463] 32-35941
1. Spiritual life. I. Title.

MILHOUSE, Paul William, 1910- 248
Doorways to spiritual living. [Dayton? Ohio, 1950] 158 p. 20 cm. [BV4501.M513] 50-29277
1. Spiritual life. I. Title.

MILLER, George Amos, bp., 1868- 248
They that hunger and thirst; studies in the life of the spirit, by George A. Miller. Garden City, N.Y., Doubleday, Doran & company, inc. 1928. vii p., 2 l., 171 p. 19 1/2 cm. [BV4501.M535] 28-23574
1. Spiritual life. 2. Mystician. I. Title.

MILLMAN, Daniel. 291.4'48
Way of the peaceful warrior : a basically true story / Dan Millman. 1st ed. Los Angeles : J. P. Tarcher ; Boston : distributed by Houghton Mifflin, c1980. 210 p. ; 22 cm. [BL624.M53 1980] 79-66725 ISBN 0-87477-121-8 : 10.00
1. Millman, Daniel. 2. Spiritual life. I. Title.

THE minister's spiritual life.
Austin, Texas, Firm Foundation [c1959] 109p.
1. Spiritual life. I. McMillan, Edward Washington, 1889-

MOFFATT, John Edward, 1894- 248
Echoes eternal; thoughts on our eternal interests, by J. E. Moffatt, S.J. Milwaukee, The Bruce publishing company [c1935] ix, 155 p. 19 cm. [BX2350.M665] 35-10873
1. Spiritual life. I. Title.

MONTCHEUIL, Yves de.
For men of action. South Bend, Ind., Fides, 1963. 162 p. 21 cm. 68-74606
1. Spiritual life. I. Title.

MOORE, William Thomas, 1832- 230.
Man preparing for other worlds; or, The spiritual man's conflicts and final victory; a study of man in the light of the Bible, science and experience, by William Thomas Moore ... Saint Louis, Christian publishing company, 1904. 1 p. l., v-xxv, 482 p. 20 cm. [BX7321.M65] 4-7703
1. Spiritual life. I. Title.

MOORE, Willis Luther, 1856- 211
Spirituel gravity, one hundred years of youth and the eternal life [by] Willis Luther Moore ... Pasadena, Calif., The Spirituel gravity press, 1924. 2 p. l., v, 153 p. 21 cm. [BL2775.M6] 25-7864
I. Title.

MOSELEY, Joel Rufus, 1870- 248
Manifest victory; a quest and a testimony, by J. R. Moseley. New York and London, Harper & brothers [1941] xv p., 1 l., 238 p. 19 1/2 cm. "First edition." [BV4501.M777 1941] 41-5086
1. Spiritual life. I. Title.

MOSELEY, Joel Rufus, 1870- 248
Manifest victory, a quest and a testimony, by J. R. Moseley. Rev. and enl. ed. New York and London, Harper & brothers [1947] xvi p., 1 l., 297 p. 20 cm. [BV4501.M777 1947] 47-2608
1. Spiritual life. I. Title.

MOSELEY, Joel Rufus, 1870- 248
Perfect everything. [1st ed.] St. Paul, Mascalester Park Pub. Co. [1949] 156 p. 20 cm. [BV4501.M778] 51-31772
1. Spiritual life. I. Title.

MOSELEY, John Reed. 248
Manifest victory; a quest and testimony, by

J. R. Moseley. New York and London, Harper & brothers [c1941] xv p., 1 l., 238 p. 19 1/2 cm. "First edition." [BV4501.M777 1941] 41-5086
1. Spiritual life. I. Title.

MUDGE, James, 1844-1918. 242
The land of faith, by James Mudge ... Cincinnati, Jennings and Pye; New York, Eaton and Mains [1903] 184 p. 15 x 12 cm. (On cover: Little books on devotion) [BV4832.M7] 3-16567
1. Spiritual life. I. Title.

MUDGE, James, 1844-1918. 242
The life of love, by James Mudge ... Cincinnati, Jennings & Pye; New York, Eaton & Mains [1902] 140 p. 15 x 12 cm. (Little books on devotion) [BV4832.M77] 2-5207
1. Spiritual life. I. Title.

MUHAIYADDEEN, M. R. Bawa. 291.4'4
A book of God's love / by M.R. Bawa Muhaiyaddeen. Philadelphia, PA : Fellowship Press, c1981. 115 p. : ill., port. ; 14 cm. Discourses spoken in Tamil in Philadelphia during February 1980. [BL624.M82] 19 81-4503 ISBN 0-914390-19-8 : 7.95
1. Spiritual life. 2. God—Love. 3. Love. I. Title.

MUHLEN, Heribert. 248
A charismatic theology : initiation in the spirit / [by] Heribert Muhlen ; [translated from the German by Edward Quinn and Thomas Linton]. London : Burns & Oates ; New York : Paulist Press, 1978. 360 p. ; 32 cm. Translation of Einubung in die christliche Grunderfahrung. Includes bibliographical references. [BV4503.M7613] 78-320580 ISBN 0-8091-2101-8 pbk. : 9.95
1. Spiritual life. 2. Pentecostalism. I. Title.

MURRAY, Andrew, 1828-1917. 248
The spiritual life, by Andrew Murray ... Philadelphia, G. W. Jacobs & co., 1898. 2 p. l., 243 p. 18 cm. [BV4501.M8S6 1898] 98-1750
1. Spiritual life. I. Title.

MURRAY, Andrew, 1828-1917. 248
The treasury of Andrew Murray. Introd. by Ralph G. Turnbull. Westwood, N.J., F. H. Revell Co. [1952] 255 p. 21 cm. [BV4501.M8T65] 52-4966
1. Spiritual life. I. Title.

NADZO, Stefan C. 291.4'48
There is a way : meditations for a seeker / Stefan C. Nadzo ; artwork by Nancy Nadzo. [Franklin, Me.] : Eden's Work, c1980. 129 p. : ill. ; 22 cm. [BL624.N3] 19 80-66831 ISBN 0-937226-00-9 : 3.95
1. Spiritual life. I. Title.

NEVILLE, Robert C. 291.5
Soldier, sage, saint / Robert C. Neville. New York : Fordham University Press, 1978. xi, 141 p. ; 24 cm. Includes index. Bibliography: p. 133-135. [BL624.N47] 77-75798 ISBN 0-8232-1035-9 : 15.00. ISBN 0-8232-1036-7 pbk : 7.50
1. Spiritual life. I. Title.

NICHOLS, R. Eugene. 289.9
Esoteric keys to personal power / by R. Eugene Nichols. Lakemont, Ga. : CSA Press, c1977. 141 p. ; 21 cm. Includes bibliographical references. [BL624.N5] 76-56593 ISBN 0-87707-186-1 : 2.95
1. Spiritual life. 2. New Thought. I. Title.

NOUWEN, Henri J. M. 248'.4
Reaching out : the three movements of the spiritual life / Henri J. M. Nouwen. 1st ed. Garden City, N.Y. : Doubleday, 1975. 120 p. ; 22 cm. Includes bibliographical references. [BV4501.2.N68] 74-9460 ISBN 0-385-03212-9 : 5.95
1. Spiritual life. I. Title.

ORCHARD, William Edwin, 1877- 248
The way of simplicity; a guide for the perplexed, by W. E. Orchard, D. D. New York city, E. P. Dutton & co., inc. [c1935] vii, 321 p. 20 cm. "First edition." [BX2350.O7 1935] 35-1822
1. Spiritual life. I. Title.

PARKER, Fitzgerald Sale, 1863- 248
The spiritual life; studies in Christian experience, by Fitzgerald Sale Parker ... Nashville, Tenn., Cokesbury press, 1926. vii, 154 p. 19 cm. [BV4501.P265] 26-12877
I. Title.

PEEKE, George Hewson, 1833-
The spiritual body in relation to the divine law of life [by] Rev. George H. Peeke. Boston, R. G. Badger [c1912] 207 p. 20 cm. 12-27811 1.50
I. Title.

PEERS, Edgar Allison. 242'.1
Behind that wall; an introduction to some classics of the interior life. Freeport, N.Y., Books for Libraries Press [1969, c1948] 181 p. 23 cm. (Essay index reprint series) Contents.Contents.—Introduction: Behind that wall.—St. Augustine: The city of God.—St. Bernard: The book of the love of God.—Ramon Lull: The book of the lover and the beloved.—The imitation of Christ.—Jan van Ruysbroeck: The seven steps of the ladder of spiritual love.—The cloud of unknowing.—St. Ignatius of Loyola: Spiritual exercises.—St. Peter of Alcantara: The golden treatise of mental prayer.—St. Teresa of Jesus: The interior castle.—St. John of the Cross: Songs of the soul.—St. Francis of Sales: Introduction to the devout life.—Jeremy Taylor: Holy living.—Henry Vaughan: The flint flashing fire.—Thomas Traherne: Poems. Includes bibliographies. [BV4818.P4 1969] 72-90672
I. Title.

PERRY, Bliss, 1860-
The amateur spirit, by Bliss Perry. Boston and New York, Houghton, Mifflin and company, 1904. ix p., 2 l., [3]-164 p., 1 l. 20 cm. [PS2545.P4A7] 4-28230
I. Title.
Contents omitted.

*PERRY, Thomas Charles. d. 1959. 248.2
Practicing Jesus' way of life. New York, Exposition [1967] 178p. 21cm. (EP45656) 4.50
1. Spiritual life. I. Title.

PIERCE, B[enjamin] W[ashington].
Foregleams in nature of redemption in Christ; or, The spiritual remedial system foreshadowed in the physical. Rev. and enl. ed. By B. W. Pierce ... Kansas City, Mo., For the author by The Hudson-Kimberly pub. co., 1902. 212, [1] p. front. (port.) 20 1/2 cm. 2-20346
I. Title.

PIERCE, Benjamin Washington.
Foregleams in nature of redemption in Christ; or, The spiritual remedial system foreshadowed in the physical. St. Louis, Mo., Christian pub. co., 1900. 155 p. front. (port.) 12 degrees. 0-6292
I. Title.

*PINK, Arthur W. 248.4
Spiritual union and communion / Arthur W. Pink. Grand Rapids : Baker Book House, 1976 c1971. 165 p. ; 22 cm. Includes index [BV4501.2P554] ISBN 0-8010-6893-2 pbk. : 2.95
1. Spiritual life. 2. Trinity. I. Title.
L.C. card no. for original edition: 72-160817.

PINK, Arthur W. 248
Spiritusal growth : growth in grace, or Christian Progress / by Arthur W. Pink. Grand Rapids : Baker Book House, c1976. 200p. ; 22 cm. Includes index. [BV4501.2] ISBN 0-8010-6862-2 pbk. : 3.95
1. Spritual life. I. Title.
L.C. card no. for original ed. 77-139863.

PINK, Arthur Walkington, 1886-1952. 248
Spiritual growth; growth in grace, or Christian progress. Grand Rapids, Mich., Baker Book House [1971] 193 p. 23 cm. [BV4501.2.P553 1971] 77-139863 ISBN 0-8010-6862-2 4.95
1. Spiritual life. I. Title.

PINK, Arthur Walkington, 1886-1952. 248.4
Spiritual union and communion. Grand Rapids, Baker Book House [1971] 160 p. 23 cm. [BV4501.2.P554] 72-160817 ISBN 0-8010-6893-2 4.95
1. Spiritual life. 2. Trinity. I. Title.

POWERS, Thomas E 248
First questions on the life of the Spirit. [1st ed.] New York, Harper [1959] 241p. 22cm. Includes bibliography. [BV4501.2.P6] 59-7159
1. Spiritual life. I. Title.

POWERS, Thomas E. 248'.4
Invitation to a great experiment : exploring the possibility that God can be known / Thomas E. Powers. 2d ed. Garden City, N.Y. : Doubleday, 1979. xii, 226 p. ; 22 cm. First ed. published in 1959 under title: First questions on the life of the Spirit. Bibliography: p. [171]-185. [BV4501.2.P6 1979] 77-26518 ISBN 0-385-14187-4 : 8.95
1. Spiritual life. 2. God—Knowableness. I. Title.

PRATHER, Hugh. 291.4
The quiet answer / Hugh Prather. 1st ed. Garden City, N.Y. : Doubleday, 1982. xii, 164 p. ; 21 cm. "A Dolphin book." [BL624.P697] 19 80-2979 ISBN 0-385-17605-8 pbk. : 5.95
1. Spiritual life. I. Title.

PRATHER, Hugh. 291.4'48
There is a place where you are not alone / Hugh Prather. Garden City, N.Y. : Doubleday, 1980. p. cm. (A Dolphin book) [BL624.P72] 19 80-912 ISBN 0-385-14778-3 : 5.95
1. Prather, Hugh. 2. Spiritual life. I. Title.

PRESCOTT, Houston. 131'.32
Vibrations of higher consciousness / Houston Prescott. 1st paperback ed. Louisville, Ky. : Cosmic Science, 1978. 100 p. ; 22 cm. [BL624.P73] 78-67067 ISBN 0-932536-01-8 : 3.70
1. Spiritual life. I. Title.

PURDY ALEXANDER C. 270
Pathways to God, by Alexander C. Purdy. New York, The Womans press, 1922. 5 p. l., 3-204 p. 20 cm. [BR125.P83] 22-25416
I. Title.

PURITY of heart is to will one thing; spiritual preparation for the office of confession; tr. from the Danish with an introductory essay by Douglas V. Steere. New York, Harper [1956] 220p. (Harper Torchlight books, TL4) 'Included in ... [the author's] Edifying addresses ... (Opbyggelige taler)'
1. Spiritual life. I. Kierkegaard, Soren Aabye, 1813-1855. II. Steere, Douglas Van, 1901- tr.

PURITY of heart is to will one thing; spiritual preparation for the office of confession; tr. from the Danish with an introductory essay by Douglas V. Steere. New York, Harper [1956] 220p. (Harper Torchlight books, TL4) 'Included in... [the author's] Edifying addresses... (Opbyggelige taler)'
1. Spiritual life. I. Kierkegaard, Soren Aabye, 1813-1855. II. Steere, Douglas Van, 1901- tr.

QUADRUPANI, Carlo Giuseppe.
Light and peace; instructions for devout souls to dispel their doubts and allay their fears. By R. P. Quadrupani ... Translated from the French, with an introduction by the Most Rev. P. J. Ryan ... 10th ed. St. Louis, Mo. and London, B. Herder book co., 1930. viii, 193 p. 18 cm. "The present translation has been made from the twentieth French edition and has been collated with the thirty-second edition of the original Italian published at Naples 1818."--Translator's pref., signed: I. M. O'R. tr. Translation of Documenti per tranquillare le anime. [BX2185.Q3] A 34
1. Spiritual life. I. O'R., I. M., tr. II. I. M. O'R., tr. III. Title.

RAJANEESH, Acharya, 1931- 299'.93
The great challenge : a Rajneesh reader / by Bhagwan Shree Rajneesh. 1st Evergreen ed. New York : Grove Press, 1982. 211 p. ; 20 cm. (An Evergreen book) (Grove Press Eastern philosophy and literature series) [BL624.R3313 1982] 19 81-47642 ISBN 0-394-17934-X (pbk.) : 9.95
1. Spiritual life. I. Title. II. Series.

RAJANEESH, Acharya, 1931- 291.4
Hammer on the rock / Bhagwan Shree Rajneesh ; photos. by Swami Shiva Murti ; compilation, editing, and commentary by Ma Prem Maneesha. 1st Evergreen ed. New York : Grove Press, 1979, c1976. p. cm. Reprint of the ed. published by Rajneesh Foundation, Poona, India. [BL624.R332 1979] 79-52012 ISBN 0-394-17090-3 : 8.95
1. Spiritual life. I. Prem Maneesha, Ma. II. Title.

RAJANEESH, Acharya, 1931- 299'.93
Nirvana, the last nightmare / Bhagwan Shree Rajneesh ; compilation and editing, Ma Yoga Pratima ; design, Swami Anand Yatri. 1st U.S. ed. Los Angeles : Wisdom Garden Books, 1981, c1976. p. cm. [BL624.R335 1981] 19 81-13068 ISBN 0-914794-37-X : 8.95
1. Spiritual life. 2. Nirvana. I. Yoga'Pratima, Ma. II. Title.
Publisher's address Box 29448, Los Angeles, CA 90029.

RAM Dass. 294
Grist for the mill / by Ram Dass, in collaboration with Stephen Levine. Santa Cruz, Calif. : Unity Press, 1977. 173 p. : ill. ; 22 cm. (The Mindfulness series) [BP610.R3514] 76-40447 ISBN 0-913300-17-9 : 7.95. ISBN 0-913300-16-0 pbk. : 3.95
1. Ram Dass. 2. Spiritual life. I. Levine, Stephen, joint author. II. Title.

RAYMOND, George Lansing, 1839-1929. 252.
Suggestions for the spiritual life; college chapel talks, by George Lansing Raymond ... New York and London, Funk & Wagnalls company, 1912. 337 p. 20 cm. [BV4310.R3] 12-24636
I. Title.

RIGGS, Ralph M 1895- 248.4'8'99
Living in Christ; our identification with Him, by Ralph M. Riggs. Springfield, Mo., Gospel Pub. House [1967] 96 p. 19 cm. [BV4509.5.R5] 67-25874
1. Spiritual life. 2. Identification (Religion) I. Title.

RUDHYAR, Dane, 1895- 128
Beyond individualism : the psychology of transformation / Dane Rudhyar. Wheaton, Ill. : Theosophical Pub. House, c1979. xiii, 148 p. : ill. ; 21 cm. (A Quest book) Includes bibliographical references and index. [BL624.R79] 78-64906 ISBN 0-8356-0518-3 : 4.75
1. Spiritual life. 2. Self-realization. 3. Theosophy. I. Title.

RUDRANANDA, Swami, 1928-1973. 294.5'4
Spiritual cannibalism / Swami Rudrananda (Rudi) ; pref. by Gaetano Maida ; foreword by Michael Shoemaker. Woodstock, N.Y. : Overlook Press, 1978. xi, 196 p. : ill. ; 22 cm. (A RudraGroup book) [BL624.R8 1978] 77-20738 ISBN 0-87951-069-2 : 10.95. ISBN 0-87951-074-9 pbk. : 4.95
1. Spiritual life. I. Title.

RUNG, Albert. 264.
Meditations for the laity, for every day in the year, by the Rev. Albert Rung. St. Louis, Mo. and London, B. Herder book co., 1927. x, 532 p. 22 cm. [BX2182.R7] 27-24120
I. Title.

RUSH, Benjamin, 1869- 248
The road to fulfillment [by] Benjamin Rush. New York and London, Harper & brothers [1942] xxi, 226 p. 19 1/2 cm. "First edition." Bibliography: p. 225-226. [BV4501.R78] 42-24210
1. Spiritual life. I. Title.

SAMPSON, Tom. 248'.4
Cultivating the presence : a spiritual guide for a journey toward the presence of God / Tom Sampson. New York : Crowell, c1977. xv, 212 p. ; 21 cm. Includes index. Bibliography: p. 198-203. [BV4501.2.S17] 76-27316 ISBN 0 ISBN 0-690-01205-5 : 8.95 ISBN 0-690-01206-3 pbk. : 3.25
1. Spiritual life. 2. Devotional literature. I. Title.

SANGSTER, Margaret Elizabeth (Munson) Mrs., 1838-1912. 235
When angels come to men, by Margaret E. Sangster ... New York, London [etc.] Fleming H. Revell company [1903] 156 p. 20 cm. [BT966.S3] 3-7790
I. Title.

SANTAYANA, George, 1863-
Platonism and their spiritual life, by George Santayana. New York, C. Scribner's sons, 1927. 2 p. l., 94 p., 1 l. 19

1/2 cm. Printed in Great Britain. [B517.S3] 27-16463
1. Spiritual life. I. Title.

SATSANG / 294.5'4'3
editor Vasant V. Paranjpe. 1st ed. Madison, Va. : Fivefold Path, c1976- v. ; 28 cm. Includes index. [BL624.S27] 75-39508 12.00 (v. 1)
1. Spiritual life. I. Paranjpe, Vasant Vithal, 1921-

SATYA Bharti, Ma. 299'.93
Death comes dancing : celebrating life with Bhagwan Shree Rajneesh / Ma Satya Bharti. London ; Boston : Routledge & Kegan Paul, 1981. viii, 183 p. ; 22 cm. [BL624.S28] 19 80-41144 ISBN 0-7100-0705-1 pbk. : 9.95
1. Satya Bharti, Ma. 2. Rajaneesh, Acharya, 1931- 3. Spiritual life. I. Title.

SAVARY, Louis M. 248.3'2
Prayerways for those who fell discouraged or distraught, frightened or frustrated, angry or anxious, powerless or purposeless, over-extended or under-appreciated, burned out or just plain worn out / Louis M. Savary, Patricia H. Berne. 1st ed. San Francisco : Harper & Row, c1980. p. cm. [BV4501.2.S276 1980] 80-7737 ISBN 0-06-067068-1 : 8.95
1. Spiritual life. 2. Conduct of life. I. Berne, Patricia H., joint author. II. Title.

SCHNEIDER, Joseph, 1824-1884.
Helps to a spiritual life; for religious and for all persons in the world who desire to serve God fervently; from the German of Rev. Joseph Schneider, S. J., with additions by Rev. Ferrol Girardey, C. SS. R. New York, Cincinnati [etc.] Benziger brothers, 1903. viii, 257 p. 20 cm. [BN2350.S3] 3-9571
I. Girardey, Ferreol, 1839-1930. II. Title.

SCHRYVERS, Joseph, 1876- 248
The gift of oneself; from the French of the Reverend Joseph Schryvers, C. SS. R.; translated by a religious of Carmel, Bettendorf, Iowa. Bettendorf, Ia., Carmel [c1934] 6 p. l., 9-239 p. 20 cm. [BX2350.S32] 34-16864
1. Spiritual life. I. A religious of Carmel, Bettendorf, Ia., tr. II. Title.

SCHWIMMER, Josephine (Betz-Hermann) Mrs. 1868- 133
Rays of light ... about cartology, astronomy, physiology, physiognomy, phrenology, chirography, philosophy and palmistry, magic arts, spiritualism and hypnotism, by Madam Josephine Schwimmer known and born Betz Hermann ... [Chicago, The Henneberry co., 1903] 319 p. front. (port.) illus. 20 cm. [BF1861.S4] 4-9137
I. Title.

THE science of spirtual alchemy; a semiprivate text expecially prepared for neophytes entering the August Fraternity for study and training. Quakertown, Penna. Philosophical Pub. Co. [1959] 235p. 24cm.
1. Spiritual life. I. Clymer, Reuben Swinburne, 1878-

SECRETS of Christian living.
ondensed book)
1. Spiritual life. I. Meyer, Frederick Brotherton, 1847-1929.

SEIFERT, Harvey. 248'.4
Liberation of life : growth exercises in meditation and action / Harvey & Lois Seifert. Nashville : The Upper Room, c1976. 112 p. ; 22 cm. [BV4501.2.S42] 76-46880
1. Spiritual life. I. Seifert, Lois, joint author. II. Title.

SHEVCHUK, Tetiana. 248
Born of the spirit, by Tania Kroiter Bishop. New York, Philosophical Library [1968] 80 p. 22 cm. [BV4510.2.S3] 68-13394
1. Spiritual life. I. Title.

SHOEMAKER, Samuel Moor, 1893- 248
By the power of God. [1st ed.] New York, Harper [1954] 158p. 20cm. [BV4501.S474] 54-9654
1. Spiritual life. 2. Evangelistic work. I. Title.

SIKORSKY, Igor Ivan, 1889- 232.952
The invisible encounter. New York, C. Scribner's Sons, 1947. 120 p. 20 cm. [BV4501.S478] 47-11689
1. Spiritual life. 2. Jesus Christ—Temptation. I. Title.

SIMMONS, Joe. 291.4'4
The warrior : brief studies in the sources of spiritual mastery, sport, and military power / Joe Simmons. Washington, D.C. : University Press of America, c1982. A-C p., 165, [10] p. ; 22 cm. Bibliography: p. [171]-[175] [BL624.S534 1982] 19 81-40925 ISBN 0-8191-2294-7 (pbk.) : 9.50 ISBN 0-8191-2293-9 : 20.50
1. Spiritual life. 2. Soldiers—Religious life. 3. Physical education and training. I. Title.

SIMONS, George F. 248'.4
Journal for life : discovering faith and values through journal keeping / George F. Simons. Chicago : Life in Christ, c1975- v. ; 23 cm. Contents.—pt. 1. Foundations. [BV4509.5.S55] 75-17161 ISBN 0-914070-07-X
1. Spiritual life. 2. Diaries—Authorship. I. Title.

A simple way of love,
by a Poor Clare; edited and introduced by Columba Cary-Elwes. Westminister, Md., Newman Press, 1949. vii, 104 p. 17 cm. A 50
1. Spiritual life. I. A Poor Clare. II. Cary-Elwes, Columba, Father, ed.

SINKLER, Lorraine. 248'.4
The alchemy of awareness / Lorraine Sinkler. 1st ed. New York : Harper & Row, c1977. ix, 149 p. ; 21 cm. [BL624.S58 1977] 76-62957 ISBN 0-06-067387-7 : 5.95
1. Spiritual life. I. Title.

SLOAN, William Niccolls, 1849-
Spiritual conquest along the Rockies, by Rev. William Niccolls Sloan... New York, Hodder & Stoughton, George H. Doran company [c1913] viii p., 2 l., 242 p. incl. tables. 20 cm. 13-25353 1.25
I. Title.

SMITH, Oswald J. 248
The spirit-filled life, by Oswald J. Smith... New York, N.Y., The Christian alliance publishing co. [c1926] 2 p. l., 7-126 p. 18 cm. [BV4501.S685] 26-15436
I. Title.

SMITH, Ronald Gregor. 248
Still point, an essay in living, by Ronald Maxwell [pseud.] London, Nisbet [1943] 74 p. 20 cm. [BV4501.S688] 44-26459
1. Spiritual life. 2. Clergy — Religious life. I. Title.

SOLOMON, Paul. 131'.32
The seven terraces / Paul Solomon. Millbrae, Calif. : Celestial Arts, 1979, c1978. p. cm. Bibliography: p. [BL624.S63] 78-54480 ISBN 0-89087-230-9 pbk. : 3.95
1. Spiritual life. 2. Meditation. I. Title.

SOLOV'EV, Vladimir Sergieevich, 1853-1900. 248
God, man and the church; the spiritual foundations of life, by Vladimir Solovyev; translated by Donald Attwater. Milwaukee, The Bruce publishing company [1938] xvii p., 1 l., 21-192 p. 21 cm. "This translation has been from the French version of Father George Tsebricov and the Abbe Alfred Martin."--Translator's pref. [BV5082.S58] 40-9276
1. Spiritual life. I. Attwater, Donald, 1892- tr. II. Title.

SPIRITUAL maxims,
Newly translated and edited. Springfield, Ill., Templegate [1961] xiii, 299p. 17cm. (Orchard Series)
1. Spiritual life. I. Grou, Jean Nicholas, 1731-1803.

SPRAGUE, Frank Headley, 1861- 126
Spiritual consciousness, by Frank H. Sprague ... Wollaston, Mass., F. H. Sprague, 1898. 238 p. 20 1/2 cm. [BF639.S7] 99-97
1. Spiritual life. I. Title.

STARCKE, Walter. 248.8'3
The ultimate revolution. [1st ed.] New York, Harper & Row [1969] 155 p. 22 cm. [BV4501.2.S73] 73-85058 4.95
1. Spiritual life. 2. Youth—Conduct of life. I. Title.

STEERE, Douglas Van, 1901- 248
On beginning from within, by Douglas V. Steere ... New York and London, Harper & brothers [1943] xvii p., 1 l., 149 p. 19 1/2 cm. "First edition." [BV4501.S7937] 44-33
1. Spiritual life. 2. Devotion. I. Title.

STEVENS, Dan E. 294.5'448
Man's search for certainty / by Dan E. Stevens. New York : Dodd, Mead, c1980. p. cm. [BL624.S73] 80-15743 ISBN 0-396-07860-5 : 9.95
1. Meher Baba, 1894-1969. 2. Spiritual life. I. Title.

STEVENS, Henry D.
A boy's life; its spiritual ministry. Boston, J. H. West co. [1899] 1 p. l., 118 p., 1 l. 16 degrees. (Life series) 99-1909
I. Title.

STEVENS, Maria. Mrs. 248
The progressive experience of the heart, under the discipline of the Holy Ghost, from regeneration to maturity. By Mrs. Maria Stevens. With a preface by Bishop Wm. R. Nicholson ... Philadelphia, J. Hammond, 1877. viii, 9-239 p. 20 cm. [BV4501.S7945] 40-37750
1. Spiritual life. 2. Regeneration (Theology) I. Title.

STREITFELD, Harold S. 294.5'2
God's plan : the complete guide to the future / by Harold Streitfeld. Oakland, Calif. : Raja Press, c1981. xv, 142 p. : ill. ; 22 cm. Includes bibliographical references. [BL624.S77] 19 81-80768 ISBN 0-9605926-0-1 (pbk.) : 6.95
1. Streitfeld, Harold S. 2. Spiritual life. 3. God. I. Title.
Publisher's address: 5534 Fremont St., Oakland, CA 94608

STUART, Vincent. 291.4'2
Changing mind / Vincent G. Stuart. Boulder : Shambhala ; New York : distributed by Random House, 1981. 74 p. ; 21 cm. [BL624.S78] 19 80-53447 ISBN 0-87773-206-X : 5.95
1. Spiritual life. 2. Occult sciences. I. Title.

*SUBRAMUNIYA, Master. 294.54
The search is within, by Master Subramuniya. San Francisco, Calif., Comstock House, [1973, c1972] 70 p., 14 cm. "A western mystic's simple guidelines for spiritual living." [BL1228] 2.00 (pbk.)
1. Spiritual life. 2. Direction, spiritual. I. Title.

*SULLIVAN, Daniel A. 248
Our bad, our good, our God [by] Daniel A. Sullivan. [1st. ed.] Hicksville, N.Y. Exposition Press [1974] 80 p. 22 cm. [BR110] ISBN 0-682-48000-2 4.50
1. Spiritual life. 2. Christian life. I. Title.

TALLING, Marshall P., 1857-
The science of spiritual life; an application of scientific method in the exploration of spiritual experience, by Marshall P. Talling ... New York, Chicago [etc.] Fleming H. Revell company [c1912] 320 p. 21 cm. 13-1164
I. Title.

THOMAS, Cordelia, Mrs. 922.773
The sheaf; or, The work of God in the soul; as illustrated in the personal experience of Mrs. Cordelia Thomas ... Boston, H. V. Degen, 1852. 1 p. l., viii, [9]-155 p. 15 1/2 cm. [BX8495.T55A3] 37-7019
1. Spiritual life. I. Title.

THOMAS, George Ernest, 1907- 248.27
Disciplines of the spiritual life. [Nashville] Abingdon [c.1963] 96p. 19cm. (Faith for life ser.) 63-23648 1.25 pap.,
1. Spiritual life. I. Title.

THOMAS, George Ernest, 1907- 248
.
Disciplines of the spiritual life. New York, Published for the Cooperative Publication Association by Abingdon Press [1963] 96 p. 19 cm. (Faith for life series) [BV5031.2.T5] 63-23648
1. Spiritual life. I. Title.

THOMPSON, George B., 1862-
The ministry of the Spirit, by G. B. Thompson ... Washington, D.C., South Bend, Ind. [etc.] Review and herald publishing assn. [c1914] 223 p. 18 1/2 cm. $0.75 14-13567
I. Title.

THURIAN, Max 248.2
Modern man and spiritual life. New York, Association [1963] 80p. 19cm. (World Christian bks., 2d ser., no. 46) 64-157 1.25 pap.,
1. Spiritual life. I. Title.

TIEDEMAN, Karl, 1890- 248
The holy cross; some ideals of the spiritual life, by Karl Tiedemann ... London, The Faith press, ltd. Milwaukee, The Morehouse publishing co. [1935] 2 p. l., 100 p. 16 1/2 cm. "First published, March, 1935." [BV4501.T53] 36-16430
1. Spiritual life. I. Title.

TITTLE, Ernest Fremont, 1885- 270
The religion of the spirit; studies in faith and life, by Ernest Fremont Tittle. New York, Cincinnati, The Abingdon press [c1928] 327 p. 19 1/2 cm. [BR125.T58] 28-4251
1. Spiritual life. I. Title.

TITTMANN, George Fabian. 248
Is religion enough? The challenge of the Gospel. Greenwich, Conn., Seabury Press, 1962. 177 p. 22 cm. [BV4501.2.T57] 62-17082
1. Spiritual life. I. Title.

TOZER, Aiden Wilson, 1897- 248
The divine conquest. Introd. by William L. Culbertson. New York, Revell [1950] 128 p. 20 cm. [BV4501.T755] 50-10877
1. Spriitual life. I. Title.

TWING, Carolinn E[dna] S[kinner] 1844-
Experiences of Samuel Bowles ... in spirit life; or, Life as he now sees it from a spiritual stand-point. Written through the mediumship of Carrie E. S. Twing ... Springfield, Mass., Star publishing company, 1880. 56 p. 19 1/2 cm. 5-20030
I. Title.

TWING, Carolinn E[dna] S[kinner] 1844-
Experiences of Samuel Bowles ... in spirit life; or, Life as he now sees it from a spiritual stand-point. New ed., with supplement. Written through the mediumship of Carrie E. S. Twing ... Springfield, Mass., Star publishing company, c1881. cover-title, 64, 27 p. 19 cm. Errors in paging. 5-20031
I. Title.

UNDERHILL, Evelyn 248
The golden sequence; a fourfold study of the spiritual life. New York, Harper [1960, c.1933] 123p. 21cm. (Harper Torchbooks/The Cloister Library TB 68) 1.25 pap.,
1. Spiritual life. 2. Mysticism. 3. Prayer. I. Title.

UNDERHILL, Evelyn, 1875- 248
The golden sequence; a fourfold study of the spiritual life, by Evelyn Underhill ... New York, E. P. Dutton & co., inc. [c1933) xiv. 196 p. 19 1/2 cm. "The first and last sections of this book incorporate the substance of a few passages which have already appeared in a paper on 'God and spirit' ... printed in Theology; and in an article on 'Prayer and the divine immanence' contributed to the Expository times."--Pref. "First edition." [BV4501.U46 1933] 33-4054
1. Spiritual life. 2. Mysticism. 3. Prayer. I. Title.
Contents omitted.

UNDERHILL, Evelyn, 1875- 248
The house on the soul, by Evelyn Underhill. New York, E. P. Dutton & co., inc. [c1930] 119 p. 17 cm. [BV4501.U47] 30-7516
1. Spiritual life. I. Title.

UNDERHILL, Evelyn, 1875- 248
The life of the spirit and the life of to-day, by Evelyn Underhill ... New York, E. P. Dutton & company [c1922] xi p. 1 l., 311 p. 21 cm. Partly reprinted from the Fortnightly review and the Hibbert journal.

"Principal works used or cited": p. 300-305. [BV4501.U5] 22-20918
1. Spiritual life. I. Title.

UNDERHILL, Evelyn, 1875- 290
Man and the supernatural, by Evelyn Underhill ... New York, E. P. Dutton & company [c1928] xi p., 1 l.,252 p. 19 1/2 cm. Bibliography: p. 243-247. [BL100.U6 1928] 28-4891
1. Spiritual life. 2. Supernatural. I. Title.

UNDERHILL, Evelyn, 1875- 248
Mixed pasture; twelve essays and addresses, by Evelyn Underhill ... New York, Longmans, Green and co., 1933. xi, [1], 233, [1] p. 19 cm. Printed in Great Britain. [BV4501.U52] 34-3496
1. Spiritual life. 2. Mysticism. I. Title.
Contents omitted.

UNDERHILL, Evelyn, 1875- 248
The spiritual life, By Evelyn Underhill. New York, London, Harper & brothers [1937] x p., 2 l., 15-142 p. incl. front., illus. 19 1/2 cm. Illustrated lining-papers. "First edition." "The substance of this book was originally presented in the autumn of 1966, as four broadcast talks."--Pref. "Books on the spiritual life": p. 141-143. [BV4501.U524 1937a] 37-28762
1. Spiritual life. I. Title.

UNDERHILL, Evelyn, 248.42081
1875-1941.
The Evelyn Underhill reader, compiled by Thomas S. Kepler. New York, Abingdon Press [1962] 238 p. 24 cm. [BV4501.U455] 62-7438
1. Spiritual life. 2. Mysticism. I. Title.

UNDERHILL, Evelyn, 1875-1941.
The fruits of the spirit. Light of Christ, with a memoir by Lucy Menzies. Abba: meditations based on the Lord's Prayer. New York, D. McKay [1962] 1 v. (various pagings) 17 cm. 63-59541
1. Spiritual life. 2. Lord's Prayer. 3. Mysticism. 4. Retreats. I. Title. II. Title: Light of Christ. III. Title: Abba: meditations on the Lord's prayer.

UNDERHILL, Evelyn, 1875-1941.
The golden sequence; a fourfold study of the spiritual life. [1st Harper Torchbook ed.] New York, Harper [1960] xii, 193 p. 21 cm. (Harper Torchbooks. The Cloister library, TB68)
1. Spiritual life. 2. Mysticism. 3. Prayer. I. Title.

UNDERHILL, Evelyn, 1875-1941. 248
Mixed pasture; twelve essays and addresses. Freeport, N.Y., Books for Libraries Press [1968] xi, 233 p. 22 cm. (Essay index reprint series) Reprint of the 1933 ed. Contents.Contents.—The philosophy of contemplation (Counsell memorial lecture,1930).—What is sanctity?—Spiritual life.—Some implicits of Christian social reform.—The will of the voice.—The Christian basis of social action.—The ideals of the ministry of women.—The spiritual significance of the Oxford Movement.—St. Francis and Franciscan spirituality (Walter Seton memorial lecture, 1933)—Richard the hermit.—Walter Hilton.—Finite and infinite: a study of the philosophy of Baron Friedrich von Hugel.—Additional note: Baron von Hugel as a spiritual teacher. [BV4501.U52 1968] 68-8501
1. Spiritual life. 2. Mysticism. I. Title.

UNDERHILL, Evelyn, 1875-1941. 248
The spiritual life. New York, Harper [1963?] 127, [1] p. 14 cm. "Books on the spiritual life": p. 127-[128] [BV4501] 63-6840
1. Spiritual life. I. Title.

VAN ZELLER, Hubert, 1905-
We sing while there's voice left. New York, Sheed and Ward [1957] x, 198 p. 20 cm.
1. Spiritual life. I. Title.

VASUDEVADAS. 294.5'44
A time for eternity / Vasudevadas. 1st ed. Bedford, Va. : Prema Dharmasala and Fellowship Assn. Pub., 1976. 85 p. : port. ; 22 cm. [BL624.V36] 76-45579
1. Spiritual life. I. Title.

VERNET, Felix. 248
... Medieval spirituality, by Felix Vernet ... Translated by the Benedictines of Talacre. London, Sands & co.; St. Louis, Mo., B. Herder [1930] 237, [1] p. 19 cm. (Catholic library of religious knowledge, xiii) Bibliography: p. 237. [BX880.C3 vol.xiii] (282.08) 32-6361
1. Spiritual life. 2. Mysticism. 3. Monasticism and religious orders. 4. Church history—Middle ages. I. Talacre abbey. II. Title.

VICTIMS of love; 248
the spiritual life as it can be lived in the world, by a member of the "Associazione delle vittime per la santa chiesa", with a foreword by Benedict Williamson ... St. Louis, Mo. and London, B. Herder book co., 1927. xvii, 96 p. 19 1/2 cm. [BX2350.V5] 27-22568
I. Associazione delle vittime per la santa chiesa. II. Williamson, Benedict, 1868-

VON HILDEBRAND, Dietrich, 1889-
Transformation in Christ; on the Christian attitude of wind. Baltimore, Helicon press [1960] ix, 406 p. 23 cm. Translation of Die umgestaltung in Christus.
1. Spiritual life. I. Title.

WATTS, Alan Wilson, 1915- 191
1973.
Om, creative meditations / Alan Watts. Millbrae, Calif. : Celestial Arts, c1980. p. cm. [BL624.W37 1980] 79-54101 ISBN 0-89087-257-0 pbk. : 5.95
1. Spiritual life. 2. Meditations. I. Title.

WENZLICK, William.
The greatest good of mankind: physical or spiritual life, by William Wenzlick... Chicago, The author, 1909. xxiv, 374 p. 19 1/2 cm. 9-18432
I. Title.

WESTERHOFF, John H. 248.4
The spiritual life : learning East and West / John H. Westerhoff III and John D. Eusden. New York : Seabury Press, 1982. 134 p. ; 22 cm. Bibliography: p. [133]-134. [BL624.W43 1982] 19 81-21312 ISBN 0-8164-0516-6 : 10.95
1. Spiritual life. 2. Religions. I. Eusden, John Dykstra. II. Title.

WESTWOOD, Horace, 1884- 248
This do and live, by Horace Westwood. Techniques of life for liberals. Boston, Mass., The Beacon press, inc., 1938. ix, 157 p. 19 1/2 cm. [BV4501.W48] 38-13549
1. Spiritual life. I. Title.

WHALEY, William Pearson, 248
1869-
The divinity within us, by W. P. Whaley. Nashville, Tenn., Dallas, Tex., Publishing house of the M. E. church, South, 1907. 130 p. 19 cm. [BV4501.W49] 7-40006
1. Spiritual life. I. Title.

WHERRIT, Elevnora. 248'.4
Beyond disbelief. Philadelphia, Dorrance [1971] 94 p. 22 cm. [BV4501.2.W444] 77-163918 4.00
1. Jesus Christ—Person and offices. 2. Spiritual life. I. Title.

WHITEHEAD, Carleton. 248'.4
Creative meditation / by Carleton Whitehead. New York : Dodd, Mead, [1975] 154 p. ; 21 cm. [BL624.W47] 75-4882 ISBN 0-396-07139-2 : 6.95
1. Spiritual life. 2. Success. I. Title.

WHITING, Lilian, 1859- 133.
The adventure beautiful, by Lilian Whiting... Boston, Little, Brown, and company, 1917. vii p., 1 l., 243 p. front. 19 cm. [BF1261.W48] 17-25596
1. Spiritual life. 2. Spiritualism. I. Title.
Contents omitted.

WHITING, Lilian, 1859- 248
The life radiant, by Lilian Whiting... Boston, Little, Brown, and company, 1903. viii, [2], 373 p., 1 l. 19 cm. [BF639.W56] 3-28571
1. Spiritual life. I. Title.
Contents omitted.

WHITING, Lilian, 1859- 248
The outlook beautiful, by Lilian Whiting... Boston, Little, Brown, and company, 1905. 6 p. l., 3-182 p., 1 l. 19 cm. [BF639.W57] 5-10556
1. Spiritual life. 2. Future life. I. Title.
Contents omitted.

WHITING, Lillian. 131.
From dream to vision of life, by Lilian Whiting... Boston, Little, Brown, and company, 1906. 7 p. l., 3-181 p., 1 l. 19 cm. [BF639.W54] 6-34651
1. Spiritual life. I. Title.

WIESENBERG, Charles, 1885- 248
1941.
Vital letters, a series of letters dealing with the spiritual life, written to Christians, by Charles Wiesenberg. Merchantville, N.J., Christian witness to Israel, inc., 1943. 6 p. l., 94 p. illus. (port.) 22 cm. [BV4501.W5955] 43-22337
1. Spiritual life. I. Christian witness to Israel. II. Title.

WILLIAMS, Charles Henry. 242
Spiritual thoughts for candid readers, by Rev. C. H. Williams... Brooklyn, N.Y., The Orphans' press, C. C. F. [1899] 198 p. 15 cm. [BV4832.W5] 24-13127
I. Title.

WILLIS, Frederick Milton, 212
1868-
The spiritual life, how to attain it and prepare children for it, by F. Milton Willis ... New York, E. P. Dufton & company [c1922] xi, 97 p. 19 1/2 cm. (His Sacred occultism series) [BP565.W6] 22-5312
I. Title.

*WOOD, A. Skevington 233.5
Life by the spirit (formerly pub. as Paul's Pentecost) Grand Rapids, Mich., Zondervan [1964, c.1963] 144p. 21cm. 2.50
I. Title.

WOODCOX, Benjamin Franklin. 133.
Spiritual evolution; thoughts on the evolution of spiritlife and various other subjects. By Benjamin F. Woodcox ... Battle Creek, Mich., Woodcox and Fanner [c1921] 80 p. 19 1/2 cm. [With his Fragments of spiritual knowledge ... Battle Creek Mich., c1923] [BF1301.W85] 23-5497
I. Title. II. Title: Evolution, Spiritual.

WRIGHT, Worthington, 1785- 242
1873.
Seeking and finding. Passages in the religious experience of the Rev. Worthington Wright. New York, A. D. F. Randolph & company [1885] 132 p. 17 1/2 cm. Introduction signed: Edwin S. Wright. "Obituary" (by Rev. A. T. Chester): p. [5]-8. [BX7260.W7A3] 36-28636
1. Spiritual life. I. Wright, Edwin Swift, 1815-1888, ed. II. Chester, Albert Tracy, 1812-1892. III. Title.

WUELLNER, Flora, Slosson. 248'.48
On the road to spiritual wholeness / Flora Slosson Wuellner. Nashville : Abingdon, c1978. p. cm. [BV4501.2.W83] 77-12232 pbk. : 3.95
1. Spiritual life. I. Title.

YOGANANDA, Paramhansa, 294.5'4
1893-1952.
Sayings of Paramhansa Yogananda. 4th ed. [Los Angeles, Calif.] : Self-Realization Fellowship, 1980. x, 125 p., [4] leaves of plates : ill. ; 21 cm. Third ed. published under title: Sayings of Yogananda. Includes index. [BP605.S4Y6 1980] 19 79-66287 ISBN 0-87612-115-6 : 3.95
1. Spiritual life. I. Title.

YORK quarterly
Christian spirituality to-day; essays contributed to the 'York quarterly', 1959-60, edited by the Archbishop of Canterbury. London, Faith Press; New York, Morehouse-Barlow [1961] 62 p. 19 cm. 63-60129
1. Spiritual life. 2. Asceticism-Hist. I. Ramsey, Arthur Michael, Abp. of Canterbury, 1904- ed. II. Title.

Spiritual life—Addresses, essays, lectures.

BACH, Marcus, 1906- 248
Questions on the quest : search and discovery in the world within, the world around, and worlds beyond / Marcus Bach. 1st ed. New York : Harper and Row, [c1978] p. cm. [BL624.B28 1978] 77-17042 ISBN 0-06-060320-8 : 6.95
1. Spiritual life—Addresses, essays, lectures. 2. Conduct of life—Addresses, essays, lectures. 3. Religion—Addresses, essays, lectures. I. Title.

BACH, Marcus, 1906- 248
Questions on the quest : search and discovery in the world within, the world around, and worlds beyond / Marcus Bach. 1st ed. San Francisco : Harper and Row, c1978. 159 p. : ill. ; 21 cm. [BL624.B28 1978] 77-20464 6.95
1. Spiritual life—Addresses, essays, lectures. 2. Conduct of life—Addresses, essays, lectures. 3. Religion—Addresses, essays, lectures. I. Title.

THE Common experience / 291.4'2
[compiled] by J.M. Cohen, J-F. Phipps. 1st ed. Los Angeles : J.P. Tarcher ; Boston : Distributed by Houghton Mifflin Co., c1979. 263 p. ; 21 cm. Includes index. Bibliography: p. [257]-261. [BL624.C65 1981] 19 81-16651 ISBN 0-87477-204-4 : 6.95
1. Spiritual life—Addresses, essays, lectures. 2. Salvation—Addresses, essays, lectures. I. Cohen, J. M. 1903- (John Michael), II. Phipps, J.-F. (John-Francis)

EASWARAN, Eknath. 294.5'44
The supreme ambition : life's goal & how to reach it / by Eknath Easwaran. Petaluma, Calif. : Nilgiri Press, c1982. 174 p. : ill. ; 25 cm. Essays originally published in The Little lamp. [BL624.E18] 19 81-18991 ISBN 0-915132-26-5 : 12.00 ISBN 0-915132-27-3 (pbk.) : 7.00
1. Spiritual life—Addresses, essays, lectures. I. Little lamp. II. Title.
Publisher's address: P.O. Box 477, Petaluma, CA 94953

HUNTER, John Edward, 1909- 248.4
Living the Christ-filled life; seving God wholeheartedly, by John E. Hunter. Grand Rapids, Zondervan Pub. House, [1969] 130 p. 22 cm. [BV4501.2.H853] 69-11635 2.95
1. Spiritual life—Addresses, essays, lectures. I. Title.

JOHN, Bubba Free. 299'.93
Compulsory dancing : talks and essays on the spiritual and evolutionary necessity of emotional surrender to the life-principle / by Da Free John. Rev. ed. Clearlake Highlands, Calif. : Dawn Horse Press, 1980. 157 p. : ill. ; 18 cm. Previous ed. published in 1979 as: Conversion. Includes bibliographical references. [BP610.B8124 1980] 19 80-80912 ISBN 0-913922-50-1 (pbk.) : 2.95
1. Spiritual life—Addresses, essays, lectures. I. Title.

JOHN, Bubba Free. 299'.93
The four fundamental questions : talks and essays about human experience and the actual practice of an enlightened way of life / by Da Free John. 2nd ed., rev. Clearlake Highlands, Calif. : Dawn Horse Press, 1980. 115 p. : ill. ; 18 cm. [BP610.B8135 1980] 19 81-165053 ISBN 0-913922-49-8 (pbk.) : 1.95
1. Spiritual life—Addresses, essays, lectures. I. Title.

KAUSHIK, R. P., 1926- 131'.32
Organic alchemy / R. P. Kaushik. 2d ed. Woodstock, N.Y. : Journey Publications, 1978, c1975. 110 p. ; 22 cm. [BL624.K36 1978] 77-94471 ISBN 0-918038-08-1 : 8.95 ISBN 0-918038-07-3 pbk. : 3.95
1. Spiritual life—Addresses, essays, lectures. I. Title.

†KAUSHIK, R. P., 1926- 158'.1
The ultimate transformation : talks at Anjuna Beach, Goa, India, 1973 / R. P. Kaushik. 2d ed. Woodstock, N.Y. : Journey Publications, 1977, c1974. 156 p. ; 22 cm. [BL624.K38 1977] 77-85215 ISBN 0-918038-05-7 : 8.95 ISBN 0-918038-04-9 pbk. : 3.95
1. Spiritual life—Addresses, essays, lectures. I. Title.

LIVE in the spirit; 248'.4
a compendium of themes on the spiritual life as presented at the Council on Spiritual Life. Editorial committee: Harris Jansen, chairman, Elva Hoover [and] Gary Leggett. Springfield, Mo., Gospel Pub. House [1972] 359 p. 22 cm. Sponsored by the Assemblies of God, General Council. [BV4501.2.L59] 73-154808
1. Spiritual life—Addresses, essays, lectures. I. Jansen, Harris, ed. II. Council

on Spiritual Life, Minneapolis, 1972. III. Assemblies of God, General Council.

MEDITATIONS of the 291.4'3
masters : selections / adapted by Ellen Kei Hua ; drawings by Maky. Ventura, Calif. : Thor Pub. Co., [1977] p. cm. "A Farout Press book." [BL624.M4] 76-47649 ISBN 0-87407-203-4 pbk. : 2.25
1. Spiritual life—Addresses, essays, lectures. I. Hua, Ellen Kei, 1945-

MULFORD, Prentice, 1834-1891. 299
The gift of the spirit : a selection from the essays of Prentice Mulford / with preface and introduction by Arthur Edward Waite. New York : Gordon Press, 1981. p. cm. Reprint of: 2nd and rev. ed. London : W. Rider, 1913. [BL624.M85 1981] 19 81-6411 ISBN 0-8490-0235-4 lib. bdg. : 79.95
1. Spiritual life—Addresses, essays, lectures. 2. Spiritualism—Addresses, essays, lectures. I. Title.

PALMER, Parker J. 248.4
The promise of paradox : a celebration of contradictions in the Christian life / Parker J. Palmer. Notre Dame, Ind. : Ave Maria Press, c1980. 125 p. ; 21 cm. Includes bibliographical references. [BV4501.2.P314] 19 80-68134 ISBN 0-87793-210-7 (pbk.) : 2.95
1. Spiritual life—Addresses, essays, lectures. 2. Christian communities—Addresses, essays, lectures. I. Title.

PAUL, John Haywood, 1877- 248
The way of power, a series of lectures delivered before the Japan convention for deepening of spiritual life, at Karnizawa, stenographically reported, by John Paul ... New York, Chicago [etc.] Fleming H. Revell company [c1918] 190 p. 20 cm. [BV4501.P3] 18-11318
I. Convention for deepening of spiritual life, Karnizawa, Japan. II. Title.

SACRED tradition and 248'.4
present need / edited by Jacob Needleman and Dennis Lewis. New York : Viking Press, 1975. xi, 146 p. ; 22 cm. (An Esalen book) First presented as a series of lectures sponsored by Esalen Institute in San Francisco during the summer of 1973. [BL624.S2 1975] 75-14498 ISBN 0-670-61441-6 : 10.00
1. Spiritual life—Addresses, essays, lectures. I. Needleman, Jacob. II. Lewis, Dennis. III. Esalen Institute.

SEARCH / 291.4
edited by Jean Sulzberger. 1st ed. San Francisco : Harper & Row, c1979. xix, 151 p. : ill. ; 23 cm. Includes bibliographical references. [BL624.S4 1979] 78-4430 ISBN 0-06-067766-X : 10.00 ISBN 0-06-067765-1 pbk. : 5.95
1. Spiritual life—Addresses, essays, lectures. I. Sulzberger, Jean.

SECULARIZATION and 248
spirituality. Edited by Christian Duquoc. New York, Paulist Press, [1969] viii, 179 p. 24 cm. (Concilium: theology in the age of renewal. Spirituality, v. 49) On spine: Spirituality and secularization. Bibliographical footnotes. [BV4501.2.S373] 76-103390 4.50
1. Spiritual life—Addresses, essays, lectures. 2. Secularism—Addresses, essays, lectures. I. Duquoc, Christian, ed. II. Title: Spirituality and secularization. III. Series: Concilium (New York) v. 49

STEVENSON, Herbert F., 248.42082
ed.
The ministry of Keswick; a selection from the Bible readings delivered at the Keswick Convention; 1st. ser. Grand Rapids., Mich., Zondervan [c.1963] v. 22cm. 64-426 5.95
1. Spiritual life—Addresses, essays, lectures. I. Title.
Contents omitted.

WHITE, William Allen, 1868-
A theory of spiritual progress; an address delivered before the Phi beta kappa society of Columbia university in the city of New York, by William Allen White. Emporia, Kan., The Gazette press [c1910] 3 p. l., 53 p. 19 1/2 cm. $1.00 "This edition is limited to six hundred copies, of which this copy is no. 472, and is signed by the author. 11-960
I. Title.

Spiritual life—Anglican authors.

COBURN, John B. 248.4'8'3
Twentieth-century spiritual letters; an introduction to contemporary prayer, by John B. Coburn. Philadelphia, Westminster Press [1967] 170 p. 21 cm. [BV4501.2.C62] 67-21793
1. Spiritual life—Anglican authors. I. Title.

HANKEY, Cyril Patrick 248.483
Sign posts on the Christian way; a guide to the devotional life. New York, Scribners [c.1962] 152 p. Bibl. 62-9640 2.95
1. Spiritual life—Anglican authors. I. Title.

HOSMER, Rachel. 248'.48'3
Living in the spirit / written by Rachel Hosmer, Alan Jones, and John H. Westerhoff III, with the assistance of a group of editorial advisors under the direction of the Church's Teaching Series Committee. New York : Seabury Press, 1979. p. cm. (The Church's teaching series ; 7) Includes index. Bibliography: p. [BV4501.2.H594] 79-26121 ISBN 0-8164-0424-0 : 9.50 ISBN 0-8164-2220-6 (pbk.) : 3.95
1. Spiritual life—Anglican authors. I. Jones, Alan W., 1940- joint author. II. Westerhoff, John H., joint author. III. Title. IV. Series: Church's teaching series ; 7.

HUGHSON, Shirley Carter, 248
1867-
Spiritual guidance; a study of the Godward way. West Park, N.Y., Holy Cross Press, 1948. viii, 285 p. 20 cm. [BV4501.H73] 49-4665
1. Spiritual life—Anglican authors. I. Title.

JONES, Alan W., 1940- 248'.9'3
Journey into Christ / Alan Jones. New York : Seabury Press, 1977. p. cm. "A crossroad book." Bibliography: p. [BV4501.2.J585] 76-30656 ISBN 0-8164-0338-4 : 8.95
1. Spiritual life—Anglican authors. I. Title.

SMITH, John Ferris. 248'.48'3
The bush still burns : how God speaks to us today / John F. Smith. Kansas City : Sheed Andrews and McMeel, c1978. xiv, 165 p. ; 21 cm. [BV4501.2.S5342] 77-18007 ISBN 0-8362-0761-0 : 7.95
1. Spiritual life—Anglican authors. 2. Prayer. I. Title.

SMITH, John Ferris. 248'.48'3
The bush still burns : how God speaks to us today / John F. Smith. Boston : G. K. Hall, 1979. xiv, 256 p. ; 25 cm. Large print ed. [BV4501.2.S5342 1978b] 78-10603 ISBN 0-8161-6629-3 : 11.95
1. Spiritual life—Anglican authors. 2. Prayer. 3. Large type books. I. Title.

STERLING, Chandler W., 248'.48'3
Bp., 1911-
The doors to perception, by Chandler W. Sterling. Philadelphia, United Church Press [1974] 127 p. 22 cm. "A Pilgrim Press book." Bibliography: p. 119-125. [BV4501.2.S755] 74-8032 ISBN 0-8298-0282-7 5.25
1. Spiritual life—Anglican authors. I. Title.

THORNTON, Martin 248.483
The purple headed mountain. [New York, Morehouse-Barlow, c.1962] 90p. 62-946 1.00 pap.,
1. Spiritual life—Anglican authors. I. Title.

TROTTER, Jesse M. 248.4'83
Christian wholeness : spiritual direction for today / by Jesse M. Trotter. Wilton, Conn. : Morehouse-Barlow Co., c1982. xii, 86 p. : ill. ; 22 cm. Bibliography: p. 86. [BV4501.2.T73 1982] 19 81-84718 ISBN 0-8192-1294-6 pbk. : 4.75
1. Trotter, Jesse M. 2. Spiritual life—Anglican authors. I. Title.

VOGEL, Arthur Anton. 248'.48'3
The power of His resurrection : the mystical life of Christians / Arthur A. Vogel. New York : Seabury Press, c1976. v, 106 p. ; 22 cm. "A Crossroad book." Includes bibliographical references. [BV4501.2.V57] 75-37762 ISBN 0-8164-0298-1 : 6.95
1. Spiritual life—Anglican authors. 2. Mysticism. I. Title.

Spiritual life—Anglican authors—Addresses, essays, lectures.

LAW, William, 1686-1761. 248'.9'3
Wholly for God : selections from the writings of William Law / edited by Andrew Murray. Minneapolis : Bethany Fellowship, 1976. xxxii, 328 p. ; 18 cm. (Dimension books) Reprint of the 1894 ed. published by J. Nisbet, London. Includes bibliographical references. [BV4500.L34 1976] 76-6622 ISBN 0-87123-602-8 pbk. : 2.75
1. Spiritual life—Anglican authors—Addresses, essays, lectures. I. Title.

Spiritual life—Baptist authors.

HINSON, E. Glenn. 248'.48'61
A serious call to a contemplative life-style [by] E. Glenn Hinson. Philadelphia, Westminster Press [1974] 125 p. 21 cm. Bibliography: p. [117]-121. [BV4501.2.H52] 74-9658 ISBN 0-664-24992-2 2.85 (pbk.).
1. Spiritual life—Baptist authors. 2. Contemplation. I. Title.

HOLLOWAY, Leonard L. 248'.48'6132
Encounter with God [by] Leonard L. Holloway. Old Tappan, N.J., Revell [1972] 126 p. 21 cm. [BV4501.2.H565] 70-172684 ISBN 0-8007-0493-2 3.95
1. Spiritual life—Baptist authors. 2. God—Knowableness. I. Title.

SMITH, Ralph M. G. 248.4861
Living the spirit-filled life, by Ralph M. Smith. Introd. by Wallace E. Johnson. Grand Rapids, Zondervan [c.1967] 159p. 21cm. [BV4501.2.S6] 67-11610 2.95
1. Spiritual life—Baptist authors. I. Title.

WIERSBE, Warren W. 248.4'86
Creative Christian living [by] Warren W. Wiersbe. Westwood, N.J., F. H. Revell Co. [1967] 127 p. 21 cm. [BV4501.2.W518] 67-22576
1. Spiritual life—Baptist authors. I. Title.

Spiritual life—Biblical teaching.

DAUGHTERS of St. Paul. 230'.21
Spiritual life in the Bible / by the Daughters of St. Paul. [Boston, Mass.] : St. Paul Editions, c1980. 456 p. ; 19 cm. Includes index. [BS680.S7D38 1980] 19 80-21707 ISBN 0-8198-6812-4 : 5.95 ISBN 0-8198-6813-2 (pbk.) : 4.00
1. Spiritual life—Biblical teaching. I. Title.

GRISPINO, Joseph A. tr. 220.824
Foundations of Biblical spirituality. Staten Island, N. Y., Alba [c.1965] 142p. 22cm. [BS680.S7G7] 65-15726 3.95
1. Spiritual life—Biblical teaching. 2. Bible—Theology. I. Title.

GRISPINO, Joseph A tr. 220.824
Foundations of Biblical spirituality, translated by Joseph A. Grispino. Staten Island, N.Y., Alba House [1965] 142 p. 22 cm. [BS680.S7G7] 65-15726
1. Spiritual life — Biblical teaching. Bible — Theology. I. Title.

LERRIGO, Peter H. J. 220
The stature of a perfect man; Bible studies on spiritual well-being, by P. H. J. Lerrigo, M. D. Philadelphia, Boston [etc.] The Judson press [c1920] 5 p. l., 3-192 p. 18 1/2 cm. [BR125.L62] 20-22526
I. Title.

PAUL, Marie De La Croix 221.6
Father
Spirituality of the Old Testament. Tr. [from French] by Elizabeth McCabe. St. Louis, Herder [c.1961] xvi, 247p. (Cross and crown ser. of spirituality, no. 18) 61-12115 4.25 bds.,
1. Spiritual life—Biblical teaching. 2. Bible. O. T.—Criticism, interpretation, etc. I. Title.

PAUL Marie de la Croix, 221.6
Father
Spirituality of the Old Testament; v.3. Tr. [from French] by Elizabeth McCabe; St. Louis, Herder [c.1963] 347p. 21cm. (Cross and crown ser. of spirituality, no. 24) 61-12115 4.95
1. Spiritual life—Biblical teaching. 2. Bible. O. T.—Criticism, interpretation, etc. I. Title.

PAUL Marie de la Croix, 226'.5'06
Father.
The Biblical spirituality of St. John. [Translated by John Clarke] Staten Island, N.Y., Alba House [1966] 425 p. 24 cm. Translation of L'Evangile de Jean et son temoignage spirituel. Bibliographical footnotes. [BS2615.2.P313] 66-13033
1. Bible. N.T. John—Theology. 2. Spiritual life—Biblical teaching. I. Title.

PIERSON, Arthur Tappan, 1837-
The Bible and spiritual life, by Arthur T. Pierson ... New York, Gospel publishing house [c1908] 3 p. l., 483 p. front., tables, diagrs. 21 cm. Library of Congress. 8-7870
I. Title.

STUHLMUELLER, Carroll. 248'.4
Thirsting for the Lord : essays in Biblical spirituality / Carroll Stuhlmueller ; edited by M. Romanus Penrose ; illustrated by Lillian Brule ; introd. by Alcuin Coyle. New York : Alba House, c1977. x, 322 p. : ill. ; 22 cm. Includes indexes. [BS680.S7S78] 76-51736 ISBN 0-8189-0341-4 : 7.95
1. Spiritual life—Biblical teaching. 2. Spiritual life—Catholic authors. 3. Liturgics—Catholic Church. I. Title.

Spiritual life (Buddhism)

CHOGYAM Trungpa, 294.3'4'44
Trungpa Tulku, 1939-
Cutting through spiritual materialism, by Chogyam Trungpa. Edited by John Baker and Marvin Casper. Illustrated by Glen Eddy. Berkeley, Shambhala, 1973. 250 p. illus. 22 cm. (The Clear light series) [BQ4302.C47] 73-86145 ISBN 0-87773-049-0 ISBN 0-87773-050-4 (pbk.) 3.95
1. Spiritual life (Buddhism) I. Title.

TENDZIN, Osel, 1943- 294.3'4448
Buddha in the palm of your hand / Osel Tendzin ; foreword by Chogyam Trungpa ; edited by Donna Holm. 1st ed. Boulder : Shambhala ; [New York] : Distributed in the United States by Random House, 1982. xiii, 109 p. : ill. ; 22 cm. Includes index. [BQ5660.T46 1982] 19 81-84450 ISBN 0-87773-223-X (pbk.) : 4.95 ISBN 0-394-70889-X (Random House : pbk.)
1. Spiritual life (Buddhism) 2. Buddhism—Doctrines. 3. Bka -rgyud-pa (Sect)—Doctrines. I. Holm, Donna. II. Title.

Spiritual life—Catholic authors.

ALBERIONE, Giacomo 248.8'9
Giuseppe, 1884-
Personality and configuration with Christ [by] James Alberione, [Boston, Mass.] St. Paul Eds. [c1967] 185p. 21cm. [BX2350.5.A575] 67-20459 3.00; 2.00 pap.,
1. Spiritual life—Catholic authors. 2. Personality. I. Title.

AMBRUZZI, Aloysius.
A companion to the Spiritual exercises of Saint Ignatius. With a foreword by the late Cardinal Lepicier. 3d ed. Westminster, Md., Newman Press, 1948. xviii, 348 p. 22 cm. 1. Loyola, Ignacio de, Saint, 1491-1556. Exercitia spiritualia. A 50
I. Title.

ANDRE, Marie Joseph. 248.4'8'2
Equilibrium; fidelity to nature and grace, by M. J. Andre. With a pref. by Yves Congar. [Translated by David Martin] St. Louis, B. Herder Book Co. [1968] xiv, 157 p. 21 cm. (Cross and crown series of spirituality, no. 35) [BX2350.5.A6513] 68-22585
1. Spiritual life—Catholic authors. I. Title. II. Series.

ARNAIZ BARON, Rafael, 1911- 248.2
1938
To know how to wait. Tr. by Mairin Mitchell. Westminster, Md., Newman [1964] xviii, 381p. illus., port. 14cm. 64-55964 3.50
1. Spiritual life—Catholic authors. 2. Meditation. I. Title.

AUER, Alfons 261.8
Open to the world: an analysis of lay spirituality. Tr. by Dennis Doherty, Carmel Callaghan. Baltimore, Helicon [1966] 337p. 22cm. Tr. of Weltoffener Christ. Bibl. [BX2350.5.A813] 66-25741 5.95

1. Spiritual life— Catholic authors. I. Title. Available from Taplinger in New York.

BAKEWELL, Francis F 248.482
Human living in Christ. Milwaukee, Bruce Pub. Co. [1962] 156 p. 18 cm. [BX2350.2.B3] 62-18185
1. Spiritual life—Catholic authors. I. Title.

BANDAS, Rudolph George, 248.84
1896-
The Catholic layman and holiness. Pref. by Charles P Greco. Boston, Christopher Pub. [c.1965] 335p. 21cm. [BX2350.5.B3] 65-25595 4.95
1. Spiritual life—Catholic authors. I. Title.

BAUR, Benedikt 248.482
In silence with God. Translated from the 4th German ed. by Elisabethe Corathiel-Noonan. Chicago, H. Regnery Co. [c.1960] x, 235p. 21cm. 60-9323 3.75
1. Spiritual life—Catholic authors. I. Title.

BAUR, Benedikt, 1877- 248
In silence with God. Translated from the 4th German ed. by Elisabethe Corathiel-Noonan. Chicago, H. Regnery Co., 1955. 157p. 22cm. [BX2350] 57-2506
1. Spiritual life—Catholic authors. I. Title.

BAUR, Benedikt, 1877- 248.482
In silence with God. Translated from the 4th German ed. by Elisabethe Corathiel-Noonan. Chicago, H. Regnery Co. [1960] 235p. 21cm. [BX2350.B323 1960] 60-9323
1. Spiritual life—Catholic authors. I. Title.

BEUTLER, Harold Joseph, 1906- 248
For Thee alone; conferences for religious. St. Louis, B. Herder Book Co., 1947. viii, 227 p. 21 cm. Bibliographical footnotes. [BX4210.B4] 48-125
1. Spiritual life—Catholic authors. 2. Monasticism and religious orders for women. I. Title.

BLOCKER, Hyacinth 248.4
Don't fall out the window. Cincinnati, St. Francis Bkshop. [1962] 214p. 23cm. 62-17240 3.95
1. Spiritual life—Catholic authors. I. Title.

BONAVENTURA, Saint, 248
Cardinal, 1221-1274.
The enkindling of love, also called The triple way. Adapted from the original, edited and arr. by William I. Joffe. Paterson, N. J., Saint Anthony Guild Press, 1956. xiv, 71p. 19cm. [BX2350.B6382] 56-14359
1. Spiritual life—Catholic authors. I. Title. II. Title: The triple way.

BOUYER, Louis, 1913- 248.482
Introduction to spirituality. Tr. [from French] by Mary Perkins Ryan. New York, Desclee 1961. 321p. Bibl. 61-15722 5.75
1. Spiritual life—Catholic authors. I. Title.

BOYLAN, M Eugene. 248
This tremendous lover. Westminster, Md., Newman Press, 1948 [i. e. 1947] xviii. 345 p. 22 cm. "Spiritual reading": p. 388-345. [BX2350.B645] 49-158
1. Spiritual life—Catholic authors. I. Title.

BRICE, Father, 1905- 248
In spirit and in truth; the spiritual doctrine of Saint Paul of the Cross. New York, F. Pustet Co., 1948. 357 p. 23 cm. Secular name: Frank Bernard Zurmuehlen. [BX2350.B687] 48-8053
1. Spiritual life—Catholic authors. 2. Paolo delia Croce, Saint, 1694-1775. I. Title.

BUCKLER, Henry Reginald, 248
1840-
Spiritual considerations, by Fr. H. Reginald Buckler ... New York Cincinnati [etc.] Benziger brothers, 1911. 233 p. 19 cm. [BX2350.B77] 11-5720
1. Spiritual life—Catholic authors. I. Title.

BUONO, Anthony M. 264'.02
Liturgy, our school of faith / Anthony M. Buono. New York, N.Y. : Alba House, 1982. p. cm. [BX1970.B78 1982] 19 82-16328 ISBN 0-8189-0435-6 pbk. : 6.95
1. Catholic Church—Liturgy. 2. Catholic Church—Education. 3. Spiritual life—Catholic authors. 4. Christian education. I. Title.

BURT, Donald X. 248.4'82
Colors of my days / Donald X. Burt. Collegeville, Minn. : Liturgical Press, 1980. p. cm. [BX2350.2.B867] 19 80-23754 ISBN 0-8146-1198-2 pbk. : 3.95
1. Spiritual life—Catholic authors. I. Title.

CALLENS, L J 248
Our search for God [by] L. J. Callens. Translated by David Martin. [St. Louis] Herder [1964] ix, 141 p. 21 cm. (Cross and crown series of spirituality, no. 27) Translation of Le mystere de notre intimite avec Dieu. Bibliographical footnotes. [BX2350.5.C313] 64-18771
1. Spiritual life—Catholic authors. I. Title.

CAMELI, Louis John. 248'.2'0922
Stories of paradise : the study of classical and modern autobiographies of faith / by Louis John Cameli. New York : Paulist Press, c1978. ix, 86 p. ; 23 cm. Includes bibliographical references. [BX2350.2.C3] 78-58961 ISBN 0-8091-2130-1 pbk. : 3.50
1. Spiritual life—Catholic authors. 2. Spirituality. I. Title.

CARRETTO, Carlo. 248.4'82
The Desert in the city / Carlo Carretto ; translated by Barbara Wall. New York : Crossroad, 1982, c1979. 106 p. ; 21 cm. Translation of: Il deserto nella citta. [BX2350.2.C337413 1982] 19 81-70877 ISBN 0-8245-0423-2 (pbk.) : 4.95
1. Spiritual life—Catholic authors. I. [Deserto nella citta.] English II. Title.

CARSWELL, Pamela, 1918- 248.482
Offbeat spirituality. Foreword by F. J. Sheed. New York, Sheed & Ward [1961, c.1960] 241p. 61-8501 3.95 bds.,
1. Spiritual life—Catholic authors. I. Title.

CARSWELL, Pamela Mary, 248.482
1918-
Offbeat spirituality. London and New York, Sheed and Ward [1960] 243p. 21cm. [BX2350.2.C34 1960] 61-65716
1. Spiritual life—Catholic authors. I. Title.

CARTER, Edward, 1929- 248'.48'2
Response in Christ; a study of the Christian life. Dayton, Ohio, Pflaum Press, 1969. xiv, 274 p. 22 cm. Bibliography: p. 263-267. [BX2350.2.C36] 69-20170 6.95
1. Spiritual life—Catholic authors. I. Title.

CARTER, Edward, 1929- 241'.04'2
The spirit is present; themes on Christian spirituality. Canfield, Ohio, Alba Books [1973] v, 130 p. 18 cm. [BX2350.2.C362] 72-9577 1.25 (pbk.)
1. Spiritual life—Catholic authors. I. Title.

CARTER, Edward, 1929- 240
Spirituality for modern man. Notre Dame, Ind., Fides Publishers [1971] ix, 208 p. 21 cm. Includes bibliographical references. [BX2350.2.C363] 71-142907 ISBN 0-8190-0080-9 6.50
1. Spiritual life—Catholic authors. I. Title.

CEGIELKA, Francis A 248'.8943
Spiritual theology for novices. Lodi, N. J., Immaculate Conception College [1961] 132p. 21cm. [BX4210.C37] 61-17401
1. Spiritual life—Catholic authors. 2. Monastic and religious life of women. I. Title.

CERESI, Vincenzo 248.482
Quest for holiness. [Tr. by Sister Gertrude] Staten Island, N.Y. Alba [c.1963] 288p. 21cm. Bibl. 63-21595 3.95
1. Spiritual life—Catholic authors. I. Title.

CERESI, Vincenzo. 248.482
Quest for holiness. [Translated by Sister Gertrude] Staten Island, N.Y. Alba House [1963] 288 p. 21 cm. Includes bibliography. [BX2350.5.C413] 62-21595
1. Spirtual life — Catholic authors. I. Title.

CHARDON, Louis, 1595-1651. 248
The cross of Jesus. Translated by Richard T. Murphy. St. Louis, Herder [1957- v. 21cm. (Cross and crown series of spirituality, no. 9 [BX2350.C422] 57-9133
1. Spiritual life—Catholic authors. I. Title.

CHAUTARD, Jean Baptiste, 242
1858-1935.
The soul of the apostolate. Translated, and with an introd., by Thomas Merton. Garden City, N. Y., Image Books [1961] 270p. 18cm. (A Doubleday image book, D124) [BX2183.C5 1961] 31-19283
1. Spiritual life—Catholic authors. I. Title.

CHAUTARD, Jean Baptiste, 242
abbot, 1858-1935.
The soul of the apostolate ... Authorized translation by Rev. J. A. Moran, S. M. 2d American printing, 4,000. Trappist, Ky., The Mission press for the Abbey of Gethsemani, 1941. 1 p. l., [v]-xii, 282 p. 17 1/2 cm. At head of title: Dom J. B. Chautard. [Secular name:Auguste Philogene Gustave Chautard] [BX2183.C5 1941] 44-178
1. Spirutual life—Catholic authors. I. Moran, James A.,1858-1940, tr. II. Title.

CHAUTARD, Jean Baptiste, 242
abbot, 1858-1935.
The true apostolate, from the French of Dom J. B. Chautard ... by Rev. Ferreol Girardey, c, ss, r. St. Louis, Mo. and London, B. Herder book co., 1918. 3 p. l., 195 p. 20 cm. [Secular name: Auguste Philogene Gustave Chautard] [BX2183.C5] 18-17464
1. Spiritual life—Catholic authors. I. Girardey, Ferreol, 1839-1930, tr. II. Title.

CHAUTARD, Jean Baptiste 242
[Secular name: Auguste Philogene Gustave Chautard] 1858-1935.
The soul of the apostolate. Tr. with an introd. by Thomas Merton. Garden City, N.Y., Image Books [dist. Doubleday, c.1946, 1961] 270p. (Doubleday image bk., D124) 61-19283 .85 pap.,
1. Spiritual life—Catholic authors. I. Title.

CHEVIGNARD, Bernard Marie. 234'.8
Reconciled with God, by B. M. Chevignard. Translated by Angele Demand. New York, Sheed and Ward [1967] vii, 212 p. 22 cm. Translation of Reconcilies avec Dieu. [BX2350.5.C4813] 67-21906
1. Spiritual life—Catholic authors. 2. Perfection (Catholic) I. Title.

CHRISTUS (PARIS) 248
Finding God in all things; essays in Ignatian spirituality selected from Christus. Translated by William J. Young. Chicago, H. Regnery Co., 1958. 276p. 21cm. (The Library of living Catholic thought) [BX2350.A1C45] 58-12411
1. Loyola, Ignacio de, Saint, 1491-1556. 2. Spiritual life —Catholic authors. I. Young, William John, 1885- tr. II. Title.

CLOONAN, John Joseph, 271.91
1881-
Principles of the spiritual life applied to the Daughters of charity, by John J. Cloonan, C.M. ... Emmitsburg, Md., St. Joseph's college [1942] iii, [7], 315 p. 23 1/2 cm. [BX4462.C56] 43-3313
1. Daughters of charity of St. Vincent de Paul, Emmitsburg, Md. 2. Spiritual life—Catholic authors. 3. Mysticism—Catholic church. I. St. Joseph's college, Emmitsburg, Md. II. Title.

COLIN, Louis, 1884- 248.482
The interior life. Tr. from French by Sister Maria Constance. Westminster, Md., Newman [c.]1962. 305p. 21cm. Bibl. 61-8966 4.95
1. Spiritual life—Catholic authors. I. Title.

COLIN, Louis, 1884- 248.482
The interior life. Translated from the French by Sister Maria Constance. Westminister, Md., Newman Press, 1962. 305 p. 21 cm. [BX2350.5.C583] 61-8966
1. Spiritual life — Catholic authors. I. Title.

COLOMBIERE, Claude de la 922.244
Faithful servant; spiritual retreats and letters of Blessed Claude La Colombiere. Translated [from the French] by William J. Young. St. Louis, Herder [c.1960] viii, 450p. 22cm. 60-7809 6.50
1. Spiritual life— Catholic authors. I. Title.

COURTOIS, Gaston 242
Fruitful activity; spiritual conferences for educators. Tr. [from French] by Sister Helen Madeleine. Westminister, Md., Newman [c.]1962. 140p. 21cm. 62-17189 3.00
1. Spiritual life—Catholic authors. I. Title.

COWAN, St. Michael, sister, 242
1884- comp.
Rest awhile; readings and meditations for retreats, compiled from approved sources by Sister St. Michael Cowan ... New York, Cincinnati [etc.] Benziger brothers, 1936. xi, 153 p. 20 cm. [Secular name: Rosalina Cowan] [BX2182.C65] 36-9446
1. Spiritual life—Catholic authors. 2. Meditations. I. Title.

CROSS and crown (St. 248.482
Louis)
Seeking the kingdom; a guide to Christian living. Ed. by Reginald Masterson. St. Louis, B. Herder [c.1961] 306p. 61-8041 5.25
1. Spiritual life—Catholic authors. I. Masterson, Reginald, ed. II. Title.

CUMMINGS, Charles, 1940- 248.4'82
The mystery of the ordinary / Charles Cummings. 1st ed. San Francisco : Harper & Row, c1982. x, 133 p. ; 22 cm. Includes bibliographies. [BX2350.2.C835 1982] 19 81-47846 ISBN 0-06-061652-0 : 9.57
1. Spiritual life—Catholic authors. I. Title.

CUSHING, Anthony J. 248'.48'2
Living Christian community : leader's manual / by Anthony Cushing and Daniel Thomson. New York : Paulist Press, c1978. vii, 152 p. ; 28 cm. Includes bibliographical references. [BX2350.2.C867] 78-51593 ISBN 0-8091-2097-6 pbk. : 10.00
1. Spiritual life—Catholic authors. I. Thomson, Daniel, 1952- joint author. II. Title.

CUSKELLY, Eugene James 248
Heart to know thee; a practical summa of the spiritual life. Westminster, Md., Newman [c.]1963. xvii, 317p. 23cm. Bibl. 63-12243 5.50
1. Spiritual life—Catholic authors. I. Title.

CUSKELLY, Eugene James 248
A heart to know thee; a practical summa of the spiritual life. Glen Rock, N.J., Paulist [1967, c.1963] 317p. 19cm. (Deus Bks.) Bibl. 1.45 pap.,
1. Spiritual life—Catholic authors. I. Title.

CUSKELLY, Eugene James. 248
A heart to know thee; a practical summa of the spiritual life. Westminster, Md., Newman Press, 1963. xvii, 317 p. 23 cm. Bibliographical references included in "Notes." [BX2350.5.C8] 63-12243
1. Spiritual life — Catholic authors. I. Title.

CUSKELLY, Eugene James. 248.4'82
A heart to know thee; a practical summa of the spiritual life, by E. J. Cuskelly. New York, Paulist Press [1967] xvii, 317 p. 19 cm. (Deus books) Includes bibliographical references. [BX2350.5] 67-7269
1. Spiritual life—Catholic authors. I. Title.

DANIELOU, Jean 248.482
The Christian today. Translated [from the French by Kathryn Sullivan. NewYork, Desclee, 1960[ ] 149p. 22cm. (Bibl. footnotes) 60-10016 2.75
1. Spiritual life—Catholic authors. I. Title.

DE HUECK, Catherine, 282'.092'4 B
1900-
Poustinia : Christian spirituality of the East for western man / Catherine de Hueck Doherty. Notre Dame, Ind. : Ave Maria Press, [1975] 216 p. ; 21 cm. [BX2350.2.D4] 74-19961 ISBN 0-87793-084-8 : 5.95 ISBN 0-87793-083-X pbk. : 3.50
1. De Hueck, Catherine, 1900- 2. Spiritual life—Catholic authors. I. Title.

DELAGE, Augustin, 1877- 248
Living in God, by Robert de Langeac (Fr. Delage, priest of St. Sulpice) With an introd. by Francois de Sainte-Marie. English translation by P. Moloney. Westminster, Md., Newman Press [1953] 117p. 17cm. Translation of La vie cachee en Dieu. [BX2350.D383] 53-3142
1. Spiritual life—Catholic authors. I. Title.

DEVAS, Francis. 248
The law of love; the spiritual teaching of Francis Devas, S. J.; edited with an introd. by Philip Caraman. New York, P. J. Kenedy [1954] 155 p. 20 cm. [BX2350.D47] 54-6529
1. Spiritual life—Catholic authors. I. Caraman, Phillip, 1911- ed. II. Title.

DI GIACOMO, James. 201
The longest step : searching for God / James Di Giacomo and John Walsh. [Minneapolis] : Winston Press, c1977. 94

p. : ill. ; 22 cm. (The Encounter series) Discusses various ways of coming to terms with God. [BX2350.2D5] 77-72547 ISBN 0-03-021276-6 pbk. : 2.95
1. Spiritual life—Catholic authors. 2. [Christian life.] I. Walsh, John J., 1913- joint author. II. Title.

DION, Philip E 248
Keys to the third floor; how to live religious life. New York, J.F. Wagner ,531953] 188p. 21cm. [BX2350.D52] 53-3841
1. Spiritual life—Catholic authors. I. Title.

DOBSON, Theodore Elliott. 248.3'2
How to pray for spiritual growth : a practical handbook of inner healing / Theodore E. Dobson. New York : Paulist Press, c1982. vi, 216 p. ; 21 cm. Includes bibliographies. [BX2350.2.D575] 19 81-83182 ISBN 0-8091-2419-X (pbk.) : 6.95
1. Spiritual life—Catholic authors. 2. Prayer. 3. Spiritual healing. I. Title.

DOHERTY, Barbara. 248.4'82
I am what I do : contemplation and human experience / by Barbara Doherty. Chicago, Ill. : T. More Press, c1981. 226 p. ; 21 cm. [BX2350.2.D615] 19 81-167856 ISBN 0-88347-129-9 : 10.95
1. Spiritual life—Catholic authors. 2. Experience (Religion) I. Title.

DON'T you belong to me? 248'.3
/ A monk of New Clairvaux. New York : Paulist Press, c1979. xi, 167 p. ; 23 cm. Includes bibliographical references. [BX2350.2.D643] 79-88985 ISBN 0-8091-2217-0 pbk. : 7.95
1. Spiritual life—Catholic authors. I. Monk of New Clairvaux.

DOTY, William Lodewick, 248.4'8'2
1919-
Holiness for all; Vatican II spirituality, by William L. Doty. St. Louis, B. Herder Book Co., 1969. 142 p. 18 cm. [BX2350.2.D648 1969] 71-97236 1.45
1. Vatican Council. 2d, 1962-1965. 2. Spiritual life—Catholic authors. I. Title.

DOTY, William Lodewick, 1919- 248
The on-going pilgrimage; process, psychodynamics and personal presence in the spiritual life, by William L. Doty. Staten Island, N.Y., Alba House [1970] vi, 179 p. 22 cm. [BX2350.2.D649] 78-117200 4.95
1. Spiritual life—Catholic authors. I. Title.

DREXEL, Jeremias, 1581-1638.
Heliotropium: Conformity of the human will to the divine. Edited by Ferdinand E. Bogner. New York, Devin-Adair [1958, c1912] xiv, 399 p. 20 cm. 68-42847
1. Spiritual life—Catholic authors. I. Bogner, Ferdinand Edward, 1881- ed. II. Title.

DREXEL, Jeremias, 1581-1638. 237.
The heliotropium; or, Conformity of the human will to the divine; from the Latin of Jeremias Drexelius, S.F., edited by Rev. Ferdinand E. Bogner. New York, The Devin-Adair company, 1912. xiv, 399 p. 19 1/2 cm. [BX2180.D7E5] 12-29370
1. Spiritual life—Catholic authors. I. Bogner, Ferdinand Edward, 1881- ed. II. Title.

DURRWELL, F X 248.482
In the redeeming Christ; toward a theology of spirituality, Translated by Rosemary Sheed. New York, Sheed and Ward [1963] 292 p. 22 cm. [BX2350.5.D813] 63-8545
1. Spiritual life—Catholic authors. I. Title.

EBERSCHWEILER, William 248.482
Stand strong in the Lord; spiritual conferences on the interior life. Tr. by Mary Aloysi Kiener. Foreword by Martin B. Hellriegel. Staten Island, N.Y., Alba House [dist. St. Paul Pubns., 1962] 348p. 21cm. 62-17038 4.00
1. Spiritual life—Catholic authors. I. Title.

EDMUND Rich, Saint, Abp. of 230.2
Canterbury, d.1240.
Speculum religiosorum; and, speculum ecclesie [by] Edmund of Abingdon; edited by Helen P. Forshaw. London, Oxford University Press for the Academy [1973 i.e.1974] ix, 125 p. 26 cm. (Auctores Britannici Medii Aevi, 3) Includes bibliographical references and indexes. English introd., Latin text. The original Latin text is printed parallel to the vulgate Latin text, which is a translation of an Anglo-Norman version. [BX2349.E35] 74-204756 ISBN 0-19-725935-9 16.00
1. Spiritual life—Catholic authors. I. Forshaw, Helen P., ed. II. Title. III. Title: Speculum ecclesie. IV. Series.
Distributed by Oxford University Press, N.Y.

ELBEE, Jean d'. 248'.48'2
I believe in love : retreat conferences on the interior life / Jean du Coeur de Jesus d'Elbee ; translated from the French by Marilyn Teichert, with Madeleine Stebbins. Chicago : Franciscan Herald Press, [1974] p. cm. Translation of Croire a l'amour. [BX2350.2.E413] 74-20671 ISBN 0-8199-0555-0
1. Spiritual life—Catholic authors. I. Title.

ELLIOTT, Walter, 1842-1928. 242
The spiritual life, doctrine and practise of Christian perfection, by Rev. Walter Elliott... New York, The Paulist press, 1914. viii p., 1 l., 388 p. 24 cm. [BX2182.E4] 15-2774
1. Spiritual life—Catholic authors. 2. Perfection. I. Title.

ENGLISH, John J. 248'.3
Choosing life / by John English. New York : Paulist Press, c1978. v, 229 p. ; 21 cm. [BX2350.2.E53] 78-58315 ISBN 0-8091-2113-1 pbk. : 6.95
1. English, John J. 2. Spiritual life—Catholic authors. 3. Spiritual exercises. 4. Decision-making (Ethics) I. Title.

ESCRIVA, Jose Maria. 248
The way. Foreword by Samuel Cardinal Stritch, Archbishop of Chicago. Chicago, Scepter, 1954. 256p. 16cm. [BX2350.E74 1954a] 55-19727
1. Spiritual life—Catholic authors. I. Title.

ESCRIVA, Jose Maria [Jose 248
Maria Escriva de Balaguer Albos]
The way. New York, All Saints [1963, c.1954, 1962] 268p. 17cm. (AS702) .75 pap.,
1. Spiritual life—Catholic authors. I. Title.

EVELY, Louis, 1910- 248.4'8'2
We are all brothers. Tr. by Sister Mary Agnes. [New York] Herder & Herder [1967] 108p. 21cm. Tr. of Fraternite et evangile. [BX2350.2.E8513] 67-13297 3.50
1. Spiritual life—Catholic authors. I. Title.

EVELY, Louis, 1910- 248'.48'2
We are all brothers. Translated by Sister Mary Agnes. Garden City, N.Y., Image Books, 1975 [c1967] 119 p. 18 cm. (Image, D 347) Translation of Fraternite et evangile. Reprint of the ed. published by Herder and Herder, New York. [BX2350.2.E8513 1975] 74-8533 ISBN 0-385-04830-0 1.45 (pbk.)
1. Spiritual life—Catholic authors. I. Title.

FABER, Frederick William, 248
1814-1863.
All for Jesus; edited and rev. by Maurice V. Shean. Westminster, Md., Newman Press, 1956. 254p. 23cm. [BX2182.F2 1956] 56-9995
1. Spiritual life—Catholic authors I. Title.

FABER, Frederick William, 248
1814-1863.
Growth in holiness; or, The progress of the spritual life. 9th American ed. Baltimore, Murphy [pref. 1854] 494 p. 20 cm. [BX2350.F3 1854] 49-39702
1. Spiritual life—Catholic authors. I. Title.

FOX, Matthew, 1940- 248'.48'2
A spirituality named compassion and the healing of the global village, Humpty Dumpty and us / Matthew Fox. Minneapolis : Winston Press, c1979. viii, 285 p. : ill. ; 24 cm. Includes bibliographical references. [BX2350.2.F67] 79-63231 ISBN 0-03-051566-1 pbk. : 6.95
1. Spiritual life—Catholic authors. 2. Compassion. I. Title.

FRANCOIS DE SALES, Saint, 271
bp. of Geneva, 1567-1622.
... Letters to persons in religion, translated into English by the Rev. Henry Benedict Mackey, O.S.B. With an introduction by Bishop Hedley, and facsimile of the saint's handwriting. Westminster, Md., The Newman bookshop, 1943. xxxvi, 443 p. incl. front. (facsim.) 19 1/2 cm. At head of title: St. Francis de Sales. [BX2179.F8L5 1943] 44-6968
1. Spiritual life—Catholic authors. I. Mackey, Benedict, 1846-1906. II. Title.

FRANCOIS DE SALES, Saint, 242
bp. of Geneva, 1567-1622.
The spiritual conferences of St. Francis de Sales, translated from the Annecy text of 1895 under the supervision of Abbot Gasquet and the late Canon Mackey, O.S.B. Westminster, Md., The Newman bookshop, 1943. lxxi, 406 p. 19 1/2 cm. (Half-title: Library of St. Francis de Sales) Translated by the Sisters of the visitation, Harrow-on-the-Hill. cf. p. xl. The editorial work was carried on by Mackey until his death, after which it was completed by Gasquet. "Introduction written by Cardinal Wiseman for an edition of the 'Conferences' published in 1862": p. xxxv-lxvii. [BX2179.F8V74 1948] 44-29972
1. Spiritual life—Catholic authors. I. Sisters of the visitation, Harrow-on-the-Hill, Eng., tr. II. Mackey, Benedict, 1846-1906, ed. III. Gasquet, Francis Aldan, cardinal, 1846-1929, ed. IV. Wiseman, Nicholas Patrick Stephen, cardinal, 1802-1865. V. Title.

FRANCOIS de Sales Saint,bp. 242
of Geneva 1567-1622
The secret of sanctity, according to St. Francis de Sales and Father Crasset, S. J. Translated from the French by Ella McMahon. New York, Cincinnati [etc.] Benziger brothers, 1893. 311 p. 18 cm. From St. Francis de Sales' Introduction to a devout life, and Treatise on the love of God; and from Father Crasset's Considerations cchretienne, Methode d'oraison, and edevotion du Calvaire. Analogous passages from other authors are also included. cf. Pref. 248 41-39789
1. Spiritual life—Catholic authors. I. Crasset, Jean, 1618-1692. II. McMahon, Ella, tr. III. Title.

FRANCOIS DE SAINTE MARIE,
248.482
Father
The simple steps to God. [Translator: Harold Evans] Wilkes-Barre, Pa., Dimension Books [1963] 153 p. 21 cm. (The Carmel series on Christian life, v. 1) Translation of Presence a Dieu et a sol-meme. Bibliographical footnotes. [BX2350.F733] 63-20361
1. Spiritual life — Catholic authors. 2. God — Worship and love. I. Title. II. Series.

FRANCOIS DE SALES, Saint Bp. 242
of Geneva, 1567-1622.
Spiritual conferences. Tr. from the Annecy text of 1895 under the supervision of Abbot Gasquet, Canon Mackey. Westminster, Md., Newman, 1962. lxxi, 406p. 19cm. 62-4748 3.95
1. Spiritual life—Catholic authors. I. Title.

[FRANCOIS DE SALES, Saint, 242
bp. of Geneva] 1567-1622.
The spiritual conferences, translated from the Annecy text of 1895 under the supervision of Abbot Gasquet and the late Canon Mackey, o. s. b. London, Burns & Oates, limited; New York, Cincinnati [etc.] Benziger brothers, 1906. ixxi, 406 p. 19 cm. (Half-title: Library of St. Francis de Sales) Translated by the Sisters of the visitation, Harrow-on-the-Hill. cf. p. xi. The editorial work was carried on by Mackey until his death, after which it was completed by Gasquet. "Introduction written by Cardinal Wiseman for an edition of the 'Conferences' published in 1862": p. xxxv-ixvii. [BX2179.F8V74] 38-37883
1. Spiritual life—Catholic authors. I. Sisters of the visitation, Harrow-on-the-Hill, Eng., tr. II. Mackey, Benedict, 1846-1906, ed. III. Gasquet, Francis Aldan, cardinal, 1846-1929, ed. IV. Wiseman, Nicholas Patrick Stephen, cardinal, 1802-1865. V. Title.

FRANCOIS DE SALES, Saint, 242
Bp. of Geneva, 1567-1622.
The spiritual directory of Saint Francis de Sales for people living in the world. With a commentary by Joseph E. Woods. Westminster, Md., Newman Press, [c.]1959 124p. illus. 13cm. 59-15886 2.00 flex. lea. cl.,
1. Spiritual life—Catholic authors. I. Woods, Joseph E. II. Title.

GARRIGOU-LAGRANGE, Reginald, 248
Father, 1877-
The three ways of the spiritual life; from the French. Westminster, Md., Newman Press, 1950. xii, 112 p. 19 cm. [BX2350.G336 1950] 51-5839
1. Spiritual life—Catholic authors. I. Title.

GARRIGOU-LAGRANGE, Reginald,
234
Father, 1877-
The three ages of the interior life, prelude of eternal life. Tr. by Sister M. Timothea Doyle. St. Louis, B. Herder Book Co., 1947-48. 2 v. 25 cm. Secular name: Gontran Garrigou--Lagrange. Bibliography: v. 1, p. *471]-486. [BX2350.G335] 47-16594
1. Spiritual life—Catholic authors. I. Doyle, Thimothea, Sister, 1896- tr. II. Title.

GARRIGOU-LAGRANGE, Reginald,
234
father, 1877-
The three ages of the interior life,, prelude of eternal life, by the Rev. R. Garrigou-Lagrange ... Translated by Sister M. Timothea Doyle ... St. Louis, Mo., and London, B. Herder book co., 1947- v. 24 1/2 cm. [Secular name: Gontran Garrigou-Lagrange] Bibliography: v. 1, p. [471]-486. [BX2350.G335] 47-16594
1. Spiritual life—Catholic authors. I. Doyle, Timothea, sister, 1896- tr. II. Title.

GILLIS, James Martin, 1876- 248
So near is God; essays on the spiritual life. New York, Scribner, 1953. 210p. 21cm. [BX2350.G485] 53-8785
1. Spiritual life—Catholic authors. I. Title.

GIRARDEY, Ferrol, 1839-1930, 242
comp.
Conference matter for religious, compiled by Rev. Ferrol Girardey, C. SS. R. with an introductin by Very Rev. Thos. P. Brown ... St. Louis, Mo. [etc.] B. Herder, 1914. 2 v. 21 cm. Compiled from three sources. The first--"Sentences, legons, avis du venere pere Champagnat ..." The second--" Ecole de perfection religieuse d'apres les meilleurs auteurs, surtout St. Alphonse, St. Francois de Sales,Ste. Therese," by Rev. Hippolyte Clement ... The compiler has added a dozen sketches. cf. Notice of the compiler. [BX2182.G5] 14-8719
1. Spiritual life—Catholic authors. 2. Meditatious. I. Title. II. Title: Religious, Conference matter for.

GLEASON, Robert W., 248.4'8'2
comp.
Contemporary spirituality; current problems in religious life. Edited by Robert W. Gleason. New York, Macmillan [1968] viii, 343 p. 21 cm. Bibliographical references included in "Notes" (p. 317-343) [BX2350.2.G62] 68-15937
1. Spiritual life—Catholic authors. I. Title.

GOODIER, Alban, abp., 1869- 248
1939.
The school of love, and other essays. 1st American ed. [St. Meinrad, Ind., 1947] 141 p. 18 cm. "A Grail publication." [BX2350.G66] 47-26778
1. Spiritual life—Catholic authors. I. Title.

GRANDMAISON, Leonce de, 1868- 248
1927.
Come Holy Spirit, meditations for apostles. Translated by Joseph O'Connell. Chicago, Fides Publishers Association [1956] 117p. 21cm. Translation of Ecrits spirituels, v. 3: Dernieres retraites et triduums. [BX2350.G745] 56-2752
1. Spiritual life—Catholic authors. I. Title.

GRANDMAISON, Leonce de, 248.482
1868-1927.
Send forth thy spirit. Selection of texts and introd. by M. Danielou. Translated by M. Angeline Bouchard. Notre Dame, Ind., Fides Publishers [c1962] 111 p. 21 cm. Translation of La vie interleure de l' apotre. [BX2350.5.G713] 62-20574
1. Spiritual life — Catholic authors. I. Title.

GRANDMAISON, Leonce de, 1868- 248
1927.
We and the Holy Spirit, talks to laymen; the spiritual writings of Leonce de Grandmaison. Translated by Angeline Bouchard. Chicago, Fides Publishers [1953]

223p. 21cm. Translation of Ecrits spirituels, v. 1. [BX2350.G743] 53-20711
1. Spiritual life—Catholic authors. I. Title.

GREELEY, Andrew M., 1928- 248.4'8'2
Life for a wanderer [by] Andrew M. Greeley. [1st ed.] Garden City, N.Y., Doubleday, 1969. 168 p. 22 cm. [BX2350.2.G73] 70-78701 4.95
1. Spiritual life—Catholic authors. I. Title.

GRIMAL, Julius Leo, 1867-1953. 248
The three stages of the spiritual life under the inspiration of Jesus. Translated under the direction of Joseph Buckley. Milwaukee, Bruce Pub. Co. [1956] 3v. 20cm. [BX2350.G765] 56-7737
1. Spiritual life— Catholic authors. I. Title.

GUIGO II, d.1188. 242'.1
The ladder of monks : a letter on the contemplative life and Twelve meditations / by Guigo II ; translated, with an introd. by Edmund Colledge and James Walsh. 1st ed. Garden City, N.Y. : Image Books, 1978. 157 p. ; 18 cm. Translation of Scala claustralium and Meditationes. Includes bibliographical references. [BX2349.G8513] 77-11230 ISBN 0-385-13596-3 pbk. : 2.45
1. Spiritual life—Catholic authors. 2. Meditations. I. Colledge, Edmund. II. Walsh, James, 1920- III. Guigo II, d. 1188. Meditationes. English. 1978. IV. Title.

GUIGO II, d.1188. 242
The ladder of monks : a letter on the contemplative life and Twelve meditations / by Guigo II ; translated, with an introd. by Edmund Colledge and James Walsh. Kalamazoo, Mich. : Cistercian Publications, 1981, c1978. 131 p. ; 23 cm. (Cistercian studies series ; no. 48) Translation of Scala claustralium and Meditationes. Includes bibliographical references. [BX2349.G8513 1981] 19 81-30 ISBN 0-87907-748-4 pbk. : 14.95
1. Spiritual life—Catholic authors. 2. Meditations. I. Colledge, Edmund. II. Walsh, James, 1920- III. Guigo II, d. 1188. Meditationes. English. 1981. IV. Title. V. Series.

GUILLAUME de Saint-Thierry, 1085(ca.)-1148? 201.1 s
The golden epistle: a letter to the brethren at Mont Dieu. Translated by Theodore Berkeley. Introd. by J. M. Dechanet. Spencer, Mass., Cistercian Publications, 1971. xxxiii, 117 p. 23 cm. (His The works of William of St Thierry, v. 4) (Cistercian Fathers series, no. 12) Translation of De vita solitaria. Bibliography: p. 107-109. [BX890.G848 1971 vol. 4] [BX2349] 248'.48'2 72-152482 ISBN 0-87907-312-8 ISBN 0-87907-712-3 (pbk) 7.50
1. Spiritual life—Catholic authors. I. Title.

GUILLERAND, Augustin, 1877-1945. 248.4
Where silence is praise, from the writings of Augustin Guillerand. Tr. by a monk of Parkminster. [dist. New York, Longmans, 1961, c.1960] 138p. 61-1409 2.75 bds.,
1. Spiritual life—Catholic authors. I. Title.

GUILLERAND, Augustin, 1877-1945 248.4
Where silence is praise, from the writings of Augustin Guillerand. Tr. [from French] by a monk of Parkminster. London, Darton, Longman & Todd [dist. Wilkes-Barre, Pa., Dimension Bks., 1964, c.1960] 138p. 18cm. 61-1409 2.95
1. Spiritual life—Catholic authors. I. Title.

HAUSER, Richard J. 248.4'82
In his spirit : a guide to today's spirituality / Richard J. Hauser. New York : Paulist Press, c1982. 117 p. ; 21 cm. Includes bibliographical references. [BX2350.2.H358 1982] 19 81-83187 ISBN 0-8091-2421-1 (pbk.) : 4.95
1. Spiritual life—Catholic authors. I. Title.

HEMPHILL, Basil, 1896- 248
The joy of serving God. St. Louis, B. Herder Book Co., 1948. x, 194 p. 23 cm. [BX2350.H347] 48-10168
1. Spiritual life—Catholic authors. I. Title.

HIGGINS, Nicholas. 248.482
As pilgrims and strangers. New York, P. J. Kenedy [1961] 213p. 21cm. [BX2350.2.H5] 60-14109
1. Spiritual life—Catholic authors. I. Title.

HINNEBUSCH, Paul. 248
Like the Word; to the Trinity through Christ. St. Louis, B. Herder Book Co. [1965] vi, 266 p. 21 cm. (Cross and crown series of spirituality, no. 29) Bibliographical footnotes. [BX2350.5.H56] 65-17849
1. Spiritual life — Catholic authors. I. Title. II. Series.

HINNEBUSCH PAUL 248
Like the word; to the Trinity through Christ St. Louis, B. Herder [c.1965] vi, 266p. 21cm. (Cross & crown ser. of spirtiuality, no. 29) Bibl. [BX2350.5.H56] 65-17849 4.50 bds.,
1. Spiritual life—Catholic authors. I. Title. II. Series.

HOFFMAN, Dominic M. 248'.48'2
Maturing the spirit; a continuation of spiritual growth for contemporary men and women [by] Dominic M. Hoffman. [Boston] St. Paul Editions [1973] 357 p. 22 cm. [BX2350.2.H584] 73-77628 5.00
1. Spiritual life—Catholic authors. I. Title.

HOFFMAN, Dominic M., 1913- 248.4'8'2
Beginnings in spiritual life [by] Dominic M. Hoffman. [1st ed.] Garden City, N.Y., Doubleday, 1967. 333 p. 22 cm. [BX2350.2.H58] 67-10356
1. Spiritual life—Catholic authors. I. Title.

HOFFMAN, Dominic M., 1913- 248.482
The life within; the prayer of union, by Dominic M. Hoffman. New York, Sheed [1966] xi, 242p. 22cm. [BX2350.5.H6] 66-12276 4.50
1. Spiritual life—Catholic authors. I. Title.

HOFFMAN, Dominic M., 1913- 248.4'82
Living divine love : transformation, the goal of Christian life / by Dominic M. Hoffman. Staten Island, N.Y. : Alba House, [1982] p. cm. [BX2350.2.H583 1982] 19 82-11552 ISBN 0-8189-0443-7 pbk. : 7.95
1. Spiritual life—Catholic authors. I. Title.

HOGAN, William F., 1920- 248.8'94
One and the same spirit; a book for domestic and manual workers in religious life, by William F. Hogan. Dayton, Ohio, Pflaum, 1967. xi, 164p. 21cm. [BX2385.H62] 67-29766 4.50
1. Spiritual life—Catholic authors. 2. Monastic and religious life. I. Title.

HUGEL, Friedrich, Freiherr von, 1852-1925. 241
Spiritual counsel and letters. Edited with an introductory essay by Douglas V. Steere. New York, Harper & Row [1964] viii, 184 p. 22 cm. [BX2350.H82] 64-10754
1. Spiritual life—Catholic authors. I. Title.

HURLEY, Wilfred Geoffrey, 1895- 248
Catholic devotional life [Boston] St. Paul Eds. [dist. Daughters of St. Paul c.1965] 148p. 21cm. [BX2350.H8] 65-17555 3.00;2.00 pap.,
1. Spiritual life—Catholic authors. I. Title.

HUYGHE, Gerard, Bp., 1909- . 248
Growth in the Holy Spirit. Translated by Isabel and Florence McHugh. Westminister, Md., Newman Press, 1966. xiii, 200 p. 22 cm. First published under title: Conduits par l'Esprit. Bibliographical footnotes. [BX2350.5.H813] 66-17358
1. Spiritual life — Catholic authors. 2. Faith. I. Title.

THE interior life simplified and reduced ot its fundamental principle. edited by Joseph Tissot. Translated by W. H. Mitchell 2d ed. Westminster, Md., Newman Press, 1949. xx, 292 p. 22 cm. A 51
1. Spiritual life—Catholic authors. I. Tissot, Joseph, 1840-1894, ed.

JAEGHER, Paul de. 248
The Lord is my joy. Westminster, Md., Newman Press, 1949. 182, p. 19 cm. [BX2350.J35] 49-7510
1. Spiritual life—Catholic authors. I. Title.

JAMART, Francois. 922.244
Complete spiritual doctrine of St. Therese of Lisieux. Translated by Walter Van de Putte. New York, St. Paul Publications [1961] 320p. 22cm. Translation of Mieux connaitre Sainte Therese de Lisieux. [BX4700.T5J313] 61-8203
1. Therese, Saint, 1873-1897. 2. Spiritual life—Catholic authors. I. Title.

JAMES, Bruno Scott. 242
Seeking God. [1st ed.] New York, Harper [1960] 128p. 14cm. [BX2350.2.J3] 60-15269
1. Spiritual life—Catholic authors. I. Title.

JARRETT, Bede, 1881-1934 248.8
For priests. Foreword by Robert W. Gleason. Chicago, Priory Pr. 2005 S Ashland Ave. [1965] 123p. 20cm. Articles which orig. appeared in the Homiletic and pastoral review. [BX1912.5.J3] 65-19358 3.50
1. Spiritual life—Catholic authors. 2. Catholic Church—Clergy—Religious life. I. Title.

JOHNSON, Edwin Clark. 248.4'82
The myth of the great secret : a search for spiritual meaning in the face of emptiness / by Edwin Clark Johnson. 1st ed. New York : Morrow, 1982. p. cm. [BX2350.2.J64] 19 81-11025 ISBN 0-688-00781-3 : 10.95
1. Spiritual life—Catholic authors. I. Title.

JUAN de la Cruz, Saint, 1542-1591. 242
The voice of the Spirit : the spirituality of St. John of the Cross / edited and introduced by Elizabeth Hamilton. London : Darton, Longman and Todd, 1976. 128 p. ; 19 cm. Consists of an introd. and selection of texts from the prose writings of St. John of the Cross [translated from the Spanish by the editor] as well as some of the better known poems. Bibliography: p. [128] [BX2349.J8513] 76-379874 ISBN 0-232-51349-X : £1.20
1. Spiritual life—Catholic authors. 2. Meditations. I. Hamilton, Elizabeth, 1906- II. Title.

JUAN de la Cruz, Saint, 1542-1591. 242
The voice of the spirit : the spirituality of St. John of the Cross / edited and introduced by Elizabeth Hamilton. Huntington, IN : Our Sunday Visitor, 1977c1976 127, [1] p. ; 21 cm. Bibliography: p. [128] [BX2349.J8513 1976b] 76-53609 ISBN 0-87973-686-0 pbk. : 2.95
1. Spiritual life—Catholic authors. 2. Meditations. I. Hamilton, Elizabeth, 1906- II. Title.

KELLY, Bernard J. 248.482
Joy in the spiritual life. Westminster, Md., Newman [1962] 167p. 62-2670 2.95
1. Spiritual life—Catholic authors. 2. Joy and sorrow. I. Title.

KENRICK, Edward F. 271.9069
The spirituality of the teaching sister. St. Louis, Herder [1962] 243p. 22cm. 62-10508 4.50
1. Spiritual life—Catholic authors. 2. Monastic and religious life of women. I. Title.

KIENER, Mary Aloysi, sister, 1882- 248
"Draw near to Him," by Sister Mary Aloysi Kiener ... With foreword by the Very Rev. Joseph Krouter ... New York and Cincinnati, Frederick Pustet co., inc., 1942. 165 p. front. 19 1/2 cm. [BX2350.K5] 42-18140
1. Spiritual life—Catholic authors. I. [Secular name: Mary Agnes Kisner] II. Title.

KODELL, Jerome. 248'.48'2
Responding to the Word : a Biblical spirituality / Jerome Kodell. New York : Alba House, c1978. xiii, 128 p. ; 21 cm. Includes bibliographies. [BX2350.2.K587] 77-20252 ISBN 0-8189-0360-0 pbk. : 3.95
1. Spiritual life—Catholic authors. I. Title.

KUNG, Hans, 1928- comp. 248
Life in the Spirit. New York, Sheed and Ward [1968] 157 p. 22 cm. (Theological meditations) Contents.Contents.—The one priesthood, by K. H. Schelkle.—Changes in Christian spirituality, by T. Sartory.—Celibacy, by M. Pfliegler. Bibliographical footnotes. [BX2350.2.K8] 68-14539
1. Spiritual life—Catholic authors. 2. Celibacy. I. Schelkle, Karl Hermann. Ihr alle seid Geistliche. English. 1965. II. Sartory, Thomas A. Wander christlicher Spiritualitat. English. 1968. III. Pfliegler, Michael, 1891- Der Zolibat. English. 1968. IV. Title.

LALLEMANT, Louis, 1578-1635. 248
The spiritual doctrine of Father Louis Lallemant of the Society of Jesus. Preceded by an account of his life by Father Champion. Edited by Alan McDougall. Westminster, Md., Newman Book Shop, 1946. xvi, 304 p. 19 cm. [BX2349.L] A 49
1. Spiritual life—Catholic authors. I. Title.

LAWRENCE, Emeric Anthony, 1908- 248'.48'2
Becoming a mature Christian / Emeric Lawrence. Collegeville, Minn. : Liturgical Press, c1979. xiv, 198 p. ; 23 cm. [BX2350.2.L38] 79-119494 ISBN 0-8146-1026-9 pbk. : 6.75
1. Spiritual life—Catholic authors. I. Title.

LEAHY, J Kenneth. 248
As the eagle; the spiritual writings of Mother Butler, R. S. H. M., foundress of Marymount, by a Carmelite pilgrim. New York, P. J. Kenedy [c1954] 206p. 21cm. [BX2350.B882L4] 54-11236
1. Butler, Marie Joseph, Mother, 1860-1940. 2. Spiritual life—Catholic authors. I. Title.

LECLERCQ, Jacques, 1891- 248.482
The interior life. Tr. [from French] by Fergus Murphy. New York, P. J. Kenedy [c.1961] 191p. 61-9449 3.95
1. Spiritual life—Catholic authors. I. Title.

LEHEN, Edouard de, 1807-1867. 248
The way of interior peace. Dedicated to Our Lady of peace, by Rev. Father Von Lehen, S.J. Translated from the German by a religious. With a preface by His Eminence, Cardinal Gibbons. New York, Cincinnati [etc.] Benziger brothers, 1889. 1 p. l., 5-371 p. 19 1/2 cm. Published originally in French, 1855. [BX2183.L56 1889] 39-32778
1. Spiritual life—Catholic authors. I. A religious, tr. II. Title.

LEKEUX, Martial, 1881- ed. and tr. 248.182
Short out to divine love. Texts collected, translated, and arranged in order by Martial Lekeux. Chicago, Franciscan Herld Press [1962] 320p. 21cm. [BX2350.2.A1L13] 61-11203
1. Spiritual life—Catholic authors. I. Title.

LEKEUX, Martial, 1884- ed. and tr. 248.482
Short cut to divine love. Texts collected, tr. and arr. in order by Martial Lekeux. Chicago, Franciscan Herald [c.1962] 320p. 21cm. 61-11203 4.95
1. Spiritual life—Catholic authors. I. Title.

LEKEUX, Martial, 1884- 922.245
20th century litany to the Poverello. Chicago, Franciscan Herald Press [1962] 320p. 21cm. [BX4700.F6L43] 58-8691
1. Spiritual life—Catholic authors. I. Title.

LIBERMANN, Francois Marie Paul [Name orig.: Jacob Libermann] 1802-1852 242
The spiritual letters of the Venerable Francis Libermann. Ed., tr. by Walter van de Putte, James Collery. Pittsburgh, Duquesne Univ. Pr. [1965, c.1964] xii, 420p. illus. 22cm. (Duquesne studies. Spiritan ser., v.8) Contents.v.4. Letters to clergy and religious (Nos. 76 to 184) [BX4705.L62A4] 62-12768 5.25
1. Spiritual life—Catholic authors. I. Title.

LIBERMANN, Francois Marie Paul, 1802-1852. 922.244
The spiritual letters of the Venerable Francis Libermann. Edited and translated by Walter van de Putte and James Collery. Pittsburgh, Duquesne University Press, 1962- v. illus. 22cm. (Duquesne studies. Spiritan series, v. 5) Contents.--v. 1. Letters to religious sisters and aspirants. [BX4705.L62A4] 62-12768
1. Spiritual life—Catholic authors. I. Title. II. Series.

LIBERMANN, Francois Marie 248.422
Paul [Name orig.: Jacob Libermann] 1802-1852
The spiritual letters of the Venerable Francis Libermann. Ed. tr. by Walter van de Putte, James Collery, Pittsburgh, Duquesne Univ. Pr. [c.]1963. 310p. illus. 22cm. (Duquesne studies. Spiritan ser., v. 6) Contents.v. 2, Letters to people in the world. 62-12768 4.95
1. Spiritual life—Catholic authors. I. Title.

LIGUORI, Alfonso Maria 248.482
de', Saint.
The way of St. Alphonsus Liguori. Ed. with an introd. by Barry Ulanov. New York, P. J. Kenedy [c.1961] 367p. 60-14645 4.95
1. Spiritual life—Catholic authors. I. Title.

LIGUORI, Alfonso Maria 248.482
de', Saint, 1696-1787.
The way of St. Alphonsus Liguori. Edited with an introd. by Barry Ulanov. New York, P. J. Kenedy [1961] 367p. 17cm. [BX2349.L5] 60-14645
1. Spiritual life—Catholic authors. I. Ulanov, Barry, ed. II. Title.

LISTON, Paul. 248'.48'2
Alive with God : a guide to greater faith / Paul Liston. Liguori, Mo. : Liguori Publications, c1978. 128 p. : ill. ; 22 cm. [BX1754.L555] 78-54157 ISBN 0-89243-078-8 pbk. : 2.95
1. Catholic Church—Doctrinal and controversial works, Popular. 2. Spiritual life—Catholic authors. I. Title.

LORD, Daniel Aloysuis, 248.4'8'2
1888-1955.
Letters to my Lord. Edited by Thomas Gavin. [New York] Herder and Herder [1969] 121 p. 21 cm. [BX2350.2.L64 1969] 76-87759 4.50
1. Spiritual life—Catholic authors. I. Title.

MCCAULEY, Michael F. 248'.48'2
On the run : spirituality for the seventies / edited by Michael F. McCauley. Chicago : Thomas More Press, [1974] 237 p. ; 22 cm. [BX2350.2.M23] 74-188853 ISBN 0-88347-042-X : 7.95
1. Spiritual life—Catholic authors. I. Title.

MCDONNELL, Killan. 248
Nothing but Christ; a Benedictine approach to lay spirituality. [St. Meinrad, Ind.,]Grail [1953] 185p. 21cm. [BX2350.M14] 53-12934
1. Spiritual life—Catholic authors. I. Title.

MCGLOIN, Joseph T. 248.482
Burn a little! or, What's love all about? Illus. by Don Baumgart. Milwaukee, Bruce [c.1961] 144p. illus. (His Love--and live, bk. 3) 61-17982 1.50 pap.,
1. Spiritual life—Catholic authors. I. Title.

MCGLOIN, Joseph T. 248'.48'2
Hey, why don't we try Christianity? / Joseph T. McGloin ; illustrated by Don Baumgart. Huntington, Ind. : Our Sunday Visitor, c1978. 192 p. : ill. ; 21 cm. [BX2350.2.M2513] 78-58465 ISBN 0-87973-641-0 pbk. : 3.95
1. Spiritual life—Catholic authors. I. Title.

MACK, Friedrich, 1877- 248
Splendor and strength of the inner life, by Doctor Fr. Mack ... English version by Sister Mary Aloysi Kiener ... New York and Cincinnati, Frederick Pustet co., inc., 1940. xv p., 1 l., 190 p. 19 1/2 cm. [BX2350.M182] 40-35458
1. Spiritual life—Catholic authors. I. Kiener, Mary Aloysi, sister, 1882- tr. II. Title.

MCMAHON, Edwin M., 248.4'8'2
1930-
Becoming a person in the whole Christ, by Edwin M. McMahon and Peter A. Campbell. New York, Sheed and Ward [1967] xiv, 306 p. 22 cm. [BX2350.5.M2] 67-13768
1. Spiritual life—Catholic authors. 2. Monastic and religious life—Psychology. I. Campbell, Peter A., 1935- joint author. II. Title.

MCMAHON, Edwin M., 1930- 242
The in-between; evolution in Christian faith, by Edwin M. McMahon and Peter A. Campbell. New York, Sheed and Ward [1969] 189 p. 21 cm. [BX2350.2.M264] 69-16990 4.95
1. Spiritual life—Catholic authors. I. Campbell, Peter A., 1935- joint author. II. Title.

MCNAMARA, William. 248.482
The art of being human. Milwaukee, Bruce Pub. Co. [1962] 164p. 22cm. [BX2350.2.M27] 62-20958
1. Spiritual life—Catholic authors. I. Title.

MCNAMARA, William. 248'.48'2
Mystical passion : spirituality for a bored society / by William McNamara. New York : Paulist Press, c1977. xi, 124 p. ; 23 cm. Includes bibliographical references. [BX2350.2.M276] 77-37378 pbk. : 4.95
1. Spiritual life—Catholic authors. 2. Emotions. I. Title.

MAHONEY, Florence Jerome, 248
1895-
... *Branches of the vine.* Milwaukee, The Bruce publishing company [c1936] x, 157 p. 19 cm. At head of title: Rev. F. J. Mahoney, S.J. [BX2438.M3] 36-21473
1. Spiritual life—Catholic authors. I. Title.

MALONEY, George A. 248.4'7
Prayer of the heart / George A. Maloney. Notre Dame, Ind. : Ave Maria Press, c1981. 206 p. ; 21 cm. Includes bibliographical references. [BX2350.2.M3148] 19 80-69095 ISBN 0-87793-216-6 (pbk.) : 3.95
1. Spiritual life—Catholic authors. 2. Jesus prayer. I. Title.

MARCHETTI, Albinus 248.2
Spirituality and the states of life. Tr. by Sebastian V. Ramge. Milwaukee, 1233 S. 45 St., Spiritual Life Pr., 1963. 174p. 19cm. (Way, v.1) Bibl. 63-21920 1.50
1. Spiritual life—Catholic authors. I. Title.

MARTELET, Gustave 248.482
The church's holiness and religious life. Tr. [from French] by Raymond L. Sullivant. St. Marys, Kan., 66536, Review for Religious. St. Mary's College [c.]1966. 124p. 20cm. Bibl. [BX2350.5.M293] 66-3721 2.50
1. Spiritual life—Catholic authors. 2. Manastic and religious life. 3. Church—Holiness. I. Title.

MARTIN, Alfred, 1896- 248'.4'82
The quest for security / by Alfred Martin. Chicago, Ill. : Franciscan Herald Press, 1980. p. cm. (Synthesis series) [BX2350.2.M3455] 80-13242 ISBN 0-8199-0371-X pbk. : 3.50
1. Spiritual life—Catholic authors. I. Title.

MATURIN, Basil William, 1847-
1915.
Some principles and practices of the spiritual life, by B. W. Maturin. Eleventh impression. London, New York [etc.] Longmans, Green, and co., 1916. 4 p. l., 206 p. 19 cm. Bibliographical foot-notes. A 40
1. Spiritual life—Catholic authors. I. Title.

MEAGHER, Robert E. 248.4'8'2
Beckonings; moments of faith [by] Robert E. Meagher. Art interpretations by Molly Geissler Barrett. Philadelphia, Fortress Press [1969] vii, 88 p. illus. 20 cm. [BX2350.2.M39] 70-84541 2.95
1. Spiritual life—Catholic authors. I. Title.

MEEHAN, Francis Xavier. 261.8
A contemporary social spirituality / Francis X. Meehan. Maryknoll, N.Y. : Orbis Books, c1982. x, 133 p. ; 21 cm. Bibliography: p. 129-133. [BX2350.2.M414 1982] 19 82-2253 ISBN 0-88344-022-9 pbk. : 6.95
1. Spiritual life—Catholic authors. 2. Church and social problems—Catholic Church. I. Title.

MERRY DEL VAL, Cardinal, 248.482
1865-1930
The spiritual diary of Raphael Cardinal Merry del Val, comp., ed. by Francis J. Weber. New York, Exposition [c.1964] 47p. port. 22cm. (Exposition-testament bk.) 64-56135 2.75
1. Spiritual life—Catholic authors. I. Weber, Francis J., ed. II. Title.

MERTON, Thomas 242
The new man. New York, Farrar [1962, c.1961] 248p. 62-7168 3.50 bds.,
1. Spiritual life—Catholic authors. I. Title.

MERTON, Thomas 1915- 248.482
Life and holiness. [New York] Herder & Herder [c.1963] 162p. 21cm. 63-10691 3.50
1. Spiritual life—Catholic authors. I. Title.

MERTON, Thomas 1915- 248.482
Life and holiness. Garden City, N.Y., Doubleday [1964, c.1963] 119p. 18cm. (Image bk. D183) .75 pap.,
1. Spiritual life—Catholic authors. I. Title.

MERTON, Thomas, 1915- 248.482
Life and holiness. [New York] Herder and Herder [1963] 162 p. 21 cm. Name in religion: Father Louis. [BX2350.5.M37] 63-10691
1. Spiritual life — Catholic authors. I. Title.

MERTON, Thomas, 1915-
Life and holiness. [New York] Image Books [1964] 119 p. 18 cm. 67-47331
1. Spiritual life — Catholic authors. I. Title.

MERTON, Thomas, 1915- 248
No man is an island. New York, Doubleday [1967,c.1955] 197p. 18cm. (Image bk., D231) [BX2350.M535] .95 pap.,
1. Spiritual life—Catholic authors. I. Title.

MERTON, Thomas, 1915- 248
Seeds of contemplation. [Norfolk, Conn.] New Directions [1949] 201 p. illus. 22 cm. [BX2350.M54] 49-1562
1. Spiritual life—Catholic authors. I. Title.

MERTON, Thomas, 1915- [Name 242
in religion: Father Louis]
Thoughts in solitude. Garden City, N.Y., Doubleday [1968, c.1958] 120p. 18cm. (Image bk., D247) .85 pap.,
1. Spiritual life—Catholic authors. 2. Solitude. I. Title.

MERTON, Thomas, 1915- 242
Thoughts in solitude. New York, Farrar, Straus & Cudahy [1958] 124p. 21cm. [BX2350.M543] 58-8817
1. Spiritual life—Catholic authors. 2. Solitude. I. Title.

MERTON, Thomas, 1915-
Thoughts in solitude. [New York, Dell Pub. Co., 1961] 160 p. (A Chapel book, F 132) 63-28047
1. Spiritual life — Catholic authors. 2. Solitude. I. Title.

MERTON, Thomas, 230'.2'0924 B
1915-1968.
The Asian journal of Thomas Merton. Edited from his original notebooks by Naomi Burton, Patrick Hart & James Laughlin. Consulting editor: Amiya Chakravarty. [New York, New Directions Pub. Corp., 1973] xxviii, 445 p. illus. 24 cm. (A New Directions book) Bibliography: p. 357-361. [BX2350.2.M449 1973] 71-103370 ISBN 0-8112-0464-2 12.50
1. Spiritual life—Catholic authors. 2. Meditation. I. Title.

MERTON, Thomas, 1915-1968. 248
No man is an island. [1st ed.] New York, Harcourt, Brace [1955] 264 p. 22 cm. [BX2350.M535] 55-7420
1. Spiritual life—Catholic authors. I. Title.

MERTON, Thomas, 1915- 248'.48'2
1968.
No man is an island / by Thomas Merton. New York : Harcourt Brace Jovanovich, 1978, c1955. p. cm. (A Harvest/HBJ book) [BX2350.2.M4494 1978] 78-7108 ISBN 0-15-665962-X : 3.95
1. Spiritual life—Catholic authors. I. Title.

MERTON, Thomas, 1915-1968. 248'.3
Seeds of contemplation / by Thomas Merton. Westport, Conn. : Greenwood Press, 1979, c1949. 201 p. : ill. ; 23 cm. Reprint of the ed. published by New Directions, Norfolk, Conn. [BX2350.M54 1979] 78-10255 ISBN 0-313-20756-9 lib. bdg. : 16.00
1. Spiritual life—Catholic authors. I. Title.

*MERTON, Thomas [Name in 242
religion, Father Louis] 1915-
The new man [New York] New Amer. Lib. [1963, c.1961] 141p. 18cm. (Mentor-omega bk., MP548) .60 pap.,
1. Spiritual life—Catholic authors. I. Title.

MERTON, Thomas [Name in 242
religion: Father Louis] 1915-
New seeds of contemplation. [Norfolk, Conn.] New Directions [1962, c.1961] 297p. 61-17869 4.50
1. Spiritual life—Catholic authors. I. Title.

MICHAEL, Chester P. 248
The new day of Christianity. Helicon[dist. New York, Taplinger, c.1965] 189p. 21cm. [BX2350.5.M5] 65-15042 4.50 bds.,
1. Spiritual life—Catholic authors. I. Title.

MICHAEL, Chester P. 248
The new day of Christianity [by] Chester P. Michael. Baltimore, Helicon [1965] 189 p. 21 cm. [BX2350.5.M5] 65-15042
1. Spiritual life — Catholic authors. I. Title.

MOORE, Thomas Verner, 1877- 248
Heroic sanctity and insanity; an introduction to the spiritual life and mental hygiene. New York, Grune & Stratton, 1959. 243p. 23cm. Includes bibliography. [BX2350.2.M64] 59-7827
1. Spiritual life—Catholic authors. 2. Psychiatry and religion. I. Title.

MOORE, Thomas Verner, 1877- 248
The life of man with God. [1st ed.] New York, Harcourt, Brace [1956] 402p. 22cm. [BX2350.M73] 56-7919
1. Spiritual life—Catholic authors. I. Title.

MOORE, Thomas Verner [name in 248
religion: Father Pablo Maria] 1877-
Heroic sanctity and insanity; an introduction to the spiritual life and mental hygiene. New York, Grune [1964, c.1959] 243p. 23cm. Bibl. 59-7827 5.00
1. Spiritual life—Catholic authors. 2. Psychiatry and religion. I. Title.

MOORE, Thomas Verner [Name 248.4
in religion: Pablo Maria, Father]
The life of man with God. Garden City, N. Y., Doubleday [1962, c.1956] 400p. (Image bk., D127) Bibl. 1.35 pap.,
1. Spiritual life—Catholic authors. I. Title.

MORICE, Henri, 1873- 248.482
The apostolate of moral beauty. Translated by Sister Mary Lelia. St. Louis, Herder [1961] 142p. 21cm. [BX2350.2.M663] 61-17456
1. Spiritual life—Catholic authors. I. Title.

MORK, Wulstan. 248.482
A synthesis of the spiritual life. Milwaukee, Bruce Pub Co. [1962] 283p. 18cm. Includes bibliography. [BX2350.2.M68] 62-11166
1. Spiritual life—Catholic authors. I. Title.

MULLALY, Charles J., 1877- 271.9
Spiritual reflections for sisters, by Rev. Charles J. Mullaly, S.J. New York, Apostleship of prayer, 1936- v. 14 1/2 cm. [BX4210.M8] 36-22955
1. Spiritual life—Catholic authors. 2. Monasticism and religious orders for women. I. Title.

MULLIGAN, James J. 248'.48'2
The Christian experience [by] James J. Mulligan. New York, Alba House [1973] xii, 162 p. 22 cm. Includes bibliographical references. [BX2350.2.M84] 73-4005 ISBN 0-8189-0270-1 3.95
1. Spiritual life—Catholic authors. 2. Sacraments—Catholic Church. I. Title.

MUTO, Susan Annette. 248'.48'2
Am I living a spiritual life? : Questions and answers on formative spirituality / by Susan Annette Muto and Adrian van Kaam. 1st English ed. Denville, N.J. : Dimension Books, [1978] 184 p. ; 22 cm. [BX2350.2.M88] 78-61428 ISBN 0-87193-065-X : 7.95
1. Spiritual life—Catholic authors. I. Van Kaam, Adrian L., 1920- joint author. II. Title.

NEWMAN, John Henry, 248.8'94
Cardinal, 1801-1890.
Newman the Oratorian; his unpublished Oratory papers. Edited with an introductory study on the continuity between his Anglican and his Catholic ministry by Placid Murray. Dublin, Gill and Macmillan [1969] xxv, 500 p. 23 cm. The editor's thesis—Pontificio Ateneo S. Anselmo, Rome. Bibliography: p. [xvii]-xxv. [BX2350.N38 1969] 71-10247

1. Spiritual life—Catholic authors. I. Murray, Placid, ed. II. Title.

NEWMAN, John Henry, Cardinal, 1801-1890 248
Reflections on God and self. Ed. by Lawrence F. Barmann [New York] Herder & Herder [1965] 60p. 19cm. [BX2350.5.N4] 63-18156 1.75 bds.,
1. Spiritual life—Catholic authors. I. Title.

NOTRE Dame, Ind. University. Sisters' Institute of Spirituality. 271.069
Prayer and sacrifice [by] Albert E. Bourke [and others. Notre Dame] University of Notre Dame Press, 1962. 249p. 21cm. (Religious life in the modern world: selections from the Notre Dame Institute of Spirituality, v. 4) [Notre Dame paperbooks] NDP17. 'Articles . . . previously published in the Proceeding s of the Sisters' Institute of Spirituality 1953, 1955 and 1956.' Bibliographical footnotes. [BX2385.N6] 62-6148
1. Spiritual life—Catholic authors. I. Bourke, Albert E. II. Title. III. Series.

NOUWEN, Henri J. M. 248'.48'20924 B
The Genesee diary : report from a Trappist monastery / Henri J. M. Nouwen. 1st ed. Garden City, N.Y. : Doubleday, 1976. xiv, 195 p. ; 22 cm. Includes bibliographical references. [BX4705.N87A33] 75-38169 ISBN 0-385-11368-4 : 6.95
1. Nouwen, Henri J. M. 2. Spiritual life—Catholic authors. I. Title.

NOUWEN, Henri J. M. 248.4
The Genesee diary : report from a Trappist monastery / Henri J. M. Nouwen. Garden City, N.Y. : Image Books, 1981, c1976. p. cm. "Complete and unabridged." Includes bibliographical references. [BX4705.N87A33 1981] 19 80-23632 ISBN 0-385-17446-2 : 3.95 (pbk.)
1. Nouwen, Henri J. M. 2. Spiritual life—Catholic authors. I. Title.

NOUWEN, Henri J. M. 248.4'82
Making all things new : an invitation to the spiritual life / Henri J. M. Nouwen. 1st ed. San Francisco : Harper & Row, c1981. p. cm. [BX2350.2.N674] 19 80-8897 ISBN 0-06-066326-X : 6.95
1. Spiritual life—Catholic authors. I. Title.

PAONE, Anthony J 1913- 242.2
My daily bread; a summary of the spiritual life, simplified and arranged for daily reading, reflection, and prayer. Brooklyn, Confraternity of the Precious Blood, 1954. viii, 439p. 14cm. [BX2350.P28] 54-43119
1. Spiritual life—Catholic authors. 2. Meditations. I. Title.

PARENTE, Pascal P 1890- 248
Spritual direction. St. Meinrad, Ind. [1950] vi, 109 p. 21 cm. "Grall publication." Bibliography: p. [107]-109. [BX2350.P29] 50-12987
1. Spiritual life — Catholic authors. I. Title.

PERRET, Andre S 248
Holiness of life [by] A. S. Perret. Translated by Lillian M. McCarthy. St. Louis. Herder [1964] 166 p. 24 cm. (Cross and crown series of spirituality, no. 28) Translation of La vie santifiee. Bibliographical footnotes. [BX2350.5.P383] 64-7635
1. Spiritual life—Catholic authors. I. Title. II. Series.

PETERS, Gerlach, 1378-1411. 232.
The divine soliloquies of Gerlac Petersen ... translated from the Latin by Monialis [pseud.] London, New York [etc.] Longmans, Green and co., 1920. xviii, [2], 108 p., 1 l. 17 cm. [BX2180.P39] 20-23037
1. Spiritual life—Catholic authors. 2. Mysticism—Middle ages. I. Monialis, pseud., tr. II. Title.

PEYRIGUERE, Albert. 248.8'943
Voice from the desert. Translated by Agnes M. Forsyth and Anne Marie de Commaille. New York, Sheed and Ward [1967] 158 p. 21 cm. "Translated from Laissez-vous salsir par le Christ." [BX2350.2.P4813] 67-13775
1. Spiritual life—Catholic authors. I. Title.

PHILIPON, Marie Michel, Father. 248
The eternal purpose; translated by John A. Otto. Westminster, Md., Newman Press, 1952. 112 p. 20 cm. [BX2350.P433] 52-7509
1. Spiritual life — Catholic authors. 2. Eternity. I. Title.

PHILIPON, Marie Michel, 1898- 248
The eternal purpose; translated by John A. Otto. Westminster, Md., Newman Press, 1952. 112p. 20cm. [BX2350.P433] 52-7509
1. Spiritual life—Catholic authors. 2. Eternity. I. Title.

PHILIPON, Marie Michel, 1898- 922.2415
The spiritual doctrine of Dom Marmion. Translated by Matthew Dillon. Westminster, Md., Newman Press [1956] 221p. 23cm. [BX4705.M411P52] 56-10000
1. Marmion, Columba, Abbot, 1858-1923. 2. Spiritual life—Catholic authors. I. Title.

PHILIPPE, Thomas, 1905- 248.4'82
The fire of contemplation : a guide for interior souls / Thomas Philippe ; translator/ed., Verda Clare Doran. New York, N.Y. : Alba House, c1981. p. cm. [BX2350.2.P486] 19 81-8099 ISBN 0-8189-0414-3 pbk. : 4.95
1. Spiritual life—Catholic authors. 2. Contemplation. I. Doran, Verda Clare. II. Title.

PICCARDA, pseud. 248
The veil of the heart. Franciscan letters of a secular missionary. From the Italian of Piccarda, translated by Clelia Maranzana. Translation edited by Frances Laughlin. Paterson, N. J., St. Anthony Guild Press [1959] 243p. illus. 19cm. 'These letters were written, from November 1945 through December 1949, by a member of a Franciscan secular institute to a young friend, Donatella.' [BX2350.2.P513] 59-3097
1. Franciscans. 2. Spiritual life—Catholic authors. I. Donatella, pseud. II. Title.

PIETRO DAMIANI, Saint 248
Selected writings on the spiritual life. Translated, with an introd., by Patricia McNulty. New York, Harper [1960] 187p. 21cm. (Classics of the contemplative life) Bibliography: p. 182-184 60-16035 5.00
1. Spiritual Life—Catholic authors. I. McNulty, Patricia, II. Title.

PLUS, Raoul, 1882- 248
Inward peace. [Translation by Helen Ramsbotham] Westminster, Md., Newman Press [1956] ix, 131p. 19cm. Bibliographical footnotes. [BX2350.P5282] 56-7081
1. Spiritual life—Catholic authors. I. Title.

PLUS, Raoul, 1882- 248
The path to the heights. Westminster, Md., Newman Press [1954] 128p. 20cm. 'Translation from the original French, Le chemin de la grandeur ... made by Wilfrid B. Kane.' [BX2350.P523] 54-3276
1. Spiritual life—Catholic authors. I. Title.

POTTER, Mary, mother, 1847-1913. 271.
The brides of Christ ... by Mother Mary Potter ... Chicago, Matro & company [c1920] 2 p. l., [1], vii, 100 p. 19 cm. (Our Lady's little library series) "Sequel to Spiritual materaity." [BX4213.P7] 20-15155
1. Spiritual life—Catholic authors. I. Title.

RADEMACHER, Arnold, 1873-1939 248.482
Religion and life. Westminster, Md., Newman Pr., 1962[c.1961] 200p. Bibl. 62-2118 3.95
1. Spiritual life—Catholic authors. I. Title.

REGAMEY, Raymond, 1900- 248.4'82
Renewal in the spirit : rediscovering the religious life / by Pius Raymond Regamey ; [translated by Dorothy L. Latz]. Authorized English ed. Boston, Mass. : St. Paul Editions, c1980. 278 p. ; 22 cm. Revised translation of La renovation dans l'esprit. Includes bibliographical references. [BX2350.2.R4213 1980] 19 80-26411 ISBN 0-8198-6402-1 : 5.95 ISBN 0-8198-6403-X pbk. : 4.95
1. Spiritual life—Catholic authors. 2. Monastic and religious life. I. Title.

ROUSTANG, Francois. 248.482
Growth in the spirit. Translated by Kathleen Pond. New York, Sheed and Ward [1966] vi, 250 p. 22 cm. Translation of Une initiation a la vie spirituelle. [BX2350.5.R5713] 65-12204
1. Spiritual life — Catholic authors. I. Title.

SAINT JURE, Jean Baptiste de, 1588-1657. 242
The secret of peace and happiness, by Father Jean Baptiste Saint-Jure and Blessed Claude de la Colombiere. Translated by Paul Garvin. Staten Island, N. Y., St. Paul Publications [c1961] 139p. 16cm. 'Extracts from Blessed Claude de la Colombiere and Ther Jean Baptiste Saint-Jure. --Dust jacket. [BX2183.S283] 61-15620
1. Spiritual life— Catholic authors. I. Colombiere, Claude de la, 1641-1682. II. Title.

SANTANER, Marie Abdon. 248.4'8'2
God in search of man. Translated by Ruth C. Douglas. Westminster, Md., Newman Press [1968] v, 218 p. 22 cm. Translation of Dieu cherche l'homme. [BX2350.5.S313] 68-21458
1. Spiritual life—Catholic authors. I. Title.

SCHEELE, Mary Augustine, sister, 1896- 242
Educational aspects of spiritual writings ... by Sister M. Augustine Scheele, O.R.F. Milwaukee, Wis., St. Joseph press, 1940. 2 p. l., [vii]-xiii, 273 p. 23 1/2 cm. Thesis (PH.D.)--Marquette university, 1939. [Secular name: Marie Ann Scheele] Contents.--Introduction, the problem.--Need for the spiritual formation of youth.--The Christian concept of human life.--The confessions of St. Augustine.-- The following of Christ.--The spiritual exercises of St. Ignatius.--A synthesis.--Bibliography (p. 236-266) Bibliography: p. 236-266. [BX2350.S23 1939] 40-34632
1. Augustinus, Aurelius, Saint, bp. of Hippo. Confessiones. 2. Imitatio Christi. 3. Loyola, Ignacio de, Saint, 1491-1556. Exercitia spiritualia. 4. Spiritual life—Catholic authors. 5. Religious education. I. Title.

SCHEURING, Tom. 282'.092'2 B
Two for joy : spirit-led journey of a husband and wife through Jesus to the Father / by Tom and Lyn Scheuring. New York : Paulist Press, c1976. v, 183 p. : ill. ; 21 cm. [BX2350.2.S32] 76-28274 ISBN 0-8091-1985-4 pbk. : 4.95
1. Scheuring, Tom. 2. Scheuring, Lyn. 3. Spiritual life—Catholic authors. 4. Christian communities. 5. Catholics in the United States—Biography. I. Scheuring, Lyn, joint author. II. Title.

SCUPOLI, Lorenzo, 1530-1610. 248'.48'2
The spiritual combat, and a Treatise on peace of the soul / by Lawrence Scupoli ; a translation, revised by William Lester, Robert Mohan. Rev. ed. New York : Paulist Press, 1978. xv, 240 p. ; 19 cm. (The Spiritual masters) Translation of Combattimento spirituale. [BX2349.S372 1978] 78-61668 ISBN 0-8091-2158-1 pbk. : 3.95
1. Spiritual life—Catholic authors. 2. Perfection (Catholic) I. Lester, James William, 1919- II. Mohan, Robert Paul, 1920- III. Title. IV. Title: Treatise on peace of the soul.

SHAMON, Albert J., Rev. 248.482
The only life. Milwaukee, Bruce Pub. Co. [c.1961] 133p. Bibl. 61-7712 3.25
1. Spiritual life—Catholic authors. I. Title.

SIMON, Raphael, Secular name: Kenneth Simon 1909- 248.4
Hammer and fire; toward divine happiness and mental health. New York, P.J. Kenedy [1959] 257 p. 22 cm. Includes bibliography. [BX2350.2.S5] 59-12900
1. Spiritual life — Catholic authors. I. Title.

SKELLY, Andrew Maria, 1855- 271.
Conferences on the interior life for sisterhoods ... by the Rev. A. M. Skelly ... St. Louis, Mo. and London, B. Herder book co., 1928-31. 4 v. front. (port.) (v. 4) 19 1/2 cm. These volumes are in good part an adaptation and an abridgment of Theologie ascetique et mystique, by Andre Marie Meynard and Mystica theoligia, by Thomas A. Vallgornera. cf. Foreword. [BX4210.S57] 28-12836
1. Spiritual life—Catholic authors. 2. Mysticism—Catholic church. I. Title.

SOUTHWELL, Robert, Saint, 1561?-1595. 248'.48'2
Two letters and Short rules of a good life. Edited by Nancy Pollard Brown. Charlottesville, Published for Folger Shakespeare Library [by] University Press of Virginia [1973] lxv, 122 p. facsim. 25 cm. (Folger documents of Tudor and Stuart civilization) Based on an early 17th century MS. acquired by the Folger Shakespeare Library, Washington, in 1964 (MS V.a. 421) Contents.Contents.—Epistle unto his father.—Short rules of a good life.—Letter to Sir Robert Cecil. Includes bibliographical references. [BX2181.S67 1973] 72-87806 ISBN 0-8139-0416-1 9.50
1. Spiritual life—Catholic authors. I. Brown, Nancy Pollard, ed. II. Title. III. Title: Epistle unto his father. IV. Title: Short rules of a good life. V. Title: Letter to Sir Robert Cecil. VI. Series.

SQUIRE, Aelred. 248'.3
Asking the fathers : the art of meditation and prayer / Aelred Squire. 2d American ed. Wilton, Conn. : Morehouse-Barlow Co., 1976, c1973. iii, 248 p. ; 22 cm. Includes bibliographical references and index. [BX2350.2.S65 1976] 77-354628 ISBN 0-8192-1221-0 : 5.95
1. Spiritual life—Catholic authors. 2. Prayer. I. Title.

STEUART, Robert Henry Joseph, 1874-1948. 248
Spiritual teaching of Father Steuart, s.j. Notes of his retreats and conferences collected and arr. by Katharine Kendall. With an introd. by H. P. C. Lyons. Westminster, Md., Newman Press [1952] 148 p. 22 cm. [BX2350.S65] 52-4526
1. Spiritual life — Catholic authors. I. Title.

STEUART, Robert Henry Joseph, 1874-1948. 248
The two voices; spiritual conferences of R. H. J. Steuart, S. J. Edited, with a memoir, by C. C. Martindale. Westminster, Md., Newman Press [1952] 274p. 22cm. [BX2350.S68] 52-14313
1. Spiritual life—Catholic authors. 2. Prayer. I. Title.

STURZO, Luigi, 1871- 248
Spiritual problems of our times, by Luigi Sturzo. New York, Toronto, Longmans, Green and co., inc., 1945. ix, 182 p. 19 1/2 cm. "First edition." [BX2350.S768] 45-10382
1. God—Proof. 2. Spiritual life—Catholic authors. I. Title.

STURZO, Luigi, 1871- 248
The true life; sociology of the supernatural, by Luigi Sturzo. Washington, D.C., The Catholic university of America press; Paterson, N.J., St. Anthony guild press, 1943. v, [1] p., 1 l., 312 p. 22 1/2 cm. "Translated from the original Italian by Barbara Barclay Carter." [BX2350.S77] A 43
1. Spiritual life—Catholic authors. 2. Sociology, Christian—Catholic authors. I. Carter, Barbara Barclay, tr. II. Title. III. Title: Sociology of the supernatural.

SULLIVAN, John J 248.482
God and the interior life; some reflections for religious on doctrine and devotion. [Boston] St. Paul Editions [1962] 283 p. 19 cm. [BX2350.2.S8] 62-22006
1. Spiritual life — Catholic authors. I. Title.

TAVARD, Georges Henri, 1922- 248'.48'2
The inner life : foundations of Christian mysticism / by George H. Tavard. New York : Paulist Press, c1976. v, 104 p. ; 19 cm. Bibliography: p. 101-104. [BX2350.2.T38] 75-32858 ISBN 0-8091-1927-7 pbk. : 1.65
1. Spiritual life—Catholic authors. I. Title.

TERESA, Saint, 1515-1582. 248.482
Interior castle. Translated and edited by E. Allison Peers, from the critical ed. of P. Silverio de Santa Teresa. Garden City, N.Y., Doubleday [1961] 235 p. 19 cm.

(Image books, D120) Translation of Les moradas. [BX2179.T4M63] 61-4019
1. Spiritual life — Catholic authors. I. Peers, Edgar Allison, ed. and tr. II. Title.

THEOLOGICAL Institute for Local Superiors, University of Notre Dame. 271.069
Prayer and sacrifice [by] Albert E. Bourke [and others. Notre Dame] University of Notre Dame Press, 1962. 249 p. 21 cm. (Religious life in the modern world, v. 4) "Articles ... previously published in the Proceedings of the Sisters' Institute of Spirituality 1953, 1955, and 1956." Bibliographical footnotes. [BX2385.T45] 62-6148
1. Spiritual life — Catholic authors. I. Bourke, Albert M. II. Notre Dame, Ind. University. III. Title. IV. Series.

THEOPHANE, the Monk. 248.4
Tales of a Magic Monastery / Theophane, the Monk. New York : Crossroad, 1981. p. cm. [BX2350.2.T486] 19 81-9765 ISBN 0-8245-0085-7 pbk. : 6.95
1. Spiritual life—Catholic authors. I. Title.

THOMPSON, Helen. 248.4'82
Journey toward wholeness : a Jungian model of adult spiritual growth / Helen Thompson. New York : Paulist Press, c1982. ix, 108 p. : ill. ; 21 cm. Bibliography: p. 107-108. [BX2350.2.T498] 19 81-83184 ISBN 0-8091-2422-X (pbk.) : 3.95
1. Thompson, Helen. 2. Spiritual life—Catholic authors. I. Title.

THOROLD, Anthony, 1896- 248
Conversation with God, by Rev. Anthony Thorold... New York, Sheed & Ward, 1940. vii, 9-94, [1] p. 17 cm. Printed in Great Britain. [Full name: Anthony Herbert Gerald Thorold] [BX2350.T45] 41-6304
1. Spiritual life—Catholic authors. I. Title.

TILMANN, Klemens, 1904- 248.83
Between God and ourselves; aids to spiritual progress. Tr. [from German] by Edward Gallagher. New York, Kenedy [c.1965] 154p. 22cm. [BX2350.5.T553] 64-24621 3.95
1. Spiritual life—Catholic authors. I. Title.

TILMANN, Klemens, 1904- 248.83
Between God and ourselves; aids to spiritual progress. Translated by Edward Gallagher. New York, Kennedy c1965] 154 p. 22 cm. Translation of Das Geistliche Gesprach. [BX2350.5.T553] 64-24621
1. Spiritual life — Catholic authors. I. Title.

TOURVILLE, Henri de 241
Letters of direction; thoughts on the spiritual life from the letters of the Abbe de Tourville.[Translated from the French by Lucy Menzies]. With an introd. by Evelyn Underhill. New York, Crowell [1959] 111p. 16cm. 59-65387 1.00 pap.,
1. Spiritual life—Catholic authors. I. Title.

TRESE, Leo John, 1902- 248.482
Everyman's road to heaven. Notre Dame, Ind., Fides [c.1961] 131p. 61-10366 2.95 bds.,
1. Spiritual life—Catholic authors. I. Title.

TRESE, Leo John, 1902- 248.482
You are called to greatness. Notre Dame, Ind., Fides [1966, c.1964] 158p. 18cm. (Dome bk., D52) .95 pap.,
1. Spiritual life—Catholic authors. I. Title.

TRESE, Leo John, 1902- 248.482
You are called to greatness Notre Dame, Ind., Fides [c.1964] 153p. 21 cm. 64-16496 3.25
1. Spiritual life—Catholic authors. I. Title.

TRESE, Leo John, 1902- 248.482
You are called to greatness [by] Leo J. Trese. Notre Dame, Ind., Fides Publisher [1964] 153 p. 21 cm. [BX2350.2.T72] 64-16496
1. Spiritual life — Catholic authors. I. Title.

TREVINO, Jose Guadalupe, 1889- 248
Rules for the spiritual life. Translated by Benjamin B. Hunt. Milwaukee, Bruce Pub. Co. [1956] 179p. 23cm. [BX2350.T713] 56-7046
1. Spiritual life—Catholic authors. I. Title.

TREVINO, Jose Guadalupe, 1889- 248
Rules for the spiritual life. Translated by Benjamin B. Hunt. Milwaukee, Bruce Pub. Co. [1956] 179 p. 23 cm. [BX2350.T713] 56-7046
1. Spiritual life — Catholic authors. I. Title.

TUNINK, Wilfrid. 232
Jesus is Lord / Wilfrid Tunink. 1st ed. Garden City, N.Y. : Doubleday, 1979. 164 p. ; 22 cm. [BT202.T84] 78-19317 ISBN 0-385-14793-7 : 7.95
1. Jesus Christ—Person and offices. 2. Spiritual life—Catholic authors. I. Title.

VAN KAAM, Adrian L., 1920- 233
Personality fulfillment in the spiritual life. by Adrian Van Kaam. [1st Amer. ed.] Wilkes-Barre, Pa., Dimension Bks. [1966] 191p. 21cm. [BX2350.2.V27 1966] 66-171950 3.95
1. Spritual life—Catholic authors. I. Title.

VAN ZELLER, Hubert, 1905 242
Moments of light. Springfield, Ill., Templegate [1963] xi, 196p. 17cm. (Golden lib.) 63-25560 3.50
1. Spiritual life—Catholic authors. I. Title.

VAN ZELLER, Hubert, 1905-
The choice of God [1st ed.] Springfield, Ill., Templegate [1956] viii, 210 p. 19 cm. Secular name: Claude Van Zeller. A59 not BX2850
1. Spiritual life — Catholic authors. I. Title. II. Series.

VAN ZELLER, Hubert, 1905- 248
The inner search. [Secular name: Claude Van Zeller] Garden City, N.Y., Doubleday [1967, c.1957] 234p. 18cm. (Image bk., D220) First pub. in Britain in 1957 by Sheed [BX2350.V224 1957a] .95 pap.,
1. Spiritual life—Catholic authors. I. Title.

VAN ZELLER, Hubert, 1905- 248
The inner search. New York, Sheed and Ward [1957] 230p. 21cm. [BX2350.V224] 57-6046
1. Spiritual life—Catholic authors. I. Title.

VINCENTIUS Ferrerius, Saint, 1350(ca.)-1419. 248
A treatise on the spiritual life. With a commentary by Julienne Morrell. Translated by the Dominican Nuns, Corpus Christi Monastery, Memlo [sic] Park, Calif. Westminster, Md., Newman Press, 1957. 175p. 22cm. Bibliographical footnotes. [BX2349.V52 1957] 57-1878
1. Splrltual life—Catholic authors. I. Morell, Jullenne, 1594-1653. II. Title.

VINCENTIUS Ferrerius, Saint, 1350(ca.)-1419. 248
Treatise on the spiritual life, by St. Vincent Ferrer ... translated from the French by the Rev. Fr. T. A. Dixon ... Westminster, Md., The Newman book shop, 1944. vii, 58 p. 20 1/2 cm. [BX2349.V52] 46-3461
1. Spiritual life—Catholic authors. I. Dixon, T. A., tr. II. Title.

VON HILDEBRAND, Dietrich, 1889- 248'.48'2
Transformation in Christ. [New ed.] Chicago, Franciscan Herald Press [1973, c1948] ix, 406 p. 23 cm. Translation of Die Umgestaltung in Christus. [BX2350.V5913 1973] 73-158305 ISBN 0-8199-0450-3 6.95
1. Spiritual life—Catholic authors. I. Title.

WALKER, David. 248.4'82
God is a sea / David Walker. New York, N.Y. : Alba House, c1981. p. cm. Bibliography: p. [BX2350.2.W33] 19 81-8072 ISBN 0-8189-0420-8 pbk. : 4.95
1. Spiritual life—Catholic authors. I. Title.

WAYWOOD, Robert J. 248'.48'2
Hanging in there with Christ, by Robert J. Waywood. Chicago, Franciscan Herald Press [1974] vii, 130 p. 22 cm. "Originally appeared as articles in the Cord." [BX2350.2.W38] 74-1367 ISBN 0-8199-0498-8 4.50
1. Spiritual life—Catholic authors. I. Title.

*WEDGE, Florence 248.4'8'2
The single woman. Pulaski, Wis., Franciscan Pubs. [1967] 64p. 19cm. .25 pap.,
1. Spiritual life—Catholic authors. 2. Woman—Religious life—Catholic authors. I. Title.

*WEDGE, Florence 248.4'8'2
You and your thoughts. Pulaski, Wis., Franciscan Pubs. [1967] 62p. 19cm. 25 pap.,
1. Spiritual life—Catholic authors. I. Title.

WHELAN, Basil, 1896- 242
Happiness with God. St. Louis, Herder [1959] 149 p. 20 cm. [BX2350.2.W5 1959] 59-2323
1. Spiritual life — Catholic authors. I. Title.

WHOM thou seekest. 248
Anonymous. New York, The Macmillan company, 1946. x, 229 p. 19 1/2 cm. "First printing." [BX2350.W5] 46-3021
1. Spiritual life—Catholic authors.

WIJNGAARDS, J. N. M. 248.4'82
Experiencing Jesus / John Wijngaards. Notre Dame, Ind. : Ave Maria Press, c1981. 176 p. ; 21 cm. Includes bibliographical references. [BX2350.2.W55] 19 81-52295 ISBN 0-87793-235-2 (pbk.) : 4.95
1. Jesus Christ—Person and offices. 2. Spiritual life—Catholic authors. 3. Christian saints. 4. Mystics. I. Title.

WROBLEWSKI, Sergius. 248.4'8'2
Christ-centered spirituality. Staten Island, N.Y., Alba House [1967] 211 p. 22 cm. Includes bibliographies. [BX2350.2.W69] 66-21813
1. Spiritual life—Catholic authors. I. Title.

ZYCHLINASKI, Aleksander. 248
... The heavenly wisdom of the saints; a practical guide to spiritual life (an authorized translation) Paterson, N.J., St. Anthony guild press, 1937. 5 p. l., 157 p. 19 1/2 cm. Illustrated t.-p. At head of title: Rev. Alexander Zychlinski, D.D. [BX2350.Z82] 38-9008
1. Spiritual life—Catholic authors. I. Rompkewska, Antonia, 1831- tr. II. Title.

Spiritual life—Catholic authors—Addresses, essays, lectures.

BUSH, Bernard J. 248'.48'2
Living in His love : essays on prayer and Christian living / Bernard J. Bush. 1st ed. Whitinsville, Mass. : Affirmation Books, c1978. 115 p. ; 21 cm. Includes bibliographical references. [BX2350.2.B87] 78-11809 3.95
1. Spiritual life—Catholic authors—Addresses, essays, lectures. 2. Prayer—Addresses, essays, lectures. I. Title.

CREATIVE formation of life and world / edited by Adrian van Kaam, Susan A. Muto. Lanham, Md. : University Press of America, 1982. p. cm. [BX2350.2.C67 1982] 19 82-16014 ISBN 0-8191-2708-6 : 27.75 ISBN 0-8191-2709-4 (pbk.) : 16.50 248.4
1. Spiritual life—Catholic authors—Addresses, essays, lectures. 2. Pastoral psychology—Addresses, essays, lectures. I. Van Kaam, Adrian L., 1920- II. Muto, Susan Annette.

†HARDON, John A. 248'.48'2
Holiness in the church / by John A. Hardon. Boston : St. Paul Editions, c1976. 179 p. : ill. ; 18 cm. [BX2350.2.H354] 76-15371 3.50 pbk. : 2.50
1. Spiritual life—Catholic authors—Addresses, essays, lectures. 2. Holiness—Addresses, essays, lectures. 3. Monastic and religious life—Addresses, essays, lectures. I. Title.

MERTON, Thomas, 1915-1968. 248.4'82
Introductions east & west : the foreign prefaces of Thomas Merton / Thomas Merton ; edited by Robert E. Daggy ; foreword by Harry James Cargas. Greensboro, N.C. : Unicorn Press, c1981. 144 p. : ill. ; 22 cm. Consists of the original prefaces, in English, which were translated into the various languages. Contents.Contents. Preface to the French edition of Exile ends in glory.—Preface to the French edition of Martha, Mary, and Lazarus.—Preface to the French edition of The ascent to truth.—Preface to the Argentine edition of The complete works of Thomas Merton.—Preface to the Japanese edition of The seven storey mountain.—Preface to the French edition of The black revolution.—Preface to the Japanese edition of Seeds of contemplation.—Preface to the Korean edition of Life and holiness.—Preface to the Spanish edition of Seeds of destruction.—Preface to the Japanese edition of Thoughts in solitude.—Preface to the Vietnamese edition of No man is an island.—Preface to the Japanese edition of The new man. "Checklist bibliography of Thomas Merton's major writings": p. 131-139. [BX2350.2.M4496] 19 80-29263 ISBN 0-87775-139-0 : 20.00 ISBN 0-87775-140-4 (pbk.)
1. Spiritual life—Catholic authors—Addresses, essays, lectures. I. Daggy, Robert E. II. Title.
Contents omitted. Contents omitted.

MERTON, Thomas, 1915-1968. 230'.2
Love and living / Thomas Merton ; edited by Naomi Burton Stone & Patrick Hart. New York : Farrar, Straus, and Giroux, c1979. 232 p. ; 21 cm. [BX1751.2.M47 1979] 79-14717 ISBN 0-374-19237-5. : 8.95
1. Catholic Church—Doctrinal and controversial works—Catholic authors—Addresses, essays, lectures. 2. Spiritual life—Catholic authors—Addresses, essays, lectures. I. Stone, Naomi Burton. II. Hart, Patrick, Brother. III. Title.

MERTON, Thomas, 1915-1968. 248'.08
The power and meaning of love / Thomas Merton. London : Sheldon Press, 1976. [7], 151 p. ; 21 cm. This edition is a selection of essays from the author's work Disputed questions. Contents.Contents.—The power and meaning of love.—A Renaissance hermit.—Philosophy of solitude.—Light in darkness.—The primitive Carmelite ideal.—Christianity and totalitarianism. [BX2350.2.M4495 1976] 76-381863 ISBN 0-85969-063-6. ISBN 0-85969-067-9 pbk.
1. Spiritual life—Catholic authors—Addresses, essays, lectures. I. Title.

NOUWEN, Henri J. M. 248'.89
Clowning in Rome : reflections on solitude, celibacy, prayer, and contemplation / Henri J. M. Nouwen. 1st ed. Garden City, N.Y. : Image Books, 1979. 110 p. ; 21 cm. [BX2350.2.N67] 78-22423 ISBN 0-385-15129-2 : 3.95
1. Spiritual life—Catholic authors—Addresses, essays, lectures. 2. Monastic and religious life—Addresses, essays, lectures. I. Title.

SPIRITUALITY and originality. [Pittsburgh, PA : Institute of Formative Spirituality, Duquesne University], 1980. 172 p. ; 23 cm. (Studies in formative spirituality ; v. 1, no. 1) Cover title. Bibliography: p. 167-172. [BX2350.2.S628] 80-114640 5.00 248.4'82
1. Spiritual life—Catholic authors—Addresses, essays, lectures. 2. Spirituality—Addresses, essays, lectures. 3. Image of God—Addresses, essays, lectures. 4. Spiritual direction—Addresses, essays, lectures. I. Title. II. Series.

SPIRITUALITY and the desert experience. [Pittsburgh, PA] : Institute of Formative Spirituality, Duquesne University, 1980. p. 182-320 ; 23 cm. (Studies in formative spirituality ;) ISSN v. 1 0193-2748) Cover title. Bibliography: p. [313]-320. [BX2350.2.S629] 19 80-126768 5.00 248.4
1. Spiritual life—Catholic authors—Addresses, essays, lectures. 2. Deserts (in religion, Folk-lore, etc.)—Addresses, essays, lectures. 3. Solitude—Addresses, essays, lectures. 4. Alienation (Theology)—Addresses, essays, lectures. 5. Reconciliation—Addresses, essays, lectures. I. Title. II. Series.

Spiritual life—Catholic authors—Collected works.

JEAN de Saint-Samson, Brother, 1571-1636. 248'.48'2
Prayer, aspiration, and contemplation : [selections] from the writings of John of St. Samson, O. Carm., mystic and charismatic / translated and edited by Venard Poslusney. Staten Island, N.Y. : Alba House, [1975] vi, 212 p. : port. ; 21 cm.

Bibliography: p. [211]-212. [BX2349.J4513] 74-30340 ISBN 0-8189-0300-7 pbk. : 3.95
1. Jean de Saint-Samson, Brother, 1571-1636. 2. Spiritual life—Catholic authors—Collected works. 3. Prayer—Collected works. 4. Contemplation—Collected works. I. Poslusney, Venard, ed. II. Title.

LEGERE, J. Roy, 1922- 248.4'82
Commissioned by the Lord himself / J. Roy Legere. Somers, CT : Apostolic Formation Center for Christian Renew-All, c1979. 167 p. ; 23 cm. Includes bibliographical references. [BX2350.2.L4383] 79-55369 ISBN 0-935488-00-6 : 7.95 ISBN 0-935488-01-4 pbk. : 3.95
1. Spiritual life—Catholic authors—Collected works. I. Title.
Publisher's Address : Box 355, Somers, CT 06071

RAHNER, Karl, 1904- 248.4'82
Prayers and meditations : an anthology of the spiritual writings of Karl Rahner / Karl Rahner ; edited by John Griffiths. New York : Seabury Press, 1980. p. cm. "A Crossroad book." Includes index. Bibliography: p. [BX2350.2.R34213] 80-17264 ISBN 0-8164-0458-5 : 8.95 ISBN 0-8164-2284-2 pbk. : 3.95
1. Spiritual life—Catholic authors—Collected works. I. Griffiths, John. II. Title.

Spiritual life—Catholic authors—Early works to 1800.

ROLLE, Richard, of Hampole, 1290?-1349. 248.4'82
The fire of love and The mending of life / by Richard Rolle ; translated with an introduction by M. L. del Mastro. 1st ed. Garden City, N.Y. : Image Books, 1981. 280 p. ; 18 cm. Translation of Incendium amoris and Emendatio vitae. Bibliography: p. [279]-280. [BX2349.R67413] 19 81-68128 ISBN 0-385-15839-4 (pbk.) : 4.95
1. Spiritual life—Catholic authors—Early works to 1800. 2. God—Worship and love—Early works to 1800. 3. Love (Theology)—Early works to 1800. I. Del'Mastro, M. L. II. Rolle, Richard, of Hampole, 1290?-1349. De emendacione vita. English. 1981. III. [Incendium amoris.] English IV. Title. V. Title: Fire of love.

Spiritual life—Catholic Church.

MCELHONE, James Francis, 1890- 271
Spirituality for postulate, novitiate, scholasticate. Notre Dame, Ind., Ave Maria Press [1955] 196p. 22cm. [BX2350.M146] 55-9482
1. Spiritual life—Catholic Church. 2. Monastic and religious life. I. Title.

SAMSON, Henri. 248.482
Spiritual insights of a practicing psychiatrist. [Translated from the French by Paul Garvin] Staten Island, N. Y., Alba House [1966] 200 p. 22 cm. Translation of Propos spirituels d'un psychiatre. [BX2350.5.S273] 66-17218
1. Spiritual life—Catholic Church. 2. Jesus Christ—Ascension. I. Title.

Spiritual life—Christian Church (Disciples of Christ) authors.

PAULSELL, William O. 248'.48'66
Taste and see : a personal guide to the spiritual life / William O. Paulsell. Nashville : Upper Room, c1976. 88 p. ; 20 cm. [BV4501.2.P356] 76-5634
1. Spiritual life—Christian Church (Disciples of Christ) authors. I. Title.

Spiritual life—Collected works.

ARNOLD, Eberhard, 1883-1935. 248
Inner land: a guide into the heart and soul of the Bible. Rifton, N.Y., Plough Pub. House, 1974- p. cm. Translation of Innenland: ein Wegweiser in die Seele der Bibel. Contents.Contents.—v. 1. The inner life. [BV4495.A7413] 74-18433 ISBN 0-87486-178-0 (v. 1)
1. Spiritual life—Collected works. I. Title.

BUBBA Free John. 299
The four fundamental questions : talks and essays about human experience and the actual practice of an enlightened way of life / by Da Free John. 1st ed. Clearlake Highlands, Calif. : Dawn Horse Press, 1980. 101 p. : ill. ; 18 cm. [BP610.B8135] 79-92923 ISBN 0-913922-49-8 (pbk.) : 1.95
1. Spiritual life—Collected works. I. Title.

A Great treasury of Christian spirituality : classic readings in the life of faith and the love of God / compiled by Edward Alcott. St. Paul : Carillon Books, 1978. xii, 189 p. ; 22 cm. Includes bibliographical references. [BV4495.G83] 78-59319 ISBN 0-89310-039-0 : 8.95. 248'.2
1. Spiritual life—Collected works. I. Alcott, Edward.

WYON, Olive, 1890- 248.4
Teaching toward Christian perfection, introducing three spiritual classics. [New York, Woman's Div. of Christian Service, Bd. of Missions, Methodist Church [c.1963] 200p. illus. 19cm. Bibl. 63-8291 1.00 pap.,
1. Spiritual life—Collections. I. Title.
Contents omitted.

WYON, Olive, 1890- 248.4
Teachings toward Christian perfection, introducing three spiritual classics. [New York, Woman's Division of Christian Service, Board of Missions, Methodist Church, 1963] 200 p. illus. 19 cm. [BV4515.W9] 63-8291
1. Spiritual life — Collections. I. Title.

Spiritual life—Comparative studies.

HIXON, Lex. 291.4'2
Coming home : the experience of enlightenment in sacred traditions / Lex Hixon. 1st ed. Garden City, N.Y. : Anchor Press/Doubleday, 1978. 233 p. : ill. ; 18 cm. Bibliography: p. [229]-233. [BL624.H55] 77-77656 ISBN 0-385-12907-6 pbk. : 2.95
1. Spiritual life—Comparative studies. I. Title.

Spiritual life—Friend authors.

PARKER-RHODES, Arthur Frederick Parker, 1914- 248'.48'96
Wholesight : the spirit quest / by Frederick Parker-Rhodes. Wallingford, Pa. : Pendle Hill Publications, c1978. 30 p. ; 19 cm. (Pendle Hill pamphlet ; 217 ISSN 0031-4250s) [BX7738.P37] 77-95406 ISBN 0-87574-217-3 : pbk. : 1.10
1. Spiritual life—Friend authors. I. Title.

Spiritual life—Friend authors—Addresses, essays, lectures.

FRIENDS search for wholeness / John L. Bond, editor. Richmond, Ind. : Friends United Press, c1978. xiv, 186 p. ; 22 cm. [BV4501.2.F764] 78-62765 ISBN 0-913408-42-5 : 8.95 248'.48'96
1. Spiritual life—Friend authors—Addresses, essays, lectures. I. Bond, John L.

NEWBY, James R. 248
Reflections from the light of Christ : five Quaker classics / by James R. Newby. Richmond, Ind. : Friends United Press, c1980. xv, 110 p. ; 22 cm. Includes bibliographical references. [BX7615.N48] 19 80-7477 ISBN 0-913408-55-7 : 6.95
1. Friends, Society of—Addresses, essays, lectures. 2. Spiritual life—Friend authors—Addresses, essays, lectures. I. Title.

Spiritual life—Friend authors—Collected works.

TRUEBLOOD, David Elton, 1900- 248.4'896
The best of Elton Trueblood : an anthology / edited and with an introd. by James R. Newby. 1st. ed. Nashville, Tenn. : Impact Books, [1979] 205 p. ; 24 cm. Bibliography: p. [199]-202. [BV4501.2.T74] 79-49226 ISBN 0-914850-86-5 : 8.95
1. Spiritual life—Friend authors—Collected works. I. Newby, James R. II. Title.

Spiritual life—Hindu authors.

AKHILANANDA, Swami. 294.5'44
Spiritual practices. Introd. by Walter G. Muelder. Boston, Branden Press [1972] 125 p. 23 cm. Includes bibliographical references. [BL1228.A34] 78-175140 ISBN 0-8283-1350-4 7.50
1. Spiritual life—Hindu authors. I. Title.

AKHILANANDA, Swami. 294.5'44
Spiritual practices, by Swami Akhilananda. Memorial ed. with reminiscences by his friends. Edited by Alice Mary Stark and Claude Alan Stark. Cape Cod, Mass., C. Stark [1974] 225 p. port. 23 cm. "Writings of Swami Akhilananda": p. 221. Includes bibliographical references. [BL1228.A34 1974] 74-76003 ISBN 0-89007-001-6 8.50
1. Akhilananda, Swami—Addresses, essays, lectures. 2. Spiritual life—Hindu authors. I. Title.

JONES, Franklin. 294.5'4'4
The knee of listening. [Los Angeles] Ashram [1972] 271 p. port. 23 cm. [BL1228.J65] 72-83720 ISBN 0-87707-093-8 6.95
1. Spiritual life—Hindu authors. I. Title.

RAMANA, Maharshi. 181'.4
The spiritual teaching of Ramana Maharshi. Foreword by C. G. Jung. Berkeley, Shambala, 1972. x, 125 p. port. 22 cm. (The Clear light series) [BL1228.R32] 79-189853 ISBN 0-87773-024-5 1.95
1. Spiritual life—Hindu authors. I. Title.

Spiritual life (Hinduism)

BUCK, Harry Merwyn. 294.3'444
Spiritual discipline in Hinduism, Buddhism, and the West / Harry M. Buck. Chambersburg, Pa. : Anima Books, 1981. vi, 69 p. : ill. ; 22 cm. (Focus on Hinduism and Buddhism) Bibliography: p. [66]-67. [BL1228.B83] 19 81-13035 ISBN 0-917946-02-2 : 25.00 ISBN 0-89012-022-6 : 3.00
1. Spiritual life (Hinduism) 2. Spiritual life (Buddhism) 3. Spiritual life (Hinduism)—Study and teaching—Audio-visual aids. 4. Spiritual life (Buddhism)—Study and teaching—Audio-visual aids. I. Title. II. Series.
Publisher's address: P. O. Box 220, St. George, UT 84770

†MEHER Baba, 1894-1969. 294.5'4
The path of love / Meher Baba. New York : S. Weiser, 1976. 102 p. ; 23 cm. [BL1228.M4 1976] 76-15540 ISBN 0-87728-309-5 : 3.95
1. Spiritual life (Hinduism) I. Title.

MUKTANANDA Paramhamsa, Swami. 294.5'6 B
Guru: Chitshaktivilas; the play of consciousness. [1st ed.] New York, Harper & Row [1971] xxx, 175 p. illus. 22 cm. [BL1175.M77A313 1971] 77-148442 ISBN 0-06-066045-7 5.95
1. Muktananda Paramhamsa, Swami. 2. Spiritual life (Hinduism) I. Title.

MUKTANANDA Paramhamsa, Swami. 294.5'42
Reflections of the self / Swami Muktananda. [South Fallsburg, N.Y. : SYDA Foundation, c1980] 205 p. ; 22 cm. Includes bibliographical references. [BL1228.2.M8413] 19 80-50391 pbk. : 5.95
1. Spiritual life (Hinduism) I. Title.
Publisher's address P. O. Box 605, South Falsburg, NY 12779

MUKTANANDA Paramhamsa, Swami. 294.5'43
The spiritual instructions of Swami Muktananda. Edited, with introd. and epilogue, by Bubba Free John (Franklin Jones) [1st ed.] Lower Lake, Calif., Dawn Horse Press [1974] xv, 15 p. ports. 22 cm. Includes bibliographical references. [BL1228.M83] 73-86295 ISBN 0-913922-02-1 1.50
1. Spiritual life (Hinduism) I. Jones, Franklin, ed. II. Title.

MUKTANANDA Paramhamsa, Swami. 294.5'43
Play of consciousness = Chitshakti vilas / Swami Muktananda. [2d ed.]. San Francisco : Harper & Row, 1978. xl, 322 p., [3] leaves of plates : ill. ; 22 cm. Translation of Citsakti vilasa. Includes index. [BL1228.M813 1978] 78-62769 ISBN 0-914602-37-3 pbk. : 5.95
1. Muktananda Paramhamsa, Swami. 2. Spiritual life (Hinduism) I. Title. II. Title: Chitshakti vilas.

[ORGESATHER, John B] 1867- 129.
The dawn of God's day; or, The day of Brahma, by Tussaloosa [pseud.] ... Chicago, Ill., 1917. vi, 91 p. diagr. 19 cm. [BL515.O8] 18-1239
I. Title.

RAJANEESH, Acharya, 1931- 294.5'44
The psychology of the esoteric / Bhagwan Shree Rajneesh ; edited by Ma Satya Bharti. 1st U.S. ed. New York : Harper & Row, 1978, c1973. viii, 168 p. ; 20 cm. (Harper colophon books.) Previous ed. published under title: The inward revolution. [BL1228.R28 1978] 78-110747 ISBN 0-06-090616-2 : 3.95
1. Spiritual life (Hinduism) 2. Meditation (Hinduism) I. Satya Bharti, Ma. II. Title.

RAMA, Swami, 1925- 294.5'42
Living with the Himalayan masters : spiritual experiences of Swami Rama / edited by Swami Ajaya. Honesdale, Pa. : Himalayan International Institute of Yoga Sciences & Philosophy, c1978. xix, 490 p., [2] leaves of plates : ill. ; 24 cm. [BL1228.R317] 78-103055 ISBN 0-89389-034-0 : 13.95
1. Rama, Swami, 1925- 2. Spiritual life (Hinduism) 3. Himalaya Mountains—Description and travel. I. Ajaya, Swami, 1940- II. Title.

RAMA, Swami, 1925- 294.5'42
Living with the Himalayan masters : spiritual experiences of Swami Rama / edited by Swami Ajaya. Honesdale, Pa. : Himalayan International Institute of Yoga Science & Philosophy, c1980. xv, 490 p., [4] leaves of plates : ill. ; 23 cm. [BL1228.R317 1980] 19 80-82974 ISBN 0-89389-070-7 (pbk.) : 7.50
1. Rama, Swami, 1925- 2. Spiritual life (Hinduism) I. Ajaya, Swami, 1940- II. Title.

RUPAGOSVAMI, 16thcent. 294.5'44
The nectar of instruction ; an authorized English presentation of Srila Rupa Gosvami's Sri Upadesamrta / with the original Sanskrit text, roman transliterations, synonyms, translations and elaborate purports by A. C. Bhaktivedanta Swami Prabhupada. New York : Bhaktivedanta Book Trust, 1976c1975 ix, 130 p., [2] leaves of plates : ill. ; 18 cm. Includes bibliographical references and indexes. [BL1228.R8613] 75-39755 ISBN 0-912776-85-4 pbk. : 1.95
1. Spiritual life (Hinduism) 2. Krishna—Cult. I. Bhaktivedanta Swami, A. C., 1896- II. Title.

Spiritual life (Hinduism)—Addresses, essays, lectures.

GAYATRI Devi, 1906- 294.5'4
One life's pilgrimage : addresses, letters, and articles by the first Indian woman to teach Vedanta in the west / Srimata Gayatri Devi. Cohasset, Mass. : Vedanta Centre, c1977. ix, 341 p. : ill. ; 21 cm. [BL1228.G39] 77-150793 4.95
1. Spiritual life (Hinduism)—Addresses, essays, lectures. I. Title.

†MUKTANANDA Paramhamsa, Swami. 294.5'4
Selected essays / Muktananda ; edited by Paul Zweig. 1st ed. New York : Harper & Row, c1976. xiv, 173 p. : ports. ; 20 cm. [BL1228.M825 1976] 76-9994 ISBN 0-06-069860-8 : 3.95
1. Spiritual life (Hinduism)—Addresses, essays, lectures. I. Title.

SATCHIDANANDA, Swami. 294.5'44
Beyond words / Swami Satchidananda ; edited by Lester Alexander ; drawings by Peter Max. 1st ed. New York : Holt, Rinehart and Winston, c1977. 182 p. : ill. ; 24 cm. [BL1228.S27] 76-29896 ISBN 0-03-020871-8 : 7.95 ISBN 0-03-016911-9 pbk. : 4.95
1. Spiritual life (Hinduism)—Addresses, essays, lectures. 2. Conduct of life—Addresses, essays, lectures. I. Title.

Spiritual life (Hinduism)—History.

SIVARAM, Mysore, 1905- 294.5'4
Ananda and the three great acharyas / M. Sivaram. New Delhi : Vikas Pub. House, c1976. [10], 165 p. ; 22 cm. Bibliography: p. [7] (1st group) [BL1228.S588] 76-901494 Rs35.00
1. Sankaracarya. 2. Ramanuja, founder of sect. 3. Madhva, 13th cent. 4. Spiritual life (Hinduism)—History. I. Title.

Spiritual life—History

COGNET, Louis, 1917- 248.2
Post- Reformation spirituality. Translated from the French by P. Hepburne Scott. [1st American ed.] New York, Hawthorn Books [1959] 143p. 22cm. (The Twentieth century encyclopedia of Catholicism, v. 41. Section 4: The means of redemption) Translation of De la devotion moderne a la spritualite francaise. Includes bibliography. [BV4490.C613] 59-14522
1. Spiritual life—Hist. 2. Spiritual life—Catholic authors. I. Title.

Spiritual life—History of doctrines.

BARRACHINA, Ignatius 281.4
Spiritual doctrine of St. Augustine. Tr. [from Spanish] by Edward James Schuster. St. Louis, B. Herder [c.1963] xvi, 264p. 21cm. (Cross & crown ser. of spirituality, no. 25) Bibl. 63-19829 4.75
1. Augustinus Aurelius, Saint Bp. of Hippo Bp. of Hippo. 2. Spiritual life—History of doctrines. I. Title. II. Series.

CHARMOT, Francois 230.0922
Ignatius Loyola and Francis de Sales: two masters, one spirituality. Tr. [from French] by Sister M. Renelle. St. Louis, B. Herder [c. 1966] x, 251p. 21cm. (Cross and crown ser. of spirituality, no. 32) Bibl. [BX4700.L7C53] 66-17096 4.75
1. Loyola, Ignaio de, Saint, 1491-1556. 2. Francois de Sales, Saint, Bp. of Geneva, 1567-1622. 3. Spiritual life—History of doctrines. I. Title. II. Series.

CHARMOT, Francois. 230.0922
Ignatius Loyola and Francis de Sales: two masters, one spirituality [by] F. Charmot. Translated by Sister M. Renelle. St. Louis, B. Herder Book Co. [1966] x, 251 p. 21 cm. (Cross and crown series of spirituality, no. 32) Translation of Deux maitres, une spiritualite: Ignace de Loyola, Francois de Sales. Bibliography: p. 250-251. [BX4700.L7C53] 66-17096
1. Loyola, Ignacio de. Saint, 1491-1556. 2. Francois de Sales, Saint, Bp. of Geneva, 1567-1622. 3. Spiritual life — History of doctrines. I. Title. II. Series.

CLANCY, Thomas H. 234
The conversational word of God : a commentary on the doctrine of St. Ignatius of Loyola concerning spiritual conversation, with four early Jesuit texts / Thomas H. Clancy. St. Louis : Institute of Jesuit Sources, 1978 xii, 71 p. ; 23 cm. (Study aids on Jesuit topics ; no. 8) Includes bibliographical references. [BX2350.2.C54] 78-51343 ISBN 0-912422-34-3 : 2.50
1. Loyola, Ignacio de, Saint, 1491-1556. 2. Spiritual life—History of doctrines. I. Title. II. Series.

FEYS, Jan, 1933- 291.4'2
The yogi and the mystic : a study in the spirituality of Sri Aurobindo and Teilhard de Chardin / Jan Feys. 1st ed. Calcutta : Firma KLM, 1977. xv, 371 p. ; 21 cm. Includes index. Bibliography: p. [341]-344. [BL624.F48] 77-905631 7.00
1. Ghose, Aurobindo, 1872-1950. Essays on the Gita. 2. Teilhard de Chardin, Pierre. Le milieu divin. 3. Mahabharata. Bhagavadgita. 4. Spiritual life—History of doctrines. 5. Christianity—Philosophy. I. Title.
Distributed by South Asia Books

FINLEY, James. 248'.2
Merton's Palace of Nowhere : a search for God through awareness of the true self / James Finley ; with a foreword by Henri Nouwen. Notre Dame, Ind. : Ave Maria Press, c1978. 158 p. ; 21 cm. Includes bibliographical references. 78-58738 ISBN 0-87793-159-3 pbk. : 2.95
1. Merton, Thomas, 1915-1968. 2. Spiritual life—History of doctrines. I. Title.

HISTORY of Christian 248
spirituality; v.1 [by] Louis Bouyer [others. New York, Desclee, 1964, c.1963] v. 23cm. Contents.v.1. The spirituality of the New Testament and the fathers, by L. Bouyer. Bibl. 63-16487 9.50
1. Spiritual life—History of doctrines. I. Bouyer, Louis, 1913-

HOLMES, Urban Tigner, 1930- 248
A history of Christian spirituality : an analytical introduction / Urban T. Holmes III. New York : Seabury Press, 1980. x, 166 p. ; 22 cm. Includes bibliographies and index. [BV4490.H63] 80-12870 ISBN 0-8164-0141-1 : 10.95
1. Spiritual life—History of doctrines. I. Title.

IMITATING Christ, 248'.09
by Edouard Cothenet [and others] Translated by Simone Inkel and Lucy Tinsley. With a pref. by John L. Boyle. St. Meinrad, Ind., Abbey Press, 1974. xiii, 122 p. 21 cm. (Religious experience series, v. 5) "Translation of the article 'Imitation du Christ' and of the second part of the article 'Imitation du Christ (livre)' which first appeared in the Dictionnaire de spiritualite, Paris, Beauchesne, 1971, vol. 7, deuxieme partie, cols. 1536-1601 and 2355-2368 respectively." Bibliography: p. 118-122. [BT304.2.I4613] 73-94173 ISBN 0-87029-029-0 3.95 (pbk.)
1. Jesus Christ—Example. 2. Spiritual life—History of doctrines. I. Cothenet, Edouard.

JETTE, Fernand. 922.271
The spiritual teaching of Mary of the Incarnation. Translation by Mother M. Herman. New York, Sheed and Ward [1963] 180 p. 21 cm. Translation of La voi de la saintete d'apres Marie de l'Incarnation. [BX4705.M36J43] 63-8535
1. Marie de l'Incarnation, Mother, 1599-1672. 2. Spiritual life — History of doctrines. I. Title.

MEHER Baba, 1894-1969. 294.5'42
The mastery of consciousness : an introduction and guide to practical mysticism and methods of spiritual development / as given by Meher Baba ; compiled and edited by Allan Y. Cohen. 1st ed. New York : Harper & Row, 1977. xx, 202 p. ; 21 cm. (Harper colophon books ; CN 371) Bibliography: p. [175]-183. [BL624.M43 1977] 76-55500 ISBN 0-06-090371-6 : 3.95
1. Meher Baba, 1894-1969. 2. Spiritual life—History of doctrines. 3. Mysticism—History. I. Cohen, Allen Y., 1939- II. Title.

PENNING de Vries, 271'.5'024
Piet.
Discernment of spirits, according to the life and teachings of St. Ignatius of Loyola. Translated by W. Dudok Van Heel. [1st ed.] New York, Exposition Press [1973] 252 p. 22 cm. (An Exposition-Testament book) Bibliography: p. 247-248. [BX2350.2.P4193] 72-90063 ISBN 0-682-47592-0 8.00
1. Loyola, Ignacio de, Saint, 1491-1556. 2. Spiritual life—History of doctrines. I. Title.

REID, John Kelman Sutherland. 232
Our life in Christ. Philadelphia, Westminster Press [1963] 148 p. 23 cm. (The Library of history and doctrine) [BV4490.R4] 63-9063
1. Jesus Christ — Person and offices. 2. Spiritual life — History of doctrines. I. Title.

RICHARD, Lucien 230'.4'20924
Joseph.
The spirituality of John Calvin / Lucien Joseph Richard. Atlanta : John Knox Press, [1974] 207 p.; 23 cm. Includes index. Bibliography: p. 195-203. [BV4490.R5] 73-16920 pbk. : 5.00 ISBN 0-8042-0711-9
1. Calvin, Jean, 1509-1564. 2. Spiritual life—History of doctrines. I. Title.

SAWARD, John. 248.4
Perfect fools : folly for Christ's sake in Catholic and orthodox spirituality / John Saward. Oxford ; New York : Oxford University Press, 1980. p. cm. Includes index. Bibliography: p. [BX2350.2.S27] 80-40164 ISBN 0-19-213230-X : 26.95
1. Spiritual life—History of doctrines. 2. Folly. I. Title.

SHEPPARD, Lancelot Capel, 248'.09
1906-
Spiritual writers in modern times, by Lancelot Sheppard. [1st ed.] New York, Hawthorn Books [1967] 125, [3] p. 21 cm. (The Twentieth century encyclopedia of Catholicism, v. 42. Section 4: The means of redemption) Bibliography: p. [127]-[128] [BV4490.S48] 65-13397
1. Spiritual life—History of doctrines. I. Title. II. Series: The Twentieth century encyclopedia of Catholicism, v. 42

WELCH, John. 248.2
Spiritual pilgrims : Carl Jung and Teresa of Avila / John Welch. New York : Paulist Press, c1982. x, 228 p., ; 21 cm. Includes index. Bibliography: p. 221-223. [BL624.W39 1982] 19 82-80164 ISBN 0-8091-2454-8 (pbk.) : 8.95
1. Jung, C. G. (Carl Gustav), 1875-1961. 2. Teresa, of Avila, Saint, 1515-1582. Moradas. 3. Spiritual life—History of doctrines. I. Title.

WILLIAMS, Rowan, 1950- 248'.09
Christian spirituality : a theological history from the New Testament to Luther and St. John of the Cross / Rowan Williams. Atlanta : John Knox Press, 1980, c1979. p. cm. British ed. published in 1979 under title: The wound of knowledge. Includes index. Bibliography: p. [BV4490.W54 1980] 19 80-82190 ISBN 0-8042-0660-0 : 16.50 (est.) ISBN 0-8042-0508-6 (pbk.) : 9.95 (est.)
1. Spiritual life—History of doctrines. I. Title.

Spiritual life—History of doctrines—17th century.

HAMBRICK-STOWE, 248.4'0974
Charles E.
The practice of piety : Puritan devotional disciplines in seventeenth-century New England / by Charles E. Hambrick-Stowe. Chapel Hill : Published for the Institute of Early American History and Culture, Williamsburg, Virginia by the University of North Carolina Press, c1982. p. cm. Includes index. [BV4490.H3] 19 81-19806 ISBN 0-8078-1518-7 : 28.00
1. Spiritual life—History of doctrines—17th century. 2. Puritans—New England. 3. New England—Religious life and customs. I. Institute of Early American History and Culture (Williamsburg, Va.) II. Title.

Spiritual life—History of doctrines—20th century.

FARICY, Robert L., 1926- 248.4
The spirituality of Teilhard de Chardin / [Robert Faricy]. Minneapolis, Minn. : Winston Press, c1981. 126 p. ; 22 cm. Bibliography: p. 110-112. [BX2350.2.F37] 19 81-51160 ISBN 0-86683-608-X pbk. : 5.95
1. Teilhard de Chardin, Pierre. 2. Spiritual life—History of doctrines—20th century. I. Title.

Spiritual life (Lamaism)

RAMACHANDRA Rao, 294.3'4'43
Saligrama Krishna, 1926-
Tibetan meditation : theory and practice / S. K. Ramachandra Rao. New Delhi : Arnold-Heinemann, 1979. 112 p. ; 22 cm. [BQ7805.R35] 79-900596 7.50
1. Spiritual life (Lamaism) 2. Lamas—Tibet—Biography. I. Title.
Distributed by Humanities Press, Atlantic Highlands, NJ Distributed by Humanities Press, Atlantic Highlands, NJ

Spiritual life—Lutheran authors.

HOLTMERMANN, Carla 248.4'8'41
Released and radiant. Westwood, N.J., Revell [1967] 60p. 17cm. [BV4501.2.H58] 67-14776 1.50 bds.,
1. Spiritual life—Lutheran authors. I. Title.

MCFADYEN, John Edgar.
In the hour of silence, by John Edgar McFadyen... Chicago, New York [etc.] F. H. Revell company, 1902. 212 p. 19 cm . "This little volume is a group of brief meditations on some of the things that pertain to the spiritual life."--Pref. 3-26341
I. Title.

Spiritual life-Meditations and Contemplations.

MERTON, Thomas 242
Thoughts in solitude. [New York, Dell 1961, c.1956, 1958] 160p. (Chapel bk. F132) .50 pap.,
1. Spiritual life—Meditations and comtemplations. I. Title.

Spiritual life—Methodist authors.

BRIGHTMAN, Edgar 248'.4
Sheffield, 1884-1953.
The spiritual life / Edgar Sheffield Brightman. New York : AMS Press, [1979] p. cm. Reprint of the 1942 ed. published by Abingdon-Cokesbury Press, New York, which was issued as the Cole lectures of 1942, Vanderbilt University. Includes index. [BV4501.B735 1979] 75-3086 ISBN 0-404-59085-3 : 22.00
1. Spiritual life—Methodist authors. I. Title. II. Series: The Cole lectures. Vanderbilt University, 1942.

DAWSON, Grace (Strickler) 248.42
1891-
For a deeper life. New York, Abingdon Press [1963] 112 p. 20 cm. Includes bibliography. [BV4509.5D3] 63-8667
1. Spiritual life — Methodist authors. 2. Prayer. I. Title.

DUMOND, Charles E. 248.4'8'76
Depth discipleship. by Charles E. DuMond. Introd. by Anna B. Mow. Grand Rapids. Zondervan [1967] 126p. 22cm. [BV4501.2.D75] 67-11620 2.95 bds.,
1. Spiritual life—Methodist authors. I. Title.

DUNNAM, Maxie D. 248.4'876
Alive in Christ : the dynamic process of spiritual formation / Maxie Dunnam. Nashville : Abingdon, c1982. 160 p. ; 21 cm. [BV4501.2.D766 1982] 19 81-20631 ISBN 0-687-00993-6 : 7.95
1. Spiritual life—Methodist authors. I. Title.

KIRK, Albert Emmanuel, 248.4
1880-
A consciousness of God; a study of the essence of genuine religion. Foreword by Gordon B. Thompson. New York, Exposition [c.1962] 159p. 21cm. (Exposition-Testament bk.) 62-21056 3.50
1. Spiritual life—Methodist authors. I. Title.

KIRK, Albert Emmanuel, 248.4
1880-
A consciousness of God; a study of the essence of genuine religion. Foreword by Gordon B. Thompson. [1st ed.] New York, Exposition Press [1962] 159p. 21cm. (An Exposition Testument book) [BV4501.2.K5] 62-21056
1. Spiritual life—Methodist authors. I. Title.

Spiritual life—Middle Ages.

FRANCESCO D'ASSISI, 922.245
Saint, 1182-1226.
Memorable words of Saint Francis. Collected and annotated by Alexandre Masseron. Translated from the French by Margaret Sullivan. Chicago, Franciscan Herald Press [1963] viii, 123 p. 21 cm. "Abbreviations of references to source material": p. vi. [BX890.F669] 63-21390
1. Spiritual life — Middle Ages. I. Masseron, Alexandre, 1880-1959. II. Title.

FRANCESCO D'ASSISI, 922.245
Saint, 1182-1226
Memorable words of Saint Francis. Collected, annotated by Alexandre Masseron. Tr. from French by Margaret Sullivan. Chicago, Franciscan Herald [c.1963] viii, 123p. 21cm. Bibl. 63-21390 3.50
1. Spiritual life—Middle Ages. I. Masseron, Alexandre, 1880-1959. II. Title.

HUGO of Saint-Victor, 1096or7-1141. 248.22
Hugh of Saint-Victor; selected spirtual writings. Translated by a religious of C. S. M. V. With an introd. by Aelred Squire. New York, Harper & Row [1962] 196 p. illus. 21 cm. (Classics of the contemplative life) [BV5080.H77] 62-21139
1. Spiritual life—Middle Ages. I. Title.
Contents omitted.

MASSERON, Alexandre, 1880-1959. 922.245
Memorable words of Saint Francis. Collected and annotated by Alexandre Masseron. Translated from the French by Margaret Sullivan. Chicago, Franciscan Herald Press [1963] viii, 123 p. 21 cm. "Abbreviations of references to source material": p. vi. [BX890.F669] 63-21390
1. Spiritual life — Middle Ages. I. Title.

Spiritual life—Middle Ages, 600-1500.

ETHELRED, Saint, 1109?-1166. 230'.2'08 s
Spiritual friendship / translated by Mary Eugenia Laker. [Kalamazoo, Mich.] : Cistercian Publications, 1974. 144 p. ; 23 cm. (Aelred of Rievaulx ; v. 2) (Cistercial Fathers series ; no. 5) Translation of De spirituali amicitia. Stamped on t.p.: Cistercian Publications, Kalamazoo, Mich. Includes index. Bibliography: p. 137-139. [BX890.E83 1974 vol. 2] [BX2349] 248'.48'2 75-152480 ISBN 0-87907-205-9 : 7.95. pbk.
1. Spiritual life—Middle Ages, 600-1500. 2. Friendship. I. Title.

SCHMIEL, David. 201'.1'0924
Via propria and via mystica in the theology of Jean le Charlier de Gerson. [St. Louis, Mo., O. Slave, ltd., 1969] vii, 107 p. 22 cm. (Concordia Seminary. School of Graduate Studies. Graduate study, no. 10) Originally presented as the author's thesis, Concordia Theological Seminary, St. Louis. Bibliography: p. [104]-107. [BX4705.G45S27 1969] 75-19933
1. Gerson, Joannes, 1363-1429. 2. Spiritual life—Middle Ages, 600-1500. 3. Mysticism—Middle Ages, 600-1500. I. Title. II. Series: Concordia Theological Seminary, St. Louis. School of Graduate Studies. Graduate study, no. 10

Spiritual life—Middle Ages, 600-1500—Addresses, essays, lectures.

MEDIEVAL and renaissance spriituality. 940.105 s
Edited by Paul Maurice Clogan. Denton, North Texas State University, 1973. xii, 248 p. 24 cm. (Medievalia et humanistica, new ser., no. 4) Includes bibliographical references. [D111.M5 n.s. no. 4] [BV4490] 914'.03'1 74-159039 ISBN 0-913904-00-7
1. Spiritual life—Middle Ages, 600-1500—Addresses, essays, lectures. 2. Civilization, Medieval—Addresses, essays, lectures. I. Clogan, Paul Maurice, ed. II. Title. III. Series.

Spiritual life - Miscellanea.

MARY Cecilia, sister, 1890- 271.
Efficiency in the spiritual life, by Sister Mary Cecilia ... New York and Cincinnati, Frederick Pustet co. (inc.) 1921. xiv p., 2 l. 19-201 p. 19 1/2 cm. [Secular name: Mary Monica Koehler] [BX4210.M3] 21-5411
I. Title.

MURPHY, Joseph, 1898- 242
Within you is the power ; (around the world with Dr. Murphy) / by Joseph Murphy. Marina del Ray Calif : DeVorss, c1977,1978 printing. 277p. ; 22 cm. Includes bibliographical references. [BF1999.M823] 77-86026 ISBN 0-87516-247-9 pbk. : 6.00
1. Spiritual life — Miscellanea. I. Title.

SPIRITUAL emphasis conference. 267.306373
Christ's adequacy for human needs; report of the nationwide series of Spiritual emphasis conferences held during the season 1934-35, under the auspices of the Commission on message and purpose of the National council of the Young men's Christian association of the U.S.A., edited by George Irving. New York, Association press [c1935] 79 p. 23 cm. [Message and purpose paper no. 12] [BV1010.S615 1934/35] 40-23871
I. Irving, George, ed. II. Young men's Christian associations. Commission on message and purpose. III. Title.

Spiritual life—Mormon authors.

DUNN, Paul H. 248.4'8933
Horizons / Paul H. Dunn. Salt Lake City, Utah : Bookcraft, c1981. viii, 171 p. ; 23 cm. [BX8656.D852] 19 81-65718 ISBN 0-88494-423-9 pbk. : 6.50
1. Spiritual life—Mormon authors. I. Title.

DUNN, Paul H. 248.4'8933
Life planning / Paul H. Dunn & Richard M. Eyre. Salt Lake City, Utah : Bookcraft, c1979. 103 p. ; 24 cm. [BX8656.D8525] 79-52230 ISBN 0-88494-374-7 pbk. : 4.95
1. Spiritual life—Mormon authors. I. Eyre, Richard M., joint author. II. Title.

LINDSTROM, Dan. 248.4'8933
Sun, shade 'n rain : moods of life / Dan Lindstrom ; foreword by Paul H. Dunn. Salt Lake City, Utah : Bookcraft, c1980. 94 p., [1] leaf of plates : ill. ; 23 cm. [BX8656.L56] 19 80-67359 ISBN 0-88494-405-0 pbk. : 3.95
1. Lindstrom, Dan. 2. Spiritual life—Mormon authors. I. Title.

MCCONKIE, Joseph F. 248'.2
Seeking the spirit / Joseph F. McConkie. Salt Lake City : Deseret Book Co., 1978 p. cm. Includes index. [BX8656.M28] 78-13372 ISBN 0-87747-721-3 : 5.95
1. Spiritual life—Mormon authors. 2. Revelation (Mormonism) I. Title.

MAXWELL, Neal A. 248.4'8933
Notwithstanding my weakness / Neal A. Maxwell. Salt Lake City, Utah : Deseret Book Co., 1981. ix, 129 p. ; 24 cm. Includes index. [BX8656.M37] 19 81-65352 ISBN 0-87747-855-4 : 6.95
1. Spiritual life—Mormon authors. I. Title.

Spiritual life—Mormon authors—Addresses, essays, lectures.

DUNN, Paul H. 248'.48'933
Look at your world / Paul H. Dunn, Maurine Ward. Salt Lake City : Bookcraft, 1978. viii, 209 p. ; 24 cm. [BX8656.D853] 78-66824 ISBN 0-88494-353-4 pbk. : 4.95
1. Spiritual life—Mormon authors—Addresses, essays, lectures. I. Ward, Maurine, joint author. II. Title.

MONSON, Thomas S., 1927- 248'.48'933
Be your best self / Thomas S. Monson. Salt Lake City : Deseret Book Co., 1979. 209 p. : ill. ; 24 cm. Includes index. [BX8656.M65] 79-54782 ISBN 0-87747-787-6 : 6.95
1. Spiritual life—Mormon authors—Addresses, essays, lectures. I. Title.

Spiritual life—Orthodox Eastern authors.

THE Ancient Fathers of the desert : 248.4'819
translated narratives from the Evergetinos on passions and perfection in Christ / by Archimandrite Chrysostomos. Brookline, Mass. : Hellenic College Press, 1980. p. cm. Translation of Mikros Euergetenos. Includes index. [BX382.M5413] 19 80-28253 ISBN 0-916586-77-4 : 8.00 pbk. : 4.95
1. Chrysostomos, Archimandrite. 2. Spiritual life—Orthodox Eastern authors.

BLOOM, Anthony, 1914- 242
Meditations on a theme: a spiritual journey, by Metropolitan Anthony (Archbishop Anthony Bloom). London, Oxford, Mowbrays, 1972. [9], 125 p. 19 cm. [BX382.B56] 72-195708 ISBN 0-264-64571-5 £0.60
1. Spiritual life—Orthodox Eastern authors. I. Title.

EVDOKIMOFF, Paul 248.2
The struggle with God, by Paul Evdokimov. Tr. by Sister Gertrude. Glen Rock, N.J., Paulist [1966] vi, 218p. 21cm. (Exploration bks.) Tr. of Les ages de la vie spirituel. Bibl. [BX382.E813] 66-24895 2.95 pap.,
1. Spiritual life—Orthodox Eastern authors. I. Title.

JOANNES, Climacus, Saint, 6th cent. 248
The ladder of divine ascent. Translated by Archimandrite Lazarus Moore. With an introd. by M. Heppell. New York, Harper [1959] 270p. illus. 21cm. (Classics of the contemplative life) Errata leaf inserted. Bibliographical footnotes. [BX382.J613 1959a] 59-10331
1. Spiritual life—Orthodox Eastern authors. I. Title.

JOANNES Climacus, Saint, 6thcent. 248'.48'19
The ladder of divine ascent / St. John Climacus. Rev. ed. Boston : Holy Transfiguration Monastery, 1978. xlv, 274 p. : ill. ; 23 cm. Translation of Scala paradisi. Includes bibliographical references and index. [BX382.J613 1978] 79-83920 ISBN 0-913026-07-7 : 12.00
1. Spiritual life—Orthodox Eastern authors. I. Title.

PAAVALI, Abp. of Karelia and All Finland, 1914- 230'.19
The faith we hold / Archbishop Paul of Finland ; translated from the Finnish by Marita Nykanen and Esther Williams. Crestwood, N.Y. : St. Vladimir's Seminary Press, 1980. p. cm. Translation of Miten uskomme. [BX320.2.P3313] 80-10404 ISBN 0-913836-61-3 pbk. : 3.95
1. Orthodox Eastern Church—Doctrinal and controversial works. 2. Spiritual life—Orthodox Eastern authors. I. Title.

THE Way of a pilgrim and The pilgrim continues his way : 248'.48'19
a new translation / by Helen Bacovcin. Garden City, N.Y. : Image Books, 1978. 196 p. ; 18 cm. Translation of Otkrovennye rasskazy strannika dukhovnomu svoemu ottsu. [BX382.O8513] 76-52000 ISBN 0-385-12400-7 pbk. : 2.45
1. Spiritual life—Orthodox Eastern authors. 2. Jesus prayer. I. Bacovcin, Helen, 1934-

Spiritual life—Poetry.

ELLARD, Virginia G.
The unity of life and spirit [poems] by Virginia G. Ellard. New York, The Grafton press [c1906] 4 p. l., 56 p. 16 1/2 x 13 1/2 cm. 6-7731
I. Title.

[PRENTISS, Elizabeth (Payson)] Mrs. 1818-1878.
Golden hours: hymns and songs of the Christian life. By the author of "Stepping heavenward" ... New York, A. D. F. Randolph & company [1874] 3 p. l., v-viii, 200 p. 19 cm. Caption title: Religious poems. Published first in 1873 under title: Religious poems. [PS2655.P5G6] 28-22649
1. Spiritual life—Poetry. I. Title.

[PRENTISS, Elizabeth (Payson) Mrs.] 1818-1878.
Religious poems, By the author of "Stepping heavenward". New York, A. D. F. Randolph & company [1873] viii, 200 p. 19 cm. Published in 1874 under title: Golden hours; hymns and songs of the Christian life. [PS2655.P5R4] 28-22650
1. Spiritual life—Poetry. I. Title.

Spiritual life—Popular works.

THE choice of God.
Springfield, Ill., Templegate, [1956] viii, 210p. 19cm.
1. Spiritual life—Popular works. I. Van Zeller, Hubert, 1905-

SPRINGLER, Augustine Joseph, 1878-
An ABC of the spiritual life. Milwaukee, Bruce Publishing Co., [1958] vii, 136 p. 21 cm.
1. Spiritual life-Popular works. I. Title.

Spiritual life—Society of Friends authors.

BRINTON, Howard Haines, 1884- 248'.48'96
Quaker journals; varieties of religious experience among Friends [by] Howard H. Brinton. Wallingford, Pa., Pendle Hill Publications [1972] xiv, 130 p. 23 cm. Bibliography: p. 122-129. [BX7738.B74] 78-188399 ISBN 0-87574-952-6 4.75
1. Spiritual life—Society of Friends authors. I. Title.

FOSTER, Richard J. 248'.48'96
Celebration of discipline : the paths to spiritual growth / Richard J. Foster. 1st ed. San Francisco : Harper & Row, c1978. x, 179 p. ; 21 cm. [BV4501.2.F655 1978] 77-20444 ISBN 0-06-062831-6 : 6.95
1. Spiritual life—Society of Friends authors. I. Title.

Spiritual life (Zen Buddhism)

ELIOT, Alexander. 294.3'4'40924 B
Zen edge / Alexander Eliot. London : Thames and Hudson, c1976. 136 p. ; 23 cm. [BQ9288.E43] 76-382477 ISBN 0-500-01171-0 : £4.00
1. Eliot, Alexander. 2. Spiritual life (Zen Buddhism) I. Title.

ELIOT, Alexander. 294.3'4'40924 B
Zen edge / Alexander Eliot ; introd. by Taitetsu Unno. 1st American ed. New York : Seabury Press, 1979, c1976. 136 p. ; 21 cm. (A Continuun book) [BQ9288.E43 1979] 78-21701 ISBN 0-8164-9355-3 pbk.: 3.95
1. Eliot, Alexander. 2. Spiritual life (Zen Buddhism) I. Title.

LU, K'uan Yu, 1898- 294.3'9
Practical Buddhism [by] Lu K'uan Yu (Charles Luk) [1st U.S. ed.] Wheaton, Ill., Theosophical Pub. House [1973, c1971] x, 167 p. 23 cm. [BQ9288.L83 1973] 72-91124 ISBN 0-8356-0212-5 5.95
1. Han-shan, 1546-1623. 2. Spiritual life (Zen Buddhism) 3. Enlightenment (Zen Buddhism) 4. Zen Buddhism—China. I. Title.

MAEZUMI, Hakuyu Taizan. 294.3'444
The hazy moon off enlightenment : on Zen practice III / Hakuyu Taizan Maezumi and Bernard Tetsugen Glassman. Los Angeles : Center Publications, c1977. xii, 194 p. : ill. ; 23 cm. (The Zen writings series) Includes indexes. [BQ9288.M33] 77-81974 ISBN 0-916820-05-X pbk. : 5.95
1. Spiritual life (Zen Buddhism) 2. Enlightenment (Zen Buddhism) I. Glassman, Bernard Tetsugen, joint author. II. Title. III. Series.

MOUNTAIN, Marian. 294.3'927
The Zen environment : the impact of Zen meditation / by Marian Mountain ; with an introduction by Dainin Katagiri Roshi and a foreword by Robert M. Pirsig. 1st ed. New York : W. Morrow, 1982. 264 p. ; 22 cm. Includes bibliographical references and index. [BQ9288.M68 1982] 19 81-11210 ISBN 0-688-00350-8 : 12.50
1. Spiritual life (Zen Buddhism) 2. Zen Buddhism. I. Title.

Spiritual life (Zen Buddhism)—Addresses, essays, lectures.

KAPLEAU, Philip, 1912- 294.3'4
Zen : dawn in the West / Philip Kapleau ; with a foreword by Albert Low. 1st ed. Garden City, N.Y. : Anchor Press, 1979. xx, 311 p. : ill. ; 22 cm. "Companion volume to The three pillars of Zen." Includes index. Bibliography: p. [277]-288. [BQ9288.K36] 77-27676 ISBN 0-385-14273-0 : 10.95
1. Spiritual life (Zen Buddhism)—Addresses, essays, lectures. 2. Zen Buddhism—Addresses, essays, lectures. I. Title.

KAPLEAU, Philip, 1912- 294.3'4
Zen : dawn in the West / Philip Kapleau ; with a pref. by Albert Low. 1st ed. New York : Anchor Books, 1980, c1979. 311 p. ; 18 cm. "Companion volume to the three pillars of Zen" Includes index. [BQ9288.K36] ISBN 0-385-14274-9 pbk. : 5.95
1. Spiritual life (Zen Buddhism) - Addresses, essays, lectures. 2. Zen Buddhism -Addresses, essays, lectures. I. Title.
L.C. card no. for 1979 Anchor Press/Doubleday ed.: 77-27676

ON Zen practice / 294.3'927 edited by Hakuyu Taizan Maezumi and Bernard Tetsugen Glassman. Los Angeles : Zen Center of Los Angeles, 1977,c1976. 2 v. : ill. ; 23 cm. (Zen writings series ; v. 1-2) Vol. 2 has subtitle: Body, breath, and mind. Includes bibliographical references and index. [BQ9288.O53] 77-70251 ISBN 0-916820-02-5 (v. 1). ISBN 0-916820-04-1 (v. 2) : pbk. : 4.00(per vol.)
1. Spiritual life (Zen Buddhism)—Addresses, essays, lectures. 2. Meditation (Zen Buddhism)—Addresses, essays, lectures. I. Maezumi, Hakuyu Taizan. II. Glassman, Bernard Tetsugen. III. Zen Center of Los Angeles. IV. Title. V. Series.

Spiritualism.

ABBOTT, Anne. 133.
The two worlds of attraction, by Anne Abbott. Boston, Mass., The Christopher publishing house [c1921] 183 p. 20 cm. "I lay no claim to the book in any way, save that...it came through my hand."--Foreword, signed: Anne Abbott. [BF1301.A13] 21-8597
1. Spiritualism. I. Title.

ABBOTT, David Phelps, 1863-
Behind the scenes with the mediums, by David P. Abbott. Chicago, The Open court publishing company; [etc., etc.] 1907. 2 p. l., [iii]-vi, 328 p. 20 1/2 cm. [BF1289.A2 1907] 7-27622
1. Spiritualism. I. Title.

ABER, William W. 133.
The dawn of another life; this book is wholly written by the star circle in full form materializations through the mediumship of William W. Aber ... [Kansas City? Mo., c1910] 327 p. incl. port. 22 1/2 cm. $1.50 [BF1301.A15] 10-15677
1. Spiritualism. I. Title.

[ABERNATHY, Elza Emmitt] 133.9 1879-
Great moments in spiritualism. A book of wisdom and knowledge of things to come. By Esnneegaapea [pseud. Denver, Esnneegaapea, inc., 19 v. illus., port. 21 cm. [BF1261.A2] 48-15435
1. Spiritualism. I. Title.

ADAMS, John Stowell. 133.
Answers to seventeen objections against spiritual intercourse and inquiries relating to the manifestations of the present time. By John S. Adams... New York, Boston, Fowlers and Wells, 1853. 3 p. l., [5]-86 p. 19 cm. [BF1251.A22] 10-32968
1. Spiritualism. I. Title.

ADAMS, John Stowell. 133.
A rivulet from the ocean of truth; an authentic and interesting narrative of the advancement of a spirit from darkness to light. Proving, by an actual instance, the influence of man, on earth, over the departed. With introductory and incidental remarks, by John S. Adams... Boston, B. Marsh, 1854. 72 p. 23 cm. [BF1291.A25] 11-3618
1. Spiritualism. I. Title.

ADAMS, John Stowell, 133. d.1893.
A letter to the Chestnut st. Congregational church, Chelsea, Mass., in reply to its charge of having become a reproach to the cause of truth, in consequence of a change of religious belief. By John S. Adams... Boston, B. Marsh, 1854. 50 p. 23 cm. [BF1275.B6A4] 28-15455
1. Spiritualism. I. Title.

ALBERTSON, Edward. 133.9
Seances and sensitives for the millions. Los Angeles, Sherbourne Press [1968] 120 p. 21 cm. [For the millions series, FM-16] [BF1261.2.A4] 68-11847
1. Spiritualism. I. Title.

ALDRICH, Bess Streeter. 133.901'3
The case for an afterlife. New York, Lancer [1968] 191p. 18cm. (74-956) .75 pap.,
1. Spiritualism. 2. Reincarnation. I. Title.

ALLEN, James Madison. 133.
Essays philosophical and practical, from the higher life, through the mediumship of James Madison Allen ... Springfield, Mo., J. M. and T. M. Allen, 1896. 92 p. 20 cm. Cover-title: Earnest words. Messages from the spiritual congress. [BF1301.A3] 13-10003
1. Spiritualism. I. Title. II. Title: Earnest words.
Contents omitted.

ALLEN, Maurice, 1886- 133.93
Our invisible friends, by Maurice Allen, with a foreword by Ralph Waldo Trine. A scientific experiment with the spirit world. New York, Liveright publishing corporation [1943] 267 p.21 cm. [BF1301.A33] 43-17479
1. Spiritualism. I. Title.

[ALPI, Mrs. Fannie 133.93 Francis]
The dawn is come, by spirit John. San Francisco, Calif., California press [c1934] 1 p. l., 157 p. 19 cm. "Reverend Mary Alice Mortensen ... through her trance mediumship [gave] these messages ... to me from my beloved son."-Introd., signed: Fannie F. Alpi. [BF1301.A37] (159.96173) 35-2126
1. Spiritualism. I. Mortensen, Mrs. Mary Alice. II. Title.

AMBLER, R.P. 133.
Elements of spiritual philosophy; being an exposition of interior principles. Written by spirits of the sixth circle. R.P. Ambler, medium. Springfield, Mass., R.P. Ambler, 1852. 76 p. 22 cm. [BF1251.A4] 10-32967
1. Spiritualism. I. Title.

AMBLER, R.P. 133.
The spiritual teacher; comprising a series of twelve lectures on the nature and development of the spirit. Written by spirits of the sixth circle. R.P. Ambler, medium... New York, R.P. Ambler, 1852. 16, 149, [1] p. 18 cm. [BF1291.A5] 11-2607
1. Spiritualism. I. Title.

ANDERSON, Roy Allan 133.9
Secrets of the spirit world. Mountain View, Calif., Pacific Pr. Pub. [1966] 92p. 19cm. [BF1031.A48] 66-18870 .30 pap.,
1. Spiritualism. I. Title.

ANDREWS, Marietta 133. Minnigerode Mrs.
The darker drink, by Marietta Minnigerode Andrews ... Boston, R. G. Badger [c1922] 2 p. l., 3-122 p. 21 cm. [BF1301.A55] 22-13009
1. Spiritualism. I. Title.

ARMSTRONG, Beulah. 133.93
Living toward mastership, arranged by Beulah Armstrong. Los Angeles, Calif., De Vorss & co. [c1937] 3 p. l., 121 p. 20 1/2 cm. Purports to be conversations with the author's mother after her death, received through a medium. cf. Pref. "First edition." [BF1301.A63] [159.96173] 42-7867
1. Spiritualism. I. Title.

ARNOLD, Adelaide, 1868- 133.
The gift of healing and spiritual science as taught by Christ, by Adelaide Arnold... Boston, Mass., Publication office Puritan linotype [c1913] 169 p. front. (port.) 20 cm. $1.00 [BF1272.A7] 14-2528
1. Spiritualism. 2. Mental healing. I. Title.

ARNOLD, Levi McKeen, 1813- 133.93 1864.
The history of the origin of all things, including The life of Jesus of Nazareth, as revealed to L. M. Arnold. New York, Vantage Press [1957] 704p. 21cm. 'A reprint of the 1852-1853 editions.' [BF1311.J5A73 1957] 55-8623
1. Spiritualism. I. Title.

ARNOLD, Levi McKeen, 1813-1864.
History of the origin of all things, given by the Lord our God through Levi M. Arnold, 1852. Revised by him through Anna A. MacDonald, 1936. Edited by Robert T. Newcomb. Kentfield, California, W-M Publishing Trust, 1961] 426 p. 24 cm. NUC67
1. Spiritualism. I. Title.

ARNOLD, Levi McKeen, 1813- 133. 1864.
The history of the origin of all things; continued from the first volume already published; and enlarged ... being now devoted to the history of the world ... By God's spirit; delivered in writing, to L. M. Arnold, medium. [New York, Fowlers and Wells] 1852. 116 p. 24 cm. [BF1311.J5A7] [BF1311.J5A73] 133. 10-33693
1. Spiritualism. I. Title.

ARNOLD, Levi McKeen, 1813- 133. 1864.
The history of the origin of all things; continued from the first volume already published; and enlarged ... being now devoted to the history of the world ... By God's spirit; delivered in writing, to L. M. Arnold, medium. [New York, Fowlers and Wells] 1852. 116 p. 23 1/2 cm. [With his The history of the origin of all things; including the history of man, from his creation to his finality. [New York? 1852] [BF1311.J5A7] [BF1311.J5A73] 133. 10-33693
1. Spiritualism. I. Title.

ARNOLD, Levi McKeen, 1813- 133. 1864.
The history of the origin of all things. [Second series] Delivered by the Lord Jesus Christ ... Written down by the medium ... L. M. Arnold ... In the year of God's grace, 1852. First printed in 1853. [New York, Stereotype association, c1853] 212 p. 22 cm. (With his The history of the origin of all things; including the history of man, from his creation to his finality. [New York?] 1852] In three books, each with special t.-p. Contents.bk. 1. A history of spirit-life, and of Paradise ... Also, a book of hymns.--bk. 2. A history of the relations of matter to life, and of bodies to spirits and to God.--bk 3. A history of the progress of man's spirit in the world of the future life. [BF1311.J5A73] 10-33694
1. Spiritualism. I. Title.

ARNOLD, Levi McKeen, 1813- 133.96 1864.
History of the origin of all things, given by the Lord thy God through His holy medium, L. M. Arnold, Poughkeepsie, N.Y. ... 1851; revised by Him through His holy medium Anola, Asheville, N.C., 1936; edited by Robert T. Newcomb. [Asheville, N.C., Biltmore press, 1936] 2 v. 23 1/2 cm. [BF1311.J5A73 1936] [159.96173] 37-6445
1. Spiritualism. I. MacDonald, Anna Addams, 1871- II. Newcomb, Robert Thomas, 1914- ed. III. Title.

ARSCOTT, Albert John 133.93 Loram, 1883-
Proof of a life beyond. Copyright ... by Albert J. L. Arscott. K[ansas] C[ity] Mo., Printed by Warden-Glore printing service, c 1937. 4 p. l., 122 p. ports. 19 cm. [BF1261.A7] 159.96173 38-2107
1. Spiritualism. I. Title.

[ARTHUR, William] 133.
Our unseen companions, by Sancho Quixote [pseud.] New York, W. Arthur [c1896] xiv, [15]-265 p. 19 1/2 cm. [BF1042.A76] CA 11
1. Spiritualism. I. Title.

ASSOCIATION of Spiritualists 289 of Mantua.
Organization and platform of principles of the Association of Spiritualists, Mantua, Portage County, Ohio. Garrettsville, Ohio, W. Peirce, printer, 1880. 80 p. 14 cm. [BX9798.S7A8] 48-33774
I. Title.

BABBITT, Edwin Dwight, 1828- 133.
Religion as revealed by the material and spiritual universe ... By Edwin D. Babbitt. New York, Babbitt & co. [c1881] vi. [7]-365 p. illus. (incl. ports.) 20 cm. [BF1251.B22] 1034678
1. Spiritualism. I. Title.

BACH, Marcus, 1906- 291.42
Spiritual breakthroughs for our time. [1st ed.] Garden City, N. Y., Doubleday, 1965. vi, 162 p. 22 cm. [BF1999.B2] 65-22578
I. Title.

BACH, W H. 133.
Mediumship and its development, and how to mesmerize to assist development, by W. H. Bach ... Saint Paul, Minn., W. H. Bach, 1893. 65 p. 18 cm. [BF1286.B2] 11-4766
1. Spiritualism. I. Title.

[BAILEY, Daniel E] 133.
Thoughts from the inner life ... Boston, Colby & Rich, 1886. 224 p. front. (port.) 22 cm. Introduction signed: D. E. Bailey. [BF1301.S9] 10-33691
1. Spiritualism. I. Title.

BAILEY, Wilson Gill, 1865- 133.
No, not dead; they live! a study of personal immortality from the standpoint of a physician and surgeon, by Wilson G. Bailey, M.D. [Camden, N. J., I. F. Huntzinger co., c1923] 2 p. l., xi, 254 p. front. (port.) 20 cm. [BF1261.B26] 23-8889
1. Spiritualism. I. Title.

BAILIE, Alfred J 133.9
Spiritualism exposed; or, The inner circle. [1st ed.] New York, Vantage Press [c1957] 91p. illus. 21cm. [BF1301.B15] 58-30005
1. Spiritualism. I. Title.

BAIRD, Alexander T ed. 133.072
One hundred cases for survival after death. New York, B. Ackerman [1944] 224 p. 24 cm. Bibliography: p. 223-224. [BF1261.B264 1944] 44-9591
1. Spiritualism. I. Title.

BAKER, Clara Worth. 133.9
Where are the dead? Can we communicate with them? In search of a lost wisdom ... [San Diego? Calif., 1950] xv. 118 p. 23 cm. [BF1261.B266] 50-2071
1. Spiritualism. I. Title.

BALDWIN, George Colfax, 133. 1817-1899.
... *The witch of Endor,* and modern spiritism. A lecture, by Geo. C. Baldwin ... Troy, N. Y., Times book printing establishment, 1872. 33 p. 22 cm. At head of title: The fifteenth of the series of Sabbath evening lectures, on "Misunderstooc Scriptures." [BF1042.B2] 27-12425
1. Spiritualism. I. Title.

BALFOUR, George William, 133. 1853-
... *The Ear of Dionysius:* farther scripts affording evidence of personal survival, by the Right Hon. G. W. Balfour; with a discussion of the evidence by Miss F. Melian Shawell [!] and a reply by Mr. Balfour. Reprinted by authority from the proceedings of the Society for psychical research. New York, H. Holt and company, 1920. 3 p. l., 3-134 p. illus. 19 1/2 cm. (The psychic series) [BF1301.B2] 20-20213
1. Spiritualism. 2. Psychical research. I. Stawell, Florence Melian. II. Society for psychical research, London. III. Title.

BALLOU, Adin, 1803-1890. 133.
An exposition of views respecting the principal facts, causes, and peculiarities involved in spirit manifestations; together with interesting phenomenal statements and communications. by Adin Ballou ... Boston, B. Marsh, 1852. vi, [7]-256 p. 17 1/2 cm. [BF1251.B25] 10-34679
1. Spiritualism. I. Title.

BALLOU, Adin, 1803-1890. 133.
An exposition of views respecting the principal facts, causes and peculiarities involved in spirit manifestations, together with interesting phenomenal statements and communications. by Adin Ballou ... 2d ed. Boston, B. Marsh, 1853. xii, 258 p. front. (port.) 19 1/2 cm. [BF1251.B25 1853] 28-7134
1. Spiritualism. I. Title.

BAMBER, L Mrs. Kelway, 133.91
Claude's book, ed. by L. Kelway-Bamber, with an introduction letter from Sir Oliver Lodge. New York, H. Holt and company, 1919. xxiii, 136 p. 19 1/2 cm. Records of spiritualistic seances and letters. [BF1301.B23] 19-26570
1. Spiritualism. 2. European war, 1914-1918—Personal narratives, English. I. Bamber, Claude H. Kelway, 1895-1915. II. Title.

BARBANELL, Maurice. 133.9
This is spiritualism. London, Tandem; New York, Award [1967,c.1959] 160p. 18cm. (A286X) [BF1261.2 B3] .60 pap.,
1. Spiritualism. I. Title.

BARBER, Charles Fitch. 133.93
Our garden, and glimpses through it's secret gate [by] Charles Fitch Barber; photographs by the author. Poland, Or., Binfords & Mort [c1939] 135, [1] p. plates, 2 port. (incl. front.) 20 1/2 cm. [(150.96173] [BF1283.B35A3] 39-20423
1. Spiritualism. I. Title.

BARKER, Elsa.
Last letters from the living dead man, written down by Elsa Barker, with an introduction. New York, M. Kennerley, 1919. 240 p. 19 cm. $1.50 "The third and last of the Living dead man series, was written between February, 1917, and February, 1918." The author states that these spiritualistic messages are from Judge David P. Hatch, of Los Angeles. [BF1391.B3 1919] 19-11582
1. Spiritualism. 2. European war, 1914-1918—Miscellanea. I. Hatch, David Patterson. II. Title.

BARKER, Elsa Mrs. 133.91
Letters from a living dead man, written down by Elsa Barker; with an introduction. New York, M. Kennerley, 1914. 3 p. l., 5-291 p. 19 1/2 cm. [BF1301.B3 1914 a] 14-8217
1. Spiritualism. I. Title.

BARKER, Elsa. 133.96
Letters from a living dead man, written down by Elsa Barker; with an introduction. New York, E. P. Dutton & company [c1920] 3 p. l., 5-291 p. 19 1/2 cm. [BF1301.B3 1920] [159.96173] 40-21009
1. Spiritualism. I. Title.

BARKER, Elsa Mrs.
War letters from the living dead man, written down by Elsa Barker, with an introduction. New York, M. Kennerley, 1915. 3 p. l., 318 p. port. 19 cm. The author states that these spiritualistic messages are from Judge David P. Hatch, of Los Angeles. [BF1310.B32 1915] 15-23633
1. Spiritualism. 2. European war, 1914-1918—Miscellanea. I. Hatch, David Patterson. II. Title.

BARNARD, Henry E. 133.9
Evolutionistic spirtualism, the new religion--a scientific ladder to heaven. New York, Carlton [c.1963] 65p. 21cm. (Reflection bk.) 2.00
I. Title.

BARNES, Ernest William, 1874-
... *Spiritualism and the Christian faith,* by the Reverend E.W. Barnes ... London, New York [etc.] Longmans, Green and co., 1918. 60 p. 20 cm. (Liverpool diocesan board of divinity publications. XVIII) A 20
1. Spiritualism. I. Title.

BARNES, Mary Stephenson. 133.93
Long distance, still calling. Los Angeles, De Vorss [1952] 143 p. 21 cm. [BF1301.B355] 53-20858
1. Spiritualism. I. Title.

BARNES, Mary Stephenson. 133.93
Long distance calling, a record of other world communications through automatic writing, by Mary Stephenson Barnes. New York, The William-Frederick press, 1945. ix, [1] p., 1 l., 114 p. front. (facsim.) 24 cm. [BF1301.B35] 45-3773
1. Spiritualism. I. Title.

BARRETT, Florence 133.93
Elizabeth (Perry) Lady ed.
Personality survives death; messages from Sir William Barrett, edited by his wife, with a foreword by Canon R. J. Campbell, D. D. ... London, New York [etc.] Longmans, Green and co. [1937] xivi, 203, [1] p. front. (port.) 19 cm. "Communications from the late Sir William Barrett ... to his wife through the mediumship of Mrs. Osborne Leonard."--Foreword. "First published, 1937." [BF1311.B3B3] 159.96173 38-16335
1. Barrett, Sir William Fletcher, 1844-1925. 2. Spiritualism. I. Leonard, Glady's Osborne. Mrs. II. Title.

BARRETT, Harrison Delivan, 133.
1863-1911? ed.
Life work of Mrs. Cora L. V. Richmond, Comp. and ed. by Harrison D. Barrett. Published under the auspices of the National spiritualists association of the U.S.A. Chicago, Hack & Anderson, printers, 1895. xvii, 759 p. 3 port. (incl. front.) 21 cm. [BF1283.R45B3] 14-15342
1. Richmond, Mrs. Cora L. v. (Scott) 1810- 2. Spiritualism. I. Title.

BARRETT, J O. 133.
The Gadarene: or, Spirits in prison. By J. O. Barrett and J. M. Peebles ... Boston, Colby and Rich, 1874. 232 p. 20 cm. [BF1251.B32] 10-34681
1. Spiritualism. I. Peebles, James Martin, 1822- joint author. II. Title.

BARRETT, Joseph O. 920.9
The spiritual pilgrim: a biography of James M. Pebbles By J. O. Barrett ... 2d ed. Boston, W. White and company, 1872. 303 p. front. (port.) 22 cm. [BF1283.P4B3 1872] 32-5794
1. Pebbles, James Martin, 1822-1922. 2. Spiritualism. I. Title.

BARRETT, Joseph O. 133.
The spiritual pilgrim: a biography of James M. Pebbles. By J. O. Barrett ... 3d ed. Boston, W. White and company. 1872. 303 p. front. (port.) 22 cm. [BF1283.P4B] A 23
1. Pebbles, James Martin, 1822-1922. 2. Spiritualism. I. Title.

BARRETT, Joseph O. 920.9
The spiritual pilgrim: a biography of James M. Pebbles. By J. O. Barrett ... 4th ed. Boston. Colby & Rich. 1872. 303 p. front. (port.) 22 cm. [BF1283.P4 B3 1878] 32-4056
1. Pebbles, James Martin, 1822-1922. 2. Spiritualism. I. Title.

BARRETT, William Fletcher, 133.
Sir 1844-1925.
On the threshold of the unseen; an examination of the phenomena of spiritualism and of the evidence for survival after death, by Sir William F. Barrett ... London, K. Paul, Trench, Trubner & co., ltd.; New York, E. P. Dutton & co., 1917. xx, 336 p. 19 cm. [BF1061.B3] 17-25450
1. Spiritualism. 2. Psychical research. I. Title.

BARRETT, William Fletcher, 133.07
Sir 1844-1925.
On the threshold of the unseen; an examination of the phenomena of spiritualism and of the evidence for survival after death, by Sir William F. Barrett ... with an introduction by James H. Hyslop ... New York, E. P. Dutton & company [1920] xviii, 336. p. 21 cm. "First printing, November, 1917 ... Fourth, July, 1920." [BF1031.B3 1920] 32-6439
1. Spiritualism. 2. Psychical research. I. Title.

BARRINGTON, Arthur H. 133.
Anti-Christian cults. An attempt to show that spiritualism, theosophy, and Christian science are devoid of supernatural powers and are contrary to the Christian religion. By A. H. Barrington ... With a commendatory by the Bishop of Milwaukee. Milwaukee, Wis., The Young churchman co.; [etc., etc., c1898] 170 p. 19 cm. [BF1042.B25] 10-22940
1. Spiritualism. 2. Theosophy. 3. Christian science. I. Title.

BARTLETT, George C. 133.
The Salem seer. reminiscences of Charles H. Foster, by George C. Bartlett. New York. Lovell, Gestefeld & company [1891] 157 p. front. (port.) 20 cm. [BF1283.F65B3] 26-0958
1. Foster, Charles Henry, 1833-1885. 2. Spiritualism. I. Title.

BARTLETT, George C. 920.9
The Salem seer, reminiscences of Charles H. Foster, by George C. Bartlett. New York, United States book company [1891] 157 p. front. (port.) 19 cm. Cover-title: Spiritualism: the Salem seer, reminiscences of Charles H. Foster. [BF1283.F65B3 1891a] 34-13035
1. Foster, Charles Henry, 1833-1885. 2. Spiritualism. I. Title.

BATCHELDER, Lottie L. 133.93
Psychic revealments comprising a series of lectures on the nature and development of the spirit, written on black paper independently through the psychic power of Dr. H. Robert Moore and presented to Lottie Batchelder ... [San Diego, Printed by Arts & crafts press, 1944] vii, 128 p. illus. (port.) 21 1/2 cm. "First edition." [BF1261.B28] 45-1478
1. Spiritualism. I. Moore, H. Robert. II. Title.

BATES, Emily Katharine. 133.
Do the dead depart? and other questions, by E. Katharine Bates ... New York, Dodge publishing company [c1908] 263 p. 20 cm. [BF1261.B3] 8-28314
1. Spiritualism. I. Title.

BATES, Emily Katharine. 133.
Our living dead; some talks with unknown friends, by E. Katharine Bates. With a reface by Major-General Sir Alfred E. Turner ... 2d impression. London, K. Paul, Trench, Trubner & co., ltd; New York, E. P. Dutton and co., 1917. 160 p. 15 cm. [BF1261.B33] 22-800
1. Spiritualism. I. Title.

BATTEN, John, pseud., ed. 133.9
The opening door; communications from Henry Manning, Charles Kingsley. Samuel Wilberforce, Thomas More, and others, edited by John Batten. London, K. Paul, Trench, Trubner & co., ltd.; New York, E. P. Dutton & co., 1918. ix, 99 p. 19 cm. "The letters printed in this volume were addressed to my wife and myself, and received by inspirational writing through the hand of Mary Fuller ... For obvious reasons we have adopted pseudonyms both for ourselves and for Miss 'Fuller'."--Introd. [BF1301.B37] 32-4068
1. Spiritualism. I. Title.

BAUGH, R P 1839- 133
Book of heavenly teachings, by R. P. Baugh. Dallas, Tex., Johnston printing & adv. co., 1912. 2 p. l., [7]-120 p. pl. 23 cm. [BF1272.B3] 18-4896
1. Spiritualism. I. Title.

BAXTER, Florence. 133.93
Many roads, many mansions; a journey in faith, by Florence and Robert Baxter. Limited ed. Toronto, Akashie Publications [1957] 182p. 23cm. [BF1301.B373] 57-46322
1. Spiritualism. I. Baxter, Robert writer on religion joint author. II. Title.

BAXTER, Francis K. 133
Does telepathy explain spiritualism? By Francis K. Baxter ... New York, Chicago [etc.] Fleming H. Revell company [c1920] 224 p. 19 1/2 cm. [BF1171.B3] 20-20211
1. Spiritualism. 2. Thought-transference. I. Title.

BEACH, Emily J. 133.
The unsealed book; or, Sequel to "Misunderstood." By E. J. Beach ... Boston, The author, 1877. 502 p. 22 1/2 cm. [BF1291.B35] 11-4773
1. Spiritualism. I. Title.

BEARD, Paul 133.9013
Survival of death: for and against. London, Hodder & Stoughton [1966] xi, 177p. 21cm. Bibl. [BF1031.B32] 66-70586 5.00
1. Spiritualism. 2. Future life. I. Title.
Available from Hillary House, New York.

BEATTY, James McGregor. 133.
Pesky problems for positive preachers, by James McGregor Beatty ... New York, The Torch press, inc., 1921. xvi, 17-136 p. 20 1/2 cm. Avertising matter: p. 132-136. [BF1275.C5B4] 21-10273
1. Spiritualism. I. Title.

BECKER, Henry J. 133
Dr. Becker's brownies rummaging among the mediums of modern spiritualism, their confederates and their baggage. By Dr. Lit [pseud.] ... v. 1- [Huntington, Ind., M. F. Keiter] 1900. v. illus. 19 1/2 cm. [BF1272.B4] 0-2493
1. Spiritualism. I. Title.

BEECHER, Charles, 1815-1900. 133.
A review of the "spiritual manifestations." Read before the Congregational association of New York and Brooklyn, By Charles Beecher ... New York, G.P. Putnam & co., 1853. viii, [9]-75 p. 19 cm. [BF1042.B4] 10-29941
1. Spiritualism. I. Title.

BEECHER, Charles, 1815-1900. 133.
Spiritual manifestations. By Charles Beecher ... Boston, Lee & Shepard; New York, C.T. Dillingham, 1879. 1 p. l., 7-322 p. incl. map. 20 cm. [BF1251.B42] 10-34682
1. Spiritualism. I. Title.

BEHR, Herman, ed. 133.9
... *The new divinity;* lectures by Henry Ward Beecher, John Wycliffe, John Bunyan, Martin Luther, Mary Baker, G. Eddy, Emmanuel Swedenborg, and others; with a foreword, edited and published by Herman Behr. New York, H. Behr; London, K. Paul, Trench, Trubner & co., ltd. [c1929] xi, 251 p. 22 1/2 cm. (His Transcendental series. v. 1) Spiritualistic messages. [BF1290.B4 vol. 1] 30-23055
1. Spiritualism. I. Beecher, Henry Ward, 1813-1887. II. Title.

BEHR, Herman, 1847- 133.9
Letters from eternity, by Abraham Lincoln, George Washington, Benjamin Franklin, John Knox, Thomas Carlyle, Percy Bysshe Shelley, with a foreword, edited and published by Herman Behr. New York, H. Behr; London, K. Paul, Trench, Trubner & co., ltd. [c1930] vii, 92 p. 19 1/2 cm. [BF1290.B35] 30-28325
1. Spiritualism. I. Title.

BEIGHLE, Nellie (Craib) 133.
Mrs. 1851-
Book of knowledge; psychic facts, by Dr. Nellie Beighle ... [New York] For the author by the Alliance publishing co. [c1903] 3 p. l., 534 p. front., plates, ports. 24 1/2 cm. [BF1283.B4] 3-32537
1. Spiritualism. I. Title.

BEIGHLE, Nellie (Craib) 133.
Mrs. 1851-
Book of knowledge, psychic facts; by Dr. Nellie Beighle ... 3d ed. [San Francisco] Hicks-Judd company, 1911. 3 p. l., 561 p. plates, ports. 24 cm. [BF1283.B43] 12-932
1. Spiritualism. I. Title.

BELL. CLARK, 1832-1918, ed. 133.
Spiritism, hypmotism and telepathy, as involved in the case of Mrs. Leonora E. Piper and the Society of psychical research, by Clark Bell ... and the discussion thereon by Thompson day Hudson, LL. D., and more than twenty observers ... 2d ed. ... New York, Medico-legal journal, 1904. 3 p. l., 191 p. front., illus. (ports.) 23 cm. [BF1283.P6B3 1904] 4-29369
1. Piper, Leonora E. Mrs. 2. Spiritualism. 3. Hypnotism. 4. Thought-transference. I. Hudson, Thomson Jay, 1834-1903. II. Title.

BELLEGAY, Michael M. 133.9
Man's eternal progress; scientific, religious, informative fundamentals of every day's life. New York, Vantage Press [1952] 151 p. 22 cm. [BF1261.B38] 52-6964
1. Spiritualism. I. Title.

*BELT, Guy Chester, 133.9
d.1969.
Love's answer from eternity. With a foreword by Virginia Schroeder. New York, Exposition Pr. [1973] 92 p. 21 cm. [BF1301] ISBN 0-682-47696-X 4.00
1. Belt, Jeanne Claire. 2. Spiritualism. 3. Spirit writing. I. Title.

BENEDICT, Anna Louise. 133.93
Mrs.
The continuity of life, by Anna Louise Benedict. Boston, The Christopher publishing house [c1933] 171 p. 22 cm. [BF1301.B38] 159.96173 33-19232
1. Spiritualism. I. Title.

BENEDICT, Anna Louise. 133.98
Mrs.
The continuity of life, by Anna Louise Benedict. Boston, Chapman and Grimes [c1940] 95 p. 21 cm. "New edition." [BF1301.B33 1940] 159.96173 41-8431
1. Spiritualism. I. Title.

BENOLIEL, Evangeline. 133.93
Apart, yet not afar [by] Evelyn Benton Seeley [pseud.] New York, Vantage Press [1951] 128 p. 23 cm. [BF1301.B384] 51-14513
1. Spiritualism. I. Title.

BERNICIE, Lillian. 133.
The book of Clifford, or, "The soul of my son speaketh to me"; from the original dictation as transcribed without alterations, by Lillian Bernice. Boston, New York, The Cornhill publishing company, 1922. xviii, 199 p. 20 cm. [BF1301.B42] 22-19627
1. Spiritualism. I. Bland, Clifford. II. Title.

BIRD, J. Malcolm, 1886- 133.
My psychic adventures, by J. Malcolm Bird ... New York, Scientific American publishing co., 1924. 2 p. l., [iii]-iv p., 1 l., 309 p. front. (port.) 20 cm. Published 1923. [BF1286.B5] 23-16089

1. Spiritualism. 2. Psychical research. I. Title.

BIRD, James Malcolm, 1886- 133.
"Margery" the medium, by J. Malcolm Bird ... Boston, Small, Maynard & company [c1925] 1 p. l., v-xi, 518 p. front., plates, ports., facsims., diagrs. 21 cm. [BF1283.C85B5] 25-8086
1. Crandon, Mrs. Mina (Stinson) 2. Spiritualism. I. Title.

BIRD, James Malcolm, 1886- 133.
My psychic adventures, by J. Malcolm Bird ... New York, Scientific American publishing co., 1924. 2 p. l., [iii]-iv p., 1 l., 309 p. front. (port.) 19 1/2 cm. Published 1923. [BF1286.B5] 23-16089
1. Spiritualism. 2. Psychical research. I. Title.

BISHOP, Richmond Leander, 1868- 133.
The divine gift of mediumship; lectures on the problems of life, given by Richmond L. Bishop at the School of natural science, Boston, Massachusetts, 1914-1915. Boston, Christopher publishing house [c1915] 4 p. l., [13]-195 p. front. port.) 19 cm. $1.00 [BF1286.B55] 15-16789
1. Spiritualism. I. Title.

BISHOP, Richmond Leander, 1868- 133.9
The divine gift of mediumship; lectures on the problems of life given by Richmond L. Bishop, at the School of natural science Boston. 2d ed., 1918. Boston, Christopher publishing house [1918] 4 p. l., [13]-195 p. front. (port.) 19 1/2 cm. [BF1286.B55 1918] 32-4076
1. Spiritualism. I. Title.

BLACKMORE, Simon Augustine, 1848- 133.
Spiritism, facts and frauds, by Simon Augustine Blackmore, S. J. With an introduction by the Right Rev. Joseph Schrembs ... New York, Cincinnati [etc.] Benziger brothers. 1924. 535 p. 20 1/2 cm. [BF1261.B47] 25-1673
1. Spiritualism. I. Title.

BLAKE, Cornelia F. 261
The kingdom of God, its whereabouts, whence we come; whither we go [by] Cornelia F. Blake. Los Angeles, Cal. [c1922] 1 p. l., 5-82 p. 17 1/2 cm. [BT94.B6] ca 23
1. Spiritualism. I. Title.

BLAND, Thomas Augustus, 1830- FIC
"In the world celestial" by T. A. Bland ... With an introduction by Rev. H. W. Thomas ... 4th ed. Chicago, T. A. Bland & co., 1905. 7 p. l., [9]-159, [2] p. front. 18 cm. [PZ3.B61 I5] 133.9 32-19532
1. Spiritualism. I. Title.

BODIN, Edward Longstreet, 1894- 133.93
Upper purgatory. Daytons Beach, Fla., College Pub. Co. [1955] 159p. 23cm. [BF1301.B53] 55-32819
1. Spiritualism. I. Title.

BODIN, Edward Longstreet, 1894- 133.93
Upper purgatory. Daytons Beach, Fla., College Pub. Co. [1955] 159p. 23cm. [BF1301.B53] 55-32819
1. Spiritualism. I. Title.

BOGERT, Cornelia H. 133.93
With brushes of comet's hair; a record of psychic paintings and their interpretations through Emma Merrill, an artist of old New England, and an ancient Persian. Introd. by Hereward Carrington. New York, Exposition Press [1950] 165 p. plates. 23 cm. [BF1347.B6] 50-7685
1. Spiritualism. I. Merrill, Emma, 1681-1702. II. Title.

BOND, Frederick Bligh, 1864- 133.93
The secret of immortality, by Frederick Bligh Bond ... Boston, Mass., Marshall Jones company [c1934] 2 p. l., viii, 189 p. illus., diagrs. 21 1/2 cm. J. A. Bartlett, using the name, John Alleyne, was the automatist. [BF1301.B55] [[159.96173]] 34-29172
1. Spiritualism. 2. Automatism. I. Bartlett, John Allen. II. Title.

BORGIA, Anthony V 133.93
Life in the world unseen. Foreword by John Andersen.[1st American ed.] New York, Citadel Press [1957] 191p. 19cm. [BF1311.B4B6 1957] 58-2144
1. Benson, Robert Hugh, 1871-1914. 2. Spiritualism. I. Title.

BOWERS, Edwin Frederick, 1871- 133.9
Spiritualism's challenge; submitting to modern thinkers conclusive evidence of survival, by Dr. Edwin F. Bowers ... New York, N.Y., National library press [c1936] 5 p. l., 294 p. 22 cm. [BF1261.B6] 159.9617 39-24338
1. Spiritualism. I. Title.

[BOYLAN, Grace (Duffie)] 1861?-1935. 133.93
Thy son liveth; messages from a soldier to his mother. Boston, Little, Brown and company, 1943. vi p., 1 l., 84 p. 17 1/2 cm. First published in 1918. [D639.P8B65 1943] 43-8577
1. Spiritualism. 2. European war, 1914-1918. I. Title.

BRACE, Josephine M. Mrs. 133.
The descending light; a series of lessons from higher intelligences on the philosophy of life ... by Mrs. Josephine M. Brace ... [Chicago, Press of J. F. Higgins, [c1922] 334 p. front. (port.) 21 cm. [BF1301.B6] 22-19626
1. Spiritualism. I. Title.

BRACE, Josephine M. 133.9
Powers within the mind; a series of lessons from higher intelligences on the philosophy of life. [1st ed.] Los Angeles, De Vorss [1952] 151 p. 21 cm. [BF1301.B62] 52-64336
1. Spiritualism. I. Title.

BRACE, Josephine McHugh, 1879-1928. 133
The great white light; a series of lessons on the proper use of your power of thought, from higher intelligences on the philosophy of life ... Los Angeles, Harmonial Philosophy [1956] 151p. 22cm. [BF1301.B614] 56-38468
1. Spiritualism. I. Title.

BRACE, Josephine McHugh, 1879-1928. 133.9
Powers within the mind; a series of lessons from higher intelligences on the philosophy of life. [1st ed.] Los Angeles, De Vorss [1952] 151p. 21cm. [BF1301.B62] 52-64336
1. Spiritualism. I. Title.

BRACKETT, Edward Augustus, 1818-1908. 133.
Materialized apparitions: if not beings from another life, what are they? By E. A. Brackett. Boston, Colby and Rich, 1886. 182 p. 20 cm. [BF1383.B8] 10-33711
1. Spiritualism. I. Title.

BRACKETT, Edward Augustus, 1818-1908. 133.9
The world we live in, by E. A. Brackett ... Boston, Banner of light publishing co., 1903. 121 p. front. (port.) diagr. 21 cm. [BF1261.B75] 32-5799
1. Spiritualism. I. Title.

BRAGDON, Claude Fayette, 1866- 133.
Oracle, arranged, ed. and introduced by Claude Bragdon. Rochester, N. Y., The Manas press, 1921. 4 p. l., 64 p. front. (port.) 17 cm. "The communications here presented ... were received through automatic writing." [BF1301.B65] 21-17647
1. Spiritualism. I. Title.

BRAGDON, Claude Fayette, 1866- 133.
Oracle [by] Claude and Eugenie Bragdon. New York, A. A. Knopf, 1941. 5 p. l., 3-72 p., 2 l. incl. facsim. front. (port.) 20 cm. "Second edition." "The communications here presented ... were received [by Mrs. Bragdon] through authomatic writing."--Introd. [BF1301.B65 1941] A 42
1. Spiritualism. I. Bragdon, Eugenie Julier (Macaulay) Mrs. d. 1920. II. Title.

[BRANNAN, H K] 133.
The guide against seducing spirits. Satanic revelation. Spritiualism exposed ... Nashville, Tenn., 1880. 76 p. 20 cm. [BF1555.B8] 11-6698

1. Spiritualism. I. Title.

[BRIGGS, G. C.] supposed author. 133.91
A true history of Jesus the Christ, being a detailed account of the manner of His birth, and of all that He did and suffered up to the time of His crucifixion. Dictated by Himself. Boston, W.F. Brown & co., printers, 1874. 96 p. 21cm. "The communications were given by ... [a] medium whilst in a state of trance." Probably written and pub. by G.C. Briggs. Work not completed in this pamphlet. "Pamphlets ... to follow ... which will continue and complete the life of Jesus, and which may be five or six in number equal to 500 or 600 pages." cf. Introd., and note on inside of cover. No more published? [BF1311.J5B8] 10-33696
1. Spiritualism. I. Title. II. Title: Jesus the Christ.

[BRILE] Tile, Mrs. 1873- 133.
Am I a human radio? By Tile Singh Bluwai [pseud.] Los Angeles, Singh Bluwai company [c1924] 221, [2] p. 20 cm. [BF1301.B68] 24-12917
1. Spiritualism. I. Title.

BRITTAN, Samuel Bryon, d.1883. 133.
The battle-ground of the spiritual reformation. By S.B. Brittan ... New York, Boston, Mass., Pub. for the author, by Colby & Rich, 1882. 2 p. l., iii-xi, 510 p. front. (port.) 19 1/2 cm. [BF1261.B8] 11-3135
1. Spiritualism. I. Title.

BRITTAN, Samuel Byron. 133.
Discussion of the facts and philosophy of ancient and modern spiritualism. By S. B. Brittan and Dr. B. W. Richmond ... New York, Partridge & Brittan, 1853. ix, [3]-377, [1] p. 23 cm. (Partridge and Brittan's spiritual library) "Originally published in the Spiritual telegraph."--p. viii. [BF1251.B82] 10-34881
1. Spiritualism. I. Richmond, B.W., joint author. II. Title.

BRITTAN, Samuel Byron. 133.9
An oral discussion of spiritualism. By S.B. Brittan and Dr. D.D. Hanson. Reported in phonetic shorthand by Charles B. Collar... New York, S.T. Munson & co., 1858. 145 p. 23 1/2 cm. [BF1041.B7] 32-6514
1. Spiritualism. I. Hanson, D.D. II. Title.

BRITTAN, Samuel Byron. 133.07
...A review of Rev. Charles Beecher's report concerning the spiritual manifestations; wherein his conclusions are carefully examined and tested by a comparison with his premises, with reason, and with the facts. By S.B. Brittan. New York, Partridge and Brittan, 1853. viii, [9]-78 p. 19 cm. (Partridge and Brittan's spiritual library) [BF1042.B4B7] 32-6517
1. Beecher, Charles, 1815-1900. A review of the spiritual manifestations. 2. Spiritualism. I. Title.

BRITTAN, Samuel Byron.
The tables turned; a brief review of Rev. C. M. Butler, D.D. By S.B. Brittan ... New York, Partridge and Brittan, 1854. 63 p. 20 1/2 cm. A review of C.M. Butler's sermon entitled "Modern necromancy." A 18
1. Butler, Clement Moore, 1810-1890. Modern necromancy. 2. Spiritualism. I. Title.

BRITTEN, Emma (Hardinge) Mrs. 133.
Modern American spiritualism; a twenty years' record of the communion between earth and the world of spirits. By Emma Hardinge. New York, The author, 1870. 2 p. l., iii-viii, 9-565 p. front., plates, ports., fold. facsim. 24 cm. Added t.-p., engr. [BF1241.B7] 10-34670
1. Spiritualism. I. Title.

BRITTEN, Emma (Hardinge) Mrs. 133.9
Modern American spiritualism; a twenty years' record of the communion between earth and the world of spirits. By Emma Hardinge. (2nd ed.) New York, The author, 1870. 3 p. l., [v]-viii, 9-565 p. front., illus., plates, ports., fold. facsim. 24 cm. Added t.-p., illustrated. [BF1241.B7 1870a] 32-19325
1. Spiritualism. I. Title.

BRITTEN, Emma (Hardinge) Mrs. 133.
Nineteenth century miracles; or, Spirits and their work in every country of the earth. A complete historical compendium of the great movement known as "modern spiritualism". By Emma Hardinge Britten ... New York W. Britten, 1884. vi, [2], 556 p. front., plates, ports., facsims. 24 cm. Printed in Great Britain. [BF1241.B8] 10-34469
1. Spiritualism. I. Title.

BRITTEN, Emma (Hardinge) Mrs., d.1899. 133.9
Modern American spiritualism; a twenty years' record of the communion between earth and the world of spirits. By Emma Hardinge. 3d ed. New York, The author, 1870. 3 p. l., [v]-viii, 9-565 p. front., illus., plates, ports., fold. facsim. 24 cm. Added t.-p., illustrated. [BF1241.B7 1870b] 32-22233
1. Spiritualism. I. Title.

BRITTEN, Emma (Hardinge) d.1899.
Modern American spiritualism: a twenty years' record of the communion between earth and the world of spirits. By Emma Hardinge. (4th ed.) New York, The author, 1870. 3 p. l., [v]-viii, 9-500 p. 1 illus. 23 1/2 cm. Added t.-p., illustrated. [BF1241B7 1870c] 46-35806
1. Spiritualism. I. Title.

[BRITTEN, William] supposed author. 133.
Art magic; or, Mundane, sub-mundane and super-mundane spiritism. A treatise in three parts and twenty-three sections; descriptive of art magic, spiritism, the different orders of spirits in the universe known to be related to, or in communication with man; together with directions for invoking, controlling, and discharging spirits, and the uses and abuses, dangers and possibilities of magical art ... New York, The author, 1876. 2 p. l., 467 p. front., illus. (incl. ports.) plates. 22 1/2 cm. Copyrighted by William Britten. Edited by Emma Hardinge Britten. [BF1251.B83] 10-34683
1. Spiritualism. 2. Magic. I. Britten, Mrs. Emma (Hardinge) ed. II. Title.

[BRITTEN, William] 133
Ghost land; or, Researches into the mysteries of occultism. Illustrated in a series of autobiographical sketches ... By the author of "Art magic"; with extracts from the records of "Magical seances," etc., etc. Tr. and ed. by Emma Hardinge Britten ... Boston, Pub. for the editor, 1876. 2 p. l., [3]-484 p., 1 l. 23 cm. [BF1611.B7] 11-14366
1. Spiritualism. I. Britten, Mrs. Emma (Hardinge) ed. II. Title.

[BRITTEN, William] supposed author. 133
Ghost land; or, Researches into the mysteries of occultism. Illustrated in a series of autobiographical sketches ... By the author of "Art magic"; with extracts from the records of "magical seances", etc., etc. Translated and edited by Emma Hardinge Britten ... Chicago, Ill., Progressive thinker publishing house, 1897. 357 p. port. 20 1/2 cm. [BF1611.B7 1897] 32-21739
1. Spiritualism. I. Britten, Mrs. Emma (Hardinge) d. 1899, ed. II. Title.

BRITTEN EMMA (HARDINGE) Mrs. 133.
Six lectures on theology and nature. i. Astronomical religion. ii. Religion of nature. iii. The Creator and His attributes. iv. Spirit--its origin and destiny. v. Sin and death. vi. Hades, the land of the dead. Together with the outline of a plan for a humane enterprise, and an autobiographical introduction. By Emma Hardinge. Reported by R.R. Hitt. [Chicago?] 1860. 100 p. front. (port.) 23 cm. [BF1291.B33] 11-4833
1. Spiritualism. I. Hitt, Robert Roberts, 1834-1906. II. Title.

BROECKLIN, Joseph von. 133.9
Psychic facts, by Joseph von Broecklin, presented without prejudice, fear or favor to intelligent humanity irrespective of race, creed or color ... Chicago, Ill., The Imperial book shop [c1910] 290 p. 23 1/2cm. [BF1042.B7] 32-21753

1. Spiritualism. I. Title.

BROWN, John, b1817. 133.
The mediumistic experiences of John Brown, the medium of the Rockies, with an introduction by Prof. J.S. Loveland. Des Moines, M. Hull & co., 1887. viii, [9]-167 p. 20 cm. [BF1283.B7] 14-15325
1. Spiritualism. I. Title.

BROWN, Rosemary. 133.9'092'4 B
Immortals by my side / Rosemary Brown. Chicago : H. Regnery Co., 1975, c1974. 239 p. ; 22 cm. Published in 1974 under title: Immortals at my elbow. [BF1283.B72A33 1975] 75-13248 ISBN 0-8092-8173-2 : 8.95
1. Brown, Rosemary. 2. Spiritualism. I. Title.

BROWNE, Lucy Lovina, Mrs. 133.9
Prophetic visions of national events, and spirit communications ... By Lucy Lovina Browne, medium ... Oakland, Cal., The author, 1882. vii, [9]-158 p. 18 cm. [BF1283.B75A3] 32-15886
1. Spiritualism. I. Title.

BRYAN, William J. 133.
The truth about spiritualism, by Wm. J. Bryan, M. D. New York, Alberta publishing company [c1918] 197 p. incl. ports. (1 mounted) 20 cm. [BF1261.B85] 18-23139
1. Spiritualism. I. Title.

BRYAN, William J. 133.
What spiritualism really is, by Thomas Carlyle in the spirit-world, and through the impressional brain of Dr. Wm. J. Bryan ... New York city, The Alberta publishing company [c1920] 236 p. incl. front., illus., ports. 20 cm. [BF1301.B75] 20-22173
1. Spiritualism. I. Carlyle, Thomas, 1795-1881. II. Title.

BUETTNER, Daisy (Gibson), 1877- 133.9
Heights of living and dying in pure spiritualism. San Francisco, Buettner Press [1952] 160 p. illus. 20 cm. [BF1261.B887] 52-29134
1. Spiritualism. I. Title.

BUETTNER, Daisy Gibson, Mrs. 1877- 133.9
The primer of pure spiritualism; a foundational text book for all spiritualists, units of the Band of pure spiritualism, and students of psychic research, by Daisy Gibson Buettner ... San Francisco, Calif., Buettner press, 1936. xviii, 196 (i. e. 208) p. incl. front. (port.) illus., plates. 21 cm. Extra numbered pages inserted. [BF1261.B89] 159.9617 36-7158
1. Spiritualism. I. Title.

BUETTNER, Daisy (Gibson) Mrs. 1877- 133.93
The spirit life of pure spiritualism; a text book on the spirit world and its relation to physical life, by Daisy Gibson Buettner ... San Francisco, Calif., Buettner press, 1939. 4 p. l., [1], xiv-xvi, 156 p. front. (port.) illus., plates. 21 cm. In three parts, each part preceded by leaf with half-title not included in the paging (3 leaves) "Instrumental materializing psychic, the Rev. James J. Dickson." [Full name: Mrs. Daisy May (Gibson) Buettner] [BF1301.B845] 159.96173 39-12723
1. Spiritualism. I. Dickson, James Jacobs, 1880- II. Title.

BURGESS, Charles A. 133.9
Pictorial spiritualism, compiled by C. A. Burgess. [Chicago] The Illinois state spiritualist association, 1922. [147] p. illus. ports. 20 x 27 1/2 cm. Cover-title: Organized spiritualism illustrated. Published... for the National spiritunlist association convention, Chicago...1922. Advertising matter interspersed. [BF1281.B8] (159.9617) 33-20341
1. Spiritualism. I. Title.

BURKE, Jane Revere, Mrs. 133.93
The bundle of life, by Jane Revere Burke ... a third series of communications believed to have come from William James. New York, E. P. Dutton & co. inc. [c1934] xiv, 178 p. incl. front. (facsim.) 19 1/2 cm. "First edition." [BF1311.J25B75] [159.96173] 34-4814
1. Spiritualism. I. James, William, 1842-1910. II. Title.

BURKE, Jane Revere, Mrs. 133.93
The immutable law; being messages on thought projection, mental control and the present crisis in human affairs, understood to be dictated by Thomas Troward ... received by Jane Revere Burke; with introductory notes by Mrs. Burke, F. Bligh Bond and Edward S. Martin. New York, E. P. Dutton & company, 1936. 2 p. l., vii-xii p., 1 l., 7-118 p. 19 1/2 cm. [BF1301.B855] [159.96173] 36-6356
1. Spiritualism. I. Troward, Thomas, 1847-1916. II. Title. III. Title: Thought projection.

BURKE, Jane Revere, Mrs. 133.9
Let us in, by Jane Revere Burke ... A record of communications believed to have come from William James; with a foreword by Edward S. Martin. New York, E. P. Dutton & co., inc. [c1931] xxi, 144 p. 19 1/2 cm. "First edition." [BF1311.J25B8] 31-31948
1. Spiritulism. I. James, William, 1842-1910. II. Title.

BURKE, Jane Revere, Mrs. 133.
Messages on healing; understood to have been dictated by William James, Sir William Osler, Andrew Jackson Davis, and others, and received by Jane Revere Burke sitting with Edward S. Martin. [Boston?] Privately printed [The Scribner press] 1936. viii, 71 p. 19 cm. [BF1311.B85] A 39
1. Spiritualism. 2. Mental healing. I. James, William, 1842-1910. II. Osler, Sir William, bart., 1849-1919. III. Davis, Andrew Jackson, 1826-1910. IV. Martin, Edward Sanford, 1856-1939. V. Title.

BURKE, Jane (Revere) Mrs. 133.
The one way, by Jane Revere Burke. New York, E. P. Dutton and company [c1922] xxi p., 1 l., 149 p. 17 1/2 cm. Messages from William James received by means of automatic writing. cf. Author's foreword. [BF1311.B86 1922] 22-7297
1. Spiritualism. I. James, William, 1842-1910. II. Title.

BURR, William Hilton, 1870- 133.91
Photographic copies of written messages from the spirit world, more than one hundred written communications from those who dwell in spirit life, including messages from Henry Ward Beecher, Robert G. Ingersoll, Susab B. Anthony, George Raines, Franklin Burr, James Breck Perkins, James A. Garfield, Elbert Hubbard, Abraham Lincoln, Ernest W. Huffcut, and many others, with commentaries concerning conditions which obtain in spirit life based upon facts gathered from these messages and from many other sources. Copyright ... by William H. Burr. Rochester, N.U., The Avondale press, c1918. 2 p., l., 107 p. illus. (incl. ports, facsims) 22 1/2 cm. [BF1301.B89] 18-16977
1. Spiritualism. I. Title.

BURTON, Eva. 133.93
A natural bridge to cross, by Eva Burton. New York, London, G. P. Putnam's sons, 1935. vi p., 1 l., 9-288 p. 21 cm. [BF1301.B93] 35-33562
1. (159.96173) 2. Spiritualism. 3. Reincarnation. 4. Automatism. I. Title.

BURTON, Eva. 133.93
Your unseen forces, by Eva Burton... New York, London, G. P. Putnam's sons, 1936. viii p., 1 l., 11-295 p. 21 cm. Spiritualistic messages received from Prentice Mulford and others by the author, through the medium, Sophie, and by automatic writing. cf. p. 15. [BF1301.B94] 36-23285
1. Spiritualism. 2. Automatism. I. Mulford, Prentice, 1834-1891. II. Title.

BUSH, Marian (Spore) 1892-1946. 133.93
They. New York, Beechhurst Press [1947] 158 p. plates (part col.) port. 24 cm. [BF1301.B97] 47-5620
1. Spiritualism. I. Title.

BUTTERWORTH, George William, 1879-
Spiritualism and religion, by G. W. Butterworth, LITT.D. London, Society for promoting Christian knowledge; New York, The Macmillan company [1944] xi, 196 p., 1 l. 22 cm. "First published 1944." Bibliographical foot-notes. A 44
1. Spiritualism. I. Title.

BYWATER, John C. 133.
The mystery solved; or, A Bible expose of the spirit rappings. Showing that they are not caused by the spirits of the dead, but by evil demons, or devils. By John C. Bywater ... Rochester, Advent harbinger office, 1852. iv, [5]-119 p. 19 cm. [BF1042.B94] 10-29942
1. Spiritualism. I. Title.

CADWALLADER, Mary E. Mrs. 133.
Hydesville in history, [by] M. E., Cadwallader ... Chicago, Ill., The Progressive thinker publishing house, 1917. 1 p. l., 62 p. front. (5 port,) pl. 20 cm. "A brief history of events connected with the Fox sisters and Hydesville cottage."--Foreword. [BF1283.F7C3] 17-23056
1. Kane, Mrs. Margaret (Fox) 1836-1883. 2. Jencken, Mrs. Catherine (Fox) 1830-1892. 3. Underhill, Mrs. Ann Leah (Fox) 1814-1891. 4. Spiritualism. I. Title.

CADWALLADER, Mary E. Mrs. 133.
Mary S. Vanderbilt, a twentieth century seer, by M. E. Cadwallader ... Chicago, Ill., The Progressive thinker publishing house [c1921] vii, 126 p. front., plates. ports. 19 cm. [BF1283.N3C3] 22-8849
1. Vanderbilt, Mrs. Mary (Scannell) 1867-1919. 2. Spiritualism. I. Title.

CAHAGNET, Louis Alphonse, 1809-1885. 133.9
The celestial telegraph; or, Secrets of the life to come, revealed through magnetism, wherein the existence, the form and the occupations, of the soul after its separation from the body are proved by many years' experiments, by the means of eight ecstatic somnambulists, who had eighty perceptions of thirty-six deceased persons of various conditions: a description of them, their conversation, etc., with proofs of their existence in the spiritual world, By L. Alph. Cahagnet. 1st American ed. New York, J. S. Redfield; Rochester, D. M. Dewey, 1851. 2 v. in 1. 19 cm. Vol. 2 without t.-p. [BF1292.C2 1851] 32-10524
1. Spiritualism. I. Title.

[CAINE, Katherine B] 133.
Light on the hidden way, with an introduction by James Freeman Clarke ... Boston, Ticknor and company, 1886. 3 p. l., [ix]-xii, [13]-183 p. 16 cm. [BF1301.C2] 12-36171
1. Spiritualism. I. Title.

CAMERON, Margaret, 1867- 133.
The seven purposes; an experience in psychic phenomena, By Margaret Cameron. New York and London, Harper & brothers [c1918] 6 p. l., 3-313, [1] p. 21 cm. [Full name: Mrs. Margaret (Cameron) Lewis] [BF1301.C3] 18-21672
1. Spiritualism. I. Title.

CAMERON, Margaret, 1867- 133.
Twelve lessons from The seven purposes, by Margaret Cameron. New York and London, Harper & brothers [c1919] 6 p. l., 63 p. 17 1/2 cm. [BF1301.C33] 19-11175
1. Spiritualism. I. Title.

CAMPBELL, John Bunyan. 133.9
Life! physical and spiritual, and the amazing powers of the cultivated and developed human soul, by which it performs the most wonderful occult phenomena and reveals the deepest mysteries. The all-absorbing and perplexing question settled at last. Scientific analysis of the whole subject of so-called modern spiritualism, explaining its human methods and manifestations and its pretended materializations, the false and the true... Development of new human faculties and wonderful powers, heretofore unknown, of vast importance in the cure of disease, prevention of death, and promotion of human happiness. Also lessons on how to get and use the power. By Prof. John Bunyan Campbell... Fairmount, Cincinnati, O., [18--] 1 p. l., [9]-227, [29], 37 p. front. (port.) 20 cm. Supplement at end contains recommendations of J. B. Campbell's publications and treatment, and proceedings of second, fourth, sixth and seventh annual conventions of vitapathic physicians, separately paged, followed by Human redemption, a lecture by J. B. Campbell (37 p.) [RZ999.C22] [159.9617] 33-18017
1. Spiritualism. I. Title.

CAMPBELL, Z. 133.
The spiritual telegraphic opposition line; or, Science and divine revelation against spiritual manifestations. By Eld. Z. Campbell. Springfield [Mass.] H. S. Taylor, 1853. 275 p. 19 1/2 cm. [BF1042.C24] 10-
1. Spiritualism. 2. Hypnotism I. Title.

CAPRON, Eliab Wilkinson. 133.9
Modern spiritualism : its facts and fanaticisms, its consistencies and contradictions / E. W. Capron. New York : Arno Press, 1976. p. cm. (The Occult) Reprint of the 1855 ed. published by B. Marsh, Boston. [BF1241.C25 1976] 75-36833 ISBN 0-405-07945-1 : 24.00
1. Spiritualism. I. Title. II. Series: The Occult (New York, 1976-)

CAPRON, Eliab Wilkinson. 133.
Modern spiritualism; its facts and fanaticisms, its consistencies and contradictions. With an appendix. By E. W. Capron. Boston, B. Marsh; New York, Partridge and Brittan; [etc., etc.] 1855. x, [11]-438 p. 19 cm. [BF1241.C25] 10-34671
1. Spiritualism. I. Title.

CARINGTON, Whately, 1892- 133.9
The foundations of spiritualism, by W. Whately Smith ... New York, E. P. Dutton & company [c1920] v, 123 p. 20 cm. [Full name: Walter Whately Carington (originally Walter Whately Smith)] [BF1261.C34 1920] 159.9617 20-21345
1. Spiritualism. I. Title.

CARINGTON, Whately, 1892- 133.9
The foundations of spiritualism, by W. Whately Smith ... London, K. Paul, Trench, Trubner &co., ltd.; New York E. P. Dutton & co., 1920. 3 p. l., 134 p. 19 cm. [Full name: Walter Whately Carington (originally Walter Whately Smith)] [BF1261.C34 1920 a] 159.9617 34-36374
1. Spiritualism. I. Title.

CARRINGTON, Hereward, 1800- 133.
The physical phenomena of spiritualism, fraudulent and genuine: being a brief account of the most important historical phenomena, a criticism of their evidential value, and a complete exposition of the methods employed in fraudulently reproducing the same, by Hereward Carrington ... Boston, H. B. Turner & co., 1907. xiii, 426 p. pl. 22 cm. [BF1371.C3] 7-17909
1. Spiritualism. I. Title.

CARRINGTON, Hereward, 1880- 133.
Eusapia Palladino and her phenomena, by Hereward Carrington ... New York, B. W. Dodge & company, 1909. xiv, 353 p. front. (port.) illus., plates. 21 cm. [BF1283.P3] 9-29965 2.00
1. Palladino, Eusapia, 1854- 2. Spiritualism. I. Title.

CARRINGTON, Hereward, 1880. 133.9
... The physical phenomena of spiritualism: being a brief account of the most important historical phenomena, with a criticism of their evidential value. By Hereward Carrington ... [3d ed.] New York, American universities publishing company. 1920. xiii, 426 p. front., plates. 21 cm. (The occult and psychical sciences [BF1371.C3 1920 a] 833.9 32-6503
1. Spiritualism. I. Title.

CARRINGTON, Hereward, 1880- 133.
The physical phenomena of spiritualism, fraudulent and genuine; being a brief account of the most important historical phenomena: a criticism of their evidential value, and a complete exposition of the methods employed in fradulently reproducing the same, by Herward Carrington ... [3d ed.] New York, Dodd, Mead & company, 1920. xiii, 426 p. 21 cm. [BF1371.C3 1920] 20-4810
1. Spiritualism. I. Title.

CARRINGTON, Hereward, 1880- 133.
Spiritualism, a fact. (Can we communicate with the dead?) By Hereward Carrington, PH. D. Boston, Mass., The Stratford company, 1925. 2 p. l., 150 p. 19 cm. Contains also "Spiritualism, a fake. (Can we communicate with the dead?) By James J. Walsh," inverted, with separate t.-p. [BF1031.C38] 25-24370
1. Spiritualism. I. Title.

CARTER, Russell Kelso, 1849- 133.
The tree of knowledge; a startling scientific

study of the original sin, and the sin of the angels, with a history of spiritism in all ages. By Captain R. Kelso Carter ... San Francisco, Cal., O. H. Elliott, 1894. 423 p. incl. front., plates. 20 x 16 cm. [BF1042.C33] 10-34900
1. Spiritualism. I. Title.

CHANEY, Robert Galen, 1913- 133.93
Mediums and the development of mediumship, by Rev. Robert G. Chaney, portraits by Gretchen. [Eaton Rapids, Mich., Psychic books, 1946] ix, [1], 11-215 p. illus. (ports.) 19 cm. "First edition." [BF1281.C5] 46-6231
1. Spiritualism. I. Title.

CHAPMAN, Herman L. 133.
The spiritualism of nature, by H. L. Chapman ... The spiritualism of nature, harmonizing the continuity of life, with eternal unchangeable law, as the source of things. Versus a personal God and creation, being a series of lectures delivered, articles and poems written as dictated of outlined by the spirit helpers. [Kalamazoo, Mich., Ihling brothers Everard co.] c1922. 3 p. l., 195, [2] p. illus. (ports.) pl. 20 cm. [BF1301.C5] 22-16239
1. Spiritualism. I. Title.

CHASE, Warren, 1813-1891. 133.
Forty years on the spiritual rostrum. By Warren Chase. A sequel to "The life line of the lone one," an autobiography of the author, as the world's child ... Boston, Colby & Rich, 1888. 324 p. front. (port.) 20 cm. [BF1283.C5A4] 14-15331
1. Spiritualism. I. Title.

CHASE, Warren, 1813-1891. 133.
The gist of spiritualism: viewed scientifically, philosophically, religiously, politically, and socially. In a course of five lectures, delivered in Washington, D. C., January, 1865. By Warren Chase ... Boston, W. White & co., 1865. 118 p. 19 cm. [BF1251.C45] 10-32966
1. Spiritualism. I. Title.

CHASE, Warren, 1813-1891. 133.
Three lectures on the harmonial philosophy, by Hon. Warren Chase ... Cleveland, O., L. E. Barnard & co.; Boston, Mass., B. Marsh, 1856. 50 p. 22 cm. [BF1291.C45] 11-4750
1. Spiritualism. I. Title.

CHILD, Asaph Bemis, 1813-1879. 133.
The bouquet of spiritual flowers; received chiefly through the mediumship of Mrs. J. S. Adams. By A. B. Child ... Boston, B. Marsh, 1856. 188 p. 19 1/2 c. [BF1291.A28] 11-4772
1. Spiritualism. I. Adams, Harriet A., "Mrs. J. S. Adams," d. 1885. II. Title.

CHILD, Asaph Bemis, 1813-1879. 133.9
The lily-wreath of spiritual communications; received chiefly through the mediumship of Mrs. J. S. Adams. By A. B. Child. New York, Partridge and Brittan; Boston, Crosby, Nichols & co., 1855. iv, 188 p. 20 cm. [BF1291.C53] 32-22228
1. Spiritualism. I. Title.

CHILD, Henry T. 133.91
Narratives of the spirits of Sir Henry Morgan, and his daughter Annie, usually known as John and Katie King. Giving an account of their earth lives, and their experiences in spirit life for nearly two hundred years. By Henry T. Child, M.D. Philadelphia, Hering, Pope & co., 1874. 100 p. 2 port. 18 1/2 cm. [BF1291.C55] 11-4834
1. Spiritualism. I. Title.

CHRISTIE, Anne. 133.9
The opening of the door, by Anne Christie and Mary Worth. Boston, Meador publishing company, 1932. 4 p. l., 11-81 p. 20 cm. Contents.The amazing discovery.--A message to the world.--The world and love. [BF1301.C52] 32-20106
1. Spiritualism. I. Worth, Mary, joint author. II. Title.

CHURCHILL, May Thirza. 248
Spirit power, by May Thirza Churchill. Buffalo, N.Y., Press of the Buffalo commercial [c1915] 3 p. l., 9-64 p. 20cm. $0.50 16-1027
I. Title.

CHURCHILL, May Thirza. 248
Spirit power, by May Thirza Churchill. New York, E.P. Dutton & co. [1917] 3 p. l., 9-64 p. 19 1/2cm. "First printing, December, 1915 ... fourth printing, July, 1917." [BV4501.C5 1917] 18-2474
I. Title.

CLARK, Uriah. 133.9
Plain guide to spiritualism. A hand-book for skeptics, inquirers, clergymen, believers, lecturers, mediums, editors, and all who need a through guide to the phenomena, science, philosophy, religion and reforms of modern spiritualism, By Uriah Clark. Boston, Mass., W. White & co., [1863] x, 11-294 p. 19 cm. [BF1251.C6] 32-15897
1. Spiritualism. I. Title.

CLODD, Edward, 1840- 133.
The question; "If a man die, shall he live again?" Job XIV. 14. A brief history and examination of modern spiritualism, by Edward Clodd: with a postscript by Professor H. E. Armstrong... New York, E. J. Clode [c1918] 313 p. 21 cm. [BF1042.C5 1918] 18-4715 2.00
1. Spiritualism. I. Title.

CLYMER, Reuben Swinburne, 1878-
True spiritualsim; also, a contradiction of the work of John E. Roberts, entitled "Spiritualism; or, Bible salvation vs. modern spiritualsim"... by Rev. R. Swinburne Clymer... Allentown, Pa., The Philosophical publishing company [c1906] 190 p. 20 cm. [BF1201.C65] 7-2066
1. Roberts, John E. Spiritualism. 2. Spiritualism. I. Title.

COAKLEY, Thomas Francis, 1880- 133.
Spiritism, the modern satanism, by Thomas F. Coakley... Chicago, Extension press [c1920] 132 p. 19 1/2 cm. [BF1042.C6] 20-6443
1. Spiritualism. I. Title.

[COCHRANE, Harriet B. Mrs. 133.
Drift, from the shore of the hereafter, by George Eliot ... transcribed by Amarauth [pseud.] [Philadelphia, H. B. Cochrane, 1883] 94 p. 19 1/2 cm. [BF1301.C6] CA11
1. Spiritualism. I. Title.

COGGESHALL, William Turner, 1824-1867. 133.
The signs of the times; comprising a history of the spirit-rappings, in Cincinnati and other places: with notes of clairvoyant revealments, by William T. Coggeshall... Cincinnati, The author, 1851. 144 p. 17 1/2 cm. [BF1241.C67] 10-34672
1. Spiritualism. I. Title.

COLIVILLE, William Wilberforce Juvenal, 1862- 133.
Universal spiritualism; spirit communion in all ages among all nations, by W. J. Colville ... New York, R. F. Fenno & company [c1906] 352 p. 20 cm. [BF1241.C7] 7-10030
1. Spiritualism. I. Title.

COMSTOCK, William Charles, 1847- 133.
A psychical experience, a man works for help with personalities in the wider life; a personal experience related by William C. Comstock. Boston, R. G. Badger [1923] 126 p. 21 cm. [BF1301.C6865] 23-11240
1. Spiritualism. I. Title.

COMSTOCK, William Charles, 1847- ed. 133.
A word for help from the wider world, ed. by William C. Comstock. Boston, R. G Badger [1920] 153 p. 15 1/2 cm. [BF1301.C69] 21-2323
1. Spiritualism. I. Title.

COMSTOCK, William Charles, 1847-1924. 133.
Man, the life free, by the authors of "Thought for help," "Will higher of God," and "man's life of purpose." William C. Comstock, amanuensis; with a foreword, by Rev. Joseph A. Milburn. Boston, R. G. Badger [1916] xxvi, 214 p. 23 cm. $1.25 [BF1301.C685] 16-19982
1. Spiritualism. I. Title.

CONFESSIONS of a medium, 133.9
with five illustrations. London, Griffith & Farran. New York, E. P. Dutton & co., 1882. xvi, 232 p. incl. front., illus. 19 cm. [R F1283. Z9 C6] 32-16706
1. Spiritualism.

CONNOR, Helen N., comp.
Broken beams from the summer-land, by many authors ... Comp. and ed. by Helen N. Connor. [Meadville? Pa.] A. Gaston [c1905] 3 p. l., [3]-147, [1] p. 21 1/2 cm. A collection of spiritualistic messages. 5-34656
I. Title.

COOK, Ellen A. Pennau, Mrs. 133.
How I discovered my mediumship, by Mrs. Cecil M. Cook, pastor and medium. The William T. Stead memorial center ... Chicago, Ill., The W.T. Stead memorial center [c1919] 3 p. l., 9-87 p. 23 cm. [BF1286.C6] 19-14329
1. Spiritualism. I. Title.

COOK, Ellen A. Peunau, Mrs. 133.9
The voice triumphant, the revelation of a medium, by Mrs. Cecil M. Cook .. New York, London, A.A. Knopf, 1931. xiv, 323 p., 1 l. front. (port.) 21 1/2 cm. [BF1283.C82A3] 31-8696
1. Spiritualism. I. Title.

COOKE, Parsons, 1800-1864. 133.9
Necromancy; or, A rap for the rappers. By Parsons Cooke. Boston, Congregational board of publication, 1857. 92 p. 17 cm. [BF1042.C75] 32-15903
1. Spiritualism. I. Title.

COOLEY, Benjamin Franklin. 133.
An exposition and explanation of the modern phenomena called spirit manifestations. Comprising the rappings, movements, writing mediums, and various other phenomena ... with extracts from different writers, of remarkable instances of presentiment, prophecying ... etc. By Benjamin Franklin Cooley ... Springfield, Mass., W. Colomy, 1852. iv, [5]-96 p. 18 cm. [BF1251.C75] 10-32965
1. Spiritualism. I. Title.

CORNING, W H. 133.
The infidelity of the times, as connected with the rappings and the mesmerists, and especially as developed in the writings of Andrew Jackson Davis. By Rev. W. H. Corning. Boston, J. P. Jewett & company: Cleveland, O., Jewett, Proctor & Worthington, 1854. 124 p. 20 cm. [BF1291.D39C8] 11-4836
1. Davis, Andrew Jackson, 1826-1910. 2. Spiritualism. I. Title.

CORSON, Hiram, 1828-1911. 133.
Spirit messages, with an introductory essay on spiritual vitality, by Hiram Corson ... Rochester, N. Y., The Austin publishing co., 1911. xv, 279 p. 20 cm. These messages were delivered through the mediumship of Mrs. Minnie Meserve Soule. [BF1301.C8] 12-760 1.25
1. Spiritualism. I. Soule, Mrs. Minnie Meserve. II. Title.

CORSON, Hiram, 1828-1911. 133.9
Spirit messages, with an introductory essay on spiritual vitality, by Hiram Corson ... New edition. Boston, Christopher publishing house, [1919] 4 p. l., [vii]-xiii, 7 p., 1 l., [5]-279 p. 21 cm. These messages were delivered through mediumship of Mrs. Minnie Meserve Soule. [BF1301.C7 1919] 32-11977
1. Spiritualism. I. Soule, Mrs. Minnie Meserve. II. Title.

COX, Edward William, 1809-1879. 133.
Spiritualism answered by science. By Edward W. Cox ... New York, H. L. Hinton, 1872. iv, [5]-79 p. 20 cm. First published in London, in 1871. [BF1051.C8] 11-2438
1. Spiritualism. 2. Psychical research. I. Title.

CRAIG, Florence M. 133.96
My journeys and experiences in the spirit world, by Florence M. Craig ... [Portland, Or., A. E. Kern, 1939?] 142 p. 17 cm. [BF1283.C82A3] 159.96173 40-25656
1. Spiritualism. I. Title.

CRAWFORD, William Jackson, 1880-1920. 133.
Hints and observations for investigating the phenomena of spiritualism, by W. J. Crawford ... New York, E. P. Dutton & company [c1918] 2 p. l., 110 p. plates, diagrs. 19 cm. [BF1261.C88] 18-22823
1. Spiritualism. I. Title.

CRENSHAW, James, 1908- 133.9
Telephone between worlds. Foreword by Gustaf Stromberg. Los Angeles, Borden Pub. Co. [1950] xix, 232 p. port. 20 cm. [BF1301.C74] 50-3674
1. Spiritualism. I. Title.

CROCKETT, Albert Stevens, 1873- 133.
Revelations of Louise, by Albert S. Crockett; with two black-and-white illustrations from photographs. New York, Frederick A. Stokes company [c1920] xxi, 234 p. port. (incl. front.) 21 cm. [BF1301.C75] 20-19174 2.75
1. Spiritualism. I. Title.

CROOKES, William, Sir, 1832-1919. 133.9'08
Crookes and the spirit world; a collection of writings by or concerning the work of Sir William Crookes, O.M., F.R.S., in the field of psychical research. Collected by R. G. Medhurst. General introd. by K. M. Goldney. Material introduced and edited by M. R. Barrington. New York, Taplinger Pub. Co. [1972] 250 p. illus. 23 cm. Includes bibliographical references. [BF1251.C79 1972] 78-185949 ISBN 0-8008-2040-1 10.00
1. Spiritualism. I. Title.

CROOKES, William, Sir 1832-1919. 133.
Researches into the phenomena of modern spiritualism, by Sir Wm. Crookes ... Rochester, N. Y., The Austin publishing company [c1904] 85 p. illus., diagrs. 18 cm. "Reprinted from 'The Quarterly journal of science' and other publications." [BF1371.C9] 4-17836
1. Spiritnalism. 2. Psychical research. I. Title.

CROSLAND, Camilla Duflour (Toulmin) "Mrs. Newton Vrosland" 1812-1895. 133.9
Light in the valley. My experiences of spiritualism. By Mrs. Newton Crosland ... London, New York, G. Routledge & co., 1857. xii, 288 p. front., illus., plates (port col.) 17 cm. [BF1251.C8] 32-10521
1. Spiritualism. I. Title.

CROSS, Harold H U. 133.9
A cavalcade of the supernatural by Harold H. U. Cross, PH. D. New York, E. P. Dutton & co., inc. [c1939] 259 p. illus., plates, diagr. 20 cm. "First edition." [BF1261.C92] 39-25826
1. Spiritualism. I. Title.

CROWELL, Eugene, 1817-1894. 133
The identity of primitive Christianity and modern spiritualism. By Eugene Crowell ... New York, G. W. Carleton & co.; [etc., etc.] 1874-75. 2 v. 24 cm. Vol. 2 published by the author. [BF1275.B5C8] 11-3422
1. Spiritualism. I. Title.

CROWELL, Eugene, 1817-1894. 133.
The spirit world: its inhabitants, nature, and philosophy. By Eugene Crowell ... Boston, Colby & Rich, 1879. xii, 197 p. 19 cm. [BF1301.K34] 11-5334
1. Spiritualism. I. Title.

CROWSON, E H.
The function of spirit in matter, by E. H. Crowson. Boston, Mass., The Stratford company, 1924. 6 p. l., 131 p. 20 cm. "Bibliographia": p. 129-131. [B841.C7] 24-10072
I. Title. II. Title: Spirit in matter.

CUMMINS, Geraldine Dorothy, 1890- 133.93
They survive; evidence of life beyond the grave from scripts of Geraldine Cummins, compiled by E. B. Gibbes. London, New York [etc.] Rider & company [1946?] 140 p. 19 cm. [BF1301.C85] 46-21787
1. Spiritualism. I. Gibbes, E. B., comp. II. Title.

CURRIE, Ian. 133.9'013
You cannot die : the incredible findings of a century of research on death / by Ian Currie. New York : Methuen, c1978. 288 p. : ill. ; 24 cm. "A Jonathan-James book." Includes bibliographical references.

[BF1261.C96] 78-16697 ISBN 0-458-93750-9 : 9.95
1. Spiritualism. 2. Death. 3. Future life. I. Title.

CURRIE, Ian. 133.9'013
You cannot die : the incredible findings of a century of research on death / by Ian Currie. New York : Playboy Paperbacks, 1981, c1980. 288 p. ; 18 cm. Includes bibliographical references. [BF1261.C96] ISBN 0-872-16791-7 pbk. : 2.50
1. Spiritualism. 2. Death. 3. Future life. I. Title.
L.C. card no. for the 1979 Methuen edition: 78-16697

[CUSHMAN, Emma (Crow)] Mrs. 133. 1839-
Insight; a record of psychic experiences; a series of questions and answers dealing with the world of facts, the world of ideals and the world of realities beyond death ... Boston, Christopher publishing house [c1918] 357 p. 21 cm. [BF1301.C9] 18-11171
1. Spiritualism. I. Title.

DADMUN, John H. 133.
Spiritualism examined and refuted; it being found contrary to Scripture, known facts and common sense ... Also a discussion of its moral claims ... by John H. Dadmun ... Philadelphia, Pa., The author, 1893. 468 p. front. (port.) 21 cm. [BF1042.D2] 10-34904
1. Spiritualism. I. Title.

DAGUE, Robert Addison. 133.
The twentieth century Bible, by Robert Addison Dague. Chicago, Ill., The Progressive thinker publishing house, 1917. 2 p. l., 3-94 p. 16 cm. [BF1261.D3] 18-19385
1. Spiritualism. I. Title.

DAICHES, Belle Turner. 133.9
Adventures in survival. Chicago, Aries Press, 1949. xi, 177 p. illus., ports. 21 cm. [BF1261.D32] 49-4506
1. Spiritualism. I. Title.

DAILEY, Abram Hoagland, 133. 1831-
Mollie Fancher, the Brooklyn enigma. An authentic statement of facts in the life of Mary J. Fancher ... By Abram H. Dailey. Brooklyn [Eagle book printing dept.] 1894. xiii, 262 p. 6 port. 21 cm. [BF1283.F2D3] 14-15340
1. Spiritualism. I. Fancher, Mary J., b. 1848. II. Title.

DALLAS, Harriet (Hughes) 133.96 Mrs.
The teaching of Platonius, received by Harriet H. Dallas ... introduction by Frederick Bligh Bond. New York, Macoy publishing company, 1932- v. illus. 23 cm. At head of title of v. 2-: Second-series. Vols. 2-3, 2d-3d ser., have imprint: Boston, Marshall Jones company. The first series contains lessons received over the ouija board. [Full name: Mrs. Harriet Louise (Hughes) Dallas] [BF1301.D2] 159.96173 33-1752
1. Spiritualism. I. Title. II. Title: Platonius, The teaching of.

DALLAS, Mary (Kyle) Mrs. 133. 1830-1897.
The freed spirit: or, Glimpses beyond the border. A collection of new and authentic occult tales from the author's personal experience and reliable private sources, by Mary Kyle Dallas ... New York, C. B. Reed, 1894. xii, 232 p. 19 cm. [BF1301.D22] 11-5325
1. Spiritualism. I. Title.

DALTON, L H. 133.
Materialization and other spiritual phenomena from a scientific standpoint; by L. H. Dalton and J. V. Wallace. Boston, A. A. Perry, 1897. 111 p. 17 cm. [BF1378.D25] 10-33710
1. Spiritualism. I. Wallace, J. V., joint author. II. Title.

DAMIANI, G. 133.
Spirit and matter. A drama, in six acts. By G. Damiani ... Boston, Colby and Rich, 1880. 96 p. 20 cm. [BF1301.D23] 12-13498
1. Spiritualism. I. Title.

DAMON, William F. 133.9
Homeward bound; a dissertation upon the relationship between atomic science and spiritualism. New York, Exposition Press [c.1959] 96p. 21cm. 59-65450 2.75
1. Spiritualism. I. Title.

DANELSON, Effa E. Mrs. 133.
Journeys through space; experiences of Effa E. Danelson. Chicago, Ill. [c1922] 96 p. 15 cm. [BF1301.D24] 22-3317
1. Spiritualism. I. Title.
Contents omitted.

DANIELS, Cora Linn (Morrison) 133 Mrs. 1852-
As it is to be. By Cora Linn Daniels ... Pub. by Cora Linn Daniels, Franklin, Mass. [Milwaukee, Wis., Press of King, Fowle & co., c1892] 3 p. l., 5-258 p. front. (port.) illus., plates. 17 cm. [BF1999.D25 1892] 20-13260
1. Spiritualism. I. Title.

DANIELS, Cora Linn (Morrison) 133 Mrs. 1852-
As it is to be, by Cora Linn Daniels ... 6th thousand. Boston, Little, Brown and company, 1900. xiii, 294 p. 18 cm. [BF1999.D25 1900] 0-5692
1. Spiritualism. I. Title.

DANIELS, J W. 133.9
Spiritualism versus Christianity; or Spiritualism thoroughly exposed. by J. W. Daniels ... New York and Auburn, Miller, Orton & Mulligan, 1856. xii, [13]-299, [1] p. front., illus., plates. 20 cm. [BF1042.D25] 32-19882
1. Spiritualism. I. Title.

DANMAR, William. 133.
Modern nirvanaism [by] Wm. Danmar ... The philosophy of life and death. Jamaica, N. Y. city, W. Danmar [1920] cover-title, 176 p. diagrs. 24 cm. Second edition; 1st edition published in 1914. [BF1261.D25 1920] 20-20348
1. Spiritualism. 2. Psychical research. 3. Cosmology. I. Title.

DANSKIN, Washington A.
How and why I became a spiritualist. [By] Wash, A, Danskin ... Boston, B. Marsh; New York, S. T. Munson, 1858. 104 p. 19 cm. [BF12151.D2] 10-34685
1. Spiritualism. I. Title.

DASKIN, Washington A. 133.9
How and why I became a spiritualist. [By] Wash. A. Danskin ... 4th ed. with an appendix, giving an authentic statement of that wonderful phenomenon known as the solid iron ring manifestation. Baltimore, Md., The author, 1869. 104, iii p., 1 l., [7]-66 p. 18 cm. Matter received by the author, impressionally or inspirationally; since the 2d edition of this volume was issued: iii p., 1 l., [7]-57 p. at end. Appendix to 4th edition: p. [58]-66 at end. [BF1251.D2 1869] 32-19887
1. Spiritualism. I. Title.

THE Davenport brothers the world-renowned spiritual mediums; 133. their biography and adventures in Europe and America ... Boston, W. White and company; New York, The American news company, 1869. 426 p. incl. plates. front. (2 port.) 20 cm. [BF1283.D3D3] 11-3623
1. Davenport, Ira Erastus, 1839-1911. 2. Davenport, William Henry, 1841-1877. 3. Spiritualism.

DAVENPORT, Reuben Briggs. 133.
The death-blow to spiritualism: being the true story of the Fox sisters, as revealed by authority of Margaret Fox Kane and Catherine Fox Jencken. By Reuben Briggs Davenport. New York, G. W. Dillingham, 1888. x, [11]-247 p. 19 cm. [BF1042.D28] 10-34905
1. Spiritualism. I. Title.

DAVIS, Andrew Jackson, 1826- 133. 1910.
Answers to ever-recurring questions from the people. (A sequel to the Penetralia.) By Andrew Jackson Davis ... New York, A. J. Davis & co., 1862. iv, [5]-417 p. 19 cm. [BF1251.D26] 10-34686
1. Spiritualism. I. Title.

DAVIS, Andrew Jackson, 1826- 133. 1910.
Arabula: or, The divine guest. Containing a new collection of gospels. By Andrew Jackson Davis ... Boston, W. White & company; New York, Banner of light branch office, 1867. 403 p. 20 cm. [BF1291.D24] 11-3596
1. Spiritualism. I. Title.

DAVIS, Andrew Jackson, 1826- 133. 1910.
Beyond the valley; a sequel to "The magic staff": an autobiography of Andrew Jackson Davis ... Boston, Colby & Rich, 1885. 402 p. front., illus. 20 cm. [BF1283.D4A3] 14-15323
1. Spiritualism. I. Title.

DAVIS, Andrew Jackson, 1826- 133. 1910.
Death and the after-life. Three lectures. By Andrew Jackson Davis. Phonographically reported by Robert S. Moore. Also, A voice from the summer land. New York, A. J. Davis & co., 1866. 101 p. 18 cm. [BF1291.D25] 11-3602
1. Spiritualism. I. Title.

DAVIS, Andrew Jackson, 1826- 133. 1910.
Death and the after-life. Eight evening lectures on the summer-land. By Andrew Jackson Davis. Phonographically reported by Robert S. Moore. Also, A voice from James Victor Wilson. 4th enl. ed. Boston, W. White & company; New York, American news co., 1871. 2 p. l., [3]-210 p. front. 20 cm. [BF1291.D25 1871] 16-4812
1. Spiritualism. I. Title.
Contents omitted.

DAVIS, Andrew Jackson, 133.9 1826-1910.
Death and the after-life: eight evening lectures on the summer-land. By Andrew Jackson Davis. Phonographically reported by Robert S. Moore. Also, A voice from James Victor Wilson. 4th enl. ed. New York, A. J. Davis & co., 1874. 2 p. l., [3]-210 p. front. 20 cm. [BF1311.F8D3 1874] 32-11978
1. Spiritualism. I. Title.

DAVIS, Andrew Jackson, 133.9 1826-1910.
Death and the after-life; eight evening lectures on the summer-land. By Andrew Jackson Davis. Phonographically reported by Robert S. Moore. Also, A voice from James Victor Wilson. Rev. and enl. Rochester, N. Y., The Austin publishing co., 1911. 2 p. l., [3]-210 p. 19 cm. [BF1311.F8D3 1911] 32-11973
1. Spiritualism. I. Title.

DAVIS, Andrew Jackson, 1826- 133. 1910.
The Diakka, and their earthly victims; being an explanation of much that is false and repulsive in spiritualism. By Andrew Jackson Davis ... New York, A. J. Davis & co., 1874. 102 p. 19 cm. [BF1555.D2] 11-6678
1. Spiritualism. I. Title.

DAVIS, Andrew Jackson, 1826- 133. 1910.
The fountain: with jets of new meanings. Illustrated with one hundred and forty-two engravings. By Andrew Jackson Davis ... 1st ed. Boston, W. White & company; New York, American news co., 1870. iv p., 1 l., [7]-252 p. illus. 18 cm. [BF1291.D26] 11-3603
1. Spiritualism. I. Title.

DAVIS, Andrew Jackson, 133.9 1826-1910.
The harmonial man; or, Thoughts for the age. By Andrew Jackson Davis ... Rev., restereotyped and enl. New York, A. J. Davis & co., 1873. 167 p. 20 cm. [BF1291.D28 1873] 32-10522
1. Spiritualism. I. Title.

DAVIS, Andrew Jackson, 133.9 1826-1910.
The harmonial man; or, Thoughts for the age. By Andrew Jackson Davis ... Rev., restereotyped, and enl. Boston, Colby & Rich, 1877. 167 p. 19 cm. Imprint on cover: New York, A. J. Davis & co., 1873. [BF1291.D28 1877] 159.9617 34-13692
1. Spiritualism. I. Title.

DAVIS, Andrew Jackson, 133.9 1826-1910.
Introduction to the writings of Andrew Jackson Davis, by James Lowell Moore. Boston, The Christopher publishing house [c1930] 4 p. l., 7-190 p. front. (port.) illus. 21 cm. [BF1261.D35] 30-10359
1. Spiritualism. I. Moore, James Lowell, ed. II. Title.

DAVIS, Andrew Jackson, 1826- 133. 1910.
The magic staff; an autobiography of Andrew Jackson Davis ... New York, J. S. Brown & co.; Boston, B. Marsh, 1857. 552 p. illus., plates, 2 port. (incl. front.) 21 cm. [BF1283.D4A2] 14-15324
1. Spiritualism. I. Title.

DAVIS, Andrew Jackson, 920.9 1826-1910.
The magic staff; an autobiography of Andrew Jackson Davis ... 9th ed. Boston, W. White & company, 1871. 552 p. front. (port.) illus., plates. 19 cm. Lettered on cover: The autobiography of A. J. Davis. The magic staff. [BF1283.D4A2 1871] 32-11982
1. Spiritualism. I. Title.

DAVIS, Andrew Jackson, 920.9 1826-1910.
The magic staff; an autobiography of Andrew Jackson Davis ... 13th ed. Boston, W. White & company, 1873. 552 p. front. (port.) illus., plates. 19 cm. Lettered on cover: The autobiography of A. J. Davis. The magic staff. [BF1283.D4A2 1873] 32-11981
1. Spiritualism. I. Title.

DAVIS, Andrew Jackson, 920.9 1826-1910.
The magic staff: an autobiography of Andrew Jackson Davis ... 13th ed. New York, A. J. Davis & co., 1876. 552 p. front. (port.) illus., plates. 19 cm. Lettered on cover: The autobiography of A. J. Davis. The magic staff. [BF1283.D4A2 1876] 32-11980
1. Spiritualism. I. Title.

DAVIS, Andrew Jackson, 1826- 133. 1910.
Memoranda of persons, places, and events; embracing authentic facts, visions, impressions, discoveries, in magnetism, clairvoyance, spiritualism. Also quotations from the opposition. By Andrew Jackson Davis. With an appendix, containing Zschokke's great story of "Hortensia", vividly portraying the wide difference between the ordinary state and that of clairvoyance. Boston, W. White & company; New York, Banner of light branch office, 1868. 488 p. 20 cm. [BF1251.D28] 10-34687
1. Spiritualism. I. Zschokke, Heinrich, 1771-1848. Hortensia. II. Title.

DAVIS, Andrew Jackson, 133.9 1826-1910.
Memoranda of persons, places, and events; embracing authentic facts, visions, impressions, discoveries, in magnetism, clairvoyance, spiritualism. Also quotations from the opposition. By Andrew Jackson Davis, with an appendix, containing Zschokke's great story of "Hortensia" vividly portraying the wide difference between the ordinary state and that of clairvoyance. 2d thousand. Boston, W. White & company; New York, Banner of light branch office, 1868. 488 p. 20 cm. [BF1251.D28 1868 a] 32-10520
1. Spiritualism. I. Zschokke, Heinrich, 1771-1848. Hortensia. II. Title.

DAVIS, Andrew Jackson, 1826- 133. 1910.
Morning lectures. Twenty discourses, delivered before the Friends of progress in the city of New York, in the winter and spring of 1863. By Andrew Jackson Davis ... New York, C. M. Plumb & co.; [etc., etc.] 1865. 434 p. 20 cm. [BF1291.D29] 11-3605
1. Spiritualism. I. Title.

DAVIS, Andrew Jackson, 1826- 133. 1910.
The penetralia: being harmonial answers to important questions. By Andrew Jackson Davis ... Boston, B. Marsh, 1856. 328 p. 23 cm. [BF1291.D3 1856] 11-3606
1. Spiritualism. I. Title.

DAVIS, Andrew Jackson, 133.9 1826-1910.
The penetralia: being harmonial answers to important questions. By Andrew Jackson

Davis ... 4th ed. Boston, B. Marsh, 1860. 328 p. 24 cm. [BF1291.D3 1860] 32-10516
1. Spiritualism. I. Title.

DAVIS, Andrew Jackson, 1826-1910. 133.9
The penetralia: being harmonial answers to important questions. By Andrew Jackson Davis ... Rev., restereotyped, and enl. Boston, Banner of light publishing company [c1872] 4 p., 1 l., [9]-516 p. 20 cm. [BF1291.D3 1872 a] 32-10517
1. Spiritualism. I. Title.

DAVIS, Andrew Jackson, 1826-1910. 133.
The penetralia; being harmonial answers to important questions. By Andrew Jackson Davis ... Rev., restereotyped, and enl. Boston, W. White and company; New York, Banner of light branch office, 1872. 4 p., 1 l., [9]-516 p. 20 cm. [BF1291.D3 1872] 11-3615
1. Spiritualism. I. Title.

DAVIS, Andrew Jackson, 1826-1910. 133.
The philosophy of spiritual intercourse: being an explanation of modern mysteries. By Andrew Jackson Davis ... Rev., restereotyped, and enl. Boston, W. White and company; New York, American news company, 1872. ix, [10]-399 p. 20 cm. [BF1251.D3 1872] 10-32964
1. Spiritualism. I. Title.

DAVIS, Andrew Jackson, 1826-1910. 133.9
The philosophy of spiritual intercourse: being an explanation of modern mysteries. By Andrew Jackson Davis ... Rev., stereotyped, and enl. ... Boston, Colby & Rich, 1890. ix, [1], [11]-399 p. illus. 20 cm. [BF1251.D3 1890] 32-11974
1. Spiritualism. I. Title.

DAVIS, Andrew Jackson, 1826-1910. 133.
The philosophy of spiritual intercourse, being an explanation of modern mysteries. By Andrew Jackson Davis ... New York Boston [etc.] Fowlers & Wells, 1856. 176 p. 23 cm. On cover: Mail edition. Cover dated 1855. [BF1251.D3 1856] 10-34688
1. Spiritualism. I. Title.

DAVIS, Andrew Jackson, 1826-1910. 133.9
The present age and inner life; a sequel to spiritual intercourse. Modern mysteries classified and explained. By Andrew Jackson Davis ... [Hartford, C. Partridge [c1853] 281 p. illus. 23 cm. [BF1251.D32 1853] 32-21758
1. Spiritualism. I. Title.

DAVIS, Andrew Jackson, 1826-1910. 133.
The present age and inner life; ancient and modern spirit mysteries classified and explained. A sequel to Spiritual intercourse. Rev. and enl. By Andrew Jackson Davis ... Boston, New York, W. White and company, 1869. 424 p. front. (port.) illus. 19 cm. [BF1251.D32] 10-34689
1. Spiritualism. I. Title.

DAVIS, Andrew Jackson, 1826-1910. 133.9
The present age and inner life; ancient and modern spirit mysteries classified and explained. A sequel to Spiritual intercourse. Revised and enlarged. By Andrew Jackson Davis ... 3d rev. ed. Boston, W. White & company; New York, agents--American news company, 1873. 424 p. illus. 20 cm. [BF1251.D32 1873] 32-10519
1. Spiritualism. I. Title.

DAVIS, Andrew Jackson, 1826-1910. 133.
A stellar key to the summar land. By Andrew Jackson Davis ... pt.1. Illustrated with diagrams and engravings of celestial scenery. Boston, W. White & company; New York, Banner of light branch office, 1867. viii, [5]-202 p. incl. front., illus. 20 cm. No more published? [BF1291.D35] 11-3620
1. Spiritualism. I. Title.

DAVIS, Andrew Jackson, 1826-1910. 133.
Views of our heavenly home. A sequel to A stellar key to the summer-land. By Andrew Jackson Davis ... Boston, Colby & Rich, 1878. viii, [9]-290 p. incl. illus., pl. 20 cm. [BF1291.D36] 11-3621
1. Spiritualism. I. Title.

DAVIS, Dixon Louis. 133.
Anthropomorphism dissected, and spiritualism vindicated. By Dixon L. Davis ... Boston, B. Marsh, 1859. xi, 13-90 p. front. (port.) 20 cm. [BF1251.D36] 1-21183
1. Spiritualism. I. Title.

DAVIS, James Ernest, 1887- 133.9
Man being revealed; a study of the science of spirit and its application toward man's revealment, by James E. Davis and Helen Newcastle. [1st ed.] New York, Exposition Press [1956] 111p. illus. 21cm. [BF1261.2.D3] 56-12366
1. Spiritualism. I. Newcastle, Helen, joint author. II. Title.

DAVISON, Charles Wright. 133.
God wrote His gospel in His nature, as plainly shown by Jesus; a philosophy of life, that is the philosophy of nature, that is the philosophy of man ... C. Wright Davison, amanuensic author. Los Angeles, Calif., The Austin publishing co. [c1923] 20 p. l., [43]-190 p., 1 l. 20 cm. "This is a companion volume to Wm. T. Stead's book, Julia's 'after death'." [BF1301.D242] 23-9866
1. Spiritualism. I. Title.

DE ANGUERRE, Charles Edgar. 133.
Do we live again? Man the molecule, phantasmal thanatology, by Charles Edgar De Anguerre ... Chicago, Ill. The Molecule syndicate, 1922. 231 p. incl. front., pl., ports. 20 cm. [BF1301.D245] 22-3125
1. Spiritualism. I. Title.

*DE GROOT, Wilson 133.9
The golden ladder; messages from beyond, by Wilson De Groot through the pen of JewellL. Williams. New York, Exposition [1966] 77p. 21cm. (EP44121) 3.50
1. Spiritualism. 2. Automatic writing. I. Williams, Jewell L. (De Groot) II. Title.

DE KOVEN, Anna (Farwell) "Mrs. Reginald De Koven," 1860- 133.
A cloud of witnesses, by Anna de Koven (Mrs. Reginald De Koven) with an introduction by James H. Hyslop ... New York, E. P. Dutton & company [c1920] xiv, 273 p. 21 cm. [BF1301.D27] 20-4626
1. Spiritualism. I. Title.

DE WETTER, Louise Hurlbutt. 133.93
The kingdom and the power; lessons in faith and in living, selected by Louise Hurlbutt de Wetter. [Rev. ed., with added material] New York, Pageant Press [1957] 173p. 21cm. [BF1301.D46 1957] 57-8218
1. Spiritualism. I. Title.

DEWEY, Daisy. 133.
Problems of your generation. The author claims but to have been privileged to transmit the following chapters, Daisy Dewey. New York, The Arden press, 1910. 104 p. 20 cm. [BF1301.D45] 10-13188 1.00
1. Spiritualism. I. Title.

[DEWEY, Dellon Marcus] 133.
... History of the strange sounds or rappings, heard in Rochester and western New-York, and usually called the mysterious noises! Which are supposed by many to be communications from the spirit world, together with all the explanation that can as yet be given of the matter. Rochester, D. M. Dewey, 1850. 1 p. l., ii. [13]-79, [1] p. incl. plan. 20 cm. At head of title: Authorized edition. On cover: New edition, with additions. Preface signed: D. M. Dewey. [BF1283.F7D5 1850 a] 39-24023
1. Spiritualism. 2. Fox family. I. Title.

DE WITT, Cornelia. Mrs. 133.
The hereafter; or, Life on the other side. By Mrs. Cornelia De Witt. Titusville [Pa.] E. C. Bell, printer, 1879. cover-title, 54 p. 21 cm. [BF1301.D47] 11-5327
1. Spiritualism. I. Title.

DINGLE, Theola (Atkinson) Mrs. 1885- 289.9
The hidden secrets of creation revealed, by Theola Dingle ... Los Angeles, Calif, Circle of the star [c1931] 129 p. front. (port.) 16 cm. [Name originally: Mrs. Maud (Atkinson) Dingle] [BR126.D52] 32-4548
1. Spiritualism. I. Title.

DIXON-SMITH, Roy. 133.93
New light on survival. London, New York, Rider [1952] 328 p. illus. 24 cm. [BF1261.D58] 52-4421
1. Spiritualism. I. Title.

DO the dead return? 133
A true story of startling seances in San Francisco ... San Francisco, Crown publishing company, 1900. 62 p. front., illus. (ports.) 17 cm. [BF1272.D6] 0-5943
1. Spiritualism.

DODD, Alfred.
The immortal master, by Alfred Dodd; being a study of the greatest genius of the English-speaking race, the creator of the English renaissance, "Shake-speare," from a new angle in the knowledge that he possessed an experimental familiarity with the supernormal hitherto unsuspected, with some remarkable evidence indicating his interest today in "this royal throne of kings, his [!] sceptre'd isle, this earth of majesty, this seat of Mars, this other Eden, demi-paradise" ... London, New York [etc.] Rider & co. [1943] 108 p. 2 illus., ports., facsim. 22 cm. A43
1. Shakespeare, William—Authorship—Baconian theory. 2. Spiritualism. I. Title.

DODS, John Bovee, 1795-1872. 133.
Spirit manifestations examined and explained. Judge Edmonds refuted; or, An exposition of the involuntary powers and instincts of the human mind. By John Bovee Dobs ... New York. De Witt & Davenport [c1854] xii, [13]-252 p. 18 cm. [BF1042.D64] 10-34906
1. Spirtualism. I. Title.

DOTEN, Elizabeth, b.1829.
The inner mystery. An inspirational poem. By Lizzie Doten. Boston, Adams and company, 1868. 2 p. l., [7]-34 p. 19 1/2 cm. Delivered "at a festival commemorative of the twentieth anniversary of the advent of modern spiritualism ..." March 31, 1868. [PS1549.D5] 27-12761
I. Spiritualism—Poetry. II. Title.

DOTEN, Elizabeth, b.1829.
The inner mystery. An inspirational poem. By Lizzie Doten. Boston, Adams and company, 1868. 2 p. l., [7]-34 p. 19 1/2 cm. Delivered "at a festival commemorative of the twentieth anniversary of the advent of modern spiritualism ..." March 31, 1868. [PS1549.D5] 27-12761
I. Spiritualism—Poetry. II. Title.

DOW, James L. 133.
Ten test circles; or, The law of conditions, by Jas. L. Dow. Being the result of ten circles held under various conditions for the purpose of studying their effect upon spirit manifestations, and the moral effect of the same upon those composing the circle. Duluth, Minn., Globe printing company, 1893. 173 p. 17 1/2 cm. [BF1286.D7] 11-4767
1. Spiritualism. I. Title.

[DOWDEN, Hester] 133.93
The book of Johannes, by Peter Fripp. London, New York [etc.] Rider & company [1945?] 98 p. 22 cm. Communicated through the medium Hester Dowden. [BF1301.D58] 45-22086
1. Spiritualism. I. Fripp, Peter. II. Title.

DOWDING, Hugh Caswall Tremenheere Dowding, baron, 1882- 133.93
Lychgate, by Air Chief Marshal Lord Dowding ... London, New York [etc.] Rider & co. [1945] 128 p. 19 cm. Cover-title: Lychgate, the entrance to the path. First published in September, 1945. [BF1261.D76] 45-10443
1. Spiritualism. I. Title.

DOWDING, Hugh Caswall Tremenheere Dowding, baron, 1882- 133.93
Many mansions, by Air Chief Marshal Lord Dowding. London, New York [etc.] Rider & co. [1943] 112 p. 19 cm. Bibliography: p. 21-24. [BF1261.D765 1943] 44-2048
1. Spiritualism. I. Title.

DOWNING, Mary Samuel. 133.93
Creation. [1st ed.] New York, Vantage Press [1957] 67p. 21cm. [BF1301.D585] 56-12203
1. Spritualism. I. Title.

DOYLE, Arthur Conan, Sir, 1859- 133.
The case for spirit photography, by Arthur Conan Doyle; with corroborative evidence by experienced researchers and photographers. New York, George H. Doran company [c1923] x p., 1 l., 13-132 p. ports., facsims. 21 cm. $1.50. Plates printed on both sides. Edited by Fred Barlow. cf. Pref. [BF1381.D6 1923] 23-6853
1. Spiritualism. I. Barlow, Fred, ed. II. Title.

DOYLE, Arthur Conan, Sir, 1859- 133.
The history of spiritualism, by Arthur Conan Doyle ... London, New York [etc.] Cassell and company, ltd. [1926] 2 v. fronts., plates, ports. 24 cm. [BF1241.D6] 26-14130
1. Spiritualism. I. Title.

DOYLE, Arthur Conan, Sir, 1859- 133.
The vital message, by Arthur Conan Doyle ... London, New York [etc.] Hodder and Stoughton [1919] 6 p. l., 15-227, [1] p. plates, ports. 19 cm. [BF1261.D6] 19-18853
1. Spiritualism. I. Title.

DOYLE, Arthur Conan, Sir, 1859- 133.
The wanderings of a spiritualist, by Arthur Conan Doyle ... New York, George H. Doran company [c1921] xi, [2], 15-299 p. front., plates, ports. 21 1/2 cm. $2.50. [BF1283.D5A3 1921 a] 22-9954
1. Spiritualism. 2. Australia—Descr. & trav. I. Title.

DOYLE, Arthur Conan, Sir, 1859-1930. 133
The new revelation, by Arthur Conan Doyle ... New York, George H. Doran company [c1918] viii p., 2 l., 13-122 p. 19 1/2 cm. [BF1272.D7 1918] 18-11168
1. Spirtualism. I. Title.

DOYLE, Arthur Conan, Sir, 1859-1930. 133.
Pheneas speaks; direct spirit communications in the family circle, reported by Arthur Conan Doyle ... New York, George H. Doran company [c1927] xi p., 2 l., 17-199 p. front. (5 port.) 19 1/2 cm. [BF1301.D6 1927 a] 27-15503
1. Spiritualism. I. Title. II. Title: Spirit communications in the family circle.

DOYLE, Arthur Conan, Sir, 1859-1930. 133.
The vital message, by Arthur Conan Doyle ... New York, George H. Doran company [c1919] vii p., 1 l., 11-164 p. plates. 19 1/2 cm. [BF1261.D6] 19-19864
1. Spiritualism. I. Title.

DRAKE, Maud Eugenia (Barrock) Lord, Mrs. 1852- 133.
Psychic light the continuity of law and life. By Mrs. Maud Lord-Drake. Kansas City, Mo., Press of The F.T. Riley pub co., 1904. 596. vii p. incl. front., illus. ports. 22 cm. 3 p. l., 305 p. col. front., illus. 19 cm. [BF1286.D76] 4-3574
1. Spiritualism. I. Title.

DRANE, Dora. Mrs. 133.93
Inevitable voyage; or, Both banks of the Styx; recounting experiences of four unwilling and four willing travelers who crossed, by one called David; with added personal narratives of six who made the journey, received through Dora Drane. [New Rochelle, N.Y. c1935] 52 p. 16 1/2 cm. [BF1311.F8D7] [159.96173] 36-6975
1. Spiritualism. 2. Automation. I. Title.

DRESSER, Charlotte Elizabeth, 1875- 133.91
Life here and hereafter, a sequel or second volume of "Spirit world and spirit life", automatic writing received mostly through the pencil of Charlotte E. Dresser ("Sis") edited by Fred Rafferty ("F. R.") Author's ed. San Jose, Calif., Cosmos publishing co. [c1927] 1 p. l., [5]-272 p. 20 1/2 cm. [BF1301.D72] 27-2056

1. Spiritualism. I. Rafferty, Fred, 1863- ed. II. Title.

DRESSER, Charlotte 133.91
Elizabeth, 1875-
Spirit world and spirit life; descriptions received through automatic writing by C. E. D.; ed. by F. R. Los Angeles, Calif., J. F. Rowny press, 1922. 3 p. l., 9-265 p. 20 1/2 cm. [BF1301.D7] 23-5495
1. Spiritualism. I. Rafferty, Fred, 1863- ed. II. Title.

DROUET, Bessie (Clarke) 133.9
Mrs.
Station Astral, by Bessie Clarke Drouet ... New York, London, G. P. Putnam's sons, 1932. xi, 290 p. front., plates, ports. 21 cm. [BF1283.D7A3] 32-21309
1. Spiritualism. II. Title.

DUNCAN, Victoria Helen
(Macfarlane) 1898- defendant.
The trial of Mrs. Duncan, edited, with a foreword, by C. E. Bechhofer Roberts ... and a note on the Old Bailey, by Helena Normanton. London, New York [etc.] Jarrolds, limited, 1945. 352 p. front., plates. ports. 21 1/2 cm. [The Old Bailey trial series. General editor: C. E. B. Roberts. 3] Plan on lining-papers. The trial on conspiracy to contravene the provisions of section 4 of the witchcraft act of 1735 was held in the Central criminal court, London, Mar. 23-Apr. 3, 1944. A 46
1. Spiritualism. I. Roberts, Carl Eric Bechhofer, 1894- ed. II. Normanton, Helena. III. London. Central criminal court. IV. Title.

DUNNINGER, Joseph. 133.9
Inside the medium's cabinet [by] Joseph Dunninger. New York, D. Kemp and company [c1935] vi p., 2 l., 228 p. plates. 20 cm. "First edition." [BF1042.D8] 159.9617 36-8082
1. Spiritualism. I. Title.

DUNRAVEN, Windham Thomas 133.9
Wyndham-Quin, 4th Earl of, 1841-1926.
Experiences in spiritualism with Mr. D. D. Home / Viscount Adare ; with an introd. by James Webb. New York : Arno Press, 1976. p. cm. (The Occult) Reprint of the 1871 ed. published in London. [BF1301.D8 1976] 75-36824 ISBN 0-405-07937-0 : 11.00
1. Home, Daniel Dunglas, 1833-1886. 2. Spiritualism. I. Title. II. Series: The Occult (New York, 1976-)

*DURANT, Richard 291.23
Spiritual evolution via cause and effect. New York, Vantage [c.1965] 127p. 21cm. 2.95 bds.,
I. Title.

EATON, William Dunseath. 133.
Spirit life; or, Do we die? By William Dunseath Eaton... Chicago, Stanton and Van Vliet co. [c1920] 272 p. 20 cm. [BF1261.E17] 21-244
1. Spiritualism. I. Title.

*EBON, Martin. ed. 133.9
True experiences in communicating with the dead. [New York] New Amer. Lib. [1968, c.1962] 127p. 18cm. (Signet mystic, P3393) .60 pap.,
1. Spiritualism. I. Title.

EDELWEISS, pseud. 133.
Spiritism, by Edelweiss. New York, United States book company, successor to J. W. Lovell company [c1891] 135 p. 19 cm. (On cover: Lovell's literature series, no. 185) [BF1261.E2] 11-3140
1. Spiritualism. I. Title.

EDMONDS, John Worth, 1799- 133.
1874.
Spiritualism. By John W. Edmonds and George T. Dexter, M.D. With an appendix, by Nathaniel P. Tallmadge ... New York, Partridge & Brittan, 1853-55. 2 v. fronts., port., facsims. 22 cm. Vol. 2, 2d edition. [BF1291.E25] 11-4815
1. Spiritualism. I. Dexter, George T., spiritualist, joint author. II. Tallmadge, Nathaniel Pitcher, 1795-1864. III. Title.

EDMONDS, John Worth, 1799- 133.93
1874.
Spiritualism. By John W. Edmonds and George T. Dexter, M.D., with an appendix, by Nathaniel P. Tallmadge ... 9th ed. New York, Partridge & Brittan, 1854. vi, [7]-505 p. incl. illus., facsims. front. 23 cm. [BF1291.E251854] 34-36355
1. Spiritualism. I. Dexter, George T., spiritualist, joint author. II. Tallmadge, Nathaniel Pitcher, 1795-1864. III. Title.

EDWARDS, Frederick, 1863- 133.93
1948.
Trevenen; a text and study of survival and communication. Editor, Elizabeth R. Satterthwait. New York, J. Felsberg [1950] ix, 275 p. ports. 22 cm. [BF1286.E3] 51-21154
1. Edwards, Frederick Trevenen, d. 1918. 2. Spiritualism. I. Title.

EDWARDS, Helen. 133.9
The dawn of a new day, by Helen Edwards. Boston, The Christopher publishing house [1947] ix, 10-430 p. 24 cm. [BF1261.E3] 47-18153
1. Spiritualism. I. Title.

EDWARDS, Henry James, 1893-
The mediumship of Jack Webber, by Harry Edwards ... New York, E. P. Dutton & co., inc., 1941. 119 p. 36 pl. (incl. ports.) on 18 l. 22 cm. Printed in Great Britain. A 42
1. Webber, John Boaden, 1907-1940. 2. Spiritualism. I. Title.

ELLIS, Edith, 1876- 133.93
Love in the afterlife, by Wilfred Brandon, transcribed by Edith Ellis. [1st ed.] New York, C. & R. Anthony, 1956. 159p. 21cm. (A Master publication) [BF1301.E46] 57-22421
1. Spiritualism. I. Title.

ELLIS, Edith, 1876- 133.98
We knew these men, by Wilfred Brandon, transcribed by Edith Ellis. New York, A. A. Knopf, 1942. 3 p. l., v-xvi, 241 p., 1 l. 21 cm. "First edition." [BF1301.E47] [159.96173] 42-2991
1. Spiritualism. I. Title.

ELMORE, Ellaine. 133.9
There is no death. Boston, Christopher Pub. House [1955] 127p. 21cm. [BF1261.2.E4] 55-14538
1. Spiritualism. I. Title.

EMMONS, Samuel Bulfinch. 133
Spiritualism exposed. By S. B. Emmons. New York, United States book company [c1889] 288 p. 19 1/2 cm. [BF1042.E45] 32-22230
1. Spiritualism. I. Title.

[ERICKSON, Elsa Forssell] 133.93
1885-
A boy who came home, by William F. Ericson. New York, 1947. 63 p. port. 19 cm. Messages allegedly received by Elsa F. Ericson from her son after his death. [BF1311.E7E7] 47-26329
1. Spiritualism. I. Ericson, William Forssell, 1921-1943. II. Title.

ERICSON, Elsa Forssell, 1885-
The clear mind, by William F. Ericson. Dictated to Elsa F. Ericson. New York, 1949. 63 p. port. 19 cm. "Book given to me through automatic writing by my son." A 51
1. Spiritualism. I. Ericson, William Forssell, 1921-1943. II. Title.

[ERWIN, Augusta] 133.93
Post mortem opinions, by Theodore Roosevelt. Sioux City, Ia., American metaphysical association [c1920] x, 176 p. 20 cm. Messages from the spirit of Theodore Roosevelt written down by Augusta Erwin. cf. Publisher's notice. [BF1301.E53] [[159.96173]] 41-39766
1. Spiritualism. I. Roosevelt, Theodore, pres. U.S., 1858-1919. II. American metaphysical association. III. Title.

ERWOOD, William Joseph, 1874- 133
Psychic power and how to unfold it; being five lessons on mediumship and its laws, by Will J. Erwood ... [Rochester, N.Y., Burnett printing co., c1922] 79 p. 19 1/2 cm. [BF1272.E78] CA 23
1. Spiritualism. I. Title.

ESSAYS on various 133.93
subjects: intended to elucidate the cuases of the changes coming upon all the earth at this present time, and the nature of the calamities that are so rapidly approaching. by Joshua Carver, Franklin, etc.. etc. Given through a lady. New York, The proprietor, 1861. 200 p. 21 cm. No [BF1235.S65] 159.961M3 34-13684 34
1. Spiritualism.

ESSAYS on various subjects
intended to elucidate the causes of the changes coming upon all the earth at this present time, and the nature of the calamities that are so rapidly approaching. By Joshua, Cuvier, Franklin, etc. ... etc. Given through a lady, who wrote "Communications from the Spirit World" ... etc. New York, Sold by D. Appleton & company. 1861. 200 p. 22 1/2 cm. [BF1291E7] 11-4821
1. Spiritualism.

ESTABROOKS, George Hoben, 133.9
1895-
Spiritism. [1st ed.] New York, E. P. Dutton, 1947. 254 p. 22 cm. Bibliography: p. [237]-244. [BF1261.E8] 47-30608
1. Spiritualism. I. Title.

ESTES, L Frances, ed. 133.
Prehistoric times; or, Milestones in the evolution of man. Our book: Hattie M. Tirrell, Annie B. Leonard, Eleanor N. Foster, L. Frances Estes. [Boston, Christopher publishing house, c1923] 11 p. l., 261 p. 21 1/2 cm. "A book from the psychic plane", the subject matter relating to the Lemurians, the Atlanteans, and the aborigines of North America. Prepared for publication by L. Frances Estes. cf. Pref. [BF1301.E6] 23-15279
1. Spiritualism. I. Tirrell, Mrs. Hattie M., joint ed. II. Leonard, Mrs. Annie B., joint ed. III. Foster, Mrs. Eleanor N., joint ed. IV. Title. V. Title: Milestones in the evolution of man.

EVANS, Frederick William, 133.9
1808-1893.
Spiritualism on trial; containing the arguments of Rev. F. W. Evans in the debate on spiritualism between him and Mr. A. J. Fishback, held in Osceola, Iowa, commencing Nov. 18, and closing Nov. 28, 1874. Cincinnati, Printed by Hitchcock & Walden, 1875. 432 p. 18 cm. [BF1041.E8] 32-21767
1. Spiritualism. I. Fishback, A. J. II. Title.

EVANS, Henry Ridgely, 1861-
Hours with the ghosts; or, Nineteenth century witchcraft. Illustrated investigations into phenomena of spiritualism and theosophy, by Henry Ridgely Evans ... Chicago, Laird & Lee [c1897] 302 p. incl. illus., plates, ports., facsims., diagrs. front. 20 1/2 cm. [Lee's library of occult science] [BF1289.E8] 11-4745
1. Blavatsky, Helene Petrovna (Halin-Halin) 1831-1891. 2. Spiritualism. 3. Theosophy. I. Title.
Contents omitted

EVANS, Henry Ridgely, 1861-
The spirit world unmasked; illustrated investigations into the phenomena of spiritualism and theosophy, by Henry Ridgely Evans ... Chicago, Laird & Lee [1902] 302 p. incl. illus., plates, ports., facsims. front. 19 1/2 cm. "List of works consulted": p. 298-302. Issued in 1897 under title: Hours with the ghosts. [BF1289.E85] 2-20068
1. Blavatsky, Helene Petrovna (Halin-Halin) 1831-1891. 2. Spiritualism. 3. Theosophy. I. Title.

EVARTS, Lewis L. 133.
Has spiritualism any foundation in the Bible? By L. L. Evarts ... [Shamokin, Pa., J. T. Shoener, Printer] c1894] 57 p. 18 cm. [BF1275.B5E8] 11-3423
1. Spiritualism. I. Title.

THE evolution of the 133.
universe; or, Creation according to science, transmitted from Michael Faraday ... Los Angeles, Calif., Cosmos publishing co., 1924. 3 p. l., v-xv, 17-176 p. front., plates, ports. 20 cm. By the "Mystic scribe" and the "Mystic helper". cf. Foreword. [BF1311.S4E8] 24-19840
1. Faraday, Michael, 1791-1867. 2. Spiritualism. I. The Mystic scribe. II. The Mystic helper.

EWER, Ferdinand Cartwright,
1826-1883.
The eventful nights of August 20th and 21st, 1854; and how Judge Edmonds was hocussed; or, Fallibility of "spiritualism" exposed. By F. C. Ewer New York, S. Hyeston, 1855. 106 p. 19 cm. [BF1289.E87] 11-4746
1. Spiritualism. I. Title.

EWER, Ferdinand Cartwright,
1826-1883.
Two eventful nights, or, The fallibility of "spiritualism" exposed. By F. C. Ewer. New York, H. Dayton, 1856. 106 p. 18 cm. [BF1289.E88] 11-4747
1. Spiritualism. I. Title.

FAIRFIELD, Francis Gerry, 133.
1844-1887.
Ten years with spiritual mediums: an inquiry concerning the etiology of certain phenomena called spiritual. By Francis Gerry Fairfield. New York, D. Appleton and company, 1875. 182 p. 19 cm. [BF1286.F22] 11-4768
1. Spiritualism. I. Title.

FALCON, Joseph, medium. 133.9
Tale of two worlds. Boston, Christopher Pub. House [1950] 168 p. 21 cm. [BF1283.F18A3] 50-6463
1. Spiritualism. I. Title.

FARNESE, A. 133.9
A wanderer in the spirit lands. By Franchezzo. Transcribed by A. Farnese ... Chicago, The Progressive thinker publishing house, 1901. 5 p. l., 286 p. 21 cm. First published London, 1896. [BF1301.F25 1901] 32-21776
1. Spiritualism. I. Title.

[FARRINGTON, Elijah] 133.
Revelations of a spirit medium; or, Spiritualistic mysteries exposed. A detailed explanation of the methods used by fraudulent mediums. By A Medium [pseud.] St. Paul, Minn., Farrington & co., 1891. vi, [7]-324 p. incl. plates. 19 cm. By Elijah Farrington and Charles F. Pidgeon. [BF1042.F3 1891] 11-4748
1. Spiritualism. I. Pidgeon, Charles F., joint author. II. Medium, A., pseud. III. Title.

[FARRINGTON, Elijah] 133.
Revelations of a spirit medium; facsimile edition, with notes, bibliography, glossary and index, by Harry Price ... and Eric J. Dingwall ... London, K. Paul, Trench, Trubner & co., ltd.; New York, E. P. Dutton & co., 1922. lxiv p.; facsim.: cover, vi, [7]-327, [1] p. incl. plates. 22 cm. Elijah Farrington and Charles F. Pidgeon claimed copyright of the original edition "as the authors of the work." With reproduction of original t.-p.: Revelations of a spirit medium; or, Spiritualistic mysteries exposed. A detailed explanation of the methods used by fraudulent mediums. By A. Medium. St. Paul, Minn., Farrington & co., 1891. "Bibliographical note [concerning this book]": p. xi-xv. Bibliography: p. xxxi-lix. [BF1042.F3 1922] 23-10608
1. Spiritualism. I. Pidgeon, Charles F., joint author. II. Price, Harry, ed. III. Dingwall, Eric John, joint ed. IV. Medium, A., pseud. V. Title.

FEARNLEY, J. R. 133.9
The way through / by J. R. Fearnley. London ; New York : Regency Press, 1975. 68 p. ; 19 cm. [BF1272.F37] 75-327464 ISBN 0-7212-0389-2 : £1.20
1. Spiritualism. 2. Conduct of life. I. Title.

FEELY, Joseph Martin. 133.82
Electrograms from Elysium; a study on the probabilities in postmortuary communication through the electronics of telepathy and extrasensory perception, including the code of anagrams in the purported sender's name. [Rochester? N. Y.] 1954. 342p. 24cm. [BF1290.F4] 54-32506
1. Spiritualism. I. Title.

FEILDING, Everard, 133.91072
1867-1936.
Sittings with Eusapia Palladino & other studies. Introd. by E. J. Dingwall, New Hyde Park, N.Y., University Books [1963] 324 p. illus. 24 cm. [BF1030.P3F42] 63-18682
1. Palladino, Eusapia, 1854-1918. 2. Spiritualism. I. Title.

FEILDING, Everard 133.91072
[Francis Henry Everard Joseph Feilding] *Sittings with Eusapia Palladino &* other studies. Introd. by E. J. Dingwall. New

Hyde Park, N.Y., University Bks. [c.1963] 324p. illus. 24cm. 63-18682 10.00
1. Palladino, Eusapia, 1854-1918. 2. Spiritualism. I. Title.

FERGUSON, Jesse Babcock. 133.
Divine illumination. Discourses on the ministry of angels: the idea of endless wrong an abomination: self knowledge the knowledge of spiritual communion: immortality is life in God: Melchisideck, or divinity in man: God will teach His creatures. By J. B. Ferguson. Nashville, J. F. Morgan, printer, 1855. v, [7]-96 p. 21 cm. [With his Spirit communion: a record of communications from the spirit-spheres. Nashville, 1854] [BF1291.F8] 11-4818
1. Spiritualism. I. Title.

FERGUSON, Jesse Babcock, d.1870. 133.
Spirit communion; a record of communications from the spirit-spheres, with incontestible evidence of personal identity, presented to the public, with explanatory observations, by J. B. Ferguson. Nashville, Union and American steam press, 1854. 276 p. 21 cm. [BF1291.F8] 11-4816
1. Spiritualism. I. Title.

FERGUSON, Jesse Babcock, d.1870, ed. 133.
Spirit communion. A record of communications through H. B. Champion. With explanatory observations by J. B. Ferguson. Rev. ed. [by Marjus C. C. Church] Parkersburg (W.Va.] Printed by Globe press, 1888. ix, 261 p. 25 cm. "Preface to revised edition" signed: M.C.C. Introduction signed: J.B.F. Sermons, by Rev. J. B. Ferguson: p. [197]-242. [BF1301.C45] 11-5824
1. Spiritualism. I. Champton, H. B. II. Church, Marius C. C. III. Title.

FIFIELD, George Edward. 220
The law of spiritual transformation [by] George Edward Fifield, D.D. Boston, R. G. Badger [c1929] 57 p. 20 1/2 cm. [BR125.F425] 29-4595
I. Title.

FINCK, Susan J. 133.
Lifting the veil: or, Interior experiences and manifestations. By Susan J. and Andrew A. Finck... Boston, Colby & Rich, 1887. 300 p. front., plates, ports. 20 1/2 cm. Pages 299-300 contain testimonials. [BF1261.F4] 11-3141
1. Spiritualism. I. Finck, Andrew A., joint author. II. Title.

FINDLAY, James Arthur, 1883- 133.9
The rock of truth; or, Spiritualism, the coming world religion. By J. Arthur Findlay ... Philadelphia, David McKay company, 1933. 321 p. front. (port.) 22 cm. "1st impression, August 1933 ... 11th impression, September 1963." "A continuation of On the edge of the etheric."--Foreword. [BF1261.F52 1963j] (159.9617) 34-32381
1. Spiritualism. 2. Christianity—Controversial literature. 3. Religions. I. Title.

FISCHER, Emily Lorena (Coleman) Mrs. 1868- 133
A visit to the astral plane; or, Another proof of life beyond the grave, by Emily L. Fischer ... Philadelphia, Pa., E.L. Fischer [c1914] 52 p., 1 l. 17 1/2 cm. [BF1272.F5] 14-12511 0.25
1. Spiritualism. I. Title.

FITZGERALD, Byron John, 1885- 133.9
A new text of spiritual philosophy and religion. [2d ed.] Oakland, Calif., Universal Church of the Master [1954] 193p. 21cm. [BF1261.2.F56 1954] 54-39026
1. Spiritualism. I. Title.

FITZ-GIBBON, Ralph Edgerton. 133.9
The man with two bodies. New York, Vantage Press [c1952] 137p. 28cm. [BF1383.F57] 52-9684
1. Spiritualism. I. Title.

FLAGSTAD, O A. 133.9
The dead. Boston, Christopher [1950] 95 p. port. 21 cm. [BF1261.F58] 50-1759
1. Spiritualism. I. Title.

FLETCHER, Anna Louise (Paine) 133.
Death unveiled. Washington, 1929. 96 p. 23 cm. [BF1261.F59] 51-47465
1. Spiritualism. I. Title.

[FLETCHER, Augusta W.] 133.
The other world and this. A compendium of spiritual laws ... New York, C. B. Reed, 1893. 278 p. 18 1/2 cm. (New White cross literature. no. 1) Copyrighted by Augusta W. Fletcher, M.D. [BF1261.F6] 11-3142
1. Spiritualism. 2. Mind and body. I. Title.

FLETCHER, James Henry. 133.
Spiritualism; its truth, helpfulness and danger, by James Henry Fletcher. New York city, The Occult book concern [c1915] xvi p. 1 l, 254 p. front. (port.) 20 cm. $1.50 [BF1261.F6] 15-19305
1. Spiritualism. I. Title.

FLOURNOY, Theodore, 1854-1920 133.9
From India to the planet Mars, a study of a case of somnambulism with glossolalia. Introd. by C. T. K. Chari. New Hyde Park, N. Y., University Bks. [c.1963] 457p. illus. 22cm. 63-16228 10.00
1. Smith, Helene. 2. Spiritualism. 3. Somnamnulism. 4. Glossolalia. I. Title.

FLOURNOY, Theodore, 1854-1920. 133.
From India to the planet Mars; a tudy of a case of somnambulism, with glossolalia; by Th. Flournoy...tr. by Daniel B. Vermilye. New York and London, Harper & brothers, 1900. xix, [1], 446, [1] p. illus., plates, facsims. 19 1/2 cm. [BF1311.M4F6] 0-4703
1. Spiritualism. 2. Somnambulism. I. Vermilye, Daniel B., tr. II. Title.

FORD, Arthur A. 133.
Spiritual vibrations, by H. P. Blavatsky, through Arthur A. Ford as medium to the Open circle ... New York, H. P. B. publishers, inc. [c1926] 2 p. l., viii, 83 p. 18 cm. [BF1311.B65F6] 42-43849
1. Blavatsky, Helene Petrovna (Hahn-Hahn) 1831-1891. 2. Spiritualism. I. Title.

FORD, Arthur A. 133.9'1
Unknown but known; my adventure into the meditative dimension, by Arthur Ford. [1st ed.] New York, Harper & Row [1968] 161 p. 22 cm. Bibliographical references included in "Notes" (p. 153-155) [BF1283.F63A3] 68-29570 4.95
1. Spiritualism. I. Title.

FORNELL, Earl Wesley. 920.913391
The unhappy medium; spiritualism and the life of Margaret Fox. Drawings by Lowell Collins. Austin, University of Texas Press [1964] x, 204 p. illus., ports. 24 cm. Bibliography: p. [183]-190. [BF1283.F7F6] 64-10317
1. Kane, Margaret (Fox) 1836-1893. 2. Spiritualism. 3. Fox family. I. Title.

FORSTER, Thomas Gales, 1816-1886. 133.
Unanswerable logic; a series of spiritual discourses, given through the mediumship of Thomas Gales Forster. Boston, Colby & Rich, 1887. 438 p. front. (port.) 20 cm. "Introduction" signed: Carrie Grimes Forster. [BF1261.F73] 11-3144
1. Spiritualism. I. Title.

FOSTER, Charles Henery. 133.
The common-sense philosophy of spirit or psychology, written from spirit impression, by Charles H. Foster ... San Francisco, 1901. 4 p. l., [5]-395 p. front. (port.) illus., plates. 18 cm. [BF1301.F75] 1-31439
1. Spiritualism. I. Title.

FOSTER, Ethel (Field) Mrs. 1883- 133.93
A light to your candle, by Hayward Grayland and Ethel Field Foster ... Los Angeles, Calif., DeVorss & co. [c1937] 4 p. l., 11-127 p. 20 cm. "I present these lessons as having come not from me but through me [From the spirit known as Hayward Grayland]"--Introd., signed; Ethel Field Foster. [Full name: Mrs. Mary Ethel (Field) Foster] [BF1301.F77] 159.96173 38-3313
1. Spiritualism. I. Title.

FOX, Nettie Pease. Mrs. 133.9
Mysteries of the border land: or, The conscious side of unconscious life life [by] Mrs. Nettie Pease Fox ... Ottumwa, Ia., D. M. & N. P. Fox, 1883. viii, [9]-536 p. 20 cm. [BF1301.F78] 32-19330
1. Spiritualism. I. Title.

FOX, Nettie Pease. Mrs.
The phantom form: experiences in earth and spirit life. A true life history, communicated by a spirit through the trance mediumship of Mrs. Nettie Pease Fox ... Newton, Ia., D. M. Fox, 1881. viii, [9]-169 p. 22 cm. 8-11370
I. Title.

FRANCIS, John Reynolds
The encyclopedia of death and life in the spirit-world. Opinions experiences from eminent sources. By J. R. Francis ... Chicago, The Progressive thinker publishing house, 1893-1900. 3 v. front. (v. 1-2, ports) illus. 20 cm. Jun
I. Title.

[FRANKE, Willibald] 133.
Voices from another world; the waking dreams and metaphysical phantasies of a non-spiritualist, edited by F. Guris [pseud.] authorized translation by Lilian A. Xlare. New York, Dodd, Mead and company, 1923. xv, 243 p. 22 cm. [BF1303.F7 1923 a] 23-17490 3.00
1. Spiritualism. 2. Subconsciousness. I. Clare, Lilian A., tr. II. Title.

FREDERICK, James Mack Henry, 1863-1942. 133.93
The silver cord, or, Life here and hereafter, with forty-one full page illustrations ... by James M. H. Frederick and Olga A. Tildes. Boston, The Christopher publishing house [1946] xiv p., 1 l., 17-602 p. fronts., plates, ports. 24 cm. "Suggested readings": p. 602. [BF1261.F76] 46-1834
1. Spiritualism. I. Tides, Olga A., joint author. II. Title.

FRIKELL, Samri. 133.
Spirit mediums exposed, by Samri Frikell; with special chapters, affidavits, and letters by the world-famed Houdini; an introduction by the famous magician, Howard Thurston; and a full account of the author's adventures with the international leader of the spiritualists, Sir Arthur Conan Doyle ... New York, N. Y., New metropolitan fiction, inc., c1930. 96 p. illus. 31 cm. Contains advertising matter. On cover: A Macfadden publication. [BF1042.F7] 30-8841
1. Spiritualism. 2. Clairvoyance. I. Title.

FROM beyond; 133.9
extracts from messages of comfort and inspiration, received from a loved one waiting on the other side, by Mrs. F., with an introduction by John Clair Minot. Boston, Mass., The Stratford company [c1930] 3 p. l., iii, 97 p. 20 cm. [BF1301.F85] 30-11834
1. Spiritualism. I. F., Mrs.

FROM Planet Pluto with brotherly love. 133
Los Angeles, DeVorss; distributed by A. J. Brown [196-?] 32 p. 16 cm. [BF1311.P6F7] 75-15985
1. Spiritualism.

FROOM, LeRoy Edwin, 1890-
Spiritualism today. Illustrated by John Gourley. Washington, Review and herald pub. association [1963] 64 p. illus. 18 cm. 64-27541
1. Spiritualism. I. Title.

FROOM, LeRoy Edwin, 1890-
Spiritualism today. Illustrated by John Gourley. Washington, Review and herald pub. association [1963] 64 p. illus. 18 cm. 64-27541
1. Spiritualism. I. Title.

FROST, George Edwin. 133.9
Immortality and the cause of spiritualism, by George Edwin Frost. Portland, Or., 1934. 3 p. l., 108 p. 21 cm. [BF1261.F8] 159.9617 34-31436
1. Spiritualism. I. Title.

FULLER, Elizabeth, 1946- 133.9'3
Poor Elizabeth's almanac / Elizabeth Fuller. New York, N.Y. : Berkley Pub. Corp. : distributed by Putnam, c1980. 103 p. ; 23 cm. [BF1311.F7F84] 19 80-127800 ISBN 0-425-04603-6 : 9.95 pbk. : 2.25
1. Franklin, Benjamin, 1706-1790. 2. Fuller, Elizabeth, 1946- 3. Spiritualism. I. Franklin, Benjamin, 1706-1790. II. Title.

FULLER, George Albion. 133.91
Wisdom of the ages; revelations from Zertonlem, the prophet of Tlaskanata, automatically transcribed by George A. Fuller, M. D. Introduction by Miss Susie C. Clark. Boston, Banner of light publishing company, 1901. viii, 211 p. 21 cm. [BF1301.F9] 1-30284
1. Spiritualism. I. Title.

FULLER, George Albion. 133.91
Wisdom of the ages; revelations from Zertonlem the prophet of Tlaskanata, automatically transcribed by George A. Fuller, M. D. Introduction by Miss Susie C. Clark. Boston, Christopher publishing house [c1916] viii, 211 p. 21 cm. [BF1301.F9 1916] 16-10457 1.25
1. Spiritualism. I. Title.

[FULLER, Ira C] 133.9
Poems and essays from many authors of this and earlier centuries, given by them through the organism of a modern psychic. Author's edition. Buffalo, C. W. Moulton, 1897. vi, [7]-128 p. incl. front. (port.) 20 cm. [BF1290.F8 1897] 32-19883
1. Spiritualism. I. Title.

FUNK, Isaac Kaufman, 1839-1912. 133.
The psychic riddle, by Isaac K. Funk ... New York and London, Funk & Wagnalls company, 1907. iii, 243 p. 20 cm. [BF1261.F87] 7-8500
1. Spiritualism. 2. Psychical research. I. Title.

FUNK, Isaac Kaufman, 1839-1912. 133.
The widow's mite and other psychic phenomena, by Isaac K. Funk ... New York and London, Funk & Wagnalls company, 1904. 1 p. l., xiv, 538 p. illus. 23 cm. Bibliography (partial): p. 523-534. [BF1031.F88] 4-11204
1. Spiritalism. 2. Psychical research. I. Title.

FUNK, Issac Kaufman, 1839-1912. 133.
The widow's mite, and other psychic phenomena, by Isaac K. Funk ... 3d ed. New York and London, Funk & Wagnalls company, 1911. xvi, 560 p. illus. 23 cm. "Bibliography--(partial)": p. 545-556. [BF1031.F884] 11-6019
1. Spiritualism. 2. Religion and science—1900- I. Title.

FURTHER communications from the world of spirits, 133.
on subjects highly important to the human family. By Joshua. Solomon. and others. Given through a lady. New York, Pub. for the proprietor. A. J. Brandy, printer, 1861. 2 p. l., [iii]-vi, [5]-174 p. 23 cm. By the author of "Communications from the spirit world." [BF1291.F84] 11-4822
1. Spiritualism. I. Communications from the spirit world, Author of.

FURTHER communications from the world of spirits, 133.
on subjects highly important to the human family. By Joshua, Solomon. and others. Including the Rights of man. by George Fox. Given through a lady. 2d ed. New York, Pub. for the proprietor, 1862. 2 p. l., [iii]-vi, [5]-174, 16 p. 23 cm. "An essay on the rights of man, by George Fox. Given through a lady New York, Printed by A. J. Brady, 1861": 16 p. at end. [BF1291.F85] 11-4823
1. Spiritualism. I. Communications from the spirit world, Author of.

GAFFIELD, Erastus Celley, 1840- 133.
A celestial message; a relation of the observations and experiences of a philosopher and poet in the spirit world, recorded by Erastus C. Gaffield. Private ed. Boston, Lee and Shepard, 1902. xiii, 133 p. 20 cm. [BF1301.G22] 2-7119
1. Spiritualism. I. Title.

GARLAND, Hamlin, 1860-1940. 133.
The shadow world, by Hamlin Garland... New York and London, Harper & brothers, 1908. iv p., 2 l., 3-294 p., 1 l. 19 1/2 cm. [BF1261.G2] 8-29371
1. Spiritualism. 2. Psychical research. I. Title.

[GARRETSON, James Edmund] 1828-1895. 133.
Nineteenth century sense; the paradox of

spiritualism. By John Darby [pseud.] Philadelphia [etc.] J. B. Lippincott company, 1887. vii, 222 p. 18 cm. [BF1031.G21] 10-29916
1. Spiritualism. 2. Rosicrucians. I. Title.

GARRETSON, James Edmund, 1828-1895. 133.
Nineteenth century sense: being the paradox of Spiritus sanctus and of Rosicrucianism. By J. E. Garretson, M. D. (John Darby). 2d ed. Philadelphia, J. B. Lippincott company, 1893. 250 p. 17 1/2 cm. [BF1031.G23] 10-29917
1. Spiritualism. 2. Rosicrucians. I. Title.

GARRETT, Eileen Jeanette (Lyttle) 1893- 133.9'1'0924 B
Many voices; the autobiography of a medium, by Eileen J. Garrett. With an introd. by Allan Angoff. New York, Putnam [1968] 254 p. 22 cm. [BF1283.G29A3] 68-20947
1. Spiritualism. I. Title.

GARRETT, Eileen Jeanette (Lyttle) Mrs. 1893- 920.9
My life as a search for the meaning of mediumship, by Eileen J. Garrett. New York, Oquaga press, 1939. 3 p. l., 224, [1] p. 22 1/2 cm. [BF1283.G3A3] 40-1487
1. Spiritualism. I. Title.

GARRETT, Eileen Jeanette Lyttle, 1893-1970. 133.9'1'0924 B
My life as a search for the meaning of mediumship / Eileen J. Garrett. New York : Arno Press, 1975. p. cm. (Perspectives in psychical research) Reprint of the 1939 ed. published by Oquaga Press, New York. [BF1283.G3A3 1975] 75-7380 ISBN 0-405-07030-6 : 13.00
1. Garrett, Eileen Jeanette Lyttle, 1893-1970. 2. Spiritualism. I. Title. II. Series.

[GARRETT, Julia E.] 133.
Mediums unmasked. An expose of modern spiritualism, by an ex-medium. Los Angeles, Cal., H. M. Lee & bro., 1892. 56 p. 17 cm. Author's name on cover. [BF1042.G23] 10-34909
1. Spiritualism. I. Title.

[GARRETT, Julia H.] Mrs. 133.
Mediums unmasked. An expose of modern spiritualism, by an ex-medium. Los Angeles, Cal., H. M. Lee & bro., 1892. 56 p. 17 cm. Author's name on cover. [BF1042.G23] 10-34909
1. Spiritualism. I. Title.

[GASTON, Henry A.] 133.
Mars revealed; or, Seven days in the spirit world; containing an account of the spirit's trip to Mars, and his return to earth ... By a spirit yet in the flesh ... San Francisco, Pub. for the writer, by A.L. Bancroft & co., 1880. 208 p. 22 1/2 cm. [BF1311.M4G2] 10-33697
1. Spiritualism. I. Title.

GENERAL Assembly of Spiritualists. 133.9
Manual of Spiritualism. 1948 ed. New York [1948] 139 p. 23 cm. Cover title: Spiritualist manual. [BX9798.S7G4 1948] 48-4090
1. Spiritualism. I. Title.

GILLINGHAM, James. 133.
Eight days with the spiritualists: or, What led me to the subject--what I heard--what I saw--and my conclusions. By James Gillingham ... Chard, T. Young, printer; [etc., etc.] 1872. 73 p. 19 cm. [BF1251.G48] 10-34690
1. Spiritualism. I. Title.

GLADSTONE, William Louis, 1875 133.
Spiritualism and a guide to mediumship, by Prof. W. Gladstone. Illuminating, instructive, inspiring; new light upon subjects of great interest to mankind ... [St. Louis Wilson pringing company, c1916] c3 p. l., 11-335 p. incl. facsim. 23 cm. [BF1286.G6] 16-20525 5.00
1. Spiritualism. I. Title.

GLEASON, Samuel Wight. 133.91
The spirit home; a closet companion. Dedicated to mothers and their children. Given by spirits from the highter sphere, through Samuel Wight Gleason, writing medium. Boston, Mass., 1852. 1 p., l., iii, [7]-241 p. 21 cm. [BF1291.G55] 11-4824
1. Spiritualism. I. Title.

GODDARD, John, 1839-
Right and wrong unveilings of the spiritual world, by Rev. John Goddard. New York city, New-church board of publication. 1912. 4 p. l., 3-78 p. 19 cm. 13-1397
I. Title.

GOFF, William M. 133
The mirror of life, sunshine and darkness, a book for the people who think, pub. by William M. Goff. Words of wisdom from the world of spirits. Modern-scientific spiritualism. [Wilmington, Del., Mercantile printing co., c1919] 2 p. l., xi, 114 p. 19 cm. [BF1272.G6] 20-2048
1. Spiritualism. I. Title.

[GONZALES, Ambrosio Jose] 133.
Heaven revealed. A series of authentic spirit-messages, from a wife to her husband, proving the sublime nature of true spiritualism. Washington [McQueen & Wallace, printers] 1889 68 p. 17 cm. Copyright by A. J. Gonzales. [BF1301.G6] 21-1969
I. Title.

GOODENOW, Juliet S. 133.
Vanishing night; a series of letters given through telepathic correspondence to Juliet S. Goodenow, by the late Frederic William Henry Myers ... Los Angeles, Cal., Time-mirror press, 1923. 155 p. 20 cm. [BF1301.G75] 23-12538
1. Spiritualism. I. Myers, Frederic William Henry, 1843-1901. II. Title.

GOODWILL, Anna. 133.93
... Trismegetus revealed, a royal romance and play upon words assembled by the ghost writers and transcribed by A. Goodwill. [Jackson Heights, N.Y.] A Goodwill [1943] 1 p. l., 954 p. 26 1/2 cm. At head of title: RR. [BF1301.G76] 43-14126
1. Spiritualism. 2. Automatism. I. Title.

GOODWILL, Anna, 1876- 133.93
Ecce Homo! Behold--the Man! Day by day cosmic wireless with an addenda of prescience, transcribed by Anna Goodwill. New York, Margent Press, 1947. 484 p. front. 25 cm. At head of title: RR. Sequel to Trismegetus revealed. Bibliography: p. 464. [BF1301.G755] 47-11754
1. Spiritualism. 2. Automatism. I. Title.

GOODWILL, Anna, 1876- 133.93
The record of a mystic; day by day cosmic wireless in two books: "Ecce Homo" [and] "One thing needful." [1st, restricted ed.] New York, Universum Book Pub. Co. [1952] 483, 348 p. illus. 27 cm. "In direct sequence to ... [the author's] Trismegetus revealed." [BF1301.G757] 52-33495
1. Spiritualism. I. Title.

GORDON, Ellen. 261
Prophecies by Ezra, received through Ellen Gordon ... New York, N. Y., Heiss publishing house [c1927] 74 p. 17 cm. [BR123.G56] 27-15639
1. Spiritualism. I. Title. II. Title: Ezra, Prophecies by.

GORDON, William Robert, 1811-1897. 133.
A three-fold test of modern spiritualism. By William R. Gordon ... New-York, C. Scribner, 1856. xvii, [19]-408 p. 20 cm. [BF1042.G65] 10-34910
1. Spiritualism. I. Title.

GRAEBNER, Theodore Conrad, 1876- 133.
Spiritism; a study of its phenomena and religious teachings, by the. Graebner ... St. Louis, Mo., Concordia publishing house, 1919. 128 p. 20 cm. [BF1261.G5] 20-3579
1. Spiritualism. I. Title.

GRANT, Miles. 133.9
Spiritualism unveiled, and shown to be the work of demons: an examination of its origin, morals, doctrines, and politics. By Miles Grant ... Boston, The "Crisis" office [1866] 1 p. l., 77, 32, 32, 32 p. 17 cm. [BF1042.G73] 32-35934
1. Spiritualism. I. Title.
Contents omitted.

GRAVES, Lucien Chase, 1849- 133.
The natural order of spirit; a psychic study and experience, by Lucien C. Graves ... Boston, Sherman. French & company, 1915. 3 p. l., v, [8] p., 1 l., 365 p. port. 21 cm. [BF1261.G6] 15-19302 1.50
1. Spiritualism. I. Title.

GRAY, James M. 1851- 133.
Spiritism and the fallen angels in the light of the Old. and New Testaments, by James M. Gray ... New York, Chicago [etc.] Fleming H. Revell company [c1920] 3 p. l., 9-148 p. 20 cm. [BF1275.B5G7] 21-3786
1. Spiritualism. I. Title.

GREBER, Johannes. 159.9617072
Communication with the spirit world; a nattative of scientific investigations and experiences, of a Catholic priest, with practical teachings from spiritual planes clarifying the Sacred Scriptures, by Johannes Greber. Translated from the German. New York, N. Y., Macoy publishing company, 1932. 1 p. l., v, 429 p. 23 cm. [BF1263.G73] 133.90702 32-35901
1. Spiritualism. I. Title.

[GREEN, Harriet L Mrs. 133.
Think on these things ... Pasadena, Calif., Star-news publishing company, 1921. 2 p. l., 62 p. 20 cm. On t.-p.: H. F. Copyright ... by Harriet L. Green. "The messages herein recorded were received by me through so-called automatic writing." [BF1343.G7] 21-16238
1. Spiritualism. I. Title.

GREY, Pamela Wyndham) Grey, viscountess, 1871- 133.
The earthen vessel a volume dealing with spirit-comminication received in the form of book-tests, by Pamela Glenconner, with a preface by Sir Oliver Lodge ... New York, John Lane company; London, John Lane, 1921. xxvi p., 1 l., 29-155 p. 20 cm. [Full name: Pamela Genevieve Adelaide (Wyndham) Grey, viscountess Grey] [BF1301.G8 1921 a] 21-4732
1. Spiritualism. I. Title. II. Title: Book-tests.

GREY, Pamela (Wyndham) Grey, viscountess, 1871- 133.
The earthen vessel;a volume dealing with spirit-communication received in the form of books-tests, by Pamela Glenconner, with a preface by Sir oliver Lodge ... London, John Lane; New York, John Lane company, 1921. xxvi p., 1 l., 29-155, [1] p. 2 port. (incl. front.) 20 cm. [Full name: Pamela Genevieve Adelaide (Wyndham) rey viscountess Grey] [BF1301.G8 1921] 21-2977
1. Spiritualism. I. Title. II. Title: Book-tests.

GREYER, Bertha Anna, Mrs. 133.
The universal treasure casket; or, Book of wisdom and knowledge, containing how she became a medium, or experiences in the study of occult science, and many formulas from which to choose a profession, with poems, by Bertha A. Greyer. Boston, Press of S. J. Parkhill & co. [1900] ix, [11]-96 p. front., pl. 20 cm. [BF1301.G84] 0-6225
1. Spiritualism. I. Title.

GRIDLEY, Josiah A. 133.
Astounding facts from the spirit world. Witnessed at the house of J. A. Gridley, Southampton, Mass., by a circle of friends, embracing the extremes of good and evil. The great doctrines of the Bible, such as the resurrection, day of judgment, Christ's second coming, defended, and ... unfolded by the spirits, with many hundreds of ... questions answered from the same source ... Southampton, Mass., J. A. Gridley, 1854. 287 p. fold. diagr. 19 cm. [BF1291.G8] 11-4825
1. Spiritualism. I. Title.

GRIMES, James Stanley, 1807-1903. 133.9
Great discussion of modern spiritualism, between Prof. J. Stanley Grimes and Leo Miller, esq. at the Melodeon, Boston, every evening during the second week in March, 1860 ... Reported. verbatim, for the "Banner of light". Boston, Berry, Colby & company, 1860. 167 p. 2 l. 24 cm. [BF1041.G7] 32-21735
1. Spiritualism. I. Miller, Leo. II. Title.

GRINNELL, John C. 133.
The ordeal of life, graphically illustrated in the experiences of fifteen hundred individuals promiscuously drawn from all nations, religions, classes, and conditions of men ... given psychometrically, through the mediumship of Dr. John C. Grinnell, in presence of the compiler, Thomas B. Hazard. [Boston] W. White an[d] [c] ompany; New York, The American news company, 1870. 130 p. front. (facsim.) col. pl. 25 cm. [BF1291.G85] 10-38818
1. Spiritualism. I. Hazard, Thomas Robinson, 1797-1886, comp. II. Title.

[GROVE, Harriet (McCrory)] Mrs. 1874- ed. 133.91
Gone west, by a soldier doctor, ed. by H. M. G. and M. M. H. With a preface by Frederick W. Kendall. New York, A. A. Knopf, 1919. 103 p. 19 cm. Spiritualistic messages edited by Harriet McCrory Grove and Mattie Mitchell Hunt. [BF1301.G87] 19-11794
1. Spiritualism. I. Hunt, Mattie (Mitchell) Mrs, 1868- joint ed. II. Title.

GRUMBINE, Jesse Charles Fremont 133.
The spirit world. Where and what it is. The abode of the departed. A revealment. By J. C. F. Grimbine. Boston, Mass., The Order of the white rose [c1909] 69 p. 17 x 14 cm. [BF1261.G7] 12-32975
1. Spiritualism. I. Title.

GUYARD, Jules. 133
The dead, by Jules Guyard... Philadelphia, Printed by the Bingham company [c1926] 3 p. l., 154 p. 20 1/2 cm. [BF1040.G65] 27-3045
1. Spiritualism. I. Title.

HABERSTROH, Ernest. 133.
Divine revelations; messages dictated by the divine planetary spirit rulers and their messengers, received by Ernest Haberstroh, ed. by John F. Sanders. 1st ed. Rosenburg, Ore. [Sun printing co., c1922] 139 p. 21 1/2 cm. [BF1301.H25] 22-20141
1. Spiritualism. I. Sanders, John F., ed. II. Title.

[HABERSTROH, Ernest] 133.
The divine revelations 2d and enl. ed.) by John F. Sanders Boston, The Christopher publishing house [c1926] 2 p. l., [7]-232 p. 20 1/2 cm. "All of these messages were received through the instrumentality of... Ernest Haberstroh."--Pref. [BF1301.H25 1926] 26-4284
1. Spiritualism. I. Sanders, John F., ed. II. Title.

HADLEY, Helen L. 133.9
Love that reaches a star; excerpts from letters received from Helen Taber by her mother, automatically written through the hand of Helen L. Hadley. [New Bedford, Mass., Printed by Vining press, c1931] 59 p. 15 1/2 cm. [BF1311.T3H3] 31-10009
1. Spiritualism. I. Taber, Helen, 1894-1914. II. Title.

HAINES, Frederick Henry. 133
A voice from Heaven; the return of "G. V. O."... written by Frederick H. Haines... Watford, Herts,. The Pure thought press [1932?] 138 p. 1 l., pl. 19 1/2 cm. (The spiritual wisdom series, no. 3) [BF1311.O8H3] 32-11665
1. Spiritualism. I. Owen, George Vale, 1869-1931. II. Title.

HALCYONE, Ruth. 133.
Music of the spheres received by radio of the spheres [by] Ruth Halcyone. [Los Angeles, House of Ralston, inc., c1927] 2 p. l., [3]-73, [1] p. 19 cm. [BF1301.H27] 27-9591
1. Spiritualism. I. Title.

*HALDEMAN, I. M. 235.
Can the dead communicate with the living? / I. M. Haldeman. Grand Rapids : Baker Book House, 1976. 138p. ; 18 cm. (Direction books) [BT962] ISBN 0-8010-4141-4 pbk. : 1.25.
1. Spiritualism. I. Title.

HALDEMAN, Isaac Massey, 1845- 133.
Can the dead communicate with the living? By I. M. Haldeman... New York, Chicago [etc.] Fleming H. Revell company [c1920] 138 p. 19 1/2 cm. [BF1261.H22] 20-20212
1. Spiritualism. I. Title.

HALL, Manly Palmer. 133
Unseen forces; nature spirits, thought forms, ghosts and specters, the dweller on the threshold, by Manly P. Hall. 3d rev. ed. Los Angeles, Calif., Hall publishing co.,

1929. 1 p. l., 5-62 p. 17 cm. Advertising matter: p. 56-62. [BF1999.H336 1929] ca 30
1. Spiritualism. 2. Psychical research. I. Title.

HALL, Thomas Bartlett. 133.
The purity and destiny of modern spiritualism; light for the seeker, hope for the weary hearted. From the pen of Thomas Bartlett Hall. Boston, Cupples and Schoenhof [c1899] 310 p. front. (port.) 22 cm. Title vignette. [BF1261.H25] Mar
1. Spiritualism. I. Title.

[HALL, Thomas Bartlett] 133.
Three articles on modern spiritualism, by a Bible spiritualist. Boston, Crosby and Nichols, 1863. v, [7]-74 p. 19 1/2 cm. [BF1251.H22] 10-34692
1. Spiritualism. I. Title.

HALL, Thomas Bartlett. 133.
Three articles on modern spiritualism. Second series. [By] Thomas B. Hall. Boston, A. Williams and company, 1882. 72 p. 19 1/2 cm. [BF1251.H24] 10-34693
1. Spiritualism. I. Title.

HALLOCK, Robert T. 133.
The road to spiritualism. Being a series of four lectures, delivered at the opening of the New York lyceum, by Dr. R. T. Hallock ... New York, The Spiritual telegraph office, 1858. 60 p. 21 1/2 cm. [BF1251.H28] 10-34694
1. Spiritualism. I. Title.

HALSTED, Carolyn Spencer. 133.
Book of revelations, by Carolyn Spencer Halsted ... New York J. F. Tapley co., 1922. 96 p. 19 cm. [BF1261.H28] 22-10877
1. Spiritualism. I. Title.

HAMMOND, Charles. 133.
Light from the spirit world. Comprising a series of articles on the condition of spirits, and the development of mind in the rudimental and second spheres. Being written wholly by the control of spirits ... C. Hammond, medium. Rochester, N.Y., Printed for the proprietor, by W. Heughes, 1852. 2 p. l., [ix]-xii, [13]-268 p. 17 cm. [BF1291.H22] 11-4837
1. Spiritualism. I. Title.

HAMMOND, Charles, 133.9
spiritualist.
Light from the spirit world. Comprising a series of articles on the condition of spirits, and the development of mind in the rudimental and second spheres. Being written wholly by the control of spirits ... C. Hammond, medium. 2d ed. Rochester, D. M. Dewey, 1852. viii, [9]-263 p. 18 cm. [BF1291.H22 1852 a] 32-21737
1. Spiritualism. I. Title.

HAMMOND, Charles. 133.
Light from the spirit world. The pilgrimage of Thomas Paine, and others to the seventh circle in the spirit world. Rev. C. Hammond, medium. Rochester, D. M. Dewey; New York, Fowler & Wells; [etc., etc.] 1852. x, [11]-264 p. incl. diagr. front. (port.) 18 cm. [BF1291.H25 1852] 11-4826
1. Spiritualism. I. Title.

HAMMOND, Charles. 133.
Light from the spirit world. The pilgrimage of Thomas Paine, and others, to the seventh circle in the spirit world. Rev. C. Hammond, medium. 4th thousand. Rochester, D. M. Dewey; New York, Fowler & Wells; [etc., etc.] 1852. x, [11]-264 p. incl. diagr. 19 1/2 cm. [BF1291.H25 1852 a] 11-4827
1. Spiritualism. I. Title.

HAMMOND, William Alexander, 133.
1828-1900.
Spiritualism and allied causes and conditions of nervous derangement. by William A. Hammond ... New York. G. P. Putnam's sons, 1876. xii, 366 p. illus. 20 cm. [BF1042.H22] 11-2449
1. Spiritualism. 2. Nervous system—Diseases. I. Title.

HANSON, E. F 1853- 133.9
Demonology or spiritualism, ancient and modern, by Eld. E.F. Hanson... Belfast, Me., The author, 1884. 2 p. l., 11-310 p. front. (port.) 20 cm. Bibliography: p. 12-14. [BF1042.H24] 34-18409
1. Spiritualism. I. Title.

HARDWICKE, Henry. 133.9
Voices from beyond, by Henry Hardwicke, M.D. [Niagara Falls, N.Y., Harkell company, c1930] 3 p., l., 125 p. 20 cm. [BF1286.H3] 30-10030
1. Spiritualism. I. Title.

HARE, Robert, 1781-1858. 133.
Experimental investigation of the spirit manifestations, demonstrating the existence of spirits and their communion with mortals. Doctrine of the spirit world respecting heaven. hell, morality, and God. Also the influence of Scripture on the morals of Christians. By Robert Hare ... New York, Partridge & Brittan, 1855. 3 p. l., 5-460, [2] p. iv. pl., 2 port. 22 cm. [BF1251.H32] 10-34605
1. Spiritualism. I. Title.

HARTMAN, Joseph. 133.93
Facts and mysteries of spiritism: learned by a seven years' experience and investigation. With a sequel. By Joseph Hartman ... Philadelphia, T. W. Hartley & co., 1885. xii, 13-378 p. 20 cm. [BF1283.H25A3] 32-35949
1. Spiritualism. I. Title.

HATCH, Benjamin Franklin.
Spiritualists' iniquities unmasked, and the Hatch divorce case. By B. F. Hatch. ... New York, The author, 1859. 52 p. 22 1/2 cm. [BF1289.H3] 16-9628
1. Spiritualism. I. Title.

HAYDEN, William Benjamin, 133.
1816-1893.
On the dangers of modern spiritualism. By William B. Hayden ... 4th ed., rev. New York, New church tract society, 1870. 137, [1] p. 18 1/2 cm. [BF1042.H4] 11-2451
1. Spiritualism. 2. New Jerusalem church. I. Title.

HAYDEN, William Benjamin, 133.
1816-1893.
On the phenomena of modern spiritualism. By William B. Hayden ... Boston, O. Clapp, 1855. 137 p. 18 cm. A comparison of spiritualism with the doctrines of Swedenborg. With this is bound: Some account of Emanuel Swedenborg and his writings [by Oliver Prescott Hiller] Boston, 1854. [BF1251.H42] 10-34696
1. Spiritualism. 2. New Jerusalem church. I. Title.

HAYDEN, William Benjamin, 133.9
1816-1893.
On the phenomena of modern spiritualism. By William B. Hayden ... 2d ed. Boston, O. Clapp, 1855. 137 p. 18 cm. A comparison of spiritualism with the doctrine of Swedenborg. With this is bound: Some account of Emanuel Swedenborg and his writings [by Oliver Prescot Hiller] Boston, O. Clapp, 1854. [BF1251.H42 1855 a] 32-32106
1. Spiritualism. 2. New Jerusalem church. I. Title.

HAYDEN, William Benjamin, 133.9
1816-1893.
On the phenomena of modern spiritualism. By William B. Hayden ... 3d ed. Boston, O. Clapp, 1859. 137 p. 18 1/2 cm. A comparison of spiritualism with the doctrines of Swedenborg. [BF1251.H42 1859] 32-35935
1. Spiritualism. 2. New Jerusalem church. I. Title.

HAYNES, Carlyle Boynton, 133.
1882-
Spiritualism versus Christianity; an account of the origin, the history, the work, the character, and the destiny of the remarkable movement which at the present time is attracting the attention of the world, by Carlyle B. Haynes ... Nashville, Tenn., Fort Worth, Tex. [etc.] Southern publishing association, c1918. 128 p. incl. front., illus. 20 1/2 cm. [BF1261.H3] 18-11295
1. Spiritualism. I. Title.

[HAYWARD, Aaron S.] 133.
An epitome of spiritualism and spirit magnetism; their verity, practicability, conditions and laws. By the author of "Vital magnetic cure" ... etc. Boston, Colby and Rich [c1876] 2 p. l. [3]-111 p. 19 cm. [BF1251.H45] 10-34697
1. Spiritualism. I. Title.

[HAYWARD, Aaron S.] 133.9
Nature's laws in human life: an exposition of spiritualism; embracing the various opinions of extremists, pro and con; together with the author's experience. By the author of "Vital magnetic cure." 2d ed. Boston, W. White and company, 1873. vii, [9]-308 p. 20 cm. [BF1251.H48 1873] [(159.9517)] 32-35955
1. Spiritualism. I. Title.

[HAYWARD, Aaron S.]
Nature's laws in human life: an exposition of spiritualism; embracing the various opinions of extremists, pro and con; together with the author's experience. By the author of "Vital magnetic cure." Boston, W. White and company; New York, The American news company, 1872. vii, [9]-308 p. 19 1/2 cm. [FB1251.H48] 10-34693
1. Spiritualism. I. Title.

HAYWARD, J. K. 133
A rebuttal of spiritism et al. By J. K. Hayward ... New York, P. Eckler, 1903. v, 7-457 p. 20 1/2 cm. [B825.H4] 3-13382
1. Spiritualism. I. Title.

HAZARD, Thomas Robinson, 133.9
1797-1886.
An examination of the Bliss imbroglio, both in its spiritual and legal aspect; to which is supplemented what occurred at an interesting spirit seance, entitled A family re-union. By Thomas R. Hazard. Boston, Colby & Rich, 1878. 139 p. diagr. 15 cm. [BF1283.B6H3] 32-35931
1. Bliss, James A. 2. Spiritualism. I. Title. II. Title: The Bliss imbrogilo.

THE heart of a father; 133.
a human document by a well-known public man. With a preface by Sir James Marchant II.D., and others . Boston and New York, Houghton Mifflin company, 1924. ix, [1] p., 1 l., 75, [1] p. 17 cm. [BF1301.H35] 25-3469
1. Spiritualism.

HEGY, Reginald. 133.9
A witness through the centuries, by Dr. Reginald Hegy. New York, E. F. Dutton & co., inc. [c1935] 3 p. l, 13-230 p. 19 1/2 cm. "First edition." [BF1261.H42] 35-2684
1. Spiritualism. 2. Automatism. I. Title.

HELLEBERG, Carl Gustaf, 133.
comp.
A book written by the spirits of the so-called dead, with their own materialized hands, by the process of independent slate-writing, through Mrs. Lizzie S. Green and others, as mediums. Comp. and arranged by C. G. Helleberg ... Cincinnati, 1883. vi, 241 p. 2 pl., 2 port. (incl. front.) 20 1/2 cm. [BF1301.G78] 11-5329
1. Spiritualism. I. Title.

HENSLOW, George, 1835- 133.
The proofs of the truths of spiritualism, by the Rev. Prof. G. Henslow ... With fifty-one illustrations. London, K. Paul, Trench, Trubner & co. ltd. New York, E. P. Dutton & co., 1919. v, iv, [vii]-xii, 255 p. front., plates, ports., facsims. 19 1/2 cm. [BF1301.H52] 20-26320
1. Spiritualism. I. Title.

HENSLOW, George, 1835- 133.91
The religion of the spirit world written by the spirits themselves, by the Rev. Prof. G. Henslow ... New York, Dodd, Mead and company, 1920. xxx, 265 p. 20 cm. $2.00. [BF1301.H53] 20-15944
1. Spiritualism. I. Title.

HENSLOW, George, 1835-1925. 133.9
The proofs of spirit forces, by the Rev. Prof. G. Henslow ... with fifty-one wonderful illustrations. 3d ed. rev. Chicago, Ill., The Marlowe press [c1920] 317 p. incl. plates. pl. 20 cm. [BF1261.H43 1920] 32-35393
1. Spiritualism. I. Title.

HENSLOW, George, 1835- 133.93
1925.
The religion of the spirit world, written by the spirits themselves, by the Rev. Prof. G. Henslow ... Chicago, Ill., The Marlowe press [c1920] 1 p. l., v-viii, 223 p. 20 cm. [BF1301.H53 1920a] [159.96173] 32-35963
1. Spiritualism. I. Title.

HERBINE, Charlotte G. 133.
The meeting of the spheres; or, Letters from Doctor Coulter, ed. by Charlotte G. Herbine. New York, Brentano's, 1919. x, 316, [1] p. 23 1/2 cm. "This classic psychic literature contains the most remarkable messages from the world of real life that lies beyond what men call death."--Publishers' weekly, May 24, 1919. [BF1301.H55] 19-9153
1. Spiritualism. I. Title.

HEREDIA, Carlos Maria de. 133.
Spiritism and common sense, by C. M. de Heredia ... New York, P. J. Kenedy & sons [1922] xv p., 1 l., 220 p., 1 l. front. (port.) plates. 20 cm. "List of books consulted": p. 207-220. [BF1042.H45] 23-291
1. Spiritualism. I. Title.

HERMANN, Jacob Rudolph. 133.
Immortality victorious; a glimpse of the life beyond, a new light on psychology, sociology and spiritualism and the dangers of ignorance, and address to the American people, by J. R. Hermann. Portland, Or., Western states publishing company [c1924] 131 p. front., plates, ports. 23 cm. "Author's edition, one thousand copies." [BF1301.H59] 24-10615
1. Spiritualism. I. Title.

HICKS, Betsey Belle, 1878- 133.
The bugle: reveille in the life beyond; a bit of comfort to soldiers' mothers, wives and friends, by Kendall Lincoln Achorn, assisted, by Betsey B. Hicks. New York, George H. Doran company [c1918] xiii p., 1 l., 17-108 p. 20 cm. [BF1301.H6] 18-18345
1. Spiritualism. I. Achorn, Kendall Lincoln, 1882-1916. II. Title.

HICKS, Marcella DeCou. Mrs. 133.9
Eternal verities, by Marcella DeCou Hicks ... Chicago, G. Engelke, 1937. 3 p. l., 5-192, [1] p. front. (port.) 21 cm. [BF1261.H44] 159.9617 37-21911
1. Spiritualism. I. Title.

HILL, John Arthur, 1872- 133.9
Spiritualism: its history, phenomena and doctrine, by J. Arthur Hill ... With an introduction by Sir Arthur Conan Doyle. London, New York [etc.] Cassell and company, ltd., 1918. xxii, 270 p. 21 cm. "Chapter X of part I appeared as an article, in slightly different form, in the Occult review for August, 1917, and chapter VI of part II appeared in the Hibbert journal for October, 1916."--Pref. "Glossary": p. 261-264. [BF1261.H6 1918] 32-21764
1. Spiritualism. I. Title.

HILL, John Arthur, 1872- 133.
Spiritualism: its history, phenomena and doctrine, by J. Arthur Hill ... with an introduction by Sir Arthur Conan Doyle. New York, George H. Doran company [c1919] xxiii p., 1 l., 25-316 p. 21 1/2 cm. "Chapter X of part I appeared as an article, in slightly different form, in the Occult review for August, 1917, and chapter VI of part II appeared in the Hibbert journal for October, 1916."--Pref. [BF1261.H6 1919] 19-4421
1. Spiritualism. I. Title.

HILL, John Arthur, 1872- 133.
Spiritualism and psychical research, by J. Arthur Hill ... London [etc.] T. C. & E. C. Jack; New York, Dodge publishing co. [1913] iii, [1], 5-93, [1] p. 16 1/2 cm. (On cover: The people's books) [BF1261.H5] 14-939
1. Spiritualism. 2. Psychical research. I. Title.

HILLMAN, Hugh H. 133
In yellow light, received by Hugh H. Hillman, from the spiritual world. San Francisco, Calif., Occult book publishing co., 1927. 284 p. front. (port.) plates. 19 1/2 cm. [BF1999.H6] 28-8947
1. Spiritualism. I. Title.

A history of the recent developments in spiritual manifestations, in the city of Philadelphia; 133.
by a member of the first circle, instituted in the month of October, 1850. Philadelphia, G. S. Harris, printer, 1851. 108 p. 18 1/2 cm. [BF1251.H67] 10-34699
1. Spiritualism.

HOFFMAN, Charles F. 133.9
A message to you, by Charles F. Hoffman.

Boston, The Christopher publishing house [c1930] 271 p. 21 cm. Spirit messages from Harriet Beecher Stowe received through the medium, Charles F. Hoffman. cf. Pref. [BF1311.S6H6] 30-13135
1. Spiritualism. I. Title.

HOLE, Donald. 133.
Spiritualism and the church, by the Rev. Donald Hole ... Milwaukee, Wis., Morehouse publishing co. [c1929] 4 p. l., [3]-121, [1] p. 19 cm. [BF1261.H65] 29-5190
1. Spiritualism. I. Title.

HOLMS, A. Campbell. 133
The fundamental facts of spiritualism, by A. Campbell Holms... Jamaica, N.Y., The Occult press [c1927] 79 p. 16cm. Advertising matter: p. 78-79. [BF1272.H65] 27-8131
1. Spiritualism. I. Title.

HOLZER, Hans W., 1920- 133.9
Life after death; the challenge and the evidence, by Hans Holzer. Indianapolis, Bobbs-Merrill Co. [1969] 175 p. 22 cm. [BF1261.2.H57] 69-13093 5.00
1. Spiritualism. I. Title.

HOME, Daniel Dunglas, 1833-1886. 133.
Incidents in my life. By D. D. Home... New-York, Carleton; [etc., etc.] 1863-72. 2 v. 19 cm. On verso of t.-p. of [v. 1]: Printed from the author's advance sheets. This vol. includes the "Introduction to the American edition", by J. W. Edmonds. Vol. 2 published in London, printed by Whittingham and Wilkins. [BF1283.H7] 11-4808
1. Spiritualism. I. Title.

HOME, Daniel Dunglas, 1833-1886. 133.
Lights and shadows of spiritualism. By D. D. Home... New York, G. W. Carleton & co., 1877. 2 p. l., [vii]-xii, [13]-483 p. 19 cm. [BF1241.H76] 10-34673
1. Spiritualism. I. Title.

HOME, Daniel Dunglas, 1833-1886. 133.9
Lights and shadows of spiritualism. By D. D. Home... New York, G. W. Carleton & co., 1879. 1 p. l., [vii]-xii, [13]-483 p. 19 cm. [BF1241.H76 1879] 32-30366
1. Spiritualism. I. Title.

HOOD, Frances Arabella (Jones) Mrs. 1853- 133.
Revelations and repudiations of great minds discarnate. Transcribed by their avator, Frances A. Hood. La Crosse, Wis., The Compendium company, 1920. 227 p. 20 cm. [BF1301.H7] 21-233
1. Spiritualism. I. Title.

HOOD, Frances Arabella (Jones) Mrs. 1853- 133.
Revelations and repudiations of great minds discarnate. A compendium of truth, transcribed by their amanuensis, Frances A. Hood. Only authorized version. La Crosse, Wis., The Compendium company, 1922. 3 p. l., 5-323 p. 19 1/2 cm. [BF1301.H7 1922] 22-15589
1. Spiritualism. I. Title.

[HORN, Henry] ed. 133.
Strange visitors; a series of original papers, embracing philosophy, science, government ... By the spirits of Irving, Willis, Thackeray ... and others now dwelling in the spirit world. Dictated through a clairvoyant while in an abnormal or trance state. New York, Carleton; [etc., etc.] 1869. viii, [9]-249, [1] p. 19 cm. "Introduction. By the editor", signed: Henry J. Horn. [BF1291.H8] 11-4838
1. Spiritualism. I. Title.

[HORN, Henry J.] ed. 133.93
Strange visitors: a series of original papers, embracing philosophy, science, government ... By the spirits of Irving, Willis, Thackeray ... and others now dwelling in the spirit world. Dictated through a clairvoyant, while in an abnormal or trance state. 4th ed. Boston, W. White and company, 1873. viii, 9-249, [1] p. 20 cm. "Introduction. By the editor", signed: Henry J. Horn. [BF1291.H8 1873] [159.96173] 34-36361
1. Spiritualism. I. Title.

[HORN, Henry J.] ed. 133.93
Strange visitors: a series of original papers, embracing philosophy, science, government ... By the spirits of Irving, Willis, Thackeray ... and others now dwelling in the spirit world. Dictated through a clairvoyant, while in an abnormal or trance state. 5th ed. Boston, Colby and Rich, 1884. viii, 9-249, [1] p. 20 cm. "Introduction. By the editor," signed: Henry J. Horn. [BF1291.H8 1884] [159.96173] 34-36362
1. Spiritualism. I. Title.

HORN, S. G., Mrs. 133.
The next world interviewed, by Mrs. S. G. Horn ... New York, T. R. Knox & co., 1886. 2 p. l., ii, 252 p. 18 1/2 cm. [BF1301.H8] 11-5330
1. Spiritualism. I. Title.

HORN, Susan G. Mrs. 133.9
The next world interviewed, by Mrs. S. G. Horn ... Chicago, The Progressive thinker publishing house, 1896. 2 p. l., ii p., 1 l., [4], 252 p. 20 cm. First edition: 1885. Lettered on cover: The Progressive thinker library. [BF1301.H8 1896] 32-33257
1. Spiritualism. I. Title.

HOTCHKISS, Samuel. 133.
The progressive age of reason, by Samuel Hotchkiss... Downsville, N.Y., The author [1910] 1 p. l., 643 p. 19 1/2 cm. [BF1261.H7] 10-19197 1.75
1. Spiritualism. I. Title.

HOUDINI, Harry, 1874-1928. 133.
A magician among the spirits, by Houdini... New York and London, Harper & brothers, 1924. xix p., 3 l., 294 p. front., illus., plates. ports. facsim. diagr. 24 1/2 cm. [BF1042.H6] 24-10324
1. Spiritualism. I. Title.

HOUSE, Agnes Augusta, 1884- 133.93
How to get to heaven, by Agnes A. House and Jenny J. Andersen. [Albany?] c1951- v. illus. 22cm. [BF1301.H82] 52-16009
1. Spiritualism. I. Andersen, Jenny J., 1886- joint author. II. Title.

HOUTS, Margaret Scott.
Messages from beyond; narrated experiences of life after death. [3d, rev, ed.] New York, Exposition [c1962] 346 p. "The first ed. was pub. in 1912 under the title: Voices from the open door." 63-23368
1. Spiritualism. I. Title. II. Title: Voices from the open door.

HOWARD, Austin Marlow, 1872-1943. 133.93
Messages for better living from the spirit world. Los Angeles, Wetzel Pub. Co. [1949] 264 p. 21 cm. [BF1301.H83] 49-25050
1. Spiritualism. I. Title.

HOWARD, Ezra Lee, 1869- 133.93
My adventure into spiritualism, by E. Lee Howard, D.D. New York, The Macmillan company, 1935. 5 p. l., 118 p. front. 19 1/2 cm. [BF1283.H77A3 1935] [159.96173] 35-2873
1. Spiritualism. I. Title.

HOWARD, J. N. 133.9
Modern spiritualism exposed; or The Bible vs. modern spiritualism. By J. N. Howard ... Moundsville, W. Va., Gospel trumpet publishing company, 1903. 155 p. incl. front. (port.) 18 1/2 cm. [BF1042.H63] [159.9617] 32-35948
1. Spiritualism. I. Title. II. Title: Bible vs. modern spiritualism.

HOWELL, Wallace S, 1885- 133.93
I know. New York, Vantage Press [1951] 2 v. ports. 23 cm. Vol. 2 has imprint: Lebanon, Ohio. Lebanon Press. Contents.v. 1. A manual of life.--v. 2. A culture of life. [BF1261.H73] 51-3671
1. Spiritualism. I. Title.

HUBBARD, George Henry, 1857- 220
Spiritual power at work: a study of spiritual forces and their application by George Henry Hubbard. New York, E. P. Dutton and company, 1903. x, 343 p. 19 1/2 cm. [BR125.H83] 3-12281
I. Title.

HUBBELL, Gabriel G. 133.
Fact and fancy in spiritualism, theosophy, and psychical research, by G. G. Hubbell ... Cincinnati, The R. Clark company, 1901. vi, [7]-208 p. 21 cm. [BF1261.H87] 1-13709
1. Blavatsky, Helene Petrovna (Hahn-Hahn) 1831-1891. 2. Spiritualism. 3. Theosophy. 4. Psychical research. I. Title.

HULL, Daniel. 920.
Moses Hull, compiled and written by Daniel Hull and others. Wellesley, Mass., Pub. by the Maugus printing company, 1907. 1 p. l., 7-104, [2] p. 21 1/2 cm. [BF1027.H8H8] 44-39797
1. Hull, Moses, 1835-1907. 2. Spiritualism. I. Title.

HULL, Moses. 133.
Encyclopedia of Biblical spiritualism; or, A concordance to the principal passages of the Old and New Testament Scriptures which prove or imply spiritualism; together with a brief history of the origin of many of the important books of the Bible. By Moses Hull ... Chicago, M. Hull & co., 1895. 1 p. l., xvii, 13-385 p. front. (port.) 20 cm. [BF1275.B5H77] 11-3586
1. Spiritualism. I. Title.

HULL, Moses. 133.
Which: spiritualism or Christianity? A friendly correspondence between Moses Hull, spiritualist, and W. F. Parker, Christian ... Boston, W. White and company, 1873. 178 p. 19 1/2 cm. [BF1275.C5H8] 11-3592
1. Spiritualism. I. Parker, W. F., of Cedar Hill, Ky. II. Title.

HULL, Moses, 1835- 133.
The contrast: evangelicalism and spiritualism compared. by Moses Hull ... Boston, W. White and company, 1873. 236 p. 19 1/2 cm. [BF1275.B5H74] 11-3587
1. Spiritualism. 2. Bible and spiritualism. I. Title.

HULL, Moses, 1835- 133.9
The contrast: evangelicalism and spiritualism compared. by Moses Hull ... 2d ed. Boston, W. White and company, 1873. 236 p. 19 1/2 cm. [BF1275.B5H74 1873 a] 32-21770
1. Spiritualism. I. Title.

HULL, Moses, 1835- 133.
A debate on spiritualism between Moses Hull (representing spiritualism) and Eld. W. R. Covert (representing Christianity) held at Anderson, Ind., Oct. 5, 6, 7 and 8, 1897 ... Chicago, Ill., The Progressive thinker publishing house, 1899. 106 p. front. (port.) 20 cm. (With Smyth, Alexander. The occult life of Jesus of Nazareth ... Chicago, Ill., 1899] [BF1311.J587] 99-3144
1. Spiritualism. I. Covert, W. R. II. Title.

HULL, Moses, 1835- 133.
The question settled. A careful comparision of Biblical and modern spiritualism. By Rev. Moses Hull ... Boston, W. White and company; New York, The American news company, 1869. 235 p. 19 1/2 cm. [BF1275.B5H82] 11-3589
1. Spiritualism. I. Title.

HULL, Moses, 1835- 133.9
The question settled. A careful comparison of Biblical and modern spiritualism. By Rev. Moses Hull ... Boston, W. White and company; New York, The American news company, 1870. 235 p. 19 1/2 cm. [BF1275.B5H82 1870] 32-21757
1. Spiritualism. I. Title.

HULL, Moses, 1835- 133.
Two in one; or, The question of the spiritualism of the Bible settled, together with a series of startling contrasts between creedal Christianity and the facts and philosophy of modern spiritualism. By Moses Hull ... Chicago, M. Hull & co., 1895. 4, 11-462 p. front. (port.) 20 cm. Includes the author's two works: "The question settled" and "The contrast," with exception of the prefaces, title-pages and table of contents. cf. Pref. [BF1275.B5H85] 11-3590
1. Spiritualism. 2. Bible and spiritualism. I. Title.

HULL, Moses, 1835-1907. 133.9
Encyclopedia of Biblical spiritualism; or, A concordance to the principal passages of the Old and New Testament Scriptures which prove or imply spiritualism. Together with a brief history of the origin of many of the important books of the Bible. [n.p., 1962] 2 v. (iii, 385 p.) port. 21 cm. [BF1275.B5H77] 63-2452
1. Spiritualism. 2. Bible and spiritualism. I. Title.

HUMPHREY, Oscar W. 133.
The mystic world: a literal narrative of strange mystical occurrences, rare materializations, voice seances, clairvoyance ... etc. The locket prophecy. [By] O. W. Humphrey ... [Washington, D. C., Press of the Law reporter co.] 1897. 3 p. l., 68 p. pl., port. 23 cm. [BF1261.H95] 11-3146
1. Spiritualism. I. Title.

HUMPHREYS, Eliza M. J. (Gollan), Mrs. 133.
The truth of spiritualism, by "Rita" (Mrs. Desmond Humphreys) Philadelphia and London, J. B. Lippincott company, 1920. 174, [1] p. 19 1/2 cm. [BF1261.H98 1920] 20-7778
1. Spiritualism. I. Title.

HYMA, Albert, 1893- 236
Eternal life; a historical analysis of the relation between Christianity and spiritualism, by Albert Hyma ... Ann Arbor, Mich., The Craft press, 1939. 139 p. 23 cm. [BT901.H95] 39-18645
1. Spiritualism. 2. Future life. I. Title.

"I heard a voice": 133.
or, The great exploration, by a king's counsel and doctor of laws. New York, E. P. Dutton and company [1918] 4 p. l., 272 p. 20 cm. [BF1301.I2] 19-6509
1. Spiritualilsm. I. Title: The great exploration.

INVITATION from the planet Venus. 133
Los Angeles, DeVorss; distributed by A. J. Brown [196-?] 20 p. 16 cm. [BF1311.V4I58] 71-15984
1. Spiritualism.

IOWA conference of spiritualists. 133.9063777
... Proceedings of the convention preceding the organization of the conference; its contents, officers, lectures by C. W. Stewart, Mrs. C. L. V. Richmond, Mrs. Nettie Pease Fox, and Dr. Juliet H. Severance. Poems, invocations, and answers to questions, by Mrs. Cora L. V. Richmond, address to spiritualists, by the president. Appendix: containing a discourse by James A. Garfield, through Mrs. Richmond, delivered at Des Moines, Nov. 22, 1882. Subject: "The mission and destiny of our country", also name poems of the members of the executive board. All stenographically reported by C. Y. Richmond, of Chicago. Ottumwa, Ia., Spiritual offering publishing house, 1883. 1 pl. l., 154 p. 23 1/2 cm. [BF1231.I 6 1883] [159.9617063777] 33-16699
1. Garfield, James Abram, pres. U.S., 1831-1881. 2. Spiritualism. I. Title.

IRION, Clyde. 133.9
The profit and loss of dying. Los Angeles, DeVorss, 1969. 152 p. 20 cm. [BF1261.2.I7] 73-79229
1. Spiritualism. 2. Death. I. Title.

IRVING, Kate. 133.
Clear light from the spirit world. By Kate Irving. New York, G. W. Carleton & co.; [etc., etc.] 1884. vi, [7]-201 p. 19 cm. [BF1301.I7] 11-5332
1. Spiritualism. I. Title.

JACOBY, Samuel A. 133.9
The immortality of the soul, written down by Samuel A. Jacoby and inspired by Henry K. Wakamussen in spirit ... Los Angeles, Calif., The Austin publishing co. [c1931] 166 p. front. (port.) 23 cm. [BF1311.W3J3] 31-24606
1. Spiritualism. I. Title.

JACOBY, Samuel A. 133.93
Voices from the spirit land. Los Angeles [1949] 413 p. port. 24 cm. [BF1301.J15] 49-24904
1. Spiritualism. I. Title.

JAMES, Edward. 133.
We never die; an investigation into the future life of man, by Edward James. Chicago, Ill., 1921. 107 p. 19 cm. [BF1261.J3] 21-20290

1. Spiritualism. I. Title.

JAMES G. Blaine on the money 133. *question, and other psychic articles.* Minneapolis, Minn., Etna publishing company [c1896] 62 p. 20 cm. [BF1301.J2] ca 10
1. Spiritualism.

JAMISON, Alcinous Burton, 133. 1851-
The making of a super-race, by Alcinous B. Jamison ... New York city, N. Y., The author, c1926. xi, 226 p. front. (port.) 21 cm. [BF1261.J35] 27-2982
1. Spiritualism. I. Title.

JAMISON, Alcinous Burton, 133. 1851-
Man: whence and whither? by Alcinous B. Jamison ... with an introduction by John Emery McLean ... New York, The author, c1922. 144 p. 21 cm. [BF1261.J4] 22-18546
1. Spiritualism. I. Title.

JAMISON, Alcinous Burton, 133.9 1851-
Spiritman's place and function in nature, by Alcinous B. Jamison ... New York city N. Y., The author, c1933. 258, [1] p. front. (port.) 21 cm. [BF1261.J43] 159.9617 33-21152
1. Spiritualism. 2. Future life. I. Title.

JANNING, Edward A. 133.93
Whether you believe or not. Boston, Christopher Pub. House [1949] 127 p. illus. 21 cm. [BF1261.J44] 49-11602
1. Spiritualism. I. Title.

JENKINS, Sephora Bettes. 133.
Ye shall know the truth [by] Sephora Bettes Jenkins. Boston, R. G. Badger [c1924] 152 p. facsim. 21 cm. [BF1301.J4] 25-2858
1. Spiritualism. I. Title.

JENNEY, Shirley Carson. 133.93
The fortune of eternity, by Percy Bysshe Shelley, taken through the clairaudience of Shirley Carson Jenney ... New York, The William-Frederick press, 1945. 3 p. l., 9-124 p. 22 1/2 cm. [BF1301.J43] 45-3832
1. Spiritualism. I. Shelley, Percy Bysshe, 1792-1822. II. Title.

... Jesus Christ, 133.9
a fiction founded upon the life of Apollonius of Tyana. The pagan priests of Rome originated Christianity. New and startling disclosures by its founders, and full explanations by ancient spirits ... Transcribed by M. Faraday. Springfield, Mass., Star publishing co. [1883] cover-title, iii, 208 p. 19 cm. At head of title: no. 5. [BF1291.J4] 32-35933
1. Spiritualism. I. Faraday, Michael, 1791-1867.

JEWETT, Pendie L. 133.
Spiritualism and charlatanism; or, The tricks of the media. Embodying an expose of the manifestations of modern spiritualism by a committe of business men of New-York. By Pendie L. Jewett ... New-York, S. W. Green, printer, 1873. 83 p. 19 cm. [BF1042.J6] 11-2452
1. Spiritualism. I. Title.

JOHNSON, George Lindsay, 133.9 1853-
Does man survive? The great problem of the life hereafter and the evidence for its solution, by George Lindsay Johnson ... New York and London, Harper & brothers, 1936. 3 p. l., 13-384 p. 1 illus., plates. 23 cm. "Origfinally published in England under the title: The great problem and the evidence for its solution." [BF1031.J6] 159.9617 36-18961
1. Spiritualism. 2. Future life. I. Title. II. Title: The great problem of the life hereafter and the evidence for its solution.

[JOHNSON, Maud Lalita 133.93 (Shlaudeman) Mrs.] 1875-
Transmitted light; Latoo [pseud.] the instrument; Lalita [pseud.] the recorder. [Laguna Beach, Calif., The Order of loving service, c1937] 3 p. l., 3-132 p. 21 cm. [BF1301.J6] 159.96173 37-17372
1. Spiritualism. I. Latto, psued. II. Title.

JONES, Amanda Theodocia, 133. 1835-
A psychic autobiography, by Amanda T. Jones ... with introduction by James H. Hyslop ... New York, Greaves publishing company [c1910] 455 p. front., ports. 20 cm. [BF1283.J7A3] 10-29100
1. Spiritualism. I. Title.

JONES, Amanda Theodocia, 920.9 1835-
A psychic autobiography by Amanda T. Jones ... with introduction by James H. Hyslop ... London, W. Rider & son, ltd.; New York, Greaves publishing company [1911] 455 p. front., ports. 30 cm. [BF1283.J7A3 1911] 32-21746
1. Spiritualism. I. Title.

JORDAN, Alfred McKay, Mrs. 133.93
Science from the unseen, a series of spirit communications, compiled by Mrs. Alfred McKay Jordan. New York, House of Field-Doubleday, inc. [1945] 3 p. l., 9-208 p. 20 1/2 cm. [BF1301.J65] 45-22160
1. Spiritualism. I. Title.

JUDSON, Abby Ann, b.1835. 133.9
Why she became a spiritualist; twelve lectures delivered before the Minneapolis association of spiritualist by Abby A. Judson ... November 30, 1890-February 15, 1891. 2d ed. Boston, Colby & Rich, 1892. 6 p. l., [11]-263 p. front. (port.) 19 cm. [BF1261.J9 1892] 32-30367
1. Spiritualism. I. Title.

JUDSON, Abby Ann, 1835- 133.9 1902.
The bridge between two worlds, by Abby A. Judson ... Minneapolis, The author; A. Roper, printer, 1894. 217 p. front. (port.) 20 cm. [BF1261.J85] 32-33251
1. Spiritualism. I. Title.

JUDSON, Abby Ann, 1835-1902. 133
A happy year; or, Fifty-two letters to the Banner of light. By Abby A. Judson ... Published by the author. Newark, N. J., Baker printing co., 1899. 178 p. front. (port.) 20 cm. Letters relating chiefly to spiritualism. [BF1272.J9] 99-943
1. Spiritualism. I. Title.

JUDSON, Abby Ann, 1835-1902. 133.
Why she became a spiritualist: twelve lectures delivered before the Minneapolis association of spiritualists, by Abby A. Judson ... November 30, 1890-March 15, 1891. Minneapolis, A. Roper, printer, 1891. 6 p. l., [11]-263 p. front. (port.) 19 cm. [BF1261.J9] 11-3147
1. Spiritualism. I. Title.

[KANE, Alice L]
Echoes from the spirit world. Topeka, Kan., Crane & co., 1899. 142 p., 1 l. port. 12 degree. Jan
I. Title.

KANT, Immanuel, 1724-1804. 110
Traume eines Geistersehers ; Der Unterschied der Gegenden im Raume / Immanuel Kant ; unter Verwendung d. Textes von Karl Vorlander mit e. Einl. hrsg. von Klaus Reich. Hamburg : Meiner, 1975. xviii, 96 p. ; 19 cm. (Philosophische Bibliothek ; Bd. 286) Includes bibliographical references and indexes. [B2793.A3 1975] 75-521673 ISBN 3-7873-0311-1 : DM14.00
1. Swedenborg, Emanuel, 1688-1772. 2. Spiritualism. 3. Metaphysics. I. Kant, Immanuel, 1724-1804. Der Unterschied der Gegenden im Raume. 1975. II. Title.

KARITZKY, Alma L., 1916- 133.9
Angels within call, by Alma L. Karitzky. A book of challenging revelations of "life after death." New York city, House of Field, inc. [c1941] 160 p. 20 cm. [BF1301.K24] 42-25204
1. Spiritualism. I. Title.

KATES, George Whitfield, 133. 1845-
The philosophy of spiritualism, a series of essays upon fundamental topics, by George W. Kates; a compendium of essential dicussion for a clearer understanding of what spiritualism reveals; and its great value to humanity. Boston, Christopher publishing house [c1916] 235 p. front. (port.) 21 cm. [BF1261.K2] 16-17483 1.00
1. Spiritualism. I. Title.

KEITH, Cassius Clay, 1867- 133.93
Voices of the night; an answer to man's unsolved problems, by Dr. C. C. Keith. Kansas City, Mo., Burton publishing company [c1937] 2 p. l., 7-103 p. 21 cm. [BF1999.K4] 159.96173 39-4710
1. Spiritualism. I. Title.

KELSO, John R. 133.
Spiritualism sustained, in five lectures. By John R. Kelso, A. M. New York, Printed at the Truth seeker office [c1886] 245 p. 19 cm. [BF1261.K3] 11-3148
1. Spiritualism. I. Title.

KENDRICK, Blanche V W. 133.98 Mrs.
Broadcasts to America from unseen friends, by the hand of Blanche V. W. Kendrick ... Boston, B. Humphries, inc. [c1941] 135 p. 21 cm. [BF1290.K4] 189.96173 41-8430
1. Spiritualism. I. Title.

KENNEDY, Edith Ann.
God and I through seance. [1st ed.] New York, Vantage Press [1966] 119 p. 67-100264
1. Spiritualism. 2. Mediums. I. Title.

KERNAHAN, Coulson, 1858- 133.
Spiritualism; a personal experience and a warning, by Coulson Kernahan ... New York, Chicago [etc.] Fleming H. Revell company [c1920] 59 p. 20 cm. [BF1042.K4] 20-17391
1. Spiritualism. I. Title.

KIDD, Almira. 133.
Occultism, spiritism, materialism. Demonstrated by the logic of facts: showing disembodied man and spirit phases. Also, the immediate condition affecting man after death ... By Almira Kidd ... Boston, Colby & Rich, 1879. 156 p. 19 1/2 cm. [BF1251.K46] 10-34700
1. Spiritualism. I. Title.

KIDD, Almira. 133.
Psychology; re-incarnation; soul, and its relations; or, The laws of being: showing the occult forces in man; that intelligence manifests without material; and the most important things to know ... By Almira Kidd. Boston, Colby & Rich, 1878. 127 p. 19 1/2 cm. [BF1231.K48] 10-34701
1. Spiritualism. I. Title.

KIDDLE, Henry, 1824-1891, 133. ed.
Spiritual communications. Presenting a revelation of the future life, and illustrating and confirming the fundamental doctrines of the Christian faith. Ed. by Henry Kiddle ... New York, The Authors' publishing company, 1879. 350 p. 19 cm. [BF1291.K46] 11-4840
1. Spiritualism. I. Title.

[KIMBALL, Grace Lucia 220 (Atkinson) Mrs., 1875-1923.
Living waters; or, Messages of joy; with an introduction by Dwight Goddard. New York, Brentano's [c1919] x p., 1 l., 140 p. 19 1/2 cm. [BR125.K49 1919] 20-2428
1. Spiritualism. I. Goddard, Dwight, 1861- II. Title.

KIMBALL, Grace Lucia 220 (Atkinson) Mrs., 1875-1923.
Living waters; or, Messages of joy, by Grace Atkinson Kimball. Akron, O., Sun publishing co. [c1925] 1 p. l., iii p., 1 l., 128 p. 14 cm. "Published anonymously in 1919."--Note. [BR125.K49 1925] 25-7957
1. Spiritualism. I. Title.

KING, Basil, 1859-1928. 133.
The abolishing of death, by Basil King ... New York, Cosmopolitan book corporation, 1919. 5 p. l., 3-197 p. 19 1/2 cm. [BF1301.K5] 19-15716
1. Spiritualism. I. Title.

KING, John Sumpter, 1843- 133.
Dawn of the awakened mind, by John S. King... New York, The James A. McCann company, 1920. 7 p. l., xvii-xxix, 451 p. front., pl., ports., facsims. 22 cm. [BF1261.K5] 20-8351
1. Spiritualism. I. Title.

KING, Maria M., Mrs. 133.
Real life in the spirit land. Being life experiences, scenes, incidents, and conditions, illustrative of spirit life, and the principles of the spiritual philosophy Given inspirationally, by Mrs. Maria M. King... vol, I) Boston, W. White and company; New York, The American news company, 1870. x, [11]-209 p. 19 1/2 cm. [BF1291.K52] CA 11
1. Spiritualism. I. Title.

KING, Maria M., Mrs. 133.9
Real life in the spirit land. Being life experiences, scenes, incidents and conditions, illustrative of spirit life, and the principles of the spiritual philosophy. Given inspirationally by Mrs. Maria M. King... Vol. I. 5th ed. Hammonton, N.J., A. J. King; Boston, Colby and Rich; [etc., etc.] 1892. x p., 1 l., [13]-209 p. front. 20 cm. No more published. [BF1291.K52 1892] 32-35932
1. Spiritualism. I. Title.

KING, Nell. 133.93
When the heavens speak, by Nell King. Boston, B. Humphries, inc. [1944] 108 p. 21 cm. "Dictated to me by automatic writing by my son who died in 1941." [BF1301.K53] 44-10779
1. Spiritualism. I. Title.

KINGSLEY, Adelaide Delia 133.91 (Nichols) Mrs., 1844-
Sky lines, by Adelaide D. Kingsley. Boston, The Christopher publishing house [c1924] 108 p. 21 cm. "These poems have been prepared on the astral plane especially for this book and given automatically by us to our inspired medium Adelaide D. Kingsley."--Note. [BF1301.K55] 24-30394
1. Spiritualism. I. Title.

KLINE, Magdalena. Mrs. 133.
A compilation of the lectures given by the spirit-band through the mediumship of Mrs. Magdalena Kline, and which is called the everlasting gospel ... Vol. I. Boston, Colby & Rich, 1882. 488 p. 23 cm. No more published? [BF1291.K65] 11-4341
1. Spiritualism. I. Title.

KNIGHT, Ralph, 1895- 133.9'0924
Learning to talk to the world beyond; an introduction to the joy of immortality. [Harrisburg, Pa.] Stackpole Books [1969] 189 p. 25 cm. [BF1283.K55A3] 69-16149 6.50
1. Spiritualism. I. Title.

[KOSANKE, Martha] 133.93
The light of truth, by Elizabeth Ann Greenwood [pseud.] A primer in spiritual understanding. [Grand Rapids, Printed by the Cargill company, 1943] 187, [1] p. illus. (port.) 20 cm. [BF1301.K66] 44-2449
1. Spiritualism. I. Title.

KRAFT, Frederick A. 1871- 133.
"Dorio"; a practical and timely expose of spiritualism, by F. A. Kraft, M. D. Milwaukee, Wis., The Memorial publishers [c1926] 144 p. 2 port. (incl. front.) 20 cm. [BF1261.K7] 26-21638
1. Spiritualism. I. Title.

KROLL, Robert C comp. 133.
Spirit philosophy of Robert G. Ingersoll and Rev. Charles Haddon Spurgeon, together with post-mortem reveries of Jack Carpenter. Comp. from the record of the Scientific seance circle ... Comp. and pub. by Robert C. Kroll. St. Louis, Mo. [c1919 v. 22 cm. [BF1301.K8] 19-9462
1. Spiritualism. I. Scientific seance circle. II. Title.

KURTH, Hanns, 1904- 133.9'013
Glimpses of the beyond; the extraordinary experiences of people who have crossed the brink of death and returned [by] Jean-Baptiste Delacour. Translated from the German by E. B. Garside. New York, Delacorte Press [1974] xi, 216 p. 21 cm. Translation of Aus dem Jenseits zuruck, published in 1973. Bibliography: p. 215-216. [BF1263.K8713] 74-8054 ISBN 0-440-03287-3 5.95
1. Spiritualism. I. Title.

LAMBERTON, Helen C. 133.93
High endeavor, a help in daily living [by] Helen C. Lamberton and Stella Sands. [Westminster, Md.] 1944. xii, 169 p. 19 cm. [BF1301.L35] 44-28735
1. Spiritualism. I. Sands, Stella, joint author. II. Title.

LANDAKER, Genevieve. 133.9
Do the dead return? Boston, Christopher Pub. House [1948] 63 p. 21 cm. [BF1261.L16] 48-3680
1. Spiritualism. I. Title.

LANDAKER, Genevieve. 133.9
Meet a guardian angel. Boston, Christopher Pub. House [1948] 100 p. 21 cm. "Books mentioned": p. 99. [BF1261.L18] 48-6840
1. Spiritualism. I. Title.

LANE, Anne (Wintermute) Mrs. 133.
Life in the circles, further lessons received through automatic writing, by Anne W. Lane and Harriet Blaine Beale. New York, Dodd, Mead and company, 1920. 4 p. l., 192 p. 20 cm. "A continuation of the lessons published in the book entitled "To walk with God.'"--Pref. [BF1343.L25] 20-19176 1.25
1. Spiritualism. I. Beale, Harriet Stanwood (Blaine) Mrs. 1872- joint author. II. Title.

LANE, Anne (Wintermute) Mrs. 133.
To walk with God; an experience in automatic writing, by Anne W. Lane and Harriet Blaine Beale. New York, Dodd, Mead and company, 1920. 3 p. l., iii-viii, 120 p. 19 cm. [BF1343.L3] 20-6367
1. Spiritualism. I. Beale, Harriet Stanwood (Blaine) Mrs. 1872- joint author. II. Title.

LANE, Charles Martin, 1865-
The theory of spiritualism, by Charles M. Lane. St. Louis, Mo., Evergreen publishing co. [c1907] 2 p. l., [7]-373, [3] p. 20 cm. 7-17910
I. Title.

LAPPONI, Giusepee, 1851-1906. 133.
Hypnotism and spiritism; a critical and medical study, by Dr. Joseph Lapponi ... tr. from the 2d rev. ed., by Mrs. Philip Gibbs. New York, Longmans, Green, and co., 1907. xi, 273 p. 20 cm. Bibliography: p. 263-264. [BF1042.L32 1907] 7-11197
1. Spiritualism. 2. Hypnotism. I. Gibbs, Agnes Mary (Rowland) "Mrs. Philip Gibbs," tr. II. Title.

LARKIN, Clarence, 1850- 235
The spirit world, by Clarence Larkin ... Fox Chase, Philadelphia, Pa., C. Larkin [c1921] 4 p. l., 158 p. front., illus. 21 cm. [BT961.L3] 21-7875 1.50
I. Title.

LATCHAW, Daniel S. 133.9
A book of revelation from the ethereal plane. Philadelphia, Dorrance [1971] v, 221 p. 22 cm. [BF1311.F8L38] 70-140969 ISBN 0-8059-1526-5 4.95
1. Spiritualism. 2. Future life. I. Title.

LAWRENCE, Edward, 133.9'09 fl.1921-1936.
Spiritualism among civilised and savage races; a study in anthropology. Freeport, N.Y., Books for Libraries Press [1971] xii, 112 p. illus. 23 cm. Reprint of the 1921 ed. Includes bibliographical references. [BF1261.L25 1971] 76-160980 ISBN 0-8369-5848-9
1. Spiritualism. I. Title.

LAWRENCE, Ida (Eckert) Mrs. 133. 1864- ed.
Aubrey messages; evidence of life, memory, affection after the change called death ... Los Angeles, Calif., The Austin publishing company, 1928. 212 p. front., ports. 21 cm. [BF1311.P4L3] 29-4338
1. Peacock, Aubrey Eckert Lawrence, 1882-1924. 2. Spiritualism. I. Title.

LAWRENCE, James. 133.
Angel voices from the spirit world: glory to God who sends them. Essays taken indiscriminately from a large amount written under angel influence, by James Lawrence... Cleveland, O., Nevins brothers, 1874. xviii, [19]-400 p. front. (port.) 19 1/2 cm. [BF1301.L45] 44-10236
1. Spiritualism. I. Title.

LAWRENCE, L. A. "Mrs. Cornelius W. Lawrence." 133.
"Do they love us yet!" By Mrs. Cornelius W. Lawrence." New York, J. Miller, 1879. 8 p. l., [3]-234 p. 20 cm. Preface signed: L A. Lawrence. [BF1301.L4] 11-5336
1. Spiritualism. I. Title.

LAWTON, George, 1900- 133.9
The drama of life after death; a study of the spiritualist religion, by George Lawton. New York, H. Holt and company [c1932] xxvii, 668 p. front., illus., plates, ports. 22 cm. (Half-title: Studies in religion and culture. American religion series, vi) Issued also as thesis (PH. D) Columbia university. Music: p. 216-222. Bibliography: p. 631-653. [BX9798.S7L3 1932 a] 32-23852
1. Spiritualism. I. Title.

LAY, Wilfrid, 1872- 133
Man's unconscious spirit; the psychoanalysis of spiritism, by Wilfrid Lay ... New York, Dodd, Mead and company, 1921. 2 p. l., 7-337 p. 20 cm. [BF1031.L35] 21-5839 2.00
1. Spiritualism. 2. Psychoanalysis. I. Title.

LEADBEATER, Charles Webster, 1847-1934. 133.9
Saved by a ghost : true tales of the occult / by Charles W. Leadbeater ; cover art by Jane A. Evans. 1st Quest book ed. Wheaton, Ill. : Theosophical Pub. House, 1979. vi, 265 p. ; 18 cm. (A Quest book) First published under title: The perfume of Egypt. Contents.Contents.—The perfume of Egypt.—The forsaken temple.—The major's promise.—A test of courage.—An astral murder.—A triple warning.—The concealed confession.—Jagannath: a tale of hidden India.—The baron's room.—Saved by a ghost. [BF1272.L4 1979] 79-9981 ISBN 0-8356-0526-4 pbk. : 5.50
1. Spiritualism. I. Title.

LEAF, Horace. 133.
What is this spiritualism! By Horace Leaf. New York, George H. Doran company [c1919] v p. 1 l., 9-185 p. 21 cm. [BF1261.L3] 19-5688 1.50
1. Spiritualism. I. Title.

LEAN, Florence (Marryat) Church, "Mrs. Francis Lean," 1837-1899. 133.
The spirit world, by Florence Marryat ... New York, C. B. Reed, 1894. 272 p. 19 cm. [BF1261.L38] 11-3149
1. Spiritualism. I. Title.

LEAN, Florence (Marryat) Church, Mrs. 1837-1899. 133.
There is no death, by Florence Marryat ... New York, J. W. Lovell company [c1891] 265 p. 19 cm. (On cover: Lovell's international series. 159) [BF1261.L43] 11-3150
1. Spiritualism. I. Title.

LEANDER, Normon. 133.
True spiritualism. By Normon Leander. Philadelphia, King & Baird, printers, 1875. 72 p. 17 cm. [BF1261.L45] 11-3151
1. Spirtualism. I. Title.

LE BEAU, Mary, pseud. 133.8
Beyond doubt a record of psychic experience. [1st ed.] New York, Harper [1956] 179p. 22cm. [BF1301.L48] 55-11476
1. Spiritualism. I. Title.

LENZNER, Emilie. 133.
The Book of Christ Jesus; teachings given from souls of spiritual realms, unfolding to mortals the true laws of light, love and purity of God's great universe, by Emilie Lenzner [New Orleans, The American printing co., c1924] 147, [1] p. incl. illus., pl., port. 24 1/2 cm. Lettered on cover: The teachings of Christ Jesus. [BF1301.L55] 24-31609
1. Spiritualism. I. Title.

LEONARD, John Calvert. 133.
The higher spiritualism; the philosophy and teachings of spiritualism from the point of view of accepted philosophy and science, by John C. Leonard. New York, F. H. Hitchcock [c1927] 4 p. l., 3-466 p. 22 cm. "Selected books for a study of spiritualism": p. 458-460. [BF1261.L47] 27-24111
1. Spiritualism. I. Title.

LESTER, Reginald Mounstephens. 133.9
In search of the hereafter; a personal investigation into life after death. New York, W. Funk [1953] 241p. 21cm. [BF1301.L56 1953] 53-5694
1. Spiritualism. I. Title.

LEUTE, Karl M. 133.
Afterworld effects; a psychic manuscript obtained by Karl M. Leute and Clyde S. Ricker ... Boston, The Christopher publishing house [c1922] 4 p. l., [7]-135 p. 21 cm. (Afterworld series, pt. I) [BF1301.L68] 22-20151
1. Spiritualism. I. Ricker, Clyde S., joint author. II. Title.

LEVERE, Rose, comp. 133.91
A modern spiritualistic classic; scientific proofs of another life. A series of essays comprising unique lessons of daily life, written by eminent persons after passing from mortal to spirit life. Comp. by Rose Levere ... The entire contents of this book written and sketched independently by spirits. New York, The Spiritual science company, 1913. 7 p. l., 231 p. front., plates, ports. (1 col.) 20 cm. $1.00 [BF1301.L6] 13-22856
1. Spiritualism. I. Title. II. Title: Scientific proofs of another life.

LEVETT, Carl David. 133.9
Crossings, a transpersonal approach / Carl Levett. Ridgefield, Conn. : Quiet Song, [1974] ca. 200 p. ; 22 cm. [BF1283.L43A32] 74-17597 ISBN 0-915054-01-9 : 8.50. ISBN 0-915054-02-7 pbk. : 3.50
1. Levett, Carl David. 2. Spiritualism. I. Title.
Publisher's address: 84 Riverside Drive, Ridgefield, Ct 06877.

LEWIS, Edwin W. 133.
The spiritual reasoner. by Edwin W. Lewis... Watkins, N.Y., Pub. for the author, 1855. 256 p. 18 1/2 cm. [BF1291.L65] 11-4842
1. Spiritualism. I. Title.

THE lifted veil; 133.
or, The hereafter revealed to reform the world, by a psychic. [New York] The International society of applied psychology, 1922. viii, 55, [5] p. 20 cm. [BF1301.L7] 23-7564
1. Spiritualism.

LILJENCRANTS, Johan, baron, 1885- 133.
Spiritism and religion. "Can you talk to the dead?" including a study of the most remarkable cases of spirit control, by Baron Johan Liljencrants ... with foreword by Maurice Francis Egan ... New York, The Devin-Adair co. c1918] 3 p. l., v-vii, 295, [1] p. 24 cm. Bibliographical note. Issued also as thesis (PH. D.) Catholic university of America, being no. 11 Universitas catholica Americae, Washingtonil, S. Facultas theologica, 1917-1918. [Full name: Karl Johan Edvard Liljencrants] Bibliography: p. [282]-286. [BF1261.L52] 19-245
1. Spiritualism. I. Title.

LILLIE, Harriet E. 133.
Flowers of thought: messages from a friend in spirit life to Harriet E. Lillie. [Boston, c1923] 3 p. l., 137 p. 20 cm. [BF1301.L715] 23-10035
1. Spiritualism. I. Title.

LILLIE, R Shepard. Mrs. 133.
The religious conflict of the ages: and other addresses, by the guides of Mrs. R. Shepard Lillie. Boston, Colby & Rich, 1889. 143 p. 20 cm. [BF1301.L72] 11-5337
1. Spiritualism. I. Title.

LILLIE, R Shepard. Mrs.
Two chapters from the book of my life, with poems, by R. Shepard Lillie. Boston, J. Wilson and son, 1889. xiv, 229 p. front. (port.) 21 cm. [PS2246.L48] 28-7940
1. Spiritualism. I. Title.

LINTON, Charles. 149
The healing of the nations. By Charles Linton ... With an introduction and appendix, by Nathaniel P. Tallmadge ... 2d ed. New York, Society for the diffusion of spiritual knowledge, 1855. 537 p. 2 port. (incl. front.) 22 cm. [BF1291.L75 1855] 11-4828
1. Spiritualism. I. Tallmadge, Nathaniel Pitcher, 1795-1864. II. Title.

LINTON, Charles. 149
The healing of the nations. by Charles Linton ... With an introduction and appendix, by Nathaniel P. Tallmadge ... 3d. ed. New York, Society for the diffusion of spiritual knowledge, 1855. 537 p 2 port. (incl. front.) 23 cm. [BF1291.L75 1855 a] 11-4829
1. Spiritualism. I. Tallmadge, Nathaniel Pitcher, 1795-1864. II. Title.

LINTON, Charles. 133.93
The healing of the nations. By Charles Linton ... With an introduction and appendix, by Nathaniel P. Tallmadge ... 4th ed. New York, S. T. Munson, 1858. 537 p. 24 cm. [BF1291.L75 1858] 159.96173 34-36364
1. Spiritualism. I. Tallmadge, Nathaniel Pitcher, 1795-1864. II. Title.

LINTON, Charles. 149
The healing of the nations. Second series. By Charles Linton ... Philadelphia, The author, 1864. viii, [9]-363 p. front. (port.) 24 cm. [BF1291.L76 1864] 11-4751
1. Spiritualism. I. Title.

LIPPITT, Francis James, 1812-1902. 133.
Physical proofs of another life, given in letters to the Seybert commission; by Francis J. Lippitt ... Washington, D. C., A. S. Witherbee & co., 1888. 65 p. incl. illus., facsims. 21 cm. [BF1029.L7] 10-29931
1. Spiritualism. 2. Future life. I. Title.

LITCHFIELD, Beals Ensign, 1823- 920.9
Autobiography of Beals E. Litchfield; or, Forty years intercourse with the denizens of the spirit world and inspirational poems by the same author. Ellicottville, N. Y., B. E. Litchfield, 1893. xv, [17]-486 p. front. (port.) 22 cm. [BF1283.L5A3] 32-35954
1. Spiritualism. I. Title.

LOCKWOOD, William Maynard, 1835- 133
The molecular hypothesis of nature; the relation of its principles to continued existence and to the philosophy of spiritualilsm. By Prof. W. M. Lockwood ... [Chicago? c1895] 57 p. 20 cm. [BF1272.L8] ca 11
1. Spiritualism. I. Title.

LODGE, Oliver Joseph, Sir 1851- 133.
Raymond; or, Life and death, with examples of the evidence for survival of memory and affection after death, by Sir Oliver J. Lodge. With eighteen illustrations. New York, George H. Doran company [c1916] xi, 404 p. front., 1 illus., plates, ports. 22 cm. The book is named after the author's son who was killed in the war. The first part contains extracts from his letters. "The second part gives specimens of what at present are considered by most people unsual communications ... The third part [Life and death] ... is of a more expository character." cf. Pref. [BF1261.L82 1916 a] 17-213
1. Spiritualism. 2. Future life. 3. European war, 1914-1918—Personal narratives, English. I. Lodge, Raymond, 1889-1915. II. Title.

LOMBROSO, Cesare, 1835-1909.
After death--what? Spiritistic phenomena and their interpretation, by Cesare Lombroso ... Rendered into English by William Sloane Kennedy ... Illustrated by photographs, diagrams, etc. Boston, Small, Maynard & company [c1909] xii p., 1 l., 364 p. front., illus., plates, ports. 22 cm. [BF1264.L8] 9-28193 2.50
1. Spiritualism. I. Kennedy, William Sloane, 1850- tr. II. Title.

"LONG distance, please," 133.93
by J. H. Los Angeles, Calif., DeVorss & co. [c1936] 2 p. l., 9-128 p. 21 cm. "First edition." [BF1261.L86] 159.96173 37-17379
1. Spiritualism. 2. Automatism. 3. Reincarnation. I. H., J.

LONGLEY, Mary Theresa (Shelhamer) Mrs. 1853- 133.93
Teachings and illustrations as they emanate from the spirit world. Methods of concentration--application and demonstration of spirit workers--how they build homes, temples, heal the soul-sick who come to their worlds from earth--how worlds are made. By Mrs. Mart T. Longley. Chicago, The Progressive thinker publishing house, 1908. 5 p. l., [9]-222 p. 2 port. (incl. front.) 20 cm. [BF1031.L86] 159.96173 32-35956
1. Spiritualism. I. Title.

LONGRIDGE, George, 1856-
Spiritualism and Christianity, by George Longridge ... London [etc.] A. R. Mowbray & co., ltd.; Milwaukee, The Morehouse publishing co. [1919] 2 p. l., 52 p. 17 cm. A 20
1. Spiritualism. I. Title.

LOOMIS, Bess Bingaman, 1884- 133.93
The return of Benjamin Franklin [by] Bess B. Loomis and Arthur J. Burks. St. Louis, State Pub. Co. [1955] 207p. 22cm. [BF1311.F7L6] 55-33686
1. Franklin, Benjamin, 1706-1790. 2. Spiritualism. I. Burks, Arthur J., 1898- joint author. II. Title.

LORD, John. 133.9
Modern spiritualism, scientifically demonstrated to be a mendacious hambug, in a series of letters to Professor Robert Hare ... Also some communications written for the Spiritual telegraph and other papers therewith connected. By John Lord ... Portland, Printed by B. Thurston, 1856. xii, [13]-127 p. 21 cm. "Communications written for the Spiritual telegraph and other papers", omitted. cf. p. 126. [BF1042.L6] 159.9617 33-24132
1. Spiritualism. I. Hare, Robert, 17814-1858. II. Title.

LOVELAND, J S. 133.
Mediumship: a course of seven lectures, delivered at the Mount Pleasant park camp-meeting, during the month of August, 1888. Also, a lecture on the perpetuity of spiritualism, given at the same place, on the last Sunday of the camp-meeting. By Prof. J. S. Loveland. Chicago, Ill., M. Hull & co., 1889. vii p., 1 l., [11]-248 p. 20 cm. [BF1286.L84] 11-3611
1. Spiritualism. I. Title.

LOVELAND, J S b.1818. 133.
An essay on mediumship. By Prof. J. S. Loveland. Columbus, O., Light of truth publishing company, 1897. 160 p. incl. front. (port.) 18 cm. (On cover: Light of truth library. vol. i, no. 4) [BF1286.L8] 11-4771
1. Spiritualism. I. Title.

[LUDINGTON, James] 201
Various revelations. With an account of the Garden of Eden, and the settlement of the eastern continent, as related by the leaders of the wandering tribes. From the age of Enoch, Seth, and Noah, to the birth of Jesus of Nazareth, as related by Mary his mother, and Joseph the foster-father; with a confirmation of his crucifixion and resurrection, as related by Pilate and the different apostles. Also, an account of the settlement of the North American continent, and the birth of the individualized spirit which has followed ... Also, many important reports from statesmen, poets, and scientists, from clergymen and warriors, who have attained to honorable position in the annals of American history. Boston, 1876. 391 p. incl. front. 24 cm. [BF1291.L85] 16-8282
1. Spiritualism. I. Title.

LUMS, Dyer Daniel. 133.
The "Spiritual" delusion; its methods, teachings, and effects. The philosophy and phenomena critically examined. By Dyer D. Lum ... Philadelphia, J. B. Lippincott & co., 1873. 252 p. 19 1/2 cm. [BF1042.L85] 11-3117
1. Spiritualism. I. Title.

[LUNT, Edward D.]
Mysteries of the seance and tricks and traps of bogus mediums: a plea for honest mediums and clean work, by a life-long spiritualist... Boston, Mass., Lunt bros., 1903. 1 p. l., 64 p. 20 cm. [BF1289.L8] 11-3613
1. Spiritualism. I. Title.

*LUPIEN, Louis H. 133.9
Prophecies and revelations by Hemaka. Boston, Christopher Pub. [c.1964] 75p. 21cm. 64-23500 2.75
1. Spiritualism. I. Title.

LUPIEN, Louis H 1894-- 133.9
Prophecies and revelations by Hemaks. By Louis H. Lupien. Boston, Christopher Pub. House [1964] 75 p. 21 cm. [BF1261.2.L78] 64-23500
1. Spiritualism. I. Title.

LUPIEN, Louis H 1894- 133.93
The unlocked truth according to Hemaka. New York, Vantage Press [1954] 80p. 22cm. [BF1261.2.L8] 54-8348
1. Spiritualism. I. Title.

MCARTHUR, Paul. 133.
Text book, ritual, valuable data, and selected poems, for public workers in the organized movement of modern spiritualism, by Paul McArthur ... adopted and published by Progressive spiritualist association of Mo., May 23rd, 1908. [St. Louis] 1908. 78 p. 19 cm. [BF1261.M24] 8-22531
1. Spiritualism. I. Title.

MCBRIDE, Andrew Jackson. 133.
Light from the spirit world; or, Revelations from the spirits of George Washington, John Wesley, Rev. John Fox, of Boston; Joel West, of Illinois; and others; on various subjects, through Andrew Jackson McBride, medium ... Cincinnati, J. West, 1856. x, 11-268 p. illus. 18 1/2 cm. [BF1291.M22] 11-4752
1. Spiritualism. I. Title.

MCCABE, Margaret Virginia. 133.
Life forces, by Margaret Virginia McCabe ... Washington, D.C., Press of J. F. Sheiry, 1899. 87 p. 18 cm. [BF1261.M26] 99-3160
1. Spiritualism. I. Title.

MCCOMAS, Henry Clay, 1875- 133.9
Ghosts I have talked with, by Henry C. McComas ... Baltimore, The Williams & wilkins company, 1935. vii, 192 p. 21 cm. [BF1031.M27] 35-18961
1. Spiritualism. 2. Psychical research. I. Title.

MCDONALD, Donald William, 1847- 133.
What we are and what we will be. Positive proof of identity. Individuality and immortality of man. Biblictic, scientific, with witnesses. And we will know each other there--spirits made perfect. Family circles eternal in the heavens. By Donald W. McDonald. Nashville, Tenn., 1909. 224 p. front. (port.) 19 1/2 cm. $1.50 Cover-title: The knowen, what we are and will be. [BF1261.M265] 9-25294
1. Spiritualism. I. Title.

MCDONALD, William, b.1820. 133.
Spiritualism identical with ancient sorcery, New Testament demonology, and modern witchcraft; with the testimony of God and man against it. By W. M'Donald. New York, Carlton & Porter, 1866. 212 p. 17 1/2 cm. [BF1042.M15] 11-2442
1. Spiritualism. I. Title.

MCDONALD, William, b.1820. 133.909
Spiritualism identical with ancient sorcery, New Testament demonology, and modern witchcraft: with the testimony of God and man against it. By W. M'Donald. New York, Nelson & Phillips; Cincinnati, Hitchcock & Walden [1866] 212 p. 18 cm. [BF1042.M15 1866a] [159.961709] 32-35019
1. Spiritualism. I. Title.

[MACE, Elizabeth H., Mrs.] 133.
The Grey ladye. By herself. Salem, O., Press of C. M. Day, 1896. 2 p. l., [7]-66 p. 20 cm. Treats of spiritualism. [BF1301.M22] 10-33680
1. Spiritualism. I. Title.

MCEVILLY, Mary A. 133.
Meslom's messages from the life beyond, by Mary A. McEvilly. New York, Brentano's [c1920] xvii, 139 p. 19 cm. [BF1301.M28] 20-6732
1. Spiritualism. I. Title.

MCEVILLY, Mary A. 133.
To woman from Meslom; a message from Meslom in the life beyond, received automatically by Mary McEvilly... with a preface by Walter Franklin Prince... New York. Brentano's [c1920] 3 p. l., ix-xxii, 108 p. 19 cm. [BF1301.M27] 20-22174
1. Spiritualism. I. Title.

MCGEHEAN, George. 133.
True spirit return [by] George McGehean, Lois McGehean. Cincinnati, O., Spiritualistic publishing co. [c1922] 2 p. l., 286 p. front., ports. 18 cm. Cover-title: True spirit return as told me by my mother from heaven above. [BF1301.M28] 23-586
1. Spiritualism. I. McGehean, Lois, joint author. II. Title.

MCGINNIS, Lillie. 133.
From the land o' the leal; being a book automatically and inspirationally written between the dates of March 15th, 1913, and March 15th, 1914. By Lillie McGinnis. Consisting of the experiences of all classes, after awakening to consciousness after the change of death. [Chicago, The Blakely printing co., c1915] 152 p. front. (port.) 19 1/2 cm. $1.00 [BF1301.M3] 16-3635
1. Spiritualism. I. Title.

MCHARGUE, Georgess. 133.9
Facts, frauds, and phantasms; a survey of the spiritualist movement. [1st ed.] Garden City, N.Y., Doubleday [1972] viii, 296 p. illus. 22 cm. Bibliography: p. [281]-284. [BF1261.2.M24] 73-180090 4.95
1. Spiritualism. I. Title.

MCKENZIE, J. Hewat. 133.
Spirit intercourse, its theory and practice, by J. Hewat McKenzie. New York, M. Kennerley, 1917. vii, [1], 295 p. illus., plates. 19 cm. "Literature": p. 294-295. [BF1261.M27] 17-30022
1. Spiritualism. I. Title.

MCMAHAN, Myrl (Edwards) 133.072
Plif. [1st ed.] New York, Exposition Press [1955] 102p. 21cm. A nontechnical report of the author's experiences in psychic phenomena. [BF1301.M2814] 54-13425
1. Spiritualism. I. Title.

MADDEN, Alfred. 133
Lifting the veil, a brief outline of spirituality, by Alfred Madden. Phoenix, Ariz., The author [c1920] 88 p. 1 illus. (port.) 19 1/2 cm. [BF1272.M25] 20-14230
1. Spiritualism. I. Title.

MAGNUSSEN, Julius, 1882- 133.
God's smile, by Julius Magnussen, tr. by Daniel Kilham Dodge. New York [etc.] D. Appleton and company, 1920. ix, 184, [1] p. 19 1/2 cm. [BF1308.S3M33] 20-13992
1. Spiritualism. I. Dodge, Daniel Kilham, tr. II. Title.

MAHAN, Asa, 1800-1889. 133.
Modern mysteries explained and exposed ... By Rev. A. Mahan ... Boston, J. P. Jewett and company; New York, Sheldon, Lamport and Blakeman; [etc., etc.] 1855. xv, 466 p. 20 cm. [BF1042.M2] 11-2443
1. Davis, Andrew Jackson, 1826-1910. Principles of nature. 2. Swendenborg, Emanuel, 1688-1772. 3. Spiritualism. I. Title.
Contents omitted.

MAHONY, Patrick, 1911- 133
Out of the silence, a book of factual fantasies; with a foreword by Maurice Maeterlinck. New York, Storm, 1948. xi, 180 p. 22 cm. [BF1261.M285] 48-11996
1. Spiritualism. I. Title.

*MANDEL, Henry A., 1894- 133.9
Banners of light; the first time the truth has been given from the spirit world. New York, Vantage [1973] 528 p. 21 cm. [BF1251] ISBN 0-533-00511-6 6.95
1. Spiritualism. 2. Psychical research. I. Title.

MARCHANT, James, Sir 1867- ed. 289.
Survival, by Sir Oliver Lodge ... Stanley De Brath ... Lady Grey of Fallodon ... [and others] edited by Sir James Marchant. London and New York, G. P. Putnam's sons [c1924] 5 p. l., 199, [1] p. 20 cm. [BF1235.M3] 24-32093
1. Spiritualism. I. Lodge, Oliver Joseph, Sir 1851- II. De Brath, Stanley. III. Grey, Pamela (Wyndham) Grey, viscountess, 1871- IV. Title.

MARSH, Luther Rawson, 1813-1902. 133.
... *Voice of the patriarchs.* Conversations with the chief characters of the Bible, held by Luther R. Marsh, through the medial power of Clarisa J. Huyler. Taken down as spoken, by Emma E. Law ... Author's ed. Buffalo, N. Y., C. A. Wenborne, 1889. xxiii, 382 p. 20 cm. (His Glimpses in the upper spheres ... v. 1) [BF1301.M33] 22-6783
1. Spiritualism. 2. Bible. I. Title.

MARTIN, Jacob, Mrs. 133.
Guide-posts to immortal roads. By Mrs. Jacob Martin. Boston, Colby & Rich, 1882. 74 p. 18 1/2 cm. [BF1261.M3] 11-3152
1. Spiritualism. I. Title.

MARVIN, Frederic Rowland, 1847-1918. 133.
The philosophy of spiritualism and the pathology and treatment of mediomania. Two lectures. By Frederic R. Marvin ... Read before the New York liberal club, March 20 and 27, 1874. New York, A. K. Butts & co., 1874. 68 p. illus. (incl. facsims.) 19 cm. [BF1042.M34] 11-2444
1. Spiritualism. 2. Insanity. I. Title.

MASKELYNE, John Nevil, 1839-1917. 133.
Modern spiritualism. A short account of its rise and progress, with some exposures of so-called spirit media. By John Nevil Maskelyne ... London, For the author by F. Warne and co.; New York, Scribner, Welford, and Armstrong [1876] viii, 182 p. facsims. 17 cm. [BF1042.M36] 11-2445
1. Spiritualism. I. Title.

MASSACHUSETTS association of the New Jerusalem. 133.
The pythonism of the present day. The response of the ministers of the Massachusetts association of the New Jerusalem to a resolution to that association requesting their consideration to what is usually known as modern spirtualism... Boston, G. Phinney, 1858. 1 p. l., 50 p. 19 1/2 cm. Signed: Warren Goddard. Printed by order of the association. [BF1042.M37] 6-26361
1. Spiritualism. I. Goddard, Warren, d. 1889. II. Title.

[MAST, Isaac Newton] 1844- 133.
The continuity of human and spiritual life. Being thoughts from the realms of each, by those who dwell in each. Ottumwa, Ia., For I. N. Mast, 1892. 191 p. 20 cm. [BF1261.M35] 4-23381
1. Spiritualism. I. Title.

MATHISON, Volney G
How to achieve past life recalls. [Quincy, Mass., Institute of Physical and Mental Development] 1956. 66 p. 68-96939
1. Spiritualism. I. Title.

MATTISON, Hiram, 1811-1868. 133.
Spirit rapping unveiled! An expose of the origin, history, theology and philosophy of certain alleged communications from the spirit world, by means of "spirit rapping", "medium writing", "physical demonstrations", etc. ... By Rev. H. Mattison ... New York, Mason brothers, 1853. 192 p. illus. 18 cm. [BF1042.M38] 11-2573
1. Spiritualism. I. Title.

MATURIN, Edith (Money) "Mrs. Fred Maturin." 133.
Rachel comforted; conversations of a mother in the dark with her child in the light. By Mrs. Fred Maturin; with a preface by W. T. Stead. New York, Dodd, Mead and company, 1920. 252 p., 1 l. 21 cm. $2.00 [BF1301.M45 1920a] 20-16938
1. Spiritualism. I. Title.

MEAD, Emily W. Mrs. 1820- 133.
In the beginning; a book for the new era, by Mrs. Emily W. Mead. [Santa Cruz, Cal., Sentinel pub. co., 1910] 229, [1] p. 19 1/2 cm. Two pencil drawings inserted. [BF1301.M5] 11-22016 2.00
1. Spiritualism. I. Title.

MEISSNER, Sophie (Radford) de. Mme. 133.
There are no dead, by Sophie Radford de Meissner ... Boston, Sherman, French & company, 1912. 4 p. l., 116 p. 20 cm. [BF1301.M6] 13-1073 1.00
1. Spiritualism. I. Title.

MERCEDIS, Tusschuna. 133.93
... *Stepping stones to divine intervention* for universal human welfare, received by Seeress Tusschuna Mercedis ... New York, N. Y., New era divine light publishers [c1933] xiii, 76 p. 20 cm. (Divine thought, light and life series, book 1) [BF1301.M63] 159.96173 34-5798
1. Spiritualism. I. Title.

MILBURN, Lucy McDowell, Mrs. 133.
The classic of spiritism, by Lucy McDowell Milburd. London, K. Paul, Trench, Trubner & co., ltd. New York, E. P. Dutton & co., 1922. vii, [1], 226 p. 19 1/2 cm. [BF1275.B5M5] 22-8981
1. Spiritualism. I. Title.

MILBURN, Lucy McDowell, Mrs. 133.
The classic of spiritism, by Lucy McDowell Milburn ... New York, The Dacrow corporation; [etc., etc.] 1922. 3 p. l., v-vii, 226 p. 19 cm. [BF1275.B5M5 1922a] 22-15590
1. Spiritualism. 2. Bible and spiritualism. I. Title.

MILLER, James D. 1895- 133.
The guiding light, by James D. Miller. Boston, The Christopher publishing house [c1922] 58 p. 21 cm. [BF1288.M4] CA 23
I. Title.

MILLER, Paul. 133.9
The invisible presence / by Paul Miller. London : Psychic Press, 1976 [i.e. 1977] 208 p. ; 20 cm. [BF1261.2.M54] 77-366174 ISBN 0-85384-046-6 : £2.50
1. Spiritualism. I. Title.

MITCHELL, David. 133.
A key to the spiritual palace. by David Mitchell. Columbus, J. Geary, son & co., 1855. 97 p. 21 1/2 cm. Cover has imprint: Columbus, J. P. Santmyer, 1856; also copyright date, 1856. Embraces "two prominent subjects...Spiritual manifestations and the prophecies of the Bible."--p. 4. [BF1251.M6] 10-34706
1. Spiritualism. 2. Prophecies. I. Title.

MITCHELL, Thomas, Rev. 133.
Key to ghostism. Science and art unlock its mysteries. By Rev. Thomas Mitchell ... New York, S. R. Wells & co., 1880. 2 p. l., [iii]-xii, [13]-249 p. 19 1/2 cm. [BF1042.M65] 11-2420
1. Spiritualism. I. Title.

MITCHELL, Thomas, Rev. 133.
Non spiritus. The philosophy of spiritualism. By Rev. Thomas Mitchell ... Albany, N.Y., Printed by Weed, Parsons and company, 1872. 168 p. 17 cm. [BF1042.M68] 11-2421
1. Spiritualism. I. Title.

MONROE, John Walker, 1901- 133.93
1943.
My travels in the far off beyond. [Clarksburg? W.Va.] c1950. 306 p. ports. 24 cm. [BF1283.M58A3] 51-29677
1. Spiritualism. I. Title.

MOORE, Margaret Gordon.
Things I can't explain, by Margaret Gordon Moore. London, New York [etc.,] Rider & co., [1944] 64 p. front pl., ports. 19 cm. A 44
1. Spiritualism. I. Title.

MORRIS, Robert Overton, 133.
1871-
Awful thoughts, or, Taming man [by] Robert Morris; a phenomenon that is interesting two worlds. Boston, The Roxburgh publishing company, inc. [c1917] 203 p. 20 cm. [BF1301.M73] 17-4992
1. Spiritualism. I. Title.

MORRISON, A. B. 133.
Spiritualism and necromancy. By Rev. A. B. Morrison ... Cincinnati, Hitchcock and Walden; New York, Nelson and Phillips, 1873. 1 p. l., iii, 3-203 p. 17 1/2 cm. Introduction signed: Benj. St. James Fry. [BF1042.M84] 11-2422
1. Spiritualism. I. Title.

MORSE, James Johnson, 1849- 133.
Practical occultism; a course of lectures through the trance mediumship of J. J. Morse. With a preface by William Emmette Coleman. San Francisco, Cal., "Carrier dove" publishing house; [etc., etc.] 1888. 159 p. 20cm. [BF1261.M85] 11-3153
1. Spiritualism. I. Title.

MORTENSEN, Mary Alice. Mrs. 133.
Acredios, the veil lifted; a series of remarkable trance communications through the mediumship of Mary Alice Mortensen; stenographically reported by Elfrieda Neville ... Los Angeles, Cal., Austin publishing company [c1921] 192 p. 19cm. [BF1301.M75] 21-11049
1. Spiritualism. I. Neville, Mrs. Elfrieda. II. Title.

MORTON, Albert, ed. 133.9
"Know thyself." Psychic studies, spiritual science, and "The higher aspects of spiritualism" ... Albert Morton, editor and publisher. San Francisco, Cal. [18-] 2 p. l., 22, 288 p. port. 29 cm. [BF1023.M6] [159.9617] 32-35951
1. Spiritualism. I. Title.

[MOSES, William Stainton] 133.9
1840-1892.
Higher aspects of spiritualism. By M. A. (Oxon) [pseud.] ... London, E. W. Allen & co.; Boston, Colby & Rich;[etc., etc.] 1880. 124 p. 19 cm. [BF1261.M88] [159.9617] 33-16690
1. Spiritualism. I. Title.

MULDOON, Sylvan Joseph, ed. 133
Psychic experiences of famous people. [Chicago] Aries Press [1947] [2] l., iii-xv, 200 p. 22 cm. [BF1277.A1M8] 47-7711
1. Spiritualism. I. Title.

MULDOON, Sylvan Joseph. 133.93
Sensational psychic experiences ... by Sylvan Muldoon ... Darlington, Wis., The New horizon publishers 1941 v. 23 cm. (On cover: Psychic series, v. 1) Reproduced from type-written copy. "First edition." [BF1023.M77] 199.96173 42-4528
1. Spiritualism. I. Title.

MULHOLLAND, John, 1898- 133.9
Beware familiar spirits / John Mulholland. New York : Arno Press, 1975, c1938. p. cm. (Perspectives in psychical research) Reprint of the ed. published by Scribner, New York. [BF1261.M93 1975] 75-7388 ISBN 0-405-07036-5 : 20.00
1. Spiritualism. I. Title. II. Series.

MULHOLLAND, John, 1898- 133.9
Beware familiar spirits, by John Mulholland. New York, C. Scribner's sons; London, C. Scribner's sons, ltd., 1938. x, 342 p. illus. 22 cm. [BF1261.M93] 159.9617 39-95
1. Spiritualism. I. Title.

MULHOLLAND, John, 1898- 133.9
Beware familiar spirits / by John Mulholland. New York : Scribner, [1979], c1938. 331 p. : ill. ; 21 cm. (The Scribner library ; 860) Includes index. [BF1261.M93 1979] 78-66328 ISBN 0-684-16181-8 : 5.95
1. Spiritualism. I. Title.

MUNDELL, Charles Samuel, 133.
1895-
Our Joe; or, Why we believe our brother lives! By Charles S. Mundell. Los Angeles, Calif., The Austin publishing company [c1922] 219 p. front., illus., ports. 20 cm. [BF1301.M78] 22-7679
1. Spiritualism. 2. Mundell, Joseph Harvey, 1900-1921 I. Title.

MUZZY, Florence Emlyn 133.323
(Downs) Mrs. 1851-1939.
Beyond the sunset; study, dedicated to seekers for truth by one who seeks; compiled and arranged from origianl notes of one called Lynd by Florence E. D. Muzzy ... [New York, c1939] 4 p. l., 208 p. 23 cm. [BF1301.M85] 159.961323 40-30437
1. Spiritualism. 2. Automatism. I. Title.

MYERS, Gustavus, 1872- 133.
Beyond the borderline of life, by Gustavus Myers; a summing up of the results of the scientific investigation of psychic phenomena, with an account of Professor Botazzi's experiments with Eusapia Paladino, and an abstract of the report of the cross-references by Mrs. Piper, Mrs. Verrall and otherswhich so influenced Sir Oliver Lodge in his decision in favor of the spiritistic hypothesis. Boston, The Ball publishing co., 1910. 2 p. l., 7-249 p. 20 cm. [BF1051.M8] 10-17977
1. Spiritualism. 2. Psychical research. I. Title.

MYERS, John, 1895- 133.9
My life with the old masters. [1st ed.] New York, Exposition Press [1967] x, 221 p. illus. (part col.) 22 cm. (An Exposition-banner book) [BF1261.2.M9] 67-6586
1. Spiritualism. I. Title.

NASH, Harold L. 1892- 133.93
The dawn of a conviction, by Harold L. Nash. Boston, The Christopher publishing house [1942] 5 p. l., 5-80, [1] p. front. (port.) 23 1/2 cm. [BF1301.N3] 43-698
1. Spiritualism. I. Title.

NATIONAL federation of 289.9
spiritual science churches.
Textbook of spiritual science, National federation of spiritual science churches. Los Angeles, Calif. [1932] 2 p. l., 7-110 p. 24 cm. [BX9798.S7N3] 33-6356
1. Spiritualism. I. Title. II. Title: Spiritual science, Textbook of.

NATIONAL Spiritualist 252.
Association.
Spiritualist manual. Revision of July, 1928. 4th ed. Washington, 1928. 199 p. illus. 23 cm. [BX978.S7N35 1928] 52-46465
1. Spiritualism. I. Title.

NATIONAL spiritualist 133.9
association.
Spiritualist manual, issued by the National sppiritualists' association of the United States of America (a religious corporation) 600 Pennsylvania avenue, S. E., Washington, D. C. [Baltimore, Day printing company] 1911. 164 p. front., 2 pl. (incl. ports.) 23 cm. Newspapers clippings inserted. [BX9798.S7N35] 33-30630
1. Spiritualism. I. Title.

NATIONAL spiritualist 133.9
association.
Spiritualist manual issued by the National spiritualist association of the United States of America (a religious body) incorporated under the laws of the District of Columbia, 600 Pennsylvania avenue, S. E., Washington D. C. ... [Chicago, Press of Printing products corporation] 1934. 200 p. front., 2 pl. (incl. ports.) 23 cm. "First edition published Jan., 1911 ... fifth edition published Jan., 1934." [BX9798.S7N35 1934] 159.9617 38-22100
1. Spiritualism. I. Title.

NATIONAL spiritualist 289.9
association.
Spiritualist manual, issued by the National spiritualist association of the United States of America (a religious body) incorporated under the laws of the District of Columbia ... [Chicago, Printing products corporation] 1940. 210 p. front., 2 pl. (incl. ports.) 2o cm. "1st ed. published Jan., 1911 ... 6th ed. published Jan., 1940." [BX9798.S7N35 1940] 40-6016
1. Spiritualism. I. Title.

NELSON, Geoffrey K. 133.9
Spiritualism and society, by Geoffrey K. Nelson. New York, Schocken Books [1969] xi, 307 p. 23 cm. Based on the author's theses (M.Sc. and Ph.D.) University of London. Bibliography: p. 289-302. [BF1261.2.N4 1969b] 69-17196 7.50
1. Spiritualism. I. Title.

NEWHOUSE, Mildred (Sechler) 133.9
Mrs., 1909-
Natives of eternity, an authentic record of experiences in realms of super-physical consciousness, by Flower A. Newhouse. Santa Barbara, Calif., J. F. Rowny press [c1937] xii p., 1 l., 15-90 p. front., plates. 24 cm. [BF1261.N4] [159.9617] 38-10003
1. Spiritualism. I. Title.

[NEWTON, Alonzo Eliot] 1821- 133.
1889.
Tract[s] no. 1- [Boston, Bela Marsh, 186-?- v. 17 1/2 cm. No. 1 signed: A.E.N. (i.e. Alonzo Eliot Newton] [BF1272.N4] 45-45689
1. Spiritualism. I. Title.
Contents omitted.

THE next beyond.. 133.
Annonymous. Boston, The Christopher publishing house [c1921] 109 p. 20 cm. [BF1301.N58] 21-12368
1. Spiritualism.

NICHOLS, Thomas Low, 133.9'092'2
1815-1901.
A biography of the brothers Davenport / T. L. Nichols. New York : Arno Press, 1976. p. cm. (The Occult) Reprint of the 1864 ed. published by Saunders, Otley, London. [BF1283.D3N6 1976] 75-36912 ISBN 0-405-07969-9 : 20.00
1. Davenport, Ira Erastus, 1839-1911. 2. Davenport, William Henry, 1841-1877. 3. Spiritualism. I. Title. II. Series: The Occult (New York, 1976-)

NIXON, Jabez Hunt. 133.
Beyond the vail. This publication is a sequel to "Rending the vail". Being a compilation, with notes and explanations, by Jabez Hunt Nixon, of narrations and illustrations of spirit experiences, spoken, written and made by full-form visible materializations ... Kansas City, Mo., Hudson-Kimberly publishing company, 1901. 500 p. incl. front. (port.) illus. 24 cm. [BF1301.A2] 2-2462
1. Spiritualism. I. Title.

NIXON, Jabez Hunt. 133.9
The guiding star to a higher spiritual condition, sequel number two to "Rending the vail", produced in the same way and by means of the same combined mediumship W. W. Aber (phenomenal) J. H. Nixon (mental) Boston, Eastern publishing company [c1905] iii p., 1 l., 7-427 p. col. front., plates, ports. (part col.) facsim. 23 cm. [BF1301.N6] 32-6487
1. Spiritualism. I. Aber, William W., medium. II. Title.

NIXON, Jabez Hunt. 133.
The mystical quadruple interrogatory. How? What?? Whence??? Whither???? Concerning the existence of man ... and all life, so far answered by ... this book as to suggest for an appropriate title, to-wit: Rending the vail. This volume is a compilation by J. H. Nixon of psychic literature, mostly given by spirits through and by means of full-form visible materializations, at seances of ...the Aber intellectual circle, the medium being William W. Aber ... Kansas City, Mo., Hudson-Kimberley publishing co., 1899. 2 p. l., 3-507 p. front., (port.) illus. (incl. facsims.) 23 cm. [BF1301.A22] 99-5528
1. Spiritualism. I. Aber, William W., 1861- II. Title. III. Title: Rending the vail.

NIXON, Jabez Hunt. 133.
The mystical quadruple interrogatory. How? What?? Whence??? Whither???? Concerning the existence of man ... and all life, so far answered by ... this book as to suggest for an appropriate title, to-wit: Rending the vail. This volume is a compilation by J. H. Nixon of psychic literature, mostly given by spirits through and by means of full-form visible materializations, at seances of ... the Aber intellectual circle, the medium being William W. Aber ... Kansas City, Mo., Hudson-Kimberley publishing co., 1899. 2 p. l., 3-507 p. front (port.) illus. (incl. facsims.) 23 cm. [BF1301.A22] 99-5528
1. Spiritualism. I. Aber, William W., 1861- II. Title. III. Title: Rending the vail.

NORMAN, Ernest L
Cosmic continuum. Santa Barbara, Calif., Unarius [c1960] 263 p. 22 cm. 68-13463
1. Spiritualism. I. Title.

NORMAN, Ernest L
The Elysium; parables of light. Glendale, Calif., R. E. Norman [1956] 71 p. illus. 23 cm. 68-62799
1. Spiritualism. I. Title.

NORMAN, Ernest L
The infinite contact. Santa Barbara, Calif., Unarius Journal [1960] 292 p. 22 cm. "Six booklets bound under one cover." 68-62832
1. Spiritualism. I. Title.

NORMAN, Ernest L 133.93
The pulse of creation series. [Los Angeles, New Age Pub. Co., c1956- v. illus. 23cm. Contents.v. 1. The voice of Venus, clairvoyantly and clairaudiently received through E. L. Norman. [BF1301.N65] 57-23351
1. Spiritualism. I. Title.

NORMAN, Ernest L
The voice of Venus, clairvoyantly and clairaudiently received through Ernest L. Norman. 3. ed. [Santa Barbara, Calif., Unarius [c1956] 198 p. illus., port. 23 cm. (His The pulse of creation series. v. 1) 68-13679
1. Spiritualism. I. Title.

NOURSE, Laura A. (Barney) 133.
Sunderlin, Mrs. 1836-
Penclings from immortality. A collection of writings from inspiration. Also writings copied from words seen clairvoyantly upon the wall ... through the medium and clairvoyant, Mrs. Laura A. Sunderlin. Maquoketa, Ia., Swigart & Sargent, printers, 1876. 1 p. l., [iv]-vii, [7]-202 p.

front. (port.) 18 cm. [BF1301.N7] 15-14016
1. Spiritualism. I. Title.

O'DONNELL, Elliot, 1872- 133.
The menace of spiritualism, by Elliot O'Donnell ... with a foreword by Father Bernard Vaughan, S.J. New York, Frederick A. Stokes company [c1920] xii p., 2 l., 206 p. 19 1/2 cm. [BF1042.O3 1920 a] 20-6366
1. Spiritualism. I. Title.

OLCOTT, Henry Steel, 1832- 133.9 1907.
People from the other world. Profusely illustrated by Alfred Kappes, and T. W. Williams. With an introd. to the new ed. by Terence Barrow. Rutland, Vt., C. E. Tuttle Co. [1972] xii, 492 p. illus. 20 cm. Reprint of the 1875 ed., with a new introd. Bibliography: p. 489-492. [BF1251.O4 1972] 74-152114 ISBN 0-8048-0979-8 8.95
1. Spiritualism. I. Title.

OLCOTT, Henry Steel, 1832- 133. 1907.
People from the other world. By Henry S. Olcott, profusely illustrated by Alfred Kappes, and T. W. Williams ... Hartford, Conn., American publishing company, 1875. xv, [16]-492 p. incl. illus., plates, ports., facsims. front., pl. 21 cm. Bibliography: p. 489-492. [BF1251.O4] 10-34872
1. Spiritualism. I. Title.

OLIPHANT, Laurence, 1829-1888.
Scientific religion; or, Higher possibilities of life and practice through the operation of natural forces. By Laurence Oliphant. With an appendix by a clergyman of the Church of England. Authorized American ed. Buffalo, C. A. Wenborne, 1889. 1 p. l., xv p., 1 l., 473 p. 22 cm. Preface signed: Rosamond Oliphant. Appendix 2 by Haskett Smith. [BF605.O5 1889] 26-9040
1. Spiritualism. 2. Mysticism. I. Oliphant, Rosamond Dale (Owen) Mrs. 1846- ed. II. Smith, Haskett, 1847-1906. III. Title.

OLSON, Mary. 133.9
Expose, by Mary Olson. New York city, N.Y., Typecraft publishing co. [1945] 3 p. l., 9-172 p., 1 l. 1 illus., diagrs. 19 cm. [BF1261.O4] 46-1139
1. Spiritualism. I. Title.

OSTBY, Ole A 1862- 133.
An awakening to the universe, by Dr. O. A. Ostby, (1st ed.) Minneapolis, Minn. [c1927] vii, [1], 367 p. 20 cm. [BF1261.O7] 27-9445
1. Spiritualism. I. Title.

... Our unseen guest; 133.93
introduction by Stewart Edward White. Los Angeles, Borden publishing company, 1943. 7 p. l., 3-319, [1] p. 20 cm. At head of title: Darby & Joan. [BF1343.O8 1943] 43-6959
1. Spiritualism.

OUR unseen guest ... 133.
New York and London, Harper & brothers [c1920] 5 p. l., 3-319, [1] p. 21 cm. [BF1343.O8] 20-3803
1. Spiritualism.

OWEN, George Vale, 1869- 133.91 1931.
The life beyond the veil; spirit messages received and written down by the Rev. G. Vale Owen ... with an appreciation by Lord Northcliffe and an introduction by Sir Arthur Conan Doyle ... ed. by H. W. Engholm ... New York, George H. Doran company [c1921] 2 v. 20 cm. Contents.--i. The lowlands of heaven.--ii. The highlands of heaven. [BF1301.O8 1921] 21-8602
1. Spiritualism. I. Engholm, H. W., ed. II. Title.

OWEN, James J., b.1827. 133.91
Psychography; marvelous manifestations of psychic power given through the mediumship of Fred P. Evans, known as the "independent slate-writer." ByJ. J. Owen ... San Francisco, The Hicks-Judd co. [c1893] 214 p. incl. illus., pl. front. (port.) 26 cm. [BF1301.E87] 11-14355
1. Spiritualism. I. Evans, Frederick P. II. Title.

OWEN, James J b.1827. 133.
Spiritual fragments, by J. J. Owen ... San Francisco, The Rosenthal-Saalburg co., 1890. 260 p. front. (port.) 20 cm. [BF1261.O9] 11-3154
1. Spiritualism. I. Title.

OWEN, Robert Dale, 1801- 133. 1877.
The debatable land between this world and the next, with illustrative narrations; by Robert Dale Owen ... New York, G. W. Carleton & co.; [etc., etc.] 1872. Apparitions. 1 p. l., [v]-xxii, [23]-542 p. illus. (incl. facsims.) 19 cm. [BF1251.O75] 10-34873
1. Spiritualism. I. Title.

OWEN, Robert Dale, 1801- 133. 1877.
Footfalls on the boundary of another world. With narrative illustrations. By Robert Dale Owen ... Philadelphia, J. B. Lippincott & co., 1860. 528 p. 2 facsim. 19 cm. "List of authors cited": p. 13-16. [BF1251.O8] 10-32956
1. Spiritualism. 2. Apparitions. I. Title.

OWEN, Robert Dale, 1801- 133.9 1877.
Footfalls on the boundary of another world. With narrative illustrations. By Robert Dale Owen ... Philadelphia, J. B. Lippincott & co., 1863. 528 p. facsims. 19 cm. "List of authors cited": p. 13-16. [BF1251.O82 1863] 159.9617 33-11048
1. Spiritualism. 2. Apparitions. I. Title.

OWEN, Robert Dale, 1801- 133. 1877.
Footfalls on the boundary of another world. With narrative illustrations. By Robert Dale Owen ... Philadelphia, J. B. Lippincott & co., 1865 [c1859] 528 p. 2 facsim. 19 cm. "List of authors cited": p. 13-16. [BF1251.O83] 10-32957
1. Spiritualism. 2. Apparations. I. Title.

OWEN, Theresa D. 133.
The message of love and hope, received through independent writing, by Theresa D. Owen. [Chicago, c1923] vi, 140 p. 20 cm. [BF1301.O84] 23-18401
1. Spiritualism. I. Title.

PADGETT, James E. 1852- 133.93 1923.
The true gospel revealed again from Jesus, through James E. Padgett. [Washington, L. R. Stone, c1941] 3 p. l., vii, iii, xii, 360, [2] p. port. 23 cm. [BF1301.P25] [159.96173] 42-19855
1. Spiritualism. I. Title.

PAGE, Charles Grafton, 1812- 1868.
Psychomancy. Spirit-rappings and table-tippings exposed. By Prof. Charles G. Page ... New-York. D. Appleton and company, 1853. 96 p. illus. 18 1/2 cm. [BF1289.P22] 11-4749
1. Spiritualism. I. Title.

[PAGET, Fannie Ruthven] 133.
How I know that the dead are alive. Washington, D.C., Plenty publishing company [c1917] 253 p. front. (port.) 24 cm. Lettered on cover: By Fannie Ruthven Paget. [BF1283.P25A3] 17-8091
1. Spiritualism. I. Title.

PALMSTIERNA, Erik Kule, 133.93 friherre, 1877-
Horizons of immortality, a quest of reality [by] Erik Palmstierna. New York, Coward-McCann, inc [c1938] vi, 281 p. 22 cm. "The messages...have reached us through the instrumentality of Mrs. Alexander Fachiri (Adila Fuchiri, the violinist)." [BF1311.F25P3 1938] [(159.96173)] 38-9996
1. Spiritualism. 2. Automatism. I. Fachiri, Mrs. Adila, 1889- II. Title.

PATON, Lewis Bayles, 1864-1932.
Spiritism and the cult of the dead in antiquity, by Lewis Bayles Paton ... New York, The Macmillan company, 1921. ix, p., 2 l., 325 p. 23 cm. Bibliographical foot-notes. [BF1241.P3] 21-19217
1. Spiritualism. 2. Dead, The. 3. Ancestor-worship. 4. Funeral rites and ceremonies. I. Title.

PEARCE, William John, 1905- 133.9
The hidden truth / by W. J. Pearce. London ; New York : Regency Press, 1974. 238 p. ; 23 cm. [BF1261.2.P37] 74-196613 ISBN 0-7212-0338-8 : £3.00
1. Spiritualism. I. Title.

PEARSALL, Ronald, 133.9'0942 1927-
The table-rappers. New York, St. Martin's Press [1973, c1972] 258 p. illus. 23 cm. Bibliography: p. 241-243. [BF1261.P29 1973] 72-92008 6.95
1. Spiritualism. I. Title.

PEEBLES, James Martin, 1822- 133.
Seers of the ages: embracing spiritualism, past and present. Doctrines stated and moral tendencies defined. By J. M. Peebles ... 3d ed. Boston, W. White and company; New-York, The American news company, 1870. x, [11]-376 p. 23 cm. [BF1241.P35 1870] 10-32972
1. Spiritualism. I. Title.

PEEBLES, James Martin, 1822- 133.
Seers of the ages: embracing spiritualism, past and present. Doctrines stated and moral tendencies defined. By J. M. Peebles ... 8th ed. Boston, Banner of light publishing co., 1898. x p., 1 l., 13-376 p. front. (port.) 24 cm. "Names of the principal authors consulted": p. 173 [i. e. 373]-376. [BF1241.P35 1898] 17-14869
1. Spiritualism. I. Title.

PEEBLES, James Martin, 1822- 133.
Spirit mates, their origin and destiny, sex-life, marriage, divorce, by J. M. Peebles ... also, a symposium, by forty noted Writers, spirit mates--their pre-existence, earth pilgrimages, reunions in spirit-life, ed. and arraged by Robert Sudall. Battle Creek, Mich., Peebles' publishing company [c1909] 2 p. l., vii-xvi, 318 p. 24 cm. p. [309]-318, advertising matter. [BF1275.M3P3] 9-29401 1.25
1. Spiritualism. 2. Marriage. 3. Sudall, Robert. I. Title.

PEEBLES, James Martin, 1822- 133.
What is spiritualism, who are these spiritualists, and what has spiritualism done for the world? By J. M. Peebles ... [Battle Creek, Mich.] Peebles institute print, 1903. 131 p. front. (port.) 23 cm. [BF1241.P37] 4-34598
1. Spiritualism. I. Title.

PEEBLES, James Martin, 1822- 133.
What is spiritualism? Who are these spiritualist? and What can spiritualism do for the world? By J. M. Peebles ... 5th ed., rev. and enl. ... Battle Creek, Mich., Peebles publishing co. [c1910] 1 p. l., iii p., 1 l., [iii]-v, [1], 7-238 p. front. (port.) 24 cm. [BF1261.P4] 10-27708 0.75
1. Spiritualism. I. Title.

PEEBLES, James Martin, 1822- 133. 1922.
Immortality, and our employments hereafter. With what a hundred spirits, good and evil, say of their dwelling places. By J. M. Peebles ... Boston, Colby and Rich, 1880. 296 p. 24 cm. [BF1291.P37] 11-4762
1. Spiritualism. I. Title.

PEEBLES, James Martin, 920.9 1822-1922.
The practical of spiritualism. Biographical sketch of Abraham James. Historic description of his oil-well discoveries in Pleasantville, Pa., through spirit direction. By J. M. Peebles ... Chicago, Horton & Leonard, printers, 1868. 85 p. 24 cm. [BF1283.J3P4] 33-20368
1. James, Abraham, b. 1827. 2. Spiritualism. I. Title.

PEEBLES, James Martin, 1822- 133. 1922.
Seers of the ages: embracing spiritualism, past and present. Doctines stated and moral tendencies defined. By J. M. Peebles ... 2d ed. Boston, W. White and company; New-York, The American news company, 1869. x, [11]-376 p. 23 cm. [BF1241.P35 1869] 10-32974
1. Spiritualism. I. Title.

PEEBLES, James Martin, 133.909 1822-1922.
Seers of the ages; embracing spiritualism, past and present. Doctrines stated and moral tendencies defined. By J. M. Peebles ... 4th ed. London, J. Burns; Boston, W. White and company, 1870. x p., 1 l., 13-376 p. 22 cm. "Names of the principal authors consulted": p. 373-376. 159.961709
1. Spiritualism. I. Title.

PEEBLES, James Martin, 133.9 1822-1922.
A series of seven essays upon spiritualism vs. materialism. Appearing in the Free thought magazine. By J. M. Peebles ... Battle Creek, Mich., Dr. Peebles institute of health publishing co., 1902. 95 p. incl. front. (port.) 25 cm. [BF1261.P34] 159.9617 33-20343
1. Spiritualism. 2. Materialism. I. Free thought magazine. II. Title. III. Title: Spiritualism vs. materialism.

PEEBLES, James Martin, 1822- 133. 1922.
The spirit's pathway traced; did it pre-exist and does it reincarnate again into mortal life? By J. M. Peebles ... Battle Creek, Mich., Dr. Peebles institute of health [c1906] 207 p. front. (port.) 24 cm. Pages [197]-207 contain book notices, etc. [BF1261.P35] 7-6170
1. Spiritualism. I. Title.

PEEBLES, James Martin, 1822- 133. 1922.
Witch-poison and the antidote, or Rev. Dr. Baldwin's sermon on witchcraft, spiritism, hell and the devil re-reviewed. By J. M. Peebles ... Troy, N. Y., The Troy children's progressive lyceum, 1872. 94 p. 22 cm. [BF1042.B23] 27-10794
1. Baldwin, George Colfax, 1817-1899. The witch scence in 1st Samuel. 2. Spiritualism. I. Title.

PEMBER, George Hawkins. 133.
Earth's earliest ages and their connection with modern spiritualism and theosophy, by G. H. Pember ... New York, Chicago [etc.] Fleming H. Revell company [19-] x, 480, [1] p. 20 cm. Revised and enlarged edition of "Earth's earliest ages and their lessons for us", published in 1876. cf. Pref. [BF1275.B5P4] 16-18852
1. Spiritualism. 2. Bible and spiritualism. I. Title.

PENNSYLVANIA. 11-15003
University. Seybert commission for investigating modern spiritualism.
Preliminary report of the Commission appointed by the University of Pennsylvania to investigate modern spiritualism, in accordance with the request of the late Henry Seybert. Philadelphia, J. B. Lippincott company, 1887. 159 p. illus. 22 cm. [BF1029.S4 1887]
1. Spiritualism. I. Title.

PENNSYLVANIA. 133.9072
University. Seybert commission for investigating modern spiritualism.
Preliminary report of the Commission appointed by the University of Pennsylvania to investigate modern spiritualism in accordance with the request of the late Henry Seybert. Philadelphia, J. B. Lippincott company, 1887. 160 p. illus. 22 cm. 159.9617072
1. Spiritualism. I. Title.

PETERSILEA, Carlyle, 1844- 133. 1903.
Letters from the spirit world. Written through the mediumship of Carlyle Petersilea, by his father, Franz Petersilea, and other spirit celebrities. Chicago, The Progressive thinker publishing house, 1905. 2 p. l., [3]-238 p. front. (port.) 20 1/2 cm. [BF1301.P48] 5-7574
1. Spiritualism. I. Petersilea, Franz. II. Title.

PETERSON, Flora (Culp) 133.9
Life and she. Boston, Christopher Pub. House [1960] 166p. 21cm. 60-6476 3.00
1. Spiritualism. I. Title.

PETERSON, Lewis. 133.91
Advanced soul science, written automatically through the hand of an agnostic under the influence of Alice Van Wyk Fisher operating for Lucelia A. Lovejoy, the inspirer of what is herein set forth; written for Lewis Peterson, who was selected to compiled and edit the work. Los Angeles, Calif., Austin publishing co., 1926. 9 p. l., [21]-142 p. 21 cm. Alice Van Wyk Fisher and Lucelia A. Lovejoy are both described in the text as "excarnate". [BF1301.P495] 26-10871
1. Spiritualism. I. Lovejoy, Lucelia A. II. Title.

PETERSON, Lewis, ed. 133.
Beyond the river, by Lucelia A. Lovejoy,

thru the hand of J. D., ed. and pub. by Lewis Peterson. Effingham, Ill. [c1918] 112 p. front. 20 cm. [BF1301.P5] 18-16979
1. Spiritualism. I. Lovejoy, Lucelia A. II. D., J. III. J. D. IV. Title.

PETTIS, Olive G Mrs. d.1884. 133.
The historical life of Jesus of Nazareth, and extracts from the apostolic age. Given by themselves through the inspiration of Olive G. Pettis ... Providence, A. C. Greene, printer, 1870-71. 2 v. in 1. 22 cm. On cover: Jesus and the apostolic age. Binder's title: Jesus of Nazareth. Vol. 2 has title: Further communications concerning the historical life of Jesus of Nazareth, and extracts from the apostolic age. Also published separately [Boston] 1896. "Erratum" slip inserted before t.-p. of v. 2. [BF1311.J5P4] 18-27486
1. Jesus Christ—Spiritualistic interpretations. 2. Spiritualism. I. Title. II. Title: Further communications.

PHILPOTT, Anthony J. 130
The quest for Dean Bridgman Conner, by Anthony J. Philpott. Boston, J. W. Luce and company, 1915. viii, 251 p. 19 cm. The search was made under the clairvoyant instructions of the famous medium, Mrs. Leonora E. Piper, and under the guidance of Dr. Richard Hodgson, secretary of the American branch of the Society for psychical research. cf. Introd. [BF1283.C8P5] 15-27909
1. Conner, Dean Bridgman, d. 1895. 2. Spiritualism. I. Title.

PIERCE, Dorothy, pseud. 133.
Thy brother shall rise again, by Dorothy Pierce. Boston, Mass., The Christopher publishing house [c1921] 151 p. 20 cm. [BF1301.P55] 21-12370
1. Spiritualism. I. Title.

PIKE, James Albert, Bp., 1913-1969. 133.9
The other side; an account of my experiences with psychic phenomena, by James A. Pike, with Diane Kennedy. [1st ed.] Garden City, N.Y., Doubleday, 1968. x, 398 p. 22 cm. Bibliography: p. [387]-396. [BF1277.P5A3] 68-29044 5.95
1. Spiritualism. 2. Psychical research. I. Title.

PINCOCK, Jenny O'Hara, Mrs. 133.9
The trails of truth [by] Jenny O'Hara Pincock. Los Angeles, Calif., The Austin publishing company [c1930] 396 p. 2 port. (incl. front.) 20 cm. [BF1301.P58] 30-17620
1. Spiritualism. I. Title.

[PLUMMER, George Winslow] 1876- 133.
A brief course in mediumship, by Khei F. R. C., O-X [pseud.] Being a series of instructions given to neophytes of Metorpolitan college, S. . R. . I. . A. . and now done into print by permission of the brotherhood. New York city, The Macoy publishing and Masonic supply co., 1915. 2 p. l., [3]-79 p., 1 l. illus. 17 1/2cm. $1.00. Two blank pages at end for "Notes." [BF1286.P7] 17-1631
1. Spiritualism. I. Title.

PODMORE, Frank, 1856-1900 133.91
Mediums of the 19th century; 2v. New Hyde Park, N.Y., University Bks. [c.] 1968. 2v. (307 374p & 24cm. First pub. in London in 1902 under title: Modern spiritualism. Bibl. 63-10384 20.00, set, bxd.
1. Spiritualism. I. Title.

PODMORE, Frank, 1856-1910. 133.91
Mediums of the 19th century. New Hyde Park, N.Y., University Books [1963] 2 v. 24 cm. First published in London in 1902 under title: Modern spiritualism. [BF1261.P7] 63-10384
1. Spiritualism. I. Title.

PODMORE, Frank, 1856-1910. 133.9'013
The newer spiritualism / Frank Podmore. New York : Arno Press, 1975. p. cm. (Perspectives in psychical research) Reprint of the 1910 ed. published by T. F. Unwin, London. [BF1261.P73 1975] 75-7392 ISBN 0-405-07041-1 : 18.00
1. Spiritualism. I. Title. II. Series.

PODMORE, Frank, 1856-1910. 133.9072
The newer spiritualism, by Frank Podmore ... New York, H. Holt and company, 1911. 320 p. illus., diagr. 23 cm. [BF1031P73 1911] 33-20335
1. Spiritualism. 2. Psychical research. I. Title.

PORTER, James, 1808-1888. 133.
The spirit rappings, mesmerism, clairvoyance, visions, revelations, startling phenomna, and infidelity of the rapping fraternity, calmly considered, and exposed By Rev. James Porter ... Boston, J. P. Magee [pref. 1853] 54 p. 19 cm. [BF1042.P7] 11-2424
1. Spiritualism. I. Title.

POST, Isaac, 1798-1872. 133.93
Voices from the spirit world, being communications from many spirits. By the hand of Isaac Post, medium. Rochester, N. Y., C. H. McDonell, printer, 1852. xiv, [17]-256 p. 18 cm. [BF1301.P73] 159.96173 33-29417
1. Spiritualism. I. Title.

POST, Samuel. 133.
... An exposition of modern spiritualism, showing its tendency to a total annihilation of Christianity. With other miscellaneous remarks and criticisms, in support of the fundamental principles of the Christian religion. By Samuel Post ... New-York, J. Egbert, printer, 1861. cover-title, 86 p. 23 cm. At head of title: Mail edition. [BF1042.P76] 11-2425
1. Spiritualism. I. Title.

POTTER, Reuben. 133.93
A voice from the heavens; or, Stellar & celestial worlds, by Reuben Potter. San Francisco, Cal., Carrier dove printing and publishing co., 1890. 10 p. l., 118 p. front. (port.) illus. 20 cm. [BF1301.P76] 159.96173 33-29280
1. Spiritualism. I. Title.

THE powers of the air; 133.
or, Spiritualism: what it is, and what it is not. By one who has had much painful experience during a period of over four years ... Dayton, O., United brethren publishing house, 1867. 6, [vii]-xii, 13-376 p. 17 cm. [BF1042.P8] 11-2426
1. Spiritualism.

PRELLS, Theresa C 1894- 133.9
Jacob's ladder; a step by step intimate and instructive true story of spiritual guidance and survival after death. Rockford, Ill., Bellevue Books [1956] 60p. illus. 23cm. [BF1261.2.P7] 56-9698
1. Spiritualism. I. Title.

THE Progressive annual for 1862[-1863] 133.
Comprising an almanac, a spiritualistic register, and a general calendar of reform. Published at the office of "The Herald of progress" ... New York, A. J. Davis & co. [1862-63] 2 v. 19 cm. [BF1272.P7] ca 11
1. Spiritualism.

PROGROFF, Ira, 1921-
The image of an oracle; a report on research into the mediumship of E.J. Garrett. New York, Helix Press Book, Garrett Publications, 1964. 372 p. 22 cm. 66-8098
1. Garrett, Eileen Jeanette (Lyttle) 1893- 2. Spiritualism. I. Title.

PROSKAUER, Julien J. 133.9
Spook crooks! Exposing the secrets of the prophet-eers who conduct our wickedest industry. By Julien J. Proskauer ... profusely illustrated by James and Howard Savage ... New York, Chicago, A. L. Burt company [c1932] 300 p. front. (port.) illus. 22 cm. "Frontispiece of the author after the original etching by Streuber." [BF1042.P84] 32-10844
1. Spiritualism. 2. Swindlers and swindling. I. Title.

PROSKAUER, Julien J., 1893- 133.9
The dead do not talk [by] Julien J. Proskauer. New York and London, Harper & brothers [1946] xvii p., 1 l., 198 p. 21 cm. "First edition." [BF1042.P83] 46-7977
1. Spiritualism. I. Title.

PSYCHIC golden threads.
'Summerland,' Howell Hill, Cheam (Sy.) J. A. Baker [1957] 176p. 19cm.
1. Spiritualism. I. Baker, John Alfred.

A psychic vigil in three watches. 133.9
New York, McBride, Nast & company, 1917. xi, 233, [1] p. 20 cm. Foreword signed Y [i. e. A. B. F. Young] Printed in England. "Second edition (Methuen & co. ltd.) 1917." First edition privately printed in 1896, edited by Rev. H. R. Haweis. cf. Foreword. [BF1261.P75 1917 a] 159.9617 33-29428
1. Spiritualism. I. Young, Alexander Bell Filson, 1876- ed.

PSYCHIC world religion. 133.9
Los Angeles, Art Buckwalter Report, Research and Review Service [1974] 80 p. 28 cm. Cover title. [BF1261.2.P85] 74-170964
1. Spiritualism. 2. Prophecies (Occult sciences)

PSYCHIC world religion. 133.9
Los Angeles, Art Buckwalter Report, Research and Review Service [1974] 80 p. 28 cm. Cover title. [BF1261.2.P85] 74-170964
1. Spiritualism. 2. Prophecies (Occult sciences)

PUTNAM, Allen, comp. 133
Flashes of light from the spirit-land, through the mediumship of Mrs. J. H. Conant. Comp. by Allen Putnam ... Boston, W. White and company, 1872. 404 p. 20 cm. [BF1291.C76] 11-4835
1. Spiritualism. I. Conant, Frances Ann (Crowell) "Mrs. J. H. Conant," b. 1831. II. Title.

PUTNAM, Allen, 1802-1887. 133.
Bible marvel workers, and the power which helped or made them perform mighty works, and utter inspired words: together with some personal traits and characteristics of prophets, apostles, and Jesus; or, new readings of "the miracles." By Allen Putnam ... Boston, Colby and Rich, 1873. 238 p. 20 cm. [BF1275.B5P8] 11-3591
1. Spiritualism. 2. Miracles. 3. Bible and spiritualism. I. Title.

PUTNAM, Allen, 1802-1887. 149
Natty, a spirit: his portrait and his life. By Allen Putnam ... Boston B. Marsh; New York Partridge and Brittan, c1856. 4 p. l., 175 p. 19 cm. [BF1291.P86] 11-4763
1. Spiritualism. I. Title.

PUTNAM, Allen, 1802-1887. 133.
Post-mortem confessions: being letters written through a mortal's hand by spirits who, when in mortal, were officers of Harvard college: with comments, by Allen Putnam ... Boston, Colby & Rich, 1886. 118 p., 1 l. 20 cm. [BF1301.P9] 5-20021
1. Spiritualism. I. Title.

PUTNAM, Allen, 1802-1887. 133.
Spirit works; real but not miraculous. A lecture read at the City hall in Roxbury, Mass. ... September 21st, 1853. By Allen Putnam. Boston, B. Marsh, 1853. 52 p. 23 cm. [BF1272.P88] 11-3415
1. Spiritualism. I. Title.

RAISTRICK, James. 133.9
Behold light beameth down from the spirit land of love. The holy banner of truth from an allwise God, undefiled by man; and the only true guide from God for all mankind; received by spirit intercourse. Published by James Raistrick. Bradford, W. Lobley, printer, 1865. 2 p. l., [7]-371 p. 20 cm. [BF1291.R2] 32-33252
1. Spiritualism. I. Title.

RAMSAY, E. W. 133.9
My psychic quest; the story of a search in spiritualism, by E. W. Ramsay. 2d impression. London, New York [etc.] Rider & company [1943] 96 p. 19 cm. [BF1261.R16] 44-29219
1. Spiritualism. I. Title.

RAMSDELL, Elizabeth. 149
Spirit life of Theodore Parker, as narrated by Himself, through the mediumship of Miss Elizabeth Ramsdell. Boston, The author, 1870. 84 p. 20 cm. [BF1291.R22] 11-4765
1. Spiritualism. I. Title.

RAMSDELL, Sarah A. 133.93
Food for the million; or, Thoughts from beyond the borders of the material. By Theodore Parker, through the hand of Sarah A. Ramsdell, medium ... Boston, The author, 1875. vi, 3-156 p. 18 cm. [BF1311.P3R3] 159.96173 33-29423
1. Spiritualism. I. Parker, Theodore, 1810-1860. II. Title.

RAMSDELL, Sarah A. 133.
The lessons of the ages, by Theodore Parker. Through the inspiration of Miss S. A. Ramsdell ... Boston, Pub. for the author, 1882. 175 p. 19 cm. [BF1301.R22] 10-33682
1. Spiritualism. I. Title.

RAMSDELL, Sarah A. 149
Science made easy. By Theodore Parker, through the mediumship of Sarah A. Ramsdell ... Philadelphia, E. R. Ramsdell, 1878. 233 p. 18 x 14 cm. [BF1291.R28] 11-3595
1. Spiritualism. I. Title.

RAMSDELL, Sarah A. 133.93
Spirit life of Theodore Parker, through the inspiration of Sarah A. Ramsdell. Boston, Press of Rand, Avery & co., 1876. 84 p. 20 cm. [BF1311.P3R33] 159.96173 33-29418
1. Parker, Theodore, 1810-1860. 2. Spiritualism. I. Title.

RAMSEY, William. 133.
Spiritualism, a satanic delusion and a sign of the times. By William Ramsey ... Ed. with a preface, by H. C. Hastings ... Peace Dale, R. I., H. L. Hastings, 1856. iv, [9]-122 p. 19 cm. [BF1042.R2 1856] 11-2429
1. Spiritualism. I. Hastings, Horace Lorenzo, ed. II. Title.

RAMSEY, William. 133.
Spiritualism, a satanic delusion and a sign of the times. By William Ramsey ... Ed. with a preface, by H. L. Hastings ... Boston, Scriptural tract repository, H. L. Hastings, 1868. iv, [9]-122 p. 17 cm. [BF1042.B2 1868] 40-25653
1. Spiritualism. I. Hastings, Horace Lorenzo, 1832- ed. II. Title.

RAMSEY, William.
Spiritualism, a satanic delusio and a sign of the times. By Willam Ramsey ... Ed. with a preface, by H. L. Hastings ... Providence, R. I., H. L. Hastings; N[ew] Y[ork] G. W. Young; [etc., etc.] 1861. vii, [9]-122, [2], 8 p. 18 cm. "An outline of the coast of man, by a voyager": 8 p. at end following advertising matter. 6-26909
I. Hastings, Horace L., ed. II. An outline of the coast of man. III. Title.

RAMSEY, William. 133.
Spiritualsm, a satanic delusion and a sign of the times. By William Ramsey ... Ed. with a preface, by H. L. Hastings ... Rochester, N. Y., H. L. Hastings, 1857. iv, [9]-122 p. 18 cm. First published in 1856. [BF1042.R2 1857] 11-2428
1. Spiritualism. I. Hastings, Horace Lorenzo, ed. II. Title.

RANDALL, Edward Caleb, 1860- 133.
Frontiers of the after life [by] Edward C. Randall. New York, A. A. Knopf, 1922. 213 p. 20 cm. [BF1261.R175] 22-17548
1. Spiritualism. I. Title.

RANDALL, Edward Caleb, 1860- 133.
The future of man, meta-pschic, by Edward C. Randall ... Buffalo, N. Y., O. Ulbrich company, 1908. 238 p. 21 cm. [BF1261.R18] 8-36721
1. Spiritualism. I. Title.

RANDALL, Edward Caleb, 1860- 133.
Life's progression; research in metaphysics, by Edward C. Randall. Buffalo, N. Y., The H. B. Brown co., 1906. 200 p. 20 cm. [BF1301.R24] 6-16487
1. Spiritualism. I. Title.

[RANDOLPH, Paschal Beverly] b.1825. 149
Dealings with the dead; the human soul, its migrations and its transmigrations. Penned by the Rosicrucian ... Utica, N. Y., M. J. Randolph, 1861-'62. 2 p. l., [3]-268 p. 19 cm. Preface signed: G. D. S. [BF1291.R3] 11-4755
1. Spiritualism. I. Title.

THE rappers: 133.
or, The mysteries, fallacies, and absurdities of spirit-rapping, table-tipping, and entrancement. By a searcher after truth. New-York, H. Long & brother [c1854] x,

[11]-282 p. front., pl. 20 cm. [BF1251.R25] 10-34874
1. Spiritualism. I. A searcher after truth, pseud.

RAUPERT, John Godfrey Ferdinand, 1858-1929. 133.
Modern spiritism; a critical examination of its phenomena, character, and teaching, in the light of the known facts, by J. Godfrey Raupert. 2d ed. St. Louis, Mo., & Freiburgh (Baden), B. Herder; [etc., etc.] 1909. vi p., 1 l., 261 p. 19 cm. [BF1261.R2 1909] 9-4134
1. Spiritualism. I. Title.

RAUPERT, John Godfrey Ferdinand, 1858-1929. 133.
The new black magic and the truth about the ouija-board, by J. Godfrey Raupert ... New York, The Devin-Adair company [c1919] 2 p. l., vi-vii p., 2 l., 3-243 p. 19 cm. [BF1042.R35] 19-14225
1. Spiritualism. I. Title.

REALITY ... 133.93
[Boston] Priv. print. [The Merrymount press] 1933. 2 p. l., 267 p. 20 cm. Messages from a "friend so recently gone to the new life." [BF1301.R35] 159.96173 33-22791
1. Spiritualism.

REICHEL, Willy. 133.9'092'4 B
An occultist's travels / by Willy Reichel. Philadelphia : Running Press, [1975] 244 p. ; 22 cm. Originally published in 1908. [BF1241.R3 1975] 74-31539 ISBN 0-914294-10-5 pbk. : 3.95
1. Reichel, Willy. 2. Spiritualism. I. Title.

REICHEL, Willy. 133.
An occultist's travels, by Willy Reichel ... New York, R. F. Fenno & company [c1908] 1 p. l., ii, 9-244 p. 2 port. (incl. front.) 20 cm. "The first portion of the present work has already appeared in Paris under the title of (Frederick Gittler, publisher), and in Germany under that of (Leipzig, Oswald Mutze), also in abridged form in England, as 'Occult experiences' (London, Office of Light)"--Pref. [BF1241.R3] 8-25375
1. Spirtualism. I. Title.

REIMER, John B. 133.9
The diary of a spiritualist, together with comments on the happenings therein described, by John B. Reimer ... Forest Hills, N.Y., J. B. Reimer, c1930. 188 p. front. (port.) illus. 20 cm. The author's seances with William H. Lake. "Written and published for private circulation." [BF1283.L3R4] 31-1106
1. Spiritualism. I. Lake, William H. II. Title.

REMARKABLE visions. 133.93
Comprising highly important revelations concerning the life after death. From the German ... Boston, Jordan and company, 1844. 1 p. l., [vii]-viii, [9]-92 p. front. 19 1/2 cm. [BF1311.F8R4] [159.96173] 33-30629
1. Spiritualism. 2. Future life.

REMBERT, S. S. 133.
The philosophy of life as evolved by modern science: lecture delivered in Texas, in 1860, by S. S. Rembert ... Memphis, Printed by Blelock & co., 1866. xv, [17]-324 p. front. (port.) 19 cm. One leaf, "Errors and corrections", inserted between pages [ii-iii] [BF1251.R4] 10-31796
1. Spiritualism. I. Title.

REMINGTON, Maud. 133.93
Growth of spiritual power, as revealed to Maud Remington by the spiritual teachers Jennie and Master Juana Ashawaska. [1st ed.] New York, Vantage Press [1957] 282p. 21cm. [BF1301.R36] 56-12782
1. Spiritualism. I. Title.

REMMERS, John Henry. 133.
Is death the end? by John Henry Remmers ... Dayton, O., Progressive publications, inc. [c1928] 199 p. 19 1/2 cm. [BF1261.R4] 29-15312
1. Spiritualism. I. Title.

A return of departed spirits of the highest characters of distinction as well as the indiscriminate of all nations, 133.
into the bodies of the "Shakers," or, "United society of believers in the second advent of the Messiah." By an associate of said society ... Philadelphia, J. R. Colon, 1843. viii, [9]-52 p. 14 1/2 cm. [BF1251.R45] 1-19060
1. Spiritualism.

RICHARDS, Laura Jane, 1874- 133.9
The coming generation; the musical education of children [by] Laura J. Richards. Los Angeles, Calif., The Austin publishing company [c1931] 2 p. l., 7-147 p. 22 cm. "Editorial note" signed: B. F. Austin. [BF1275.E4R5] 31-29139
1. Spiritualism. 2. Children. I. Austin, Benjamin Fish, 1850- ed. II. Title. III. Title: The musical education of children.

RICHARDSON, John Emmett,- 1853- 133
The great known. Rev. ed. By J. E. Richardson... [Hollywood, Calif.] The Great school of natural science [c1928] 384 p. 21 cm. (Harmonic series, vol. IV) [BF1999.H38 vol. 4 1928] 28-14914
1. Spiritualism. I. Title.

RICHARDSON, John Emmett, 1853- 133
The great known; or, What science knows of the spiritual world... by J. E. Richardson... Hollywood, Calif., The Royal press, 1924. 3 p. l., 5-407 p. 20 cm. (Harmonic series, vol. IV) [BF1909.H33 vol. 4] 24-23631
1. Spiritualism. I. Title.

RICHARDSON, John Emmett, 1853-1935. 133
The great known; what natural science knows of the spiritual world. [Los Gatos, Calif.] Great School of Natural Science [1956] 396p. 21cm. (Harmonic series, v. 4) [BF1999.R458] 56-2401
1. Spiritualism. I. Title.

RICHARDSON, John Emmett, 1853-1935. 133
The great known; what natural science knows of the spiritual world. [Los Gatos, Calif.] Great School of Natural Science [1956] 398p. 21cm. (Harmonic series, v. 4) [BF1999.R458] 56-2401
1. Spiritualism. I. Title.

RICHMOND, Almon Benson. 133.
What he saw at Cassadaga Lake; 1888. Addendum to a review in 1887 of the Seybert commissioners' report. By A. B. Richmond ... Boston, Colby & Rich, 1889. 163 p. incl. facsims. front. 19 1/2 cm. [BF1030.S4R5] 11-15000
1. Spiritualism. 2. Pennsylvania. University. Seybert commission for investigating modern spiritualism. I. Title.

RICHMOND, Almon Benson. 133.9072
What I saw at Cassadaga lake; a review of the Seybert commissioners' report. By A. B. Richmond ... 3d ed. Boston, Colby & Rich, 1890. 2 v. in l. front., illus. (facsims.) 19 1/2 cm. Volume two: ... Addendum. [BF1030.S4R5 1890] (159.9617072) 33-28519
1. Spiritualism. 2. Pennsylvania. University. Seybert commission. 3. Investigating modern spiritualism. I. Title.

RICHMOND, Cora L. V. (Scott) Mrs., 1840- 133
My experiences while out of my body and my return after many days, by Rev. Cora L. V. Richmond. [Boston, Christopher press, c1915] 76 p. 20 1/2 cm. $1.00 [BF1272.R5] 15-28154
1. Spiritualism. I. Title.

RICHMOND, Cora L. V. (Scott) Mrs., 1840- 133.
The soul: its nature, relations, and expressions in human embodiments. Given through Mrs. Cora L. V. Richmond, by her guides. Chicago, Ill., The Spiritual publishing co., 1887. 117, [1] p. 23 1/2 cm. [BF1301.R53] 10-33683
1. Spiritualism. 2. Reincarnation. I. Title.

[RICHMOND, Cora Linn Victoria (Scott) Mrs.] 1840-1923. 133.93
Discourses through the mediumship of Mrs. Cora L. V. Tappan. The new science. Spiritual ethics. Boston, Colby & Rich, 1876. [722] p. 19 cm. Various pagings. [BF1291.R47] (159.96173) 34-36369
1. Spiritualism. I. Title.

RICHMOND, Cora Linn Victoria (Scott) Mrs., 1840-1923. 133.93
The nature of spiritual existence, and spiritual gifts, given through the mediumship of Mrs. Cora L. V. Richmond. Reported and published by G. H. Hawes. San Francisco, Women's co-operative printing office, 1884. 2 p. l., 172 p. 23 1/2 cm. [BF1301.R523] (159.96173) 34-10930
1. Spiritualism. I. Hawes, G. H. II. Title.

RICHMOND, Cora Linn Victoria Scott, Mrs., 1840-1923. 133.93
Ouina's canoe and Christmas offering, filled with flowers for the darlings of earth, given through her medium "Water Lily" (Mrs. Cora L. V. Richmond) Ottumwa, Ia., D. M. & N. P. Fox, 1882. 160 p. 22 cm. [BF1301.R525] (159.96173) 33-24153
1. Spiritualism. I. Title.

RICHMOND, Cora Linn Victoria (Scott) 1840-1923. 133.
The soul; its nature, relations, and expressions in human embodiments. Given through Mrs. Cora L. V. Richmond, by her guides. Chicago, Ill., The Spiritual publishing co., 1887. 117, [1] p. 23 1/2 cm. [BF1301.R53] 10-33683
1. Spiritualism. 2. Reincarnation. I. Title.

RICHMOND, Cora Linn Victoria Scott, Mrs., 1840-1923. 133.923
Voices from life's thither side. Is materialization true? With eleven other lectures of great interest. Given in Chicago, Ill., by and through the trance-mediumship of Mrs. Cora L. V. Richmond. Boston, Colby & Rich, 1885. 185 p. 19 1/2 cm. [BF1301.R54] [159.961723] 33-29426
1. Spiritualism. I. Title.

RICHMOND, Cora Linn Victoria (Scott) Mrs., 1840-1923. 133.96
The weekly discourse; containing spiritual sermons, by the guides of Mrs. Cora L. V. Richmond. [n.p.] 1888-91. 3 v. 23 cm. Title from cover. Contents.[v. 1] March 4. 88-Feb. 17. 89.--[v. 2] Feb. 24. 89--Feb. 16. 90.--[v. 3] Feb. 23. 90--Feb. 15. 91. [BF1301.R55] [159.96173] 33-39244
1. Spiritualism. I. Title.

RICHMOND, Thomas, b.1796. 133.
God dealing with slavery. God's instrumentalities in emancipating the African slave in America. Spirit messages from Franklin, Lincoln, Adams, Jackson, Webster, Penn, and others, to the author, Thomas Richmond. Chicago, Religio-philosophical publishing house, 1870. 6 p. l., [9]-236 p. front. (port.) 19 1/2 cm. [BF1291.R5] 3-31798
1. Spiritualism. I. Title.

RIDER, Fremont, 1885- 133.
Are the dead alive? The problem of physical [!] research that the world's leading scientists are trying to solve, and the progress they have made, by Fremont Rider; with statements of their personal belief by Sir Oliver Lodge, Andrew Lang, Count Leo Tolstoi ... and others. New York, B. W. Dodge & company, 1909. xvi, 372 p. front., illus., plates. ports., facsims. 22 cm. [Full name: Arthur Fremont Rider] [BF1261.R5] 9-15095
1. Spiritualism. 2. Psychical research. I. Title.

RIVAIL, Hippolyte Leon Denizard, 1803-1869. 133.9'1
Experimental spiritism. Book on mediums; or, Guide for mediums and invocators: containing the special instruction of the spirits on the theory of all kinds of manifestations; the means of communicating with the invisible world; the development of mediumship; the difficulties and the dangers that are to be encountered in the practice of spiritism, by Allan Kardec. Translated by Emma A. Wood. New York, S. Weiser [1970] 458 p. 21 cm. On spine: The book of mediums. Translation of Spiritisme experimental. [BF1288.R6 1970] 77-16630 7.50
1. Spiritualism. I. Title. II. Title: The book of mediums.

[RIVAIL, Hippolyte Leon Denizard] 1803-1869. 133.
Experimental spiritism. Book on mediums; or, Guide for mediums and invocators: containing the special instruction of the spirits on the theory of all kinds of manifestations ... the development of mediumship; the difficulties and the dangers that are to be encountered in the practice of spiritism, By Allan Kardec [pseud.] Tr. by Emma A. Wood. Boston, Colby and Rich, 1874. 1 p. l., 458 p. 20 cm. [BF1288.R6] 11-4814
1. Spiritualism. I. Wood, Emma A., tr. II. Title.

[RIVAIL, Hippolyte Leon Denizard] 1803-1869. 133.9
Experimental spiritism. Book on mediums; or, Guide for mediums and invocators: containing the special instruction of the spirits in the theory of all kinds of manifestations ... the development of mediumship; the difficulties and the dangers that are to be encountered in the practice of spiritism. By Allan Kardec [pseud.] Translatee by Emma A. Wood. 2d thousand. Boston, Colby and Rich, 1874. 1 p. l., 458 p. 20 cm. [BF1288.R6 1874 a] 32-32117
1. Spiritualism. I. Wood, Emma A., tr. II. Title.

[RIVAIL, Hippolyte Leon Denizard] 1803-1869. 133.9
Experimental spiritism. Book of mediums; or, Guide for mediums and invocators: containing the special instruction of the spirits on the theory of all kinds of manifestations ... the development of mediumship; the difficulties and the dangers that are to be encountered in the practice of spiritism. By Allan Kardec [pseud.] Translated by Emma A. Wood. 4th ed. Boston, Colby and Rich, 1884. 1 p. l., 458 p. 20 cm. [BF1288.R6 1884] 32-32118
1. Spiritualism. I. Wood, Emma A., tr. II. Title.

[RIVAIL, Hippolyte Leon Denizard] 1803-1869. 133.9
Experimental spiritism. Book on mediums; or, Guide for the spirits on the theory of all kinds of manifestations ... the development of mediumship; the difficulties and the dangers that are to be encountered in the practice of spiritism. By Allan Kardec [pseud.] Translated by Emma A. Wood. 6th ed. Boston, Colby & Rich, 1894. 1 p. l., 458 p. 22 cm. [BF1288.R6 1894] 159.9617 34-10931
1. Spiritualism. I. Wood, Emma A., tr. II. Title.

[RIVAIL, Hippolyte Leon Denizard] 1803-1869.
Spiritualist philosophy. The spirits' book. Containing the principles of spiritist doctrine ... according to the teaching of spirits of high degree, transmitted through various mediums, collected and set in order by Allan Kardec [pseud.] Tr. from the hundred and twentieth thousand by Anna Blackwell. Boston, Colby and Rich, 1875. 24, xlix, [1], 438 p. incl. front. (port.) 21 cm. [BF1292.R53] 3-19928
1. Spiritualism. I. Blackwell, Anna, tr. II. Title.

ROBBINS, Anne Manning. 133
Both sides of the veil; a personal experience, by Anne Manning Robbins. Boston, Sherman, French & company, 1909. 4 p. l., vii-xii p., 1 l., 15-258 p. ports., facsims. 20 cm. [BF1283.P6R6] 9-26326 1.25
1. Piper, Mrs. Leonora E. 2. Spiritualism. I. Title.

ROBBINS, Anne Manning. 133
... Past and present with Mrs. Piper, by Anne Manning Robbins ... New York, H. Holt and company, 1922. 2 p. l., iii-iv, 280 p. front., ports. 20 cm. (The psychic series) Part i is rewritten, with great abbreviation and some trifling expansion from the author's Both sides of the veil. cf. Pref. [BF1283.P6R65] 22-19729
1. Piper, Mrs. Leonora E. 2. Spiritualism. I. Title.

ROBERTS, Jane, 1929- 133.9'1
The Seth material. Englewood Cliffs, N.J., Prentice-Hall [1970] xiv, 304 p. illus., ports. 24 cm. [BF1286.R57 1970] 75-112971 ISBN 0-13-807198-5 7.95
1. Spiritualism. 2. Reincarnation. I. Seth. II. Title.

[ROBERTS, Jonathan M] 1821-1888. 133.
Antiquity unveiled. Ancient voices from the spirit realms disclose the most startling revelations, proving Christianity to be of heathen origin ... Philadelphia, Oriental publishing co., 1892. xvi, 608 p. front. (port.) plates. 20 cm. "... A compilation of

communications from ancient spirits with explanatory remarks and suggestions by the late Jonathan M. Roberts.--Pref. of 2d ed., p. 14. [BF1301.R6 1892] 10-33687
1. Spiritualism. I. Title.

[ROBERTS, Jonathan M] 1821- 1888. 133.
Antiquity unveiled. Ancient voices from the spirit realms disclose the most startling revelations, proving Christianity to be of heathen origin ... 2d ed. Philadelphia, Oriental publishing co., 1894. xvi, 608 p. front. (port.) plates. 20 cm. " ... A compilation of communications from ancient spirits with explanatory remarks and suggestions by the late Jonathan M. Roberts."--Pref., p. 14. [BF1301.R6 1894] 10-33686
1. Spiritualism. I. Title.

[ROBERTS, Jonathan M] 1821- 1888. 133.
Antiquity unveiled. Disclosing the origin of Christianity. The most startling revelations from occult sources proving Christianity to be the child of paganism. [Abridged ed.] Philadelphia, Oriental publishing co., 1894. viii, [9]-172 p., 1 l., 565-608 p. front. (port.) illus., pl. 19 cm. " ... A compilation of communications from ancient spirits with explanatory remarks and suggestions by the late Jonathan M. Roberts."--Pref., p. 14. [BF1301.R6 1894a] 10-33688
1. Spiritualism. I. Title.

[ROBERTSON, Helen Field] 1896- 133.
The letters of a woman who was, by the woman. Minneapolis, Minn., W. H. Robertson, 1917. 1 p. l., [5]-122 p. 20 cm. [BF1301.R65] 17-12373 1.50
1. Spiritualism. 2. Future life. I. Title.

ROBERTSON, James, spiritualist. 133.9
Spiritualism; the open door to the unseen universe, being thirty years of personal observation and experience concerning intercourse between the material and spiritual worlds, by James Robertson. London, L. N. Fowler & co.; New York, Fowler & Wells co., 1908. x, 413 p. front. (port.) 19 cm. [BF1283.R65A3] 159.9617 33-29425
1. Spiritualism. I. Title.

ROBERTSON, Mabel Nixon. Mrs. 133.98
"The other side God's door"; messages from Lord Kitchener, Mary Baker Eddy, and others, by Mabel Nixon Robertson ... London, K. Paul, Trench, Trubner & co., ltd.; New York, E. P. Dutton & co., 1920. 5 p. l., 158 p. illus. 19 cm. [BF1301.R66] 159.96173 33-29414
1. Spiritualism. I. Title.

ROBINSON, Almadora Mead. 133.
Divine science, by Miss A. M. Robinson ... Valhalle, N. Y., Robinson publishing company [c1920] 155 p. incl. plates. 20 cm. [BF1261.R6] 20-23199
1. Spiritualism. I. Title.

ROBINSON, William Ellsworth, prestidigitateur. 133.
Spirit slate writing and kindred phenomena, by William E. Robinson ... sixty-two illustrations. New York city, Munn & company, 1898. v, 148 p. front., illus. 19 1/2 cm. [BF1042.R6] 98-1882
1. Spiritualism. 2. Conjuring. I. Title.

ROGERS, Edward Coit. 133.
A discussion on the automatic powers of the brain; being a defence against Rev. Charles Beecher's attack upon the Philosophy of mysterious agents, in his Review of "Spirtual manifestations." By E. C. Rogers... Bosotn, J. P. Jewett and company; Cleveland, O., Jewett, Proctor & Worthington: [etc., etc.] 1853. 64 p. 20 cm. [BF1042.R7] 11-2432
1. Beecher, Charles, 1815-1900. A review of the "spirtual manifestations". 2. Spiritualism. I. Title.

ROGERS, Edward Coit. 133.
A discussion on the automatic powers of the brain; being a defence against Rev. Charles Beecher's attack upon the Philosophy of mysterious agents, in his Review of "spiritual manifestations." By E. C. Rogers... Boston, J. P. Jewett and company; Cleveland, O., Jewett, Proctor & Worthington; [etc., etc.] 1856. 64 p. 21 cm. [With his Philosophy of mysterious agents, human and mundane. Boston, 1856] First published in 1853. [BF1251.R7] 11-2431
1. Beecher, Charles, 1815-1900. A review of the "spiritual manifestations." 2. Spiritualism. I. Title.

ROGERS, Rochester H. 1880- 133.93
Nathaniel. Boston, Christopher Pub. House [1950] 96 p. illus. 21 cm. [BF1286.R6] 50-3496
1. Spiritualism. I. Title.

ROHLFING, Charles. 133.9
God's way of life, by Charles Rohlfing. Boston, The Christopher publishing house [1947] 115 p. ports. 20 cm. [BF1261.R65] 47-17995
1. Spiritualism. I. Title.

ROSMINI SERBATI, Antonio, 1797-1855. 2710.698
Counsels to religious superiors. Selected, edited, and translated by Claude Leetham. Westminster, Md., Newman Press [1961] 177p. 23cm. [BX2438.R6] 60-14829
1. Spiritual I. Title.

ROSS, Joel H. 248
The spirit world; or, The caviler answered. By Joel H. Ross ... New York, M. W. Dodd, 1852. iv, [5]-284 p. 16 cm. [BV4921.R55] 33-24160
1. Spiritualism. I. Title.

RULOF, Jozef, 1898- 133.93
My revelations to the peoples of the earth, by Jozef Rulof; translation by O. V. Gundlach of the book: De volkeren der aarde door gene zijde bezien, published in 1941, the Hague, Netherlands. White Plains, N.Y., Rulof brothers, 1947. 400 p. front. (port.) 22 cm. "First edition." [BF1308.D8R815] 47-3878
1. Spiritualism. I. Gundlach, Oscar V., 1896- tr. II. Title.

RUNDQUIST, Alfred. 133.
The occult powers of modern spiritualism, designed as a popular treatise ... written and published by Alfred Rundquist ... Chicago, Ill., 1925. 120 p. 20 cm. [BF1261.R8] 25-11339
1. Spiritualism. I. Title.

[RUSH, Mary (Wheeler) Mrs. 1872- 133.93
Show me the way; spirit counsels for right living [by] Herodius. Boston, The Christopher publishing house [c1935] 2 p. l., 7-98 p. 20 cm. "Messages ... sent through inspiration and by the use of automatic writing from one in spirit, Herodius, by name."--Foreword. [BF1301.R8] 159.96173 35-4769
1. Spiritualism. I. Herodius. II. Title.

RUSSELL, Beatrice K 133.3
The Lincoln way; nine messages of timely warning and advice received from Abraham Lincoln on America's present dilem.na and future destiny. Cleveland, Lincoln Philosophical Research Foundation [1955] 63p. 23cm. [BF1311.L45R8] 56-26191
1. Lincoln, Abraham, Pres. U. S., 1809-1865. 2. Spiritualism. I. Title.

[RUTHERFORD, Joseph F.] 1869- 133.9
Can? The living talk with the dead?? A clear explanation of spiritism. Brooklyn, International Bible students association [c1920] 125 p. 19 1/2 cm. [BF1042.R8] [159.9617] A 22
1. Spiritualism. I. Title.

[RUTHERFORD, Joseph F.] 1869- 133.
Talking with the dead? Brooklyn, N.Y., International Bible students association [c1920] 155 p. illus. 21 1/2 cm. Advertising matter: p. 151-155. [BF1261.R9] 20-6731
1. Spiritualism. I. Title.

SADLER, William Samuel, 1875- 133.
The truth about spiritualism, by William S. Sadler ... Chicago, A. C. McClurg & co., 1923. vii, 211 p. 20 cm. [BF1042.S3] 23-17895
1. Spiritualism. I. Title.

SADONY, Joseph A 133.8
Gates of the mind; the proven psychic discoveries of Joseph Sadony. [2d, enl. ed.] New York, Exposition Press [1964] 143 p. 21 cm. [BF1283.S24A3] 64-6618
I. Title.

SAGE, Michel, 1863-1931. 920.
Mrs. Piper & the Society for psychical research; translated & slightly abridged from the French of M. Sage by Noralie Robertson, with a preface by Sir Oliver Lodge. New York, Scott-Thaw co., 1904. xxiv 187, [1] p. 19 cm. [BF1283.P6S2] 4-16274
1. Piper, Lenora E. 2. Spiritualism. I. Robertson, Noralie, tr. II. Title.

SAGE, Michel, 1863-1931. 920.
Mrs. Piper & the Society for psychical research; translated & slightly abridged from the French of M. Sage by Noralie Robertson, with a preface by Sir Oliver Lodge. New York, Scott-Thaw co., 1904. xxiv, 187, [1] p. 19 cm. [BF1283.P6S2] 4-16274
1. Robertson, Noralie, tr. 2. Spiritualism. 3. Piper, Mrs. Leonora E. I. Title.

SALMINEN, Immanuel. 133.9
...Essence of life in psychic phenomena; when vision is false of withered then knowledge perishes, by Immanuel Salminen. Brooklyn, N.Y., Finnish newspaper co. [c1938] 205 p. 20 1/2 cm. [BF1261.S28] (159.9617) 38-16333
1. Spiritualism. I. Title.

SAMSON, George Whitefield, 1819-1896. 133.
The physical in spiritualism; or, The spiritual medium not psychical, but physical. Illustrated by attested facts in universal history and confirmed by the ruling philosophy of all ages, presented in a series of letters to a young friend. Philadelphia. J. B. Lippincot, 1881. 185 p. 18 cm. [BF1251.S18] 52-53280
1. Spiritualism. I. Title.

SAMSON, George Whitefield, 1819-1896. 133.
Physical media in spiritual manifestations. The phenomena of responding tables and the planchette and their physical cause in the nervous organism, illustrated from ancient and modern testimonies. By G. W. Samson... Philadelphia, J. B. Lippincott & co., 1869. viii, [9]-185 p. 17 cm. Published in 1852 under title: "To daimonion," or The spiritual medium. Republished with an additional chapter, in 1860, as: Spiritualism tested... [BF1251.S2] 1-9408
1. Spiritualism. I. Title.

SAMSON, George Whitefield, 1819-1896. 133.
Spiritualism tested; or, The facts of its history classified, and their cause in nature verified from ancient and modern testimonies. By George W. Samson... Boston, Gould and Lincoln; New York, Sheldon and company; [etc., etc.] 1860- viii, [9]-185 p. 17 cm. Published in 1852 under title: "To daimonion", or The spiritual medium. The present edition contains an additional chapter. Republished in 1869, as Physical media in spiritual manifestations... [BF1251.S23] 10-32952
1. Spiritualism. I. Title.

[SAMSON, George Whitefield] 1819-1896. 133.
"To daimonion," or The spiritual medium. Its nature illustrated by the history of its uniform mysterious manifestation when unduly excited. In twelve familiar letters to an inquiring friend. By Traverse Oldfield [pseud.] Boston, Gould and Lincoln, 1852. viii, [9]-157. p. 16 cm. Republished with an additional chapter, under title: Spiritualism tested... Boston, 1800; and later as Physical media in spiritual manifestations... Philadelphia, 1809. [BF1251.S25] 10-32953
1. Spiritualism. I. Title.

[SAMSON, George Whitefield] 1819-1896. 133.9
"To daimonion", or The spiritual medium. Its nature illustrated by the history of its uniform mysterious manifestation when unduly excited. In twelve familiar letters to an inquiring friend. By Traverse Oldfield [pseud.] Boston, Gould and Lincoln, 1853. viii, [9]-157 p. 17 cm. Republished with an additional chapter under title: Spiritualism tested... Boston, 1800; and later as Physical media in spiritual manifestations... Philadelphia, 1869. [BF1251.S25 1853] [159.9617] 33-16700
1. Spiritualism. I. Title. II. Title: The spiritual medium.

[SARGENT, Epes] 1813-1880. 133.
Planchette; or, The despair of science. Being a full account of modern spiritualism, its phenomena, and the various theories regarding it. With a survey of French spiritism. Boston, Roberts brothers, 1869. 2 p. l., iii-xii, 404 p. 16 1/2 cm. (Half-title: Handy-volume series, no. III) Preface signed: E. S. [BF1251.S3] 10-34875
1. Spiritualism. I. Title.

[SARGENT, Epes] 1813-1880. 133.9
Planchette; or, The despair of science. Being a full account of modern spiritualism, its phenomena and the various theories regarding it. With a survey of French spiritism ... Boston, Roberts brothers, 1887. xii, 404 p. 16 1/2 cm. (On cover: Handy-volume series) Preface signed: E. S. [BF1251.S3 1887] 30-33496
1. Spiritualism. I. Title.

SARGENT, Epes, 1813-1880. 133.93
The proof palpable of immortality; being an account of the materialization phenomena of modern spiritualism. With remarks on the relations of the facts to theology, morals, and religion. By Epes Sargent ... Boston, Banner of light publishing co., 1901. 2 p. l., [iii]-viii, 9-238 p. diagr. 19 cm. [BF1378.S3] [159.96173 33-20352
1. Spiritualism. I. Title.

SARGENT, Epes, 1813-1880. 133.
The proof palpable of immortality; being an account of the materialization phenomena of modern spiritualism. With remarks on the relations of the facts to theology, morals, and religion. By Epes Sargent... 3d ed. Boston, Colby and Rich, 1881. 2 p. l., [iii]-viii, 9-238 p. front. (port.) 19 1/2 cm. [BF1378.S3 1881] 44-14746
1. Spiritualism. I. Title.

SARGENT, Epes, 1813-1880. 133.
The scientific basis of spiritualism. By Epes Sargent ... Boston, Colby and Rich, 1881 [1880] 372 p. 19 cm. [BF1261.S3] 11-3402
1. Spiritualism. I. Title.

SARGENT, Epes, 1813-1880. 133.9
The scientific basis of spiritualism. By Epes Sargent ... 2d ed. Boston, Colby and Rich, 1881. 372 p. 20 cm. [BF1261.S3 1881 a] [159.9617 33-20355
1. Spiritualism. I. Title.

SARGENT, Epes, 1813-1880. 133.9
The scientific basis of spiritualism. By Epes Sargent ... 6th ed. Boston, Banner of light publishing co. [1891] 396 p. 20 cm. [BF1261.S32] [159.9317 33-20360
1. Spiritualism. I. Title.

SATURN, planet of peace, sends warning. 133 Los Angeles, DeVorss; distributed by A. J. Brown [196-?] 31 p. 16 cm. [BF1311.S3S3] 72-15987
1. Spiritualism.

SAVAGE, Minot Judson, 1841- 1918. 133.
Can telepathy explain? Results of psychical research by Minot J. Savage ... New York and London, G. P. Putnam's sons, 1902. xvi p., 1 l., 243 p. 18 cm. "A partial list of books": p. 233-238. [BF1261.S36] 2-30275
1. Spiritualism. 2. Psychical research. I. Title.

SAVAGE, Minot Judson, 1841- 1918. 133.
Can telepathy explain? Results of psychical research, by Minot J. Savage ... New York and London, G. P. Putnam's sons, 1903. xvi p., 1 l., 243 p. 18 cm. "Published, November 1902. Reprinted, February, 1903; October, 1903." "A partial list of books": p. 233-238. [BF1261.S36 1903] 27-21563
1. Spiritualism. 2. Psychical research. I. Title. II. Title: Telepathy.

SAVAGE, Minot Judson, 1841- 1918. 237.2
Life beyond death, being a review of the world's beliefs on the subject, a consideration of present conditions of thought and feeling, leading to the question

as to whether it can be demonstrated as a fact, to which is added An appendix containing some hints as to personal experiences and opinions, by Minot Judson Savage ... New York & London, G. P. Putnam's sons, 1900. 2 p. l., iii-xv, 836 p. 21 1/2 cm. [BF1031.S3 1900] [159.9617] 33-20354
1. Spiritualism. 2. Future life. 3. Psychical research. I. Title.

SAVAGE, Minot Judson, 1841-1918. 133.
Life beyond death, being a review of the world's beliefs on the subject, a consideration of present conditions of thought and feeling, leading to the question as to whether it can be demonstrated as a fact, to which is added An appendix containing some hints as to personal experiences and opinions, by Minot Judson Savage ... New York & London, G. P. Putnam's sons, 1902. 2 p. l., iii-xv, 336 p. 21 1/2 cm. [BF1031.S3 1902] 33-38487
1. Spiritualism. 2. Future life. 3. Psychical research. I. Title.

SAVAGE, Minot Judson, 1841-1918. 237.2
Life beyond death, being a review of the world's beliefs on the subject, a consideration of present conditions of thought and feeling, leading to the question as to whether it can be demonstrated as a fact, to which is added an appendix containing some hints as to personal experiences and opinions, by Minot Judson Savage ... New York & London, G. P. Putnam's sons, 1903. 2 p. l., iii-xv, 336 p. 21 1/2 cm. [BF1031.S3 1903] [159.9617] 36-4266
1. Spiritualism. 2. Future life. 3. Psychical research. I. Title.

SAVAGE, Minot Judson, 1841-1918. 133.
Psychics: facts and theories. By Rev. Minot J. Savage ... Boston, Mass., Arena publishing company, 1893. x, [5]-153 p. 20 cm. [BF1261.S39 1893] 30-5369
1. Spiritualism. 2. Psychical research. I. Title.

SAVAGE, Minot Judson, 1841-1918. 133.
Psychics: facts and theories. By Rev. Minot J. Savage. Boston, G. H. Ellis, 1899. x, [5]-153 p. 20 cm. [BF1261.S39] 2-20338
1. Spiritualism. 2. Psychical research. I. Title.

SCHEUING, Herman Aloysius, 1872- 133.
The psychology of mediumship (Two worlds in o,e) by H. Scheuing... Columbus, O., The F. J. Heer printing co., 1923. 142 p. 20 cm. [BF1286.S3] 23-12758
1. Spiritualism. I. Title. II. Title: Two worlds in one.

SCHLESINGER, Julia, Mrs. 133.
Workers in the vineyard. A review of the progress of spiritualism, biographical sketches, lectures, essays and poems. By Julia Schlesinger ... San Francisco, Cal., 1896. 2 p. l., [13]-290 p. front., ports. 26 cm. On cover, "vol. 2," No more published? [BF1281.S4] 11-14354
1. Spiritualism. 2. Spiritualism—Biog. I. Title.

SCOTT, Catharine Amy (Dawson) Mrs. 133.
Is this Wilson? Messages accredited to Woodrow Wilson, received by Mrs. C. A. Dawson Scott, with an introduction by Edward S. Martin. New York, E. P. Dutton & co. inc. [c1929] 165 p. 20 cm. [BF1311.W53S4] 29-2490
1. Wilson, Woodrow, pres. U. S., 1856-1924. 2. Spiritualism. I. Title.

SCOTT, Elizabeth A. 133.93
The tree of life. New York, Vantage [c.1961] 120p. 3.00 bds.,
1. Spiritualism. 2. Automatic writing. I. Title.

SEABORNE, Frederick. 133.
The lost New Testament book, restored through spirit agency; professedly a continuation of the Acts of the Apostles down to the death of St. Peter and St. Paul, by Luke, and given to the world by Spirit Theophilus, through the hand of the psychic, Frederick Seaborne. Los Angeles, Calif., The Austin publishing company [c1920] 58, [1] p. 20 cm. [BF1311.B5S4] 21-465
I. Title.

SEWALL, May (Wright) Mrs. 1844-1920. 133.
Neither dead nor sleeping, by May Wright Sewall; with an introduction by Booth Tarkington. Indianapolis, The Bobbs-Merrill company [c1920] 22 p. l., 320 p. 20 cm. [BF1301.S4] 20-8214
1. Spiritualism. I. Title.

SEYMOUR, Charles J. 133.
This spiritualism; results of an inquiry. By Charles J. Seymour. London, New York [etc.] Longmans, Green and co. [1940] 4 p. l., 143 p. 19 cm. "First published 1940." [BF1261] A41
1. Spiritualism. I. Title.

[SHAW, Bradley] comp. 133.
Mediums and their dupes. A complete exposure of the chicaneries of professional mediums, and explanations of spiritual phenomena ... San Francisco, Waldteufel, 1887. 54 p. 22 cm. On cover: By Bradley Shaw. [BF1042.S5] 11-2433
1. Spiritualism. I. Title.
Contents omitted.

SHELHAMER, Mary Theresa. 133.
Outside the gates; and other tales and sketches. By a band of spirit intelligences, through the mediumship of Mary Theresa Shelhamer ... Boston, Colby and Rich, 1887. 515 p. 19 1/2 cm. [BF1301.S56] 10-33689
1. Spiritualism. I. Title.

SHELTON, Harriet M. 133.93
Abraham Lincoln returns. New York, Evans Pub. Co., 1957. 232 p. illus. 22 cm. [Psychic library series] [BF1311.S45S5] 58-11268
1. Spiritualism. 2. Lincoln, Abraham, Pres. U.S. 1809-1865 I. Title.

SHERMAN, Harold Morrow, 1898-
You live after death. New York, C & R Anthony [1966, c1949] 205 p. 21 cm. 68-29210
1. Spiritualism. I. Title.

SHERMAN, Harold Morrow, 1898- 133.9
You live after death. New York, Creative Age Press, 1949. 205 p. 21 cm. [BF1261.S53 1949] 49-1594
1. Spiritualism. I. Title.

SHERMAN, Lois. 133.93
Experiences from "Over there", by Lois Sherman. Los Angeles, Calif., Press of Wetzel publishing co., inc. [c1933] 4 p. l., 11-146, [1] p. 19 1/2 cm. [BF1301.S572] (159.96173) 34-10062
1. Spiritualism. I. Title.

SHERMAN, Loren Albert. 133.
Science of the soul. A scientific demonstration of the existence of the soul of man as his conscious individuality independently of the physical organism: of the continuity of life and the actuality of spirit return. By Loren Albert Sherman. Port Huron, Mich., The Sherman company, 1895. xvi, [17]-114 p. incl. illus., ports., facsims. ports. 20 cm. [BF1261.S55] 11-3155
1. Spiritualism. I. Title.

SHERMAN, M. L. 133.
The gospel of nature. By M. L. Sherman and Wm. F. Lyon ... Chicago, Hazlitt & Reed, 1877. 483 p. 20 cm. "The ideas were given in a series of lectures through the organism of M. L. Sherman", medium, and written by W. F. Lyon. cf. Pref. [BF1291.S5] 11-4831
1. Spiritualism. I. Lyon, William F. II. Title.

SHERMAN, M. L. 133.
The hollow globe; or, The world's agitator and reconciler. A treatise on the physical conformation of the earth. Presented through the organism of M. L. Sherman, M.D., and written by Prof. Wm. F. Lyon. Chicago, Religio-philosophical publishing house, 1871. viii, [9]-447 p. illus. 20 cm. [BF1291.S55] 11-4830
1. Spiritualism. I. Lyon, William F. II. Title.

SHERMAN, M. L. 133.
The hollow globe; or, The world's agitator and reconciler. A treatise on the physical conformation of the earth. Presented through the organism of M. L. Sherman, M.D., and written by Prof. Wm. F. Lyon. [2d ed.] Chicago, Sherman & Lyon, 1875. viii, [9]-455 p. illus. 20 cm. [BF1291.S55 1875] 16-23730
1. Spiritualism. I. Lyon, William F. II. Title.

SHERWOOD, Jane. 133.93
The country beyond; a study of survival and rebirth, by Jane Sherwood. London, New York [etc.] Rider & co. [1945] 144 p. diagrs. 19 1/2 cm. [BF1261.S56] 45-7319
1. Spiritualism. I. Title.

SHINDLER, Mary Dana, Mrs., 1810-1883. 133.9072
A southerner among the spirits; a record of investigations into the spiritual phenomena, by Mrs. Mary Dana Shindler ... 2d ed. Boston, Colby & Rich [18- xii, [13]-169 p. 20 cm. [Full name: Mrs. Mary Stanley Bunce (Palmer) Dana Shindler] [BF1283.5A32] [159.9617072] 33-24146
1. Spirtualism. I. Title.

SHINDLER, Mary Dana, Mrs., 1810-1883. 133.9072
A southerner among the spirits; a record of investigations into the spiritual phenomena, by Mrs. Mary Dana Shindler ... Memphis, Tenn., Southern Baptist publication society, 1877. xii, [13]-169 p. 19 1/2 cm. [Full name: Mrs. Mary Stanley Bunce (Palmer) Dana Shindler] [BF1283.S5A3] [159.9617072 33-24145
1. Spiritualism. I. Title.

[SHIPPEN, Edward] b.1820? 133.
Woman, and her relations to humanity. Gleams of celestial light on the genesis and development of the body, soul, and spirit, and consequent moralization of the human family ... The true religion: magnetism--materialization--reincarnation. Boston, Colby & Rich, 1892. 2 p. l., [iii]-xx,[3]-180 p. 2 port. (incl. front.) 21 cm. [BF1301.S58] 18-15931
1. Spiritualism. I. Title.

[SIMON, Otto Torney] 1860- 133.91
The message of Anne Simon. Boston, R. G. Badger [c1920] 145 p. front. (port.) illus. 23 cm. Spiritualistic messages received by Otto Torney Simon. [BF1301.S6] 20-1535
1. Spiritualism. I. Simon, Mrs. Anne (McConnor) 1870-1916. II. Title.

[SIMON, Otto Torney] 1860- 133.91
The second message of Anne Simon. Boston, R. G. Badger [c1920] 157 p. 22 1/2 cm. Spititualistic messages received by Otto Torney Simon. [BF1301.S62] 20-21306
1. Spiritualism. I. Simon, Mrs. Anne (McConnor) 1870-1916. II. Title.

SMITH, Callie Margaret. 133.
Faith, Christ and truth, by Callie Margaret Smith. Boston, The Christopher publishing house [c1924] 142 p. 19 1/2 cm. [BF1301.S625] 24-29860
1. Spiritualism. I. Title.

SMITH, Cora (Kincannon) Mrs. 133.9
A key to the development of your psychic powers; interesting, startling, thrilling; stories of spirit power and spirit phenomena, by Cora Kincannon Smith... [Spokane, Inland-American printing company, c1931] 7 p. l., 109 p. front., pl., ports., facsim. 19 1/2 cm. "First edition." [BF1283.S6A3] 31-10633
1. Spiritualism. I. Title.

SMITH, Hester Travers, Mrs. 133.
OscarWilde from purgatory, psychic messages edited by Hester Travers Smith...with a preface by Sir William F. Barrett F. R. S. New York, H. Holt and company [1926] xii, 179 p. front. (port.) illus. (facsims.) 22 cm. Printed in Great Britain. [BF1311.W5M6 1926] 27-23489
1. Wilde, Oscar, 1854-1900. 2. Spiritualism. I. Title.

SMITH, Hester Travers, Mrs. 133.
Voices from the void; six years' experience in automatic communications, by Hester Travers Smith; with introduction by Professor Sir W. F. Barrett, F.R.S. New York, E. P. Dutton & company [c1919] xviii p., 1 l., 164 p. 19 cm. [BF1343.S6] 20-274
1. Spiritualism. I. Title.

SMITH, Julia A. (Norcross) Crafts. 133.
The reason why; or, Spiritual experiences of Mrs. Julia Crafts Smith, physician, assisted by her spirit guides. Boston, The author, 1881. vi, 7-187 p. front. (port.) 19 1/2 cm. [BF1301.S63] 10-33690
1. Spiritualism. I. Title.

SMITH, Julia A. (Norcross) Crafts. Mrs. 133.
The reason why; or, Spiritual experiences of Mrs. Julia Crafts Smith, physician, assisted by her spirit guides. Boston, The author, 1881. vi, 7-187 p. front. (port.) 19 1/2 cm. [BF1301.S63] 10-33690
1. Spiritualism. I. Title.

SMITH, Julia A. (Norcross) Crafts. Mrs. 133.93
The reason why; or, Spiritual experiences of Mrs. Julia Crafts Smith, physician, assisted by her spirit guides. Boston, The author, 1893. vi, 7-201 p. front. (port.) 20 cm. "Contents" on p. [2] of cover. [BF1301.S63 1893] 159.96173 34-15714
1. Spiritualism. I. Title.

[SMITH, Myrtle] Mrs. 133.93
Betty's proof of spirit return. "A child shall lead them" By Betty Smith, through the hand of her mother. Los Angeles, Calif., The Austin publishing co. [c1932] 127 p. incl. front. (port.) 19 1/2 cm. "Copyright 1932 by Myrtle Smith." [BF1301.S6333] 159.96173 34-1745
1. Spiritualism. I. Title.

*SMITH, Susy. 133.9
Widespread psychic wonders. New York, Ace Books [1974? c1970] 190 p. 18 cm. (The Exorcism series, book V) [BF1286] 1.25 (pbk.)
1. Spiritualism. I. Title.

SMITH, W.A. 133.9
This is perfection, by W.A. Smith. [1st ed.] New York, American Press [1966) 115 p. 21 cm. [BF1261.2.S6] 66-18788
1. Spiritualism. I. Title.

SNELL, Joy. 133.9
The ministry of angels, here and beyond [1st American ed.] New York, Citadel Press [1959] 190 p. 24 cm. [BF1283.S64A3 1959] 59-8907
1. Spiritualism. I. Title.

SNIPES, Joseph Franklin. 133.
Fifty years in psychic research; a remarkable record of phenomental facts, by Joseph F. Snipes. Boston, Mass., Chapple publishing company, ltd. [c1927] 483 p. front., ports. 28 cm. [BF1301.S635] 28-5568
1. Spiritualism. I. Title.

SNOW, Charles Miles, 1868- 133.
On the throne of sin; spiritism and the nature of man as related to demonism, witchcraft, and modern spiritualism, by Charles M. Snow ... Takoma Park, Washington, D. C., South Bend, Ind. [etc.] Review and herald publishing association [c1927] 222 p. incl. front. (port.) 1 illus. 21 cm. [BF1042.S65] 27-23397
1. Spiritualism. I. Title.

SNOW, Herman, b.1812, ed. 133.93
Visions of the beyond, by a seer of to-day; or, Symbolic teaching from the higher life Edited by Herman Snow 3d ed. Boston, Colby & Rich, 1888. 186 p. 20 cm. Given chiefly through the mediumship of Mrs. Anna D. Loucks. [BF1301.L88 1888] 159.96173 34-36377
1. Spiritualism. I. Loucks, Anna Danforth, Mrs. d. 1893. II. Title.

SNOW, Herman, b.1812, ed. 133.
Visions of the beyond, by a seer of to-day; or, Symbolic teaching from the higher life. Ed. by Herman Snow. Boston, Colby & Rich; San Francisco, Cal., H. Snow, 1877. 186 p. 20 cm. Given chiefly through the mediumship of Mrs. Anna D. Loucks. [BF1301.L88] 11-6880
1. Spiritualism. I. Loucks, Anna Danforth, Mrs. d. 1893. II. Title.

SNOW, Herman, b.1812, ed. 133.93
Visions of the beyond, by a seer of to-day;

or, Symbolic teachings from the higher life. Edited by Herman Snow. 2d ed. Boston, Colby & Rich, 1887. 136 p. 20 cm. Given chiefly through the mediumship of Mrs. Anna D. Loucks. [BF1301.L88 1887] 159.96173 34-36376
1. Spiritualism. I. Loucks, Anna Danforth, Mrs. d. 1893. II. Title.

SOME account of the vampires of Onset, past and present. Boston, New England news company, 1892. 80, [2] p. 23 cm. Imprint covered by label: Boston, Press of S. Woodberry & co., 1892. [BF1289.S7] 11-22225
1. Spiritualism. I. Title: Vampires of Onset, Some account of the.

SOME revelations as to "Raymond"; an authoritative statement, by A plain citizen ... London, K. Paul, Trench, Trubner & co., ltd.; New York, E. P. Dutton & co. [191-?] 245 p. 19 1/2 cm. A 21
1. Lodge, Sir Oliver Joseph, 1851- 2. Raymond. A plain citizen. 3. Spiritualism.

SPIRITUAL exposition of the prophetic scriptures, of the New Testament, received by J. M. Brown, E. H. Baxter, E. A. Benedict ... [etc.] Auburn, N.Y., E. H. Baxter and E. A. Benedict, 1850. 120 p. 20 cm. [BF1291.S74] 11-4846 133.
1. Spiritualism.

SPIRITUAL instructions received at the meetings of one of the circles formed in Philadelphia, for the purpose of investigating the philosophy of spiritual intercourse. Published for the benefit of the Harmonial benevolent association. Philadelphia, For sale by A. Comfort, 1852. 180 p. 16 1/2 cm. [BF1291.S76] 11-4847 133.
1. Spiritualism.

SPRAGUE, Eli Wilmot, 1847- 133.
All the spiritualism of the Christian Bible and the Scripture directly opposing it, by Rev. E. W. Sprague ... [Chicago, The Regan printing house, c1922] 392 p. front. (port.) 19 1/2 cm. [BF1275.B5S6] 22-24884
1. Spiritualism. I. Title.

SPRAGUE, Eli Wilmot, 1847- 133.
A future life demonstrated; or, Twenty-seven years a public medium, by E. W. Sprague ... [Detroit] E. W. Sprague, 1908. vi, [7]-862 p. 2 port. 20 cm. [BF1283.S7] 8-29859
1. Spiritualism. I. Title.

SPRAGUE, Eli Wilmot, 1847- 133.9
Letters from heaven, a modern revelation, by Spirit Clarissa Adelia Sprague, automatically written through the hand of her husband, the Reverend E. W. Sprague. Grand Rapids, Mich., E. W. Sprague, 1931. 4 p. l., [11]-151, [6] p. ports. 19 1/2 cm. [BF1311.S656] 31-16280
1. Spiritualism. I. Sprague, Mrs. Clarissa Adelia, d. 1929. II. Title.

SPRAGUE, Eli Wilmot, 1847- 133.
Spirit mediumship. Its various phases. How developed and safely practiced. A compendium of psychic science. For seances, circles and individual use. The medium's companion and guide. By Rev. E. W. Sprague ... Detroit, Mich., E. W. Sprague [c1912] 4 p. l., [5]-137 p. port. 19 1/2 cm. $1.25. p. 135-137, advertising matter. [BF1286.S7] 12-17265
1. Spiritualism. I. Title.

SPRAGUE, Eli Wilmot, 1847- 133.9
Spirit obsession. A false doctrine and a menace to modern spiritualism. By Rev. E. W. Sprague ... Detroit, Mich., The author, 1915. 153 p. front. (port.) 19 1/2 cm. [BF1275.S6S6] [159.9617] 34-36380
1. Spiritualism. I. Title.

STALEY, Amelia Fargo. Mrs. 133.
The leading of a minister, by Amelia Fargo Staley. Boston, The Christopher publishing house [c1922] 135 p. 21 cm. [BF1301.S64] 22-10109
1. Spiritualism. I. Title.

STALEY, Amelia Fargo. Mrs. 133.
The psychic flame, by Amelia Fargo Staley ... Boston, The Christopher publishing house [c1924] 192 p. front. (port.) 21 1/2 cm. [BF1301.S642] 24-8261
1. Spiritualism. I. Title.

STEAD, Estelle Wilson. 920.
My father, personal & spiritual reminiscences, by Estelle W. Stead. New York, George H. Doran company, 1913. xii, 351 p. front., plates. ports. 23 cm. "Printed in England." [PN5123.S7S7] 14-2957
1. Stead, William Thomas, 1849-1912. 2. Spiritualism. I. Title.

STEAD, W. T. memorial center. 133.9
The key to communication. New York city, W. T. Stead memorial center [1942] xxv, 86 p. 2 port (incl. front.) 19 cm. [BF1261.S698] 159.9617 42-6183
1. Spiritualism. I. Title.

STEAD, W. T., memorial center, Chicago.
God's world ... a treatise on spiritualism founded on transcripts of shorthand notes taken down, over a period of five years, in the scance-room of the William T. Stead memoiral center (a religious body incorporated under the statutes of the state of Illinois) Mrs. Cecil M. Cook, medium and pastor. Comp. and written by Lloyd Kenyon Jones. Chicago, Ill., The William T. Stead memorial center [c 1918]- v. ports. 23 cm. [BF1228.S75] 19-1662
1. Spiritualism. I. Jones, Lloyd Kenyon. II. Cook, Ellen A. Pennau Mrs. III. Title.

STEAD, W. T., memorial center, Chicago. 133.
Healing forces; a volume of the "table-top" treatise of the Wm. T. Stead memorial center. Mrs. Cecil M. Cook, pastor and medium. Written by Lloyd Kenyon Jones. Chicago, Ill., The William T. Stead memorial center [c1919] 1 p. l., 56 p. 24 cm. (On cover: Stead center table-top home study series) [BF1275.H357] 19-10072
1. Spiritualism. I. Jones, Lloyd Kenyon. II. Cook, Ellen A. Mrs. III. Title.

STEAD, W. T., memorial center, Chicago.
The world next-door, based on teachings received in seance-room of the William T. Stead memorial center, and dealing with conditions in the spirit-spheres, and with natural law, and the nature of matter, ether and energy. Comp. and written by Lloyd Kenyon Jones. Chicago, Ill., The William T. Stead memorial center [c1920] 94 p. 22 cm. (On cover: Stead center table-top home study series) [BF1228.S77] 20-6998
1. Spiritualism. I. Jones, Lloyd Kenyon. II. Title.

STEAD, W. T., memorials center, Chicago. 133.
Development of mediumship; a volume of the "tabletop" treatises of the Wm. T. Stead memoiral center, Mrs. Cecil M. Cook, pastor and medium, written by Lloyd Kenyon Jones. Chicago, Ill., The William T. Stead memorial center [c1919] 59 p. 35 cm. (On cover: Stead center table-top home study series) [BF1286.S8] 19-7804
1. Spiritualism. I. Jones, Lloyd Kenyon. II. Cook, Ellen A. Pennau Mrs. III. Title.

[STEAD, William Thomas] 1849-1912. 133.9
After death, a personal narrative; new and cheaper edition of "Letters from Julia." New York, John Lane company, 1907. xxx, 187, [1] p. 14 cm. Printed in London. Preface signed: William T. Stead. First edition, December 1897; sixth edition, November 1905. "The companions of the rosary": p. 185-[188] [BF1301.S65 1907] 32-4065
1. Spiritualism. I. Title. II. Title: Letters from Julia.

STEAD, William Thomas, 1849-1912. 133.9
Borderland; a casebook of true supernatural stories. Introd. to the American ed. by Leslie Shepard. New Hyde Park, N.Y., University Books [1970] xxiv, 344 p. 22 cm. Reprint of the 1897 ed. issued under title: Real ghost stories. Originally issued in two volumes as Real ghost stories, 1891, and More ghost stories, 1892. [BF1261.S75 1970] 69-16361 5.95
1. Spiritualism. I. Title.

STEAD, William Thomas, 1849-1912. 133.
How I know that the dead return, by William T. Stead; an account of the remarkable personal experiences of the author which dispelled all doubt in his mind as to the reality of a future life. Boston, The Ball publishing co., 1909. 3 p. l., 50 p. 20 cm. [BF1261.S7] 9-12077
1. Spiritualism. I. Title.

STEAD, William Thomas, 1849-1912. 133.
Real ghost stories, collected and edited by William T. Stead. New ed., re-arranged and introduced by Estelle W. Stead. New York, George H. Doran company, 1921. 1 p. l., [v]-viii p., 4 l., [17]-256 p. 19 cm. A reissue of a collection published in 1891-92 in two volumes, the first entitled Real ghost stories, the second, More ghost stories. The contents of the two volumes, slightly curtailed, were later brought out as one book. cf. Introd. [BF1261.S75] 21-18001
1. Spiritualism. I. Stead, Estelle W., ed. II. Title.

STEARN, Jess. 133.9'1'0924 B
A matter of immortality : dramatic evidence of survival / Jess Stearn. 1st ed. New York : Atheneum Publishers, 1976. 300 p. ; 22 cm. [BF1283.M587S73 1976] 76-11543 ISBN 0-689-10721-8 : 9.95
1. Moreno, Maria. 2. Spiritualism. I. Title.

STEARN, Jess. 133.9'1'0924
A matter of immortality : dramatic evidence of survival / Jess Stearn. 1st ed. New York : New American Library, 1977,c1976. 245p. ; 18 cm. [BF1283.M587S73 1976] ISBN 0-451-07652-4 pbk. : 1.95
1. Moreno, Maria. 2. Spritualism. I. (A Signet Book) II. Title.
L.C. card no. for 1976 Atheneum ed:76-11543.

STEBBINS, Giles Badger, 1817-1900. 133.
After dogmatic theology, what? Materialism, or a spiritual philosophy and natural religion. By Giles B. Stebbins ... Boston, Colby and Rich, 1880. 144 p. 20 cm. [BF1261.S8] 11-3156
1. Spiritualism. I. Title.

STEMMAN, Roy, 1942- 133.9
Spirits and spirit worlds / by Roy Stemman. Garden City, N.Y. : Doubleday, 1976, c1975. 142 p. : ill. ; 28 cm. (A New library of the supernatural) [BF1261.S83 1976] 75-16751 7.95
1. Spiritualism. I. Title. II. Series.

STEMMER, Charles C 1883- 920.91339
A brand from the burning, from the depths of despair to the gates of heaven. Boston, Christopher Pub. House [1959] 132 p. illus. 21 cm. Autobiographical. [BF1261.2.S77] 50-6923
1. Spiritualism. I. Title.

STERN, Henry L., 1899- 133.9'1'0924 B
Help from beyond / by Henry L. Stern. New York : Walker, 1974. 177 p. ; 24 cm. [BF1283.S84A34 1974] 73-90380 ISBN 0-8027-0444-1 : 7.95
1. Stern, Henry L., 1899- 2. Spiritualism. I. Title.

STEVENS, Leon Herbert, 1888- 133.
Letters from Roy; or, The spirit voice, by Leon H. Stevens; being a series of messages received during daily communication with Leroy S. Stevens, who passed to spirit life on March thirtieth, 1916. Boston, Christopher publishing house [c1917] 1 p. l., [5]-114 p. incl. front. (port.) 21 cm. [BF1301.S7] 17-29750 1.00
1. Stevens, Leroy Sylvan, 1895-1916. 2. Spiritualism. I. Title.

STEVENS, Leon Herbert, 1888- 133.
The second letters from Roy, by Leon H. Stevens, further progress in the messages from the life beyond, as coming from Leroy S. Stevens, who since his passing, has given us the previous book, called "Letters from Roy." Boston, Christopher publishing house [c1918] 179 p. 1 l. front.(port.) 21 cm. [BF1301.S73] 18-22880 1.25
1. Stevens, Leroy Sylvan, 1895-1916. 2. Spiritualism. I. Title.

STILES, Joseph D. 133.
Twelve messages from the spirit of John Quincy Adams, through Joseph D. Stiles, medium, to Josiah Brigham ... Boston, B. Marsh, 1859. xxiii, 459 p. facsims. 24 cm. [BF1291.S85] 11-5298
1. Spiritualism. I. Brigham, Josiah. II. Title.

STODDART, Jane T. 133.
The case against siritualism, by Jane T. Stoddart. London, New York [etc.] Hodder and Stoughton, 1919. 6 p. l., 17-171, [1] p. 19 1/2 cm. [BF1261.S87] 20-4476
1. Spiritualism. I. Title.

STOOPS, Ella. 133.
Some psychic messages, by Ella Stoops. Boston, The Christopher publishing house [c1925] 52 p. 21 cm. [BF1301.S78] 25-11532
1. Spiritualism. I. Title.

STRAUBE, Carl Frederick. 133.9
Actual spirit messages from life beyond, by Carl F. Straube. [Pittsburg, Herbick & Held printing co., c1931] 1 p.l.139, [1]p. 19 1/2 cm. [BF1301.S83] 31-4951
1. Spiritualism. I. Title.

STREET, J. C.
The hidden way across the threshold; or, The mystery which hath been hidden for ages and generations. An explanation of the concealed forces in every man to open the temple of the soul and to learn the guidance of the unseen hand. Illustrated and made plain with as few occult phrases as possible, by J. C. Street ... Boston, Lee and Shepard, 1888. xi, 598 p. front., illus., plates, diagrs. 22 1/2 cm. [BF1999S8] 10-24999
1. Spiritualism. I. Title.

STRESAU, Marion. 133.9'092'4 B
Tomorrows unlimited. Boston, Branden Press [1973] 143 p. illus. 22 cm. [BF1286.S8] 72-91222 ISBN 0-8283-1486-1 5.95 (pbk.)
1. Stresau, Jan, 1939-1967. 2. Spiritualism. I. Title.

SUPLER, Albert J. 133.
Voices from beyond the vale, by Albert J. Supler ... Oklahoma City, Okla., Joslyn engraving co., [1928] 2 p. l., 135 p. pl., ports. 22 cm. "Messages ... received through trance mediums, Mrs. L. D. McMasters and Tressis Washburn." [BF1290.S8] 28-29462
1. Spiritualism. I. Title.

SWEET, Elizabeth, Mrs. 133.
The future life: as described and portrayed by spirits, through Mrs. Elizabeth Sweet. Boston, New York, W. White and company, 1869. 1 p. l., 408 p. 19 1/2 cm. Introduction by J. W. Edmonds. [BF1291.S88] 11-4757
1. Spiritualism. I. Title.

SWEETSER, Lewis Hobart, 1868- 133.93
the inner voice reveals, by Lewis H. Sweetser. Los Angeles, Calif., De Vorss & co. [1943] 4 p. l., 11-148 p. 20 1/2 cm. "First edition." [BF1301.S92] 44-19613
1. Spirtualism. 2. New thought. I. Title.

SYLVESTER, Arline. 133.9
Who, me? Yes, you! / By Arline Sylvester. Boston : Branden Press, [1975] 153 p. ; 22 cm. [BF1261.S95] 74-82230 ISBN 0-8283-1581-7 : 4.95
1. Spiritualism. I. Title.

TAYLOR, William George Langworthy, 1859- 133.9
Immortality, an essay on some of its vital, moral, and physical aspects, by W. G. Langworthy Taylor ... Boston, B. Humphries, inc. [c1937] 623 p. 20 1/2 cm. [BF1261.T25] [159.9617] 38-5176
1. Spiritualism. I. Title.

TERHUNE, Anice Morris (Stockton) 133.03
Across the line, by Albert Payson Terhune, with notes and comments by Anice Terhune, and with a foreword by Rev. Dr. Joseph R. Sizoo ... New York, The Dryden press [1945] 1 p. l., v-vi p., 2 l., 116 p. 21 cm. Includes "Across the line; rough notes for an article by Albert Payson Terhune made some time before his death February 18, 1942" (1 l., p. 1-10) and "Notes and comments by Anice Terhune" (p. [11]-116) [BF1261.T28] 46-389

1. Spiritualism. I. Terhune, Albert Payson, 1872-1942. II. Title.

TERRY, Alfred Howe, 1883- 133
The light bearers, and other lectures ... by Alfred H. Terry. [Washington, Hayworth publishing house, c1918] 96 p. port. 18 cm. [BF1272.T4] 18-11074
1. Spiritualism. I. Title.
Contents omitted

TERRY, Alfred Howe, 1883- 133
Spiritualism, what is it? By Alfred H. Terry ... [Washington, D. C., Hayworth publishing house, c1922] 4 p. l., 7-116 p. 17 cm. [BF1272.T45] 22-11867
1. Spiritualism. I. Title.

THEOBALD, Morell. 133.93
Spirit workers in the home circle; an autobiographic narrative of psychic phenomena in family daily life, extending over a period of twenty years, by Morell Theobald, F.C.A. Boston, Mass., Colby and Rich, 1887. xii p., 2 l., 310 p. plan. facsims. (part fold.) 22 cm. Printed in Great Britain. [BF1261.T3 1887 a] [159.961730 34-36385
1. Spiritualism. I. Title.

THIEBAULT, Jules. 133.
The vanished friend, evidence, theoretical and practical, of the survival of human identity after death, from the French of Jules Thiebault, foreword by Margaret Deland ... New York, E. P. Dutton & company [c1920] xxii p., 1 l., 226 p. incl. front., illus., ports. 21 cm. [BF1261.T4] 20-9418
1. Spiritualism. I. Title.

THOMAS, Charles Drayton, 1867-
From life to life; a story of family reunion after death, by Rev. Charles Drayton Thomas. London, New York [etc.] Rider & co. [1946] 80 p. 19 cm. A 47
1. Spiritualism. 2. Psychical research. I. Title.

THOMAS, Franklin Alonzo, 1867- 133
How to hold circles for developing mediumship at home, by Franklin A. Thomas ... [Boston, Machine composition co., printer, 1920] 5 p. l., 87 p. 19 cm. [BF1272.T5 1920] 20-8354
1. Spiritualism. I. Title.

THOMAS, Franklin Alonzo, 1867- 133.
Philosophy and phenomena of spiritualism, by Franklin A. Thomas ... Brookline, Mass., F. A. Thomas [c1922] 471 p. 20 cm. [BF1261.T42] 22-24259
1. Spiritualism. I. Title.

THOMAS, John F. 133.9072
Beyond normal cognition; an evaluative and methodological study of the mental content of certain trance phenomena, by John F. Thomas ... with a foreword by Professor William McDougall ... [Boston] Boston society for psychic research, 1937. xiii p., 1 l., 319 p. diagrs. 23 1/2 cm. "The study was made under university direction and was accepted as a doctor's thesis in a university Department of psychology."--Pref. "Publication of Boston society for psychic research." [BF1031.T54] [159.9617072] 37-32416
1. Spiritualism. 2. Psychical research. I. Boston society for psychic research. II. Title.

THOMAS, John F. 133
Case studies bearing upon survival, by John F. Thomas. Boston, Boston society for psychic research, 1929. 150 p. 23 cm. [BF1321.T5] 29-13315
1. Spiritualism. 2. Psychical research. I. Title.

THOMAS, John Frederick, 1874-1940. 133.9072
Beyond normal cognition; an evaluative and methodological study of the mental content of certain trance phenomena, by John F. Thomas ... with a foreword by Professor William McDougall ... [Boston] Boston society for psychic research, 1937. xiii p., 1 l., 319 p. diagrs. 23 1/2 cm. "The study was made under university direction and was accepted as a doctor's thesis in a university Department of psychology."--Pref. "Publication of Boston society for psychic research." [BF1031.T54] [159.96] 37-32416
1. Spiritualism. 2. Psychical research. I. Boston society for psychic research. II. Title.

THOMAS, Joseph Hromas. 133
The spirtual mysteries revealed unto man, being a record of messages involuntarily received while in full consciousness. By Joseph Hromas Thomas. Aberdeen, Wash., J. H. Thomas [c1924] 2 p. l., [7]-120 p. 21 1/2 cm. [BF1623.R7T5] 24-16632
I. Title.

THOMSON, Mary. 133.9'1'0924 B
To Elsie with love : an adventure into the unknown / by Mary Thomson. London ; New York : Regency Press, 1975. 160 p., plate : port. ; 23 cm. [BF1283.N3T47] 75-325201 ISBN 0-7212-0395-7 : 12.95
1. Nash, Elsie. 2. Spiritualism. I. Title.

THORNDYKE, E. P., Mrs.
Astrea, or Goddess of justice. By Mrs. E. P. Thorndyke... San Franciso, A. M. Slocum, printer, 1881. 104, [2] p. 23 cm. Poems. [PS3059.T4] 31-17964
1. Spiritualism. I. Title.

THURSTON, Herbert, 1856-1939. 133.9
The church and spiritualism, by Herbert Thurston, S.J. Milwaukee, The Bruce publishing company [c1933] xxi, 384 p., 1 l., 22 cm. [Science and culture series] [BF1275.C3T5] [159.9617] 33-14280
1. Spiritualism. 2. Catholic church—Doctrinal and controversial works—Catholic authors. I. Title.

TIFFANY, Joel. 133.
The astral world, higher occult powers; clairvoyance, spiritism, mediumship, and spirit-healing fully explained, by Joel Tiffany; introduction by Phenix. 3d ed. Chicago, Ill., de Laurence, Scott & company, 1910. ix, 17-224 p. front. 20 cm. $2.00. [BF1261.T5] 10-16965
1. Spiritualism. I. Title.

TIFFANY, Joel, 1811-1893. 133.9
Lectures on spiritualism, being a series of lectures on the phenomena and philosophy of development, individualism, spirit, immortality, mesmerism, clairvoyance, spiritual manifestations, Christianity, and progress, delivered at Prospect street church, in the city of Cleveland, during the winter and spring of 1851, by J. Tiffany. Cleveland, J. Tiffany, 1851. 331 p., 1 l. 19 cm. [BF1251.T48] [159.9617] 34-36387
1. Spiritualism. I. Title.

TIFFANY, Joel, 1811-1893. 133.9
Spiritualism explained: being a series of twelve lectures delivered before the New York conference of spiritualists, by Joel Tiffany, in January 1856. With an introduction by "Phoenix". Reported phonographically by Graham and Ellinwood. 2d ed. New York, Graham and Ellinwood, 1856. ix, [11]-206 p. 22 cm. [BF1251.T5 1856 a] [159.9617] 34-36389
1. Spiritualism. I. Title.

*TIMMONS, Tim. 133.9
Chains of the spirit, a manual for liberation. Washington, D.C., Cannon Press, [1973] 86 p., 20 cm. [BF1251] ISBN 0-913686-07-7 1.25 (pbk.)
1. Spiritualism. I. Title.

TITUS, Justin E. 133.9
The lost word; an inward search for an imperishable seed; unveiling the birth processes and growth patterns of an immortal man [by] Justin E. Titus. Lakemont, Ga., CSA Press, 1967. 222 p. illus., port. 23 cm. [BF1999.T55] 67-29384
1. Spiritualism. I. Title.

TORREY, Reuben Archer, 1856- 231
The God of the Bible; the God of the Bible as distinguished from the God of "Christian science", the God of "new thought", the God of spiritualism, the God of "Theosophy", the God of Unitarianism, the God of "the new theology", the God of modern philosophy, and the God of modernism in general. By R. A. Torrey... New York, George H. Doran company [c1923] ix p., 2 l., 15-246 p. 19 1/2 cm. [BT101.T65] 23-10250
I. Title.

TOUEY, John P. 133.
Are mediums really witches: or, The vexed question of spiritism [by] John P. Touey... Lancaster, Pa., Wickersham press, 1927. ix, 119 p. front., plates. 19 1/2 cm. Bibliographical foot-notes. [BF1042.T6] 27-14183
1. Spiritualism. I. Title.

TOWARDS the hereafter;
with a special inquiry into spiritual healing. [1st. Amer. ed.] New York, Citadel Press [1957, c1956] 191p. illus. 21cm. Sequel to In search of the hereafter.
1. Spiritualism. 2. Mental healing. I. Lester, Reginald Mounstephens.

TOWNSEND, Harry Brayton, 1873- 133.
Leaves from heaven, a message of God, a word from heaven, by Harry Brayton Townsend. Boston, Mass., The Christopher publishing house [c1921] 3 p. l., [5]-76 p. 20 cm. $1.50 Spiritualistic message from Clara Townsend sent through Ethel G. Casterline. cf. Dedication. [BF1301.T6] 21-4487
1. Spiritualism. I. Title.

TREWHITT, Paul W. 133.
A study in spirit wisdom, written and comp. by Paul W. Trewhitt. Automatic writing. Washington, D.C., The Temple publishing company, c1921. 4 p. l., 11-240 p. 19 1/2 cm. [BF1301.T68] 22-795
1. Spiritualism. I. Title.

TRUE, Minnehaha Howard, Mrs. 1860- 133.
Messages from higher spheres, through the mediumship of and inspirationally given by M. Howard True, received and recorded verbatim in the dictaphone ... [Red Bluff, Cal.] The author, 1912. 3 p. l., [iii]-iv p., 1 l., 193 p. front. (port.) 20 1/2 cm. $1.00 [BF1301.T7] 12-21421
1. Spiritualism. I. Title.

TRUESDELL, John W. 133.9
The bottom facts concerning the science of spiritualism; derived from careful investigations covering a period of twenty-five years, by John W. Truesdell. With many descriptive illustrations. New York, G. W. Dillingham, 1892. xv, 17-331 p. illus. 19 1/2 cm. [BF1301.T67] [159.9617] A 14
1. Spiritualism. I. Title.

TRUESDELL, John W. 133
The bottom facts concerning the science of spiritualism: derived from careful investigations covering a period of twenty-five years, by John w. Truesdell ... New York, G. W. Carleton & co.; London, S. Low & co., 1883. xv, 17-331 p. illus., plates. 19 cm. Cover-title: Spiritualism; bottom facts. [BF1031.T67 1883] 46-35807
1. Spiritualism. I. Title.

TUBBY, Gertrude Ogden. 133.
James H. Hyslop--X; his book, a cross reference record, collated and annotated by Gertrude Ogden Tubby ...with a preface by Weston D. Bayley, M.D. York, Pa., The York printing company, 1929. 424 p. illus. 23 cm. "This volume is the first collection of the Hyslop material which has been collated, and it is actually only the later and minor portion of the mass of psychical material Miss Tubby has accumulated since ... 1920."--Pref. [BF1311.H88T8] 29-6154
1. Hyslop, James Hervey, 1854-1920. 2. Spiritualism. I. Title.

TUTTLE, Hudson, 1836- 133.
Arcana of spiritualism; a manual of spiritual science and philosophy, by Hudson Tuttle. Chicago, Ill., J. R. Francis; [etc., etc.] 1904. 351 p. incl. front., port. 20 cm. Rewritten; first edition published in 1871. [BF1251.T8 1904] 4-20704
1. Spiritualism. I. Title.

TUTTLE, Hudson, 1836-1910. 133.
Arcana of spiritualism: a manual of spiritual science and philosophy. By Hudson Tuttle ... Boston, Adams & co., 1871. 455 p. front. (port.) 19 1/2 cm. [BF1251.T8 1871] 10-34877
1. Spiritualism. I. Title.

TUTTLE, Hudson, 1836-1910. 133.
The ethics of spiritualism; a system of moral philosophy founded on evolution and the continuity of man's existence beyond the grave. By Hudson Tuttle ... Chicago, Religio-philosophical publishing house, 1878. ix, [11]-155 p. 19 cm. [BF1275.E8T8] 11-3594
1. Spiritualism. I. Title.

TUTTLE, Hudson, 1836-1910. 133.9
Medium and its laws; its conditions and cultivation. By Hudson Tuttle. 6th ed. Chicago, The Progressive thinker publishing house; Berlin Heights, O., H. Tuttle, 1904. 1 p. l., 186 p. 20 cm. [BF1286.T85 1904] [159.9617] 34-15706
1. Spiritualism. I. Title.

TUTTLE, Hudson, 1836-1910. 133.9
The philosophy of spirit, and the spirit-world. By Hudson Tuttle ... London, H. A. Copley; Berlin Heights, O., H. Tuttle; [etc., etc.] 1896. 1 p. l., [c]-ix, [1], 207 p. illus. 21 cm. [BF1261.T78] [159.9617] 33-35473
1. Spiritualism. I. Title.

TUTTLE, Hudson, 1836-1910. 133.93
... Scenes in the spirit world; or, Life in the spheres. By Hudson Tuttle ... New York, Partridge and Brittan, 1855. 143 p. 19 cm. (Partridge and Brittan's spiritual library) With Child, A.B. ABC of life ... Boston, 1862. [AC5.C55] [159.96173] 34-18484
1. Spiritualism. 2. Future life. I. Title.

TWIGG, Ena. 133.9'1'0924 B
Ena Twigg, medium, by Ena Twigg with Ruth Hagy Brod; introduction by Mervyn Stockwood. London, New York, W. H. Allen, 1973. xix, 295 p. 23 cm. [BF1283.T95A3 1973] 73-158703 ISBN 0-491-00903-8 £3.00
1. Twigg, Ena. 2. Spiritualism. I. Brod, Ruth Hagy. II. Title.

TWIGG, Ena. 133.9'1'0924 B
Ena Twigg: medium, by Ena Twigg, with Ruth Hagy Brod. Introd. by Mervyn Stockwood. New York, Hawthorn Books [1972] xviii, 297 p. 22 cm. [BF1283.T95A3 1972] 72-1970 6.95
1. Twigg, Ena. 2. Spiritualism. I. Brod, Ruth Hagy. II. Title.

TWING, Carolinn Edna (Skinner) Mrs., 1844- 133.
Contrasts in spirit life; and recent experiences of Samuel Bowles ... in the first five spheres. Also a thrilling account of the late President Garfield's reception in the spirit world. Written through the hand of Carrie E. S. Twing ... Springfield, Mass., Star publishing company [c1881] 142 p. 18 1/2 cm. [BF1301.T82] 10-33692
1. Spiritualism. I. Title.

TWING, Carolinn Edna Skinner, Mrs., 1844- 133.
Golden gleams from the heavenly light. By Spirit Samuel Bowles ... Mrs. Carolinn E. S. Twing, medium. Springfield, Mass., The Star publishing company [c1898] 2 p. l., 119 p. 19 1/2 cm. [BF1301.T87] CA 11
1. Spiritualism. I. Title.

TWING, Carolinn Edna (Skinner) Mrs., 1844- 133.93
... Interviews with spirits, Joan of Arc.--Napoleon Bonaparte [and others] ... Mr. Bowles reports his own progress in spirit-life. By Samuel Bowles ... Carrie E. S. Twing, medium. Springfield, Mass., Star publishing company [1885?] 1 p. l., ii-iii, 207 p. 20 cm. At head of title: No. 3. [BF1301.T885] [159.96173] 34-14470
1. Spiritualism. I. Title.

TYLAR, William. 133.
The great Bournemouth mystery. The spirit of Irene speaks ... Bournemouth, W. Tylar, 1923. 3-127 p. front. (port.) illus. 19 cm. Illustrated lining-papers. On cover: First edition. Blank pages for "notes" (119-125) [BF1301.T9] 23-11537
1. Spiritualism. I. Title. II. Title: The spirit of Irene.

UNDERHILL, Ann Leah, 1814-1890. 133.9
The missing link in modern spiritualism / A. Leah Underhill. New York : Arno Press, 1976, c1885. p. cm. (The Occult) Reprint of the ed. published by T. R. Knox, New York. [BF1283.F7U6 1976] 75-36923 ISBN 0-405-07977-X : 28.00
1. Fox family. 2. Spiritualism. I. Title. II. Series: The Occult (New York, 1976-)

UNDERHILL, Ann Leah (Fox) Mrs. 1814-1891. 133.
The missing link in modern spiritualism. By A. Leah Underhill, of the Fox family. Rev. and arranged by a literary friend. New York, T. R. Knox & co., 1885. xii p.,

1 l., 477 p. incl. illus., plans, facsims. front., ports. 20 1/2 cm. [BF1283.F7U6] 11-4738
1. Fox family. 2. Spiritualism I. Title.

UNDERWOOD, Sara A. 133.91
(Francis) Mrs. 1838-
Automatic or spirit writing, with other psychic experiences, by Sara A. Underwood. With an introduction by B. F. Underwood. Chicago, Ill., T. G. Newman, 1896. 352 p. incl. front. (port.) facsims. 19 1/2 cm. [BF1261.U5] 11-3404
1. Spiritualism. I. Title.

...*THE unseen doctor,* 133.
formerly published in England as One thing I know; or, The power of the unseen. Authorized ed., with preface by J. Arthur Hill. New York, H. Holt and company; [etc., etc., c1920] 2 p. l., iii-x p., 1 l., xi-xiv, 142 p. 19 1/2 cm. (The psychic series) $1.75 By "E. M. S." [BF1286.O5 1920] 20-15457
1. Spiritualism. I. S., Miss E. M. II. E. M. S., Miss. III. Hill, John Arthur, 1872-

VAY, Adelina Barone 133.9
Wurmbrand-Sluppach, 1840-1925.
Spirit, power and matter, ed. by Catharina, Adelma and Oedoen Vay; tr. by Robert E. Shiller and Grace H. Shiller. Cleveland, c1948. x, 181 p. illus. 18 cm. [BF1303.V32] 49-22067
1. Spiritualism. I. Title.

VINCENT, Howell Smith. 133.9
Lighted passage, by Howell S. Vincent, D.D. Philadelphia, Dorrance and company [1943] xiv, [2], 17-240 p., 1 l. illus. (facsim.) diagrs. 19 cm. [BF1261.V5] 43-14922
1. Spiritualism. I. Title.

[VON Ravn, Clara Iza
(Tibbetts)] Mrs. 1870-
The scribe of a soul, by Clara Iza Price, introduction by Professor A. Van der Naillen ... Seattle, Wash., Denny-Coryell company, 1901. 201 p. 17 1/2 cm. [Z3.V894Se] 1-7315
1. Spiritualism. I. Van der Naillen, Albert, 1830- ed. II. Title.

VON KLENNER, Katharine 133.
(Evans) baroness.
The greater revelation; messages from the unseen world received through automatic writing in various languages [!] including Chinese and Japanese, in the chirography and with verified signatures of those sending the messages. By Baroness Katharine Evans von Klenner ... New York, Siebel publishing corporation, 1925. ix, p., 1 l., 259 p. illus. (facsims.) 21 cm. [BF1301.V65] 25-8286
1. Spiritualism. I. Title.

WADE, Alda Madison, 1883- 133.9
At the Shrine of the Master; glimpses of immortality. Philadelphia , Dorrance [1953] 302p. illus. 20cm. [BF1261.W15] 52-13094
1. Spiritualism. 2. Tampa, Fla. Shrine of the Master Church. I. Title.

WADE, Alda Madison, 1883- 133.93
Evidences of immortality. [2d ed.] Boston, Christopher Pub. House [1956] 168p. illus. 21cm. [BF1301.W12 1956] 56-23998
1. Spiritualism. I. Title.

WADE, Alda Madison, 1883- 133.93
Evidences of immortality, by Alda Madison Wade ... New York, William-Frederick press, 1943. 4 p. l., 152 p. front. (port.) 20 cm. "First edition." [BF1301.W12] 44-3715
1. Spiritualism. I. Title.

WALLACE, Alfred Russel, 133.
1823-
A defence of modern spiritualism. By Alfred R. Wallace...With a preface by Epes Sargent. 4th thousand. Boston, Colby and Rich, 1874. iv, [5]-63 p. 19 1/2 cm. [BF1251.W16] 10-34878
1. Spiritualism. I. Title.

WALLACE, Alfred Russel, 133.9
1823-1913.
On miracles and modern spiritualism / Alfred Russel Wallace. New York : Arno Press, 1975. p. cm. Reprint of the 1896 ed. published by G. Redway, London. [BF1251.W2 1975] 75-7409 ISBN 0-405-07338-0 : 14.00
1. Spiritualism. 2. Miracles. I. Title.

WALLACE, Alfred Russel, 133.9
1823-1913.
The psycho-physiological sciences, and their assailants. Being a response, by Alfred R. Wallace...Professor J. R. Buchanan...Darius Lyman...Epes Sargent...to the attacks of Prof. W. B. Carpenter...and others. Boston, Colly & Rich, 1878. vi, [7]-216 p. 18 1/2 cm. [BF1041.W3] [159.9617] 34-15703
1. Carpenter, William Benjamin, 1813-1885. 2. Spiritualism. I. Buchanan, Joseph Rodes, 1814-1899. II. Lyman, Darious, 1821?-1892. III. Sargent, Epes, 1813-1880. IV. Title.
Contents omitted.

WALLACE, Mary Bruce, Mrs. 133.
The coming light; sequel to The thinning of the veil, by Mary Bruce Wallace... New York, Dodd, Mead and company, 1925. xii, 196 p. 19 1/2 cm. [The deeper issues series] $1.25 [BF1301.W22 1925] 25-8870
1. Spiritualism. I. Title.

WALLACE, Mary Bruce, Mrs. 133.
The thinning of the veil; a record of experience, by Mary Bruce Wallace, with foreword by J. Bruce Wallace, M.A. London, J. M. Watkins; New York, Dodd, Mead and company, 1919. xxiv, 120 p. 17 cm. [Deeper issues series] [BF1301.W2 1919] 19-7803
1. Spiritualism. I. Title.

WALLACE, Mary Bruce, Mrs. 133.
The thinning of the veil; a record of experience, by Mary Bruce Wallace, with foreword by J. Bruce Wallace, M.A. New York, Dodd, Mead and company, 1919. xxi, 99 p. 19 1/2 cm. [BF1301.W2 1919a] 19-7802
1. Spiritualism. I. Title.

WALLIS, Eleanor 133.9
Our thin-air friends; a remarkable documentation of the reality of the invisible world, as proven by communications with the dead. New York, America [1962, c.1961] 132p. 22cm. 61-17245 3.00
1. Spiritualism. I. Title.

WALRATH, M. E. 133.
History of the earth's formation. Its first inhabitance in connection with the explanation of the Bible. By a convocation of God's messengers, through the mediumship of M. E. Walrath. New-York, Printed for the author, 1868. viii, 633 p. 25 1/2 cm. [BF1291.W24] 11-4758
1. Spiritualism. I. Title.

WALSH, James Joseph, 1865- 133.
Spiritualism, a fake. (Can we communicate with the dead?) By James J. Walsh ... Boston, Mass., The Stratford company, 1925. 2 p. l., 132 p. 19 cm. Contains also "Spiritualism, a fact. (Can we communicate with the dead?) By Hereward Carrington", inverted, with separate t.-p. [BF1031.C38] 25-24369
1. Spiritualism. I. Title.

WARD, Ellen E., Mrs. 133.93
Angels messages, through Mrs. Ellen E. Ward, as a medium. Nashville, Tenn., Wheeler, Marshall & Bruce, printers, 1875. 408 p. 19 1/2 cm. [BF1291.W27] (159.96173] 33-38489
1. Spiritualism. I. Title.

WARD, John Sebastian 133.93
Marlow, 1885-
Gone west; three narratives of after-death experiences, communicated through the mediumship of J. S. M. Ward ... 6th thousand. London, New York [etc.] Rider & company [1944] 188 p. illus. (plan) diagrs. 19 cm. "First published autumn 1917 ... fifth impression summer 1944." [BF1301.W223 1944] 44-13791
1. Spiritualism. I. Title.

WARMAN, Edward Barrett. 133.
... *Spiritism,* by Edward B. Warman ... Chicago, A. C. McClurg & co., 1910. ix, 11-62 p. front. (port.) 20 cm. (Half-title: Psychic science series, no. vi) $0.35. Series title also at head of t.-p. [BF1261.W2] 10-23753
1. Spiritualism. I. Title.

[WARREN, Jennie (Reed)] 133.
The new revelation of the will of God, concerning the educating and cultivating the mind here on earth, by the angel world ... vol. I[-II] Utica, N.Y., T. J. Griffiths, printer, 1871-77. 2 v. 19 1/2 cm. No more published? [BF1291.W28] CA 11
1. Spiritualism. I. Title.

WASHBURN, Owen Redington, 133.93
1866-
The discovered country, by Owen Redington Washburn ... Philadelphia, The David McKay company [1939] vii, 9-160 p. 19 cm. "Printed in Great Britain." [BF1283.W35A3] [159.96173] 39-16668
1. Spiritualism. I. Title.

WASHBURN, Owen Redington, 133.93
1866- comp.
Who are these? Writings from psychic sources, presented by Owen Redington Washburn. Philadelphia, David McKay company [c1941] 1 p. l., v-vii, 155 p. 19 cm. [BF1290.W3] [159.96173] 41-4807
1. Spiritualism. I. Title.

WASSON, John Bourbon. 133.
Modern spiritualism laid bare, unmasked, dissected, and viewed from spiritualists' own teachings, and from Scriptural standpoints ... Complete in two parts: part second ... containing autobiographical sketches of the ... author ... Dr. John Bourbon Wasson ... San Francisco, Bacon & company, printers, 1887. 322 p. incl. front., illus., ports. 20 cm. [BF1042.W3] 11-2572
1. Spiritualism. I. Title.

WATSON, Albert Durrant, 133.
1859-
Birth through death, the ethics of the twentieth plane; a revelation received through the psychic consciousness of Louis Benjamin, reported by Albert Durrant Watson ... New York, The James A. McCann company, 1920. 4 p. l., 374 p. 20 1/2 cm. [BF1301.W23] 20-21214
1. Spiritualism. I. Benjamin, Louis. II. Title.

WATSON, Albert Durrant, 133.
1859-
The twentieth plane; a psychic revelation reported by Albert Durrant Watson ... Philadelphia, G. W. Jacobs & company [c1919] 312 p. 20 1/2 cm. One leaf laid in. "Recounts solely as evidence, the extraordinary recent conversations with great men of the past."--Publishers' weekly, May 3, 1919. [BF1301.W25] 19-8474
1. Spiritualism. I. Title.

WATSON, Samuel. 133.
The religion of spiritualism. Its phenomena and philosophy. By Samuel Watson... New York, Printed for the author by E. O. Jenkins, 1880. 399 p. 19 cm. [BF1261.W3] 11-3405
1. Spiritualism. I. Title.

WATSON, Samuel, 1813- 133.9072
The clock struck one, and Christian spiritualist: being a synopsis of the investigations of spirit intercourse by an Episcopal bishop, three ministers, five doctors, and others, at Memphis, Tenn., in 1855... By the Rev. Samuel Watson ... Louisville, Ky., J. P. Morton and company, 1878. xxxiv, [35]-208 p. front. (port.) 19 1/2 cm. [BF1251.W28] (159.9617072) 33-38464
1. Spiritualism. I. Title.

WATSON, Samuel, 1813- 133.
The clock struck three, being a review of Clock struck one, and reply to it. Part II. Showing the harmony between Christianity, science, and spiritualism. By Samuel Watson. Chicago, S. S. Jones, 1874. xiii, [15]-352 p. front. (port.) 20 cm. [BF1251.W32] 11-3121
1. Spiritualism. I. Title.

WATSON, Samuel, 1813- 133.
Clock struck two, and Christian spiritualist: being a review of the reviewers of the "Clock struck one," charges, etc., with recent investigations of spiritualism. By Samuel Watson. Memphis, Boyle & Chapman, 1873. 96 p. 20 1/2 cm. [BF1251.W3] 11-3120
1. Spiritualism. I. Title.

WATSON, Samuel, 1813- 133.9
The religion of spiritualism, its phenomena and philosophy. By Samuel Watson... 3d ed. New York, Printed for the author by E. O. Jenkins, 1884. 423 p. front. (port.) 19 1/2 cm. [BF1261.W3 1884] (159.9617) 33-39257
1. Spiritualism. I. Title.

WATSON, Samuel, 1813- 133.9
The religion of spiritualism, its phenomena and philosophy. By Samuel Watson... 4th ed. Boston, Banner of light publishing co., 1896. 423 p. illus. 20 cm. [BF1261.W3 1896] (159.9617) 33-38463
1. Spiritualism. I. Title.

WEBB, Blanche A. 133.8
The radian flame, by Blanche A. Draper [pseud.] Foreword by Edward L. Bodin. Daytona Beach, Fla., College Pub. Co. [c1956] 157 p. 24 cm. [BF1261.2.W4] 57-3122
1. Spiritualism. I. Title.

WEIL, Samuel. 133.
The religion of the future, or, Outlines of spiritual philosophy, by Rev. Samuel Weil. Boston, Arena publishing company, 1894. 3 p. l., 267 p. 20 cm. [BF1261.W4] 4-6865
1. Spiritualism. I. Title.

WEIMAR, James A. 133.
The mysteries and revelations of spiritism and mediumship and its kindred subjects viewed in the light of the Bible and personal investigation ... By J. A. Weimar ... [Fort Wayne, Ind., Press of the Journal company, c1898] xix, [1] 317, [1] p., 1 l., front. (port.) illus. 20 cm. [BF1042.W4] 98-200
1. Spiritualism. I. Title.

WEISS, Sara. 133.
Decimon Huydas, a romance of Mars; a story of actual experiences in Ento (Mars) many centuries ago given to the psychic Sara Weiss and by her transcribed automatically under the editorial direction of spirit Carl De L'Ester; illustrated with six original drawings. Rochester, N.Y., The Austin publishing company, 1906. 207 p. front. (port.) 6 pl. 20 1/2 cm. [BF1311.M4W35] 7-523
1. Spiritualism. I. Title. II. Title: Mars, A romance of.

WEISS, Sara. 133.
Journeys to the planet Mars; or, Our mission to Ento (Mars) being a record of visits made to Ento (Mars) by Sara Weiss, psychic, under the guidance of a spirit band... transcribed automatically by Sara Weiss under the editorial direction of (spirit) Carl De L'Ester...Illustrated by thirteen original drawings. 2d ed. Rochester, N.Y., The Austin publishing company, 1905. 3 p. l., [iii]-vi, 548 p. front., plates. 19 cm. [BF1311.M4W4 1905] 5-24199
1. Spiritualism. I. Title.

WELLNER, Catherine. 133.
Enroute of a soul, by Catherine Wellner ... Boston The Christopher publishing house [c1925] 137 p. 21 cm. [BF1301.W37] 25-11531
1. Spiritualism. I. Title.

WELLS, Helen (Butler) 133.93
1854-1940.
Spiritual America as seen from the other side, dictated by invisible teachers, clairaudiently received by Helen Wells, transcribed by a class of eight students ... Boston, R. G. Badger [c1927] 10 p. l., 17-200 p. 21 1/2 cm. At end: The end of volume I. No more published? [BF1301.W383] 33-34666
1. Spiritualism. I. Title.

WELLS, Helen (Butler) 133.93
1854-1940.
Beyond the eyes of man; or, The astronomy of earth, by Dr. Alonzo P. Mathewson ... clairaudiently received by Helen Wells. [Jamaica, N.Y.] c1932. 107 p. front. (port.) 21 1/2 cm. [BF1311.M45W38] [159.96173] 32-34239
1. Spiritualism. I. Mathewson, Alonzo P. II. Title. III. Title: The astronomy of earth.

WELLS, Helen (Butler) 1854- 133.9
1940.
The bridge of love, by a lover; automatically and clairaudiently received from Bertrand L. Wells by Helen Wells. [Floral Park, N.Y., Mayflower press, 1920] 115 p. incl. front. (port.) 21 1/2 cm. [BF1301.W375] 31-4280

1. Spiritualism. I. Wells, Bertrand Laurence, 1878-1913. II. Title.

WELLS, Helen (Butler) 1854-1940. 133.9
The hidden path; text book for psychic development, by Cornelius Jensen, received by Helen Wells. [Floral Park, N.Y., c1930] 6 p. l., 15-107 p. 21 1/2 cm. Cover-title. "These thirty lessons were received automatically by Helen Wells, president of the Spiritual and ethical society of New York city, through the hand control of the invisible dictator Cornelius Jansen."--1st prelim. leaf. [BF1311.J3W4] 31-7526
1. Spiritualism. I. Jansenius, Cornelius, bp., 1585-1638. II. Title.

WELLS, Helen (Butler) 1854-1940. 133.9
The hidden path; text book for psychic development, by Cornelius Jensen, received by Helen Wells. [Floral Park, N.Y., c1930] 6 p. l., 15-107 p. 21 1/2 cm. Cover-title. "These thirty lessons were received automatically by Helen Wells, president of the Spiritual and ethical society of New York city, through the hand control of the invisible dictator Cornelius Jansen."--1st prelim. leaf. [BF1311.J3W4] 31-7526
1. Spiritualism. I. Jansenius, Cornelius, bp., 1585-1638. II. Title.

WELLS, Helen (Butler) 1854-1940. 133.9
Life, before and after earth's expression, dictated by Alonzo P. Mathewson, clairaudiently received by Helen Wells, 1929 ... New York city, The Spiritual and eithical society, inc. [c1930] 108, [1] p. 16 1/2 cm. (The Little blue booklet series, vol. VI) [BF1311.M45W4] 31-7530
1. Spiritualism. I. Mathewson, Alonzo P. II. Title.

WELLS, Helen (Butler) 1854-1940. 133.9
The three modern musketeers, dictated by themselves, clairaudiently received by Helen Wells. [New York, Printed by Polytype co., inc.] c1931. 1 p. l., 5-114 p. ports. 21 1/2 cm. Messages received from Bertrand L. Wells, Carlton Childs and Patsy. [BF1301.W385] 31-34217
1. Spiritualism. I. Title.

WELLS, Helen (Butler) Mrs., 1862- 133.93
Beyond the eyes of man: or, The astronomy of earth, by Dr. Alonzo P. Mathewson ... clairaudiently received by Helen Wells. [Jamaica, N.Y.] c1932. 107 p. front. (port.) 21 1/2 cm. [BF1311.M45W38] 159.96173 32-34239
1. Spiritualism. I. Mathewson, Alonzo P. II. Title. III. Title: The astronomy of earth.

WELLS, Helen (Butler) Mrs., 1862- 133.9
The bridge of love by a lover; automatically and clairaudiently received from Bertrand L. Wells by Helen Wells. [Floral Park, N.Y., Mayflower press, 1930] 115 p. incl. front. (port.) 21 1/2 cm. [BF1301.W375] 31-4280
1. Spiritualism. I. Wells, Bertrand Laurence, 1878-1912. II. Title.

WELLS, Helen (Butler) Mrs., 1862- 133.9
The hidden path; text book for psychic development, by Cornelius Jansen, received by Helen Wells. [Floral Park, N.Y., c1930] 6 p. l., 15-107 p. 21 1/2 cm. Cover-title. "These thirty lessons were received automatically by Helen Wells, president of the Spiritual and ethical society of New York city, through the hand control of the invisible dictator Cornelius Jansen."--1st prelim. leaf. [BF1311.J3W4] 31-7526
1. Spiritualism. I. Jansenius, Cornelius, bp., 1585-1638. II. Title.

WELLS, Helen (Butler) Mrs., 1862- 133.9
Life, before and after earth's expression, dictated by Alonzo P. Mathewson, clairaudiently received by Helen Wells, 1929 ... New York city, The Spiritual and ethical society, inc. [c1930] 108, [1] p. 16 1/2 cm. (The little blue booklet series, vol. vi) [BF1311.M45W4] 31-7530
1. Spiritualism. I. Mathewson, Alonzo P. II. Title.

WELLS, Helen (Butler) Mrs., 1862- 133.93
Spiritual America as seen from the other side, dictated by invisible teachers, clairaudiently reissued by Helen Wells, transcribed by a class of eight students ... Boston, R. G. Badger [c1927]- v. 21 1/2 cm. [BF1301.W736] [[159.96173]] 33-34666
1. Spitirualism. I. Title.

WELLS, Helen (Butler) Mrs., 1862- 133.9
The three modern musketeers, dictated by themselves, clairaudiently received by Helen Wells. [New York, Printed by Polytype co., inc.] c1931. 1 p. l., 5-114 p. ports. 21 1/2 cm. Messages received from Bertrand L. Wells, Carlton Childs and Patsy. [BF1301.W385] 31-34217
1. Spiritualism. I. Title.

WELLS, Helen (Melchers) 1891- 133.93
Adventures in the spirit world. [1st ed.] New York, Vantage Press [1957] 50p. illus. 21cm. [BF1301.W386] 56-12771
1. Spiritualism. I. Title.

WELLS, Helen (Melchers) 1891- 133.93
Adventures in the spirit world. [1st ed.] New York, Vantage Press [1957] 50 p. illus. 21 cm. [BF1301.W386] 56-12771
1. Spiritualism. I. Title.

WEST, Simeon Henry, 1827- 133.
Goddena, the unknown god, by S. H. West ... [Bloomington, Ill., Pantograph printing stationery co., 1917] 153 p. front., ports. 20 cm. [BF1301.W4] 17-23955
1. Spiritualism. I. Title.

WESTWOOD, Horace, 1884- 133.9
There is a psychic world; introd. by John Haynes Holmes. New York, Crown Publishers [1949] xix, 206 p. 22 cm. "Suggested reading": p. 204-206. [BF1301.W413] 49-10994
1. Spiritualism. I. Title.

WETHERBEE, John. 133.
"Shadows": being a familiar presentation of thoughts and experiences in spiritual matters, with illustrative narrations. By John Wetherbee ... Boston, Colby & Rich, 1885. 288 p. front. (port.) 19 1/2 cm. [BF1261.W46] 11-3406
1. Spiritualism. I. Title.

WETZEL, Delia M. 133.
Divine love and the possibilities of life; comprises a historical account of ancient times, blending into a knowledge of the Supreme as accorded. Received inspirationally between June 30 and August 30, 1922. By Delia M. Wetzel. Los Angeles, Calif., The Austin publishing company [c1922] 88, [3] p. incl. front. port. 18 cm. [BF1301.W42] 23-1543
1. Spiritualism. I. Title.

WEYANT, Helen. 133.
Letters from spirit people to earth friends demonstrating Christ's teachings through spirit return, by Dr. Helen Weyant. Los Angeles, Cal., The Austin publishing co. [c1919] 80 p. 19 1/2 cm. [BF1301.W45] 19-18956
1. Spiritualism. I. Title.

WHITE, George Starr, 1866- 133.
The guiding power; or, The plan of the universe. A true narrative explaining many mysteries of everyday life, by George Starr White... [Los Angeles, Phillips printing co., c1929] 4 p. l., 13-72 p. port. 10 cm. [BF1272.W4] 29-12695
1. Spiritualism. I. Title.

WHITE, Stewart Edward, 1873- 133.93
Across the unknown, by Stewart Edward White and Harwood White... New York, E. P. Dutton & company, inc., 1939. 336 p. diagrs. 19 1/2 cm. Transmitted by Betty [pseud.] cf. Author's note. "First edition." 159.96173
1. Spiritualism. I. White, Harwood Arend, 1897- joint author. II. White, Mrs. Elizabeth Calvert (Grant) 1881- III. Title.

WHITE, Stewart Edward, 1873- 133.93
The Betty book, excursions into the world of other-consciousness, made by Betty [pseud.] between 1919 and 1936, now recorded by Stewart Edward White. New York, E. P. Dutton & company, 1937. 302 p. 19 1/2 cm. "First edition." [BF1301.W5954] 159.96173 37-8526
1. Spiritualism. I. White, Mrs. Elizabeth Calvert (Grant) 1881- II. Title.

WHITE, Stewart Edward, 1873- 133.93
...The road I know... New York, E. P. Dutton and company, inc., 1942. 253 p. 21 cm. "First eidtion." [BF1301.W5955] [159.96173] 42-9994
1. Spiritualism. I. Title.

WHITE, Stewart Edward, 1873- 133.93
... The stars are still there. New York, E. P. Dutton & company, 1946. 191 p. 21 cm. "First edition." [BF1261.W464] 46-245
1. Spiritualism. I. Title.

WHITE, Stewart Edward, 1873- 133.93
The unobstructed universe, by Stewart Edward White. New York, E. P. Dutton and company, inc., 1940. 320 p. 20 1/2 cm. "First eiditon." [BF1261.W465 1940] (159.96173) 40-31655
1. Spiritualism. I. Title.

WHITE, Stewart Edward, 1873-1946.
Across the unknown, by Stewart Edward White and Harwood White. New York, E. P. Dutton [1962] 336 p. diagrs. 20 cm. Transmitted by Betty [pseud.] cf. Author's note. 67-32538
1. Spiritualism. I. White, Harwood Arend, 1897- joint author. II. White, Elizabeth Calvert (Grant) 1881- III. Title.

WHITE, Stewart Edward, 1873-1946.
The Betty book; excursions into the world of other-consciousness, made by Betty [pseud.] between 1918 and 1936; now recorded by Stewart Edward White. New York, Dutton [c1965] 302 p. 20 cm. 67-34687
1. Spiritualism. I. White, Elizabeth Calvert (Grant) 1881-1939. II. Title.

WHITE, Stewart Edward, 1873-1946. 133.93
The job of living. [1st ed.] New York, E. P. Dutton, 1948. 196 p. port. 20 cm. "Stewart Edward White, his later years: a personal impression by Mrs. Leslie F. Kimmell": p. 13-19. [BF1301.W59544] 48-7164
1. Spiritualism. I. Kimmell, Susan C. II. Title.

WHITE, Stewart Edward, 1873-1946.
The unobstructed universe. New York, Dutton, 1959. 320 p. 19 cm. (Dutton Everyman Paperback)
1. Spiritualism. I. Title.

WHITE, Stewart Edward, 1873-1946. 133.93
With folded wings, by Stewart Edward White ... New York, E. P. Dutton & co., 1947. xiii, 236 p. 19 1/2 cm. Based on communications received by the author through the medium-ship of Betty [i.e. Mrs. Elizabeth White] cf. Introd. "First edition." [BF1301.W5956] 47-3109
1. Spiritualism. I. White, Elizabeth Calvert (Grant) 1881-1939. II. Title.

WHITING, Albert Bennet, 1835-1871. 133.
Evidences of modern spiritualism, being a debate held at Decatur, Michigan, March 12th, 13th, and 14th, 1861, between Mr. A. B. Whiting and Rev. Jos. Jones, upon the question "Resolved, that the origin of modern spiritual phenomena is entirely hypothetical, and therefore, the revelations from that source are not at all reliable." Reported by C. C. Flint ... Chicago, S. P. Rounds, steam printing house, 1861. 114 p., 1 l. 21 1/2 cm. [BF1251.W58] 11-3122
1. Spiritualism. I. Jones, Rev. Joseph. II. Flint, Chambers C., reporter. III. Title.

WHITING, Lilian. 133.
They who understand, by Lilian Whiting ... Boston, Little, Brown, and company, 1919. 4 p. l., 200 p. 19 cm. $1.25 [BF1261.W55] 19-5066
1. Spiritualism. I. Title.

[WHITING, Lilian] 1859- 133.
After her death; the story of a summer, by the author of "The world beautiful"... Boston, Roberts brothers, 1897. 137 p. front. (port.) 17 1/2 cm. [BF1261.W5] CA 12
1. Spiritualism. I. Title.

WHITING, Lilian, 1859- 133
The spiritual significance; or, Death as an event in life, by Lilian Whiting... Boston, Little, Brown, and company, 1900. 3 p. l., [iii]-vii p., 2 l. [13]-393 p. 18 cm. [BF1031.W5] 1-29406
1. Spiritualism. I. Title.

[WHITING, Lillian] 1859-1942. 133.
After her death, the story of a summer. By the author of "The world beautiful" ... Boston, Roberts brothers, 1897. 180 p. front. (port.) 17 1/2 cm. [BF1261.W5 1897 a] 46-44858
1. Spiritualism. I. Title.

WHITING, Rachel Augusta, comp. 920.
Golden memories of an earnest life. A biography of A. B. Whiting: together with selections from his poetical compositions and prose writings. Comp. by his sister, R. Augusta Whiting. Introduction by Rev. J. M. Peebles... Boston, W. White and company, 1872. 293 p. front. (port.) 18 1/2 cm. [BF1283.W55W5] 15-13518
1. Whiting, Albert Bennet, 1835-1871. 2. Spiritualism. I. Title.

WHITMORE, Clara Helen, 1865- 133.
Jo, the Indian friend, by Clara H. Whitmore... Boston, The Christopher publishing house [c1925] 52 p. 21 cm. [BF1301.W596] 25-6894
1. Spiritualism. I. Title.

WICKLAND, Carl August, 1861- 133.9
The gateway of understanding, by Carl A. Wickland ... in collaboration with Nelle M. Watts [and] Celia L. Goerz. Los Angeles, Calif., National psychological institute, incorporated, 1934. 7 p. l., xvii-xx, 313 p. front. (ports.) plates. 20 1/2 cm. [BF1261.W556] [159.9617] 34-2164
1. Spiritualism. I. Watts, Mrs. Nelle Minnetta (Yates) 1868- joint author. II. Goerz, Mrs. Celia Loretta (Krehbiel) 1886- joint author. III. Title.

WICKLAND, Carl August, 1861- 133.
Thirty years among the dead, by Carl A. Wickland ... in collaboration with Nelle M. Watts, Celia L. Goerz, Orlando D. Goerz. Los Angeles, National psychological institute, inc., 1924. 5 p. l., [13]-390 p. pl. (2 port.) 23 1/2 cm. [BF1301.W597] 25-217
1. Spiritualism. I. Title.

WIGGIN, Frederick Alonzo. 133.
The living Jesus; the words of Jesus of Nazareth uttered through the medium Frederick A. Wiggin, from February 11 to June 1, 1921. New York, G. Sully and company, 1921. xliii p., 1 l., 213 p. front. (port.) 21 cm. [BF1311.J5W5] 21-22088
1. Spiritualism. I. Title.

WILLARD, Winifred. 133.93
From the seventh plane; inter-world messages [by] Winifred Willard. Chicago, The Aries press [1946] 3 p. l., 5-251 p., 1 l. 23 1/2 cm. [BF1301.W617] 47-16314
1. Spiritualism. I. Title.

WILLIAMS, Gail. 133.
Fear not the crossing, written down by Gail Williams. New York, E. J. Clode [c1920] 1 p. l., 5-126 p. 19 cm. [BF1301.W62] 20-1895
1. Spiritualism. I. Title.

[WILLIAMSON, M. J.] 133.
The invisibles: an explanation of phenomena commonly called spiritual. Philadelphia, J. B. Lippincott & co., 1867. 331 p. 19 1/2 cm. [BF1251.W7] 11-3123
1. Spiritualism. I. Title.

WILLIAMSON, M. J. 133.
Modern diabolism; commonly called modern spiritualism: with new theories of light, heat, electricity, and sound. By M. J. Williamson. New York, J. Miller, 1873. vii, [9]-401 p. 19 cm. [BF1042.W7] 11-2437
1. Spiritualism. I. Title.

WILLS, Arthur J. 133.072
Life, now and forever, a summary of psychic research, its new discoveries and their meanings. Written and compiled by Arthur J. Wills ... with 8 illustrations. London, New York [etc.] Rider & co., ltd. [1942]. 184 p. plates. 22 1/2 cm. "List of valuable publications": p. 183-184. [BF1261.W57] 43-1847
1. Spiritualism. I. Title.

WILSON, Ebenezer. V. 133.
The truths of spiritualism. Immortality proved beyond a doubt by living witnesses. By E. V. Wilson ... Chicago, Hazlitt & Reed, printers, 1876. x, 11-400 p. 29 cm. [BF1251.W74] 11-3124
1. Spiritualism. I. Title.

WILSON, Henry Blauvelt, 133.
1870-1923.
Ghosts or gospels; the methods of spiritualism in healing compared with the methods of Christ, by Henry B. Wilson ... a guide to the use of our psychic powers ... Boonton, N.J., The Nazarene press, c1922. 3 p. l., 130, [2] p. 19 1/2 cm. "Bibliography and review": p. [111]-130. [BF1261.W6] 23-10034
1. Spiritualism. I. Title.

WILSON, John K. 133.
Death; the meaning and result. By John K. Wilson ... Lily Dale, N.Y., The Sunflower publishing co., 1901. xxiii, 25-559 p. front. (port.) 20 cm. [BF1301.W7] May
1. Spiritualism. I. Title.

WILSON, R. P. 133.93
...Discourses from the spirit-world, dictated by Stephen Olin, through Rev. R. P. Wilson, writing medium ... New York, Partridge and Brittan, 1853. xiii, 197 p. 19 1/2 cm.. (Partridge and Brittan's spiritual library) [BF1291.W5 1853] [159.96173] 34-14471
1. Spiritualism. I. Olin, Stepeh, 1797-1851. II. Title.

WILSON, R. P. 149
... Discourses from the spirit-world, dictated by Stephen Olin, through Rev. R. P. Wilson, writing medium ... New York, Patridge and Brittan, 1855. xii, 197 p. 18 1/2 cm. (Partridge and Brittan's spiritual library) [BF1291.W5] 27-10769
1. Spiritualism. I. Olin, Stephen, 1797-1851. II. Title.

WILTSE, May Barnard.
Theorem or teleology of spiritualism, by May Barnard Wiltse. New Rockford, N.D. [Eddy County provost] 1909. 91 p. 18 1/2 cm. 9-14070
I. Title.

WITLEY L. V. H. 133.
The ministry of the unseen; a personal experience of, and testimony to, love from beyond the veil, by L. V. H. Witley ... New York, London [etc.] Fleming H. Revell company [1926] 124 p. 19 1/2 cm. Bibliographical foot-notes. [BF1301.W77] 28-4438
1. Spiritualism. I. Title.

WOLFE, Napoleon Bonaparte. 133.9
Startling facts in modern spiritualism. by N. B. Wolfe ... Cincinnati, 1874. xxvii, 543 p. front., illus. (incl. plan, music) ports. 20 1/2 cm. [BF1251.W76] [159.9617] 34-13046
1. Spiritualism. I. Title.

WOOD, Edward Cope. 133.93
The "how" of divine revelation, its method and technique, with special reference to the Hosean communications, by Edward Cope Wood. Camden, N.J., "Pyne Poynt" [c1940] 95 p. 23 1/2 cm. [BF1275.C5W6] [159.96173] 40-8093
1. Spiritualism. I. Title.

WOOD, Edward Cope. 133.9
A personal testimony to life after death, being expierences in the worlds of spirit and of matter. Philadelphia, Dorrance [1963] 77 p. illus. 21 cm. [BF1311.F8W6] 63-20594
1. Spiritualism. 2. Future life. I. Title.

WOOD, Frederic Herbert, 133.03
1880-
This Egyptian miracle; or, The restoration of the lost speech of ancient Egypt by supernormal means, recorded and edited by Frederic H. Wood ... Philadelphia, David McKay company [1940] 6 p. l., 17-256 p. illus. (music) 19 cm. "The language spoken in partial trance by 'Rosemary' (a pseudonym) adopted by ... [a] cultured English girl) ... claims to be ... the spoken language of the people of Egypt during the XVIIIth dynasty." --p. 19. Bibliography: p.25. [BF1311.E45W6] [159.96173] 41-9160
1. Spiritualism. 2. Egyptian language. I. Title.

WOODMAN, Jabez C. 133.
A reply to William T. Dwight, D.D., on spiritualism. Three lectures. By Jabez C. Woodman ... Portland [Me.] G. R. Davis & brother; New York, C. Partridge; [etc., etc.] 1857. 83, [1] p. 22 cm. [BF1275.B5W8] 11-3425
1. Dwight, William Theodore, 1795-1865. 2. Spiritualism. 3. Bible and spiritualism. I. Title.

WOODMAN, Jabez C. 133.9
A reply to William T. Dwight, D.D., on spiritualism. Three lectures. By Jabez C. Woodman ... Stereotype ed. Boston, B. Marsh, 1858. 1 p. l., [5]-96 p. 19 1/2 cm. [BF1275.B5W8 1858] [159.9617] 34-13683
1. Dwight, William Theodore, 1795-1865. 2. Spiritualism. 3. Bible and spiritualism. I. Title.

THE work and office of the 133.
holy angels here on earth and in paradise, comp. by one who has seen and heard ... Boston, R. G. Badger [c1922] 77 p. 19 cm. [BF1301.W6] 22-14370
1. Spiritualism.

WRIGHT, Alfred Askin. 133.
Momentous memoirs, by Alfred Askin Wright ... Boston, The Christopher publishing house [c1923] 316 p. 21 cm. [BF1301.W87] 23-6520
1. Spiritualism. I. Title.

WRIGHT, Alfred Askin. 133.
Spiritual science, the universal religion, by Alfred A. Wright ... New York, A. A. Wright [c1917] x p., 1 l., 11-149 p. front. (port.) plates. 19 cm. [BF1261.W9] 17-24120
1. Spiritualism. I. Title.
Contents omitted.

WRIGHT, Alfred Askin, 133.93
1869-
Ghosts. New York, Paebar Co., 1948. 154 p. 22 cm. [BF1277.A1W7] 49-8060
1. Spiritualism. I. Title.

WRIGHT, Alfred Askin, 133.93
1869-
Invited guests, by Alfred Askin Wright ... Boston, Mass., House of Edinboro [1946] 251 p. 20 1/2 cm. [BF1301.W868] 46-19277
1. Spiritualism. I. Title.

WRIGHT, J. Clegg.
Body and soul. A course of lectures delivered in the trance state through the mediumistic organization of J. Clegg Wright. Amelia, O., J. C. Wright, 1902. x, 9-146 pp. front. (port.) 22 cm. 2-5203
1. Spiritualism. I. Title.

WRIGHT, Marcenus R. K., 133.
1830-
The only hope: or, Time reveals all. By Marcenus R. K. Wright ... Detroit, W. Graham, printer, 1877. 89 p. 18 1/2 cm. [BF1272.W8] 11-3420
1. Spiritualism. I. Title.

WRIGHT, Marcenus Rodolphus 133.
Kilpatrick, 1830-
The mastereon, or Reason and recompense, a revelation concerning the laws of mind and modern mysterious phenomena, by Marcenus R. K. Wright ... Chicago, S. S. Jones & co., 1872. xvii, [18]-259 p. front. (port.) 19 cm. [BF1251.W8] 11-3125
1. Spiritualism. I. Title.

YINGLING, Emma Katherine, 133.9
1888-
Manna. [rev. ed.] Boston, Christopher Pub. House [1951] 78 p. 21 cm. [BF1261.Y5] 51-37805
1. Spiritualism. I. Title.

YOST, Casper Salathiel, 133.
1864-
Patience Worth: a psychic mystery, by Casper S. Yost. New York, H. Holt and company, 1916. iv p., 1 l., 290 p. 19 1/2 cm. [BF1301.W865Y6] 16-5963
1. Worth, Patience. 2. Spiritualism. I. Curran, Mrs. Pearl Lenore (Pullard) 1883- II. Title.

YOUNG, James H., comp. 133.
Rules and advice for those desiring to form circles, where, thru developed media, they may commune with spirit friends. Together with a declaration of principles and belief, and hymns and songs for circle and social singing. Comp. by James H. Young... Onset, Mass., Onset publishing company, 1889. 64 p. 18 cm. On cover: Fourth thousand, revised and enlarged. [BF1286.Y6] 11-3612
1. Spiritualism. I. Title.

ZOLLNER, Johann Karl 133.9'01'5
Friedrich, 1834-1882.
Trancendental physics / Johann Carl Friedrich Zollner. New York : Arno Press, 1976. p. cm. (The Occult) Reprint of the 1888 ed. published by Colby & Rich, Boston. Translated from v. 3 of Wissenschaftliche Abhandlungen. [BF1383.Z8 1976] 75-36924 ISBN 0-405-07978-8 : 12.00
1. Spiritualism. I. Title. II. Series: The Occult (New York, 1976-)

ZOLLNER, Johann Karl 133.
Friedrich, 1834-1882.
Transcendental physics. An account of experimental investigations from the scientific treatises of Johann Carl Friedrich Zollner. Tr from the German, with a pref. and appendices, by Charles Carleton Massey. 2d ed. Boston, Colby & Rich, 1881. 218 p. illus. 19 cm. [BF1383.Z8 1881a] 48-32670
1. Spiritualism. I. Massey, Charles Carleton, tr. II. Title.

ZOLLNER, Johann Karl 133.
Friedrich, 1834-1882.
Transcendental physics. An account of experimental investigations from the scientific treatise of Johann Carl Zollner ... Tr. from the German, with a preface and appendices, by Charles Carleton Massey ... Boston, Colby & Rich, 1881. 218 p. incl. plates. front. 19 1/2 cm. [BF1383.Z8] 10-33713
1. Spiritualism. I. Massey. Charles Carleton, tr. II. Title.

ZOLLNER, Johann Karl 133.922
Friedrich, 1834-1882.
Transcendental physics. An account of experiemntal investigations from the scientific treatises of Johann Carl Friedrich Zollner ... Translated from the German, with a preface and appendices, by Charles Carleton Massey 4th ed. Boston, Banner of light publishing co., 1901. 218 p. incl. 10 pl. (1 double) front. 19 1/2 cm. [BF1383.Z8 1901] [159.961722] 34-13042
1. Spiritualism. I. Massey, Charles Carleton, tr. II. Title.

ZYMONIDAS, Allessandro. 133.
Normal and abnormal evolution, by Allessandro Zymonidas. London and Chicago, The Spiritual ray publications [1921] x, 198 p. front. 19 1/2 cm. [BF1261.Z9] 21-16731
1. Spiritualism. I. Title.

Spiritualism—Addresses, essays, lectures.

EBON, Martin, comp. 133'.08
The psychic reader. New York, World Pub. Co. [1969] xiii, 226 p. 22 cm. [BF1261.2.E2] 69-18535 4.95
1. Spiritualism—Addresses, essays, lectures. I. Title.

HALFYARD, Samuel Follet, 1871-
The spiritual basis of man and nature, by Samuel F. Halfyard ... Chncinnati, Jennings and Graham; New York, Eaton and mains [c1909] 252 p. 20 cm. $1.00 "The essays which compose this volume have grown out of talks to college students."--Pref. 9-22197
I. Title.

Spiritualism—Africa—Bibliography.

ZARETSKY, Irving I. 016.1339'09'6
Bibliography on spirit possession and spirit mediumship. Comp. by Irving I. Zaretsky. Berkeley. Dept. of Anthrop. Univ. of Calif. [1967, c1966] xvi, 106p. 28cm. [Z6879.A3Z3] 66-26923 3.75 pap.,
1. Spritualism—Africa—Bibl. 2. Occult sciences—Africa—Bibl. I. Title.

ZARETSKY, Irving I. 016.1339'096
Spirit possession and spirit mediumship in Africa and Afro-America : an annotated bibliography / Irving I. Zaretsky, Cynthia Shambaugh. New York : Garland Pub., 1978. xxii, 443 p. ; 23 cm. (Garland reference library of social science ; v. 56) Previous ed. published in 1966 under title: Bibliography on spirit possession and spirit mediumship. [Z6878.S8Z36 1978] [BF1242.A35] 78-4181 ISBN 0-8240-9823-4 : 30.00
1. Spiritualism—Africa—Bibliography. 2. Spiritualism—America—Bibliography. I. Shambaugh, Cynthia, joint author. II. Title.

Spiritualism—Bibliography

LOVI, Henrietta. 016.
Best books on spirit phenomena, 1847-1925; notes describing representative volumes; belief--unbelief--disbelief [by] Henrietta Loui. Boston, R. G. Badger [c1925] 94 p. 22 cm. "Selected bibliography of spirit phenomena": p. 89-90. [Z6878.S8L9] 25-24685
1. Spiritualism—Bibl. I. Title.

Spiritualism—Biography.

COPPER, Arnold. 133.9'092'6
Psychic summer / Arnold Copper and Coralee Leon. New York : Dial Press, 1976. 184 p. ; 24 cm. [BF1283.C823A36] 76-40420 ISBN 0-8037-7182-7 : 7.95
1. Copper, Arnold. 2. Spiritualism—Biography. I. Leon, Coralee, joint author. II. Title.

COPPER, Arnold. 133.9'092'6
Psychic summer / Arnold Copper and Coralee Leon. New York : Dell Pub. Co., 1977c1976. 250p. ; 18 cm. (A Dell Book) [BF1283.C823A36] ISBN 0-440-17166-0 pbk. : 1.95
1. Copper, Arnold. 2. Spiritualism-Biography. I. Leon, Coralee, joint author. II. Title.
L.C. card no. for 1976 Dial Press ed.:76-40420.

Spiritualism—Brazil.

ST. Clair, David. 133.9
Drum and candle. [1st ed.] Garden City, N.Y., Doubleday, 1971. 304 p. illus. 22 cm. [BF1261.2.S25] 79-131103 6.95
1. Spiritualism—Brazil. 2. Umbanda (Cultus) I. Title.

Spiritualism—Case studies.

JAY, Carroll E. 133.9'092'6
Gretchen, I am / Carroll E. Jay ; introd. by Ian Stevenson. 1st ed. New York : Wyden Books : trade distribution by Simon and Schuster, c1977. xv, 304 p. ; 21 cm. Bibliography: p. [303]-304. [BF1353.J39] 77-13784 8.95
1. Jay, Carroll E. 2. Jay, Dolores. 3. Spiritualism—Case studies. 4. Xenoglossy—Case studies. 5. Hypnotism—Case studies. I. Title.

JAY, Carroll E. 133.9'092'6
Gretchen, I am / Carroll E. Jay ; introd. by Ian Stevenson. 1st ed. New York : Avon Books, 1979, c1977. 288p. ; 18 cm. Bibliography:p. 287-288. [BF1353.J39] ISBN 0-380-42820-2 pbk. : 2.25
1. Jay, Carroll. 2. Jay, Dolores. 3. Spiritualism — case studies. 4. Xenoglossy — Case studies. 5. Hypnotism — Case studies. I. Title.
L.C.card no. for 1977 Wyden Books ed.:77-13784.

LONDON Dialectical Society. 133.9
Report on spiritualism of the committee of the London Dialectical Society. New York : Arno Press, 1976. p. cm. (The Occult) Reprint of the 1871 ed. published by Longmans, Green, Reader and Dyer, London. [BF1029.L82 1976] 75-36849 ISBN 0-405-07965-6 : 24.00

1. Spiritualism—Case studies. I. Title. II. Series: The Occult (New York, 1976-)

Spiritualism—Controversial literature.

DAVENPORT, Reuben Briggs. 133.9
The death-blow to spiritualism / Reuben Briggs Davenport. New York : Arno Press, 1976. p. cm. (The Occult) Reprint of the 1888 ed. published by G. W. Dillingham, New York, under title: The death-blow to spiritualism: being the true story of the Fox sisters, as revealed by authority of Margaret Fox Kane and Catherine Fox Jencken. [BF1042.D28 1976] 75-36836 14.00
1. Kane, Margaret (Fox) 1836-1893. 2. Jencken, Catherine (Fox) 1839-1892. 3. Spiritualism—Controversial literature. I. Title. II. Series: The Occult (New York, 1976-)

ERNEST, Victor H. 133.9
I talked with spirits [by] Victor H. Ernest. Wheaton, Ill., Tyndale House Publishers [1970] 89 p. 22 cm. [BF1042.E7] 78-112665 ISBN 0-8423-1550-0 2.95
1. Spiritualism—Controversial literature. 2. Demonology. I. Title.

[FARRINGTON, Elijah] 133.9
Revelations of a spirit medium / [edited by] Harry Price and Eric J. Dingwall. New York : Arno Press, 1975. p. cm. (Perspectives in psychical research) Written by E. Farrington and C. F. Pidgeon. Reprint of the 1922 ed. published by K. Paul, Trench, Trubner, London, and E. P. Dutton, New York. Bibliography: p. [BF1042.F3 1975] 75-7395 ISBN 0-405-07044-6 : 22.00
1. Spiritualism—Controversial literature. I. Price, Harry, 1881-1948. II. Dingwall, Eric John. III. Pidgeon, Charles F., joint author. IV. Title. V. Series.

HOME, Daniel Dunglas, Mrs. 133.9
D. D. Home, his life and mission / Mme. Dunglas Home. New York : Arno Press, 1976. p. cm. (The Occult) Reprint of the 1888 ed. published by Trubner & Co., London. [BF1027.H65H6 1976] 75-36844 ISBN 0-405-07956-7 : 24.00
1. Home, Daniel Dunglas, 1833-1886. 2. Spiritualism—Controversial literature. I. Title. II. Series: The Occult (New York, 1976-)

HOUDINI, Harry, 1874-1926. 133.9
A magician among the spirits. New York, Arno Press, 1972 [c1924] xix, 294 p. illus. 24 cm. [BF1042.H6 1972] 71-140606 ISBN 0-405-02801-6 15.00
1. Spiritualism—Controversial literature. I. Title.

†HULL, Burling. 133.9
The billion dollar bait / by Burling "Volta" Hull ; edited by A. Joseph Candalino. Deland, Fla. : Volcanda Associates, c1977. 205 p. : ill. ; 23 cm. [BF1042.H76] 78-101007 pbk. : 6.50
1. Spiritualism—Controversial literature. I. Candalino, A. Joseph. II. Title.
Publisher's address: Rte. 4, Box 632, Deland, FL 32720 Publisher's address: Rte. 4, Box 632, Deland, FL 32720

KEENE, M. Lamar. 133.9'1'0924 B
The psychic Mafia / by M. Lamar Keene, as told to Spraggett, with a foreword by William V. Rauscher. New York : St. Martin's Press, c1976. 177 p. : ill. ; 22 cm. Bibliography: p. 165-177. [BF1042.K28] 75-40793 7.95
1. Keene, M. Lamar. 2. Spiritualism—Controversial literature. I. Spraggett, Allen, joint author. II. Title.

MATTISON, Hiram, 1811-1868. 133.
Spirit-rapping unveiled! An expose of the origin, history, theology and philosophy of certain alleged communications from the spirit world, by means of spirit rapping, medium writing, physical demonstrations, etc. A new ed. with an appendix, containing replies to Professor Brittan and the Tribune, and reviews of the explanatory theories of Rev. Dr. Pond, Dr. Rogers, Rev. Abel Stevens, Rev. James Porter, Rev. Charles Beecher, Dr. Dods, Professor Faraday, etc. New York, J. C. Derby, 1855. 240 p. illus. 20 cm. [BF1042.M38 1855] 50-41205
1. Spiritualism—Controversial literature. I. Title.

THE Mediums and the 133.9
conjurors / with an introd. by James Webb. New York : Arno Press, 1976. p. cm. (The Occult) Reprint of Modern spiritualism, by J. N. Maskelyne, first published in 1876 by F. Warne, London; of Expose of the Davenport brothers, by Herr Dobler, first printed in 1869 by D. & J. Allen, Belfast; and of Spirit-mediums and conjurors, by G. Sexton, first published in 1873 by J. Burns, London. [BF1042.M46 1976] 75-36909 ISBN 0-405-07967-2 : 18.00
1. Davenport, Ira Erastus, 1839-1911. 2. Davenport, William Henry, 1841-1877. 3. Spiritualism—Controversial literature. 4. Spiritualism. 5. Conjuring. I. Maskelyne, John Nevil, 1839-1917. Modern spiritualism. 1976. II. Dobler, Herr. Expose of the Davenport brothers. 1976. III. Sexton, George. Spirit-mediums and conjurors. 1976. IV. Series.

PROSKAUER, Julien J., 1893- 133.9
1958.
Spook crooks! Exposing the secrets of the prophet-eers who conduct our wickedest industry. Profusely illustrated by James and Howard Savage. New York, A. L. Burt Co. Ann Arbor, Mich., Gryphon Books, 1971 [c1932] 300 p. illus., port. 22 cm. [BF1042.P84 1971] 70-162517
1. Spiritualism—Controversial literature. 2. Swindlers and swindling. I. Title.

UNGER, Merrill Frederick, 133.9
1909-
The haunting of Bishop Pike; a Christian view of The other side [by] Merrill F. Unger. Wheaton, Ill., Tyndale House Publishers [1971] 115 p. 22 cm. Includes bibliographical references. [BF1042.U5 1971] 76-144329 ISBN 0-8423-1340-0 2.95
1. Pike, James Albert, Bp., 1913-1969. 2. Pike, James Albert, Bp., 1913-1969. The other side. 3. Spiritualism—Controversial literature. I. Title.

WHELPLEY, Theresa A. 133.9
Unmasking the spirits / Theresa A. Whelpley. Washington : Review and Herald Pub. Association, 1978. 77 p. ; 19 cm. [BF1042.W55] 76-53273 pbk. : 0.85
1. Spiritualism—Controversial literature. I. Title.

Spiritualism—Dictionaries.

BLUNSDON, Norman. 133.903
A popular dictionary of spiritualism. [1st American ed.] New York, Citadel Press [1963] 255, [1] p. 20 cm. Bibliography: p. 237-[256] [BF1025.B58] 63-16730
1. Spiritualism — Dictionaries. I. Title.

WEDECK, Harry Ezekiel, 133'.03
1894-
Dictionary of spiritualism, by Harry E. Wedeck. New York, Philosophical Library [1971] vi, 390 p. 22 cm. [BF1025.W4] 73-104365 ISBN 0-8022-2039-8 10.00
1. Spiritualism—Dictionaries. I. Title.

Spiritualism—Drama.

NICKERSON, Converse Ennis. 133.
"The birth of modern spiritualism" (the message of Hydesville) A drama in three acts, by Converse E. Nickerson ... Wakefield, Mass., Camden publishing company, printers. c1937. 20 p. 20 1/2 cm. [BF1272.N5] 45-44699
1. Spiritualism—Drama. I. Title.

Spiritualism—Fiction.

JOHNSON, George Lindsay, 1854-
The weird adventures of Professor Delapine of the Sorbonne, by George Lindsay Johnson ... London, G. Routledge & sons, limited; New York, E. P. Dutton and co.; [etc., etc.] 1916. xii, 344 p. 19 cm. A22
1. Spiritualism—Fiction. I. Title.

Spiritualism—Florida—Cassadaga.

HARROLD, Robert, 133.9'09759'21
1951-
Cassadaga : an inside look at the South's oldest psychic community : with true experiences of people who have been there / by Robert Harrold ; [line drawings by Evelyn Fatigati]. Miami : Banyan Books, c1979. p. cm. Bibliography: p. [BF1242.U6H37] 79-20718 ISBN 0-916224-49-X pbk. : 3.95
1. Spiritualism—Florida—Cassadaga. 2. Cassadaga, Fla.—History. I. Title.

Spiritualism—History.

BRITTEN, Emma Hardinge, 133.9
d.1899.
Nineteenth century miracles : or, Spirits and their work in every country of the earth / Emma Hardinge Britten. New York : Arno Press, 1976. p. cm. (The Occult) Reprint of the 1884 ed. published by W. Britten, New York. [BF1241.B72 1976] 75-36831 ISBN 0-405-07943-5 : 33.00
1. Spiritualism—History. I. Title. II. Series: The Occult (New York, 1976-)

DOYLE, Arthur Conan, 133.9'09
Sir, 1859-1930.
The history of spiritualism / Arthur Conan Doyle. New York : Arno Press, 1975, c1926. p. cm. (Perspectives in psychical research) Reprint of the 2 v. ed. published by G. H. Doran Co., New York. [BF1241.D6 1975] 75-7375 ISBN 0-405-07025-X : 18.00
1. Spiritualism—History. I. Title. II. Series.

JACKSON, Herbert 133.9'2'0922 B
G.
The spirit rappers [by] Herbert G. Jackson, Jr. [1st ed.] Garden City, N.Y., Doubleday, 1972. 226 p. 22 cm. Bibliography: p. [221]-226. [BF1283.F7J33] 71-171300 6.95
1. Jencken, Catherine Fox, 1836-1892. 2. Fox, Margaret, 1833-1893. 3. Underhill, Ann Leah, 1814-1890. 4. Spiritualism—History. I. Title.

STOBART, Mabel Annie 133.9'09
(Boulton) 1862-1954.
Torchbearers of spiritualism, by Mrs. St. Clair Stobart. Port Washington, N.Y., Kennikat Press [1971] 231 p. front. 22 cm. Reprint of the 1925 ed. Bibliography: p. 230-231. [BF1241.S8 1971] 70-118550
1. Spiritualism—History. I. Title.

Spiritualism—Juvenile literature.

ANDREAE, Christine. 133.9
Seances & spiritualists. [1st ed.] Philadelphia, Lippincott [1974] 157 p. illus. 21 cm. (The Weird and horrible library) Bibliography: p. 151-153. Describes the various aspects of spiritualism and some of its more famous practitioners. [BF1261.2.A5] 74-8044 ISBN 0-397-31555-4 5.15; 1.95 (pbk.)
1. Spiritualism—Juvenile literature. 2. [Spiritualism.] I. Title.

Spiritualism—Language.

PRATT, Joseph 133.9'1'014
Gaither, 1910-
On the evaluation of verbal material in parapsychology [by] J. G. Pratt. New York, Parapsychology Foundation [1969] 78 p. 23 cm. (Parapsychological monographs, no. 10) Bibliographical footnotes. [BF1311.L25P7] 70-94866
1. Spiritualism—Language. I. Title. II. Series.

Spiritualism—Mediumship.

THEMASCUS, Hazel G. 133.91
My mystic beam discloses. New York, Vantage Press [c.1961] 146p. 3.00 bds.,
1. Spiritualism—Mediumship. 2. Clairvoyance. I. Title.

Spiritualism Mirror-writing.

TAYLOR, William George 920.9
Langworthy, 1859-
Katie Fox, epochmaking medium and the making of the Fox-Taylor record, by W. G. Langworthy Taylor ... New York, London, G. P. Putnam's sons, 1933. xxv p., 1 l., 29-326 p. front., plates, ports., plan, facsims. 22 1/2 cm. [BF1283.F7T3] 33-30688
1. Jencken, Mrs. Catherine (Fox) 1839-1892. 2. Spiritualism s Mirror-writing I. Title. II. Title: Fox-Taylor record.

Spiritualism—Miscellanea.

†HARBER, Francis, 1913- 133.9
The soul and life after death : questions and answers / by Francis Harber. 1st ed. Brooklyn, N.Y. : T. Gaus, c1977. x, 112 p. ; 23 cm. [BF1272.H245] 77-84782 12.00
1. Spiritualism—Miscellanea. 2. Spirits—Miscellanea. 3. Future life—Miscellanea. I. Title.
Publisher's address: 30 Prince St.,Brooklyn, NY 11201

Spiritualism—Periodicals

GALLERY of spirit art;
an illustrated magazine devoted to and illustrative of spirit photography, spirit painting, the photographing of materialized forms and every form of spirit art. Aug. 1882-Nov. 1883. Brooklyn, C. R. Miller. 112 p. illus., ports. 26 cm. Subtitle varies. No more published? [BF1001.G34] 49-36029
1. Spiritualism—Period.

[HOUTS, Margaret J. Mrs.] 1838-

Voices from the open door. v. 1- Cleveland, O., [The Open door publishing company] c1912- v. 17 cm. Caption title. Vol. 1 also issued in 12 parts. "This...is a plain narration of facts as related by reliable, intelligent people that have liad off their natural bodies and passed into the inner world."--Pref., v. 1. [BF1001.V6] 20-5317
1. Spiritualism—Period. I. Title.

THE Sacred circle.
Editors: Judge Edmonds, Dr. Dexter, O. G. Warren ... New York, Partridge & Brittan, 1855- v. fronts. (ports.) 22 cm. I. C. Copy imperfect? Title-page of v. 2 wanting? [BF1001.S35] 47-33342
1. Spiritualism—Period. I. Edmonds, John Wroth, 1799-1874, ed. II. Dexter, George T., joint ed. III. Warren, Owen Grenliffe, joint ed.

... The Spiritual 289.
telegraph. Ed. by S. B. Britain. New series ... New York, Partridge & Brittan, 1853-57. 9 v. 19 cm. (Partridge and Brittan's spiritual library) Vol. IX has title: ... The Telegraph papers. Ed. by S. B. Brittan. New York, C. Partridge, 1857. (Charles Partridge's spiritual library) A compilation of "all the more interesting articles" which appeared in the weekly journal of the same name. cf. Publishers' announcement in vol. I. Vols. I-VIII were issued quarterly. [BF1235.S7] 10-32978
1. Spiritualism—Period. I. Brittan, Samuel Byron, ed.

... Spiritualist register,
with a calendar and speakers' almanac ... Facts, philosophy, statistics (!) of spiritualism. U. Clark, ed. ... Auburn, N.Y., U. Clark; [etc., etc., 18 v. 14 1/2 cm. annual. CA 7
I. Clark, Uriah, ed.

Spiritualism—Psychic phenomena.

CAMPBELL, Anna Zimdars, 133.93
1875-
Dearest mother: letters from a departed son. New York, Exposition Press, [c.1961] 60p. 2.50
1. Spiritualism—Psychic phenomena. I. Title.

Spiritualism—Puerto Rico.

MORALESDORTA, Jose. 133.9
Puerto Rican espiritismo : religion and psychotherapy / Jose Morales-Dorta. 1st ed. New York : Vantage Press, c1976. 106 p. : ill. ; 22 cm. Includes bibliographical references. [BF1242.P9M67] 76-368299 ISBN 0-533-01721-1 : 4.95
1. Spiritualism—Puerto Rico. 2. Spiritualism—New York (City) 3. Puerto Ricans in New York (City) I. Title.

Spiritualism—Study and teaching.

NATIONAL spiritualist 133.9
association.
Spiritualist lyceum manual, for use in spiritualist progressive lyceums, compiled

from various sources by Verna K. Kuhlig, national superintendent, Bureau of lyceums, of the National spiritualist association. Washington, D.C., National spiritualist association of the United States of America [1944] 245, [9] p. front., pl., ports. 19 cm. "Suggested literature": p. 173, 245. [BF1272.N3] 44-47710
1. Spiritualism—Study and teaching. I. Kuhlig, Verna K., comp. II. Title.

Spiritualism Supernatural.

GASPARIN, Agenor Etienne comte de 1810-1871.
Science vs. modern spiritualism. A treatise on turning tables, the supernatural in general, and spirits. Tr. from the French Count Agenor de Gasparin by E. W. Robert with an introduction by Rev. Robert Baird New York Kiggins & Kellogg, 1857. 2 v. 20 cm. [BF1232.G25] 11-3129
1. Spiritualism sSupernatural 2. Supernatural I. Robert E. W., tr. II. Title.

Spiritualism—United States.

BRITTEN, Emma (Hardinge) d.1899. 133.9'0973
Modern American spiritualism; a twenty years' record of the communion between earth and the world of spirits. New introd. by E. J. Dingwall. New Hyde Park, N.Y., University Books [1970] xviii, 565 p. illus., ports. 25 cm. Reprint of the 3d ed. published in 1870. [BF1241.B7 1970] 78-129514 12.50
1. Spiritualism—U.S. I. Title.

BROWN, Slater, 1896- 133.9'0973
The heyday of spiritualism. New York, Hawthorn Books [1970] 264 p. illus. 24 cm. Bibliography: p. [249]-256. [BF1241.B75] 71-109094 6.95
1. Spiritualism—U.S. I. Title.

HOLZER, Hans W., 1920- 133.9
The spirits of '76 : a psychic inquiry into the American Revolution / Hans Holzer. Indianapolis : Bobbs-Merrill, c1976. xi, 177 p. ; 22 cm. [BF1311.U5H64] 76-24401 ISBN 0-672-51884-8 : 7.95
1. Spiritualism—United States. 2. Ghosts—United States. 3. United States—History—Revolution, 1775-1783—Miscellanea. I. Title.

Spiritualism—United States—History.

MOORE, Robert Laurence. 133
In search of white crows : spiritualism, parapsychology, and American culture / R. Laurence Moore. New York : Oxford University Press, 1977. p. cm. Includes index. Bibliography: p. [BF1242.U6M66] 76-51720 ISBN 0-19-502259-9 : 11.95
1. Spiritualism—United States—History. 2. Psychical research—United States—History. I. Title.

Spiritualism—United States—Juvenile literature.

RASKIN, Joseph. 133.9'024'054
Strange shadows : spirit tales of early America / Joseph and Edith Raskin ; illustrated by William Sauts Bock. New York : Lothrop, Lee & Shepard Co., c1977. 128 p. : ill. ; 22 cm. Bibliography: p. [127]-128. The experiences of the Fox sisters, Mollie Fancher, Nettie Colburn, and others who seemed to be in contact with the spirit world in eighteenth- and nineteenth-century America. [BF1242.U6R37] 76-54515 ISBN 0-688-41795-7 : 5.75 ISBN 0-688-51795-1 lib.bdg. : 4.99
1. Spiritualism—United States—Juvenile literature. 2. [Spiritualism.] I. Raskin, Edith, joint author. II. Bock, William Sauts, 1939- III. Title.

Spiritualism—Wales.

SKULTANS, Vieda. 133.9'09429
Intimacy and ritual; a study of spiritualism, mediums and groups. London, Boston, Routledge & K. Paul [1974] vii, 106 p. 22 cm. Bibliography: p. 101-104. [BF1261.2.S56] 73-87318 ISBN 0-7100-7760-2 8.25
1. Spiritualism—Wales. I. Title.

Spiritualism—Year-books.

NATIONAL spiritualist association. 289.
Year book of the National spiritualist association of the United States of America ... Washington, D. C., National spiritualist association. v. ports. 16 cm. [BX9798.S7A16] 40-16569
1. Spiritualism—Year-books. I. Title.

THE Year-book of spiritualism for 1871. Presenting the status of spiritualism for the current year throughout the world; philosophical, scientific, and religious essays; review of its literature; history of American associations; state and local societies; progressive lyceums; lecturers, mediums; and other matters relating to the momentous subject. By Hudson Tuttle and J. M. Peebles. Boston, W. White and company; [etc., etc.] 1871. 246 p. 21 1/2 cm. [BF1001.Y4] 11-5299
1. Spiritualism—Year-books. I. Tuttle, Hudson, 1836-1910, ed. II. Peebles, James Martin, 1822-1922, joint ed.

Spiritualists—Connecticut—Biography.

LEVETT, Carl David. 133.9'2
Crossings : a transpersonal approach / Carl D. Levett. 2d ed. West Dennis, Mass. : C. Stark, [1977] c1974. p. cm. [BF1283.L43A32 1977] 76-51798 ISBN 0-89007-401-1 : 8.50. ISBN 0-89007-402-X pbk. : 4.50
1. Levett, Carl David. 2. Spiritualists—Connecticut—Biography. 3. Spiritualism. I. Title.

Spiritualists—Florida—Biography.

CLARK, Clare A. 133
Psychic adventures and the unseen world / [by Clare A. Clark]. St. Petersburg, Fla. : Valkyrie Press, c1977. 122 p. ; 22 cm. [BF1283.C548A36] 76-42918 ISBN 0-912760-33-8 pbk. : 3.50
1. Clark, Clare A. 2. Spiritualists—Florida—Biography. I. Title.

Spiritualists—United States—Biography.

CHAPLIN, Annabel. 133.9'013'0926 B
The bright light of death / by Annabel Chaplin. Marina del Rey, Calif. : DeVorss, c1977. xii, 133 p. ; 22 cm. [BF1283.C485A33] 77-75169 ISBN 0-87516-230-4 pbk. : 3.00
1. Chaplin, Annabel. 2. Spiritualists—United States—Biography. I. Title.

JONES, Amanda Theodocia, 1835-1914. 133.9'1'0924 B
A psychic autobiography / Amanda T. Jones. New York : Arno Press, 1980, c1910. p. cm. (Signal lives) Reprint of the ed. published by Greaves Pub. Co., New York. [BF1283.J7A3 1980] 79-8798 ISBN 0-405-12845-2 : 42.00
1. Jones, Amanda Theodocia, 1835-1914. 2. Spiritualists—United States—Biography. I. Title. II. Series.

WHITFIELD, Joseph. 133.9'3
The treasure of El Dorado : featuring "the Dawn Breakers" / by Joseph Whitfield. Washington : Occidental Press, 1977. 213 p. : ill. ; 22 cm. [BF1283.W543A37] 77-89125 ISBN 0-911050-44-2 : 8.95
1. Whitfield, Joseph. 2. Spiritualists—United States—Biography. I. Title.

Spiritualists—United States—Biography—Juvenile literature.

EDMONDS, I. G. 133.9'1'0922
The girls who talked to ghosts : the story of Katie and Margaretta Fox / by I. G. Edmonds. New York : Holt, Rinehart, and Winston, c1979. 160 p. : ill. ; 22 cm. Includes index. Bibliography: p. [151]-156. A biography, with emphasis on the early years, of the Fox sisters who claimed to communicate with ghosts. Their experiences led to the founding of the Spiritualist movement. [BF1283.F7E35] 920 B 78-14089 ISBN 0-03-042691-X : 6.95
1. Jencken, Catherine Fox, 1836-1892—Juvenile literature. 2. Fox, Margaret, 1833-1893—Juvenile literature. 3. [Jencken, Catherine Fox, 1836-1892.] 4. [Fox, Margaret, 1833-1893.] 5. Spiritualists—United States—Biography—Juvenile literature. 6. Spiritualism—History—Juvenile literature. 7. [Spiritualists.] I. Title.

Spirituality.

ALEKSANDR Mikhailovich grand duke of Russia, 1866-1933. 248
Spiritual education, by Alexander, grand duke of Russia. New York, N.Y. Lucis publishing company, 1930. 4 p. l., 11-104 p. 18 1/2 cm. [BV4510.A365] 30-24104
1. Spirituality. 2. Soul. 3. Spiritual life. I. Title.

ALLCHIN, A. M. 248
The world is a wedding : explorations in Christian spirituality / by A. M. Allchin. New York : Oxford University Press, 1978. p. cm. Includes index. [BV4501.2.A38] 78-16888 ISBN 0-19-520079-9 : 7.95
1. Spirituality. I. Title.

AUMANN, Jordan. 248
Christian spirituality East & West [by] Jordan Aumann, Thomas Hopko [and] Donald G. Bloesch. Chicago, Priory Press [1968] 203 p. 23 cm. (Institute of Spirituality. Special lectures, v. 3, 1967) Includes bibliographical references. [BV4509.5.A9] 68-29598 5.95
1. Spirituality. I. Hopko, Thomas. II. Bloesch, Donald G., 1928- III. Title. IV. Series.

AUMANN, Jordan. 248.4
Spiritual theology / Jordan Aumann. Huntington, Ind. : Our Sunday Visitor ; London : Sheed & Ward, c1980. 456 p. ; 23 cm. Includes bibliographical references and index. [BX2350.2.A83] 19 79-88516 ISBN 0-87973-588-0 pbk. : 18.95
1. Spirituality. 2. Spiritual life—Catholic authors. I. Title.

BERDIAEV, Nikolai Aleksandrovich, 1874-1948. 128
The realm of spirit and the realm of Caesar / by Nicolas Berdyaev ; translated by Donald A. Lowrie. Westport, Conn. : Greenwood Press, 1975, c1952. 182 p. ; 22 cm. Reprint of the 1953 ed. published by Harper, New York. Translation of TSarstvo dukha i tsarstvo kesaria. Reprint of the 1953 ed. published by Harper, New York. [B4238.B43T83 1975] 74-1554 ISBN 0-8371-7395-7 lib.bdg. : 10.75
1. Spirituality. 2. Civilization—Philosophy. 3. Socialism. I. Title.

BOSCH, David Jacobus. 266'.023
A spirituality of the road / David J. Bosch ; introd. by Cornelius J. Dyck. Scottdale, Pa. : Herald Press, 1979. 92 p. ; 20 cm. (Missionary studies ; no. 6) Includes bibliographical references. [BV4501.2.B648] 79-10856 ISBN 0-8361-1889-8 : 3.95
1. Bible. N.T. 2 Corinthians—Criticism, interpretation, etc. 2. Spirituality. 3. Missionaries. I. Title. II. Series.

BRUNTON, Paul. 248
A message from Arunachala, by Paul Brunton ... New York, E. P. Dutton & co., inc. [c1936] 223 p. incl. front. 20 cm. "First edition." [BV4501.B7568] 36-18691
1. Spirituality. I. Title. II. Title: Arunachala, A message from.

CORBISHLEY, Thomas. 230'.2'0924
The spirituality of Teilhard de Chardin. Paramus, N.J., Paulist Press [1971] 126 p. 18 cm. Includes bibliographical references. [B2430.T374C63 1971b] 72-78440 1.45
1. Teilhard de Chardin, Pierre. 2. Spirituality. I. Title.

FOX, Matthew, 1940- 291.4'2
Whee! We, wee, all the way home : a guide to the new sensual spirituality / by Matthew Fox. [Wilmington, N.C.] : Consortium, c1976. xiv, 226 p. : ill. ; 23 cm. Bibliography: p. 216-217. [BV4501.2.F67] 76-19775 ISBN 0-8434-0606-2 : 10.00
1. Spirituality. 2. Ecstasy. I. Title.

GUIBERT, Joseph de. 248
The theology of the spiritual life; translated by Paul Barrett. New York, Sheed and Ward, 1953. 382p. 22cm. Translation of Theologia spiritualis, ascetica et mystica. [BX2350.G7913] 53-9804
1. Spirituality. 2. Asceticism—Catholic Church. 3. Mysticism—Catholic Church. I. Title.

HOLLAND, Jack H., 1922- 233
Man's victorious spirit; how to release the victory within you, by Jack H. Holland. Monterey, Calif., Hudson-Cohan Pub. Co., 1971. 127 p. 23 cm. [BV4501.2.H54] 76-179668 ISBN 0-87852-001-5 2.95
1. Spirituality. I. Title.

KEATING, Thomas. 248.3'4
The heart of the world : a spiritual catechism / Thomas Keating, as told to John Osborne. New York : Crossroad, 1981. 82 p. ; 22 cm. Bibliography: p. 81-82. [BV4501.2.K37] 19 81-684 ISBN 0-8245-0014-8 : 8.95
1. Spirituality. 2. Contemplation. I. Osborne, John 1952- II. Title.

LITTLEFAIR, Duncan Elliot, 1912- 233
The glory within you: modern man and the spirit, by Duncan E. Littlefair. Philadelphia, Westminster Press [1973] 218 p. 22 cm. Includes bibliographical references. [BV4501.2.L56] 72-8972 ISBN 0-664-20960-2
1. Spirituality. I. Title.

MACGOWAN, Robert. 248
The making of the spiritual mind, by Robert MacGowan. ... New York [etc.] Fleming H. Revell company [c1940] 127 p. 19 1/2 cm. [BV4501.M266] 40-4986
1. Spirituality. I. Title.

MACGOWAN, Robert. 248
Roads to reality, by Robert MacGowan ... New York [etc.] Fleming H. Revell company [c1941] 122 p. 19 1/2 cm. [BV4501.M267] 41-8459
1. Spirituality. I. Title.

MASSON, Thomas Lansing, 1866-1934. 220
Why I am a spiritual vagabond, by Thomas L. Masson. New York and London, The Century co. [c1925] xvi, 351 p. 19 1/2 cm. [BR125.M472] 25-7868
1. Spirituality. I. Title.

MEEHAN, Francis Joseph Gallagher, 1881- 133
The temple of the spirit. [1st ed.) New York, E. P. Dutton, 1948. 183 p. 22 cm. [BJ1493.M4] 48-1011
1. Spirituality. I. Title.

MULLER, Robert. 261.8
New Genesis : shaping a global spirituality / Robert Muller. 1st ed. Garden City, N.Y. : Doubleday, 1982. xvii, 192 p. ; 22 cm. [BV4501.2.M76 1982] 19 81-43925 ISBN 0-385-18123-X : 14.95
1. Spirituality. I. Title.

SCHAEFFER, Francis August. 248'.4
True spirituality [by] Francis A. Schaeffer. Wheaton, Ill., Tyndale House Publishers [1971] 180 p. 22 cm. [BV4501.2.S285] 73-183269 ISBN 0-8423-7350-0 ISBN 0-8423-7351-9 (pbk.) 3.50
1. Spirituality. I. Title.

SEWARD, Theodore Frelinghuysen, 1835-1902. 220
Spiritual knowing; or, Bible sunshine; the spiritual gospel of Jesus the Christ. By Theodore F. Seward ... New York and London, Funk & Wagnalls company, 1901. xi, 155 p. 19 1/2 cm. [BR125.S42] 1-29572
1. Spirituality. I. Title.

SIMPSON, William Gayley, 1892- 248
Toward the rising sun, by William Gayley Simpson; with a biographical sketch by Jerome Davis. New York, The Vanguard press [c1935] 122 p. port. 19 1/2 cm. "For further reading": p. 111-122. [BV4501.S56] 35-3213
1. Spirituality. 2. Idealism. I. Davis, Jerome, 1891- II. Title.

THE Spirituality of Western Christendom / introd. by Jean Leclerq : edited by E. Rozanne Elder. Kalamazoo : 230

Published for the Medieval Institute & the Institute of Cisterian Studies, Western Michigan University, [by] Cisterian Publications, 1976. xxxv, 217 p. ; 23 cm. (Cistercian studies series ; no. 30) "A special volume of the series: Studies in medieval culture." Includes bibliographical references. [BV4490.S73] 76-22615 ISBN 0-87907-987-8 pbk. : 7.95
1. Spirituality. I. Elder, Ellen Rozanne. II. Studies in medieval culture. III. Series.

STUART, Janet Erskine, 1857-1914. 248
Highways and by-ways in the spiritual life, by Janet E. Stuart, with a preface by His Eminence Cardinal Bourne ... ed. by M. Monahan. London, New York [etc.] Longmans, Green and co., 1923. viii, 210 p. 19 cm. [BX2350.S7] 23-18113
I. Monahan, Maud, ed. II. Title.

TOZER, Aiden Wilson, 1897- 248
The pursuit of God; introd. by Samuel M. Zwemer. Harrisburg, Pa., Christian Publications [1948] 128 p. 20 cm. [BV4817.T6] 48-28189
1. Spirituality. 2. God—Worship and love. I. Title.

WADDELL, David, 1811-
The stability of the covenant of grace, and other poems. By David Waddell. New York, 1881. xii, 232 p. 17 1/2 cm. [PS3129.W15] 31-14591
1. Spirituality. I. Title.

WAKEFIELD, Gordon Stevens. 248
The life of the spirit in the world of today, [by] Gordon S. Wakefield. [New York] Macmillan [1969] xi, 176 p. 18 cm. Bibliographical footnotes. [BV4501.2.W28] 69-10929
1. Spirituality. I. Title.

YOUTZ, Herbert Alden, 1867- 270
The supremacy of the spiritual; essays toward the understanding and attainment of spiritual personality. By Herbert Alden Youtz... New York, The Macmillan company, 1924. 183 p. 20 cm. [BR125.Y65] 24-25198
1. Spirituality. I. Title.

Spirituality—Addresses, essays, lectures.

THE Concrete Christian life. 248.4
Edited by Christian Duquoc. [New York] Herder and Herder [1971] 154 p. 23 cm. (Concilium: theology in the age of renewal. Spirituality, v. 69) On cover: The New concilium: religion in the seventies. Includes bibliographical references. [BV4501.2.C647] 78-168653 2.95
1. Spirituality—Addresses, essays, lectures. I. Duquoc, Christian, ed. II. Series: Concilium (New York) v. 69.

THE Journey of Western spirituality 248.2
/ edited by A.W. Sadler. Chico, Calif. : Scholars Press, c1981. xii, 222 p. ; 24 cm. (The Annual publication of the College Theology Society (1980)) Includes bibliographical references. [BV4501.2.J673] 19 81-5831 ISBN 0-89130-506-8 pbk. : 18.00
1. Spirituality—Addresses, essays, lectures. I. Sadler, A. W. 1928- (Albert William),

ROCHE de Coppens, Peter. 248.2
The spiritual perspective : key issues and themes interpreted from the standpoint of spiritual consciousness / Peter Roche de Coppens. Washington, D.C. : University Press of America, c1980. p. cm. [BV4501.2.R6195] 80-487 ISBN 0-8191-1017-5 : 16.75 ISBN 0-8191-1018-3 pbk. : 7.75
1. Spirituality—Addresses, essays, lectures. 2. Man—Addresses, essays, lectures. I. Title.

WESTERN spirituality : 230
historical roots, ecumenical routes / edited by Matthew Fox. Notre Dame, Ind. : Fides/Claretian, c1979. viii, 440 p. ; 20 cm. Includes bibliographical references and index. [BV4501.2.W435] 79-18312 ISBN 0-8190-0635-1 : 9.95
1. Spirituality—Addresses, essays, lectures. I. Fox, Matthew.

Spirituality—Bibliography.

WEBORG, John. 016.248'4
Where is it written? : An introductory, annotated bibliography in spirituality / by John Weborg. Chicago : Franciscan Herald Press, [1978] p. cm. (Synthesis series) Bibliography: p. [Z7776.5.W4] [BV4501.2] 78-5178 ISBN 0-8199-0739-1 : 0.65
1. Spirituality—Bibliography. I. Title.

Spirituality—Collected works.

THE Fire and the cloud : 230'.2
an anthology of Catholic spirituality / edited by David A. Fleming. New York : Paulist Press, c1978. xiii, 370 p. ; 23 cm. Includes bibliographical references. [BV4495.F57] 77-83582 ISBN 0-8091-2065-8 pbk. : 9.95
1. Spirituality—Collected works. I. Fleming, David A.

Spirituality—History.

GANNON, Thomas M. 248'.09
The desert and the city; an interpretation of the history of Christian spirituality, by Thomas M. Gannon and George W. Traub. [New York] Macmillan [1969] xiii, 338 p. 22 cm. Bibliographical references included in "Notes": p. [293]-327. [BV4490.G26] 69-10502
1. Spirituality—History. I. Traub, George W., joint author. II. Title.

HOLMES, Chauncey D. 209
Christian spirituality in geologic perspective / Chauncey Holmes. Philadelphia : Dorrance, [1975] 116 p. ; 22 cm. Includes bibliographical references. [BV4490.H6] 75-313613 ISBN 0-8059-2136-2 : 4.95
1. Spirituality—History. 2. Theology. I. Title.

Spirituals (songs)—Bibliography.

JACKSON, Irene V. 016.7836'75
Afro-American religious music : a bibliography and a catalogue of gospel music / compiled by Irene V. Jackson. Westport, Conn. : Greenwood Press, 1979. xiv, 210 p. : facsim. ; 24 cm. Includes music and indexes. [ML128.S4J3] 78-60527 ISBN 0-313-20560-4 lib. bdg. : 19.95
1. Spirituals (songs)—Bibliography. 2. Gospel music—Bibliography. 3. Afro-American music—Bibliography. I. Title.

Spirituals (Songs)—History and criticism.

CONE, James H. 783.6'7'09
The spirituals and the blues : an interpretation / James H. Cone. Westport, Conn. : Greenwood Press, 1980, c1972. viii, 152 p. ; 23 cm. Reprint of the ed. published by Seabury Press, New York. Includes bibliographical references. [ML3556.C66 1980] 19 80-19382 ISBN 0-313-22667-9 lib. bdg. : 17.50
1. Spirituals (Songs)—History and criticism. 2. Blues (Songs, etc.)—United States—History and criticism. I. Title.

DIXON, Christa. 783.6'7
Negro spirituals : from Bible to folk song / Christa K. Dixon. Philadelphia : Fortress Press, c1976. x, 117 p. ; 22 cm. Includes indexes. [ML3556.D58] 75-36444 ISBN 0-8006-1221-3 : 3.25
1. Spirituals (Songs)—History and criticism.

LOVELL, John, 1907- 783.6'7'0973
Black song : the forge and the flame : the story of how the Afro-American spiritual was hammered out / John Lovell, Jr. New York : Schirmer Books, 1980, c1972. p. cm. Reprint of the ed. published by Macmillan, New York. Bibliography: p. [ML3556.L69 1980] 80-15646 ISBN 0-02-871900-X pbk. : 6.95
1. Spirituals (Songs)—History and criticism. I. Title.

Spirituals (Songs)—Texts.

CHILDREN, go where I send thee : 783.6'72
an American spiritual / illustrated by Kathryn Shoemaker. Minneapolis, Minn. : Winston Press, c1980. [32] p. : col. ill. ; 16 x 24 cm. The text of an American spiritual, originally sung by slave congregations on Christmas Eve. [PZ8.3.C4337] 19 79-55960 ISBN 0-03-056673-8 pbk. : 6.95
1. Spirituals (Songs)—Texts. 2. Christmas music—Texts. 3. [Spirituals (Songs)] 4. [Christmas music.] I. Shoemaker, Kathryn E., ill.

Spokane. Holy Names College.

DE FREES, Madeline [Name in religion: Mary Gilbert, Sister] 377.8273
Later thoughts from the springs of silence, by Sister Mary Gilbert. Indianapolis, Bobbs [c.1962] 222p. 22cm. 62-19310 3.95
1. Spokane. Holy Names College. I. Title.

Sponsa regis—Addresses, essays, lectures.

BLOW the trumpet at the new moon : 248.8'943
a Sisters today jubilee / [edited] by Daniel Durken. Collegeville, Minn. : Liturgical Press, [1979] p. cm. "Collection of editorials, essays, interviews, and poetry ... selected from the pages of Sponsa regis/Sisters today." Includes index. [BX4200.B58] 80-10806 ISBN 0-8146-1016-1 pbk. : 6.95
1. Sponsa regis—Addresses, essays, lectures. 2. Monasticism and religious orders for women—Addresses, essays, lectures. 3. Monastic and religious life of women—Addresses, essays, lectures. I. Durken, Daniel.

Sponsors.

BAILEY, Derrick Sherwin, 1910- 265.1
Sponsors at baptism and confirmation; an historical introduction to Anglican practice. New York, Macmillan [1953] xiii, 162p. 19cm. Bibliography:p. 146-151. [BX5149.B2B2] 53-6323
1. Sponsors. 2. Baptism—Anglican communion. 3. Confirmation—Anglican communion. I. Title.

Sprague, Philo Woodruff, 1852-1927.

PHILO Woodruff Sprague; 922
the collected essays of eight intimate associates, with a foreword by his bishop for forty-three years. [Boston] Priv. print., 1927. 74 p. incl. front. (port.) 20 cm. [BX5995.S78P5] 28-4500
1. Sprague, Philo Woodruff, 1852-1927.

SPRAGUE, Philo Woodruff, 1852-1927. 225
... *The influence of Christianity of fundamental human institutions*, by Philo W. Sprague ... New York, Chicago [etc.] Fleming H. Revell company [c1925] 185 p. 19 1/2 cm. (The Bohlen lectures, 1924) [BR121.S75] 25-20607
I. Title.

Sprague, William Buell, 1795-1876.

BRONSON, Oliver, 1826-1860.
Sermons by the late Rev. Oliver Bronson, with a memoir of his life, by William B. Sprague, D. D. Albany, W. B. Sprague, jr., 1861. 1 p. l., ii, 342 p. 20 1/2 cm. 5-18820
1. Sprague, William Buell, 1795-1876. I. Title.

[WEST, George Montgomery] 922
The living martyr and the unholy alliance; or, Calumny exposed, truth defended, and character vindicated by irrefutable evidence ... Albany, Printed by H. J. Hastings, 1850. 84 p. 23 cm. Erratum slip inserted. Signed: George Montgomery West. "The controversy ... between Dr. Sprague and Dr. West."--p. 4. [BX5995.W47A5] 36-1483
1. Sprague, William Buell, 1795-1876. 2. Albany. Second Presbyterian church. Impostures and calumnies of George Montgomery West. I. Title.

Spring, Samuel, 1746-1819. A friendly dialogue ... upon the nature of duty.

TAPPAN, David, 1752-1803. 264
Two friendly letters from Toletus to Philalethes, or from the Rev. David Tappan to the Rev. Samuel Spring, containing remarks on the sentiments and reasonings of the latter, in his Dialogue on the nature of duty. Newbury-port: Printed by John Mycall McDCC,LXXXV. 136 p. 18 1/2 cm. "Appendix, (number 2,) By the author of 'The sacrifice of the wicked explained and distinguished'" (i.e. Joseph Dana): p. [115]-119. "Appendix, (number II.) A letter from Toletus to Amartolos, containing brief remarks on the 'Private conference' between him and Philalethes": p. [120]-136. [BT700.S7T3] [AC901.W3 vol. 133, no. 7] 233 40-36598
1. Spring, Samuel, 1746-1819. A friendly dialogue ... upon the nature of duty. 2. Man (Theology)—Early works to 1800. I. Dana, Joseph, 1742-1827. II. Title.

Springer, Helen Emily (Chairman) 1868-1949.

SPRINGER, John McKendree, Bp., 1873- 922.773
I love the trail: a sketch of the life of Helen Emily Springer. Publisher's agencies: Congo Book Concern, Nashville [etc. Nashville? 1952] 176 p. illus. 24 cm. [BV3505.S6S6] 52-27463
1. Springer, Helen Emily (Chairman) 1868-1949. I. Title.

Springfield, Ill. St. Paul's church.

HAUGHTON, Edward, 1869- comp. 283.77356
The parish of Saint Paul's church, Springfield, Illinois, compiled by Edward Haughton, rector. One hundred years, 1835-1935. Springfield, Ill., Hartman-Jefferson printing co. [1935] 79, [1] p. front., illus. (incl. ports.) pl. 24 cm. [Full name: Edward John Haughton] [BX5980.S6S3] 36-18302
1. Springfield, Ill. St. Paul's church. I. Title.

Springfield, Mass.—Churches.

DOUGLASS, Harlan Paul, 1871- 277.
The Springfield church survey; a study of organized religion with its social background, by H. Paul Douglass ... New York, George H. Doran company [c1926] xxiv p., 2 l., 33-445 p. front., plates, tables (1 fold.) diagrs. 22 1/2 cm. "The Institute of social and religious research ... is responsible for this publication." [BR560.S7D6] 26-7591
1. Springfield, Mass.—Churches. 2. Springfield, Mass.—Soc. condit. 3. Social surveys. I. Institute of social and religious research. II. Title.

Springfield, Mass. First church of Christ.

[EDWARDS, Jonathan] 1703-1758. 922.
A letter to the author of the pamphlet Called An Answer [!] to the Hampshire Narrative ... Boston: Printed in the Year 1737. 1 p. l., 84 p. 17 cm. A justification of the Hampshire county ministers who disapproved of the settlement of Rev. Robert Breck at Springfield. Errata slip mounted on p. 84. [BX7260.B63E4] 27-6603
1. Breck, Robert, 1713-1784. 2. Springfield, Mass. First church of Christ. I. Title.

Springfield, Mass. Trinity Methodist church.

WAGNER, H. Hughes, 1903-
Trinity's first century [by] H. Hughes Wagner. Published in connection with the centennial celebration of Trinity Methodist church, Springfield, Massachusetts. Springfield, Mass., McLoughlin bros., inc. [pref. 1944] 4 p. l., 207 p. illus. (incl. ports., facsim.) diagr. 21 1/2 cm. Title vignette. A 45
1. Springfield, Mass. Trinity Methodist church. I. Title.

Springfield, Mo. Central Bible Institute.

CUP. 207.778
Springfield, Mo. v. illus. 28 cm. "By the sentors of Central Bible Institute." [BV4070.C39313] 52-41388
1. Springfield, Mo. Central Bible Institute.

Springfield, OH. First Evangelical Lutheran chur ch.

RINKLIFF, George Louis. 284.1771491
The First Evangelical Lutheran church of Springfield, a centennial history, by George L. Rinkliff. Philadelphia, Pa., Published by Muhlenberg press for the First Evangelical Lutheran church of Springfield, O. [c1941] 202 p. plates, ports. 23 cm. [BX8076.S75R5] 42-484
1. Springfield, O. First Evangelical Lutheran church. I. Title.

Springs (in religion, folk-lore, etc.)

SMITH, James Reuel, 1852-1935.
Springs and wells in Greek and Roman literature, their legends and locations, by James Reuel Smith; with two illustrations. New York and London, G. P. Putnam's sons, 1922. xxiii p., 1 l., 722 p. 2 pl. (incl. front.) 20 cm. [DE31.S6] 22-8269
1. Springs (in religion, folk-lore, etc.) 2. Mythology, Classical. I. Title.

Spurgeon, Charles Haddon, 1834-1892.

ADCOCK, Elver F. 920.
Charles H. Spurgeon, prince of preachers, by E. F. Adcock. Anderson, Ind., Gospel trumpet company [c1925] 116 p. incl. front. (port.) illus. 19 cm. [BX6495.S7A8] 26-2
1. Spurgeon, Charles Haddon, 1834-1892. I. Title.

BACON, Ernest Wallace. 253.7'0924 (B)
Spurgeon, heir of the Puritans [by] Ernest W. Bacon. [1st U. S. A. ed.] Grand Rapids, Mich., W. B. Eerdmans Pub. Co. [1968, 1967] 184 p. port. 23 cm. Bibliography: p. 178-179. [BX6495.S7B3] 67-30115
1. Spurgeon, Charles Haddon, 1834-1892. I. Title.

BACON, Ernest Wallace. 253.7'0924
Spurgeon, heir of the Puritans [by] Ernest W. Bacon. [1st U.S.A. ed.] Grand Rapids, Mich., Eerdmans [1968, c1967] 184p. port. 23cm. Bibl. [BX6495.S7B3] (B) 67-30115 3.95
1. Spurgeon, Charles Haddon, 1834-1892. I. Title.

CONWELL, Russell Herman, 1843-1925. 922.642
Life of Charles Haddon Spurgeon, the world's great preacher. By Russell H. Conwell ... [Philadelphia] Edgewood publishing co., 1892. 616 p. incl. illus., plates, ports. front. 20 cm. [BX6495.S7C6] 36-24851
1. Spurgeon, Charles Haddon, 1834-1892. I. Title.

*DAY, Richard Ellsworth 251.'0092'4
The shadow of the broad brim : the life story of Charles Hadden Spurgeon, heir of the Puritans. Grand Rapids : Baker Book House, 1976c1934. 236p. : ill., ports. ; 20 cm. [BX6495.S7.] [B] ISBN 0-8010-2855-8 pbk. : 3.95.
1. Spurgeon, Charles Haddon, 1834-1892. 2. Preaching. I. Title.

DAY, Richard Ellsworth. 922.642
The shadow of the broad brim; the life story of Charles Haddon Spurgeon, heir of the Puritans, by Richard Ellsworth Day. Philadelphia, Boston [etc.] The Judson press [1934] 6 p. l., 3-236 p. front., plates. ports. 20 cm. [BX6495.S7D3] 34-13521
1. Spurgeon, Charles Haddon, 1834-1892. I. Title.

FULLERTON, William Young, 1857-1932. 253.70924 B
Charles Haddon Spurgeon; a biography. Chicago, Moody Press [1966] 283 p. 23 cm. (The Tyndale series of great biographies) "First published, 1920." [BX6495.S7F8 1966] 66-8933
1. Spurgeon, Charles Haddon, 1834-1892. I. Title. II. Series.

HANDFORD, Thomas W. 922.642
Spurgeon. Episodes and anecdotes of his busy life. With personal reminiscences. By Thomas W. Handford... Chicago, Morrill, Higgins & co., 1892. 5 p. l., 9-256 p. incl. plates, ports. front. 20 cm. (On cover: Idylwild series. I. 10) [BX6495.S7H3 1892] 36-21123
1. Spurgeon, Charles Haddon, 1834-1892. I. Title.

HANDFORD, Thomas W. 922.642
Spurgeon. Episodes and anecodtes of his busy life. With persona- reminiscences. By Thomas W. Handford... 20th thousand. Chicago, W. B. Conkey company [c1894] 5 p. l., 9-256 p. incl. plates. ports. front. 21 cm. (On cover: Franklin series, v. I, no. I) [BX6495.S7H3 1894] 36-21122
1. Spurgeon, Charles Haddon, 1834-1892. I. Title.

HAYDEN, Eric W. 269
Spurgeon on revival; a Biblical and theological approach. Grand Rapids, Mich., Zondervan [c.1962] 144p. 23cm. 62-52736 2.95
1. Spurgeon, Charles Haddon, 1834-1892. 2. Evangelistic work. I. Title.

KRUPPA, Patricia Stallings, 1936- 286'.1'0924 B
Charles Haddon Spurgeon : a preacher's progress / Patricia Stallings Kruppa. New York : Garland Pub., 1982. p. cm. (Modern British history) Includes index. Bibliography: p. [BX6495.S7K78 1982] 19 81-48362 ISBN 0-8240-5158-0 : 60.00
1. Spurgeon, Charles Haddon, 1834-1892. 2. Baptists—Clergy—Biography. 3. Clergy—England—Biography. I. Title. II. Series.

NEEDHAM, George Carter, 1840-1902. 922.642
The life and labors of Charles H. Spurgeon, the faithful preacher, the devoted pastor, the noble philanthropist, the beloved college president, and the voluminous writer, autor, etc., etc. Compiled and edited by Geo. C. Needham ... Boston, D. L. Guernsey, 1882. xx, 693 p. front., illus., plates, ports. 23 cm. [BX6495.S7N4 1882] 36-24853
1. Spurgeon, Charles Haddon, 1834-1892. I. Title.

NEEDHAM, George Carter, 1840-1902. 922.642
The life and labors of Charles H. Spurgeon, the faithful preacher, the devoted pastor, the noble philanthropist, the beloved college president, and the voluminous writer, author, etc., etc. By Geo. C. Needham ... Enl. ed. Boston, D. L. Guernsey, 1884. xxvi, 631 p. incl. front., illus. plates. ports. 23 cm. [BX6495.S7N4 1884] 36-24852
1. Spurgeon, Charles Haddon, 1834-1892. I. Title.

PIERSON, Arthur Tappan, 1837-1911. 920.
From the pulpit to the palm-branch; a memorial of C. H. Spurgeon, sequel to the sketch of his life, entitled "From the usher's desk to the Tabernacle pulpit": five memorial sermons by Rev. A.T. Pierson, D.D. Descriptive account of Mrs. Spurgeon's long illness, and partial recovery; his last month at Mentone [!] including verbatim reports of the last two addresses given by him, and the last two articles he wrote, with the official report of the services in connection with his funeral. New York, A. C. Armstrong and son, 1892. 281 p. incl. front., illus. (incl. ports., facsims.) 19 cm. [BX6495.S7P5] 3-22478
1. Spurgeon, Charles Haddon, 1834-1892. I. Title.

PIKE, Godfrey Holden, 1836- 920.
Charles Haddon Spurgeon, preacher, author, philanthropist; with anecdotal reminiscences, by G. Holden Pike ... Introduction by William Cleaver Wilkinson and concluding chapters by James C. Fernald. New York [etc.] Funk & Wagnalls company, 1892. xiv, 397 p. 2 port. (incl. front.) 19 1/2 cm. [BX6495.S7P55] 12-37598
1. Spurgeon, Charles Haddon, 1834-1892. I. Wilkinson, William Cleaver, 1833-1920. II. Fernald, James Champlin, 1838-1918. III. Title.

SHINDLER, Robert. 922.642
From the usher's desk to the tabernacle pulpit; the life and labors of Charles Haddon Spurgeon, by Rev. Robert Shindler ... New York, A. C. Armstrong and son, 1892. xii, 316 p. incl. front., illus. (incl. ports., facsim.) 19 cm. [BX6495.S7S4 1892a] 36-21125
1. Spurgeon, Charles Haddon, 1834-1892. I. Title.

SMITH, Joseph Manton. 922.642
The Essex lad who became England's greatest preacher. The life of Charles Haddon Spurgeon, for young people. By J. Manton Smith ... With thirty-five illustrations. New York, American tract society [1892] 169 p. front. (port.) illus. (incl. facsims.) 19 1/2 cm. [BX6495.S7S5] 36-24265
1. Spurgeon, Charles Haddon, 1834-1892. I. American tract society. II. Title.

SPURGEON, Charles Haddon, 1834-1892. 922.642
C. H. Spurgeon's autobiography, edited and condensed from the 4 original volumes, 1500 pages, by David Otis Fuller ... Grand Rapids, Zondervan publishing house [1946] 4 p. l., 11-148 p. 20 cm. [BX6495.S7A25] 47-16317
I. Fuller, David Otis, 1903- II. Title.

SPURGEON, Charles Haddon, 1834-1892. 920.
The letters of Charles Haddon Spurgeon, collected and collated by his son, Charles Spurgeon. London, New York [etc.] Marshall brothers, limited [1923] 224 p. front. (port.) facsim. 22 cm. [BX6495.S7A3] 24-24266
I. Spurgeon, Charles, 1856- ed. II. Title.

SPURGEON, Charles Haddon, 1834-1892. 264.
Prayers from metropolitan pulpit; C. H. Spurgeon's prayers. New York, Chicago [etc.] Fleming H. Revell company [c1906] 160 p. 19 1/2 cm. [BV250.S6] 6-27360
I. Title.

[STEVENSON, George John] 1818-1888. 922.642
Sketch of the life and ministry of the Rev. C. H. Spurgeon. From original documents. Including anecdotes and incidents of travel; biographical notices of former pastors; historical sketch of Park-street chapel; and an outline of Mr. Spurgeon's articles of faith. New York, Sheldon, Blakeman & co.; Chicago, S. C. Griggs & co., 1858. 141 p. incl. front. (port.) illus. 20 cm. [BX6495.S7S8 1858] 33-32833
1. Spurgeon, Charles Haddon, 1834-1892. I. Title.

[STEVENSON, George John] 1818-1888. 922.642
Sketch of the life and ministry of the Rev. C. H. Spurgeon. From original documents. Including anecdotes and incidents of travel; biographical notices of former pastors; historical sketch of Park-street chapel; and an outline of Mr. Spurgeon's articles of faith. New York, Sheldon and company; Boston, Gould & Lincoln; [etc., etc.] 1859. 141 p. incl. front. (port.) illus. 20 cm. [BX6495.S7S8 1859] 36-28831
1. Spurgeon, Charles Haddon, 1834-1892. I. Title.

WAYLAND, Heman Lincoln, 1830-1898. 922.642
Charles H. Spurgeon: his faith and works. By H. L. Wayland. Philadelphia, American Baptist publication society [1892] 317 p. incl. illus., plates, ports., facsim. front. (map) pl., 2 port 19 1/2 cm. [BX6495.S7W3] 36-28832
1. Spurgeon, Charles Haddon, 1834-1892. I. American Baptist publication society. II. Title.

YARROW, William H. 922.
... The life and work of Charles H. Spurgeon, by Rev. William H. Yarrow. With an introduction by John Stanford Holme ... New York, I. K. Funk & co., c1880. cover-title, 1 p. l., [5]-100 p. illus. (incl. port., facsim.) 22 1/2 cm. (The standard series. Class M. 1 (Biography) no. 46) [BX6495.S7Y3] 9-23218
1. Spurgeon, Charles Haddon, 1834-1892. I. Title.

Spurgeon, Charles Haddon—Sermons.

*ADAMS, Jay E. 251
Sense appeal in the sermons of Charles Haddon Spurgeon / Jay E. Adams. Grand Rapids : Baker Book House, 1976 c1975. [viii], 62 p. ; 22 cm. (Studies in preaching ; 1) Bibliography: pp. 60-62. [BV4222] ISBN 0-8010-0102-1 pbk. : 1.95
1. Spurgeon, Charles Haddon—Sermons. 2. Preaching. I. Title.

Spurgeon, Thomas, 1856-1917.

FULLERTON, William Young, 1857- 920.
Thomas Spurgeon; a biography by W. Y. Fullerton ... London, New York [etc.] Hodder and Stoughton, 1919. xiii, 304 p. front. (port.) illus., pl., port., group. 19 cm. [BX6495.S6F8] 19-13067
1. Spurgeon, Thomas, 1856-1917. I. Title.

Spurling, Richard G., 1858-1935.

MARSHALL, June Glover. 289.9 B
A biographical sketch of Richard G. Spurling, Jr. / by June Glover Marshall. Cleveland, Tenn. : Pathway Press, [1974] 29 p. : port. ; 16 cm. [BX7020.Z8S685] 74-27630
1. Spurling, Richard G., 1858-1935. I. Title.

Sri Varadarajaswami Temple.

RAMAN, K. V., 1934- 954'.82
Sri Varadarajaswami Temple, Kanchi : a study of its history, art, and architecture / K. V. Raman. 1st ed. New Delhi : Abhinav Publications, 1975. x, 206 p., [12] leaves of plates : ill. ; 25 cm. "This book formed the subject matter of ... [the author's] dissertation for the degree of the doctor of philosophy of the University of Madras." Includes index. Bibliography: p. [190]-194. [BL1227.C66R35] 75-907263 18.00
1. Sri Varadarajaswami Temple. 2. Temples, Hindu—India—Conjeeveram.

Ssu shih erh chang ching—Commentaries.

HSUAN-HUA, 1908- 294.3'8
A general explanation of The Buddha speaks, The sutra in forty-two sections / by Hsuan Hua ; translated by Bhikshuni Heng ChAih ; reviewed by Bhikshuni Heng ChAing ; edited by Kuo Chou Rounds ; certified by Bhikshuni Heng Yin. 1st ed. [San Francisco] : Buddhist Text Translation Society, 1977. 94 p., [4] leaves of plates : ill. ; 22 cm. Cover title: Sutra in forty-two sections. [BQ2117.H78] 78-100311 ISBN 0-917512-15-4 : 4.25
1. Ssu shih erh chang ching—Commentaries. I. Rounds, Kuo Chou. II. Ssu shih erh chang ching. English. 1977. III. Title.

Ssu shu.

LEGGE, James, 1815-1897. 181.1
The Chinese classics: a translation by James Legge ... New York, Hurd and Houghton: [etc., etc.] 1870. xii, [13]-163, xii, [13]-219 p. 22 cm. No more published in this edition. [PL3277.E22L4 1876] 16-18665
1. Ssu shu. 2. Confucius. 3. Mencius. 4. Chinese literature—Translations into English. 5. English literature—Translations from Chinese. I. Title.

Stabler, Edward, 1769-1831.

STABLER, William, 1795-1852. 922.8673
A memoir of the life of Edward Stabler, late of Alexandria in the District of Columbia; with a collection of his letters, By his son, William Stabler ... Philadelphia, Printed by J. Richards, 1846. 312 p. 19 cm. [BX7795.S7S7] 35-22119
1. Stabler, Edward, 1769-1831. I. Title.

Stackhouse, Russell Orr, 1932-1954.

STACKHOUSE, Mildred (Orr) 920
God's plan for Russ; a mother's story of her gifted son's life. [1st ed.] New York, Exposition Press [1956] 98p. 21cm. [CT275.S636S8] 56-10977
1. Stackhouse, Russell Orr, 1932-1954. I. Title.

Stafford, Conn.—Church history.

FOSTER, Isaac, 1725-1807. 261
A defence of religious liberty; comprehending, i. The introduction; containing a true state of the matters judged upon by the late Consociation, from their rise until laid before that venerable body. ii. Protestation against the doings and procedure of Consociation at West-Stafford, with the reasons of it at large. iii. Strictures on the report of a certain anonymous committee. Concluding with, An address to the reverend elders of the late Consociation at Stafford, and An address to the people of the late Connecticut. By Isaac Foster, A. M., Pastor of the church of West-Stafford ... Massachusetts-Bay: Worcester, Printed by Isaiah Thomas, 1780. 192 p. 20 cm. "Appendix: containing a renunciation of Saybrook platform, (usually so called) with reasons of it", signed Dan Foster, 1779: p. 159-192. [BX7260.F6A3] 27-10776
1. Stafford, Conn.—Church history. 2. Congregational churches in Connecticut. I. Foster, Dan, 1748-1810. II. Title.

Stafford, Conn. First Congregational church.

GROBEL, Kendrick, 1908- 285.8746
History of the First church of Stafford, Connecticut, known as "The Stafford street Congregational church," from its birth, 1723, to its death, 1892, by Kendrick Grobel ... Stafford Springs, The Women's council of the Congregational church, 1942. 87 p. front., pl. 23 cm. Cover-title: The First church of Stafford, Connecticut. Bibliography: p. 81-86. [BX7255.S77F54] 43-14080
1. Stafford, Conn. First Congregational church. I. Stafford Springs, Conn. Congregational church. Women's council. II. Title.

Stafford, Eng. King Edward VI School.

GILMORE, Conal Gregory. 261
History of King Edward VI School, Stafford Oxford, Printed at the University Press by C. Batey, 1953. 137p. illus. 23cm. [LF795.S73G5] 56-46773
1. Stafford, Eng. King Edward VI School. I. Title.

Stagaard, George Hansen.

STAGAARD, George Hansen. 209'.2'4 B
Pursuer or pursued [incidents from my life, by George Hansen Stagaard as told through P. P. W. New York, Loizeaux Bros., 1954?] 31 p. 17 cm. (Treasury of truth, no. 200) Cover title. [BR1725.S73A33] 75-304115
1. Stagaard, George Hansen. I. P. P. W. II. W., P. P. III. Title. IV. Series.

Stagg, Harry P., 1898-

O'BRIEN, Bonnie Ball. 286'.1'0924 B
Harry P. Stagg : Christian statesman / Bonnie Ball O'Brien. Nashville : Broadman Press, c1976. 190 p. : ill. ; 21 cm. Bibliography: p. 190. [BX6495.S744O25] 76-18622 ISBN 0-8054-7215-0 pbk. : 3.00
1. Stagg, Harry P., 1898- 2. Baptists—Clergy—Biography. 3. Clergy—New Mexico—Biography.

Stahl, Ana Christina (Carlsen)

WESTPHAL, Barbara Osborne. 922.685
Ana Stahl of the Andes and Amazon. Illustrated by Vernon Nye. Mountain View, Calif., Pacific Press Pub. Association [1960] 127 p. illus. 23 cm. [BV2853.P7S83] 60-16412
1. Stahl, Ana Christina (Carlsen) 2. Missions — Peru. I. Title.

Stalcup, Joseph Cole, 1851-

STALCUP, Lena (Van Aken) Mrs. 1873- comp. 922.673
The life and labors of Joseph Cole Stalcup, compiled by Lena V. Stalcup. Oklahoma City, Baptist general convention of Oklahoma, 1937. xiv, 90 p. incl. front. (port.) 20 cm. [Full name: Mrs. Lena Caroline (Van Aken) Stalcup) [BX6495.S746S7] 37-38548
1. Stalcup, Joseph Cole, 1851- 2. Baptists—Oklahoma. I. Title.

Stam, John Cornelius, 1907-1934.

ENGLISH, Eugene Schuyler, 1899- 922
By life and by death; excerpts and lessons from the diary of John C. Stam. by E. Schuyler English... Grand Rapids, Mich., Zondervan publishing house [c1938] 4 p. l., v-xii, [13]-62 p. illus. (facsim.) ports. 19 1/2 cm. "By life, or by death": 1st prelim. leaf. [BV3427.S8E5] 38-39120
1. Stam, John Cornelius, 1907-1934. I. Title.

HUIZENGA, Lee S., 1881- 922
John and Betty Stam, martyrs, by Lee S. Huizenga ... A short story of the life and death of Mr. and Mrs. John C. Stam ... Written by a friend of both families with permission of both families. Introduction by Will H. Houghton ... preface by Jacob Stam ... Grand Rapids, Mich., Zondervan publishing house, c1935. 3 p. l., 11-64 p. front., illus. (incl. ports., map) 20 cm. [BV3427.S8H8] 36-7149
1. Stam, John Cornelius, 1907-1934. 2. Stam, Mrs. Elisabeth Alden (Scott) 1906-1934. I. Title.

TAYLOR, Mary Geraldine (Guinness) 922
The triumph of John and Betty Stam, Philadelphia, China Inland Mission, 1949. 129 p. ports. 21 cm. [BV3427.S8T3 1949] 51-32750
1. Stam, John Cornelius, 1907-1934. 2. Stam, Elizabeth Alden (Scott) 1906-1934. 3. Missions—China. I. Title.

TAYLOR, Mary Geraldine (Guinness) "Mrs. Howard Taylor." 922
The triumph of John and Betty Stam, by Mrs. Howard Taylor ... Philadelphia [etc.] China inland mission, 1935. 6 p. l., 125, [2] p. front., ports. 19 1/2 cm. [BV3427.S8T3] 35-10724
1. Stam, John Cornelius, 1907-1934. 2. Stam, Mrs. Elisabeth Alden (Scott) 1906-1934. 3. Missions—China. I. Title.

Stamping Ground Baptist Church.

SINGER, J. W., 1905- 286'.1'769425
A history of the Baptist Church at the Stamping Ground, Ky., 1795- by J. W. Singer. Rev. and enl. [Stamping Ground, Ky.] 1970. 278 p. illus., ports. 24 cm. [BX6480.S84S5] 71-118990
1. Stamping Ground Baptist Church. I. Title.

Stamps, Ellen de Kroon, 1940-

STAMPS, Ellen de Kroon, 1940- 269'.2'0922 B
My years with Corrie / Ellen de Kroon Stamps. Old Tappan, N.J. : F. H. Revell Co., c1978. 128 p. ; 22 cm. [BR1725.S733A35] 78-13979 ISBN 0-8007-0957-8 : 5.95
1. Stamps, Ellen de Kroon, 1940- 2. Ten Boom, Corrie. 3. Christian biography—United States. I. Title.

STAMPS, Ellen de Kroon, 1940- 269'.2'0922 B
My years with Corrie / Ellen de Kroon Stamps. Boston : G. K. Hall, 1979, c1978. xii, 254 p. ; 24 cm. "Published in large print." [BR1725.S733A35 1979] 79-18310 ISBN 0-8161-6773-7 lib. bdg. : 11.95
1. Stamps, Ellen de Kroon, 1940- 2. Ten Boom, Corrie. 3. Christian biography—United States. 4. Large type books. I. Title.

Stan-Padilla, Viento, 1945-

STAN-PADILLA, Viento, 1945- 299'.7
Dream feather / Viento Stan-Padilla ; illustated by the author. San Rafael, Calif. : Dawne-Leigh Publications, 1980. p. cm. [E99.Y3S79] 79-26213 ISBN 0-89742-035-7 : 10.95 ISBN 0-89742-034-9 (pbk.) : 7.95
1. Stan-Padilla, Viento, 1945- 2. Yaqui Indians—Art. 3. Yagui Indians—Religion and mythology. 4. Indians of North America—Religion and mythology. 5. Spiritual life. I. Title.

Stanchfield, Wilma.

STANCHFIELD, Wilma. 248'.24 B
Struck by lightning, then by love / Wilma Stanchfield, with Helen Kooiman Hosier. Nashville : T. Nelson, c1979. 180 p. ; 21 cm. [BV4935.S66A37] 79-13763 ISBN 0-8407-5690-9 : 4.95
1. Stanchfield, Wilma. 2. Converts—United States—Biography. I. Hosier, Helen Kooiman, joint author. II. Title.

Standing, Joseph, 1855?-1879.

NICHOLSON, John, 1839-1909. 922.8373
The martyrdom of Joseph Standing; or, The murder of a "Mormon" missionary. A true story. Also an appendix, giving a succint [!] description of the Utah penitentiary and some data regarding those who had, up to date of this publication, suffered incarceration through the operations of the anti-"Mormon" crusade, begun in 1884. Written in prison, by John Nicholson ... Salt Lake City, Utah, The Deseret news co., printers, 1886. 2 p. l., [3]-160 p. 18 1/2 cm. [BX8095.S77N5] 36-31807
1. Standing, Joseph, 1855?-1879. 2. Utah. State prison, Salt Lake City. I. Title.

Stanford, Frank W., 1862-1948.

ABRAM, Victor P 232.6
The restoration of all things. Amherst, N. H., Kingdom Press [1962] 149p. 21cm. 'The first eleven chapters ... appeared as successive monthly instalments in the Standard during 1951 and 1952.' [BV3785.S18A65] 62-18059
1. Stanford, Frank W., 1862-1948. 2. Second Advent. I. Title.

Stanford, John, 1754-1834.

SOMMERS, Charles George, 1793-1868. 922.673
Memoir of the Rev. John Stanford, D.D., late chaplain to the humane and criminal institutions in the city of New-York. By Charles G. Sommers ... Together with an appendix, comprising brief memoirs of the late Rev. John Williams, the Rev. Thomas Baldwin, D.D., and the Rev. Richard Furman ... New-York, Swords, Stanford, and co., 1835. xix, [13]-417 p. front. (port.) 2 pl., facsim. 19 1/2 cm. [BX6495.S75S6] 36-24864
1. Stanford, John, 1754-1834. 2. Williams, John, 1767-1825. 3. Baldwin, Thomas, 1753-1825. 4. Furman, Richard, 1755-1825. I. Title.

Stanford University. Stanford Memorial Church.

STANFORD University. Publications Service. 917.94'73
Stanford Memorial Church / prepared by the Stanford University Publications Service. 2d ed. [Stanford, Calif.] : The University, [1974] 27 p., [2] leaves of plates : ill. (some col.) ; 23 cm. [NA5235.S72S72 1974] 74-195997
1. Stanford University. Stanford Memorial Church. I. Title.

Stanislaus, Sister, 1863-1949.

LANCASTER, Vincentine. 922.244
Katie Malone, in religion Sister Stanislaus; a biography. St. Louis, Marillac Provincial House [1963?] viii, 83 p. illus., ports. 17 cm. [BX4705.S795L3] 67-38551
1. Stanislaus, Sister, 1863-1949. I. Title.

Stanislaw Kostka, Saint, 1550-1568

KANE, William Terence, 1880- 922.
For greater things; the story of Saint Stanislaus Kostka, by William T. Kane, S. J. With a preface by James J. Daly, S. J. St. Louis, Mo. [etc.] B. Herder, 1915. xi p., 1 l., 99 p. front. (port.) 20 cm. [BX4700.S7K3] 15-22696
1. Stanislaw Kostka, Saint, 1550-1568 I. Title.

KERNS, Joseph E 922.2438
Portrait of a champion; a life of St. Stanley Kostka. Westminster, Md., Newman Press, 1957. 278p. 23cm. Includes bibliography. [BX4700.S7K4] 57-8613
1. Stanislaw Kostka, Saint, 1550-1568. I. Title.

THE life of St. Stanislaus Kostka, of the Society of Jesus, patron of novices. Tr. from the French. 1st Amer. ed. Baltimore, J. Murphy & co., 1850. 144 p. front. 16 degree. Contents.--Life of St. Stanislaus Kostka.--A short novena in honor of Saint Stanislaus Kostka--Litany of Saint Stanislaus Kostka.--Three prayers to be recited each day in honor of Saint Stanislaus.--A short novena in honor of St. Stanislaus or Saint Aloysius.--Litany of Saint Aloysius.--A favorite devotion of Saint Pius v.--Prayer to recite before the image of Jesus crucified.--Indulgences, granted by ... Pius viii.--Remarkable epochs in the life of Saint Saint Stanislaus.--Index. 1-6085

MONAHAN, Maud. 922.
On the King's highway; the story of Saint Stanislaus, by Maud Monahan. Illustrated by Robin. [New York, London, etc., Longmans, Green and company, 1927] 58, [2] p. illus. 22 x 18 cm. [BX4700.S7M6] 28-28254 1.40
1. Stanislaw Kostka, Saint, 1550-1568. I. Title.

SIGISMUND, brother. 922.2433
The lad who hiked to heaven, a story of St. Stanislaus Kostka, S.J., by Brother Sigismund, C.S.C. Illustrations by students of Sister M. Edna, C.S.C. Notre Dame, Ind., Dujarie press [1945] 2 p. l., 122 p. illus. 22 1/2 cm. [BX4700.S7S5] 46-12027
1. Stanislaw Kostka, Saint, 1550-1568. I. Title.

UMINSKI, Sigmund H. 282'.0924 B
No greater love; a story of Saint Stanislaus Kostka, by Sigmund H. Uminski. With a foreword by John Cardinal Krol. New York, Polish Publication Society of America [1969] xv, 57 p. illus. 23 cm. (Saints who made history) [BX4700.S7U4] 70-97138 3.00
1. StanisOaw Kostka, Saint, 1550-1568. I. Title.

Stanislaw Kostka, Saint, 1550-1568 — Juvenile literature.

SIGISMUND, Brother. 92
The lad who hiked to heaven; a story of Saint Stanislaus Kostka. Illus. by Carolyn Lee Jagodits. Rev. Notre Dame, Ind., Dujarie Press, 1966. 93 p. illus. 24 cm. [BX4700.S7S5 1966] 66-12691
1. Stanislaw Kostka, Saint, 1550-1568—Juvenile literature. I. Title.

SIGISMUND, Brother, Brother 92
The lad who hiked to heaven; a story of Saint Stanislaus Kostka. Illus. by Carolyn Lee Jagodits. Rev. Notre Dame, Ind., Dujarie Pr., 1966 [c.1945, 1966] 93p. illus. 24cm. [BX4700.S7S5] 66-12691 2.25
1. Stanislaw Kostka, Saint, 1550-1568 — Juvenile literature. I. Title.

Stanley, Arthur Penrhyn, 1815-1881.

BRADLEY, George Granville, 1821-1903. 922.
Recollections of Arthur Penrhyn Stanley, late dean of Westminster. Three lectures delivered in Edinburgh in November 1882, by George Granville Bradley ... New York, C. Scribner's sons, 1883. 1 p. l., v-xiv p., 1 l., 142 p. 20 cm. [BX5199.S8B7 1883 a] 15-22636
1. Stanley, Arthur Penrhyn, 1815-1881. I. Title.

ERNLE, Rowland Edmund Prothero, baron, 1851-1937. 922.
The life and correspondence of Arthur Penrhyn Stanley, late dean of Westminster, by Rowland E. Prothero ... With the co-operation and sanction of the Very Rev. G. G. Bradley ... New York, C. Scribner's sons, 1894. 2 v. fronts., plates, ports. 24 cm. The first seven chapters are based upon the work of Dean Bradley. cf. Pref. [BX5199.S8E7] 4-16987
1. Stanley, Arthur Penrhyn, 1815-1881. I. Bradley, George Granville, 1821-1903. II. Title.

ERNLE, Rowland Edmund Prothero, baron, 1852-1937. 922.
The life and correspondence of Arthur Penrhyn Stanley, late dean of Westminster. by Rowland E. Prothero ... With the co-operation and sanction of the Very Rev. G. G. Bradley ... New York, C. Scribner's sons, 1894. 2 v. fronts., plates, ports. 24 cm. The first seven chapters are based upon the work of Dean Bradley. cf. Pref. [BX5199.S8E7] 4-16968
1. Stanley, Arthur Penrhyn, 1815-1881. I. Bradley, George Granville, 1821-1903. II. Title.

HUMPHREY, Frances A. 922.
Dean Stanley with the children, by Mrs. Frances A. Humphrey; five of Dean Stanley's sermons to children, with an introduction by Canon Farrar. Boston, D. Lothrop and company [c1884] 185 p. incl. front., illus., plates, ports. 28 1/2 cm. [BX5199.S8H8] 12-34313
1. Stanley, Arthur Penrhyn, 1815-1881. 2. Children's sermons. I. Title.

Stanley, Clarence Ballard, 1889-1969.

CARRAWAY, W. B. 286'.1'0924 B
Mr. Benevolence of Association Baptists; a biography of Clarence Ballard Stanley, by W. B. Carraway. [Texarkana, Ark., 1974] 100 p. illus. 23 cm. [BX6495.S755C37] 74-80033
1. Stanley, Clarence Ballard, 1889-1969. I. Title.

Stanton, William A., 1870-1910.

KANE, William Terence, 1880- 922.
A memoir of William A. Stanton, S. J., by William T. Kane, S. J., with an introduction by the Most Reverend J. J. Harty ... St. Louis, Mo., and London, B. Herder book co., 1918. 6 p. l., 262 p. pl., 2 port. (incl. front.) 20 cm. [BX4705.S8K8] 18-8198
1. Stanton, William A., 1870-1910. I. Title.

Stapleton, Staten Island, Churches, Roman Cathol ic-Immaculate Conception.

STAPLETON, S.I. Immaculate Conception Church.
History of the parish of Immaculate Conception on the occasion of the 75th anniversary, 1887-1962. Stapleton, S.I., [1962] 248 p. illus., ports., facsim. 28 cm. Includes bibliographies. 65-62720
1. Stapleton, S.I.—Churches, Roman Catholic-Immaculate Conception. I. Title.

Stapleton, Thomas, 1535-1598.

O'CONNELL, Marvin Richard. 274.2
Thomas Stapleton and the Counter Reformation. New Haven, Yale University Press, 1964. xii, 221 p. 23 cm. (Yale publications in religion,9) "Bibliographical note": p. [211]-213. [BX4705.S812O2] 64-12656
1. Stapleton, Thomas, 1535-1598. 2. Counter-Reformation — England. I. Title. II. Series.

Stapleton, Thomas, 1535-1598. A fortress of the faith.

FULKE, William, 1538-1589. 283.082
Stapleton's Fortress overthrown. A rejoinder to Martiall's Reply. A discovery of the dangerous rock of the popish church commended by Sanders By William Fulke ...Edited for the Parker society, by the Rev. Richard Gibbings ... Cambridge [Eng.] Printed at the Universtiy press, 1848. viii p., 1 l., 412 p. 23 cm. (Half-title: The Parker society. [Publications. v. 24]) Leaf inserted after p. viii has caption: Fulke's works, vol. ii. Includes reprints of original title-pages. "A catalogue of ... popish books ... answered": p. [3]-4. [BX5035.P2 vol. 24] A 33
1. Stapleton, Thomas, 1535-1598. A fortresse of the faith. 2. Martiall, John, 1534-1597. A replie to Mr. Calfhill's blasphemous answer made against Treatise of the crosse." 3. S 4. Sanders, Nicholas, 1530?-1581. 5. Sanders, Nicholas, 1830?-1581. I. Gibbings, Richard, 1813-1888 ed. II. Title.

FULKE, William, 1538-1589. 283.082
Stapleton's Fortress overthrown. A rejoinder to Martiall 's Reply. A discovery of the dangerous rock of the popish church commended by Sanders. By William Fulke ... Edited for the Parker society, by the Rev. Richard Gibbings ... Cambridge [Eng.] Printed at the University press, 1848. viii p., 1 l., 412 p. 23 cm. (Half-title: The Parker society. [Publications, v. 18]). Leaf inserted after p. viii has caption: Fulke's works, vol. II. Includes reprints of original title-pages. "A catalogue of ... popish books ... answered": p. [3]-4. [BX5035.P2] 282 A C
1. Stapleton, Thomas, 1535-1598. A fortress of the faith. 2. Martiall, John, 1534-1597. A replie to M. Calfhill's blasphemous answer made against "Treatise of the crosse." 3. Sanders, Nicholas, 1530?-1581. I. Gibbings, Richard, 1813-1888, ed. Union theol. sem. Library. II. Title.

Star of Bethlehem.

BOA, Kenneth. 232.9'2
The return of the star of Bethlehem / Kenneth Boa and William Proctor. 1st ed. Garden City, N.Y. : Doubleday, 1980. viii, 205 p. ; 22 cm. "A Doubleday-Galilee original." Bibliography: p. [183]-205. [BT315.2.B57] 79-8548 ISBN 0-385-15454-2 : 8.95
1. Star of Bethlehem. I. Proctor, William, joint author. II. Title.

Star of Bethlehem—Juvenile literature.

BRANLEY, Franklyn Mansfield, 1915- 232.92
The Christmas sky, by Franklyn M. Branley. Illus. by Blair Lent. New York, Crowell [1966]*v. (unpaged) col. illus. 24cm. [BT315.2.B67] 66-76879 3.75
1. Star of Bethlehem—Juvenile literature. I. Lent, Blair, illus. II. Title.

Starbuck, Edwin Diller, 1866-1947.

BOOTH, Howard J. 200'.1'9
Edwin Diller Starbuck, pioneer in the psychology of religion / Howard J. Booth. Washington, D.C. : University Press of America, c1981. p. cm. Bibliography: p. [BL43.S85B66] 19 80-5731 ISBN 0-8191-1703-X (pbk.) : 13.00 ISBN 0-8191-1702-1 : 24.50
1. Starbuck, Edwin Diller, 1866-1947. 2. Psychology, Religious. I. Title.

Stars (in religion, folk-lore, etc.)

LUM, Peter, 1911- 291.2127
The stars in our heaven, myths and fables; drawings by Anne Marie Jauss. [New York] Pantheon [1948] 245 p. charts. 25 cm. [GR625.L8] 48-10648
1. Stars (in religion, folk-lore, etc.) I. Title.

Stars on Sunday.

MAX-WILSON, Peter. 791.45'7
Stars on Sunday / [by] Peter Max-Wilson ; [photographs Brian Jeeves, Alan Harbour, Brian Cleasby]. Pinner : Pentagon, 1976. [163] p. : ill. (some col.), ports. (some col.) ; 26 cm. "Stars on Sunday is a Yorkshire Television Programme; producer, Peter Max-Wilson." Includes ten short talks delivered by Dr. Donald Coggan, Archbishop of Canterbury. [BV656.3.M39] 77-354256 ISBN 0-904288-09-9 : £4.95
1. Stars on Sunday. 2. Television in religion—England—Yorkshire. I. Coggan, Frederick Donald, 1909- II. Title.

State aid to education—Australia.

ALBINSKI, Henry Stephen. 329.9'94
The Australian Labor Party and the aid to parochial schools controversy, by Henry S. Albinski. University Park, Pennsylvania State University, 1966. 55 p. 23 cm. (The Pennsylvania State University studies, no. 19) Bibliographical references included in "Notes" (p. 50-55) [LC509.A75] 67-63886
1. Labor Party (Australia) 2. Catholic Church in Australia—Education. 3. State aid to education—Australia. I. Title. II. Series: Pennsylvania. State University. The Pennsylvania State University studies, no. 19.

State, The.

LEWIS, Tayler, 1802-1877 261
A discourse on the true idea of the state as a religious institution, together with the family and the church, ordained of God. Delivered Sept. 5, 1843, before hte Porter rhetorical society of the Theological seminary, Andover, Mass. By Taylor Lewis... Andover, Allen, Morrill and Wardwell; New York, M. H. Newman, 1843. 56 p. 24 cm. [BR115.P7L4] 35-37805
1. State, The. 2. Church and state. I. Title.

ROTMANN, Bernhard, ca.1495-1535? 261.7'092'4
Earthly and temporal power; translated and edited by George Albert Moore. Chevy Chase, Md., Country Dollar Press [1950] x, [xi], xi b-xi d, xiii-xx, 81 p. 28 cm. (The Moore series of English translations of source books) "Collector's edition ... limited to fifty (50) signed and numbered copies ... No. 27. [Signed]: G. A. Moore." German and English. Bibliography: p. xi d. [JC141.R63] 51-7395
1. State, The. 2. Anabaptists. I. Moore, George Albert, 1893- ed. and tr. II. Title.

States, New.

APTER, David Ernest, 1924-
Political religion on the new nations. Berkeley, Calif., Institute of Industrial Relations and Institute of International Studies, University of California, 1964. [57]-104 p. 27 cm. (California. University. Institute of Industrial Relations. Reprint no. 233) "Reprinted ... from Old societies and new states, edited by Clifford Geertz ... 1963." NUC66
1. States, New. 2. Theocracy. 3. Asia — Religion. 4. Africa — Religion. I. Title. II. Series.

States, Small.

ECONOMIC consequences of the size of nations; proceedings of a conference held by the International Economic Association. Edited by E. A. G. Robinson. New York, St. Martin's Press, 1960. xxii, 446p. diagrs., tables. 23cm.
1. States, Small. 2. Economic development. I. International Economic Association. II. Robinson, Edward Austin Gossage, ed.

Statesmen—Canada—Biography.

BAKER, William M., 1943- 328.71'092'4 B
Timothy Warren Anglin, 1822-96, Irish Catholic Canadian / William M. Baker. Toronto ; Buffalo : University of Toronto Press, c1977. xiv, 336 p., [4] leaves of plates : ill. ; 24 cm. Originally presented as the author's thesis, University of Western Ontario. Includes bibliographical references and index. [F1033.A532B34 1977] 76-49480 ISBN 0-8020-5368-8 : 22.50
1. Anglin, Timothy Warren, 1822-1896. 2. Statesmen—Canada—Biography. I. Title.

Statesmen—Israel—Biography.

DAYAN, Moshe, 1915- 221.9'5
Living with the Bible / Moshe Dayan. New York : W. Morrow, 1978. 232 p. : ill. ; 26 cm. Includes index. [BS1197.D35] 78-52478 ISBN 0-688-03361-X : 14.95
1. Dayan, Moshe, 1915- 2. Bible. O.T.—History of Biblical events. 3. Statesmen—Israel—Biography. 4. Palestine—Antiquities. I. Title.

Stations of the Cross.

ABT, Emmanuel. 266.
The way of the cross. For the priest, the religious, and all other souls especially consecrated to God, or who aspire to perfection. Translated from the French of Le Pere Abt...By P.P.S. Baltimore, The Baltimore publishing company, 1888. v. 7-56 p. 13 cm. [BX2040.A6] 39-15990
1. Stations of the cross. I. SPP., tr. II. PPS., tr. III. Title.

BALTHASAR, Hans Urs von, 1905- 232.96'3
The way of the cross. Drawings by Joseph Hegenbarth. Translated by Rodelinde Albrecht and Maureen Sullivan. [New York] Herder and Herder [1969] 30 p. illus. 20 cm. Translation of Der Kreuzweg der St-Hedwigs Kathedrale in Berlin. [BX2040.B313 1969b] 69-17500 2.50
1. Stations of the Cross. I. Title.

BERNARDINI statuary company, New York 704
A few select specimens of the sculptors art in stations of the way of the cross. [Catalogue] New York 1 v. illus. 31 cm. Only latest issue in Library is kept on shelf. [NK1657.B4] CA 17
1. Stations of the cross. I. Title.

BLUNT, Hugh Francis, 1877- 264.02
The road of pain; considerations on the drama of the stations of the cross, by the Reverend Hugh F. Blunt. ... New York city, J. F. Wagner, inc. [c1937] v. 194 p. 19cm. [BX2040.B45] 38-1727
1. Stations of the cross. I. Title.

BORIES, Marcel. 232.96
Life through the cross; meditation on the Way of the Cross based on the seven sacraments. Translated by Kathryn Sullivan. New York, Desclee [1954?] 111p. 19cm. Translation of Ma vie par la croix. [BX2040] 56-3536
1. Stations of the Cross. 2. Sacraments—Catholic Church. I. Title.

BREIG, Joseph Anthony, 1905- 249
The family and the Cross; the Stations of the Cross and their relation to family life. Illustrated by Margaret Goldsmith. Chicago, H. Regnery Co., 1959. 83p. illus. 20cm. [BX2040.B7] 59-7861
1. Stations of the Cross. 2. Family—Religious life. I. Title.

BUETOW, Harold A 232.96
To Calvary with Christ. Milwaukee, Bruce Pub. Co. [1960] 136p. illus. 20cm. [BX2040.B76] 60-7392
1. Stations of the Cross. I. Title.

BUISSINK, P J. 264.02
Frequent journeys to Calvary; various exercises for the Way of the Cross.

Milwaukee, Bruce [1950] vi, 186 p. 23 cm. [BX2040.B78 1950] 50-6078
1. Stations of the Cross. 2. Catholic Church—Prayer-books and devotions—English. I. Title. II. Title: Various exercises for the Way of the Cross.

BUISSINK, P J. 264.02
Frequent journeys to Calvary; or, Various exercises for the way of the cross, by Rev. P. J. Buissink ... with supplement of several popular forms. 1st American ed. Grand Rapids, Mich., F. H. McGough & son, 1935. 149 p. 22 cm. [BX2040.B78] 36-7302
1. Stations of the cross. 2. Catholic church—Prayer-books and devotions—English. I. Title. II. Title: Various exercises for the way of the cross.

ELSNER, Paul J. 232.96
By Thy holy cross; considerations on the Stations of the Cross. Milwaukee, Bruce [1950] 69 p. 19 cm. [BX2040.E55] 50-6411
1. Stations of the Cross. I. Title.

HAMMES, John A. 232.963
To help you follow the way of the Cross: brief meditations drawn from the Scriptures. Milwaukee, Bruce [c.1964] vi, 120p. 16cm. 64-13748 1.50 pap.,
1. Stations of the Cross. I. Title.

HARTMANN, Helen Louise. 232.96
Journey of love; the Way of the Cross through the eyes of a mother, by Helen Louise Hartmann and Janice Brickey. Paterson, N.J., St. Anthony Guild Press [1960] 99p. illus. 16cm. [BX2040.H27] 60-14147
1. Stations of the Cross I. Brickey, Janice, Joint author. II. Title.

HOUSELANDER, Frances Caryll. 232.96
The way of the cross; written and illustrated by Caryll Houselander. New York, Sheed & Ward, 1955. 173p. illus. 20cm. [BX2040.H68] 55-7479
1. Stations of the Cross. I. Title.

LYNCH, Flann. 242
Come, take up your cross : the practical responsibilities of Christians today / Flann Lynch. Notre Dame, Ind. : Ave Maria Press, 1978, c1976. 95 p. : ill. ; 19 cm. [BX2040.L94 1978] 77-608263 ISBN 0-87793-144-5 pbk. : 2.95
1. Stations of the Cross. I. Title.

MARMION, Columba Abbot [secular name: Joseph Marmion] 232.96
The Way of the Cross, its efficacy and practice. Translated from the French by a nun of Tyburn Convent. St. Louis, B. Herder [1960] 39p. 17cm. 60-2685 .85 pap.,
1. Stations of the Cross. I. Title.

MUELLER, Joseph, 1868- 266.
Via salutis; or, Various methods of the exercise of the way of the cross ... by Rev. Jospeh Mueller, O. S. B. New York Christian press association publishing company, 1903 245 p. 13 x 8 cm. [BX2040.M8] 3-8671
1. Stations of the cross. I. Title.

ROBIN, Jean, 1890- 232.96
The royal road of the holy cross, by Abbe Jean Robin; authorized translation by M. R. Glover; illustrations by C. Bosseron Chambers. New York, P. J. Kenedy & sons [c1937] 6 p. l., 3-146 p. front., plates. 19 cm. [Full name: Jean Alphonse Charles Robin] [BX2040.R572] 37-12793
1. Stations of the cross. I. Glover, Marie Roberts, 1890- tr. II. Title.

ROPER, Anita, 1908- 242
The fifteenth station. With an epilogue by Karl Rahner. Translated by M. Dolores Sablone. [New York] Herder and Herder [1967] 108 p. 22 cm. Translation of Die 14 Stationen im Leben des NN. [BV2040.R613] 67-22226
1. Stations of the Cross. I. Title.

SHEEN, Fulton John, Bp., 1895- 232.96
The way of the cross. Garden City, N.Y., Garden City Books [1956? c1932] unpaged. illus. 13 cm. [BX2040] 56-286
1. Stations of the Cross. I. Title.

THE Stations of the cross. 264.
According to the method of St. Alphonsus Liguori, the method of St. Francis of Assisi, and the eucharistic method. With the Stabat mater in Latin and English ... New York, Cincinnati [etc.] Benziger brothers, 1900. 149 p. incl. front., plates. 12 1/2 cm. [BX2040.V45] 0-1888
1. Stations of the cross. 2. Stations of the cross. I. Liguori, Alfonso Maria de'Saint, 1696-1787. II. Francesco d'Assisi, Saint, 1182-1226. III. Liguori, Alfonso Maria de'Saint, 1696-1787. IV. Francesco d'Assisi, Saint, 1182-1226.

**STATIONS of the Cross for children.* 247.92
Written, illus. by the Daughters of St. Paul. Boston, St. Paul Eds. [dist. Daughters of St. Paul, c.1965] 30p. illus. (pt. col.) 18cm. .15 pap.,

THAYER, Mary Dixon. 266.
A child's way of the cross, by Mary Dixon Thayer. New York, The Macmillan company, 1928. 65 p. incl. plates. 19 cm. [BX2040.T5] 28-9962
1. Stations of the cross. I. Title.

VAN ZELLER, Hubert, 1905- 232.96
Approach to Calvary. New York, Sheed and Ward [1961] 128 p. illus. 10 cm. Secular name: Calude Van Zeller. [BX2040.V3] 61-7282
1. Stations of the Cross. I. Title. II. Series.

VAN ZELLER, Hubert, 1905-
The Way of the Cross; designs and text, by Dom Hubert van Zeller. Springfield, Ill., Templegate [1958] 1 v. (unpaged) illus. 18 cm.
1. Stations of the Cross. I. Title.

VEUTHEY, Leon. 232.96
The Way of the Cross. Translated by Theodoric Kernel. Chicago, Franciscan Herald Press [c1956] 106p. illus. 20cm. (Franciscan spirituality, no.3) [BX2040.V42] 57-1029
1. Stations of the Cross. I. Title.

VEUTHEY, Leon. 232.96
The Way of the Cross. Translated by Theodoric Kernel. Chicago, Franciscan Herald Press [c1956] 106 p. illus. 20 cm. (Franciscan spirituality, no. 8) [BX2040.V42] 57-1029
1. Stations of the Cross. I. Title.

[VIA crucis] The stations of the cross. According to the method of St. Alphonsus Liguori, the method of St. Francis of Assisi, and the Eucharistic method . . . New York, Cincinnati [etc.] Benziger bros., 1900. 149 pp. illus. 32. Copyright by Benziger bros., New York. 1900, class A, no. 6183, Feb. 26; 2 copies rec'd Feb. 26, 1900. Apr

WASHINGTON, D.C. Sulpician seminary. 264.02
The way of the cross in the seminary. Washington, D.C., Sulpician seminary [c1935] 71 p. illus. 15 cm. [BX2040.W3] 35-15606
1. Stations of the cross. I. Title.

THE Way of the Cross.
Edited by Louis F. Hartman, C. SS. R. New York, J. J. Crawley, 1956. [80]p. illus. (part col.) 14cm.
1. Stations of the Cross. I. Liguori, Alfonso Maria de', Saint, 1696-1787. II. Hartman, Louis F., ed. and tr.

Stations of the Cross-Meditations.

THE Way of the Cross of Our Lord and Savior Jesus Christ. With woodcuts by Michael Biggs. Chicago, Scepter [1959] 77p. illus. 19cm. (Sharon selection)
1. Stations of the Cross-Meditations. I. Guardini, Romano, 1885-

Staughton, William, 1770-1829.

LYND, Samuel W. 920.
Memoir of the Rev. William Staughton, D.D. By Rev. S. W. Lynd ... Boston, Lincoln, Edmands, & co.; Cincinnati, Hubbard and Edmands, 1834. vi, [7]-311, [1] p. front. (port.) 19 cm. [BX6495.S76L9] 7-23373
1. Staughton, William, 1770-1829. I. Title.

Staunton, Va.—Biography.

SECOND Presbyterian Church, Staunton, Va. 285'.1755'911
A history of the Second Presbyterian Church, Staunton, Virginia, 1875-1975. Staunton, Va. : The Church, c1975. 76 p. : ill. ; 24 cm. Includes index. [BX9211.S8S4 1975] 75-332489
1. Second Presbyterian Church, Staunton, Va. 2. Staunton, Va.—Biography. I. Title.

Stead, William Thomas, 1849-1912.

STEAD, Estelle Wilson. 920.
My father, personal & spiritual reminiscences, by Estelle W. Stead. New York, George H. Doran company, 1913. xii, 351 p. front., plates. ports. 23 cm. "Printed in England." [PN5123.S7S7] 14-2957
1. Stead, William Thomas, 1849-1912. 2. Spiritualism. I. Title.

STEAD, William T[homas] 1849-
The crucifixion: a narrative of Jesus' last week on earth; founded on the Oberammergau passion play. Chicago, Davis & co., 1900. 2 p. l., 225 p. 12 degrees. Jul
I. Title.

Stearns, George Munroe, 1831-1894.

JOHNSON, Clifton, 1865- 920
The parson's devil, by Clifton Johnson, the life story of George M. Stearns, one of the ablest, wittiest, and best loved of American lawyers; illustrated by Peter Newell. New York, Thomas Y. Crowell company [c1927] 8 p. l., 3-296 p. incl. front., plates. 21 cm. [CT275.S67J6] 27-1673
1. Stearns, George Munroe, 1831-1894. I. Title.

Stearns, Samuel Horatio, 1801-1837.

[STEARNS, William Augustus] 1805-1876. 922.573
Life of Rev. Samuel H. Stearns, late minister of the Old South church in Boston. New ed. Boston, J. Munroe and company, 1846. viii, 244 p. 20 cm. Preface signed: W. A. Stearns. [BX7260.S75S8 1846] 36-16666
1. Stearns, Samuel Horatio, 1801-1837. I. Title.

Stebbins, Horatio, 1821-1902.

MURDOCK, Charles Albert, 1841- 922.
Horatio Stebbins, his ministry and his personality, by Charles A. Murdock. Boston and New York, Houghton Mifflin company, 1921. x p., 1 l., 269, [1] p. incl. front. (port.) 22 cm. [BX9869.S7M7] 21-21577
1. Stebbins, Horatio, 1821-1902. I. Title.

Steckley, Anna Marie, 1917-

STECKLEY, Anna Marie, 1917- 280'.4 B
A song in the night : the true story of how the assurance of faith sustained a life through widowhood, tragedy, and illness / Anna Marie Steckley. Elgin, Il : Brethren Press, [1981] p. cm. [BR1725.S736A37] 19 80-29321 ISBN 0-87178-806-3 pbk. : 2.50
1. Steckley, Anna Marie, 1917- 2. Christian biography—United States. I. Title.

Steelberg, Wesley Rowland.

SUMRALL, Lester Frank, 1913- 922.89
'All for Jesus'; the life story of Wesley Rowland Steelberg. Springfield, Mo., Gospel Pub. House [1955] 260p. illus. 20cm. [BX6198.A7S8] 56-17683
1. Steelberg, Wesley Rowland. I. Title.

Steele, Harvey, 1911-

STEELE, Harvey, 1911- 266'.2'0924 B
Agent for change; the story of Pablo Steele as told to Gary MacEoin. Maryknoll, N.Y., Orbis Books [1973] xvi, 175 p. 22 cm. [HN32.S79] 72-85797 ISBN 0-88344-006-7 4.50
1. Steele, Harvey, 1911- I. MacEoin, Gary, 1909- II. Title.

Steensma, John.

STEENSMA, Juliana. 266.5'1519
The quality of mercy. Richmond, John Knox Press [1969] 143 p. illus., ports. 21 cm. [HV1559.K8S73] 69-13271 3.95
1. Steensma, John. 2. Physically handicapped—Rehabilitation—Korea. 3. Missions—Korea. I. Title.

Stehle, Aurelius, 1877-1930, comp.

CATHOLIC church. Liturgy and ritual. Ceremonial of bishops. 264.
Manual of episcopal ceremonies. Based on the caermoniale episcoporum, decrees of the Sacred congregation of rites, etc. and approved authors. Compiled by Rev. Aurelius Stehle ... [2d ed.] Beatty, Pa., St. Vincent archabbey press, 1916. 3 p. l., [ix]-xvi, 377 p. illus., diagrs. 23 cm. "Laying of the corner-stone of a church, performed by a bishop": 20 p. laid in. [BX1971.A25 1916] 16-11980
1. Stehle, Aurelius, 1877-1930, comp. I. Title.

Stein, Edith, 1891-1942.

BORDEAUX, Henry, 1870- 922.243
Edith Stein: thoughts on her life and times. Translated by Donald and Idella Gallagher. Milwaukee, Bruce Pub. Co. [c1959] 87p. 22cm. Translation of La vie pathetique d'edith Stein. Includes bibliography. [BX4705.S814B63] 59-14276
1. Stein, Edith, 1891-1942. I. Title.

FABREGUES, Jean de. 248.2460924
Edith Stein. [Translated from the French by Donald M. Antoine] Staten Island, N.Y., Alba House [1965] 138 p. 20 cm. Translation of La conversion d'Edith Stein. [BX4705.S814F313] 65-25849
1. Stein, Edith, 1891-1942. 2. Converts, Catholic. I. Title.

GRAEF, Hilda C 922.243
The scholar and the cross; the life and work of Edith Stein. London, New York, Longmans, Green [1955] 234p. illus. 23cm. [BX4705.S814G7 1955a] 55-2959
1. Stein, Edith, 1891-1942. I. Title.

GRAEF, Hilda C 922.243
The scholar and the cross; the life and work of Edith Stein. Westminster, Md., Newman Press, 1955. 234p. illus. 22cm. [BX4705.S814G7] 54-12447
1. Stein, Edith, 1891-1942. I. Title.

POSSELT, Teresia Renata de Spiritu Sancto, Sister, 1891- 922.243
Edith Stein; translated by Cecily Hastings and Donald Nicholl. London, New York, Sheed and Ward [1952] 238 p. illus. 21 cm. Secular name: Teresia Posselt. [BX4705.S814P63 1952] 52-2160
I. Stein, Edith, 1891-1942. II. Title.

POSSELT, Teresia Renata de Spiritu Sancto, Sister, 1891- 922.243
Edith Stein; translated by Cecily Hastings and Donald Nicholl. New York, Sheed and Ward, 1952. 238 p. illus. 21 cm. Secular name: Teresia Posselt. [BX4705.S814P63 1952 a] 52-4323
I. Stein, Edith, 1891-1942. II. Title.

ROBERTO, Brother, 1927- 922.243
The broken lamp; a story of Edith Stein. Illus. by Anthony Joyce. Notre Dame, Ind., Dujarie Press [1957] 94p. illus. 24cm. [BX4705.S814R6] 58-290
1. Stein, Edith, 1891-1942. I. Title.

Steinberg, Milton, 1903-1950.

NOVECK, Simon. 296.6'1'0924 B
Milton Steinberg : portrait of a rabbi / by Simon Noveck. New York : Ktav Pub. House, c1978. xii, 353 p., [8] leaves of plates : ill. ; 24 cm. Includes index. Bibliography: p. 330-337. [BM755.S67N68] 77-25943 ISBN 0-87068-444-2 : 12.50
1. Steinberg, Milton, 1903-1950. 2. Rabbis—United States—Biography.

Steiner, Rudolf, 1861-1925.

MCKNIGHT, Floyd, 1901- 149'.3
Rudolf Steiner and anthroposophy. New York, Anthroposophical Society in America [1967] 44 p. illus., port. 18 cm. [BP595.M3] 67-5589
1. Steiner, Rudolf, 1861-1925. 2. Anthroposophy. I. Title.

SPRING, Henry Powell, 1891- 212
Challenge to think, by Powell Spring ... Winter Park, Fla., The Rollins press, inc., 1942. xvi, 331 p. 1 illus. 20 1/2 cm. "Notes and partial bibliography": [323]-329. "A selected bibliography of writings by Rudolf Steiner": p. 330-331. [BP595.S6] 42-5461
1. Steiner, Rudolf, 1861-1925. 2. Anthroposophy. I. Title.

SPRING, Henry Powell, 1891- 212
Essays on human science, by Powell Spring ... Winter Park, Fla., The Orange press, 1943. 3 p. l., v-viii, 360 p. plates. 20 cm. Bibliography: p. 353-360. [BP595.S62] 43-14539
1. Steiner, Rudolf, 1861-1925. 2. Anthroposophy. I. Title.

STEFFEN, Albert, 1884- 921.3
In memoriam, Rudolf Steiner, by Albert Steffen; translated from the German by Olin D. Wannamaker. New York city, AnthropoSophic press, 1931. 3 p. l., [9]-44 p. 23 cm. "First edition." [B3333.Z7S66] 32-2253
1. Steiner, Rudolf, 1861-1925. I. Wannamaker, Olin Dantzier, tr. II. Title.

STEINER, Rudolf, 1861- 212
A road to self-knowledge, described in eight meditations, by Rudolph Steiner. London and New York, G. P. Putnam's sons, 1918. x, 124 p. 19 cm. "Authorized English translation, edited by H. Colleson." [BP565.S66] 20-6574
I. Title.

STEINER, Rudolf, 1861-1925. 921.3
The course of my life. Rev. translation by the authorized translator, Olin D. Wannamaker. New York, Anthroposophic Press, 1951. 376 p. illus. 24 cm. [BP595.S895A32] 51-7011
I. Title.

STEINER, Rudolf, 1861-1925. 193 B
The course of my life. Rev. translation by the authorized translator, Olin D. Wannamaker. [2d ed.] New York, Anthroposophic Press [1970, c1951] 358 p. ports. 25 cm. Translation of Mein Lebensgang. [BP595.S854883 1970] 78-121898

WACHSMUTH, Guenther, 1893- 921.3
The life and work of Rudolf Steiner from the turn of the century to his death. Translated by Olin D. Wannamaker and Reginald E. Raab. 2d ed., supplemented and expanded, of the volume published in 1941 under the title Die Geburt der Geisteswissenshaft (The birth of spiritual science) New York, Whittier Books [1955] 594p. illus. 25cm. [BP595.S895W35] 55-14834
1. Steiner, Rudolf, 1861-1925. 2. Anthroposophy. I. Title.

Steinkraus, Walter.

STEVEN, Hugh. 266'.023'0922 B
The measure of greatness. Old Tappan, N.J., F. H. Revell Co. [1973] 158 p. 21 cm. [BV3680.N52S88] 73-14950 ISBN 0-8007-0634-X 2.50 (pbk.)
1. Steinkraus, Walter. 2. Steinkraus, LaVonne. 3. Missions—New Guinea. I. Title.

Steno, Nicolaus, Bp., 1638-1686.

CIONI, Aaffaello 922.2489
Niles Stensen, scientist-bishop. Tr. [from Italian] by Genevieve M. Camera. Pref. by John LaFarge. New York, Kenedy [c.1962] 192p. 22cm. 62-16530 3.95
1. Steno, Nicolaus, Bp., 1638-1686. I. Title.

Stephan, Martin, 1777-1846.

FORSTER, Walter Otto. 284.1778
Zion on the Mississippi; the settlement of the Saxon Lutherans in Missouri, 1839-1841. Saint Louis, Concordia Pub. House, 1953. xiv, 606p. illus., ports., maps (part fold.) facsims. 24cm. An expansion and revision of 'the study ... originally prepared as a doctoral dissertation at Washington University in Saint Louis.' Bibliography: p. 584-594. [BX8061.M7F6] 53-9271
1. Stephan, Martin, 1777-1846. 2. Lutheran Church—Missouri Synod—Hist. 3. Lutherans in Missouri. 4. Germans in Missouri. I. Title. II. Title: Saxon Lutherans in Missouri.

Stephen, Saint, martyr

[COREY, George W]
St. Stephen ii. or, The deil among the dimecrats ... In seven cantos. By Spike Rider [pseud.] Cheyenne, Wyo., Daily Sun steam printing house, 1888. 166 p. 18 cm. 6-45583
I. Title.

KILGALLEN, John J. 226'.6'06
The Stephen speech : a literary and redactional study of Acts 7, 2-53 / [di] John Kilgallen. Rome : Biblical Institute Press, 1976. xiii, 187 p. ; 24 cm. (Analecta biblica ; 67) "Developed from a doctoral dissertation entitled A literary and redactional study of Acts 7, 2-53 (Pontifical Biblical Institute, Roma, 1974)" Includes indexes. Bibliography: p. [165]-170. [BS2625.2.K5] 77-364631
1. Stephen, Saint, Martyr. 2. Bible. N.T. Acts VII, 2-53—Criticism, interpretation, etc. I. Title. II. Series.

SIMON, Marcel. 225.92
St. Stephen and the Hellenists in the primitive church. London, New York, Longmans, Green [1958] 130 p. 21 cm. (The Haskell lectures, 1956) Includes bibliography. [BS2520.S8S5] 59-16126
1. Stephen, Saint, martyr I. Title.

Stephens family.

NAVESINK, N.H. All Saints' Memorial Church in the Highlands of Navesink.
All Saints' Memorial Church in the Highlands of Navesink, 1864-1964; [a centennial history. n.p., 1964] 56 p. illus. 22 cm. Includes Stephens family history. 66-41267
1. Stephens family. I. Title.

Stephenson, Colin.

STEPHENSON, Colin. 283'.092'4 B
Merrily on high. [1st American ed.] New York, Morehouse-Barlow Co. [1973, c1972] 192 p. 22 cm. [BX5199.S819A33 1973] 73-166415 ISBN 0-8192-1152-4 4.95
1. Stephenson, Colin. I. Title.

Stephenson, Percival William, 1888-1962.

COLE, Edmund Keith, 1919- 266.3'0924 B
Sincerity my guide; a biography of the Right Reverend P. W. Stephenson (1888-1962) by Keith Cole. [Melbourne, Church Missionary Historical Publications Trust] 1970. 127 p. illus., ports. 19 cm. (Great Australian missionaries) Includes bibliographical references. [BX5720.S8C64] 72-864218
1. Stephenson, Percival William, 1888-1962. I. Title.

Stepinac, Aloysius, Cardinal, 1898-1960.

O'BRIEN, Anthony Henry. 922.2497
Archbishop Stepinac, the man and his case; foreword by John C. McQuaid. Westminster, Md. Newman Bookshop, 1947. x, 100p. ports. 21 cm. [DR359.S75O2] 47-11257
1. Stepinac, Aloysius., Abp. I. Title.

RAYMOND, Father, 1903- 262'.135'0924 B
The man for this moment [by] M. Raymond. Staten Island, N.Y., Alba House [1971] xvii, 345 p. illus. 22 cm. Half-title: The life and death of Aloysius Cardinal Stepinac. [BX4705.S823R39] 77-169142 ISBN 0-8189-0220-5 6.95
1. Stepinac, Aloysius, Cardinal, 1898-1960. I. Title. II. Title: The life and death of Aloysius Cardinal Stepinac.

Sterling, Chandler W., Bp., 1911-

STERLING, Chandler W., Bp., 1911- 283'.092'4 B
Beyond this land of whoa, by Chandler W. Sterling. Philadelphia, United Church Press [1973] 141 p. 22 cm. "A Pilgrim Press book." [BX5995.S786A32] 73-5904 ISBN 0-8298-0261-4 4.95
1. Sterling, Chandler W., Bp., 1911- I. Title.

Sterlization (Birth control)—Moral and religious aspects—Catholic Church.

BOYLE, John P. 261.8'34'26
The sterlization controversy : a new crisis for the Catholic hospital? / By John P. Boyle. New York : Paulist Press, c1977. ix, 101 p. ; 21 cm. (An Exploration book) Includes bibliographical references and index. [RD585.B69] 77-7378 ISBN 0-8091-2016-X pbk. : 3.50
1. Sterlization (Birth control)—Moral and religious aspects—Catholic Church. 2. Catholic hospitals. I. Title.

Stern, Henry L., 1899-

STERN, Henry L., 1899- 133.9'1'0924 B
Help from beyond / by Henry L. Stern. New York : Walker, 1974. 177 p. ; 24 cm. [BF1283.S84A34 1974] 73-90380 ISBN 0-8027-0444-1 : 7.95
1. Stern, Henry L., 1899- 2. Spiritualism. I. Title.

Sterry, Peter, 1613-1672.

PINTO, Vivian de Sola. 928.2
Peter Sterry, Platonist and Puritan, 1613-1672; a biographical and critical study with passages selected from his writings by Vivian de Sola Pinto... Cambridge [Eng.] The University press, 1934. xiii, 242 p. front. (facsim.) 23 cm. Includes facsimile reproduction of t.-p. of "A discourse of the freedom of the will", London, 1675. "Passages selected from the writing of Peter Sterry": p. [119]-202. Bibliography: p. [223]-235. [PR3717.S15Z8] [922.542] 34-23303
1. Sterry, Peter, 1613-1672. I. Title.

Stetson, Mrs. Augusta Emma (Simmons) 1842?-1928.

KREISCHER, Louise, comp. 922.85
Our teacher, Augusta E. Stetson, C. S. D., by some of Mrs. Stetson's students, and an article from the Radio guide, July 1926. Compiled by LouiseKreischer and Bertha Hamilton. [New York, The Riverside printing service] 1932. 3 p. l., 59 p. front. (port.) illus. 19 cm. [BX6996.S7K7] 33-5390
1. Stetson, Mrs. Augusta Emma (Simmons) 1842?-1928. I. Hamilton, Bertha, joint comp. II. Radio guide. III. Title.

NEW York city Christian science institute. 922.
A tribute of love and gratitude to our faithful teacher, Augusta E. Stetson, C.S.D. [New York] New York city, Christian science institute [c1919] 1 p. l., [5]-8 p., 2 l., x p., 1 l., [11]-221 p. illus. (facsims.) col. pl., ports. 17 1/2 cm. Stetson, Mrs. Augusta Emma (Simmons) [BX6996.S7N4 1919] 20-4897
I. Title.

NEW York city Christian science institute. 922.
A tribute of love and gratitude to our faithful teacher, Augusta E. Stetson, C.S.D. principal of the New York city Christian science institute... 2d ed. ... New York and London, G. P. Putnam's sons, 1921. 291 ports, facsims. 17 1/2 cm. [BX6996.S7N4 1921] 21-4815
1. Stetson, Mrs. Augusta Emma (Simmons) 1842?-1928. I. Title.

NEW York city Christian science institute.
Vital issues in Christian science; a record of unsettled questions which arose in the year 1909, between the directors of the Mother church, the First church of Christ, scientist, Boston, Massachusetts, and First church of Christ, scientist, New York city, eight of its nine trustees and sixteen of its practitioners. [By] New York city Christian science institute, Augusta E. Stetson, C.S.D., principal. With facsimiles of excerpts and letters of Mary Baker Eddy. 3d thousand. New York and London, G. P. Putnam's sons, 1914. vii, 405 p. incl. facsims. 22 cm. [BX6931.N4 1914a] 14-9368
1. Stetson, Mrs. Augusta Emma (Simmons) 1842?-1928. 2. Christian science. I. Eddy, Mrs. Mary (Baker) 1821-1910. II. Title.

NEW York city Christian science institute.
Vital issues in Christian science, a record of unsettled questions which arose in the year 1909, between the directors of the Mother church, the First church of Christ, scientist, Boston, Massachusetts, and First church of Christ, scientist, New York city, eight of its nine trustees and sixteen of its practitioners. [By] New York city Christian science institute, Augusta E. Stetson, C.S.D., principal; with facsimiles of excerpts and letters of Mary Baker Eddy. 5th thousand. New York and London, G. P. Putnam's sons, 1917. vii, 405 p. incl. facsims. 22 cm. [BX6931.N4 1917] 29-24241
1. Stetson, Mrs. Augusta Emma (Simmons) 1842?-1928. 2. Eddy, Mrs. Mary (Baker) 1821- 1910. 3. Christian science. I. Title.

[STETSON, Augusta Emma (Simmons) Mrs.] comp. 922.
Correspondence of interest to the members of the Choral society of the New York city Christian science institute, and letters, essays, poems, etc., on Christian science as taught by Mary Baker Eddy. [New York, New York city Christian science institute, c1918] 1 p. l., iii, 174 p. 18 cm. Foreword signed: Augusta E. Stetson. [BX6996.S7A5] 18-18800
I. New York city Christian science institute. II. Title.

SWIHART, Altman K. 289.5
Since Mrs Eddy, by Altman K. Swihart. New York, H. Holt and company [c1931] xii, 402 p. 2 port. (incl. front.) 22 1/2 cm. (Half-title: Studies in religion and culture. American religion series, III) Bibliography: p. 337-357. [BX6997.S8] 31-16855
1. Stetsom, Mrs. Augusta Emma (Simmons) 1842?-1928. 2. Bill, Mrs. Annie Cecilia (Bulmer) 1865?- 3. Christian science. I. Title.
Contents omitted.

SWIHART, Altman K., 1903- 289.5
Since Mrs. Eddy, by Altman K. Swihart... New York, H. Holt and company [1931] xii, 402 p., 1 l., 2 port. (incl. front.) 21 1/2 cm. (Half-title: Studies in religion and culture. American religion series, III) Thesis (PH.D.)--Columbia university, 1931. Vita. Published also without thesis note. Bibliography: p. [335]-357. [BX6997.S8 1921] 31-31952
1. Stetson, Mrs. Augusta Emma (Simmons) 1842?-1928. 2. Bill, Mrs. Annie Cecilia (Bulmer) 1853?- 3. Christian science. I. Title.
Contents omitted.

Steuben Baptist association.

CARTER, Thomas William. 286.
Centennial history of the Steuben Baptist association and of its original churches and pioneer pastors. [By] Thomas William Carter. Bath, N. Y. [The Courier press] 1917. 105, [6] p. plates, ports. 23 cm. [BX6209.S8C3] 18-6302
1. Steuben Baptist association. I. Title.

Steven, Norma.

STEVEN, Norma. 248'.833
Please, can I come home? No, you can't come home! Old Tappan, N.J., F. H. Revell Co. [1973] 126 p. illus. 19 cm.

Exchange of letters between the author and her daughter Wendy. [BJ1681.S73] 73-6794 ISBN 0-8007-0619-6 1.95 (pbk.)
1. Steven, Norma. 2. Steven, Wendy. 3. Young women—Conduct of life. I. Steven, Wendy. II. Title.

Stevens, Beulah Fern, 1937-

STEVENS, Beulah Fern, 1937- 248'.4
Dear Georgia ... / by Beulah Fern Stevens. Nashville : Southern Pub. Association, c1978. p. cm. [BV4501.2.S758] 78-13546 ISBN 0-8093-0851-7 pbk : 0.50
1. Stevens, Beulah Fern, 1937- 2. Christian life—1960- I. Title.

Stevens, Leroy Sylvan, 1895-1916.

STEVENS, Leon Herbert, 1888- 133.
Letters from Roy; or, The spirit voice, by Leon H. Stevens; being a series of messages received during daily communication with Leroy S. Stevens, who passed to spirit life on March thirtieth, 1916. Boston, Christopher publishing house [c1917] 1 p. l., [5]-114 p. incl. front. (port.) 21 cm. [BF1301.S7] 17-29750 1.00
1. Stevens, Leroy Sylvan, 1895-1916. 2. Spiritualism. I. Title.

STEVENS, Leon Herbert, 1888- 133.
The second letters from Roy, by Leon H. Stevens, further progress in the messages from the life beyond, as coming from Leroy S. Stevens, who since his passing, has given us the previous book, called "Letters from Roy." Boston, Christopher publishing house [c1918] 179 p. 1 l. front.(port.) 21 cm. [BF1301.S73] 18-22880 1.25
1. Stevens, Leroy Sylvan, 1895-1916. 2. Spiritualism. I. Title.

Stevenson, Dwight Eshelman, 1906-

DWIGHT E. Stevenson : 230
a tribute by some of his former students / editor, William R. Barr. Lexington, Ky. : Lexington Theological Seminary, 1975. 67 p. ; 25 cm. On spine: Stevenson tribute volume. Contents.Contents.—White, R. C. Dwight E. Stevenson, teacher of preachers.—Reid, M. K. On identifying the word of God today.—Spainhower, J. I. It occurs to me.—Blanton, Betty L. God's continuing incarnation through us.—Wilson, G. H. Always a pilgrim?—Barr, W. R. The presentation of Christ.—Pierson, R. M. A selected listing of some of the literary productions of Dwight E. and Deloris Stevenson. Includes bibliographical references. [BR50.D85] 75-330964
1. Stevenson, Dwight Eshelman, 1906- 2. Stevenson, Dwight Eshelman, 1906- —Bibliography. 3. Theology. I. Stevenson, Dwight Eshelman, 1906- II. Barr, William R. III. Title: Stevenson tribute volume.

Stevenson, William, 1768-1857.

VERNON, Walter N. 922.773
William Stevenson, riding preacher. Dallas, Southern Methodist Univ. Pr. [c.]1964. xiii, 78p. illus., facsims. 23cm. Bibl. [BX8495.S767V4] 65-1232 1.45 pap.,
1. Stevenson, William, 1768-1857. I. Title.

Stevenson, William Barron, 1869- joint author.

YOUNG, Robert, 1882-1888. 220.5'203
Young's Analytical concordance to the Bible : containing about 311,000 references subdivided under the Hebrew and Greek originals with the literal meaning and pronunciation of each : based upon the King James version / by Robert Young ; rev. by William B. Stevenson and David Wimbish. Nashville : T. Nelson Publishers, 1980. 1236 p. in various pagings ; 28 cm. [BS425.Y7 1980] 19 80-29084 ISBN 0-8407-4985-6 : 18.95
1. Stevenson, William Barron, 1869- joint author. 2. Wimbish, David, joint author. 3. Bible—Concordances, English. 4. Hebrew language—Dictionaries—English. 5. Greek language, Biblical—Dictionaries—English. I. Title. II. Title: Analytical concordance to the Bible.

Stewardship, Christian.

AGAR, Frederick Alfred, 1872- 248
The stewardship of life; by Frederick A. Agar. New York, Chicago, etc. Fleming H. Revell company, [c1920] 107 p. 19 cm. [BV4501.A4] 20-2496
I. Title.

AGAR, Frederick Alfred, 1872- 248
The stewardship of life, by Frederick A. Agar. New York, Chicago [etc.] Fleming H. Revell company [c1924] 2 p. l., 113 p. 19 cm. [BV4501.A4 1924] 25-4422
I. Title.

ALDERFER, Helen, ed. 248.8
A farthing in her hand; stewardship for women. Scottdale, Pa., Herald Pr. [c.1964] vi, 222p. 18cm. Bibl. [BV772.A46] 64-23376 3.50
1. Stewardship, Christian. 2. Woman—Religious life. I. Title.

AMMERMAN, Leila Tremaine. 223'.7'06
The golden ladder of stewardship. Natick, Mass., W. A. Wilde Co. [1962] 66p. 20cm. [BV772.A48] 62-13688
1. Stewardship, Christian. I. Title.

ANDERSON, Robert Phillips, 1866- 254
Studies in stewardship, by Rev. Robert P. Anderson ... Boston, Chicago, United society of Christian endeavor [c1923] 95 p. 18 cm. [BV772.A5] 24-678
I. Title.

APPLEGARTH, Margaret Tyson, 1886- 254.8
Twelve baskets full. [1st ed.] New York, Harper [1957] 245p. 22cm. [BV772.A65] 56-12059
1. Stewardship, Christian. I. Title.

APPLEGARTH, Margaret Tyson, 1886- 254.8
Twelve baskets full, by Margaret T. Applegarth. Grand Rapids, Mich., Baker Book House [1973, c1947] 245 p. 19 cm. [BV772.A65 1973] 2.95 (pbk.)
1. Stewardship, Christian. I. Title.
L.C. card no. for original ed.: 56-12059.

BALCOMB, Raymond E. 254.8
Stir what you've got! and other stewardship studies [by] Raymond E. Balcomb. Nashville, Abingdon Press [1968] 160 p. 21 cm. [BV772.B25] 68-17443
1. Stewardship, Christian. I. Title.

BALDWIN, Maud Junkin. 268.
Using our heavenly Father's gifts; stewardship lessons for juniors, by Maud Junkin Baldwin. Philadelphia, The Westminister press, 1924. 56 p. 19 cm. "Reference books for teachers": p. 6. [BV1546.B39] 24-18297
I. Title.

BERNER, Carl W. 248
The power of pure stewardship [by] Carl W. Berner, Sr. St. Louis, Concordia Pub. House [1970] 125 p. illus. 21 cm. [BV772.B38] 77-126536
1. Stewardship, Christian. I. Title.

BOCKELMAN, Eleanor. 259
The stewardess. Columbus, Ohio, Wartburg Press [1956] 71p. 20cm. [BV772.B6] 56-57288
1. Stewardship, Christian. 2. Woman—Religious life. I. Title.

BRATTGARD, Helge, 1920- 248
God's stewards; a theological study of the principles and practices of stewardship. Translated by Gene J. Lund. Minneapolis, Augsburg Pub. House [c1963] 248 p. 23 cm. Full name: Heige Axel Kristian Brattgard. Bibliography: p. 241-248. [BV772.B68] 63-16594
1. Stewardship, Christian. I. Title.

BRAZELL, George. 248.6
This is stewardship. Springfield, Mo., Gospel Pub. House [1962] 127 p. 20 cm. Includes bibliographies. [BV772.B7] 62-20510
1. Stewardship, Christian. I. Title.

BROWN, L. David. 248'.6
Take care : a guide for responsible living / L. David Brown. Minneapolis : Augsburg Pub. House, c1978. 142 p. ; 20 cm. [BV772.B74] 78-52200 ISBN 0-8066-1665-2 pbk. : 2.95
1. Stewardship, Christian. I. Title.

BUCK, Carlton C 254.8
At the Lord's treasury; a stewardship manual. St. Louis, Bethany Press [1959] 192p. 16cm. Includes bibliography. [BV772.B77] 58-59535
1. Stewardship, Christian. I. Title.

BURKHALTER, Frank Elisha, 1880- 248
Living abundantly, a study in Christian stewardship [by] Frank E. Burkhalter ... Nashville, Tenn., The Sunday school board of the Southern Baptist convention [1942] 144 p. 19 cm. Bibliography: p. 143-144. [BV770.B77] 42-18907
1. Stewardship, Christian. I. Southern Baptist convention. Sunday school board. II. Title.

CALKINS, Harvey Reeves.
Stewardship starting points; an introduction, by Harvey Reeves Calkins. [Chicago] The Epworth league of the Methodist Episcopal church [c1916] 112 p. 15 cm. 16-20312 0.35
I. Title.

CARROLL, Ramon Leonard. 248.4'8'99
Stewardship: total-life commitment. [1st ed.] Cleveland, Tenn., Pathway Press [1967] 144 p. 22 cm. [BV772.C37] 67-26668
1. Stewardship, Christian. 2. Christian life. I. Title.

CASEMORE, Robert.
There were twelve; a collection of twelve stewardship plays. Edited, and with an introduction by Malcolm D. Blackburn. [New York, Published for the Dept. of Stewardship and Benevolence, by the Office of Publication and Distribution, National Council of the Churches of Christ in the U.S.A., c1964] c. 238 p. 66-32216
1. Stewardship, Christian. 2. Religious drama. I. Title.

CHRISTIAN stewardship and church finance. 261.8
Foreword by J. D. Grey. Grand Rapids, Zondervan Pub. House [1953] 153p. 20cm. [BV770.E4] [BV770.E4] 254 53-28736 53-28736
1. Stewardship, Christian. I. Ellis, Hallett West, 1882-

CHURCH, Pharcellus, 1801-1886. 254
The philosophy of benevolence. By Pharcellus Church ... New-York, Leavitt, Lord & co. Boston, Crocker & Brewster, 1836. vi, [7]-355 p. 19 1/2 cm. [BV770.C55] 43-27315
1. Stewardship, Christian. I. Title.

CLINARD, Turner Norman. 248'.4
Responding to God : the life of stewardship / by Turner N. Clinard ; [book design by Dorothy Alden Smith]. 1st ed. Philadelphia : Westminster Press, c1980. 118 p. ; 21 cm. Includes bibliographical references. [BV772.C56] 79-24762 ISBN 0-664-24292-8 pbk. : 6.95
1. Stewardship, Christian. I. Title.

CONRAD, Paul H 254
This way to a thriving church. New York, Abingdon-Cokesbury Press [1947] 96 p. diagr. 23 cm. [BV772.C65] 48-5654
1. Stewardship, Christian. I. Title.

COOPER, Claire (Hill) Mrs. 1891- 248
Not your own [by] Claire Hill Cooper. Nashville, Tenn., The Sunday school board of the Southern Baptist convention [c1937] 110 p. 19 cm. [BV772.C755] 37-29371
1. Stewardship, Christian. 2. Religious education. I. Title.

COWLING, Ellis, 1905- 254.8
Let's think about money. New York, Abingdon Press [1957] 95p. 19cm. [BV772.C76] 57-1588
1. Stewardship, Christian. I. Title.

CRAWFORD, Julius Earl. 254
The call to Christian stewardship, by Julius Earl Crawford. Nashville, Tenn., Dallas, Tex. [etc.] Publishing house of the M. E. church, South, Lamar & Barton, agents, 1924. 131 p. 20 cm. Bibliography: p. 130-131. [BV771.C8] 24-15691
I. Title.

CUNNINGHAM, Richard B. 248'.6
Creative stewardship / Richard B. Cunningham. Nashville : Abingdon, c1979. 128 p. ; 20 cm. (Creative leadership series) Includes bibliographical references. [BV772.C779] 79-973 ISBN 0-687-09844-0 pbk. : 4.95
1. Stewardship, Christian. 2. Christian giving. 3. Church finance. I. Title. II. Series.

CUSHMAN, Ralph Spaulding, bp., 1879- 254
The message of stewardship; a book for daily devotions and class study, by Ralph S. Cushman. New York, Cincinnati, The Abingdon press [c1922] 240 p. 17 cm. [BV772.C8] 22-23920
1. Stewardship, Christian. 2. Meditations. I. Title.

CUSHMAN, Ralph Spaulding, bp., 1879- 254
The message of stewardship, a book for daily devotions and class study. A complete revision. [By] Ralph Spaulding Cushman. New York, Nashville, Abingdon-Cokesbury press [1946] 256 p. illus. 17 cm. [BV772.C8 1946] 46-20694
1. Stewardship, Christian. 2. Meditations. I. Title.

CUSHMAN, Ralph Spaulding, 1879- 262.
The new Christian; studies in stewardship (revised) by Ralph S. Cushman. New York city, Interchurch press [c1920] 10, [4], 13-146 p. 18 cm. [BX8339.C7 1920] 20-9053
1. Stewardship, Christian. I. Title.

CUSHMAN, Ralph Spaulding, bp., 1879- 254
Will a man rob God? Four studies in Christian stewardship, by Ralph Spaulding Cushman ... New York, Nashville, Abingdon-Cokesbury press [1942] 75, [1] p. 19 1/2 cm. [BV770.C8] 42-22632
1. Stewardship, Christian. I. Title.

*DAVIDS, David E. 248.42
Christian Stewardship. New York, Carlton [c.1965] 67p. 21cm. (Reflection bk.) 2.00
I. Title.

DAVIDS, David E
Christian stewardship, by David E. Davids. New York, Carlton Press [1965] 67 p. 21 cm. (A Reflection book) NUC67
1. Stewardship, Christian. I. Title.

DICK, Opal Wheeler. 254
5 little pennies and how they grew, by Opal Wheeler Dick, illustrated by Virginia Lohmon. Washington, D.C., Review and herald publishing association [1946] 90 p. illus. 23 1/2 cm. [BV772.D45] 47-519
1. Stewardship, Christian. I. Title.

DIETZE, Charles E., 1919- 248'.6
God's trustees, to whom much is given / Charles E. Dietze. Saint Louis, Mo. : Bethany Press, c1976. 92 p. ; 22 cm. Includes bibliographical references. [BV772.D46] 75-43848 ISBN 0-8272-1216-X pbk. : 3.95
1. Stewardship, Christian. I. Title.

DOLLAR, Truman. 248'.6
How to carry out God's stewardship plan. Nashville, T. Nelson [1974] 191 p. 21 cm. Bibliography: p. 189-191. [BV772.D73] 74-840 6.95
1. Stewardship, Christian. I. Title.

DYCK, Cornelius J. 248
They gave themselves; lessons in Christian stewardship, Newton, Kan., Faith and Life Pr., 724 Main [1965] 111, [1]p. 17cm. Bibl. [BV772.D9] 64-8699 .40 pap.,
1. Stewardship, Christian. I. Title.

EGGERICHS, Fred W., 1912- 248'.6
A bag without holes : how to prepare for your family, your finances, your future / by Fred W. Eggerichs, with Bernard Palmer. Minneapolis : Bethany Fellowship, [1975] 95 p. ; 21 cm. [BV772.E4] 74-23435 ISBN 0-87123-532-3 ; 2.25
1. Stewardship, Christian. I. Title.

ELY, Virginia, 1899- 248.42
Stewardship: witnessing for Christ. [Westwood, N.J.] Revell [c.1962] 96p. 20cm. 62-10736 1.95
1. Stewardship, Christian. I. Title.

ESPIE, John C. 248'.6
Opportunities in stewardship for concerned Christians in a local church / John C. Espie, Thomas C. Rieke. Nashville : Discipleship Resources, c1975. 148 p. : ill. ; 28 cm. Includes index. Bibliography: p. 145. [BV772.E83] 75-10371
1. Stewardship, Christian. I. Rieke, Thomas C., joint author. II. Title.

EVANS, Silas, 1876- 248
The currency of the invisible; a spiritual interpretation of stewardship, by Silas Evans ... introduction by David McConaughy ... New York, Chicago [etc.] Fleming H. Revell company [c1925] 96 p. 20 cm. [BV4501.E8] 25-20509
I. Title.

FISHER, Wallace E. 248'.6
All the good gifts : on doing Biblical stewardship / Wallace E. Fisher. Minneapolis : Augsburg Pub. House, c1979. 111 p. ; 20 cm. Bibliography: p. 109-111. [BV772.F48] 79-50077 ISBN 0-8066-1702-0 pbk. : 2.95
1. Stewardship, Christian. 2. Christian giving. I. Title.

FISHER, Wallace E. 248'.6
A new climate for stewardship / Wallace E. Fisher. Nashville : Abingdon Press, c1976. 127 p. ; 19 cm. [BV772.F5] 76-109 ISBN 0-687-27723-X : 3.95
1. Stewardship, Christian. I. Title.

FLYNN, Leslie B. 254.8
Your God and your gold. Grand Rapids, Mich., Zondervan [c.1961] 137p. 61-66732 2.50 bds.,
1. Stewardship, Christian. I. Title.

FOLLOWING St. Francis, 248.482
no. 5.
Stewardship. Pulaski, Wis., Franciscan Pubs. [c.1966] 48p. 19cm. .25 pap.,
I. Title.

FOUND faithful; 261.8
Christian stewardship in personal and church life. Nashville, Broadman Press [1953] 142p. illus. 19cm. [BV772.M55] 254 53-12600
1. Stewardship, Christian. I. Moore, Merrill Dennis, 1904-

FREEMAN, John Davis, 1884- 254
More than money, by John D. Freeman ... Nashville, Tenn., The Sunday school board of the Southern Baptist convention [c1935] 154 p. 19 cm. Bibliography: p. 154. [BV770.F7] 36-729
1. Stewardship, Christian. I. Title.

GARRISON, Winfred Ernest, 1874-
Stewards of the grace of God, by Winfred E. Garrison. [Indianapolis, Dept. of Evangelism, United Christian Missionary Society, 196-] Unpaged. Cover title. 67-25584
1. Stewardship, Christian. I. Title.

GOOD stewards. 261.8
Nashville, Broadman Press [1953] 141p. 20cm. Includes bibliography. [BV772.D48] [BV772.D48] 254 53-12597 53-12597
1. Stewardship, Christian. I. Dillard, James Edgar, 1879-

HARRELL, Costen Jordan, 254.8
1885-
Stewardship and the tithe. Nashville, Abingdon-Cokesbury Press [1953] 61p. 20c4. [BV772.H225] 54-3107
1. Stewardship, Christian. I. Title.

HARTMAN, Levi Balmer, 1838- 254
1907.
The business aspect of Christian stewardship, by L. B. Hartman ... Philadelphia, American Baptist publication society, 1907. vi, 7-89 p. 17 cm. [BV770.H3] 7-7183
1. Stewardship, Christian. I. Title.

HASTINGS, Robert J 248.486
The Christian man's world; a study of the total stewardship of life for Baptist men [by] Robert J. Hastings. Memphis, Brotherhood Commission, SBC, 1964. 94 p. illus. 22 cm. Bibliography: p. 93-94. [BV772.H32] 64-54538
1. Stewardship, Christian. I. Title.

HASTINGS, Robert J. 254.8
My money and God. Nashville, Broadman Press [c.1961] 127p. Bibl. notes: p.126-127. 61-5393 2.50
1. Stewardship, Christian. I. Title.

HATCH, Clarence W 1903-1960. 254
Stewardship enriches life. Rev. by Mildred Hatch. Anderson, Ind., Warner Press [1962] 96p. 21cm. [BV772.H34 1962] 62-13335
1. Stewardship, Christian. I. Title.

HATCH, Clarence W 1903-1960. 254
Stewardship enriches life. Anderson, Ind., Warner Press [1951] 107 p. 20 cm. [BV772.H34] 51-13778
1. Stewardship, Christian. I. Title.

HICKERSON, May Josephine 254.8
(compere.)
These dared to share. [Teacher's ed.] Nashville, Broadman Press [1952] 102 p. illus. 20 cm. [BV772.H5] 52-38081
1. Stewardship, Christian. I. Title.

HOWELL, Roy Wilbur 254.8
Saved to serve; accent on stewardship. Grand Rapids, Mich., Baker Bk. [c.]1965. 132p. 20cm. Bibl. [BV772.H63] 65-28579 1.95 pap.,
1. Stewardship, Christian. I. Title.

JONES, George Curtis, 1911- 261.8
Christian stewardship: what are you worth? St. Louis, Bethany Press [1954] 159p. 20cm. [BV772.J6] 254 54-2649
1. Stewardship, Christian. I. Title. II. Title: What are you worth?

KANTONEN, Taito Almar 1900- 261.8
A theology for Christian stewardship. Philadelphia, Muhlenberg Press [1956] ix, 126p. 21cm. Bibliographical footnotes. [BV772.K26] 254 56-9341
1. Stewardship, Christian. 2. Theology, Doctrinal. I. Title.

KAUFFMAN, Milo, 1898- 261.8
The challenge of Christian stewardship. Scottdale, Pa., Herald Press [1955] xii, 180p. 21cm. (The Conrad Grebel lectures for 1953) Bibliography: p. 169-175. [BV772.K3] 254 55-9814
1. Stewardship, Christian. I. Title. II. Series.

KEECH, William J. 250
The life I owe; Christian stewardship as a way of life. Valley Forge, Judson [c.1963] 108p. 21cm. Bibl. 63-13989 1.50 pap.,
1. Stewardship, Christian. I. Title.

KUNTZ, Kenneth A. 250
Wooden chalices, new ideas for stewardship. St. Louis, Bethany [c.1963] 192p. 23cm. Bibl. 62-22316 3.50
1. Stewardship, Christian. I. Title.

LACY, Mary Lou. 248.4
Springboard to discovery. Richmond, John Knox Press [1965] 92 p. 21 cm. [BV772.L3] 65-10277
1. Stewardship, Christian. I. Title.

LAUBACH, Frank Charles, 261.85
1884-
What Jesus had to say about money. Grand Rapids, Mich., Zondervan [c.1966] 63p. 21cm. [BV772.L36] 64-8845 1.00 pap.,
1. Stewardship, Christian. I. Title.

LAUBACH, Frank Charles, 1884-
What Jesus had to say about money, by Frank C. Laubach. Grand Rapids, Zondervan Pub. House [1966] 63 p. 21 cm.
1. Stewardship, Christian. I. Title.

LAUBACH, Frank Charles, 261.85
1884-
What Jesus had to say about money, by Frank C. Laubach. Grand Rapids, Zondervan Pub. House [1966] 63 p. 21 cm. [BV772.L36] 64-8845
1. Stewardship, Christian. I. Title.

LAYTON, Mac, 1931- 248.6
This grace also. 1st ed. Dallas, Christian Pub. Co. [c1964] xi, 279 p. 23 cm. Includes bibliographical references. [BV772.L38] 65-5011
1. Stewardship, Christian. I. Title.

LINDHOLM, Paul R
Manual on Christian stewardship and church finances. 3d ed. New York, World horizons, 1961 xxi, 330 p. illus. 19 cm. (A World horizons book) Cover title: Christian stewardship and church finance. Includes bibliography. 63-26706
1. Stewardship, Christian. 2. Church finance. I. Title.

LOVEJOY, Luther Ellsworth, 1864-
1936.
... *Stewardship for all of life,* by Luther E. Lovejoy ... New York, Cincinnati, The Methodist book concern [c1924] 144 p. 19 cm. (Life and service series) "Approved by the Committee on curriculum of the Board of Sunday schools of the Methodist Episcopal church." Bibliography: p. 15. [BX8225.L6] 24-28698
I. Title.

MCBAIN, John M. 248'.6
It is required of stewards [by] John M. McBain. Nashville, Tenn., Broadman Press [1972] 128 p. 20 cm. [BV772.M27] 72-79172 ISBN 0-8054-8505-8
1. Stewardship, Christian. I. Title.

MCCALL, Duke K. 254
God's hurry. Nashville, Broadman Press [1949] xxiv, 120 p. 20 cm. Bibliography: p. 118-120. [BV772.M28] 50-3646
1. Stewardship, Christian. I. Title.

MCCONNELL, Francis John, 261
bp., 1871-
Christian materialism; inquiries into the getting, spending and giving of money, By Francis John McConnell. New York, Friendship press [c1936] xiii, 167 p. 20 cm. [BV770.M24] 36-18863
1. Stewardship, Christian. I. Title.

MCEACHERN, Ted. 248
Being there for others. Nashville, Abingdon Press [1967] 158 p. illus. 19 cm. Bibliography: p. 157-158. [BV4501.2.M23] 67-24330
1. Stewardship, Christian. 2. Christian life—Methodist authors. I. Title.

MCGEACHY, Pat, 1929- 248'.6
Traveling light / Pat McGeachy. Nashville : Abingdon Press, [1975] 112 p. ; 19 cm. Includes bibliographical references. [BV772.M3514] 75-17572 ISBN 0-687-42530-1 pbk. : 3.25
1. Stewardship, Christian. I. Title.

MCMULLEN, John S. 250
Stewardship unlimited, a cooperative text, pub. for the Cooperative Pubn. Assn. Richmond, Va., John Knox [1962, c.1961] 94p. 20cm. (Faith for life ser.) 62-19445 1.00, 1.25 pap., after Jan. 1,
1. Stewardship, Christian. I. Title.

MACNAUGHTON, John H. 248'.6
Stewardship-myth and methods : a program guide for ministers and lay leaders / John H. MacNaughton. New York : Seabury Press, [1975] xv, 137 p. ; 21 cm. "A Crossroad book." [BV772.M355] 75-5878 ISBN 0-8164-2112-9 pbk. : 3.95
1. Stewardship, Christian. 2. Church finance. I. Title.

*MARTIN, Alfred. 220'.07
Not my own; total commitment in stewardship. Chicago, Moody [1968] 126p. 18 cm. (MP33-528) .50 pap.,
I. Title.

MEANS, Frank K. 254
Give ye! A study of stewardship and missions, by Frank K. Means ... Nashville, Tenn., Broadman press [1944] ix p., 1 l., 166 p. 19 cm. Bibliographical foot-notes. [BV770.M4] 44-47812
1. Stewardship, Christian. I. Title.

MEDLIN, Josephine (Riley) 254
Mrs.
The Steward family, by Josephine Riley Medlin. Nashville, Tenn., Broadman press [1942] 3 p. l., 9-73 p. illus. 20 cm. [BV772.M4] 42-14148
1. Stewardship, Christian. I. Title.

MILLER, Basil William, *254.8
1897-
Treasury of stewardship illustrations; 164 sparkling illustrations of march to fame and infamy. [1st ed.] Kansas City, Mo., Beacon Hill Press [1952] 192 p. 20 cm. [BV772.M5] 52.9724
1. Stewardship, Christian. 2. Homiletical illustrations. I. Title.

MOORE, Merrill Dennis, 261.8
1904-
Found faithful; Christian stewardship in personal and church life. Nashville Convention Press [1958, c1953] 146p. illus. 20cm. [BV772.M55 1958] 254 58-10985
1. Stewardship, Christian. I. Title.

MORRILL, Guy Louis. 254
More stewardship stories, by Guy L. Morrill ... New York and London, Harper & brothers [c1941] vii p., 1 l., 11-96 p. 18 1/2 cm. "First edition." [BV772.M57] 41-3152
1. Stewardship, Christian. I. Title.

MORRILL, Guy Louis. 254
Stewardship stories, by Guy L. Morrill ... New York, George H. Doran company [c1927] x p., 1 l., 13-91 p. illus. 19 cm. [BV772.M58] 27-24941
I. Title.

MURRAY, Andrew, 1828-1917. 254
Money: thoughts for God's stewards, by Rev. Andrew Murray ... New York, Chicago [etc.] Fleming H. Revell company, 1897. 96 p. 16 x 10 cm. [BV772.M8] 40-23867
1. Stewardship, Christian. I. Title.

NASH, Gerald R. 248
Investment, the miracle offering, by Gerald R. Nash, Lois M. Parker. Mountain View, Calif., Pacific Pr. [c.1965] xii, 146p. illus. 22cm. [BV772.N3] 65-21139 3.25
1. Stewardship, Christian. I. Parker, Lois M., joint author. II. Title.

NASH, Gerald R. 248
Investment, the miracle offering, by Gerald R. Nash and Lois M. Parker. Mountain View, Calif., Pacific Press Pub. Association [1965] xii, 146 p. illus. 22 cm. [BV772.N3] 65-21139
1. Stewardship, Christian. I. Parker, Lois M, joint author. II. Title.

OLSON, Raymond M 254.8
Stewards appointed; ten studies in Christian stewardship based on Luther's small catechism. Minneapolis, Augsburg Pub. House [1958] 141p. 20cm. Includes bibliography. [BV772.O6] 58-10319
1. Luther, Martin. Catechismus, Kleiner. 2. Stewardship, Christian. I. Title.

OWNBEY, Richard L. 254
A Christian and his money. Nashville, Abingdon-Cokesbury Press [1947] 124 p. 18 cm. [BV772.O85] 47-27304
1. Stewardship, Christian. I. Title.

PETRY, Ronald D., 1934- 248'.6
Partners in creation : stewardship for pastor and people / by Ronald D. Petry. Elgin, Ill. : Brethren Press, c1980. 126 p. ; 21 cm. Bibliography: p. [125]-126. [BV772.P45] 79-21770 ISBN 0-87178-688-5 pbk. : 4.95
1. Stewardship, Christian.

PIAT, Stephane Joseph, 254.8
1899-
Riches and the spirit. Translated from the French by Paul J. Oligny. Chicago, Franciscan Herald Press [1958] 254p. 21cm. [BV772.P483] 58-12950
1. Stewardship, Christian. I. Title.

PIERCE, Earle Vaydor, 1869- 254
The supreme beatitude, by Earle V. Pierce ... New York, London [etc.] Fleming H. Revell company [1947] 208 p. 21 cm. [BV772.P5] 47-3915
1. Stewardship, Christian. I. Title.

PIPER, Otto A 1891- 248
The Christian meaning of money, by Otto A. Piper. Englewood Cliffs, N J., Prentice-Hall [1965] xii, 116 p. 21 cm. (Library of Christian stewardship, LCS-3) Bibliographical footnotes. [BV772.P53] 65-16594
1. Stewardship, Christian 2. Wealth, Ethics of. I. Title.

POTEAT, Edwin McNeill, 1861- 254
The withered fig tree; studies in stewardship, by Edwin McNeill Poteat ... Philadelphia, Boston [etc.] The Judson press [c1921] 4 p. l., 74 p. 19 cm. "Selected bibliography": p. 72-74. [BV772.P6] 21-16491
I. Title.

RANSOME, William Lee, 1879- 254
Christian stewardship and Negro Baptists, by W. L. Ransome ... Richmond, Virginia, National ministers' institute, Virginia union university. Richmond, Va., Brown print shop, inc., 1934. 193 p. 20 cm. "A short bibliography": p. 190. [BV772.R25] 36-30056
1. Stewardship, Christian. 2. Baptists, Negro. 3. Baptists—Missions. I. National ministers' institute, Virginia. Union university, Richmond. II. Title.

RAY, George McNeill. 254.8
Tall in His presence; a manual of Christian stewardship. Greenwich, Conn., Seabury Press, 1961. 127p. 20cm. [BV772.R28] 61-9108
1. Stewardship, Christian. I. Title.

RAYZOR, James Newton, 1858- 254
"Stewardship born of God", by J. N. Rayzor ... Dallas, Tex., Baptist standard publishing company, 1922. 7 p. l., 13-58 p. 17 cm. [BV772.R3] 22-7868
I. Title.

REBOK, Denton Edward, 1897- 254.8
God's gold in my hand. Mountain View, Calif., Pacific Press Pub. Association [c1959] 82p. illus. 19cm. [BV772.R34] 59-9707
1. Stewardship, Christian. 2. Tithes. I. Title.

REIN, Remus C 1905- 248
Adventures in Christian stewardship. Saint Louis, Mo., Concordia Pub. House [c1955] 100p. illus. 22cm. [BV772.R4] 55-11139
1. Stewardship, Christian. I. Title.

SACRIFICE and song. 261.8
[Teacher's ed.] Nashville, Broadman Press [1953] 136p. 20cm. 'A publication of the Woman's Missionary Union, Birmingham, Alabama.' [BV772.F35] [BV772.F35] 254 53-9362 53-9362
1. Stewardship, Christian. I. Farmer, Foy (Johnson) 1887-

SALSTRAND, George A E 1908- 261.8
The story of stewardship in the United States of America. Grand Rapids, Baker Book House, 1956. 169p. illus. 23cm. Includes bibliography. [BV772.S3] [BV772.S3] 254 56-7586 56-7586
1. Stewardship, Christian. I. Title.

SAYERS, Carl R 254.8
Tithing and the church's mission, by Carl R. Sayers and Bertram T. White. Pref. by Richard S. Emrich. New York, Morehouse-Barlow Co. [1962] 65p. illus. 19cm. [BV772.S33] 62-19256
1. Stewardship, Christian. I. White, Bertram T., joint author. II. Title.

SELLS, James William. 248'.6
A partner with the living Lord / James William Sells. Nashville : Upper Room, c1975. 112 p. ; 22 cm. [BV772.S44] 75-21628 1.95
1. Stewardship, Christian. 2. Christian life—Methodist authors. I. Title.

SHEDD, Charlie W. 248'.6
The exciting church where they give their money away / Charlie W. Shedd. Waco, Tex. : Word Books, c1975. 88 p. : ill. ; 21 cm. [BV772.S518] 75-19904 3.95
1. Stewardship, Christian. 2. Christian giving. I. Title.

SHEDD, Charlie W. 254.8
How to develop a tithing church. Nashville, Abingdon Press [c.1961] 123p. 61-2942 1.25 pap.,
1. Stewardship, Christian. I. Title.

SHEDD, Charlie W. 254.8
How to develop a tithing church. New York, Abingdon Press [1961] 123 p. 19 cm. [BV772.S52] 61-2942
1. Stewardship, Christian. I. Title.

SIMPSON, John Ernest, 1889- 254
Faithful also in much; a history of man in his relation to his possessions and his God, by John E. Simpson ... New York [etc.] Fleming H. Revell company [1942] 96 p. 19 cm. [BV770.S523] 42-12990
1. Stewardship, Christian. I. Title.

SIMPSON, John Ernest, 1889- 254
Great stewards of the Bible. New York, F. H. Revell Co. [1947] 98 p. 20 cm. [BV772.S53] 47-6812
1. Stewardship, Christian. 2. Bible—Biog. I. Title.

SIMPSON, John Ernest, 1889- 254
"He that giveth"; a study of the stewardship of money as taught in Scripture, by John E. Simpson ... New York [etc.] Fleming H. Revell company [c1935] 92 p. 19 1/2 cm. [BV770.S525] 36-724
1. Stewardship, Christian. I. Title.

SIMPSON, John Ernest, 1889- 248
Into my storehouse; a treasure chest of stewardship materials, By John E. Simpson, D. D., with graded memory course by W. J. Harper McKnight, D. D. New York [etc.] Fleming H. Revell company [c1940] 192 p. 22 1/2 cm. [BV772.S55] 40-35807
1. Stewardship, Christian. I. McKnight, William James Harper, 1900- II. Title.

SIMPSON, John Ernest, 1889- 266
Stewardship and the world mission, by John E. Simpson. D.D. New York, London [etc.] Fleming H. Revell company [1944] 78 p. 1 illus. 19 1/2 cm. [BV770.S528] 44-6073
1. Stewardship, Christian. 2. Missions, Foreign. I. Title.

SLY, Florence M
Your family and Christian stewardship. St.Louis, Bethany Press, 1958. 96 p. (A Bethany course in Christian living)
1. Stewardship, Christian. I. Title.

SMITH, Paul G. 248'.6
Managing God's goods, by Paul G. Smith. Nashville, Southern Pub. Association [1973] 126 p. illus. 21 cm. [BV772.S614] 73-84597 ISBN 0-8127-0036-8 1.95 (pbk.)
1. Stewardship, Christian. I. Title.

SMITH, Roy Lemon, 1887- 261.8
Stewardship studies. Nashville, Abingdon Press [1954] 256p. 21cm. [BV772.S615] [BV772.S615] 254 54-8242 54-8242
1. Stewardship, Christian. I. Title.

SORENSON, Charles M. 248'.6
Stewardship upside down : a new and exciting design for nurturing commitment to the Christian cause / Charles M. Sorenson. New York : Hawthorn Books, [1975] 76 p. ; 21 cm. Bibliography: p. 74-76. [BV772.S63 1975] 74-22914 ISBN 0-8015-7144-8 pbk. : 2.95
1. Stewardship, Christian. 2. Christian life—1960- 3. Church renewal. I. Title.

SPEER, Michael L. 332'.024
A complete guide to the Christian's budget / Michael L. Speer. Nashville : Broadman Press, [1975] 170 p. ; 19 cm. Includes bibliographical references. [BV772.S64] 74-80341 ISBN 0-8054-5227-3 pbk. : 1.95
1. Stewardship, Christian. 2. Finance, Personal. I. Title.

SWADLEY, Elizabeth. 248.4'8'6132
Acknowledging my stewardship. [Teacher's ed.] Nashville, Convention Press [1967] x, 86 p. 20 cm. "Church study course [of the Sunday School Board of the Southern Baptist Convention] This book is number 2084 in category 20, section for intermediates." Bibliographical footnotes. [BV772.S88] 68-12129
1. Stewardship, Christian. 2. Christian giving. I. Southern Baptist Convention. Sunday School Board. II. Title.

THOMAS, Winburn T ed. 248
Stewardship in mission [edited] by Winburn T. Thomas. Authors: Elmer J. F. Arndt [and others] Englewood Cliffs, N.J., Prentice-Hall [1964] xiv, 114 p. 21 cm. (Library of Christian stewardship, LCS-2) Bibliographical footnotes. [BV772.T48] 64-20978
1. Stewardship, Christian. I. Title.

THOMPSON, Thomas K 254.8
Handbook of stewardship procedures, by T. K. Thompson. Englewood Cliffs, N.J., Prentice-Hall [1964] x, 115 p. 21 cm. (Library of Christian stewardship, LCS-1) "An annotated bibliography": p. 59-72. [BV772.T46] 64-20977
1. Stewardship, Christian. 2. Church finance. I. Title.

THOMPSON, Thomas K ed. 248
Stewardship illustration, edited by T. K. Thompson. Englewood Cliffs, N.J., Prentice-Hall [1965] xvi, 112 p. 21 cm. (Library of Christian stewardship, v. 4) [BV772.T49] 65-16587
1. Stewardship, Christian. I. Title.

THOMPSON, Thomas K., ed. 248
Stewardship illustrations. Englewood Cliffs, N.J., Prentice [c.1965] xvi, 112p. 21cm. (Lib. of Christian stewardship, v.4) [BV772.T49] 65-16587 2.95; 1.50 pap.,
1. Stewardship, Christian. I. Title.

THOMPSON, Thomas K ed. 248
Stewardship in contemporary life, edited by T. K. Thompson. New York, Association Press [1965] 190 p. 21 cm. Contents.CONTENTS. -- Motives for giving in the New Testament, by T. M. Taylor. -- Corporate stewardship, by J. C. McLelland. -- The ethics of promotion, by J. M. Gustafson. -- The denominational structure, by S. P. Austin. Includes bibliographical references. [BV772.T47] 65-11094
1. Stewardship, Christian. I. Title.

THOMPSON, Thomas K ed. 254.8
Stewardship in contemporary theology. New York, Association Press [1960] 252 p. 20 cm. Include bibliography. [BV772.T47] 60-6564
1. Stewardship, Christian. I. Title.

VAIL, Albert Lenox, 1844-
Stewardship among Baptists, by Albert L. Vail ... Philadelphia, American Baptist publication socity, 1913. x p., 1 l., 140 p. 20 cm. $0.75 14-677
I. Title.

VELAZCO MEDINA, Jose Luis, 261
1926-
What's mine? what's yours? New Yrok, Friendship [1966] 63p. 16cm. (Questions for Christians, no. 7) Bibl. [BV772.V35] 66-1132 .65 pap.,
1. Stewardship, Christian. I. Title. II. Series.

VERSTEEG, John M. 254
The deeper meaning of stewardship, by John M. Versteeg. New York, Cincinnati, The Abingdon press [c1923] 218 p. 19 cm. Bibliography: p. 217-218. [BV772.V4] 23-3454
I. Title.

VERSTEEG, John Marinus, 1888- 254
Save money! [By] John M. Versteeg ... New York, Cincinnati [etc.] The Abingdon press [c1939] 126 p. 19 1/2 cm. "Official text for the United stewardship council of the United States and Canada." [BV772.V43] 39-20409
1. Stewardship, Christian. I. United stewardship council of the United States and Canada. II. Title.

VERSTEEG, John Marinus, 1888- 254
When Christ controls; stewardship messages, by John M. Versteeg. New York, Nashville, Abingdon-Cokesbury press [1943] 148 p. 19 1/2 cm. "War edition." [BV772.V45] 43-16163
1. Stewardship, Christian. I. Title.

WALLACE, Helen Kingsbury 248.84
Stewardship for today's woman. [Westwood, N. J.] Revell [c. 1960] 94p. Bibl.: p.93-94 20cm. 60-13093 1.75
1. Stewardship, Christian. 2. Woman—Religious life. I. Title.

WEBER, Herman Carl, 1873- 254
The horizons of stewardship, by Herman C. Weber ... New York [etc.] Fleming H. Revell company [c1938] 119 p. diagrs. 19 1/2 cm. [BV770.W42] 38-34321
1. Stewardship, Christian. I. Title.

WELLMAN, Sterrie Austin, 250
1879-
Your stewardship and mine, its blessings and responsibilities. Washington, Review and Herald Pub. Association [1950] 192 p. 20 cm. [BV770.W45] 50-1765
1. Stewardship, Christian. I. Title.

WENGER, A. Grace 248.4
Stewards of the gospel; a resource book for the study of Christian stewardship. Illus. by Jan Gleysteen. Scottdale, Pa., Herald Pr. [c.1964] 126p. illus. 20cm. Bibl. 64-20135 1.00 pap.,
1. Stewardship, Christian. I. Title.

WENGER, A Grace. 248.4
Stewards of the gospel; a resource book for the study of Christian stewardship, by A. Grace Wenger. Illustrated by Jan Gleysteen. Scottdale, Pa., Herald Press [1964] 126 p. illus. 20 cm. 29 p. 22 cm. Bibliography: p. 126. Leader's guide. Scottdale, Pa., Herald Press. [1964] [BV772.W43] 64-20135
1. Stewardship, Christian. I. Title.

WERNING, Waldo J 248
The stewardship call; an approach to personal and group stewardship based on the concept of Christian vocation [by] Aldo J. Werning. Saint Louis, Concordia Pub. House [1965] 186 p. 21 cm. Bibliography: p. 185-186. [BV772.W44] 65-6734
1. Stewardship, Christian. I. Title.

WERNING, Waldo J. 248.6
Where does the money go? The Christian philosophy of money and a practical approach for Christian family budgeting, by Waldo J. Werning. [St. Louis, Church-Craft Pictures, inc., 1964] 85 p. 23 cm. Bbiliography: p. 85. [BV773.W445] 67-6140
1. Stewardship, Christian. 2. Christian giving. I. Title.

WHITE, Ellen Gould (Harmon) 254
Mrs., 1827-1915.
Counsels on stewardship; a compilation from the writings of Ellen G. White ... Takoma Park, Washington, D.C., Review and herald publishing assn. [c1940] 377 p. 19 cm. (Ministerial reading course selection for 1940) [BX6111.W482] 40-7850
1. Stewardship, Christian. 2. Seventh-day Aventists. 3. Tithes. I. Title.

WILSON, Bert, 1878- 200
The Christian and his money problems, by Bert Wilson ... New York, George H. Doran company [c1923] xii, [2], 15-236 p. 20 cm. Bibliography: p. 235-236. [BR115.W4W5] 23-12204
1. Stewardship, Christian. I. Title.

WILSON, Bert, 1878- 254
Progressive stewardship, by Bert Wilson ... Indianapolis, Ind., Unified promotion [1941?] 67 p. 20 1/2 cm. [BV772.W5] 41-13616
1. Stewardship, Christian. I. Title.

WRIGHT, Carter, Mrs. 1876- 254
Stewardship and Christmas stories. Nashville, Broadman Press [1947] 81 p. 19 cm. [BV772.W67] 48-15703
1. Stewardship, Christian. I. Title.

*YOUNG, Samuel. 254-8
Giving and living : foundations for Christian Stewardship / by Samuel Young. Grand Rapids : Baker Book House, 1976c1974. 94p. ; 20cm. Bibliography: p. 93-94. [BV772] ISBN 0-8010-9911-0 pbk. : 1.95
1. Stewardship, Christian. I. Title.

Stewardship, Christian—Addresses, essays, lectures.

BARFOOT, Earl F. 248'.6
What does the Lord want / Earl F. Barfoot, editor. Nashville, : Tidings, [1974] 55 p. ; 19 cm. [BV772.B27] 74-80892 pbk. : 1.25.
1. Stewardship, Christian—Addresses, essays, lectures. 2. Laity—Addresses, essays, lectures. I. Title.

THE Earth is the Lord's 248'.6
: essays on stewardship / edited by Mary Evelyn Jegen and Bruno Manno. New York : Paulist Press, c1978. ix, 215 p. ; 21 cm. Includes bibliographical references. [BV772.E2] 77-83588 ISBN 0-8091-2067-4 pbk. : 4.95
1. Stewardship, Christian—Addresses, essays, lectures. I. Jegen, Mary Evelyn. II. Manno, Bruno V.

JESUS, dollars and sense 248'.6
: a practical and effective stewardship guide for clergy and lay leaders / edited by Oscar C. Carr, Jr. ; foreword by Furman C. Stough. New York : Seabury Press, c1976. p. cm. "A Crossroad book." [BV772.J45] 76-14362 ISBN 0-8164-2132-3 pbk. : 3.95
1. Protestant Episcopal Church in the

U.S.A.—Sermons. 2. Stewardship, Christian—Addresses, essays, lectures. 3. Stewardship, Christian—Sermons. 4. Sermons, American.

Stewardship, Christian—Biblical teaching.

KAUFFMAN, Milo, 1898- 248'.6
Stewards of God. Scottdale, Pa., Herald Press, 1975. 264 p. 22 cm. Includes bibliographical references. [BV772.K33] 74-13130 ISBN 0-8361-1747-6 5.95
1. Stewardship, Christian—Biblical teaching. I. Title.

USSERY, Annie (Wright) 254.8
Christian sharing of possessions. [Nashville] Convention Press [1961] 141 p. 10 cm. Includes bibliography. [BV772.U8] 61-11006
1. Stewardship, Christian — Biblical teaching. I. Title.

Stewardship, Christian—Handbooks, manuals, etc.

NATIONAL Catholic Stewardship Council. 248'.6
Stewardship of money : a manual for parishes. Washington : National Catholic Stewardship Council, 1975. 64 p. : ill. ; 28 cm. Bibliography: p. 62-64. [BV772.N325 1975] 75-34042
1. Stewardship, Christian—Handbooks, manuals, etc. I. Title.

TRIMBLE, Henry Burton.
... The Christian motive and method in stewardship, by Henry Burton Trimble. Nashville, Tenn., Cokesbury press, 1929. 227 p. 19 cm. (Leadership training series. Standard training series) Series title in part at head of t.-p. [BC4501.T78] 29-12413
I. Title.

Stewardship, Christian — Juvenile literature.

MCCAW, Mabel (Niedermeyer) 248.4
This is God's world. Illustrated by Gedge Harmon. St. Louis, Bethany Press [c.1949, 1959] 94p. illus. 22cm. 60-6826 1.75 bds.,
1. Stewardship, Christian—Juvenile literature. I. Title.

MOON, Floyce (Orr) j248
A horse named Amber [by] Floyce Moon. [Teacher's ed.] Nashville, Convention Press [1965] ix, 97 p. illus. 19 cm. "Helps for the teacher": [(15] p.) bound between p. 46-47. [BV772.M54] 65-15603
1. Stewardship, Christian — Juvenile literature. I. Title.

NIEDERMEYER, Mabel A. 248
This is God's world; a book on Christian stewardship for boys and girls, by Mabel A. Niedermeyer, illustrated by Gedge Harmon. St. Louis, Mo., The Bethany press [1946] 63 p. illus. (part col.) 20 cm. [BV772.N5] 47-16459
1. Stewardhsip, Christian—Juvenile literature. I. Title.

ROBINSON, Emma Amelia, 1863- 262.
Stewardship stories for boys and girls, by Emma A. Robinson. New York, Joint centenary committee, Methodist Episcopal church, Methodist Episcopal church, South [c1918] 2 p. l., 3-70 p. 18 cm. [BX8339.R6] 19-11790
I. Methodist Episcopal church. Joint centenary committee. II. Title.

WILLIAMSON, Robert Donald. 171.
Stewardship in life of youth, by Robert Donald Williamson and Helen Kingsbury Wallace ... introduction by Helen B. Montgomery. New York, Chicago [ect.] Fleming H. Revell company [c1926] 88 p., 19 1/2 cm. "Reading list": p. 88. [BV4531.W515] 26-14440
I. Wallace, Helen Kingsbury, joint author. II. Title.

Stewardship, Christian — Sermons.

CLEARWATERS, Richard V 254.8
Stewardship sermonettes. Grand Rapids, Baker Book House, 1955. 120p. 21cm. [BV772] 55-12086
1. Stewardship, Christian—Sermons. 2. Baptists—Sermons. 3. Sermons, American. I. Title.

CLEARWATERS, Richard V 254.8
Stewardship sermonettes. Wheaton, Ill., Van Kampen Press [1955] 120p. 20cm. [BV772.C54] 55-33689
1. Stewardship. Christian—Sermons. 2. Baptists—Sermons. 3. Sermons, American. I. Title.

CROWE, Charles M. 252.07
Stewardship sermons. Nashville, Abingdon Press [c.1960] 141p. 21cm. 60-12072 2.50
1. Stewardship, Christian—Sermons. 2. Methodist Church—Sermons. 3. Sermons, American. I. Title.

HOBBS, Herschel H 261.8
The gospel of giving. Nashville, Broadman Press [c1954] 146p. 20cm. [BV772.H52] 254 55-24353
1. Stewardship, Christian—Sermons. 2. Baptists—Sermons. 3. Sermons, American. I. Title.

KNUDSEN, Raymond B. 248'.6
Developing dynamic stewardship / Raymond B. Knudsen. Nashville : Abingdon, c1978. 127 p. ; 19 cm. [BV772.K58] 78-7846 ISBN 0-687-10500-5 pbk. : 3.95
1. Stewardship, Christian—Sermons. 2. Sermons, American. I. Title. II. Title: Dynamic stewardship.

MCKAY, Arthur R. 250
Servants and stewards; the teaching and practice of stewardship. Geneva Pr. dist. Philadelphia, Westminster, c.1963 76p. 20cm. hristian. 63-12597 1.25
I. Title.

MESSAGES on 248.4'8'608
stewardship, by K. Owen White, Herschel H. Hobbs, J. Ralph Grant, and others. Grand Rapids, Baker Book House, 1963. 141 p. 20 cm. [BV772.M48] 63-23043
1. Stewardship, Christian — Sermons. I. White, Kenneth Owen. 1902.

OLFORD, Stephen F. 248'.48'61
The grace of giving; thoughts on financial stewardship [by] Stephen Olford. Grand Rapids, Mich., Zondervan Pub. House [1972] 134, [2] p. 18 cm. (Zondervan books) Bibliography: p. [135]-[136] [BV772.O58] 72-83872 pap. 0.95
1. Stewardship, Christian—Sermons. 2. Baptists—Sermons. 3. Sermons, American. I. Title.

REEVE, Jack V., ed. 254.8
A God to glorify, through Christian stewardship. St. Louis, Bethany [c.1964] 160p. 23cm. Bibl. 64-20802 2.95
1. Stewardship, Christian—Sermons. 2. Sermons, American. 3. Disciples of Christ—Sermons. I. Title.

REEVE, Jack V ed. 254.8
A God to glorify, through Christian stewardship. Edited by Jack Reeve. St. Louis, Bethany Press [1964] 160 p. 23 cm. Bibliographical footnotes. [BV772.R36] 64-20802
1. Stewardship, Christian — Sermons. 2. Sermons, American. 3. Disciples of Christ — Sermons. I. Title.

THE stewardship of God's tomorrow . . .selected sermons from the stewardship preaching fellowship. New York, Presbyterian Church in the U. S. A. General Council, Committee on United Promotion [195-] 59p. 23cm.
I. Presbyterian Church in the U. S. A. General Council. Committee on United Promotion.

20 stewardship sermons, 248.6
by pastors of the Evangelical Lutheran Church Minneapolis, Augusburg Pub. House [1954] 227p. 21cm. [BV772.T9] 54-13222
1. Stewardship, Christian—Sermons. 2. Lutheran Church—Sermons. 3. Sermons, American. I. Evangelical Lutheran Church.

WILLIAMSON, E. Stanley, comp. 248'.6
Faithful to the Lord. Compiled by E. Stanley Williamson. Nashville, Broadman Press [1973] 122 p. 21 cm. [BV772.W49] 72-97607 ISBN 0-8054-2219-6 3.95
1. Baptists—Sermons. 2. Stewardship, Christian—Sermons. 3. Sermons, American. I. Title.

Stewardship, Christian—Study and teaching.

CRAWFORD, Julius Earl. 248
The stewardship life; an elective course for young people and adults, approved as a supplementary text in the Standard training series, by Julius Earl Crawford ... edited by E. B. Chappell. Nashville, Tenn., Cokesbury press, 1929. 176 p. 19 cm. [BV4501.C76] 29-22314
I. Chappell, Edwin Barfield, 1853- ed. II. Title.

KEECH, William J 250
Our church plans for missionary and stewardship education. Valley Forge [Pa.] Judson Press [1963] 104 p. illus. 19 cm. [BV602.K4] 62-17000
1. Stewardship, Christian — Study and teaching. 2. Missions — Study and teaching. I. Title.

LEE, Julia Tolman. 254
The spirit of service, seven lessons on Christian stewardship for class and discussion groups, arranged by Julia Tolman Lee ... New York, Chicago [etc.] Fleming H. Revell company [c1922] 1 p. l., 5-62 p. 19 1/2 cm. "A short reading list": p. 61-62. [BV772.L4] 23-987
I. Title.

MCRAE, Glenn, 1887- 261.8
Teaching Christian stewardship. St. Louis, Bethany Press [1954] 158p. 20cm. [BV772.M357] [BV772.M357] 254 54-37559 54-37559
1. Stewardship, Christian—Study and teaching. I. Title.

O'CONNELL, Hugh J., 1910- 248.6
Stewardship; call to a new way of life [by] Hugh J. O'Connell. Liguori, Mo., Liguorian Books [1969] 192 p. 18 cm. (Catholic living series, v. 10) [BV772.O3] 75-97517 1.00
1. Stewardship, Christian—Study and teaching. I. Title.

REIN, Remus C 1905- 254.8
First fruits: God's guide for giving. Saint Louis, Concordia Pub. House [1959] 111p. 22cm. [BV772] 59-16764
1. Stewardship, Christian—Study and teaching. I. Title.

SIMPSON, John Ernest, 1889- 248
This world's goods; a study of stewardship as it is related to life today, by John E. Simpson ... New York [etc.] Fleming H. Revell company [c1939] 96 p. 19 1/2 cm. [BV770.S535] 39-9782
1. Stewardship, Christian—Study and teaching. I. Title.

Stewart, Andrew G.

STEWART, Andrew G. 266'.6'70924 B
In letters of gold; heroism for God in the South Seas [by] Andrew G. Stewart. Mountain View, Calif., Pacific Press Pub. Association [1973] 128 p. illus. 22 cm. (A Destiny book, D-143) [BV3676.S8A33] 73-87368
1. Stewart, Andrew G. I. Title.

STEWART, George, 1892- 270
The crucifixion in our street, by George Stewart ... New York, George H. Doran company [c1927] viii p., 1 l., 11-170 p. 20 cm. [BR125.S836] 27-3249
I. Title.

Stigmata.

GALGANI, Gemma, Saint, 1878-1903. 922.245
Portrait of Saint Gemma, a stigmatic, by Sister Saint Michael. Foreword by J. F. Minihan. New York, Kenedy [1950] xviii, 248 p. ports., facsim. 21 cm. Bibliography: p. 247-248. [BX4700.G22A44] 51-45
I. Saint Michael, Sister. II. Title.

*GIGLIOZZI, Giovanni 271.36
Padre Pio, a pictorial biography. Tr. [from Italian] by Oscar DeLiso. New York, Pocket Bks. [1966, c.1965] 128p. illus., ports. 18cm. (75177) First pub. in 1965 by Phaedra under the title: I monili dello sposo (Cardinal ed., 75177) .75 pap.,
1. Guiseppe, Francesco, 1887- 2. Stigmata. I. Title.

Stigmatization.

BIOT, Rene, 1889- 231.73
The enigma of the stigmata. Tr. from French by P. J. Hepburne-Scott. New York, Hawthorn [c.1962] 157p. 22cm. (Twentieth cent. encyclopedia of Catholicism, v. 57. Sect. 5: The life of faith) Bibl. 62-21734 3.50 bds.,
1. Stigmatization. I. Title.

BIOT, Rene, 1889- 231.73
The enigma of the stigmata. Translated from the French by P. J. Hepburne-Soctt. [1st ed.] New York, Hawthorn Books [1962] 157 p. 22 cm. (The Twentieth century encyclopedia of Catholicism, v. 57. Section 5: The life of faith) [BV5091.S7B53] 62-21734
1. Stigmatization. I. Title.

BOYER, Onesime Alfred, 1874- 922.273
She wears a crown of thorns; Marie Rose Ferron (1902-1936) known as "Little Rose," the stigmatized ecstatic of Woonsocket, R.I. By Rev. O. A. Boyer ... 3d ed. Ellenburg, N.Y., The author, 1944. xv, 286 p. front., plates, ports. 21 1/2 cm. "Some literature on mysticism": p. 221-225. [BX4705.F445B6 1944] 44-31993
1. Ferron, Marie Rose, 1902-1936. 2. Stigmatization. I. Title.

BOYER, Onesimus Alfred, 1874- 922.273
She wears a crown of thorns; Marie Rose Ferron (1902-1936) known as 'Little Rose,' the stigmatized ecstatic of Woonsocket, R. I. By Rev. O. A. Boyer... 3d ed. Ellenburg, N. Y., The author, 1944. xv, 286p. front., plates(ports. 22cm. 'Some literature on mysticism' : p. 221-225. [BX4705.F445B6 1944] 44-31993
1. Ferron, Marie Rose, 1902-1936. 2. Stigmatixation. I. Title.

BOYER, Onesimus Alfred, 1874- 922.273
She wears a crown of thorns Marie Rose Ferron (1902-1936) known as 'Little Rose,' the stigmatized ecstatic of Woonsocket, R. I. [4th ed.] New York, Benziger Bros., 1949. 364p. illus. 22cm. [BX4705.F445B6 1955] 55-36607
1. Ferron, Marie Rose, 1902-1966. 2. Stigmatization. I. Title.

GRAEF, Hilda C. 922.243
The case of Therese Neumann. Westminster, Md., New man Press, 1951. xix, 162 p. 23 cm. Bibliographical footnotes. [BX4705.N47G7] 51-10857
1. Neumann, Therese, 1898- 2. Stigmatization. I. Title.

HOVRE, Eugene de. 922.243
The riddle of Konnersreuth, by Eugene canon De Hovre translated by Reverend P. M. Van Dorpe, S.T.B. Chicago, Ill., Benedictine press [c1933] 396, [3] p. incl. illus., ports. 19 cm. Translation of Therese Neumann, het levend raadael van Konnersreuth. [BX4705.N47H6] 33-33273
1. Neumann, Therese, 1898- 2. Stigmatisation. I. Van Dorpe, Paul Mary, 1899- tr. II. Title.

HOWE, Frances R. 922.2493
A visit to Bois d'Haine, the home of Louise Lateau ... By Frances R. Howe ... Baltimore, Kelly, Piet and company, 1878. xiv, 269 p., 1 l. front. 19 1/2 cm. "Revised from the 'Ave Maria'." [BX4705.L3H7] 37-11154
1. Lateau, Louise, 1850-1883. 2. Stigmatization. I. Title.

LAMA, Fredrich, ritter von, 1876- 922.243
Further chronicles of Therese Neumann, by Fredrich ritter von Lama; translated by Albert Paul Schimberg. Milwaukee, New York [etc.] The Bruce publishing company [c1932] vii, [5], 259 p. front., pl. 20 cm. [BX4705.N47L33] 32-9245
1. Neumann, Therese, 1898- 2. Stigmatization. I. Schimberg, Albert Paul, tr. II. Title.

LAMA, Friedrich, ritter, von, 1876- 922.
Therese Neumann; a stigmatist of our days, by Friedrich ritter von Lama, translated by Albert Paul Schimberg. Milwaukee, Wis., New York [etc.] The Bruce publishing company c[1929] 5 p. l., 249 p. pl. 2 port. (incl. front.) 21 cm. "References": p. [243]-249. [BX4705.N47L32] 30-3995
1. Neumann, Therese, 1898- 2. Stigmatization. I. Schimberg, Albert Paul, tr. II. Title.

LAMA, Friedrich, ritter von, 1876- 922.243
Therese of Konnersreuth; a new chronicle, by Friedrich ritter von Lama; translated by Albert Paul Schimberg. Milwaukee, The Bruce publishing company [c1935] xiii p., 1 l., 267 p. front., plates, ports. 20 cm. [BX4705.N47L35] 35-10466
1. Neumann, Therese, 1898- 2. Stigmatization. I. Schimberg, Albert Paul, tr. II. Title.

MESSMER, Josef. 922.
A visit to the stigmatized seer, Therese Neumann, by Msgr. Joseph Messmer [and] Rt. Rev. Bishop Sigismund Waltz, D. D.; translated from the German by a member of the Dominican order. Chicago, Ill., John P. Daleiden co. [c1929] 117 p. front. (port.) 20 cm. "The message of Konnersreuth, by the Right Reverend Bishop Sigismund Waltz": p. 79-110. Translated of Die stigmatislerte seherin, Theresia Neumann. [BX4705.N47M4] 29-15060
1. Neumann, Therese, 1898- 2. Stigmatization. 3. Miracles. I. Waitz, Siegmund, bp., 1864- II. A member of the Dominican order, tr. III. Title.

[MOEWS, Guy Albert] 1904- 922.243
Soldiers saw Resl. Cincinnati, O., St. Francis book shop [1947] 71 p. front., plates, ports. 17 cm. On cover: Story of Theres Neumann. [BX4705.N47M6] 47-3879
1. Neumann, Therese, 1808- 2. Stigmatization. I. Title.

PROSERPIO, Leone, bp., 1878- 922.245
St. Gemma Galgani [by] the Rt. Rev. Dr. Leo Proserpio ... with a foreword by His Excellency the Most Rev. Dr. Leo Peter Kierkels ... Milwaukee, The Bruce publishing company [c1940] xx, 212 p. incl. front. (port.) 21 cm. (Half-title: Science and culture series; Joseph Husslein ... general editor) [BX4700.G22P7] 40-10687
1. Galgani, Gemma, Saint, 1878-1903. 2. Stigmatization. I. Title.

SCHIMBERG, Albert Paul, 1885- 922.243
The story of Therese Neumann. Bruce paperback pub. in collaboration with All Saints. New York. [1962,c.1947] 211p. 17cm. (AS-233) .50 pap.,
1. Neuman, Therese, 1898- 2. Stigmatization. I. Title.

SCHIMBERG, Albert Paul, 1885- 922.243
The story of Therese Neumann. Milwaukee, Bruce Pub. Co. [1947] ix, 232 p. illus., ports. 21 cm. [BX4705.N47S34] 47-12337
1. Neumann, Therese, 1898- 2. Stigmatization. I. Title.

SIWEK, Paul. 922.243
The riddle of Konnersreuth, a psychological and religious study; translated by Ignatius McCormick. Milwaukee, Bruce Pub. Co. [1953] xvi, 228p. 23cm. Translation and revision of Une stigmatisee de nos jours. Bibliographical footnotes. [BX4705.N47S52] 53-13490
1. Neumann, Therese, 1898- 2. Stigmatization. I. Title.

TEODOROWICZ, Jozef, abp., 1864- 922.243
Mystical phenomena in the life of Theresa Neumann, by Most Reverend Josef Teodorowicz ... translated by Rev. Rudolph Kraus ... St. Louis, Mo., and London, B. Herder book co., 1940. xi, 519 p. 22 1/2cm. [BX4705.N47T42] 40-4930
1. Neumann, Therese, 1898 2. Stigmatization. I. Kruas, Rudolph, 1895- tr. Translation of Konnersreuth im lichte der mystik and psychologie. II. Title.

THE two stigmatists,
Padre Pio and Teresa Neumann; containing the autobiography of Teresa Neumann, a critical account of the phenomena in her life and a comparison with Padre Pio. A reply to the apostles of hysteria. 2d ed. St. Paul, Radio Replies Press Society, [1956?] xxxii, 212p. illus. 22cm.
1. Neumann, Therese, 1898- 2. Pio da Pietralcina, Father, 1887- 3. Stigmatization. I. Carty, Charles Mortimer. II. Neumann, Therese, 1898-

Stiles, Ezra, 1727-1795.

STILES, Isaac, 1697-1760. 252.
A sermon preached by the Reverend Isaac Stiles, A.M., pastor of the church in North-Haven, at the ordination of his son Ezra Stiles, A.M., to the pastoral charge of the church and congregation meeting in Clark street, Newport, October 22, 1755. [Four lines of Bible quotations] Newport, Rhode Island; Printed by J. Franklin, at the Town-school-house [1755] 2 p. l., 33 p. 20 cm. Signatures: 2 leaves (t.-p.: dedication) unsigned, A-H2, leaf, unsigned. [BX7233.S782S4] 31-4014
1. Stiles, Ezra, 1727-1795. 2. Ordination sermons. I. Title.

Stillemans, Joseph F., ed.

MERCIER, Desire Felicien Francois Joseph, cardinal, 1851-1926.
Cardinal Mercier; pastorals, letters allocutions, 1914-1917; with a biographical sketch and foreword by Rev. Joseph F. Stillemans ... New York, P. J. Kenedy & sons, 1917. xix, 258 p. col. front. (port.) 20 cm. [D622.M47] 18-14960
1. Stillemans, Joseph F., ed. I. Title.

Stilling of the storm (Miracle)—Juvenile literature.

WARREN, Mary 231.73
The little boat that almost sank. Illus. by Kveta Rada [St. Louis] Concordia [c.1965] [32]p. col. illus. 21cm. (Arch bks., set 2, no.59-1111) On cover: How Jesus stopped the storm [BS2401.W3] 64-23371 .35 pap.,
1. Stilling of the storm (Miracle)—Juvenile literature. I. Title. II. Title: How Jesus stopped the storm.

Stinespring, William Franklin, 1901- —Bibliography.

THE Use of the Old Testament 225
in the New and other essays; studies in honor of William Franklin Stinespring. Edited by James M. Efird. Durham, N.C., Duke University Press, 1972. xv, 332 p. illus. 25 cm. Contents.Contents.—Smith, D. M., Jr. The use of the Old Testament in the New.—Tucker, G. M. The Rahab saga (Joshua 2): some form-critical and traditio-historical observations.—Eakin, F. E., Jr. Spiritual obduracy and parable purpose.—Williams, D. L. The Israelite cult and Christian worship.—Cresson, B. C. The condemnation of Edom in post-exilic Judaism.—Polley, M. E. H. Wheeler Robinson and the problem of organizing an Old Testament theology.—Pope, M. H. A divine banquet at Ugarit.—Strugnell, J. "Of cabbages and kings"—or queans: notes on Ben Sira 36:18-21.—Brownlee, W. H. Anthropology and soteriology in the Dead Sea scrolls and in the New Testament.—Wintermute, O. A study of gnostic exegesis of the Old Testament.—Charlesworth, J. H. Ba'uta [romanized form] in earliest Christianity.—Anderson, H. The Old Testament in Mark's Gospel.—Efird, J. M. Note on Mark 5:43.—Davies, W. D. The moral teaching of the early church.—Bibliography (p. xiv-xv) [BS2387.U8] 70-185463 ISBN 0-8223-0288-8
1. Stinespring, William Franklin, 1901- —Bibliography. 2. Bible. N.T.—Relation to O.T.—Addresses, essays, lectures. I. Stinespring, William Franklin, 1901- II. Efird, James M., ed.

Stirling, Scot. University. Library.

SHERINGTON, Nick. 016.335'83
A handlist of anarchist material in the library of the University of Stirling / compiled by Nick Sherington. Brighton : Smoothie Publications, 1976. 9 p. ; 30 cm. (Smoothie's alternative indexing series) Cover title. [Z7164.A52S48] [HX826] 77-359445 ISBN 0-903612-36-4 : £0.80
1. Stirling, Scot. University. Library. 2. Anarchism and anarchists—Bibliography. I. Stirling, Scot. University. Library. II. Title.

Stob, Henry, 1908- —Bibliography.

GOD and the good : 230
essays in honor of Henry Stob / edited by Clifton Orlebeke and Lewis Smedes. Grand Rapids : Eerdmans, [1975] 227 p. : port. ; 23 cm. Bibliography of Henry Stob compiled by Peter DeKlerk": p. 221-227. [BR50.G538] 74-31479 ISBN 0-8028-3454-X : 6.95
1. Stob, Henry, 1908- —Bibliography. 2. Theology—Addresses, essays, lectures. I. Stob, Henry, 1908- II. Orlebeke, Clifton, ed. III. Smedes, Lewis B., ed.
Contents omitted.

Stockbridge Indians—Missions.

HOPKINS, Samuel, 1693-1755. 266'.5'87441
Historical memoirs relating to the Housatonic Indians. Boston, S. Kneeland, 1753. New York, W. Abbatt, 1911. [New York, Johnson Reprint Corp., 1972] 198 p. facsims. 24 cm. Reprint of the 1911 ed., which was issued as Extra number 17 of The Magazine of history with notes and queries. [E99.S8H7 1972] 72-2288 9.00
1. Sergeant, John, 1710-1749. 2. Stockbridge Indians—Missions. I. Title. II. Series: The Magazine of history with notes and queries. Extra numbers, 17.

Stockton, Calif. College of the Pacific. Morris chapel.

RITTER, Ovid Herbert, 1883- 726.41
Morris chapel, by Ovid H. Ritter. Stockton, Calif., College of the Pacific, 1946. 91 p. incl. illus., plates (1 col.) 18 1/2 cm. [NA5235.S75R5] 47-15845
1. Stockton, Calif. College of the Pacific. Morris chapel. I. Title.

Stockton, Calif. St. Mary of the Assumption.

BONTA, Robert Eugene. 282.7948
The cross in the valley; the history of the establishment of the Catholic Church in the northern San Josquin Valley of California up to 1863. [Fresno, Calif.] Academy of California Church History [1963] xxi, 308 p. illus., ports., mpas. 22 cm. Bibliography: p. 265-278. [BX4603.S8S2] 63-23225
1. Stockton, Calif. St. Mary of the Assumption. 2. Catholic Church in San Joaquin Valley, Calif. I. Title.

Stoddard, David Tappan, 1818-1857.

THOMPSON, Joseph Parrish, 1819-1879. 922.573
Memoir of Rev. David Tappan Stoddard, missionary to the Nestorians. By Joseph P. Thompson ... New York, Sheldon, Blakeman & company; Boston, Gould & Lincoln; [etc., etc.] 1858. vi, [7]-422 p. front., illus. (incl. port.) 19 1/2 cm. [BV2628.N5S8 1858] 37-18692
1. Stoddard, David Tappan, 1818-1857. 2. Missions—Nestorians. I. Title.

THOMPSON, Joseph Parrish, 1819-1879. 922.573
Memoirs of the Rev. David Tappan Stoddard, missionary to the Nestorians. By Joseph P. Thompson ... Boston, The American tract society [c1858] vi, [7]-422 p. front., illus. (incl. port.) 19 1/2 cm. [BV2628.N5S8 1858a] 32-29695
1. Stoddard, David Tappan, 1818-1857. 2. Missions—Nestorians. I. American tract society. II. Title.

Stoddard, Solomon, 1643-1729

COFFMAN, Ralph J. 285'.8'0924 B
Solomon Stoddard / by Ralph J. Coffman. Boston : Twayne Publishers, 1978. 224 p. : ill. ; 21 cm. (Twayne's United States authors series : TUSAS 295) Includes index. Bibliography: p. 215-219. [BX7260.S816C63] 78-5520 ISBN 0-8057-7198-0 lib. bdg. : 9.95
1. Stoddard, Solomon, 1643-1729

Stoddart, Charles, 1806-1842.

WOLFF, Joseph, 1795-1862.
Narrative of a mission to Bokhara, in the years 1843-1845, to ascertain the fate of Colonel Stoddart and Captain Conolly; by The Rev. Joseph Wolff ... New York, Harper & brothers, 1845. xxi, [1], [23]-384 p. 5 pl. (incl. front.) 4 port. 23 cm. Appendix: I. The three liturgies of St. Chrysostom, St. Basil, and St. Gregory, with various rites and ceremonies of the Greek church, and separate prayers. II. Narrative of events which happened to Dr. Wolff at Bokhara, and on his journey thence to Teheraun; by Abdul Wahab. III. Digest of English policy relative to Asiatic state, by Captain Conolly. [DK878.W8] 5-7325
1. Stoddart, Charles, 1806-1842. 2. Conolly, Arthur, 1807-1842? 3. Bokhara—Descr. & trav. 4. Asia, Central—Descr. & trav. I. Title.

Stoics

ALSTON, Leonard, 1875-
Stoic and Christian in the second century; a comparison of the ethical teaching of Marcus Aurelius with that of contemporary and antecedent Christianity, by Leonard Alston ... London, New York and Bombay, Longmans, Green and co., 1906. ix, 146 p. 1 l. 20 1/2 cm. "Originally intended for the Burney prize."-Pref. Appendix: some brief biographical notes. [BJ212.A4] 7-11201
1. Stoics 2. Christian ethics. 3. Aurelius Antoninus, Marcus, emperor of Rome. I. Title.

ARNOLD, Edward Vernon, 1857-1926.
Roman Stoicism; being lectures on the history of the Stoic philosophy, with special reference to its development within the Roman empire, by E. Vernon Arnold... Cambridge [Eng.] The University press, 1911. ix, [1] p., 1 l., 468 p. 28 cm. Bibliography: p. [437]-450. [B528.A7] A 11
1. Stoics. I. Title.

BEVAN, Edwyn Robert, 1870-
Stoics and sceptics; four lectures delivered in Oxford during Hilary term 1913 for the common university fund, by Edwyn Bevan. Oxford, Clarendon press, 1913. 152 p. 23 cm. [B528.B4] A 14
1. Stoics. 2. Skeptics (Greek philosophy) I. Title.

BROWN, James Baldwin, 1820-1884. 188
Stoics and saints; lectures on the later heathen moralists, and on some aspects of the life of the mediaeval church. Freeport, N.Y., Books for Libraries Press [1972] viii, 296 p. 22 cm. (Essay index reprint series) Reprint of the 1893 ed. Includes bibliographical references. [BR163.B7 1972] 72-4500 ISBN 0-8369-2936-5 11.50
1. Stoics. 2. Saints. 3. Religious thought—Middle Ages. I. Title.

BROWN, James Baldwin, 1820-1884. 270.
Stoics and saints; lectures on the later heathen moralists and on some aspects of the life of the mediaeval church. By the late James Baldwin Brown... New York, Macmillan and co., 1893. viii, 296 p. 23 cm. "Note by the editor: signed: E.B.B. [i.e. Elizabeth Baldwin Brown] [BR163.B7 1893a] 39-5064
1. Stoics. 2. Saints. 3. Religious thought—Middle ages. I. Brown, Mrs. Elizabeth Baldwin, ed. II. Title.

BUSSELL, Frederick William, 1862-
... Marcus Aurelius and the later Stoics, by F. W. Bussell ... New York, C. Scribner's sons, 1910. xi, 302 p. 19 cm. (Added t.-p.:

The world's lpoch-makers) Series title also at head of t.-p. A10
1. Stoics. 2. Aurelius Antoninus, emperor of Rome, 121-180. I. Title.

CAPES, William Wolfe, 1834-1914.
...Stoicism. By Rev. W.W. Capes... London, Society for promoting knowledge. New York, Pott, Young, & co., 1380. 255 p. 17 cm. (Chief ancient philosophies) [B528.C3] 1-27160
1. Stoics. I. Title.

DAVIS, Charles Henry Stanley, 1840-1917.
Greek and Roman stoicism and some of its disciples; Epictetus, Seneca and Marcus Aurelius, by Chas. H Stanley Davis Boston, H. B. Turner & co., 1903. viii, 269 p. 20 cm. [B528.D4] 3-2503
1. Epictetus. 2. Seneca Lucius Annaeus, B. C. 4-a. d. 65. 3. Aurelius Antoninus, Marcus emperor of Rome. 4. Stoics. I. Title.

HICKS, Robert Drew, 1850-
... Stoic and Epicurean, by R. D. Hicks ... New York, C. Scribner's sons, 1910. xix, 412 p. 21 cm. (Epochs of philosophy) "Select bibliography": p. 401-404. [B528.H6] 10-6721
1. Stoics. 2. Epicurus. 3. Philosophy, Ancient. I. Title.

HOLLAND, Frederic May, 1836-1908.
The reign of the Stoics. History. Religion. Maxims of self control, self culture, benevolence, justice. Philosophy. With citations of authors quoted from on each page. By Frederic May Holland ... New York, C. P. Somerby, 1879. viii p., 1 l., [1]-248 p. 19 1/2 cm. "Authorities": p. [231]-236. [B528.H7] 11-6699
1. Stoics. I. Title.

MURRAY, Gilbert, 1866-
The stoic philosophy; Conway memorial lecture delivered at South Place institute on March 16, 1915, by Gilbert Murray ... New York and London, G. P. Putnam's sons, 1915. 74 p. 20 cm. References: p. 66-67. Appendices: a. Biographical and bibliographical notes concerning Moncure Daniel Conway.--b. The Conway memorial lectureship. [Full name: George Gilbert Aime Murray] [B528.M8 1915 a] 15-14382
1. Stoics. I. Title.

SENECA, Lucius Annaeus. 170
Seneca's morals. By way of abstract. To which is added, a discourse, under the title of An after-thought By Sir Roger L'Estrange... 6th American ed. Philadelphia, Grigg & Elliott, 1834. xvi, [17]-359 [1] p. 15 1/2 cm. [BJ214.S4M6 1834] 33-30880
1. Stoics. 2. Conduct of life. I. L'Estrange, Sir Roger, 1616-1704. comp. II. Title.
Contents omitted.

WENLEY, Robert Mark, 1861-1929.
Stoicism and its influence, by R. M. Wenley... Boston, Mass., Marshall Jones company, [c1924] xi, 194 p. 19 cm. (Half--title: Our debt to Greece and Rome; editors, G. D. Hadzsits...D. M. Robinson) Bibliography: p. 182-186. [B528.W35] 25-1034
1. Stoics. I. Title.

Stoics—History

JACKSON, William Taylor, 1839- 170
Seneca and Kant; or, An exposition of stoic and rationalistic ethics, with a comparison and criticism of the two systems; by Rev. W. T. Jackson ... Dayton, O., United brethren publishing house, 1881. 3 p. l., [v]-vi p., 2 l., [11]-109 p. 20 cm. [BJ214.S5J3] 7-13316
1. Kant, Immanuel, 1724-1804. 2. Seneca, Lucius Annaeus. 3. Stoics—Hist. 4. Ethics. I. Title.

Stokes, James, 1841-1918.

OBER, Frank W., ed.
James Stokes, pioneer of Young men's Christian associations, by his associates in more than half a century of world service to young men. Frank W. Ober, editor... New York, Association press, 1921. x p., 1 l., 235 p. front., plates, ports. 21 1/2 cm. [BV1265.S603] 21-5547
1. Stokes, James, 1841-1918. 2. Young men's Christian associations. I. Title.

OBER, Frank W. ed.
James Stokes, pioneer of Young men's Christian association, by his associates in more than half a century of world service to young men. Frank W. Ober, editor... New York, Association press, 1921. x p., 1 l., 235 p. front., plates, ports. 22 cm. [BV1265.S6O3] 21-5547
1. Stokes, James, 1841-1918. 2. Young men's Christian associations. I. Title.

Stoles.

SENECA, Lucius Annaeus. 170
Seneca's morals by way of abstract. To which is added, a discourse, under the title of An after thought. By Sir Roger L'Estrange, knt. Keene, (N.H.) Printed by John Prentise, and sold at his book-store, 1806. xiv, [15]-372 p. front., 3 pl. 18 cm. Imperfect: frontispiece and 2 plates wanting. [BJ214.S4M6 1806] 1-27159
1. Stoles. 2. Conduct of life. I. L'Estrange, Sir Roger, 1616-1704, comp. II. Title.
Contents omitted.

Stone, Alvan, 1807-1833.

WRIGHT, David. 922.673
Memoir of Alvan Stone, of Goshen, Mass., by David Wright ... Boston, Gould, Kendall and Lincoln; Hartford, Canfield and Robins; [etc., etc.] 1837. 2 p. l., [9]-256 p. 16 cm. [BX6495.S797W7] 36-24861
1. Stone, Alvan, 1807-1833. I. Title.

Stone, Barton Warren, 1772-1844.

DUNLAVY, John, 1769-1826. 230'.9'8
The manifesto. [1st AMS ed.] New York, AMS Press [1972] vi, 520 p. 22 cm. Reprint of the 1818 ed. [BX9771.D9 1972] 74-134416 ISBN 0-404-08460-5 21.00
1. Stone, Barton Warren, 1772-1844. 2. Shakers. I. Title.

DUNLAVY, John, 1769-1826. 289.
The manifesto, or A declaration of the doctrine and practice of the church of Christ. By John Dunlavy ... Printed at Pleasant-Hill, Ky., mdcccxviii. New York, Reprinted by E. O. Jenkins, 1847. viii, 486 p. 24 cm. "The substance of a letter to Barton W. Stone": p. [411]-486. [BX9771.D9] 31-54
1. Stone, Barton Warren, 1773-1844. 2. Shakers. I. Title.

DUNLAVY, John, 1769-1826. 230.98
Plain evidences, by which the nature and character of the true church of Christ may be known and distinguished from all others. Taken from a work entitled "The manifesto, or, A declaration of the doctrines and practice of the church of Christ"; published at Pleasant Hill, Kentucky, 1818. By John Dunlavy ... Albany, Printed by Hoffman and White, 1834. 120 p. 19 cm. "Extracts from a letter addressed to Barton W. Stone, by John Dunlavy": p. [105]-119. [BX9771.D93 1934a] 33-17071
1. Stone, Barton Warren, 1772-1844. 2. Shakers. I. Title.

WARE, Charles Crossfield, 1886- 922.673
Barton Warren Stone, pathfinder of Christian union; a story of his life and times, by Charles Crossfield Ware; with introduction by Elmer Ellsworth Snoddy ... St. Louis, Mo., The Bethany press [c1932] xiv, 357 p. front., plates, ports., facsims. 22 1/2 cm. Bibliography: p. 345-349. [BX7343.S8W3] 32-30916
1. Stone, Barton Warren, 1772-1844. I. Title.

WEST, William Garrett. 922.673
Barton Warren Stone; early American advocate of Christian unity. Nashville, Disciples of Christ Historical Society, 1954. xvi, 245p. port. 25cm. Bibliography:p. 227-237. [BX7343.S8W4] 54-12928
1. Stone, Barton Warren, 1772-1844. I. Title.

Stone, Carrie, 1843-1853.

CARRIE; or, The child of the parsonage. 922
An authentic memoir ... New York, Stanford and Swords, 1854. 146 p. 16 cm. [BR1715.S87C3] 37-19957
1. Stone, Carrie, 1843-1853. I. Title: The child of the parsonage.

Stone, James Kent, 1840-1921.

BURTON, Katherine (Kurz) 1890- 922.273
No shadow of turning; the life of James Kent Stone (Father Fidelis of the Cross) by Katherine Burton. New York, Toronto, Longmans, Green and co., 1944. 5 p. l., 243 p. front. (port.) 21 1/2 cm. "First edition." [BX4705.S835B8] 44-9589
1. Stone, James Kent, 1840-1921. I. Title.

SMITH, Walter George, 1854-1924. 922
Fidelis of the Cross, James Kent Stone, by Walter George Smith ... and Helen Grace Smith, with 14 illustration. New York, London, G. P. Putnam's sons, 1926. xvi, 467 p. front., plates, ports. 24 cm. [BX4705.S835S6] 26-11728
1. Stone, James Kent, 1840-1921. I. Smith, Helen Grace, 1865- joint author. II. Title.

Stone, Richard Cecil, b. 1798.

STONE, Richard Cecil, b.1798.
Life-incidents of home, school and church, (autobiographical.) In seventeen years of instruction in schools and academies--in extensive labors and travels--in forty years' work in the ministry--in social, moral and historical correspondence--and in literary and scientific lectures. By Richard Cecil Stone ... Saint Louis, Southwestern book and publishing company, 1874. viii, 352 p. front. (port.) 17 1/2 cm. E 13
1. Stone, Richard Cecil, b. 1798. I. Title.

Stone Ridge, N. Y.—Genealogy

CHURCH records
[compiled by] Kenneth E. Hasbrouck. New Paltz [1956?] 5v. in 1. 29cm. Title from cover of [Part 1] Contents.[Part 1] Marriages, 1796-1859; members, 1797-1826; deaths, 1855-1871.--[Part 2] Baptisms: v. 1, 1746-1769. v.2, 1769-1787. [v.3] 1772-1806. [v.4] 1806- 1860.
1. Stone Ridge, N. Y.—Geneal. I. Stone Ridge, N. Y. Marbletown Reformed Dutch Church. II. Hasbrouck, Kenneth Edward, 1916- comp.

Stoner, David, 1794-1826.

[DAWSON, William] 1773-1841. 922.
Memoirs of the Rev. David Stoner: containing copious extracts from his diary and epistolary correspondence ... 1st American, from the 2d English ed. New-York, J. Emory and B. Waugh, 1832. 286 p. 14 cm. Preface signed: William Dawson, John Hannah. [BX8495.S78D3 1832] 43-26598
1. Stoner, David, 1794-1826. 2. Hannah, John, 1792-1867, joint author. I. Title.

[DAWSON, William] 1773-1841. 922.742
Memoirs of the Rev. David Stoner: containing copious extracts from his diary and epistolary correspondence ... Revised by Thomas O. Summers. Nashville, Tenn., E. Stevenson & F. A. Owen, agents, for the Methodist Episcopal church, South, 1855. xiv, 15-282 p. 15 cm. Preface signed: William Dawson, John Hannah. [BX8495.S78D3 1855] 34-41700
1. Stoner, David, 1794-1826. I. Hannah, John, 1792-1867, joint author. II. Summers, Thomas Osmond, 1812-1882, ed. III. Title.

Stonor family.

STONOR, Robert Julian, 1909- 282.42
Stonor, a Catholic sanctuary in the Chilterns from the fifth century til to-day. Newport, Mon., R. H. Johns, 1951. 400 p. illus. 23 cm. [BX1494.C5S8] 51-38718
1. Stonor family. 2. Catholics in England. 3. Persecution. I. Title.

Storey, Del.

STOREY, Del. 269'.2'0924 B
Collision course / by Del Storey, with Laura Watson. Plainfield, N.J. : Logos International, c1977. xiv, 123 p. ; 21 cm. [BR1725.S825A34] 77-71143 ISBN 0-88270-230-0 pbk. : 2.95
1. Storey, Del. 2. Clergy—United States—Biography. I. Watson, Laura, joint author. II. Title.

Stork, Charles Augustus Gottlieb, 1764-1831.

MORRIS, John Gottlieb, 1803-1895.
The Stork family in the Lutheran church: or, Biographical sketches of Rev. Charles Augustus Gottlieb Stork, Rev. Theophilus Stork, D.D., and Rev. Charles A. Stork, D.D., by John G. Morris ... Philadelphia, Lutheran publication society [c1886] 263 p. front. (2 port.) 19 1/2 cm. 12-36862
1. Stork, Charles Augustus Gottlieb, 1764-1831. 2. Stork, Theophilus, 1814-1874. 3. Stork, Charles Augustus, 1838-1883. 4. Stork family. I. Title.

Storr, Harry, 1875-1918.

O'RORKE, Benjamin Garniss, 1875-1918. 922.
A soldier and a man; a sketch of the life and work of Lieut.-Colonel H. Storr ... By B. G. O'Rorke ... With a preface by the Archbishop of York ... London, New York [etc.] Longmans, Green and co., 1919. ix, 121 p. front. (port.) 19 cm. [BX5199.S83O7] 19-17826
1. Storr, Harry, 1875-1918. I. Title.

Storrs, Richard Salter, 1787-1873.

PARK, Edwards Amasa, 1808-1900. 922.573
A sermon preached in Braintree, Mass., August 15, 1873, at the funeral of Rev. Richard Salter Storrs, D. D. By Prof. Edwards A. Park. Boston, A. Mudge & son, printers, 1874. 95 p. front. (port.) 23 cm. "Appendix" (p. [79]-95) includes account of Dr. Storrs' closing days and of his funeral. [BX7260.S85P3 1874 a] 36-25370
1. Storrs, Richard Salter, 1787-1873. 2. Funeral sermons. I. Title.

Story sermons.

BROWN, David M. 1949- (David Mark), 251
Dramatic narrative in preaching / by David M. Brown. Valley Forge, PA : Judson Press, [1981] p. cm. Bibliography: p. [BV4307.S7B76] 19 81-8345 ISBN 0-8170-0911-6 : 4.95
1. Story sermons. 2. Preaching. I. Title.

CALAWAY, Bernie L. 251'.08
Forty-four fun fables / by Bernie L. Calaway. Wilton, Conn. : Morehouse-Barlow Co., c1982. vi, 72 p. ; 22 cm. [BV4307.S7C34 1982] 19 81-84714 ISBN 0-8192-1296-2 pbk. : 4.95
1. Story sermons. 2. Animals, Legends and stories of. I. Title.

COZAD, Simeon Earl. 252
The second book of story talks, by Simeon E. Conzad ... New York, Round table press, inc., 1936. ix p., 1 l., 13-205 p. 20 cm. [BV4315.C66] 36-19821
I. Title.

HERBST, Winfrid. 230.
"Tell us another!" Stories told by Uncle Joe, by Winfrid Herbst, S.D.S. St. Nazianz, Wis., The Society of the Divine Savior, 1925. 147 p. illus. 18 1/2 cm. [BX2371.H4] 25-20422
I. Title.

JUNIPER, Daniel. 251'.08
Along the water's edge : stories that challenge and how to tell them / by Daniel Juniper ; with a preface by Morton T. Kelsey. New York : Paulist Press, c1982. x, 115 p. : ill. ; 21 cm. [BV4307.S7J86

1982] 19 81-84348 ISBN 0-8091-2395-9 (pbk.) : 5.95
1. Story sermons. 2. Story-telling in Christian education. I. Title.

MCKAY, Claude Allen.
Finding out God's secrets, and 43 other story-sermons, by Claude Allen McKay. New York, Cincinnati, The Abingdon press [c1916] 160 p. 17 1/2 cm. 16-16555 0.50
I. Title.

MCKAY, Claude Allen.
Finding out God's secrets, and 43 other story-sermons, by Claude Allen McKay. New York, Cincinnati, The Abingdon press [c1916] 160 p. 17 1/2 cm. 16-16555 0.50
I. Title.

Story-telling.

ARNOTE, Thelma. 268.69
The story hour leadership manual [by] Thelma Arnote ... Nashville, Tenn., The Sunday school board of the Southern Baptist convention [1944] 146 p. 20 cm. "Additional helps on subjects discussed" at end of each chapter. [BV1472.A75] 44-22354
1. Story-telling. I. Southern Baptist convention. Sunday school board. II. Title.

BOYD, Eleanor Herr, Mrs. 221.
How Granny told the Bible stories, by Eleanor H. Boyd. New York, The Book stall [c1921] 177 p. incl. plates. 24 cm. [BS551.B63] 22-2487
I. Title.

CATHER, Katherine Dunlap. 268
Mrs.
... Religious education through story-telling, by Katherine D. Cather. New York, Cincinnati. The Abingdon press [c1925] 219 p. 20 cm. (The Abingdon religious education texts, D. G. Downey, general editor. Community training school series, N. E. Richardson, editor) "Helpful books": p. 218-219. [BV1472.C25] 25-4631
1. Story-telling. 2. Religious education. I. Title.

CATHER, Katherine Dunlap. 268
Mrs.
Story telling for teachers of beginners and primary children, by Katherine Dunlap Cather. A textbook in the standard course in teacher training, outlined and approved by the Sunday school council of evangelical denominations. Third year specialization series. New York, Printed for the Teacher training publishing association by the Caxton press [c1921] 144 p. illus. (music) 17 cm. [BV1472.C3] 21-18516
1. Story-telling. I. Title.

FARMER, Beulah Maude 267
(Hollabaugh) "Mrs. T. H. Farmer," 1893 comp.
The B. Y. P. U. story hour, by Mrs. T. H. Farmer ... a manual for leaders of the Story hour with stories for a year's program ... Oklahoma City, Okla., Baptist book store, c1929. 64 p. 22 cm. [BV1472.F3] 29-10657
1. Story-telling. 2. Religious education. I. Baptist young people's union of America. II. Title.

HADLEY, Henry Harrison. 277.
The blue badge of courage, by Henry H. Hadley. Akron, O., New York [etc.] The Saalfield publishing co., 1902. xi, 13-468 p. front., plates, ports. 19 cm. "Story of the wonderful...experiences of my life...I have endeavored to show...what young men...whose lives are blasted by drink and kindred sins may do."--Introd. [BV2650.H3] 2-20248
I. Title.

HANNAN, Jerome Daniel, 1896 238.
Teacher tells a story; story-lessons in conduct and religion for every day in the school year; containing also teachers' help for use with "Religion hour: book one Story-lessons in conduct and religion". By Rev. Jerome D. Hannan, D. D. New York, Cincinnati [etc.] Benziger brothers, 1925. v. 19 cm. [BX925.H3] 26-1
1. Story-telling. 2. Religious education. 3. Catholic church—Education. I. Title.

HOUGHTON, Louise (Seymour) 220.
Mrs., 1838-1920.
How to tell Bible stories, by Louise Seymour Houghton. With introduction by Rev. T. T. Munger, D.D. Second edition with an appendix. New York, Charles Scribner's sons, 1929. xv, 205 p. 19 cm. Bibliography: p. 287-289. [[BS546.H]] A 31
I. Title.

MAY, William J. 220.95
Bible stories and how to tell them, by William J. May ... Nashville, Tenn., Cokesbury press, 1930. 239 p. 20 1/2 cm. [BS546.M3] 30-32856
1. Story-telling. 2. Religious education. 3. Bible—History of Biblical events. I. Title.

ROYAL, Claudia. 268.69
Storytelling. Nashville, Broadman Press [1956, c1955] 132p. illus. 21cm. [BV1472.R66] 56-1570
1. Story-telling. 2. Religious education. I. Title.

SPALDING, Arthur Whitefield, 264
1877-
Christian story-telling and stories for parents, teachers, and students, by Arthur Whitefield Spalding ... Mountain View, Calif., Portland, Ore., [etc.] Pacific press publishing association [c1928] 3 p. l., 5-123 p. illus. 20 1/2 cm. "Good books on story telling": p. 123. [BV1472.S6] 28-20328
1. Story-telling. 2. Religious education. I. Title.

SPALDING, Arthur 808.543
Whitefield, 1877-1954
Christian storytelling. Rev., enl. by Eric B. Hare. Mountain View, Calif., Pacific Pr. [1966] 187p. 22cm. First pub. in 1928 under title: Christian storytelling and stories for parents, teachers, and students. [BV1534.3.S6 1966] 66-26928 3.25
1. Story-telling. 2. Religious education. I. Hare, Eric B., ed. II. Title.

TRALLE, Henry Edward, 268.69
1867-
Story-telling lessons, by Henry Edward Tralle ... Philadelphia, Boston [etc.] The Judson press [1934] 4 p. l., 108 p. 19 cm. (Half-title: Judson training manuals for the school of the church) "Second revision and reissue, September, 1934." [LB1042.T7 1934] 35-1016
1. Story-telling. 2. Religious education. I. Title.

Story-telling (Christian theology)

[AMOS, Mary Jane (Davies)] 923
Mrs. 1872-
"Blessed are the pure in heart"; or, The story of Mary Jane, by Mary S. Collins [pseud.] Boston, Meador publishing company, 1940. 122 p. front. (port.) 20 cm. Autobiography. [BR1725.A66A3] 40-4794
I. Title. II. Title: The story of Mary Jane. III. Title: Mary Jane, The story of.

...A child's story of the New Testament in words of one syllable; with thirty-nine illustrations. Philadelphia, H. Altemus company [c1900] viii, 9-112 p. incl. col. pl. 19 cm. (Altemus' one syllable series) 9-7556

...A child's story of the New Testament in words of one syllable; with thirty-nine illustrations. Philadelphia, H. Altemus company [c1909] viii, 9-112 p. col. front., illus., col. pl. 19 1/2 cm. (Altemus' one syllable series) 9-17216

... A child's story of the Old Testament pin words of one syllabe; with twenty-nine illustrations. Philadelphia, H. Altemus company [c1900] 3 p. l., 5-116 p. col. front., illus., col. pl. 19 1/2 cm. (Altemus' one syllable series) 9-7427

... A child's story of the Old Testament in words of one syllabe with thirty-nine illustrations. Philadelphia, H. Altemus company [c1909] 4 p. l., 5-116 p. col. front., illus., col. pl. 19 1/2 cm. (Altemus' one syllable series). 9-17215

COBBIN, Ingram, 1777-1851. 225.
The child's story of the New Testament; explaining in simple language in a manner to interest children, the wonderful truths as taught by Christ and his apostles, by Rev. Ingram Cobbin ... [Philadelphia? 1901] 3 p. l., 9-250 p. incl. illus., col. plates, map. col. front. 24 1/2 cm. [BS2401.C55] 1-25503
I. Title.

LATHBURY, Mary A.
Child's story of the Bible; with introduction by ... J. H. Vincent ... Boston, De Wolfe, Fiske & co. [1898] x p., 1 l., 267, [1] p. illus. 8 degree. Nov
I. Title.

LAWLER, Michael G. 230
Raid on the inarticulate : an invitation to adult religion / Michael G. Lawler. Washington, D.C. : University Press of America, c1980. xi, 156 p. ; 21 cm. Bibliography: p. 153-155. [BT78.L34] 19 80-1438 ISBN 0-8191-1899-0 pbk. : 7.75
1. Story-telling (Christian theology) I. Title.

NAVONE, John J. 230
The Jesus story : our life as story in Christ / by John Navone. Collegeville, Minn. : Liturgical Press, 1980. p. cm. Bibliography: p. [BT78.N38] 79-25026 pbk. : 8.50
1. Jesus Christ—Person and offices. 2. Story-telling (Christian theology) I. Title.

SHEA, John. 231
Stories of God : an unauthorized biography / by John Shea. Chicago : Thomas More Press, c1978. 203 p. ; 22 cm. Includes bibliographical references. [BR118.S47] 78-303611 ISBN 0-88347-085-3 : 8.95
1. Story-telling (Christian theology) 2. Theology. I. Title.

STRETTON, Hesba.
The child's story of the beautiful life of Jesus told in simple language, adapted to all ages, but especially to the young ... By Hesba Stretton ... Hartford, Conn., Hartford publishing company [1902] 249 p. incl. col. front.,illus., pl. col. pl. 25 cm. 2-25431
I. Title.

Story-telling in Christian education.

BENTLEY, Joseph. 220
How to sleep on a windy night, by Joseph Bentley; with an introduction by F. W. Norwood ... Philadelphia, Henry Altemus company [c1928] 158 p. incl. front. (port.) 20 cm. Stories and lessons. [BR125.B458] 28-16653
I. Title.

DYE, Eva May.
Bolenge; a story of Gospel triumphs on the Congo, by Mrs. Royal J. Dye. Cincinnati, O., Foreign Christian missionary society [c1909] 225 p. plates, ports., maps, plan. 19 1/2 cm. 10-17590
I. Title.

GRIGGS, Patricia, 1935- 268'.6
Using storytelling in Christian education / Patricia Griggs ; photography by Scott Griggs. Nashville : Abingdon, c1981. 63 p. : ill. ; 28 cm. Bibliography: p. 63. [BV1534.3.G74] 19 80-26468 ISBN 0-687-43117-4 pbk. : 4.95
1. Story-telling in Christian education. I. Title.

[RANYARD, Ellen Henrietta
(White) Mrs.] 1810-1879.
The Book and its story; a narrative for the young. On occasion of the jubilee of the British and foreign Bible society. By L. N. R., with an introductory preface by the Rev. T. Phillips ... 1st American, from 11th London ed. Philadelphia, Parry & McMillan, 1854. 463 p. front., illus. (incl. ports.) 20 cm. 17-14852
I. Phillips, Thomas. Rev. II. Title.

Story, Thomas, 1662-1742.

DALGLISH, Doris N. 289.6'0922
People called Quakers, by Doris N. Dalglish. Freeport, N.Y., Books for Libraries Press [1969] 169 p. 23 cm. (Essay index reprint series) Reprint of the 1938 ed. Contents.Contents.—The first Quaker poet.—An American saint.—A digression on women and the eighteenth century.—A neighbour of Wordsworth.—A friend from France.—Convert and critic. [BX7791.D3 1969] 78-90628
1. Story, Thomas, 1662-1742. 2. Woolman, John, 1720-1772. 3. Wilkinson, Thomas, 1751-1836. 4. Grellet, Stephen, 1773-1855. 5. Stephen, Caroline Emelia, 1834-1909. 6. Friends, Society of—Biography. I. Title.

LEA, John William, 1870- 220
The Book of books and its wonderful story; a popular handbook for colleges, Bible classes, Sunday schools, and private students, by John W. Lea. Philadelphia, The J. L. Winston company, 1922. xv, [1], 351 p. incl. front., illus. 24 cm. Bibliography: p. 343-345. [BS475.L4] 22-17394
I. Title.

LOGAN, James, 1674-1751. 922.
The correspondence of James Logan and Thomas Story, 1724-1741, edited by Norman Penney ... Philadelphia, Pa., Friends' historical association [c1927] 2 p. l., 100 p. 24 cm. [BX7795.L6A3] 27-3829
I. Story, Thomas, 1662-1742. II. Penney, Norman, 1858- ed. III. Title.

STORY, Thomas, 1662-1742. 922.
The life of Thomas Story, carefully abridged; in which the principal occurrences and the most interesting remarks and observations are retained. By John Kendall. Philadelphia, Printed by J. Crukshank, 1805. 346 p. 18 cm. [BX7795.S82A3 1805] 9-30727
I. Kendall, John, 1726-1815, ed. II. Title.

Stover, George Gilbert, 1853-1875.

MULLINS, George Gatewood. 922.
My life is an open book. By Chaplain G. G. Mullins ... St. Louis, J. Burns, 1883. xv, 17-331 p. incl. front., port. 20 cm. A biography of "Berty" Stover, the "boy preacher" of the Christian church, and sermons by the author. [BX7343.S84M8] 12-36940
1. Stover, George Gilbert, 1853-1875. 2. Disciples of Christ—Sermons. 3. Sermons, American. I. Title.

Stow, Baron, 1801-1869.

SKINNER, Otis Ainsworth, 269
1807-1861.
Letters to Rev. B. Stow, R. H. Neale, And R. W. Cushman, on modern revivals. By Otis A. Skinner. Boston, A. Tompkins, 1842. iv, [7]-144 p. 19 1/2 cm. [BV3790.S6] 37-39293
1. Stow, Baron, 1801-1869. 2. Neale, Rollin Heber, 1808-1879. 3. Cushman, Robert Woodward, 1800-1868. 4. Revivals. I. Title.

STOCKBRIDGE, John Calvin, 922.673
1818-1896.
The model pastor. A memoir of the life and correspondence of Rev. Baron Stow, D.D., late pastor of the Rowe street Baptist church, Boston. By John C. Stockbridge, D.D. Boston, Lee and Shepard; New York, Lee, Shepard and Dillingham, 1871. 376 p. front. (port.) pl. 20 cm. [BX6495.S798S8 1871] 32-33645
1. Stow, Baron, 1801-1869. I. Title.

STOCKBRIDGE, John Calvin, 1818-1896. 922.673
A model pastor. A memoir of the life and correspondence of Rev. Baron Stow, D.D., by John C. Stockbridge, D.D. A new, illustrated ed. with biographical appendix. Boston, Lee and Shepard, 1894. 392 p. font., plates, ports. 21 cm. [BX6495.S798S8 1894] 32-33646
1. Stow, Baron, 1801-1869. I. Title.

Stowe School, Buckingham, Eng.

ANNAN, Noel Gilroy Annan, Baron, 1916- 261
The headmaster; Roxburgh of Stowe and his influence in English education [by] Noel Annan. New York, Schocken Books [1966] xiii, 216 p. 22 cm. First published in London in 1965 under title: Roxburgh of Stowe. Roxburgh, John Fergusson, 1888-1954. Bibliographical footnotes. [LF795.B87934R63 1966] 66-16310
1. Stowe School, Buckingham, Eng. I. Title.

Strachan, John, Bp., 1778-1867.

HENDERSON, John L. H. 283'.0924 B
John Strachan, 1778-1867 [by] J. L. H. Henderson. [Toronto] University of Toronto Press [1969] 112 p. 21 cm. (Canadian biographical studies) Includes bibliographical references. [BX5620.S75H4] 70-408188 4.50
1. Strachan, John, Bp., 1778-1867.

Strachan, Robert Kenneth, 1910-1965.

ELLIOT, Elisabeth. 266'.023'0924 B
Who shall ascend; the life of R. Kenneth Strachan of Costa Rica. [1st ed.] New York, Harper & Row [1968] xii, 171 p. map (on lining paper), ports. 22 cm. [BV2843.C7S75] 68-11732
1. Strachan, Robert Kenneth, 1910-1965. 2. Missions—Costa Rica. I. Title.

ROBERTS, W. Dayton. 269'.2
Revolution in evangelism; the story of Evangelism-in-depth in Latin America. [by] W. Dayton Roberts. Foreword by Leighton Ford. Chicago, Moody [1967] 127p. 18cm. (Christian forum bks.) [BV3777.L3R6] 67-26295 1.25 pap.,
1. Strachan, Robert Kenneth, 1910-1965. 2. Evangelistic work—Latin American. 3. Latin America Mission. I. Title. II. Title: Evangelism-in-depth.

ROBERTS, W. Dayton. 266'.023'0924 B
Strachan of Costa Rica; missionary insights and strategies, by W. Dayton Roberts. Grand Rapids [1971] 187 p. 21 cm. (Christian world mission books) [BV2843.C7S78] 78-163657 2.95
1. Strachan, Robert Kenneth, 1910-1965. I. Title.

Strambi, St. Vincent Mary,

LEABEL, Pius A
St. Vincent Strambi's guide to sacred eloguence. From the Italian of St. Vincent Mary Strambi, passionist and afterward Bishop of Macerata and Tolentino. St. Meinrad, Ind., Abbey Press, 1962. ix, 138 p. 19 cm. 65-70534
1. Strambi, St. Vincent Mary, 1745- Guide to sacred eloquence. 2. Sermons — Composition and delivery. I. Title. II. Title: Guide to sacred eloquence.

ST. Vincent Strambi's guide to sacred eloquence. From the Italian of St. Vincent Mary Strambi, passionist and afterward Bishop of Macerata and Tolentino. St. Meinrad, Ind., Abbey Press, 1962. ix, 138 p. 19 cm. 65-70534
1. Strambi, St. Vincent Mary, 1745- Guide to sacred eloquence. 2. Sermons — Composition and delivery. I. Title: Guide to sacred eloquence.

Strambi, Vincenzo Maria, Saint, 1745-1824.

GRASHOFF, Raphael. 922.245
"I'll not be a traitor!" The story of the Passionist bishop, St. Vincent Mary Strambi. St. Meinrad, Ind., The Grail ['1951] 68 p. illus. 20 cm. [BX4700.S77G7] 52-6865
1. Strambi, Vincenzo Maria, Saint, 1745-1824. I. Title.

MCDEVITT, Herbert, father, 1881- 922.245
Blessed Vincent Maria Strambi, by Herbert McDevitt, C.P. Union City, N.J., St. Michael's monastery [1925] 2 p. l., [3]-57 p. front., illus. (incl. ports.) 15 cm. [Secular name: Charles A. McDevitt] [BX4705.S84M3] 37-21101
1. Strambi, Vincenzo Maria, bp., 1745-1824. I. Title.

Strang, James Jesse, 1813-1856.

FITZPATRICK, Doyle C. 289.3'0924 B
The King Strang story; a vindication of James J. Strang, the Beaver Island Mormon King, by Doyle C. Fitzpatrick. [1st ed.] Lansing, Mich., National Heritage, 1970. xxviii, 289 p. illus., facsims., geneal. table, map (on lining papers), ports. 24 cm. [BX8680.S88S84] 70-140603 7.95
1. Strang, James Jesse, 1813-1856. 2. Beaver Island, Mich.—History. I. Title.

QUAIFE, Milo Milton, 1880- 289.3
The kingdom of Saint James; a narrative of the Mormons, by Milo M. Quaife ... New Haven, Yale university press; London, H. Milford, Oxford university press, 1930. 5 p. l., 284 p. front. (port.) plates, facsims. 24 cm. "The present volume in the eleventh work published by the Yale university press on the Amasa Stone Mather memorial publication fund." "Sources of information": p. 184-194. [BX8695.S8Q3] 30-10360
1. Strang, James Jesse, 1813-1856. 2. Beaver island, Mich.—Hist. 3. Mormons and Mormonism. I. Yale university. Amasa Stone Mather memorial publication fund. II. Title.

RIEGEL, Oscar Wetherhold, 1902- 922.8373
Crown of glory, the life of James J. Strang, Moses of the Mormons, by O. W. Riegel. New Haven, Yale university press, 1935. 4 p. l., 281 p. front. (port.) 24 cm. "Published on the foundation established in memory of Amasa Stone Mather of the class of 1907, Yale college."--1st prelim. leaf. "Sources of information": p. [274]-276. [BX8695.S8R5] 35-23615
1. Strang, James Jesse, 1813-1856. 2. Mormons and Mormonism. 3. Beaver island, Mich.—Hist. I. Title.

STRANG, James Jesse, 1813.1856. 922.8373
Diary. Deciphered, transcribed, introduced, and annotated by Mark A. Strang. With a foreword by Russell B. Nye. [East Lansing] Michigan State University Press [1961] xiv, 78 p. port., facsim. 22 cm. Bibliography: p. 65-78. [BX8680.S88S8] 60-16420
I. Title.

Stratford, Conn. Christ Church.

CAMERON, Kenneth Walter, 1908- 283'.746'9
The genesis of Christ Church, Stratford, Connecticut, pre-Revolutionary Church of England; background and earliest annals, commemoration of the two hundred fiftieth anniversary. With a detailed index. An appendix by Carolyn Hutchens. Hartford, Transcendental Books [1972] 64 l. illus., facsims. 29 cm. Includes bibliographical references. [BX5980.S88C5 1972] 72-195488
1. Stratford, Conn. Christ Church. I. Title.

Stratford-upon-Avon—History—Sources.

CHURCH of the Holy Trinity, Stratford-upon-Avon. 283'.424'8
The vestry minute-book of the Parish of Stratford-on-Avon from 1617 to 1699 A.D. New York, AMS Press [1971] 158 p. 23 cm. Reprint of the 1899 ed. [DA690.S92C46 1971] 72-142244 ISBN 0-404-00366-4
1. Stratford-upon-Avon—History—Sources. I. Title.

Straughn, James Henry, Bp., 1877-

STEPHENSON, Frank W. 287'.7'0924
For such a time: Bishop James H. Straughn, A.B., B.S.T., D.D., LL.D.; a brief account of Bishop Straughn's life and his part in bringing the Methodist Protestant Church into the Methodist Church, by Frank W. Stephenson. [Grand Rapids? 1967] 64 p. illus., ports. 21 cm. [BX8495.S79S7] 67-8469
1. Straughn, James Henry, Bp., 1877- 2. Methodist Church (United States)—History. I. Title.

Strauss, David Friedrich, 1808-1874.

CROMWELL, Richard S. 230'.092'4 B
David Friedrich Strauss and his place in modern thought, by Richard S. Cromwell. Foreword by Wilhelm Pauck. Fair Lawn, N.J., R. E. Burdick [1974] 232 p. 23 cm. "A Carl Hermann Voss book." Bibliography: p. 219-224. [BX4827.S8C76 1974] 73-88620 ISBN 0-913638-05-6 12.50
1. Strauss, David Friedrich, 1808-1874. I. Title.

HARRIS, Horton. 230'.092'4 B
David Friedrich Strauss and his theology. Cambridge [Eng.] University Press, 1973. xv, 301 p. illus. 22 cm. (Monograph supplements to the Scottish journal of theology) Bibliography: p. 295-298. [BX4827.S8H33] 72-93137 ISBN 0-521-20139-X
1. Strauss, David Friedrich, 1808-1874. I. Title. II. Series: Scottish journal of theology. Monograph supplements.
Distributed by Cambridge University Press, New York, 16.00.

MASSEY, Marilyn Chapin, 1942- 232.9'01
Christ unmasked : the meaning of The life of Jesus in German politics / Marilyn Chapin Massey. Chapel Hill : University of North Carolina Press, c1983. p. cm. (Studies in religion) Includes index. Bibliography: p. [BT301.S73M37 1983] 19 82-8547 ISBN 0-8078-1524-1 : 25.00
1. Strauss, David Friedrich, 1808-1874. Das Leben Jesu. 2. Jesus Christ—Biography. 3. Christian biography—Palestine. 4. Germany—Politics and government—1806-1848. I. Title.

Streitfeld, Harold States

STREITFELD, Harold S. 294.5'2
God's plan : the complete guide to the future / by Harold Streitfeld. Oakland, Calif. : Raja Press, c1981. xv, 142 p. : ill. ; 22 cm. Includes bibliographical references. [BL624.S77] 19 81-80768 ISBN 0-9605926-0-1 (pbk.) : 6.95
1. Streitfeld, Harold S. 2. Spiritual life. 3. God. I. Title.
Publisher's address: 5534 Fremont St., Oakland, CA 94608

Stresau, Jan, 1939-1967.

STRESAU, Marion. 133.9'092'4 B
Tomorrows unlimited. Boston, Branden Press [1973] 143 p. illus. 22 cm. [BF1286.S8] 72-91222 ISBN 0-8283-1486-1 5.95 (pbk.)
1. Stresau, Jan, 1939-1967. 2. Spiritualism. I. Title.

Stress (Psychology)

WISE, Robert L. 248.4
How not to go crazy : finding stability in unstable times / Robert L. Wise. Irvine, Calif. : Harvest House Publishers, c1980. 158 p. ; 21 cm. Includes bibliographical references. [BF575.S75W57] 19 80-80459 ISBN 0-89081-237-3 (pbk.) : 3.95
1. Stress (Psychology) 2. Identity (Psychology) 3. Self-actualization (Psychology) 4. Christian life—1960- I. Title.

Strickland, Henry Benjamin, 1884-1944.

FOSTER, John J., 1912- 282'.0924 B
A priest for all men; the life of Henry B. Strickland, by John J. Foster. Lebanon, Penn., Holy Name Society, Assumption B.V.M. Church [1971] 160 p. illus., facsim., ports. 23 cm. Bibliography: p. 160. [BX4705.S8433F68] 77-158664 3.00
1. Strickland, Henry Benjamin, 1884-1944. I. Title.

Strict Congregational churches in Connecticut.

BLAKE, Silas Leroy, 1834-1902.
The separates; or, Strict Congregationalists of New England. by Rev. S. Leroy Blake ... with an introduction by Prof. Williston Walker, D.D. Boston, Chicago, The Pilgrim press [1902] "Principal authorities consulted": p. 10-12. [BX7252.S4B6] 2-23421
1. Strict Congregational churches in Connecticut. 2. Congregational churches in New England. 3. Connecticut—Church history. I. Title.

Strict Congregational churches in Connecticut—Catachisms and creeds.

FROTHINGHAM, Ebenezer, 1717?-1798. 285.
The articles of faith and practice, with the covenant, that is confessed by the separate churches of Christ in general in this land. Also a discourse, holding forth the great privileges of the church of Jesus Christ, and the same privileges vindicated from the Sacred Scriptures; and some points of practice in the church of Christ, that are in great dispute between the learned and unlearned, fairly settled in a line of divine truth. Written by Ebenezer Frothingham. [Eleven lines of Biblical quotations] Newport: Printed by L. Franklin, 1750. 432 p., 1 l., 15 cm. Signatures: A-Z4, Aa-Zz4, Aaa-Hhh4, leaf (Errata) unsigned. Imperfect: p. 187-190 wanting; supplied by photostat. [BX7230.F7]
1. Strict Congregational churches in Connecticut—Catachisms and creeds. 2. Covenants (Church polity) I. Title.

Strict Congregational churches in Connecticut—Doctrinal and controversial works.

WINDHAM county association of Congregational ministers, Windham co., Conn. 285.8746
A letter from the associated ministers of the county of Windham, to the people in the several societies in said county. Boston, N.E. Printed and sold by J. Draper, in Newbury-street. M,DCC,XLV. 52 p. 22 cm. [BX7230.W55] [AC901.W3 vol. 107] 27-21556
1. Strict Congregational churches in Connecticut—Doctrinal and controversial works. 2. Connecticut—Church history. I. Title.

Stritch, Samuel Alphonsus, Cardinal, 1887-1958.

BUEHRLE, Marie Cecilia, 1887- 922.273
The Cardinal Stritch story. Milwaukee, Bruce Pub. Co. [1959] 197p. illus. 22cm. [BX4705.S844B8] 59-12941
1. Stritch, Samuel Alphonsus, Cardinal, 1887-1958. I. Title.

Strong, Augustus Hopkins, 1836-1921.

HENRY, Carl Ferdinand Howard, 1913- 230
Personal idealism and Strong's theology. Wheaton, Ill., Van Kampen Press [1951] 233 p. 24 cm. Bibliography: p. 230-233. [BT75.S874H4] 51-8679
1. Strong, Augustus Hopkins, 1836-1921. 2. Personalism. I. Title.

STRONG, Augustus Hopkins, 1836-1921. 230'.61'0924 B
Autobiography of Augustus Hopkins Strong / edited by Crerar Douglas. Valley

Forge, PA : Judson Press, 1981. p. cm. Includes bibliographical references and index. [BX6495.S7985A32] 19 81-5970 ISBN 0-8170-0916-7 : 25.00
1. Strong, Augustus Hopkins, 1836-1921. 2. Theologians—United States—Biography. 3. Baptists—Clergy—Biography. 4. Clergy—United States—Biography. I. Douglas, Crerar. II. Title.

STRONG, Augustus Hopkins, 1836-1921. 230
What shall I believe? A primer of Christian theology, by Augustus Hopkins Strong ... New York, Chicago [etc.] Fleming H. Revell company [c1922] 118 p. 19 1/2 cm. [BT77.S75] 22-14222
I. Title.

Strong, Charles, 1844-1942.

BADGER, Colin Robert, 1906- 285'.2'0924 B
The Reverend Charles Strong and the Australian Church [by] C. R. Badger. Melbourne, Abacada Press [on behalf of the Charles Strong Memorial Trust, 1971] 335 p. illus., ports. 23 cm. Includes bibliographical references. [BR1725.S84B3] 72-883252 ISBN 0-909505-00-4 8.50
1. Strong, Charles, 1844-1942. 2. Australian Church. I. Title.

Strong, June.

STRONG, June. 248'.833 B
Journal of a happy woman. Nashville, Southern Pub. Association [1973] 160 p. 23 cm. Includes bibliographical references. [BX6193.S77A3] 73-80238 ISBN 0-8127-0072-4 4.95
1. Strong, June. I. Title.

Strossmayer, Josip Juraj, Bp., 1815-1905.

SIVRIC, Ivo. 262'.5'20924 B
Bishop J. G. Strossmayer; new light on Vatican I. Chicago, Franciscan Herald Press [1974, i.e.1975] p. [BX4705.S845S56] 73-22014 ISBN 0-8199-0491-0 8.95
1. Strossmayer, Josip Juraj, Bp., 1815-1905. 2. Vatican Council, 1869-1870.

Structural anthropology—Addresses, essays, lectures.

FONCTION symbolique. 306'.4
Between belief and transgression : structuralist essays in religion, history, and myth / edited by Michel Izard and Pierre Smith ; translated by John Leavitt ; with an introduction by James A. Boon. Chicago : University of Chicago Press, 1982. xx, 276 p. : ill. ; 23 cm. (Chicago originals) Translation of: La Fonction symbolique. Includes bibliographies and index. [GN362.F6613 1982] 19 81-16377 ISBN 0-226-38861-1 : 20.00
1. Structural anthropology—Addresses, essays, lectures. 2. Rites and ceremonies—Addresses, essays, lectures. 3. Symbolism—Addresses, essays, lectures. 4. Religion—Addresses, essays, lectures. I. Izard, Michel. II. Smith, Pierre. III. Title. IV. Series.

Structural drawing.

BISHOP, Carlton Thomas, 1882- 25-6060
Structural drafting and the design of details, by Carlton Thomas Bishop... 2d ed., rev. Appendix added on hip and valley rafters. Total issue, seven thousand. New York, J. Wiley and sons, inc.; [etc., etc] 1925. 2 p. l., iii-xiii, 362 p. incl. illus., tables, diagrs. 20 1/2 x 27 1/2 cm. [T355.B5 1925]
1. Structural drawing. I. Title.

Structuralism.

STRUCTURAL analysis and 220.6
Biblical exegesis : interpretational essays / by R. Barthes ... [et al.] ; translated by Alfred M. Johnson, Jr. Pittsburgh : Pickwick Press, 1974. p. cm. (Pittsburgh theological monograph series ; no. 3) Translation of Analyse structurale et exegese biblique. Bibliography: p. [BS531.A513] 74-31334 ISBN 0-915138-02-6 : 6.95
1. Bible. O.T. Genesis XXXII, 23-33—Criticism, interpretation, etc. 2. Bible. N.T. Mark V, 1-20—Criticism, interpretation, etc. 3. Structuralism. I. Barthes, Roland. II. Title. III. Series.

Structuralism (Literary analysis)

PATTE, Daniel. 220.6'3
Structural exegesis : from theory to practice / Daniel Patte, Aline Patte. Philadelphia : Fortress Press, c1978. p. cm. Includes bibliographical references and index. [BS476.P33] 78-54557 ISBN 0-8006-0524-1 : 8.95
1. Bible—Hermeneutics. 2. Structuralism (Literary analysis) I. Patte, Aline, joint author. II. Title.

POLZIN, Robert. 808
Biblical structuralism : method and subjectivity in the study of ancient texts / by Robert M. Polzin. Philadelphia : Fortress Press, c1977. vii, 216 p. : ill. ; 22 cm. (Semeia supplements) Includes index. Bibliography: p. 202-214. [BS1415.2.P64] 76-15895 ISBN 0-8006-1506-9 : 5.95
1. Bible. O.T. Job—Criticism, interpretation, etc. 2. Structuralism (Literary analysis) I. Title. II. Series.

Structuralism (Literary analysis)—Addresses essays lectures.

†THE New Testament and 225.6
structuralism : a collection of essays / by Corina Galland ... [et al.] ; edited and translated by Alfred M. Johnson, Jr. Pittsburgh : Pickwick Press, 1976. ix, 338 p. : ill. ; 22 cm. (Pittsburgh theological monograph series ; 11) "Originally published in 1971 as number 22 (June) issue of Langages, entitled Semiotique narrative : recits Bibliques." Includes index. Bibliography: p. 325-332. [BS2325.N48] 76-25447 ISBN 0-915138-13-1 pbk. : 7.95
1. Bible. N.T.—Criticism Textual—Addresses essays lectures. 2. Structuralism (Literary analysis)—Addresses essays lectures. I. Galland, Corina. II. Johnson, Alfred M., 1942- III. Series.

Stuart family.

SANDERS, Robert Stuart. 285.10924
The Reverend Robert Stuart, D. D., 1772-1856, a pioneer in Kentucky Presbyterianism, and his descendants. Louisville, Ky., Dunne Press, 1962. 167p. illus. 24cm. [BX9225.S788S3] 62-6330
1. Stuart, Robert, 1772-1856. 2. Stuart family. I. Title.

Stuart, Moses, 1780-1852.

ADAMS, Williams, 1807-1880. 016.
A discourse on the life and services of Professor Moses Stuart; delivered in the city of New York...January 25, 1852. By William Adams... New York, J. F. Trow, printer, 1852. 71 p. 23 cm. "Prof. Bela B. Edwards, D.D."; p. [65]-66. "Greek and oriental type": p. 67-71. [BV4070.A559S8] 4-24810
1. Stuart, Moses, 1780-1852. 2. Edwards, Bela Bates, 1802-1852 I. Title.

PARK, Edwards Amasa, 1808-1900. 207.
A discourse delivered at the funeral of Professor Moses Stuart. By Edwards A. Park ... Boston, Tappan & Whittemore, 1852. 56 p. 23 cm. Partial catalogue of Mr. Stuart's published writings: p. [51]-54. [BV4070.A559S82] 5-18226
1. Stuart, Moses, 1780-1852. 2. Funeral sermons. I. Title.

Stuart, Moses, 1780-1852. A letter to William E. Channing.

WHITMAN, Bernard, 1796-1834. 261.
Two letters to the Reverend Moses Stuart; on the subject of religious liberty. By Bernard Whitman. Boston, Gray and Bowen, 1830. 165, [1] p. 23 1/2 cm. Cover-title: Mr. Whitman's letters to Professor Stuart, on religious liberty. [BV741.S7W4 1830] 45-43784
1. Stuart, Moses, 1780-1852. A letter to William E. Channing. 2. Religious liberty. 3. Unitarian churches—Doctrinal and controversial works. I. Title.

WHITMAN, Bernard, 1796-1834. 261.
Two letters to the Reverend Moses Stuart; on the subject of religious liberty. By Bernard Whitman. 2d ed. Boston, Gray and Bowen, 1831. 1 p. l., [v]-vi, 162, [v]-vi p. 23 1/2 cm. Cover-title: Mr. Whitman's letters to Professor Stuart, on religious liberty. [BV741.S7W4 1831] 44-28895
1. Stuart, Moses, 1780-1852. A letter to William E. Channing. 2. Religious liberty. 3. Unitarian churches—Doctrinal and controversial works. I. Title.

Stuart, Robert, 1772-1856.

SANDERS, Robert Stuart. 285.10924
The Reverend Robert Stuart, D. D., 1772-1856, a pioneer in Kentucky Presbyterianism, and his descendants. Louisville, Ky., Dunne Press, 1962. 167p. illus. 24cm. [BX9225.S788S3] 62-6330
1. Stuart, Robert, 1772-1856. 2. Stuart family. I. Title.

Stucco—Italy—Vatican City.

SMITH, Graham, 1942- 726'.5'0945634
The Casino of Pius IV / Graham Smith. Princeton, N.J. : Princeton University Press, c1976. p. cm. Includes index. Bibliography: p. [N6920.S54] 76-3017 ISBN 0-691-03915-1 : 20.00
1. Vatican City. Casino di Pio IV. 2. Stucco—Italy—Vatican City. 3. Mural painting and decoration, Renaissance—Vatican City. 4. Mural painting and decoration—Vatican City. 5. Symbolims in art—Vatican City. I. Title.

Stuckenberg, John Henry Wilburn, 1835-1906.

EVJEN, John Oluf, 1874- 922.473
The life of J. H. W. Stuckenberg, theologian, philosopher, sociologist, friend of humanity ... by John O. Evjen ... Minneapolis, Minn., The Lutheran free church publishing company, 1938. 535 p. front., illus., ports., facsims. 23 cm. Bibliography: p. 23-24; "Articles by Dr. Stuckenberg in the Homiletic review": p. 535. [BX8080.S86E8] 38-11593
1. Stuckenberg, John Henry Wilburn, 1835-1906. I. Title.

Studd, Charles Thomas, 1860-1931.

GRUBB, Norman P. 922
C. T. Studd, athlete and pioneer, by Norman P. Grubb ... Grand Rapids, Mich., Zondervan publishing house [1941] 238 p., 1 l. front., pl., ports. 20 cm. "First published in England, November, 1932 ... Fourth impression in U.S.A. 1941." [BV3705.578G7 1941] 42-20135
1. Studd, Charles Thomas, 1860-1931. 2. Missions—Kongo, Belgian. I. Title.

GRUBB, Norman Percy, 1895- 922
After C. T. Studd. [North American ed.] Grand Rapids, Zondervan Pub. House [1946] 185 p. illus., ports., maps. 20 cm. [BV3705.S78G68 1946] 47-4693
1. Studd, Charles Thomas, 1860-1931. 2. Worldwide Evangelization Crusade. I. Title.

GRUBB, Norman Percy, 1895- 922
C. T. Studd, athlete and pioneer, by Norman P. Grubb ... Grand Rapids, Mich., Zondervan publishing house [1941] 238 p., i 1. front., pl., ports. 20 cm. "First published in England, November, 1963 ... Fourth impression in U. S. A., 1941." [BV3705.S78G7 1941] 42-20135
1. Studd, Charles Thomas, 1860-1931. 2. Missions—Kongo, Belgian. I. Title.

Studdiford, Peter Ogilvle, 1799-1866.

LAMBERTVILLE, N. J. Presbyterian church. 922.573
Memorial of Rev. Peter O. Studdiford, D. D., late pastor of the Presbyterian church of Lambertville, New Jersey, who departed this life June 5th, 1866 ... Published by the session. Philadelphia. Printed by A. Martien, 1866. 68 p. 23 cm. "Funeral sermon, by the Rev. George Hale, D. D.": p. [9]-32. "Commemorative discourse, preached at Lambertville, July 8, 1866, by the Rev. John L. Janeway, D. D.": p. [51]-68. [BX9225.S795L3] 36-22148
1. Studdiford, Peter Ogilvle, 1799-1866. 2. Funeral sermons. 3. Presbyterian church—Sermons. I. Hale, George, 1812-1888. II. Janeway, John Livington, 1815-1906. III. Title.

Student movements.

CARLING, Francis, 1945- 322.4
Move over: students, politics, religion. New York, Sheed and Ward [1969] 154 p. 22 cm. [LB3605.C33] 69-19252 3.95
1. Student movements. 2. College students—Conduct of life. I. Title.

STUDENT Christian Movement in New England.
Five experiments in campus Christian community. [Cambridge, Mass., 1962] 66 p. 24 cm. "The essays in this book were first presented at the Staff-Clergy Conference sponsored by the Student Christian Movement in New England, Janaury 24-26, 1962." 66-30295
I. Title.

Student volunteer movement for foreign missions.

STUDENT volunteer movement for foreign missions. International convention. 3d, Cleveland, 1898.
The student missionary appeal. Addresses at the third International convention of the Student volunteer movement for foreign missions, held at Cleveland, Ohio, February 22-27, 1898. New York, Student volunteer movement for foreign missions, 1898. xiii p., 2 l., 3-563 p. 24 cm. [BV2890.S8 1898] 2-17527
I. Title.

WILDER, Robert Parmelee, 1863- 266
The Student volunteer movement for foreign missions; some personal reminiscences of its origin and early history, by Robert P. Wilder, foreword by Jesse R. Wilson... New York, N.Y., The Student volunteer movement [c1935] 63 p. 19 1/2 cm. [BV2360.S8W5] 36-9459
1. Student volunteer movement for foreign missions. I. Title.

Students.

BENNETT, Margaret Elaine, 1893- 207
Beyond high school, by Margaret E. Bennett ... and Harold C. Hand ... New York and London, McGraw-Hill book company, inc. [c1938] xv, 227 p. illus. 21 cm. "Helpful reading" at end of each chapter except the first. Bibliography: p. 211-217. [LB1027.B45] 38-11288
1. Students. 2. Profession, Choice of. 3. Conduct of life. I. Hand, Harold Curtis, 1901- joint author. II. Title.

CLARK, Thomas Arkle, 1862- 170
The Sunday eight o'clock, brief sermons for the undergraduate, by Thomas Arkle Clark... Urbana, Illini publishing company, 1916. vii, 197 p. incl. front. 20 1/2 cm. [BJ1661.C55] 16-24089 1.00.
1. Students. 2. Conduct of life. I. Title.

KNOPF, Carl Summer, 1889- 371.8
The student faces life; a study of solutions; lectures delivered at the University of Redlands, March, 1931, by Carl Summer Knopf, PH. D. Philadelphia, Boston [etc.] The Judson press [c1932] 8 p. l., 3-222 p. 20 cm. [LB3605.K55] 201 32-11210
1. Students. 2. Religion—Philosophy. I. Redlands, Calif. University. II. Title.

PRITCHETT, Henry Smith, 1857- 252.
What is religion? and other student questions; talks to college students by Henry S. Pritchett ... Boston and New York, Houghton, Mifflin and company, 1906. x p., 2 l., 3-117, [1] p. 20 cm. [BV4310.P7] 6-4177
I. Title.
Contents omitted.

TRAHEY, Jane. 818.54
Life with Mother Superior. New York, Farrar, Straus and Cudahy [1962] 210 p. illus. 21 cm. Autobiographical. [LC485.T7] 62-16278
1. Students. I. Title.

Students, Jewish—Religious life.

CENTRAL Conference of American Rabbis. Youth Committee. 296.7
Working with college students, a handbook for rabbis. [New York? 1967] vi, 44 p. 22 cm. Bibliography: p. 24-27. [BM727.C4] 67-31000
1. Students, Jewish—Religious life. I. Title.

FRIEDMAN, Theodore 296.08
Letters to Jewish college students. New York, J. David [c.1965] 223p. 24cm. [BM727.F7] 65-17362 4.95, 1.95 bds., pap.,
1. Students, Jewish—Religious life. I. Title.

Students—Prayer-books and devotions—English.

BOLLINGER, Hiel De Vere, 1898- comp. 248.373
The student at prayer. Nashville, Upper room [1960] 96p. 16cm. [BV283.C7B6] 60-14671
1. Students—Prayer-books and devotions—English. I. Title.

FINEGAN, Jack, 1908- 264.1
Book of student prayers, by Jack Finegan. New York, N.Y., Association press, 1946. [100] p. 21 cm. [BV283.C7F5] 46-5768
1. Students—Prayer-books and devotions—English. I. Title.

HADDAM House, inc. 264
The student prayerbook; edited and written by a Haddam House committee, under the chairmanship of John Oliver Nelson, for personal and group devotion. New York, Association Press [1953] 237p. 20cm. (A Haddam House Book) [BV283.C7H3] 53-11972
1. Students—Prayer-books and devotions—English. I. Title.

HUSE, Dennis. 264'.02
Speak Lord, I'm listening / Dennis Huse and Geralyn Watson. Notre Dame, Ind. : Ave Maria Press, c1981. 175 p. : ill. ; 28 cm. "39 liturgies which present the gospel message in terms that upper grade and junior high school students can understand"—Cover. [BX2198.H87] 19 80-70851 ISBN 0-87793-220-4 (pbk.) : 7.95
1. Students—Prayer-books and devotions—English. I. Watson, Geralyn. II. Title.

MEDITATIONS for college students, by Donald Deffner [and others] 242.63
St. Louis, Concordia Pub. House [1961] 152p. 20cm. [BV4850.M4] 61-11242
1. Students—Prayer-books and devotions—English. I. Deffner, Donald.

SHILLONG, Eric W. 242'.2
Guiding thoughts to success and achievement : for students each day of the year / by Eric W. Shillong. Philadelphia : Dorrance, [1974] 462 p. ; 24 cm. Includes bibliographical references and index. [BV4531.2.S54] 73-91540 ISBN 0-8059-1972-4 : 10.00
1. Students—Prayer-books and devotions—English. 2. Devotional calendars. I. Title.

Students—Religious life.

BRIGHT, Bill. 267'.61
Come help change the world. Old Tappan, N.J., F. H. Revell Co. [1970] 207 p. 21 cm. Includes bibliographical references. [BV4427.B73] 70-112462 4.95
1. Campus Crusade for Christ. 2. Students—Religious life. I. Title.

CONFREY, Burton, 1898- 248
Spiritual conferences for college men [by] Burton Confrey ... Manchester, N.H., Magnificat press [c1939] 264 p. front., 2 pl. on 1 l. 23 cm. [Full name: Joseph Burton Confrey] Includes bibliographies. [BX2360.C58] 40-3535
1. Students—Religious life. 2. Young men—Religious life. I. Title.

COVINGTON, G. Edwin. 248
What they believe; a survey of religious faith among groups of college students. New York, Philosophical Library [1956] 109p. 24cm. [BT85.C6] 56-3294
1. Students—Religious life. 2. Theology, Doctrinal. I. Title.

CURRY, Albert Bruce, 1887- 267.
Facing student problems, by A. Bruce Curry, jr. ... Council of Christian associations ... New York, Association press, 1925. xxv, 156 p. 19 cm. "The Scripture text is taken from 'The New Testament, a new translation', by James Moffatt." [BV1170.C8] 25-11258
1. Students—Religious life. I. Council of Christian associations. II. Title.

DEFFNER, Donald L 248.83
Christ on campus; meditations for college life, by Donald L. Deffner. Saint Louis, Concordia Pub. House [1965] xii, 156 p. 20 cm. [BV4531.2.D42 1965] 65-24176
1. Students — Religious life. I. Title.

GARA, Matthew 248.4'8'2
Hey- lets talk it over! considerations for Catholic teens. Illus. by Dorothy Koch. North Easton, Mass., Holy Cross Pr. [1967] 111p. illus. 27cm. [BX2373.S8G32] 67-25213 3.00
1. Students—Religious life. 2. Christian life—Catholic authors. I. Title.

GLAZIER, Daniel Johnson, 1828-1855. 252.
The student-preacher: being a memoir with discourses of Daniel Johnson Glazier. By Robert Turnbull. Boston, Gould and Lincoln; New York, Sheldon, Lamport & Blakeman, 1855. 190 p. 20 cm. [BX6333.G56S7] 40-25727
I. Turnbull, Robert, 1809-1877, ed. II. Title.

GUILLET, Cephas. 171.
Talks to students about God and life [by] C. Guillet ... New York city, J. F. Guillet [1927] 3 p. l., 96 p., 1 l. 20 1/2 cm. "Second thousand."--p. [2] of cover. Talks given at Alfred university in the spring of 1925 and 1926. cf. Pref. [BV4531.G8] 43-21614
1. Students—Religious life. I. Title.

HAMILL, Robert H 248
Gods of the campus. New york, Abingdon-Cokesbury Press [1949] 126 p. 19 cm. "Written for the Methodist Student Movement." Bibliographical footnotes. [BV4531.H2] 49-5127
1. Students—Religious life. I. Title.

HARRIS, Cyril, 1891- 259
The religion of undergraduates, by Cyril Harris ... New York, C. Scribner's sons, 1925. viii p. 2 l. 3 87 p. 20 cm. [BV639.Y7H3] 25-20603
1. Students Religious life. I. Title.

INTER-COLLEGIATE Conference on Students' Religious Activities, 1st, University of Minnesota, 1958.
The First inter-collegiate conference on students' religious activities, April 18-19, 1958. [Minneapolis] University of Minnesota, 1958. 63 p. Sponsored by the Student Councils of Religion at the University of Minnesota, with the cooperation of the Minnesota-Dakota region of the National Conference of Christians and Jews and its Commission of Religious Organizations. 68-47512
1. Students—Religious life. I. Minnesota. University. Student Councils of Religion. II. Title.

KILGO, John Carlisle, bp., 1861-1922. 252.
Chapel talks, by John Carlisle Kilgo...edited by D. W. Newsom... Nashville, Tenn., Dallas, Tex. [etc.] Publishing house M.E. church, South, 1922. 173 p. front. port.) 19 1/2 cm. [BV4310.K5] 23-2669
1. Students—Religious life. I. Newsom, Dallas Walter, ed. II. Title.

KIRVAN, John J. 220.6
The restless believers, by John J. Kirvan. Glen Rock, N.J., Paulist Press [1966] ix, 109 p. 18 cm. (Deus books) [BX2373.S8K5] 66-29818
1. Students—Religious life. 2. Pastoral theology—Catholic Church. I. Title.

LARSEN, Vernon Fred, 1906- 248
... Development of a religious inventory for a specific study in higher education ... by Vernon Fred Larsen ... [Chicago] 1942. v. 63 p. incl. tables. 23 cm. Part of thesis (PH. D.)--University of Chicago, 1941. Lithoprinted. Bibliography: p. 61-63. [BV1610.L3] A 42
1. Students—Religious life. 2. Church and college. I. Title.

LEAVELL, Frank Hartwell, 1884- 248
The Master's minority. Nashville, Broadman Press [1949] 189 p. 21 cm. [BV4531.L34] 49-9574
1. Students—Religious life. I. Title.

LEMMON, Clarence Eugene, 1888- 252.066
Religion helps, by Clarence E. Lemmon. St. Louis, Mo., The Bethany press, 1942. 152 p. 20 cm. [BV4310.L44] 42-13754
1. Students—Religious life. I. Title.

MCCOY, Charles S 253.7
The gospel on campus; rediscovering evangelism in the academic community [by] Charles S. McCoy [and] Neely D. McCarter. Richmond, John Knox Press [1959] 123p. 21cm. Includes bibliography. [BV4531.2.M2] 59-6077
1. Students—Religious life. 2. Universities and colleges—Religion. 3. Evangelistic work. I. McCarter, Neely D., joint author. II. Title.

MCDOWELL, William Fraser, bp. 1858-1937. 252.
...This mind, by William Fraser McDowell... New York, Cincinnati, The Methodist book concern, [c1922] 183 p 17 1/2 cm. (The Mendenhall lectures, 8th series, delivered at De Pauw university.) [BV4310.M2] 22-16530
1. Students—Religious life. I. Title.

NATIONAL student conference, Milwaukee. 1926. 206.
Religion on the campus, the report of the National student conference, Milwaukee. Dec. 28, 1926 to Jan. 1. 1927, edited by Francis P. Miller. Council of Christian associations ... New York, Association press, 1927. x, 198 p. 19 cm. [BR41.N3] 27-10329
1. Students—Religious life. I. Council of Christian associations. II. Miller, Francis Pickens. 1895- ed. III. Title.

PRESBYTERIAN Church in the U. S. Board of Christian Education. Dept. of Campus Christian Life. 377.85
A basis for study, a theological prospectus for the campus ministry; a symposium by Presbyterian university pastors, prepared by the Dept. of Campus Christian Life, Board of Christian Education, Presbyterian Church, U. S., and the Dept. of Campus Christian Life, Board of Christian Education, United Presbyterian Church, U. S. A. [Richmond? 1959] 153p. 21cm. [BV1610.P7 1959] 59-38177
1. Students—Religious life. 2. Universities and colleges— Religion. 3. Religious education of young people. I. United Presbyterian Church in the U. S. A. Board of Christian Education. Dept. of Campus Christian. II. Title.

REED, Harold W. 248.8'3
Baccalaureate messages : for preachers, evangelists, speakers, writers / Harold W. Reed. Grand Rapids : Baker Book House, 1978, c1960. 112p. ; 18 cm. (Pocket Pulpit library) Formerly published under the title: Committed to Christ. [BV4310.R37] ISBN 0-8010-7615-3 pbk. : 1.65
1. Students — Religious life. 2. Church of the Nazarene — Sermons. 3. Sermons, American. I. Title.
L.C. card no. for 1960 original ed.: 60-2244.

REED, Harold W 248.83
Committed to Christ; messages to college youth. Grand Rapids, Baker Book House, 1960. 112p. 20cm. [BV4310.R37] 60-2244
1. Students—Religious life. 2. Church of the Nazarene—Sermons. 3. Sermons, American. I. Title.

WEEKS, S Marion. 948
The student views religion. [Nashville, Parthenon Press, 1951] 118 p. 20 cm. [BV1610.W37] 51-7795
1. Students — Religious life. 2. Religious education — U.S. I. Title.

Students' societies—United States

BABCOCK, Fern. 267.61
A new program book for student Christian associations, by Fern Babcock. New York, N.Y., Pub. for the National inter-collegiate Christian council [by the] Association press [1943] x, 116 p. incl. forms, diagrs. 23 cm. "Program resources": p. 110-115. [BV970.N3B3] 43-13886
1. Students' societies—U.S. 2. Students—Religious life. I. National intercollegiate Christian council. II. Title.

BABCOCK, Fern. 267.61
A program book for student Christian associations. [3d ed., rev.] New York, Pub. for the National Intercollegiate Christian Council [by the] Association Press, 1948. ix, 115 p. illus., map. 23 cm. "Program resources": p. 107-114. [BV970.N3B3 1948] 49-6701
1. Students' societies—U. S. 2. Students—Religious life. I. National Intercollegiate Christian Council. II. Title.

SHEDD, Clarence Prouty. 267.610973
Two centuries of student Christian movements, their origin and intercollegiate life, by Clarence P. Shedd ... New York, Association press, 1934. xxii, 466 p. 22 1/2 cm. "These studies in a somewhat different form were submitted in 1932 to the graduate faculty of Yale university in partial fulfilment of the requirements for the degree of doctor of philosophy."--Foreword. Bibliography: p. 423-444. [BV970.A1S5 1934] 35-2123
1. Students' societies—U.S. 2. Students—Religious life. 3. Students—U.S. I. Title.

Students — United States

EDWARDS, Richard Henry, 1877- 268.
... Student counseling, by Richard H. Edwards and Ernest R. Hilgard ... [Ithaca, N.Y., The Cayuga press] 1928. 64 p. diagrs. 23 cm. (Bulletin of the National council on religion in higher education, vii) "Reports from the Seminar on student personnel service ... Teachers college, Columbia university ... July 12-August 11, 1927 ... and the Personnel group ... at Lisle, New York, September 1-8, 1927." Contains bibliographies. [[BV1460.N3 no.7]] E28
1. Students—U.S. I. Hilgard, Ernest Ropiequet, joint author. II. Title.

NORTH American Student Conference on Christian Frontiers, University of Kansas, 1947-1948. 266.0637
Christian frontiers; a report of the North American Student Conference on Christian Frontiers, December 27, 1947-January 1, 1948 at the University of Kansas, Lawrence, Kansas. New York, Association Press, 1948. 116 p. 19 cm. [BV970.N6A3 1947] 50-1091
1. Students—U. S. 2. Students—Religious life. I. Title.

WHALEN, William Joseph. 248.83
Catholics on campus; a guide for Catholic students in secular colleges and universities. Milwaukee, Bruce Pub. Co. [1961] 125 p. 20 cm. [BX922.W5] 61-9581
1. Students — U.S. 2. Catholics in the U.S. 3. Newman clubs. I. Title.

WHALEN, William Joseph. 378.198
Catholics on campus: a guide for Catholic students in secular colleges and universities, by William J. Whalen. Milwaukee, Bruce Pub. Co. [1965] 125 p. 20 cm. [BX922.W5 1965] 65-23033
1. Students — U.S. 2. Catholics in the U.S. 3. Newman clubs. I. Title.

Study course books — Intermediate.

REDDING, George Walker.
Exploring the Old Testament. Nashville, Tenn., Convention Press [1964] 106 p. 67-60184
1. Study course books — Intermediate. 2. Bible. O.T. — Criticism, interpretation, etc. I. Title.

ROBERTS, Cecil A.
Letters on Christian living. Nashville, Tenn., Convention press [1965] 101 p. 67-64661
1. Study course books — Intermediates. I. Title.

Study course books-Juniors.

WILLIAMS, Margaret.
Before Jesus came. Nashville, Convention Press [c1960] 104 p. (Teacher's ed.) 68-50823
1. Study course books-Juniors. I. Title.

Study course books—Primary.

CAPELL, Evone Wood.
God wants me to learn. Leadership material: a unit to use with primary children. Nashville, Tenn., Convention press [1964] 92 p. 67-44621
1. Study course books—Primary. I. Title.

Stundists.

BRANDENBURG, Hans, 1895- 280'.4'0947
The meek and the mighty : the emergence of the evangelical movement in Russia / [by] Hans Brandenburg ; [translated from the German]. London : Mowbrays, 1976. xii, 210 p. ; 22 cm. (Keston book ; no. 7) Translation of Christen im Schatten der Macht. Includes index. Bibliography: p. 206. [BX9798.S8B713] 77-364637 ISBN 0-264-66349-7 : £3.75
1. Stundists. 2. Russia—Church history. 3. Church and state in Russia. I. Title.

Stupas—Asia, Southeastern.

GOVINDA, Anagarika Brahmacari. 726'.1'430954
Psycho-cosmic symbolism of the Buddhist stupa / Lama Anagarika Govinda. Emeryville, Calif. : Dharma Pub., c1976. xviii, 102 p. : ill. ; 21 cm. Consists of the author's Some aspects of stupa symbolism, to which is added an article originally published in 1950 in Marg under title: Solar and lunar symbolism in the development of stupa architecture. Includes bibliographical references and index. [NA6000.G68] 76-797 ISBN 0-913546-35-6 : 8.95. ISBN 0-913546-36-4 pbk. : 4.95
1. Stupas—Asia, Southeastern. 2. Buddhist art and symbolism—Asia, Southeastern. 3. Stupas—Tibet. 4. Buddhist art and symbolism—Tibet. I. Govinda, Anagarika Brahmacari. Some aspects of stupa symbolism. c1976. II. Title.

Sturge, Scott, 1968-1974.

*STURGE, Judi Hinchliffe. 155.9'37
The spirit of Scott / by Judi Hinchliffe Sturge. Pittsford, N.Y. : Judi Sturge, c1978. 163p. : ill. ; 24 cm. [BV4907] 5.95
1. Sturge, Scott, 1968-1974. 2. Chilren — Death and Future State. 3. Bereavement — Personal Narratives. I. Title.
Publisheer's address : 18 Lodge Pole Rd., Pittsford, N.Y. 14534

Sturges, A. A.

CRAWFORD, David Livingston, 1889- 266'.023'09965
Missionary adventures in the South Pacific, by David and Leona Crawford. [1st ed.] Rutland, Vt., Tuttle [1967] 280p. illus., ports. 22cm. [BV3677.C7] 67-15137 5.00
1. Sturges, A. A. 2. Sturges, Susan Thompson, 1820-1893. 3. Missions—Micronesia. I. Crawford, Leona, joint author. II. Title.

Sturlaugson, Mary Frances.

STURLAUGSON, Mary Frances. 289.3'3 B
A soul so rebellious / Mary Frances Sturlaugson. Salt Lake City, Utah : Deseret Book Co., 1980. 88 p. ; 24 cm. [BX8695.S85A37] 19 80-69271 ISBN 0-87747-841-4 : 5.95
1. Sturlaugson, Mary Frances. 2. Mormons and Mormonism—United States—Biography. I. Title.

Styler, G. M.

SUFFERING and martyrdom in the New Testament : studies presented to G. M. Styler / by the Cambridge New Testament Seminar, William Horbury, Brian McNeil. Cambridge [Eng.] ; New York : Cambridge University Press, 1980. p. cm. Includes index. [BS2545.S9S83] 19 80-40706 ISBN 0-521-23482-4 : 39.95 231'.8
1. Styler, G. M. 2. Bible. N.T.—Criticism, interpretation, etc.—Addresses, essays, lectures. 3. Suffering—Biblical teaching—Addresses, essays, lectures. 4. Martyrdom—Biblical teaching—Addresses, essays, lectures. I. Styler, G. M. II. Horbury, William. III. McNeil, Brian. IV. Cambridge New Testament Seminar.
Contents omitted.

Subjectivity.

HEROLD, Norbert. 189.4
Menschliche Perspektive und Wahrheit : zur Deutung der Subjektivitat in den philosophischen Schriften des Nikolaus von Kues / Norbert Herold. Munster, Westf. : Aschendorff, 1975. x, 120 p. ; 24 cm. (Buchreihe der Cusanus-Gesellschaft ; Bd. 6) Abridgement of the author's thesis, Munster, 1973. Includes index. Bibliography: p. 113-118. [BX4705.N58C8 Bd. 6] [B765.N54] 189.4 75-511415 ISBN 3-402-03156-6
1. Nicolaus Cusanus, Cardinal, 1401-1464. 2. Subjectivity. I. Title. II. Series: Cusanus-Gesellschaft, Vereinigung zur Forderung der Cusanusforschung. Buchreihe ; Bd. 6.

Substance (Philosophy)

THOMAS Aquinas Saint 1225-1274 111
Tractatus de substantiis separatis. Newly-established Latin text based on 12 mediaeval mss. Introd, notes by Francis J. Lescoe. West Hartford 17, Conn., St. Joseph College [c1962] x, 207p. illus. 24cm. Bibl. 62-12144 4.85
1. Substance (Philosophy) 2. Angels—Early works to 1800. I. Lescoe, Francis J., ed. II. Title.

THOMAS Aquinas Saint, 1225?-1274. 189.4
Tractatus de substantiis separatis. A newly-established Latin text based on 12 mediaeval mss., with introd. and notes by Francis J. Lescoe. West Hartford, Conn., Saint Joseph College [1962] x, 207 p. facsims. 24 cm. Bibliography: p. 181-189. [B765.T53T7 1962] 62-12144
1. Substance (Philosophy) 2. Angels — Early works to 1800. I. Lescoe, Francis J., ed. II. Title.

THOMAS Aquinas Saint 1225?-1274 111
Treatise on separate substances. A Latin-English ed. of a newly-established text based on 12 mediaeval mss. Introd, notes by Francis J. Lescoe. West Hartford, Conn., St. Joseph College [c.1963] 1v. (various pagings) facsims. 24cm. Bibl. 63-14361 7.50
1. Substance (Philosophy) 2. Angels—early works to 1800. I. Lescoe, Francis J., ed. and tr. II. Title.

THOMAS Aquinas Saint, 1225?-1274. 111
Treatise on separate substances. Translated from a newly-established Latin text based on 12 mediaeval mss., with introd. and notes, by Francis J. Lescoe. West Hartford, Conn., Saint Joseph College [c1959] x, 138 p. facsim. 23 cm. Bibliography: p. [122]-130. [B765.T53T73] 59-15370
1. Substance (Philosophy) 2. Angels — Early works to 1800. I. Lescoe, Francis J., ed and tr. II. Title.

Substance (Philosophy)—History.

STEAD, George Christopher. 212
Divine substance / Christopher Stead. Oxford : Clarendon Press, 1977. 315 p. ; 22 cm. Includes indexes. Bibliography: p. [280]-296. [B187.S8S73] 77-552626 ISBN 0-19-826630-8 : 27.50
1. Aristoteles. 2. Substance (Philosophy)—History. 3. Philosophy, Ancient—History. 4. God—History of doctrines. I. Title.
Distributed by Oxford University Press, New York, NY

Suburban churches.

CANTELON, John E. 254.2
A Protestant approach to the campus ministry. Philadelphia, Westminster [c.1964] New York, Paulist Pr. [c.1959, 1963] 127p. n3 192p. 18cm. (Deus bk.) 254.2 254.2 64-12142 .95 pap.,
1. Suburban churches. I. Greeley, Andrew M., 1928- II. Title. III. Title: The church and the n3 IV. Title: The church and the suburbs.

FACKRE, Gabriel J. 254.2'3
Second fronts in metropolitan mission, by Gabriel Fackre. Grand Rapids, Eerdmans [1968] 30 p. 21 cm. (A Reformed journal monograph) "First appeared in ... The Reformed journal." [BV637.7.F3] 68-7824 0.75
1. Suburban churches. 2. Segregation in education—Lancaster, Pa. I. Title.

GREELEY, Andrew M 1928- 254.2
The church and the suburbs. New York, Sheed & Ward [1959] 206p. 21cm. Essays. [BX1407.S8G7] 59-12089
1. Suburban churches. I. Title.

HOYES, Herbert 254.2
Spiritual suburbia: the church in a new and growing community. New York, Vantage Press [c.1959] 63p. 21cm. 2.00 bds.,
I. Title.

METZ, Donald L. 254.2'3
New congregations; security and mission in conflict, by Donald L. Metz. With a foreword by Charles Y. Glock. Philadelphia, Westminster Press [1967] 170 p. 22 cm. Bibliography: p. [161]-165. [BV637.7.M4] 67-10276
1. Suburban churches. I. Title.

NOYCE, Gaylord B. 277.3
The responsible suburban church, by Gaylord B. Noyce. Philadelphia, Westminster Press [1970] 176 p. illus. 21 cm. Includes bibliographical references. [BV637.7.N68] 71-110724 3.50
1. Suburban churches. I. Title.

SHIPPEY, Frederick Alexander, 1908- 261.83
Protestantism in suburban life [by] Frederick A. Shippey. New York, Abingdon Press [1964] 221 p. 24 cm. Bibliography: p. 203-212. [BV637.7.S46] 64-20521
1. Suburban churches. I. Title.

SPIRITUAL suburbia:
the church in a new and growing community. New York, Vantage Press [c1959] 63p.
1. Suburban churches. I. Hoyes, Herbert.

WINTER, Gibson.
The suburban captivity of the churches; and analysis of Protestant responsibility in the expanding metropolis. New York, Macmillan [c1962] 255 p. 18 cm. "Macmillan paperbacks edition 1962." Includes bibliography. 65-8202
1. Suburban churches. 2. City churches. I. Title.

WINTER, Gibson. 254.23
The suburban captivity of the churches; an analysis of Protestant responsibility in the expanding metropolis. [1st ed.] Garden City, N.Y., Doubleday, 1961. 216 p. 22 cm. Includes bibliography. [BV637.7.W5] 61-7667
1. Suburban churches. 2. City churches. I. Title.

Suburban churches—Case studies.

FRAY, Harold R. 285'.8744'4
Conflict and change in the church, by Harold R. Fray, Jr. Boston, Pilgrim Press [1969] xiv, 113 p. 21 cm. [BV637.7.F7] 73-76085 2.95
1. Newton, Mass. Eliot Church. 2. Suburban churches—Case studies. I. Title.

Success.

AUSTIN, Lou, 1891- 248
You are greater than you know. Winchester, Va., Partnership Foundation [1955] 206p. 22cm. [BJ1611.2.A8] 55-43371
1. Success. 2. Christian life. I. Title.

BUMP, Glen Hale. 248'.4
How to succeed in business without being a pagan. Wheaton, Ill., Victor Books [1974] 132 p. 18 cm. (An Input book) [HF5386.B884] 74-77451 ISBN 0-88207-712-0 1.50 (pbk.).
1. Success. I. Title.

CAMPOLO, Anthony. 248.4
The success fantasy / Anthony Campolo, Jr. ; [cover photo., by Camerique]. Wheaton, Ill. : Victor Books, c1980. 144 p. ; 21 cm. [BJ1611.2.C25] 19 79-67852 ISBN 0-88207-796-1 (pbk.) : 3.50
1. Success. I. Title.

CONN, Charles Paul. 248.4
Making it happen : a Christian looks at money, competition, and success / Charles Paul Conn. Old Tappan, N.J. : F.H. Revell Co., c1981. 123 p. ; 22 cm. [BJ1611.2.C66] 19 81-7383 ISBN 0-8007-1252-8 : 7.95
1. Success. I. Title.

CONWELL, Russell Herman 204
Acres of diamonds. With an introductory statement by Millard E. Gladfelter. Philadelphia, Winston [c.1905-1959] viii, 38p. 24cm. 59-15577 lea. cl., not for sale
1. Success. I. Title.

CONWELL, Russell Herman, 1813-1925. 252.
Acres of diamonds, by Russell H. Conwell ... His life and achievements, by Robert Shackleton; with an autobiographical note. New York and London, Harper and brothers]c1915] 6 p. l., 3-180, [1] p. plates, 2 port. (incl. front.) 19 cm. [BX6333.C6A3 1915] 15-24504
1. Success. I. Shackleton, Robert, 1860-1923. II. Title.

CONWELL, Russell Herman, 1843-1925 204
Acres of diamonds. New York, Pyramid [1966, c.1960] 64p. 17cm. (Little inspiration classic, LP8) [BX6333C6A3 1960] .35 pap.,
1. Success. I. Title.

CONWELL, Russell Herman, 1843-1925 204
Acres of diamonds. [Westwood, N.J.] Revell [1960] 64p. 17cm. (Revell inspirational classic) [BX6333.C6A3 1960] 61-318 3.95
1. Success. I. Title.

CONWELL, Russell Herman, 1843-1925. 248'.4
Acres of diamonds [by] Russell Conwell. Essay on self-reliance [by] Ralph Waldo Emerson. As a man thinketh [by] James Allen. New Canaan, Conn., Keats Pub. [1973] 131 p. 18 cm. (A Pivot family reader) (Inspiration three, v. 1) [BX6333.C6A3 1973] 74-156290 1.25 (pbk.)
1. Success. 2. Self-reliance. 3. New Thought. I. Emerson, Ralph Waldo, 1803-1882. Self-reliance. 1973. II. Allen, James, 1864-1912. As a man thinketh. 1973. III. Title. IV. Series.

CONWELL, Russell Herman, 1843-1925. 131.3
Acres of diamonds; Russell Conwell's inspiring classic about opportunity. Edited for contemporary readers by William R. Webb. With drawings by Betty Fraser. [Kansas City, Mo.] Hallmark Editions [1968] 60 p. illus. 20 cm. [BX6333.C6A3 1968] 68-19596 2.50
1. Success. I. Title.

CONWELL, Russell Herman, 1843-1925. 252.
Acres of diamonds. Some sermons on the life that now is, which point with a lively faith to the heavenly home. A lecture is included. By Russell H. Conwell ... Cleveland, O., F. M. Barton [c1905] 96 p. front. (port.) 19 1/2 cm. [BX6333.C6A3 1905] 6-624
1. Success. 2. Baptist—Sermons. 3. Sermons, American. I. Title.

COOLEY, Donald Gray, 1904- 133.3
Predict your own future. New York, W. Funk [1950] viii, 278 p. diagrs. 21 cm. Bibliography: p. 269-271. [BJ1611.C65] 50-5780
1. Success. I. Title.

CRAFTS, Wilbur Fisk, 1850- 248'.4
1922.
Successful men of to-day, and what they say of success. New York, Arno Press, 1973 [c1883] 263 p. illus. 23 cm. (Big business: economic power in a free society) Reprint of the ed. published by Funk & Wagnalls, New York. [HF5386.C892 1973] 73-2500 ISBN 0-405-05081-X 13.00
1. Success. I. Title. II. Series.

DAS, Ranendra Kumar. 170
Your hidden treasures, by Ranendra Kumar Das ... Indianapolis, Ind., Self-realization fellowship [1944] 5 p. l., 15-207 p. 20 cm. "First edition." [BJ1611.D28] 45-12607
1. Success. 2. Happiness. I. Indianapolis. Self-realization fellowship (Non-sectarian church) II. Title.

DEMOSS, Arthur. 248.4'2
How to change your world in 12 weeks [by] Arthur DeMoss & David R. Enlow. Old Tappan, N.J., F. H. Revell Co. [1969] 128 p. 21 cm. [BJ1611.2.D42] 69-12293 3.50
1. Success. I. Enlow, David R., joint author. II. Title.

DOBBERT, John. 248'.4
Give yourself a chance / John Dobbert. Old Tappan, N.J. : Revell, c1979. 160 p. ; 22 cm. [BJ1611.2.D6] 78-21106 ISBN 0-8007-0988-8 : 6.95
1. Success. 2. Christian life—1960- I. Title.

DROWN, Harold J. 248'.42
You the graduate [by] Harold J. Drown. Nashville, Abingdon Press [1974] 64 p. 20 cm. [BJ1611.D75] 73-18380 ISBN 0-687-46856-6 2.95
1. Success. 2. Conduct of life. I. Title.

DUNN, Paul H. 248'.48'93
Discovering the quality of success [by] Paul H. Dunn. Compiled by Gary Gough and Jeril Winget. Salt Lake City, Deseret Book Co., 1973. 140 p. 24 cm. [BF637.S8D74] 73-77365 ISBN 0-87747-493-1 3.95
1. Success. I. Title.

DUNN, Paul H. 248.4'8'93
Meaningful living [by] Paul H. Dunn. Illus. by Richard L. Gunn. Salt Lake City, Bookcraft, 1968. 175 p. illus. 24 cm. [BJ1611.2.D8] 68-28761 3.00
1. Success. I. Title.

ENLOW, David R. 209'.2'2 B
Saved from bankruptcy : the story of the boatbuilding Meloons / by David and Dorothy Enlow. Chicago : Moody Press, [1975] p. cm. [BR1725.M36E54] 75-23223 ISBN 0-8024-7540-X : 4.95
1. Meloon, Wilfred C. 2. The Meloon family. 3. Success. I. Enlow, Dorothy, joint author. II. Title.

FOWLER, Nathaniel Clark, 1858-
... The boy, how to help him succeed; a symposium of successful experiences, by Nathaniel C. Fowler, jr. assisted by three hundred and nineteen American men of marked accomplishment. New York, Moffat, Yard and company, 1912. 320 p. 20 cm. [BS1641.F75] E 14
1. Success. 2. Boys. I. Title.

JEWELL, Earle B., 1896- 248.4'8'3
You can if you want to! By Earle B. Jewell. [Kansas City, Mo., Midwest Pub. Co., 1968] xiii, 141 p port. 23 cm. [BJ1611.2.J4] 68-3819
1. Success. 2. Christian life—Anglican authors. I. Title.

LAURENCE, Theodor. 248'4
The miracle power of believing / Theodor Laurence. West Nyack, N.Y. : Parker Pub. Co., c1976. 204 p. ; 24 cm. [BJ1611.2.L4] 75-35831 ISBN 0-13-585810-0 : 8.95 pbk. : 2.95
1. Apostles' Creed—Miscellanea. 2. Success. 3. Creeds—Miscellanea. I. Title.
Distributed by Prentice-Hall.

LEWIS, Harve Spencer, 1883- 299
Self mastery and fate, with the cycles of life, by H. Spencer Lewis ... San Jose, Calif., Rosicrucian press, AMORC college [1929] 261 p. diagrs. 20 cm. (Rosicrucian library, v. no. 7) Pages 256-261, advertising matter. [BF1623.R7R65 vol. 7] 30-7514
1. Rosicrucians. 2. Success. I. Title.

LUNDSTROM, Lowell. 248'.4
How to enjoy supernatural prosperity / Lowell Lundstrom. Irvine, Calif. : Harvest House Publishers, c1979. 112 p. ; 21 cm. [BJ1611.2.L87] 79-87771 ISBN 0-89081-204-7 : 3.95
1. Success. 2. Christian life—1960- I. Title.

MCCLAIN, Dayton E. 287'.6'0924 B
The miracle of two cents; the story of a truly remarkable life, by Dayton E. McClain. With a foreword by Samuel Engle Burr, Jr. Edited by Henry d'Arcy. Linden, Va., Burr Publications, 1968. xii, 48 p. 23 cm. [BX8495.M15A3] 68-58719 2.45
1. Success. I. Title.

MACDOUGALL, Mary 131.3'2
Katherine.
Prosperity now. Lee's Summit, Mo., Unity Books [1969] 159 p. 20 cm. [BX9890.U5M25] 69-17412 2.95
1. Unity School of Christianity—Doctrinal and controversial works. 2. Success. I. Title.

MURPHY, Joseph, 1898- 248'.4
Great Bible truths for human problems / by Joseph Murphy. Marina del Rey, Calif. : DeVorss, 1976. 288 p. ; 20 cm. [BJ1611.2.M795] 76-19844 ISBN 0-87516-214-2 pbk. : 5.00
1. Success. I. Title.

NASH, E. J. H. 248.483
How to succeed in the Christian life. Chicago 10, 1519 North Astor Inter-Varsity Press, [1960] 16p. 13cm. .20 pap.,
I. Title.

NORVELL. 133
The occult sciences: how to get what you want through your occult powers [by] Anthony Norvell. West Nyack, N.Y., Parker Pub. Co. [1971] 220 p. 22 cm. [BJ1611.2.N69] 76-133414 ISBN 0-13-627877-9
1. Success. 2. Occult sciences. I. Title.

PEALE, Norman Vincent, 248.4
1898-
Dynamic imaging / Norman Vincent Peale. Old Tappan, N.J. : Revell, c1981. p. cm. [BJ1611.2.P37] 19 81-14382 ISBN 0-8007-1278-1 : 8.95
1. Success. I. Title.

PEALE, Norman Vincent, 248.4
1898-
Ethusiasm makes the difference. Englewood Cliffs, N.J., Prentice-Hall [1967] x, 244 p. 22 cm. 1968 ed. published under title: The new executive edition of Enthusiasm makes the difference. [BF637.S8P38] 67-26078
1. Success. 2. Enthusiasm. I. Title.

PONDER, Catherine. 222'.11'0922 B
The millionaires of Genesis, their prosperity secrets for you! / Catherine Ponder. Marina del Rey, Ca. : DeVorss, c1976. 178 p. ; 21 cm. (Her The Millionaires of the Bible) [BJ1611.2.P626] 76-19843 ISBN 0-87516-215-0 pbk. : 3.95
1. Bible. O.T.—Biography. 2. Success. 3. Patriarchs (Bible)—Biography. I. Title.

PONDER, Catherine. 248.3
Open your mind to prosperity. Unity Village, Mo., Unity Books [1971] 185 p. 20 cm. [BJ1611.P773] 79-155720 ISBN 0-87159-092-1
1. Success. I. Title.

PONDER, Catherine. 248.3
Pray and grow rich. West Nyack, N.Y., Parker Pub. Co. [1968] xxii, 228 p. 24 cm. Bibliographical footnotes. [BJ1611.P775] 68-29606 6.95
1. Success. 2. Prayer. I. Title.

PONDER, Catherine 248.4899
The prospering power of love. Lee's Summit, Mo., Unity Bks., 1966. 126p. 19cm. [BJ1611.2.P63] 66-25849 1.00 pap.,
1. Success. 2. Love. I. Title.

PROKOP, Phyllis Stillwell. 248'.4
How to wake up singing / Phyllis Stillwell Prokop. Nashville : Broadman Press, c1979. 191 p. ; 21 cm. [BJ1611.2.P76] 79-50877 ISBN 0-8054-5271-0 : 5.95
1. Success. I. Title.

RAINES, Robert Arnold. 248'.48'7
Success is a moving target / Robert A. Raines. Waco, Tex. : Word Books, c1975. 152 p. : ill. ; 23 cm. Includes bibliographical references. [BJ1611.R14] 75-10091 ISBN 0-87680-395-8 : 5.95
1. Success. 2. Christian life—Methodist authors. I. Title.

ROBERTS, Oral, ed. 248
God's formula for success and prosperity, edited by Oral Roberts and G. H. Montgomery. Tulsa, Okla., 1956. 158p. 20cm. [BJ1611.2.R57] 56-8450
1. Success. 2. Christian life. I. Montgomery, G. H. joint ed. II. Title.

ROBERTS, Oral. 248
God's formula for success and prosperity, edited by the editorial staff, Abundant life magazine. Rev. ed. Tulsa, Okla., Abundant Life Publications, 1966. 128 p. 20 cm. First ed., by O. Roberts and G. H. Montgomery, published in 1956. [BJ1611.2.R57] 66-15958
1. Success. 2. Christian life. I. Montgomery, G. H., joint author. II. Abundant life magazine. III. Title.

SCHULLER, Robert Harold. 248.4
The peak to peek principle / Robert H. Schuller. 1st ed. Garden City, N.Y. : Doubleday, 1980. xi, 177 p. ; 22 cm. [BJ1611.2.S3157] 19 80-1693 ISBN 0-385-17319-9 : 9.95
1. Success. 2. Christian life—Reformed authors. I. Title.

SILL, Sterling W. 248.4'8'93
Making the most of yourself [by] Sterling W. Sill. Salt Lake City, Bookcraft, 1971. xi, 324 p. 24 cm. [BJ1611.2.S514] 71-177292
1. Success. I. Title.

TAM, Stanley, 1915- 248.4
God owns my business, by Stanley Tam as told to Ken Anderson. Waco, Tex., Word Books [1969] 155 p. illus., ports. 23 cm. [BJ1611.T28] 69-18864 3.95
1. Success. I. Anderson, Kenneth, 1917- II. Title.

WILLINGHAM, Ronald L. 248'.4
Life is what you make it; a guide for self-discovery and goal-setting [by] Ronald L. Willingham. Introd. by Maxwell Maltz. Waco, Tex., Word Books [1973] 157 p. 23 cm. Includes bibliographical references. [BF637.S8W522] 73-77950 4.95
1. Success. 2. Psychology, Religious. I. Title.

YOUNG, Frank Rudolph. 133.8
Psychastra: key to secret ESP+Control. West Nyack, N.Y., Parker Pub. Co. [1968] xvi, 231 p. illus. 24 cm. [BF1999.Y64] 68-29607 6.95
1. Success. 2. Occult sciences. I. Title.

Success—Addresses, essays, lectures.

SILL, Sterling W. 248.4
The three infinities: to know, to do, to be [by] Sterling W. Sill. Salt Lake City, Bookcraft, 1969. xii, 355 p. port. 24 cm. [BJ1611.S535] 70-102004 3.95
1. Success—Addresses, essays, lectures. I. Title.

Success—Anecdotes, facetiae, satire, etc.

SCHULLER, Robert Harold. 248'.4
It's possible / Robert Schuller. Old Tappan, N.J. : F. H. Revell Co., c1978. 160 p. ; 22 cm. Includes index. [BJ1611.2.S29] 78-1653 ISBN 0-8007-0927-6 : 6.95
1. Success—Anecdotes, facetiae, satire, etc. I. Title.

Success—Sermons.

BAKKER, Jim. 248.4
Eight keys to success / by Jim Bakker ; edited by Jeffrey Park. Charlotte, NC : PTL Television Network, c1980. ix, 85 p. : ill. ; 18 cm. [BV4253.B33] 19 79-92249 ISBN 0-89221-071-0 (pbk.) : 2.50
1. Success—Sermons. 2. Sermons, American. I. Park, Jeffrey. II. Title.

Sudan Interior Mission.

FORSBERG, Malcolm. 266.02309624
Last days on the Nile. [1st ed.] Philadelphia, Lippincott [1966] 216 p. fold. map. 21 cm. [BV3625.S82F6] 66-25409
1. Sudan Interior Mission. 2. Missions—Sudan. I. Title.

HUNTER, James Hogg, 1890- 276.6
A flame of fire; the life and work of R. V. Bingham. Foreword by Donald M. Fleming, introd. by Albert D. Helser. Sudan Interior Mission [dist. Chicago, Moody Pr., c.]1961 320p. illus. maps. 61-66182 3.50
1. Bingham, Rowland Victor, 1872-1942. 2. Sudan Interior Mission. I. Title.

WALL, Martha. 276.61
Splinters from an African log. Drawings by Al Fabrizio, from photographs. Chicago, Moody [1968,c.1960] 319p. illus. 18cm. (Moody Diamonds, 20) Autobiographical. [BV3542.W3A3] 60-16878 1.29 pap.,
1. Sudan Interior Mission. 2. Missions—Africa, West. I. Title.

Suenens, Leon Joseph, Cardinal, 1904-

HAMILTON, 262'.135'0924 B
Elizabeth, 1906-
Suenens : a portrait / Elizabeth Hamilton. 1st ed. in the U.S. of America. Garden City, N.Y. : Doubleday, 1975. 283 p. ; 22 cm. Includes index. [BX4705.S8684H35 1975] 74-32571 ISBN 0-385-09907-X : 7.95
1. Suenens, Leon Joseph, Cardinal, 1904-

Suffering.

ANDRUS, Paul F., 1931- 248'.86
Why me? Why mine? : Clear thinking about suffering / Paul F. Andrus. Nashville : Abingdon Press, [1975] 112 p. ; 19 cm. Includes bibliographical references. [BT732.A52] 75-12668 ISBN 0-687-45485-9 pbk. : 2.95
1. Suffering. I. Title.

APPROACHES to the Cross.
Translated by the Earl of Wicklow. New York, Macmillan, 1960. 115p. 19cm.
1. Suffering. I. Leclercq, Jacques, 1891-

BAILEY, Jack S. 231'.8
Let not your heart be troubled : answers to the problems of human suffering / Jack S. Bailey. Bountiful, Utah : Horizon Publishers, 1977,c1976. 219 p. ; 23 cm. Includes index. [BT732.7.B3] 76-3988 ISBN 0-88290-060-9 : 3.95.
1. Suffering. 2. Consolation. I. Title.

BLAKE, Buchanan. 179
The meaning of suffering in human life, by the Rev. Buchanan Blake, D. D. Paisley, A. Gardner, 1922. 174 p. 20 cm. [BJ1409.B5] 22-9371
1. Suffering. I. Title.

BOROS, Ladislaus, 1927- 242.66
Pain and providence. Tr. by Edward Quinn. Baltimore, Helicon [1966] 131p. 21cm. Tr. of Erlostes Dasein: theologische Betrachtungen. [BT732.7.B613] 66-26629 3.50 bds.,
1. Suffering. I. Title.
Available from Taplinger, New York

BOROS, Ladislaus, 1927- 242'.6'6
Pain and Providence / by Ladislaus Boros ; translated by Edward Quinn. New York : Seabury Press, [1975] 1972. p. cm. Translation of Erlostes Dasein: theologische Betrachtungen. "A Crossroad book." [BT732.7.B613 1975] 74-26563 ISBN 0-8164-2110-2 pbk. : 2.95
1. Suffering. I. Title.

BOWKER, John 291.2'11
Problems of suffering in religions of the world. [London] Cambridge University Press [1975, c1970] xii, 318 p. 22 cm. Bibliography: p. 293-297. [BL65.S85B68] 77-93706 ISBN 0-521-09903-X

1. Suffering. I. Title.
Distributed by Cambridge University Press, N.Y. for 15.95; 4.95 (pbk.)

BRYANS, Edith Ama. 179
Thorns: the joyful mystery of pain, by E. A. Bryans, with an introduction by Father Vernon, S. D. C. London, New York [etc.] Longmans, Green and co., 1925. 4 p. l., xi-xii, 113, [1] p. 20 cm. [BJ1409.B7] 25-20428
1. Suffering. I. Title.

BRYDEN, James Davenport, 1900- 231.8
God and human suffering. Nashville, Broadman [1965, c.1953] 128p. 20cm. Bibl. [BT732.7.B7] 65-11768 1.95 bds.,
1. Suffering. I. Title.

BUTTRICK, George Arthur, 1892- 231.8
God, pain, and evil. Nashville, Abingdon Press [1966] 272 p. 24 cm. Bibliographical references included in "Notes" (p. 236-259) [BT732.7.B8] 66-16020
1. Suffering. I. Title.

CARROLL, Robert Sproul, 1869- 179
The soul in suffering; a practical application of spiritual truths, by Robert S. Carroll ... New York, The Macmillan company, 1919. 6 p. l., 241 p. 20 cm. [BJ1409.C3] 19-9930
1. Suffering. 2. Conduct of life. I. Title.

CHRISTENSON, Evelyn. 248.8'6
Gaining through losing / Evelyn Christenson ; assisted editorially by Viola Blake. Wheaton, Ill. : Victor Books, c1980. 180 p. ; 21 cm. [BV4905.2.C47] 19 80-51630 ISBN 0-88207-795-3 pbk. : 4.95
1. Suffering. 2. Resignation. I. Blake, Viola, 1921- II. Title.

CLARKSON, Edith Margaret, 1915- 242'.4
Grace grows best in winter : help for those who must suffer / by Margaret Clarkson. Grand Rapids : Zondervan Pub. House, [1975] c1972. p. cm. Large print ed. [BV4909.C56 1975] 75-25997 4.95
1. Suffering. 2. Sight-saving books. I. Title.

CROCK, Clement Henry, 1890- 248
No cross, no crown; or, Through suffering to eternal glory. New York, Society of Saint Paul [1955] 174 p. 21 cm. 'New and revised edition.'--Dust jacket. [BV4905.C693 1955] 57-3097
1. Suffering. I. Title.

DUPORTAL, Marguerite, 1869- 179
A key to happiness; the art of suffering, by Marguerite Duportal. Translated from the French by Romuald Pecasse, S.O. CIST. Milwaukee, The Bruce publishing company [1944] xviii p., 1 l., 124 p. 20 1/2 cm. (Half-title: Religion and culture series; Joseph Husslein ... general editor) Translation of De ia souffrance. [BV4905.D8] 44-4190
1. Suffering. I. Pecasse, Romualdus, 1900- tr. II. Title.

EITEN, Robert B. 248
The apostolate of suffering, by Robert B. Eiten, B.J. Detroit, Mich., Mariannhill mission society [1946] [iii]-xii, 106 p. 20 1/2 cm. "Some select books": p. 108. [BX2373.S5E5] 46-17244
1. Suffering. I. Mariannhill fathers. II. Title.

EVELY, Louis, 1910- 231'.8
Suffering. Translated by Marie-Claude Thompson. Garden City, N.Y., Doubleday [1974, c1967] 111 p. 18 cm. (Image books). [BT160.E913] ISBN 0-385-02996-9 1.45 (pbk.)
1. Suffering. 2. Theodicy. I. Title.
L.C. card number for original ed.: 67-13296.

EVELY, Louis, 1910- 231'.8
Suffering. Translated by Marie-Claude Thompson. [New York] Herder and Herder [1967] 160 p. 21 cm. [BT160.E913] 67-13296
1. Suffering. 2. Theodicy.

EVERETT, Caroline Kane (Mills) "Mrs. Leo Everett," d.1921. 179
The privilege of pain, by Mrs. Leo Everett; introduction by Kate Douglas Wiggin. Boston, Small, Maynard & company [c1920] 4 p. l., 3-105 p. 18 cm. [BJ1409.E8] 21-1052
1. Suffering. I. Title.

FEIDER, Paul A., 1951- 253.5
Arise and walk : the Christian search for meaning in suffering / Paul A. Feider. Notre Dame, IN : Fides/Claretian, c1980. 121 p. ; 20 cm. Bibliography: p. 117-121. [BT732.7.F44] 79-23622 ISBN 0-8190-0634-3 pbk. : 3.95
1. Suffering. 2. Faith-cure. I. Title.

FERGUSON, John, 1921- 291.2'11
The place of suffering. Cambridge, J. Clarke, 1972. 137 p. 23 cm. [BT732.7.F47] 73-157107 ISBN 0-227-67803-6 £1.75
1. Suffering. I. Title.

FISHER, C. William 248
Don't park here! Nashville, Abingdon [c.1962] 158p. 21cm. 62-16253 3.00
1. Suffering. 2. Conduct of life. 3. Biography. I. Title.

*GILLESE, John Patrick 240
The challenge of suffering. Pulaski, Wis., Franciscan [c.1964] 71p. 19cm. .35 pap.,
I. Title.

GILMORE, G. Don. 248.8'6
No matter how dark the valley / G. Don Gilmore. 1st ed. San Francisco : Harper & Row, c1982. p. cm. [BV4905.2.G53 1982] 19 81-20052 ISBN 0-06-063121-X : 7.64
1. Suffering. 2. Faith. I. Title.

GLOVER, Carl Archibald, 1891- 248
Victorious suffering, by Carl A. Glover. New York, Nashville, Abingdon-Cokesbury press [1943] 158 p. 20 cm. [BV4905.G58] 43-3141
1. Suffering. I. Title.

GOULOOZE, William, 1903- 248
Blessings of suffering. Grand Rapids, Baker Book House, 1954. 173 p. 20 cm. [BV4905.G63] 51-5370
1. Suffering. I. Title.

GOULOOZE, William, 1903- 248
Victory over suffering. Grand Rapids, Baker Book House, 1949. 150 p. 20 cm. Verse and prose. [BV4905.G64] 49-11715
1. Suffering. 2. Consolation. I. Title.

GOULOOZE, William, 1903-1955. 248
Grace for today. Grand Rapids, Baker Book House, 1957. 114p. 21cm. [BV4905.G636] 57-9383
1. Suffering. I. Title.

GOULOOZE, William, 1903-1955. 248
My second valley. Grand Rapids, Baker Book House, 1955 [c1953] 170p. 21cm. [BV4905.G638] 57-2583
1. Suffering. I. Title.

GRAHAM, Billy, 1918- 248.8'6
Till Armageddon : a perspective on suffering / Billy Graham. Waco, Tex. : Word Books, c1981. 224 p. ; 24 cm. Includes bibliographical references and index. [BT732.7.G7] 19 80-51485 ISBN 0-8499-0195-2 : 8.95
1. Suffering. I. Title.

HARRINGTON, Vernon Charles, 1871-1942. 179
The problem of human suffering looked at from the standpoint of a Christian, by Vernon C. Harrington... [Burlington, Vt., The Lane press, 1944] 5 p. l., 148 p. 19 cm. "Memorial edition...edited by Elizabeth Bowles Harrington." [BJ1409.H35 1944] 44-25992
1. Suffering. 2. Good and evil. I. Harrington, Elizabeth (Bowles) ed. II. Title.

HARRITY, Michael. 242'.4
Thoughts on suffering, sorrow, and death. Huntington, Ind., Our Sunday Visitor [1973] 96 p. 18 cm. [BT732.7.H3] 73-86976 ISBN 0-87973-812-X
1. Suffering. 2. Meditations. I. Title.

HERHOLD, Robert M. 248'.86
The promise beyond the pain / Robert M. Herhold. Nashville : Abingdon, c1979. 111 p. ; 20 cm. [BT732.7.H4] 79-895 ISBN 0-687-34331-3 : 6.95
1. Suffering. I. Title.

HEYNEN, Ralph 248.4
Building your spiritual strength. Grand Rapids, Mich., Baker Bk. [1965] 111p. 21cm. [BV4905.2.H47] 65-18262 2.95
1. Suffering. 2. Consolation. I. Title.

HINTON, James, 1822-1875. 179
The mystery of pain; a book for the sorrowful. By James Hinton ... New York, D. Appleton and company, 1872. 2 p. l., 101 p. 18 cm. [BJ1409.H5 1872] 38-33110
1. Suffering. I. Title.

HINTON, James, 1822-1875. 179
The mystery of pain; a book for the sorrowful, by James Hinton ... New York, D. Appleton, 1892. 2 p. l., 101 p. 18 1/2 cm. First edition published in 1866. [BJ1409.H5 1892] 4-10395
1. Suffering. I. Title.

HOFFMAN, Dona, 1932- 242'.4
Yes, Lord / Dona Hoffman. St. Louis : Concordia Pub. House, [1975] p. cm. Includes correspondence between the author and Paul G. Bretscher. [BV4909.H6] 74-30867 ISBN 0-570-03195-8 pbk. : 3.95
1. Hoffman, Dona, 1932- 2. Bretscher, Paul G. 3. Suffering. 4. Consolation. I. Bretscher, Paul G. II. Title.

HOFFMAN, Herman S., bp.1841- 170
The gift of suffering; or, Meditations on the mystery of pain, by Bishop H. S. Hoffman... New York, Eaton & Mains; Cincinnati, Jennings & Graham [c1912] 150 p. 19 cm. [BJ1408.H6] 12-18154 0.75
1. Suffering. I. Title.

HONG, Edna (Hatlestad) 1913- 231'.8
Turn over any stone, by Edna Hong. Designed and illustrated by Don Wallerstedt. Minneapolis, Augsburg Pub. House [1970] 173 p. illus. 24 cm. [BV4909.H64] 77-121966 4.95
1. Suffering. 2. Consolation. I. Title.

HYGONET, Bernard. 248.4
Deliver us from evil. Translated from the French by Sister M. Bernarda. Chicago, Franciscan Herald Press [c1958] 125p. 18cm. [BX2373.S5H9] 58-13684
1. Suffering. I. Title.

IKIN, Alice Graham, 1895- 248
Victory over suffering; glimpses into a mystery. Foreword by J. B. Philips. Introd. by Edward Ely. Great Neck, N. Y., Channel Press [1961] 144p. 21cm. [BV4909.I4 1961] 61-7572
1. Suffering. I. Title.

JONES, Eli Stanley, 1884- 179.9
Christ and human suffering [by] E. Stanley Jones. New York, Cincinnati [etc.] The Abingdon press [c1933] 231 p. 20 cm. [BJ1409.J6] 33-23034
1. Suffering. I. Title.

JONES, Eli Stanley, 1884- 179.9
Christ and human suffering [by] E. Stanley Jones. New York, Cincinnati [etc., The Abingdon press, 1933] 2 p. l., 7-235 p. 20 cm. "First edition printed July, 1963 ... fourth printing, September, 1963" [BJ1409.J6 1933] 34-6974
1. Suffering. I. Title.

JONES, Eli Stanley, 1884- 179.9
Christ and human suffering [by] E. Stanley Jones. New York, Cincinnati [etc.] The Abingdon press [1933] 2 p. l., 7-235 p. 19 1/2 cm. "First edition printed July, 1933 ... fourth printing, September, 1933." [BJ1409.J6 1933b] 34-6974
1. Suffering. I. Title.

JOWETT, John Henry, 1864-1923. 252.058
The school of Calvary; or, Sharing His suffering. Grand Rapids, Baker Book House, 1956. 125p. 18cm. 'Reprint of the original edition ... London ... 1911.' [BX7233] 55-10431
1. Suffering. 2. Congregational churches—Sermons. 3. Sermons, English. I. Title. II. Title: Sharing His suffering.

JUD, Gerald John. 248
The shape of crisis and tragedy; an adult resource book [by] Gerald J. Jud. Boston, United Church Press [c1965] 124 p. illus. 21 cm. [BT732.7.J8] 65-14278
1. Suffering. I. Title.

KELLY, Mary Ellen, 1922- 616.72
But with the dawn, rejoicing. Milwaukee, Bruce Pub. Co. [1959] 182p. 22cm. Autoniographical. [BX2373.S5K38] 59-10531
1. Suffering. 2. Arthritis—Personal narratives. I. Title.

KENNEDY, John S 242.4
The common cross. New York, McMullen Books [1954] 141p. 20cm. [BX2373.S5K4] 54-7090
1. Suffering. I. Title.

KEPPLER, Paul Wilhelm von, bp., 1852-1926. 248
The school of suffering; a companion book to "More joy," by the Rt. Rev. Paul Wilhelm von Keppler ... translated by August F. Brockland. St. Louis, Mo., and London, B. Herder book co., 1929. v, 188 p. 19 1/2 cm. [BX2350.K47] 29-1305
1. Suffering. I. Brockland, August F., tr. II. Title.

LECLERQ, Jacques, 1891- 248
Approaches to the cross. Tr. from French by the Earl of Wicklow. New York, Macmillan, 1963. 115p. 20cm. 63-5310 2.50 bds.,
1. Suffering. I. Title.

LOCKYER, Herbert. 242'.4
Dark threads the weaver needs / Herbert Lockyer. Old Tappan, N.J.: F. H. Revell Co., c1979. 127 p. ; 22 cm. [BT732.7.L63] 78-11620 ISBN 0-8007-0977-2 : 5.95
1. Suffering. I. Title.

LOVASIK, Lawrence George, 1913- 248.376
Jesus, joy of the suffering [Boston] St. Paul Eds. [dist. Daughters of St. Paul, c.1964] 229p. 19cm. 64-17752 2.50; 1.50 pap.,
1. Suffering. 2. Catholic Church—Prayer-books and devotions—English. I. Title.

MCASTOCKER, David Plante, 1884- 179
The joy of sorrow, by David P. McAstocker, S.J. New York, Milwaukee [etc.] The Bruce publishing company [c1936] vii, 178 p. 19 cm. [BJ1409.M3] 36-17610
1. Suffering. I. Title.

MACGUIRE, Meade. 248
Does God care? By Meade MacGuire ... Mountain View, Calif., Omaha, Nebr. [etc.] Pacific press publishing association [1942] 91 p. 18 1/2 cm. [BV4905.M18] 42-14680
1. Suffering. I. Title.

MCLARRY, Newman R 242.4
When shadows fall. Nashville, Broadman Press [1960] 60p. 16cm. [BV4909.M3] 60-9534
1. Suffering. I. Title.

MASTON, Thomas Bufford, 1897- 242'.4
God speaks through suffering / T. B. Maston. Waco, Tex. : Word Books, c1977. 95 p. ; 21 cm. [BV4909.M38] 77-76349 ISBN 0-8499-2802-8 pbk. : 3.25
1. Suffering. 2. Consolation. I. Title.

MASTON, Thomas Bufford, 1897- 231'.8
Suffering, a personal perspective, [by] T. B. Maston. Nashville, Broadman Press [1967] vii, 87 p. 21 cm. [BV4905.2.M3] 68-11848
1. Suffering. I. Title.

MINCHIN, Gerald H., 1901- 242.4
Bow in the cloud [by] Gerald H. Minchin. Washington, Review and Herald Pub. Association [1968] 160 p. 21 cm. Bibliography: p. 159-60. Bibliographical footnotes. [BV4909.M5] 68-18367
1. Suffering. I. Title.

MOHLER, James A. 231'.8
The sacrament of suffering / James Aylward Mohler. Notre Dame, Ind. : Fides/Claretian, c1979. viii, 170 p. ; 20 cm. Includes index. Bibliography: p. 160-165. [BT732.7.M63] 79-15738 ISBN 0-8190-0632-7 : 5.95
1. Suffering. I. Title.

NEFF, Merlin L 242.4
Triumphant in suffering. Mountain View, Calif., Pacific Press Pub. Association [1954] 120p. 21cm. [BV4596.A3N4] 54-10676
1. Suffering. I. Title.

OTTERSTAD, Robert L. 242.4
They came to a place; meditations on human suffering. Minneapolis, Augsburg [c.1962] 47p. 21cm. 62-9091 1.25
1. Suffering. I. Title.

PASTORELLI, France. Mme. 179
Strength out of suffering [by] France Pastorelli; a translation of Servitude et grandeur de la maladie. Boston, New York, Houghton Mifflin company, 1936. 2 p. l., 7-223, [1] p. 20 cm. Autobiographical. Translated by Alice Debenham. London edition (G. Allen & Unwin ltd.) has title: The glorious bondage of illness. [BJ1409.P34 1936 a] 36-27351
1. Suffering. I. Debenham, Alice, 1867- tr. II. Title.

RAYMOND, Father, 1903- 248.8
This is your tomorrow ... and today. Milwaukee, Bruce Pub. Co. [1959] 207p. illus. 24cm. [BV4909.R3] 59-9719
1. Suffering. I. Title.

REGAMEY, Raymond, 1900- 248
The cross and the Christian; translated by Angeline Bouchard. St. Louis, B. Herder Book Co. [1954] 177p. 21cm. (Cross and crown series of spirituality, no. 2) Translation of La croix du Christ et celle du chretien. [BX2373.S5R413] 54-7327
1. Suffering. 2. Atonement. 3. Christian life—Catholic authors. I. Title.

RHEA, Carolyn. 242.4
Healing in His wings. New York, Grosset & Dunlap [1968] 95 p. 17 cm. (The Family inspirational library) [BV4909.R5] 68-31348 1.95
1. Suffering. 2. Consolation. I. Title.

ROBINSON, Henry Wheeler, 1872- 179
Suffering, human and divine, by H. Wheeler Robinson...introduction by Rufus M. Jones... New York, The Macmillan company, 1939. xx p., 1 l., 230 p. 20 1/2 cm. [Great issues of life series] "Published September, 1939. First printing." "Some books about suffering": p. 225. [BJ1409.R57] 39-27996
1. Suffering. 2. Providence and government of God. 3. Atonement. I. Title.

ROBINSON, Henry Wheeler, 1872-1945. 221.8179
The cross in the Old Testament. Philadelphia, Westminster Press [1955?] 192p. 22cm. 'Originally printed under the titles The cross of Job (1916), The cross of the servant (1926), and The cross of Jeremiah (1925). [BS1199.S8R6] 56-5103
1. Suffering. 2. Job, the patriarch. 3. Servant of Jehovah. 4. Jeremiah, the prophet. I. Title.

SCHAEFFER, Edith. 242'.4
Affliction / Edith Schaeffer. Old Tappan, N.J. : F. H. Revell Co., c1978. 253 p. ; 24 cm. [BV4909.S33] 78-7993 ISBN 0-8007-0926-8 : 7.95
1. Suffering. 2. Consolation. I. Title.

SCHEMMER, Kenneth E. 248.8'6
Between faith and tears / Kenneth E. Schemmer. Nashville : T. Nelson, c1981. 131 p. ; 20 cm. Includes bibliographical references. [BT732.7.S36] 19 81-1467 ISBN 0-8407-5770-0 pbk. : 3.95
1. Suffering. 2. Spiritual healing. 3. Consolation. I. Title.

SCHUKNECHT, Joseph J. 1859- 922.
A suffering Job of the twentieth century, by Joseph J. Schuknecht ... Cleveland, O., The Evangelical press [c1928] 116 p. incl. front. (port.) plates. 20 cm. [BX8495.S355A3] 29-1986
I. Title.

SELLERS, James Earl 233.2
When trouble comes; a Christian view of evil, sin, and suffering. Nashville, Abingdon Press [c.1960] 128p. 20cm. 60-5476 2.00 bds.,
1. Suffering. I. Title.

SIMMONS, Henry C. 248'.86
Valuing suffering as a Christian : some psychological perspectives / Henry C. Simmons. Chicago : Franciscan Herald Press, [1976] p. cm. (Synthesis series) [BT732.7.S57] 76-43247 ISBN 0-8199-0708-1 pbk. : 0.65
1. Fromm, Erich, 1900- 2. Suffering. I. Title.

SINKS, Perry Wayland. 200
In the refiner's fire; the problem of human suffering ... By Perry Wayland Sinks ... Chicago, The Bible institute colportage association [c1911] 88 p. 20 1/2 cm. 11-11254 0.50
I. Title.

SMITH, Helen (Reagan) 248.8'6
Jesus stood by us. Nashville, Tenn., Broadman Press [1970] 143 p. 21 cm. Bibliography: p. 143. [BV4905.2.S6] 70-113218 3.75
1. Suffering. 2. Consolation. I. Title.

SOCKMAN, Ralph Washington, 1889- 231.8
The meaning of suffering. Nashville, Abingdon [1962, c.1961] 143p. 21cm. (112) Bibl. 1.25 pap.,
1. Suffering. I. Title.

SOCKMAN, Ralph Washington, 1889- 231.8
The meaning of suffering. [New York] Woman's Division of Christian Service, Board of Missions, the Methodist Church [1961] 143 p. 20 cm. Includes bibliography. [BV4909.S6] 61-5637
1. Suffering. I. Title.

SOCKMAN, Ralph Washington, 1889-
The meaning of suffering. Nashville, Abingdon [c1961] xii, 143 p. 64-46349
1. Suffering. I. Title.

SOLLE, Dorothee. 248'.3
Suffering / by Dorothee Soelle ; translated by Everett R. Kalin. Philadelphia : Fortress Press, c1975. 178 p. ; 24 cm. Translation of Leiden. Includes bibliographical references. [BT732.7.S6513] 75-13036 ISBN 0-8006-0419-9 : 8.95
1. Suffering. I. Title.

STRINGFELLOW, William. 248
A second birthday. [1st ed.] Garden City, N.Y., Doubleday, 1970. 203 p. 22 cm. [BT732.7.S75] 75-116256 5.95
1. Suffering. 2. Faith-cure. I. Title.

TAYLOR, Michael J., comp. 231'.8
The mystery of suffering and death. Michael J. Taylor, editor. Staten Island, N.Y., Alba House [1973] xi, 203 p. 23 cm. [BT732.7.T38] 72-13294 ISBN 0-8189-0263-9 5.95
1. Suffering. 2. Theodicy. 3. Death. I. Title. Contents omitted.

TAYLOR, Michael J., comp. 231'.8
The mystery of suffering and death. Michael J. Taylor, editor. Garden City, N.Y., Image Books, 1974 [c1973] 228 p. 18 cm. [BT732.7.T38 1974] 74-177305 ISBN 0-385-09556-2 1.75 (pbk.)
1. Suffering. 2. Theodicy. 3. Death. I. Title. Contents omitted.

TEILHARD de Chardin, Pierre. 233
On suffering / Pierre Teilhard de Chardin. 1st U.S. ed. New York : Harper & Row, [1974?] 120 p. ; 15 cm. Translation of Sur la souffrance. [BV4909.T4413 1974] 75-18606 ISBN 0-06-068211-6
1. Suffering. I. Title.

VAN ZELLER, Hubert 1905- 248
Suffering in other words; a presentation for beginners. Springfield, Ill., Templegate [1964] 96 p. 20 cm. 96 p. 20 cm. (His[In other words series]) (His [In other words series]) [BT732.7.V3] 65-3298
1. Suffering. I. Title.

VIEUJEAN, Jean 231.8
Love, suffering, providence. Tr. [from French] by Joan Marie Roth. Westminster, Md., Newman, 1966 [c.1964] xvi, 134p. 21cm. Bibl. [BT732.7.V513] 66-16571 3.50
1. Suffering. I. Title.

WALKER, William Bruce. 248
Victory over suffering. Butler, Ind., Higley Press [1958] 156 p. 20 cm. [BV4909.W2] 58-33247
1. Suffering. I. Title.

WEATHERHEAD, Leslie Dixon. 179
Why do men suffer? [By] Leslie D. Weatherhead ... New York, Cincinnati [etc.] The Abingdon press [c1936] 224 p. 19 1/2 cm. [BJ1409.W4 1936] 36-5245
1. Suffering. I. Title.

WEATHERHEAD, Leslie Dixon, 1893- 248.42
Salute to a sufferer; an attempt to offer the plain man a Christian philosophy of suffering. New York, Abingdon [1963, c.1962] 95p. 20cm. 63-8669 2.00 bds.,
1. Suffering. I. Title.

WEATHERHEAD, Leslie Dixon, 1893- 231.8
Why do men suffer? Nashville, Abingdon Press [1961, c.1936] 224p. (Apex bks. E 8) 1.25 pap.,
1. Suffering. I. Title.

WILDER-SMITH, A. E. 231'.8
The paradox of pain [by] A. E. Wilder Smith. [1st ed.] Wheaton, Ill., H. Shaw Publishers [1971] 132, [1] p. 21 cm. Bibliography: p. 132-[133] [BT732.7.W53] 71-165790 ISBN 0-87788-667-9
1. Suffering. 2. Good and evil. 3. Providence and government of God. I. Title.

WILDS, Louis Trezevant, 1885- 248
Why good people suffer, by L. T. Wilds, D.D. Richmond, Va., John Knox press [1944] 47 p. 19 cm. [BV4905.W63] 44-8058
1. Suffering. I. Title.

*WOODS, B. W. 231'.8
Understanding suffering Grand Rapids, Baker Book House [1974] 176 p. 18 cm. Includes bibliographical references [BT160] ISBN 0-8010-9551-4 2.45 (pbk.)
1. Suffering. 2. Theodigy. I. Title.

YANCEY, Philip. 248'.86
Where is God when it hurts? / By Philip Yancey. Grand Rapids, Mich. : Zondervan Pub. House, c1977. p. cm. Includes bibliographical references. [BT732.7.Y36] 77-12776 ISBN 0-310-35410-2 5.95 ISBN 0-310-35411-0 pbk. : 2.95
1. Suffering. I. Title.

ZEOLI, Anthony. 248
Why do Christians suffer? By Anthony Zeoli ... Waterloo, Ia., Cedar book store [1943] 226 p. 18 1/2 cm. [BV4905.Z4] 44-1321
1. Suffering. I. Title.

Suffering—Addresses, essays, lectures.

CREATIVE suffering: 231'.8
the ripple of hope [by] Alan Paton [and others. Boston] Pilgrim Press [1970] 122 p. ports. 21 cm. [BV4905.2.C7] 79-106559 ISBN 8-298-01529- 2.25
1. Suffering—Addresses, essays, lectures. I. Paton, Alan.

THE Language of the cross 232.9'63
/ edited by Aelred Lacomara. Chicago : Franciscan Herald Press, c1977. vii, 149 p. ; 21 cm. [BT431.L37] 76-43287 ISBN 0-8199-0617-4 : 6.95
1. Jesus Christ—Passion—Addresses, essays, lectures. 2. Suffering—Addresses, essays, lectures. I. Lacomara, Aelred.

REMLER, Francis Joseph, 1874- 242
Why must I suffer? (Reprinted from Franciscan herald) A book of light and consolation, by Rev. F. J. Remler ... Chicago, Ill., Franciscan herald press [c1923] 4 p. l., 5-84 p. front. 17 1/2 cm. [BV4905.R5] 23-16789
I. Title.

Suffering — Biblical teaching.

BERTRANGS, A. 220.8
The Bible on suffering. Tr. by F. Vander Heijden. De Pere, Wis., St. Norbert Abbey Pr. [c.]1966. 62p. 17cm. Bibl. [BT732.7.B413] 66-16990 .95 pap.,
1. Suffering — Biblical teaching. I. Title.

BERTRANGS, A. 220.8
The Bible on suffering, by A. Bertrangs. Translated by F. Vander Heijden. De Pere, Wis., St. Norbert Abbey Press, 1966. 62 p. 17 cm. Bibliographical references included in "Notes" (p. [57]-62) [BT732.7.B413] 66-16990
1. Suffering — Biblical teaching. I. Title.

THE elements of pain and conflict in human life, considered from a Christian point of view; being lectures delivered at the Cambridge summer meeting 1916, by members of the University. Cambridge, University press, 1916. vi p., 1 l., 206 p. 19 1/2 cm. "Prefactory note" signed: V. H. Stanton. Contents.Theism and modern thought by W. R. Sorley.--Human freedom, by J. W. Oman.--The problem of the existence of moral evil, by F. R. Tennant. --The problem of suffering, by the Rev. Dr. Tennant.--The doctrine of providence, by V. H. Stanton.--Prayer, by the Rev. Dr. Stanton.--War, by J. W. Owan.--Competition between individuals and classes, considered from the Christian point of view, by W. M. Ede.--Competition between nations, considered from the Christian point of view, by W. M. Ede. 17-1918
I. Stanton, Vincent Henry, 1846- II. Cambridge University.

KAISER, Walter C. 224'.307
A Biblical approach to personal suffering / by Walter C. Kaiser, Jr. Chicago : Moody Press, c1982. p. cm. Includes bibliographical references. [BS1535.2.K34] 19 82-2232 ISBN 0-8024-4634-5 pbk. : 4.95
1. Bible. O.T. Lamentations—Criticism, interpretation, etc. 2. Suffering—Biblical teaching. I. Title.

PROUDFOOT, Merrill. 248
Suffering: a Christian understanding. Philadelphia, Westminster Press[1964] 194 p. 21 cm. [BS2655.S8P7] 64-23954
1. Suffering—Biblical teaching. 2. Bible. N.T. Epistles of Paul—Criticism, interpretation, etc. I. Title.

SIMUNDSON, Daniel J. 231'.8
Faith under fire : Biblical interpretations of suffering / Daniel J. Simundson. Minneapolis : Augsburg Pub. House, c1980. 158 p. ; 20 cm. [BS680.S854S57] 79-54119 ISBN 0-8066-1756-X pbk. : 4.95
1. Suffering—Biblical teaching. I. Title.

Suffering—Biblical teaching—Addresses, essays, lectures.

GERSTENBERGER, Erhard. 231'.8
Suffering / Erhard S. Gerstenberger and Wolfgang Schrage ; translated by John E. Steely. Nashville : Abingdon, c1980. 272 p. ; 22 cm. (Biblical encounters series) Translation of Leiden. [BS680.S854G4713] 79-20499 ISBN 0-687-40574-2 pbk. : 8.95
1. Suffering—Biblical teaching—Addresses, essays, lectures. I. Schrage, Wolfgang, joint author. II. Title. III. Series.

SUFFERING and martyrdom in the New Testament 231'.8
: studies presented to G. M. Styler / by the Cambridge New Testament Seminar, William Horbury, Brian McNeil. Cambridge [Eng.] ; New York : Cambridge University Press, 1980. p. cm. Includes index. [BS2545.S9S83] 19 80-40706 ISBN 0-521-23482-4 : 39.95
1. Styler, G. M. 2. Bible. N.T.—Criticism, interpretation, etc.—Addresses, essays, lectures. 3. Suffering—Biblical teaching—Addresses, essays, lectures. 4. Martyrdom—Biblical teaching—Addresses, essays, lectures. I. Styler, G. M. II. Horbury, William. III. McNeil, Brian. IV. Cambridge New Testament Seminar. Contents omitted.

Suffering—Meditations.

STEDMAN, Ray C. 223'.107
Expository studies in Job : behind suffering / Ray C. Stedman. Waco, Tex. : Word Books, c1981. 216 p. ; 21 cm. (A Discovery Bible study book) [BS1415.4.S67] 19 80-54546 ISBN 0-8499-2932-6 (pbk.) : 5.95
1. Bible. O.T. Job—Meditations. 2. Suffering—Meditations. I. Title. II. Series.

Suffering—Moral and religious aspects.

BONAR, Horatius, 1808-1889. 242'.4
When God's children suffer / Horatius Bonar ; introduction by George Sweeting ; illustrations by Ron McCarty. New Canaan, Conn. : Keats Pub., 1981. 125 p., [5] leaves of plates : ill. ; 21 cm. (A Shepherd illustrated classic) Originally published as: Night of weeping. London :

Nisbet, 1846. [BV4905.B56 1981] 19 80-84441 ISBN 0-87983-245-2 (pbk.) : 5.95
1. Suffering—Moral and religious aspects. 2. Consolation. I. [Night of weeping] II. Title. III. Series.

Suffering of God.

KITAMORI, Kazo, 1916- 231
Theology of the pain of God [Tr. from Japanese] Richmond, Va., Knox [c.1965] 183p. 21cm. Bibl. [BT153.S8K513] 65-20544 4.50
1. Suffering of God. I. Title.

OHLRICH, Charles, 1954- 231'.8
The suffering God : hope and comfort for those who hurt / Charles Ohlrich ; foreword by Philip Yancey. Downers Grove, Ill. : InterVarsity Press, c1982. 130 p. ; 18 cm. Includes bibliographical references. [BT153.S8O35] 19 82-7815 ISBN 0-87784-376-7 (pbk.) : 4.95
1. Suffering of God. 2. Suffering—Religious aspects—Christianity. I. Title.

Suffering—Religious aspects—Christianity.

HARRINGTON, Vernon C[harles]
The problem of human suffering looked at from the standpoint of a Christian. Chicago, New York [etc.] F. H. Revell co., 1899. 5 p. l., 157 p. 12 degrees. Jul
I. Title.

HITCHENS, Kate, Mrs. 922.773
1862-
Christian castle building; or, Lersons learned in suffering. By Mrs. Kate Hitchens. McKeesport, Daily news publishing house, 1890. vii, 256 p. port. 18 cm. Autobiography. [BR1725.H57A3 1890] 38-3208
I. Title.

ISRAEL, Martin. 248.8'6
The pain that heals : the place of suffering in the growth of the person / Martin Israel. New York : Crossroad, 1982, c1981. 192 p. ; 21 cm. [BV4909.I86 1982] 19 81-70881 ISBN 0-8245-0437-2 (pbk.) : 6.95
1. Suffering—Religious aspects—Christianity. I. Title.

LYONNARD, Jean, 1819-1887.
The apostleship of suffering, by Father John Lyonnard ... Rev. with additional matter after the author's final edition, from the translation by Lady Herbert. Philadelphia, Messenger of the Sacred Heart, 1890. ix, [1], 317 p. 18 1/2 cm. (Sacred Heart library, 2d year, nos. 2-3]) Contents.pt. 1. The divine mission of suffering.--pt. 2. The apostolic uses of suffering. 3-3106
I. Title.

Suffering—Religious aspects—Christianity—Addresses, essays, lectures.

KOSICKI, George W., 1928- 248.8'6
The good news of suffering : mercy and salvation for all / George W. Kosicki. Collegeville, Minn. : Liturgical Press, c1981. 87 p. ; 18 cm. [BV4909.K65] 19 81-13644 ISBN 0-8146-1240-7 pbk. : 1.95
1. Suffering—Religious aspects—Christianity—Addresses, essays, lectures. I. Title.

Suffering—Sermons.

PREACHING on suffering and 242'.4
a God of love / Henry James Young, editor ; with a foreword by Nathan A. Scott, Jr. ; and contributions by George Thomas ... [et. al.]. Philadelphia : Fortress Press, c1977. p. cm. Includes bibliographical references. [BV4909.P73] 77-15250 ISBN 0-8006-1332-5 pbk. : 3.50
1. Suffering—Sermons. 2. Sermons, American—Afro-American authors. I. Young, Henry J., 1943- II. Thomas, George.
Contents Omitted

SHEPARDSON, Daniel.
The suffering Savior, and other sermons. Chicago, New York [etc.] F. H. Revell co. [1898] 144 p. port. 12c. Nov
I. Title.

Suffering—Spiritual consolation.

*CLARKSON, E. Margaret. 248.8
God's hedge; help for those who must suffer. Chicago, Moody [1968] 62p. illus. 22 cm. .95 pap.,
1. Suffering—Spiritual consolation. I. Title.

Suffern, N.Y. Christ Evangelical Lutheran Church.

GROTTKE, Theodore L 284.174728
A history of Christ Evangelical Lutheran Church, Airmont, Suffern, New York, formerly Ramapo Lutheran Church, organized June 14, 1715, Mahwah, New Jersey. Prepared by Theodore L. and Erna H. Grottke. [Suffern, N.Y., 1965] 69 p. illus., maps, port 23 cm. "Presented on the occasion of the 250th anniversary of the congregation, June 14, 1965." Includes bibliographies. [BX8076.S85C5] 66-31561
1. Suffern, N.Y. Christ Evangelical Lutheran Church. I. Grottke, Erna H., joint author. II. Title.

Sufism.

ARASTEH, A. Reza. 297'.4
Growth to selfhood : a Sufi contribution / A. Reza Arasteh. London ; Boston : Routledge & Kegan Paul, 1980. xii, 145 p. ; 22 cm. Bibliography: p. 144-145. [BP189.6.A72] 79-41238 ISBN 0-7100-0355-2 pbk. : 7.50
1. Sufism. 2. Self realization. I. Title.

AS-SUFI, 'Abd al-Qadir. 297'.4
The way of Muhammad / 'Abd al-Qadir as-Sufi. Berkeley [Calif.] : Diwan Press, c1975. 202 p. : diagrs. ; 21 cm. (The Sufic path series) [BP189.6.S85] 75-8119 5.95
1. al-Shadhiliyah. 2. Sufism. I. Title.

BAKHTIAR, Laleh. 297'.4
Sufi : expressions of the mystic quest / [by] Laleh Bakhtiar. London : Thames and Hudson, 1976. 120 p. : ill. (some col.), plans, ports. (chiefly col.) ; 26 cm. (Art and imagination) Bibliography: p. 120. [BP189.3.B34] 76-377195 ISBN 0-500-81015-X : £2.50
1. Sufism. I. Title.

BURCKHARDT, Titus. 297'.4
An introduction to Sufi doctrine / Titus Burckhardt ; translated [from the French] by D. M. Matheson. Wellingborough : Thorsons, 1976. 126 p. ; 22 cm. Translation of Du soufisme. Includes bibliographical references. [BP189.3.B8713] 77-363283 ISBN 0-7225-0333-4 : £2.25
1. Sufism. I. Title. II. Title: Sufi doctrine.

*BURKE, Omar Michael. 297.4
Among the dervishes; an account of travels in Asia and Africa, and four years studying the dervishes, sufis and fakirs, by living among them by O. M. Burke. 1st edition New York, E. P. Dutton and Co. 1975. 203 p. 21 cm. Bibliography: pp 201-203. [BP189.2] ISBN 0-525-47386-6 3.95 (pbk.)
1. Sifism. I. Title.

FARID al-Din Attar 13thcent. 131
The conference of the birds, a Sufi allegory; being an abridged version of Farid-ud-din Attar' Mantiq-ut-Tayr, by R. P. Masani, M. A. London, New York [etc.] H. Milford, Oxford university press, 1924. xi, 128 p. 19 cm. [BP175.M9F3] 26-11264
1. Sufism. I. Rustamji Pestonji Masani, 1876- tr. II. Title.

FARZAN, Massud, comp. 297'.4
The tale of the reed pipe; teachings of the Sufis. [1st ed.] New York, Dutton, 1974. xxi, 104 p. 19 cm. [BP189.F34 1974] 74-166175 ISBN 0-525-47362-9 1.95 (pbk.).
1. Sufism. I. Title.

FATEMI, Nasrollah 297'.4
Saifpour, 1911-
Love, beauty, and harmony in Sufism / Nasrollah S. Fatemi, Faramarz S. Fatemi, Fariborz S. Fatemi. South Brunswick [N.J.] : A. S. Barnes, c1978. p. cm. Includes bibliographical references and index. [BP188.9.F36] 78-54329 ISBN 0-498-02248-X : 12.95
1. Sufism. 2. Sufi poetry, Persian—History and criticism. I. Fatemi, Faramarz S., joint author. II. Fatemi, Fariborz S., joint author. III. Title.

FATEMI, Nasrollah 297'.4
Saifpour, 1911-
Sufism : message of brotherhood, harmony, and hope / Nasrollah S. Fatemi, Faramarz S. Fatemi, Fariborz S. Fatemi. South Brunswick : A. S. Barnes, c1976. 243 p. ; 22 cm. Includes bibliographical references and index. [BP188.9.F37] 75-29692 ISBN 0-498-01869-5 : 12.00
1. Sufism. 2. Sufi poetry, Persian—History and criticism. I. Fatemi, Faramarz S., joint author. II. Fatemi, Fariborz S., joint author. III. Title.

FEILD, Reshad. 297'.4'0924
The invisible way / by Reshad Feild. 1st ed. New York : Harper & Row, c1979. p. cm. [BP189.62.F44] 78-19501 ISBN 0-06-062587-2. : 7.95
1. Sufism. I. Title.

FEILD, Reshad. 297'.4'0924 B
The last barrier / Reshad Feild ; illustrated by Salik Chalom. 1st ed. New York : Harper & Row, c1976. 183 p. : ill. ; 21 cm. [BP189.6.F44 1976] 75-9345 ISBN 0-06-062585-6 : 8.95
1. Feild, Reshad. 2. Sufism. I. Title.

FEILD, Reshad. 297'.4'0924 B
The last barrier / Reshad Feild ; illustrated by Salik Chalom. London : Turnstone Books, 1976. [7], 183 p. : ill. ; 20 cm. [BP189.6.F44 1976b] 77-362800 ISBN 0-85500-063-5 : £2.95
1. Feild, Reshad. 2. Sufism. 3. Sufism—Biography. I. Title.

GURU Bawa, Shaikh 297'.4
Muhaiyaddeen.
God, his prophets and his children / M. R. Bawa Muhaiyaddeen. Philadelphia : Fellowship Press, c1978. vii, 255 p. : ill. ; 21 cm. [BP189.62.G87] 78-12891 ISBN 0-914390-09-0 pbk. : 3.95
1. Sufism. I. Title.

INAYAT Khan, 1882-1926. 297'.4
Cosmic language. Tucson, Ariz., Omen Press, 1972. 131 p. 21 cm. "Consists of addresses given by Hazrat Inayat Khan to his pupils during the summer school at Suresnes in 1924." [BP189.3.I5 1972] 72-195007 ISBN 0-912358-02-5 1.95
1. Sufism. I. Title.

INAYAT Khan, 1882-1926. 297'.4
The soul, whence and whither / by Hazrat Inayat Khan. New Lebanon, N.Y. : Sufi Order Publications, 1977. 190 p. ; 22 cm. Includes index. [BP189.3.I52 1977] 78-100154 ISBN 0-930872-01-0 pbk. : 4.95
1. Sufism. I. Title.

INAYAT Khan, 1882-1927. 297'.43
Gayan ; Vadan ; Nirtan / Inayat Khan. Lebanon Springs, N.Y. : Sufi Order Publications, 1980. viii, 295 p. ; 15 cm. (The Collected works of Hazrat Inayat Khan) (Series: Inayat Khan, 1882-1927. Works.) [BP189.62.I4582 1980] 19 80-52801 ISBN 0-930872-21-5 : 10.00 ISBN 0-930872-16-9 pbk. : 5.95
1. Sufism. I. [Selections.] 1980 II. Title. III. Series. IV. 1980.
Publisher's address: Box 568, Lebanon Springs, NY 12114

INAYAT KHAN, 1882-1926. 297.4
The Sufi message of Hazvat Inayat Khan. London, Published for International Headquarters of the Sufimovement, Geneva, by Barrie and Rockliff [dist. New York, Citadel Press, 1960, i.e., 1961] 240p. illus., port. Contents.v. 1. The way of illumination. The inner life. The soul, whence and whither? The purpose of life. 61-100 6.00
1. Sufism. I. Title.

INAYAT Khan, Pir Vilayat. 297'.4
Toward the one. [1st ed.] New York, Harper & Row [1974] A-G, 678 p. illus. 21 cm. (Harper colophon books) Bibliography: p. 658-663. [BP189.62.I54 1974] 73-7132 ISBN 0-06-090352-X 5.75 (pbk.)
1. Sufism. I. Title.

*JALALV-D-DIN MUHAMMAD I 297.4
RUMI, Mavlana
Teachings of Rumi: The masnavi of Mavlana Jalalv-d-Din M. Translated and abridged by E. H. Whinfield. 1st. ed. New York, E. P. Dutton & Co., 1975 xii, 330 p. 21 cm. [BP189.62] ISBN 0-525-47387-4 3.95 (pbk.)
1. Jalal al—Din Rumi, Mavlana, 1207-1273 2. Sufism. I. Whinfield, E. H. Trans. II. Title.

LEWIS, Samuel L., 1896- 297'.4
1971.
Toward spiritual brotherhood. [Novato, Calif., Prophecy Pressworks, 1971?] xvii, 101 p. illus. 22 cm. [BP189.2.L49] 74-157561 2.50
1. Sufism. I. Title.

LINGS, Martin. 297'.4
What is Sufism? / Martin Lings. Berkeley : University of California Press, 1975. 133 p. ; 23 cm. Includes bibliographical references and indexes. [BP189.L5] 75-317448 ISBN 0-520-02794-9 : 8.50
1. Sufism. I. Title.

LINGS, Martin. 297'.4
What is Sufism? / Martin Lings. 1st California paperback ed. Berkeley : University of California Press, 1977, c1975. 133 p. ; 21 cm. Includes bibliographical references and indexes. [BP189.L5 1977] 77-362607 ISBN 0-520-03171-7 pbk. : 2.95
1. Sufism. I. Title.

MANIRI, Sharaf al-Din 297'.4
Ahmad ibn Yahya, d.1380?
The hundred letters / Sharafuddin Maneri ; translation, introd., and notes by Paul Jackson ; pref. by Syed Hasan Askari ; foreword by Bruce Lawrence. New York : Paulist Press, c1980. xix, 458 p. ; 23 cm. (The Classics of Western spirituality) Includes bibliographical references and indexes. [BP189.6.M3613] 79-56754 ISBN 0-8091-2229-4 pbk. : 7.95 7.95
1. Sufism. I. Jackson, Paul, 1937- II. Title. III. Series: Classics of Western spirituality.

MUHAIYADDEEN, M. R. Bawa. 297'.4
Four steps to pure iman : explanations of a painting / by M.R. Bawa Muhaiyaddeen. 2nd ed. Philadelphia, Pa. : Fellowship Press, c1970 (1981 printing) 68 p. : ill. ; 20 cm. Includes index. [BP189.2.M79 1970] 19 81-1429 2.00
1. Sufism. I. Title.

MUHAIYADDEEN, M. R. Bawa. 297'.4
The wisdom of man : selected discourses / by M. R. Bawa Muhaiyaddeen. Philadelphia, Pa. : Fellowship Press, c1980. p. cm. [BP189.M7] 19 80-20541 ISBN 0-914390-16-3 : 4.95
1. Sufism. I. Title.

MUHAIYADDEEN, Sheikh 297'.4
Muhammad.
God, his prophets, and his children / M. R. Bawa Muhaiyaddeen. Philadelphia : Fellowship Press, c1976, 1978 printing. p. cm. [BP189.62.M83] 78-12891 ISBN 0-914390-09-0 : pbk. : 3.95
1. Sufism. I. Title.

MUHAIYADDEEN, Sheikh 297'.4
Muhammad.
The guidebook to the true secret of the heart / M. R. Bawa Muhaiyaddeen. Philadelphia : Bawa Muhaiyaddeen Fellowship, c1976- v. : ill. ; 21 cm. [BP189.3.M82] 75-44557 ISBN 0-914390-07-4 pbk. : 3.95 (v. 1)
1. Sufism. I. Title.

N 297'.4
Sufism / Javad Nurbakhsh. New York : Khaniqahi-Nimatullahi Publications, c1982. 126 p. ; 21 cm. [BP189.N88 1982] 19 82-156083 3.95
1. Sufism. I. Title.

NICHOLSON, Reynold Alleyne, 297
1868-
The idea of personality in Sufism: three lectures delivered in the University of London, by Reynold A. Nicholson ... Cambridge [Eng.] The University press, 1923. 4 p. l., 77 p. 19 1/2 cm. [BP175.M9N4] 23-18953
1. Sufism. I. Title. II. Title: Personality in Sufism.

NICHOLSON, Reynold Alleyne, 297
1868-
Studies in Islamic mysticism, by Reynold Alleyne Nicholson ... Cambridge [Eng.] The University press, 1921. xi p., 1 l., 282 p. 23 1/2 cm. [BP175.M9N5] 23-5382
1. Abu sa'Id bn Abi 'l-Khair (Eazl Ullah) 968-1049. 2. 'Abd al-Karim ibn Ibrahim, al-Jili, b. 1365 or 66. 3. 'Umar ibn Ali,

called Ibn al-Farid, 1181-1235. 4. Sufism. I. Title. II. Title: Islamic mysticism.

NICHOLSON, Reynold Alleyne, 1868-1945. 297'.4
The mystics of Islam / by Reynold A. Nicholson. New York : Schocken Books, 1975. 178 p. ; 21 cm. Reprint of the 1963 ed. published by Routledge & Kegan Paul, London, of a work first published in 1914. Includes index. Bibliography: p. 169-171. [BP189.N49 1975] 75-10713 ISBN 0-8052-0492-X pbk. : 2.45
1. Sufism. I. Title.

NICHOLSON, Reynold Alleyne, 1868-1945. 297'.4
The mystics of Islam / by Reynold Alleyne Nicholson. London ; Boston : Routledge and K. Paul, 1975. vii, 178 p. ; 19 cm. Reprint of the 1914 ed. published by G. Bell, London. Includes index. Bibliography: p. 169-171. [BP189.N49 1975b] 75-327476 ISBN 0-7100-1892-4. ISBN 0-7100-8015-8 pbk. : £1.00
1. Bibliography: p. 169-171. 2. Sufism. I. Title.

NICHOLSON, Reynold Alleyne, 1868-1945 297.4
Studies in Islamic mysticism, by Reynold Alleyne Nicholson . . . Cambridge [Eng.] Univ. Pr., 1921. Reprinted 1967. xii p., 1 l., 282p. 24cm. [BP189.N5] 23-5382 8.50
1. Abu Sa'id ebn Abi al-Kheyr, 987-1049-1235. 2. al-JIIL, 'Abd al-Karim ibn Ibrahim, b. 1365 or 6. 3. Ibn al-Farid, 'Umar ibn 'Ali, 1181 or 2. 4. Sufism. I. Title. II. Title: Islamic mysticism.
Available from Cambridge Univ. Pr., N.Y.

NICHOLSON, Reynold Alleyne, 1868-1945.
Studies in Islamic mysticism. Cambridge, University Press, 1921; reprinted, 1967. xii, 282 p. 22 cm. 68-62499
1. Fazl, Ullah, Abu Sa'id Abi'l-Khair, 968-1049. 2. Al-Jili, 'Abd al-Karim ibn Ibrahim, b. 1365 or 66. 3. Ibn al-Farid, 'Umar ibn Ali, 1181-1235. 4. Sufism. I. Title.

NURBAKHSH, Javad. 297'.4
In the paradise of the Sufis / Javad Nurbakhsh ; translated from the original Persian. New York : Khaniqahi-Nimatullahi Publications, c1979. 125 p. : ill. ; 21 cm. Includes bibliographical references. [BP189.5.N8713] 79-83588 ISBN 0-933546-01-7 : 3.95
1. Sufism. I. Title.

NURBAKHSH, Javad. 297'.4
In the tavern of ruin : seven essays on Sufism / Javad Nurbakhsh. New York : Khaniqahi-Nimatullahi Publications, c1978. 135 p. ; 21 cm. [BP189.N87] 78-102838 pbk. : 3.95
1. Sufism. I. Title.
Publisher's address: 306 W. 11th St., New York, NY 10014

NURBAKHSH, Javad. 297'.4
What the Sufis say / Javad Nurbakhsh ; translated from the original Persian. New York : Khaniqahi-Nimatullahi Publications, c1980. 143 p. ; 21 cm. Includes bibliographical references. [BP189.62.N8713] 19 79-56614 ISBN 0-933546-02-5 pbk. : 3.95
1. Sufism. 2. Sufi poetry, Persian—Terminology. I. Title.
Publisher's address: 306 W. 11th St., New York, NY 10014

RICE, Cyprian 297.4
The Persian Sufis. London, G. Allen & Unwin [dist. New York, Hillary, c.1964] 104). 19cm. [BP189.R5] 65-273 3.00 bds.,
1. Sufism. 2. Mystcism—Iran. I. Title.

SCHIMMEL, Annemarie. 297'.4
Mystical dimensions of Islam. Chapel Hill, University of North Carolina Press [1975] xxi, 506 p. illus. 25 cm. Bibliography: p. 437-467. [BP189.2.S34] 73-16112 ISBN 0-8078-1223-4 : 14.95
1. Sufism. I. Title.

SCHUON, Frithjof, 1907- 297
Islam and the perennial philosophy / [by] Frithjof Schuon ; translated [rom the French MS.] by J. Peter Hobson ; preface by Seyyed Hossein Nasr. [London] : World of Islam Festival Publishing Company Ltd, 1976. xii, 217 p. ; 23 cm. Includes index. [BP189.3.S38] 76-375638 ISBN 0-905035-06-2 : £6.00. ISBN 0-905035-22-4 pbk.
1. Sufism. I. Title.

SHAH, Idries, 1924- 297'.07
A perfumed scorpion : the way to the way / by Idries Shah. 1st U.S. ed. San Francisco : Harper & Row, c1981. 192 p. ; 21 cm. [BP189.2.S52 1981] 19 81-48214 ISBN 0-06-067254-4 pbk. : 5.95
1. Sufism. I. Title.

SHAH, Idries, Sayed, 1924- 828'.9'1408
The subtleties of the inimitable Mulla Nasrudin, by Idries Shah. Drawings by Richard Williams and Richard Purdum. [1st ed.] New York, Dutton, 1973. 174 p. illus. 19 cm. [BP189.62.S5 1973b] 74-182285 ISBN 0-525-47354-8 1.95
1. Sufism. I. Title.

SHAH, Idries, Sayed, 1924- 181.5
The Sufis. Introd. by Robert Graves. [1st ed.] Garden City, N. Y., Doubleday, 1964. xxvi, 403 p. front. 22 cm. Bibliographical footnotes. [BP189.S38] 64-11299
1. Sufism. I. Title.

SHAH, Idries, Sayed, 1924- 297'.4
The way of the Sufi. New York, Dutton, 1969 [c1968] 287 p. 22 cm. Bibliography: p. 36-48. [BP189.S388 1969] 71-92615 6.95
1. Sufism. I. Title.

SHAH, Ikbal Ali, sirdar. 297'.4
Islamic sufism. New York, S. Weiser, 1971. 299 p. 21 cm. Reprint of the 1933 ed. [BP189.S3883] 70-166410 ISBN 0-87728-161-0 2.50
1. Sufism. I. Title.

SHAH, Indries, Sayed, 1924- 297'.4
Learning how to learn : psychology and spirituality in the Sufi way / by Indries Shah. 1st U.S. ed. San Francisco : Harper & Row, 1981, c1980. p. cm. [BP189.2.S5 1981] 19 80-8892 ISBN 0-06-067255-2 pbk. : 6.95
1. Sufism. I. Title.

SIRAJ ul-Din, Abu Bakr. 297'.2
The book of certainty, by Abu Bakr Siraj Ed-Din. New York, S. Weiser, 1970. 108 p. front. 21 cm. Includes bibliographical references. [BP189.S46 1970] 71-138082 3.00
1. Sufism. I. Title.

SMITH, Margaret. 922.
Rabi'a the mystic & her fellow-saints in Islam; being the life and teachings of Rabi'a al-'Adwiyya al-Qaysiyya of Basra together with some account of the place of the women saints in Islam, by Margaret Smith... Cambridge, Eng., The University press, 1928. xxv, 219, [1] p. 22 1/2 cm. "Survey of sources": p. [xiii]-xxv; "List of authors quoted": p. [205]-209. [BP80.R3S6] 29-10771
1. Rabi'ah, al-'Adawiyah, d. 801? 2. Saints, Mohammedan. 3. Sufism. 4. Saints, Women. I. Title.

SMITH, Margaret, 1884- 297'.4
Readings from the mystics of Islam; translations from the Arabic and Persian, together with a short account of the history and doctrines of Sufism and brief biographical notes on each Sufi writer. London, Luzac & Co., 1972. v, 144 p. 19 cm. Includes bibliographical references. [BP189.23.S64 1972] 73-169376 ISBN 0-7189-0162-2
1. Sufism. I. Title.
Distributed by Rowman & Littlefield, 8.50; pbk. 3.25.

STODDART, William. 297'.4
Sufism : the mystical doctrines and methods of Islam / by William Stoddart ; with a foreword by R. W. J. Austin. Wellingborough : Thorsons, 1976. 91 p. : ill., facsim. ; 23 cm. Includes index. Bibliography: p. 85-86. [BP189.S74] 76-368448 ISBN 0-7225-0305-9 : £3.25
1. Sufism. I. Title.

STOLK, Sirkar van, 1894-1963. 297'.4'0924 B
Memories of a Sufi sage, Hazrat Inayat Khan / by Sirkar van Stolk, with Daphne Dunlop. 2d ed. The Hague : East-West Publications Fonds, c1975. 208 p. : ill. ; 21 cm. "List of books by Hazrat Inayat Khan": p. 206-208. [BP80.I55S8 1975] 75-328485 ISBN 0-8476-1052-7 7.25
1. Inayat Khan, 1882-1926. 2. Stolk, Sirkar van, 1894-1963. 3. Sufism. I. Dunlop, Daphne, joint author. II. Title.
Distributed by Rowman & Littlefield.

TRIMINGHAM, John Spencer. 297.4
The Sufi orders in Islam, by J. Spencer Trimingham. London, Oxford Univ. Pr. [1973, c.1971] viii, 333 p. geneal. tables. 20 cm. index. (Galaxy Book, GB390) Bibl: p. [282]-299. [BP189.T7] 77-582531 ISBN 0-19-501662-9 pap., 2.95
1. Sufism. I. Title.
Available from the publisher's New York office.

Sufism—Addresses, essays, lectures.

THE Elephant in the dark, and other writings on the diffusion of Sufi ideas in the West / by Idries Shah and others ; Leonard Lewin, editor. 2d ed. New York : E. P. Dutton, 1976. vi, 154 p. ; 21 cm. First ed. published in 1972 under title: The diffusion of Sufi ideas in the West. Contents.Contents.—Christianity, Islam and the Sufis: Shah, I. The elephant in the dark. Sanchez, I. Christian mysticism and the Sufis.—Sufi study material: Sufi Abdul-Hamid First statement. Shah I. The teaching story.—On Idries Shah and contemporary Sufism: Lessing, D. An ancient way to new freedom. Courtland, L. F. A visit to Idries Shah. Williams, P. An interview with Idries Shah.—On the diffusion of Sufi ideas in the West. Foster, W. Sufi studies today. Imdad Hussein Sheikh el-Qadiri. Sufi thought. A session with a Western Sufi. Bibliography: p. 153-154. [BP189.2.L48 1976] 75-34151 ISBN 0-525-47372-6 pbk. : 4.95 297'.4
1. Sufism—Addresses, essays, lectures. I. Shah, Idries, Sayed, 1924- II. Lewin, Leonard. III. Lewin, Leonard, comp. The diffusion of Sufi ideas in the West.

INAYAT-KHAN, Fazal. 297'.4
Old thinking, new thinking : a Sufi prism / by Fazal Inayat-Khan. 1st ed. San Francisco : Harper & Row, c1978. p. cm. [BP189.6.I55 1978] 77-7831 ISBN 0-06-064086-3 pbk. : 6.95
1. Sufism—Addresses, essays, lectures. I. Title.

LEWIN, Leonard, comp. 297'.4
The diffusion of Sufi ideas in the West; an anthology of new writings by and about Idries Shah. Edited by L. Lewin. Boulder, Colo., Keysign Press, 1972. 212 p. 21 cm. (The Transmission of wisdom, v. 1) Contents.Contents.—An interview with Idries Shah, by P. Williams.—An ancient way to new freedom, by D. Lessing.—A visit to Idries Shah, by L. F. Courtland.—Sufi study material.—How they see us, by B. Kolinski.—A reconnaissance; why I traveled, by Taslim.—Dervish ritual, by A. Archer-Forbes.—Perfecting of man, by D. R. Forbes.—A sort of monks, by J. Grant.—Social mysticism, by R. Fischer.—Trail of the Damascus blade, by C. P. Stone.—The mystics choose a king, by M. Brackett.—The festival of Dervishes, by A. Samuelson.—Mystical virtue, by M. L. Isher.—The Sufi way, by A. L. M. Farris.—The pattern of the Sufis, by A. C. Butterfield. [BP189.2.L48] 74-182745 2.85
1. Sufism—Addresses, essays, lectures. I. Shah, Idries, Sayed, 1924- II. Title.

NASR, Seyyed Hossein. 297'.4
Sufi essays. Albany, State University of New York Press [1973, c1972] 184 p. 23 cm. Includes bibliographical references. [BP189.N38 1973] 72-11566 ISBN 0-87395-233-2 8.95
1. Sufism—Addresses, essays, lectures. I. Title.

NASR, Seyyed Hossein. 297'.4
Sufi essays / by Seyyed Hossein Nasr. New York : Schocken Books, 1977, c1972. 184 p. ; 2l cm. Reprint of the ed. published by G. Allen and Unwin, London. Includes bibliographical references and index. [BP189.N38 1977] 76-39629 pbk. : 3.75
1. Sufism—Addresses, essays, lectures. I. Title.

RAJANEESH, Acharya, 1931- 297.4
Until you die : discourses on the Sufi way / given by Rajneesh ; compilation, Swami Amrit Pathik ; editing, Ma Yoga Anurag. Poona : Rajneesh Foundation, c1976. ix, 261 p., [1] leaf of plates : ports. ; 22 cm. [BP189.62.R34] 77-900984 Rs75.00
1. Sufism—Addresses, essays, lectures. I. Title.

SUFI studies: East and West; a symposium in honor of Idries Shah's services to Sufi studies by twenty-four contributors marking the 700th anniversary of the death of Jalaluddin Rumi (A.D. 1207-1273) Edited by L. F. Rushbrook Williams. [1st ed.] New York, Dutton [1973] xxxvi, 260 p. 22 cm. Includes bibliographical references. [BP80.S483S9] 73-178387 ISBN 0-525-21195-0 10.00 297'.4
1. Shah, Idries, Sayed, 1924- —Addresses, essays, lectures. 2. Sufism—Addresses, essays, lectures. I. Shah, Idries, Sayed, 1924- II. Jalal al-Din Rumi, Mawlana, 1207-1273. III. Williams, Laurence Frederic Rushbrook, 1890- ed.

Sufism—Africa—History.

MARTIN, Bradford G. 297'.4
Muslim brotherhoods in nineteenth century Africa / B. G. Martin. Cambridge, [Eng.] ; New York : Cambridge University Press, 1976. p. cm. (African studies series ; 18) Includes index. Bibliography: p. [BP188.8.A44M37] 75-35451 ISBN 0-521-21062-3 : 24.00
1. Sufism—Africa—History. 2. Africa—History—19th century. I. Title. II. Series.

Sufism—Biography.

BREWSTER, David Pearson, 1930- 297'.4'0924 B
Al Hallaj : Muslim mystic and martyr : translated extracts with a short biography and bibliography / D. P. Brewster Christchurch : University of Canterbury, Dept. of Philosophy and Religious Studies, 1976. 51 p. ; 21 cm. (Occasional papers in religious studies) Includes bibliographical references. [BP80.H27B73] 77-366228
1. al-Hallaj, al-Husayn ibn Mansur, 858 or 9-922. 2. Sufism—Biography. I. Title. II. Series.

IBN al-'Arabi, 1165-1240. 297'.4
Sufis of Andalusia; the Ruh al-quds and al-Durrah al-fakhirah of Ibn 'Arabi. Translated with introd. and notes by R. W. J. Austin. With a foreword by Martin Lings. Berkeley, University of California Press [1972, c1971] 173 p. illus. 23 cm. Translation of the biographical portion of [Ruh al-Quds (romanized form)] and of extracts from [al-Durrah al-fakhirah (romanized form)]. Bibliography: p. 161-162. [BP189.4.I13 1972] 77-165230 ISBN 0-520-01999-7 8.75
1. Sufism—Biography. 2. Muslims in Spain—Biography. I. Ibn al-'Arabi, 1165-1240. al-Durrah al-fakhirah. English. Selections. 1972. II. Title.

INAYAT Khan, Pir Vilayat. 297'.4'0924 B
The message in our time : the life and teaching of the Sufi master, Pir-o-murshid Inayat Khan / by Pir Vilayat Inayat Khan. 1st ed. San Francisco : Harper & Row, c1978. x, 442 p. : ill. ; 24 cm. Includes bibliographical references and index. [BP80.I55I52 1979] 78-4751 ISBN 0-06-064237-8 : 14.95
1. Inayat Khan, 1882-1926. 2. Sufism—Biography. I. Title.

MASSIGNON, Louis, 1883-1962. 297'.6 B
The passion of al-Hallaj : mystic and martyr of Islam / Louis Massignon ; translated from the French with a biographical foreword by Herbert Mason. Princeton, N.J. : Princeton University Press, [1980] c1979. p. cm. (Bollingen series ; 98) Translation of La Passion de Husayn Ibn Mansur Hallaj. Contents.Contents.—v. 1. The life of al-Hallaj. [BP80.H27H3713 1980] 80-11085 ISBN 0-691-09910-3 (v. 1) : 125.00
1. Hallaj, al-Husayn ibn Mansur, 858 or 9-922. 2. Sufism—Biography. 3. Sufism. I. Title. II. Series.

NIZAMI, Khaliq Ahmad. 297'.64'0924
The life and times of Shaikh Farid-ud-Din

Gang-i-Shakar / by Khaliq Ahmad Nizami ; with a foreword by Sir Hamilton Gibb. 1st Pakistani ed. Lahore : Universal Books, 1976. x, 144 p. ; 24 cm. Reprint of the 1955 ed. published from Aligarh, India. Includes index. Running title: Life of Shaikh Farid-'ud-din Ganj-i Shakar. Bibliography: p. [125]-132. [BP80.F3N5 1976] 77-930059 Rs45.00
1. Farid-uddin, Shaikh, called Ganj-i Shakar, 1175?-1265. 2. Sufism—Biography. I. Title. II. Title: Life of Shaikh Farid-'ud-din Ganj-i Shakar.

Sufism—Collected works.

HUGHES, Catharine, 1935- comp. 297'.4
The secret shrine: Islamic mystical reflections. Edited and with photos. by Catharine Hughes. New York, Seabury Press [1974] 1 v. (unpaged) illus. 21 cm. "A Crossroad book." [BP189.62.H83] 74-12106 ISBN 0-8164-2101-3
1. Sufism—Collected works. I. Title.

LEWIS, Samuel L., 1896-1971. 297'.4
In the garden / Samuel L. Lewis (Sufi Ahmed Murad, Chisti). New York : Harmony Books, c1975. 288 p. : ill. ; 20 cm. Bibliography: p. 286-287. [BP189.62.L48 1975] 75-27184 ISBN 0-517-52412-0 : 5.00
1. Sufism—Collected works. I. Title.

Sufism—Early works to 1800.

AL-KALABADHI, Muhammed ibn Ibrahim, 10th cent. 297'.4
The doctrine of the Sufis = Kitab al-ta'arruf li-madhhab ahl al-tasawwuf / translated from the Arabic of Abu Bakr al-Kalabadhi by A. J. Arberry. Cambridge ; New York : Cambridge University Press, 1977. xviii, 173 p. ; 23 cm. Reprint of the 1935 ed. published by University Press, Cambridge. Includes bibliographical references and index. [BP189.26.K3813 1977] 76-58075 ISBN 0-521-21647-8 : 14.50 ISBN 0-521-29218-2 pbk. : 4.95
1. Sufism—Early works to 1800. I. Arberry, Arthur John, 1905-1969. II. Title.

HUJVIRI, 'Ali ibn 'Usman, d.ca.1072. 297'.4
The Kashf al-mahjub : the oldest Persian treatise on Sufiism / written by Ali ibn Uthman al-Hujwiri ; translated by Reynold A. Nicholson ; with a foreword by Shahidullah Faridi. Lahore : Islamic Book Foundation, 1976. xxiv, 446 p. ; 22 cm. "Reprint of rare Islamic books." Reprint of the 1911 ed. published by E. J. Brill. Leyden. Includes t.p. of the original with imprint Leyden, E. J. Brill, 1911. Includes bibliographical references and index. [BP188.9.H8413 1976] 76-930137 Rs60.00 ($6.00 U.S.)
1. Sufism—Early works to 1800. I. Nicholson, Reynold Alleyne, 1868-1945. II. Title.

IBN al-'Arabi, 1165-1240. 297'.4
The bezels of wisdom / Ibn al'Arabi ; translation and introd. by R.W.J. Austin ; pref. by Titus Burckhardt. New York : Paulist Press, c1980. xviii, 302 p. ; 23 cm. (The Classics of Western spirituality) Translation of Fusus al-hikam. Includes indexes. Bibliography: p. 285-287. [BP189.26.I2513 1980] 19 80-83892 ISBN 0-8091-2331-2 (pbk.) : 7.95 ISBN 0-8091-0313-3
1. Sufism—Early works to 1800. I. Austin, R. W. J. II. [Fusus al-hikam.] English III. Title.

IBN al-'Arabi, 1165-1240. 297'.4
The bezels of wisdom / Ibn al'Arabi ; translation and introd. by R.W.J. Austin ; pref. by Titus Burckhardt. New York : Paulist Press, c1980. xviii, 302 p. ; 23 cm. (The Classics of Western spirituality) Translation of Fusus al-hikam. Includes indexes. Bibliography: p. 285-287. [BP189.26.I2513 1980] 19 80-83892 ISBN 0-8091-2331-2 (pbk.) : 7.95
1. Sufism—Early works to 1800. I. Austin, R. W. J. II. [Fusus al-hikam.] English III. Title.

IBN al-'Arabi, 1165-1240. 297'.4
Journey to the Lord of Power : a Sufi manual on retreat / by Muhyidin Ibn 'Arabi ; with extracts of a commentary by 'Abdul-Karim Jili and an introd. by Muzaffereddin al-Jerrahi ; translated by Terri Harris. New York : Inner Traditions International, 1981, c1980. p. cm. Translation of Risalat al-anwar. [BP188.9.I2513] 19 81-28 ISBN 0-89281-018-1 pbk. : 7.95
1. Sufism—Early works to 1800. I. Jili, 'Abd al-Karim ibn Ibrahim, b. 1365 or 6. Selections. 1980. II. [Risalat al-anwar.] English III. Title.

IBN 'Ata' Allah, Ahmad ibn Muhammad, d.1309. 297'.4
The book of wisdom / Ibn 'Ata' Illah. Intimate conversations / K[h]waja Abdullah Ansari ; introd., translation, and notes of The book of wisdom by Victor Danner and of Intimate conversations by Wheeler M. Thackston ; pref. by Annemarie Schimmel. New York : Paulist Press, c1978. xvii, 233 p. ; 23 cm. (The Classics of Western spirituality) Translation of Ibn 'Ata' Allah's al-Hikam al-'Ata'iyah and of al-Ansari's Munajat. Includes bibliographies and indexes. [BP189.62.I2613 1978] 79-101197 ISBN 0-8091-2182-4 pbk. : 6.95
1. Sufism—Early works to 1800. I. Danner, Victor, 1926- II. Thackston, Wheeler M., 1944- III. al-Ansari al-Harawi, 'Abd Allah ibn Muhammad, 1006-1089. Munajat. English. c1978. IV. Title. V. Title: Intimate conversations. VI. Series.

'IRAQI, Fakhr al-Din Ibrahim, d.1289? 297'.4
Divine flashes / Fakhruddin 'Iraqi ; translation and introduction by William C. Chittick and Peter Lamborn Wilson ; preface by Seyyed Hossein Nasr. New York : Paulist Press, c1982. xvi, 178 p. : ill. ; 23 cm. (The Classics of Western spirituality) Translation of: Lama'at. Includes indexes. Bibliography: p. 168-169. [BP188.9.I6813 1982] 19 82-80859 ISBN 0-8091-2373-8 (pbk.) : 7.95
1. Sufism—Early works to 1800. I. Chittick, William C. II. Wilson, Peter Lamborn. III. [Lama'at.] English IV. Title. V. Series.

AL-KALABADHI, Muhammad ibn Ibrahim, 10thcent. 297'.4
The doctrine of the Sufis / [translated from the Arabic of Abu Bakr al-Kalabadhi, by Arthur John Arberry. New York : AMS Press [1976] p. cm. Translation of al-Ta'arruf li-madhhab ahl al-tasawwuf. Reprint of the 1935 ed. published by University Press, Cambridge. [BP189.26.K3813 1976] 75-41003 ISBN 0-404-14637-6 : 14.00
1. Syfism—Early works to 1800. I. Title.

AL-SUHRAWARDI, 'Abd al-Qahir ibn 'abd Allah, 1097-1168. 297'.4
A Sufi rule for novices = Kitab adab al-muridin of Abu al-Najib al-Suhrawardi / an abridged translation and introd. by Menahem Milson. Cambridge, Mass. : Harvard University Press, 1975. vi, 93 p. ; 22 cm. (Harvard Middle Eastern studies ; 17) Bibliography: p. 85-88. [BP189.6.S8713] 74-27750 ISBN 0-674-85400-4 : 8.95 ISBN 0-674-85403-9 pbk. : 1.95
1. Sufism—Early works to 1800. I. Milson, Menahem. II. Title. III. Series.

SULAMI, Muhammad ibn al-Husayn, d.1021. 297'.4
The book of Sufi chivalry : lessons to a son of the moment : Futtuwah / by Ibn al-Husayn al-Sulami. New York : Inner Traditions, [1982] p. cm. Translation of: Futuwah. [BP189.6.S8813] 19 82-2943 ISBN 0-89281-031-9 : 10.95 ISBN 0-89281-032-7 (pbk.) : 8.95
1. Sufism—Early works to 1800. 2. Futuwwa (Islamic order)—Early works to 1800. I. [Futuwah.] English II. Title.

Sufism—Egypt.

GILSENAN, Michael. 297'.4
Saint and Sufi in modern Egypt: an essay in the sociology of religion. Oxford, Clarendon Press, 1973. 248 p. illus. 23 cm. (Oxford monographs on social anthropology) Bibliography: p. [242]-246. [BP189.7.S5G55] 74-157832 ISBN 0-19-823181-4
1. al-Shadhiliyah. 2. al-Radi, Salamah, 1866 or 7-1939. 3. Sufism—Egypt. I. Title.
Distributed by Oxford University Press; 15.25.

WINTER, Michael. 297'.4'0924
Society and religion in early Ottoman Egypt : studies in the writings of 'Abd al-Wahhab al-Sharani / Michael Winter. New Brunswick [N.J.] : Transaction Books, c1982. x, 345 p. ; 24 cm. (Studies in Islamic culture and history) Includes index. Bibliography: p. 318-326. [BP80.S5W57 1982] 19 81-3042 ISBN 0-87855-351-7 : 39.95
1. Sha'rani, 'Abd al-Wahhab ibn Ahmad, 1493 (ca.)-1565 or 6. 2. Sufism—Egypt. I. Title. II. Series.
Publisher's address Bldg. 4051, Rutgers-State Univ. New Burnswick, NJ 08903.

Sufism—India.

SUBHAN, John A. 297.4
Sufism, its saints and shrines; an introduction to the study of Sufism with special reference to India, by John A. Subhan. New York, S. Weiser, 1970. viii, 412 p. illus. 21 cm. [BP188.8.I4S9 1970] 73-142499 ISBN 0-87728-039-8 8.50
1. Sufism—India. I. Title.

Sufism—India—Biography.

SCHIMMEL, Annemarie. 297.4'092'2 B
Pain and grace : a study of two mystical writers of eighteenth-century Muslim India / by Annemarie Schimmel. Leiden : E. J. Brill, 1976. xiv, 310 p. ; 25 cm. (Studies in the history of religions, supplements to Numen ; 36) Includes indexes. Bibliography: p. [291]-296. [BP80.K54S34] 77-351051 ISBN 9-00-404771-9
1. Khvajah Mir, 1719?-1785?—Religion and ethics. 2. 'Abd al-Latif, Shah, ca. 1689-ca. 1752—Religion and ethics. 3. Sufism—India—Biography. I. Title. II. Series.

Sufism—Iran.

CORBIN, Henry. 297'.4
The men of light in Iranian sufism / Henry Corbin ; translated from the French by Nancy Pearson. Boulder, Colo. : Shambhala ; [New York] : distributed by Random House, 1977. p. cm. Translation of L'homme de lumiere dans le soufisme iranien. "A Far West book." Includes index. Bibliography: p. [BP188.8.I55C6713] 77-6013 ISBN 0-394-73441-6 pbk. : 6.95
1. Sufism—Iran. I. Title.

SPIRITUAL body and celestial Earth : from Mazdean Iran to Shi'ite Iran / [edited by] Henry Corbin ; translated from the French by Nancy Pearson. Princeton, N.J. : Princeton University Press, c1977. xviii, 351 p., [1] leaf of plates : ill. ; 25 cm. (Bollingen series ; XCI, 2) Translation of Terre celeste et corps de resurrection. Includes index. Bibliography: p. 333-341. [BP188.8.I55T4713] 76-45919 ISBN 0-691-09937-5 : 14.50 297'.4
1. Sufism—Iran. I. Corbin, Henry. II. Series.

Sufism—Miscellanea.

MUHAIYADDEEN, M. R. Bawa. 297'.4
My love you my children : stories for children of all ages / by M.R. Bawa Muhaiyaddeen. [Philadelphia, PA] : Fellowship Press, 1981. p. cm. A collection of fables written by a Sufi holy man reflecting the lore and teachings of Sufism. [BP189.62.M626] 19 81-9847 ISBN 0-914390-20-1 : 17.95
1. Sufism—Miscellanea. 2. [Sufism.] 3. [Fables.] I. Title.
Publisher's address: 5820 Overbrook Ave., Carriage House, Philadelphia, PA 19131

Sufism—Prayer-books and devotions.

FRIEDLANDER, Shems. 297'.4'3
Ninety-nine names of Allah : the beautiful names = [Asma' al-husna (romanized form)] / Shems Friedlanders, al-Hajj Shaikh Muzaffereddin ; calligraphy, Hamid al-Amidi ; Arabic and Turkish translation, Tevfik Topuzoglu. 1st ed. New York : Harper & Row, 1978. 128 p. ; 16 cm. (Harper colophon books ; CN621) English or Arabic. [BP189.62.F74 1978] 78-19234 ISBN 0-06-090621-9 : 3.95
1. Sufism—Prayer-books and devotions. I. Muzaffereddin, al-Hajj Shaikh, joint author. II. al-Amidi, Hamid. III. Title. IV. Title: Asma' al-husna.

INAYAT Khan, 1882-1927. 297'.43
The bowl of saki : thoughts for daily contemplation from the sayings and teachings of Hazrat Inayat Khan. Lebanon Springs, N.Y. : Sufi Order Publications, 1980. 132 p. ; 14 cm. (The collected works of Hazrat Inayat Khan) [BP189.62.I46 1980] 19 81-116606 ISBN 0-930872-20-7 (pbk.) : 4.95
1. Sufism—Prayer-books and devotions. I. Title. II. Series: Inayat Khan, 1882-1927. Works. III. 1980.
Publisher's address: P. O. Box 86 E Rte. 3, Santa Fe, NM 87501

INAYAT, Taj, 1943- 297'.4
The crystal chalice : spiritual themes for women / Taj Inayat, with contributions by Hayat Abuza ... [et al.]. New Lebanon, N.Y. : Sufi Order Publications, 1979. 151 p. : ill. ; 21 cm. Includes bibliographies. [BP189.62.I45] 79-105496 ISBN 0-930872-08-8 pbk. : 4.75
1. Sufism—Prayer-books and devotions. 2. Women, Muslin—Prayer-books and devotions. I. Title.

SHAH, Idries, 1924- 297'.4
Seeker after truth : a handbook / by Idries Shah. 1st U.S. ed. San Francisco : Harper & Row, c1982. p. cm. [BP189.62.S49 1982] 19 82-48401 ISBN 0-06-067257-9 : 6.67
1. Sufism—Prayer-books and devotions. I. Title.

Sufism—Prayer-books and devotions—English.

INAYAT Khan, 1882-1927. 297'.43
Nature meditations. Lebanon Springs, N.Y. : Sufi Order Publications, 1980. 128 p. : ill. ; 18 cm. (The collected works of Hazrat Inayat Khan) [BP189.62.I516 1980] 19 80-126102 ISBN 0-930872-12-6 pbk. : 5.00
1. Sufism—Prayer-books and devotions—English. I. Title. II. Series: Inayat Khan, 1882-1927. Collected works of Hazrat Inayat Khan.

Sufism—Psychology.

INAYAT Khan, 1882-1927. 150.19'088297
Spiritual dimensions of psychology / Hazrat Inayat Khan. Santa Fe, NM, Sufi Order Publications, 1981. x, 242 p. ; 22 cm. (The Collected works of Hazrat Inayat Khan) (Series: Inayat Khan, 1882-1927. [Works.) Includes index. [BP189.65.P7815 1981] 19 80-54830 ISBN 0-930872-24-X (pbk.) : 7.95
1. Sufism—Psychology. I. Title. II. Series. III. (Series: 1980] Collected works of Hazrat Inayat Khan.)
Publisher's address P. O. Box 86E, Rte 3, Santa Fe, NM 87501.

Sufism—Punjab.

SHARDA, Sadhu Ram, 1927- 297'.4
Sufi thought : *its development in Panjab and its impact on Panjabi literature, from Baba Farid to 1850 A.D.* by S. R. Sharda. With a foreword by Surindar Singh Kohli. [1st ed. New Delhi] Munshiram Manoharlal Publishers [1974] xxiv, 288 p. maps. 23 cm. Bibliography: p. [270]-279. [BP188.8.I42P867] 74-900478
1. Sufism—Punjab. 2. Panjabi poetry—History and criticism. I. Title.
Distributed by South Asia Books, 11.50.

Sufism—Quotations.

THE Wisdom of the Sufis / compiled by Kenneth Cragg. New York : New Directions, c1976. 94 p. ; 21 cm. [BP189.62.W57] 76-7032 ISBN 0- 297'.4

8112-0626-2 : 7.00 ISBN 0-8112-0627-0 pbk. :
1. Sufism—Quotations. I. Cragg, Kenneth.

THE Wisdom of the *Sufis* compiled by Kenneth Cragg. London : Sheldon Press, 1976. vii, 94 p. ; 20 cm. Includes bibliographical references. [BP189.62.W57 1976b] 77-364798 ISBN 0-85969-080-6 : £1.50 297'.4'08
1. Sufism—Quotations. I. Cragg, Kenneth.

Sufism—Tanzania.

NIMTZ, August H. 322'.1
Islam and politics in East Africa : the Sufi order in Tanzania / August H. Nimtz, Jr. Minneapolis : University of Minnesota Press, c1980. p. cm. Includes index. Bibliography: p. [BP188.8.T34N55] 80-429 ISBN 0-8166-0963-2 : 20.00
1. Sufism—Tanzania. 2. Islam and politics—Tanzania. 3. Tanzania—Politics and government. I. Title.

Suger, Abbot of Saint Denis, 1081-1151.

ROCKWELL, Anne F. 282'.0924 B
Glass, stones & crown; the Abbe Suger and the building of St. Denis [by] Anne Rockwell. [1st ed.] New York, Atheneum, 1968. 80 p. illus. 25 cm. The life and accomplishments of the religious leader who used his power to unite nobles and peasants under the King of the Franks, and helped begin the powerful French empire of the twelfth century. His rebuilding of St. Denis established the Gothic design in church architecture. [DC89.7.S8R6] 92 AC 68
1. Suger, Abbot of Saint Denis, 1081-1151. 2. Saint-Denis, France (Benedictine abbey) I. Title.

Suger, Abbot of Saint Denis, 1081-1151—Juvenile literature.

ROCKWELL, Anne F. 271'.1'0924' B
Glass, stones & crown; the Abbe Suger and the building of St. Denis [by] Anne Rockwell. [1st ed.] New York, Atheneum, 1968. 80 p. illus. 25 cm. [DC89.7.S8R6] 68-12241
1. Suger, Abbot of Saint Denis, 1081-1151—Juvenile literature. 2. Saint-Denis, France (Benedictine abbey)—Juvenile literature. I. Title.

Sugg's Creek Cumberland Presbyterian Church, Wilson Co., Tenn.

PARTLOW, Thomas E. 285'.1768'54
Sugg's Creek Cumberland Presbyterian Church : an early history / by Thomas E. Partlow. Lebanon, Tenn : Partlow, 1974. 52 p. : ill. ; 27 cm. Includes index. Bibliography: p. 44-45. [BX9211.W634S936] 75-305491
1. Sugg's Creek Cumberland Presbyterian Church, Wilson Co., Tenn. 2. Wilson Co., Tenn.—Biography. I. Title.

Suicide.

GURNHILL, James. 179.
The morals of suicide, by Rev. J. Gurnhill ... London, New York [etc.] Longmans, Green and co., 1900. x, 227 p. 20 cm. [HV6545.G9] 10-20956
1. Suicide. I. Title.

INGERSOLL, Robert Green, 1833-1899. 179.
Is suicide a sin? Robert G. Ingersoll's famous letter. Replies by Mgr. Thos. Ducey ... Nym Crinkle [pseud.] ... Madison C. Peters ... Wm. Q. Judge ... C. Wilfred Mowbray ... John T. Nagle ... And Col. Ingersoll's brilliant rejoinder ... Prefaced by a startling chapter, Great suicides of history! Schopenhauer's celebrated essay "On suicide." Extracts from Omar Khayyam ... New York, Standard publishing company, 1894. 95 p. 19 cm. [HV6545.I 4] 10-20957
1. Suicide. I. Title.

INGERSOLL, Robert Green, 1833-1899. 179.7
Is suicide a sin! Robert G. Ingersoll's famous letter. Replies by eminent men and Col. Ingersoll's brillang rejoinder. Prefaced by a stratling chapter, Great sucides of history! New York, Holland publishing company [1895] 95 p. 20 cm. (On cover: Holland library, no. 3) Portrait on cover. On cover: Thirtieth thousand. [HV6545.I 4 1895] 34-11164
1. Suicide. I. Title.

INGERSOLL, Robert Green, 1833-1899. 179.
Is suicide a sin? Robert G. Ingersoll's famous letter. Replies by eminent men and Col. Ingersoll's brilliant rejoinder. Preface by a startling chapter, Great suicides of history.! New York, P. Eckler [1899!] 95 p. 20 cm. Author's portrait on cover. On verso of t.-p.:The Holland library. [HV6545.I 5] 20-22183
1. Suicide. I. Title.

PEDERSON, Duane. 261.8'33'1522
Going sideways : hope, love, life versus suicide / Duane Pederson and Helen W. Kooiman. New York : Hawthorn Books, [1974] viii, 135 p. ; 21 cm. Includes bibliographical references. [HV6545.P43] 74-335 ISBN 0-8015-3056-3 : 2.95
1. Suicide. 2. Suicide—Prevention—United States—Directories. I. Kooiman, Helen W., joint author. II. Title.

STEVENS, John, 1919- 248'.86
Suicide : an illicit lover / John Stevens. Denver : Heritage House Publications, c1976. 150 p. ; 18 cm. [HV6545.S794] 76-7690 2.95
1. Suicide. I. Title.

Sukkoth—Addresses, essays, lectures.

GOODMAN, Philip, 1911- comp. 296.4'33
The Sukkot and Simhat Torah anthology. [1st ed.] Philadelphia, Jewish Publication Society of America, 1973. xxxiii, 475 p. illus. 25 cm. Bibliography: p. [459]-475. [BM695.S8G66] 72-14058 ISBN 0-8276-0010-0 7.50
1. Sukkoth—Addresses, essays, lectures. 2. Simhat Torah—Addresses, essays, lectures. I. Title.

Sukkoth—Juvenile literature.

ADLER, David A. 296.4'33
The house on the roof : a Sukkot story / by David A. Adler ; pictures by Marilyn Hirsh. New York : Bonim Books, c1976. [32] p. : col. ill. ; 26 cm. [BM107.A34] 76-19014 ISBN 0-88482-905-7 : 5.95
1. Sukkoth—Juvenile literature. I. Hirsh, Marilyn. II. Title.

CEDARBAUM, Sophia N. 296.4
Sukos and Simchas Torah. festivals of thanksgiving. Pictures by Clare and John Ross. [New York] Union of Amer. Hebrew Congregations [c.1961] 30p. col. illus. 61-9696 .59 bds.,
1. Sukkoth—Juvenile literature. I. Title.

EDELMAN, Lily. 296.433
The sukkah and the big wind. With illus. by Leonard Kessler. [New York] United Synagogue Commission on Jewish Education, c1956. unpaged. illus. 28cm. [BM695.S8E3] 56-44770
1. Sukkoth—Juvenile literature. I. Title.

SIMON, Norma 296.433
Our first Sukkah. Illus. by Ayala Gordon. [New York 27] 3080 Bway. United Synagogue Commission on Jewish Education, c.1959. unpaged. illus. (col.) 25x15cm. 59-12530 .95 bds.,
1. Sukkoth—Juvenile literature. I. Title.

SIMON, Norma. 296.433
Our first Sukkah. Illus. by Ayala Gordon. [New York] United Synagogue Commission on Jewish Education, c1959. unpaged. illus. 25 cm. [BM695.S8S5] 59-12530
1. Sukkoth — Juvenile literature. I. Title.

Suku (African tribe)—Religion

MILLROTH, Berta, 1914- 299.6
Lyuba; traditional religion of the Sukuma. [Uppsala] 1965. 217p. 32cm. (Studia ethnographica Upsaliensia, 22) Akademisk avhandling--Uppsala. Without thesis statement. Bibl. [BL2480.S8M5] 65-83266 15.00 pap.,
1. Suku (African tribe)—Religion 2. Sunworship. I. Title. II. Series.
American distributor: Heinman, New York, N.Y. 10021

Sukyo Mahikari.

DAVIS, Winston Bradley. 299'.56
Dojo : magic and exorcism in modern Japan / Winston Davis. Stanford, Calif. : Stanford University Press, 1980. xvi, 332 p. : ill. ; 23 cm. Includes bibliographical references and index. [BL2228.S94D38] 19 79-64219 ISBN 0-8047-1053-8 : 18.50
1. Sukyo Mahikari. 2. Exorcism. I. Title.

Sullivan, Catherine, 1886-1969.

MEYERS, Bertrande. 271'.979'0924 B
Always springtime. Saint Louis, Marillac Towers Press [1969] 174 p. 22 cm. [BX4705.S869M4] 79-102726
1. Sullivan, Catherine, 1886-1969. I. Title.

Sullivan, James J., 1855-1927.

[REGAN, Mary Barbara, sister] 1866- 922.273
Memoir of Very Reverend J. J. Sullivan, C.M., late director of the Daughters of charity. St. Louis, Mo. [A. B. Dewes printing co., 1930] 194 p. front., ports. 20 cm. [BX4705.S87R4] 37-18687
1. Sullivan, James J., 1855-1927. I. Title.

SULLIVAN, James L. 286'.132'0924 B
God is my record / James L. Sullivan. Nashville : Broadman Press, [1974] 145 p. : ill. ; 21 cm. [BX6495.S799A33] 74-78609 ISBN 0-8054-5134-X : 3.95
1. Sullivan, James L. 2. Southern Baptist Convention. Sunday School Board. I. Title.

Sullivan, John, 1861-1933.

MCGRATH, Fergal, 1895- 922.2415
Father John Sullivan, S.J., by Fergal McGrath, S.J. ... London, New York [etc.] Longmans Green and co. [1941] vii p., 1 l., 285 p. front., ports. 21 cm. "Printed in the United States of America." [Full name: Joseph Stanislaus Fergal McGrath] [BX4705.S875M3] A 42
1. Sullivan, John, 1861-1933. I. Title.

Sullivan, Leon Howard, 1922- —Quotations.

SULLIVAN, Leon Howard, 1922- 242
Philosophy of a giant; quotations. Compiled and edited by Edna C. Wells. Philadelphia, Progressive Ventures Printers [1973] 72 p. illus. 14 x 22 cm. On cover: Meditation. Bibliography: p. 70-71. [BX6455.S84A5] 73-76352
1. Sullivan, Leon Howard, 1922- —Quotations. I. Title. II. Title: Meditation.

Sulpicians.

POURRAT, Pierre, 1871- 922.244
Father Olier, founder of St. Sulpice; from the French of the Very Rev. Pierre Pourrat ... by the Rev. W. S. Reilly ... Roland park, Baltimore, Md., The Voice publishing company [c1932] 223 p. front., ports. 20 cm. [BX4705.O48P63] 33-3812
1. Olier, Jean Jacques, 1608-1657. 2. Sulpicians. I. Reilly, Wendell Stephen, 1875- tr. II. Title.

Sulpicians in the United States

HERBERMANN, Charles George, 1840-1916. 203
The Sulpicians in the United States, by Charles G. Herbermann ... New York, The Encylcopedia press [c1916] xi, 360 p. front., plates, ports. 22 cm. Bibliography: p. xi. [BX4060.H4] 16-23063
I. Title.

RUANE, Joseph William, 1904- 271.750973
... The beginning of the Society of St. Sulpice in the United States (1791-1829) by Joseph William Ruane ... Washington, D. C., The Catholic university of America, 1935. cx, 266 p., 1 l. illus. (plan) 23 cm. (The Catholic university of America. Studies in American church history. vol. xxii) Thesis (PH. D.)--Catholic university of America, 1935. Vita. "Essays on the sources": p. 216-221. [BX4060.R8 1935] 85-9369
1. Sulpicians in the U. S. I. Title.

Sulzberger, Cyrus Leo, 1912-

SULZBERGER, Cyrus Leo, 1912- 242
Go gentle into the night / C. L. Sulzberger. Englewood Cliffs, N.J. : Prentice-Hall, c1976. 152 p. ; 22 cm. Includes index. [BL560.S94] 75-42344 ISBN 0-13-357293-5 : 6.95
1. Sulzberger, Cyrus Leo, 1912- 2. Prayer. 3. Prayers. 4. Religion. 5. Death. I. Title.

Sumerian language—Texts.

NESBIT, William Marsiglia, 1881- 222.
... Sumerian records from Drehem, by William M. Nesbit ... New York, Columbia university press, 1914. xiv, 71 p. 10 pl. 24 cm. (Columbia university oriental studies, vol. viii) [PJ4075.N4] [PJ25.C6 vol. 8] 15-2779
1. Sumerian language—Texts. 2. Babylonia—Comm. I. Title.

Sumerians—Religion.

COHEN, Mark E. 299'.9
Balag-compositions : Sumerian lamentation liturgies of the second and first millennium B.C. / by Mark E. Cohen. Malibu, Calif. : Undena Publications, 1974, c1975. 32 p. ; 28 cm. (Sources and monographs) (Sources from the ancient Near East ; v. 1, fasc. 2) Includes bibliographical references. [BL1615.C58] 75-321040 ISBN 0-89003-003-0
1. Sumerians—Religion. 2. Laments. I. Title. II. Series.

KRAMER, Samuel Noah, 1897- 299'.2
The sacred marriage rite; aspects of faith, myth, and ritual in ancient Sumer. Bloomington, Indiana University Press [1969] xv, 170 p. illus. 22 cm. "An expanded version of the Patten lectures delivered at Indiana University ... 1968." Bibliographical references included in "Notes" (p. 135-161) [BL1615.K7] 73-85090 7.50

1. Sumerians—Religion. 2. Sacred marriage (Mythology) I. Title.

Summary of the Law (Theology)

MCGARRIGLE, Francis Joseph, 1888- 241

The two commandments of Christ. Milwaukee, Bruce Pub. Co. [1962] 198 p. 23 cm. [BV4714.M3] 62-16839
1. Summary of the Law (Theology) I. Title.

Summer Institute of Linguistics.

COWAN, George M. 266'.023
The word that kindles : people and principles that fueled a worldwide Bible translation movement / by George M. Cowan. Chappaqua, N.Y. : Christian Herald Books, [1979] p. cm. [BS449.C68] 78-64837 ISBN 0-915684-47-0 pbk. : 4.95

1. Summer Institute of Linguistics. 2. Bible—Translating. 3. Linguistics. 4. Illiteracy. 5. Wycliffe Bible Translators. I. Title.

Summerfield, John, 1798-1825.

HOLLAND, John, 1794-1872. 922.773
Memoirs of the life and ministry of the Rev. John Summerfield, a.m. By John Holland. With an introductory letter by James Montgomery. Together with letters and reminiscences not before published ... 8th ed. New York, J. K. Wellman, 1846. 4 p. l., 3-460 p. front. (port.) 21 1/2 cm. [BX8495.S87H6 1846] 37-7020
1. Summerfield, John, 1796-1825. I. Title.

HOLLAND, John, 1794-1872. 922.773
Memoirs of the life and ministry of the Rev. John Summerfield, a.m. By John Holland. With an introductory letter by James Montgomery. Abridged, with additional letters and reminiscences. New York, American tract society [1850] 339 p. front. (port.) 19 1/2 cm. [BX8495.S87H6 1850] 37-7024
1. Summerfield, John, 1798-1825. I. American tract society. II. Title.

WILLETT, William Marinus, 922.773
1803-1895.
A new life of Summerfield. By William M. Willett... Philadelphia, J. B. Lippincott & co., 1857. 256 p. front. (port.) 22 cm. [BX8495.S87W5] 37-7021
1. Summerfield, John, 1798-1835. I. Title.

Summerhill School, Leiston, Eng.

WALMSLEY, John, 1947- 261
Neill & Summerhill: a man and his work: a pictorial study. Harmondsworth, Penguin, 1969. [96] p. (chiefly illus.). 20 cm. (Penguin education specials) (Penguin education.) [LF795.L692953W3 1969b] 79-574622 ISBN 0-14-080134-0 7/-
1. Summerhill School, Leiston, Eng. 2. Neill, Alexander Sutherland, 1883- I. Title.

Summers, Ray.

NEW Testament studies : 225.6
essays in honor of Ray Summers in his sixty-fifth year / edited by Huber L. Drumwright and Curtis Vaughan. Waco, Tex. : Markham Press Fund, c1975. xii, 195 p., [1] leaf of plates : port. ; 24 cm. Bibliography: p. 177-195. [BS2395.N56] 75-29815
1. Summers, Ray. 2. Summers, Ray—Bibliography. 3. Bible. N.T.—Criticism, interpretation, etc.—Addresses, essays, lectures. I. Summers, Ray. II. Drumwright, Huber L. III. Vaughan, Curtis.

Sumrall, Ken.

SUMRALL, Ken. 289.9 B
From glory to glory / by Ken Sumrall with Robert Paul Lamb. 1st ed. St. Simons Island, Ga. : Souls Books, 1980. v, 185 p. : ill. ; 21 cm. [BX8769.Z8S957] 19 80-51487 ISBN 0-935452-01-X : 3.95
1. Sumrall, Ken. 2. Liberty Fellowship of Churches and Ministers—Clergy—Biography. 3. Liberty Church, Pensacola, Fla. 4. Liberty Bible College, Pensacola, Fla. 5. Clergy—United States—Biography. I. Lamb, Robert Paul, joint author. II. Title.

Sumrall, Lester Frank, 1913-

SUMRALL, Lester 269'.2'0924 B
Frank, 1913-
Run with the vision / Lester Sumrall, with J. Stephen Conn. Plainfield, N.J. : Logos International, c1977. vi, 161 p., [3] leaves of plates : ill. ; 21 cm. [BV3785.S78A37] 77-87596 pbk. : 2.95
1. Sumrall, Lester Frank, 1913- 2. Evangelists—United States—Biography. I. Conn, J. Stephen, joint author. II. Title.

Sun.

MORRIS, Herbert William, 219
1818-1897.
The celestial symbol interpreted; or, The natural wonders and spiritual teachings of the sun, as revealed by the triumphs of modern science. By Herbert W. Morris ... Philadelphia, Cincinnati, O. [etc.] J. C. McCurdy & co., 1883. 704 p. incl. front., illus., plates (part col.) diagrs. 2 pl. (1 col.) 23 cm. "The plan ... is this: Each particular analogy is ... enunciated, and forms ... a distinct chapter, in which, first, are ... described the natural phenomena ... then the spiritual parallel to ... the Sun of righteousness." --Pref. [BS655.M7] 31-5416
1. Jesus Christ. 2. Sun. 3. Analogy (Religion) I. Title.

OLCOTT, William Tyler, 291.2127
1873-1936.
Sun lore of all ages; a collection of myths and legends concerning the sun and its worship, by William Tyler Olcott ... With 30 full-page illustrations and several drawings. New York and London, G. P. Putnam's sons, 1914. xiii, 346 p. front., illus., plates, coats of arms. 24 cm. Bibliography: p. 329-331. [BL325.S8O5] 14-8216
1. Sun. 2. Sun-worship. 3. Mythology. I. Title.

Sun (in religion, folk-lore, etc.)

OLCOTT, William Tyler, 291.2'12
1873-1936
Myths of the sun (Sun lore of all ages); a collection of myths and legends concerning the sun and its worship. [Magnolia, Mass., Peter Smith, 1968,c.1914] 307p. 19cm. (Capricorn bk. rebound) First pub. in 1914 under title: Sun lore of all ages. Bibl. [BL325.S8O5 1967] 68-2765 4.00
1. Sun (in religion folk-lore etc.) 2. Mythology. I. Title.

OLCOTT, William Tyler, 291.2'12
1873-1936.
Myths of the sun (Sun lore of all ages); a collection of myths and legends concerning the sun and its worship. New York, Capricorn Books [1967, c1914] 307 p. 19 cm. First published in 1914 under title: Sun lore of all ages. Bibliographical footnotes. [BL325.S8O5 1967] 68-2765
1. Sun (in religion folk-lore, etc.) 2. Mythology. I. Title.

OLCOTT, William Tyler, 291.2'12
1873-1936.
Sun lore of all ages; a collection of myths and legends concerning the sun and its worship. Boston, Milford House [1973] p. Reprint of the 1914 ed. published by Putnam, New York. Bibliography: [BL325.S8O5 1973] 73-13711 ISBN 0-87821-181-0 30.00 (lib. bdg.)
1. Sun (in religion, folk-lore, etc.) I. Title.

PALMER, Abram Smythe. 291.1'3
The Samson-saga and its place in comparative religion / Abram Smythe Palmer. New York : Arno Press, 1977. xii, 267 p., [2] leaves of plates : ill. ; 21 cm. (International folklore) Reprint of the 1913 ed. published by I. Pitman, London. Includes index. Bibliography: p. x. [BS580.S15P34 1977] 77-70613 ISBN 0-405-10112-0 : 17.00
1. Samson, Judge of Israel. 2. Sun (in religion, folk-lore, etc.) I. Title. II. Series.

PURUCKER, Gottfried de, 1874- 299
1942.
The four sacred seasons / G. de Purucker. Pasadena, Calif. : Theosophical University Press, 1979. x, 87 p. ; 18 cm. [BP573.S95P87 1979] 79-63565 ISBN 0-911500-83-9 : 4.50 ISBN 0-911500-84-7 pbk. : 2.75
1. Sun (in religion, folk-lore, etc.) 2. Theosophy. I. Title.

Sun (in religion, folk-lore, etc.)—Juvenile literature.

BAYLOR, Byrd. 291.1'3
The way to start a day / by Byrd Baylor ; illustrated by Peter Parnall. New York : Scribner, c1978. [30] p. : col. ill. ; 26 cm. Text and illustrations describe how people all over the world celebrate the sunrise. [BL325.S8B34] 78-113 ISBN 0-684-15651-2 : 7.95
1. Sun (in religion, folk-lore, etc.)—Juvenile literature. 2. Sun worship—Juvenile literature. 3. [Sun (in religion, folk-lore, etc.)] I. Parnall, Peter. II. Title.

Sun lore.

LUOMALA, Katharine. 291.2127
Oceanic, American Indian, and African myths of snaring the sun, by Katharine Luomala ... Honolulu, Hawaii, The Museum, 1940. 1 p. l., ii, [3]-58 p. illus. (maps) 25 1/2 cm. (Bernice P. Bishop museum. Bulletin 168) "Literature cited": p. 53-58. [GN670.B4 no. 168] [BL325.S8L8] (572.996) 43-8788
1. Sun lore. I. Title. II. Title: Snaring the sun.

Sun lore—Juvenile literature.

HELFMAN, Elizabeth S. 398'.362
Signs and symbols of the sun, by Elizabeth S. Helfman. New York, Seabury Press [1974] 192 p. illus. 24 cm. "A Clarion book." Bibliography: p. [188-189] Explores man's symbolic and mythical representation of the sun in art, crafts, literature, and religion from prehistory to the present day. [BL325.S8H44] 73-20121 ISBN 0-8164-3122-1 8.95
1. Sun lore—Juvenile literature. 2. Sun-worship—Juvenile literature. 3. [Sun lore.] I. Title.

Sun-worship.

HAWKES, Jacquetta 291.212
(Hopkins) 1910-
Man and the sun. New York, Random [c.1962] 277p. illus. 22cm. 62-8448 5.00 bds.,
1. Sun-worship. 2. Sun lore. I. Title.

[TITCOMB, Sarah 291.2127
Elizabeth] 1841-1895.
Aryan sun-myths the origin of religions; with an introduction by Charles Morris... Troy, N.Y., Nims and Knight, 1889. 192 p. 19 1/2 cm. "List of books consulted": p. [21]-25. [BL325.S8T5 1889] 31-5279
1. Sun-worship. 2. Religions. I. Title.

TITCOMB, Sarah 291.2127
Elizabeth, 1841-1895.
Aryan sun-myths the origin of religions, by Sarah E. Titcomb...With an introduction by Charles Morris... Boston, Pub. by the author, sold by Estes and Lauriat [1890] 192 p. 19 cm. "List of books consulted": p. [21]-25. [BL325.S8T5 1890] 31-5278
1. Sun-worship. 2. Religions. I. Title.

Sunbury and Erie railroad company.

PHILADELPHIA. Councils.
Report of the sub-committee deputed to visit Erie, etc., on the subject of a proposed subscription by the councils of the city of Philadelphia to the capital stock of the Sunbury and Erie rail road company. Submitted to the general joint special committee of councils, December 14, 1852. Philadelphia, Crissy & Markley, printers, 1852. 2 p. l., [3]-92 p. front. (fold. map) 23 cm. Report prepared by George Griscom. A 19
1. Sunbury and Erie railroad company. I. Griscom, George. II. Title.

Sundar Singh, 1889-

ANDREWS, Charles Freer, 1871- 922
Sadhu Sundar Singh; a personal memoir, by C. F. Andrews. New York and London, Harper & brothers, 1934. xvi p., 1 l., 205 p. 19 1/2 cm. "First edition." Bibliography: p. 203-205. [BV5095.S8A7 1934 a] 34-37468
1. Sundar Singh, 1889- I. Title.

PARKER, Rebecca J. Arthur 922
Parker. "Mrs.
Sadhu Sundar Singh, called of God, by Mrs. Arthur Parker ... New York, Chicago [etc.] Fleming H. Revell company [c1920] xvi, 144 p. incl. front., illus. (facsim.) ports. 20 cm. [BV5095.S8P3] 20-20538
1. Sundar Singh, 1889- I. Title.

STREETER, Burnett Hillman, 922
1874-
The message of Sadhu Sundar Singh, a study in mysticism on practical religion, by B. H. Streeter ... and A. J. Appasamy ... New York, The Macmillan company, 1921. xiii, 3-209 p. 19 1/2 cm. English edition appeared under title: The Sadhu: a study in mysticism and practical religion. [BV5095.S8S8 1921a] 21-9736
1. Sundar Singh. 1889- I. Appammy, Alyadural Jesudama, joint author. II. Title.

Sunday.

AMERICAN and foreign Sabbath
union.
Permanent Sabbath documents of the American and foreign Sabbath union. Boston, Perkins & Whipple, 1851. 2 p. l., [3]-60, 52, [2], [9]-40, 97, 86, 76 p. 20 cm. "Constitution": verso of t.-p. "Extracts from reports": 76 p. at end. [BV107.A65] 39-811
1. Sunday. I. Title.

BACON, Leonard Woolsey, 263.
1830-1907.
The Sabbath question: Sunday observance and Sunday laws, a sermon and two speeches by Leonard Woolsey Bacon ... Six sermons on the Sabbath question by the late George Blagden Bacon ... New York, G. P. Putnam's sons, 1882. 263 p. 18 cm. [BV130.B3] 15-24964
1. Sunday. 2. Sunday legislation. I. Bacon, George Blagden, 1836-1876. Six sermons on the Sabbath question. II. Title. III. Title: Sunday observance and Sunday laws.

BIGELOW, Abijah, 1775-1860.
The Sabbath. A poem. In two parts. By Abijah Bigelow ... Worcester, Printed by H. J. Howland, 1842. vi, [7]-56 p. 19 cm. [PS1098.B2283 1842] 20-13415
1. Sunday. I. Title.

CARVER, William Owen, 1868- 263
Sabbath observance; the Lord's day in our day [by] W. O. Carver ... Nashville, Tenn., The Broadman press [c1940] 89 p. 20 cm. (My covenant series. book 6) Text on lining-paper. [BV110.C36] 41-4431
1. Sunday. I. Title.

CASEBOLT, D. E., 1927- 263
Saturday or Sunday? : Letter to a Sunday-keeping minister / by D. E. Casebolt. Nashville : Southern Pub. Association, c1978. p. cm. [BV113.C33] 78-8672 ISBN 0-8127-0182-8 pbk. : 0.75
1. Sunday. 2. Sabbath. 3. Law and gospel. I. Title.

THE Christian sabbath, its 263
history, authority, duties, benefits, and civil relations. A series of discourses by the Rev. N. L. Rice, D.D., the Rev. William Hague, D.D., The Rev. Hervey D. Ganse [and others] ... With a sketch of the Sabbath reform by the secretary of the New York Sabbath committee. New York, R. Carter & brothers, 1863. 271 p. 19 1/2 cm. [BV110.C5] 45-33998
1. Sunday. I. Rice, Nathan Lewis, 1807-1877. II. Hague, William, 1808-1887. III. Ganse, Hervey Doddridge, 1822-1891.

COTTON, Paul, 1901- 263
From Sabbath to Sunday; a study in early Christianity [by] Paul Cotton, PH.D. Bethlehem, Pa., Times publishing company, 1933. 184 p. 21 cm. [Full name: John Paul Cotton] "Selected bibliography": p. 179-182. [BV110.C67 1933] 33-37183
1. Sunday. 2. Sabbath. 3. Christianity and other religions—Judaism. I. Title.

CRAFTS, Wilbur Fisk, 1850- 263.
1922.
The Sabbath for man, a study of the origin, obligation, history, advantages and present state of Sabbath observance, with special references to the rights of workingmen,

based on Scripture, literature and especially on a symposium of correspondence with persons off all nations and denominations, by Rev. Wilbur F. Crafts ... New York, London, Funk & Wagnalls, 1885. 638 p. incl. illus., map. 20 cm. [BV130.C73 1885] 15-22023
1. Sunday. I. Title.

CRAFTS, Wilbur Fisk, 1850-1922. 263.
The Sabbath for man, a study of the origin, obligation, history, advantages and present state of Sabbath observance, with special reference to the rights of workingmen, based on Scripture, literature, and especially on a symposium of correspondence with persons of all nations and denominations 6th ed., rev. and enl., by Rev. Wilbur F. Crafts. ... New York, The Baker & Taylor co., c1892. 672 p. incl. illus., map. 20 cm. [BV130.C73 1892] 15-22024
1. Sunday. I. Title.

CRAFTS, Wilbur Fisk, 1850-1922. 263.
The Sabbath for man, a study of the origin, obligation, history, advantages and present state of Sabbath observance, with special references to the rights of workingmen, based on Scripture, literature, and especially on a symposium of correspondence with person of all nations and denominations Rev. and enl. 10th ed. ... By Rev. Wilbur F. Crafts ... Washington, D. C., The International reform bureau [c1894] 672 p. incl. illus., maps. 20 cm. [BV130.C72 1894 a] 15-22025
1. Sunday. I. Title.

CRAFTS, Wilbur Fisk, 1850-1922. 263.
The Sabbath for man, a study of the origin, obligation, history, advantages and present state of Sabbath observance, with special reference to the rights of workingmen, based on Scripture, literature, and especially on a symposium of correspondence with persons of all nations and denominations; rev. and enl., 7th ed. .. By Rev. Wilbur F. Crafts. Baltimore, Authors' union [1894] 672 p. illus (incl. double map) 20 cm. [BV130.C73 1894] 24-19614
1. Sunday. I. Title.

CRAGIN, Laura Ella. 221.
Sunday story hour, by Laura Ella Cragin ... illustrated by Helen W. Cooke. New York, Hodder & Stoughton, George H. Doran company [c1917] xi p., 2 l., 17-204 p. front., plates. 20 cm. Many of the stories were written for the Beginner's leaflets, issued by the Presbyterian boards. cf. Foreword. [BV4571.C8] 17-13402
I. Title.

DAVIS, William Watters, ed. 263
The day of worship, edited by W. W. Davis. New York, The Macmillan company, 1932. xii p., 1 l., 164 p. 20 cm. [BV110.D35] 32-2135
1. Sunday. I. Title.

DICKENS, Charles, 1812-1870. 263.
Sunday under three heads. As it is. As Sabbath bills would make it. As it might be made. By Charles Dickens (Timothy Sparks.) New York, P. Eckler [1894] 64 p. incl. front. (port.) illus. 3 pl. 20 cm. Illustrated t.-p. [BV130.D5] 26-7337
1. Sunday. I. Title.

DILL, James Renwick. 263.
Christian government and the Sabbath, by James Renwick Dill ... Philadelphia, Harper & brother company, printers, c1903. 2 p. l., 140 p. front. (port.) illus. 18 cm. [BV130.D53] 3-3538
1. Sunday. I. Title.

EARLE, Alice (Morse) 1851-1911. 277.4
The Sabbath in Puritan New England. Detroit, Singing Tree Press, 1968. viii, 335 p. 21 cm. Title page includes original imprint: New York, Scribner, 1891. Reprint of the 1891 ed. [F7.E14 1968] 68-17961
1. Sunday. 2. New England—Social life and customs—Colonial period, ca. 1600-1775. I. Title.

EARLE, Alice (Morse) 1851-1911. 277.4
The Sabbath in Puritan New England. Williamstown, Mass., Corner House Publishers, 1969. viii, 335 p. 22 cm. Reprint of the 1891 ed. [F7.E14 1969] 76-15961 8.50
1. Sunday. 2. New England—Social life and customs—Colonial period, ca. 1600-1775. I. Title.

EARLE, Alice (Morse) 1851-1911. -263.4
The Sabbath in Puritan New England, by Alice Morse Earle. New York, C. Scribner's sons, 1891. viii, 335 p. 19 cm. [F7.E14] 4-4189
1. Sunday. 2. New England—Soc. life & cust. I. Title.

EARLE, Alice (Morse) Mrs. 1853-1911. 263.40974
The Sabbath in Puritan New England, by Alice Morse Earle. New York, C. Scribner's sons, 1891. viii, 335 p. 19 cm. [F7.E14] 4-4189
1. Sunday. 2. New England—Soc. life & cust. I. Title.

FISHER, William Logan, 1781-1862. 263
History of the institution of the Sabbath Day, being a plea for liberty of conscience in opposition to Sabbath conventions. Philadelphia, Merrihew & Thompson, printers, 1846. 60 p. 18 cm. "In part, extracted from a larger work, entitled, "The history of the Sabbath Day, its uses and abuses.'" [BV110.F52] 50-45671
1. Sunday. I. Title.

FLOODY, Robert John, 1859- 263
Scientific basis of Sabbath and Sunday; a new investigation after the manner and methods of modern science, revealing the true origin and evolution of the Jewish Sabbath and the Lord's day, for the purpose of ascertaining their real significance and proper observance, by the Rev. Robert John Floody... With introduction by G. Stanley Hall... 2d and rev. ed. Boston, H.B. Turner & co., 1906. xvii, 359 p. 20 1/2 cm. [BV110.F64 1906] 6-46335
1. Sunday. 2. Sabbath. I. Title.

FREDRICK, William. 263
Three prophetic days: or, Sunday the Christian's Sabbath. Showing the requirements of the Mosaic law and comparing what should have occurred during the week of the Passover, with what was done by Jesus and His apostles, as recorded in the New Testament ... By Wm. Fredrick ... Clyde, O., The author [1900] 230 p. 19 cm. [BV110.F7] 0-3191
1. Sunday. I. Title.

FROM Sabbath to Lord's Day 263
: a Biblical, historical, and theological investigation / edited by D.A. Carson. Grand Rapids, Mich. : Zondervan, c1982. 444 p. ; 21 cm. Includes bibliographical references and indexes. [BV111.F76 1982] 19 81-16343 ISBN 0-310-44531-0 pbk. : 10.95
1. Sunday. 2. Sabbath. I. Carson, D. A.

GAMBLE, Samuel Walter, 1852- 263
Sunday, the true Sabbath of God; or, Saturday proven to be neither the Sabbath of the Old Testament, nor the Sabbath of the ancients, who lived before the Christian era. Being a complete refutation of the Saturday-Sabbath heresy, and a vindication of the changeableness of the day of the Sabbath. By Samuel Walter Gamble ... Cincinnati, Jennings & Pye; New York, Eaton & Mains [c1900] 203 p. fold. chart. 19 cm. [BV110.G3] 1-29191
1. Sunday. 2. Sabbath. I. Title.

HOW shall we keep Sunday? 263.4
An answer in four parts ... Boston, The Free religious association, 1877. v, 99 p. 19 1/2 cm. [BV130.H65 1877] 33-25250
1. Sunday. 2. Sunday legislation—Massachusetts. I. Whipple, Charles King. II. Savage, Minot, Judson, 1841-1918. III. Pratt, Charles E. IV. Gannett, William Channing, 1840-1923. V. Free religious association, Boston.
Contents omitted.

HOW shall we keep Sunday? 263.4
An answer in four parts ... Boston, Published for the Free religious association by James W. West co., 1898. vi, 7-100 p. 19 1/2 cm. [BV130.H65 1898] 33-25251
1. Sunday. 2. Sunday legislation—Massachusetts. I. Whipple, Charles King. II. Savage, Minot, Judson, 1841-1918. III. Pratt, Charles E. IV. Hoag, William. V. Gannett, William Channing, 1840-1823. VI. Free religious association, Boston.
Contents omitted.

HUESTIS, Charles Herbert. 263
Sunday in the making; a historical and critical study of the Sabbath principle in inheritance and development, by Charles Herbert Huestis. New York, Cincinnati [etc.] The Abingdon press [c1929] 256 p. 19 1/2 cm. [BV110.H68] 29-16500
1. Sunday. 2. Sabbath. I. Title.

HUTCHISON, James Patterson.
Our obligations to the day of rest and worship, by Rev. James Patterson Hutchison ... Boston, R. G. Badger; [etc., etc., c1916] 4 p. l., 7-136 p. 20 cm. (Lettered on cover: Library of religious thought) 16-23972 1.00
I. Title.

HYLAN, John Perham, 1870-
Public worship; a study in the psychology of religion, by John P. Hylan. Chicago, The Open court pub. co.; London, K. Paul, Trench, Trubner & co., ltd., 1901. 2 p. l., 94 p. 20 cm. (The religion of science library, no. 50) Bibliography: p. 92-94. 2-6068
1. Sunday. 2. Worship. I. Title.

KIESLING, Christopher. 263'.3
The future of the Christian Sunday. New York, Sheed & Ward [1970] 142 p. 21 cm. [BV130.K5] 71-106155 ISBN 8-362-12290-4.50
1. Sunday. 2. Christianity—20th century. I. Title.

LEWIS, Abram Herbert, 1836-
Swift decadence of Sunday. What next? Plainfield, N.J., American Sabbath tract society, 1899. 1 p. l., vi p., 1 l., 273 p. 12° 99-2430
I. Title.

MARTIN, Renwick Harper, 1872- 263
The day; a manual on the Christian Sabbath, by R. H. Martin, D.D.; with an introduction by the Rev. Joseph R. Sizoo ... Pittsburgh, Pa., National reform association, 1933. 6 p. l., 190 p. incl. maps. front. (port.) 24 cm. [BV110.M45] 34-1020
1. Sunday. 2. Sunday legislation—U.S. I. Title.

MARTIN, Renwick Harper, 1872- 263
Six studies on the Day, by R. H. Martin ... Pittsburgh, Pa., The National reform association [pref. 1935] cover-title, 100 p. illus. (maps) 21 cm. Text on p. [2] of cover. [BV110.M46] 36-9771
1. Sunday. 2. Sunday legislation—U.S. I. Title. II. Title: Day, Six studies on the.

M'OWAN, Peter. 263
Practical considerations on the Christian Sabbath. By Rev. Peter M'Owan. New York, G. Lane & P. P. Sandford, 1843. 2 p. l., 7-200 p. 16 cm. [BV110.M35 1843] 20-17717
1. Sunday. I. Title.

M'OWAN, Peter. 263
Practical considerations on the Christian Sabbath. By Rev. Peter M'Owan. New York, Lane & Scott, 1851. 1 p. l., 7-200 p. 15 17 cm. [BV110.M35 1851] 20-17718
1. Sunday. I. Title.

PARKER, Johns Dempster, 1831-1909. 263
The Sabbath transferred, by Rev. Johns D. Parker, PH. D., with an introduction by Rev. F. N. Peloubet ... East Orange, N. J., J. D. Parker & company, 1900. 151 p. 19 cm. [BV110.P3 1900] 0-2300
1. Sunday. I. Title.

PARKER, Johns Dempster, 1831-1909. 263
The Sabbath transferred, by Rev. Johns D. Parker, PH. D.; with an introduction by Rev. F. N. Peloubet ... 2d ed., rev. and enl. East Orange, N. J., J. D. Parker & company, 1902. 242 p. front. (port.) 19 cm. [BV110.P3 1902] 3-602
1. Sunday. I. Title.

PORTER, Harry Boone 263.3
The day of light; the Biblical and liturgical meaning of Sunday. Greenwich, Conn., Seabury Press, 1960[ ] 86p. 22cm. Bibl. footnotes, 60-4401 1.75 pap.,
1. Sunday. I. Title.

PRIZE essays on the 263.04
temporal advantages of the Sabbath, considered in relation to the working classes ... Philadelphia, Presbyterian board of publication [185-?] 3 v. in 1 front., plates. 20 cm. Contents.--Heaven's antidote to the curse of labour; or, The temporal advantages of the Sabbath, considered in relation to the working classes. By John Allen Quinton.--The torch of time, or The temporal advantages of the Sabbath, considered in relation to the working classes. By David Farquhar.--The pearl of days, or, The advantages of the Sabbath to the working classes. By a labourer's daughter [i. e., Barbara H. Farquhar] [BV113.P75] 37-14665
1. Sunday. I. Quinton, John Allan. II. Farquhar, David. III. Farquhar, Barbara H. IV. Presbyterian church in the U. S. A. (Old school) Board of publication.

QUINTON, John Allan. 263
Heaven's antidote to the curse of labor; or, The temporal advantages of the Sabbath, considered in relation to the working classes. By John Allan Quinton. With a prefatory notice by Rev. S. H. Tyng, D. D. New York, S. Hueston, 1850. xii, [13]-155 p. incl. front., plates. 15 cm. [BV110.Q5] 41-81273
1. Sunday. I. Title.

RIDDLE, Marion, 1898- 263.3
The Lord's Day not a Sabbath Day; a discussion of Sunday worship from a historical standpoint. Los Angeles, Bedrock Press [1947] 94 p. 21 cm. [BV110.R47] 48-15927
1. Sunday. I. Title.

RORDORF, Willy. 263'.3'09015
Sunday; the history of the day of rest and worship in the earliest centuries of the Christian church. [Translated by A. A. K. Graham from the German] Philadelphia, Westminster Press [1968] xvi, 335 p. 22 cm. Bibliographical footnotes. [BV111.R613] 68-15920
1. Sunday. I. Title.

RORDORF, Willy. 263'.3'09075
Sunday; the history of the day of rest and worship in the earliest centuries of the Christian church. [Translated by A. A. K. Graham from the German] Philadelphia, Westminster Press [1968] xvi, 335 p. 22 cm. Bibliographical footnotes. [BV111.R613] 68-15920
1. Sunday.

THE sacredness of the 285.
Sabbath. A review of the case of Robert P. Nevin, in the presbytery of Allegheny. By a member of presbytery ... Allegheny, Pa., Ogden & Vance, printers, 1876. 49 p. 17 cm. [BX9193.N4S3] 37-37671
1. Nevin, Robert Peebles, 1820-1908. 2. Sunday. I. A member of presbytery. II. Presbyterian church in the U.S.A. Presbytery of Allegheny.

STRAW, Walter E. 263
Origin of Sunday observance in the Christian church, by Walter E. Straw ... Takoma Park, Washington, D.C., Review and herald publishing association [c1939] 3 p. l., 9-118 p. 19 1/2 cm. (Ministerial reading course. Selection for 1940, Ministerial association of Seventh-day Adventists) [BV125.S74] 39-34132
1. Sunday. 2. Seventh-day Adventists—Doctrinal and controversial works. I. Title.

SUNDERLAND, Byron, 1819-1900.
... *The Lord's day--or man's?* A public discussion between Byron Sunderland, D.D., and W. A. Croffut. PH.D., at Washington, D.C., as reported in the Washington daily post from January 27 to April 17, 1896. (With sundry recent poems.) New York, Truth seeker company [1897] ix, 152 p. 19 cm. [BV130.S7] 44-53534
1. Sunday. I. Croffut, William Augustus, 1835-1915. II. Title.

TREVELYAN, William Bouverie, 1853- 263
Sunday, by the Rev. W. B. Trevelyan ... London, New York [etc.] Longmans, Green, and co., 1902. xii, 307 p. 19 1/2 cm. (Half-title: The Oxford library of

practical theology) Title vignette. [BV110.T7] 3-7077
1. Sunday. I. Title.

UNITED Lutheran church in America. 263
The Sunday problem: a study book for groups and individuals; four points of view and a conclusion: The Jewish Sabbath, The Christian Lord's day, The "blue law" Sabbath, The modern Sunday, The conclusion. Philadelphia, Pa., The United Lutheran publication house [c1923] 70 p. 20 cm. [BV110.U6] 23-9682
I. Title.

VANKIRK, John M. 263.3
Thirteen chapters on First day observance, by John M. Vankirk, LL.D. Des Moines, Ia., Christian index, publishing company, 1898. 220 p. 20 1/2 cm. [BV110.V3] 98-197
1. Sunday. I. Title.

WARD, Miley H. 263
Space-age Sunday. New York, Macmillan [c.]1960. 160p. (Bibl. footnotes) endpaper map 22cm. 60-10617 3.95
1. Sunday. I. Title.

WILLISON, John, 1680-1750.
A treatise concerning the sanctification of the Lord's day, wherein the morality of the Sabbath, or the perpetual obligation of the fourth commandment, is maintained against adversaries; and the religious observation of the Lord's day, or first day of the week as our Christian Sabbath, is strongly pressed by Scripture arguments. Containing also, many special directions and advices for the better performing the most necessary and comprehensive duty of Sabbath-sanctification. To which are added (by way of appendix) Meditations for the Sabbath day, taken from the author's manuscripts ... By the Reverend Mr. John Willison ... Philadelphia, Printed by W. Young, bookseller and stationer, at the corner of Chestnut and Second streets, M.DCC.LXXXVIII. xvi, [25]-315 p. 18 cm. [BV109.W7] 45-34436
1. Sunday. I. Title.

WODEHOUSE, Helen. 252.
Sunday talks to teachers, by Helen Wodehouse, D. PHIL. New York, The Macmillan company, 1921. 126 p. 19 1/2 cm. [BV4316.T4W6] 21-16732
I. Title.

Sunday-evening services.

RILEY brothers, New York 264
Solved; or, The Sunday evening problem. To which is added hints on the purchase of lantern outfits and instruction to operate. New York, Bradford, Eng. Riley brothers, c1895. 64 p. illus. 15 1/2 cm. Text on p. [2] and [3] of cover. [BV27.R5] 45-31517
1. Sunday evening services. 2. Lantern projection. I. Title.

SCOTT, Herbert Morgan, 1918- 264
How to increase Sunday night attendance. Independence, Mo., Herald Pub. House,.1948. 160 p. illus. 21 cm. (The Priesthood library) [BV27.S36] 48-11075
1. Sunday-evening services. 2. Church attendance. 3. Reorganized Church of Jesus Christ of Latter-Day Saints. I. Title.

Sunday—History.

SPENCER, Frederick Joseph, 1848-
Sunday the seventh day, its history and origin proved by the testimony of antiguarian research, bronze antiques, the imperial laws of Rome, the ancient Saxon gospels ... and the united testimony of the early fathers ... By F. Joseph Spencer. v. 1- ... Fruitvale, near San Francisco, Cal., Office of "Sunday the seventh day;" [etc., etc.] c1904- v. front. (port.) illus. 16 cm. "Earthquake edition." 7-23075
I. Title.

WIGLEY, John. 263'.4'0941
The rise and fall of the Victorian Sunday / John Wigley. Manchester : Manchester University Press, c1980. 216 p. ; 23 cm. Includes bibliographical references and index. [BV130.W55] 19 81-110089 ISBN 0-7190-0794-1 : 49.00
1. Sunday—History. 2. Sunday legislation—England. 3. England—Religious life and customs. I. Title.
Distributed by Humanities Press, 171 First Ave., Atlantic Highlands, NJ 07716

Sunday legislation.

HARRIS, Groege Emrick, 1827-1911.
A treatise on Sunday laws. The Sabbath--the Lord's day, its history and observance. Civil and criminal ... By George E. Harris ... Rochester, N. Y., The Lawyers' co-operative publishing co., 1892. xxiii, 338 p. 24 cm. 12-32780
1. Sunday legislation. 2. Sunday legislation—U. S. I. Title.

LEWIS, Abram Herbert, 1836-1908. 263.
A critical history of Sunday legislation from 321 to 1888 A. D., by A. H. Lewis... New York, D. Appleton and company, 1888. x p., 1 l., 279 p. 19 cm. [BV133.L4 1888] 13-22657
1. Sunday legislation. I. Title.

LEWIS, Abram Herbert, 1836-1908. 263.
Sunday legislation; its history to the present time and its results, by Abram Herbert Lewis... New ed., rev. to date and enl. New York, D. Appleton and co., 1902. xv, 297 p. 19 cm. [BV133.L4 1902] 2-3565
1. Sunday legislation. I. Title.

LONGACRE, Charles Smull. 263.
The church in politics, by Charles S. Longacre ... Washington, D. C., Peekskill, N. Y. [etc.] Review and herald publishing association [1927] 128 p. incl. front., illus. 19 cm. Two poems. "America the beautiful," by Katherine Lee Rates, and "A nation weeps," by C. P. Bollman, printed on back cover. [BV133.L6] 28-3084
1. Sunday legislation. I. Title.

WEISS, Edward Benjamin, 1899-
"Never on Sunday? A study on Sunday retailing. New York, Doyle, Dane, Bernbach inc., 1962. 84 p. 63-72923
1. Sunday legislation. I. Doyle, Dane, Bernbach, inc. II. Title.

Sunday legislation—Congresses.

INTERNATIONAL congress on Sunday rest. 10th, St. Louis, 1904.
Sunday rest in the twentieth century; containing an account of the International Sunday rest congress at St. Louis; the various papers and addresses presented at it; sketches of the societies which united in holding it; and portraits and autographs of the leading advocates of Sunday rest; edited: Dr. Alexander Jackson ... Cleveland, O., The International federation of Sunday rest associations of America, 1905. 499 p. front. (port.) illus. 20 cm. [HD5114.A3I6 1904] 6-16490
1. Sunday legislation—Congresses. I. Labor laws and legislation—Congresses. II. Jackson, Alexander, ed. III. Title.

INTERNATIONAL congress on Sunday rest. 14th, Oakland, Cal., 1915.
Sunday the world's rest day; an illustrated story of the fourteenth International Lord's day congress held in Oakland, California, July 27th to August 1st, 1915, during the Panama-Pacific international exposition; ed. by a committee of seven appointed by the Congress, Duncan J. McMillan, chairman, Alexander Jackson, secretary ... New York city, Pub. for the New York Sabbath committee by Doubleday, Page & company, Garden City, N.Y., 1916. xiv, 622 p. front., illus., pl., ports., diagrs. 19 1/2 cm. $1.50 [HD5114.A3I6 1915] 16-14306
1. Sunday legislation—Congresses. 2. Labor laws and legislation—Congresses. I. McMillan, Duncan James, 1846- II. Jackson, Alexander. III. Title.

INTERNATIONAL congress on Sunday rest. 7th, Chicago, 1893.
The Sunday problem; its present day aspects, physiological, industrial, social, political, and religious; papers presented at the International congress on Sunday rest, Chicago, Sept. 28-30, 1893. Boston, J. H. Earle, 1894. 5. 9-338 p. 19 cm. [HD5114.A3I6 1893] 13-18535
1. Sunday legislation—Congresses. 2. Labor laws and legislation—Congresses I. Title.

Sunday legislation—Great Britain.

SUNDAY work; seven pamphlets, 1794-1856. 331.2'574 New York, Arno Press, 1972. 1 v. (various pagings) 23 cm. (British labour struggles: contemporary pamphlets 1727-1850) Contents.Contents.—The grounds of complaint against the practice of Sunday baking [first published 1794].—A sketch of an act of Parliament to permit, under certain regulations, in wet and casual harvests, the appropriation of two Sundays in a year, for the purpose of carrying and securing corn, by J. R. Head [first published 1797].—Remarks on the regulation of railway travelling on Sundays [first published 1836].—The substance of a lecture delivered at the Guildhall, Worcester, on Monday, November 7, 1836, by J. Davies [first published 1837].—The Sabbath railway system practically discussed, by J. Bridges [first published 1847].—Sunday trading in London, by W. Rivington [first published 1856].—A plea for national holy days, by J. Manners [first published 1843] [HD5114.G8S94] 72-2547 ISBN 0-405-04438-0 12.00
1. Sunday legislation—Great Britain. I. Title. II. Series.

Sunday legislation—United States

BLAKELY, William Addison, ed. 263.8
American state papers and related documents on freedom in religion. 4th rev. ed. Washington, Published for the Religions Liberty Association by the Review and Herald, 1949. 915 p. illus., ports. 23 cm. First ed. published in 1891 under title: American state papers bearing on Sunday legislation. [BV133.B6 1949] 50-206
1. Sunday legislation—U. S. 2. Religious liberty—U. S. 3. Ecclesiastical law—U. S. I. Title.

BLAKELY, William Addison, ed. 263.
... American state papers bearing on Sunday legislation, compiled and annotated by William Addison Blakely ... New York and Washington, National religious liberty association, 1891. 2 p. l., [3]-360 p., 1 l., [361]-368 p. 24 cm. At head of title: Legislative, executive, judicial. [BV133.B6 1891] 43-47493
1. Sunday legislation—U.S. 2. Religious liberty—U.S. 3. Ecclesiastical law—U.S. I. Religious liberty association, Washington, D.C. II. Title.

BLAKELY, William Addison, ed. 263.
... American state papers bearing on Sunday legislation. Rev. and enl. ed. Compiled and annotated by William Addison Blakely. Revised edition edited by Willard Allen Colcord ... Foreword by Judge Thomas M. Cooley ... Washington, D.C., The Religious liberty association, 1911. 800 p. illus. (maps) 22 1/2 cm. At head of title: Legislative, executive, judicial. [BV133.B6 1911] 11-20528
1. Sunday legislation—U.S. 2. Religious liberty—U.S. 3. Ecclesiastical law—U.S. I. Colcord, Willard Allen, 1860- ed. II. Religious liberty association, Washington, D.C. III. Title.

BLAKELY, William Addison, ed. 263.8
American state papers on freedom in religion. 3d. rev. ed. First edition compiled by William Addison Blakely ... [Takoma Park, Washington, Pub. for the Religious liberty association, Washington, D.C., by the Review and herald, 1943. 688 p. incl. front., illus. (incl. ports.) 23 1/2 cm. Published in 1891 under title: American state papers bearing on Sunday legislation. [BV133.B6 1943] 43-14734
1. Sunday legislation—U.S. 2. Religious liberty—U.S. 3. Ecclesiastical law—U.S. I. Religious liberty association, Washington, D.C. II. Title.

COHEN, Richard, 1923- 330.9'73 S
Sunday in the sixties. [New York, AMS Press, 1973, c1962] p. (Public affairs pamphlet no. 327) Reprint of the ed. published by Public Affairs Committee, New York. [HC101.P78 no. 327] 73-12329
1. Sunday legislation—United States. I. Title. II. Series: Public affairs pamphlets (New York), no. 327.

KAPLAN, Samuel Abraham, 323.442
1890-
Can persecution arise in America? [by] S. A. Kaplan. Washington, Pub. for the Religious Liberty Assn. by Review & Herald [1966] 128p. illus. 21cm. 66-8084 1.00 pap.,
1. Sunday legislation—U. S. 2. Religious liberty—U. S. 3. Sabbath (Judaism) I. Title.

RINGGOLD, James Trapier, 1852-1898.
Sunday, Legal aspects of the first day of the week. By James T. Ringgold ... Jersey City, N. J., F. D. Linn & co., 1891. xxii, 321 p. 25 cm. 15-22175
1. Sunday legislation—U. S. I. Title.

WYLIE, Richard Cameron, 1846-1928.
Sabbath laws in the United States. By R. C. Wylie, D.D. With an introduction by the Rev. S. F. Scovel, D.D. Pittsburgh, Pa., The National reform association, 1905. 1 p. l., viii, 240 p. map. 23 1/2 cm. 36-12271
1. Sunday legislation—U.S. I. Title.

Sunday school board.

LEAVELL, Landrum Pinson, 1874- 263
Pupil life, with hints to teachers, by L. P. Leavell ... Nashville, Tenn., Sunday school board, Southern Baptist convention [c1919] 135 p. 20 cm. [BV1520.L45] 19-13531
1. Sunday school board. I. Southern Baptist convention. II. Title.

Sunday school buildings.

ATKINSON, Charles Harry, 1894- 268.2
Building and equipping for Christian education. New York, Published for the Bureau of Church Building and the Dept. of Administration and Leadership of the National Council of the Churches of Christ in the U. S. A., by the Office of Publication and Distribution [c1956] 87p. illus. 30cm. [BV1528.A8] 56-12731
1. Sunday-school buildings. I. Title.

EVANS, Herbert Francis. 268.
The Sunday school building and its equipment, by Herbert Francis Evans ... Chicago, Ill., The University of Chicago press [c1914] xv, 116 p. illus. (incl. plans) 18 cm. (Half-title: The university of Chicago publications in religious education. Principles and methods of religious education, ed. by T. G. Soures) [BV1528.E8] 14-22326
1. Sunday school buildings. I. Title.

INTERNATIONAL council of religious education. 268.2
Building and equipment for Christian education ... Chicago, Ill., The International council of religious education, c1941. 56 p. illus. (incl. plans) 22 1/2 cm. (Service bulletin no. 8) Bibliography: p. 56. [BV1528.I5] 42-1300
1. Sunday-school buildings. I. Title.

LAWRENCE, Marion, 1850-1924. 726.
... Housing the Sunday school; or, A practical study of Sunday school buildings, by Marion Lawrence ... Philadelphia, The Westminster press, 1911. 4 p. l., 5-146 p. front., illus. (incl. plans) plates. 23 cm. (Modern Sunday school manuals, ed. by C. F. Kent) [NA4890.L2] 11-10632 2.00
1. Sunday-school buildings. I. Title.

METHODIST Church (United States) Dept. of Architecture.
Church school planning. Philadelphia [1962] 66 p. illus., tables, plans. 28 cm. Includes bibliography. 65-70581
1. Sunday school buildings. 2. Church architecture. I. Title.

METHODIST Church (United States) Dept. of Architecture.
Church school planning. [Rev. ed.] Philadelphia [1963] 92 p. illus., tables, plans. 28 cm. Includes bibliography. 65-71005

1. Sunday school buildings. 2. Church architecture. I. Title.

Sunday school—Junior.

TRENT, Robbie, 1894- ed.
A book about Jesus; Junior pupil, year one, book two. Written by Mary Jane Haley. 60 p. (Southern Baptist Sunday School series) 68-18250
1. Sunday school—Junior. I. Haley, Mary Jane. II. Title. III. Title: Nashville, IV. Series.

TRENT, Robbie, 1894- ed.
Eleven-year teacher, book one. For use with How we got our Bible. Written by Robbie Trent and Harriett H. Maffett. Nashville, Sunday School Board of the Southern Baptist Convention, c1962. 96 p. (Southern Baptist Sunday School series) 68-18275
1. Sunday school—Junior. I. Maffett, Harriett H. II. Title. III. Series.

TRENT, Robbie, 1894- ed.
God of all the earth; Junior pupil, year one, book three. Written by Phyllis Woodruff Sapp and Robbie Trent. Nashville, Sunday School Board of the Southern Baptist Convention, c1961. 61 p. (Southern Baptist Sunday School series) 68-18235
1. Sunday school—Junior. I. Sapp, Phyllis Woodruff, 1908- II. Title. III. Series.

TRENT, Robbie, 1894- ed.
How God meets needs; Junior pupil, year two, book one. Written by Prova Stevens. Nashville, Sunday School Board of the Southern Baptist Convention, c1961. 61 p. (Southern Baptist Sunday School series) 68-18249
1. Sunday school—Junior. I. Stevens, Prova. II. Title. III. Series.

TRENT, Robbie, 1894- ed.
How we got our Bible; Junior pupil, year three, book one. Written by Robbie Trent and Harriett H. Maffett. Nashville, Sunday School of the Southern Baptist Convention, c1962. 60 p. (Southern Baptist Sunday School series) 68-181774
1. Sunday school—Junior. I. Maffett, Harriett H. II. Title. III. Series.

TRENT, Robbie, 1894- ed.
My responsibilities; Junior pupil, year two, book four. Written by Robert L. Bishop. Nashville, Sunday School Board of the Southern Baptist Convention, c1961. 60 p. (Southern Baptist Sunday School series) 68-17851
1. Sunday school—Junior. I. Bishop, Robert L. II. Title. III. Series.

TRENT, Robbie, 1894- ed.
Nine Bible heroes; Junior pupil, year one, book four. Written by Harriett H. Maffett. Nashville, Sunday School Board of the Southern Baptist Convention, c1961. 61 p. (Southern Baptist Sunday School series) 68-18751
1. Sunday school—Junior. I. Maffett, Harriett H. II. Title. III. Series.

TRENT, Robbie, 1894- ed.
Nine-year teacher, book four. For use with Nine Bible heroes. Written by Harriett H. Maffett. Nashville, Sunday School Board of the Southern Baptist Convention, c1961. 96 p. (Southern Baptist Sunday School series) 68-17890
1. Sunday school—Junior. I. Maffett, Harriett H. II. Title. III. Series.

TRENT, Robbie, 1894- ed.
Nine-year teacher, book three. For use with God of all the earth; Junior pupil, year one, book three. Written by Mary Jane Haley. Nashville, Sunday School Board of the Southern Baptist Convention, c1961. 96 p. (Southern Baptist Sunday School series) 68-17898
1. Sunday school—Junior. I. Haley, Mary Jane. II. Title. III. Series.

TRENT, Robbie, 1894- ed.
Nine-year teacher, book two. For use with A book about Jesus. Written by Mary Jane Haley. Nashville, Sunday School Board of the Southern Baptist Convention, 1960. 96 p. (Southern Baptist Sunday School series) 68-18176
1. Sunday school—Junior. I. Haley, Mary Jane. II. Title. III. Series.

TRENT, Robbie, 1894-
Simon Peter's friend; Junior pupil, year two, book two. Written by Robbie Trent. Nashville, Sunday School Board of the Southern Baptist Convention, c1960. 60 p. (Southern Baptist Sunday School series) 68-17926
1. Sunday school—Junior. I. Title. II. Series.

TRENT, Robbie, 1894- ed.
Ten-year teacher; book four. For use with My responsibilities. Written by Robert L. Bishop and William N. McElrath. Nashville, Sunday School Board of the Southern Baptist Convention, c1961. 96 p. (Southern Baptist Sunday School series) 68-18000
1. Sunday school—Junior. I. Bishop, Robert L. II. McElrath, William N. III. Title. IV. Series.

TRENT, Robbie, 1894- ed.
Ten-year teacher, book one. For use with How God meets needs. Written by Prova Stevens. Nashville, Sunday School Board of the Southern Baptist Convention, c1961. 96 p. (Southern Baptist Sunday School series) 68-18752
1. Sunday School—Junior. I. Stevens, Prova. II. Title. III. Series.

TRENT, Robbie, 1894- ed.
Ten-year teacher, book two. For use with Simon Peter's friend. Written by Myrtle Owens Looney. Nashville, Sunday School Board of the Southern Baptist Convention, c1960. Nashville, Sunday School Board of the Southern Baptist Convention, c1961. 96 p. 96 p. (Southern Baptist Sunday School series) 68-24742
1. Sunday school—Junior. 2. Sunday school—Junior. I. Looney, Myrtle Owens.n3 II. Trent, Robbie, 1894- ed. III. Cannon, Anne Cary. IV. Title. V. Title: Ten-year teacher, book three. VI. Series. VII. Southern Baptist Sunday School series

TRENT, Robbie, 1894- ed.
A Treasure book; Junior pupil, year one book one. Written by Harriett H. Maffett. Nashville, Sunday School Board of the Southern Baptist Convention, c1960. 60 p. (Southern Baptist Sunday School series) 68-26219
1. Sunday school—Junior. I. Maffett, Harriett H. II. Title. III. Series.

TRENT, Robbie, 1894- ed.
What is God like?; Junior pupil, year two, book three. Written by Anne Cary Cannon. Nashville, Sunday School Board of the Southern Baptist Convention, c1961. 60 p. (Southern Baptist Sunday School series- 68-17925
1. Sunday school—Junior. I. Cannon, Anne Cary. II. Title. III. Series.

Sunday-school literature.

BAILEY, Carolyn Sherwin. 252
Stories for Sunday telling, by Carolyn Sherwin Bailey ... Boston, New York [etc.] The Pilgrim press [c1916] ix, 219 p. 18 cm. [BV4315.B35] 16-22746 1.00
1. Sunday-school literature. I. Title.

NAGY, Paul, jr. 268.76
... There's a song in the air; a dramatic Christmas service for Sunday school or public school assembly, by Paul Nagy, jr. ... Boston, Mass., Los Angeles, Cal., Baker's plays [1945] 20 p. 18 1/2 cm. (Baker's religious plays and pageants) [PN6120.C5N26] 45-22150
I. Title.

WILD flowers;
or, The May day walk. Written for the American Sunday school union... Philadelphia, American Sunday school union, 1827. 122 p. incl. front. 14 cm. [PZ6.W644] 22-10924
I. American Sunday-school union.

WILD flowers;
or, The May day walk. Written for the American Sunday school union... Philadelphia, American Sunday school union, 1827. 122 p. incl. front. 14 cm. [PZ6.W644] 22-10924
I. American Sunday-school union.

Sunday school literature—Bibliography

BOSTON. South Congregational church. 016
Catalogue of the South Congregational Sunday school library, Union-Park street, Boston. Boston, Printed by J. Wilson and son, 1878. 47 p. 16 1/2 cm. [Z1037.B79] 2-26674
1. Sunday school literature—Bibl. I. Title.

BROOKLYN. First Reformed Dutch church. Sunday-school library. 016.
Descriptive catalogue of the library of the Sunday-school attached to the First Ref. Dutch church. Brooklyn, E.D. ... By the superintendent. New York, J.A. Gray, printer, 1860. 65 p. 15cm. [Z881.B8678] 8-23318
1. Sunday-school literature—Bibl. I. Title.

CONNECTICUT congregational club, Hartford. 016
List of books approved by the Sunday school book commission of the Connecticut congregational club, including the general list, revised to 1892 and the annual supplements since ... Hartford, Conn., Hartford seminary press, 1896. cover-title, 47, [1], 8, 10, 6, 6 p. 20 1/2 cm. The list and supplements are separately paged. [Z1037.C765] 40-21738
1. Sunday-school literature—Bibl. I. Title.

GOODENOUGH & Woglom co. 016
Selected list of approved books for Sunday-school and parish libraries ... New York, Goodenough & Woglom co., 1902. cover-title, [3]-34 p. 23 cm. [Z1037.Z9G64 1902] 2-17286
1. Sunday-school literature—Bibl. I. Title.

NEW York. Church of the holy communion. Sunday-school library. 016.
...Catalogue of books in the library of the Sunday-school of the Church of the holy communion... New York, American church press co., 1871. 68 p. 19 1/2 cm. [Z881.N6284] 8-25097
1. Sunday school literature—Bibl. I. Title.

WASHINGTON, D.C. All Souls' church. Sunday school. Library. 016
Catalogue of the library of All Soul's Sunday school, Washington, D.C. [Washington, 1893] 30 p. 16 1/2 cm. [Z1037.W25'93] 7-13714
1. Sunday-school literature—Bibl. I. Title.

WASHINGTON, D.C. All Souls' church. Sunday school. Library. 016
Catalogue of the library of All Soul's Sunday school, Washington, D.C. [Washington] 1907. 40 p. 16 1/2 cm. By C. W. Perley. [Z1037.W25'07] 7-13715
1. Sunday-school literature—Bibl. I. Perley, Clarence Warner, 1867- II. Title.

Sunday School—Primary.

BAKER, Delores, ed.
The Bible tells me; Primary pupil, year three, book two, Written by Mrs. Ray Summers. Nashville, Sunday School Board of the Southern Baptist Convention, c1960. 52 p. (Southern Baptist Sunday School series) 68-69105
1. Sunday School—Primary. I. Summers, Mrs. Ray. II. Title. III. Series.

BAKER, Delores, ed.
Eight-year teacher; book four. For use with This is my Father's world. Written by Virginia Roberts and Donald Minton. Nashville, Sunday School Board of the Southern Baptist Convention, c1961. 96 p. (Southern Baptist Sunday School series) 68-79537
1. Sunday School—Primary. I. Roberts, Virginia. II. Minton, Donald. III. Title. IV. Series.

BAKER, Delores, ed.
Eight-year teacher, book one. For use with We learn about Jesus. Written by Dr. Floy Barnard. Nashville Sunday School Board of the Southern Baptist Convention, c1960. 96 p. (Southern Baptist Sunday School series) 68-68833
1. Sunday School—Primary. I. Barnard, Floy Merwyn. II. Title. III. Series.

BAKER, Delores, ed.
Eight-year teacher, book two. For use with The Bible tells me. Written by Mrs. Ray Summers. Nashville, Sunday School Board of the Southern Baptist Convention, c1960. 96 p. (Southern Baptist Sunday School series) 68-69288
1. Sunday School—Primary. I. Summers, Mrs. Ray. II. Title. III. Series.

BAKER, Delores, ed.
Friends wherever we are; Primary pupil, year two, book three. Written by Mrs. Ray Summers. Nashville, Sunday School Board of the Southern Baptist Convention, c1961. 1 v. (unpaged) (Southern Baptist Sunday School series) 68-80284
1. Sunday School—Primary. I. Summers, Mrs. Ray. II. Title. III. Series.

BAKER, Delores, ed.
God's plan for His friends; Primary pupil year two, book four. Written by Mrs. Maynard Hadley and Mrs. Robert Jackson. Nashville, Sunday School Board of the Southern Baptist Convention, c1961. 1 v. (unpaged) (Southern Baptist Sunday School series) 68-76717
1. Sunday School—Primary. I. Hadley, Mrs. Maynard. II. Jackson, Mrs. Robert. III. Title. IV. Series.

BAKER, Delores, ed.
God's plan for me; Primary pupil, year three, book three. Written by Dr. Floy M. Barnard. Nashville, Sunday School Board of the Southern Baptist Convention. c1960. 1 v. (unpaged) (Southern Baptist Sunday School series) 68-68831
1. Sunday School—Primary. I. Barnard, Floy Merwyn. II. Title. III. Series.

BAKER, Delores, ed.
My book about friends; Primary pupil, year one, book one. Written by Mrs. Ray Summers. Nashville, Sunday School Board of the Southern Baptist Convention, c1960. 1 v. (unpaged) (Southern Baptist Sunday school series) 68-68830
1. Sunday School—Primary. I. Summers, Mrs. Ray. II. Title. III. Series.

BAKER, Delores, ed.
My book about God and me; Primary pupil, year one, book two. Written by Edna Campbell Horton and Roberta Hadley. Nashville, Sunday School Board of the Southern Baptist Convention, c1960. 1 v. (unpaged) (Southern Baptist Sunday School series) 68-76299
1. Sunday School—Primary. I. Horton, Edna Campbell. II. Hadley, Roberta. III. Title. IV. Series.

BAKER, Delores, ed.
My book about growing up; Primary pupil, year one, book four. Written by Mrs. Ray Summers. Nashville, Sunday School Board of the Southern Baptist Convention, c1961. 1 v. (unpaged) (Southern Baptist Sunday School series) 68-79090
1. Sunday School—Primary. I. Summers, Mrs. Ray. II. Title. III. Series.

BAKER, Delores, ed.
My book about happy times; Primary pupil, year one, book three. Written by Kate Chenault Maddry and Allene Bryan. Nashville, Sunday School Board of the Southern Baptist Convention, c1961. 1 v. (unpaged) (Southern Baptist Sunday School series) 68-76153
1. Sunday School—Primary. I. Maddry, Kate Chenault. II. Bryan, Allene. III. Title. IV. Series.

BAKER, Delores, ed.
Seven-year teacher, Book four. For use with God's plan for His friEnds. Written by Mrs. Maynard Hadley and Mrs. Robert Jackson. Nashville, Sunday School Board of the Southern Baptist Convention, c1961. 96 p. (Southern Baptist Sunday School series) 68-77897
1. Sunday School—Primary. I. Hadley, Mrs. Maynard. II. Jackson, Mrs. Robert. III. Title. IV. Series.

BAKER, Delores, ed.
Seven-year teacher, book three. For use with Friends wherever we are. Written by Mrs. Ray Summers. Nashville, Sunday School Board of the Southern Baptist Convention, c1961. 96 p. (Southern Baptist Sunday School series) 68-81760
1. Sunday School—Primary. I. Summers, Mrs. Ray. II. Title. III. Series.

BAKER, Delores, ed.
Seven-year teacher, book two. For use with Friends of Jesus. Written by Mayola

Johns Clark. Nashville, Sunday School Board of the Southern Baptist Convention, c1960. 96 p. (Southern Baptist Sunday School series) 68-71020
1. Sunday School—Primary. I. Clark, Mayola Johns. II. Title. III. Series.

BAKER, Delores, ed.
Seven-year teacher, book one. For use with Friends at work and worship. Written by Edna Campbell Horton ancd Roberta Hadley. Nashville, Sunday School Board of the Southern Baptist Convention, 1960. 96 p. (Southern Baptist Sunday School series) 68-79433
1. Sunday School—Primary. I. Horton, Edna Campbell II. Hadley, Roberta. III. Title. IV. Series.

BAKER, Delores, ed.
Six-year-teacher, book one. For use with My book about friends. Nashville, Sunday School Board of the Southern Baptist Convention c1960. 96 p. (Southern Baptist Sunday School series) 68-98786
1. Sunday school—Primary. I. Summers, Mrs. Ray. II. Title. III. Series.

BAKER, Delores, ed.
Six-year-teacher, book four. For use with My book about growing up. Written by Mrs. Ray Summers. Nashville, Sunday School Board of the Southern Baptist Convention, c1961. 96 p. (Southern Baptist Sunday School series) 68-79842
1. SundaySchool—Primary. I. Summers, Mrs. Ray. II. Title. III. Series.

BAKER, Delores, ed.
Six-year-teacher, book three. For use with My book about happy times. Written by Kate Chenault Maddry and Allene Bryan. Nashville, Sunday School Board of the Southern Baptist Convention, c1961. 96 p. (Southern Baptist Sunday School series) 68-77309
1. Sunday School—Primary. I. Maddry, Kate Chenault. II. Bryan, Allene. III. Title. IV. Series.

BAKER, Delores, ed.
This is my Father's world; Primary pupil, year three, book four. Written by Virginia Roberts and Donald Minton. Nashville, The Sunday School Board of the Southern Baptist Convention, c1961. 1 v. (unpaged) (Southern Baptist Sunday School Series) 68-75939
1. Sunday School—Primary. I. Roberts, Virginia. II. Minton, Donald. III. Title. IV. Series.

BAKER, Delores, ed.
We learn about Jesus; Primary pupil, year three, book one. Written by Dr. Floy Barnard.) Nashville, Sunday School Board of the Southern Baptist Convention, c1960. 1 v. (unpaged) (Southern Baptist Sunday School series) 68-68832
1. Sunday School—Primary. I. Barnard, Floy Merwyn. II. Title. III. Series.

Sunday-school superintendents.

BROWN, Frank Llewellyn, 1863-1922. 268
... The superintendent and his work, by Frank L. Brown ... authorized and issued by the Board of Sunday schools of the Methodist Episcopal church ... [Chicago] Printed for the Board by Jennings and Graham [c1911] 312 p. 18 cm. (The Worker and his work series; text-books for the correspondence study courses of the Board of Sunday schools [v. 7]) Contains bibliographies. [BV1531.B7] 12-1135
1. Sunday-school superintendents. I. Methodist Episcopal church. Board of Sunday schools. II. Title.

JONES, Idris W 268.333
The superintendent plans his work. Philadelphia, Judson Press [1956] 88p. 19cm. [BV1531.J58] 56-13457
1. Sunday-school superintendents. I. Title.

LEAVITT, Guy P 368.3
Superintend with success. Illustrated by Robert E. Haffman. Cincinnati, Standard Pub. Co. [1960] 143p. illus. 28cm. [BV1531.L4] 64-1
1. Sunday-school superintendants. I. Title.

LEAVITT, Guy P. 268'.1
Superintend with success / written by Guy P. Leavitt ; revision by A. Leon Langston ; illustrated by Pat Karch. Rev. Cincin[n]ati, Ohio : Standard Pub., c1980. 144 p. : ill. ; 28 cm. [BV1531.L4 1980] 19 79-66658 ISBN 0-87239-377-1 pbk. : 6.50
1. Sunday-school superintendents. I. Langston, A. Leon. II. Title.

PEPPER, John Robertson, 1850-1931. 268
Thrity years at the superintendent's desk, lessons learned and noted, by J. R. Pepper. New York, Chicago [etc.] Fleming H. Revell company [c1910] 58 p. 19 cm. [BV1531.P45] 10-12319
1. Sunday-school superintendents. I. Title.

SLOAN, Patrick James, 1874-
The Sunday-school director's guide to success, by Rev. Patrick J. Sloan... New York, Cincinnati [etc.] Benziger brothers, 1909. xxv, 271 p. 18 1/2 cm. 9-7555
I. Title.

WELLS, Amos Russel, 1862-
Sunday-school essentials; what every Sunday-school teacher and superintendent needs the most in order to win success, by Amos R. Wells ... Boston and Chicago, W. A. Wilde company [c1911] 253 p. 19 1/2 cm. $1.00. Partly reprinted from various periodicals. 12-6252
I. Title.

WESTING, Harold J. 268'.1
The super superintendent / Harold J. Westing. Denver, Colo. : Accent Books, c1980. 159 p. : ill. ; 19 cm. (Accent teacher training series) Includes bibliographical references. [BV1531.W46] 19 80-66721 ISBN 0-89636-057-1 pbk. : 3.95
1. Sunday-school superintendents. I. Title. II. Series.

Sunday-school teachers.

AXTELL, James Wickleff. 268.
The superintendent's handbook ... containing the lesson text, the golden text, review suggestions ... for every Sunday in the year ... prepared by J. W. Axtell ... Nashville, Tenn., The Cumberland press, 1903 3i. e. 1902]- v. 14 x 8 cm. [BV1531.A3] 2-27530
I. Title.

AXTELL, James Wickleff. 268.
The superintendent's handbook ... containing the lesson text, the golden text, review suggestions ... for every Sunday in the year ... prepared by J. W. Axtell ... Nashville, Tenn., The Cumberland press, 1903 3i. e. 1902]- v. 14 x 8 cm. [BV1531.A3] 2-27530
I. Title.

BARTOW, Harry Edwards. 268
The superintendent's guide by Harry Edwards Bartow ... Philadelphia, American Sunday-school union [c1916- v. 15 cm. [BV1520.B3] 16-22697
I. Title.

BARTOW, Harry Edwards. 268
The superintendent's guide by Harry Edwards Bartow ... Philadelphia, American Sunday-school union [c1916- v. 15 cm. [BV1520.B3] 16-22697
I. Title.

BERGER, William Francis. 268.
The Sunday-school teacher as a soul-winner, by William Francis Berger, A. M. New York, Chicago [etc.] Fleming H. Revell company [c1925] 140 p. 20 cm. [BV1534.B4] 25-20423
I. Title.

BROWN, Frank Llewellyn, 1863-
...The superintendent and his work, by Frank L. Brown...authorized and issued by the Board of Sunday schools of the Methodist Episcopal church... Chicago, Printed for the board by Jennings and Graham [c1911] 312 p. 18 cm. (The worker and his work series; text-books for the correspondence study courses of the Board of Sunday schools [v. 7]) Contains bibliographies. 12-1135 0.50
I. Methodist Episcopal church. Board of Sunday schools. II. Title.

BROWN, Frank Llewellyn, 1863-
...The superintendent and his work, by Frank L. Brown...authorized and issued by the Board of Sunday schools of the Methodist Episcopal church... Chicago, Printed for the board by Jennings and Graham [c1911] 312 p. 18 cm. (The worker and his work series; text-books for the correspondence study courses of the Board of Sunday schools [v. 7]) Contains bibliographies. 12-1135 0.50
I. Methodist Episcopal church. Board of Sunday schools. II. Title.

BROWN, Frank Llewellyn, 1863-1922. 268.
...The superintendent, by Frank L. Brown. New York, Cincinnati, The Methodist book concern [c1922] 383 p. 17 cm. (The worker and work series; H. H. Meyer, editor) First published under title: The superintendent and his work. Bibliography at end of each chapter. [BV1531.B6] 22-12183
I. Title.

BROWN, Frank Llewellyn, 1863-1922. 268.
...The superintendent, by Frank L. Brown. New York, Cincinnati, The Methodist book concern [c1922] 383 p. 17 cm. (The worker and work series; H. H. Meyer, editor) First published under title: The superintendent and his work. Bibliography at end of each chapter. [BV1531.B6] 22-12183
I. Title.

DUCKERT, Mary. 268'.432
Help! I'm a Sunday school teacher. Illustrated by Don Patterson. Philadelphia, Westminster Press [1969] 125 p. illus. 21 cm. [BV1534.D82] 77-83133 1.85
1. Sunday-school teachers. I. Title.

DUNN, Frank E. 268
The ministering teacher / Frank E. Dunn. Valley Forge, PA : Judson Press, c1982. 111 p. : ill. ; 22 cm. Includes bibliographical references. [BV1534.D837 1982] 19 82-15257 ISBN 0-8170-0958-2 : 5.95
1. Sunday-school teachers. 2. Pastoral theology. I. Title.

LESHER, W. Richard, 1924- 268'.6
Tips for teachers / W. Richard Lesher. Mountain View, Calif. : Pacific Press Pub. Association, c1980. 109 p. ; 18 cm. [BV1534.L445] 80-12823 ISBN 0-8163-0365-7 pbk. : 4.50
1. Sunday-school teachers. 2. Christian education—Teaching methods. I. Title.
Distributed by the Greater New York Bookstore, 12 W. 40th St., New York, NY

MCCARTHY, David S. 268'.6
Memo to a weary Sunday school teacher / David S. McCarthy. Valley Forge, Pa. : Judson Press, c1978. 95 p. ; 21 cm. Includes bibliographical references. [BV1534.M15] 77-92877 ISBN 0-8170-0773-3 : pbk. : 4.95
1. Sunday-school teachers. I. Title.

MCKINNEY, Alexander Harris, 1858- 268.
The Sunday-school teacher at his best, by A. H. McKinney... New York, Chicago [etc.] Fleming H. Revell company [c1915] 107 p. 18 1/2 cm. [BV1534.M27] 16-1709 0.50
I. Title.

RICHARDS, Lawrence O. 268'.6
You, the teacher, by Lawrence O. Richards. Chicago, Moody Press [1972] 124 p. illus. 22 cm. (Effective teaching series) [BV1534.R43] 72-77942 ISBN 0-8024-9829-9 1.95
1. Sunday-school teachers. I. Title.

ROADS, Charles.
Teacher-training for the Sunday-school; embracing studies in human nature, Sunday school organization and principles of teaching, by the Rev. Charles Roads ... with an introduction by the Rev. Thomas B. Neely ... New York, Eaton & Mains. Cincinnati, Jennings & Pye [1902] 95 p. diagr. 19 cm. 3-253
I. Title.

SISEMORE, John T. 268'.6
Rejoice, you're a Sunday school teacher! / John T. Sisemore ; [ill. by Ron Hester]. Nashville : Broadman Press, c1977. 94 p. : ill. ; 20 cm. [BV1534.S553] 76-20053 ISBN 0-8054-5147-1 : 3.25
1. Sunday-school teachers. I. Title.

SUMMERS, Thomas Osmond, 1812-1887.
The Sunday-school teacher; or, The catechetical office. By Thos. O. Summers. Richmond, Va., & Louisville, Ky., J. Early, 1853. 144 p. 15 1/2 cm. 16-12486
I. Title.

TIDWELL, Josiah Blake, 1870-
The Sunday school teacher magnified, by J. B. Tidwell ... New York, Chicago [etc.] Fleming H. Revell company [c1918] 143 p. 19 1/2 cm. [BV1530.T5] 19-464
I. Title.

TRULL, George Harvey, 1873- 268.
The Sunday-school teacher and the program of Jesus, by George H. Trull and Jay S. Stowell. Philadelphia, The Westminster press, 1915. 160 p. 20 cm. Bibliography at end of each chapter. [BV1534.T65] 15-11020
I. Stowell, Jay Samuel, 1883- joint author. II. Title.

WELLS, Amos Russel, 1862-
Ten don'ts for Sunday-school teachers, by Amos R. Wells. Philadelphia, The Westminster press, 1913. 74 p. 14 cm. $0.25. 14-2534
I. Title.

Sunday-school teachers—Prayer-books and devotions—English.

ALDEN, Joseph.
Hand-book for Sunday-school teachers... New York, Eaton & Mains; Cincinnati, Jennings & Pye [1900] 222 p. 18 cm. Copyright by William Alden, U.S. Class A, 1900, no. 16645, July 6; 2 copies rec'd June 25, 1901. 1-17611
I. Title.

ANDERSEN, Richard, 1931- 268'.4
Devotions for church school teachers / Richard Andersen. St. Louis : Concordia Pub. House, c1976. p. cm. [BV4596.S9A5] 76-2158 ISBN 0-570-03722-0 pbk. : 1.75
1. Sunday-school teachers—Prayer-books and devotions—English. I. Title.

ANDERSEN, Richard, 1931- 268
Inspirational meditations for Sunday school teachers / by Richard Andersen. St. Louis, MO : Concordia Pub. House, c1980. 47 p. ; 21 cm. [BV4596.S9A53] 80-10114 ISBN 0-570-03810-3 pbk. : 1.95
1. Sunday-school teachers—Prayer-books and devotions—English. I. Title.

ANDERSEN, Richard, 1931- 242'.69
A little library of inspiration for Sunday school teachers / Richard Andersen. St. Louis : Concordia Pub. House, c1982. 45 p. ; 21 cm. [BV4596.S9A54 1982] 19 81-12492 ISBN 0-570-03846-4 pbk. : 1.95
1. Sunday-school teachers—Prayer-books and devotions—English. I. Title.

BAYLY, Joseph T. 268'.6
I love to tell the story / Joseph Bayly ; [edited by Linda Girard]. Elgin, Ill. : D. C. Cook Pub. Co., c1978. 61 p. ; 22 cm. (Ideabooks) [BV4596.S9B38] 78-61299 ISBN 0-89191-162-6 pbk. : 1.50
1. Sunday-school teachers—Prayer-books and devotions—English. I. Title.

Sunday-school union of the Methodist Episcopal church.

SMITH, Daniel, 1806-1852. 225.92
The life of John the Baptist. By Rev. Daniel Smith...Revised by the editors. New York, T. Mason and G. Lane, for the Sunday school union of the Methodist Episcopal church, 1840. 108 p. incl. front. map. 14 1/2 cm. [BS2456.S5] 39-8950
1. Sunday-school union of the Methodist Episcopal church. I. John the Baptist. II. Title.

SMITH, Daniel, 1806-1852. 225.92
The life of St. Paul. By Rev. Daniel Smith... New York, Pub. by T. Mason and G. Lane, for the Sunday school union of the Methodist Episcopal church, 1839. 175 p. incl. front. map. 14 1/2 cm. [BS2505.S45] 922.1 34-16733
1. Paul, Saint, apostle. 2. Sunday school union of the Methodist Episcopal church. I. Title.

Sunday-school—United States.

RICE, Edwin Wilbur, 1831- 922.
After ninety years, by Edwin Wilbur Rice. Philadelphia, American Sunday-school union [c1924] 167 p. front., ports. 22 cm. [BX7260.R4A4] 24-20787
I. Title.

RICE, Edwin Wilbur, 1831- 268
1929.
The Sunday school movement 1780-1917, and the American Sunday-School Union 1817-1917. New York, Arno Press, 1971 [c1917] 501 p. illus. 23 cm. (American education: its men, ideas, and institutions. Series II) [BV1515.R5 1971] 70-165728 ISBN 0-405-03717-1
1. American Sunday-School Union. 2. Sunday-school—United States. I. Title. II. Series.

Sunday-Schools.

[ALDEN, Isabella (Macdonald) "Mrs. G. R. Alden," 1841-
The teacher's helper. By Pansy [pseud.]... Boston, D. Lothrop and company [c1880] vii, 9-243 p. 18 1/2 cm. Cover-title: The S. S. teacher's helper. [LC381.A35] E 15
1. Sunday schools. I. Title.

ALEXANDER, John l. 1878- 268.
1932.
The boy and the Sunday school a manual of principle and method for the work of the Sunday school with teen age boys [by] John L. Alexander ... introduction by Marion Lawrance ... New York [etc.] Association press, 1913. 284 p. 17 1/2 cm. Bibliography at the end of each chapter. [BV1575.A6] 13-18041
1. Sunday-schools. I. Title.

ALEXANDER, John L., 1878-1932.
The secondary division organized for service; a manual of present and future organization for the teen years in the Sunday school, by John L. Alexander ... introduction by Marion Lawrence ... New York, Chicago [etc.] Fleming H. Revell company [c1916] 92 p. 18 1/2 cm. [BV1547.A6] 17-
1. Sunday-schools. I. International Sunday-school association. II. Title.

ANDERSON, Andy, 1927- 268'.8'6132
Where action is / Andy Anderson with Eugene Skelton. Nashville : Broadman Press, c1976. 158 p. : ill. ; 21 cm. [BV1523.A7A52] 76-11988 ISBN 0-8054-6212-0 : 4.95
1. Anderson, Andy, 1927- 2. Bible—Study. 3. Sunday—schools. 4. Church growth. I. Skelton, Eugene, joint author. II. Title.

ARCHIBALD, Ethel Jessie, 268.
1881-
The primary department, by Ethel J. Archibald. Philadelphia, The Sunday school times company [c1907] vi, 91 p. plates, 18 1/2 cm. (On cover: The "Times" handbooks for Sunday-school workers, no. 4) [BV1538.A7] 7-17354
1. Sunday-schools. I. Title.

ARCHIBALD, George Hamilton.
The modern Sunday-school; its theory and practice, by George Hamilton Archibald... New York & London, The Century co. [c1926] ix, 206 p. 19 1/2 cm. Bibliography at end of most of the chapters. [BV1820.A65] 36-9710
1. Sunday-schools. I. Title.

ATKINSON, William Ezra, 1858-
comp.
The value of the Sunday school, contributed by more than one hundred people representing every state in the union; comp. by William E. Atkinson. New York, Chicago [etc.] Fleming H. Revell company [c1922] 124 p. front. 20 cm. [BV1507.A3] 23-480
I. Title.

ATKINSON, William Ezra, 1858-
comp.
The value of the Sunday school, contributed by more than one hundred people representing every state in the union; comp. by William E. Atkinson. New York, Chicago [etc.] Fleming H. Revell company [c1922] 124 p. front. 20 cm. [BV1507.A3] 23-480
I. Title.

AXTELL, James Wickleff. 268
Grading the Sunday school; the outcome of organization, by J. W. Axtell ... Nashville, Tenn., The Cumberland press, 1904. 121 p. 18 cm. "A bibliography of grading": p. 107-111. [BV1520.A8] 4-82681
1. Sunday-schools. I. Title.

AXTELL, James Wickleff. 268
The organized Sunday school; a working manual for officers, by J. W. Axtell. Nashville, Tenn., The Cumberland press, 1901. 111 p. 1 illus., pl. 18 cm. [BV1520.A85] 25-12033
1. Sunday-schools. I. Title.

BALDWIN, Josephine L. 268.
Introduction and use of the graded lessons, international course; junior manual, prepared by Josephine L. Baldwin; approved by Committee on curriculum, Board of Sunday schools, Methodist Episcopal church, Henry H. Meyer, editor. New York, Cincinnati, The Methodist book concern [c1915] 191 p. 19 cm. "The Berean graded lessons, international course." [BV1546.B3] 15-18961
1. Sunday-schools. I. Meyer, Henry Herman, 1874- ed. II. Title.

BARCLAY, Wade Crawford, 268.
1874-
... The adult worker and his work, by Wade Crawford Barclay ... authorized and issued by the Board of Sunday schools of the Methodist Episcopal church ... [Chicago] Printed for the board by Jennings and Graham [c1910] 276 p. incl. form. 19cm. (The worker and his work series; a correspondence study course for Sunday school workers. [v. 6] Contains bibliographies. [BV1550.B3] 19-1138
1. Sunday schools. I. Methodist Episcopal church. Board of Sunday schools. II. Title.

BARCLAY, Wade Crawford, 262.
1874-
... First standard manual of teacher training, by Wade Crawford Barclay. New York and Cincinnati, The Methodist book concern [c1915] 2 v. maps. 20cm. Paged continuously. "References for supplementary reading" at end of each chapter. Contents.pt. I. The Bible--pt. II. The pupil, the teacher, and the school. [BV1533.B3 1915] [416960] 16-274
1. Sunday-schools. 2. Bible—Study. I. Title.

BARCLAY, Wade Crawford, 1874- 268
... The pupil, the teacher and the school, by Wade Crawford Barclay Nashville, Tenn., Dallas, Tex. [etc] Publishing house of the M. E. Church, South, Smith & Lamar, agents [c1918-] v. 20cm. "References for supplementary reading" at end of each chapter. [BV1520.B2] 18-23140
1. Sunday-schools. 2. Religious education. I. Title.

*BARLOW, Fred S. 268.0973
Reap ten tips for Sunday school enlargement campaigns by Fred M. Barlow. Des Plaines, Ill., Regular Baptist Press, 1974 60 p. illus. 19 cm. [BV1516] 1.50 (pbk.)
1. Sunday-schools. I. Title.

BARNETTE, Jasper Newton, 268.861
1887-
Associational Sunday school work [by] J. N. Barnette ... Nashville, Tenn., Sunday school board of the Southern Baptist convention [c1933] 154 p. incl. forms. 19 cm. [BX6228.B8] 34-32721
1. Sunday-schools. 2. Rural churches. 3. Southern Baptist convention. I. Title.

BARNETTE, Jasper Newton, 268
1887-
A church using its Sunday school; adapted for Sunday schools organized on the class basis, by J. N. Barnette. Nashville, Tenn., The Sunday school board of the Southern Baptist convention [c1937] 178 p. diagrs. 19 cm. [BV1520.B28] 37-21919
1. Sunday-schools. I. Title.

BEAUCHAMP, Harvey, 1866- 268
The graded Sunday school: a text book on Sunday school organization and management, by H. Beauchamp ... Nashville, Tenn., Sunday school board, Southern Baptist convention [c1910] 222 [2] p. illus. (incl. plans) 19 cm. "Helpful books for Sunday school workers": [2] p. at end. [BV1520.B4] 10-26255
1. Sunday-schools. I. Title.

BENSON, Clarence H. 266
The Sunday school in action, by Clarence H. Benson ... Chicago, The Bible institute colportage ass'n [c1932] 327 p. incl. illus., diagrs., forms. plates. 20 cm. Bibliography: p. 326-327. [BV1520.B45] 22-8290
1. Sunday-schools. I. Title.

BENSON, Clarence H. 268
The Sunday school in action, by Clarence H. Benson ... Chicago, The Bible institute colportage ass'n.[c1941] 327 p. incl. illus., plans, diagrs., forms. plates. 20 cm. "Fourth printing, revised, 1941." Bibliography: p. 326-327. [BV1520.B45 1941] 41-24217
1. Sunday-schools. I. Bible institute colportage association, Chicago. II. Title.

BENSON, Clarence Herbert, 268
1879-
The Sunday school in action, by Clarence H. Benson ... Chicago, The Bible institute colportage ass'n [c1932] 327 p. incl. illus., forms, diagrs. plates. 20 cm. Bibliography: p. 326-327. [BV1520.B45] 32-8290
1. Sunday-schools. I. Title.

BENSON, Clarence Herbert, 268
1879-
The Sunday school in action, by Clarence H. Benson ... Chicago, The Bible institute colportage ass'n [c1941] 327 p. incl. illus., plans, forms, diagrs. plates. 20 cm. "Fourth printing, revised, 1941." Bibliography: p. 326-327. [BV1520.B45 1941] 41-24217
1. Sunday-schools. I. Title.

BENSON, Clarence Herbert, 268
1879-
Sunday school success. 3d rev. Wheaton, Ill., Evangelical Teacher Training Assn. [1964] 96p. 23cm. (Evangelical Teacher Training Assn. Certificate ser., unit 6) Bibl. 64-13765 price unreported
1. Sunday-schools. I. Title.

BETTS, Anna (Freelove) Mrs. 268.
... The nursery child in the church school, by Anna Freelove Betts. New York, Cincinnati [etc.] The Abingdon press [c1930] 194 p. front., illus. 21 cm. (The Abingdon religious education texts, J. W. Langdale, general editor, G. H. Betts, associate editor) "Music: rhythms and songs": p. 173-190. "References" at end of some of the chapters. [Full name: Mrs. Anna Marie (Freelove) Betts] [BV1540.B45] 30-6734
1. Sunday-schools. 2. Nursery schools. 3. Religious education. I. Title.

BLACK, Israel Putnam, 1845- 268.
1903.
Practical primary plans for primary teachers of the Sunday-school. Rev. and enl., by Israel P. Black. With an appendix containing a list of helpful books and applicances. New York, Chicago [etc.] Fleming H. Revell company [1930] 4 p. l., 7-264 p. pl. 20 cm. [BV1538.B6 1903] 4-2150
1. Sunday-schools. I. Title.

BLAZIER, Kenneth D. 268'.1
Building an effective church school : guide for the superintendent and board of

Christian education / Kenneth D. Blazier. Valley Forge, Pa. : Judson Press, c1976. 64 p. : ill. ; 22 cm. Includes bibliographical references. [BV1521.B5] 75-42018 ISBN 0-8170-0708-3 pbk. : 1.95
1. Sunday-schools. I. Title.

BOVARD, William Sherman, 1864- 268.
Adults in the Sunday school; a field and a force, by William Sherman Bovard ... New York, Cincinnati, The Abingdon press [c1917] 196 p. front., plates. 19 1/2 cm. [BV1550.B6] 17-23302
1. Sunday-Schools. I. Title.

BOWEN, Cawthon Asbury, 1885- 268.6
Literature and the Christian life, by C. A., Bowen. Nashville, Tenn., Cokesbury press [c1937] 128 p. 17 cm. [BV1558.B62] 37-14725
1. Sunday schools 2. Religious education. I. Title.

BOWER, Robert K. 268.1
Administering Christian education; principles of administration for ministers and Christian leaders, by Robert K. Bower. Grand Rapids, W. B. Eerdmans Pub. Co. [1964] 227 p. illus., forms. 24 cm. Bibliography: p. 219-223. [BV1521.B6] 64-22018
1. Sunday-schools. 2. Religious education. I. Title.

BRABHAM, Mouzon William, 1885- 268
The Sunday school at work in town and country, by William Mouzon Brabham ... with an introduction by Rev. E. B. Chappell, D.D. New York, George H. Doran company [c1922] xix p., 2 l., 21-217 p. incl. plans. front., plates, diagrs. 20 cm. Contains bibliographies. [BV1520.B68] 28-1227
1. Sunday-schools. I. Title.

BRADNER, Lester, 1867- 268
Organizing the smaller Sunday school; a study in grading, by Lester Bradner ... Milwaukee, The Young churchman co., 1917. ix, 111 p. diagrs. 19 cm. Contains references. [BV1520.B7] 17-20428 0.75
1. Sunday-schools. I. Title.

BRECK, Flora Elizabeth, 1886- 268
Sunday-school ideas (for church and Sunday-school) Boston, W. A. Wilde Co. [1958] 90p. illus. 23cm. [BV1520.B713] 58-12416
1. Sunday-schools. I. Title.

BREWBAKER, Charles Warren, 1869- 268.
The adult program in the church school, by Charles W. Brewbaker ... New York, Chicago [etc.) Fleming H. Revell company [c1925] 3 p. l. 5-139 p. 19 1/2 cm. [BV1550.B65] 26-20809
1. Sunday-schools. I. Title.

BREWBAKER, Charles Warren, 1869- 268
A program for Sunday-school management, by Charles W. Brewbaker ... New York, Chicago [etc.] Fleming H. Revell company [c1922] 122 p. 19 cm. "List of helpful books": p. 120-122. [BV1520.B715] 23-478
1. Sunday-schools. I. Title.

BREWER, Abraham Titus, 1841-1933.
How to make the Sunday school go, by A. T. Brewer ... New York, Eaton & Mains; Cincinnati, Curtis & Jennings [c1897] 191 p. incl. front. 18 cm. E12
1. Sunday-schools. I. Title.

BROWN, Ario Ayres, 1883- 268
...Teacher's guide to the organizaiton and administration of the Sunday school (Cuninggim-North) by Ario Ayres Brown. New York, Cincinnati, The Methodist book concern; Nashville, Dallas, Smith & Lamar [c1920] 92 p. illus. (plans) 18 1/2 cm. (Training courses for leadership, ed. by H. H. Meyer and E. D. Chappell) Contains references. [BV1520.B73] 20-14751
1. Sunday-schools. I. Title.

BROWN, Frank Llewellyn, 1863-1922.
The city Sunday-school: its work, growth, possibilities. With an appendix showing forms, letters, and blanks which have been used with success. By Frank L. Brown ... Philadelphia, Sunday school times co., 1906. 70 p. 19 cm. On cover: The "Times" handbooks for Sunday-school workers. Number 1. A 17
1. Sunday-schools. I. Title.

BROWN, Frank Llewellyn, 1863-1922.
The Sunday-school and the home, by Frank L. Brown... Philadelphia, Pa., The Sunday school times company [c1907] 68 p. 18 1/2 cm. 10-9217
I. Title.

BROWN, Frank Llewellyn, 1863-1922.
Sunday-school officers manual; the training of officers and committees, a practical course for Sunday school leaders, by Frank L. Brown ... New York, Cincinnati, The Abingdon press [c1916] 254 p. 17 1/2 cm. Containes bibliographies. [BV1530.B85] 16-6911 0.50
1. Sunday-schools. I. Title.

BROWN, Joseph, 1837-1918. 268.
Sabbath-school missions in Wisconsin; a record of fifteen years of Sabbath-school mission work done in Wisconsin, in which the needs and the triumphs of the work are made known, by Rev. Joseph Brown... Philadelphia, Presbyterian board of publication and Sabbath-achool work, 1904. xv, 163 p. 16 pl., 2 port. (incl. front.) 20 cm. [BV1516.A2W6] 4-27365
1. Sunday-schools. 2. Missions—Wisconsin. 3. Presbyterian church in Wisconsin. I. Title.

BROWN, Lowell E. 268
Your Sunday school can grow : guidelines for building a better Sunday school / by Lowell E. Brown with Bobbie Reed. Glendale, Calif. : G/L Regal Books, [1974] 120 p. : ill. ; 20 cm. (An ICL insight book) At head of title: Grow. [BV1521.B73] 74-79564 ISBN 0-8307-0309-8 pbk. 2.25
1. Sunday-schools. I. Title. II. Title: Grow.

BROWN, Marianna Catherine, d.1916. 268
Sunday-school movements in America, by Marianna C. Brown. New York, Chicago [etc.] Fleming H. Revell co., 1901. 269 p. 19 1/2 cm. Thesis (PH. D.)--Columbia university, 1902. Bibliography: p. 246-257. [BV1520.B76] 1-31831
1. Sunday-schools. I. Title.

BROWN, William Herbert, 1864- 268
Activities for active Bible classes, by Will H. Brown... Cincinnati, O., The Standard publishing company [c1926] 111 p. 29 cm. [BV1520.B765] 26-17493
1. Sunday-schools. I. Title.

BRUCE, Gustav Marius, 1879- 268.841
Ten studies on the Sunday school, by Gustav M. Bruce ... published under the auspices of the Board of elementary Christian education of the Norwegian Lutheran church of America. Minneapolis, Minn., Augsburg publishing house, 1931. 95 p. 20 1/2 cm. "References for further study" at end of each chapter except the last. [BX8013.B7] 31-5534
1. Sunday-schools. I. Norwegian Lutheran church. Board of elementary Christian education. II. Title.

BRYAN, Allene. 268
Primary Sunday school work, by Allene Bryan. Nashville, Tenn., The Sunday school board of the Southern Baptist convention [c1941] 149 p. 18 1/2 cm. [BV1545.B77] 42-22960
1. Sunday-schools. I. Southern Baptist convention. Sunday school board. II. Title.

BRYAN, Joseph Harris, 1862- 268.434
The organized adult Bible class, by J. H. Bryan. St. Louis, Mo., Christian publishing company [1909] 163 p. illus. 18 cm. [BV1550.B7] 9-7564
1. Sunday-schools. I. Title. II. Title: Bible class, The organized adult.

BRYNER, Mary Foster. 268.
The elementary division organized for service, by Mary Foster Bryne. New York, Chicago [etc.] Fleming H. Revell company [c1917] 127 p. 19 cm. Plans for the elementary division of the Sunday school. cf. Foreword. "Book list": p. 120-127. [BV1538.B7] 17-4887
1. Sunday-schools. I. Title.

BULLARD, Asa, 1804-1888.
Fifty years with the Sabbath schools. By Rev. Asa Bullard ... Boston, Lockwood, Brooks and company, 1876. 336 p. front. (port.) 20 cm. E 18
1. Sunday-schools. I. Title.

BURKE, Verdia. 268
Building a better Sunday school. St. Louis, Bethany Press [1950] 96 p. 20 cm. Includes bibliographies. [BV1520.B777] 50-2516
1. Sunday-schools. I. Title.

BURROUGHS, Prince Emanuel, 1871- 268
Building a successful Sunday school, by P. E. Burroughs ... New York, Chicago [etc.] Fleming H. Revell company, [1921] 192 p. froms. 19 1/2 cm. [BV1520.B79] 21-21581
1. Sunday-schools. I. Title.

BURROUGHS, Prince Emanuel, 1871- 268
The present-day Sunday school, studies in its organization and management, by P. E. Burroughs ... New York, Chicago, [etc.] Fleming H. Revell company, [c1917] 214 p. illus. (incl. plans) 19 1/2 cm. Contains "reference". [BV1520.B8] 17-15563
1. Sunday-schools. I. Title.

BURTON, Ernest DeWitt, 1856-1925. 268
Principles and ideals for the Sunday school; an essay in religious pedagogy, by Ernest DeWitt Burton & Shailer Mathews... Chicago, The University of Chicago press, 1903. vii, 207 p. 20 cm. [BV1520.B78] 3-13941
1. Sunday schools. I. Mathews, Shailer, 1863- joint author. II. Title.

CALDWELL, Irene Catherine]Smith: 1917- 268
Solving church school problems. Anderson, Ind., Warner Press [1944] 128 p. diagrs. 19 cm. "For further study" at end of each chapter. [BV1520.C3] 44-44878
1. Sunday-school. I. Title.

CALLARMAN, Eva Avis 1890-1934.
How to improve your Sunday school by Eva Callarman St. Louis The [bethany press 1934 91 p. incl. forms. 17 cm. "Approved as a textbook in leadership training by the Department of religious education, Disciples of Christ." "References for additional reading" at end of each chapter. A 36
1. Sunday-schools. I. Disciples of Christ. Dept. of religious education. II. Title.

CAMPBELL, Doak Sheridan, 1888- 268.6
When do teachers teach? [By] Doak S. Campbell ... Nashville, Tenn., The Sunday school board of the Southern Baptist convention [c1935] 110 p. 19 cm. The author has rewritten his revision and abridgment of H. C. Trumbull's "Teaching and teachers" which was published in 1934 under the joint authorship of H. C. Trumbull and D. S. Campbell with the title "When do teachers teach?" "Selected references": p. 108-110. [BV1534.C25] 36-8083
1. Sunday-schools. 2. Teaching. I. Trumbull, Henry Clay, 1830-1903 Teaching and teachers. II. Title.

CAMPBELL, Oscar Pierce, 1888- 268.333
The superintendent wants to know; a handbook for the layman serving as church school superintendent, by Oscar P. Campbell... Philadelphia, Boston [etc.] The Judson press [c1937] 81 p. diagrs. 19 1/2 cm. "References for further study" at end of each chapter; "The superintendent's library": p. [80]-81. [BV1531.C35] 38-8797
1. Sunday schools. I. Title.

CHALMERS, William Everett, 1868- ed. 268
Church school objectives, "bigger and better Sunday schools"; a manual of study and work for the workers' conference of the Sunday school, ed. by William E. Chalmers. Philadelphia, Boston [etc.] The Judson press, [c1922] 4 p. l., 160 p. 20 cm. [BV1520.C5] 22-19971
1. Sunday-schools. I. Title.

CHALMERS, William Everett, 1868- ed. 268
A church school program, "better and bigger church schools"; a manual of study and work for the workers conference of the Sunday school, edited by William E. Chalmers. Philadelphia, Boston [etc.] The Judson press [c1923] 4 p. l., 157 p. 20 cm. Contains bibliographies. [BV1520.C52] 23-16094
1. Sunday-schools. I. Title.

CHALMERS, William Everett, 1868-1928, ed. 268
The Baptist Sunday school standard manual by J. M. Gurley, J. D. Collins, A. A. Holtz ... [and others] ed, by William E. Chalmers, D. D. Philadelphia, Boston [etc.] American Baptist publication society [c1917] iv p., 2 l., 3-162 p. 18 cm. [BX6223.C5] 17-29544
1. Sunday-schools. I. Title.
Contents omitted.

CHALMERS, William Everett, 1868-1928, ed. 268
Church school objectives, "bigger and better Sunday schools"; a manual of study and work for the workers' conference of the Sunday school, Edited by William E. Chalmers. Philadelphia, Boston [etc.] The Judson press [c1922] 4 p. l., 160 p. 20 cm. "Erratum" leaf inserted. "Books you need": p. 149-153. [BV1520.C5 1922 a] 24-18831
1. Sunday-schools. I. Title.

CHAPMAN, John Wilbur, 1859-1918. 263
The spiritual life of the Sunday school. By Rev. J. Wilbur Chapman ... Boston and Chicago, United society of Christian endeavor [1899] 62 p. 17 1/2 cm. "The four chapters of this book appeared in four different articles in the Sunday school times." [BV1520.C55] 99-3746
1. Sunday-schools. I. International society of Christian endeavor. II. Title.

CHURCH of Jesus Christ of latter-day saints. Deseret Sunday school union. 268
Latter-day saints' Sunday school treatise. Salt Lake City, Deseret Sunday school union, 1896. 124 p. 19 cm. [BX8610.A47] 18-8641
1. Sunday-schools. 2. Mormons and Mormonism—Education. I. Title.

CLACK, Henry P.
Songs and praises for revivals, Sunday schools, singing schools, and general church work. Dallas, Tex., H.P. Clack, 1899. 144 p. incl. port. 12 cm. 0-4418
I. Title.

CLARK, Joseph, 1854- 268.435
The extension arm of the Sunday school; a new study of the enlarged field of the Home department. A manual for Home department workers. By Dr. Joseph Clark... Elgin, Ill., David C. Cook publishing company [c1929] 85 p. illus. 17 cm. [BV1578.C6] 30-11387
1. Sunday-schools. I. Title. II. Title: Home department, A new study of the enlarged field of the.

CONVENTION normal manual for Sunday-school workers; Baptist first standard course in three divisions ... Nashville, Tenn., Sunday-school board, Southern Baptist convention [c1909] 224 p. illus. (maps) 17 1/2 cm. Advertising matter: p. 221-224. [BV1520.C6] 9-16790 268
1. Sunday-schools. I. Spilmau, Bernard Washington, 1871- II. Leavell, Landrum Pinsou, 1874-1929. III. Moore, Hight C., 1871-
Contents omitted.

COOK, David C. 268.
Successful adult Bible classes and what they are doing; also reports from Sunday school superintendents on adult Bible class work and its needs and conditions of the work as seen by adult Bible class teachers of the ordinary sort, by David C. Cook ... Chicago, New York [etc.] David C. Cook publishing company, 1906. 96 p. incl. illus., forms. 21 1/2 x 17 1/2 cm. "Class printing matter": p. 69-96. [BV1550.C6] 7-1941
1. Sunday-schools. 2. Bible—Study. I. Title.

COOPER, James Alfred, 1822-1898. 268.37
Counsels to Sunday school teachers on

personal improvement and practical efficiency ... By J. A. Cooper ... 4th thousand. London, Sunday school union; New York, T. Nelson & sons [1871?] viii, 123 p. 18 cm. Bibliography: p. 39-42, [120]-123. [BV1534.C62] 37-8047
1. Sunday-schools. I. Title.

COPE, Henry Frederick, 1870-1913. 268
The modern Sunday school in principle and practice, by Henry Frederick Cope ... New York, Chicago [etc.] Fleming H. Revell company [c1907] 3 p. l., 9-206 p. 20 cm. [BV1520.C65] 7-20534
1. Sunday-schools. I. Title.

COPE, Henry Frederick, 1870-1923. 268
Efficiency in the Sunday school, by Henry Frederick Cope ... New York, Hodder & Stoughton, George H. Doran company [c1912] viii, 253 p. 21 cm. "A working library on religious education": p. 234-241. Partly reprinted from various periodicals. [BV1520.C635] 12-27814
1. Sunday-schools. I. Title.

COPE, Henry Frederick, 1870-1923. 268
The modern Sunday school and its present day task, by Henry Frederick Cope. [Rev. ed.] New York, Chicago [etc.] Fleming H. Revell company [c1916] 252 p. diagr. 19 cm. [BV1520.C64] 16-21245
1. Sunday-schools. I. Title.

COPE, Henry Frederick, 1870-1923. 268
Organizing the church school; a comprehensive scheme for religious educational activities for children and youth, by Henry Frederick Cope. New York, George H. Doran company [c1923] viii, p., 1 l., 11-255 p. tables. 20 cm. Contains bibliographies. [BV1520.C67] 23-8307
1. Sunday-schools. I. Title.

CRAFTS, Sara J (Timanus) Mrs.
The infant class; hints on primary religious instruction, by Sara J. Timanus ... Ed., with an introduction, by Edward Eggleston ... Chicago, Adams, Blackmer, & Lyon publishing co., 1870. iv, [2], [7]-108 p. diagrs. 18 cm. E 10
1. Sunday schools. I. Eggleston, Edward, 1837- ed. II. Title.

CRAIG, John Bradford, 1877- 268
Bible school teacher's handbook, by J. Brad Craig ... Nashville, Tenn., Cokesbury press, 1926. x, 218 p. 17 cm. Good books for children to read": p. 208-212. [BV1520.C7] 27-1933
1. Sunday-schools. 2. Religious education. I. Title.

CRAIG, John Bradford, 1877- 263
Bible school teacher's handbook, by J. Brad Craig... Nashville, Tenn., Cokesbury press, 1926. x, 218 p. 17 cm. "Good books for children to read": p. 208-212. [BV1520.C7] 27-1933
1. Sunday-schools. 2. Religious education. I. Title.

CRAIG, John Bradford, 1877- 268.
Life problems ... for pupils of the junior high school or the intermediate department of the church Bible school, by J. Brad Craig ... pupil's textbook. Nashville, Tenn., Cokesbury press, 1930- v. illus. (maps) 17 cm. [BV1548.C7] 30-8911
1. Sunday-schools. 2. Religious education. I. Title.

*CRISCI, Elizabeth W. 268
Creative sunday schools, [by] Elizabeth W. Crisci. Grand Rapids, Baker Book House, [1975] 107 p. 20 cm. [BV1515] ISBN 0-8010-2371-8 1.95 (pbk.)
1. Sunday-schools. 2. Religious education. I. Title.

CULLY, Iris V. 268
New life for your Sunday school / Iris V. Cully. New York : Hawthorn Books, c1976. viii, 117 p. ; 22 cm. Includes index. [BV1521.C84 1976] 75-28684 ISBN 0-8015-5366-0 : 5.95
1. Sunday-schools. 2. Christian education. I. Title.

CUNINGGIM, Jesse Lee, 1870- 268
... The organization and administration of the Sunday school, by Jesse L. Cunningim and Eric M. North. Approved by the Committee on curriculum of the Board of Sunday schools of the Methodist Episcopal church and the Committee on curriculum of General Sunday school board of the Methodist Episcopal church. South. New York, Cincinnati, The Methodist book concern; Nashville, Dallas [etc.] Smith & Lamar [c1919] 155 p. illus. (plans) 19 cm. (Training courses for leadership, ed. by [H. H. Meyer and E. B. Chappell) "References" at end of chapters. [BV1520.C8] 19-3298
1. Sunday-schools. I. North, Eric McCoy, 1888- joint author. II. Title.

CURTISS, Phebe A. Mrs. 268.
The primary department, by Phebe A. Curtiss ... Philadelphia, The Westminister press, 1918. 102 p. 19 cm. "Books for each chapter": p. 99-102. [BV1545.C8] 19-11001
1. Sunday-schools. I. Title.

DADMUN, Frances May, 1875- 268.
Living together; a manual for teachers of children of primary grade, prepared especially for pupils seven years of age, by Frances M. Dadmun. Boston, Mass., The Beacon press, inc. [c1915] xxxvi, 233 p. 21 cm. (Half-title: The New beacon course of graded lessons) Reprinted in part from "Scattered seeds". [BV1545.D3] 15-24016 0.75
1. Sunday-schools. 2. Story-telling. I. Title.

DAMM, John Silber, ed.
The teaching of religion. Edited by John S. Damm with the assistance of Walter R. Bouman [and others] River Forest, Ill. Lutheran Education Association, 1965. viii, 107 p. 23 cm. (Lutheran Education Association. Yearbook, 22d, 1965) Includes bibliographical references. 67-83057
1. Sunday-schools. 2. Religious education. 3. Church schools. I. Title.

DENNEN, Ernest Joseph, 1866-
The Sunday school under scientific management, by Ernest J. Dennen; with introduction by William E. Gardner ... Milwaukee, The Young churchman co., 1914. 5 p. l., 147 p. 19 cm. "The material contained in these pages was ... delivered as a course of six lectures: first, to a class at the Cambridge school for church workers in July, 1912; then, in amplified form, to a class at the Massachusetts diocesan training school for Sunday school teachers."--Pref. 14-9776
I. Title.

DOANE, W[illiam] H[oward] 1831- 783.
Glorious praise; specially prepared for use in the prayer meeting, the church service, the young people's meetings, the Sunday school, the evangelistic and other religious gatherings, by W. H. Doane, MUS, DOC., assisted by W. J. Kirkpatrick. Louisville, Ky., Harvey & Burnett [1904] 256 p. 21 cm. [M2117.D631] 4-28403
I. Kirkpatrick, William J., joint author. II. Title.

DOBBINS, Gaines Stanley, 1886- 268.6
The improvement of teaching in the Sunday school, by Gaines S. Dobbins ... Nashville, Tenn., The Sunday school board of the Southern Baptist convention [1943] 170 p. 19 cm. [BV1534.D6] 43-15340
1. Sunday-schools. 2. Religious education—Teaching methods. I. Southern Baptist convention. Sunday school board. II. Title.

DOBBINS, Gaines Stanley, 1886- 268
The school in which we teach [by] G. S. Dobbins ... Nashville, Tenn., The Sunday school board of the Southern Baptist convention [c1934] 144 p. 19 cm. "Books for further reading": p. 138-141. "Sunday school board publications": p. 141-142. [BX6223.D6] 35-2622
1. Sunday-schools. 2. Religious education. I. Title.

DONNELLY, Harold Irvin, 1892- 268
Administering the senior department of the church school, a text-book in the Standard leadership training curriculum, outlined and approved by the International council of religious education. by Harold I. Donnelly. Philadelphia, printed for the Leadership training publication association by the Westminster press, 1931. 195 p. diagrs. 20 cm. "Reference library suggested for use with the class": p. 16-18; "Selected bibliography": p. 189-195. [BV1549.D6] 31-11798
1. Sunday-schools. 2. Religious education. I. International council of religious education. II. Title.

DUCKERT, Mary. 268
Help! I run a Sunday school. Illustrated by Donald W. Patterson. Philadelphia, Westminster Press [1971] 128 p. illus. 21 cm. [BV1521.D82] 77-158124 ISBN 0-664-24930-2
1. Sunday-schools. I. Title.

DUDDY, Frank E. 268
A new way to solve old problems, by Frank E. Duddy... New York, C. Scribner's sons, 1921. x p., 1 l., 50 p. illus. (forms) 19 1/2 cm. "List of books and lessons found useful": p. 49-50. [BV1520.D8] 21-10603
1. Sunday-schools. I. Title.

EDWARDS, Gus Callaway, 1886-
The country town Sunday school, by Gus. C. Edwards. Clarkesville, Ga., Legal publishing company [c1915] 120 p. front., plates. 19 cm. $1.25 Some of the plates accompanied by leaf with descriptive letterpress. 15-14499
I. Title.

ENTZMINGER, Louis 268
The Sunday school transformed, by Louis Entzminger. Philadelphia, The Sunday school times company [c1925] 179 p. incl. forms. 19 1/2 cm. [BV1520.E6] 26-1336
1. Sunday-schools. I. Title.

FARIS, John Thomson, 1871- ed. 268
The Sunday school at work, by Philip E. Howard, Amos R. Wells, Rev. A. H. McKinney ... [and others] ed. by John T. Faris, D D. Philadelphia, The Westminster press, 1914. 359 p. 20 cm. Title within double line border. [BV1520.F3 1914] 14-7894 1.25
1. Sunday-schools. I. Howard, Philip Eugene, 1870- II. Title.

FARIS, John Thomson, 1871- ed. 263
The Sunday school at work, by Philip E. Howard, Amos R. Wells, Rev. A. H. McKinney ... [and others] ed. by John T. Faris, D. D. Philadelphia, The Westminster press, 1916. 452 p. 20 cm. Bibliography: p. 445-452. [BV1520.F3] 17-14392 1.25
1. Sunday-schools. I. Howard, Philip Eugene, 1870- II. Title.

FARIS, John Thomson, 1871-
The Sunday school at work, by Philip E. Howard, Amos R. Wells, Rev. A. H. McKinney [and others] Ed. by John T. Faris ... Philadelphia, The Westminster press, 1913. 359 p. 20 cm. [LC381.F22] E 14
1. Sunday schools. I. Title.

FEENEY, Bernard, 1843or4-1919. 238.
The Catholic Sunday school: some suggestions on its aim, work, and management, by Rev. Bernard Feeney ... with introduction by Most Rev. John Ireland ... St. Louis, Mo., and Freiburg (Baden) B. Herder, 1907. xxii, 233 p. 20 1/2 cm. "Lectures given ... during the past year, to the students of the Seminary of St. Paul."--Introd. [BX925.F4] 7-33916
1. Sunday-schools. I. Title.

FERGUSSON, Edmund Morris, 1864- 268
How to run a little Sunday school, by E. Morris Fergusson. New York, Chicago [etc.] Fleming H. Revell company [c1916] 128 p. 19 1/2 cm. $0.60 [BV1520.F4] 16-10809
1. Sunday-schools. I. Title.

FERGUSSON, Edmund Morris, 1864 268
Piloting the Sunday school; a message to superintendents, by E. Morris Fergusson ... New York, Chicago [etc.] Fleming H. Revell company [c1925] 152 p. 19 1/2 cm. [BV1520.F45] 25-9226
1. Sunday-schools. I. Title.

FERGUSSON, Edmund Morris, 1864-1934.
Church-school administration, by E. Morris Fergusson ... New York, Chicago [etc.] Fleming H. Revell company [c1929] 270 p. 19 cm. Bibliography: p. 361-394. [BV1529.F87] 23-619
1. Sunday-schools. I. Title.

FLAKE, Arthur. 268.861
Building a standard Sunday school [by] Arthur Flake... Nashville, Tenn. The Sunday school board of the Southern Baptist convention [c1934] 3 p. l., 9-172 p. incl. forms. 19 cm. "First revision in 1928; second revision in 1934." [BX6223.F6 1934] 34-39194
1. Sunday-schools. I. Title.

FLAKE, Arthur, 1862-1952. 268
The true functions of the Sunday school. Nashville, Convention Press [1957] 130 p. 20 cm. [BX6223.F62] 62-11837
1. Sunday-schools. 2. Southern Baptist Convention — Education. I. Title.

FOSTER, Eugene Clifford, 1867- 268.
The intermediate department, by Eugene C. Foster ... Philadelphia, Pa., The Westminster press, 1917. 84 p. 19 cm. Bibliography at end of most of the chapters. [BV1548.F6] 18-7384
1. Sunday-schools. I. Title.

FRAYSER, Nannie Lee, d.1924.
The Sunday school and citizenship, by Nannie Lee Frayser. Cincinnati, The Standard publishing company [c1915] 99 p. 20 cm. Bibliography at end of each chapter. [BV1615.F7] 15-17047
1. Sunday-schools. I. Title.

FRENCH, Addie Marie. 268
... All about the Sunday school, by Addie Marie French; with foreword and introductory chapter by Rev. David J. Fant, B. A. New York, Harrisburg, Christian publications, incorporated [c1934] 123 p. 24 cm. At head of title: A handbook of instruction for the administration and conduct of the average Sunday school. [BV1520.F65] 34-2439
1. Sunday-schools. I. Fant, David Jones, 1897- II. Title. III. Title: A handbook of instruction for the administration and conduct of the average Sunday school.

FRENCH, Addie Marie, 1876-1940. 268
All about the Sunday school; instructions for the conduct of an average Sunday school, courses of study, methods of teaching, departmental grading, accessories, and literature, by David J. Fant and Addie Marie French. 2d rev. ed. New York, Christian Publications [1947] 192 p. 20 cm. A revision and enlargement by Mr. Fant of the 1934 ed. on the t.-p. of which Miss French's name appeared first. Bibliography: p. 191-192. [BV1520.F65 1947] 47-6868
1. Sunday schools. I. Fant, David Jones, 1897- joint author. II. Title.

FROST, James Marion, 1849-1916. 268
The school of the church; its pre-eminent place and purpose, by J. M. Frost ... New York, Chicago [etc.] Fleming H. Revell company [c1911] 193 p. 20 cm. [BV1520.F7] 11-26969 1.00
1. Sunday-schools. I. Title.

GAGE, Albert Henry, 1878- 268
A bigger and better Sunday school, by Albert H. Gage ... introduction by W. Edward Raffety ... New York, Chicago [etc.] Fleming H. Revell company [c1927] 160 p. 20 cm. Bibliography: p. 156-160. [BV1520.G3] 27-20148
1. Sunday-schools. I. Title.

GAGE, Albert Henry, 1878- 268.146
Increasing church school attendance, by Albert H. Gage ... Grand Rapids, Mich., Zondervan publishing house [c1939] 6 p. l., 11-130, [4] p. 20 cm. Blank pages for "Notes" ([4] at end) [BV1520.G33] 39-16213
1. Sunday-schools. I. Title.

GARDNER, Lucile Blake, "Mrs. T. C. Gardner." 268.
Primary leaders manual, by Mrs. T. C. Gardner ... Dallas, Tex., The Baptist book store [c1929] 64 p. 19 1/2 cm. "Suggested books for primary leaders": p. 15. [BV1545.G25] 29-16958
1. Sunday-schools. I. Title.

GARDNER, Lucile Blake, 268.
"Mrs. T. C. Gardner."
Programs and methods for primary unions [by] Mrs. T. C. Gardner ... Dallas, Tex., c1926. 72 p. 17 cm. [BV1545.G3] 27-5883
1. Sunday-schools. I. Title.

GARDNER, William Edward, 268.
1872-
The children's challenge to the church; a study in religious nurture for rectors and teachers, by Rev. William E. Gardner ... prepared for the Sunday school commission, diocese of New York ... Milwaukee, The Young churchman company, 1913. viii, 132 p. 19 cm. Bibliography: p. 125-128. [BX5870.G3] 13-21448
1. Sunday-schools. 2. Protestant Episcopal church in the U.S.A.—Education. I. Protestant Episcopal church in the U.S.A. New York (Diocese) Sunday school commission. II. Title.

GAW, Lily (Storrs) "Mrs. Ralph H. Gaw," 1862-
God's family; a three years' graded course in mission study for children, for use in the primary Sunday school teacher training, mission bands and for mothers at home, by Mrs. Ralph H. Gaw ... Topeka, Kan., The Mail printing house [1915] 94, [1] p. illus. 24 cm. $0.50 15-10683
I. Title.

GEE, Howard James. 268
... *Methods of church school administration,* by Howard James Gee ... New York, Chicago [etc.] Fleming H. Revell company [c1920] 117 p. illus. (charts) 20 cm. At head of title: A textbook for community training schools and international and state schools of Sunday school methods. "Books for reading and further study": at end of each chapter. [BV1520.G4] 20-20829
1. Sunday-schools. I. Title.

GETMAN, Arthur Kendall, 1887- 268
The church school in action, [by] Arthur Kendall Getman. New York, Cincinnati [etc.] The Abingdon press [c1931] 178 p. 20 cm. Bibliography: p. 174-178. [BV1520.G43] 31-6403
1. Sunday-schools. 2. Religious education. I. Title.

GRAHAM, Margaret Althea, 268.424
1924-
How to win a Sunday school contest; a gold mine of successful ideas for building larger Sunday school attendance through the contest method, chosen from the many entires in the National Christian life magazine contest. Compiled and written by Margaret Graham and Nancy Bates. Wheaton, Ill., Scripture Press [1958] 108 p. illus. 26 cm. [BV1520.G67] 58-42569
1. Sunday-schools. I. Bates, Nancy, joint author. II. Title.

GREENE, Samuel Harrison, 268
1845-1920.
The twentieth century Sunday school. Sunday school board seminary lectures, course no. 3, delivered at the Southern Baptist theological seminary, Louisville, Ky., December 14-18, 1903 [by] Samuel H. Greene ... Nashville, Tenn., Sunday school board, Southern Baptist convention [1904] 151 p. front. (port.) 19 cm. [BV1520.G75] 4-0135
1. Sunday-schools. I. Title.

GRIME, William, 1898- 268.6
Modern methods in the church school, by William Grime ... foreword by Dr. Adelaide Teague Case. New York, Round table press, inc., 1934. xviii, 99 p. front. 20 cm. [BV1546.G7] 35-239
1. Sunday-schools. I. Title.

HAMILL, Howard Melancthon, 268.
1847-1915.
The Sunday school teacher. By Prof. H. M. Hamill ... 10th thousand. Nashville, Tenn., Dallas, Tex., Publishing house of the M.E. church, South, Barbee & Smith, agents, 1902. 156 p. 18 1/2 cm. "A Sunday school teacher's library": p. 153-156. [BV1534.H35] 2-18592
1. Sunday-schools. I. Title.

HANNA, Frederick Watson, 1866 268
The Sunday school; an evangelistic opportunity, by F. Watson Hannan. New York, Cincinnati, The Methodist book concern [c1920] 138 p. 17 1/2 cm. [BV1520.H3] 20-14604
1. Sunday schools. I. Title.

HARMON, Joseph, 1880- 268.6
Principles of Bible school teaching, by Joseph Harmon ... Yonkers, N. Y., General efficiency company, 1934. 76 p. illus. 19 cm. [BV1534.H356] 35-761
1. Sunday-schools. I. Title.

HARNER, Nevin Cowger, 268.841748
1901-
Factors related to Sunday school growth and decline in the Eastern synod of the Reformed church in the United States, by Nevin C. Harner ... New York city, Teachers college, Columbia university, 1931. vi, 101 p. incl. forms. 24 cm. (Teachers college, Columbia university. Contributions to education, no. 479) Published also as thesis (PH. D.) Columbia university. Bibliography: p. 101 [BX9563.H3 1931 a] [LB5.C8 no.479] 31-29653
1. Sunday-schools. 2. Reformed church in the United States. Eastern synod. 3. Churches—Pennsylvania. I. Title. II. Title: Sunday school growth and decline.

HARTSOUGH, Palmer, and Fillmore, J[ames] H.
Fillmores' Sunday-school songs. nos. 1 and 2 combined. Cincinnati and New York, Fillmore bros., 1900. [128] p. 12 degree. With music. Mar
I. Title.

HASLETT, Samuel B. 268
The pedagogical Bible school; a scientific study of the Sunday school with chief reference to the curriculum, by Samuel B. Haslett... Introduction by Pres. G. Stanley Hall... New York, London [etc.] Fleming H. Revell company [1903] 2 p. l., 383 p. 21 1/2 cm. "Bibliography : p. 349-363. [BV1520.H37] 3-31497
1. Sunday-schools. I. Title.

HAZARD, Marshall Custiss, 268.
1839-1929.
Home classes and the home department of the Sunday-school; history, purpose, plan, organization, methods, requisites and difficulties, by M. C. Hazard, PH.D. Boston, Chicago, The Pilgrim press [c1906] 192 p 19 cm. First published 1895. [BV1578.H3 1906] 6-45048
1. Sunday-schools. I. Title.

HEIM, Ralph Daniel, 1895- 268'.1
Leading a church school, by Ralph D. Heim. Philadelphia, Fortress Press [1968] x, 358 p. 23 cm. Bibliographical footnotes. [BV1521.H4] 68-16262 6.95
1. Sunday-schools. I. Title.

HEIM, Ralph Daniel, 1895- 268
Leading a Sunday church school. Philadelphia, Muhlenberg Press [1950] xi, 368 p. 22 cm. [BV1520.H39] 50-9488
1. Sunday-schools. I. Title.

HENRY, Freddie Elizabeth. 268.432
The small church at work for children, by Freddie Elizabeth Henry; C. A. Bowen, D.D., general editor. Nashville, Tenn., Cokesbury press [c1933] 125 p. 17 cm. Bibliography: p. 126. [BV1520.H43] 33-33085
1. Sunday-schools. 2. Religious education. I. Bowen, Cawthon Asbury, 1885- ed. II. Title.

HERON, Henrietta. 268
The workers' conference; how to make it go, by Henrietta Heron. Cincinnati, The Standard publishing company [c1921] 141 p. illus. 18 cm. "A suggestive list of books for the workers' library": p. 137-141. [BV1520.H5] 21-10275
1. Sunday-schools. I. Title.

HEWITT, Mildred. 268
The church school comes to life, by Mildred Hewitt. New York, The Macmillan company, 1932. xiv p., 1 l., 341 p. incl. diagrs., forms. 20 cm. Bibliography: p. 311-324; 328-333. [BV1520.H53] 32-15325
1. Sunday-schools. 2. Religious education. I. Title.

HOW to teach the little 268.
folks. The primary department. By J. Bnnet Tyler. II. Methods in the class. By Mrs. G. R. Alden. III. How to teach an infant class. By Faith Latimer. IV. Methods in mission schools. By Mrs. George Partridge. Philadelphia, Presbyterian board of publication [c1875] 72 p. 14 cm. Introductory note signed: J. B. T. [i.e. J. Bennet Tyler] [BV1538.H6] 8-14142
1. Sunday-schools. I. Tyler, J. Bennet.

HOWSE, William Lewis, 1905- 268
Those treasured hours; the adventure and dividends of Sunday school teaching. Nashville, Broadman Press [c1960] 67p. 21cm. [BV1534.H74] 60-5630
1. Sunday-schools. 2. Religious education—Teaching methods. I. Title.

*HUGHES, Ray H. 268.1
Sunday school workers' training course, no. 1., introd. course. Grand Rapids, Mich., Baker Bk. [1964, c.1955] 110p. 20cm. 1.50 pap.,
I. Title.

HURLBUT, Jesse Lyman, 1843- 262.
1930.
Hurlbut's teacher-training lessons for the Sunday school, by Jesse Lyman Hurlbut. New York, Eaton & Mains; Cincinnati, Jennings & Graham [c1908] 144 p. incl. illus., maps, plans. 20 cm. [BV1533.H8] 8-19233
1. Sunday schools. 2. Religious education. 3. Bible—Study—Text-books. I. Title. II. Title: Teacher-training lessons for the Sunday school.

HURLBUT, Jesse Lyman, 1843- 268
1930.
... *Organizing and building up the Sunday school,* by Jesse Lyman Hurlbut. New York, Eaton & Mains; Cincinnati, Jennings & Graham [c1910] 152 p. 19 cm. (Modern Sunday school manuals. [BV1520.H8] 10-15676
I. Title.

INTERNATIONAL Sunday-school association. Commission for the study of the adolescent period.
The Sunday school and the teens; the report of the Comission on adolescence authorized by the San Francisco convention of the International Sunday school association. A study of the adolescent in relationship to the home, church, Sunday school and the community: Edited by John L. Alexander ... Introduction by Edgar H. Nichols ... New York, London, Association press, 1913. xxv, 416 p. fold. diagr. 19 1/2 cm. Contains brief bibliographies. [BV1547.I6] 13-15550
1. Sunday-schools. 2. Adolescence. I. Alexander, John L., 1878-1932, ed. II. Title.

INTERNATIONAL Sunday-school 268
association. Commission for the study of the adolescent period.
The teens and the rural Sunday school; being the second volume of the report of the Commission on adolescence, authorized by the San Francisco convention of the International Sunday school association. A study of the adolescent in relation to the rural community under 2,500 population and in the open country. By the commission for the study of the adolescent in the country Sunday school. Ed. by John L. Alexander ... New York [etc.] Association press, 1914. viii, 151 p. 19 1/2 cm. $0.50. "Bibliographies": p. 149-151. [BV1555.I5] 14-11587
1. Sunday-schools. 2. Rural schools-U.S. I. Alexander, John L., 1875- ed. II. Title.

INTERNATIONAL Sunday-school convention of the United States and British American provinces. 7th, St. Louis, 1893.
Seventh International (twelfth national) and world's second Sunday school conventions, held in the exposition building, St. Louis, Missouri, U.S.A., Aug. 30, 31 and Sept. 1, 2, 3, 4 and 5, 1893 ... Chicago, Published for the Executive committees by W. B. Jacobs [1893] 456 p. 19 1/2 cm. Reported by J. Clayton Youker, Chicago. E 14
1. Sunday schools. I. Youker, J. Clayton. II. Title.

INTERNATIONAL Sunday school convention of the United States and British American provinces. 9th, Atlanta, 1899.
Ninth International (fourteenth national) Sunday school convention, held in Grand opera house, Atlanta, Ga., Wednesday, Thursday, Friday and Saturday, April 26th to 30th, 1899 ... [Atlanta?] The Executive committee [1899] 8 p. l., [9]-345 p. 20 cm. Reported by J. Clayton Youker, Chicago. E 14
1. Sunday schools. I. Youker, J. Clayton. II. Title.

IRVIN, Ida M. 268
The secretary's guide; duties and problems; the prospective school, the present school, the absent school. Prepared by Ida M. Irvin. St. Louis, Mo., Christian board of publication [c1920] 84 p. incl. forms, diagrs. 16 cm. [BV1532.I7] 21-15273
1. Sunday-schools. I. Title.

IRVIN, Ida M. 268
The workers' manual: the modern Sunday school, its organization and equipment. by Ida M. Irvin. Rev. ed. for 1920-1921. St. Louis, Mo., Christian board of publication [1921] 78 p. illus., forms. 23 cm. Preceded by "Mr. Sunday School" by H. E. Tralle. [BV1520.I 7] 21-16946
1. Sunday-schools. I. Christian board of publications, St. Louis, Mo. II. Title.

JACOBS, Alice. 268.
... *The elementary worker and his work (treating the beginner's and primary departments only.)* By Alice Jacobs and Ermina C. Lincoln; authorized and issued by the Board of Sunday schools of the Methodist Episcopal church ... Chicago ... [Cincinnati] Printed for the board by Jennings and Graham [c1911] 247 p. illus., pl. 18 cm. (The worker and his work series; text-books for the correspondence study courses of the Board of Sunday schools. [v. 2]) Contains bibliographies. [BV1538.J3] 12-1134
1. Sunday schools. I. Lincoln, Ermina Chester, 1881- joint author. II. Methodist Episcopal church. Board of Sunday schools. III. Title.

JACOBS, James Vernon, 1898- 268
1,000 plans and ideas for Sunday school workers. Grand Rapids, Zondervan Pub. House [1957] 157p. illus. 20cm. [BV1520.J2] 57-3246
1. Sunday-schools. I. Title.

JACOBS, James Vernon, 1898-
Teaching problems and how to solve them; a question and answer book. Grand Rapids, Zondervan Pub. House [c1962] 64 p. (Sunday school know-how series) 65-2403
1. Sunday schools. I. Title. II. Series.

JONES, Orabelle C. 268.432
The nursery department of the Sunday school, by Orabelle C. Jones. Nashville, Tenn., The Sunday school board of the Southern Baptist convention [1946] 7 p. l., 154 p. illus. 19 cm. "References" at end of most of the chapters. Bibliography: p. 150-154. [BV1540.J6] 47-18678
1. Sunday schools. 2. Religious education of pre-school children. I. Southern Baptist convention. Sunday school board. II. Title.

JONES, Philip Cowell. 268.333
The church school superintendent [by] Philip Cowell Jones ... New York, Cincinnati [etc.] The Abingdon press [c1939] 112 p. incl. illus., forms. 20 cm. [The Abingdon religious education texts, J. W. Langdale, general editor; Guides to Christian leadership, P. H. Vieth, editor] [BV1531.J6] 39-9928
1. Sunday-schools. I. Title.

JOSEPH, Oscar L. 268
Personal appeals to Sunday school workers, by Oscar L. Joseph ... New York, Chicago [etc.] Fleming H. Revell company [c1917] 215 p. 20 cm. "Commended books" at end of each chapter; "Notes on select books": p. 196-215. Reprinted in part from various periodicals. [BV1520.J7] 17-31918
1. Sunday-schools. I. Title.

JOY, Donald Marvin. 268
Meaningful learning in the church, by Donald M. Joy. Winona Lake, Ind., Light and Life Press [1969] 168 p. illus. 20 cm. "Commissioned as a part of the Aldersgate

Graded Curriculum project by the Aldersgate Publications Association." Bibliographical references included in "Notes" (p. 153-162) [BV1521.J65] 72-80801
1. Sunday-schools. 2. Christian education. I. Aldersgate Publications Association. II. Title.

KEARNEY, Emilie Fairchild. 262.
The teacher training class and how to conduct it, by Emilie Fairchild Kearney ... New York, Chicago [etc.] Fleming H. Revell company [c1918] 125 p. 20 cm. "Reference books for sale by Fleming H. Revell company": p. 124-125. [BV1533.K4] 18-10287
1. Sunday-schools. 2. Religious education. I. Title.

KENNEDY, M. G. Mrs. 268.
Our boys and girls; how to interest and instruct them in Bible study, by Mrs. M. G. Kennedy. Boston, Chicago, W. A. Wilde company [c1909] 122 p. 19 cm. [BV1546.K4] 9-25951
1. Sunday-schools. I. Title.

KNAPP, Ezra C. 268
The Sunday school between Sundays, by E C. Knapp ... New York, Chicago [etc.] Fleming H. Revell company [c1920] 143 p. 20 cm. [BV1520.K6] 21-3328
1. Sunday-schools. 2. Amusements. 3. Church entertainments. I. Title.

LAWRENCE, Marion, 1850-1924. 263
The church-school blue-print, by Marion Lawrence... Cincinnati, The Standard publishing company [1924] 150 p. diagrs. (1 fold.) 20 cm. [BV1520.L25] 24-15263
1. Sunday-schools. I. Title.

LAWRENCE, Marion, 1850-1924. 263
How to conduct a Sunday school; or, Twenty eight years a superintendent, by Marion Lawrence ... New York, Chicago [etc.] Fleming H. Revell company [c1905] 1 p. l., 7-279 p. illus. (music) plates, diagrs. 21 cm. [BV1520.L3 1905] 5-17292
1. Sunday-schools. I. Title.

LAWRENCE, Marion, 1850-1924. 263
How to conduct a Sunday school; or, Thirty-one years a superintendent, by Marion Lawrence ... New York, Chicago [etc.] Fleming H. Revell company [c1915] 324 p. front. (port.) illus., plates. 21 cm. Bibliography: p. 293-307 [BV1520.L3 1915] 15-14581
1. Sunday-schools. I. Title.

LAWRENCE, Marion, 1850-1924. 263
My message to Sunday school workers, by Marion Lawrence. New York, George H. Doran company [c1924] xv p., 1 l., 19-290 p. incl. front. (port.) 20 cm. [BV1520.L32] 24-20780
1. Sunday-schools. I. Title.

LAWRENCE, Marion, 1850-1924. 263
The Sunday school organized for service, by Marion Lawrence ... Boston, New York [etc.] The Pilgrim press [c1914] ix p., 1 l., 87 p. illus., fold. chart. 20 cm. [BV1520.L33] 14-13158
1. Sunday-schools. I. Title.

LEATHERWOOD, Mattie C. 268.432
The cradle roll department of the Sunday school, by Mattie C. Leatherwood. Nashville, Tenn., The Sunday school board of the Southern Baptist convention [1941] 4 p. l., 7-158 p. 18 1/2 cm. [BV1537.L4] 43-11322
1. Sunday-schools. 2. Religious education of pre-school children. I. Southern Baptists convention. Sunday school board. II. Title.

LEAVELL, Clarence Stanley, 1889- 263
The successful Sunday school at work, by C. S. Leavell ... New York, George H. Doran company [c1924] xii p., 1 l., 15-271 p. illus. (incl. plans) plates. 20 cm. [BV1520.L37] 24-27611
1. Sunday-schools. I. Title.

LEAVELL, Landrum Pinson, 1874- 263
The intermediate department of the Sunday school, by L. P. Leavell ... Nashville, Tenn., Sunday school board, Southern Baptist convention [c1918] c159 p. 19 cm. Bibliography: p. 159. [BV1520.L4] 18-5310
1. Sunday-schools. I. Title.

LEAVELL, Landrum Pinson, 1874-1929. 268.6
Some learning processes [by] L. P. Leavell ... and John L. Hill ... Nashville, Tenn., The Sunday school board of the Southern Baptist convention [c1934] 115 p. 19 cm. Published in 1919 under title: Pupil life. Revised and abridged by J. L. Hill. [BV1534.L4 1934] 34-40709
1. Sunday-schools. 2. Educational psychology. I. Hill, John Leonard, 1878- ed. II. Title.

LEAVITT, Guy P 268
How to improve my church's school, an analysis and improvement program. Cincinnati, Standard Pub. Co. [1953] 104p. 19cm. [BV1520.L38] 53-31993
1. Sunday-schools. I. Title.

LEE, Carvel 268.68
The Sunday school bulletin board guide, by Carvel and Lorita Lee. Illus. by the authors. Minneapolis, Denison [c.1963] 63p. col. illus. 28 cm. 1.85 pap.,
I. Title.

LESTER, H. A., ed.
Sunday schools and religious education; sermons and addresses, ed. by Rev. H. A. Lester ... assisted by Canon Morley Stevenson ... With an introduction by the Archbishop of Canterbury. London, New York [etc.] Longmans, Green, and co., 1913. viii, 147, [1] p. 20 cm. E 14
1. Sunday-schools. 2. Religious education. I. Stevenson, Morley, 1851- joint ed. II. Title.
Contents omitted.

LEWIS, Charles Smith, 1868- 252.
...The work of the church in the Sunday school, by the Rev. Charles Smith Lewis... Milwaukee, Pub. for the Western theological seminary, Chicago, by the Young churchman co. [1910] 57 p. 22 1/2 cm. (The Hale memorial sermon. no. 5) [BX5937.A1H3 no.5] 19-12762
I. Title.

LEWIS, Hazel Asenath, 1886- 268.
Methods for primary teachers, by Hazel A. Lewis ... a textbook in the standard course in teacher training, outlined and approved by the Sunday school council of Evangelical denominations. Third year specialization series. St. Louis, Pub. for the Teacher training publishing association by the Front rank press [c1921] 182 p. 17 cm. [BV1545.L45] 22-3319
1. Sunday-schools. I. Title.

... Life in the making, 263
by Wade Crawford Barclay, Arlo A. Brown, Alma S. Sheridan, William J. Thompson, and Harold J. Sheridan, approved by the Committee on curriculum of the Board of Sunday schools of theMethodist Episcopal church and the Committee on curriculum of the General Sunday school board of the Methodist Episcopal church, South. New York, Cincinnati, The Methodist book concern; Nashville, Dallas [etc.] Smith & Lamar [c1917] 236 p. 19 cm. (Training courses for leadership, ed. by H. H. Meyer and E. B. Chappell) [BV1520.L5] 17-30762
1. Sunday-schools. 2. Religious education. 3. Child study. I. Barclay, Wade Crawford, 1874- II. Brown, Arlo Ayres, 1883- III. Sheridan, Alma Stanley. IV. Thompson, William Joseph, 1804- V. Sheridan, Harold James.

LITTLEFIELD, Milton Smith, 1864- 268.
Hand-work in the Sunday-school, by Milton S. Littlefield. with an introduction by Patterson Du Bois. Philadelphia, The Sunday school times company [c1908] xvii, 162 p. incl. illus., maps. front., plates. 18 cm. [BV1536.L5] 8-19114
1. Sunday-schools. I. Title.

LLOYD, Mary Edna. 268.432
Nursery class teaching; religious guidance [by] Mary Edna Lloyd; edited by Lucius H. Bugbee. New York, Cincinnati [etc.] The Methodist book concern [c1934] 192 p. 21 cm. Music: p. 167-178. [BV1540.L5] 34-29171
1. Sunday-schools. 2. Nursery schools. I. Bugbee, Lucius Hatfield, 1874- ed. II. Title.

LOBINGIER, John Leslie, 1884- 268
The better church school. Boston, Pilgrim Press [1952] 152 p. 21 cm. [BV1520.L58] 52-1583
1. Sunday schools. 2. Religious education. I. Title.

LONDON, Allie Spencer. 268
The Sunday school challenge. Butler, Ind., Higley Press [1958] 157p. 20cm. [BV1520.L65] 58-1555
1. Sunday-schools. I. Title.

MCCAFFERTY, Florence. 268.
How to conduct a primary department; a manual for the use of primary workers in the Sunday school, by Florence McCafferty. Cincinnati, The Standard publishing company [c1919] 225 p. illus. 13 x 7 cm. [BV1540.M3] 19-9454
1. Sunday-schools. I. Title.

MCCALLUM, Eva Beatrice (McNown) Mrs., 1892- 268.432
Guiding nursery children in home and church (successor to the author's The nursery class of the church school) procedures, stories, songs, and verses [by] Eva B. McCallum. St. Louis, The Bethany press [c1934] 240 p. 26 cm. Music: p. 221-227. Bibliography: p. 288-240. [BV1540.M3 1934] 34-29161
1. Sunday-schools. 2. Nursery schools. I. Title.

MCCALLUM, William Cecil. 268
The graded church, by W. C. McCallum ... St. Louis, Mo., The Bethany press [c1930] 144 p. illus. (plans) diagrs. 19 1/2 cm. "Helpful reference materials": p. 140-144. [BV1520.M25] 30-8910
1. Sunday-schools. 2. Religious education. I. Title.

MCCONAUGHY, James, 1857- 268
... Sunday-school teaching and management; a first standard training course for Sunday-school workers and older pupils especially in smaller schools, by James McConaughy...with the co-operation of James L. McConaughy... and Harry Edwards Bartow... Philadelphia, American Sunday-school union [c1916] 199 p. 18 cm. (Green fund book no. 21) "Books for use with this course of study": p. [197]-199. [BV1520.M3] 16-20889
1. Sunday schools. I. McConaughy, James Lukens, 1887- II. Bartow, Harry Edwards. III. Title.

MCCRAW, Mildred C 268.4
The extension department; lifting through love. Nashville, Convention Press [1958] 150p. illus. 19cm. [BV1523.M3 1958] 59-3674
1. Sunday-schools. I. Title.

MCCRAW, Mildred C 268.422
The extension department; lifting through love. Nashville, Broadman Press [1952] 146 p. illus. 20 cm. [BV1523.M3] 52-11929
1. Sunday-schools I. Title.

MCCRAW, Mildred C 268.435
The teaching ministry of the extension visitor. Nashville, Convention Press [1959] 141p. 19cm. [BV1523.M33] 59-7079
1. Sunday-schools. I. Title.

MCELFRESH, Franklin.
...The training of Sunday school teachers and officers, by Franklin McElfresh... New York, Eaton & Mains; Cincinnati, Jennings & Graham [c1914] iii, 230 p. 19 cm. (Modern Sunday school manuals) "List of books approved by International committee on education": p. 220-230. [BV1530.M3] 14-7732
1. Sunday-schools. I. Title.

MCENTIRE, Ralph N. 268
The Sunday school secretary, by Ralph N. McEntire. New York, Cincinnati, The Methodist book concern [c1917] 152 p. illus. (illus. forms.) fold. charts. 20 cm. [BV1532.M3] 17-15561
I. Title.

*MC INTYRE, Ralph L. 268
Big ideas for small sunday schools / by Ralph L.McIntyre Grand Rapids : Baker Book House, 1976c1975. 61.p ; 20 cm. (Teaching helps series) [BV 1521] ISBN 0-8010-6005-2 pbk. : 1.50.
1. Sunday-schools. I. Title.

MCKEEVER, William Arch, 1868- 268.
...How to become an efficient Sunday school teacher, by William A. McKeever... Cincinnati, The Standard publishing company [c1915] 236 p. 19 1/2 cm. (Phillips Bible institute series of efficiency text-books for Bible schools and churches) [BV1534.M2] 15-27907
1. Sunday-schools. I. Title.

MCNATT, Elmer E 1908- 268
The Pentecostal Sunday school. [Nashville? 1952] 201p. illus. 20cm. On spine: A Sunday school concordance. [BX3795.P25M32] 53-19913
1. Sunday-schools. 2. United Pentecostal Church—Education. I. Title. II. Title: A Sunday school concordance.

MCNAUGHTON, Jeannette A. Mrs. 268.
Our junior department, by Jeannette A. McNaughton. Philadelphia, Boston [etc.] The Judson press [c1921] 108 p. 19 cm. (Half-title: Judson training manuals for the school of the church) [BV1546.M36] 22-1725
1. Sunday-schools. I. Title.

MALEHORN, Hal, 1930- 268
Over 200 ways to improve your Sunday school / by Harold Malehorn. St. Louis, MO : Concordia Pub. House, c1982. 61 p. ; 28 cm. [BV1521.M25 1982] 19 81-22101 ISBN 0-570-03857-X (pbk.) : 5.95
1. Sunday-schools. I. Title. II. Title: Over two hundred ways to improve your Sunday school.

MARQUIS, John Abner, 1861- 268.
Learning to teach from the Master teacher, by John A. Marquis ... Philadelphia, The Westminster press, 1913. x, 79 p. 19 cm. [BV1534.M35] 13-17328
1. Sunday-schools. 2. Religious education. I. Title.

MARRINAN, John J.
The children and religion, by John J. Marrinan ... [Worcester, Mass., 1913] cover-title, p. [229]-235. 23 cm. Reprinted from the Pedagogical seminary June, 1913, vol. xx. [LC381.M34] E 13
1. Sunday schools. 2. Religious education. I. Title.

MARTIN, Albert William, 1891- 268.
Worship in the Sunday school, for workers in small schools, by A. W. Martin ... Nashville, Tenn., Cokesbury press, 1930. 164 p. 19 cm. (Cokesbury series) Contains bibliographies. [BV1522.M3] 30-8387
1. Sunday-schools. 2. Worship (Religious education) I. Title.

MARTIN, Florence, 1904-
When they are nine to eleven; a junior guidance manual. Philadelphia, Board of Christian Education of the Presbyterian Church in the United States of America, 1950. vi, 68p. illus. 23cm. A53
1. Sunday-Schools. 2. Religious education of children. I. Title.

MEAD, George Whitefield, 1865- 268
Modern methods in Sunday-school work; the new evangelism, by Rev. George Whitefield Mead ... New York, Dodd, Mead and company, 1903. 3 p. l., v-xxiv, 376 p. illus. 20 cm. [BV1520.M38] 3-27915
1. Sunday-schools. I. Title.

METHODIST Episcopal church, South. General Sunday school board. 268.
Program of work B, for Sunday schools having seven organized departments and meeting in a building with at least six assembly rooms in addition to the church auditorium ... Nashville, Tenn., General Sunday school board, Methodist Episcopal church, South [c1929] 129 p. 23 cm. Leaflet no. 553. [BX8223.M4] 29-18638
1. Sunday-schools. I. Title.

METHODIST Episcopal church, South. General Sunday school board. 268.
Program of work C, for Sunday schools having four organized departments in addition to the Nursery department, and meeting in a building with at least three assembly rooms in addition to the church auditorium ... Nashville, Tenn., General Sunday school board, Methodist Episcopal

church, South [c1929] 82 p. 23 cm. "Leaflet no. 553." [BX8223.M4 2] 29-18903
1. Sunday-schools. I. Title.

MEYER, Henry Herman, 1874- 268
... The graded Sunday school in principle and practice, by Henry H. Meyer. New York, Eaton & Mains; Cincinnati, Jennings & Graham [c1910] viii, 241 p. 19 cm. (Modern Sunday school manuals) "Selected bibliography": p. 239-241. [BV1520.M4 1910] 10-11170
1. Sunday-schools. I. Title.

MEYER, Henry Herman, 1874- 268
... The graded Sunday school in principle and practice, by Henry H. Meyer. Rev. ed. New York, Eaton & Mains; Cincinnati, Jennings & Graham [c1912] x, 263 p. 19 cm. (Modern Sunday school manuals) "Selected bibliography": p. 261-263. [BV1520.M4 1912] 13-361
1. Sunday-schools. I. Title.

MEYER, Henry Herman, 1874-
The lesson handbook, a concise commentary on the International Sunday school lessons for the entire year based on the text of the American standard Bible, by Henry H. Meyer ... New York, Eaton & Mains; Cincinnati, Jennings & Graham v. illus. (map) 15 x 8 cm. (Berean series) Subtitle varies slightly. Editors: John T. McFarland. Imprint varies: 1907- New York, Eaton & Mains.--Cincinnati, Jennings & Graham.--1912- New York and Cincinnati, The Methodist book concern. 9-27356 0.25
I. Title.

MICHAEL, Oscar Stewart, 1864- 268.
The Sunday-school in the development of the American church, by the Rev. Oscar S. Michael ... Milwaukee, The Young churchman company, 1904. 298 p. 20 cm. [BX5870.M5] 4-34576
1. Sunday-schools. I. Title.

MIDDLETON, Edwin L.
Building a country Sunday school, by E. L. Middleton ... New York, Chicago [etc.] Fleming H. Revell company [c1923] 159 p. illus., plates, plans. 19 1/2 cm. [BX1555.M5] 23-10868
I. Title.

MILLER, Basil William, 1897- 268
Putting your church school across; blueprints for growing Sunday schools, by Basil Miller ... Grand Rapids, Mich., Zondervan publishing house [1942] 106 p. 20 cm. [BV1520.M46] 42-23502
1. Sunday schools. I. Title.

MILLER, Ernest Albert. 268
Making the old Sunday school new, by Ernest Albert Miller. New York, Cincinnati, The Methodist book concern [c1917] 100 p. 17 1/2 cm. [BV1520.M5] 17-23304
1. Sunday-schools. I. Title.

MILLER, T. Franklin 268
You can have a better Sunday school. Anderson. Ind., Warner Press [dist. Gospel Trumpet Press] [c.1960] 79p. 21cm. 60-13191 1.00 pap.,
1. Sunday-schools. I. Title.

MOORE, George Voiers, 1897- 268
Improving the small church school, by George Voiers Moore ... St. Louis, Mo., The Bethany press [c1932] 5 p. l., 172 p. 20 cm. "A selected bibliography": p. 168-172. [BV1520.M65] 32-30378
1. Sunday-schools. I. Title. II. Title: Church school, Improving the small.

MOORE, Jessie Eleanor. 268.432
Experiences in the church school kindergarten, by Jessie Eleanor Moore. Boston, Chicago, Printed for the Leadership training publishing association by the Pilgrim press [c1935] 1 p. l., v-x p., 1 l., 144 p. illus. (music) 20 cm. "Editor's introduction" signed: Mary Skinner, chairman. Editorial and educational section. "This book is a companion to 'Guiding kindergarten children in the church school', by Elizabeth McE. Shields."--Author's introd. Bibliography at end of each chapter. [BV1540.M6] 35-11048
1. Sunday-schools. 2. Kindergarten. I. Skinner, Mary Elizabeth, 1886- ed. II. Title.

MOORE, Mary Hunter. 268.37
They that be teachers, by Mary Hunter Moore. Nashville, Tenn., Southern publishing association [c1937] 209 p. 20 cm. "References" at end of each chapter. [BV1534.M6] 38-2318
1. Sunday-schools. I. Title.

MORSE, F. Harvey. 268.
The men's class in action, by F. Harvey Morse ... New York, George H. Doran company [c1923] xii p., 1 l., [15]-247 p. illus. (facsims, forms) 19 1/2cm. Bibliography at end of each chapter. [BV1550.M65] 28-8310
1. Sunday-schools. I. Title.

MORSE, F. Harvey. 268.
The women's class in action, by F. Harvey Morse ... illustrated with forms, advertisements, etc. New York, George H. Doran company [c1926] xiv p., 1 l., 17-298 p. incl. illus., forms. 19 1/2 cm. Bibliography at end of each chapter. [BV1550.M67] 26-19182
1. Sunday-schools. I. Title.

NATIONAL Sunday School Association. 268
Sunday school encyclopedia. Edited by Clate A. Risley. Chicago [19 v. illus., ports. 28cm. Includes bibliographies. [BV1521.N3] 61-770
1. Sunday-schools. I. Risley, Clate A., ed. II. Title.

NATIONAL Sunday-school convention of the United States. 4th, Newark, N. J., 1869.
The third [i. e. fourth] National Sunday-school convention of the United States. 1869. Pub. by authority of the Convention. Philadelphia, J. C. Garrigues & co.; New York, Broughton & Wyman; [etc., etc., 1869] 188 p. front. (port) 23 cm. 8-25621
I. Title.

NATIONAL Sunday-school convention of the United States. 5th, Indianapolis, 1872. 268.
The fifth National Sunday-school convention, held at Indinapolis, April 16, 17, 18, 19, 1872. With an historical introduction, by the Rev. H. Clay Trumbull. New York, Pub. for the Convention by A. O. Van Lennep, 1872. 2 p. l., [9]-159, xxviii p. 23 cm. After the 5th, the convention include Canada, and are entered under heading: International Sunday-school convention of the United States and British American provinces. [BV1505.N4 5th] ca 9
I. Trumbull, Henry Clay, 1830-1903. II. Title.

NEW York state Sunday school association.
Annual report. New York [etc.] v. 22 cm. Title varies: 18 -76, Proceedings of the ... annual convention of the New York state Sunday-school teachers' association ... [1871, "Statistical report" only] 1877- Annual report of the New York state Sunday school association, and the proceedings of the ... annual convention ... [BV1503.N4] CA 8
I. Title.

NO king in Israel;
or, The importance of discipline. By a Sabbath school teacher. Revised by the editor, D. P. Kidder. New York, G. Lane & C. B. Tippett, 1844. 1 p. l., [5]-54 p. 15 cm. [BJ163.N6] 24-22596
I. Kidder, Daniel Parish, 1815-1891, ed. II. Sabbath school teacher.

OLIVER, Charles Alexander. 262.
Preparation for teaching; a standard course for teacher training, by Charles A. Oliver; approved by the Committee on education of the International Sunday school association. Philadelphia, The Westminster press, 1909. x p., 1 l., 132 p., 1 l. illus. (maps, plan) 19 cm. "Reference books": leaf at end. [BV1533.O6] 9-14939
1. Sunday-schools. I. Title.

OLMSTEAD, William Backus, 1862- 268
Handbook for Sunday-school workers, by Rev. William B. Olmstead ... introduction by Rev. J. T. Logan. Chicago, W. B. Rose [c1907] 206 p. incl. tables. pl., maps. 19 cm. [BV1520.O6] 7-39387
1. Sunday-schools. 2. Bible—Study. I. Title.

OLSON, Ove Sigfrid, 1892- 268
... Administration of the church school, by Ove S. Olson ... Recommended by the Board of Chirstian education and literature of the Augustana synod. Rock Island, Ill., Augustana book concern [1943] 115 p. incl. diagrs. forms. 19 1/2 cm. (The Augustana teacher training course) Bibliography at end of each chapter except one. [BV1520.O63] 43-5023
1. Sunday-schools. I. Evangelical Lutheran Augustana synod of North America. Board of Christian education and literature. II. Title.

PALMER, Florence Ursula. 268.
One year of Sunday school lessons for young children; a manual for teachers and parents... by Florence U. Palmer. New York, The Macmillan company; London, Macmillan & co., 1900. xvi, 226 p. illus. (incl. music) pl. 21 cm. [BV1540.P3] 0-1046
1. Sunday-schools. I. Title.

PALMER, Florence Ursula. 268.
A second year of Sunday school lessons for young children; a manual for teachers and parents, presenting a series of lessons selected, arranged, and adapted for the use of young children, by Florence U. Palmer. New York, The Macmillan company, 1908. xiv, 259 p. front., illus. (incl. music) 20 1/2 cm. [BV1545.P3] 9-6578
1. Sunday-schools. 2. Religious education. I. Title.

PALMER, Leon Carlos, 1883- 266
Church school organization and administration, by Leon C. Palmer...with foreword by Gardiner L. Tucker... Milwaukee, Wis., Morehouse publishing co. [c1930] 5 p. l., 205, [1] p. 19 1/2 cm. Contains bibliographies. [BV1520.P33] 30-11929
1. Sunday-schools. I. Title.

PALMER, Lois Sedgwick. 268.
Lesson stories for the kindergarten grades of the Bible school; general subject: God the workman, the Creator and His works... by Lois Sedgwick Palmer, kindergartner, outline by Prof. George William Pease. New York, The Macmillan company, 1908. viii, 127 p. 18 cm. Half-title:...Grade A. Bibliography: p. 125-127. [BV1540.P35] 8-20328
I. Pease, George William, 1863-1905. II. Title. III. Title: Kindergarten grades of the Bible school.

PARDEE, Richard Gay, 1811-1869. 263
The Sabbath-school index. Pointing out the history and progress of Sunday-schools, with approved modes of instruction ... By R. G. Pardee, A.M. Philadelphia, J. C. Garrigues & co., 1868. 256 p. illus. (incl. map) 17 1/2 cm. "Helps for teachers": p. 251-254. [BV1520.P34] 42-48970
1. Sunday-schools. I. Title.

PARET, William, bp., 1826-
... The place and function of the Sunday school in the church, by the Rt. Rev. William Paret ... New York, T. Whittaker [c1906] 101 p. 19 cm. (The Reinicker lectures for 1906) 6-34266
I. Title.

PARET, William, bp., 1826-1911. 268
... The place and function of the Sunday school in the church, by the Rt. Rev. William Paret ... New York, T. Whittaker [1906] 1 p. l., 5-101 p. 19 cm. (The Reinicker lectures for 1906) [BX5870.P3] 6-34266
1. Sunday-schools. I. Title.

PATTISON, Thomas Harwood, 1838-1904. 268
The ministry of the Sunday-school, by T. Harwood Pattison ... Philadelphia, American Baptist publication society, 1902. viii p., 1 l., 264 p. 20 cm. [BV1520.P36] 2-14463
1. Sunday-schools. I. Title.

PAULSON, Donna.
God speaks in the Bible. Illus. by William K. Plummer. Gustav K. Wiencke, ed. Philadelphia Lutheran Church Press [c1965] 159 p. illus. 20 cm. (Lutheran church in America. Sunday church school ser. Pupil's reader. [Grade 6:] term 1) 67-57916
I. Wiencke, Gustav K., ed. II. Title. III. Series.

PEARCE, William Cliff, 1864- 268.
The adult Bible class, its organization and work, by W. C. Pearce ... Philadelphia, The Westminster press, 1908. 87 p. incl. front., forms. map. 19 cm. Music: p. 87. [BV1550.P4 1908] 8-34614
1. Sunday-schools. I. Title.

PEARCE, William Cliff, 1864- 268.
The adult Bible class, its organization and work, by W. C. Pearce ... Philadelphia, The Westminster press, 1912. 107 p. incl. front., illus. (forms) map. 19 cm. Contains music. [BV1550.P4 1912] 12-18451
1. Sunday-schools. I. Title.

PEASE, George William, 1863-1905. 268.
An outline of a Bible-school curriculum, by George William Pease ... Chicago, The University of Chicago press, 1904. xii, 418 p. 20 cm. Contains bibliographies. [BV1559.P4] 4-34926
1. Sunday-schools. 2. Bible—Study. I. Title. II. Title: Bible-school curriculum, An outline of a.

PELL, Edward Leigh, 1861- 268.
Secrets of Sunday-school teaching, by Edward Leigh Pell ... New York, Chicago [etc.] Fleming H. Revell company [c1912] 201 p. 20 cm. [BV1534.P43] 13-745
1. Sunday-schools. I. Title.

PELOUBET, Francis Nathan, 1831-1920. 268
The front line of the Sunday school movement; the line of the vanguard of Sunday school progress, with a glimpse of ideals beyond, by Rev. F. N. Peloubet ... Boston and Chicago, W. A. Wilde company [c1904] 287 p. illus. (plans) 20 cm. [BV1520.P4] 5-2410
1. Sunday-schools. I. Title.

PEPPER, John Robertson, 1850- 268.876
Well-nigh 50 years at the superintendent's desk, by John R. Pepper. [Memphis, Tenn., Press of Early-Freeburg co., 1929] 141, [1] p., 1 l., [9] p. front., (port.) illus., plates. 20 cm. [BX8223.P4] 31-9270
1. Sunday-schools. 2. Memphis. First Methodist Episcopal church. I. Title.

PERKINS, Jeanette Eloise, 1887- 268.6
Others call it God; a unit on how the world began, by Jeanette E. Perkins ... Enid Dearborn, teacher, Elizabeth Babcock, assistant; foreword by Frank W. Herriott. New York and London, Harper & brothers, 1934. xx, 141 p. plates. 20 cm. "First edition." Music: p. 113. Bibliography: p. 138-141. [BV1545.P36] 34-28594
1. Sunday-schools. 2. Education—Experimental methods. I. Dearborn, Enid (Williams) Mrs. 1895- II. Babcock, Elizabeth, Mrs. III. Title.

PETERS, Lewis Edwin. 268
A practical handbook on Sunday-school work, by Rev. L. E. Peters ... Philadelphia, American Baptist publication society, 1900. 128 p. 18 cm. [BV1520.P45] 0-3365
1. Sunday-schools. I. Title.

PHILLIPS, William Presley, 1882- 268.434
The adult department of the Sunday school [by] William P. Phillips ... Nashville, Tenn., Sunday school board of the Southern Baptist convention [1930] 244 p. illus. (plans, forms) 20 cm. [BV1550.P5] 32-9292
1. Sunday-schools. I. Title.

PHILLIPS, William Presley, 1882- 268.43
The adult department of the Sunday school [by] William P. Phillips ... Nashville, Tenn., The Sunday school board of the Southern Baptist convention [c1935] 137 p. 19 cm. "Editor's foreword" signed: P. E. Burroughs. [BV1550.P5 1935] 35-30036
1. Sunday-schools. I. Burroughs, Prince Emanuel, 1871- ed. II. Title.

PHILLIPS, William 268.433
Presley, 1882-
The young people's department of the Sunday school [by] William P. Phillips ... Nashville, Tenn., The Sunday school board of the Southern Baptist convention [c1936] 5 p. l., [11]-140 p. incl. forms. 19 cm. [BV1549.P5] 36-16374
1. Sunday-schools. I. Southern Baptist convention. Sunday school board. II. Title.

PLUMMER, L. Flora (Fait) 268
Mrs. 1862-
The soul winning teacher, by L. Flora Plummer ... New York [etc.] Fleming H. Revell company [c1934] 192 p. 19 1/2cm. [Name originally: Lorena Florence Fait] [BV1534.P6] 35-2125
1. Sunday-schools. I. Title.

PLUMMER, L. Flora (Fait) 268'.3
1862-1945.
The spirit of the teacher. Rev. and enl. by G. R. Nash. Takoma Park, Washington, Review and Herald Pub. Association [1967] 128 p. 22 cm. Bibliographical footnotes. [BV1534.P58 1967] 67-30827
1. Sunday-schools. 2. Teachers. I. Nash, Gerald R. II. Title.

PLUMMER, L. Flora (Fait) 268.371
Mrs. 1882-
The spirit of the teacher, by L. Flora Plummer ... Takoma Park, Washington, D.C., South Bend, Ind. [etc.] Review and herald publishing assn. [c1935] 118 p. incl. front. 20cm. Name originally: Lorena Florence Fait. [BV1534.P58] 35-22955
1. Sunday-schools. 2. Teachers. I. Title.

POWELL, Robert R 268
Improving your church school; C. A. Bowen, general editor. New York, Pub. for the Co-operative Pub. Assn. by Abingdon-Cokesbury Press [1949] 160 p. 19 cm. [BV1520.P62] 49-35350
1. Sunday-school. I. Title.

POWELL, T. W.
Easy keys for busy teachers, helps for Sunday school teachers and prayermeeting leaders. By T. W. Powell ... [Chicago. Ill., Messenger publishing company, c1917] 176 p. 16 cm. E 18
1. Sunday-schools. 2. Prayer-meetings. I. Title.

PROTESTANT Episcopal church in the U. S. A. New York (Diocese) Sunday school commission.
The Crypt conference on Sunday schools, held under the auspices of the Sunday school commission, diocese of New York, May, 1901. New York [etc.] Longmans, Green and co., 1901. vii, 104 p. 19 cm. 1-25637
I. Title.

PROTESTANT Episcopal church in the U.S.A. New York (Diocese) Sunday school commission.
The Crypt conference on Sunday schools, held under the auspices of the Sunday school commission, diocese of New York, May, 1901. New York [etc.] Longmans, Green and co., 1901. vii, 104 p. 18 1/2 cm. [BX5869.N7A3 1901] 1-25637
1. Sunday-school. I. Title.

RAFFETY, William Edward, 268.333
1876-
How to lead a Bible school; friendly talks with the superintendent, by W. Edward Raffety ... Cincinnati, O., The Standard publishing company [c1936] 182 p. 20 cm. [BV1520.R27] 37-691
1. Sunday-schools. I. Title.

RAFFETY, William Edward, 263
1876-
... The smaller Sunday school makes good, by W. Edward Raffety ... Philadelphia, American Sunday-School union [c1927] 332 p. diagrs. 20 cm. (Green fund book, no. 25) "Two hundred and fifty worth-while books for Sunday-school workers": p. 302-308. [BV1520.R3] 27-14871
1. Sunday-schools. I. Title.

REIN, Remus C 1905- 268
Building the Sunday School. St. Louis, Concordia Pub. House [1950] v., 116 p. 19 cm. Includes bibliographies. [BV1520.R4] 50-11974
1. Sunday-schools. I. Title.

REXROAT, Stephen. 268
The Sunday school' spirit / Stephen Rexroat. Springfield, Mo. : Gospel Pub. House, c1979. 127 p. ; 20 cm. [BV1521.R49] 79-51833 ISBN 0-88243-594-9 pbk. : 1.50
1. Sunday-schools. I. Title.

RICE, Edwin Wilbur, 1831- 268.
The Sunday-school movement, 1780-1917, and the American Sunday-school union, 1817-1917, by Edwin Wilbur Rice ... Philadelphia, American Sunday-school union [c1917] 101 p. pl., ports. 22 cm. [BV1515.R5] 17-14395
1. Sunday-schools. 2. American Sunday-school union. I. Title.

RICE, Kenneth S 268.4
The department supervisor. Kansas City, Mo., Beacon Hill Press [1955] 124p. illus. 20cm. [BV1532] 55-14616
1. Sunday-schools. I. Title.

RICHTER, J. S. 232.
Sunday school sermonettes; a three years' course of brief and practical instructions on Catholic doctrine and practice, by Canon J. S. Richter. New York, Joseph F. Wagner, inc.; [etc., etc.] c1919. 3 p. l., 426 p. 21 1/2 cm. $2.00 [BX1754.R5] 20-1896
I. Title.

RINGLAND, Mabel Crews. 244
Tested methods for teachers of juniors, by Mabel Crews Ringland; introduction by Rev. Frank Langford ... New York, Chicago [etc.] Fleming H. Revell company [c1924] 155 p. 19 cm. [BV1546.R5] 24-23815
1. Sunday-schools. I. Title.

ROADS, Charles, 1855- 263
Problemas y metodes de la escuela dominical, por Charles Roads ... New York, Eaton & Mains; Cincinnati, Jennings & Graham [1911] 92 p. 1 l. 17 1/2 cm. [BV1520.R6] 11-20918
1. Sunday-schools. I. Title.

ROADS, Charles, 1855- 263
Sunday-school organization and methods, by Chas. Roads ... introduction by Rev. Charles J. Little ... Cincinnati, Jennings and Graham; New York, Eaton and Mains [1905] 110 p. 18 cm. [BV1520.R64] 5-9281
1. Sunday-schools. I. Little, Charles Joseph, 1840-1911. II. Title.

[ROGERS, William Osgood] 1874-
Boy's-eye views of the Sunday-school, by Pucker [pseud.] Philadelphia, The Sunday school times company [c1908] 4 p. l., 110 p. illus. 18 1/2 cm. Reprinted from the Worker. 9-35059
I. Title.

RUSSELL, James Elmer, 1872- 268
The up-to-date Sunday school, its organization and administration, by J. Elmer Russell ... New York [etc.] Fleming H. Revell company [c1932] 244 p. front. 20 cm. "For further reading" at the end of each chapter. [BV1520.R8] 32-12710
1. Sunday-schools. 2. Religious education. I. Title.

RUSSELL, Reginald Charles.
Sunday schools in Lindsey; the miserable compromise of the Sunday school. [Lindsey, Lindsey County Council Education Committee, 1965] 92 p. (His A history of schools & education in Lindsey, Lincolnshire, 1800-1902, 2) 68-19026
1. Sunday schools. I. Title.

SANDERSON, Leonard, 1914- 268
Using the Sunday school in evangelism. Vashville, Convention Press [1958] 146p. illus. 20cm. [BV1523.S2] 58-9944
1. Sunday schools. 2. Evangelistic work. I. Title.

SCHAAL, John H. 268'.6
Feed my sheep; a manual for Sunday school teachers, superintendents, and leaders. Compiled and edited by John H. Schaal. Grand Rapids, Baker Book House [1972] 162 p. 21 cm. Includes bibliographies. [BV1521.S3] 72-85717 ISBN 0-8010-7958-6 1.95
1. Sunday-schools. 2. Christian education. I. Title.

SCHAUFFLER, A[dolphus]
F[rederick] 1845- ed.
Practical helps for Sunday-school scholars, especially designed for the Scriptural education and religious nurture of the young, and to promote more regular, profitable and enjoyable use of the Bible in the home, in the Sunday school and in all young people's societies. Ed. by A. F. Schauffler ... New York, T. Nelson & sons [1902] 64 p. illus., maps. 14 1/2 cm. 2-13664
1. Sunday schools. I. Title.

SCHAUFFLER, Adolphus 268
Frederick, 1845-1919.
Pastoral leadership of Sunday school forces ... [by] A. F. Schauffler ... Nashville, Tenn., Sunday school board, Southern Baptist convention [1903] 176 p. front. (port.) diagrs. 19 cm. (Sunday school board seminary lectures, course no. 2) Delivered at the Southern Baptist theological seminary, Louisville, Ky., December, 1902. [BV1520.S27] 3-9563
1. Sunday-schools. I. Title.

SCHAUFFLER, Adolphus 268
Frederick, 1845-1919.
The teacher, the child and the Book; or, Practical suggestions and methods for Sunday-school workers. By A. F. Schauffler ... with a foreword by the late Dwight L. Moody. Boston and Chicago, W. A. Wilde company [1901] ix, 283 p. illus. 20 cm. [BV1520.S33] 2-14694
1. Sunday-schools. 2. Bible—Study. I. Title.

SCHAUFFLER, Adolphus 263
Frederick, 1845-1919.
Ways of working; or, Helpful hints for Sunday school officers and teachers. By A. F. Schauffler ... Boston, W. A. Wilde and company [1895] 212 p. illus. 20 cm. [BV1520.S35 1895] 42-40827
1. Sunday-schools. I. Title.

SCHAUFFLER, Adolphus 263
Frederick, 1845-1919.
Ways of working; or, Helpful hints for Sunday school officers and teachers. By A. F. Schauffler ... New and rev. ed. Boston and Chicago, W. A. Wilde company [1912] 238 p. illus. 20 cm. [BV1520.S35 1912] 42-40826
1. Sunday-schools. I. Title.

SCHMAUK, Theodore Emanuel, 268.
1860-1920.
... How to teach in Sunday-school, by Theodore E. Schmauk ... Philadelphia, The United Lutheran publication house [1920] x, 11-296 p. 20 cm. (Teacher-training handbook) [BV1534.S35] 20-3582
1. Sunday-schools. I. Title.

SENSABAUGH, Leonidas 268
Franklin, 1879-
...The small Sunday school, its plans and work, by I. L. Sensabaugh; approved by the Committee on curriculum of the General Sunday school board of the Methodist Episcopal church, South, as a text-book for Cokesbury training schools. Nashville, Tenne., Cokesbury press, 1924. 136 p. illus. (incl. plans) 19 1/2 cm. (Cokesbury training course, E. B. Chappell, editor) [BV1520.S4] 25-4304
1. Sunday-schools. I. Title.

SENSABAUGH, Leonidas 268.1
Franklin, 1879-
... The small Sunday school its plans and works, by L. F. Sensabaugh. Approved by the Committee on curriculum of the General Sunday school board of the Methodist Episcopal church, South, as a text-book for Cokesbury training schools. Nashville, Tenn., Cokesbury press, 1925. 136 p. illus. (incl. plans) 19 1/2 cm. (Cokesbury training course, E. B. Chappell, editor) [BV1520.S4 1925] 25-5236
1. Sunday-schools. I. Title.

SENSABAUGH, Leonidas Franklin,
1879-
...The Sunday school worker; his life and work, by L. F. Sensabaugh... Nashville, Tenn., Cokesbury press, 1926. 170 p. 19 1/2 cm. (Cokesbury training course, K. B. Chappell, editor) [BV1530.S4] 26-11927
1. Sunday-schools. I. Title.

SEXTON, Ida.
Manual work for use in Sunday schools, prepared by Ida Sexton, with foreword by the Rev. William Walter Smith... Milwaukee, The Young churchman co., 1910. vi p., 1 l., 132 p. illus. 19 1/2 cm. 10-13319
I. Smith, William Walter. II. Title.

SHAVER, Erwin Leander, 268.6
1890-
100 ways to improve your Sunday school teaching, by Erwin L. Shaver ... Elgin, Ill., David C. Cook publishing company [c1942] 4 p. l., 112 p. 19 1/2 cm. Bibliography: p. 111-112. [BV1534.S433] 44-2632
1. Sunday-schools. 2. Religious education—Teaching methods. I. Title. II. Title: Sunday school teaching.

SHAVER, Erwin Leander, 1890- 262.
Teaching adolescents in the church school; a plan-book for training leaders of youth, based on the project principle, by Erwin L. Shaver ... with an introductory note by Professor George A. Coe ... New York, George H. Doran company [c1928] xiv p., 1 l., 17-173 p. 19 1/2 cm. "General bibliography": p. 163-170. [BV1533.S47] 23-8308
1. Sunday-schools. 2. Religious education. I. Title.

SHEPHERD, Robert Perry, 262.
1867-
The teacher-training handbook revised. First standard teacher-training course [by] Robert Perry Shepherd [and] Marion Stevenson. St. Louis, Mo., Christian publishing company, 1910. 194 p. 19 cm. [BV1533.S5 1910] 11-3
1. Sunday-schools. I. Stevenson, Marion, 1861- joint author. II. Title.

SHOWALTER, J. Henry,
The song service for Sunday schools and revival meetings (no. i) Boaz, Ala., The Normal pub. co.; West Milton, O., The J. H. Showalter co. [etc. 1900] 112 p. 8°. May
I. Mosley, T. B. and II. Perry, S. J. III. Title.

SILVEY, D. O. 268
The enlisting Sunday school. Little Rock, Ark., Baptist Pubns. Comm. [c.1963] c108p. diagr. 21cm. 63-21458 1.00 pap.,
1. Sunday-chools. I. Title.

SILVEY, D O 268
The enlisting Sunday school. Little Rock, Ark., Baptist Publications Committee [c1963] 108 p. diagr. 21 cm. [BV1521.S5] 63-21458
1. Sunday-schools. I. Title.

SKINNER, Mary Elizabeth, 268
1886-
Children's work in the church, for the church without separate departments, by Mary E. Skinner; C. A. Bowen, D.D., general editor. Nashville, Tenn., Cokesbury press [c1932] 186 p. incl. illus. 19 cm. "Additional material for parents and teachers": p. 185-186. [BV1555.S5] 32-21102
1. Sunday-schools. 2. Rural churches. I. Bowen, Cawthon Asbury, 1885- II. Title.

SLATTERY, Margaret. 262.
Talks with the training class, by Margaret Slattery; introduction by Patterson Du Bois. Boston, New York [etc.] The Pilgrim press, 1906. x, [3], 84 p. 19 1/2 cm. "Reference books": 1 p. following p. x. [BV1533.S63] 6-15716
1. Sunday-schools. I. Title.

SLATTERY, Margaret. 268.
The teacher's candlestick, by Margaret Slattery. Cleveland, O., F. M. Barton company, 1909. 2 p.l., 7-53 p. 19 cm. [BV1534.S6] 9-20217
1. Sunday-schools. I. Title.

SMITH, Irene Catherine. 268
Solving church school problems, by Irene Catherine Smith. Anderson, Ind., The Warner press [1944] vi, 7-128 p. incl. forms, diagrs. 19 cm. "For further study" at end of each chapter. [BV1520.S64] 44-44878
1. Sunday-schools. I. Title.

SMITH, Una (Riddick) Mrs. 268.432
The junior department of the church school, by Una Riddick Smith. [Nashville] Printed for the Leadership training association by the Cokesbury press [c1934]

231 p. 18 cm. "Editor's introduction" signed: Erwin L. shaver, chariman, Editoral and educational section. Bibliography at end of each chapter; "Helpful books for the junior workers' library": p. 230. [BV1546.S57] 34-12015
1. Sunday-schools. 2. Religious education—Teaching methods. I. Shaver, Erwin Leander, 1890- ed. II. Title.

SMITH, William Walter.
The Sunday-school of to-day; a compendium of hints for superintendents and pastors, by the Rev. Wm. Walter Smith ... with a special chapter on Sunday-school architecture by Charles William Stoughton, A. I. A. and an introduction by the Rev. Lester Brander ... New York, Chicago [etc.] Fleming H. Revell company [c1911] 3 p. l., 5-230 p. illus. (incl. plans) plates, fold. chart. 22 cm. p$1.25 "A short bibliography for readers": p. 224-225. 12-4162
I. Stoughton, Charles William. II. Title.

SOMERNDIKE, John Mason, 1877- 377.
By-products of the rural Sunday school, by J.M. Somerndike... Philadelphia, The Westminster press, 1914. vi, 169 p. plates. 19 1/2 cm. $0.60. [BV1555.S6] 15-5868
I. Title.

SOMERNDIKE, John Mason, 1877- 268
The Sunday school in town and country, by John M. Somerndike. Philadelphia, The Westminster press, 1924. 151 p. illus., diagrs. 20 1/2 cm. "Sunday school workers' library": p. 148-151. [BV1520.S7] 24-14390
1. Sunday-schools. I. Title.

STRICKLAND, Hazel N. 268
Beginner Sunday school work, by Hazel N. Strickland and Mattie C. Leatherwood. Nashville, Tenn., The Sunday school board of the Southern Baptist convention [1943] 152 p. 19 cm. [BV1540.S75] 44-2045
1. Sunday-schools. 2. Religious education of pre-school children. I. Leatherwood, Mattie C., joint author. II. Southern Baptist convention. Sunday School board. III. Title.

STUART, George Wilse, 1911- 268'.8'6132
A guide to Sunday School enlargement. George W. Stuart, comp. Nashville, Convention Press [1968] x, 142 p. 20 cm. "Church study course [of the Sunday School Board of the Southern Baptist Convention] This book is number 1734 in category 17, section for adults and young people." Bibliographical footnotes. [BV1521.S7] 68-28773
1. Sunday-schools. I. Southern Baptist Convention. Sunday School Board. II. Title.

STUART, George Wilse, 1911- 268'.8'6132
A guide to Sunday School enlargement. George W. Stuart, compiler. [Rev.] Nashville, Convention Press [1970] vii, 134 p. illus. 20 cm. "New church study course [of the Sunday School Board of the Southern Baptist Convention] ... number 6311 in Subject area 63, Bible teaching program." Includes bibliographical references. [BV1521.S7 1970] 77-21036
1. Sunday-schools. I. Southern Baptist Convention. Sunday School Board. II. Title.

SUDLOW, Elizabeth Williams, Mrs. 268.
Primary plans for the smaller Sunday school, by Elizabeth Williams Sudlow ... Philadelphia, The Union press [c1928] 167 p. plates. 17 cm. "Some helpful books for primary workers": p. 165-166. [BV1545.S85] 28-24040
1. Sunday-schools. I. Title.

SUDLOW, Elizabeth Williams, Mrs. 268.432
Sunday school babies, how-to-do-it plans for cradle roll workers, by Elizabeth Williams Sudlow. Elgin, Ill., David C. Cook publishing company [c1929] 80 p. illus. 18 cm. [BV1537.S82] 30-9421
I. Title.

SUDLOW, Elizabeth (Williams) 1878- 268.
All about the primary, by Elizabeth Williams Sudlow. Milwaukee, Wis., Hammond publishing co., 1909. 141 p. 15 1/2 cm. [BV1545.S8 1909] 9-30421
1. Sunday-schools. 2. Religious education of children. I. Title.

SUDLOW, Elizabeth (Williams) 1878- 268.432
All about the primary, by Elizabeth Williams Sudlow. [Milwaukee, c1932] 137 p. 15 cm. "Revised edition." Bibliography: p. 27-28. [BV1545.S8 1932] 32-13149
1. Sunday-schools. 2. Religious education of children. I. Title.

SUNDAY school times. 268.
... Preparing and teaching the lesson. The two prize winners: "How I prepare my lesson for teaching", by Mrs. G. A. Stead; "How I teach the lesson in class", by Miss N. Grace Cooledge together with selections from twenty-one other articles offered in the competition. Philadelphia, The Sunday school times company [c1923] 1 p. l., 5-130 p. 20 cm. At head of title: The Sunday school times prize contest articles. [BV1534.S87] 24-1277
1. Sunday-schools. I. Stead, Mrs. G. A. II. Cooledge, N. Grace. III. Title. IV. Title: The Sunday school times prize contest articles.

THE Superintendent's almanac 268.
for ... a manual for the Bible school superintendent ... Cincinnati, O., The Standard publishing company [c1928- v. illus. 23 cm. Editors: 1928- E. R. Errett, G. P. Leavitt. [BV1531.S7] 28-2835
1. Sunday-schools. I. Errett, Edwin R., ed. II. Leavitt, Guy P., joint ed.

THE superintendent's guide 268.
for Sunday school year aim, means, program ... St. Louis, Mo., Christian board of publication [c192 v. 16 cm. Editors: Ida M. Irvin. [BV1531.S75] 21-15728
1. Sunday-schools. I. Irvin, Ida M., ed.

SUTHERLAND, Angelyn B 268
How to run a Sunday school. [Westwood, N.J.] Revell [1956] 160 p. 20 cm. [BV1520.S83] 56-10897
1. Sunday-schools. I. Title.

SWANSON, Lawrence F 268
Build an approved Sunday Bible school. Chicago, Baptist Conference Press [c1957] 167 p. illus. 20 cm. Includes bibliography. [BV1520.S88] 57-14491
1. Sunday-schools. I. Title.

THE teacher and the class;
a symposium on Sunday-school teaching. New York, Chicago [etc.] F. H. Revell company [c1895] 1 p. l., 5-130 p. 17 1/2 cm. E 13
1. Sunday schools.
Contents omitted.

THOMAS, Marion. 268.
... The primary worker and work, by Marion Thomas. New York, Cincinnati, The Abingdon press [c1920] 160 p. 17 cm. (The worker and work series, H. H. Meyer, editor) [BV1545.T57] 20-3807
1. Sunday-schools. I. Title.

THORNTON, Edwin William, 1863- 268.6
How to teach, by E. W. Thornton; revised by C. J. Sharp. Cincinnati, O., The Standard publishing company [c1943] 128 p. diagrs. 19 cm. "Revision (and condensation) of the book formerly entitled 'Common sense'." --Foreword. "Helpful books" at end of some of the chapters. [BV1534.T472] 44-23925
1. Sunday-schools. 2. Religious education—Teaching methods. I. Sharp, Cecil James, 1876- II. Title.

TIBBITTS, Fred Lyman, 1892- 268.4
Platooning the church school, by F. Lyman Tibbitts, Ed. Tulsa, Okla., Burkhart press [c1934] 3 p. l., 5-86 p. diagrs. 20 1/2 cm. [BV1520.T5] 35-8398
1. Sunday-schools. 2. Platoon schools. I. Title.

TODD, John, 1800-1873. 263
The Sabbath school teacher: designed to aid in elevating and perfecting the Sabbath school system. By Rev. John Todd... Northampton, J. H. Butler; Philadelphia, W. Marshall & co.; [etc., etc.] 1837. xiii, 15-432 p. 19 cm. [BV1520.T6 1837] 24-16993
1. Sunday-schools. 2. Religious education. I. Title.

TODD, John, 1800-1873. 263
The Sabbath school teacher; designed to aid in elevating and perfecting the Sabbath school system, by John Todd...Author's ed. Northampton [Mass.] Bridgman and Childs, 1869. 336 p. front. (port.) 19 1/2 cm. [BV1520.T6 1869] 24-19610
1. Sunday-schools. 2. Religious education. I. Title.

TOWNER, Walter 268
Guiding a church school. Nashville, Abingdon [c.1961, 1963] 192p. 23cm. 63-19032 2.00 pap.,
1. Sunday-schools. I. Title.

TOWNER, Walter. 268
Guiding a church school. New York, Abingdon Press [1963] 192 p. 23 cm. [BV1521.T6] 63-19032
1. Sunday-schools. I. Title.

TOWNS, Elmer L. 268
How to grow an effective Sunday school / Elmer L. Towns. Denver, Colo. : Accent Books, c1979. 160 p. ; 19 cm. (Accent teacher training series) Includes bibliographies. [BV1521.T626] 79-51836 ISBN 0-89636-028-8 pbk. : 3.95.
1. Sunday-schools. 2. Sunday-schools—Growth. I. Title. II. Series.

TOWNS, Elmer L. 268
The successful Sunday school and teachers guidebook / Elmer Towns. Carol Stream, Ill. : Creation House, 1976. 400 p. : ill. ; 24 cm. Includes index. [BV1521.T628 1976] 75-23009 ISBN 0-88419-118-4 pbk. : 6.95
1. Sunday-schools. 2. Christian education. I. Title.

TRAINING the teacher, 262.
by A. F. Schauffler, D.D., Antoinette Abernethy Lamoreaux, Martin G. Brumbaugh, PH.D., LL.D., Marion Lawrence; supplementary chapters by Charles A. Oliver, Ira Maurice Price, PH.D. Approved as a first standard course by the Committee on education, International Sunday school association. Philadelphia, The Sunday school times company [c1908] iii, 5-272 p. illus. (maps) 18 cm. Title within line border. [BV1533.T73] 8-29858
1. Sunday-schools. 2. Bible—Study. I. Schauffler, Adolphus Frederick, 1845-1919. II. Lamoreaux, Antoinette Abernethy, III. III. Brumbaugh, Martin Grove, 1862-1930. IV. Lawrance, Marion, 1850-1924.

TRUMBULL, Henry Clay, 1830-1903.
The origin and expansion of the Sunday-school, by H. Clay Trumbull. Being an excerpt from "Yale lectures on the Sunday-school" by the same author. Philadelphia, The Sunday school times co., 1906. 2 p. l., 3-142 p. 20 cm. 6-23285
I. Title.

TRUMBULL, Henry Clay, 1830-1903. 268
...The Sunday-school; its origin, mission, methods, and auxiliaries ... By H. Clay Trumbull ... Philadelphia, J. D. Wattles, 1893. xiii, 415 p. incl. front. (facism) 21 1/2 cm. (The Lyman Beecher lectures before Yale divinity school for 1888) At head of title: Yale lectures on the Sunday-school. "Bibliographical index": p. 381-392. [BV1520.T7 1893] 39-5818
1. Sunday-schools. 2. Preaching. 3. Theology, Pastoral. I. Title. II. Title: Yale lectures on the Sunday-school.

TRUMBULL, Henry Clay, 1830-1903. 268.6
When do teachers teach? [By] H. Clay Trumbull and Doak S. Campbell, PH.D. Nashville, Tenn., The Sunday school board of the Southern Baptist convention [c1934] 100 p. 19 cm. A revised and abridged edition of "Teaching and teachers" by H. C. Trumbull, originally published in 1884. A discussion of teaching in the Sunday-school. of. Foreword. [BV1534.T76] 34-34764
1. Sunday-schools. 2. Teaching. I. Campbell, Doak Sheridan, 1888- ed. II. Title.

TYNG, Stephen Higginson, 1800-1885.
Forty years' experience in Sunday-schools. By Stephen H. Tyng ... New-York, Sheldon & company. Boston, Gould & Lincoln, 1860. vi, [7]-251 p. 17 cm. E 10
1. Sunday-schools. I. Title.

VAN ZYL, Henry, 1883- 268.6
Some vital aspects of teaching in Sunday schools, by Henry van Zyl, jr. ... Zeeland, Mich., Instructor publishing house, 1935. xv p., 1 l., 118 p. 1 illus., plates. diagrs. 23 1/2 cm. "Orientation in Sunday school literature": p. 1-30. [BV1534.V3] 36-6354
1. Sunday schools. I. Title.

VIETH, Paul Herman, 1895- 268
The church school: the organization, administration, and supervision of Christian education in the local church. Philadelphia, Christian Education Press [c1957] 179 p. illus. 22 cm. [BV1520.V45] 57-14607
1. Sunday-schools. I. Title.

VIETH, Paul Herman, 1895- 268
Improving your Sunday school; practical suggestions for superintendents, pastors, and others whose duty it is to supervise the teaching of religion in the local church, by Paul H. Vieth ... Philadelphia, The Westminster press, 1930. 184 p. illus., diagr. 17 1/2 cm. (On cover: Handybooks for church school leaders) [BV1520.V46] 30-17428
1. Sunday-schools. I. Title.

VINCENT, John Heyl, bp., 1832-
The church school and the Sunday-school normal guide, by John H. Vincent. New York, Hunt & Eaton. Cincinnati, Cranston & Stowe. 410 p., 1 l. 19 cm. E 15
1. Sunday schools. 2. [Sunday schools—Teaching] I. Title.

VINCENT, John Heyl, bp., 1832-1920. 268
The church school and its officers. by J. H. Vincent ... New York, Carlton & Lanahan. Cincinnati, Hitchcock & Walden; [etc., etc., 1872] 224 p. 17 cm. [BV1520.V5 1872] 40-37719
1. Sunday-schools. I. Title.

VINCENT, John Heyl, bp., 1832-1920. 268
... The church school and its officers. By J. H. Vincent ... New York, Phillips & Hunt. Cincinnati, Cranston & Stowe, 1886. 224 p. 16 1/2 cm. At head of title: Chautauqua assembly normal union. [BV1520.V5 1886] 40-37720
1. Sunday-schools. I. Title.

VINCENT, John Heyl, bp., 1832-1920. 268
The modern Sunday-school. By John H. Vincent. New York, Phillips & Hunt. Cincinnati, Cranston & Stowe, 1887. 344 p. 19 1/2 cm. [BV1520.V55 1887] 1-5711
1. Sunday-schools. I. Title.

VINCENT, John Heyl, bp., 1832-1920. 268
The modern Sunday-school, by John H. Vincent. Rev. ed. New York, Eaton & Mains. Cincinnati, Jennings & Pye [c1900] 357 p. 19 cm. Contains music. [BV1520.V55 1900] 0-6126
1. Sunday-schools. I. Title.

VINCENT, John Heyl, bp., 1832-1920. 268.07
Sunday-school institutes and normal classes. By J. H. Vincent. With an introduction by Alfred Taylor ... New York, Carlton & Lanahan. San Francisco, E. Thomas; [etc., etc., 1872] 1 p. l., 186 p. 19 cm. [BV1533.V55] 40-37724
1. Sunday-schools. 2. Religious education—Teacher training. I. Title.

WALDEN, Treadwell, 1830- 264.
The Sunday school prayer book. By Treadwell Walden ... New and rev. ed. Boston, E. P. Dutton and company, 1866. 2 p. l., [iii]-vii, 8-83 p. 17 cm. With this is bound The Sunday school chant and tune book ... Boston, 1866. [BX5873.W3 1866] 27-490
1. Sunday-schools. 2. Protestant Espicopal church in the U.S.A. Book of common prayer. I. Title.

WALTERS, Orville Selkirk, 1903- 268
Christian education in the local church [by] Orville S. Walters ... Winona Lake, Ind., Light and life press [c1939] 75 p. 19

cm. "Books for supplementary reading": p. 74-75. [BV1520.W28] 41-5572
1. Sunday-schools. I. Title.

WARDLE, Addie Grace.
History of the Sunday school movement in the Methodist Episcopal church, by Addie Grace Wardle. New York, Cincinnati, The Methodist book concern [c1918- 232 p. 23 1/2 cm. Bibliography: p. 223-225. [BX8221.W3] 18-10545
1. Sunday-schools. 2. Methodist Episcopal church. I. Title.

WARREN, Mary Sherburne. 268.432
Ways of working in the nursery department, by Mary Sherburne Warren. St. Louis, Mo., The Bethany press [c1932] viii p., 1 l., 76 p. 19 1/2 cm. Bibliography: p. 75-78. [BV1540.W3] 32-31016
1. Sunday-schools. I. Title. II. Title: The nursery department. Ways of working in.

WASHBURN, Alphonso V. 268'.1
Administering the Bible teaching program; Sunday school work, by A. V. Washburn and Melva Cook. Nashville, Convention Press [1969] x, 128 p. 20 cm. "This book is the text for course 6301 in the subject area Bible teaching program of the new church study course." [BS600.2.W33] 71-79195
1. Bible—Study. 2. Sunday-schools. I. Cook, Melva, joint author. II. Title.

WASHBURN, Alphonso V., 268'86'132 comp.
The Sunday School at work, 1966-67 Nashville, Convention Press. v. in 19 cm. annual. (Vols. for 1968/69- issued as series: Crusade of the Americas resource.) Vols. for 1968/69- issued in different editions, e. g. Adult, extension, cradle roll workers' edition. Compiler: 1966/67- A. V. Washburn. [BX6223.S85] 68-25544
1. Sunday-schools. 2. Southern Baptist Convention—Education. I. Title. II. Series: Crusade of the Americas resource

WASHBURN, Alphonso V. 268.86132 comp.
The Sunday school at work, 1966-67. Compiler: A. V. Washburn. Nashville, Convention Press [1966] x, 134 p. 20 cm. "Church study course [of the Sunday School Board of the Southern Baptist Convention] This book is number 1730 in category 17, section for adults and young people." Includes bibliographical references. [BX6223.W33] 66-20896
1. Sunday schools. 2. Southern Baptist Convention — Education. I. Southern Baptist Convention. Sunday School Board. II. Title.

WASHBURN, Alphonso V., comp. 268
The Sunday School at work. 1967-68. A. V. Washburn, compiler. Nashville, Tenn. Convention Press [1967] x. 142 p. 20 cm. "Church study course [of the Sunday School Board of the Southern Baptist Convention] This book is number 1732 in category 17, section for adults and young people." Includes bibliographical references. [BX6223.W34] 67-5603
1. Sunday schools. 2. Southern Baptist Convention — Education. I. Southern Baptist Convention. Sunday School Board. II. Title.

WASHBURN, Alphonso V. 268.86132
The sunday school program of a church [by] A. V. Washburn and staff. Nashville, Convention Press [1966] ix, 150 p. 19 cm. "Church study course [of the Sunday School Board of the Southern Baptist Convention] This book is number 31 in category 17, section for adults and young people." Bibliographical footnotes. [BV1521.W3] 66-23089
1. Sunday-schools. I. Southern Baptist Convention. Sunday School Board. II. Title.

WATTS, Joseph Thomas, 268.422 1874-
The extension department of the Sunday school [by] Joseph T. Watts, D.D. Nashville, Tenn., The Sunday school board of the Southern Baptist convention [1936] 156 p. incl. forms. 19 cm. "Copyright, 1930; revised edition, 1936." [BX6223.W35 1936] 38-3115
1. Sunday-schools. 2. Religious education. I. Southern Baptist convention. Sunday school board. II. Title.

WEIGLE, Luther Allan, 1880- 268.
Talks to Sunday-school teachers, by Luther Allan Weigle ... New York, George H. Doran company [c1920] viii p., 1 l., 11-188 p. 19 1/2 cm. Reprinted from various periodicals. Bibliography at end of each chapter. [BV1534.W4] 20-6997
1. Sunday schools. 2. Religious education. 3. Child study. I. Title.

WELLS, Amos Russel, 1862- 268.
The successful Sunday-school superintendent, by Amos R. Wells ... Philadelphia, The Westminster press, 1915. 179 p. 20 cm. Reprinted in part from the Westminster adult Bible class and the Executive. [BV1531.W4] 15-8996
1. Sunday-schools. I. Title.

WELLS, Amos Russel, 1862- 268 1933.
Sunday-school problems; a book of practical plans for Sunday-school teachers and officers, by Amos R. Wells ... Boston and Chicago, W. A. Wilde company [c1905] 297 p. 19 1/2 cm. [BV1520.W46] 5-27084
1. Sunday-schools. I. Title.

WELLS, Amos Russel, 1862- 268 1933.
Sunday-school success; a book of practical methods for Sunday-school teachers and officers, by Amos R. Wells ... New York, Chicago [etc.] Fleming H. Revell company [1897] 300 p. 18 1/2 cm. [BV1520.W47] 12-39907
1. Sunday-schools. I. Title.

WELLS, Amos Russel, 1862- 268. 1933.
The teacher that teaches, by Amos R. Wells ... Boston, Chicago, The Pilgrim press [c1907] 95 p. 19 1/2 cm. [BV1534.W45] 7-37979
1. Sunday-schools. I. Title.

WESTING, Harold J. 268'.1
Make your Sunday school grow through evaluation / Harold J. Westing. Wheaton, Ill. : Victor Books, c1976. 117 p. : forms ; 21 cm. [BV1521.W4 1976] 76-9216 ISBN 0-88207-464-4 : 1.95
1. Sunday-schools. I. Title.

WHITE, Goodrich Cook, 1889- 268.
...Teaching in the Sunday school, by Goodrich C. White... Nashville, Tenn., Cokesbury press, 1926. 211 p. 19 1/2 cm. (Training courses for leadership) "Suggestions for further reading and study": p. 201-211. [BV1534.W49] 26-19184
1. Sunday-schools. 2. Religious education. I. Title.

WILLIS, Wesley, R. 268'.09
200 years—and still counting! / Wesley R. Willis ; foreword by Clayton E. Raymond. Wheaton, Ill. : Victor Books, c1979. 132 p. ; 20 cm. [BV1521.W54] 79-92009 ISBN 0-88207-604-3 pbk. : 2.95
1. Sunday-schools. I. Title.

[WOODRUFF, Albert] 268
Kindling; or, A way to do it. By a Sabbath school teacher. With an introductory note by Rev. R. S. Storrs, jun., D.D. New York, M. W. Dodd, 1856. 384 p. 19 1/ 2 cm. On cover: The Sabbath school for man, the church, our country and the world. [BV1520.W6] 40-23872
1. Sunday-schools. I. Title.

WOODWORTH, Reginald O 268.4
How to operate a Sunday school; a handbook of practical Sunday school methods. Introd. by G. Beauchamp Vick. Grand Rapids, Zondervan Pub. House [1961] 160 p. 23 cm. [BV1521.W65] 61-1489
1. Sunday-schools. I. Title.

WORLD'S Sunday-school 268. convention. 5th, Rome, 1907.
Sunday-schools the world around; the official report of the World's fifth Sunday-school convention in Rome May 18-23, 1907. Edited by Philip E. Howard. Philadelphia, Pa., The World's Sunday-school executive committee, G. W. Bailey, chairman [c1907] xiv, 422 p. front., plates, ports., facsims. 20 1/2 cm. [BV1505.W6 1907] 7-42328
I. Howard, Philip Eugene, 1870- ed. II. Title.

WORLD'S Sunday-school 268.063 convention. 7th, Zurich, 1913.
World-wide Sunday-school work; the official report of the World's seventh Sunday-school convention, held in Zurich, Switzerland, July 8-15, 1913, ed. by Charles Gallaudet Trumbull. London, New York city, The World's Sunday-school association [1913] 664 p. front., plates, ports., facsims. 20 cm. [BV1505.W6 1913] 14-13568
1. Sunday-schools. I. Trumbull, Charles Gallaudet, 1872- ed. II. Title.

WRAY, Angelina W. 268.
The beginners' department, by Angelina W. Wray ... Philadelphia, The Sunday school times company [c1907] vi, 108 p. illus. (incl. music) 18 1/2 cm. (Lettered on cover: The "Times" handbooks for Sunday-school workers. no. 7) [BV1540.W7] 7-39400
1. Sunday-schools. I. Title.

WRAY, Angelina W 268.
The beginners' department, by Angelina W. Wray ... Philadelphia, The Sunday school times company [c1907] vi, 108 p. illus. 18 1/2 cm. (On cover: The "Times" handbooks for Sunday-school workers. No. 7) Songs, with music: p. 99-108. [BV1540.W7] 7-39400
1. Sunday-schools. 2. Religious education of pre-school children. I. Title.

Sunday-schools—Addresses, essays, lectures.

GRIFFIN, John, 1769-1834. 248
... Story of Dinah Doudney, Portsea, England. Addressed to children, by John Griffin ... Philadelphia, Sunday and adult school union [1822?] 12 p. 20 cm. ([Sunday and adult school union. Tracts] no. 28) Title vignette. Has also continuous paging. (p. [89]-100) With The life of William Kelly. Philadelphia [1822?] [BV4510.A1S8 no. 28] 26-12099
I. Title. II. Title: Dinah Doudney.

JACOBS, J. Vernon 268.081
24 talks for Sunday School workers' conferences. Grand Rapids, Mich., Zondervan [c.1961] 64p. (Sunday school know-how ser.) 1.00 pap.,
I. Title.

MCFARLAND, John Thomas, 1851-
Etchings of the Master, by John T. McFarland... New York, Eaton & Mains; Cincinnati, Jennings & Graham [c1909] vi, 297 p. 21 1/2 cm. $1.25 "About three fourths of the matter in this book was published in the Sunday school journal during 1906 and the first half of 1908."--Author's pref. 9-31954
I. Title.

MCFARLAND, John Thomas, 1851-
Etchings of the Master, by John T. McFarland... New York, Eaton & Mains; Cincinnati, Jennings & Graham [c1909] vi, 297 p. 21 1/2 cm. $1.25 "About three fourths of the matter in this book was published in the Sunday school journal during 1906 and the first half of 1908."--Author's pref. 9-31954
I. Title.

†*SUNDAY school basics /* 268
edited by Floyd D. Carey. Cleveland, Tenn. : Pathway Press, c1976. 142 p. : ill. ; 21 cm. (Church training course ; 130) Bibliography: p. 141-142. [BV1525.S78] 75-31490 ISBN 0-87148-778-0 : 2.50 ISBN 0-87148-777-2 pbk. : 1.95
1. Sunday-schools—Addresses, essays, lectures. I. Carey, Floyd D.

Sunday-schools—Blackboard drawing.

CRAFTS, Wilbur Fisk, 1850- 016. 1922.
Plain uses of the blackboard and slates, and other visible and verbal illustrations in the Sunday-school and homes. By Dr. and Mrs. Wilbur F. Crafts. Rev. and enl. 16th ed., with a new department on temperance. Cincinnati, Jennings & Pye, 1901. vi, 372 p. illus., diagrs. 19 cm. [BV1535.C7 1901] 1-22851
1. Sunday-schools—Blackboard drawing. 2. Chalk—talks. I. Crafts, Sara Jane (Timanus) "Mrs. W. F. Crafts," d. 1930. II. Title.

CRAPULLO, George Anthony, 016. 1890-
Blackboard outlines, through eye and ear to heart and mind, by George A. Crapullo, B. D., introduction by A. H. McKinney ... New York, Chicago [etc.] Fleming H. Revell company [c1924] 158 p. illus. 20 cm. [BV1535.C75] 25-2859
1. Sunday-schools—Blackboard drawing. 2. Chalk-talks. I. Title.

Sunday schools—Congresses.

BAPTIST training union, 267.136 Southwide conference. 5th, Memphis, Tenn., Dec. 31, 1940-Jan. 3, 1941.
Following the living Christ; proceedings of the fifth Southwide Baptist training union conference, Memphis, Tennessee, December 31, 1940-January 3, 1941. Auspices, the Sunday school board of the Southern Baptist convention, Nashville, Tennessee ... [Nashville, 1941] 372 p. 1 illus., diagr. 23 cm. "Following the living Christ" (song, with music): p. [7] [BX6205.B28A4 1940/41] 41-24708
1. Sunday schools—Congresses. I. Title.

INTERNATIONAL Sunday-school 268. convention of the United States and British American province. 13th, San Francisco, 1911.
Organized Sunday-school work in America, 1908-1911; triennial survey of Sunday school work including the official report of the thirteenth International Sunday school convention, San Francisco, California, June 20-27, 1911. Sunday school statistics revised to date. Chicago, The Executive committee of the International Sunday school association, 1911. 6 p. l., 9-612 p. incl. illus., plates, ports., tables. 20 cm. "Edited at and issued from the office of the Association at Chicago." [BV1505.I6 13th] 13-12057
1. Sunday-schools—Congresses. I. International Sunday-school association. II. Title.

INTERNATIONAL Sunday-school 268. convention of the United States and British American provinces. 14th, Chicago, 1914.
Organized Sunday-school work in America, 1911-1914; official report of the fourteenth International Sunday school convention, Chicago, Illinois, 1914. Triennial survey of Sunday school work, including the official report of the fourteenth International Sunday school convention, Chicago, Illinois, June 23-30, 1914. Sunday school statistics revised to date, edited by J. Clayton Youker. Chicago, The Executive committee of the International Sunday school association, 1914. 143, 143a-143b, 143-550 p. front., illus. plates, ports., tables. 20 cm. [BV1505.I6 14th] 16-4399
1. Sunday schools—Congresses. I. Youker, J. Clayton, ed. II. International Sunday-school association. III. Title.

INTERNATIONAL Sunday-school 268. convention of the United States and British American provinces. 1st, Baltimore, 1875.
The first International (sixth national) Sunday school convention held at Baltimore, Md., May 11, 12, 13, 1875. Newark, N.J., The Executive committee [1875] 167, [1] p. illus. (incl. plans) 23 cm. [With National Sunday-school convention of the United States. 5th. Indianapolis. 1872. The fifth National Sunday-school convention. New York. 1872] "Wm. F. Sherwin, editor and business manager." Advertising matter: p. 2-6, 8-9, 153-167. [BV1505.N4 5th] CA 9
1. Sunday-schools—Congresses. I. Sherwin, William Fisk, 1826-1888, ed. II. Title.

INTERNATIONAL Sunday-school 268. convention of the United States and British American provinces. 2d, Atlanta, 1878.
Second International (seventh national) Sunday-school convention of the United States and British American provinces, held in the city of Atlanta, Georgia, April 7, 18 and 19, 1878. Washington, D.C., The Executive committee, 1878. iv, 5-160 p. 23 cm. [With National Sunday-school convention of the United States. 5th, Indianapolis, 1872. The fifth National Sunday-school convention. New York, 1872] "1. Newton Baker, editor and

reporter." Advertising matter: p. 158-160. [BV1505.N4 5th] CA 9
1. Sunday-schools—Congresses. I. Baker, Isaac Newton, 1838- ed. II. Title.

INTERNATIONAL Sunday- 268.0631 school convention of the United States and British American provinces. 4th, Louisville, Ky., 1884.
Fourth International (ninth national) Sunday school convention of the United States and British American provinces held in the city of Louisville, Kentucky, June 11, 12 and 13, 1884. Published by the executive committee. Chicago, Ill., J. Guilbert, printer, 1884. 316 p. illus. (incl. music) 23 cm. Advertising matter: p. 315-316. [BV1505.I6 4th] 38-11651
1. Sunday-schools—Congresses. I. Title.

INTERNATIONAL Sunday-school 268. convention of the United States and British American provinces. 5th, Chicago, 1887.
Fifth International (tenth national) Sunday school convention of the United States and British North America provinces, held in the city of Chicago, Illinois, June 1st, 2d & 3d, 1887 ... Reported by Harry F. Lee, Chicago, arranged by Joseph B. Phipps ... Published by the Executive committee. Chicago, J. Guilbert, printer, 1887. 236 p. 22 cm. [BV1505.I6 5th] 9-31576
1. Sunday-schools—Congresses. I. Lee, Harry F. II. Phipps, Joseph B. III. Title.

WORLD'S Sunday-school 268. convention. 10th, Los Angeles, 1928.
"Thy kingdom come." The official book of the World's tenth Sunday school convention, held in Los Angeles, California, July 11-18, 1928. Edited by John T. Faris, D.D. New York city, World's Sunday school association [1928] 388 p. plates, ports. 19 1/2 cm. Plates printed on both sides. [BV1505.W6 1928] 29-25346
1. Sunday-schools—Congresses. I. Faris, John Thomson, 1871- ed. II. Title.

WORLD'S Sunday-school 268.0631 convention. 11th, Rio de Janeiro, 1932.
The living Christ in the world fellowship of religious education; official record of the eleventh World's Sunday-school convention held in Rio de Janeiro, compiled by William Charles Poole ... St. Louis, Pub. for the World's Sunday school association by the Bethany press [c1933] 351 p. front. (fold. map) plates, ports. 21 cm. [BV1505.W6 1932] 33-15282
1. Sunday-schools—Congresses. I. Poole, William Charles, comp. II. Title.

WORLD'S Sunday-school 268-0631 convention. 12th, Oslo, 1936.
Christ, the hope of the world; the official report of the twelfth World's Sunday school convention, Oslo, Norway, July, 1936, compiled by Alexander Gammie ... New York, Glasgow, World's Sunday school association [1936] x, 11-349, [3] p. front., illus., plates, ports. 19 cm. Printed in Great Britain. [BV1505.W6 1936] 37-13665
1. Sunday-schools—Congresses. I. Gammie, Alexander, comp. II. Title.

WORLD'S Sunday-school 268. convention. 8th, Tokyo, 1920.
The Sunday-school and world progress. The official book of the eighth World's Sunday school convention, held in Tokyo, Japan, October 5-14, 1920, ed. by John T. Faris ... New York city, World's Sunday school association [1922?] xiv p., 1 l., 360 p. front., plates, ports. 19 1/2 cm. [BV1505.W6 1920] 22-12766
1. Sunday-schools—Congresses. I. Faris, John Thomson, 1871- ed. II. Title.

Sunday-schools—Directories

ORGANIZED Bible Class 268.06273 Association.
Bible class directory. Washington. v. 23cm. annual. Title varies: 19-47, Directory. [BV1503.O69] 53-17014
1. Sunday-schools—Direct. I. Title.

Sunday-schools—England—History.

LAQUEUR, Thomas Walter. 301.5'8
Religion and respectability : Sunday schools and working class culture, 1780-1850 / Thomas Walter Laqueur. New Haven : Yale University Press, 1976. xv, 293 p. : ill. ; 25 cm. Includes index. Bibliography: p. [261]-287. [BV1517.G7L36] 77-354647 ISBN 0-300-01859-2 : 22.50
1. Sunday-schools—England—History. 2. Labor and laboring classes—England—History. I. Title.

Sunday-schools—Exercises, recitations, etc.

ARNOLD, Charlotte E, 1905- 264
Special programs for the Sunday school through the year. Cincinnati, Standard Pub. Co. [1952] 232 p. illus. 21 cm. [BV1572.A1A7] 268.7 52-31847
1. Sunday-schools—Exercises, recitations, etc. I. Title.

BARTHOLOMEW, John Glass, 1834-1874.
The new altar; a service book for Sunday schools, compiled mainly from the book of Rev. J. G. Bartholomew; newly arranged and with additions by Charles L. Hutchinson ... Boston and Chicago, Universalist publishing house [c1906] vi, 201 p. 18 cm. "Psalms and hymns and spiritual songs": p. [115]-198. [BX9920.B3] 6-6899
1. Sunday-schools—Exercises, recitations, etc. I. Hutchinson, Charles Laurence, 1854- comp. II. Title.

BIBLE. English. 220.52 Selections. 1937. Authorized.
High heritage; readings on the experiences of life from the Old and New Testaments and the Apocrypha, compiled by Mary Chapin White. New York, E. P. Dutton & company, 1937. xvi p., 2 l., 3-226 p. 21 cm. "First edition." [Full name: Mrs. Mary Whitney (Chapin) White] [BS391.W42] 37-15738
1. Sunday-schools—Exercises, recitations, etc. I. White, Mary (Chapin) Mrs. 1888- comp. II. Title.

BRECK, Flora Elizabeth, 268.67 1886-
Playlets and poems for church school (for teaching Bible truths) Boston, W. A. Wilde Co. [1954] 50p. 22cm. [BV1573.B7] 54-10180
1. Sunday-schools—Exercises, recitations, etc. I. Title.

BRECK, Flora Elizabeth, 268.76 1886-
Special day programs and selections, for church and Sunday school. Boston, W. A. Wilde Co. [1951] 142 p. illus. 20 cm. [BV1572.A1B7] 51-14489
1. Sunday-schools—Exercises, recitations, etc. I. Title.

BUTTERWORTH, Hezekiah, 1839-1905, ed.
Sunday school concert book; harmonized Scripture texts, with poetical illus., and appropriate selections for speaking. Twelve exercises, one for each month in the year. Boston, H. A. Young, 1872. 256 p. 18 cm. Without the music. [BV1573.B8] 52-51021
1. Sunday-schools—Exercises, recitations, etc. I. Title.

CHAMPNEY, Elizabeth 394.268 (Williams) Mrs. 1850-1922, ed.
Entertainments. Comprising directions for holiday merry makings, new programmes for amateur performances, and many novel Sunday-school exercises. Collected and edited by Lizzie W. Champney ... Boston, D. Lothrop and company [1879] vii, 9-359 p. illus. 18 cm. [PN6120.A4C5] 35-35897
1. Sunday-schools—Exercises, recitations, etc. 2. Amateur theatricals. I. Title.

CHOICE dialogues 268
for Sunday-school concerts ... Philadelphia, Garrigues brothers, 1875. 2 v. 15 1/2 cm. First and second series. Numbers evidently issued separately, with separate and continuous paging. [PN4231.C54] 25-288
1. Sunday-schools—Exercises, recitations, etc. 2. Dialogues.

CLARKE, Maurice, 1882- 268.73
Little children's praises; services of worship for kindergarten and primary children, by the Reverend Maurice Clarke, D.D. Foreword by the Very Reverend John W. Suter, D.D. New York, Morehouse-Gorham co., 1946. 64 p. incl. front. 21 cm. Includes music. "First edition of 1929 issued under the title Worship services for kindergarten and primary children ... Second edition. First printing, September, 1946." [BX5873.C65 1946] 47-932
1. Sunday schools—Exercises, recitations, etc. I. Protestant Episcopal church in the U.S.A. Liturgy and ritual. II. Title.

CLARKE, Maurice, 1882- 268.83
Prayer and praise for juniors, by the Reverend Maurice Clarke, D.D. New York, Morehouse-Gorham co., 1946. 6 p. l., 3-53 p. 21 cm. On cover: Six Christian year and four special services for the church school. "Issued originally under the title: A church school book of prayer and praise." "Third edition, first printing, October, 1946." [BX5873.C6 1946] 47-16909
1. Sunday-schools—Exercises, recitations, etc. I. Title.

DEMEREST, Ada Rose. 268
Junior worship, with programs, songs and stories, by Ada Rose Demerest ... Cincinnati, O., The Standard publishing company [c1931] 240 p. illus. 22 cm. "Hymns": p. 209-240. [BV1570.D4] ISBN 31-12029
1. Sunday-schools—Exercises, recitations, etc. 2. Worship. I. Title.

FAIR, Harold L., 1924- 242'.2
Class devotions for use with the 1981-82 International lessons / Harold L. Fair. Nashville : Abingdon, c1981. 128 p. ; 22 cm. [BV1561.F25 1981] 19 82-153154 ISBN 0-687-08621-3 pbk. : 3.95
1. International lesson annual. 2. Sunday-schools—Exercises, recitations, etc. 3. Devotional calendars. I. International lesson annual. II. Title.

FERRIS, Carrie Sivyer. 268.
The Sunday kindergarten; game, gift, and story; a manual for use in the Sunday schools and in the home, by Carrie Sivyer Ferris... Chicago, The University of Chicago press, 1909. xxvi, 271 p. incl. illus., plates. front. 20 1/2 cm. (Half-title: Constructive Bible studies, ed. by M. C. Burton [Elementary series]) Series title also on t.-p. "Books of reference": p. xxv. [BV1540.F4] 9-23249
I. Title.

HARTSHORNE, Hugh, 1885- 298.
Manual for training in worship, by Hugh Hartshorne ... New York, C. Scribner's sons [c1915] vi, 154 p. 23 cm. "Biographies of stories, sources, and prayers": p. 28-32 [BV1570.H35] 16-560
1. Sunday-schools—Exercises, recitation, etc. 2. Worship. I. Title.

HUMPHREY, Imogene.
Primary worship services, by Imogene Humphrey. Cincinnati, O., The Standard publishing company [c1926] 96 p. illus. (incl. music) 23 1/2 cm. [BX7313.H8] 26-17846
1. Sunday-schools—Exercises, recitations, etc. I. Title.

LAWRENCE, Marion, 1850-1924. 268.
Special days in the Sunday school, by Marion Lawrence ... New York, Chicago [etc.] Fleming H. Revell company [c1916] 250 p. front., illus. (music) plates. 21 cm. [BV1572.A1L3] 16-20891
1. Sunday-schools—Exercises, recitations, etc. I. Title.

NASH, Gerald R 268.6
Sabbath school special days, by Gerald R. Nash. Mountain View Calif., Pacific Press Pub. Association [1966] 178 p. illus. 22 cm. Includes music. [BX6113.N32] 66-20342
1. Sunday schools — Exercises, recitations, etc. 2. Seventh-Day Adventists — Education. I. Title.

... The Paramount children's 268. *day book;* exercises, dialogs, playlets, recitations and songs; contributors: Pearl Holloway, Carolyn Freeman, Alice L. Whitson, Sara E. Gosselink ... Chicago, Ill., Meyer & brother, c1923. 53, [10] p. 20 cm. At head of title: A Paramount line publication. Music: 8 p. at end. [BV1572.C45P3] 23-11536
1. Sunday-schools—Exercises, recitations, etc. 2. Readers and speakers—1870- I. Holloway, Pearl. II. Freeman, Carolyn. III. Whitson, Alice L. IV. Gosselink, Sara E. V. Title: Children's day book.

PHILIPPS, Martin, 1853-
Sunday school instructions for every Sunday of the year, with a short sketch of eminent saints, followed by prayers of the mass and hymns; comp. by Rev. M. Philipps. [Buffalo, N. Y., 1910] 432 p. 21 x 12 cm. 10-20507
I. Title.

REED, John J. 244
My Sabbath school scrap book, containing anniversary dialogues, addresses, recitations, &c., (in prose and verse,) with other miscellaneous pieces. By John J. Reed. New York, M. L. Byrn, 1874. xi, [12]-407 p. illus. (music) 19 cm. [PN4231.R4] 24-30037
1. Sunday-schools—Exercises, recitations, etc. 2. Dialogues. I. Title.

SLADE, Mary Bridges (Canedy) Mrs.
Sunday school entertainments. Containing exercises for Christmas and New Year; Palm Sunday and Easter; Children's day; floral concert; autumn-leaf Sunday; memorial days; and the regular Sunday school concert. By Mrs. Mary B. C. Slade ... Boston, H. A. Young and company [c1880] 128 p. 17 cm. [BV1573.S6] 12-38726
1. Sunday-schools—Exercises, recitations, etc. I. Title.

SMITH, Henry Augustine, 268.7 1874-
Worship in the church school through music, pageantry and pictures, by H. Augustine Smith... Elgin, Ill., David C. Cook publishing company [c1928] p. 3-148 incl. front. (port.) plates. 19 cm. "A master handbook of hymn stories, leadership in worship and song, religious art, choir and orchestra."--p. 3. Bibliography at end of chapters i and iv. [BV1522.S6] 30-10028
1. Sunday-schools—Exercises, recitations, etc. 2. Hymns, English—Hist. & crit. 3. Church music. 4. Religious education. I. Title.

**SUNDAY Church school for* 268.432 *4's;* class activity packet, term 1. Gerry Bream, course ed. Gisela Jordan, packet illus. Gustav K. Wiencke, ser. ed. Philadelphia, Lutheran Church Pr. [c.1966] 1v. (chiefly col. illus.) 26x34cm. (LCA Sunday church sch. ser.) 5.75 pap.,

SUNDELOF-ASBRAND, Karin. 394.268
Easy Sunday school entertainments for Easter, Christmas, Mother's day, Father's day, Children's day and Rally day, by Karin Sundelof-Asbrand. Boston, Mass., and Los Angeles, Cal. [Walter H. Baker company, c1939] 157 p. 19 cm. Contains music. [PN4231.S83] 39-17114
1. Sunday-schools—Exercises, recitations, etc. I. Title.

VINCENT, John Heyl, bp., 268.7 1832-1920.
The Sunday-school reader, for opening service and class study. Comprising a series of Scripture lessons on the life, journeys, and miracles of Jesus. By Rev. J. H. Vincent. New York, Carlton & Porter, Sunday-school union, 1866. 57 p. 18 cm. [BV1570.V55] 40-37727
1. Sunday-schools—Exercises, recitations, etc. I. Sunday-school union of the Methodist Episcopal church. II. Title.

WALKER, Mollie (Cullom) 268. Mrs., comp.
Programs, plays, songs, stories, for workers with children, comp. by Mollie Cullom Walker (Mrs. Wm. M. Walker.) Birmingham, Ala., 1921. [3]-107 p. illus. (incl. music) 23 cm. [BV1572.A1W3] 21-22090
1. Sunday schools—Exercises, recitations, etc. I. Title.

YOUNG, Henry A., comp. 394.2624
Harvest recitations. Especially adapted for Sunday-school concerts. Compiled by Henry A. Young. Boston, H. A. Young & co. [1887] [96] p. 17 cm. Various pagings. On cover: Sunday school exercises and recitations, especially arranged for Harvest Sunday. Includes six harvest exercises by Marion West [pseud.] [PN4305.H7Y6] 37-32855

1. Sunday-schools—Exercises, recitations, etc. 2. Hoyt, Mrs. G. S. I. Title.

Sunday-schools—Great Britain

POLE, Thomas, 1753-1829. 374.9'42
A history of the origin and progress of adult schools. [3d ed.] New York, A. M. Kelley, 1969. ii, 128 p. 22 cm. (The Social history of education. First series, no. 8) Reprint of the 1816 ed., with a new introd. Bibliographical footnotes. [LC361.P75 1969] 75-5597
1. Bible—Teaching—Gt. Brit. 2. Sunday-schools—Gt. Brit. 3. Education—Gt. Brit. I. Title. II. Title: Origin and progress of adult schools.

POLE, Thomas, 1753-1829.
A history of the origin and progress of adult schools; with an account of some of the beneficial effects already produced on the moral character of the labouring poor; also, considerations on the important advantages of which they are likely to be productive to society at large; with an appendix containing rules for the government of adult school societies and for the organization of the schools, &c. By Thomas Pole ... Bristol, Printed; New York, Re-printed and sold by S. Wood, 1815. iv, [5]-127 p. fold. tab. 18 cm. [LC361.P75] E 10
1. Sunday-schools—Gt. Brit. 2. Bible—Teaching—Gt. Brit. 3. Education—Gt. Brit. I. Title.

Sunday-schools—Growth.

ALLEN, Charles Livingstone, 1913- 268
How to increase your Sunday-school attendance / Charles L. Allen, Mildred Parker. Old Tappan, N.J. : Revell, c1979. 127 p. ; 22 cm. [BV1523.G75A44] 79-22655 ISBN 0-8007-1088-6 : 5.95
1. Sunday-schools—Growth. I. Parker, Mildred, joint author. II. Title.

BLAZIER, Kenneth D. 268'.1
A growing church school / Kenneth D. Blazier. Valley Forge, Pa. : Judson Press, c1978. 64 p. ; 22 cm. Bibliography: p. 63-64. [BV1523.G75B55] 77-26297 ISBN 0-8170-0785-7 pbk. : 2.50
1. Sunday-schools—Growth. I. Title.

THE Encyclopedia of Sunday schools and religious education; giving a world-wide view of the hisotry and progress of the Sunday school and the development of religious education... Editors-in-chief: John T. McFarland...Benjamin S. Winchester...Canadian editor: R. Douglas Fraser...European editor: Rev. J. William Butcher... New York, London [etc.] T. Nelson & sons [c1915] 3 v. front., illus. (incl. maps, plans, forms) plates, ports., diagrs. 24 1/2 cm. Paged continuously. [BV1510.E5] 16-1651
I. McFarland, John Thomas, 1851-1913, ed. II. Winchester, Benjamin Severance, 1868- joint ed. III. Fraser, Robert Douglas, 1849- ed. IV. Butcher, James Williams, 1857- ed.

Sunday — schools — History.

BENSON, Clarence Herbert, 1879- 268.09
A popular history of Christian education, by Clarence H. Benson ... Chicago, Moody press [c1943] 355 p. 20 cm. Cover-title: History of Christian education. Bibliography: p. 353-355. [BV1515.B4] 44-649
1. Sunday-schools—Hist. 2. Religious education—Hist. I. Title.

CONSECRATED talents; 922.773
or, The life of Mrs. Mary W. Mason. With an introduction by Bishop Janes. New York, Carlton & Lanahan; Cincinnati, Hitchcock & Walden; [etc., etc.] 1870. 285 p. front. (port.) 19 1/2 cm. [BX8495.M34C6] 36-37388
1. Mason, Mrs. Mary W. (Morgan) 1791-1868. 2. Sunday schools—Hist.

COPE, Henry Frederick, 1870-1923.
... The evolution of the sunday school, by Henry Frederick Cope ... Boston, New York [etc.] The Pilgrim press [c1911] vii p., 2 l., 3-240 p. 20 cm. (Modern Sunday-school manuals, ed. by C. F. Kent) "Some helpful books for further study": p. 231-236. 11-17464
I. Title.

FERGUSSON, Edmund Morris, 1864-1934. 268.09
Historic chapters in Christian education in America; a brief history of American Sunday school movement, and the rise of the modern church school by E. Morris Fergusson. New York [etc.] Fleming H. Revell company [c1935] 192 p. front. (port.) 19 1/2 cm. [BV1516.A1F4] 35-17659
1. Sunday-schools—Hist. I. Title.

HAENDSCHKE, Martin A
The Sunday school story; the history of the Sunday school in the Lutheran Church -- Missouri Synod. River Forest, Ill., Lutheran Education Association, 1963. xv, 137 p. illus. (Lutheran Education Association. 20th yearbook, 1963) Bibliography: p. 127-132. 65-36800
1. Sunday — schools — History. 2. Lutheran Church — Education. 3. Lutheran Church — Missouri Synod — Education. I. Title. II. Series.

INTERNATIONAL Sunday-school convention of the United States and British American provinces. 11th, Toronto, 1905. 268.
The development of the Sunday-school The official report of the eleventh International Sunday-school convention, Toronto, Canada, June 23-27, 1905. Boston, Mass., Executive committee of the International Sunday-school association, 1905. xix, [1] 716 p. illus. (incl. ports) 20 1/2 cm. [BV1505.I6 11th] 9-9500
1. Sunday-schools—Hist. I. Title.

INTERNATIONAL Sunday-school convention of the United States and British American provinces. 12th, Louisville, Ky., 1908.
Organized Sunday-school work in America, 1905-1908; triennial survey of Sunday-school work including the official report of the twelfth International Sunday school convention, Louisville, Kentucky, June 18-23, 1908. Sunday- school statistics revised to date. Chicago, The Executive committee of the International Sunday-school association, 1908. xxiv, 665 p. illus. (incl. ports.) 20 1/2 cm. "Edited ... and issued from the office of the Association at Chicago." 10-7589
I. International Sunday-school association. II. Title.

INTERNATIONAL Sunday-school convention of the United States and British American provinces. 16th, Kansas City, Mo., 1922. 268.
Organized Sunday school work in North America, 1918-1922. Official report of the sixteenth International Sunday school convention, Kansas City, Missouri, June 21-27, 1922. Ed. by Herbert H. Smith. Chicago, International Sunday school council of religious education, 1922. 4 p. l., 536 p. illus., plates, ports., fold. tab. 19 1/2 cm. [BV1505.I6 16th] 23-14353
I. Smith, Herbert Heebner, ed. II. Title.

KNOFF, Gerald E. 268'.09
The world Sunday school movement : a story of a broadening mission / Gerald E. Knoff. New York : Seabury Press, 1979. xiv, 283 p. ; 24 cm. "A Crossroad book." Includes index. Bibliography: p. 269-276. [BV1515.K58] 78-26096 ISBN 0-8164-0416-X : 13.95
1. Sunday-schools—History. I. Title.

LANKARD, Frank Glenn, 1892- 268.6
...A history of the American Sunday school curriculum, by Frank Glenn Lankard ... New York, Cincinnati, The Abingdon press [c1927] 360 p. 21 cm. (The Abingdon religious education texts; D. G. Downey, general editor. College series; G. H. Betts, editor) Thesis (PH. D.)--Northwestern university, 1926. Without thesis note. "References" at end of most of the chapters. Bibliography: p. 342-352. [BV1516.A1L3] 27-24563
1. Sunday-schools—Hist. 2. Religious education—U. S. 3. Religious education—Curricula I. Title.

ROBERT Raikes: his Sunday schools and his friends; 268.09 including historical sketches of the Sunday school cause in Europe and America. Philadelphia, American Baptist publication society [1859] 311 p. front. (port.) plates. 16 cm. [BV1518.R3R6] 33-397
1. Raikes, Robert, 1735-1811. 2. Sunday-schools—Hist. I. American Baptist publication society.

TEMPLE, Josiah Howard, 1815-1893. 268.
History of the first Sabbath school in Framingham, Mass., from 1816 to 1868; with a sketch of the rise of Sabbath schools. By J. H. Temple ... Boston, Printed for the author by Wright & Potter, 1868. 158 p. 17 1/2 cm. [BV1516.F7T4] 38-33150
1. Sunday-schools—Hist. 2. Framingham, Mass.—Church history. I. Title.

Sunday schools—Hymn-books.

ANNIVERSARY and Sabbath school hymns; 783 or, The child's Sunday school music book. Nos. 1, 2, 3, and 4, complete. New-York, G. S. Scofield, 1861. 1 p. l., 118, [2] p. 13 x 15 cm. With music. [M2193.A75H7 1861] 43-26705
1. Sunday-schools—Hymn-books. 2. Hymns, English. I. Title: The child's Sunday school music book.

AUGUSTANA, Evangelical Lutheran Church. 245.
The junior hymnal, containing Sunday school and Luther League liturgy and hymns for the Sunday school and oter gatherings, authorized by the Evangelical Lutheran Augustana Synod. Rock Island, Ill., Augustana Book Concern [1928] vii, 320 p. 14 cm. Without music. [BV410.A83] 50-40845
1. Sunday-schools—Hymn-books. I. Luther League of America. II. Title.

BLACK, James M. ed. 783.
Praise and promise, for use in Sunday-schools, prayer meetings, revivials, young people's meetings and on special occasions. Edited by J. M. Black and C. C. McCabe ... Chicago, Ill., R. R. McCabe & co., c1900. 208 p. 20 cm. With music. [M2193.B6P7] 0-4000
1. Sunday-schools—Hymn-books. 2. Hymns, English. I. McCabe, Charles Cardwell, bp., 1836-1906, joint ed. II. Title.

BOAZ, Charles, comp.
The King's message in song; for use in the Sunday school, and all the services of the church, by Rev. Charles Boaz ... Edited by T. Martin Towne ... Mattoon, Ill., C. Boaz [c1901] 128 p. 20 cm. With music. [M2493.B] Mus
1. Sunday schools—Hymn-books. I. Towne, Thomas Martin, 1835-1911 or 12, ed. II. Title.

BOE, Viglelk Engebretson, 1872- 783.7
The primary hymn book; hymns and songs for little children, by V. E. Boe. Minneapolis, Augsburg publishing house [c1936] 72 p. illus., col. plates. 22 1/2 cm. Piano accompaniment. [M2193.b67P95] 37-39090
1. Sunday-schools—Hymn-books. I. Title.

BOWDISH, T. M. ed. 783
Kingdom of song. A collection of songs for Sunday-schools, young people's societies and all religious services. Edited by T. M. Bowdish... [Toledo] The W. W. Whitney co., c1900. 192 p. 21 cm. [M2193.B] Mus
1. Sunday-schools—Hymn-books. 2. Hymns, English. I. Title.

THE call to praise; 783
a hymnal for children's division ... Philadelphia, Pa., Hall-Mack company; Chicago, Ill., National music co. [c1929] 2 p. l., 139 p. 22 cm. "Worship programs" : p. 127-137. [M2193.C2] 29-30277
1. Sunday-schools—Hymn-books. 2. Hymns, English.

COLEMAN, Robert Henry, 1869- comp. 783
Service songs, containing hymns suitable for all the services of the churches but prepared especially for use in the Sunday school, compiled and edited by Robert H. Coleman ... Dallas, Tex., R. H. Coleman [c1931] 288 p. 22 cm. [M2198.C72S5] 31-10965
1. Sunday-schools—Hymn-books. 2. Hymns, English. I. Title.

[CONVERSE, Charles Crozat] 1832-1918. 783.
The sweet singer: a collection of hymns and tunes for Sunday-schools. Together with a variety suitable for day-schools, revival occasions, and the family circle. By Karl Reden [pseud.] and S. J. Goodenough. New York, Carlton & Porter, 1863. 144 p. 11 1/2 x 15 cm. Music composed or arranged for three voices only (soprano, alto, tenor) by Charles Crozat Converse, under the pseudonyms, Karl Reden, E. C. Revons and C. O. Nevers. [M2198.C76S9] 44-31608
1. Sunday-schools—Hymn-books. I. Goodenough, S. J. II. Title.

CUMMINGS, M. Homer, comp. 783.
Songs of salvation and service, revised; a collection of gospel hymns ... comp. by M. Homer Cummings, Millard F. Compton and L. B. Bowers; musical editor, E. O. Excell ... Wheeling, W. Va., M. H. Cummings, c1922. [256] p. 21 cm. [M2198.C97S5] 22-13328
1. Sunday-schools—Hymn-books. I. Compton, Millard F., joint comp. II. Bowers, L. B., joint comp. III. Excell, Edwin Othello, 1851-1921. IV. Title.

DATE, Henry, comp. 783.
Pentecostal hymns no. 2; a winnowed collection for evangelistic services, young peoples's societies, and Sunday schools, selected by Henry Date. Music editors E. A. Hoffman and J. H. Tenney. Chicago, The Hope publishing company [c1898] [224] p. 20 cm. [M2198.D] 98-1803
1. Sunday-schools—Hymn-books. I. Hoffman, Elisha A., ed. II. Tenney, John Harrison, 1840- joint ed. III. Title.

DATE, Henry. 783.
Pentecostal hymns, number three [-number four a winnowed collection for evangelistic services, young people's societies and Sunday schools selected by Henry Date. Music editors, E. A. Hoffman, T. C. O'Kane, W. W. Bentley. Chicago, Hope publishing company [c1902-07] 2 v. in l. 21 cm. Half-title: Pentecostal hymns no. 3 and 4 combined. Paged continuously. Subtitle varies slightly. Music editors of number four: E. A. Hoffman, T. M. Towne. [M2198.D233B] 16-7630
1. Sunday-schools-Hymn-Books. 2. Hymns, English. I. Hoffman, Elisha A., 1839-1929, ed. II. O'Kane, Tullus Clinton, 1830-1912, ed. III. Bentley, W. W., ed. IV. Towne, Thomas Martin, 1835-1911 or 12. ed. V. Title.

DATE, Henry, comp. 783.
Pentecostal hymns, a winnowed collection for evangelistic services, young people's societies and Sunday-schools, selected by Henry Date. Music editors: E. A. Hoffman, W. A. Ogden [and] J. H. Tenney. Chicago, The Hope publishing company [c1894] 224 p. 20 cm. [M2198.D23P4 1894] 45-46648
1. Sunday-schools—Hymn-books. 2. Hymns, English. I. Hoffman, Elisha A., 1838-1929, ed. II. Ogden, William Augustine, 1841-1897, joint ed. III. Tenney, John Harrison, b. 1840, joint ed. IV. Title.

DUNBAR, Charles, comp. 783.
Sabbath-school gems, being a collection of favorite hymns and tunes for Sabbath-school anniversaries. Selected from the Young people's chorister, by C. Dunbar. Cincinnati, The author, 1860. cover-title, [3]-66 p. 14 1/2 cm. Music and text on p. [2]-[4] of cover. Some of the tunes have piano accompaniment. [M2198.D] 43-38216
1. Sunday-schools—Hymn-books. I. Title. II. Title: Young people's chorister.

ELDERKIN, George D. ed. 783.7
Songs of the century. [No. 1] For missionary and revival meetings, Sabbath schools and young people's societies. Edited by Geo. D. Elderkin, Jno. R. Sweney, Wm. J. Kirkpatrick, H. L. Gilmour and F. A. Hardin. Chicago, G. D. Elderkin, 1900. 234 p. 20 cm. [M2198.E3855 no.1] Mus
1. Sunday-schools—Hymn-books. I. Title.

EVANGELICAL Lutheran Church. 783
Board of Parish Education.
Children's chapel song book. Minneapolis, Augsburg Pub. House [1947] 71 p. 22 cm. With music. [M2193.E895C5] 48-23338
1. Sunday-schools—Hymn-books. I. Title.

EVANGELICAL Lutheran Church. 783.
Board of Parish education
Children's chapel song book. Minneapolis, Augsburg Pub. House [c1947] 71 p. 22 cm. With music. [M2193.E895C5] 48-23338
1. Sunday-schools—Hymn-books. I. Title.

EXCELL, Edwin Othello,221851-
1921.
The gospel hymnal for Sunday school and church work... for the Western Methodist book concern. Cincinnati, Chicago [etc.] Curtis & Jennings [1899] 240 p. 12 degree. Mar
I. Title.

FILLMORE, J. Henry. 783.
Hymns for today for Sunday schools, young people's societies, the church, the home, community welfare, associations, and patriotic meetings, by J. H. Fillmore. Cincinnati, O., Fillmore music house, c1920. 352 p. 22 cm. [M2198.F45H7] 20-7928
1. Sunday-schools—Hymn-books. I. Title.

FITZ, Asa, b., 1810, comp. 783.
My little singing book, with a supplement. For the use of Sabbath and juvenile schools., By Asa Fitz. Boston, D. S. King & co., Saxton & Peirce, 1843. 128 p. 9 x 13 cm. For 1-3 voices. [M2193.F55M7 1843] 45-27599
1. Sunday-schools—Hymn-books. 2. Hymns, English. I. Title.

FITZ, Asa, b., 1810, comp. 783.
The Sabbath school singing book, containing a selection of easy and familiar tunes, adapted to the Union Sabbath school hymn book, published by the American Sunday school union. Together with several other beautiful hymns and tunes, not before published. By Asa Fitz and E. B. Dearborn. Boston, A. B. Kidder, 1844. 96 p. 10 1/2 x 13 1/2 cm. [M2193.F55S2 1844] 45-27880
1. Sunday-schools—Hymn-books. 2. Hymns, English. I. Dearborn, E. B., joint comp. II. Title. III. Title: Union Sabbath school hymn book.

GENERAL council of the 245.2041
Evangelical Lutheran church in North America.
Sunday-school book for the use of Evangelical Lutheran congregations. (Rev. and enl.) By authority of the General council of the Evangelical Lutheran church in North America. Philadelphia, General council's publication board [c1896] iv, 319 p. 14 cm. [BX8014.A3 1896] 34-7215
1. Sunday-schools—Hymm-books. 2. Lutheran church—Hymns. 3. Hymns, English. I. Title.

GOODRICH, Alfred Bailey, 783
b.1828.
A new service and tune book, for Sunday schools. By A. B. Goodrich ... New ed., enl. New York, The Gen. Prot. Episc. S. S. union and church book society; Chicago, Street, Pearson & co. [c1866] 176 p. 14 1/2 x 11 1/2 cm. [M2193.G65N4 1866 a] 45-51860
1. Sunday-schools—Hymn-books. 2. Protestant Episcopal church in the U.S.A.—Hymns. I. General Protestant Episcopal Sunday school union and church book society. II. Title.

GOODRICH, Alfred Bailey, 783
b.1828.
A new service and tune book, for Sunday schools. By A. B. Goodrich ... New ed., enl. New York, Gen. Prot. Episc. S. S. union and church book society; Chicago, Street, Moore & co.; [etc., etc.] 1867. 176 p. 14 1/2 x 11 1/2 cm. [M2193.G65N4 1867] 45-31346
1. Sunday-schools—Hymn books. 2. Protestant Episcopal church in the U.S.A.—Hymns. I. General Protestant Episcopal Sunday school union and church book society. II. Title.

HARTSHORNE, Hugh, 1885- 298.
The book of worship of the church school, prepared by Hugh Hartshorne ... New York, C. Scribner's sons [c1915] iv p., 2 l., 3-170 p. 23 cm. Hymns (with music): p. [45]-104. [BV1570.H3] 15-27905
1. Sunday schools—Hyme-books. I. Title.

HARTSOUGH, Palmer, 1844- 783
1932, ed.
A hymnal for joyous youth, an all-purpose hymnal for church, young peoples' services and Sunday schools, edited by Rev. Palmer Hartsough, Rev. George O. Webster, Eleanor Allen Schroll and J. H. Fillmore. Scripture readings by Rev. Craig W. Schwartz ... Cincinnati, O., Fillmore music house. c1927] 288 p. 22 cm. [M2193.H35H7] 27-10636
1. Sunday-schools—Hymn-books. I. Webster, George O., joint ed. II. Schroll, Eleanor Allen, joint ed. III. Fillmore, James Henry, 1849- joint ed. IV. Schwartz, Craig W. V. Title.

HENSON, John M., comp. 783.
Billows of song, for the song service, by J. M. Henson, B. L. Whitworth, J. W. Askew [and others] ... Atlanta, Ga., The J. M. Henson music co.; Knoxville, Tenn., C. C. Maples, c1943. [160] p. 19 1/2 cm. Shape-note notation. Text of p. [2] and [3] of cover. Hymns with music, compiled by John M. Henson. [M2193.H5B5] 45-2895
1. Sunday schools—Hymn-books. 2. Hymns, English. I. Title.

THE Hosanna, 783
rev. and enl.; a song and service book for the Sunday school and home ... New York, The New-church press [c1920] v, 346 p. front. (music) 18 cm. Combines material from "The Welcome," "The Hosanna," "The New Hosanna," and "The Sunday school magnificat." cf. Foreword. Foreword signed by the Committee of the American New-church Sunday school association; Richard B. Carter, chairman. [M2193.H822] 20-23002
1. Sunday-schools—Hymn-books. I. New Jerusalem church.

HUGG, George C. comp. 783.
The crowning triumph, a new collection of sacred songs and gospel hymns. For sanctuary, Sunday-schools, prayer and praise meetings, the home circle. Anniversaries, funeral occasions, etc. By George C. Hugg & Frank L. Armstrong. Philadelphia, F. A. North & co. [1879] 112 p. 20 cm. [M2193.H89C7] 45-44598
1. Sunday-schools—Hymn-books. I. Armstrong, Frank L., joint comp. II. Title.

HULL, Asa. 783.9
Many little voices: a choice collection of songs and scriptural exercises for the primary and intermediate classes of Sunday schools. Written, arranged and compiled by Asa Hull ... New York, A. Hull; Chicago, Lyon & Healy; [etc., etc.] c1895. 160 p. 17 cm. [M2193.H] 1-12431
1. Sunday schools—Hymn books. I. Title.

HULL, Asa. 783
Many little voices; a choice collection of songs and Scriptural exercises for the primary and intermediate classes of Sunday schools. Written, arranged and compiled by Asa Hull ... Enlarged ed. New York, A. Hull, c1900. 192 p. 17 1/2 cm. [M2193.H] 0-6406
1. Sunday schools—Hymn books. I. Title.

HUTCHINS, Charles Lewis, 783.
1838-1920, ed.
The Sunday school hymnal: arranged by the Rev. Charles L. Hutchins. Buffalo, Breed, Lent & co., 1871. 2 p. l., 204 p. 19 1/2 cm. With music. [M2193.H96S8 1871] 45-44603
1. Sunday-schools—Hymn-books. 2. Hymns, English. I. Title.

HUTCHINS, Charles Lewis, 783.
1838-1920, ed.
The Sunday-school hymnal, containing also hymns suited for other occasions, compiled and edited by the Rev. Charles L. Hutchins. Ed. C. Medford, Mass., The editor, 1881. 320 p. 20 1/2 cm. With music. [M2193.H96S8 1881] 45-15264
1. Sunday-schools—Hymn-books. 2. Hymns, English. I. Title.

HYMNS for primary 783.9
worship. Philadelphia, The Westminster Press [1946] 172 p. 26 cm. Pref. signed: W. Wallace Ashley, Florence Norton, chairman, W. Lawrence Curry, musical editor [and others] "The music has been kept within the range of the children's voices." [M2193.H993] 49-4868
1. Sunday schools—Hymn-books. I. Curry, Lawrence, 1906- ed.

INTERNATIONAL society of 783.9
Christian endeavor.
Christian youth at song ... Boston, Mass., International society of Christian endeavor [1939] [96] p. 21 cm. Introduction signed: Daniel A. Poling. Hymnal, with music. [M2198.Y5C5] 39-32445
1. Sunday-schools—Hymn-books. 2. Hymns, English. I. Poling, Daniel Alfred, 1884- II. Title.

INTERNATIONAL society of 783.
Christian endeavor.
The Endeavor hymnal for young people's societies, Sunday schools and church prayer meetings. Boston and Chicago, United society of Christian endeavor [1901] 356 p. 21 cm. [M2198.Y5I68] 2-8447
1. Sunday-schools—Hymn-books. 2. Hymns, English. I. Title.

LAUFER, Calvin Weiss, 1874-
1938, ed.
The church school hymnal for youth; a book for use in worship, providing hymns, responsive readings, worship programs, prayers, and other worship materials as a part of the program of Christian education for intermediates, seniors, and young people; with supplement. Philadelphia, The Westminster press, 1938. xiv, 430 p. 21 cm. A 40
1. Sunday-schools—Hymn-books. 2. Devotional exercises. I. Title.

LORENZ, Edmund Simon, 1854- 783.
1942.
Notes of triumph: for the Sunday school. By Rev. E. S. Lorenz and Rev. I. Baltzell ... Dayton, O., United brethren publishing house, 1886. 192 p. 15 1/2 x 19 cm. Hymns, with music. [M2193.L86N6] 45-44599
1. Sunday schools—Hymn-books. 2. United brethren in Christ—Hymns. I. Baltzell, Issiah, 1832-1898. II. Title.

LOWRY, Robert, 1826-1899, 783.
ed.
Good as gold; a new collection of Sunday school songs. By Rev. Robert Lowry and W. Howard Doane. New York and Chicago, Biglow & Main [1881] 192 p. 13 1/2 x 18 cm. With music. [M2193.L932G6 1881] 45-46621
1. Sunday-schools—Hymn-books. 2. Hymns, English. I. Doane, William Howard, 1831-1915, joint ed. II. Title.

LOWRY, Robert, 1826-1899, 245.
ed.
Good as gold hymn book; a new collection of Sunday school songs. Containing the words only, from "Good as gold." By Rev. Robt. Lowry and W. Howard Doane. New York and Chicago, Biglow & Main, c1881. 160 p. 12 1/2 cm. [BV520.L6] 45-47071
1. Sunday-schools—Hymn-books. 2. Hymns, English. I. Doane, William Howard, 1831-1915, joint ed. II. Title.

LOWRY, Robert, 1826-1899, 783.
ed.
Pure gold for the Sunday school. A new collection of songs. Prepared and adapted for Sunday school exercises. By Rev. Robert Lowry and W. Howard Doane. New York and Chicago, Biglow & Main [c1871] 160 p. 14 x 17 1/2 cm. With music. [M2198.L] 43-33348
1. Sunday-school—Hymn-books. I. Doane, William Howard, 1831-1915, joint ed. II. Title.

MEREDITH, Isaac H. ed. 783
Sunday school hymns no. 1. Edited by I. H. Meredith, Grant Colfax Tullar and J. W. Lerman ... Chicago, Ills., New York, Tullar-Meredith co., c1903. 256 p. 23 cm. With music. [M2193.M559] 3-32174
1. Sunday-schools—Hymn-books. 2. Hymns, English. I. Tullar, Grant Colfax, joint ed. II. Lerman, J. W., joint ed. III. Title.

MEREDITH, Isaac Hickman, 783.7
1872- ed.
Exalt His name; a hymnal for the church school, young people's societies, and other departments of church work, edited by I. H. Meredith ... New York, N. Y., Tullar-Meredith co., c1936. 253, [3] p. 22 cm. With music. "Worship material, prepared and edited by Rev. George Orlia Webster": p. 217-253. [M2193.M55E9] 36-11232
1. Sunday-schools—Hymn-books. 2. Hymns, English. I. Webster, George Orlia. II. Title.

METHODIST Episcopal church. 783.
The centenary singer, a collection of hymns and tunes popular during the last one hundred years, compiled as directed by the music committee of the Gen. conference & Assoc. M. E. choirs for the Sunday school union. New York, Carlton & Porter; Cincinnati, Poe & Hitchcock, 1867. v, [1], 419 p. 16 cm. [M2193.M6C4] 45-46681
1. Sunday-schools—Hymn-books. 2. Hymns, English. I. Associated Methodist Episcopal choirs. II. Sunday-school union of the Methodist Episcopal church. III. Title.

METHODIST Episcopal church. 783.
The centenary singer, a collection of hymns and tunes popular during the last one hundred years, compiled as directed by the music committee of the Gen. conference & Assoc. M. E. choirs for the Sunday school union. New York, Carlton & Porter; Cincinnati, Poe & Hitchcock, 1867. v, [1], 419 p. 16 cm. [M2193.M6C4] 45-46681
1. Sunday-schools—Hymn-books. 2. Hymns, English. I. Associated Methodist Episcopal choirs. II. Sunday-school union of the Methodist Episcopal church. III. Title.

METHODIST Episcopal church 783.
The Epworth hymnal, containing standard hymns of the church, songs for the Sunday-school, songs for social services ... New York. Phillips & Hunt: Cincinnati, Cranston & Stowe, c1885. 231, [1] p. 21 cm. Prepared by a committee appointed in pursuance of the action of the General conference. With music. [M2127.E6H5] 3-16295
1. Sunday-schools—Hymn-books. 2. Methodist Episcopal church—Hymns I. Title.

[MOLDENKE, Charles Edward] 245.2
1860-1935, comp.
... Sunday school hymns ... Watchung, N.J., Elsinore press, 1908-09. 2 v. illus. (port.) 17 cm. At head of title: Villa Elsinore. Without music. [BV520.M6] 41-41804
1. Sunday-schools—Hymn-books. 2. Hymns, English. I. Title.

MURRAY, James R. b.1841. 783.
Heavenward, a choice collection of sacred songs, adapted to the wants of Sunday schools, praise meetings, and the home circle, by James R. Murray. Cleveland, O., S. Brainard's sons [c1877] 160 p. 13 1/2 x 17 cm. With music. [M2193.M97H4] 45-47885
1. Sunday-schools—Hymn-books. I. Title.

NEILSON, William H comp. 245.
Gathered leaves of Sunday school song. Comp. by Rev. Wm. H. Neilson, jr. New York and Chicago, Biglow & Main, 1876. 176 p. 15 cm. [BV520.N4] 20-23337
1. Sunday-schools—Hymn-books. 2. Hymns, English. I. Title.

ORIGINAL hymns for Sabbath 245.
schools ... Boston, Lilly, Wait, Colman & Holden, 1833. vii, [9]-96 p. 15 cm. "Hymns (with the exception of two or three) ... written expressly for this collection."--Advertisement (signed, J. S. W.) Without music. "List of contributors, intended only for friends of the compiler, and not for publication" mounted on inside of front cover. [BV520.O7] 39-10932
1. Sunday-schools—Hymn-books. 2. Hymns, English. I. W., J. S., comp. II. J. S. W., comp.

PEABODY, Andrew Preston, 245.
1811-1893, comp.
A Sunday school hymn book; with devotional services. Compiled by A. P. Peabody ... Boston and Cambridge, J. Munroe & company, 1857. viii, 192 p. 16 1/2 cm. "First published in 1840 ... reprinted with very few omissions, and a few additional hymns."--Pref. [BV520.P37 1857] 45-40608

1. Sunday schools—Hymn-books. 2. Hymns, English. I. Title.

PHILLIPS, Philip, 1834- 1895, comp. 783.
The new complete standard singer, for Sabbath schools, public worship, and special services. By Philip Phillips ... New York and London, P. Phillips & co. [c1869] 224 p. 20 cm. Issued in 7 parts, each with special t.-p. With music. [M2193.P56N4] 45-47321
1. Sunday-schools—Hymn-books. I. Title.

POPPEN, Emmanuel, 1874- ed. 783.7
Primary songs of praise for the primary department of the Sunday school and the home, edited by Emmanuel Poppen, D. D. Columbus, O., The Lutheran book concern [c1935] 22, 70, 93-94 p. 23 cm. Includes orders of service for the primary department and a selection of psalms and prayers. Also published as part of the editor's "Songs of praise for Sunday schools, church societies and the home." [Full name: Emmanuel Frederick Poppen] [M2193.P68P7] 36-1576
1. Sunday-schools—Hymn-books. 2. Lutheran church—Hymns. I. Title.

PROTESTANT Episcopal society for the promotion of evangelical knowledge, New York. 245.
Liturgy and hymns for Sunday-schools. New York, The Protestant Episcopal society for the promotion of evangelical knowledge [18-] 222 p., 1 l., 18, 16 p. 13 cm. Without music. "The church catechism" (16 p. at end) has special t.-p. [BV520.P7] 45-46425
1. Sunday-schools—Hymn-books. 2. Hymns, English. I. Title.

REFORMED church in the United States. 783
The Sunday school hymnal, with offices of devotion. Philadelphia, The Heidelberg press, 1899. [344] p. 20 1/2 cm. "The music was ... edited under the direction of Profs. Adam Gelbel and W. J. Baltwell." [M2193.R32S9 1899] 0-182
1. Sunday-schools—Hymn-books. 2. Hymns, English. I. Title.

REFORMED church in the United States. 783
The Sunday school hymnal, with offices of devotion. 50th thousand. Philadelphia, The Heidelberg press, 1900. xxii, [311], xxiii-xxxiii p. 20 1/2 cm. "The music of this hymnal was edited by Profs. Adam Geibel, W. J. Baltsell, and ... Irvin j. Morgan." [M2193.R32S9 1900] 0-5281
1. Sunday-schools—Hymn-books. 2. Hymns, English. I. Title.

ROBINSON, Charles Seymour, 1829-1899, comp. 245.
A selection of spiritual songs for the Sunday-school. Selected and arranged by Rev. Charles S. Robinson, D.D. New-York, The Century co., c1881. 1 p. l., 249 p. 13 cm. Cover-title: Spiritual songs for the Sunday school. Without music. [BV459.R68 1881] 45-47045
1. Sunday-schools—Hymn-books. 2. Hymns, English. I. Title. II. Title: Spiritual songs for the Sunday school.

ROBINSON, Charles Seymour, 1829-1899, comp. 245.
A selection of spiritual songs for the Sunday-school. Selected and arranged by Rev. Charles S. Robinson, D.D. Richmond, Va., Presbyterian committee of publication; New-York, The Century co. [1882] 1 p. l., 249 p. 13 1/2 cm. Cover-title: Spiritual songs for the Sunday school. Without music. [BV459.R68 1882] 45-47044
1. Sunday-schools—Hymn-books. 2. Hymns, English. I. Title. II. Title: Spiritual songs for the Sunday school.

RODEHEAVER, Homer Alvan, 1880- comp. 783
Progressive Sunday school songs. Compiler: Homer A. Rodeheaver; music editor: Chas. H. Gabriel; services of worship, Marion Lawrence [i.e. Lawrance]; precious Bible promises, Hugh Cork; responsive selections, La Motte Wells... Chicago, Philadelphia, The Rodeheaver co. [c1923] 1 p. l., 256 p. 20 cm. [M2193.R7P6] 23-10835
1. Sunday-schools—Hymn-books. I. Gabriel, Charles H. II. Title.

ROSBOROUGH, William, comp. 783.7
Celestial showers, no. 2. A choice collection of ascred songs, original and selected, for use in churches, Sunday schools, revivals, and young people's meetings. Arranged and selected by William Rosborough. Texarkana, Tex., W. Rosborough [c1900] [224] p. 20 cm. With music. [M2198.R] 0-2322
1. Sunday-schools—Hymn-books. I. Title.

ROWLEY, Charles, E. comp. 783.
... Victory bells, by Rev. C. E. Rowley for revival services, prayer meetings, young people's societies & the Sunday school ... Toledo, O., C. E. Rowley, c1900. cover-title, [92] p. 19 cm. With music. [M2198.R] Mus
1. Sunday-schools—Hymn—books. I. Title.

THE Sabbath school lyre, 783.
a collection of hymns and music, original and selected, for general use in Sabbath schools. Prepared for the New-England S. S. union. Boston, New England Sabbath school union [c1848] [M2193.S118] 45-46814
1. Sunday-schools—Hymn-books. 2. Hymns, English I. New England Sabbath school union.

SCHAUFFLER, Alfred Theodore, 1841or42-1915, ed. 783
Hosanna; for the Sunday school, edited by A. T. Schauffler. New York, The Century co. [c1898] 176 p. 15 1/2 x 19 cm. [M2196.S] 98-529
1. Sunday-schools—Hymn-books. 2. Hymns, English. I. Title.

[SEWALL, Frank] 1837-1915, comp. 783.
The welcome: a book of hymns, songs and lessons, for the children of the New church. 2d ed. New York, The General convention of the New Jerusalemn in the United States of America, 1869. iv p., 1 l., 7-80, 36 p. illus. 17 1/2 cm. Preface signed: F. S. (i.e. Frank Sewall] With music. [M2131.S8S5 1869a] 45-53419
1. Sunday-schools—Hymn-books. 2. Hymns, English. I. General convention of the New Jerusalemn in the U.S.A. II. Title.

SHOWALTER, Anthony J, 1858- 1924. 783.9
The highway to heaven. A new colleciton of gospel songs ...by A. J. Showalter, J. Henry Showalter, J. M. Bowman and T. B. Mosley. Dalton, Ga., The A. J. Showalter company; West Milton, O., The J. Henry Showalter co.; [etc., etc.] c1899. 224 p. 19 cm. [M2193.S] 99-847
1. Sunday-schools—Hymn-books. I. Showalter, J. Henry, joint author. II. Bowman, J. M., joint author. III. Mosley, T. B., joint author. IV. Title.

SMITH, Eleanor, 1858- comp. 783
The children's hymnal, by Eleanor Smith ... Charles H. Farnsworth ... C. A. Fullerton ... New York, Cincinnati [etc.] American book company [c1918] iv, 284 p. 21 cm. [M2193.S642C4] 19-27603
1. Sunday-schools—Hymn-books. 2. Hymns, English. I. Farnsworth, Charles Hubert, 1859- joint comp. II. Fullerton, Charles Alexander, 1861- joint comp. III. Title.

SONG-LAND messenger no. 2. 783
A new and complete collection of music for singing classes, Sunday schools, young people's meetings, and general public worship. By A. J. Showalter, J. S. Hendricks, E. B. Fowler, A. J. Robertson, and J. M. Hunt. Dallas, Tex., Showalter-Lincoln co.; Dalton, Ga., The A. J. Showalter co., c1898. [186] p. 19 cm. [M2193.S] Mus
1. Sunday-schools—Hymn-books. I. Showalter, Anthony J., 1858-1924, comp.

... Spirit and life; 783.
a collection of songs for the Sunday school, young people's societies, devotional meetings, and revival services. Prepared by Rev. E. S. Lorenz and Rev. D. E. Dortch, assisted by Rev. W. T. Dale and James H. Ruebush. Dayton, O., Lorenz & co., 1895. 192 p. 21 1/2 cm. [M2198.L862S52] 17-31260
1. Sunday-schools—Hymn-books. I. Lorenz, Edmund Simon, 1854- II. Dortch, David Elijah, 1851-

STELZER, Theodore George Wilhelm, ed. 783
A child's garden of song. Saint Louis, Concordia Pub. House [1949] 81 p. illus. 21 x 23 cm. [M2193.S78C5] 49-49072
1. Sunday-schools—Hymn-books. 2. Children's songs. I. Title.

THE Sunday school hymn book ... 12th ed. Philadelphia, American Sunday school union, 1826. 1 p. l., [v]-vi, [7]-128, 61, [3] p. 10 1/2 cm. "Appendix. Selected for adult learners by a committee of the Union adult school society," paged separately. [BV520.S77 1826] 6-26921 245.
1. Sunday-schools—Hymns-books. I. American Sunday-school union.

THE Sunday school hymn book ... 12th edition. Philadelphia, American Sunday school union, 1826. 1 p. 1 [v]-vi, [7]-128, 61, [3] p. 10 1/2 cm. "Appendix. Selected for adult learners by a committee of the Union adult school society." paged separately. 6-26921
I. American Sunday school union.

THE Sunday-school music book, enlarged. N[ew] Y[ork] M. W. Dodd, c1858. 66 p. 11 x 14 1/2 cm. [M2193.S957] 45-47336 783.
1. Sunday-schools—Hymn-books.

VESTRY songs; 783.
a collection of hymns and tunes for Sabbath schools, social meetings, and private devotions. Prepared for the Mass, Sabbath school society, and revised by the committee of publication. Boston, Massachusetts Sabbath school society, 1854. xi, 12-234 p. 16 1/2 cm. Preface signed: F. A. B. [M2193.V48 1854] 45-44606
1. Sunday-schools—Hymn-books. I. B., F. A., comp. II. F. A. B. comp. III. Massachusetts Sabbath school society.

VESTRY songs; 783.
a collection of hymns and tunes for Sabbath schools, social meetings, and private devotions. Prepared for the Mass. Sabbath school society, and revised by the committee of publication. 8th ed., rev. and enl. Boston, Massachusetts Sabbath school society [c1854] vi, 12-270 p. 16 1/2 cm. Preface signed: F.A.B. [M2193.V48 1854a] 45-51740
1. Sunday-schools—Hymn-books. I. B., F. A., comp. II. F. A. B. comp. III. Massachusetts Sabbath school society.

WATTS, Isaac, 1674-1748. 245
Questions with answers. Taken from Dr. Watts's Hymns for children. Enlarged from the London edition, and revised by the Committee of publication. Boston, Mass. Sabbath school society, 1842. 64 p. incl. front., illus. 11 1/2 cm. Prepared for the Massachusetts Sabbath school society by Asa Bullard. cf. W. M. Stone's The divine and moral songs of Isaac Watts. [PR3763.W2A665 1842] 32-13275
I. Bullard, Asa. 1804-1888, ed. II. Massachusetts Sabbath school society. III. Title.

WENDTE, Charles William, 1844- comp. 783.9
Heart and voice; a collection of songs for the Sunday school and the home, by Chas. W. Wendte, D.D. Boston, Geo. H. Ellis co., 1917. iv, [231], [341]-347 p. 21 1/2 cm. [M2193.W48H4] 32-7575
1. Sunday-schools—Hymn-books. I. Title.

WHEELER, John S. 783.
Wheeler's new songs, no. 1- Valdosta, Ga., J. S. Wheeler, 1943- v. 20 1/2-21 1/2 cm. Hymns, in shape-note notation. [M2193.W58N4] 44-52631
1. Sunday-schools—Hymn-books. 2. Hymns, English. I. Title.

Sunday schools — Hymns.

BLANKENBAKER, Frances, comp.
Primary children sing; 126 hymns and songs for use at church and home, with suggestions for visualizing and teaching the songs to primaries, compiled by Frances Blankenbaker and Lois L. Curley. Mound, Minn., Praise Book [c1962] 1 v. (unpaged) illus. With music. NUC64
1. Sunday schools — Hymns. 2. Children's songs. I. Title.

GENERAL synod of the Evangelical Lutheran church in the United States of America. 245.2041
Hymns for Sunday-schools. Published by order of the General synod of the Evangelical Lutheran church of the United States. Philadelphia, Lutheran board of publication,[1860] vi, 7-286, 46 p. 13 cm. Without music. "Appendix. Hymns for infants": 46 p. at end. [BV410.A45] 34-8077
1. Sunday-schools—Hymns. 2. Lutheran church—Hymns. 3. Hymns, English. I. Title. II. Title: Hymns for infants.

HAMERSMA, John E. ed. 783.952
Hymns for youth. Comp., ed. by John E. Hamersma, Wilma Vander Baan, Albertha Bratt. Illus. by Edgar Boeve. [n.p. Natl. Union of Christian Schls. and Eerdmans 1966 264p. col. illus. 27cm. With music. [M2193.H2H9] 66-27412 3.95
1. Sunday-schools—Hymns. 2. Hymns, English. I. Title.
Available from Eerdmans, Grand Rapids, Mich.

HULL, Asa.
Sunday school anthem and chorus book. An unique collection of easy anthems, suitable for anniversaries and all special occasions, and choruses for every day in the year, by Asa Hull. New York, A. Hull, 1901. 256 pp. 16 cm. 1-285
I. Title.

HYMNAL for juniors in worship and study. Philadelphia, Westminster c.1966. 146p. 25cm. With music. W. Lawrence Curry, musical ed. 'A number of hymns have been carried over from Hymns for juniors worship Bibl. [M2193.H97] 66-15816 1.75 783.952
1. Sunday-schools—Hymns. 2. Hymns, English. I. Curry, Lawrence, 1906- ed.

JAHSMANN, Allan Hart, ed. 783.9
Little children, sing to God! Compiled and edited by Allan Hart Jahsmann and Arthur W. Gross. Pictures by Frances Hook. Saint Louis, Concordia Pub. House [c.1960] 95p. illus. (part col.) 25cm. M60 2.95 bds.,
1. Sunday-schools—Hymns. 2. Children's songs. I. Gross, Arthur William, 1896- joint ed. II. Title.

JONES, Nettie Lou, ed. 783.95
Songs for primaries. Comp., ed.by Nettie Lou Jones, Saxe Adams. Nashville, Broadman [c.1964] vi, 160p. illus. 27cm. For church and home use. 64-4698 1.75
1. Sunday-schools—Hymns. 2. Children's songs. I. Adams, Saxe, joint editor. II. Title.

MURRAY, James Ramsey, 1841- 1905. 783
Heavenward, achoice collection of sacred songs, adapted to the wants of Sunday schools, praise meetings, and the home circle, by James R. Murray. Cleveland, O., S. Brainard's sons [c1877] 160 p. 13 1/2 x 17 cm. With music. [M2193.M97H4] 45-47885
1. Sunday-schools—Hymns. I. Title.

SCOTTISH school hymnary. Music ed. London, Oxford Univ. Pr. [dist. New York, Oxford c.] 1964. 1 v. (unpaged) 19cm. 64-56297 1.80 783.952
1. Sunday-schools—Hymns. 2. Church of Scotland—Hymns. 3. Hymns, English.

SONGS and hymns for primary children. [Ed. by W. Lawrence Curry, others] Illus. by Marian Ebert. Philadelphia, Westminster, c.1963. 159p. illus. 26cm. 63-13776 1.75 783.9
1. Sunday-schools—Hymns. 2. Children's songs. I. Curry, Lawrence, 1906- ed.

Sunday schools—Junior department

ANDERSON, Robert Phillips, 1866- 268.
Handwork for junior societies, by Rev. Robert P. Anderson ... Boston, Chicago, United society of Christian endeavor [c1921] 122 p. 17 cm. [BV1546.A6] 21-15274 0.75
I. Title.

FLYNT, Faye DeBeck.
Teaching juniors. Philadelphia, The Judson Press [1965, c1954] 96 p. 68-84997
1. Sunday schools—Junior dept. I. Title.

KOONTZ, Ida M. 268.
Junior department organization and administration, by Ida M. Koontz; a textbook in the standard course in teacher training outlined and approved by the Sunday school council of evangelical denominations. Third year specialization series. Dayton, O., Printed for the Teacher training publishing association by the Otterbein press [c1922] 128 p. 17 cm. [BV1546.K6] 22-15903
I. Title.

SODERHOLM, Marjorie Elaine.
The junior; a handbook for his Sunday school teacher. Chicago, Moody Press [c1956] 95 p. illus. 67-69060
1. Sunday-schools—Junior dept. I. Title.

Sunday-schools — Juvenile literature.

HERON, Frances (Dunlap) j268
Jay Bain, junior boy. Illustrated by Janet Smalley. New York, Abingdon Press [1963] 144 p. illus. 21 cm. [BV1521.5.H4] 63-15708
1. Sunday-schools — Juvenile literature. I. Title.

TOOKE, Mary E.
Hand in hand with the wise men; a reading and story book for young children, for use in the school and the home. Chicago and Rochester, N.Y., Williams & Rogers, 1899. 112 p. illus. 12 cm. (The wise men series) Jun
I. Title.

Sunday schools— Kindergarten.

THE good child's Sunday book.
Worcester [Mass.] S. A. Howland [1843] 24 p. illus. 10 x 8 cm. [With Happy Charles, and other stories. Worcester, Mass., 184-?] L. C. copy imperfect: p. 15-24 wanting. [PZ6.H2123] 41-40971

HAVERSTICK, Alexander Campbell.
A Sunday school kindergarten; a practical method of teaching in the infant room, by Alexander C. Haverstock ... Milwaukee, The Young churchman co., 1906. 3 p. l., 57 p. illus. 18 1/2 cm. 9-27432
I. Title.

[MORTON, William Albert] 1866-
Sunday morning in the kindergarten, illustrated lessons for the kindergarten department of the Sunday school. Salt Lake City, Utah, Deseret Sunday school union, 1916. 3 p. l., 157 p. front., illus. 20 cm. $0.75. 16-16292
I. Title.

OGLEVEE, Louise M. 268.
Cradle roll lessons, by Louise M. Oglevee; a book for the cradle roll class of the Sunday school and for little children in the home, a program for every Sunday in the year, including the Bible story, a finger-play, handwork, picture and cut-out suggestions, and songs, both words and music. Cincinnati, O., The Standard publishing company, c1924. 144 p. illus., pl. 24 cm. Music: p. 139-144. [BV1540.O5] 24-9559
I. Title.

PATTY goes to the nursery class; a year's course in twelve units for 2-and 3-year-old children. Illustrated by Faith M. Lowell. Rev. Wheaton, Ill., Scripture press, 1957. 256p. illus., music. 22cm. 'Patty sings in the nursery class': [7]p. inserted in pocket. Bibliography: p.252-254.
1. Sunday schools— Kindergarten. I. Le Bar, Mary Evelyn, 1910-

Sunday schools — Organization and conduct.

RICE, Edwin Wilbur, 1831- ed.
The Sunday-school: how to start and keep it, ed. by Edwin Wilbur Rice, D.D. Revised by the committee. Philadelphia, American Sunday-school union, 1909. 104 p. 16 cm. 0-17653
I. Title.

UNITED Presbyterian Church in the U.S.A. Board of Christian Education.
The Christian education committee in action; a study manual... Philadelphia [c1963] 96 p. 23 cm. "Resources": p. 93-96. 65-65089
1. Sunday schools — Organization and conduct. I. Title.

Sunday schools—Pennsylvania.

HARNER, Nevin Cowger, 268'.8'5733 1901-1951.
Factors related to Sunday school growth and decline in the Eastern Synod of the Reformed Church in the United States. New York, Bureau of Publications, Teachers College, Columbia University, 1931. [New York, AMS Press, 1973, c1972] vi, 101 p. illus. 22 cm. Reprint of the 1931 ed., issued in series: Teachers College, Columbia University. Contributions to education, no. 479. Originally presented as the author's thesis, Columbia. Bibliography: p. 101. [BX9563.H3 1972] 71-176839 ISBN 0-404-55479-2 10.00
1. Reformed Church in the United States. Eastern Synod. 2. Sunday schools—Pennsylvania. 3. Churches—Pennsylvania. I. Title. II. Series: Columbia University. Teachers College. Contributions to education, no. 479.

Sunday-schools—Prayers.

BEARD, Frederica, comp. 248
Prayers for use in home, school and Sunday school, selected and arranged by Frederica Beard. New York, Hodder & Stoughton, George H. Doran company [c1917] ix, [2], 15-81 p. 20 1/2 cm. $0.60 [BV265.B4] 17-24844
I. Title.

BRACHER, Marjory Louise, compiler. 264.1
Church school prayers. Philadelphia, Muhlenberg Press [c1956] 56p. 16cm. [BV283.S9B7] 55-5640
1. Sunday-schools—Prayers. I. Title.

HOWARD, Philip Eugene, 1870- 264.
Leading in prayer (a prayer before the lesson) a collection of brief prayers for use in the Sunday-school and in the home, by Philip E. Howard. Philadelphia, The Sunday school times company [c1922] iv, 153 p. 16 cm. Published in 1911 under title: A prayer before the lesson. [BV245.H6 1922] 23-704
I. Title.

KIRKPATRICK, William J.
Sunday-school praises; prepared especially for use in the Sunday-school. Cincinnati [etc.] Jennings & Pye; New York [etc.] Eaton & Mains [1900] 184 p. 8 degree. Nov
I. Title.

PELL, Edward Leigh, 1861- 264.1
The superintendent's book of prayer, by Edward Leigh Pell. Richmond, Va., Harding company, inc. [c1905] 64 p. 17 cm. [BV283.S9P4] 5-10560
1. Sunday-schools—Prayers. I. Title.

Sunday schools, Protestant—Administration.

*RANEY, L. H. 268.1
Blueprint for a balanced Sunday school, by L. H. Raney, others. Grand Rapiopds, Baker Bk. [1967] 89p. 20cm. Bibl. 1.50 pap.,
1. Sunday schools, Protestant—Administration. I. Title.

Sunday-schools—Question-books.

GORDON, Helen. 232.9076
"The way, the truth, and the life." Questions on the life of our Saviour for the use of Sunday-schools and Bible classes in the Protestant Episcopal church. By M,iss Helen Gordon. Advanced series. Boston, New York, E. P. Dutton and company, 1869. vi. 124 p. 16 cm. Illustrated t.-p. [BT307.G65] 35-32277
1. Jesus Christ—Biog—Study. 2. Sunday—Schools—Question-books. I. Title.

GORDON, Helen. 232.9076
"The way, the truth, and the life." Questions on the life of our Saviour., for the use of Sunday-schools in the Protestant Episcopal church. By Miss Helen Gordon. Primary series. Boston, New York, E. P. Dutton and company, 1869. vi, 152 p. 16 cm. Illustrated t.-p. [BT307.G63] 35-32279
1. Jesus Christ—Biog.—Study. 2. Sunday-schools—Question-books. I. Title.

IMPROVED question-book 232.9076
on the life of Christ. With the text. Arranged for classes of all ages. Philadelphia, New York, American Sunday-school inoin [1868] 134 p. 13 cm. [BT307.I 6] 35-33518
1. Jesus Christ—Biog.—Study. 2. Sunday-schools—Question-books. I. American Sunday-school union.

KNOX, Charles Eugene, 1833- 232.9 1900.
Sermons and addresses of Our Saviour. The fourth year of the graduatedSunday-school text-books. By Charles E. Knox ... New York, A. D. F. Randolph, 1866. iv, [3]-183 p. 18 cm. Title vignette. [BT307.K6] 35-28544
1. Jesus Christ—Words. 2. Sunday-schools—Question-books. I. Title.

ROBINSON, L. L. 232.9076
Questions on the life of Christ. By Miss L. L. Robinson ... Milwaukee, Wis., The Young churchman co. [c1897] 142 p. 16 1/2 cm. [BT307.R6] 35-23994
1. Jesus Christ—Biog.—Study. 2. Sunday-schools—Question-books. I. Title.

WINKLEY, Samuel Hobart, 232.9076 d.1911.
A new analytical question-book on the life and ministry of Jesus. By S. H. Winkley. Boston, Press of J. Wilson and son, 1873. 78 p. 18 cm. [BT307.W74] 35-23995
1. Jesus Christ—Biog.—Study. 2. Sunday-schools—Question-books. I. Title.

WINKLEY, Samuel Hobart, 232.90761 d.1911.
Questions concerning the Son of man. By S. H. Winkley. Boston, Unitarian Sunday-school society, 1885. viii, [9]-82 p. 18 cm. [BT307.W75] 35-29986
1. Jesus Christ—Biog.—Study. 2. Sunday-schools—Question books. I. Unitarian Sunday school society. II. Title.

Sunday-schools—Recitations, exercises, etc.

SMITH, Carrie Heckman, Mrs. 377 1870-
Keystone graded Sunday-school lessons. Beginners teachers' manual, ed. by C. R. Blackall, D.D.; prepared by Carrie H. Smith and Kate Hershey Rowland... Philadelphia, Boston [etc.] American Baptist publication society [c1912] 128 p. 21 cm. $0.75 [MT10.B62] 12-27184
1. Sunday-schools—Recitations, exercises, etc. I. Rowland, Mrs. Kate Shirley Hershey, 1855- joint author. II. Blackall, C. R., ed. III. Title.

Sunday-schools—Records.

FOX, Edgar Alonzo, 1858-
Sunday-school records, reports and recognitions, by E. A. Fox ... Philadelphia, The Sunday school times company [c1907] viii, 113 p. illus. 19 cm. (On cover: The "Times" handbooks for Sunday-school workers. no. 6) 7-26996
I. Title.

NOLAND, Emma. 268.5
The six point record system and its use. [Rev. ed., 1955] Nashville, Convention Press [1958, c1941] 139p. 20cm. [BV1527.N6 1958] 60-15018
1. Sunday-schools—Records. I. Title.

NOLAND, Emma. 268.45
The six point record system and its use [by] Emma Noland ... Nashville, Tenn., The Sunday school board of the Southern Baptist convention [c1941] 156 p. incl. forms. 20 cm. "Replaces the old text The Sunday school secretary and the six point record system which was issued under the joint authorship of Flake and Noland."--Introd. [BV1527.N6] 41-14403
1. Sunday-schools—Records. I. Flake, Arthur. The Sunday school secretary and the six point record system. II. Southern Baptist convention. Sunday school board. III. Title.

Sunday-schools—Societies.

BRAIN, Belle Marvel, 1859-
Fuel for missionary fires. Some programmes and plans for use in young people's societies, Sunday-schools, monthly missionary concerts, and mission bands. By Belle M. Brain ... Boston and Chicago, United society of Christian endeavor [c1912] 115 p. fold. pl. 15 cm. "A part of the matter in the following pages has appeared from time to time in the columns of the Sunday school times in the 'Ways of working' department." Bibliography: p. 109-115. 13-2473
I. Title.

NEW York Sunday school union society.
... Annual report of the New-York Sunday school union society ... 1st (Feb. 1817)- New-York, Printed for the Society, 18? v. tables. 21 1/2 cm. Title varies: 1st, First report of the New-York Sunday school union society ... 2d- Annual report of the New-York Sunday school union society ... [BV1503.N418] A 32
1. Sunday-schools—Societies. I. Title.

ORGANIZED Bible Class 268.06273 Association.
Report [of the] conference. Washington. v. 28 cm. annual. [BV1503.O7] 52-17242
1. Sunday-schools—Societies. I. Title.

TROY, N.Y. Sunday school association.
The ... annual report of the Board of inspectors of the Sunday school association of the city of Troy ... 1st (1817)- [n.p., 1817]- v. 21 cm. [BV1503.T8] A 32
1. Sunday-schools—Societies. I. Title.

WILLIAMSON, E. Stanley. 268.06273
Helping churches through associational Sunday school work. Nashville, Convention Press [c1959] 146 p. 29 cm. [BX6222.A1W5] 59-9966
1. Sunday schools — Societies, etc. 2. Baptist associations. I. Title.

Sunday-schools—Teaching.

AXTELL, James Wickleff. 268.
The teaching problem; a message to Sunday school workers., by J. W. Axtell ... Nashville, Tenn., The Cumberland press, 1902. 1 p. l., 152 p. illus. 18 cm. [BV1531.A83] 2-26247
I. Title.

BLACK, Israel Putnam, 1845-1903.
Practical primary plans for primary teachers of the Sunday-school, by Israel P. Black. With an appendix containing a list of helpful books, and appliances. New York, Chicago [etc.] F. H. Revell company, 1897. 5 p. l., [9]-196 p. 18 1/2 cm. Fifth preliminary leaf numbered vii. [LC381.B56] E 12
1. Sunday-schools—Teaching. I. Title.

BERGER, William Francis. 268.
The Sunday-school teacher and the Book, by William Francis Berger ... New York, Chicago [etc.] Fleming H. Revell company [c1956] 153 p. 20 cm. [BV1534.B37] 26-14438
I. Title.

BOMBERGER, John Huston, 1858-
Three thousand practical illustrations in religion and morals, a classified collection of anecdotes, incidents and thought-germs for preachers, platform speakers, Sunday school superintendents and teachers, Christian workers and Bible readers, with copious indexes: homiletic topical, textual, Biblical, biographical, junior congregation and Sunday School lesson gathered and arranged by J. H.Bomberger... Cleveland, O., Central publishing house, 1909. v, 450 p. 23 cm. 9-28185
I. Title.

BRETHREN lesson commentary on the International Sunday-school lessons for 1903. By Eld. I. Bennett Trout Elgin, Ill., Brethren Publishing house [1902] front., illus., maps, plan. 23 1/2 cm. 3-604

BUTLER, Alford Augustus, 1845-
How to study the life of Christ; a handbook for Sunday-school teachers, and

other Bible students, by the Reverend Alford A. Butler ... 2d ed. New York, T. Whittaker [c1901] 175 p. front. (map) 19 1/2 cm. 3-13573
I. Title.

CHAPMAN, Marie M. 268.6
Practical methods for Sunday School teachers. Grand Rapids, Mich., Zondervan [c.1962] 64p. 21cm. (Sunday School know-how ser.) 1.00 pap.,
I. Title.

CHURCH of the brethren. 262.
General Sunday school board.
Training the Sunday school teacher. First standard course. By E. B. Hoff, H. K. Ober, J. S. Flory, I. B. Trout. Approved by the Committee on education, International Sunday school association. Published by the General Sunday school board of the Church of the brethren. Elgin, Ill., For sale by Brethren publishing house [c1913] 288 p. illus. (maps) 18 1/2 cm. [BV1533.H6 1913] 13-12528
I. Hoff, Emanuel Buechley, 1880- joint author. II. Ober, Henry Kulp, 1878- joint author. III. Flory, John Samuel, 1866- joint author. IV. Trout, Isaiah Bennett, 1860- joint author. V. Title.

CRAFTS, Wilbur Fisk, 1850-
Through the eye to the heart; or, Eye-teaching in the Sunday-school. By Rev. W. F. Crafts. ["Callen Fisk."] With an introduction by J. H. Vincent, D. D., and an appendix for primary-class teachers by Mrs. W. F. Crafts. [Sara J. Timanus.] New York, Nelson & Phillips; Cincinnati, Hitchcock & Walden [1874?] 224 p. front., illus. 20 cm. 15-22026
I. Crafts, Sara Jane (Timanus) "Mrs. W. F. Crafts." II. Title.

DU BOIS, Patterson, 1847-1917.
The point of contact in teaching, by Patterson Du Bois ... Philadelphia, J. D. Wattles & co., 1897. vii, 86 p. 18 cm. [LC377.D84] E 10
1. Sunday-schools—[Teaching] I. Title.

EAVEY, Charles Benton, 1889-
How to be an effective Sunday School teacher. Grand Rapids. Zondervan Publishing House [1962, c1955] 89 p. 64-32668
I. Title.

*GANGEL, Kenneth O. 268.07
Sunday School Evangelism; A guide of practical helps for teaching teachers and leaders in the church educational program. Wheaton, Ill., Box 327, Evangelical Teacher Trng. Assoc., c. 1964. (various p.) Bibl. 1.35, pap., plastic bdg.
I. Title.

GROTON, William Mansfield, 1850-
ed.
The Sunday-school teacher's manual, designed as an aid to teachers in preparing Sunday-school lessons. Ed. by the Rev. William M. Groton ... Philadelphia, G. W. Jacobs & company [1909] 391 p. 21 cm. Bibliography at end of each chapter. 9-2533
I. Title.

GUILD, Clara T. 268.
The little child in Sunday school; a manual for teachers of beginners' classes (ages, four and five) by Clara T. Guild and Lillian B. Poor. Boston, Mass., The Beacon press, inc. [c1918] 220 p. 23 cm. (Half-title: The new Beacon course of graded lessons, W. I. Lawrence, F. Buck, editors) "Songs" [with music]: p. [201]-229. [BV1540.G8] 18-17915
I. Poor, Lillian B. II. Title.

HAMILL, Howard Melancthon, 1847-
Sunday-school teacher-training, by H. M. Hamill ... [Rev. ed.] Philadelphia, The Sunday school times co. [c1907] v. 110 p. 19 1/2 cm. "Reprinted from the Sunday school times." 7-24761
I. Title.

HARKER, Ray Clarkson.
The work of the Sunday-school; a manual for teachers, by Ray Clarkson Harker, D. D. New York, Chicago [etc.] Fleming H. Revell company [c1911] 2 p. l., 7-194 p. 20 cm. 11-26770 1.00
I. Title.

*JACOBS, J. Vernon 268.7
How to plan and conduct Sunday school worship services. Grand Rapids, Mich., Zondervan [c.1964] 63p. 20cm. (Sunday sch. know-how ser.) 1.00 pap.,
I. Title.

JACOBS, J. Vernon 268.081
Teaching tools for Sunday schools; teaching methods, types of lessons, and teaching materials. Grand Rapids, Mich., Zondervan [c.1963] 64p. diagrs. 21p. (Sunday school know-how ser.) 1.00 pap.,
I. Title.

JACOBS, James Vernon 268
How to increase your Sunday school attendance. Grand Rapids, Michigan, Zondervan [c.1960] 64p. 20cm. (Sunday know-how ser.) 1.00 pap.,
I. Title.

KNIGHT, Edgar Wallace, 1885-
Some principles of teaching as applied to the Sunday-school, by Edgar W. Knight ... with an introduction by Professor Franklin N. Parker ... Boston, New York [etc.] The Pilgrim press [c1915] x, 157 p. 20 cm. Contains bibliographies. 15-24846 0.75
I. Title.

LAWRENCE, Marion.
The working manual of a successful Sunday-school; being for the most part the actual working manual in use for years in the Washington street Congregational Sunday-school, Toledo, Ohio, with the addition of some features not yet in use but planned for the future, by Marion Lawrence ... New York, Chicago [etc.] F. H. Revell company [c1908] 58 p. front. 19 cm. 9-31248
I. Title.

LESTER, H. A., ed.
Sunday school teaching; its aims and its methods, ed. by the Rev. H. A. Lester ... with an introduction by the Bishop of London. London, New York [etc.] Longmans, Green and co., 1912. x, 133, [3] p. 19 cm. [London diocesan Sunday school series] "Books recommended for the Sunday school teachers' library": p. 130-131. [LC381.L56] E 12
1. Sunday schools—[Teaching] I. Title.
Contents omitted.

METCALF, Joel Hastings, 920.
1866-1925.
... *World stories,* by Joel H. Metcalf. Boston, Chicago, Unitarian Sunday-school society [c1909] 3 p. l., 118 p., 1 l., 3. p. 21 cm. (The Beacon series; a graded course of study for the Sunday School. [4a]) On cover: Teachers' edition with helper. [BX9821.B4 vol. 4a] 9-26324
I. Title.

MITCHELL, James Alexander, 268
1844-
The normal manual of modern Sunday, school method, ...By Pastor James A. Mitchell...With an introduction by the Rev. T. O. Fuller, D.D. [Memphis, Memphis S.S. publishing co.] 1919- v. 19 cm. [BV1520.M6] 19-13533
I. Title.

MULLER, G J. 221.
Junior class manual; a scholar's textbook, for study at home, and recitation and explanation in classes, by G. J. Muller; a book of essentials for pre-confirmation classes. Philadelphia, Pa., The United Lutheran publication house] 1923] 127 p. 19 cm. [BX8015.M8] 23-13821
I. Title.

OSBORN, Andrew Rule.
Method in teaching; a text-book for Sunday school teachers, by Rev. A. R. Osborn ... London, New York [etc.] H. Frowde, 1913. 151 p. illus., diagrs. 20 cm. [LC381.O8] E 13
1. Sunday school—Teaching. I. Title.

SHERIDAN, Harold James, 1885-
... *Learning and teaching,* by Harold J. Sheridan and G. C. White, approved by the Committee on curriculum of the Board of Sunday schools of the Methodist Episcopal church and the Committee on curriculum of the General Sunday school board of the Methodist Episcopal church, South. New York, Cincinnati, The Methodist book concern; Nashville, Dallas [etc.] Smith & Lamar [c1918] 207 p. 19 cm. (Training courses for leadership ed. by H. H. Meyer and E. B. Chappell) [LC3S1.S5] E 19
1. Sunday schools—[Teaching] 2. Religious education. I. White, Goodrich Cook, 1889- joint author. II. Title.

SMILEY, W B.
Teacher training manual; an outline study of the scriptures as a preparation for teaching in the Sabbath-school; prepared by W. B. Smiley... Pittsburg, Pa., United Presbyterian board of publication [c1911] 1 p. l., iii p., 2 l., 85 p. 3 maps. 18 1/2 cm. The maps are detached. E 11
1. Sunday schools—Teaching. 2. Teachers—Training—Sunday schools. I. United Presbyterian board of publication. II. Title.

SMITH, Frank Wade. 268
How to improve your Sunday school, by Frank Wade Smith ... New York, Cincinnati, The Abingdon press [c1924] 75 p. 17 cm. Contains bibliographies. [BV1520.S63] 24-12303
I. Title.

SMITH, William Walter.
Sunday school teaching; the simple elements of childstudy and religious pedagogy in popular and interesting form. Comp. from leading educators. Together with some gratuitors advice on Sunday school management, by the Rev. William Walter Smith ... Milwaukee, The Young churchman co., 1903. 166, [2] p. 19 cm. "List of reference books suggested": p. [161]-163. 3-24232
I. Title.

TOMPKINS, De Loss M.
Vest pocket commentary on Sunday school international lessons for 1899, for teachers and scholars... Chicago, F. D. Ewell, 1898. [114 pp.] 24 cm. 98-2210
I. Title.

TRALLE, Henry Edward.
Sunday school experience, by Henry Edward Tralle ... a first standard teacher-training textbook. Mexico, Mo., Hardin college press [c1913] 3 p. l., [9]-335 p. 17 1/2 cm. $0.50 13-7552
I. Title.

TRUMBULL, Henry Clay, 1830-1903.
Teaching and teachers; or, The Sunday-school teacher's teaching work and the other work of the Sunday-school teacher. By H. Clay Trumbull ... Philadelphia, J. D. Wattles, 1884. ii, 390 p. 18 1/2 cm. [LC381.T76] E13
1. Sunday-schools—[Teaching] I. Title.

URBAN, A.
Sunday school teacher's explanation of the Baltimore catechism, by the Rev. A. Urban. New York, J. F. Wagner, 1908. 437 p. 20 1/2 cm. 9-3901
I. Title.

VAN MARTER, Martha, 1839-
The primary teacher with helps and exercises, by Martha Van Marter, introduction by Jesse Lyman Hurlbut. New York, Hunt & Eaton; Cincinnati; Cranston & Curts, 1893. 166. 18 1/2 cm. [LC381.V38] E13
1. Sunday schools—Teaching. I. Title.

WEIGLE, Luther Allan, 1880- 268
... *The pupil,* by Luther A. Weigle ... Together with an appendix especially designed for church teachers. Prepared by the Parochial department of the General board of religious education. Milwaukee, Wis., The Morehouse publishing co. [c1918] 78, xviii p. 19 cm. (Protestant Episcopal church in the U.S. General board of religious education. Standard course in teacher training) At head of title: First year--unit I. Bibliography at end of each chapter. [BV1520.W42] E 21
1. Sunday schools—[Teaching] I. Title.

WEIGLE, Luther Allan, 1880- 268
... *The teacher,* by Luther A. Weigle ... Together with an appendix especially designed for church teachers. Prepared by the Parochial department of the General board of religious education. Milwaukee, Wis., The Morehouse publishing co. [c1918] 2 p. l., 85-166, xiv p. 19 cm. (Protestant Episcopal church in the U.S. General board of religious education. Standard course in teacher training) At head of title: First year--unit II. Bibliography at end of each chapter. [BV1520.W422] E 21
1. Sunday schools—[Teaching] 2. Teachers—Training [of]—[Sunday schools] I. Title.

WELLS, Amos Russel, 1862-
The ideal adult class in the Sunday-school; a manual of principles and methods, by Amos R. Wells ... Boston, New York [etc.] The Pilgrim press [c1912] 126 p. 19 1/2 cm. $0.50. 12-28367
I. Title.

WIMMS, J. H.
The way and the work; a manual of Sunday school teaching, by J. H. Wimms ... and Rev. Frederick Humphrey. Boston, The Pilgrim press; [etc., etc.] 1914. 165, [1] p. 19 cm. [LC381.W7] E14
1. Sunday schools—[Teaching] I. Humphrey, Frederick, joint author. II. Title.

WINSHIP, Albert Edward, 1845-
Methods and principles in Bible study and Sunday-school teaching; by Rev. A. E. Winship. Boston, W. A. Wilde & co., 1885. 227 p. 20 cm. E 11
1. Sunday schools—Teaching. 2. Bible—Study. I. Title.

WORKER'S training course No. 4; Sunday school evangelism. Cleveland, Pathway Press. [c1958] 125p.
I. Paulk, Earl P

Sunday-schools—[Teaching—Kindergarten methods]

FOSTER, Mary Jane (Chisholm)
Mrs. 1848-
The kindergarten of the church, by J. Chisholm Foster. New York, Hunt & Eaton; Cincinnati, Cranston & Curts, 1894. 227 p. 19 cm. E 10
1. Sunday-schools—[Teaching—Kindergarten methods] I. Title.

PROTESTANT Episcopal church in the U. S. New York, Diocese of. Sunday school commission.
Kindergarten lessons for church Sunday schools; a manual for the instruction of beginners; prepared for the Sunday school commission, Diocese of New York. Milwaukee, The Young churchman company, 1911. xxxii, 148 p. illus., diagrs. 19 cm. E 14
1. Sunday schools—[Teaching—Kindergarten methods] I. Title.

Sunday-schools—United States.

SKELTON, Eugene. 268'.0973
10 fastest-growing Southern Baptist Sunday Schools. Nashville, Broadman Press [1974] 152 p. illus. 21 cm. [BV1516.A1S56] 73-83831 ISBN 0-8054-6515-4 1.50 (pbk.)
1. Sunday-schools—United States. 2. Church growth—Case studies. I. Title.

Sunday-schools—U.S.—Case studies.

TOWNS, Elmer L. 268'.0973
The ten largest Sunday schools and what makes them grow, by Elmer L. Towns. Grand Rapids, Baker Book House [1969] 163 p. illus. 20 cm. Bibliographical footnotes. [BV1521.T63] 74-98554 1.95
1. Sunday-schools—U.S.—Case studies. I. Title.

Sunday-schools—U.S.—History.

LYNN, Robert W. 268'.0973
The big little school : two hundred years of the Sunday school / Robert W. Lynn and Elliott Wright. 2d ed., rev. and enl. Birmingham, Ala. : Religious Education Press, c1980. v, 178 p. ; 20 cm. Includes bibliographical references and indexes. [BV1516.A1L9 1980] 19 79-27864 ISBN 0-89135-021-7 : 6.95
1. Sunday-schools—United States—History. I. Wright, H. Elliott, 1937- joint author. II. Title.

Sunday-schools—Virginia.

MILLER, Minor Cline, 1889- 268'.0924
These things I remember, by Minor C. Miller, Philadelphia, Dorrance [1968] 226p. 21cm. [BV1470.3.M5A3] (B) 67-18237 4.50
1. Sunday-schools—Virginia. I. Title.

Sunday—Sermons.

BACON, George Blagden, 1836-1876. 263
The Sabbath question. Sermons preached to the Valley church, Orange, N. J., by George B. Bacon, pastor. New York, C. Scribner & co., 1868. v p., 2 l., [11]-194 p. 20 cm. [BV130.B28] 35-28815
1. Sunday—Sermons. 2. Sermons, American. I. Title.

CHAPMAN, Michael Andrew. 248
Sundays of the saints; sermon outlines for the feast days which may occur on Sundays, by the Reverend Michael Andrew Chapman ... St. Louis, Mo. and London, B. Herder book co., 1928. vii, 217 p. 19 cm. [BX1756.C5S8] 28-29359
I. Title.

HILL, Owen Aloysius, 1863- 248
Sermons for Sundays; or, The seed is the Word of God, by Owen A. Hill, S.J. St. Louis, Mo., and London, B. Herder book co., 1926. x, 373 p. 19 1/2 cm. [BX1756.H5S4 1926] 26-15362
I. Title.

RAYCROFT, Benjamin Joseph. 238.
Sermons for every Sunday in the year, dedicated to his fellow-students by the author, Rev. B. J. Raycroft, A. M. New York & Cincinnati, F. Pustet & co., 1900. 351 p. 22 cm. [BX1756.R3 1900] 0-3370
I. Title.

Sunday, William Ashley, 1862-1935.

BROWN, Elijah P. 1842- 922
The real Billy Sunday; the life and work of Rev. William Ashley, D.D., the baseball evangelist, by Elijah P. Brown, D.D. (Ram's Horn Brown)... New York, Chicago [etc.] Fleming H. Revell company [c1914] 285 p. front., plates, ports., facsims. 19 1/2 cm. [BV3785.S8B7] 14-5825
1. Sunday, William Ashley, 1862-1935. I. Title.

ELLIS, William Thomas, 1873- 922
Billy Sunday, the man and his message, by William T. Ellis ... including Mr. Sunday's autobiography, a concluding chapter by Mrs. William A. Sunday and a yoke-fellow's tribute by Homer A. Rodeheaver ... Philadelphia, Chicago [etc.] The John C. Winston company [c1936] xvi, 519 p. front., illus., plates, ports. 21 cm. "De brewer's big bosses" (words and music): p. [64] [BV3785.S8E6] 36-7658
1. Sunday, William Ashley, 1862-1935. I. Title.

FRANKENBERG, Theodore Thomas, 1877- 922
Billy Sunday, his tabernacle and sawdust trials, a biographical sketch of the famous baseball evangelist, by Theodore Thomas Frankenberg ... Columbus, O., The F. J. Heer printing co., 1917. 224 p. front., illus. plates, ports. 20 cm. [BV3785.S8F7] 17-16191 1.00
1. Sunday, William Ashley, 1863- I. Title.

FRANKENBERG, Theodore Thomas, 1877- 922
Billy Sunday, his tabernacle and sawdust trials, a biographical sketch of the famous baseball evangelist, by Theodore Thomas Frankenberg ... Columbus, O., The F. J. Heer printing co., 1917. 224 p. front., illus. plates, ports. 20 cm. [BV3785.S8F7] 17-16191 1.00
1. Sunday, William Ashley, 1863- I. Title.

FRANKENBERG, Theodore Thomas, 1877-
Spectacular career of Rev. Billy Sunday, famous baseball evangelist, by Theodore Thomas Frankenberg ... Columbus, O., McClelland & company [c1913] 231 p. front., plates, ports. 20 cm. "Authorities quoted": p. 229-231. "Publications and records consulted": p. 231. 14-550 1.00
1. Sunday, William Ashley, 1863- I. Title.

FRANKENBERG, Theodore Thomas, 1877-
Spectacular career of Rev. Billy Sunday, famous baseball evangelist, by Theodore Thomas Frankenberg ... Columbus, O., McClelland & company [c1913] 231 p. front., plates, ports. 20 cm. "Authorities quoted": p. 229-231. "Publications and records consulted": p. 231. 14-550 1.00
1. Sunday, William Ashley, 1863- I. Title.

LOCKERBIE, D. Bruce 269.20924
Billy Sunday [Waco. Tex., Word Bks., 1966, c.1965] 64p. illus., ports. 29cm. Based on the motion picture by Sacred Cinema [BV3785.S8L6] 66-1560 3.50 bds.,
I. Sunday, William Ashley, 1862-1935. II. Title.

MCLOUGHLIN, William Gerald. 922
Billy Sunday was his real name. [Chicago] University of Chicago Press [1955] 324 p. illus. 24 cm. [BV3783.S8M35] 55-5138
1. Sunday, William Ashley, 1862-1935. I. Title.

PARKER, Andrew McClean. 922
Billy Sunday meetings, by Mac Parker; reprinted from the reports of Mac Parker as they appeared in the Tampa morning tribune during the Tampa revival of March and April, 1919'... 1st ed. Tampa Tribune press, c1919. 83 p., 1 l. incl. facsim. ports. 23 cm. [BV3785.S8P2] 19-8643 0.60
1. Sunday, William Ashley, 1863- I. Title.

PARKER, Andrew McClean. 922
Billy Sunday meetings, by Mac Parker; reprinted from the reports of Mac Parker as they appeared in the Tampa morning tribune during the Tampa revival of March and April, 1919 ... 1st ed. Tampa Tribune press, c1919. 83 p., 1 l. incl. facsim. ports. 23 cm. [BV3785.S8P2] 19-8643 0.60
1. Sunday, William Ashley, 1863- I. Title.

RODEHEAVER, Homer Alvan, 1880- 922
Twenty years with Billy Sunday [by] Homer Rodeheaver. Nashville, Cokesbury press [c1936] 149 p. front., plates, ports. 19 1/2 cm. [BV3785.S8R6] 36-22369
1. Sunday, William Ashley, 1862-1935. I. Title.

SUNDAY, Helen Amelia (Thompson) 1868- 922
'Ma' Sunday still speaks; a transcription of the tape recording she made shortly before her death. Winona Lake, Ind., Winona Lake Christian Assembly [1957] 55p. illus. 18cm. [BV3785.S8S8] 57-43685
1. Sunday, William Ashley, 1862-1935. I. Title.

SUNDAY, William Ashley, 1862-1935. 922
"Billy" Sunday, the man and his message, with his own words which have won thousands for Christ, by William T. Ellis ... Authorized ed. Philadelphia, Chicago [etc.] The John C. Winston company [c1914] 482 p. front., illus., plates, ports. 22 1/2 cm. [BV3785.S8A3 1914] 14-22162
I. Ellis, William Thomas, 1873- II. Title.

SUNDAY, William Ashley, 1862-1935.
"Billy" Sunday, the man and his message, with his own words which have won thousands for Christ, by William T. Ellis ... Authorized ed. Philadelphia, The John C. Winston company [c1917] 432 p. front., illus., plates, ports. 22 cm. 17-9586
I. Ellis, William Thomas, 1873- II. Title.

THOMAS, Lee, 1918- 922
The Billy Sunday story: the life and times of William Ashley Sunday; an authorized biography. Grand Rapids, Zondervan Pub. House [1961] 256 p. illus. 23 cm. [BV3785.S8T5] 61-14864
1. Sunday, William Ashley, 1862-1935. I. Title.

THOMAS, Lee [Obra Lee Thomas] 922
The Billy Sunday story; the life and times of William Ashley Sunday; an authorized biography. Grand Rapids, Zondercan Pub. House [c.1961] 256p. illus. 61-14864 3.95
1. Sunday, William Ashley, 1862-1935. I. Title.

Sunday, William Ashley, 1862-1935- The second coming.

PRESTON, William J. 232.
Billy Sunday's doctrine conerning the second coming exposed by the voice of Scripture (a brief examination of the doctrine of William Ashley Sunday, as set forth in his book, The second coming.) by Wm. J. Preston ... [Anderson, Ind., c1924] 1 p. l., 5-141 p. 19 cm. [BT885.S87P7] 25-4419
1. Sunday, William Ashley, 1863- The second coming. I. Title.

Sunderland, Eng.—Social conditions.

ROBSON, Brian Turnbull. 301.3'64
Urban analysis: a study of city structure with special reference to Sunderland, by B. T. Robson. London, Cambridge U.P., 1969. xii, 302 p. illus., maps. 24 cm. (Cambridge geographical series, no. 1) Bibliography: p. 284-294. [HN398.S85R6] 68-25086 ISBN 0-521-07272-7 80/- ($12.50)
1. Sunderland, Eng.—Social conditions. 2. Cities and towns. 3. Human ecology. I. Title. II. Series.

Sunflower Co., Miss.—Genealogy

MARRIAGE records Sunflower county-Leflore county, Mississippi, 1844-59, 1860-71. [Greenwood? Miss, 1956] 1v. (various pagings) 28cm. Cover title.
1. Sunflower Co., Miss.—Geneal. 2. Leflore Co., Miss.—Geneal. I. Lowe, Hester R II. Sunflower Co., Miss. III. Leflore Co., Miss.

Sunrise cooperative farm community, Alicia, Mich.

IN quest of heaven;
the story of the Sunrise cooperative farm community. New York, Sunrise history pub. committee [1957] 255p. illus., port. 23cm.
1. Sunrise cooperative farm community, Alicia, Mich. I. Cohen, Joseph J

Superiors, Religious.

ALBERIONE, Giacomo Giuseppe, 1884- 248.8943
The superior follows the master, by James Alberione. Translated by a Daughter of St. Paul. [Boston] St. Paul Editions [1965] 213 p. 19 cm. [BX4212.A413] 65-24080
1. Superiors, Religious. I. Title.

COLIN, Louis, 1884- 271
The superior's handbook. Translated from the French by Fergus Murphy. Chicago, Regnery, 1955 [i. e. 1956] 144p. 23cm. [BX2438.C6] 56-4461
1. Superiors, Religious. I. Title.

FUTRELL, John Carroll. 255
Making an apostolic community of love; the role of the superior according to St. Ignatius of Loyola. St. Louis, Institute of Jesuit Sources, 1970. 231 p. 24 cm. "A condensation of a ... dissertation." Bibliography: p. 217-221. [BX2434.F87] 73-139365 8.50
1. Loyola, Ignacio de, Saint, 1491-1556. 2. Superiors, Religious. I. Title.

GALOT, Jean. 255
Inspiritor of the community; the new role of the religious superior. Staten Island, N.Y., Alba House [1971] vii, 110 p. 22 cm. Translation of Animatrice de communaute. [BX4209.G3313] 75-169147 ISBN 0-8189-0235-3 3.95
1. Superiors, Religious. I. Title.

SALMON, Pierre, Aug.23,1896- 255
The abbot in monastic tradition; a contribution to the history of the perpetual character of the office of religious superiors in the West. Translated by Claire Lavoie. Washington, Cistercian Publications, Consortium Press, 1972. xv, 160 p. 23 cm. (Cistercian studies series, no. 14) Translation of L'abbe dans la tradition monastique. Bibliography: p. 151-153. [BX2434.2.S2413 1972] 78-158955 ISBN 0-87907-814-6 9.95
1. Superiors, Religious. 2. Monasticism and religious orders—History. I. Title. II. Series.

Supernatural.

BALTAZAR, Eulalio R. 201
Teilhard and the supernatural, by Eulalio R. Baltazar. Baltimore, Helicon [1966] 336 p. 22 cm. Bibliographical footnotes. [B2430.T374B27] 66-26481
1. Teilhard de Chardin, Pierre. 2. Supernatural. I. Title.

BERGER, Peter L. 230
A rumor of angels; modern society and the rediscovery of the supernatural [by] Peter L. Berger. [1st ed.] Garden City, N.Y., Doubleday, 1969. xi, 129 p. 22 cm. Bibliographical references included in "Notes" (p. [125]-129) [BL100.B43] 69-10979 4.50
1. Supernatural. 2. Religion and sociology. I. Title.

BRABANT, Frank Herbert, 1892- 201
Religion and the mysterious, by Rev. F. H. Brabant ... London, New York [etc.] Longmans, Green and co., 1930. viii p., 2 l., 97, [1] p. 20 cm. (Half-title: Anglican library of faith and thought) [BL100.B7] 30-30524
1. Supernatural. 2. Psychology, Religious. I. Title. II. Title: Mysterious, Religion and the.

BURLAND, Cottie Arthur, 1905- 133
Beyond science; a journey into the supernatural [by] C. A. Burland. New York, Grossett & Dunlap [1973, c1972] 128 p. illus. 31 cm. [BL100.B8] 72-83611 ISBN 0-448-02157-9 9.95
1. Supernatural. 2. Occult sciences. 3. Religion. I. Title.

CASE, Shirley Jackson, 1872- 270.
Experience with the supernatural in early Chrisian times, by Shirley Jackson Case ... New York, London, The Century co. [c1929] vii, 341 p. 23 cm. [BR165.C36] 29-24029
1. Supernatural. 2. Miracles. 3. Church history—Primitive and early church. I. Title.

CASE, Shirley Jackson, 1872- 230.09
The origins of Christian supernaturalism, by Shirley Jackson Case. Chicago, Ill., The University of Chicago press [1946] vii, 239 p. 20 cm. "A survey of historical data previously used in ... Experience with the supernatural in early Christian times, published in 1929."--p. vi. Bibliographical foot-notes. [BR128.A2C3] A 46
1. Supernatural. 2. Christianity and other religions. I. Title.

CASE, Shirley Jackson, 1872-1947. 291.6'2
Experience with the supernatural in early Christian times. New York, B. Blom, 1971. vii, 341 p. 22 cm. Reprint of the 1929 ed. Includes bibliographical references. [BR128.A2C27 1971] 75-174851
1. Supernatural. 2. Christianity and other religions. I. Title.

COLVILLE, William Wilberforce Juvenal, 1862-1917. 290
Ancient mysteries and modern revelations, by W. J. Colville. New York, R. F. Fenno & company [c1910] 4 p. l., vii-xiii, 15-366 p. front. (port.) pl. 20 cm. [BL100.C6] 10-17592
1. Supernatural. 2. Religions. 3. Psychical research. I. Title.

DAVIS, Andrew Jackson, 1826-1910. 133.
The approaching crisis: being a review of Dr. Bushnell's recent lectures on supernaturalism. By Andrew Jackson Davis ... New York, The author, 1852. 221 p. 24 cm. [BF1251.D27] 27-12033
1. Bushnell, Horace, 1802-1876. 2. Supernatural. 3. Spiritualism. I. Title.

DAVIS, Andrew Jackson, 1826-1910. 133.9
The approaching crisis: being a review of Dr. Bushnell's course of lectures, on the Bible, nature, religion, skepticism, and the supernatural. By Andrew Jackson Davis ... 4th ed. Boston, Colby & Rich, Banner publishing house, 1879. 293 p. 20 cm. [BF1251.D27 1879] 32-10518

1. Bushnell, Horace, 1802-1876. 2. Supernatural. 3. Spiritualism. I. Title.

HOLBACH, Paul Henri Thiry, baron d', 1723-1789. 211
Good sense; or Natural ideas opposed to supernatural; being a translation from a work called "Le bons sens", by Baron d'Holbach ... Corrected, and carefully revised, by H. D. Robinson ... 4th ed. New York, G. W. & A. J. Matsell, 1836. xii, [iii]-vi, [17]-140 p. 19 1/2 cm. [BL2773.H63 1836] 24-21576
I. Robinson, H. D., tr. II. Title.

HOLBACH, Paul Henri Thiry, baron d', 1723-1789. 211
Good sense; or Natural ideas opposed to supernatural; being a translation from a work called "Le bons sens", by Baron d'Holbach ... Corrected, and carefully revised, by H. D. Robinson ... 4th ed. New York, G. W. & A. J. Matsell, 1836. xii, [iii]-vi, [17]-140 p. 19 1/2 cm. [BL2773.H63 1836] 24-21576
I. Robinson, H. D., tr. II. Title.

HOWITT, William, 1792-1879. 290
The history of the supernatural in all ages and nations and in all churches, Christian and pagan, demonstrating a universal faith. By William Howitt ... Philadelphia, J. B. Lippincott & co., 1863. 2 v. 19 1/2 cm. [BL100.H8 1863 a] [(133)] 32-32122
1. Supernatural. 2. Spiritualism. 3. Religions. I. Title.

HOWITT, William, 1792-1879. 290
The history of the supernatural in all ages and nations and in all churches, Christian and pagan, demostrating a universal faith. By William Howitt ... Philadelphia, J. B. Lippincott & co., 1863. 2 v. 20 cm. [BL100.H8 1863 a] 133 32-32122
1. Supernatural. 2. Spiritualism. 3. Religions. I. Title.

HURWOOD, Bernhardt J. 133.1
Passport to the supernatural; an occult compendium from all ages and many lands by Bernhardt J. Hurwood. New York, New American Lib. [1973 c.1972] 278 p. 18 cm. (A Mentor Book) Selected bibliography: p. 276-278. [BF1411.H87 1973] 78-164019 1.75 (pbk.)
1. Supernatural. I. Title.

HURWOOD, Bernhardt J. 133.1
Passport to the supernatural; an occult compendium from all ages and many lands [by] Bernhardt J. Hurwood. New York, Taplinger Pub. Co. [1972] 319 p. 22 cm. Bibliography: p. 317-319. [BF1411.H87 1972] 78-164019 ISBN 0-8008-6261-9 7.50
1. Supernatural. I. Title.

JARDINE, Robert Anderson, 1878- 922
The supernatural in a commonplace life, an autobiography by Bishop R. Anderson Jardine ... [Los Angeles, Printed at B. N. Robertson company, 1944] 212 p. incl. front. (port.) 21 cm. [BR1725.J37A3] 44-13787
I. Title.

JARDINE, Robert Anderson, 1878- 922
The supernatural in a commonplace life, an autobiography by Bishop R. Anderson Jardine ... [Los Angeles, Printed at B. N. Robertson company, 1944] 212 p. incl. front. (port.) 21 cm. [BR1725.J37A3] 44-13787
I. Title.

LESTER-GARLAND, Lester Vallis, -1860- 201
The idea of the supernatural, by L. V. Lester-Garland ... London, Society for promoting Christian Knowledge. New York, The Macmillan co., 1934. 4 p. l., 172, [2] p. 19 cm. "The treatment of the problem of evil by some modern philosophers was printed in the Hibbert journal in April 1933, and What is a miracle? in Theology in September 1933."--Pref. [BL100.L4] 35-6474
1. Supernatural. 2. Religion—Philosophy. 3. Philosophy of nature. I. Title.
Contents omitted.

MCCOSH, James, 1811.1894. 290
The supernatural relation to the natural. By the Rev. James McCosh... New York, R. Carter & brothers, 1862. vii, 300 [1] p. 19 1/2 cm. [BL100.M3] 30-9643
1. Supernatural. I. Title.

MILLS, Philo Laos. 290
The psychology of the superconscious; or, The higher phenomena of the saints and mystics viewed in the light of the counter-phenomena of the psychics and trance-mediums and vindicating the over whelming brilliancy of the divine light against its obscure and occult distortions; a theory of supraliminal intuition overpowering the trance-control and showing the transcendence of the supernatural over the rival forms of supernormal cognition; a preliminary contribution in aid of a clearer understanding of this mysterious subject, by Philo Laos Mills ... Washington, D.C., The National capital press, 1922. 84 p. 27 1/2 cm. Advertising matter: p. 82-84. Bibliographical foot-notes. [BL100.M5] 23-976
1. Supernatural. 2. Psychical research. I. Title.

MURRAY, David Ambrose, 1861-
The supernatural; or, Fellowship with God, by David A. Murray ... New York, Chicago [etc.] Fleming H. Revell company [c1917] 311 p. 21 cm. 17-11676 1.50
I. Title.

MURRAY, David Ambrose, 1861-
The supernatural; or, Fellowship with God, by David A. Murray ... New York, Chicago [etc.] Fleming H. Revell company [c1917] 311 p. 21 cm. 17-11676 1.50
I. Title.

PALMER, Francis Bolles, 1834- 231.
The supernatural revealed by nature [by] Francis B. Palmer... Boston, R. G. Badger; [etc., etc., c1917] 162 p. 19 1/2 cm. (Lettered on cover: Library of religious thought) $1.00 [BT97.P3] 17-21359
1. Supernatural. I. Title.

PHILLIPS, McCandlish, 1927- 248'.42
The Bible, the supernatural, and the Jews. New York, World Pub. Co. [1970] xiii, 366 p. 22 cm. [BF1434.U6P48] 77-92532 7.95
1. Supernatural. 2. Occult sciences—United States. 3. Judaism. 4. United States—Moral conditions. I. Title.

PHILLIPS, McCandlish, 1927- 248.4'2
The spirit world. Wheaton, Ill., Victor Books [1972] 192 p. 18 cm. (An Input book) "An abridgement of The Bible, the supernatural, and the Jews." [BF1434.U6P482] 72-77015 ISBN 0-88207-048-7 1.45
1. Supernatural. 2. Occult sciences—United States. 3. Judaism. 4. United States—Moral conditions. I. Title.

PLATT, William Henry, 1821-1898. 211
... *The philosophy of the supernatural,* by W. H. Platt ... New York, E. P. Dutton & company, 1886. 4 p. l., 342 p. 22 1/2 cm. (The Bishop Paddock lectures, 1886) [BL100.P6] 30-29964
1. Supernatural. I. Title.

Supernatural—History of doctrines.

KENNY, John Peter, 1916- 231
The supernatural : medieval theological concepts to modern. [by] J. P. Kenny. New York, Alba House [1972] xiv, 150 p. 22 cm. Bibliography: p. [145]-150. [BT745.K45] 72-3575 ISBN 0-8189-0251-5 4.95
1. Supernatural—History of doctrines. I. Title.

Supernatural in the Bible.

MIRACLES and mysteries in the Bible / Bruce Kaye and John Rogerson. 1st ed. Philadelphia : Westminster Press, [1978] 144 p. ; 21 cm. Contents.Contents.—Rogerson, J. Old Testament. Kaye, B. New Testament. Includes bibliographical references. [BS680.S86M57] 77-24077 ISBN 0-664-24179-4 pbk. : 3.95 221.6'8
1. Supernatural in the Bible. I. Rogerson, John William. The supernatural in the Old Testament. 1978. II. Kaye, Bruce. The supernatural in the New Testament. 1978.

ROGERSON, John William. 221.6'8
The supernatural in the Old Testament / by John Rogerson. Guildford : Lutterworth Press, 1976. [7], 66 p. : ill. ; 22 cm. (Interpreting the Bible) Includes bibliographical references. [BS1199.S94R63] 76-383981 ISBN 0-7188-2233-1 : £1.90
1. Bible. O.T.—Criticism, interpretation, etc. 2. Supernatural in the Bible. I. Title.

Supernatural (Theology)

BOYD, Boston Napoleon Bonapart, 1860- 220
Revised search light on the seventh day Bible and x-ray: by organic, supernatural and artificial science; discoveries of the twentieth century, by Boston Napoleon Bonapart Boyd. Greenville, N. C., 1924. 250 p. front. (port.) 21 cm. Revised edition of "Search Light on the seventh wonder." [BS530.B6 1924] 25-520
I. Title.

FLYNN, Thomas Edward, 1880-
The supernatural virtues, by the Rev. T.E. Flynn... introduction by Rev. Martin J. Scott... New York, The Macmillan co., 1928. x, 95 p. 17 cm. (Half-title: The treasury of the faith series: 18) [BV4630.F5] 28-28692
I. Title.

FLYNN, Thomas Edward, 1880-
The supernatural virtues, by the Rev. T.E. Flynn... introduction by Rev. Martin J. Scott... New York, The Macmillan co., 1928. x, 95 p. 17 cm. (Half-title: The treasury of the faith series: 18) [BV4630.F5] 28-28692
I. Title.

LUBAC, Henri de, 1896- 201
The mystery of the supernatural. Translated by Rosemary Sheed. [New York] Herder and Herder [1967] xiii, 321 p. 23 cm. Bibliographical footnotes. [BT745.L813 1967] 68-1423
1. Supernatural (Theology) I. Title.

REMLER, Francis Joseph, 1874-
Supernatural merit, your treasure in heaven. A treatise on the nature of supernatural merit and on the ways and means of securing a high degree of glory in heaven. By Rev. F. J. Remler ... St. Louis, Mo. [etc.] B. Herder, 1914. 4 p. l., vii-xx, 109 p. 15 cm. $0.15. 14-2869
I. Title.

REMLER, Francis Joseph, 1874-
Supernatural merit, your treasure in heaven. A treatise on the nature of supernatural merit and on the ways and means of securing a high degree of glory in heaven. By Rev. F. J. Remler ... St. Louis, Mo. [etc.] B. Herder, 1914. 4 p. l., vii-xx, 109 p. 15 cm. $0.15. 14-2869
I. Title.

REUTER, William Charles, 1850-
The supernatural Christ. (From a negative point of view.) By W. C. Reuter ... Cincinnati, Jennings and Graham [c1913] 88 p. front. 19 cm. $0.50 13-13135
I. Title.

REUTER, William Charles, 1850-
The supernatural Christ. (From a negative point of view.) By W. C. Reuter ... Cincinnati, Jennings and Graham [c1913] 88 p. front. 19 cm. $0.50 13-13135
I. Title.

Superstition.

BERRY, Brewton. 133
You and your superstitions, by Brewton Berry ... illustrations by L. Frederic Stephens. Columbia, Mo., Lucas brothers, 1940. 4 p. l., 11-249 p. incl. illus., pl. 21 cm. [Full name: James Brewton Berry] [BF1777.B4] 159.961 40-35456
1. Superstition. I. Title.

CALDWELL, Otis William, 1869- 133
Do you believe it? By Otis W. Caldwell ... and Gerhard E. Lundeen ... Garden City, N. Y., Doubleday, Doran & company, inc., 1934. x p., 1 l., 307 p. illus. 21 cm. "First edition." Bibliography: p. 288-300. [BF1775.C3] 159.961 34-38696
1. Superstition. 2. Errors, Popular. I. Lundeen, Gerhard Emmanuel, joint author. II. Title.

CALDWELL, Otis William, 1869- 133
Do you believe it? Curious habits and strange beliefs of civilized man, by Otis W. Caldwell ... and Gerhard E. Lundeen ... Garden City, N. Y., Garden City publishing co., inc. [1937] 3 p. l., v-x, 307 p. illus. 21 cm. "Selected bibliography dealing with superstitions and closely related ideas": p. 288-300. [BF1775.C3 1937] 159.961 37-22099
1. Superstition. 2. Errors, Popular. I. Lundeen, Gerhard Emmanuel, joint author. II. Title.

DALYELL, John Graham, Sir, bart., 1775-1851. 133.4
The darker superstitions of Scotland. Norwood, Pa., Norwood Editions, 1973. vii, 700 p. 24 cm. Reprint of the 1835 ed. printed for R. Griffin, Glasgow. Includes bibliographical references. [BF1775.D33 1973] 72-7065 45.00
1. Superstition. 2. Scotland—Social life and customs. I. Title.

†DALYELL, John Graham, Sir, bart, 1775-1851. 133.4
The darker superstitions of Scotland / by John Graham Dalyell. Folcroft, Pa. : Folcroft Editions, 1977. p. cm. Reprint of the 1835 ed. printed for R. Griffin, Glasgow. Includes bibliographical references. [BF1775.D33 1977] 77-26734 ISBN 0-8414-1863-2 lib. bdg. : 45.00
1. Superstition. 2. Scotland—Social life and customs. I. Title.

DANIELS, Cora Linn (Morrison) Mrs. 1852- ed. 133.
Encyclopeadia of superstitions folklore, and the occult sciences of the world; a comprehensive library of human belief and practice in the mysteries of life ... Editorial staff. Cora Linn Daniels ... and Prof. C. M. Stevans ... with more than one thousand eminent assistants ... Chicago and Milwaukee, J. H. Yewdale & sons co. [c1903] 3 v. fronts., illus., plates 27 cm. Paged continuously. [BF1025.D22] 3-4662
1. Superstition. 2. Folk-lore. 3. Occult sciences. I. Stevens, Charles McClellan, 1861- joint ed. II. Title.

DEERFORTH, Daniel. 001.9'6
Knock wood! Superstition through the ages. [New York] Brentano's. Detroit, Gale Research Co., 1974 [c1928] 200 p. 18 cm. [BL490.D4 1974] 79-164220 ISBN 0-8103-3964-1 11.00
1. Superstition. I. Title.

DEERFORTH, Daniel.
Knock wood! superstition through the ages. by Dr. Daniel Deerforth. [New York] Brentano's [c1928] 5 p. l., 3-200 p. 22 cm. [BL490.D4] 28-23319
1. Superstition. I. Title.

EMMONS, Samuel Bulfinch. 133
The spirit land. By S. B. Emmons. Philadelphia, J. W. Bradley, 1860. 288 p. front. 18 1/2 cm. [BF1042.E42 1860] 32-22236
1. Superstition. 2. Spiritualism. I. Title.

FIELDING, William John, 1886- 133
Strange superstitions and magical practices, by William J. Fielding ... Philadelphia, The Blakiston company [1945] xiii, 273 p. 21 cm. (Circle books) [BF1411.F5] 45-10248
1. Superstition. 2. Magic. I. Title.

[GOLDSMITH, Milton] 1861- 133
Signs, omens and superstitions, by Astra Cielo psued. ... New York, G. Sully & company [c1918] vii, 159 p. 20 cm. [BF1775.G6] 18-11172
1. Superstition. 2. Omens. I. Title.

[HOLBACH, Paul Henri Thiry, baron d'] 1723-1789. 211
Superstition in all ages. by John Meslier, a Roman Catholic priest, who ... left as his last will and testament ... the following papes, entitled Common sense, tr. from the French original, by Miss Anna Knoop. New York, Miss Anna Knoop, 1878. 339 p. front. (port.) 19 1/2 cm. The first part, "Common sense", is a translation of "Le bon sens, ou Idees naturelles opposees aux idees surnaturelles", by Baron Holbach, also published with title "Le bon sens du cure J. Meslier". The second part, "Abstract of the Testament of John

Meslier", was first published by Voltaire in 1761. cf. Voltaire, par G. Bengesco; Le libertinage, par F. Lachevre, v. 7, p. 227-246; Querard, etc. Contents.--Preface of the editor of the French edition of 1830.--Life of Jean Meslier. By Voltaire.--Common sense, by the Curate Meslier.--Abstract of the Testament of John Meslier, by Voltaire. [BL2773.H63 1878] 24-21578
1. Meslier, Jean, 1664-1733? II. Voltaire, Francois Marie Arouet de, 1694-1778. III. Knoop, Anna, d. 1889, tr. IV. Title.

[HOLBACH, Paul Henri Thiry, baron d'] 1723-1789. 211
Superstition in all ages. by John Meslier, a Roman Catholic priest, who ... left as his last will and testament ... the following papes, entitled Common sense, tr. from the French original, by Miss Anna Knoop. New York, Miss Anna Knoop, 1878. 339 p. front. (port.) 19 1/2 cm. The first part, "Common sense", is a translation of "Le bon sens, ou Idees naturelles opposees aux idees surnaturelles", by Baron Holbach, also published with title "Le bon sens du cure J. Meslier". The second part, "Abstract of the Testament of John Meslier", was first published by Voltaire in 1761. cf. Voltaire, par G. Bengesco; Le libertinage, par F. Lachevre, v. 7, p. 227-246; Querard, etc. Contents.--Preface of the editor of the French edition of 1830.--Life of Jean Meslier. By Voltaire.--Common sense, by the Curate Meslier.--Abstract of the Testament of John Meslier, by Voltaire. [BL2773.H63 1878] 24-21578
I. Meslier, Jean, 1664-1733? II. Voltaire, Francois Marie Arouet de, 1694-1778. III. Knoop, Anna, d. 1889, tr. IV. Title.

[HOLBACH, Paul Henri Thiry, baron d'] 1723-1789. 211
Superstition in all ages: by Jean Meslier, a Roman Catholic priest, who, after a pastoral service of thirty years at Etrepigny and But in Champagne, France, wholly abjured religious dogmas, and left as his last will and testament, to his parishioners, and to the world, to be published after his death, the following pages, entitled Common sense. Translated from the French original by Miss Anna Knoop. New York, P. Eckler, 1890. vi p., 1 l., [5]-339 p. front. (port.) 20 cm. (On cover: Library of liberal classics. v. 1, no. 12. 1896) Running title: Common sense. The first part is a translation of "Le bon sens du cure Meslier". by Baron d'Holbach. The second part is an abstract of the testament of John Meslier by Voltaire (p. 283-339) [BL2773.H63 1890] 24-30675
I. Meslier, Jean, 1678-1733. II. Voltaire, Francois Marie Arouet de, 1694-1778. III. Knoop, Anna, d. 1889, tr. IV. Title. V. Title: Common sense.

[HOLBACH, Paul Henri Thiry, baron d'] 1723-1789. 211
Superstition in all ages: by Jean Meslier, a Roman Catholic priest, who, after a pastoral service of thirty years at Etrepigny and But in Champagne, France, wholly abjured religious dogmas, and left as his last will and testament, to his parishioners, and to the world, to be published after his death, the following pages, entitled Common sense. Translated from the French original by Miss Anna Knoop. New York, P. Eckler, 1890. vi p., 1 l., [5]-339 p. front. (port.) 20 cm. (On cover: Library of liberal classics. v. 1, no. 12. 1896) Running title: Common sense. The first part is a translation of "Le bon sens du cure Meslier". by Baron d'Holbach. The second part is an abstract of the testament of John Meslier by Voltaire (p. 283-339) [BL2773.H63 1890] 24-30675
I. Meslier, Jean, 1678-1733. II. Voltaire, Francois Marie Arouet de, 1694-1778. III. Knoop, Anna, d. 1889, tr. IV. Title. V. Title: Common sense.

[HOLBACH, Paul Henri Thiry, baron d'] 1723-1789. 211
Superstition in all ages: a dying confession by Jean Meslier, a Roman Catholic priest, who at his death left as his "Last will and testament" this now famous manuscript as contained herein, entitled Common sense ... Tr. from the French original by Miss Anna Knoop; arranged for publication in its present form and manner with new title page and preface by Dr. L. W. De Laurence. Same to now serve as "text-book" number five, for "The Congress of ancient, diving, mental and Christian masters"; Chicago, Ill., De Laurence, Scott & co., 1910. xx, 17-339 p. front. (port.) 20 cm. $2.25 The first part, "Common sense", is a translation of "Le bon sens, ou Idees naturelles", by Baron Holbach, also published with title: Le bon sens du cure J. Meslier. The second part, "Abstract of the Testament of John Meslier", was first published by Voltaire in 1761. cf. Voltaire, par G. Bengesco; Le libertinage, par F. Lachevre, 7, p. 227-246; Barton Holbach, by M. P. Cushing, etc. [BL2773.H74] 10-17593
I. Meslier, Jean, 1664-1733? II. Voltaire, Francois Marie Arouet de, 1694-1778. III. Knoop, Anna, d. 1889, tr. IV. De Laurence, Lauron William, 1868- V. Congress of ancient, divine, mental and Christian masters. VI. Title.

[HOLBACH, Paul Henri Thiry, baron d'] 1723-1789. 211
Superstition in all ages: a dying confession by Jean Meslier, a Roman Catholic priest, who at his death left as his "Last will and testament" this now famous manuscript as contained herein, entitled Common sense ... Tr. from the French original by Miss Anna Knoop; arranged for publication in its present form and manner with new title page and preface by Dr. L. W. De Laurence. Same to now serve as "text-book" number five, for "The Congress of ancient, diving, mental and Christian masters"; Chicago, Ill., De Laurence, Scott & co., 1910. xx, 17-339 p. front. (port.) 20 cm. $2.25 The first part, "Common sense", is a translation of "Le bon sens, ou Idees naturelles", by Baron Holbach, also published with title: Le bon sens du cure J. Meslier. The second part, "Abstract of the Testament of John Meslier", was first published by Voltaire in 1761. cf. Voltaire, par. G. Bengesco; Le libertinage, par F. Lachevre, 7, p. 227-246; Barton Holbach, by M. P. Cushing, etc. [BL2773.H74] 10-17593
I. Meslier, Jean, 1664-1733? II. Voltaire, Francois Marie Arouet de, 1694-1778. III. Knoop, Anna, d. 1889, tr. IV. De Laurence, Lauron William, 1868- V. Congress of ancient, divine, mental and Christian masters. VI. Title.

[HOLBACH, Paul Henri Thiry, baron d'] 1723-1789. 210
Superstition in all ages: by Jean Meslier, a Roman Catholic priest, who, after a pastoral service of thirty years at Etrepigny and But in Champagne, France, wholly abjured religious dogmas, and left as his last will and testament to his parishioners, and to the world, to be published after his death, the following pages, entitled Common sense. Translated from the French original by Miss Anna Knoop. New York, P. Eckler, 1920. vi p., 1 l., [5]-339 p. front. (port.) 19 1/2 cm. Running title: Common sense. The first part is a translation of "Le bon sens du cure Meslier", by Baron d'Holbach. The second part is an abstract of the testament of John Meslier by Voltaire (p. 283-339) [BL2773.H63 1920] 32-35938
I. Atheism. II. Meslier, Jean, 1678-1733. III. Voltaire, Francois Marie Arouet de, 1694-1778, tr. IV. Knoop, Anna, d. 1889, tr. V. Title. VI. Title: Common sense.

[HOLBACH, Paul Henri Thiry, baron d'] 1723-1789. 210
Superstition in all ages: by Jean Meslier, a Roman Catholic priest, who, after a pastoral service of thirty years at Etrepigny and But in Champagne, France, wholly abjured religious dogmas, and left as his last will and testament to his parishioners, and to the world, to be published after his death, the following pages, entitled Common sense. Translated from the French original by Miss Anna Knoop. New York, P. Eckler, 1920. vi p., 1 l., [5]-339 p. front. (port.) 19 1/2 cm. Running title: Common sense. The first part is a translation of "Le bon sens du cure Meslier", by Baron d'Holbach. The second part is an abstract of the testament of John Meslier by Voltaire (p. 283-339) [BL2773.H63 1920] 32-35938
I. Atheism. II. Meslier, Jean, 1678-1733. III. Voltaire, Francois Marie Arouet de, 1694-1778, tr. IV. Knoop, Anna, d. 1889, tr. V. Title. VI. Title: Common sense.

HUEBNER, Louise. 133.4
Superstitions; a witchy collection of mysterious beliefs about love, money, weather, and much more. Illustrated by John Overmyer. [Kansas City, Mo.] Springbok Editions [1972] [28] p. illus. 15 cm. [BF1775.H8] 73-178977 ISBN 0-87529-256-9
1. Superstition. I. Overmyer, John, illus.

INGERSOLL, Robert Green, 1833-1899. 211
Superstition ... A lecture, by Robert G. Ingersoll. New York, C. P. Farrell, 1898. 55, 57-62 p. 21 cm. [BL2725.S8 1898] 98-1031
1. Superstition. I. Title.

[KENNEY, Eudorus Catlin] 133.
Ghosts, devils, angels and sun gods. A series of essays against superstition, by P. Rusticus [pseud.] [Baltimore? Md., c1891] cover-title, 126 p. 15 x 12 cm. [BF1042.K3] 11-2453
I. Title.

SINCLAIR, George, d.1696. 133.4
Satan's invisible world discovered. Gainesville, Fla., Scholars' Facsimiles & Reprints, 1969. xxviii, xxx, 256 p. 23 cm. Reprint of the 1685 ed., with a new introd. by C. O. Parsons. [BF1410.S5 1969] 68-17017 12.50
1. Superstition. 2. Witchcraft. I. Title.

STEVENS, Samuel Eugene, 1839-
Science and superstition [by] Samuel Eugene Stevens ... New York, Truth seeker company, 1913. 4 p. l., [11]-119 p. 20 cm. 14-3759 1.25
I. Title.

WHITMAN, Bernard, 1796-1834. 252.
A lecture on popular superstitions. By Bernard Whitman... Boston, Bowles & Dearborn, 1829. 1 p. l., [5]-66 p. 20 cm. [BF1439.W6] [AC901.M5 vol. 359] 11-6881
1. Superstition. I. Title.

[WHITTIER, John Greenleaf] 1807-1892. 272.
The supernaturalism of New England. By the author of "The stranger in Lowell." New York & London, Wiley & Putnam, 1847. ix, 71 p. 19 1/2 cm. (Half-title: Wiley & Putnam's library of American books) [BF1576.W5 1847 a] 44-10261
1. Superstition. 2. New England—Soc. life & cust. I. Title.

Superstition—Moral and religious aspects.

BAUER, Paul, 1905- 133
Wizards that peep and mutter; Christians and superstition. [1st U.S.A. ed.] Westwood, N.J., F. H. Revell Co. [1967] 160 p. illus. 21 cm. Translation of Horoskop und Talisman. [BR115.S85B33 1967] 67-4717
1. Superstition—Moral and religious aspects. I. Title.

Surangamasutra—Commentaries.

†HSUAN-HUA, 1908- 294.3'8
The Shurangama sutra / [Commentary by Hsuan Hua ; Translated from the Chinese by the Buddhist Text Translation Society]. [San Francisco] : Sino-American Buddhist Association, Buddhist Text Translation Society, 1977- v. : ill. ; 22 cm. Includes index. [BQ2127.H7813] 77-88845 ISBN 0-917512-17-0 : 8.50
1. Surangamasutra—Commentaries. I. Buddhist Text Translation Society. II. Surangamasutra. English. 1977. III. Title.

SURANGAMASUTRA. English & Khotanese. 294.3'92
The Khotanese Surangamasamadhisutra; [edited] by R. E. Emmerick. London, New York, Oxford U. P., 1970. xxv, 134 p., 20 plates. facsims. 23 cm. (London oriental series, v. 23) Khotanese translation from the original Buddhist Sanskrit text. Khotanese text with English translation on facing pages. Includes partial text of the Tibetan version. Includes bibliographical references. [BL1411.S77E53] 72-185897 ISBN 0-19-713562-5 £5.00 ($14.00 U.S.)
I. Emmerick, R. E., ed. II. Title. III. Series.

Surburban churches.

WINTER, Gibson 254.23
The suburban captivity of the churches. ; an analysis of Protestant responsibility in the expanding metropolis. New York, Macmillan [c.1962] 255p. 18cm. Bibl. 1.45 pap.,
1. Surburban churches. 2. City churches. I. Title.

Suriano, Francesco, 1549-ca. 1621

KNISELEY, S. Philip. 783.2'00924
The masses of Francesco Soriano; a style-critical study, by S. Philip Kniseley. Gainesville, University of Florida Press, 1967. 83 p. music. 23 cm. (University of Florida monographs. Humanities, no. 26) Bibliography: p. 81-83. [ML410.S963K6] 67-22198
1. Suriano, Francesco, 1549-ca. 1621 Masses. I. Title.

Surveys, Church.

IRWIN, Leonard G
Some significant findings from the North Central Alabama religious surveys. [Prepared by] Leonard G. Irwin [and] Orrin D. Morris. Atlanta, Ga., Dept. of Survey & Special Studies, Home mission board, SBC, 1964. 1 v. (various pagings) Mimeographed copy. 68-59914
1. Surveys, Church. I. Title.

IRWIN, Leonard G
Summary report of Greater Birmingham area religious survey. Atlanta, Ga., Department of Survey & Special Studies, Home Mission Board SBC, 1964. 1 v. (various pagings) 68-50656
1. Surveys, Church. I. Morris, Orrin D. II. Title.

IRWIN, Leonard G
Summary report of North Central Alabama religious survey findings. Prepared by Leonard G. Irwin [and] Orrin D. Morris. Atlanta, Ga., Department of Survey & Special Studies, Home mission board, SBC, 1964. 1 v. (various pagings) Mimeographed copy. 68-53476
1. Surveys, Church. I. Title.

NEW York. Riverside Church.
The Riverside Church survey report, 1956. [New York, 1956] 78p. front., chart. 24cm. A 57
I. Title.

Survival skills.

DARGA, Bert. 613.6'9
The survival bible : how to make it through any crisis calmly, effectively, and safely / by Bert Darga. Indianapolis : Bobbs-Merrill, [1982] p. cm. Includes index. Bibliography: p. [GF86.D37] 19 82-4261 ISBN 0-672-52707-3 pbk. : 12.95
1. Survival skills. 2. Survival and emergency equipment. I. Title.

Susanna, Saint, d. ca. 295—Drama.

JOURDAN, Adrien, pere, 1617-1692. 879.2
... *Adrein Jourdan's Susanna* (1653) a critical edition of the Latin text with a study of the play and its infleunce on Brueys's Gabinie (1699) by Sister Loyola Maria Coffey, S. S. J. Baltimore, Md., The Johns Jopkins press; London, H. Milford, Oxford university press; [etc., etc.] 1942. 127 p. 26 cm. (The Johns Hopkins studies in Romance literatures and languages, vol. xli) Issued also as thesis (PH. D.) Johns Hopkins university. Bibliography: p. 125-127. [PA8540.J7A7 1942 a] 42-142402
1. Susanna, saint, d. ca. 295—Drama. 2. Brueys, David Augustin de, 1640-1723. Gabinie. I. Coffey, Loyola Maria, sister, 1900- ed. II. Title.

JOURDAN, Adrien, pere, 1617-1692. 879.2
... *Adrien Jourdan's Susanna* (1653) a critical edition of the Latin text with a study of the play and its influence on Brueys's Gabinie (1699) by Sister Loyola Maria Coffey ... Baltimore, The Johns Hopkins press, 1942. 127 p., 1 l. 26 cm. Sister Loyola M. Coffey's thesis (PH. D.)--

Johns Hopkins university, 1939. "Reprinted from the Johns Hopkins studies in Romance literatures and languages, volume xli." Vita. Bibliography: p. 125-127. [PA8540.J7A7 1942] A 42
1. Susanna, Saint, d. ca. 295—Drama. 2. Brueys, David Augustin de, 1640-1723. Gabinie. I. Coffey, Loyola Maria, sister, 1900- ed. II. Title.

JOURDAN, Adrien, pere, 1617-1692. 872'.04
Susanna (1653); a critical edition of the Latin text with a study of the play and its influence on Brueys's Gabinie (1699), by Sister Loyola Maria Coffey, Baltimore, John Hopkins Press, 1942. [New York, Johnson Reprint Corp., 1973] p. Originally presented as the author's thesis, Johns Hopkins University. Reprint of the 1942 ed., issued in series: The Johns Hopkins studies in Romance literatures and languages, v. 41. [PA8540.J7A7 1973] 72-12597 ISBN 0-384-27960-0
1. Susanna, Saint, d. ca. 295—Drama. 2. Brueys, David Augustin de, 1640-1723. Gabinie. I. Coffey, Loyola Maria, sister, 1900- ed. II. Series: The Johns Hopkins studies in Romance literatures and languages, v. 41.

Susannis, Marquardus de, d. 1578.

STOW, Kenneth R. 262.9
Catholic thought and papal Jewry policy, 1555-1593 / by Kenneth R. Stow. New York : Jewish Theological Seminary of America, [1976] p. cm. (Moreshet ; 6) Includes index. Bibliography: p. [LAW] 76-55307 ISBN 0-87334-001-9 : 25.00
1. Susannis, Marquardus de, d. 1578. De Iudaeis. 2. Jews—Legal status, laws, etc. (Canon law) 3. Catholic Church—Relations—Judaism. 4. Judaism—Relations—Catholic Church. I. Title. II. Series: Moreshet (New York) ; 6.

Susquehanna Co., Pa.—Social conditions

INTERCHURCH world movement of North America. 261.
Susquehanna County survey by the Interchurch world movement of North America, field work done by F. E. Cholerton. New York city, Interchurch press [c1920] 52 p. incl. front. (map) illus. 20 cm. [BR555.P5S8] 20-13714
1. Susquehanna Co., Pa.—Soc. condit. 2. Social surveys. 3. Churches—Pennsylvania—Susquehanna Co. I. Cholerton, Frank Edward, 1884- II. Title.

Sustar, Bob R., 1938-1975.

†SUSTAR, Bob R., 1938-1975. 248'.86
Yet will I serve Him / Bob R. Sustar, as told to Hoyt E. Stone. Cleveland, Tenn. : Pathway Press, c1976. 105 p. : port. ; 18 cm. Autobiography. [RC280.L9S85 1976] 76-1683 ISBN 0-87148-931-7 pbk. : 1.95
1. Sustar, Bob R., 1938-1975. 2. Lymphoma—Biography. I. Stone, Hoyt E., joint author. II. Title.

Svenska Kyrkan—History.

WADDAMS, Herbert Montague. 284.1'485
The Swedish church / by H.M. Waddams. Westport, Conn. : Greenwood Press, 1981. p. cm. Reprint. Originally published: London : Society for Promoting Christian Knowledge, 1946. [BX8039.W28 1981] 19 81-7021 ISBN 0-313-22184-7 lib. bdg. : 19.75
1. Svenska Kyrkan—History. 2. Sweden—Church history. I. Title.

Swain, Clara A., 1834-1910.

WILSON, Dorothy Clarke. 266.7'6'0924
Palace of healing; the story of Dr. Clara Swain, first woman missionary doctor, and the hospital she founded. [1st ed.] New York, McGraw-Hill [1968] x, 245 p. 22 cm. [R608.S92W5] 68-22771
1. Swain, Clara A., 1834-1910. 2. Clara Swain Hospital. I. Title.

Swain, Jasper.

SWAIN, Jasper. 133.9'013
From my world to yours : a young man's account of the afterlife / by Jasper Swain ; edited by Noel Langley. New York : Walker, 1977. 101 p. ; 22 cm. Psychic conversations with the author's dead son, Mike Swain. "First published under a pseudonym in a privately-printed edition." [BF1301.S892 1977] 76-52573 ISBN 0-8027-0573-1 : 5.95
1. Swain, Jasper. 2. Swain, Mike. 3. Spirit writings. I. Swain, Mike. II. Title.

Swalm, E. J., 1897-

SWALM, E. J., 1897- 289.9 B
"My beloved brethren ...": personal memoirs and recollections of the Canadian Brethren in Christ Church, by E. J. Swalm. Nappanee, Ind., Evangel Press [1969] 156 p. illus. 21 cm. [BX9675.Z8S9] 73-172782
1. Swalm, E. J., 1897- 2. Brethren in Christ—Canada. I. Title.

Swearing.

LUCKENBACH, William Henry, 1828-1896. 179.
The folly of profanity. By Rev. W. H. Luckenbach, A.M. With an introduction by Milton Valentine ... Philadelphia Lutheran publication society, 1884. 4, v-xvi, 17-310 p. 19 1/2 cm. [BJ1535.P95L8] 12-36339
1. Swearing. 2. Christian life. I. Title.

Swedeenborg, Emanuel, 1688-1772.

KELLER, Helen Adams, 1880-
My religion, by Helen Keller; illustrations from photographs. Garden City, N. Y., Doubleday, Page & company, 1927. viii p., 1 l, 208 p. 2 port. (incl. front.) 20 cm. [BK8721.K35] 27-22433
1. Swedeenborg, Emanuel, 1688-1772. I. Title.

ODHNER, C[arl] Th[eophilus] 1863-
A brief account of the life and work of Emanuel Swedenborg, the servant of the Lord. With a sketch of his personality. By the Rev. C. Th. Odhner ... Philadelphia, Academy book room, 1893. 50 p. incl. front. (port.) 19 cm. "A visit to Emanuel Swedenborg [by a student of the University of Upsala in 1770]": p. 25-38. p. 43-50, advertising matter. 5-12176
I. Title.

Sweden—Church history.

NYVALL, David, 1863- 284.1
The Swedish Covenanters, a history by David Nyvall. Chicago, Covenant book concern [c1930] 137 p. 20 cm. [BX8049.5.N8] 30-32753
1. Sweden—Church history. 2. Revivals. 3. Swedish evangelical mission covenant of America. I. Title.

WORDSWORTH, John, bp. of Salisbury, 1843-1911.
The national church of Sweden, by John Wordsworth ... delivered in St. James' church, Chicago, 24-29th October, 1910. London [etc.] A. R. Mowbray & co. ltd.; Milwaukee, The Young churchman co., 1911. xix, 459 p. 21 1/2 cm. (The Hale lectures, 1910) [BX8039.W8] 11-35349
1. Sweden—Church history. 2. Lutheran church in Sweden. I. Title.

Sweden—History—Prophecies.

STROMMENBERG, Anders Gabriel, d.1857. 133.3'2
A prophecy concerning the Swedish monarchy; as it was related in 1809. With an introd. by William H. W. Sabine. New York [Colburn & Tegg] 1968. xii, 13 p. illus., facsim. 23 cm. Translation of De somniis futuras eventus prasagientibus dissertatio. [DL780.S7713 1968] 68-10634
1. Sweden—History—Prophecies. 2. Sweden—History—Gustavus IV Adolphus 1792-1809. I. Sabine, William Henry Waldo, 1903- ed. II. Title.

Sweden in Delaware.

WILMINGTON, Del. First Swedish Baptist church. 286.17512
First Swedish Baptist church, Wilmington, Delaware, 1889-1939. [Wilmington, Del., Lithographed by W. N. Cann, inc., 1939] 2 p. l., 3-58 p. illus (incl. ports.) 23 cm. [BX6480.W5F5] 40-2856
1. Sweden in Delaware. I. Title.

Sweden in Minnesota.

ANDERS, John Olson. 277.13
The origin and history of Swedish religious organizations in Minnesota, 1853-1885, by John Olson Anders ... Rock Island, Ill., Augustana book concern, 1932. 101, [1] p. illus. (maps) 23 cm. "An abbreviated version of a dissertation presented at the University of Minnesota [PH. D., 1930]"--Pref. [BR555.M6A62] 32-32898
1. Sweden in Minnesota. 2. Minnesota—Religion. I. Title. II. Title: Swedish religious organizations in Minnesota, 1853-1885. III. Title: Religious organizations in Minnesota, The origin and history of Swedish.

Sweden—Social life and customs

LINDEVALL, Carl August, 1863- 922.473
Reminiscences of an old clergyman, and other narratives and sketches drawn from real life, also narratives of numerous visions and other phenomena from the "unseen" world, claimed by trustworthy persons to be real experiences, indicating that there is a spiritual and supersensible world, and that human personality survives bodily death, committed to writing and edited by C. A. Lindevall ... [Rock Island, Ill., Augustana book concern, 1936] 231 p. 20 cm. [BX8080.L55A35] 37-1734
1. Sweden—Soc. life & cust. 2. Visions. I. Title.

Swedenborg, Emanuel, 1688—1772.

BARRETT, Benjamin Fiske, 1808-1892. 922.84
Life of Emanuel Swedenborg, with some account of his writings. Compiled by B. F. Barrett ... New York, S. Colman, 1841. vii, 160 p. 20 cm. [BX8748.B26] 36-31842
1. Swedenborg, Emanuel, 1688-1772. I. Title.

BARRETT, Benjamin Fiske, 1808-1892. 230.94
Swedenborg and Channing, Showing the many and remarkable agreements in the beliefs and teachings of these writers. By B. F. Barrett. Philadelphia, Claxton, Remsen & Haffelfinger, 1879. xx, 21-288 p. 20 cm. [BX8748.B28] 36-31813
1. Swedenborg, Emanuel, 1688-1772. 2. Channing, William Ellery, 1780-1842. 3. New Jerusalem church—Doctrinal and controversial works. 4. Unitarianism.—Doctrinal and controversial works. I. Title.

BEAMAN, Edmund Addison, b.1811. 289.4'0924 B
Swedenborg and the new age; or, "The Holy City New Jerusalem," ... New York, AMS Press [1971] 225 p. 22 cm. Reprint of the 1881 ed. [BX8748.B36 1971] 77-134422 ISBN 0-404-08458-3 10.00
1. Swedenborg, Emanuel, 1688-1772. I. Title. II. Title: The Holy City New Jerusalem.

BIGELOW, John, 1817-1911. 230.
The Bible that was lost and is found, by John Bigelow ... New York, New-church board of publication, 1912. 1 p. l., 120 p. front. (port.) 24 cm. "Chronological list of Swedenborg's principal theological works, translated into English": p. 119-120. Footnotes. [BX8711.B5] A13
1. Swedenborg, Emanuel, 1688-1772. I. Title.

BIGELOW, John, 1817-1911. 923.
Emanuel Swedenborg, servus domini, by John Bigelow. New York & London, G. P. Putnam's sons, 1888. 1 p. l., [xxv]-ixxxvi p. 23 cm "Literary, scientific, and philosophical works": p. ixxix-ixxxvi. [BX8748.B5] 922. S D
1. Swedenborg. Emanuel. 1688-1772. I. Title.

EVANS, Warren Felt. 230.94
The new age and its messenger. By Rev. W. F. Evans ... Boston, T. H. Carter & company; London, C. P. Alvey, 1864. 110 p. 19 cm. [BX8721.E8] 32-22238
1. Swedenborg, Emanuel, 1688-1772. 2. New Jerusalem church—Doctrinal and controversial works. I. Title.

FERBER, Adolph C. 236'.2
We are immortal / A. C. Ferber. 1st ed. Hicksville, N.Y. : Exposition Press, [1975] 143 p. ; 22 cm. (An Exposition-testament book) Includes excerpts from the works of E. Swedenborg and others. Includes bibliographical references. [BX8711.F47] 75-319949 ISBN 0-682-48288-9 : 7.00
1. Swedenborg, Emanuel, 1688-1772. 2. Future life—History of doctrines. I. Title.

FERBER, Adolph C 215
Where is heaven? [1st ed.] New York, Pageant Press [1955] 243p. 24cm. [BL240.F45] 55-7358
1. Swedenborg, Emanuel. 1688-1772. 2. Religion and science—1900- 3. Heaven. 4. Extrasensory perception. I. Title.

GOPALA, Chetti, D. 230.
New light upon Indian philosophy; or, Swedenborg and Saiva siddhanta, by D. Gopaul Chetty ... With a foreword by L. B. de Beaumont, D. SC. London and Toronto, J. M. Dent & sons, ltd. New York, E. P. Dutton & co., 1923. xxxvi, 218 p., 1 l. front. (port.) 19 cm. [BX8711.G6] 25-7414
1. Swedenborg, Emmanuel, 1688-1772. 2. Sivaism. 3. India—Religion. 4. Philosophy, Hindu. I. Title.

GOULD, Edwin Miner Lawrence, 1886- 922.
The business of living, by E. M. Lawrence Gould ... New York, The New-church press [c1926] viii p., 1 l., 103 p. 20 cm. "I have ... tried in these pages to express in popular language the essential outlines of Swedenborg's teaching."--Foreword. [BX8748.G6] 26-12969
1. Swedenborg, Emmanuel, 1688-1772. I. Title.

HEMPEL, Charles Julius, 1811-1879. 289.4
The true organization of the new church, as indicated in the writings of Emanuel Swedenborg, and demonstrated by Charles Fourier. New York, W. Radde, 1848. [New York, AMS Press, 1972] 454 p. 22 cm. [BX8711.H45 1972] 74-134424 ISBN 0-404-08464-8 18.00
1. Swedenborg, Emanuel, 1688-1772. 2. Fourier, Francois Marie Charles, 1772-1837. I. Swedenborg, Emanuel, 1688-1772. II. Fourier, Francois Marie Charles, 1772-1837. III. Title.

[HILLER, Margaret] 289.4
Religion and philosophy United; or, An attempt to show that philosophical principles form the foundation of the New Jerusalem church, as developed to the world in the mission of the Honourable Emanuel Swedenborg... Boston, Published for the subscribers, 1817. xii, [13]-55 p. 24 1/2 cm. [BX8721.H5] 5-21983
1. Swedenborg, Emanuel, 1688-1772. 2. New Jerusalem church—Doctrinal and controversial works. I. Title.

[HITCHCOCK, Ethan Allen] 1798-1870. 922.
Swedenborg, a hermetic philosopher. Being a sequel to Remarks on alchemy and the alchemists. Showing that Emanuel Swedenborg was a hermetic philosopher and that his writings may be interpreted from the point of view of hermetic philosophy. With a chapter comparing Swedenborg and Spinoza. By the author of Remarks on alchemy and the alchemists ... New York, D. Appleton & company, 1858. 352 p. 19 cm. Advertisement" signed: E. A. H. [BX8748.H5] 14-7596

1. Swedenborg, Emanuel, 1688-1772. 2. Spinoza, Benedictus de, 1632-1677. 3. Alchemy. I. Title.

HITE, Lewis Field, 1852- 922.
Swedenborg's historical position, containing the testimonies of eminent men of his own and subsequent time, by Lewis Field Hite... Boston, Massachusetts New-church union, 1928. 2 p. l., [3]-174 p. 20 1/2 cm. [BX8748.H53] 28-31133
1. Swedenborg ,Emanuel, 1688-1772. I. Title.

[HOBART, Nathaniel] 922.84
Life of Emanuel Swedenborg, with some account of his writings, together with a brief notice of the rise and progress of the New Church. Boston, Allen and Goddard, 1831. iv, [6]-188 p. 20 cm. [BX8748.H6 1831] 32-30343
1. Swendenshorg, Emanuel, 1894-1772. 2. New Jersulem church. I. Title.

HOBART, Nathaniel. 922.84
Life of Emanuel Swedenborg; with some account of his writings. By Nathaniel Hobart. 4th ed. Containing, in addition, a lecture on the mission of Swedenborg, by Sampson Reed, and an article on the New Jerusalem church, prepared for the new American cyclopedia. Boston, W. Carter & brother, 1862. iv, 246 p. front. (port.) 19 1/2 cm. [BX8748.H6 1862] 32-30344
1. Swedenborg, Emanuel, 1688-1772. 2. New Jerusalem church. I. Reed, Sampson, 1809-1880. II. Title.

HODGETTS, E. Brayley. 230.
Reasonable religion. Emanuel Swedenborg, his message & teaching, by E. Brayley Hodgetts ... London and Toronto, J. M. Dent & sons, ltd.; New York, E. P. Dutton & co., 1923. vii, 252 p. front. (port.) 22 1/2 cm. [BX8711.H6] 24-17719
1. Swedenborg, Emanuel, 1688-1772. I. Title.

INTRODUCTION to Swedenborg's religious thought. New York, Swedenborg pub. association, 1956. 235p. 21cm. 'Published some years ago under the title: 'The kingdom of heaven as seen by Swedenborg', the book hasnow been revised and condensed.'
1. Swedenborg, Emanuel, 1688—1772. 2. New Jerusalem church. I. Spalding, John Howard.

JONSSON, Inge. 289.4'0924
Emanuel Swedenborg. Translated from the Swedish by Catherine Djurklou. New York, Twayne Publishers [1971] 224 p. 21 cm. (Twayne's world authors series. Sweden, TWAS 127) Bibliography: 213-220. [BX8748.J64] 72-120397
1. Swedenborg, Emanuel, 1688-1772.

KANT, Immanuel, 1724-1804. 133.9'01
Dreams of a spirit seer, and other related writings. Translation and commentary by John Manolesco. [1st ed.] New York, Vantage Press [1969] 192 p. 21 cm. Translation of Traume eines Geistersehers. Includes bibliographical references. [B2793.E5G6 1969] 79-5058 5.00
1. Swedenborg, Emanuel, 1688-1772. 2. Metaphysics. I. Manolesco, John, tr. II. Title.

KANT, Immanuel, 1724-1804. 110
Traume eines Geistersehers ; Der Unterschied der Gegenden im Raume / Immanuel Kant ; unter Verwendung d. Textes von Karl Vorlander mit e. Einl. hrsg. von Klaus Reich. Hamburg : Meiner, 1975. xviii, 96 p. ; 19 cm. (Philosophische Bibliothek ; Bd. 286) Includes bibliographical references and indexes. [B2793.A3 1975] 75-521673 ISBN 3-7873-0311-1 : DM14.00
1. Swedenborg, Emanuel, 1688-1772. 2. Spiritualism. 3. Metaphysics. I. Kant, Immanuel, 1724-1804. Der Unterschied der Gegenden im Raume. 1975. II. Title.

KELLER, Helen. 922.84
My religion. New York, Pyramid Books [1974, c1960] 126 p. illus. 18 cm. [BX8721.K35] 74-11645 ISBN 0-515-03555-6 1.25 (pbk.)
1. Swedenborg, Emanuel, 1688-1772. I. Title.
L.C. card no. for original ed.: 62-52553.

KELLER, Helen Adams, 1880- 922.84
My religion. New York, Citadel [1964, c.1960] 157p. 19cm. (C 154) 63-21205 1.50 pap.,
1. Swedenborg, Emanuel, 1688-1772. I. Title.

KELLER, Helen Adams, 1880- 922.84
My religion. New York, Swedenborg Foundation, 1962. 208p. 19cm. [BX8721.K35 1962] 62-52553
1. Swedenborg, Emanuel, 1688-1772. I. Title.

KELLER, Helen Adams, 1880-
My religion. New York, Avon Book Division, The Hearst corporation [c1960, by Swedenborg Foundation] 157 p. 16 cm. (Bard Book, 7) 67-43535
1. Swedenborg, Emanuel, 1688-1772. I. Title.

KIP, Abraham Lincoln, 1865- 922.
The seven types of humanity and other essays, by A. L. Kip. New York, The Knickerbocker press, 1929. iii, 218 p. 20 1/2 cm. Essays dealing chiefly with the teachings of Emanuel Swedenborg. [BX8748.K55] 29-15939
1. Swedenborg, Emanuel, 1688-1772. I. Title.

MAHIN, R. Newton. 230.94
From Swedenborg; an outline of Emanuel Swedenborg's Latin testament. [1st ed.] New York, Greenwich Book Publishers [1959] 120p. 21cm. [BX8711.M32] 59-12046
1. Swedenborg, Emanuel, 1688-1772. I. Title.

MAHIN, R. Newton. 230.94
Palewings... Based on Emanuel Swedenborg's revelation of an internal of the Word. Boston, Meador Pub. Co. [1956] 524p. 21cm. [BX8711.M33] 56-25041
1. Swendenborg, Emanuel, 1688-1772. I. Title.

MERCER, Lewis Pyle, 1847-1906. 289.
Emanuel Swedenborg and the New Christian church, by Rev. L. P. Mercer ... With a fraternal address to the church universal. Chicago, Western New-church union, 1893. 109 p. 13 cm. "Swedenborg's works": p. [95]-109. [BX8723.M38] 38-20528
1. Swedenborg, Emanuel, 1688-1772. 2. New Jerusalem church. I. Title.

ODHNER, C[arl] Th[eophilus] 1863-
A brief view of the heavenly doctrines revealed in the theological writings of Emanuel Swedenborg. By C. Th. Odhner. 2d ed. Bryn Athyn, Pa., Academy book room, 1903. 1 p. l., 103 p. front. (port.) 19 1/2 cm. 5-12182
I. Title.

ODHNER, C[arl] Th[eophilus] 1863-
A brief view of the heavenly doctrines revealed in the theological writings of Emanuel Swedenborg. By C. Th. Odhner. 2d ed. Bryn Athyn, Pa., Academy book room, 1903. 1 p. l., 103 p. front. (port.) 20 cm. 5-12182
I. Title.

ODHNER, C[arl] Theophilus, 1863-
A brief view of the heavenly doctrines revealed in the theological writings of Emanuel Swedenborg. By C. Theophilus Odhner. Philadelphia, Academy book room, 1897. 105 p. 19 cm. Cover-title: A view of the New Jerusalem. 5-12181
I. Title.

ODHNER, C[arl] Theophilus, 1863-
A brief view of the heavenly doctrines revealed in the theological writings of Emanuel Swedenborg. By C. Theophilus Odhner. Philadelphia, Academy book room, 1897. 105 p. 19 cm. Cover-title: A view of the New Jerusalem. 5-12181
I. Title.

ODHNER, Hugo Ljungberg, 1891- 230.94
Spirits and men; some essays on the influence of spirits upon men, as described in the writings of Emanuel Swedenbord. Bryn Athyn, Pa., Academy Books Room [1958] 227p. 20cm. [BX8711.O3] 58-48845
1. Swedenborg, Emanuel, 1688-1772. I. Title.

PARSONS, Theophilus, 1797-1882. 289.
Outlines of the religion and philosophy of Swedenborg. By Theophilus Parsons. Boston, Roberts brothers, 1876. 318 p. 18 cm. [BX8721.P3 1876] 12-37430
1. Swedenborg, Emanuel, 1688-1772. 2. New Jerusalem church—Doctrinal and controversial works. I. Title.

PARSONS, Theophilus, 1797-1882. 230.94
Outlines of the religion and philosophy of Swedenborg. By Theophilus Parsons. Rev. and enl. ed. New York city, The New church board of publication, 1903. 382 p. 18 cm. [BX8721.P3 1903] 12-37455
1. Swedenborg, Emanuel, 1688-1772. 2. New Jerusalem church—Doctrinal and controversial works. I. Title.

PENDLETON, Charles Rittenhouse. 289.4
Space and extense in the spiritual world. Bryn Althyn, Pa., 1962. 66 p. 23 cm. [BX8711.P4] 63-36811
1. Swedenborg, Emanuel, 1688-1772. 2. Space and time. I. Title.

POND, Enoch, 1791-1882. 230.94
Swedenborgianism examined. By Enoch Pond ... Rev. ed. Boston, American tract society [1861] xi, [13]-250 p. 18 cm. The first edition was published in 1846; this is the thoroughly revised 2d ed. cf. Pref. [BX8731.P6 1861] 35-23816
1. Swedenborg, Emanuel, 1688-1772. I. American tract society. II. Title.

REDGROVE, Herbert Stanley.
Purpose and transcendentalism; an exposition of Swedenborg's philosohical doctrines in relation to modern thought, by H. Stanley Redgrove ... London, K. Paul, Trench, Trubner & co., ltd.; New York, E. P. Dutton & co. [1920] xvi, 170 p. 19 cm. [B4468.S8R4] 21-20767
1. Swedenborg, Emanuel, 1688-1772. 2. Transcendentalism. I. Title.

RENDELL, Elias De La Roche. 230.
The word and its inspiration ... By the late Rev'd E. D. Rendell ... New Haven, Conn., Connecticut New church association, 1899-1900. 3 v. 20 1/2 cm. On t.-p. of v. 1: From the second English edition; v. 2-3: From the first English edition. [BX8727.R4] 0-6694
I. Swedenborg, Emanuel, 1688-1772. II. Title.
Contents omitted.

SIGSTEDT, Cyriel Sigrid (Ljungberg Odhner) 289.4'0924 B
The Swedenborg epic; the life and works of Emanuel Swedenborg, by Cyriel Odhner Sigstedt. New York, Bookman Associates, 1952. New York, AMS Press, 1971] xvii, 517 p. illus. 23 cm. (Communal societies in America) Includes bibliographical references. [BX8748.S53 1971] 78-137269 ISBN 0-404-05999-6
1. Swedenborg, Emanuel, 1688-1772. I. Title.

SIGSTEDT, Cyriel Sigrid (Ljungberg Odhner) 922.84
The Swendenborg epic : the life and works of Emanuel Swedenborg New York, Bookman Associates, 1952. xvii, 517p. illus., ports., map (on lining papers) 14cm. List of works: p. 499-501. Bibliographical references included in Notes and references (p. 445-482) [BX8748.S53] 53-5811
1. Swedenborg, Emanuel, 1688-1772. I. Title.

SIGSTEDT, Cyriel Sigrid (Ljungberg Odhner) 289.4
Wonder footprints, stories about heaven for children, by Sigrid Odhner Sigstedt. Illustrated by Claire E. Berninger. [(Philadelphia, Printed by Blaetz brothers, inc., 1937] 2p. 1., 7-46, [2]p. illus. 26cm. 'For the six memorable relations on which these stories are based, see the work on Conjugial love, by Emanuel Swedenborg, nos. 74-82 and the True Christian religion, no. 791. --p. [48] [BX8729.H4S5] 38-13101
1. Swedenborg, Emmanuel, 1688-1772. I. Title.

SPALDING, John Howard.
Introduction to Swedenborg's religious thought. New York, Swedenborg pub. association, 1956. 235 p. 21 cm. "Published some years ago under the title: 'The kingdom of heaven as seen by Swedenborg', the book has now been revised and condensed."
1. Swedenborg, Emanuel, 1688-1772. 2. New Jerusalem church. I. Title.

SPALDING, John Howard. 230'.9'4
Introduction to Swedenborg's religious thought / John Howard Spalding. New York : Swedenborg Pub. Association, 1977. 235 p. ; 18 cm. First published in 1916 under title: The kingdom of heaven as seen by Swedenborg; rev. and condensed in 1956 by R. H. Tafel. [BX8721.S692] 77-78682 ISBN 0-87785-121-2 pbk. : 1.50
1. Swedenborg, Emmanuel, 1688-1772. 2. New Jerusalem Church—Doctrinal and controversal works. I. Tafel, Richard H. II. Title.

SWEDENBORG, Emanuel, 1688-1772.
Angelic wisdom about divine providence; new translation by W. F. Wunsch. [Standard Edition] New York, Swedenborg Foundation [1964] ix, 376 p. 66-84426
I. Title.

SWEDENBORG, Emanuel, 1688-1772. 228
Angelic wisdom concerning the divine love and the divine wisdom, by Emanuel Swedenborg; originally published in Latin at Amsterdam, 1763. Library ed. New York, The American Swedenborg printing and publishing society, 1908. xiii, 293 p. 21 1/2 cm. Translated by J. C. Ager. [BX8712.D4 1908] 10-6149
I. Ager, John Curtis, 1835-1913, tr. II. Title.

SWEDENBORG, Emanuel, 1688-1772.
Angelic wisdom concerning the divine love and the divine wisdom. Tr. from the Latin of Emanuel Swedenborg ... Originally pub. at Amsterdam MDCCLXIII. From the last London ed. New York, American Swedenborg printing and publishing society, 1872. xii, 199 p. 23 cm. One of the reprints of the London edition 0f 1843, which was revised by Dr. J. J. G. Wilkinson. cf. J. Hyde, A bibliography of the works of Emanuel Swedenborg, 1906, p. 427 (no. 2044) 17-4646
I. Wilkinson, James John Garth, 1812-1899. II. Title.

SWEDENBORG, Emanuel, 1688-1772.
Angelic wisdom concerning the divine Providence. Tr. from the Latin of Emanuel Swedenborg ... Originally pub. at Amsterdam, MDCCLXIV. From the last London ed. New York, American Swedenborg printing and publishing society, 1873. xiii, 308 p. 23 cm. 17-4663
I. Title.

SWEDENBORG, Emanuel, 1688-1772.
Angelic wisdom concerning the divine Providence. Tr. from the Latin of Emanuel Swedenborg ... Originally pub. at Amsterdam, MDCCLXIV. From the last London ed. New York, American Swedenborg printing and publishing society, 1892. 2 p. l., [vii]-xiii, 308 p. 23 cm. One of the reprints of the London edition of 1833, which was revised by A. Maxwell. cf. J. Hyde, A bibliography of the works of Emanuel Swedenborg, 1906, p. 439 (no. 2105) 17-4664
I. Maxwell, Alexander, ed. II. Title.

SWEDENBORG, Emanuel, 1688-1772. 230.94
A compendium of the theological writings of Emanuel Swedenborg. By Samuel M. Warren. 3d and rev. ed., with a biographical introduction, by Hon. John Bigelow. New York, The New Church board of publications, 1888. lxxxvi p., 1 l., 773 p. front. (port.) 23 cm. Bibliography: p. lxxix-lxxxvi. [BX8711.A7W3 1888] 4-14243
I. Warren, Samuel Mills, comp. II. Bigelow, John, 1817-1911. III. Title.

SWEDENBORG, Emanuel, 1688-1772.
A dictionary of correspondences, representatives, and significatives, derived from the Word of the Lord. Extracted from the writings of Emanuel Swedenborg. 2d ed. Boston, O. Clapp; New York, J. Allen; [etc., etc.] 1847. 4 p. l., 436 p. 19

1/2 cm. Principally an abridgment of Charles Bolles of "A new and comprehensive dictionary of correspondences, representatives, and significatives, contained in the Word of the Lord ... extracted from all the theological works of ... E. Swedenborg ... By George Nicholson." cf. Publisher's advertisement to 3d ed. of present work. 15-21991
I. Nicholson, George. II. Bolles, Charles. III. Title.

SWEDENBORG, Emanuel, 1688-1772. 228
The divine Providence, by Emanuel Swedenborg ... London and New York, F. Warne & company [1906] 2 p. l., vii-xx, 164 p. 21 1/2 cm. Translated by Isaiah Tansley. cf. Prefatory note. [BX8712.D6 1906] 30-8086
I. Tansley, Isaiah, tr. II. Title.

SWEDENBORG, Emanuel, 1688-1772. 228
The divine Providence, by Emanuel Swedenborg ... London and New York, F. Warne & company [1906] 2 p. l., vii-xx, 164 p. 21 1/2 cm. Translated by Isaiah Tansley. cf. Prefatory note. [BX8712.D6 1906] 30-8086
I. Tansley, Isaiah, tr. II. Title.

SWEDENBORG, Emanuel, 1688-1772. 228
The doctrine of life for the New Jerusalem, from the commandments of the Decalogue. Tr. from the Latin of the Honourable and learned Emanuel Swedenborg. To which is prefixed, a short account of the life of the author. Philadelphia: Printed for a member of the New Jerusalem church, by Lydia R. Bailey, no. 10, North alley, 1816. 140 p. 15 cm. One of the reprints of the London edition if 1786, which was translated by the Rev. J. Clowes. cf. J. Hyde. A bibliography of the works of Emanuel Swedenborg, 1906, p. 394 (no. 1860) Translation of Doctrina vitae pro nove Hieresolyma ex praeceptis Decalogi. [BX8712.D96 1816] 19-7113
I. Clowes, John, 1743-1831, tr. II. Title.
Contents omitted.

SWEDENBORG, Emanuel, 1688-1772. 228
The heavenly doctrine of the New Jerusalem, as revealed from Heaven. Translated from the Latin of the Hon. Emanuel Swedenborg, of the senatorial order of nobles in the kingdom of Sweden. By the Rev. John Clowes, M.A. The first American, from the fourth London edition ... Printed at Boston, by Thomas Hall: sold at his office, Dock square, and at the bookstores, MDCCXCIV. 129, [1] p. 17 1/2 cm. "Errata": p. [130] [BX8712.H] A33
I. Clowes, John, 1743-1831, tr. II. Title.

SWEDENBORG, Emanuel, 1688-1772.
Miscellaneous theological works of Emanuel Swedenborg ... New York, American Swedenborg printing and publishing society, 1871. 525, [1] p. 23 cm. 17-4658
I. Title.
Contents omitted.

SWEDENBORG, Emanuel, 1688-1772.
Miscellaneous theological works of Emanuel Swedenborg ... New York, American Swedenborg printing and publishing society, 1892. 526 p. 23 1/2 cm. 17-4659
I. Title.
Contents omitted.

SWEDENBORG, Emanuel, 1688-1772. 230.
Swedenborg's Spiritual diary, &c. [New York, 1846] 144 p. 23 cm. [With his The memorabilia ... New York, 1846] Caption title. [BX8711.A7B8] 1-22080
I. Title.

SWEDENBORG publishing association.
Annual report of the Board of managers. [Philadelphia, v. 17 1/2 cm. Issue for 1905 has also distinctive title: Is it worth while? Does it pay? [BX8703.S75A3] 7-871
I. Title.

TAFEL, Johann Friedrich Immanuel, 1796-1868. 922.84
Documents concerning the life and character of Emanuel Swedenborg; collected by Dr. J. F. I. Tafel ... Translated and revised by Rev. I. H. Smithson ... A new ed. with additions, by George Bush ... New York, J. Allen; Boston, O. Clapp, 1847. viii, [17]-232 p. front. (port.) 23 1/2 cm. (On cover: The Swedenborg library. no. 61-64) [BX8748.T3] 36-31927
1. Swedenborg, Emanuel, 1688-1772. I. Smithson, John Henry, 1808-1877, ed. and tr. II. Bush, George, 1766-1859, ed. III. Title.

TOKSVIG, Signe, 1891- 922.84
Emanuel Swedenborg, scientist and mystic. New Haven, Yale Univ. Press, 1948. 389 p. ports. 24 cm. Full name: Signe Kirstine Toksvig. Includes bibliographies. [BX8748.T65] 48-6174
1. Swedenborg, Emanuel, 1688-1772. I. Title.

TOKSVIG, Signe, 1891- 198'.5 B
Emanuel Swedenborg: scientist and mystic. Freeport, N.Y., Books for Libraries Press [1972, c1948] 389 p. ports. 22 cm. (Biography index reprint series) Includes bibliographical references. [BX8748.T65 1972] 72-5447 ISBN 0-8369-8140-5
1. Swedenborg, Emanuel, 1688-1772.

TROBRIDGE, George, 1851-1909. 922.
Emanuel Swedenborg, his life, teachings and influence, by George Trobridge ... 1st American ed.; foreword by Charles W. Harvey ... New York, The New-church press incorporated [1918] viii, 247 p. front. (port.) 19 cm. [BX8748.T8] 19-7228
1. Swedenborg, Emanuel, 1688-1772. I. Title.

TROBRIDGE, George, 1851-1909. 922.84
Swedenborg, life and teaching, by G. Trobridge ... New York, Swedenborg foundation, incorporated, 1938. 346 p., 1 l. incl. front. (port.) 17 cm. Preface to fourth edition signed: E. C. M. "This memorial edition is published in commemoration of the 250th anniversary of the birth of Emanuel Swedenborg." First published in 1907 under title: Emanuel Swedenborg, his life, teachings and influence. Advertising matter: p. 344-346. [BX8748.T8 1938] 38-25505
1. Swedenborg, Emanuel, 1688-1772. I. M., E. C., ed. II. E. C. M., ed. III. Title.

TROBRIDGE, George, 1851-1909. 922.84
Swedenborg, life and teaching. New York, Swedenborg Foundation, 1962. 298 p. illus. 20 cm. "Fifth reprint of the 1935 (fourth) edition of the Swedenborg Society of London." First published in 1907 under title: Emanuel Swedenborg, his life, teachings, and influence. [BX8748.T8 1962] 62-53182
1. Swedenborg, Emanuel, 1688-1772.

VAN DUSEN, Wilson Miles. 230'.9'4
The presence of other worlds; the psychological/spiritual findings of Emanuel Swedenborg [by] Wilson Van Dusen. New York, Harper & Row [1975, c1974] xv, 240 p., 18 cm. (Perennial Library) Includes bibliographical references. [BX8748.V3] ISBN 0-06-080342-8 1.75 (pbk.)
1. Swedenborg, Emanuel, 1688-1772. I. Title.
L.C. card no. for original ed.: 73-18684

VAN DUSEN, Wilson Miles. 230'.9'4
The presence of other worlds; the psychological/spiritual findings of Emanuel Swedenborg [by] Wilson Van Dusen. [1st ed.] New York, Harper & Row [1974] xv, 240 p. 21 cm. Includes bibliographical references. [BX8748.V3] 73-18684 ISBN 0-06-068826-2 6.95
1. Swedenborg, Emanuel, 1688-1772. I. Title.

VERY, Frank Washington, 1852-1927. 113
An epitome of Swedenborg's science, by Frank W. Very ... Boston, The Four seas company [c1927] 2 v. fronts. (v. 1, port.) plates, diagrs. 20 1/2 cm. [Q157.S9V4] 28-21160
1. Swedenborg, Emanuel, 1688-1772. I. Title.

[VETTERLING, Carl Herman] 922.84
Swedenborg the Buddhist; or, The higher Swedenborgianism, its secrets and Thibetan origin, by Philangi Dasa [pseud.] ... Los Angeles, The Buddhistic Swedenborgian brotherhood, 1887. 322 p. 25 cm. [BX8748.V4] 39-5087
1. Swedenborg, Emanuel, 1688-1772. I. Title.

WHITE, William. 922.
Life of Emanuel Swedenborg. Together with a brief synopsis of his writings, both philosophical and theological. By William White. With an introduction by B. F. Barrett. 1st American ed. Philadelphia, J. B. lippincott & co., 1866. 272 p. 19 1/2 cm. [BX8748.W53] 12-40233
1. Swedenborg, Emanuel, 1688-1772. I. Title.

WORCESTER, Benjamin, 1824-1911. 922.
The life and mission of Emanuel Swedenborg. By Benjamin Worcester ... Boston, Roberts brothers, 1883. vi p., 1 l., 473 p. front. (port.) 1 facsim. 20 cm. "Writings of Swedenborg": p. 444-452. "Biographies of Swedenborg": p. 454-456. [BX8748.W6 1883] 4-22767
1. Swedenborg, Emanuel, 1688-1772. I. Title.

WORCESTER, Benjamin, 1824-1911. 922
The life and mission of Emanuel Swedenborg, By Benjamin Worcester ... [5th ed.] Boston, Little, Brown, and company, 1901. vi p., 1 l., 473 p. front. (port.) facsim. 19 1/2 cm. "Writings of Swedenborg": p. 444-452. "Biographies of Swedenborg": p. 454-456. [BX8748.W6 1901] 4-16978
1. Swedenborg, Emmanuel, 1688-1772. I. Title.

WORCESTER, Benjamin, 1824-1911. 922.84
Swedenborg; harbinger of the new age of the Christian church, by Benjamin Worcester. Philadelphia, J. B. Lippincott company, 1910. 4 p. l., 293, [1] p. 19 1/2 cm. [BX8748.W7] 11-718
1. Swedenborg, Emanuel, 1688-1772. I. Title.

WUNSCH, William Frederic, 1882- 289.4
A practical philosophy of life, as gathered from the writings of Swedenborg, by William Frederic Wunsch. New York, The New-church press [c1937] 5 p. l., 7-98 p. 18 1/2 cm. Half-title: Four addresses. "References for quotations": p. 97-98. [BX8711.W85] 37-17938
1. Swedenborg, Emanuel, 1688-1772. I. Title.

Swedenborg, Emanuel, 1688-1772. Arcana coelestia.

ROEDER, Adolph, 1857- 230.94
Man's two memories; a study of Emanuel Swedenborg's teachings concerning them, by Adolph Roeder. New York, The New-church press, [c1931] 4 p. l., 135 p. 21 1/2 cm. [BX8712.A89R6] 31-11185
1. Swedenborg, Emanuel, 1688-1772. Arcana coelestia. 2. Memory. 3. Mind and body. I. Title.

WUNSCH, William Frederic, 1882- 228
The world within the Bible; a handbook to Swedenborg's Arcana coelestia, by William F. Wunsch. New York, The New-church press [c1929] 5 p. l., [3]-161 p. 21 1/2 cm. [BX8712.A89W8] 29-12999
1. Swedenborg, Emanuel, 1688-1772. Arcana coelestia. I. Title.

Swedenborg, Emanuel, 1688-1772—Bibliography

NEW Jerusalem church.
Descriptive catalogue of New Church books and tracts, American and foreign, containing Swedenborg's works ... and works of other authors, including juvenile and Sunday school books, tracts. ... etc. [New York, New Church Board of publication] 1873. 71 p. 19 cm. A 10
1. Swedenborg, Emanuel, 1688-1772—Bibl. 2. New Jerusalem church—Bibl. I. Title.

SWEDENBORG foundation, incorporated. 922.
Who was Swedenborg, and what are his writings? With catalogue of the theological writings of Emanuel Swedenborg. New York, The American Swedenborg printing and publishing society [190-?] 21 p. 17 1/2 cm. Signed: The American Swedenborg printing and publishing society. "Theological works of Emanuel Swedenborg": p. [9]-20. [BX8748.S93] [Z8855.S97] 5-12382
1. Swedenborg, Emanuel, 1688-1772—Bibl. I. Title.

Swedenborg, Emanuel, 1688-1772—Dictionaries, indexes, etc.

SWEDENBORG, Emanuel, 1688-1772. 230.94
A dictionary of correspondence, representatives, and significatives, derived from the Word of the Lord. Extracted from the writings of Emanuel Swedenborg. New York, Swedenborg Foundation, 1962. 453 p. 20 cm. (A Book for Bible readers) "Second photo offset reprint of the thirteenth edition (1931)" Principally an abridgment, by Charles Bolles, of "A new and comprehensive dictionary of correspondence, representatives, and significatives, contained in the World of the Lord . . . Faithfully extracted from all the theological works of the Hon. Emanuel Swedenborg . . . by George Nicholson." [VX8711.A7N4 1962] 62-53179
1. Swedenborg, Emanual, 1688-1772 — Dictionaries, indexes, etc. 2. Correspondence, Doctrine of. I. Nicholson, George, d. 1819. II. Bolles, Charles. 1802-1854. III. Title.

SWEDENBORG, Emanuel, 1688-1772. 230.94
A dictionary of correspondences, representatives, and significatives, derived from the Word of the Lord. Extracted from the writings of Emanuel Swedenborg. 3d ed. Boston, O. Clapp, 1860. 453 p. 20 cm. "Principally an abridgment" by Charles Bolles of "A new and comprehensive dictionary of correspondences, representatives, and significatives, contained in the Word of the Lord ... extracted from all the theological works of ... E. Swedenborg ... By George Nicholson". cf. Publisher's advertisement. [BX8711.A7N4 1860] 15-21990
1. Swedenborg, Emanuel, 1688-1772—Dictionaries, indexes, etc. 2. Correspondences, Doctrine of. I. Nicholson, George, d. 1819. II. Bolles, Charles, 1802-1854. III. Title.

Swedenborg, Emanuel, 1688-1772—Influence.

MORRIS, Herbert Newall, 1871- 700'.9
Flaxman, Blake, Coleridge, and other men of genius influenced by Swedenborg; together with Flaxman's allegory of the "Knight of the blazing cross". [Folcroft, Pa.] Folcroft Library Editions, 1973. viii, 166 p. illus. 34 cm. Reprint of the 1915 ed. published by New-Church Press, London. Chapters originally published in 1909 and 1910 in the New Church young people's magazine. Contents.Contents.—John Flaxman, R.A.—Flaxman's "Knight of the blazing cross".—William Blake.—Samuel Taylor Coleridge.—Hiram Powers.—Henry Septimus Sutton.—Ralph Waldo Emerson.—James John Garth Wilkinson.—The Brownings. [BX8748.M7 1973] 73-619 ISBN 0-8414-1515-3 (lib. bdg.)
1. Swedenborg, Emanuel, 1688-1772—Influence. I. Flaxman, John, 1755-1826. Knight of the blazing cross. 1973. II. Title.

Swedenborg, Emanuel, 1688-1772. The Apocalypse revealed.

REVELATION; 228
an independent compendium of the "Apocalypse revealed". Lancaster, Pa., The Neighborly library, 1936. 3 p. l., 94 p. 17 1/2 x 15 1/2 cm. [BX8712.A69R4] (230.94) 37-1390
1. Swedenborg, Emanuel, 1688-1772. The Apocalypse revealed. I. Bible. N.T. Revelation—Commentaries. II. Bible—Commentaries—N.T. Revelation.

Swedenborg, Emanuel. The true Christian religion.

SWEDENBORG, Emanuel, 1688-1772.
The true Christian religion; containing the universal theology of the New church, foretold by the Lord in Daniel, VII. 13, 14, and in the Apocalypse, XXI. 1, 2. Tr. from the Latin of Emanuel Swedenborg ... New York, American Swedenborg printing and publishing society, 1871. 3 p. l., [iii]-xviii, 982 p. 23 cm. One of the reprints of the London edition of 1846, which was revised by H. Butter. cf. J. Hyde. A bibliography of the works of Emanuel Swedenborg, 1906, p. 553 (no. 2745) "The coronis, or appendix, to The true Christian religion": p. 817-883. 17-4655
1. Butter, Henry, ed. II. Title.

SWEDENBORG, Emanuel, 1688-1772.
The true Christian religion; containing the universal theology of the New church, foretold by the Lord in Daniel, VII. 13, 14, and in the Apocalypse, XXi. 1, 2. Tr. from the Latin of Emanuel Swedenborg ... New York, American Swedenborg printing and publishing society, 1873. 3 p. l., [iii]-xviii, 982 p. 23 1/2 cm. One of the reprints of the London edition of 1846, which was revised by H. Butter. cf. J. Hyde, A bibliography of the works of Emanuel Swedenborg, 1906, p. 553 (no. 2745) "The cornois, or appendix, to The true Christian religion": p. 817-883. 17-4653
I. Butter, Henry, ed. II. Title.

SWEDENBORG, Emanuel, 1688-1772.
The true Christian religion; containing the universal theology of the New church, foretold by the Lord in Daniel, VII. 13, 14, and in the Apocalypse, XXI. 1, 2. Tr. from the Latin of Emanuel Swedenborg ... New York, American Swedenborg printing and publishing society, 1886. 3 p. l., [iii]-xviii, 982 p. 23 1/2 cm. "The cornois, or appendix, to The true Christian religion": p. 817-883. 17-4652
I. Title.

SWEDENBORG, Emanuel, 1688-1772.
The true Christian religion; containing the universal theology of the New church, foretold by the Lord in Daniel, VII. 13, 14, and in the Apocalypse, XXI. 1, 2. Tr. from the Latin of Emanuel Swedenborg ... New York, American Swedenborg printing and publishing society, 1892. 2 p. l., [iii]-xviii, 982 p. 23 cm. One of the reprints of the London edition of 1846, which was revised by H. Butter. cf. J. Hyde, A bibliography of the works of Emanuel Swedenborg, 1906, p. 553 (no. 2745) "The coronis, or appendix, to The true Christian religion": p. 817-883. 17-4654
I. Butter, Henry, ed. II. Title.

SWEDENBORG, Emanuel, 1688-1772.
The true Christian religion: containing the universal theology of the New church, foretold by the Lord in Daniel VII. 13, 14; and in Revelation XXI. 1, 2. By Emanuel Swedenborg ... Rotch ed. Boston, Massachusetts New-church union, 1903. 1 p. l., xvii, 4, [1014]-1057, [1099]-1106 p. 18 1/2 cm. Selected portions from Swedenborg's last work, The true Christian religion. 4-35577
I. Title.

WILDE, Arthur.
True Christian religion, a digest of Emanuel Swedenborg's The true Christian religion; prepared originally as a talking book for the blind. New York, Swedenborg Foundation, 1956. 80 p. port. 19 cm. 68-47572
1. Swedenborg, Emanuel. The true Christian religion. I. Title.

Swedes in New Jersey.

RACCOON, N. J. Swedish Lutheran church. 284.774981
The records of the Swedish Lutheran churches at Raccoon and Penns Neck, 1713-1786 ... translated and compiled by the Federal writers project of the Works progress administration, state of New Jersey: with an introduction and notes by Dr. Amandus Johnson ... [Elizabeth, N. J., Colby and McGowan, inc.] 1938. 2 p. l., xv p., 1 l., 387 p. front. (facsims.) 24 cm. (American guide series) "Sponsored by the New Jersey commission to commemorate the 300th anniversary of the settlement by the Swedes and Finns on the Delaware, D. Stewart Craven, chairman." [BX8076.R27S8] 39-24680
1. Swedes in New Jersey. 2. Finns in New Jersey. 3. Registers of births, etc.—New Jersey. I. Penns Neck, N. J. Swedish Lutheran church. II. Johnson, Amandus, 1877- ed. III. Federal writers' project, New Jersey. IV. Title.

Swedes in the United States

STEPHENSON, George Malcolm, 1883- 277.3
The religious aspects of Swedish immigrations; a study of immigrant churches, by George M. Stephenson ... Minneapolis, The University of Minnesota press, 1932. viii p., 1 l., 542 p. front., ports. 24 cm. Bibliography: p. 479-510. [BR563.S8S7] 32-5258
1. Swedes in the U. S. 2. Sects—U. S. I. Title.

Swedish Americans.

STEPHENSON, George Malcolm, 1883-1958. 280'.09174'397
The religious aspects of Swedish immigration. New York, Arno Press, 1969. viii, 542 p. 24 cm. (The American immigration collection) Reprint of the 1932 ed. Bibliography: p. 479-510. [BR563.S8S7 1969] 69-18790
1. Swedish Americans. 2. Sects—United States. I. Title.

STEPHENSON, George Malcolm, 1883-1958. 280'.0973
The religious aspects of Swedish immigration; a study of immigrant churches. Minneapolis, University of Minnesota Press, 1932. [New York, AMS Press, 1972] viii, 542 p. illus. 23 cm. Bibliography: p. 479-510. [BR563.S8S7 1972] 71-137294 ISBN 0-404-06257-1
1. Swedish Americans. 2. Sects—United States. I. Title.

Swedish evangelical mission covenant of America.

BOWMAN, Charles Victor, 1868- 277.
The Mission covenant of America, by C. V. Bowman ... Chicago, Ill., The Covenant book concern [c1925] 223 p. plates. 21 cm. [BV2766.L8B6] 26-1331
1. Swedish evangelical mission covenant of America. I. Title.

Swedish evangelical mission covenant of America—Addresses, essays, lectures.

NYVALL, David, 1863- 252.047
Beacon lights; three addresses and an essay, by David Nyvall; translated from the Swedish by E. Gustav Johnson. Chicago, North park college alumni association, 1933. 61 p. incl. port. 21 cm. [BX8049.5.N78] 33-4716
1. Swedish evangelical mission covenant of America—Addresses, essays, lectures. I. Johnson, E. Gustav, 1893- tr. II. Title.

NYVALL, David, 1863- 252.047
Beacon lights; three addresses and an essay, by David Nyvall; translated from the Swedish by E. Gustav Johnson. Chicago, North park college alumni association, 1933. 61 p. incl. port. 21 cm. [BX8049.5.N78] 33-4716
1. Swedish evangelical mission covenant of America—Addresses, essays, lectures. I. Johnson, E. Gustav, 1893- tr. II. Title.

Sweeney, Zachary Taylor, 1849-1926.

ERRETT, Isaac, 1820-1888. 220
The querists' drawer, a discussion of difficult subjects and passages of the Scriptures, by Isaac Errett ... arranged and ed. by Z. T. Sweeney. Cincinnati, The Standard publishing company [c1910] 335 p. 20 1/2 cm. 10-14498 1.50
1. Sweeney, Z. T., ed. I. Title.

MCALLISTER, Lester G. 286'.6'0924(B)
Z. T. Sweeney: preacher and peacemaker, by Lester G. McAllister. St. Louis, Christian Board of Publication [1968] 128 p. port. 23 cm. Bibliography: p. 123-124. [BX7343.S94M3] 68-5649
1. Sweeney, Zachary Taylor, 1849-1926.

SWEENEY, Zachary Taylor, 1849- ed. 230.
New Testament Christianity ... Edited by Z. T. Sweeney. Columbus, Ind., Printed for the editor [c1923- v. 20 cm. [BX7321.S8] 24-995
I. Title.

Sweet, William Warren, 1881-1959.

ASH, James L., 1945- 277.3'0092'4 B
Protestantism and the American university : an intellectual biography of William Warren Sweet / by James L. Ash, Jr. ; foreword by Martin E. Marty. Dallas : SMU Press, 1982. p. cm. Includes index. Bibliography: p. [BR139.S93A83 1982] 19 82-10629 ISBN 0-87074-183-7 : 15.00
1. Sweet, William Warren, 1881-1959. 2. Church historians—United States—Biography. I. Title.

Swieson, Eddy, 1932-

SWIESON, Eddy, 1932- 285'.131'0924 B
When the angels laughed / Eddy Swieson tells his story with Howard Norton. Plainfield, N.J. : Logos International, c1977. x, 126 p., [3] leaves of plates : ill. ; 21 cm. [BX9225.S93A36] 77-20584 ISBN 0-88270-264-5 pbk. : 2.95
1. Swieson, Eddy, 1932- 2. Presbyterian Church—Clergy—Biography. 3. Clergy—United States—Biography. I. Norton, Howard Melvin, joint author. II. Title.

Swift, Job, 1743-1804.

SWIFT, Job, 1743-1804. 252.
Discourses on religious subjects, by the late Rev. Job Swift, D.D To which are prefixed sketches of his life and character, and a sermon, preached at West-Rutland, on the occasion of his death, by the Rev. Lemuel Haynes... Middlebury, Vt., Printed by Huntington and Fitch, 1805. xii, [13]-300 p. 17 1/2 cm. [BX7233.S8D5] A 35
1. Swift, Job, 1743-1804. 2. Congregational churches—Sermons. 3. Sermons. American. I. Haynes, Lemuel, 1753-1833. II. Title.

Swift, Jonathan, 1667-1745.

BRADY, Frank, comp. 230'.0942
Twentieth century interpretations of Gulliver's travels; a collection of critical essays. Englewood Cliffs, N.J., Prentice-Hall [1968] viii, 118 p. 21 cm. (Twentieth century interpretations) (A Spectrum book.) Includes bibliographical references. [PR3724.G8B7] 68-23699 3.95
1. Swift, Jonathan, 1667-1745. Gulliver's travels. I. Title.

Swing, David, 1830-1894.

MCCLURE, James B., ed.
Ingersoll's new departure. Replies to his famous lecture "What shall we do to be saved," by Prof. David Swing, Bishop Fallows, Dr. H. W. Thomas, Prof. Curtis, Dr. Lorimer, Dr. Courtney, and others. With the lecture appended. ed. by J. B. McClure. Chicago, Rhodes & McClure. 1880. viii, 17-92, 32 p. 20 cm. 4-36778
I. Swing, David, 1830-1894. II. Courtney, Frederick, 1837- III. Curtis, Samuel Ives. 1844- IV. Fallows, Samuel, 1835- V. Lorimer, George Claude, 1838-1904. VI. Thomas, Hiram Washington. VII. Title.

NEWTON, Joseph Fort, 1876- 922
David Swing, poet-preacher, by Joseph Fort Newton. Chicago, The Unity publishing co., Abraham Lincoln centre, 1909. 273 p. 2 pl., 2 port. (incl. front.) 24 1/2 cm. Bibliography: p. [11]-12. [BR1725.S9N4] 8-37339
1. Swing, David, 1830-1894. I. Title.

PATTON, Francis Landey, 1843-1932. 285.
Before the Synod of Illinois, North. In the matter of the appeal of Francis L. Patton against the decision of the presbytery of Chicago, in the case of David Swing. Appellant's argument. Chicago, Ills., Beach, Barnard & co.'s printing house, 1872. 68 p. 23 cm. Errata slip inserted. [BX9193.S9P3] 39-7838
1. Swing, David, 1830-1894. 2. Presbyterian church in the U. S. A. Presbyterian of Chicago. I. Presbyterian church in the U. S. A. Synod of Illinois. II. Title.

PRESBYTERIAN church in the U.S.A. Presbyteries. Chicago. 285.
The trial of the Rev. David Swing, before the Presbytery of Chicago. Edited by a committee of the Presbytery ... Chicago, Jansen, McClurg & co., 1874. 1 p. l., 286 p. 24 cm. [BX9193.S9A3] 44-24097
1. Swing, David, 1830-1894. I. Title.

Swithun, Saint, Bp. of Winchester, d. 862.

EARLE, John, 1824-1903, comp. 270.3'092'4 B
Gloucester fragments. [Folcroft, Pa.] Folcroft Library Editions, 1974. vii, 4, 116 p. 34 cm. Reprint of the 1861 ed. published by Longman, Green, Longman, and Roberts, London. Contents.Contents.—Facsimile of some leaves in Saxon handwriting on Saint SwiEhun, copied by photozincography.—Leaves from an Anglosaxon translation of the life of S. Maria Agyptiaca, with a translation and notes, and a photozincography facsimile. [BX4700.S86E2 1974] 74-18301 ISBN 0-8414-3989-3 (lib. bdg.)
1. Swithun, Saint, Bp. of Winchester, d. 862. I. Title.

Sycamore United Presbyterian church, Sycamore township, Hamilton co., O.

MORROW, Josiah, 1838-1928. 285.477177
History of the Sycamore Associate reformed church, now United Presbyterian. By Josiah Morrow ... [Cincinnati? 1930] 52 p. front. (port.) 26 1/2 cm. "Publications of the Historical and philosophical society of Ohio, 1930." [BX9211.S86U6] 31-13056
1. Sycamore United Presbyterian church, Sycamore township, Hamilton co., O. I. Historical and philosophical society of Ohio. Publications. II. Title.

Sychar, Woman of (Biblical character)

[ALDEN, Joseph] 232.95
Jesus and the woman of Sychar. Written for the Massachusetts Sabbath school society, and revised by the Committee of publication. Boston, Massachusetts Sabbath school society, 1845. 54 p. incl. front., illus. 14 1/2 cm. [BT309.A45] 35-34741
1. Sychar, Woman of (Biblical character) I. Massachusetts Sabbath school society. Committee of publication. II. Title.

TAYLOR, William Mackergo, 1829-1895. 232.95
Jesus at the well, John iv. 1-42, By William M. Taylor, D.D. New York, A. D. F. Randolph & company [1884] 3 p. l., [3]-128 p. 17 cm. [BT309.T3] 35-34740
1. Sychar, Woman of (Biblical character) I. Title.

Sydenstricker, Absalom, 1852-1931.

BUCK, Pearl (Sydenstricker) Mrs. 1892- 922
Fighting angel; portrait of a soul ... by Pearl S. Buck ... New York, Reynal & Hitchcock [c1936] 3 p. l., [9]-302 p. 22 cm. "A John Day book." "Fighting angel, the biography of the author's father, is a companion volume to The exile, which is a biography of her mother. Together they form a work to be entitled The spirit and the flesh."--1st prelim. leaf. [BV3427.S85B8 1936] 37-27009
1. Sydenstricker, Absalom, 1852-1931. 2. Missions—China. I. Title.

BUCK, Pearl (Sydenstricker) 1892- 922
... The spirit and the flesh. New York, The John Day company [1944] 378 p. 21 cm. At head of title: Pearl S. Buck. Contains

Fighting angel and The exile, biographies of the author's father and mother, respectively. [BV3427.S85B85] 44-3294
1. Sydenstricker, Absalom, 1852-1931. 2. Sydenstricker, Caroline (Stulting) 1857-1921. I. Title. II. Title: Fighting angel; portrait of a soul. III. Title: The exile.

Sydenstricker, Mrs. Caroline (Stulting) 1857-1921.

BUCK, Pearl (Sydenstricker) 920.7
Mrs. 1892-
The exile, by Pearl S. Buck ... New York, Reynal & Hitchcock [c1936] 3 p. l., [9]-315 p. 22 cm. A biography of the author's mother. A John Day book. [BV3427.S852B8] 36-3511
1. Sydenstricker, Mrs. Caroline (Stulting) 1857-1921. 2. Missions—China. I. Title.

Sydney. Wayside Chapel.

NOFFS, Ted. 259
The Wayside Chapel; a radical Christian experiment in today's world. Valley Forge, Judson Press [1970, c1969] 192 p. 19 cm. Includes bibliographical references. [BV2656.S9W37] 79-121054
1. Sydney. Wayside Chapel. 2. City missions—Sydney. I. Title.

Sykes, Norman, 1897-1961.

BENNETT, Gareth Vaughan, 274.2
ed.
Essays in modern English church history, in memory of Norman Sykes, ed. by G. V. Bennett, J. D. Walsh. New York, Oxford [c.]1966. x, 227p. 23cm. Bibl. [BR755.B4] 66-10794 5.75
1. Sykes, Norman, 1897-1961. 2. Gt. Brit.—Church history—Modern Period—Addresses. essays, lectures. I. Walsh, John Dixon, joint author. II. Title.

Sykes, Norman, 1897- Old priest and new presbyter.

PECK, Arthur Leslie, 1902-
Anglicanism and episcopacy; a re-examination of evidence. With special reference to Professor Norman Sykes' Old priest and new presbyter, together with an essay on validity. London, Faith Press; New York, Morehouse-Gorham [1958] viii, 104p. 23cm. A60
1. Sykes, Norman, 1897- Old priest and new presbyter. 2. Church of England. 3. Episcopacy. I. Title.

Sylvester II, pope, d. 1003.

THE peasant boy who became Pope: story of Gerbert. London, New York, Abelard-Schuman [1958] xi, 179p. 16 plates. 20cm.
1. Sylvester II, pope, d. 1003. I. Lattin, Harriet (Pratt) 1898-

Symbolism.

ADDINGTON, Jack Ensign. 220.6'4
The hidden mystery of the Bible. New York, Dodd, Mead [1969] ix, 276 p. 21 cm. Bibliography: p. 275-276. [BS534.A28] 70-93549 5.00
1. Bible—Criticism, interpretation, etc. 2. Symbolism. I. Title.

AMBAUEN, Andrew Joseph, 1847-
The world's symbolism; or, Nature voices and other voices; being a collection of symbols and emblems for the instruction and entertainment of many, both young and old, by Rev. Andrew Joseph Ambauen... Chicago, Ill., J.S. Hyland & co., 1916. 240 p. front. plates 19 1/2 cm. 16-15069
I. Title.

BEVAN, Edwyn Robert, 291.3'7
1870-1943.
Symbolism and belief. Port Washington, N.Y., Kennikat Press [1968] 391 p. 23 cm. (Essay and general literature index reprint series.) (Gifford lectures, 1933-34) Reprint of the 1938 ed. Bibliographical footnotes. [BL603.B4 1968] 68-26211
1. Symbolism. 2. Belief and doubt. 3. God—Knowableness—Addresses, essays, lectures. 4. Religion—Philosophy. I. Title. II. Series.

CHURCHWARD, Albert.
The signs and symbols of primordial man; being an explanation of the evolution of religious doctrines from the eschatology of the ancient Egyptians, by Albert Churchward ... With 186 illustrations. London, S. Sonnenschein & co., lim.; New York, E.P. Dutton & company, 1910. xxiii, 499, [1] p. illus., 17 pl. (part col., part fold., incl. front.) fold map. 25 1/2cm. [BL603.C5] 11-1005
1. Symbolism. 2. Freemasons. 3. Egypt—Religion. 4. Eschatology. 5. Religion, Primitive. I. Title.

CHURCHWARD, Albert. 291.2'09
The signs and symbols of primordial man : the evolution of religious doctrines from the eschatology of the ancient Egyptians / by Albert Churchward. Westport, Conn. : Greenwood Press, 1978. xxvii, 501 p., [19] leaves of plates (3 fold.) : ill. ; 24 cm. Reprint of the 1913 ed. published by Allen & Unwin, London. Includes index. [BL603.C5 1978] 75-104257 ISBN 0-8371-3908-2 lib.bdg. : 38.50
1. Freemasons. 2. Symbolism. 3. Egypt—Religion. 4. Eschatology, Egyptian. I. Title.

COPE, Gilbert Frederick 246
Symbolism in the Bible and the church. New York, Philosophical Library [1959] 287p. 23cm. (bibl. footbotes)illus. 59-65286 10.00
1. Symbolism. I. Title.

DUNBAR, Helen Flanders, 1902-
Symbolism in medieval thought and its consummation in the Divine comedy, by H. Flanders Dunbar ... New Haven, Yale university press; London, H. Milford, Oxford university press, 1929. 2 p. l., [ix] xvii, 563 p. front., diagrs. 25 cm. Published also as thesis (PH. D.) Columbia university. Bibliography: p. [515]-553. [PQ4406.D8 1929 a] 29-21282
1. Symbolism. 2. Dante—Allegory and symbolism. 3. Dante. Divina commedia. 4. Philosophy, Medieval. 5. Symbolism in literature. 6. Mysticism—Middle ages. I. Title.

ELIADE, Mircea, 1907- 291.37
Images and symbols; studies in religious symbolism. Translated by Philip Mairet. New York, Sheed & Ward [1961] 189 p. 22 cm. Includes bibliography. [BL600.E413] 61-7290
1. Symbolism. I. Title.

EWER, Mary Anita, 1892- 149.3
A survey of mystical symbolism ... by Mary Anita Ewer. London, Society for promoting Christian knowledge; New York, The Macmillan co., 1933. 2 p. l., 234 p., 2 1, 20 cm. Thesis (PH. D.)--Columbia university, 1963. Vita. "Selected bibliogrpahy": p. 213-231. [BL625.E8 1933] 33-32392 33-32892
1. Symbolism. 2. Mysticism. I. Title. II. Title: Mystical symbolism.

FARBRIDGE, Maurice Harry, 1896-
Studies in Biblical and Semitic symbolism, by Maurice H. Farbridge ... London, K. Paul, Trench, Trubner & co., ltd.; New York, E. P. Dutton & co., 1923. xiv p., 4 l., 288 p. 21 cm. (Half-title: Trubner's oriental series) [BL603.F26] 24-2332
1. Symbolism. 2. Jews—Religion. 3. Animal-worship. 4. Funeral rites and ceremonies. I. Title.

FARRINGTON, Marie L.
Facing the sphinx. By Marie L. Farrington ... San Francisco, Cal., The author, 1889. xii, 13-207 p. front., illus., diagrs. 19 cm. "The only aim of this book is to foster the study of symbolism, and of the inner interpretation of the so-called Sacred Scriptures."--p. vii. [BL603.F3] 31-13160
1. Symbolism. 2. Religion, Primitive. I. Title.

FINGESTEN, Peter. 704.948
The eclipse of symbolism. [1st ed.] Columbia, S.C., University of South Carolina Press [1970] 172 p. illus. 21 cm. Includes bibliographical references. [BL603.F55] 77-86194 6.95
1. Symbolism. I. Title.

FIRTH, Raymond William, 301.2'1
1901-
Symbols: public and private [by] Raymond Firth. Ithaca, N.Y., Cornell University Press [1973] 469 p. 23 cm. (Symbol, myth, and ritual series) Bibliography: p. 429-456. [BL600.F55 1973] 72-11806 ISBN 0-8014-0760-5
1. Symbolism. I. Title.

GILLIG, Ethel M
Christian symbolism; a manual of study for laymen. [Berkeley, Calif.] 1961. 120 1. illus. 29 cm. (Theses, Pacific school of religion, 1961:6) Bibliography: p. [114]-120. 63-12435
I. Title.

GOBLET d'Alviella, Eugene 246
Felicien Albert, comte, 1846-1925.
The migration of symbols. With an introd. by Sir George Birdwood. New York, B. Franklin [1972] xxiii, 277 p. illus. 23 cm. (Burt Franklin: research & source works series. Art history & reference series, 36) Reprint of the 1894 ed. [BL603.G6 1972] 76-154638 ISBN 0-8337-0762-0
1. Symbolism. I. Title.

GOBLET D'ALVIELLA, Eugene 246
Feliclen Albert, comte, 1846-1925.
The migration of symbols. With an introd. by Sir George Birdwood. New York, University Books [1956] 277p. illus. 22cm. 'A faithful reproduction of the whole of the original as published at Westminster in 1894.' [BL603.G6 1956] 56-78284
1. Symbolism. I. Title.

THE golden well; [291.37]
an anatomy of symbols. New York, Sheed and Ward, 1950. xiv, 191 p. 21 cm. Bibliographical footnotes. [BF1623.S9D6 1950a] 704.946 50-10712
1. Symbolism. I. Donnelly, Dorothy (Boillotat), 1903-

GOLDSMITH, Elizabeth 291.3'7
Edwards, 1860-
Ancient pagan symbols, by Elisabeth Goldsmith. New York, Putnam, 1929. [New York, AMS Press, 1973] xxxvii, 220 p. illus. 19 cm. [BL600.G6 1973] 77-168153 ISBN 0-404-02861-6 8.75
1. Symbolism. 2. Mythology. 3. Art and mythology. I. Title.

GOLDSMITH, Elizabeth 291.3'7
Edwards, 1860-
Ancient pagan symbols / by Elisabeth Goldsmith. Detroit : Gale Research Co., 1976, c1929. xxxvii, 220 p., [12] leaves of plates : ill. ; 23 cm. Reprint of the ed. published by Putnam, New York. Includes index. [BL600.G6 1976] 68-18025 ISBN 0-8103-4140-9 : 8.00
1. Symbolism. 2. Mythology. 3. Art and mythology. I. Title.

GOLDSMITH, Elizabeth Edwards, 264
1860-
Ancient pagan symbols, by Elizabeth Goldsmith; with forty-eight illustrations. New York, London, G. P. Putnam's sons, 1929. xxxvii, 220 p. front., illus., plates. 17 cm. A companion volume to the author's Sacred symbols in art. Much of the material used has been derived from a larger work, Life symbols. cf. Pref. [BL600.G6] 29-7583
1. Symbolism. 2. Mythology. 3. Art and mythology. I. Title.

GOLDSMITH, Elizabeth Edwards,
1860-
Life symbols as related to sex symbolism; a brief study into the origin and significance of certain symbols which have been found in all civilisations, such as the cross, the circle, the serpent, the triangle, the tree of life, the swastika, and other solar emblems, showing the unity and simplicity of thought underlying their use as religious symbols, by Elizabeth E. Goldsmith ... with more than 100 illustrations. New York & London, G. P. Putnam's sons, 1924. xxviii, 455 p. front., illus., plates. 24 cm. [CB475.G6] 24-28976
1. Symbolism. 2. Mythology. I. Title.

HALL, Adelaide Susan, Mrs.,
1857- comp.
A glossary of important symbols in their Hebrew, pagan and Christian forms; compiled by Adelaide S. Hall... Boston, Bates & Guild co., 1912. 4 p. l., 193 p. 19 cm. Bibliography: 4th prelim. leaf. A 13
1. Symbolism. I. Title.

HALL, Manly Palmer. 133
The occult anatomy of man; to which is added a treatise on occult masonry, by Manly P. Hall. 3d rev. ed. Los Angeles, Calif., Hall publishing company, 1929. 60 p. 17 cm. Advertising matter: p. 54-60. [BF1999.H333 1929] ca 30
1. Symbolism. 2. Freemasons—Symbolism. I. Title.

HASTINGS, Ila. 220.64
Bible symbols. Eugene, Or., 1958. 51p. 20cm. [BS477.H33] 58-40288
1. Symbolism. 2. Bible—Dictionaries. I. Title.

INMAN, Thomas, 1820-1876. 291.5
Ancient pagan and modern Christian symbolism. Rev. and enl. With an essay on Baal worship, on the Assyrian sacred "grove," and other allied symbols, by John Newton. 4th ed. Kennebunkport, Me., Milford House, 1970. xxxix, 147 p. 200 illus. 23 cm. Reprint of the 1922 ed. [BL603.I54 1970] 70-88627
1. Symbolism. 2. Christian art and symbolism. I. Newton, John, M.R.C.S.E. II. Title.

INMAN, Thomas, 1820-1876. 290
Ancient pagan and modern Christian symbolism. By Thomas Inman ... Rev. and enl. With an essay on Baal worship, on the Assyrian sacred "grove", and other allied symbols. By John Newton ... 4th ed. With two hundred illustrations. New York, Peter Eckler publishing company, 1922. xxxix, 147 p. illus., xix pl. on 11 l. (incl. front.) 21 cm. [BL85.I 6 1922] 24-17447
1. Symbolism. 2. Christian art and symbolism. I. Newton, John, M. R. C. S. E. II. Title.

INMAN, Thomas, 1820-1876. 291
Ancient pagan and modern Christian symbolism / by Thomas Inman. Kennebunkport, Me. : Longwood Press, 1979. p. cm. Reprint of the 4th ed., rev. and enl. (1884) published by J. W. Bouton, New York. Includes index. [BL603.I54 1979] 77-6998 ISBN 0-89341-301-1 : 25.00
1. Symbolism. 2. Christian art and symbolism. I. Title.

INSTITUTE for Religious 291.37
and Social Studies, Jewish Theological Seminary of America.
Religious symbolism. Edited by F. Ernest Johnson. New York, Institute for Religious and Social Studies; distributed by Harper [c1955] ix, 263p. 21cm. (Religion and civilization series) Includes bibliographies. [BL600.I5] 54-7119
1. Symbolism. 2. Christian art and symbolism. 3. Rites and ceremonies. I. Johnson, Frederick Ernest, 1884- ed. II. Title. III. Series.

INSTITUTE for Religious 291.3'7
and Social Studies. Jewish Theological Seminary of America.
Religious symbolism. Edited by F. Ernest Johnson. Port Washington, N.Y., Kennikat Press [1969, c1955] ix, 263 p. 23 cm. (Essay and general literature index reprint series.) (Religion and civilization series) "Based on lectures given at the Institute for Religious and Social Studies of the Jewish Theological Seminary of America during the winter of 1952-1953." Contents.Contents.—The foundations of Christian symbolism, by C. C. Richardson.—The liturgical revival in Protestantism, by M. P. Halverson.—Symbolism in Catholic worship, by D. J. Sullivan.—Symbolism and Jewish faith, by A. J. Heschel.—Religious symbols crossing cultural boundaries, by D. J. Fleming.—Theology and symbolism, by P. J. Tillich.—A psychologist's view of religious symbols, by G. Watson.—Symbolism in contemporary church architecture, by A. A. Dirlam.—Religious use of the dance, by T. Shawn.—Religious symbolism in contemporary literature, by N. A. Scott, Jr.—Developments in religious drama, by M. Wefer.—The future of religious symbolism, a Jewish view, by M. M. Kaplan.—The future of religious symbolism, a Catholic view, by J. LaFarge.—The future of religious symbolism, a Protestant view, by S. R. Hopper. Includes bibliographical references. [BL600.I5 1969] 68-26191

1. Symbolism. 2. Christian art and symbolism. 3. Rites and ceremonies. I. Johnson, Frederick Ernest, 1884- ed. II. Title. III. Series.

KATZENELLENBOGEN, Adolf 704.948
Edmund Max, 1901-
Allegories of the virutes and vices in mediaeval art from early Christian times to the thirteenth century [Tr. from German by Alan J. P. Crick] New York, Norton [c.1964] 102 p. 48 plates on 241. 20 cm. (Studies of the Warburg inst., v.10; Norton lib., N243) Bibl. 2.45 pap.,
1. Symbolism. I. Crick, Alan J. P., tr. II. Title.

LEWIS, Ralph M. 291.37
Behold the sign; a book of ancient symbolism, by Ralph M. Lewis... San Jose, Calif., Supreme grand lodge of AMORC, Printing and publishing dept. [1944] 99 p. illus. 20 cm. (Rosicrucian library. Vol. X) "First edition." [BF1623.R7 R65 vol. 10] [133.02] 44-30695
1. Symbolism. 2. Rosicrucians. I. Title.

MACKENZIE, Donald Alexander, 1873-
The migration of symbols and their relation to beliefs and customs, by Donald A. Mackenzie... London, K. Paul, Trench, Trubner & co., ltd.; New York, A. A. Knopf, 1926. xvi, 219 p. incl. plates, front., illus., plates. 27 1/2 cm. (Half-title: The history of civilization. [Pre-history and antiquity]) [BL603.M3] 26-8213
1. Symbolism. I. Title.

MACKENZIE, Donald 291.3'7
Alexander, 1873-1936.
The migration of symbols and their relations to beliefs and customs. New York, Knopf, 1926. Detroit, Gale Research Co., 1968. xvi, 219 p. illus. 22 cm. Bibliographical footnotes. [BL603.M3 1968] 68-18029
1. Symbolism. I. Title.

MACKENZIE, Donald 291.3'7
Alexander, 1873-1936.
The migration of symbols and their relations to beliefs and customs. New York, AMS Press [1970] xvi, 219 p. illus. 23 cm. Reprint of the 1926 ed. Includes bibliographical references. [BL603.M3 1970] 73-121283 ISBN 0-404-04136-1
1. Symbolism. I. Title.

MAY, Rollo, ed. 246
Symbolism in religion and literature. New York, G. Braziller, 1960. 253 p. 22 cm. Six of the nine "essays ... were originally published in Daedalus, the journal of the American Academy of Arts and Sciences, in the issue devoted to 'Symbolism in religion and literature' (vol. 87, no. 3)" [BL600.M35] 59-8842
1. Symbolism. 2. Symbolism in literature. I. Title.

MEAGHER, James Luke.
The temples of the eternal; or, The symbolism of churches. The mystic meanings of the houses of God and the wonderful lessons written in the God-given plans, divisions, decoration, and rites of the tabernacle, temple and church buildings... By Rev. Jas. L. Meagher... New York, Christian press association [c1913] 8 p. l., 15-513 p. incl. illus., plates. 19 1/2 cm. 13-2540
I. Title.

MORO, Louis. 133.335
A romance of Mother Nature and Father Time. [1st ed.] New York, Pageant Press [1956] 347p. illus. 24cm. [BF1623.S9M6] 56-9457
1. Symbolism. I. Title.

MUKERJEE, Radhakamal, 291.37
1889-
The symbolic life of man. Bombay, Hind Kitabs [dist. New York, W. S. Heinman, 1959, i.e.1961] 294p. 25cm. Bibl. footnotes. 60-52160 8.00
1. Symbolism. I. Title.

MURRAY-AYNSLEY, Harriet 291.3'7
Geogiana (Manners-Sutton) 1827?-1898.
Symbolism of the East and West. With introd. by Sir George C. M. Birdwood. Port Washington, N.Y., Kennikat Press [1971] xxiv, 212 p. illus. 23 cm. "First published in 1900." Includes bibliographical references. [CB475.M8 1971] 74-118538 ISBN 0-8046-1162-9
1. Symbolism. 2. Folk-lore. I. Title.

MURRAY-AYNSLEY, Harriet 291.3'7
Georgiana Maria (Manners-Sutton) 1827?-1898.
Symbolism of the East and West. With introd. by Sir George C. M. Birdwood. London, G. Redway, 1900. Detroit, Gale Research Co., 1971. xxiv, 212 p. illus. 24 cm. "A facsimile reprint." Includes bibliographical references. [GR67.M8 1900a] 77-141748
1. Symbolism. 2. Folk-lore. 3. Man—Migrations. I. Title.

OBEYESEKERE, Gananath. 306'.6
Medusa's hair : an essay on personal symbols and religious experience / Gananath Obeyesekere. Chicago : University of Chicago Press, c1981. xiii, 217 p. : ill. ; 23 cm. Includes index. Bibliography: p. 207-211. [BL600.O23] 19 80-27372 ISBN 0-226-61600-2 : 26.00
1. Symbolism. 2. Hair (in religion, folk-lore, etc.) 3. Kataragama, Ceylon—Religious life and customs. I. Title.

O'MALLEY, William J. 220.6
Scripture & myth / William J. O'Malley. New York, N.Y. : Paulist Press, c1980. 168 p. : ill. ; 25 cm. (His The Living Word ; v. 1) (Series: O'Malley, William J. Living Word.) [BS537.O43] 19 80-80534 ISBN 0-8091-9558-5 (pbk.) : 4.95
1. Bible—Language, style. 2. Symbolism. 3. Symbolism in the Bible. 4. Myth. 5. Myth in the Bible. I. Title. II. Series.

OUR Christian symbols
... illustrated by Harold Minton. [Enl. ed.] Philadelphia, Christian Education Press [1956] viii, 86p. illus. (part col.) 22cm. Bibliography: p. 81.
I. Rest, Friedrich, 1913-

POTTENGER, Milton Alberto.
Symbolism, a treatise on the soul of things; how the natural world is but a symbol of the real world ... The pack of playing cards, or book of fifty-two, an ancient masonic Bible; each card a symbol of universal law. The United States a masonic nation, whose duty and history are read in these ancient sacred symbols. By Milton Alberto Pottenger ... Sacramento, Cal., Symbol publishing company [c1905] xix, 275 p. incl. front. (port.) illus. 2 fold. charts. 27 cm. 5-23650
I. Title.

POTTENGER, Milton Alberto.
Symbolism, a treatise on the soul of things; how the natural world is but a symbol of the real world ... The pack of playing cards, or book of fifty-two, an ancient masonic Bible; each card a symbol of universal law. The United States a masonic nation, whose duty and history are read in these ancient sacred symbols. By Milton Alberto Pottenger ... Sacramento, Cal., Symbol publishing company [c1905] xix, 275 p. incl. front. (port.) illus. 2 fold. charts. 27 cm. 5-23650
I. Title.

REEVES, Marjorie. 246'.55
The Figurae of Joachim of Fiore, by Marjorie Reeves and Beatrice Hirsch-Reich. Oxford, Clarendon Press, 1972. [xxiii], 350 p. illus. 24 cm. (Oxford-Warburg studies) Bibliography: p. [xix]-[xxi] [BV150.J63R4] 73-162381 ISBN 0-19-920038-6 £10.00
1. Joachim, Abbot of Fiore, 1132 (ca.)-1202. Liber figurarum. 2. Symbolism. 3. Trinity—Early works to 1800. 4. History (Theology) I. Hirsch-Reich, Beatrice. II. Title. III. Series.

REST, Friedrich, 1913-
Our Christian symbols illus. by Harold Minton. Enl. ed. Philadelphia, Christian Education Press [1956] viii, 86p. illus. (part col.) 22cm. Bibliography: p. 81.
I. Title.

SCHUYLEMAN, John Louis, 220.6
1875-
Symbolisms of the Bible, by John L. Schuyleman. Boston, Meador publishing company, 1942. 224 p. 20 cm. [BS477.S4] 42-12087
1. Symbolism. I. Title.

SHANNON, Richard. 135.4
The book of peace; or, The way of within called the glorious threefold path, the way of the true self. Designed by the author. [1st ed.] Garden City, N.Y., Doubleday, 1971. 1 v. (unpaged) illus. 24 cm. [BF1623.S9S47] 72-144230 6.00
1. Symbolism. I. Title.

SNYDER, William Richard. 291.37
The sun, the cross, and the soul of man; fact and faith find harmony. [1st ed.] New York, Exposition Press [1965] 302 p. illus. 22 cm. Bibliography: p. [301]-302. [BL603.S66] 65-4090
1. Symbolism. I. Title.

STEINER, Rudolf, 1816- 133.3'3
1925.
Occult signs and symbols. New York, Anthroposophic Press [1972] 60 p. illus. 19 cm. "Four lectures ... given in Stuttgart, September 13-16, 1907; translated from German shorthand reports unrevised by the lecturer (vol. 101 in the Bibliographic survey, 1961) by Sarah Kurland, with emendations by Gilbert Church." [BF1623.S9S76] 72-76474
1. Symbolism. I. Title.

SYMBOLS, signposts of devotion
... illustrated by Bodo Jose Weber and Ernst A. Pickup. Nashville, Tenn., The Upper Room [1956] 96p. illus. (part col.) 19cm.
1. Symbolism. 2. Signs and symbols. I. McGee, Ratha Doyle.

TRUMBULL, Henry Clay, 1830- 291.
1903.
The covenant of salt as based on the significance and symbolism of salt in primitive thought, by H. Clay Trumbull ... New York, C. Scribner's sons, 1899. x, 184 p. 21 cm. Bibliographical foot-notes. [BL617.T83] 0-22
I. Title. II. Title: Salt, The covenant of.

WESTROPP, Hodder M.
Ancient symbol worship; influence of the phallic idea in the religions of antiquity, by Hodder M. Westropp and C. Staniland Wake. With an introduction, additional notes, and an appendix by Alexander Wilder. Second ed, illus. New York, Humanities [1972] 6.50

[WHITNEY, Charles Frederick]
Indian designs and symbols. [Salem, Mass., Newcomb & Gauss co., printers, c1936] 1 p. l., 57 p. incl. illus., pl. 19 cm. "Copyright 1936 by Charles Frederick Whitney." [E98.A7W6 1936] [NK1177.W5]
1. Indians of North America—Art. 2. Symbolism. I. Title.

WILSON, Walter Lewis, 1881- 220.6
This means that, by Walter Lewis Wilson ... Kansas City, Mo., The W. & M. publications [1943] 286, [4] p. 23 cm. "Compendium of types, shadows, signs, and symbols ... for the Bible student, a fairly complete explanation of the Scripture passages."--Foreword. [BS477.W5] 43-14923
1. Symbolism. 2. Bible—Dictionaries. 3. Typology (Theology) I. Title.

WILSON, Wlater Lewis, 1881- 220.6
Wilson's dictionary of Bible types. Grand Rapids, Eerdmans [c1957] 519 p. 23 cm. [BS477.W53] 57-14495
1. Symbolism. 2. Bible — Dictionaries. 3. Typology (Theology) I. Title. II. Title: Dictionary of Bible types.

ZACHAR, Louis A. 133
Symbols versus cymbals, by Louis A. Zachar. Rochester, N.Y., The Black faun press, 1941. 2 p. l., x p., 1 l., 52 p., 1 l., 19 1/2 cm. "250 copies have been printed...This copy is number 25." [BF1999.Z27] [159.961] 42-488
I. Title.

ZACHAR, Louis A. 133
Symbols versus cymbals, by Louis A. Zachar. Rochester, N.Y., The Black faun press, 1941. 2 p. l., x p., 1 l., 52 p., 1 l., 19 1/2 cm. "250 copies have been printed...This copy is number 25." [BF1999.Z27] [159.961] 42-488
I. Title.

Symbolism—Addresses, essays, lectures.

BEVAN, Edwyn Robert, 1870- 121
1943.
Symbolism and belief / by Edwyn Bevan. Folcroft, Pa. : Folcroft Library Editions, 1976. p. cm. Reprint of the 1938 ed. published by Macmillan, New York, and issued as the 1933-1934 Gifford lectures. Includes index. [BL603.B4 1976] 76-18183 ISBN 0-8414-3240-6 lib. bdg. : 30.00
1. Symbolism—Addresses, essays, lectures. 2. Belief and doubt—Addresses, essays, lectures. 3. God—Knowableness—Addresses, essays, lectures. 4. Religion—Philosophy—Addresses, essays, lectures. I. Title. II. Series: Gifford lectures ; 1933-1934.

Symbolism—Dictionaries.

COOPER, J. C., fl.1972- 301.2'1
An illustrated encyclopaedia of traditional symbols / J. C. Cooper. London : Thames and Hudson, c1978. 208 p. : ill. ; 25 cm. Bibliography: p. 203-207. [BL603.C66] 78-55429 ISBN 0-500-01201-6 : 14.95
1. Symbolism—Dictionaries. 2. Signs and symbols—Dictionaries. I. Title.
Distributed by Norton, NYC

GASKELL, George Arthur 290.3
Dictionary of all scriptures and myths. New York, Julian Press [c.] 1960. 844p. 26cm. Published in 1923 under title: A dictionary of the sacred language of all scriptures and myths. 60-9923 15.00
1. Symbolism—Dictionaries. I. Title.

VRIES, Ad de. 423
Dictionary of symbols and imagery / Ad de Vries. Amsterdam ; London : North-Holland Pub. Co., 1974. 523 p. ; 23 cm. Distributed in the U.S.A. by American Elsevier Publishing Company, New York. [BL600.V74] 73-86087 ISBN 0-444-10607-3 (American Elsevier) : 38.50
1. Symbolism—Dictionaries. I. Title.

Symbolism—History.

SMITH, Henry James.
Illustrated symbols and emblems of the Jewish, early Christian, Greek, Latin, and modern churches. Philadelphia, T. S. Leach & co., 1900. viii, 224 numb l., illus., fol. 0-2469
I. Title.

SWIATECKA, M. Jadwiga. 201'.4
The idea of the symbol : some nineteeth century comparisons with Coleridge / M. Jadwiga Swiatecka. Cambridge [Eng.] : New York : Cambridge University Press, 1980. viii, 213 p. ; 23 cm. Includes index. Bibliography: p. 197-210. [BV150.S89] 79-19802 ISBN 0-521-22363-6 : 26.95
1. Coleridge, Samuel Taylor, 1772-1834—Allegory and symbolism. 2. Coleridge, Samuel Taylor, 1772-1834—Influence. 3. Symbolism—History. 4. Symbolism in literature. 5. English literature—19th century—History and criticism. I. Title.

Symbolism in architecture—Scotland—Orkney.

WORDEN, Ian P. 726'.5'0941132
The round church of Orphir, Orkney / by Ian P. Worden. Cambridge : Institute of Geomantic Research, 1976. 5 p., plate : ill., plan ; 30 cm. (Occasional paper - Institute of Geomantic Research ; no. 6 ISSN 0308-1966s) [NA5481.O74W67]177-373205.ISBN 0-905376-04-8
1. Orphir Church. 2. Symbolism in architecture—Scotland—Orkney. I. Title. II. Series: Institute of Geomantic Research. Occasional paper — Institute of Geomantic Research ; no. 6.

Symbolism in art.

KATZENELLENBOGEN, Adolf 704.948
Edmund Max, 1901-
Allegories of the virtues and vices in mediaeval art from early Christian times to the thirteenth century [by] Adolf Katzenellenbogen. [Translated by Alan J. P. Crick] New York, W. W. Norton [1964] vii, 102, xiviii p. illus., facsims. 20 cm.

(The Norton library, N243) Bibliographical footnnotes. [N7740.K313] 65-1559
1. Symbolism in art. 2. Virtues in art. 3. Vices in art. 4. Art. Medieval. I. Title.

VOIGT, Robert J 246
Symbols in Christian art. Somerset, Ohio, Rosary Pfess [1950] 52 p. illus. 18 cm. [N7740.V58] 50-746
1. Symbolism in art. I. Title.

Symbolism in the Bible.

BARTLETT, Harriet (Tuttle) Mrs. 1860-
An esoteric reading of Biblical symbolism, by Harriet Tuttle Bartlett. San Francisco, Philopolis press, 1916. 3 p. l., 166, [1] p. diagr. 20 cm. 16-19473 1.50
I. Title.

HODSON, Geoffrey. 220.6'4
The hidden wisdom in the Holy Bible. Wheaton, Ill., Theosophical Pub. House [1967- v. illus. 21 cm. (A Quest book) Vol. 1: revised. Contents.Contents.—[1] An examination of the idea that the contents of the Bible are partly allegorical.—v. 2-3. The golden grain of wisdom in the Book of Genesis. Includes bibliographies. [BS534.H67 1967] 67-8724 ISBN 0-8356-0005-X (v. 2) 2.75 (v. 3)
1. Bible. O.T. Genesis—Miscellanea. 2. Symbolism in the Bible. I. Title.

MACKY, Peter W. 220.6'4
The pursuit of the divine snowman / Peter Macky. Waco, Tex. : Word Books, c1977. 240 p. ; 23 cm. Includes bibliographies. [BS477.M33] 76-19540 ISBN 0-87680-484-9 : 6.95
1. Symbolism in the Bible. 2. Symbolism. I. Title.

SCHOFF, Wilfred Harvey, 1874- 221
The ship "Tyre"; a symbol of the fate of conquerors as prophesied by Isaiah, Ezekiel and John and fulfilled at Nineveh, Babylon and Rome; a study in the commerce of the Bible, by Wilfred H. Schoff. New York [etc.] Longmans, Green and co., 1920. 157 p. plates. 24 cm. Advertising matter: p. 157. [BS680.C6S3] 20-18184 2.00
I. Title.

Symbolism, Jewish — Juvenile literature.

GOLDMAN, Alex J
A child's dictionary of Jewish symbols. Illustrated by Joseph Kastner. New York, P. Feldheim [1965] 94 p. illus. 26 cm. 66-37868
1. Symbolism, Jewish — Juvenile literature. 2. Symbolism — Juvenile literature. 3. Rites and ceremonies — Jews. 4. Rites and ceremonies. I. Title.

Symbolism—Miscellanea.

PETTIS, Charles Roberts, 135.4 1948-
Cosmic geometry : Tantric transformations / by Charles R. Pettis III and Sina Pettis. Ithaca, N.Y. : [Bliss Press], c1976. 49 p. (on double leaves) : ill. ; 21 cm. Issued in portfolio. "130 copies of this book were hand-crafted with Caslon Old Style type and printed on handmade Hosho paper." Bibliography: p. 49. [BF1623.S9P47] 77-150094
1. Symbolism—Miscellanea. I. Pettis, Sina, 1950- joint author. II. Title.

Symbolism of colors.

SEXSON, W. Mark. 133
The power of color, by Mark Sexson. Boston, The Christopher publishing house [c1938] xi, 13-138 p. 20 cm. [BF1623.O6S45] [159.961] 38-20146
1. Symbolism of colors. I. Title.

SEXSON, William Mark, 1877- 133
The power of color, by Mark Sexson. Boston, The Christopher publishing house [1938] xi, 13-138 p. 20 cm. [BF1623.C6S45] 159.961 38-20146
1. Symbolism of colors. I. Title.

ZARCHY, Harry. 133.3
Color and the Edgar Cayce readings, by Roger Lewis. Virginia Beach, Va., A.R.E. Press [1973] 48 p. 23 cm. Bibliography: p. 47-48. [BF1027.C3Z37] 73-175202 ISBN 0-87604-068-7 1.25
1. Cayce, Edgar, 1877-1945. 2. Symbolism of colors. I. Title.

Symbolism of numbers.

ADAMS, Mary, 1873- 133.335
Count your numbers, and Keep on counting. [Rev. and enl. ed.] Chicago, Aries Press, 1948. 201 p. illus. 21 cm. Full name: Mary Coleman Adams. [BF1623.P9A335] 49-17642
1. Symbolism of numbers. I. Title. II. Title: Keep on counting.

ADAMS, Mary, 1873- 133.335
Count your numbers and make your numbers count, by Mary Adams; numerology is a practical aid to every-day living. Chicago, The Aries press [c1937] 96 p. 1 l. illus. 19 cm. [Full name: Mary Coleman Adams] [BF1629.P9A34] 87-14728
1. Symbolism of numbers I. Title.

ADAMS, Mary, 1873- 133.335
Keep on counting; a handbook of advanced numerology, by Mary Adams... Chicago, The Aries press [c1939] 96 p. illus. 19 cm. "A companion volume is "Count your numbers." [Full name: Mary Coleman Adams] [BF1623.P9A35] 159.961335 39-14092
1. Symbolism of numbers. I. Title.

BIBLE. N.T. Greek. 1934. 225.48
The New Testament in the original Greek; the text established by Ivan Panin by means of Bible numerics. [Oxford] Print, priv. for the editor [by the University press] 1934- v. 17 cm. On cover: Numeric Greek New Testament. "Corrigenda" slip mounted on p. [1] of v. 1. [BS1965 1934] 34-22208
1. Symbolism of numbers. I. Bible. Greek. N.T. 1934. II. Panin, Ivan, 1855- ed. III. Title. IV. Title: Bible numerics. V. Title: Numeric Greek testament.

BOYILE, Zeolia J. 133
The fundamental principles of the Yi-king, Tao, and the Cabbalas of Egypt and the Hebrews, by Zeolia J. Boyile. The switchboard of the universe ... Cover design by Avela J. Boyile. New York, Azoth publishing company [c1920] 3 p. l., [5]-67 p. 25 cm. "Authorities consulted":p. 11-12. [BF1623.P9B6] 20-13331
1. Symbolism of numbers. 2. Yih-king. 3. Cabala. 4. Occult of sciences. I. Title.

BULLINGER, Ethelbert William, 1837-1913. 220.6'8
Number in Scripture; its supernatural design and spiritual significance. Grand Rapids, Kregel Publications [1967] viii, 303 p. illus. 23 cm. Reprint of the 1894 ed. Bibliographical footnotes. [BS534.B83] 67-26498
1. Symbolism of numbers. 2. Symbolism in the Bible. 3. Bible—Criticism, interpretation, etc. I. Title.

CLAIGH, Roberleigh H. 133.3'35
Letters in action / by Roberleigh H. Claigh ; illustrated by Robert Hurzt Gran[i]te. Los Angeles, CA. : Astro Press, c1976. 144 p. : ill. ; 28 cm. Bibliography: p. 141. [BV1623.P9C58] 76-13296 ISBN 0-89322-002-7 : 6.95
1. Symbolism of numbers. I. Title.

COLEMAN, Eleanor. 133.335
Simplified numerology; how to analyze yourself and others, by Eleanor Coleman... Fort Wayne, Ind., Eleanor Coleman [1940] 59 p. 19 1/2 cm. [BF1623.P9C74] [159.961335] 42-33855
1. Symbolism of numbers. I. Title.

EISEN, William. 133.3'35
The English cabalah / by William Eisen. 1st ed. Marina Del Rey, CA : DeVorss, c1980- v. : ill. ; 24 cm. Contents.Contents.—v. 1. The mysteries of Pi. [BF1611.E37] 19 79-57053 ISBN 0-87516-390-4 (v. 1) : 16.95
1. Cabala. 2. Symbolism of numbers. I. Title.

GARDNER, Martin, 1917- 133.3'35
The incredible Dr. Matrix / Martin Gardner. New York : Scribner, [1976] p. cm. [BF1623.P9G24] 76-16860 ISBN 0-684-14669-X : 8.95
1. Symbolism of numbers. I. Title.

GOODMAN, Morris C. 133.3'359
Modern numerology, by Morris C. Goodman. New York, Fleet Press Corp. [1968, c1945] 157 p. 21 cm. [BF1623.P9G6 1968] 67-31524
1. Symbolism of numbers. I. Title.

GOODMAN, Morris C. 133.335
Modern numerology; the last word on numbers, by Morris C. Goodman ... New York, B. Ackerman, incorporated [1945] 157 p. incl. front. 21 cm. [BF1623.P9G6] 46-241
1. Symbolism of numbers. I. Title.

GOODMAN, Morris C 133.335
Numerology; what is your lucky number? New York, Permabooks [1949, c1945] 190 p. 17 cm. (Permabooks, P 37) "Previously pulished under the title Modern numerology." [BF1623.P9G6 1949] 49-53970
1. Symbolism of numbers. I. Title.

GRUNER, Mark. 133.3'35
Mark Gruner's Numbers of life : an introduction to numerology / by Mark Gruner and Christopher K. Brown. 1st ed. New York : Taplinger Pub. Co., 1978, c1977. p. cm. First published under title: Numbers of life. [BF1623.P9G77 1978] 78-57560 ISBN 0-8008-5639-2 : 9.95. pbk. : 4.95
1. Symbolism of numbers. I. Brown, Christopher K., joint author. II. Title. III. Title: Numbers of life.

HAMON, Louis, 1866-1936. 133.335
Cheiro's book of numbers, by Cheiro. New York, Arc Books [1964] 188 p.illus., port. 19 cm. "1170." [BF 1623.P9H3] 64-11269
1. Symbolism of numbers. I. Title. II. Title: Book of numbers.

HITCHCOCK, Helyn. 133.3'35
Helping yourself with numerology. West Nyack, N.Y., Parker Pub. Co. [1972] 238 p. illus. 24 cm. [BF1623.P9H44] 72-172406 ISBN 0-13-386771-4 6.95
1. Symbolism of numbers. I. Title.

HOPPER, Vincent Foster, 133.335 1906-
Medieval number symbolism, its sources, meaning, and influence on thought and expression, by Vincent Foster Hopper ... New York, Columbia university press, 1938. xii p., 2 l., [3]-241 p. 22 cm. (Half-title: Columbia university studies in English and comparative literature. no. 132) Issued also as thesis (PH.D.) Columbia university. Bibliography: p. [213] -232. [BF1623.P9H53 1938a] [159.961335] 39-1970
1. Symbolism of numbers. 2. Mysticism—Middle ages. I. Title.

HULL, Marion McHenry, 220.8133335 1872-
The God-breathed book; a study in Bible numbers, by Marion McH. Hull ... Grand Rapids, Mich., Zondervan publishing house [c1933] 3 p. l., 5-50 p. 19 1/2 cm. [B534.H78] 39-3
1. Sympolism of numbers. 2. Bible—Miscellanes. I. Title.

KINNEY, LeBaron Wilmont, 220.6 1876-
The greatest thing in the universe; the living Word of God, by LeBaron W. Kinney. New York city, Loizeaux brothers, Bible truth depot [c1939] 201 p. 21 cm. [BS534.K5] 39-31303
1. Symbolism of numbers. 2. Bible—Criticism, interpretation, etc. I. Title.

[KNIGHT, Stuart Walter] 133.395 1884-
Know your numbers, by Ali Memmet, cf. [pseud.] ... Boston, Mass., Athena publishers [1942] 95 p. 19 cm. Cover-title: Know your numbers; the nature of numbers revealed. [BF1623.P9K55] 42-25388
1. Symbolism of numbers. I. Title.

LIU, Da. 133.3'3
I ching numerology : based on Shao Yung's classic Plum blossom numerology / Da Liu. 1st ed. San Francisco : Harper & Row, c1979. xiii, 145 p. : ill. ; 21 cm. Includes bibliographical references. [BF1623.P9L58 1979] 77-20459 ISBN 0-06-061668-7 : 4.95
1. Shao Yung, 1011-1077. I ching mei hua shu. 2. Symbolism of numbers. I. Shao Yung, 1011-1077. I ching mei hua shu. II. Title.

MELTON, Roy. 133.335
Metaphysics of numerology ... by Roy Melton, Ms. D., with an introduction by Eugene P. Cantwell ... Boston, The Christopher publishing house [c1934- v. 21 cm. [BF1623.P9M4] 159.961335 34-2167
1. Symbolism of numbers. I. Title.

MICHELL, John 133.3'359
City of revelation; on the proportions and symbolic numbers of the cosmic temple. New York, Ballantine Books [1973, c1972] xiii, 203 p. illus. 18 cm. [BF1623.P9M48] 1.50 (pbk.)
1. Symbolism of numbers. I. Title.
L.C. card no. for the hardbound (London) edition: 72-192290.

MICHELL, John F. 135.4
City of revelation; on the proportions and symbolic numbers of the cosmic temple [by] John Michell. [1st American ed.] New York, D. McKay Co. [1972] 176 p. illus. 24 cm. [BF1623.P9M48 1972b] 72-88116 5.95
1. Symbolism of numbers. I. Title.

[MILLER, Laurel] 133
Kabbalistic numerology; or, The true science of numers, letters, words and their astrological allocations according to the Kabbala; including the art of the name horoscope and divination by numbers ... New York, Metaphysical publishing co. [c1921] 76 p. front. (port.) fold. chart, diagr. 18 1/2 cm. [BF1623.P9M5] 22-285
1. Symbolism of numbers. 2. Astrology. I. Title.

MOLINARO, Ursule. 133.3'359
Life by the numbers; a basic guide to learning your life through numerology. New York, Morrow, 1971. 158 p. 22 cm. [BF1623.P9M6] 72-151907 5.95
1. Symbolism of numbers. I. Title.

OLD, Walter Gorn, 1864- 133.3'35
The kabala of numbers; the original source book in numerology, by Sepharial. New and expanded one-volume ed. New York, S. Weiser, 1970. vi, 387 p. illus. 24 cm. [BF1623.P9O6 1970] 75-131208 ISBN 0-87728-024-X 8.50
1. Symbolism of numbers. I. Title.

[OLD, Walter Gorn] 1864- 133
The kabala of numbers ... a handbook of interpretation; by Sepharial [pseud.] New ed., enl. and rev. 53Philadelphia, David McKay company [1928] 2 v. in 1. diagrs. 20 cm. [BF1623.P9O6 1928] 29-16763
1. Symbolism of numbers. I. Title.

OLD, Walter Gorn, 1864- 133.3'35
The Kabala of numbers : a handbook of interpretation / by Sepharial [i.e. W. G. Old]. San Bernardino, Calif. : Borgo Press, 1980. p. cm. Reprint of the new ed., enl. and rev., published by D. McKay, Philadelphia, 1928. [BF1623.P9O6 1980] 19 80-53342 lib. bdg. : 12.95
1. Symbolism of numbers. I. Title.

OLD, Walter Gorn, 1864- 133.335
The numbers book; the science of numerology, by Sepharial [pseud.] London, New York, W. Foulsham [1957] 128p. 19cm. [BF1623.P9O62] 58-24912
1. Symbolism of numbers. I. Title.

OLD, Water Gorn, 1864- 133.3'35
The kabala of numbers, a handbook of interpretation, by Sepharial. New ed., enl. and rev. Hollywood, Calif., Newcastle Pub. Co. [1974- v. illus. 22 cm. (A Newcastle occult book P-27) Reprint of the 1928 ed. published by D. McKay Co., Philadelphia. [BF1623.P9O6 1974] 74-6128 ISBN 0-87877-027-5
1. Symbolism of numbers. I. Title.

OMARR, Sydney 133.335
Thought dial. Introd. by Carl Payne Tobey. [6th ed.] St. Paul, Minn., Llewellyn [1963, c.1962] 172p. 20cm. 8.00
1. Symbolism of numbers. I. Title.

OMARR, Sydney 133.335
Thought dial. Introd. by Carl Payne Tobey.

1967 ed. Hollywood, Calif., Wilshire [1967, c.1962] 173p. illus. 21cm. 2.00 pap.,
1. Symbolism of numbers. I. Title.

OMARR, Sydney. 133.335
Thought dial. Introd. by Carl Payne Tobey. [3d ed. Hollywood, Calif., 9th House Pub. Co., 1959] 168p. 20cm. [BF1623.P9O64 1959] 60-2420
1. Symbolism of numbers. I. Title.

OMARR, Sydney. 133.3'35
The thought dial way to a healthy and successful life. With an introd. by Carl Payne Tobey. [New York] New American Lib. [1973, c.1969] 174 p. 18 cm. (Signet mystic, Q5369) "A Stuart L. Daniels book." "Parts of this book have appeared in a previous publication by the author called Thought dial." [BF1623.P9065] pap., 0.95
1. Symbolism of numbers. I. Title.

OMARR, Sydney. 133.3'35
The thought dial way to a healthy and successful life. With an introd. by Carl Payne Tobey. [1st ed.] New York, Hawthorn Books [1969] 206 p. 27 cm. "A Stuart L. Daniels book." "Thought dial": 1 leaf in pocket. "Parts of this book have appeared in a previously published volume [by the author] called Thought dial." [BF1623.P9O65] 69-16024 8.95
1. Symbolism of numbers. I. Title.

STAINAKER, Leo, 1897- 220.8133335
Mystic symbolism in Bible numerals. Philadelphia, Dorrance [1952] 148 p. 20 cm. [BS680.C2S8] 52-13775
1. Symbolism of numbers. 2. Bible — Criticism, interpretation, etc. I. Title.

STEIN, Sandra Kovacs. 133.3'354
Love numbers : a numerological guide to compatibility / by Sandra Kovacs Stein and Carol Ann Schuler. New York : Putnam, c1980. 264 p. ; 24 cm. Bibliography: p. 264. [BF1623.P9S784 1980] 80-17391 ISBN 0-399-12518-3 : 11.95
1. Symbolism of numbers. 2. Love. I. Schuler, Carol Ann, 1946- joint author. II. Title.

STEWART, Eva (Southgate) Mrs. 220.6
The ancient cipher; or, "God's wisdom in a mystery", by Eva Southgate Stewart ... New York, London, G. P. Putnam's sons, 1932- v. 22 cm. [BS534.S73] 32-7801
1. Symbolism of numbers. I. Title.

STRAYHORN, Lloyd, 1944- 133.3'35
Numbers and you : a numerology guide for everyday living / by Lloyd Strayhorn. New York : Yama Pub. Co., c1980. p. cm. [BF1623.P9S82] 80-18386 ISBN 0-937290-02-5 pbk. : 10.00
1. Symbolism of numbers. I. Title.
Publisher's address 2266 Fifth Ave., N0. 136, New York, NY 10037.

STRICKLAND, Walter William, Sir bart., 1851- 133.335
The great divide, by W. W. Strickland ... New York, B. Westermann co., inc., 1931. 374, [1] p. plates, ports. 19 cm. [BF1623.P9S85] [159.961335] 32-33249
1. Poe, Edgar Allan, 1809-1849. 2. Symbolism of numbers. 3. Platenists. 4. Mysticism. I. Title.
Contents omitted.

TAYLOR, Ariel Yvon. 133.335
Character grams; a divining rod to human nature the world over; entertainment for one or twenty; an answer to your query, who? what? when? where? and why? By Ariel Yvon Taylor in collaboration with H. Warren Hyer [pseud.] New York, R. Long & R. R. Smith, 1934. 2 p. l., 7-141 p. 19 1/2 cm. [BF1623.P9T25] [159.961335] 34-5307
1. Symbolism of numbers. I. Settles, Warren William, 1879- joint author. II. Title.

[UPJOHN, James A.] 232
The name counted; Jesus, 888... by the author of "The number counted." Appleton, Wis., Post publishing co., 1883. 1 p. l., 160 p., 1 l. 19 1/2 cm. [BT295.U6] 38-10401
1. Jesus Christ—Miscellanea. 2. Symbolism of numbers. I. Title.

VARLEY, Desmond. 133.3'359
Seven : the number of creation / Desmond Varley. London : G. Bell, 1976. 179 p. : ill. ; 23 cm. Includes index. Bibliography: p. 174. [BF1623.P9V35] 76-379878 ISBN 0-7135-1947-9 : £4.95
1. Symbolism of numbers. 2. Seven (The number) 3. Creation—Miscellanea. I. Title.

VAUGHAN, Richard Blackmore, 1916- 133.3'354
Numbers as symbols of self-discovery; everything you ever wanted to know about anybody. Graphics by John Sarando. Brooklyn, N.Y., Phantasy Press [1973] 450 p. 23 cm. [BF1623.P9V38] 73-78043 8.95
1. Symbolism of numbers. I. Title.

WINTERBURN, Katherine. 133.335
A key to the riddle of your life; an introduction to spiritual mathematics. New York, Whittier Books [c1958] 192 p. illus. 23 cm. [BF1623.P9W63] 59-289
1. Symbolism of numbers. I. Title.

Sympathy.

COLLINS, Gary R. 248.4
The joy of caring / Gary R. Collins. Waco, Tex. : Word Books, c1980. 198 p. ; 21 cm. Includes bibliographical references and index. [BV4647.S9C64] 19 80-52130 ISBN 0-8499-2928-8 (pbk.) : 5.95
1. Sympathy. I. Title.

MCNEILL, Donald P. 248.4
Compassion, a reflection on the Christian life / text by Donald P. McNeill, Douglas A. Morrison, Henri J.M. Nouwen ; drawings by Joel Filartiga. 1st ed. Garden City, N.Y. : Doubleday, 1982. xii, 142 p. : ill. ; 22 cm. [BV4647.S9M38] 19 81-65660 ISBN 0-385-17699-6 : 12.95
1. Sympathy. 2. Christianity and justice. I. Morrison, Douglas A. II. Nouwen, Henri J. M. III. Filartiga, Joel. IV. Title.

THE power of sympathy:
or, The triumph of nature. Founded in truth ... Printed at Boston, by Isaiah Thomas and company. Sold at their bookstore, no. 45, Newbury street. And at said Thomas's bookstore in Worcester, mdcclxxxix. 2 v. in 1. front. 18 cm. Listed anonymously in Sabin, Bibl. amer., v. 15, p. 377. Attributed to William Hill Brown, the earlier attribution to Mrs. Sarah Wentworth (Apthorp) Morton having apparently been based on insufficient evidence. cf. Emily Pendleton and Milton Ellis, "Philenia", Orono, Me., 1931, p. 38, 109-112: Milton Ellis, "The author of the first American novel", in American literature, v. 4, 1933, p. 359-368. [PS700.A1P67 1789] 9-3029
I. Brown, William Hill, 1766-1793, supposed author.

Sympathy—Juvenile literature.

MONCURE, Jane Belk. 241'.699
Caring / by Jane Belk Moncure ; illustrated by Helen Endres. Elgin, Ill. : Child's World, 1980. p. cm. (What does the Bible say?) [BV4647.S9M66] 80-14200 ISBN 0-89565-166-1 : 4.95
1. Sympathy—Juvenile literature. 2. Empathy—Juvenile literature. I. Endres, Helen. II. Title. III. Series.

Synagogue.

ENELOW, Hyman Gerson, 1876-
The synagogue in modern life; a series of sermons, by Rabbi H. G. Enelow, D.D. New York, Temple Emanu-El, 1916. 94 p. 17 1/2 cm. 17-8247
I. Title.

KAPLOUN, Uri. 296.6'5
The synagogue. Philadelphia, Jewish Publication Society of America [1973] 119 p. illus. 21 cm. (JPS popular Judaica library) Bibliography: p. 117. [BM653.K26] 72-13537 ISBN 0-8276-0012-7 pap 3.95
1. Synagogues. 2. Jewish art and symbolism. I. Series: Jewish Publication Society of America. JPS popular Judaica library.

KOHN, Joshua. 296.6'5
The synagogue in Jewish life. New York, Ktav Pub. House [1973] 246 p. illus. 21 cm. Bibliography: p. 231-237. [BM653.K6] 72-5826 ISBN 0-87068-096-X 3.95 (pbk.)
1. Jews. Liturgy and ritual. 2. Synagogue. I. Title.

LUKOMSKII, Georgil Kresent'evich, 1884- 726.3
Jewish art in European synagogues (from the Middle Ages to the eighteenth century) London, New York, Hutchinson [1947] 182 p. plates, plans. 26 cm. Bibliography: p. 59-62. [NA4690.L8] 47-7217
1. Synagogues. 2. Art, Jewish—Hist. I. Title.

RIVKIN, Ellis, 1918-
Ben Sira and the nonexistance of the Synagogue: a study in historical method. [New York, Macmillan, 1963] 321-354 p. 22 cm. Repr.: Silver. Daniel Jeremy, ed. In the time of harvest. 65-34959
1. Synagogue. 2. Apocryphal Books — Ecclesiasticus. I. Title.

SPICKER, Max, 1858-1912. 783
The synagogical service ... Edited and in part composed by Max Spicker (musical director) and the Rev. William Sparger (cantor) of Temple Emanu-el. New York, G. Schirmer, c1901. 2 v. 27 cm. Contents.--pt. I. Service for Sabbath eve.--pt. II. Service for Sabbath morning. [M2017.6.S75] 2-8472
I. Sparger, William. II. Jews. Liturgy and ritual. III. New York (City) Temple Emanu-El. IV. Title.

SUKENIK, Eleazar Lipa, 1880- 726.3
Ancient synagogues in Palestine and Greece, by E. L. Sukenik ... London, Pub. for the British academy by H. Milford, Oxford university press, 1934. viii p., 4 l., 90 p. 1 l. front., illus. (incl. plans) xix pl. (incl. fold. map) on 10 l. 24 1/2 cm. (The Schweich lectures of the British academy, 1930) [NA4690.S8] 34-11241
1. Synagogues. I. Title.

YESHIVA Synagogue Council. 296.6
Annual convention. New York City. v. Illus. 28cm. English and Hebrew, the latter inverted with separate t. p. [LD6371.Y43A26] 53-36876
I. Title.

Synagogue Addresses, essays, lectures.

ANCIENT synagogues, 296'.09'01
the state of research / edited by Joseph Gutmann. Chico, CA : Scholars Press, c1981. p. cm. (Brown Judaic studies ; no. 22) Includes index. Bibliography: p. [BM653.A5] 19 81-5252 ISBN 0-89130-467-3 pbk. : 14.00
1. Synagogues—Addresses, essays, lectures. 2. Jewish art and symbolism—Addresses, essays, lectures. 3. Judaism—Liturgy—Addresses, essays, lectures. 4. Synagogue architecture—Addresses, essays, lectures. I. Gutmann, Joseph. II. Title. III. Series.
Publisher's address: 101 Salem St., Chico, CA 95926.

GUTMANN, Joseph, comp. 726'.3
The synagogue : studies in origins, archaeology, and architecture / selected with a prolegomenon by Joseph Gutmann. New York : Ktav Pub. House, [1975] xxxi, 359 p. : ill. ; 24 cm. (The Library of Biblical studies) English or German. Bibliography: p. xxx-xxxi. [BM653.G87] 74-34065 ISBN 0-87068-265-2 : 25.00
1. Synagogues—Addresses, essays, lectures. 2. Synagogue architecture—Addresses, essays, lectures. I. Title. II. Series.
Contents omitted.

Synagogue-Adminstration and organization.

FRANKLIN, Leo Morris, 1870- 296
The rabbi, the man and his message, by Leo M. Franklin ... New York, Behrman's Jewish book house, 1938. xix, 122 p. 19 cm. [BM652.F7] 39-2411
1. Synagogues—Administration and organization. 2. Wise, Isaac Mayer, 1819-1900. I. Hebrew union college, Cincinnati. II. Title.
Contents omitted

KATZ, Irving I 296.65
Successful synagogue administration, by Irving I. Katz, Myron E. Schoen. New York, Union of Amer. Hebrew Cong. [c.1963] 200p. illus. 23cm. 63-10407 2.00 pap.,
1. Synagogues—Organization and administration. I. Schoen, Myron E., jointauthor. II. Title.

LEIPZIGER, Emil William, 1877- 296
The rabbi and his flock, by Emil W. Leipziger ... New York, Behrman's Jewish book house, 1940. xxi, 91 p. 19 cm. [BM652.L35] 40-34358
1. Synagogues—Administration and organization. I. Title.

NEW York board of Jewish ministers. 296
Problems of the Jewish ministry. Published by the New York board of Jewish ministers... [New York?] 1927. 5 p. l., 255, [2] p. 23 1/2 cm. Preface signed: Israel Goldstein, president New York board of Jewish ministers. [BM652.N4] 39-1501
1. Synagogues—Administration and organization. I. Goldstein, Israel, 1896- II. Title.
contents omitted.

ROSENAU, William, 1865- 290
The rabbi in action; alumni course of lectures delivered at the Hebrew union college, during the scholastic year 1935-1936, by William Rosenau ... New York, Bloch publishing company, 1937. xvii p., 1 l., 124 p. 19 cm. [BM652.R6] 38-2028
1. Synagogues—Administration and organization. I. Hebrew union college, Cincinnati. II. Title.

SCHWARZ, Jacob David, 1883- 296
Adventures in synagogue administration, by Rabbi Jacob D. Schwarz ... Cincinnati, Commission on synagogue activities, The Union of American Hebrew congregations, 1936. iv, 75 p. 23 cm. [BM653.S35] 37-2624
1. Synagogue-Adminstration and organization. I. Title.

SCHWARZ, Jacob David, 1883- 296
Financial security for the synagogue, by Rabbi Jacob D. Schwarz ... Cincinnati, Commission on synagogue activities, The Union of American Hebrew congregations, 1935. iv, 79 p. incl. forms. 23 cm. [BM653.S36] 37-2623
1. Synagogues—Administration and organization. I. Title.

SCHWARZ, Jacob David, 1883- 296.6
The life and letters of Montgomery Prunejuice; illustrated by Russell Newton Roman. New York, Union of American Hebrew Congregations [c1957] 246p. illus. 21cm. [BM653.S363] 58-22710
1. Synagogues—Organization and administration. 2. Reform Judaism. I. Title.

SCHWARZ, Jacob David, 1883- 296
New trustees for a new age, by Rabbi Jacob D. Schwarz ... Cincinnati, Commission on syngogue activities, The Union of American Hebrew congregations, 1938. vi, 90 p. 20 cm. [BM653.S365]
1. Synagogues—Administration and organization. I. Title.

SCHWARZ, Jacob David, 1883- 296
The synagogue in modern Jewish life, by Rabbi Jacob D. Schwarz ... Cincinnati, Commission on synagogue activities, The Union of American Hebrew congregations, 1939. viii, 79 p. 20 cm. [BM653.S368] 39-24406
1. Synagogues—Administration and organization. I. Title.

Synagogue architecture.

DE BREFFNY, Brian. 296.6'5
The synagogue / Brian de Breffny ; photography by George Mott. 1st American ed. New York : Macmillan, 1978. 215 p. : ill. ; 28 cm. Includes bibliographical references and index. [NA4690.D4 1978] 78-7583 18.95
1. Synagogue architecture. 2. Synagogues—History. I. Title.

NATIONAL Conference and Exhibit on Synagogue Architecture and Art. 726'.3'097307401444
Proceedings. New York, Union of American Hebrew Congregations. v. 28cm. Each vol. has also a distinctive title: 1957, The American synagogue, a progress report. [NA4690.N3] 58-46291
1. Synagogue architecture. I. Union of

American Hebrew Congregations. II. Title. III. Title: The American synagogue, aprogress report.

Synagogue architecture—Bibliography.

BLACK, Linda Perlis. 016.3092 s *Synagogue architecture and planning* : an annotated bibliography / Linda Perlis Black. Monticello, Ill. : Council of Planning Librarians, 1978. 24 p. ; 28 cm. (Exchange bibliography - Council of Planning Librarians ; 1469) Cover title. [Z5942.C68 no. 1469] [Z5943.S9] [NA4690] 016.726'3 78-103394 2.50
1. Synagogue architecture—Bibliography. I. Title. II. Series: Council of Planning Librarians. Exchange bibliography ; 1469.

Synagogue architecture—Europe.

WISCHNITZER, Rachel 726.3094 (Bernstein) 1885- *The architecture of the European synagogue,* by Rachel Wischnitzer. [1st ed.] Philadelphia, Jewish Publication Society of America, 1964. xxxii, 312 p. illus. 19 x 27 cm. Bibliography: p. 299-300. [NA4690.W49] 64-16754
1. Synagogue architecture — Europe. 2. Synagogues — Europe. I. Title.

Synagogue architecture—Illinois—Exhibitions.

FAITH & 726'.3'09773074017311 *form* : an exhibition / organized by the Maurice Spertus Museum of Judaica ; introductory material, Arthur M. Feldman, Grace Cohen Grossman. Chicago : Spertus College Press, 1976. 101 p. : ill. ; 22 x 28 cm. Contents.Contents.—Gutstein, M. A. The roots and the branches.—Rader, L. W. Synagogue architecture in Illinois. Includes bibliographical references. [NA5230.I3F34] 77-356182
1. Maurice Spertus Museum of Judaica. 2. Synagogue architecture—Illinois—Exhibitions. 3. Jews in Chicago—History. I. Maurice Spertus Museum of Judaica. II. Gutstein, Morris Aaron, 1905- The roots and the branches. 1976. III. Rader, Lauren Weingarden. Synagogue architecture in Illinois. 1976.

Synagogue architecture—Spain.

HALPERIN, Don A. 726'.3'0946 *The ancient synagogues of the Iberian peninsula,* by Don A. Halperin. Gainesville, University of Florida Press, 1969. 86 p. illus., plans. 23 cm. (University of Florida monographs. Social sciences, no. 38) Bibliography: p. 85-86. [NA4690.H3] 78-625777 2.00
1. Synagogue architecture—Spain. 2. Synagogue architecture—Portugal. I. Title. II. Series: Florida. University, Gainesville. University of Florida monographs. Social sciences, no. 38

Synagogue architecture—United States

JEWISH Theological 726.30973 Seminary of America. Jewish Museum. *Recent American synagogue architecture* [Exhibition] organized by Richard Meier. [New York, Author 1963] 63p. illus., facsim., plans. 24cm. Bibliography. 63-22379 2.00
1. Synagogue architecture—U. S. I. Title. Contents omitted.

WISCHNITZER, Rachel 726.3 (Bernstein) 1885- *Synagogue architecture in the United States;* history and interpretation. Philadelphia, Jewish Publication Society of America, 1955. 204p. illus. 23x29cm. (The Jacob R. Schiff library of Jewish contributions to American democracy) Includes bibliographies. [NH4690.W5] 55-8422
1. Synagogue architecture—U. S. I. Title.

Synagogue architecture—United States—Exhibitions.

TWO hundred 726'.3'097307401444 *years of American synagogue architecture* : [exhibition], the Rose Art Museum, Brandeis University, Waltham, Massachusetts, [March 30 to May 2, 1976] . Waltham, Mass. : American Jewish Historical Society, c1976. 63 p. : ill. ; 25 cm. Bibliography: p. 55-63. [NA4690.T86] 76-15469
1. Brandeis University, Waltham, Mass. Rose Art Museum. 2. Synagogue architecture—United States—Exhibitions. 3. United States—Religious life and customs—Exhibitions. I. Brandeis University, Waltham, Mass. Rose Art Museum. II. American Jewish Historical Society.

Synagogue art, American.

KAMPF, Avram 704.94896 *Contemporary synagogue art;* developments in the United States, 1945-1965. New York, Union of Amer. Hebrew Cong. [c.1966] xii. 276p. illus. 29cm. Bibl. [N7415.K35] 65-25292 10.00
1. Synagogue art, American. 2. Synagogue architecture—U.S. I. Title.

KAMPF, Avram. 704.94896 *Contemporary synagogue art;* developments in the United States, 1945-1965. New York, Union of American Hebrew Congregations [1966] Westminster, Md., Newman Press, 1966. vii, 276 p. illus. 29 cm. x. 96 p. 22 cm. Bibliography: p. 261-263. [N7415.K35] [BV30,K313] 263.9 65-25202 66-20035
1. Synagogue art, American. 2. Synagogue architecture — U.S. 3. Church year. I. Kampmann, Theoderich. II. Title. III. Title: The year of the church;

Synagogue art—Venice—Exhibitions.

JEWISH art treasures 709'.45'31 *in Venice.* [Edited by the Venice Jewish Community] New York, International Fund for Monuments [1973?] 94 p. illus. (part col.) 24 cm. Added t.p.: Tesori d'arte ebraica a Venezia; text in English and Italian. [NK1672.J48] 74-177364
1. Synagogue art—Venice—Exhibitions. 2. Synagogues—Venice—Exhibitions. 3. Jews in Venice. I. Comunita israelitica di Venezia.

Synagogue History.

BALTIMORE. Beth Tfiloh 296 congregation. *15th anniversary, memorial history, Beth Tfiloh congreations...* Baltimore, Md., 1936. 88 p. incl. illus., plates, ports. 23 1/2 cm. Foreword signed: Michael Miller, editor. [BM225.B2B4] 39-10278
I. Miller, Michael, 1889- ed. II. Title.

EISENBERG, Azriel Louis, 296.6'5 1903- *The synagogue through the ages,* by Azriel Eisenberg. New York, Bloch Pub. Co. [1974] vi, 206 p. illus. 24 cm. Bibliography: p. 195-197. A history of the synagogue emphasizing its importance in the lives of the Jewish people through the ages. [BM653.E35] 73-77284 ISBN 0-8197-0291-9 12.50
1. Synagogues—History. 2. [Synagogues—History.] 3. [Judaism.] I. Title.

MARCUS, Jacob Rader, 1896- 296 *Three hundred years in America in Katz,* Irving I The Beth El story ... Detroit, Wayne Univ. Press, 1955. [BM225.D44K3] 55-7560
I. Title.

Synagogue Hungary.

HELLER, Imre. 296.6'5'094391 *The synagogues of Hungary: an album* [by] Imre Heller and Zsigmond Vajda. Edited by Randolph L. Braham with the collaboration of Ervin Farkas. New York, [Published for] World Federation of Hungarian Jews [by] Diplomatic Press, 1968. x, 197, xxxi p. illus. 22 x 30 cm. Added t.p. in Hebrew. Added t.p. in Hungarian: A Magyarorszagi zsinagogak albuma. English, Hebrew, and Hungarian. Bibliography: p. 63. [DB906.5.H4] 68-56000
1. Synagogues—Hungary. I. Vajda, Zsigmond, joint author. II. World Federation of Hungarian Jews. III. Title. IV. Title: Bate ha-keneset be-Hungaryah: albom. V. Title: A Magyarorszagi zsinagogak albuma.

Synagogue music.

IDELSOHN, Abraham Zebi, 1882-1938, ed. *The Jewish song book for synagogue, school and home, covering the complete Jewish religious year.* 3d ed., enl. and rev. Musical editor: Baruch Joseph Cohon. [Cincinnati, Publications for Judaism, c1961] xi, 548 p. 25 cm. Added t.p. in Hebrew. Words part English and part Hebrew transliterated. Pref. remarks signed by A. Irma Cohon, ed. 63-30066
1. Synagogue music. I. Cohon, Baruch Joseph, ed. II. Title.

WEISGAL, Adolph J *Shirei Hayyim ve-emunah.* Songs of life and faith. [Baltimore? 1950] score (128 p.) 31 cm. For 1-4 solo voices or chorus, acc. and unacc.; principally Hebrew words. [M2079.5.W4S4] 52-37263
1. Synagogue music. I. Title. II. Title: Songs of life and faith.

Synagogue music—Day of atonement services.

SALAMAN, Charles Kensington, 783. 1814-1901, comp. *... The day of atonement,* compiled by Mr. Charles Kensington Salaman; re-arranged & edited by Dr. C. G. Verrinder. London & New York, Novello, Ewer & co. [187-?] 2 p. l., 71 p. 19 x 28 cm. (West London synagogue of British Jews. [Publications] v. 5 & 6) Published also in an enlarged edition. Score: solo voices, mixed chorus and organ; Hebrew words (transliterated) [M2017.6.S23D3] 45-28955
1. Synagogue music—Day of atonement services. I. Verrinder, Charles Garland, 1835 or 6, ed. and arr. II. Title.

SALAMAN, Charles Kensington, 783. 1814-1901, comp. *... The day of atonement,* compiled by Mr. Charles Kensington Salaman; re-arranged & edited by Dr. C. G. Verrinder. London & New York, Novello, Ewer & co. [187-?] 3 p. l., 226 p. 19 x 28 cm. (West London synagogue of British Jews, [Publications] v. 5 & 6) Score: Solo voices, mixed chorus and organ; Hebrew words (transliterated) [M2017.6.S23D3] 45-28956
1. Synagogue music—Day of atonement services. I. Verrinder, Charles Garland, 1835 or 6 ed. and arr. II. Title.

SCHLESINGER, Sebastian 783.296 Benson, 1837-1917. *Complete musical service for Day of atonement;* evening, morning, afternoon, memorial and concluding, according to the Union prayer book. By S. Schlesinger. New York, Cincinnati; The Jewish book concern, Bloch publishing company [c1901] 169 p. 32 1/2 x 25 1/2 cm. On spine: Atonement music. With piano accompaniment. Words partly in English and partly in Hebrew (transliterated) [M2017.6.S34C6] 2-14247
1. Synagogue music—Day of atonement services. I. Jews. Liturgy and ritual. Day of atonement prayers. II. Title. III. Title: Atonement music.

Synagogue music—History and criticism

WERNER, Eric. 783.9 *In the choir loft;* a manual for organists and choir directors in American synagogues. New York, Union of American Hebrew Congregations [1957] 54p. music. 25cm. Bibliography: p. 37-48. [ML3195.W4] 57-37467
1. Synagogue music—Hist. & crit. I. Title.

Synagogue music — Morning services.

SCHWARTZ, Jacob, 1888- *Shiro B'nai Jeshurun.* Composed, compiled, and arranged by Jacob Schwartz. New York, Bloch, 1952. v. illus. 32 cm. At head of title: A century of synagogue liturgical music. For cantor, solo voices, chorus (SATB) and organ. Hewbrew words transliterated. Contents.Contents. -- v. 1. A complete Rosh Hashonoh morning service. [M2186.S474] 52-39470
1. Synagogue music — Morning services. I. Title.

Synagogue music — Sabbath services.

FROMM, Herbert. *Adath Israel,* Friday eve service for cantor, mixed voices and organ, according to the newly revised Union prayer book, by Herbert Fromm. New York city, Transcontinental music corporation [1943] 59 p. 26 1/2 cm. [M2187.F76A3] 45-18601
1. Synagogue music—Sabbath services. I. Jews. Liturgy and ritual. Sabbath prayers. II. Title.

SYNAGOGUE music by contemporary composers : an anthology of 38 compositions for the Sabbath Eve service, almost all of which were composed for the Park Avenue Synagogue, New York City, at the invitation of Cantor David J. Putterman. New York, G. Schirmer [1951] score (354 p.) 27 cm. Principally for solo voice, chorus (SATB) and organ. Words partly in Hebrew transliterated, partly in English, partly in both. [M2187.S9] 52-32740
1. Synagogue music — Sabbath services.

WEINBERG, Jacob, 1879- *Sabbath morning service (Shabath baarets) for cantor (baritone), mixed chorus and organ,* by Jacob Weinberg ... Op. 41. New York, Bloch publishing company [1939] 80 p. 23 cm. Hebrew words (transliterated) and English translation. "Performing time ... 49 minutes." [M2187.W44S3] 45-28168
1. Synagogue music—Sabbath service. I. Title. II. Title: Shabath baarets.

Synagogue music (Scores)

EPHROS, Gershon, 1890- ed. 783. *Cantorial anthology of traditional and modern synagogue music,arr. for cantor and choir with organ acc.,* with an introd. by A. Z. Idelsohn. New York, Bloch Pub. Co., 1929- v. 27 cm. At head of title: Contents.--v. 1. Rosh hashonoh.--v. 2. Yom kippur.--v. 3. Sholosh r'golim. [M2186.E5C2] 48-38695
1. Synagogue music (Scores) I. Title.

Synagogue music (Scores)—New Year services.

SANDBERG, Mordechai, 1897- 783. *A little Palestinian New Year's festival,* by Mordecai Sandberg. Limited facsimile ed. New York and Jerusalem, Institute of new music [1946] 5 v. in 1. 32 cm. Cover-title. Portrait on p. [3] of cover. Words in Hebrew (transliterated) Contents.[v.] 1. Zeman simchathenu. (The season of our gladness) For baritone and piano.--[v.] 2. "In Thy pavillion, O Eternal ..." For oboe or soprano and string orchestra.--[v.] 3. "Happy is everyone who reveres the Eternal"; for soprano and piano.--[v.] 4A. Orah "Elul." "I am my beloved's and my beloved is mine." For violin, cello and piano.--[v.] 4B. Orah "Elul"; for mixed chorus and piano.--[v.] 5. Kaddish; for cello or trombone and piano. [M2017.6.S27L5] 47-4883
1. Synagogue music (Scores)—New Year services. I. Title.

Synagogue music (Scores)—Sabbath services.

COOPERSMITH, Harry, 1902- 783. ed. *Sabbath service in song.* Friday evening: Gershon Esphros. Sabbath morning: Jacob Beimel. Ed. and supplemented with congregational songs by Harry Coopersmith. New York, Behrman House, 1948. 128 p. 29 cm. "Words in Hebrew, with transliteration. Title transliterated: Manginot shabot. [M2017.6.C8S3] 49-56224

1. Synagogue music (Scores)—Sabbath services. I. Ephros, Gershon, 1890- II. Beimel, Jacob, d. 1944. III. Title.

Synagogue New York (City).

FINE, Jo Renee. 296.6'5'097471
The synagogues of New York's Lower East Side / photos. by Jo Renee Fine ; text by Gerard R. Wolfe. New York : New York University Press, 1977. p. cm. Bibliography: p. [BM225.N49F46] 75-15126 ISBN 0-8147-2559-7 : 17.50
1. Synagogues—New York (City) 2. Judaism—New York (City) 3. Jews in New York (City)—History. 4. Lower East Side, New York—History. I. Wolfe, Gerard R., 1926- II. Title.

Synagogue seating.

LITVIN, Baruch, ed. 296.65
The sanctity of the synagogue; the case for mechitzah, separation between men and women in the synagogue, based on Jewish law, history of philosophy, from sources old and new. [1st ed.] New York [Spero Foundation] 1959. xxiii, 442, 99p. illus. 24cm. Added t. p. in Hebrew. Articles in English, Hebrew or Yiddish. Errata slip mounted on p. 92 (3d group) [BM653.2.L56] 59-15959
1. Synagogue seating. I. Title.

LITVIN, Baruch, ed.
The sanctity of the synagogue; the case for mechitzah, separation between men and women in the synagogue, based on Jewish law, history of philosophy, from sources old and new. [2d ed.] New York, 1962. xxiii, 442, 99 p. illus. 24 cm. Added t.p. in Hebrew. Articles in English, Hebrew or Yiddish. 65-27206
1. Synagogue seating. I. Title.

LITVIN, Baruch, ed.
The sanctity of the synagogue; the case for mechitzah, separation between men and women in the synagogue, based on Jewish law, history of philosophy, from sources old and new. [2d ed.] New York, 1962. xxiii, 442, 99 p. illus. 24 cm. Added t.p. in Hebrew. Articles in English, Hebrew or Yiddish. 65-27206
1. Synagogue seating. I. Title.

Synagogue United States.

AMERICAN synagogue 296.6'7
directory, with an international synagogue and U.S. book dealer supplement. 1957- New York. v. 24 cm. [BM205.A6] 57-34944
1. Synagogues—U.S.

Synanon (Foundation)

MITCHELL, Dave. 071'.9462
The Light on Synanon : how a country weekly exposed a corporate cult—and won the Pulitzer Prize / Dave Mitchell, Cathy Mitchell, and Richard Ofshe. 1st Wideview Books ed. [S.l.] : Wideview Books, 1982, c1980. viii, 307 p., [8] p. of plates : ill. ; 21 cm. Includes index. [PN4899.P575P65 1982] 19 81-68437 ISBN 0-87223-761-3 pbk. : 7.50
1. Synanon (Foundation) 2. Point Reyes light. I. Mitchell, Cathy. II. Ofshe, Richard. III. Title.

Synanon (Foundation)—History.

GERSTEL, David U., 1945- 362.2'93'06079493
Paradise, Incorporated—Synanon : a personal account / by David U. Gerstel. Novato, CA : Presidio Press, c1982. x, 288 p. ; 22 cm. Bibliography: p. 283-288. [HV5800.S93G47 1982] 19 82-312 ISBN 0-89141-112-7 : 15.95
1. Synanon (Foundation)—History. I. Title.

Syncretism, Religious.

CHRISTO-PAGANISM;
a study of Mexican religious syncretism. [New Orleans, Tulane University of Louisiana, Middle American Research institute] 1957. 179p. illus. 'Preprinted from: Tulane University of Louisiana. Middle American Research Institute. Publication 19, p. 105-180.' Includes bibliography.
1. Syncretism, Religious. 2. Mexico—Religion. 3. Supernatural. I. Madsen, William.

Synesius, of Cyrene, Bishop of Ptolemais.

BREGMAN, Jay. 186'.4
Synesius of Cyrene, philosopher-bishop / Jay Bregman. Berkeley : University of California Press, c1982. xi, 206 p. ; 25 cm. (The transformation of the classical heritage ; 3) Includes index. Bibliography: p. 185-193. [BR1720.S9B72 1982] 19 81-10293 ISBN 0-520-04192-5 : 25.00
1. Synesius, of Cyrene, Bishop of Ptolemais. I. Title. II. Series.

GARDENER, Alice, 1854-1927. 281.
... Synesius of Cyrene, philosopher and bishop. By Alice Gardner ... Pub. under the direction of the Tract committee. London. Society for promoting Christian knowledge; New York. E. & J. B. Young & co., 1886. xii, 179, [1] p. 17 cm. (The Fathers for English readers) [BR1705.F4S8] 20-17700
1. Synesius, Cyrenneus, bp. of Ptolemais. 2. Society for promoting Christian knowledge. London. Tract committee. I. Title.

Synod for the Norwegian Evangelical Lutheran Church in America.

NORWEGIAN synod of the American Evangelical Lutheran church. 284.7
Grace for grace; brief history of the Norwegian synod, Published in grateful commemoration of the ninetieth anniversary of its founding in the year eighteen hundred and fifty-three and the twenty-fifth anniversary of its reorganization in nineteen hundred and eighteen as the Norwegian synod of the American Evangelical Lutheran church. Mankato, Minn., Lutheran synod book company, 1943. vii, 211 p. incl. plates, ports. plates. 20 1/2 cm. [BX8055.N6A5] 43-11432
1. Synod for the Norwegian Evangelical Lutheran church in America. I. Title.

PREUS, Johan Carl Keyser, 1881- ed. 284.7
Norsemen found a church; an old heritage in a new land. J. C. K. Preus, editor; T. F. Gullixson [and] E. C. Reinertson, associate editor [s] Minneapolis, Augsburg Pub. House [1953] x, 427p. maps (on lining papers) facsims. 22cm. 'Prepared on the occasion of the centennial of the founding of the Synod for the Norwegian Evangelical Lutheran Church in America. 1853-1953.' Bibliography: p. 419-427. [BX8052.P7] 53-3690
1. Synod for the Norwegian Evangelical Lutheran Church in America. I. Title.

Synod of the Reformed Presbyterian Church of North America — History

MCFEETERS, James Calvin, 1848-
The Covenanters in America; the voice of their testimony on present moral issues, reasons for the hope and work of the Reformed Presbyterian Church. Philadelphia, Press of Spangler & Davis, 1892. 235p. 18cm. [BX8992.M3] 60-58370
1. Synod of the Reformed Presbyterian Church of North America —Hist. I. Title.

RICHMOND (Diocese). Synod, 4th, 1966. 277.55451
Fourth Synod of the Diocese of Richmond. Celebrated by John J. Russell, Bishop of Richmond, together with the clergy, religious, and laity of the Diocese in Sacred Heart Cathedral, Richmond, Virginia, December 5, 1966. [Richmond, Diocese of Richmond, 1967? c1966] x, 86 p. 23 cm. [BX1417.R5A47 1966] 70-259761
I. Richmond (Diocese). Bishop, 1958- (J. J. Russell) II. Richmond (Diocese)

Synoptic problem.

HAWKINS, John Caesar, Sir, 4th bart., 1837-1929. 225.
Horse synopticae; contributions to the study of the synoptic problem, by the Rev. Sir John C. Hawkins, bart. ... 2d ed., rev. and supplemented. Oxford, Clarendon press, 1909. xvi, 223, [1] p. 22 1/2 cm. [BS2555.H25 1909] A 11
I. Title.
Contents omitted.

LONGSTAFF, Thomas Richmond Willis. 226'.3'06
Evidence of conflation in Mark? : A study in the synoptic problem / Thomas R. W. Longstaff. Missoula, Mont. : Scholars Press for the Society of Biblical Literature, c1977. x, 245 p. ; 22 cm. (Society of Biblical Literature dissertation series ; no. 28) Originally presented as the author's thesis, Columbia University, 1973. Bibliography: p. 237-245. [BS2585.2.L66 1977] 76-40001 ISBN 0-89130-086-4 pbk. : 6.00
1. Bible. N.T. Mark—Criticism, interpretation, etc. 2. Synoptic problem. I. Title. II. Series: Society of Biblical Literature. Dissertation series ; no. 28.

LUMMIS, Edward William, 1867-
How Luke was written (considerations affecting the two-document theory with special reference to the phenomena of order in the non-Marcan matter common to Matthew and Luke] by E. W. Lummis... Cambridge [Eng.] The University press, 1915. vii, [1], 141 p. 19 1/2 cm. 16-3932
I. Title.

MONAGHAN, Forbes J. 226'.06'6
Reflections on the synoptic gospels, and their special design [by] Forbes J. Monaghan. Staten Island, N.Y., Alba House [1970] xvii, 204 p. 22 cm. Includes bibliographical references. [BS2555.5.M65] 70-110595 4.95
1. Synoptic problem. I. Title.

PATTON, Carl Safford, 1866-1939 226
Sources of the synoptic Gospels, by Carl S. Patton . . . New York, London, Macmillan 1915; New York, Johnson Reprint, 1967. xiii, 263p. 23cm. (Half-title: Univ. of Mich. studies. Humanistic ser., vol. v.) The author's doctoral dissertation, Univ. of Mich., but not pub. as a thesis, [BS2555.P35] 15-19244 20.00 pap.,
I. Title.

STOLDT, Hans-Herbert. 226'.306
History and criticism of the Marcan hypothesis / Hans-Herbert Stoldt ; translated and edited by Donald L. Niewyk ; introd. by William R. Farmer. Macon, Ga. : Mercer University Press ; Edinburgh : T. & T. Clark, c1980. xviii, 302 p. ; 24 cm. Translation of Geschichte und Kritik der Markushypothese. Includes indexes. Bibliography: p. [281]-283. [BS2585.2.S7613] 19 80-82572 ISBN 0-86554-002-0 : 18.95
1. Bible. N.T. Mark—Criticism, interpretation, etc. 2. Synoptic problem. I. Niewyk, Donald L., 1940- II. [Geschichte und Kritik der Markushypothese.] English III. Title.

TYSON, Joseph B. 220.2'08 s
Synoptic abstract / by Joseph B. Tyson and Thomas R. W. Longstaff, assisted by Elizabeth A. Tipper and L. Marvin Guier. Wooster, Ohio : Biblical Research Associates, c1978. x, 193 p. ; 23 cm. (The Computer Bible ; v. 15) Includes bibliographical references. [BS421.C64 vol. 15] [BS2555.2] 226'.1 79-100392 ISBN 0-930734-00-9 : 15.00
1. Synoptic problem. I. Longstaff, Thomas R. W., joint author. II. Title. III. Series.

Synoptic problem—Congresses.

JOHANN Jakob Griesbach Bicentenary Colloquium, 1776-1976, Munster,Ger., 1976. 225'.6
J. J. Griesbach, synoptic and text critical studies, 1776-1976 / edited by Bernard Orchard and Thomas R. W. Longstaff. Cambridge [Eng.] ; New York : Cambridge University Press, 1978. xvi, 224 p. ; 24 cm. (Monograph series - Society for New Testament Studies ; 34) "Selected papers from the Johann Jakob Griesbach Bicentenary Colloquium, 1776-1976, held at Munster (Westf.) 26-31 July 1976 ... on the theme Johann Jakob Griesbach and the development of the investigation of the synoptic problem, 1776-1976." Includes bibliographical references and index. [BS2351.G7J64 1976] 77-27405 ISBN 0-521-21706-7 : 19.95
1. Griesbach, Johann Jakob, 1745-1812—Congresses. 2. Bible. N.T.—Criticism, interpretation, etc.—Congresses. 3. Bible. N.T.—Criticism, Textual—Congresses. 4. Synoptic problem—Congresses. I. Orchard, Bernard, Father, 1910- II. Longstaff, Thomas R. W. III. Title. IV. Series: Studiorum Novi Testamenti Societas. Monograph series ; 34.

Syphillis.

FRACASTORO, Girolamo, 1483-1553. 616.951
The sinister shepherd: a translation of Girolamo Fracastoro's Sphilidis: sive, De morbo gallico libri tres by William Van Wych. Los Angeles, The Primavera press, 1934. xxii [2], 85, [3] p. illus. 25 cm. Author's portrait on t.-p. "One thousand copies printed by Ward Ritchie, 1934." "Introduction is a translation of an article by Dr. Albert Garrigues. entitled Fracastor, chantre de la sy phills, which appeared in Aesculape, number 4, April, 1925" "The origin of the French disease" (p. 81-85) is from Uldrich von Hutten's De guala medicina et morbo gallico, Jo Schoeffer, Mainz, 1519. which appeared in Aesculape, vol. 7, no. 4, April, 1926. [PA8520.F7A66 1934] [RC201.A2F72] 879.1 35-5908
1. Syphillis. I. Van Wyck, William, 1883- tr. II. Title.

Syria—Religion.

BLISS, Frederick Jones, 1859- 275.
...The religions of modern Syria and Palestine; lectures delivered before Lake Forest college on the foundation of the late William Bross, by Frederick Jones Bliss... New York, C. Scribner's sons, 1912. xvi, 354 p. front., pl. 19 1/2 cm. (Half title: The Bross library. vol. v) At head of title: The Bross lectures... 1906. [BL2340.B6] 12-
1. Syria—Religion. 2. Palestine—Religion. I. Title.

BLISS, Frederick Jones, 1859-1937. 200'.9569
The religions of modern Syria and Palestine; lectures delivered before Lake Forest College on the foundation of the late William Bross. New York, Scribner, 1912. [New York, AMS Press, 1972] xiv, 354 p. front. 23 cm. Original ed. issued as v. 5 of the Bross library. [BL2340.B6 1972] 76-39454 ISBN 0-404-00897-6 20.00
1. Syria—Religion. 2. Palestine—Religion. I. Title. II. Series: The Bross library, v. 5.

CATHOLIC Church. Syrian rite. Liturgy and ritual. Kthobe Dkhourobo. English. 264.025
The Holy Mass according to the the Syrian rite of Antioch, with Anaphora of the Twelve Apostles. Translated into English by Joseph Redlinger. Issued by Andrew C. Shashy for the benefit of Syrians of Oriental rites. Jacksonville, Fla., 1955. 50p. illus., port. 16cm. 'The prayers and responses of the congregation are in Syriac rendered in Roman letters.' [BX1995.S9A26] 55-5779
I. Redinger, Joseph, 1875- ed. and tr. II. Title.

Syria—Social life and customs

RIHBANY, Abraham Mitrie, 1869- 232.9
The Christ story for boys and girls, by Abraham Mitrie Rihbany; illustrated by Gustaf Tenggren. Boston and New York, Houghton Mifflin company [c1923] viii p., 2 l., 239 p. col. front., illus., col. plates. 21 cm. An adaptation for young readers of the author's Syrian Christ. [BT302.B5] 23-17325
1. Jesus Christ—Biog.—Juvenile literature. 2. Syria—Soc. life & cust. 3. Palestine—Soc. life & cust. I. Title.

RIHBANY, Abraham Mitrie, 1869- 232.
The Syrian Christ, by Abraham Rihbany. Boston and New York, Houghton Mifflin company, 1916. xi, [1], 425, [1] p., 1 l. 21 cm. "The central purpose of this publication is ... to give the oriental background of certain Scriptural passages, whose correct understanding depends upon knowledge of their original environment."--p. 408. [BT301.R55] 16-21561
1. Jesus Christ—Biog. 2. Syria—Soc. life & cust. 3. Palestine—Soc. life & cust. I. Title.

Syrian Church—History.

MCCULLOUGH, William Stewart, 1902- 270.2'0935
A short history of Syriac Christianity to the rise of Islam / W. Stewart McCullough. Chico, Calif. : Scholars Press, c1980. p. cm. (Polebridge books ; no. 4) Includes index. Bibliography: p. [BX173.2.M3] 19 80-29297 ISBN 0-89130-453-3 : 29.95
1. Syrian Church—History. 2. Church history—Primitive and early church, ca. 30-600. I. Title. II. Series.

Szold, Henrietta, 1860-1945.

LEVINGER, Elma (Ehrlich) 1887- 922.96
Fighting angel; the story of Henrietta Szold, by Elma Ehrlich Levinger. Drawings by Jean Rosenbaum. New York, Behrman house, 1946. 191 p. front. (port.) illus. 21 1/2 cm. [DS151.S9L4] 46-22684
1. Szold, Henrietta, 1860-1945. I. Title.

Tabernacle.

BENJAMIN, Charles Thomas, 1877-
The fall of David's tabernacle, rebuilt by Christ, by Charles T. Benjamin. New York, Press of the Reliance printing co., 1908. 160 p., 1 l. front. (port.) 19 cm. 8-20158
I. Title.

CALDECOTT, W Shaw. 296
The Tabernacle; its history and structures, by the Rev. W. Shaw Caldecott ... With a preface by the Rev. A. H. Sayce ... Philadelphia, The Union press, 1904. xix, [1], 236 p. front., illus., plates, map. tables, diagrs. 20 cm. Also publish London, Religious tract society, 1904. [BM654.C3] 5-19563
1. Tabernacle. I. Title.

CHAMBERS, Laurence T. 296.6
Tabernacle studies. Grand Rapids, Zondervan Pub. House [c1958] 137p. illus. 20cm. [BM654.C47] 59-29216
1. Tabernacle. I. Title.

CLARKE, Edith Goreham. 263'.042
Tabernacle talks for young people, by E. Goreham Clarke. New York, Loizeaux Bros. [1954?] 127 p. 17 cm. (Treasury of truth, no. 206) [BM654.C55] 75-304239 0.50
1. Tabernacle. I. Title. II. Series.

COWAN, Aldworth. 221.6'4
God's tent : the tabernacle for today / Aldworth Cowan. Old Tappan, N.J. : Revell, c1980. 138 p. : ill. ; 22 cm. Bibliography: p. 137-138. [BM654.C68 1980] 19 81-179729 ISBN 0-8007-1269-2 : 6.95
1. Jesus Christ—Person and offices. 2. Bible. O.T. Exodus—History of Biblical events. 3. Tabernacle. I. Title.

DE CHARMS, George, 1889- 246'.9
The tabernacle of Israel. [1st ed.] New York, Pageant Press International Corp. [1969] 293 p. illus. (part col.) 21 cm. [BM654.D37] 77-76583 7.95
1. Tabernacle. I. Title.

DOLMAN, Dirk Hermanis. 296
Simple talks on the tabernacle; a type of Christ and his church, by D. H. Dolman ... Introduction by Wilbur M. Smith ... Grand Rapids, Mich., Zondervan publishing house [c1941] 6 p. l., 11-228 p. front. (port.) illus. 20 cm. [BM654.D6] 42-595
1. Tabernacle. 2. Typology (Theology) I. Title.

FULLER, Charles Edward, 1887- 221.93
The tabernacle in the wilderness; edited by Grace L. and Daniel P. Fuller. [Westwood, N. J.] F. H. Revell Co. [c1955] 96p. illus. 20cm. [BM654.F8] 55-6632
1. Tabernacle. 2. Typology (Theology) I. Title.

KIENE, Paul F. 296.4
The tabernacle of God in the wilderness of Sinai / Paul F. Kiene ; translated by John S. Crandall. Grand Rapids : Zondervan Pub. House, c1977. 176 p. : ill. ; 29 cm. Translation of Das Heiligtum Gottes in der Wuste Sinai. Bibliography: p. 176. [BM654.K4813] 77-12986 ISBN 0-310-36200-8 : 14.95
1. Tabernacle. I. Title.

KIMBER, John Shober. 220.93
Tabernacle talks, by John Shober Kimber. Los Angeles, Calif., The Oriental missionary society [c1931] xv, 97 p. front., plates (1 col.) 19 1/2 cm. [BM654.K5] 31-20640
1. Tabernacle. I. Title.

MCCORD, Iris Ikeler. 296
The tabernacle; its God-appointed structure and service, by Iris Ikeler, McCord. Chicago, The Bible institute colportage ass'n [c1927] 72 p. incl. 1 illus. pl. 19 cm. [BM654.M3] 27-18813
1. Tabernacle. I. Title.

MENSCH, Ernest Cromwell, 1891- 221.93
King Solomon's "first" temple. San Francisco [1947] 365 p. illus., maps. 22 cm. [BM654.M4] 48-12628
1. Tabernacle. 2. Jerusalem. Temple. I. Title.

MOUNT, Ralph Holmes, 1910-
The law prophesied, 2d ed. [n.p.] R. H. Mount, Jr., c1963. 205 p. illus. Bibliography: p. 198. 67-23795
1. Tabernacle. I. Title.

NEW York. Broadway tabernacle church.
History of the Broadway tabernacle of New York city, by L. Nelson Nichols, deacon and chairman of the Historical committee. Rev. Allan Knight Chalmers, D.D., L.L.D., minister. New Haven, Conn., The Tuttle, Morehouse and Taylor co., 1940. 4 p. l. 219 p. front., plates, ports. 24 cm. On cover: The Broadway tabernacle, New York city, 1840-1940. A 41
I. Nichols, Leon Nelson 1898- comp. II. Title.

NICHOLSON, Wallace B 1903- 296
The Hebrew sanctuary; a study in typology. Grand Rapids, Baker Book House, 1951. 67 p. 22 cm. [BM654.N5] 51-6813
1. Tabernacle. 2. Typology (Theology) I. Title.

RIDOUT, Samuel, 1855-1930. 296.6
Lectures on the Tabernacle. New York, Loizeaux Bros. [1952] 519p. illus. 19cm. (Bible truth library) [BM654.R56] 54-31947
1. Tabernacle. I. Title.

[RUSSELL, Charles Taze] 1852-1916. 289.
Tabernacle shadows of the "better sacrifices". A helping hand for the royal priesthood. Brooklyn, N. Y., Watch tower Bible and tract society, 1910. 3 p. l., 11-131 p. incl. illus., plates. front. 16 cm. [With his Studies in the Scriptures. Series i. The plan of the ages. Brooklyn, 1910] [BX8526.R7 1910] 11-27665
1. Tabernacle. I. Title.

[RUSSELL, Charles Taze] 1852-1916. 289.9
Tabernacle shadows of the "better sacrifices". A helping hand for the royal priesthood. Brooklyn, London [etc.] International Bible students association, 1914. 3 p. l., 11-131 p. incl. illus., plates. front. 19 cm. [With his Studies in the Scriptures. Series v. The at-one-ment between God and man. Brooklyn, London [etc.] 1914] [BX8526.R7 1914 a ser. 5] 34-16731
1. Tabernacle. I. Title.

[RUSSELL, Charles Taze] 1852-1916. 289.9
Tabernacle shadows of the "better sacrifices". A helping hand for the royal priesthood. Philadelphia, Pa., P. S. L. Johnson, 1937. vi, 11-168 p. incl. front., illus., plates. 18 cm. Author's foreword signed: Charles T. Russell. Editor's preface signed: Paul S. L. Johnson. [BX8526.R78 1937] 38-1724
1. Tabernacle. 2. Typology (Theology) I. Johnson, Paul Samuel Leo, 1873- ed. II. Title.

SOLTAU, Henry W., 1805-1875. 296.4
The holy vessels and furniture of the Tabernacle. [1st American ed.] Grand Rapids, Mich., Kregel Publications [1969] 148 p. 10 col. illus. 24 cm. Reprinted from the 1851 ed., published under title: The holy vessels and furniture of the Tabernacle of Israel. [BM654.S55 1969] 74-85428 4.95
1. Tabernacle. I. Title.

SOLTAU, Henry W., 1805-1875. 291.3'5
The Tabernacle, the priesthood and the offerings. [Illustrated ed.] Grand Rapids, Mich., Kregel Publications [1972?] xii, 474 p. illus. 22 cm. Includes bibliographical references. [BM654.S56] 72-88590 ISBN 0-8254-3703-2 5.95
1. Tabernacle.

WINROD, Frances.
The tabernacle, temple and throne, by Mrs. Gerald B. Winrod, TH. B. Wichita, Kan., Defender publishers [c1934] 2 p. l., 7-74 p. illus. 21 cm. [BM654.W53] 42-39883
1. Tabernacle. I. Title.

ZEHR, Paul M., 1936- 296.6'5
God dwells with his people : a study of Israel's ancient tabernacle / Paul M. Zehr ; introd. by Myron S. Augsburger. Scottdale, Pa. : Herald Press, 1981. 210 p. ; 25 cm. Includes index. Bibliography: p. 198-204. [BM654.Z43 1981] 19 80-22701 ISBN 0-8361-1939-8 (pbk.) : 7.95 ($9.20 Can)
1. Jesus Christ—Person and offices. 2. Tabernacle. I. Title.

Tabernacle—Desecration.

MILGROM, Jacob, 1923- 221.4'4
Studies in Levitical terminology. Berkeley, University of California Press, 1970- v. 27 cm. (University of California publications. Near Eastern studies, v. 14) Contents.Contents.—1. The encroacher and the Levite. The term 'Aboda. Bibliography (p. 91-94) [PJ4801.M5] 76-626141 ISBN 0-520-09308-9 (v. 1) 5.50 (v. 1)
1. P document (Biblical criticism) 2. Tabernacle—Desecration. 3. Levites. 4. 'Avodah (The word) I. Title. II. Series: California. University. University of California publications. Near Eastern studies, v. 14

Tabernacle—Meditations.

WEMP, C. Sumner. 296.6'5
Teaching from the tabernacle / C. Sumner Wemp. Chicago : Moody Press, c1976. 125 p. : ill. ; 22 cm. [BM654.W43] 76-3794 ISBN 0-8024-8563-4 pbk. : 2.25
1. Tabernacle—Meditations. I. Title.

Tabernacle—Miscellanea.

CORNWALL, E. Judson. 222'.12
Let us draw near / Judson Cornwall. Plainfield, N.J. : Logos International, c1977. 168 p. : ill. ; 21 cm. [BM654.C67] 77-24832 ISBN 0-88270-226-2 : 2.95
1. Bible. O.T. Exodus XXV-XXX—Miscellanea. 2. Tabernacle—Miscellanea. I. Title.

Tabernacle—Study and teaching.

MAXFIELD, Heln Adell, 1894- 268.61
The Tabernacle; director's manual. Grand Rapids, Zondervan [1950] 180 p. 20 cm. [BM654.M36] 50-4560
1. Paton, John Gibson, 2. Tabernacle—Study and teaching. I. Title.

Table-talk.

LUTHER, Martin, 1483-1546.
Conversations with Luther, selections from recently published sources of the Table talk, translated and edited by Preserved Smith...and Herbert Percival Gallinger... Boston, New York [etc.] The Pilgrim press [1915] xxvii, 260 p. front., plates, ports. 19 cm. "Bibliographical note": p. 252-253. [BR332.T4S5] 16-912
1. Table-talk. I. Smith, Preserved, 1880- ed. and tr. II. Gallinger, Herbert Percival, 1860- joint ed. and tr. III. Title.

LUTHER, Martin, 1483-1546. 230'.4'1
Conversations with Luther : selections from recently published sources of the table talk / translated and edited by Preserved Smith and Herbert Percival Gallinger. New Canaan, Conn. : Keats Pub., 1979. xxx, 260 p., [4] leaves of plates : ill. ; 22 cm. (A Shepherd illustrated classic) Cover title: Table talk. First published in 1915. Includes index. Bibliography: p. 252-253. [BR332.T4S5 1979] 79-64830 ISBN 0-87983-209-6 : 5.95
1. Table-talk. I. Smith, Preserved, 1880-1941. II. Gallinger, Herbert Percival, 1869- III. Title. IV. Title: Table talk.

LUTHER, Martin, 1483-1546. 244
The table talk of Martin Luther, edited with an introd. by Thomas S. Kepler. [1st American ed.] New York, World Pub. Co. [1952] xxiii, 345p. 16cm. (World devotional classics) Based on the English translation of William Hazlitt.' [BR332.T4H3 1952] 52-10322
1. Table-talk. I. Title.

*TABLE talks; 248.42
gifts of God for every family. Minneapolis, Augsburg, c.1965. 32p. col. illus. 28x42cm. Based on material furnished by Harold J. Belgum; illus. by John Mosand. 3.25, pap., wire bdg.,

Tacoma. Epworth Methodist church.

POLLOM, Noah Doc.] 1868- 287.6797
... *Epworth Methodist church, golden jubilee.* Tacoma, Wash., 1939. cover-title, 96 p. illus. (incl. ports.) 23 1/2 cm. At head of title: 1889, 1839. Includes advertising matter. [BX8481.T3E7] 42-34985
1. Tacoma. Epworth Methodist church. I. Title.

Tagore, Rabindranath, Sir, 1861-1941.

SRIVASTAVA, A. K. 294.5'2'11
God and its relation with the finite self in Tagore's philosophy / by A. K. Srivastava. 1st ed. Delhi : Oriental Publishers, 1976. 11, 166 p. ; 23 cm. Includes index. Bibliography: p. 159-162. [BL1205.S7] 76-902831 Rs40.00
1. Tagore, Rabindranath, Sir, 1861-1941. 2. God (Hinduism)—History of doctrines. 3. Self (Philosophy)—History. I. Title.

TAGORE, Rabindranath, Sir 208.1
The religion of man, being the Hibbert lectures for 1930. Beacon Baeacon [1961, c.1931] 239p. (BP125) 1.65 pap.,
I. Title.

TAGORE, Rabindranath, Sir, 1861-1941. 181'.4
Sadhana; the realisation of life. Tucson [Ariz.] Omen Press, 1972. xi, 164 p. 21 cm. Reprint of the 1913 ed. [BL1146.T3S2 1972] 72-194121 ISBN 0-912358-03-3 1.95
I. Title.

Tahara, Yoneko.

TAHARA, Yoneko. 248'.246'0924 B
Yoneko, daughter of happiness / by Yoneko Tahara ; as told to Bernard Palmer. Chicago : Moody Press, c1976. 173 p. ; 22 cm. [BV4935.T28A38] 76-19009 ISBN 0-8024-9811-6 : 5.95
1. Tahara, Yoneko. 2. Conversion. I. Palmer, Bernard Alvin, 1914- II. Title.

Taigi, Anna Maria, 1769-1837.

BALZOFLORE, Filippo, 1831-1877. 922.245
The life of the venerable servant of God Anna Maria Taigi. Translated from the Italian of the Very Rev. Philip Balzofiore, D.D., of the Order of St. Augustine. By a religious of the same order. Philadelphia, E. Cummiskey, 1872. xvi, 17-166 p. incl. front. (port.) 16 1/2 cm. Translator's preface signed: T. C. Middleton, C.S.A. [BX4705.T25B3] 37-18501
1. Taigi, Anna Maria, 1769-1837. I. Middleton, Thomas Cooke, 1842-1923, tr. II. Title.

BESSIERES, Albert, 1877- 922.245
Wife, mother, and mystic (blessed Anna-Maria Taigi) Translated by Stephen Rigby; edited by Douglas Newton. Westminster, Md., Newman Press [1952] 256p. illus. 19cm. Translation of La bienheureuse Anna Maria Taigi. [BX4705.T25B43] 52-13325
1. Taigi, Anna Maria, 1769-1837. I. Title.

THOMPSON, Edward Healy, 1813- ed.
The life of the venerable Anna Marie Taigi, the Roman matron. (1769-1837.) Ed. by Edward Healy Thompson ... New York, Cincinnati, F. Pustet; [etc., etc.] 1874. xxiii, 414 p. front. (port.) 18 cm. (Half-title: Library of religious biography ... vol. V) 12-39607
I. Title.

Tait, Catharine (Spooner) 1819-1878.

TAIT, Archibald Campbell, abp. of Canterbury, 1811-1882. 920.
Catharine and Craufurd Tait, wife and son of Archibald Campbell, archbishop of Canterbury; a memoir, edited, at the request of the archbishop, by the Rev. Wm. Benham ... With two portraits engraved by Jeens. American ed. New York, Macmillan & co., 1880. xvi, 395, [1] p. 2 port. (incl. front.) 19 1/2 cm. "Preafce to American edition" signed: F. D. H. The Archbishop of Canterbury's memoirs of his wife and son, together with his wife's recollections, and extracts from letters and journals. [CT788.T24T3 1880] 43-9343
1. Tait, Catharine (Spooner) 1819-1878. 2. Tait, Craufurd, 1849-1878. I. Benham, William, 1831-1910, ed. II. H., F. D., ed. III. F. D. H., ed. IV. Title.

Taita (Bantu tribe)—Religion.

HARRIS, Grace Gredys, 1926- 299'.6
Casting out anger : religion among the Taita of Kenya / Grace Gredys Harris. Cambridge ; New York : Cambridge University Press, 1978. xi, 193 p., [4] leaves of plates : ill. ; 24 cm. (Cambridge studies in social anthropology ; 21) Includes index. Bibliography; p. 186-188. [BL2480.T27H37] 77-80837 ISBN 0-521-21729-6 : 19.95
1. Taita (Bantu tribe)—Religion. I. Title.

Taiwan—Religion.

GATES, Alan Frederick, 1931- 299'.51'0951249
Christianity and animism in Taiwan / Alan Frederick Gates. San Francisco : Chinese Materials Center, 1980. ix, 262 p., [5] leaves of plates : ill. ; 22 cm. (Occasional series - Chinese Materials and Research Aids Service Center, inc. ; no. 40) Includes index. Bibliography: p. 247-256. [BL1975.G37] 79-124483 ISBN 0-89644-573-9 : 14.50
1. Taiwan—Religion. 2. Animism. 3. Missions—Taiwan. 4. Missions—Theory. 5. Powers (Christian theology) I. Title. II. Series: Chinese Materials and Research Aids Service Center. Occasional series ; no. 40.

Takahashi, Reiji, 1930-

HENDRICKS, Kenneth C. 266'.009'52
Shadow of his hand; the Reiji Takahashi story, by KNneth C. Hendricks. St. Louis, Bethany Pr. [1967] 202p. 22cm. [BV3457.T28H4] 67-15864 3.45 pap.,
1. Takahashi, Reiji, 1930- 2. Missions—Japan. I. Title.

Takayama, Ukon, 1562-1615.

LAURES, John, 1891- 922.252
Two Japanese Christian heroes: Justo Takayama Ukon and Gracia Hosokawa Tamako. [Tokyo, Rutland, Vt.] Bridgeway Press [1959] 128p. illus. 20cm. [BV3457.T3L3] 58-14205
1. Takayama, Ukon, 1562-1615. 2. Hosokawa, Garasha, 1563-1600. I. Title.

T'al-an, China. Home of Onesiphorus.

ALBUS, Harry James, 1920- 922.651
Twentieth-century Onesiphorus, the story of Leslie M. Anglin and the Home of Onesiphorus. Grand Rapids, Eerdmans, 1951. 160 p. illus., ports. 20 cm. [BV3427.A53A7] 51-10560
1. Anglin, Leslie M., 1882-1942. 2. T'al-an, China. Home of Onesiphorus. I. Title.

Talansi (African tribe)—Religion.

FORTES, Meyer. 299'.63
Oedipus and Job in West African religion / by Meyer Fortes. New York : Octagon, 1981, c1959. 81 p. ; 21 cm. Reprint. Originally published: Cambridge, Eng. : University Press, 1959. [BL2480.T3F6 1981] 19 81-2631 ISBN 0-374-92820-7 : 13.50 13.50
1. Talansi (African tribe)—Religion. 2. Fate and fatalism. I. Title.

Talbot, Edward Stuart, bp. of Winchester, 1844-1934.

STEPHENSON, Gwendolen. 922.34[illegible]
Edward Stuart Talbot, 1844-1934, [illegible] Gwendolen Stephenson. London, Soci[illegible]y for promoting Christian knowledge; [illegible]w York, The Macmillan company [1936] iii, 352 p. front., ports. 23 cm. "First published in 1936." [BX5199.T275S8] 36-34831
1. Talbot, Edward Stuart, bp. of Winchester, 1844-1934. I. Society for promoting Christian knowledge, London. II. Title.

Talbot, Ethelbert, Bp., 1848-1928.

BARNES, Calvin Rankin, 1891- 922.373
Ethelbert Talbot, 1848-1928, missionary bishop, diocesan bishop, presiding bishop. Philadelphia, Church Historicl Society [1955] 51p. illus:, ports. 23cm. (Church Historical Society. Publication no. 41) 'Reprinted from Historical magazine, volume xxiv (1955) pages 141-185. [BX5995.T22B3] 55-4033
1. Talbot, Ethelbert, Bp., 1848-1928. I. Title.

Talbot, John. 1645-1727.

PENNINGTON, Edgar Legare, 1891- 922.373
Apostle of New Jersey, John Talbot, 1645-1727, by Edgar Legare Pennington ... with foreword by the historiographer of the diocese of New Jersey ... Philadelphia, The Church historical society [c1938] xii p., 2 l., [3]-217 p. 23 cm. (Church historical society. Philadelphia. Publication no. 10) Contents.--book 1. Biography of John Talbot.--Book. 2. Letters of John Talbot.--book 3. Excerpts from the Journal of George Keith.--Book 4. Bibliography (p. 187 202) [BX5995.T23P4] 38-31813
1. Talbot, John. 1645-1727. I. Keith, George, 1639?-1716. II. Title.

Talbot, Louis Thompson, 1889-1976.

TALBOT, Carol. 269'.2'0924 B
For this I was born / by Carol Talbot. Chicago : Moody Press, c1977. p. cm. Bibliography & filmography: p. [BR1725.T23T34] 77-10537 ISBN 0-8024-2822-3 pbk. : 4.95
1. Talbot, Louis Thompson, 1889-1976. 2. Clergy—United States—Biography. I. Title.

Talbot, Matthew, 1856-1925.

DOHERTY, Edward Joseph, 1890- 922.2415
Matt Talbot. Milwaukee, Bruce Pub. Co. [1953] 200p. 21cm. [BX4705.T27D55] 53-11076
1. Talbot, Matthew, 1856-1925. I. Title.

DOLAN, Albert Harold. 922.2415
We knew Matt Talbot; visits with his relatives and friends. Englewood, N. J. Carmelite Press [1948] ix, 129 p. illus., ports. 20 cm. [BX4705.T27D62] 48-19582
1. Talbot, Matthew, 1856-1925. I. Title.

ERNEST, Brother, 1897- 922.2415
Through the dark night, a story of Matt Talbot. Illus. by Brother Bernard Howard. Notre Dame, Ind., Dujarie Press [1952] 88 p. illus. 24 cm. [BX4705.T27E7] 52-39270
1. Talbot, Matthew, 1856-1925. I. Title.

GOLLAND TRINDADE, Henrique Heitor, Bp., 1897- 922.2415
Matt Talbot, worker and penitent; his life as seen through Franciscan eyes. Translated from the Portuguese by Conall O'Leary. Paterson, N. J., St. Anthony Guild Press, 1953 [i. e. 1954] 126p. illus. 20cm. [BX4705.T27G7] 54-24800
1. Talbot, Matthew, 1856-1925. I. Title.

PURCELL, Mary. 922.2415
Matt Talbot and his times; with a foreword by Richard J. Cushing. Archbishop of Boston. [1st American ed.] Westminster, Md., Newman Press, 1955. 278p. illus. 20cm. [BX4705.T27P8] 55-7054
1. Talbot, Matthew, 1856-1925. I. Title.

PURCELL, Mary, 1906- 282'.092'4 B
Matt Talbot and his times / by Mary Purcell ; with a foreword by Dermot Ryan. Rev. ed. Chicago : Franciscan Herald Press, [1977] p. cm. [BX4705.T27P8 1977] 77-3556 ISBN 0-8199-0657-3 : 4.95
1. Talbot, Matthew, 1856-1925. 2. Catholics in Dublin—Biography. 3. Dublin—Biography. I. Title.

The talents (Parable)—Juvenile literature.

KRAMER, Janice 226
Eight bags of gold: Matthew 25: 14-30 for children. Illus. by Sally Mathews. St.Louis, Concordia, c.1964 [32]p. col. illus. 21cm. (Arch bks.) 64-16985 .35 pap.,
1. The talents (Parable)—Juvenile literature. I. Title.

Tales, African.

WHITELEY, W H ed. 298.2
A selection of African prose, compiled by W. H. Whiteley. Oxford, Clarendon Press, 1964. 2 v. 23 cm. (Oxford library of African literature) Contents.Contents. -- 1. Traditional oral texts. -- 2. Written prose. Bibliographical footnotes. [PL8013.E5W4] 66-2290
1. Tales, African. 2. African literature — Translations into English. 3. English literature — Translations from African. I. Title.

Tales, American.

CRABBE, George, 1754-1832.
Tales. By the Rev. George Crabbe ... New-York: Published by James Eastburn, 86, Broadway, corner of Wall-street, 1813. 2 v. 18 cm. In verse. [PR4512.T3 1813] 24-31519
I. Title.

GLASS, Theodore, 1896- 133
Tales of cosmic wisdom, by Theodamus [pseud.] Illustrated by the author. [1sted.] Los Angeles, House-Warven [c1949] 92 p. illus. 26 cm. (Gusto classics) [BF1999.G56] 51-21842
I. Title.

LIVNE, Zvi, 1891- JUV
The children of the cave: a tale of Israel and of Rome [by] Zvi Livne (Lieberman); illustrated by Victor G. Ambrus, English translation by Zipora Raphael. London, Oxford U.P., 1969. [5], 168 p. illus. 22 cm. [P 7.L764Ch3] 220.9 70-491976 17/6
I. Title.

RASKIN, Joseph. 133.1'29'73
Ghosts and witches aplenty; more tales our settlers told [by] Joseph and Edith Raskin. Illustrated by William Sauts Bock. New York, Lothrop, Lee & Shepard Co. [1973] 128 p. illus. 22 cm. Thirteen tales of ghosts, devils, and witches collected from early American diaries, documents, and records. [PZ8.1.R225Gh] 398.2 73-4949 ISBN 0-688-41554-7 4.50
1. Tales, American. 2. [Folklore—United States.] I. Raskin, Edith, joint author. II. Bock, William Sauts, 1939- illus. III. Title. Library binding 4.14; ISBN 0-688-51554-1.

SPILLMANN, Joseph, 1842-1905.
Children of Mary, a tale of the Caucasus, by Rev. Joseph Spillmann, S.J. Tr. from the German by Miss Helena Long. St. Louis, Mo., B. Herder, 1896. 122 p. 17 1/2 cm. (Added t.-p.: Tales of foreign lands, vol. III) 12-38944
I. Long, Helena, tr. II. Title.

Tales, American—North Carolina.

HARDEN, John William, 1903- 133.1
Tar Heel ghosts. With drawings by Lindsay McAlister. Chapel Hill, University of North Carolina Press [1954] 178 p. illus. 22 cm. [GR110.N8H3] 54-13061
1. Tales, American—North Carolina. 2. Ghost stories. I. Title.

Tales, Hasidic.

BUBER, Martin 296
Tales of the Hasidim [Tr. by Olga Marx] New York, Schocken Books [1961, c.1947, 1948] 2v. 355p; 352p. Contents.v.1, Early masters. v.2, Later masters. (Schocken paperback SB1; SB2) Bibl. 1.65, pap., ea.
1. Tales, Hasidic. I. Marx, Olga, 1894- tr. II. Title.

DOB Baer ben Samuel. 296.8'33
In praise of Baal Shem Tov [Shivhei ha-Besht]; the earliest collection of legends about the founder of Hasidism. Translated and edited by Dan Ben-Amos & Jerome R. Mintz. Bloomington, Indiana University Press [1970] xxx, 352 p. 25 cm. Translation of Shivhe ha-Besht. (romanized form) Bibliography: p. [273]-279. [BM755.I8D613] 76-98986 17.50
1. Israel ben Eliezer, Ba'al Shem Tob, called Besht, 1700 (ca.)-1760. 2. Tales, Hasidic. I. Ben-Amos, Dan, ed. II. Mintz, Jerome R., ed. III. Title.

LANGER, Mordecai Georgo, 1894-1943. 296.833
Nine gates to the Chassidic mysteries, by Jiri Langer. Translated by Stephen Jolly. [1st ed.] New York, D. McKay Co. [1961] 266p. 21cm. [BM532.L313] 61-7986
1. Tales, Hasidic. I. Title. II. Title: Translation of Devet bran.

LANGER, Mordecai Georgo, 1894-1943. 296.8'33
Nine gates to the Chassidic mysteries / by Jiri Langer ; translated by Stephen Jolly. New York : Behrman House, [1976] c1961. p. cm. (A Jewish legacy book) Translation of Devet bran. [BM532.L313 1976] 76-5859 ISBN 0-87441-241-2 pbk. : 3.95
1. Tales, Hasidic. I. Title.

LEVIN, Meyer, 1905- 398.35
Classic Hassidic tales; marvellous tales of Rabbi Israel Baal Shem and of his greatgrandson, Rabbi Nachman, retold from Hebrew. Yiddish, and German sources. Illus. by Marek Szwarc. New York, Citadel [1966, c.1932] xvii, 357p. illus., fold. map. 21cm. First pub. in 1932 under title: The golden mountain. Includes 26 legendary tales about Rabbi Israel and 11 tales by Rabbi Nachman. [BM755.I8L4 1966] 67-63 2.45 pap.,
1. Israel ben Eliezer. Ba'al-Shem Tob, called Besht, 1700 (ca.)-1760. 2. Tales, Hasidic. I. Nahman ben Simhah, of Bratzlav, 1770?-1810? II. Title.

LEVIN, Meyer, 1905- 398.2
Classic Hassidic tales : marvellous tales of Rabbi Israel Baal Shem and of his great-grandson, Rabbi Nachman, retold from Hebrew, Yiddish, and German sources / by Meyer Levin ; illustrated by Marek Szwarc. New York : Penguin Books, 1975. xx, 357 p. : ill. ; 20 cm. First published in

1932 under title: The golden mountain. Includes 26 legendary tales about Rabbi Israel and 11 tales by Rabbi Nachman. [BM532.L423 1975] 75-318799 ISBN 0-14-004042-0 pbk. 3.95
1. Israel ben Eliezer, Ba'al Shem Tob, called BeSHT, 1700 (ca.)-1760. 2. Tales, Hasidic. I. Nahman ben Simhah, of Bratzlav, 1770?-1810? II. Title.

NAHMAN ben Simhah, of Bratzlav, 1770?-1810? 892.4'3'3
The tales / Nahman of Bratslav ; translation, introd., and commentaries by Arnold J. Band ; pref. by Joseph Dan. New York : Paulist Press, c1978. xix, 340 p. ; 24 cm. (The Classics of Western spirituality) Translation of Sipure ma'asiyot. Includes indexes. Bibliography: p. 325-327. [BM 532.N33 1978] 78-53433 ISBN 0-8091-0238-2 pbk. : 6.95
1. Tales, Hasidic. I. Band, Arnold J. II. Title. III. Series.

NAHMAN ben simhah, of Bratzlav 1770?-1810?
The tales of Rabbi Nachman [by] Martin Buber. Translated from the German by Maurice Friedman. Bloomington, Indiana University Press [c1956] 214 p. 22 cm. 63-34476
1. Tales, Hasidic. I. Buber, Martin, 1878- II. Title.

NAHMAN Ben Simhah, of Bratzlav 1770?-1810? 296
The tales of Rabbi Nachman [by] Martin Buber. Translated from the German by Maurice Friedman. New York, Horizon Press [1956] 214p. 22cm. [BM532.N33] 56-12329
1. Tales, Hasidic. I. Buber. Martin. 1878- II. Title.

NAHMAN Ben Simhah, of Bratzlav 7702-1810? 296
The tales of Rabbi Nachman [by] Martin Buber. Tr. from German by Maurice Friedman [Gloucester. Mass., P. Smith, 1966, c.1956] 214p. 21cm. (Midland bk., MB33 rebound) [BM532.N33] 4.00
1. Tales. Hasidic. I. Buber, Martin, 1878. II. Title.

RABBI Eizik : FIC
Hasidic stories about the Zaddik of Kallo / translated from the Hungarian with an introd. and notes by Andrew Handler. Rutherford : Fairleigh Dickinson University Press, c1977. p. cm. Bibliography: p. [BM532.R28] 894'.511'3008 75-5245 ISBN 0-8386-1739-5 12.00
1. Taub, Eizik, 1751-1821—Legends. 2. Tales, Hasidic. 3. Jew in Nagykallo, Hungary—Literary collections. I. Handler, Andrew, 1935- II. Neumann, Albert, d. 1943. III. Szabolcsi, Lajos. IV. Patai, Jozsef, 1882-1953.
Contents omitted

RABINOWICZ, Harry M 1919- 296.833
The slave who saved the city, and other Hassidic tales. Drawings by Ahron Gelles. New York, A. S. Barnes [1960] 192p. illus. 21cm. (A Wonderful world book) [BM532.R3] 60-10202
1. Tales, Hasidic. I. Title.

RABINOWICZ, Harry M., 1919- 296.833
The slave who saved the city, and other Hassidic tales. Drawings by Ahron Gelles. New York, A. S. Barnes [c.1960] 192p. illus. 21cm. (A Wonderful world book) 60-10202 2.95
1. Tales, Hasidic. I. Title.

STEINSALZ, Adin. 296.8'33
Beggars and prayers : Adin Ateinsaltz retells the tales of Rabbi Nachman of Bratslav ; translated by Yehuda Hanegbi ... [et al.] ; edited by Jonathan Omer-Man. New York : Basic Books, c1979. vi, 186 p. ; 22 cm. [BM532.S73] 78-54502 ISBN 0-465-00579-9 : 8.95
1. Tales, Hasidic. I. Nahman ben Simhah, of Bratzlav, 1770?-1810? II. Title.

Tales, Hasidic—History and criticism.

BERGER, Alan L., 1939- 296.7'1
Witness to the sacred : Hasidic tales and normalized mystical experience / Alan L. Berger. Chico, Calif. : New Horizons Press, 1977. p. cm. Includes bibliographical references and index. [BM532.B46] 77-11871 ISBN 0-914914-11-1. ISBN 0-914914-10-3 pbk. : 3.00
1. Tales, Hasidic—History and criticism. 2. Mysticism—Judaism. I. Title.

Tales, Hawaiian.

THRUM, Thomas George, 1843-1932, comp. 299'.9
Hawaiian folk tales : a collection of native legends / compiled by Thos. G. Thrum. New York : AMS Press, [1978] c1907. p. cm. Reprint of the ed. published by A. C. McClurg, Chicago. [GR385.H3T4 1978b] 75-35211 ISBN 0-404-14234-6 : 20.00
1. Tales, Hawaiian. 2. Legends, Hawaiian. I. Title.

Tales, Jewish.

BIN Gorion, Micha Joseph, 1865-1921. 398.2
Mimekor Yisrael : classical Jewish folktales / collected by Micha Joseph Bin Gorion ; edited by Emanuel bin Gorion ; translated by I. M. Lask ; with introd. by Dan Ben-Amos. Bloomington : Indiana University Press, [1976] p. cm. Includes index. Bibliography: p. [BM530.B4913 1976] 74-15713 ISBN 0-253-15330-1 : 42.50
1. Tales, Jewish. 2. Legends, Jewish. 3. Aggada—Translations into English. I. Title.

†FRIEDLANDER, Gerald, 1871-1923, ed. and tr. 398.2
The Jewish fairy book / translated and adapted by Gerald Friedlander. Great Neck, N.Y. : Core Collection Books, 1977. 188 p. ; 20 cm. (Children's literature reprint series) Reprint of the 1920 ed. published by F. A. Stokes Co., New York. Presents twenty-three tales from various Jewish writings retold in a modern setting. [BM530.F74 1977] 77-89718 ISBN 0-8486-0215-3 : 16.75
1. Tales, Jewish. 2. Fairy tales. 3. [Folklore, Jewish.] 4. [Fairy tales.] I. Title. II. Series.

GAER, Joseph, 1897- 296
The unconquered; adapted folklore legends, by Joseph Gaer; illustrated by Aaron J. Goodelman. Cincinnati, The Sinai press [c1932] xii, 359 p. incl. illus., plates. 22 cm. Descriptive letterpress on recto of the plates. [BM530.G3] 33-1340
1. Tales, Jewish. 2. Legends, Jewish. I. Title.

GATES to the Old City : 296.1
a book of Jewish legends / [selected by] Raphael Patai. Detroit : Wayne State University Press, 1981. li, 807 p. ; 24 cm. Includes index. Bibliography: p. 749-765. [BM530.G37 1981] 19 80-66154 ISBN 0-8143-1679-4 : 27.50
1. Bible. O.T.—Legends. 2. Aggada—Translations into English. 3. Tales, Jewish. 4. Legends, Jewish. 5. Tales, Hasidic. I. Patai, Raphael, 1910-

GERSHATOR, Phillis. 296.1'2 B
Honi and his magic circle / by Phillis Gershator ; pictures by Shay Rieger. 1st ed. Philadelphia : Jewish Publication Society of America, 1980, c1979. [48] p. : col. ill. ; 24 cm. Retells the wondrous deeds of Honi the Circle Maker who wandered over the land of ancient Israel planting carob seeds. [BM530.H66G47] 92 79-84731 ISBN 0-8276-0167-0 : 6.95
1. Honi ha-Meaggel, 1st cent. B.C.—Juvenile literature. 2. [Honi ha-Meaggel, 1st cent. B.C.] 3. [Jews—Biography.] 4. Talmud—Biography—Juvenile literature. 5. Tales, Jewish. 6. [Folklore, Jewish.] I. Rieger, Shay. II. Title.

GLENN, Mendel Gershon, 1896- ed. and tr. 296
Jewish tales and legends; Supplentary readings to the Torah, selected and translated by Mendel G. Glenn. New York, Star Hebrew book co. [c1929] x, 11-443 p. 21 cm. "Tales and legends from the Talmud and midrash ... chronologically arranged and translated into the modern."--Author's note. "Original and secondary sources": p. vi. [BM530.G58] 30-7735
1. Tales, Jewish. 2. Legends, Jewish. 3. Bible—History of Biblical events. I. Title.

GRAND, Ben Zion, 1879- 296.1
And I will make of thee a great nation; tales from Jewish history illuminating the spiritual and cultural heritage of Israel from the days of Abraham to the present, for students and laymen. New York, William-Frederick Press, 1952. 198 p. 24 cm. [PN6071.J5G7] 52-9946
1. Tales, Jewish. I. Title.

HALPERN, Salomon Alter. 296
Tales of faith. [Jerusalem] Boys Town Jerusalem Publishers; [sole dist.: P. Feldheim. New York] 1968. 216p. 22cm. Bibl. [BM530.H3] HE68 3.75
1. Tales, Jewish. 2. Legends, Jewish. I. Title.

HURWITZ, Hyman, 1770-1844, comp. and tr.
Hebrew tales; selected and translated from the writings of the ancient Hebrew sages. To which is prefixed an essay on the uninspired literature of the Hebrews. By Hyman Hurwitz... New York, Spalding & Shepard, 1847. xiii p., 1 l., 171 p. 19 1/2 cm. 47-39379
1. Tales, Jewish. I. Title.

ISAACS, Abram Samuel, 1852-1920. 296.1
Stories from the rabbis. New York, B. Blom, 1972. 222 p. 18 cm. Reprint of the 1911 ed. Contents.Contents.—The Faust of the Talmud.—The wooing of the princess.—The Rip Van Winkle of the Talmud.—Rabbinical romance.—The shepherd's wife.—The repentant rabbi.—The inheritance.—Elijah in the legends.—When Solomon was King.—Rabbinical humor.—The Munchausen of the Talmud.—The rabbi's dream.—The gift that blessed.—In the sweat of thy brow.—A four-leaved clover.—The expiation.—A string of pearls.—The vanished bridegroom.—The lesson of the harvest. [BM530.I8 1972] 79-175868 12.50
1. Tales, Jewish. I. Title.

†KAHAN, Israel Meir, 1838-1933. FIC
The stories and parables of the Hafetz Hayyim / gathered and arranged by David Zaretsky ; translated from the Hebrew by Charles Wengrov. Jerusalem ; New York : Feldheim Publishers, c1976. 207 p. ; 24 cm. Translation of Mishle ha-"Hafets Hayim." [BM530.K2813 1976] 296.7'4 77-551136 7.50
1. Tales, Jewish. 2. Parables, Jewish. I. Zaretsky, David. II. Title.

LURIE, Rose G
The great march; post-Biblical Jewish stories. Illus. by Todros Geller. [Rev. ed.] 2 v. illus. 24 cm. (Union graded series) 67-8817
1. Tales, Jewish. 2. Children's stories. I. Union of American Hebrew Congregations. II. Title.

LURIE, Rose G
The great march; post-Biblical Jewish stories. Illus. by Todros Geller. [Rev. ed.] New York, Union of American Hebrew Congregations, 1931 [i.e. 1961, c1955] 2 v. illus. 24 cm. (Union graded series) 67-8817
1. Tales, Jewish. 2. Children's stories. I. Union of American Hebrew Congregations. II. Title.

LURIE, Rose G. 296
The great march; post-Biblical Jewish stories, by Rose G. Lurie; illustrations by Todros Geller. Cincinnati, Dept. of synagogue and school extension of the Union of American Hewbrew congregations, 1931. x p., 1 l., 228 p. illus. 24 1/2 cm. Illustrated lining-papers. [RM107.L8] 31-32321
1. Tales, Jewish. 2. Children's stories. I. Union of American Hebrew congregations. Dept. of synagog and school extension. II. Title.

MARENOF, Martha, comp. JUV
Stories round the year; from Rosh Hashanah to Shavuot. Illus. by Frances H. Quint. [2d ed., rev.] Detroit, Dot Publications, 1969. 159 p. illus. 24 cm. Thirty-three traditional and modern tales for the various holidays of the Jewish calendar. Included are "A Runaway Dreidel" for Hanukah, "Haman's Reward" for Purim, and "Moses and the Birds" for Shavuot. [BM107.M3 1969] 398.2'09176'6 70-12656 3.75
1. Tales, Jewish. 2. [Folklore—Jews.] I. Quint, Frances H., illus. II. Title.

POSY, Arnold, 1893-
Israeli tales and legends. [Rev. ed.] New York, J. David [1966] 270 p. illus. 23 cm. 68-14374
1. Tales, Jewish. I. Title.

PROSE, Francine, 1947- 398.2'094
Stories from our living past. Edited by Jules Harlow. Associate editor, Seymour Rossel. Illustrated by Erika Weihs. New York, Behrman House [1974] 127 p. illus. (part col.) 26 cm. Twenty-eight Jewish tales with morals, including "Daniel in the Lion's Den," "The King's Garden," and "The Goat that Made the Stars Sing." [BM107.P73] 74-8514 ISBN 0-87441-081-9 3.95
1. Tales, Jewish. 2. Religious education, Jewish—Text-books for children. 3. [Jewish way of life—Fiction.] I. Weihs, Erika, illus. II. Title.

SERWER, Blanche Luria. 398.2'094
Let's steal the moon; Jewish tales, ancient and recent, retold by Blanche Luria Serwer. Illustrated by Trina Schart Hyman. [1st ed.] Boston, Little, Brown [1970] 88 p. col. illus. 25 cm. Eleven traditional tales from Jewish folklore of the Middle East and Europe. [BM107.S45] 398.2 71-105750 3.95
1. Tales, Jewish. 2. [Folklore—Jews.] I. Hyman, Trina Schart, illus. II. Title.

SILVERMAN, William B *296.42
Rabbinic stories for Christian ministers and teachers. New York, Abingdon Press [1958] 221 p. 22 cm. [PN6071.J5S49] 58-7436
1. Tales, Jewish. I. Title.

SILVERMAN, William B. 296.1
Rabbinic wisdom and Jewish values / William B. Silverman. Rev. ed. New York : Union of American Hebrew Congregations, c1971. 221 p. ; 22 cm. First ed. published in 1958 under title: Rabbinic stories for Christian ministers and teachers. Includes index. [BM530.S49 1971] 75-314804
1. Tales, Jewish. 2. Tales, Hasidic. I. Title.

WEYNE, Arthur. 296
The treasure chest; tales and legends from Jewish lore, by Arthur Weyne. New York, Judea publishing corporation [c1941] xv, 208 p. illus. 22 1/2 cm. [BM580.W4] 41-26021
1. Tales, Jewish. 2. Legends, Jewish. I. Title.

Tales, Latin.

GESTA Romanorum. English. 873'.03
Gesta Romanorum; or, Entertaining moral stories; invented by the monks as a fireside recreation, and commonly applied in their discourses from the pulpit: whence the most celebrated of our own poets and others, from the earliest times, have extracted their plots. Translated from the Latin, with preliminary observations and copious notes, by Charles Swan. Rev. and corr. by Wynnard Hooper. New York, AMS Press [1970] lxxvi, 425 p. 23 cm. Reprint of the 1894 ed. Includes bibliographical references. [PA8323.E5S9 1970] 75-136377 ISBN 0-404-50009-9
1. Tales, Latin. I. Swan, Charles, tr. II. Hooper, Wynnard, ed.

Tales, Oriental.

THREE unknown Buddhist stories in an Arabic version. 294.3'8
Introd., text & translation by S. M. Stern & Sofie Walzer. Columbia, University of South Carolina Press [1971] 38 p. 23 cm. Arabic text reproduced from ms. copy. Stories incorporated in Ibn Babawayh's Kamal al-din wa-tamam al-ni'mah (romanized form), from which the editors have extracted them. [GR265.T5 1971] 72-189034 ISBN 0-87249-211-7 4.95
1. Tales, Oriental. 2. Legends, Buddhist. I. Stern, Samuel Miklos, 1920-1969, tr. II. Walzer, Sophie, tr. III. Ibn Babwayh, Muhammad ibn 'Ali, d. 991 or 2. Kamal al-din wa-tamam al-ni'mah. English & Arabic. 1971.

Tales, Sufi.

INAYAT Khan, 1882-1927. 297'.4
Tales / told by Hazrat Inayat Khan. New

Lebanon, N.Y. : Sufi Order Publications, 1980. xxii, 261 p. : ill. ; 23 cm. (The Collected works of Hazrat Inayat Khan) [PN6071.S8515 1980] 19 80-52548 ISBN 0-930872-15-0 (pbk.) : 7.95
1. Tales, Sufi. I. Title. II. Series: Inayat Khan, 1882-1927. Collected works of Hazrat Inayat Khan.
Publisher's address P. O. Box 568, Lebannon Springs, NY 12114.

Tales, Yoruba.

COURLANDER, Harold, 1908- 299'.6
Tales of Yoruba gods and heroes. Decorations by Larry Lurin. New York, Crown Publishers [1973] vii, 243 p. illus. 24 cm. Bibliography: p. 241-243. [GR360.Y6C68 1973] 72-84307 ISBN 0-517-50063-9 5.95
1. Tales, Yoruba. 2. Mythology, Yoruba. I. Title.

Talismans.

BEARD, Charles Relly, 1891-1958. 133.4'43
Lucks and talismans; a chapter of popular superstition. New York, B. Blom, 1972. xix, 258 p. 21 cm. Reprint of the 1934 ed. Bibliography: p. 249-258. [BF1561.B35 1972] 72-80494
1. Talismans. 2. Superstition. I. Title.

BEARD, Charles Relly, 1891-1958. 133.4'4
Lucks and talismans; a chapter of popular superstition. London, S. Low, Marston. Detroit, Singing Tree Press, 1972. xix, 258 p. 22 cm. Reprint of the 1934 ed. Bibliography: p. 253-258. [BF1561.B35 1972b] 74-174903
1. Talismans. 2. Superstition. I. Title.

GILES, Carl H. 133.4'4
Bewitching jewelry : jewelry of the black arts / Carl H. Giles and Barbara Ann Williams. South Brunswick : A. S. Barnes, c1976. 159 p., [4] leaves of plates : ill. ; 26 cm. Includes index. Bibliography: p. 147-153. [BF1561.G54 1976] 74-30726 ISBN 0-498-01654-4 : 14.50
1. Talismans. 2. Amulets. 3. Jewelry—Miscellanea. I. Williams, Barbara, 1944- joint author. II. Title.

OLD, Walter Gorn, 1864- 133.4'4
The book of charms and talismans, by Sepharial. New York, Arc Books [1969] 118 p. illus. 18 cm. [BF1561.O4 1969] 70-84400 ISBN 0-668-02010-5 0.95 (pbk)
1. Talismans. 2. Charms. 3. Symbolism of numbers. I. Title.

PAVITT, William Thomas. 133.4'4
The book of talismans, amulets and zodiacal gems, by William Thomas & Kate Pavitt. London, W. Rider, 1914. Detroit, Tower Books, 1971. xix, 292 p. illus. 23 cm. Bibliography: p. 283-284. [BF1561.P38 1971] 72-157497
1. Talismans. 2. Amulets. 3. Zodiac. 4. Gems. I. Pavitt, Kate, joint author. II. Title.

PAVITT, William Thomas. 133.4'4
The book of talismans, amulets, and zodiacal gems, by William Thomas & Kate Pavitt. [3d rev. ed.] New York, S. Weiser [1970] xii, 292 p. illus. 23 cm. Reprint of the 1929 ed. [BF1561.P38 1970] 77-16448 6.50
1. Talismans. 2. Amulets. 3. Zodiac. 4. Gems. I. Pavitt, Kate, joint author. II. Title.

PAVITT, William Thomas.
The book of talismans, amulets and zodiacal gems, by William Thomas & Kate Pavitt ... Philadelphia, D. McKay [1915] xix, 292 p. col. front., 10 pl. 23 cm. Printed in Plymouth, Eng., 1914. Bibliography: p. 283-284. A 15
1. Talismans. 2. Amulets. 3. Gems. I. Pavitt, Kate, joint author. II. Title. III. Title: Zodiacal gems.

POULE noire. English. 133.4'4
The black pullet; science of magical talisman. New York, S. Weiser, 1972. 80 p. illus. 22 cm. Translation of La poule noire. [BF1561.P6813] 78-190080 ISBN 0-87728-176-9
1. Talismans. 2. Occult sciences. I. Title.

Tallis, Thomas, 1505 (ca.)-1585.

DOE, Paul. 783'.092'4 B
Tallis / Paul Doe. 2d ed. London ; New York : Oxford University Press, 1976. 71 p. ; 22 cm. (Oxford studies of composers ; 4) Music. "List of works": p. 66-71. [ML410.T147D6 1976] 76-361379 ISBN 0-19-314122-1 : 5.50
1. Tallis, Thomas, 1505 (ca.)-1585. I. Title. II. Series.

Tallmadge, Benjamin, 1725-1786.

BUELL, Samuel, 1716-1798.
Christ the grand subject of gospel-preaching; the power of God, manifested in the work of faith; and unbelief under the gospel, lamented. A sermon, preach'd at Brook-Haven, on Long-island, October 23, 1754. At the ordination of Mr. Benjamin Tallmadge. By Samuel Buell, A. M. pastor of the church at East-Hampton, Long island. Together with a discourse on ordination: the charge, and exhortation to the people. Published at the desire of the hearers ... New-York: Printed and sold, by J. Parker, and W. Weyman, at the new-printing-office in Beaver-street, Mdcclv. 2 p. l., [3]-62 p. 21 cm. Half-title: Mr. Buell's sermon. The nature of ordination ... by Ebenezer Prime (p. [29]-53), and An exortation to the people ... By James Brown (p. [55]-62), each have special t.-p. A31
1. Tallmadge, Benjamin, 1725-1786. I. Prime, Ebenezer, 1700-1779. II. Brown, James, 1721?-1788. III. Title.

Talmage, James Edward, 1862-1933.

TALMAGE, James Edward, 1862-
Jesus the Christ; a study of the Messiah and His mission according to Holy Scriptures both ancient and modern, by James E. Talmage ... Pub. by the church. 2d ed., 6th to 15th thousand inclusive. Salt Lake City, Utah, The Deseret news, 1915. xi, 804 p. 20 cm. "The book is published by the Church of Jesus Christ of Latter-day saints."--Pref. 16-691
I. Title.

TALMAGE, James Edward, 1862-
Jesus the Christ; a study of the Messiah and His mission according to Holy Scriptures both ancient and modern, by James E. Talmage ... Pub. by the church. 3d ed., 16th to 20th thousand inclusive. Salt Lake City, Utah, The Deseret news, 1916. xi, 804 p. 20 cm. "The book is published by the church of Jesus Christ of Latter-day saints."--Pref. 16-10810
I. Title.

TALMAGE, James Edward, 1862-
Jesus the Christ; a study of the Messiah and His mission according to Holy Scriptures, both ancient and modern, by James E. Talmage ... Pub. by the church. 4th ed., 21st to 25th thousand inclusive. Salt Lake City, Utah, The Deseret news, 1916. xi, 804 p. 20 cm. "The book is published by the Church of Jesus Christ of Latter-day saints."--Pref. 16-24943
I. Title.

TALMAGE, John R., 1911- 289.3'3 B
The Talmage story; life of James E. Talmage - educator, scientist, apostle [by] John R. Talmage. Salt Lake City, Bookcraft, 1972. 246 p. illus. 24 cm. [BX8695.T25T34] 77-189831
1. Talmage, James Edward, 1862-1933. I. Title.

Talmage, John Van Nest, 1819-1892.

FAGG, John Gerardus, 1860-1917. 922.551
Forty years in south China: the life of Rev. John Van Nest Talmage, D. D. By Rev. John Gerardus Fagg ... New York, A. D. F. Randolph & company [1894?] 301 p. front., plates, ports. 20 cm. [BX9225.T28F3] 36-22116
1. Talmage, John Van Nest, 1819-1892. I. Title.

Talmage, Thomas De Witt, 1832-1902.

ADAMS, Charles Francis, 1869- 285.
The life and sermons of Rev. T. DeWitt Talmage, by Charles Francis Adams... Chicago, M. A. Donohue & co. [c1902] xvi, 13-50, 29-252, 23-192 p. front. (port) plates 20 cm. [BX9225.T3A6] 3-17066
1. Talmage, Thomas De Witt, 1832-1902 2. Presbyterian church—Sermons. I. Title.

BANKS, Charles Eugene, 1852-1932. 285.
Authorized and authentic life and works of T. De Witt Talmage, by Charles Eugene Banks ... assisted by Geo. C. Cook and Marshall Everett [pseud.] ... Chicago, The Bible house, 1902. 479 p. incl. front., plates, ports. 24 1/2 cm. [BX9225.T3B3] 2-16762
1. Talmage, Thomas De Witt, 1832-1902. I. Cook, George Cram, 1873-1924, joint author. II. Neil, Henry, 1863- joint author. III. Title.

INGERSOLL, Robert Green, 1833-1899. 211
Six interviews with Robert G. Ingersoll on six sermons by The Rev. T. De Witt Talmage, D.D. To which is added A Talmagian catechism. Stenographically reported by I. Newton Baker. Washington, D.C., C. P. Farrell, 1882. xii p., 1 l., 15-443 p. 20 cm. [BL2725.S5 1882] [AC8.I6272 no.5] 041 44-12885
1. Talmage, Thomas De Witt, 1832-1902. 2. Free thought. I. Title.

LOBB, John, 1840-1921. 922.573
The life and death of Rev. T. DeWitt Talmage, D D. By Rev. John Lobb ... New York, J. S. Ogilvie publishing company [1902] 1 p. l., [7]-222 p. 19 cm. [BX9225.T3L6] 36-22117
1. Talmage, Thomas DeWitt, 1832-1902. I. Title.

PRESBYTERIAN church in the U.S.A. Presbyteries. Brooklyn. 285.
Report of proceedings in the Talmage case, before the Presbytery of Brooklyn. 1879. New York city, N. Tibbals & sons [1879?] cover-title, 767 p. 21 cm. [BX9193.T3A3] 1-14625
1. Talmage, Thomas De Witt, 1832-1902. I. Title.

TALMAGE, Thomas De Witt, 1832-1902. 243
Fifty short sermons, by T. De Witt Talmage; compiled by his daughter, May Talmage. New York, George H. Doran company [c1923] vi p., 1 l., 9-294 p. 20 cm. [BX9178.T3F4] 23-10249
I. Talmage, May, comp. II. Title.

TALMAGE, Thomas De Witt, 1832-1902. 243
Fifty short sermons, by T. De Witt Talmage; compiled by his daughter, May Talmage. New York, George H. Doran company [c1923] vi p., 1 l., 9-294 p. 20 cm. [BX9178.T3F4] 23-10249
I. Talmage, May, comp. II. Title.

TALMAGE, Thomas De Witt, 1832-1902. 285.
... Life and teachings of Rev. T. De Witt Talmage ... embracing the richest and most brilliant utterances given to the world during his phenomenal career, by Rev. T. De Witt Talmage ... with an introduction by Rev. Russell H. Conwell ... Memorial volume. Philadelphia, National publishing co. [1902] 1 p. l., xiv, 17-511 p. incl. illus., plates. front., plates., ports. 23 1/2 cm. [BX9225.T3A35] 2-14597
I. Title.

TALMAGE, Thomas De Witt, 1832-1902. 243
New Tabernacle sermons, by T. De Witt Talmage ... delivered in the Brooklyn tabernacle ... New York, E. B. Treat, 1886. vi, 7-410 p. incl. front., (port.) 19 1/2 cm. Lettered on cover: Treasury series. [BX9178.T3N4 1886a] 29-24782
I. Title.

TALMAGE, Thomas De Witt, 1832-1902. 243
New tabernacle sermons, by T. De Witt Talmage, D.D., delivered in the Brooklyn tabernacle. Garden City, N.Y., Doubleday, Doran & company, inc., 1929. 1 p., l., [v]-vi, [7]-410 p. 19 1/2 cm. [BX9178.T3N4 1929] 29-7828
I. Title. II. Title: Tabernacle sermons.

WARREN, William Nixon.
The illustrious life of T. De Witt Talmage, the greatly beloved divine, by William Nixon Warren ... including extracts from his most eloquent sermons and lectures and tributes on his life from the world's greatest men ... [Chicago, Monarch book co., 1902] 2 p. l., 7-12, [2], 25-464 p. incl. front., pl., port. 25 cm. Subject entries: Talmage, Thomas De Witt, 1832-1902. 2-19008
I. Title.

Talmud.

AUERBACH, Charles.
The Talmud, a gateway to the common law. Cleveland, Press of Western Reserve University, 1952. 49p. 24cm. Reprinted from the Western Reserve law review, June, 1951. A54
1. Talmud. 2. Jewish law. 3. Common law—U.S. I. Title.

*BULKA, Reuven P., Rabbi. 296.12
The wit and wisdom of the Talmud, by Rabbi Dr. Reuven P. Bulka. Illustrations by Jeff Hill. Mount Vernon, N.Y., Peter Pauper Press, [1974] 62 p. illus. 19 cm. [BM504.5] 1.95
1. Talmud. I. Title.

COHEN, Abraham, 1887- 296
Everyman's Talmud. London, J. M. Dent; New York, E. P. Dutton [1949] xii, 403 p. facsim. 19 cm. "A summary of the teachings of the Talmud on religion, ethics, folk-lore, and jurisprudence." "Selected bibliography": p. xxxix-xii. [BM504.C6 1949a] 49-48032
1. Talmud. 2. Jews—Religion. 3. Ethics, Jewish. 4. Jews—Soc. life & cust. I. Title.

COHEN, Abraham, 1887- 296
Everyman's Talmud; with an introd. to the new American ed. Boaz Cohen. New York, E. P. Dutton, 1949. xii, 403 p. 21 cm. "A summary of the teachings of the Talmud on religion, ethics, folk-lore, and jurisprudence." "Selected bibliography": p. xxxix-xii. [BM504.C6 1949] 49-9302
1. Talmud. 2. Jews—Religion. 3. Ethics, Jewish. 4. Jews—Soc. life & cust. I. Title.

DARMESTETER, Arsene, 1846-1888. 296
The Talmud, by Arsene Darmesteter, tr. from the French by Henrietta Szold. Philadelphia, The Jewish publication society of America [191-] 97 p. 19 cm. Translated from the author's Reliques scientifiques. cf. Prefatory note. [BM504.D3] 19-5550
1. Talmud. I. Szold, Henrietta, 1860- tr. II. Title.

DEUTSCH, Emanuel Oscar Menahem, 1829-1873. 296
The Talmud, by Emanuel Deutsch. Philadelphia, The Jewish publication society of America [191-] 2 p. l., [3]-107 p. 19 cm. "Reprinted from 'Literary remains of the late Emanuel Deutsch,' London. 1874." [BM504.D4] 19-5549
1. Talmud. I. Title.

KAPLAN, Julius, 1885- 296
The redaction of the Babylonian Talmud, by Julius Kaplan, PH. D. New York, Bloch publishing company, 1933. 4 p. l., 356 p. 25 cm. Chapters i-xii issued also as thesis (PH. D.) Columbia university. "Works quoted or referred to in this book": p. 347-350. [BM504.K28 1933] 33-25959
1. Talmud. I. Title.

KATZ, Mordecai.
Protection of the weak in the Talmud. New York, AMS Press, 1966 [c1925] 87 p. (Columbia University oriental studies, v. 24) Bibliography: p. 85-87. 67-95779
1. Talmud. 2. Jewish law. I. Title. II. Series.

KATZ, Mordecai. 016.
... Protection of the weak in the Talmud, by Mordecai Katz ... New York, Columbia university press, 1925. 5 p. l., 87 p. 23 cm. (Columbia university oriental studies, vol. xxiv) Published also as thesis (PH. D.) Columbia university, 1925. Bibliography: p.

85-87. [BM509.L3K3 1925 a] [PJ25.C6 vol. xxiv] 26-5706
1. Talmud. 2. Jews—Law. I. Title.

MAHAN, William Dennes, 1824-1906. 232.
Archaeological writings of the Sanhedrin and Talmuds of the Jews. Translated from manuscripts in Constantinople and the records of the senatorial docket, taken from the Vatican in Rome. Being the official documents made in these courts in the days of Jesus Christ. Translated by Drs. McIntosh and Twyman. Also important extracts taken from the ante-Nicene fathers and the works of Eusebius. Compiled by Rev. W. D. Mahan and Elder J. W. Damon. St. Louis, Mo., Pub. for the compilers by Christian publishing co. [1887] 569 p., 2 l. 20 1/2 cm. Issued in part under the title The archko volume. This work is considered a forgery by Dr. Montague R. James in his Apocryphal New Testament, Oxford, 1924, p. 90. [BT441.A2M3 1887] 1-3496
I. Damon, J. W. II. McIntosh, M. III. Twyman, T. H., joint tr. IV. Title.

MAHAN, William Dennes, 1824-1906. 232.
The archaeological and the historical writings of the Sanhedrin and Talmuds of the Jews, translated from the ancient parchments and scrolls at Constantinople and the Vatican at Rome; an official record made by the enemies of Jesus of Nazareth in His day. Positively guaranteed to be accurate and authentic. The most interesting history of Jesus extant. By Rev. W. D. Mahan ... Chicago, Ill., The de Laurence company, 1923. 3 p. l., 313 p. 19 1/2 cm. "1923 de Laurence American edition de luxe." Issued in part under the title The archko volume. This work is considered a forgery by Dr. Montague R. James in his Apocryphal New Testament, 1924, p. 90. [BT441.A2M3 1923] 25-2269
I. McIntosh, M. II. Twyman, T. H. III. Title.

MAHAN, William Dennes, 1824-1906. 232.
Archaeological writings of the Sanhedrin and Talmuds of the Jews, taken from the ancient parchments and scrolls at Constantinople and the Vatican at Rome, being the record made by the enemies of Jesus of Nazareth in his day. The most interesting history ever read by man. By W. D. Mahan ... St. Louis, Pub. for the author by Perrin & Smith, 1884. 352 p. 21 cm. This work is considered a forgery by Dr. Montague R. James in his Apocryphal New Testament, Oxford, 1924, p. 90. [BT441.A2M3 1884] 29-24270
I. Title.

[MAHAN, William Dennes] 1824-1906. 232.
The archko volume; or, The archeological writings of the Sanhedrin and Talmuds of the Jews. (Intra secus.) These are the official documents made in these courts in the days of Jesus Christ. Translated by Drs. McIntosh and Twyman ... From manuscripts in Constantinople and the records of the senatorial docket taken from the Vatican at Rome. Philadelphia, Antiquarian book company [1913] 1 p. l., vii-viii, 9-248 p. front. 17 1/2 cm. Compiled by W. D. Mahan. Published under various titles. Generally regarded as spurious. cf. James, M. R. Apocryphal New Testament, Oxford, 1924, p. 90, and Goodspeed, E. J. Strange new gospels, Chicago, 1931, chapter v. [BT441.A2M3 1913] 13-15805
I. McIntosh, M. II. Twyman, T. H. III. Title.
Contents omitted.

[MAHAN, William Dennes] 1824-1906. 232.
The archko volume; or, The archeological writings of the Sanhedrin and Talmuds of the Jews. (Intra secus) These are the official documents made in these courts in the days of Jesus Christ. Translated by Drs. McIntosh and Twyman ... From manuscripts in Constantinople and the records of the senatorial docket taken from the Vatican at Rome. Philadelphia, Antiquarian book company [1913] 1 p. l., vii-viii, 9-248 p. front. 17 1/2 cm. Compiled by W. D. Mahan. This work is considered a forgery by Dr. Montague R. James in his Apocryphal New Testament, Oxford, 1924, p. 90. [BT441.A2M3 1913] 13-15805
I. McIntosh, M. II. Twyman, T. H. III. Title.
Contents omitted.

[MAHAN, William Dennes] 1824-1906. 232.
The arshko volume, translated from ancient manuscripts at the Vatican of Rome, and the Seraglio library at Constantinople, by Drs. McIntosh and Twyman. Grand Rapids, Mich., The Classic press [1925?] 150 p. 16 cm. Cover title: Archko library. Compiled by W. D. Mahan. This work is considered a forgery by Dr. Montague R. James in his Apocryphal New Testament, Oxford, 1924, p. 90. [BT441.A2M3 1925] 27-2264
I. McIntosh, M. II. Twyman, T. H. III. Title.
Contents omitted.

MIELZINER, Moses, 1828-1903. 296
Introduction to the Talmud. Historical and literary introduction. Legal hermeneutics of the Talmud. Talmudical terminology and methodology. Outline of Talmudical ethics. Appendix Key to the abbreviations used in the Talmud and its commentaries. By M. Mielziner ... Cincinnati and Chicago, The Bloch printing company, 1894. xii, 293 p. 22 cm. Bibliography: p. [93]-102. [BM504.M5 1894] 27-2973
1. Talmud. I. Title.

MIELZINER, Moses, 1828-1903. 296
Introduction to the Talmud; historical and literary introduction, legal hermeneutics of the Talmud, Talmudical terminology and methodology, outlines of Talmudical ethics. Appendix: Key to the abbreviations used in the Talmud and its commentaries, by . Mielziner ... 2d rev. ed. New York and London, Funk & Wagnalls company, 1903. 8 p. l., 297 p. 21 cm. [BM504.M5 1903] 3-2132
1. Talmud. I. Title.

MIELZINER, Moses, 1828-1903. 296
Introduction to the Talmud; historical and literary introduction, legal hermeneutics of the Talmud, Talmudical terminology and methodology, outlines of Talmudical ethics, by M. Mielziner ... 3d ed., with additional notes by Dr. Joshua Bloch and Dr. Louis Finkelstein. New York, Bloch publishing company, inc., 1925. xiv, 395 p. 21 cm. Bibliography: p. [98]-102. [BM504.M5 1925] 27-67
1. Talmud. I. Bloch, Joshua, 1890- II. Finkelstein, Louis, 1895- III. Title.

PICK, Bernhard, 1842-1917. 232
Jesus in the Talmud; his personality, his disciples and his sayings, by Bernhard Pick ... Chicago [etc.] The Open court publishing company, 1913. 5 p. l., [3]-100, [3] p. 18 cm. [BT520.P52] 13-25392
1. Jesus Christ. 2. Talmud. I. Title.

RODKINSON, Michael Levi, 1845-1904. 296
The history of the Talmud, from the time of its formation, about 200 B.C., up to the present time ... By Michael L. Rodkinson ... New York, New Talmud publishing company [1903] 2 v. in 1. port., facsims. 27 1/2 cm. Forms vols. 19 and 20 of the New edition of the Babylonian Talmud, English translation. Appended: Synopsis of subjects. [Name originally: Michael Levi Frumkin] Contents.I. Its development and the persecutions since its birth up to date, including all religious disputes and brief biographies of the separated sects.--II. The historical and literary introduction to the new edition: Ethics, method, with illustrations, criticism, etc. "Bibliography of modern works and monographs on Talmudic subjects": v. 2, p. 58-70. [BM504.R6] 3-32538
1. Talmud. I. Title.

RODKINSON, Michael Lewy, 1843or4-1904. 296
The history of the Talmud, from the time of its formation, about 200 B.C., up to the present time... By Michael L. Rodkinson... New York, New Talmud publishing company [1903] 2 v. in 1. port., facsims. 27 1/2 cm. Appended: Synopsis of subjects. Contents.I. Its development and the persecutions since its birth up to date, including all religious disputes and brief biographies of the separated sects.--II. The historical and literary introduction to the new edition: Ethics, method, with illustrations, criticism, etc. "Bibliography of modern works and monographs on Talmudic subjects": vol. II, p. 58-70. Forms vols. XIX and XX of the New edition of the Babylonian Talmud, English translation. [BM504.R6] 3-32538
1. Talmud. I. Title.

SHOHET, David Menahem, 1888- 296.1'8 S
The Jewish court in the Middle Ages : studies in Jewish jurisprudence according to the Talmud, Geonic, and Medieval German responsa / by David Menahem Shohet. New York : Hermon Press, 1974. xv, 224 p. ; 24 cm. (Studies in Jewish jurisprudence ; v. 3) Reprint of the 1931 ed. published in New York. Originally presented as the author's thesis, Columbia University, 1931. Includes index. Bibliography: p. 211-216. [LAW] 296.1'8 74-79442 ISBN 0-87203-049-0 11.50
1. Jews—History—70-1789. 2. Talmud. 3. Courts, Jewish. 4. Jewish law. 5. Responsa. I. Title. II. Series.

STRACK, Hermann Leberecht, 1848-1922. 296
Introduction to the Talmud and Midrash, by Hermann L. Strack; authorized translation on the basis of the author's revised copy of the fifth German edition. Philadelphia, Jewish publication society of America, 1931. xvii, 374 p. 23 1/2 cm. Bibliography: p. xv-xvi. [BM504.S73] 32-991
1. Talmud. 2. Midrash. I. Title.

TALMUD. Berakoth.
The Babylonian Talmud: Tractate Brakot; translated into English for the first time, with introduction, commentary, glossary and indices, by the Rev. A. Cohen ... Cambridge, [Eng.] The University press, 1921. xxxix, [1], 460 p. 23 cm. [BM500.C6] 21-21403
I. Cohen, Abraham, 1887- tr. II. Title.

TALMUD. Chagigah. 296
... A translation of the treatise Chagigah from the Babylonian Talmud, with introduction, notes, glossary, and indices, by the Rev. A. W. Streane ... Cambridge, University press, 1891. xvi, 166 p. 23 cm. At head of title: [BM506.C5E5 1891] 17-24373
I. Streane, Annesley William, ed. II. Title. III. Title: Chagigah.

TALMUD. English. 296
New edition of the Babylonia Talmud. Original text edited, corrected, formulated, and translated into English by Michael L. Redkinson, 1st ed., rev. and corr. by the Rev. Dr. Isaac M. Wise ... 2d ed., re-ed., rev. and enl. Boston, The Talmud society, 1918. 20 v. in 10, port., facsim. 24 1/2 cm. On cover: v. 1-10. Vol. 16 has half-title only; v. 19-20 have special title-pages only. Vols. 1-2, 11-12, 13-14, 15-16 are paged continuously. The last two chapters of v. 10 are bound in the front of vol. 11. [BM500.R] A 41
I. Title.

TALMUD. English. 296
New edition of the Babylonian Talmud. English translation. Original text edited, formulated, and punctuated by Michael L. Redkinson ... New York, New Amsterdam book company [c1896-c1903] 20 v. in 18 front., (v. 1, 15, 17-18) plates, poets, incicsm, 28 cm. Title of v. 2-15; 17-18: New edition of the Babylonian Talmud. Original text, edited, corrected, formulated, and translated into English by Michael L. Redkinson. Vol. 16 has half-title only: v. 19-20 have special title-pages only. Vols. 1-2, 11-12, 13-14, 15-16 are paged continuously. Vols. 1-2 revised and corrected by I. M. Wise; revised by Godfrey Taubenhaus. Vols. 2-20 have imprint: New York, New Talmud publishing company. Contents.Section Moed (Festivals)--v. 1-2 Tract Sabbath. c1896--v. 3. Tract Erubin. c1897--v. 4. Tracts Shekalim and Rosh Hashana. Hebrew and English. c1896--v. 5. Truce pesachim. c1896--v. 6. Tracts Yomah and Hugign. c1896--v. 7. Tracts Betzah. Succah and Moed Katan. c1899--v. 8. Tracts Tannith, Megilla, and Ebel Rabbathi or Semaboth. c1899. [BM500.R6] 7-28727
I. Redkinson, Michael Lewy, 1843 or 4-1904, ed. II. Wise, Issac Mayer, 1819-1900, ed. III. Taubenhaus, Godfrey, ed. IV. Title.

TALMUD, English. Selections. 296
The Babylonian Talmud in selection, edited and translated from the original Hebrew and Aramic by Leo Auerbach. New York, Philosophical library [1944] 286 p. 20 1/2 cm. [BM502.A8] 44-7600
I. Auerbach, Leo, ed. and tr. II. Title.

TALMUD. English. Selections.
... The essence of the Talmud [ed. by] Theodore M. R. von Keler. Girard, Kan., Haldeman-Julius company [c1922] 64 p. 13 cm. (Ten cent pocket series, no. 218, ed. by E. Haldeman-Julius) [BM502.V6] 47-43112
I. Von Keler, Theodore Maximilian R., 1877-1927, ed. II. Title.

TALMUD. English. Selections.
Selections from the Talmud. Being specimens of the contents of that ancient book, its commentaries, teachings, poetry, and legends. Also, brief sketches of the men who made and commented upon it. Translated from the original, by H. Polano ... Philadelphia, Claxton, Remsen & Haffelfinger, 1876. viii. [17]-382 p. 24 cm. [BM502.P6 1876] 30-33840
I. Polano, Hymen. tr. II. Title.

TALMUD, English. Selections.
Tales and maxims from the Talmud; selected, arranged and tr, with an introduction by Rev. Samuel Rapaport ...together with "An essay on the Talmud" by the late Emanuel Deutsch. London, G. Routledge & sons, limited; New York, E. P. Dutton & co., 1910. 4 p. 1., 237, [1] p. 20 cm. (On cover: The Semitic series) [BM502.R3] 10-27710
I. Rapaport, Samuel, 1837-1923, ed. and tr. II. Deutsch, Emanuel Oscar Menahem, 1829-1873. III. Title.

TALMUD. English. Selections.
Tales and maxims from the Talmud: selected, arranged and tr., with an introduction by Rev. Samuel Rapaport ... together with "An essay on the Talmud" by the late Emanuel Deutsch. London, G. Routledge & sons, limited; New York, The Block publishing co., 1910. 4 p. 1., 237, [1] p. 20 cm. (On cover: This Semitic series) [BM502.R3 1910a] 24-11631
I. Rapaport,Samuel, 1837-1923, ed. and tr. II. Deutsch, Emanuel Oscar Menahem, 1829-1873 III. Title.

TALMUD. English. Selections.
The Talmud. Selections from the contents of that ancient book ... Also, brief sketches of the men who made and commented upon it. Translated from the orignal, by H. Polano ... Philadelphia, E. S. Stuart [1884] xi, 359 p. front. (fold. plan) 2 pl., plan. 19 cm. [BM502.P6 1884] 9-22514
I. Polano, Hymen, tr. II. Title.

TALMUD. English. Selections.
The Talmud. Selections from the contents of that ancient book ... Also, brief sketches of the men who made and commented upon it. Translated from the orignal, by H. Polano ... Philadelphia, E. S. Stuart [1884] xi, 359 p. front. (fold. plan) 2 pl., plan. 19 cm. [BM502.P6 1884] 9-22514
I. Polano, Hymen, tr. II. Title.

TALMUD. English. Selections. 296
The Talmud for every Jew; readings in the Talmud, with a brief commentary by Rabbi Ralph Simon ... New York city, The National academy for adult Jewish studies under the auspices of the Jewish theological seminary of America [194-?] 3 p. 1., 97 numb. 1. 28 cm] "Preliminary edition." [BM502.S5] 47-11913
I. Simon, Ralph, ed. II. National academy for adult Jewish studie. III. Jewish theological seminary of America. IV. Title.

TALMUD. English. Selections.
The Talmud; selections from the contents of that ancient book, its commentaries, teaching, poetry and legends. Also, brief sketches of the men who made and commented upon it. Tr. from the original by H. Polano. London, New York, F. Warne, 1894. xi, 328 p. 18 cm. (The Chandos classics) [BM502.P6 1894] 48-43445
I. Polano, Hymen, tr. II. Title. III. Series.

TALMUD. English. Selections. 296
The Talmudic anthology, tales and teachings of the rabbis, a collection of parables, folk-tales, fables, aphorism [sic] epigrams, sayings, anecdotes, proverbs and exegetical interpretations, selected and edited by Louis I. Newman ... in collaboration with Samuel Spitz. New York, Behrman house, inc., 1945. xxxiv (i.e. xxxvi) p., 1 l., 570 p. 23 1/2 cm. Bibliography: p. 567-570. [BM502.N4] 45-9682
I. Newman, Louis Israel, 1898- ed. II. Spitz, Samuel, joint ed. III. Title.

TALMUD. English. Selections. 296
A Talmudic miscellany ... or, A thousand and one extracts from the Talmud, the Midrashim and the Kabbalah, comp. and tr. by Paul Isaac Hershon ... with introductorypreface by the rv. F. W. Farrar ... With notes and copious indexes. boston, Houghton, Mifflin & co., 1880. 5 p. 1., v-xxvii,361 p. 21 cm. (Half-title: English and foreign philosophical library. Vo. xix) [BM495.T3 1880] 17-31581
I. Midrash. English. Selections. II. Hershon, Paul Isaac, 1817-1888, comp. III. Title.

TALMUD. English. Selections.
Talmudic pearls, comp. by Barnet Hodes, LL. B. Chicago, Ill., A. Blackwood & co. [c1922] 2 p. 1., 50 p. 18 cm. [BM502.H6] 22-13472
I. Hodes, Barnet, 1900- comp. II. Title.

TALMUD. English. Selections.
Talmudic sayings, selected and arranged under appropriate headings, by Rabbi Henry Cohen. 2d ed. New York, Block publishing company, 1910. viii, 72 p. 17 1/2 cm. 10-23347
I. Cohen, Henry, ed. II. Title.

TALMUD. English. Selections.
Wit and wisdom of the Talmud; edited by Madison C. Peters ... With an introduction by Rabbi H. Pereira Mendes. New York, The Baker & Taylor co. [1900] 169 p. 20 cm. [BM502.P4] 0-6474
I. Peters, Madison Clinton, 1859-1918. II. Title.

TALMUD. English. Selections.
Wit and wisdom of the Talmud; edited by Madison C. Peters ... With an introduction by Rabbi H. Pereira Mendes. New York, The Baker & Taylor co. [1900] 169 p. 20 cm. [BM502.P4] 0-6474
I. Peters, Madison Clinton, 1859-1918. II. Title.

TALMUD, Selections.
The Talmudic anthology; tales and teachings of the rabbis; a collection of parables, folktales, fables ... Selected and edited by Louis I. Newman in collaboration with Samuel Spitz. [New York] Behrman House [1962] xxxiv, 570 p. 63-73794
I. Newman, Louis Israel, 1893- II. Title.

TALMUD. Selections. English. 296
The Babylonian Talmud in selection, edited and translated from the original Hebrew and Aramic by Leo Auerbach. London, New York [etc.] Skeffington & son, ltd. [194-] 152 p. 19 cm. [BM502.A8] 46-36444
I. Auerbach, Leo, ed. and tr. II. Title.

TALMUD. Selections. English.
... *The essence of the Talmud* [ed. by] Theodore M. R. von Keler. Girard, Kan., Haldeman-Julius company, [c1922] 64 p. 13 cm. (Ten cent pocket series, no. 218, ed. by E. Haldeman-Julius) [BM502.V6] CA 23
I. Von Keler, Theodore Maximillian R., 1877- ed. II. Title.

TALMUD. Selections. English.
Selections from the Talmud. Being specimens of the contents of that ancient book, its commentaries, teachings, poetry, and legends. Also brief sketches of the men who made and commented upon it. Translated from the original, by H. Polano ... Philadelphia, Claxton, Remsen & Haffelfinger, 1876. viii, [17]-382 p. 23 1/2 cm. [BM502.P6 1876] 30-33840
I. Polano, Hymen, tr. II. Title.

TALMUD. Selections. English.
Tales and maxims from the Talmud; selected, arranged and tr., with an introduction by Rev. Samuel Rapaport ... together with "An essay on the Talmud" by the late Emanuel Deutsch. London, G. Routledge & sons, limited New York, E. P. Dutton & co., 1910. 4 p. l., 237, [1] p. 19 1/2 cm. (Lettered on cover: The Semitic series) [BM502.R3] 10-27710
I. Rapaport, Samuel, 1837- ed. and tr. II. Deutsch, Emanuel Oscar Menahem, 1829-1873. III. Title.

TALMUD. Selections. English.
Tales and maxims from the Talmud; selected, arranged and tr., with an introduction by Rev. Samuel Rapaport ... together with "An essay on the Talmud" by the late Emanuel Deutsch. London, G. Routledge & sons, limited. New York, The Block publishing co., 1910. 4 p. l., 237, [1] p. 19 1/2 cm. (On cover: The Semitic series) [BM502.R3 1910a] 24-11631
I. Rapaport, Samuel, 1837- ed and tr. II. Deutsch, Emanuel Oscar Menahem, 1829-1873. III. Title.

TALMUD. Selections. English.
Tales and maxims from the Talmud, by Rev. Samuel Rapaport ... 2d series. London, G. Routledge & sons, limited. New York, The Bloch publishing co., 1912. vii, 165 p. 19 1/2 cm. (Lettered on cover: The Semitic series) 15-14851
I. Rapaport, Samuel, 1837- ed. and tr. II. Title.

TALMUD. Selections. English.
The Talmud. Selections from the contents of that ancient book ... Also, brief sketches of the men who made and commented upon it. Translated from the original, by H. Polano ... Philadelphia, E. S. Stuart, [1884] xi, 350 p. front. (fold. plan) 2 pl., plan. 19 cm. [BM502.P6 1884] 9-22514
I. Polano, Hymen, tr. II. Title.

TALMUD. Selections. English.
A Talmudic miscellany ... or, A thousand and one extracts from Talmud, the Midrashim and the Kabbalah, comp. and tr. by Paul Isaac Hershon ... with introductory preface by the Rev. F. W. Farrar ... notes and copious indexes. Boston, Houghton, Mifflin & co., 1880. 5 p. l., v-xxvii, 361 p. 20 1/2 cm. (Half-title: English and foreign philosophical library. vol. xix) [BM502.H4] 17-31581
I. Midrash. Selections. English. II. Cabala. Selections. English. III. Hershon, Paul Isaac, 1817-1888, comp. IV. Title.

TALMUD. Selections. English.
Talmudic pearls, comp. by Barnet Hodes, LL. B. Chicago, Ill., A. Blackwood & co. [c1922] 2 p. l., 50 p. 18 cm. [BM502.H6] 22-13472
I. Hodes, Barnet, comp. II. Title.

TALMUD. Selections. English.
Wit and wisdom of the Talmud; edited by Madison C. Peters ... With an introduction by Rabbi H. Ereira Mendes. New York, The Baker & Taylor co. [1900] 169 p. 19 1/2 cm. [BM502.P4] 0-6474
I. Peters, Madison Clinton, 1859-1918. II. Title.

TALMUD. Selections. English.
Wit and wisdom of the Talmud; edited by Madison C. Peters ... With an introduction by Rabbi H. Ereira Mendes. New York, The Baker & Taylor co. [1900] 169 p. 19 1/2 cm. [BM502.P4] 0-6474
I. Peters, Madison Clinton, 1859-1918. II. Title.

TALMUD Yerushalmi. 296.1'24
Berakot. English.
The Talmud of Jerusalem. Translated for the first time by Moses Schwab. Vol. I. Berakhoth. New York, Hermon Press [1969] iv, 188 p. 25 cm. No more published. Reprint of the 1886 ed. Includes bibliographical references. [BM498.5.E52S3 1969] 77-76173 6.95
I. Schwab, Moise, 1839-1918, tr. II. Title.

TALMUD Yerushalmi. English. 296.1
Selections.
The Talmud of Jerusalem; with a pref. by Dagobert D. Runes. New York, Wisdom Library [1956] 160p. 19cm. 'The text of these selections is based upon the translations from the original Hebrew and Aramaic by Professor H. Polano.' [BM502.P62 1956] 56-14440
I. Polano, Hymen tr. II. Title.

TALMUD Yerushalmi. *296.1
English. Selections.
The Talmud of Jerusalem: with a pref. by Dagobert D. Runes. New York, Wisdom Library [1956] 160 p. 19 cm. "The text of these selections is based upon the translations from the original Hebrew and Aramaic by Professor H. Polano." [BM502.P62 1956] 56-14440
I. Polano, Hymen tr. II. Title.

TAUBENHAUS, Godfrey. 296
Echoes of wisdom; or, Talmudic sayings with classic, especially Latin, parallelisms, by G. Taubenhaus ... Brooklyn, Haedrich & sons' print [c1900] 2 p. l., 106 p. 1 l. 17 1/2 cm. Talmudic sayings in English and Hebrew. "The present volume, comprising Talmudic sayings beginning with Aleph', is the first of a proposed series to come forth is alphabetical order, and on the same plan."--Pref. No more published? [BM502.T3] 9-2781
I. Talmud. Selections. English. II. Title.

Talmud—Addresses, essays, lectures.

EXPLORING the Talmud / 296.1'2
edited by Haim Z. Dimitrovsky. New York : Ktav Pub. House, 1976- p. cm. Contents.Contents.—v. 1. Education. Includes bibliographical references. [BM500.2.E88] 76-7449 ISBN 0-87068-254-7 20.00 (v. 1)
1. Jews—Education—History—Addresses, essays, lectures. 2. Talmud—Addresses, essays, lectures. 3. Jewish learning and scholarship—History—Addresses, essays, lectures. I. Dimitrovsky, Hayim Zalman.

TALMUD, Ta'anit. 296.1'25
The treatuse Ta'anit of the Babylonian Talmud. Critically ed. provided with a tr, notes by Henry Malter. Philadelphia, Jewish Pubn. Soc. [1967] xlii, 481p. 20cm. (JPS lib. of Jewish classics, 2) [BM506.T2E5 1967] HE67 4.50 bds.,
I. Talmud. Ta'anit. English. II. Malter, Henry, 1864-1925, ed. III. Title.

Talmud—Biography

KOLATCH, Alfred J 1916- 296.12
Who's who in the Talmud, by Alfred J. Kolatch. New York, J. David [1964] 315 p. facsims. 23 cm. [BM501.15.K6] 64-24891
1. Talmud—Biog. 2. Talmud—Introductions. I. Title.

Talmud—Biography—Juvenile literature.

GERSHATOR, Phillis. 296.1'2 B
Honi and his magic circle / by Phillis Gershator ; pictures by Shay Rieger. 1st ed. Philadelphia : Jewish Publication Society of America, 1980, c1979. [48] p. : col. ill. ; 24 cm. Retells the wondrous deeds of Honi the Circle Maker who wandered over the land of ancient Israel planting carob seeds. [BM530.H66G47] 92 79-84731 ISBN 0-8276-0167-0 : 6.95
1. Honi ha-Meaggel, 1st cent. B.C.—Juvenile literature. 2. [Honi ha-Meaggel, 1st cent. B.C.] 3. [Jews—Biography.] 4. Talmud—Biography—Juvenile literature. 5. Tales, Jewish. 6. [Folklore, Jewish.] I. Rieger, Shay. II. Title.

Talmud — Commentaries.

GROZOVSKY, Ruvin.
Hidushe rabi Reuven. New York, Balshan [1964- v. Contents.Contents. -- v. 1. Bava kama, Bava mezi'a, Bava batra ve-Sukah. 66-71752
1. Talmud — Commentaries. I. Title.

Talmud—Criticism, interpretation, etc.

BOKSER, Ben Zion, 1907- 296.12
Wisdom of the Talmud. New York, Citadel [1962, c.1951] 176p. 21cm. (C-103) 62-17830 1.50 pap.,
1. Talmud—Criticism, interpretation, etc. I. Title.

BOKSER, Ben Zion, 1907- 296
The wisdom of the Talmud; a thousand years of Jewish thought. New York, Philosophical Library [1951] 180 p. 21 cm. [BM504.B6] 51-14677
1. Talmud—Criticism, Interpretation, etc. I. Title.

JACOBS, Louis. 296.1'2507
Teyku : the unsolved problem in the Babylonian Talmud : a study in the literary analysis and form of the Talmudic argument / by Louis Jacobs. London ; New York : Cornwall Books, c1981. 312 p. ; 25 cm. [BM503.6.J33] 19 80-70887 ISBN 0-8453-4501-X : 20.00
1. Talmud—Criticism and interpretation. 2. Jewish law—Interpretation and construction. 3. Teku (The Aramaic word) I. Title.

THE student's guide through the Talmud. Translated from the Hebrew, edited and critically annotated by Jacob Shachter. [2nd ed.] New York, Feldheim [1960] xxviii, 290p. Errata slip inserted. Title of original Hebrew: Mavo ha-Talmud. Bibliographical footnotes.
1. Talmud—Criticism, interpretation, etc. I. Chajes, Zebi Hirsch, 1805-1855. II. Shachter, Jacob, 1887- ed.

UNTERMAN, Isaac, 1889- 296.1
The Talmud, origin and devedopment, methods and systems, causes and results, contents and significance, with commentaries, interpretations, glossary, and indices. [1st ed.] New York, Record Press, 1952. xv, 351 p. 24 cm. Bibliography: p. 320-328. [BM504.U5] 52-800
1. Talmud — Criticism, interpretation, etc. I. Title.

Talmud—Criticism, interpretation, etc.—Addresses, essays, lectures.

GUTTMANN, Alexander. 296
Studies in Rabbinic Judaism / by Alexander Guttmann. New York : Ktav Pub. House, 1976. p. cm. Includes bibliographical references. [BM500.2.G87] 76-6553 17.50
1. Talmud—Criticism, interpretation, etc.—Addresses, essays, lectures. 2. Judaism—History—Talmudic period, 10-425—Addresses, essays, lectures. I. Title.

Talmud—History

ADLER, Morris. 296.1
The world of the Talmud. Washington, B'nai B'rith Hillel Foundations, 1958. 148p. 19cm. (Hillel little books, v.4) [BM501.A3] 57-12179
1. Talmud—Hist. I. Title. II. Series.

ADLER, Morris. 296.12
The world of the Talmud. 2d ed. New York, Schocken Books [1963] 156 p. 21 cm. (Schocken paperbacks, SB58) Bibliography: p. 155-156. [BM501.A3 1963] 63-18390
1. Talmud—History. I. Title.

Talmud — Introductions.

MIELZINER, Moses, 1828- 296.1'206
1903.
Introduction to the Talmud. [4th ed.] New York, Bloch Pub. Co. [1969] xiv, 415 p. 22 cm. Reprint of the 3d ed., 1925, with a new bibliography, 1925-1967, by Alexander Guttmann. Includes bibliographical references. [BM503.5.M5 1969] 68-29908
1. Talmud—Introductions. I. Title.

NEUSNER, Jacob, 1932- 296.1'206'6
Invitation to the Talmud; a teaching book. [1st ed.] New York, Harper & Row [1973] xxii, 263 p. 22 cm. Bibliography: p. [247]-255. [BM503.5.N48] 73-6343 ISBN 0-06-066098-8 7.95
1. Talmud—Introductions. I. Title.

SILVERSTONE, Harry. 296
A guide to the Talmud, by Harry Silverstone ... Baltimore, Md., The Romm press, inc. [1942] ix, 11-144 p. 23 1/2 cm. [BM504.S5] 42-21472
1. Talmud—Introductions. I. Title.

STEINSALZ, Adin. 296.1'206'6
The essential Talmud / Adin Steinsaltz ; translated from Hebrew by Chaya Galai.

New York : Basic Books, c1976. vi, 296 p. ; 22 cm. Includes index. [BM503.5.S8] 75-36384 ISBN 0-465-02060-7 : 10.00
1. Talmud—Introductions. I. Title.

STEINSALZ, Adin. 296.1'2
The essential Talmud / Adin Steinsaltz : translated from the Hebrew [MS.] by Chaya Galai. London : Weidenfeld and Nicolson, 1976. vi, 296 p. ; 22 cm. Includes index. [BM503.5.S8 1976] 77-365182 ISBN 0-297-77180-9 : £6.75
1. Talmud—Introductions. I. Title.

STRACK, Hermann Leberecht, 296.12
1848-1922.
Introduction to the Talmud and Midrash. New York, Meridian Books [1959, c1931] 371 p. 20 cm. ([Jewish Publication Society series] JP8) Includes bibliography. [BM503.5.S73 1959] 59-7191
1. Talmud—Introductions. 2. Midrash.

STRACK, Hermann Leberecht, 1848-
1924.
Introduction to the Talmud and Midrash. New York, Harper & Row [1965, c1931] 364 p. 21 cm. (Harper torchbooks. Temple library, TB808L) Includes bibliography. 66-91744
1. Talmud — Introductions. 2. Midrash. I. Title.

TRATTNER, Ernest Robert, 296.1
1898-
Understanding the Talmud. New York, T. Nelson [1955] 211 p. 22 cm. [BM504.T7] 55-10608
1. Talmud—Introductions. I. Title.

TRATTNER, Ernest 296.1'206
Robert, 1898-
Understanding the Talmud / by Ernest R. Trattner. Westport, Conn. : Greenwood Press, 1978 c1955. 211 p. ; 22 cm. Reprint of the ed. published by T. Nelson, New York. Bibliography: p. 203-205. [BM503.5.T7 1978] 77-27887 ISBN 0-313-20253-2 lib.bdg. : 17.50
1. Talmud—Introductions. I. Title.

UNTERMAN, Isaac, 1889- 296.1'2
The Talmud; an analytical guide to its history and teachings. New York, Bloch Pub. Co. [1971, c1952] xv, 351 p. 21 cm. Bibliography: p. 320-328. [BM503.5.U57 1971] 73-148291 ISBN 0-8197-0189-0
1. Talmud—Introductions.

Talmud—Legends.

†NISSIM ben Jacob ben 296.1
Nissim ibn Shahin, 11thcent.
An elegant composition concerning relief after adversity / by Nissim ben Jacob ibn Shahin ; translated from the Arabic with introd. and notes by William M. Brinner. New Haven : Yale University Press, 1977. xxxiii, 196 p. ; 22 cm. (Yale Judaica series ; v. 20) Translation of Ibn Shahin's Book of comfort, known as Hibur yafe meha-yeshu'ah. Includes index. Bibliography: p. 178-182. [BM530.N4813] 78-100075 ISBN 0-300-01952-1 : 12.50
1. Talmud—Legends. I. Brinner, William M. II. Title. III. Title: Book of comfort. IV. Series.

RAISIN, Jacob Salmon, 1877- 296
Twice-told Talmud tales, by Jacob S. Raisin ... New York, Behrman's Jewish book shop, 1929. xi, 13-186 p. illus. 21 cm. [BM504.5.R3] 30-1406
I. Title. II. Title: Talmud tales.

Talmud. Minor tractates. Avot de-Rabbi Nathan—Criticism, interpretation, etc.

SALDARINI, Anthony J. 296.1'23
Scholastic rabbinism : a literary study of the Fathers according to Rabbi Nathan / by Anthony J. Saldarini. Chico, CA : Scholars Press, c1982. x, 161 p. ; 23 cm. (Brown Judaic studies ; no. 14) Bibliography: p. 155-161. [BM506.4.A943S24 1924] 19 81-13564 ISBN 0-89130-523-8 pbk. : 12.00
1. Talmud. Minor tractates. Avot de-Rabbi Nathan—Criticism, interpretation, etc. 2. Ethics, Jewish. I. Title. II. Series.

Talmud—Study—Text-books.

NEUSNER, Jacob, 1932- 296.1'206
Learn Talmud / by Jacob Neusner ; [designed by Ed Schneider ; illustrated by Jim Hellmuth]. New York : Behrman House, c1979. 166 p. : ill. ; 24 cm. Includes passages and vocabulary in English and Hebrew or Aramaic. A study of the Talmud that applies traditional values to modern life. [BM504.7.N48] 79-9415 ISBN 0-87441-292-7 pbk. : 4.95
1. Talmud—Study—Text-books. 2. [Talmud.] 3. [Jewish religious eductaion.] I. Hellmuth, Jim. II. Title.

Talmud—Theology.

BELKIN, Samuel. 296.3'8
In His image : the Jewish philosophy of man as expressed in rabbinic tradition / by Samuel Belkin. Westport, Conn. : Greenwood Press, [1979] c1960. p. cm. Reprint of the ed. published by Abelard-Schuman, London, New York, in series: Ram's horn books. Includes indexes. Bibliography: p. [BM627.B49 1979] 78-10192 ISBN 0-313-21234-1 lib. bdg. : 22.75
1. Talmud—Theology. 2. Man (Jewish theology) I. Title.

COHEN, Abraham, 1887- 296.1'2
Everyman's Talmud / by A. Cohen ; with an introd. to the new American ed. by Boaz Cohen. New York : Schocken Books, 1975. p. cm. Reprint of the 1949 ed. published by E. P. Dutton, New York. "A summary of the teachings of the Talmud on religion, ethics, folk-lore, and jurisprudence." Bibliography: p. [BM504.3.C63 1975] 75-10750 ISBN 0-8052-0497-0 pbk. : 6.95
1. Talmud—Theology. 2. Jewish law. I. Title.

MARMORSTEIN, Arthur, 1882- 296.3
1946.
Studies in Jewish theology; the Arthur Marmorstein memorial volume. Edited by J. Rabbinowitz and M. S. Lew. Freeport, N.Y., Books for Libraries Press [1972, c1950] xlvi, 228, 92 p. front. 23 cm. (Essay index reprint series) English and Hebrew. Contents.Contents.—The master, an appreciation, by the editors.—My father, a memoir, by E. Marmorstein.—Bibliography of the works of Arthur Marmorstein (p. [xxvi]-xlvi).—The background of the Haggadah.—The unity of God in rabbinic literature.—The imitation of God (Imitatio Dei) in the Haggadah.—The Holy Spirit in rabbinic legend.—The doctrine of the resurrection of the dead in rabbinic theology.—Participation in eternal life in rabbinic theology and in legend.—Judaism and Christianity in the middle of the third century.—ha-Emunah be-netsah Yisrael bi-derashot ha-Tana'im veha-Amora'im (romanized form)—Ra'ayon ha-ge'ulah be-agadat ha-Tana'im veha-Amora'im (romanized form)—Ma'amar 'al 'erkah ha-histori shel ha-agadah (romanized form) Bibliography: p. [xxvii]-xlvi. [BM177.M37 1972] 76-39174 ISBN 0-8369-2702-8
1. Talmud—Theology. 2. Aggada. I. Title.

Talmud—Theology—Addresses, essays, lectures.

UNDERSTANDING the 296.1'206'6
Talmud / selected with introductions by Alan Corre. New York : Ktav Pub. House, 1975. xii, 468 p. ; 23 cm. Includes bibliographical references. [BM496.5.U52] 78-138459 ISBN 0-87068-140-0 : 15.00 pbk. : 5.95
1. Talmud—Theology—Addresses, essays, lectures. 2. Rabbinical literature—History and criticism—Addresses, essays, lectures. I. Corre, Alan D.

Talmud Torahs—Curricula.

UNION of orthodox Jewish 296
congregations of America.
A model program for the Talmud Torah, a handbook for rabbis, principals, teachers, officers and lay members of the board of Jewish education. Prepared and published by the Union of orthodox Jewish congregations of America. New York, N.Y., [1942] x, 11-205 p. 22 cm. On cover: Edited by Rabbi Leo Jung and Joseph Kaminetsky. [BM103.U5] 43-13888
1. Talmud Torahs—Curricula. I. Jung, Leo, 1892- ed. II. Kaminetsky, Joseph, joint ed. III. Title.

Talmud Yerushalmi—Commentaries.

TALMUD Yerushalmi. 296.1'2407
The Talmud of the land of Israel : a preliminary translation and explanation / translated by Jacob Neusner. Chicago : University of Chicago Press, <1982- > v. <34 > ; 24 cm. (Chicago studies in the history of Judaism) Includes indexes. Contents.Contents. — v. 34. Horayot and Niddah Bibliography: v. 34, p. 225-231. [BM498.5.E5 1982] 19 81-13115 ISBN 0-226-57619-1 (set) : 25.00
1. Talmud Yerushalmi—Commentaries. I. Neusner, Jacob, 1932- II. Title. III. Series.

Taney, Roger Brooke, 1777-1864.

[MURRAY, Nicholas] 1802-1861. 282
Romanism at home. Letters to the Hon. Roger B. Taney ... by Kirwan [pseud.] New York, Harper & brothers, 1852. xi, [13]-272 p. 19 cm. [BX1765.M85] 35-33519
1. Taney, Roger Brooke, 1777-1864. 2. Catholic church—Doctrinal and controversial works—Protestant authors. I. Title.

Tangier, Va. Swain Memorial Methodist Church.

GEORGE, Lawrence W 287.675516
This is Tangier Island and its church [by] L. W. George. [Martinsville, Va.] Radio Fellowship [1965] 51 p. illus., port. 22 cm. 66-5536
1. Tangier, Va. Swain Memorial Methodist Church. I. Title.

Tankas (Tibetan scrolls)

LAUF, Detlef 704.948'9'4392309515
Ingo.
Secret revelation of Tibetan thangkas = Verborgene Botschaft tibetischer Thangkas : picture meditation and interpretation of Lamaist cult paintings : this work is based on the John Gilmore Ford Collection / Detlef-Ingo Lauf ; [ins Engl. ubertr. von J. A. Underwood]. Freiburg im Breisgau : Aurum-Verlag, 1976. 167 p. : numerous ill. (some col.) ; 30 cm. Parallel German text with English translation. Includes bibliographical references. [N8193.3.L356T54] 77-552535 ISBN 3-591-08025-X : DM85.00
1. Tankas (Tibetan scrolls) 2. Art, Lamaist—Tibet. 3. Buddhist art and symbolism—Tibet. I. Ford, John Gilmore, 1928- II. Title. III. Title: Verborgene Botschaft tibetischer Thangkas.

Tannaim.

GUTTMANN, Alexander. 296.1'23
Rabbinic Judaism in the making; a chapter in the history of the Halakhah from Ezra to Judah I. Detroit, Wayne State University Press, 1970. xx, 323 p. 24 cm. Bibliography: p. 298-309. [BM501.2.G85 1970] 69-10525 ISBN 0-8143-1382-5 17.95
1. Tannaim. I. Title.

MOORE, George Foot, 296'.09'015
1851-1931.
Judaism in the first centuries of the Christian era, the age of the Tannaim. New York, Schocken Books [1971, c1927-30] 2 v. 21 cm. (Schocken paperbacks on Jewish life and religion) Includes bibliographical references. [BM177.M62] 72-146791 ISBN 0-8052-0294-3 (v. 1) ISBN 0-8052-0295-1 (v. 2) 4.50 (each)
1. Tannaim. I. Title.

SANDERS, E. P. 296.3
Paul and Palestinian Judaism : a comparison of patterns of religion / E. P. Sanders. 1st American ed. Philadelphia : Fortress Press, 1977. xviii, 627 p. ; 24 cm. Includes indexes. Bibliography: p. 557-582. [BM177.S2 1977] 76-62612 ISBN 0-8006-0499-7 : 25.00
1. Dead Sea scrolls—Criticism, interpretation, etc. 2. Bible. O.T. Apocrypha—Criticism, interpretation, etc. 3. Apocryphal books (Old Testament)—Criticism, interpretation, etc. 4. Bible. N.T. Epistles of Paul—Theology. 5. Tannaim. I. Title.

Tannaim—Juvenile literature.

NEUSNER, Jacob, 1932- 296.6'1
Meet our sages / by Jacob Neusner ; [illustrated by Jim Hellmuth]. New York : Behrman House, c1980. 128 p. : ill. ; 24 cm. [BM501.2.N48] 80-12771 ISBN 0-87441-327-3 pbk. : 4.95
1. Tannaim—Juvenile literature. 2. Aggada—Juvenile literature. I. Hellmuth, Jim. II. Title.

Tanner, Annie Clark, 1864-1941.

TANNER, Annie 289.3'092'4 B
Clark, 1864-1941.
A mormon mother; an autobiography. [1st rev. ed.] [Salt Lake City] Tanner Trust Fund, University of Utah Library [1973] xxix, 346 p. 23 cm. (Utah, the Mormons, and the West) [BX8695.T27A33 1973] 73-86679 10.00
1. Tanner, Annie Clark, 1864-1941. I. Title. II. Series.

Tannyhill, Samuel Woodrow, 1929-1956.

FAGAL, William A 248.2'46'0924
Three hours to live, by William A. Fagal. Mountain View, Calif., Pacific Press Pub. Association [c1967] 63 p. 18 cm. [BV4935.T35F3] 67-29979
1. Tannyhill, Samuel Woodrow, 1929-1956. I. Title.

Tantrism.

AGEHANANDA Bharati. Swami 294
The Tantric tradition. London, Rider [New York, Hillary House, 1966. c.]1965. 350p. tables. 22cm. Bibl. [BL1495.T3A35] 66-2336 8.50
1. Tantrism. I. Title.

AGEHANANDA Bharati, 294.5'92
Swami, 1923-
The Tantric tradition / Agehananda Bharati. Westport, Conn. : Greenwood Press, 1977. 349 p. ; 23 cm. Reprint of the 1965 ed. published by Rider, London. Includes index. Bibliography: p. 303-336. [BL1245.T3A64 1977] 77-7204 ISBN 0-8371-9660-4 lib.bdg. : 19.75
1. Tantrism. 2. Tantric Buddhism. I. Title.

GUNTHER, Bernard. 294.5'514
Neo-tantra : Bhagwan Shree Rajneesh on sex, love, prayer, and transcendence / by Bernard Gunther (Swami Deva Amit Prem) ; photographed by Swami Krishna Bharti. 1st ed. New York : Harper & Row, c1980. 120 p. : ill. ; 24 cm. Based on selections from writings of A. Rajaneesh. [BL1245.T3G85 1980] 79-3591 ISBN 0-06-064140-1 : 6.95
1. Tantrism. I. Rajaneesh, Acharya, 1931- II. Krishna Bharti, Swami. III. Title.

RAJANEESH, Acharya, 1931- 294
The book of the secrets : discourses on "Vigyana Bhairava tantra" ; Bhagwan Shree Rajneesh ; compilation, Ma Yoga Astha ; editor, Ma Ananada Prem. New York : Harper & Row, 1980, c1976. 398 p. ; 18 cm. ("A Harper Colophon Book") Volume 3 of discourses on "Vigyana Bhairava Tantra" (in five volumes) [BL1245.T3R33] ISBN 0-06-090754-1 pbk. : 5.95
1. Tantrism. 2. Meditation. I. Title.
L.C. card no. for 1976 Harper & Row ed.: 75-36733

TANTRAS. 294.3282
Hevajratantrarajanama.
The Hevajra Tantra; a critical study, by D. L. Snellgrove. London, New York, Oxford University Press, 1959. 2 v. illus. 26 cm. (London oriental series, v. 6) Contents.-- v. 1. Introduction and translation. -- v. 2. Sanskrit and Tibetan texts (including commentary, the Yogaratnamaia, by Krisnacaryapada) Bibliography: v. 1, p. xiii-xv. [BL1411.T3E57] 60-282
I. Snellgrove, David L. ed. and tr. II. Krisnacaryapada. Yogaratnamaia. III. Title. IV. Series.

TANTRAS. Kularnavatantra. 294
Kularnava tantra / John Woodroffe and M. P. Pandit ; [introd. by Arthur Avalon]. [Madras : Ganesh, 1974 128 p. ; 22 cm. Label on t.p.: Distributed by Vedanta Press, Hollywood. Includes bibliographical references. [BL1135.T47A38] 75-554059 4.00
I. Woodroffe, John George, Sir, 1865-1966. II. Pandit, Madhav Pundalik, 1918- III. Title.

Tantrism—Addresses, essays, lectures.

RAJANEESH, Acharya, 1931- 294
The book of the secrets : discourses on "Vigyana Bhairava Tantra" / Bhagwan Shree Rajneesh ; compilation, Ma Yoga Astha ; editors, Ma Ananda Prem, Swami Ananda Teerth. London : Thames and Hudson, 1976- v. ; 21 cm. [BL1245.T3R33 1976] 77-356775 ISBN 0-500-27076-7 (v. 1) : £3.95 (v. 1)
1. Tantrism—Addresses, essays, lectures. 2. Meditation—Addresses, essays, lectures. I. Title.

RAJNEESH, Bhagwan Shree. 294
The book of the secret -I : discourses on "Vigyana Bhairava tantra" / Bhagwan Shree Rajneesh ; compilation, Ma Yoga Astha ; editors, Ma Ananda Prem, Swami Ananda Teerth. New York : Harper and Row, 1977. 402p. ; 21 cm. (Harper Colophon Books) [BL1245.T3R33] ISBN 0-06-090564-6 pbk. : 3.95
1. Tantrism — Addresses, essays, lectures. 2. Meditation — Addresses, essays, lectures. I. Title.
L.C. card no. for 1976 Thames and Hudson (London) ed.: 77-356775.

Tantrism, Buddhist.

CHANG, Ch'eng-chi, ed. 291.322
Teachings of Tibetan yoga. Translated and annotated by Garma C. C. Chang. New Hyde Park, N.y., University Books [1963] 128 p. 24 cm. Contents.The teaching of Mahamundra. -- The epitome of an introduction to the six yogas of Naropa. [BL1480.C513] 62-22082
1. Tantrism, Buddhist. 2. Yoga. I. Nadapada. II. Title. III. Title: Tibetan yoga.

DASGUPTA, Shashibhusan. 294.3'92
An introduction to Tantric Buddhism / Shashi Bhushan Dasgupta ; foreword by Herbert V. Guenther. Berkeley, Calif. : Shambhala, 1974. xi, 211 p. ; 22 cm. Reprint of the 1958 ed. published by Calcutta University Press, Calcutta. Includes index. Bibliography: p. [199]-204. [BQ8915.4.D37 1974] 74-75094 ISBN 0-87773-052-0 pbk. : 3.95
1. Tantric Buddhism. I. Title.

GUENTHER, Herbert V. 294.5'92
The Tantric view of life, by Herbert V. Guenther. Berkeley [Calif.] Shambala, 1972. x, 168 p. illus. 26 cm. (The Clear light series) Bibliography: p. 158-159. [BQ8918.3.G8 1972] 78-146511 ISBN 0-87773-028-8 8.50
1. Tantrism, Buddhist. I. Title.

WAYMAN, Alex. 294.3'8
The Buddhist Tantras; light on Indo-Tibetan esotericism. New York, S. Weiser, 1973. xiii, 247 p. illus. 24 cm. Includes bibliographical references. [BQ8915.4.W39] 73-79801 ISBN 0-87728-223-4 12.50
1. Tantric Buddhism. I. Title.

Tantrism, Buddhist-Essence, genius, nature.

GUENTHER, Herbert V. 294.392
Treasures on the Tebetan middle way / Herbert V. Guenther 2nd edition. Berkeley : Shambhala [1976] x, 156p. ; 21 cm. (Clear light) Includes bibliographical references and index. [BL1495.T3G78] 75-40260 ISBN 0-87773-002-4 pbk. : 4.50
1. Tantrism, Buddhist-Essence, genius, nature. I. Title.

Tantrism, Buddhist Rituals.

TANTRAS. 294.3'8
Candamaharosanatantra. English & Sanskrit.
The Candamaharosana Tantra, chapters I-VIII. A critical edition and English translation [by] Christopher S. George. New Haven, Conn., American Oriental Society, 1974. x, 135 p. 26 cm. (American Oriental series, 56) Introductory matter in English. Includes the Tibetan text of the Candamaharosanatantra. Bibliography: p. 126-129. [BQ3340.C352E53] 74-182286 14.50
1. Candamaharosana—Cult. 2. Tantric Buddhism—Rituals. I. George, Christopher S., ed. II. Tantras. Candamaharosanatantra. Tibetan. 1974. III. Title. IV. Series.

Tantrism, Buddhist—Tibet.

BLOFELD, John Eaton 294.3'4'42
Calthorpe, 1913-
The Tantric mysticism of Tibet; a practical guide, by John Blofeld. [1st ed.] New York, Dutton, 1970. 257 p. illus. 22 cm. Bibliography: p. 253. [BL1433.3.T3B55 1970b] 76-119478 ISBN 0-525-21423-2 6.95
1. Tantric Buddhism—Tibet. I. Title.

WENTZ, Walter Yeeling 294.3'92
Evans.
The Tibetan book of the great liberation; or, The method of realizing Nirvana through knowing the mind; preceded by an epitome of Padma-Sambhava's biography [by Yeshey Tshogyal] and followed by Guru Phadampa Sangay's teachings, according to English renderings by Sardar Bahadur S. W. Laden La and by the Lamas Karma Sumdhon Paul, Lobzang Mingyur Dorje, and Kazi Dawa-Samdup; introductions, annotations and editing by W. Y. Evans-Wentz, with psychological commentary by C. G. Jung. London, New York [etc.] Oxford U.P., 1968. lxiv, 261 p. 10 plates, illus., ports. 21 cm. [BL1495.T3W4 1968] 71-464839 ISBN 0-19-680696-8 19/6
1. Tantrism, Buddhist—Tibet. 2. Nirvana. 3. Yoga (Buddhist tantrism) I. Padma Sambhava, ca.717-ca.762. II. Ye-ses-mtsho-rgyal, 8th cent. III. Phadampa Sangay, fl. 1100. IV. Jung, Carl Gustav, 1875-1961. V. Title.

Tantrism—Pictorial works.

MOOKERJEE, Ajitcoomar. 294.5'5
Tantra asana; a way to self-realization [by] Ajit Mookerjee. New York, George Wittenborn, Inc. [1971] 161 p. illus. (part col.) 32 cm. Bibliography: p. [141]-174. [BL1245.T3M6] 79-153698
1. Tantrism—Pictorial works. I. Title.

Taoism.

BLOFELD, John Eaton 299'.514
Calthorpe, 1913-
The secret and sublime: Taoist mysteries and magic, by John Blofeld. London, Allen & Unwin, 1973. 3-217 p. illus. 23 cm. Bibliography: p. 9. [BL1920.B56] 73-163668 ISBN 0-04-181019-8
1. Taoism. I. Title.
Distributed by Verry, 12.50.

BLOFELD, John Eaton 299'.514
Calthorpe, 1913-
Taoism : the road to immortality / John Blofeld. Boulder, Colo. : Shambhala, 1978. ix, 195 p., [2] leaves of plates : ill. ; 22 cm. [BL1920.B57] 77-90882 ISBN 0-87773-116-0 : 4.95
1. Taoism. I. Title.

CHANG, Chung-yuan, 1907- 299.514
Creativity and Taoism; a study of Chinese philosophy, art, & poetry. New York, Julian [c.1963] 241p. illus. 25cm. Bibl. 62-21446 6.50
1. Taoism. 2. Creation (Literary, artistic, etc.) 3. China—Intellectual life. I. Title.

HALL, Manley Palmer, 1901-
The white bird of Tao. A seminar of three classes given at Los Angeles in the summer of 1962. Los Angeles, Philosophical Research Society [c1964] 51 p. illus. Reproduced from type-written copy. 68-90821
1. Taoism. 2. Lao-tzu. I. Title.

HUANG, Al Chung-liang. 299'.514
Living Tao : still visions and dancing brushes / by Al Chung-liang Huang and Si Chi Ko. Millbrae, Calif. : Celestial Arts, 1976. p. cm. [BL1920.H84] 76-11338 ISBN 0-89087-127-2 pbk. : 5.95
1. Taoism. I. Ko, Si Chi. II. Title.

KALTENMARK, Max. 299'.514'2
Lao Tzu and Taoism. Translated from the French by Roger Greaves. Stanford, Calif., Stanford University Press, 1969. vi, 158 p. 23 cm. Bibliography: p. [151]-152. [BL1930.K313] 69-13179 5.95
1. Lao-tzu. 2. Taoism. I. Title.

KENNEY, Edward Herbert, 299.514
1891-
A Taoist notebook, by Edward Herbert [pseud.] New York, Grove Press [1960] 80 p. 18 cm. (The Wisdom of the East series, WP-2) Includes bibliography. [BL1920.K4 1960] 60-13788
1. Taoism. I. Title.

LAO-TZU. 299.5
The wisdom of Laotse, tr., ed. and with an introd. and notes by Lin Yutang. New York, Modern Library [1948] xx, 326 p. 19 cm. (The Modern library of the world's best books [262]) Contains the "Book of Tao," each chapter of which is followed by a comparable passage from Chuangtse's writings; supplemented by "Prolegomea" and "Imaginary conversations between Laotso and Confucius" by Chuangtse. [BL1900.L3L5] 49-341
I. Lin, Yu-t'ang, 1895- ed. and tr. II. Chuang-Tro III. Title.

LAO-TZU. 299.5
The wisdom of Laotse, tr., ed. and with an introd. and notes by Lin Yutang. New York, Modern Library [1948] xx, 326 p. 19 cm. (The Modern library of the world's best books [262]) Contains the "Book of Tao," each chapter of which is followed by a comparable passage from Chuangtse's writings; supplemented by "Prolegomea" and "Imaginary conversations between Laotso and Confucius" by Chuangtse. [BL1900.L3L5] 49-341
I. Lin, Yu-t'ang, 1895- ed. and tr. II. Chuang-Tro III. Title.

LAO-TZU. 299'.5148'2
The wisdom of Laotse / translated, edited, and with an introd. and notes by Lin Yutang. Westport, Conn. : Greenwood Press, [1979] c1948. Translation of Tao te ching. Reprint of the ed. published by Random House, New York in series: The Modern library of the world's best books. Contains the "Book of Tao," each chapter of which is followed by a comparable passage from Chuangtse's writings; supplemented by "Prolegomena" and "Imaginary conversations between Laotse and Confucius" by Chuangtse. [BL1900.L26E5 1979] 78-12160 ISBN 0-313-21164-7 lib. bdg. : 20.50
I. Lin, Yutang, 1895-1976. II. Chuang-tzu. III. Title.

LAO-TZU. 299'.5148'2
The wisdom of Laotse / translated, edited, and with an introd. and notes by Lin Yutang. Westport, Conn. : Greenwood Press, [1979] c1948. Translation of Tao te ching. Reprint of the ed. published by Random House, New York in series: The Modern library of the world's best books. Contains the "Book of Tao," each chapter of which is followed by a comparable passage from Chuangtse's writings; supplemented by "Prolegomena" and "Imaginary conversations between Laotse and Confucius" by Chuangtse. [BL1900.L26E5 1979] 78-12160 ISBN 0-313-21164-7 lib. bdg. : 20.50
I. Lin, Yutang, 1895-1976. II. Chuang-tzu. III. Title.

LAO-TZU. 299.5
Laotzu's Tao and wu-wei. 2d ed. rev. and enl. A new translation by Bhiksu Wai-tao and Dwight Goddard. Interpretive essays by Henry Borel. Outline of Taoist philosophy and religion, by Dr. Kiang Kang-flu. Santa Barbara, Calif., D. Goddard, 1935. 2 p. l., 7-149 p. 19 cm. Contents.--Laotzu's Tao-teh-king; a new translation from the Chinese by Wai-tao and Dwight Goddard.--Essays interpreting Taoism, by Henry Borel; translated by M. E. Reynolds.--Historical essays, by Dr. Kiang-hu. [BL1900.L3G6 1935] 36-9710
1. Taoism. I. Hui-tao, tr. II. Goddard, Dwight, 1861-1839, joint tr. III. Borel, Henri, 1869-1933. IV. Reynolds, Mabel Edith (Galsworthy) Mrs. 1871- tr. V. Kiang, K'ang-hu, 1883- VI. Title. VII. Title: Tao and wu-wei. VIII. Title: Wu-wei.

LAO-TZU. 299.5
Laotzu's Tao and wu-wei. 2d ed., rev. and enl. A new translation by Bhikshu Wai-tao and Dwight Goddard. Interpretive essays by Henri Borel. Outline of Taoist philosophy and religion by Dr. Kiang Kang-hu. Thetford, Vt., D. Goddard, 1939. 139 p. 19 cm. Contents.--Laotzu's Tao-teh-king; a new translation from the Chinese by Wai-tao and Dwight Goddard.--Essays interpreting Taoism, by Henri Borel; translated by M. E. Reynolds.--Historical essays, by Dr. Kiang Kang-hu. [BL1900.L3G6 1939] 39-11744
1. Taoism. I. Hui-tao, tr. II. Goddard, Dwight, 1861- joint tr. III. Borel, Henri, 1869-1933. IV. Reynolds, Mabel Edith (Galsworthy) Mrs. 1871- tr. V. Kiang, K'ang-hu, 1883- VI. Title. VII. Title: Tao and wu-wei. VIII. Title: Wu-wei.

LIU, Da. 299'.514
The Tao and Chinese culture / Da Liu. New York : Schocken Books, [1979] p. cm. Includes index. Bibliography: p. [BL1920.L56] 78-26767 ISBN 0-8052-3714-3 : 14.50
1. Taoism. I. Title.

[LU, Yen] b.798. 299'.514
The secret of the golden flower : a Chinese book of life / translated and explained by Richard Wilhelm ; commentary by C. G. Jung ; [translated into English by Cary F. Baynes]. New York : Causeway Books, [1975] xix, 151 p., 10 leaves of plates : ill. ; 24 cm. Translation of T'ai i chin hua tsung chih. Reprint of the 1931 ed. published by K. Paul, Trench, Trubner, London; with new introd. [BL1900.L83B3 1975] 74-98765 ISBN 0-88356-036-4 : 7.95
1. Taoism. 2. China—Religion. I. Wilhelm, Richard, 1873-1930. II. Jung, Carl Gustav, 1875-1961. III. Title.

MCNAUGHTON, William, 299'.514
1933- comp.
The Taoist vision. [Ann Arbor] University of Michigan Press [1971] 90 p. illus. 22 cm. (Ann Arbor paperbacks) [BL1920.M3] 70-143183 ISBN 0-472-09174-3 4.95
1. Taoism. I. Title.

POLITELLA, Joseph, 1910- 299'.5
Taoism and Confucianism. Iowa City, Iowa, Sernoll [1967] 161 p. 22 cm. (Crucible books) "Annotated bibliography": p. 152-153. [BL1920.P57] 67-5683
1. Taoism. 2. Confucianism. I. Title.

QUENTIN, A. P. 922.
A Taoist pearl, by A. P. Quentin. London, Society for promoting Christian knowledge; New York [etc.] The Macmillan co. [1928] xv, [1] 143, [1] p. front., illus. 19 cm. Half-title: A Taoist pearl; the life story of a Chinese convert. [BV3427.H7Q8] 29-14372
1. Haiao Chih Shan. 2. Taoism. I. Title.

SASO, Michael R. 299'.514'38
Taoism and the rite of cosmic renewal [by] Michael R. Saso. [Pullman] Washington State University Press [1972] 120 p. illus. 23 cm. Bibliography: p. 115-120. [BL1920.S27] 72-189459 4.00
1. Taoism. I. Title.

SASO, Michael R. 299'.514'0924 B
The teachings of Taoist Master Chuang / Michael Saso. New Haven : Yale University Press, 1978. xiii, 317 p. : ill. ; 22 cm. Includes index. Bibliography: p. 297-301. [BL1940.C47S27] 76-58919 ISBN 0-300-02080-5 : 17.50
1. Chuang, Ch'en Teng-yun, 1911-1976. 2. Taoism. I. Title.

SIU, Ralph Gun Hoy, 181'.09'514
1917-
Ch'i: a neo-Taoist approach to life [by] R. G. H. Siu. Cambridge, Mass., MIT Press [1974] 351 p. illus. 21 cm. Includes bibliographical references. [BL1923.S58] 74-1139 ISBN 0-262-19123-7 10.00
1. Taoism. I. Title.

T'AI shang kan ying p'ien. English & Chinese. 299'.514
Treatise on response & retribution [by] Lao Tze. Translated from the Chinese by D. T. Suzuki & Paul Carus. Containing introd., Chinese text, verbatim translation, translation, explanatory notes and moral tales. Edited by Paul Carus. With sixteen plates by Chinese artists and a front. by Keichyu Yamada. [3d pbk. ed.] LaSalle, Ill., Open Court Pub. Co., 1973 [c1906] 139 p. illus. 21 cm. (Open Court paperbacks) At head of title in characters: T'ai shang kan ying p'ien. [BL1900.T3S8 1973] 74-155276 ISBN 0-87548-244-9 1.95 (pbk.).
1. Taoism. I. Lao-tzu. II. Suzuki, Daisetz Teitaro, 1870-1966, tr. III. Carus, Paul, 1852-1919, ed. IV. Title.

T'AI I CHIN HUA TSUNG CHIH. 299.51
The secret of the golden flower, a Chinese book of life. Translated and explained by Richard Wilhelm, with a European commentary by C. G. Jung. [Translated into English by Cary F. Baynes] New York, Wehman Bros. [1955] ix, 151p. illus., plates. 23cm. [BL1900.T25B3 1955] 55-12925
1. Taoism. 2. China— Religion. I. Wilhelm, Richard, 1873-1960, ed. and tr. II. Jung, Carl Gustav, 1875- III. Title.

T'AI I CHIN HUA TSUNG CHIH. 1962 299.51
The secret of the golden flower, a Chinese book of life Translated and explained by Richard Wilhelm, with a foreword and commentary by C. G. Jung. And a part of the Chinese meditation text The book of consciousness and life, with a foreword by Salome Wilhelm. [Translated from the German by Cary F. Baynes. New, rev. and augm. ed.] New York, Harcourt, Brace & World [1962] xvi, 149 p. illus. 22 cm. [BL1900.T25B3] 62-10499
1. Taoism. 2. China — Religion. I. Wilhelm, Richard, 1873-1930, ed. and tr. II. Jung, Carl Gustav, 1875-1961. III. Liu, Huayang, fi 1794. IV. Title. V. Title: The book of consciousness and life.

T'AI-SHANG KAN-YING P'LEN. 299.
... *T'ai-shang kan-ying p'ien;* treatise of the Exalted one on response and retribution; translated from the Chinese by Teitaro Suzuki and Dr. Paul Carus; containing introduction, Chinese text, verbatim translation, translation, explanatory notes and moral tales, edited by Dr. Paul Carus. With sixteen plates by Chinese artists and a frontispiece by Keichyu Yamada. Chicago, Ill., The Open court publishing co.; London, K. Paul, Trench, Trubner & co., ltd., 1906. 3 p. l., [3]-139. p. front., illus., plates. 21 cm. [BL900.T3S8] 6-28775
1. Taoism. I. Suzuki, Dr isiz Teitaro, 1870- tr. II. Carus, Paul, 1852-1919, ed. and tr. III. Title.

UNDERWOOD, Horace Grant, 1859-1916. 294
The religions of eastern Asia, by Horace Grant Underwood, D.D. New York, The Macmillan company, 1910. ix, 267 p. 20 1/2 cm. "Authorities cited": p. ix. [BL1055.U6] 10-3300
1. Taoism. 2. Shinto. 3. Shamanism. 4. Confucius and Confucianism. 5. Buddha and Buddhism. 6. Christianity and other religions. I. Title.

WATTS, Alan Wilson, 1915-1973. 299'.514
Tao : the watercourse way / by Alan Watts, with the collaboration of Al Chung-liang Huang ; additional calligraphy by Lee Chih-chang. 1st ed. New York : Pantheon Books, [1975] xxvi, 134 p. : ill. ; 24 cm. Bibliography: p. 129-134. [BL1920.W37 1975] 74-4762 ISBN 0-394-48901-2 : 6.95
1. Taoism. 2. Chinese language—Writing. I. Huang, Al Chung-liang. II. Title.

*WIEGER, Leo. 181.'09'514
Taoism : the philosphy of China / by Leo Wieger ; edited by Charles Lucas ; graphic design by David Paul Kaplan. Burbank, Calif. : O'hara Publications, 1976. 192p. : ill. ; 23 cm. (Literary links to the Orient) [BL1920] 76-4285 pbk. : 4.95
1. Taoism. I. Lucas, Charles, ed. II. Title.

Taoism—China—Addresses, essays, lectures.

CREEL, Herrlee Glessner, 1905- 320.5'0951
What is Taoism? And other studies in Chinese cultural history [by] Herrlee G. Creel. Chicago, University of Chicago Press [1970] vii, 192 p. 24 cm. Contents.—What is Taoism?—The great clod.—On two aspects in early Taoism.—On the origin of Wu-wei.—The meaning of Hsing-ming.—The Fa-chia: "Legalists" or "Administrators"?—The beginnings of bureaucracy in China: the origin of the Hsien.—The role of the horse in Chinese history. Includes bibliographical references. [BL1925.C7 1970] 77-102905 ISBN 0-226-12041-4
1. Taoism—China—Addresses, essays, lectures. 2. China—Politics and government—Addresses, essays, lectures. I. Title.

Taoism—Collected works.

HUGHES, Catharine, 1935- comp. 181'.09'514
Shadow and substance: Taoist mystical reflections, edited and with photos. by Catharine Hughes. New York, Seabury Press [1974] [125] p. illus. 21 cm. "A Crossroad book." [BL1900.A1H8] 74-12189 ISBN 0-8164-2104-8 2.95
1. Taoism—Collected works. I. Title.

Taoism—Congresses.

INTERNATIONAL Conference on Taoist Studies, 2d, Chino, Japan, 1972. 299'.514
Facets of Taoism : essays in Chinese religion / edited by Holmes Welch, Anna Seidel. New Haven : Yale University Press, 1979. 301 p. ; 24 cm. Includes bibliographical references and index. [BL1899.5.I57 1972] 77-28034 ISBN 0-300-01695-6 : 22.50
1. Taoism—Congresses. 2. China—Religion—Congresses. I. Welch, Holmes. II. Seidel, Anna K. III. Title.

Taoism—Sacred books.

LAO-TZU. 299.514
The book of Tao. Translation by Frank J. MacHovec. Mount Vernon, N. Y., Peter Pauper Press [1962] 61p. illus. 19cm. [BL1900.L3M3] 62-4768
I. MacHovec, Frank J., tr. II. Title.

THE Sacred books of China: The texts of Taoism. Translated by James Legge. New York, Dover Publications [1962] 2 v. 22 cm. (The sacred books of the East, v. 39—40) "An unabridged and unaltered republication of the work first published ... in 1891." Contents.Contents.—pt. 1. The Tao te ching of Lao Tzu. The writings of Chuang Tzu (books I-XVII)—pt. 2. The writings of Chuang Tzu (books XVIII-XXXIII) The T'ai Shang Tractate of Actions and their retributions. Appendices I-VIII. [BL1900.A1S3 1962] 62-53181 299.51482
1. Taoism—Sacred books. I. Chuang-tzu. Writings. Works. English. 1962. II. Legge, James, 1815-1897, tr. III. Lao-tzu. Tao te ching. English. 1962. IV. Thai-Shang Tractate of Actions and their Retribution. T'ai shang kan ying p'ien. English. 1962. V. Title: The texts of Taoism. VI. Series: The sacred books of the East (New York) v. 39-40.

THE sacred books of China: The texts of Taoism, translated by James Legge ... Oxford, The Clarendon press, 1891. 2 v. 23 cm. (Added t.-p.: The sacred book of the East ... vol. XXXIX-XL) Contents.I. The Tao teh king. The writings of Kwang-tsze, books I-XVII.--II. The writings of Kwang-tsze, books XVII-XXXIII. The Thai-shang, tractate of actions and their retributions. Appendixes I-VIII. [BL1010.S3 vol. 39-40] 33-9264 299.5
1. Taoism—Sacred books. I. Lao-tze. Tao te ching. II. Chuang-tzfi. III. Tai-shang yan-ying p'len. IV. Legge, James, 1815-1897, tr.

SACRED books of China (The): The texts of Taoi'sm; 2 pts. Tr. by James Legge [Gloucester, Mass., P. Smith, 1964] 2 v. (396; 336 p.) 22 cm. (Sacred books of the east, v. 39-40) Unabridged unaltered re-pubn. of the work first pub. in 1891 by Oxford. Contents.Contents—pt. 1. the Tao te chingof Lao Tzu. The writings of Chuang Tzu (books i-xviii)—pt. 2. the writings of Chuang Tzu (books xviii-xxxiii) the T'ai shang tractate of actions and their retributions. Appendices i-viii. set, 8.00 299.51482
1. Taoism—Sacred books. I. Lao-tzu. Tao te ching. II. Chuang-tzu. III. Trai shang kan ying p'ien. IV. Legge, James, 1815-1897, tr. V. Title: The texts of Taoism. VI. Series: The sacred books of the East (New York) v. 39-40

TAOIST texts : ethical, political, and speculative / [compiled and translated] by Frederic Henry Balfour. New York : Gordon Press, 1975. vi, 118 p. : ill. ; 24 cm. First published in 1884. Contents.Contents.—The Tao Te ching.—The Yin fu ching.—The T'ai hsi ching.—The Hsin yin ching.—The Ta t'ung ching.—The Ch'in wen tung.—The Ch'ing ching ching.—Huai-nan tzu. A chapter from the Hung lieh chuan.—The Su shu.—The Kan ying pien. Includes bibliographical references. [BL1900.A1T28 1975] 75-3878 ISBN 0-87968-191-8 299'.5148'2
1. Taoism—Sacred books. I. Balfour, Frederic Henry.

Taoists—Hawaii—Biography.

LAI, Bessie C. 299'.514'0924 B
Ah Ya, I still remember / by Bessie C. Lai. Taipei : Meadea Enterprise Co., c1976. 173 p. ; 20 cm. Added title in Chinese romanized: Chi nien fu ch'in Huang Shih-hsi. [BL1940.W66L34] 77-358819
1. Wong, Sai Hee, 1857-1927. 2. Taoists—Hawaii—Biography. I. Title.

Tapia, Gonzalo de, 1561?-1594.

SHIELS, William Eugene. 922.272
... *Gonzalo de Tapia (1561-1594)* founder of the first permanent Jesuit mission in North America [by] W. Eugene Shiels ... New York, The United States Catholic historical society, 1934. ix, 198 p. maps. 23 cm. (United States Catholic historical society. Monograph series, XIV) Half-title: Historical records and studies. Bibliography: p. 180-195. [F1230.T26] [E184.C3U6 vol. 14] (973.062) 34-8045
1. Tapia, Gonzalo de, 1561?-1594. 2. Jesuits in Mexico. I. Title.

SHIELS, William Eugene, 1897- 266'.272'1 B
Gonzalo de Tapia (1561-1594) : founder of the first permanent Jesuit mission in North America / W. Eugene Shiels. Westport, Conn. : Greenwood Press, 1978. ix, 198 p. : maps ; 22 cm. Reprint of the 1934 ed. published by the United States Catholic Historical Society, New York, which was issued as 14 of the Society's Monograph series. Includes index. Bibliography: p. 180-195. [F1219.3.M59T367 1978] 74-12835 ISBN 0-8371-7758-8 lib.bdg. : 15.50
1. Tapia, Gonzalo de, 1561?-1594. 2. Indians of Mexico—Missions. 3. Jesuits—Mexico—Biography. 4. Jesuits—Missions. I. Title. II. Series: United States Catholic Historical Society. Monograph series ; 14.

Tappan, Arthur, 1786-1865.

WINTER, Rebecca J. 248'.5'0922 B
The night cometh : two wealthy evangelicals face the nation / Rebecca J. Winter. South Pasadena, Calif. : William Carey Library, c1977. xii, 84 p. ; 22 cm. Includes index. Bibliography: p. 78-80. [BR1643.A1W56] 77-87594 ISBN 0-87808-429-0 pbk. : 2.95
1. Tappan, Arthur, 1786-1865. 2. Tappan, Lewis, 1788-1873. 3. Evangelicalism—United States—Biography. 4. Philanthropists—United States—Biography. I. Title.

Tappan, David, 1752-1803

[SPRING, Samuel] 1746-1819. 233
A friendly dialogue, in three parts, between Philalethes & Toletus, upon the nature of duty ... Newbury-port: Printed and sold by John Mycall, 1784. 160, 32 p. 17 cm. "Toletus represents the Reverend David Tappan ... Philalethes ... the Reverend Samuel Spring."--p. [4] "A private conference between Philalethes & Amartolos": 32 p. at end. [BT700.S7] 40-36597
1. Tappan, David, 1752-1803 2. Man (Theology)—Early works in 1800. I. Title.

Tappan, David, 1752-1803. Two friendly letters from Toletus to Philalethes.

SPRING, Samuel, 1746-1819. 233
Moral disquisitions: and strictures on the Rev. David Tappan's Letters to Philalethes. By Samuel Spring, A.M., pastor of the North church in Newburyport ... Newburyport, Printed and sold by John Mycall, M,DCC,LXXXIX. 252 p. 16 cm. Tappan's Letters are in answer to Spring's "A friendly dialogue ... upon the nature of duty". "Structures on Mr. D.'s reply" (i.e. J. Dana's reply to Spring's Dialogue, appended to Tappan's Letters): p. 236-244. [BT700.S7T35 1789] 40-36599
1. Tappan, David, 1752-1808. Two friendly letters from Toletus to Philalethes. 2. Dana, Joseph, 1742-1827. 3. Man (Theology)—Early works to 1800. I. Title.

SPRING, Samuel, 1746-1819. 233
Moral disquisitions: and strictures on the Rev. David Tappan's Letters to Philalethes. By Samuel Spring, A.M., pastor of the North churh in Newburyport ... 2d ed. Exeter [Mass.]: Printed by Charles Norris & co. ... 1815. 247 p. 16 1/2 cm. Tappan's Letters are in answer to Spring's "A friendly dialogue ... upon the nature of duty". "Structures on Mr. D.'s reply" (i.e. J. Dana's reply to Spring's Dialogue, appended to Tappan's Letters): p. 220-228. [BT700.S7T35 1815] 40-36600
1. Tappan, David, 1752-1803. Two friendly letters from Toletus to Philalethes. 2. Dana, Joseph, 1742-1827. 3. Man [Theology)—Early works to 1800. I. Title.

Tappan, David Stanton.

TAPPAN, Luella Rice.
David Stanton Tappan, Grandfather's China story, 1906-1950, as told by Grandmother Luella Rice Tappan. [Duarte, Calif., Westminster Gardens] 1966. vi, 62 p. illus. 22 cm. 68-65107
1. Tappan, David Stanton. 2. Missions—Hainan. 3. Presbyterian Church—Missions. I. Title. II. Title: Title: Grandfather's China story, 1906-1950.

Tappan family.

TAPPAN, Sarah (Homes) Mrs., 1748-1826. 920.7
Memoir of Mrs. Sarah Tappan: taken in part from the Home missionary magazine, of November, 1828, and printed for distribution among her descendants ... New-York, West & Trow, printers, 1834. 150 p. front. (port.) 19 1/2 cm. "Family record": p. 119-150. Preface signed: L. T. [i.e. Lewis Tappan] [BR1725.T25A4] 10-12537
1. Tappan family. I. Tappan, Lewis, 1788-1873, ed. II. Title.

Tappan, N. Y. Reformed church.

COLE, David, 1822-1903. 289
History of the Reformed church of Tappan, N. Y. Prepared for its two hundredth anniversary by Rev. David Cole ... New York, Press of Stettiner, Lambert & co., 1894. iv, [2], 168 p. front., illus., plates, ports., plan, facsims. 26 1/2 cm. [B X9531.T3C6] 20-8494
1. Tappan, N. Y. Reformed church. I. Title.

TAPPAN, N.Y. Reformed church. 285.7747
Two hundred and fifty years of service, 1694-1944 ... Tappan, N.Y., Tappan Reformed church [1944] 2 p. l., 57, [1] p., 1 l. illus. (incl. ports.) 26 cm. "Four hundred copies ... Number 18." [BX9531.T3A5] 45-18215
I. Title.

Tara (goddess)—Cult—Tibet.

BEYER, Stephan. 294.3'4'38
The cult of Tara; magic and ritual in Tibet. Berkeley, University of California Press [1974, c1973] xxi, 542 p. 25 cm. (Hermeneutics: studies in the history of religions, 1) Bibliography: p. 503-519. [BQ4710.T34T53] 74-186109 ISBN 0-520-02192-4 20.00
1. Tara (goddess)—Cult—Tibet. 2. Buddha and Buddhism—Rituals. I. Title. II. Series.

BEYER, Stephan. 294.3'4'38
The cult of Tara : magic and ritual in Tibet / by Stephen Beyer. Berkeley : University of California Press, 1978, c1974. xxi, 542p. : ill. ; 23 cm. Includes index. Bibiliography: p. 503-519. [BQ4710.T34T53] ISBN 0-520-03635-2 pbk. : 7.95
1. Tara (goddess) — Cult — Tibet. 2. Buddha and Buddhism — Rituals. I. Title.
L.C. card no. for 1974 hardcover ed.: 74-186109.

Tarasco Indians.

CARRASCO Pizana, Pedro 1921- 972
Tarascan folk religion an analysis of economic, social, and religious interactions. [Robert Wauchope, editor] New Crleans, 1952. 63p. 27cm. Cover title. 'Preprinted from Publication 17, pages 1-64, Middle American Institute, the Tulane University of Louisiana.' Bibliography: p.60-61. [F1221.T3C3] 299.7 970.62 53-9433
1. Tarasco Indians. I. Title.

TARASCAN folk religion,
an analysis of economic, social, and religious interactions. [Robert Wauchope, editor] New Orleans, 1957. 63p. (Synoptic studies of Mexican culture, p. 1-63) Issued as Publication 17, pages 1-64 of Tulane University of Louisiana. Middle American Research Institute. Bibliography: p. 60-61.
1. Tarasco Indians. I. Carrasco Pizana, Pedro, 1921-

Targum Johnathan.

CHURGIN, Pinkhos, 1894- 28-9075
Targum Jonathan to the Prophets, by Pinkhos Churgin. New Haven, Yale university press, 1907 [i.e. 1927] 152 p. 25cm. (Yale oriental series--Researches xiv) Thesis (PH. D.)--Yale university, 1922. Thesis note on label mounted on half-title.
1. Targum Johnathan. I. Title.

Tarot.

BUESS, Lynn M. 133.3'2424
The tarot and transformation, by Lynn M. Buess. Tarot illus. [by] Roxana R. Donegan. Lakemont, Ga., Tarnhelm Press [1973] 256 p. illus. 21 cm. [BF1879.T2B83] 73-77608 ISBN 0-87707-123-3 2.95
1. Tarot. I. Title.

BUTLER, Bill. 133.3'2424
Dictionary of the tarot / Bill Butler. New York : Schocken Books, 1975. 253, [1] p. : ill. ; 21 cm. Bibliography: p. 253-[254] [BF1879.T2B87] 74-9230 7.95
1. Tarot. I. Title.

CAMPBELL, Joseph, 1904- 133.3'2424
Tarot revelations / Joseph Campbell, Richard Roberts ; introduction by Colin Wilson. [San Francisco : Alchemy Books, 1980, c1979. ix, 294 p. : ill. ; 21 cm. Cover title. Includes bibliographical references. [BF1879.T2C28] 19 80-50329 pbk. : 5.95
1. Tarot. I. Roberts, Richard. II. Title.

CASE, Paul F. 133.
An introduction to the study of the tarot, by Paul F. Case ... New York, Azoth publishing company, 1920. 4 p. l., 5-59 p. diagr. 25 cm. [BF1879.T2C3] 20-12202
1. Tarot. I. Title.

CASE, Paul Foster, 1884- 133.324
The tarot, a key to the wisdom of the ages. New York, Macoy Pub. Co., 1947. 214 p. illus. 24 cm. [BF1879.T2C32] 48-12895
1. Tarot. I. Title.

CASE, Paul Foster, 1884-1954. 133.3'2424
The oracle of Tarot in Qabalah; authorized religious practices and teachings of B.O.T.A., based upon the Holy Qabalah and Tarot. Completely rev. and enl. ed. Los Angeles, Builders of the Adytum, 1969. 1 v. (various pagings) illus. 29 cm. [BF1879.T2C316 1969] 77-268701
1. Tarot. 2. Cabala. I. Builders of the Adytum. II. Title.

CAVENDISH, Richard. 133.3'2424
The Tarot / Richard Cavendish. 1st U.S. ed. New York : Harper & Row, 1975. 191 p. : ill. (some col.) ; 29 cm. Includes index. Bibliography: p. 186. [BF1879.T2C36 1975] 75-848 ISBN 0-06-010688-3 : 19.95
1. Tarot. I. Title.

CONNOLLY, Eileen. 133.3'2424
Tarot : a new handbook for the apprentice / Eileen Connolly. 1st ed. North Hollywood, Calif. : Newcastle Pub. Co., 1979. x, 244 p. : ill. ; 26 cm. [BF1879.T2C58] 79-15303 ISBN 0-87877-345-2 : 14.95. ISBN 0-87877-045-3 pbk. : 7.95
1. Tarot. I. Title.

CONNOLLY, Eileen. 133.3'2424
Tarot, a new handbook for the apprentice / Eileen Connolly. San Bernardino, Calif. : Borgo Press, 1980 [1979] p. cm. Reprint of the 1st ed. published by Newcastle Pub. Co., North Hollywood, Calif. Includes index. [BF1879.T2C58 1980] 19 80-22271 ISBN 0-89370-645-0 : 15.95
1. Tarot. I. Title.

CONSTANT, Alphonse Louis, 1810-1875. 135.4
The magical ritual of the sanctum regnum interpreted by the Tarot trumps. Translated from the MSS. of Eliphaz Levi and edited by W. Wynn Westcott. New York, S. Weiser [1971, c1970] x, 108 p. 8 col. plates. 19 cm. First published in 1896. [BF1879.T2C6 1971] 79-27709 ISBN 0-87728-034-7 7.50
1. Tarot. I. Westcott, William Wynn, 1848-1925, ed. II. Title.

CROWLEY, Aleister, 1875-1947. 133.3'2424
The book of Thoth; a short essay on the Tarot of the Egyptians, being the Equinox, volume III, no. 5, by the Master Therion. Artist executant: Frieda Harris. New York, S. Weiser, 1969. xii, 287 p. illus. (part col.) 24 cm. Reprint of the 1944 ed. [BF1879.T2C7 1969] 79-16399 12.95
1. Tarot. I. Harris, Frieda, illus. II. Title.

D'AGOSTINO, Joseph D. 133.3'2424
Tarot : the royal path to wisdom / by Joseph D. D'Agostino. 1st ed. New York : S. Weiser, 1976. 132 p. : ill. ; 18 cm. Errata slip inserted. [BF1879.T2D3] 76-15549 ISBN 0-87728-329-X : 2.95
1. Tarot. I. Title.

D'AGOSTINO, Joseph D. 133.3'2424
Tarot : the royal path to wisdom / by Joseph D. D'Agostino. 1st ed. New York : S. Weiser, 1976. 132 p. : ill. ; 18 cm. Errata slip inserted. [BF1879.T2D3] 76-15549 ISBN 0-87728-329-X : 2.95
1. Tarot. I. Title.

DEQUER, John H. 133
Arrows of light from the Egyptian tarot; a practical application of the Hermetic system of names and numbers, based upon the teaching of the Brotherhood of light, by John H. Dequer. New York, N. Y., The author [c1930] 263 p. col. front., illus., plates, diagrs. 24 cm. "References": p. 262-263. [BF1879.T2D43] 30-22738
1. Tarot. 2. Symbolism of numbers. 3. Names, Personal. 4. Occult sciences. 5. Astrology. I. Title.

DOANE, Doris Chase. 133.3'.2424
How to read tarot cards / Doris Chase Doane and King Keyes. New York : Barnes & Noble Books, 1979, 1967. 207p. : ill. ; 21 cm. [BF1879] ISBN 0-06-463481-7 pbk. : 2.95
1. Tarot. I. Keyes, King, joint author. II. Title.
L.C. card no. for 1967 Parker ed.:67-19976.

DOANE, Doris Chase 133.3'2424
Tarot-card spread reader [by] Doris Chase Doane, King Keyes. West Nyack, N. Y., Parker [1967] 207p. illus. 24cm. Ancient Egyptian tarot card set: (21p.) inserted at end. [BF1879.T2D6] 67-19976 5.95
1. Tarot. I. Keyes, King, joint author. II. Title.
Available from Prentice, Englewood Cliffs, New Jersey.

DOUGLAS, Alfred. 133.3'2424
The tarot; the origins, meaning and uses of the cards. Illustrated by David Sheridan. New York, Taplinger [1972] 249 p. illus. 22 cm. Bibliography: p. 240-243. [BF1879.T2D68 1972b] 72-2202 ISBN 0-8008-7547-8 7.95
1. Tarot.

DOUGLAS, Alfred, 1942- 133.3'2424
The tarot; the origins, meaning and uses of the cards. Illus. by David Sheridan. [Harmondsworth] Penguin Books [1973 c.1972] 249 p. illus. 18 cm. Bibliography: p. 240-243. [BF1879.T2D68 1973] ISBN 0-14-003737-3
I. Title.
Distributed by Penguin, Baltimore for 1.45 (pbk). L.C. card for original ed.: 72-2202.

FULLWOOD, Anna (Mebane) Mrs. 1870- 133
The flaming sword, written by Nancy Fullwood ... New York, Macoy publishing co., 1935. 2 p. l., 9-59 p. 21 cm. [BF1999.F78] 159.961 35-10725
1. Tarot. I. Title.

FULLWOOD, Anna (Mebane) Mrs. 1870- 133
The tower of light, written by Nancy Fullwood. New York, Macoy publishing co., 1931. 2 p. l., 7-120 p. 21 cm. " ... A limited edition consisting of five hundred copies only, was first printed from the type of which this copy is number 274." Signed by the author. "A further revelation of the light of Sano Tarot, as set forth in the book, "The song of Sano Tarot'." [BF1999.F83] 31-33001
1. Tarot. I. Title.

GETTINGS, Fred. 133.3'2424
The book of tarot. London, New York, Hamlyn, 1973. 144 p. illus. (some col.), facsims., ports. 29 cm. Bibliography: p. [144] [BF1879.T2G47] 74-161147 ISBN 0-600-31327-1 £1.75
1. Tarot. I. Title.

GRAVES, Frederick David, 1943- 133.3'2424
The windows of tarot [by] F. D. Graves. Dobbs Ferry, N.Y., Morgan & Morgan [1973] 95 p. illus. 22 cm. Bibliography: p. 95. [BF1879.T2G67] 73-85990 ISBN 0-87100-027-X 2.95
1. Tarot. I. Title.

GRAY, Eden. 133.3'2424
A complete guide to the tarot. New York, Crown [1970] 160 p. illus. (part col.) 26 cm. Bibliography: p. 157. [BF1879.T2G68 1970] 70-108086 6.95
1. Tarot. I. Title.

GRAY, Eden. 133.3'2424
Mastering the tarot; basic lessons in an ancient, mystic art. New York, New American Library [1973 c1971] 221 p. illus. 18 cm. [[BF1879.T2G69]] 1.25 (pbk.)
1. Tarot. I. Title.
L.C. card no. for original ed. 78-168322.

GRAY, Eden. 133.3'2424
Mastering the tarot; basic lessons in an ancient, mystic art. [New York, Crown, 1971] 152 p. illus. 26 cm. [BF1879.T2G69] 78-168322 5.95
1. Tarot. I. Title.

HAICH, Elizabeth. 133.3'2424
The wisdom of the tarot / by Elizabeth Haich ; translated by D. Q. Stephenson. 1st American ed. New York : ASI Publishers, 1975. p. cm. Translation of Tarot. [BF1879.T2H3313 1975] 75-22379 ISBN 0-88231-018-6 : 12.95
1. Tarot. I. Title.

HALL, Manly Palmer, 1901- 133.3'2424
The tarot : an essay / by Manly P. Hall ; accompanied by reproductions of the seventy-eight special tarot ill. designed by J. Augustus Knapp and Manly P. Hall. Los Angles : Philosophical Research Society, 1978. 34 p., [10] leaves of plates : ill. ; 23 cm. [BF1879.T2H35] 77-90441 ISBN 0-89314-382-0 pbk. : 2.50
1. Tarot. I. Knapp, J. Augustus. II. Title.

HOELLER, Stephan A. 133.3'2424
The royal road : a manual of Kabalistic meditations on the tarot / Stephan A. Hoeller. Wheaton, Ill. : Theosophical Pub. House, c1975. xx, 119 p. : ill. ; 21 cm. (A Quest book) [BF1879.T2H6] 75-4244 ISBN 0-8356-0465-9 : 2.95
1. Tarot. 2. Cabala. I. Title.

HOLY Order of MANS. 135.4
Jewels of the wise. San Francisco : Holy Order of MANS, c1974. 197 p. : ill. ; 21 cm. [BF1879.T2H64 1974] 75-309845 pbk. : 3.50
1. Tarot. I. Title.

HOY, David. 133.3'2424
The meaning of Tarot. Nashville, Aurora Publishers [1971] x, 168 p. illus. 23 cm. [BF1879.T2H69] 79-128449 ISBN 0-87695-073-X
1. Tarot. I. Title.

HUMPHREY, Christopher Carter, 1939- 133.3'2424
The book of one : introducing the tarot of the Holy Grail / by Christopher Carter Humphrey. Stillwater, OK : Thales Microuniversity Press, c1977. 93 p. : ill. ; 27 cm. (Speakers of the sun series ; v. 1) Forty copies printed no. 4. [BF1879.T2H84] 76-44860 ISBN 0-914312-09-X : 20.00
1. Tarot. 2. Occult sciences. I. Title.

HUSON, Paul. 135.4
The devil's picturebook: the compleat guide to tarot cards: their origins and their usage. New York, Putnam [1971] 256 p. illus. 22 cm. Bibliography: p. 252-256. [BF1879.T2H86] 77-157064 6.95
1. Tarot. I. Title.

INNES, Brian. 133.3'2424
The Tarot : how to use and interpret the cards / Brian Innes. New York : Arco Pub. Co., 1978, c1977. 88, [1] p. : ill. ; 30 cm. Bibliography: p. [89] [BF1879.T2156 1978] 77-27587 ISBN 0-668-04552-3 : 10.00
1. Tarot. I. Title.

KAPLAN, Stuart R. 133.3'2424
The encyclopedia of tarot / Stuart R. Kaplan. 1st ed. New York : U.S. Games Systems, c1978. xv, 387 p. : ill. (some col.) ; 28 cm. Includes index. Bibliography: p. 347-376 [BF1879.T2K28] 77-94173 ISBN 0-913866-11-3 : 14.95
1. Tarot. I. Title.

KAPLAN, Stuart R. 133.3'2424
Tarot cards for fun and fortune telling; illustrated guide to the spreading and interpretation of the popular 78-card tarot IJJ deck of Muller & Cie, Switzerland, by S. R. Kaplan. [1st ed.] New York, U.S. Games Systems, Inc. [1970] 96 p. illus. 24 cm. Bibliography: p. 96. [BF1879.T2K3] 71-119490
1. Tarot. I. Title.

KAPLAN, Stuart R. 133.3'2424
Tarot classic. New York, Grosset & Dunlap [1973, c.1972] xv, 240 p. illus. 21 cm. "A selective, annotated bibliography": p. 204-232. [BF1879.T2K32] 74-183028 ISBN 0-448-11544-1 2.95 (pbk.)
1. Tarot. I. Title.

LAURENCE, Theodor. 135.4
How the tarot speaks to modern man. [Harrisburg, Pa.] Stackpole Books [1972] 216 p. illus. 20 cm. [BF1879.T2L37] 79-179607 ISBN 0-8117-0858-6 6.50
1. Tarot. I. Title.

MATHERS, S. Liddell MacGregor. 133.3'2424
The tarot; its occult signification, use in fortune-telling, and method of play, etc., by S. L. MacGregor Mathers. New York, S. Weiser, 1969. 35, [1] p. illus. 22 cm. Bibliography: p. [36] [BF1879.T2M37] 71-17150 1.00
1. Tarot. I. Title.

MORGAN, Frederick, 1922- 133.3'2424
The tarot of Cornelius Agrippa / by Frederick Morgan. 1st ed. Sand Lake, N.Y. : Sagarin Press, c1978. [54] p. : ill. ; 23 cm. "Illustrations ... from the Gioseppe Maria Mitelli deck of tarot cards engraved

in 1664." [BF1879.T2M67] 77-94782 ISBN 0-915298-11-2 pbk. : 4.00
1. Tarot. I. Title.

MULLER, Marcia. FIC
Ask the cards a question / Marcia Muller. 1st ed. New York : St. Martin's Press, c1982. 169 p. ; 22 cm. [PS3563.U397A9 1982] 813'.54 19 81-21554 ISBN 0-312-05653-2 : 10.95
I. Title.

NICHOLS, Sallie. 133.3'2424
Jung and Tarot : an archetypal journey / Sallie Nichols ; with an introduction by Laurens van der Post. New York : S. Weiser, 1980. xv, 393 p., [25] p. of plates : ill. (some col.) ; 24 cm. Includes bibliographical references. [BF1879.T2N52] 19 80-53118 ISBN 0-87728-480-6 : 24.95
1. Jung, C. G. (Carl Gustav), 1875-1961. 2. Tarot. I. Title.
Publisher's address: Box 612, York Beach, ME 03910

RAINE, Kathleen Jessie, 1908- 821'.8
Yeats, the tarot, and the Golden Dawn, by Kathleen Raine. [Dublin] Dolmen Press [1972] 60, [31] p. illus. 25 cm. (New Yeats papers, 2) Imprint covered by label: Distributed in the U.S.A. by Humanities Press, New York. Includes bibliographical references. [PR5908.O25R3] 73-166426 ISBN 0-85105-195-2 £2
1. Yeats, William Butler, 1865-1939—Supernatural element. 2. Hermetic Order of the Golden Dawn. 3. Tarot. I. Title. II. Series.

SADHU, Mouni 133.324
The Tarot; a contemporary course of the quintessence of hermetic occultism. London, G. Allen & Urwin [dist. New York, Hillary, 1964, c.1962 494p. illus. 25cm. Bibl. 64-1422 12.50
1. Tarot. I. Title.

STEIGER, Brad. 133.324'24
The tarot [by] Brad Steiger & Ron Warmoth New York, Award Books [1973? c.1969] 168 p. 18 cm. [BF1879.T2S7] pap., 0.95
1. Tarot. I. Warmoth, Ron, joint author.

TESSIER, Albert Denis. 133.324
Tarosophy, the esoteric doctrine of the tarot; a course of study in tarot symbolism, interpretation and delineation. Los Angeles, c1956. 143 l. illus. 30cm. [BF1879.T2T4] 57-18419
1. Tarot. I. Title.

THIERENS, A. E. 133.3'2424
Astrology & the tarot / A. E. Thierens ; introd. by A. E. Waite. Hollywood, Calif. : Newcastle Pub. Co., [1975] p. cm. (A Newcastle occult book ; P-31) Reprint of the 1930 ed. published by D. McKay Co., Philadelphia, under title: The general book of the tarot. [BF1879.T2T47 1975] 74-31486 ISBN 0-87877-031-3 pbk. : 2.95
1. Tarot. 2. Astrology. I. Title.

THIERENS, A. E. 133.3'2424
Astrology & the tarot / A. E. Thierens ; introd. by A. E. Waite. San Bernardino, Calif. : Borgo Press, 1980. p. cm. Reprint of the 1930 ed. published by D. McKay, Philadelphia, under title: The general book of the tarot. [BF1879.T2T47 1980] 19 80-53344 10.95
1. Tarot. 2. Astrology. I. Title.

USPENSKII, Petr Dem'ianovich, 1878-1947. 133.3'2424
The symbolism of the tarot : philosophy of occultism in pictures and numbers / P. D. Ouspensky ; translated by A. L. Pogossky. New York : Dover Publications, 1976. 63 p. ; 22 cm. Set of 22 tarot cards prepared by P. C. Smith, under the supervision of A. E. Waite, reproduced on the covers. Unabridged and corrected republication of the work first published in 1913 by Trood Print. and Pub. Co., St. Petersburg, Russia. [BF1879.T2U7813 1976] 75-31286 ISBN 0-486-23291-3 pbk. : 1.50
1. Tarot. I. Title.

USSHER, Arland. 133.3'2424
The XXII keys of the tarot. The designs drawn by Leslie MacWeeney. [New ed., reset] Dublin] Dolmen Press; [distributed in the U.S.A. by Dufour Editions, Chester Springs, Pa., 1969] 54 p. illus. 23 cm. [BF1879.T2U8] 79-5851 3.95
1. Tarot. I. Title.

WAITE, Arthur Edward, 1857-1942. 133.3'2424
The pictorial key to the tarot; being fragments of a secret tradition under the veil of divination. With 78 plates, illustrating the greater and lesser arcana, from designs by Pamela Colman Smith. Introd. by Paul M. Allen. Blauvelt, N.Y., Rudolf Steiner Publications, 1971. xii, 340 p. illus. 18 cm. (Steinerbooks) Bibliography: p. 319-340. [BF1879.T2W3 1971] 79-175056 1.95
1. Tarot. I. Title.

WAITE, Arthur Edward, 1857-1942. 133.324
The pictorial key to the tarot; being fragments of a secret tradition under the veil of divination. With 78 plates, illustrating the greater and lesser arcana, from designs by Pamela Colman Smith. New York, University Books [1959] 344 p. illus. 19 cm. Includes bibliography. [BF1879.T2W3 1959] 59-15903
1. Tarot. I. Title.

WAITE, Arthur Edward, 1857-1942. 133.3'2424
The pictorial key to the tarot : being fragments of a secret tradition under the veil of divination / by Arthur Edward Waite ; with 78 plates, illustrating the greater and lesser arcana, from designs by Pamela Colman Smith ; introd. by Paul M. Allen. New York : Harper & Row, c1980. p. cm. Reprint of the 1971 ed. published by Steiner Publications, Blauvelt, N.Y., issued in Steinerbooks series. Bibliography: p. [BF1879.T2W3 1980] 79-3596 ISBN 0-06-068945-5 pbk. : 4.95
1. Tarot. I. Title.

Tarot and sex.

LAURENCE, Theodor. 133.3'2424
The sexual key to the tarot. [New York] New American Library [1973, c1971] 128 p. illus. 18 cm. [BF1879.T2L38] 1.25 (pbk.)
1. Tarot and sex. I. Title.

LAURENCE, Theodor. 133.3'2424
The sexual key to the tarot. [1st ed.] New York, Citadel Press [1971] 121 p. illus. 22 cm. [BF1879.T2L38] 70-29950 ISBN 0-8065-0242-8 5.95
1. Tarot and sex. I. Title.

Tarrants, Thomas A.

TARRANTS, Thomas A. 248'.2 B
The conversion of a Klansman : the story of a former Ku Klux Klan terrorist / Thomas A. Tarrants III. 1st ed. Garden City, N.Y. : Doubleday, 1979. x, 130 p. ; 22 cm. "A Doubleday-Galilee original." [BV4935.T37A33] 78-74713 ISBN 0-385-14926-3 : 7.95
1. Tarrants, Thomas A. 2. Ku Klux Klan (1915-) 3. Converts—United States—Biography. I. Title.

Tarthang Tulku.

ANNALS of the Nyingma lineage in America. 294.3'923 [Berkeley, Calif.] : Dharma Pub., 1975- v. : ill. ; 28 cm. Contents.Contents.—v. 1. 1969-1975. [BQ7662.2.A56] 75-323606 ISBN 0-913546-23-2
1. Tarthang Tulku. 2. Rnin-ma-pa (Sect)—United States—History.

Tate, Archibald Campbell, Abp. of Canterbury, 1881-1882.

MARSH, Peter T. 283'.0924
The Victorian church in decline; Archbishop Tait and the Church of England, 1868-1882 [by] P. T. Marsh. [Pittsburgh] University of Pittsburgh Press [1969] x, 344 p. illus., port. 23 cm. Bibliography: p. 328-335. [BX5199.T278M3 1969b] 72-80032 8.95
1. Tate, Archibald Campbell, Abp. of Canterbury, 1881-1882. 2. Church of England—History. I. Title.

Tate, Charles Spencer, 1865-

BAYLISS, Edward Ebenezer, 1843- 922
The transformation of Tate, by E.E. Bayliss ... Boston, Mass., J.H. Earle & company, [1903.] 23 p. illus. 15 1/2 cm. [BV3785.T27B3] 37-36755
1. Tate, Charles Spencer, 1865- I. Title.

TATE, Charles Spencer, 1865- 922
Pickway; a true narrative. By Charles Spencer Tate. Chicago, The Golden rule press, 1905. 3 p. l., 9-159 p. front., illus., ports. 19 1/2 cm. [BV3785.T27A3] 5-13948
I. Title.

Tatianus, 2d century Diatessuron.

HOBSON, Alphonzo Augustus.
The Diatessaron of Tatian and the synoptic problem; being an investigation of the Diatesseron for the light which it throws upon the solution of the problem of the origin of the synoptic Gospels, by A. Augustus Hobson, PH.D. Chicago, The University of Chicago press, 1904. 81 p. 24 cm. (On cover: The University of Chicago...Historical and linguistic studies in literature related to the New Testament; issued under the direction of the Department of Biblical and patristic Greek. Second series: Linguistic and exegetical studies, v. 1, pt. III) "List of works and authors": p. 7-8. [BS2554.S8T6] 4-27970
1. Tatianus, 2d cent. Diatessuron. I. Title.

Tau (The Greek letter)

VORREUX, Damien. 246'.558
A Franciscan symbol, the Tau : history, theology, and iconography / Damien Vorreux ; translation from the French, Marilyn Archer and Paul Lachance. Chicago : Franciscan Herald Press, [1980] p. cm. (Tau series ; no. 4) (The Presence of Saint Francis) Translation of Un Symbole franciscain, le Tau. [BV160.V6713] 79-23214 ISBN 0-8199-0791-X : 6.95
1. Francisco d'Assisi, Saint, 1182-1226. 2. Tau (The Greek letter) I. Title. II. Series: Presence of Saint Francis.

Taub, Eizik, 1751-1821—Legends.

RABBI Eizik : FIC
Hasidic stories about the Zaddik of Kallo / translated from the Hungarian with an introd. and notes by Andrew Handler. Rutherford : Fairleigh Dickinson University Press, c1977. p. cm. Bibliography: p. [BM532.R28] 894'.511'3008 75-5245 ISBN 0-8386-1739-5 12.00
1. Taub, Eizik, 1751-1821—Legends. 2. Tales, Hasidic. 3. Jew in Nagykallo, Hungary—Literary collections. I. Handler, Andrew, 1935- II. Neumann, Albert, d. 1943. III. Szabolcsi, Lajos. IV. Patai, Jozsef, 1882-1953.
Contents omitted

Taxation.

KAUFMAN, Donald D. 261.8'73
What belongs to Caesar? A discussion on the Christian's response to payment of war taxes, by Donald D. Kaufman. Scottdale, Pa. Herald Press [1970, c1969] 128 p. 20 cm. Bibliography: p. 105-122. [HJ2305.K3] 70-109939
1. Taxation. 2. Tax evasion. I. Title.

Taxation—Great Britain—History

LUNT, William Edward, 1882- ed.
The valuation of Norwich; edited by W. E. Lunt... Oxford, The Clarendon press, 1926. xv, 870 p. fold. map. 23 cm. "The valuation of Norwich [1254] takes its name from Walter Suffield, bishop of Norwich...one of three English prelates charged with the collection of the tenth which gave rise to the valuation...The occasion of the assessment was the levy of a tax imposed on the English clergy by Innocent IV, at the instance of Henry III, with the consent of the English prelates."--p. 52-58. "Abbreviations used in the citation of titles and bibliography of books cited": p. 621-636. [BX1495.N6L8] 27-15505
1. Taxation—Gt. Brit.—Hist. 2. Gt. Brit.—Church history—Sources. 3. Catholic church—Finance. I. Title.

Taxation, Papal.

LUNT, William Edward, 1882-1956. 254.8'0942
Accounts rendered by papal collectors in England, 1317-1378. Transcribed with annotations and introd. by William E. Lunt. Edited, with additions and revisions by Edgar B. Graves. Philadelphia, American Philosophical Society, 1968. liv, 579 p. facsims. 31 cm. (Memoirs of the American Philosophical Society, v. 70) Includes bibliographical references. [BX1950.L78] 67-19647
1. Catholic Church—Finance. 2. Catholic Church. Camera Apostolica. 3. Catholic Church—History—Sources. 4. Taxation, Papal. I. Graves, Edgar B., ed. II. Title. III. Title: Papal collectors in England. IV. Series: American Philosophical Society, Philadelphia. Memoirs, v. 70.

LUNT, William Edward, 1882-1956. 254
Financial relations of the papacy with England. Cambridge, Mass., Mediaeval Academy of America, 1939-62. 2 v. 26 cm. (Mediaeval academy of America. Publication no. 33, 74. Studies in Anglo-papal relations during the middle ages, 1-2) Series: Mediaeval Academy of America. Studies in Anglo-papal relations during the Contents.Contents. -- [1] To 1327. -- [2] 1327-1534. Bibliography: v. 1, p. 687-721. Bibliographical footnotes. [BR747.A1M4 vol. 1-2] 39-29743
1. Taxation, Papal. 2. Taxation — Gt. Brit. — Hist. 3. Catholic Church — Relations — Gt. Brit. 4. Gt. Brit. — Relations (general) with Catholic Church. 5. Annates. I. Title. II. Series.

Tay, John.

ENGEN, Sadie Owen. 266'.673 B
John Tay, messenger to Pitcairn / by Sadie Owen Engen. Mountain View, Calif. : Pacific Press Pub. Association, c1981. p. cm. (Trailblazer series) The lives of the people of Pitcairn Island, and in a special way two young boys, are profoundly affected by the visit of John Tay who spreads the word of the Seventh-day Adventists. [BV3680.P52T393] 92 19 80-26401 pbk. : 5.95
1. Tay, John. 2. [Tay, John.] 3. Missionaries—Pitcairn Island—Biography—Juvenile literature. 4. Missionaries—United States—Biography—Juvenile literature. 5. Seventh-Day Adventists—Missions—Pitcairn Island. 6. [Missionaries.] 7. [Seventh-Day Adventists.] 8. [Pitcairn Island.] I. Title.

Taylor, Benjamin, 1786-1848.

EDMUNDS, Edward. 922.
Memoir of Elder Benjamin Taylor, aminister of the Christian connexion, and pastor of the Bethel church in Providence, R. I. By E. Edmunds ... Boston, G. W. White, printer, 1850. vi, [7]-144 p. front. (port.) 18 cm. [BX6793.T3E4] 25-2738
1. Taylor, Benjamin, 1786-1848. I. Title.

Taylor, Blaine, 1933-

TAYLOR, Blaine, 1933- 251'.08
Real life, real faith / Blaine E. Taylor. Nashville : Abingdon, c1980. 96 p. ; 23 cm. [BV4225.2.T39] 79-26235 ISBN 0-687-35586-9 pbk. : 6.95
1. Taylor, Blaine, 1933- 2. Homiletical illustrations. I. Title.

Taylor, Charles, 1871-

TAYLOR, Charles Forbes, 1899- 922
The gospel wagon, by Charles Forbes Taylor ... New York, Chicago [etc.] Fleming H. Revell company [c1928] 96 p. front. 19 cm. A recital of the making of an evangelist. [BV3785.T3T3] 28-29575
1. Taylor, Charles, 1871- I. Title.

Taylor, Charles, 1931-

WRIGHT, Larry. 124
Teleological explanations : an etiological analysis of goals and functions / Larry Wright. Berkeley : University of California Press, c1976. ix, 153 p. ; 23 cm. Includes bibliographical references and index. [BD541.W74] 75-17284 ISBN 0-520-03086-9 : 10.00
1. Taylor, Charles, 1931- The explanation of behaviour. 2. Teleology. 3. Causation. 4. Psychology. 5. Motivation (Psychology) I. Title.

Taylor, Charles Forbes, 1890-

NYGAARD, Norman Eugene, 1897- 922
The crusading Taylors, evangelists extraordinary. New York, Greenberg [1950] 96 p. illus., ports. 28 cm. [BV3785.T3N9] 50-9533
1. Taylor, Charles Forbes, 1890- 2. Taylor, Laurie Forbes, 1901 or 2- I. Title.

TAYLOR, Charles Forbes, 1899- 243
Everlasting salvation: gospel addresses, by Charles Forbes Taylor ... New York, Chicago [etc.] Fleming H. Revell company [c1925] 128 p. 19 1/2 cm. [BV3797.T26] 25-20421
I. Title.

TAYLOR, Charles Forbes, 1899- 243
Everlasting salvation: gospel addresses, by Charles Forbes Taylor ... New York, Chicago [etc.] Fleming H. Revell company [c1925] 128 p. 19 1/2 cm. [BV3797.T26] 25-20421
I. Title.

TAYLOR, Charles Forbes, 1899- 922
Up to now; a story of crowded years, by Charles Forbes Taylor. New York [etc.] Fleming H. Revell company [c1938] 140 p. front., ports. 19 1/2 cm. [BV3785.T3U6] 38-19612
I. Title.

Taylor, Charles Lincoln, 1901-

AMERICAN Association of Theological Schools. 230'.07
Horizons of theological education: essays in honor of Charles L. Taylor, edited by John B. Coburn, Walter D. Wagoner [and] Jesse H. Ziegler. Dayton, Ohio [1966] xvii. 133 p. 27 cm. "Published [also] in paper covers as vol. II, number 4 of Theological education." Includes bibliographical references. [BV4020.A63] 67-3969
1. Taylor, Charles Lincoln, 1901- 2. Theology — Study and teaching — Addresses, essays, lectures. I. Coburn, John B., ed. II. Wagoner, Walter D., joint ed. III. Ziegler, Jesse H., joint ed. IV. Taylor, Charles Lincoln, 1901- V. Title.
Contents omitted

Taylor, Edward, 1642-1729.

GRABO, Norman S. 922.573
Edward Taylor. New York, Twayne Publishers [1962, c1961] 192 p. 21 cm. (Twayne's United States authors series, 8) Includes bibliography. [BX7260.T28G7 1962] 61-15668
1. Taylor, Edward, 1642-1729.

TAYLOR, Edward, 1642-1729. 818.1
Diary. Edited with an introd. by Francis Murphy. Springfield, Mass., Connecticut Valley Historical Museum, 1964. 40 p. 28 cm. "Originally published in the Proceedings of the Massachusetts Historical Society, xviii, 1880." Bibliographical footnotes. [BX7260.T28A3] 65-1311
I. Murphy, Francis E. X., ed. II. Title.

TAYLOR, Edward, 1642-1729. 264'.36
Edward Taylor vs. Solomon Stoddard : the nature of the Lord's Supper / edited by Thomas M. & Virginia L. Davis. Boston : Twayne Publishers, [1981] p. cm. (The Unpublished writings of Edward Taylor ; v. 2) (Twayne's American literary manuscripts series) (Series: Taylor, Edward, 1642-1729. Unpublished writings of Edward Taylor ; v. 2.) Includes bibliographical references. [BV824.T39 1981] 19 80-29343 ISBN 0-8057-9653-3 : 30.00
1. Taylor, Edward, 1642-1729. 2. Stoddart, Solomon, 1643-1729. 3. Lord's Supper—Early works to 1800. I. Stoddard, Solomon, 1643-1729. II. Davis, Thomas Marion. III. Davis, Virginia L. IV. Title. V. Series.

TAYLOR, Edward, 1642-1729.
A transcript of Edward Taylor's Metrical history of Christianity, by Donald E. Stanford. [n.p., c1962] 440 p. Microfilm on 1 reel. 65-54039
I. Title.

Taylor, Edward Thompson, 1798-1871.

COLLYER, Robert, 1823-1912. 922
Father Taylor [by] Robert Collyer. Boston, American Unitarian association, 1906. 3 p. l., 58 p. front. (port.) 21 cm. [BV2678.T3C7] 6-42972
1. Taylor, Edward Thompson, 1798-1871. I. Title.

HAVEN, Gilbert, bp., 1821-1880. 922
... *Incidents and anecodotes of Rev. Edward T. Taylor,* for over forty years pastor of the Seaman's Bethel, Boston. By Rev. Gilbert Haven ... and Hon. Thomas Russell ... Boston, B. B. Russell; San Francisco, A. L. Bancroft & co., 1872. 445 p. plates, 2 port. (incl. front.) 19 1/2 cm. [BV2678.T3H3] 17-
1. Taylor, Edward Thompson, 1796-1871. I. Russell, Thomas, 1825-1887, joint author. II. Title.

Taylor, George Braxton, 1860-1942—Juvenile literature.

MONSELL, Helen Albee, 1895- 92
The story of Cousin George. Illustrated by William Moyers. Birmingham, Ala., Woman's Missionary Union [1961] 122p. illus. 21cm. [BV3705.T3M6] 61-12680
1. Taylor, George Braxton, 1860-1942—Juvenile literature. I. Title.

Taylor, James Barnett, 1804-1871.

TAYLOR, George Boardman, 1832-1907. 922.673
Life and times of James B. Taylor. By George B. Taylor. With an introduction by J. B. Jeter, D.D. Philadelphia, The Bible and publication society [c1872] 359 p. front. (port.) 19 1/2 cm. [BX6495.T39T3] 36-24274
1. Taylor, James Barnett, 1804-1871. I. Title.

Taylor, James Brainerd, 1801-1829.

RICE, John Holt, 1777-1831. 922.573
Memoir of James Brainerd Taylor. By John Holt Rice, D.D. and Benjamin Holt Rice, D.D. 1st edition. New York, Jocelyn, Darling & co., 1833. 2 p. l., [3]-330 p. front. (port.) 18 1/2 cm. [BX9225.T36R5 1833] 36-31466
1. Taylor, James Brainerd, 1801-1829. I. Rice, Benjamin Holt, 1782-1856, joint author. II. Title.

RICE, John Holt, 1777-1831. 285.
Memoir of James Brainerd Taylor. By John Holt Rice, D.D. and Benjamin Holt Rice. D.D. 2d stereotype ed., rev. under the sanction of the surviving compiler. New York, The American tract society [1833] 441 p. front. (port.) 15 1/2 x 9 1/2 cm. [BX9225.T36R5 1833a] 7-41876
1. Taylor, James Brainerd, 1801-1829. I. Rice, Benjamin Holt, 1782-1856, joint author. II. Title.

TAYLOR, James Brainerd, 1801-1829. 922.573
A new tribute to the memory of James Brainerd Taylor. New York, J. S. Taylor, 1838. xi, [13]-440 p. 19 1/2 cm. Added t.-p. engraved. Selections from the letters and diary of J. B. Taylor. [BX9225.T36A6] 36-22115
I. Title.

Taylor, James Hudson, 1832-1905.

BROOMHALL, Marshall. 922.742.
Hudson Taylor, The man who believed God, by Marshall Broomhall ... London,Philadelphia [etc.] The China inland mission, 1929. xii, 244 p. front. (port.) illus. (facsim.) 19 1/2 cm. [BV3427.T3B7 1929b] 31-7669
1. Taylor, James Hudson, 1833-1905. 2. Missions—China. I. Title.

HUNNEX, Gloria G. Mrs. 922.
James Hudson Taylor, pioneer missionary of inland China, by Gloria G. Hunnex. Anderson, Ind., Gospel trumpet company [c1925] 154 p. front. (port.) illus. 19 cm. [BV3427.T3H8] 23-6644
1. Taylor, James Hudson, 1832-1905. I. Title.

MILLER, Basil William, 1897- 922.742
J. Hudson Taylor, for God and China. Grand Rapids, Zondervan Pub. House [1948] 136 p. 20 cm. [BV3427.T3M5] 48-8077
1. Taylor, James Hudson, 1832-1905. I. Title.

POLLOCK, John Charles 922.742
Hudson Taylor and Maria; pioneers in China. Grand Rapids, Mich., Zondervan [1967] 207p. 21cm. Bibl. [BV3427.T3P6] 1.95 pap.,
1. Taylor, James Hudson, 1832-1905. 2. Taylor, Maria (Dyer) I. Title.

TAYLOR, Frederick Howard. 922.
Hudson Taylor and the China inland mission; the growth of a work of God ... by Dr. and Mrs. Howard Taylor. 4th impression. London, Morgan & Scott, ld.; Philadelphia [etc.] China inland mission, 1920. xi, [1], 640 p. front., ports., fold. map. 22 cm. Sequel to "Hudson Taylor in early years: the growth of a soul". [BV3427.T3T35] 21-5096
1. Taylor, James Hudson, 1832-1905. 2. Missions—China. I. Taylor, Mary Geraldine (Guinness) "Mrs. Howard Taylor," joint author. II. Title.

TAYLOR, Frederick Howard. 922.
Hudson Taylor in early years; the growth of a soul ... by Dr. and Mrs. Howard Taylor, with introduction by Mr. D. E. Hoste ... 6th impression. London, Philadelphia [etc.] The China inland mission [1923] xxi, 511 p. front, illus. (plan) plates, ports, fold. map. 22 cm. [BV3427.T3T3 1923] 25-10864
1. Taylor, James Hudson, 1832-1905. 2. Missions—China. I. Taylor, Mary Geraldine (Guinness) "Mrs. Howard Taylor," joint author. II. Title.

TAYLOR, Frederick Howard. 922.742
Hudson Taylor's spiritual secret, by Dr. and Mrs. Howard Taylor ... London, Philadelphia [etc.] China inland mission, 1932. 178 p., 1 l. incl. front. (port.) 22 1/2 cm. "Printed in the United States." [BV3427.T3T37] 33-11726
1. Taylor, James Hudson, 1832-1905. I. Taylor, Mary Geraldine (Guinness) "Mrs. Howard Taylor," joint author. II. Title.

TAYLOR, Frederick Howard 266.00924
J. Hudson Taylor; a biography. by Dr. and Mrs. Howard Taylor. Foreword by Arthur F. Glasser. Chicago, Moody [c.1965] xi, 366p. port. 23cm. (Tyndale ser. of great biogs.) [BV3427.T3T38] 66-32 4.95
1. Taylor, James Hudson, 1832-1905. 2. Missions—China. I. Taylor, Mary Geraldine (Guinness) joint author. II. Title.

Taylor, James Hudson, 1832-1905—Juvenile literature.

KIEFER, James S. j 92
Apostle to inland China; the story of J. Hudson Taylor, by James S. and Velma B. Kiefer. Illustrated by Adrian Beerhorst. Grand Rapids, Baker Book House, 1965. 63 p. illus. 20 cm. (Valor series, 11) [BV3427.T3K5] 65-29831
1. Taylor, James Hudson, 1832-1903 — Juvenile literature. 2. Missions — China — Juvenile literature. I. Kiefer, Velma B., joint author. II. Title.

Taylor, James Monroe, 1848-1916.

HAIGHT, Elizabeth Hazelton, 1872- 920
The life and letters of James Monroe Taylor; the biography of an educator, by Elizabeth Hazelton Haight... New York, E. P. Dutton & company [c1919] xi p., 1 l., 391 p. front., plates. ports. 22 cm. "Partial list of writings of James Monroe Taylor": p. 381-387. [LD7182.7.H2] 19-14687
1. Taylor, James Monroe, 1848-1916. I. Title.

Taylor, Jeremy, Bp. of Down and Connor, 1613-1667.

BROWN, William James, 1889- 922.
... *Jeremy Taylor,* by W. J. Brown ... London, Society for promoting Christian knowledge; New York and Toronto. The Macmillan co., 1925. 4 p. l., 224 p. 20 cm. (English theologians) Printed in India. Taylor's works: p. 211-213. Bibliography: p. 214-217. [BX5199.T3B8] 26-14390
1. Taylor, Jeremy, bp. of Down and Connor, 1613-1667. I. Title.

GOOSE, Edmund William, Sir, 1849-1928. 283'.0924
Jeremy Taylor. New York, Greenwood Press, 1968 [c1904] xi, 234 p. 19 cm. [BX5199.T3G6 1968] (B) 68-28590
1. Taylor, Jeremy, Bp. of Down and Connor, 1613-1667.

GOSSE, Edmund William, Sir, 1849-1928. 283'.0924 B
Jeremy Taylor. New York, Macmillan, 1904. Grosse Pointe, Mich., Scholarly Press, 1968. xi, 234 p. 20 cm. (English men of letters) [BX5199.T3G6 1968b] 71-5151
1. Taylor, Jeremy, Bp. of Down and Connor, 1613-1667.

GOSSE, Edmund William, Sir 1849-1928. 922.
... *Jeremy Taylor,* by Edmund Gosse. New York, The Macmillan company; London, Macmillan & co., ltd., 1904. xi, 234 p. 20 cm. (Half-title English men of letters, ed. by John Morley) Series title also at head of t.-p. [BX5199.T3G6 1904 a] [PR3729.T13Z7 1904] 4-1683
1. Taylor, Jeremy bp. of Down and Connor, 1613-1667. I. Title.

HUGHES, Henry Trevor 922.342
The piety of Jeremy Taylor. New York, St. Martin's Press, 1960[ ] 183p. Bibl.: p.178-180 and bibl. notes. 60-50586 5.75
1. Taylor, Jeremy, Bp. of Down and Conner, 1613-1667. 2. Piety. I. Title.

HUNTLEY, Frank Livingstone, 1902- 283'.0924
Jeremy Taylor and the Great Rebellion; a study of his mind and temper in controversy. Ann Arbor, University of Michigan Press [1970] ix, 131 p. 22 cm. Bibliography: p. 113-125. [BX5199.T3H82] 72-107975 ISBN 0-472-08470-4 7.50
1. Taylor, Jeremy, Bp. of Down and Connor, 1613-1667. I. Title.

ROSS Williamson, Hugh, 1901- 283'.092'4 B
Jeremy Taylor. [Folcroft, Pa.] Folcroft Library Editions, 1973. p. Reprint of the 1952 ed. published by Dobson, London, in series: A Pegasus biography. [BX5199.T3R65 1973] 73-15705 20.00
1. Taylor, Jeremy, Bp. of Down and Connor, 1613-1667.

ROSS Williamson, Hugh, 1901- 283'.092'4 B
Jeremy Taylor / Hugh Ross Williamson. Norwood, Pa. : Norwood Editions, 1975. 179 p., [5] leaves of plates : ill. ; 24 cm. Reprint of the 1952 ed. published by D. Dobson, London, in series: A Pegasus biography. Includes index. Bibliography: p. 176. [BX5199.T3R65 1975] 75-31842 ISBN 0-88305-778-6 : 25.00
1. Taylor, Jeremy, Bp. of Down and Connor, 1613-1667.

STRANKS, Charles James. 283'.092'4 B
The life and writings of Jeremy Taylor, by C. J. Stranks. [Folcroft, Pa.] Folcroft Library Editions, 1973. p. Reprint of the 1952 ed. published by S.P.C.K., London,

for the Church Historical Society. [BX5199.T3S8 1973] 73-11259 25.00
1. Taylor, Jeremy, Bp. of Down and Connor, 1613-1667. I. Church Historical Society (Gt. Brit.) II. Title.

Taylor, Jeremy, Bp. of Down and Connor, 1613-1667—Bibliography.

GATHORNE-HARDY, Robert, 1902- 016.283'0924
A bibliography of the writings of Jeremy Taylor to 1700, with a section of Tayloriana. By Robert Gathorne-Hardy and William Proctor Williams. Dekalb, Northern Illinois University Press [1971] xi, 159 p. port. 25 cm. "An expansion and revision of Robert Gathorne-Hardy's original bibliography which appeared in 1930 as part of Logan Pearsall Smith's The golden grove." [Z8861.8.G35 1971] 71-149932 ISBN 0-87580-023-8
1. Taylor, Jeremy, Bp. of Down and Connor, 1613-1667—Bibliography. I. Williams, William Proctor, 1939- joint author. II. Title.

TAYLOR, Jeremy, bp. of Down and Connor, 1613-1667. 208.1
The Golden grove; selected passages from the sermons and writings of Jeremy Taylor. Edited by Logan Pearsall Smith, with a bibliography of the works of Jeremy Taylor by Robert Gathorne-Hardy. Oxford, The Clarendon press, 1930. lxiii, 330 p., 1 l. incl. front. port. 19 1/2 cm. [PR3729.T13A6 1930] 31-3379
1. Taylor, Jeremy, bp. of Down and Connor, 1613-1667—Bibl. I. Smith, Logan Pearsall, 1865- ed. II. Gathorne-Hardy, Robert, 1902- III. Title.

WILLIAMS, William Proctor, 1939- 016.283'092'4 B
Jeremy Taylor, 1700-1976 : an annotated checklist / compiled by William P. Williams. New York : Garland Pub., 1979. p. cm. (Garland reference library of the humanities ; v. 177) Includes indexes. [Z8861.8.W54] [BX5199.T3] 78-68302 ISBN 0-8240-9756-4 : 12.00
1. Taylor, Jeremy, Bp. of Down and Connor, 1613-1667—Bibliography. 2. Theology—17th century—Bibliography. 3. Theology, Anglican—Bibliography. I. Title.

Taylor, Jim.

ADAMS, Norman, fl.1972- 289.9
Goodbye, beloved Brethren. Aberdeen, Impulse Publications Ltd, 1972. 162, [5] p. illus., facsim., ports. 20 cm. Bibliography: p. [162] [BX8809.T39A63] 73-162292 ISBN 0-901311-13-8 £2.50
1. Taylor, Jim. 2. Plymouth Brethren. I. Title.

Taylor, John, 1624-1761. The Scripture doctrine of original sin.

NILES, Samuel, 1674-1762. 283.
The true Scripture doctrine of original sin stated and defended. In the way of remarks on a late piece, intitled, "The Scripture-doctrine of original sin proposed to free and candid examination. By John Taylor. The second edition." To which is premised a brief discourse on the decrees of God, in general, and on the election of grace, in particular. Being, the substance of many meditations, in the course of a long life, and now published as his Boston, N. E. Printed and sold by S. Kneeland, opposite to the probate-office in Queen-street. 1757. 3 p. l., 320 p. 18 1/2 cm. [BT720.T33N5 1757] 45-48582
1. Taylor, John, 1624-1761. The Scripture doctrine of original sin. 2. Sin, Original. I. Title.

Taylor, John, 1752-1835.

TAYLOR, John, 1752-1835. 286'.173
A history of ten Baptist churches / John Taylor. New York : Arno Press, 1980. 302 p. ; 21 cm. (The Baptist tradition) Reprint of the 1827 ed. printed by W. H. Holmes, Bloomfield, Ky. [BX6248.V8T33 1980] 79-52609 ISBN 0-405-12474-0 : 22.00
1. Taylor, John, 1752-1835. 2. Baptists—Virginia—History. 3. Baptists—Kentucky—History. 4. Virginia—Church history. 5. Kentucky—Church history. 6. Baptists—Clergy—Biography. 7. Clergy—Virginia—Biography. 8. Clergy—Kentucky—Biography. I. Title. II. Series: Baptists tradition.

Taylor, John, 1808-1887.

ROBERTS, Brigham Henry, 1857-1933 922.8373
The life of John Taylor, third president of the Church of Jesus Christ of Latter-Day Saints. Salt Lake City, Bookcraft [1963] 499p. illus., ports. 24cm. 63-5946 price unreported
1. Taylor, John, 1808-1887. I. Title.

ROBERTS, Brigham Henry, 1857-1933. 922.
The life of John Taylor, third president of the Church of Jesus Christ of latterday saints. By B. H. Roberts ... Salt Lake City, Utah, G. Q. Cannon & sons, co., 1892. xiv, p., 1 l., [17]-468 p. front., plates, ports. 24 cm. [BX8695.T3R6] 44-26537
1. Taylor, John, 1808-1887. I. Title.

TAYLOR, Samuel Woolley, 1907- 289.3'3 B
The Kingdom or nothing : the life of John Taylor, militant Mormon / by Samuel W. Taylor. New York : Macmillan, c1976. x, 406 p. ; 24 cm. Includes index. Bibliography: p. 386-396. [BX8695.T3T39] 75-38962 ISBN 0-02-616600-3 : 8.95
1. Taylor, John, 1808-1887. 2. Mormons and Mormonism—History. I. Title.

Taylor, John. 1808-1887—Juvenile literature.

NEELEY, Deta Petersen. 922.8373
A child's story of the prophet John Taylor, by Deta Petersen Neeley and Nathan Glen Neeley. Salt Lake City. Printed by the Deseret News Press, 1960. 140p. illus. 20cm. [BX8695.T3N4] 61-22320
1. Taylor, John. 1808-1887—Juvenile literature. I. Neeley, Nathan Glen, joint author. II. Title.

Taylor, June Filkin, 1938-

TAYLOR, June Filkin, 1938- 242'.4
But for our grief : how comfort comes / June Filkin Taylor. 1st ed. Philadelphia : A. J. Holman Co., c1977. 129 p. ; 22 cm. Includes bibliographical references. [BJ1487.T375] 77-3345 ISBN 0-87981-078-5 pbk. : 3.45
1. Taylor, June Filkin, 1938- 2. Grief. 3. Consolation. I. Title.

Taylor, Mrs. Sarah Louisa (Foote) 1809-1836.

JONES, Lot, d.1865. 922
Memoir of Mrs. Sarah Louisa Taylor; or, An illustration of the work of the Holy Spirit, in awakening, renewing, and sanctifying the heart. By Lot Jones ... New York, J. S. Taylor; Boston, Weeks, Jordan, and co.; [etc., etc.] 1838. 3 p. l., [v]-xii, [13]-324 p. front. (port.) 20 cm. Added t.-p., engraved. [BR1725.T33J6] 33-8156
1. Taylor, Mrs. Sarah Louisa (Foote) 1809-1836. I. Title.

Taylor, Nathaniel William, 1786-1858.

MACWHORTER, Alexander, 1822-1880. 261
Yahveh Christ, or, The memorial name. By Alexander MacWhorter...with introductory letter by Nathaniel W. Taylor... Boston, Gould and Lincoln; New York, Sheldon, Blakeman & co.; [etc., etc.] 1857. x, [11]-179 p. 18 1/2 cm. [BT180.N2M3] 22-15338
1. Taylor, Nathaniel William, 1786-1858. I. Title.

MEAD, Sidney Earl, 1904- 922.573
Nathaniel William Taylor, 1786-1858, a Connecticut liberal, by Sidney Earl Mead. Chicago Ill., The University of Chicago press [1942] xi, 250 p. front. (port.) 23 cm. "List of the manuscript materials used in this study": p. 243-246. Bibliographical foot-notes. [BX7260.T32M35] 42-50728
1. Taylor, Nathaniel William, 1786-1858. I. Title.

MEAD, Sidney Earl, 1904- 285'8'0924
Nathaniel William Taylor, 1786-1858; a Conneticut liberal [Hamden, Conn.] Archon, 1967 [c.1942] xi, 259p. 23cm. Bibl. [BX260.T32M35 1967] 67-15932 7.00
1. Taylor, Nathaniel William, 1786-1858. I. Title.

NELSON, Levi, 1779-1855. 233.
A letter to the theological professors at New Haven, concerning their supposition that God may not have been able to prevent sin in a moral system; with an appendix. Also, a few thoughts on the origin of sin. By Levi Nelson ... Norwich [Conn.] J. G. Cooley, 1848. 87 p. 23 cm. [BT715.N4] 41-33062
1. Taylor, Nathaniel William, 1786-1858. 2. Sin. 3. Providence and government of God. I. Title.

Taylor, Richard 1805?-1873.

MEAD, Arthur David, 1888- 266.30924
Richard Taylor, missionary tramper, by A. D. Mead. Wellington, A. H. & A. W. Reed [1966] 272p. illus., maps, port. 23cm. [BV3667.T3M4] 66-7850 6.50
1. Taylor, Richard 1805?-1873. 2. Missions—New Zealand. 3. Maoris. I. Title.
Available from Tri-Ocean in San Francisco.

Taylor, William, bp., 1821-1902

DAVIES, Edward, 1830- 922.76
The Bishop of Africa; or, The life of William Taylor, D. D. With an account of the Congo county. and mission, By Rev. E. Davies ... Published for the benefit of the building and transit fund of William Taylor's missions. Reading, Mass., Holiness book concern [1885] x, [11]-192 p. front. (port.) 19 cm. [BX8495.T3D3] 37-7003
1. Taylor William bp., 1821-1902. 2. Missions—Africa, West. 3. Methodist Episcopal church—Missions. I. Title.

PAUL, John Haywood, 1877- 922.
The soul digger; or, Life and times of William Taylor, by John Paul ... Upland, Ind., Taylor university press [c1928] 318 p. front., ports. 21 cm. [BX8495.T3P3] 28-13131
1. Taylor, William, bp., 1821-1902 I. Title.

TAYLOR, William, 1821-1902. 922.
Story of my life; an account of what I have thought and said and done in my ministry of more than fifty-three years in Christian lands and among the heathen ... by William Taylor. Edited by John Clark Ridpath; copiously embellished with original engravings and sketches by Frank Beard. New York, Hunt & Eaton, 1895. 3 p. l., [5]-750 p. incl. front., illus., plates, facsim. 26 1/2 cm. [BX8495.T3A3] 15-7539
I. Ridpath, John Clark, 1840-1900, ed. II. Title.

Taylors. First Baptist Church—History

FLYNN, Jean Martin, 1917- 286'.1757'27
History of the First Baptist Church of Taylors, South Carolina. [Clinton, S.C.] Jacobs Bros., 1964. vii, 133 p. illus., ports. 24 cm. Bibliographical references included in "Footnotes" (p. 118-130) [BX6480.T38F54] 68-67
1. Taylors. First Baptist Church—History. I. Title.

Tazewell, Charles.

GRAY, Patricia (Clark)
The littlest angel; a Christmas play in one act. Based on a story by Charles Tazewell. Chicago, The Dramatic Publishing Co. [c1964] 20 p. 19 cm. 66-18812
1. Tazewell, Charles. I. Title.

Tchividjian, Gigi.

TCHIVIDJIAN, Gigi. 248.4
A woman's quest for serenity / by Gigi Tchividjian. Old Tappan, N.J. : F. H. Revell Co., c1981. 158 p. ; 22 cm. [BV4501.2.T34] 19 80-25103 ISBN 0-8007-1183-1 : 7.95
1. Tchividjian, Gigi. 2. Christian life—1960- I. Title.

Te Deum laudamus.

MORGAN, Dewi 223.2
But God comes first, a meditation on the Te Deum. Foreword by the Bishop of London. Longmans. [dist. New York, McKay, c.1962] 96p. 61-66825 1.50; .90 pap.,
1. Te Deum laudamus. 2. Meditations. I. Title.

Teacher of Righteousness.

CARMIGNAC, Jean. 296.81
Christ and the Teacher of Righteousness; the evidence of the Dead Sea scrolls. Translated from the French by Katharine Greenleaf Pedley. Baltimore, Helicon Press [1962] 168p. 23cm. Translation of: Le Docteur de Justice et Jesus Christ. Includes bibliography. [BM175.Q6C33] 62-11183
1. Teacher of Righteousness. 2. Jesus Christ—Person and offices. I. Title.

EWING, Upton Clary 221.4
The prophet of the Dead Sea Scrolls. New York, Philosophical [c.1963] 148p. 22cm. Bibl. 62-21558 3.75
1. Teacher of Righteousness. 2. Dead Sea scrolls. I. Title.

Teachers.

BIBLE. English. 1901. Authorized. 220.52
The teachers' Bible; containing the Old and New Testaments according to the authorized version, together with a selection of new and revised helps to Bible study, a new concordance, elementary introduction to the Hebrew and Greek languages, and indexed Bible atlas. London, S. Bagster and sons, limited; New York, J. Pott & co. [c1901] [1388] p. plates. (part col.) maps. plans, facsims, double tab., diagr. 22 cm. Various pagings. [BS185.1901.L63] 1-14640
I. Title.

FELDMAN, Abraham Jehiel, 1893-
Choice passages in the Holy Scriptures; a teacher's guide. Selected and titled by A. J. Feldman. Hartford, Conn., Temple Beth Israel, 1965. 57 p. 23 cm. 67-79511
I. Title.

IN the service of God; 248
translated by Sister Mary Charitas ... edited by Edward A. Fitzpatrick. Milwaukee, The Bruce publishing company [c1938] xvii, 188 p. 16 cm. "The book in its German form was ... prepared for and issued under the auspices of the Society of German Catholic women teachers of Muenster in Westphalia."--Introd. [BX2373.T4E62] 38-16152
1. Teachers. 2. Meditations. I. Verein katholischer deutscher lehrernnen. II. Mary Charitas, sister, 1893- tr. III. Fitzpatrick, Edward Augustus, 1884- ed. Translation of Engeldienst! 52 betrachtungen fiber den ersiehlichen beruf der christilchen lehrerin.

Teachers' institutes—[Michigan]

MICHIGAN Christian teachers' institute. 377.
Six lectures delivered at the Michigan Christian teachers' institute, held at Grand Rapids, Mich., October 1 and 2, 1914. Kalamazoo, Mich., Dalm printing co. [1915] 108 p. 23 1/2 cm. [LC586.C4M5] E 15
1. Teachers' institutes—[Michigan] I. Christian Reformed church. II. Title.

Teachers—Meditations.

[BRANSIET, Philippe] 1792-1874. 242.6
As stars for all eternity; meditations for teachers. Rev. by Brother Francis Patrick [for] the Brothers of the Christian Schools. Milwaukee, Bruce Pub. Co. [1959] 255p. 18cm. 'Abridged and revised edition of Considerations for Christian teachers.' [BX2373.T4B7] 59-13017
1. Teachers— Meditations. I. Francis Patrick, Brother, 1884- ed. II. Brothers of the Christian Schools. III. Title.

DALY, Lowrie John 242.694
Meditation for educators, by Lowrie J. Daly, Mary Virgene Daly. Introd. by Paul C. Reinert. New York, Sheed [c.1965] 176p. 21cm. [BX2373.T4D3] 65-20865 3.95
1. Teachers—Meditations. I. Daly, Mary Virgene, joint author. II. Title.

DALY, Lowrie John. 242.694
Meditations for educators, by Lowrie J. Daly and Mary Virgene Daly. With an introd. by Paul C. Reinert. New York, Sheed and Ward [1965] 176 p. 21 cm. [BX2373.T4D3] 65-20865
1. Teachers — Meditations. I. Daly, Mary Virgene, joint author. II. Title.

Teachers of exceptional children.

HARING, Norris Grover, 1923- 371.9
Attitudes of educators toward exceptional children / Norris G. Haring, George G. Stern, William M. Cruickshank ; including lectures by Georgie Lee Abel ... [et al.]. Westport, Conn. : Greenwood Press, [1978] c1958. xv, 238 p. ; 24 cm. Reprint of the ed. published by Syracuse University Press, Syracuse, which was issued as no. 3 of Syracuse University special education and rehabilitation monograph series. Includes bibliographical references. [LC3965.H28 1978] 77-25983 ISBN 0-313-20070-X lib.bdg. : 18.75
1. Teachers of exceptional children. I. Stern, George G., joint author. II. Cruickshank, William M., joint author. III. Title. IV. Series: Syracuse University. Special education and rehabilitation monograph series ; 3.

Teachers of socially handicapped children, Training of—United States.

STOREN, Helen Frances. 371.9'6
The disadvantaged early adolescent; more effective teaching [by] Helen F. Storen. New York, McGraw-Hill [1968] xvi, 117 p. 22 cm. (McGraw-Hill series in education) Bibliography: p. 111-114. [LC4091.S7] 68-13528
1. Teachers of socially handicapped children, Training of—United States. 2. Socially handicapped children—Education—United States. I. Title.

Teachers—Prayer book and devotions

*MAINPRIZE, Donald Charles 242
Good morning, lord meditations for teacher Grand Rapids, Baker Book House, [1974] lv. (unpaged) 19 cm. [BV4832] ISBN 0-8010-5959-3 1.95
1. Teachers—Prayer book and devotions I. Title.

Teaching.

BRADFORD, Reed H. 371.1'001
A teacher's quest [by] Reed H. Bradford. [1st ed. Provo, Utah] Brigham Young University Press [1971] 77 p. illus. 23 cm. [BX8695.B65A3] 72-178774
1. Teaching. I. Title.

BROTHERS of the Christian schools. 377
Elements of practical pedagogy, by the Brothers of the Christian schools. New York, La Salle bureau of supplies, 1905. 3 p. l., v-xx, [2], 304 p. 20 cm. [LB1025.B86] 6-1282
1. Teaching. I. Title.

FRITZ, Dorothy Bertolet. 268.6
Ways of teaching; a book concerning approaches to and techniques of teaching, with an emphasis on the learner. For teachers, group leaders and Philadelphia, Published for the Cooperative Publication Association by the Westminster Press [1965] 111 p. 21 cm. [LB1025.F86] 65-17002
1. Teaching. I. Title.

GILSON, Etienne Henry, 1884- 377.82
The eminence of teaching in Disputed questions in education. New York, Catholic Textbook Division, Doubleday [1954- [LC485.D57] 54-1725
I. Title.

[GRAHAM, Constantius] 1851- 238.
The young Christian teacher encouraged; or, Objections to teaching answered ... With an introduction by the Right Reverend John L. Spalding ... By B. C. G. St. Louis, Mo., B. Herder, 1903. xxii, 381 p. 20 cm. Based upon a work by Frere Exuperien, entitled "Motives of encouragement for young teachers: or, Objections to teaching answered", published in Paris in 1866, cf. Pref. [BX925.G7] 3-15187
I. Prats de Mollo, Exupere de, 1837- II. Title.

JACOBS, J. Vernon 268.43
Teaching problems and how to solve them; a question and answer book. Grand Rapids, Mich., Zondervan [c.1962] 64p. 21cm. (Sunday sch. know-how ser.) 1.00 pap.,
I. Title.

MCKINNEY, Alexander Harris, 1858- 268.
A top notch teacher; an inspirational handbook for church-school teachers, leaders of clubs, and all others interested in religious education, by A. H. McKinney... Boston, Chicago, W. A. Wilde company [c1925] 254 p. 19 1/2 cm. [BV1534.M28] 26-3506
1. Teaching. 2. Religious education. I. Title.

*STAINBACK, Arthur House 268.6
Illustrating the lesson. 1965 ed. Westwood, N.J., Revell [c.1964] 122p. 22cm. 1.50 pap.,
I. Title.

Teaching of the twelve apostles.

VOKES, Frederick Ercolo.
The riddle of the Didache, fact or fiction, heresy or Catholicism? By E. E. Vokes ... Published for the Church historical society. London, Society for promoting Christian knowledge; New York, The Macmillan co. [1938] v. [1], 222 p. 22 1/2 cm. "First published 1938." A 39
1. Teaching of the twelve apostles. I. Title.

Teaching teams.

HELLER, Melvin P. 371.3'0282
Team teaching; a rationale, by Melvin P. Heller. Dayton, Ohio, National Catholic Educational Association; [distributed by G. A. Pflaum Publisher, 1967] 47 p. illus., port. 22 cm. (NCEA papers, no. 2) Bibliography: p. 47. [LC461.N432 no. 2] 67-26588
1. Teaching teams. I. Series: National Catholic Educational Association. NCEA papers, no. 2.

Technical assistance, American—Spanish America.

TECHNICAL assistance by religious agencies in Latin America. 266
[Chicago] University of Chicago Press [1956] 139p. illus. 24cm. [HC60.M24] 278 56-6643
1. Technical assistance, American—Spanish America. 2. Missions—Spanish America. I. Maddox, James Gray, 1907-

Technical education.

YOUNG men's Christian associations. International committee. Educational dept.
Education and railroad men; hints, suggestions and outlines for conducting educational privileges in railroad Young men's Christian associations; pre- pared by the Educational department in co-operation with the international railroad secretaries, railroad officials and others. George B. Hodge, educational secretary. New York, Young men's Christian association press, 1908. 2 p. l. 59 p. 19 1/2 cm. [LC589.Y4] 8-29077
1. Technical education. I. Title.

Technology and ethics.

BECK, Hubert F. 261.8'3
The age of technology [by] Hubert F. Beck. Art work by Art Kirchhoff. St. Louis, Concordia Pub. House [1970] 133 p. illus. 18 cm. (The Christian encounters) Bibliography: p. 131-133. [BJ59.B4 1970] 79-112440
1. Technology and ethics. I. Title. II. Series.

COULSON, Charles Alfred. 261.5
Faith and technology, by C. A. Coulson. Being the inaugural lecture of the Luton Industrial College, delivered 14th September, 1968. [Nashville, Upper room, 1971] 31 p. 19 cm. [BJ59.C65 1971] 70-24927
1. Technology and ethics. I. Luton Industrial College. II. Title.

FARAMELLI, Norman J. 261.8'3
Technethics; Christian mission in an age of technology [by] Norman J. Faramelli. New York, Friendship Press [1971] 160 p. 18 cm. Bibliography: p. 157-160. [BJ59.F37] 77-146630 ISBN 0-377-01001-4 1.75
1. Technology and ethics. I. Title.

KINGREY, David W. 241
Now is tomorrow : crucial questions for space-age Christians / by David W. Kingrey and Marion F. Baumgardner. Richmond, Ind. : Friends United Press, c1975. xiv, 91 p. : ill. ; 21 cm. [BJ59.K55] 75-34946 3.45
1. Technology and ethics. 2. Religion and science—1946- I. Baumgardner, Marion F., joint author. II. Title.

TO love or to perish: 261.8'3
the technological crisis and the churches. Edited by J. Edward Carothers [and others] New York, Friendship Press [1972] 152 p. 21 cm. "Report of the U.S.A. Task Force on the Future of Mankind and the Role of the Christian Churches in a World of Science-based Technology." [BJ59.T6] 72-1150[illegible]
1. Technology and ethics. I. Carothers, J. Edward, ed. II. U.S.A. Task Force on the Future of Mankind and the Role of the Christian Churches in a World of Science-based Technology.

WILKES, Keith. 179
Religion and technology. Oxford, Eng., New York, Religious Education Press [1972] xii, 177 p. 18 cm. (Man and religion series, 7) Includes bibliographical references. [BJ59.W54 1972] 79-134732 ISBN 0-08-016560-5 ISBN 0-08-006804-9 (pbk)
1. Technology and ethics. I. Title.

Teed, Cyrus Reed, 1839-1908.

WEIMAR, J. Augustus. 299
Koreshanity, the new age religion, by the Koreshan Foundation. [Miami, Printed by Center Print. Co., 1971] viii, 171 p. ports. 23 cm. "The divine and Biblical credentials of Dr. Cyrus R. Teed (Koresh), by J. Augustus Weimar": p. 1-141. [BP605.K6W43] 70-158993
1. Teed, Cyrus Reed, 1839-1908. 2. Koreshanity. I. Koreshan Foundation. II. Title.

Teen Challenge.

BARTLETT, Bob. 259
The Soul Patrol: "Here comes the God Squad." With Jorunn Oftedal. Plainfield, N.J., Logos International [1970] 170 p. 21 cm. [BV4447.B37] 71-107609 3.95
1. Teen Challenge. 2. Church work with youth—Philadelphia. I. Title.

BLANCHARD, Leora M. 259
Teen-age tangles; a teacher's experiences with live young people, by Leora M. Blanchard. Philadelphia, [The Union press c1923] v. 122 v. 19 cm. [BV4447.B6] 23-6351
I. Title.

GRABER, Edith 268.433
Choice; a study guide on teenage issues. Drawings by Robert W. Regier. Newton, Kans., Faith & Life Pr., [c.1963] 144p. 23cm. Bibl. .75 pap.,
I. Title.

Tegakouita, Catherine, 1656-1680.

DAUGHTERS of St. Paul. 282'.092'4 B
Blessed Kateri Tekakwitha, Mohawk maiden / by the Daughters of St. Paul. Boston, Mass. : Daughters of St. Paul, c1980. 92 p. : ill. ; 19 cm. [E90.T2D38 1980] 19 80-20403 ISBN 0-8198-1100-9 : 3.75 ISBN 0-8198-1101-7 (pbk.) : 2.95
1. Tegakouita, Catherine, 1656-1680. 2. Mohawk Indians—Biography. 3. Christian biography—New York (State) I. Title.

Tegh Bahadur, 9th guru of the Sikhs, 1621-1675.

JOHAR, Surinder Singh. 294.6'61
Guru Tegh Bahadur : a biography / Surinder Singh Johar. New Delhi : Abhinav Publications, 1976 262 p., [1] leaf of plates : ill. ; 22 cm. Includes index. Bibliography: p. 245-249. [BL2017.9.T4J64] 75-908901 11.50
1. Tegh Bahadur, 9th guru of the Sikhs, 1621-1675. 2. Sikh gurus—Biography. I. Title.
Distributed by South Asia Books Columbia, Mo.

Tegh Bahadur, 9th guru of the Sikhs, 1621-1675—Addresses, essays, lectures.

GERU Tegh Bahadur : 294.6'61 B
background and the supreme sacrifice : a collection of research articles / edited by Gurbachan Singh Talib. Patiala : Punjabi University, 1976. xvi, 250 p. ; 25 cm. (Guru Tegh Bahadur's martyrdom tercentenary memorial series) Includes bibliographical references. [BL2017.9.T4G86] 77-900595 Rs30.00
1. Tegh [illegible] dur, 9th [illegible] of the Sikhs, 1621-16[illegible]—Addresses, essays, lectures. 2. Sikh gurus—Biography—Addresses, Essays, lectures. 3. Sikhism—Addresses essays, lectures. I. Talib, Gurbachan Singh, 1911- II. Series: Guru Tegh Bahadara tiji shahidi shatabadi prakashana lari.

Teilhard de Chardin, Pierre.

ALLER, Catherine. 215
The challenge of Pierre Teilhard de Chardin. 2d ed. New York, Exposition Press [1967] 62 p. 21 cm. [B2430.T373P57 1967] 67-3843
1. Teilhard de Chardin, Pierre. Le phenomene humain. I. Title.

BALTAZAR, Eulalio R. 201
Teilhard and the supernatural, by Eulalio R. Baltazar. Baltimore, Helicon [1966] 336 p. 22 cm. Bibliographical footnotes. [B2430.T374B27] 66-26481
1. Teilhard de Chardin, Pierre. 2. Supernatural. I. Title.

BRAVO, Francisco, 1934- 230
Christ in the thought of Teilhard de Chardin. Translated by Cathryn B. Larme. Notre Dame, Ind., University of Notre Dame Press [1967] xviii, 163 p. 22 cm. Translation of Cristo en el pensamiento del padre Teilhard de Chardin. Includes bibliographical references. [B2430.T374B6813] 67-22140
1. Teihard de Chardin, Pierre. I. Title.

CORBISHLEY, Thomas. 230'.2'0924
The spirituality of Teilhard de Chardin. Paramus, N.J., Paulist Press [1971] 126 p. 18 cm. Includes bibliographical references. [B2430.T374C63 1971b] 72-78440 1.45
1. Teilhard de Chardin, Pierre. 2. Spirituality. I. Title.

CRESPY, Georges. 230'.0924
From science to theology; an essay on Teilhard de Chardin. Translated by George

H. Shriver. Nashville, Abingdon Press [1968] 174 p. 21 cm. Translation of De la science a la theologie. Bibliography: p. 169-170. [B2430.T374C683] 68-25367 4.00
1. Teilhard de Chardin, Pierre. I. Title.

CULLITON, Joseph T. 201
A processive world view for pragmatic Christians / by Joseph T. Culliton. New York : Philosophical Library, c1975. 302 p. ; 22 cm. Includes bibliographical references. [BD331.C84] 75-3781 ISBN 0-8022-2170-X : 12.50
1. Teilhard de Chardin, Pierre. 2. Dewey, John, 1859-1952. 3. Reality. 4. Evolution. 5. Christianity—Philosophy. 6. Pragmatism. I. Title.

DEVAUX, Andre A. 201
Teilhard and womanhood, by Andre A. Devaux. Translated by Paul Joseph Oligny and Michael D. Meilach. New York, Paulist Press [1968] vii, 83 p. 19 cm. (Deus books) Translation of Teilhard et la vocation de la femme. [B2430.T374D483] 68-31259 0.95
1. Teilhard de Chardin, Pierre. 2. Woman. I. Title.

DIMENSIONS of the future; 248
the spirituality of Teilhard de Chardin. Edited by Marvin Kessler and Bernard Brown. Washington, Corpus Books [1968] viii, 216 p. 21 cm. Bibliographical references included in "Notes" (p. 189-207) [B2430.T374D5] 68-25584 5.95
1. Teilhard de Chardin, Pierre. I. Kessler, Marvin, ed. II. Brown, Bernard, 1936- ed.

FARICY, Robert L., 1926- 248.4
The spirituality of Teilhard de Chardin / [Robert Faricy]. Minneapolis, Minn. : Winston Press, c1981. 126 p. ; 22 cm. Bibliography: p. 110-112. [BX2350.2.F37] 19 81-51160 ISBN 0-86683-608-X pbk. : 5.95
1. Teilhard de Chardin, Pierre. 2. Spiritual life—History of doctrines—20th century. I. Title.

HEFNER, Philip J. 201
The promise of Teilhard; the meaning of the twentieth century in Christian perspective, by Philip Hefner. [1st ed.] Philadelphia, Lippincott [1970] 127 p. 21 cm. (The Promise of theology) Bibliography: p. 125-127. [B2430.T374H37] 79-118976 3.95
1. Teilhard de Chardin, Pierre. I. Title.

JONES, David Gareth. 201
Teilhard de Chardin: an analysis and assessment [by] D. Gareth Jones. Grand Rapids, Eerdmans [1970, c1969] 72 p. 21 cm. Includes bibliographical references. [B2430.T374J6 1970] 70-127933 1.25
1. Teilhard de Chardin, Pierre.

KENNEY, W. Henry, 1918- 215
A path through Teilhard's Phenomenon [by] W. Henry Kenney. Dayton, Ohio, Pflaum Press, 1970. xii, 284 p. 21 cm. (Themes for today) Bibliography: p. 267-279. [B2430.T373P65] 69-20172 2.95
1. Teilhard de Chardin, Pierre. Le phenomene humain. I. Title.

KING, Ursula. 291.4'2
Towards a new mysticism : Teilhard de Chardin and Eastern religions / Ursula King. New York : Seabury Press, c1980. 318 p. ; 22 cm. "A Crossroad book." Includes index. Bibliography: p. 293-306. [BL80.2.K56] 80-17260 ISBN 0-8164-0475-5 : 14.95
1. Teilhard de Chardin, Pierre. 2. Religions. 3. Mysticism. I. Title.

KLAUDER, Francis J. 201'.1
Aspects of the thought of Teilhard de Chardin, by Francis J. Klauder. North Quincy, Mass., Christopher Pub. House [1971] 151 p. 21 cm. Includes bibliographical references. [B2430.T374K57] 70-155359 ISBN 0-8158-0259-5 4.95
1. Teilhard de Chardin, Pierre. I. Title.

KOPP, Josef Vitalis. 213.5
Teilhard de Chardin; a new synthesis of evolution [by] Joseph V. Kopp. Glen Rock, N.J., Paulist Press [1964] 72 p. 18 cm. (Deus books) Translation of Entstehung and Zukunft des Menschen; Pierre Tellhard de Chardin und sein Weltbild. [QE707.T4K63] 65-3171
1. Tellhard de Chardin, Pierre. I. Title.

LUBAC, Henri de, 1896- 230.2'0924
The religion of Teilhard de Chardin. Translated by Rene Hague. Garden City, N.Y., Image Books [1968, c1967] 432 p. 18 cm. Translation of La pensee religieuse du pere Teilhard de Chardin. Bibliographical references included in "Notes" (p. [319]-422) [B2430.T374L783 1968] 68-7165 1.65
1. Teilhard de Chardin, Pierre. I. Title.

LUBAC, Henri de, 1896- 230.20924
Teilhard de Chardin: the man and his meaning. Tr. [from French] by Rene Hague. [1st Amer. ed.] New York, Hawthorn [c.1964, 1965] x, 203p. 22cm. Bibl. [B2430.T374L813] 65-22914 4.95
1. Teilhard de Chardin, Pierre. I. Title.

LUBAC, Henri de, 1896- 230.20924
Teilhard de Chardin the man and his meaning. Translated by Rene Hague, [1st American ed.] New York Hawthorn Books [1965] x, 203 p. 22 cm. Translation of La priere du Pere Teilhard de Chardin. Bibliographical footnotes. [B2430.T374L813] 65-22914
1. Teilhard de Chardin, Pierre. I. Title.

LUBAC, Henri de, 1896- 201
Teilhard explained. Translated by Anthony Buono. New York, Paulist Press [1968] xi, 115 p. 19 cm. (Deus books) Translation of Teilhard, missionaire et apologiste. "List of Teilhard's works": p. 91-94. Bibliographical references included in "Notes" (p. 95-115) [B2430.T374L833] 68-16677
1. Teilhard de Chardin, Pierre. I. Title.

LUBAC, Henri Henri de, 1896- 230'.2'0924
The religion of Teilhard de Chardin. Tr. by Rene Hague. New York, Desclee [1967] 380p. 22cm. Tr. of La pensee religieuse du pere Teilhard de Chardin. [B2430.T374L783 1967a] 67-17675 5.95
1. Teilhard de Chardin, Pierre. I. Title.

MARTIN, Maria Gratia. 248.4'8'20924
The spirituality of Teilhard de Chardin. Westminster, Md., Newman Press [1968] xii, 122 p. 21 cm. Bibliography: p. 119-122. [B2430.T374M27] 68-16674
1. Teilhard de Chardin, Pierre. I. Title.

MEILACH, Michael D., comp. 201
There shall be one Christ, edited by Michael D. Meilach. Saint Bonaventure, N.Y., Franciscan Institute, Saint Bonaventure University, 1968. viii, 85 p. 23 cm. Cover has subtitle: A collection of essays on Teilhard de Chardin. Bibliographical footnotes. [B2430.T374M38] 68-7926 1.50
1. Teilhard de Chardin, Pierre. I. Title.

MOONEY, Christopher F. 1925- 232
Teilhard de Chardin and the mystery of Christ. New York, Harper [c. 1964-1966] 287p. port. 22cm. Bibl. [B2430.T374M63] 66-15050 6.00
1. Teilhard de Chardin, Pierre. I. Title.

MOONEY, Christopher F., 1925- 232
Teilhard de Chardin and the mystery of Christ. Garden City, N. Y., Doubleday [1968, c.1964] 318p. 18cm. (Image bk. D252) Bibl. [B2430.T374M63] 66-15050 1.35 pap.,
1. Teilhard de Chardin, Pierre. I. Title.

MOONEY, Christopher F 1925- 232
Teilhard de Chardin and the mystery of Christ [by] Christopher F. Mooney. [1st ed.] New York, Harper & Row [1966] 287 p. port. 22 cm. Bibliography: p. 264-277. [B2430.T374M63] 66-15050
1. Teilhard de Chardin, Pierre. I. Title.

MOONEY, Christopher F., 1925- 230.2
Teilhard de Chardin and the mystery of Christ. Garden City, N. Y., Doubleday [1968, c1964] 318 p. (Image books, D252) Bibliography: p. [289]-304. [B2430.T34M606]
1. Teilhard de Chardin, Pierre. I. Title.

MURRAY, Michael H 230.20924
The thought of Teihard de Chardin; an introduction [by] Michael H. Murray. New York, Seabury Press [1966] x, 177 p. 22 cm. [B2430.T374M8] 66-13466
1. Teilhard de Chardin, Pierre. I. Title.

MURRAY, Michael H. 230.20924
The thought of Teilhard de Chardin; an introduction. New York, Seabury [c. 1966] x, 177p. 22cm. [B2430.T374M8] 66-13466 4.95
1. Teilhard de Chardin, Pierre. I. Title.

NORTH, Robert Grady, 1916- 233
Teilhard and the creation of the soul. Introd. by Karl Rahner. Milwaukee, Bruce [1967] xiv, 317p. 23cm. (St. Louis Univ. (Saint Marys) theol. studies. 5) Index of Teilhard writings: p. 308-317. Bibl. [B2430.T374N6] 67-15250 7.95
1. Teilhard de Chardin, Pierre. 2. Soul. I. Title. II. Series.

SPEAIGHT, Robert, 1904- 230.2'0924
Teilhard de Chardin: re-mythologization; three papers on the thought of Teilhard de Chardin presented at a symposium at Seabury-Western Theological Seminary, Evanston, Illinois, September, 1968. By Robert Speaight, Robert V. Wilshire [and] J. V. Langmead Casserley. [Chicago, Argus Communications, 1970] 101 p. illus. 23 cm. (Peacock books) Cover title: Chardin: remytholi[sic]gization. Includes bibliographical references. [B2430.T374S75] 73-113275 2.45
1. Teilhard de Chardin, Pierre. I. Wilshire, Robert V. II. Casserley, Julian Victor Langmead, 1909- III. Title. IV. Title: Chardin: remytholi[sic]gization.

TEILHARD de Chardin, Pierre. 271'.5'0924
Letters from Hastings, 1908-1912. Introd. by Henri de Lubac.(Translated by Judith de Stefano New York] Herder and Herder [1968] 206 p. 21 cm. Translation of 70 letters from the 1st part of the author's Lettres d'Hastings et de Paris, 1908-1914. Bibliographical footnotes. [B2430.T374A413] 68-9137 4.95
I. Title.

TEILHARD de Chardin, Pierre. 271'.5'0924
Letters from Paris, 1912-1914. Introd. by Henri de Luba.(Annotation by Auguste Demoment and Henri de Lubac.(Translated by Michael Mazzarese [New York] Herder and Herder [1967] 157 p. 21 cm. Portion of the author's Lettres d'Hastings et de Paris, 1908-1914, published in 1965. Bibliographical footnotes. [B2430.T374A42] 67-17626
I. Lubac, Henri de, 1896- ed. II. Title.

TOWERS, Bernard. 230.20924
Teilhard de Chardin. Richmond, Knox [1966] xi, 45p. 19cm. (Makers of contemp. theol.) Bibl. [B2430.T374T6] 66-15515 1.00 pap.,
1. Teilhard de Chardin, Pierre. I. Title.

Teilhard de Chardin, Pierre—Addresses, essays, lectures.

COUSINS, Ewert H., comp. 230
Process theology: basic writings. Edited by Ewert H. Cousins. New York, Newman Press [1971] vii, 376 p. 23 cm. Contents.Contents.—Preface, by E. H. Cousins.—Introduction: process models in culture, philosophy, and theology, by E. H. Cousins.—Process thought: a contemporary trend in theology, by W. N. Pittenger.—Faith and the formative imagery of our time, by B. E. Meland.—The development of process philosophy, by C. Hartshorne.—Whitehead's method of empirical analysis, by B. M. Loomer.—God and the world, by A. N. Whitehead.—Philosophical and religious uses of "God," by C. Hartshorne.—The reality of God, by S. M. Ogden.—A Whiteheadian reflection on God's relation to the world, by W. E. Stokes.—The world and God, by J. B. Cobb.—God and man, by D. D. Williams.—The new creation, by B. E. Meland.—Bernard E. Meland, process thought, and the significance of Christ, by W. N. Pittenger.—The human predicament, by H. N. Wieman.—Teilhard de Chardin and the orientation of evolution: a critical essay, by T. Dobzhansky.—My universe, by P. Teilhard de Chardin.—The cosmic Christ, by H. de Lubac.—Cosmology and Christology, by N. M. Wildiers.—The problem of evil in Teilhard's thought, by G. Crespy.—Teilhard de Chardin and Christian spirituality, by C. F. Mooney.—Teilhard's process metaphysics, by I. G. Barbour.—Bibliography on process theology (p. 351-369) Includes bibliographies. [BT83.6.C68] 78-171961 4.95
1. Teilhard de Chardin, Pierre—Addresses, essays, lectures. 2. Process theology—Addresses, essays, lectures. I. Title.

Teilhard de Chardin, Pierre. Le phenomene humain.

ALLER, Catherine 215
The challenge of Pierre Teilhard de Chardin. New York, Exposition [c.1964] 56p. 21cm. 64-1039 3.00
1. Teilhard de Chardin, Pierre. Le phenomene humain. I. Title.

Teilhard de Chardin, Pierre—Theology.

FARICY, Robert L 1926- 230.2'0924
Teilhard de Chardin's theology of the Christian in the world, by Robert L. Faricy. New York, Sheed and Ward [1967] xviii, 235 p. 22 cm. Bibliography: p. 217-226. [[B2430.T374F37]] 67-13767
1. Teilhard de Chardin, Pierre—Theology. I. Title.

LEPP, Ignace, 1909-1966. 230'.2'0924
The faith of men; meditations inspired by Teilhard de Chardin. Translated by Bernard Murchland. New York, Macmillan [1967] 117 p. 22 cm. Translation of Teilhard et la foi des hommes. [B2430.T374L43] 67-24287
1. Teilhard de Chardin, Pierre—Theology. I. Title.

Telchin, Stan, 1925-

TELCHIN, Stan, 1925- 248.2'46
Betrayed! / Stan Telchin. Lincoln, VA : Chosen Books Pub. Co., [981] p. cm. Includes index. Bibliography: p. [BV2623.A1T44] 19 81-10043 ISBN 0-912376-68-6 : 7.95
1. Telchin, Stan, 1925- 2. Telchin, Judy. 3. Telchin, Ethel. 4. Converts from Judaism—Biography. I. Title.

Teleology.

BUCKLEY, Joseph, 1905- 124
Man's last end, with a foreword by Reginald Garrigou-Lagrange. St. Louis, B. Herder Book Co., 1949. xii. 249 p. 22cm. Bibliography : p. 234-237. [BD541.B8] 49-3694
1. Teleology. I. Title.

CAILLIET, Emile, 1894- 124
The recovery of purpose. [1st ed.] New York, Harper [1959] 192p. 22cm. Includes bibliography. [BD541.C12] 59-14530
1. Teleology. 2. Providence and government of God. I. Title.

COLLOQUE, Orrok, 1877- 124
The concept purpose; a philosophical thesis, by the Rev. Orrok Colloque, PH. D. Limited ed. New York, E. S. Gorham, 1904. 4 p. l., 3-57 p. diagrs. 25 cm. "Accepted in partial fulfillment of the requirements for the degree of doctor of philosophy, by the Graduate school of New York university, in 1904." Bibliography: p. 56-57. [BD541.C6] 6-3633
1. Teleology. I. Title.

HUMAN destiny.
[New York] New American Library [1956] 189p. 18cm. (A Mentor book, MD165)
1. Teleology. 2. Religion and science—1900- 3. Evolution. I. Lecomte du Notly, Pierre, 1883-1947.

JANET, Paul Alexandre Rene, 1823-1899. 124
Final causes. By Paul Janet ... Tr. from the 2d ed. of the French by William Affleck, B. D. With preface by Robert Flint ... 2d ed. New York, C. Scribner's sons, 1883. xxii p., 1 l., 520 p. 23 cm. [BD542.J3 1883] 4-5450
1. Teleology I. Affleck, William, tr. II. Title.

LECOMTE du Novy, Pierre, 1883- 110
...Human destiny. New York, London

[etc.] Longmans, Green and co., 1947. xix, [2], 289 p. 21 cm. Illustrated lining-papers. "First edition." [BD511.L4] 47-1523
1. Teleology. 2. Religion and science—1900- 3. Evolution. I. Title.

MCEWEN, William P. 124
Enduring satisfaction; a philosophy of spiritual growth. New York, Philosophical Library [1949] xxiii, 370 p. 23 cm. Bibliography: p. 355-364. [BD541.M3] 50-6006
1. Teleology. 2. Religion—Philosophy. I. Title.

SHEBBEARE, Charles John. 124
The challenge of the universe, a popular restatement of the argument from design, by the Rev. Charles J. Shebbeare ... London, Society for promoting Christian knowledge; New York, The Macmillan company, 1918. xxiv, 244, [1] p. 22 cm. [BD541.S5] 19-11433
1. Teleology. I. Title. II. Title: Argument from design.

SHEBBEARE, Charles John, 1865- 211
The revelation of God in nature; a discussion between the Rev. C. J. Shebbeare ... and Joseph McCabe ... with introduction by Professor Clement C. J. Webb. New York & London, G. P. Putnam's sons, 1924. 210 p. ports. 22 cm. [BL2778.S53] 24-3855
1. Teleology. I. McCabe, Joseph, 1867- II. Title.

WALCOTT, Gregory Dexter, 1869- 124
The rationality of the world. [Brooklyn? N.Y.] 1950. 64 p. 22 cm. Bibliographical footnotes. [BD541.W27] 51-29435
1. Teleology. 2. Reason. I. Title.

WARD, Leo Richard, 1893- 124
God and world order; a study of ends in nature. St. Louis, Herder [1961] 222 p. 22 cm. [BD541.W32] 61-13709
1. Teleology. 2. Causation. I. Title.

WARREN, Howard Crosby, 1867- 124
A study of purpose. By Harold [!] C. Warren ... [New York, 1916] cover-title, 5-72 p. 24 1/2 cm. Stamped over author's name: Howard C. Warren, Princeton, New Jersey. Reprinted from the Journal of philosophy, psychology and scientific methods, vol. XIII, no. 1, Jan. 6; no. 2, Jan. 20; no. 3, Feb. 3, 1916. [BD541.W25] E 16
1. Teleology. I. Title. II. Title: Purpose, A study of

WOODFIELD, Andrew. 124
Teleology / Andrew Woodfield. Cambridge ; New York : Cambridge University Press, 1976. p. cm. Based on the author's thesis, St. John's College, Oxford. Includes index. Bibliography: p. [BD541.W63] 75-44574 ISBN 0-521-21102-6 : 17.95
1. Teleology. I. Title.

WRIGHT, Larry. 124
Teleological explanations : an etiological analysis of goals and functions / Larry Wright. Berkeley : University of California Press, c1976. ix, 153 p. ; 23 cm. Includes bibliographical references and index. [BD541.W74] 75-17284 ISBN 0-520-03086-9 : 10.00
1. Taylor, Charles, 1931- The explanation of behaviour. 2. Teleology. 3. Causation. 4. Psychology. 5. Motivation (Psychology) I. Title.

Teleology — Addresses, essays, lectures.

CANFIELD, John V ed. 124
Purpose in nature. Edited by John V. Canfield. Englewood Cliffs, N.J., Prentice-Hall [1966] viii, 111 p. 22 cm. (Contemporary perspectives in philosophy series) Bibliography: p. 109-111. [BD541.C17] 66-18159
1. Teleology—Addresses, essays, lectures. I. Title.

Teleology—History

HURLBUTT, Robert H. 211.3
Hume, Newton, and the design argument, by Robert H. Hurlbutt, III. Lincoln, University of Nebraska Press [1965] xiv, 221 p. 24 cm. Bibliographical footnotes. [BD541.H8] 65-10047
1. Newton, Isaac, 1642-1727. 2. Hume, David, 1711-1776. 3. Teleology — Hist. I. Title. II. Title: The design argument.

Telephone in church work.

DOWDY, Augustus W. 254'.0028
Phone power / Augustus W. Dowdy, Jr. Valley Forge, PA. : Judson Press, [1975] 96 p. ; 18 cm. Includes index. Bibliography: p. 92-94. [BV656.4D68] 74-22368 ISBN 0-8170-0652-4 : 2.95
1. Telephone in church work. I. Title.

METCALF, Harold E 253.7
The magic of telephone evangelism, by Harold E. Metcalf. Atlanta, Southern Union Conference [of Seventh-Day Adventists, 1967] 448 p. illus. 21 cm. [BV656.4.M4] 68-801
1. Telephone in church work. I. Title. II. Title: Telephone evangelism.

Television in religion.

BLUEM, A. William. 207
Religious television programs; a study of relevance, by A. William Bluem. New York, Hastings House [1969] viii, 220 p. illus. 22 cm. (Communication arts books) Includes bibliographical references. [BV656.3.B55] 68-31687 4.95
1. Television in religion. I. Title.

HOLLAND, Daniel W. 253'.028
Using nonbroadcast video in the church / Daniel W. Holland, J. Ashton Nickerson, Terry Vaughn. Valley Forge, PA : Judson Press, c1980. 126 p. : ill. ; 22 cm. Bibliography: p. 99-105. [BV656.3.H64] 80-15004 ISBN 0-671-32939-1 pbk. : 5.95 5.95
1. Television in religion. I. Nickerson, J. Ashton, joint author. II. Vaughn, Terry, joint author. III. Title.

KABLER, Ciel Dunne. 254.3
Telecommunications and the church / by Ciel Dunne Kabler ; [illustrated by Mark Johnson]. Virginia Beach, Va. : Multi Media Pub., c1979. xvi, 166 p. : ill. ; 23 cm. Bibliography: p. 145-148. [BV656.3.K32] 79-83510 9.95
1. Television in religion. I. Title.
P.O. Box 1041, Virginia Beach, Va.

MCNULTY, Edward N., 1936- 268'.635
Television, a guide for Christians / Ed McNulty. Nashville : Abingdon, c1976. 96 p. : ill. ; 21 cm. Bibliography: p. 94-96. [BV656.3.M3] 76-1990 ISBN 0-687-41220-X pbk. : 3.50
1. Television in religion. I. Title.

PARKER, Everett C. 254.3
Religious television; what to do and how. New York, Harper [c.1961] 244p. 61-5265 4.00 bds.,
1. Television in religion. I. Title.

PARKER, Everett C 254.3
The television-radio audience and religion [by] Everett C. Parker, David W. Barry [and] Dallas W. Smythe. New York, Harper [1955] xxx, 464p. diagrs., tables. 25cm. (Studies in the mass media of communication) Bibliography: p. 15. Bibliographical footnotes. [BV656.3.P3] [BV656.3.P3] 259 55-8526 55-8526
1. Television in religion. 2. Radio in religion. 3. U. S.—Religion. I. Title. II. Series.

RELIGIOUS TV;
a handbook for Rabbis and religious organizations, sponsored by The New York Board of Rabbis and The American Jewish Committee. [New York, 1957] 52p. illus. 22cm.
1. Television in religion.

Television in religion—England—Yorkshire.

MAX-WILSON, Peter. 791.45'7
Stars on Sunday / [by] Peter Max-Wilson ; [photographs Brian Jeeves, Alan Harbour, Brian Cleasby]. Pinner : Pentagon, 1976. [163] p. : ill. (some col.), ports. (some col.) ; 26 cm. "Stars on Sunday is a Yorkshire Television Programme; producer, Peter Max-Wilson." Includes ten short talks delivered by Dr. Donald Coggan, Archbishop of Canterbury. [BV656.3.M39] 77-354256 ISBN 0-904288-09-9 : £4.95
1. Stars on Sunday. 2. Television in religion—England—Yorkshire. I. Coggan, Frederick Donald, 1909- II. Title.

Television in religion—United States.

JABERG, Gene. 253
The video pencil : cable communications for church and community / Gene Jaberg, Louis G. Wargo, Jr. Lanham, MD : University Press of America, c1980. iii, 147 p. ; 24 cm. Includes bibliographical references and index. [BV656.3.J32] 19 80-7951 ISBN 0-8191-1085-X : 15.00 ISBN 0-8191-1086-8 pbk. : 7.75
1. Television in religion—United States. 2. Community antenna television—United States. I. Wargo, Louis G. II. Title.

SHAW, Horace John, 1909- 286.7'3 B
The bishop : the story of A.A. Leiske and the unique telecast—"The American Religious Town Hall Meeting" / Horace J. Shaw. Mountain View, Calif. : Pacific Press Pub. Association, 1981. p. cm. [BV3785.L36S5] 19 81-11191 ISBN 0-8163-0444-0 pbk. : 4.95
1. Leiske, Albert A., 1901- 2. American Religious Town Hall Meeting (Television program) 3. Television in religion—United States. 4. Evangelists—United States—Biography. I. Title.

Television—Programmes, Religions.

SHEEN, Fulton John, Bp., 1895-
Life is worth living. Fourth series. illus. by Dik Browne. New York, McGraw-Hill [1956] 285p. 21cm. Transcribed from tape recordings of the author's television talks.
1. Television—Programmes, Religions. I. Life is worth living (Television program) II. Title.

SHEEN, Fulton John, Bp. 1895-
Life is worth living. Fourth series, illus. by Dik Browne. New York, McGraw-Hill [1956] 285 p. 21 cm. Transcribed from tape recordings of the author's television talks.
1. Television — Programmes, Religions. I. Life is worth living (Television program) II. Title.

Tell Beit Mirsim, Palestine.

†KYLE, Melvin Grove, 1858-1933. 221.9'3
Excavating Kirjath-Sepher's ten cities / Melvin Grove Kyle. New York : Arno Press, 1977 [c1934] 203 p., [10] leaves of plates : ill. ; 24 cm. (America and the Holy Land) Reprint of the ed. published by Eerdmans, Grand Rapids, in series: The James Sprunt lectures, 1932. [DS110.T393K94 1977] 77-70714 ISBN 0-405-10262-3 : 14.00
1. Kyle, Melvin Grove, 1858-1933. 2. Bible. O.T.—Antiquities. 3. Tell Beit Mirsim, Palestine. 4. Palestine—Antiquities. I. Title. II. Series. III. Series: The James Sprunt lectures ; 1932.

Tell en-Nasbeh, Palestine.

BADE, William Frederic, 1871- 296
Excavations at Tell en-Nasbeh, 1926 and 1927, a preliminary report, by William Frederic ... Berkeley, Calif., 1928. 56 p. front. (double map) illus. (incl. plans) 23 cm. ([Berkeley, Calif. Pacific school of religion] Palestine institute publication, no. 1) "Seven hundred and fifty copies of this report were printed." [DS101.B4 no. 1] 29-20899
1. Tell en-Nasbeh, Palestine. I. Title.

Tellez, Gabriel, 1570?-1648—Criticism and interpretation—Bibliography.

AN annotated, 016.862'3
analytical bibliography of Tirso de Molina studies, 1627-1977 / Vern G. Williamsen, general editor ; Walter Poesse, compiler. Columbia : University of Missouri Press, 1979. xv, 238 p. ; 24 cm. "A project of the Research Committee on the Comediantes, the Division of Sixteenth- and Seventeenth-Century Spanish Drama of the Modern Language Association of America." Includes indexes. [Z8864.A55] [PQ6436] 78-19640 ISBN 0-8262-0265-9 : 25.00
1. Tellez, Gabriel, 1570?-1648—Criticism and interpretation—Bibliography. I. Williamsen, Vern G. II. Poesse, Walter. III. Modern Language Association of America. Division of 16th- and 17th-Century Spanish Drama. Research Committee.

Tempel gesellschaft—Doctrinal and controversial works.

HOFFMANN, Christoph, 1815-1885. 289.
Missives, treating of the temple and the sacraments, the dogma of the trinity and the divinity of Christ; and the reconciliation of man with God. By the late Rev. Christopher Hoffmann ... Translated from the German. [Buffalo, P. Paulus] 1905. 67 p. 22 1/2 cm. Translation of Uber den tempel und die sacramente, dreieinigkelt und gotthelt Christi. [BX9798.T39H62] 46-33170
1. Tempel gesellschaft—Doctrinal and controversial works. I. Title.

Temperance.

BIRMINGHAM, James. 922.
A memoir of the Very Rev. Theobald Mathew, with an account of the rise and progress of temperance in Ireland. By the Rev. James Bermingham ... Edited by P. H. Morris, M. D., and by whom is added The evil effects of frunkenness physiologically explained. New-York, A. V. Blake, 1841. xix, [15]-216 p. 19 cm. [HV5032.M3B5 1841] 26-16990
1. Mathew, Theobald, 1790-1856. 2. Temperance. 3. Alcohol—Physiological effect. I. Morris, P. H. II. Title.

BRAIN, Belle Marvel, 1859- 178.
Weapons for temperance warfare; some plans and programmes for use in young people's societies ... By Belle M. Brain ... Boston and Chicago, United society of Christian endeavcr [c1897] 107 p. 16 cm. "List of books, leaflets, magazines, music, etc. to which reference has been made": p. 103-107. [HV5072.B8] 10-1629
1. Temperance. I. Title.

BURNS, Dawson. 178.
The bases of the temperance reform; an exposition and appeal. With replies to numerous objections. By Rev. Dawson Burns ... New York, National temperance society and publication house, 1873. 224 p. 19 1/2 cm. [HV5035.B8] 10-2092
1. Temperance. I. Title.

CAMPBELL, Mary J. 275.
The power-house at Pathankot; what some girls of India wrought by prayer, by Mary J. Campbell... Philadelphia, Pa., The Board of foreign missions of the United Presbyterian church of North America [c1918] ix p., 3 l., 17-192 p. front., plates, ports. 19 cm. [BV3265.C33] 18-11077
1. Temperance. 2. Missions—India. I. Title.

CAMPBELL, Mary Jane, 1865- 275.
The power-house at Pathankot; what some girls of India wrought by prayer, by Mary J. Campbell ... Philadelphia, Pa., The Board of foreign missions of the United Presbyterian church of North America [c1918] ix p., 3 1.,17-192 p. front., plates, ports. 19 cm. [BV3265.C33] 18-11077
1. Temperance. 2. Missions—India. I. Title.

[CASTLE, Robert Mason] 1873- 178.
"As ye sow." Los Angeles, Cal., Pictorial press, c1911. 1 p. l., [5]-174 p. illus. 18 x 24 cm. Added t.p., illus.: "As ye sow" ... life's certain admonitions; illustrations by C. D. Rhodes, trruisms by R. M. Castle. [HV5072.C35] 11-26277 1.00
1. Temperance. I. Rhodes, C. D. illus. II. Title.

CLARKE, McDonald, 1798-1842.
Death in disquise; a temperance poem. From the mss. of Mr. McDonald Clarke. Boston, B. B. Mussey, 1833. 1 p. l, [5]-36 p. 16 1/2 cm. [PS1299.C58D4 1833] 21-19360
I. Title.

COLLIER, Francis James. 178.
Temperance truth for the young and old, by Rev. Francis J. Collier ... Philadelphia, A. T. Zeising & co., printers, 1884. 84, iv p. 19 cm. "The greater part of this little book was published in the "Daily local news" of West Chester, Pa., and in the "Chester County archive" of Downington, Pa."--p. [3] [HV5296.C65] 9-33845
1. Temperance. I. Title.

COOK, Silas Arthur, 1875- 178.
Christian patriotism in temperance reform, by S. Arthur Cook. Philadelphia, Boston [etc.] The Griffith and Rowland press [1916] 3 p. l., 58 p. 19 1/2 cm. $0.10 "Acknowledgment and bibliography": p. 57-58. [HV5296.C77] 16-23943
1. Temperance. 2. Liquor problem. I. Title.

CRAFTS, Wilbur Fisk, 1850- 178.
1922.
The two chains; or, The twenty-nine articles of temperance. By Rev. W. F. Crafts ... New York, National temperance society and publication house, 1878. iv, 5-66 p. 19 cm. [HV5296.C8] 9-33847
1. Temperance. I. Title.

CRAFTS, Wilbur Fisk, 1850- 178.
1922.
What the temperance century has made certain in regard to intemperance and other social problems of the Anglo-Saxon nations, with a symposium of suggestions, for the new century, By Rev. Wilbur Fisk Crafts ... New York [etc.] Funk & Wagnalls, c1885. xi, 12-192 p. incl. front. (port.) diagrs. 19 cm. (On cover:Temperance library no. 1) [HV5025.C7] 10-1902
1. Temperance. I. Title.

CROSS, Marcus E. 178.
The mirror of intemperance, an history of the temperance reform. To which is added, The life and death of King Alcohol, and original and selected anecdotes. By Rev. Marcus E. Cross ... 2d ed. Philadelphia, J. T. Lange, 1850. x, ii-240 p. 20 cm. [HV5295.C8] 10-7166
1. Temperance. I. Title.

CROSS, Marcus E. 178.
The mirror of intemperance, and history of the temperance reform. To which is added, The life and death of King Alcohol and original and selected anecdotes. By Rev. Marcus E. Cross ... Philadelphia, J. T. Lange, 1849. x 11-240 p. 20 cm. [HV5295.C78] 10-7165
1. Temperance. I. Title.

DAVIS, Edith (Smith) Mrs. 178.
1859- comp.
A compendium of temperance truth largely contributed by the counselors of the Department of scientific temperance investigation and of scientific temperance instruction of the World's and National woman's Christian temperance union. Comp. by Mrs. Edith Smith Davis ... [Evanston, Ill.] National woman's Christian temperance union [1916?] 3 p. l., [9]-240 p. 1 illus. 23 cm. [HV5060.D18] 16-8350
1. Temperance. 2. Alcoholism. I. Title.

DAVIS, Edith (Smith) Mrs. 178.
1859-
... A manual for the public schools explaining the use of the graded set of charts and giving supplementary lessons to aid in the teaching of the nature and effects of alcohol and tobacco, by Edith Smith Davis ... Evanston, Ill., National woman's Christian temperance union [c1913] 152 p. incl. charts. 22 cm. [HV5060.D2] 13-2443 0.50
1. Temperance. I. Title.

DOUTNEY, Thomas N., 1846-
Thomas N. Doutney: his life-struggle and triumphs, also a vivid pen-picture of New York, together with a history of the work he has accomplished as a temperance reformer. Written by himself. Profusely illustrated. Battle Creek, Mich., W. C. Gage & sons, printers, 1893. 1 p. l., xiv, 544 p. front. (port.) pl. 24 1/2 cm. 3-3183
I. Title.

EATON, Ephraim Llewellyn, 178.
1846-
Winning the fight against drink; the history, development, rational basis, moral, financial, economic, and scientific appeal of the temperance reform, in which every phase of the subject is fully considered. By E. L. Eaton, D.D. Cincinnati, Jennings and Graham; New York, Eaton and Mains [c1912] 344 p. 19 1/2 cm. "Temperance and prohibition literature": p. 9; "Temperance and prohibition books": p. 10. [HV5296.E3] 12-12512 1.00
1. Temperance. I. Title.

EDWARDS, Justin, 1787-1853. 178.
The temperance manual, by Rev. Justin Edwards, D. D. New-York, American tract society [1847?] 99, [1] p. 15 1/2 cm. [HV5060.E32] 1-1448
1. Temperance. I. Title.

EDWARDS, Justin, 1787-1853. 178
The temperance manual. By Rev. Justin Edwards, D. D. New York, American tract society [185-?] 95 p. 15 1/2 cm. [HV5060.E323] 36-24129
1. Temperance. I. Title.

HEARN, Charles Aubrey, 1907- 177
Alcohol and Christian influence. Nashville, Convention Press [1957] 138p. illus. 20cm. [HV5060.H44] 178.1 57-20156
1. Temperance. I. Title.

HEARN, Charles Aubrey, 1907- 178
Alcohol the destroyer [by] C. Aubrey Hearn ... Nashville, Tenn., The Sunday school board of the Southern Baptist convention [1943] 149 p. front., illus. 19 cm. Bibliography: p. 142-144. [HV5060.H45] 43-3724
1. Temperance. I. Southern Baptist convention. Sunday school board. II. Title.

HOMAN, J A. 178.
Prohibition, the enemy of temperance; an exposition of the liquor problem... by Rev. J. A. Homan. Cincinnati, Christian liberty bureau [1910] 116 p. 23 1/2 cm. [HV5088.H7] A10
1. Temperance. 2. Liquor problem—U.S. 3. Prohibition—U.S. I. Title.

HOOTON, Caradine R. 261.83
What shall we say about alcohol? Nashville, Abingdon Press [1960] 127 p. 20 cm. [HV5186.H6] 60-6931
1. Temperance. I. Title.

HUBBARD, Thomas Franklin, 178.
1880-
The temperance program, by Evangelist Thos. F. Hubbard. Galesburg, Ill., Wagoner printing company, 1915. 218 p. incl. illus. (1 col.) port. 20 cm. $1.25 [HV5072.H77] 15-10305
1. Temperance. I. Title.

HUNT, Thomas Poage, 1794- 285.
1876.
Life and thoughts of Rev. Thomas P. Hunt. An autobiography... Wilkes-Barre, Pa., R. Baur & son, 1901. vii, 400 p. front. (port.) pl. 21 1/2 cm. Compiled by S. C. Hunt. [BX9225.H8A3] 1-18710
1. Temperance. I. Hunt, S. C., comp. II. Title.

KELLOGG, John Harvey, 1852- 178.
The physical, moral and social effects of alcoholic poison as a beverage and as a medicine. By J. H. Kellogg, M. D. Battle Creek, Mich., Office of the Health reformer, 1876. viii, 9-125 p. 18 cm. [HV5060.K5] 10-2118
1. Temperance. 2. Alcohol—Pysiological effect. I. Title.

LOFTON, George Augustus, 178.
1839-1914.
Habitual drinking and its remedy. By Rev. George A. Lofton ... Memphis, Tenn., Southern Baptist publication society, 1874. xii, [9]-99 p. 15 x 12 cm. [HV5296.L8] 10-12938
1. Temperance. I. Title.

MONTGOMERY, Hugh, 1839- 178.
The way out, a solution of the temperance question, by Rev. Hugh Montgomery; with an introduction by Daniel Dorchester, D. D. New York, Hunt & Eaton; Cincinnati, Cranston & Curts [c1895] 320 p. 20 cm. [HV5296.M65] 12-36866
1. Temperance. 2. Prohibition. I. Title.

MOODY, Dwight Lyman, 1837- 178.
1899.
Moody's talks on temperance, with anecdotes and incidents in connection with the Tabernacle temperance work in Boston. Comp. and ed. by Rev. James B. Dunn. New York, National temperance society and publication house, 1877. 2 p. l., [3]-248 p. front. (port.) pl. 19 cm. [HV5296.M7] 10-12942
1. Temperance. I. Dunn, James B., comp. II. Title.

MORSE, A. L. 178.
The battle to save; or, Lost and rescued ... By Rev. A. L. Morse ... Contains thrilling thoughts from God's word and great minds, and ninety plain questions and Bible answers ... Introduction by M. R. Drury, D.D., illustrated by Chas. M. Auer and Ed. Clement. Cincinnati, O., New York, N.Y. [etc.] Methodist book concern, 1903. 3 p. l., [v]-xvi, 17-268 p. front. (port.) illus., plates. 18 1/2 cm. With music. Original copyright 1895. [HV5296.M8] 3-17578
1. Temperance. I. Title.

PETERSEN, LaMar, 289.3'092'4 B
1910-
Hearts made glad : the charges of intemperance against Joseph Smith the Mormon prophet / LaMar Petersen ; drawings by Linda Marion. [Salt Lake City : Petersen], c1975. iv, 258 p. : ill. ; 23 cm. Includes index. Bibliography: p. 245-253. [BX8695.S6P39] 75-21678
1. Smith, Joseph, 1805-1844. 2. Temperance. I. Title.

THE potent enemies of 178.
America laid open: being some account of the baneful effects attending the use of distilled spirituous liquors, and the slavery of the Negroes; to which is added, the happiness attending life, when dedicated to the honour of God, and good of mankind, in the sentiments of some persons of emience near the close of their lives, viz. the Earl of Essex, Count Oxcistern, H. Grotius, D. Brainard, John Lock, &c. Philadelphia, Printed by J. Crukshank [1774] 1 p. l., 48, 83, 16 p. 16 cm. Contents.--The mighty destroyer displaye, in some account of the dreadfull havock made by the mistaken use as well as abuse of distilled spirituous liquors. By a lover of mankind [A. Beneset] ... Philadelphia, 1774.--Thoughts upon slavery. By John Wesley ... Philadelphia, 1774.-- ... Extracts of some letters ... [of David Brainard, also The experience of some men of note expressed near the conclusion of their days] [HV5295.P6] 10-17385
1. Temperance. 2. Slavery. I. Beneset, Anthony, 1713-1784. II. Wesley, John, 1708-1791. III. Brainerd, David, 1718-1747.

THE potent enemies of 178.
America laid open: being some account of the beneful effects attending the use of distilled spirituous liquors, and the slavery of the negroes. Philadelphia: Printed by Joseph Crukshank in Market-street, between Second and Third streets [1774] 2 p. l., [3]-48, 83 p. 17 cm. Each part has separate t.-p. Contents.--The mighty destroyer displayed, in some account of the dreadful havock made by the mistaken use as well as abuse of distilled spirituous liquors. By a lover of mankind [Anthony] Benezet] Philadelphia, 1774.--Thoughts upon slavery. By John Wesley. Philadelphia, 1774. [HV5295.P62] 7-29407
1. Temperance. 2. Slavery.

PRENTICE G. H. comp. 178.
Constitutional prohibition, the best remedy for the drink evil of modern times. Herewith demonstrated by the opinions of leading representatives of the professional and public life of Kansas, the first state to adopt and try this new policy. Collected and ed. by Rev. G. H. Prentice. With an introductory poem by Rev. A.S. Holland. Gilbertsvill, N. Y., Otsego journal presses, 1889 cover-title, 49 p. 22 cm. Text is continued on page 3 of cover. [HV5089.P7] 20-611
1. Temperance. 2. Prohibition—Kansas. I. Holland, A. S. II. Title.

RANKIN, George Clark, 1849- 178.
1915.
Two nights in the bar-rooms, and what I saw. The villainies of the liquor-shop handled without gloves. By G. C. Rankin ... Nashville, Tenn., Southern Methodist publishing house, Printed for the author, 1887. 106, [3] p. incl. double tab. 19 cm. [HV5296.R3] 10-12944
1. Temperance. I. Title.

RAYMOND, Irving Woodworth, 241
1898-
The teaching of the early church on the use of wine and strong drink. New York, AMS Press [1970] 170 p. 23 cm. (Studies in history, economics and public law, no. 286) Reprint of the 1927 ed. Originally presented as the author's thesis, Columbia, 1927. Bibliography: p. 156-164. [HV5186.R3 1970] 79-120207 ISBN 0-404-51286-0
1. Temperance. 2. Christian ethics—Early church, ca. 30-600. I. Title. II. Series: Columbia studies in the social sciences 286

REGAN, John. 178.
Tragedies of the liquor traffic, a non-sectarian, non-political appeal against the use of intoxicating liquors ... by John Regan ... with life sketches of Neal Dow, John P. St. John, John B. Gough and Father Mathew. Chicago, J. Regan & co. [c1917]. 188 p. incl. front., illus., pl. 19 1/2 cm. [HV5072.R3] 17-23969
1. Temperance. I. Title.

RITCHIE, William. 178.
Scripture testimony against intoxicating wine. By the Rev. William Ritchie ... New York, National temperance society and publication house, 1866. 213 p. 16 cm. [HV5182.R5] 15-22915
1. Temperance. I. Title.

ROBINSON, John Bunyan, 1834- 178.
The serpent of Sugar Creek colony, a temperance narrative of pioneer life in Ohio. By Rev. J. B. Robinson ... Philadelphia, Pa., G. W. Johnson, printer, 1885. 128 p. front., illus., pl., port. 16 1/2 cm. [HV5068.R65] 22-3174
1. Temperance. I. Title.

SMALL, Samuel White, 1851- 178.
The white angel of the world, that foretells the freedom of the nations from the evils of strong drink. By Rev. Sam'l W. Small...John P. St. John, Miss Frances E. Willard, Mother Stewart, Charles Morris. Lynn, Mass., A. W. Atkinson [c1893] v, 7-623 p. front., illus., plates, ports. 23 cm. [HV5292.S6] 10-7155
1. Temperance. I. Morris, Charles, 1833-1922. II. St. John, John Pierce, 1833-1916. III. Willard, Frances Elizabeth, 1839-1896. IV. Stewart, Mrs. Eliza (Daniel) 1816-1908. V. Title.

SMALL, Samuel White, 1851- 178.
1931.
The white angel of the world, that foretells the freedom of the nations from the evils of strong drink. By Rev. Sam'l W. Small...in collaboration with Charles Morris, esq. Philadelphia, Pa., Peerless publishing co. [c1891] v, 7-603 p. front., illus., plates, ports. 23 cm. [HV5292.S58] 10-7154
1. Temperance. I. Morris, Charles, 1833-1922. II. Title.

SOUTHERN Baptist 178.1
convention. Sunday school board. Baptist training union dept.
Youth looks at liquor, compiled by the Training union department of the Baptist Sunday school board. Nashville, Broadman press. 1944 51 p. 19 cm. "A series of addresses given by fifteen young people ... in the Better speakers' tournament of the southwide training union assembly at Ridgecrest in the summer of 1943."--Introd. [HV5060.S665] 44-14071
1. Temperance. I. Title.

STEVENS, Lillian M N (Ames) 178.
Mrs. 1844-1914.
What Lillian M. N. Stevens said [comp. by] Anna A. Gordon. Evanston, Ill., National woman's Christian temperance union, 1914. v, 88 p. front. (port.) 19 cm. Selections from addresses delivered before annual conventions of the National woman's Christian temperance union 1899-1913. [HV5296.S7] 14-20401 0.50
1. Temperance. I. Gordon, Anna Adams, 1853- comp. II. Title.

THE temperance text-book; 178.
a collecction of facts and interesting anecdotes, illustrating the evils of intoxicating drinks ... Philadelphia, Brown & Sinquet; New York, Howe & Bates, 1836. 154 p. 15 1/2 cm. [HV5072.T5] 10-1881

1. Temperance.

THOUGHTS on the evils of 178. *drunkenness, and the blessings of temperance,* suggested to the members of the total abstinence societies, established during the mission, by the Passionist fathers, as a means to reclaim drunkards... New York, P. O'Shea, 1868. 1 p. l., [5]-65, [1] p. 15 1/2 cm. [HV5296.T6] 9-33861
1. Temperance.

TINLING, Christine Isabel, 178
1869-
Temperance tales, for the Loyal temperance legion [by] Christine I. Tinling. Evanston, Ill., National woman's Christian temperance union [c1913] 49 p. 22 cm. $0.10 [HV5068.T5] 13-8926
1. Temperance. I. Title.

TUCKER, David N 1834- 178.
A struggle for life and victory through the Lamb, by D. N. Tucker. Sycamore, Ill., Baker & Arnold, 1879. iv, [5]-64 p. 20 cm. [HV5296.T8] 10-12950
1. Temperance. I. Title.

VANDERSLOOT, Jacob Samuel, 178.
1834-1882.
The true path; or, Gospel temperance; being the life, work and speeches of Francis Murphy, Dr. Henry A. Reynolds, and their co-laborers. Embracing also a history of the Women's Christian temperance union. By Rev. J. Sam'l Vandersloot... New York, H. S. Goodspeed & co.; Boston, Crocker & co.; [etc., etc.] c1878] xi p., 1 l., 13-642 p. incl. plates, ports., front., port. 19 1/2 cm. [HV5292.V3] 10-7143
1. Murphy, Francis, 1836-1907. 2. Reynolds, Henry Augustus, 1839- 3. Temperance. 4. Woman's Christian temperance union. I. Title.

VANDERSLOOT, Jacob Samuel, 178.
1834-1882.
The true path; or, The Murphy movement and gospel temperance. A complete history of the...great reformatory wave now deluging our land; together with the biography, addresses, incidents and anecdotes of Francis Murphy... By Rev. J. Saml. Vandersloot... Philadelphia, W. Flint; Minneapolis, Minn., Haber brothers; [etc., etc.] 1877. 2 p. l., [3]-408 p. front., (port.) 19 cm. [HV5292.V28] 10-7144
1. Murphy, Francis, 1836-1907. 2. Temperance. I. Title.

WESTERMAN, John. 178'.1
Liquor and commonsense. [Melbourne] Joint Board of Christian Education of Australia and New Zealand [1968?] 20 p. 21 cm. [HV5258.W46] 72-436193 0.20
1. Temperance. I. Joint Board of Christian Education of Australia and New Zealand. II. Title.

WILLARD, Warren Wyeth, 1905- 922
Steeple Jim, by Warren Wyeth Willard, foreword by Robert Dick Wilson... Princeton, N.J., Princeton publishing house, 1929. xv, 301 p. front., ports. 21 cm. "The biography of James Alfred Parker."--Introd. Bibliography included in introduction. [BV4935.P3W5] 30-8277
1. Parker, James Alfred, 1880-1929. 2. Temperance. 3. Steeple-jacks. 4. Evangelistic work. I. Title.

WOOLLEY, John Granville, 178.
1850-1922.
The sower, by John G. Woolley. Chicago, The Church press [c1898] 1 p. l., 83 p. pl. 16 1/2 x 13 cm. [HV5296.W83] 46-35569
1. Temperance. I. Title.

Temperance—Addresses, essays, lectures.

BACON, Leonard, 1802-1881. 178.
A discourse on the traffic in spirituous liquors, delivered in the Center church, New Haven, February 6, 1838, by Leonard Bacon. With an appendix, exhibiting the present state and influence of the traffic in the city of New Haven. New Haven, Printed by B. L. Hamlen, 1838. 54 p. 22 cm. [HV5295.B23] 46-40330
1. Temperance—Addresses, essays, lectures. 2. Liquor traffic—New Haven. I. Title.

BANKS, Louis Albert, 1855- 178.
The saloon-keeper's ledger; a series of temperance revival discourses, by Rev. Louis Albert Banks ... with introduction by the Rev. Theodore L. Cuyler ... New York, London and Toronto, Funk & Wagnalls company, 1895. 129 p. 19 1/2 cm. [HV5296.B28] 9-33824
1. Temperance—Addresses, essays, lectures. I. Title.

BANKS, Louis Albert, 1855- 178.
Seven times around Jericho; a series of temperance revival discourses, by Rev. Louis Albert Banks ... with introduction by the Rev. C. H. Mead ... New York, London and Toronto, Funk & Wagnalls company, 1896. 134 p. 19 1/2 cm. [HV5296.B3] 9-33825
1. Temperance—Addresses, essays, lectures. I. Title.

CLOPTON, Abner W. comp. 178.
Wisdom's voice to the rising generation being a selection of the best addresses and sermons on intemperance, from Dwight, Rush, Kittredge, Porter, Beecher, Sprague and others... By Abner W. Clopton and Eli Ball... Philadelphia, Pub. by the compilers [18--] vi, [2] 172 p. 18 cm. [HV5035.C6] A 14
1. Temperance—Addresses, essays, lectures. I. Ball, Eli. II. Title.

GOUGH, John Bartholomew, 178.
1817-1886.
Platform echoes: or, Leaves from my note-book of forty years. Comprising living truths for head and heart ... By John B. Gough ... With an introduction and sketch of Mr. Gough's life and work, by Rev. Lyman Abbott ... With a portrait of the author, and two hundred and twenty-seven engravings ... Hartford, Conn., A. D. Worthington & co., 1885. xxviii, 29-639 p. incl. illus., plates. front. (&ort.) 23 cm. Added t.-p., illustrated. [HV5296.G78] 9-33853
1. Temperance—Addresses, essays, lectures. I. Abbott, Lyman, 1835-1922. II. Title.

GOUGH, John Bartholomew, 178
1817-1886.
Platform echoes: or, Living for head and heart ... by John B. Gough ... With a history of Mr. Gough's life and work, by Rev. Lyman Abbott, D. D. Superbly illustrated with two hundred and twenty-five engravings ... Hartford, Conn., A. D. Worthington & co., 1890. xxviii, 29-639 p. incl. illus., plates. 23 cm. Added t.-p., illustrated: Platform echoes, or, Leaves from my note-book of forty years. [HV5296.G78 1890] 36-16722
1. Temperance—Addresses, essays, lectures. I. Abbott, Lyman, 1835-1922. II. Title.

THE great awakening on 178. *temperance,* and The great controversy, Romanism, Protestantism and Judaism. A series of lectures, papers and biographies from the ablest advocates of tem perance, and prominent clergymen of the Roman Catholic, Protestant and Jewish churhces ... St. Louis, Anchor publishing company, 1878. 386, [2], 241, [3] p. incl. ports. 22 cm. [HV5186.G8] 10-4669
1. Temperance—Addresses, essays, lectures. 2. Catholic church—Doctrinal and controversial works.

HALL, Newman, 1816-1902. 178.
Newman Hall in America. Rev. Dr. Hall's lectures on Temperance and Missions to the masses; also, an oration on Christian liberty; together with his reception by the New York Union league club. Reported by Wm. Anderson. [New York] New York news company, 1868. 137 p. 19 1/2 cm. Full name: Christopher Newman Hall [HV5296.H2] 10-7133
1. Temperance—Addresses, essays, lectures. 2. Missions. 3. Liberty. I. [Full name: Christopher Newman Hall] II. Title.

NATIONAL temperance society 178.
and publication house, New York.
Temperance sermons, delivered in response to an invitation of the National temperance society and publication house. New York, The National temperance society and publication house [1873] 2 p. l., [9]-400 p. 18 1/2 cm. [HV5060.N34] 45-37960
1. Temperance—Addresses, essays, lectures. I. Title.

Contents omitted.

OHIO anti-saloon league. 178.
The saloon must go! Anti-saloon contest selections, nos. 1 and 2. For use in anti-saloon contests conducted by young people's societies of Christian endeavor, Epworth leagues, Baptist young people's unions ... and other organizations, and adapted for public and private readings and all non-partisan anti-saloon agitation ... Columbus, O., The Ohio anti-saloon league, 1895. cover-title, 1 l. p., 5-120, [2], 7-96 p. 18 1/2 cm. [HV5296.O48] 43-36883
1. Temperance—Addresses, essays, lectures. I. Title.

PALFREY, John Gorham, 1796- 178.1
1881.
Discourses on intemperance, preached in the church in Brattle square, Boston, April 5, 1827, the day of annual fast, and April 8, the Lord's day following. By John G. Palfrey... [Boston] N. Hale, 1827. 111 p. 16 cm. [HV5295.P3] 33-38078
1. Temperance—Addresses, essays, lectures. I. Title.

Temperance and religion.

COME, Arnold B 178.1
Drinking; a Christian position. Philadelphia, Westminister Press [1964] 84 p. 19 cm. (Christian perspectives on social problems) [HV5175.C6] 64-12779
1. Temperance and religion. I. Title.

TILSON, Charles Everett. 177
Should Christians drink? Nashville, Abingdon Press [1957] 128p. 20cm. [HV5175.T5] 178.1 57-6122
1. Temperance and religion. I. Title.

Temperance — Biblical arguments.

BEEBE, George Monroe. 178.
Bible temperance is not total abstinence, by George Monroe Beebe ... Ellenville, N.Y., G. M. Beebe & co., 1918. ix, 358 p. 19 1/2 cm. [HV5183.B4] 18-2027
1. Temperance—Biblical arguments. I. Title.

BIBLE. English. Selections.
1910.
The Holy Bible repudiates "prohibition"; compilation of all verses containing the words "wine" or "strong drink," proving that the Scriptures commend and command the temperate use of alcoholic beverages. With comment by George G. Brown. Louisville, Ky., G. G. Brown [1910] 103 p. port. 22 cm. [HV5183.B6] 10-19635
1. Temperance — Biblical arguments. 2. Prohibition. I. Brown, George Garvin, b. 1846. II. Title.

BIBLE. Selections. English. 178.
1910.
The Holy Bible repudiates "prohibition"; compilation of all verses containing the words "wine" or "strong drink," proving that the Scriptures commend and command the temperate use of alcoholic beverages ... With comment by George Brown. Louisville, Ky., G. G. Brown [1910] 103 p. port. 22 cm. [HV5183.B6] 10-19635
1. Temperance—Biblical arguments. 2. Prohibition. I. Brown, George Garvin, 1846- II. Title.

COLLINS, Almer M. 178
Bible temperance; a critical study of the wines of the Old and New Testaments, including sacramental wine, together with several chapters of the different phases of the temperance reform, and many beautiful temperance gems by the world's most famous authors; by A. M. Collins ... Cincinnati, Standard publishing company, 1882. 200 p. 19 cm. [HV5182.C8] 10-333
1. Temperance—Biblical arguments. 2. Temperance. I. Title.

DODSHON, Joseph Henry, 178.1
1868- comp.
God's word and man's; abstience, temperance and excess (first survey) by the Rev. Dr. Joseph H. Dodshon ... with William P. Taylor. New York, R. Long & R. R. Smith, inc., 1932. 3 p. l., 58 p. 20 cm. Contents.pt. i. God's word; the Bible--texts.--pt. ii. Man's word; notable quotations. [HV5060.D6] 32-17277
1. Temperance—Biblical arguments. 2. Quotations. I. Taylor, William Patterson, 1864- joint comp. II. Title. III. Title: Bible. English. Selections. 1932.

DUFFIELD, George, 1794-1868. 178
The Bible rule of temperance; total abstinence from all intoxicating drink. By Geo. Duffield ... New York, National temperance society and publication house, 1868. viii p., 1 l., 9-206 p. 16 cm. [HV5182.D8] 10-4650
1. Temperance—Biblical arguments. I. Title.
Contents omitted.

ELLIS, John, b.1815.
A reply to "The Academy's" review of "The wine question in light of the new dispensation." By John Ellis ... New York, Pub. by the author. 1883. 1 p. l., 270 p. 19 1/2 cm. [HV5184.E6] 6-24612
1. Temperance—Biblical arguments. 2. New Jerusalem church. I. Title.

ELLIS, John, b.1815.
The wine question in the light of the new dispensation. A controversy, in which the views of his opponents are fairly and fully represented in their own language. By John Ellis ... Five works in one volume ... New York, The author, 1886. 736 p. illus. 19 cm. Each part has special t.-p. Contents."Pure wine--fermented wine and other alcoholic drinks," first published in 1880.--"The wine question in the light of the new dispensation," first published in 1882.--"Reply to the Academy's review," first published in 1883.-- "Intoxicants, prohibition, and our New Church periodicals during 1884-85," published in 1885.--"Deterioration of the Puritan stock," first published in 1884. [HV5184.E7] 10-4506
1. Temperance—Biblical agruments. 2. New Jerusalem church. I. Title.

EMERSON, Edward Randolph, 178.
1856-
A lay thesis on Bible wines. by Edward R. Emerson ... [New York] Merrill & Baker, 1902. 63 p. 19cm. [HV5183.E5] 4-28236
1. Temperance—Biblical arguments. 2. Wine and wine making. I. Title.

[ENGLISH, Francis M.] 178.
Prohibition a fallacy, a fanaticism, and an absurdity ... Because contrary to the teachings of the Bible. Jerseyville, Ill., Commercial book and job printing office, 1890. 2 p. l., 104 p. 19 1/2 cm. Preface signed: Francis M. English. [HV5183.E6] 10-4664
1. Temperance—Biblical arguments. 2. Prohibition. I. Title.

FERRIN, Clark Elam, 1848- 178.
1881.
The wine texts of the Bible, each arranged under the Hebrew or Greek word translated wine in that text; showing the different kinds of wine, their nature and uses, with a few notes, preface, introduction and conclusion. By Rev. C. E. Ferrin. New York, Lovell, Adam, Wesson & co., 1877. 72 p. 13 cm. [HV5182.F5] 10-4651
1. Temperance—Biblical arguments. I. Title.

GREGORY, John, of Woburn, 178
Mass.
The bramble. To which is added a letter to Rev. Thomas Whittermore, an answer to the hoe, a sermon on temperance in all things, delivered at Woburn, Stoneham, and New Rowley, and a reply to certain editions who noticed The bramble532d. ed.] By John Gregory ... Pub. by an association of gentlemen in Woburn, Mass. Methuen [Mass.] S. J. Varney, printer, 1837. viii, [9]-114 p. 18 cm. [HV5182.G83] 9-33806
1. Temperance—Biblical arguments. 2. Oakes, George P. The hoe, designed to uproot "The bramble ... I. Title.

GRIFFING, C. S. S. 178.
Christianity not a temperance religion. Jesus of Nazareth did not institute the eucharist, nor make wine at a wedding feast. A new departure by the church necessary and practical. As maintained in an address by C. S. S. Griffing, at Columbus, Ohio, July 26th, 1876. Rev. and

enl. Columbus, O., L. G. Thrall & co., 1879. 60 p. 22 cm. [HV5183.G8] 10-4665
1. Temperance—Biblical arguments. I. Title.

HALL, Newman, 1816-1902.
The scriptural claims of total abstinence. By Newmann Hall, LL.B. New York, National temperance society, 1868. 62, [2] p. 16 1/2 cm. Full name: Christopher Newman Hall [HV5258.H2] 10-4901
1. Temperance—Biblical arguments. 2. Temperance. I. [Full name: Christopher Newman Hall] II. Title.

JEFFRIES, James J. 178.
Temperance vs. prohibition, from the standpoint of the Bible and Bible only, by James J. Jeffries ... Los Angeles, Cal., J. J. Jeffries [c1914] 3 p. l., 67 p. 15 cm. [HV5183.J4] 14-18495 0.25
1. Temperance—Biblical arguments. 2. Prohibition. I. Title.

KERR, Edith A. 220.8'394'1
Alcohol and the scriptures by Edith A. Kerr. With introduction by A. T. Stevens. 2d. ed. rev. and enl. Melbourne, Temperance Committee of the Presbyterian Church of Victoria, 1968. 44 p. 21 cm. Bibliography: p. 42. [HV5182.K43 1968] 77-359108 0.35
1. Temperance—Biblical arguments. I. Presbyterian Church of Victoria. Temperance Committee. II. Title.

LEES, Frederic Richard, 1815-1897. 178
The temperance Bible-commentary; giving at one view, version, criticism, and exposition, in regard to all passages of Holy Writ bearing on 'wine' and 'strong drink,' or illustrating the principles of the temperance reformation. By Dr. Frederic Richard Lees, F.S.A., and Rev. Dawson Burns ... New York, Sheldon & co. [etc.] 1870. xiviii, 469 p. 23 cm. "First American edition, with a new preface by Tayler Lewis." [HV5182.L4 1870] 17-31860
1. Temperance—Biblical arguments. 2. Bible—Commentaries. I. Burns, Dawson, 1828-1909, joint author. II. Lewis, Tayler, 1802-1877, ed. III. Title.

MACLEAN, John, 1800-1886.
An examination of the essays Bacchus [by R. B. Grindrod] and Anti- Bacchus [by Benjamin Parsons] ... By John Maclean ... Princeton, Printed by J. Bogart, 1841. 140 p., 1 l. 23 cm. Published originally in the Princeton review. [HV5184.M2] 10-4507
1. Grindrod, Ralph Barnes Bacchus. 2. Parsons, Benjamin, 1797-1855. Anti-Bacchus. 3. Temperance—Biblical arguments. I. Title.

MAIR, John, 1798-1877. 178
Nephaleia; or, Total abstinence from intoxicating liquors in man's normal state of health, the doctrine of the Bible, in a series of letters, with addenda ... (with colored plates of the stomach, as affected by strong drink.) ... By John Mair ... New York, Sheldon & company; Boston, Gould & Lincoln; [etc., etc.] 1861. 300, [2] p. illus., col. pl. 19 1/2 cm. [HV5182.M3] 10-4654
1. Temperance—Biblical arguments. I. Title.

PATTON, William, 1798-1879. 178
The laws of fermentation and the wines of the ancients. By Rev. William Patton ... New York, National temperance society and publication house, 1871. 129 p. 20 cm. [HV5182.P3] 10-4655
1. Temperance—Biblical arguments. I. Title.

RAGSDALE, John Thomas, 1851- 178.2
The Bible on temperance; against prohibition, by J. T. Ragsdale, sr. Boston, The Chistopher publishing house [c1931] 99 p. 21 cm. [HV5183.R3] 32-2643
1. Temperance—Biblical arguments. 2. Prohibition. I. Title.

SAMSON, George Whitefield, 1819-1896. 178
The divine law as to wines; established by the testimony of sages, physicians, and legislators against the use of fermented and intoxicating wines; confirmed by their provision of unfermented wines to be used for medicinal and sacramental purposes. By G. W. Samson... New York, National temperance society and publication house, 1880. 326 p. illus. 19 1/2 cm. [HV5182.S2] 10-4657
1. Temperance—Biblical arguments. I. Title.

SAMSON, George Whitefield, 1819-1896. 178.1
The divine law as to wines; established by the testimony of sages, physicians, and legislators against the use of fermented and intoxicating wines; confirmed by their provision of unfermented wines to be used for medicinal and sacramental purposes. By G. W. Samson... New York, National temperance society and publication house, 1881. 467 p. 19 1/2 cm. [HV5182.S2 1881] 36-16745
1. Temperance—Biblical arguments. I. Title.

SAMSON, George Whitefield, 1819-1896. 178
The divine law as to wines. Established by the testimony of sages, physicians, and legislators against the use of fermented and intoxicating wines, confirmed by Egyptian, Greek, and Roman methods of preparing unfermented wines for festal, medicinal, and sacramental uses. By Dr. G. W. Samson... Philadelphia, J. B. Lippincott & co., 1885. iv, 513 p. 19 1/2 cm. [HV5182.S22] 10-4658
1. Temperance—Biblical arguments. I. Title.

SHERMAN, Josiah Patterson, 1860-
The dry side of a wet subject ... By Josiah P. Sherman. Camden, N.J., The Bethany press, 1920. 143 p. incl. front. (port.) illus. 17 1/2 cm. [HV51S2.S5] 20-12468
1. Temperance—Biblical arguments. I. Title.

SIKES, J. R. 178
The Biblical reason why prohibition is wrong; or, What the Bible teaches with regard to the use and abuse of wine and strong drink ... By Rev. J. R. Sikes ... [Rev.] Loudonville, O., P. H. Stauffer, 1886. 1 p. l., vii-x, 11-116 p. 20 cm. [HV5182.S6] 10-4667
1. Temperance—Biblical arguments. 2. Prohibition. I. Title.

SIKES, J. R. 178.
The Biblical reason why prohibition is wrong. In four parts. Comprising a complete text book of the Bible teaching on the use and abuse of wine and strong drink ... A discussion of the non-intoxicating wine theory and other miscellaneous matter bearing on the subject of prohibition. By Rev. J. R. Sikes ... [2d ed.] Loudonville, O., P. H. Stauffer, 1887. 169, 66, 86 p., 1 l., 170 p. front. (port.) plates. 20 cm. [HV5183.S62] 10-4529
1. Temperance—Biblical arguments. 2. Prohibition. I. Title.

SIKES, J. R. 178.
Pen pictures of prohibition and prohibitionists. By Rev. J. R. Sikes ... Loudonville, O., P. H. Stauffer, 1887. 1 p. l., iv, 5-57 p. 14 cm. [HV5089.S54] 18-21287
1. Temperance—Biblical arguments. 2. Prohibition. I. Title.

STUART, Moses, 1780-1852. 178
Essay on the prize-question, whether the use of distilled liquors, or traffic in them, is compatible, at the present time, with making a profession of Christianity? By Moses Stuart ... New-York, J. P. Haven; Boston, Perkins & Marvin; [etc., etc.] 1830. 70 p. 21 cm. [HV5182.S8] 10-4683
1. Temperance—Biblical arguments. I. Title.

THAYER, William Makepeace, 1820-1898.
Communion wine and Bible temperance. Being a review of Dr. Thos. Laurie's article in the Bibliotheca sacra, of January, 1869. By Rev. William M. Thayer. New York, National temperance society and publication house, 1869. 90 p. 19 1/2 cm. [HV5184.T4] 10-4509
1. Laurie, Thomas, 1821-1897. What wine shall we use at the Lord's supper? 2. Temperance—Biblical arguments. I. Title.

VAN BUREN, J. M. 178.
Gospel temperance. By Rev. J. M. Van Buren. New York, National temperance society and publication house, 1877-84. 2 v. 19 cm. Pt. 2 has title: Gospel temperance, a new principle. Pt. 1 contains chapters I-XIX, iv, 5-114 p: pt. 2, chapters XXI-XXIII, cover-title, 123-251 p. Between p. 128 and 129 are inserted p. 127a-127d. [HV5182.V3] 6-38808
1. Temperance—Biblical arguments. I. Title.

WASSON, Edmond Atwill, 1864- 178.
Religion and drink, by the Rev. E. A. Wasson ... New York, Burr printing house, 1914. 301 p. 21 cm. $1.25. [HV5183.W26] 14-12525
1. Temperance—Biblical arguments. I. Title.

WHITMORE, Orin Beriah, 1851-
Bible wines vs. the saloon keeper's Bible; a study of the two-wine theory of the Scriptures and an arraignment of the argument for Biblical sanction of the use of intoxicants. By Rev. Orin B. Whitmore...With an introduction by the Rev. W. H. G. Temple... Seattle, Press of the Alaska printing co., 1911. 3 p. l., 115 p., 1 l. 23 cm. [HV5180.W6] 11-18999
1. Temperance—Biblical arguments. I. Title.

WILKERSON, David R. 241'.6'81
Sipping saints / David Wilkerson. Old Tappan, N.J. : Spire Books, c1978. 127 p. ; 18 cm. [HV5180.W62] 78-17876 ISBN 0-8007-8338-7 pbk. : 1.95
1. Temperance—Biblical arguments. 2. Alcoholism and religion. I. Title.

Temperance — Bibliography

METHODIST Church (United States) Division of Alcohol Problems and General Welfare.
Alcohol problems and general welfare; comprehensive resource list. [Washington, D.C., 1964] 1 v. (various pagings) 28 cm. 65-76898
1. Temperance — Bibl. 2. Church and social problems — Bibl. I. Title.

Temperance—Congresses.

NATIONAL temperance congress, New York, 1890. 178.
Proceedings of the National temperance congress, held in the Broadway tabernacle, New York ...June 11th and 12th, 1890 ... New York [and] London, Funk & Wagnalls, 1891. xiii, 406 p. 20 cm. [HV5288.1890.N3] 9-18251
1. Temperance—Congresses. I. Title.

Temperance—Drama.

THE wine cup; 244
or Saved at last. A temperance sketch, in two scenes. New York, Happy hours company [1876] 8 p. 19 cm. (The amateur stage.) [HV5069.W58] 27-10304
1. Temperance—Drama.

Temperance—Exercises, recitations, etc.

CROCKETT, Harriet Pritchard, comp. 178.
Manual for teaching temperance in daily vacation Bible and week day religious schools, compiled by Harriet Pritchard Crockett. Evanston, Ill., National woman's Christian temperance union, c1927. 63, [1] p. illus. 23 cm. Contains bibliographies. [HV5060.C93] 27-12349
1. Temperance—Exercises, recitations, etc. 2. Temperance—Study and teaching. I. Woman's Christian temperance union. II. Title.

MARSH, John, 1788-1868, comp. 178.
The temperance speaker, compiled from various sources for the use of bands of hope, juvenile temperance associations, cadets of temperance, &c., in their monthly and weekly meetings. By Rev. John Marsh ... New York, American temperance union, 1860. 70, [2] p. 20 cm. [HV5071.M3] 16-9105
1. Temperance—Exercises, recitations, etc. 2. Readers and speakers 1800-1870. I. Title.

Temperance—Fiction.

BIGHAM, Robert W. 178.
Wine and blood. By the Rev. Robert W. Bigham ... Ed. by T. O. Summers, D. D. Nashville, Tenn., Southern Methodist publishing house, 1879. 208 p. 17 cm. A temperance story. [HV5068.B6] 10-313
1. Temperance—Fiction. I. Summers, Thomas Osmond, 1812-1882. ed. II. Title.

BRIDGES, James F. 178.1
Who is to blame! By J. F. Bridges ... illustrated by Ransom D. Marvin ... [Glendale, Calif., The Church press, c1938] 95, [1] p. illus. 19 cm. [HV5068.B78] 38-39091
1. Temperance—Fiction. I. Title.

BROWN, Thurlow Weed, d.1866. 269
Why I am a temperance man; a series of letters to a friend. Together with Tales and sketches from real life, and Hearthstone reveries. By Turlow W. Brown... Auburn, Derby and Miller; Buffalo, Derby, Orton and Mulligan; [etc., etc.] 1853. viii, [9]-384 p. front. (port.) plates. 20 cm. [BV5068.B8] 10-2125
1. Temperance—Fiction. I. Title.

THE family temperance meeting: or, An illustration of the nature, symptoms, and danger of intemperance. By the author of "Sabbath school teacher's visits." Boston, J. Loring, 1830. 147, [1] p. incl. front. 16 cm. [HV5068.F2] 10-608 178.
1. Temperance—Fiction. I. Sabbath school teacher's visits, author of.

MANN, Cyrus, 1785-1859. 178.
The Clinton family: or, The history of the temperance reformation. By Rev. Cyrus Mann...Written for the Massachusetts Sabbath school society, and rev. by the Committee of publication. Boston, Massachusetts Sabbath school society, 1833. vii, [12]-263 p. incl. front., illus. 15 cm. [HV5068.M3] 10-614
1. Temperance—Fiction. I. Massachusetts Sabbath school society. Committee of publication. II. Title.

[PEARL, Cyril] 178.
Tales of intemperance. By an observer. Written for the Massachusetts Sabbath school society, and rev. by the committee of publication. Boston, Massachusetts Sabbath school society, 1836. 1 p. l., [vi]-v p., 1 l., [9]-99 p. front. 15 cm. [HV5068.P5] 10-617
1. Temperance—Fiction. I. Massachusetts Sabbath school society. II. Title.
Contents omitted.

THE unjust judge; 178
or, The evils of intemperance on judges, lawyers, and politicians. By a member of the Ohio bar... Mansfield, O. [Printed at the Western branch book concern of the Wesleyan Methodist connection of America] 1854. 352 p. 17 1/2 cm. [HV5068.U55] 41-34231
1. Temperance—Fiction. I. A member of the Ohio bar.

Temperance—History

ARMSTRONG, Lebbeus, 1775-1860. 178.
The temperance reformation: its history, from the organization of the first temperance society to the adoption of the liquor law of Maine, 1851; and the consequent influence of the promulgation of that law on the political interest of the state of New York, 1852. By Rev. Lebbeus Armstrong ... New York, Boston [etc.] Fowlers and Wells, 1853. xvi, 17-408 p. 20 cm [HV5291.A8] 10-3880
1. Temperance—Hist. 2. Liquor problem—U.S. I. Title.

CHALFANT, Harry Malcolm, 1869- 178.
Father Penn and John Barleycorn, by Harry Malcolm Chalfant ... Harrisburg, Pa., The Evangelical press [c1920] 291 p. illus., plates. 20 cm. [HV5090.P4C5] 20-22553
1. Temperance—Hist. 2. Liquor problem—Pennsylvania. I. Title.

HOBBS, Charles Albert.
The boys of Princeville; or, Temperance reform in the fifties; illustrations by Jane H. Allen. Philadelphia, American Baptist

pub. society [1898] 152 p. illus. 12 cm. Oct
I. Title.

SHAW, James. 178.
History of the great temperance reforms of the nineteenth century, exhibiting: the evils of intemperance,--the methods of reform,--the Woman's crusade,--and the coming conflict on the temperance question ... By Rev. James Shaw. For the author. Cincinnati, O., Hitchcock & Walden; [etc., etc., c1875] 1 p. l., ix, [1], [9]-505 p. front., plates, ports. 22 cm. [HV5292.S5] 10-7153
1. Temperance—Hist. I. Title.

[STEVENSON, Katharine Lent] 1853-
A brief history of the Woman's Christian temperance union; outline course of study for local unions.' Evanston, Ill., The Union signal, c1907. 117 p. 20 cm. References--suggested topics--questions: p. 81-93. 7-11008
I. Title.

Temperance—Societies.

CATHOLIC total abstinence union of America. 178.
... *Annual convention.* Cambridge. v. illus. (ports.) 27 cm. At head of title: Catholic total abstinence union of America. Advertising matter interspersed. [HV5287.C3A3] ca 14
1. Temperance—Societies. I. Title.

WOMAN'S Christian Temperance Union. 178.
Report of the annual meeting. [Evanston? Ill.] v. 20-23 cm. Title varies: 18 Minutes.--Reports (varies alightly) [HV5227.W5A3] 52-15119
1. Temperance—Societies. I. Title.

WORLD'S woman's Christian temperance union. 178.
Report made to the first convention of the World's women's Christian temperance union, held in Boston, U.S.A., Nov. 10-19, 1891. By its secretary, Mary Clement Leavitt. Boston, A. Mudge & son, printers, 1891. 72 p. 23 cm. [HV5227.W5A7] CA 10
1. Temperance—Societies. I. Leavitt, Mrs. Mary Greenleaf (Clement) 1830- II. Title.

Temperance—Songs and music.

GORDON, Anna Adams, 1853-1931, comp. 783.
Marching songs for young crusaders. Temperance songs for the Cold water army. By Anna A. Gordon ... Chicago, Woman's temperance publishing association [c1885] 62 p., 1 l. 17 x 13 1/2 cm. Close score (SATB), or for solo voice with piano accompaniment. [M2198.G65M3] 44-31495
1. Temperance—Songs and music. 2. Sunday-schools—Hymn-books. I. Woman's temperance publishing association. II. Title.

HOWER, Charles P. comp. 783.
... *Francis Murphy gospel temperance hymns,* with sketch of the great reformer's life. Compiled and published by Chas. P. Hower and Jno. L. Linton ... Philadelphia, Gumpert & bro., prs., 1877. viii, 88 p. 13 1/2 cm. Text on p. [3] of cover. Without music. [M2198.H83F7] 45-43128
1. Temperance—Songs and music. 2. Hymns, English. I. Linton, John L., joint comp. II. Murphy, Francis, 1836-1907. III. Title.

PLIMPTON, Job, arr. 783.
The Washington choir, original and selected music: with an accompaniment for the piano-forte or organ. Composed, selected, arranged, and adapted to the cause of total abstinence. By J. Plimpton ... Boston, Printed for the author by Kidder and Wright, 1843. cover-title, 79, [1] p. 25 cm. In 2 parts, each with special t.-p. For 1-4 voices. [M2198.P73W3] 45-28150
1. Temperance—Songs and music. I. Title.

ROOT, George Frederick, 1820-1895. 783.
The musical foundation, enlarged; a collection of temperance music, for public and social meetings and the home circle. To which is appended the odes of the Good templars. By Geo. F. Root. Cincinnati, New York [etc.] The John Church company [1895] 126 p. 17 cm. [M2198.R76M9 1895] 45-46634
1. Temperance—Songs and music. 2. International order of Good templars—Songs and music. 3. Hymns, English. I. Title.

Temperance—Study and teaching.

PALMER, Bertha Rachael, 1880- 178.1
A syllabus in alcohol education. By Bertha Rachael Palmer... [2d ed.] [Evanston, Ill.] The Dept. of scientific temperance instruction of the National woman's Christian temperance union [c1934] 53 p. 22 cm. "Research work and preparation of material done in the Alcohol investigation library of the Scientific temperance federation, Boston, Massachusetts, 1933." Bibliography: p. 51-53. [HV5128.U6P3 1934] 34-6132
1. Temperance—Study and teaching. 2. Alcohol—Physiological effect. I. Title. II. Title: Alcohol education.

Temperance (Virtue)

CHERESO, Cajetan. 241.68
The virtue of honor and beaty according to St. Thomas Aquinas; an analysis of moral beauty. River Forest, Ill., 1960. xviii, 89 p. 23 cm. (The Aquinas library) Bibliography: p. 86-89. [BV4647.T4C5] 64-56370
1. Thomas Aquinas, Saint — Ethics. 2. Temperance (Virtue) I. Title.

Templars.

ADDISON, Charles Greenstreet, d.1866. 271'.79
The Knights Templar history / by C. G. Addison ; enl. from the research of numerous authors ... the whole affording a complete history of Masonic knighthood from the origin of the orders to the present time, adapted to the American system by Robert Macoy. 1st AMS ed. New York : AMS Press, 1978. 637 p. : ill. ; 23 cm. Reprint of the 1912 ed. published by Macoy Pub. and Masonic Supply Co., New York. Includes index. [CR4743.A4 1978] 76-29832 ISBN 0-404-15407-7 : 47.50
1. Freemasons. Knights Templars. 2. Templars. I. Macoy, Robert, 1815-1895. II. Title.

FREEMASONS. Massachusetts and Rhode Island. Grand commandery of Knights templars.
Grand commandery of Knights templars, Massachusetts and Rhode Island. 1805-1905. Clebration of centennial anniversary, in Boston, May 24, 1905. Published by order of the Grand commandery. [Central Falls, R. I., Press of E. L. Freeman & sons, 1905] x, 293 p. front., plates (1 col.) ports. 25 cm. Plate representing centennial medal is accompanied by leaf of descriptive letterpress. 5-36309
I. Title.

KREAMER, George W. comp.
St. John's commandery no. 4, Knights templar, Philadelphia; a condensed history from its organization June 10, 1819 to October, 1901, comp. by Sir George W. Kreamer, recorder. [Philadelphia? 1901] 337 p. incl. front., pl., port. 20 cm. 2-8168
I. Title.

MARTIN, Edward James. 271'.79
The trial of the Templars / by Edward J. Martin. 1st AMS ed. New York : AMS Press, 1978. 94 p. ; 28 cm. Reprint of the 1928 ed. published by G. Allen & Unwin, London. Includes bibliographical referenes and index. [CR4749.M3 1978] 76-29845 ISBN 0-404-15424-7 : 14.50
1. Templars. I. Title.

PANCOAST, Chalmers Lowell, 1880- 366.1
Templar tales; "Your pot of gold", by Sir Knight Chalmers Lowell Pancoast...Dedicated to freemasonry "the maker of men"... New York, N.Y., The Gettinger press, 1935. ix, 182 p. 21 cm. "Author's first edition. This 'first edition' has been printed especially for advance subscribers. Each copy being numbered and autographed by the author..." This copy neither numbered nor autographed. [HS745.P32] 35-1987
1. Templars. I. Title.

SIMON, Edith, 1917- 255'.79
The piebald standard : a biography of the Knights Templars / by Edith Simon. 1st AMS ed. New York : AMS Press, 1978, c1959. xi, 312 p., [8] leaves of plates : ill. ; 23 cm. Reprint of the ed. publishedby Cassell, London. Includes index. Bibliography: p. 301-302. [CR4743.S5 1978] 76-29836 ISBN 0-404-15419-0 : 32.00
1. Templars. I. Title.

Templars—History.

CAMPBELL, George Archibald, 1900- 271'.79
The Knights Templars. New York : AMS Press, [1980] p. cm. Reprint of the 1937 ed. published by Duckworth, London. Includes index. Bibliography: p. [CR4743.C27 1980] 78-63330 ISBN 0-404-17005-6 : 28.50
1. Templars—History. I. Title.

FREEMASONS. Illinois. Knights Templars. Grand Commandery.
History of the Grand Commandery of Knights Templar of the State of Illinois, from October 27,A.D. 1857 to October 25, A.D. 1881. [Chicago] 1885. 380 p. ports. 23 cm. [HS757.I3A5] 49-31902
I. Title.

Templars in England.

PARKER, Thomas William, 1921- 271
The Knights Templars in England. Tucson, Univ. of Ariz. Pr. [c.]1963. 195p. 24cm. Bibl. 63-11983 5.00
1. Templars in England. I. Title.

Templars of honor and temperance.

TEMPLE of honor illustrated. 178. A complete illustrated exposition of the subordinate temple and first three degrees of the order of the Templars of honor and temperance, commonly called the Temple of honor ... By a templar of fidelity and past worthy chief templar. Chicago, E. A. Cook, 1881. 155 p. illus. 19 cm. [HV5287.T43T5] CA 10
1. Templars of honor and temperance.

Templars of honor and temperance—Rituals.

TEMPLARS of honor and temperance. Supreme council. 178.
Installation, dedication, funeral and other ceremonies; together with rules, instructions, etc. for the use of deputies. Prepared and pub. by a committee appointed by the Supreme council of the Templars of honor and temperance. Cincinnati, Printed by Marshall & Langtry, 1855. 79, [1] p. 18 cm. [HV5287.T43A5 1855] 10-4857
1. Templars of honor and temperance—Rituals. I. Title.

Templars—Spain—Aragon.

FOREY, Alan John. 271'.79
The Templars in the Corona de Aragon [by] A. J. Forey. London, Oxford University Press, 1973. xi, 498 p. maps. 23 cm. (University of Durham. Publications) Bibliography: p. 455-470. [CR4755.S6A724 1973] 73-163691 ISBN 0-19-713137-9
1. Templars in Aragon. I. Title. II. Series: Durham, Eng. University. Publications.
Distributed by Oxford University Press N.Y. 30.00.

Temple Baptist Church, Colorado Springs.

TUCKER, Michael R. 286'.1788'56
The church that dared to change / Michael R. Tucker. Wheaton, Ill. : Tyndale House Publishers, 1975. x, 129, [2] p. ; 21 cm. Bibliography: p. [131] [BX6480.C65T456] 74-21971 ISBN 0-8423-0280-8 : 2.95
1. Temple Baptist Church, Colorado Springs. 2. Church renewal—Case studies. I. Title.

Temple Beth El of Northern Westchester, Chappaqua, N.Y.

TEMPLE Beth El of Northern Westchester, Chappaqua, N.Y. 296'.09747'277
Temple Beth El, 1972. [Editor: Alice Wolff Ozaroff. Chappaqua, N.Y., 1974] 1 v. (unpaged) illus. 27 cm. Cover title. [BM225.C35T456 1974] 74-80959
1. Temple Beth El of Northern Westchester, Chappaqua, N.Y. 2. Jews in Chappaqua, N.Y. I. Ozaroff, Alice Wolff, ed.

Temple Beth El, Rochester, N.Y.

ELKINS, Dov Peretz. 296
Humanizing Jewish life / Dov Peretz Elkins. South Brunswick : A. S. Barnes, 1976. p. cm. Includes index. Bibliography: p. [BM723.E5] 75-38456 ISBN 0-498-01912-8 : 9.95
1. Temple Beth El, Rochester, N.Y. 2. Elkins, Dov Peretz. 3. Jewish way of life. 4. Fellowship (Judaism) I. Title.

Temple, Ezra, 1865 or 6-1946.

DEN HARTOG, Egbert, 1892- 922.673
The tramp preacher. [New Sharan? Iowa, 1952, '1949] 214 p. illus. 20 cm. [BV3785.T36D4] 52-44002
1. Temple, Exra, 1865 or 6-1946. I. Title.

Temple, Frederick, abp. of Canterbury, 1821-1902.

SANDFORD, Ernest Gray, 1839-1910. 922.
Frederick Temple; an appreciation, by E. G. Sandford ... with a biographical introduction by William Temple ... London, Macmillan and co., limited; New York, The Macmillan company, 1907. ixvi p., 1 l., 318 p. 3 port. (incl. front.) 28 cm. "Archdeacon Sandford's 'Appreciation' was first published in Memoirs of Archbishop Temple ... 1906. Republished, with introduction by W. Temple 1907." [BX5199.T4S4] 8-12582
1. Temple, Frederick, abp. of Canterbury, 1821-1902. I. Temple William, abp. of Canterbury, 1881- II. Title.

SANDFORD, Ernest Grey, 1839-1910, ed. 922.
Memoirs of Archbishop Temple, by seven friends, edited by E. G. Sanford ... With photogravure and other illustrations ... London, Macmillan and co., limited; New York, The Macmillan company, 1906. 2 v. 6 pl., 5 port. (incl. fronts) 23 cm. Contents.I. Preface. Memoir of earlier years, 1821-1848, by the Rev. J. M. Wilson. Memoirs of the Education office period, 1848-1857, by H. J. Roby. Rugby memoir, 1857-1869, by F. E. Kitchener. Exeter memoir, 1869-1885, by the Venerable E. G. Sandford.--II. London memoir, 1885-1896, by the Venerable H. E. J. Bevan. Canterbury memoir, 1896-1902, by the Venerable H. M. Spooner. The primacy, 1896-1902, by the Right Rev. George Forrest Browne. Editor's supplement. [BX5199.T4S3] 6-15106
1. Temple, Frederick, abp. of Canterbury, 1821-1902. I. Title.

Temple, Frederick, Abp. of Canterbury, 1821-1902—Manuscripts—Indexes.

LAMBETH Palace. Library. 016.283'092'4
Index to the letters and papers of Frederick Temple, Archbishop of Canterbury, 1896-1902 in Lambeth Palace Library / by Melanie Barber. London : Mansell, 1975. xii, 160 p. ; 29 cm. (Calendars and indexes to the letters and papers of the Archbishops of Canterbury in Lambeth Palace Library ; v. 1) [Z6616.T29L35 1975] [BX5199.T4] 75-321735 ISBN 0-7201-0520-X : 24.00
1. Temple, Frederick, Abp. of Canterbury, 1821-1902—Manuscripts—Indexes. 2. Lambeth Palace. Library. I. Barber, Melanie. II. Title: Index to the letters and papers of Frederick Temple ... III. Series:

Lambeth Palace. Library. Calendars and indexes to the letters and papers of the Archbishops of Canterbury in Lambeth Palace Library ; v. 1.
Distributed by International Scholarly Book Services. Distributed by International Scholarly Book Services.

Temple Israel, New Rochelle, N.Y.

SHANKMAN, Jacob K. 296.6'5'09747277
The history of Temple Israel of New Rochelle, New York / by Jacob K. Shankman. New Rochelle, N.Y. : The Temple, c1977. 187 p., [8] leaves of plates : ill. ; 26 cm. [BM225.N442T457] 77-72427
1. Temple Israel, New Rochelle, N.Y. 2. Jews in New Rochelle, N.Y.—History. I. Title.

Temple Israel of Greater Miami.

TEBEAU, Charlton W. 296'.09759'381
Synagogue in the central city : Temple Israel of Greater Miami, 1922-1972. [by] Charlton W. Tebeau. Coral Gables, Fla., University of Miami Press [1972] 172 p. illus. 24 cm. [BM225.M5T4] 72-85107 ISBN 0-87024-239-3 7.95
1. Temple Israel of Greater Miami. 2. Jews in Miami, Fla. I. Title.

Temple Mount, Jerusalem.

CORNFELD, Gaalyahu, 1902- 915.694'4
The mystery of the Temple Mount; new guidebook to discovery [by] Gaalyah Cornfeld. Tel Aviv, New York, Bazak Israel Guidebook Publishers [1972] 112 p. illus. (part col.) 24 cm. [DS109.8.T45C67] 73-950215 IL15.00
1. Temple Mount, Jerusalem. I. Title.

Temple of God.

BARROIS, Georges Augustin, 1898- 262
Jesus Christ and the temple / by Georges Barrois. Crestwood, N.Y. : St. Vladimir's Seminary Press, 1980. p. cm. Includes bibliographical references. [BS680.T4B37] 19 80-19700 ISBN 0-913836-73-7 pbk. : 5.95
1. Temple of God. I. Title.

CAPT, E. Raymond. 222'.5095
King Solomon's Temple / by E. Raymond Capt. ; cover and original ill. by J. A. Dryburgh. Thousand Oaks, Calif. : Artisan Sales, c1979. 96 p. : ill ; 22 cm. [BS680.T4C36] 19 79-54774 ISBN 0-934666-05-9 pbk. : 3.00
1. Temple of God. I. Title.
Publisher's address: Box 1497, Thousand Oaks, CA 91360

LIGNEE, Hubert 233
The living temple. Baltimore, Helicon [1966] 107p. 18cm. (Living word ser., 5) Tr. of Le temple nouveau. [BS680.T4L523] 66-9663 1.25 pap.,
1. Temple of God. I. Title.
Available from Taplinger, New York.

LIGNEE, Hubert 221.87261
The temple of Yahweh. Baltimore, Helicon [1966] 128p. 18cm. (Living word ser., 2) Tr. of Le temple du Seigneur & Vers le sanctuaire du Ciel. [BS680.T4L513] 66-9664 1.25 pap.,
1. Temple of God. I. Lignee, Hubert. Vers le sanctuaire du Ciel. II. Title.
Available from Taplinger, New York.

Temple, William, Abp. of Canterbury, 1881-1944.

FLETCHER, Joseph Francis, 1905- 922.342
William Temple, twentieth-century Christian. New York, Seabury Press, 1963. 372 p. 21 cm. Includes bibliography. [BX5199.T42F5] 63-12587
1. Temple, William, Abp. of Canterbury, 1881-1944. I. Title.

IREMONGER, Frederic Athelwold, 1878- 922.342
William Temple, Archbishop of Canterbury; his life and letters. London, New York, Oxford Univ. Press [1948] xv, 663 p. plates, ports. 22 cm. "[List of] portraits of William Temple": p. 638. [BX5199.T4217] 48-9469
1. Temple, William, Abp. of Canterbury, 1881-1944. I. Title.

IREMONGER, Frederick Athelwold, 1878- 283'.092'4
William Temple, Archbishop of Canterbury; his life and letters Abridged ed. by D. C. Somervell. London, New York, Oxford University Press, 1963. 292 p. 20 cm. (Oxford AErbacks, no 59) [BX5199.T42I72] 64-1859
1. 1. Temple, William, Abp. of Canterbury, 1881-1944. I. Title.

TEMPLE, William, Abp. of Canterbury, 1881-1944 922.342
Some Lambeth letters. Ed. by F. S. Temple. New York, Oxford [c.]1963. xv, 198p. illus., ports., facsim. 22cm. 63-3709 4.80
I. Title.

TEMPLE, William, Abp. of Canterbury, 1881-1944. 922.342
Some lambeth letters. Edited by F. S. Temple. London, New York, Oxford University Press, 1963. xv, 198 p. illus., ports., facsim. 22 cm. [BX5199.T42A42] 63-3709
I. Title.

Temples.

LUNDWALL, Nels Benjamin, 1884- comp. 289.3
Temples of the Most High ... N. B. Lundwall, compiler and publisher. Salt Lake City, Utah, 1941. x, 358 p. incl. col. front., illus. (1 col.; incl. ports. plans) 23 cm. [BX8643.T4L8] 44-26685
1. Mormons and Mormonism. 2. Temples. I. Title.

REMEY, Charles Mason, 1874- 726.1
Architectural compositions in the Indian style; designs for temples and shrines, by Charles Mason Remey. [Boston, The Tudor press] 1923. 12 p. l., 75 pl. 32 cm. Each group of designs preceded by half-title not included in collation. [NA4621.R4] 24-17887
1. Temples. 2. Architecture, Indic. I. Title.

RIPLEY, M. M.
The world's worship in stone; temple, cathedral, and mosque. One hundred and fifty engravings from the best artists. With descriptive text by M. M. Ripley ... Boston, Estes and Lauriat, 1880. 2 p. l., [vii]-viii, 9-176 p. front., illus. 33 cm. [NA4601.R5] 11-35000
1. Temples. 2. Cathedrals. 3. Mosques. I. Title.

SCHMIDT, Paul Frederic, 1925- 915'.04427
Temple reflections / Paul F. Schmidt. 1st ed. Albuquerque : Hummingbird Press, 1980. 103 p. : ill. ; 25 cm. [NA4620.S35] 19 80-80346 ISBN 0-912998-04-0 : 16.50 ISBN 0-912998-05-9 pbk. : 6.50
1. Temples. 2. Mosques. I. Title.

Temples—Asia, Southeastern.

LOUIS-FREDERICK pseud. 726.10959
The art of Southeast Asia: temples and sculpture. Foreword by Jeannine Auboyer. [Translated from the French by Arnold Rosin] New York, H. N. Abrams [1965?] 434 p. illus., maps, plans. 32 cm. Translation of Sud-Est asiatique: ses temples, ses sculptures. Bibliography: p. 425-427. [NA5960.L653] 65-19228
1. Temples—Asia, Southeastern. 2. Sculpture—Asia, Southeastern. I. Title.

Temples, Buddhist—China.

PRIP-MOLLER, Johannes, 1889-1943- 726'.7799'430951
Chinese Buddhist monasteries; their plan and its function as a setting for Buddhist monastic life. [2d ed.] Hong Kong, Hong Kong Univ. Pr. [1967] 396p. illus. (pt. col.), facsims., map, plans (pt. col.), ports. 39cm. Buddhist hymn with music: p. 357. [NA6040.P7 1967] 68-2487 50.00
1. Temples, Buddhist—China. 2. Monasticism and religious orders, Buddhist. I. Title.
Available from Oxford Univ. Pr., New York.

Temples—Cambodia—Angkor.

KRASA, Miloslav 726.14
The temples of Angkor; monuments to a vanished empire. Photos. by Jan Cifra. [Tr. by Joy Turner] London. A. Wingate [dist. New York, Tudor, 1964, c. 1963] 211, [61] p. illus., plates, port., col. maps (pt. fold) 28cm. Bibl. 64-1799 9.95
1. Temples—Cambodia—Angkor. 2. Sculpture—Angkor, Cambodia. 3. Art, Khmer. I. Title.

Temples—China—Jehol.

MONTELL, Gosta.
The Chinese lama temple, Potala of Jehol; exhibition of historical and ethnographical collections made by Dr. Gosta Montell, member of Dr. Sven Hedin's expeditions, and donated by Vincent Bendix. Chicago, A. Century of progress exposition [c1932] 64 p. front. (port.) illus., plan. 24 cm. Illustrated on t.-p. Chapter i by Sven Hedin. cf. p. 11. Preface signed: Sven Hedin. A 34
1. Temples—China—Jehol. 2. Lamaism. I. Hedin, Sven Anders, 1865- II. Chicago. Century of progress international exposition, 1933-1934. III. Title.

Temples, Chinese—California.

WELLS, Mariann Kaye. 917.94
Chinese temples in California. [San Francisco, R and E Research Associates, 1971] iii, 108 p., [22] p. of illus. 29 cm. Reprint of the ed. originally presented as the author's thesis, University of California, 1962. Bibliography: p. 102-108. [BL1950.U6W4 1971] 72-155650
1. Temples, Chinese—California. I. Title.

Temples—Egypt.

MURRAY, Margaret Alice. 726'.1'931
Egyptian temples / by Margaret A. Murray. New York : AMS Press, 1977. x, 246 p., [32] leaves of plates : ill. ; 23 cm. Reprint of the 1931 ed. published by S. Low, Marston, London. Includes index. Bibliography: p. 239. [NA215.M8 1977] 75-41203 ISBN 0-404-14708-9 : 18.50
1. Temples—Egypt. 2. Egypt—Antiquities. I. Title.

OTTO, Eberhard, 1913- 709'.32
Ancient Egyptian art: the cults of Osiris and Amon. Photos. by Max Hirmer. [Translated by Kate Bosse Griffiths] New York, Abrams [1967] 144 p. illus. (part col.), maps, plans. 27 cm. Translation of Osiris und Amon: Kult und heilige Statten. Bibliography: p. 143-144. [DT62.T4O83 1967] 67-26469
1. Temples—Egypt. 2. Osiris. 3. Amon (Egyptian deity) I. Title.

Temples, Greek.

AYRTON, Elizabeth. 726.1
The Doric temple. Photos. by Serge Moulinier. New York, C. N. Potter [c1961] xiv, 227 p. illus., plates. 28 cm. [NA275.A9] 61-14830
1. Temples, Greek. 2. Columns, Doric. I. Title.

GRINNELL, Isabel Hoopes. 726'.1'208
Greek temples. New York, 1943. [New York] Arno Press, 1974. xxi, 59 p. illus. 32 cm. At head of title: The Metropolitan Museum of Art. Includes bibliographies. [NA275.G7 1974] 79-168420 ISBN 0-405-02258-1 20.00
1. New York (City). Metropolitan Museum of Art. 2. Temples, Greek. I. New York (City). Metropolitan Museum of Art.

GRINNELL, Isabel Hoopes. 726.12
... *Greek temples,* by Isabel Hoopes Grinnell. New York, 1943. xxi, 59, [1] p. illus. (incl. plans) LIV pl. on 28 l. 36 cm. At head of title: The Metropolitan museum of art. Map on lining-papers. Includes bibliographies. [NA275.G7] 43-16467
1. Temples. Greek. I. New York. Metropolitan museum of art. II. Title.

SCULLY, Vincent Joseph, 1920- 726.1'2'08
The earth, the temple, and the gods : Greek sacred architecture / Vincent Scully. Rev. ed. New Haven : Yale University Press, c1979. p. cm. Includes bibliographical references and index. [NA275.S3 1979] 79-12717 ISBN 0-300-02397-9 pbk. : 35.00
1. Temples, Greek. I. Title.

†TOMLINSON, Richard Allan. 726'.1'208
Greek sanctuaries / R. A. Tomlinson. New York : St. Martin's Press, 1976. 150 p., [14] leaves of plates (2 fold.) : ill. ; 26 cm. Includes bibliographical references and index. [NA275.T65 1976b] 76-27588 16.95
1. Temples, Greek. I. Title.

Temples, Hindu.

MICHELL, George. 726'.1'45
The Hindu temple : an introduction to its meaning and forms / George Michell. 1st U.S. ed. New York : Harper & Row, c1977. 192 p. : ill. ; 25 cm. (Icon editions) Includes index. Bibliography: p. [185]-186. [NA6002.M52 1977] 77-82075 ISBN 0-06-435750-3 : 22.50
1. Temples, Hindu. 2. Symbolism in architecture—India. I. Title.

MICHELL, George. 726'.1'450954
The Hindu temple : an introduction to its meaning and forms / George Michell. London : Elek, 1977. 192 p. : ill. ; 25 cm. Includes indexes. Bibliography: p. [185]-186. [BL1227.A1M52 1977] 78-301590 ISBN 0-236-40088-6 : 22.50
1. Temples, Hindu. I. Title.
Available from Harper Row

Temples, Hindu—India.

BALASUBRAHMANYAM, S. R. 726'.1'45
Early Chola art [by] S. R. Balasubrahmanyam. Bombay, New York, Asia Pub. House [c1966- v. illus., facsims., map, plans. 25 cm. v. 1: Rs60 Bibliographical footnotes. [NA6002.B3] S A
1. Temples, Hindu—India. 2. Cholas. I. Title.

Temples, Hindu—India—Conjeeveram.

RAMAN, K. V., 1934- 954'.82
Sri Varadarajaswami Temple, Kanchi : a study of its history, art, and architecture / K. V. Raman. 1st ed. New Delhi : Abhinav Publications, 1975. x, 206 p., [12] leaves of plates : ill. ; 25 cm. "This book formed the subject matter of ... [the author's] dissertation for the degree of the doctor of philosophy of the University of Madras." Includes index. Bibliography: p. [190]-194. [BL1227.C66R35] 75-907263 18.00
1. Sri Varadarajaswami Temple. 2. Temples, Hindu—India—Conjeeveram.

Temples, Hindu—India—South India—Addresses, essays, lectures.

SOUTH Indian temples : 294.53
an analytical reconsideration / edited by Burton Stein. New Delhi : Vikas Pub. House, c1978. 155 p. : diagrs., map ; 25 cm. Includes bibliographical references and index. [BL1227.S65S68] 77-907846 ISBN 0-7069-0581-4 : 12.50
1. Temples, Hindu—India—South India—Addresses, essays, lectures. I. Stein, Burton, 1926-
Intl. Pub. Serv., 114 E. 32nd St., NY, NY 10016

Temples—India.

FERGUSSON, James, 1808-1886. 726'.1'4
Archaeology in India, with especial reference to the works of Babu

Rajendralala Mitra / James Fergusson. New Delhi : K. B. Publications, 1974. vii, 115 p. : ill. ; 23 cm. "1st Indian reprint." First published in 1884. Includes bibliographical references. [NA6002.F44 1974] 74-904007 10.00
1. Mitra, Rajendralala, Raja, 1824-1891. 2. Temples—India. 3. Cave temples—India. I. Title.
Distributed by South Asia Books.

LOUIS-FREDERIC, pseud. 726.10954
The art of India: temples and sculpture. Introd. by Jean Naudou. [Translated from the French by Eva M. Hooykaas and A. H. Christie] New York, H. N. Abrams [1960] 464p. illus., maps, plans. 32cm. 59-12873 17.50
1. Temples—India. 2. Sculpture—India. I. Title.

MEHTA, Rustam Jehangir, 1912- 726'.1'40954
Masterpieces of Indian temples / introd. and notes on plates by Rustam J. Mehta. Bombay : D. B. Taraporevala Sons, 1974i.e.1976 67, 100 p. (chiefly ill.) ; 29 cm. [NA6002.M44] 75-901641 15.00
1. Temples—India. I. Title.
Distributed by International Pubns. Service, New York.

MONOD-BRUHL, Odette. 722.41
Indian temples; 135 photographs chosen and annotated. With a pref. by Sylvain Levi. [English translation by Roy Hawkins. 2d ed. London] Oxford University Press [1952, c1951] 1v. illus. 25cm. Translation of Aux Indes; sanctuaires. [NA6001.M6513 1952] 53-6574
1. Temples—India. 2. Sculpture—India. I. Title.

Temples—India—Bengal.

DATTA, Bimal Kumar, 1920- 726'.1'45095414
Bengal temples / Bimal Kumar Datta ; with a foreword by Suniti Kumar Chatterji. New Delhi : Munshiram Manoharlal Publishers, 1975, c1974. x, 88 p., [14] leaves of plates : ill., map ; 25 cm. Includes bibliographical references and index. [NA6007.B4D38 1975] 75-904212 16.00
1. Temples—India—Bengal. I. Title.
Distributed by South Asia Books, Columbia, Mo.

Temples—India—Orissa.

DEHEJIA, Vidya. 726'.1'4095413
Early stone temples of Orissa / Vidya Dehejia. Durham, N.C. : Carolina Academic Press, c1979. vi, 217 p. : ill. ; 25 cm. Includes index. Bibliography: p. [209]-212. [NA6007.O74D43 1979] 78-54434 ISBN 0-89089-092-7 : 24.95
1. Temples—India—Orissa. I. Title.

Temples—India—South India.

SRINIVASAN, K. R., 1910- 726'.1'409548
Temples of South India. New Delhi, National Book Trust, India; [chief stickists in India: India Book House, Bombay, 1972] 223 p. illus. (pt. col.) 21 cm. (India—the land and people) [NA6007.S6S67] 72-906086
1. Temples—India—South India. I. Title.
Available from Verry, Mystic, Conn., for 3.75. ISBN 0-8426-0511-8.

VENKATARAMAN, Balasubrahmanyam, 1925- 726'.1'509548
Temple art under the Chola queens / B. Venkataraman. Faridabad : Thomson Press (India), Publication Division, 1976. xx, 154 p., 28 leaves of plates : ill. ; 25 cm. Includes index. Bibliography: p. 126. [NA6007.S6V46] 76-904390 Rs80.00
1. Temples—India—South India. 2. Architecture, Chola. I. Title.

Temples—Japan—Kroto.

BUDDIST temples in Japan: Kroto. 294.30035 [Photgs. by Yoshio Watanabe, Yukio Futagawa. Dist. New York, Perkins Oriental, 1962, c.1961] 311 p. illus. (pt. col.) 36 cm. Japanese text. English title on box. 4-page leaflet inserted "An English language supplement to Buddist temples of Japan: Kroto. J62 18.00, bxd.
1. Temples—Japan—Kroto. 2. Temples—Buddhist. I. Watanabe, Yoshio, 1907- II. Fukuyama, Toshio, 1905-

Temples—Japan—Nara (City)

BUDDHIST temples in Japan: Nara. 294.30035 [Photogs. by Ken Domon, others. Dist. New York, Perkins Oriental, 1962, c.1961] 315p. illus. (pt. col.) 36cm. Japanese text. English title on box. 4-page leaflet inserted 'An English language supplement to Buddhist temples of Japan: Nara.' J62 18.00, bxd.
1. Temples—Japan—Nara (City) 2. Temples, Buddhist. I. Domon, Ken, 1909- II. Fukuyama, Toshio, 1905-

OOKA, Minoru, 1900- 726'.1'43095218
Temples of Nara and their art. Translated by Dennis Lishka. [1st English ed.] New York, Weatherhill [1973] 184 p. illus. (part col.) 24 cm. (The Heibonsha survey of Japanese art, v. 7) Translation of Nara no tera. [NA6057.N3O5513] 72-78601 ISBN 0-8348-1010-7 8.95
1. Temples—Japan—Nara (City) 2. Temples, Buddhist—Japan—Nara (City) I. Title. II. Series.

Temples, Mormon.

ANDREW, Laurel B. 726'.58'9373
The early temples of the Mormons : the architecture of the Millennial Kingdom in the American West / Laurel B. Andrew. Albany : State University of New York Press, 1977. p. cm. Includes bibliographical references. [NA4829.M67A53] 77-23971 ISBN 0-87395-358-4 : 15.00
1. Temples, Mormon.

HEINERMAN, Joseph. 248'.2
Temple manifestations / Joseph Heinerman. Manti, Utah : Mountain Valley Publishers, 1974. 185 p. ; 21 cm. Includes bibliographical references. [BX8643.T4H44] 74-193174 2.95
1. Temples, Mormon. I. Title.

PACKER, Boyd K. 230'.933
The holy temple / Boyd K. Packer ; ill. by Darrell Thomas. Salt Lake City, Utah : Bookcraft, c1980. x, 274 p. : ill. ; 23 cm. Cover title: You may claim the blessings of the holy temple. Includes index. [BX8643.T4P32] 19 80-69100 ISBN 0-88494-411-5 : 7.95
1. Church of Jesus Christ of Latter-Day Saints—Doctrinal and controversial works. 2. Temples, Mormon. I. Title. II. Title: You may claim the blessings of the holy temple.

Temples, Roman—Great Britain

LEWIS, Michael Jonathan Tauton 726.1207
Temples in Roman Britian, by M. J. T. Lewis Cambridge, Cambridge., 1966. xvi, 218p. illus., 4 plates, maps, plans, tables, diagrs. 26cm. (Cambridge classical studies) Bibl. [NA323.L4] 66-2517 9.50
1. Temples, Roman—Gt. Brit. I. Title. II. Series.

Temples, Roman—Lebanon.

TAYLOR, George. 726'.1'207095692
The Roman temples of Lebanon; a pictorial guide. [Beirut, Dar el-Machreq Pub., 1967] Imprint covered by label: Argonaut, Chicago. 133p. illus. 28cm. English & French. Bibl. ref. [NA335.L37T3] 68-3544 price unreported
1. Temples, Roman—Lebanon. I. Title.

Temples, Sikh—Great Britain.

JANJUA, Harbhajan Singh. 294.6'3'502541
Sikh temples in the U.K. & the people behind their management / [by Harbhajan Singh Janjua]. London : Jan Publications, 1976. vi, 106 p. : ill., ports. ; 23 cm. [BL2018.36.G7J36] 76-373636 ISBN 0-905454-00-6 : £2.50
1. Temples, Sikh—Great Britain. I. Title.

Temptation.

THE age-temptation of American Christians; 268.3 and Christ's own method of gaining the victory and the kingdom. Together with some introductory and illustrative chapters. Introductory note by William S. Tyler. New York, A. D. F. Randolph and co. [1880] viii p., 1 l., 166 p. 19 cm. [BT726.A2] 40-24815
1. Temptation.

BECK, Hubert F. 232.9'5
Into the wilderness : dialogue meditations on the temptations of Jesus / by Hubert F. Beck and Robert L. Otterstad. Philadelphia : Fortress Press, [1974] c1975. vi, 90 p. ; 22 cm. Includes index. [BT355.B4] 74-80417 ISBN 0-8006-1082-2 pbk. : 2.75
1. Jesus Christ—Temptation. 2. Temptation. I. Otterstad, Robert L., joint author. II. Title.

BOROS, Ladislaus, 1927- 233
In time of temptation. Translated by Simon and Erika Young. [New York] Herder and Herder [1968] 112 p. 21 cm. Translation of In der Versuchung. [BT725.B6313 1968b] 68-55983 3.95
1. Temptation. 2. Perfection (Catholic) I. Title.

BUNTAIN, Ruth Jaeger. 248'.48'673
The Christian & temptation / Ruth Jaeger Buntain. Washington, D.C. : Review and Herald Pub. Association, c1978. 62 p. ; 18 cm. [BT725.B86] 78-9036 pbk. : 0.85
1. Temptation. 2. Christian life—Seventh-Day Adventist authors. I. Title.

DURHAM, Charles, 1939- 248.8'6
Temptation, help for struggling Christians / Charles Durham. Downers Grove, Ill. : InterVarsity Press, c1982. 166 p. ; 21 cm. Includes bibliographical references. [BT725.D87 1982] 19 82-153 ISBN 0-87784-382-1 : 4.95
1. Temptation. I. Title.

GORDON, Samuel Dickey, 1859- 248
Quiet talks about the tempter, by S. D. Gordon ... New York, Chicago [etc.] Fleming H. Revell company [c1910] 249 p. 19 cm. [BV4501.G59] 10-24733 0.75
1. Temptation. 2. Conduct of life. I. Title.

HALL, Arthur Crawshay Alliston, bp., 1847-1930. 232.952
... Christ's temptation and ours, by the Rt. Rev. A. C. A. Hall... New York, London and Bombay, Longmans, Green, and co., 1897. xvii, [1] p., 2 l., [3]-255 p. 18 cm. (The baldwin lectures, 1895) [BT855.H3] 35-31620
1. Jesus Christ—Temptation. 2. Temptation. I. Title.

HANSON, James H 232.952
Through temptation; a series of messages based on Genesis 3 and Matthew 4. Minneapolis, Augsburg Pub. House [1959] 79p. 20cm. [BT725.H2] 59-6984
1. Temptation. 2. Jesus Christ—Temptation. I. Title.

HOWARD, Philip Eugene, 1870-
Temptation; what it is and how to meet it, by Philip E. Howard. Philadelphia, The Sunday school times company, 1911. iv, 92 p. 17 cm. $0.50. 12-305
I. Title.

HUGHSON, Shirley Carter.
The welfare of the soul; practical studies in the life of temptation, by Shirley C. Hughson...with a preface by the Rev. Alfred G. Mortimer... New York [etc.] Longmans, Green, and co., 1910. xiv, 216 p. 19 1/2 cm. 10-4595
I. Title.

[HUME, Jean B.]
Amethyst Gray: the evangelist's temptation. By Julien Viclare [pseud.] [Buffalo, N.Y., Press of A. H. Morey printing company, 1902] 2 p. l., 272 p. 23 cm. 3-9621
I. Title.

JONES, George Curtis, 1911- 233
Strongly tempted, by G. Curtis Jones. Cleveland, World Pub. Co. [1968] x, 150 p. 21 cm. Bibliography: p. 144-150. [BT725.J6] 68-26841 4.50
1. Temptation. I. Title.

LE QUEUX, William.
If sinners entice thee. New York, G. W. Dillingham co., 1899. 286 p. pl. 12°. Mar
I. Title.

MUMFORD, Bob. 233
The purpose of temptation. Old Tappan, N.J., Revell [1973] 156 p. illus. 21 cm. "Adapted from the popular tape series: The purpose and principle of temptation." [BT725.M85] 73-15622 ISBN 0-8007-0633-1 2.95
1. Temptation. I. Title.

REMLER, Francis Joseph, 1874- 233.2
Why am I tempted? By F. J. Remler, C.M. Paterson, N.J., St. Anthony guild press, 1938. vi p., 1 l., 110 p. 20 cm. [BT725.R4] 38-33187
1. Temptation I. Title.

SCROGGIE, William Graham, 1877-1958. 232.9'5
Tested by temptation / by W. Graham Scroggie. Grand Rapids, Mich. : Kregel Publications, [1980] 76 p. ; 19 cm. (W. Graham scroggie library series) (Series: Scroggie, William Graham, 1877-1958. W. Graham Scroggie library series.) Reprint of the 1923 ed. published by Pickering and Inglis, London. [BT355.S37 1980] 79-2559 pbk. : 2.50
1. Jesus Christ—Temptation. 2. Temptation. I. Title. II. Series.

*WEDGE, Florence 233.2
What are temptations? Pulaski, Wis., Franciscan Pubs. [1966, c.1965] 56p. 19cm. .25 pap.,
I. Title.

WINES, Enoch Cobb, 1806-1879. 233.2
An essay on temptation. By E. C. Wines, D.D. Philadelphia Presbyterian board of publication [c1865] 144 p. 18 cm. [BT725.W5] 40-24817
1. Temptation. I. Presbyterian church in the U.S.A. (Old school) Board of publication. II. Title.

WOOD, Frederick Ponsonby, 1884- 233.2
Temptation; how to win through, by Frederick P. Wood ... Grand Rapids, Mich., Zondervan publishing house [c1937] 66 p. 19 1/2 cm. [BT725.W6] 37-140897
1. Temptation. I. Title.

YOHN, Rick. 248'.4
How to overcome temptation / Rick Yohn. Nashville : T. Nelson, c1978. 165 p. ; 21 cm. Includes index. Bibliography: p. 163-165. [BT725.Y63] 78-3672 ISBN 0-8407-5645-3 pbk. : 3.95
1. Temptation. I. Title.

Temptation—Biblical teaching.

IERSEL, Bastiaan Martinus Franciscus van. 233
The Bible on the temptations of man. Tr. by F. Vander Heijden. De Pere, Wis., St. Norbert Abbey Pr. [c.] 1966. 88p. 17cm. [BT725.1313] 66-16991 .95 pap.,
1. Temptation—Biblical teaching. I. Title.

IERSEL, Bastiaan Martinus Franciscus van. 233
The Bible on the temptations of man, by B. van Iersel. Translated by F. Vander Heijden. De Pere, Wis., St. Norbert Abbey Press, 1966. 88 p. 17 cm. [BT725.I 313] 66-16991
1. Temptation — Biblical teaching. I. Title.

Ten Boom, Corrie.

BROWN, Joan Winmill. 269'.2'0924 B
Corrie, the lives she's touched / Joan Winmill Brown. Old Tappan, N.J. : F. H. Revell Co., c1979. 160 p. : ill. ; 26 cm. Includes index. [BR1725.T35B76] 79-20893 ISBN 0-8007-1049-5 : 8.95 ISBN 0-8007-1050-9 (pbk.) : 4.95
1. Ten Boom, Corrie. 2. Christian biography—Netherlands. I. Title.

CARLSON, Carole C. 284'.2'0924
Corrie ten Boom, the authorized biography / Carole C. Carlson ; with a special tribute by Billy Graham. Old Tappan, N.J. : F.H. Revell Co., c1983. p. cm. Includes

bibliographical references. [BR1725.T35C37 1983] 19 82-13330 ISBN 0-8007-1293-5 : 12.95
1. Ten Boom, Corrie. 2. Christian biography. I. Title.

TEN Boom, Corrie. 269'.2'0924 B
He sets the captive free / Corrie ten Boom. Old Tappan, N.J. : Revell, c1977. p. cm. (Her Jesus is victor) [BR1725.T35A33] 78-1503 ISBN 0-8007-0929-2 : 4.95
1. Ten Boom, Corrie. 2. Christian biography—Netherlands. 3. World War, 1939-1945—Personal narratives, Dutch. 4. Ravensbruck (Concentration camp) 5. Christian life—1960- I. Title. II. Series.

TEN BOOM, Corrie. 269'.2'0924 B
Clippings from my notebook : writings and sayings collected / by Corrie ten Boom. Nashville : T. Nelson, c1982. 127 p. : col. ill. ; 23 cm. [BX9479.T46A32 1982] 19 82-6278 ISBN 0-8407-4102-2 : 14.95
1. Ten Boom, Corrie. 2. Reformed (Reformed Church)—Netherlands—Biography. 3. Christian life—Reformed authors. I. Title.

TEN BOOM, Corrie. 269'.2'0924 [B]
He sets the captive free / Corrie Ten Boom. Old Tappan, N.J. : Revell, 1978, c1977 93 p. ; 20 cm. (Her Jesus is victor) [BR1725.T35A33] 77-99134 ISBN 0-8007-0929-2 : 4.95
1. Ten Boom, Corrie. 2. Christian biography—Netherlands. 3. World War, 1939-1945—Personal narratives, Dutch. 4. Ravensbruck (Concentration camp) 5. Christian life—1960- I. Title. II. Series.

TEN BOOM, Corrie. 269'.2'0924 B
A tramp finds a home / Corrie ten Boom ; photos. by Ross Busby. Old Tappan, N.J. : Revell, c1978. 62 p. : ill. ; 18 cm. (New life ventures) [BR1725.T35A365] 78-52040 ISBN 0-8007-9008-1 pbk. : 0.95
1. Ten Boom, Corrie. 2. Christian biography—United States. I. Title.

TEN BOOM, Corrie. 269'.2'0924 B
A tramp finds a home / Corrie ten Boom. Old Tappan, N.J. : Revell, c1978. p. cm. (New life ventures) [BR1725.T35A365] 78-1504 ISBN 0-8007-8368-9 pbk. : 1.25
1. Ten Boom, Corrie. 2. Christian biography—United States. I. Title.

TEN BOOM, Corrie. 269'.2'0924 B
Tramp for the Lord [by] Corrie ten Boom, with Jamie Buckingham. Fort Washington, Pa., Christian Literature Crusade [1974] 192 p. illus. 21 cm. [BR1725.T35A37] 74-5205 ISBN 0-8007-0665-X 5.95
1. Ten Boom, Corrie. I. Buckingham, Jamie, joint author. II. Title.

TEN BOOM, Corrie. 269'.2'0924 B
Tramp for the Lord / by Corrie ten Boom, with Jamie Buckingham. Boston : G. K. Hall, 1974. xx, 305 p. 25 cm. Large print ed. [BR1725.T35A37 1974b] 74-20672 ISBN 0-8161-6259-X
1. Ten Boom, Corrie. 2. Sight-saving books. I. Buckingham, Jamie, joint author. II. Title.

Ten Commandments.

BACH, W H.
The ten commandments analyzed. Lily Dale, N. Y., W. H. Bach, 1899. 88 p. port. 16 cm. 99-6
I. Title.

CHAINEY, George.
The ten commandments; an interpretation; or, The constitution of the spiritual universe. Chicago, Stockham pub. co. [1900] 130 p. front. 24 degree. 1-29283
I. Title.

*DEANE, John 241.52
Love's imperative; a meditation on the Ten Commandments. Chicago, Moody [c.1965] 61p. illus. 21cm. Cover title: Devotionals: Love's imperatives. 1.00 pap.,
I. Title.

FERRELL, Pauline Glover.
The eleventh commandment, [1. ed.] New York City, Pageant press [1965] 50 p. 21 cm. 66-36579
1. Ten Commandments. I. Title.

HOOPES, Wilford Lawrence, 1863-
The code of the spirit; an interpretation of the decalogue, by Wilford L. Hoopes... Boston, Sherman, French & company, 1911. 4 p. l., 154 p. 19 1/2 cm. 11-1219 1.20
I. Title.

THE laws of the King;
or, Talks on the commandments, by a religious of the Society of the Holy Child Jesus. New York, Cincinnati [etc.] Benziger brothers, 1910. 199 p. front., plates. 18 cm. 10-15678

SCHENCK, Ferdinand Schureman, 1845-
The ten commandments and the Lord's prayer; a sociological study, by Ferdinand S. Schenck ... [New ed.] New York and London, Funk & Wagnalls company, 1902. 3 p. 1., 245 p. 20 cm. 2-23927
I. Title.

Ten (The number)

MANLEY, Thomas R. 133.3'359
Ten : the amazing evidence for astronumerology / by Thomas R. Manley. Parsons, W. Va. : McClain Printing Co., 1980. iv, 188 p. ; 22 cm. [BF1623.P9M36] 19 79-92707 ISBN 0-87012-374-2 : 10.00
1. Ten (The number) 2. Symbolism of numbers. I. Title.

Ten virgins.

COLMAN, Benjamin, 1673-1747. 226.8
Practical discourses on the parable of the ten virgins. Being a serious call and admonition to watchfulness and diligence in preparing for death and judgment. By Bejamin Colman, D. D. pastor of the church in battle-street, Boston. The 2d ed. Boston, N. E., Printed and sold by Rogers and Fowle in Queen-street next to the prison, and J. Edwards in Cornhill, mdccxlvii. 1 p. l., vi, 344 p. 20 cm. Signatures: A4, B-X3, Y1. Pages 238-239 erroneously numbered 240-241. Contains a portrait of the author, inserted as frontispiece. --Copy 2. 21 cm. Mounted on the fly-leaf is an autograph letter from the author, presenting this copy to the Rev. Solomon William of Lebanon. --Another issue, 21 cm. Manuscript note on t.-p.: These discourses first published about 1707. Pages 238-240 erroneously numbered 240-242. Contains a folded plate (The parable of the ten virgins) inserted as frontispiece. [BT378.T4C6 1747a] 3-16594
1. Ten virgins. I. Title.

Ten virgins—Sermons.

SEISS, Joseph Augustus, 1823-1904. 226.8
The parable of the ten virgins: in six discourses. And a sermon on the judgeship of the saints. By Joseph A. Seiss... Philadelphia, Smith, English & co.; Boston, Gould & Lincoln;[etc., etc.] 1862. 189 p. 19 1/2 cm. [BT378.T4S4] 35-29034
1. Ten virgins—Sermons. 2. Lutheran church—Sermons. 3. Sermons, American. I. Title.

Tenafly, N.J. Church of the Atonement.

VAUGHAN, Samuel S. 283'.749'21
The little church; one hundred years at the Church of the atonement, 1868-1968, Tenafly, New Jersey, by Samuel S. Vaughan. [1st ed. Tenafly, N.J., 1969] 123 p. illus., ports. 22 cm. [BX6081.T4C488] 72-11393
1. Tenafly, N.J. Church of the Atonement. I. Title.

Tengren, Gustaf, 1896-

MOORE, Clement Clarke, 1779-1863.
The night before Christmas; illustrated by Gustaf Tenggren. New York, Simon and Schuster [1951] unpaged. illus. 29 cm. (A Big golden book, 474)
1. Tenggren, Gustaf, 1896- illus. PZ8.3.M782N 42 I. Title.

Tennant, Frederick Robert, 1866-

SCUDDER, Delton Lewis, 1906- 201
Tennant's philosophical theology, by Delton Lewis Scudder ... New Haven, Yale university press; London, H. Milford, Oxford university press, 1940. xiv, 278 p., 1 l. diagrs. 24 cm. (Half-title: Yale studies in religious education. xiii) "The substance of this book constitutes 'A dissertation presented to ... the Graduate school of Yale university ... for the degree of doctor of philosophy' (May, 1969)"--Pref. "Acknowledgments": p. [277]-278. Bibliography: p. [259]-273. [BL51.T42S3 1969] 40-14172
1. Tennant, Frederick Robert, 1866- 2. Theism. 3. Experience (Religion) I. Title.

Tennent, Gilbert, 1703-1764. The danger of an uncoverted ministry.

THE querists, part iii.
or, An extract of sundry passages taken out of Mr. G. Tennent's sermon preached at Nottingham, of the danger of an uncovereted ministry. Together with some scruples propos'd in proper queries raised on each remark. By the same hands with the former. [Five lines of quotation] Philadelphia: Printed by B. Franklin in Market-street. 1741. 150 p. 16 cm. Signatures: A-T4 (T4 (probably blank) wanting) The date of imprint was printed 1740 and corrected by impressing the figure 1 over the 0, apparently by hand. cf. The Curtis collection of Franklin imprints. "The querists, or, An extract of sundry passages taken out of Mr. Whitefield's printed sermons, jounrals and letters ... By some churchmembers of the Presbyterian persuasion ... Philadelphia, 1740", has been attributed to Thomas Evans of Pencader. cf. R. Webster's History of the Presbyterian church in America, 1875, p. 158; Evans' Amer. bibl., v. 2, p. 166. [BV659.T4Q4] 31-11211
1. Tennent, Gilbert, 1703-1764. The danger of an uncovered ministry. I. Evans, Thomas, d. 1743.

TENNENT, Gilbert, 1703-1764.
The examiner, examined; or, Gilbert Tennent, harmonious. In answer to a pamphlet entitled, The examiner; or, Gilbert against Tennent, being a vindication of the Rev. Gilbert Tennent and his associates, together with six rev. ministers of Boston, from the unjust reflections cast upon them by the author of that anonymous pamphlet, together with some remarks upon The querist's, the third part, and other of their performances ... The whole essay is submitted to the decision of truth and common sense. By Gilbert Tennent ... Philadelphia, Printed and sold by W. Bradford, 1743. 146 p., 1 l. 16 cm. 11-13450
I. Title.

Tennent, Gilbert, 1703-1764. The late association for defence, encourag'd; or, The lawfulness of a defensive war.

[SMITH, John] 1722-1771. 289.
The doctrine of Christianity, as held by the people called Quakers, vindicated: in answer to Gilbert Tennent's sermon on the lawfulness of war. [Twelve lines of Biblical quotations] Philadelphia: Printed by Benjamin Franklin, and David Hall, MDCCXLVIII. iv, 56 p. 20 1/2 cm. Signatures: 2 leaves unsigned, B-H4. Preface signed: John Smith, Philadelphia, 11th Mo. 25. 1747-8. In answer to "The late association for defence, encourag'd; or, The lawfulness of a defensive war ... By Gilbert Tennent. Philadelphia [1747]" Smith's work was, in turn, answered by Tennent in "The late association for defence farther encouraged: or, Defensive war defended ... Philadelphia, 1748." [BX7748.W2S6 1748] 30-21379
1. Tennent, Gilbert, 1708-1764. The late association for defence, encourg'd; or, The lawfulness of a defensive war. 2. War. 3. Friends, Society of—Doctrinal and controversial works. I. Title.

[SMITH, John] fl.1748. 230.
The doctrine of Christianity, as held by the people called Quakers, vindicated: in answer to Gilbert Tennent's sermon on the lawfulness of war. The 2d ed. ... Philadelphia: Printed by Benjamin Franklin, and David Hall, 1748. iv, 56 p. 20 1/2 x 12 1/2 cm. Preface signed: John Smith, Philadelphia, 11th mo. 25. 1747-8. In answer to "The late association for defence, encourag'd; or, The lawfulness of a defensive war ... By Gilbert Tennent. Philadelphia [1747]" Smith's work was, in turn, answered by Tennent in "The late association for defence farther encouraged; or, Defensive war defended ... Philadelphia, 1748." [BX7730.S55 1748] 19-20293
1. Tennent, Gilbert, 1703-1764. The late association for defence, encourag'd; or, The lawfulness of a defensive war. 2. Friends, Society of—Doctrinal and controversial works. I. Title.

Tennent, N.J. Old Tennent church.

SMITH, Henry Goodwin, 1860- 285.174946
The history of the "Old Scots" church of Freehold, from the Scotish immigration of 1685 till the removal of the church under the ministry of the Rev. William Tennent, jr. By Henry Goodwin Smith... Freehold, N.J., Transcript printing house, 1895. 52, viii p., front., illus. (map) plates, facsims. 24 1/2 cm. [BX9211.T4O6] 40-2579
1. Tennent, N.J. Old Tennent church. I. Title.

Tennent, William, 1705-1777.

[BOUDINOT, Elias] 1740-1821 922.573
Life of the Rev. William Tennent, formerly Pastor of the Presbyterian church at Freehold, in Jersey.. 370 in which is contained... an account of his being three days in a trance, and apparently lifeless. Hartford, S. Andrus and son, 1845. 128 p. 12 1/2 cm. [BX9225.T4B6 1845] 36-221205
1. Tennent, William, 1705-1777. I. Title.

[BOUDINOT, Elias] 1740-1821. 922.
A memoir of the Rev. William Tennent, minister of Freshold, Monmouth county, N.J., first published in the Evangelical magazine ... Springfield [N.J.] G. W. Callender [1822] 67 p. 15 cm. [BX9225.T4B6 1822] 12-24839
1. Tennent, William, 1705-1777. I. Title.

[BOUDINOT, Elias] 1740-1821. 922.573
Memoirs to the life of the Rev. William Tennent, formerly pastor of the Presbyterian church at Freehold, in New Jersey; in which is contained...an account of his being three days in a trance and apparently lifeless: extracted from the "Evangelical intelligencer" for the year 1806. York, Printed and published by W. Alexander & son (etc.) 1822. vii, (9)-125 p. 15 1/2 cm. [BX9225.T4B6 1822 a] 36-31934
1. Tennent, William, 1705-1777. I. Title.

Tennessee—Church history.

NORTON, Herman Albert. 280'.09768
Religion in Tennessee, 1777-1945 / Herman A. Norton. 1st ed. Knoxville : University of Tennessee Press : Tennessee Historical Commission, c1981. p. cm. (Tennessee three star books) Includes index. Bibliography: p. [BR555.T2N67] 19 81-1562 ISBN 0-87049-317-5 : 8.50 ISBN 0-87049-318-3 (pbk.) : 3.50
1. Tennessee—Church history. I. Title. II. Series.

Tenney, Merrill C.

CURRENT issues in 220.6'6
Biblical and patristic interpretation; studies in honor of Merrill C. Tenney presented by his former students. Edited by Gerald F. Hawthorne. Grand Rapids, Eerdmans [1975] 377 p. port. 25 cm. "Select bibliography of the writings of Merrill C. Tenney": p. 19-20. [BS413.C8] 74-19326 ISBN 0-8028-3442-6 9.95
1. Tenney, Merrill C. 2. Bible—Addresses, essays, lectures. 3. Theology—Early church, ca. 30-600—Addresses, essays, lectures. I. Tenney, Merrill Chapin, 1904- II. Hawthorne, Gerald F., 1925- ed.

Tennyson, Alfred Tennyson, 1st baron, 1809-1892. Idylls of the King.

EVANS, Morris Owen, 1857- 220
The healing of the nations, by Morris O. Evans ... Boston, R. G. Budger [c1922] 3 p. l., ix-x p., 1 l., 13-246 p. 21 1/2 cm. "In the interweaving of Lord Tennyson's poems with the treatment of my theme the object was ... to trace the organic development of Christian thought and ideals from medieval times to the present day along the lines of the laureate's own conception of the movements of history. [BR125.E8] 24-4638
1. Tennyson, Alfred Tennyson, 1st baron, 1809-1892. Idylls of the King. 2. Religion. I. Title.

Tennyson, Alfred Tennyson 1st barran, 1809-1892.

HORTON, Robert Forman, 1855-1934.
Alfred Tennyson. A saintly life. By Robert F. Horton ... London, J. M. Dent & co.; New York, E. P. Dutton & co., 1900. xi, [1], 328, [1] p. incl. front. (port.) plates, port. 18 cm. A 36
I. Tennyson, Alfred Tennyson, baron, 1809-1892. II. Title.

ROBINSON, Edna Moore, 1885-
... *Tennyson's use of the Bible,* by Edna Moore Robinson ... Baltimore, The Johns Hopkins press, 1917. 3 p. l., v-ix, 110 p. 24 cm. (Hesperia: Ergilzungarelhe: schriften zur englischen philologie, hrsg. von James W. Bright ... 4. hft.) (Hesperia: erganzungarelhe: schriften zur englischen philologie, hrsq . [PR5592.P5R6] 17-11456
1. Tennyson, Alfred Tennyson, 1st baron, 1800-1892. 2. Bible in literature. I. Title.

SINNETT, Alfred Percy, 1840-1921. 821'.8
Tennyson, an occultist, as his writings prove. London, Theosophical Pub. House, 1920. New York, Haskell House Publishers, 1972. 89 p. 23 cm. [PR5592.O25S5 1972] 72-2102 ISBN 0-8383-1485-6
1. Tennyson, Alfred Tennyson, Baron, 1809-1892. 2. Occultism in literature. I. Title.

TENNYSON, Alfred Tennyson, 1st baron, 1809-1892.
The Holy Grail, by Alfred lord Tennyson; with drawings by W. L. Taylor. Boston, D. Lothrop company [c1892] [60] p., 1 l. front., illus., plates. 23 cm. [PR5559.H5] 29-27724
I. Taylor, William Ladd, 1854-1926, illus. II. Title.

TENNYSON, Alfred Tennyson, 1st baron, 1809-1892.
The Holy Grail, by Alfred lord Tennyson; with drawings by W. L. Taylor. Boston, D. Lothrop company [c1892] [60] p., 1 l. front., illus., plates. 23 cm. [PR5559.H5] 29-27724
I. Taylor, William Ladd, 1854-1926, illus. II. Title.

TENNYSON, Alfred Tennyson, 1st baron, 1809-1892.
... *The Holy Grail;* edited, with introduction and notes by Sophie Jewett ... New York, Boston [etc.] Silver, Burdett and company [1901] 132 p. incl. front. 18 cm. (The Silver series of English and American classics) [PR5559.H6J4] 1-17625
I. Jewett, Sophie, 1861-1909, ed. II. Title.

TENNYSON, Alfred Tennyson, 1st baron, 1809-1892.
... *The Holy Grail;* edited, with introduction and notes by Sophie Jewett ... New York, Boston [etc.] Silver, Burdett and company [1901] 132 p. incl. front. 18 cm. (The Silver series of English and American classics) [PR5559.H6J4] 1-17625
I. Jewett, Sophie, 1861-1909, ed. II. Title.

TENNYSON, Alfred Tennyson, 1st baron, 1809-1892.
The Holy Grail [by] Alfred Tennyson. New York and Boston, H. M. Caldwell co. [1904] 2 p. l., 83 p. front. 15 1/2 cm. [PR5559.H5 1904] 4-23755
I. Title.

TENNYSON, Alfred Tennyson, 1st baron, 1809-1892.
The Holy Grail [by] Alfred Tennyson. New York and Boston, H. M. Caldwell co. [1904] 2 p. l., 83 p. front. 15 1/2 cm. [PR5559.H5 1904] 4-23755
I. Title.

TENNYSON, Alfred Tennyson, 1st baron, 1809-1892.
... *The Holy Grail,* by Alfred lord Tennyson, ed. for school use by John H. Collins ... Chicago, Ill., Loyola university press, 1924. 64 p. illus. (incl. port.) 19 cm. (Loyola English classics) "Reference list": p. 59-60. [PR5559.H6C6] 24-5922
I. Collins, John H., ed. II. Title.

TENNYSON, Alfred Tennyson, 1st baron, 1809-1892.
... *The Holy Grail,* by Alfred lord Tennyson, ed. for school use by John H. Collins ... Chicago, Ill., Loyola university press, 1924. 64 p. illus. (incl. port.) 19 cm. (Loyola English classics) "Reference list": p. 59-60. [PR5559.H6C6] 24-5922
I. Collins, John H., ed. II. Title.

TENNYSON, Alfred Tennyson, 1st baron, 1809-1892.
The Holy Grail, and other poems. By Alfred Tennyson ... Boston, Fields, Osgood, & co., 1870. 202 p. 18 1/2 cm. "From advance sheets ... simultaneously with its publication in England." Differs from the English edition in paging and arrangement of contents. First leaf, advertisement. [PR5559.H5 1870 a] 15-8671
I. Title.
Contents omitted.

TENNYSON, Alfred Tennyson, 1st baron, 1809-1892.
The Holy Grail, and other poems. By Alfred Tennyson ... Boston, Fields, Osgood, & co., 1870. 202 p. 18 1/2 cm. "From advance sheets ... simultaneously with its publication in England." Differs from the English edition in paging and arrangement of contents. First leaf, advertisement. [PR5559.H5 1870 a] 15-8671
I. Title.
Contents omitted.

TENNYSON, Alfred Tennyson, 1st baron, 1809-1892.
The Holy Grail, and other poems. By Alfred Tennyson ... Boston, J. E. Tilton and company, 1870. 151 p. 19 cm. 1st edition, London, 1870. Contains twenty-four poems not found in the authorized edition printed the same year by Fields, Osgood & co. [PR5559.H5 1870] 15-8670
I. Title.

TENNYSON, Alfred Tennyson, 1st baron, 1809-1892.
The Holy Grail, and other poems. By Alfred Tennyson ... Boston, J. E. Tilton and company, 1870. 151 p. 19 cm. 1st edition, London, 1870. Contains twenty-four poems not found in the authorized edition printed the same year by Fields, Osgood & co. [PR5559.H5 1870] 15-8670
I. Title.

Tennyson, Alfred Tennyson, baron, In memoriam.

RADER, William, 1862-
The elegy of faith; a study of Alfred Tennyson's In memoriam, by William Rader. New York, T. Y. Crowell and company, 1902. 2 p. l., 56, [1] p. 20 cm. [PR5562.R3] 1-19595
1. Tennyson, Alfred Tennyson, baron, In memoriam. 2. Religion in literature. I. Title.

Tenrikyo—Doctrines.

KANO, Matao. 299'.5619
The mysteries of destiny / written by Matao Kano ; English version translated from the Japanese by Yama Trans. 1st American ed. Torrance, CA : Yama Trans Co., c1981. xii, 199 p. ; 22 cm. (Matao Kano's Destiny series ; v. 1) (Series: Kano, Matao. Destiny series ; v. 1.) Translation of: Ummei no shimpi. [BL2222.T4K3613 1981] 19 82-138743 ISBN 0-942512-00-6 : 12.95
1. Tenrikyo—Doctrines. 2. Fate and fatalism—Religious aspects—Tenrikyo. I. [Ummei no shimpi.] English II. Title. III. Series.
Publisher's address : 24228 Hawthorne Rd., Torrance, CA 90505.

Tepecano Indians—Rites and ceremonies.

MASON, John Alden, 1885-1967. 299'.7
The ceremonialism of the Tepecan [by] John Alden Mason [and] George Agogino. [Portales] Eastern New Mexico University, Paleo-Indian Institute, 1972. 44 p. illus. 26 cm. (Eastern New Mexico University. Contributions in anthropology, v. 4, no. 1) Bibliography: p. 43-44. [F1221.T37M37 1972] 74-621111
1. Tepecano Indians—Rites and ceremonies. 2. Indians of Mexico—Rites and ceremonies. I. Agogino, George, joint author. II. Title. III. Series: Contributions in anthropology, v. 4, no. 1.

Teresa Margherita del Sacro Cuore di Gesu. Saint, 1747-1770.

GABRIELE di Santa Marie Maddelena Father 271.9710924 (B)
From the Sacred Heart to the Trinity; [the spiritual itinerary of St. Teresa Margaret of the Sacred Heart] by Father Gabriel of St. Mary Magdalene. Translated by Sebastian V. Ramge. Milwaukee, Spiritual Life Press, 1965. 75 p. 22 cm. "The original French, Du sacre-Coeur a la Trinite, appeared in Ephemerides carmeliticae, vol. III (1949) pp. 337-296." [BX4700.T43G33] 65-24751
1 Teresa Margherita del Sacro Cuore di Gesu. Saint, 1747-1770. I. Title.

STANISLAO DI SANTA TERESA, padre. 922.245
St. Theresa Margaret of the Sacred Heart of Jesus (Anna Maria Redi) adapted from the Italian "Un angelo del Carmelo" of Friar Stanislaus of St. Theresa ... by Msgr. James F. Newcomb ... New York, Chicago [etc.] Benziger brothers, 1934. xii, 254, [1] p. front. (port.) 19 cm. [BX4700.T43S8] 35-245
*1. *Teresa Margherita del Sacro Cuore di Gesh, Saint, 1747-1770. I. Newcomb, James Francis, 1885- tr. II. Title.*

TERESA Margaret Sister. 922.245
God is love; St. Teresa Margaret: her life. Milwaukee, Spiritual Life Press, 1964. 168 p. port. 23 cm. [BX4700.T43T4] 64-21566
1 Teresa Margherita del Sacro Cuore de Gosu, Saint, 1747-1770. I. Title.

Teresa, Mother, 1910-

DOIG, Desmond. 266'.2'0924 B
Mother Teresa, her people and her work / Desmond Doig ; photos. by Raghu Rai ... [et al.]. 1st U.S. ed. New York : Harper & Row, c1976. 175 p. : ill. (some col.) ; 25 cm. [BX4406.5.Z8D65 1976] 75-39857 ISBN 0-06-060560-X : 15.00
1. Teresa, Mother, 1910- I. Title.

DOIG, Desmond. 266'.2'0924 B
Mother Teresa, her people and her work / Desmond Doig. 1st paperback ed. San Francisco : Harper & Row, [1980], c1976. p. cm. [BX4406.5.Z8D65 1980] 19 80-19610 ISBN 0-06-061941-4 : 9.95
1. Teresa, Mother, 1910- 2. Nuns—India—Biography. I. Title.

GONZALEZ-BALADO, Jose Luis. 266'.2'0924 B
Always the poor : Mother Teresa, her life and message / Jose Luis Gonzalez-Balado. Liguori, Mo. : Liguori Publications, c1980. 112 p. : ill. ; 18 cm. Revised translation of Madre Teresa de los pobres mas pobres. "Resources: film and cassette tapes": p. 112. [BX4406.5.Z8G6513] 19 80-83484 ISBN 0-89243-134-2 (pbk.) : 2.50
1. Teresa, Mother, 1910- 2. Nuns—India—Calcutta—Biography. 3. Calcutta—Biography. I. Title.

GORREE, Georges, 1908- 266'.2'0924 B
Love without boundaries : Mother Teresa of Calcutta / by Georges Gorree and Jean Barbier ; translated by Paula Speakman. Huntington, Ind. : Our Sunday Visitor, c1974. 96 p. : ill. ; 18 cm. Translation of Amour sans frontiere. [BX4406.5.Z8G6713 1974b] 75-37364 ISBN 0-87973-679-8 : 1.50
1. Teresa, Mother, 1910- 2. Missionaries of Charity. I. Barbier, Jean, fl. 1940- joint author. II. Title.

MCGOVERN, James. 266'.2'0924 B
To give the love of Christ : a portrait of Mother Teresa and the Missionaries of Charity / by James McGovern. New York : Paulist Press, c1978. 109 p. ; 19 cm. (Emmaus books) [BX4705.T4455M32] 77-14832 ISBN 0-8091-2076-3 pbk. : 1.95
1. Teresa, Mother, 1910- 2. Missionaries of Charity—History. 3. Nuns—India—Calcutta—Biography. 4. Calcutta—Biography. I. Title.

MUGGERIDGE, Malcolm, 1903- 266.2'0924 [B]
Something beautiful for God; Mother Teresa of Calcutta. New York, Ballantine [1973, c.1971] 156 p. illus. (1 col.) ports. 21 cm. [BX4406.5.Z8M8] ISBN 0-345-03276-4 2.00 (pbk.)
1. Teresa, Mother, 1910- 2. Missionaries of Charity. I. Title.
L.C. card no. for the hardbound ed.: 77155106.

MUGGERIDGE, Malcolm, 1903- 266.2'0924 B
Something beautiful for God; Mother Teresa of Calcutta. New York, Harper & Row [1971] 156 p. illus. 23 cm. [BX4406.5.Z8M8 1971b] 77-155106 5.95
1. Teresa, Mother, 1910- 2. Missionaries of Charity. I. Title.

SERROU, Robert. 266'.2'0924 B
Teresa of Calcutta : a pictorial biography / Robert Serrou ; with a foreword by Malcolm Muggeridge. New York : McGraw-Hill, [1980] p. cm. [BX4406.5.Z8S47] 80-18477 ISBN 0-07-056319-5 : 14.95 ISBN 0-07-056318-7 (pbk.) : 9.95
1. Teresa, Mother, 1910- 2. Nuns—India—Calcutta—Biography. 3. Calcutta—Biography. I. Title.

Teresa, Mother, 1910- —Juvenile literature.

LEE, Betsy, 1949- 266'.2'0924 B
Mother Teresa : caring for all God's children / by Betsy Lee ; illustrated by Robert Kilbride. Minneapolis, Minn. : Dillon Press, c1981. 47 p. : col. ill. ; 24 cm. (Taking part books) A biography of the nun whose many years of working with poor and outcast people has been recognized with the 1980 Nobel Peace Prize. [BX4406.5.Z8L43] 92 19 80-20286 ISBN 0-87518-205-4 : 6.95
1. Teresa, Mother, 1910- —Juvenile literature. 2. Missionaries of Charity—Juvenile literature. 3. [Teresa, Mother, 1910-] 4. Nuns—India—Biography—Juvenile literature. 5. [Nuns.] I. Kilbride, Robert. II. Title.

Teresa, Saint, 1515-1582.

AUCLAIR, Marcelle, 1899- 922.246
St. Teresa of Avila. Translation by Kathleen Pond; With a pref. by Andre Maurois. [New York] Pantheon [1953] 437p. illus. 22cm. Translation of La vie de sainte Therese d'Avila. [BX4700.T4A813] 53-6126
1. Teresa, Saint, 1515-1582. I. Title.

BEEVERS, John. 922.246
St. Teresa of Avila. [1st ed.] Garden City, N. Y., Hanover House [1961] 191p. 22cm. [BX4700.T4B37] 61-12492
1. Teresa, Saint, 1515-1582. I. Title.

BERTRAND, Louis, 1866- 922.
Saint Theresa of Avila, translated from the French of Louis Bertrand ... by Marie Louise Hazard. New York, The Society for the propagation of the faith, 1929. xviii, 301 p. front. 21 cm. [Full name: Louis Marie Emile Bertrand] Bibliography: p. 295-296. [BX4700.T4B45] 29-28968
1. Teresa, Saint, 1515-1582. I. Hazard, Marie Louise, tr. II. Title.

BRICE, father, 1905- 922.246
Teresa, John, and Therese, a family portrait of three great Carmelites: Teresa of Avila, John of the Cross, Therese of

Lisieux. By Rev. Fr. Brice, C.P. New York and Cincinnati, F. Pustet co., inc., 1946. 336 p. 23 1/2 cm. [Secular name: Frank Bernard Zurmuehlen] [BX3255.B7] 47-816
1. Teresa, Saint, 1515-1582. 2. Juan de la Cruz, Saint, 1542-1591. 3. Therese, Saint, 1873-1897. 4. Carmelites—Biog. I. Title.

CASTRO Albarren, A de 922.246
The dust of her sandals, by A. De Castro Albarran, translated by Sister Mary Bernarda ... New York, Cincinnati [etc.] Benziger brothers, 1936. 202, [1] p. incl. plates. 20 cm. [BX4700.T4C28] 36-18297
1. Teresa, Saint, 1515-1582. I. Welch, Mary Bernarda, sister, 1892- tr. II. Title.

CASTRO Albarren, Aniceto de 922.246
The dust of her sandals, by A. De Castro Albarran, translated by Sister Mary Bernarda ... New York, Cincinnati [etc.] Benziger brothers, 1936. 202, [1] p. incl. plates. 20 cm. [BX4700.T4C28] 36-18297
1. Teresa, Saint, 1515-1582. I. Welch, Mary Bernarda, sister, 1892- tr. II. Title.

CHESTERTON, Ada E.]Jones: 922.
"Mrs. Cecil Chesterton."
... *St. Teresa.* Garden City, N.Y. Doubleday, Doran and company, inc., 1928. 3 p. l., 273 p. 19 cm. At head of title: Mrs. Cecil Chesterton. [BX4700.T4C5] 28-17429
1. Teresa, Saint, 1515-1582. I. Title.

CLISSOLD, Stephen. 282'.092'4 B
St Teresa of Avila / Stephen Clissold. New York : Seabury Press, 1982, c1979. xv, 272 p. : map ; 22 cm. Includes bibliographical references and index. [BX4700.T4C55 1982] 19 81-9304 ISBN 0-8164-2223-0 pbk. : 8.95
1. Teresa, of Avila, Saint, 1515-1582. 2. Christian saints—Spain—Biography. I. Title.

DEVOTIONS in honor of Saint Teresa of Jesus, compiled for the tercentenary of her canonization. Wheeling, W. Va., Carmelite monastery [c1922] 3 p. l., 9-62 p. front., plates. 15 cm. [BX2167.T4D4] 23-8749
1. Teresa, Saint, 1515-1582.

DICKEN, E W Trueman. 922.246
The crucible of love; a study of the mysticism of St. Teresa of Jesus and St. John of the Cross. New York, Sheed and Ward [1963] xv, 548 p. illus., ports., facisms. 22 cm. Bibliography: p. 524-525. [BX4700.T4D5] 63-18069
1. Teresa, Saint, 1515-1582. 2. Juan de la Cruz, Saint, 1542-1591. 3. Mysticism — Catholic Church. I. Title.

DONZE, Mary Terese. 282'.092'4 B
Teresa of Avila / Mary Terese Donze. New York ; Ramsey, N.J. : Paulist Press, c1982. 200 p. ; 21 cm. Bibliography: p. 199-200. [BX4700.T4D63 1982] 19 81-85380 ISBN 0-8091-2434-3 (pbk.) : 5.95
1. Teresa, of Avila, Saint, 1515-1582. 2. Christian saints—Spain—Avila—Biography. 3. Avila (Spain)—Biography. I. Title.

GABRELE di Santa Maria Maddalena, Father.
St. Teresa of Jesus. Translated from the Italian by a Benedictine of Stanbrook Abbey. Westminister, Md., Newman Press, 1949. xii, 123 p. 23 cm. Bibliographical footnotes. A 50
1. Teresa, Saint, 1515-1582. I. Title.

GILMAN, Mary Rebecca 922.246
(Foster) "Mrs. Bradley Gilman". 1859-
... *Saint Theresa of Avila,* by Mrs. Bradley Gilman. Boston, Roberts brothers, 1889. xii, 203 p. 18 cm. (Half-title: Famous women) "List of authorities": p. [xi]-xii. [BX4700.T4G5] 4-16959
1. Teresa, Saint, 1515-1582. I. Title.

HAMILTON, Elizabeth, 922.246
1906-
Saint Teresa, a journey to Spain. New York, Scribner [1959] 192p. illus. 22cm. Includes bibliography. [BX4700.T4H3] 59-12684
1. Teresa, Saint, 1515-1582. I. Title.

KELLY, Joseph Patrick, 922.246
1902-
Meet Saint Teresa, an introduction to La Madre of Avila. New York, F. Pustet Co., 1958. 212p. illus. 21cm. Includes bibliography. [BX4700.T4K4] 58-49284
1. Teresa, Saint, 1515-1582. I. Title.

LOWRY, Walker. 271'.971'024 B
Teresa de Jesus : a secular appreciation / Walker Lowry. [New York : Lowry], 1977. 91 p. ; 27 cm. 125 copies. [BX4700.T4L68] 77-150320
1. Teresa, Saint, 1515-1582. 2. Christian saints—Spain—Avila—Biography. 3. Avila, Spain—Biography. I. Title.

LUCAS DE SAN JOSE, 1872- 922.
St. Teresa's book-mark; a meditative commentary, by Rev. Father Luke of St. Joseph ... tr. by a friend for Carmel of St. Louis. [St. Louis, H. S. Collins printing co.] c1919 130 p. front. (port.) illus. (coat of arms) 20 cm. "Poems composed by St. Teresa of Jesus, translated by Benedicatines of Stanbrook, Eng.": p. [121]-130. (Secular name: Jose Tristany) [BX4700.T4L8] 19-9547
1. Teresa, Saint, 1515-1582. I. Olivares, Lenore de, tr. II. Title. III. Title: Translation of Glosa a una letrilla de Santa Teresa de Jesus.

MARIE, Joseph, pere. 922.
Popular life of Saint Teresa of Jesus. Translated from the French of l'Abbe Marie Joseph, of the Order of Carmel, by Annie Porter. With a preface by the Rt. Rev. Monsignor Thomas S. Preston ... New York, Cincinnati [etc.] Benziger brothers, 1884. 174 p. front. 20 cm. [BX4700.T4M32] 41-31764
1. Teresa, Saint, 1515-1582. I. Porter, Annie, tr. II. Title.

MULLANY, Katherine Frances. 922.
Teresa of Avila, the woman; a study, by Katherine F. Mullany ... New York and Cincinnati, Frederick Pustet co. (inc.) 1929. ix, 115 p. front. (port.) 17 cm. Published 1928. [BX4700.T4M8] 28-29788
1. Teresa, Saint, 1515-1582. I. Title.

NEVIN, Winifred. 922.24
Heirs of St. Teresa of Avila. Milwaukee, Bruce Pub. Co. [1959] 147p. 22cm. [BX3255.N4] 59-10219
1. Teresa, Saint, 1515-1582. 2. Carmelites Biog. I. Title.

NEVIN, Winifred. 922.246
Teresa of Avila, the woman. Milwaukee, Bruce Pub. Co. [1956] 169p. 22cm. [BX4700.T4N4] 56-7036
1. Teresa, Saint, 1515-1582. I. Title.

O'BRIEN, Kate, 1897- 922.246
Teresa of Avila. New York, Sheed & Ward [1951]wc96p. iii 19cm. (Personal portraits) [BX4700.T4O2] 51-13840
1. Teresa. Saint, 1515-1582. I. Title.

O'BRIEN, Kate, 1898- 922.246
Teresa of Avila. New York, Sheed & Ward [1951] 96 p. illus. 29 cm. (Personal portraits) [BX4700.T4O2] 51-13840
1. Teresa, Saint, 1515-1582. I. Title.

OSUNA, Francisco de, 149.3
d.ca.1540.
The third spiritual alphabet, by Fray Francisco de Osuna; translated from the Spanish by a Benedictine of Stanbrook, with an introduction by Father Cuthbert, O. S. F. C., and notes showing the influence of the book on St. Teresa. New York, Cincinnati [etc.] Benziger brothers [1931] 2 p. l., vii-xxxvi, 490 p. 1 l. 23 cm. [BV5080.O83] 32-22676
1. Teresa, Saint, 1515-1582. 2. Mysticism—Catholic church. 3. Meditation. I. A Benedictine of Stanbrook, tr. II. Title.

OSUNA, Francisco de, 149.
d.ca.1840.
The third spiritual alphabet, tr. from the Spanish by a Benedictine of Stanbrook, with an introd. by Father Cuthbert, o. s. f. c., and notes showing the influence of the book of St. Teresa. Westminster, Md., Newman Bookshop, 1948. xxxvi, 490 p. 22 cm. Translation of Tercera parte d'l libro liamado Abecedario espual. [BV5080.O] A 48
1. Teresa, Saint, 1515-1582. 2. Mysticism—Catholic Church. 3. Meditation. I. A Benedictine of Stanbrook, tr. II. Title.

PAPASOGLI, Giorgio. 922.246
St. Teresa of Avila. Translated from the Italian by G. Anzilotto. New York, Society of St. Paul [c1959] 408p. illus. 22cm. Includes bibliography. [BX4700.T4P313] 58-12223
1. Teresa. Saint. 1515-1582. I. Title.

PEERS, Edgar Allison. 271.73
Handbook to the life and times of St. Teresa and St. John of the Cross. Westminster, Md., Newman Press [1954] vii, 277p. 23cm. Bibliographical footnotes. [BX3206] 54-10164
1. Teresa, Saint, 1515-1582. 2. Juan de la Cruz, Saint, 1542-1591. 3. Camelites—Hist. I. Title.

PEERS, Edgar Allison. 922.246
Mother of Carmel, a portrait of St. Teresa of Jesus, by E. Allison Peers. New York, Morehouse-Gorham co., 1946. xi p., 1 l., 220 p. 20 1/2 cm. Companion volume to the author's Spirit of flame. cf. Foreword. [BX4700.T4P4] 46-3611
1. Teresa, Saint, 1515-1582. I. Title.

RAMGE, Sebastian V. 922.246
An introduction to the writings of Saint Teresa. Chicago, Regnery [c.]1963. 135p. 21cm. Bibl. 63-20527 3.95 bds.,
1. Teresa, Saint, 1515-1582. I. Title.

SACKVILLE-WEST, Victoria 922.246
Mary, Hon., 1892-
... *The eagle and the dove,* a study in contrasts: St. Teresa of Avila, St. Theresa of Lisieux. Garden City, New York, Doubleday, Doran & co., inc., 1944. 4 p. l., 175 p. 21 cm. At head of title: V. Sackville-West. "First edition." [BX4700.T4S25 1944] 44-2447
1. Teresa, Saint, 1515-1582. 2. Therese, Saint, 1873-1897. I. Title.

SCHMID, Evan 1920- 922.246
The eagle of Avila: a story of Saint Teresa, Illus. by Judith E. Quinn. Notre Dame, Dujarie Press [1956] 94p. illus. 24cm. [BX4700.T4S35] 56-23346
1. Teresa Saint, 1545-1582. I. Title.

TERESA, Saint, 1515-1582. 208.1
The complete works of Saint Theresa of Jesus; tr. from the critical ed. of P. Silverio de Santa Teresa and ed. by E. Allison Peers. New York, Sheed & Ward, 1916. 3 v. 23 cm. Contents.v. 1. General introduction. Life. Spiritual relations-v. 2. Book called Way of perfection. Interior castle. Conceptions of the love of God. Exclamations of the soul to God.--v. 3. Book of the foundations. Minor prose works. Poems. Documents. Indices. "Select bibliography": p. 379-387. [BX890.T] A 48
I. Peers, Edgar Allison, ed. and tr. II. Title.

TERESA, Saint, 1515-1582. 242
The interior castle; or, The mansions. Done into English by a Discaleed Carmelite. Westminister, Md., The Newman Bookshop [1945] 122, vi p. front. 22 cm. Translation of El castillo interior; o, Las moradas. [BX2179.T] A 50
I. Title. II. Title: The mansions.

TERESA, Saint, 1515-1582. 242
The interior castle; or, The mansions. Done into English by a Discaleed Carmelite. Westminister, Md., The Newman Bookshop [1945] 122, vi p. front. 22 cm. Translation of El castillo interior; o, Las moradas. [BX2179.T] A 50
I. Title. II. Title: The mansions.

TERESA, Saint, 1515-1582. 922.246
The letters of Saint Teresa of Jesus. Translated and edited by E. Allison Peers, from the critical ed. of P. Silverio de Santa Teresa. Westminster, Md., Newman Press [1950] 2 v. (xii, 1006 p.) 22 cm. [BX4700.T4A31] 52-8915
I. Title.

TERESA, Saint, 1515-1582.
The life of Saint Teresa of Avila, by herself. Tr. with an introd. by J. M. Cohen. [Harmondsworth, Eng.] Penguin Books [1957] 316 p. 18 cm. (The Penguin classics, L73)
I. Cohen, John Michael, tr. II. Title.

TERESA, Saint, 1515-1582. 922.246
The life of St. Teresa of Avila, including the relations of her spiritual state, written by herself. Translated from the Spanish by David Lewis. With an introd. by David Knowles. Westminster, Md., Newman Press [1962] 432 p. 20 cm. The Orchard books) [BX4700.T4A2 1962] 62-51605
I. Lewis, David, 1814-1895, tr. II. Title.

TERESA Saint 1515-1582.
The life of Teresa of Jesus; the autobiography of St. Teresa of Avila, translated and ed. by E. Allison Peers from the critical ed. of P. Silverio de Santa Teresa. Garden City, N.Y., Image Books [1960] 397 p. 18 cm. (A Doubleday image book, D96) Translation of: La vida de la madre Teresa de Jesus. 63-59413
I. Peers, Edgar Allison, ed. II. Title.

TERESA, Saint, 1515-1582. 922.
St. Teresa of Jesus of the Order of Our Lady of Carmel, embracing the life, relations, maxims and foundations, with a map and illustrations, introduction by Walter Elliott, C. S. P., edited by John J. Burke, C. S. P. New York, The Columbus press, 1911. lxxix, 727 p. xxvii double pl., double map. 24 1/2cm. [BX4700.T4A2 1911] 12-1018
I. Burke, John Joseph, 1875-1936, ed. II. Title.

TERESA of Avila.
Translated by Kathleen Pond. With a preface by Andre Maurois. Garden City, N. Y., Image books (Doubleday co.) [1959, c1953] 480p. 18cm. (Image D79) Translation of La vie de Sainte Therese d' avila.
1. Teresa, Saint, 1515-1582. I. Auclair, Marcelle, 1899-

THOMAS, Father, ed. 922.246
St. Teresa of Avila studies in her life, doctrine, and times. Ed. by Father Thomas, Father Gabriel, Westminster, Md., Newman [1964] 249p. plates, ports. 23cm. Bibl. 64-969 4.75
1. Teresa, Saint. 1515-1582. 2. Mysticism—History of doctrines. I. Gabriele di Santa Maria Maddalena, Father Gabriel, joint ed. II. Title.

THOMAS, Father, ed. 922.246
St. Teresa of Avila; studies in her life, doctrine, and times. Edited by Father Thomas and Father Gabriel. Westminster, Md., Newman Press [1963] 249 p. plates, ports. 23 cm. Includes bibliographical references. [BX4700.T4T5] 64-969
1. Teresa, Saint, 1515-1582. 2. Mysticism — History of doctrines. I. Gabriele di Santa Maria Maddelena, Father, joint ed. II. Title.

WALSH, William Thomas, 922.246
1891-
Saint Teresa of Avila, a biography by William Thomas Walsh. Milwaukee, Bruce publishing company [1943] xii p., 1 l., 502 p. front., pl., ports. 24 cm. (On cover: Science and culture series) Bibliographical foot-notes. [BX4700.T4W3] 43-14534
1. Teresa, Saint, 1515-1582. I. Title.

Teresa, Saint, 1515-1582—Addresses, essays, lectures.

SPIRITUAL direction / 248.4
John Sullivan, editor. Washington, D.C. : ICS Publications, 1980. ix, 230 p. ; 21 cm. (Carmelite studies) Includes bibliographical references. [BX2438.S64] 19 80-26654 ISBN 0-9600876-8-0 pbk. : 6.95
1. Teresa, Saint, 1515-1582—Addresses, essays, lectures. 2. Juan de la Cruz, Saint, 1542-1591—Addresses, essays, lectures. 3. Therese, Saint, 1873-1897—Addresses, essays, lectures. 4. Spiritual direction—History—Addresses, essays, lectures. 5. Carmelites—Spiritual life—Addresses, essays, lectures. I. Sullivan, John, 1942- II. Series.

Teresa, Saint, 1515-1582. Camino de perfeccion.

GABRIELE di Santa 271.9710924
Marie Maddelena Father
The way of prayer; a commentary on St. Teresa's "Way of perfection," by Father Gabriel of St. Mary Magdalen. Translated by the Carmel of Baltimore. Milwaukee, Spiritual Life Press, 1965. 143 p. 22 cm. [BX2179.T4C373] 65-24750
1. Teresa, Saint, 1515-1582. Camino de perfeccion. I. Title.

TERESA of Avila, Saint 1515-82 248
The way of perfection. Tr. [from Spanish] ed. by E. Allison Peers. From the critical ed. of P. Silverio De Santa Teresa, C.D. Garden City, N.Y., Doubleday [1964] 280p. 18cm. (Image bk. D 176) .85 pap.,
I. Title.

Teresa, Saint, 1515-1582-Drama.

LA Madre;
a play about Teresa of Avila. New York, S. French [c1959] 143, [1]p. illus., music. 19cm.
1. Teresa of Avila, Saint, 1515-1582—Drama. I. Mary Francis, Sister, P. C.

Teresa, Sister, originally Marie Francoise Therese Martin, 1873-1897.

CLARKE, John P. ed. 922.
Blessed Therese of the Child Jesus "The Little sister of missionaries", edited by Reverend John P. Clarke ... New York, Little flower shop [1923]. 3 p. l, vii, 110 p. plates, 2 port. (incl. front.) 19 1/2 cm. Lettered on cover: Her little way, Blessed Therese of the Child Jesus. [BX4705.T45C6] 23-17898
1. Teresa, Sister, originally Marie Francoise Therese Martin, 1873-1897. I. Title.

SOCIETY for the propagation of the faith. 922
Shower of roses upon the missions: spiritual and temporal favors obtained through the intercession of Blessed Teresa, the Little sister of the missionaries, 1909-1923. New York, N. Y., The Society for the propagation of the faith [c1924] 2 p. l., vii-x, 108 p. plates, ports. 20 cm. One hundred authentic letters of testimony received by the Carmelite nuns of Lisicux. cf. Foreword. [BX4705.T45S6] 24-10057
1. Teresa, Sister, originally Marie Francoise Therese Martin, 1873-1897. I. Title.

Terling, Eng.—Rural conditions.

WRIGHTSON, Keith. 301.35'2'094267
Poverty and piety in an English village : Terling, 1525-1700 / Keith Wrightson, David Levine. New York : Academic Press, 1979. xii, 200 p. ; 24 cm. (Studies in social discontinuity) Includes index. Bibliography: p. 187-196. [HN398.T45W74] 78-22536 ISBN 0-12-765950-1 : 17.00
1. Terling, Eng.—Rural conditions. 2. Villages—England—History—Case studies. 3. Poor—England—Terling—Case studies. 4. Reformation—England—Terling. I. Levine, David, 1946- joint author. II. Title. III. Series.

Terminal care.

ELLIOTT, Neil. 174'.24
The gods of life. New York, Macmillan [1974] xii, 180 p. 21 cm. Includes bibliographical references. [R726.8.E4] 74-11215 ISBN 0-02-535200-8 5.95
1. Terminal care. 2. Euthanasia. 3. Aged—Medical care—United States. 4. Aged—United States. I. Title.

KOPP, Ruth Lewshenia, 1947- 248.8'6
Encounter with terminal illness / Ruth Lewshenia Kopp, with Stephen Sorenson. Grand Rapids, MI : Zondervan Pub. House, c1980. 238 p. ; 24 cm. [R726.8.K66] 19 80-10982 ISBN 0-310-41600-0 : 8.95
1. Terminal care. 2. Death—Psychological aspects. 3. Terminal care—Moral and religious aspects. 4. Christian life—1960- I. Sorenson, Stephen, joint author. II. Title.

Terminal care—Moral and religious aspects.

COLEN, B. D. 174'.2
Karen Ann Quinlan : dying in the age of eternal life / B. D. Colen. New York : Nash Pub., c1976. 204 p. ; 22 cm. Includes index. [R726.C64] 76-7144 ISBN 0-8402-1368-9 : 7.95
1. Quinlan, Karen Ann. 2. Terminal care—Moral and religious aspects. 3. Death. 4. Coma—Biography.

SHERRILL, John L. 241'.6424
Mother's song / John Sherrill. Lincoln, Va. : Chosen Books, c1982. 134 p. ; 23 cm. [R726.S53 1982] 19 82-9527 ISBN 0-912376-80-5 lib. bdg. : 7.95
1. Sherrill, Helen Hardwicke. 2. Terminal care—Moral and ethical aspects. 3. Right to die—Religious aspects—Christianity. 4. Pneumonia—Patients—United States—Biography. I. Title.
Publisher's address: Lincoln, VA 22078.

VEATCH, Robert M. 174'.24
Death, dying, and the biological revolution : our last quest for responsibility / Robert M. Veatch. New Haven : Yale University Press, 1976. ix, 323 p. ; 25 cm. Includes index. Bibliography: p. 307-318. [R726.V4] 75-43337 ISBN 0-300-01949-1 : 12.95
1. Terminal care—Moral and religious aspects. 2. Medical policy—United States. 3. Death. I. Title.

Terminal care—Moral and religious aspects—Congresses.

MORAL, ethical, and legal issues in the neurosciences / edited by T.P. Morley. Springfield, Ill. : Thomas, c1981. p. cm. Proceedings of a symposium held within the 15th Canadian Congress of Neurological Sciences, Ottawa, June 1980. Includes index. Bibliography: p. [R726.M67] 19 81-9352 ISBN 0-398-04586-0 : 14.50 174'.24
1. Terminal care—Moral and religious aspects—Congresses. 2. Brain death—Congresses. 3. Neurology—Moral and religious aspects—Congresses. 4. Neurologists—Malpractice—Canada—Congresses. 5. Death—Proof and certification—Canada—Congresses. I. Morley, T. P. (Thomas P.) II. Canadian Congress of Neurological Sciences Ottawa, Ont. (15th : 1980 : Ottawa, Ont.)

Terra-cottas, Etruscan.

MALLE, Quentin Froebel. 292.218
Votive religion at Caere: prolegomena, by Quentin F. Maule and H. R. W. Smith. Berkeley, University of California Press, 1959. x, 128p. illus., plates. 26cm. (University of California publications in classical archaeology, v. 4, no. 1) Includes bibliographies. [DE1.C3 vol. 4, no. 1] A59
1. Terra-cottas, Etruscan. 2. Cerveteri, Italy—Antiq. 3. Votive offerings. 4. Etrurians— Religion. I. Smith, Henry Roy William, 1891- joint author. II. Title. III. Series: California. University. University of California publications in classical archaeology, v. 4, no. 1

Terra-cottas, Greek.

VAN BUREN, Elizabeth (Douglas). 726'.1'20938
Greek fictile revetments in the archaic period, by E. Douglas Van Buren. Washington, McGrath Pub. Co., 1973. xx, 208 p. illus. 27 cm. Reprint of the 1926 ed. published by J. Murray, London. Includes bibliographical references. [NA270.V3 1973] 73-129561 ISBN 0-8434-0150-8 65.00
1. Terra-cottas, Greek. 2. Architecture, Greek. 3. Temples—Greece. I. Title.

Terra-cottas, Greek—Sicily.

VAN BUREN, Elizabeth (Douglas) 726'.1'0938
Archaic fictile revetments in Sicily and Magna Graecia, by E. Douglas Van Buren. Washington, McGrath Pub. Co., 1973. xx, 168 p. illus. 27 cm. Reprint of the 1923 ed. [NB158.5.S52V36 1973] 75-119282 ISBN 0-8434-0149-4 45.00
1. Terra-cottas, Greek—Sicily. 2. Terra-cottas, Greek—Magna Graecia. 3. Temples, Greek—Sicily. 4. Temples,Greek—Magna Graecia. 5. Sicily—Antiquities, Greek. 6. Magna Graecia—Antiquities, Greek. I. Title.

Terrien, Samuel L., 1911- — Addresses, essays, lectures.

ISRAELITE wisdom : theological and literary essays in honor of Samuel Terrien / edited by John G. Gammie ... [et al.]. Missoula, MT : Scholars Press for Union Theological Seminary, c1977. p. cm. Includes index. Bibliography: p. [BS1455.I84] 77-17862 ISBN 0-89130-208-5 ISBN pbk. : 15.00 223
1. Terrien, Samuel L., 1911- —Addresses, essays, lectures. 2. Bible. O.T. Prophets—Criticism, interpretation, etc.—Addresses, essays, lectures. 3. Wisdom literature—Criticism, interpretation, etc.—Addresses, essays, lectures. I. Terrien, Samuel L., 1911- II. Gammie, John G.

Terry, Mary, 1690-1708.

REYNOLDS, Thomas, 1667?-1727. 922.347
Practical religion exemplify'd in the lives of Mrs. Mary Terry, who died Decemb. 8th. 1708. in the eighteenth year of her age. and Mrs. Clissovld. who departed this life the 12th of Decemb. 1711. in the twenty ninth year of her age. By Thomas Reynolds. Recommended by Increase Mather, D.D. London, printed 1712; reprinted at Boston in N.E. by John Allen, for Samuel Gerrish, at the Sign of the buck. 1713. 4 p. l., 109 p. 13 1/2 x 8 cm. Title within mourning border. [BR1713.R4 1713] 2-28229
1. Terry, Mary, 1690-1708. 2. Clissould, Mrs.—, 1683?-1711. I. Title.

Tertullianus, Quintus Septimius Florens.

BRAY, Gerald Lewis. 230'.1'30924
Holiness and the will of God : perspectives on the theology of Tertullian / Gerald Lewis Bray. Atlanta : John Knox Press, 1979. xii, 179 p. ; 22 cm. (New foundations theological library) Includes indexes. "List of Tertullian's works": p. [169]-170. [BR65.T7B754 1979] 79-5211 ISBN 0-8042-3705-0 : 18.50
1. Tertullianus, Quintus Septimius Florens. I. Title.

TERTULLIANUS, Quintus Septimius Florens. 230
Tertullian concerning the resurrection of the flesh, by A. Souter, D.LITT. London, Society for promoting Christian knowledge; New York, The Macmillan company, 1922. xxiv, 205 [1] p. 19 cm. (Translations of Christian literature. ser. II, Latin texts) [BR45.T62T45] 22-19557
I. Souter, Alexander, 1873- tr. II. Title.

TERTULLIANUS, Quintus Septimius Florens. 239.
Tertullian On the testimony of the soul and On the "prescription" of heretics, translated into English by T. Herbert Bindley ... London [etc.] Society for promoting Christian knowledge; New York, E. S. Gorham, 1914. xi, [1], 13-96 p. 17 cm. (Early church classics) [BR60.E3T4] 22-6508
I. Bindley, Thomas Herbert, 1861- tr. II. Title.

TERTULLIANUS, Quintus Septimius Florens. 230
Tertullian's treatises, Concerning prayer, Concerning baptism, tr. by Alexander Souter, D.LITT. London, Society for promoting Christian knowledge; New York, The Macmillan company, 1919. xvii, 19-75, [1] p. 19 cm. (Translations of Christian literature. ser. II, Latin texts) [BR45.T62T5] 20-6943
I. Souter, Alexander, 1873- tr. II. Title.

WARFIELD, Benjamin Breckinridge, 1851-1921. 230.1'3'0922
Studies in Tertullian and Augustine. Westport, Conn., Greenwood Press [1970] v, 412 p. 23 cm. Reprint of the 1930 ed. Includes bibliographical references. [BR1720.T3W3 1970] 73-109980
1. Tertullianus, Quintus Septimius Florens. 2. Augustinus, Aurelius, Saint, Bp. of Hippo—Addresses, essays, lectures. 3. Trinity—History of doctrines. 4. Knowledge, Theory of (Religion) 5. Pelagianism. I. Title.

WARFIELD, Benjamin Breckinridge, 1851-1921. 231
Studies in Tertullian and Augustine, by Benjamin Breckinridge Warfield ... New York, London [etc.] Oxford university press, 1930. v, 412 p. 24 cm. "Prefatory note" signed: Ethelbert D. Warfield, William Park Armstrong, Caspar Wistar Hodge, committee. Contents.--Tertullian and the beginnings of the doctrine of the Trinity.--Augustine. Augustine's doctrine of knowledge and authority.--Augustine and his "Confessions".--Augustine and the Pelagian controversy. [BR1720.T3W3] [189.2] 31-1501
1. Tertullianus, Quintus Septimium Florena. 2. Augustinus, Aurellus. Saint, bp. of Hippo. 3. Trinity. 4. Knowledge, theory of. 5. Pelagianism. I. Warfield, Ethelbert Dudley, 1861- ed. II. Title.

Test act, 1673.

[MATTHEWS, Albert] 1860- 261.
A sacrament certificate 1673. Reprinted from the Publications of the Colonial society of Massachusetts, vol. XIII. Cambridge, J. Wilson and son, 1910. 1 p. l., 119-126 p. double front. (facsim.) 24 1/2 cm. [BR757.M4] 11-18222
1. Test act, 1673. 2. Catholics in England. I. Title.

Testerman, Jean.

TESTERMAN, Jean. 248'.4
Eagle's wings. Anderson, Ind., Warner Press [1973] 107 p. 19 cm. Includes bibliographical references. [BR1725.T38A33] 73-8533 ISBN 0-87162-156-8 2.50 (pbk.)
1. Testerman, Jean. 2. Christian life—1960- I. Title.

Tettemer, John Moyniahn, 1876-1949.

TETTEMER, John Moynihan, 1876-1949. 271'.62'024 B
I was a monk; the autobiography of John Tettemer. Edited by Janet Mabie, with a foreword by Jean Burden and an introd. by John Burton. Wheaton, Ill. [Published by Pyramid Publications for the Theosophical Pub. House, 1974, c1951] 255 p. 18 cm. (Re-quest books) [BX4668.3.T47A34 1974] 73-89888 ISBN 0-8356-0300-8 1.25 (pbk.)
1. Tettemer, John Moyniahn, 1876-1949. I. Title.

Texas—Biography

BURLESON, Georgiana (Jenkins) Mrs. comp. 920.
The life and writings of Rufus C. Burleson, d. d., ll. d., con- taining a biography of Dr. Burleson by Hon. Harry Haynes; funeral occasion, with sermon, addresses, resolutions, etc.; selected "chapel talks" ... Dr. Burleson as a preacher, with selected sermons ... Compiled and published by Mrs. Georgia J. Burleson. [Waco! Tex.] 1901. xxii, 887 p. incl. front., illus., ports. 24 cm. "'The old guard' biographies, by Dr. Burleson": p. [661]-744. [BX6495.B8B8] 2-6243
1. Burleson, Rufus Columbus, 1823-1901. 2. Texas—Biog. I. Haynes, Harry. II. Title.

Texas Christian University, Fort Worth. Graduate School—Dissertations.

TEXAS Christian University, Fort Worth. 013'.37'9
Theses and dissertations accepted by Texas Christian University: the Graduate School and Brite Divinity School, 1909-1972. Centennial ed. Fort Worth, 1973. xiv, 166 p. 23 cm. [Z5055.U5T4715] 73-85413 2.00 (pbk.)
1. Texas Christian University, Fort Worth. Graduate School—Dissertations. 2. Brite Divinity School—Dissertations. I. Title.

Texas—Church history.

HELD, John Adolf, 1869- 277.64
Religion a factor in building Texas; a study of religion as it has affected the life of the early colonies in Texas...A discussion of the forces that affect life generally--

education, social life, and the political factors that make up the body politic, with the spiritual forces that have tremendously affected later life. By John A. Held... San Antonio, The Naylor company, 1940. xviii, 167 p. front., plates, ports. 21 cm. Bibliography: p. [153]-156. [BR555.T4H4] 40-10847
1. Texas—Church history. I. Title.

RED, William Stuart. 277.
The Texas colonists and religion, 1821-1836; a centennial tribute to the Texas patriots who shed their blood that we might enjoy civil and religious liberty. [By] William Stuart Red. Austin, Tex., E. L. Shettles [c1924] viii, 149 p. illus. (facsims.) pl. 24 cm. [BR555.T4R4] 24-14892
1. Texas—Church history. 2. Church and state in Texas. I. Title.

SMITH, Jesse Guy. 277.64
Heroes of the saddle bags; a history of Christian denominations in the Republic of Texas. San Antonio, Naylor Co. [1951] ix, 234 p. map (on lining papers) 22 cm. Bibliography: p. 210-227. [BR555.T4S6] 51-4527
1. Texas—Church history. 2. Texas—Hist.—Revolution, 1835-1836. 3. Texas—Hist.—Republic, 1836-1846. 4. Sects—Texas. I. Title.

Texas—History

KNIGHTS of Columbus. Texas state council. Historical commission. 976.4
Our Catholic heritage in Texas, 1519-1936; prepared under the auspices of the Knights of Columbus of Texas, Paul J. Foik ... editor ... Austin, Von Boeckmann-Jones company, 1936- v. fronts. (ports.) plates, fold. maps. 27 cm. [F386.K66] [BX1415.T4K6] 36-18384
1. Texas—Hist. 2. Catholics in Texas. 3. Indians of North America—Missions. I. Castañeda, Carlos Eduardo, 1896- II. Folk, Paul Joseph, 1880- ed. III. Title.
Contents omitted.

Thacher, Peter, 1677-1739.

[SEARES, Alexander] fl.1720. 289
An account of the reasons why a considerable number (about fifty, whereof ten are members in full communion) belonging to the New North congregation in Boston, could not consent to Mr. Peter Thacher's ordination there. Who has left his flock at Weymouth, and accepted of a call in Boston, without the approbation, and contrary to the advice of the ministers in this town ... [Boston] Printed in the year 1720. 3 p. l., 56, [1] p. 16 cm. Declarations, documents and letters (some of which are signed by Alexander Seares and Increase Mather) in opposition to the ordination of Peter Thacher. cf. Holmes, T. J. Increase Mather, v. 1, p. [5]-7. [BX9861.B7N45] 24-17630
1. Thacher, Peter, 1677-1739. 2. Boston. New North Church. I. Mather, Increase, 1639- 1723. II. Title.

Thailand—Religion.

CADET, J. M., 1935- FIC
The Ramakien : the Thai epic [by] J. M. Cadet. Illustrated with the bas-reliefs of Wat Phra Jetubon, Bangkok. [1st ed.] Tokyo, Palo Alto, Calif., Kodansha International [1971] 256 p. illus. 30 cm. A retelling of the Thai version of Valmiki's Ramayana. Bibliography: p. 251-252. [PZ4.C1274Ram] [PR6053.A335] 294.5'922 70-128685 ISBN 0-87011-134-5 14.50 (U.S.)
I. Valmiki. Ramayana. English. II. Rammakian. English. III. Title.

TAMBIAH, S. J. 294.3'09593
Buddhism and the spirit cults in north-east Thailand, [by] S. J. Tambiah. New York: Cambridge University Press, [1975 c1970] xi., 388 p.: illus., maps; 23 cm. (Cambridge studies in social anthropology; no. 2) [BL2075.T3] 73-108112 ISBN 0-521-09958-7 6.95 (pbk.)
1. Thailand—Religion. 2. Buddha and Buddhism—Relations. I. Title.

Thanksgiving day.

WEDEL, Cynthia C. 268.61
Celebrating Thanksgiving; a Christian education unit for kindergarten, by Cynthia C. Wedel... New York, N.Y., The National council, Protestant Episcopal church [c1941] 82 p. diagrs. 21 1/2 cm. [Christian education units] "Source materials": p. 10-13. [BV1540.W4] [268.76] 41-13118
1. Thanksgiving day. I. Title.

Thanksgiving Day Addresses.

HUGHES, Edwin Holt, bp., 1866- 261.
Thanksgiving sermons, by Edwin Holt Hughes... Cincinnati, Jennings and Graham; New York, Eaton and Mains [c1909] 246 p. 19 cm. [BV4305.H8] 9-28184
1. Thanksgiving day addresses. 2. Methodist church—Sermons. 3. Sermons, American. I. Title.

LORD, Willis, 1809-1888. 261.
Our national preeminence and its true source. A sermon preached on Thanksgiving day, Nov. 25, 1847, in the Seventh Presbyterian church, Philadelphia. By the pastor, Rev. Willis Lord ... Philadelphia, W. S. Martien, 1848. 64 p. 15 cm. [BV4305.L6] 39-8939
1. Thanksgiving day addresses. I. Title.

MATHER, Cotton, 1663-1728. 252.
The wonderful works of God commemorated; praises bespoke for the God of Heaven in a Thanksgiving sermon, delivered on Decemb. 19, 1689, containing just reflections upon the excellent things done by the great God, more generally in creation and redemption, and in the government of the world; but more particularly in the remarkable revolutions of providence which are every where the matter of present observation. With a postscript giving an account of some very stupendous accidents which have lately happened in France. To which is added a sermon preached unto the convention of the Massachuset-Colony in New-England. With a short narrative of several prodigies which New England hath of late had the alarms of heaven in. Boston, Printed by S. Green & sold by J. Browning, 1690. 62 (i.e. 64), 26 (i.e. 36), 5 p. 15 cm. "The way to prosperity; a sermon preached to the honorable convention" has special t.p. and separate paging. Imperfect: all after p. 62 wanting. [BX7233.M32W6] 50-52272
1. Thanksgiving Day Addresses. I. Title. II. Title: The way to prosperity.

ROGERS, John, 1712-1789. 252.
Three sermons on different subjects and occasions, The first, On the pleasure which affects the hearts of virtuous men, at the view of publick happiness; particularly when they meet in the house of God, to give thanks for his favours. The second, On the vanity of prayer and fasting; when these are not joined with reformation of manners. The last. On the terribleness, and the moral cause of earthquakes; delivered at Leominster, by John Rogers ... Boston, Printed by Edes & Gill for S. Kneeland in Queen-street, 1756. 1 p. l., 5-61 p. 18 cm. [BX7233.R5T5] 25-22630
1. Thanksgiving day addresses. 2. Earthquakes. I. Title.

SKINNER, Thomas Harvey, 1791-1871. 261.70973
Religion and liberty. A discourse delivered Dec. 17, 1840; the day appointed for public thanksgiving by the governor of New York. By Thomas H. Skinner. New York, Wiley and Putnam, 1841. vii, [9]-77 p. 19 1/2 cm. [BV4305.S5] 15-25966
1. Thanksgiving day addresses. 2. Church and state in the U.S. I. Title.

Thanksgiving scroll—Criticism, interpretation, etc.

KITTEL, Bonnie Pedrotti. 296.1'55
The hymns of Qumran : translation and commentary / Bonnie Pedrotti Kittel. Chico, Calif. : Scholars Press, c1981. xi, 222 p. ; 22 cm. (Dissertation series - Society of Biblical Literature ; no. 50 ISSN 0145-269Xs) Selected hymns in English and Hebrew, commentary in English. Originally presented as the author's thesis, Graduate Theological Union, 1975. Includes indexes. Bibliography: p. 213-216. [BM488.T5K57 1981] 80-11616 ISBN 0-89130-397-9 pbk. : 13.50
1. Thanksgiving scroll—Criticism, interpretation, etc. 2. Hymns, Hebrew—History and criticism. I. Thanksgiving scroll. English & Hebrew. Selections. 1980. II. Title. III. Series: Society of Biblical Literature. Dissertation series ; no. 50.

MANSOOR, Menahem, ed. and tr. 296.4
Thanksgiving scroll. English. Grand Rapids, Eerdmans, 1961. xi, 227 p. 25 cm. (Studies on the texts of the desert of Judah, v. 3) Bibliography: p. [197]-208. [BM488.T5A3 1961] 61-1542
I. Title. II. Title: The Thanksgiving hymns.

Thatcher, Moses, 1842-1909.

REASONER, Calvin. 922.8373
Church and state; the issue of civil and religious liberty in Utah; a testimonial in behalf of civil liberty and the American state as separate from the church. Salt Lake City [1896] 139p. 23cm. Cover title: The late manifesto in politics; practical working of counsel in relation to civil and religious liberty in Utah. [BX8695.T5R4] 55-48891
1. Thatcher, Moses, 1842-1909. 2. Church and state in Utah. I. Title.

Theater—History—Medieval, 500-1500.

MEZIERES, Philippe de, 1327?-1405. 792.1'0909'351
Figurative representation of the Presentation of the Virgin Mary in the temple. Translated and edited by Robert S. Haller. Introd. by M. Catherine Rupp. Lincoln, University of Nebraska Press [1971] xliv, 97 p. illus. 24 cm. Cover title: The Presentation play. Texts in Latin or French, with English translations. Contents.Contents.—The Presentation play.—A Letter and a Note concerning the Presentation play.—Mary's early life from Philippe's Book of the sacrament of marriage.—Bibliography (p. 95) [PA8552.M445F4 1971] 71-125315 ISBN 0-8032-0780-8 7.95
1. Mary, Virgin—Drama. 2. Theater—History—Medieval, 500-1500. 3. Theaters—Stage-setting and scenery. I. Mezieres, Philippe de, 1327?-1405. Festum praesentationis Beatae Mariae. English & Latin. 1971. II. Title. III. Title: The Presentation play.

Theater — Moral and religious aspects.

BAKER, Richard, Sir, 1568-1645. 792'.013
Theatrum redivivum; or, The theatre vindicated. Introductory note by Peter Davison. New York, Johnson Reprint Corp., 1972. 141 p. 16 cm. (Theatrum redivivum) Running title: The theatre vindicated. "Written in response to Prynne's Histrio-mastix." Reprint of the 1662 ed. printed by T. R. for F. Eglesfield, London (Wing B513) [PN2047.B3 1972] 76-175650 13.50
1. Prynne, William, 1600-1669. Histrio-mastix. 2. Theater—Moral and religious aspects. I. Prynne, William 1600-1669. Histrio-mastix. II. Title. III. Title: The theatre vindicated.

BALE, John, Bp. of Ossory, 1495-1563. 792'.013
The epistle exhortatory of an English Christian, by Henry Stalbrydge (John Bale). "Reply to Gosson," by Thomas Lodge. Introductory notes by Peter Davison. New York, Johnson Reprint Corp., 1972. 28 l., 48 p. 16 cm. (Theatrum redivivum) Reprint of The epistle exhortatorye of an Englyshe Christiane, published at Antwerp, 1544, (STC1291), and of A reply to Stephen Gosson's Schoole of abuse in defence of poetry, musick, and stage plays, published 1579-80 (STC 16663) [PN2047.B43 1972] 70-175662 12.00
1. Theater—Moral and religious aspects. I. Gosson, Stephen, 1554-1624. The schoole of abuse. II. Lodge, Thomas, 1558?-1625. A reply to Stephen Gosson's Schoole of abuse. 1972. III. Title. IV. Title: Reply to Gosson.

BEDFORD, Arthur, 1668-1745. 792'.013
The evil and danger of stage-plays. With a pref. for the Garland ed. by Arthur Freeman. New York, Garland Pub., 1974. 12, 227 p. 18 cm. (The English stage: attack and defense, 1577-1730) Reprint of the 1706 ed. printed by W. Bonny, Bristol, Eng. [PN2047.B46 1974] 72-170479 ISBN 0-8240-0626-7 22.00
1. Theater—Moral and religious aspects. I. Title. II. Series.

BEDFORD, Arthur, 1668-1745. 792'.013
Serious reflections on the scandalous abuse and effects of the stage, A second advertisement concerning the profaneness of the play-house, and A sermon preached in the parish-church of St. Butolph's Aldgate. With a pref. for the Garland ed. by Arthur Freeman. New York, Garland Pub., 1974. 11, [26], 44, 16, 40 p. 21 cm. (The English stage: attack and defense, 1577-1730) Reprint of 3 works: the 1st printed in 1705, by W. Bonny, Bristol; the 2d printed in 1705; the 3d printed in 1730, by C. Ackers, London. [PN2047.B49 1974] 78-170475 ISBN 0-8240-0624-0
1. Church of England—Sermons. 2. Theater—Moral and religious aspects. 3. Theater—England—History—Sources. 4. Sermons, English. I. Bedford, Arthur, 1668-1745. A second advertisement concerning the profaneness of the play-house. 1974. II. Bedford, Arthur, 1668-1745. A sermon preached in the parish-church of St. Butolph's Aldgate. 1974. III. Title. IV. Title: A second advertisement concerning the profaneness of the play-house. V. Title: A sermon preached in the parish-church of St. Butolph's Aldgate. VI. Series.

BEDFORD, Arthur, 1668-1745. 792'.013
A serious remonstrance in behalf of the Christian religion. With a pref. for the Garland ed. by Arthur Freeman. New York, Garland Pub., 1974. 11, xx, 383 p. 21 cm. (The English stage: attack and defense, 1577-1730) Reprint of the 1719 ed. printed by J. Darby, London. Includes bibliographical references. [PN2047.B5 1974] 79-170478 ISBN 0-8240-0625-9 22.00
1. Theater—Moral and religious aspects. I. Title.

COLLIER, Jeremy, 1650-1726. 792'.013
A defence of the Short view of the profaneness and immorality of the English stage. With a pref. for the Garland ed. by Arthur Freeman. New York, Garland Pub., 1972. 6, 139 p. 19 cm. (The English stage: attack and defense, 1577-1730) Reprint of the 1699 ed. "Wing C5248." [PN2047.C62C624 1972] 72-170444 ISBN 0-8240-0613-5 22.50 (ea.)
1. Congreve, William, 1670-1729. Amendments upon Mr. Collier's false and imperfect citations. 2. Vanbrugh, John, Sir, 1664-1726. A short vindication of The relapse and the The provoked wife. 3. Theater—Moral and religious aspects. 4. Theater—England. I. Title. II. Series.
Set of 50 volumes; $1050.00.

COLLIER, Jeremy, 1650-1726. 792'.013
A second defence of the Short view of the prophaneness [sic] and immorality of the English stage. With a pref. for the Garland ed. by Arthur Freeman. New York, Garland Pub., 1972. 6, 142 p. 22 cm. (The English stage: attack and defense, 1577-1730) Reprint of the 1700 ed. "Wing C5262." [PN2047.C62D72 1972] 76-170445 ISBN 0-8240-0617-8
1. Drake, James, 1667-1707 The antient and modern stages survey'd. 2. Theater—Moral and religious aspects. 3. Theater—England. I. Title. II. Series.

COLLIER, Jeremy, 1650-1726. 792'.013'0942
A short view of the immorality and profaneness of the English stage. With a pref. for the Garland ed. by Arthur Freeman. New York, Garland Pub., [1973 c1972] 6, 288 p. 19 cm. (The English stage: attack and defense, 1577-1730)

Reprint of the 1698 ed. "Wing C5263." [PN2047.C6 1972] 70-170438 ISBN 0-8240-0605-4 22.00 ea.
1. Theater—Moral and religious aspects. 2. Theater—England. I. Title. II. Series.
Part of a 50 volume series selling for 1,050.00.

COLLIER, Jeremy, 1650-1726. 792'.013
A short view of the immorality and profaneness of the English stage. New York, AMS Press [1974] 288 p. 23 cm. Reprint of the 3d ed. printed for S. Keble, London, 1698. [PN2047.C6 1974] 74-3401 ISBN 0-404-01619-7 10.00
1. Theater—Moral and religious aspects. 2. Theater—England. I. Title.

COLLIER tracts, 1703-1708. 792'.013
With a pref. for the Garland ed. by Arthur Freeman. New York, Garland Pub., 1973. 1 v. (various pagings) 22 cm. (The English stage: attack and defense, 1577-1730) Reprint of Mr. Collier's dissuasive from the play-house, by Jeremy Collier, first printed in 1703, for R. Sare, London; of The person of quality's answer to Mr. Collier's letter, by John Dennis, first printed in 1704 by the Booksellers of London and Westminster, London; of A representation of the impiety & immorality of the English stage (anonymous), first printed in 1704, and sold by J. Nutt, London; of Some thoughts concerning the stage (anonymous), first printed in 1704, and sold by J. Nutt, London; of The stage-beaux toss'd in a blanket, by Thomas Brown, first printed in 1704, and sold by J. Nutt, London; and of A farther vindication of the short view of the profaneness and immorality of the English stage, by Jeremy Collier, first printed in 1708, for R. Sare, London. [PN2047.C69 1973] 70-170462 ISBN 0-8240-0618-6 22.00
1. Theater—Moral and religious aspects. I. Title. II. Series.
Part of a 50 volume series selling for 1050.00.

COLLIER tracts, 1698. 792'.013
With a pref. for the Garland ed. by Arthur Freeman. New York, Garland Pub., 1974. [161] p. 22 cm. (The English stage: attack and defense, 1577-1730) Reprint of the 1698 editions of The immorality of the English pulpit (anonymous), printed in London; of A letter to A. H. Esq., concerning the stage (attributed to Charles Hopkins), printed for A. Baldwin, London (Wing M 2033); of A letter to Mr. Congreve on his pretended amendments (anonymous), printed for S. Keble, London (Wing L1713a); of Some remarks upon Mr. Collier's defence of his short view of the English stage (anonymous), printed for A. Baldwin, London (Wing S4605); of The occasional paper: number IX, containing some considerations about the danger of going to plays, by Richard Willis, Bishop of Winchester, printed for M. Wotton, London; and of A vindication of the stage (anonymous), printed for J. Wild, London (Wing V532) Includes bibliographical references. [PN2047.C68 1974] 76-170453 ISBN 0-8240-0610-0 22.00
1. Theater—Moral and religious aspects. 2. Theater—England—History—Sources. I. Title. II. Series.

CRASHAW, William, 1572-1626. 230'.2
The sermon preached at the cross, Feb. 14, 1607. Introductory note by Peter Davison. New York, Johnson Reprint Corp., [1973 c.1972] 174 p. 22 cm. (Theatrum redivivum) Reprint of the 1608 ed. imprinted by H. L. for E. Weaver, London under title: The sermon preached at the crosse, Feb. xiiij. 1607 (STC 6027) Includes bibliographical references. [BX1763.C65 1972] 70-175654 14.50
1. Catholic Church—Doctrinal and controversial works—Protestant authors. 2. Theater—Moral and religious aspects. I. Title.

DENNIS, John, 1657-1734. 792'.013
The usefulness of the stage. With a pref. for the Garland ed. by Arthur Freeman. New York, Garland Pub., [1972, i.e. 1973] 6, [8], 143 p. 19 cm. (The English stage: attack and defense, 1577-1730) Reprint of the 1698 ed. "Wing D1046." [PN2047.C62D4 1972] 71-170441 ISBN 0-8240-0609-7 22.00 ea.
1. Collier, Jeremy, 1650-1726. A short view of the immorality and profaneness of the English stage. 2. Theater—Moral and religious aspects. 3. Theater—England. I. Title. II. Series.
Part of a 50 volume series selling for 1050.00 a set.

DRAKE, James, 1667-1707. 792'.013
The antient and modern stages survey'd. With a pref. for the Garland ed. by Arthur Freeman. New York, Garland Pub., 1972. 6, [32], 367 p. 19 cm. (The English stage: attack and defense, 1577-1730) Reprint of the 1699 ed. "Wing D2123." [PN2047.C62D7 1972] 70-170446 ISBN 0-8240-0615-1 22.00 ea.
1. Collier, Jeremy, 1650-1726. A short view of the immorality and profaneness of the English stage. 2. Theater—Moral and religious aspects. 3. Theater—England. I. Title. II. Series.
Part of a 50 volume series selling for 1050.00 a set.

FEILDE, John, d.1588. 792'.013
A godly exhortation by occasion of the late judgement of God, showed at Paris-garden, the thirteenth day of January, by John Field. A sermon preached at Paul's Cross, 3 November, 1577, by T. W. Introductory notes by Peter Davison. New York, Johnson Reprint Corp., [1973 c1972] 1 v. (various pagings) 16 cm. (Theatrum redivivum) Running title of A godly exhortation: The wofull crie at Parris garden. Reprint of A godly exhortation by occasion of the late judgement of God, shewed at Parris-garden, printed by R. Walde-graue and H. Carre, London, 1583, (STC 10845), and of A sermon preached at Pawles Crosse on Sunday the Thirde of November, 1577, imprinted by F. Coldock, London, 1578 (STC 25406) [PN2047.F36 1972] 75-175658 15.00
1. Theater—Moral and religious aspects. I. T. W. II. W., T. III. White, Thomas, 1550?-1624. A sermon preached at Pawles Crosse on Sunday the thirde of November, 1577. 1972. IV. Title. V. Title: A sermon preached at Paul's Cross, 3 November, 1577. VI. Title: The wofull crie at Parris garden.

FILMER, Edward, fl.1707. 792'.013
A defence of plays. With a pref. for the Garland ed. by Arthur Freeman. New York, Garland Pub., 1972. 5, 167 p. 18 cm. (The English stage: attack and defense, 1577-1730) Reprint of the 1707 ed. [PN2047.C62F5 1972] 70-170449 ISBN 0-8240-0619-4 22.00 (Part of 50 vol. series)
1. Collier, Jeremy, 1650-1726. A short view of the immorality and profaneness of the English stage. 2. Theater—Moral and religious aspects. 3. Theater—England. I. Title. II. Series.
Set 1050.00.

GOSSON, Stephen, 1554-1624. 792'.013'0942
Playes confuted in five actions. With a pref. for the Garland ed. by Arthur Freeman. New York, Garland Pub., 1973. 6 [122] p. 19 cm. (The English stage: attack and defense, 1577-1730) Reprint of the 1582 ed. "STC 12095." [PN2047.G6 1972] 74-170407 ISBN 0-8240-0589-9 22.00 ea.
1. Theater—Moral and religious aspects. 2. Theater—England. I. Title. II. Series.
Part of a 50 volume series selling for 1,050.00

GOSSON, Stephen, 1554-1624. 792'.013
Plays confuted in five actions. Introductory note by Peter Davison. New York, Johnson Reprint Corp., [1973 c.1972] 1 v. (unpaged) 17 cm. (Theatrum redivivum) Reprint of the 1582 ed. published by T. Gosson, London, under title: Playes confuted in fiue actions; with new introd. "S.T.C. no. 12095." [PN2047.G6 1972b] 79-175659 11.00
1. Theater—Moral and religious aspects. I. Title.

HEIDEGGER, John James, 1659?-1748. 792'.013
Heydegger's letter to the Bishop of London [by] John James Heidegger. A seasonable apology for Mr. H—g—r [by] P. W. The conduct of the stage considered. With a pref. for the Garland ed. by Arthur Freeman. New York, Garland Pub., 1973. 6, 8, 26, 43 p. 22 cm. (The English stage: attack and defense, 1577-1730) Reprint of the 3 works, the 1st originally printed in 1724 for N. Cox, London; the 2d originally printed in 1724 for A. Moor, London; and the 3d originally printed in 1721 for E. Matthews, London. [PN2047.H35] 72-170487 ISBN 0-8240-0628-3 22.00 ea.
1. Theater—Moral and religious aspects. I. A seasonable apology for Mr. H—g—r. 1973. II. The conduct of the stage considered. 1973. III. Title. IV. Series.
Part of a 50 vol. series selling for 1,050.00.

HEYWOOD, Thomas, d.1641. 792'.013
An apology for actors, by Thomas Heywood. A refutation of the Apology for actors, by I. G. (John Greene?) Introductory notes by J. W. Binns. New York, Johnson Reprint Corp., [1973 c.1972] 1 v. (various pagings) 22 cm. (Theatrum redivivum) Reprint of An apology for actors, printed by N. Okes, London, 1612 (STC 13309), and of A refutation of the Apology for actors, imprinted at London by W. White, 1615 (STC 12214) [PN2047.H4 1972] 73-175660 16.50
1. Heywood, Thomas, d. 1641. An apology for actors. 2. Theater—Moral and religious aspects. I. I. G. II. G., I. III. Green, John, fl. 1615. A refutation of the Apology for actors. 1972. IV. Title. V. Title: A refutation of the Apology for actors.

HEYWOOD, Thomas, d.1641. 792'.013
An apology for actors, by Thomas Heywood. A refutation of the Apology for actors, by I. G. With a pref. for the Garland ed. by Arthur Freeman. New York, Garland Pub., 1973. 7, [64], 62 p. 23 cm. (The English stage: attack and defense, 1577-1730) "The author, 'I. G.,' is sometimes identified as John Green or Greene (e.g. STC of 1926)"—pref. Reprint of 2 works, the 1st printed in 1612 by N. Okes, London (STC 13309); and the 2d imprinted in 1615 by W. White; sold by T. Langley, London (STC 12214) [PN2047.H4 1973] 74-170415 ISBN 0-8240-0595-3
1. Theater—Moral and religious aspects. 2. Theater—England—History. I. I. G. II. G., I. III. Green, John, fl. 1615. A refutation of the Apology for actors. 1973. IV. Title. V. Title: A refutation of the Apology for actors. VI. Series.

LAW, William, 1686-1761. 792'.013
The absolute unlawfulness of the stage-entertainment fully demonstrated [by] William Law. The stage defended [by] John Dennis. Law outlaw'd [by] Mrs. S. O. With a pref. for the Garland ed. by Arthur Freeman. New York, Garland Pub., 1973. 7, 50, xii, 34, 15 p. 22 cm. (The English stage: attack and defense, 1577-1730) Reprint of 3 works, the 1st printed in 1726 for W. and J. Innys, London; the 2d printed in 1726 for N. Blandford, London; and the 3d printed in 1726 for the benefit of the Candle-Snuffers, London. [PN2047.S7 1973] 72-170495 ISBN 0-8240-0632-1 22.00 ea.
1. Theater—Moral and religious aspects. I. Dennis, John, 1657-1734. The stage defended. 1973. II. Law outlaw'd. 1973. III. Title. IV. Series.
Part of a 50 vol. series selling for 1,050.00.

MR. William Prynn, his defence of stage-plays, anonymous. 792'.013
The vindication of William Prynne by William Pryne. Theatrum redivivum; or, The theatre vindicated by Sir Richard Baker. With a pref. for the Garland ed. by Arthur Freeman. New York, Garland Pub., 1973. 7, 8, 141 p. 21 cm. (The English stage: attack and defense, 1577-1730) Reprint of the 1649 ed. of Mr. William Prynn, his defence of stage-plays, printed in London; of the 1649 broadside of The vindication of William Prynne; and of the 1662 ed. of Theatrum redivivum, printed by T. R. for F. Eglesfield, London. [PN2047.M5 1973] 79-170427 ISBN 0-8240-0598-8
1. Prynne, William, 1600-1669. Histrio-mastix. 2. Theater—Moral and religious aspects. I. Prynne, William, 1600-1669. The vindication of William Prynne. 1973. II. Baker, Richard, Sir, 1568-1645. Theatrum redivivum. 1973. III. Title. IV. Series.

MR. William Prynn, his defence of stage-plays, anonymous. 792'.013
The vindication of William Prynne [by] William Prynne. Theatrum redivivum; or, The theatre vindicated [by] Sir Richard Baker. With a pref. for the Garland ed. by Arthur Freeman. New York, Garland Pub., 1973. 7, 8, 141 p. 21 cm. (The English stage: attack and defense, 1577-1730) Reprint of the 1649 ed. of Mr. William Prynn, his defence of stage-plays, printed in London; of the 1649 broadside of The vindication of William Prynne; and of the 1662 ed. of Theatrum redivivum, printed by T. R. for F. Eglesfield, London. [PN2047.M5 1973] 76-170429 ISBN 0-8240-0598-8 22.00
1. Prynne, William, 1600-1669. Histrio-mastix. 2. Theater—Moral and religious aspects. I. Prynne, William, 1600-1669. The vindication of William Prynne. 1973. II. Baker, Richard, Sir, 1568-1645. Theatrum redivivum. 1973. III. Title. IV. Series.

NORBERG, Janet Louise, 1925-
From opposition to appropriation: the resolution of Southern Baptist conflict with dramatic forms, 1802-1962. [Iowa City] 1964. 437 l. illus. 28 cm. Thesis (Ph.D.) -- University of Iowa. 65-110050
1. Theater — Moral and religious aspects. 2. Southern Baptist Convention. 3. Theater — U.S. — Hist. I. Title.

OLDMIXON, John, 1673-1742. 792'.013
Reflections on the stage. With a pref. for the Garland ed. by Arthur Freeman. New York, Garland Pub., 1972. 6, 194 p. illus. 19 cm. (The English stage: attack and defense, 1577-1730) Reprint of the 1699 ed. "Wing O262." [PN2047.O5 1972] 73-170447 ISBN 0-8240-0616-X 22.50 (ea.)
1. Collier, Jeremy, 1650-1726. A short view of the immorality and profaneness of the English stage. 2. Theater—Moral and religious aspects. 3. Theater—England. I. Title. II. Series.
Set of 50 volumes: 1050.00.

PHILOMUSUS, S. 792'.013
Mr. Law's Unlawfulness of the stage entertainment examin'd [by] S. Philomusus. The Entertainment of the stage. Anonymous. Some few hints, in defence of dramatical entertainments [by] Allan Ramsay. With a pref. for the Garland ed. by Arthur Freeman. New York, Garland Pub., 1974. p. cm. "The Entertainment of the stage" attributed to George Anderson. Cf. pref. Reprint of 3 works: the 1st, printed and sold by J. Roberts, London, 1726; the 2d, printed by J. Davidson, Edinburgh, 1727; and the 3d published in 1728? [PN2047.P53 1974] 76-170496 ISBN 0-8240-0633-X 22.00
1. Law, William, 1686-1761. The absolute unlawfulness of the stage-entertainment fully demonstrated. 2. Theater—Moral and religious aspects. I. Anderson, George, 1676-1756. II. Ramsay, Allan, 1685-1758. Some few hints, in defence of dramatical entertainments. 1974. III. The Entertainment of the stage. 1974. IV. Title.

PRYNNE, William, 1600-1669. 792'.013
Histrio-mastix; the player's scourge or, actor's tragedy. Introductory note by Peter Davison. New York, Johnson Reprint Corp., 1972. 2 v. (1006 p.) 22 cm. (Theatrum redivivum) Reprint of the 1633 ed. printed by E. A. and W. I. for M. Sparke, London (STC 20464a) [PN2047.P7 1972] 75-175666 50.00
1. Theater—Moral and religious aspects. 2. Theater—England—History. I. Title.

PRYNNE, William, 1600-1669. 792'.013
Histriomastix. With a pref. for the Garland ed. by Arthur Freeman. New York, Garland Pub., 1974. 7, 1006 p. 22 cm. (The English stage: attack and defense, 1577-1730) Reprint of the 1633 ed. printed by E. A. and W. I. for Michael Sparke, London. "STC 20464a." [PN2047.P7 1974] 75-170418 ISBN 0-8240-0596-1 22.00
1. Theater—Moral and religious aspects. 2. Theater—England—History.

RAINOLDS, John, 1549-1607. 792'.013
Th'overthrow of stage-playes, by John Rainoldes, William Gager, and Alberico Gentili. With a pref. for the Garland ed. by Arthur Freeman. New York, Garland Pub., 1974. 7, 190, 36 p. 18 cm. Reprint of the 1599 ed. published by R. Schilders,

Middleburgh, with the addition of sheets A-E reprinted from the 1600 ed. English and Latin. STC 20616. [PN2047.R3 1974] 70-170414 ISBN 0-8240-0594-5 22.00
1. Theater—Moral and religious aspects. I. Gager, William, fl. 1580-1619. II. Gentili, Alberico, 1552-1608. III. Title.

RAINOLDS, John, 1549-1607. 792'.013
The overthrow of stage-plays, by the way of controversy between D. Gager and D. Rainolds. Introductory note by J. W. Binns. New York, Johnson Reprint Corp., 1972. 190 p. 22 cm. (Theatrum redivivum) "Comprises two long English letters written in July 1592 and May 1593, from John Rainolds ... to William Gager ...; together with four Latin letters exchanged between John Rainolds and Albericus Gentilis." Reprint of Th'overthrow of stage-playes, published by R. Schilders, Middleburg, 1599 (S.T.C. no. 20616) [PN2047.R3 1972] 79-175667 13.50
1. Gager, William, fl. 1580-1619. 2. Theater—Moral and religious aspects. I. Gager, William, fl. 1580-1619. II. Gentili, Alberico, 1552-1608. III. Title.

REES, James, 1802-1885. 822.3'3
Shakespeare and the Bible, to which is added prayers on the stage, proper and improper; Shakespeare's use of the sacred name of Deity; the stage viewed from a scriptural and moral point; the old mysteries and moralities, the precursors of the English stage. Philadelphia, Claxton, Remsen & Haffelfinger, 1876. [Folcroft, Pa.] Folcroft Library Editions, 1973. [PR3012.R4 1973] 72-14367 ISBN 0-8414-1348-7
1. Shakespeare, William, 1564-1616—Knowledge—Bible. 2. Theater—Moral and religious aspects. I. Title.

REES, James, 1802-1885. 822.3'3
Shakespeare and the Bible, to which is added prayers on the stage, proper and improper; Shakespeare's use of the sacred name of Deity; the stage viewed from a scriptural and moral point; the old mysteries and moralities—the precursors of the English stage. Philadelphia, Claxton, Remsen & Haffelfinger, 1876. [New York, AMS Press, 1972] 188 p. illus. 19 cm. [PR3012.R4 1972] 70-174307 ISBN 0-404-05235-5
1. Shakespeare, William, 1564-1616—Religion and ethics. 2. Theater—Moral and religious aspects. 3. Bible and literature. I. Title.

ROUSSEAU, Jean Jacques, 1712-1778 792'.013
Politics and the arts; letter to M. d'Alembert on the theatre. Tr., with notes, introd., by Allan Bloom. Ithaca, N. Y. Cornell Univ. Pr. [1968,c.1960] xxxviii, 153p. 19cm. (CP71) Tr. of J. J. Rousseau, citoyen de Geneve a Mr. d'Alembert. Includes d'Alembert's article Geneva, which appeared in v. 7 (1757) of l'Encyclopedie, to which the letter is a critical response. Bibl. refs. included in Translator's notes [PN2051.R713] 1.95 pap.,
1. Theater—Moral and religious aspects. I. Alembert, Jean Lerond d', 1717-1783. II. Title.

ROUSSEAU, Jean Jacques, 1712-1778. 792.013
Politics and the arts, letter to M. d'Alembert on the theatre. Translated, with notes and an introd., by Allan Bloom. Glencoe, Ill., Free Press [1960] xxxviii, 153p. 22cm. (Agora editions) Translation of J. J. Rousseau, citoyen de Geneve, a M'. d Alembert. Includes d Alembert's article Geneva, which appeared in v. 7 (1757) of PEncyclopedle, to which the letter is a critical response. Bibliographical references included in 'Translator's notes' (p. 149-153) [PN2051.R713] 60-7093
1. Theater—Moral and religious aspects. I. Alembert, Jean Lerond d;, 1717-1783. II. Title.

SALVIANUS, 5th,cent. 792'.013
A second and third blast of retrait from plaies and theaters, by Anthony Munday. With a pref. for the Garland ed. by Arthur Freeman. New York, Garland Pub., 1973. 6, 128 p. 18 cm. (The English stage: attack and defense 1577-1730) Facsimile reprint. Original t.p. reads: A second and third blast of retrait from plaies and theaters: the one whereof was sounded by a reuerend Byshop dead long since; the other by a worshipful and zealous gentleman now alive; one showing the filthines of plaies in times past; the other the abhomination of theaters in the time present ... Set forth by Anglo-phile Eutheo ... Allowed by authority, 1580. "The second blast" is a translation of Book 6 of De gubernatione Dei by Salvianus. "The first blast" is S. Gosson's The school of abuse. [PN2051.S2 1973] 77-170405 ISBN 0-8240-0587-2 22.00
1. Theater—Moral and religious aspects. I. Munday, Anthony, 1553-1633. II. Gosson, Stephen, 1554-1624. The school of abuse. III. Title. IV. Series.

SALVIANUS, 5thcent. 792'.013
A second and third blast of retreat from plays and theatres, by Salvian and "Anglophile-Eutheo". Introductory note by J. W. Binns. New York, Johnson Reprint Corp., [1973 c.1972] 128 p. 16 cm. (Theatrum redivivum) "The first blast" is S. Gosson's The school of abuse. "The second blast" is a translation of Book 6 of De gubernatione Dei by Salvianus. "The third blast" was written by A. Munday under the pseud. Anglo-phile Eutheo. Reprint of the 1580 ed. imprinted by H. Denham, London under title: A second and third blast of retrait from plaies and theaters (S.T.C. no. 21677). [PN2051.S2 1972] 76-175669 12.50
1. Theater—Moral and religious aspects. I. Munday, Anthony, 1553-1633. II. Gosson, Stephen, 1554-1624. The schoole of abuse. III. Title.

SETTLE, Elkanah, 1648-1724. 792'.013
A defence of dramatick poetry; and, A farther defence of dramatick poetry. With a pref. for the Garland ed. by Arthur Freeman. New York, Garland Pub., 1972. 6, 118, 72 p. 19 cm. (The English stage: attack and defense, 1577-1730) Attributed to E. Filmer. Cf. Wing F905, F906. Also attributed to T. Rymer, Cf. Brit. Mus. Cat. Reprint of 2 works first published in 1698. [PN2047.C62S4 1972] 75-170450
1. Collier, Jeremy, 1650-1726. A short view of the immorality and profaneness of the English stage. 2. Theater—Moral and religious aspects. 3. Theater—England. I. Filmer, Edward, fl. 1707. A defence of dramatick poetry. II. Filmer, Edward, fl. 1707. A farther defence of dramatick poetry. III. Rymer, Thomas, 1641-1713. A defence of dramatick poetry. IV. Rymer, Thomas, 1641-1713. A farther defence of dramatick poetry. V. Settle, Elkanah, 1648-1724. A farther defence of dramatick poetry. 1972. VI. Title. VII. Title: A farther defence of dramatick poetry. VIII. Series.

THE Stage acquitted. 792'.013
Anonymous. With a pref. for the Garland ed. by Arthur Freeman. New York, Garland Pub., 1972. 185 p. 18 cm. (The English stage: attack and defense, 1577-1730) Reprint of the 1699 ed. "Wing S5160." [PN2047.R52S7 1972] 77-170448 ISBN 0-8240-0614-3 22.00
1. Ridpath, George, d. 1726. The stage condemn'd. 2. Theater—Moral and religious aspects. 3. Theater—England. I. Title. II. Series.

STUBBES, Phillip. 792'.013
The anatomie of abuses. With a pref. for the Garland ed. by Arthur Freeman. New York, Garland Pub., 1973. 1 v. (unpaged) 18 cm. (The English stage: attack and defense, 1577-1730) Reprint of the 1583 ed. printed at London, by R. Jones. [PN2047.S8 1973] 71-170409 ISBN 0-8240-0590-2 22.00
1. Theater—Moral and religious aspects. 2. Theater—England. I. Title. II. Series.

STUBBES, Phillip. 792'.013
The second part of the anatomie of abuses. With a pref. for the Garland ed. by Arthur Freeman. New York, Garland Pub., 1973. 1 v. (unpaged) 18 cm. (The English stage: attack and defense 1577-1730) Reprint of the 1583 ed. printed by R. W. for W. Wright, London. [PN2047.S82 1973] 73-4399 ISBN 0-8240-0591-0 22.00
1. Theater—Moral and religious aspects. 2. Theater—England. I. Title. II. Series.

A Treatise of daunces. 792'.013
Anonymous. A godly exhortation, by John Field. With a pref. for the Garland ed. by Arthur Freeman. New York, Garland Pub., 1974. 8, [37], 8, [40] p. 18 cm. (The English stage: attack and defense, 1577-1730) Reprint of A Treatise of daunses, wherin it is shewed, that they are as it were accessories and depedants (or thinges annexed) to whoredome: where also by the way is touched and proued, that playes are ioyned and knit togeather in a rancke or rowe with them. 1581; and of A godly exhortation by occasion of the late iudgement of God shewed at Parris-garden, the thirteenth day of Ianvarie ... by Iohn Field. London, Printed by R. Walde-graue, for H. Carre, 1583. (STC 10845) [PN2047.T7 1974] 78-170408 ISBN 0-8240-0588-0
1. Theater—Moral and religious aspects. 2. Dancing—Moral and religious aspects. I. Feilde, John, d. 1588. A godly exhortation by occasion of the late iudgement of God, shewed at Parris-garden, the thirteenth of Ianvarie. 1974. II. Title. III. Title: A godly exhortation by occasion of the late iudgement of God, shewed at Parris-garden, the thirteenth day of Ianvarie. IV. Series.

VANBRUGH, John, Sir, 1664-1726. 792'.013
A short vindication of The relapse and The provok'd wife. With a pref. for the Garland ed. by Arthur Freeman. New York, Garland Pub., [1973 c1972] 6, 79 p. 19 cm. (The English stage: attack and defense, 1577-1730) Reprint of the 1698 ed. "Wing V59." [PN2047.C62V3 1972] 75-170442 ISBN 0-8240-0612-7 22.00 ea.
1. Collier, Jeremy, 1650-1726. A short view of the immorality and profaneness of the English stage. 2. Theater—Moral and religious aspects. 3. Theater—England. I. Title. II. Series. Complete series of 50 volumes sold for 1,050.

VISITS from the shades. 792'.013
Anonymous. With a pref. for the Garland ed. by Arthur Freeman. New York, Garland Pub., 1972. 6, 147 p. 22 cm. (The English stage: attack and defense, 1577-1730) Reprint of the 1704 ed. [PN2047.V5 1972] 70-170473 22.50 (ea.)
1. Theater—Moral and religious aspects. 2. Theater—England. I. Title. II. Series. Set of 50 volumes; $1050.00

Theatines.

KUNKEL, Paul Aloysius, 1901- 271.79
... The Theatines in the history of Catholic reform before the establishment of Lutheranism ... by Paul A. Kunkel. Washington, D. C., The Catholic university of America press, 1941. ix, 184 p. 23 cm. Thesis (PH. D.)--Catholic university of America, 1941. Reproduced from type-written copy. Bibliography: p. 171-184. [BX4080.T45K8] A 41
1. Theatines. 2. Catholic church—Hist. I Title.

Thecla, Saint—Juvenile literature.

PANUNZI, Paul. 92 (j)
Love as strong as death; the story of St. Thecla. Translated and illustrated by the Daughters of St. Paul. [Boston] St. Paul Editions [1966] 80 p. illus. 22 cm. [BR1720.T33P3] 66-30822
1. Thecla, Saint—Juvenile literature. I. Title.

Theism.

ABBOT, Francis Ellingwood, 1836-1903. 211
Scientific theism, by Francis Ellingwood Abbot. Boston, Little, Brown, and company, 1885. xxiii, 219 p. 20 cm. At head of title: Organic scientific philosophy. Founded on a lecture given by the author before the Concord summer school of philosophy, July 30, 1885. ef. Preface. [BL206.A3] 30-30816
1. Theism. I. Title. II. Title: Organic scientific philosophy.

ABBOT, Francis Ellingwood, 1836-1903. 211'.3
Scientific theism / by Francis Ellingwood Abbot. 1st AMS ed. New York : AMS Press, 1979. xxiii, 219 p. ; 19 cm. (Philosophy in America) At head of title: Organic scientific philosophy. Reprint of the 1885 ed. published by Macmillan, London. [BL200.A3 1979] 75-3012 ISBN 0-404-59004-7 : 21.50
1. Theism. I. Title. II. Title: Organic scientific philosophy.

[ANDERSON, Louis Francis] 1859- 211
Prolegomena to theism [New York, Press of Andrew H. Kellogg co., c1910] 70 p. 21 cm. Preface signed: Jestus. [BL200.A6] 10-30585
1. Theism. I. Title.

BALFOUR, Arthur James Balfour, 1st earl of, 1848-1930. 211
Theism and humanism; being the Gifford lectures delivered at the University of Glasgow, 1914, by the Rt. Hon. Arthur James Balfour ... New York, Hodder & Stoughton, George H. Doran company [1915] xv p., 1 l., 19-274 p. 21 1/2 cm. [BL200.B2] 10-23375
1. Theism. 2. Humanism. I. Title.

BALFOUR, Arthur James Balfour, 1st earl of, 1848-1930. 211
Theism and thought, a study in familiar beliefs, being the second course of Gifford lectures delivered at the University of Glasgow, 1922-23, by Arthur James Balfour, earl of Balfour ... New York, George H. Doran company [c1924] xii p., 1 l., 15-288 p. 21 cm. "Probability, calculable and intuitive (reprinted from Theism and humanism)": p. 255-264. [BL200.B3 1924] 24-3012
1. Theism. 2. Philosophy and religion. I. Title.

BARR, Thomas E.
The gist of it: a philosophy of human life. By Rev. Thomas E. Barr, B. A. With an introductory note by Rev. D. S. Gregory ... New York, A. C. Armstrong & son, 1887. xxxiii, 350 p. 19 cm. [BD555.B25] 13-18890
1. Theism. I. Title.

BOWNE, Borden Parker, 1847-1910. 211
Philosophy of theism, by Borden P. Bowne ... New York, Harper & brothers, 1887. x p., 1 l., 269 p. 22 cm. [BL200.B6] 30-30818
1. Theism. I. Title.

BOWNE, Borden Parker, 1847-1910. 211
Studies in theism. By Borden P. Bowne ... New York, Phillips & Hunt; Cincinnati, Hitchcock & Walden, 1879. vi, 444 p. 20 cm. [BL200.B65 1879] 30-30817
1. Theism. I. Title.

BOWNE, Borden Parker, 1847-1910. 211
Studies in theism. By Borden P. Bowne ... New York, Phillips & Hunt; Cincinnati, Cranston & Stowe [1907] vi, 444 p. 19 cm. [BL200.B65 1907] 7-25071
1. Theism. I. Title.

BOWNE, Borden Parker, 1847-1910. 211
Theism, by Borden P. Browne ... comprising the Deems lectures for 1902. New York, Cincinnati [etc.] American book company [1902] xii, 323 p. 22 cm. [Charles L. Deems lectureship of philosophy] "This work is a revision and extension of my ... 'Philosophy of theism'." [1887] [BL200.B7] 3-862
1. Theism. I. Title.

BROSNAN, William Joseph, 1864- 231
God and reason; some theses from natural theology, by William J. Brosnan ... New York, Fordham university press, 1924 1 p.

l., 227 p. 22 cm. Bibliography: p. 15-20. [BL200.B766] 33-1364
1. Theism. I. Title.

BROSNAN, William Joseph, 1864- 211
God infinite, the world and reason; some theses from natural theology, by William J. Brosnan ... New York, Fordham university press, 1943. viii, 246 p. 21 1/2 cm. "First edition." Bibliography: p. 31-34. [BL200.B77] 43-6591
1. Theism. 2. Creation. 3. Natural theology. I. Title.

CAVERNO, Charles, 1832-1916. 211
Theism et als, by Rev. Charles Caverno ... New York, London [etc.] The Abbey press [1902] vii, [9]-246 p. 20 cm. [BL200.C3] 2-16437
1. Theism. I. Title.
Contents omitted

CHAMPNESS, Ernest F. 211
Must we part with God? A short study in theism, by Ernest F. Champness; introduction by John W. Graham ... New York, The Macmillan company, 1925. 100 p. 20 cm. Published first under title: The significance of life, London, 1923. [BL200.C5 1925] 25-2862
1. Theism. I. Title.

COBBE, Frances Power, 1822-1904. 204
The religious demands of the age: a reprint of the preface to the London edition of the collected works of Theodore Parker, By Frances Power Cobbe. Boston, Walker, Wise and company, 1863. 63 p. 19 1/2 cm. [BX9815.P3 1863 a] 43-48091
1. Parker, Theodore, 1810-1860. 2. Theism. I. Title.

COCKER, Benjamin Franklin, 1821-1883.
The theistic conception of the world. An essay in opposition to certain tendencies of modern thought. By B. F. Cocker ... New York, Harper & brothers, 1875. x, [11]-426 p. 21 cm. [BD555.C5] 20-6268
1. Theism. I. Title.

DIMAN, Jeremiah Lewis, 1831-1881. 211
The theistic argument as affected by recent theories; a course of lectures delivered at the Lowell institute in Boston, by J. Lewis Diman ... Boston, Houghton, Mifflin and company, 1881. viii, 392 p. 20 cm. Preface signed: George F. Fisher. [BL200.D5] 30-28763
1. Theism. I. Title. II. Title: Lowell institute lectures, 1880.

DOLE, George Henry.
Divine selection; or, The survival of the useful; prologue to a system of philosophy from the standpoint of the theist [by] George Henry Dole. New York, The New-church board of publication, 1903. 130 p. 18 cm. 3-81969
I. Title.

FENN, William Wallace, 1862-1932. 211'.3
Theism; the implication of experience. Edited by Dan Huntington Fenn. Peterborough, N.H., Noone House, 1969. xv, 198 p. 24 cm. Bibliographical references included in "Notes" (p. 193-196) [BT102.F37] 68-57276 5.00
1. Theism. 2. God—Proof. I. Title.

FOSTER, Randolph Sinks bp. 1820-1903 211
... Theism. Cosmic theism; or, The theism of nature, By Rev. Randolph S. Foster ... New York, Hunt & Eaton; Cincinnati, Cranston & Stowe, 1889. xii, [5]-450, 4 p. 24 cm. (His Studies in theology. [ii]) "Works referred to in this treatise": 4 p. at end. [BT15.F7 vol. 2] 230.081 37-11159
1. Theism. 2. God (Theory of knowledge) I. Title. II. Title: Cosmic theism.

FRASER, Alexander Campbell, 1819-1914.
Philosophy of theism; being the Gifford lectures delivered before the University of Edinburgh in 1894-95, first series, by Alexander Campbell Fraser ... New York, Scribner's 1895. 3 p. l., 306 p. 21 cm. A 22
1. Theism. 2. Religion—Philosophy. I. Gifford lectures, 1894-95. II. Title.

FRASER, Alexander Campbell, 1819-1914.
Philosophy of theism; being the Gifford lectures delivered before the University of Edinburgh in 1895-96, second series, by Alexander Campbell Fraser ... New York, Scribner's, A 22
1. Theism. 2. Religion—Philosophy. I. Gifford lectures, 1895-96. II. Title.

FRIESE, Philip Christopher. 261
Semitic philosophy: showing the ultimate social and scientific outcome of original Christianity in its conflict with surviving ancient heathenism. By Philip C. Friese. Chicago, S. C. Griggs & company, 1890. xvi, 247 p. 20 cm. [HN31.F7] 12-20773
1. Theism. 2. Civilization, Christian. I. Title.

FULLERTON, George Stuart, 1859-1925. 211
A plain argument of God, by George Stuart Fullerton ... Philadelphia, J. B. Lippincott company, 1889. 110 p. 19 cm. [BL200.F8] 30-28765
1. Theism. I. Title.

HACKETT, Stuart Cornelius. 211
The resurrection of theism; prolegomena to Christian apology. Chicago, Moody Press [1957] 381p. 24cm. Includes bibliography. [BL200.H2] 57-3368
1. Theism. I. Title.

HARRIS, Samuel, 1814-1899. 211
The philosophical basis of theism; an examination of the personality of man to ascertain his capacity to know and serve God, and the validity of the principles underlying the defence of theism, by Samuel Harris ... New York, Charles Scribner's sons. 1883. xxii p., 1 l., 564 p. 24 cm. [BD555.H24] [BL200.H3] E 16
1. Theism. 2. Knowledge, Theory of. I. Title.

HARTSHORNE, Charles, 1897- 211
Man's vision of God and the logic of theism. Hamden, Conn., Archon [dist. Shoe String] 1964[c.1941] xxi, 360p. 21cm. Bibl. 64-24714 10.00
1. Theism. 2. God—Proof. I. Title.

HARTSHORNE, Charles, 1897- 211
Man's vision of God, and the logic of theism, by Charles Hartshorne ... Chicago, New York, Willett, Clarke & company, 1941. xxi p., 1 l., 360 p. 21 cm. [BL200.H35] 41-51847
1. Theism. 2. God—Proof. I. Title.

HAWKINS, Denis John Bernard, 1906-- 211
The essentials of theism. London, New York, Sheed & Ward, 1949. v. 151 p. 19 cm. [BL200.H38 1949] 49-49251
1. Theism. I. Title.

HAWKINS, Denis John Bernard, 1906-1964. 211'.3
The essentials of theism. Westport, Conn., Greenwood Press [1973, c1949] v, 151 p. 20 cm. [BL200.H38 1973] 72-9373 ISBN 0-8371-6579-2 8.50
1. Theism. I. Title.

IVERACH, James, 1839-1922. 211.
Theism in the light of present science and philosophy, by James Iverach ... New York, The Macmillan company; London, Macmillan & co., ltd., 1899. 2 p. l., vii-x p., 1 l. 330 p. 20 cm. [BL200.I 8] 0-503
1. Theism. 2. Religion and science—1860-1899. I. Deems lectures. New York university. II. Title.

JONES, Jesse Henry, 1836-1904.
Know the truth; a critique on the Hamiltonian theory of limitation, including some strictures upon the theories of Rev. Henry L. Mansel and Mr. Herbert Spencer. By Jesse H. Jones ... New York, Hurd and Houghton; Boston, Nichols and Noyes, 1865. ix, 225 p. 19 cm. [BD555.J7] 11-24749
1. Hamilton, Sir William, 9th bart., 1788-1856. 2. Mansel Henry Longueville, 1820-1871. 3. Spencer, Herbert, 1820-1903. 4. Theism. I. Title.

KEYSER, Leander Sylvester, 1856- 211
A system of natural theism, by Leander S. Keyser ... Burlington, Ia., The German literary board, 1917. 144 p. 20 cm. Bibliography: p. 12-13. [BL200.K4] 17-30760
1. Theism. I. Title.

KEYSER, Leander Sylvester, 1856- 211
A system of natural theism, by Leander S. Keyser ... 2d ed., rev. Burlington, Ia., The Lutheran literary board, 1927. 159 p. 20 cm. Bibliography: p. 152-155. [BL200.K4 1927] 27-14219
1. Theism. I. Title.

KNIGHT, William Angus, 1836-1916. 211
Aspects of theism, by William Knight ... London and New York, Macmillan and co., 1893. x, 220 p. 23 cm. Lectures, enlarged with addenda, delivered in 1890 at the Theological college, Salisbury, and in 1891 in London.--Pref. [BL200.K6] 30-28769
1. Theism. I. Title.

LAIRD, John, 1887- 211
Mind and deity; being the second series of a course of Gifford lectures on the general subject of metaphysics and theism given in the University of Glasgow in 1940, by John Laird ... New York, N.Y., Philosophical library [1944] 2 p. l., 7-322 p. 22 1/2 cm. "First published in [London] 1941." Bibliographical foot-notes. [BL200.L27 1944] 44-45318
1. Theism. 2. Idealism. 3. God—Proof. I. Title.

LAIRD, John, 1887-1946. 211'.3
Mind and deity; being the second series of a course of Gifford lectures on the general subject of metaphysics and theism given in the University of Glasgow in 1940. [Hamden, Conn.] Archon Books, 1970. 322 p. 22 cm. ([Gifford lectures, 1940]) Reprint of the 1941 ed. Includes bibliographical references. [BL200.L27 1970] 70-114424
1. Theism. 2. Idealism. 3. God—Proof. I. Title. II. Series.

LAIRD, John, 1887-1946. 211'.3
Theism and cosmology, being the first series of a course of Gifford lectures on the general subject of metaphysics and theism given in the University of Glasgow in 1939. Freeport, N.Y., Books for Libraries Press [1969] 325 p. 23 cm. (Essay index reprint series.) (Gifford lectures, 1939) Reprint of the 1940 ed. Bibliographical footnotes. [BL200.L3 1969] 74-84317
1. Theism. 2. God—Proof. 3. Cosmology. I. Title. II. Series.

MASCALL, Eric Lionel, 1905- 211'.3
Existence and analogy; a sequel to 'He who is', by E. L. Mascall. [Hamden, Conn.] Archon, 1967. xix, 188p. 22cm. Reprint of the 1949 ed. Bibl. [BL200.M318 1967] 67-14497 5.00
1. Theism. 2. Existentialism. 3. Analogy (Religion) I. Title.

MASCALL, Eric Lionel, 1905-
Existence and analogy; a sequel to "He who is." London, New York, Longmans, Green [1949] xix, 188 p. 23 cm. "Large portions of chapters v and vii were originally published as an article in Laudate for December 1943. Chapter III and part of chapter IV are based on papers read to the Origen Society at Oxford." Bibliographical footnotes. A 51
1. Theism. 2. Existentialism. 3. Analogy (Religion) I. Title.

MASCALL, Eric Lionel, 1905- 211'.3
He who is; a study in traditional theism, by E. L. Mascall. [Hamden, Conn.] Archon Books, 1970 [c1966] xviii, 238 p. 20 cm. Bibliography: p. 227-234. [BL200.M32 1970] 76-95026
1. Theism. I. Title.

MASCALL, Eric Lionel, 1905- 211
He who is; a study in traditional theism, by E. L. Mascall ... London, New York [etc.] Longmans, Green and co. [1943] xiii, [1], 210 p. 22 1/2 cm. "First published 1943." Bibliography: p. 200-208. [BL200.M32] 44-977
1. Theism. I. Title.

MICOU, Richard Wilde, 1848-1912. 211
Basic ideas in religion; or, Apologetic theism, by Richard Wilde Micou ... edited by Paul Micou ... New York [etc.] Association press, 1916. xxii, 496 p. 22 1/2 cm. Bibliography: p. 475-478. Bibliographical foot-notes. [BL200.M5] 16-2582
1. Theism. I. Micou, Paul, 1885- ed. II. Title. III. Title: Apologetic theism.

MILL, John Stuart, 1806-1873. 211
Theism. Edited with an introd. by Richard Taylor. New York, Liberal Arts Press [1957] xx, 98p. 21cm. (The Library of liberal arts, no. 64) 'Reprinted from the fourth edition of [the author's] Three essays on religion (London, 1875).' Bibliography: p. xx. [BL200.M56 1957] 57-2053
1. Theism. I. Title.

MUIR, Pearson M' Adam, 1846-1924.
Modern substitutes for Christianity, by Pearson M'Adam Muir ... New York and London, Hodder and Stoughton [1910] viii, 262 p. 19 cm. (Half-title: ... The Baird lecture 1909) Contents.--i. Popular impeachments of Christianity.--ii. Morality without religion.--iii. The religion of the universe.--iv. The religion of humanity.--v. Theism withouf Christ.--vi. The tribute of criticism to Christ. A 12
1. Theism. 2. Ethical culture movement. 3. Pantheism. 4. Positivism. 5. Atheism—History. I. Title.

NEWMAN, John Henry, Cardinal, 1801-1890. 163
An essay in aid of a grammar of assent; with an introd. by Etienne Gilson. Garden City, N. Y., Image Books [1955] 396p. 18cm. (A Doubleday image book, D19) [BR100.N4 1955] [BR100.N4 1955] 201 55-14909 55-14909
1. Theism. 2. Faith. I. Title. II. Title: Grammar of assent.

NEWMAN, John Henry, Cardinal, 1801-1890. 230'.2
An essay in aid of a grammar of assent. Westminster, Md., Christian Classics, 1973. viii, 503 p. 21 cm. (His The Works of Cardinal Newman) On spine: Grammar of assent. [BR100.N4 1973] 73-85623 8.75
1. Theism. 2. Faith. I. Title. II. Title: Grammar of assent.

NEWMAN, John Henry, cardinal, 1801-1890. 239
An essay in aid of a grammar of assent, by John Henry cardinal Newman ... New ed. London and New York, Longmans, Green and co., 1892. viii, 503 p. 19 cm. [BR100.N4 1892] 20-17716
1. Theism. 2. Faith. I. Title. II. Title: Grammar of assent.

NEWMAN, John Henry, cardinal, 1801-1890. 239
An essay in aid of a grammar of assent, by John Henry cardinal Newman ... New impression. London, New York [etc.] Longmans, Green, and co., 1901. viii, 503, [1] p. 19 cm. (On cover: The works of Cardinal Newman) [[BR100.N]] A 33
1. Theism. 2. Faith. I. Title. II. Title: Grammar of assent.

NEWMAN, John Henry, Cardinal, 1801-1890. 201
An essay in aid of a grammar of assent. New ed., ed. with a pref. and introd. by Charles Frederick Harrold. New York, Longmans, Green, 1947. xxii, 394 p. 21 cm. "A select bibliography": p. xxi-xxii. [BR100.N4 1947] 163 47-11560
1. Theism. 2. Faith. I. Harrold, Charles Frederick, 1897- ed. II. Title. III. Title: Grammar of assent.

NEWMAN, John Henry, Cardinal, 1801-1890. 230'.2
An essay in aid of a grammar of assent / by John Henry Newman ; with an introd. by Nicholas Lash. Notre Dame, Ind. : University of Notre Dame Press, 1979. viii, 396 p. ; 22 cm. Includes bibliographical references and index. [BR100.N4 1979] 79-114636 ISBN 0-268-00999-6 : 15.95
1. Theism. 2. Faith. I. Title. II. Title: Grammar of assent.

OWEN, Huw Parri. 211
Concepts of deity [by] H. P. Owen. [New York] Herder and Herder [1971] xi, 174 p. 22 cm. (Philosophy of religion series) Bibliography: p. 166-172. [BL200.O9] 72-150307 7.95
1. Theism. 2. God—History of doctrines. I. Title.

PARKER, Theodore, 1810-1860. 204
Theism, atheism and the popular theology, by Theodore Parker; edited with a preface, by Charles W. Wendte. Boston, American Unitarian association [1907] 9 p. l., 389 p. 21 cm. [His Works. Centenary ed. v. 2] "It is this normal and universal religion of mankind which the discourses collected in the present volume are intended to set forth and sustain."--Editor's pref. [BX9815.P3 1907 vol. 2] A 12
1. Theism. 2. Atheism—Controversial literature. 3. Theology. I. Wendte, Charles William, 1844-1931, ed. II. Title.

PATTON, Francis Landey, 1843-
Notes from lectures on theistic conception of the universe ... by Francis L. Patton. [Princeton, N. J., 1883] cover-title, 56, 10 p. 21 cm. [BD555.P3] 20-6264
1. Theism. I. Title.

PETTY, Orville Anderson, 1874- 231
Common sense and God; a critique of naturalism, by Orville A. Petty. New Haven, 1936. xiv, 195, [1] p. diagr. 21 cm. [BT010.P4] 36-5964
1. Theism. 2. Humanism—20th cent. 3. Naturalism. I. Title.

[ROMANES, George John] 1848-1894. 211
A candid examination of theism. By Physicus [pseud.] Boston, Houghton, Osgood, & company, 1878. xviii, 197 p. 21 cm. (Half-title: The English and foreign philosophical library. Vol. XIII) [BL200.R6 1878] 43-35282
1. Theism. I. Title.

RUST, Eric Charles. 200'.1
Religion, revelation & reason / by Eric C. Rust. Macon, Ga. : Mercer University Press, c1981. vi, 186 p. ; 24 cm. Includes index. [BT102.R87] 19 81-2760 ISBN 0-86554-006-3 : 14.50
1. Theism. 2. Philosophical theology. I. Title. II. Title: Religion, revelation, and reason.

SAVAGE, Minot Judson, 1841-1918. 231
Belief in God: an examination of some fundamental theistic problems. By M. J. Savage. To which is added an address on The intellectual basis of faith, by W. H. Savage. 2s ed. Boston, G. H. Ellis, 1881. 4 p. l., [13]-176 p. 19 1/2 cm. [BT101.S13 1881] 33-22235
1. Theism. 2. God. 3. Unitarian churches—Sermons. 4. Sermons, American. I. Savage, William Henry, 1833-1907. II. Title.

SCUDDER, Delton Lewis, 1906- 201
Tennant's philosophical theology, by Delton Lewis Scudder ... New Haven, Yale university press; London, H. Milford, Oxford university press, 1940. xiv, 278 p., 1 l. diagrs. 24 cm. (Half-title: Yale studies in religious education. xiii) "The substance of this book constitutes 'A dissertation presented to ... the Graduate school of Yale university ... for the degree of doctor of philosophy' (May, 1969)"--Pref. "Acknowledgments": p. [277]-278. Bibliography: p. [259]-273. [BL51.T42S3 1969] 40-14172
1. Tennant, Frederick Robert, 1866- 2. Theism. 3. Experience (Religion) I. Title.

SETH, Pringle Pattison, Andrew 1856-1931.
Two lectures on theisms delivered on the occasion of the sesquicentennial celebration of Princeton university, by Andrew Seth ... New York, C. Scribner's sons, 1897. 2 p. l., 64 p. 19 cm. (On cover: Princeton lectures) [BD555.S4] 11-24642
1. Theism. I. Title.

SHEPHERD, John J. 211'.3
Experience, inference, and God / John J. Shepherd. New York : Barnes & Noble, 1975. 190 p. ; 23 cm. (Library of philosophy and religion) Based on a doctoral thesis prepared at the University of Lancaster. Includes index. Bibliography: p. [185]-187. [BT102.S49 1975] 75-317435 ISBN 0-06-496235-0 : 16.50
1. Theism. 2. God. 3. Natural theology. I. Title.

SIMONS, Minot, 1868- 211
A modern theism, by Minot Simons ... Boston, Mass., The Beacon press, inc. [c1931] vii, 207 p. 20 1/2 cm. "Made up for the most part from sermons delivered in the Church of All souls, Unitarian, New York city." [BL200.S5] 32-459
1. Theism. 2. Sermons, American. 3. Unitarian church—Sermons. I. Title.

STORR, Vernon Faithfull, 1869-
... *The being of God,* by the Rev. Vernon F. Storr ... London, New York [etc.] Longmans, Green and co., 1922. 75, [1] p. 18 cm. (Liverpool diocesan board of divinity publications, XXVI) "Books recommended": last page. A 23
1. Theism. I. Title.

STORR, Vernon Faithfull, 1869-
... *The moral argument for theism,* by the Rev. Vernon F. Storr ... London, New York [etc.] Longmans, Green & co., 1921. 59, [1] p. 18 1/2 cm. (Liverpool diocesan board of divinity publications, XXIV) "Books recommended": last page. A 22
1. Theism. 2. Ethics. I. Title.

STORRS, Richard Salter, 1821-1900.
The recognition of the supernatural in letters and in life: an oration, by Richard S. Storrs ... New York, A. D. F. Randolph & company [c1881] 57 p. 25 cm. [BD555.S7] 11-24644
1. Theism. 2. Religion—Addresses, essays, lectures. I. Title.

TAYLOR, Alfred Edward, 1869-1945. 231
Does God exist? By A. E. Taylor ... New York, The Macmillan company, 1947. vii, 172, [1] p. 19 1/2 cm. "First [American] printing." "Bibliography": p. [173] [BL200.T36 1947] 47-1689
1. God—Proof. 2. Theism. I. Title.

TIGERT, John James, 1856-1906. 211
Theism; a survey of the paths that lead to God, chiefly in the light of the history of philosophy, by Jno. J. Tigert ... Nashville, Tenn., Dallas, Tex., Publishing house of the M. E. church, South, Barbee & Smith, agents, 1901. xviii, 351 p. 19 cm. [BL200.T5] 7-9536
1. Theism. 2. Natural theology. 3. Philosophy. I. Title.

[VAN Gelder, Martinus] 1854-
"The night of truth," by Erardus Sagra [pseud.]... Philadelphia, Penna., The Progressive publishing company [c1909] 69 p. 22 cm. [BD708.V3] 20-6274
1. Theism. 2. Truth. I. Title.

WALKER, Aaron, 1826-
Physiology and psychology; or, The vital and physical force philosophies of creation and thought discussed, compared and contrasted, by Elder Aaron Walker. Indianapolis, The Hollenbeck press, 1900. iv p., 1 l., 200 p. front. (port.) 20 cm. [BD555.W2] Feb
1. Theism 2. Psychology. 3. Creation. I. Title.

WHARTON, Francis, 1820-1889. 211
A treatise on theism, and on the modern skeptical theories. By Francis Wharton ... Philadelphia, J. B. Lippincott & co.; London, Trubner & co., 1859. 395 p. 19 1/2 cm. [BL200.W5] 30-28780
1. Theism. 2. Skepticism. I. Title.

WICKLINE, W. A. 211
A man-made God; a study of tolerance and understanding the goals of our modern education, by W. A. Wickline. [Oberlin, O., Wickline & son, c1941] 79 p. 17 1/2 cm. [BL200.W55] 41-18936
1. Theism. I. Title.

Theism—Addresses, essays, lectures.

DONNELLY, John, comp. 211'.3
Logical analysis and contemporary theism. New York, Fordham University Press, 1972. xi, 337 p. 23 cm. Contents.Contents.—On proofs for the existence of God, by J. F. Ross.—Two criticisms of the cosmological argument, by W. L. Rowe.—The argument from design, by R. G. Swinburne.—The claims of religious experience, by H. J. N. Horsburgh.—Ineffability, by W. P. Alston.—The divine simplicity, by D. C. Bennett.—Necessary being, by J. H. Hick.—A new theory of analogy, by J. F. Ross.—Hume on evil, by N. Pike.—The perfect goodness of God, by A. Plantinga.—C. B. Martin's contradiction in theology, by W. L. Rowe.—Divine foreknowledge and human freedom, by A. Kenny.—Some puzzles concerning omnipotence, by G. I. Mavrodes.—The paradox of the stone, by C. W. Savage.—Creation ex nihilo, by J. Donnelly.—The miraculous, by R. F. Holland.—On miracles, by P. J. Dietl.—The tacit structure of religious knowing, by J. H. Gill.—On the observability of the self, by R. M. Chisholm.—Re-examining Kierkegaard's "Teleological suspension of the ethical," by J. Donnelly. Includes bibliographical references. [BL200.D6] 77-168693 ISBN 0-8232-0940-7 12.50
1. Theism—Addresses, essays, lectures. I. Title.

FRASER, Alexander Campbell, 1819-1914. 211
Philosophy of theism / by Alexander Campbell Fraser. New York : AMS Press, 1979. 303 p. ; 18 cm. "Delivered before the University of Edinburgh in 1894-95." Reprint of the 1895 ed. published by W. Blackwood and Sons, Edinburgh, which was issued as the 1894-1895 Gifford lectures. Includes index. [BL200.F7 1979] 77-27228 ISBN 0-404-60453-6 : 22.50
1. Theism—Addresses, essays, lectures. 2. Religion—Philosophy—Addresses, essays, lectures. I. Title. II. Series: Gifford lectures ; 1894-1895.

Theism — Congresses.

MONSON, Charles H ed. 211.3
Great issues concerning theism, edited and with an introd. by Charles H. Monson, Jr. Salt Lake City, University of Utah Press [1965] 164 p. 20 cm. (Utah. University. The great issues forum, 1964-1965- Errata slip inserted. Bibliographical footnotes. [BT102.A1M6] 65-26132
1. Theism — Congresses. I. Title. II. Series.

Theism—History—20th century.

EATON, Jeffrey C. 230
The logic of theism : an analysis of the thought of Austin Farrer / Jeffrey C. Eaton. Lanham, MD : University Press of America, c1980. xxiv, 262 p. ; 23 cm. Includes bibliographical references. [BT102.F33E27] 19 80-67260 ISBN 0-8191-1337-9 : 19.25 ISBN 0-8191-1338-7 (pbk.) : 10.50
1. Farrer, Austin Marsden. 2. Theism—History—20th century. 3. Philosophical theology—History—20th century. I. Title.

Theism—History—Addresses, essays, lectures.

HARTSHORNE, Charles, 1897- 201
Aquinas to Whitehead : seven centuries of metaphysics of religion / by Charles E. Hartshorne. Milwaukee : Marquette University Publications, 1976. 54 p. ; 19 cm. (The Aquinas lecture ; 1976) Includes bibliographical references. [BL200.H32] 76-5156 ISBN 0-87462-141-0 : 4.00
1. Theism—History—Addresses, essays, lectures. I. Title. II. Series.

Theobald, Abp. of Canterbury, d. 1161.

SALTMAN, Avrom. 282'.0924 B
Theobald, Archbishop of Canterbury. New York, Greenwood Press, 1969. xvi, 594 p. illus. 23 cm. (University of London historical studies, 2) Reprint of the 1956 ed. Part 2 (p. [179]-556): Introduction to the charters.—Texts of the charters.—Supplementary documents.—Manuscripts. [BX4705.T482S3 1969] 69-14068
1. Theobald, Abp. of Canterbury, d. 1161. 2. Gt. Brit.—Church history—Sources. I. Series: London. University. Historical studies, 2

Theocracy.

RUTHERFORD, Joseph Franklin, 1869- 289.9
Government; the indisputable evidence showing that the peoples of earth shall have a righteous government and explaining the manner of its establishment, by J. F. Rutherford... Brooklyn, N.Y. [etc.] International Bible students association, Watch tower Bible and tract society [c1928] 3 p. l., 9-363 p. incl. illus., col. plates. 19 cm. "2,457,500 edition." [BX8526.R864 1928e] [220.1] 38-12908
1. Theocracy. 2. Bible—Prophecies. 3. Jehovah's witnesses. I. Title.

THEARCH society. 289.9
The new theocracy; Thearch society ... the absolute reign of God. The new and final church of Christ Jesus, regenerated--completed. [New York, Thearch society, c1936] 146 p., 1 l. 17 cm. "Copyright ... by Dunscombe Moore." [BX9798.T45A3] 36-13076
I. Moore, Dunscombe. II. Title.

[THOMASON, Adam Peter] 1865-
On the road to theocracy, divine government ... Chicago, Ill., The Christ brotherhood, 1924. 128 p. 15 cm. "Prefatory" signed: Adam Peter Thomason. [BX6600.C5T5] 38-24297
I. Christ brotherhood. II. Title.

Theocritus. Epigrammata.

SMUTNY, Robert Jaroslav, 1919- 292.211
The text history of the Epigrams of Theocritus. Berkeley, University of California Press, 1955. [6], 29-94p. 24cm. (University of California publications in classical philology, v. 15, no. 2) Based on thesis, University of California. Bibliorphical references included in 'Notes' (p. 87-94) Bibliography: 6th prelim. page. [PA25.C3 vol. 15, no.2] A55
1. Theocritus. Epigrammata. I. Title. II. Series: California, University. University of California publications in classical philology. v. 15, no. 2

Theodicy.

ARMOUR, John M. 231.8
Mercy, its place in the divine government. By John M. Armour ... Boston, Bradley & Woodruff [1891] 244 p. 21 cm. [BT160.A7] 40-24462
1. Theodicy. 2. God—Mercy. I. Title.

BELLAMY, Joseph, 1719-1790. 231.
Four sermons on the wisdom of God in the permission of sin, by Joseph Bellamy ... Morris-town [Pa.] Printed by Henry P. Russell, for Cornelius Davis, N. York, 1804. 130 p. 18 cm. [BT160.B4] A 34
1. Theodicy. 2. Sin. 3. Sermons, American. I. Title.

BLACK, Hubert 231.8
Good God! Cry or credo? Nashville. Abingdon [1966] 144p. 20cm. Bibl. [BT160.B5] 66-21967 2.75
1. Theodicy. I. Title.

BLEDSOE, Albert Taylor, 1809-1877. 231.8
A theodicy; or, Vindication of the divine glory, as manifested in the constitution and government of the moral world. By Albert Taylor Bledsoe... New York, Carlton & Phillips 1854. 1 p. l., [5]-365 p. 24 cm. [BT160.B6 1854] 31-
1. Theodicy. I. Title.

BLOOD, Benjamin Paul, 1832-1919. 231.8
Optimism the lesson of ages. A compendium of democratic theology, designed to illustrate necessities whereby all things are as they are, and to reconcile the discontents of men with the perfect love and power of ever-present God. Written by Benjamin Blood ... Boston, B. Marsh, 1860. 132 p. 19 1/2 cm. [BT160.B65] 40-23724
1. Theodicy. I. Title. II. Title: Democratic theology, A compendium of.

BRYDEN, James Davenport, 1900- 231.8
Letters to Mark on God's relation to human suffering. [1st ed.] New York,

Harper [1953] 150p. 20cm. [BT160.B75] 52-11437
1. Theodicy. 2. Suffering. I. Title.

BURTON, Warren, 1800-1866. 231.8
Cheering views of man and Providence, drawn from a consideration of the origin, uses, and remedies of evil. By Warren Burton. Boston, Carter, Hendee and co., 1832. xi, [1], 264 p. 17 cm. [BT160.B8] 40-23725
1. Theodicy. 2. Good and evil. I. Title.

ELPHINSTONE, Andrew, 1918- 231'.8 1975.
Freedom, suffering and love / [by] Andrew Elphinstone. London : S.C.M. Press, 1976. xii, 147 p. ; 23 cm. [BT160.E45] 77-357905 ISBN 0-334-00502-7 : £4.50
1. Theodicy. 2. Suffering. I. Title.

FITCH, William. 231'.8
God and evil; studies in the mystery of suffering and pain. Grand Rapids, Eerdmans [1967] 183 p. 19 cm. (The Elmore Harris series, no. 1) [BT160.F5] 67-19317
1. Theodicy. 2. Good and evil. 3. Suffering. I. Title. II. Series.

FORSYTH, Peter Taylor, 1848- 231. 1921.
The justification of God; lectures for war-time on a Christian theodicy, by P. T. Forsyth ... New York, C. Scribner's sons, 1917. viii, 282 p., 1 l., 19 1/2 cm. (Half-title: Studies in theology) Bibliography: 1 leaf at end. [BT160.F7] 17-9816
1. Theodicy. I. Title.

FRENCH, Daniel H. 231.8
From Eden to glory, or Footsteps of mercy. By Rev. Daniel H. French ... New York, A. D. F. Randolph & company [1889] 220 p. 19 cm. [BT160.F8] 40-23726
1. Theodicy. I. Title. II. Title: Footsteps of mercy.

GALLAHUE, Alpheus 231.8 Cornelius, 1817-1894.
Theodicy; or, A vindication of the wisdom and goodness of God as manifested in the admission and sufferance of moral evil which rendered the atonement with all its benefits possible, by Rev. A. C. Gallahue ... New York, The author [1892] v, [7]-82 p. 13 cm. [BT160.G2] 40-23727
1. Theodicy. 2. Good and evil. I. Title.

GALLIGAN, Michael. 231'.8
God and evil / by Michael Galligan. New York : Paulist Press, 1976. vii, 80 p. ; 18 cm. Includes bibliographical references. [BT160.G24 1976] 75-36172 ISBN 0-8091-1925-0 pbk. : 1.65
1. Theodicy. I. Title.

GLENN, Paul Joseph, 1893- 231.8
Theodicy, a class manual in the philosophy of deity, by Paul J. Glenn ... St. Louis, Mo. and London, B. Herder book co., 1938. x, 300 p. 19 cm. [BT160.G5] 38-3604
1. Theodicy. 2. God. I. Title.

GREEN, Peter, 1871- 231.8
The problem of evil: being an attempt to shew that the existence of sin and pain in the world is not inconsistent with the goodness and power of God, by the Rev. Peter Green ... London, New York [etc.] Longmans, Green and co., 1920. viii, 205, [1] p. 20 cm. [BT160.G7] A 20
1. Theodicy. 2. Good and evil. I. Title.

HEATH, Thomas Richard, 231'.8 1920-
In face of anguish, by Thomas R. Heath. New York, Sheed and Ward [1966] ix, 212 p. 22 cm. Includes bibliographical references. [BT160.H4] 66-22015
1. Theodicy. I. Title.

HICK, John 231.8
Evil and the God of Love. New York, Harper [c.1966] xii, 403p. 22cm. Bibl. [BT160.H5] 66-20778 6.95
1. Theodicy. I. Title.

HICK, John. 231.8
Evil and the God of Love. [1st ed.] New York, Harper & Row [1966] xii, 403 p. 22 cm. Bibliographical footnotes. [BT160.H5] 66-20778
1. Theodicy. I. Title.

†HUGHES, Philip Edgcumbe. 216
Hope for a despairing world : the Christian answer to the problem of evil / Philip E. Hughes. Grand Rapids : Baker Book House, c1977. 125 p. ; 20 cm. (A Canterbury book) Includes bibliographical references. [BT160.H83] 78-101254 pbk. : 3.95
1. Theodicy. 2. Good and evil. 3. Providence and government of God. I. Title.

KUSHNER, Harold S. 296.3'11
When bad things happen to good people / Harold S. Kushner. New York : Schocken Books, 1981. vii, 149 p. ; 21 cm. [BM645.P7K87] 19 81-40411 ISBN 0-8052-3773-9 : 10.95
1. Kushner, Harold S. 2. Theodicy. I. Title.

LEIBNIZ, Gottfried 231'.8 Wilhelm, von, Freiherr, 1646-1716.
Theodicy, abridged. Edited, abridged, and with an introd. by Diogenes Allen. [Translated by E. M. Huggard] Indianapolis, Bobbs-Merrill, 1966. xx, 176 p. 21 cm. (The Library of liberal arts, 121) Translation of Essais de theodicee sur la bonte de Dieu, la liberte de l'homme et l'origine du mal. Bibliographical references included in "Notes" (p. xvii-xx) [BT160.L4563 1966] 67-4155
1. Theodicy. 2. Theism. 3. Free will and determinism. I. Allen, Diogenes, ed. II. Title.

LITTLETON, Mary Brabson. Mrs. 214
Whence cometh victory! By Mary Brabson Littleton, 2d ed. [Baltimore, John Murphy company, printers, c1918] 109 p. 18 cm. [BT135.L5] 19-15930
I. Title.

MCGILL, Arthur Chute. 231'.8
Suffering: a test of theological method [by] Arthur C. McGill. Philadelphia, Geneva Press [c1968] 128 p. illus. 21 cm. (Decade books) [BT160.M28] 68-10189
1. Theodicy. 2. Suffering. I. Title.

MADDEN, Edward H. 231'.8
Evil and the concept of God, by Edward H. Madden and Peter H. Hare. Springfield, Ill., [1968] vii, 142 p. 24 cm. (American lecture series. Publication no. 706. A monograph in the Bannerstone division of American lectures in philosophy) Includes bibliographical references. [BT160.M29] 67-27930
1. Theodicy. I. Hare, Peter H., joint author. II. Title.

MARITAIN, Jacques, 1882- 231.8
God and the permission of evil. Tr. by Joseph W. Evans. Milwaukee, Bruce [c.1966] ix,121p. illus. 21cm. (Christian culture and phil. ser.) Bibl. [BT160.M313] 66-17003 3.75
1. Theodicy. I. Title. II. Series.

ONE body, one gospel, one world; the Christian mission today. London; New York, International Missionary Council [1959] 56p. 19cm. Second printing of 1958 edition.
I. Newbigin, James Edward Lesslie, Bp.

PALMER, Bryon. 231.
God's white throne; a rational, evangelical theodicy, by the Rev. Byron Palmer... 3d ed. Cincinnati; Press of Jennings and Graham, 1904. 226 p. front. (port.) 20 1/2 cm. [BT160.P2] 5-27081
1. Theodicy. I. Title.

PETITPIERRE, Ferdinand 231. Oliver, 1722-1790.
Thoughts on the divine goodness, relative to the government of moral agents, particularly displayed in future rewards and punishments ... Translated from the French of Ferdinand Oliver Petitpierre, formerly minister of Chaux-de-Fond. Walpole, N. H., Printed for Thomas & Thomas, by D. and T. Carlisle, 1801. vi, [7]-237 p. 18 cm. [BT160.P4 1801] 41-30183
1. Theodicy. 2. God-Goodness. I. Title.

PETITPIERRE, Ferdinand 231. Oliver, 1722-1790.
Thoughts on the divine goodness, relative to the government of moral agents, particularly displayed in future rewards and punishments ... Translated from the French of Ferdinand Oliver Petitpierre ... Montpelier [Vt.] Printed by G. W. Hill, 1828. iv, [5]148 p. 18 cm. [BT160.P4] 40-37283
1. Theodicy. 2. God-Goodness. I. Title.

SCHILLING, Sylvester Paul, 231'.8 1904-
God and human anguish / S. Paul Schilling. Nashville : Abingdon, c1977. 304 p. ; 22 cm. Includes bibliographical references and indexes. [BT160.S33] 77-5857 ISBN 0-687-14909-6 : 11.95
1. Theodicy. 2. Good and evil. I. Title.

SCHWARZBAUM, Haim.
The Jewish and Moslem versions of some theodicy legends. [Berlin, 1959] 119-169 p. 24 cm. Repr.: Fabula 3. 66-71324
1. Theodicy. I. Title.

SIMON, Ulrich E. 231'.8
A theology of Auschwitz : the Christian faith and the problem of evil / Ulrich Simon. Atlanta : J. Knox Press, 1979, c1967. 160 p. ; 21 cm. Includes bibliographical references. [BT160.S54 1979] 78-24507 ISBN 0-8042-0724-0 pbk. : 3.95
1. Theodicy. 2. Good and evil. 3. Oswiecim (Concentration camp) I. Title.

SONTAG, Frederick. 231'.8
God, why did You do that? Philadelphia, Westminster Press [1970] 172 p. 19 cm. Bibliography: p. 169-172. [BT160.S64] 71-114715
1. Theodicy. I. Title.

WENHAM, John William. 231'.8
The goodness of God [by] John W. Wenham. Downers Grove, Ill., InterVarsity Press [1974] 223 p. 21 cm. Includes bibliographical references. [BT160.W45 1974] 74-93141 ISBN 0-87784-764-9 2.95 (pbk.)
1. Theodicy. I. Title.

WENHAM, John William. 231'.8
The goodness of God [by] J. W. Wenham. London, Inter-Varsity Press, 1974. 223 p. 20 cm. Includes bibliographical references and index. [BT160.W45 1974b] 74-174681 ISBN 0-85111-736-8
1. Theodicy. I. Title.
Distributed by Inter-Varsity Press, Downers Grove, Ill. 2.95 (pbk.)

YOUNG, John, 1805-1881. 231.8
The mystery; or, Evil and God. By John Young... Philadelphia, J. B. Lippincott and company, 1856. viii p., 1 l., 11-343 p. 20 cm. English edition, 1870, published under title: The creator and the creation. [BT160.Y7] 40-24788
1. Theodicy. 2. Good and evil. I. Title. II. Title: Evil and God.

Theodicy—Addresses, essays, lectures.

GEACH, Peter Thomas. 231'.8
Providence and evil / Peter Geach. Cambridge [Eng.] ; New York : Cambridge University Press, 1977. xxii, 153 p. ; 21 cm. (Stanton lectures ; 1971-2) Includes bibliographical references and index. [BT160.G3] 76-28005 ISBN 0-521-21477-7 : 12.50
1. Theodicy—Addresses, essays, lectures. I. Title. II. Series.

Theodicy—History of doctrines.

GRIFFIN, David, 1939- 231'.8
God, power, and evil : a process theodicy / by David Ray Griffin. Philadelphia : Westminster Press, c1976. p. cm. Includes bibliographical references and index. [BT160.G74] 76-21631 ISBN 0-664-20753-7 : 17.50
1. Theodicy—History of doctrines. 2. Theodicy. 3. Process theology. I. Title.

Theodicy—History of doctrines—20th century.

CONCETTA, Sister, D.S.P., 231'.8 1916-
God and the problem of evil / by Concetta Bellegia. Boston, Mass. : Daughters of St. Paul, 1981. p. cm. Bibliography: p. [BT160.C63] 19 80-20906 ISBN 0-8198-3007-0 : 3.75 ISBN 0-8198-3008-9 (pbk.) : 2.50
1. Maritain, Jacques, 1882-1973. 2. Theodicy—History of doctrines—20th century. 3. Providence and government of God—History of doctrines—20th century. 4. Good and evil—History of doctrines—20th century. I. Title.

Theodore, Saint, abp. of Canterbury, 602-690.

REANY, William, 1887- 922.242
St. Theodore of Canterbury, by William Reany, D.D. St. Louis, Mo., and London, B. Herder book co., 1944. ix, 227 p. 21 cm. Bibliography: p. 200-212. [BX4700.T44R4] 44-2160
1. Theodore, Saint, abp. of Canterbury, 602-690. I. Title.

Theodorus, Bp of Mopsuestia, d. ca. 428.

NORRIS, Richard Alfred, Jr. 232.9
Manhood and Christ; a study in the Christology of Theodore of Mopsuestia. Oxford, Clarendon Pr. [New York, Oxford, c.]1963. xv, 274p. 23cm. Bibl. 63-2531 6.10
1. Theodorus, Bp of Mopsuestia, d. ca. 428. 2. Jesus Christ—History of doctrines. I. Title.

NORRIS, Richard Alfred. 232.9
Manhood and Christ; a study in the Christology of Theodore of Mopsuestia. Oxford, Clarendon Press, 1963. xv, 274 p. 23 cm. Based on thesis, Oxford University. Bibliography: p. [263]-269. [BR1720.T35N6] 63-2531
1. Theodorus, Bp. of Mopsuestia, d. ca. 428. 2. Jesus Christ — History of doctrines. I. Title.

Theodorus, bp. of Mopsuestia, d. ca. 428. Liber ad baptizandos.

REINE, Francis Joseph. 265.3
The eucharistic doctrine and liturgy of the mystagogical catecheses of Theodore of Mopsuestia, by Francis J. Reine ... Washington, D.C., The Catholic university of America press, 1942. xix, 204 p. IV pl. on 3 l., 23 1/2 cm. (Added t.-p.: The Catholic university of America. Studies in Christian antiquity, ed. by Johannes Quasten ... no. 2) Thesis (S.T.D.)--Catholic university of America, 1942. Bibliography: p. xv-xix. [BR65.T7574R54] A 43
1. Theodorus, bp. of Mopsuestia, d. ca. 428. Liber ad baptizandos. 2. Lord's supper—Hist. 3. Lord's supper (Liturgy) 4. Liturgies, Early Christian. I. Title.

Theodorus Studita, Saint, 759?-826.

GARDNER, Alice, 281.9'092'4 B 1854-1927.
Theodore of Studium; his life and times. New York, B. Franklin Reprints [1974] xiii, 284 p. illus. 23 cm. (Burt Franklin research & source works series. Philosophy & religious history monographs, 151) Reprint of the 1905 ed. published by E. Arnold, London. "The published works of Theodore": p. 271-277. Includes bibliographical references. [BR1720.T38G3 1974] 72-82007 ISBN 0-8337-1280-2 12.00
1. Theodorus Studita, Saint, 759?-826. 2. Byzantine Empire—Politics and government.

Theodosius I, the Great, Emperor of Rome, 346?-395.

KING, Noel Quinton 270.2
The Emperor Theodosius and the establishment of Christianity. Philadelphia, Westminster Pr. [1961, c.1960] 135p. map. (Lib. of hist. and doctrine) Bibl. 61-11847 4.00
1. Theodosius I, the Great, Emperor of Rome, 346?-395. 2. Church history—Primitive and early church. 3. Church and state—Hist. I. Title.

Theologians.

BONEY, William Jerry. 230.2'0922
The new day; Catholic theologians of the renewal. Edited by Wm. Jerry Boney and Lawrence E. Molumby. Richmond, John Knox Press [1968] 142 p. 21 cm. Includes bibliographical references. [BT28.B62] 68-13664
1. Catholic Church—Biography. 2. Theologians. 3. Theology, Doctrinal—History—20th century. I. Molumby, Lawrence E., joint author. II. Title.

FLETCHER, William C. 230.0904
The moderns: molders of contemporary theology. Grand Rapids, Mich., Zondervan [c.1962] 160p. 23cm. 62-13173 3.00
1. Theologians. 2. Theology, Doctrinal—Hist.—20th cent. I. Title.

GRANFIELD, Patrick 230'.0922
Theologians at work. New York, Macmillan [1967] xxvi, 262p. 21cm. Interviews. [BT28.G7 1967] 67-27515 5.95
1. Theologians. 2. Theology, Doctrinal—Hist.—20th Century. I. Title.
Contents omitted.

HUNT, George Laird, ed. 284.04
Ten makers of modern Protestant thought: Schweitzer, Rauschenbusch, Temple, Kirkegaard, Barth, Brunner, Niebuhr, Tillich, Bultmann, Buber. New York, Association Press [1958] 126 p. 18 cm. (An Association Press reflection book) [BX4825.H8] 58-6478
1. Theologians. I. Title.

HUNT, George Laird, comp. 230
Twelve makers of modern Protestant thought. Edited with introd. by George L. Hunt. New York, Association Press [1971] 140 p. 18 cm. 1958 ed. published under title: Ten makers of modern Protestant thought. Contents.Contents.—Albert Schweitzer, by H. A. Rodgers.—Walter Rauschenbusch, by R. T. Handy.—Soren Kierkegaard, by F. J. Denbeaux.—Karl Barth, by T. F. Torrance.—Reinhold Niebuhr, by C. Welch.—Paul Tillich, by R. C. Johnson.—Rudolph Bultmann, by C. Michalson.—Martin Buber, by W. E. Wiest.—Dietrich Bonhoeffer, by T. A. Gill.—Martin Heidegger, by J. Macquarrie.—Jurgen Moltmann, by D. L. Migliore.—Alfred North Whitehead, by J. B. Cobb, Jr. Includes bibliographical references. [BX4825.H8 1971] 70-152897 ISBN 0-8096-1824-9 2.25
1. Theologians. I. Title.

JOURNEYS : 230'.2'0922 B
the impact of personal experience on religious thought / edited by Gregory Baum. New York : Paulist Press, c1975. vi, 271 p. ; 23 cm. [BX4651.2.J68] 75-31401 ISBN 0-8091-0204-8 : 10.95 ISBN 0-8091-1909-9 pbk. : 6.95
1. Catholic Church—Biography. 2. Theologians. I. Baum, Gregory, 1923-

KERSHNER, Frederick Doyle, 922
1875-
Pioneers of Christian thought. Indianapolis, The Bobbs-Merrill company [c1930] 6 p. l., xv-xvi p., 1 l., 19-373 p. 22 1/2 cm. At head of title: Frederick D. Kershner. "First edition." [BR1700.K4] 30-24606
1. Theologians. 2. Theology,Doctrinal—Hist. I. Title.

KERSHNER, Frederick 230'.0922
Doyle, 1875-1953.
Pioneers of Christian thought [by] Frederick D. Kershner. Freeport, N.Y., Books for Libraries Press [1968, c1930] 373 p. 23 cm. (Essay index reprint series) Contents.Contents.—Philo.—Paul of Tarsus.—Marcion.—Origen.—Athanasius.—Theodore.—Augustine.—Anselm.—Abelard.—Aquinas.—Erasmus.—Luther.—Calvin.—Arminius.—Schleiermacher.—Ritschl.—Bibliography (p. 351-355) [BR1700.K45 1968] 68-57327
1. Theologians. 2. Theology, Doctrinal—History. I. Title.

MODERN theologians: 200'.922
Christians and Jews; introduction to the works of Martin Buber [and others] Editor: Thomas E. Bird. Notre Dame [Ind.] University of Notre Dame Press [1967] xii, 224 p. 21 cm. (Theology today, v. 2) Contents.Contents.—Theologians of dialogue: Martin Buber, by L. D. Streiker. John Courtney Murray, by T. T. Love. Josef Hromadka, by C. C. West.—Theologians of the life of the church: Bernard Haring, by S. O. Weselowsky. Edward Schillebeeckx, by M. J. Houdijk. John A. T. Robinson, by L. D. Streiker.—Theologians of intellectual renewal: Bernard Lonergan, by F. E. Crowe. John Hick, by L. D. Streiker.—Theologians of mystical experience: Abraham Josua Heschel, by F. A. Rothschild. Henri de Lubac, by W. C. Russell.—Bibliography (p. 201-224) [BT28.M6] 68-696
1. Theologians. 2. Theology, Doctrinal—History—20th century.

PAUL, father, 1876- 922.2
The doctors of the church, by the Reverend Father Paul, O, S. F. C. with a preface by the Most Reverend Thomas Leighton Williams ... New York, Cincinnati [etc.] Benziger brothers, 1931. xiv, 181 p. front. 19 cm. "Printed in Great Britain." [Secular name: Edward John Thorpe] [BX4669.P3] 33-23531
1. Theologians. I. Title.

PEERMAN, Dean G., ed. 230.0922
A handbook of Christian theologians, edited by Dean G. Peerman and Martin E. Marty. Cleveland, World Pub. Co. [1965] 506 p. 21 cm. "Companion volume to A handbook of Christian theology." Includes bibliographical references. [BT28.P36] 65-18010
1. Theologians. I. Marty, Martin E., 1928- joint ed. II. Title.

REINISCH, Leonhard, ed. 230.0904
Theologians of our time: Karl Barth [others] Foreword by Charles H. Henkey [Notre Dame, Ind.] Univ of Notre Dame Pr. [c.1964] x, 235p. 21cm. Orig. pub. in Munich in 1960. Bibl. [BT28.R413] 64-17067 2.25
1. Theologians. 2. Theology, Doctrinal—Hist.—20th cent. I. Title.

REINISCH, Leonhard, ed. 230.0904
Theologians of our time: Karl Barth [and others] Foreword by Charles H. Henkey. [Notre Dame, Ind.] University of Notre Dame Press [1964] x, 235 p. 21 cm. ([Theology today, v. 1]) Bibliography: p. 203-235. [BT28.R413] 64-17067
1. Theologians. 2. Theology, Doctrinal—History—20th century. I. Title.

SZYMANOWSKI, Stephen Korwin, 1854-
The evolution of a theologian, by Stephen K. Szymanowski... Boston, Sherman, French & company, 1913. 4 p. l., 350 p. 21 cm. 14-23 2.00
I. Title.

Theologians, American.

CATHOLIC Theological Society of America.
Directory of American Catholic theologians. Supplement of the Proceedings of the seventh annual convention. [Yonkers, N.Y., St. Joseph's Seminary] 1963. 114 p. 23 cm. 64-62378
1. Theologians, American. I. Title.

FERM, Vergilius Ture Anselm, 922
ed.
Contemporary American theology; theological autobiographies, edited by Vergilius Ferm. New York, Round table press, inc., 1932-33. 2 v. 22 cm. "Principal publications" at end of each "autobiography". [BR525.F4] 33-2542
1. Theologians, American. I. Title.

SOPER, David Wesley, 230.0973
1910-
Major voices in American Theology. Philadelphia, Westminster Press [1953-55] 2 v. 21 cm. Contents.Contents.—[v. 1] Six contemporary leaders.—v. 2. Men who shape belief. [BR569.S65] 52-13140
1. Theologians, American. 2. Theology, Doctrinal—History—U. S. I. Title. II. Title: Men who shape belief.

Theologians—France—Biography.

ELLUL, Jacques. 261.8
Perspectives on our age : Jacques Ellul speaks on his life and work / Jacques Ellul ; edited by William H. Vanderburg ; translated from the French by Joachim Neugroschel. New York : Seabury Press, 1981. 111 p. ; 22 cm. [BX4827.E5A3413] 19 81-368 ISBN 0-8164-0485-2 : 10.95
1. Ellul, Jacques. 2. Theologians—France—Biography. I. Vanderburg, William H. II. Title.

Theologians, German—Correspondence, reminiscences, etc.

BARTH, Karl, 1886- 922.4494
Revolutionary theology in the making: Barth-Thurneysen correspondent, 1914-1925. Tr. [from German] by James D. Smart. Richmond, Va., Knox [1964] 249p. 21cm. Pt. I was orig. pub. as Die Anfange, pages 831-864 in Antwort, 1956. Part II was orig. pub. as Lebendige Vergangenheit, pages 7-173 in Gottesdienst-Menschendienst. 1958. 64-10771 5.00
1. Theologians, German—Correspondence, reminiscences, etc. I. Turneysen, Eduard, 1888- II. Title.

Theologians—Switzerland—Basel—Biography.

BUSCH, Eberhard, 230'.092'4 B
1937-
Karl Barth : his life from letters and autobiographical texts / Eberhard Busch ; translated by John Bowden. Philadelphia : Fortress Press, c1976. xvii, 569 p. : ill. ; 23 cm. Translation of Karl Barths Lebenslauf. Includes bibliographical references and indexes. [BX4827.B3B86313] 76-15881 ISBN 0-8006-0485-7 : 19.95
1. Barth, Karl, 1886-1968. 2. Theologians—Switzerland—Basel—Biography. 3. Basel—Biography.

Theologians—Switzerland—Correspondence.

BARTH, Karl, 230'.044'0922 B
1886-1968.
Karl Barth-Rudolf Bultmann letters, 1922 to 1966 / edited by Bernd Jaspert ; translated and edited by Geoffrey W. Bromiley. Grand Rapids, Mich. : Eerdmans, c1981. p. cm. Translation of: Briefe. Bd. 1. Karl Barth-Rudolf Bultmann Briefwechsel, 1922-1966. Includes bibliographies and index. [BX4827.B3A4 1981] 19 81-17246 ISBN 0-8028-3536-8 : 13.95
1. Barth, Karl, 1886-1968. 2. Bultmann, Rudolf Karl, 1884-1976. 3. Theologians—Switzerland—Correspondence. 4. Theologians—Germany (West)—Correspondence. I. Bultmann, Rudolf Karl, 1884-1976. II. Jaspert, Bernd. III. Bromiley, Geoffrey William. IV. [Correspondence.] English. Selections V. Title. VI. Title: Barth-Bultmann letters.

BARTH, Karl, 230'.044'0924 B
1886-1968.
Letters, 1961-1968 / Karl Barth ; translated and edited by Geoffrey W. Broniley. Grand Rapids, Mich. : Eerdmans, c1980. xv, 382 p. ; 24 cm. Translation of Briefe 1961-1968. Includes indexes. Bibliography: p. 381-382. [BX4827.B3A4 1980] 19 80-29140 18.95
1. Barth, Karl, 1886-1968. 2. Theologians—Switzerland—Correspondence. I. Fangmeier, Jurgen. II. Stoevesandt, Hinrich. III. Bromiley, Geoffrey William. IV. Title.

Theologians—United States.

SOPER, David Wesley, 230'.0922
1910-
Major voices in American theology. Port Washington, N.Y., Kennikat Press [1969, c1953-55] 2 v. 22 cm. (Essay and general literature index reprint series) Contents.Contents.—[1] Six contemporary leaders.—v. 2. Men who shape belief. [BR569.S652] 72-86060 ISBN 0-8046-0587-4
1. Theologians—United States. 2. Theology, Doctrinal—History—United States. I. Title. II. Title: Six contemporary leaders. III. Title: Men who shape belief.

Theologians—United States—Biography.

BROWN, Robert 230'.134'0924 B
McAfee, 1920-
Creative dislocation : the movement of grace / Robert McAfee Brown. Nashville : Abingdon, 1980. 144 p. ; 21 cm. (Journeys in faith) [BX9225.B7617A4] 80-16433 ISBN 0-687-09826-2 pbk. : 7.95
1. Brown, Robert McAfee, 1920- 2. Theologians—United States—Biography. I. Title. II. Series.

PAUCK, Wilhelm, 230'.092'4 B
1901-
Paul Tillich, his life & thought / Wilhelm & Marion Pauck. 1st ed. New York : Harper & Row, c1976- v. : ill. ; 22 cm. Contents.Contents.—v. 1. Life. Includes bibliographical references and index. [BX4827.T53P28 1976] 74-25709 ISBN 0-06-066474-6 (v. 1) : 15.00
1. Tillich, Paul, 1886-1965. 2. Theologians—United States—Biography. 3. Theologians—Germany—Biography. I. Pauck, Marion, joint author.

PELOTTE, Donald E. 261.7'092'4
John Courtney Murray : theologian in conflict / by Donald E. Pelotte. New York : Paulist Press, c1976. xi, 210 p. ; 24 cm. Includes index. Bibliography: p. 191-206. [BX4705.M977P44] 76-18046 ISBN 0-8091-0212-9 : 9.95
1. Murray, John Courtney. 2. Catholic Church—Biography. 3. Theologians—United States—Biography.

STRONG, Augustus 230'.61'0924 B
Hopkins, 1836-1921.
Autobiography of Augustus Hopkins Strong / edited by Crerar Douglas. Valley Forge, PA : Judson Press, 1981. p. cm. Includes bibliographical references and index. [BX6495.S7985A32] 19 81-5970 ISBN 0-8170-0916-7 : 25.00
1. Strong, Augustus Hopkins, 1836-1921. 2. Theologians—United States—Biography. 3. Baptists—Clergy—Biography. 4. Clergy—United States—Biography. I. Douglas, Crerar. II. Title.

TILLICH, Hannah. 910'.4
From place to place : travels with Paul Tillich, travels without Paul Tillich / Hannah Tillich. New York : Stein and Day, 1976. 223 p. : ill. ; 24 cm. [BX4827.T53T52] 75-34490 ISBN 0-8128-1902-0 : 10.00
1. Tillich, Paul, 1886-1965. 2. Tillich, Hannah. 3. Theologians—United States—Biography. 4. Wives—United States—Biography. I. Title.

WHITE, William, 285'.731'0924 B
1934-
Van Til, defender of the faith : an authorized biography / William White, Jr. Nashville : T. Nelson Publishers, c1979. 233 p., [4] leaves of plates : ill. ; 21 cm. Includes bibliographical references. [BX9225.V37W47] 79-9732 ISBN 0-8407-5670-4 pbk. : 4.95
1. Van Til, Cornelius, 1895- 2. Theologians—United States—Biography. I. Title.

WHITTAKER, 230'.58'0924 B
Frederick William, 1913-
Samuel Harris, American theologian / by Frederick William Whittaker. 1st ed. New York : Vantage Press, c1982. xiii, 268 p. : port. ; 21 cm. Includes index. Bibliography: p. 257-264. [BX7260.H22W47 1982] 19 81-65257 ISBN 0-533-04969-5 : 10.00
1. Harris, Samuel, 1814-1899. 2. Theologians—United States—Biography. 3. Congregational churches—Clergy—Biography. 4. Clergy—United States—Biography. I. Title.

Theologic seminaries, Catholic.

CATHOLIC University of 207
America. Conference on the Curriculum of the Minor Seminary, 1955.
Curriculum of the minor seminary: social studies, Greek, and the general curriculum; the proceedings of the Sixth Annual Conference on the Curriculum of the Minor Seminary, conducted at the Catholic University of America, May 13, 14, 15, 1955. Edited by Roy J. Deferrari. Washington, Catholic University of America Press, 1956. iv, 81p. 22cm. Includes bibliographies. [BX905.C3 1955] 56-1552
1. Theologic seminaries, Catholic. 2. Greek language—Study and teaching. 3. Social science—Study and teaching (Secondary) I. Deferrari, Roy Joseph, 1890- ed. II. Title.

RICHMOND. Union 207.75523
Theological Seminary.
The days of our years, 1812-1962; the historical conuocations held April 24-27, 1962 as a feature of the celebration of the sessuicentennial of Union Theological Seminary in Virginia Richmond [1962?] 91 p. 26 cm. Contents.The first years, by E. T. Thompson. -- Times of crisis, by F. B. Lewis. -- Rebuilding, by J. Appleby. -- The twentieth century, by E. T. Thompson. [BV4070.R665] 66-39503

I. Title.

Theological education—Africa.

TAYLOR, Theophilus, 1909-
Survey of theological education in overseas seminaries in Africa and Asia to which the United Presbyterian commission on Ecumenical mission and relations is related. [n. p., 1962] 141 p. 29 cm. "An abbreviated edition for restricted circulation." 65-23970
1. Theological education—Africa. 2. Theological education—Asia. 3. Missions—Educational work. 4. United Presbyterian church in the U.S.A.—Missions—Africa. 5. United Presbyterian church in the U.S.A.—Missions—Asia. I. United Presbyterian Church in the U.S.A. Commission on Ecumenical Mission and Relations. II. Title.

Theological education, Baptist.

ELLIOT, Leslie Robinson, 1886-
The training of Southern Baptist ministers; Founder's day address. Fort Worth, Texas, Southwestern Baptist Theological Seminary, 1960. 53 p. 67-67872
1. Theological education, Baptist. I. Title.

Theological education — Directories

AMERICAN Association of Theological Schools.
AATS directory 1964, including aids in the choice of a theological school. [Dayton, O., 1964] 128 p. 23 cm. NUC65
1. Theological education — Direct. I. Title.

Theological libraries,

ALDRICH, Ella Virginia, 1902- 026.2
Using theological books and libraries [by] Ella v. Aldrich [and] Thomas Edward Camp. Illustrated by John Chase. Englewood Cliffs, .J., Prentice-Hall [1963] [Z675.T4A4] 63-13208
1. Theological libraries. 2. Religion-Bibi. I. Camp, Thomas Edward, joint author. II. Title.

BARBER, Cyril J. 016.2
The minister's library, by Cyril J. Barber. Foreword by Merrill F. Unger. Grand Rapids, Baker Book House [1974] xiii, 378 p. illus. 27 cm. [Z675.T4B3] 73-92977 ISBN 0-8010-0598-1 9.95
1. Theological libraries. I. Title.

BARBER, Cyril J. 016.2
The minister's library. Cyril J. Barber. Grand Rapids, Mich. : Baker Book House, 1982. 76 p. ; 26 cm. Includes indexes. [Z675.T4B3 Suppl] 19 82-142899 ISBN 0-8010-0813-1 (pbk.) : 5.95
1. Theological libraries. 2. Theology—Bibliography. I. Title.

THE International theological library. Edited by Charles A. Briggs and Stewart D. F. Salmond. New York, C. Scribner's sons, 1892. v. 8 cm. 1-1237

SONNE, Niels Henry, 1907-
Current trends in theological libraries. [Urban, Ill., University of Illionois Graduate School of Library Science] 1960. 131-283 p. 23 cm. (Library trends, v. 9, no. 2)
1. Theological libraries, I. Title. II. Series.

Theological libraries—Australia—Directories.

DRAKEFORD, Paul. 026'.2'02594
The Australian & New Zealand theological library directory / edited by Paul Drakeford. Melbourne : P. D. Drakeford, 1974. 88 p. ; 24 cm. Spine title: The ANZ theological library directory. Limited ed. of 500 copies. "ANZ theological library directory addendum": 3 p. inserted. Includes index. Bibliography: p. 66-72. [Z675.T4D7] 75-321122 ISBN 0-9599515-1-2 : 6.00
1. Theological libraries—Australia—Directories. 2. Theological libraries—New Zealand—Directories. I. Title. II. Title: The ANZ theological library directory.

Theological libraries—Directories.

RUOSS, George Martin. 027.6'7'025
A world directory of theological libraries, by G. Martin Ruoss. Metuchen, N.J., Scarecrow Press, 1968. 220 p. 23 cm. [Z675.T4R8] 68-12632
1. Theological libraries—Directories. I. Title.

Theological school inventory.

DITTES, James E. 207
Vocational guidance of theological students; a manual for the use of the Theological school inventory [by] James E. Dittes. [Dayton, Ohio, Ministry Studies Board, 1964] 1 v. (various pagings) illus. 28 cm. "The Theological school inventory was developed in research conducted by Educational Testing Service, directed by Frederick R. Kling, supported by Lilly Endowment, inc." [BV4011.4.D5] 254 68-2363
1. Theological school inventory. I. Title.

Theological seminaries.

CATHOLIC University of America. Conference on the Curriculum of the Minor Seminary, 1954.
Curriculum of the minor seminary: religion, Greek, and remedial rading; the proceedings of the fifth annual Conference on the Curriculum of the Minor Seminary conducted at the Catholic University of America, May 14, 15, 16, 1954. Edited by Roy J. Deferrari. Washington, Catholic University of America Press, 1955. iii, 59p. 23cm. Includes bibliographies. A 55
1. Theological seminaries. 2. Religious education. 3. Greek language—Study and teaching. 4. Reading— Remedial teaching. I. Deferrari, Roy Joseph, 1890- ed. II. Title.

DANIEL, William Andrew, 1895- 207'.73
The education of Negro ministers, by W. A. Daniel. Based upon a survey of theological schools for Negroes in the United States made by Robert L. Kelly and W. A. Daniel. New York, J. & J. Harper Editions [1969] vii, 187 p. 22 cm. Bibliography footnotes. [BV4080.D3 1969b] 70-98002
1. Theological seminaries. 2. Theology—Study and teaching. 3. Negroes—Education. I. Title.

DANIEL, William Andrew, 1895- 207.
The education of Negro ministers, byW. A. Daniel; based upon a survey of theological schools for Negroes in the United States made by Robert L. Kelly and W. A. Daniel. New York, George H. Doran company [c1925] vii p., 2 l., 13-187 p. 20 cm. "The Institute of social and religious research ... is responsible for this publication. [BV4080.D3] 25-15962
1. Theological seminaries. 2. Theology—Study and teaching. 3. Negroes—Education. I. Institute of social and religious research. II. Title. III. Title: Negro ministers, The education of.

DANVILLE, Ky. Theological seminary of the Presbyterian church in the U. S. A.
Addresses delivered at the inauguration of the professors in the Danville theological seminary, October 13, 1853. Printed at the request of the directors then present. Cincinnati, Printed by T. Wrighton, 1854. cover-title, 74 p. 29 cm. [BV4079.D825 1853] 24-14639
I. Young, John Clarks, 1860-1867. II. Brackenridge, Robert Jefferson. 1800-1877. III. Humphery, Edward Peter, 1860-1867. IV. Title.
Contents omitted.

DE WITT, William Converse, 1860- 252.
... The work of the church in theological seminaries in the United State of America, by the Rev. William Converse De Witt ... Preached at S. Paul's church, Chicago, Septuagesima Sunday, February 12, 1911. Milwaukee, Pub. for the Western theological seminary, Chicago, by the Young churchman co. [1911] 58 p. fold. tab. 23 cm. (The Hale memorial sermon. no. 6) [BX5937.A1H3 no. 6] 19-12763
I. Title.

THE education of American ministers ... New York, Institute of social and religious research [c1934] 4 v. diagrs., forms. 23 1/2 cm. Vol. IV lithographed. "The study ... has been made under the joint auspices of the Conference of theological seminaries in the United States and Canada, and the Institute of social and religious research."--Foreword. Contents.--I. Ministerial education in America, summary and interpretation, by W. A. Brown.--II. The profession of the ministry, its status and problems, by M. A. May, in collaboration with W. A. Brown, F. K. Shuttleworth, J. A. Jacobs, and Charlotte V. Feeney.-- III. The institutions that train ministers, by M. A. May, in collaboration with W. A. Brown, Charlotte V. Feeney, R. B. Montgomery, and F. K. Shuttleworth.--IV. Appendices, by M. A. May and F. K. Shuttleworth. A brief bibliography (p. 275-280) [BV4080.E4] 34-5799 207.73
1. Theological seminaries. 2. Theology—Study and teaching. I. Institute of social and religious research. II. Conference of theological seminaries and colleges in the United States and Canada. III. May, Mark Arthur, 1891- IV. Brown, William Adams, 1865- V. Shuttleworth, Frank Kayley, 1899-
contents omitted

FOSTER, Frank Clifton, 1894- 207
Field work and its relation to the curriculum of theological seminaries [by] Frank C. Foster ... Johnson City, Conn., Muse-Whitlock co., printers, 1932. 103 p. fold. tab. 24 cm. Thesis (PH. D.)--Columbia university, 1934. Vita. "The major part of this dissertations has appeared as chapter x of vol. iii of The education of American ministers published by the Institute of social and religious research for whom the study was made."--Pref. Bibliography: p. 93-98. [BV4030.E42 1932] 34-40490
1. Theological seminaries. 2. Theology—Study and teaching. I. Title.

GOLDEN Gate Baptist Theological Seminary.
The master plan; projection 74. [Mill Valley, Golden Gate Seminary, 1965] 1 v. (unpaged) 68-2976
1. Theological seminaries. I. Title.

GRIER, James Alexander, 1846-
Pastoral homilies, delivered as commencement addresses to the graduating classes of the Allegheny theological seminary, by James A. Grier ... Introduction by John McNaugher ... Pittsburgh, Pa., United Presbyterian board of publication, 1909. vii, 168 p. front. (port.) 19 cm. $1.00. 10-1357
I. Title.

HARTFORD theological seminary, Hartford, Conn. 207.7463
A memorial of the semi-centenary celebration of the Theological institute of Connecticut. Hartford, Conn., Press of the Case Lockwood & Brainard company, 1884. 146 p. 24 cm. On cover Semi-centenary Hartford theological seminary. "At the annual meeting of the Pastorial Union of Connecticut ... May 8, 1884. Rev. Graham Taylor. Rev. Jhn H. Goodell, and J. M. Allen esq ... were appointed a committee to publish ... the proceedings of the semi-centennial celebration of the Theological insdtitute of Connecticut."--Prefatory note. [BV4070.H3665 1884] 36-2432
I. Taylor, Graham, 1851- II. Pastoral union of Connecticut. III. Title.

KELLY, Robert Lincoln, 1865- 207
Theological education in America; a study of one hundred sixty-one theological schools in the United States and Canada, by Robert L. Kelly ... with a foreword by Rt. Rev. Charles Henry Brent ... New York, George H. Doran company [c1924] xix p., 1 l., 23-456 p. illus. (maps) plates, diagrs. 23 cm. Authorized by the Institute of social and religious research and directed by the Council of church boards of education. cf. Introd. [BV4030.K4] 24-18270
1. Theological seminaries. 2. Theology—Study and teaching. I. Institute of social and religious research. II. Council of church boards of education. III. Title. IV. Title: Theological schools in the United States and Canada.

NEW York. Union theological seminary. 207.7471
The dedication of the new buildings of the Union theological seminary in the city of New York, November 27, 28 and 29, 1910. New York [1910?] 167 p. front., pl. 25 cm. [BV4070.U635 1910] CA 12
I. Title.

NEW York. Union theological seminary. 016.
... Exercises connected with the inauguration of the Rev. Daniel Johnson Fleming ... The Rev. Harry Frederick Ward ... the Rev. Eugene William Lyman ... at the opening service of the eighty-third academic year of the Seminary, September twenty-sixth, nineteen hundred and eighteen; together with an address given at the eighty-second commencement, May fourteenth, nineteen hundred and eighteen, by the Rev. Henry Preserved Smith ... [New York, The Union theological seminary in the city of New York] 1918. 65 p. 23 cm. (On cover: Union theological seminary bulletin. vol. II, no. 1. Nov. 1918) At head of title: The Union theological seminary in the city of New York. [BV4070.U635 1918] 19-18762
I. Fleming, Daniel Johnson, 1877- II. Ward, Harry Frederick, 1873- III. Lyman, Eugene William, 1872- IV. Smith, Henry Preserved, 1847- V. Title.

NEW York. Union theological seminary. 016.
... Exercises connected with the inauguration of the Rev. Daniel Johnson Fleming ... The Rev. Harry Frederick Ward ... the Rev. Eugene William Lyman ... at the opening service of the eighty-third academic year of the Seminary, September twenty-sixth, nineteen hundred and eighteen; together with an address given at the eighty-second commencement, May fourteenth, nineteen hundred and eighteen, by the Rev. Henry Preserved Smith ... [New York, The Union theological seminary in the city of New York] 1918. 65 p. 23 cm. (On cover: Union theological seminary bulletin. vol. II, no. 1. Nov. 1918) At head of title: The Union theological seminary in the city of New York. [BV4070.U635 1918] 19-18762
I. Fleming, Daniel Johnson, 1877- II. Ward, Harry Frederick, 1873- III. Lyman, Eugene William, 1872- IV. Smith, Henry Preserved, 1847- V. Title.

RICHMOND. Union theological seminary. 207.755451
Centennial general catalogue of the trustees, officers, professors and alumni of Union theological seminary in Virginia, 1807-1907. Edited by Walter W. Moore and Tilden Scherer. Richmond, Va., Printed by Whittet & Shepperson, [1908] 189 p. front., plates. ports. 24 cm. Based upon a former general catalogue compiled by the late Rev. Benjamin M. Smith, published in 1884, before the removal of the seminary from Hampden-Sidney to Richmond. cf. Pref. [BV4070.R64 1907] 8-30160
I. Moore, Walter William, 1857-1926. ed. II. Scherer, Tilden, 1876- joint ed. III. Title.

RICHMOND. Union theological seminary. 207.
Exercises in connection with the inauguration of the Rev. Walter W. Moore, DD., LL.D., as president of Union theological seminary, Richmond, Va., May 9, 1905. Richmond, Va., Press of L. D. Sullivan & co. [1905?] 50 p. 23 1/2 cm. [BV4070.R668 1905] 45-26719
I. Moore, Walter William, 1857-1926. II. Title.

RICHMOND. Union theological seminary. 207.
Exercises in connection with the inauguration of the Rev. Walter W. Moore, DD., LL.D., as president of Union theological seminary, Richmond, Va., May 9, 1905. Richmond, Va., Press of L. D. Sullivan & co. [1905?] 50 p. 23 1/2 cm. [BV4070.R668 1905] 45-26719
I. Moore, Walter William, 1857-1926. II. Title.

SPRAGUE, William Buell, 1795-1876. 016.
A discourse addressed to the alumni of the Princeton theological seminary, April 30, 1862, on occasion of the completion of its first half century. By William B. Sprague, D.D. With an appendix, containing notices of the other commemorative exercises. Albany, Steam press of Van Benthuysen, 1862. 72 p. 23 1/2 cm. On cover: The Princeton semi-centennial jubilee, MDCCCLXII. [BV4070.P765 1862] 7-34865
1. Princeton theological seminary. II. Title.

SPRAGUE, William Buell, 1795-1876. 016.
A discourse addressed to the alumni of the Princeton theological seminary, April 30, 1862, on occasion of the completion of its first half century. By William B. Sprague, D.D. With an appendix, containing notices of the other commemorative exercises. Albany, Steam press of Van Benthuysen, 1862. 72 p. 23 1/2 cm. On cover: The Princeton semi-centennial jubilee, MDCCCLXII. [BV4070.P765 1862] 7-34865
I. Princeton theological seminary. II. Title.

WAGONER, Walter D 207'.11
The seminary: Protestant and Catholic, by Walter D. Wagoner. New York, Sheed and Ward [1966] xxiii, 256 p. 22 cm. Includes bibliographical references. [BV4020.W3] 66-22029
1. Theological seminaries. 2. Catholic Church—Relations—Protestant churches. 3. Protestant churches—Relations—Catholic Church. I. Title.

WAGONER, Walter D. 207'.11
The seminary: Protestant and Catholic, by Walter D. Wagoner. New York, Sheed and Ward [1966] xxiii, 256 p. 22 cm. Includes bibliographical references. [BV4020.W3] 66-22029
1. Catholic Church—Relations—Protestant churches. 2. Theological seminaries. 3. Protestant churches—Relations—Catholic Church. I. Title.

Theological seminaries—Accreditation.

ACCREDITING Association of Bible Colleges.
Official listing of member schools and officers of the executive committee. Providence. v. 28cm. [BV4019.A52] 59-27167
1. Theological seminaries—Accreditation. I. Title.

MINOR Seminary Conference. 11th, Catholic University of America, 1960. 207
Self-evaluation in the minorseminary; the proceedings of the Eleventh Seminary Conference, conducted at the Catholic University of America, May 13, 14, 15, 1960. Ed. by Cornelius M. Cuyler. Washington, D.C., Catholic Univ. of America Press [c.]1961. v, 70p. Bibl. 61-10774 1.50 pap.,
1. Theological seminaries—Accreditation. I. Cuyler, Cornelius M., ed. II. Title.

MINOR Seminary Conference. 11th, Catholic University of America, 1960. 207
Self-evaluation in the minor seminary; the proceedings of the Eleventh Minor Seminary Conference, conducted at the Catholic University of America, May 13, 14, 15, 1960. Edited by Cornelius M. Cuyler. Washington, Catholic University of America Press, 1961. v. 70p. 22cm. Includes bibliographical references. [BX903.M425 1960] 61-1077
1. Theological seminaries—Accreditation. I. Cuyler, Cornelius M., ed. II. Title.

Theological seminaries, Baptist.

JOINT Survey Commission of the Baptist Inter-convention Committee. 207.73
The Negro Baptist ministry; an analysis of its profession, preparation, and practices, by Ira De A. Reid. Report of a survey conducted by the Joint Survey Commission of the Baptist Inter-convention Committee: the American Baptist Convention, the National Baptist Convention [and] the Southern Baptist Convention. [Philadelphia, H. and L. Advertising Co.] 1951[i.e. 1952] 145p. 28cm. [BV4080.J6] 52-67070
1. Theological seminaries, Baptist. 2. Baptists, Negro— Education. I. Reid, Ira De Augustine, 1901- II. Title.

Theological seminaries—California—Berkeley.

THE Graduate 207'.794'67
Theological Union; its participants and their ecclesiastical heritage. Edited by Elizabeth Kelley Bauer and Florence Noyce Wertz. [Berkeley, Calif.] Graduate Theological Union Guild, 1970. 50 p. illus. 24 cm. [BV4070.G7664] 75-21850
1. Graduate Theological Union. 2. Theological seminaries—California—Berkeley. I. Bauer, Elizabeth (Kelley), ed. II. Wertz, Florence Noyce, ed. III. Graduate Theological Union Guild.

Theological seminaries (Canon law)

COX, Joseph Godfrey, 1903-
... The administration of seminaries; historical synopsis and commentary ... by Joseph Godfrey Cox ... Washington, D. C., The Catholic university of America, 1931. vi, 124 p. 23 cm. (The Catholic university of America. Canon law studies. no. 67) Thesis (j. c. d.)--Catholic university of America, 1931. "Biographical note." Bibliography: p. 112-115. 32-8
1. Theological seminaries (Canon law) 2. Catholic church. Codex juris canonici. C. 1352-1371: De seminariis. I. Title. II. Title: Seminaries, The administration of.

MANNING, Timothy. 207
... Clerical education in major seminaries, its nature and application ... by Timothy Manning ... [Paterson, N.J., St Anthony guild press] 1946. 61 p. 23 1/2 cm. Extract from thesis--Pontificia universita gregorians. Bibliography: p. 54-60. [BX1939.S45M3] 47-22709
1. Theological seminaries (Canon law) 2. Theology—Study and teaching—Catholic church. I. Title.

Theological seminaries, Catholic.

CATHOLIC University of America. Conference on the Curriculum of the Minor Seminary, 1951.
The curriculum of the minor seminary; the proceedings of a Conference on the Curriculum of the Minor Seminary, conducted at the Catholic University of America, May 4, 5, 6, 1951. Edited by Michael J. McKeough. Washington, Catholic University of America Press, 1952. iv, 99 p. tables. 23 cm. Bibliographical footnotes. A 52
1. Theological seminaries, Catholic. 2. Theology—Study and teaching—Catholic Church. I. McKeough, Michael John, 1891- ed. II. Title.

CATHOLIC University of America. Conference on the Curriculum of the Minor Seminary, 1952.
Latin and English syllabi in the minor seminary; the proceedings of a Conference on the Curriculum of the Minor Seminary, conducted at the Catholic University of America. May 9, 10, 11, 1952. Edited by Roy J. Deferrari. Washington, Catholic University of America Press, 1953. iv, 94p. 28cm. A 53
1. Theological seminaries, Catholic. 2. Latin language—Study and teaching. 3. English language—Study and teaching. I. Deferrari, Roy Joseph, 1890- ed. II. Title.

D'ARCY, Paul F., 1921- 248.892
The genius of the apostolate; personal growth in the candidate, the seminarian, and the priest, by Paul F. D'Arcy, Eugene C. Kennedy. Foreword by Bishop O'Donnell. New York, Sheed [c.1965] xiii, 273p. 22cm. Bibl. [BX900.D3] 65-24690 5.50
1. Theological seminaries, Catholic. 2. Catholic Church—Clergy—Apointment, call and election. 3. Seminarians. I. Kennedy, Eugene C., joint author. II. Title.

D'ARCY, Paul F 1921- 248.892
The genius of the apostolate; personal growth in the candidate, the seminarian, and the priest, by Paul F. D'Arcy and Eugene C. Kennedy. Foreword by Bishop O'Donnell. New York, Sheed and Ward [1965] xiii, 273 p. 22 cm. Bibliography: p. 264-268. [BX900.D3] 65-24690
1. Theological seminaries, Catholic. 2. Catholic Church — Clergy — Appointment, call and election. 3. Seminarians. I. Kennedy, Eugene C., joint author. II. Title.

ELLIS, John Tracy, 1905- 207'.11'2
Essays in seminary education. Notre Dame, Ind., Fides Publishers [1967] x. 278 p. 22 cm. Bibliographical footnotes. [BX900.E47] 67-24811
1. Theological seminaries, Catholic. 2. Theology—Study and teaching—Catholic Church. I. Title. II. Title: Seminary education.

ELLIS, John Tracy, 1905- 207'.11'2
Essays in seminary education. Notre Dame, Ind., Fides Publishers [1967] x, 278 p. 22 cm. Bibliographical footnotes. [BX900.E47] 67-24811
1. Theological seminaries, Catholic. 2. Theology—Study and teaching—Catholic Church. I. Title. II. Title: Seminary education.

LEE, James Michael, ed. 207
Seminary education in a time of change, ed. by James Michael Lee, Louis J. Putz. Contributors: John Tracy Ellis [others] Foreword by Joseph Cardinal Ritter. Introd. by Frank Norris [Notre Dame, Ind.] Fides [c.]1965. xii, 590p. 24cm. Bibl. [BX900.L4] 65-13797 7.95
1. Theological seminaries, Catholic. I. Putz, Louis J., joint ed. II. Ellis, John Tracy, 1905- III. Title.

LEE, James Michael, ed. 207
Seminary education in a time of change, edited by James Michael Lee and Louis J. Putz. Contributors: John Tracy Ellis [and others] Foreword by Joseph Cardinal Ritter. Introd. by Frank Norris. [Notre Dame, Ind.] Fides Publishers, 1965. xii, 590 p. 24 cm. Bibliographical footnotes. [BX900.L4] 65-13797
1. Theological seminaries, Catholic. I. Putz, Louis J., joint ed. II. Ellis, John Tracy, 1905- III. Title.

MINOR Seminary Conference. 1st, Catholic University of America, 1950. 207.73
The organization and administration of the minor seminary; the proceedings of a Conference on the Organization and Administration of the Minor Seminary, conducted at the Catholic University of America on May 19, 20, 21, 1950. Edited by Roy J.Deferrari. Washington, Catholic University of America Press, 1951. iv, 91p. 23cm. Includes bibliographies. [BX905.M5 1950] A51
1. Theological seminaries, Catholic. I. Deferrari, Roy Joseph, 1890- ed. II. Title.

MINOR Seminary Conference. 2d, Catholic University of America. 1951. 207.73
The curriculum of the minor seminary; the proceedings of a Conference on the Curriculum of the Minor Seminary, conducted at the Catholic University of America, May 4, 5, 6, 1951. Edited by Michael J. McKeough. Washington, Catholic University of America Press, 1952. iv, 99p. tables. 23cm. Bibliographical footnotes. [BX905.M5 1951] A52
1. Theological seminaries, Catholic. 2. Theology—Study and teaching— Catholic Church. I. McKeough, Michael John, 1891- ed. II. Title.

MINOR Seminary Conference. 3d, Catholic University of America. 1952. 207.73
Latin and English syllabi in the minor seminary; the proceedings of a Conference on the Curriculum of the Minor Seminary, conducted at the Catholic University of America, May 9, 10, 11, 1952. Edited by Roy J. Deferrari. Washington, CatholicUniversity of America Press, 1953. iv, 94p. 28cm. [BX905.M5 1952] A53
1. Theological seminaries, Catholic. 2. Latin language—Study and teaching. 3. English language—Study and teaching. I. Deferrari, Roy Joseph, 1890- ed. II. Title.

MINOR Seminary Conference. 4th, Catholic University of America. 1953. 207.73
Latin and religion syllabi in the minor seminary; the proceedings of a Conference on the Curriculum of the Minor Seminary, conducted at the Catholic University of America, May 8, 9, 10, 1953. Edited by Roy J. Deferrari. Washington, Catholic University of America Press, 1954. v. 77p. 23cm. [BX905.M5 1953] A54
1. Theological seminaries, Catholic. 2. Latin language—Study and teaching. 3. Theology—Study and teaching. I. Deferrari, Roy Joseph, 1890- ed. II. Title.

MINOR Seminary Conference. 5th, Catholic University of America. 1954. 207.73
Curriculum of the minor seminary: religion, Greek, and remedial reading; the proceedings of the Fifth Annual Conference on the Curriculum of the Minor Seminary, conducted at the Catholic University of America, May 14, 15, 16, 1954. Edited by Roy J. Deferrari. Washington, Catholic University of America Press, 1955. iii, 59p. 23cm. Includes bibliographies. [BX905.M5 1954] A55
1. Theological seminaries, Catholic. 2. Religious education [of young people] 3. Greek language—Study and teaching. 4. Reading—Remedial teaching. I. Deferrari, Roy Joseph, 1890- ed. II. Title.

MINOR Seminary Conference. 6th, Catholic University of America, 1955. 207.73
Curriculum of the minor seminary: social studies, Greek, and the general curriculum; the proceedings of the Sixth Annual Conference on the Curriculum of the Minor Seminary, conducted at the Catholic University of America, May 13, 14, 15, 1955. Edited by Roy J. Deferrari. Washington, Catholic University of America Press, 1956. iv, 81p. 22cm. Includes bibliographies. [BX905.M5 1955] 56-1552
1. Theological seminaries, Catholic. 2. Greek language—Study an teaching. 3. Social sciences—Study and teaching (Secondary) I. Deferrari, Roy Joseph, 1890- ed. II. Title.

MINOR Seminary Conference. 7th, Catholic University of America, 1956. 207.73
Curriculum of the minor seminary: natural sciences and curriculum review; the proceedings of the Seventh Annual Minor Seminary Conference on the Curriculum of the Minor Seminary, conducted at the Catholic University of America, May 11, 12, 13, 1956. Edited by Cornelius M. Cuyler. Washington, Catholic University of America Press, 1957. iv, 97p. 22cm. Includes bibliographical references. [BX905.M5 1956] 57-793
1. Theological seminaries, Catholic. 2. Science—Study and teaching (Secondary) I. Cuyler, Cornellus M., ed. II. Title.

MINOR Seminary Conference, 8th, Catholic University of America, 1957. 207.73
Curriculum of the minor seminary: natural sciences and modern languages; the proceedings of the Eighth Annual Minor Seminary Conference on the Curriculum of the Minor Seminary, conducted at the Catholic University of America, May 17, 18, 19, 1957. Edited by Cornelius M. Cuyler. Washington, Catholic University of America Press, 1958. v. 87p. 22cm. Includes bibliographies. [BX905.M5 1957] 57-59522
1. Theological seminaries, Catholic. 2. Science—Study and teaching (Secondary) 3. Languages, Modern—Study and teaching. I. Cuyler, Cornelius M., ed. II. Title.

MINOR Seminary Conference. 9th, Catholic University of America, 1958. 207.73
Curriculum of the minor seminary: mathematics and speech training; the proceedings of the Ninth Annual Minor Seminary Conference on mathematics and speech training, conducted at the Catholic University of America, May 9, 10, 11, 1958. Ed. by Cornelius M. Cuyler. Washington, Catholic University of America Press, 1959. vi, 103p. 22cm.

Includes bibliographical references. [BX905.C3 1958] 59-2837
1. Theological seminaries, Catholic. 2. Mathematics—Study and teaching. 3. Languages, Modern—Study and teaching. I. Cuyler, Cornelius M., ed. II. Title.

MINOR Seminary Conference, Catholic University of America.
Some answers to current criticism of the minor seminary; proceedings. Edited by Rev. Cornelius M. Cuyler. Washington, Catholic University of America Press [c1967] viii, 114 p. 22 cm. 68-100046
1. Theological seminaries, Catholic. I. Cuyler, Cornelius M., ed. II. Title.

POOLE, Stafford 207.11
Seminary in crisis. [New York] Herder & Herder [c.1965] 190p. 21cm. Bibl. [BX900.P6] 65-20558 3.95
1. Theological seminaries. Catholic. 2. Theology—Study and teaching—Catholic Church. I. Title.

Theological seminaries, Catholic — Congresses.

CHRISTOPHER Study Week. 207.112 2d, New York, 1964.
Apostolic renewal in the seminary in the light of Vatican Council II; the papers of the 2nd Christopher Study Week, July 20-24, 1964 with the conclusions of the 1st and 2nd Christopher Study Weeks. Edited by James Keller [and] Richard Armstrong. New York, Christophers [1965] 305 p. 17 cm. [BX900.C48 1964] 65-5585
1. Theological seminaries, Catholic — Congresses. I. Keller, James Gregory, 1900- ed. II. Armstrong, Richard G., ed. III. Title.

MINOR Seminary Conference, 207.73 Catholic University of America
Proceedings. 16th, May 14-16, 1965. Ed. by Rev. Cornclius M. Cuyler. Washington, D.C., Catholic Univ. [c.1965] 101p. 22cm. annual. Ea. vol. has a distinctive title: 1965: Programs and procedures of the Minor Seminary [BX903.M425] 61-66767 2.75 pap.,
1. Theological seminaries, Catholic—Congresses. I. Catholic University of America. II. Title.

MINOR Seminary Conference, 207.73 Catholic University of America.
Proceedings. 17th. Washington, Catholic Univ. of Amer. Pr. [1967] v. 22cm. annual. Each vol. has also a distinctive title. 1966. Some answers to current criticism of the Minor Seminary Issued by the cont. under earher names: 1950, Conf. on the Org. and Admin. of the Minor Seminary; 1951-55, Cont. on the Curriculum of the Minor Seminary 1956-57, Minor Seminary Cont. on the Curriculum of the Minor Seminary. 1966. Minor Seminary Cont. [BX903.M425] 61-66767 3.50 pap.,
1. Theological seminaries, Catholic—Congresses. I. Catholic University of America. II. Title.

MINOR Seminary Conference, 207.73 Catholic University of America
Proceedings. 18th-1967 Washington. Catholic Univ. Pr. v. 22cm. annual. Each v. has also a distinctive title. Issued by the conf. under earlier names: 1950, Conference on the Organization and Administration of the Minor Seminary-1951-55, Conference on the Curriculum of the Minor Seminary; 1956-57, Minor Seminary Conference on the Curriculum of the Minor Seminary. Ed. 1967: C. M. Cuyler [BX903.M425] 61-66767 3.95 pap.,
1. Theological seminaries, Catholic—Congresses. I. Catholic University of America. II. Title.

Theological seminaries — Directories

SMITH, C Stanley.
Protestant theological seminaries and Bible schools in Asia, Africa, the Middle East, Latin America, the Caribbean and Pacific areas; a directory compiled by C. Stanley Smith and Herbert F. Thomson. Edited by Frank W. Price. New York, Missionary Research Library, 1960. viii, 50 p. (MRL directory series, no. 12)
1. Theological seminaries — Direct. 2. Theology — Study and teaching. I. Thomson, Herbert F., joint comp. II. New York. Missionary Research Library. III. Title.

Theological seminaries, Methodist.

METHODIST Church (United States) Commission on Theological Education.
A survey of ten theological schools affiliated with the Methodist Church, under the auspices of The Commission on Theological Education, The Board of Education, and the Association of Methodist Theological Schools. Nashville, Department of Educational Institutions (General) Board of Education of the Methodist Church. [n. d.] 448 p. profiles. 22 cm. Cover title: A survey of theological education in the Methodist Church. 66-17071
1. Theological seminaries, Methodist. I. Association of Methodist Theological Schools. II. Title. III. Title: A survey of theological education in the Methodist Church.

Theological seminaries, Methodist—History.

MCCULLOH, Gerald O. 207'.73
Ministerial education in the American Methodist movement / by Gerald O. McCulloh. Nashville, Tenn. : United Methodist Board of Higher Education and Ministry, Division of Ordained Ministry, c1980. p. cm. (An informed ministry, 200 years of American Methodism ; no. 1) Includes index. Bibliography: p. [BX8219.M32] 19 80-69028 ISBN 0-938162-00-4 pbk. : 3.95
1. Theological seminaries, Methodist—History. 2. Theological seminaries—United States—History. 3. Theology, Methodist—United States—History. I. Title. II. Series: Informed ministry, 200 years of American Methodism ; no. 1.
Publisher's address: Box 871, Nashville, TN 37202

Theological seminaries, Minor.

MINOR Seminary Conference, Catholic University of America.
A continuing study of outcomes. (The proceedings of the Annual Minor Seminary (Conference...1962.) Edited by Reverend Cornelius M. Cuyler... Washington, D.C., Cath. Univ. of Amer. Pr., 1963. vi, 95 p. 22 cm. 65-35422
1. Theological seminaries, Minor. I. Cuyler, Cornelius M., ed. II. Title. III. Title: Outcomes, A continuing study of.

MINOR Seminary Conference, Catholic University of America.
Minor Seminary Conference: academic program of the minor seminary (May 8, 9, and 10, 1964) Edited by Cornelius M. Cuyler. Washington, D.C., Cath. Univ. of Amer. Press, 1964. vii, 105 p. 22 cm. 65-85238
1. Theological seminaries, minor. I. Cuyler, Cornelius, ed. II. Title. III. Title: Academic program of the minor seminary.

MINOR Seminary Conference, Catholic University of America.
Minor seminary conference on outcomes. The proceedings of the twelfth Minor Seminary Conference... May 12, 13, 14, 1961. Edited by Cornelius M. Cuyler. Washington, D.C., Cath. Univ. of Amer. Press, 1961. v, 90 p. 22 cm. 65-33910
1. Theological seminaries, minor. I. Cuyler, Cornelius M., ed. II. Title. III. Title: Outcomes.

Theological seminaries, Protestant.

"IMPORTANT correspondence," concerning the Presbyterian theological seminary of the North-west, between Rev. Willis Lord ... Jesse L. Williams ... twocommittees of the directory and others, and Mr. Cyrus H. McCormick ... Rev. N. L. Rice ... and others. New York, A. C. Rogers, printer, 1869. 94 p., 1 l. 23 cm. Reprinted in part from the North-western Presbyterian and other periodicals. 16-21162
I. Lord, Willis, 1809-1888. II. Williams, Jesse Lynch, 1807-1886. III. McCormick, Cyrus Hall, 1809-1884. IV. Rice, Nathan Lewis, 1807-1877.

PHILADELPHIA (Mt. Airy) 207. Lutheran theological seminary.
The Philadelphia seminary biographical record, 1864-1923; ed. by Luther D. Reed, '95. Mt. Airy, Philadelphia, 1923. 271 p. incl. illus., plates, ports. front. 24 cm. Plates printed on both sides. "Issued by the Seminary and the Alumni association." [BV4070.P659A2 1923] 23-11899
I. Reed, Luther Dotterer, 1873- ed. II. Philadelphia (Mt. Airy) Lutheran theological seminary. Alumni association. III. Title.

PROTESTANT theological 207 *seminaries and Bible schools in Asia, Africa, the Middle East, Latin America, the Caribbean and Pacific areas;* a directory. 1960- New York, Missionary Research Library. v. 27cm. (MRL directory series) [BV2030.N43] 61-1632
1. Theological seminaries, Protestant. I. New York, Missionary Research Library. II. Series: New York, Missionary Research Library, MRL directory series

Theological seminaries, Protestant—Directories.

SMITH, Charles Stanley, 207'.11 1890?-1959.
Protestant theological seminaries and Bible schools in Asia, Africa, the Middle East, Latin America, the Caribbean and Pacific areas; a directory. Compiled by C. Stanley Smith and Herbert F. Thomson. Edited by Frank W. Price. New York, Missionary Research Library, 1960. viii, 50 p. 28 cm. (MRL directory series, no. 12) [BV2030.N43 no. 12] 77-234260 2.00
1. Theological seminaries, Protestant—Directories. 2. Bible colleges—Directories. I. Thomson, Herbert F., joint author. II. Title. III. Series: New York. Missionary Research Library. MRL directory and survey series, no. 12

Theological seminaries—Sermons.

MADSON, Norman Arthur, 252.041 1886-
Evening bells at Bethany. Mankato, Minn., Lutheran Synod Book Co. [1948] viii, 152 p. illus. 21 cm. Forty-two devotional addresses delivered at Bethany Lutheran College, Mankato, Minn., Oct. 2, 1946-Dec. 7, 1947. [BV4316.T5M32] 48-3496
1. Theological seminaries—Sermons. I. Title.

Theological seminaries—United States

ANDOVER theological 016. seminary.
General catalogue. Boston [etc.] 18-1927] v. 23-25 cm. Issued triennially 1815-57, inclusive; subsequent issues in 1867, 1870, 1880, 1908 and 1927. Title varies: 18 General catalogue. 18-70, Triennial catalogue. 1880-1927, General catalogue. Vols. for 18-80 published in Andover. No more published. [BV4070.A54] 7-42200
I. Title.

ANDOVER theological 016. seminary.
General catalogue of Andover theological seminary, 1927, with biographical data for 1909-1927, supplementing the General catalogue of 1908; compiled by the Reverend Owen H. Gates... Boston, Mass., The Fort Hill press, S. Usher [1927] v., 151 p. 23 cm. [BV4070.A541 1927] 29-15143
I. Gates, Owen Hamilton, 1862- comp. II. Title.

ANDOVER theological 016. seminary.
General catalogue of the Theological seminary, Andover, Mass., 1880. Andover, Printed by W. F. Draper, 1883. xx, 355, [l] p. 24 1/2 cm. [BV4070.A541] 7-42200
I. Title.

ANDOVER theological 016. seminary.
General catalogue of the Theological seminary, Andover, Massachusetts, 1808-1908. Boston, Mass., T.Todd, printer [1909] viii, stop. front, pl., ports 23 1/2 cm. "There have been eighteen previous general catalogues of the Seminary, beginning in 1815, and continuing triennially until 1857, inclusive; subsequent issues were in 1867, 1870 and 1880 (published 1883) ... The present catalogue ... is based upon the edition of 1880."--Pref., signed C. C. Carpenter. [BV4070.A541] 9-20769
I. Carpenter, Charles Carroll, 1836-1918, comp. II. Title.

CHICAGO. Presbyterian 378 theological seminary.
General catalogue of the McCormick theological seminary of the Presbyterian church, Chicago, Illinois. Chicago, McCormick theological seminary, 1912. xx p., 1 l., 242 p. 23 cm. On cover: 1830-1912. [Education BV4070.P664 1912] [[BV4070.M24]] E 18
I. Title.

CLARK, Calvin Montague, 1862-
History of Bangor theological seminary, by Calvin Montague Clark... Boston, New York [etc.] The Pilgrim press [1916] xix, 408 p. front., plates, ports. 21 1/2 cm. "Lecturers": p. 391-395. At head of title: 1816-1916. Lettered on cover: Centennial commemoration. 16-22749 2.00
I. Title.

CLARK, Calvin Montague, 1862-
History of Bangor theological seminary, by Calvin Montague Clark... Boston, New York [etc.] The Pilgrim press [1916] xix, 408 p. front., plates, ports. 21 1/2 cm. "Lecturers": p. 391-395. At head of title: 1816-1916. Lettered on cover: Centennial commemoration. 16-22749 2.00
I. Title.

FREEMAN, Z comp.
Manual of American colleges and theological seminaries: giving statistical statements of their origin, endowments, libraries, students, alumni, &c., with supplementary notes. By Rev. Z. Freeman, A. M. Rochester, Steam press of A. Strong & co., 1856. 72 p. 22 cm. E 15
1. Theological seminaries—U. S. 2. Universities and colleges—U. S. I. Title.

HARTFORD theological 016. seminary, Hartford, Conn.
General catalog of Hartford theological seminary, formerly]1834-1885: the Thiological institute of Connecticut, 1834-1927; Henry Lincoln Bailey , editor [Hartford] The Seminary, 1927. 375 p. 22 cm. [BV4070.H34 1927] 30-9667
I. Bailey, Henry Lincoln, 1865- II. Title.

HARVARD university. Divinity 016. school.
General catalogue of the Divinity school of Harvard university. 1898-19 Cambridge [Mass.] The University, 1898-19 v. 24 cm. [BV4070.H44] 7-42197
I. Title.

LANE theological seminary, 016. Cincinnati.
General catalogue of Lane theological seminary. 1828-1881. Cincinnati, Elm street printing company, 1881. 69 p. 23 cm. [BV4070.L343] 15-21994
I. Title.

LINDBECK, George A. 207'.73
University divinity schools : a report on ecclesiastically independent theological education / by George Lindbeck, in consultation with Karl Deutsch and Nathan Glazer. [New York] : Rockefeller Foundation, 1976. vii, 107 p. ; 28 cm. (Working papers - the Rockefeller Foundation) Includes bibliographical references. [BV4030.L53] 76-3506
1. Theological seminaries—United States. 2. Theology—Study and teaching—United States. I. Deutsch, Karl Wolfgang, 1912- II. Glazer, Nathan. III. Title. IV. Series: Rockefeller Foundation. Working papers — the Rockefeller Foundation

MCCORMICK theological 207.7731 seminary, Chicago.
General catalogue of the McCormick theological seminary of the Presbyterian church, Chicago, Illinois. Chicago, McCormick theological seminary, 1912. xx p., 1 l., 242 p. 23 cm. On cover: 1830-1912. [BV4070.M347] E 13
I. Title.

MCCORMICK Theological 207.7731 seminary, Chicago.
General catalogue of the Presbyterian

theological seminary, Chicago ... formerly McCormick theological seminary. Chicago, Presbyterian theological seminary, 1928. xxv p., 1 l., 363 p. 24 1/2 cm. [BV4070.M347 1928] 33-17735
I. Title.

NEW York. Union theological seminary. 016.
General catalogue of the Union theological seminary in the city of New York, 1836-1918: comp. by Rev. Charles Ripley Gillett ... New York, 1919. xl, 555 p. 23 cm. (On cover: Union theological seminary bulletin, vol. II, no. 4) [BV4070.U64 1918] 19-12584
I. Gillett, Charles Ripley, 1855- comp. II. Title.

NEW York. Union theological seminary. 016.
General catalogue of Union theological seminary in the city of New-York. 1836-1876. New York, S. W. Green, printer, 1876. 170 p. 23 cm. Compiled by Edwin F. Hatfield. [BV4070.U64 1876] 4-33139
I. Hatfield, Edwin Francis, 1807-1883, comp. II. Title.

NEW York. Union theological seminary. 016.
General catalogue of Union theological seminary in the city of New York, 1836-1897; comp. by Rev. Charles Ripley Gillett ... [New York, The Trow print] 1898. xvi, 312 p. 23 cm. [BV4070.U64 1897] 4-33140
I. Gillett, Charles Ripley, 1855- comp. II. Title.

NEW York. Union theological seminary.
Services in Adams chapel at the dedication of the new buildings of the Union theological seminary, 1200 Park avenue, New York city. December 9, 1884. New York, Printing house of W. C. Martin, 1885. 82 p. front., pl. 23 cm. E 15
I. Title.

NEW York. Union theological seminary. 207.7471
Union theological seminary in the city of New York. One hundredth anniversary. 1836-1936. New York, 1936. 72 p. 23 cm. [BV4070.U665 1966] 39-6140
I. Title.

PRINCETON theological seminary. 207.
General catalogue, 1894. Philadelphia, J. B. Rodgers printing co., 1894. 440 p., 1 l. front., 3 pl. 25 cm. Compiled by Joseph H. Dulles. [BV4070.P74] 7-42095
I. Dulles, Joseph Heatly, 1853- comp. II. Title.

ROCHESTER theological seminary, Rochester, N.Y. 207.
... General catalogue, 1850 to 1910. [5th ed.] Rochester, N.Y., E. R. Andrews printing co., 1910. xxii, 326 p. 24 1/2 cm. "Previous editions appeared in 1869, 1876, 1889 and 1900." [BV4070.R742 1910] E 10
I. Title.

WILSON, J Christy, 1891- ed. 207
Ministers in training; a review of field work procedures in theological education, by the directors of field work in the seminaries of the Presbyterian Church, U. S. A., representatives of the boards of the church and other specialists. [Princeton, N. J.] Directors of field work in the theological seminaries of the Presbyterian Church, U. S. A., 1957. xii, 177p. 24cm. Bibliography: p. 171-172. [BV4020.W5] 57-3054
1. Theological seminaries— U. S. 2. Theology—Study and teaching—Presbyterian Church. I. Title. II. Title: Field work procedures in theological education.

Theological seminaries—United States—Directories

WHITE, Alex Sandri 207.73025
Guide to religious education: the directory of seminaries, Bible colleges, and theological schools covering the USA and Canada. 1965-1966 ed. Allenhurst, N. J., Aurea Pubns., c.1965. 82.1 30cm. [BV4030.W46] 65-5823 4.95 pap.,
1. Theological seminaries—U.S.—Direct. I. Title.

Theological seminary libraries.

KORTENDICK, James Joseph, 1907- 026.2
The library in the Catholic theological seminary in the United States. Washington, D.C., Catholic Univ. [1965, c.1963] xi, 353p. 23cm. (Catholic Univ. Studies in lib. sci., no. 3) Bibl. [Z675.T4K6] 65-24301 7.25 pap.,
1. Theological seminary libraries. I. Title. II. Series.

Theological seminiaries, Catholic—Congresses.

MINOR Seminary Conference, Catholic University of America. 207.73
Proceedings. 1st-1950- Washington, Catholic University Press. v. 23 cm. annual. Each vol. has also a distinctive title. Issued by the conference under earlier names: 1950, Conference on the Organization and Administration of the Minor Seminary; 1951-55, Conference on the Curriculum of the Minor Seminary; 1956-57, Minor Seminary Conference on the Curriculum of the Minor Seminary. [BX903.M425] 61-66767
1. Theological seminiaries, Catholic—Congresses. I. Title. II. Title: Catholic University of America.

Theological seventeen.

THE faith of a modern Christian; papers by the Theological seventeen ... Columbus, O., Stoneman press, 1922. 143 p. 19 cm. [BR50.F3] 23-9678 204
1. Theological seventeen.

Theological virtues.

ENGEMANN, Antonellus. 241
The new song; faith, hope, and charity in Franciscan spiritualtiy. Translated from the German by Isabel and Florence McHugh. Chicago, Franciscan Herald Press [1964] ix, 140 p. 21 cm. Bibliographical references included in "Notes" (p. 129-136) [BV4635.E513] 64-14255
1. Theological virtues. 2. Franciscans. I. Title.

GARRIGOU-LAGRANGE, Reginald, 1877- 234.1
The theological virtues. Translated by Thomas a Kempis Reilly. St. Louis, Herder [1965-] v. 24 cm. Contents.v. 1. On faith; a commentary on St. Thomas' Theological summa, IaIIaa qq. 62, 65, 68: IIaIIaa qq. 1-16. Bibliographical footnotes. [BV4635.G313] 64-8560
1. Thomas Aquinas, Saint, 1225?-1274 — Ethics. 2. Theological virtures. I. Title.

GENNARO, Camillus 241
Faith, hope, love. Tr. by Bruno Cocuzzi, Matthias Montgomery. Milwaukee, Spiritual Life Pr., 1223 S. 45 St. [c.]1965. 150p. 19cm. (The Way, v.2.) Bibl. [BV4635.G413] 64-66113 1.75 pap.,
1. Theological virtues. I. Title.

Theological virtues—Biblical teaching.

BAAB, Otto Justice,
The theology of the Old Testament. New York, Abingdon Press [1960] 287p. 21cm. (Apex books, E-1) This is a reprint of the 1949 edition.
I. Title.

GUARDINI, Romano, 1885- 241
The word of God on faith, hope and charity. Translated by Stella Lange. Chicago, H. Regnery Co., 1963. 113 p. 21 cm. Translation of Drei Schriftauslegungen. [BV4635.G813] 63-12895
1. Theological virtues — Biblical teaching. I. Title.

THEOLOGY of the Old Testament. William G. Heidt, translator. [Collegeville, Minn.] Liturgical Press, 1956. xx, 476p.
I. Heinisch, Paul, 1878-

A theology word book of the Bible. New York, Macmillan, 1956 [c1950] 290p.
I. Richardson, Alan, 1905- ed.

A theology word book of the Bible. New York, Macmillan, 1956 [c1950] 290p.
I. Richardson, Alan, 1905- ed.

Theologicans—France—Tours—Biography.

MACDONALD, Allan John Macdonald, 1887- 230'.2'0924 B
Berengar and the reform of sacramental doctrine / by A. J. Macdonald. Merrick, N.Y. : Richwood Pub. Co., [1977] xii, 444 p. ; 23 cm. Reprint of the 1930 ed. published by Longmans, Green, London. Includes index. Bibliography: p. [415]-430. [BX4705.B32M3 1977] 77-10031 ISBN 0-915172-25-9 lib.bdg. : 28.50
1. Berengarius, of Tours, 1000 (ca.)-1088. 2. Theologicans—France—Tours—Biography. 3. Tours—Biography. 4. Lord's Supper—History. I. Title.

Theology.

ALLEN, Alexander Viets Griswold, 1841-1908. 230
The continuity of Christian thought: a study of modern theology in the light of its history, by Alexander V. G. Allen ... Boston, New York, Houghton, Mifflin and company, 1884. xviii,438 p. 10 1/2 cm. Lectures delivered in Philadelphia on the foundation of the late John Bohlen, 1883. (botanic) medicine. Cf. Pref. [BT21.A4 1884] 4-4033
1. Theology. I. Title.

AMES, William, 1576-1633. 191
Technometry / William Ames ; translated, with introd. and commentary, by Lee W. Gibbs. Philadelphia : University of Pennsylvania Press, 1979. xii, 202 p. ; 24 cm. (The Twenty-fourth publication in the Haney Foundation series, University of Pennsylvania) Translation of Guilielmi Amesii Technometria. A revision of the translator's thesis, Harvard. Includes bibliographical references and index. [BR118.A4513 1979] 78-65117 ISBN 0-8122-7756-2 : 14.95
1. Theology. 2. Philosophy. I. Gibbs, Lee W. II. Title.

AUSTIN, William H. 230'.01
Waves, particles, and paradoxes [by] William H. Austin. Houston, Tex., William Marsh Rice University, 1967. 103 p. 23 cm. (Monograph in philosophy) (Rice University studies, v. 53, no. 2) Bibliographical references included in "Notes" (p. 99-103) [HS36.W65 vol. 53 no. 2] 67-9342
1. Theology. 2. Paradox. I. Title. II. Series. III. Series: William Marsh Rice University, Houston, Tex. Monograph in philosophy.

BELL, Hermon Fiske, 1880- 230
An introduction to theology, by Hermon F. Bell ... New York, The author [c1924] 205 p. 20 cm. [BT77.B45] 24-11893
I. Title.

BROWN, James 111.1
Kierkegaard, Heidegger, Buber and Barth: subject and object in modern theology. (Orig. title: Subject and object in modern theology.) New York, Collier [1962, c.1955] 192p. 18cm. (AS256Y) Bibl. .95 pap.,
1. Theology. 2. Religion—Philosophy. I. Title.

BROWN, James, minister.
Kierkegaard, Heidegger, Buber and Barth: Subject and object in modern theology. New York, Collier [1962, c1955] 192 p. 18 cm. (The Croall lectures, 1953) "Originally published as Subject and object in modern theology." On cover: Collier books. 64-7802
1. Theology. 2. Religion — Philosophy. I. Title. II. Title: Subject and object in modern theology. III. Series.

CARTER, Samuel Thomson, 1840-
Wanted--a theology, by Samuel T. Carter, D. D. New York and London, Funk & Wagnalls company, 1908. 144 p. 20 cm. 8-17230
I. Title.
Contents omitted.

CHENU, Marie Dominique, 1895- 201
Is theology a science? Translated from the French by A. H. N. Green-Armytage. [1st ed.] New York, Hawthorn Books [1959] 126p. 21cm. (The Twentieth century encyclopedia of Catholicism, v. 2. Section I: Knowledge and faith) Includes bibliography. [BR118.C433] 59-6732
1. Theology. I. Title.

CLARKE, James Freeman, 1810-1888.
Ten great religions: an essay in comparative theology. By James Freeman Clarke ... Boston, Houghton, Osgood and company, 1880. x, 528 p. front. 20 1/2 cm. 15-28218
I. Title.

CLARKE, William Newton, 1841-1912. 230.
The use of the Scriptures in theology; the Nathaniel William Taylor lectures for 1905 given before the Divinity school of Yale university, by William Newton Clarke ... New York, C. Scribner's sons, 1905. viii p., 1 l., 170 p. 19 cm. [BT78.C5] 5-29970
I. Title.

CONNER, J.M. 230
Outlines of Christian theology, or, Theological hints, by J.M. Conner ... Little Rock, Ark., Brown printing company, 1896. 309 p. 20 cm. [BT77.C73] 26-12103
1. Theology. I. Title.

CRANOR, Phoebe. 230
Why did God let grandpa die? / Phoebe Cranor. Minneapolis : Bethany Fellowship, c1976. 128 p. ; 18 cm. (Dimension books) [BR96.C72] 76-17737 ISBN 0-87123-603-6 pbk. : 1.95
1. Theology. 2. Children—Religious life. I. Title.

DAVIS, Humphrey. 133
A treatise by way of a dialogue on cause and effect, illustrating the true science of astronomy. Also electricity, attraction, animal magnetism, repulsion and the true science of theology ... By Humphrey Davis, jr. New Bedford [Mass.] Printed for the author, 1856. 56 p. 23 cm. [X3.D28] 23-3044
I. Title.

DELK, Edwin Heyl. 230
The need of a restatement of theology [by] Edwin Heyl Delk ... Philadelphia, Pa., The Lutheran publication society [c1917] iv, 5-57 p. 18 cm. "The substance of this essay was first given in a lecture to the students of the Lutheran theological seminary at Gettysburg, Pennsylvania. It was afterward expanded and appeared in printed from in the Lutheran quarterly."--Foreword. [BT80.D4] 17-21852 0.50
I. Title.

DEWEY, Robert D
The language of faith; a course for ninth and tenth grades. [Teacher's book.] Decorations by Roger Martin. Boston, United Press [1963] Boston, United Church Press [1963] 126 p. illus. 26 cm. 96 p. illus. 21 cm. 65-98376
1. Theology. I. Title. II. Title: [Student's resource book]

DRUMMOND, Henry, 1851-1897. 261
The new evangelism, and other addresses, by Henry Drummond ... New York, Dodd, Mead and company, 1899. 5 p. l., [3]-284 p. 19 1/2 cm. [BR85.D75] 99-5823
1. Theology. 2. Natural selection. 3. Christianity. 4. Regeneration, (Theology) 5. Missions, Foreign. 6. Religion and science. 7. Soul. I. Title.
Contents omitted.

*DUDDE, John H. 208.1
Truth is the word of God; theological realism. St. Petersburg, Fla., Great Outdoors [c.1964] 199p. 22cm. 1.50 pap.,
I. Title.

DUDDLE, John H 1889-
Truth is the word of God; theological realism. St. Petersburg, Fla., Great Outdoors Pub. Co. [1964] 199 p. 23 cm. 67-8959
I. Title.

DWIGHT E. Stevenson : 230
a tribute by some of his former students / editor, William R. Barr. Lexington, Ky. : Lexington Theological Seminary, 1975. 67 p. ; 25 cm. On spine: Stevenson tribute volume. Contents.Contents.—White, R. C.

Dwight E. Stevenson, teacher of preachers.—Reid, M. K. On identifying the word of God today.—Spainhower, J. I. It occurs to me.—Blanton, Betty L. God's continuing incarnation through us.—Wilson, G. H. Always a pilgrim?—Barr, W. R. The presentation of Christ.—Pierson, R. M. A selected listing of some of the literary productions of Dwight E. and Deloris Stevenson. Includes bibliographical references. [BR50.D85] 75-330964
1. Stevenson, Dwight Eshelman, 1906- 2. Stevenson, Dwight Eshelman, 1906- — Bibliography. 3. Theology. I. Stevenson, Dwight Eshelman, 1906- II. Barr, William R. III. Title: Stevenson tribute volume.

DWIGHT, Timothy, 1752-1817. 260
Theology; explained and defended, in a series of sermons; by Timothy Dwight...with a Memoir of the life of the author... 9th ed. New Haven, T. Dwight & son, 1836. 4 v. 23 cm. Memoir by the author's son, Sereno E. Dwight. [BT75.D9 1836] 27-7863
1. Theology. I. Dwight, Sereno Edwards, 1786-1850, ed. II. Title.

EBELING, Gerhard, 1912- 201'.1
The study of theology / Gerhard Ebeling ; translated by Duane A. Priebe. [Philadelphia : Fortress Press, 1978] p. cm. Translation of Studium der Theologie. Bibliography: p. [BR118.E2413] 78-5393 ISBN 0-8006-0529-2 pbk. : 9.95
1. Theology. I. Title.

EICKENBERG, Charles. 016.
Twelve object lessons of Scripture ... By Charles Eickenberg, illustrated by Naomi Frances Kim. [Chicago, Langston press, c1922] v. illus. 16 1/2 cm. [BV1535.E5] ca23
I. Title.

FISHER, Neal F. 1936- 230'.76
(Neal Floyd),
Context for discovery / Neal F. Fisher. Nashville : Abingdon, c1981. p. cm. (Into our third century) [BT75.2.F57] 19 81-7929 ISBN 0-687-09620-0 pbk. : 4.50
1. Theology. 2. Theology, Methodist. I. Title. II. Series.

FORSYTH, Peter Taylor, 1848-
Theology in church and state, by Peter Taylor Forsyth ... New York and London, Hodder and Stoughton, 1915. xxvi, 328 p. 20 1/2 cm. 16-12554
I. Title.

FOX, Douglas A., 1927- 201'.1
Mystery and meaning : personal logic and the language of religion / Douglas A. Fox. Philadelphia : Westminster Press, [1975] 189 p. ; 21 cm. Includes bibliographical references. [BR118.F74] 75-15738 ISBN 0-664-24768-7 pbk. : 4.95
1. Theology. I. Title.

*FUNK, Robert W., ed. 208
Journal for theology and the church, v.2: translating theology into the modern age, ed. [by] Robert W. Funk [others. Tr. from German by Charles E. Carleston, others] New York, Harper [c.]1965. 179p. 21cm. (Harper torchbks., Cloister lib., TB252L) 1.95 pap.,
I. Title.

*FUNK, Robert W., ed. 208
Journal for theology and the church; 1 [Magnolia, Mass., P. Smith, 1966, c.] 1965. xi, 183p. 21cm. (Harper torchbk., Cloister lib. rebound) Orig. pub. in Tubingen by J. C. B. Mohr (Paul Siebeck) 4.00
I. Title.
Contents omitted.

*FUNK, Robert W., ed. 208
Journal for theology and the church; v.2. Edit. bd.: Robert W. Funk [others] [Magnolia, Mass., P. Smith, 1966, c.1965] (Torchbks., Cloister lib., TB252L rebound) Tr. from German by Charles E. Carlston, others Contents.contents—v. 2 Translating theology into the modern age Bibl. 4.00
I. Title.

GOD, secularization, and 201'.1
history; essays in memory of Ronald Gregor Smith. Edited by Eugene Thomas Long. [1st ed.] Columbia, University of South Carolina Press [1974] xii, 161 p. 22 cm. [BR50.G545] 73-15712 ISBN 0-87249-293-1 7.95
1. Smith, Ronald Gregor. 2. Smith, Ronald Gregor—Bibliography. 3. Theology. I. Smith, Ronald Gregor. II. Long, Eugene Thomas, ed.
Contents omitted.

GROFF, Warren F. 248'.48'65
Story time : God's story and ours / Warren F. Groff. Elgin, Ill. : Brethren Press, [1974] 141 p. ; 18 cm. Includes bibliographical references. [BR118.G68] 74-23540 ISBN 0-87178-815-2
1. Theology. 2. Christian life—Church of the Brethren authors. I. Title.

HEBBLETHWAITE, Brian. 291.2
The problems of theology / Brian Hebblethwaite. Cambridge [Eng.] ; New York : Cambridge University Press, 1980. viii, 164 p. ; 21 cm. Includes index. Bibliography: p. 158-161. [BR118.H423] 79-41812 ISBN 0-521-23104-3 : 19.50 ISBN 0-521-29811-3 pbk. : 6.95
1. Theology. I. Title.

HENRY, Carl Ferdinand 230 s
Howard, 1913-
God who speaks and shows : / Carl F. H. Henry. Waco, Tex. : Word Books, c1976- v. in ; 24 cm. (His God, revelation, and authority ; v. 1-) Contents.Contents.—[1] Preliminary considerations.—[2] Fifteen theses. v. Includes bibliographies and indexes. [BR1640.A25H45 vol. 1-2, etc.] [BR118] 230 77-353143 12.95
1. Theology. 2. Christianity—Philosophy. 3. Revelation. I. Title.

HILTNER, Seward, 1909- 200'.1
Theological dynamics. Nashville, Abingdon Press [1972] 224 p. 24 cm. Includes bibliographical references. [BR118.H53] 76-186829 ISBN 0-687-41465-2 5.75
1. Theology. 2. Psychology, Religious. I. Title.

HOLMES, Thomas, D.D.
Light in dark places; theological nuts, philosophically cracked, on the rock of the Scriptures, with the hammer of common sense. Ann Arbor, Mich., The Inland press, 1898. xxi, [1], 285 p. port. 12. Aug
I. Title.

HOVEY, Alvah, 1820-
Manual of Christian theology. 2d ed. New York, Boston [etc.] Silver, Burdett & co. [1900] xxvii, 472 p. 8° Nov
I. Title.

HOVEY, Alvah, 1820-1903. 260
Manual of systematic theology, and Christian ethics. By Alvah Hovey... Philadelphia, New York [etc.] American Baptist publication society [18-] vii, [1], [9] -437 p.23 cm. Reprint of 1877 edition, with addition of a "Scriptural index" by E. F. Merriam. [BT75.H813] 20-23089
1. Theology. 2. Christian ethics. I. Title.

HOVEY, Alvah, 1820-1903. 260
Manual of systematic theology, and Christian ethics. By Alvah Hovey... Boston, 1877. vii, [1], [9]-416 p. 24 cm. [BT75.H8] 20-23091
1. Theology. 2. Christian ethics. I. Title.

HYDE, William De Witt, 1858- 225
1917.
Outlines of social theology, by William De Witt Hyde ... New York and London, Macmillan and co., 1895. ix, 260 p. 20 cm. [BR121.H9] 12-34543
I. Title. II. Title: Social theology, Outlines of.

JOHANNES VON KASTL, 15thcent.
Unpublished theological writings of Johannes Castellensis [edited by] Clemens Stroick. Ottawa, University of Ottawa Press, 1964. ix, 200 p. (Universite d'Ottawa. Publications seriees, 73) 64-52707
I. Stroick, Clemens. II. Title.

JOHNSON, Early Ashby, 1917- 230
The crucial task of theology. Richmond, John Knox Press [1958] 222p. 21cm. Includes bibliography. [BT40.J6] 58-7773
1. Theology. 2. Knowledge, Theory of (Religion) I. Title.

JOURNAL for Theology and 220.08
the Church; v. 1. [Tr. from German] Edit. bd.: Robert W. Funk, chm.; Frank M. Cross [others] Ed.: Robert W. Funk. Tubingen, J. C. B. Mohr; New York, Harper [c.1965] 183p. 21cm. (Harper torchbks.; the cloister lib./TB251L) Contents.v. 1. The Bultmann school of biblical interpretation: new directions. Bibl. 1.95 pap.,

KAINZ, Howard P., 1933- 230
Wittenberg, revisited : a polymorphous critique of religion and theology / Howard P. Kainz. Washington, D.C. : University Press of America, c1981. 214 p. ; 23 cm. Includes bibliographical references. [BX1751.2.K28 1981] 19 81-40729 ISBN 0-8191-1949-0 : 20.75 ISBN 0-8191-1950-4 pbk. : 10.25
1. Catholic Church—Doctrinal and controversial works. 2. Bible—Meditations. 3. Theology. 4. Religion. I. Title.

LATOURELLE, Rene. 201
Theology: science of salvation. Translated by Mary Dominic. Staten Island, N.Y., Alba House [1969] xii, 276 p. 22 cm. Translation of Theologie, science du salut. Includes bibliographies. [BR118.L313] 79-94697 5.95
1. Theology. I. Title.

MCCONNELL, Francis John, 225
bp., 1871-
... *Public opinion and theology,* by Francis John McConnell... New York, Cincinnati, The Abingdon press [c1920] 259 p. 19 1/2 cm. (The Earl lectures of the Pacific school of religion, 1920) [BR121.M253] 20-9414
I. Title.

MAINS, George Preston, 1844- 225
1930.
Modern thought and traditional faith, by George Preston Mains. New York, Eaton & Mains; Cincinnati, Jennings & Graham [c1911] xxi, 279 p. 22 1/2 cm. Bibliography: p. 269-271. [BR121.M352] 11-2008
1. Theology. I. Title.

MAN and his happiness;
by a group of theologians; translated by Charles Miltner. Chicago, Ill., Fides [1956] xxxix, 420p. 20cm. (Theology Library, 3) Includes bibliography.
I. Henry, Antonin Marcel, 1911- ed.

MICKS, Marianne H. 230
Introduction to theology. New York, Seabury [1967,c.1964] xiv, 204p. 21cm. (SP40) [BT77.M524] 64-19622 2.25 pap.,
1. Theology. I. Title.

NELSON, Levi, 1779-1855.
Letters to the Christian public, concerning unscriptural speculations in theology. By Levi Nelson ... Hartford, Press of Case, Tiffany and company, 1851. 128 p. 22 cm. [BX7139.N4] 25-12617
I. Title.

*NEWMAN, Paul S., comp. 230
In God we trust; America's heritage of faith. compiled by Paul S. Newman. Designed by Herman Zuckerman. Norwalk, Conn., Published by the C. R. Gibson Company, [1974] 89 p. col. illus. 21 cm. Bibliography: p. 89 [BT77] 73-88091 ISBN 0-8378-1754-4 3.95
1. Theology 2. United States—Social life and customs. I. Title.

PANNENBERG, Wolfhart, 230'.01
1928-
Theology and the philosophy of science / by Wolfhart Pannenberg ; translated by Francis McDonagh. Philadelphia : Westminster Press, c1976. p. cm. Translation of Wissenschaftstheorie und Theologie. Includes index. [BR118.P2713 1976] 76-20763 ISBN 0-664-21337-5 : 17.50
1. Theology. 2. Religion and science—1946- I. Title.

POTTHOFF, Harvey H. 230.7
Current theological thinking: an elective unit for adults, with Leader's guide by Howard M. Ham. Nashville, Abingdon [1963, c.1962] 64p. 23cm. .75 pap.,
I. Title.

POTTHOFF, Harvey H. 230.7
Current theological thinking: an elective unit for adults, with Leader's guide by Howard M. Ham. Nashville, Abingdon [1963, c.1962] 64p. 23cm. .75 pap.,
I. Title.

PROCELUS, Lycius, surnamed
Diadochus.
"Divine arithmetic" a subject long since forgotten. A translation by A. C. Ionides. London, John Lane; New York, John Lane company, 1917. 138 p. 23 cm. Added t.-p.: The elements of theology, by Proclus. E 19
1. Theology. I. Ionides, A. C., tr. II. Title.

REVUE de theologie et de 205
philosophie; ser. 1, v. 1-44, 1868-1911. Geneve, H. Georg. 1868-1911, New York, Johnson Reprint, 1966. 44v. (various p.) 21cm. 1,230.00; 1.100.000; 25.00 set, set, pap., ea., pap.,

SELTZER, Lewis B. 1847-
Truth, not legend; reason, not superstition; by Louis B. Seltzer. Boston, The Roxburgh publishing co. [c1912] 1 p. l., 5-124 p. 20 cm. $1.00 12-25096
I. Title.

SHEETS, William B. 211
God and church apart, by W. B. Sheets; the two theologies, natural theology, scriptural theology ... [Quincy, Ill., The Royal printing co., inc., c1925] 63 p. 21 1/2 cm. [BL2780.S5] 25-15858
I. Title.

SHEETS, William B. 211
God and church apart, by W. B. Sheets ... Rev. ed. ... [Quincy, Ill., The Royal printing co., inc., c1926] 96 p. 23 cm. [BL2780.S5 1926] 27-11312
I. Title.

SHINN, Asa, 1781-1853. 231.8
On the benevolence and rectitude of the Supreme Being. By Asa Shinn ... Baltimore, Book committee of the Methodist Protestant church; Philadelphia, J. Kay, jun. & brother, 1840. x, 11-408 p. 20 cm. [BT160.S5] 40-23730
1. Theology. I. Title.

SLOAN, Harold Paul. 220
Historic Christianity and the new theology, by Harold Paul Sloan... Louisville, Ky., Pentecostal publishing company, 1922. 208 p. 19 1/2 cm. [BR125.S54] 23-13027
I. Title.

SLOAN, Harold Paul. 220
Historic Christianity and the new theology, by Harold Paul Sloan... Louisville, Ky., Pentecostal publishing company, 1922. 208 p. 19 1/2 cm. [BR125.S54] 23-13027
I. Title.

SONG, Choan-Seng, 1929- 230
The compassionate God / C.S. Song. Maryknoll, NY : Orbis Books, c1982. xiii, 284 p. ; 24 cm. Includes bibliographical references and index. [BR118.S66] 19 81-16972 ISBN 0-88344-095-4 pbk. : 12.95
1. Theology. 2. Religions. I. Title.

TAYLOR, T. B. 236
Old theology turned upside down or right side up; by a Methodist preacher; or, Eight lectures:--six on the resurrection of the dead, one on the second coming of Christ, and one on the last day judgment ... By Rev. T. B. Taylor ... Fort Scott, Kans., Monitor publishing company, 1871. 209 p., 1 l., 18 1/2 cm. "The magnetic forces of the universe": p. 171-209. [BT821.T26 1871] 26-12108
I. Title.

THEOLOGIA deutsch. 242
Theologia germanica: which setteth forth many fair lineaments of divine truth, and faith very lofty and lovely things touching a perfect life. Ed. by Dr. Pfeiffer from the only complete manuscript yet known. Tr. from the German by Susanna Winkworth. With a preface by the Rev. Charles Kingsley ... and a letter to the translator by the Chevalier Bunsen ... and an introduction by Professor Calvin E. Stowe, D.D. Andover, W. F. Draper; Boston, J. P. Jewett & co., 1856. lxxii, 203 p. 18 cm. [BV4834.T47 1856] 16-24025
I. Pfeiffer, Franz, 1815-1868, ed. II. Winkworth, Susanna, 1820-1884, tr. III. Title.

THEOLOGY, a course for 260
college students. [Syracuse? N.Y., 1952- v. 24 cm. Contents. -- v. 1. Christ as Prophet and King [by] J. J. Fernan. [BX904.T45] 52-4093
1. Theology. 2. Catholic Church — Doctrinal and controversial works.

THOMAS Aquinas, Saint, 1225?-1274. 230.
The "Summa theologica" of St. Thomas Aquinas ... literally translated by Fathers of the English Dominican province ... London [etc.] R. & T. Washburne, ltd.; New York [etc.] Benziger brothers; [etc., etc.] 1912-25. 21 v. 21 cm. The Supplement "was compiled probably by Fra Raimalde da Piperno."--pt. III, no. 4, p. 98. Imprint varies slightly; later volumes have London, Burns, Oates & Washburne, ltd.; [etc., etc.] [BX1749.T5] 29-30635
I. Dominicans in Great Britain. II. Reginaldus de Piperno, 13th cent. III. Title.

THORNTON, Martin. 201
The function of theology. [New York] Seabury Press [1968] 184 p. 23 cm. (The Library of practical theology) [BR118.T5 1968b] 68-25318 3.95
1. Theology. I. Title.

TICHENOR, Henry M. 211
Tales of theology, Jehovah, Satan and the Christian creed, by Henry M. Tichenor. St. Louis, Mo., The Melting pot publishing co. [c1918] 2 p. l., 580 p. front. (port.) 18 1/2 cm. $2.50. [BL2775.T55] 19-68
I. Title.

TILLICH, Paul, 1886- 230.4
Ultimate concern; Tillich in dialogue. [Ed. by] D. Mackenzie Brown. New York, Harper [1965] xvi, 234p. 22cm. Ed. from tape recordings made during a seminar held at Union of Calif, Santa Barbara, in the spring of 1964. Bibl. [BX4811.T5] 65-15389 3.95
1. Theology. 2. Protestantism. I. Brown, Donald Mackenzie, 1908- ed. II. California. University, Santa Barbara. III. Title. IV. Title: Tillich in dialogue.

WOLFARD, Nathan Dordwin, 1852.
Popular manual of theology. by Nathan D. Wolfard ... Reading, Pa., I. M. Beaver, 1908. viii, [9]-181 p. front. (port.) 20 1/2 cm. 8-20331
I. Title.

Theology—16th century.

BORNKAMM, Heinrich, 1901- 230.4
The heart of Reformation faith; the fundamental axioms of Evangelical belief. Translated by John W. Doberstein. [1st ed.] New York, Harper & Row [1965] 126 p. 22 cm. Translation of Das bleibende Recht der Reformation. Bibliographical references included in "Notes" (p. 123-124) [BT27.B613] 65-15388
1. Theology—16th century. 2. Protestantism. I. Title.

HODGSON, Francis, 1805-1877.
An examination of the system of new divinity; or, New school theology. By Rev. Francis Hodgson ... New York, T. Mason and G. Lane, 1839. 416 p. 19 cm. 17-17496
I. Title.

PAUCK, Wilhelm, 1901- comp. 230.4'1
Melanchthon and Bucer. Philadelphia, Westminster Press [1969] xx, 406 p. 24 cm. (The Library of Christian classics, v. 19) Contents.Contents.—Loci communes theologici, by P. Melanchthon.—De regno Christi, by M. Bucer.—Selected bibliography (p. 395-399) [BR336.L62 1969] 69-12309 ISBN 6-642-20193- 7.50
1. Theology—16th century. I. Melanchthon, Philipp, 1497-1560. Loci communes theologici. II. Butzer, Martin, 1491-1551. De regno Christi. III. Title. IV. Series.

Theology—17th century—Bibliography.

WILLIAMS, William Proctor, 1939- 016.283'092'4 B
Jeremy Taylor, 1700-1976 : an annotated checklist / compiled by William P. Williams. New York : Garland Pub., 1979. p. cm. (Garland reference library of the humanities ; v. 177) Includes indexes. [Z8861.8.W54] [BX5199.T3] 78-68302 ISBN 0-8240-9756-4 : 12.00
1. Taylor, Jeremy, Bp. of Down and Connor, 1613-1667—Bibliography. 2. Theology—17th century—Bibliography. 3. Theology, Anglican—Bibliography. I. Title.

Theology—19th century

PFLEIDERER, Otto, 1839-1908. 209
The development of theology in Germany since Kant; and its progress in Great Britain since 1825, by Otto Pfleiderer ... Translated under the author's supervision by J. Frederick Smith. 2d ed., with an appendix. London, S. Sonnenschein & co.; New York, Macmillan & co., 1893. 2 p. l., ix-xii, 456 p. 24 cm. [Library of philosophy, ed. by J. H. Muirhead] [BT27.P5 1898] 35-32563
1. Theology—19th cent. I. Smith, John Frederick, tr. II. Title.

PFLEIDERER, Otto, 1839-1908. 209
The development of theology in Germany since Kant and its progress in Great Britain since 1825, by Otto Pfleiderer ... Translated under the author's supervision by J. Frederick Smith. 3d ed., with an appendix. London, S. Sonnenschein & co., ltd.; New York, The Macmillan co., 1909. 2 p. l., ix-xii, 456 p. 24 cm. [Library of philosophy, ed. by J. H. Muirhead] [BT27.P5 1909] 10-7941
1. Theology—19th cent. I. Smith, John Frederick, tr. II. Title.

PFLEIDERER, Otto, 1839-1908. 230
The development of theology in Germany since Kant and its progress in Great Britain since 1825, by Otto Pfleiderer ... Translated under the author's supervision by J. Frederick Smith. London, G. Allen & Unwin, ltd.; New York, The Macmillan company [1923?] viii, 456 p. 23 cm. (Half-title: Library of philosophy, ed. by J. H. Muirhead) "First published October 1890, second edition March 1896, third edition July 1909, reprinted September 1923." On jacket: Fourth impression. [BT27.P5 1923] 35-23985
1. Theology—19th cent. I. Smith, John Frederick, tr. II. Title.

Theology—19th century—Bibliography.

MCCULLOH, Gerald W. 016.23
A bibliography of dissertations in nineteenth century theology, 1960-1976, accepted by doctoral institutions in the United States and Canada / Gerald W. McCulloh. [s.l.] : McCulloh, c1976. iii, 29 leaves ; 28 cm. Includes index. [Z7751.M14] [BR45] 77-362608
1. Theology—19th century—Bibliography. 2. Religions—Bibliography. 3. Dissertations, Academic—United States—Bibliography. 4. Dissertations, Academic—Canada—Bibliography. I. Title: A bibliography of dissertations in nineteenth century theology, 1960-1976 ...

Theology—20th century

AUBREY, Edwin Ewart, 1896- 230
Living the Christian faith [by] Edwin Ewart Aubrey ... New York, The Macmillan company, 1939. xi p., 1 l., 118 p. 20 cm. "Published March, 1939. First printing." [BR479.A8] 39-10090
1. Theology—20th cent. 2. Christianity—20th cent. I. Title.
Contents ommitted.

BERGER, Peter L. 200'.1
The heretical imperative : contemporary possibilities of religious affirmation / Peter L. Berger. 1st ed. Garden City, N.Y. : Anchor Press, 1979. xv, 220 p. ; 22 cm. Includes bibliographical references and index. [BT28.B43 1979] 78-20106 ISBN 0-385-14286-2 : 9.95
1. Theology—20th century. 2. Religion and sociology. 3. Experience (Religion) 4. Religions. I. Title.

CARMODY, John, 1939- 230'.009'047
Theology for the 1980s / by John Carmody. 1st ed. Philadelphia : Westminster Press, c1980. p. cm. Includes index. Bibliography: p. [BT28.C35] 19 80-19349 ISBN 0-664-24345-2 : 9.50
1. Theology—20th century. I. Title.

CHAMPION, John Benjamin, 1868- 260
More than atonement: a study in genetic theology, by John B. Champion ... Harrisburg, Pa., The Evangelical press [c1927] 459 p. 24 cm. [BT75.C3] 27-17090
I. Title.

CHRISTIANITY and the contemporary scene, edited by Randolph Crump Miller and Henry H. Shires. Jubilee volume on the fiftieth anniversary of the Church divinity school of the Pacific, Berkeley, California, 1943. New York, Morehouse-Gorham co. [1943] vii, 231 p. 22 cm. Bibliography at end of most of the essays. [BR479.C395] 43-15823 204
1. Theology—20th cent. 2. Berkeley, Calif. Church divinity school of the Pacific. I. Miller, Randolph Crump, 1910- ed. II. Shires, Henry Herbert, 1886- joint ed.
Contents omitted.

CONNOLLY, James M. 230.2
The voices of France; a survey of contemporary theology in France. New York, Macmillan [c.]1961. 231p. Bibl. 61-6686 5.50
1. Theology—20th cent. 2. Catholic Church—Doctrinal and controversial works. 3. Theologians, French. I. Title.

DILLENBERGER, John. 230'.09
Contours of faith; changing forms of Christian thought. Nashville, Abingdon Press [1969] 176 p. 21 cm. Bibliography: p. 166-168. [BT80.D47] 69-18451 ISBN 0-687-09588-3 4.00
1. Theology—20th century. 2. Theology, Doctrinal—History—Modern period, 1500- I. Title.

FACKRE, Gabriel J. 201
Humiliation and celebration; post-radical themes in doctrine, morals, and mission, by Gabriel Fackre. New York, Sheed and Ward [1969] viii, 307 p. 22 cm. Includes bibliographical references. [BT28.F3] 72-82605 6.95
1. Theology—20th century. I. Title.

HAMILTON, Kenneth 230.0904
Revolt against heaven; an enquiry into anti-supernaturalism. Grand Rapids, Mich., Eerdmans [1966,c.1965] 193p. 21cm. Bibl. [BT28.H3] 65-25189 2.45 pap.,
1. Theology —20th cent. I. Title.

HAMILTON, William, 1924- 230
The new essence of Christianity. [Rev. ed.] New York, Association Press [1966] 159 p. 20 cm. Includes bibliographical references. [BR481.H25 1966] 66-18857
1. Theology—20th century. 2. Christianity—20th century. I. Title.

HAMILTON, William, 1924- 230
On taking God out of the dictionary. New York, McGraw-Hill [1974] 255 p. 23 cm. [BR481.H26] 73-19691 ISBN 0-07-025802-3 8.95
1. Theology—20th century. 2. Christianity—20th century. I. Title.

HAMILTON, William Hughes, 1924- 208.1
The new essence of Christianity. New York, Association [c.1961] 159p. Bibl. 61-14172 3.00 bds.,
1. Theology—20th cent. 2. Christianity—20th cent. I. Title.

HARVEY, Van Austin 230.0904
The historian and the believer; the morality of historical knowledge and Christian belief. New York, Macmillan [c.1966] xv,301p. 22cm. Bibl. [BT28.H34] 66-14692 6.95
1. Theology—20th cent. 2. Bible—Criticism, interpretation, etc.—Hist. 3. History—Philosophy. I. Title.

HENRY, Carl Ferdinand Howard, 1913- ed. 230.082
Christian faith and modern theology: contemporary evangelical thought [by] J. Oliver Buswell, Jr. [and others] Edited by Carl F. H. Henry. [1st ed.] New York, Channel Press [1964] xi, 426 p. 25 cm. Bibliography: p. 421-426. [BR118.H45] 63-23360
1. Theology—20th cent. 2. Evangelicalism. I. Buswell, James Oliver. II. Title. III. Title: Contemporary evangelical thought.

HENRY, Carl Ferdinand Howard, 1913- ed. 230.04
Contemporary evangelical thought [by] Andrew W. Blackwood [and others] Great Neck, N. Y., Channel Press [1957] 320p. 24cm. Includes bibliography. [BR118.H46] 57-7630
1. Theology—20th cent. 2. Evangelicalism. I. Title.

HENRY, Carl Ferdinand Howard, 1913- 253
Evangelical responsibility in contemporary theology. Grand Rapids, Eerdmans [1957] 89 p. 19 cm. (Pathway books; a series of contemporary evangelical studies) [B479.H44] 57-13036
1. Theology—20th cent. 2. Evangelicalism. I. Title.

HENRY, Carl Ferdinand Howard, 1913- 230.01
Frontiers in modern theology Chicago, Moody [1966. c1964. 1965] 160p. 18cm. (Christian forum bks.) Bibl. [BT28.H394 1966] 66-6298 1.45 pap.,
1. Theology—20th cent. I. Title.

HERZOG, Frederick. 261
Justice church : the new function of the church in North American Christianity / Frederick Herzog. Maryknoll, N.Y. : Orbis Books, [1980] p. cm. Includes bibliographical references. [BT28.H43] 80-15091 ISBN 0-88344-249-3 pbk. : 6.95
1. Theology—20th century. 2. Church. 3. Liberation theology. I. Title.

HUGHES, Philip Edgcumbe, ed. 230.08
Creative minds in contemporary theology; a guidebook to the principal teachings of Karl Barth, G. C. Berkouwer, Emil Brunner, Rudolf Bultmann, Oscar Cullmann, James Denney, C. H. Dodd, Herman Dooyeweerd, P. T. Forsyth, Charles Gore, Reinhold Niebuhr, Pierre Teilhard de Chardin, and Paul Tillich. Grand Rapids, Eerdmans [1966] 488 p. 24 cm. Includes bibliographies. [BT28.H8] 64-22029
1. Theology—20th century. I. Title.

HUGHES, Philip Edgcumbe, ed. 230'.0922
Creative minds in contemporary theology; a guidebook to the principal teachings of Karl Barth, G. C. Berkouwer, Dietrich Bonhoeffer, Emil Brunner, Rudolf Bultmann, Oscar Cullmann, James Denney, C. H. Dodd., Herman Dooyeweerd, P. T. Forsyth, Charles Gore, Reinhold Niebuhr, Pierre Teilhard de Chardin, and Paul Tillich. 2d, rev. ed. Grand Rapids, Eerdmans [1969] 522 p. 24 cm. Includes bibliographies. [BT28.H8 1969] 74-3017 6.95
1. Theology—20th century. I. Title.

LIGHTNER, Robert Paul. 230
Neo-evangelicalism. Findlay, Ohio, Dunham Pub. Co. [1961?] 170p. 20cm. Includes bibliography. [BR479.L5] 62-37726
1. Theology—20th cent. 2. Evangelicalism. I. Title.

LIGHTNER, Robert Paul 230
Neo-evangelism [2d ed.] Des Plaines, Ill., Regular Baptist Pr. [1965] 190p. 20cm. Bibl. [BR479.L5] 65-3741 2.95
1. Theology—20th cent. 2. Evangelism. I. Title.

MCCLENDON, James William. 280'.4'0922
Pacemakers of Christian thought. Nashville, Broadman Press [1962] 68p. 20cm. (A Broadman starbook) Includes bibliography. [BX4825.M3] 62-9198
1. Theology—20th cent. 2. Theologians. I. Title.

MCCOY, Charles S. 200'.1
When gods change : hope for theology / Charles S. McCoy. Nashville : Abingdon, c1980. 255 p. ; 22 cm. Includes bibliographical references and index. [BT28.M24] 79-27890 ISBN 0-687-45000-4 pbk. : 7.95
1. Theology—20th century. 2. Pluralism (Social sciences) 3. Liberty. I. Title.

MACFARLAND, Charles Stedman, 1866- 016.62
The Christian faith in a day of crisis, by Charles S. Macfarland... New York [etc.] Fleming H. Revell company [c1939] 2 p. l., 7-226 p. 19 1/2 cm. Book reviews. Bibliography: p. 223. [BR479.M24] 39-10370
1. Theology—20th cent. 2. Religious

thought—20th cent. 3. Books—Reviews. I. Title.

MACFARLAND, Charles Stedman, 1866- 016.62
Contemporary Christian thought, by Charles S. Macfarland... New York [etc.] Fleming H. Revell company [c1936] viii, 204 p. 19 1/2 cm. Book reviews. Bibliography: p. [197]-199. [BR479.M25] 36-3818
1. Theology—20th cent. 2. Religious thought—20th cent. 3. Books—Reviews. I. Title.

MACFARLAND, Charles Stedman, 1866- 230
Current religious thought: a digest, by Charles S. Macfarland... New York, London [etc.] Fleming H. Revell company [c1941] 185 p. 19 1/2 cm. "Volumes discussed": p. 9-10. [BR479.M253] 41-8454
1. Theology—20th cent. 2. Religious thought—20th cent. 3. Books—Reviews. I. Title.

MCFARLAND, Charles Stedman, 1866- 200
A digest of Christian thinking, by Charles S. Macfarland... New York [etc.] Fleming H. Revell co. [1942] 192 p. 19 cm. "Volumes surveyed": p. 11-12. [BR479.M255] 42-14257
1. Theology—20th cent. 2. Religious thought—20th cent. 3. Books—Reviews. I. Title.

MACFARLAND, Charles Stedman, 1866- 016.62
A survey of religious literature ... by Charles S. Macfarland ... New York, London [etc.] Fleming H. Revell company [1943] 157 p. 19 cm. "Volumes surveyed": p. 11-12. [BR479.M258] 43-16426
1. Theology—20th cent. 2. Religious thought—20th cent. 3. Books—Reviews. I. Title.

MACFARLAND, Charles Stedman, 1866- 016.62
Trends of Christian thinking, by Charles S. Macfarland... New York [etc.] Fleming H. Revell company [c1937] 207 p. 19 1/2 cm. Book reviews. Bibliography: p. 201-202. [BR479.M26] 37-5963
1. Theology—20th cent. 2. Religious thought—20th cent. 3. Books—Reviews. I. Title.

MARLE, Rene. 230
Identifying Christianity / by Rene Marle ; translated by Jeanne Marie Lyons. St. Meinrad, Ind. : Abbey Press, 1975. xi, 175 p. ; 21 cm. (A Priority edition) Translation of La Singularite chretienne. Includes bibliographical references. [BT28.M27713] 75-209 ISBN 0-87029-043-6 : 4.75
1. Theology—20th century. I. Title.

MARSH, Spencer. 209'.73
God, man, and Archie Bunker / Spencer Marsh ; foreword by Carroll O'Connor. 1st ed. New York : Harper & Row, [1975] xiv, 104 p., [1] leaf of plates : ill. ; 21 cm. [BT28.M279 1975b] 74-25694 ISBN 0-06-065423-6 : 5.95 ISBN 0-06-065422-8 pbk. : 2.95
1. All in the family. 2. Theology—20th century. I. Title.

MORGAN, John Vyrnwy, 1860- ed. 230
Theology at the dawn of the twentieth century; essays on the present status of Christianity and its doctrines; edited with an introduction by J. Vyrnwy Morgan, D.D. Boston, Small, Maynard & company, 1901. xiiv, 544 p. 24 cm. [BR479.M7] 1-11879
1. Theology—20th cent. I. Title.

NASH, Arnold Samuel, ed. 200
Protestant thought in the twentieth century: whence & whither? New York, Macmillan, 1951. xii, 296 p. 21 cm. Contents.Contents.—America at the end of the Protestant era, by A. S. Nash. —The study of the Old Testament, by G. E. Wright.—The study of the New Testament, by F. V. Filson.—The philosophy of religion, by G. F. Thomas.—Systematic theology, by W. M. Horton.—Christian ethics by W. Beach and J. C. Bennett.—Church history, by G. H. Williams.—Pastoral theology and psychology, by S. Hiltner.—Preaching, by C. W. Gilkey.—Christian education, by H. S. Smith.—Reunion and the ecumenical movement, by H. S. Leiper.—Christianity and other religions, by J. A. Mackay. Includes bibliographies. [BR479.N3] 51-11218
1. Theology—20th century. 2. Protestantism. 3. Religious thought—20th century. I. Title.

O'BRIEN, Elmer ed. 230.209045
Theology in transition; a bibliographical evaluation of the 'decisive decade,' 1954-1964 [New York] Herder & Herder [1965] 282p. 22cm. (Contemp. theol., v.1) Bibl. [BT28.O2] 65-13486 5.95
1. Theology—20th cent. 2. Theology—Bibl. I. Title.

ODEN, Thomas C. 230
Agenda for theology / Thomas C. Oden. 1st ed. San Francisco : Harper & Row, c1979. xiii, 176 p. ; 21 cm. Bibliography: p. 171-176. [BT28.O33 1979] 78-19506 ISBN 0-06-066347-2 pbk. : 7.95
1. Theology—20th century. I. Title.

O'MEARA, Thomas F., 1935- 230'.09'04
Projections; shaping an American theology for the future. Edited by Thomas F. O'Meara and Donald M. Weisser. [1st ed.] Garden City, N.Y., Doubleday, 1970. vi, 233 p. 22 cm. Includes bibliographical references. [BT28.O5] 71-89086 5.95
1. Theology—20th century. 2. Religious thought—U.S. I. Weisser, Donald M., joint author. II. Title.

PAGE, Robert Jeffress, 1922- 283
New directions in Anglican theology; a survey from Temple to Robinson New York, Seabury [1965] viii, 208p. 22cm. Bibl. [BT28.P3] 65-21312 4.95
1. Theology—20th cent. 2. Theology, Doctrinal—Hist.—Gt. Brit. I. Title. II. Title: Anglican theology.

PENNSYLVANIA. University. Bicentennial Conference. 200
Religion and the modern world, by Jacques Maritain [and others] Port Washington, N.Y., Kennikat Press [1969, c1941] 192 p. 25 cm. (Essay and general literature index reprint series) [BR41.P4 1969] 68-26204
1. Theology—20th century. I. Maritain, Jacques, 1882- II. Title.

PENNSYLVANIA. University. Bicentennial conference. 206.373
... *Religion and the modern world,* by Jacques Maritain, Joseph L. Hromadka, William J. McGarry [and others] ... Philadelphia, University of Pennsylvania press, 1941. 3 p. l., 192 p. 24 cm. At head of title: University of Pennsylvania. Bicentennial conference. [BR41.P4 1941] 41-6144
1. Theology—20th cent. I. Maritain, Jacques, 1882- II. Hremadka, Josef Luki, 1889- III. McCarry, William James, 1894- IV. Title.
Contents omitted.

POTTHOFF, Harvey H
Current theological thinking; an elective unit for adults by Harvey H. Potthoff. With leader's guide by Howard M. Ham. New York, Abingdon [1962] 64 p. 68-62225
1. Theology—20th cent. I. Title.

REPORT of seminar...
June 4-23, 1956. Nashville, Tenn. [1956] 1v. illus. 28cm. Various pagings. 'Under the direction of the Department of the Christian family, The Board of Education, The Methodist Church.' Includes questionaires. Reviews of books and films: p.38-45.
I. Boston University. School of Theology. Seminar on the Church and Family Life, 1956.

SCHILLING, Sylvester Paul, 1904- 230
Contemporary continental theologians. Nashville, Abingdon [c.1966] 288p. 24cm. [BT28.S37] 66-10854 5.00
1. Theology — 20th cent. I. Title.

SCHILLING, Sylvester Paul, 1904- 230
Contemporary continental theologians [by] S. Paul Schilling. Nashville, Abingdon Press [1966] 288 p. 24 cm. [BT28.S37] 66-10854
1. Theology—20th cent. I. Title.

SHORT, Robert L. 230'.09'04
Something to believe in : Is Kurt Vonnegut the exorcist of Jesus Christ Superstar? / Robert Short. New York : Harper & Row, [1978] p. cm. Includes bibliographical references. [BR115.C8S53] 75-36754 ISBN 0-06-067381-8 pbk. : 4.95 ISBN 0-06-067380-X : 8.95
1. Vonnegut, Kurt—Religion and ethics. 2. Blatty, William Peter. The exorcist. 3. Jesus Christ superstar [Motion picture] 4. Theology—20th century. 5. Christianity and culture. 6. United States—Popular culture. I. Title.

STREYFFELER, Alan. 261
Prophets, priests, and politicians. Valley Forge, Judson Press [1971] 160 p. 23 cm. Bibliography: p. 153-158. [BT28.S74] 71-129487 ISBN 0-8170-0502-1 4.95
1. Theology—20th century. 2. Secularism. 3. Christianity and politics. I. Title.

SYKES, Stephen. 230
An introduction to Christian theology today. Atlanta, John Knox Press [1974, c1971] 153 p. 21 cm. First published under title: Christian theology today. Bibliography: p. 149-153. [BT28.S93 1974] 73-16911 ISBN 0-8042-0474-8 3.50
1. Theology—20th century. I. Title.

THEOLOGY and life.
With an introd. by C. J. Stranks. London, A. R. Mowbray; New York, Morehouse-Gorham [1957] 128p. 19cm. (Sermons of today series, 3)
I. Henson, Herbert Hensley, of Durham, Bp. 1863-1947.

THEOLOGY and life.
With an introd. by C. J. Steranks. London, A. R. Mowbray; New York, Morehouse--Gorham [1957] 128p. 19cm. (Sermons of today series, 3)
I. Henson, Herbert Hensley, Bp. of Durham, 1863-1947.

THIELICKE, Helmut, 1908- 230 s
Prolegomena: the relation of theology to modern thought forms. Translated and edited by Geoffrey W. Bromiley. Grand Rapids, Eerdmans [1974] 420 p. 25 cm. (His The evangelical faith, v. 1) Includes bibliographical references. [BT75.2.T4513 vol. 1] [BT28] 230'.09'04 74-7011 ISBN 0-8028-2342-4
1. Theology—20th century. I. Title.

TRACY, David. 230
Blessed rage for order, the new pluralism in theology / David Tracy. New York : Seabury Press, [1975] p. cm. "A Crossroad book." Includes index. [BT28.T65] 75-8803 ISBN 0-8164-0277-9 : 12.95
1. Theology—20th century. 2. Religion and language. I. Title.

TYPES of modern theology;
Schleiermacher to Barth. New York, Scribner [1958] vii, 333p. 22cm. (Croall lectures, 1933)
I. Mackintosh, Hugh Ross, 1870-1936.

VOGEL, Arthur Anton 230.0904
The next Christian epoch. New York, Harper [c.1966] xii, 111p. 22cm. Bibl. [BT28.V6] 66-12647 3.50 bds.,
1. Theology—20th cent. I. Title.

VOGEL, Arthur Anton. 230.0904
The next Christian epoch, by Arthur A. Vogel. [1st ed.] New York, Harper & Row [1966] xii, 111 p. 22 cm. Bibliographical footnotes. [BT28.V6] 66-12647
1. Theology—20th cent. I. Title.

WOLF, Donald J., ed. 282.082
Current trends in theology, ed. by Donald J. Wolf, James V. Schall. Garden City, N.Y., Doubleday [c.]1965. 285p. 22cm. Bibl. [BT28.W6] 65-12362 4.95
1. Theology—20th cent. 2. Catholic Church—Addresses, essays, lectures. I. Schall, James V., joint ed. II. Title.

WOLF, Donald J., ed: 282.082
Current trends in theology, ed. by Donald J. Wolf, James V. Schall. Garden City, N.Y., Doubleday [1966, c.19658] 274p. 18cm. (Image bks., D202) Bibl. [BT28.W6] 65-12362 .85 pap.,
1. Theology—20th cent. 2. Catholic Church—Addresses, essays, lectures. I. Schall, James V., joint ed. II. Title.

ZAHRNT, Heinz, 1915- 211
What kind of God? A question of faith. [1st U.S. ed.] Minneapolis, Augsburg Pub. House [1972, c1970] 279 p. 23 cm. Translation of Gott kann nicht sterben. Includes bibliographical references. [BT28.Z2813 1972] 77-176102 ISBN 0-8066-1209-6
1. Theology—20th century. 2. God. I. Title.

Theology—20th century—Addresses, essays, lectures.

ADAMS, F. W.
Theological criticisms; or, Hints of the philosophy of man and nature. In six lectures. To which are appended two poetical scraps, and dogmas of infidelity. By F.W. Adams, M.D. Montpelier, J.E. Thompson, 1843. xv, [17]-216, 32 p. 19 cm. 2-8982
I. Title.

BARTH, Karl, 1886- 208.1
Against the stream; shorter post-war writings, 1946-52. [Edited by Ronald Gregor Smith] New York, Philosophical Library [1954] 252p. port. 23cm. 'Bibliography of Karl Barth's writings in English': p. [247]-248. [BX9410.B3] 54-2880
1. Theology—20th cent.—Addresses, essays, lectures. 2. Reformed Church—Addresses, essays, lectures. I. Title.

BARTH, Karl, 1886- 261.704
Community, state, and church; three essays. [Tr. from German] Introd. by Will Herberg. [Gloucester, Mass., Peter Smith, 1961, c.]1960. 193p. (Anchor books, A221 rebound in cloth) 3.00
1. Theology—20th cent.—Addresses, essays, lectures. 2. Reformed Church—Addresses, essays, lectures. I. Title.

BARTH, Karl, 1886-1968. 261.704
Community, state, and church; three essays. With an introd. by Will Herberg. [1st ed.] Garden City, N.Y., Doubleday, 1960. 193 p. 18 cm. (Anchor books, A221) Translated from the German. Contents.Contents.—Gospel and law.—Church and state.—The Christian community and the civil community.—Bibliography (p. 191-193) [BX9410.B323] 60-13233
1. Reformed Church—Addresses, essays, lectures. 2. Theology—20th century—Addresses, essays, lectures. I. Title.

THE Context of contemporary theology; essays in honor of Paul Lehmann. Edited by Alexander J. McKelway and E. David Willis. Atlanta, John Knox Press [1974] 270 p. 21 cm. [BT10.C64] 73-16916 ISBN 0-8042-0513-2 10.00 230
1. Lehmann, Paul Louis, 1906- —Addresses, essays, lectures. 2. Theology—20th century—Addresses, essays, lectures. I. Lehmann, Paul Louis, 1906- II. McKelway, Alexander J., ed. III. Willis, Edward David, ed.
Contents omitted

DECONSTRUCTION and theology / Thomas J.J. Altizer ... [et al.] New York : Crossroad, 1982. ix, 178 p. ; 21 cm. Includes bibliographical references. [BT28.D38 1982] 19 82-1377 ISBN 0-8245-0475-5 : 14.95 ISBN 0-8245-0412-7 pbk. : 5.95 230
1. Theology—20th century—Addresses, essays, lectures. I. Altizer, Thomas J. J.

STIRRINGS : 200
essays Christian and radical / edited by John J. Vincent. London : Epworth Press, 1976. 128 p. ; 22 cm. (City soundings) [BT28.S69] 76-381620 ISBN 0-7162-0265-4 : £1.00
1. Theology—20th century—Addresses, essays, lectures. I. Vincent, John J.

THEOLOGIANS in transition : The Christian century "How my mind has changed" series / edited by James M. Wall ; with an introduction by Martin E. Marty. New York : Crossroad, c1981. p. cm. Twenty essays originally published in The Christian century in 1980 and 1981. [BR50.T42158] 19 81-9875 ISBN 0-8245-0101-2 : 14.95 ISBN 0-8245-0103-9 pbk. : 7.95 230'.09'04
1. Theology—20th century—Addresses,

essays, lectures. 2. Theologians—Addresses, essays, lectures. I. Wall, James McKendree, 1928- II. Christian century.

THEOLOGICAL crossings 200'.1
[by] Robert McAfee Brown [and others] Edited by Alan Geyer and Dean Peerman. Grand Rapids, Eerdmans [1971] 155 p. ports. 21 cm. Essays, originally published in the Christian century as the 4th of a decennial series of articles entitled How my mind has changed. [BR50.T422] 79-168439 2.95
1. Theology—20th century—Addresses, essays, lectures. I. Brown, Robert McAfee, 1920- II. Geyer, Alan F., ed. III. Peerman, Dean G., ed. IV. The Christian century.

Theology—20th century—Bibliography.

SCHMEMANN, Alexander, 1921- 016.2
Russian theology 1920-1965 , a bibliographical survey [Richmond] Union Theological Seminary in Virginia, 1969. 35, 14 p. 28 cm. (Union Theological Seminary in Virginia. Annual bibliographical lecture, 7th, 1969) Cover title. Bibliography: p. [1]-14 (2d group) [Z7751.S4] 77-16858
1. Theology—20th century—Bibliography. 2. Religious thought—Russia—Bibliography. I. Title. II. Series: Richmond. Union Theological Seminary. Annual bibliographical lecture, 7th, 1969

Theology—Abbreviations.

TAYLOR, John Thomas, 1947- 200'.1'48
An illustrated guide to abbreviations, for use in religious studies / prepared by John T. Taylor ; edited by John L. Sayre. Enid, Okla. : Seminary Press, 1976. iii, 70 p. ; 28 cm. Includes index. [BR96.5.T39] 76-14705 ISBN 0-912832-13-4 pbk. : 5.00
1. Theology—Abbreviations. 2. Religion—Abbreviations. I. Title.

Theology—Abstracts.

MAGILL, Frank Northen, 1907- ed. 208.2
Masterpieces of Catholic literature in summary form, edited by Frank N. Magill with associate editors A. Robert Caponigri [and] Thomas P. Neill. New York, Harper & Row [1965] xxvi, 1134, v p. 24 cm. "Acknowledgments" (biographical): p. [v]-xii. [BX885.M2] 63-20740
1. Theology—Abstracts. 2. Catholic literature—Abstracts. I. Title.

MAGILL, Frank Northen, 1907- ed. 208.22
Masterpieces of Christian literature in summary form, ed. by Frank N. Magill with Ian P. McGreal. New York, Harper [c.1963] xxix, 1193, v p. 24cm. 63-10622 3.95
1. Theology—Abstracts. 2. Protestantism—Collections. I. Title.

PRINCETON Theological Seminary. 260.016
Catalogue of doctoral dissertations, 1944-1960. Princeton, N. J., 1962. 119 p. 24 cm. [BR53.P7] 64-326
1. Theology—Abstracts. 2. Dissertations, Academic—U.S.—Abstracts. I. Title.

Theology—Addresses, essays, lectures.

ADAMS, James Luther, 1901- 230
On being human religiously : selected essays in religion and society / James Luther Adams ; edited and introduced by Max L. Stackhouse. Boston : Beacon Press, c1976. xxx, 257 p. ; 21 cm. Includes bibliographical references and index. [BR50.A28] 75-36037 ISBN 0-8070-1122-3 : 9.95
1. Theology—Addresses, essays, lectures. 2. Social ethics—Addresses, essays, lectures. 3. Liberty—Addresses, essays, lectures. I. Stackhouse, Max L. II. Title.

ADAMS, James Luther, 1901- 230.04
Taking time seriously. [Articles] Glencoe, Ill., Free Press [1957] 74p. 24cm. [BR123.A35] 57-4296
1. Theology—Addresses, essays, lectures. I. Title.

'AND other pastors of thy flock,' 204
a German tribute to the Bishop of Chichester, edited by Franz Hildebrandt. Cambridge [eng.] Printed for subscribers at the University press, 1942. x, 175, [1] p. 20 cm. Bibliographical foot-notes. [BR50.A55] 43-14915
1. Bell, George Kennedy Allen, bp. of Chichester, 1883- 2. Theology—Addresses, essays, lectures. I. Hildebrandt, Franz, ed.
Contents omitted.

ANDERSON, Galusha, 1832-1918. 261
Science and prayer, and other papers, by Galusha Anderson ... Boston, New York [etc.] The Pilgrim press [1915] 6 p. l., 3-259 p. 21 cm. Reprinted in part from various sources. [BR85.A6] 15-28094
1. Clarke, William Newton, 1841-1912. The use of the Scriptures in theology. 2. Theology—Addresses, essays, lectures. I. Title.
Contents omitted.

ANDERSON, James Norman Dalrymple. 230
A lawyer among the theologians, by Norman Anderson. [1st American ed.] Grand Rapids, W. B. Eerdmans Pub. Co. [1974, c1973] 240 p. 20 cm. Includes bibliographical references. [BR85.A623 1974] 73-21894 ISBN 0-8028-1565-0 3.95 (pbk.)
1. Jesus Christ—Resurrection. 2. Theology—Addresses, essays, lectures. I. Title.

ASIAN Christian theology : emerging themes 230'.095
/ edited by Douglas J. Elwood. Rev. ed. of What Asian Christians are thinking. Philadelphia : Westminster Press, c1980. 342 p. ; 23 cm. Includes index. Bibliography: p. [337]-340. [BR50.W48 1980] 19 80-21228 ISBN 0-664-24354-1 : 14.95
1. Theology—Addresses, essays, lectures. 2. Christianity—Asia—Addresses, essays, lectures. I. Elwood, Douglas J. II. What Asian Christians are thinking.

BARTH, Karl, 1886-1968. 230
Final testimonies / by Karl Barth ; edited by Eberhard Busch ; translated by Geoffrey W. Bromiley. Grand Rapids : Eerdmans, c1977. 67 p. ; 22 cm. Translation of Letzte Zeugnisse. [BR85.B41913 1977] 77-8088 ISBN 0-8028-3497-3 : 3.95
1. Theology—Addresses, essays, lectures. I. Title.
Contents omitted

BERTRAM, Robert W. ed. 250.08
The lively function of the Gospel; essays in honor of Richard R. Caemmerer on completion of 25 years as professor of practical theology at Concordia Seminary, Saint Louis. St. Louis, Concordia [c.1966] ix, 196p. front. 24cm. Bibl. [BR50.B44] 66-19143 5.00
1. Theology—Addresses, essays, lectures. I. Caemmerer,Richard Rudolf, 1904- II. Title.

BERTRAM, Robert W. 250.08
The lively function of the Gospel; essays in honor of Richard R. Caemmerer on completion of 25 years as professor of practical theology at Concordia Seminary, Saint Louis. Robert W. Bertram, editor. Saint Louis, Concordia Pub. House [1966] ix. 196 p. 24 cm. Bibliographical footnotes. [BR50.B44] 66-19143
1. Theology — Addresses, essays, lectures. I. Caemmerer, Richard Rudolf, 1904- II. Title.
CONTENTS OMITTED

BOROS, Ladislaus, 1927- 230
You can always begin again / Ladislaus Boros ; translated by David Smith. New York : Paulist Press, c1977. 94 p. ; 19 cm. (A Deus book) Translation of Gedanken uber das Christliche. [BR85.B74513 1977] 76-49324 ISBN 0-8091-2006-2 pbk. : 1.75
1. Theology—Addresses, essays, lectures. I. Title.

BOSWORTH, Edward Increase, 1861-1927. 230.04
The Christian religion and human progress, being the spring lectures at the School of Religion, Athens, Greece, together with a selection from the published and unpublished addresses of Edward Increase Bosworth. Ed., with an introductory note, by Ernest Pye. New York, Bosworth Memorial Committee of the Board of Sponsors [1948] xi, 328 p. port. 24 cm. "A companion volume to [the editor's] The biography of a mind: Bosworth of Oberlin." [BR85.B75] 48-7486
1. Theology—Addresses, essays, lectures. 2. Progress. I. Pye, Ernest, 1881- ed. II. Title.

BROWN, Robert McAfee, 1920- 201'.1
The pseudonyms of God. Philadelphia, Westminster Press [1972] 234 p. 21 cm. Includes bibliographical references. [BR85.B839] 77-178813 ISBN 0-664-20930-0 ISBN 0-664-24948-5 (pbk)
1. Theology—Addresses, essays, lectures. 2. Church and the world—Addresses, essays, lectures. I. Title.

BROWN, William Bryant.
The problem of final destiny; studied in the light of revised theological statement. New York, T. Whittaker, 1900. 319 p. 12 cm. Aug
I. Title.

BULTMANN, Rudolf Karl, 1884- 230
Essays, philosophical and theological. New York, Macmillan [1955] xi, 337p. 22cm. (The Library of philosophy and theology) Translation by J. C. G. Greig of the author's Glauben und Verstehen: gesammelte Aufsatze, II. [BT15.B] A56
1. Theology—Addresses, essays, lectures. 2. Philosophy, Modern—Addresses, essays, lectures. I. Title. II. Series.

BULTMANN, Rudolf Karl, 1884- 230'.08
Faith and understanding, [by] Rudolf Bultmann. Edited with an introd. by Robert W. Funk. Translated by Louise Pettibone Smith. [1st U.S. ed.] New York, Harper & Row [1969- v. 22 cm. Essays. Translation of Glauben und verstehen. Bibliographical footnotes. [BT15.B8213] 69-10471 7.50
1. Bible—Theology. 2. Theology—Addresses, essays, lectures. I. Title.

CAPECELATRO, Alfonso, cardinal, 1824-1912.
Christ, the church, and man. An essay on new methods in ecclesiastical studies & worship, with some remarks on a new apologia for Christianity in relation to the social question. By His Eminence, Cardinal Capecelatro, archbishop of Capus. London, Burns & Oates; St. Louis, Mo., B. Herder 1909. 3-78 p. front. (port.) 19 cm. A 10
1. Theology—Addresses, essays, lectures. 2. Catholic church. I. Title.

THE Carey memorial lectures. 201'.1'08
Delivered at the annual sessions of Baltimore Yearly Meeting, 1947-1971. [Compiled by Benjamin H. Branch, Jr. Lincoln? Va., 1972] viii, 103 p. 24 cm. [BR50.C37] 72-192655
1. Theology—Addresses, essays, lectures. I. Branch, Benjamin Harrison, 1919- comp. II. Friends, Society of. Baltimore Yearly Meeting.

CATHOLIC Theological Society of America. 282.06273
Proceedings of the annual convention. [Washington] v. 23cm. Title varies slightly. [BX810.C285] 53-17016
1. Theology— Addresses, essays, lectures. 2. Catholic Church—Addresses, essays, lectures. I. Title.

... Christ and modern thought. 201
With a preliminary lecture on the methods of meeting modern unbelief, by Joseph Cook. Boston, Roberts brothers, 1881. [iii]-lvii, 315 p. 18 cm. (Boston Monday lectures, 1880-1881) Contents.Preliminary lecture: Methods of meeting modern unbelief, by Joseph Cook.--I. The seen and the unseen, by Rt. Rev. Thomas M. Clark.--II. Moral law in its relations to physical and science and to popular religion, by President E. G. Robinson.--III. Christianity and the mental activity of the age, by Rev. Thomas Guard.--IV. The place of conscience, by Rev. Mark Hopkins.--V. Development: Its nature: what it can do and what it cannot do, by Rev. James McCosb.--VI. A calm view of the temperance question, by Chancellor Howard Crosby.--VII. Old and New theologies, by Rev. George R. Crooks.--VIII. Facts as to divorce in New England, by Rev. Samuel W. Dike.--IX. Significance of the historic element to scripture, by Rev. J. B. Thomas.--X. The theistic basis of evolution by Rev. John Cotton Smith. [AC5.C] A 34
1. Theology—Addresses, essays, lectures. I. Cook, Joseph, 1838-1901.

CHRISTIAN belief and this world.
Greenwich, Conn. Seabury Press, 1957. 156p. 22cm. (The Firth lectures in the University of Nottingham, 1955)
1. Theology—Addresses, essays, lectures. I. Vidler, Alexander Roper, 1899- II. Series.

CHRISTIAN history and interpretation; 230
studies presented to John Knox. Ed. by W. R. Farmer, C. F. D. Moule, R. R. Niebuhr. Cambridge [Eng.] Univ. Pr., 1967. xxxv, 428p. port. 24cm. [BR50.C52] 67-15306 9.50
1. Knox, John, 1900- 2. Theology—Addresses, essays, lectures. I. Knox, John, 1900- II. Farmer, William Reuben. ed. III. Moule, Charles Francis Digby, ed. IV. Niebuhr, Richard R. ed.
Available from Cambridge Univ. Pr., New York.

CLARKE, William Newton, 1841-1912. 261
Immortality, a study of belief, and earlier addresses, by William Newton Clarke. New Haven, Yale university press; London, H. Milford, Oxford university press, 1920. xiii p., 1 l., 132 p., 1 l. 20 1/2 cm. "Published on the fund given to the Yale university press in memory of M. A. K." [BR85.C53] 20-15458
1. Theology—Addresses, essays, lectures. I. Title.

CLUTTON-BROCK, Arthur, 1868-1924. 210
Essays on religion. With an introd. by Canon B. H. Streeter. Freeport, N.Y., Books for Libraries Press [1969] xxvi, 171 p. 23 cm. (Essay index reprint series) Reprint of the 1926 ed. [BR85.C536 1969] 79-84302
1. Theology—Addresses, essays, lectures. I. Title.

CLUTTON-BROCK, Arthur, 1868-1924. 201'.1
More essays on religion. With an introd. by B. H. Streeter. Freeport, N.Y., Books for Libraries Press, [1971] vii, 215 p. 23 cm. (Essay index reprint series) Reprint of the 1928 ed. Contents.Contents.—Crashaw's Christmas poems.—Christina Rossetti.—The Rev. Robert Herrick.—Ecclesiastical art.—"Restoration and renovation."—The problem of evil.—Creative religion.—An unborn Catholicism.—The pursuit of happiness.—The problem of Martha.—On Jonahs.—The remedy.—Sheep without a shepherd.—The kingdom of heaven. [BR85.C54 1971] 76-156632 ISBN 0-8369-2349-9
1. Theology—Addresses, essays, lectures. I. Title.

COBBE, Frances Power, 1822-1904. 200
Darwinism in morals, and other essays. Freeport, N.Y., Books for Libraries Press [1972] 399 p. 22 cm. (Essay index reprint series) Reprint of the 1872 ed. Contents.Contents.—Darwinism in morals.—Hereditary piety.—The religion of childhood.—An English Broad churchman.—A French theist.—The devil.—A pre-historic religion.—The religions of the world.—The religions of the East.—The religion and literature of India.—Unconscious cerebration.—Dreams, as illustrations of involuntary cerebration.—Auricular confession in the Church of England.—The evolution of morals and religion. Includes bibliographical references. [BR85.C544 1972] 72-3306 ISBN 0-8369-2895-4
1. Theology—Addresses, essays, lectures. 2. Religions—Addresses, essays, lectures. I. Title.

COGGAN, Frederick Donald, 1909- 230'.3
Convictions / by Donald Coggan. Grand Rapids : Eerdmans, c1975. 320 p. ; 23 cm. [BX5199.C567A33] 75-42458 ISBN 0-8028-3481-7 : 9.95
1. Coggan, Frederick Donald, 1909- 2. Theology—Addresses, essays, lectures. 3. England—Biography. I. Title.

COLESTOCK, Henry Thomas. 261
The changing view-point in regligious

thought, and other short studies in present religious problems, by Henry Thomas Colestock ... New York, E. B. Treat & company, 1901. 306 p. 19 cm. "Some of the chapters ... were first contributed to various periodicals ..."--Note. [BR85.C64] 1-31708
1. Theology—Addresses, essays, lectures. I. Title.

COLLEGE Theology Society. 201'.1
That they may live: theological reflections on the quality of life; [proceedings] George Devine, editor. Staten Island, N.Y., Alba House [1972] viii, 306 p. 21 cm. Proceedings of the national convention of the College Theology Society, held in St. Paul, Minn., Apr. 12-14, 1971. Includes bibliographical references. [BR50.C588] 72-3488 ISBN 0-8189-0243-4 3.95
1. Theology—Addresses, essays, lectures. I. Devine, George, 1941- ed. II. Title.

COLLEGE Theology Society. 201
Theology in revolution; [proceedings] George Devine, editor. Staten Island, N.Y., Alba House [1970] xi, 286 p. 21 cm. "Based on the Society's last annual convention in Chicago, April 6-8, 1969." Includes bibliographical references. [BR50.C59] 71-110590 ISBN 8-18-901764-3.95
1. Theology—Addresses, essays, lectures. I. Devine, George, 1941- ed. II. Title.

CONTEMPORARY American 230'.0973
theologies II : a book of readings / edited by Deane William Ferm. New York : Seabury Press, 1982. x, 374 p. ; 21 cm. [BT80.C66 1982] 19 82-5744 ISBN 0-8164-2407-1 : 15.95
1. Theology—Addresses, essays, lectures. I. Ferm, Deane William, 1927- II. Title: Contemporary American theologies 2.

COOK, Joseph, 1838-1901. 230
... Orthodoxy, with preludes on current events. By Joseph Cook ... Boston, J. R. Osgood and company, 1878. 2 p. l., 7-8, 343 p. 19 1/2 cm. (His Boston Monday lectures) [Name originally: Flavius Josephus Cook] [BT78.C65] 34-4755
1. Theology—Addresses, essays, lectures. 2. Parker, Theodore, 1810-1860. I. Title.

CORNELL, George W. 200'.1
The untamed God / George W. Cornell. 1st ed. New York : Harper & Row, [1975] 152 p. ; 21 cm. Includes index. Bibliography: p. [143]-146. [BR85.C783 1975] 74-25690 ISBN 0-06-061582-6 : 7.95
1. Theology—Addresses, essays, lectures. I. Title.

CREATION, Christ, and culture 230
: studies in honour of T. F. Torrance / edited by Richard W. A. McKinney. Edinburgh : Clark, 1976. ix, 321 p., plate : port. ; 23 cm. Contents.Contents.—Clements, R. E. Covenant and Canon in the Old Testament.—Black, M. The New Creation in I Enoch.—Barbour, R. S. Creation, wisdom, and Christ.—Heron, A. Logos, image, son.—Ritschl, D. Some comments on the backbround and influence of Augustine's Lex Aeterna doctrine.—Jenson, R. W. The body of God's presence.—MacKinnon, D. M. The relation of the doctrines of the Incarnation and the Trinity.—Galloway, A. D. Creation and covenant.—Moltmann, J. Creation and redemption.—O'Donoghue, N. D. Creation and participation.—Jaki, S. L. Theological aspects of creative science.—Langford, T. A. Authority, community, and church.—Houston, J. Precepts and counsels.—McDonagh, E. Morality and prayer.—McIntyre, J. Theology and method.—Jungel, E. The truth of life.—McKinney, R. W. A. Historical relativism, the appeal to experience and theological reconstruction.—Sykes, S. W. Life after death.—Thomas, J. H. The problem of defining a theology of culture with reference to the theology of Paul Tillich.—Newbigin, L. All in one place or all of one sort? Bibliography: p. 307-321. [BR50.C66] 76-379213 ISBN 0-567-01019-8 : £5.60
1. Torrance, Thomas Forsyth, 1913- 2. Torrance, Thomas Forsyth, 1913- — Bibliography. 3. Theology—Addresses, essays, lectures. I. Torrance, Thomas Forsyth, 1913- II. McKinney, Richard W. A.

CREATIVITY and method : 230'.2
essays in honor of Bernard Lonergan, S.J. / edited by Matthew L. Lamb. Milwaukee, Wis. : Marquette University Press, 1981. x, 584 p. : port. ; 24 cm. Includes bibliographical references and index. [BR50.C663] 19 81-80327 ISBN 0-87462-533-5 : 24.95
1. Catholic Church—Addresses, essays, lectures. 2. Lonergan, Bernard J. F.—Addresses, essays, lectures. 3. Theology—Addresses, essays, lectures. 4. Philosophy—Addresses, essays, lectures. I. Lonergan, Bernard J. F. II. Lamb, Matthew L.

CUSHMAN, Robert Earl, ed. 230.082
The heritage of Christian thought; essays in honor of Robert Lowry Calhoun. Edited by Robert E. Cushman and Egil Grislis. [1st ed.] New York, Harper & Row [1965] ix, 243 p. port. 25 cm. Contents.-- Preface, by R. E. Cushman. -- A biographical sketch. To recall in gratitude Robert Lowry Calhoun. By V. Corwin. -- The sense of tradition in the ante-Nicene church, by A. C. Outler. -- St. Anselm on the harmony between God's mercy and God's justice, by G. S. Heyer, Jr. -- The a priori in St. Thomas' theory of knowledge, by G. A. Lindbeck. -- The role of consensus in Richard Hooker's method of theological enquiry, by E. Grislis. -- Spinoza on theology and truth, by W. A. Christian. -- Pascal's wager argument, by R. Hazelton. -- The hermeneutics of holiness in Wesley, by C. Michalson. -- Original sin and the enlightenment, by C. A. Holbrook -- The Christology of Paul Tillich, by R. E. Cushman. -- Two models of transcendence: An inquiry into the problem of theological meaning, by G. D. Kaufman. -- Analogy as a principle of theological method historically considered, by N. C. Nielsen, Jr. -- Modern Papal social teaching, by R. P. Ramsey. -- A select bibliography of Robert Lowry Calhoun's writings, by R. P. Morris and J. E. McFarland (p. 239-243) Bibliographical footnotes. [BR50.C8] 65-15390
1. Theology — Addresses, essays, lectures. I. Calhoun, Robert Lowry, 1896- II. Grislis, Egil, joint ed. III. Title.

CUSTANCE, Arthur C. 230 s
The Virgin birth and the Incarnation / by Arthur C. Custance ; ill. by the author. Grand Rapids : Zondervan Pub. House, c1976. p. cm. (His The doorway papers ; v. 5) "Each of these papers was previously published separately." Bibliography: p. [BS543.A1C87 vol. 5] [BR85] 230 76-14968 8.95
1. Theology—Addresses, essays, lectures. I. Title.
Contents omitted. Contents omitted.

DIMENSIONS in religious 230
education / contributors, Avery Dulles ... [et al.] ; edited by John R. McCall. Havertown, Pa. : CIM Books, c1973. iv, 183 p. ; 26 cm. Includes bibliographical references. [BR50.D52] 75-322209
1. Theology—Addresses, essays, lectures. 2. Christian education—Addresses, essays, lectures. I. Dulles, Avery Robert, 1918- II. McCall, John R., 1920-

DINGWELL, James Davidson. 220
The closing century's heritage, by Rev. J. D. Dingwell ... New York, Chicago [etc.] Fleming H. Revell company [c1899] 108 p. 20 cm. [BR125.D62] 99-2651
1. Theology—Addresses, essays, lectures. I. Title.

DOING theology in new places 230
/ edited by Jean-Pierre Jossua and Johann Baptist Metz. New York : Seabury Press, 1979. 114 p. ; 23 cm. (Concilium : religion in the seventies ; 115) "A Crossroad book." Includes bibliographical references. [BR75] ISBN 0-8164-2611-2 pbk. : 4.95
1. Theology—Addresses, essays, lectures. I. Jossua, Jean-Pierre. II. Metz, Johannes Baptist. III. Series: Concilium (New York) ; 115.

DRUMMOND, Henry, 1851-1897. 261
...Addresses. Philadelphia, Henry Altemus company [1898?] viii, [4], 11-363 p. 16 cm. [BR85.D68 1898B] 24-21559
1. Theology—addresses, essays, lectures. I. Title.
Contents omitted.

DRUMMOND, Henry, 1851-1897. 261
Addresses by Henry Drummond... Philadelphia, H. Altemus, 1891. 244 p. 15 cm. [BR85.D68 1891] 12-81879
1. Theology—addresses, essays, lectures. I. Title.
Contents omitted.

DRUMMOND, Henry, 1851-1897.
Drummond's address ... Chicago, W. B. Conkey Co. [1960] 155 p. 18 cm. 67-96899
1. Theology — Addresses, essays, lectures. I. Title.

DRUMMOND, Henry, 1851-1897. 240
Drummond's addresses... Chicago, W. B. Conkey company [1900] 155 p. front. (port.) 3 pl. 16 cm. [BR85.D68 1900] 4-13553
1. Theology—addresses, essays, lectures. I. Title.
Contents omitted.

THE Dynamic in Christian 200'.1
thought. Edited by Joseph Papin. [Villanova, Pa.] Villanova University Press [1970] vii, 291 p. 23 cm. (The Villanova University symposium, v. 1, 1968) Includes bibliographical references. [BR50.D9] 70-107942 ISBN 0-87723-008-0
1. Theology—Addresses, essays, lectures. I. Papin, Joseph, 1914- ed. II. Title. III. Series.

DYNAMICS of the faith; 201'.1
evangelical Christian foundations, edited by Gene Miller, Max Gaulke [and] Donald Smith. [Houston, Gulf-Coast Bible College, 1972] 304 p. ports. 23 cm. Includes bibliographies. [BR50.D93] 72-193745 4.95
1. Theology—Addresses, essays, lectures. I. Miller, Gene, 1929- ed. II. Gaulke, Max R., ed. III. Smith, Donald, June 15, 1935- ed.

EBELING, Gerhard, 1912- 231
God and word. [Tr. by James W. Leitch from the German] Philadelphia, Fortress [1967] vii, 53p. 20cm. (Earl lects., 1966) [BT80.E213] 67-14623 1.50 bds.,
1. Theology—Addresses, essays, lectures. I. Title. II. Series.

ECCLESIASTICAL History 270'.08 s
Society, London.
Popular belief and practice; papers read at the ninth summer meeting and the tenth winter meeting of the Ecclesiastical History Society. Edited by G. J. Cuming and Derek Baker. Cambridge [Eng.] University Press, 1972. xii, 330 p. 23 cm. (Studies in church history, 8) Includes bibliographical references. [BR141.S84 vol. 8] [BR50] 201'.1 77-155583 ISBN 0-521-08220-X
1. Theology—Addresses, essays, lectures. 2. Religion—Addresses, essays, lectures. I. Cuming, G. J., ed. II. Baker, Derek, ed. III. Title. IV. Series: Studies in church history (London), 8.

EDWARDS, Bela Bates, 1802- 261
1852.
Writings of Professor B. B. Edwards, with a memoir by Edwards A. Park ... Boston, J. P. Jewett and company; Cleveland, O., Jewett, Proctor, and Worthington;[etc., etc.] 1853. 2 v. 18 1/2 cm. [BR85.E45] 42-6185
1. Theology—Addresses, essays, lectures. I. Park, Edwards Amasa, 1808-1900. II. Title.

ELLER, Vernard. 230'.044
Thy kingdom come : a Blumhardt reader / by Vernard Eller. Grand Rapids, Mich. : Eerdmans, c1980. p. cm. [BR85.E48] 19 80-19328 ISBN 0-8028-1854-4 : 4.95
1. Theology—Addresses, essays, lectures. I. Blumhardt, Johann Christoph, 1805-1880. II. Blumhardt, Christoph, 1842-1919. III. Title.

ELLUL, Jacques. 230'.42'0924
In season, out of season : an introduction to the thought of Jacques Ellul / translated by Lani K. Niles and based on interviews by Madeleine Garrigou-Lagrange. 1st U.S. ed. San Francisco : Harper & Row, c1982. p. cm. Translation of: A temps et a contretemps. [BR85.E4914 1982] 19 82-47743 ISBN 0-06-062239-3 : 6.68
1. Theology—Addresses, essays, lectures. I. Garrigou-Lagrange, Madeleine. II. [A temps et a contretemps.] English III. Title.

ESSAYS in honor of Joseph P. 230
Brennan / by members of the faculty, Saint Bernard's Seminary ; edited by Robert F. McNamara. Rochester, N.Y. : The Seminary, 1976, c1977. 158 p. ; 22 cm. "The sheaf, Bicentennial issue, (part one)." Contents.Contents.—Turvasi, F. Charles Briggs, a pioneer of theological ecumenism.—Healy, J., Carm, O. Empathy with the cross.—Falcone, S. A. The kind of bread we pray for in the Lord's prayer.—Kelly, J. G. The interpretation of Amos 4:13 in the early Christian community.—Jankowiak, J. M. The American seminary.—Graf, W. Some reflections on reconciliation.—Pennington, J. G. Fulton John Sheen, a chronology and bibliography.—Brennan, J. P. Some hidden harmonies of the Fifth Book of Psalms. Includes bibliographical references. [BR50.E84] 76-51644
1. Brennan, Joseph P.—Addresses, essays, lectures. 2. Sheen, Fulton John, Bp., 1895- Bibliography. 3. Theology—Addresses, essays, lectures. I. Brennan, Joseph P. II. McNamara, Robert Francis, 1910- III. St. Bernard's Seminary, Rochester, N.Y. IV. The Sheaf.

ESSAYS on the works of 199'.492
Erasmus / edited by Richard L. DeMolen. New Haven : Yale University Press, 1978. p. cm. Includes index. [PA8518.A1E8] 78-3481 ISBN 0-300-02177-1 : 16.00
1. Erasmus, Desiderius, d. 1536—Criticism and interpretation—Addresses, essays, lectures. 2. Thompson, Craig Ringwalt, 1911- 3. Theology—Addresses, essays, lectures. I. DeMolen, Richard L. II. Title.

FAITH and order 230.082
findings; the final report of the theological commissions to the Fourth World Conference on Faith and Order, Montreal, 1963. Minneapolis, Augsburg [c.1963] 31, 62, 63, 64p. 22cm. (Faith and order paper, no. 37-40) On jacket: Ed. by Paul S. Minear. Bibl. 63-16608 4.50
1. Theology—Addresses, essays, lectures. 2. Institutionalism (Religion)—Addresses, essays, lectures. 3. Worship—Addresses, essays, lectures. 4. Church—Addresses, essays, lectures. 5. Tradition (Theology)—Addresses, essays, lectures. I. World Conference on Faith and Order, 4th, Montreal, 1963. II. Minear, Paul Sevier, 1906- ed. III. Series.
Contents omitted.

FARRER, Austin Marsden. 230
Interpretation and belief / Austin Farrer ; edited by Charles C. Conti ; foreword by E. L. Mascall. London : SPCK, 1976. xiv, 210 p. ; 23 cm. Includes bibliographical references. [BR85.F37] 76-379459 ISBN 0-281-02889-3 : £5.95
1. Theology—Addresses, essays, lectures. I. Title.

FEINER, Johannes, ed. 230.2082
Theology today. Edited by Johannes Feiner, Josef Trutsch, and Franz Bockle. Translated by Peter White and Raymond H. Kelly. Milwaukee, Bruce Pub. Co. [1965- v. 22 cm. Translation of Fragen der Theologie heute. Contents.v. 1. Renewal in dogma. Bibliography: v. 1, p. 245-276. [BT10.F353] 64-24337
1. Theology—Addresses, essays, lectures. 2. Catholic Church—Addresses, essays, lectures. I. Trutsch, Josef, joint ed. II. Bockle, Franz, joint ed. III. Title.

FERM, Vergilius Ture 230.081
Anselm, 1896-
Toward an expansive Christian theology. New York, Philosophical [c.1964] xv, 186p. illus. 21cm. Bibl. 64-16459 5.00 bds.,
1. Theology—Addresses, essays, lectures. I. Title.

FERM, Vergilius Ture 230.081
Anselm, 1896-
Toward an expansive Christian theology, by Vergilius Ferm. New York, Philosophical Library [1964] xv, 186 p. illus. 21 cm. Bibliographical references included in "Notes" (p. 169-177) [BT80.F4] 64-16359
1. Theology—Addresses, essays, lectures. I. Title.

FERM, Vergilius Ture 201'.1
Anselm, 1896-1974.
Philosophy beyond the classroom / by Vergilius Ferm. North Quincy, Mass. : Christopher Pub. House, [1974] 407 p. ; 25

cm. Includes bibliographies. [BR85.F415] 74-75159 ISBN 0-8158-0314-1 : 12.95
1. Theology—Addresses, essays, lectures. I. Title.

FERRELL, John Appley, 1865-
Meliorism; a series of theological essays, written in an effort to point out to the reader a more reasonable and satisfactory interpretation of the ideas of God the universe, and the hereafter, and to put him in touch with the progressive thought of the present relative to these ideas. By John Appley Ferrell... [Sedan, Kan., J. A. Ferrell, c1914] 83 p. 19 cm. "In the main, articles taken from the Meliorist."--Adv. following p. 83. 14-9868 0.50
I. Title.

FINNEY, Charles Grandison, 1792-1875. 230
The heart of truth : Finney's lectures on theology / by Charles G. Finney. New bicentennial ed. Minneapolis : Bethany Fellowship, 1976. 248 p. ; 21 cm. Originally published in 1840 under title: Skeletons of a course of theological lectures. [BR85.F427 1976] 75-46128 ISBN 0-87123-226-X pbk. : 3.50
1. Theology—Addresses, essays, lectures. 2. Christian ethics—Addresses, essays, lectures. I. Title.

FISHER, George Park, 1827-1909. 261
Discussions in history and theology, by George P. Fisher... New York, C. Scribner's sons, 1880. x, 555 p. 22 cm. [BR85.F45] 12-32196
1. Theology—Addresses, essays, lectures. I. Title.

FLEW, Antony Garrard Newton, 1923- 210
The presumption of atheism and other philosophical essays on God, freedom, and immortality / Antony Flew. New York : Barnes & Noble, 1976. 183 p. ; 23 cm. Includes index. Bibliography: p. [176]-180. [BR85.F54 1976b] 76-361131 ISBN 0-06-492119-0 : 20.00
1. Theology—Addresses, essays, lectures. 2. Immortality—Addresses, essays, lectures. I. Title: The presumption of atheism ...

FORLINES, Charles Edward, 1868-1944. 230.77
Finding God through Christ; lectures and sermons by Charles Edward Forlines ... Arranged and edited by Richard Larkin Shpley, with a biographical sketch by Fred Garrigus Holloway ... New York, Nashville, Abingdon-Cokesbury press. 1947 207 p. 20 1/2 cm. [BR123.F6] 47-716
1. Theology—Addresses, essays, lectures. 2. Baccalaureate addresses—Westminster theological seminary, Westminster, Md. I. Shipley, Richard Larkin, ed. II. Title.

FOSBROKE, Hughell E. W. 208.1
God in the heart of things. Introductory memoir by Stephen F. Bayne, Jr. Edward French, ed. Greenwich, Conn., Seabury [c.] 1962. 152p. 62-9615 3.75 bds.,
1. Theology—Addresses, essays, lectures. I. Title.

FOUR faces of Christian ministry; essays in honor of A. Dale Fiers. 253
Essyas, by Granville T. Walker [and others] With a biographical essay by Robert I. Friedly. St. Louis, Bethany Press [1973] 64 p. port. 21 cm. [BR50.F63] 73-9560 ISBN 0-8272-1005-1 1.95
1. Theology—Addresses, essays, lectures. 2. Fiers, Alan Dale. I. Fiers, Alan Dale. II. Walker, Granville T.
Contents omitted.

FROM faith to faith : 220'.6
essays to honor of Donald G. Miller on his seventieth birthday / edited by Dikran Y. Hadidian. Pittsburgh : Pickwick Press, 1979. p. cm. (Pittsburgh theological monograph series ; 31) "Bibliography of Donald G. Miller": p. [BS540.F75] 79-23408 ISBN 0-915138-38-7 pbk. : 14.50
1. Miller, Donald G.—Addresses, essays, lectures. 2. Miller, Donald G.—Bibliography. 3. Bible—Criticism, interpretation, etc.—Addresses, essays, lectures. 4. Theology—Addresses, essays, lectures. I. Hadidian, Dikran Y. II. Series.

FULLERTON, Kemper, 1865- 252.5
Essays & sketches; Oberlin, 1904-1934, by Kemper Fullerton. New Haven, Pub. for Oberlin college by Yale university press; London, H. Milford, Oxford university press, 1938. x, 284 p., 1 l. 26 cm. "Essays and sketches, most of which are definitely connected with the noon-hour chapel service in Oberlin college."--Foreword. [BV4310.F8] 39-1969
1. Theology—Addresses, essays, lectures. 2. Oberlin college. I. Title.

FULLERTON, Kemper, 1865-1940. 208
Essays & sketches, Oberlin, 1904-1934. Freeport, N.Y., Books for Libraries Press [1971, c1938] x, 284 p. 23 cm. (Essay index reprint series) [BV4310.F8 1971] 70-156644 ISBN 0-8369-2361-8
1. Oberlin College. 2. Theology—Addresses, essays, lectures. I. Title.

THE Future of our religious past; essays in honour of Rudolf Bultmann. 200.9
Edited by James M. Robinson. Translated by Charles E. Carlston and Robert P. Scharlemann. New York, Harper & Row [1971] xi, 372 p. port. 22 cm. Translation of selected papers from Zeit und Geschichte. Contents.Contents.—Exegesis: Eschatology and history in the light of the Dead Sea scrolls, by N. A. Dahl. Eschatological expectation in the proclamation of Jesus, by W. G. Kummel. Some thoughts on the theme 'The doctrine of reconciliation in the New Testament,' by E. Kasemann. The theological aspects of primitive Christian heresy, by H. Koester. Logoi sophon: on the Gattung of Q, by J. M. Robinson. [Baptisma metanoias eis aphesin amarteion (romanized form)], by H. Thyen. Peter's confession and the Satan saying: the problem of Jesus' messiahship, by E. Dinkler. The risen Lord and the earthly Jesus: Matthew 28.16-20, by G. Bornkamm. The mother of wisdom, by H. Conzelmann.—Theology and philosophy: Time and word, by G. Ebeling. The hermeneutical problem, by E. Fuchs. Dietrich Bonhoeffer and Rudolf Bultmann, by G. Krause. The debt and responsibility of theology, by F. Gogarten. From the last Marburg lecture course, by M. Heidegger. Philosophical meditation on the seventh chapter of Paul's Epistle to the Romans, by H. Jonas.—List of English works and translations (p. [351]-357) [BR50.B849132 1971] 70-148440 18.95
1. Theology—Addresses, essays, lectures. I. Bultmann, Rudolf Karl, 1884- II. Robinson, James McConkey, 1924- ed.

GABRIEL, Ralph Henry, 1890- ed. 201'.1
Christianity and modern thought, by Charles R. Brown [and others] Edited with a foreword by Ralph H. Gabriel. Freeport, N.Y., Books for Libraries Press [1973] p. (Essay index reprint series) Reprint of the 1924 ed. [BR50.G2 1973] 72-10705 ISBN 0-8369-7217-1
1. Theology—Addresses, essays, lectures. I. Brown, Charles Reynolds, 1862-1950. II. Title.

GARDNER-SMITH, Percival, 1888- ed. 260
The roads converge; a contribution to the question of Christian reunion, by members of Jesus College, Cambridge. Introd. by C. H. Dodd. New York, St. Martin's [1964, c.]1963. x, 253p. 23cm. Bibl. 64-10301 7.00 bds.,
1. Theology—Addresses, essays, lectures. 2. Christianity—Addresses, essays, lectures. I. Cambridge. University. Jesus College. II. Title.

GARRETT Biblical institute, Evanston, Ill. 204
The theological school to-day; addresses given on the occasion of the inauguration of President Frederick Carl Eiselen and the sixty-eight annual commencement of Garrett Biblical institute. Evanston, Ill., Garrett Biblical institute, [1924?] 106 p. 22 1/2 cm. Contents.The theological school to-day, by F. C. Eiselen.--The teacher, by E. H. Hughes.--The making of the prophet, by L. H. Hough.--Christian service, by James Moffatt.--Essentials of a world religion, by J. E. Crowther.--Christian controversy, by F. J. McConnell.--Address at the naming of the Charles Macaulay Stuart chapel, by H. G. Smith.--The charge to the President, by John Thompson. [BV4070.G265 1924] 41-17716
1. Elselen, Frederick Carl, 1872-1937. 2. Theology—Addresses, essays, lectures. I. Title.

GARRISON, Winfred Ernest, 1874- 208
Variations on a theme: "God saw that it was good." St. Louis, Bethany Press [1964] 208 p. 23 cm. Bibliographical references included in footnotes. [BT80.G37] 64-12009
1. Theology — Addresses, essays, lectures. I. Title.

GARRISON, Winfred Ernest, 1874- 208
Variations on a theme: 'God saw that it was good.' St. Louis, Bethany [c.1964] 208p. 23cm. Bibl. 64-12009 3.50
1. Theology—Addresses, essays, lectures. I. Title.

GLADSTONE, William Ewart, 1809-1898. 200'.1
Later gleanings. A new series of Gleanings of past years: theological and ecclesiastical. Freeport, N.Y., Books for Libraries Press [1972] 426 p. 23 cm. (Essay index reprint series) Reprint of the 1897 ed. Includes bibliographical references. [BR85.G53 1972] 72-8478 ISBN 0-8369-7314-3
1. Theology—Addresses, essays, lectures. I. Title.

GOD and the good : 230
essays in honor of Henry Stob / edited by Clifton Orlebeke and Lewis Smedes. Grand Rapids : Eerdmans, [1975] 227 p. : port. ; 23 cm. Bibliography of Henry Stob compiled by Peter DeKlerk": p. 221-227. [BR50.G538] 74-31479 ISBN 0-8028-3454-X : 6.95
1. Stob, Henry, 1908- —Bibliography. 2. Theology—Addresses, essays, lectures. I. Stob, Henry, 1908- II. Orlebeke, Clifton, ed. III. Smedes, Lewis B., ed.
Contents omitted.

GODWIN, William, 1756-1836. 230
Essays / by William Godwin. Folcroft, Pa. : Folcroft Library Editions, 1977. viii, 293 p. ; 23 cm. Reprint of the 1873 ed. published by H. S. King, London. Contents.Contents.—Preliminary essay.—Preface to essay I.—On a state of future retribution.—On the present life of man considered as a state of probation for a future world.—On contrition.—On the death of Jesus considered as an atonement for sin.—On providence.—Note to essay V (fragment).—On the question, what shall we do to be saved? (fragment).—On faith and works.—On the character of Jesus.—On the history and effects of the Christian religion. [BR85.G577 1977] 77-23245 ISBN 0-8414-4502-8 : 35.00
1. Theology—Addresses, essays, lectures. I. Title.

GORDON College of Theology and Missions 207.744
Gordon 75th anniversary war. [Wenham, Mass., Gordon College and Gordon Divinity School, 1964] 1 v. (unpaged) illus., ports. 28 cm. Cover title. [BV4070.G7565 1964] 66-53513
I. Gordon College of Theology and Missions. Divinity School. II. Title.

THE Gospel as history / 230
edited by Vilmos Vajta. Philadelphia : Fortress Press, [1975] viii, 247 p. ; 22 cm. (The Gospel encounters history series) Includes bibliographical references. [BR50.G584] 74-263348 ISBN 0-8006-0410-5 : 10.95
1. Theology—Addresses, essays, lectures. I. Vajta, Vilmos. II. Series.

GREEN, Beriah, 1795-1874. 261
The miscellaneous writings of Beriah Green. Whitesboro [N.Y.] The Oneida institute, 1841. vii, 408 p. 19 1/2 cm. [BR85.G645] 45-51719
1. Theology—Addresses, essays, lectures. I. Oneida institute, Whitesboro, N.Y. II. Title.

GUERRY, William Alexander, 1861-1928. 230'.3'08
A 20th century prophet : being the life and thought of William Alexander Guerry, eighth Bishop of South Carolina / edited by Edward B. Guerry. Sewanee, Tenn. : University Press, c1976. 199 p. [1] leaf of plates : ports. ; 24 cm. Includes bibliographical references. [BX5995.G9A25 1976] 76-382338
1. Theology—Addresses, essays, lectures. I. Guerry, Edward B., 1902- II. Title.

HANS Kung, his work and his way / edited by Hermann Haring 230.2'0924
and Karl-Josef Kuschel ; bibliography by Margret Gentner ; translated by Robert Nowell. Garden City, N.Y. : Image Books, 1980, c1979. 254 p. ; 18 cm. Translation of Hans Kung : weg und werk. Bibliography: p. [187]-254. [BX4705.K76H3613 1980] 79-8702 ISBN 0-385-15852-1 pbk. : 4.50
1. Kung, Hans, 1928- —Addresses, essays, lectures. 2. Kung, Hans, 1928- —Bibliography. 3. Theology—Addresses, essays, lectures. I. Kung, Hans, 1928- II. Haring, Hermann, 1937- III. Kuschel, Karl-Josef, 1948-

HARD questions / 230
edited by Frank Colquhoun. [1st American ed.]. Downers Grove, Ill. : InterVarsity Press, 1977, c1976. 131 p. ; 21 cm. Includes bibliographical references. [BR96.H32 1977] 77-150604 ISBN 0-87784-720-7 : 2.95
1. Theology—Addresses, essays, lectures. I. Colquhoun, Frank.

HARTT, Julian Norris. 230
The restless quest / Julian N. Hartt. Philadelphia : United Church Press, [1975] 189 p. 21 cm. "A Pilgrim Press book." Includes bibliographical references. [BR85.H29] 74-26836 ISBN 0-8298-0289-4 : 6.95
1. Theology—Addresses, essays, lectures. I. Title.

HARVARD university. Divinity school. 207.744
The Harvard divinity school bulletin; issue containing the annual lectures and book reviews. Cambridge, Mass., Harvard university press [19- v. 21 cm. (On cover: Official register of Harvard university) [BV4070.H423] 45-27720
1. Theology—Addresses, essays, lectures. 2. Books—Reviews. I. Title.

HEALEY, Francis G. 201.1
What theologians do [by] P. R. Ackroyd [and others] Edited by F. G. Healey. Grand Rapids, Eerdmans [1971, c1970] 354 p. 22 cm. First published in London in 1971 under title: Preface to Christian studies. Includes bibliographies. [BR118.H42 1971b] 75-162040
1. Theology—Addresses, essays, lectures. I. Ackroyd, Peter R. II. Title.

HEDGE, Frederic Henry, 1805-1890, ed. 204
Recent inquiries in theology, by eminent English churchmen;being "essays and reviews." 2d American, from the 2d London ed. With an appendix. Edited with an introduction, by Rev. Frederic H. Hedge, D.D. Boston, Walker, Wise, and company, 1861. xiv, 498 p. 20 cm. [BR85.H4] 15-
1. Theology—Addresses, essays, lectures. I. Title.
Contents omitted.

HEDGE, Frederic Henry, 1805-1890. 261
Ways of the spirit, and other essays. By Frederic Henry Hedge ... Boston, Roberts brothers, 1877. 2 p. l, 367 p. 18 1/2 cm. [BR85.H53] 12-34065
1. Theology—Addresses, essays, lectures. I. Title.

HEFNER, Philip J., ed. 208.2
The scope of grace; essays on nature and grace in honor of Joseph Sittler, Philadelphia, Fortress [1964] x, 310p. port. 22cm. Bibl. 64-23065 4.95
1. Theology—Addresses, essays, lectures. 2. Sittler, Jooseph. I. Sittler, Joseph. II. Title.

HERZOG, Frederick, comp. 201'.1'08
Theology of the liberating word. Nashville, Abingdon Press [1971] 123 p. 23 cm. Translation of articles selected from Evangelische Theologie, with an introd. by the compiler. Contents.Contents.—Introduction: A new church conflict? By F. Herzog.—God, as a word of our language; for Helmut Gollwitzer on his sixtieth birthday, by E. Jungel.—From the Word to

the words; Karl Barth and the tasks of practical theology, by H.-D. Bastian.—The living God; a chapter of Biblical theology, by H.-J. Kraus.—Paul's doctrine of justification: theology or anthropology? By H. Conzelmann. Includes bibliographical references. [BR50.H425] 78-141148 ISBN 0-687-41534-9 2.75
1. Theology—Addresses, essays, lectures. I. Evangelische Theologie. II. Title.

HOLMER, Paul L. 230
The grammar of faith / Paul L. Holmer. 1st ed. San Francisco : Harper & Row, c1978. p. cm. [BR85.H574] 78-3351 ISBN 0-06-064003-0 : 10.00
1. Theology—Addresses, essays, lectures. I. Title.

HUNTER, Archibald Macbride. 230
Jesus : Lord and Saviour / [by] A. M. Hunter. London : S.C.M. Press, 1976. vii, 182 p. ; 22 cm. Includes bibliographical references. [BR85.H743] 77-355602 ISBN 0-334-00804-2 : 2.50
1. Theology—Addresses, essays, lectures.

HUNTER, Archibald Macbride. 230
Jesus, Lord and Saviour / A. M. Hunter. 1st American ed. Grand Rapids : Eerdmans, 1978, c1976. vi, 181 p. ; 22 cm. Includes bibliographical references. [BR85.H743 1978] 78-19193 ISBN 0-8028-1755-6 pbk. : 4.95
1. Theology—Addresses, essays, lectures. I. Title.

HUTTON, Richard Holt, 1826-1897. 261
Theological essays, by Richard Holt Hutton ... 3d ed.--rev. London and New York, Macmillan and co., 1888. xivi, 424 p. 19 cm. [BR85.H83 1888] 38-37827
1. Theology—Addresses, essays, lectures. I. Title.

INTERGERINI parietis septum (Eph. 2:14) : essays / presented to Markus Barth on his sixty-fifth birthday ; edited by Dikran Y. Hadidian. Pittsburgh, Pa. : Pickwick Press, 1980. p. cm. (Pittsburgh theological monograph series ; 33) Includes one essay in French and one in German. "Bibliography of Markus Barth": p. [BR50.I57] 19 81-284 ISBN 0-915138-42-5 : 15.95 230
1. Barth, Markus—Addresses, essays, lectures. 2. Theology—Addresses, essays, lectures. I. Barth, Markus. II. Hadidian, Dikran Y. III. Title. IV. Series.

IRONSIDE, Henry Allan, 1876-1951. 252
Miscellaneous papers. New York, Loizeaux Bros. [1945] 2v. 20cm. [BR85.I7] 54-37436
1. Theology—Addresses, essays, lectures. I. Title.

JENKINS, David E. 200
The contradiction of Christianity / [by] David E. Jenkins. London : S.C.M. Press, 1976. viii, 162 p. ; 23 cm. (Edward Cadbury lectures ; 1974) Includes bibliographical references and index. [BR85.J44] 76-375639 ISBN 0-334-00289-3 : £4.50
1. Theology—Addresses, essays, lectures. I. Title. II. Series.

JERUSALEM and Athens; 201'.1
critical discussions on the theology and apologetics of Cornelius Van Til. Edited by E. R. Geehan. [Nutley, N.J.] Presbyterian and Reformed Pub. Co., 1971. xv, 498 p. 23 cm. Includes bibliographical references. [BR50.J4] 78-155779 9.95
1. Van Til, Cornelius, 1895- 2. Van Til, Cornelius, 1895- —Bibliography. 3. Theology—Addresses, essays, lectures. I. Geehan, E. R., ed.

JOHN Paul II, Pope, 1920- 230'.2
Ireland, "In the footsteps of St. Patrick" / John Paul II ; compiled and indexed by the Daughters of St. Paul. Boston, MA : St. Paul Editions, c1979. 141 p., [8] leaves of plates : ill. ; 19 cm. Includes index. [BX1755.J645] 79-24934 ISBN 0-8198-0624-2 : 3.95 ISBN 0-8198-0625-0 pbk. : 2.95
1. Theology—Addresses, essays, lectures. 2. Ireland—Moral conditions—Addresses, essays, lectures. I. Daughters of St. Paul. II. Title. III. Title: "In the footsteps of St. Patrick."

JONES, Rufus Matthew, 1863-1948, ed. 201
Religious foundations, by A. Clutton-Brock [and others] Edited by Rufus M. Jones. Freeport, N.Y., Books for Libraries Press [1973] p. (Essay index reprint series) Reprint of the 1923 ed. [BR50.J6 1973] 73-1195 ISBN 0-518-10057-X
1. Theology—Addresses, essays, lectures. I. Clutton-Brock, Arthur, 1868-1924. II. Title.

JUBILEE : 260
a study resource for the bicentennial / contributors, Walter Rauschenbusch ... [et al.] ; study guide, Mark Matheny. Nashville : Upper Room, c1976. x, 101 p. ; 20 cm. Bibliography: p. 100-101. [BR50.J8] 75-39964 2.50
1. Theology—Addresses, essays, lectures. I. Rauschenbusch, Walter, 1861-1918.
Contents omitted.

KERR, Hugh Thomson, 1909- 230
Our life in God's light : essays / by Hugh T. Kerr ; edited by John M. Mulder. 1st ed. Philadelphia : Westminster Press, c1979. 349 p. : ill. ; 21 cm. "Bibliography of the writings of Hugh T. Kerr": p. 325-349. [BR50.K39] 78-24089 ISBN 0-664-21372-3 : 12.50 ISBN 0-664-24235-9 pbk. : 7.95
1. Kerr, Hugh Thomson, 1909- —Addresses, essays, lectures. 2. Kerr, Hugh Thomson, 1909- —Bibliography. 3. Theology—Addresses, essays, lectures. 4. Theology today—Addresses, essays, lectures. I. Mulder, John M., 1946- II. Title.

KOYAMA, Kosuke, 1929- 230'.0959
Waterbuffalo theology / Kosuke Koyama. Maryknoll, N.Y. : Orbis Books, [1974] ix, 239 p. : ill. ; 22 cm. Includes bibliographical references. [BR85.K68 1974] 74-80980 ISBN 0-88344-702-9 : 4.95
1. Theology—Addresses, essays, lectures. I. Title.

KUITERT, Harminus Martinus. 230
The necessity of faith : or, Without faith you're as good as dead / by Harry M. Kuitert ; translated by John K. Tunistra. Grand Rapids, Mich. : W. B. Eerdmans Pub. Co., c1976. 159 p. ; 18 cm. Translation of Zonder geloof vaart niemand wel. Bibliography: p. 154-159. [BR85.K8413] 76-17837 ISBN 0 ISBN 0-8028-1616-9 pbk. : 3.95
1. Theology—Addresses, essays, lectures. I. Title.

KUNG, Hans, 1928- 230
Consensus in theology? : A dialogue with Hans Kung, Edward Schillebeeckx / by Hans Kung, EdwardSchillebeeckx, and David Tracey ... [et al.] ; edited by Leonard Swidler. 1st ed. Philadelphia : Westminster Press, c1980. viii, 165 p. ; 23 cm. "Originally published as Journal of ecumenical studies 17, no. 1 (Winter 1980)." Includes bibliographical references. [BR50.K75] 80-63585 ISBN 0-664-24322-3 : 11.95
1. Kung, Hans, 1928- —Addresses, essays, lectures. 2. Schillebeeckx, Edward Cornelis Florentius Alfons, 1914- —Addresses, essays, lectures. 3. Theology—Addresses, essays, lectures. I. Schillebeeckx, Edward Cornelis Florentius Alfons, 1914- joint author. II. Swidler, Leonard J. III. Journal of ecumenical studies. IV. Title.

KUNG, Hans, 1928- 230
Consensus in theology? : A dialogue with Hans Kung, Edward Schillebeeckx / by Hans Kung, Edward Schillebeeckx, and David Tracey ... [et al.] ; edited by Leonard Swidler. 1st ed. Philadelphia : Westminister Press, c1980. viii, 165 p. ; 23 cm. "Originally published as Journal of ecumenical studies 17, no. 1 (Winter 1980)." Includes bibliographical references. [BR50.K75] 19 80-65385 ISBN 0-664-24322-3 : 12.95
1. Kung, Hans, 1928- —Addresses, essays, lectures. 2. Schillebeeckx, Edward Cornelis Florentius Alfons, 1914- —Addresses, essays, lectures. 3. Theology—Addresses, essays, lectures. I. Schillebeeckx, Edward Cornelis Florentius Alfons, 1914- joint author. II. Swidler, Leonard J. III. Journal of ecumenical studies. IV. Title.

LASH, Nicholas. 230
Theology on Dover Beach / Nicholas Lash. New York : Paulist Press, c1979. 187 p. ; 22 cm. Includes bibliographical references and index. [BR85.L425 1979] 79-88760 ISBN 0-8091-2241-3 pbk. : 9.95
1. Theology—Addresses, essays, lectures. I. Title.

LEIBRECHT, Walter, ed. 230.04
Religion and culture; essays in honor of Paul Tillich. [1st ed.] New York, Harper [1959] xi, 399p. port. 25cm. Bibliographical references included in 'Notes' (p.355-363) 'A bibliography of Paul Tillich, complied by Peter H. John': p.367-396. [BR50.L38] 58-5193
1. Tillich, Paul, 1886- 2. Theology—Addresses, essays, lectures. 3. Civilization, Modern—Addresses, essays, lectures. I. Title.

LEIBRECHT, Walter, ed. 230
Religion and culture; essays in honor of Paul Tillich. Edited by Walter Leibrecht. Freeport, N.Y., Books for Libraries Press [1972, c1959] xi, 399 p. port. 24 cm. (Essay index reprint series) Bibliography: p. 367-396. [BR50.L38 1972] 78-167376 ISBN 0-8369-2558-0
1. Theology—Addresses, essays, lectures. 2. Civilization, Modern—Addresses, essays, lectures. I. Tillich, Paul, 1886-1965. II. Title.

LEWIS, C. S. 1898-1963. (Clive Staples), 230
The visionary Christian : 131 readings from C.S. Lewis / selected and edited by Chad Walsh. New York : Macmillan, c1981. p. cm. Bibliography: p. [BR85.L4846 1981] 19 81-11770 ISBN 0-02-570540-7 : 10.95
1. Theology—Addresses, essays, lectures. I. Walsh, Chad, 1914- II. Title.

LEWIS, Clive Staples, 1898- 204
The weight of glory, and other addresses. New York, Macmillan Co., 1949. 66 p. 20 cm. "Published in England under the title, Transposition and other addresses." Contents.--The weight of glory.--Transposition.--Membership.--Learning in war-time.--The inner ring. [BR123.L485 1949a] 49-6869
1. Theology—Addresses, essays, lectures. I. Title.

LEWIS, Clive Staples, 1898-1963. 201
God in the dock; essays on theology and ethics, by C. S. Lewis. Edited by Walter Hooper. Grand Rapids, Eerdmans [1970] 346 p. 23 cm. Includes bibliographical references. [BR85.L484] 70-129851 6.95
1. Theology—Addresses, essays, lectures. I. Title.

LEWIS, Clive Staples, 1898-1963. 230
The weight of glory, and other addresses / C. S. Lewis. Rev. and expanded ed. / edited, and with an introd., by Walter Hooper. New York : Macmillan, c1980. p. cm. Contents.Contents.—The weight of glory.—Learning in war-time.—Why I am not a pacifist.—Transposition.—Is theology poetry?—The inner ring.—Membership.—On forgiveness.—A slip of the tongue. [BR50.L396 1980] 80-18792 ISBN 0-02-095980-X pbk. : 1.95
1. Theology—Addresses, essays, lectures. I. Hooper, Walter. II. Title.

LONNING, Per 210.81
The dilemma of contemporary theology prefigured in Luther, Pascal, Kierkegaard, Nietzsche. [Oslo] Universitetsforlaget; New York, Humanities, 1964, c.1962] 139p. illus. 23cm. (Scandinavian univ. bks.) 64-5569 3.00 bds.,
1. Theology—Addresses, essays, lectures. I. Title.

LONNING, Per. 210.81
The dilemma of contemporary theology prefigured in Luther, Pascal, Kierkegaard, Nietzsche. [Olso] Universitetsforlaget; New York, Humanities Press, 1962 [i.e. 1964] 139 p. illus. 23 cm. (Scandinavian university books) [BT15.L6] 64-5569
1. Theology — Addresses, essays, lectures. I. Title.

LONNING, Per 208
Off the beaten path [by] Per Lonning. [Tr. by J. M. Moe, H. George Anderson. 1st ed.] New York, Harper [1966] ix, 176p. 22cm. Portions have appeared in Norwegian in two volumes, Kan kirken moderniseres? and Utenfor allfarvei. [BR85.L83] 66-20780 4.50
1. Theology — Addresses, essays, lectures. I. Title.

LONNING, Per. 208
Off the beaten path [by] Per Lonning. [Translated by J. M. Moe and H. George Anderson. 1st ed.] New York, Harper & Row [1966] ix, 176 p. 22 cm. "Portions...have appeared in Norwegian in two volumes, Kan kirken moderniseres? ...and Utenfor allfarvel." [BR85.L83] 66-20780
1. Theology — Addresses, essays, lectures. I. Title.

LOUTH, Andrew. 230
Theology and spirituality : a paper read by Andrew Louth to the Origen Society in St. John's College on 30 October 1974 ; also, Contemporary doctrinal criticism and Catholic theology : an article first published in Faith and Unity, Autumn 1975. Oxford : S.L.G. Press, 1976. [2], 24 p. ; 21 cm. (Fairacres publications ; 55 ISSN 0307-1405s) [BT80.L68]i76-368449 ISBN 0-7283-0057-5 : £0.35
1. Theology—Addresses, essays, lectures. 2. Spirituality—Addresses, essays, lectures. I. Title.

LUCAS, John Randolph. 230
Freedom and grace : essays / by J. R. Lucas. Grand Rapids : Eerdmans, 1976. xiv, 138 p. ; 23 cm. [BR50.L77 1976] 75-43843 ISBN 0-8028-3482-5 : 7.95
1. Theology—Addresses, essays, lectures. I. Title.

LUCAS, John Randolph. 230
Freedom and grace / essays by J. R. Lucas. London : SPCK, 1976. xiv, 138 p. ; 22 cm. Includes bibliographical references. [BR85.L878] 76-376729 ISBN 0-281-02932-6 : £3.95
1. Theology—Addresses, essays, lectures. I. Title.

MACDONALD, George, 1824-1905. 230
Life essential : the hope of the Gospel / George MacDonald ; edited by Rolland Hein. Wheaton, Ill. : H. Shaw Publishers, c1974. 102 p. ; 22 cm. (The Wheaton literary series) Abridgment of The hope of the Gospel. [BR85.M162 1974] 74-16732 ISBN 0-87788-499-4 : 1.95
1. Theology—Addresses, essays, lectures. I. Hein, Rolland. II. Title.

MCKIM, Randolph Harrison, 1842-1920. 225
Present-day problems of Christian thought, by Randolph Harrison McKim... New York, T. Whittaker [c1900] 4 p. l., [3]-317 p. 19 1/2 cm. [BR121.M325] 1-29211
1. Theology—Addresses, essays, lectures. I. Title.
Contents omitted.

MANDEVILLE, Bernard, 1670-1733. 201'.1
Free thoughts on religion, the church, and national happiness / by Bernard Mandeville. Delmar, N.Y. : Scholars' Facsimiles & Reprints, [1977] p. cm. Photoreprint of the 1720 ed. printed by T. Jauncy, London. [BR75.M28 1977] 77-17171 ISBN 0-8201-1300-X lib.bdg. : 35.00
1. Theology—Addresses, essays, lectures. 2. Political science—Addresses, essays, lectues. I. Title.

MARTY, Martin E. 1928- ed. 230.08
New theology. no. 1- New York, Macmillan. 1964 v. 18 cm. Editors: 1964- M. E. Marty and D. G. Peerman. Consists of reprints from various religious journals. [BR53.N5] 64-3132
1. Theology — Addresses, essays, lectures. 2. Christianity — 20th cent. — Addresses, essays, lectures. I. Peerman, Dean G., ed. II. Title.

MARTY, Martin E., 1928- ed. 230.082
New theology, no. 1, Ed. by Martin E. Marty, Dean G. Peerman. New York, Macmillan [1967] v. 19cm. (MP 08742) Bibl. [BR53.M37] 64-3132 1.95 pap.,
1. Theology—Addresses, essays, lectures. 2. christianity—20th Cent. —Addresses, essays, lectures. I. Peerman, Dean G., joint ed. II. Title.

MARTY, Martin E., 1928- 230.082
ed.
New theology no. 1, Ed. by Martin E. Marty, Dean G. Peerman. New York, Macmillan [c.1964] 256p. 18cm. (147) Bibl. 64-3132 1.95 pap.,
1. Theology—Addresses, essays, lectures. 2. Christianity—20th cent.—Addresses, essays, lectures. I. Peerman, Dean, G., joint ed. II. Title.

MARTY, Martin E., 1928- 230.082
ed.
New theology, no. 3. Ed. by Martin E. Marty, Dean G. Peerman. New York, Macmillan [c.1966] 190p. 18cm. (08741) Bibl. [BR53.M37] 64-3132 1.95 pap.,
1. Theology—Addresses, essays, lectures. 2. Christianity—20th cent.—Addresses, essays, lectures. I. Peerman, Dean G., joint ed. II. Title.

MARTY, Martin E., 1928- 230.082
ed.
New theology, no. 2. Ed. by Martin E. Marty. Dean G. Peerman. New York, Macmillan [c.1965] 316p. 18cm. (185) Bibl. [BR53.M37] 64-3132 1.95 pap.,
1. Theology—Addresses, essays, lectures. 2. Christianity—20th cent.—Addresses, essays, lectures. I. Peerman, Dean G., joint ed. II. Title.

MATTHEWS, Walter Robert, 230.04
1881-
God and this troubled world; essays in spiritual construction, by W. R. Matthews . preface to the American edition by the author. New York, E. P. Dutton & co., inc. [c1934] xvii, 243 p. 20 1/2 cm. "First edition." London edition (Nisbet and co., ltd.) has title: Essays in construction. [BT15.M3 1934a] 34-33076
1. Theology—Addresses, essays, lectures. I. Title.

MAURICE, Frederick 230.04
Denison, 1805-1872.
Theological essays. Introd. by Edward F. Carpenter. New York, Harper [c1957] 331p. illus. 21cm. [BR85.M33 1957a] 58-5194
1. Theology—Addresses, essays, lectures. I. Title.

MICHALSON, Carl. 230
The witness of radical faith / by Carl Michalson. Nashville : Tidings, [1974] 108 p. ; 19 cm. [BR85.M479] 74-80895 pbk. : 1.75
1. Theology—Addresses, essays, lectures. I. Title.

MIGUEZ Bonino, Jose. 230
Room to be people : an interpretation of the message of the Bible for today's world / Jose Miguez Bonino ; translated by Vickie Leach. Philadelphia : Fortress Press, c1979. 80 p. ; 22 cm. Translation of Espacio para ser hombres. [BR85.M48513] 78-14662 ISBN 0-8006-1349-X : 3.95
1. Theology—Addresses, essays, lectures. I. Title.

MOLTMANN, Jurgen. 201'.1
Hope and planning. [1st U.S. ed.] New York, Harper & Row [1971] viii, 228 p. 22 cm. "Translated by Margaret Clarkson from selections from the German Perspektiven der Theologie; gesammelte Aufsatze." Includes bibliographical references. [BT15.M6132 1971] 79-124703 6.50
1. Theology—Addresses, essays, lectures. I. Title.

MOLTMANN, Jurgen. 230
Religion, revolution, and the future. Translated by M. Douglas Meeks. New York, Scribner [1969] xvii, 220 p. 24 cm. Bibliographical footnotes. [BT15.M62] 69-17053 5.95
1. Theology—Addresses, essays, lectures. I. Title.

MONTGOMERY, John Warwick. 230.4'1
History & Christianity. Downers Grove, Ill., InterVarsity Press [1971] 110 p. 18 cm. Contains 4 articles published Dec. 1964 to Mar. 1965 in His magazine. Includes bibliographical references. [BR85.M615 1971] 78-160367 ISBN 0-87784-437-2
1. Theology—Addresses, essays, lectures. I. Title.

MOON, Sun Myung. 230
Christianity in crisis: new hope. [Washington] HSA-UWC, 1974. ix, 123 p. illus. 19 cm. Translation of 3 speeches from the author's 1973 tour delivered Oct. 20, 21, and 28, 1973. Contents.Contents.—God's hope for man.—God's hope for America.—The future of Christianity. [BR85.M617] 74-76156
1. Theology—Addresses, essays, lectures. I. Title.

MOON, Sun Myung. 230'.9'9
New hope; twelve talks. [Washington] Holy Spirit Association for the Unification of World Christianity [1973] xi, 103 p. port. 22 cm. [BR85.M618] 73-88416
1. Theology—Addresses, essays, lectures. I. Title.

MOONEY, Christopher F., 201'.1
1925-
The making of man; essays in the Christian spirit, by Christopher F. Mooney. New York, Paulist Press [1971] vii, 181 p. 21 cm. Includes bibliographical references. [BR85.M62] 72-147906 2.95
1. Theology—Addresses, essays, lectures. I. Title.

MOORE, Basil, comp. 230'.0968
The challenge of Black theology in South Africa. Atlanta, John Knox Press [1974, c1973] xii, 156 p. 22 cm. First published in 1973 under title: Black theology. Includes bibliographical references. [BR50.M63 1974] 73-16918 ISBN 0-8042-0794-1 4.95
1. Theology—Addresses, essays, lectures. 2. Blacks—South Africa—Religion—Addresses, essays, lectures. I. Title.

MORGAN, Everett J., comp. 201
Christian witness in the secular city. Compiled and edited by Everett J. Morgan. Chicago, Loyola University Press [1970] 12, 352 p. 23 cm. Includes bibliographical references. [BR50.M64] 75-133951
1. Theology—Addresses, essays, lectures. I. Title.

MYERS, Jacob Martin, 1904- 208.1
ed.
Theological and missionary studies in memory of John Aberly. Edited by J. M. Myers, O. Reimherr [and] H. N. Bream. Gettysburg, Pa., Printed by Times and News Pub. Co., 1965. vii, 152 p. port. 24 cm. (Gettysburg theological studies,2) Contents.Contents omitted. Bibliographical footnotes. [BR50.M84] 65-16692
1. Theology — Addresses, essays, lectures. 2. Missions — Addresses, essays, lectures. 3. Aberly, John, 1867-1963. I. Reimherr, Otto, 1917- joint ed. II. Bream, H. N., joint ed. III. Aberly, John, 1867-1963. IV. Title. V. Series.

NATIONAL Holiness 230
Association.
Projecting our heritage; papers and messages delivered at the centennial convention of the National Holiness Association, Cleveland, Ohio, April 16-19, 1968. Compiled by Myron F. Boyd and Merne A. Harris. Kansas City, Mo., Beacon Hill Press of Kansas City [1969] 157 p. 20 cm. [BT10.N35] 75-79957
1. Theology—Addresses, essays, lectures. 2. Sanctification—Addresses, essays, lectures. I. Boyd, Myron F., comp. II. Harris, Merne A., comp. III. Title.

NEAL, Marie Augusta. 261.8
A socio-theology of letting go : the role of a First World church facing Third World peoples / by Marie Augusta Neal. New York : Paulist Press, c1977. vii, 118 p. ; 21 cm. (An Exploration book) Bibliography: p. 112-118. [BR85.N28] 76-50953 ISBN 0-8091-2012-7 pbk. : 3.95
1. Theology—Addresses, essays, lectures. 2. United States—Religion—1945- —Addresses, essays, lectures. 3. Church and social problems—Addresses, essays, lectures. I. Title.

THE New life : 230
readings in Christian theology / Millard J. Erickson, editor. Grand Rapids : Baker Book House, c1979. 524 p. ; 22 cm. Includes bibliographical references. [BR53.N49] 79-122112 ISBN 0-8010-3340-3 : 10.95
1. Theology—Addresses, essays, lectures. I. Erickson, Millard J.

NEW theology. 230.08
no. 5- 1968- New York, Macmillan. v. 18cm. Eds.: 1964-68 M. E. Marty, D. G. Peerman. Consists of reprints from various religious journals. [BR53.N5] 64-3132 1.95 pap.,
1. Theology—Addresses, essays, lectures. 2. Christianity—20th cent.—Addresses, essays, lectures. I. Marty, Martin E., 1928- ed. II. Peerman, Dean G. ed.

NEWTON, William Wilberforce, 204
1843-1914.
Essays of today; religious and theological. Boston, A. Williams, 1879. 253 p. 21 cm. [BR85.N55]
1. Theology—Addresses, essays, lectures. I. Title.

NO famine in the land : 230
studies in honor of John L. McKenzie / edited by James W. Flanagan, Anita Weisbrod Robinson. Missoula, Mont. : Published by Scholars Press for the Institute for Antiquity and Christianity—Claremont, c1975. xii, 349 p. : ill. ; 24 cm. Contents.Contents.—Munson, T. N. Biographical sketch of John L. McKenzie.—Robinson, A. W. Letters from life.—Freedman, D. N. The Aaronic benediction (numbers 6:24-26).—Bellefontaine, E. The curses of Deuteronomy 27.—Mendenhall, G. E. Samuel's "broken rib".—Blenkinsopp, J. The quest of the historical Saul.—Flanagan, J. W. Judah in all Israel.—Murphy, R. E. Wisdom and Yahwism.—Vawter, B. Prophecy and the redactional question.—Wicker, K. O. First century marriage ethics.—Fitzmyer, J. A. Reconciliation in Pauline theology.—Brown, R. E. Luke's method in the Annunciation narratives of chapter one.—Crossan, J. D. Jesus and pacifism.—Funk, R. W. The significance of discourse structure for the study of the New Testament.—Sloyan, G. S. Postbiblical development of the Petrine Ministry.—Cooke, B. The "war-myth" in 2nd century Christian teaching.—Burkhart, J. E. Authority, candor, and ecumenism.—Baum, G. An ecclesiological principle.—Cahill, P. J. Myth and meaning.—Robinson, J. M. The internal word in history. "A bibliography of the books, articles, and reviews of John L. McKenzie, by Donald H. Wimmer": p. 301-322. [BR50.N55] 75-33108 ISBN 0-89130-051-1 : 7.00
1. McKenzie, John L. 2. McKenzie, John L.—Bibliography. 3. Theology—Addresses, essays, lectures. I. McKenzie, John L. II. Flanagan, James W. III. Robinson, Anita Weisbrod. IV. Institute for Antiquity and Christianity.

NOGAR, Raymond J. 230
The Lord of the absurd [by] Raymond J. Nogar. [New York] Herder & Herder [1966] 157p. 21cm. [BT80.N6] 66-22608 3.95
1. Theology — Addresses, essays, lectures. I. Title.

NORRIS, John, 1657-1711. 230
Treatises upon several subjects, 1698 / John Norris. New York : Garland Pub., 1978. 4, 506 p. ; 19 cm. (British philosophers and theologians of the 17th & 18th centuries) Reprint of the 1698 ed. printed for S. Manship, London. [BR75.N67 1978] 75-11244 ISBN 0-8240-1796-X : 29.50
1. Theology—Addresses, essasy, lectures. 2. Religion—Philosophy—Addresses, essays, lectures. 3. Conduct of life—Addresses, essays, lectures. I. Title. II. Series.

NORRIS, Richard Alfred, 230.08
ed.
Lux in lumine; essays to honor W. Norman Pittenger, ed. by R. A. Norris, Jr. New York, Seabury [1966] vi, 186p. 22cm. Bibl. [BR50.N58] 66-16650 4.50
1. Theology—Addresses, essays, lectures. 2. Pittenger, William Norman, 1905—Bibl. I. Pittenger, William Norman, 1905- II. Title.
Contents omitted.

NOYES, John Humphrey, 230.9'9
1811-1886.
The Berean. Male continence. Essay on scientific propagation. New York, Arno Press, 1969. viii, 504, 24, 32 p. 24 cm. (Religion in America) Reprint of the 1847, 1872, and 1875 ed., respectively. [BR85.N68 1969] 74-83431
1. Theology—Addresses, essays, lectures. I. Noyes, John Humphrey, 1811-1886. Male continence. 1969. II. Noyes, John Humphrey, 1811-1886. Essay on scientific propagation. 1969. III. Title. IV. Title: Male continence. V. Title: Essay on scientific propagation.

NOYES, John 335'.9'74764
Humphrey, 1811-1886.
"The way of holiness" : a series of papers formerly published in the Perfectionist, at New Haven / by John H. Noyes. Westport, Conn. : Hyperion Press, 1976. p. cm. (The Radical tradition in America) Reprint of the 1838 ed. published by J. H. Noyes, Putney, Vt. [BR85.N69 1976] 75-337 ISBN 0-88355-240-X : 17.50
1. Theology—Addresses, essays, lectures. I. Title.

OUR common history as 230
Christians : essays in honor of Albert C. Outler / edited by John Deschner, Leroy T. Howe, and Klaus Penzel. New York : Oxford University Press, 1975. xxi, 298 p. ; 22 cm. [BR50.O7] 74-83988 ISBN 0-19-501865-6 : 9.50
1. Outler, Albert Cook, 1908- 2. Outler, Albert Cook, 1908- —Bibliography. 3. Theology—Addresses, essays, lectures. I. Deschner, John. II. Howe, Leroy T., 1936- III. Penzel, Klaus.
Contents omitted

PAGE, Kirby, 1890-1957. 230
Kirby Page and the social gospel : an anthology / edited, with an introd., by Charles Chatfield and Charles DeBenedetti. New York : Garland Pub., 1976. p. cm. (The Garland library of war and peace) Bibliography: p. [BR85.P23 1976] 70-147695 ISBN 0-8240-0451-5 lib.bdg. : 25.00
1. Page, Kirby, 1890-1957. 2. Page, Kirby, 1890-1957—Bibliography. 3. Theology—Addresses, essays, lectures. 4. Church and social problems—Addresses, essays, lectures. I. Title. II. Series.

PANNENBERG, Wolfhart, 1928- 230
Faith and reality / [by] Wolfhart Pannenberg ; translated [from the German] by John Maxwell. London : Search Press ; Philadelphia : Westminster Press, 1977. ix, 138 p. ; 23 cm. Translation of Glaube und Wirklichkeit. [BR85.P2613 1977b] 77-379729 ISBN 0-85532-378-7 pbk. : 5.45
1. Theology—Addresses, essays, lectures. I. Title.

PERSPECTIVES on 230'.044
evangelical theology : papers from the thirtieth annual meeting of the Evangelical Theological Society / Kenneth S. Kantzer, Stanley N. Gundry, editors. Grand Rapids, Mich. : Baker Book House, c1979. x, 289 p. ; 23 cm. Includes bibliographical references and index. [BR50.P45] 80-114075 ISBN 0-8010-5413-3 pbk. : 9.95
1. Theology—Addresses, essays, lectures. 2. Evangelicalism—Addresses, essays, lectures. I. Kantzer, Kenneth S. II. Gundry, Stanley N. III. Evangelical Theological Society.

PHELPS, Austin, 1820-1890. 208.
My note-book; fragmentary studies in theology and subjects adjacent thereto, by Austin Phelps ... New York, C. Scribner's sons, 1891. ix, 324 p. front. (port.) 20 cm. [BR85.P55] 12-37604
1. Theology—Addresses, essays, lectures. I. Title.

PHELPS, Austin, 1820-1890. 208.
My study, and other essays, by Austin Phelps ... New York, C. Scribner's sons, 1886. vi p., 1 l., 319 p. 20 cm. [BR85.P56] 12-37571
1. Theology—Addresses, essays, lectures. I. Title.

PRENTER, Regin, 1907- 230.41082
The Word and the Spirit; essays on inspiration of the Scriptures. Tr. by Harris E. Kaasa. Minneapolis, Augsburg [c.1965] 163p. 22cm. [BR85.P653] 65-12135 4.00
1. Theology—Addresses, essays, lectures. I. Title.

THE Princeton review. 285
Essays, theological and miscellaneous, reprinted from the Princeton review. Second series. Including the contributions

of the late Rev. Albert B. Dod, D.D. New York and London, Wiley and Putnam, 1847. 3 p. l., 612 p. 24 1/2 cm. [BR45.P72] ISBN 42-41958
1. Theology—Addresses, essays, lectures. 2. Presbyterian church—Addresses, essays, lectures. I. Dod, Albert Baldwin, 1805-1845. II. Title.

THE Princeton review. 285
Theological essays: reprinted from the Princeton review. New York & London, Wiley and Putnam, 1846. iv p., 1 l., 705 p. 24 cm. [BR45.P7] 42-41959
1. Theology—Addresses, essays, lectures. 2. Presbyterian church—Addresses, essays, lectures. I. Title.

PRINCETON theological seminary. 204
Biblical and theological studies, by the members of the faculty of Princeton theological seminary; published in commemoration of the one hundredth anniversary of the founding of the seminary. New York, C. Scribner's sons, 1912. 5 p. l., [3]-634 p. ii pl. (1 fold.) 24 cm. Bibliographical foot-notes. [BR50.P7] 12-10660
1. Theology—Addresses, essays, lectures. I. Title.
Contents omitted.

PROBLEMI e prospettive di teologia fondamentale. 230'.01
Problems and perspectives of fundamental theology / edited by Rene Latourelle and Gerald O'Collins ; translated by Matthew J. O'Connell. New York : Paulist Press, c1982. iv, 412 p. ; 23 cm. Translation of: Problemi e prospettive di teologia fondamentale. Includes bibliographical references and index. [BR50.P73813 1982] 19 82-81192 ISBN 0-8091-2466-1 (pbk.) : 12.95
1. Theology—Addresses, essays, lectures. 2. Theology, Catholic—Addresses, essays, lectures. I. Latourelle, Rene. II. O'Collins, Gerald. III. Title.

THE Process of religion; 200'.1
essays in honor of Dean Shailer Mathews. Edited by Miles H. Krumbine. Freeport, N.Y., Books for Libraries Press [1972] viii, 266 p. port. 23 cm. (Essay index reprint series) Reprint of the 1933 ed. Contents.Contents.—Shailer Mathews, a biographical note, by R. E. Mathews.—Theology and the social process, by E. E. Aubrey.—Whither historicism in theology, by S. J. Case.—Confused Protestantism, by J. W. Nixon.—Some reflections on the progress and decline of religion in New England, by D. C. Macintosh.—The philosophy of Protestantism in its relation to industry, by C. A. Ellwood.—The social and the individual in religion, by D. A. McGregor.—Truth and paradox, by L. H. Hough.—The validity of the concept of revelation in an empirical age, by W. M. Horton.—Theological contexts and patterns, by J. W. Buckham.—The plight of mechanism, by R. M. Vaughan.—The New Testament and the origin of Jesus (a study in social interpretation) by E. W. Parsons.—The renaissance of religion, by A. E. Haydon. [BR50.P75 1972] 71-38776 ISBN 0-8369-2667-6
1. Theology—Addresses, essays, lectures. 2. Religion—Addresses, essays, lectures. I. Mathews, Shailer, 1863-1941. II. Krumbine, Miles Henry, 1891- ed.

THE process of religion: 204
essays in honor of Dean Shailer Mathews, edited by Miles H. Krumbine ... New York, The Macmillan company, 1933. viii, 266 p. front. (port.) 20 cm. [BR50.P75] 33-13342
1. Mathews Shailer, 1863- 2. Theology—Addresses, essays, lectures. 3. Religion—Addresses, essays, lectures. I. Krumbine, Miles Henry, 1891- ed.
Contents omitted.

RAHNER, Karl, 1904- 248
Christian at the crossroads. New York : Seabury Press [1976c1975] 95p. ; 21 cm. (Crossroad book) [BR85.R237] 75-29634 ISBN 0-8164-1204-9 : 5.95
1. Theology-Addresses, essays, lectures. 2. Monastic and religious life-Addresses, essays, lectures. I. Title.

RAHNER, Karl, 1904- 230
Opportunities for faith; elements of a modern spirituality. Translated by Edward Quinn. New York, Seabury Press [1975, c1974] x, 229 p. 22 cm. Translation of Chancen des Glaubens. "A Crossroad book." Bibliography: p. [227]-229. [BR85.R22913 1975] 74-13973 ISBN 0-8164-1180-8 8.95
1. Theology—Addresses, essays, lectures. I. Title.

RASHDALL, Hastings, 1858-1924. 230
Ideas and ideals. Selected by H. D. A. Major and F. L. Cross. Freeport, N.Y., Books for Libraries Press [1968] 238 p. 22 cm. (Essay index reprint series) Reprint of 1928 ed. Contents.Contents.—The validity of religious experience.—The rights of the state.—The rights of the church.—The rights of the individual.—The idea of progress.—Modernism.—The life of Newman.—George Tyrrell.—The atonement.—The scholastic theology.—The alleged immanence of God.—The metaphysic of Mr. Bradley. [BR85.R25 1968] 68-16970
1. Theology—Addresses, essays, lectures. I. Major, Henry Dewsbury Alves, 1872- ed. II. Cross, Frank Leslie, 1900- ed. III. Title.

RECENT inquiries in 204
theology, by eminent English churchmen; being "Essays and reviews." 2d American, from the 2d London ed. With an appendix. Edited, with an introduction, by Rev. Frederic H. Hedge, D.D. Boston, Walker, Wise, and company, 1861. xiv, 498 p. 20 cm. [BR50.E78 1861 a] 15-13990
1. Theology—Addresses, essays, lectures. I. Hedge, Frederick Henry, 1805-1890, ed.
Contents omitted.

THE religious aspects of the 204
age, with a glance at the church of the present and the church of the future, being addresses delivered at the anniversary of the Young men's Christian union of New York, on the 13th and 14th days of May, 1858. By Samuel Osgood, D.D., T. J. Sawyer, D.D., Rev. O. B. Frothingham ... Hon. Horace Greeley [and others] ... 2d ed. New York, Thatcher & Hutchinson, 1858. 2 p. l., [iii]-vi, [5]-179, 7 p. 19 cm. "Publisher's preface" signed: Martin Thatcher, Orren Hutchinson. "Constitution, officers and life members of the Young men's Christian union of New York": 7 p. at end. [BR50.R4 1858] 31-14797
1. Theology—Addresses, essays, lectures. I. Thatcher, Martin ed. II. Hutchinson, Orren, joint ed. III. Young men's Christian union, New York. IV. Greeley, Horace, 1811-1872.

THE religious aspects of the 204
age, with a glance at the church of the present and the church of the future, being addresses delivered at the anniversary of the Young men's Christian union of New York, on the 13th and 14th days of May, 1858. By Samuel Osgood, D.D., T. J. Sawyer, D.D., Rev. O. B. Frothingham ... Hon. Horace Greeley [and others] New York, Thatcher & Hutchinson. 1858. 2 p. l., [iii]-vi, [5]-179 p. 19 cm. "Publisher's preface" signed: Martin Thatcher, Orren Hutchinson. [BR50.R4 1858] 33-10382
1. Theology—Addresses, essays, lectures. I. Thatcher, Martin, ed. II. Hutchinson, Orren, joint ed. III. Young men's Christian union, New York. IV. Greeley, Horace, 1811-1872.

RICHARDS, James McDowell, 1902- 201'.1
Change and the changeless; articles, essays, and sermons. Decatur, Ga., Columbia Theological Seminary, 1972. 90 p. 23 cm. Contents.Contents.—Chronology of J. McDowell Richards.—Reflections on Armistice Day.—Brothers in black.—Christian church in a world at war.—A condemnation of mob violence.—Woodrow Wilson—the Christian and the churchman.—God's commandment for His people.—A call to civil obedience and racial good will.—A prayer of invocation.—The strange story of our times.—The relevance of the Gospel.—The Holy Spirit and the church.—The church and its ministry.—World missions—a Christian imperative.—The theological seminary as a graduate professional school.—Change, and the changeless. [BR85.R53] 72-87843
1. Theology—Addresses, essays, lectures. I. Title.

SCHARLEMANN, Martin Henry 230.41
Toward tomorrow. Saint Louis, Mo., Concordia Pub. House [c.]1960. 160p. 21cm. (bibl.) 60-4034 1.95 pap.,
1. Theology—Addresses, essays, lectures. 2. Lutheran Church—Doctrinal and controversial works. I. Title.

SCHILLEBEECKX, Edward Cornelius Florentinius Alfons, 1914- 201'.1
The understanding of faith: interpretation and criticism [by] Edward Schillebeeckx. Translated by N. D. Smith. New York, Seabury Press [1974] p. cm. "A Crossroad book." Translation of Geloofsverstaan. Includes bibliographical references. [BR85.S274313] 74-12465 ISBN 0-8164-1185-9 6.95
1. Theology—Addresses, essays, lectures. 2. Hermeneutics—Addresses, essays, lectures. I. Title.

SCHNEIDER, Reinhold, 1903-1958. 230
Messages from the depths : selections from the writings of Reinhold Schneider / edited by Curt Winterhalter ; translated by Robert J. Cunningham. Chicago : Franciscan Herald Press, [1977] p. cm. Translation of Worte aus der Tiefe. Bibliography: p. [BR85.S27613] 77-12809 ISBN 0-8199-0683-2 pbk. : 4.95
1. Theology—Addresses, essays, lectures. I. Title.

SCIENCE, faith, and 230
revelation : an approach to Christian philosophy / edited by Bob E. Patterson. Nashville : Broadman Press, c1979. xi, 371 p. ; 24 cm. Festschrift in honor of Eric Charles Rust. "Publications by Eric C. Rust": p. 369-371. [BR50.S26] 79-50751 ISBN 0-8054-1809-1 pbk. : 8.95
1. Rust, Eric Charles—Addresses, essays, lectures. 2. Theology—Addresses, essays, lectures. I. Patterson, Bob E. II. Rust, Eric Charles.

SCOTT, Milton Robinson, b.1841. 234.
Essay on truth, by Milton R. Scott ... Newark, O. [1903] 120 p. 17 1/2 cm. [BR125.S338] 3-24548
1. Theology—Addresses, essays, lectures. I. Title.

SELWYN, Edward Gordon, 1885- ed. 201'.1
Essays Catholic & critical, by members of the Anglican communion. 3d ed. Freeport, N.Y., Books for Libraries Press [1971] xxxii, 456 p. 23 cm. (Essay index reprint series) "First published 1926." Contents.Contents.—The emergence of religion, by E. O. James.—The vindication of religion, by A. E. Taylor.—Authority: Authority as a ground of belief, by A. E. J. Rawlinson. The authority of the church, by W. L. Knox.—The Christian conception of God, by L. S. Thornton.—The Christ of the synoptic Gospels, by Sir E. C. Hoskyns.—The incarnation, by J. K. Mozley.—Aspects of man's condition: Sin and the fall, by E. J. Bicknell. Grace and freedom, by J. K. Mozley.—The atonement, by K. E. Kirk.—The resurrection, by E. G. Selwyn.—The spirit and the church in history, by E. Milner-White.—The Reformation, by A. H. Thompson.—The origins of the sacraments, by N. P. Williams.—The Eucharist, by W. Spens. Includes bibliographical references. [BR50.S43] 75-142695 ISBN 0-8369-2075-9
1. Theology—Addresses, essays, lectures. I. Title.

SEWALL, Frank, 1837-
The pulpit and modern thought, by Frank Sewall, D.D.; being three lectures delivered before the theological school of the New church in Cambridge, Mass., May, 1905. I. The pulpit and philosophy. II. The pulpit and psychology. III. The pulpit and sociology. Boston, Massachusetts New-church union [1905?] iv, 63 p. 23 1/2 cm. 6-26087
I. Title.

SIMPSON, Robert L. ed. 208
One faith: its Biblical, historical, and ecumenical dimensions; a series of essays in honor of Stephen J. England on the occasion of his seventieth birthday. Robert L. Simpson, editor. Enid, Okla., Phillips Univ. Pr., 1966. ix, 135p. port. 24cm. Bibl. [BR50.S53] 66-27821 2.50
1. England, Stephen Jackson, 1895- 2. Theology — Addresses, essays, lectures. I. England, Stephen Jackson, 1895- II. Title.
Contents omitted.

SMITH, George, 1800-1868. 204
Elements of divinity. A series of lectures on Biblical science, theology, church history, and homiletics. Designed for candidates for the ministry and other students of the Bible. By George Smith ... Revised by Thomas O. Summers, D.D. Nashville, Tenn., A. H. Redford, agent, for the M.E. church, South, 1875. xvi, 17-592 p. 19 cm. [BR85.S487 1875] 37-7765
1. Theology—Addresses, essays, lectures. I. Summers, Thomas Osmond, 1812-1882, ed. II. Title.

SMITH, Goldwin, 1823-1910. 201'.1'08
Guesses at the riddle of existence, and other essays on kindred subjects. Freeport, N.Y., Books for Libraries Press [1972] ix, 244 p. 23 cm. (Essay index reprint series) Reprint of the 1897 ed. Contents.Contents.—Guesses at the riddle of existence.—The church and the Old Testament.—Is there another life?—The miraculous element in Christianity.—Morality and theism. [BR85.S488 1972] 72-8529 ISBN 0-8369-7326-7
1. Theology—Addresses, essays, lectures. I. Title. II. Title: The riddle of existence, and other essays on kindred subjects.

SMITH, Henry Boynton, 1815-1877. 204
Faith and philosophy: discourses and essays by Henry S. Smith... edited with an introductory notice by George L. Prentiss... New York, Scribner, Armstrong & co., 1877. 2 p. l., [iii]-xiv p., 1 l., 496 p. 23 1/2 cm. [BR85.S5] 40-21021
1. Theology—Addresses, essays, lectures. I. Prentiss, George Lewis, 1816-1906, ed. II. Title.
Contents omitted.

SMITH, John, 1618-1652. 230'.08
Select discourses / John Smith ; a facsimile reproduction with an introd. by C. A. Patrides. Delmar, N.Y. : Scholars' Facsmiles & Reprints, 1979. xiv, liii, 526 p. ; 23 cm. Photoreprint of the 1660 ed. printed by F. Flesher for W. Morden, London. Includes bibliographical references. [BR75.S66 1979] 79-15690 ISBN 0-8201-1335-2 : 48.00
1. Theology—Addresses, essays, lectures. I. Title.

SMITH, John, 1618-1652. 230'.08
Select discourses, 1660 / John Smith. New York : Garland Pub., 1978. liii, 526 p. ; 23 cm. (British philosophers and theologians of the 17th & 18th centuries) Reprint of the 1660 ed. printed by F. Flesher for W. Morden, London. [BR75.S66 1978] 75-11252 ISBN 0-8240-1803-6 : 29.50
1. Theology—Addresses, essays, lectures. I. Title. II. Series.

SPALDING, John Lancaster, abp., 1840-1916. 261
Religion, agnosticism and education, by J. L. Spalding... 2d ed. Chicago, A. C. McClurg & co., 1903. 285 p., 1 l. 18 cm. [BR85.S55 1903] 15-20475
1. Theology—Addresses, essays, lectures. 2. Agnosticism. 3. Education—Addresses, essays, lectures. I. Title.
Contents omitted.

SPENCER, Sidney, 1888- 230.04
The deep things of God; essays in liberal religion. London, Allen & Unwin [dist. Mystic, Conn., Verry, 1965] 118p. 19cm. [BR85.S634] 2.00 bds.,
1. Theology—Addresses, essays, lectures. I. Title.

SPIRIT and light : 230
essays in historical theology / edited by Madeleine L'Engle and William B. Green. New York : Seabury Press, c1976. p. cm. "Crossroad books." [BR50.S67] 76-17834 ISBN 0-8164-0310-4 : 8.95
1. West, Edward N. 2. Theology—Addresses, essays, lectures. I. L'Engle, Madeleine. II. Green, William B., 1927-

SQUIER, Miles Powell, 1792-1866. 261
The miscellaneous writings of Miles P. Squier ... with an autobiography, edited and supplemented by Rev. James B. Boyd

... Geneva, N.Y., Press of R. L. Adams & son [1867] 408 p. front. (port.) 20 1/2 cm. [BR85.S72] 4-33768
1. Theology—Addresses, essays, lectures. I. Boyd, James Robert, 1804-1890, ed. II. Title.

STANLEY, Arthur Penrhyn, 1815-1881. 261
Christian institutions; essays on ecclesiastical subjects, by Arthur Penrhyn Stanley ... New York, Harper & brothers, 1881. xii, 326 p. 19 1/2 cm. [BR85.S73 1881] A 32
1. Theology—Addresses, essays, lectures. I. Title.

STANLEY, Arthur Penrhyn, 1815-1881. 261
Christian institutions; essays on ecclesiastical subjects, by Arthur Penrhyn Stanley ... New York, C. Scribner's sons, 1881. xiv, 396 p. 21 1/2 cm. [BR85.S73 1881a] 42-29626
1. Theology—Addresses, essays, lectures. I. Title.

STANLEY, Arthur Penrhyn, 1815-1881. 208.
Christian institutions; essays on ecclesiastical subjects, by Arthur Penrhyn Stanley ... New York, Harper & brothers, 1881. xii, 326 p. 19 1/2 cm. [BR85.S73 1881] A 32
1. Theology—Addresses, essays, lectures. I. Title.

STOB, Henry, 1908- 230'.57
Theological reflections : essays on related themes / by Henry Stob. Grand Rapids, Mich. : Eerdmans, c1981. ix, 267 p. ; 23 cm. [BR85.S79] 19 81-1472 ISBN 0-8028-1881-1 : 11.95
1. Theology—Addresses, essays, lectures. I. Title.

STRONG, Augustus Hopkins, 1836-1921. 261
Christ in creation and ethical monism, by Augustus Hopkins Strong ... Philadelphia, The Roger Williams press, 1899. xix, 524 p. 22 1/2 cm. [BR85.S8] 9-13045
1. Theology—Addresses, essays, lectures. 2. Monism. I. Title.

STUDIES honoring Ignatius 230
Charles Brady, Friar Minor / edited by Romano Stephen Almagno and Conrad L. Harkins. St. Bonaventure, N.Y. : Franciscan Institute, 1976. 494 p. : port. ; 25 cm. (Franciscan Institute publications : Theology series ; no. 6) English, French, German, Italian, or Spanish. Includes bibliographical references. [BR50.S819] 76-1318
1. Brady, Ignatius C. 2. Brady, Ignatius C.—Bibliography. 3. Theology—Addresses, essays, lectures. I. Brady, Ignatius C. II. Almagno, Romano Stephen. III. Harkins, Conrad L. IV. Series: St. Bonaventure University, St. Bonaventure, N.Y. Franciscan Institute. Theology series ; no. 6.

SWANDER, John I. 1833-
The Mercersburg theology, by Rev. John I. Swander ... a course of lectures delivered in the Theological seminary of the Reformed church in the United States, at Lancaster, Pa., on the foundation of the Swander lectureship, and pub. under the direction of the Faculty. Philadelphia, Reformed church publication board, 1909. 316 p. 19 1/2 cm. (On back of cover: The Swander memorial lectures, 1908) 12-12945
I. Title.

TAYLOR, Isaac, 1787-1865. 261
Logic in theology, and other essays. By Isaac Taylor. With a sketch of the life of the author and a catalogue of his writings. New York, W. Gowans, 1860. 297, [3] p. 20 1/2 cm. [BR85.T3 1860] 7-31937
1. Theology—Addresses, essays, lectures. I. Title.
Contents omitted.

TEILHARD de Chardin, Pierre. 201'.1
Christianity and evolution. Translated by Rene Hague. [1st American ed.] New York, Harcourt Brace Jovanovich [1971] 255 p. 21 cm. "A Helen and Kurt Wolff book." Translation of Comment je crois. Includes bibliographical references. [BR85.T3313 1971] 78-162798 ISBN 0-15-117850-X
1. Theology—Addresses, essays, lectures. I. Title.

TEILHARD de Chardin, Pierre. 230.2
How I believe. Translated by Rene Hague. New York, Harper & Row [1969] 91 p. 19 cm. (Perennial library, 156) Translation of Comment je crois. [B2430.T373C593] 76-7823 0.75
1. Theology—Addresses, essays, lectures. I. Title.

TEMPLE, William, abp. of York, 1881- 261
Essays in Christian politics and kindred subjects, by William Temple, bishop of Manchester. London, New York [etc.] Longmans, Green and co., ltd., 1927. vii, 228 p. 22 1/2 cm. [BR85.T4] 27-12719
1. Theology—Addresses, essays, lectures. I. Title.

TEMPLE, William, abp. of Canterbury, 1881- 208.
Essays in Christian politics and kindred subjects, by William Temple, bishop of Manchester. London, New York [etc.] Longmans, Green and co., ltd., 1927. vii, 228 p. 22 1/2 cm. [BR85.T4] 27-12719
1. Theology—Addresses, essays, lectures. I. Title.

THEOLOGICAL study today; 250
addresses delivered at the seventy-fifth anniversary of the Meadville theological school, June 1-3, 1920. Chicago, Ill., The University of Chicago press [c1921] xii, 215 p. 20 cm. [BV4020.T5] 21-11646
I. Meadville theological school, Meadville, Pa.

THEOLOGY and church in times of change. 201
[Essays in honor of John Coleman Bennett] Edited by Edward Le Roy Long, Jr. and Robert T. Handy. Philadelphia, Westminster Press [1970] 304 p. 24 cm. Contents.Contents.—Theology and the Gospel: Reflections on theological method, by R. M. Brown.—Deossification of theological obstacles in view of ecumenism, by B. Haring.—God, Torah, and Israel, by A. J. Heschel.—Theology, the churches, and the ministry, by G. W. Webber.—Theological ethics: Retrospect and prospect, by R. L. Shinn.—Aspects of the interpenetration of religion and politics, by D. E. Sturm.—Theology and international relations, by K. W. Thompson.—The eclipse of a public: Protestant reflections on religion and public education, 1940-1968, by R. W. Lynn.—Jerusalem and Athens in transition, by J. A. Martin, Jr.—John Coleman Bennett: Theologian, churchman, and educator, by R. Niebuhr.—The theology of John Coleman Bennett, by D. D. Williams.—A select bibliography of the writings of John Coleman Bennett, by R. F. Beach (p. [267]-304) Includes bibliographical references. [BR50.T429] 78-96699 ISBN 6-642-08819- 10.00
1. Bennett, John Coleman, 1902- —Bibliography. 2. Theology—Addresses, essays, lectures. I. Bennett, John Coleman, 1902- II. Long, Edward Le Roy, ed. III. Handy, Robert T., ed.

THEOLOGY and discovery : 230'.2
essays in honor of Karl Rahner, S.J. / edited by William J. Kelly. Milwaukee, Wis. : Marquette University Press, c1980. 365 p. : port. ; 24 cm. Includes bibliographical references and indexes. [BR50.T4296] 19 80-82361 ISBN 0-87462-521-1 : 24.95
1. Rahner, Karl, 1904- —Addresses, essays, lectures. 2. Theology—Addresses, essays, lectures. I. Rahner, Karl, 1904- II. Kelly, William J., 1924-

THEOLOGY and modern life; 200
essays in honor of Harris Franklin Rall. Edited by Paul Arthur Schilpp. Freeport, N.Y., Books for Libraries Press [1970] x, 297 p. port. 23 cm. (Essay index reprint series) Reprint of the 1940 ed. Contents.Contents.—Harris Franklin Rall, by I. G. Whitchurch.—Our immortality, by S. S. Cohon.—The significance of critical study of the Gospels for religious thought today, by F. C. Grant.—The Christian doctrine of man, by A. C. Knudson.—Facing the problem of evil, by F. J. McConnell.—The realistic movement in religious philosophy, by E. W. Lyman.—The meaning of rational faith, by P. A. Schilpp.—Interpreting the religious situation, by I. G. Whitchurch.—The kingdom of God and the life of today, by C. C. McCown.—The church and social optimism, by S. Mathews.—The church, the truth, and society, by E. S. Brightman.—Let the church be the church! By E. F. Tittle.—Bibliography of the writings of Harris Franklin Rall (p. 285-297) [BT10.T53 1970] 70-117852
1. Theology—Addresses, essays, lectures. I. Rall, Harris Franklin, 1860-1964. II. Schilpp, Paul Arthur, 1897- ed.

THEOLOGY and modern life; 204
essays in honor of Harris Franklin Rall, edited by Paul Arthur Schilpp. Chicago, New York, Willett, Clark & company, 1940. x p., 1 l., 297 p. front. (port.) 20 1/2 cm. Contents.Harris Franklin Rall, by I. G. Whitchurch.--Our immortality, by S. S. Cohon.--The significance of critical study of the Gospels for religious thought today, by F. C. Grant.--The Christian doctrine of man, by A. C. Knudson.--Facing the problem of evil, by F. J. McConnell.--The realistic movement in religious philosophy, by E. W. Lyman.--The meaning of rational faith, by P. A. Schilpp.--Interpreting the religious situation, by I. G. Whitchurch.--The kingdom of God and the life of today, by C. C. McCown.--The church, the truth, and society, by E. S. Brightman.--Let the church be the church! By E. F. Tittle.--Bibliography of the writings of Harris Franklin Rall (p. 285-297) Bibliographical references in "Notes" at end of most of the chapters. [BT10.T53] 40-8892
1. Rall, Harris Franklin, 1870- 2. Theology—Addresses, essays, lectures. I. Schilpp, Paul Arthur, 1897- ed.

THIELICKE, Helmut, 1908- 207.6
Between heaven and earth; conversations with American Christians. Tr. [from German] ed. by John W. Doberstein. New York, Harper [c.1965] xvii, 192p. 22cm. Bibl. [BR123.T453] 65-10703 3.75
1. Theology—Addresses, essays, lectures. I. Title.

THIELICKE, Helmut, 1908- . 207.6
Between heaven and earth; conversations with American Christians. Translated and edited by John W. Doberstein. [1st ed.] New York, Harper & Row [1965] xvii, 192 p. 22 cm. Translation of Gesprache Uber Himmel und Erde. Bibliographical footnotes. [BR123.T453] 65-10703
1 Theology — Addresses, essays, lectures. I. Title.

THIELICKE, Helmut, 1908- 230
Between heaven and earth : conversations with American Christians / by Helmut Thielicke ; translated and edited by John W. Doberstein. Westport, Conn. : Greenwood Press, 1975, c1965. xvii, 192 p. ; 22 cm. Translation of Gesprache uber Himmel und Erde. Reprint of the ed. published by Harper & Row, New York. Includes bibliographical references and index. [BR85.T48413 1975] 73-16609 ISBN 0-8371-7185-7 lib.bdg. : 12.00
1. Theology—Addresses, essays, lectures. I. Title.

THIELICKE, Helmut, 1908- 230
Between heaven and earth : conversations with American Christians / by Helmut Thielicke ; translated and edited by John W. Doberstein. Westport, Conn. : Greenwood Press, 1975, c1965. xvii, 192 p. ; 22 cm. Translation of Gesprache uber Himmel und Erde. Reprint of the ed. published by Harper & Row, New York. Includes bibliographical references and index. [BR85.T48413 1975] 73-16609 ISBN 0-8371-7185-7
1. Theology—Addresses, essays, lectures. I. Title.

THIELICKE, Helmut, 1908- 231
The hidden question of God / by Helmut Thielicke. Grand Rapids, Mich. : Eerdmans, c1976. p. cm. Translation of Die geheime Frage nach Gott. Translated and edited by G. W. Bromiley. [BR85.T4813] 76-44492 ISBN 0-8028-1661-4 pbk. : 3.95
1. Theology—Addresses, essays, lectures. I. Title.

THIRD world theologies / 230
edited by Gerald H. Anderson and Thomas F. Stransky. New York : Paulist Press, c1976. viii, 254 p. ; 19 cm. (Mission trends ; no. 3) Bibliography: p. 250-254. [BR50.T47] 76-24451 ISBN 0-8091-1984-6 pbk. : 3.45
1. Theology—Addresses, essays, lectures. I. Anderson, Gerald H. II. Stransky, Thomas F.

THOMSON, Edward, bp., 1810-1870. 204
Essays, moral and religious. By E. Thomson, D.D. ... edited by Rev. D. W. Clark, D.D. Cincinnati, Published by L. Swormstedt & A. Poe for the Methodist Episcopal church, 1856. 374 p. 19 cm. [AC8.T46] 32-19447
1. Theology—Addresses, essays, lectures. I. Clark, Davis Wasgatt, bp., 1812-1871. II. Title.

TILLICH, Paul, 1886-1965. 230.0924
On the boundary; an autobiographical sketch. New York, Scribner [1966] 104 p. 22 cm. "A revision, newly translated, of Part I of [the author's] The interpretation of history." Bibliography: p. 102-104. [BX4827.T53A33] 66-18546
1. Theology—Addresses, essays, lectures. 2. Protestantism—Addresses, essays, lectures. I. Title.

TRANSCENDENCE and immanence: reconstruction in the light of process thinking; 200'.1
festschrift in honour of Joseph Papin. Edited by Joseph Armenti. [Saint Meinrad, Ind.] Abbey Press [1972- v. port. 23 cm. Contents.Contents.—v. 1. Curran, C. E. The present state of Catholic moral theology. Baltazar, E. R. Process thinking in theology. Gustafson, J. M. Toward ecumenical Christian ethics: some brief suggestions. Swidler, L. Aufklarung Catholicism's mass reforms. Tavard, G. H. Can the ministry be reconstructed? Bonniwell, B. L. Transmaterial time in psychology. Schmemann, A. Crisis in theology and liturgy: orthodox insight. Katsh, A. I. Hebraic studies in early America. Peter, C. J. Christian eschatology and a theology of exceptions, part I. Blake, E. C. Ecumenism, structured and unstructured. Schoonenberg, P. The transcendence of God, part I. Beniak, V. Umriet' doma. Allen-Shore, L. From the garden of Slovakia ... Includes bibliographical references. [BR50.T715] 72-83737
1. Theology—Addresses, essays, lectures. I. Papin, Joseph, 1914- II. Armenti, Joseph, ed.

TROELTSCH, Ernst, 1865-1923. 230'.08
Writings on theology and religion / Ernst Troeltsch ; translated and edited by Robert Morgan and Michael Pye. Atlanta : John Knox Press, 1977, c1976. p. cm. "The first three essays ... translated ... from Gesammelte Schriften II, Tubingen, 1913 and 1922 ... The fourth was published separately." Bibliography: p. [BR85.T7613] 77-79596 ISBN 0-8042-0554-X : 17.50
1. Troeltsch, Ernst, 1865-1923—Addresses, essays, lectures. 2. Theology—Addresses, essays, lectures. I. Title.
Contents omitted

TUFTS papers on religion; 204
a symposium by Clarence R. Skinner, Bruce W. Brotherston, John M. Ratcliff [and others] ... Boston, Mass., Universalist publishing house, 1939. 77 p. 20 cm. "Written from the point of view of the personal experience of men who teach in the School of religion at Tufts college."--Introd. [BR50.T8] 39-14231
1. Theology—Addresses, essays, lectures. I. Skinner, Clarence Russell, 1881- II. Tufts college. Crane theological school.
Contents omitted.

VALEN-SONDSTAAN, Olav 230
The word that can never die. Tr. [from Norwegian] by Norman A. Madson, Sr., Ahlert H. Strand. [Licensed Eng. ed.] St. Louis, Concordia [1966, c. 1949] 164p. 24cm. Lects. delivered in Sweden in 1947. [BT80.V313] 66-22419 3.95
1. Theology—Addresses, essays, lectures. I. Title.

WALVOORD, a tribute / 230'.044
edited by Donald K. Campbell. Chicago :

Moody Press, c1982. p. cm. Includes bibliographical references. [BR50.W33] 19 81-1688 ISBN 0-8024-9227-4 : 12.95
1. Walvoord, John F. Addresses, essays, lectures. 2. Theology—Addresses, essays, lectures. I. Walvoord, John F. II. Campbell, Donald K.

WHITEHOUSE, Walter Alexander. 230'.044
Creation, science, and theology : essays in response to Karl Barth / by W. A. Whitehouse. Grand Rapids, Mich. : Eerdmans, 1981. p. cm. Bibliography: p. [BX4827.B3W47] 19 80-29332 ISBN 0-8028-1870-6 : 10.95
1. Barth, Karl, 1886-1968—Addresses, essays, lectures. 2. Barth, Karl, 1886-1968—Bibliography. 3. Theology—Addresses, essays, lectures. I. Title.

WILDER, Amos Niven, 1895- 201
Theopoetic : theology and the religious imagination / by Amos Niven Wilder. Philadelphia : Fortress Press, c1976. vi, 106 p. ; 20 cm. Includes bibliographical references. [BR85.W5657] 75-36458 ISBN 0-8006-0435-0 : 4.95
1. Theology—Addresses, essays, lectures. 2. Imagination—Addresses, essays, lectures. I. Title. II. Title: Theology and the religious imagination.

WILSON, James Maurice, 1836-1931. 201
Essays and addresses; an attempt to treat some religious questions in a scientific spirit. Freeport, N.Y., Books for Libraries Press [1973] p. (Essay index reprint series) [BR85.W585 1973] 73-1193 ISBN 0-518-10070-7
1. Theology—Addresses, essays, lectures. I. Title.

WOOD, Frederic C. 230
Living in the now; spirit-centered faith for 20th century man, by Frederic C. Wood, Jr., New York, Association Press [1970] 159 p. 21 cm. Includes bibliographical references. [BR123.W68] 74-93428 4.95
1. Theology—Addresses, essays, lectures. I. Title.

THE Word in the world; 201'.1
essays in honor of Frederick L. Moriarty, S.J. Edited by Richard J. Clifford & George W. MacRae. [Cambridge, Mass.] Weston College Press, 1973. x, 282 p. port. 23 cm. [BR50.W63] 72-97356 3.50 (pbk.)
1. Moriarty, Frederick L. 2. Moriarty, Frederick L.—Bibliography. 3. Theology—Addresses, essays, lectures. I. Moriarty, Frederick L. II. Clifford, Richard J., ed. III. MacRae, George W., ed. Publisher's Address: 3 Phillips Place Cambridge, Mass. 02138.

A World more human, a church more Christian. 201'.1
George Devine, editor-in-chief. New York, Alba House [1973] vi, 195 p. 22 cm. "Annual publication of the College Theology Society," i.e. based in part on the proceedings of the Society's annual convention, held in Los Angeles in 1972. Includes bibliographical references. [BR50.W634] 73-9512 ISBN 0-8189-0265-5 3.95
1. Theology—Addresses, essays, lectures. I. Devine, George, 1941- ed. II. College Theology Society.

YALE university. Divinity school.
Education for Christian service, by members of the faculty of the Divinity school of Yale university; a volume in commemoration of its one hundredth anniversary. New Haven, Yale university press, 1922. viii, 348 p., 1 l. 23 1/2 cm. [BV4019.Y3] 23-21493
1. Theology—Addresses, essays, lectures. I. Title.
Contents omitted.

ZATKO, James J., comp. 230'.2
The valley of silence; Catholic thought in contemporary Poland, edited by James J. Zatko. Notre Dame [Ind.] University of Notre Dame Press [1967] xiv, 391 p. illus. 24 cm. Includes bibliographical references. [BT10.Z3] 67-12125
1. Catholic Church in Poland—Addresses, essays, lectures. 2. Theology—Addresses, essays, lectures. I. Title.

Theology, Anglican—Addresses, essays, lectures.

CHURCH of England. Archbishops' Commission on Christian Doctrine. 230'.3
Christian believing : the nature of the Christian faith and its expression in Holy Scripture and creeds : a report / by the Doctrine Commission of the Church of England. London : S.P.C.K., 1976. xii, 156 p. ; 22 cm. [BX5131.2.C53 1976] 76-370993 ISBN 0-281-02937-7 : £2.50
1. Bible—Criticism, interpretation, etc.—Addresses, essays, lectures. 2. Theology, Anglican—Addresses, essays, lectures. 3. Creeds—Addresses, essays, lectures. I. Title.

Theology, Anglican—History—19th century—Addresses, essays, lectures.

F.D. Maurice : 230'.3'0924
a study / Frank McClain, Richard Norris, John Orens. Cambridge, MA : Cowley Publications, c1982. xvii, 93 p. ; 22 cm. Includes bibliographical references. [BX5199.M3F18 1982] 19 82-70636 ISBN 0-936384-05-0 (pbk.) : 5.00
1. Maurice, Frederick Denison, 1805-1872—Addresses, essays, lectures. 2. Theology, Anglican—History—19th century—Addresses, essays, lectures. I. Norris, Richard Alfred. Maurice on theology. 1982. II. McClain, Frank Mauldin. Maurice on women. 1982. III. Orens, John. Maurice on prayer. 1982. Contents omittted. Publisher's address: 980 Memorial Dr., Cambridge, MA 02138.

Theology, Baptist—History—20th century.

THOMPSON, James J., 1944- 286'.132
Tried as by fire : Southern Baptists and the religious controversies of the 1920s / James J. Thompson, Jr. Macon, GA : Mercer University Press, c1982. xv, 224 p. ; 24 cm. Revision of thesis (Ph.D.)—University of Virginia, 1971. Includes indexes. Bibliography: p. [217]-219. [BX6207.S68T47 1982] 19 82-8056 ISBN 0-86554-032-2 : 13.95
1. Southern Baptist Convention—History—20th century. 2. Theology, Baptist—History—20th century. I. Title.

Theology — Bibliography

AIDS to a theological library 016.2
/ edited by John B. Trotti. Missoula, Mont. : Published by Scholars Press for the American Theological Library Association, c1977. viii, 69 p. ; 22 cm. (Library aids ; no. 1) A revision of Library check list, by the American Association of Theological Schools. [Z7751.A52 1977] [BR118] 76-54173 ISBN 0-89130-127-5
1. Theology—Bibliography. 2. Religions—Bibliography. I. Trotti, John B. II. American Association of Theological Schools. Library check list. III. American Theological Library Association. IV. Title. V. Series.

AMERICAN Theological Library Association. 016.2
A bibliography of post-graduate masters' theses in religion; prepared by the Committee on a Master List of Research Studies in Religion. Niels H. Sonne, editor. [Chicago, Distributed by American Library Association] 1951. xi, 82 p. 28 cm. [Z7751.A64] 52-1356
1. Theology—Bibliography. 2. Dissertations, Academic—United States—Bibliography. I. Sonne, Niels Henry, 1907- ed.

ANDOVER Newton Theological School, Newton Center, Mass.
Theological bibliographies: essential books for a minister's library [edited by Normak K. Gottwald. Newton Center] 1963. 138 p. 22 cm. (The Andover Newton quarterly, old ser., v. 56, no. 1) Cover-title. NUC64
1. Theology — Bibl. I. Gottwald, Norman Karol, 1926- ed. II. Title.

ANDOVER theological seminary. Library. 016.
Catalogue of the library belonging to the theological institution in Andover. Andover, Printed by Flagg and Gould, 1819. 161 p. 24 cm. [Z881.A553] 8-23177
1. Theology—Bibl. I. Title.

BASIC books for the minister's library 016.2
/ compiled by members of the summer 1978 class in the minister's library ; edited by John L. Sayre. 2d ed. Enid, Oklahoma : Seminary Press, 1978. iii, 22 leaves ; 28 cm. [Z7751.B34 1978] [BR118] 79-10136 ISBN 0-912832-18-5 pbk. : 2.00
1. Theology—Bibliography. I. Sayre, John L., 1924-

BOLLIER, John A., 1927- 016.23
The literature of theology : a guide for students and pastors / John A. Bollier. 1st ed. Philadelphia : Westminster Press, c1979. 208 p. ; 21 cm. Includes index. [Z7751.B67] [BR118] 78-10962 ISBN 0-664-24225-1 pbk. : 5.95
1. Theology—Bibliography. I. Title.

BOOKS to read; 016.
a reference list of inexpensive literature for students of Christianity, with a prefatory note by the Archbishop of York 2d ed. London, New York [etc.] Longmans, Green, and co., 1914. 48 p. 18 1/2 cm. Introduction signed: W. Temple. [Z7751.B72] 14-17920
1. Theology—Bibl. 2. Religious literature—Bibl. I. Lang, Cosmo Gordon, abp. of York, 1864- II. Temple, William, 1881-

BOSTON. General theological library.
Catalogue of the General theological library, Boston, Massachusetts; a dictionary catalogue of religion, theology, sociology and allied literature. Boston, Mass., The Fort Hill press [c1913] 4 p. l., 5 313 p. 25 1/2 cm. $1.00. "The catalogue lists books in the English language only."--Pref. [Z7755B85] 14-319
1. Theology—Bibl. 2. Religious literature—Bibl. I. Title.

BRANSON, Mark Lau. 016.2
The reader's guide to the best evangelical books / Mark Lau Branson. 1st ed. San Francisco : Harper & Row, c1982. p. cm. [Z7751.B77 1982] [BR118] 19 81-48205 ISBN 0-06-061046-8 pbk. : 5.95
1. Theology—Bibliography. 2. Evangelicalism—Bibliography. 3. Bibliography—Best books—Theology. 4. Bibliography—Best books—Evangelicalism. I. Title.

BUCKMINSTER, Joseph Stevens, 1784-1812. 016.
Catalogue of the library of the late Rev. J. S. Buckminster. Boston, Printed by J. Elliot jun., 1812. 66 p. 23 cm. 1,136 entries. [Z997.B926] 12-30134
1. Theology—Bibl. I. Title.

CALIFORNIA. University. Library. 016.
... Catalogue of the theological library presented by Andrew S. Hallidie ... Berkeley, 1886. 50 p. 23 cm. (Its Library bulletin, no. 7) Supplement to the Report of the secretary of the Board of regents [1886] [Z7755.C15] [Z881.C153 no. 7] 016. 1-15621
1. Theology—Bibl. I. Title.

CENTER for Reformation Research. 016.23
Evangelical theologians of Wurttemberg in the sixteenth century : a finding list of CRR holdings. St. Louis : Center for Reformation Research, 1975. 57 p. ; 22 cm. (Sixteenth century bibliography ; 3) [Z7751.C38 1975] [BR118] 76-355415 2.00
1. Theology—Bibliography. 2. Theologians—Wurttemberg—Biography. I. Title. II. Series.

DEITRICK, Bernard E., 1930- 016.2
A basic book list for church libraries / by Bernard E. Deitrick. Bryn Mawr, PA : Church and Synagogue Library Association, c1977. 16 p. ; 28 cm. (A CSLA bibliography) [Z7751.D36] [BR118] 77-4093 ISBN 0-915324-10-5 : 1.75
1. Theology—Bibliography. 2. Religion—Bibliography. 3. Bibliography—Best books—Theology. 4. Bibliography—Best books—Religion. 5. Libraries, Church—Book lists. I. Title. II. Series: Church and Synagogue Library Association. CSLA bibliography.

ESSENTIAL books for a pastor's study. 016.2
Richmond, Union Theological Seminary. 71p. 23cm. First ed. published in 1954. Title varies: Essential books for a pastor's library. 60-11917 1.00 pap.,
1. Theology—Bibl. I. Richmond, Union Theological Seminary.

FUERST, Bartholomew, 1919-
Seminarian's reading list ... Theology list. Revised edition, 1964. St. Meinrad, Ind., Abbey press publications, 1964. 54 p. 19 cm. 66-60487
1. Theology — Bibliography. 2. Seminarians — Books and reading. I. Title.

FUERST, Bartholomew, 1919-
Seminarian's reading list ... Theology list. Revised edition, 1964. St. Meinrad, Ind., Abbey press publications, 1964. 54 p. 19 cm. 66-60487
1. Theology — Bibliography. 2. Seminarians — Books and reading. I. Title.

HURST, John Fletcher, bp., 1834-1903. 016.
Bibliotheca theologica; a select and classified bibliography of theology and general religious literature, by John F. Hurst, LL. D. New York, C. Scribner's sons, 1883. xvi, 417 p. 24 cm. [Z7751.H96] 1-13538
1. Theology—Bibl. 2. Religious liter... re—Bibl. I. Title.

HURST, John Fletcher, Bp., 1834-1903. 016.2
Literature of theology : a classified bibliography of theological and general religious literature / by John Fletcher Hurst. Boston : Longwood Press, 1977. p. cm. Reprint of the 1896 ed. published by Hunt & Eaton, New York. Includes indexes. [Z7751.H97 1977] [BR118] 77-85625 ISBN 0-89341-196-5 lib.bdg. : 50.00
1. Theology—Bibliography. I. Title.

HURST, John Fletcher, bp., 1834-1903. 016.
Literature of theology; a classified bibliography of theological and general religious literature, by John Fletcher Hurst. New York, Hunt & Eaton; Cincinnati, Cranston & Curts, 1896. xv, [1] 757 p. 24 cm. [Z7751.H97] 1-13539
1. Theology—Bibl. I. Title.

HURST, John Fletcher Hurst, Bp., 1834-1903. 016.2
Literature of theology; a classified bibliography of theological and general religious literature. Boston, Milford House [1972] xv, 757 p. 22 cm. Reprint of the 1896 ed. [Z7751.H97 1972] 71-186789 ISBN 0-87821-096-2
1. Theology—Bibliography. I. Title.

HURTER, Hugo, 1832-1914.
Nomenclator literarius theologiae catholicae theologos exhibens aetate, ratione, disciplinis distinctos. New York, Burt Franklin [1962] 5 v. in 6. 24 cm. (Burt Franklin bibliographical and reference series, no. 39) Reprint of Inssbruck edition of 1906-26. Vol. 1 is ed. 4, cura Fr. Pangerl S. J. 1926; vols. 2-5 are ed. 3. 1906-11. Each volume also has special title page. 63-23777
1. Theology — Bibliography. 2. Catholic literature — Bibliography. I. Pangerl, Franz, 1879- ed. II. Title.

MALCOM, Howard, 1799-1879. 016.
An index to the principal works in every department of religious literature. Embracing nearly seventy thousand citations, alphabetically arranged under two thousand heads. By Howard Malcom ... 2d ed., with addenda ... Philadelphia, J. B. Lippincott & co., 1870. 1 p. l., 5-488, 6 p. 23 1/2 cm. [Z7751.M241] 1-13579
1. Theology—Bibl. 2. Religious literature—Bibl. I. Title.

MALCOM, Howard, 1799-1879. 016.
Theological index. References to the principal works in every department of religious literature. Embracing nearly seventy thousand citations, alphabetically arranged under two thousand heads. By Howard Malcom ... Boston, Gould and Lincoln; [etc., etc.] 1868. 1 p. l., 5-489 p.

24 cm. Advertisement: p. 489. [Z7751.M24] 1-13578
1. Theology—Bibl. 2. Religious literature—Bibl. I. Title.

MORRIS, Raymond P. 016.2
A theological book list. Produced by the Theological Education Fund of the International Missionary Council for theological seminaries and colleges in Africa, Asia, Latin America, and the Southwest Pacific. Oxford, Blackwell; Naperville, Ill., Allenson: distributors [1960] 242p. 28cm. 60-3685 6.00
1. Theology—Bibl. I. International Missionary Council. Theological Education Fund. II. Title.

NEW York. Union Theological 016.2
Seminary.
A basic bibliography for ministers, selected and annotated by the faculty. [2d ed.] New York] [1960] 139p. 23cm. [Z7751.N4 1960] 60-53204
1. Theology—Bibl. I. Title.

PITTSBURGH. Western 016.
theological seminary.
... *Bibliography.* [Pittsburgh, Press of Pittsburgh printing company, 1918] cover-title, 76 p. 24 cm. (The bulletin of the Western theological seminary ... vol. x, no. 1. Oct., 1917) "The best literature in the various departments of theology."--Foreword. [Z7751.P62] 18-10942
1. Theology—Bibl. 2. Bibliography—Best books—Theology. I. Title.

PRESBYTERIAN church in the U. S.
A. Board of publication.
Descriptive catalogue of the publications of the Presbyterian board of publication, with alphabetical index. Philadelphia, 1880. 528 p. 18 cm. A 10
1. Theology—Bibliography. 2. Presbyterian—Bibliography. I. Title.

PRESBYTERIAN church in the U. S.
A. (Old school) Board of publication.
Numerical, alphabetical and descriptive catalogues of the publications of the Presbyterian board of publication, No. 821. Chestnut street, Philadelphia. [Philadelphia, 1866?] 9, 42-432 p. 18 cm. A 10
1. Theology—Bibliography. 2. Presbyterian—Bibliography. I. Title.

PRESBYTERIAN church in the
United States of America, Board of publication.
Descriptive catalogue of the publicatons of the Presbyterian board of publication, with priced alphabetical index. Philadelphia, 1871. 508 p. 18 cm. A 10
1. Theology—Bibliography. 2. Presbyterian—Bibliography. I. Title.

PRINCETON theological seminary.
Library.
Catalogue of the library of Princeton theological seminary. Part 1. Religious literature. Princeton, N. J., C. S. Robinson & co., 1886. xv, 453 p., 1 l. 24 cm. No more published. [Z7755.P94] 2-562
1. Theology—Bibl. 2. Church history—Bibl. I. Title.

RICHMOND. Union Theological 016.2
Seminary.
Essential books for a postor's library; basic and recommended works, selected and annotated by the faculty of Union Theological Seminary. 2d ed. Richmond [1955] 54p. 23cm. Cover title. [Z7751.R5 1955] 55-43262
1. Theology—Bibl. I. Title.

RICHMOND, Va. Union 016.
theological seminary. Library.
Catalogue of the library belonging to the Union theological seminary in Prince Edward, Va. Richmond, Printed by J. Macfarlan, 1833. 107 p. 21 1/2 cm. [Z881.R536] 8-36973
1. Theology—Bibl. I. Title.

ROBERTS, William Henry, 1844-
1920.
List of books intended as an aid in the selection of a pastor's library. By W. H. Roberts. Princeton, The Princeton press, 1885. 24 p. 20 cm. A reissue of the edition of 1884 which had "Princeton theological seminary" on t.-p. in place of author. A 10
1. Theology—Bibliography. I. Princeton theological seminary. II. Title.

SAYRE, John L., 1924- 016.2
Tools for theological research / compiled and edited by John L. Sayre and Roberta Hamburger. 3d rev. ed. Enid, Okla. : Seminary Press, 1975. p. cm. Includes index. [Z7751.S37 1975] [BR118] 75-23362 ISBN 0-912832-11-8 pbk. : 3.00
1. Theology—Bibliography. 2. Religion—Bibliography. I. Hamburger, Roberta, joint author. II. Title.

SAYRE, John L., 1924- 016.2
Tools for theological research / compiled and edited by John L. Sayre and Roberta Hamburger. 4th rev. ed. Enid, Okla. : Seminary Press, 1976. v, 85 p. ; 22 cm. Includes index. [Z7751.S37 1976] [BR118] 76-14703 ISBN 0-912832-14-2 pbk. : 3.00
1. Theology—Bibliography. 2. Religion—Bibliography. I. Hamburger, Roberta, joint author. II. Title.

SAYRE, John L., 1924- 016.2
Tools for theological research / compiled and edited by John L. Sayre and Roberta Hamburger. 6th rev. ed. Enid, Okla. : Seminary Press, 1981. v, 104 p. ; 22 cm. Includes index. [Z7751.S37 1981] [BR118] 19 81-9359 ISBN 0-912832-20-7 : pbk : 4.50
1. Theology—Bibliography. 2. Religion—Bibliography. I. Hamburger, Roberta. II. Title.
Publisher's address : Box 2218 University Station, Enid, OK 73701

SCM Press. Editorial Dept. 016.2
Religion and theology : a select book guide / compiled by the Editorial Department of SCM Press. London : S.C.M. Press, 1976. 80 p. ; 23 cm. Includes index. [Z7751.S23 1976] [BR118] 76-368452 ISBN 0-334-02302-5 : £0.50
1. Theology—Bibliography. 2. Religion—Bibliography. I. Title.

SMITH, Harry Denman, 1866- 016.2
1933.
A preacher's first books, by Harry D. Smith. Cincinnati, O., The Standard publishing company [c1933] 80 p. 17 cm. "A group of books which should be in the libraries of all ministers."--Editor's note, signed: E. W. Thornton. [Z7751.S65] 34-1746
1. Theology—Bibl. 2. Preaching—Bibl. 3. Bibliography—Best books—Theology. I. Thornton, Edwin William, 1863- ed. II. Title.

SMITH, Wilbur Moorehead, 253
1894-
The minister in his study, by Wilbur M. Smith. Chicago, Moody Press [1973] 128 p. 22 cm. Includes bibliographical references. [Z7751.S66] 73-7329 ISBN 0-8024-5295-7 3.95
1. Theology—Bibliography. 2. Bibliography—Best books—Theology. I. Title.

TIBBALS, Cyrus F. 016.
A thesaurus of the best theological, historical, and biographical literature, with a complete index of subjects, authors and titles, compiled and edited by Cyrus F. Tibbals. New York, London, Funk & Wagnalls, 1891. vi, [5]-549 p. 25 cm. [Z7751.T55] 2-7243
1. Theology—Bibl. 2. History—Bibl. 3. Biography—Bibl. I. Title.

Theology — Bibliography — Catalogs.

ANDOVER theological 016.
seminary. Library.
Catalogue of the library of the Theol. seminary in Andover, Mass. By Oliver A. Taylor, M.A. Andover, Printed by Gould & Newman, 1838. viii, [9]-531 p. 23 1/2 cm. [Z881.A554] 8-23178
1. Theology—Bibl.—Catalogs. I. Taylor, Oliver Alden. 1801-1851. II. Title.

BOSTON. Theological library.
Catalogue of books, in the Theological library, in the town of Boston. March 1, 1808. Boston. Snelling and Simons, printers, Devonshire-street, 1808. 33 p. 17 1/2 cm. A34
1. Theology—Bibliography—Catalogs. I. Title.

CAMERON, Kenneth Walter, 016.2
1908-
Index of the pamphlet collection of the Diocese of Connecticut. Hartford, Conn., The Historiographer, 1958. 169. illus. 29cm. 'A short-title list of the 3,000 tracts (some of them duplicates) in the first one hundred and eighty-eight volumes in the Archieves of the Diocese of Connecticut, housed in the Trinity College Library in Hartford.' [Z7755.C2] 59-24853
1. Theology—Bibl.—Catalogs. I. Protestant Episcopal Church in the U. S. A. Connecticut (Diocese) II. Trinity College, Hartford. Library. III. Title.

CHURCH club of New York. 016.62
Library.
The library of the Church club of New York; a selected list. [New York, 1933?] cover-title, 23 p. 22 1/2 x 10 cm. "A list of books that may be borrowed from the Club library." [Z7755.N54] 33-37944
1. Theology—Bibl.—Catalogs. I. Title.

HISTORICAL Foundation of 016.23
the Presbyterian and Reformed Churches.
Historical Foundation holdings of eighteenth-century American publications / compiled by Ruth D. See ; prepared in the office of Mary G. Lane, research librarian, the Historical Foundation of the Presbyterian and Reformed Churches. Montreat, N.C. : The Foundation, 1976. 100 p. ; 27 cm. (Historical Foundation working bibliographies) Includes index. [Z7751.H65 1976] [BR118] 77-351275
1. Presbyterian Church in the United States (General)—Bibliography—Catalogs. 2. Reformed Church in the United States—Bibliography—Catalogs. 3. Historical Foundation of the Presbyterian and Reformed Churches. 4. Theology—Bibliography—Catalogs. I. See, Ruth Douglas, 1910- II. Title. III. Series: Historical Foundation of the Presbyterian and Reformed Churches. Historical Foundation working bibliographies.

JARVIS, Samuel Farmar, 1786- 016.
1851.
A catalogue of the entire library of the late Rev. Samuel Farmar Jarvis ... of Middletown, Connecticut, to be sold at auction ... November 4, 1851, and following evenings, by Lyman & Rawdon ... New-York. [New York] H. F. Snowden, printer, 1851. vi, 219, [1] p. 23 cm. Interleaved. Date, November 4, mounted over original date, October 14. Prices and purchasers noted in manuscript. Compiled by J. Sabin. [Z997.J38] 7-6197
1. Theology—Bibl.—Catalogs. I. Sabin, Joseph, 1821-1881. II. Title.

NEW York (City). Union 016.2
Theological Seminary. Library.
Alphabetical arrangement of main entries from the shelf list / Union Theological Seminary Library, New York City. Boston : G. K. Hall, 1960. 10 v. ; 37 cm. [Z7755.N534 1960] [BR118] 75-313282
1. New York (City). Union Theological Seminary. Library. 2. Theology—Bibliography—Catalogs. I. Title.

NEW York. Union Theological
Seminary. Library.
Alphabetical arrangement of main entries from the shelf list. Boston, G. K. Hall, 1960. 10 v. 36 cm. 65-111023
1. Theology — Bibl. — Catalogs. I. Title.

NEW York. Union theological
seminary. Library.
... *Catalogue of the McAlpin collection of British history and theology,* compiled and edited by Charles Ripley Gillett ... New York, 1927- v. 24 1/2 cm. At head of title: The Union theological seminary in the city of New York. Running title: McAlpin collection. [Z7757.E5N5] 29-29688
1. Theology—Bibl.—Catalogs. 2. Gt. Brit.—Hist.—Bibl. I. Gillett, Charles Ripley, 1855- II. McAlpin, David Hunter, 1816-1901. III. Title. IV. Title: McAlpin collection.

ST. Paul Seminary, St. 016.91603
Paul. Library.
Catalogue. St. Paul, Brown, Treacy & Sperry Co., printers, 1902. 122p. 22cm. [Z881.S157] 3-19591
1. Theology-Bibl.—Catalogs. I. Title.

SCRIBNER, firm, publishers, New
York. (1898. Charles Scribner's sons)
Classified and descriptive catalogue of new and standard works in all departments of religious literature, including philosophy, published and imported by Charles Scribner's sons. New York, C. Scribner's sons, 1898. cover-title, 80 p. 22 cm. [Z7755.Z9S4 1898] 1-10210
1. Theology—Bibl.—Catalogs. 2. Philosophy—Bibl.—Catalogs. 3. Catalogs, Publishers'—U. S. I. Title.

Theology—Bibliography—Union lists.

ALHADEF, John J. 016.2
National bibliography of theological titles in Catholic libraries [John J. Alhadef, compiler] Los Gatos, Calif., Alma College, 1965- v. 22 x 33 cm. Vol. 1 has title: Jesuit theological library author catalog: Alma College. Vol. 3 has imprint: Berkeley, Calif., Catholic Microfilm Center, Graduate Theological Union Library. [Z7755.A6] 76-16969
1. Theology—Bibliography—Union lists. I. Alma College, Los Gatos, Calif. Library. II. Title. III. Title: Jesuit theological library author catalog: Alma College.

SUFFOLK parochial 018'.1'094264
libraries : a catalogue. London : Mansell on behalf of St. Edmundsbury and Ipswich Diocesan Parochial Libraries Committee, 1977. 129 P. : ill. ; 29 cm. [Z7751.S84] [BR118] 78-305114 ISBN 0-7201-0704-0 lib.bdg. : 26.00
1. Theology—Bibliography—Union lists. 2. Church history—Bibliography—Union lists. 3. Libraries, Church—England—Suffolk. 4. Catalogs, Union—England—Suffolk. I. St. Edmundsbury and Ipswich Diocesan Parochial Libraries Committee.
Distributed by Merrimack Book Service

Theology—Bio-bibliography

SMITH, Joseph. 016.2896
bookseller
Bibliotheca anti-Quakeriana; or, A catalogue of books adverse to the Society of Friends, alphabetically arranged; with biographical notices of the authors, together with the answers which have been given to some of them by Friends and others, by Joseph Smith. London, J. Smith, 1873; New York, Kraus Reprint, 1968. 474p. 22cm. Bound with the 1968 reprint ed. Bibliotheca Quakeristica, a bibliography of miscellaneous literature relating to the Friends (Quakers), chiefly written by persons, not members of their Society; also of publications by authors in some way connected; and biographical notices, by Joseph Smith. London, J. Smith, 1883. 32p. 22cm. A10 18.00
1. Theology—Bio-bibl. 2. Friends, Society of—Bio-bibl. I. Title.

SMITH, Joseph, 016.2896
bookseller.
Bibliotheca anti-Quakeriana; or, A catalogue of books adverse to the Society of Friends. Alphabetically arranged; with biographical notices of the authors ... London, 1873. New York, Kraus Reprint Co., 1968. 474 p. 23 cm. Bound with the author's Bibliotheca Quakeristica. London, 1883. New York, Kraus Reprint Co., 1968. [Z7845.F8S6 1968] 78-643
1. Friends, Society of—Bibliography. 2. Theology—Bio-bibliography. I. Title.

Theology—Caricatures and cartoons.

RICHARDS, Alun. 201
God—alive! [By] Alun Richards, Edna Lambert, and Les George. Philadelphia, Westminster Press [1973] 182 p. illus. 23 cm. [BR96.R48] 73-9980 ISBN 0-664-24978-7
1. Theology—Caricatures and cartoons. I. Lambert, Edna, joint author. II. George, Les, joint author. III. Title.

Theology—Catalogs.

*UNION Theological 016.2
Seminary. New York City
Alphabetical arrangement of main entries from the shelf list, Union Theological Seminary Library, New York; 10v. Boston,

G. K. Hall, 1965, 10v. (various p.) 41cm. 975.00 set,
1. Theology—Catalogs. 2. Theology—Bibl. I. Title.

Theology, Catholic.

AN American Catholic 238'.2
catechism / [edited by George J. Dyer]. New York : Seabury Press, [1975] xii, 308 p. ; 22 cm. "A Crossroad book." Includes index. [BX1751.2.A795] 75-7786 ISBN 0-8164-1196-4 : 10.00 ISBN 0-8164-2588-4 pbk. : 4.95
1. Catholic Church—Doctrinal and controversial works. 2. Theology, Catholic. I. Dyer, George J., 1927-

BAUSCH, William J. 230'.2
Positioning : belief in the mid-seventies / William J. Bausch. Notre Dame, Ind. : Fides Publishers, [1975] viii, 176 p. ; 23 cm. Includes bibliographical references. [BX1751.2.B33] 75-5679 ISBN 0-8190-0606-8 : 7.95
1. Theology, Catholic. 2. Theology, Doctrinal. I. Title.

CHILSON, Richard. 230'.2
The faith of Catholics. New York, Paulist Press [1972] vi, 182 p. 19 cm. (Deus books) [BX1751.2.C45] 72-81229 1.25
1. Theology, Catholic. I. Title.

CHILSON, Richard. 230'.2
An introduction to the faith of Catholics / Richard Chilson. Newly rev. and expanded. New York : Paulist Press, c1975. xi, 303 p. : ill. ; 19 cm. (Deus books) Edition of 1972 published under title: The faith of Catholics. [BX1751.2.C45 1975] 75-329397 ISBN 0-8091-1907-2 pbk. : 2.45
1. Theology, Catholic. I. Title.

THE Development of 230
fundamental theology. Edited by Johannes B. Metz. New York, Paulist Press [1969] viii, 180 p. 24 cm. (Concilium: theology in the age of renewal. Fundamental theology, v. 46) Bibliographical footnotes. [BX1747.D48] 74-92116 4.50
1. Theology, Catholic. 2. Apologetics—History. I. Metz, Johannes Baptist, 1928- ed. II. Series: Concilium: theology in the age of renewal, v. 46

DEVINE, George, 1941- 248'.48'2
Transformation in Christ. Staten Island, N.Y., Alba House [1972] xii, 163 p. 23 cm. Includes bibliographical references. [BX1751.2.D395] 70-39884 ISBN 0-8189-0240-X 3.95
1. Theology, Catholic. 2. Christian life—Catholic authors. I. Title.

EBNER, James H. 230'.2
God present as mystery : a search for personal meaning in contemporary theology / by James H. Ebner ; [foreword by Andrew M. Greeley]. Winona, Minn. : St. Mary's College Press, c1976. 168 p. ; 21 cm. Includes bibliographical references and index. [BX1751.2.E25] 76-13750 ISBN 0-88489-084-8 pbk. : 4.95
1. Theology, Catholic. 2. Theology, Doctrinal—Popular works. I. Title.

FRIES, Heinrich 230.2
Bultmann-Barth and Catholic theology. Tr., introd. [by] Leonard Swidler. Pittsburgh. Duquesne [1967] 182p. 22cm. (Duquesne studies. Theological ser., 8) Bibl. [BX4827.B78F73] 67-9153 4.50
1. Bultmann, Rudolf Karl, 1884- 2. Barth, Karl, 1866- 3. Theology, Catholic. I. Title. II. Series.

GAFFNEY, James. 230'.2
Focus on doctrine / by James Gaffney. New York : Paulist Press, [1975?] 148 p. ; 18 cm. (Paulist Press/Deus book) "The articles ... originally appeared in Service, vol. 1." Bibliography: p. 141-148. [BX1751.2.G26] 74-28635 ISBN 0-8091-1863-7 pbk. : 1.65
1. Theology, Catholic. I. Title.

HARDON, John A. 230'.2
The Catholic catechism / John A. Hardon. 1st ed. Garden City, N.Y. : Doubleday, 1975. 623 p. ; 22 cm. Includes bibliographical references and index. [BX1751.2.H36] 73-81433 ISBN 0-385-08039-5 : 9.95
1. Catholic Church—Doctrinal and controversial works—Catholic authors. 2. Theology, Catholic. I. Title.

HELLWIG, Monika. 230'.2
Understanding Catholicism / Monika K. Hellwig. New York : Paulist Press, c1981. 200 p. ; 21 cm. Includes index. Bibliography: p. 192. [BX1751.2.H45] 19 81-80047 ISBN 0-8091-2384-3 pbk. : 4.95
1. Theology, Catholic. I. Title.

HIRE, Richard P. 230'.2
Our Christian faith : one, holy, catholic, and apostolic / Richard P. Hire. Huntington, IN : Our Sunday Visitor, c1977. 320 p. ; 21 cm. [BX1751.2.H57] 76-56918 ISBN 0-87973-855-3 pbk. : 4.95
1. Theology, Catholic. I. Title.

LANG, Martin A. 230'.2
The inheritance: what Catholics believe, by Martin A. Lang. Dayton, Ohio, G. A. Pflaum, 1970. 128 p. illus. 18 cm. (Christian identity series) (Witness book, CI 7) Bibliography: p. 124-125. [BX1751.2.L34] 71-114723 0.95
1. Theology, Catholic. I. Title.

LINDBECK, George A. 230.2
The future of Roman Catholic theology; Vatican II - catalyst for change [by] George A. Lindbeck. Philadelphia, Fortress Press [1970] xvi, 125 p. 22 cm. Includes bibliographical references. [BX830 1962.L513] 75-83678 4.75
1. Vatican Council. 2d, 1962-65. 2. Catholic Church—Relations—Protestant churches. 3. Theology, Catholic. 4. Protestant churches—Relations—Catholic Church. I. Title.

O'COLLINS, Gerald. 230'.01
Fundamental theology / Gerald O'Collins. New York : Paulist Press, c1981. 283 p. ; 23 cm. Includes bibliographical references and index. [BX1751.2.O29] 19 80-82809 ISBN 0-8091-2347-9 (pbk.) : 7.95
1. Theology, Catholic. I. Title.

PESCH, Otto Hermann. 230'.2
Questions and answers : a shorter Catholic catechism / Otto Pesch. Chicago : Franciscan Herald Press, [1976?] p. cm. Translation of Kleines katholisches Glaubensbuch. [BX1754.P4613] 76-23402 2.95
1. Theology, Catholic. I. Title.

PRINCIPLES of Catholic 230'.2
theology : a synthesis of dogma and morals / Edward J. Gratsch, editor ... [et al.]. New York, N.Y. : Alba House, c1981. xii, 410 p. ; 21 cm. Includes bibliographical references and indexes. [BX1751.2.P74] 19 80-26272 ISBN 0-8189-0407-0 pbk. : 10.95
1. Theology, Catholic. 2. Christian ethics—Catholic authors. I. Gratsch, Edward J.

RAHNER, Karl, 1904- 230'.2
Theological investigations. Translated with an introd. by Cornelius Ernst. Baltimore, Helicon Press [1961- v. 22 cm. Vol. 7-8 has imprint: London, Darton, Longman & Todd; New York, Herder and Herder. Vol. 13 published by Seabury Press, New York, as a Crossword book. Vol. 11 has imprint: London, Darton, Longman & Todd; New York, Seabury Press. Translation of Schriften zur Theologie. Translators vary. Contents.Contents.—v. 1. God, Christ, Mary, and grace.—v. 2. Man in the church.—v. 3. The theology of the spiritual life.—v. 4. More recent writings.—v. 5. Later writings.—v. 6. Concerning Vatican Council II.—v. 7. Further theology of the spiritual life, 1.—v. 8. Further theology of the spiritual life, 2.— —v. 11. Confrontations 1. —v. 13. Theology, anthropology, christology. Bibliographical footnotes. [BX1751.2.R313] 61-8189 ISBN 0-232-35616-5 (v. 6)
1. Catholic Church—Doctrinal and controversial works.—Catholic authors. 2. Theology, Catholic. I. Title.

SIMPSON, William John Sparrow.
Broad church theology, by W. J. Sparrow Simpson, D.D. London, R. Scott; Milwaukee, Wis., The Morehouse publishing co., 1919. xiv, 130 p., 1 l. 19 1/2 cm. (Half-title: Handbooks of Catholic faith and practice) "Index of authors quoted": 1 leaf at end. [BX5117.S6] 20-7671
I. Title.

THE Teaching of Christ : 230'.2
a Catholic catechism for adults / edited by Ronald Lawler, Donald W. Wuerl, Thomas Comerford Lawler. Huntington, IN : Our Sunday Visitor, c1976. 640 p. ; 22 cm. Includes indexes. Bibliography: p. 582-612. [BX1751.2.T4] 75-34852 ISBN 0-87973-899-5 : 9.95 ISBN 0-87973-858-8 pbk. : 5.95
1. Theology, Catholic. I. Lawler, Ronald David, 1926- II. Wuerl, Donald W. III. Lawler, Thomas Comerford.

*WEIGEL, Gustave 230.2
Catholic theology in dialogue. New York, Harper [1965, c.1960, 1961] 126p. 21cm. (Harper torchbks.; Cathedral lib., TB301) .95 pap.,
I. Title.

Theology, Catholic—Addresses, essays, lectures.

BAUM, Gregory, 1923- 230'.2
New horizon: theological essays. New York, Paulist Press [1972] viii, 152 p. 18 cm. (Deus books) "The articles [were] for the most part previously published in The Ecumenist." [BX1756.B349N48] 74-188284 1.45
1. Theology, Catholic—Addresses, essays, lectures. I. Title.

JOHN Paul II, Pope, 1920- 230'.2
U.S.A.—the message of justice, peace, and love : pastoral visit of Pope John Paul II, October 1-7, 1979 / compiled and indexed by the Daughters of Sa. Paul. Boston : St. Paul Editions, 1980, c1979. 315 p., [24] leaves of plates : ill. ; 19 cm. Reprint from L'Osservatore romano, English weekly edition. Includes index. [BX1755.J65] 79-24936 ISBN 0-8198-0630-7 : 5.95 ISBN 0-8198-0631-5 pbk. : 4.95
1. Theology, Catholic—Addresses, essays, lectures. 2. United States—Religion—1945- —Addresses, essays, lectures. I. Daughters of St. Paul. II. Title.

MCGINN, John T., comp. 201'.1
Doctrines do grow; a challenge to believers, edited by John T. McGinn. New York, Paulist Press [1972] v, 118 p. 19 cm. (Deus books) Includes bibliographical references. [BX1751.2.M254] 75-180542 1.45
1. Theology, Catholic—Addresses, essays, lectures. I. Title.

Theology, Catholic—Bio-bibliography.

CENTER for 016.23'02'0922
Reformation Research.
Early sixteenth century Roman Catholic theologians and the German Reformation : a finding list of CRR holdings. Saint Louis : Center for Reformation Research, 1975, c1974. 55 p. ; 22 cm. (Sixteenth century bibliography ; 2) [Z7837.C45 1975] [BX1749] 75-315894
1. Theology, Catholic—Bio-bibliography. 2. Reformation—Germany—Bio-bibliography. I. Title. II. Series.

Theology, Catholic—Collected works.

KASCHMITTER, William A. 230'.2
The spirituality of Vatican II : conciliar texts concerning the spiritual life of all Christians / assembled and annotated by William A. Kaschmitter. Huntington, Ind. : Our Sunday Visitor, inc., [1975] 271 p. ; 24 cm. Includes index. [BX1747.5.K37] 74-29344 ISBN 0-87973-868-5 : 7.95
1. Vatican Council. 2d, 1962-1965. 2. Theology, Catholic—Collected works. I. Vatican Council. 2d, 1962-1965. II. Title.

SEGUNDO, Juan Luis. 230'.2
A theology for artisans of a new humanity. [Maryknoll, N.Y.] Orbis Books [1973- v. 24 cm. Translation of Teologia abierta para el laico adulto. Includes bibliographical references. [BX1751.2.A1S413] 73-160586 ISBN 0-88344-480-1 6.95 per vol.
1. Theology, Catholic—Collections. I. Title.

Theology, Catholic—History.

AURICCHIO, John. 201
The future of theology. Staten Island, N.Y., Alba House [1970] 486 p. 22 cm. Bibliography: p. [441]-486. [BX1747.A8] 69-15853 6.95
1. Theology, Catholic—History. I. Title.

MCCOOL, Gerald A. 230'.2
Catholic theology in the nineteenth century : the quest for a unitary method / Gerald A. McCool. New York : Seabury Press, 1977. p. cm. "A Crossroad book." Includes bibliographical references and index. [BX1747.M25] 76-30493 ISBN 0-8164-0339-2 : 14.95
1. Theology, Catholic—History. 2. Theology, Doctrinal—History—19th century. I. Title.

MILET, Jean. 306'.6
God or Christ? : the excesses of Christocentricity / Jean Milet. New York : Crossroad, 1981. p. cm. Translation of: Dieu ou le Christ? Includes bibliographical references and index. [BX1751.2.M5213] 19 81-5566 ISBN 0-8245-0104-7 : 12.95
1. Theology, Catholic—History. 2. Sociology, Christian (Catholic) I. [Dieu ou le Christ?] English II. Title.

SCHOOF, T. Mark, 1933- 201'.1
A survey of Catholic theology, 1800-1970 [by] Mark Schoof. With an introd. by E. Schillebeeckx. Translated by N. D. Smith. Glen Rock, N.J., Paulist Newman Press [1970] 275 p. 21 cm. Translation of Aggiornamento. Includes bibliographical references. [BX1747.S313] 79-133569 4.95
1. Catholic Church—Doctrinal and controversial works—Catholic authors. 2. Theology, Catholic—History. I. Title.

Theology, Catholic—History—19th century.

O'MEARA, Thomas F., 1935- 230'.2
Romantic idealism and Roman Catholicism : Schelling and the theologians / Thomas Franklin O'Meara. Notre Dame : University of Notre Dame Press, c1982. ix, 231 p. ; 24 cm. Includes index. Bibliography: p. 224-227. [BX1747.O6 1982] 19 81-40449 ISBN 0-268-01610-0 : 20.00
1. Tubingen School (Catholic theology) 2. Schelling, Friedrich Wilhelm Joseph von, 1775-1854. 3. Theology, Catholic—History—19th century. I. Title.

Theology, Catholic—History—20th century.

CARMODY, John, 1939- 230'.2
Contemporary Catholic theology : an introduction / John Tully Carmody and Denise Lardner Carmody. 1st ed. San Francisco : Harper & Row, c1980. 252 p. ; 24 cm. Includes bibliographies and index. [BX1747.C35 1980] 19 80-7743 ISBN 0-06-045215-3 : 8.95
1. Theology, Catholic—History—20th century. 2. Theology, Doctrinal—History—20th century. I. Carmody, Denise Lardner, 1935- joint author. II. Title.

Theology, Catholic—Quotations, maxims, etc.

NOBILE, Philip, comp. 200
Catholic nonsense. Drawings by Kieran Quinn. [1st ed.] Garden City, N.Y., Doubleday, 1970. 155 p. illus. 18 cm. [BX1755.N55] 76-116240 3.95
1. Theology, Catholic—Quotations, maxims, etc. I. Title.

Theology—Collected works—16th century

ARMINIUS, Jacobus, 1560- 208.1
1609.
The works of James Arminius ... Translated from the Latin, in three volumes. The first and second, by James Nichols ... The third, with a sketch of the life of the author, by Rev. W. R. Bagnall ... Auburn and Buffalo, Derby, Miller and Orton, 1853. 3 v. 23 cm. Volumes 2 and 3 have imprint: Auburn, Derby and Miller; Buffalo, Derby, Orton and Mulligan. [BX6195.A65 1853] 34-23410
1. Theology—Collected works—16th cent. I. Nichols James, 1785-1861, tr. II. Bagnall, William R., d. 1892, tr. III. Title.

ARMINIUS, Jacobus, 1560-1609. 208.1
Writings. Translated from the Latin, in three volumes, the first and second by James Nichols, the third by W. R. Bagnall; with a sketch of the life of the author. Grand Rapids, Baker Book House, 1956. 3v. 24cm. Photolithoprinted from the author's Works, published in 1853. [BX6195.A65 1956] 56-7575
1. Theology—Collected works—16th cent. I. Title.

CALVIN, Jean, 1509-1564. 201'.1
John Calvin: selections from his writings. Edited and with an introd. by John Dillenberger. Garden City, N.Y., Anchor Books, 1971. viii, 590 p. 18 cm. Bibliography: p. [574]-575. [BX9420.A32D54] 72-123715 2.45
1. Reformed Church—Collected works. 2. Theology—Collected works—16th century. I. Dillenberger, John, ed.

HOOKER, Richard, 1553or4-1600. 230'.3
The Folger Library edition of the works of Richard Hooker / W. Speed Hill, general editor. Cambridge : Belknap Press of Harvard University Press, 1976- c1975- p. cm. Contents.Contents.—v. 1- . Of the laws of ecclesiastical polity. Includes bibliographical references and index. [BX5037.A2 1976] 76-24879 ISBN 0-674-63205-2 (v.1-2) : 60.00(set)
1. Church of England—Collected works. 2. Theology—Collected workks—16th century. I. Hill, William Speed, 1935- II. Title.

JEWEL, John, bp. of Salisbury, 1522-1571. 208.1
The works of John Jewel ... Edited for the Parker society, by the Rev. John Ayre ... Cambridge [Eng.] Printed at the University press, 1845-50. 4 v. 26 1/2 cm. (Half-title: The Parker society. [Publications, v. 23-26]) Additional half-title pages for the four volumes bound in back of v. 4. Include reprints of original title-pages. Contents.I. A sermon preached at Paul's cross. Correspondence with Dr. Cole. The reply to Harding's Answer ...--II. The reply to Harding's Answer ... [cont.] An exposition upon the two Epistles to the Thessalonians. Sermons. A treatise of the sacraments.--III. Apologia Ecclesiae anglicanae. An apology of the Church of England [a translation of the Latin Apologia, by Anne, lady Bacon] The defence of the Apology, parts i-iii. [Reply to attacks by M. Harding]--IV. Biographical memoir of John Jewel. The defence of the Apology, parts IV-VI. The epistle to Scipio. A view of a seditious bull. A treatise on the Holy Scriptures. Letters and miscellaneous pieces. [BX5035.P2] (283.082) A C
1. Church of England—Collected works. 2. Catholic church—Doctrinal and controversial works—Protestant authors. 3. Harding, Thomas, 1516-1572. 4. Cole, Henry, 1500?-1580. 5. Catholic church. Pope, 1566-1572 (Plus V) Regnans in excelsis. 6. Theology—Collected works—16th cent. 7. Lord's supper—Anglican communion. I. Ayre, John, 1801-1869, ed. II. Title.

JUAN de la Cruz, Saint, 1542-1591. 149'.3
Darkness and light; selections from St. John of the Cross. Edited by Catharine Hughes. New York, Sheed & Ward [1972] 41 p. illus. 28 cm. (Mysticism and modern man) [BX890.J62413 1972] 72-6269 ISBN 0-8362-0502-2 2.95
1. Catholic Church—Collected works. 2. Theology—Collected works—16th century. 3. Mysticism—Collected works. I. Hughes, Catharine, 1935- ed. II. Title.

KARLSTADT, Andreas Rudolf, 1480(ca.)-1541. 230'.08
Karlstadt's battle with Luther : documents in a liberal-radical debate / edited by Ronald J. Sider. Philadelphia : Fortress Press, c1977. p. cm. Includes index. Bibliography: p. [BR301.K3] 77-78642 ISBN 0-8006-1312-0 pbk. : 5.95
1. Karlstadt, Andreas Rudolf, 1480 (ca.)-1541. 2. Luther, Martin, 1483-1546. 3. Theology—Collected works—16th century. 4. Reformation—History—Sources. I. Sider, Ronald J. II. Luther, Martin, 1483-1546. Selections. 1977. III. Title.

LUTHER, Martin 208.1
Luther's works. Companion volume. Luther the expositor, introduction to the Reformer's exegetical writings [edited] by Jaroslav Pelikan. Saint Louis, Concordia Pub. House [c.1959] xiii, 286p. 24cm. 55-9893 4.00
1. Theology—Collected works—16th cent. 2. Lutheran Church—Collected works. I. Pelikan, Jaroslav, ed. II. Lehmann, Helmut T., ed. III. Title.

LUTHER, Martin 208.1
Luther's works. v. 9, Lectures on Deuteronomy [edited by] Jaroslav Pelikan and Daniel Poellot. Saint Louis, Concordia Pub. House [c.1960] x, 334p. 24cm. 55-9893 6.00
1. Theology—Collected works—16th cent. 2. Lutheran Church—Collected works. I. Pelikan, Jaroslav, ed. II. Lehmann, Helmut., ed. III. Title.

LUTHER, Martin 208.1
Luther's works. v. 34, Career of the reformer IV. Edited by Lewis W. Spitz. Philadelphia, Muhlenberg Press [c.1960] xvii, 387p. 24cm. 55-9893 5.00
1. Theology—Collected works—16th cent. 2. Lutheran Church—Collected works. I. Pelikan, Jaroslav, ed. II. Lehmann, Helmut T., ed. III. Title.

LUTHER, Martin, 1483-1546. 208
D. Martin Luther's Werke; kritische Gesammtausgabe. Weimar, H. Bohlau, 1883-19 v. in illus., facsims., music, ports. 27 cm. Section 1, v.: sections 2-4 have special titles. Section 1, v. 7. 10-11, 15- ; sections 2-4 published by H. Bohlaus Nachf. -- -- Revisionsnachtrag. Weimar, H. Bohlaus Nachf., 19 v. 28 cm. Contents. -- [1. Abt. Schriften] Bd. Contents.Contents. -- [1, Abt. Schriften] [2. Abt.] Tischreden. 6 v. -- [3. Abt.] Die deutsche Bibel. [4. Abt.] Briefwechsel. Bibliographical footnotes. [BR330.A2 1883] 5-33483
1. Theology — Collected works — 16th cent. 2. Luthern Church — Collected works. I. Title.

LUTHER, Martin, 1483-1546 208.1
Luther's works; v.53. Ed. by Ulrich S. Leupold. General ed.: Helmut T. Lehmann. Philadelphia, Fortress [c.1965] xx, 356p. 24cm. Contents.v.53. Liturgy and hymns. Amer. ed., tr. based on the Weimar ed. of 1883. Bibl. 55-9893 6.00
1. Theology—Collected works—16th cent. 2. Lutheran Church—Collected works. 3. Bible—Criticism, interpretation, etc.—Hist. I. Leupold, Ulrich S., ed. II. Title.

LUTHER, Martin, 1483-1546 208.1
Luther's works, v.48. Ed. by Helmut T. Lehmann. Philadelphia, Fortress [c.1963] 426p. 24cm. Contents.v.48: Letters, 1. Ed., tr. by Gottfried G. Krodel. Bibl. 55-9893 6.00
1. Theology—Collected works—16th cent. 2. Lutheran Church—Collected works. 3. Bible—Criticism, interpretation, etc.—Hist. I. Krodel, Gottfried G., ed., tr. II. Lehmann, Helmut T., ed. III. Title.

LUTHER, Martin, 1483-1546 208.1
Martin Luther, selections from his writings. Ed., introd. by John Dillenberger. Chicago, Quadrangle [c.1961] 526p. 8.00
1. Theology—Collected works—16th cent. 2. Lutheran Church—Collected works. I. Dillenberger, John, ed. II. Title.

LUTHER, Martin, 1483-1546. 208.1
Martin Luther, selections from his writings. Edited and with an introd. by John Dillenberger. [1st ed.] Garden City, N.Y., Doubleday, 1961. xxxiii, 526 p. 19 cm. (Anchor books, A271) [BR331.E5D5] 61-9503
1. Lutheran Church—Collected works. 2. Theology—Collected works—16th century. I. Dillenberger, John, ed.

LUTHER, Martin, 1483-1546. 230.4'1
Readings in Luther for laymen. With introductions and notes by Charles S. Anderson. Minneapolis, Augsburg Pub. House [1967] ix, 304 p. 22 cm. Bibliographical footnotes. [BR331.E5A6] 67-25367
1. Lutheran Church—Collected works. 2. Theology—Collected works—16th century. I. Anderson, Charles S., comp. II. Title.

LUTHER, Martin., 1483-1546 23.0410924
Selected writings of Martin Luther. Theodore G. Tappert, ed. Philadelphia, Fortress [1967] 4v. 18cm. Includes music. Contents.v. 1.] 1517-1520.--[v.2.] 1520-1523.--[v.3.] 1523-1526--[v.4.] 1529-1546 Bibl. [BR331.E5T32] 67-25835 2.95 pap., ea.,; 10.00 set, bxd.
1. Theology—Collected works—16th cent. 2. Lutheran Church—Collected works. I. Tappert, Theodore Gerhardt, 1904- ed. II. Title.

LUTHER, Martin, 1483-1546 208.1
Works; v.7. Jaroslav Pelikan, ed. Walter A. Hansen, assoc. ed. St. Louis, Concordia [c.1965] x, 406p. 24cm. Contents.v.7. Lectures on Genesis, chapters 38-44, tr. by Paul D. Pahl. Bibl. 55-9893 6.00
1. Theology—Collected works—16th cent. 2. Lutheran Church—Collected works. 3. Bible—Criticism. interpretation, etc.—Hist. I. Pelikan, Jaroslav, 1923-ed. II. Hansen, Walter A., ed. III. Title. IV. Title: Lectures on Genesis.

LUTHER, Martin, 1483-1546 208.1
Works; v.8. Jaroslav Pelikan ed. Walter A. Hansen, assoc. ed. St. Louis, Concordia [c.1966] viii, 360p. 24cm. Contents.v.8. Lectures on Genesis chapters 45-50, tr. by Paul D. Pahl. Bibl. 55-9893 6.00
1. Theology — Collected works — 16th cent. 2. Lutheran Church — Collected works. 3. Bible — Criticism. Interpretation, etc. — Hist. I. Pelikan, Jaroslay, 1923- ed. II. Hansen, Walter A., ed. III. Title. IV. Title: Lectures on Genesis.

LUTHER, Martin, 1483-1546. 208.1.
Works. v. 2, lectures on Genesis, chapts 6-14. Jaroslav Pelikan, ed.; Daniel E. Poellot, ass't. ed. St. Louis, Concordia [c.1960] 433p. Bibl. 55-9893 6.00
1. Theology—Collected works—16th cent. 2. Lutheran Church—Collected works. I. Pelikan, Jaroslav, 1923- ed. II. Title.

LUTHER, Martin, 1483-1546 208.1
Works; v.26. Ed.: Jaroslav Pelikan; assoc. ed.: Walter A. Hansen [Tr. from German by Jaroslav Pelikan] St. Louis, Concordia [c.1963] 492p. 24cm. Contents.v.26, Lectures on Galatians 1535, chapters 1-4. Bibl. 55-9893 6.00
1. Theology—Collected works—16th cent. 2. Lutheran Church—Collected works. 3. Bible—Cricism, interpretation, etc.—Hist. I. Pelikan, Jaroslav, 1923- ed. II. Hansen, Walter A., ed. III. Title. IV. Title: Lectures on Galatians.

LUTHER, Martin, 1483-1546 208.1
Works, v.37. General ed.: Holmut T. Lehmann. Philadelphia, Muhlenberg [c.1961] 406p. Contents.v.37. Word and sacrament, ed. by Robert H. Fischer. 55-9893 5.00
1. Theology—Collected works—16th cent. 2. Lutheran Church—Collected works. I. Title.

LUTHER, Martin, 1483-1546 208.1
Works; v.45. Ed. by Walther I. Brandt. General ed.: Helmut T. Lehmann. Philadelphia, Muhlenberg [c.1962] 424p. 24cm. Contents.v.45. The Christian in society, 2. Bibl. 55-9893 6.00
1. Theology—Collected works—16th cent. 2. Lutheran Church—Collected works. 3. Bible—Criticism, interpretation, etc.—Hist. I. Brandt, Walther I., ed. II. Lehmann, Helmut T., ed. III. Title.

LUTHER, Martin, 1483-1546 208.1
Works. Ed.: Jaroslav Pelikan, Walter A. Hansen. St. Louis, Concordia [1967] v. 24cm. Contents.v. 30. The Catholic epistles. Pub. jointly by Concordia Pub. House & Fortress Pr. Bibl. 55-9893 6.00
1. Theology—Collected works—16th cent. 2. Lutheran Church—Collected works. 3. Bible—Criticism, interpretation, etc.—Hist. I. Leupold, Uirich S., ed. II. Pelikan, Jaroslav, ed. III. Hane)0sen, Walter A., ed. IV. Title.

LUTHER, Martin, 1483-1546. 208.1
Works. Edited by Jaroslav Pelikan. Saint Louis, Concordia Pub. House [1955- v. 24cm. Contents.v. 12. Selected Psalms, I. [BR330.E5 1955] 55-9893
1. Theology— Collected works—16th cent. 2. Lutheran Church—Collected works. I. Pellkan, Jaroslav, 1923- ed. II. Title.

LUTHER, Martin, 1483-1546 208.1
Works. Ed. by Jaroslav Pelikan, Walter A. Hansen. St. Louis, Concordia [1968- v. 24cm. Contents.v. 5. Lectures on Genesis, chapters 26-30. [BR330.E5 1955] 55-9893 6.00
1. Theology—Collected works—16th cent. 2. Lutheran Church—Collected works. 3. Bible—Criticism, interpretation, etc.—Hist. I. Pelikan, Jaroslav, 1923- ed. II. Hansen, Walter A. ed. III. Title.

LUTHER, Martin, 1483-1546. 208.1
Works. Edited by Jaroslav Pelikan. Saint Louis, Concordia Pub. House [1955- v. 1, 1958] Saint Louis, Concordia Pub. House [1959] v. 24cm. xiii, 286p. 24cm. Vols. 31- edited by Harold J. Grimn. [and others] General editor: Helmut T. Lehmann. Vols. 31- have imprint: Philadelphia, Muhlenberg Press. Bibliographical footnotes. [BR330.E5 1955] 55-9893
1. Theology—Collected works—16th cent. 2. Lutheran Church—Collected works. 3. Bible—Criticism, interpretation, etc.—Hist. I. Pelikan, Jaroslav, 1923- ed. II. Lehmann, Helmut T., ed. III. Title. IV. Title: — Companion volume. V. Title: Luther the expositor.

MARBECK, Pilgram, d.1556. 230'.4'3
The writings of Pilgram Marpeck / translated and edited by William Klassen and Walter Klaassen. Kitchener, Ont. ; Scottdale, Pa. : Herald Press, 1978. 612 p. ; 23 cm. (Classics of the radical Reformation ; 2) Includes indexes. Bibliography: p. 589-592. [BT15.M28 1978] 77-87419 ISBN 0-8361-1205-9 : 24.95
1. Theology—Collected works—16th century. 2. Anabaptists—Collected works. I. Klassen, William. II. Klaassen, Walter, 1926- III. Title. IV. Series.

MARTIN Luther,
selections from his writings. Edited and with an introd. by John Dillenberger. Chicago, Quadrangle Books [1961] xxxiii, 526p. 22cm. Includes bibliography.
1. Theology—Collected works—16th cent. 2. Lutheran Church—Collected works. I. Luther, Martin, 1483-1546. II. Dillenber, John, ed.

MELANCHTHON, Philipp, 1497-1560.
Opera quae supersunt omnia, editit Carolus Gottlieb Bretschneider. Halis Saxonum, C. A. Schwetschke, 1834-60. [New York Johnson Reprint Corp., 1963] 28 v. 26 cm. (Corpus reformatorum. v. 1-28) Vols. 16-28: Post Carol. Gott. Bretschneiderum edidit Henricus Ernestus bindseil. Original imprint of v. 19-23 is: Brunsvigae, apud C. A. Schwetschke. "Indices": v. 10, p. 324-455. 66-53810
1. Theology — Collected works — 16th cent. 2. Lutheran Church-Collected works. I. Bretschneider, Karl Gottlieb, 1776-1848, ed. II. Bindseil, Heinrich Ernst, 1803-1876, ed. III. Title.

MELANCHTHON, Philipp, 1497-1560. 230.41
Selected writings. Translated by Charles Leander Hill. Edited by Elmer Ellsworth Flack and Lowell J. Satre. Minneapolis, Augsburg Pub. House [1962] 190p. 22cm. Bibliography: p. 189-190. [BR336.A33 1962] 62-9092
1. Theology— Collected works—16th cent. 2. Lutheran Church—Collected works. I. Hill, Charles Leander, tr. II. Flack, Elmer Ellsworth, 1894- ed. III. Satre, Lowell J., ed. IV. Title.

MELANCHTHON, Philipp, 1497-1560. 230'.4'1
Selected writings / Melanchthon ; translated by Charles Leander Hill ; edited by Elmer Ellsworth Flack and Lowell J. Satre. Westport, Conn. : Greenwood Press, 1978, c1962. xiv, 190 p. ; 23 cm. Reprint of the ed. published by Augsburg Pub. House, Minneapolis. Bibliography: p. 189-190. [BR336.A33 1978] 78-5175 ISBN 0-313-20384-9 lib.bdg. : 15.25
1. Lutheran Church—Collected works. 2. Theology—Collected works—16th century. I. Flack, Elmer Ellsworth, 1894- II. Satre, Lowell J.

RUPP, Ernest Gordon, comp. 270.6'0924 B
Martin Luther. Edited by E. G. Rupp and Benjamin Drewery. New York, St.

Martin's Press [1970] xii, 179, [1] p. 21 cm. (Documents of modern history) Bibliography: p. [180] [BR331.E5R86 1970b] 79-124955 6.00
1. Lutheran Church—Collected works. 2. Theology—Collected works—16th century. I. Drewery, Benjamin, joint comp. II. Luther, Martin, 1483-1546.

TERESA, Saint, 1515-1582. 248
The collected works of St. Teresa of Avila / translated by Kieran Kavanaugh and Otilio Rodriguez. Washington : Institute of Carmelite Studies, 1976- v. ; 22 cm. Contents.Contents.—v. 1. The book of her life. Spiritual testimonies. Soliloquies. Includes bibliographical references and index. [BX890.T353 1976] 75-31305 ISBN 0-9600876-2-1 : 4.95
1. Catholic Church—Collected works. 2. Theology—Collected works—16th century.

TERESA, Saint, 1515-1582. 201'.1
The prison of love; selections from St. Teresa of Avila. Edited by Catharine Hughes. New York, Sheed & Ward [1972] [80] p. chiefly illus. 28 cm. (Mysticism and modern man) [BX890.T39 1972] 72-6606 ISBN 0-8362-0503-0 2.95
1. Catholic Church—Collected works. 2. Theology—Collected works—16th century. 3. Mysticism—Collected works. I. Hughes, Catharine, 1935- ed. II. Title.

TYNDALE, William, d. 1536. 208.1
The work of William Tyndale. Ed., introd. by G. E. Duffield. Pref. by F. F. Bruce. Philadelphia, Fortress [c.1965] x1, 406p. facsim., port. 23cm. (Courtenay lib. of Reformation classics) Bibl. [BR75.T77] 65-3003 6.25
1. Theology—Collected works—16th cent. I. Duffield, Gervase E., ed. II. Title.

VIO, Tommaso de, called Gaetano, Cardinal, 1469-1534. 230
Cajetan responds : a reader in Reformation controversy / edited and translated by Jared Wicks. Washington : Catholic University of America Press, c1978. ii, 292 p. ; 24 cm. Bibliography: p. 245-253. [BX890.V59 1978] 77-22666 ISBN 0-8132-0545-X : 19.95
1. Theology—Collected works—16th century. 2. Protestantism—Controversial literature—Collected works. I. Wicks, Jared, 1929- II. Title.
Contents omitted

YODER, John Howard, comp. 284'.3
The legacy of Michael Sattler. Trnaslated and edited by John H. Yoder. Scottdale, Pa., Herlad Press, 1973. 183 p. illus. 23 cm. (Classics of the Radical Reformation, 1) Bibliography: p. 178-182. [BX4929.Y6 1973] 72-6333 ISBN 0-8361-1187-7 9.95
1. Theology—Collected works 16th century. 2. Anabaptists—Collected works. I. Sattler, Michael, 1527. II. Title. III. Series.

ZWINGLI, Ulrich, 1484-1531. 230'.4
Huldrych Zwingli / [edited by] G. R. Potter. New York : St. Martin's Press, [1978] p. cm. (Documents of modern history) Bibliography: p. [BR346.A2513 1978] 78-5311 ISBN 0-312-39633-3 : 19.95
1. Reformed Church—Collected works. 2. Theology—Collected works—16th century. I. Potter, George Richard, 1900-

Theology—Collected works—17th century

BAXTER, Richard, 1615-1691.
Select practical writings of Richard Baxter, with a life of the author. By Leonard Bacon. New Haven, Durrie & Peck, 1831. 2 v. port. 24 cm. [BX5200.B35 1831] 48-35432
1. Theology—Collected works—17th cent. I. Bacon, Leonard, 1802-1881. II. Title.

BULL, George, bp. of St. David's, 1634-1710. 252.
The works of George Bull, D. D., lord bishop of St. David's, collected and revised by the Rev. Edward Burton ... To which is prefixed the life of Bishop Bull, by Robert Nelson ... Oxford, Clarendon press, 1827. 7 v. in 8. 22 cm. [BR75.B65 1827] 12-31048
1. Bull, George, bp. of St. David's, 1934-1710. 2. Theology—Collected works—17th cent. 3. Church of England—Collected works. I. Burton, Edward, 1794-1836, ed. II. Nelson, Robert, 1656-1715. III. Title.

CHILLINGWORTH, William, 1602-1644. 283'.092'4 B
The works of William Chillingworth. New York, AMS Press [1972] 3 v. 23 cm. Reprint of the 1938 ed. [BX5037.C48 1972] 72-946 ISBN 0-404-01570-0 21.00 ea.
1. Church of England—Collected works. 2. Catholic Church—Doctrinal and controversial works. 3. Theology—Collected works—17th century.
62.50 a set.

DELL, William, d.1670? 208.1
The works of William Dell, minister of the gospel and master of Gonvil and Caius college, in Cambridge. Philadelphia: Published by Joseph Sparpless [i. ed. Sharpless] no. 30, Arch street, 1816. vii p., 1 l., [11]-592 p. 22 cm. [BR75.D35] 37-30799
1. Theology—Collected works—17th cent. I. Title.
Contents omitted.

FOX, George, 1624-1691. 289.6'092'4
The works of George Fox. New York : AMS Press, [1975] p. cm. Reprint of the 1831 ed. published by M. T. C. Gould, Philadephia. Contents.Contents.—v. 1-2. A journal or historical account of the life, travels, sufferings, Christian experiences, and labour of love in the work of the ministry of that ancient, eminent, and faithful servant of Jesus Christ, George Fox.—v. 3. The great mystery of the great whore unfolded; and Antichrist's kingdom revealed unto destruction.—v. 4-6. Gospel truth demonstrated, in a collection of doctrinal books, given forth by that faithful minister of Jesus Christ, George Fox: containing principles essential to Christianity and salvation, held among the people called Quakers.—v. 7-8. A collection of many select and Christian epistles, letters and testimonies, written on sundry occasions, by that ancient, eminent, faithful Friend and minister of Christ Jesus, George Fox. [BX7617.F54 1975] 72-154113 ISBN 0-404-09350-7 : 30.00
1. Friends, Society of—Collected works. 2. Theology—Collected works—17th century.

GOUGE, Thomas, 1609-1681.
The works of the late reverend and pious Mr. Thomas Gouge ... In six parts ... To which is prefixed, an account of the author's life. Albany, George Lindsay, E. & E. Hosford, printers, 1815. x, [11]-540, [2] p. 22 cm. [BX5200.G6] A34
1. Theology—Collected works—17th century. I. Title.
Contents omitted

HALES, John, 1584-1656. 208
The works of John Hales. New York, AMS Press [1971] 3 v. in 2. 18 cm. Reprint of the 1765 ed., originally published under title: The works of the ever memorable John Hales of Eaton. Includes bibliographical references. [BR75.H32 1971] 77-131037 ISBN 0-404-03050-5
1. Theology—Collected works—17th century.

HALL, Joseph, Bp. of Norwich, 1574-1656. 208
The works of the Right Reverend Joseph Hall. A new ed., rev. and corrected with some additions, by Philip Wynter. New York, AMS Press [1969] 10 v. 23 cm. Reprint of the 1863 ed. Includes bibliographical references. [BX5037.H26 1969] 76-86830
1. Church of England—Collected works. 2. Theology—Collected works—17th century. I. Wynter, Philip, 1793-1871, ed. II. Title.

HOOKER, Thomas, 1586-1647. 230'.5'8
Thomas Hooker : writings in England and Holland, 1626-1633 / edited, with introductory essays, by George H. Williams ... [et al.]. Cambridge : Harvard University Press, 1975. viii, 435 p., [1] leaf of plates : ill. ; 24 cm. (Harvard theological studies ; 28) Includes indexes. "A bibliography of the published writings of Thomas Hooker": p. 390-425. [BX7117.H58 1975] 75-30570 ISBN 0-674-88520-1 : 10.00
1. Hooker, Thomas, 1586-1647. 2. Hooker, Thomas, 1586-1647—Bibliography. 3. Theology—Collected works—17th century. 4. Congregational churches—Collected works. I. Williams, George Huntston, 1914- II. Title. III. Series.
Contents omitted

LAUD, William, Abp. of Canterbury, 1573-1645. 230'.3'08
The works of the Most Reverend Father in God, William Laud, D.D. New York : AMS Press, [1975] p. cm. (LACT ; #11) Reprint of the 1847-1860 ed. published by J. H. Parker, Oxford. Contents.Contents.—v. 1. Sermons.—v. 2. Conference with Fisher.—v. 3. Devotions, diary, and history.—v. 4. History of troubles and trial, &c.—v. 5 [pt. 1] History of his chancellorship. pt. 2. Accounts of province, &c.—v. 6. pt. 1. Miscellaneous papers. Letters. pt. 2. Letters. Notes on Bellarmine.—v. 7. Letters. [BX5037.L3 1975] 74-5373 ISBN 0-404-52120-7 : 270.00
1. Church of England—Collected works. 2. Theology—Collected works—17th century. I. Title. II. Series: The Library of Anglo-Catholic theology ; #11.

LEIGHTON, Robert, abp. of Glasgow, 1611-1684. 208.1
The select works of Archbishop Leighton. Prepared for the practical use of private Christians. With an introductory view of the life, character, and writings of the author. By George B. Cheever. Boston, Pierce & Parker; New York, H.C. Sleight; [etc., etc.] 1832. ix, [61]-569 p. front. (port.) 23 cm. [BX5255.L42] 33-16020
1. Theology—Collected works—17th cent. 2. Episcopal church in Scotland—Collected works. I. Cheever, George Barrell, 1807-1890. II. Title.

LEIGHTON, Robert, abp. of Glasgow, 1611-1684. 208.
The whole works of Robert Leighton ... to which is prefixed, A life of the author, by John Norman Pearson ... With a table of the texts of Scripture, and an index of the subjects, compiled expressly for this edition. New York, J. C. Riker; Philadelphia, G. S. Appleton, 1844. 800 p. 23 1/2 cm. Combines the London edition, 1835, and the Edinburgh edition, 1840. cf. Notice. "Appendix. Life of Archbishop Leighton: by James Alkman": p. [739]-767. [BX5255.L4 1844] 38-33104
1. Theology—Collected works—17th cent. 2. Episcopal church in Scotland—Collected works. I. Pearson, John Norman, 1787-1865. II. Alkman, James, 1779?-1860. III. Title.

LEIGHTON, Robert, abp. of Glasgow, 1611-1684. 208.1
The whole works of Robert Leighton ... To which is prefixed, a life of the author, by John Norman Pearson ... With a table of the texts of Scripture, and an index of the subjects, compiled expressly for this edition. New York, J. C. Riker; Philadelphia, G. S. Appleton, 1846. 800 p. 23 1/2 cm. Combines the London edition, 1835, and the Edinburgh edition, 1840. cf. Notice. [BX5255.L4 1846] 34-10129
1. Theology—Collected works—17th cent. 2. Episcopal church in Scotland—Collected works. I. Pearson, John Norman, 1787-1865. II. Title.

LEIGHTON, Robert, abp. of Glasgow, 1611-1684. 208.1
The whole works of Robert Leighton ... To which is prefixed, a life of the author, by John Norman Pearson ... With a table of the texts of Scripture, and an index of the subjects, compiled expressly for this edition. New York, J. C. Riker; Philadelphia, G. S. Appleton, 1851. 800 p. 23 1/2 cm. Combines the London edition, 1835, and the Edinburgh, 1840. cf. Notice. [BX5255.L4 1831] 33-12083
1. Theology—Collected works—17th cent. 2. Episcopal church in Scotland—Collected works. I. Pearson, John Norman, 1787-1865. II. Title.

QUAKER classics in brief. Wallingford, Pa. : Pendle Hill Publications, 1978. xii, 153 p. ; 23 cm. [BX7615.Q34] 78-57741 ISBN 0-87574-904-6 pbk. : 2.75 230'.96
1. Friends, Society of—Collected works. 2. Theology—Collected works—17th century. I. Penn, William, 1644-1718. No cross, no crown. 1978. II. Barclay, Robert, 1648-1690. Theologia vere Christiana apologia. English. 1978. III. Penington, Isaac, 1616-1679. The inward journey of Isaac Penington. 1978.
Contents omitted

SCOUGAL, Henry, 1650-1678. 208
The works of the Rev. Henry Scougal ... Together with his funeral sermon by the Rev. Dr. Gairden; and an account of his life, and writings. Philadelphia, J. Kay, jun. and brother; Pittsburgh, J. I. Kay & co. [183-?] xii, [13]-272 p. 15 cm. [BR75.S3] 15-24963
1. Theology—Collected works—17th cent. I. Garden, George, 1649-1723. II. Title.

TAYLOR, Jeremy, Bp. of Down and Connor, 1613-1667. 208.1
The house of understanding; selections from the writings of Jeremy Taylor by Margaret Gest. Philadelphia, University of Pennsylvania Press, 1954. x, 118p. port. 24cm. Bibliography: p. 116-118. [BR75.T28] 54-5011
1. Theology— Collected works—17th cent. 2. Church of England—Collected works. I. Title.

TAYLOR, Jeremy, Bp. of Down and Connor, 1613-1667. 230'.3
Jeremy Taylor: a selection from his works made by Martin Armstrong. Waltham Saint Lawrence, Berkshire, Golden Cockerel Press, 1923. [Folcroft, Pa., Folcroft Library Editions, 1972] p. [BR75.T29 1972] 72-13174 ISBN 0-8414-1165-4 (lib. bdg.)
1. Church of England—Collected works. 2. Theology—Collected works—17th century. I. Armstrong, Martin Donisthorpe, 1882- ed.

TAYLOR, Jeremy, bp. of Down and Connor, 1613-1667. 252.
Selections from the works of Jeremy Taylor. With some account of the author and his writings. Boston, Little, Brown, and company, 1865. vi, 7-306 p. 20 cm. [BR75.T3] 20-11819
1. Theology—Collected works—17th cent. I. Title.

WHICHCOTE, Benjamin, 1609-1683. 230'.3
The works / Benjamin Whichcote. New York : Garland Pub., 1976. p. cm. (British philosophers and theologians of the 17th & 18th centuries ; no. 64) Reprint of the 1751 ed. printed by J. Chalmers for A. Thomson, Aberdeen. [BX5037.W53 1976] 75-11265 ISBN 0-8240-1814-1 lib. bdg. : 25.00 per vol.
1. Church of England—Collected works. 2. Theology—Collected works—17th century. I. Title. II. Series.

Theology—Collected works—18th century.

LAW, William, 1686-1761. 208.1
The pocket William Law. With a foreword by the Archbishop of York. Edited by Arthur W. Hopkinson. Philadelphia, Westminster Press [1950] 160p. 20cm. [BR75.L344] 52-6520
1. Theology—Collected works—18th cent. I. Title.

LAW, William, 1688-1761. 230'.3'08
The power of the spirit : selections from the writings of William Law / edited by Andrew Murray. Minneapolis : Bethany Fellowship, 1977. xv, 218 p. ; 18 cm. (Dimension books) (Classics of devotion) Reprint of the 1896 ed. published by J. Nisbet. [BR75.L346 1977] 76-57110 ISBN 0-87123-463-7 pbk. : 2.25
1. Theology—Collected works—18th century. I. Title. II. Series.

LESSING, Gotthold Ephraim, 1729-1781. 230.081
Theological writings; selections in translation with an introductory essay, by Henry Chadwick. Stanford, Calif. Stanford University Press [1957] 110p. 23cm. (A Library of modern religious thought) Bibliography: p. 107. [BR75.L47 1957] 57-9374
1. Theology—Collected works—18th cent. I. Title.

PENN, William, 1644-1718. 289.6
The select works of William Penn. 4th ed. London, Printed and sold by W. Phillips, G. Yard, 1825. New York, Kraus Reprint Co., 1971. 3 v. 24 cm. [BX7617.P5A1 1971] 73-154550
1. Friends, Society of—Collected works. 2. Penn, William, 1644-1718. 3. Theology—Collected works—18th century. I. Title.

PENN, William, 1644-1718. 289.6
The witness of William Penn / edited with an introd., Frederick B. Tolles and E. Gordon Alderfer. New York : Octagon Books, 1980, c1957. xxx, 205 p. ; 21 cm. Selected passages from the author's works. Reprint of the ed. published by Macmillan, New York. Bibliography: p. 203-205. [BX7617.P5W52 1980] 79-27856 ISBN 0-374-97950-2 lib. bdg. : 13.50
1. Friends, Society of—Collected works. 2. Theology—Collected works—18th century. I. Tolles, Frederick Barnes, 1915- II. Alderfer, Everett Gordon, 1915- III. Title.

SWEDENBORG, Emanuel, 1688-1772. 230'.9'4
The four doctrines : the Lord, Sacred Scripture, life, faith / by Emanuel Swedenborg ; English translation by John Faulkner Potts ; edited by Alice Spiers Sechrist. New York : Swedenborg Foundation, 1976. 328 p. ; 18 cm. Translation of Doctrina Novae Hierosolymae de Domino, Doctrina Novae Hierosolymae de Scriptura Sacra, Doctrina Novae Hierosolymae de fide, and Doctrina vitae pro Noya Hierosolyma ex praeceptis decalogi. [BX8711.A25 1976] 76-151239 ISBN 0-87785-064-X pbk. : 1.25
1. New Jerusalem Church—Doctrinal and controversial works. 2. Theology—Collected works—18th century. I. Title.

SWEDENBORG, Emanuel, 1688-1772. 230'.94
The four leading doctrines of the New Church, signified by the New Jerusalem in the revelation: being those concerning the Lord, the Sacred Scripture, faith, and life. New York, American Swedenborg Print. and Pub. Society, 1882. [New York, AMS Press, 1971] 247 p. 22 cm. Translations of Doctrina Novae Hierosolymae de Domino, Doctrina Novae Hierosolymae de Scriptura Sacra, Doctrina Novae Hierosolymae de fide, and Doctrina vitae pro Nova Hierosolyma ex praeceptis decalogi. [BX8711.A25 1971] 71-134426 ISBN 0-404-08466-4
1. New Jerusalem Church—Doctrinal and controversial works. 2. Theology—Collected works—18th century. I. Title.

SWEDENBORG, Emanuel, 1688-1772. 230'.9'408
Miscellaneous theological works of Emanuel Swedenborg / translation by John Whitehead. Standard ed. New York : Swedenborg Foundation, [1976] vii, 634 p. ; 22 cm. Contents.Contents.—The New Jerusalem and its heavenly doctrine.—A brief exposition of the doctrine of the new church.—The intercourse between the soul and the body.—The white horse mentioned in the Apocalypse, Chap.XIX.—Appendix to the treatise on The white horse.—The earths in the universe.—The last judgment.—Continuation concerning the last judgment. [BX8711.A25 1976b] 76-46143 ISBN 0-87785-071-2. ISBN 0-87785-070-4 (student)
1. New Jerusalem Church—Doctrinal and controversial works. 2. Theology—Collected works—18th century. I. Title.

SWEDENBORG, Emanuel, 1688-1772.
[Theological works] Boston and New York, Houghton Mifflin and company, 1907. 32 v. 19 cm. Rotch edition. Special t.-p. to each part of [v. 22] and to 2d part of [v. 23] Contents.[v. 1-19] The heavenly arcana disclosed ... which are in Genesis ([v. 1-11]) [and] in Exodus ([v. 12-19])--[v. 20] Index to ... The heavenly arcana.--[v. 21] Heaven and its wonders and hell.--[v. 22] Miscellaneous works: [pt. 1] Final judgment; [pt. 2] The white horse; [pt. 3] Earths in the universe; [pt. 4] Summary exposition.--[v. 23, pt. 1] The four doctrines of the New Jerusalem. [pt. 2] The New Jerusalem and its heavenly doctrine.--[v. 24, pt. 1] Angelic wisdom concerning the divine love and concerning the divine wisdom.--[pt. 2] The intercourse between the soul and the body.--[v. 25] Angelic wisdom concerning the divine providence.--[v. 26-28] The Apocalypse revealed.--[v. 29] The delights of wisdom pretaining to marriage love.--[v. 30-32] The true Christian religion. 13-11913
I. Title.

SWENDENBORG, Emanuel, 1688-1772. 198'.5
The essential Swedenborg: basic teachings of Emanuel Swedenborg, scientist, philosopher, and theologian. Selected and edited and with an introd. by Sig Synnestvedt. [New York] Swedenborg Foundation [1970] 202 p. 21 cm. "The theological writings of Emanuel Swedenborg": p. 181-190. [BX8711.A25 1970] 70-110362
1. New Jerusalem Church—Doctrinal and controversial works. 2. Theology—Collected works—18th century. I. Synnestvedt, Sigfried T., comp. II. Title.

WESLEY, John, 1703-1791. 230'.7'108
Fire of love : the spirituality of John Wesley / [selected by] Gordon Wakefield. New Canaan, Conn. : Keats Pub., 1977, c1976. 124 p. ; 18 cm. (A Pivot family reader) Includes bibliographies. [BX8217.W54W3 1977] 76-58765 1.95
1. Methodist Church—Collected works. 2. Theology—Collected works—18th century. I. Title.

WESLEY, John, 1703-1791. 230'.7
John and Charles Wesley : selected prayers, hymns, journal notes, sermons, letters and treatises / edited, with an introduction, by Frank Whaling ; preface by Albert C. Outler. New York : Paulist Press, c1981. xx, 412 p. ; 24 cm. (The Classics of Western spirituality) Includes indexes. Bibliography: p. 389-393. [BX8217.W54W45 1981] 19 81-82207 ISBN 0-8091-0318-4 : 11.95 ISBN 0-8091-2368-1 pbk. : 7.95
1. Methodist Church—Collected works. 2. Church of England—Collected works. 3. Theology—Collected works—18th century. I. Wesley, Charles, 1707-1788. Selections. 1981. II. Whaling, Frank, 1934- III. [Selections.] 1981 IV. Title. V. Series.

WESLEY, John, 1703-1791. 208
John Wesley; [a representative collection of his writings] Edited by Albert C. Outler. New York, Oxford University Press, 1964. xvi, 516 p. 24 cm. (A Library of Protestant thought) Bibliography: p. 500-506. [BX8217.W54O8] 64-15525
1. Theology—Collected works—18th century. 2. Methodist Church—Collected works. I. Outler, Albert Cook, 1908- ed. II. Title. III. Series.

WESLEY, John, 1703-1791. 287
John Wesley / John W. Drakeford, editor. Nashville : Broadman Press, c1979. 414 p. ; 24 cm. (Christian classics) Includes bibliographical references. [BX8217.W54D7] 78-59981 ISBN 0-8054-6536-7 : 24.95
1. Methodist Church—Collected works. 2. Theology—Collected works—18th century. I. Drakeford, John W. II. Title. III. Series. Publisher's Address : 127 Ninth Ave., Nashville, TN 37234

WESLEY, John, 1703-1791. 230'.7
The John Wesley treasury / Erwin Paul Rudolph, editor. Wheaton, Ill. : Victor Books, c1979. 96 p. ; 18 cm. (Great Christian classics series) Abridged selections from Wesley's sermons, letters, and journals. Bibliography: p. 95-96. [BX8217.W54R82] 78-66035 ISBN 0-88207-517-9 pbk. : 1.75
1. Methodist Church—Collected works. 2. Theology—Collected works—18th century. I. Rudolph, Erwin Paul, 1916- II. Title. III. Series.

WESLEY, John, 1703-1791. 287
Selections from the writings of the Rev. John Wesley ... compiled and arranged with a preface by Herbert Welch ... [Rev. ed.] New York, Cincinnati, The Methodist book concern [c1918] 405 p. front., pl., ports., facsim. 19 cm. [BX8217.W54W4 1918] 18-16479
1. Theology—Collected works—18th cent. 2. Methodism—Collected works. I. Welch, Herbert, bp., 1862- comp. II. Title.

WESLEY, John, 1703-1791. 230'.7
The works of John Wesley / edited by Frank Baker. Oxford ed. Oxford : Claredon Press ; New York : Oxford University Press, c1980- p. cm. Includes index. Contents.Contents.— —v. 26. Letters II, 1740-1755. [BX8217.W5 1980] 79-40591 ISBN 0-19-812546-1 : 37.50
1. Methodist Church—Collected works. 2. Theology—Collected works—18th century. I. Baker, Frank, 1910-

Theology — Collected works — 19th century

ALEXANDER, Archibald, 1772-1851. 285
Practical truths. By the Rev. Archibald Alexander... consisting of his various writings for the American tract society, and correspondence from the Society's formation in 1825, to his death in 1851. New York, The American tract society [1857] 396 p. front. (port.) 19 1/2 cm. [BR85.A4] 36-5016
1. Theology—Collected works—19th cent. 2. Presbyterian church—Collected works. I. American tract society. II. Title.

CURRENT discussions in theology. 208.2 By Professors ... of Chiicago theological seminary ... Chicago, F. H. Revell, 1883-90. 7 v. 20 cm. On cover (v. 2-7): Annual theological review. Vols. 5-7 have imprint: Boston and Chicago, Congregational Sunday-school and publishing society. Contents.--i. Present state of Old Testament studies, by S. I. Curtizs Church history, with some notice of auxillary studies, by H. M. Scott. Present theological tendencies, and the influences producing them, by G. N. Boardman.--ii. Present state of Old Testament studies; history of Israel, by S. I. Curtiss. Present state of New Testament study, by J. T. Hyde. The most recent history of doctrine; or, The present state of theology and theological parties in Germany and German-Switzerland, by H. M. Scott. Theisru and revelation, by G. N. Boardman. Current preaching; its matter, manner, tendencies and conditions of power, by F. W. Fisk. Present church work, by G. B. Willcox.--iii. Present state of Old Testament studies, by S. I. Curtiss. Present state of New Testament study, by J. T. Hyde. The most recent studies in church history, with some of the more important results, by H. M. Scott. Christian dogmatics, apologetics and morals, by G. N. Boardman. Homiletics: theoretical and practical, by F. W. Fisk. Recent studies in pastoral theology, by G. B. Willcox.--iv. Present state of Old Testament studies, by S. I. Curtiss. Present state of New Testament study, by H. M. Scott. The most recent studies in church history, with some of the more important results, by H. M. Scott. Dogmatic theology, apologetics, theism and ethics, by G. N. Boardman. Homiletics: theoretical and practical, by F. W. Fisk. Recent studies in pastroal theology, by G. B. Willcox.--v. Present state of Old Testament studies, by S. I. Curtiss. Present state of New Testament studies, by G. H. Gilbert. The most recent studies in church history, with some of the more important results, by H. M. Scott. Theism, apologetics, dogmatic theology and ethics, by G. N. Boardman. Recent studies in pastoral theology, by G. B. Willcox. Homiletics: theoretical and practical, by F. W. Fisk.--vi. Present state of Old Testament studies, by S. I. Curtiss. Present state of New Testament studies, by G. H. Gilbert. Present state of studies in church history, by H. M. Scott. Present state of studies in natural and revealed theology, by G. N. Boardman. Present state of studies in homiletics, by F. W. Fisk. Present state of studies in pastroal theology, by G. B. Willcox.--vii. Present state of Old Testament studies, by S. I. Curtiss. Present state of New Testament studies, by G. H. Gilbert. Present state of studies in church history, by H. M. Scott. Present state of studies in natural and revealed theology, by G. N. Boardman. Present state of studies in homiletics, by F. W. Fisk. Present state of studies in pastoral theology, by G. B. Willcox. [BR45.C8] 41-31801
1. Theology—Collections—19th cent. 2. Theology—Bibl. I. Chicago theological seminary.

DRUMMOND, Henry, 1851-1897. 208.1
Henry Drummond: an anthology, edited, and with the story of his life by James W. Kennedy. Introd. by Samuel M. Shoemaker. [1st ed.] New York, Harper [c1953] 253p. illus. 22cm. [BR85.D696] 52-10673
1. Theology—Collected works—19th cent. I. Kennedy, James William, 1905- ed. II. Title.

GRUNDTVIG, Nicolai Frederik Severin, 1783-1872. 230'.4'10924 B
Selected writings / N. F. S. Grundtvig ; edited and with an introd. by Johannes Knudsen ; translated by Johannes Knudsen, Enok Mortensen, Ernest D. Nielsen. Philadelphia : Fortress Press, c1976. vii, 184 p. ; 22 cm. Includes index. Bibliography: p. 182. [BX8011.G78213 1976] 76-7873 ISBN 0-8006-1238-8 : 5.95
1. Lutheran Church—Collected works. 2. Theology—Collected works—19th century.

[HASTED, Frederick] b.1793. 208.
[Theological miscellanies] [Buffalo? 1866?] 1 l., 49 p., 1 l., 4 p. 22 cm. Binder's title. A collection of miscellanies signed by Frederick Hasted, dated between 1863 and 1866. The second item is undated. [BR85.H3] 45-25367
1. Theology—Collected works—19th cent. I. Title.

[HASTED, Frederick] b.1793. 208.
Writings, etc. [Buffalo? 186-] [497] p. 22 cm. Binder's title. Various pagings. A collection of tracts, letters and poems, most of which are signed by Frederick Hasted and dated between 1860 and 1863. [BR85.H32] 45-45678
1. Theology—Collected works—19th cent. I. Title.

JACKSON, Rebecca, 1795-1871. 298'.8
Gifts of power : the writings of Rebecca Jackson, black visionary, Shaker eldress / edited, with an introduction, by Jean McMahon Humez. Amherst : University of Massachusetts Press, 1981. p. cm. Bibliography: p. [BX9771.J3 1981] 19 81-4684 ISBN 0-87023-299-1 : 20.00
1. Shakers—Collected works. 2. Theology—Collected works—19th century. I. Humez, Jean McMahon, 1944- II. Title.

JAY, William, 1769-1853.
Standard works of the Rev. William Jay ... comprising all his works known in this country; and, also, several which have not, heretofore, been presented to the American public ... Baltimore, Plaskitt & co., and Armstrong & Plaskitt, 1832. 3 v. 23 cm. Contents.I. Morning and evening exercises.--II. Short discourses to be read in families. The Christian contemplated, in a course of lectures. Prayers.-- III. Sermons. Life of Winter. Memoirs of John Clark. A charge to the wife of a minister. The wife's advocate, &c. [BX5200.J3 1832] 44-43235
1. Theology—Collected works—19th cent. I. Title.

JAY, William, 1769-1853.
Standard works of the Rev. William Jay ... comprising all his works known in this country; and, also, several which have not, heretofore, been presented to the American public ... Baltimore, J. Plaskitt, 1835. 3 v. front. (port.) 23 cm, Contents.I. Morning and evening exercises.--II. Short discourses to be read in families. The Christian contemplated, in a course of lectures. Prayers.-- III. Sermons. Life of Winter. Memoirs of John Clark. A charge to the wife of a minister. The wife's advocate, &c. [BX5200.J3 1835] 44-43237
1. Theology—Collected works—19th cent. I. Title.

KIERKEGAARD, Soren Aabye, 1813-1855. 204
... The present age and two minor ethico-religious treatises; translated by Alexander Dru and Walter Lowrie. London, New York [etc.] Oxford university press, 1940. xii, 163, [1] p. 19 cm. At head of title: Kierkegaard. "The present age" ... first appeared ... March 1846. It ... fromed the last part of a review of a novel, The two ages." [BR85.K458] 41-2050
1. Theology—Collected works—19th cent. I. Dru, Alexander, tr. II. Lowrie, Walter, 1868- tr. III. Title.
Contents omitted.

MACKINTOSH, Charles Henry, 1820-1896. 220.6'6
The Mackintosh treasury : miscellaneous writings / by C. H. Mackintosh. Neptune, N.J. : Loizeaux Bros., [1976] p. cm. First published in 1898 under title: The miscellaneous writings of C. H. Mackintosh. [BR85.M18 1976] 75-44323 ISBN 0-87213-609-4 : 12.95
1. Theology—Collected works—19th century. I. Title.

MACKINTOSH, Charles Henry, 1820-1896. 208.1
Miscellaneous writings. New York, Loizeaux Bros. [1951] 6 v. 17cm. Contents.v. 1. The all sufficiency of Christ.--v. 2. The Lord's coming.--v. 3. The assembly of God.--v. 4. The great commission.--v. 5. Elijah the Tiahbite.--v. 6. Life and times of David. [BR85.M18] 55-16561
1. Theology—Collected works—19th century. I. Title.

MACKINTOSH, Charles Henry, 1820-1896. 230'.9
Short papers : reprinted from Things new and old / by C. H. Mackintosh. Sunbury, Pa. : Believers Bookshelf, c1975. 2 v. ; 21 cm. [BR85.M19 1975] 75-29527
1. Theology—Collected works—19th century. I. Things new and old. II. Title.

NEVIN, John Williamson, 1803-1886. 230'.5'733
Catholic and Reformed : selected theological writings of John Williamson Nevin / edited by Charles Yrigoyen, Jr. and George H. Bricker. Pittsburgh : Pickwick Press, 1978. ix, 411 p. : port. ; 22 cm. (Pittsburgh original texts & translations series ; 3) Includes bibliographical references. [BX9559.N48 1978] 78-2567 ISBN 0-915138-37-9 : 9.50
1. Reformed Church in the United States—Doctrinal and controversial works—Collected works. 2. Theology—Collected works—19th century. 3. Mercersburg theology—Collected works. I. Yrigoyen, Charles, 1937- II. Bricker, George H. III. Title.

NEWMAN, John Henry, Cardinal, 1801-1890. 230'.2'08
Characteristics from the writings of John Henry Newman : being selections personal, historical, philosophical, and religious, from his various works / arranged by William Samuel Lilly, with the author's approval. Folcroft, Pa. : Folcroft Library Editions, 1976. p. cm. Reprint of the 1875 ed. published by Scribner, Wilford & Armstrong, New York. Includes bibliographical references and index. [BX890.N39 1976] 76-45366 ISBN 0-8414-5813-8 lib. bdg. : 40.00
1. Catholic Church—Collected works. 2. Theology—Collected works—19th century. I. Title.

NEWMAN, John Henry, Cardinal, 1801-1890. 208
Essays and sketches. [Edited by Charles Frederick Harrold] Westport, Conn., Greenwood Press [1970, c1948] 3 v. 23 cm. Contents.Contents.—v. 1. Personal and literary character of Cicero, 1824. Poetry, with reference to Aristotle's Poetics, 1829. Primitive Christianity, 1833-36. The rationalistic and the Catholic tempers contrasted, 1835. Holy Scripture in its relation to the Catholic Creed, 1838. Prospects of the Anglican Church, 1839.—v. 2. The theology of St. Ignatius, 1839. Catholicity of the Anglican Church, 1840. Private judgement, 1841. The Tamworth Reading Room, 1841. Milman's view of Christianity, 1841. Rise and progress of universities (Selections from the original discourses) 1856.—v. 3. The church of the Fathers, 1833. The last years of St. Chrysostom, 1859-60. Benedictine schools, 1858-59. An internal arguement for Christianity, 1866. Includes bibliographical references. [BX890.N415 1970] 76-98785
1. Catholic Church—Collected works. 2. Theology—Collected works—19th century. I. Harrold, Charles Frederick, 1897-1948, ed.

NEWMAN, John Henry, Cardinal 1801-1890. 081
The essential Newman. Edited by Vincent Ferrer Blehl. [New York] New American Library [1963] 350 p. 18 p. (A Mentor-Omega book, MT488) "A bibliographical note": p. 340-341. [BX890.N417] 63-25953
1. Theology — Collected works — 19th cent. 2. Catholic Church — Collected works. I. Blehl, Vincent Ferrer, ed. II. Title.

NEWMAN, John Henry, Cardinal 1801-1890.
Works. [Westminster, Md., Christian Classics, 1966- v. 21 cm. Title from spine, Each vol. has special t.p. Each work reprinted from an earlier ed. Contents.Contents. -- [1] Fifteen sermons preached before the University of Oxford. -- [2] Lectures on the doctrine of justification. -- [3] Discourses addressed to mixed congregations.- 67-54104
1. Theology — Collected works — 19th cent. 2. Catholic Church — Collected works. I. Title.

PALLOTTI, Vincenzo, Saint, 1795-1850. 282.08
Complete writings. Baltimore, Pallottine Fathers & Brothers Press, 1968- v. 24 cm. Contents.—v. 1. Pious Society of the Catholic Apostolate. Bibliographical footnotes. [BX890.P25] 68-7190
1. Catholic Church—Collected works. 2. Theology—Collected works—19th century.

[PENNOCK, Ames Castle] 1815- 208.1
Fragments of thought upon theology, science, morals and men. Omaha, Neb., Douglas print. co., 1900. 25 v. in 1. ports. 20 cm. Volume of 25 pieces, published 1867-99, at different places, bound together with above t.-p. and a table of contents. Author's name on t.-p. of most of the pieces. [BR85.P45] 0-4766
1. Theology—Collected works—19th cent. I. Title.
Contents omitted.

SPURGEON, Charles Haddon, 1834-1892. 252.06
The treasury of Charles H. Spurgeon. Introd. by Wilbur M. Smith. [Westwood, N.J.] F.H. Revell Co. [1955] 256p. 21cm. [BX6217.S67] 55-9251
1. Theology—Collected works—19th cent. 2. Baptists—Collected works. I. Title.

SPURGEON, Charles Haddon, 1834-1892 252.06
The treasury of Charles H. Spurgeon. Introd. by Wilbur M. Smith. Grand Rapids, Mich., Baker Bk. [1967,c.1955] 256p. 20cm. (Treasury ser.) [BX6217.S67] 1.95 pap.,
1. Theology—Collected works—19th cent. 2. Baptists—Collected works. I. Title.

TOLSTOI, Lev Nikolaevich, graf 210.81
Lift up your eyes; the religious writings of Leo Tolstoy. Introd. by Stanley R. Hopper. New York, Julian Press, [c.] 1960. 581p. port. 21cm. 59-15567 5.95
1. Theology—Collected works—19th cent. I. Title.

WALTHER, C. F. W. 1811-1887. (Carl Ferdinand Wilhelm), 230'.41322
Convention essays / Aug. R. Suelflow, translator. St. Louis : Concordia Pub. House, c1981. 192 p. : port. ; 24 cm. (Selected writings of C.F.W. Walther) (Series: Walther, C. F. W. (Carl Ferdinand Wilhelm), 1811-1887. Selections. English. 1981.) Includes bibliographical references. [BX8011.W28213 1981] 19 81-3096 ISBN 0-570-08277-3 : 12.95
1. Lutheran Church—Collected works. 2. Theology—Collected works—19th century. I. Suelflow, August Robert, 1922- II. [Essays.] English. Selections. III. Title. IV. Series.

WALTHER, C. F. W. 1811-1887. (Carl Ferdinand Wilhelm), 230'.41322
Convention essays / Aug. R. Suelflow, translator. St. Louis : Concordia Pub. House, c1981. p. cm. (Selected writings of C.F.W. Walther) (Series: Walther, C. F. W. (Carl Ferdinand Wilhelm), 1811-1887. Selections. English. 1981.) [BX8011.W28213 1981] 19 81-3096 ISBN 0-570-08277-3 : 12.95
1. Lutheran Church—Collected works. 2. Theology—Collected works—19th century. I. Suelflow, August Robert, 1922- II. [Essays.] English. Selections. III. Title. IV. Series.

WALTHER, C. F. W. 1811-1887. (Carl Ferdinand Wilhelm), 230'.41322
Editorials from Lehre und Wehre / Herbert J.A. Bouman, translator. St. Louis : Concordia Pub. House, c1981. p. cm. (Selected writings of C.F.W. Walther) (Series: Walther, C. F. W. (Carl Ferdinand Wilhelm), 1811-1887. Selections. English. 1981.) Bibliography: p. [BX8011.W28213 1981b] 19 81-3095 ISBN 0-570-08280-3 : 12.95
1. Lutheran Church—Collected works. 2. Theology—Collected works—19th century. I. [Essays.] English. Selections II. Lehre und Wehre. III. Title. IV. Series.

WHEDON, Daniel Denison, 1808-1885. 230'.7
Essays, reviews, and discourses, by Daniel D. Whedon. With a biographical sketch by his son, J. S. Whedon, and his nephew, D. A. Whedon. Freeport, N.Y., Books for Libraries Press [1972] 352 p. 23 cm. (Essay index reprint series) Reprint of the 1887 ed. [BX8217.W7 1972] 72-8504 ISBN 0-8369-7339-9
1. Methodist Church—Collected works. 2. Theology—Collected works—19th century. I. Title.

WILLIAMS, William R., 1804-1885. 208.1
Miscellanies, by William R. Williams. New York, E. H. Fletcher, 1850. 5 p. l., [3]-391 p. 22 1/2 cm. "The discourses, reviews, and sermons ... have, several of them, been already issued separately."--Pref. Includes "Note to the third edition". [BR85.W58 1850] 39-433
1. Theology—Collected works—19th cent. I. Title.

WILLIAMS, William R., 1804-1885. 208.1
Miscellanies, by William R. Williams. 2d ed. New York, E. H. Fletcher, 1851. 5 p. l., [3]-391 p. 20 cm. "The discourses. reviews, and sermons ... have, several of them, been already issued separately."--Pref. Includes "Note to the third edition". [BR85.W58 1851] 39-434
1. Theology—Collected works—19th cent. I. Title.

Theology—Collected works—20th century.

ARNOLD, Eberhard, 1883-1935 270.1
Lectures and writings: v. 2 & 4 [Rifton, N.Y.] Plough [1962] 123;96p. 18cm. Contents.2. The early Christians, after the death of the apostles [Tr. from German by J. S. Hoyland E. Wilms, K. E. Hasenberg] 4. The peace of God [Tr. from German by K. E. Hasenberg] Bibl. pap., v.2, 1.50; v.4, 1.25, plastic bdg.
1. Theology—Collected works—20th cent. I. Title.

BALTHASAR, Hans Urs von, 1905- 230'.2'08
Hans Urs von Balthasar [compiled by Martin Redfern] London, New York, Sheed & Ward, 1972. 126 p. 20 cm. (Theologians today: a series selected and edited by Martin Redfern) (Series: Redfern, Martin Theologians today.) [BX891.B33] 72-2166 ISBN 0-7220-7240-6 3.95
1. Catholic Church—Collected works. 2. Theology—Collected works—20th century. I. Series.
Pbk; 1.95, ISBN 0-7220-0538-3; Contents omitted.

BONHOEFFER, Dietrich, 1906-1945. 230'.092'4 B
True patriotism; letters, lectures, and notes, 1939-45, from the Collected works of Dietrich Bonhoeffer, volume III. Edited and introduced by Edwin H. Robertson. Translated by Edwin H. Robertson and John Bowden. [1st U.S. ed.] New York, Harper and Row [1973] 256 p. 21 cm. Includes bibliographical references. [BX4827.B57A2513 1973] 73-6421 ISBN 0-06-060801-3 6.95
1. Bonhoeffer, Dietrich, 1906-1945. 2. Lutheran Church—Collected works. 3. Theology—Collected works—20th century. I. Robertson, Edwin Hanton, ed. II. Title.

BONHOEFFER, Dietrich, 1906-1945. 230.4'1
The way to freedom; letters, lectures, and notes, 1935-1939, from the Collected works of Dietrich Bonhoeffer, volume II. Edited and introduced by Edwin H. Robertson. Translated by Edwin H. Robertson and John Bowden. [1st U.S. ed.] New York, Harper & Row [1966] 272 p. 22 cm. Bibliographical footnotes. [BX8011.B65 1966] 67-11501
1. Lutheran Church—Collected works. 2. Theology—Collected works—20th century. I. Robertson, Edwin Hanton, ed. II. Title.

BULGAKOV, Sergei Nikolaevich, 1871-1944. 230'.1'93
A Bulgakov anthology / Sergius Bulgakov ; edited by James Pain and Nicholas Zernov. Philadelphia : Westminster Press, 1976. p. cm. Bibliography: p. [BX480.B78 1976] 76-23245 ISBN 0-664-21338-3 : 12.50
1. Orthodox Eastern Church, Russian—Collected works. 2. Bulgakov, Sergei Nikilaevich, 1871-1944. 3. Theology—Collected works—20th century. I. Title.

BULGAKOV, Sergei Nikolaevich, 1871-1944. 230'.1'93
A Bulgakov anthology / Sergius Bulgakov ; edited by James Pain and Nicolas Zernov. London : SPCK, 1976. xxv, 191, [2] p. ; 22 cm. Bibliography: p. [193] [BX480.B78 1976b] 76-379873 ISBN 0-281-02933-4 : £5.50
1. Orthodox Eastern Church, Russian—Collected works. 2. Bulgakov, Sergei Nikolaevich, 1871-1944. 3. Orthodox Eastern Church, Russian—Biography. 4. Theology—Collected works—20th century. I. Title.

CARNELL, Edward John, 1919-1967. 230
The case for biblical Christianity. Edited by Ronald H. Nash. Grand Rapids, Mich., W. B. Erdmans Pub. Co. [1969] 186 p. 22 cm. Contents.Contents.—Christian fellowship and the unity of the church.—The nature of the unity we seek.—Conservatives and liberals do not need each other.—Orthodoxy: cultic vs. classical.—On faith and reason.—Becoming acquainted with the person of God.—On Reinhold Niebuhr and Billy Graham.—Reinhold Niebuhr's view of Scripture.—Niebuhr's criteria of verification.—Reflections on aspects of a Christian ethic.—The virgin birth of Christ.—Jesus Christ and man's condition.—Reflections on contemporary theology.—The government of the church.—The case for orthodox theology.—The fear of death and the hope of the resurrection.—Bibliography of books and articles by Edward John Carnell (p. 183-186) Bibliographical footnotes. [BT15.C3] 68-20584 3.50
1. Theology—Collected works—20th century. I. Title.

CONGAR, Yves Marie Joseph, 1904- 261
Christians active in the world [by] Yves Congar. Translated by P. J. Hepburne-Scott. [New York] Herder and Herder [1968] viii, 227 p. 22 cm. Translation of Sacerdoce et laicat, second half. Includes bibliographical references. [BX891.C5813 1968] 67-14142 5.95
1. Catholic Church—Collected works. 2. Theology—Collected works—20th century. I. Title.

CONGAR, Yves Marie Joseph, 1904- 208
A gospel priesthood [by] Yves Congar. Translated by P. F. Hepburne-Scott. [New York] Herder and Herder [1967] 250 p. 22 cm. Translation of Sacerdoce et laicat. Bibliography: p. 237-241. [BX891.C5813] 67-14143
1. Theology—Collected works—20th cent. 2. Catholic Church—Collected works. I. Title.

CONGAR, Yves Marie Joseph, 1904- 230'.2'08
Yves M.-J. Congar, O.P. [compiled by Martin Redfern] London, New York, Sheed & Ward, 1972. 128 p. 20 cm. (Theologians today: a series selected and edited by Martin Redfern) (Series: Redfern, Martin. Theologians today.) [BX891.C62] 72-2167 ISBN 0-7220-7241-4 3.95
1. Catholic Church—Collected works. 2. Theology—Collected works—20th century. I. Series.
Pbk; 1.95, ISBN 0-7220-0533-2; Contents omitted.

DURRWELL, F. X. 230'.2'08
F. X. Durrwell, C.S.S.R. [compiled by Martin Redfern] London, New York, Sheed & Ward, 1972. 125 p. 20 cm. (Theologians today: a series selected and edited by Martin Redfern) Contents.Contents.—The Resurrection of Christ, birth of the Church.—The Sacrament of Scripture.—The Mass in our lives.—Creation and the apostolate. [BX891.D87] 72-2163 ISBN 0-7220-7242-2 £1.25
1. Catholic Church—Collected works. 2. Theology—Collected works—20th century. I. Redfern, Martin. Theologians today.

FLOROVSKII, Georgii 230'.193
Vasel'evich, 1893-
Ways of Russian theology / Georges Florovsky ; general editor, Richard S. Haugh ; translated by Robert L. Nichols. Belmont, Mass. : Nordland Pub. Co., c1979- v. ; 22 cm. (Collected works of Georges Florovsky ; v. 5) Translation of Puti russkogo bogosloviia. Includes bibliographical references. [BX260.F55 vol. 5] 19 78-78267 ISBN 0-913124-23-0 (v. 1) : 27.50
1. Orthodox Eastern Church—Collected works. 2. Theology—Collected works—20th century. I. Title.

FLOROVSKII, Georgii 230'.1'908
Vasil'evich, 1893-
Collected works of Georges Florovsky. Belmont, Mass., Nordland Pub. Co. [1972- v. 23 cm. Contents.Contents.—v. 1. Bible, church, tradition: an Eastern Orthodox view. [BX260.F55] 72-197090
1. Orthodox Eastern Church—Collected works. 2. Theology—Collected works—20th century. I. Title.

FORSYTH, Peter Taylor, 230.3'08
1848-1921.
The creative theology of P. T. Forsyth; selections from his works. Edited by Samuel J. Mikolaski. Grand Rapids, Mich., Eerdmans [1969] 264 p. 22 cm. Bibliography: p. 262-264. [BX7117.F6 1969] 68-16257 6.95
1. Theology—Collected works—20th century. 2. Congregational churches—Collected works. I. Title.

FORSYTH, Peter Taylor, 1848- 248
1921.
The cure of souls; an anthology of P. T. Forsyth's practical writings, with an appraisement by Harry Escott. [Rev. and enl. ed.] Grand Rapids, W. B. Eerdmans Pub. Co. [1971, c1970] xxii, 128 p. 19 cm. First ed. published in 1948 under title: Peter Taylor Forsyth: director of souls. Includes bibliographical references. [BR85.F593 1971] 74-142905 ISBN 0-04-248008-6
1. Theology—Collected works—20th century. 2. Congregational churches—Collected works. I. Escott, Harry, ed. II. Title.

FORSYTH, Peter Taylor, 201'.1
1848-1921.
The Gospel and authority; a P. T. Forsyth reader. Edited by Marvin W. Anderson. Minneapolis, Augsburg Pub. House [1971] 199 p. 22 cm. Contents.Contents.—The evangelical churches and the higher criticism.—The distinctive thing in Christian experience.—Revelation and the Bible.—A rallying ground for the free churches.—The church's one foundation.—Authority and theology.—The cross as the final seat of authority.—The soul of Christ and the cross of Christ. [BX7117.F62] 72-159014 ISBN 0-8066-1136-7 5.59
1. Theology—Collected works—20th century. 2. Congregational churches—Collected works. I. Title.

HALLINAN, Paul J. 282'.73
Days of hope and promise. The writings and speeches of Paul J. Hallinan. Edited by Vicent A. Yzermans. A memoir by Joseph L. Bernardin. A tribute by John Tracy Ellis. Collegeville, Minn., Liturgical Press [1973] xviii, 228 p. illus. 24 cm. [BX891.H3] 73-75293 ISBN 0-8146-0424-2 6.95
1. Catholic Church—Collected works. 2. Theology—Collected works—20th century. I. Title.
Publisher's Address: St. John's Abbey Collegeville, Minn. 56521.

JARRETT, Bede, 1881- 230.2081
1934.
Bede Jarrett anthology. Edited by Jordan Aumann. Dubuque, Priory Press, 1961. 506 p. 23 cm. [BX890.J35] 64-937
1. Catholic Church—Collected works. 2. Theology—Collected works—20th cent. I. Title.

JOANNES XXIII, Pope, 1881- 282
1963
A Pope John memorial miniature. [New York, Random House, 1966] 4 v. ports. 97 mm. Contents.CONTENTS. -- [1] Wisdom: a memorable collection of wise sayings that will long linger in the world touched by this great man. -- [2] Wit; a collection of sayings and anecdotes showing the lighter side of the pontiff. -- [3] Faith: excerpts from Pope John's Pacem in terris, which so moved the hearts and minds of the world. -- [4] Eulogies offered by leading dignitaries as the world mourned the loss of Pope John XXIII. [BX891.J6] 66-18333
1. Catholic Church — Collected works. 2. Theology — Collected works — 20th cent. 3. Bibliography and miniature editions — Specimens. I. Catholic Church. Pope, 1938-1963 (Joannes XXIII) Paceum in terris (11 Apr. 1963) English. II. Title.

JOHN Paul II, Pope, 1920- 230'.2
Toward a philosophy of praxis : an anthology / Karol Wojtyla (Pope John Paul II) ; edited by Alfred Bloch and George T. Czuczka. New York : Seabury Press, 1980. p. cm. [BX1751.2.J64] 19 80-21239 ISBN 0-8164-0463-1 : 10.95
1. Catholic Church—Collected works. 2. Theology—Collected works—20th century. I. Bloch, Alfred, 1922- II. Czuczka, George T. III. Title.

JONES, Eli Stanley, 1884- 201'.1
Selections from E. Stanley Jones; Christ and human need. Compiled by Eunice Jones Mathews and James K. Mathews. Nashville, Abingdon Press [1972] 255 p. 23 cm. [BR85.J63] 76-173952 ISBN 0-687-37426-X 4.95
1. Methodist Church—Collected works. 2. Theology—Collected works—20th century. I. Title.

KEE, Alistair, 1937- comp. 230
A reader in political theology. Philadelphia, Westminster Press [1975, c1974] xiii, 171 p. 22 cm. [BT28.K4 1975] 74-19047 ISBN 0-664-24816-0
1. Theology—20th century—Collected works. I. Title.

KNUTSON, Kent S. 230'.4'1
Gospel, church, mission / Kent S. Knutson. Minneapolis : Augsburg Pub. House, c1976. 160 p. ; 21 cm. "Bibliography of Kent S. Knutson material": p. 140-160. [BX8011.K55] 75-40632 ISBN 0-8066-1522-2 : 4.95
1. Lutheran Church—Collected works. 2. Theology—Collected works—20th century. 3. Knutson, Kent S. 4. Knutson, Kent S.—Bibliography. I. Title.

KUNG, Hans, 1928- 230'.2'08
Hans Kung [compiled by Martin Redfern] London, New York, Sheed & Ward, 1972. 128 p. 20 cm. (Theologians today: a series selected and edited by Martin Redfern) (Series: Redfern, Martin. Theologians today.) Contents.Contents.—Justification and sanctification according to the New Testament.—Liturgical reform and Christian unity.—Freedom in the world.—Truthfulness as a demand of the message of Jesus. [BX891.K83] 72-2159 ISBN 0-7220-7243-0 £1.25
1. Catholic Church—Collected works. 2. Theology—Collected works—20th century. I. Series.

LEWIS, Clive Staples, 1898- 201
1963.
C. S. Lewis; five best books in one volume. [Christianity today ed.] New York, Iversen Associates, 1969. vii, 520 p. 22 cm. On spine: The best of C. S. Lewis. Contents.Contents.—The Screwtape letters.—The great divorce.—Miracles.—The case for Christianity.—Christian behaviour. [BR83.L48] 72-93142
1. Church of England—Collected works. 2. Theology—Collected works—20th century. I. Title: The best of C. S. Lewis.

LEWIS, Clive Staples, 230'.092'4
1898-1963.
The joyful Christian : one hundred readings from C. S. Lewis. New York : Macmillan Pub. Co., c1977. p. cm. Bibliography: p. [BX5037.L4 1977] 77-21685 ISBN 0-02-570900-3 : 7.95
1. Church of England—Collected works. 2. Theology—Collected works—20th century. 3. Christian life—Anglican authors—Collected works. I. Title.

LEWIS, Clive Staples, 230'.092'4
1898-1963.
The joyful Christian : 127 readings from C. S. Lewis. Boston : G. K. Hall, 1978, c1977. xvii, 421 p. ; 24 cm. Large print ed. Bibliography: p. 417-421. [BX5037.L4 1978] 78-10549 ISBN 0-8161-6634-X : 13.50
1. Church of England—Collected works. 2. Theology—Collected works—20th century. 3. Christian life—Anglican authors—Collected works. 4. Large type books. I. Title.

LEWIS, Clive Staples, 230'.08
1898-1963.
A mind awake; an anthology of C. S. Lewis, edited by Clyde S. Kilby. [1st American ed.] New York, Harcourt, Brace & World [1969, c1968] 252 p. 21 cm. [BT15.L48 1969] 70-78866
1. Theology—Collections—20th century. I. Kilby, Clyde S., ed. II. Title.

LEWIS, Clive Staples, 1898- 230
1963.
A mind awake : an anthology of C. S. Lewis / edited by Clyde S. Kilby. 1st Harvest/HBJ ed. New York : Harcourt Brace Jovanovich, 1980, c1968. 252 p. ; 21 cm. (A Harvest/HBJ book) [BT15.L48 1980] 80-14133 7.95
1. Theology—Collected works—20th century. I. Kilby, Clyde S. II. Title.

LONERGAN, Bernard J. F. 230'.2'08
A second collection; [papers] by Bernard J. F. Lonergan. Edited by William F. J. Ryan and Bernard J. Tyrrell. Philadelphia, Westminster Press [1975, c1974] 300, [2] p. 23 cm. Bibliography: p. [302] [BX891.L644 1975] 74-14798 ISBN 0-664-20721-9 12.00
1. Catholic Church—Collected works. 2. Theology—Collected works—20th century. I. Title.

LUBAC, Henri de, 1896- 230'.2'08
Henri de Lubac, S.J. [compiled by Martin Redfern] London, New York, Sheed & Ward, 1972. 127 p. 20 cm. (Theologians today: a series selected and edited by Martin Redfern) (Series: Redfern, Martin. Theologians today.) [BX891.L8] 72-2164 ISBN 0-7220-7244-9 3.95
1. Catholic Church—Collected works. 2. Theology—Collected works—20th century. I. Series.
Pbk; 1.95, ISBN 0-7220-0539-3. Contents omitted. Contents omitted.

LUBAC, Henri de, 1896- 230'.2'08
Henri de Lubac, S.J. [compiled by Martin Redfern] London, New York, Sheed & Ward, 1972. 127 p. 20 cm. (Theologians today: a series selected and edited by Martin Redfern) (Series: Redfern, Martin. Theologians today.) Contents.Contents.—Christianity and history.—The sacraments as instruments of unity.—Ludwig Feuerbach, protagonist of atheist humanism.—The family of God. [BX891.L8] 72-2164 ISBN 0-7220-7244-9 £1.25
1. Catholic Church—Collected works. 2. Theology—Collected works—20th century. I. Series.

LUCCOCK, Halford Edward, 230.7
1885-1960
Halford Luccock treasury. Ed. by Robert E. Luccock. Nashville, Abingdon [c.1950-1963] 446p. illus. 24cm. 63-11378 6.00
1. Theology—Collected works—20th cent. I. Title.

LUCCOCK, Halford Edward, 230.7
1885-1960.
Halford Luccock treasury. Edited by Robert E. Luccock. New York, Abingdon Press [1963] 446 p. illus. 24 cm. [BX8217.L8] 63-11378
1. Theology — Collected works — 2oth cent. I. Title.

MAIER, Walter Arthur, 230'.41322
1893-1950.
The best of Walter A. Maier / [edited by] Paul L. Maier. St. Louis, Mo. : Concordia Pub. House, [1981] c1980. 248 p. : ill. ; 24 cm. Bibliography of the writings of Walter A. Maier: p. 246-248. [BR50.M224 1981] 19 80-23684 ISBN 0-570-03823-5 pbk.: 7.95
1. Lutheran Church—Collected works. 2. Theology—Collected works—20th century. I. Maier, Paul L. II. Title.

MURRAY, John, 1898- 285'.2'0924
1975.
Collected writings of John Murray : professor of systematic theology, Westminster Theological Seminary, Philadelphia, Pennsylvania, 1937-1966. Edinburgh ; Carlisle, Pa. : Banner of Truth Trust, 1976- v. ; 24 cm. Contents.Contents.—v. 1. The claims of truth.—v. 2. Select lectures in systematic theology. [BX8915.M87 1976] 77-376336 ISBN 0-85151-241-0 (v. 1) : write for information
1. Presbyterian Church—Collected works. 2. Theology—Collected works—20th century.

PAULSON, Eric Edwin 248.08
Thunder in the wilderness; evangelical essays in an age of doubt. Minneapolis, Augsburg [1965] 283p. 22cm. [BX8011.P3] 65-28345 3.50
1. Theology—Collected works—20th cent. 2. Lutheran Church—Collected works. I. Title.

RAHNER, Karl, 1904- 208.1
Inquiries [New York] Herder & Herder [c.1964] viii, 462p. 22cm. Studies which appeared separately in the series Quaestiones disputatae as nos. 1. 10, 9, 4, 11. [BX891.R3] 64-20435 8.00
1. Theology—Collected works—20th cent. 2. Catholic Church—Collected works. I. Title.
Contents omitted

RAHNER, Karl, 1904- 230'.2'08
Karl Rahner, S.J. [compiled by Martin Redfern] London, New York, Sheed & Ward, 1972. 128 p. 20 cm. (Theologians today: a series selected and edited by Martin Redfern) (Series: Redfern, Martin. Theologians today.) Contents.—The propect for Christianity.—The sacrifice of the Mass.—The inspiration of the Bible.—Action in the Church. Includes bibliographical references. [BX891.R32] 72-2165 ISBN 0-7220-7245-7 £1.65
1. Catholic Church—Collected works. 2. Theology—Collected works—20th century. I. Series.

RAHNER, Karl, 1904- 230'.2
A Rahner reader. Edited by Gerald A. McCool. New York, Seabury Press [1975] xxviii, 381 p. 24 cm. "A Crossroad book." Bibliography: p. 363-372. [BX891.R253 1975] 74-16138 ISBN 0-8164-1173-5 ISBN 0-8164-2107-2 (pbk.)
1. Catholic Church—Collected works. 2. Theology—Collected works—20th century. I. McCool, Gerald A., ed. II. Title.

RAHNER, Karl, 1904- 230'.2
A Rahner reader / edited by Gerald A. McCool. New York : Crossroad, 1981, c1975. p. cm. Reprint. Originally published: New York : Seabury Press, 1975. [BX891.R253 1981] 19 81-17394 ISBN 0-8245-0370-8 pbk. : 13.50
1. Catholic Church—Collected works. 2. Theology—Collected works—20th century. I. McCool, Gerald A. II. Title.

RAMSEY, Arthur Michael, 230'.3
Abp. of Canterbury, 1904-
Canterbury pilgrim / Michael Ramsey. New York : Seabury Press, [1974] x, 188 p. : ill. ; 22 cm. "A Crossroad book." [BX5037.R28] 74-20800 ISBN 0-8164-1192-1 : 7.95
1. Church of England—Collected works. 2. Theology—Collected works—20th century. I. Title.

ROBINSON, John Arthur 230'.3
Thomas, Bp., 1919-
The roots of a radical / John A. T. Robinson. New York : Crossroad Pub. Co., 1981. viii, 168 p. ; 22 cm. Includes index. Bibliography: p. 164-166. [BR85.R64] 19 80-26002 ISBN 0-8245-0028-8 : 10.95
1. Church of England—Collected works. 2.

Theology—Collected works—20th century. I. Title.

SCHILLEBEECKX, Edward 230'.2'08
Cornelius Florentinius Alfons, 1914-
Edward Schillebeeckx, O.P. [compiled by Martin Redfern] London, New York, Sheed and Ward, 1972. 128 p. 20 cm. (Theologians today: a series selected and edited by Martin Redfern) (Series: Redfern, Martin. Theologians today.) Contents.Contents.—The Sacraments: an encounter with God.—Marriage in the Divine Revelation of the Old Testament.—Revelation, scripture, tradition, and teaching authority.—Secular worship and Church liturgy. Includes bibliographical references. [BX891.S354] 72-2162 ISBN 0-7220-7246-5 £1.25
1. Catholic Church—Collected works. 2. Theology—Collected works—20th century. I. Series.

SCHWEITZER, Albert, 1875- 232
1965.
The theology of Albert Schweitzer for Christian inquirers, by E. N. Mozley. With an epilogue by Albert Schweitzer. New York, Macmillan, 1951 [c1950] vii, 117 p. 20 cm. [BR85.S295 1951] 51-1674
1. Jesus Christ—Messiahship. 2. Theology—Collected works—20th century. 3. Eschatology. I. Mozley, Edward Newman, 1875- II. Title.

SHEED, Francis Joseph, 230'.2'08
1897-
F. J. Sheed [compiled by Martin Redfern.] London, New York, Sheed and Ward, 1972. 127 p. 20 cm. (Theologians today: a series selected and edited by Martin Redfern) (Series: Redfern, Martin. Theologians today.) Contents.Contents.—Man and his context.—Born of a woman.—Scripture in the Church.—Mass and Eucharist. [BX891.S53] 72-2161 ISBN 0-7220-7247-3 £1.25
1. Catholic Church—Collected works. 2. Theology—Collected works—20th century. I. Series.

SHEPPARD, Hugh Richard 208.1
Lawrie, 1880-1937.
The best of Dick Sheppard (H. R. L. Sheppard) Edited, with an introd., by Halford E. Luccock. [1st ed.] New York, Harper [1951] xx, 162 p. 21 cm. Bibliography: p. [v] [BX5037.S45] 51-9056
1. Theology—Collected works—20th cent. 2. Church of England—Collected works. I. Title.

SITTLER, Joseph. 230'.41
Grace notes and other fragments / Joseph A. Sittler. Philadelphia : Fortress Press, c1981. p. cm. [BT15.S585] 80-8055 ISBN 0-8006-1404-6 : 5.50
1. Lutheran Church—Collected works. 2. Theology—Collected works—20th century. I. Title.

SMITH, Frederick 230'.9'33
Madison, 1874-1946.
The writings of President Frederick M. Smith / edited by Norman D. Ruoff. Independence, Mo. : Herald Pub. House, c1978- v. : ill. ; 20 cm. Articles first published in the Saints herald. Contents.Contents.—v. 1. His theology and philosophy.—v. 2. Educating, nurturing, and upholding. [BX8674.S63 1978] 78-6428 ISBN 0-8309-0215-5 pbk. : 6.50
1. Reorganized Church of Jesus Christ of Latter-Day Saints—Collected works. 2. Theology—Collected works—20th century. I. Ruoff, Norman D.

STANILOAE, Dumitru. 230'.19498
Theology and the church / Dumitru Staniloae ; translated by Robert Barringer ; foreword by John Meyendorff. Crestwood, N.Y. : St. Vladimir's Seminary Press, 1980. p. cm. Collection of essays translated from various Romanian journals. Includes bibliographical references. [BX695.S7] 19 80-19313 ISBN 0-913836-69-9 pbk. : 7.95
1. Orthodox Eastern Church, Romanian—Collected works. 2. Theology—Collected works—20th century. I. Title.

STUMP, V. L., 1885-1943. 289.9
Time for everything under the sun : on the life and times of V. L. Stump, a gifted minister and able editor / compiled and edited by Ruth Stump Whittenburg. New York : Philosophical Library, c1980. xiv, 363 p., [5] leaves of plates : ports. ; 22 cm. [BX9675.S78 1980] 79-84856 ISBN 0-8022-2351-6 : 17.50
1. Brethren in Christ—Collected works. 2. Stump, V. L., 1885-1943. 3. Theology—20th century—Collected works. I. Whittenburg, Ruth Stump. II. Title.

SUENENS, Leon Joseph, 230'.2'08
Cardinal, 1904-
Ways of the spirit : the spirituality of Cardinal Suenens / drawn from the writings of Cardinal Suenens and edited with an introd. by Elizabeth Hamilton. New York : Seabury Press, 1976. 123, [1] p. ; 21 cm. "A Crossroad book." Bibliography: p. 123-[124] [BX891.S85] 76-46307 ISBN 0-8164-1218-9 : 5.95
1. Catholic Church—Collected works. 2. Theology—Collected works—20th century. I. Hamilton, Elizabeth, 1906- II. Title.

SUENENS, Leon Joseph, 230'.2'08
Cardinal, 1904-
Ways of the spirit : the spirituality of Cardinal Suenens / drawn from the writings of Cardinal Suenens and edited with an introduction by Elizabeth Hamilton. London : Darton, Longman and Todd, 1976. 124 p. ; 19 cm. Bibliography: p. 123-[124] [BX891.S85 1976b] 77-368905 ISBN 0-232-51359-7 : £1.20
1. Catholic Church—Collected works. 2. Theology—Collected works—20th century. I. Hamilton, Elizabeth, 1906- II. Title.

SUHARD, Emmanuel 282'.08
Celestin, Cardinal, 1874-1949.
The responsible church; selected texts of Cardinal Suhard. Compiled by Olivier de la Brosse. Notre Dame, Ind., Fides Publishers [1967] 258 p. 23 cm. Abridged translation of Vers une eglise en etat de mission. Bibliographical footnotes. [BX890.S843 1967b] 68-15355
1. Catholic Church—Collected works. 2. Theology—Collected works—20th century. I. Title.

TOZER, Aiden Wilson, 230'.99
1897-1963.
A treasury of A. W. Tozer : a collection of Tozer favorites / introd. by Warren W. Wiersbe. Grand Rapids, Mich. : Baker Book House, c1980. 296 p. ; 23 cm. [BX6700.T69 1980] 19 80-118204 ISBN 0-8010-8851-8 : 8.95
1. Christian and Missionary Alliance—Collected works. 2. Theology—Collected works—20th century. I. Title.

TWENTIETH century 230'.09'04
theology in the making. Edited by Jaroslav Pelikan. Translated by R. A. Wilson. [1st Harper pbk. ed.] New York, Harper & Row [1971] 3 v. 21 cm. Selections from the 2d ed. of Die Religion in Geschichte und Gegenwart. Contents.Contents.—v. 1. Themes of biblical theology.—v. 2. The theological dialogue: issues and resources.—v. 3. Ecumenicity and renewal. Includes bibliographies. [BR45.R4235] 72-178974 ISBN 0-06-139220-0 (v. 1) ISBN 0-06-131613-X (v. 1. pbk.)
1. Theology—20th century—Collections. I. Pelikan, Jaroslav Jan, 1923- ed.

WARFIELD, Benjamin 230.5'1
Breckinridge, 1851-1921.
Selected shorter writings of Benjamin B. Warfield, edited by John E. Meeter. Nutley, N.J., Presbyterian and Reformed Pub. Co., 1970-73. 2 v. 23 cm. Includes bibliographical references. [BX8915.W3] 76-110499 7.50 (v. 1) 8.95 (v. 2)
1. Presbyterian Church—Collected works. 2. Theology—Collected works—20th century.

Theology—Collected works—Early church.

AMBROSIUS, Saint, 230.1'4'0924
Bp. of Milan.
Letters. Translated by Mary Melchior Beyenka. [Reprinted with corrections] Washington, Catholic University of America [1967, c1954] xix, 515 p. 22 cm. (The Fathers of the Church, a new translation, v. 26) Contents.Letters to emperors.--Letters to bishops.--Synodal letters.--Letters to Priests.--Letters to his sister.--Letters to layment. Bibliography: p. xiv. [BR60.F3A5612] 67-28583
1. Theology—Collected works—Early church. I. Title. II. Series.

AMBROSIUS, Saint Bp.ofMilan.
Opera. New York, Johnson Reprint Corp. [1962- v. tables. (Corpvs scriptorvm ecclesiasticorvm latinorvm, v. 32, 62, 64, 78,-79) Editors vary. Imprint varies. Some vols. are reprints of ed. Vienna 1897-1919. Contents.-pt. 1. Exameron. De paradiso. De Cain et Abel. De Noe. De Abraham. De Isaac. De bono mortis.-pt. 2. De Iacob. De Ioseph. De partriarchis. De fvga saecvli. De interpellatione Iob et David. De apologia David Apologia David altera. De Helia t Ieivnio. De Nabvthae. De Tobia. Tobia.-pt. 4. Expositio evangelii secvndvm Lvcan.-pt. 5. Expositio psalmi 118.-pt. 6. Explanatio psalmorvm 12.-pt. 8. De fide(Ad gratianvm Avgvstvm) Recensvit O. Faller. 1962.-pt. 9. De spiritu sancto; libri tres. De incarnationis dominicae sacramento. Recensvit O. Faller. 1964. 68-78904
1. Theology-Collected works-Early church. I. Title. II. Series.

ATHENAGORAS, 2ndcent. 281.
Athenagoras. Edited for schools and colleges by F. A. March, L.L. D. With explanatory notes by W. B. Owen ... New York, Harper & brothers, 1876 1 p. l., vi p., 1 l. [9]-262 p. 19 1/2 cm. (Half-title: Douglass series of Christian Greek and Latin writers, vol. IV) [BR60.D6 vol. 4] 4-22513
1. Theology—Collected works—Early church. I. March, Francis Andrew, 1825-1911, ed. II. Owen, William Baxter, 1843-1917. III. Title.

AUGUSTINUS, Aurelius, 281.4
Saint, Bp. of Hippo.
An Augustine sunthesis, arranged by Erich Przywara. New York, Harper [1958] xii, 495p. 21cm. (Harper torchbooks, TB35. Cathedral library) [BR65.A52E6 1958] 58-7110
1. Theology—Collected works—Early church. I. Przywara, Erich, 1889- comp. II. Title.

AUGUSTINUS, Aurelius, 281.4
Saint, bp. of Hippo.
An Augustine synthesis, arranged by Erich Prrzywara, s. j.; introduction by C. C. Martindale, s. j. New York, Sheed & Ward inc., 1936. xvi, 495, [1] p. 22 cm. [BR65.A52E6 1936] 36-12674
1. Theology—Collected works—Early church. I. Przywara, Erich, 1869- comp. II. Title.

AUGUSTINUS, Aurelius, 281.4
Saint, Bp. of Hippo.
Basic writings of Saint Augustine, ed. with an introd. and notes by Whitney J. Oates. New York, Random House [1948] 2 v. 24 cm. Contents.1. The Confessions. Twelve treatiers.--v. 2. The city of God. On the Trinity. [BR65.A52E6 1948] 49-02
1. Theology—Collected works—Early church. I. Oates, Whitney Jennings. 1904- ed. II. Title.

AUGUSTINUS, Aurelius, 281.4
Saint, Bp. of Hippo.
Earlier writings; selected and translated with introductions by John H. S. Burleigh. Philadelphia, Westminster Press [1953] 413p. 24cm. (The Library of Christian classics, v. 6) Bibliography: p.407. [BR65.A52E6 1953] 53-13043
1. Theology—Collected works—Early church. I. Title. II. Series.

AUGUSTINUS, Aurelius, 189.2
Saint, Bp. of Hippo.
Introduction to the philosophy of Saint Augustine; selected readings and commentaires [by] John A. Mourant. University Park, Pennsylvania State University Press [1964] ix. 366 p. 24 cm. Half title: Philosophy of St. Augustine. Writings of St. Augustine": p. 355-356. Bibliography: p. 360-362. [BR65.A52E6] 64-15064
1. Theology — Collected works — Early church. 2. Philosophy — Collected works. I. Mourant, John Arthur, 1903- ed. II. Title. III. Title: Philosophy of St. Augustine.

AUGUSTINUS Aurelius Bp. of 281.4
Hippo
St. Augustine [pamphs. 12-13 Boston] St. Paul eds. [dist. Daughters of St. Paul, 1963] 2v. 18cm. Selections from the works of the Fathers in pamphlet form. 63-23668 .50 pap., ea.,
1. Theology—Collected works—Early church. I. Title.
Contents omitted.

AUGUSTINUS, Aurelius, Bp. 281.4
of Hippo
Selected writings. Ed., introd. by Roger Hazelton. Cleveland, World [c.1962] 312p. 18cm. (Meridian Living age bks., LA37) Bibl. 62-13383 1.65 pap.,
1. Theology—Collected works—Early church. I. Hazelton, Roger, 1909- ed. II. Title.

AUGUSTINUS, Aurelius, 281.4
Saint, Bp. of Hippo.
Selected writings. Edited and with an introd. by Roger Hazelton. Cleveland, Meridian Books [1962] 312p. 18cm. (Living age books, LA37) Bibliography: p. 311-312. [BR65.A52E6 1962] 62-13383
1. Theology— Collected works—Early church. I. Hazelton, Roger, 1909- ed. II. Title.

AUGUSTINUS, Aurelius, 281.4
Saint, Bp. of Hippo.
Treatises on various subjects; translated by Mary Sarah Muldowney [and others] Edited by Roy J. Deferrari. New York, Fathers of the Church, inc., 1952. viii, 479p. 22cm. (The Fathers of the church, a new translation, v. 16) [BR60.F3A83] 53-287
1. Theology—Collected works—Early church. I. Title.
Contents omitted.

AUGUSTINUS, Aurelius, 281.4
Saint, Bp. of Hippo.
Treatises on various subjects. Translated by Mary Sarah Muldowney [and others] Edited by Roy J. Deferrari. Washington, Catholic University of America Press [1965, c1952] viii, 479 p. 22 cm. (The Fathers of the church, a new translation, v. 16) At head of title: Volume 14. Includes bibliographies. [BR60.F3A833] 65-18319
1. Theology—Collected works—Early chruch. I. Title. II. Series: The Fathers of the church, a new translation, v. 16
Contents omitted

AUGUSTINUS, Aurelius, 281.4
Saint, Bp. of Hippo.
Writings of Saint Augustine. [New York, Cima Pub. Co., 19 v. 22 cm. (The Father of the Church, a new translation) Includes bibliographies. [BR60.F3A8] 48-11583
1. Theology—Collected works—Early church. I. Title. II. Series.
Contents omitted

AUGUSTINUS, Aurelius, 281.4
Saint, Bp. of Hippo.
Later works. Selected and translated with introductions by John Burnaby. Philadelphia, Westminster Press [1955] 359 p. 24 cm. (The Library of Christian classics, v. 8) Contents.Contents.—The Trinity.—The Spirit and the letter.—Ten homilies on the First epistle general of St. John.—Select bibliography (p. 349-351) [BR65.A52E6 1955] 55-5022
1. Theology—Collected works—Early church. I. Burnaby, John, ed. and tr. II. Series: The Library of Christian classics (Philadelphia) v. 8

AUGUSTINUS, Aurelius, 189.2
Saint,Bp. of Hippo
The essential Augustine. Selected, commentary by Vernon J. Bourke [New York] New Amer. Lib. [c.1964] 272p. 18cm. (Mentor-Omega bk. MT601) [BR65.A52E6] 64-8194 .75 pap.,
1. Theology—Collected works—Early church. I. Bourke, Vernon Joseph, 1907- ed. II. Title.

BASILIUS, Saint, the 281.4
Great, Abp. of Caesarea, 330(ca.)-379.
Writings. [New York, Fathers of the Church, inc., 1950- v. 22 cm. (The Fathers of the Church, a new translation. v. 9 Contents.v. 1. Ascetical works, translated by Sister M. Monica Wagner. Bibliography: v. 1, p. 6. [BR60.F3B3] 50-10735
1. Theology—Collected works—Early church. I. Title. II. Series.

BASILIUS, Saint, the 281.4
Great, Abp. of Caesarea, 330(ca.)-379
St. Basil. [Boston, Daughters of St. Paul, 1963] 3v. (various p.) 18cm. (Selections from the works of the Fathers of the church in pamphlet form) Vols. 1-3

translated by Sister M. Monica Wagner. Selections from St. Basilius' Writings issued in the ser.: The Fathers of the church, a new translation. 62-16942 v.1, pap., .35; v.2,3, ea., .50
1. Theology—Collected works—Early church. I. Title.
Contents omitted.

CYPRIANUS, Saint, Bp. of Carthage.
Opera omnia. Recensuit et commentario critico instruxit Guilelmus Hartel. Vindobonae, Apud C. Geroldi filium, 1868-71; New York, Johnson Reprint Corp. [1965] 3 v. diagrs. 22 cm. (Corpus scriptorum ecclesiasticorum latinorum, v. 3) 67-77061
1. Theology — Collected works — Early church. I. Title.

CYPRIANUS, Saint. Bp. of Carthage.
S. Thasci Caecili Cypriani Opera omnia. Recensvit et commentario critico instrvxit Gvilelmvs Hartel. New York, Johnson Reprint Corp. [1965] 3 v. (Corpvs scriptorvm ecclesiasticorvm latinorvm, v. 3) Reprint of the 1868 Vienna ed. 68-25132
1. Theology—Collected works—Early church. I. Hartel, Wilhelm August, ritter von, 1839-1907, ed. II. Title.

CYRILLUS, Saint, Bp. of Jerusalem, 315(ca.)-386.
Catechetical lectures, with a rev. translation, introd., notes and indices, by Edwin Hamilton Gifford. Select orations [and] Select letters of Saint Gregory Nazianzen, translated by Charles Gordon Browne and James Edward Swallow. [Grand Rapids, Eerdmans, 1955] ix, 498 p. 25cm. (A Select library of Nicene and post-Nicene Fathers of the Christian Church. Second series, v.7) Each part has separate title page. A55
1. Theology—Collected works—Early church. 2. Catechetical sermons. I. Gregorius Nazianzenus, Saint, Patriarch of Constantinople. II. Title. III. Series: A Select library of Nicene and post-Nicene Fathers of the Christian Church. Second series (Grand Rapids) v. 7

GREGORIUS, Saint, Bp. of Nyssa, fl.379-394.
Select writings and letters; translated, with prolegomena, notes and indices, by William Moore [and others. Grand Rapids, Eerdmans, 1954] 566p. 25cm. (A Select library of Nicene and post-- Nicene Fathers of the Christian Church. Second series, v. 5) A54
1. Theology—Collected works—Early church. I. Title. II. Series: A Select library of Nicene and post-Nicene Fathers of the Christian Church. Second series (Grand Rapids) v. 5

GREGORIUS, Saint, Bp. of Tours, 538-594. 281.4
Gregory of Tours; selections from the minor works, translated by William C. McDermott. Philadelphia, University of Pennsylvania Press, 1949. xi, 109 p. 21 cm. (Pennsylvania. University. Dept. of History. Translations and reprints from the original sources of history, ser. 3, v. 4) Contents.Introduction.--Gregory's prefaces.--The miracles of St. Martin.--The lives of the Fathers.--The Seven Sleepers of Ephesus.--The Seven Wonders of the World.--Bibliography and abbreviations (p. 100-106) [D101.P4 ser. 3, vol. 4] [BR65.G583E64] 49-49067
1. Theology—Collected works—Early church. I. McDermott, William Coffman, 1907- tr. II. Title. III. Series.

HIERONYMUS, Saint. 239
Saint Jerome, dogmatic and polemical works. Tr. by John N. Hritzu. Washington, D.C., Catholic Univ. [c.1965] xix, 410p. 22cm. (Fathers of the church, a new tr., v.53) Bibl. [BR60.F3H52] 65-20802 7.55
1. Theology—Collected works—Early church. I. Hritzu John Nicholas tr. (Series) II. Title.

HIERONYMUS, Saint. 239
Saint Jerome, dogmatic and polemical works. Translated by John N. Hritzu. Washington, Catholic University of America Press [1965] xix, 410 p. 22 cm. (The Fathers of the church, a new translation, v. 53) Bibliographical footnotes. [BR60.F3H52] 65-20802
1. Theology — Collected works — Early church. I. Hritzu, John Nicholas, tr. II. Title. III. Series.

JUSTINUS Martyr, Saint. 281.3
Saint Justin Martyr: The first apology, the second apology, dialogue with Trypho, exhortation to the Greeks, discourse to the Greeks, the monarchy, or the rule of God, by Thomas B. Falls. Washington, Catholic University of America Press [1965, c1948] 486 p. 22 cm. (The Fathers of the church, a new translation, v. 6) Bibliographical footnotes. [BR60.F3J8] 65-18317
1. Theology — Collected works — Early church. I. Falls, Thomas B. II. Title. III. Series.

JUSTINUS Martyr, Saint. 281.3
Saint Justin Martyr: The first apology, The second apology, Dialogue with Trypho, Exhortation to the Greeks, Discourse to the Greeks, The monarchy; or, The rule of God, by Thomas B. Falls. New York, Christian Heritage [1949] 486 p. 22 cm. (The Fathers of the Church, a new translation) Half title: Writings of Saint Justin Martyr. Includes bibliographies. [BR60.F3J8] 49-48169
1. Theology—Collected works—Early church. I. Falls, Thomas B. II. Title. III. Series.

LACTANTIUS, Lucius Caecilius Firmianus 281.3
Minor works. Tr. by Sister Mary Francis McDonald. Washington, D.C., Catholic Univ. of Amer Pr. [c.1965] x, 248p. 22cm. (Fathers of the church, a new tr., v.54) Bibl. [BR60.F3L33] 65-6715 5.80
1. Theology—Collected works—Early church. I. McDonald, Mary Francis, Sister, 1920- tr. (Series) II. Title.

MARTINUS, Saint, Abp. of Braga, d.580 281.4
Opera omnia; edidit Claude W. Barlow. Published for the American Academy in Rome. New Haven, Yale University Press, 1950. xii, 328 p. diagrs. 25 cm. (Papers and monographs of the American Academy in Rome, v. 12) Bibliography: p. 305-306. [BR65.M39] 50-10338
1. Theology—Collected works—Early church. I. Barlow, Claude W., ed. II. Title. III. Series: American Academy in Rome. Papers and monographs, v. 12

SALVIANUS, 5thcent. 281.2'082
Salviani presbyteri massiliensis Opera omnia. Recensvit et commentario critico instrvxit Franciscvs Pavly. Vindobonae, apvd. C. Geroldi filivm, 1883; New York, Johnson Reprint 1968 xvi, 359, [1] p. 23cm. (Added t.-p.: Corpvs scriptorvm eccelsiasticorvm latinorvm. . . vol. VIII) [BR60.C6vol. 8] AC34 20.00 pap.,
1. Theology—Collected works—Early church. I. Pauly, Franz, 1827- ed. II. Title.

SEDULIUS, 5thcent. 281.2'082
Sedvlii Opera omnia. Recensvit et commentario critico instrvxit Iohannes Huemer. Accedvnt excerpta ex Remigii Expositione in Sedvlii Paschale carmen. Vindobonae, apvd C. Geroldi filivm, 1885; New York, Johnson Reprint. 1968. 2p. 1., xlvii, [1] p., 1 1., [2] 414p. diagr. 23cm. (Added t.-p.: Corpvs scriptorvm ecclesiasticorvm latinorvm . . . vol. x) [BR60C6 vol.10] AC34 25.00 pap.,
1. Theology—Collectedworks—Early church. I. Remigius, of Auxerre, 9th cent. II. Huemer, Johann, 1849-1915, ed. III. Title.

TERTULLIANUS, Quintus Septimius Florens. 281.1
Disciplinary, moral, and ascetical works. Translated by Rudolph Arbesmann, Sister Emily Joseph Daly [and] Edwin A. Quain. New York, Fathers of the Church, inc., 1959. 323 p. 22 cm. (The Fathers of the church, a new translation, v. 40) Includes bibliographies. [BR60.F3T38] 60-281
1. Theology — Collected works — Early church. I. Title. II. Series.
Contents omitted.

TERTULLIANUS, Quintus Septimius Florens. 281.1
Disciplinary, moral, and ascetical works. Translated by Rudolph Arbesmann, Sister Emily Joseph Daly [and] Edwin A. Quain. New York, Fathers of the Church, inc., 1959. 323 p. 22 cm. (The Fathers of the church, a new translation, v. 40) Contents.Contents.—Foreword, by R. J. Deferrari.—To the martyrs.—Spectacles.—The apparel of women.—Prayer.—Patience.—The chaplet.—Flight in time of persecution. Includes bibliographies. [BR60.F3T38] 60-281
1. Theology—Collected works—Early church. I. Title. II. Series.

TERTULLIANUS, Quintus Septimius Florens. 281.
The select works of Tertullian. Edited for schools and colleges by F. A. March, LL.D. With an introduction by Lyman Coleman ... New York, Harper & brothers, 1876. iv p., 1 l., vii, [9]-250 p. 19 1/2 cm. (Half-title: Douglass series of Christian Greek and Latin writers, vol. III) [BR60.D6 vol. 3] 4-22514
1. Theology—Collected works—Early church. I. March, Francis Andrew, 1825-1911, ed. II. Title.

TERTULLIANUS, Quintus Septimius Florens. 281.3
Tertullian: Apologetical works, and Minucius Felix: Octavius; translated by Rudolph Arbesmann, Sister Emily Joseph Daly [and] Edwin A. Quain. New York, Fathers of the Church, inc., 1950. xix, 430 p. 22 cm. (The Fathers of the Church, a new translation, v. 10) Includes bibliographies. [BR60.F3T4] 51-9180
1. Theology—Collected works—Early church. 2. Apologetics—Early church. I. Minucius Felix, Marcus. Octavius. II. Series.

Theology—Collected works—Early church, ca. 30-600.

AMBROSIUS, Saint, Bp. of Milan. 201'.1
Seven exegetical works. Translated by Michael P. McHugh. Washington, Catholic University of America Press in association with Consortium Press [1972] viii, 486 p. 22 cm. (The Fathers of the church, a new translation, v. 65) Contents.Contents.—Isaac, or the soul.—Death as a good.—Jacob and the happy life.—Joseph.—The patriarchs.—Flight from the world.—The prayer of Job and David. Bibliography: p. vi-vii. [BR65.A313E55 1972] 71-157660 ISBN 0-8132-0065-2 15.85
1. Theology—Collected works—Early church, ca. 30-600. I. Title. II. Series.

AUGUSTINUS, Aurelius, Saint, Bp. of Hippo. 230'.14
Augustine / Douglas L. Anderson, editor. [Nashville] : Broadman Press, c1979. 416 p. ; 24 cm. (Christian classics) Contents.Contents.—The confessions.—The enchiridion of faith, hope, and charity.—The city of God.—A sermon. [BR65.A52E6 1979] 78-59977 ISBN 0-8054-6539-1 (set) : 24.95
1. Theology—Collected works—Early church, ca. 30-600. I. Anderson, Douglas L. II. Title. III. Series.

AUGUSTINUS, Aurelius, Saint, Bp. of Hippo. 230'.1'4
An Augustine reader. Edited, with an introd., by John J. O'Meara. [1st ed.] Garden City, N.Y., Image Books [1973] 556 p. 19 cm. (An Image book original, D322) Bibliography: p. [545]-553. [BR65.A52E6 1973] 73-80800 ISBN 0-385-06585-X 2.45
1. Theology—Collected works—Early church, ca. 30-600. I. O'Meara, John Joseph, comp. II. Title.

AUGUSTINUS, Aurelius, Saint, Bp. of Hippo. 242
The confessions. [Translated by Edward Bouverie Pusey] The city of God. [Translated by Marcus Dods] On Christian doctrine. [Translated by J. F. [i.e. J.] Shaw] Chicago, Encyclopedia Britannica [1955, c1952] x, 698 p. 25 cm. (Great books of the Western World, v. 18) Bibliographical footnotes. [AC1.G72 vol. 18] 55-10327
1. Theology—Collected works—Early church, ca. 30-600. I. Pusey, Edward Bouverie, 1800-1882, tr. II. Dods, Marcus, 1786-1838, tr. III. Shaw, James Johnston, 1845-1910, tr. IV. Augustinus, Aurelius, Saint, Bp. of Hippo. The city of God. 1955. V. Augustinus, Aurelius, Saint, Bp. of Hippo. On Christian doctrine. 1955. VI. Title: The city of God.

AUGUSTINUS, 230.1'4'0924
Aurelius, Saint, Bp. of Hippo.
Writings of Saint Augustine. Washington, Catholic University of America Press, 1966- c1947- v. 22 cm. (The Fathers of the church, a new translation, v. 2, 12, 21) Contents.Contents.— —v. 4. Christian instruction. Admonition and grace. The Christian combat. Faith, hope and charity.—v. 5. Confessions. —v. 9- Letters. Includes bibliographies. [BR60.F3A82] 66-20314
1. Theology—Collected works—Early church, ca. 30-600. I. Series: The Fathers of the church, a new translation, v. 2 [etc.]

CYRILLUS, Saint, Bp. of Jerusalem, 315(ca.)-386. 281'.4
The works of Saint Cyril of Jerusalem. Translated by Leo P. McCauley and Anthony A. Stephenson. Washington, Catholic University of America Press [1969-70] 2 v. 22 cm. (The Fathers of the church, a new translation, v. 61, 64) Contents.Contents.—v. 1. General introduction. The introductory lecture (Procatechesis). Lenten lectures (Catecheses).—v. 2. Lenten lectures (Katecheseis). Mystagogical lectures (Katecheseis mystagogikai). Sermon on the paralytic (Homilia eis ton paralytikon ton epi ten Kolymbethran). Letter to Constantius (Epistole pros Konstantion). Fragments. Indices. Includes bibliographical references. [BR60.F3C92] 68-55980 ISBN 0-8132-0061-X (v. 1) ISBN 0-8132-0064-4 (v. 2) 8.50 (v. 1) 8.65 (v. 2)
1. Theology—Collected works—Early church, ca. 30-600. I. Series: The fathers of the church, a new translation, v. 61, [etc.]

DIONYSIUS Areopagita, Pseudo- 281'.4
The works of Dionysius the Areopagite / now first translated into English from the original Greek by John Parker. Merrick, N.Y. : Richwood Pub. Co., 1976. 2 v. in 1 ; 21 cm. Reprint of the 1897-1899 ed. published by James Parker & Co., London. Includes bibliographical references and index. [BR65.D62E5 1976] 76-15013 ISBN 0-915172-13-5 lib.bdg. : 25.00
1. Theology—Collected works—Early church, ca. 30-600. I. Parker, John, Rev. II. Title.

A Lost tradition : 270.1
women writers of the early Church / Patricia Wilson-Kastner ... [et al.]. Washington, D.C. : University Press of America, c1981. p. cm. Contents.Contents.—Perpetua: Introduction ; Account of her martyrdom / Rosemary Rader — Proba: Introduction / G. Ronald Kastner and Ann Millin. Cento / Jeremiah Reedy — Egeria: Introduction ; Account of her pilgrimage / Patricia Wilson-Kastner — Eudokia: Introduction ; Life of St. Cyprian of Antioch / G. Ronald Kastner. Includes bibliographical references. [BR60.L59] 19 80-6290 ISBN 0-8191-1642-4 : 18.50 ISBN 0-8191-1643-2 (pbk.) : 9.75
1. Theology—Collected works—Early church, ca. 30-600. I. Wilson-Kastner, Patricia.

ORIGENES. 230'.1'3
Origen / translation and introd. by Rowan A. Greer ; pref. by Hans Urs von Balthasar. New York : Paulist Press, c1979. xvi, 293 p. ; 23 cm. (The Classics of Western spirituality) Contents.Contents.—An Exhortation to martyrdom.—On Prayer.—On First principles: Book IV.—The prologue to the commentary on the Song of songs.—Homily XXVII on Numbers. Includes bibliographical references and index. [BR65.O52 1979] 79-84886 ISBN 0-8091-2198-0 (pbk) : 7.95
1. Theology—Collected works—Early church, ca. 30-600. I. Title. II. Series: Classics of Western spirituality.

VICTORINUS, C. Marius. 231
Theological treatises on the Trinity / Marius Victorinus ; translated by Mary T. Clark. Washington : Catholic University of America Press, c1981. xiii, 371 p. ; 22 cm. (The Fathers of the church, a new translation ; 69) Translation of Opera theologica. Includes indexes. Bibliography: p. ix-xi. [BR65.V532E5 1981] 79-15587 ISBN 0-8132-0069-5 : 24.95
1. Theology—Collected works—Early

church, ca. 30-600. 2. Trinity—Collected works. 3. Arianism—Collected works. I. Clark, Mary T., 1913- II. [Selected works.] English. 1981 III. Title. IV. Series.

Theology — Collected works — Middle Ages.

ANSELM, Saint, Abp. of Canterbury, 1033-1109. 189'.4
Theological treatises. Editors: Jasper Hopkins [and] Herbert Richardson. Cambridge, Harvard Divinity School Library [1965-67] 3 v. 28 cm. [B765.A82E57] 67-1355
1. Theology — Collected works — Middle Ages. 2. Catholic Church — Collected works. I. Hopkins, Jasper, ed. II. Richardson, Herbert Warren, ed. III. Title.

FRANCESCO d'Assisi, Saint, 1182-1226. 282
The writings of Saint Francis of Assisi, newly translated into English, with an introduction and notes, by Father Paschal Robinson ... Philadelphia, The Dolphin press, 1906. xxxii, 208 p. front., pl., facsims. 19 cm. Half-title within ornamental border. Bibliography: p. [189]-195. [BX890.F665 1906] 6-717
1. Theology—Collected works—Middle ages. 2. Catholic church—Collected works. I. Robinson, Paschal, 1870- tr. II. Title.

GERSON, Joannes, 1363-1429.
OEuvres completes [de] Jean Gerson. Introd., texte et notes par Mgr Glorieux. Paris, New York, Desclee [1961, c1960] v. 23 cm. Contents.-- v. 1. Introduction generale. -- v. 2. L'oeuvre Epistolaire. -- v. 3. L'oeuvre magistrale (87-105) -- v. 4. L'oeuvre poetique (106-206) v. 6. L'oeuvre ecclesiologique (253a-291) Includes bibliographies. [BX890.G42] 64-6465
1. Theology — Collected works — Middle Ages. 2. Catholic Church — Collected works. I. Glorieux, Palemon, 1892- ed. II. Title.

THOMAS Aquinas Saint, 1225?-1274. 208.1
Introduction to Saint Thomas Aquinas, ed., with an introd., by Anton C. Pegis. New York, Modern Library [1948] xxx, 690 p. 19 cm. (The Modern library of the world's best books [259]9 "Selections ... from Basic writings of St. Thomas Aquinas ... published in 1945." Bibliography: p. 682-690. [BX890.T62E6 1948] 48-2954
1. Theology—Collected works—Middle Ages. I. Pegis, Anton Charles, 1905- ed. II. Title.

THOMAS Aquinas. Saint, 1225?-1274. 208.1
Theological texts. Selected and translated with notes and an introd. by Thomas Gilby. London, New York, Oxford University Press, 1955. xvii, 423p. 19cm. 'Biographical and bibliographical note': p. [xv]-xvii. Bibliographical footnotes. [BX890.T62E6 1955] 55-14254
1. Theology—Collected works— Middle Ages. I. Title.

THOMAS Aquines Saint 1225?-1274. 208.1
Selected writings. Edited by M. C. D'Arcy. New York, Dutton, 1950. xiv, 283 p. 19 cm. (Everyman's library, 953 A. Philosophy and theology) Includes bibliographies. [AC1.E8] 50-11232
1. Theology — Collected works — Middle Ages. 2. Catholic Church — Collected works. I. Title.

THOMAS Aquinas Saint, 1225?-1274. 230'.2
An Aquinas reader. Edited, with an introd., by Mary T. Clark. [1st ed.] Garden City, N.Y., Image Books, 1972. 597 p. 19 cm. (An Image book original) Bibliography: p. [555]-575. [BX890.T62E6 1972] 72-76709 ISBN 0-385-02505-X 2.45
1. Catholic Church—Collected works. 2. Theology—Collected works—Middle Ages. I. Clark, Mary T., R.S.C.J., ed. II. Title.

WYCLIFFE, John., d.1384 208
Latin works; v. 1-34. [London, Pub. for the Wyclif Soc. by Trubner, 1883-1922] New York, Johnson Reprint, 1967. 22v. in 34 illus. 24cm. Cover title. Vs. 20-22 have imprint: Pub. for the Vyclif Soc. by C. K. Paul. [BR75.W8] 53-57104 560.00 set,; 17.00 ea.,
1. Theology—Collected works—Middle Ages. I. Wyclif Society, London. II. Title.

Theology—Collected works—Middle Ages, 600-1500.

ANSELM, Saint, Abp. of Canterbury, 1033-1109. 230
Trinity, incarnation, and redemption; theological treatises. Edited with introd. by Jasper Hopkins and Herbert Richardson. New York, Harper & Row [1970] xxii, 199 p. 21 cm. (Harper Torchbooks, TB 1513) [B765.A82E575 1970] 71-111082 2.75
1. Catholic Church—Collected works. 2. Theology—Collected works—Middle Ages, 600-1500. I. Title.

BONAVENTURA, Saint, Cardinal, 1221-1274. 230'.2
Bonaventure / translation and introd. by Ewert Cousins ; pref. by Ignatius Brady. New York : Paulist Press, c1978. xx, 353 p. ; 23 cm. (The Classics of Western spirituality) Translated from the Latin. Includes indexes. Contents.Contents.—The soul's journey into God.—The tree of life.—The life of St. Francis. Bibliography: p. 329-333. [BX890.B6731313 1978] 78-60723 ISBN 0-8091-0240-4 : 9.95 ISBN 0-8091-2121-2 pbk. : 6.95
1. Catholic Church—Collected works. 2. Theology—Collected works—Middle Ages, 600-1500. I. Cousins, Ewert H. II. Title. III. Series.

GUILLAUME de Saint-Thierry, 1085(ca.)-1148? 201'.1 s
The works of William of St. Thierry. Spencer, Mass., Cistercian Publications, 1971- [c1970- v. 23 cm. (Cistercian Fathers series, no. 3, 12,) Vol. distributed by Consortium Press, Washington. Contents.Contents.—v. 1. On contemplating God. Prayer. Meditations. —v. 3. The enigma of faith.—v. 4. The golden epistle. [BX890.G848 1971] 72-181841 ISBN 0-87907-300-4
1. Catholic Church—Collected works. 2. Theology—Collected works—Middle Ages, 600-1500. I. Title.

OBERMAN, Heiko Augustinus. 230'.09'02
Forerunners of the Reformation : the shape of late medieval thought / Heiko Augustinus Oberman ; illustrated by key documents ; [translations by Paul L. Nyhus]. 1st Fortress Press ed. Philadelphia : Fortress Press, 1981. p. cm. Includes index. Bibliography: p. [BT10.O23 1981] 19 81-66518 ISBN 0-8006-1617-0 pbk. : 11.95
1. Theology—Collected works—Middle Ages, 600-1500. 2. Theology, Doctrinal—History—Middle Ages, 600-1500. I. Title.

ROLLE, Richard, of Hampole, 1290?-1349. 230'.2
Selected works of Richard Rolle, hermit / transcribed with an introd. by G. C. Heseltine. Westport, Conn. : Hyperion Press, 1979. p. cm. Reprint of the 1930 ed. published by Longmans, Green, London, New York. Bibliography: p. [BX890.R59 1979] 78-20488 ISBN 0-88355-865-3 : 23.50
1. Catholic Church—Collected works. 2. Theology—Collected works—Middle Ages, 600-1500. I. Heseltine, George Coulehan, 1895- II. Title.

A Scholastic miscellany : Anselm to Ockham / edited and translated by Eugene R. Fairweather. Ichthus ed. Philadelphia : Westminster Press, [1981?] 457 p. ; 22 cm. (The Library of Christian classics) Includes bibliographies and indexes. [BX880.S37 1981] 19 82-138386 ISBN 0-664-24418-1 : 11.95 230'.2'0902
1. Catholic Church—Collected works. 2. Theology—Collected works—Middle Ages, 600-1500. I. Fairweather, Eugene Rathbone.

SYMEON, the New Theologian, Saint, 949-1022. 231
The practical and theological chapters & the three theological discourses / Symeon the New Theologian ; translated, with an introduction by Paul McGuckin. Kalamazoo, Mich. : Cistercian Publications, 1982. p. cm. (Cistercian studies series ; 41) [BX890.S95 1982] 19 81-18126 ISBN 0-87907-841-3 : 17.95 ISBN 0-87907-941-X pbk. : 8.00
1. Theology—Collected works—Middle Ages, 600-1500. I. Title. II. Series.

THOMAS, Aquinas, Saint, 1225?-1274. 230'.2
St. Thomas Aquinas, theological texts / selected and translated with notes and an introduction by Thomas Gilby. 1st Labyrinth Press ed. Durham, N.C. : Labyrinth Press, 1982. xvii, 423 p. ; 23 cm. Reprint: London : Oxford University Press, 1955. Includes bibliographical references and index. [BX890.T62E6 1982] 19 81-14270 ISBN 0-939464-01-2 : 12.50
1. Catholic Church—Collected works. 2. Theology—Collected works—Middle Ages, 600-1500. I. Gilby, Thomas, 1902- II. [Selections.] English. 1982 III. Title.
Publisher's address: P.O. Box 2124, Durham, NC 27701

THOMAS Aquinas Saint, 1225?-1274. 230'.2
Pattern for a Christian, according to St. Thomas Aquinas / by A. I. Mennessier; introd. by M. D. Chenu ; translated by Nicholas Halligan. New York : Alba House, [1975] xi, 225 p. ; 21 cm. Translation of L'homme chretien. Includes bibliographical references. [BX890.T62E6 1975] 74-23677 ISBN 0-8189-0299-X pbk. : 4.95
1. Catholic Church—Collected works. 2. Theology—Collected works—Middle Ages, 600-1500. I. Mennessier, Ignatius, 1902-1965. II. Halligan, Francis Nicholas, 1917- tr. III. Title.

WYCLIFFE, John, d.1384. 230
Wycliffe : select English writings / edited by Herbert E. Winn ; with a pref. by H. B. Workman. New York : AMS Press, [1976] p. cm. Reprint of the 1929 ed. published by Oxford University Press, London. [BR75.W84 1976] 75-41303 ISBN 0-404-14635-X : 14.00
1. Theology—Collected works—Middle Ages, 600-1500. I. Title.

Theology — Collections.

CALVIN, Jean, 1509-1564. 248
The piety of John Calvin : an anthology illustrative of the spirituality of the reformer / translated and edited by Ford Lewis Battles ; music edited by Stanley Tagg. Grand Rapids : Baker Book House, c1978. 180 p. : music ; 23 x 27 cm. "Metrical psalms translated by Calvin," for unison chorus with keyboard acc.: p. 137-165. Includes bibliographical references and index. [BX9420.A32B3 1978] 77-88698 ISBN 0-8010-0701-1 : 9.95
1. Reformed Church—Collected works. 2. Theology—Collected works. I. Battles, Ford Lewis. II. Title.

CHRISTIANITY and crisis. 230'.08
Witness to a generation; significant writings from Christianity and crisis, 1941-1966, edited by Wayne H. Cowan. With a pref. by Herbert Butterfield. Indianapolis, Bobbs-Merrill [1966] xxi, 272 p. 24 cm. [BT10.C5] 66-29152
1. Theology—Collections. I. Cowan, Wayne H., ed. II. Title.

ESSAYS in modern theology and related subjects, gathered and published as a testimonial to Charles Augustus Briggs, D.D., D. LITT., graduate professor of theological encyclopedia and symbolics in the Union theological seminary in the city of New York, on the completion of his seventieth year, January 15, 1911, by a few of his pupils, colleagues and friends. New York, C. Scribner's sons. 1911. xvi p, 1 l., 347 p. 2 pl. 23 1/2 cm. [BR50.E85] 11-3361 204
1. Briggs, Charles Augustus, 1841-1913. 2. Theology—Collections.
Contents omitted.

FAIRWEATHER, Eugene Rathbone, ed. 283
The Oxford movement. Edited by Eugene R. Fairweather. New York, Oxford University Press, 1964. xvi, 400 p. 24 cm. (A Library of Protestant thought) Bibliography: p. 385-392. [BX5099.F3] 64-19451
1. Theology — Collections. 2. Oxford movement. I. Title. II. Series.

FERM, Robert L., ed. 230.082
Readings in the history of Christian thought. New York, Holt, Rinehart and Winston [1964] xix, 619 p. 24 cm. Bibliography: p. 613-619. [BT10.F4] 64-10211
1. Theology—Collections. I. Title.

FICKER, Victor B., comp. 208
The revolution in religion. Edited by Victor B. Ficker [and] Herbert S. Graves. Columbus, Ohio, Merrill [1973] vi, 169 p. 23 cm. Contents.Contents.—Leary, J. P. The revolution in religion.—Harrington, M. Religion and revolution.—Gelpi, D. Religion in the age of Aquarius.—Berrigan, D. Conscience, the law, and civil disobedience.—Rose, S. C. The coming confrontation on the church's war investments.—Hadden, J. K. Clergy involvement in civil rights.—Groppi, J. E. The church and civil rights.—Newsweek. Verdict at First Baptist.—Bloy, M. B., Jr. The counter-culture: it just won't go away.—Forman, J. The Black manifesto.—McIntire, C. Christian manifesto.—Sandeen, E. R. Fundamentalism and American identity.—Kuhn, H. B. Obstacles to Evangelism in the world.—Zahn, G. C. A religious pacifist looks at abortion.—The Lutheran Church-Missouri Synod. Abortion: theological, legal, and medical aspects.—Bayer, C. H. Confessions of an abortion counselor.—Osborn, R. T. Religion on the campus.—Ficker, V. B. The search for meaning. Includes bibliographical references. [BR50.F46] 73-75682 ISBN 0-675-08932-8
1. Theology—Collections. 2. Church and social problems—Collections. 3. Christianity—20th century—Collections. I. Graves, Herbert S., 1914- joint comp. II. Title.

THE Fundamentals, 230
a testimony to the truth ... Compliments of two Christian laymen. Chicago, Ill., Testimony publishing company (not inc.) [1910-15] 12 v. 18 1/2 cm. Includes bibliographies. [BR45.F8] 43-40693
1. Theology—Collections.

THE Fundamentals / 230
compiled by R. A. Torrey and others ; rev. under direction of Charles L. Feinberg. Grand Rapids : Kregel Publications, 1979, c1958. p. cm. Revision of the 1958 ed. published under title: The Fundamentals for today, which was first published in 1910-1915 under title: The Fundamentals. [BR45.F8 1979] 79-15007 ISBN 0-8254-3814-4 : 7.95
1. Theology—Collected works. 2. Fundamentalism. I. Torrey, Reuben Archer, 1856-1928. II. Feinberg, Charles Lee. III. The Fundamentals for today.

GALLOWAY, Allan Douglas, 1920- ed. 230.082
Basic readings in theology. London, Allen & Unwin [dist. New York. Humanities, c.1964] 316p. 23cm. Bibl. [BT10.G3] 64-7244 7.50
1. Theology—Collections. I. Title.

GALLOWAY, Allan Douglas, 1920- ed. 230'.08
Basic readings in theology. Edited by A. D. Galloway. Cleveland, Meridian Books [1968, c1964] 316 p. 21 cm. Includes bibliographical references. [BT10.G3 1968] 68-15658
1. Theology—Collections. I. Title.

KAGAWA, Toyohiko 230
Kagawa, Japanese prophet, his witness in life and word. [Edited by] Jessie M.Trout. New York, Association Press [1960] 80p. [2p. bibl. notes] 19cm. (World Christian books, no. 30. Second series) 60-6574 1.00 pap.,
1. Theology—Collected works. I. Trout, Jessie M., ed. II. Title.

KERR, Hugh Thomson, 1909- ed. 230.08
Readings in Christian thought, edited by Hugh T. Kerr. Nashville, Abingdon Press [1966] 382 p. 26 cm. [BR50.K4] 66-14992
1. Theology—Collections. I. Title.

LEITH, John H., ed. 238.082
Creeds of the churches; a reader in Christian doctrine from the Bible to the present. Chicago, Aldine [c.1963] 589p. 22cm. 7.50

1. Theology—Collections. 2. Creeds—Collections. I. Title.

LEITH, John H., ed. 238.082
Creeds of the churches; a reader in Christian doctrine from the Bible to the present. Garden City, N. Y., Doubleday [c.]1963. 589p. 18cm. (Anchor bk., A312) 63-10439 1.95 pap.,
1. Theology—Collections. 2. Creeds—Collections. I. Title.

LEITH, John H ed.
Creeds of the churches; a reader in Christian doctrine from the Bible to the present. Chicago, Aldine [c1963] xiv, 589 p. 22 cm. Includes bibliographies. 65-18368
1. Theology — Collections. 2. Creeds — Collections. I. Title.

LEITH, John H ed. 238.062
Creeds of the churches; a reader in Christian doctrine from the Bible to the present. [1st ed.] Garden City, N.Y., Anchor Books, 1963. 589 p. 18 cm. (Anchor, A312) [BT990.A1L4] 63-10439
1. Theology — Collections. 2. Creeds — Collections. I. Title.

LUTHER, Martin, 1483-1546 230.41
Early theological works. Ed., tr. by James Atkinson. Philadelphia, Westminster [c.1962] 380p. 24cm. (Lib. of Christian classics, v. 16) Bibl. 62-12358 6.50
1. Theology—Collected works. I. Atkinson, James, 1914- ed. and tr. II. Title. III. Series.
Content omitted.

LUTHER, Martin, 1483-1546 208.1
Works: v.4. St. Louis, Concordia [c.1964] 443p. 24cm. Contents.v.4. Lectures on Genesis, chapters 21-25. Bibl. 55-9893 6.00
1. Theology—Collected works. 2. Bible—Criticism. interpretation, etc.—Hist. I. Pelikan. Jaroslav. 1923- ed. II. Hansen, Walter A., ed. III. Title. IV. Title: Lectures on Genesis.

MACQUARRIE, John, comp. 201
Contemporary religious thinkers from idealist metaphysicians to existential theologians, selected and introduced by John Macquarrie. [1st ed.] New York, Harper & Row [1968] xii, 285 p. 21 cm. (Harper forum books) [BR50.M2] 68-11747
1. Theology—Collections. 2. Religion—Philosophy—Collections. I. Title.

METHODIST Publishing House, 208.2 Nashville.
Training series A. [Nashville] Personnel and Public Relations Division, Methodist Publishing House, 1953- v. 28cm. Contents.Course 1. An outline and bibliographical guide for the study of the living non-Christian religions of the world, by J. M. Batten.--Course 2. An outline and bibliographical guide for the study of the history of the Christian church. by J. M. Batten.-- Course 7. The Methodist Publishing House, Its organisation and function. Includes bibliography. [BR45.M36] 54-19592
1. Theology—Collections. I. Title.

MILLER, William Robert. 230'.08 comp.
The new Christianity; an anthology of the rise of modern religious thought, Ed., introds. by William Robert Miller. [New York, Dell, 1968,c.1967] xxi, 393p. 20cm. (Delta bk., 6317) Bibl. [BR115.C8W5 1967] 2.45 pap.,
1. Theology—Collections. I. Title.

MILLER, William Robert, 230'.08 comp.
The new Christianity; an anthology, of the rise of modern religious thought, edited and with introductions by William Robert Miller. New York, Delacorte Press [1967] xxi, 303 p. 21 cm. Includes bibliographies. [BT10.M] 67-14998
1. Theology — Collections. I. Title.

NEWTON, Sir Isaac, 1642-1727.
Theological manuscripts, selected and edited with an introd. by H. McLachlan. Liverpool, University Press, 1950. vii, 147 p. 23 cm. A51
1. Theology — Collected works. I. Title.

OBERMAN, Heiko Augustinus, 230.08 ed.
Forerunners of the Reformation: the shape of late medieval thought illustrated by key documents. Translations by Paul L. Nyhus. [1st ed.] New York, Holt, Rinehart and Winston [1966] x, 333 p. 22 cm. Bibliography: p. 319-327. [BT10.O23] 66-13496
1. Theology — Collections. I. Title.

PRINCETON Theological 016. Seminary.
Princeton pamphlets. no. 1- Princeton, N. J., 1948- no. 24 cm. Title varies: no. 1- Princeton Seminary pamphlets. [BV4070.P713] 49-2799
1. Theology—Collections. I. Title.

WELCH, Claude, ed. and 232.082 tr.
God and Incarnation in mid-nineteenth century German theology: G. Thomasius, I. A. Dorner, A. E. Biedermann. New York, Oxford, 1965. viii, 391p. 24cm. (Lib. of Protestant thought) Bibl. [BT10.W4] 65-18230 7.00
1. Theology—Collections. 2. Theology, Doctrinal—Hist.Germany. 3. Theology, Doctrinal—Hist.—19th. cent. I. Thomasius, Gottfried, 1802-1875. II. Dorner, Isaak August, 1809-1884. III. Biedermann, Aloys Emanuel, 1819-1885. IV. Title. V. Series.

WICKS, Robert S., ed. 230.082
The edge of wisdom; a source book of religious and secular writers. New York, Scribners [1965, c.1964] xv, 278p. 24cm. [BT10.W55] 64-24235 3.50 pap.,
1. Theology—Collections I. Title.

WIRT, Sherwood Eliot, 201'.1'08 comp.
Great reading from Decision: selections from the first ten years of publication. Edited by Sherwood E. Wirt and Mavis R. Sanders. Minneapolis, World Wide Publications [1970] 432 p. illus. (part col.) 23 cm. [BR50.W56] 75-141316 4.95
1. Theology—Collections. I. Sanders, Mavis R., joint comp. II. Decision. III. Title.

Theology—Collections—Catholic authors.

DANIEL-ROPS, Henry, 1901- 230.2 ed.
The Twentieth century encyclopedia of Catholicism. [Edited by Henri Daniel-Rops. New York, Hawthorn Books, 1958- v. 21 cm. 1 v. (unpaged) 21 cm. Half title; each vol. has also special t. p. Index to the first sixteen volumes. Joseph W. Sprug, index editor. [New York] Hawthorn Books [1959] 58-14327
1. Theology — Collections — Catholic authors. I. Title.

DANIEL-ROPS, Henry, 1901- 230.2 ed.
The Twentieth century encyclopedia of Catholicism. [Edited by Henri Daniel-Rops. New York, Hawthorn Books, 1958- v. 21 cm. v. 21 cm. (BX841.T85 Index Half title: each vol. has also special t. p. -- Index ... Joseph W. Sprug, index editor. [New York] Hawthorn Books [1959- Cover title. Indexes issued semi-annually with annual cumulations. 58-14327
1. Theology — Collections — Catholic authors. I. Title.

PEGIS, Anton Charles, 1905- 208.2 ed.
The wisdom of Catholicism. [1st Modern Library giant ed.] New York, Modern Library [1955] 988 p. 21 cm. (The modern library of the world's best books [G56]) [BX880] 55-6396
1. Theology—Collections—Catholic authors. 2. Catholic literature. I. Title.

PEGIS, Anton Charles, 1905- 208.2 ed.
The wisdom of Catholicism. New York, Random House [1949] xxix, 968 p. 24 cm. (The Random House lifetime library) Bibliography: p. 985-968. [BX880.P36] 49-9822
1. Theology—Collections—Catholic authors. 2. Catholic literature. I. Title.

TWENTIETH century 230.2
Catholicism; a periodical supplement to The Twentieth Century Ency. of Catholicism. No. 2 Ed.: Lancelot Sheppard. Managing ed.: Paul Fargis. European ed.: Arthur Coppotelli. New York, Hawthorn [c.1965] 248p. 21cm. Bibl. [BX841.T85] 58-14327 6.00 bds.,
1. Theology—Collections—Catholic authors.

WOODS, Ralph Louis, 1904- 230.2 ed.
A treasury of Catholic thinking. Introd. by James M. Gillis. New York [Apollo Eds., 1962, c.1953] 378p. (A-36) 1.95 pap.,
1. Theology—Collections—Catholic authors. I. Title.

WOODS, Ralph Louis, 1904- 230.2 ed.
A treasury of Catholic thinking. Introd. by James M. Gillis. New York, Crowell [1953] 378p. 24cm. [BX880.W65] 53-8443
1. Theology—Collections—Catholic authors. I. Title.

Theology—Collections—Puritan authors.

EMERSON, Everett H., 285'.9'08 1925-
English Puritanism from John Hooper to John Milton [by] Everett H. Emerson. Durham, N.C., Duke University Press, 1968. xii, 313 p. ports. (on lining paper) 25 cm. Bibliography: p. [295]-306. [BX9313.E4] 68-29664 10.00
1. Theology—Collections—Puritan authors. 2. Puritans—Collections. I. Title.

Theology — Collections — Reformed authors.

BEARDSLEE, John W., III 230.4208 ed. and tr.
Reformed dogmatics: J. Wollebius. G. Voetius, F. Turretin. New York, Oxford [c.]1965. xi,471p. 24cm. (Lib. of Protestant thought) Bibl. [BX9409.B4] 65-28036 2.50
1. Theology—Collections—Refrmed authors. 2. Reformed Church—Collections. I. Wolleb. Johannes, 1586-1629. Compendium theologiae Christianae. II. Voet, Giisbert, 1589-1676. Selectae disputationes theologicae. III. Turrettini, Francois. 1623-1687. Institutio theologiae elencticae. IV. Title. V. Series.
Contents omitted.

BEARDSLEE, John W ed. 230.4208 and tr.
Reformed dogmatics: J. Wollebius, G. Voetius [and] F. Turretin. Edited and translated by John W. Beardslee, III New York, Oxford University Press, 1965. xi. 471 p. 24 cm. (A Library of Protestan thought) [BX9409.B4] 65-28036
1. Theology — Collections — Reformed authors. 2. Reformed Church — Collections. I. Wolleb, Johannes, 1586-1629. Compendium thelogiae Christianae. II. Voet, Gijsbert, 1589-1676. Selectac Disputations theologicae. III. Turrettini, Francois, 1623-1687. Institutio theologiae elencticae. IV. Title. V. Series.
Contents omitted.

Theology—Congresses.

INTERNATIONAL 230'.2'0924 s Lonergan Congress, St. Leo College, 1970.
Foundations of theology. Edited by Philip McShane. [American ed. Notre Dame, Ind.] University of Notre Dame Press [1972, c1971] xx, 257 p. 23 cm. (Papers from the International Lonergan Congress, 1970, v. 1) Includes bibliographical references. [BX4705.L7133157 1970, Vol. 1] 230'.2'0924 76-167705 ISBN 0-268-00456-0 10.00
1. Lonergan, Bernard J. F.—Congresses. 2. Theology—Congresses. I. McShane, Philip, ed. II. Title. III. Series.

INTERNATIONAL 230'.2'0924 Lonergan Congress, St. Leo College, 1970.
Papers from the International Lonergan Congress, 1970. Edited by Philip McShane. [American ed.] Notre Dame, Ind.] University of Notre Dame Press [1972-c1971 v. 23 cm. [BX4705.L7133157 1970] 74-166474 10.00 (v. 1)
1. Lonergan, Bernard J. F.—Congresses. 2. Theology—Congresses. I. McShane, Philip, ed.

Theology—Dictionaries.

ABBOTT, Lyman, 1835-1922, 220. ed.
A dictionary of religious knowledge, for popular and professional use; comprising full information on Biblical, theological, and ecclesiastical subjects. With several hundred maps and illustrations. Edited by the Rev. Lyman Abbott, assisted by the Rev. T.J. Conant, D.D. New York, Harper & brothers [c1902] xv, [1], 1074 p. illus. (incl. maps, plans) 25 1/2 cm. [BR95.A3 1902] 2-28398
1. Theology—Dictionaries. 2. Religion—Dictionaries. I. Conant, Thomas Jefferson, 1802-1891. II. Title.

BAKER'S dictionary of 203
theology. Everett F. Harrison, editor-in-chief; Geoffrey W. Bromiley, associate editor; Carl F. H. Henry, consulting editor. Grand Rapids, Baker Book House, 1960. 566 p. 25 cm. Includes bibliography. [BR95.B25] 60-7333
1. Theology—Dictionaries. I. Harrison, Everett Falconer, 1902- ed. II. Title: Dictionary of theology.

BENHAM, William, 1831-1910. 220.
The dictionary of religion: an encyclopedia of Christian and other religious doctrines, denominations, sets, heresies, ecclesiastical terms, history, biography, etc., etc. Edited by the Rev. William Benham ... London, New York [etc.] Cassell & company, limited, 1887. iv, 1148 p. illus. 24 cm. [BR95.B4] 1-2112
1. Theology—Dictionaries. 2. Religion—Dictionaries. I. Title.

BENTON, Angelo Ames, 283'.03 1837-1912, ed.
The church cyclopaedia : a dictionary of church doctrine, history, organization, and ritual ... designed especially for the use of the laity of the Protestant Episcopal Church in the United States of America / edited by A. A. Benton. Detroit : Gale Research Co., 1975, c1883. 810 p. ; 23 cm. Reprint of the ed. published by M. H. Mallory, New York. [BR95.B5 1975] 74-31499 ISBN 0-8103-4204-9 : 28.00
1. Protestant Episcopal Church in the U.S.A.—Dictionaries. 2. Theology—Dictionaries. I. Title.

BLUNT, John Henry, 1823- 200'.3 1884.
Dictionary of sects, heresies, ecclesiastical parties, and schools of religious thought. London, Rivingtons, 1874. Detroit, Gale Research Co., 1974. viii, 648 p. 23 cm. [BR95.B6 1974] 74-9653 ISBN 0-8103-3751-7 28.50
1. Theology—Dictionaries. 2. Sects—Dictionaries. I. Title.

BLUNT, John Henry, 1823- 200'.3 1884.
Dictionary of sects, heresies, ecclesiastical parties, and schools of religious thought. Edited by John Henry Blunt. Ann Arbor, Mich., Gryphon Books, 1971. viii, 648 p. 22 cm. Reprint of the 1874 ed. [BR95.B6 1971] 71-107136
1. Theology—Dictionaries. 2. Sects—Dictionaries. I. Title.

BLUNT, John Henry, 1823- 280.3 1884.
Dictionary of sects, heresies, ecclesiastical parties and schools of religious thought, edited by the Rev. John Henry Blunt... New ed. London and New York, Longmans, Green, and co., 1891. viii, 647, [1] p. 27 1/2 cm. [BR95.B6 1891] 31-4594
1. Theology—Dictoraries. 2. Sects. I. Title.

BOUYER, Louis, 1913- 230.203
Dictionary of theology. Tr. [from French] by Charles Underhill Quinn. [New York, Desclee, 1966, c.1965] xi, 470p. 25cm. [BR95.B6413] 66-13370 9.75
1. Theology—Dictionaries. 2. Catholic Church—Dictionaries. I. Title.

BUCK, Charles, 1771-1815. 220.
A theological dictionary: containing definitions of all religious terms; a comprehensive view of every article in the system of divinity; an impartial account of all the principal denominations ... together with an accurate statement of the most remarkable transactions and events recorded in ecclesiastical history. By Charles Buck ... 1st American, from the 2d

London, edition. Philadelphia, Whitehall: from the W. W. Woodward, no. 52, corner of Chesnut and Second streets, 1807. Dickinson, printer. 2 v. 22 cm. [BR95.B75 1807] 27-11366
1. Theology—Dictionaries. I. Title.

BUCK, Charles, 1771-1815. 220.
A theological dictionary: containing definitions of all religious terms: a comprehensive view of every article in the system of divinity: an impartial account of all the principal denominations ... together with an accurate statement of the most remarkable transactions and events recorded in ecclesiastical history. By Charles Buck ... 2d American from the 2d London edition. Philadelphia: Printed for W. W. Woodward, no. 52, corner of Chesnut and Second street. Borwn & Merritt printers, no. 24 cm. Church-alley. 1810. 2 v. 22 cm. [BR95.B75 1810] 27-11364
1. Theology—Dictionaries. I. Title.

BUCK, Charles, 1771-1815. 220.
A theological dictionary, containing definitions of all religious terms; a comprehensive view of every article in the system of divinity, an impartial account of all the principal denominations which have subsisted in the religious world, from the birth of Christ to the present day: together with an accurate statement of the most remarkable transactions and events recorded in ecclestical history. By Charles Buck. Two volumes in one. Third American, from the third London edition, with additions. Also, An account of the Cumberland Presbyterians in the United States. Philadelphia, Printed for W. W. Woodward, 1814. iv, 476 p. 23 cm. [BR95.B] A 34
1. Theology—Dictionaries. I. Title.

BUCK, Charles, 1771-1815. 220.
A theological dictionary, containing definitions of all religious terms: a comprehensive view of every article in the system of divinity: an impartial account of all the principal denominations ... together with an accurate statement of the most remarkable transactions and events, recorded in ecclesiastical history. By Charles Buck ... 5th American, from the 3d London edition, with additions. Also an account of the Cumberland Presbyterians in the United States. Philadelphia, Printed for W. W. Woodward, no. 52, south west corner of Chesnut and Second streets, 1818. W. Hill Woodward, printer. 2 v. in 1. 23 cm. [BR95.B75 1818] 27-11365
1. Theology—Dictionaries. I. Title.

BUCK, Charles, 1771-1815. 220.
A theological dictionary, containing definitions of all religious terms: a comprehensive view of every article in the system of divinity: an impartial account of all the principal denominations ... together with an accurate statement of the most remarkable transactions and events, recorded in ecclesiastical history. By the late Rev. Charles Buck. Scott's 2d American from the last London edition; with extensive additions and improvements. Philadelphia, E. T. Scott, 1823. 592 p. 22 cm. [BR95.B75 1823] 27-11382
1. Theology—Dictionaries. I. Title.

BUCK, Charles, 1771-1815. 220.
A theological dictionary, containing definitions of all religious terms; a comprehensive view of every article in the system of divinity; an impartial account of all the principal denominations ... together with an accurate statement of the most remarkable transactions and events recorded in ecclesiastical history. By the late Rev. Charles Buck ... Woodward's enlarged and improved American, from the last London edition; to which is added, an account of the Cumberland Presbyterians, and an appendix, containing an account of the Methodist Episcopal church in the United States, &c. Philadelphia, W. W. Woodward, 1825. 2 v. in 1. front. (ports.) 22 cm. [BR95.B75 1825] 27-11367
1. Theology—Dictionaries. I. Title.

BUCK, Charles, 1771-1815. 220.
... A theological dictionary, containing definitions of all religious terms: a comprehensive view of every article article in the system of divinity: an impartial account of all the principal denominations ... together with an accurate statement of the most remarkable transactions ad events recorded in ecclesiastical history. By the Rev. Charles Buck. New American, from the latest London edition. Revised and improved ... by the Rev. George Bush, A. M. With an Appendix, containing a late account of the Methodist Episcopal church in America, and of the Associated Methodist. Philadelphia, J. Kay, jun. & co.: Pittsburgh, J. J. Kay & co., 1830. 463 p. front. (port.) 23 cm. At head of title: Kay's improved & enlarged edit. [BR95.B75 1830] 27-11384
1. Theology—Dictionaries. I. Bush, George, 1796-1859, ed. II. Title.

BUCK, Charles, 1771-1815. 220.
A theological dictionary, containing definitions of all religious terms; a comprehensive view of every article in the system of divinity; an impartial account of all the principal denominations ... together with an accurate statement of the most remarkable transactions and events recorded in ecclesiastical history. By the Rev. Charles Buck. New American, from the latest London edition. Revised and improved ... by the Rev. George Bush ... Philadelphia, J. Kay, jun. & co.; Pittsburgh J. J. Kay & co., 1831. 472 p. front. 24 cm. [BR95.B75 1831] 27-11369
1. Theology—Dictionaries. I. Bush, George, 1796-1859, ed. II. Title.

BUCK, Charles, 1771-1815. 220.
... A theological dictionary: containing definitions of all religious terms; a comprehensive view of every article in the system of divinity, an impartial account of all the principal denominations ... together with an accurate statement of the most remarkable transactons and events recorded in the ecclesiastical history. By the Rev. Charles Buck. New American, from the latest London ed. Rev. and improved by the addition of many new articles ... By the Rev. George Bush, A. M. With an appendix ... Philadelphia, J. J. Woodward, Pittsburgh, Sold by J. J. Kay & co., 1835. 472 p. front., plates. 23 cm. [BR95.B75 1835] 15-22821
1. Theology—Dictionaries. I. Bush, George, 1796-1859, ed. II. Title.

BUCK, Charles, 1771-1815. 220.
A theological dictionary, containing definitions of all religious terms; a comprehensive view of every article in the system of divinity. An impartial account of all the principal denominations ... together with an accurate statement of the most remarkable transactions and events recorded in ecclesiastical history. By the Rev. Charles Buck. New American from the latest London edition. Revised, and improved ... by the Rev. George Bush ... Corrected to 1836. Philadelphia, J. J. Woodward, 1836. 472 p. front. 23 cm. [BR95.B75 1836] 27-11368
1. Theology—Dictionaries. I. Bush, George, 1796-1859, ed. II. Title.

BUECHNER, Frederick, 1926- 203
Wishful thinking; a theological ABC. [1st ed.] New York, Harper & Row [1973] xii, 100 p. 22 cm. [BR95.B785 1973] 72-9872 ISBN 0-06-061155-3 4.95
1. Theology—Dictionaries. I. Title.

A Catholic dictionary of 230.203
theology; a work projected with the approval of the Catholic hierarchy of England and Wales. London, New York, Nelson [1962- v. illus. 27cm. Contents.v. 1. Abandonment-casuistry. Includes bibliographies. [BR95.C27] 62-52257
1. Theology—Dictionaries. 2. Catholic Church—Dictionaries.

CATHOLIC dictionary of 230.203
theology (A); a work projected with the approval of the Catholic hierarchy of England and Wales. New York, Nelson [c.1962] 332p. illus. 27cm. Contents.v.1. Abandonment--easuistry. Bibl. 62-52257 9.25
1. Theology—Dictionaries. 2. Catholic Church—Dictionaries.

CATHOLIC dictionary of 230.203
theology (A); a work projected with the approval of the Catholic hierarchy of England and Wales. London, New York, Nelson [1967] v. illus. 27cm. Contents.v.2.Cathechism-heaven. Bibl. [BR95.C27] 62-52257 15.00
1. Theology — Dictionaries. 2. Catholic Church — Dictionaries.

THE Catholic encyclopedia for 031
school and home. New York, McGraw-Hill [1965] 12 v. illus. (part col.) maps, ports. 25 cm. Bibliography: v. 12, p. [1]-86. [BX841.C36] 65-20114
1. Catholic Church—Dictionaries. 2. Theology—Dictionaries. 3. Encyclopedias and dictionaries. I. Title: The contemporary church.

CHRISTIAN word book 230'.03
[by] J. Sherrell Hendricks [and others] Nashville, Abingdon Press [1969, c1968] 320 p. 24 cm. [BR95.C53 1969] 69-19739 ISBN 6-87076-498- 3.95
1. Theology—Dictionaries. I. Hendricks, John Sherrell, 1931-

CHRISTIAN word book. 230'.03
[Nashville] Graded Press [1968] 320 p. 23 cm. Prepared by the Editorial Division, Methodist Board of Education for use in the United Methodist Church. Authors: J. Sherrell Hendricks and others. [BR95.C53] 70-302
1. Theology—Dictionaries. I. Hendricks, John Sherrell, 1931- II. United Methodist Church (United States) Board of Education. Editorial Division.

THE Concise Oxford dictionary 203
of the Christian Church / edited by Elizabeth A. Livingstone. 2d ed. abridged. Oxford [Eng.] ; New York : Oxford University Press, 1978 vi, 570 p. ; 21 cm. An abridgement of the 2d ed. of The Oxford dictionary of the Christian Church. [BR95.O82 1977] 77-30192 ISBN 0-19-211549-9 : 14.95
1. Theology—Dictionaries. I. Livingstone, Elizabeth A. II. The Oxford dictionary of the Christian Church.

CORPUS dictionary of Western 203
churches. Edited by T. C. O'Brien. Washington, Corpus Publications [1970] xviii, 820 p. 25 cm. Includes bibliographical references. [BR95.C67] 78-99501 25.00
1. Theology—Dictionaries. I. O'Brien, Thomas C., ed.

CULLY, Iris V 203
An introductory theological wordbook, by Iris V. and Kendig Brubaker Cully. Philadelphia, Westminister Press [1963] 204 p. 21 cm. [BR95.C8] 64-10033
1. Theology — Dictionaries. I. Cully, Kendig Brubaker, joint author. II. Title. III. Title: An introductory theological wordbook,

DAVIS, John Jefferson. 230'.07
Theology primer : resources for the theological student / John Jefferson Davis. Grand Rapids, Mich. : Baker Book House, c1981. 111 p. ; 22 cm. Bibliography: p. 67-111. [BR95.D38] 19 81-67093 ISBN 0-8010-2912-0 (pbk.) : 5.95
1. Theology—Dictionaries. 2. Theologians—Biography. 3. Theology—Bibliography. I. Title.

DICTIONARY of church terms 203
and symbols. Comp. by Loice Gouker. Ed. by Carl F. Weidmann. Designed by Tyyne Hakola. Norwalk, Conn., C. R. Gibson [1964] 69p. illus. 18cm. 64-18545 price unreported
1. Theology—Dictionaries. I. Gouker, Loice, comp. II. Title: Church terms and symbols.

DOUGLAS, James Dixon. 203
The new international dictionary of the Christian church. J. D. Douglas, general editor. Earle E. Cairns, consulting editor. Grand Rapids, Zondervan Pub. Co. [1974] xii, 1074 p. 25 cm. Includes bibliographical references. [BR95.D68] 74-8999 24.95
1. Theology—Dictionaries. I. Title.

ENCYCLOPEDIA of theology 201'.1
: the concise Sacramentum mundi / edited by Karl Rahner. New York : Seabury Press, [1975] xiv, 1841 p. ; 24 cm. "A Crossroad book." Contains revised articles from Sacramentum mundi, together with articles from Lexikon fur Theologie und Kirche and Theologisches Taschenlexikon, and new articles. [BR95.E48] 74-33145 ISBN 0-8164-1182-4 : 32.50
1. Theology—Dictionaries. I. Rahner, Karl, 1904- ed.

ENCYCLOPEDIC dictionary of 201
Christian doctrine. Edited by John P. Bradley. Gastonia, N.C., Good Will Publishers [1970] 3 v. (xi, 1304, iii p.) illus. (part col.), facsims., ports. (part col.) 25 cm. (The Catholic layman's library, v. 7-9) Includes bibliographies. [BR95.E49] 78-92779
1. Theology—Dictionaries. I. Bradley, John P., ed. II. Title. III. Series.

FERM, Vergilius Ture Anselm, 203
1896-
Concise dictionary of religion; a lexicon of Protestant interpretation, by Vergilius Ferm. New York, Philosophical Library [1964? c1951] ix, 283 p. 22 cm. First published in 1951 under title: A Protestant dictionary. "Revised edition."--Dust jacket. [BR95.F37] 64-4055
1. Theology—Dictionaries. 2. Protestants—Dictionaries. I. Title.

FERM, Vergilius Ture Anselm, 203
1896-
A Protestant dictionary. New York, Philosophical Library [1951] 283 p. 22 cm. [BR95.F37] 51-14412
1. Theology—Dictionaries. 2. Protestantism—Dictionaries. I. Title.

FUNK, E P ed. 220.3
Encyclopedia of Biblical examples & illustrations demonstrated by the Scriptures. Carefully arranged and prepared by Rev. E. P. Funk ... Harrisburg, Pa., 1881. 56 p. 15 cm. "Second edition." [BR95.F83 1881] 37-38002
1. Theology—Dictionaries. I. Title.

A Handbook of Christian 230.03
theology; definition essays on concepts and movements of thought in contemporary Protestantism. New York, Meridian Books [1958] 380 p. 18 cm. (Living age books, LA18) Edited by Marvin Halverson and Arthur A. Cohen. [BR95.H3] 57-10852
1. Theology—Dictionaries. I. Halverson, Marvin, 1913- ed. II. Cohen, Arthur Allen, 1928- ed.

HANDBOOK of Christian 230.03
theology (A); definition essays on concepts and movements of thought in contemporary Protestantism. Cleveland, World [1965, c.1958] 380p. 21cm. Ed. by Marvin Halverson, Arthur A. Cohen. [BR95.H3] 5.00
1. Theology—Dictionaries. I. Halverson, Marvin, 1913- ed. II. Cohen, Arthur A., ed.

HARDON, John A. 282'.03
Modern Catholic dictionary / John A. Hardon. 1st ed. Garden City, N.Y. : Doubleday, 1980. xii, 635 p. ; 24 cm. [BX841.H36] 77-82945 ISBN 0-385-12162-8 : 14.95
1. Catholic Church—Dictionaries. 2. Theology—Dictionaries. I. Title.

HARVEY, Van Austin. 230.03
A handbook of theological terms [by] Van A. Harvey. New York, Macmillan [1964] 253 p. 18 cm. "168." [BR95.H32] 64-25193
1. Theology—Dictionaries. I. Title.

HOBBS, Herschel H. 230
A layman's handbook of Christian doctrine / Herschel H. Hobbs. Nashville : Broadman Press, [1974] 142 p. ; 20 cm. [BR96.H55] 74-78615 ISBN 0-8054-1927-6 pbk. : 2.50
1. Theology—Dictionaries. I. Title.

HOOK, Walter Farquhar, 1798- 220.
1875.
A church dictionary. By Walter Farquhar Hook...6th ed. Revised and adapted to the Protestant Episcopal church in the United States of America, by a presbyter of said church. Philadelphia, E. H. Butler & co., 1854. 3 p. l., 580 p. 23 cm. [BR95.H6 1854] 32-16678
1. Theology—Dictionaries. 2. Church of England—Dictionaries. 3. Protestant Episcopal church in the U.S.A.—Dictionaries. I. Title.

JACKSON, Samuel Macauley, 203
1851-1912, ed.
The concise dictionary of religious knowledge and gazetteer, edited by Rev. Samuel Macauley Jackson ... associate

editor; Rev. Talbot Wilson Chambers ... and Rev. Frank Hugh Foster ... 3d ed., throughly rev. New York, The Christian literature co., 1898. 2 p. l., 996, xi, 34 p. v fold. maps. 26 cm. [BR95.J4 1898] 4-4012
1. Theology—Dictionaries. 2. Religion—Dictionaries. I. Chambers, Talbot Wilson, 1819-1896, joint ed. II. Foster, Frank Hugh, 1851-1935, joint ed. III. Title.

JACKSON, Samuel Macauley, 1851-1912, ed. 200.3
Schaff-Herzog encyclopedia. Grand Rapids, Mich, Baker, 1949-50. 13 v. 25 cm. Vols. 2-12 have abbreviated title which varies slightly; v. 13; Index by George William Gilmore. "Editor-in-chief of supplementary volumes, Lefferts A. Loetscher." [[BR95.S]] A51
1. Theology — Dictionaries. I. Title. II. Title: The new Schaff-Herzog encyclopedia of religious knowledge, embracing Biblical, historical, doctrinal, and practical theology, and Biblical, theological, and ecclesiastical biography from the earliest times to the present day; based on the 3d ed. of the Realencyklopadic founded by J. J. Herzog, and edited by Albert Hauke, prepared by more than six hundred scholars and specialists under the supervision of Samuel Macauley Jackson (editor-in-chief) with the assistance of Charles Colebrook Sherman and George William Gilmore (associate editors) and [others]

KERR, James S. 203
A Christian's dictionary; 1,600 names, words and phrases [by] James S. Kerr and Charles Lutz. Philadelphia, Fortress Press [1969] viii, 178 p. 22 cm. Bibliographical references included in "Acknowledgments" (p. vii-viii) [BR95.K4] 74-84542 2.95
1. Theology—Dictionaries. I. Lutz, Charles, joint author. II. Title.

LEE, Frederick George, 1832-1902. 200'.3
A glossary of liturgical and ecclesiastical terms. London, B. Quaritch, 1877. Detroit, Tower Books, 1971. xxxix, 452 p. illus. 23 cm. Bibliography: p. [xxxi]-xxxix. [BR95.L4 1971] 76-174069
1. Theology—Dictionaries. 2. Liturgical objects—Dictionaries. I. Title.

LEON-DUFOUR, Xavier. 220.3
Dictionary of Biblical theology. Edited under the direction of Xavier Leon-Dufour, translated under the direction of P. Joseph Cahill. 2d ed. rev. and enl. Revisions and new articles translated by E. M. Stewart. New York, Seabury Press [1973] xxxii, 711 p. 24 cm. "A Crossroad book." Translation of Vocabulaire de theologie biblique. [BS543.A1L413 1973] 73-6437 ISBN 0-8164-1146-8 17.50
1. Bible—Dictionaries. 2. Bible—Theology. 3. Theology—Dictionaries. I. Title.

LEON-DUFOUR, Xavier comp. 220.3
Dictionary of Biblical theology. Translated from the French under the direction of Joseph Cahill. New York, Desclee Co., 1967. xxix, 617 p. 25 cm. Translation of Vocabulaire de theologie biblique. [BS543.A1L43] 67-30761
1. Bible—Dictionaries. 2. Bible—Theology. 3. Theology—Dictionaries. I. Title.

LUTHERAN cyclopedia / 284'.1'03
Erwin L. Lueker, editor. Rev. ed. St. Louis : Concordia Pub. House, [1975] xiv, 845 p. ; 26 cm. [BX8007.L8 1975] 75-2096 ISBN 0-570-03255-5 : 24.95
1. Lutheran Church—Dictionaries. 2. Theology—Dictionaries. I. Lueker, Erwin Louis, 1914- ed.

MALLOCH, James M., D.D. comp. 203
A practical church dictionary. Ed. by Kay Smallzried. New York, Morehouse [c.1964] xiv, 520p. 25cm. Bibl. 64-23926 13.95
1. Theology—Dictionaries. 2. Anglican Communion—Dictionaries. I. Title.

MONSER, J W
An encyclopaedia on the evidences; or, masterpieces of many minds. Grand Rapids, Baker Book House, 1961. 671 p. 67-8494
1. Theology — Dictionaries. 2. Philosophy — Dictionaries. I. Title. II. Title: Masterpieces of many minds.

THE oxford dictionarry of the Christian Church, edited by F. L. Cross London, New York, Oxford University Press, [c1958] xix, 1492p. 25cm. 'First published 1957; reprinted (with corrections) 1958.' Includes bibliographical references.
1. Theology—Dictionaries. I. Cross, Frank Leslie, 1900- ed.

THE Oxford dictionary of the Christian Church, edited by F. L. Cross. 203
London, New York, Oxford University Press, 1957. xix, 1492 p. 25 cm. Includes bibliographical references. [BR95.O8] 57-4541
1. Theology—Dictionaries. I. Cross, Frank Leslie, 1900- ed.

THE Oxford dictionary of the Christian Church, edited by F. L. Cross. 203
London, New York, Oxford University Press [1966] xix, 1492 p. 25 cm. Includes bibliographical references. [BR95.O8 1966] 72-443015 unpriced
1. Theology—Dictionaries. I. Cross, Frank Leslie, 1900- ed.

PURVIS, John Stanley, 1890- 203
Dictionary of ecclesiastical terms. London, New York, T. Nelson [1962] vii, 204p. 22cm. [BR95.P8] 62-51845
1. Theology—Dictionaries. I. Title. II. Title: Ecclesiastical terms.

RAHNER, Karl, 1904- 230'.2'0321
Dictionary of theology / Karl Rahner, Herbert Vorgrimler ; [English translation by Richard Strachan ... et al.] 2nd ed. New York : Crossroad, 1981. p. cm. Translation of: Kleines theologisches Worterbuch. [BR95.R313 1981] 19 81-5492 ISBN 0-8245-0040-7 : 24.50
1. Catholic Church—Dictionaries. 2. Theology—Dictionaries. I. Vorgrimler, Herbert. II. Strachan, Richard. III. [Kleines theologisches Worterbuch.] English IV. Title.

RAHNER, Karl, 1904- 230.203
Theological dictionary [by] Karl Rahner [and] Herbert Vorgrimler. Edited by Cornelius Ernst. Translated by Richard Strachan. [New York] Herder and Herder [1965] 493 p. 22 cm. Translation of Kleines theologisches Worterbuch. [BR95.R313] 65-26562
1. Catholic Church—Dictionaries. 2. Theology—Dictionaries. I. Vorgrimler, Herbert, joint author. II. Title.

RICHARDSON, Alan, 1905- 230'.03
A dictionary of Christian theology. Philadelphia, Westminster Press [1969] xii, 364 p. 26 cm. Includes bibliographical references. [BR95.R47] 69-19153 8.50
1. Theology—Dictionaries. I. Title.

SACRAMENTUM mundi; 203
an encyclopedia of theology. [Edited by Karl Rahner and others. New York] Herder and Herder [1968- v. 27 cm. Includes bibliographies. [BR95] 68-25987
1. Theology—Dictionaries. I. Rahner, Karl, 1904- ed.

SCHAFF-HERZOG encyclopedia. 203
The new Schaff-Herzog encyclopedia of religious knowledge, embracing Biblical, historical, doctrinal, and practical theology, and Biblical, theological, and ecclesiastical biography from the earliest times to the present day; based on the 3d ed. of the Real encyklopadie founded by J.J. Herzog, and edited by Albert Hauck, prepared by more than six hundred scholars and specialists under the supervision of Samuel Macauley Jackson (editor-in-chief) with the assistance of Charles Colebrook Sherman and George William Gilmore (associate editors) and others. Grand Rapids, Mich., Baker, 1949-50. Grand Rapids, Mich., Baker, 1955. 13v. 23cm. 2 v .(xx, 1205p.) 25cm. Vols. 2-12 have abbreviated title which varies slightly; v. 13: Index by George William Gilmore.--Twentieth century encyclopedia of religious knowledge. An extension of The new Schaff-Herzog encyclopedia of religious knowledge. Editor-in-chief: Uefferts A. Loetscher. Includes bibliographies. A51
1. Theology—Dictionaries. I. Jackson, Samuel Macauley, 1851-1912. bd. II. Udetscher, Leffert Augustine, 1904- ed. III. Title.

SCHAFF-HERZOG encyclopedia. 220.
The new Schaff-Herzog encyclopedia of religious knowledge, embracing Biblical, historical, doctrinal, and practical theology and Biblical, theological, and ecclesiastical biography from the earliest times to the present day, based on the third edition of the Realencyklopadie founded by J. J. Herzog, and edited by Albert Hauck, prepared by more than six hundred scholars and specialists under the supervision of Samuel Macauley Jackson ... (editor-in-chief) with the assistance of Charles Colebrook Sherman and George William Gilmore ... (associate editors) and [others] ... New York and London, Funk and Wagnalls company [1908-c14] 13 v. 27 1/2 cm. Vols. II-XII have abbreviated title which varies slightly; vol. XIII: Index, by George William Gilmore. [BR95.S43] 8-20152
1. Theology—Dictionaries. I. Herzog, Johann Jakob, 1805-1882. II. Schaff, Philip, 1819-1893. III. Hauck, Albert, 1845-1918. IV. Jackson, Samuel Macauley, 1851-1912, ed. V. Sherman, Charles Colebrook, 1860-1927, joint ed. VI. Gilmore, George William, 1858-1933, joint ed. VII. Title.

SCHAFF-HERZOG encyclopedia. 220.
A religious encyclopedia: or, Dictonary of Biblical, historical, doctrinal, and practical theology. Based on the Real-encyklopadie of Herzog, Plitt and Hauck. Ed. by Philip Schaff ... Associate editors: Rev. Samuel M. Jackson ... and Rev. D. S. Schaff ... New York, Funk & Wagnalls [1882-84] 3 v. 28 1/2 cm. Paged continuously. [BR95.S4] 1-11171
1. Theology—Dictionaries. I. Herzog, Johann Jakob, 1805-1882. II. Schaff, Philip, 1819-1893, ed. III. Jackson, Samuel Macauley, 1851-1912, joint ed. IV. Schaff, David Schley, 1852- joint ed. V. Title.

SHANNON, Ellen C. 203
A layman's guide to Christian terms, by Ellen C. Shannon. South Brunswick [N.J.] A. S. Barnes [1969] 347 p. 22 cm. Bibliography: p. 347. [BR95.S45] 69-15776 10.00
1. Theology—Dictionaries. I. Title.

SLEIGH, William Willcocks, b.1796. 268
The Christian's defensive dictionary. Being an alphabetical refutation of the general objections to the Bible... By W. W. Sleigh... Philadelphia, E. C. Biddle, 1837. 437, [1] p. front. (fold. geneal. tab.) 18 cm. "A sketch of the author's life": p. [7]-19. [BR95.S55] 35-35227
1. Theology—Dictionaries. 2. Bible—Dictionaries. I. Title.

STEWART, William, 1910- 260'.3
50 key words: the church. Richmond, Va., John Knox Press [1970] 84 p. 20 cm. On spine: Fifty key words: church. [BR95.S76] 79-82935 1.65
1. Theology—Dictionaries. I. Title. II. Title: The church.

STUBER, Stanley Irving, 1903- ed. 203
The illustrated Bible and church handbook, edited by Stanley I. Stuber. New York, Association Press [1966] 532 p. illus., ports. 24 cm. [BR95.S79] 66-11794
1. Theology — Dictionaries. I. Title.

STUBER, Stanley Irving, 1903- ed. 203
The illustrated Bible and church handbook / edited by Stanley I. Stuber. New York : Galahad Books, [197-] c1966. 532 p. : ill. ; 24 cm. Originally published by Association Press. Includes index. [BR95.S79 1970z] 73-79814 ISBN 0-88365-024-X : 7.95
1. Theology—Dictionaries. I. Title.

WATSON, Richard, 1781-1833. 220.3
A Biblical and theological dictionary: explanatory of the history, manners, and customs of the Jews, and neighbouring nations. With an account of the most remarkable places and persons mentioned in Sacred Scripture; an exposition of the principal doctrines of Christianity; and notices of Jewish and Christian sects and heresies. By Richard Watson. [Revised by the American editors]... New York, Pub. by B. Waugh and T. Mason, for the Methodist Episcopal church, 1832. 2 p. l., 1003 p. fold. maps (incl. front.) 23 1/2 cm. "Only that part of the work from the eight hundred and forty second page has been printed under the superintendence of the present editor; the former part having passed through the press previous to the last general conference."--Advertisement to the American edition, signed: N. Bangs. [BR95.W45 1882] 15-24171
1. Theology—Dictionaries. 2. Bible—Dictionaries. I. Bangs, Nathan, 1778-1862. II. Title.

WATSON, Richard, 1781-1833. 220.3
A Biblical and theological dictionary: explanatory of the history, manners and customs of the Jews, and neighbouring nations. With an account of the most remarkable places and persons mentioned in Sacred Scripture; an exposition of the principal doctrines of Christianity: and notices of Jewish and Christian sects and heresies. By Richard Watson. [Revised by the American editors]... New York, Pub. by B. Waugh and T. Mason, for the Methodist Episcopal church, 1833. 2 p. l., 1003 p. fold. maps. 23 cm. "Only that part of the work from the eight hundred and forty second page has been printed under the superintendence of the present editor."--Advertisement to the American edition, signed: N. Bangs. [BR95.W45 1833] 32-10509
1. Theology—Dictionaries. 2. Bible—Dictionaries. I. Bangs, Nathan, 1778-1862. II. Title.

WHITE, Richard Clark, 1926- 203
The vocabulary of the church: a pronunciation guide. New York, Macmillan, 1960. xiv, 178 p. 22 cm. [BR95.W53] 60-11810
1. Theology — Dictionaries. I. Title.

WRIGHT, Charles Henry Hamilton, 1836-1909, ed. 203
A Protestant dictionary, containing articles on the history, doctrines, and practices of the Christian Church, edited by Charles H. H. Wright and Charles Neil. London, Hodder and Stoughton, 1904. Detroit, Gale Research Co., 1972. xv, 832 p. illus. 23 cm. Includes bibliographical references. [BR95.W7 1972] 73-155436 27.50
1. Catholic Church—Doctrinal and controversial works—Protestant authors. 2. Theology—Dictionaries. 3. Protestantism—Dictionaries. I. Neil, Charles, 1841- joint ed. II. Title.

Theology—Dictionaries—German.

MOSSE, Walter M. 203
A theological German vocabulary; German theological key words illustrated in quotations from Martin Luther's Bible and the Revised standard version, by Walter M. Mosse. New York, Octagon Books, 1968 [c1955] viii, 148 p. 21 cm. [BR95.M6 1968] 68-15887
1. Theology—Dictionaries—German. 2. German language—Dictionaries—English. I. Title.

ZIEFLE, Helmut W., 1939- 203'.31
Dictionary of modern theological German / Helmut W. Ziefle. Grand Rapids, Mich. : Baker Book House, c1982. 199 p. ; 22 cm. [BR95.Z53 1982] 19 82-70464 ISBN 0-8010-9929-3 (pbk.) : 9.95
1. Theology—Dictionaries—German. 2. German language—Dictionaries—English. 3. German language—Terms and phrases. I. Title.

Theology, Doctrinal.

ABAILARD, Pierre, 1079-1142. 230'.2
Sic et non : a critical edition / Peter Abailard ; [edited by] Blanche B. Boyer and Richard McKeon. Chicago : University of Chicago Press, 1975. p. cm. Includes indexes. [BT70.A2 1975] 74-7567 ISBN 0-226-00058-3
1. Theology, Doctrinal. I. Boyer, Blanche Beatrice. II. McKeon, Richard Peter, 1900- III. Title.

ADAMS, Nehemiah, 1806-1878. 230
Evenings with the doctrines. By Nehemiah Adams... Boston, Gould and Lincoln. New York, Sheldon and company; [etc., etc.] 1861. viii p. 1 l., [11]-415 p. 20 1/2 cm. [BT75.A2] 39-5051
1. Theology, Doctrinal. I. Title.

AGAT'ANGEGHOS. 230.1'62
The teaching of Saint Gregory; an early Armenian catechism. Translation and

commentary by Robert W. Thomson. Cambridge, Mass., Harvard University Press, 1970. 206 p. 24 cm. (Harvard Armenian texts and studies, 3) Translation of Vardapetowt'iwn Srboyn Grigori (romanized form) which forms part 2 of the author's Patmowt'iwn (romanized form) Bibliography: p. 184-190. [BT70.A3813 1970] 78-115482 ISBN 0-674-87038-7 8.00
1. Gregorius Illuminator, Saint. 2. Theology, Doctrinal. 3. Theology, Doctrinal—History—Armenia. I. Thomson, Robert W., 1934- ed. II. Title. III. Series.

AMES, William, 1576-1633 230
The marrow of theology. Tr. from the 3d Latin ed., 1629, by John D. Eusden. Boston, Pilgrim Pr. [1968] xiii, 353p. port. 23cm. [Milestone lib.] Tr. of Medulla theologica. Bibl. [BT70.A5513] 67-26186 7.95
1. Theology, Doctrinal. I. Eusden, John Dykstra. ed. II. Title.

ANDERSON, Robert T 1928- 230
An introduction to Christianity [by] Robert T. Anderson [and] Peter B. Fischer. New York, Harper & Row [1966] x 234 p. 23 cm. Includes bibliographies. [BT75.2.A5] 66-11260
1. Theology. Doctrinal. I. Fischer, Peter B., joint author. II. Title.

ANDERSON, Tony Marshall, 1888-
Our holy faith. Compiled and edited by T. M. Anderson. Kansas City, Mo., Printed for Asbury College by Beacon Hill Press [c1965] 347 p. 22 cm. Bibliography: p. 347. 68-76551
1. Theology, Doctrinal, 2. Sanctification. I. Title.

ARMSTRONG, George Dodd, 1813- 230 1899.
The theology of Christian experience, designed as an exposition of the "common faith" of the church of God. By Geo. D. Armstrong ... New York, C. Scribner, 1858. ix p., 1 l., 13-342 p. 19 1/2 cm. [BT75.A64] 45-27211
1. Theology, Doctrinal. I. Title.

AUBREY, Edwin Ewart. 230
Present theological tendencies, by Edwin Ewart Aubrey ... New York and London, Harper & brothers, 1936. x, 245 p. 20 cm. "First edition." [BT28.A8] 36-3817
1. Theology, Doctrinal. I. Title.

AULEN, Gustaf Emanuel 230 Hildebrand, Bp., 1879-
The faith of the Christian church. Translated from the 5th Swedish ed. by Eric H. Wahlstrom. Philadelphia, Muhlenberg Press [c1960] 403p. 22cm. Translation of Den allmllnneliga kristna tron. Includes bibliography. [BT75.A763 1960] 61-5302
1. Theology, Doctrinal. I. Title.

AULEN, Gustaf Emanuel 230 Hildebrand, Bp., 1879-
The faith of the Christian church; tr. from the 4th Swedish ed. by Eric H. Wahlstrom and G. Everett Arden. Philadelphia, Muhlenberg Press [c1948] 457 p. 24 cm. [BT75.A763] 48-8897
1. Theology. Doctrinal. I. Wahistrom, Eric Herbert, tr. II. Title.

AUSTIN, Samuel, 1760-1830. 230
Dissertations upon several fundamental articles of Christian theology. By Samuel Austin ... Worcester, Printed by W. Manning [1826] 260 p. 25 cm. [BT75.A8] 39-5052
1. Theology, Doctrinal. 2. Atonement. I. Title.

BAKER, Charles F. 230
A dispensational theology, by Charles F. Baker. Pref. by Peter Veltman. Grand Rapids, Mich., Grace Bible College Publications [1971] xiii, 688 p. 25 cm. Bibliography: p. 659-666. [BT75.2.B3] 71-150312 ISBN 0-912340-01-0 9.95
1. Theology, Doctrinal. 2. Dispensationalism. I. Title.

BANCROFT, Emery H. 230
Christian theology, systematic and Biblical, arranged and compiled by Rev. Emery H. Bancroft ... Bible School Park, N.Y., Echoes publishing company [c1930] 2 p. l., [iii]-xxviii, 351 p. 23 1/2 cm. Bibliography: p. 350-351. [BT77.B3 1930] 30-33233
1. Theology, Doctrinal. I. Title.

BANCROFT, Emery Herbert. 230
Christian theology, systematic and Biblical / by Emery H. Bancroft. 2d rev. ed. / edited by Ronald B. Mayers. Grand Rapids : Zondervan Pub. House, c1976. 410 p. ; 23 cm. Includes bibliographical references and index. [BT77.B3 1976] 76-150619
1. Theology, Doctrinal. I. Mayers, Ronald B. II. Title.

BANCROFT, Emery Herbert. 230
Elemental theology, doctrinal and conservative, written and edited by Rev. Emery H. Bancroft ... Binghamton, N.Y., Conservative book and Bible publishing company [c1932] 4 p. l., [xiii]-xxviii p., 1 l., 309, [1] p. 23 1/2 cm. Bibliography: p. 304-306. [BT75.B17] 33-3807
1. Theology, Doctrinal. I. Title.

BANCROFT, Emery Herbert. 230
Elemental theology, doctrinal and conservative, written and edited by Rev. Emery H. Bancroft ... Johnson City, N.Y., Baptist Bible seminary book room [1945] xxii p., 1 l., 326 p. 23 1/2 cm. "Second edition." Bibliography: p. 319-322. [BT75.B17 1945] 45-16320
1. Theology, Doctrinal. I. Title.

BANCROFT, Emery Herbert. 230
Elemental theology, doctrinal and conservative / Emery H. Bancroft ; Ronald B. Mayers, editor. 4th ed. Grand Rapids : Zondervan Pub. House, 1977. 399 p. ; 23 cm. [BT75.B17 1977] 77-154061 9.95
1. Theology, Doctrinal. I. Mayers, Ronald B. II. Title.

BANGS, Nathan, 1778-1862. 230
The errors of Hopkinsianism detected and refuted. In six letters to the Rev. S. Williston ... By Nathan Bangs ... New-York; Printed for the author, by John C. Totten, no. 9 Bowery ... 1815. xi, [18]-324 p. 18 1/2 cm. [BX7251.B29] 7-39361
1. Theology, Doctrinal. 2. Hopkins, Samuel, 1721-1803. I. Williston, Seth, 1770-1851. II. Title. III. Title: Hopkinsianism, The errors of.

BANKS, John Shaw, 1835-1917. 230
A manual of Christian doctrine. By the Rev. John S. Banks ... 1st American from 4th English ed. Edited, with introduction and additions, by Jno. J. Tigert ... Nashville, Tenn., Publishing house Methodist Episcopal church, South, Barbee & Smith, agents, 1897. xxi, 391 p. 19 cm. "Literature" at end of most of the chapters. [BT75.B2] 39-5053
1. Theology, Doctrinal. I. Tigert, John James, 1856-1906, ed. II. Title.

BARRY, Mack C. 230
Every wind of doctrine. Boston, Christopher Pub. House [1952] 155 p. 21 cm. [BT78.B27] 52-25939
1. Theology, Doctrinal. I. Title.

BARTH, Karl, 1886- 230
Church dogmatics; a selection. Introd. by Helmut Gollwitzer. Tr. [from German] ed. by G. W. Bromiley [Gloucester, Mass., Peter Smith, 1963, c.1961] 262p. 21cm. (Harper torchbk., Cloister lib., TB95 rebound) 3.50
1. Theology, Doctrinal. I. Title.

BARTH, Karl, 1886- 230
Church dogmatics; a selection. Introd. by Helmut Gollwitzer. Tr. [from German] ed. by G. W. Bromiley. New York, Harper & Row [1962, c.1961] 262p. 21cm. (Harper torchbks. TB95: Cloister lib.) 1.50 pap.,
1. Theology, Doctrinal. I. Title.

BARTH, Karl, 1886- 230
Church dogmatics. [Authorised translation by G. T. Thomson. New York, Scribner, 1955- v. in 23cm. Half title: each pt. has also special t.p. Contents.v. 1. The doctrine of the word of God. 2 pts. [BT75.B283] 57-1428
1. TeOlogy, Doctrinal. I. Title.

BARTH, Karl, 1886-
Church dogmatics; a selection, with an introduction by Helmut Gollwitzer. Translated and edited by G. W. Bromiley. New York, Harper [1962] viii, 262 p. (Harper torchbooks, TB95. The Cloister library) NUC63
1. Theology, Doctrinal. I. Bromiley, Geoffrey William, ed. and tr. II. Title.

BARTH, Karl, 1886- 238.1
Dogmatics in outline. Translated by G. T. Thomson. [1st American ed.] New York, Philosophical Library [1949] 155 p. 22 cm. [BT77.B345] 49-10669
1. Theology, Doctrinal. 2. Apostles' Creed. I. Title.

BARTH, Karl, 1886-1968. 230
Karl Barth, preaching through the Christian year : a selection of exegetical passages from the Church dogmatics by Karl Barth / taken from the English translation edited by G. W. Bromiley and T. F. Torrance ; selected by John McTavish and Herold Wells. Grand Rapids : Eerdmans, [1978] p. cm. [BT75.B2834 1978] 77-16275 ISBN 0-8028-1725-4 : 5.95
1. Theology, Doctrinal. I. McTavish, John. II. Wells, Harold. III. Title.

BARTON, George Aaron, 1859- 230
Christ and evolution; a study of the doctrine of redemption in the light of modern knowledge, by George A. Barton ... Philadelphia, University of Pennsylvania press, 1934. xi, 166 p. 21 cm. [BT77.B35] 35-68
1. Theology, Doctrinal. 2. Christianity—20th cent. 3. Redemption. 4. Kingdom of God. 5. Religion and science—1900- I. Title.

BATTLES, Ford Lewis. 230'.42
Analysis of the Institutes of the Christian religion of John Calvin / Ford Lewis Battles, assisted by John Walchenbach. Grand Rapids, Mich. : Baker Book House, c1980. 421 p. ; 22 cm. "Errata" slip mounted on p. [10] Includes bibliographical references. [BX9420.I69B37] 19 79-57385 ISBN 0-8010-0766-6 (pbk.) : 10.95
1. Calvin, Jean, 1509-1564. Institutio Christianae religionis 2. Reformed Church—Doctrinal and controversial works. 3. Theology, Doctrinal. I. Walchenbach, John, joint author. II. Title.

BAUM, Gregory, 1923- 230.2
Man becoming; God in secular language. [New York] Herder and Herder [1970] xiv, 285 p. 22 cm. Includes bibliographical references. [BT75.2.B35] 71-110889 6.95
1. Theology, Doctrinal. I. Title.

BEARD, Richard, 1799-1880. 260
Lectures on theology. By Richard Beard ... Second series. Nashville, Board of publication of the Cumberland Presbyterian church, 1873. 572 p. 23 cm. [BT75.B3 2d ser.] 3-25939
1. Theology, Doctrinal. 2. Cumberland Presbyterian church—Doctrinal and controversial works. I. Cumberland Presbyterian board of publication. II. Title.

BECKWITH, Clarence Augustine, 260 1849-1931.
Realities of Christian theology; an interpretation of Christian experience, by Clarence Augustine Beckwith ... Boston and New York, Houghton, Mifflin and company, 1906. xiv, [2], 406 p., 1 l. 20 cm. [BT75.B33] 6-37867
1. Theology, Doc..inal. I. Title.

BENNET, Moses P. 230
Lectures on theology: or, Dissertations on some of the most important doctrines of the Christian religion. By The rev. Moses P. Bennet ... Kittanning, Pa., Printed for the author by Copley, Croll, & co., 1826. vi, [7]-286 p. diagr. 19 cm. [BT75.B35] 44-34875
1. Theology, Doctrinal. I. Title.

BERKHOF, Hendrikus. 230
Christian faith : an introduction to the study of the faith / Hendrikus Berkhof ; translated by Sierd Woudstra. Grand Rapids : Eerdmans, c1979. p. cm. Translation of Christelijk geloof. Includes index. [BT75.2.B4713] 79-12673 ISBN 0-8028-3521-X : 12.95
1. Theology, Doctrinal. I. Title.

BERKHOF, Louis, 1873- 230
Manual of Reformed doctrine, by Louis Berkhof ... Grand Rapids, Mich., Wm. B. Eerdmans publishing co., 1838. 372 p. 21 cm. Based on the author's "Reformed dogmatics." "Refernces for further study" at the end of each chapter. [BT75.B36 Manual] 40-16250
1. Theology, Doctrinal. 2. Reformed church—Doctrinal and controversial works. I. Title.

BERKHOF, Louis, 1873- 230
Reformed dogmatics, by Louis Berhof ... Grand Rapids, Mich., Wm. B. Eerdmans publishing co., 1932. 3 v. 24 cm. Bibliography (p. 351-358) [BT75.B36] 32-2484
1. Theology, Doctrial. I. Title.
Contents omitted.

BERKHOF, Louis, 1873- 230
Summary of Christian doctrine for senior classes. by Louis Berkhof ... Grand Rapids, Mich. Wm. B. Eerdmans publishing co., 1938. 5 p. l., 198 p. 20 cm. "My 'Manual of Reformed doctrine' ... in an abrigded form."--Pref. [BT75.B362] 40-16845
1. Theology, Doctrinal. 2. Reformed church—Doctrinal and controversial works. 3. Religious education—Text-books for young peoples. I. Title.

BERKHOF, Louis, 1873- 230
Systematic theology, by L. Berkhof ... 2d rev. and enl. ed. Grand Rapids, Mich., Wm. B. Eerdmans publishing company, 1941. 759 p. 24 cm. Previously published under title: Reformed dogmatics. Bibliography: p. 739-745. [BT75.B38] 41-24701
1. Theology, Doctrinal. 2. Reformed church—Doctrinal and controversial works. I. Title.

BERKHOF, Louis, 1873- 230
Systematic theology, by L. Berkhof ... 2d rev. and enl. ed. Grand Rapids, Mich., Um B. Eerdmans publishing company, 1941. 750 p. 23 1/2 cm. Previously published under title: Reformed dogmatics. Textual aid to Systematic theology; a practical handbook ... with all the essential proof texts, covering each doctrine and classified by subjects, printed in full and giving Bible references. Grand Rapids, Mich., Wm. B. Eerdmans publishing co., 1942. p. 1., 11-122 p. 20 cm. Bibliography: p. 739-745. [BT75.B38] 41-24701
1. Theology, Doctrinal. 2. Reformed church—Doctrinal and controversal works. I. Title.

BIBLE. N. T. English. 1955. 230.7 Authorized.
Selections from John Wesley's Notes on the New Testament, systematically arr. with explanatory comments [by] John Lawson. Chicago, A. R. Allenson [1955] 219p. 20cm. [BX8330.W36] 55-1584
1. Theology. Doctrinal. 2. Methodist Church—Doctrinal and controversial works. I. Wesley, John, 1703-1791. II. Lawson, John. III. Title.

BINNEY, Amos.
The theological compend: containing a system of divinity, or a brief view of the evidences, doctrines, morals, and institutions of Christianity ... New York, T. Mason & G. Lane, 1840. 128 p. 24*. 1-5189
I. Title.

BINNEY, Amos, 1802-1878. 230
Binney's Theological compend improved, containing a synopsis of the evidences, doctrines, morals and institutions of Christianity. Designed for Bible classes, theological students, and young preachers. By Rev. Amos Binney and Rev. Daniel Steele ... New York, Nelson & Phillips; Cincinnati, Hitchcock & Walden, 1875. 195 p. 18 cm. [BT77.B5 1875] 1-5193
1. Theology. Doctrinal. I. Steele, Daniel, 1824-1914, joint author. II. Title. III. Title: Theological compend improved.

BINNEY, Amos, 1802-1878. 230
The theological compend: containing a system of divinity; a brief view of the evidence, doctrines, morals, and institutions of Christianity. Designed for the benefit of families, Bible classes, and Sunday School. By Amos Binney ... New York, Carlton & Porter, 1857. 128 p. 16 cm. [BT77.B5 1857] 41-40819
1. Theology, Doctrinal. I. Title.

BINNEY, Amos, 1802-1878. 230
The theological compend: containing a system of divinity, or a brief view of the evidences, doctrines, morals, and institutions of Christianity. Designed for the benefit of families, Bible classes, and Sunday schools. By Amos Binney ... New

York, G. Lane & P. P. Sandford, for the Methodist Episcopal church, 1842. 128 p. 14 cm. [BT77.B5 1842] 38-33124
1. Theology, Doctrinal. I. Title.

BINNEY, Amos, 1802-1878. 230
The theological compend: containing a system of divinity, or a brief view of the evidences, doctrines, morals, and institutions of Christianity. Designed for the benefit of families, Bible classes, and Sunday schools. By Amos Binney ... Rev. ed. Nashville, Tenn., Publishing house of the Methodist Episcopal church, South, Barbee & Smith, agents, 1898. 160 p. 16 cm. [BT77.B5 1898] 1-29439
1. Theology. Doctrinal. I. Title.

BLACKWELL, Thomas, 1660?- 1728. 230
Forms sacra, or, A sacred platform of natural and revealed religion ; exhibiting, a Scriptural and rational account of these three important heads, 1st. Of creation ... 2dly. Of the whole complex eternal plans of divine predestination ... 3dly. Of the wise divine procedure in accomplishing each part ... By the pious and learned Thomas Blackwell, to which is now added, an introduction ... By Simon Williams ... Boston; Printed by William M'Alpine, for the Rev. Mr. Williams, of Windham. M, DCC, LXXIV. 1774. xvii, [1], xviii, vii, 8-830, [1] p. 16 cm. Includes List of subscribers. First published in Edinburgh in 1710, with title: Schema sacrum; or, A sacred scheme of natural and revealed religion ... [BT70.B6 1774a] 26-1591
1. Theology, Doctrinal. I. Williams, Simon, 1729-1793, ed. II. Title.

BLACKWELL, Thomas 1660?-1728 230
Schema sacrum: or, A sacred scheme of natural and revealed religion. By Thomas Blackwell. Lancaster [Pa.]: Printed by Francis Bailey, at the printing and post-offices, near the market, MDCCLXXVI. 1776. 3 p. l., iv, 331, xxix p. 16 1/2 cm. Added t.-p., with title: Schema sacrum: or, A sacred scheme of natural and revealed religion: making a Scriptural rational account of these three heads: as first, of creation ... And secondly, of the whole complex eternal scheme of divine predestination ... And thirdly, of the wise divine procedure in accomplishing the whole parts of the foresaid scheme. First published in Edinburgh in 1710. "List of subscribers": xxix p. at end. [BT70.B6 1776] 22-821
1. Theology, Doctrinal. I. Title.

BLOESCH, Donald G., 1928- 230 s
God, authority, and salvation / Donald G. Bloesch. 1st ed. San Francisco : Harper & Row, c1978. xii, 265 p. ; 24 cm. (His Essentials of evangelical theology ; v. 1) Includes bibliographical references and indexes. [BR1640.A25B57 vol. 1] [BT75.2] 230 77-15872 ISBN 0-06-060798-X : 12.95
1. Theology, Doctrinal. 2. Evangelicalism. I. Title.

BOETTNER, Loraine. 230
Studies in theology. Grand Rapids, W. B. Eerdmans Pub. Co., 1947. 351 p. 24 cm. Chap. 1, 4 & 5 also pub. separately; chap. 2 & 3 appeared serially in Christianity today, 1937, and the Evangelical quarterly, London, 1938-39, respectively. [BT75.B58] 47-29563
1. Theology, Doctrinal. I. Title.
Contents omitted.

BONAVENTURA, Saint, cardinal, 1221-1274. 230.2
Breviloquium, by St. Bonaventure, translated by Erwin Esser Nemmers ... St. Louis, Mo. and London, B. Herder book co., 1946. xxii, 248 p. 21 cm. "Bibliographical notations: p. xvii-xvii. [BX1749.B62] 46-23336
1. Theology, Doctrinal. 2. Catholic church—Doctrinal and controversial works. I. Nemmers, Erwin Esser, 1916- tr. II. Title.

BOSLEY, Harold Augustus, 1907- 230
A firm faith for today. [1st ed.] New York, Harper [1950] 283 p. 22 cm. Bibliography: p. 273-278. [BT75.B59] 50-6190
1. Theology, Doctrinal. I. Title.

BOYCE, James Petigru, 1827- 1888. 230
Abstract of systematic theology, by James P. Boyce ... Printed (not published) for the exclusive use of his pupils. Louisville, Ky., C. T. Dearing, 1882. 3 p. l., [4]-514 p. 23 cm. [BT75.B6] 39-5055
1. Theology, Doctrinal. 2. Baptists—Doctrinal and controversial works. I. Title.

BRAATEN, Carl E., 1929- 236
The future of God; the revolutionary dynamics of hope [by] Carl E. Braaten. [1st ed.] New York, Harper & Row [1969] 186 p. 21 cm. Bibliographical references included in "Notes" (p. [167]-181) [BT75.2.B68] 69-17024 5.95
1. Theology, Doctrinal. 2. Eschatology. 3. Hope. 4. Revolution (Theology) I. Title.

BRADLEY, Rolland, 1896- 230
Our basic faith. [Austin, Tex.] Von Boeckmann-Jones Co., 1964. x 122 p. 19 cm. Bibliographical footnotes. [BT78.B72] 64-8144
1. Theology, Doctrinal. 2. Religions. I. Title.

BRECKINRIDGE, Robert Jefferson, 1800-1871. 260
The knowledge of God, objectively considered, being the first part of theology considered as a science of positive truth, both inductive and deductive. By Robert J. Breckinridge ... New York, R. Carter & brothers, 1858. 530 p. 24 cm. Contined by the author's The knowledge of God, subjectively considered ... 1859. [BT75. B77] 39-5060
1. Theology, Doctrinal. 2. Presbyterian church—Doctrinal and controversial works. I. Title.

BRECKINRIDGE, Robert Jefferson, 1800-1871. 260
The knowledge of God, subjectively considered, being the second part of theology considered as a science of positive truth, both inductive and deductive. By Robert J. Breckinridge ... New York, R. Carter & brothers; Louisville, A. Davidson, 1859. xvi, 697 p. 24 cm. A continuation of the author's The knowledge of God, objectively considered ... 1858. [BT75.B78] 39-5061
1. Theology, Doctrinal. 2. Presbyterian church—Doctrinal and controversial works. I. Title.

BROMILEY, Geoffrey William. 230'.092'4
Introduction to Karl Barth / by Geoffrey W. Bromiley. Grand Rapids : Eerdmans, c1979. p. cm. [BT75.B286B76] 79-15397 ISBN 0-8028-1804-8 pbk. : 7.95
1. Barth, Karl, 1886-1968. Die Kirchliche Dogmatik. 2. Theology, Doctrinal. I. Title.

BROWN, William Adams, 1865- 260
Christian theology in outline, by William Adams Brown... New York, C. Scribner's sons, 1906. xiv, [2], 468 p. 22 1/2 cm. "A classified bibliography": p. [427]-454. [BT75.B83] 6-44353
1. Theology, Doctrinal. I. Title.

BROWN, William Adams, 1865- 230
Modern theology and the preaching of the gospel, by William Adams Brown... New York, C. Scribner's sons, 1914. viii p., 1 l., 274 p. 19 1/2 cm. Published in the Biblical world for 1913-14. ef. Pref. [BT75.B834] 14-15195
1. Theology, Doctrinal. I. Title.

BROWN, William Adams, 1865- 1943. 230
Christian theology in outline / by William Adams Brown. New York : AMS Press, 1976. xiv, 468 p. ; 19 cm. Reprint of the 1906 ed. published by Scribner, New York. Includes index. "A classified bibliography": p. [427]-454. [BT75.B83 1976] 75-41044 ISBN 0-404-14648-1 : 26.00
1. Theology, Doctrinal. I. Title.

BRUNNER, Heinrich Emil, 1889- 230.08
The scandal of Christianity; the gospel as stumbling block to modern man [by] Emil Brunner. Richmond, Va., Knox [c.1965] 115p. 19cm. Five lect. delivered as the Robertson lectures, Trinity College, Glasgow, March, 1948. [BT75.B847] 65-12729 1.25 pap.,
1. Theology, Doctrinal. 2. Apologetics—20th cent. I. Title.

BRUNNER, Heinrich Emil, 1889- 230
The scandal of Christianity. Philadelphia, Westminster Press [1951] 116 p. 20 cm. (The Andrew C. Zenos memorial lectures. 1946) [BT75.B847] 51-12829
1. Theology. Doctrinal. 2. Apologetics—20th cent. I. Title.

BRUNNER, Heinrich Emil, 1889- 230
The word and the world, by Emil Brunner ... New York, C. Scribner's sons, 1931. 126, [1] p. 19 cm. Printed in Great Britain. "Lectures ... delivered in King's college [London] in March of this year [1931]"--Pref. "The interest in the dialectical theology ... encourages me to give these lectures to the public."--Pref. [BT15.B7] 32-6320
1. Theology, Doctrinal. I. Title. II. Title: Dialectical theology.

BRUNNER, Heinrich Emil, 1889- 1966. 230
Dogmatics. Translated by Olive Wyon. Philadelphia, Westminster Press [1950- v. 24 cm. Contents.Contents.—v. 1. The Christian doctrine of God. —v. 3. The Christian doctrine of the church, faith, and the consummation. [BT75.B842] 50-6821
1. Theology, Doctrinal. I. Title.

BUBE, Richard H 1927- 230
To every man an answer; a systematic study of the scriptural basis of Christian doctrine. Chicago, Moody Press [1955] 510p. 24cm. [BT75.B848] 55-4050
1. Theology, Doctrinal. I. Title.

BUEL, Samuel, 1815-1892. 230
A treatise of dogmatic theology, by the Rev. Samuel Buel ... New York, T. Whittaker, 1890. 2 v. 23 cm. [BT75.B85] 39-5065
1. Theology, Doctrinal. 2. Protestant Episcopal church in the U. S. A.—Doctrinal and controversial works. I. Title.

BURI, Fritz, 1907- 230
Theology of existence, Tr. by Harold H. Oliver, Gerhard Onder. Greenwood, S. C., Attic Pr., 1965. xiv, 112p. 23cm. Bibl. [BT75.2.B7813] 65-29261 4.00
1. Theology, Doctrinal. 2. Existentialism. I. Title.

BURNS, Lytle, 1858- 230
Bible truth presented in prose and poetry, by Lytle Burns. A dissertation in line with the teaching of the ancient Waldenses, also the doctrinal teachings of the reformers, Luther, Calvin and Toplady of the Church of England. Nashville, Baird-Ward press, 1942. 5 p. l. 9-115 p. front. (port.) 20 cm. [BT85.B8] 46-36733
1. Theology, Doctrinal. I. Title.

BURROW, Reuben, 1798-1868. 230
Medium theology. Lectures of Rev. Reuben Burrow ... With autobiographical sketch and short, account of funeral. Arranged and prepared by his son, Rev. A. G. Burrow ... Nashville, Tenn., Printed at the Cumberland Presbyterian publishing house, 1881. viii, 9-628 [1] p. 23 1/2 cm. [TB75.B9] 39-8926
1. Theology, Doctrinal. 2. Cumberland Presbyterian church—Doctrinal and controversial works. I. Burrow, Allen G. II. Title.

BUSWELL, James Oliver, 1895- 230
A systematic theology of the Christian religion. Grand Rapids, Zondervan Pub. House [1962-63] 2 v. 23 cm. [BT75.2.B8] 62-16807
1. Theology, Doctrinal. I. Title.

BUSWELL, James Oliver, 1895- 230
A Systematic theology of the Christian religion. Grand Rapids, Zondervan Pub. House [1962-63] 2 v. 23 cm. [BT75.2.B8] 62-16807
1. Theology, Doctrinal. I. Title.

BUTLER, John Jay, 1814-1891. 230
Natural and revealed theology. A system of lectures, embracing the divine existence and attributes; authority of the Scriptures; Scriptural doctrine; institutions and ordinances of the Christian church. By John J. Butler ... Dover [N.H.] Freewill Baptist printing establishment, W. Burr, printer, 1861. xxiii, [25]-456 p. 22 1/2 cm. [BT75.B95] 39-5066
1. Theology, Doctrinal. I. Title.

BUTTRICK, George Arthur, 1892- 230
So we believe, so we pray. Nashville, Abingdon [1962, c.1951] 256p. (Apex bks., H2) Bibl. 1.25 pap.,
1. Theology, Doctrinal. 2. Lord's prayer. I. Title.

BUTTRICK, George Arthur, 1892- 230
So we believe, so we pray. New York, Abingdon-Cokesbury [1951] 256 p. 23 cm. "References": p. 233-248. [BT75.B96] 51-9467
1. Theology, Doctrinal. 2. Lord's prayer. I. Title.

BYRUM, Russell R. 260
Christian theology; a systematic statement of Christian doctrine for the use of theological students, by Russell R. Byrum ... Anderson, Ind., Gospel? trumpet company [c1925] 680 p. 23 cm. [BT75.B97] 25-20285
1. Theology, Doctrinal. I. Title.

CALVIN, Jean, 1509-1564. 230'.4'2
Institution of the Christian religion : embracing almost the whole sum of piety & whatever is necessary to know the doctrine of salvation : a work most worthy to be read by all persons zealous for piety, and recently published ; Preface to the most Christian King of France, wherein this book is offered to him as a confession of faith / John Calvin of Noyon, author ; translated and annotated by Ford Lewis Battles. Atlanta : John Knox Press, 1975. p. cm. Translation of Christianae religionis institutio ... published in 1536. Includes indexes. [BX9420.I65 1975] 74-3718 ISBN 0-8042-0489-6 : 9.95
1. Reformed Church—Doctrinal and controversial works. 2. Theology, Doctrinal. I. Battles, Ford Lewis. II. Title.

CAMBRON, Mark G 1911- 230
Bible doctrines; beliefs that matter. Introd. by Herbert Lockyer. Grand Rapids, Zondervan Pub. House [1954] 288p. 23cm. [BT75.C18] 55-248
1. Theology, Doctrinal. I. Title.

CAMBRON, Mark Gray, 1911- 230
Bible doctrines beliefs that matter. Introd. by Herbert Lockyer. Grand Rapids, Zondervan Pub. House [1954] 288p. 23cm. [BT75.C18] 55-248
1. Theology, Doctrinal. I. Title.

CAMPBELL, George, 1719-1796 230
Lectures on systematic theology and pulpit eloquence, by the late George Campbell ... To which are added, Dialogues on eloquence by M. de Fenelon ... Edited by Henry J. Ripley. Boston, Lincoln and Edmands 1832. vi, [7]-206 iv, [2] 7-102 p. 23 1/2 cm. Lectures composed for the students of divinity to Marischal college, and first delivered in 1772 and 1773 cf. Advertisement. "Dialogues concerning eloquence in general ...by M. de Fenelon", translated and edited by William Stevenson has special t.-p. and separate paging. [BT75.C2 1832] 31-11670
1. Theology, Doctrinal. 2. Preaching. 3. Oratory. I. Fehelon, Francois de Salignac de La Mothe, 1651-1715. Dialogues sur l'eloquence. II. Title. III. Title: Dialogues concerning eloquence.

CAMPBELL, Reginald John, 1867- 230
The new theology, by R. J. Campbell... New York, The Macmillan company, 1907. ix, 258 p. 20 cm. [BT78.C2] 7--11604
1. Theology, Doctrinal. I. Title.

CARR, James B
Basic Bible doctrines. Manhattan, Kan., Manhattan Bible College Press, 1966. 204 p. 68-29509
1. Theology, Doctrinal I. Title.

CATLIN, Jacob, 1758-1826. 230
A compendium of the system of divine truth: contained in a series of essays; in which the principal subjects contained in the Holy Scriptures, are carefully arranged, briefly discussed and improved, by Jacob Catlin ... Hartford, George Goodwin & sons .....printers, 1818. viii, 314, [2] p. 18 cm. "Subscribners' names": 2 p. at end. [BT77.C2] a 32
1. Theology, Doctrinal I. Title.

CATLIN, Jacob, 1758-1826. 230
A compendium of the system of divine truth, contained in a series of essays, in

which the principal subjects contained in the Holy Scriptures, are carefully arranged briefly discussed, and improved. By Jacob Catlin ... Middletown, Printed by E. & H. Clark, 1824. viii, [13]-304 p. 18 cm. [BT77.C25 1824] 41-33317
1. Theology, Doctrinal. I. Title.

CATLIN, Jacob, 1758-1826. 230
A compendium of the system of divine truth, by Jacob Catlin ... to which is added appropriate questions .. 3d ed. Boston, Doctrinal tract and book society, 1851. viii, 302 p. 20 cm. [BT77.C25 1851] 39-803
1. Theology, Doctrinal. I. Doctrinal tract and book society, Boston. II. Title.

CHAFER, Lewis Sperry, 1871- 230
Systematic theology. Dallas, Dallas Seminary Press 1947-48 8 v. port. 24 cm. Contents.--v. 1. Prolegomenao Biology. Theology proper.--v. 2. Anegelogy. Anthropology. Hamartiology.--v. 3. Soteriology.--v. 4. Ecclesiology. Eschatology.--v. 5. Christology.--v. 6. Phenmatoilogy.--v. 7. Doctrinal summarization.--v. 8. Biographical sketch and indexes. [BT75.C28] 49-5285
1. Theology, Doctrinal. I. Title.

CHAFER, Lewis Sperry, 1871-1952.
Systematic theology, Dallas, Tex., Dallas Seminary Press [1964, c1947-48] 8 v. port. Contents.Contents.--v.1. Prolegomena. Bibliology. Theology proper.--v.2. Angelology. Anthropology. Hamartiology.--v.3. Soteriology.--v.4. Ecclesiology. Eschatology.--v.5. Christology.--v.6. Pneumatology.--v.7. Doctrinal summarization.--v.8. Biographical sketch and index. 68-31500
1. Theology, Doctrinal. I. Title.

CHANDLER, S C. 230
The theology of the Bible, or, The true doctrines of the Christian faith plainly stated and defended; with a Key to the Revelations[!] By S. C. Chandler ... New-York, The author 1853. iv, [5]-408 p. front. (port.) 20 cm. [BT75.C4] 39-5067
1. Theology, Doctrinal. 2. Bible—Theology. 3. Bible. N. T. Revelation—Criticism, interpretation, etc. 4. Bible—Criticism, interpretation, etc.—N. T. Revelation. I. Title.

CHAPELL, Frederick Leonard, 1836-1900. 260
Biblical and practical theology, by Rev. F. L. Chapell. Philadelphia, H. Chapell, 1901. viii, 307 p. illus. 20 cm. [BT75.C43] 1-30708
1. Theology, Doctrinal. 2. Theology, Practical. I. Title.

CLARK, William Crawford, 1849- 230
The Christian faith; a handbook of Christian teaching, by W. C. Clark... Boston, Sherman, French & company, 1915. 6 p. l., 347 p. 20 1/2 cm. [BT77.C5] 15-1232
1. Theology, Doctrinal. I. Title.

CLARKE, Adam, 1760?-1832. 230
Christian theology, by Adam Clarke...Selected from his published and unpublished writings and systematically arranged; with a life of the author; by Samuel Dunn... New York, T. Mason and G. Lane, 1840. 438 p. 18 1/2 cm. "Second edition." [BT75.C53 1840] 33-2237
1. Theology, Doctrinal. I. Title.

CLARKE, William Newton, 1841-1912. 280
An outline of Christian theology. For the use of students in Hamilton, N. Y. By William N. Clarke. Cambridge, J. Wilson and son, 1894. 2 p. l., 444 p. 24 cm. [BT75.C55 1894] 39-5789
1. Theology, Doctrinal. I. Title.

CLARKE, William Newton, 1841-1912. 230
An outline of Christian theology, by William Newton Clarke ... New York, C. Scribner's sons, 1898. ix, 488 p. 21 cm. [B755.C55 1808] 4-4036
1. Theology, Doctrinal. I. Title.

CLARKE, William Newton, 1841-1912. 230
An outline of Christian theology, by William Newton Clarke ... 6th ed. New York, C. Scribner's sons, 1899. ix, 488 p. 21 1/2 cm. [BT75.C55 1899] 15-23424
1. Theology, Doctrinal. I. Title.

CLINE, Colin Marion, 1873- 230
A manual of Christian theology, Prepared for the use of the students in the Western Baptist theological seminary, Portland, Oregon, by Colin Marion Cline... [Portland, Or., Cutler printing company, 1936] 7 p. l., [3]-346 p. 20 1/2 cm. [BT75.C57] 41-38405
1. Theology, Doctrinal. 2. Baptists—Doctrinal and controversial works. I. Portland, Or. Western Baptist theological seminary. II. Title.

COBB, Howell, b.1795. 230
An examination of the origin, progress and unity of the church of God; together with its doctrines, institutions and ordinances: exhibiting the connection of its various dispensations in the development of the plan of human salvation; with an appendix containing the religious principles of the church. The whole comprising a system of general theology. By Howell Cobb. Georgia [New York, E. O. Jenkins, printer] 1854. x, 11-253 p. 23 cm. [BT75.C6] 39-5070
1. Theology, Doctrinal. I. Title.

COMO, John Freeman. 230.4
In the light of the supernatural; or, Some difficulties in Christian theology removed, by Rev. John F. Como ... Boston, The Christopher publishing house [c1930] 69 p. 21 cm. [BR125.C675] 30-10516
I. Title.

CONE, James H. 200
A Black theology of liberation [by] James H. Cone. [1st ed.] Philadelphia, Lippincott [1970] 254 p. 21 cm. (C. Eric Lincoln series in Black religion) [BT78.C59 1970] 74-120333 5.50
1. Theology, Doctrinal. 2. Freedom (Theology) 3. Negroes—Religion. I. Title. II. Series.

CONNER, Walter Thomas, 1877- 230
Christian doctrines [by] W.T. Conner ... Nashville, Tenn., Broadman press [c1937] 4 p. l., 7-349 p. 20 cm. Published, 1924, under title: A system of Christian doctrine. [BT75.C65 1937] 37-22925
1. Theology, Doctrinal. I. Title.

CONNER, Walter Thomas, 1877- 230
The gospel of redemption, by Walter T. Conner. Nashville, Tenn., Broadman press [1945] 6 p. l., 369 p. 20 cm. "A revision and enlargement of some things that I published...[in] my former book, A system of Christian doctrine."--Pref. [BT75.C63] 45-15772
1. Theology, Doctrinal. I. Title.

COSTAS, Peter J 230
The voice of the living God; a study of the Biblical basis of various Christian beliefs today. [1st ed.] New York, Exposition Press [1956] 182p. 21cm. [BT78.C7] 56-11584
1. Theology, Doctrinal. I. Title.

CULLMANN, Oscar. 230
Christ and time; the primitive Christian conception of time and history. Translated from the German by Floyd V. Filson. Philadelphia, Westminster Press [1950] 253 p. 21 cm. Bibliographical footnotes. [BT78.C83] 50-6855
1. Theology, Doctrinal. 2. Church history—Philosophy. 3. Salvation. I. Title.

CULLMANN, Oscar. 230
Christ and time; the primitive Christian conception of time and history. Translated from the German by Floyd V. Filson. Rev. ed. Philadelphia, Westminster Press [1964] xvi, 253 p. 21 cm. [BT78.C83 1964] 64-2336
1. Theology, Doctronal. 2. Church history — Philosophy. 3. Salvation. I. Title.

CURTIS, Olin Alfred, 1850-1918. 260
The Christian faith personally given in a system of doctrine, by Olin Alfred Curtis ... New York, Eaton & Mains; Cincinnati, Jennings & Graham [c1905] xi, 541 p. 24 cm. [BT75.C78] 5-31859
1. Theology, Doctrinal. I. Title.

DABNEY, Robert Lewis, 1820-1898. 230'.5'1
Lectures in systematic theology. Grand Rapids, Zondervan Pub. House [1972] 903 p. 25 cm. Reprint of the 1878 ed. published under title: Syllabus and notes of the course of systematic and polemic theology taught in Union Theological Seminary, Virginia. [BT75.D2 1972] 73-171200 12.95
1. Presbyterian Church—Doctrinal and controversial works. 2. Theology, Doctrinal. I. Title.

DABNEY, Robert Lewis, 1820-1898. 230
Syllabus and notes of the course of systematic and polemic theology taught in Union theological seminary, Virginia. By R. L. Dabney, D. D. Published by the students. Richmond, Shepperson & Graves, printers, 1871. iv p., 2 l., 3-323 p. 24 cm. [BT75.D2] 39-5071
1. Theology, Doctrinal. 2. Presbyterian church—Doctrinal and controversial works. I. Title.

DAGG, John Leadley, 1794-1884. 260
Manual of theology. Charelston, S. C., Southern Baptist Publication Society, 1859. 2 v. in 1. port. 23 cm. [BT75.D23 1859] 51-50036
1. Theology, Doctrinal. 2. Baptist—Doctrinal and controversial works. I. Title.

DAGG, John Leadley, 1794-1884. 230
A manual of theology. By J. L. Dagg ... Charleston, Southern Baptist publication society, 1857. xii, 13-379 p. 23 cm. [BT75.D23 1857] 39-7011
1. Theology, Doctrinal. 2. Baptists—Doctrinal and controversial works. I. Southern Baptist publication society. II. Title.

DAGG, John Leadley, 1794-1884. 230
Manual of theology. A treatise on Christian doctrine. By J. L. Dagg ... Philadelphia, American Baptist publication society [c1871] xii, 13-379 p. 23 cm. [BT75.D23 1871] 39-7012
1. Theology, Doctrinal. 2. Baptists—Doctrinal and controversial works. I. American Baptist publication society. II. Title.

DAGG, John Leadley, 1794-1884. 230
Manual of theology / J. L. Dagg. New York : Arno Press, 1980. 379, 312 p. : port. ; 23 cm. (The Baptist tradition) Reprint of the 1858-1859 ed. published by Southern Baptist Publication Society, Charleston, S.C. Contents.Contents.—pt. 1. A treatise on Christian doctrine.—pt. 2. A treatise on church order. [BT75.D23 1980] 79-52592 ISBN 0-405-12459-7 : 50.00
1. Baptists—Doctrinal and controversial works. 2. Baptists—Government. 3. Theology, Doctrinal. 4. Sacraments—Baptists. I. Title. II. Series: Baptist tradition.

D'ARCY, Charles Frederick, abp. of Armagh, 1859-
Christianity and the supernatural, by Charles F. D'Arcy ... London, New York [etc.] Longmans, Green and co., 1909. 127 p. 18 cm. (Half-title: Anglican church handbooks) A 34
1. Theology, Doctrinal. 2. Apologetics. I. Title.

[DAY, Edward] b.1759? 230
The independent credends in theology, accompanied by annotations and explanatory ovservations, illustrative thereof, compiled in part, from the works of many celebrated authors, historical, polemic and theological, being and humble attempt to reconcile the salvation of all men, with the attributes of God, and the Scriptures of truth, on the principles of common sense, with references to each subject or section, not originally intended for publication, but prepared for the private use of the writer ... By a country layman aged 73 years. Baltimore, Printed for the author, 1832. 58 p., 1 l. 24 cm. Preface signed: Edward Day. [BT85.D2] 40-21302
1. Theology, Doctrinal. 2. Universalism. I. Title.

DE BLOIS, Austen Kennedy, 1866- ed. 230
The evangelical faith; a series of papers by Professors in the Eastern Baptist theological seminary, edited by President Austen Kennedy de Blois. Philadelphia, Boston [etc.] The Judson press [1931] 3 p. l. 274 p. 20 cm. [BT75.D4] 31-34504
1. Theology, Doctrinal. 2. Christinity. I. Philadelphia. Eastern Baptist theological seminary. II. Title.

DEITZ, Archibald Edwin, 1869- 230
Exploring the deeps; studies in theology, by Archibald E. Deitz ... New York [etc.] Fleming H. Revell company [c1935] 121 p. 20 cm. [BT75.D44] 35-1735
1. Theology, Doctrinal. I. Title.

DENIS, Henri, priest. 230
Where is theology going? Translated by Theodore DuBois. Westminster, Md., Newman Press [1968] v, 106 p. 21 cm. Translation of Pour une prospective theologique. [BT78.D413] 68-20851
1. Theology, Doctrinal. I. Title.

DE WOLF, Lotan Harold, 1905- 230
The case for theology in liberal perspective. Philadelphia, Westminster Press [1959] 206 p. 21 cm. Includes bibliography. [BT75.2.D4] 59-6062
1. Theology, Doctrinal. 2. Liberalism (Religion) I. Title.

DICK, John, 1764-1833. 230
Lectures on theology, by the late Rev. John Dick ... Published under the superintendence of his son, with a preface, memoir, &c by the American editor ... New York, R. Carter & brothers, 1851. 2 v. in 1. front. (port.) 24 cm. "The first edition was published at Edinburgh in 1834."--Pref., signed J. F. [BT75.D5 1851] 32-31800
1. Theology, Doctrinal. 2. Presbyterian church—Doctrinal and controversial works. I. Dick, Andrew Coventry. II. F., J., ed. III. J., F., ed. IV. Title.

DICK, John, 1764-1833. 230
Lectures on theology. By the late Rev. John Dick ... Published under the superintendence of his son. With a preface, memoir, &c., by the American editor ... Philadelphia, F. W. Greenough, 1839. 2 v. 24 cm. "The first edition was published at Edinburgh in 1834."--Pref., signed: J. F. [BT75.D5 1839] 45-51834
1. Theology, Doctrinal. 2. Presbyterian church—Doctrinal and controversial works. I. Dick, Andrew Coventry. II. F., J., ed. III. J. F., ed. IV. Title.

THE Divine principle. 230
[Washington] Holy Spirit Association for the Unification of World Christianity [1973] 643 p. port. 24 cm. Translation of Wolli haeje. [BT75.2.W6313] 73-78869
1. Theology, Doctrinal. 2. History (Theology) I. Segye Kidokkyo T'ongil Sillyong Hyophoe.

DIXON, John W. 230
The physiology of faith : a theory of theological relativity / John W. Dixon, Jr. 1st ed. San Francisco : Harper & Row, c1979. p. cm. Bibliography: p. [BT75.2.D59 1979] 79-1782 ISBN 0-06-061926-0. : 15.00
1. Theology, Doctrinal. I. Title.

DONNE, John, 1573-1631. 230
Essays in divinity, edited by Evelyn M. Simpson. Oxford, Clarendon Press, 1952. xxix, 137 p. facsim. 23 cm. [BT70.D65] 52-9892
1. Theology, Doctrinal. I. Title.

DORCHESTER, Daniel, 1827-1907. 230
Concessions of "liberalists" to orthodoxy. By Daniel Dorchester, D. D. Boston, D. Lothrop and company [1878] 343 p. 18 cm. [BT78.D6] 40-15248
1. Theology, Doctrinal. 2. Philosophy and religion. I. Title.

DOWNS, Francis Shunk, 1885- 230
The heart of the Christian faith, by Francis Shunk Downs ... New York American tract society [c1937] 200 p. 30 cm. [BT77.D65] 37-6562
1. Theology, Doctrinal. I. Title.

DRURY, Augustus Waldo, 1851-
Outlines of doctrinal theology, with

preliminary chapters on theology in general and theological encyclopedia, by A. W. Drury... Dayton, O., The Otterbein press, 1914. 256 p. illus. 20 cm. 14-3108
I. Title.

DUNS, Joannes, Scotus, 1265?-1308? 230'.2
God and creatures; the quodlibetal questions [by] John Duns Scotus. Translated with an introd., notes, and glossary by Felix Alluntis and Allan B. Wolter. [Princeton, N.J.] Princeton University Press, 1975. xxxiv, 548 p. 25 cm. Translation of Quodlibeta. Includes bibliographical references. [BX1749.D8213] 73-2468 ISBN 0-691-07195-0 25.00
1. Theology, Doctrinal. I. Alluntis, Felix, tr. II. Wolter, Allan Bernard, 1913- tr. III. Title. IV. Title: The quodlibetal questions.

DUNS, Joannes, Scotus, 1265?-1308?. 230'.2
God and creatures : the quodlibetal questions / John Duns Scotus ; translated with and introd., notes, and glossary by Felix Alluntis and Allan B. Wolter. Washington, D.C. : Catholic University of America Libraries, 1981, c1975. p. cm. Translation of Quodlibeta. Reprint of the ed. published by Princeton University Press, Princeton, N.J. Includes bibliographical references and indexes. [BX1749.D8213 1981] 19 80-28098 ISBN 0-8132-0557-3 : price unreported.
1. Theology, Doctrinal. I. Alluntis, Felix. II. Wolter, Allan Bernard, 1913- III. [Quodlibeta.] English IV. Title.

DWIGHT, Timothy, 1752-1817. 260
Theology; explained and defended, in a series of sermons; by Timothy Dwight... With a memoir of the life of the author... Middletown, Conn. Printed by Clark and Lyman, for Timothy Dwight, New Haven. 1818-19. 5 v. front. (port.) 23 cm. Portrait by Trumbull. Memoir by his son Sererno E. Dwight. [BT75.D9 1818] 3-27852
1. Theology, Doctrinal. I. Trumbull, John, 1756-1843, illus. II. Dwight, Sereno Edwards, 1786-1850, ed. III. Title.

DWIGHT, Timothy, 1752-1817. 260
Theology; explained and defended, in a series of sermons; by Timothy Dwight...with a Memoir of the life of the author... 3d ed. New Haven, S. Converse, 1823. 4 v. front. (port.) 22 1/2 cm. Portrait of Trumbull. Memoir by the author's son, Sereno E. Dwight. [BT75.D9 1823] 27-7862
1. Theology, Doctrinal. I. Trumbull, John, 1756-1843, illus. II. Dwight, Sereno Edwards, 1786-1850, ed. III. Title.

DWIGHT, Timothy, 1752-1817. 260
Theology; explained and defended, in a series of sermons; by Timothy Dwight...with a Memoir of the life of the author... 6th ed. New York, G. & C. & H. Carvill, 1829. 4 v. 23 cm. Memoir by the author's son, Sereno E. Dwight. [BT75.D9 1829] 27-7864
1. Theology, Doctrinal. I. Dwight, Sereno Edwards, 1786-1850, ed. II. Title.

EDGREN, John Alexis, 1839-1908. 230
Fundamentals of faith; translation from Swedish by J. O. Backlund. Chicago, Baptist Conference Press, 1948. 207 p. port. 20 cm. ([Baptist General Conference of America] Centenary series) Translation of Bibliak troelra. [BT77.E22] 48-5870
1. Theology, Doctrinal. I. Title. II. Series.

EDWARDS, Francis Henry, 1897- 230
The joy in creation and judgment / F. Henry Edwards. Independence, Mo. : Herald Pub. House, c1975. 255 p. ; 21 cm. Includes bibliographical references and index. [BT75.2.E38] 75-12821 ISBN 0-8309-0147-7 : 10.00
1. Theology, Doctrinal. I. Title.

AN elementary course of 230
Biblical theology, translated from the work of Professors Storr and Flatt, with additions by S. S. Schmucker ... 2d ed. Andover [Mass.] Gould and Newman; New-York, Griffin, Wilcox and co., 1836. xvi, [17]-605 p. 23 cm. The author's Doctrinae christianae pars theoretica, 1793, was translated by Flatt, 1803, under title: Lehrbuch der christlichen dogmatik. Schmucker translated this into English, 1826, in 2 volumes; the second edition is condensed from the first. [BT75.S77 1836] [Storr, Gottlob Christian,] 39-10312 1746
1. Theology, Doctrinal. I. Flatt, Karl Christian, 1772-1843, ed. and tr. II. Schmucker, Samuel Simon, 1790-1873, ed. and tr.

ELY, Ezra Stiles, 1786-1861. 260
A synopsis of didactic theology. By the Rev. Ezra Stiles Ely ... Philadelphia, J. Crissy, 1822. v, [7]-803 (i.e. 308) p. 18 1/2cm. Page 308 incorrectly numbered 803. [BT75.E5] 39-11827
1. Theology, Doctrinal. 2. Presbyterian church—Doctrinal and controversial works. I. Title.

EMBRY, James Crawford, bp., 1834-1897. 230
Digest of Christian theology, designed for the use of beginners, in the study of theological science. By Rev. J.C. Embry, d.d. Philadelphia, A.M.E. book concern, 1890. viii, 298 p. 18cm. [BT77.E5] 39-7016
1. Theology, Doctrinal. 2. Methodist church—Doctrinal and controversial works. I. Title.

EMMONS, Nathanael, 1745-1840. 260
A system of divinity, by Nathanael Emmons ... Edited by Jacob Ide ... Boston, Crocker & Brewster, 1842. 2 v. 23 1/2 cm. [BT75.E55] 42-40819
1. Theology, Doctrinal. 2. Ide, Jacob, 1785-1880, ed. I. Title.

EVANS, William, 1870- 230
The great doctrines of the Bible. Section two. By Rev. William Evans ... Chicago, The Bible institute colportage association [1912] 275 p. 23 1/2 cm. The first chapter of this book: "The doctrine of God" (p. 1-48) was issued in 1911 with title "The great doctrines of the Bible. Section one." [BT77.E82] 12-10659
1. Theology, Doctrinal. I. Bible institute colportage association, Chicago. II. Title.

FACKRE, Gabriel J. 230
The Christian story : a narrative interpretation of basic Christian doctrine / by Gabriel Fackre. Grand Rapids : W. B. Eerdmans Pub. Co., c1978. p. cm. [BT75.2.F33] 78-15087 ISBN 0-8028-1735-1 pbk. : 3.95
1. Theology, Doctrinal. I. Title.

FAIRBAIRN, Andrew Martin, 1838-1912. 232.
The place of Christ in modern theology, by A. M. Fairbairn ... New York, C. Scribner's sons, 1903. xxiii, 556 p. 22 cm. "This book appears as the Morse lecture."--Pref. [BT201.F3 1903] 39-5795
1. Jesus Christ—Person and offices. 2. Theology, Doctrinal. 3. Bible. N. T.—Criticism, interpretation, etc.—Hist. 4. Bible—Criticism, interpretation, etc.—Hist.—N. T. I. Title.

FAIRCHILD, James Harris, 1817-1902. 260
Elements of theology, natural and revealed. By James H. Fairchild ... Oberlin, O., E. J. Goodrich [1892] xv, 358 p. 23 cm. [BT75.F2] 37-20277
1. Theology, Doctrinal. I. Title.

FANT, David Jones, 1897- ed. 230
Foundations of the faith; twelve studies in the basic Christian revelation. Westwood, N. J., Revell ['1951] 189 p. 21 cm. [BT75.F25] 51-14857
1. Theology, Doctrinal. I. Title.

FEINER, Johannes. 230
The common catechism : a book of Christian faith / [edited by Johannes Feiner and Lukas Vischer ; with the cooperation of Josef Blank ... et al.] New York : Seabury Press, 1975. xxv, 690 p. ; 22 cm. "A Crossroad book." Translation of Neues Glaubensbuch: der gemeinsame christliche Glaube. Includes index. [BT75.2.F4213] 75-1070 ISBN 0-8164-0283-3 : 10.95
1. Theology, Doctrinal. I. Vischer, Lukas, joint author. II. Title.

FERNAN, John Joseph, 1908- 230.2
Theology, a course for college students. [Syracuse? N. Y., 1952-55] 4v. maps (on lining papers, v. 3) 24cm. Contents.v. 1. Christ as prophet and king.--v. 2. Christ. our high priest.--v. 3. The mystical Christ.--v. 4. Christ in His Members, by B. J. Murray, J. J. Ferman, and E. J. Messemer. [BX904.F4] 52-4098
1. Theology, Doctrinal. 2. Catholic Church—Doctrinal and controversial works. I. Murray, Bernard J. II. Title.

FERRE, Nels Fredrick Solomon, 1908- 230
Searchlights on contemporary theology. New York, Harper [c.1961] 241p. Bibl. 61-7355 4.50 bds.,
1. Theology, Doctrinal. I. Title.

FESSENDEN, Thomas, 1739-1813. 230
A theoretic explanation of the science of sanctity. According to reason, Scripture, common sense, and the analogy of things; containing an idea of God; of his creations, and kingdoms; of the Holy Scriptures; of the Christian Trinity, and of the Gospel system. By Thomas Fessenden, A.M., pastor of the church in Walpole, (New Hampshire.)... Printed by William Fessenden, for the author. Brattleboro. 1804. viii, [9]-308, [4] p. 19 cm. [BR121.F55] 9-5868
1. Theology, Doctrinal. I. Title.

FIELD, Benjamin, d.1869. 230
The student's handbook of Christian theology. New ed. Edited, with extensive additions, by John C. Symons. With an introd. by L. Tyerman. Freeport, Pa., Fountain Press [1949] xxxii, 332 p. 19 cm. Original imprint covered by label, as above. [BT75.F45 1949] 49-2428
1. Theology, Doctrinal. I. Symons, John C., ed. II. Title.

FIELD, Benjamin, d. 1869. 230
The student's handbook of Christian theology. New ed., edited, with extensive additions by John C. Symons. Also considerable new material never heretofore published, added to the chapter, The final perseverance of the saints, by Peter Wiseman. Freeport, Pa., Fountain Press [1955] 332p. 21cm. [BT75.F45 1955] 55-27321
1. Theology, Doctrinal. I. Title.

FINNEY, Charles Grandison, 1792-1875. 260
Lectures on systematic theology; by the Rev. Charles G. Finney ... Edited by Pres. J.H. Fairchild. Oberlin, O., E.J. Goodrich, 1878. xxi, 622 p. front. (port.) 23cm. "Prepared from the English edition [of 1851] by a process of condensation, omitting ... repetitions of the argument ... and other parts not essential to the expression or elucidation of the doctrine."--Note by the editor. [BT75.F5 1878] 37-21080
1. Theology, Doctrinal. I. Fairchild, James Harris, 1817-1902, ed. II. Title.

FISHER, George Park, 1827-1909. 230
...History of Christian doctrine, by George Park Fisher... New York, C. Scribner's sons, 1896. xv, 583 p. 21 cm. (Half-title: The international theological library, ed. by C. A. Briggs and S. D. F. Saimond. iv) Series title also at head of t.-p. [BT21.F5] 4-4037
1. Theology, Doctrinal. I. Title.

FITZWATER, Perry Braxton, 1871-
Christian theology; a systematic presentation. 2d ed. Grand Rapids, W. B. Eerdmans Pub. Co. [1958, c1948] 567 p. 23 cm. 63-16148
1. Theology, Doctrinal. I. Title.

FITZWATER, Perry Braxton, 1871- 230
Christian theology, a systematic presentation. Grand Rapids, W. B. Eerdmans Pub. Co., 1948. 552 p. 24 cm. [BT75.F57] 48868
1. Theology, Doctrinal. I. Title.

FOSTER, Robert Verrell, 1845-1914. 260
Systematic theology, by Robert Verrell Foster ... Nashville, Tenn., Cumberland Presbyterian publishing house, 1898. xxii, 868 p. 24 cm. [BT75.F7] 98-1510
1. Theology, Doctrinal. 2. Presbyterianism. I. Title.

FRANKLIN, Marion Clyde. 230
The chain that saves, by M. C. Franklin ... Greenville, Tex. [M. C. Franklin] 1933. 181 p. diagr. 20 cm. [BT77.F7] 33-31103
1. Theology, Doctrinal. I. Title.

FULLER, Andrew, 1754-1815.
Dialogues, letters, and essays, on various subjects. To which is annexed, An essay on truth: containing an inquiry into its nature and importance; with the causes of error, and the reasons of its being permitted. By Andrew Fuller. Hartford: Published by Oliver D. Cooke. J. Seymour, printer, New York. 1810. iv, [5]-258 p. 19 cm. A 23
1. Theology, Doctrinal. 2. Truth. I. Title.

FULLER, T. 230
The sword of the spirit, or Theology and orthodoxy made plain. Containing a selection and arrangement of the fundamental doctrines of the Scriptures. By T. Fuller. New York, N. Tibbals & sons, 1883. x, [5]-354 p. 19 cm. [BT77.F8] 40-21296
1. Theology, Doctrinal. 2. Bible—Indexes, Topical. I. Title. II. Title: Theology and orthodoxy made plain.

GAMERTSFELDER, Solomon J 1851- 230.79
Systematic theology. Harrisburg, Pa., Evangelical Pub. House, 1938 [c1921] xvi, 619 p. 23 cm. [BT75.G22] 51-52155
1. Theology, Doctrinal. 2. Evangelical Church—Doctrinal and controversial works. I. Title.

GELPI, Donald L., 1934- 230
Experiencing God : a theology of human experience / by Donald L. Gelpi. New York : Paulist Press, c1978. v, 406 p. ; 23 cm. Cover title: Experiencing God, a theology of human energence. Includes bibliographical references and index. [BT75.2.G44] 77-14854 ISBN 0-8091-2061-5 pbk. : 10.00
1. Theology, Doctrinal. 2. Holy Spirit. 3. Experience (Religion) 4. Pentecostalism. 5. Philosophy, American. I. Title.

GERAHRT, Emanuel Vogel, 1817-1904. 230
Institutes of the Christian religion. by Emauel V. Gerhart ... with an introduction by Philip Schaff ... 1. Source of theological knowledge. 2. Principle of Christian doctrine. 3. Doctrine on God. 4. Doctrine on creation and providence. New York, A. C. Armstrong & son, 1891. xxvii, 754 p. 22 cm. A projected second volume was published only with the 1894 edition. [BT75.G3 1891] 39-5796
1. Theology, Doctrinal. 2. Reformed church Doctrinal and controversial works. I. Title.

GERHART, Emanuel Vogel, 1817-1904. 230
Institutes of the Christian religion, by Emanuel V. Gerhart ... with an introduction by Philip Schaff ... New York [etc.] Funk & Wagnalls company [1894] 2 v. 22 cm. Contents.--.1. The source of theological knowledge. The Christ iden: or, The principle of Christian doctrine. The doctrine on God. The doctrine on creation and providence.--ii. Anthropology; or, Doctrine on the Admaic race. Jesus Christ. The Holy Spirit. Personal salvation. the last things. [BT75.G3 1894] 30-5797
1. Theology, Doctrinal. 2. Reformed church—Doctrinal and controversial works. I. Title.

GILL, Jerry H. 230
Toward theology / Jerry H. Gill. Washington, D.C. : University Press of America, c1982. x, 118 p. ; 22 cm. [BT75.2.G55 1982] 19 82-45009 ISBN 0-8191-2430-3 : 17.50 ISBN 0-8191-2429-X (pbk.) : 17.50
1. Theology, Doctrinal. I. Title.

GIRARDEAU, John Lafayette, 1825-1898. 260
Discussions of theological questions. By John L. Girardeau ... edited by Rev. George A. Blackburn ... Richmond, Va., The Presbyterian committee of publication [1905] vi p., 1 l., 534 p. 20 cm. [BT75.G45] 41-39777
1. Theology, Doctrinal. I. Blackburn, George Andrew, 1861-1918- ed. II. Presbyterian church in the U. S. Executive committee of publication. III. Title.

GLADDEN, Washington, 1836-1918. 230
How much is left of the old doctrines? A book for the people, by Washington Gladden. Boston and New York, Houghton, Mifflin and company, 1899. iv

p., 1 l., 321, [1] p. 19 cm. [BT77.G5] 0-136
1. Theology, Doctrinal. I. Title.

GOD in His World. 269
New York, Abingdon Press [1956] 176p. 21cm. [BT77] [BT77] 253 56-7759 56-7759
1. Theology, Doctrinal. 2. Evangelistic work. I. Duthie, Charles S

GOODWIN, Henry Martyn, 1820- 233 1893.
Christ and humanity; with a review, historical and critical, of the doctrine of Christ's person. By Henry M. Goodwin. New York, Harper & brothers, 1875. xxv p., 1 l., 404 p. 20 cm. [BT231.G57] 37-8748
1. Jesus Christ—Person and offices. 2. Theology, Doctrinal. I. Title.

GRAVES, Henry Clinton, 1830- 230
Handbook of Christian doctrine, by Henry C. Graves ... prepared for the classroom and the use of students. This work is based upon the "Manual of Christian theology" by Alvah Hovey ... with the special permission and approval of its author. Philadelphia, American Baptist publication society, 1903. xi, 13-176 p. 20 cm. [BT77.G8] 3-30967
1. Hovey, Alvah, 1820-1908. Manual of Christian theology. 2. Theology, Doctrinal. I. Title.

GRAY, Albert Frederick, 1886- 230
Christian theology ... by Albert F. Gray ... Anderson, Ind., The Warner press [1944-46] 2 v. 21 cm. [BT75.G7] 44-9177
1. Theology, Doctrinal. 2. Church of God (Anderson, Ind.)—Doctrinal and controversial works. I. Title.

GREGORIUS, Saint, bp. of 239. Nyssa, fl.379-394
The Catechetical oration of Gregory of Nyssa, edited by James Herbert Srawley ... Cambridge [eng.] University press, 1903. i, 181, [1] p. 20 cm. (Half-title: Cambridge paristic texts) "Books ... for reference": p. i. [BR60.C3G7] 9-25190
1. Theology, Doctrinal. I. Srawley, James Herbert, 1868- ed. II. Title.

HAAS, John Augustus William, 230 1862-1937.
What is revelation? A system of Christian truth [by] John A. W. Haas...with a foreword by Dr. Emil E. Fischer. Boston, Mass., The Stratford company [c1937] 2 p. l., viii, 175 p. 19 1/2 cm. Bibliography: p. 167. [BT75.H2] 38-740
1. Theology, Doctrinal. 2. Revelation. I. Fischer, Emil Eisenhardt, 1882- ed. II. Title.

[HALL, Edwin] 1802-1877. 230
Digest of studies and lectures in theology... Auburn [N.Y.] W.J. Moses, 1866. 212 p. 23 cm. "An outline of the studies and lectures in the Department of Christian theology...in Auburn theological seminary." [BT77.H2] 39-7823
1. Theology, Doctrinal. 2. Congregational churches—Doctrinal and controversial works. I. Title.

HALL, Francis Joseph, 1857- 260
Introduction to dogmatic theology, by the Rev. Francis J. Hall... New York [etc.] Longmans, Green, and co., 1907. xliii, 273 p. 20 cm. (Lettered on cover: Dogmatic theology. v. 1.) "Literature of dogmatic theology": p. 250-273. [BT75.H3 vol. 1] 7-14566
1. Theology, Doctrinal. I. Title. II. Title: Dogmatic theology.

[HALL, Francis Joseph] 1857- 260 1932.
Theological outlines 2d ed., rev. throughout. Milwaukee, Wis., The Young churchman co.; London, W. Walker, 1905-15] 3 v. 19 1/2 cm. Half-title. "Index of author": v. 1, p. [149]-156; v. 2, p. [141]-150; v. 3, p. [125]-130. Contents.v. 1. The doctrine of God.--v. 2. The doctrine of man and of the God-man--v. 3. The doctrine of the church and of last things. [BT75.H35 1903] 5-20745
1. Theology, Doctrinal. 2. Protestant Episcopal church in the U.S.A.—Cotrinal and controversial works. I. Title.

HALL, Francis Joseph, 1857- 230 1932.
Theological outlines, by the Rev. Francis J. Hall...revised by the Rev. Frank Hudson Hallock... 3d ed. Milwaukee, Wis, The Morehouse publishing co [c1933] xiv p., 1 l., 336 p. 22 cm. Bibliography: p. [307]-326. [BT75.H35 1933] 33-33890
1. Theology, Doctrinal. 2. Protestant Episcopal church in the U.S.A.—Doctrinal and controversial works. I. Hallock, Frank Hudson, 1877- ed. II. Title.

HALL, Francis Joseph, 1857- 230 1932.
Theological outlines... By the Rev. Francis J. Hall... Milwaukee, Wis., The Young churchman co., 1892-95. 3 v. 18 cm. Contents.--v. 1. The doctrine of God. 1892.--v. 2. The doctrine of man and of the God-man. 1894.--v. 3. The doctrine of the church and of last things. 1895. [BT75.H25 1892] 5-21279
1. Theology, Doctrinal. 2. Protestant Episcopal church in the U.S.A.—Doctrinal and controversial works. I. Title.

HAMILTON, Peter Napier. 230'.0924
The living God and the modern world; Christian theology based on the thought of A. N. Whitehead, by Peter Hamilton. Philadelphia, United Church Pr. [1968,c.1967] 256p. 21cm. Bibl. [BT75.2.H35 1968] 67-28283 2.95 pap.,
1. Whitehead, Alfred North, 1861-1947. 2. Theology, Doctrinal. 3. Process theology. I. Title.

HANSON, Paul D. 230
Dynamic transcendence : the correlation of confessional heritage and contemporary experience in a Biblical model of divine activity / Paul D. Hanson. Philadelphia : Fortress Press, c1978. p. cm. Includes bibliographical references and index. [BS543.H36] 78-54552 ISBN 0-8006-1338-4 pbk. : 4.95
1. Bible—Theology. 2. Theology, Doctrinal. I. Title.

HANSON, Richard Patrick 230'.3'08 Crosland.
The attractiveness of God; essays in Christian doctrine [by] R. P. C. Hanson. Richmond, Va., John Knox Press [1973] 202 p. 23 cm. Includes bibliographical references. [BT75.2.H37 1973] 73-5345 ISBN 0-8042-0473-X 9.95
1. Theology, Doctrinal. I. Title.

HAROUTUNIAN, Joseph, 1904- 230
God with us; a theology of transpersonal life. Philadelphia, Westminister Press, [1965] 318 p. 21 cm. Bibliographical references included in "notes" (p. [305]-314) [BT78.H29] 65-19279
1. Theology, Doctrinal. I. Title.

HARSHA, William Willett, 230 1820?-1900.
Heavenly light for earthly firesides ... By Rev. W. W. Harsha ... Chicago, S. M. Kennedy, 1868. x ii, [13]-427 p. 23 cm. [BT75.H5] 39-7348
1. Theology, Doctrinal. 2. Presbyterian church—Doctrinal and controversial works. I. Title.

HEADLAM, Arthur Cayley, bp. 230 of Gloucester, 1862-
Christian theology; the doctrine of God, by the Rt. Rev. Arthur C. Headlam ... Oxford, Clarendon press, 1934. x, 482 p. 1 l. 23 cm. "The outcome of lectures ... delivered to theological students ... in King's college, London, and ... in the University of Oxford."--Pref. "The present work may be looked upon as complete in itself. It discusses somewhat fully the sources of our theological knowledge and the Christian doctrine of God."--p. vi. "Literature": p. 3-4. [BT75.H52] A 35
1. Theology, Doctrinal. 2. Authority (Religion) 3. God. 4. Church of England—Doctrinal and controversial works. I. Title.

HEINECKEN, Martin J. 230
We believe and teach / Martin J. Heinecken ; Harold W. Rast, editor. Philadelphia : Fortress Press, c1980. p. cm. (Heritage of faith series) [BT75.2.H44] 80-16363 ISBN 0-8006-1387-2 : 3.95
1. Theology, Doctrinal. I. Rast, Harold W. II. Title. III. Series.

HELFFENSTEIN, Samuel, 1775- 230 1866.
The doctrines of divine revelation, as taught in the Holy Scriptures, exhibited, illustrated, and vindicated. Designed for the use of Christians generally, and for young men, preparing for the gospel ministry, in particular. By the Rev. Samuel Helffenstein, D.D. Philadelphia, J. Kay, jun. & brother; Pittsburg, C. H. Kay & co., 1842. viii, 9-394 p. front. (port.) 23 c. [BT75.H54] 39-7350
1. Theology, Doctrinal. 2. Reformed church in the United States—Doctrinal and controversial works. I. Title.

HODGE, Archibald Alexander, 230 1823-1886.
Outlines of theology. Grand Rapids, Mich., Zondervan Pub. House [1972] 678 p. 23 cm. Reprint of the rewritten and enl. ed. of 1879. [BT75.H6 1972] 73-150624 9.95
1. Presbyterian Church—Doctrinal and controversial works. 2. Theology, Doctrinal. I. Title.

HODGE, Archibald Alexander, 230 1823-1886
Outlines of theology. By the Rev. A. Alexander Hodge ... New York, R. Carter & brothers, 1860. x, [11]-522 p. 24 cm. [BT75,H6 1860] 39-7022
1. Theology, Doctrinal. 2. Presbyterian church—Doctrinal and controversial works. I. Title.

HODGE, Archibald Alexander, 230 1823-1886.
Outlines of theology. Rewritten and enlarged. By Archibald Alexander Hodge ... New York, R. Carter and brothers, 1879. 678 p. 23 1/2 cm. [BT75.H6 1879] 39-7023
1. Theology, Doctrinal. 2. Presbyterian church—Doctrinal and controversial works. I. Title.

HODGE, Archibald Alexander, 230 1823-1886.
Outlines of theology. Grand Rapids, W.B. Eerdmans Pub. Co., 1949. 678 p. 23 cm. Reproduction of the Rewritten and enl. ed. published in New York in 1879. [BT75.H6 1949] 49-50171
1. Theology, Doctrinal. 2. Presbyterian Church—Doctrinal and controversial works. I. Title.

HODGE, Charles, 1797-1878. 230
Systematic theology. By Charles Hodge ... New York, C. Scribner and company; London and Edinburgh, T. Nelson and sons, 1872-73. 3 v. 24 1/2 cm. Vol. 3 has imprint: New York, Scribner, Armstrong, and co.; London and Edinburgh, T. Nelson and sons. Index ... New York, Scribner, Armstrong, and company; London and Edinburgh, T. Nelson and sons, 1873. 1 p. l., 81 p. 24 1/2 cm. Bibliographical footnotes. [BT75.H63] 45-41149
1. Theology, Doctrinal. 2. Prebyterian church—Doctrinal and controversial works. I. Title.

HOEKSEMA, Herman. 230
Reformed dogmatics. Grand Rapids, Reformed Free Pub. Association [1966] xvii, 917 p. 23 cm. Bibliography: p. 915-917. [BT75.2.H6] 66-24047
1. Theology, Doctrinal. I. Title.

HOLGATE, Jerome Bonaparte. 230
Moral science; a new theology, deduced from the Bible ... By Jerome B. Holgate ... Utica, N.Y., Curtiss & Childs, printers, 1878-87. 5 v. 20 1/2 x 24 cm. Cover-title. Pts. 1-4, paged continuously, were originally issued in 14 numbers. No. 1 has special t.p., with imprint: Lansingburgh, N.Y., and Defiance, O., The author, 1875. Pt. 5 has cover-title and special t.-p.: Moral science: deduced from the Bible. The true theology ... By Jerome B. Holgate ... Utica, N.Y., L. C. Childs & son, printers, 1887. [BT85.H6] 45-26574
1. Theology, Doctrinal. 2. Christian ethics. I. Title.

HOPKINS, Samuel, 1721-1803. 230
The system of doctrines, contained in divine revelation, explained and defended. Showing their consistence and connection with each other. To which is added, a Treatise on the millennium. By Samuel Hopkins, D.D. pastor of the First Congregational church in Newport... Printed at Boston, by Isaiah Thomas and Ebenezer T. Andrews,[proprietors of the work.] At Faust's statute, no. 45, Newbury street. Sold at their bookstore, and by said Thomas, at his bookstore in Worcester. MDCCXCIII. 2 v. 21 1/2 cm. [BT70.H6] 5-1544
1. Theology, Doctrinal. I. Title.

HORTON, Walter Marshall, 230 1895-
Christian theology, an ecumenical approach. Rev. and enl. ed. New York, Harper [1958] 320p. illus. 22cm. Includes bibliography. [BT75.H68 1958] 57-149036
1. Theology, Doctrinal. 2. Ecumenical movement. I. Title.

HORTON, Walter Marshall, 230 1895-
Christian theology, an ecumenical approach. [1st ed.] New York, Harper [1955] 304p. 22cm. Includes bibliography. [BT75.H68] 54-12329
1. Theology, Doctrinal. 2. Ecumenical movement. I. Title.

HOULDEN, James Leslie. 230
Patterns of faith : a study in the relationship between the New Testament and Christian doctrine / J. L. Houlden. Philadelphia : Fortress Press, c1977. 87 p. ; 20 cm. Includes bibliographical references and index. [BT78.H67] 76-55829 ISBN 0-8006-0493-8 pbk. : 3.25
1. Bible. N.T.—Criticism, interpretation, etc. 2. Theology, Doctrinal. I. Title.

HOVEY, Alvah, 1820-1903. 230
Outlines of Christian theology; for the use of students in the Newton theological institution. By Alvah Hovey... Boston, Printed for the author by G. C. Rand & Avery, 1861. 206 p. 24 cm. "List of theological writers": p. 11-17. [BT75.H82] 20-17711
1. Theology, Doctrinal. 2. Baptists—Doctrinal and controversial works. I. Title.

HUFFMAN, Jasper Abraham, 230 1880-
The meanings of things believed by Christians. Winona.Lake, Ind., Standard Press [1953] 184p. 20cm. [BT75.H9] 53-29144
1. Theology, Doctrinal. I. Title.

HUGHES, Henry Maldwyn, 1875- 230
Basic beliefs; an introduction to Christian doctrine, by H. Maldwyn Hughes... New York, Cincinnati [etc.] The Abingdon press [c1929] 282 p. 19 1/2 cm. Bibliography: p. 219-221. [BT77.H8] 29-28338
1. Theology, Doctrinal. I. Title.

IN understanding be men.
A handbook on Christian doctrine for non-theological students. [5th ed.] Chicago, Inter-Varsity Press, 1958. x, 208p. 20cm. Includes bibliography.
1. Theology, Doctrinal. I. Hammond, Thomas Chatterton, 1877-

IRRELIGIOUS reflections of the Christian church. Naperville, Ill., SCM Book Club [1959] 128p. 19cm. (Religious Book Club edition, 128)
1. Theology, Doctrinal. I. Pelz, Werner.

JACOBS, Henry Eyster, 1844- 260
A summary of the Christian faith, by Henry Eyster Jacobs ... Philadelphia, General council publication house, 1905. xii, 637 p. 23 cm. "An attempt is here made to restate the doctrines of the Christian faith upon the basis of the Lutheran confessions."--Pref. [BT75.J2] 5-34658
1. Theology, Doctrinal. 2. Lutheran church—Doctrinal and controversial works. I. Title.

JAMES, Edwin Oliver, 1886- 230.2
The Christian faith in the modern world; a study in scientific theology, by E. O. James ... London [etc.] A. R. Mowbray & co. ltd.; Milwaukee, U. S. A., The Morehouse publishing co [1930] xi, 259, [1] p. 19 cm. Bibliography at end of each chapter. [BT75.J2] 31-17190
1. Theology, Doctrinal. 2. Religion and science—1900- 3. Bible—Criticism, interpretation, etc. I. Title.

JARRATT, Devereux, 1733- 922. 1801.
Thoughts on some important subjects in divinity; in a series of letters to a friend.

By the Rev. Devereux Jarratt ... Baltimore: Printed by Warner & Hanna, 1806. 84 p. 16 cm. [With his The life of the Reverend Devereux Jarratt. Baltimore, 1806] [BX5995.J27A2] 34-11519
1. Theology, Doctrinal. I. Title.

JEMISON, T Housel. 230.67
Christian beliefs; fundamental Biblical teachings for Seventh-Day Adventist college classes, by T. H. Jemison. Prepared by the Dept. of Education, General Conference of Seventh-Day Adventists. Mountain View, Calif., Pacific Press Pub. Association [1959] 481p. 23cm. Includes bibliography. [BX6154.J4] 59-14248
1. Theology, Doctrinal. 2. Seventh-Day Adventists—Doctrinal and controversial works. I. Seventh-Day Adventists. General Conference, Dept. of Education. II. Title.

JENKINS, Daniel Thomas, 230.08
1914-ed.
The scope of theology. Cleveland, World [1968,c.1965] 270p. 270p. 21cm. (Meridian bk., M254) Bibl. [BT75.2.J4] 65-25777 2.95 pap.,
1. Theology, Doctrinal. I. Title.

JOHNSON, Elias Henry, 1841- 230
1906.
Outline of systematic theology. By E. H. Johnson ... Philadelphia, American Baptist publication society [1891] xv, 17-304 p. 23 cm. Bibliography: p. [17]-18. [BT75.J6 1891] 39-5800
1. Theology, Doctrinal. 2. Baptists—Doctrinal and controversial works. I. American Baptist publication society. II. Title.

JOHNSON, Elias Henry, 1841- 230
1906.
An outline of systematic theology, by E. H. Johnson ... [2d ed.] and of Ecclesiology, by Henry G. Weston ... Philadelphia, American Baptist publication society, 1895. 2 p. l., iii-xviii, 383 p. 23 cm. Bibliography: p. 2. [BT75.J6 1895] 39-5799
1. Theology, Doctrinal. 2. Baptists—Doctrinal and controversial works. 3. Church polity. I. Weston, Henry Griggs, 1820-1909. II. American Baptist publication society. III. Title.

JOYCE, J Daniel. 230
The living Christ in our changing world. St. Louis, Bethany Press [1962] 95p. 20cm. [BT80.J68] 62-17917
1. Theology, Doctrinal. 2. Christian life. 3. Sermons, American. I. Title.

KAUFMAN, Edmund George. 230
Basic Christian convictions, by Edmund G. Kaufman. North Newton, Kan., Bethel College [1972] xxiv, 338 p. 24 cm. Includes bibliographies. [BT75.2.K36] 72-86406 6.50
1. Theology, Doctrinal. I. Title.

KAUFMAN, Edmund George. 230
Basic Christian convictions, by Edmund G. Kaufman. North Newton, Kan., Bethel College [1972] xxiv, 338 p. 24 cm. Includes bibliographies. [BT75.2.K36] 72-86406 6.50
1. Theology, Doctrinal. I. Title.

KAUFMAN, Gordon D. 230
Systematic theology : a historicist perspective / by Gordon D. Kaufman. New York : Scribner, c1978. xxiv, 543 p. ; 21 cm. Includes bibliographical references and index. [BT75.2.K38 1978] 78-50761 ISBN 0-684-15796-9 pbk. : 7.95
1. Theology, Doctrinal. I. Title.

KAUFMAN, Gordon D. 230
Systematic theology; a historicist perspective, by Gordon D. Kaufman. New York, Scribner [1969, c1968] xxii, 543 p. 24 cm. Bibliographical footnotes. [BT75.2.K38 1969] 68-27789 8.95
1. Theology, Doctrinal. I. Title.

KEDNEY, John Steinfort, 1819- 230
1911.
Christian doctrine harmonized and its rationality vindicated, by John Steinfort Kedney ... New York and London, G. P. Putnam's sons, 1889. 2 v. 25 cm. [BT75.K2] 39-5801
1. Theology, Doctrinal. I. Title.

KENT, John, 19thcent. 230
The Divine being and other realities of the Scriptures. By John Kent. Philadelphia, L. Kent., printer, 1882. 158 p. 24 cm. [BT85.K3] 40-21303
1. Theology, Doctrinal. I. Title.

KEPLER, Thomas Samuel, 230.082
1897 comp.
Contemporary religious thought, an anthology, compiled by Thomas S. Kepler ... New York, Nashville, Abingdon-Cokesbury press [c1941] 423 p. 23 1/2 cm. "Biographical index of authors": p. 409-419. Bibliography: p. 405-408. [BT75.K4] 41-25071
1. Theology, Doctrinal. 2. Religious thought—20th cent. I. Title.

KERR, I. C. 230
The true philosophy of life as it related to the present and the future, viewed in the light of reason and revelation. By L. C. Kerr ... [Belmont? O.] 1897. 435 p. 20 1/2 cm. [BT78.K4] 40-15260
1. Theology, Doctrinal. I. Title.

KEYSER, Cassius Jackson, 230
1862-
The new infinite and the old theology, by Cassius J. Keyser ... New Haven, Yale university press; [etc., etc.] 1915. v p., 1 l., 117 p. 19 1/2 cm. [BT85.K4] 15-16250
1. Theology, Doctrinal. I. Title.

KIM, Young Oon. 230
Unification theology & Christian thought / Young Oon Kim. 1st ed. New York : Golden Gate Pub. Co., 1975. xi, 302 p. ; 21 cm. Includes bibliographies and index. [BT75.2.K53] 74-32590
1. Segye Kidokkyo T'ongil Sillyong Hyophoe—Doctrinal and controversial works. 2. Theology, Doctrinal. 3. Theology, Doctrinal—History. I. Title.

KINNEBREW, J. H. 230
The theology of fatherhood, psychologically, metaphysically, and ethically considered. A new theology, in which is developed a new theory of original sin, atonement, justification, etc., by the Rev. J. H. Kinnebrew ... Nashville, Tenn., Southern Methodist publishing house, printed for the author, 1883. 120 p. 19 cm. "The contents of this little volume were delivered in the Baptist church at Rome, Ga. ... as lectures."--Pref. [BT78.K5] 40-15261
1. Theology, Doctrinal. I. Title.

KNAPP, Georg Christian, 1753- 260
1825.
Lectures on Christian theology, by George Christian Knapp. Tr. by Leonard Woods, jun. ... New-York, G. & C. & H. Carvill, 1831-33. 2 v. 23 cm. [BT75.K64] 20-19114
1. Theology, Doctrinal. I. Woods, Leonard, 1807-1878, tr. II. Title.

KNAPP, Georg Christian, 1753- 230
1825.
Lectures on Christian theology. By George Christian Knapp ... Translated by Leonard Woods, jun. ... 2d American ed., reprinted from the last London ed. Philadelphia, T. Wardle, 1845. 572 p. 25 cm. [BT75.K64 1845] 35-22780
1. Theology, Doctrinal. I. Woods, Leonard, 1807-1878, tr. II. Title.

KNAPP, Georg Christian, 1753- 260
1825.
Lectures on Christian theology. By George Christian Knapp ... Tr. by Leonard Woods, jun. ... 6th American ed., reprinted from the last London ed. Philadelphia, J. W. Moore, 1856. 572 p. 24 cm. [BT75.K64 1856] 20-19115
1. Theology, Doctrinal. I. Woods, Leonard, 1807-1878, tr. II. Title.

KNAPP, Georg Christian, 1753- 230
1825.
Lectures on Christian theology. By George Christian Knapp ... Translated by Leonard Woods, jun. ... 7th American ed., reprinted from the last London ed. Philadelphia, J. W. Moore, 1858. 572 p. 24 cm. [BT15.K64 1858] 35-22779
1. Theology, Doctrinal. I. Woods, Leonard, 1807-1878, ed. II. Title.

KNOX, Loren Laertes, 1811- 230
1901.
Evangelical rationalism; or, A consideration of truths practically related to man's probation. By Loren L. Knox, D. D. Cincinnati, Hitchcock and Walden; New York, Nelson & Phillips, 1879. 250 p. 18 cm. A refutation of the doctrine of probation after death. [BT78.K7] 40-15262
1. Theology, Doctrinal. 2. Probation after death. 3. Reward (Theology) I. Title.

KNUDSON, Albert Cornelius, 231
1873-
The doctrine of God [by] Albert C. Knudson ... New York, Cincinnati [etc.] The Abingdon press [c1930] 434 p. 22 cm. "This is the first of two independent volumes that together will cover the field of Christian theology. The second volume will be entitled The doctrine of redemption."--Pref. [BT75.K67] 30-24005
1. God. 2. Theology, Doctrinal. I. Title.
Contents omitted.

KNUDSON, Albert Cornelius, 234.3
1873-
The doctrine of redemption [by] Albert C. Knudson ... New York, Cincinnati [etc.] The Abingdon press [c1933] 512 p. 22 cm. "A companion volume to "The doctrine of God."--Pref. [BT75.K675] 33-22173
1. Theology, Doctrinal. 2. Redemption. I. Title.
Contents omitted.

KNUTSON, Kent S. 201'.1
The shape of the question; the mission of the church in a secular age [by] Kent S. Knutson. Minneapolis, Augsburg Pub. House [1972] 128 p. 20 cm. [BT75.2.K58] 72-78558 ISBN 0-8066-1225-8 2.50
1. Theology, Doctrinal. 2. Christianity—20th century. I. Title.

LAWSON, John. 230
Comprehensive handbook of Christian doctrine. Englewood Cliffs, N.J., Prentice-Hall [1967] xiii, 287 p. 24 cm. Includes bibliographies. [BT75.2.L38] 67-10011
1. Theology, Doctrinal. I. Title.

LEE, Luther, 1800-1889. 230.7
Elements of theology, or, An exposition of the divine origin, doctrines, morals and institutions of Christianity. By Rev. Luther Lee ... New York, Miller, Orton & Mulligan; Syracuse, N.Y., S. Lee, 1856. viii, 580 p. 23 cm. [BR121.L4 1856] 36-4658
1. Theology, Doctrinal. 2. Methodist Episcopal church—Doctrinal and controversial works. I. Title.

LEE, Luther, 1800-1889. 230.7
Elements of theology, or, An exposition of the divine origin, doctrines, morals and institutions of Christianity. By Rev. Luther Lee ... 2d ed. ... Syracuse, N.Y., S. Lee, 1859. viii, 584 p. 23 cm. [BR121.L4 1859] 36-6874
1. Theology, Doctrinal. 2. Methodist Episcopal church—Doctrinal and controversial works. I. Title.

LEE, Luther, 1800-1889. 230.7
Elements of theology; or, An exposition of the divine origin, doctrines, morals and institutions of Christianity, by Rev. Luther Lee ... 11th ed. Syracuse, N.Y., A. W. Hall, 1892. xii, 584 p. 23 cm. [BR121.L4 1892] 36-4659
1. Theology, Doctrinal. 2. Methodist Episcopal church—Doctrinal and controversial works. I. Title.

LE GUILLOU, M. J. 230
Christ and church; a theology of the mystery, by M. J. Le Guillou. Pref. by M. D. Chenu. Foreword by J. Bosc. Translated by Charles E. Schaldenbrand. New York, Desclee Co., 1966 [c1963] 375 p. 22 cm. Bibliographical footnotes. [BT75.2.L413] 66-17859
1. Theology, Doctrinal. 2. Mystery. I. Title.

LESCOE, Francis J. 110
God as first principle in Ulrich of Strasburg / by Francis J. Lescoe. New York : Alba House, c1979. xvi, 276 p. : facsims. ; 23 cm. Expanded version of the author's thesis, Toronto. "The edited text Summa de bono, liber quartus, tractatus primus": p. 145-242. Includes index. Bibliography: p. 242-260. [BX1749.U383L47 1979] 79-4140 ISBN 0-8189-0385-6 : 11.95
1. Ulrich von Strassburg, d. 1277. Summa de bono. 2. Theology, Doctrinal. 3. Philosophy. I. Ulrich von Strassburg, d. 1277. Summa de bono. Book 4, tractate 1. 1979. II. Title.

LEWIS, Ernest Ridley. 230
Give heed unto reading; a book of organic theology for the clergy, by the Rev. E. Ridley Lewis...with a foreword by the Bishop of Swansea and Brecon. London and Oxford, A. R. Mowbray & co., limited; New York, Morehouse-Gorham co. [1943] 135 p. 19 cm. "First published in 1943." "A select bibliography": p. 134-135. [BT75.L47] 44-38728
1. Theology, Doctrinal. 2. Church of England—Doctrinal and controversial works. I. Title.

LINDSELL, Harold, 1913- 230
A handbook of Christian truth, by Harold Lindsell and Charles J. Woodbridge. Westwood, N. J., F. H. Revell Co. [1952] 351p. 21cm. [BT75.L55] 53-9083
1. Theology, Doctrinal. I. Woodbridge, Charles Jahleel, 1902- joint author. II. Title.

LOBSTEIN, Paul, 1850-1922. 230
An introduction to Protestant dogmatics, by Dr. P. Lobstein ... Authorized translation from the original French edition by Arthur Maxon Smith, PH. D. [Chicago] , The translator, printed at the University of Chicago press [c1902] xxi, 275 p. 21 cm. [BT65.L8] 3-2198
1. Theology, Doctrinal. I. Smith, Arthur Maxson, tr. II. Title.

LONERGAN, Bernard J. F. 201
Doctrinal pluralism, by Bernard Lonergan. Milwaukee, Marquette University Press, 1971. 75 p. 19 cm. (The Pere Marquette theology lectures, 1971) Includes bibliographical references. [BT75.2.L58] 70-155364 ISBN 0-87462-220-4
1. Theology, Doctrinal. 2. Pluralism. I. Title. II. Series.

LORD, Willis, 1809-1888. 230
Christian theology for the people. By Willis Lord ... New York, R. Carter and brothers, 1875. xv, [17]-623 p. 24 cm. [BT75.L8] 39-5804
1. Theology, Doctrinal. 2. Presbyterian church—Doctrinal and controversial works. I. Title.

LOWREY, Asbury. 230.7
Positive theology: being a series of dissertations on the fundamental doctrines of the Bible; the object of which is to communicate truth affirmatively, in a style direct and practical. By Rev. Asbury Lowrey ... Cincinnati, Printed at the Methodist book concern, for the author, 1853. 333 p. 19 cm. [BT75.L85] 33-8324
1. Theology, Doctrinal. I. Title.

MCCALLUM, James Ramsay. 230
Abelard's Christian theology / by J. Ramsey McCallum. Merrick, N.Y. : Richwood Pub. Co., 1976. vii, 117 p. ; 23 cm. Reprint of the 1948 ed. published by Blackwell, Oxford. Includes a translation of a substantial portion of Abelard's Theologiae christianae. Includes index. Bibliography: p. 115-116. [BT70.M23 1976] 76-1128 ISBN 0-915172-07-0 lib.bdg. : 12.50
1. Abailard, Pierre, 1079-1142. Theologiae christiane. 2. Theology, Doctrinal. I. Abailard, Pierre, 1079-1142. Theologiae chritianae. English. Selections. 1976. II. Title.

MCCARTY, W. A. 230
Doctrines for the times. By Rev. W. A. M'cCarty ... assisted by Rev. T. R. M'cCarty ... Atlanta, Ga., The Foote & Davies company, 1895. 251 p. 23 cm. [BT78.M15] 40-15263
1. Theology, Doctrinal. I. McCarty, T. R., joint author. II. Title.

MACCOLL, Alexander, 1866- 230
A working theology, by Alexander MacColl. New York, C. Scribner's sons, 1909. vii p., 1 l., 99 p. 19 1/2 cm. [BT78.M2] 9-6470
I. Title.

MCDONALD, James Porter, 230.53
1861-
Bible studies in Christian doctrines; or, Studies in theology, by Rev. J. P. McDonald. [Nashville, Tenn., Printed by the Cumberland Presbyterian publishing house, 1939] 1 p. l., 5-326 p. 18 cm. [BX8975.M3] 40-8174
1. Theology, Doctrinal. 2. Cumberland

Presbyterian church—Doctrinal and controversial works. I. Title.

MCDOWELL, John, 1780-1863. 230
Theology, in a series of sermons, in the order of the Westminster shorter catechism. By John M'Dowell... Elizabeth-Town [N.J.] M. Hale, 1825-26. 2 v. 22 1/2 cm. [BT75.M15] 39-7025
1. Theology, Doctrinal. 2. Presbyterian church—Doctrinal and controversial works. I. Title.

MCGUIRE, Ulysses Melville, 1856-1939. 230
In clearer light, by U. M. McGuire, edited by Wm. H. Strain ... [Bloomington? Ind., 1945] xii, 129 p. ports. 22 1/2 cm. "Privately published as a memorial to John McGuire Strain." [BT78.M25] 45-9406
1. Theology, Doctrinal. 2. Strain, John McGuire, 1935-1944. I. Strain, William Hunter, ed. II. Title.

MACINTOSH, Douglas Clyde, 1877- 260
Theology as an empirical science, by Douglas Clyde Macintosh ... New York, The Macmillan company, 1919. xvi p., 1 l., 270 p. 21 cm. [BT75.M2] 19-11655
1. Theology, Doctrinal. 2. Experience (Religion). 3. Theology—Methodology. I. Title.

MACINTOSH, Douglas Clyde, 1877-1948. 230
Theology as an empirical science / Douglas Clyde Macintosh. New York : Arno Press, 1980, [c1919] xvi, 270 p. ; 23 cm. (The Baptist tradition) Reprint of the ed. published by Macmillan, New York. Includes index. [BT75.M2 1980] 79-52601 ISBN 0-405-12466-X : 20.00
1. Theology, Doctrinal. 2. Experience (Religion) 3. Theology—Methodology. I. Title. II. Series: Baptist tradition.

MCKELWAY, Alexander J. 230
The Systematic theology of Paul Tillich, a review and analysis. Richmond, Knox [c.1964] 280p. 21cm. Bibl. 64-13969 5.50
1. Tillich, Paul, 1886- Systematic theology. 2. Theology, Doctrinal. I. Title.

MACKENZIE, William Douglas, 1859-
The final faith: a statement of the nature and authority of Christianity as the religion of the world, by W. Douglas Mackenzie... New York, The Macmillan company, 1910. xvi, 243 p. 22 1/2 cm. A 10
1. Theology, Doctrinal. 2. Christianity. I. Title.

MACQUARRIE, John. 230
Principles of Christian theology / John Macquarrie. 2d ed. New York : Scribner, c1977. xiii, 544 p. ; 24 cm. Includes bibliographical references and index. [BT75.2.M3 1977] 76-23182 ISBN 0-684-14776-9 : 15.00. ISBN 0-684-14777-7 pbk. : 6.95
1. Theology, Doctrinal. I. Title.

MARTIN, Earl L. 230
Toward understanding God, by Earl Martin ... Anderson, Ind., Gospel trumpet company [1942] xii, 13-255 p. 21 cm. [Christian life library series, ed. by H. L. Phillips] [BT75.M38] 42-17888
1. Theology, Doctrinal. I. Title.

MARTIN, Earl Leslie, 1892- 230
Toward understanding God, by Earl Martin ... Anderson, Ind., Gospel trumpet company [1942] xii, 13-255 p. 21 cm. [Christian life library series, ed. by H. I. Phillips] [BT75.M38] 42-17888
1. Theology, Doctrinal. I. Title.

MASCALL, Eric Lionel, 1905-
Via media; an essay in theological synthesis. Greenwich, Conn., Seabury press [1957] xvi, 171p. 19cm. Bibliography: p. 166-168.
1. Theology, Doctrinal. I. Title.

MEAD, Charles Marsh, 1836-1911. 230
Irenic theology; a study of some antitheses in religious thought, by Charles Marsh Mead ... New York and London, G. P. Putnam's sons, 1905. x p., 1 l., 375 p. 21 cm. [BT78.M4] 5-36319
1. Theology, Doctrinal. I. Title. II. Title: Antitheses in religious thought.
Contents omitted.

MELANCHTHON, Philipp, 1497-1560. 230.41
The Loci communes of Philip Melanchthon, with a critical introduction by the translator, Charles Leander Hill ... and a special introduction by Dean E. E. Flack ... Boston, Meador publishing company [c1944] 274 p. 20 1/2 cm. Bibliographical foot-notes. "Bibliographia Melanchthoniana": p. 268-274. [BR336.L62] 45-1360
1. Theology, Doctrinal. 2. Lutheran church—Doctrinal and controversial works. I. Hill, Charles Leander, tr. II. Title.

MELANCHTHON, Philipp, 1497-1560 230.4
Melanchthon on Christian doctrine: Loci communes, 1555. Tr., ed. by Clyde L. Manschreck. Introd. by Hans Engelland. New York, Oxford [c.]1965. lvii, 356p. 24cm. (Lib. of Protestant thought) Bibl. [BR336.L62M3] 65-20803 7.00
1. Theology, Doctrinal. 2. Lutheran Church—Doctrinal and controversial works. I. Manschreck, Clyde Leonard, 1917- ed. II. Title. III. Title: Loci communes, 1555. (Series)

MELANCHTHON, Philipp, 1497-1560. 230.4
Melanchthon on Christian doctrine: Loci communies, 1555. Translated and edited by Clyde L. Manschreck. Introd. by Hans Engelland. New York, Oxford University Press, 1965. lvii, 356 p. 24 cm. (A Library of Protestant thought) Bibliography: p. 345-348. [BR336.L62M3] 65-20803
1. Theology, Doctrinal. 2. Lutheran Church—Doctrinal and controversial works. I. Manschreck, Clyde Leonard, 1917- ed. II. Title. III. Title: Loci communes, 1555.

MELLENBRUCH, Parl Leslie, 1896- 230.4
The doctrines of Christianity, a handbook of evangelical theology, by Parl L. Mellenbruch ... New York, Chicago [etc.] Fleming H. Revell company [c1931] xxvi, 257 p. 21 cm. [BT75.M4] 31-13979
1. Theology, Doctrinal. I. Title.

MENNONITE church. Board of missions and charities. 230.97
The message and the message-bearer; setting forth in simple form the teachings of the Word of God and the character of the people who should make this message known to the world. Published under the auspices of the Mission committee of the Mennonite board of missions, and charities ... Scottdale, Pa., Mennonite publishing house, 1919. 156 p. 19 cm. [BX8121.A5 1919] 20-4900
1. Mennonites—Doctrinal and controversial works. 2. Theology, Doctrinal. I. Title.

MENNONITE church. General conference. 230.97
Bible doctrine; a treatise on the great doctrines of the Bible pertaining to God, angels, Satan, the church, and the salvation, duties and destiny of man, compiled by a committee appointed by Mennonite general conference Daniel Kauffman, editor ... Scottdale, Pa., Mennonite publishing house, 1914. 701 p. 22 1/2 cm. [BX8121.A52] 14-18107
1. Mennonites—Doctrinal and controversial works. 2. Theology, Doctrinal. I. Kauffman, Daniel, bp., ed. II. Title.

MERSCH, Emile, 1890-1940. 232
The theology of the mystical body; translated by Cyril Vollert. St. Louis, Herder, 1951. 663 p. 24 cm. [BX1751.M516] 51-7383
1. Theology, Doctrinal. 2. Catholic Church — Doctrinal and controversial works. 3. Jesus Christ — Mystical body. I. Title.

MIDDLETON, H. W. 230
The truth unmasked and error exposed in theology and metaphysics, moral government, and moral agency. By Elder H. W. Middleton ... Philadelphia, J. B. Lippincott & co., 1858. 314 p. 19 1/2 cm. [BT78.M62] 40-15264
1. Theology, Doctrinal. I. Title.

MILEY, John, 1813-1895. 230
Systematic theology ... By John Miley ... Neu York, Hunt & Eaton. Cincinnati, Cranston & Stowe, 1892-94. 2 v. 23 1/2 cm. (Added t.-p.: Library of Biblical and theological literature, ed. by G. R. Crooks. V-VI) Vol. II has imprint: New York, Hunt & Eaton; Cincinnati, Cranston & Curts. [BT5.M55] 39-7027
1. Theology, Doctrinal. 2. Methodist church—Doctrinal and controversial works. I. Title.

MILLER, John Allen, 1866-1936! 230.65
Christian doctrine; lectures and sermons. A memorial volume of selected lectures and sermons by the late Dr. J. Allen Miller ... Ashland, O., The Brethren publishing company, 1946. xvi, 346 p. incl. front. (port.) 23 1/2 cm. "Sponsored by the National ministerial association of the Brethren church." [BX7821.M5] 46-21258
1. The Brethren church (Progressive Dunkers)—Doctrinal and controversial works. 2. Theology, Doctrinal. I. Title.

MILNE, Bruce. 230
Know the truth : a handbook of Christian belief / Bruce Milne ; foreword by J.I. Packer. Downers Grove, Ill. : InterVarsity Press, c1982. p. cm. Includes index. [BT75.2.M49 1982] 19 82-4711 ISBN 0-87784-392-9 : 6.95
1. Theology, Doctrinal. I. Title.

MITCHELL, Thomas. 230
The gospel crown of life; a system of philosophical theology, by Thomas Mitchell ... Albany, J. Munsell, printer, 1851. xvii, viii, 417 p. front. (port.) 19 1/2 cm. [BT75.M6] 39-5080
1. Theology, Doctrinal. I. Title.

MOODY, Dale. 230
The word of truth : a summary of Christian doctrine based on Biblical revelation / Dale Moody. Grand Rapids, Mich. : W. B. Eerdmans Pub. Co., c1981. xii, 628 p. ; 24 cm. Includes bibliographical references and indexes. [BT75.2.M59] 19 80-19103 ISBN 0-8028-3533-3 : 23.95
1. Theology, Doctrinal. I. Title.

MOORE, Robert Braden, 1835-1906. 230
Old tabernacle theology for New Testament times, by R. Braden Moore, D. D. Philadelphia, Presbyterian board of publication and Sabbath-school work [1894] 440 p. 23 cm. [BT78.M8] 40-15266
1. Theology, Doctrinal. I. Presbyterian church in the U. S. A. Board of publication. II. Title.

MUELLER, John Theodore, 1885- 230
Christian dogmatics; a handbook of doctrinal theology for pastors, teachers and laymen, by John Theodore Mueller ... St. Louis, Mo., Concordia publishing house, 1934. xxiii, 665 p. 24 cm. An epitome of F. A. O. Pieper's "Christian dogmatik." cf. Foreword. [BT75.P55] 34-32378
1. Theology, Doctrinal. I. Pieper, Franz August Otto, 1852-1931 Christliche dogmatik. II. Title.

MULFORD, Elisha, 1833-1885. 230
The republic of God. An institute of theology. By Elisha Mulford, LL. D. Boston, Houghton, Mifflin and company, 1881. 2 p. l., [iii]-viii, 260 p., 1 l. 22 cm. [BT75.M75 1881] 4-4039
1. Theology, Doctrinal. 2. Protestant Episcopal church in the U. S. A.—Doctrinal and controversial works. I. Title.

MULFORD, Elisha, 1833-1885. 230
The republic of God. An institute of theology. By Elisha Mulford, LL. D. 5th thousand, rev. Boston and New York, Houghton, Mifflin and company, 1897. 2 p. l., [iii]-viii, 260 p., 1 l. 22 cm. [BT75.M75 1897] 4-10394
1. Theology, Doctrinal. I. Title.

MULLINS, Edgar Young, 1860-1928. 260
The Christian religion in its doctrinal expression, by Edgar Young Mullins ... Philadelphia, New York [etc.] Roger Williams press [1917] xxiv, 514 p. 24 cm. [BT75.M8] 17-28792
1. Theology, Doctrinal. I. Title.

NEWMAN, John Henry, Cardinal 1801-1890 230.2
The heart of Newman, a synthesis arranged by Erich Przywara. Introd. by H. Francis Davis. Springfield, Ill., Templegate [1963] xx, 361p. port. 17cm. Pub. in 1931 under title: A Newman synthesis. 63-25651 3.95
1. Theology, Doctrinal. I. Przywara, Erich, 1889- comp. II. Title.

NOORE, Gerardus Cornelis van, 1861-1946. 282
Dogmatic theology; translated and revised by John J. Castelot [and] William R. Murphy. Westminster, Md., Newman Press, 1955- v. 24cm. Contents.v.1. The true religion; from the 5th ed. edited by J. P. Verhaar. Includes bibliographies. [BX1751.N7] 55-10552
1. Theology, Doctrinal. 2. Catholic Church—Doctrinal and controversial works. I. Title.

NOORT, Gerardus Cornelis van, 1861-1946. 282
Dogmatic theology, v. 3. tr. and rev. by John J. Castelot, William R. Murphy. Westminster, Md., Newman Press [c.]1961. 420p. Contents.v. 3. The sources of revelation; Divine Faith. Bibl. 55-10552 7.50 rev
1. Theology, Doctrinal. 2. Catholic Church—Doctrinal and controversial works. I. Title.

NOORT, Gerardus Cornelis van, 1861-1946. 282
Dogmatic theology; translated and revised by John J. Castelot [and] William R. Murphy. Westminster, Md., Newman Press, 1955- v. 24cm. Contents.v. 1. The true religion.-- v. 2. Christ's church. Includes bibliographies. [BX1751.N7] 55-10552
1. Theology, Doctrinal. 2. Catholic Church— Doctrinal and controversial works. I. Title.

NORTON, John, 1606-1663. 230'.58
The orthodox evangelist. New York : AMS Press, [1981] p. cm. (A Library of American Puritan writings ; v. 11) Reprint. Originally published: London : Printed by J. Macock for H. Cripps, 1654. Includes index. [BT70.N8 1981] 19 78-280 ISBN 0-404-60811-6 : 57.50
1. Theology, Doctrinal. I. Title. II. Series.

OMAN, John Wood, 1860-
Grace and personality, by John Oman ... 2d ed., rev. Cambridge, The University press, 1919. xvi, 302 p. 20 cm. A 20
1. Theology, Doctrinal. 2. Religion—Addresses, essays, lectures. I. Title.

OMAN, John Wood, 1860-1939. 230
Grace and personality. [New York] Association [1961, c.1917] 255p. (Giant reflection bks., 701) 61-14175 1.50 pap.,
1. Theology, Doctrinal. I. Title.

OOSTERZEE, Johannes Jacobus van, 1817-1882. 230
Christian dogmatics: a text-book for academical instruction and provate study. / By J. J. van Oosterzee...Translated from the Dutch by John Watson Watson...and Maurice J. Evans... New York Scribner, Armstrong & co., 1874 2v. 25 cm. (Added t.-p.: Theological and philosophical library...ed. by H.B. Smith and Philip Schaff) Paged continously...Bibliographies interspersed. [BT75.O65] 35-22745
1. Theology, Doctrinal I. Watson, John Watson d. 1889, tr. II. Evans, Maurice J., joint tr. III. Title.

ORR, James, 1844-1913.
Sidelights on Christian doctrine, by James Orr ... New York, A. C. Armstrong & son, 1909. 4 p. l., 183 p. 23 cm. A 11
1. Theology, Doctrinal. I. Title.
Contents omitted.

OSBORN, Loran David, 1863- 230
The recovery & restatement of the gospel, by Loran David Osborn, PH. D. Chicago, The University of Chicago press, 1903. xxvi, 253 p. 20 cm. Issued also as thesis (PH. D.) University of Chicago. [BT75.O8 1903] 3-18662
1. Theology, Doctrinal. 2. Theology, Doctrinal—Hist. 3. Bible. N. T.—Theology. 4. Bible—Theology—N. T. I. Title.

OSTERHAVEN, M. Eugene 1915- (Maurice Eugene), 230'.57
The faith of the Church : a Reformed perspective on its historical development / M. Eugene Osterhaven. Grand Rapids, Mich. : Eerdmans, c1982. p. cm. Includes

bibliographical references. [BX9571.O84] 19 82-5061 ISBN 0-8028-1916-8 : 11.95
1. Theology, Doctrinal. 2. Reformed Church—Doctrinal and controversial works. I. Title.

PARMELEE, J H., Rev. 230
Problems in theology. By Rev. J. H. Parmelee. Boston, G. J. Stiles, printer, 1886. 1 p. l., 199 p. 20 cm. [BT78.P2] 37-39622
1. Theology, Doctrinal. I. Title.

PEARLMAN, Myer, 1898- 230
Knowing the doctrines of the Bible, by Myer Pearlman. Springfield, Mo., The Gospel publishing house [1939] 1 p. l., v-xiv, 15-399 p. 20 cm. "Second edition." [BT75.P4 1939] 41-19459
1. Theology, Doctrinal. I. Title.

PECOCK, Reginald, 1395?-1460? 230
The donet, By Reginald Pecock ... now first ed. from ms. Bodl. 916 and collated with The poore mennis myrrour (British museum, Addl. 37788) by Elsie Vaughan Hitchcock ... London, Pub. for the Early English text society, by H. Milford, Oxford university press, 1921. xxxii, 270 p., 1 l. front. (facsim.) 23 cm. (Half-title: Early English text society. Original series, no. 156) Early English text society's List of publications, etc. (8 p.) at end. Intended as a simple statement of Christian doctrine, in form of dialogue between father and son, written about 1445. Condemmed to be burned. A supplement "The folewer to The conet," forms no. 164 of the series [PR1119.A2 no. 156] 22-5093
1. Theology, Doctrinal. I. Hitchcock, Elise Vaughan, ed. II. Title. III. Title: The poore mennis myrrour.

PECOCK, Reginald, 1395?-1460? 230
The folewer to the Donet, by Reginald Pecock ... now first edited from Brit, mus. roy. ms. 17 D. ix, with an introduction on Pecock's language and style by Elsie Vaughan Hitechcock ... London, Pub. for the Early English text society, by H. Milford, Oxford university press, 1924. ixxx, 263, [1] p. front. (facsim.) 23 cm. (Half-title: Early English text society. Original series, no. 164. 1924 (for 1923)) Composed about 1454. A supplement to the author's Donet, an introduction to Christian doctrine. written about 1445. Ije parti (p. 181-227) contains. "Answers to arguments against the Four tables." The Donet forms no. 156 of the same series. Early English text society's List of publications, etc. (8 p.) at end. [PR1119.A2 no. 164] 24-13716
1. Theology, Doctrinal. I. Hitchcock, Elsie Vaughan, ed. II. Title.

PECOCK, Reginald, 1395?-1460? 230
The reule of Crysten religioun, by Reginald Pecock ... now first edited from Pierpont Morgan ms. 519 by William Cabell Green ... London, Pub. for the Early English text society by H. Milford, Oxford university press, 1927. xxxi, 539 p. front. (facsim.) 23 cm. (Half-title: Early English text society. Original series, no. 171. 1927 (for 1926)) Early English text society's List of publications, etc. (8 p.) at end. [PR1119.A2 no. 171] 28-10528
1. Theology, Doctrinal. 2. Christian life. I. Greet, William Cabell, ed. II. Title.

PENDLETON, James Madison, 230
1811-1891.
Christian doctrines: a compendium of theology, by J. M. Pendleton ... Philadelphia, American Baptist publication society [c1906] 426 p. 20 cm. First published 1878. [BT77.P4] 6-9692
1. Theology, Doctrinal. I. Title.

PETRUS THOMAE, ca.1280- 230.2
ca.1340.
Quodlibet. Edited by Sister M. Rachel Hooper and Eligius M. Buytaert. St. Bonaventure, N.Y., Franciscan Institute, 1957. xiv, 242 p. 24 cm. (Franciscan Institute publications. Text series, no. 11) Text based chiefly on MS. 1494, fol. 67-103, of the Nationalbibliothek, Vienna. Includes bibliographical references. [BX1749.P46] 75-261555
1. Catholic Church—Doctrinal and controversial works. 2. Theology, Doctrinal. I. Hooper, Mary Rachel, ed. II. Buytaert, Eloi Marie, 1913- ed. III. Vienna. Nationalbibliothek. MSS. (1494) IV. Title. V. Series: St. Bonaventure University, St. Bonaventure, N.Y. Franciscan Institute. Text series, no. 11

PIEPER, Franz August Otto, 230
1852-1931.
Christian dogmatics. Saint Louis, Concordia Pub. House, 1950-57. 4v. 24cm. Vol. 4: Index. Bibliographical footnotes. [BT75.P53] 50-8650
1. Theology. Doctrinal. 2. Lutheran Church—Doctrinal and controversial works. I. Title.

PITTENGER, W. Norman 1905- 230'.2
(William Norman)
Catholic faith in a process perspective / Norman Pittenger. Maryknoll, NY : Orbis Books, [1981] p. cm. Bibliography: p. [BT75.2.P57] 19 81-9615 ISBN 0-88344-091-1 pbk. : 6.95
1. Theology, Doctrinal. 2. Process theology. I. Title.

PORTEOUS, Alvin C., 1922- 201'.1
The search for Christian credibility; explorations in contemporary belief [by] Alvin C. Porteous. Nashville, Abingdon Press [1971] 207 p. 20 cm. Includes bibliographical references. [BT75.2.P67] 74-148069 ISBN 0-687-37121-X
1. Theology, Doctrinal. I. Title.

PREMM, Mathias, 1890- 230.2
Dogmatic theology for the laity. Staten Island, N. Y., Alba [1967] 456p. 23cm. Tr. of Weltuberwindender Glaube. [BX1751.2.P713] 67-21425 9.50
1. Theology, Doctrinal. 2. Catholic Church—Doctrinal and controversial work. I. Title.

PRENTER, Regin, 1907- 230
Creation and redemption. Tr. by Theodor I. Jensen. Philadelphia, Fortress [1967] xi, 596p. 23cm. Bibl. [BT75.2.P713] 66-17342 9.00
1. Theology, Doctrinal. I. Title.

PRICE, Richard, 1723-1791.
Sermons on the Christian doctrine, as received by the different denominations of Christians. By Richard Price ... With an appendix, occasioned by Dr. Priestley's letters to the authors. Boston, Printed and published by Wells and Lilly, 1815. 120 p. 22 cm. [BX5261.P] A 32
1. Theology, Doctrinal. I. Title.

PRINCIPLES of Christian 181.4
theology New York, Scribners [c.1966] xiv, 477p. 24cm. Bibl. [B] 7.95; 3.95 pap.,
1. Theology, Doctrinal. I. Macquarrie, John

PURKISER, W T ed. 230.99
Exploring our Christian faith. W. T. Purkiser, editor [and others] Kansas City, Mo., Beacon Hill Press [1960] 615p. 23cm. Includes bibliography. [BT75.2.P85] 60-10576
1. Theology, Doctrinal. 2. Church of the Nazarene—Doctrinal and controversial works. I. Title.

PURKISER, W. T. 230
God, man & salvation : a Biblical theology / by W. T. Purkiser, Richard S. Taylor, Willard H. Taylor. Kansas City, Mo. : Beacon Hill Press of Kansas City, c1977. 732 p. ; 23 cm. Includes indexes. Bibliography: p. 715-732. [BS543.P87] 77-70038 ISBN 0-8341-0440-7 : 16.95
1. Bible—Theology. 2. Theology, Doctrinal. I. Taylor, Richard Shelley, 1912- joint author. II. Taylor, Willard H., joint author. III. Title.

RAHNER, Hugo, 1900- 230
A theology of proclamation. Tr. by Richard Dimmler [others] Adapted by Joseph Halpin. [New York] Herder & Herder [1968] 216p. 22cm. Tr. of Eine Theologie der Verkundigung. Bibl. [BT78.R2813] 67-29677 5.95
1. Theology, Doctrinal. 2. Communication (Theology) 3. Preaching. I. Halpin, Joseph. II. Title.

RAHNER, Karl, 1904- 230'.2
Foundations of Christian faith : an introduction to the idea of Christianity / Karl Rahner ; translated by William V. Dych. New York : Seabury Press, 1978. xv, 470 p. ; 24 cm. "A Crossroad book." Translation of Grundkurs des Glaubens. [BT75.2.R3313] 77-13336 ISBN 0-8164-0354-6 : 17.50
1. Theology, Doctrinal. I. Title.

RAHNER, Karl, 1904- 230'.2
Foundations of Christian faith : an introduction to the idea of Christianity / Karl Rahner ; translated by William V. Dych. New York : Crossroad, 1982, c1978. xv, 470 p. ; 23 cm. Translation of: Grundkurs des Glaubens. [BT75.2.R3313 1982] 19 82-4663 ISBN 0-8245-0523-9 (pbk.) : 12.95
1. Catholic Church—Doctrinal and controversial works—Catholic authors. 2. Theology, Doctrinal. I. [Grundkurs des Glaubens.] English II. Title.

RALL, Harris Franklin, 1870- 230
The God of our faith. New York, Abingdon Press [1955] 158p. 21cm. [BT75.R16] 55-10271
1. Theology, Doctrinal. 2. God. I. Title.

RALSTON, Thomas Neely, 1806- 230
1891.
Elements of divinity; or, A concise and comprehensive view of Bible theology; comprising the doctrines, evidences, morals, and institutions of Christianity; with appropriate questions appended to each chapter. By Thomas N. Ralston ... Edited by T. O. Summers, D. D. Nashville, Tenn., A. H. Redford, 1871. 1023 p. 24 cm. [BT75.R2 1871] 25-4658
I. Summers, Thomas Osmond, 1812-1882, ed. II. Title.

RALSTON, Thomas Neely, 1806- 230
1891.
Elements of divinity, by Thomas N. Ralston, D. D. A concise and comprehensive view of Bible theology; comprising the doctrines, evidences, morals, and institutions of Christianity; with appropriate questions appended to each chapter; edited by T. O. Summers, D. D. Rev., with introduction. Nashville, Tenn., Cokesbury press, 1924. 1 p. l., 1023 p. 24 cm. [BT75.R2 1924] 25-2856
1. Theology, Doctrinal. I. Summers, Thomas Osmond, 1812-1882, ed. II. Title.

RALSTON, Thomas Neely, 1806- 230
1891.
Elements of divinity; or, A course of lectures, comprising a clear and concise view of the system of theology as taught in the Holy Scriptures; with appropriate questions appended to each lecture, by Rev. Thomas N. Ralston ... Louisville, Ky., Morton & Griswold, 1847. iv, [5]-463 p. 24 cm. [BT75.R2 1847] 25-4656
1. Theology, Doctrinal. I. Title.

RAMSDELL, Edward Thomas. 230
The Christian perspective. New York, Abingdon-Cokesbury Press [1950] 218 p. 22 cm. Bibliographical footnotes. [BT75.R213] 50-6922
1. Theology, Doctrinal. I. Title.

RAYMOND, Miner, 1811-1897. 230
Systematic theology. By Miner Raymond ... Cincinnati, Hitchcock and Walden; New York, Nelson and Phillips, 1877-79. 3 v. 23 cm. Vol. iii has imprint: Cincinnati, Hitchcock and Walden; New York, Phillips and Hunt. [BT75.R23] 39-7030
1. Theology, Doctrinal. 2. Methodist church—Doctrinal and controversial works. I. Title.

REED, David Allen. 230
Outline of the fundamental doctrines of the Bible, by David Allen Reed ... New York, Chicago [etc.] Fleming H. Revell company [1893] 107 p. 19 cm. Interleaved. [BT77.R37] 41-33818
1. Theology, Doctrinal. I. Title.

**REVUE Thomiste;* 282.05
revue doctrinale de theologie et de philosophie; v.1-48. New York, Kraus Reprint, 1965. 48v. (various p.) 23cm. For the years 1893-1948, excluding 1915-1917 and 1940-1945 when pubn. was suspended. set, 1,100.00; set, pap., 990.00; ea., pap., 22.50

RICHEY, Thomas, d.1905. 230
Truth and counter truth; by the Rev. Thomas Richey, D.D. New York, J. Pott & co., 1900. vii, [4], [13]-118 p. 18 1/2 cm. [BT77.R5] 31-9269
1. Theology, Doctrinal. I. Title.

ROBERTS, James Deotis. 230
A Black political theology, by J. Deotis Roberts. Philadelphia, Westminster Press [1974] 238 p. 19 cm. Includes bibliographical references. [BT75.2.R6] 74-4384 ISBN 0-664-24988-4 3.95 (pbk.).
1. Theology, Doctrinal. 2. Negroes—Religion. I. Title.

ROBERTSON, Frederick William,
1816-1853.
Sermons on Christian doctrine, by Frederick W. Robertson. London, J. M. Dent & co.; New York, E. P. Dutton [1906] 349, [1] p. 18 cm. (Half-title: Everyman's library, ed. by Ernest Rhys. Theology & philosophy) "Works of F. W. Robertson": p. 8. A 22
1. Theology, Doctrinal. I. Title.

ROBINSON, Ezekiel Gilman, 230
1815-1894.
Christian theology, by Ezekiel Gilman Robinson... Rochester, N.Y., Press of E. R. Andrews [1894] viii, 385 p. 23 1/2 cm. [BT75.R7] 39-5809
1. Theology, Doctrinal. 2. Baptists—Doctrinal and controversial works. I. Title.

RYAN, Michael D., 230'.09'04
comp.
The contemporary explosion of theology : ecumenical studies in theology / Langdon Gilkey ... [et al.] ; edited and introduced by Michael D. Ryan. Metuchen, N.J. : Scarecrow Press, 1975. viii, 190 p. ; 22 cm. Includes bibliographical references and index. [BT75.2.R9] 74-34125 ISBN 0-8108-0794-7 : 7.50
1. Theology, Doctrinal. 2. Theology, Doctrinal—History—20th century. I. Gilkey, Langdon Brown, 1919- II. Title.

SAWYER, Elbert Henry, 1843- 230
The science of religion, by Elbert H. Sawyer ... Philadelphia, Chicago [etc.] The John C. Winston company [c1936] xv, 392 p. 21 cm. "General references": p. 391-392. [BT77.S3] 36-25819
1. Theology, Doctrinal. I. Title.

SCHEEBEN, Matthias Joseph, 282
1835-1888.
A manual of Catholic theology, based on Scheeben's "Dogmatik," by Joseph Wilhelm ... and Thomas B. Scannell ... with a preface by Cardinal Manning ... 2d ed. New York, The Catholic publication society co., 1899-1901. 2 v. 23 cm. Contents.i. The sources of theological knowledge, God, creation and the supernatural order.--ii. The fall, redemption, grace, the church and the sacraments, the last things. [BX1751.S25] 5-20037
1. Theology, Doctrinal. 2. Catholic church—Doctrinal and controversial works. I. Wilhelm, Joseph, tr. II. Scannell, Thomas Bartholomew, 1854-1917, joint tr. III. Title.

SCHLEIERMACHER, Friedrich 230
Ernst Daniel, 1768-1834.
The Christian faith / by Friedrich Schleiermacher ; edited by H. R. Mackintosh and J. S. Stewart. Philadelphia : Fortress Press, 1976. xii, 760 p. ; 23 cm. Translation of the 2d ed. of Der christliche Glaube. Includes bibliographical references and indexes. [BT75.S58513 1976] 76-53313 ISBN 0-8006-0487-3
1. Theology, Doctrinal. I. Title.

SCHLEIERMACHER, Friedrich 230
Ernst Daniel, 1768-1834.
The theology of Schleiermacher; a condensed presentation of his chief work, "The Christian faith", by George Cross ... Chicago, Ill., The University of Chicago press [1911] xi, 344 p. 20 cm. "Works of reference": p. 335-337. [BT75.S5C74] 11-13345
1. Theology, Doctrinal. I. Cross, George, 1862- II. Title.

SCHMAUS, Michael, 1897- 230.2
Dogma. [Translated by Ann Laeuchli, and others] New York, Sheed and Ward [1968- v. 21 cm. "A project of John XXIII Institute, Saint Xavier College, Chicago." Translation of Der Glaube der Kirche. Contents.Contents.—v. 1. God in revelation.—v. 2. God and creation.—v. 3. God and His Christ.—v. 4. The Church: its origin and structure. Includes bibliographical references. [BT75.2.S3513] 68-26033 ISBN 0-8362-0385-2 (v. 3) 3.95 per vol.

1. Theology, Doctrinal. I. John XXIII Institute, Chicago.

SCHMUCKER, Samuel Simon, 1799-1873. 230.41
Elements of popular theology, with special reference to the doctrines of the reformation, as avowed before the Diet at Augsburg, in mdxxx. Designed chiefly for private Christians and theological students. By S. S. Schmucker ... 3d ed., with numerous additions. Baltimore, Printed and published at publication rooms; New York, D. Appleton & co. and Saxton & Dayton; [etc., etc.] 1842. xii, 396 p. 18 cm. "Formula for the government and discipline of the Evangelical Lutheran church. [Published by the General synod of said church.]": p. [355]-388. "Constitution of the General synod of the Evan. Luth. church in the United States of North America": p. 389-396. [BX8065.S445 1842] 38-29419
1. Theology, Doctrinal. 2. Augsburg confession. 3. Lutheran church—Doctrinal and controversial works. 4. Lutheran church—Government. I. General synod of the Evangelical Lutheran church in the United States of America. II. Title.

SCHOONENBERG, Piet J. A. M., 1911- 232
The Christ; a study of the God-man relationship in the whole of creation and in Jesus Christ [by] Piet Schoonenberg. [Translated by Della Couling. New York] Herder and Herder [1971] 191 p. 22 cm. Translation of Hij is een God van mensen. Includes bibliographical references. [BT202.S3613] 74-127874 8.50
1. Jesus Christ—Person and offices. 2. Theology, Doctrinal. I. Title.

SCOTT, Thomas, 1747-1821. 230
Essays on the most important subjects in religion. By Thomas Scott ... 1st American, from the 3d London ed. ... Whitehall: Printed for W. W. Woodward, no. 52, corner of Second and Chestnut streets, Philadelphia ...... 1806. 1 p. l., ii, [2], [9]-366, [4] p. 18 1/2 cm. [BT70.S35 1806] 43-41747
1. Theology, Doctrinal. I. Title.

SELBIE, William Boothby, 1862-
Evangelical Christianity, its history and witness; a series of lectures delivered at Mansfield college, Oxford, in the Hilary term, 1911, ed. by W. B. Selbie... London, New York [etc.] Hodder and Stoughton [1911] xii, 256 p. 20 cm. Contents.Introduction.--I. The Protestant idea of church and ministry as rooted in early Christianity, by J. Vernon Bartlet--II. The Church of England, by A. J. Carlyle.--III. The Presbyterian churches, by John Oman--IV. The Congregational churches, by F. J. Powicke.--V. The Baptist churches, by Newton H. Marshall.--VI. The Society of Friends, by Edward Grubb.--VII. The Methodist churches, by A. S. Peake. A 13
1. Theology, Doctrinal. 2. Christian union. I. Bartlet, James Vernon, 1863- II. Carlyle, A. J., 1861- III. Oman, John Wood, 1860- IV. Powicke, Frederick J. V. Marshall, Newton H. VI. Grubb, Edward. VII. Peake, Arthur Samuel, 1865- VIII. Title.

SELWYN, Edward Gordon, 1885- 260
The approach to Christianity, by Edward Gordon Selwyn... London, New York [etc.] Longmans, Green and co., 1925. 2 p. l., vii-xv, 286 p. 22 1/2 cm. [BT75.S626] 25-19204
1. Theology, Doctrinal. 2. Apologetics—20th cent. 3. Church of England—Doctrinal and controversial works. I. Title.

SHEDD, William Greenough Thayer, 1820-1894. 230
Dogmatic theology, by William G. T. Shedd ... New York, C. Scribner's sons, 1888-94 3 v. 23 cm. Vol. III has subtitle: Supplement. Bibliography at beginning of some of the chapters. [BT75.S63] 39-5814
1. Theology, Doctrinal. 2. Presbyterian church in the U.S.A.—Doctrinal and controversial works. I. Title.

SHEDD, William Greenough Thayer, 1820-1894. 230'.5
Dogmatic theology / by William G. T. Shedd. 2d ed. Nashville : T. Nelson, c1980. 3 v. : port. ; 21 cm. [BT75.S63 1980] 19 80-19709 ISBN 0-8407-5223-7 (v. 1) ISBN 0-8407-5743-3 (pbk. : v. 1) set : 37.50

1. Presbyterian Church in the U.S.A.—Doctrinal and controversial works. 2. Theology, Doctrinal. I. Title.

SHEED, Francis Joseph, 1897- 230
God and the himan condition; v. 1 [by] F. J. Sheed. New York, Sheed [1966] 301p. 22cm. Contents.v. 1. God and the human mind. [BT75.2.S5] 66-22027 5.00
1. Theology, Doctrinal. I. Title.

SHELDON, Henry Clay, 1845-1928. 260
System of Christian doctrine. By Henry C. Sheldon ... Cincinnati, Jennings and Pye; New York, Eaton and Mains [c1903] xi, 635 p. 24 cm. [BT75.S64] 4-9127
1. Theology, Doctrinal. I. Title.

SIMMONS, Thomas Paul. 230.6
A systematic study of Bible doctrine; a logical arrangement and a diligent treatment of the teachings of God's holy word for the average preacher and the studious layman, by Thomas Paul Simmons... Ashland, Ky., Baptist book and Bible house, 1936. ix, 11-505 p. 23 cm. Advertising matter: p. 504-505. [BX6331.S5] 36-9711
1. Theology, Doctrinal. 2. Baptists—Doctrinal and controversial works. I. Title.

SINGMASTER, John Alden, 1852-1926. 260
A handbook of Christian theology, by J. A. Singmaster. Philadelphia, The United Lutheran publication house [c1927] 308 p. 22 1/2 cm. [BT75.S65] 27-16135
1. Theology, Doctrinal. I. Title. II. Title: Christian theology, A handbook of.

SLAATTE, Howard Alexander. 201'.1
The paradox of existentialist theology; the dialectics of a faith-subsumed reason-in-existence [by] Howard A. Slaatte. New York, Humanities Press, 1971 [i.e. 1972] xv, 254 p. 24 cm. Bibliography: p. 233-245. [BT84.S57] 75-172936 ISBN 0-391-00161-2 7.50
1. Theology, Doctrinal. 2. Existentialism. I. Title.

SLAATTE, Howard Alexander. 230'.044
The paradox of existentialist theology : the dialectics of a faith-subsumed reason-in-existence / Howard A. Slaatte. Washington, D.C. : University Press of America, c1982. xv, 254 p. ; 22 cm. Reprint. Originally published: New York : Humanities Press, 1971 [i.e. 1972] Sequel to: The pertinence of the paradox. Includes indexes. Bibliography: p. 233-245. [BT84.S57 1982] 19 81-43508 ISBN 0-8191-2187-8 : 21.50 ISBN 0-8191-2188-6 (pbk.) : 11.00
1. Theology, Doctrinal. 2. Existentialism. I. Slaate, Howard Alexander. The pertinence of the paradox. II. Title.

SMITH, Harold D 230
A criticism of Christian dogma; a plea for a revitalized morality based on rational principles, by Harold D. Smith. [1st ed.] New York, Exposition Press [1964] 119 p. 21 cm. Bibliography: [117]-119. [BT75.2.S6] 65-2514
1. Theology, Doctrinal. I. Title.

SMITH, Henry Boynton, 1815-1877. 230
System of Christian theology [by] Henry B. Smith... edited by William S. Karr... New York, A. C. Armstrong and son, 1884. xiv, 630 p. 24 1/2 cm. [BT75.S66 1884] 39-7033
1. Theology, Doctrinal. 2. Congregational churches—Doctrinal and controversial works. I. Karr, William Stevens, 1829-1888, ed. II. Title.

SMITH, Henry Boynton, 1815-1877. 230
System of Christian theology, by Henry B. Smith...edited by William S. Karr ... 4th ed., rev. With an introduction by Thomas S. Hastings... New York, A. C. Armstrong and son, 1890. xx, 641 p. 23 cm. [BT75.S66 1890] 39-7034
1. Theology, Doctrinal. 2. Congregational churches—Doctrinal and controversial works. I. Karr, William Stevens, 1829-1888, ed. II. Hastings, Thomas Samuel, 1827-1911, ed. III. Title.

SMITH, Samuel Stanhope, 1750-1819. 230
A comprehensive view of the leading and most important principles of natural and revealed religion; digested in such order as to present to the pious and reflecting mind, a basis for the superstructure of the entire system of the doctrines of the gospel. By the Rev. Samuel Stanhope Smith ... New-Brunswick [N. J.]: Printed and published by Deare & Myer, 1815. vii, [1] p., 1 l., [3]-543 p. 22 cm. [BT75.S67 1815] 39-5816
1. Theology, Doctrinal. 2. Presbyterian church in the U. S. A.—Doctrinal and controversial works. I. Title.

SMITH, Samuel Stanhope, 1750-1819. 230
A comprehensive view of the leading and most important principles of natural and revealed religion: digested in such order as to present to the pious and reflecting mind, a basis for the superstructure of the entire system of the doctrines of the gospel. By the Rev. Samuel Stanhope Smith ... 2d ed.--with additions. New-Brunswick [N. J.]: Printed and published by Deare & Myer, 1816. 544 p. 22 cm. [BT75.S67 1816] 39-10941
1. Theology, Doctrinal. 2. Presbyterian church in the U. S. A.—Doctrinal and controversial works. I. Title.

SMITH, William Edward, 1881- 230
God's creation and salvation, by William Edward Smith. Boston, Meador publishing company, 1938. 327 p. front. (port.) 21 cm. [BT75.S675] 38-18155
1. Theology, Doctrinal. I. Title.

SMITH, William Martin, 1872- 230
Bible doctrines, by William M. Smith ... 2d ed. (rev.) Westfield, Ind., Union Bible seminary, 1934. 223 p. 21 cm. [BT77.S63] 35-2623
1. Theology, Doctrinal. I. Title.

SONG, Choan-Seng, 1929- 230
Third-eye theology : theology in formation in Asian settings / Choan-Seng Song. Maryknoll, N.Y. : Orbis Books, c1979. xiii, 274 p. ; 24 cm. Includes bibliographical references. [BT78.S66] 79-4208 ISBN 0-88344-474-7 pbk. : 9.95
1. Theology, Doctrinal. 2. Christianity and other religions. 3. Asia—Religion. 4. Asia—Civilization. I. Title.

SPALDING, Joshua, 1760-1825. 230
The divine theory; a system of divinity, founded wholly upon Christ; which by one principle, offers an explanation of all the works of God. By Joshua Spalding ... Elizabeth-town (N.J.) Printed by Shepard Kollock, nearly opposite the academy. 1808-12. 2 v. 21 cm. [BT75.S68] 44-52874
1. Theology, Doctrinal. I. Title.

SPARKES, Vernone M., 1938- 230
The theological enterprise, by Vernone M. Sparkes. [Independence, Mo., Herald Pub. House, 1969] 272 p. 21 cm. Includes bibliographical references. [BT75.2.S65] 73-89842 5.95
1. Theology, Doctrinal. I. Title.

SPROULL, Thomas, 1803-1892. 230
Prelections on theology, by Rev. Thomas Sproull ... Pittsburgh, Printed by Myers, Shinkle & co., 1882. viii, 455 p. front. (port.) 23 1/2 cm. [BT75.S7] 39-7035
1. Theology, Doctrinal. 2. Presbyterian church—Doctrinal and controversial works. I. Title.

SPURRIER, William Atwell.
Guide to the Christian faith, an introduction to Christian doctrine. New York, Scribner [1963, c1952] xii, 242 p. 21 cm. Bibliography: p. 239-240. 68-19633
1. Theology, Doctrinal. I. Title.

STAFFORD, Thomas Polhill, 1866- 230
A study of Christian doctrines, by T. P. Stafford ... Kansas City, Mo., Western Baptist publishing company, 1936. 6 p. l., 15-645 p. 23 cm. [BT75.S73] 36-20699
1. Theology, Doctrinal. I. Title.

STEARNS, Lewis French, 1847-1892. 230
Present day theology; a popular discussion of leading doctrines of the Christian faith, by Lewis French Stearns ... with a biographical sketch by George L. Prentiss ... New York, C. Scribner's sons, 1893. xxiv, 568 p. front. (port.) 21 cm. [BT75.S75] 39-7036
1. Theology, Doctrinal. 2. Congregational churches—Doctrinal and controversial works. I. Prentiss, George Lewis, 1816-1903. II. Title.

STEVENS, George Barker, 1854-1906. 230
Doctrine and life; a study of some of the principal truths of the Christian religion in their relation to Christian experience, by George B. Stevens ... New York Boston [etc.] Silver, Burdett & company, 1895. 3 p. l., v-vi, 247 p. 20 cm. [BT78.S8] 40-20157
1. Theology, Doctrinal. I. Title.

STEVENS, William Wilson.
The doctrines of the Christian religion. Clinton, Mississippi College [1965] 251 p. 67-841
1. Theology, Doctrinal. 2. Christianity. I. Title.

STEVENS, William Wilson. 230
Doctrines of the Christian religion. Grand Rapids, Eerdmans [1967] 435 p. 24 cm. Bibliography: p. 411-413. [BT75.2.S7] 67-13977
1. Theology, Doctrinal. I. Title.

STEWART, Marshall Bowyer, 1880-
In other words; reflections on Christian theology, by the Rev. Marshall Bowyer Stewart. West Park, N.Y., Holy cross press, 1941. 78 p. 20 cm. A 41
1. Theology, Doctrinal. I. Title.

STORR, Gottlob Christian, 1746-1805. 230
An elementary course of Biblical theology, translated from the work of Professors Storr and Flatt, with additions by S. S. Schmucker ... 2d ed. Andover [Mass.] Gould and Newman; New-York, Griffin, Wilcox and co., 1836. xvi, [17]-605 p. 23 cm. The author's Doctrine christianae pars theoretica. 1793, was translated by Flatt, 1803, under title: Lehrbuch der christichen dogmatik. Schmucker translated this into English, 1826, in 2 volumes; the second edition is condensed from the first. [BT75.S77 1836] 39-10312
1. Theology, Doctrinal. I. Flatt, Karl Christian, 1772-1843, ed. and tr. II. Schmucker, Samuel Simon, 1799-1873, ed. and tr. III. Title.

STRONG, Augustus Hopkins, 1836-1921. 230
Lectures on theology. By Augustus Hopkins Strong. Printed for the use of students in the Rochester theological seminary. Rochester, Press of E. R. Andrews, 1876. xvi, 271 p. 24 cm. Bibliographies interspersed. [BT75.S8] 39-7372
1. Theology, Doctrinal. 2. Baptists—Doctrinal and controversial works. I. Rochester theological seminary, Rochester, N.Y. II. Title.

STRONG, Augustus Hopkins, 1836-1921. 260
Outlines of systematic theology, designed for the use of theological students, by Augustus Hopkins Strong ... Philadelphia, The Griffith & Rowland press [1906] xxviii, 274 p. 23 1/2 cm. "The present work contains the substance of my 'systematic theology' It omits all bibliographical and illustrative material, and confines itself to bare statements of doctrine."--Introd. note. [BT75.S85] 8-30158
1. Theology, Doctrinal. I. Title.

STRONG, Augustus Hopkins, 1836-1921.
Systematic theology; a compendium designed for the use of theological students . . . Philadelphia, The Judson Press [1960, c1907] xxviii, 1166 p. 24 cm. "The present work is a revision and enlargement of my 'Systematic theology,' first published in 1886. " -- Pref.
1. Theology, Doctrinal. 2. Baptists — Doctrinal and controversial works. I. Title.

STRONG, Augustus Hopkins, 1836-1921. 230
Systematic theology; a compendium and commonplace-book designed for the use of theological students, by Augustus Hopkins Strong ... Rochester, Press of E. R. Andrews, 1886. xxix p., 1 l., 758 p. 25 cm.

"Text-books in theology": p. 28. [BT75.S83 1886] 39-7846
1. Theology, Doctrinal. 2. Baptists—Doctrinal and controversial works. I. Title.

STRONG, Augustus Hopkins, 1836-1921. 230
Systematic theology; a compendium and commonplace-book designed for the use of theological students, by Augustus Hopkins Strong ... Philadelphia, Griffith & Rowland press [1907-09] 3 v. 24 cm. Vol. 2 published by the American Baptist publication society, Philadelphia. "The present work is a revision and enlargement of my 'Systematic theology', first published in 1886."--Pref. Contents.I. The doctrine of God.--II. The doctrine of man.--III. The doctrine of salvation. [BT75.S83 1907] 7-37983
1. Theology, Doctrinal. 2. Baptists—Doctrinal and controversial works. I. Title.

STROOP, John Ridley, 1897- 230
God's plan and me. Nashville [1950- v. 20 cm. Contents.book 1. Jesus' mission and method. [BT77.S77] 51-18847
1. Theology, Doctrinal. I. Title.

STROUP, George W., 1944- 230
The promise of narrative theology : recovering the gospel in the church / George W. Stroup. Atlanta : John Knox Press, c1981. 288 p. ; 21 cm. Includes bibliographical references and indexes. [BT75.2.S76] 19 80-84654 ISBN 0-8042-0683-X : 8.50 (pbk.)
1. Theology, Doctrinal. 2. Identification (Religion) 3. Revelation. I. Title.

STUMP, Joseph, 1866- 230.41
The Christian faith; a system of Christian dogmatics, by Joseph Stump ... New York, The Macmillan company, 1932. x p., 1 l., 463 p. diagr. 22 cm. Bibliography: p. 429-455. [BT75.S88] 32-22365
1. Theology, Doctrinal. 2. Lutheran church—Doctrinal and controversial works. I. Title.

STUMP, Joseph, 1866- 230.41
The Christian faith, a system of Christian dogmatics, by Joseph Stump ... [Philadelphia, The Muhlenberg press, 1942] x p., 1 l., 463 p. diagr. 22 1/2 cm. Bibliography: p. 429-455. [BT75.S88 1942] 42-25391
1. Theology, Doctrinal. 2. Lutheran church—Doctrinal and controversial works. I. Title.

A syllabus of lectures, 230
on the most important subjects in theology. [n.p.] Minerva office, 1812. 2 p. l., [3]-101 p. 19 1/2 cm. [BT77.S8] 38-33878
1. Theology, Doctrinal.

TALBOT, Louis Thompson, 1889- 230.076
Bible questions explained, over Radio station KMPC, Beverly Hills, California, by Louis T. Talbot ... Los Angeles, Calif. [1938] 275 p. 19 cm. [BT77.T3] 39-3906
1. Theology, Doctrinal. I. Title.

TANQUEREY, Adolphe, 1854-1932. 230.2
A manual of dogmatic theology. Translated by John J. Byrnes. New York, Desclee Co., 1959. 2 v. 22 cm. Translation of Brevior synopsis theologiae dogmaticae. Bibliographical footnotes. [BX1751.T313 1959] 59-13235
1. Theology, Doctrinal. 2. Catholic Church — Doctrinal and controversial works. Full name: Adolphe Alfred Tanquerey. I. Title.

TERRY, Milton Spenser, 1840-1914. 260
Biblical dogmatics; an exposition of the principal doctrines of the Holy Scriptures, by Milton S. Terry ... New York, Eaton & Mains; Cincinnati, Jennings & Graham [c1907] xviii, 608 p. 23 1/2 cm. "Select bibliography": p. 583-593. [BT75.T38] 7-16991
1. Theology, Doctrinal. 2. Bible—Theology. I. Title.

THEOLOGICAL evolution: 230
or, Dissertations containing suggestions for a system of Biblical interpretation, based on catholic-evangelic or broad-church principles. The introduction by Rev. Charles P. McCarthy ... New York, Shea & Jenner, 1880. 2 p. l., [vii]-viii, [9]-158 p. 18 cm. [BT78.T35] 40-19048
1. Theology, Doctrinal. I. McCarthy, Charles P.

THIELICKE, Helmut, 1908- 230
The evangelical faith. Translated and edited by Geoffrey W. Bromiley. Grand Rapids, Eerdmans [1974- v. 25 cm. Translation of Der evangelische Glaube. Contents.Contents.—v. 1. Prolegomena: the relation of theology to modern thought forms. Includes bibliographical references. [BT75.2.T4513] 74-7010 ISBN 0-8028-2342-4 (v. 1)
1. Theology, Doctrinal. I. Title.

THIESSEN, Henry Clarence. 230
Lectures in systematic theology / by Henry Clarence Thiessen. Rev. / by Vernon D. Doerksen. Grand Rapids : Eerdmans, c1979. xii, 450 p. ; 24 cm. Published in 1949 under title: Introductory lecture in systematic theology. Includes indexes. Bibliography: p. 401-407. [BT75.T39 1979] 79-17723 13.95
1. Theology, Doctrinal. I. Doerksen, Vernon D. II. Title.

THIESSEN, Henry Clarence, 1885- 230
Introductory lectures in systematic theology. Grand Rapids, Eerdmans, 1949. 574 p. 23 cm. Based on the author's syllabus, An outline of lectures in systematic theology. [BT75.T39] 49-50070
1. Theology, Doctrinal. I. Title.

THOMAS Aquinas Saint, 1225?-1274. 230.2
Compendium of theology; tr. by Cyril Vollert. St. Louis, B. Herder Book Co., 1947. xx, 366 p. 22 cm. Bibliography: p. 345-348. [BX1749.T36] 48-5510
1. Theology, Doctrinal. 2. Catholic Church—Doctrinal and controversial works. I. Vollert, Cyril O., 1901- tr. II. Title.

THOMAS Aquinas. Saint, 1225?-1274 230.2
Summa theologiae. Latin text and English tr., introds., notes, appendices, glossaries. London, Eyre & Spottiswoode; New York, McGraw. v. 23cm. Contents.v.8 (1a. 44-49) Creation, variety, and evil, ed., tr. by Thomas Gilby.--v. 19 (1a2ae.22-30; The emotions, ed., tr. by Eric D'Arcy. Bibl. [BX1749.T48 1964] 63-11128 6.75 v.8,; 6.00 v.19,
1. Theology, Doctrinal. I. Title.

THOMAS Aquinas Saint 1225?-1274 230.203
Summa Theologiae, vs. 18; 42, 60. Latin text, English tr., introds., notes., appendices, glossaries. Blackfriars, london, eyre & spottiswood; new york, mcgraw 1966. 3 v. (various p) 23 cm Contents.—v. 18 (ia2ae 18-21) Principles of murality, ed. tr. by Thomas Gilby. v. 42 (2a 2ae) 123.140) courage, ed., tr. by Antony Ross. p. 6 Walsh—v.60 (3a. 84-90) the Sacrament of penace, ed. tr by Reginald masterson, T.C. O'Brien. Bibl. [bx1749.t48] 63-11128 19 & 42 ea., 6.75 v. 60 7.00
1. theology, doctrinal. I. Title.

THOMAS, Aquinas, Saint, 1225?-1274 230.2
Summa theologiae. Latin text, English tr., introd., notes, appendices & glossary. London, Eyre & Spottiswoode; New York, McGraw [1966] 23cm. Contents.v.33, 2a2ae. 17-22: Hope, ed., tr., William J. Hill. Bibl. [BX1749.T48] 63-11128 6.75
1. Theology, Doctrinal. I. Title.

THOMAS Aquinas Saint, 1225?-1274. 230.2
Summa theologiae. General editor: Thomas Gilby. Garden City, N.Y., Image Books [1969- v. 18 cm. The Blackfriars English translation. Contents.Contents.—v. 1. The existence of God (pt. 1, questions 1-13) Bibliographical footnotes. [BX1749.T5 1969] 70-84399 1.45 (v. 1)
1. Theology, Doctrinal. I. Gilby, Thomas, 1902- ed. II. Title.

THOMAS AQUINAS, Saint, 1225?-1274 230.2
Summa theologica [vs. 1, 2, 13] Latin text and English tr., introds., notes, appendices, glossaries. Blackfriars. London, Eyre & Spottiswoode: dist. New York, McGraw [1964] 3v. (various p.) 23cm. Bibl. 63-11128 v.1, 5.50; vs.2 & 13, ea., 6.75
1. Theology, Doctrinal. I. Title.

THOMAS AQUINAS, Saint, 122?-1274 230.2
Summa theologiae. Latin text and English tr., introds., notes, appendices, glossaries. New York, McGraw; London, Eyre & Spottiswoode [1967] v. 23cm. Contents.v.5 (Ia. 19-26) God's will and providence, ed., tr. by Thomas Gilby.--v.10 (Ia. 65-74) Cosmogony, ed., tr. by William A. Wallace. Bibl. [BX1749.T48 1964] 63-11128 v.5, 6.75; v.10,p7.25
1. Theology, Doctrinal. I. Title.

THOMAS AQUINAS, Saint, 1225?-1274 230.2
Summa theologiae. Latin text. English tr., introd., notes, appendices & glossary. London, Eyre & Spottiswoode; New York, McGraw [1966] 23cm. Contents.v.46, 2a2ae. 179-182: Action and contemplation, ed. tr., Jordan Aumann. Bibl. [BX1749.T48] 63-1128 6.00
1. Theology, Doctrinal. I. Title.

THOMPSON, John Samuel, b.1787. 230
A course of critical lectures, or, Systematical theology, in four parts, viz: Theology, Demonology, Christology, and Anthropology. By the Rev. John S. Thompson ... 3d ed., greatly enlarged and improved ... Rochester, N.Y., Printed for the author by L. W. Sibley, 1824. xvi, 240 p. 22 1/2 cm. [BT75.T4] 39-8952
1. Theology, Doctrinal. 2. Universalist church—Sermons. I. Title. II. Title: Systematical theology.

THORNTON, Thomas C. 1794-1860. 230
Theological colloquies; or, A compendium of Christian divinity, speculative and practical, founded on Scripture and reason. Designed to aid heads of families, young men about to enter the ministry, and the youth of both sexes, in their efforts to obtain and communicate a knowledge of true piety. By Thomas C. Thornton... Baltimore, Lewis & Coleman, 1837. xvi, [13]-723 p. 24 cm. [BT75.T5] 39-7848
1. Theology, Doctrinal. 2. Methodist church—Doctrinal and controversial works. I. Title.

TILLICH, Paul, 1886-1965. 230'.0924
Systematic theology. [Chicago] University of Chicago Press [1967, c1951-63] 3 v. in 1. 24 cm. [BT75.2.T5 1967] 66-20786
1. Theology, Doctrinal. I. Title.

TILLICH, Paul, 1886-1965. 230
Systematic theology. Chicago, University of Chicago Press [1951-63] 3 v. 24 cm. Contents.Contents.—v. 1. Reason and revelation. Being and God.—v. 2. Existence and the Christ.—v. 3. Life and the spirit. History and the kingdom of God. [BT75.T56] 51-2235
1. Theology, Doctrinal.

TRACY, David. 230
The analogical imagination : David Tracy. by David Tracy. New York : Crossroad, 1981. xiv, 467 p. ; 24 cm. Includes bibliographical references and indexes. [BT75.2.T645] 19 81-629 ISBN 0-8245-0122-5 : 17.50
1. Theology, Doctrinal. I. Title.

TYLER, Bennet, 1783-1858. 230
Lectures on theology. By Rev. Bennet Tyler ... With a memoir, by Rev. Nahum Gale, D.D. Boston, J. E. Tilton & company, 1859. 395 p. front. (port.) 23 cm. [BT75.T8] 39-7852
1. Theology, Doctrinal. 2. Congregational churches—Doctrinal and controversial works. I. Gale, Nahum, 1812-1876. II. Title.

VALENTINE, Milton, 1825-1906. 230
Christian theology, by Milton Valentine ... Philadelphia, Lutheran publication society [1906] 2 v. 23 1/2 cm. Preface by M. H. Valentine. "These volumes are the outgrowth and expansion of the author's 'Outlines of theology'."--Pref. [BT75.V2] 6-46336
1. Theology, Doctrinal. I. Title.

VAN BUREN, Paul Matthews, 1924- 230
Discerning the way : a theology of the Jewish Christian reality / Paul M. Van Buren. New York : Seabury Press, 1980. vii, 207 p. ; 22 cm. "A Crossroad book." Includes bibliographical references and indexes. [BT78.V28] 19 79-27373 ISBN 0-8164-0124-1 : 9.95
1. Theology, Doctrinal. 2. Christianity and other religions—Judaism. 3. Judaism—Relations—Christianity. I. Title.

VAN DUSEN, Henry Pitney, ed. 230
Ventures in belief; Christian convictions for a day of uncertainty [by] Reinhold Niebuhr, Francis J. McConnell, Henry Sloan Coffin [and others], Henry P. Van Dusen, editor. New York, London, C. Scribner's sons, 1930. vi, p., 2 l., 242 p. 20 cm. "These papers have been collected and are issued under the auspices of the Student Christian association movement in America." [BT77.V3] 30-16462
1. Theology, Doctrinal. I. Student Christian association movement of America. II. Title.

VERITY, George Bersford, 1887- 230
Life in Christ; a study of coinherence. Greenwich, Conn., Seabury Press [1954] 224p. 20cm. [BT75.V44 1954] 54-13344
1. Theology. Doctrinal. I. Title. II. Title: Coinherence.

VERITY, Geroge Beresford 1887- 230
Life in Christ; a study of coinherence. London, New York, Longmans, Green [1954] 224p. 20cm. [BT75.V44 1954a] 55-153
1. Theology, Doctrinal. I. Title. II. Title: Coinherence.

VIA media
an essay in theological synthesis. Greenwich, Conn., Seabury press [1957] xvi, 171p. 19cm. Bibliography: p. 166-168.
1. Theology, Doctrinal. I. Mascall, Eric Lionel, 1905-

VIDLER, Alexander Roper, 1899- 230
Christian belief; a course of open lectures delivered in the University of Cambridge. New York, Scribner [1950] 129 p. 22 cm. Includes btbliographical references. [BT75.V48] 50-13220
1. Theology, Doctrinal. I. Title.

VOIGT, Andrew George, 1859-1933. 260
Biblical dogmatics, by Andrew George Voigt ... Columbia, S.C., Press of Lutheran board of publication [c1917] 3 p. l., [v]-xx, 244 p. 20 1/2 cm. [BT75.V8] 17-25448
1. Theology, Doctrinal. 2. Lutheran church—Doctrinal and controversial works. I. Title.

WAINWRIGHT, Geoffrey, 1939- 230
Doxology : the praise of God in worship, doctrine, and life : a systematic theology / by Geoffrey Wainwright. New York : Oxford University Press, 1980. p. cm. Includes indexes. Bibliography: p. [BT75.2.W34 1980] 80-11886 ISBN 0-19-520192-2 : 24.95
1. Theology, Doctrinal. 2. Liturgics. I. Title.

WAKEFIELD, Samuel, 1799-1895. 230
A complete system of Christian theology; or, A concise comprehensive, and systematic view of the evidences, doctrines, morals, and institutions of Christianity. By Samuel Wakefield ... New York, Carlton & Porter, 1862. 663, [1] p. 23 1/2 cm. [BT75.W2 1862] 39-7039
1. Theology, Doctrinal. 2. Methodist church—Doctrinal and controversial works. I. Title.

WAKEFIELD, Samuel, 1799-1895. 230
A complete system of Christian theology; or, A concise, comprehensive, and systematic view of the evidences, doctrines, morals, and institutions of Christianity. By Samuel Wakefield ... Pittsburgh, J. L. Read & son, 1869. 663, [1]p. 23 1/2 cm. On cover: Revised edition. [BT75.W2 1869] 39-7040
1. Theology, Doctrinal. 2. Methodist church—Doctrinal and controversial works. I. Title.

WALKER, Cornelius, 1819-1907. 230
Outlines of Christian theology, by Rev. Cornelius Walker ... New York, T.

Whittaker, 1894. vi, 256 p. 20 1/2 cm. [BT75.W23] 39-7041
1. Theology, Doctrinal. 2. Protestant Episcopal church in the U.S.A.—Doctrinal and controversial works. I. Title.

WALKER, Henry Martyn, 1838- 241
The Law of love called the Golden rule... [by] H. M. Walker. Lancaster, O., Democrat print [1914] 57 p. 18 cm. Issued also in the author's "Theological views...A volume made of tracts and circulars first printed at intervals and given away from 1900 to 1917," p. [205]-276. [BV4715.W3] 19-19170
I. Title.

WARFIELD, Benjamin Breckinridge, 1851-1921. 260
Biblical doctrines, by Benjamin Breckinridge Warfield ... New York [etc.] Oxford university press, 1929. v, 665 p. 24 cm. "Prefatory note" signed Ethelbert D. Warfield, William Park Armstrong, Caspar Wistar Hodge. "List of other articles on Biblical doctrines": p. 665. [BT75.W28] 29-14370
1. Theology, Doctrinal. I. Warfield, Ethelbert Dudley, 1861- ed. II. Title.

[WATERS, Cyrus] d.1853. 230
Reflections upon some prominent religious doctrines; and an appeal from Calvinism and Arminianism to reason and written revelation. By Elder Plummer Waters and son ... Ellicotts Mills [Md.] J. Schofield, 1854. v, [7]-333, vi, [7]-47, [1] p. 19 cm. "The following posthumous work ... was written by Dr. Cyrus Waters."--Pref. "Addendum, by Elder P. Waters, chiefly consists of reflections on the controverted doctrines of election, predestination and reprobation": vi, [7]- 47, [1] p. at end. [BT78.W25] 40-23084
1. Theology, Doctrinal. 2. Calvinism. 3. Arminianism—Controversial literature. I. Waters, Plummer. II. Title.

WATSON, Richard, 1781-1833. 230
Theological institutes; or, A view of the evidences, doctrines, morals and institutions of Christianity. By Richard Watson... New York, Pub. by W. Waugh and T. Mason, for the Methodist Episcopal church, 1834. 2 v. 22 1/2 cm. First edition published in 6 parts, 1823-29. [BR121.W35 1834] 34-8878
1. Theology, Doctrinal. 2. Apologetics—19th cent. 3. Christian ethics. 4. Church polity. 5. Sacraments. I. Title.

WATSON, Richard, 1781-1833. 230
Theological institutes; or, A view of the evidences, doctrines, morals, and institutions of Christianity. By Richard Watson. A new ed., carefully rev.; with a complete index of Scriptural texts, an index of Greek terms, and a copious analtyical index, by Thomas O. Summers. Nashville, Tenn., Pub. by E. Stevenson & F. A. Owen, agents, for the Methodist Episcopal church, South, 1857. viii, 9-771 p. 24 1/2 cm. First edition published in 6 parts, 1823-29. [BR121.W35 1857] 34-8377
1. Theology, Doctrinal. 2. Apologetics—19th cent. 3. Christian ethics. 4. Church polity. 5. Sacraments. I. Summers, Thomas Osmond, 1812-1882. II. Title.

WEATHERHEAD, Leslie Dixon, 1893- 230
The Christian agnostic [by] Leslie D. Weatherhead. New York, Abingdon Press [1965] 368 p. 23 cm. Bibliographical footnotes. [BT78.W4] 65-26733
1. Theology, Doctrinal. I. Title.

WEAVER, Jonathan, bp., 1824-1901, ed. 230
Christian doctrine a comprehensive treatise on systematic and practical theology. By thirty-seven different writers. Edited by Bishop Jonathan Weaver ... Dayton, O., United brethren publishing house, 1889. 1 p. l., ix-xvi, 17-611 p. 20 1/2 cm. [BT75.W3] 39-8956
1. Theology, Doctrinal. 2. United brethren in Christ—Doctrinal and controversial works. I. Title.

WEBER, Otto, 1902-1966. 230
Foundations of dogmatics / by Otto Weber ; translated and annotated by Darrell L. Guder. Grand Rapids, Mich. : Eerdmans, c1981- p. cm. Includes indexes. Translation of: Grundlagen der Dogmatik. [BT75.2.W413 1981] 19 81-7852 ISBN 0-8028-3554-6 : 25.00
1. Theology, Doctrinal. 2. Theology, Doctrinal—History. I. [Grundlagen der Dogmatik.] English II. Title.

WENGER, John Christian, 1910- 230.97
Introduction to theology; an interpretation of the doctrinal content of Scripture, written to strengthen a childlike faith in Christ. Prepared at the request of the Publishing Committee of Mennonite Publication Board. Scottdale, Pa., Herald Press, 1954. 418p. illus. 24cm. [BT75.W36] 53-9049
1. Theology. Doctrinal. 2. Mennonite Church—Doctrinal and controversial works. I. Title.

WESLEY, John, 1703-1791. 230.71
A compend of Wesley's theology; edited by Robert W. Burtner and Robert E. Chiles. Nashville, Abingdon Press [1954] 302p. 24cm. Biblipgraphy: p. 291-292. [BX8217.W54B8] 54-5227
1. Theology, Doctrinal. 2. Methodist Church— Doctrinal and controversial works. I. Burtner, Robert Wallace, ed. II. Chiles, Robert Eugene, ed. III. Title.

WESLEY, John, 1703-1791. 230'.7
John Wesley's theology : a collection from his works / edited by Robert W. Burtner and Robert E. Chiles. Nashville : Abingdon, 1982. p. cm. Originally published: A compend of Wesley's theology. Nashville : Abingdon Press, [1954] Includes indexes. Bibliography: p. [BX8217.W54B82 1982] 19 82-6735 ISBN 0-687-20529-8 pbk. : 7.95
1. Methodist Church—Doctrinal and controversial works. 2. Theology, Doctrinal. I. Burtner, Robert Wallace. II. Chiles, Robert Eugene. III. [Selections.] 1982 IV. Title.

WESTON, Frank, bp. of Zanzibar, 1871-
The revelation of eternal love; Christianity stated in terms of love, by Frank Weston ... London, Mowbray; Milwaukee, Morehouse [1920] 2 p. l., 192 p. 19 cm. A 21
1. Theology, Doctrinal. 2. Love. I. Title.

WHALE, John Seldon, D. D. 1896- 230
Christian doctrine: eight lectures delivered in the University of Cambridge to undergraduates of all faculties. [reissue, New York4 Cambridge, 1963. 196p. 19cm. Bibl. 1.25 pap.,
1. Theology, Doctrianal. I. Title.

WHALE, John Seldon, D. D. 1896- 230
Christian doctrine: eight lectures delivered in the University of Cambridge to undergraduates of all faculties. [reissue, New York4 Cambridge, 1963. 196p. 19cm. Bibl. 1.25 pap.,
1. Theology, Doctrianal. I. Title.

WHALE, John Seldon, 1896-
Christian doctrine: eight lectures delivered in the University of Cambridge to undergraduates of all faculties. Cambridge [Eng.] University Press, 1963. 196 p. 19 cm. Bibliography: p. 188-90. 67-15760
1. Theology, Doctrinal. I. Title.

WHALE, John Seldon, 1896- 230
Christian doctrine; eight lectures delivered in the University of Cambridge to undergraduates of all faculties, by J. S. Whale ... Cambridge [Eng.] The University press, 1941. 196, [1] p. 19 1/2 cm. Bibliography: p. 188-190. [BT75.W45] 42-4101
1. Theology, Doctrinal. I. Title.

WHALE, John Seldon, 1896- 230
Christian doctrine, by J. S. Whale ... New York, The Macmillan company; Cambridge, Eng., The University press, 1941. 196, [1] p. 21 cm. "Reprinted November, 1941." [BT75.W45 1941a] 42-9225
1. Theology, Doctrinal. I. Title.

[WHELPLEY, Samuel] 1766-1817.
The triangle. Second series of numbers. By Investigator [pseud.] New-York, Printed and published for the author, Van Winkle & Wiley, printers, 1816. iv, [5]-84 p. 22 1/2 cm. Attributed to Wheeler in Cushing, Initials and pseudonyms. [BX7251.W45] A 33
1. Theology, Doctrinal. I. Title. II. Title: Hopkinsianism.

WILEY, Henry Orton, 1877- 230
Christian theology, by H. Orton Wiley. Kansas City, Mo., Beacon Hill Press of Kansas City [1969] 3 v. 24 cm. Reprint of the 1940 ed. Bibliography: v. 3, p. 394-436. [BT75.W5 1969] 75-14807
1. Theology, Doctrinal. I. Title.

WILEY, Henry Orton, 1877- 230
Christian theology ... by H. Orton Wiley ... Kansas City, Mo., Nazarene publishing house [1940] 2 v. 23 1/2 cm. Imprint covered by label: Kansas City, Mo., Kingshighway press. [BT75.W5] 43-45083
1. Theology, Doctrinal. I. Title.

WILLIAMS, Ernest Swing, 1885- 230.99
Systematic theology. Springfield, Mo., Gospel Pub. House [1954, c1953] 3v. illus. 20cm. [BT75.W53] 54-37091
1. Theology, Doctrinal. 2. Assemblies of God, General Council—Doctrinal and controversial works. I. Title.

WINGREN, Gustaf, 1910- 230.41
Gospel and church. Tr. [from Swedish] by Ross Mackenzie. Philadelphia, Fortress [1965, c.1964] viii, 271p. 22cm. Bibl. [BT75.2.W5613] 64-18152 6.25
1. Theology, Doctrinal. 2. Law and gospel. I. Title.

WINSLOW, Hubbard, 1799-1864. 230
The Christian doctrines. By Rev. Hubbard Winslow ... Boston, Crocker and Brewster, 1844. xii, [13]-360 p. 20 cm. [BT75.W7] 39-8957
1. Theology, Doctrinal. 2. Congregational churches—Doctrinal and controversial works. I. Title.

ZERBE, Alvin Sylvester, 1847- 230.4
The Karl Barth theology; or, The new transcendentalism, by Alvin Sylvester Zerbe... Cleveland, O., Central publishing house [c1930] xviii, 279 p. 22 cm. "Chief works of Karl Barth and Barthians": p. xi-xii. [BX4827.B3Z4] 31-3390
1. Barth, Karl, 1886- 2. Theology, Doctrinal. 3. Transcendentalism. I. Title.

Theology, Doctrinal, 1888-

HERRMANN, Wilhelm, 1846-1922. 230
Systematic theology (Dogmatik) by Wilhelm Herrmann, translated by Nathaniel Micklem ... and Kenneth A. Saunders ... New York, The Macmillan company, 1927. 2 p. l., [7]-152 p. 20 cm. [BT77.H42] 27-3388
1. Theology, Doctrinal, 1888- I. Micklem, Nathaniel, tr. II. Saunders, Kenneth, A., tr. III. Title.

Theology, Doctrinal—20th century

COONEY, Cyprian. 230.2
Understanding the new theology. Milwaukee, Bruce Pub. Co. [1968, c1969] xii, 193 p. 22 cm. Includes bibliographies. [BX1751.2.C65] 68-55278 4.95
1. Catholic Church—Doctrinal and controversial works—Catholic authors. 2. Theology, Doctrinal—20th century. I. Title.

LEITCH, Addison H. 230.0904
Winds of doctrine; the theology of Barth, Brunner, Bonhoeffer, Bultmann, Niebuhr, Tillich. Westwood, N.J., Revell [c.1966] 62p. 21cm. [BT28.L4] 66-17050 2.50 bds.,
1. Theology, Doctrinal—20th cent. I. Title.

PORTEOUS, Alvin C. 230.0904
Prophetic voices in contemporary theology; the theological renaissance and the renewal of the church. Nashville, Abingdon [c.1966] 224p. 21cm. Bibl. [BT28.P6] 66-15000 4.00
1. Theology, Doctrinal—20th cent. I. Title.

Theology, Doctrinal—20th Century—Addresses, essays, lectures.

ROBINSON, James McConkey, 1924- ed. 230.82
The later Heidegger and theology, ed. by James M. Robinson, John B. Cobb, Jr. New York, Harper [c.1963] xii, 212p. 22cm. (New frontiers in theology: discussions among German and Amer. theologians, v. 1) Bibl. 63-10506 4.50
1. Heidegger, Martin, 1889- 2. Theology, Doctrinal—20th cent.—Addresses, essays, lectures. I. Cobb, John B., joint ed. II. Title. III. Series.

ROBINSON, James McConkey, 1924- ed. 230.82
The later Heidegger and theology, edited by James M. Robinson [and] John B. Cobb, Jr. [1st ed.] New York, Harper & Row [1963] xii, 212 p. 22 cm. (New frontiers in theology: discussions among German and American theologians, v. 1) Bibliographical footnotes. [B3279.H49R6] 63-10506
1. Heidegger, Martin, 1889- 2. Theology, Doctrinal — 20th Cent. — Addresses, essays, lectures. I. Cobb, John B., joint ed. II. Title. III. Series.

ROSE, Delbert R
Theology as we preach it. [Wilmore, Ky.] 1966. 1 v. (various pagings) Metz-Rothwell Lectures, Bethany Nazarene College, February 24, 25, 1966. Bibliographical footnotes. 68-68856
1. Theology, Doctrinal—20th Century—Addresses, essays, lectures. I. Title.

Theology, Doctrinal—Addresses, essays, lectures.

ARNDT, Elmer J F. ed. 230.41
The heritage of the Reformation; essays commemorating the centennial of Eden Theological Seminary. New York, R. R. Smith, 1950. 264 p. 23 cm. [BT10.A7] 50-1259
1. Theology, Doctrinal—Addresses, essays, lectures. 2. Evangelical and Reformed Church—Addresses, essays, lectures. 3. Eden Theological Seminary, St. Louis. I. Title.
Contents Omitted.

BALTHASAR, Hans Ure von, 1905- 232.2
Word and revelation. [Translated by A. V. Littledale with the cooperation of Alexander Dru. New York] Herder and Herder [1964] 191 p. 22 cm. (His Essays in theology, 1) Translation of Verbum caro. [BT80.B333] 64-19725
1. Theology, Doctrinal—Addresses, essays, lectures. 2. Communication (Theology) I. Title.

BALTHASAR, Hans Urs von, 1905- 230'.2
The von Balthasar reader / Hans Urs von Balthasar ; edited by Medard Kehl and Werner Loser ; translated by Robert J. Daly and Fred Lawrence. New York : Crossroad, 1982. xiv, 437 p. ; 24 cm. Translation of: In der Fulle des Glaubens. Includes index. Bibliography: p. [432]-434. [BX1751.2.B23413 1982] 19 82-5193 ISBN 0-8245-0468-2 : 24.50
1. Catholic Church—Doctrinal and controversial works—Catholic authors—Addresses, essays, lectures. 2. Theology, Doctrinal—Addresses, essays, lectures. I. [In der Fulle des Glaubens.] English II. Title.

BALTHASAR, Hans Urs von, 1905- 230.2081
Word and redemption. [Translated by A. V. Littledale in cooperation with Alexander Dru. New York] Herder and Herder [1965] 175 p. 22 cm. (His Essays in theology, 2) Translation of Verbum caro. Bibliographical footnotes. [BT80.B333 1965] 65-14591
1. Theology, Doctrinal—Addresses, essays, lectures. I. Title.

BARTH, Karl, 1886- 230.082
God here and now. Tr. by Paul M. van Buren. New York, Harper [c.1964] xviii, 108p. 22cm. (Religious perspectives, v.9 [i. e. 10]) 64-10750 3.75
1. Theology, Doctrinal—Addresses, essays, lectures. I. Title. II. Series.

BARTH, Karl, 1886- 230.082
God here and now. Translated by Paul M. van Buren. [1st ed.] New York, Harper & Row [1964] xviii, 108 p. 22 cm. (Religious perspectives, v. 9 [i.e. 10]) [BT80.B353] 64-10750

1. Theology, Doctrinal — Addresses, essays, lectures. I. Title. II. Series.

BARTH, Karl, 1886- 230.81
Theology and church; shorter writings, 1920-1928. Translated by Louise Pettibone Smith. With an introd. by T. F. Torrance. [1st American ed.] New York, Harper & Row [1962] 358p. 22cm. Bibliographical footnotes. [BT80.B373] 62-14572
1. Theology, Doctrinal—Addresses, essays, lectures. I. Title.

BEARDSLEE, William A ed. 230.08
America and the future of theology, edited by William A. Beardslee. Philadelphia, Westminster Press [1967] 206 p. 21 cm. (Adventures in faith) includes bibliographical references. [BT15.B4] 67-11861
1. Theology, Doctrinal — Addresses, essays, lectures. 2. U.S. — Religion — Addresses, essays, lectures. I. Title.
Contents omitted

BOWDEN, John Stephen, 230'.08
comp.
A reader in contemporary theology, ed. by John Bowden, James Richmond. Philadelphia, Westminster [1967] 190p. 19cm. Bibl. [BT10.B6 1967 a] 67-16281 1.95 pap.,
1. Theology, Doctrinal—Addresses, essays, lectures. I. Richmond, James, 1931- joint comp. II. Title.

BRAATEN, Carl E., 1929- 230
The futurist option, by Carl E. Braaten and Robert W. Jenson. New York, Newman Press [1970] vi, 183 p. 21 cm. Includes bibliographical references. [BT15.B66] 73-127792 2.95
1. Theology, Doctrinal—Addresses, essays, lectures. I. Jenson, Robert W. II. Title.

BURKE, Thomas Patrick, 1934- 230
ed.
The Word in history; the St. Xavier symposium, edited by T. Patrick Burke. New York, Sheed and Ward [1966] ix, 180 p. 22 cm. "[Symposium] held at Saint Xavier College, Chicago, March 31st to April 3rd, 1966, under the auspices of the John XXIII Institute." Includes bibliographical references. [BT80.B8] 66-27571
1. Theology, Doctrinal—Addresses, essays, lectures. I. St. Xavier College, Chicago. II. John XXIII Institute, Chicago. III. Title.

CALLAHAN, Daniel J., 230'.08
comp.
God, Jesus, and Spirit. Edited by Daniel Callahan. [New York] Herder and Herder [1969] xix, 352 p. 22 cm. A collection of articles which originally appeared in the Commonweal, 1967-68. Bibliographical footnotes. [BT10.C3] 70-75256 8.50
1. Theology, Doctrinal—Addresses, essays, lectures. I. The Commonweal. II. Title.

CHRISTIAN theology : 230
an introduction to its traditions and tasks / edited by Peter G. Hodgson and Robert H. King. Philadelphia : Fortress Press, c1982. xi, 353 p. ; 23 cm. Includes bibliographies and index. [BT80.C49 1982] 19 81-71388 ISBN 0-8006-1676-6 : 15.95
1. Theology, Doctrinal—Addresses, essays, lectures. I. Hodgson, Peter Crafts, 1934- II. King, Robert Harlen, 1935-

CHRISTIANITY today. 230.082
Basic Christian doctrines by Oswald T. Allis [others] Ed. by Carl F. H. Henry. New York, Holt [c.1962] 302p. 24cm. (Contemporary evangelical thought) First pub. as a ser. in Christianity today. Bibl. 62-18752 6.00
1. Theology, Doctrinal—Addresses, essays, lectures. I. Christianity today. II. Henry, Carl Ferdinand Howard, 1913- ed.

CHRISTIANITY today. 230.082
Basic Christian doctrines [by] Oswald T. Allis [and others] Edited by Carl F. H. Henry. [1st ed.] New York, Holt, Rinehart and Winston [1962] 302p. 24cm. (Contemporary evangelical thought) 'First published as a series in Christianity today.' [BT80.C5] 62-18752
1. Theology, Doctrinal— Addresses, essays, lectures. I. Henry, Carl Ferdinand Howard, 1913- ed. II. Title.

COBB, John B. 230
God and the world, by John B. Cobb, Jr. Philadelphia, Westminster Press [1969] 138, [1] p. 21 cm. Bibliography: p. [139] [BT75.2.C6] 69-11374 ISBN 6-642-48608-2.95
1. Theology, Doctrinal—Addresses, essays, lectures. I. Title.

COMMUNITY of the 230.082
Resurrection
Mirfield essays in Christian belief. London, Faith Pr. New York, Morehouse [1963, c.1962] 308p. 23cm. Bibl. 63-2424 5.00
1. Theology, Doctrinal—Addresses, essays, lectures. I. Title.

*DENNEY, James. 230
Studies in theology : lectures delivered in Chicago Theological Seminary. Grand Rapids : Baker Book House, 1976 xxvii, 272p. : port. ; 20 cm. (Notable books on theology) Includes bibliographical references. [BT75] ISBN 0-8010-2850-7 pbk. : 3.95.
1. Theology, Doctrinal-Addresses, essays, lectures. I. Title.

EBELING, Gerhard, 1912- 230.082
Word and faith. Tr. [from German] by James W. Leitch. Philadelphia, Fortress [c.1963] 442p. 23cm. Bibl. 63-13878 6.25
1. Theology, Doctrinal—Addresses, essays, lectures I. Title.

EBELING, Gerhard, 1912- 230.082
Word and faith. [1st English ed. Translated by James W. Leitch] Philadelphia, Fortress Press [1963] 442 p. 23 cm. Bibliography: p. [16] Bibliographical footnotes. [BT15.E213] 63-13878
1. Theology, Doctrinal—Addresses, essays, lectures. I. Title.

EBELING, Gerhard, 1912- 230
The word of God and tradition; historical studies interpreting the divisions of Christianity. Translated by S. H. Hooke. Philadelphia, Fortress Press [1968] 272 p. 21 cm. Translation of Wort Gottes und Tradition. Bibliographical references included in "Notes" (p. 237-261) [BT15.E2413] 68-29130 3.95
1. Theology, Doctrinal—Addresses, essays, lectures. 2. Tradition (Theology)—Addresses, essays, lectures. I. Title.

FINNEY, Charles Grandison, 230
1792-1875.
Finney's systematic theology / Charles Finney ; edited by J. H. Fairchild. Abridged. Minneapolis : Bethany Fellowship, 1976. xx, 435 p. ; 22 cm. First published in 1846 under title: Finney's Lectures on systematic theology. [BT80.F5 1976] 76-3500 ISBN 0-87123-153-0 pbk. : 4.95
1. Theology, Doctrinal—Addresses, essays, lectures. 2. Christian ethics—Addresses, essays, lectures. I. Title.

GARDNER, Percy, 1846- 225
Modernity and the churches; by Percy Gardner, LITT.D. London, Williams & Norgate. New York, G. P. Putnam's sons, 1909. xviii, 314 p. 19 cm. (Half-title: Crown theological library. Vol. XXIX) [BR121.G3] 230 ISBN W 10-63
1. Theology, Doctrinal—Addresses, essays, lectures. 2. Church of England—Doctrinal and controversial works. I. Title.

GLADDEN, Washington, 1836-1918.
Burning questions of the life that now is and that which is to come. By Washington Gladden. New Yorks, The Century co., 1890. 3 p. l., 248 p. 19 cm. A 34
1. Theology, Doctrinal—Addresses, essays, lectures. I. Title.

GLADDEN, Washington, 1836- 230
1918.
Present day theology, by Washington Gladden. Columbus, O., McClelland & company [c1913] vii, 220 p. 21 cm. [BT77.G6] 13-21781
1. Theology, Doctrinal—Addresses, essays, lectures. 2. Congregationalism. I. Title.
Contents omitted.

GLEASON, Robert W. ed. 230.208
A theology reader. New York, Macmillan [c.1966] xii,333p. 21cm. Bibl. [BT80.G5] 66-14691 6.95
1. Theology, Doctrinal—Addresses, essays, lectures. I. Title.

GLEASON, Robert W ed. 230.208
A theology reader, edited py Robert W. Gleason. New York, Macmillan [1966] xii, 333 p. 21 cm. Includes bibliographical references. [BT80.G5] 66-14691
1. Theology. Doctrinal — Addresses, essays, lectures. I. Title.

GOODSELL, Daniel Ayres, bp., 230
1840-1909.
The things which remain; an address to young ministers, by Daniel A. Goodsell ... Cincinnati, Jennings & Pye; New York, Eaton & Mains [c1904] 63 p. 18 cm. [BT80.G6] 4-6885
1. Theology, Doctrinal. Addresses, essays, lectures. I. Title.

GORDON, George Angier, 1853- 248
1920.
Ultimate conceptions of faith, by George A. Gordon ... Boston and New York, Houghton. Mifflin and company, 1903. xix, 390, [1] p. 20 cm. "This book contains the lectures delivered in the autumn of 1902 in Yale university on the Lyman Beecher foundation."--Pref. [BT771.G68] 3-21733
1. Theology, Doctrinal—Addresses, essays, lectures. I. Title.

HANSON, Richard Patrick 230
Crosland, ed.
Difficulties for Christian belief, edited by R. P. C. Hanson. London, Melbourne [etc.] Macmillan; New York, St. Martin's Press, 1967. [6], 154 p. 19 cm. (B 67-548) Bibliography: p. [150]-151. [BT80.H26 1967] 67-10580
1. Theology, Doctrinal — Addresses, essays, lectures. I. Title.

HARENBERG, Werner, 1929- 230.2
Der Spiegel on the New Testament; a guide to the struggle between radical and conservative in European university and parish. Translated by James H. Bruteness. [New York] Macmillan [1970] x, 246 p. 21 cm. Translation of Jesus und die Kirchen. A series of articles which appeared in Der Spiegel in 1960. Bibliography: p. [240]-246. [BT202.H27513] 75-99022 6.95
1. Jesus Christ—Person and offices—Addresses, essays, lectures. 2. Theology, Doctrinal—Addresses, essays, lectures. I. Title.

HEIM, Karl, 1874- 230
The new divine order, by Karl Heim ... English translation by E. P. Dickie ... with a foreword by Professor H. R. Mackintosh, D.D. New York and London, Harper & brothers [1930] 124 p. 19 1/2 cm. Printed in Great Britain. [BT15.H4] 31-15104
1. Theology. Doctrinal—Addresses, essays, lectures. 2. Faith—cure. 3. Eschatology. 4. Christianity. I. Dickie, Edgar Primrose, tr. II. Title.

HENRY, Carl Ferdinand 230'.08
Howard, 1913- comp.
Fundamentals of the faith [by] Gordon H. Clark [and others] Edited by Carl F. H. Henry. Grand Rapids, Zondervan Pub. House [1969] 291 p. 24 cm. (Contemporary evangelical thought) Each essay also published separately in Christianity today as a pamphlet bind-in, Sept. 1965-Aug. 1968. Contents.Contents.—Revealed religion, by G. H. Clark.—God, his names and nature, by H. B. Kuhn.—The triune God, by S. J. Mikolaski.—The creation of matter, life, and man, by A. H. Leitch.—Jesus Christ, his life and ministry, by J. Schneider.—Jesus Christ, the divine redeemer, by C. D. Linton.—The Holy Spirit, by G. W. Bromiley.—Christ and his church, by M. L. Loane.—The new birth, by B. Graham.—The Reformed doctrine of sanctification, by C. N. Weisiger, 3d.—Heaven or hell? By F. C. Kuehner.—The second advent of Christ, by W. M. Smith.—The glorious destiny of the believer, by M. C. Tenney. Includes bibliographies. [BT10.H4] 72-81056 5.95
1. Theology, Doctrinal—Addresses, essays, lectures. I. Clark, Gordon Haddon. II. Christianity today. III. Title.

HODGE, Archibald Alexander, 230.5
1823-1886.
Popular lectures on theological themes. By the Rev. Archibald Alexander Hodge ... Philadelphia, Presbyterian board of publication [1887] 472 p. 21 1/2 cm. [BT75.H62] 22-21898
1. Theology, Doctrinal—Addresses, essays, lectures. 2. Presbyterian church—Doctrinal and controversial works. I. Presbyterian church in the U.S.A. Board of publication. II. Title.

KASPER, Walter. 230'.2
An introduction to Christian faith / Walter Kasper ; [translated by V. Green]. New York : Paulist Press, 1980. ix, 210 p. ; 22 cm. Translation of: Einfuhrung in den Glauben. Includes bibliographical references and index. [BT80.K3713 1980] 19 80-82808 ISBN 0-8091-2324-X (pbk.) : 4.95
1. Theology, Doctrinal—Addresses, essays, lectures. 2. Faith—Addresses, essays, lectures. I. [Einfuhrung in den Glauben.] English II. Title.

KEDNEY, John Steinfort, 230.3
1819-1911.
Mens Christi and other problems in theology and Christian ethics. By John Steinfort Kedney ... Chicago, S. C. Griggs and company, 1891. 3 p. l., 201 p. 20 cm. "The first five of the lectures ... were delivered in December, 1890, before the students of the Episcopal theological seminary at Cambridge, Massachusetts ... The sixth lecture was delivered in ... 1889 before the Summer school of theology at Sewanee, Tennessee."--Pref. [BT15.K4] 40-16557
1. Theology, Doctrinal—Addresses, essays, lectures. 2. Protestant Episcopal church in the U. S. A.—Doctrinal and controversial works. I. Title.

KIMMEL, William 230.082
Breyfogel, 1908- ed.
Dimensions of faith; contemporary prophetic Protestant theology. [By] Karl Barth [and others] Edited by William Kimmel and Geoffrey Clive. With a foreword by James Luther Adams. New York, Twayne Publishers [1960] 507p. 21cm. Includes bibliography. [BT10.K5] 60-8551
1. Theology, Doctrinal—Addresses, essays, lectures. I. Clive, Geoffrey, 1927- joint ed. II. Title.

KRONER, Richard, 1884- 230
Between faith and thought: reflections and suggestions. New York, Oxford, 1966. ix, 203p. 21cm. [BT80.K7] 66-22264 4.95
1. Theoiogy, Doctrinal — Addresses, essays, lectures. I. Title.

KRONER, Richard, 1884- 230
Between faith and thought: reflections and suggestions. New York, Oxford University Press, 1966. ix, 203 p. 21 cm. [BT80.K7] 66-22264
1. Theology, Doctrinal — Addresses, essays, lectures. I. Title.

KRONER, Richard, 1884- 230
Between faith and thought : reflections and suggestions / Richard Kroner. Westport, Conn. : Greenwood Press, 1975, c1966. ix, 203 p. ; 21 cm. Reprint of the ed. published by Oxford University Press, New York. Includes index. [BT80.K7 1975] 75-3995 ISBN 0-8371-7430-9 lib.bdg. : 12.00
1. Theology, Doctrinal—Addresses, essays, lectures. I. Title.

KUNG, Hans, 1928- ed. 231
The unknown God? New York, Sheed and Ward [1967, c1966] 158 p. 22 cm. (Theological meditations) Translations of three volumes originally published separately in German. [BT80.K8] 66-22028
1. Theology, Doctrinal—Addresses, essays, lectures. I. Moller, Joseph. Are we searching for God? II. Haag, Herbert. The God of the beginnings and of today. III. Hasenhuttl, Gotthold. Encounter with God. IV. Title.
Contents omitted

KUNG, Hans, 1928- 231
The unknown, God! New York, Sheed and Ward [1967, c1966] 158 p. 22 cm. (Theological meditations) Translations of three volumes originally published separately in German. Contents.CONTENTS. -- Preface, by H. Kung. -- The God of the beginnings and of today, by H. Hang. -- Encounter with God, by G. Hasenhuttl, Notes (p. 1550158) [BT80.K8] 66-22023
1. Theology, Doctrinal — Addresses, essays, lectures. I. Muller, Joseph. Are we searching for God? II. Hand, Herbert. The God of the beginnings and of today. III. Ilasenuhuttl, Gotthold. Encounter with God. IV. Title.

KUNG, Hans, 1928- ed. 231
The unknown God? New York, Sheed and Ward [1967, c1966] 158 p. 22 cm. (Theological meditations) Translations of three volumes originally published separately in German. Contents.Contents.—Preface, by H. Kung.—Are we searching for God? By J. Moller.—The God of the beginnings and of today, by H. Haag.—Encounter with God, by G. Hasenhuttl. Notes (p. 155-158) [BT80.K8] 66-22028
1. Theology, Doctrinal—Addresses, essays, lectures. I. Moller, Joseph. Fragen wir nach Gott? English. 1967. II. Haag, Herbert. Am Morgan der zeit. English. 1967. III. Hasenhuttl, Gotthold. Der unbkannte Gott. english. 1967. IV. Title.

LAETSCH, Theodore 230.41
Ferdinand Karl, 1877- ed.
The abiding word; an anthology of doctrinal essays for the year 1945-1946, v. 3. St. Louis, Concordia Pub. House, 1960. At head of title: The Centennial series. Bibl. 47-19571 4.75 rev
1. Theology, Doctrinal—Addresses, essays, lectures. 2. Evangelical Lutheran Synod of Missouri, Ohio, and Other States—Doctrinal and controversial works. 3. Lutheran Church—Doctrinal and controversial works. I. Title.

LAETSCH, Theodore 230.41
Ferdinand Karl, 1877- ed.
... The abiding word; an anthology of doctrinal essays for the year 1945 ... edited by Theodore Laetsch ... Saint Louis, Concordia publishing house, 1946- v. 24 cm. At head of title: The Centennial series. Bibliography: v. 1, p. 583-587. [BT10.L3] 47-19571
1. Theology, Doctrinal—Addresses, essays, lectures. 2. Evangelical Lutheran synod of Missouri, Ohio, and other states—Doctrinal and controversial works. 3. Lutheran church—Doctrinal and controversial works. I. Title.

LEE, Robert Greene, 1886- 230.04
Great is the Lord. [Westwood, N. J.] F. H. Revell Co. [1955] 160p. 21cm. [BT15.L38] 55-5393
1. Theology. Doctrinal—Addresses, essays, lectures. I. Title.

LOWRIE, Walter, 1868- 230.41
Our concern with the theology of crisis; the fundamental aspects of the dialectical theology associated with the name of Karl Barth, appreciatively presented as our possible theology with the query whether it be not our only positive possibility; the crisis of society and of the church understood as the crisis of the individual before God. by Walter Lowrie ... Boston, Meador publishing company, 1932. 214 p. 21 cm. (The Bohlen lectures for 1932) Bibliography: p. 19-22. [BT78.L6] 32-81747
1. Barth, Karl, 1886- 2. Theology, Doctrinal—Addresses, essays, lectures. I. Title. II. Title: The theology of crisis, Our concern with. III. Title: Dialectical theology.

MACKINTOSH, Hugh Ross, 1870- 261
Some aspects of Christian belief, by H. R. Mackintosh... New York, George H. Doran company [1924] x, 306 p. 20 1/2 cm. Printed in Great Britain. [BR85.M2] 24-13369
1. Theology, Doctrinal—Addresses, essays, lectures. 2. Philosophy and religion. I. Title.

MACQUARRIE, John.
Studies in Christian existentialism; lectures and essays by John Macquarrie. Philadelphia, Westminster Press [1965] xiv, 477 p. 24 cm. 68-63378
1. Theology, Doctrinal—Addresses, essays, lectures. 2. Existentialism. I. Title.

MACQUARRIE, John. 230
Studies in Christian existentialism; lectures and essays. Philadelphia, Westminster Press [1966, c1965] 278 p. 21 cm. [BT80.M 1966a] 66-21808
1. Theology, Doctrinal—Addresses, essays, lectures. I. Title.

MAN'S need and God's gift : 230
readings in Christian theology / Millard J. Erickson, editor. Grand Rapids, Mich. : Baker Book House, 1977,c1976 382 p. ; 22 cm. Includes bibliographical references. [BT80.M36] 77-150993 ISBN 0-8010-3324-1 : 7.95
1. Theology, Doctrinal—Addresses, essays, lectures. I. Erickson, Millard.

MICHALSON, Carl. 230
Worldly theology; the hermeneutical focus of an historical faith. New York, Scribner [1967] xii, 243 p. 24 cm. Bibliographical references included in "Notes" (p. 227-238) [BT15.M48] 67-21348
1. Theology, Doctrinal—Addresses, essays, lectures. I. Title.

MILFORD, Theodore Richard. 230
Foolishness to the Greeks. Greenwich, Conn., Seabury Press [1953] 112p. 23cm. [BT15.M5] 54-2078
1. Theology, Doctrinal—Addresses, essays, lectures. I. Title.

MONTEFIORE, Hugh 230.081
Awkward questions on Christian love. Philadelphia, Westminster [1965, c.1964] 124p. 19cm. (Adventures in faith) Bibl. [BV4639.M586] 65-15073 1.45 pap.,
1. Theology, Doctrinal—Addresses, essays, lectures. 2. Love (Theology)—Addresses, essays, lectures. I. Title.

NINETEENTH century 230'.044
evangelical theology / Fisher Humphreys, editor. Nashville, Tenn. : Broadman Press, c1981. 415 p. ; 24 cm. (Christian classics) Includes bibliographical references. [BT10.N56] 19 79-55535 ISBN 0-8054-6547-2 : price unreported.
1. Theology, Doctrinal—Addresses, essays, lectures. 2. Evangelicalism—Addresses, essays, lectures. I. Humphreys, Fisher. II. Title. III. Series.

NOVAK, Michael. 230
A time to build; [essays] New York, Macmillan [1967] xii, 493 p. 21 cm. Includes bibliographical references. [BT15.N6] 67-23484
1. Theology, Doctrinal—Addresses, essays, lectures. I. Title.

OGDEN, Schubert Miles, 1928- 230
The reality of God, and other essays, by Schubert M. Ogden. [1st ed.] New York, Harper [1966] xii, 237p. 22cm. Bibl. [BT80.04] 66-20783 6.00
1. Theology, Doctrinal — Addresses, essays, lectures. I. Title.

O'NEILL, Joseph Eugene, 230.2082
1910- ed.
The encounter with God; aspects of modern theology. Foreword by John Courtney Murray. New York, Macmillan [c.1960-1962] 205p. 22cm. Bibl. 62-19426 4.00
1. Theology, Doctrinal—Addresses, essays, lectures. I. Title.

PANNENBERG, Wolfhart, 201'.1
1928-
Basic questions in theology; collected essays. Translated by George H. Kehm. Philadelphia, Fortress Press [1970-71] 2 v. 23 cm. Translation of Grundfragen systematischer Theologie. Includes bibliographical references. [BT80.P3413] 79-123505 9.75 per vol.
1. Theology, Doctrinal—Addresses, essays, lectures. I. Title.

PANNENBERG, Wolfhart, 201'.1
1928-
The idea of God and human freedom. Philadelphia, Westminster Press [1973] ix, 213 p. 22 cm. Translation of 1 essay by the author from Terror und Spiel and 5 essays from his Gottesgedanke und menschliche Freiheit. Also published as v. 3 of his Basic questions in theology. Includes bibliographical references. [BT80.P34133] 73-3165 ISBN 0-664-20971-8 6.95
1. Theology, Doctrinal—Addresses, essays, lectures. 2. Christianity—Philosophy—Addresses, essays, lectures. I. Title.

PEERMAN, Dean G. ed. 230'.08
Frontline theology, ed. by Dean Peerman. Introd. essay by Martin E. Marty. Richmond. Knox [1967] 172p. 21cm. [BT80.P4] 67-10615 4.50
1. Theology. Doctrinal —Addresses, essays, lectures. I. Title.

PITTENGER, William Norman, 230
1905-
Christian affirmations. New York, Morehouse-Gorham Co., 1954. 159p. 21cm. [BT15.P55] 55-15152
1. Theology, Doctrinal—Addresses, essays, lectures. 2. Worship. I. Title.

PITTENGER, William Norman, 230
1905-
Theology and reality; essays in restatement. Greenwich, Conn., Seabury Press, 1955. 235p. 22cm. [BT15.P554] 55-6356
1. Theology. Doctrinal—Addresses, essays, lectures. I. Title.

POND, Enoch, 1791-1882. 230
Lectures on Christian theology. By Enoch Pond ... 4th ed. Boston, Congregational publishing society, 1875. xxiv, [25]-784 p. 24 cm. [BT15.P6 1875] 35-25177
1. Theology, Doctrinal—Addresses, essays, lectures. I. Title.

RALSTON, Thomas Neely, 1806- 230
1891.
Elements of divinity; or, A course of lectures, comprising a clear and concise view of the system of theology as taught in the Holy Scriptures; with appropriate questions appended to each lecture, by Rev. Thomas N. Ralston ... Cincinnati, Poe & Hitchcock, 1861. iv, [5]-463 p. front. (port.) 24 cm. [BT75.R2 1861] 25-4657
I. Title.

RAMSEY, Ian T. 230.3
On being sure in religion [London] Univ. of London, Athlone Pr. [dist. New York, Oxford, c.]1963. vii, 92p. 21cm. Rev. and slightly expanded version of the Frederick Denison Maurice lects. for 1961-2, given at King's Coll., London. Bibl. 64-21 2.00 bds.,
I. Theology, Doctrinal—Addresses, essays, lectures. II. Title. III. Title: Being sure in religion.

RAMSEY, Paul, ed. [Full 230.08
name: Robert Paul Ramsey]
Faith and ethics; the theology of H. Richard Niebuhr [by] Waldo Beach [others] New York, Harper [1965, c.1957] 306p. port. 20cm. (Harper torchbk. TB129L) [BX4827.N47R3] 1.95 pap.,
1. Niebuhr, Helmut Richard, 1894- 2. Niebuhr, Helmut Richard, 1894- —Bibl. 3. Theology, Doctrinal—Addresses, essays, lectures. I. Title.

RAMSEY, Paul, ed.
Faith and ethics; the theology of H. Richard Niebuhr [by] Waldo Beach [and others] New York, Harper [1965, c1957] xii, 314, 10 p. port. (Harper Torchbooks) Bibliography of H. Richard Niebuhr's writings: p. 291-306. 66-43975
1. Niebuhr, Helmut Richard, 1894-1962. 2. Niebuhr, Helmut Richard, 1894-1962 — Bibl. 3. Theology, Doctrinal — Addresses, essays, lectures. I. Beach, Waldo. II. Title.

RAMSEY, Paul [Robert Paul 230.08
Ramsey]
Faith and ethics; the theology of H. Richard Niebuhr [by] Waldo Beach [others] Ed. Paul Ramsey [Gloucester, Mass., P. Smith, 1965, c.1957] xii, 314p. port. 21cm. (Harper torchbk., Cloister lib., TB129L rebound) Bibl. [BX4827.N47R3] 4.00
1. Niebuhr, Helmut Richard, 1894- 2. Niebuhr, Helmut Richard, 1894- —Bibl. 3. Theology, Doctrinal—Addresses, essays, lectures. I. Title.

RANDOLPH, Alfred Magill, 230
bp., 1836-1918.
Reason, faith and authority in Christianity, being the Paddock lectures for 1901-02, by Alfred Magill Randolph ... New York, T. Whittaker [c1902] 272 p. 21 cm. (On cover: The Bishop Paddock lectures for 1901-02) "These lectures ... were delivered before the students and professors in the chapel of the General theological seminary in New York in December, 1901, and February, 1902."--Pref. [BT15.R25] 3-860
1. Theology, Doctrinal—Addresses, essays, lectures. I. Title.

RELTON, Herbert Maurice, 230.09
1882-
Studies in Christian doctrine. London, Macmillan; New York, St. Martin's Press, 1960. 269p. 23cm. Includes bibliography. [BT15.R4 1960] 60-50585
1. Theology, Doctrinal—Addresses, essays, lectures. 2. Theology, Doctrinal—Hist. I. Title.

RICHARDSON, Herbert Warren. 230
Toward an American theology [by] Herbert W. Richardson. [1st ed.] New York, Harper & Row [1967] xii, 170 p. 22 cm. Bibliographical footnotes. [BT15.R5] 67-14942
1. Theology, Doctrinal—Addresses, essays, lectures. I. Title.

RODDY, Clarence 230.082
Stonelynn, ed.
Things most surely believed. [Westwood, N.J.] Revell [1963] 191 p. 21 cm. 63-10395
1. Theology, Doctrinal—Addresses, essays, lectures. I. Title.

SAYERS, Dorothy Leigh, 1893- 230
Creed or chaos? [1st American ed.] New York, Harcourt, Brace [1949] 85 p. 21 cm. Contents.The greatest drama ever staged.--The triumph of Easter.--Strong meat.--The dogma is the drama.--Creed or chaos?--Why work?--The other six deadly sins. [BT15.S3 1949] 49-7768
1. Theology, Doctrinal—Addresses, essays, lectures. I. Title.

SAYERS, Dorothy Leigh, 1893- 208
1957.
Christian letters to a post-Christian world; a selection of essays. Selected and introduced by Roderick Jellema. Grand Rapids, Eerdmans [1969] xiii, 236 p. illus. (part col.), port. 23 cm. Contents.Contents.—Selections from The Pantheon papers.—The greatest drama ever staged.—Strong meat.—The dogma is the drama.—What do we believe?—Creed or chaos?—A vote of thanks to Cyrus.—The dates in The Red-Headed League.—Towards a Christian aesthetic.—Creative mind.—The image of God.—Problem picture.—Christian morality.—The other six deadly sins.—Dante and Charles Williams.—The writing and reading of allegory.—Oedipus simplex.—The Faust legend and the idea of the devil. Bibliographical footnotes. [BT15.S27 1969] 67-19331 6.95
1. Theology, Doctrinal—Addresses, essays, lectures. I. Jellema, Roderick, ed. II. Title.

SAYERS, Dorothy Leigh, 201'.1
1893-1957.
The whimsical Christian : 18 essays / by Dorothy L. Sayers. 1st Macmillan ed. New York : Macmillan, 1978, c1969. x, 275 p. ; 22 cm. Previous ed. published under title: Christian letters to a post-Christian world. [BT15.S27 1978] 78-5613 ISBN 0-02-606930-X : 7.95
1. Theology, Doctrinal—Addresses, essays, lectures. I. Title.

SHEBBEARE, Charles John, 230
1865-
Religion in an age of doubt, by the Rev. Charles J. Shebbeare ... New York, Chicago, Fleming H. Revell company [1914?] 1 p. l., vii-xx, 219 p. illus. (music) 22 1/2 cm. (Lettered on cover: Library of historic theology. Editor, Wm. C. Piercy, M.A.) Imprint covered by label: New York, S. R. Leland. The substance of the book was delivered in the form of lectures to the vacation term of Biblical study in the Divinity school at Cambridge in 1911. cf. Pref. [BT15.S45] 34-4492
1. Theology, Doctrinal—Addresses, essays, lectures. I. Title.

SHEDD, William Greenough 230.51
Thayer, 1820-1894.
Theological essays, by William G. T. Shedd ... New York, Scribner, Armstrong & company, 1877. vii, 1 l., 7-383 p. 21 1/2 cm. [BT15.S5] 40-16579
1. Theology, Doctrinal—Addresses, essays, lectures. 2. Presbyterian church—Doctrinal and controversial works. I. Title.
Contents omitted.

SKINNER, Thomas Harvey, 230.5
1791-1871.
Discussions in theology. By Thomas H. Skinner ... New York, A. D. F. Randolph, 1868. 3 p. l., 287 p. 19 1/2 cm. "A second edition" of miscellanies collected from periodicals. cf. Pref. "Erratum": slip inserted between 2d and 3d prelim. leaves. [BT15.S6] 40-16581
1. Theology, Doctrinal—Addresses, essays,

lectures. 2. Presbyterian church—Doctrinal and controversial works. I. Title.

SOUTH church lectures: 230.64
discourses upon Christian doctrine. Delivered in the South Baptist church, New York, on Sabbath evenings, from January to April, 1863. By clergymen of New York ... New York, R. Carter & brothers, 1865. vi p., 1 l., [9]-431 p. 19 1/2 cm. [BT10.S6] 40-16586
1. Theology, Doctrinal—Addresses, essays, lectures.
Contents omitted.

TENNEY, Merrill Chapin, 230.082
1904- ed.
The word for this century [by] Carl F. H. Henry [and others] New York, Oxford University Press, 1960. 184 p. 20 cm. Includes bibliography. [BT15.T4] 60-5275
1. Theology, Doctrinal — Addresses, essays, lectures. 2. Evangelicalism. I. Henry, Carl Ferdinand Howard, 1913- II. Title.

TORRANCE, Thomas Forsyth, 230
1913-
Theology in reconstruction Grand Rapids, Mich., Eerdmans [1966, c.1965] 288p. 23cm. Bibl. [BT80.T6] 66-2894 5.00 bds.,
1. Theology, Doctrinal—Addresses, essays, lectures. I. Title.

TRUTH and life, an outline 230.2
of modern theology [by] Donal Flanagan [and others. 1st. American ed.] Milwaukee, Bruce Pub. Co. [1969, c1968] xi, 213 p. 20 cm. Bibliographical footnotes. [BT80.T7 1969] 69-12674 4.95
1. Theology, Doctrinal—Addresses, essays, lectures. 2. Christian life—Catholic authors. I. Flanagan, Donal, 1929-

TUCKLEY, Henry. 230
Questions of the heart. How reason helps faith to answer them. By Henry Tuckley ... Cincinnati, Cranston & Curts; New York, Hunt & Eaton, 1892. 2 p. l., 3-257 p. 20 cm. [BT15.T8] 39-8954
1. Theology, Doctrinal—Addresses, essays, lectures. I. Title.

VAN BUREN, Paul Matthews, 230'.08
1924-
Theological explorations [by] Paul M. van Buren. New York, Macmillan [1968] 181 p. 22 cm. Includes bibliographies. [BT80.V34] 68-16766
1. Theology, Doctrinal—Addresses, essays, lectures. I. Title.

VINTON, Alexander Hamilton, 231
1807-1881.
... Four lectures delivered in the Church of the Holy Trinity, Philadelphia, in the year 1877, on the foundation of the late John Bohlen, esq. By Alexander H. Vinton, D. D. 2d ed. New York, T. Whittaker, 1887. 130 p. 19 1/2 cm. (Bohlen lectures, inaugural series) [BT15.V5 1887] 40-17573
1. Theology, Doctrinal—Addresses, essays, lectures. 2. Protestant Episcopal church in the U.S.A.—Doctrinal and controversial works. I. Title.

WALKER, Henry Martyn, 1838- 239
Theological views, by H. M. Walker, A.M. A volume made of tracts and circulars, first printed at intervals and given away, from 1900 to 1917. [Lancaster, O., H. B. Walker, 1918?] 3 p. l., [5]-351 p. 19 1/2 cm. [BT15.W3] 20-1593
1. Theology, Doctrinal—Addresses, essays, lectures. I. Title.

WARFIELD, Benjamin 230.51
Breckinridge, 1851-1921.
Biblical and theological studies edited by Samuel G. Craig. Philadelphia, Presbyterian and Reformed Pub. Co., 1952. 580 p. illus. 21 cm. [BT15.W34] 52-6506
1. Theology, Doctrinal — Addresses, essays, lectures. 2. Presbyterian Church — Doctrinal and controversial works. I. Title.

WARFIELD, Benjamin 230
Breckinridge, 1851-1921.
Biblical foundations. Grand Rapids, Eerdmans [1958] 350 p. 23 cm. (Selected theological studies) [BT15.W343 1958] 58-13059
1. Theology, Doctrinal — Addresses, essays, lectures. I. Title.

WARFIELD, Benjamin 230
Breckinridge, 1851-1921.
Studies in theology, by Benjamin Breckinridge Warfield ... New York [etc.] Oxford university press, 1932. v, 671 p. 24 cm. "Prefatory note" signed: Ethelbert D. Warfield, William Park Armstrong, Caspar Wistar Hodge, committee. "List of other studies in theology": p. 667-671. [BT15.W35] 32-14463
1. Theology, Doctrinal—Addresses, essays, lectures. I. Warfield, Ethelbert Dudley, 1861- ed. II. Title.

WILDER, Amos Niven, 1895- 230
Otherworldliness and the New Testament. [1st ed.] New York, Harper [1954] 124p. 20cm. [BT15.W5] 54-11661
1. Theology, Doctrinal— Addresses, essays, lectures. I. Title.

WILES, Maurice F. 230
The remaking of Christian doctrine / by Maurice Wiles. Philadelphia : Westminster Press, c1978. p. cm. "Lectures delivered in the University of Cambridge in the Michaelmas Term, 1973." Includes bibliographical references and indexes. [BT80.W52 1978] 78-5800 ISBN 0-664-24217-0 pbk. : 5.95
1. Theology, Doctrinal—Addresses, essays, lectures. I. Title.

WILES, Maurice F. 230
Working papers in doctrine / [by] Maurice Wiles. London : S.C.M. Press, 1976. ix, 213 p. ; 23 cm. Contents.Contents.—Some reflections on the origins of the doctrine of the Trinity.—Eternal generation.—In defence of Arius.—The doctrine of Christ in the patristic age.—The nature of the early debate about Christ's human soul.—The theological legacy of St. Cyprian.—One baptism for the remission of sins.—The consequences of modern understanding of reality for the relevance and authority of the tradition of the early Church in our time.—The unassumed is the unhealed.—Does Christology rest on a mistake?—Religious authority and divine action.—Jerusalem, Athens, and Oxford.—The criteria of Christian theology. Includes bibliographical references and index. [BT80.W53] 76-376862 ISBN 0-334-01807-2 : £4.95
1. Theology, Doctrinal—Addresses, essays, lectures. I. Title.

WILLIAMS, John Milton, 230.58
1817-1900.
Rational theology; or, Ethical and theological essays, by John Milton Williams, A.M. Chicago, C. H. Kerr & company; Boston, G. H. Ellis, 1888-96. 2 v. front. (port.: v. 2) 20 cm. Vol. II has imprint: Chicago, C. H. Kerr & company. "Largely reprints of articles...contributed to the Bibliotheca sacra and Yale review."--Vol. II, p. 5. [BT15.W7] 40-17567
1. Theology, Doctrinal—Addresses, essays, lectures. 2. Christian ethics—Addresses, essays, lectures. 3. Congregational churches—Doctrinal and controversial works. I. Title.

WOOD, Charles James. 230
Survivals in Christianity, studies in the theology of divine immanence; special lectures delivered before the Episcopal theological school at Cambridge, Mass., in 1892, by Charles James Wood. New York and London, Macmillan and co., 1893. ix, 317 p. 20 cm. Bibliography:p. 295-300. [BT15.W8] 45-34010
1. Theology, Doctrinal—Addresses, essays, lectures. I. Title.

Theology, Doctrinal—Africa—History.

POBEE, J. S. 201'.1
Toward an African theology / John S. Pobee. Nashville : Abingdon, c1979. 174 p. ; 22 cm. Includes index. Bibliography: p. 157-159. [BT30.A4P62] 78-21080 ISBN 0-687-42420-8 : 5.95
1. Theology, Doctrinal—Africa—History. 2. Akans (African people)—Religion. 3. Black theology. I. Title.

Theology, Doctrinal—Africa—History—Congresses.

PAN African Conference of 276
Third World Theologians, Accra, 1977.
African theology en route : papers from the Pan African Conference of Third World Theologians, December 17-23, Accra, Ghana / edited by Kofi Appiah-Kubi and Sergio Torres. Maryknoll, NY : Orbis Books, c1979. x, 214 p. ; 24 cm. Includes bibliographical references. [BT30.A4P36 1977] 78-10604 ISBN 0-88344-010-5 pbk. : 7.95
1. Theology, Doctrinal—Africa—History—Congresses. I. Appiah-Kubi, Kofi. II. Torres, Sergio. III. Title.

Theology, Doctrinal—Asia—Addresses, essays, lectures.

LIVING theology in Asia 230'.095
/ edited by John C. England. U.S. ed. Maryknoll, N.Y. : Orbis Books, 1982, c1981. p. cm. Bibliography: p. [BT30.A8L58 1982] 19 82-2288 ISBN 0-88344-298-1 pbk. : 9.95
1. Theology, Doctrinal—Asia—Addresses, essays, lectures. I. England, John C.

Theology, Doctrinal—Bibliography

LANE, William Coolidge, 016.
1859-1931.
... Catalogue of a collection of works on ritualism and doctrinal theology, presented by John Harvey Treat. By William Coolidge Lane ... Cambridge, Mass., Library of Harvard university, 1889. cover-title, 29 p. 25 cm. (Harvard university. Library, Bibliographical contributions, no. 36) [Z1009.H33] [Z7751.L26] 2-21315
1. Theology, Doctrinal—Bibl. 2. Ritualism—Bibl. 3. Treat, John Harvey, 1839-1908. I. Title.

Theology, Doctrinal—Case studies.

CHRISTIAN theology : 230
a case method approach / editors, Robert A. Evans, Thomas D. Parker ; consulting editors, Keith R. Bridston, John B. Cobb, Jr., Gordon D. Kaufman. 1st ed. New York : Harper & Row, c1976. p. cm. (A Harper forum book) Includes bibliographies. [BT78.C455 1976] 76-9963 ISBN 0-06-062251-2 : 10.00. ISBN 0-06-062252-0 pbk. : 4.95
1. Theology, Doctrinal—Case studies. I. Evans, Robert A., 1937- II. Parker, Thomas D.

Theology, Doctrinal—Collected works.

CUSHMAN, Robert Earl. 230
Faith seeking understanding : essays theological and critical / by Robert E. Cushman. Durham, N.C. : Duke University Press, 1981. xv, 373 p. ; 24 cm. Includes bibliographical references and index. [BT15.C87] 19 80-69402 ISBN 0-8223-0444-9 : 19.75
1. Theology, Doctrinal—Collected works. 2. Theology, Doctrinal—History—Collected works. 3. Ecumenical movement—History—Collected works. I. Title.

Theology, Doctrinal—Early works to 1800.

THOMAS, Aquinas, Saint, 230'.2
1225?-1274.
Summa theologica / St. Thomas Aquinas ; translated by Fathers of the English Dominican Province. Complete English ed. Westminster, Md. : Christian Classics, 1981, c1948. 5 v. (xix, 3057 p.) ; 25 cm. Translation of: Summa theologica. Reprint. Originally published: New York : Benziger Bros., 1947-1948. Vol. 5 includes index. [BX1749.T5 1981] 19 81-68580 ISBN 0-87061-063-5 : 195.00 (set)
1. Catholic Church—Doctrinal and controversial works—Catholic authors. 2. Theology, Doctrinal—Early works to 1800. I. Dominicans. English Province. II. [Summa theologica.] English III. Title.

ZWINGLI, Ulrich, 1484- 230'.42
1531.
Commentary on true and false religion / Ulrich Zwingli ; edited by Samuel Macauley Jackson and Clarence Nevin Heller. Durham, N.C. : Labyrinth, 1981, c1929. p. cm. Translation of: De vera et falsa religione commentarius. Reprint. Originally published: The Latin works and the correspondence of Huldreich Zwingli, v. 3, issued under title: The Latin works of Huldreich Zwingli. Philadelphia : Heidelberg Press, 1929. Includes index. [BT70.Z8713 1981] 19 81-8272 ISBN 0-939464-00-4 pbk. : pbk. : 15.95
1. Theology, Doctrinal—Early works to 1800. I. Jackson, Samuel Macauley, 1851-1912. II. Heller, Clarence Nevin. III. [De vera et falsa religione commentarius.] English IV. Title.
Publisher's address : P. O. Box 2124, Durham, NC 27701.

Theology, Doctrinal—England—History—17th century.

GEORGE, Timothy. 285'.9'0924
John Robinson and the English separatist tradition / by Timothy George. Macon, Ga. : Mercer University Press, c1982. p. cm. (NABPR dissertation series ; no. 1) Originally presented as the author's thesis (D.D.)—Harvard Divinity School. Includes index. Bibliography: p. [BX9339.R55G46 1982] 19 82-14201 ISBN 0-86554-043-8 : 16.95
1. Robinson, John, 1575?-1625. 2. Theology, Doctrinal—England—History—17th century. 3. Separatists—History—17th century. 4. Theology, Puritan—England—History—17th century. I. Title. II. Series.

Theology, Doctrinal—History

BENARD, Edmond Darvil. 922.242
A preface to Newman's theology, by Rev. Edmond Darvil Benard ... St. Louis, Mo. and London, B. Herder book co., 1945. xv, 234 p. 21 cm. Bibliography: p. [208]-223. [BX4705.N5B4] 45-926
1. Newman, John Henry, cardinal, 1801-1890. 2. Theology, Doctrinal—Hist. 3. Dogma. I. Title.

BERKHOF, Louis, 1873- 230
Reformed dogmatics, by Louis Berhof ... Historical (history of dogma) Grand Rapids, Mich., Wm. B. Eerdmans publishing co., 1937. 3 p. l., 11-296 p. 24 cm. Includes bibliographies. [BT75.B37] 40-16249
1. Theology, Doctrinal—Hist. 2. Reformed church—Doctrinal and controversial works. I. Title.

BROMILEY, Geoffrey 230'.09
William.
Historical theology : an introduction / by Geoffrey W. Bromiley. Grand Rapids : Eerdmans, c1978. p. cm. Includes indexes. [BT21.2.B74] 77-17030 ISBN 0-8028-3509-0 : 15.95
1. Theology, Doctrinal—History. I. Title.

BULL, Robert J. 230'.09
Tradition in the making [by] Robert J. Bull. Philadelphia, Geneva Press [1967, c1968] 128 p. 21 cm. (Decade books) [BT21.2.B8] 68-10624
1. Theology, Doctrinal—History. I. Title.

BURKILL, T. Alec. 201'.1'09
The evolution of Christian thought, by T. A. Burkill. Ithaca [N.Y.] Cornell University Press [1971] x, 504 p. 24 cm. Bibliography: p. 487-488. [BT21.2.B86] 76-127601 ISBN 0-8014-0581-5 12.50
1. Theology, Doctrinal—History. I. Title.

CASE, Shirley Jackson, 230.09
1872-
Highways of Christian doctrine, by Shirley Jackson Case ... Chicago, New York, Willett, Clark & company, 1936. vii p., 1 l., 201 p. 21 cm. "Lowell institute lectures delivered in King's chapel, Boston, Massachusetts, April 27 to May 1, 1936."--Pref. "Selected bibliography": p. 193-196. [BT21.C3] 36-28597
1. Theology, Doctrinal—Hist. I. Lowell institute lectures, 1936. II. Title.

*CHARROUX, Robert. 291
Masters of the world. Translated by Lowell Blair. [New York] Berkley Pub. Co. [1974, c1967] xi, 252 p. illus. 18 cm. (A Berkley medallion book) [BT22] ISBN 0-425-02710-4 1.50 (pbk.)
1. Theology, Doctorinal—History. I. Title.

CHRISTIANITY and history 230.09
... Lectures ... delivered at the Washington Cathedral Library ... 1948-

Authorized recording and production by Henderson Services. Washington [1950- v. ir 28 cm. (Christianity and modern man, course 3) Cover title. Contents.pt. 1. The Christian movement in history: A. The historical Jesus and the Christian revelation, by A. T. Mollegen and S. Brown-Serman. B. The development of Christian thought, by C. L. Stanley. 2 v. [BT21.C5] 51-33006
1. Theology, Doctrinal—Hist. 2. Religious thought—Hist. 3. Jesus Christ—Messiahship. 4. Christianity—Origin. I. Mollegen, Albert T. II. Series.

CONGAR, Yves Marie Joseph, 1904- 230'.09
A history of theology [by] Yves M. J. Congar. Translated and edited by Hunter Guthrie. [1st ed. in the U.S.A.] Garden City, N.Y., Doubleday, 1968. 312 p. 22 cm. "Based on the article Theologie ... which first appeared in volume 15 of Dictionnaire de theologie catholique." Includes bibliographical references. [BT21.2.C6] 68-19008 5.95
1. Theology, Doctrinal—History. I. Title.

CONTEMPORARY Theology Institute, 2d, Loyola College, Montreal, 1965. 230'.09
The convergence of traditions, Orthodox, Catholic, Protestant. Edited by Elmer O'Brien. [New York] Herder and Herder [1967] 141 p. 22 cm. (Contemporary theology, v. 2) Sponsored by Dept. of Theology, Loyola College. Bibliographical footnotes. [BT22.C65] 67-25880
1. Theology. Doctrinal—Hist. 2. Theology, Eastern Church. 3. Theology, Catholic. 4. Theology, Protestant. I. O'Brien, Elmer, ed. II. Loyola College, Montreal. Dept. of Theology. III. Title.

CONTEMPORARY Theology Institute, 2d, Loyola College, Montreal, 1965. 230'.09
The convergence of traditions, Orthodox, Catholic, Protestant. Edited by Elmer O'Brien. [New York] Herder and Herder [1967] 141 p. 22 cm. (Contemporary theology, v. 2) Sponsored by Dept. of Theology, Loyola College. Bibliographical footnotes. [BT22.C65 1965] 67-25880
1. Theology, Doctrinal—History. 2. Theology, Eastern Church. 3. Theology, Catholic. 4. Theology, Protestant. I. O'Brien, Elmer, ed. II. Loyola College, Montreal. Dept. of Theology. III. Title.

CRAPSEY, Algernon Sidney, 1847-1927. 230
The re-birth of religion; being an account of the passing of the old and coming of the new dogmatic, by Algernon Sidney Crapsey ... New York, John Lane company; London, John Lane, 1907. 323 p. 20 cm. [BT28.C7] 8-1487
1. Theology, Doctrinal—Hist. 2. Dogma. I. Title.

CURTISS, George Lewis, 1835-1898. 230.09
... Evolution of Christian doctrines, or, Outline lectures on the history of Christian doctrines. Used in the senior class of the School of theology of De Pauw university. By George L. Curtiss ... [Terre Haute, Ind.] The author [1891] 1 p. l., iv, 228, v. p. 20 cm. (De Pauw university series) [BT21.C8] 39-24021
1. Theology, Doctrinal—Hist. I. Title.

AN essay on the development of Christian doctrine, with a foreword by Gustave Weigel.*arden City, N. Y., Image Books [c1960] 434p.
1. Theology, Doctrinal—Hist. 2. Catholic Church—Doctrinal and controversial works—Catholic authors. I. Newman, John Henry, Cardinal, 1801-1890.

ESSAY on the development of Christian doctrine. London, New York, Sheed and Ward [1960] xi, 320p. 18cm. (The New ark library)
1. Theology, Doctrinal—Hist. 2. Catholic Church—Doctrinal and controversial works—Catholic authors. I. Newman, John Henry, Cardinal, 1801-1890.

FISHER, George Park, 1827-1909. 230'.09
History of Christian doctrine / by George Park Fisher. New York : AMS Press, [1976] p. cm. Reprint of the 1901 ed. published by Scribner, New York, in series: International theological library. [BT21.F5 1976] 75-41095 ISBN 0-404-14663-5 : 32.50
1. Theology, Doctrinal—History. I. Title.

GARDNER, Percy, 1846- 230
Evolution in Christian doctrine, by Percy Gardner ... London, Williams and Norgate. New York, G. P. Putnam's sons, 1918. xiii, 241 p. 19 cm. (Half-title: Crown theological library, vol. XLI) [BT21.G3] 18-26478
1. Theology, Doctrinal—Hist. I. Title.

GONZALEZ, Justo L. 230'.09
A history of Christian thought [by] Justo L. Gonzalez. Nashville, Abingdon Press [1970-75] 3 v. 24 cm. Contents.Contents.—v. 1. From the beginnings to the Council of Chalcedon.—v. 2. From Augustine to the eve of the Reformation.—v. 3. From the Protestant Reformation to the twentieth century. Includes bibliographical references. [BT21.2.G6] 74-109679 ISBN 0-687-17174-1 (v. 1) 9.00 (v. 1) varies
1. Theology, Doctrinal—History. I. Title.

HAGENBACH, Karl Rudolf, 1801-1874. 280
A text-book of the history of doctrines. By Dr. K. R. Hagenbach... The Edinburgh translation of C. W. Buch, revised with large additions from the fourth German edition, and other sources. By Henry B. Smith... New York, Sheldon & co.; Boston, Gould & Lincoln, 1861-62. 2 v. 24 cm. Bibliography: v. 1, p. 30-42. [BT21.H22 1861] 33-16029
1. Theology, Doctrinal—Hist. I. Buch, Carl W., tr. II. Smith, Henry Boynton, 1815-1877, ed. III. Title.

HAGENBACH, Karl Rudolf, 1801-1874. 280
A text-book of the history of doctrines. By Dr. K. R. Hagenbach... The Edinburgh translation of C. W. Buch, revised with large additions from the fourth German edition and other sources. By Henry B. Smith... New York, Sheldon & company; Boston, Gould & Lincoln, 1864, '62. 2 v. 24 cm. Bibliography: p. 30-42. [BT21.H22 1864] 33-16028
1. Theology, Doctrinal—Hist. I. Buch, Carl W., tr. II. Smith, Henry Boynton, 1815-1877, ed. III. Title.

HAGGLUND, Bengt, 1920- 230'.09
History of theology. Translated by Gene J. Lund. St. Louis, Concordia Pub. House [1968] 425 p. 24 cm. Translation of Teologins historia. [BT21.2.H313] 68-13365
1. Theology, Doctrinal—History. I. Title.

HARNACK, Adolf von, 1851-1930 230.09
History of dogma. Tr. from 3d German ed. by Neil Buchanan [Gloucester, Mass., Peter Smith, 1961] 7 v. in 4. various p. (Dover bks. rebound) Bibl. 18.00 set
1. Theology, Doctrinal—Hist. I. Title.

HARNACK, Adolf von, 1851-1930. 230.09
Outlines of the history of dogma. Translated by Edwin Knox Mitchell. With an introd. by Philip Rieff. [Boston] Starr King Press [c1957] 567p. 22cm. [BT21.H27 1957a] 58-26851
1. Theology, Doctrinal—Hist. I. Title.

HARNACK, Adolf von, 1851-1930. 230.09
Outlines of the history of dogma. Translated by Edwin Knox Mitchell. With an introd. by Philip Rieff. Boston, Beacon Press [1957] xii, [25], 567p. 21cm. (Beacon paperback no. 49) [BT21.H27 1957] 57-3270
1. Theology, Doctrinal—Hist. I. Title.

HARNACK, Adolf von, 1851-1930. 230.9
Outlines of the history of dogms, by Dr. Adolf Harnack ... translated by Edwin Knox Mitchell ... New York, London and Toronto, Funk & Wagnalls company, 1893. xii, 567 p. 21 cm. [BT21.H27] 39-24773
1. Theology, Doctrinal—Hist. I. Mitchell, Edwin Knox, 1853-1934, tr. II. Title.

HENEGHAN, John Joseph. 230.09
... The progress of dogma according to Anselm of Havelberg, by John J. Heneghan ... [New York, The Paulist press, 1943] viii, 56 p. 25 cm. At head of title: Pontificia universitas Gregoriana. "A doctoral dissertation in the Faculty of sacred theology of the Pontifica: Gregorian university, Rome." Bibliography: p. 55-56. [BX4705.A62H4] 44-471
1. Anselnans, bp. of Havelberg, d. 1158. 2. Theology, Doctrinal—Hist. 3. Dogma. I. Title.

HORDERN, William. 230'.09
A layman's guide to Protestant theology. Rev. ed. New York, Macmillan [1968] xx, 265 p. 22 cm. Bibliography: p. 259-262. [BT21.2.H67 1968] 68-11862
1. Theology, Doctrinal—History. 2. Theology, Protestant. I. Title.

HORDERN, William. 230.09
A layman's guide to protestant theology. New York, Macmillan, 1955. 222 p. 22 cm. [BT21.H67] 55-14264
1. Theology, Doctrinal—History. I. Title.

HORDERN, William Edward 230.09
A layman's guide to protestant theology. New York, Macmillan [1962, c.1955] 222p. 18cm. (110) 1.45 pap.,
1. Theology, Doctrinal—Hist. I. Title.

JONES, Ora L. 230.61
How the Baptists got their doctrines; a restatement of some almost forgotten church history and doctrines that should be remembered, by Ora L. Jones. Detroit, Harlo Press [1966] 227 p. 23 cm. [BX6331.2.J6] 66-26929
1. Theology, Doctrinal—History. 2. Baptists—Doctrinal and controversial works. I. Title.

KENT, John H. S. 230'.09'03
The end of the line? : the development of Christian theology in the last two centuries / John H. S. Kent. 1st Fortress Press ed. Philadelphia : Fortress Press, c1982. x, 134 p. ; 22 cm. Originally published: Christian theology in the eighteenth to the twentieth centuries. In: A History of Christian doctrine. Edinburgh : Clark, 1978, p. [459] -591. Includes index. Bibliography: p. [132] -133. [BT21.2.K46 1982] 19 82-7263 ISBN 0-8006-1652-9 pbk. : 5.95
1. Theology, Doctrinal—History. I. [Christian theology in the eighteenth to the twentieth centuries] II. Title.

KLOTSCHE, Ernest Heinrich, 1875-1937. 230.03
The history of Christian doctrine, by E. H. Klotsche ... Last chapter by Prof. J. Theodore Mueller ... Burlington, Ia., The Lutheran literary board, 1945. 2 p. l., vii-xvi, 349 p. 23 1/2 cm. [BT21.K48] 45-3683
1. Theology, Doctrinal—Hist. I. Mueller, John Theodore, 1885- II. Title.

KLOTSCHE, Ernest Heinrich, 1875-1937. 230'.09
The history of Christian doctrine / E. H. Klotsche ; with additional chapters by J. Theodore Mueller and David P. Scaer. Rev. ed. Grand Rapids, Mich. : Baker Book House, 1979. xvii, 387 p. ; 22 cm. (Twin brooks series) [BT21.K48 1979] 79-127388 ISBN 0-8010-5404-4 : 6.95
1. Theology, Doctrinal—History. I. Mueller, John Theodore, 1885- joint author. II. Scaer, David P., 1936- joint author. III. Title.

KRONER, Richard, 1884- 201
Speculation and revelation in the age of Christian philosophy. Philadelphia, Westminster Press [1959] 269p. 24cm. (His Speculation and revelation in the history of philosophy) Includes bibliography. [BT23.K7] 59-9947
1. Theology, Doctrinal— Hist. 2. Philosophy—Hist. I. Title.

LOHSE, Bernhard, 1928- 230'.09
A short history of Christian doctrine. Translated by F. Ernest Stoeffler. Philadelphia, Fortress Press [1966] xiv, 304 p. 23 cm. Translation of Epochen der Dogmengeschichte. Bibliography: p. 267-273. [BT21.2.L613] 66-21732
1. Theology, Doctrinal—History. I. Title.

LOHSE, Bernhard, 1928- 230'.09
A short history of Christian doctrine / Bernhard Lohse ; translated by F. Ernest Stoeffler. Philadelphia : Fortress Press, 1978,c1966. xiii, 304p. ; 22 cm. Translation of Epochen der Dogmengeschicte. Bibliography: p. 267-273. [BT212.L613] ISBN 0-8006-1341-4 pbk. : 6.50
1. Theology, Doctrinal — History. I. Title.
L.C.card no. for 1966 hardcover ed.: 60-21732

MCGIFFERT, Arthur Cushman, 1861-1933.
A history of Christian thought. New York, Scribner's [c1960-61] 2 v. 21 cm. Contents.--I. Early and Eastern; from Jesus to John of Damascus.--II. The West; from Tertullian to Erasmus. 68-56221
1. Theology, Doctrinal—Hist. 2. Religious thought—Hist. I. Title.

MCGIFFERT, Arthur Cushman, 1861-1933. 230
A history of Christian thought, by Arthur Cushman McGiffert ... New York, London, C. Scribner's sons, 1932-33. 2 v. 21 1/2 cm. Contents.--I. Early and Eastern, from Jesus to John of Damascus. Bibliography (p. 333-344)--II. The West, from Tertullian to Erasmus. Bibliography (p. 397-411) [BT21.M15] 32-8444
1. Theology, Doctrinal—Hist. 2. Religious thought—Hist. I. Title.

MCGIFFERT, Arthur Cushman, 1861-1933. 209
The rise of modern religious ideas, by Arthur Cushman McGiffert. New York, The Macmillan company, 1915. x p., 2 l., 315 p. 19 1/2 cm. "This volume is based upon the Earl lectures, given before the Pacific theological seminary, at Berkeley, California, in September, 1912."--Pref. [BT27.M3] 15-2864
1. Theology, Doctrinal—Hist. 2. Philosophy and religion. I. Title.

MARNACK, Adolf von 1851-1930. 230
History of dogma. Tr. from the 3d German ed., by Neil Buchanan. New York, Dover [1961] 4 v. various p. (T904, T905, T906, T907) 2.50 pap., ea.,
1. Theology, Doctrinal—Hist. I. Title.

MEANS, Stewart, 1852- 234.2
Faith; an historical study, by Stewart Means; with an introduction by Erwin R. Goodenough. New York, The Macmillan company, 1933. xiii p., 2 l., 334 p. 22 1/2 cm. [BT771.M37] 33-14052
1. Theology, Doctrinal—Hist. 2. Church history. 3. Christianity. 4. Faith. I. Title.

MOBERLY, George, bp. of Salisbury, 1803-1885. 232.97
The sayings of the great forty days, between the resurrection and ascension, regarded as the outlines of the kingdom of God, in five discourses: with an examination of Mr. Newman's theory of developments. By George Moberly ... From the 2d London ed. Philadelphia, H. Hooker, 1850. 273 p. 20 cm. "The doctrine of development": p. [195]-231. [BT485.M6 1850] 35-22136
1. Jesus Christ—Forty days. 2. Theology, Doctrinal—Hist. 3. Newman, John Henry, cardinal, 1801-1890. An essay on the development of Christian doctrine. I. Title.

MOZLEY, John Kenneth, 1883- 230
The beginnings of Christian theology, by J. K. Mozley ... Cambridge [Eng.] The University press, 1931. x, 137, [1] p. 19 cm. "Eight talks, given by invitation of the British broadcasting corporation on Sundays during August and September 1930."--Pref. On cover: Christian theology. [BT21.M6] 31-30916
1. Theology, Doctrinal—Hist. 2. Church history—Primitive and early church. I. Title. II. Title: Christian theology.

MUNSCHER, Wilhelm, 1766-1814. 230
Elements of dogmatic history. By William Muenscher ... Translated from the second edition of the original German. By James Murdock ... New-Haven, A. H. Maltby, 1830. 208 p. 20 cm. On label mounted on spine: Murdock's Elements of Christian dogmatic history. Translation of Lehrbuch der christlichen dogmengeschichte. Includes bibliographical references. [BT21.M82] 45-51826
1. Theology, Doctrinal—Hist. I. Murdock, James, 1776-1856, tr. II. Title. III. Title: Dogmatic history.

[NEVE, Juergen Ludwig] 1865-1943 230.09
A history of Christian thought [v.1. Rev.

ed.] by Otto W. Heick. Philadelphia, Fortress [c.1965] 508p. 24cm. In the earlier ed. Neve's name appeared first on the title page. Bibl. [BT21.N482] 65-23839 8.75
1. Theology, Doctrinal—Hist. I. Heick, Otto William. II. Title.

NEVE, Juergen Ludwig, 1865-1943. 230.09
A history of Christian thought, by Otto W. Heick. Philadelphia, Fortress Press [1965- v. 24 cm. In the earlier edition Neve's name appeared first on the title page. Includes bibliographies. [BT21.N482] 65-23839
1. Theology, Doctrinal — Hist. I. Heick, Otto William. II. Title.

NEVE, Juergen Ludwig 1865-1943 Heick, Otto William 230.09
a history of christian thought; v. 2 by Otto W. Heick. Philadelphia, Fortress [c.1966] x 517 p. 24 cm -continues the work beg. by Juergen Ludwig Neve and Otto W. H first published in 1943. bibl. [BT21.N482] 66-23839 7.75
1. theology, doctrinal—hist. I. Title.

NEVE, Juergen Ludwig, 1865-1943. 230.09
A history of Christian thought, by Dr. J. L. Neve ... With contributions by the Reverend O. W. Heick ... on the middle ages and Catholicism. Philadelphia, Pa., The United Lutheran publication house [1943-46] 2 v. 24 cm. Vol. 2 has also special title: History of Protestant theology, by O. W. Heick, PH.D. With contributions by Dr. J. L. Neve on the post-reformation developments and first fundamental steps into the modern age; and imprint: Philadelphia, The Muhlenberg press. Includes bibliographies. [BT21.N48] 44-3802
1. Theology, Doctrinal—Hist. I. Heick, Otto William. II. Title.

NEWMAN, John Henry, cardinal, 1801-1890. 230
An essay on the development of Christian Doctrine, by John Henry cardinal Newman. 16th impression. London, New York [etc.] Longmans, Green and co., 1920. xvi, 445 p., 1 l. 19 1/2 cm. [BT21.N5 1920] 26-26914
1. Theology, Doctrinal—Hist. 2. Catholic church—Doctrinal and controversial works—Catholic authors. I. Title.

ORR, James, 1844-1913. 230.09
The progress of dogma, being the Elliot lectures, delivered at the Western Theological Seminary, Allegheny, Penna., U.S.A., 1897. Grand Rapids, Eerdmans, 1952. 365p. 22cm. [BT21] 52-9919
1. Theology, Doctrinal—Hist. I. Title.

OTTEN, Bernard John, 1862-1930. 230
A manual of the history of dogmas ... by Rev. Bernard J. Otten ... St. Louis, Mo., and London, B. Herder, 1917-18. 2 v. 23 cm. Contents.--v. 1. The development of dogmas during the patristic age, 100-869--v. 2. The development of dogmas during the middle ages and after, 890-1907. Bibliography: v. 1, p. xi-xiv; v. 2, p. v-vii. [BT21.Q8] 17-23554
1. Theology, Doctrinal—Hist. I. Title.

PELIKAN, Jaroslav, 1923- 230.41
From Luther to Kierkegaard; a study in the history of theology. [2d. ed.] St. Louis, Concordia [1963, c.1950] xiii, 171p. 21cm. Bibl. 63-15352 1.75 pap.,
1. Theology, Doctrinal—Hist. 2. Philosophy, Modern—Hist. 3. Lutheran Church—Hist. I. Title.

PELIKAN, Jaroslav Jan, 1923- 230.2
The Christian tradition; a history of the development of doctrine [by] Jaroslav Pelikan. Chicago, University of Chicago Press [1971- v. 24 cm. Contents.Contents.—v. 1. The emergence of the Catholic tradition (100-600) Bibliography: v. 1, p. 358-376. [BT21.2.P42] 79-142042 ISBN 0-226-65370-6
1. Theology, Doctrinal—History. I. Title.

PELIKAN, Jaroslav Jan, 1923- 230.41
From Luther to Kierkegaard; a study in the history of theology. Saint Louis, Concordia Pub. House [1950] vii. 71 p. 21 cm. Bibliographical references included in "Notes" (p. 121-166) [BT27.P4] 50-58133
1. Theology, Doctrinal—Hist. 2. Philosophy, Modern—Hist. 3. Lutheran Church—Hist. I. Title.

PELIKAN, Jaroslav Jan, 1923- 230.41
From Luther to Kierkegaard; a study in the history of theology, [2d ed.] Saint Louis, Concordia Pub. House [1963, c1950] xiii, 171 p. 21 cm. Bibliographical references included in "Notes" (p.121-166) [BT27.P4] 63-15352
1. Theology, Doctrinal—Hist. 2. Philosophy, Modern—Hist. 3. Lutheran Church—Hist. I. Title.

PELIKAN, Jaroslav Jan, 1923- 230
Historical theology: continuity and change in Christian doctrine [by] Jaroslav Pelikan. New York, Corpus [1971] xxiii, 228 p. 24 cm. (Theological resources) Bibliography: p. 219-223. [BT21.2.P43 1971b] 77-93572 ISBN 0-664-20909-2 9.95
1. Theology, Doctrinal—History. I. Title.

PICKMAN, Edward Motley, 1886- 230.09
The sequence of belief; a consideration of religious thought from Homer to Ockham. New York, St. Martin's Press [1962] ix, 741p. 22cm. Bibliography: p.727-730. [BT21.2.P5] 61-6699
1. Theology, Doctrinal—Hist. 2. Religious thought—Hist. I. Title.

PRIESTLEY, Joseph, 1733-1804. 907'.2'024 s
An history of the corruptions of Christianity, 1782. New York, Garland Pub., 1974. p. cm. (The Life & times of seven major British writers. Gibboniana 10-11) Reprint of the 1782 ed. printed by Piercy and Jones for J. Johnson, Birmingham, Eng. Includes bibliographies. [DG206.G5G52 vol. 10-11] [BT20] 273 74-14853 ISBN 0-8240-1347-6 22.00
1. Theology, Doctrinal—History. 2. Heresies and heretics—History. I. Title. II. Series: Gibboniana 10-11.

SEEBERG, Reinhold, 1859-1935. 230.09
Text-book of the history of doctrines. Translated by Charles E. Hay. Grand Rapids, Baker Book House, 1952. 2v. in 1. 23cm. Contents.v. 1. History of doctrines in the ancient church.--v. 2. History of doctrines in the middle and early modern ages. Bibliographical footnotes. [BT21.S] A53
1. Theology, Doctrinal—Hist. I. Title.

SEEBERG, Reinhold, 1859-1935. 230.09
Text-book of the history of doctrines. Translated by Charles E. Hay. Grand Rapids, Baker Book House, 1956. 2 v. in 1. 23cm. Contents.v. 1. History of doctrines in the ancient church.--v. 2. History of doctrines in the middle and early modern ages. Bibliographical footnotes. [BT21.S4 1956] 56-7584
1. Theology, Doctrinal— Hist. I. Title.

SEEBERG, Reinhold, 1859-1935. 230
Text-book of the history of doctrines, by Dr. Reinhold Seeberg ... Revised, 1904, by the author. Translated by Charles E. Hay ... Philadelphia, Pa., Lutheran publication society [c1905] 2 v. 21 cm. Contents.--v. 1. History of doctrines in the ancient church.--v. 2. History of doctrines in the middle and modern ages. [BT21.S4] 5-30051
1. Theology, Doctrinal—Hist. I. Hay, Charles Ebert, 1851-1934, tr. II. Title.

SHEDD, William Greenough Thayer, 1820-1894.
A history of Christian doctrine. By William G. T. Shedd ... New York, C. Scribner, 1863. 2 v. 23 cm. Contains bibliographies. [BT21.S45 1863] 1-11893
1. Theology, Doctrinal—Hist. I. Title.

SHELDON, Henry Clay, 1845-1928. 230.09
History of Christian doctrine, by Henry C. Sheldon ... 2d ed. New York, Harper & brothers, 1895. 2 v. 21 cm. Contents.I. From A.D. 90 to 1517.--II. From A.D. 1517-1895. [BT21.S5 1895] 39-25250
1. Theology, Doctrinal—Hist. I. Title.

SHELDON, Henry Clay, 1845-1928. 230
History of Christian doctrine, by Henry C. Sheldon ... 4th ed. New York, Eaton & Mains; Cincinnati, Jennings & Graham [c1906] 2 v. 21 cm. Contents.I. From A.D. 90 to 1517.--II. From A.D. 1517 to 1905. [BT21.S5 1906] 6-17853
1. Theology, Doctrinal—Hist. I. Title.

SHELDON, Henry Clay, 1845-1928. 230.09
History of Christian doctrine, A.D. 90-1517. By Prof. H. C. Sheldon. [Boston] Boston university, 1881. 417 p. 19 1/2 cm. Later editions include a second volume, continuing the work from 1517 to date of publication. [BT21.S5 1881] 39-25249
1. Theology, Doctrinal—Hist. I. Title.

TILLICH, Paul, 1886- 230.09
A history of Christian thought. Recorded and edited by Peter H. John. 2d ed. [Providence? R.I.] 1956. 309 p. 28 cm. "Lectures ... stenographically recorded and transcribed during the spring semester, 1953, at Union Theological Seminary in New York." [BT21.T5 1956] 57-32588
1. Theology, Doctrinal—Hist. I. Title.

TILLICH, Paul, 1886-1965. 230'.09
A history of Christian thought. [2d ed., rev. and] edited by Carl E. Braaten. New York, Harper & Row [1968] xvii, 300 p. 22 cm. Lectures delivered in 1953 at Union Theological Seminary, New York, recorded and originally edited by P. H. John. [BT21.2.T5 1968] 68-17592
1. Theology, Doctrinal—History. I. Title.

TILLICH, Paul, 1886-1965. 230'.09
A history of Christian thought, from its Judaic and Hellenistic origins to existentialism. Edited by Carl E. Braaten. [New York] Simon and Schuster [1972] xlii, 550 p. 21 cm. (A Touchstone book) Previously published in two separate volumes entitled A history of Christian thought and Perspectives on 19th and 20th century Protestant theology. Includes bibliographical references. [BT21.2.T53] 72-171021 ISBN 0-671-21426-8 4.95
1. Theology, Doctrinal—History. I. Braaten, Carl E., 1929- ed. II. Tillich, Paul, 1886-1965. Perspectives on 19th and 20th century Protestant theology. 1972. III. Title. IV. Title: Perspectives on 19th and 20th century Protestant theology.

TIXERONT, Joseph, 1856-1925.
History of dogmas, by J. Tixeront, translated from the 5th French ed. by H. L. B. ... St. Louis, Mo., and Freiburg (Baden) B. Herder, 1910-16. 3 v. 20 1/2 cm. Contents.I. The Antenicene theology.--II. From St. Athanasius to St. Augustine (318-430)--III. The end of the patristic age (430-800) [BT23.T52] 10-30041
1. Theology, Doctrinal—Hist. I. Brianceau, Henry L., tr. II. Title.

WENLEY, Robert Mark, 1861-1929.
Contemporary theology and theism, by R. M. Wenley ... New York, C. Scribner's sons, 1897. x p., 1 l., 202 p. 19 1/2 cm. [BT28.W4] 45-40060
1. Ritschi, Albrecht Benjamin, 1822-1889. 2. Theology, Doctrinal—Hist. 3. Theism. I. Title.

WILES, Maurice F. 230
Jerusalem, Athens, and Oxford, by Maurice Wiles, an inaugural lecture delivered before the University of Oxford on 18 May, 1971. Oxford, Clarendon Press, 1971. 21 p. 22 cm. Includes bibliographical references. [BT21.2.W54] 72-188636 ISBN 0-19-951289-2 £0.40
1. Theology, Doctrinal—History. I. Title.

Theology, Doctrinal—History—16th century.

HUGHES, Philip Edgcumbe. 230'.09'03
Theology of the English reformers. Grand Rapids, Eerdmans [1966, c1965] 283 p. 23 cm. Bibliographical footnotes. [BT27.H8 1966] 67-1745
1. Theology, Doctrinal—History—16th century. 2. Theology, Anglican. I. Title.

REARDON, Bernard M. G. 230'.09'031
Religious thought in the Reformation / by Bernard M. G. Reardon. London ; New York : Longman, 1981. p. cm. Includes indexes. Bibliography: p. [BT27.R36] 19 80-40861 ISBN 0-582-49030-8 : 25.00 ISBN 0-582-49031-6 (pbk.) : 12.95
1. Theology, Doctrinal—History—16th century. I. Title.

Theology, Doctrinal — History — 17th century

ALLISON, Christopher FitzSimons, 1927- 230.309032
The rise of moralism; the proclamation of the Gospel from Hooker to Baxter [by] C. F. Allison. New York, Seabury Press [1966] xii, 250 p. 23 cm. "Select bibliography": p. [239]-244. [BT27.A4 1966a] 66-22996
1. Theology, Doctrinal—History—17th century. 2. Theology, Anglican. I. Title.

MCADOO, Henry Robert, Bp. of Ossory 230.3018
The spirit of Anglicanism: a survey of Anglican theological method in the seventeenth century. New York, Scribners [c.1965] ix, 422p. 22cm. (Hale lects. of Seabury-Western Theological Seminary) Bibl. [BT27.M22] 65-16696 5.95
1. Theology, Doctrinal—Hist.—17th cent. 2. Theology—Methodology. I. Title. II. Title: Anglican theological method. III. Series: Seabury-Western Theological Seminary, Evanston, Ill. The Hale lectures

MCADOO, Henry Robert, Bp. of Ossory.
The spirit of Anglicanism: a survey of Anglican theological method in the seventeenth century [by]Henry R. McAdoo. New York, Scribner [1965] ix, 422 p. 22 cm. (The Hale lectures of Seabury-Western Theological Seminary) Bibliography: p. 415-417.
1. Theology, Doctrinal — Hist. — 17th cent. 2. Theology — Methodology. I. Anglican theological method. (Series: Seabury-Western Theological Seminary, Evanston, Ill. The Hale lectures) II. Title.

MCADOO, Henry Robert, Bp. of Ossory. 230.3018
The spirit of Anglicanism: a survey of Anglican theological method in the seventeenth century [by]Henry R. McAdoo. New York, Scribner [1965] ix, 422 p. 22 cm. (The Hale lectures of Seabury-Western Theological Seminary) Bibliography: p. 415-417. [BT27.M22 1965a] 65-16696
1. Theology, Doctrinal — Hist. — 17th cent. 2. Theology — Methodology. I. Anglican theological method. (Series: Seabury-Western Theological Seminary, Evanston, Ill. The Hale lectures) II. Title.

Theology, Doctrinal—History—19th-20th centuries.

*CHARLES, Rodger 230
The church and the world, by Rodger Charles S. J. General editor: Edward Yarnold. Notre Dame, Ind., Fides Publishers [1973] 89, [4] p. 18 cm. (Theology today series no. 43) [BT28] ISBN 0-85342-333-4 0.95 (pbk.)
1. Theology. Doctrinal—History—19th-20th centuries. I. Yarnold, Edward. ed. II. Title.

Theology, Doctrinal—History—19th century.

AARFLOT, Andreas, 1928- 230'.4'10924
Hans Nielsen Hauge, his life and message / Andreas Aarflot. Minneapolis : Augsburg Pub. House, c1979. 208 p. ; 22 cm. Translation of Hans Nielsen Hauge: liv og budskap, an abridgement and revision of the author's thesis. [BX8080.H3A62213] 77-84101 ISBN 0-8066-1627-X : 8.95
1. Hauge, Hans Nielsen, 1771-1824. 2. Theology, Doctrinal—History—19th century. I. Title.

BARTH, Karl, 1886- 230.0903
The humanity of God [Reissue] Richmond, Va., Knox [1963, c.1960] 96p. 21cm. 1.50 pap.,
1. Theology, Doctrinal—Hist.—19th cent. 2. Theology, Doctrinal—Hist.—20th cent. 3. Liberty. I. Title.

BARTH, Karl, 1886-1968. 230.0903
The humanity of God. Richmond, John Knox Press [1960] 96 p. 21 cm. Contents.Contents.—Evangelical theology in the 19th century—The humanity of God.—The gift of freedom. [BT28.B273] 60-5479
1. Theology, Doctrinal—History—19th century. 2. Theology, Doctrinal—History—20th century. 3. Freedom (Theology) I. Title.

COOPER, John Charles. 230
The roots of the radical theology. Philadelphia, Westminster Press [1967] 172 p. 21 cm. Bibliographical references included in "Notes" (p. [160]-172) [BT28.C6] 67-12013
1. Theology, Doctrinal—History—19th century. 2. Theology, Doctrinal—History—20th century. 3. Death of God theology. I. Title.

FITZER, Joseph, 1939- 230
Moehler and Baur in controversy, 1832-38: romantic-idealist assessment of the Reformation and Counter-Reformation. Tallahassee, Fla., American Academy of Religion, 1974. 116 p. 23 cm. (AAR studies in religion, no. 7) Includes bibliographical references. [BT28.F48] 74-77619 ISBN 0-88420-111-2 3.00 (pbk.)
1. Mohler, Johann Adam, 1796-1838. 2. Baur, Ferdinand Christian, 1792-1860. 3. Theology, Doctrinal—History—19th century. I. Title. II. Series: American Academy of Religion. AAR studies in religion, no. 7.

HERON, Alasdair. 230'.044'0904
A century of Protestant theology / by Alasdair I. C. Heron. Philadelphia : Westminster Press, c1980. ix, 229 p. ; 21 cm. Includes bibliographies and indexes. [BT28.H425] 80-17409 ISBN 0-664-24346-0 : 8.95
1. Theology, Doctrinal—History—19th century. 2. Theology, Doctrinal—History—20th century. 3. Theology, Protestant—History. I. Title.

IDINOPULOS, Thomas A., comp. 230'.09'04
The erosion of faith; an inquiry into the origins of the contemporary crisis in religious thought, by Thomas A. Idinopulos. Chicago, Quadrangle Books, 1971. xii, 265 p. 22 cm. Contents.Contents.—The theology of feeling, by F. Schleiermacher.—The theology of the individual, by S. Kierkegaard.—The theology of the word, by K. Barth.—The theology of correlation, by P. Tillich.—Theocentric humanism: the Thomistic philosophy of Jacques Maritain.—The theology of Godmanhood, by N. Berdyaev.—The theology of dialogue, by M. Buber.—Theologians in a world come of age.—Bibliography (p. 253-258) [BT28.I34 1971] 74-152094 ISBN 0-8129-0197-5 8.95
1. Theology, Doctrinal—History—19th century. 2. Theology, Doctrinal—History—20th century. I. Title.

PITTENGER, William Norman, 1905- 230'.09'04
Reconceptions in Christian thinking, 1817-1967 [by] W. Norman Pittenger New York, Seabury Press [1968] 127 p. 22 cm. (The Paddock lectures, 1967) [BT28.P53] 68-11591
1. Theology, Doctrinal—History—19th century. 2. Theology, Doctrinal—History—20th century. I. Title. II. Series.

WEAVER, Jonathan, 1824-1901.
Christian theology a concise and practical view of the cardinal doctrines and institutions of Christianity by Jonathan Weaver ... Dayton, O., United Brethren publishing house, 1900. xiii, 381 p. 21 cm. 9-29356
I. Title.

WELCH, Claude. 209'.034
Protestant thought in the nineteenth century. New Haven, Yale University Press, 1972- v. 24 cm. Contents.Contents.—v. 1. 1799-1870. Includes bibliographical references. [BT28.W394] 72-75211 ISBN 0-300-01535-6 12.50
1. Theology, Doctrinal—History—19th century. 2. Theology, Protestant—History. I. Title.

Theology, Doctrinal—History—20th century.

BARNETTE, Henlee H. 230'.09'04
The new theology and morality, by Henlee H. Barnette. Philadelphia, Westminster Press [1967] 120 p. 21 cm. Bibliographical references included in "Notes" (p. [109]-120) [BT28.B27] 67-11671
1. Theology, Doctrinal—History—20th century. 2. Christian ethics. I. Title.

BERKOUWER, Gerrit Cornelis, 1903- 230
A half century of theology : movements and motives / by G. C. Berkhouwer ; translated and edited by Lewis B. Smedes. Grand Rapids : Eerdmans, c1977. 268 p. ; 22 cm. Translation of Een halve eeuw theologie. Includes index. [BT28.B44713] 76-56798 pbk. : 4.95
1. Theology, Doctrinal—History—20th century. I. Title.

CONN, Harvie M. 230'.09'04
Contemporary world theology; a layman's guidebook, by Harvie M. Conn. [Nutley, N.J.] Presbyterian and Reformed Pub. Co., 1973. x, 155 p. 21 cm. Includes bibliographical references. [BT28.C56] 72-97711 2.95 (pbk.)
1. Theology, Doctrinal—History—20th century. I. Title.

CONN, Harvie M. 230'.09'04
Contemporary world theology : a layman's guidebook / by Harvie M. Conn. 2d rev. ed. [Nutley, N.J.] : Presbyterian and Reformed Pub. Co., 1974, c1973. x, 155 p. ; 21 cm. Includes bibliographical references and index. [BT28.C56 1974] 75-317574 2.95
1. Theology, Doctrinal—History—20th century. I. Title.

CONN, Harvie M. 230'.09'04
Contemporary world theology; a layman's guidebook, by Harvie M. Conn. [Nutley, N.J.] Presbyterian and Reformed Pub. Co., 1973. x, 155 p. 21 cm. Includes bibliographical references. [BT28.C56] 72-97711 2.95
1. Theology, Doctrinal—History—20th century. I. Title.

CONN, Harvie M. 230'.09'04
Contemporary world theology : a layman's guidebook / by Harvie M. Conn. 2d rev. ed. [Nutley, N.J.] : Presbyterian and Reformed Pub. Co., 1974, c1973. x, 155 p. ; 21 cm. Includes bibliographical references and index. [BT28.C56 1974] 75-317574 2.95
1. Theology, Doctrinal—History—20th century. I. Title.

COOPER, John Charles. 230'.09'04
Radical Christianity and its sources. Philadelphia, Westminster Press [1968] 171 p. 21 cm. Bibliographical references included in "Notes" (p. [151]-164) [BT28.C58] 68-21411 5.95
1. Theology, Doctrinal—History—20th century. 2. United States—Religion—1946- 3. Christianity—20th century. 4. Death of God theology. I. Title.

DE WOLF, Lotan Harold 230.09
Present trends in Christian thought. New York, Association Press [c.1960] 128p. 16cm. (an Association Press reflection book) (bibl. notes) 60-6569 .50 pap.,
1. Theology, Doctrinal—Hist.—20th cent. 2. Religious thought—20th cent. I. Title.

FUNK, Robert Walter, 1926- 230.0904
Language, hermeneutic, and word of God; the problem of language in the New Testament and contemporary theology [by] Robert W. Funk. [1st ed.] New York, Harper & Row [1966] xvi, 317 p. 22 cm. Bibliographical footnotes. [BT28.F8] 66-20776
1. Jesus Christ—Parables. 2. Theology, Doctrinal—History—20th century. 3. Communication (Theology) 4. Religion and language. I. Title.

GEFFRE, Claude. 230'.09'04
A new age in theology / by Claude Geffre ; translated by Robert Shillenn, with Francis McDonagh and Theodore L. Westow. New York : Paulist Press, [1974] v, 119 p. ; 20 cm. Translation of Un nouvel age de la theologie. Includes bibliographical references. [BT28.G3613] 74-12634 ISBN 0-8091-1844-0 pbk. : 3.95
1. Theology, Doctrinal—History—20th century. 2. Theology, Catholic—History. I. Title.

HAMILTON, Kenneth. 230'.09'04
What's new in religion? A critical study of new theology, new morality, and secular Christianity. Grand Rapids, Eerdmans [1968] 176 p. 22 cm. Bibliography: p. 175-176. [BT28.H32] 67-28382
1. Theology, Doctrinal—History—20th century. I. Title.

HENRY, Carl Ferdinand Howard, 1913- 230.0904
Fifty years of Protestant theology. Boston, Wilde [1950] 113 p. 20 cm. Bibliographical footnotes. [BT28.H39] 50-10665
1. Theology. Doctrinal—Hist.—20th cent. I. Title.

HENRY, Carl Ferdinand Howard, 1913- ed. 232
Jesus of Nazareth, Saviour and Lord [by] Paul Althaus [and others] Edited by Carl F. H. Henry. Grand Rapids, Eerdmans [1966] viii, 277 p. 24 cm. (Contemporary evangelical thought) Bibliography: p. 265-271. [BT28.H396] 66-18727
1. Theology, Doctrinal—History—20th century. 2. Theology, Doctrinal—Addresses, essays, lectures. I. Title.

HENRY, Carl Ferdinand Howard, 1913- 230
The Protestant dilemma; an analysis of the current impasse in theology. Grand Rapids, W.B. Eerdmans Pub. Co., 1949 [i.e. 1948] 248 p. 21 cm. [BT28.H4] 49-7368
1. Theology, Doctrinal—Hist.—20th cent. I. Title.

HERZOG, Frederick 230.0904
Understanding God, the key issue in present-day Protestant thought. New York, Scribners [1966] 191p. 22cm. Bibl. [BT28.H44] 66-25565 4.50
1. Theology, Doctrinal—Hist. — 20th cent. 2. God—History of doctrines. I. Title.

HORTON, Walter Marshall, 1895- 230
Theology in transition, by Walter Marshall Horton ... New York and London, Harper & brothers [1943] xxix, 196, [10] p. 19 1/2 cm. An abbreviated reprint of the author's A psychological approach to theology and Realistic theology. cf. Pref. to new ed. "First edition." [BT28.H62] 43-15114
1. Theology, Doctrinal—Hist.—20th cent. 2. Psychology, Religious. 3. Liberalism (Religion) I. Horton, Walter Marshall, 1895- A psychological approach to theology. II. Horton, Walter Marshall, 1895- Realistic theology. III. Title.

JENKINS, David E. 231
Guide to the debate about God, by David E. Jenkins. Philadelphia, Westminster Press [1966] 111 p. 19 cm. (Adventures in faith) Includes bibliographical references. [BT28.J4] 66-13083
1. Theology, Doctrinal—History—20th century. I. Title. II. Title: The debate about God.

JONG, Pieter de 230.4
Evangelism and contemporary theology; a study of the implications for evangelism in the thoughts of six modern theologians. Nashville 1908 Grand Ave. Tidings. [c. 1962] 116p. 22cm. Bibl. 62-13349 1.25 pap.,
1. Theology, Doctrinal—Hist.—20th cent. 2. Evangelistic work. I. Title.

KELSEY, David H. 220.1'3
The uses of Scripture in recent theology / by David H. Kelsey. Philadelphia : Fortress Press, [1975] ix, 227 p. ; 24 cm. Includes index. Bibliography: 218-224. [BT89.K44] 74-26344 ISBN 0-8006-0401-6 : 11.95
1. Bible—Evidences, authority, etc.—History of doctrines. 2. Theology, Doctrinal—History—20th century. 3. Theology, Protestant. I. Title.

LANGFORD, Thomas A. 230'.0942
In search of foundations; English theology, 1900-1920 [by] Thomas A. Langford. Nashville, Abingdon Press [1969] 319 p. 24 cm. Bibliography: p. 299-311. [BT28.L3] 79-84720 6.95
1. Theology, Doctrinal—History—20th century. 2. Theology, Doctrinal—History—Gt. Brit. I. Title.

LUTHERAN Church in America. Task Group for Long-Range Planning. 201
Theology; an assessment of current trends; report. Edward W. Uthe, director. Philadelphia, Fortress Press [1968] ix, 164 p. 21 cm. Bibliography: p. 159-164. [BT28.L88] 68-55757 2.25
1. Theology, Doctrinal—History—20th century. I. Uthe, Edward W. II. Title.

MARLE, Rene. 220.6'3
Introduction to hermeneutics. [Translated by E. Froment and R. Albrecht. New York, Herder and Herder [1967] 128 p. 21 cm. [BS4.76.M2813] 66-13071
1. Bible—Hermeneutics. 2. Theology, Doctrinal—History—20 century. I. Title.

MASCALL, Eric Lionel, 1905- 230'.09'04
Theology and the future [by] E. L. Mascall. [1st American ed.] New York, Morehouse-Barlow [1968] 183 p. 19 cm. (Charles A. Hart memorial lectures, 1968) Bibliographical footnotes. [BT28.M29 1968] 72-190
1. Theology, Doctrinal—History—20th century. I. Title. II. Series.

MAURO, Philip, 1859- 230
The number of man, the climax of civilization [by] Philip Mauro ... New York, Chicago [etc.] Fleming H. Revell company [1909] 359 p. 20 1/2 cm. [BT28.M3 1909] 9-30146
1. Theology, Doctrinal—Hist.—20th cent. 2. Religion and science—1900- I. Title.

MEEKS, M. Douglas. 230'.092'4
Origins of the theology of hope [by] M. Douglas Meeks. Foreword by Jurgen Moltmann. Philadelphia, Fortress Press [1974] xiv, 178 p. 24 cm. Bibliography: p. 164-174. [BX4827.M6M43] 73-88351 ISBN 0-8006-0265-X 8.50
1. Moltmann, Jurgen. 2. Theology, Doctrinal—History—20th century. 3. Hope—History of doctrines. I. Title.

MEHTA, Ved Parkash. 230.0904
The new theologian [by] Ved Mehta, New York, Harper [1968,c.1965] 217p. 20cm. (Colophon Bks. CN 131) [BT28.M4] 66-13913 2.45 pap.,
1. Bonhoeffer, Dietrich, 1906-1945. 2. Theology, Doctrinal—Hist.—20th cent. I. Title.

MEHTA, Ved Parkash. 230.0904
The new theologian [by] Ved Mehta. [1st ed.] New York, Harper & Row [1966, c1965] 217 p. 22 cm. [BT28.M4] 66-13913
1. Bonhoeffer, Dietrich, 1906-1945. 2. Theology, Doctrinal — Hist. — 20th cent. I. Title.

MILLER, William Robert. 209'.04
Goodbye, Jehovah; a survey of the new directions in Christianity. New York, Walker [1969] 206 p. 22 cm. Includes bibliographical references. [BT28.M53] 69-11834 5.95
1. Theology, Doctrinal—History—20th century. 2. Christianity—20th century. I. Title.

NEW directions in theology today. 230.0904 William Hordern, editor. [Philadelphia, Westminster Press, 1966- v. 21 cm. Contents.Contents.—v. 1. Introduction, by W. Hordern.—v. 2. History and hermeneutics, by C. E. Braaten.—v. 3. God and secularity, by J. Macquarrie.—v. 4. The church, by C. W. Williams.—v. 5. Christian life, by P. Hessert.—v. 6. Man: the new humanism, by R. L. Shinn. Includes bibliographical references. [BT28.N47] 66-15544
1. Theology, Doctrinal—History—20th century. I. Hordern, William, ed.

NICHOLLS, William. 210
Systematic and philosophical theology. Harmondsworth, Penguin, 1969. 363 p. 18 cm. (Pelican books, A1048.) (The Pelican guide to modern theology, v. 1) Bibliography: p. 349-352. [BT28.N5] 70-446866 ISBN 1-402-10482- 10/-
1. Theology, Doctrinal—History—20th century. I. Title. II. Series.

RAMM, Bernard, 1916- 230.0904
A handbook of contemporary theology. Grand Rapids, Mich., Eerdmans [c.1966]

141p. 22cm. Bibl. [BT28.R3] 65-28565 1.95 pap.,
1. Theology, Doctrinal—Hist.—20th cent. I. Title. II. Title: Contemporary theology.

RAMM, Bernard, 1916- 230.0904
A handbook of contemporary theology. Grand Rapids, Eerdmans [1966] 141 p. 22 cm. Bibliographical references included in "List of abbreviations" (p. 139-141) [BT28.R3] 65-28565
1. Theology, Doctrinal—Hist.—20th cent. I. Title. II. Title: Contemporary theology.

RAMSEY, Arthur 230'.09'04
Michael, Abp. of Canterbury, 1904-
God, Christ, and the world; a study in contemporary theology. [1st American ed.] New York, Morehouse-Barlow Co. [1969] 125 p. 19 cm. Bibliography: p. [119]-121. [BT28.R34 1969b] 75-3935
1. Theology, Doctrinal—History—20th century. I. Title.

REYMOND, Robert L. 230'.09'04
Introductory studies in contemporary theology [by] Robert L. Reymond. [Philadelphia] Presbyterian and Reformed Pub. Co. [1968] 242 p. 20 cm. Includes bibliographical references. [BT28.R48] 68-25834
1. Theology, Doctrinal—History—20th century. I. Title.

RICHARDSON, Alan, 1905- 230.0904
Religion in contemporary debate. Philadelphia, Westminster [1966] 124p. 20cm. Lects. given in Queen's College Hall, Dundee, between November 17 and 24, 1965. [BT28.R5 1966] 66-22987 2.75
1. Theology, Doctrinal—Hist—20th cent. I. Title.

ROBINSON, James 230'.09'04
McConkey, 1924-
Theology as history, edited by James M. Robinson [and] John B. Cobb, Jr. [1st ed.] New York, Harper & Row [1967] x, 276 p. 22 cm. (New frontiers in theology: discussions among Continental and American theologians, v. 3) Contents.Revelation as word and as history, by J. M. Robinson. -- Focal essay: The revelation of God in Jesus of Nazareth, by W. Pannenberg. -- The meaning of history, by M. J. Buss -- Revelation and resurrection, by K. Grobel. -- The character of Pannenberg's theology, by W. Hamilton. -- Past, present, and future, by J. B. Cobb. -- Response to the discussion, by W. Pannenberg. Includes bibliographical references. [BT28.R58] 67-14936
1. Pannenberg, Wolfhart, 1928- 2. Theology, Doctrinal — Hist. — 20th cent. 3. History (Theology) — History of doctrines. I. Cobb, John B., joint author. II. Title. III. Series. IV. Series: New frontiers in theology. v. 3

RUMSCHEIDT, Martin. 230'.09'04
Revelation and theology: an analysis of the Barth-Harnack correspondence of 1923 [by] H. Martin Rumscheidt. Cambridge [Eng.] University Press, 1972. x, 219 p. 22 cm. (Monograph supplements to the Scottish journal of theology) Bibliography: p. 216-217. [BT28.R85] 78-166947 ISBN 0-521-08365-6 £3.40 ($11.95 U.S.)
1. Barth, Karl, 1886-1968. 2. Harnack, Adolf von, 1851-1930. 3. Theology, Doctrinal—History—20th century. I. Title. II. Series: Scottish journal of theology. Monograph supplements.

SENARCLENS, Jacques de, 1914- 230
Heirs of the Reformation. Tr. [from French] ed. by G. W. Bromiley. Foreword by T. F. Torrance. Philadelphia, Westminster [1964, c.1959] 343p. 23cm. (Lib. of hist. and doctrine) Bibl. 63-20956 6.50
1. Theology, Doctrinal—Hist.—20th cent. I. Title.

SHINER, Larry E. 230.0904
The secularization of history; an introduction to the theology of Friedrich Gogarten [by] Larry Shiner. Nashville, Abingdon Press [1966] 236 p. 23 cm. Bibliography: p. 223-228. [BX4827.G6S48] 66-22918
1. Gogarten, Friedrich, 1887- 2. Theology, Doctrinal—History—20th century. I. Title.

SMART, James D. 230'.0904
The divided mind of modern theology, Karl Barth and Rudolf Bultmann, 1908-1933, by James D. Smart. Philadelphia, Westminster Press [1967] 240 p. 24 cm. Bibliographical references included in "Notes" (p. [229]-238) [BT28.S6] 67-10614
1. Barth, Karl, 1886- 2. Bultmann, Rudolf Karl, 1884- 3. Theology, Doctrinal—History—20th century. I. Title.

SPERNA WEILAND, Jan. 230'.09'04
New ways in theology [by] J. Sperna Weiland. Translated by N. D. Smith. Glen Rock, N.J., Newman Press [1968] xv, 222 p. 22 cm. Translation of Orientatie. Includes bibliographies. [BT28.S6513 1968] 68-55398 5.95
1. Theology, Doctrinal—History—20th century. I. Title.

SUTPHIN, Stanley T. 230'.0904
Options in contemporary theology / Stanley T. Sutphin. Washington : University Press of America, 1978,c1977. iv, 175 p. ; 22 cm. Includes bibliographical references and index. [BT28.S87] 78-100404 ISBN 0-8191-0277-6 pbk. : 8.65
1. Theology, Doctrinal—History—20th century. I. Title.

VAHANIAN, Gabriel, 1927- 231.0904
No other god. New York, G. Braziller [1966] xii, 114 p. illus. 21 cm. "References": p. 103-114. [BT28.V3] 66-28591
1. Theology, Doctrinal—History—20th century. 2. Death of God theology. I. Title.

VIDLER, Alexander Roper, 230.0904
1899-
20th century defenders of the faith [by] Alex R. Vidler. New York, Seabury [c.1965] 127p. 20cm. (Robertson lects. 1964) Title. (Series: Robertson lectures, 1964) Bibl. [BT28.V5] 65-29702 2.50 bds.,
1. Theology, Doctrinal—Hist.—20th cent. 2. Apologetics—Hist. I. Title. II. Series.

VIDLER, Alexander Roper, 230.0904
1899-
20th century defenders of the faith [by] Alec R. Vidler New York, Seabury Press [1965] 127 p. 20 cm. (Robertson lectures [1964]) Bibliographical footnotes. [BT28.V5] 65-29702
1. Theology, Doctrinal — Hist. — 20th cent. 2. Apologetics — Hist. I. Title. II. Series: Robertson lectures, 1964

VOELKEL, Robert T. 230'.0924 B
The shape of the theological task, by Robert T. Voelkel. Philadelphia, Westminster Press [1968] 171 p. 21 cm. Bibliographical references included in "Notes" (p. [165]-171) [BX4827.H44V6] 68-10986
1. Herrmann, Wilhelm, 1846-1922. 2. Theology, Doctrinal—History—20th century. I. Title.

WEST, Charles C. 261.7
Communism and the theologians; study of an encounter. New York, Macmillan [1963, c.1958] 399p. 23cm. 63-2966 1.95 pap.,
1. Theology, Doctrinal—Hist.—20th cent. 2. Communism and religion. 3. Christianity—Philosophy. I. Title.

WILLIAMS, Daniel Day, 1910- 230
What present-day theologians are thinking. Rev. ed. [New York] Harper [1959] 190 p. 20 cm. Includes bibliography. [BT28.W55 1959] 58-13946
1. Theology, Doctrinal — Hist. — 20th cent. 2. Religious thought — 20th cent. I. Title.

WILLIAMS, Daniel Day, 230'.0904
1910-
What present-day theologians are thinking. 3d ed., rev. New York, Harper & Row [1967] 227 p. 21 cm. (Harper chapelbooks, CB32) Includes bibliographies. [BT28.W55 1967] 67-1206
1. Theology, Doctrinal—History—20th century. 2. Religious thought—20th century. I. Title.

WILLIAMS, Daniel Day, 1910- 230
What present-day theologians are thinking. [1st ed.] [New York] Harper [1952] 158 p. 20 cm. [BT28.W55] 52-8494
1. Theology, Doctrinal—History—20th cent. 2. Religious thought—20th cent. I. Title.

WILLIAMS, Daniel Day, 230'.0904
1910-1973.
What present-day theologians are thinking / Daniel Day Williams. Rev. ed. Westport, Conn. : Greenwood Press, [1978] c1959. p. cm. Reprint of the ed. published by Harper, New York. Bibliography: p. [BT28.W55 1978] 78-16410 ISBN 0-313-20587-6 lib.bdg. : 15.25
1. Theology, Doctrinal—History—20th century. 2. Religious thought—20th century. I. Title.

WINGREN, Gustaf, 1910- 230
Theology in conflict; Nygren, Barth, Bultmann. Translated by Eric II. Wahlstrom. Philadelphia, Muhlenberg Press [1958] 170 p. 21 cm. Translation of Teologiens metodfraga. [BT28.W573] 58-5750
1. Nygren, Anders Bp., 1890- 2. Barth, Karl, 1886- 3. Bultmann, Rudolf Karl, 1884- 4. Theology, Doctrinal — Hist. — 20th cent. 5. Law and gospel. I. Title.

Theology, Doctrinal—History—20th century—Addresses, essays, lectures.

ROBINSON, James McConkey, 230
1924- ed.
The later Heidegger and theology / edited by James M. Robinson, John B. Cobb, Jr. Westport, Conn. : Greenwood Press, 1979, c1963. xii, 212 p. ; 23 cm. Reprint of the 1st ed. published by Harper & Row, New York, which was issued as v. 1 of New frontiers in theology. Includes bibliographical references. [B3279.H49R6 1979] 78-23619 ISBN 0-313-20783-6 : 17.75
1. Heidegger, Martin, 1889-1976—Addresses, essays, lectures. 2. Theology, Doctrinal—History—20th century—Addresses, essays, lectures. I. Cobb, John B. II. Title. III. Series: New frontiers in theology ; v. 1.

TENSIONS in 230'.09'04
contemporary theology / edited by Stanley N. Gundry and Alan F. Johnson foreword by Roger Nicole. Chicago : Moody Press, c1976. 366 p. ; 24 cm. Includes bibliographies and index. [BT28.T4] 76-7629 ISBN 0-8024-8585-5 : 8.95
1. Theology, Doctrinal—History—20th century—Addresses, essays, lectures. I. Gundry, Stanley N. II. Johnson, Alan F.

A World of grace : 230'.2'0924
an introduction to the themes and foundations of Karl Rahner's theology / edited by Leo J. O'Donovan. New York : Crossroad, 1981, c1980. p. cm. Bibliography: p. [BX4705.R287W67 1981] 19 81-5441 ISBN 0-8245-0406-2 pbk. : 9.95
1. Rahner, Karl, 1904- —Addresses, essays, lectures. 2. Theology, Doctrinal—History—20th century—Addresses, essays, lectures. I. O'Donovan, Leo J.

Theology, Doctrinal—History—Addresses, essays, lectures.

FINLAYSON, R. A. 230.09
The story of theology, by R. A. Finlayson. Chicago, Inter-Varsity Pr. [1964, c.1963] 55p. 22cm. Bibl. 64-4510 1.25 pap.,
1. Theology, Doctrinal—Hist.—Addresses, essays, lectures. I. Title.

A History of Christian 230'.09
doctrine : in succession to the earlier work of G. P. Fisher, published in the International technological library series / edited by Hubert Cunliffe-Jones, assisted by Benjamin Drewery. 1st Fortress Press ed. Philadelphia : Fortress Press, 1980, c1978. x, [iii], 601 p. ; 22 cm. Includes indexes. Bibliography: p. [xiii] [BT21.2.H57 1980] 79-21689 ISBN 0-8006-0626-4 : 29.95
1. Theology, Doctrinal—History—Addresses, essays, lectures. I. Cunliffe-Jones, Hubert. II. Drewery, Benjamin. III. Fisher, George Park, 1827-1909. History of Christian doctrine.

Theology, Doctrinal—History—America—Congresses.

THEOLOGY in the Americas 230'.097
/ edited by Sergio Torres and John Eagleson. Maryknoll, N.Y. : Orbis Books, c1976. xxviii, 438 p. ; 22 cm. Includes papers prepared for a conference held in Detroit, August 1975. Includes bibliographical references. [BT30.A5T46] 76-22545 ISBN 0-88344-479-8 : 12.95. pbk. :
1. Theology, Doctrinal—History—America—Congresses. I. Torres, Sergio. II. Eagleson, John.

Theology, Doctrinal—History—Asia—Addresses, essays, lectures.

ASIAN voices in 230'.095
Christian theology / edited and with an introd. by Gerald H. Anderson. Maryknoll, N.Y. : Orbis Books, c1976. 321 p. ; 22 cm. Bibliography: p. 264-321. [BT30.A8A78] 75-13795 ISBN 0-88344-017-2 : 15.00. ISBN 0-88344-016-4 pbk. : 7.95
1. Theology, Doctrinal—History—Asia—Addresses, essays, lectures. I. Anderson, Gerald H.

Theology, Doctrinal—History—Early church.

BIRDSALL, James Neville, ed.
Biblical and patristic studies in memory of Robert Pierce Casey. Edited by J. Neville Birdsall and Robert W. Thomson. Freiburg, New York, Herder [1963-) 269 p. port., facsims. 22 cm. NUC64
1. Casey, Robert Pierce, 1897-1959. 2. Theology, Doctrinal—History—Cearly church. I. Thomson, Robert W., joint ed. II. Title.

CARPENTER, Levy Leonidas. 232.
Primitive Christian application of the doctrine of the servant, by Levy Leonidas Carpenter ... with an introduction by Allen H. Godbey ... Durham, N. C., Duke university press, 1929. 3 p. l., [v]-xxi, 185 p. 20 cm. (Half-title: Duke university publications) "Written originally as a doctoral dissertation at the Graduate school of Yale university."--Pref. "Select bibliography": p. 171-177. [BT198.C3] 29-8707
I. Title.

CONE, Orello, 1835-1905 230.12
The Gospel and its earliest interpretations; a study of the teaching of Jesus and its doctrinal transformations in the New Testament, by Orello Cone, p.p. New York, London, G. P. Putnam's sons, 1893. vii, 413 p. 21 cm. [BT24.C6] 39-24765
1. Jesus Christ Teachings 2. Theology, Doctrinal—Hist.—Early church. 3. Bible, N.T.—Theology. 4. Bible—Theology—N.T. I. Title.

EDWARDS, Lyford Paterson, 1882-
... The transformation of early Christianity from an eschatological to a socialized movement ... by Lyford Paterson Edwards. Menasha, Wis., George Banta publishing company, 1919. 2 p. l., 94 p. 24 cm. Thesis (PH.D.)--University of Chicago, 1919. [BT25.E3] 20-1301
1. Theology, Doctrinal—Hist.—Early church. 2. Eschatology—History of doctrines. 3. Sociology, Christian—Early church. I. Title.

KELLY, John Norman 230.11
Davidson.
Early Christian doctrines. New York, Harper [1959, c1958] 500p. 22cm. Includes bibliography. [BT25.K4] 58-12933
1. Theology, Doctrinal—Hist.—Early church. I. Title.

KELLY, John Norman Davidson.
Early Christian doctrines. 2d ed. New York, Harper [c1960] xi, 500 p. Includes bibliography. 65-95001
1. Theology, Doctrinal — History — Early church. I. Title.

KELLY, John Norman 230.11
Davidson.
Early christian doctrines / by J.N.D. Kelly. New York : Harper and Row, 1978 xii,511p. ; 20 cm. [BT25.K4] ISBN 0-06-064334-X pbk. : 6.95
1. Theology, Doctrinal — History — Early Church. I. Title.
L.C. card no. for 1959 Harper and Row ed. :58-12933.

LADNER, Gerhart Burian, 1905- 230.09
The idea of reform, its impact on Christian thought and action in the age of the Fathers. [Rev. ed.] New York, Harper [1967,c.1959] 561p. 21cm. (Torchbook, TB149) Bibl. [BT25.I.3] 3.75 pap.,
1. Theology, Doctrinal—Hist.—Early church. 2. Title. I. Title.

LADNER, Gerhart Burian, 1905- 230.09
The idea of reform; its impact on Christian thought and action in the age of the Fathers [Magnolia, Mass., Peter Smith, 1968,c. 1959] 553p. 23cm. Bibl. [BT25.L3 1959] 5.75
1. Theology, Doctrinal—Hist.—Early church. I. Title.

LADNER, Gerhart Burian, 1905- 230.09
The idea of reform, its impact on Christian thought and action in the age of the Fathers. Cambridge, Harvard University Press, 1959. 553p. 23cm. Includes bibliography. [BT25.L3 1959] 59-6159
1. Theology, Doctrinal—Hist.—Early church. I. Title.

LADNER, Gerhart Burian, 1905- 230'.09'015
The idea of reform; its impact on Christian thought and action in the age of the Fathers [by] Gerhart B. Ladner. [Rev. ed.] New York, Harper & Row [1967] x, 561 p. 21 cm. (Harper torchbooks, TB149) Bibliography: p. 469-489. Bibliographical footnotes. [BT25.L3 1967] 68-732
1. Theology, Doctrinal—Hist.—Early church. I. Title.

MELLONE, Sydney Herbert, 1869- 230
Leaders of early Christian thought. Boston, Beacon Press [1955] 243p. 23cm. [BT23] 55-14644
1. Theology, Doctrinal—Hist.—Early church. I. Title.

NORRIS, Richard Alfred. 231.09
God and world in early Christian theology [by] R. A. Norris, Jr. New York, Seabury Press [1965] x, 177 p. 22 cm. Bibliography: p. 173-177. [BT25.N6] 65-21311
1. Theology, Doctrinal — Hist. — Early church. 2. God — History of doctrines. 3. Creation — History of doctrines. I. Title.

PRESTIGE, George Leonard, 1889- 281.1
Fathers and heretics; six studies in dogmatic faith with prologue and epilogue ... by G. L. Presige, D.D. London, Society for promoting Christian knowledge; New York, The Macmillan company [1940] vii, 432 p. 22 cm. (The Bampton lectures, 1940) "First published 1940." [BR45.B3 1940] (230.082) 43-13867
1. Theology, Doctrinal—Hist.—Early church. 2. Fathers of the church. 3. Heresies and heretics—Early church. I. Title.

WATERMAN, Lucius, 1851- 265.
The primitive tradition of the Eucharistic Body and Blood, by Lucius Waterman ... New York [etc.] Longmans, Green and co., 1919. xv, 270 p. 19 1/2 cm. [The Paddock lectures for 1918-1919] $2.00 [BV825.W3] 19-13463
I. Title.

WERNER, Martin, 1887- 230.1
The formation of Christian dogma; an historical study of its problem. Boston, Beacon [1965, c.1957] 352p. 21cm. (BP191) [BT23.W413] 2.45 pap.,
1. Theology, Doctrinal—Hist.—Early Church. I. Title.

WERNER, Martin, 1887-
The formation of Christian dogma, an historical study of its problem. Rewritten in shortened form by the author from his Die Enstehung des christlichen Dogmas, and translated, with an introd. by S.G.F. Brandon. Boston, Beacon Press [1965] 352 p. (BP 191) Copyright 1957; first published as Beacon paperback 1965. 68-99735
1. Theology, Doctrinal—Hist.—Early church. I. Title.

WERNER, Martin, 1887- 230.1
The formation of Christian dogma; an historical study of its problem. New York, Harper [1957] 352 p. illus 23 cm. "Rewritten in shortened form by the author from his Die Entstehung des christlichen Dogmas, and translated, with an introduction by S. G. F. Brandon." [BT23.W413] 57-10528
1. Theology, Doctrinal — Hist. — Early church. I. Title.

WILLIAMS, Robert R. 281.1
A guide to the teachings of the early church Fathers. Grand Rapids, Eerdmans [1960] 224 p. 23 cm. Includes bibliography. [BT25.W5] 60-6401
1. Theology, Doctrinal — Hist. — Early church. 2. Fathers of the church. I. Title.

WOLFSON, Harry Austryn, 1887- 230
The philosophy of the Church fathers; v.1. 2d ed. rev. Cambridge, Mass., Harvard, 1964. v. 23cm. (His Structure and growth of philosophic systems from Plato to Spinoza, 3) Contents.v.1. Faith, Trinity, Incarnation. Bibl. 64-5600 10.00
1. Theology, Doctrinal—Hist.—Early church. 2. Incarnation—History of doctrines. 3. Trinity—History of doctrines. 4. Heresies and heretics—Early church. I. Title.

WOLFSON, Harry Austryn, 1887- 230
The philosophy of the church fathers. Cambridge, Harvard University Press, 1956- v. 23 cm. (His Structure and growth of philosophic systems from Plato to Spinoza, 3) Contents.v. 1. Faith, Trinity, Incarnation. Bibliographical footnotes. [BT25.W6] 56-5176
1. Theology, Doctrinal — Hist. — Early church. 2. Christian literature, Early — Hist. & crit. 3. Christianity — Philosophy. 4. Trinity — History of doctrines. 5. Heresies and heretics — Early church. I. Title.

Theology, Doctrinal—History—Early church, ca. 30-600.

BARR, Robert R. 230.11
Main currents in early Christian thought, by Robert Barr. Pref. by Jean Danielou. Glen Rock, N.J., Paulist Press [1966] vi, 122 p. illus. 20 cm. (Guide to the Fathers of the church, 1) Bibliographical footnotes. [BT25.B24] 66-22055
1. Theology, Doctrinal—History—Early church, ca. 30-600. I. Title.

DUNN, James D. G., 1939- 201'.1
Unity and diversity in the New Testament : an inquiry into the character of earliest Christianity / by James D. G. Dunn. Philadelphia : Westminster Press, c1977. p. cm. Includes index. Bibliography: p. [BS2397.D85] 77-22598 ISBN 0-664-21342-1 : 19.50
1. Bible. N.T.—Theology. 2. Theology, Doctrinal—History—Early church, ca. 30-600. I. Title.

MORE, Paul Elmer, 1846-1937. 232
Christ the Word. New York, Greenwood Press [1969, c1927] vii, 343 p. 23 cm. Bibliographical footnotes. [BT201.M67 1969] 72-88913 ISBN 0-8371-2244-9
1. Jesus Christ—Person and offices. 2. Theology, Doctrinal—History—Early church, ca. 30-600. I. Title.

PFLEIDERER, Otto, 1839-1908. 225.9'24
Lectures on the influence of the apostle Paul on the development of Christianity : delivered in London and Oxford in April and May, 1885 / by Otto Pfleiderer ; translated by J. Frederick Smith. [1st AMS ed.] [New York : AMS Press, 1979] vii, 292 p. ; 18 cm. Reprint of the 1885 ed. published by Williams and Norgate, London, which was issued as the 1885 Hibbert lectures. [BS2651.P4 1979] 77-27166 ISBN 0-404-60406-4 : 22.50
1. Paul, Smith, apostle. 2. Bible. N.T. Epistles of Paul—Theology. 3. Theology, Doctrinal—History—Early church, ca. 30-600. I. Title. II. Series: Hibbert lectures (London) ; 1885.

RICHARDSON, Alan, 1905-1975. 230'.09'015
Creeds in the making : a short introduction to the history of Christian doctrine / Alan Richardson. 1st Fortress Press ed. Philadelphia : Fortress Press, 1981, c1935. 128 p. ; 18 cm. [BT25.R52 1981] 19 81-43073 ISBN 0-8006-1609-X pbk. : 5.95
1. Theology, Doctrinal—History—Early church, ca. 30-600. I. Title.

TURNER, Henry Ernest William, 1907- 230'.08 s
The pattern of Christian truth : a study in the relations between orthodoxy and heresy in the early chuch / H. E. W. Turner. New York : AMS Press, 1978. xvi, 508 p. ; 23 cm. Reprint of the 1954 ed. published by A. R. Mowbray, London, which was issued as Bampton lectures, 1954. Includes bibliographical references and indexes. [BT25.T87 1978] 273'.1 77-84707 ISBN 0-404-16114-6 : 34.50
1. Theology, Doctrinal—History—Early church, ca. 30-600. 2. Heresies and heretics—Early church, c. 30-600. I. Title. II. Series: Bampton lectures, 1954.

WILLIS, John Randolph. 230'.1'1
A history of Christian thought : from apostolic times to Saint Augustine / John R. Willis. 1st ed. Hicksville, N.Y. : Exposition Press, c1976. 410 p. ; 24 cm. (An Exposition-university book) Includes index. Bibliography: p. 389-397. [BT25.W53] 76-16237 ISBN 0-682-48583-7 : 16.00
1. Theology, Doctrinal—History—Early church, ca. 30-600. I. Title.

WOLFSON, Harry Austryn, 1887- 230
The philosophy of the Church fathers. 3d ed., rev. Cambridge, Harvard University Press [1970- v. 23 cm. (His Structure and growth of philosophic systems from Plato to Spinoza, 3) Contents.Contents.—v. 1. Faith, Trinity, Incarnation. Includes bibliographical references. [BT25.W63] 70-119077 ISBN 0-674-66551-1 12.50
1. Theology, Doctrinal—History—Early church, ca. 30-600. 2. Incarnation—History of doctrines. 3. Trinity—History of doctrines. 4. Heresies and heretics—Early church, ca. 30-600. I. Title.

Theology, Doctrinal—History—Early church ca. 30-600—Addresses, essays, lectures.

TEXTS and testaments : 230
critical essays on the Bible and early church fathers : a volume in honor of Stuart Dickson Currie / edited by W. Eugene March. San Antonio : Trinity University Press, c1980. xiii, 321 p. : port. ; 24 cm. "Written work, Stuart Dickson Currie": p. [301]-302. Includes bibliographical references and indexes. [BS511.2.T47] 19 79-92585 ISBN 0-911536-80-9 : 15.00
1. Currie, Stuart Dickson, 1922-1975—Addresses, essays, lectures. 2. Bible—Criticism, interpretation, etc.—Addresses, essays, lectures. 3. Theology, Doctrinal—History—Early church ca. 30-600—Addresses, essays, lectures. 4. Church history—Primitive and early church, ca. 30-600—Addresses, essays, lectures. I. March, Wallace Eugene, 1935- II. Currie, Stuart Dickson, 1922-1975.

WILES, Maurice F. 230
The Christian fathers / Maurice Wiles. [2nd ed.] New York : Oxford University Press, 1982, c1966. 190 p. ; 21 cm. Includes index. Bibliography: p. 186-187. [BT25.W47 1982] 19 81-16881 ISBN 0-19-520260-0 pbk. : 5.95
1. Theology, Doctrinal—History—Early church, ca. 30-600—Addresses, essays, lectures. 2. Fathers of the church. I. Title.

Theology, Doctrinal—History—Europe.

HORTON, Walter Marshall, 1895- 230
Contemporary continental theology; an interpretation for Anglo-Saxons [by] Walter Marshall Horton ... New York and London, Harper & brothers, 1938. xxi p., 1 l., 246 p. 19 1/2 cm. "First edition. Bibliography: p. 234-239. [BT28.H6] 38-23014
1. Theology, Doctrinal—Hist.—Europe. 2. Theologians, European. I. Title.

Theology, Doctrinal—History—Germany.

BARTH, Karl, 1886-1968. 230'.09'034
Protestant theology in the nineteenth century; its background & history. Valley Forge [Pa.] Judson Press [1973, c1972] 669 p. 23 cm. "The first complete translation of Die protestantische Theologie im 19. Jahrhundert." Includes bibliographical references. [BT30.G3B313 1973] 72-1956 ISBN 0-8170-0572-2 15.00
1. Theology, Doctrinal—History—Germany. 2. Theology, Doctrinal—History—18th century. 3. Theology, Doctrinal—History—19th century. 4. Theology, Protestant—Germany. I. Title.

BARTH, Karl, 1886-1968. 230.4
Protestant thought: from Rousseau to Ritschl, being the translation of eleven chapters of Die protestantische Theologie im 19. Jahrhundert. [Translated by Brian Cozens] New York, Harper [1959] 435 p. 22 cm. Includes bibliography. [BT30.G3B313 1959] 59-10931
1. Theology, Doctrinal—History—Germany. 2. Theology, Doctrinal—History—18th century. 3. Theology, Doctrinal—History—19th century. I. Title.

BARTH, Karl, 1886-1968. 230.4
Protestant thought: from Rousseau to Ritschl; being the translation of eleven chapters of Die protestantische Theologie im 19. Jahrhundert. [Translated by Brian Cozens. New York] Simon and Schuster [1969, c1959] 435 p. 21 cm. Bibliography: p. [423]-425. Bibliographical footnotes. [BT30.G3B313 1969] 70-4455 2.95
1. Theology, Doctrinal—History—Germany. 2. Theology, Doctrinal—History—18th century. 3. Theology, Doctrinal—History—19th century. I. Title.

BARTH, Karl, 1886-1968. 230
Protestant thought: from Rousseau to Ritschl, being a translation of eleven chapters of Die protestantische Theologie im 19. Jahrhundert. [Translated by Brian Cozens] Freeport, N.Y., Books for Libraries Press [1971, c1959] 435 p. 23 cm. (Essay index reprint series) Bibliography: p. [423]-425. [BT30.G3B313 1971] 73-142606 ISBN 0-8369-2102-X
1. Theology, Doctrinal—History—Germany. 2. Theology, Doctrinal—History—18th century. 3. Theology, Doctrinal—History—19th century. 4. Theology, Protestant—Germany. I. Title.

NUELSEN, John Louise, bp., 1867-
Some recent phases of Germany theology, by John L. Nuelsen ... Cincinnati, Jennings and Graham; New York, Eaton and Mans [1908] 114 p. 21 cm. "The following three lectures were delivered at the Bible institute, at Lakeside, O., in August, 1907."--Foreword. [BT30.G3N8] 8-7161
1. Theology, Doctrinal—Hist.—Germany. 2. Bible—Criticism, interpretation, etc.—Hist. I. Title.
Contents omitted.

Theology, Doctrinal—History—Great Britain

HORTON, Walter Marshall, 1895- 230
Contemporary continental theology; an interpretation for Anglo-saxons [by] Walter Marshall Horton ... New York and London, Harper & brothers, 1938. xix p., 1 l., 186 p. 20 cm. "First edition." [BT30.G7H6] 36-25271
1. Theology, Doctrinal—Hist.—Gt. Brit. 2. Theologians, English. I. Title.

NEW, John F H 230.0942
Anglican and Puritan; the basis of their opposition, 1558-1640 [by] John F. H. New. Stanford, Calif., Stanford University Press, 1964. 140 p. 23 cm. Bibliographical references included in "Notes" (p. [115]-132) [BR756.N48] 64-12075
1. Theology, Doctrinal — Hist. — Gt. Brit. I. Title.

RAMSEY, Arthur Michael, Abp. of York, 1904- 230.3
An era in Anglican theology, from Gore to Temple; the development of Anglican theology between Lux Mundi and the Second World War, 1889-1939. New York, Scribners [c.1960] ix, 192p. Bibl. footnotes 22cm. (The Hale memorial lectures of Seabury-Western Theological Seminary, 1959) 60-14014 3.50
1. Theology, Doctrinal—Hist.—Gt. Brit. 2. Theology, Doctrinal—Addresses, essays, lectures. I. Title.

RAMSEY, Arthur Michael, 230.3
Abp. of Canterbury, 1904-
An era in Anglican theology, from Gore to Temple; the development of Anglican theology between Lux Mundi and the Second World War, 1889-1939. New York, Scribner [1960] 192 p. 22 cm. (The Hale memorial lectures of Seabury-Western Theological Seminary, 1959) Includes bibliography. [BT30.G7R3] 60-14014
1. Theology, Doctrinal — Hist. — Gt. Brit. I. Title.

Theology, Doctrinal—History—India.

BOYD, Robin H. S., 230'.0954
1924-
India and the Latin captivity of the Church; the cultural context of the Gospel [by] R. H. S. Boyd. [London] Cambridge University Press [1974] xiv, 151 p. 23 cm. (Monograph supplements to the Scottish journal of theology no. 3) Includes bibliographical references. [BR1155.B66] 73-86049 ISBN 0-521-20371-6
1. Theology, Doctrinal—History—India. I. Title. II. Series: Scottish journal of theology. Monograph supplements, no. 3. Distributed by Cambridge University Press, New York; 10.50.

Theology, Doctrinal—History—Japan.

MICHALSON, Carl. 230.0952
Japanese contributions to Christian theology. Philadelphia, Westminster Press [1960] 192p. 21cm. Includes bibliography. [BT30.J3M5] 60-7487
1. Theology, Doctrinal—Hist.—Japan. I. Title.

Theology, Doctrinal—History—Middle Ages.

OBERMAN, Heiko 230.0902
Augustinus
The harvest of medieval theology; Gabriel Biel and late medieval nominalism. Cambridge, Mass., Harvard [c.]1963. xv, 495p. illus. 24cm. (Robert Troup Paine prize-treatise, 1962) Bibl. 63-9553 9.25
1. Biel, Gabriel, d. 1495. 2. Theology, Doctrinal—Hist.—Middle Ages. 3. Nominalism. I. Title. II. Series.

OBERMAN, Heiko 230'.09'02
Augustinus.
The harvest of medieval theology; Gabriel Biel and late medieval nominalism.[Rev. ed.] Grand Rapids, Eerdmans [1967] xv, 495p. 22cm. (Robert Troup Paine prizetreatise, 1962) Bibl. [BT26.O2] 67-19313 3.95 pap.,
1. Biel, Gabriel, d. 1495. 2. Theology, Doctrinal—Hist.—Middle Ages. 3. Nominalism. I. Title. II. Series.

OBERMAN, Heiko 230'.09'02
Augustinus.
The harvest of medieval theology; Gabriel Biel and late medieval nominalism. [Rev. ed.] Grand Rapids, W. B. Eerdmans Pub. Co. [1967] xv, 495 p. 22 cm. (The Robert Troup Paine prize-treatise, 1962) Bibliography: p. 431-456. [BT26.O2] 67-19313
1. Biel, Gabriel, d. 1495. 2. Theology, Doctrinal—Hist.—Middle Ages. 3. Nominalism. I. Title. II. Series.

OBERMAN, Heiko 230.0902
Augustinus.
The harvest of medieval theology; Gabriel Biel and late medieval nominalism. Cambridge, Harvard University Press, 1963. xv, 495 p. illus. 24 cm. (The Robert Troup Paine prize-treatise, 1962) Bibliography: p. 431-456. [BT26.O2] 63-9553
1. 1. Biel, Gabriel, d. 2. Theology, Doctrinal — Hist. — Middle Ages. 3. Nominalism. I. Title. II. Series.

Theology, Doctrinal—History—Middle Ages, 600-1500.

CHENU, Marie Dominique, 1895- 230
Nature, man, and society in the twelfth century; essays on new theological perspectives in the Latin West, by M. D. Chenu, with a pref. by Etienne Gilson. Selected, edited, and translated by Jerome Taylor and Lester K. Little. Chicago, University of Chicago Press [1968] xxi, 361 p. 25 cm. Translation of nine essays selected from La theologie au douzieme siecle. Bibliographical footnotes. [BT26.C513] 68-15574
1. Theology, Doctrinal—History—Middle Ages, 600-1500. 2. Philosophy, Medieval—History. 3. Scholasticism—History. I. Title.

CHENU, Marie Dominique, 1895- 230
Nature, man and society in the twelfth century : essays on new theological perspectives in the Latin West / M.D. Chenu, with a preface by Etienne Gilson. Selected, edited and translated by Jerome Taylor and Lester K. Little. Chicago, London : University of Chicago Press, 1979 c1968. Transltion of nine essays selected from La theologie au douzieme siecle. Includes bibliographical references and index,. [BJ26.C513] 68-15574 ISBN 0-226-10255-6 pbk. : 7.95
1. Theology Doctrinal — History — Middle Ages 600-1500 2. Philosophy, Medieval — History 3. Scholasticism — History I. Title.

EVANS, Gillian. 230
Old arts and new technology : the beginnings of theology as an academic discipline / by G. R. Evans. Oxford [Eng.] : Clarendon Press ; New York : Oxford University Press, 1980. p. cm. Includes index. [BT26.E9] 79-42788 ISBN 0-19-826653-7 : 29.95
1. Theology, Doctrinal—History—Middle Ages, 600-1500. I. Title.

PELIKAN, Jaroslav Jan, 230 s
1923-
The growth of medieval theology (600-1300) / Jaroslav Pelikan. Chicago : University of Chicago Press, c1978. p. cm. (His The Christian tradition ; 3) Includes indexes. Bibliography: p. [BT21.2.P42 vol. 3] [BT26] 230'.09'02 78-1501 ISBN 0-226-65374-9 : 17.50
1. Theology, Doctrinal—History—Middle Ages, 600-1500. I. Title.

Theology, Doctrinal—History—Modern period, 1500-

LIVINGSTON, James C., 1930- 201
Modern Christian thought: from the Enlightenment to Vatican II [by] James C. Livingston. New York, Macmillan [1971] xvi, 523 p. ports. 24 cm. Includes bibliographies. [BT28.L55] 76-121675
1. Theology, Doctrinal—History—Modern period, 1500- I. Title.

Theology, Doctrinal—History—Modern periodicals

CREED, John Martin. 232.8
The divinity of Jesus Christ: a study in the history of Christian doctrine since Kant Hulsean lectures, 1936, by John Martin Creed ... Cambridge [Eng.] The University press, 1938. x, 146 p., 1 l. 21 cm. [BT198.C7] 39-631
1. Jesus Christ—Divinity. 2. Theology, Doctrinal—Hist.—Modern period. I. Hulsean lectures, 1936. II. Title.

Theology, Doctrinal—History—.Sweden.

FERRE, Nels Fredrick 230.09485
Solomon, 1908-
Swedish contributions to modern theology, with special reference to Lundensian thought, by Nels F. S. Ferre. With a new chapter, Developments in Swedish theology, 1939-1966 by William A. Johnson. New York, Harper [1967,c.1939] x, 304p. 21cm. (Torchbk., TB147) [BT30.S8F4] 2.45 pap.,
1. Theology, Doctrinal—Hist.—Sweden. I. Title.

FERRE, Nels Fredrick 230.00485
Solomon, 1908-
Swedish contributions to modern theology, with special reference to Lundensian thought, by Nels F.S. Ferre... New York, London, Harper & brothers [c1939] x p., 1 l., 250 p. diagrs. 21 1/2 cm. "First edition." Bibliography: p. 243-247. [BT30.S8F4] 39-31178
1. Theology, Doctrinal—Hist.—.Sweden. I. Title.

FERRE, Nels Fredrick 230'.09485
Solomon, 1908-
Swedish contributions to modern theology, with special reference to Lundensian thought [by] Nels F.S. Ferré. With a new chapter, "Developments in Swedish theology, 1939-1966," by William A. Johnson. New York, Harper & Row [1967] x, 304, 6 p. 21 cm. (Harper torchbooks, TB147) Bibliography: p. 296-301. [BT30.S8F4] 67-9656
1. Theology. Doctrinal—Hist.—Sweden. I. Title.

WINGREN, Gustaf, 230.4'1'0924
1910-
An exodus theology; Einar Billing and the development of modern Swedish theology. Translated by Eric Wahlstrom. Philadelphia, Fortress Press [1969] viii, 181 p. port. 22 cm. Translation of Einar Billing. En studie i svensk teologi fore 1920. Bibliography: p. 173-174. [BX8080.B47W513] 69-14616 4.75
1. Billing, Einar, Bp., 1871-1939. 2. Theology, Doctrinal—History—Sweden. I. Title.

Theology, Doctrinal—History—U.S.

AHLSTROM, Sydney E. 230'.0973
comp.
Theology in America; the major Protestant voices from puritanism to neo-orthodoxy. Edited by Sydney E. Ahlstrom. Indianapolis, Bobbs-Merrill Co. [1967] 630 p. 21 cm. (The American heritage series, 73) Bibliographical footnotes. Bibliography: p. 93-107. [BT30.U55A6] 67-21401
1. Theology. Doctrinal—Hist.—U. S. 2. Theology—Collections—Protestant authors. I. Title.

FOSTER, Frank Hugh, 230.0973
1851-1935.
The modern movement in American theology: sketches in the history of American Protestant thought from the civil war to the world war, by Frank Hugh Foster. New York [etc.] Fleming H. Revell company [c1939] 219 p. 21 cm. "Andover Newton theological school ... Stephen Green lectures for 1934-35."--Foreword, signed: John Gardener Greene. "A continuation ... of ... "Genetic history of the New England theology'."--F oreword. "References" at end of most of the Chapters. [BT30.U6F6] 39-14095
1. Theology, Doctrinal—Hist.—U. S. 2. New England theology. I. Greene, John Gardner. ed. II. Title.

GIBSON, Raymond E. 230
God, man, and time; human destiny in American theology [by] Raymond E. Gibson. Philadelphia, United Church Press [1966] 187 p. 21 cm. Bibliographical references included in "Notes" (p. 179-187) [BT821.2.G5] 66-17662
1. Theology, Doctrinal — Hist. — U.S. 2. Man (Theology) — History of doctrines. 3. Eschatology — History of doctrines. I. Title.

MILLER, Randolph Crump, 230'.0973
1910-
The American spirit in theology. Philadelphia, United Church Press [1974] 252 p. 22 cm. "A Pilgrim Press book." Bibliography: p. 241-244. [BT30.U6M54] 74-11099 ISBN 0-8298-0285-1 8.50
1. Theology, Doctrinal—History—United States. 2. Empiricism. 3. Process philosophy. I. Title.

SONTAG, Frederick. 230'.0973
The American religious experience; the roots, trends, and future of American theology, by Frederick Sontag and John K. Roth. [1st ed.] New York, Harper & Row [1972] xiii, 401 p. 22 cm. Bibliography: p. [387]-394. [BT30.U6S65 1972] 73-163164 10.95
1. Theology, Doctrinal—History—U.S. 2. Philosophy, American. I. Roth, John K., joint author. II. Title.

WILLIAMS, Daniel Day, 207'.744'5
1910-
The Andover liberals; a study in American theology. New York, Octagon Books, 1970 [c1941] viii, 203 p. 24 cm. Thesis—Columbia University, 1941. Bibliography: p. [193]-199. [BV4070.A56W5 1970] 79-111636
1. Andover Theological Seminary. 2. Theology, Doctrinal—History—U.S. I. Title.

Theology, Doctrinal—Introductions.

ALEXANDER, Anthony F., 230.2
1920-
College dogmatic theology. Chicago, Regnery, 1962. 267p. 21cm. 62-15609 3.00
1. Theology, Doctrinal—Introductions. I. Title.

BARTH, Karl 230.081
Evangelical theology, an introduction. Tr. [from German] by Grover Foley. Garden City, Doubleday [1964, c.1963] 184p. 19cm. (Anchor Bk. A408) 1.25 pap.,
1. Theology, Doctrinal—Introductions. I. Title.

BARTH, Karl, 1886-1968. 230.081
Evangelical theology, an introduction. Translated by Grover Foley. [1st ed.] New York, Holt, Rinehart and Winston [1963] xiii, 206 p. 22 cm. Translation of Einfuhrung in die evangelische Theologie. "The first five lectures of this volume were delivered under the auspices of the Divinity School, the University of Chicago, and were 'The Annie Kinkead Warfield lectures of 1962' at the Princeton Theological Seminary." [BT65.B313] 63-7268
1. Theology, Doctrinal—Introductions. I. Title.

BARTH, Karl, 1886-1968. 230
Evangelical theology : an introduction / Karl Barth ; translated by Grover Foley. Grand Rapids, Mich. : Eerdmans, [1979] c1963. p. cm. Translation of Einfuhrung in die evangelische Theologie. "The first five lectures of this volume were delivered under the auspices of the Divinity School, the University of Chicago, and were 'The Annie Kinkead Warfield Lectures of 1962' at the Princeton Theological Seminary." Reprint of the 1st ed. published by Holt, Rinehart and Winston, New York. [BT65.B313 1979] 79-16735 ISBN 0-8028-1819-6 pbk. : 5.95
1. Theology, Doctrinal—Introductions. I. Title.

CORDUAN, Winfried. 230'.01
Handmaid to theology : an essay in philosophical prolegomena / Winfried Corduan ; foreword by Norman L. Geisler. Grand Rapids, Mich. : Baker Book House, c1981. 184 p. ; 22 cm. Includes index. Bibliography: p. 179. [BT65.C64 1981] 19 82-125335 ISBN 0-8010-2468-4 (pbk.) : 7.95
1. Theology, Doctrinal—Introductions. 2. Philosophical theology. I. Title.

DAVIS, Charles 230.2
Theology for today. New York, Sheed [1963, c. 1962] 310p. 22cm. ibl. 63-8550 5.00
1. Theology, Doctrinal—Introductions. I. Title.

FENTON, Joseph Clifford. 230.2
The concept of sacred theology [by] Joseph Clifford Fenton... Milwaukee, The Bruce publishing company [c1941] xi p., 1 l., 276 p. 22 cm. "A development of a doctoral dissertation completed ten years ago at Rome, while the author was a student priest at the Angelico."--Introd. Bibliographical foot-notes. [BX1751.F43] 41-22507
1. Theology, Doctrinal—Introductions. 2. Theology, Doctrinal—Hist. 3. Catholic church—Doctrinal and controversial works. I. Title.

FOSTER RANDOLPH SINKS bp. 230
1820-1903
... *Prolegomena.* Philosophic basis of theology; or, Rational principles of religious faith. By Rev. Randolph S. Foster ... New York, Hunt & Eaton; Cincinnati, Cranston & Stowe, 1889. 2 p. l., viii, [5]-344 p. 24 cm. (His Studies in theology. [1]) [BT15.F7 vol. 1] 230.081 37-11155
1. Theology, Doctrinal—Introductions. I. Title. II. Title: Philosophic basic of theology.

GERHART, Emanuel Vogel, 1817- 230
1904.
Prolegomena to Christian dogmatics, by Prof E. V. Gerhart, D. D. Lancaster, Pa.,

Printed by the Lecture printing society of the Theological seminary of the Reformed church, 1891. 2 p. l., [3]-136 p. 24 cm. [BT65.G3] 39-32774
1. Theology, Doctrinal—Introductions. I. Title.

JESSOP, Thomas Edmund, 1896- 230
An introduction to Christian doctrine. New York, T. Nelson [1961, c.1960] 133p. Bibl. 61-2472 3.00
1. Theology, Doctrinal—Introductions. I. Title.

KAISER, Edwin G 1893- 230
Sacred doctrine: an introduction to theology. Westminster, Md., Newman Press, 1958. 344p. 24cm. [BT65.K2] 57-11816
1. Theology, Doctrinal—Introductions. 2. Catholic Church— Doctrinal and controversial works. I. Title.

LAWSON, John. 230
Introduction to Christian doctrine / by John Lawson. Wilmore, Ky. : Asbury Pub. Co., c1980. p. cm. Reprint of the 1967 ed. published by Prentice-Hall, Englewood Cliffs, N.J., under title: Comprehensive handbook of Christian doctrine. Includes index. [BT65.L38 1980] 19 80-24909 ISBN 0-937336-01-7 : 8.95
1. Theology, Doctrinal—Introductions. 2. Theology, Methodist. I. Title.
Publisher's address: P. O. Box 7, Wilmore, KY 40390

MARSHALL, I. Howard 230.02
Christian beliefs: a brief introduction. Chicago, Intervarsity Pr. [c.1963] 96p. 18cm. (Christian bks. for the mod. world) Bibl. 63-23670 1.25 pap.,
1. Theology, Doctrinal—Introductions. I. Title.

MARSHALL, I. Howard. 230'.02'02
Pocket guide to Christian beliefs / I. Howard Marshall. 3d ed. Downers Grove, Ill. : InterVarsity Press, 1978. 144 p. ; 18 cm. First ed. published in 1963 under title: Christian beliefs. Includes indexes. Bibliography: p. 140-141. [BT65.M3 1978] 78-2077 ISBN 0-87784-504-2 : pbk. : 2.95
1. Theology, Doctrinal—Introductions. I. Title.

REID, Gavin. 201'.1
Living the new life / Gavin Reid. Nashville : Abingdon, 1979, c1977. 128 p. ; 20 cm. [BT65.R43 1979] 78-11980 ISBN 0-687-22370-9 pbk. : 4.50 pbk. : 4.50
1. Theology, Doctrinal—Introductions. 2. Christian life—Anglican authors. I. Title.

ROARK, Dallas M., 1931 230
The Christian faith : an introduction to Christian thought / Dallas M. Roark. Grand Rapids, Mich. : Baker Book House, 1977,c1969. 352p. ; 20 cm. Includes indexes. Bibliographical footnotes. [BT65.R6] ISBN 0-8010-7652-8 pbk. : 4.95
1. Theology, Doctrinal-Introductions. I. Title.
L.C. card no. for 19699 Broadman Press ed.: 69-14369.

ROARK, Dallas M., 1931- 230
The Christian faith [by] Dallas M. Roark. Nashville, Broadman Press [1969] 328 p. 22 cm. Bibliographical footnotes. [BT65.R6] 69-14369 7.50
1. Theology, Doctrinal—Introductions. I. Title.

SMITH, Henry Boynton, 1815-1877. 230
Introduction to Christian theology. Comprising, i. A. General introduction. ii. The special introduction; or, The prolegomena of systematic theology. By Henry B. Smith... Edited by William S. Karr... New York, A. C. Armstrong & son, 1883. viii, 237 p. 19 1/2 cm. "Errate": slip inserted on p. [vii] [BT65.S55] 41-31828
1. Theology, Doctrinal—Introductions. I. Karr, William Stevens, 1829-1888, ed. II. Title.

TRESE, Leo John, 1902- 230.2
The faith and Christian living, four-volume religion program. [Discussion questions by James Carroll. Notre Dame, Ind., Fides c.1963] 4v. (various p.) 18cm. (Fides dome bks., D-21, 22, 23, 24) Reprinting of The faith explained, Many are one, More than many sparrows, and Everyman's road to heaven, by L. J. Trese, and of God so loved the world, by J. J. Castelot. Contents.v.1. The Creed, summary of the faith.--v.2. Salvation, history and the Commandments, by L. J. Trese, J. J. Castelot.--v.3. The sacraments and prayer.--v.4. Guide to Christian living. 63-11404 1.25 pap., ea.,
1. Theology, Doctrinal—Introductions. I. Title.

TRESE, Leo John, 1902- 230.2
The faith and Christian living, four-volume religion program. [Discussion questions by James Carroll. Notre Dame, Ind., Fides Publishers, 1963] 4 v. 18 cm. (A Fides dome book) A reprinting of The faith explained, Many are one, More than many sparrows, and Everyman's road to heaven, by L. J. Trese and J. J. Castelot -- v.3. The sacraments and prayer. -- v. 4. Guide to Christian living. [BT77.T76] 63-11404
1. Theology, Doctrinal — Introductions. I. Title.

WEIDNER, Revere Franklin, 1851-1915. 230
An introduction to dogmatic theology. Based on Luthardt. By Revere Franklin Weidner ... Rock Island, Ill., Augustana book concern, 1888. 3 p. l., [5]-260 p. 20 1/2 cm. (Added t.-p.: A system of dogmatic theology. Based on Luthardt and Krauth. By Revere Franklin Weidner ... I) [BT65.W4 1888] 38-4779
1. Theology, Doctrinal—Introductions. 2. Lutheran church—Doctrinal and controversial works. I. Luthardt, Christoph Ernst, 1823-1902. Kompendium der dogmatik. II. Title.

WEIDNER, Revere Franklin, 1851-1915. 230
An introduction to dogmatic theology. Based on Luthardt. By Revere Franklin Weidner ... 2d ed., rev. Rock Island, Ill., Lutheran Augustana book concern, 1895. 287 p. 20 cm. (Added t.-p.: A system of dogmatic theology. Based on Luthardt and Krauth. By Revere Franklin Weidner ... I) [BT65.W4 1895] 38-4778
1. Theology, Doctrinal—Introduction. 2. Lutheran church—Doctrinal and controversial works. I. Luthardt, Christoph Ernst, 1823-1902. Kompendium der dogmatik. II. Title.

WHITE, Hugh Vernon, 1889- 230
Truth and the person in Christian theology; a theological essay in terms of the spiritual person. New York, Oxford University Press, 1963. 240 p. 21 cm. [BT75.2.W5] 63-12821
1. Theology, Doctrinal — Introductions. I. Title.

Theology, Doctrinal—Miscellanea.

MCGINLEY, John. 238
Catechism for theologians : the foundations for meaningful Jewish/Christian dialogue / John McGinley. Washington, D.C. : University Press of America, c1981. p. cm. [BT78.M395] 19 81-40063 ISBN 0-8191-1595-9 (pbk.) : 6.00
1. Theology, Doctrinal—Miscellanea. 2. Christianity and other religions—Judaism—Miscellanea. 3. Judaism—Relations—Christianity—Miscellanea. I. Title.

Theology, Doctrinal—New England—History—17th century.

BURG, B. R. 1938- (Barry Richard), 285.8'32'0924
Richard Mather / by B.R. Burg. Boston : Twayne, c1982. p. cm. (Twayne's United States authors series ; TUSAS 429) Includes index. Bibliography: p. [BX7260.M368B86] 19 82-932 ISBN 0-8057-7364-9 : 16.50
1. Mather, Richard, 1596-1669. 2. Theology, Doctrinal—New England—History—17th century. I. Title. II. Series.

Theology, Doctrinal—New England—History—18th century.

CONFORTI, Joseph A. 230'.58
Samuel Hopkins and the New Divinity movement : Calvinism, the Congregational Ministry, and reform in New England between the Great Awakenings / Joseph A. Conforti. Grand Rapids, Mich. : Christian University Press : available from Erdmans, 1982, c1981 viii, 241 p. ; 22 cm. Includes index. Bibliography: p. 233-236. [BX7260.H6C66] 19 80-28268 ISBN 0-8028-1871-4 : 16.95
1. Hopkins, Samuel, 1721-1803. 2. Theology, Doctrinal—New England—History—18th century. 3. Congregationalism—History—18th century. I. Title. II. Title: New Divinity movement.

Theology, Doctrinal—Outlines, syllabi, etc.

HALL, Francis J[oseph] 1857-
Theological outlines... By the Rev. Francis J. Hall... Milwaukee, Wis., The Young churchman co., 1892-95. 3 v. 18 cm. Contents.The doctrine of God. 1892.--v. 2. The doctrine of man and of the God-man. 1894.--v. 3. The doctrine of the church and of last things. 1895. 5-21279
I. Title.

SPYKMAN, Gordon J. 230'.02'02
Christian faith in focus, by Gordon J. Spykman. Grand Rapids, Baker Bk. [1967] 164p. 20cm. [BT77.3.S6] 67-29071 1.95 pap.,
1. Theology, Doctrinal—Outlines, syllabi, etc. I. Title.

STRENG, William D. 209'.04
In search of ultimates, by William D. Streng. Minneapolis, Augsburg Pub. House [1969] xi, 156 p. illus. 22 cm. Includes bibliographies. [BT77.3.S7] 69-14182 2.50
1. Theology, Doctrinal—Outlines, syllabi, etc. 2. Discussion in religious education. I. Title.

TURNBULL, Ralph G. 230.0202
What Christians believe. Grand Rapids, Mich., Baker Bk. [c.]1965. 86p. 22cm. (Bible companion ser. for lesson and sermon prep.) [BT77.3.T8] 65-29502 1.00 pap.,
1. Theology, Doctrinal—Outlines, syllabi, etc. I. Title.

Theology, Doctrinal—Poetry.

LITTLE, William Herbert, 1876- 230
God's plan for man; Christian doctrines in verse. [1st ed.] New York, Pageant Press [1959] 152p. 21cm. [BS85.L5] 59-13333
1. Theology, Doctrinal—Poetry. I. Title.

Theology, Doctrinal—Popular works.

AASENG, Rolf E. 230'.41
Basic Christian teachings / Rolf Aaseng. Minneapolis : Augsburg Pub. House, c1982. 111 p. ; 20 cm. [BT77.A18] 19 81-52276 ISBN 0-8066-1908-2 pbk. : 3.95
1. Theology, Doctrinal—Popular works. I. Title.

ANDERSON, Ardis Leroy, 1924- 230
The way / A. L. Anderson. Milwaukee : Northwestern Pub. House, 1979. 72 p. ; 16 cm. [BT77.A47] 78-61258 ISBN 0-8100-0006-7 pbk. : 1.75
1. Theology, Doctrinal—Popular works. I. Title.

ANDERSON, Margaret J. 230
Bible doctrines for teenagers, by Margaret J. Anderson. Grand Rapids, Zondervan Pub. House [1968] 93 p. 20 cm. [BT77.A48] 67-22694
1. Theology, Doctrinal—Popular works. I. Title.

ANDERSON, Phoebe M. 207
Teach what you preach : the great commission and the good news / Phoebe M. Anderson, Thomas R. Henry. New York : Pilgrim Press, c1982. ix, 182 p. ; 21 cm. Bibliography: p. 177-179. [BT77.A49 1982] 19 81-22700 ISBN 0-8298-0481-1 pbk. : 8.95
1. Theology, Doctrinal—Popular works. 2. Christian education—Philosophy. 3. Developmental psychology. I. Henry, Thomas R., 1943- II. Title.

BAKER, Charles F 230
Bible truth what we believe and why we believe it. Milwaukee, Milwaukee Bible College [1956] 123p. 20cm. [BT77.B26] 57-28034
1. Theology, Doctrinal—Popular works. I. Title.

BAKER, John Austin. 231
The foolishness of God. Atlanta, J. Knox [1975, c1970] 409 p. 22 cm. Includes bibliographical references. [BT77.B27 1975] 74-3714 ISBN 0-8042-0489-6 9.95
1. Theology, Doctrinal—Popular works. I. Title.

BARNEY, Kenneth D. 230
You'd better believe it! / Kenneth D. Barney ; adapted from The fundamentals of the faith by Donald Johns. Springfield, Mo. : Gospel Pub. House, c1975. 126 p. ; 18 cm. (Radiant books) [BT77.B334] 75-22608 ISBN 0-88243-887-5 pbk. : 1.25
1. Theology, Doctrinal—Popular works. 2. Christian life—1960- I. Johns, Donald. The fundamentals of the faith. II. Title.

BARREAU, Jean Claude. 230
The faith of a pagan. Translated by Jules G. Viau. New York, Paulist Press [1968] v, 89 p. 19 cm. Translation of La foi d'un paien. [BT77.B3423] 68-20850
1. Theology, Doctrinal—Popular works. I. Title.

BARREAU, Jean Claude 230.2
The good news of Jesus. Tr. [from French] by Roma Rudd Turkel. New York, Paulist [c.1964, 1965] 159p. 18cm. (Deus bks.) [BT77.B3363] 65-21763 .95 pap.,
1. Theology. Doctrinal—Popular works. I. Title.

BARRETT, Charles D., 1933- 230
Understanding the Christian faith / Charles D. Barrett. Englewood Cliffs, N.J. : Prentice-Hall, [1980] p. cm. Includes index. Bibliography: p. [BT77.B343] 79-24858 ISBN 0-13-935882-X : 13.95
1. Theology, Doctrinal—Popular works. 2. Religion. I. Title.

BARRETT, J. Edward, 1932- 230
Faith in focus : a compact introduction to Christian theology / J. Edward Barrett. Washington, D.C. : University Press of America, c1981. xii, 117 p. ; 22 cm. [BT77.B344] 19 81-40167 ISBN 0-8191-1878-8 : 17.75 ISBN 0-8191-1879-6 (pbk.) : 7.75
1. Theology, Doctrinal—Popular works. I. Title.

BEARD, Richard, 1799-1880.
Lectures on theology. By Richard Beard, D.D. ... First series. Nashville, Committee of publication, 1874. viii, 9-500 p. 23 cm. 3-25938
I. Title.

BEARD, Richard, 1799-1880.
Lectures on theology. By Richard Beard, D.D. ... Third series. Nashville, Board of publication of the Cumberland Presbyterian church, 1875. 572 p. 23 cm. 3-25940
I. Title.

BEAVEN, Robert Haddow. 230
In Him is life; a fresh approach to the Christian faith, by Robert Haddow Beaven. New York, Nashville, Abingdon-Cokesbury press [1946] 188 p. 19 1/2 cm. [BT77.B38] 46-342
1. Theology, Doctrinal—Popular works. 2. Christianity—Essence, genius, nature. I. Title.

BENTLEY, William W., 1911- 230
The simple story of the universe : revealing the reasons for everything (based on the word of God) / by William W. Bentley, Jr. 1st ed. La Jolla, Calif. : Truth Publishers, c1979. xi, 77 p. ; 23 cm. Includes bibliographical references. [BT77.B43] 78-65456 ISBN 0-9602182-1-1 : 5.95
1. Theology, Doctrinal—Popular works. I. Title.

BERRY, William G. 230
To be honest. Philadelphia, Westminster [c.1965] 2159p. 19cm. (Adventures in faith) Bibl. [BT77.B46] 65-19778 1.45 pap.,
1. Theology, Doctrinal—Popular works. I. Title.

BEYER, Douglas. 230
Basic beliefs of Christians / Douglas Beyer. Valley Forge, Pa. : Judson Press, c1981. 64 p. ; 22 cm. [BT77.B48] 19 80-25500 ISBN 0-8170-0896-9 pbk. : 3.50
1. Theology, Doctrinal—Popular works. I. Title.

BLAKELY, Hunter Bryson, 1894- 231
I wager on God. Richmond, John Knox

Press [1956] 207 p. 21 cm. [BT77.B56] 56-8849
1. Theology, Doctrinal—Popular works. I. Title.

BOA, Kenneth. 230
God, I don't understand / Kenneth Boa. Wheaton, Ill. : Victor Books, c1975. 154 p. : ill. ; 21 cm. (An Input book) Includes bibliographical references. [BT77.B63] 75-173 ISBN 0-88207-722-8 pbk. : 2.25
1. Theology, Doctrinal—Popular works. I. Title.

BOOTH, Charles Octavius, 1845-. 230
Plain theology for plain people. By C. W. [!] Booth, d.d. Philadelphia, American Baptist publication society [1890] 205 p. 18 1/2 cm. [BT77.B7] 39-7007
1. Theology. Doctrinal. Popular works. I. American Baptist publication society. II. Title.

BOOTHE, Charles Octavius, b.1845. 230
Plain theology for plain people. By C. W. [!] Booth [!] D.D. Philadelphia, American Baptist publication society [1890] 205 p. 18 1/2 cm. [BT77.B7] 39-7007
1. Theology, Doctrinal—Popular works. I. American Baptist publication society. II. Title.

BRANDEIS, Donald Asa, 1928- 230.6
A faith for modern man. Grand Rapids, Mich., Baker Bk. House [c.]1961. 129p. 61-18798 2.95 bds.,
1. Theology, Doctrinal—Popular works. I. Title.

BRIGHT, Bill. 248.4
Handbook of concepts for living : a compilation of the nine transferable concepts / by Bill Bright. San Bernandino, CA : Here's Life Publishers, c1981. 359 p. : ill. ; 21 cm. Spine title: Concepts for living. "A Campus Crusade for Christ book." [BT77.B77] 19 81-67818 ISBN 0-86605-011-6 (pbk.) : 6.95
1. Theology, Doctrinal—Popular works. 2. Witness bearing (Christianity) 3. Evangelistic work. 4. Christian life—1960- I. Title.

BROWN, Robert McAfee, 1920- 220.6
The Bible speaks to you. Philadelphia, Westminster Press [1955] 320 p. 22 cm. [BS538.B74] 55-7089
1. Bible—Criticism, interpretation, etc. 2. Theology, Doctrinal—Popular works. I. Title.

BRUNNER, Heinrich Emil, 1889- 230
Our faith, by Emil Brunner. Tr. by John W. Rilling. New York, Scribners [1963] 153p. 21cm. (SL87) 1.25 pap.,
1. Theology, Doctrinal—Popular works. I. Rilling, John William, 1906- tr. II. Title.

BRUNNER, Heinrich Emil, 1889-
Our faith, by Emil Brunner. Translated by John W. Rilling. New York, C. Scribner's sons [foreword 1962, c1936] x, 153 p. 20 cm. Translation of Unser Glaube. 65-92928
1. Theology, Doctrinal — Popular works. I. Title.

BRUNNER, Heinrich Emil, 1889- 230
Our faith, by Emil Brunner ... translated by John W. Rilling. New York, C. Scribner's sons, 1936. x p., 1 l., 153 p. 20 cm. [BT77.B865] 36-37285
1. Theology. Doctrinal—Popular works. I. Rilling, John William, 1906- tr. II. Title.

BURKHEAD, Jesse DeWitt. 230
"Theology for the masses", or, Bible truths for all men. By J. DeWitt Burkhead ... Atlanta, Ga., J. P. Harrison & co., printers, 1888. x, [9]-343 p. front. (port.) 20 1/2 cm. [BT77.B87] 39-7340
1. Theology, Doctrinal—Popular works. 2. Presbyterian church—Doctrinal and controversial works. I. Title.

CADOUX, Cecil John, 1883- 230
The case for evangelical modernism; a study of the relation between Christian faith and traditional theology, by Cecil John Cadoux ... Chicago, New York, Willett. Clark & company, 1939. xii p., 1 l., 191 p. 21 cm. Based on four lectures delivered in the University college of North Wales at Bangor, 1967, cf. Pref. [BT77.C18 1939] 39-31181
1. Theology, Doctrinal—Popular works. 2. Christianity—20th cent. I. Title.

CAIRD, George B. 230
The truth of the gospel. London, New York, Oxford University Press, 1950. vii, 168 p. 20 cm. (A Primer of Christianity, pt. 3) [BT77.C19] 50-12101
1. Theology, Doctrinal—Popular works. 2. Apologetics—20th cent. I. Title. II. Series.

CAIRD, George Bradford. 230
The truth of the gospel. London, New York, Oxford University Press, 1950. vii, 168p. 20cm. (A Primer of Christianity, pt. 3) [BT77.C19] 50-12101
1. Theology, Doctrinal— Popular works. 2. Apologetics—20th cent. I. Title. II. Series.

CALKINS, Wolcott, 1831-1924. 230
Keystones of faith, or, What and why we believe, by Wolcott Calkins ... New York, The Baker and Taylor co. [1888] viii, [9] 179 p. 19 cm. [BT77.C2] 39-7009
1. Theology Doctrinal—Popular works. 2. Congregational churches—Doctrinal and controversial works. I. Title. II. Title: What and why we believe.

CALVIN, Jean, 1509-1564. 230.42
Instruction in faith (1537) tr. with a historical foreword and critical and explanatory notes by Paul T. Fuhrmann. Philadelphia, Westminster Press [1949] 96 p. 20 cm. [BT70.C25] 49-10385
1. Theology, Doctrinal—Popular works. 2. Reformed Church—Doctrinal and controversial works. I. Title.

CAMPBELL, Donald James, Bp. 230
If I believe. Philadelphia, Westminster Press [1959] 157p. 20cm. [BT77.C22] 59-8071
1. Theology, Doctrinal—Popular works. I. Title.

CAPON, Robert Farrar. 230
Hunting the divine fox; images and mystery in Christian faith. New York, Seabury Press [1974] 167 p. 22 cm. "A Crossroad book." [BT77.C227] 73-17891 ISBN 0-8164-0252-3 5.95
1. Theology, Doctrinal—Popular works. I. Title.

CAPON, Robert Farrar. 818'.5'408
An offering of uncles; the priesthood of Adam and the shape of the world. New York, Sheed and Ward [1967] v, 182 p. 21 cm. [BT77.C23] 67-13758
1. Theology, Doctrinal—Popular works. I. Title.

CAPON, Robert Farrar. 230'.3
An offering of uncles : the priesthood of Adam and the shape of the world / Robert Farrar Capon. New York : Crossroad, 1982, c1967. v, 182 p. ; 21 cm. Reprint. Originally published: New York : Sheed and Ward, c1967. [BT77.C23 1982] 19 81-70386 ISBN 0-8245-0422-4 (pbk.) : 5.95
1. Theology, Doctrinal—Popular works. I. Title.

CASSELS, Louis 230
Christian primer. Garden City, N. Y. Doubleday [1967,c.1964] 108p. 21cm. (Waymark bk., W3) Bibl. 1.45 pap.,
1. Theology, Doctrinal—Popular works. 2. Christian life. I. Title.

CASSELS, Louis. 230
Christian primer. [1st ed.] Garden City, N. Y., Doubleday, 1964. 108 p. 22 cm. Bibliography: p. [105]-108. [BT77.C24] 64-13848
1. Theology, Doctrinal—Popular works. 2. Christian life. I. Title.

CHAFER, Lewis Sperry, 1871-1952. 230
Major Bible themes; 52 vital doctrines of the Scripture simplified and explained. Rev. by John F. Walvoord. Grand Rapids, Mich., Zondervan Pub. House [1974] 374 p. 23 cm. [BT77.C452] 73-17641 5.95
1. Theology, Doctrinal—Popular works. I. Walvoord, John F. II. Title.

CHALMERS, Randolph Carleton 248.42
A faith for you. Richmond, Va., John Knox [1962, c.1960] 118p. 'First pub. in 1960, under the title A gospel to proclaim.' Bibl. 62-8223 1.50 pap.,
1. Theology, Doctrinal—Popular works. I. Title.

CHAPMAN, Colin Gilbert. 230
An Eerdmans' handbook : the case for Christianity / Colin Chapman. 1st American ed. Grand Rapids, Mich. : W.B. Eerdmans Pub. Co., 1981. 313 p. : ill. (some col.) ; 23 cm. Includes bibliographical references and index. [BT77.C4544 1981] 19 81-9704 ISBN 0-8028-3547-3 : 19.95
1. Theology, Doctrinal—Popular works. I. Title. II. Title: Case for Christianity.

CHRISTIAN, C. W. 230
Shaping your faith; a guide to a personal theology [by] C. W. Christian. Waco, Tex., Word Books [1973] 254 p. 23 cm. Bibliography: p. 242-245. [BT77.C458] 72-84156 5.95
1. Theology, Doctrinal—Popular works. I. Title.

COGSWELL, William, 1787-1850. 230.076
The theological class book; containing a system of divinity, in the form of question and answer, accompanied with Scripture proofs, designed for the benefit of theological classes, and the higher classes in Sabbath schools. By William Cogswell.. Boston, Crocker and Brewster; New York, J. Leavitt, 1832. 1 p. l., [v]-vii, [1] ll, 172 p. 15 1/2 cm. [BT77.C6] 39-7342
1. Theology, Doctrinal—Popular works. I. Title.

COLE, C. Donald. 238'.11
"I believe— " / by C. Donald Cole. Chicago : Moody Press, c1982. p. cm. Includes bibliographical references. [BT993.2.C64] 19 81-22297 ISBN 0-8024-0353-0 pbk. : 2.50
1. Apostles' Creed. 2. Theology, Doctrinal—Popular works. I. Title.

COLEMAN, Michael Edward. 230
Faith under fire, by Michael Coleman... New York, C. Scribner's sons, 1942. x p., 1 l., 160 p. 21 cm. [BT77.C68] 42-12941
1. Theology, Doctrinal—Popular works. 2. Church of England—Doctrinal and controversial works. I. Title.

COMPEND of Bible truth. 230
Philadelphia, Presbyterian board of publication, 1845. iv, 186 p. 11 cm. [BT77.C7] 39-7821
1. Theology, Doctrinal—Popular works. I. Presbyterian church in the U. S. A. (Old school) Board of publication.

COOK, Walter L. 248.83
What can I believe? talks to youth on the Christian faith. Nashville Abingdon [c.1965] 112p. 20cm. [BT77.C747] 65-20360 2.00
1. Theology, Doctrinal—Popular works. I. Title.

COOPER, David Lipscomb, 1886- 230
...What men must believe, by David L. Cooper... Los Angeles, Calif., Biblical research society [c1943] xxii, 507 p. incl. front. (map) illus., fold. diagrs. 20 1/2 cm. Includes hymns (words and piano accompaniment) Bibliography: p. 506-507. [BT77.C75] 44-3291
1. Theology, Doctrinal—Popular works. I. Biblical research society. II. Title.

COOPER, David Lipscomb, 1886- 230
...What men must believe (abridged) by David L. Cooper... Los Angeles, Calif., Biblical research society, c1943. 271, [1] p. illus. (incl. map) fold. diagr. 20 1/2 cm. Includes hymns (words and piano accompaniment) [BT77.C752] 44-26530
1. Theology, Doctrinal—Popular works. I. Biblical research society. II. Title.

COTTAM, Joseph Almond, 1881- 230
Know the truth, by J. Almond Cottam, PH. D. New York, American tract society [c1940] 259 p. 30 cm. [BT77.C77] 40-11601
1. Theology, Doctrinal—Popular works. I. American tract society. II. Title.

COURTENAY, Walter Rowe, 1902- 230
"I believe, but ...!" A reaffirmation of faith. Richmond, John Knox Press [1950] 182 p. 21 cm. "References and acknowledgments": p. 173-182. [BT77.C79] 50-7761
1. Theology, Doctrinal—Popular works. I. Title.

COX, David, 1920- 230
What Christians believe. London, Darton, Longman & Todd [dist. Westminster, Md., Canterbury, c.1963] ix, 187p. 19cm. A 63 2.75 bds.,
1. Theology, Doctrinal—Popular works. I. Title.

CRACRAFT, John W. 230
The old paths: the essential and the important truths of the gospel. by the Rev. J. W. Cracraft ... Cincinnati, R. Clarke & co., 1870. vi p. 1 l., 226 p. 20 cm. [BT77.C8] 39-7010
1. Theology, Doctrinal—Popular works. I. Title.

CUSKELLY, Eugene James 230.2
God's gracious design; a new look at Catholic doctrine. Westminster, Md., Newman, 1965. x,311p. 23cm. Bibl. [BX1754.C83] 65-25979 5.95
1. Theology, Doctrinal—Popular works. I. Title.

DAVIS, Charles 230.2
The study of theology. New York, Sheed [1962] 348p. 23cm. 63-4548 5.00
1. Theology, Doctrinal—Popular works. I. Title.

DAVIS, Charles, S. T. L. 200
The study of theology. London, New York, Sheed and Ward [1962] 348 p. 23 cm. Essays. [BT77.D3] 63-4548
1. Theology, Doctrinal — Popular works. I. Title.

DEJEAN, Edgar K. 230
Tom, Dick, and Jane in theology land / with Edgar DeJean. Corte Madera, Calif. : Omega Books, c1976. 109 p. ; 22 cm. Includes bibliographical references. [BT77.D395] 76-24109 ISBN 0-89353-010-7 pbk. : 4.00
1. Theology, Doctrinal—Popular works. I. Title.

DEPUY, Norman R. 230
Help in understanding theology : creation, Christ, God, church, bible, holy spirit / Norman R. DePuy. Valley Forge, PA : Judson Press, c1980. 110 p. ; 22 cm. [BT77.D397] 79-20120 ISBN 0-8170-0847-0 pbk. : 3.95
1. Theology, Doctrinal—Popular works. I. Title.

DE'SANTO, Charles. 230
Dear Tim : letters on basic Christian beliefs from a father to his maturing son / Charles P. De Santo. Scottdale, Pa. : Herald Press, 1982. 199 p. ; 20 cm. A series of letters explaining Christian beliefs about Christ, God, human nature, the church, and Christian life. [BT77.D34] 19 81-23744 ISBN 0-8361-1991-6 : 7.95 ($9.55 Can)
1. Theology, Doctrinal—Popular works. 2. Christian life—1960- 3. [Theology.] 4. [Christian life.] I. Title.

DE WOLF, Lotan Harold, 1905- 230
A theology of the living church. [1st ed.] New York, Harper [1953] 383p. 25cm. [BT77.D4] 53-5989
1. Theology, Doctrinal—Popular works. I. Title.

DIBRANDI, Herman A. 230
Introduction to Christian doctrine / Herman A. diBrandi. New York : Morehouse-Barlow Co., c1976. iv, 90 p. ; 19 cm. Bibliography: p. 89-90. [BT77.D45] 75-43430 ISBN 0-8192-1194-X pbk. : 3.50
1. Theology, Doctrinal—Popular works. I. Title.

DIETRICH, Suzanne de. 230
God's word in today's world. Valley Forge, Judson Press [1967] 110 p. 20 cm. (Lake view books) [BT77.D47] 67-25894
1. Theology, Doctrinal — Popular works. 2. Bible — Theology. I. Title.

DILLARD, J L. 230
Elements of medium theology. By Rev. J. L. Dillard ... Nashville, Tenn., Published for the author by the Cumberland Presbyterian board of publication, 1874. 498 p. 20 cm. [BT77.D5] 39-7014
1. Theology, Doctrinal—Popular works. 2. Presbyterian church—Doctrinal and controversial works. I. Cumberland Presbyterian board of publication. II. Title. III. Title: Medium theology, Elements of.

A doctrinal guide, 230
for the convert and the anxious inquirer.

By a clergyman ... New York, J. Leavitt; Boston, Crocker & Brewster, 1832. 2 p. l., [3]-294 p. 16 cm. [BT77.D6] 39-7344
1. Theology, Doctrinal—Popular works. I. A clergyman.

DUTHIE, Charles S. 230
Outline of Christian belief, by Charles S. Duthie. Nashville, Abingdon Press [1968] 116 p. 21 cm. A series of articles which appeared in The British Weekly from Oct. 1966 to June 1967. Bibliography: p. [115]-116. [BT77.D8] 68-7990 2.75
1. Theology, Doctrinal—Popular works. I. The British weekly. II. Title.

EASTON, William Burnet, 1905- 230
Basic Christian beliefs. Philadelphia, Westminster Press [1957] 196p. 21cm. [BT77.E14] 57-8930
1. Theology, Doctrinal—Popular works. I. Title.

EASTON, William Burnet, 1905- 230
... The faith of a Protestant. New York, The Macmillan company, 1946. xi, 76 p. 19 1/2 cm. "First printing." At head of title: W. Burnet Easton, jr. [BT77.E15] 46-1418
1. Theology, Doctrinal—Popular works. 2. Protestantism. I. Title.

EBERSOLE, Mark C. 230
Christian faith and man's religion. New York, Crowell [1961] 206 p. 21 cm. Includes bibliography. [BT77.E18] 61-14526
1. Theology, Doctrinal—Popular works. 2. Religious thought—Modern period. 3. Religion. I. Title.

EDINGTON, Andrew. 230
The big search. [1st ed.] New York, Pageant Press [1955] 51p. 21cm. [BT77.E24] 55-10115
1. Theology, Doctrinal—Popular works. I. Title.

ENGLISH, Eugene Schuyler, 1899- 230
Things surely to be believed ... by E. Schuyler English ... New York, N.Y., Our hope press (A. C. Gaebelein, inc.) [1947] ix, 307 p. 20 1/2 cm. (His A primer of Bible doctrine. Vol. I) "Copyright, 1946." "The contents of this volume originally appeared in the magazine, Our hope ... under the general title, 'A primer of Bible doctrine'."--Pref. Bibliography: p. [291]-296. [BT77.E55] 47-18683
1. Theology, Doctrinal—Popular works. I. Title.

EVANS, William, 1870-1950. 230
The great doctrines of the Bible / by William Evans. Enl. ed. / with eighty additional entries by S. Maxwell Coder. Chicago : Moody Press, [1974] 325 p. ; 24 cm. Includes index. [BT77.E82 1974] 74-185534 ISBN 0-8024-3301-4 : 5.95
1. Bible—Theology. 2. Theology, Doctrinal—Popular works. I. Coder, Samuel Maxwell, 1902- II. Title.

FERGUSON, Sinclair B. 230'.52
Know your Christian life : a theological introduction / Sinclair B. Ferguson ; foreword by J.I. Packer. Downers Grove, Ill. : InterVarsity Press, 1981. p. cm. Previously published as: The Christian life, 1981. [BT77.F38 1981] 19 81-18588 ISBN 0-87784-371-6 pbk. : 5.95
1. Theology, Doctrinal—Popular works. 2. Christian life—Presbyterian authors. I. [Christian life] II. Title.

FERRE, Nels Frederick Solomon, 1908- 230
Pillars of faith. [1st ed.] New York, Harper [1948] 128 p. 20 cm. "Written for the Wells lectures at Texas Christian University and for the Gay lectures at the Southern Baptist Theological Seminary." [BT77.F4] 48-5147
1. Theology, Doctrinal—Popular works. I. Title.

FICHTER, Joseph Henry, 1908- 230.2
Christianity, an outline of dogmatic theology for laymen, by Joseph H. Fichter, S.J. St. Louis, Mo., and London, B. Herder book co., 1946. ix, 267 p. 21 cm. [BX1754.F5] 46-5089
1. Theology, Doctrinal—Popular works. 2. Catholic church—Doctrinal and controversial works, Popular. I. Title.

*FINE, Herbert J. 233
Tomorrow is ours. New York, Vantage [1968] 51p. 21cm. 2.75 bds.,
1. Theology, Doctrinal—Popular works. I. Title.

FINEGAN, Jack 230
First steps in theology. New York, Association Press [c.1960] 128p. 16cm. (An Association Press reflection book) 'A reflection book drawn from the author's Beginning in theology.' 60-12719 .50 pap.,
1. Theology, Doctrinal—Popular works. I. Title.

FINEGAN, Jack, 1908- 230
Beginnings in theology. New York, Association Press [c1956] 244p. 20cm. [BT77.F5] 56-5029
1. Theology, Doctrinal—Popular works. I. Title.

FINEGAN, Jack, 1908- 230
Step by step in theology; adapted from Jack Finegan's First steps in theology. Prepared by Hal and Jean Vermes. New York, Association [c.1962] 120p. 26cm. (Association programed instruction bk.) 62-11032 3.00 pap.,
1. Theology, Doctrinal—Popular works. I. Vermes, Hal G. II. Vermes, Jean Campbell (Pattison) III. Title.

FOWLER, Clifton Lefevre, 1882- 230
Fundamental facts of the faith [by] Clifton L. Fowler ... Denver, Maranatha press [c1936] 274 p. 20 cm. [BT77.F59] 36-30341
1. Theology, Doctrinal—Popular works. I. Title.

FROST, Henry Weston, 1858- 230
About the old faith; meditations upon important Christian truths, by Henry W. Frost. New York [etc.] Fleming H. Revell company [c1937] 128 p. 20 cm. [BT77.F74] 37-10145
1. Theology, Doctrinal—Popular works. I. Title.

FURNESS, John Malcolm. 230
Vital doctrines of the faith, by Malcolm Furness. [1st U.S. ed.] Grand Rapids, Eerdmans [1974, c1973] 128 p. 18 cm. Includes bibliographical references. [BT77.F84 1974] 73-22310 ISBN 0-8028-1573-1 2.45 (pbk.)
1. Theology, Doctrinal—Popular works. I. Title.

GILBERT, James Eleazer, 1839-1909. 230
Biblical doctrine; adult probationer's second book, by Rev. J. E. Gilbert ... New York, Eaton & Mains; Cincinnati, Jennings & Pye [c1904] 75 p. 18 cm. "Reading course": p. 74-75. [BT77.G45] 4-9134
1. Theology, Doctrinal—Popular works. I. Title.

GILBERT, Jesse Samuel, 1846-1906. 230
The old paths. By Rev. Jesse S. Gilbert ... with a preface by Rev. J. T. Crane, D. D. Newark, N. J., Ward & Tichenor, 1875. ix, [5]-158 p. 19 cm. [BT77.G46] 38-37835
1. Theology, Doctrinal—Popular works. I. Title.
Contents omitted.

GILKEY, Langdon Brown, 1919- 230
Message and existence : an introduction to Christian theology / Langdon Gilkey. New York : Seabury Press, c1979. p. cm. "A Crossroad book." [BT77.G478] 79-17612 ISBN 0-8164-0450-X : 10.95
1. Theology, Doctrinal—Popular works. I. Title.

GILLQUIST, Peter E. 230
The physical side of being spiritual / by Peter E. Gillquist. Grand Rapids : Zondervan, c1979. p. cm. [BT77.G48] 79-12096 ISBN 0-310-36950-9 : 6.95
1. Theology, Doctrinal—Popular works. 2. Evangelicalism. I. Title.

GRAEF, Hilda C. 230.2
Adult Christianity. Chicago, Franciscan Herald [1966] 140p. 21cm. [BX1754.G6845] 65-22872 3.50
1. Theology, Doctrinal—Popular works. I. Title.

GRAFF, John Franklin, 1828- 230
"Graybeard's" lay sermons. Being a summary of the great doctrines of Holy Scripture as interpreted and illustrated by the Scriptures themselves. By John Franklin Graff ("Graybeard") Philadelphia, J. B. Lippincott & co., 1877. 505 p. front. (port.) 20 cm. Articles that appeared in the Philadelphia press, February 1874 to March 1876. cf. Pref. [BT77.G75] 39-7347
1. Theology, Doctrinal—Popular works. I. Title.

GRAHAM, William Franklin, 1918-
Peace with God. New York, Pocket Books [1963, c1953] 248 p. (Permabook, M 4003) 65-51022
1. Theology, Doctrinal — Popular works. I. Title.

GRAHAM, William Franklin, 1918- 230
Peace with God. [1st ed.] Garden City, N.Y., Doubleday, 1953. 222 p. 22 cm. [BT77.G78] 53-5967
1. Theology, Doctrinal—Popular works. I. Title.

GRANT, Frederick Clifton, 1891- 230
Basic Christian beliefs. New York, Macmillan, 1961 [c.1960] 126p. Bibl. 61-14707 2.95
1. Theology, Doctrinal—Popular works. I. Title.

GRAY, Henry David, 1908- 200
The theology for Christian youth. Hartford, Independent Press [1970] 144 p. 19 cm. Bibliography: p. 140-142. [BT77.G82 1970] 70-16620
1. Theology, Doctrinal—Popular works. I. Title.

GRAY, Henry David, 1908- 230
A theology for Christian youth, by Henry David Gray. New York, Nashville, Abingdon-Cokes bury press, c1941. 144 p. 20 cm. "Some readable books": p. 140-142. [BT77.G82] 41-2737
1. Theology, Doctrinal—Popular works. I. Title.

GRAY, James Martin, 1851-1935. 230.0714
Scripture truth course; Scripture truth simplified and explained for young Christians, by Rev. James M. Gray ... Chicago, Ill., The Moody Bible institute of Chicago, Correspondence school [c1937] 68 p. 21 cm. "Rev. Wm. H. Lee Spratt ... is entitled to the credit for preparing Dr. Gray's material for ... use."--Introd. [BT77.G825] 37-39472
1. Theology, Doctrinal—Popular works. I. Spratt, William Henry Lee, 1903- ed. II. Title.

GREELEY, Andrew M., 1928- 230'.2
The great mysteries : an essential of catechism / Andrew M. Greeley. New York : Seabury Press, [1976] p. cm. "A Crossroad book." Bibliography: p. [BT77.G837] 76-13208 ISBN 0-8164-0309-0 : 7.95. ISBN 0-8164-2128-5 pbk. : 3.95
1. Theology, Doctrinal—Popular works. 2. Theology, Catholic. I. Title.

GREEN, Joseph Franklin 230
Faith to grow on. Nashville, Broadman Press [c.1960] 123p. 21cm. 60-9532 2.50 bds.,
1. Theology, Doctrinal—Popular works. I. Title.

GREEN, Joseph Franklin, 1924- 230
The heart of the Gospel [by] Joseph F. Green. Nashville, Broadman Press [1968] 128 p. 21 cm. [BT77.G842] 68-20675
1. Theology, Doctrinal—Popular works. I. Title.

HAND, John Raymond, 1886- 280
Revealed unto babes, by John Raymond Hand... Chicago, Polzin press [1938] 147 p. 22 1/2 cm. "First printing, September, 1938." [BT77.H26] 38-39119
1. Theology, Doctrinal—Popular works. I. Title.

HANSON, Anthony Tyrell. 230
Reasonable belief : a survey of the Christian faith / A. T. Hanson and R. P. C. Hanson. Oxford ; New York : Oxford University Press, 1980. p. cm. Includes index. Bibliography: p. [BT77.H264] 80-40481 ISBN 0-19-213235-0 : 24.95
1. Theology, Doctrinal—Popular works. I. Hanson, Richard Patrick Crosland, joint author. II. Title.

HARKNESS, Georgia Elma, 1891- 230
Beliefs that count. New York, Abingdon Press [1961] 125 p. 20 cm. [BT77.H268] 61-65438
1. Theology, Doctrinal—Popular works. I. Title.

HARKNESS, Georgia Elma, 1891- 230
Our Christian hope [by] Georgia Harkness. New York, Abingdon Press [1964] 176 p. 21 cm. Bibliographical footnotes. [BT77.H269] 64-19346
1. Theology, Doctrinal—Popular works. I. Title.

HARKNESS, Georgia Elma, 1891- 230
Understanding the Christian faith, by Georgia Harkness. New York, Nashville, Abingdon-Cokesbury press [1947] 187 p. 19 1/2 cm. [BT77.H27] 47-659
1. Theology, Doctrinal—Popular works. I. Title.

HARKNESS, Georgia Elma, 1891- 230
What Christians believe [by] Georgia Harkness. New York, Abingdon Press [1965] 72 p. 19 cm. [BT77.H273] 65-15232
1. Theology, Doctrinal — Popular works. I. Title.

HARNER, Nevin Cowger, 1901- 230
I believe, a Christian faith for youth. Philadelphia, Christian Education Press [1950] 127 p. 21 cm. [BT77.H282] 50-6216
1. Theology, Doctrinal—Popular works. I. Title.

HARTZLER, John Ellsworth, 1879- 230
The supremacy of Christianity, a study of the Christian way. [Hartford] The author, 1946. 390 p. 20 cm. [BT77.H288] 47-23929
1. Theology, Doctrinal—Popular works. I. Title.

HASCALL, Daniel, 1782-1852. 239
The elements of theology, or The leading topics of Christian theology, plainly and Scripturally set forth, with the principal evidences of divine revelation concisely stated, with questions; for the use of families, Bible classes, and seminaries of learning. By Daniel Hascall, A. M. New York, L. Colby & co., 1846. ix, 261 p. 16 cm. [BT77.H3] 39-7349
1. Theology, Doctrinal—Popular works. 2. Baptists—Doctrinal and controversial works. I. Title.

HEATON, Charles Henry, 1886- 230
Revealed knowledge; seeing is believing; by faith we understand. [By] Charles Henry Heaton, D.D. Butler, Ind., The Higley press [1943] 159 p. 19 1/2 cm. [BT77.H38] 43-6705
1. Theology, Doctrinal—Popular works. 2. Apologetics—20th cent. I. Title.

HECK, James Arthur, 1892- 230
A theology for laymen. Harrisburg, Pa., Evangelical Press [1956] 185p. 18cm. 'First appeared as a series of fifty-three weekly columns in the Telescope-messenger ... during the year 1955, under the title, Fireside talks on our Christian beliefs.' [BT77.H39] 56-58925
1. Theology, Doctrinal—Popular works. I. Title.

HELLWIG, Monika. 200
What are the theologians saying? Dayton, Ohio, Pflaum Press, 1970. xiv, 98 p. 21 cm. Bibliography: p. 97-98. [BT77.H413] 78-114694 1.50
1. Theology, Doctrinal—Popular works. I. Title.

HENDERLITE, Rachel 230.4
Forgiveness and hope; toward a theology for Protestant Christian education. Richmond, Va., Knox [1966,c.1961] 127p. 21cm. (Aletheia ed.) Bibl. [BT78.H44] 61-13518 1.45 pap.,
1. Theology, Doctrinal—Popular works. 2. Religious education. I. Title.

HEUSS, John, 1908- 230
Have a lively faith. New York, Morehouse [c.1963] 191p. 21cm. 63-21702 4.95
1. Theology. Doctrinal—Popular works. I. Title.

HIGDON, David Andrew, 1871- 230
The end of the world and the world to come, by the Rev. D. A. Higdon ... Louisville, Ky., The Standard printing company, incorporated, 1936. 4 p. l., [3]-218 p. 22 cm. "The teachings of the Bible relating to God's purpose towards man."--Introd. [BR125.H64] 36-20420
1. Theology, Doctrinal—Popular works. 2. Eschatology. I. Title.

HILL, John Godfrey, 1870-
... Christianity for to-day; a brief study of our Christian faith, by John Godfrey Hill ... New York, Cincinnati, The Methodist book concern [c1924] 139 p. 19 cm. (Studies in Christian faith) "Approved by the Committee on curriculum of the Board of Sunday schools of the Methodist Episcopal church." "Suggested readings" at end of each chapter. [BX8225.H5] 24-28699
1. Theology, Doctrinal—Popular works. I. Title.

HOBBS, Herschel H. 230
Fundamentals of our faith. Nashville, Broadman Press [1960] x, 161p. Includes bibliography. 20cm. 60-5200 1.95 pap.,
1. Theology, Doctrinal—Popular works. I. Title.

HOBBS, Herschel H. 230.6
What Baptists believe. Nashville, Broadman [c.1964] 128p. 20cm. (Broadman inner circle bk.) 64-12411 1.50 bds.,
1. Theology, Doctrinal—Popular works. 2. Baptists—Doctrinal and controversial works. I. Title.

HODGSON, Leonard, 1889- 230.08
Christian faith and practice; seven lectures. Grand Rapids, Mich., Eerdmans [1965, c.1950] xii, 113p. 20cm. [BT77.H55] 65-9540 2.50
1. Theology, Doctrinal—Popular works. I. Title.

HODGSON, Leonard, 1889- 230
Christian faith and practice; seven lectures. New York, Scribner, 1951. 116 p. 23 cm. [BT7.H55] 51-12463
1. Theology, Doctrinal—Popular works. I. Title.

HOOD, Frederic. 230
God's plan. With a foreword by the Bishop of London. London, New York, Longmans, Green [1955] 93p. 17cm. [BT77.H595] 55-4297
1. Theology, Doctrinal—Popular works. I. Title.

HOPKINS JOSIAH, 1786-1862. 230
The Christian's instructor. Containing a summary explanation and defence of the doctrines and duties of the Christian religion. By Rev. Josiah Hopkins... 3d ed.,--rev. and enl. Auburn, N.Y., J. C. Derby & co.; New-York, M. H. Newman & co.; [etc., etc.] 1847. xii, [13]-336 p. front. (port.) 20 cm. [BT77.H6 1847] 39-8937
1. Theology, Doctrinal—Popular works. 2. Presbyterian church—Doctrinal and controversial works. I. Title.

HORTON, Walter Marshall, 230
1895-
Our Christian faith. Boston, Pilgrim Press, 1947. xxi, 124 p. 20 cm. "In the original edition, this book was addressed to the laity of one particular denomination [Congregational] ... [This] revised edition is definitely non-sectarian in treatment."--Dust jacket. [BT77.H64 1947] 47-12165
1. Theology, Doctrinal—Popular works. I. Title.

HUGGENVIK, Theodore, 1889- 230.41
We believe; an elementary re-affirmation of the fundamentals of the evangelical Christian religion. Minneapolis, Augsburg Pub. House [1950] x, 149 p. 22 cm. "Parts of this handbook ... were published as a series of articles in the Lutheran teacher from October, 1948, to and including October, 1949." [BT77.H79] 50-14975
1. Theology. Doctrinal—Popular works. 2. Lutheran Church—Doctrinal and controversial works. 3. Luther, Martin. Catechismus, Kleiner. I. Title.

HUMPHREYS, Fisher. 230
Thinking about God : an introduction to Christian theology / Fisher Humphreys. New Orleans : Insight Press, [1974] 224 p. 22 cm. Includes bibliographical references. [BT77.H83] 74-81556 ISBN 0-914520-00-8 : 5.00
1. Theology, Doctrinal—Popular works. I. Title.

HUNT, Earl G. 230'.76
I have believed : a bishop talks about his faith / Earl G. Hunt, Jr. ; foreword by James S. Stewart. Nashville, Tenn. : Upper Room, c1980. 175 p. ; 23 cm. Includes bibliographical references. [BT77.H837] 19 80-50240 ISBN 0-8358-0401-1 6.95 ISBN 0-8358-0403-8 pbk. : 4.50
1. Theology, Doctrinal—Popular works. I. Title.
Publisher's address 1908 Grand Ave., Nashville, TN 37202.

HUNT, F. Olen. 230
Heaven is my home, by F. Olen Hunt, Sr. [1st ed.] Atlanta, Spiritual Life Publishers [1967] xi, 106 p. 22 cm. [BT77.H84] 67-18480
1. Theology, Doctrinal—Popular works. I. Title.

HUNTER, Archibald Macbride. 230
Taking the Christian view [by] A. M. Hunter. Atlanta, John Knox Press [1974] viii, 84 p. 21 cm. [BT77.H85 1974] 73-16919 ISBN 0-8042-0721-6
1. Theology, Doctrinal—Popular works. 2. Christian life—1960- I. Title.

INMAN, Lee Bertram, 1892- 230
The hand of God... by Lee B. Inman. [Rice Lake, Wis., 1943] 2 p. l., 7-220 p., 1 l. illus. 21 cm. [BT77.I5] 43-13274
1. Theology, Doctrinal—Popular works. I. Title.

IRESON, Gordon Worley. 230
Strange victory; the gospel of the resurrection [by] Gordon W. Ireson. New York, Seabury Press [1970] 128 p. 21 cm. (A Seabury paperback SP 69) Includes bibliographical references. [BT77.I67] 70-120367
1. Theology, Doctrinal—Popular works. I. Title.

IRONSIDE, Henry Allan, 1876- 230
Great words of the gospel, by H. A. Ironside... Chicago, Ill., Moody press [1944] 3 p. l., 9-124 p. 17 cm. [Moody colportage library, no. 188] Addresses delivered in most part at the Moody memorial church, Chicago. [BT77.I7] 44-30709
1. Theology, Doctrinal—Popular works. 2. Sermons, American. I. Title.

IRONSIDE, Henry Allan, 1876- 230
1951.
Sailing with Paul; simple papers for young Christians. [1st ed.] New York, Loizeaux Bros. [1953] 78p. 19cm. [BT77.I74] 54-43122
1. Theology, Doctrinal—Popular works. I. Title.

*ISSETT, Lu Nell. 230
Color me legitimate [first ed.] Van Nuys, Calif., Bible Voice Books, [1975] 88 p. 18 cm. Includes bibliographical references. [BT771.2] 1.50 (pbk.)
1. Theology, Doctrinal—Popular works. I. Title.
Pub. address: P.O. Box 7491 91409.

JACOBS, Charles Michael, 230
1875-1938.
The way, a little book of Christian truth... By Charles M. Jacobs. Philadelphia, Pa., The Castle press [1922] v, 7-178 p. 19 cm. [BT77.J17] 22-17796
1. Theology, Doctrinal—Popular works. I. Title.

JACOBS, Henry Eyster, 1844- 230
1932.
Elements of religion, by Henry Eyster Jacobs ... Philadelphia, G. W. Frederick, 1894. 298 p. 20 cm. [BT77.J2] 39-7353
1. Theology, Doctrinal—Popular works 2. Lutheran church—Doctrinal and controversial works. I. Title.

JANSEN, G. M. A. 230
An existential approach to theology [by] G. M. A. Jansen. Milwaukee, Bruce Pub. Co. [1966] xii, 128 p. 23 cm. (Impact books) Bibliography: p. 125-126. [BT77.J3] 66-26657
1. Theology, Doctrinal—Popular works. I. Title.

JENSON, Robert W. 230
Story and promise; a brief theology of the gospel about Jesus, by Robert W. Jenson. Philadelphia, Fortress Press [1973] ix, 198 p. 20 cm. Includes bibliographies. [BT77.J38] 72-87060 ISBN 0-8006-0143-2 3.95
1. Theology, Doctrinal—Popular works. I. Title.

KALLAS, James G. 230
A layman's introduction to Christian thought, by James Kallas. Philadelphia, Westminster Press [1969] 140 p. 21 cm. [BT77.K23] 69-16919 2.45
1. Theology, Doctrinal—Popular works. I. Title.

KAVANAUGH, James J. 233
Man in search of God, by James J. Kavanaugh. New York, Paulist Press [1967] 109 p. illus. 19 cm. (Deus books) [BT77.K26] 67-23600
1. Theology, Doctrinal—Popular works. I. Title.

KENNEDY, Dennis James, 1930- 230
Truths that transform / D. James Kennedy. Old Tappan, N.J. : F. H. Revell Co., [1974] 160 p. ; 26 cm. Includes index. [BT77.K277] 74-20923 ISBN 0-8007-0655-2 : 4.95
1. Theology, Doctrinal—Popular works. I. Title.

KENNEDY, Dennis James, 1930- 230
Why I believe / D. James Kennedy. Waco, Tex. : Word Books, c1980. 164 p. ; 23 cm. Includes bibliographical references. [BT77.K278] 19 79-67668 ISBN 0-8499-0194-4 : 6.95
1. Theology, Doctrinal—Popular works. I. Title.

KERN, Horatio G. 230
Mysteries of godliness. By Horatio G. Kern ... Philadelphia, J. B. Lippincott & co., 1882. 204 p. 19 cm. [BT77.K3] 39-7355
1. Theology, Doctrinal—Popular works. I. Title.

KING, Rachel Hadley, 1904- 230
Theology you can understand. New York, Morehouse-Gorham Co. [1956] 223p. illus. 21cm. [BT77.K4] 56-9732
1. Teeology, Doctrinal—Popular works. I. Title.

KNUDSEN, Ralph Edward, 1897- 230
Christian beliefs. Philadelphia, Judson Press [1947] 177 p. 20 cm. Bibliography: p. 177. [BT77.K5] 47-11786
1. Theology, Doctrinal—Popular works. I. Title.

KOEHLER, Alfred W. 230
Light from above; Christian doctrine explained and applied. Saint Louis, Mo., Concordia Pub. House [c.1960] 165p. 23cm. 60-50142 1.50 pap.,
1. Theology, Doctrinal—Popular works. I. Title.

KOEHLER, Edward Wilhelm 230.41
August, 1875-
A summary of Christians doctrine; a popular presentation of the teachings of the Bible, By Edward W. A. Koehler ... River Forest, Ill., Koehler publishing company [c1939] xv, 292 p. 24 cm. Bibliography: p. 281. [BX8065.K56] 39-14018
1. Theology, Doctrinal—Popular works. 2. Lutheran church—Doctrinal and controversial works. I. Title.

KOEHLER, Edward Wilhelm 230.41
August, 1875-1951.
A summary of Christian doctrine; a popular presentation of the teachings of the Bible. 2d rev. ed. prepared for publication by Alfred W. Koehler. Detroit, L. H. Koehler [1952] 328 p. 24 cm. [BX8065.K58 1952] 52-22789
1. Theology, Doctrinal—Popular works. 2. Lutheran Church—Doctrinaland controversial works. I. Title.

KRIEG, Carl E. 230
What to believe? : The questions of Christian faith / Carl E. Krieg. Philadelphia : Fortress Press, [1974] viii, 113 p. ; 19 cm. [BT77.K65] 74-80415 ISBN 0-8006-1085-7 pbk. : 3.25
1. Theology, Doctrinal—Popular works. 2. Apologetics—20th century. I. Title.

KURTZ, Robert Merrill, 1871- 260
A Christian layman's handbook, by Robert M. Kurtz ... New York, American tract society [c1937] 72 p. 17 cm. [BT77.K8] 38-2116
1. Theology, Doctrinal—Popular works. I. Title.

LAVIK, John Rasmus, 1881- 230.41
The way, the truth, and the life; the basic teachings of the Bible concerning God, man, and the way of salvation Minneapolis, Augsburg Pub. House [1957] 258p. 23cm. [BT77.L32] 57-9724
1. Theology, Doctrinal —Popular works. 2. Lutheran Church—Doctrinal and controversial works. I. Title.

LAWSON, John. 201'.1
An evangelical faith for today. Nashville, Abingdon Press [1972] 95 p. 19 cm. Bibliography: p. 93-95. [BT77.L325] 75-186826 ISBN 0-687-12180-9
1. Theology, Doctrinal—Popular works. 2. Evangelicalism. I. Title.

LEITCH, Addison H. 230
Interpreting basic theology, Great Neck, N.Y., Channel Pr. [c.1961] 208p. 61-17159 3.50 bds.,
1. Theology, Doctrinal—Popular works. I. Title.

LESLIE, Charles W. 248.4
God is a spirit. Boston, Christopher [c.1965] 94p. 21cm. [BT77.L347] 65-21527 2.95
1. Theology, Doctrinal—Popular works. I. Title.

LESLIE, Charles W 248.4
God is a spirit, by Charles W. Leslie. Boston, Christopher Pub. House [1965] 94 p. 21 cm. [BT77.L347] 65-21527
1. Theology, Doctrinal — Popular works. I. Title.

LEWIS, C. S. 1898-1963. 230
(Clive Staples),
Mere Christianity : a revised and enlarged edition, with a new introduction, of the three books, The case for Christianity, Christian behaviour, and Beyond personality / by C.S. Lewis. Old Tappan, N.J. : F.H. Revell, [1982], c1952. 352 p. ; 24 cm. Rev. ed. first published in 1952. Large print ed. [BT77.L348 1982] 19 81-13972 ISBN 0-8007-1289-7 : 12.95
1. Theology, Doctrinal—Popular works. 2. Apologetics—20th century. 3. Large type books. I. Title.

LEWIS, Charles Smith, 1868- 230
Some foundation truths of the Christian faith, by Charles Smith Lewis... Philadelphia, G. W. Jacobs & co. [1923] 3 p. l., 144 p. 19 1/2 cm. [BT77.L35] 23-15073
1. Theology, Doctrinal—Popular works. I. Title.

LEWIS, Edwin, 1881- 230.76
Great Christian teachings; a book for study classes [by] Edwin Lewis... New York, Cincinnati [etc.] The Methodist book concern [1933] 121 p. 17 1/2 cm. "Approved by the Committee on curriculum of the Board of education of the Methodist Episcopal church." "Recommended readings": p. 107. [BT77.L37] ,3-23039
1. Theology, Doctrinal—Popular works. 2. Methodist church—Doctrinal and controversial works. I. Methodist Episcopal church. Board of education. II. Title.

LEWIS, Gordon Russell, 1926- 230
Decide for yourself; a theological workbook [by] Gordon R. Lewis. Downers Grove, Ill., Inter-Varsity Press [1970] 174 p. 21 cm. Includes bibliographical references. [BT77.L43] 71-116046
1. Theology, Doctrinal—Popular works. I. Title.

LITTLE, Ganse. 230
Beliefs that matter. Philadelphia, Westminster Press [1957] 142p. 21cm. [BT77.L55] 57-9603
1. Theology, Doctrinal—Popular works. I. Title.

LITTLE, Paul E. 230
Know what you believe [by] Paul E. Little. Wheaton, Ill., Scripture Press Publications [1970] 192 p. 18 cm. Includes

bibliographical references. [BT77.L555] 76-105667
1. Theology, Doctrinal—Popular works. I. Title.

LONG, Abram Miller, 1895- 230
Pillars of the Christian faith. New York, F. H. Ravell Co. [1947] 189 p. 21 cm. [BT77.L6] 47-29969
1. Theology, Doctrinal—Popular works. I. Title.

MACCARTY, Skip. 230
Who am I? : A christian guide to meaning and identity / Skip MacCarty. Washington : Review and Herald Pub. Association, c1979. 191 p. ; 21 cm. Includes bibliographical references. [BT77.M128] 78-24079 pbk. : 4.95
1. Theology, Doctrinal—Popular works. 2. Man (Christian theology) 3. Identification (Religion) I. Title.

MCCOMB, John Hess, 1898- 230
God's purpose in this age, by John Hess McComb ... New York [etc.] Fleming H. Revell company [c1941] 93 p. 19 1/2 cm. [BT77.M13] 41-23374
1. Theology, Doctrinal—Popular works. I. Title.

MACKEY, James Patrick 230
The grace of God, the response of man a study in basic theology [by] J. P. Mackey. Albany, Magi Bks. [c.1966] 192p. 21cm. First ed., 1966, has title: Life and grace. [BT77.M155 1966] 67-21468 3.95
1. Theology, Doctrinal— Popular works. I. Title.

MCKOWN, Edgar Monroe, 1896- 230
Understanding Christianity; a study of our Christian heritage, by Edgar M. McKown and Carl J. Scherzer. New York, Ronald Press Co. [1949] vii, 162 p. 21 cm. (Series in religion) Bibliography: p. 149-151. [BT77.M16] 49-8029
1. Theology, Doctrinal—Popular works. I. Scherzer, Carl J., joint author. II. Title. III. Series.

MACLENNAN, David Alexander, 1903- 200
Let's take another look; basic beliefs reinterpreted, by David A. MacLennan. Waco, Tex., Word Books [1970] 125 p. 21 cm. Originally published in The Link as a series of articles entitled Faith reinterpreted. Includes bibliographical references. [BT77.M163] 75-122495 2.95
1. Theology, Doctrinal—Popular works. I. Title.

MACPHAIL, James Russell. 230
The Way, the Truth, and the Life; an outline of Christian doctrine. New York, Oxford University Press, 1954. 208p. 20cm. [BT77.M165] 54-6910
1. Theology, Doctrinal—Popular works. I. Title.

MCQUARRIE, John. 230
The faith of the people of God; a lay theology. New York, Scribner [1973? c.1972] 191 p. 21 cm. (Lyceum Editions, SL367) Bibliography: p. 181-187. [BT77.M166] 72-1224 ISBN 0-68413060-2 2.45 (pbk.)
1. Theology, Doctrinal—Popular works. I. Title.

MAPLE, James. 230
Discourses on Christian doctrine. By Elder James Maple ... Springfield, O., Gospel herald office, 1851. 1 p. l., [v]-viii, 208 p. 19 cm. [BT77.M2] 39-7359
1. Theology, Doctrinal—Popular works. I. Title.

MARTIN, Earl Leslie, 1892- 230
What a Christian should believe, by Earl L. Martin. Anderson, Ind., Gospel trumpet company [1928] 120 p. 18 1/2 cm. [BT77.M25] 28-25771
1. Theology, Doctrinal—Popular works. 2. Church of God (Anderson, Ind.)—Doctrinal and controversial works. I. Title.

MARTIN, Walter Ralston, 1928- 230
Essential Christianity; a handbook of basic Christian doctrines. Grand Rapids, Zondervan Pub. House [1962] 114p. 21cm. [BT77.M28] 62-51869
1. Theology, Doctrinal— Popular works. I. Title.

MEYER, John C., 1934- 230
Christian beliefs and teachings / John C. Meyer. Washington, D.C. : University Press of America, c1981. p. cm. [BT77.M48] 19 81-40353 ISBN 0-8191-1757-9 : 17.25 ISBN 0-8191-1758-7 (pbk.) : 7.75
1. Theology, Doctrinal—Popular works. I. Title.

MILLER, Allen O 230
Invitation to theology; resources for Christian nurture and discipline. Philadelphia, Christian Education Press [1958] 278p. 21cm. Includes bibliography. [BT77.M53] 58-11704
1. Theology, Doctrinal—Popular works. 2. Religious education. I. Title.

MILLER, Park Hays, 1879- 230
Christian doctrine for Sunday school teachers. Boston, W. A. Wilde Co. [1947] 105 p. 20 cm. [BT77.M54] 48-15930
1. Theology, Doctrinal—Popular works. I. Title.

MILLER, Samuel Martin, 1890- 230.41
The Word of Truth; the gospel of your salvation. Rock Island, Ill., Augustana Book Concern [1952] 158 p. 20 cm. [BT77.M57] 52-7237
1. Theology, Doctrinal — Popular works. 2. Lutheran Church — Doctrinal and controversial works. I. Title.

MISSIONARY Society of Connecticut. 230
A summary of Christian doctrine and practice, designed especially for the use of the people in the new settlements of the United States of America. Hartford, Printed by Hudson & Goodwin, 1804. 63 p. 23 cm. [BT77.M58] 49-39176
1. Theology, Doctrinal—Popular works. I. Title.

MONFORT, Francis Cassatte, 1844- 220
Applied theology, by Rev. F. C. Monfort ... Cincinnati, Monfort & company [c1904] 234 p. 19 cm. [BR125.M75] 4-36947
1. Theology. Docitinali—Popular works. I. Title. II. Title: Theology, Applied.

MORGAN, Dewi. 261.8
God and sons. New York, Weybright and Talley [1968, c1967] 165 p. 22 cm. Bibliographical footnotes. [BT77.M83 1968] 68-28269 6.50
1. Theology, Doctrinal—Popular works. I. Title.

MOSLEY, Nicholas, 1923- 230
Experience and religion; a lay essay in theology. Philadelphia, United Church Pr. [1967,c.1965] 156p. 20cm. [BT77.M87 1967] 67-22945 1.95 pap.,
1. Theology, Doctrinal — Popular works. 2. Experience (Religion) I. Title.

MURPHY, Chuck, 1922- 248'.48'3
There's no business like God's business. Nashville, Abingdon Press [1974] ix, 128 p. 19 cm. [BT77.M92] 73-20312 ISBN 0-687-41632-9 2.95 (pbk.)
1. Theology, Doctrinal—Popular works. 2. Christian life—Anglican authors. I. Title.

NORDEN, Rudolph F. 230
The Gospel: love it & live it [by] Rudolph F. Norden. St. Louis, Concordia Pub. House [1973] 79 p. 19 cm. [BT77.N67 1973] 72-94850 ISBN 0-570-03146-X
1. Theology, Doctrinal—Popular works. I. Title.

NORRIS, Richard Alfred. 230'.3
Understanding the faith of the Church / written by Richard A. Norris, with the assistance of a group of editoral advisors under the direction of the Church's teaching series committee. New York : Seabury Press, c1979. xvi, 262 p. ; 22 cm. (The Church's teaching series ; 4) Includes index. Bibliography: p. 255. [BT77.N68] 79-4039 ISBN 0-8164-0421-6 : 9.50. ISBN 0-8164-2217-6 pbk. : 3.95
1. Theology, Doctrinal—Popular works. I. Title. II. Series: Church's teaching series ; 4.

OGILVIE, Lloyd John. 230'.51
Ask Him anything : God can handle your hardest questions / Lloyd J. Ogilvie. Waco, Tex. : Word Books, c1981. 244 p. ; 23 cm. Includes bibliographical references. [BT77.O35] 19 81-51224 ISBN 0-8499-0281-9 : 8.95
1. Theology, Doctrinal—Popular works. 2. Christian life—Presbyterian authors. I. Title.

ORR, James Edwin, 1912- 230
Faith that makes sense. Valley Forge [Pa.] Judson [1962, c.1960] 109p. 19cm. 62-14809 1.45 pap.,
1. Theology, Doctrinal—Popular works. I. Title.

ORR, William Fridell, 1907- 230
Great beliefs of the church, by William F. Orr ... Philadelphia, Board of education of the Presbyterian church in the United States of America [1946] 61 p. 18 1/2 cm. "This little book grew out of a Westminster fellowship summer conference at Grove City, Pennsylvania, in 1945."--Editor's note. [BT77.O75] 47-18887
1. Theology, Doctrinal—Popular works. I. Title.

OUTLER, Albert Cook, 1908- 230'.7'1
Theology in the Wesleyan spirit / Albert C. Outler. Nashville : Tidings, [1975] ix, 101 p. ; 19 cm. Includes bibliographical references. [BX8331.2.O9] 74-24509
1. Methodist Church—Doctrinal and controversial works. 2. Theology, Doctrinal—Popular works. I. Title.

OWEN, Bob. 248'.83
Jesus is alive and well (what Jesus People really believe). Pasadena, Calif., Compass Press [1972] 127 p. illus. 18 cm. [BT77.O86] 72-182095 1.25
1. Theology, Doctrinal—Popular works. 2. Jesus people. I. Title.

PALMER, Albert Wentworth, 1879- 230
The light of faith; an outline of religious thought for laymen, by Albert W. Palmer ... New York, The Macmillan company, 1945. ix, 156 p. 19 1/2 cm. "First printing." "Notes and references": p. 149-152. [BT77.P25] 45-9044
1. Theology, Doctrinal—Popular works. I. Title.

PEARSON, Roy Messer, 1914- 230
The believer's unbelief; a layman's guide through Christian doubts. New York, Nelson [c.1963] 175p. 22cm. Bibl. 63-10926 3.95
1. Theology, Doctrinal—Popular works. I. Title.

PEARSON, Roy Messer, 1914- 230
The beliver's unbelief; a layman's guide through Christian doubts. New York, T. Nelson [1963] 175 p. 22 cm. [BT77.P37] 63-10926
1. Theology, Doctrinal—Popular works. I. Title.

PIKE, James Albert, Bp., 1913- 230
What is this treasure? New York, Harper [c.1966] 90p. 22cm. [BT77.P47] 66-11484 3.00 bds.,
1. Theology, Doctrinal — Popular works. I. Title.

PIKE, James Albert, Bp., 1913-1969. 230'.0924
If this be heresy [by] James A. Pike. [1st ed.] New York, Harper & Row [1967] x, 205 p. 22 cm. Bibliographical footnotes. [BT77.P46] 67-21551
1. Theology, Doctrinal—Popular works. I. Title.

PIKE, James Albert, Bp., 1913-1969. 230
What is this treasure? [By] James A. Pike. [1st ed.] New York, Harper & Row [1966] 90 p. 22 cm. [BT77.P47] 66-11484
1. Theology, Doctrinal—Popular works. I. Title.

PITCAIRN, Theodore. 230
My Lord and my God; essays on modern religion, the Bible, and Emanuel Swedenborg. [1st ed.] New York, Exposition Press [1967] ix, 298 p. illus. (part col.), col. ports. 21 cm. [BX8721.2.P5] 67-9668
1. New Jerusalem Church—Doctrinal and controversial works. 2. Theology, Doctrinal—Popular works. I. Title.

PITTENGER, William Norman, 1905- 230
The Christan way in a modern world, by W. Norman Pittenger ... Louisville, Ky., The Cloister press [1944] 5 p. l., iii, 194 p. 19 cm. "Books for further reading": p. 192-193. [BT77.P5] 44-3805
1. Theology, Doctrinal—Popular works. I. Title.

PLUMER, William Swan, 1802-1880. 230
Truths for the people; or, Several points in theology plainly stated, for beginners. By William S. Plumer, D.D. New York, American tract society [1875] 227 p. 19 1/2cm. [BT77.P6] 39-7360
1. Theology, Doctrinal—Popular works. 2. Presbyterian church—Doctrinal and controversial works. I. American tract society. II. Title.

POTTER, John, of Fayette county, Pa. 230
An inquiry concerning the most important truths, namely: What God is--where He dwells--what that knowledge of God and Christ is, which is life eternal: what the otonement is, and for whom made: how an interest therein is obtained, and respecting predestination and the Methodist doctrine concerning it. By John Potter ... [Uniontown? Pa.] J. & T. Patton, printers, 1820. xii, 251 p. 19 cm. [BT77.P67] 39-10935
1. Theology, Doctrinal—Popular works. I. Title.

POWELL, Ivor 230
This I believe; the essential truths of Christianity. Grand Rapids, Mich., Zondervan Pub. House [1961] 222p. 61-1490 2.50
1. Theology, Doctrinal—Popular works. I. Title.

*POWELL, John Joseph, 1925- 230
A reason to live! A reason to die! [by] John Powell, S. J. Niles, Ill., Argus Communications [1972] 207 p. illus. (some col.) 23 cm. [BT77] 2.95
1. Theology, Doctrinal—Popular works. I. Title.

POWERS, Joseph M., 1926- 234
Spirit and sacrament; the humanizing experience, by Joseph M. Powers. New York, Seabury Press [1973] x, 211 p. 22 cm. (A Continuum book) [BT77.P7] 72-10566 ISBN 0-8164-1121-2 6.95
1. Theology, Doctrinal—Popular works. 2. Life. I. Title.

PRENTER, Regin, 1907- 230
The church's faith; a primer of Christian beliefs. Translated by Theodor I. Jensen. Philadelphia, Fortress Press [1968] xxxii, 224 p. 18 cm. (A Fortress paperback original) Translation of Kirkens tro: en kristenlaere for laegfolk. [BT77.K4313] 68-17708 2.75
1. Theology, Doctrinal—Popular works. I. Title.

PURDY, Alexander Converse, 1890- 230
Pathways to God, by Alexander C. Purcy. New York, The Womans press, 1922. 5 p. l., 3-204 p. 19 1/2 cm. [BT77.P8] 22-25416
1. Theology, Doctrinal—Popular works. I. Title.

RALL, Harris Franklin, 1870- 230
The Christian faith and way. New York, Pub. for Cooperative Pub. Assn., by Abingdon-Cokesbury Press [1947] 126 p. 17 cm. "Suggestions for further reading": p. 124. [BT77.R27] 48-1768
1. Theology, Doctrinal—Popular works. I. Title.

RALL, Harris Franklin, 1870- 230
A faith for today [by] Harris Franklin Rall. New York, Cincinnati [etc.] The Abingdon press [c1936] 284 p. 22 cm. Includes bibliographies. [BT77.R3] 36-28596
1. Theology, Doctrinal—Popular works. I. Title.

RAWLINSON, Alfred Edward John, bp. of Derby, 1884- 230
Religious reality; a book for men, by A. E. J. Rawlinson ... With a preface by the Bishop of Lichfield. London, New York [etc.] Longmans, Green and co., 1918. xi, 183 p. 19 cm. [BT77.R346] 18-18686

1. Theology, Doctrinal—Popular works. I. Title.

RAYMOND, Father, 1903- 230.2
The mysteries in your life [by] M. Raymond. Milwaukee, Bruce Pub. Co. [1965] 200 p. 23 cm. [BX1754.R37] 65-20547
1. Theology, Doctrinal — Popular works. 2. Catholic Church — Doctrinal and controversial works, Popular. 3. Mystery. I. Title.

RAYMOND,M, Father 1903- 230.2
The mysteries in your life. Milwaukee, Bruce [c.1965] vi, 200p. 24cm. [BX1754.R37] 65-20547 4.25
1. Theology, Doctrinal—Popular works. 2. Catholic Church—Doctrinal and controversial works, Popular. 3. Mystery. I. Title.

READ, David Haxton Carswell. 230
The Christian faith. New York, Scribner [c1956] 175p. 18cm. [BT77.R36 1956] 56-7129
1. Theology, Doctrinal—Popular works. I. Title.

READ, David Haxton Carswell.
The Christian faith. London, English Universities Press [1965] ix, 175 p. (The teach yourself books) 68-6038
1. Theology, Doctrinal—Popular works. I. Title. II. Series.

REID, John, Rev. 230
A pocket system of theology for Sabbath-school teachers and church-members generally. By The Rev. John Reid ... with an introduction by the Rev. John Hall, D.D. Philadelphia, Presbyterian board of publication [1884] 1 p. l., iv. 3-246 p. 18 cm. [BT77.R4] 39-10476
1. Theology, Doctrinal—Popular works. 2. Presbyterian church—Doctrinal and controversial works. I. Presbyterian church in the U.S.A. Board of publication. II. Title.

REST, Karl H A 230
Put your faith to work [by] Karl H. A. Rest. Philadelphia, Muhlenberg Press [1956] xii, 186 p. 20 cm. Bibliographical footnotes. [BT77.R43] 56-9338
1. Theology, Doctrinal — Popular works. 2. Church membership. I. Title.

ROBERTSON, Norvell, 1796-1879. 230
Church-members' hand-book of theology, by Norvell Robertson ... Memphis, Tenn., Published for the author, by the Southern Baptist publication society, 1874. 4 p. l., 7-323 p. 20 cm. [BT77.R6] 39-7366
1. Theology, Doctrinal—Popular works. 2. Baptists—Doctrinal and controversial works. I. Southern Baptist publication society. II. Title.

ROBINSON, Godfrey Clive. 230
Here is the answer [by] Godfrey C. Robinson [and] Stephen F. Winward. Valley Forge, Judson Press [1970, c1949] 110 p. 20 cm. [BT77.R627] 70-123472 2.50
1. Theology, Doctrinal—Popular works. I. Winward, Stephen F., joint author. II. Title.

ROBINSON, John Arthur Thomas, Bp., 1919- 230
But that I can't believe! [By] John A. T. Robinson [New York] New American Library [1967] 170 p. 21 cm. (Perspectives in humanism) Bibliographical footnotes. [BT77.R63 1967] 67-24793
1. Theology, Doctrinal—Popular works. I. Title. II. Series.

ROBINSON, Wayne Bradley, 1936- 230
Questions are the answer : believing today / by Wayne Bradley Robinson ; [ill. by Sandy Bauer]. New York : Pilgrim Press, c1980. xiii, 110 p. : ill. ; 23 cm. Discussion questions, Bible verses, and text explore the nature of faith. [BT77.R64] 80-36780 ISBN 0-8298-0409-9 (pbk.) : 5.95
1. Theology, Doctrinal—Popular works. 2. [Faith.] 3. [Christian life.] I. Title.

RUPERT, Hoover. 230
What's good about God? Nashville, Abingdon Press [1970] 173 p. 21 cm. Includes bibliographical references. [BT77.R86] 70-124749 ISBN 6-87448-700-4.50
1. Theology, Doctrinal—Popular works. I. Title.

SCHROEDER, W. Widick. 230
Where do I stand? : living thelogical options for contemporary Christians / W. Widick Schroeder and Keith A. Davis. Rev. ed. Chicago : Exploration Press, [1975] ix, 157 p. ; 23 cm. (Studies in ministry and parish life) Includes bibliographical references. [BT77.S384 1975] 75-5284 ISBN 0-913552-02-X : 7.50 pbk. : 4.00
1. Theology, Doctrinal—Popular works. I. Davis, Keith A., joint author. II. Title. III. Series.

SCHROEDER, W. Widick. 230
Where do I stand? Living theological options for contemporary Christians, by W. Widick Schroeder and Keith A. Davis. Chicago, Exploration Press [1973] ix, 158 p. 28 cm. [BT77.S384] 72-97252 3.00
1. Theology, Doctrinal—Popular works. I. Davis, Keith A., joint author. II. Title.

SCHROEDER, W. Widick. 230
Where do I stand? : Living theological options for contemporary Christians / W. Widick Schroeder and Keith A. Davis. 3d ed. Chicago : Exploration Press, c1978. ix, 158 p. ; 23 cm. (Studies in ministry and parish life) Includes bibliographical references. [BT77.S384 1978] 78-59809 ISBN 0-913552-12-7. ISBN 0-913552-13-5 pbk. : Price unreported.
1. Theology, Doctrinal—Popular works. I. Davis, Keith A., joint author. II. Title. III. Series.

SCRIVEN, Charles. 230
The demons have had it : a theological ABC / by Charles Scriven. Nashville : Southern Pub. Association, c1976. 125 p. ; 21 cm. Includes bibliographical references. [BT77.S386] 76-2926 ISBN 0-8127-0111-9
1. Theology, Doctrinal—Popular works. I. Title.

SEELY, Amos W. 230
Doctrinal thoughts, by Rev. Amos W. Seely... New-York, F. McElroy, printer, 1861. 102 p. 17 cm. [BT77.S4] 39-7844
1. Theology, Doctrinal—Popular works. I. Title.

SESSLER, Jacob John, 1899- 231
The fact of God, a study book for young people and adults, by Jacob J. Sessler ... with an introduction by Norman Vincent Peale. New York [etc.] Fleming H. Revell company [1944] 159 p. 19 1/2 cm. [BT77.S44] 44-4407
1. Theology, Doctrinal—Popular works. 2. God. I. Title.

SETZER, J. Schoneberg. 230
What's left to believe? [By] J. Schoneberg Setzer. Nashville, Abingdon Press [1968] 236 p. 25 cm. [BT77.S45] 68-11473
1. Theology, Doctrinal—Popular works. I. Title.

SHAW, John Arthur. 260
Some features of the faith; a popular discussion of certain cardinal points of Christian doctrine, by John Arthur Shaw ... Milwaukee, The Young churchman co., 1902. 306 p. 19 cm. [BT75.S627] 2-26079
1. Theology, Doctrinal—Popular works. I. Title.

SHROYER, Montgomery J., 1888- 230
.
The authority of the Bible in Christian belief. Nashville, Tidings [1961] 72 p. 19 cm. [BT77.S53] 61-9130
1. Theology, Doctrinal — Popular works. I. Title.

SIRE, James W. 230
Beginning with God : a basic introduction to the Christian faith / James W. Sire. Downers Grove, Ill. : InterVarsity Press, c1981. p. cm. Bibliography: p. [BT77.S56] 19 81-14305 ISBN 0-87784-369-4 : 3.50
1. Theology, Doctrinal—Popular works. I. Title.

SMART, James D. 230
The ABC's of Christian faith, by James D. Smart. Philadelphia, Westminster Press [1968] 140 p. 19 cm. [BT77.S58] 68-13958
1. Theology, Doctrinal—Popular works. I. Title.

SMART, James D. 230
What a man can believe [by] James D. Smart ... Philadelphia, The Westminster press [c1943] 2 p. l., 3-252 p. 20 1/2 cm. [BT77.S585] 44-3804
1. Theology, Doctrinal—Popular works. I. Title.

SMART, Moses Mighels, 1812-1885. 230
A brief view of Christian doctrine, by Moses M. Smart... Lowell, N. L. Dayton, 1843. 330 p. 16 1/2 cm. "Errata" slip inserted at end. [BT77.S6] 39-7371
1. Theology, Doctrinal—Popular works. I. Title.

SNOWDEN, James Henry, 1852-1936. 230
The basal beliefs of Christianity, by James H. Snowden ... New York, The Macmillan company, 1911. ix p., 2 l., 252 p. 20 cm. "Bibliographical note": p. 244-247. [BT77.S65] 11-1324
1. Theology, Doctrinal—Popular works. I. Title.

SOPER, Donald Oliver, 1903-
Popular fallacies about the Christian faith. [London, New York, Epworth Press, 1957] 128 p. 18 cm. (Wyvern Brooks, 8)
1. Theology, Doctrinal. Popular works. 2. Religious thought — 20th century. I. Title.

SPENCE, Walter, 1867- 230
Back to Christ; some modern forms of religious thought, by Walter Spence. Chicago, A. C. McClurg & co., 1900. vi p., 1 l., [11]-222 p. 19 1/2 cm. [BT77.S7] 0-2754
1. Theology, Doctrinal—Popular works. I. Title.

SPENCER, Bonnell. 230'.3
God who dares to be man : a theology for prayer and suffering / Bonnell Spencer ; foreword by Paul Moore, Jr. New York : Seabury Press, 1980. p. cm. (A Crossroad book) Includes bibliographical references and indexes. [BT77.S713] 80-16833 ISBN 0-8164-0478-X : 12.95
1. Theology, Doctrinal—Popular works. 2. Spiritual life—Anglican authors. I. Title.

SPURRIER, William A. 230
Guide to the Christian faith, an introduction to Christian doctrine. New York, Scribner [c.1952] xii, 242p. 21cm. (Scribner library SL19) 1.25 pap.,
1. Theology, Doctrinal—Popular works. I. Title.

SPURRIER, William Atwell. 230
Guide to the Christian faith, an introduction to Christian doctrine. New York, Scribner, 1952. 242 p. 21 cm. [BT77.S72] 52-554
1. Theology, Doctrinal — Popular works. I. Title.

STANFIELD, James Monroe. 230
Corner stones of faith, being the witness of the Bible brought to bear on the vital questions of the Christian religion. The Bible collected, quoted, and focused on each subject; explained, discussed and applied; laying a foundation for a sound faith. By J. M. Stanfield ... With an introduction by Ernest C. Wareing ... Grant Rapids, Mich., Wm. B. Eerdmans publishing company, 1938. 227 p. 20 cm. [BT77.S73] 38-17245
1. Theology, Doctrinal—Popular works. I. Title.

STEEVES, Paul D. 230
Getting to know your faith / Paul Steeves. Downers Grove, Ill. : InterVarsity Press, c1977. 126 p. : forms ; 21 cm. Includes bibliographical references. [BT77.S733] 76-55555 ISBN 0-87784-629-4 pbk. : 2.95
1. Theology, Doctrinal—Popular works. I. Title.

STEINMANN, Jean. 230.2
A Christian faith for today. Translated by Edmond Bonin. Paramus, N.J., Newman Press [1969] v, 135 p. 21 cm. Translation of Une foi chretienne pour aujourd'hui. Bibliographical footnotes. [BT77.S73513] 70-79038 4.50
1. Theology, Doctrinal—Popular works. I. Title.

STERLING, Chandler W., Bp., 1911- 230
The eighth square, by Chandler Sterling. Artwork and cover design by Don Crouse. Ambler, Pa., Trinity Press [1970] xii, 106 p. illus. 22 cm. [BT77.S737] 75-111643
1. Theology, Doctrinal—Popular works. I. Title.

STOTT, John R. 230
Basic Christianity. [1st ed., reprinted] Grand Rapids, Eerdmans [1958] 144 p. 18 cm. (Eerdmans pocket editions) [BT77.S74 1958] 58-13513
1. Theology, Doctrinal — Popular works. I. Title.

STRENG, William D. 230
Faith for today : a brief outline of Christian thought / William D. Streng. Minneapolis : Augsburg Pub. House, c1975. 64 p. ; 20 cm. [BT77.S743] 75-2843 ISBN 0-8066-1488-9 pbk. : 1.25
1. Theology, Doctrinal—Popular works. I. Title.

STRINGFELLOW, William. 241
Free in obedience. New York, Seabury Press, 1964. 128 p. 20 cm. [BT77.S745] 64-10142
1. Theology, Doctrinal — Popular works. I. Title.

SUTER, John Wallace. 1890- 230.3
To know and believe; a senior high school resource book. Greenwich, Conn., Seabury Press [1958] 81 p. 21 cm. (The Seabury series, R-10) [BX5930.S8] 58-9266
1. Theology, Doctrinal-Popular works. 2. Protestant Episcopal Church in the U.S.A.—Doctrinal and controversial works. I. Title.

SWANN, Doris Cutter. 230
Bible teachings. Nashville, Broadman Press [1970] 46 p. 21 cm. [BT77.S785] 79-117309
1. Theology, Doctrinal—Popular works. I. Title.

SWEAZEY, George Edgar, 1905- 230
The Christian answer to life's urgent questions. St. Louis, Bethany [c.1962] 192p. 23cm. 62-8757 3.50
1. Theology, Doctrinal—Popular works. I. Title.

TANNER, Jacob, 1865- 230.41
Exploring God's word; a study guide to Bible teachings. Minneapolis, Augsburg Pub. House [1950] viii, 168 p. 22 cm. [B[cpp.T325] 50-10774
1. Theology, Doctrinal — Popular works. 2. Lutheran Church — Doctrinal and controversial works. I. Title.

TANNER, Jacob, 1865- 230
Helps for Bible readers, by Jacob Tanner ... Minneapolis, Minn., Augsburg publishing house [1931] 64 p. 19 cm. [BT77.T33] 43-18831
1. Theology, doctrinal—Popular works. I. Title.

TAVARD, Georges Henri, 1922- 230
Meditation on the word; perspectives for a renewed theology, by George H. Tavard. Glen Rock, N.J., Paulist Press Paperback [1968] v, 169 p. 21 cm. [BT77.T34] 68-24813 3.50
1. Theology, Doctrinal—Popular works. I. Title.

THIELICKE, Helmut, 1908- 238'.11
I believe; the Christian's creed. Translated by John W. Doberstein and H. George Anderson. Philadelphia, Fortress Press [1968] xvi, 256 p. 22 cm. Translation of Ich glaube. Das Bekenntnis der Christen. Bibliographical footnotes. [BT993.2.T543] 68-23991 2.50
1. Apostles' Creed. 2. Theology, Doctrinal—Popular works. I. Title.

THOMAS, Edgar Garfield, 1880- 230
High points in the higher life, by Edgar Garfield Thomas ... [Fort Lauderdale, Fla., 1943] 77 p. 23 cm. Portrait on t.-p. [BT77.T45] 43-13348
1. Theology, Doctrinal—Popular works. 2. Baptists—Doctrinal and controversial works. I. Title.

THOMAS, Owen C. 230
Introduction to theology [by] Owen C. Thomas. Cambridge, Mass., Greeno, Hadden [1973] 218 p. 23 cm. Bibliography: p. 216-218. [BT77.T455] 73-76599 ISBN 0-913550-02-7

1. Theology, Doctrinal—Popular works. I. Title.

THOMPSON, Egbert Herron, 1895- 230
The kingdom of heaven. [1st ed.] New York, Pageant Press, 1955. 58p. 21cm. [BT77.T48] 54-10887
1. Theology, Doctrinal—Popular works. I. Title.

THURIAN, Max. 230
Love and truth meet. Translated by C. Edward Hopkin. Philadelphia, Pilgrim Press [1968] x, 166 p. 22 cm. Translation of Amour et verite se rencontrent. [BT77.T4913] 68-59100 6.50
1. Theology, Doctrinal—Popular works. I. Title.

TOWNSEND, Luther Tracy, 1838-1922. 230.02
Elements of general and Christian theology. By L. T. Townsend ... New York, Nelson & Phillips; Cincinnati, Hitchcock & Walden, 1879. 79 p. diagrs. 17 cm. Published in 1873 under title: Outlines of theology. [BT77.T7] 39-7849
1. Theology, Doctrinal—Popular works. 2. Methodist church—Doctrinal and controversial works. I. Title.

TOWNSEND, Luther Tracy, 1838-1922. 230.02
Outlines of theology. By L. T. Townsend ... New York, Nelson & Phillips; Cincinnati, Hitchcock & Walden [1873] 79 p. diagrs. 17 cm. (On cover: Normal outline series) Published in 1879 under title: Elements of general and Christian theology. On cover: Outlines of Christian theology. [BT77.T72] 39-7851
1. Theology, Doctrinal—Popular works. 2. Methodist church—Doctrinal and controversial works. I. Title.

TRUEMPER, David G. 230'.41
Keeping the faith : a guide to the Christian message / David G. Truemper and Frederick A. Niedner, Jr. Philadelphia : Fortress Press, c1981. p. cm. [BT77.T77] 19 81-43072 ISBN 0-8006-1608-1 : 5.95
1. Lutheran Church—Doctrinal and controversial works. 2. Theology, Doctrinal—Popular works. I. Niedner, Frederick A., 1945- II. Title.

TURNER, John Clyde, 1878- 234
Soul-winning doctrines. [Rev. ed.] Nashville, Convention Press [1955, c1943] 116 p. 19 cm. [BT77.T8] 58-11353
1. Theology, Doctrinal — Popular works. I. Title.

TURNER, John Clyde, 1878- 231
Soul-winning doctrines, by J. Clyde Turner ... Nashville, Tenn., The Sunday school board of the Southern Baptist convention [1943] 133 p. 19 1/2 cm. [BT77.T8] 43-13671
1. Theology, Doctrinal—Popular works. I. Southern Baptist convention. Sunday school board. II. Title.

TURNER, John Clyde, 1878- 230.6
These things we believe. Nashville, Conventions Press [1956] 134 p. 20 cm. [BT77.T83] 56-23822
1. Theology Doctrinal — Popular works. 2. Baptists — Doctrinal and controversial works. I. Title.

UNGERSMA, Aaron J 1905- 230
Handbook for Christian believers [by] A. J. Ungersma. Richmond, John Knox Press [1964] x, 215 p. 21 cm. (Aletheia paperbacks) [BT77.U5 1964] 64-16285
1. Theology, Doctrinal — Popular works. 2. Christianity — 20th cent. I. Title.

UNGERSMA, Aaron J., 1905- 230
Handbook for Christian believers; faith explained for today's needs. [1st ed.] Indianapolis, Bobbs-Merrill [1953] 215 p. 21 cm. [BT77.U5] 53-5233
1. Theology, Doctrinal—Popular works. 2. Christianity—20th century. I. Title.

VARILLON, Francois, 1905- 230.2
Announcing Christ through Scripture to the church [Tr. from French] by Stephen Deacon, Jennifer Nicholson] Westminster, Md., Newman, 1964. 503p. 23cm. Bibl. 64-2531 6.95
1. Theology, Doctrinal—Popular works. I. Title.

VASSADY, Bela. 230
Light against darkness. Philadelphia, Christian Education Press [1961] 176 p. 21 cm. [BT77.V34] 61-13471
1. Theology, Doctrinal — Popular words. 2. Christianity — Essence, genius, nature. I. Title.

VIA media;
an essay in theological synthesis. London, New York, Longmans, Green [1956] xvi, 171p. 19cm. Bibliography: p. 166-168. Bibliographical references also included in footnotes.
1. Theology, Doctrinal—Popular works. I. Mascall, Eric Lionel, 1905-

WAGNER, James Edgar, 1900- 230
Incarnation to ascension: a pastoral interpretation. Philadelphia, Christian Educ. Pr. [dist. United Church Pr., c.1962] 111p. 20cm. 62-18103 2.50
1. Theology, Doctrinal—Popular works. I. Title.

WAGNER, James Edgar, 1900- 230
Incarnation to ascension: a pastoral interpretation. Philadelphia, Christian Education Press [1962] 111 p. 20 cm. [B777.W25] 62-18103
1. Theology, Doctrinal — Popular works. I. Title.

WAHKING, Harold L. 230.6
Being Christlike [by] Harold L. Wahking. Nashville, Tenn., Broadman Press [1970] 96 p. illus. 19 cm. (Being books) Includes bibliographical references. [BT77.W27] 73-113216
1. Theology, Doctrinal—Popular works. 2. Youth—Religious life. I. Title.

WALTERS, Dick H., 1907- 230.02
Our Christian doctrine course [a Bible doctrine manual) twenty-seven lessons; a course presenting the subject of Christian doctrine in complete outline form, according to the six divisions of systematic theology, together with Scripture references and exercises, prepared by D. H. Walters ... Grand Rapids, Mich., Zondervan publishing house [1942] 92, 97-149 p. 27 x 20 cm. Work sheets for classwork: p. 97-149. [BT77.W3] 43-697
1. Christian Reformed church—Doctrinal and controversial works. 2. Theology, Doctrinal—Popular works. I. Title.

WARD, William B. 230
Beliefs that live. Richmond, Va., John Knox [c.1963] 126p. 21cm. 63-13832 1.75 pap.,
1. Theology, Doctrinal—Popular works. I. Title.

WARD, William B. 230
Beliefs that live. Richmond, John Knox Press [1963] 126 p. 21 cm. [BT77.W33] 63-13832
1. Theology, Doctrinal — Popular works. I. Title.

WATTS, Ewart G., 1915- 252'.07'6
Bench marks of faith, by Ewart G. Watts. Study aids by John P. Gilbert. Nashville, Tidings [1974] 104 p. 19 cm. Includes bibliographical references. [BT77.W37] 73-90773 1.25 (pbk.).
1. Theology, Doctrinal—Popular works. 2. Christian life—Methodist authors. I. Gilbert, John Peyton, 1936- II. Title.

WILLIAMS, Carl Carnelius, 1903- 230
Things most surely believed. Anderson, Ind., Gospel Trumpet Co. [1955] 144p. 19cm. [BT77.W55] 55-28918
1. Theology, Doctrinal— Popular works. 2. Church of God (Anderson, Ind.)—Doctrinal and controversial works. I. Title.

WILLIAMS, Howard, 1918-
Down to earth; an interpretation of Christ. Naperville, ,Ill., SCM Book Club [1964] 127 p. 68-49964
1. Theology, doctrinal-Popular works. I. Title.

WILLIAMS, John Rodman. 230
10 teachings / J. Rodman Williams. Carol Stream, Ill. : Creation House, [1974] 121 p. ; 18 cm. (New leaf library) [BT77.W57] 73-82858 ISBN 0-88419-051-X : 1.95
1. Theology, Doctrinal—Popular works. I. Title.

WILLIAMSON, Isaac Dowd, 1807-1876. 230
Rudiments of theological and moral science. By Rev. I. D. Williamson ... Cincinnati, Williamson & Cantwell, 1870. viii, 9-377 p. front. (port.) 20 1/2 cm. [BT77.W7] 39-7853
1. Theology, Doctrinal—Popular works. I. Title.

WILSON, Frank Elmer, bp., 1885- 230.3
Faith and practice, by the Right Reverend Frank E. Wilson ... New York, Morehouse-Gorham co., 1939. 320 p. 22 cm. [BX5930.W483] 39-6947
1. Theology, Doctrinal—Popular works. 2. Protestant Episcopal church in the U.S.A.—Doctrinal and controversial works. I. Title.

WILSON, Frank Elmer, bp., 1885- 290.3
Faith and practice, by the Right Reverend Frank E. Wilson ... Textbook ed. New York, Morehouse-Gorham co., 1941. 340 p. 21 1/2 cm. [BX5930.W483 1941] 42-2838
1. Theology, Doctrinal—Popular works. 2. Protestant Episcopal church in the U.S.A.—Doctrinal and controversial works. I. Title.

WINWARD, Stephen F. 230.4
A modern ABeCedary for Protestants. New York, Association [1964, c.1963] 128p. 24cm. 64-11595 3.50
1. Theology, Doctrinal—Popular works. I. Title.

WOLF, Barbara, 1924- 230'.33
Journey in faith : an inquirer's program / Barbara Wolf. Rev. ed. New York : Seabury Press, 1982. 131 p. ; 21 cm. [BT77.W75 1982] 19 82-145510 ISBN 0-8164-2402-0 (pbk.) : 5.95
1. Theology, Doctrinal—Popular works. I. Title.

WRIGHT, Robert Joseph. 230
Synopsis of a Christian theology. By R. J. Wright ... Philadelphia, Published for the author by J. B. Lippincott & co., 1881. 144 p. 15 1/2 cm. [BT77.W8] 39-7854
1. Theology, Doctrinal—Popular works. I. Title.

YLVISAKER, Nils Martin, 1882- 230.41
No other way, by N. M. Ylvisaker. Minneapolis, Augsburg publishing house, 1938. xv, 255 p. 20 1/2 cm. [BX8065.Y5] 39-2578
1. Theology, Doctrinal—Popular works. 2. Lutheran church—Doctrinal and controversial works. I. Title.

ZACHMAN, Harry L. 230
...Messages on Christian beliefs. New York, Fortuny's [c1941] 218 p. 20 1/2 cm. "First edition." [BT77.Z3] 41-18789
1. Theology, Doctrinal—Popular works. I. Title.

Theology, Doctrinal—Popular works—Addresses, essays, lectures.

THE Christian faith; 230
essays in explanation and defence. Edited by W. R. Matthews. Freeport, N.Y., Books for Libraries Press [1971] 339 p. 23 cm. (Essay index reprint series) Reprint of the 1936 ed. Includes bibliographical references. [BT77.C46 1971] 73-152162 ISBN 0-8369-2348-0
1. Theology, Doctrinal—Popular works—Addresses, essays, lectures. I. Matthews, Walter Robert, 1881- ed.

COFFIN, Henry Sloane, 1877-1954. 230
Some Christian convictions; a practical restatement in terms of present-day thinking. Freeport, N.Y., Books for Libraries Press [1972] ix, 222 p. 23 cm. (Essay index reprint series) Reprint of the 1915 ed. [BT77.C59 1972] 79-167328 ISBN 0-8369-2763-X
1. Theology, Doctrinal—Popular works—Addresses, essays, lectures. I. Title.

PITTENGER, William Norman, 1905- 230
Unbounded love : God and man in process, with study guide / by Norman Pittenger. New York : Seabury Press, c1976. x, 115 p. ; 21 cm. (The First Stephen Fielding Bayne memorial lectures) "A Crossroad book." [BT77.P56] 76-2083 ISBN 0-8164-2119-6 pbk. : 3.95
1. Theology, Doctrinal—Popular works—Addresses, essays, lectures. 2. Process theology—Addresses, essays, lectures. I. Title. II. Series: Stephen Fielding Bayne memorial lectures ; 1st.

Theology, Doctrinal—Popular works—Handbooks, manuals, etc.

EERDMANS' handbook to 230
Christian belief / edited by Robin Keely. 1st American ed. Grand Rapids, Mich. : Eerdman's, 1982. p. cm. Includes index. [BT77.E35 1982] 19 82-7282 ISBN 0-8028-3577-5 : 24.95
1. Theology, Doctrinal—Popular works—Handbooks, manuals, etc. I. Keely, Robin.

Theology, Doctrinal—Popular works—Juvenile literature.

SCHOOLLAND, Marian M., 1902- 230
Leading little ones to God : a child's book of Bible teachings / Marian M. Schoolland ; illustrations by Paul Stoub. Rev. ed. Grand Rapids, Mich. : W.B. Eerdmans Pub. Co., 1981, c1962. x, 173 p. : col. ill. ; 26 cm. [BT77.S375 1981] 19 81-186464 ISBN 0-8028-4029-9 : 12.95
1. Theology, Doctrinal—Popular works—Juvenile literature. 2. Children—Prayer-books and devotions—English. I. Title.

SPEERSTRA, Karen. 230
I believe : a child's guide to understanding basic Christian beliefs / written by Karen Speerstra ; illustrated by Erin Leigh. St. Louis, Mo. : Concordia Pub. House, c1980. [23] p. : ill. ; 21 x 26 cm. Explains basic beliefs of Christianity, including God as Creator, The Trinity, the prophets, teachings of Jesus, and the Holy Spirit. [BT77.S69] 79-28846 ISBN 0-570-03493-0 pbk. : 2.50
1. Theology, Doctrinal—Popular works—Juvenile literature. 2. Children—Prayer books and devotions—English. 3. [Theology.] I. Leigh, Erin. II. Title.

Theology, Doctrinal—Southern States—History.

HOLIFIELD, E. Brooks. 277'.5
The gentlemen theologians : American theology in Southern culture, 1795-1860 / E. Brooks Holifield. Durham : Duke University Press, 1978. x, 262 p. ; 25 cm. Includes bibliographical references and indexes. [BR535.H57] 78-59580 ISBN 0-8223-0414-7 : 14.75
1. Theology, Doctrinal—Southern States—History. 2. Religious thought—Southern States. I. Title.

Theology, Doctrinal—Study and teaching.

EMPIE, Paul C. 230'.2
Lutherans and Catholics in dialogue : personal notes for a study / by Paul C. Empie ; edited by Raymond Tiemeyer. Philadelphia : Fortress Press, c1981. x, 150 p. ; 18 cm. [BX8063.7.C3E47] 19 80-69754 ISBN 0-8006-1449-6 : 3.95
1. Lutheran Church—Relations—Catholic Church—Study and teaching. 2. Catholic Church—Relations—Lutheran Church—Study and teaching. 3. Theology, Doctrinal—Study and teaching. I. Tiemeyer, Raymond. II. Title.

Theology, Doctrinal—United States—History—20th century.

FACKRE, Gabriel J. 230'.044
The Religious Right and Christian faith / by Gabriel Fackre. Grand Rapids, Mich. : Eerdmans, c1982. xiii, 126 p. : ill. ; 22 cm. Includes bibliographical references and index. [BT30.U6F33 1982] 19 82-2488 ISBN 0-8028-3566-X : 8.95
1. Falwell, Jerry. 2. Moral Majority, Inc. 3. Theology, Doctrinal—United States—History—20th century. 4. Fundamentalism—History—20th century. 5. Christianity and politics—History—20th century. I. Title.

FERM, Deane William, 1927- 230'.0973
Contemporary American theologies : a critical survey / Deane William Ferm. New York : Seabury Press, 1981. p. cm. Includes index. Bibliography: p. [BT30.U6F4] 19 81-5678 ISBN 0-8164-2341-5 pbk. : 8.95
1. Theology, Doctrinal—United States—History—20th century. I. Title.

Theology — Early church.

AUGUSTINUS, Aurelius, Saint, Pp. of Hippo. 242
Confessions and Enchiridion, newly translated and edited by Albert C. Outler. Philadelphia, Westminster Press [1955] 423p. 24cm. (The Library of Christian classics, v. 7) Bibliography: p.413-416. [BR65.A6E5 1955] 55-5021
1. Theology—Early church. I. Augustinus, Aurelius. Saint, Bp. of Hippo. II. Outler, Albert Cook, 1908- ed. and tr. III. Title. IV. Series: The Library of Christian classics (Philadelphia) v. 7

AUGUSTINUS, Aurelius, Saint, bp. of Hippo. 230.11
Faith, hope and charity, tr. and annotated by Louis A. Arand. Westminster, Md., Newman Bookshop, 1947. [4] l., 3-165 p. 23 cm. (Ancient Christian writers; the works of the Fathers in translation, no. 3) Translation of Enchiridion de fide, spe et caritate. Bibliographical references included in "Notes" (p. [113]-147) [BR65.A7E5 1947] 47-5546
1. Theology—Early church. I. Arand, Louis A., 1892- ed. and tr. II. Title. III. Series.

AUGUSTINUS, Aurelius, Saint, Bp. of Hippo.
Of true religion. Introd. by Louis O. Mink, translated by J. H. S. Burleigh. Chicago, H. Regnery [c1959] xix, 107 p. 17 cm. (Gateway edition, 6042) NUC63
1. Theology — Early church. I. Title.

Theology—Early church, ca. 30-600—Addresses, essays, lectures.

CURRENT issues in 220.6'6
Biblical and patristic interpretation; studies in honor of Merrill C. Tenney presented by his former students. Edited by Gerald F. Hawthorne. Grand Rapids, Eerdmans [1975] 377 p. port. 25 cm. "Select bibliography of the writings of Merrill C. Tenney": p. 19-20. [BS413.C8] 74-19326 ISBN 0-8028-3442-6 9.95
1. Tenney, Merrill C. 2. Bible—Addresses, essays, lectures. 3. Theology—Early church, ca. 30-600—Addresses, essays, lectures. I. Tenney, Merrill Chapin, 1904- II. Hawthorne, Gerald F., 1925- ed.

Theology, Eastern church.

LOSSKY, Vladimir, 1903-1958. 230'.1'09
Orthodox theology : an introdution / Vladimir Lossky ; translated by Ian and Ihita Kesarcodi-Watson. Crestwood, NY : St. Vladimir's Seminary Press, 1978. 137 p. ; 22 cm. Chapters 1-4 were originally published in Messager de l'Exarchat du patriarche russe en Europe occidentale, 1964-1965, as a series of related pieces under title: Theologie dogmatique. Contents.Contents.—Faith and theology.—The two monotheisms.—The creation.—Original sin.—Christological dogma.—Image and likeness. Includes bibliographical references. [BX320.2.L6713] 78-1853 ISBN 0-913836-43-5 pbk. : 4.50
1. Theology, Eastern church. 2. Theology, Doctrinal. I. Title.

MEYENDORFF, Jean, 1926- 230'.1'9
Byzantine theology : historical trends and doctrinal themes / John Meyendorff. 1st ed. New York : Fordham University Press, 1974. 243 p. ; 22 cm. Includes index. Bibliography: p. [229]-237. [BX320.2.M47] 72-94167 ISBN 0-8232-0965-2 : 20.00
1. Theology, Eastern Church. I. Title.

MEYENDORFF, Jean, 1926- 232
Christ in Eastern Christian thought [by] John Meyendorff. Washington, Corpus Books [1969] ix, 218 p. 21 cm. Translation of Le Christ dans la theologie byzantine. Includes bibliographical references. [BT198.M4313] 78-76472
1. Jesus Christ—History of doctrines. 2. Theology, Eastern Church. I. Title.

MEYENDORFF, Jean, 1926- 232
Christ in Eastern Christian thought / John Meyendorff. [2d ed.] Crestwood, N.Y. : St. Vladimir's Seminary Press, 1975. p. cm. Translation of Le Christ dans la theologie byzantine. Includes bibliographical references and index. [BT198.M4313 1975] 75-31979 ISBN 0-913836-27-3 : 5.95
1. Jesus Christ—History of doctrines. 2. Theology, Eastern Church. I. Title.

OUSPENSKY, Leonide. 230'.1'9
Theology of the icon / Leonid Ouspensky. Crestwood, N.Y. : St. Vladimir's Seminary Press, 1978. 232 p., [12] leaves of plates : ill. ; 22 cm. Stamped on t.p.: Translated by Elizabeth Meyendorff. Translation of Essai sur la theologie de l'icone dans l'Eglise orthodoxe. Bibliography: p. 231-232. [BX323.O8513] 77-11882 ISBN 0-913836-42-7 pbk. : 7.95
1. Theology, Eastern church. 2. Icons—Cult. 3. Orthodox Eastern Church and art. I. Title.

Theology, Eastern church—Addresses, essays, lectures.

ALLCHIN, A. M. 230
The kingdom of love and knowledge : the encounter between Orthodoxy and the West / A.M. Allchin. New York : Seabury Press, 1982, c1979. 214 p. ; 22 cm. Includes bibliographical references and index. [BX325.A44 1982] 19 81-8995 ISBN 0-8164-2354-7 : 14.95
1. Church of England—Addresses, essays, lectures. 2. Theology, Eastern church—Addresses, essays, lectures. 3. Theology, Anglican—Addresses, essays, lectures. 4. Theology—20th century—Addresses, essays, lectures. I. Title.

MEYENDORFF, Jean, 1926- 230'.1'9
Living tradition : orthodox witness in the contemporary world / John Meyendorff. Crestwood, N.Y. : St. Vladimir's Seminary Press, 1978. 202 p. ; 22 cm. Includes bibliographical references. [BX320.2.M475] 78-2031 ISBN 0-913836-48-6 pbbk. : 5.95
1. Theology, Eastern church—Addresses, essays, lectures. I. Title.

ORTHODOX synthesis : 230'.19
the unity of theological thought : an anthology published in commemoration of the fifteenth anniversary of Metropolitan Philip as Primate of the Antiochian Orthodox Christian Archdiocese of North America / Joseph J. Allen, editor. Crestwood, N.Y. : St. Vladimir's Seminary Press, 1981. p. cm. Includes bibliographical references. [BX320.2.O76] 19 81-5674 ISBN 0-913836-84-2 pbk. : 8.95
1. Philip, Metropolitan. 2. Theology, Eastern church—Addresses, essays, lectures. I. Allen, Joseph J. II. Philip, Metropolitan.
Publisher' address 575 Scrasdale Rd., Crestwood, NY 10707. Publisher's address: 575 Scarsdale Rd., Crestwood, NY 10707

ORTHODOX theology and 281.9
diakonia : essays in honor of His Eminence Archbishop Iakovos on the occasion of his seventieth birthday / edited by Demetrios J. Constantelos. Brookline, Mass. : Hellenic College Press, 1981. p. cm. Includes index. [BX320.2.O77] 19 81-6811 ISBN 0-916586-79-0 : Write for information. ISBN 0-916586-80-4 pbk. : Write for information.
1. Orthodox Eastern Church—History—Addresses, essays, lectures. 2. Orthodox Eastern Church—Relations—Addresses,essays, lectures. 3. Iakovos, Archbishop of the Greek Orthodox Archdiocese of North and South America—Addresses, essays, lectures. 4. Theology, Eastern Church—Addresses,essays, lectures. I. Iakovos, Archbishop of the Greek Orthodox Archdiocese of North and South America. II. Constantelos, Demetrios J.

VERHOVSKOY, Serge S., 1907- 281.9
The light of the World : Essays on Orthodox Christianity / Serge S. Verhovskoy ; [editor Theodore Bazil]. Crestwood, N.Y. : St. Vladimir's Seminary Press, c1982. p. cm. "The first three articles: 'Orthodoxy,' 'Christ,' 'Christianity' are translated from Russian." Includes bibliographical references. [BX325.V47 1982] 19 82-16963 ISBN 0-88141-004-7 pbk. : 6.95
1. Orthodox Eastern Church—Addresses, essays, lectures. 2. Theology, Eastern church—Addresses, essays, lectures. I. Title.

Theology, Eastern church—History.

MALONEY, George A., 1924- 230'.1'909
A history of Orthodox theology since 1453 / by George A. Maloney. Belmont, Mass. : Nordland Pub. Co., 1977 388 p. ; 23 cm. Includes bibliographical references and index. [BX320.2.M34] 75-27491 ISBN 0-913124-12-5 : 22.50
1. Theology, Eastern church—History. I. Title.

Theology for the laity—Addresses, essays, lectures.

KNOX, Ronald Arbuthnott, 1888-1857.
In soft garments, a collection of Oxford conferences. New York, Sheed and Ward, 1958. ix, 214 p. 21 cm. Lectures delivered during the years 1926 to 1938 when the author was chaplain at Oxford. 65-5115
1. Theology for the laity—Addresses, essays, lectures. I. Title.

NOYES, George Rapall, 1798-1868, ed. 204
A collection of theological essays from various authors. With an introduction by George R. Noyes... 7th ed. Boston, American Unitarian association, 1880. xlvi p., 1 l., 512 p. 19 1/2 cm. [BR50.N65 1880] 26-21523
I. Title.

Theology-History

ALLEN, Alexander Viets Griswold, 1841-1908. 230
The continuity of Christian thought: a study of modern theology in the light of its history, by Alexander V. G. Allen ... [14th impression] Boston and New York. Houghton, Mifflin and company, 1900. xxviii, 445 p. 20 1/2 cm. [Bohlen lectures, 1883] [BT21.A4 1900] 4-10392
1. Theology-Hist. I. Title.

CHURCH at work in the world 266.2
(The); selections for a readings course on the theology history and methods of the mission apostolate, contributed by Ronan Hoffman [others]. ed. by Edward A. Freking [others] Cincinnati, 5100 Shattue Ave. Catholic Students' Mission Crusade, [c.1961] 141p. (CSMC five-hour ser.) 1.00 pap.,

GREAVES, Richard L. 230'.52
Theology and revolution in the Scottish reformation : studies in the thought of John Knox / by Richard L. Greaves. Grand Rapids, Mich. : Christian University Press, c1980. xi, 280 p. ; 21 cm. Includes index. Bibliography: p. 262-274. [BX9223.G73] 80-15338 ISBN 0-8028-1847-1 pbk. : 9.95
I. Knox, John, 1505-1572. II. Title.

O'CALLAGHAN, Michael C. 230'.2
Unity in theology : Lonergan's framework for theology in its new context / Michael C. O'Callaghan ; foreword by Bernard Lonergan. Lanham, Md. : University Press of America, 1980. p. cm. Originally presented as the author's thesis, Tubingen. Includes index. Bibliography: p. [BX4705.L7133O27 1980] 19 80-8177 ISBN 0-8191-1151-1 lib. bdg. : 24.50 ISBN 0-8191-1152-X (pbk.) : 16.75
1. Lonergan, Bernard J. F. 2. Theology—History. 3. Theology—Methodology. I. Title.

SLATER, Thomas, 1855-
A short history of moral theology, by Rev. Thomas Slater... New York, Cincinnati [etc.] Benziger brothers, 1909. 53 p. 22 1/2 cm. Bibliography: p. 51-53. 9-26330 0.50
I. Title.

WERNER, Karl, 1821-1888 282.09
Geschichte der katholischen theologie. Seit dem Trienter konzil bis zur gegenwart. Von dr. Karl Werner ... 2. Aufl. Munchen und Leipzig, R. Oldenbourg 1889; New York, Johnson Reprint. 1966 2p. 1., viii, 656p. 22cm. (Added t.-p.: Geschichte der wissenschaften in Deutschland. Neuere zeit. 6. bd.) [BX1747.W4] 25.00
1. Theology—Hist. 2. Catholic church—Hist. I. Title.

Theology—History—17th century

REX, Walter 230.0924
Essays on Pierre Bayle and religious controversy. The Hague, M. Nijhoff [New York, Humanities, c.1965] xv,271p. port. 24cm. (Intl. archives of the hist. of ideas, 8) Bibl. [BX9419.B3R4] 66-1628 9.50
1. Bayle, Pierre, 1647-1706. 2. Theology—Hist.—17th cent. I. Title. II. Title: Title. (Series: Archives internationales d'histoire des idees, 8)

Theology, Internal—Popular works.

HALSEY, Leroy Jones, 1812-1896. 230
Living Christianity; or, Old Truths restated. By the Rev. Leroy J. Halsey ... Philadlphia, Presbyterian board of publication [c 88] 310 p. 19 cm. [BT77.H25] 39-7020
1. Theology, Internal—Popular works. 2. Presbyterian church—Doctrinal and controversal works. I. Presbyterian church in the U.S.A. Board of publication. II. Title.

Theology—Juvenile literature.

BECK, Hubert F. 230
What should I believe? : Sorting out today's bewildering Christian beliefs / Hubert F. Beck. St. Louis : Concordia Pub. House, c1980. 112 p. ; 23 cm. Discusses current forms of religious expression, many of which have been repeatedly propagated and rejected since the time of Christ. [BR125.5.B42] 80-16439 ISBN 0-570-03800-6 pbk. : 4.95
1. Theology—Juvenile literature. 2. [Theology.] I. Title.

NAVE, Orville James, 1841-
Theology for young people ... for instruction in religious doctrines and history, by Orville J. Nave ... Los Angeles, Cal., College association publishing company [c1910] 201 p. illus. 24 cm. (Home school series) 10-5252 1.25
I. Title.

Theology. Lutheran.

ANDERSON, Charles S. 230'.4'1
Faith and freedom : the Christian faith according to the Lutheran Confessions / Charles S. Anderson. Minneapolis : Augsburg Pub. House, c1977. 160 p. ; 20 cm. Bibliography: p. 158-160. [BX8068.A1A5] 76-27087 ISBN 0-8066-1558-3 pbk. : 3.95
1. Lutheran Church—Catechisms and creeds. 2. Theology, Lutheran. 3. Justification. I. Title.

GRITSCH, Eric W. 230'.4'1
Lutheranism : the theological movement and its confessional writings / Eric W. Gritsch and Robert W. Jenson. Philadelphia : Fortress Press, c1976. x, 214 p. ; 24 cm. Includes index. [BX8065.2.G74] 76-7869 ISBN 0-8006-0458-X : 7.50
1. Theology, Lutheran. I. Jenson, Robert W., joint author. II. Title.

LUTHER College, Decorah, Iowa Dept. Of Religion
Theological perspectives; a discussion of contemporary issues in Lutheran theology. Decorah, Iowa, Luther College Press [1963?] vi, 86 p. 23 cm. "Originally delivered as public lectures in the fall of 1962." 66-226
I. Title.

MONTGOMERY, John Warwick. 230'.4'1
Crisis in Lutheran theology; the validity and relevance of historic Lutheranism vs.

its contemporary rivals. With a pref. by J. A. O. Preus. Grand Rapids, Baker Book House [1967] 2 v. 22 cm. Bibliography: v. 2, p. 166-168. Bibliographical footnotes. [BX8065.2.M6] 67-6517
1. Theology, Lutheran. 2. Theology, Doctrinal—Hist.—20th cent. I. Title.

MONTGOMERY, John Warwick. 230'.4'1
Crisis in Lutheran theology; the validity and relevance of historic Lutheranism vs. its contemporary rivals. With a pref. by J. A. O. Preus. [2d ed., rev., with additional material] Minneapolis, Bethany Fellowship [1973] 2 v. 22 cm. Contents.Contents.—v. 1. Essays.—v. 2. An anthology. Bibliography: v. 2, p. 166-168. [BX8065.2.M6 1973] 73-161393 ISBN 0-87123-073-9 1.95 (v.1), (pbk); 2.95 (v.2) (pbk)
1. Theology, Lutheran. 2. Theology, Doctrinal—History—20th century. I. Title.

MONTGOMERY, John Warwick. 230'.4'1
Crisis in Lutheran theology; the validity and relevance of historic Lutheranism vs. its contemporary rivals. With a pref. by J. A. O. Preus. Grand Rapids, Baker Book House [1967] 2 v. 22 cm. Bibliography: v. 2, p. 166-168. Bibliographical footnotes. [BX8065.2.M6] 67-6517
1. Theology, Lutheran. 2. Theology, Doctrinal—History—20th century. I. Title.

THEOLOGICAL perspectives; a discussion of contemporary issues in Lutheran theology. Decorah, Iowa, Luther College Press [1963?] vi, 86 p. 23 cm. "Originally delivered as public lectures in the fall of 1962." 66-226

Theology, Lutheran—Addresses, essays, lectures.

THE Lutheran Church, past and present / edited by Vilmos Vajta. Minneapolis : Augsburg Pub. House, c1977. vii, 392 p. ; 22 cm. Translation of Die Evangelisch-Lutherische Kirche, Vergangenheit und Gegenwart. Bibliography: p. 371-380. [BX8018.L7613] 76-46120 ISBN 0-8066-1573-7 : 9.50 284'.1'09
1. Lutheran Church—History—Addresses, essays, lectures. 2. Theology, Lutheran—Addresses, essays, lectures. I. Vajta, Vilmos.

STUDIES in Lutheran hermeneutics / edited by John Reumann in collaboration with Samuel H. Nafzger and Harold H. Ditmanson. Philadelphia : Fortress Press, c1979. x, 370 p. ; 24 cm. Includes bibliographical references. [BS476.S84] 78-14673 ISBN 0-8006-0534-9 : 14.95 220.6'3
1. Bible—Hermeneutics—Addresses, essays, lectures. 2. Theology, Lutheran—Addresses, essays, lectures. I. Reumann, John Henry Paul. II. Nafzger, Samuel H. III. Ditmanson, Harold H.

Theology, Lutheran—Germany—Bibliography—Catalogs.

CENTER for Reformation Research. 016.2304'1
Gnesio-Lutherans, Philippists, and Formulators : a finding list of CRR holdings. Saint Louis, Mo. : Center for Reformation Research, 1977. iv, 78 p. ; 22 cm. (Sixteenth century bibliography ; 8) [Z7845.L9C45 1977] [BX8065.2] 77-369200
1. Center for Reformation Research—Bibliography. 2. Theology, Lutheran—Germany—Bibliography—Catalogs. 3. Reformation—Bibliography—Catalogs. I. Title. II. Series.

Theology, Lutheran—History.

PREUS, Robert D., 1924- 230'.4'1
The theology of post-Reformation Lutheranism [by] Robert D. Preus. Saint Louis, Concordia Pub. House [1970-72] 2 v. 24 cm. Contents.Contents.—[1] A study of theological prolegomena.—v. 2. God and His creation. Bibliography: v. 1, p. 421-435; v. 2, p. [259]-264. [BX8065.2.P7 1970] 70-121877 ISBN 0-570-03226-1 (v. 2)
1. Theology, Lutheran—History. I. Title.

Theology, Lutheran—History.—Addresses, essays, lectures.

TWO kingdoms and one world / edited by Karl H. Hertz. Minneapolis : Augsburg Pub. House, c1976. 379 p. ; 22 cm. Bibliography: p. 375-377. [BX8066.A1T85] 76-3852 ISBN 0-8066-1538-9 : 9.50 261
1. Theology, Lutheran—History.—Addresses, essays, lectures. 2. Christianity and politics—History—Addresses, essays, lectures. 3. Church and the world—History—Addresses, essays, lectures. 4. Social ethics—Addresses, essays, lectures. I. Hertz, Karl H.

Theology, Lutheran—United States—Collections.

TAPPERT, Theodore Gerhardt, 1904- comp. 230'.4'173
Lutheran confessional theology in America, 1840-1880. Edited by Theodore G. Tappert. New York, Oxford University Press, 1972. viii, 364 p. 24 cm. (A Library of Protestant thought) Contents.Contents.—Krauth, C. P. The conservative Reformation and its confessions.—Walther, C. F. W. The kind of confessional subscription required.—Fritschel, S. The doctrinal agreement essential to church unity.—Krauth, C. P. The right relation to denominations in America.—Fritschel, G. Concerning objective and subjective justification.—Walther, C. F. W. God's grace alone the cause of man's election. Election is not in conflict with justification.—Loy, M. Is God's election arbitrary or in view of faith?—Krauth, C. P. Issues in the controversy over predestination.—Walther, C. F. W. Theses on the church and ministry. The proper form of a local congregation.—Krauth, C. P. Fundamental principles of faith and church polity.—Loy, M. The significance of ordination to the ministry.—Walther, C. F. W. The laity in the government of the congregation.—Loy, M. Restoration of the cultus in the Lutheran Church.—Fritschel, S. A proper understanding of freedom in worship.—An order of service for Sundays and festivals.—Selected bibliography (p. 353-358) [BX8065.T33] 72-81463 10.75
1. Theology, Lutheran—United States—Collections. 2. Theology—19th century—Collections. I. Title. II. Series.

Theology—Manuscripts—Catalogs.

STRATFORD, Jenny. 016.282
Catalogue of the Jackson Collection of manuscript fragments in the Royal Library Windsor Castle : with a memoir of Canon J.E. Jackson and a list of his works / by Jenny Stratford. London ; New York : Academic Press, 1982. xiii, 106 p., 10 p. of plates : ill. ; 24 cm. Includes bibliographical references and index. [Z6611.T3S77 1981] [BX1970] 19 81-66309 ISBN 0-12-672980-8 : 19.50
1. Catholic Church—Liturgy—Manuscripts—Catalogs. 2. Jackson, John Edward, 1805-1891—Library—Catalogs. 3. Jackson, John Edward, 1805-1891—Bibliography. 4. Windsor Castle. Royal Library—Catalogs. 5. Theology—Manuscripts—Catalogs. I. Windsor Castle. Royal Library. II. Title.

Theology, Methodist.

STOKES, Mack B. 230'.7
The Bible in the Wesleyan heritage / Mack B. Stokes. Nashville, TN : Abingdon, 1981, c1979. 95 p. ; 20 cm. [BS500.S83 1981] 19 80-23636 ISBN 0-687-03100-1 pbk. : 3.95
1. Wesley, John, 1703-1791. 2. Bible—Criticism, interpretation, etc.—History. 3. Theology, Methodist. I. Title.

WHITE, Hamilton, 1834-
"The new theology," by a Methodist layman, by Hamilton White... New York, Baltimore [etc.] Broadway publishing co., 1910. 206 p. front. 20 cm. $1.25 11-568
I. Title.

Theology-Methodology.

BAILEY, Charles James Nice. 230
Ground work for comparative metatheology; a roadmap for ecumenical analytics. Ann Arbor, University Microfilms, 1965. xi, 435 p. (on double leaves) illus. 22 cm. Supplement. [Ann Arbor, University Microfilms, 1965] S-40 p. (on double leaves) 22 cm. Bibliographical references includes in "Notes" (p. S-81--S-88) BT78.B25 Suppl. Bibliographical references included in "Notes" (p. [861]-432]) [BT78.B25] 65-2555
1. Theology—Methodology. I. Title. II. Title: Methatheology.

BOX, Hubert Stanley, 1904- ed. 201.8
The priest as student, by various writers, edited by Hubert S. Box ... London, Society for promoting Christian knowledge; New York, The Macmillan company [c1939] vii, 380 p. 22 cm. "First published, 1939." Bibliography at end of some of the chapters. [BR118. B6 1939] 40-11396
1. Theology—Methodology. I. Society for promoting Christian knowledge, London. II. Title.
Contents omitted.

CARNES, John Robb, 1924- 230
Axiomatics and dogmatics / John R. Carnes. New York : Oxford University Press, 1982. p. cm. (Theology and scientific culture ; 4) Includes indexes. Bibliography: p. [BR118.C23 1982] 19 82-12537 ISBN 0-19-520377-1 : 13.95
1. Theology—Methodology. 2. Axioms. 3. Knowledge, Theory of (Religion) 4. Christianity and language. 5. Theology, Doctrinal. I. Title. II. Series.

CASSIDORUS, Flavius Magnus Aurelius Senator ca.487-ca.580 878.02
An introduction to divine and human readings. Tr., introd., notes by Leslie Webber Jones. New York, Octagon, 1966 [c.1946] xvii, 233p. illus. 24cm. (Records of civilization: sources and studies, no. 40) Bibl. [PA6271.C4152] 66-16002 8.00
1. Theology—Methodology. 2. Classification of sciences. I. Jones, Leslie Webber, 1900- ed. and tr. II. Title.

CASSIN-SCOTT, Jack. 271.069
Cassiodori Senatoris Institutiones, ed. from the manuscripts by R.A.B. Mynors. [New York] Oxford Univ. Press [1961] 193p. 3.40
1. Theology—Methodology. 2. Classification of sciences. I. Mynors, Roger Aubrey Baskerville, ed. II. Title.

CASSIODORUS Senator, Flavius Magnus Aurelius
Cassiodori Senatoris Institutiones, edited from the manuscripts by R. A. B. Mynors. 1 vi, 193, [1] p. diagrs. 20 cm. 68-100433
1. Theology-Methodology. 2. Classification of sciences. I. Mynors, Roger Aubrey Baskerville, ed. II. Title. III. Title: Oxford,

CLARK, Gordon Haddon 230
Karl Barth's theological method. Philadelphia. Presbyterian & Reformed, 1963. 229p. 24cm. Bibl. 63-12648 apply
1. Barth, Karl, 1886- 2. Theology—Methodology. I. Title.

EBELING, Gerhard, 1912- 230
Theology and proclamation; dialogue with Bultmann. Tr. byJohn Riches. Philadelphia, Fortress [1966] 186p. 21cm. Bibl. [BX4827.B78E213] 66-7851 3.95 bds.,
1. Bultmann, Rudolf Karl, 1884- 2. Theology—Methodology. I. Title.

ECKARDT, Arthur Roy, 1918- comp. 230'.08
The theologian at work; a common search for understanding, edited by A. Roy Eckardt. [1st ed.] New York, Harper & Row [1968] xxx, 253 p. 21 cm. (Harper forum books) [BR118.E25] 68-11745
1. Theology—Methodology. I. Title.

ELLICOTT, Charles John, bp. of Gloucester, 1819-1905. 208
Foundations of sacred study. Five addresses by C.J. Ellicott... Published under the direction of the Tract committee. London [etc.] Society for promoting Christian knowledge; New York, E. & J.B. Young & co., 1893. 188 p. 17 1/2 cm. [BR118.E65] 42-27238
1. Theology—Methodology. I. Society for promoting Christian knowledge, London. Tract committee. II. Title.

FARLEY, Edward, 1929- 230'.01'8
Ecclesial reflection : an anatomy of theological method / Edward Farley. Philadelphia : Fortress Press, c1982. xix, 380 p. ; 24 cm. Includes bibliographical references and index. [BR118.F35] 19 81-43088 ISBN 0-8006-0670-1 : 29.95
1. Theology—Methodology. I. Title.

FLEMING, Bruce C. E., 1950- 230'.044
Contextualization of theology / Bruce C. E. Fleming. Pasadena, CA : William Carey Library, 1980. p. cm. Includes indexes. Bibliography: p. [BR118.F6] 80-174 ISBN 0-87808-431-2 : 8.95
1. Theology—Methodology. 2. Missions—Theory. I. Title.

HAGENBACH, Karl Rudolf, 1801-1874. 208
Theological encyclopaedia and methodology. On the basis of Hagenbach. By George R. Crooks, D.D., and John F. Hurst, D.D. New ed., rev. New York, Hunt & Eaton; Cincinnati, Cranston & Curts, 1894. 3 p. l., [3]-627 p. 23 1/2 cm. (Added t.-p.: Library of Biblical and theological literature, ed. by George R. Crooks...and John F. Hurst...vol. iii) [BR118.H22 1894] 30-12093
1. Theology—Methodology. 2. Theology—Bibl. I. Crooks, George Richard, 1822-1897, ed. and tr. II. Hurst, John Fletcher, bp., 1834-1903, joint ed. and tr. III. Title.

HAGENBACH, Karl Rudolf, 1801-1874. 208
Theological encyclopaedia and methodology. On the basis of Hagenbach. By George R. Crooks, D.D., and John F. Hurst, D.D New ed., revised. New York, Hunt & Eaton; Cincinnati, Cranston & Curtis [1895?] 4 p. l., [3]-627 p. 24 cm. (Added t.-p.: Library of Biblical and theological literature, ed. by George R. Crooks...and John F. Hurst...vol. III) [BR118.H22 1895] 30-12934
1. Theology—Methodology. 2. Theology—Bibl. I. Crooks, George Richard, 1822-1897, ed. and tr. II. Hurst, John Fletcher, bp., 1834-1903, joint ed. and tr. III. Title.

HAGENBACH, Karl Rudolf, 1801-1874. 208
Theological encylopaedia and methodology. On the basis of Hagenbach. By George R. Crooks, D.D., and John F. Hurst, D.D. New York, Phillips & Hunt; Cincinnati, Walden & Stowe, 1884. iv p., 2 l., [3]-596 p. 23 1/2 cm. (Added t.-p.: Library of Biblical and theological literature, ed. by George R. Crooks...and John F. Hurst...vol. III) Bibliographies interspersed. [BR118.H32 1884] 33-12087
1. Theology—Methodology. 2. Theology—Bibl. I. Crooks, George Richard, 1822-1897, ed. and tr. II. Hurst, John Fletcher, bp., 1834-1903, joint ed. and tr. III. Title.

HALL, Charles A. M. 230.01
The common quest, theology and the search for truth. Philadelphia, Westminster [1965, c.1961] 332p. 24cm. [BR118.H35] 65-19780 8.50
1. Theology—Methodology. I. Title.

HARTT, Julian Norris. 200'.1'8
Theological method and imagination / Julian N. Hartt. New York : Seabury Press, c1977. p. cm. "A Crossroad book." [BR118.H37] 76-49901 ISBN 0-8164-0335-X : 12.95
1. Theology—Methodology. I. Title.

HEFNER, Philip J 230.0924
Faith and the vitalities of history: a theological study based on the work of Albrecht Ritschl [by] Philip Hefner. [1st ed.] New York, Harper & Row [1966] xi, 192 p. port. 22 cm. (Makers of modern theology) Bibliography: p. 187-190. [BX4827.R5H4] 66-15038
1. Ritschl, Albrecht Benjamin, 1822-1889. 2. Theology — Methodology. 3. History (Theology) 4. Theology — 20th cent. I. Title.

HOLMES, Urban Tigner, 1930- 230
To speak of God; theology for beginners [by] Urban T. Holmes, III. New York, Seabury Press [1974] xix, 153 p. 22 cm. "A Crossroad book." [BR118.H64] 74-8917 ISBN 0-8164-1169-7 6.95
1. Theology—Methodology. I. Title.

JENNINGS, Theodore W. 201'.1
Introduction to theology : an invitation to reflection upon the Christian mythos / Theodore W. Jennings, Jr. Philadelphia : Fortress Press, c1976. viii, 184 p. ; 22 cm. Includes bibliographical references and index. [BR118.J44] 76-7867 ISBN 0-8006-1234-5 : 5.95
1. Theology—Methodology. I. Title.

JOHNSON, William Alexander 201
On religion: a study of theological method in Schleiermacher and Nygren. Leiden, E. J. Brill [New York, Humanities, 1966, c.1964] x, 167p. 25cm. Bibl. [BR118.J6] 65-4258 5.00
1. Schleiermacher, Friedrich Ernst Daniel, 1768-1834. 2. Nygren, Anders, Bp., 1890- 3. Theology — Methodology. I. Title.

JOURNET, Charles. 201.8
The wisdom of faith, an introduction to theology; translated by R. F. Smith. Westminster, Md., Newman Press, 1952. 225 p. 23 cm. Translation of Introduction a la theologie. [BR118.J67] 52-7508
1. Theology—Methodology. 2. Catholic Church—Doctrinal and controversial works. I. Title.

KAUFMAN, Gordon D. 230
An essay on theological method / by Gordon D. Kaufman. Missoula, Mont. : Published by Scholars Press for the American Academy of Religion, c1975. p. cm. (AAR studies in religion ; no. 11) Includes bibliographical references. [BR118.K38] 75-31656 ISBN 0-89130-046-5 : 4.20
1. Theology—Methodology. I. Title. II. Series: American Academy of Religion. AAR studies in religion ; no. 11.

KAUFMAN, Gordon D. 230
An essay on theological method / by Gordon D. Kaufman. Missoula, Mont. : Published by Scholars Press for the American Academy of Religion, c1975. xiii, 72 p. ; 24 cm. (AAR studies in religion ; no. 11) Includes bibliographical references. [BR118.K38] 75-31656 ISBN 0-89130-046-5 : 4.20
1. Theology—Methodology. I. Title. II. Series: American Academy of Religion. AAR studies in religion ; no. 11.

KUYPER, Abraham, 1837-1920. 208
Encyclopedia of sacred theology; its principles; by Abraham Kuyper ... tr. from the Dutch by Rev. J. Hendrik De Vries; with an introduction by Professor Benjamin B. Warfield ... New York, C. Scribner's sons, 1898. xxv, 683 p. 23 cm. [BR118.K83] 98-371
1. Theology—Methodology. I. Title.

LONERGAN, Bernard J. F. 230'.2'018
Method in theology, [by] Bernard J. F. Lonergan. London, Darton, Longman and Todd, 1972. xii, 405 p. 23 cm. Includes bibliographical references. [BR118.L65 1972b] 72-195722 ISBN 0-232-51139-X
1. Theology—Methodology. I. Title.
Available from Herder & Herder, 10.00, ISBN 0-07-073198-5.

LONERGAN, Bernard J. F. 200'.1'8
Method in theology [by] Bernard J. F. Lonergan. [New York] Herder and Herder [1972] xii, 405 p. 22 cm. Includes bibliographical references. [BR118.L65] 78-181008 10.00
1. Theology—Methodology. I. Title.

MCCLENDON, James William. 209'.2'2 B
Biography as theology; how life stories can remake today's theology [by] James Wm. McClendon, Jr. Nashville, Abingdon Press [1974] 224 p. 22 cm. Includes bibliographical references. [BR118.M28] 74-9715 ISBN 0-687-03540-6 13.95; 4.95 (pbk.).
1. Theology—Methodology. 2. Christian biography. 3. Christian ethics. I. Title.

METHODIST Church (United States) Commission on Ministerial Training. 287
The student's handbook, issued by the General Conference Commission on Ministerial Training ... for the guidance of those taking the undergraduate and accepted supply courses, 1941- Nashville, Methodist Pub. House. v. 20 cm. Subtitle varies slightly. Issue for 1941 pub. under the commission's earlier name: Commission on Courses of Study. [BX8219.A65] 42-10934
1. Theology—Methodology. I. Title.

METHODIST church (United States) Commission on ministerial training. 287
The student's handbook, issued by the General conference commission on courses of study of the Methodist church for the guidance of those taking the undergraduate course ... Nashville, New York [etc.] The Methodist publishing house [1941] 459 p. 19 1/2 cm. Includes bibliographies. [BX8219.A65 1941] 42-10934
1. Theology—Methodology. I. Title.

METHODIST church (United States) Commission on ministerial training. 287
The student's handbook, issued by the Commission on ministerial training of the Methodist church for the guidance of candidates taking the required courses ... Nashville, New York [etc.] The Methodist publishing house [1945] vii, 406 p. diagrs. 19 1/2 cm. "Revised edition." Includes bibliographies. [BX8219.A65 1945] 45-18416
1. Theology—Methodology. I. Title.

METHODIST Episcopal church. General conference commission on courses of study. 287.607
Directions and helps; examination for reception on trial into the annual conference, issued by the General conference commission on courses of study, Methodist Episcopal church, Bishop Edwin H. Hughes, chairman, Bishop Francis J. McConnell, vice-chairman, Prof. Harris Franklin Rall, secretary ... [and others] Allan MacRossie, executive secretary ... New York, Cincinnati [etc.] The Methodist book concern] 1937. 194 p. illus. 19 cm. Includes bibliographies. [BX8219.A4 1937] 37-18647
1. Theology—Methodology. I. Hughes, Edwin Holt, bp., 1866- II. MacRossie, Allan. III. Title.

METHODIST Episcopal church. General conference commission on courses of study. 207
Directions and helps for the first[-fourth] year conference course of study, issued by the General conference commission on courses of study, Methodist Episcopal church, Bishop Edwin H. Hughes, chairman, Bishop Francis J. McConnell, vice-chairman, Prof. Harris Franklin Rall, secretary ... [and others] Allan MacRossie, executive secretary ... New York, Cincinnati [etc.] The Methodist book concern, 1937. 4 v. illus. 16 cm. Includes bibliographies. [BX8219.A5 1937] 37-18646
1. Theology—Methodology. I. Hughes, Edwin Holt, bp., 1866- II. MacRossie, Allan. III. Title.

METHODIST Episcopal church. General conference commission on courses of study. 287.607
Directions and helps for the first ... [-fourth] years local preachers' course of study, issued by the General conference commission on courses of study, Methodist Episcopal church, Bishop Edwin H. Hughes, chairman, Bishop Francis J. McConnell, vice-chairman, Prof. Harris Franklin Rall, secreataty ... [and others] Allan MacRossie, executive secretary ... New York, Cincinnati [etc.] The Methodist book concern [c1933] 2 v. 10 cm. Includes bibliographies. [BX8219.A5 1933] 33-10566
1. Theology—Methodology. I. Hughes, Edwin Holt, bp., 1866- II. MacRossie, Allan. III. Title.

METHODIST Episcopal church. General conference commission on courses of study. 287.607
Directions and helps for the first[-fourth] years local preachers' course of study, issued by the General conference commission on courses of study, Methodist Episcopal church, Bishop Edwin H. Hughes, chairman, Bishop Francis J. McConnell, vice-chairman, Prof. Harris Franklin Rall, secretary ... [and others] Allan MacRossie, executive secretary ... New York, Cincinnati [etc.] The Methodist book concern, 1937. 2 v. 16 cm. Includes bibliographies. [BX821.A54 1937] 37-23520
1. Theology—Methodology. I. Hughes, Edwin Holt, bp., 1866- II. MacRossie, Allan. III. Title.

OMMEN, Thomas B. 230
The hermeneutic of dogma / by Thomas B. Ommen. Missoula, Mont. : Published by Scholars Press for the American Academy of Religion, 1976c1975 xii, 250 p. ; 22 cm. (Dissertation series - American Academy of Religion ; no. 11) Originally presented as the author's thesis, Marquette University, 1973. Bibliography: p. 243-250. [BR118.O49 1975] 75-29493 ISBN 0-89130-039-2 pbk. : 4.50
1. Theology—Methodology. 2. Hermeneutics. 3. Dogma. I. Title. II. Series: American Academy of Religion. Dissertation series — American Academy of Religion ; no. 11.

RAMM, Bernard L., 1916- 230'.044
After fundamentalism : the future of evangelical theology / Bernard Ramm. 1st ed. San Francisco : Harper & Row, c1982. p. cm. Includes index. Bibliography: p. [BR118.R33 1982] 19 82-47792 ISBN 0-06-066789-3 : 14.37
1. Barth, Karl, 1886-1968. 2. Theology—Methodology. 3. Evangelicalism. 4. Enlightenment. 5. Modernist-fundamentalist controversy. I. Title.

RAMSEY, Ian T 230.01
Models and mystery. London, New York, Oxford University Press, 1964. ix, 74 p. 19 cm. (The Whidden lectures, 1963) Bibliographical footnotes. [BR118.R34] 64-2871
1. Theology — Methodology. I. Title. II. Series.

SCHLEIERMACHER, Friedrich Ernst Daniel, 1768-1834. 230.01
Brief outline on the study of theology. Translated, with introductions and notes, by Terrence N. Tice. Richmond, John Knox Press [1966] 132 p. 21 cm. "Bibliographical note": p. 127-128. [BR118.S3513] 66-10301
1. Theology—Methodology. I. Title.

Theology—Methodology—Addresses, essays, lectures.

CROWE, Frederick E. 230'.2
The Lonergan enterprise / Frederick E. Crowe. [Cambridge, Mass.] : Cowley, [c1980] xxi, 121 p. ; 22 cm. "Originally [presented as] the St. Michael's lectures, delivered at Gonzaga University in 1979." Includes bibliographical references and index. [BR118.C75] 19 80-51569 ISBN 0-936384-02-6 (pbk.) : 5.00
1. Lonergan, Bernard J. F.—Addresses, essays, lectures. 2. Theology—Methodology—Addresses, essays, lectures. 3. Theology, Catholic—Addresses, essays, lectures. I. Title.
Publisher's address: 980 Memorial Dr., Cambridge, MA 02138

MELAND, Bernard Eugene, 1899- 201'.8
Fallible forms and symbols : discourses on method in a theology of culture / Bernard E. Meland. Philadelphia : Fortress Press, c1976. xvi, 206 p. ; 24 cm. Includes bibliographical references and index. [BR118.M44] 76-7868 ISBN 0-8006-0453-9 : 11.95
1. Theology—Methodology—Addresses, essays, lectures. I. Title.

WILES, Maurice F. 201'.1
What is theology? / Maurice Wiles. London ; New York : Oxford University Press, 1976. viii, 117 p. ; 21 cm. "Based on lectures ... given ... at King's College, London ... and in the University of Oxford." Includes index. Bibliography: p. [112]-114. [BR118.W58] 77-360493 ISBN 0-19-213525-2 : 5.25 ISBN 0-19-289066-2 pbk. : 2.50
1. Theology—Methodology—Addresses, essays, lectures. I. Title.

Theology—Methodology—History.

CLAYTON, John Powell. 230'.044
The concept of correlation : Paul Tillich and the possibility of a mediating theology / by John Powell Clayton. Berlin ; New York : W. de Gruyter, 1980. p. cm. (Theologische Bibliothek Topelmann ; Bd. 37) Includes index. Bibliography: p. [BX4827.T53C56] 80-11208 ISBN 3-11007-914-3 : 51.25
1. Tillich, Paul, 1886-1965. 2. Theology—Methodology—History. I. Title.

HEFNER, Philip J. 230.0924
J.Ritschl, Albrecht Benjamin 1822-1899
Faith and the vitalities of history; a theological study based on the work of albrecht ritschl. New York, Harper [c.1966] xi, 192 p. port. 22 cm (Makers mod. theol.) bibl. [bx4827.r5h4-] 66-15038 4.50
1. Theology-Methodology. History (Theology. Theology. Theology—20th cent. I. Title.

JOHNSON, Wayne G. 230'.092'2
Theological method in Luther and Tillich : law-gospel and correlation / Wayne G. Johnson. Washington, D.C. : University Press of America, c1981. x, 194 p. ; 23 cm. Bibliography: p. 187-194. [BR333.2.J63] 19 80-5691 ISBN 0-8191-1895-8 : 20.25 ISBN 0-8191-1896-6 (pbk.) : 10.25
1. Luther, Martin, 1483-1546—Theology. 2. Tillich, Paul, 1886-1965. 3. Theology—Methodology—History. I. Title.

Theology—Methodology—History—Addresses, essays, lectures.

CROWE, Frederick E. 230'.072
Method in theology : an organon for our time / by Frederick E. Crowe. Milwaukee, Wis. : Marquette University Press, c1980. 65 p. ; 19 cm. (The 1980 Pere Marquette theology lecture) Includes bibliographical references. [BR118.C76] 19 80-81015 ISBN 0-87462-519-Xx 6.95
1. Lonergan, Bernard J. F.—Addresses, essays, lectures. 2. Theology—Methodology—History—Addresses, essays, lectures. I. Title. II. Series: Pere Marquette theology lectures ; 1980.

Theology—Middle Ages.

MCCRACKEN, George Englert, 1904- ed. 230.082
Early medieval theology. Newly translated and edited by George E. McCracken in collaboration with Allen Cabaniss. Philadelphia, Westminster Press [1957] 430p. 24cm. (The Library of Christian classics, v. 9) Includes bibliographies. [BR50.M18 1957] 57-5015
1. Theology—Middle Ages. I. Title. II. Series.

Theology—Middle Ages, 600-1500.

PREUS, James Samuel. 221.6
From shadow to promise; Old Testament interpretation from Augustine to the young Luther. Cambridge, Mass., Belknap Press of Harvard University Press, 1969. vii, 301 p. 22 cm. A revision of the author's thesis, Harvard Divinity School. Bibliography: p. [285]-293. [BR333.5.B5P7 1969] 69-12732 7.50
1. Luther, Martin, 1483-1546. 2. Bible. O.T.—Criticism, interpretation, etc. 3. Theology—Middle Ages, 600-1500. I. Title.

Theology—Miscellanea.

ACKERMAN, George Everett.
Old thoughts in new dress; or, Today's theology for laymen, by the Rev. Geo. E. Ackerman... Louisville, Ky., Pentecostal publishing company [1915] 154 p. 19 1/2 cm. $0.50. 15-5397
I. Title.

ASKING them questions; 230
new series, edited by Ronald Selby Wright. London, New York, Oxford University Press, 1972- v. 19 cm. Bibliography: v. 1, p. [159]-160. [BR96.A833] 72-190704 ISBN 0-19-213423-X £1.00
1. Theology—Miscellanea. I. Wright, Ronald Selby, 1908- ed.

AUGUSTINE, Saint, Bishop of Hippo. 270 s
Eighty-three different questions / Saint Augustine ; translated by David L.

Mosher. Washington, D.C. : Catholic University of America Press, c1981. p. cm. (The Fathers of the Church ; v. 70) Translation of: De diversis quaestionibus LXXXIII. Includes indexes. Bibliography: p. [BR60.F3A8243] [BR65.A6544] 230'.14 19 81-2546 ISBN 0-8132-0070-9 : 19.50
1. Theology—Miscellanea. 2. Philosophy—Miscellanea. I. [De diversis quaestionibus octoginta tribus.] English II. Title. III. Series.

AUGUSTINE, Saint, Bishop of Hippo. 270 s
Eighty-three different questions / Saint Augustine ; translated by David L. Mosher. Washington, D.C. : Catholic University of America Press, 1982, c1981. p. cm. (The Fathers of the Church ; v. 70) Translation of: De diversis quaestionibus LXXXIII. Includes indexes. Bibliography: p. [BR60.F3A8243] [BR65.A6544] 230'.14 19 81-2546 ISBN 0-8132-0070-9 : 24.95
1. Theology—Miscellanea. 2. Philosophy—Miscellanea. I. [De diversis quaestionibus octoginta tribus.] English II. Title. III. Series.

BECON, Thomas, 1512-1567. 230'.3
The demaundes of the Holy Scripture : London, 1577 / Thomas Becon. Norwood, N.J. : W.J. Johnson ; Amsterdam : Theatrum Orbis Terrarum, 1979. ca. 100 p. ; 16 cm. (The English experience, its record in early printed books published in facsimile ; no. 907) Reprint of the 1577 ed. printed by J. Day, London, with title: The demaundes of Holy Scripture. Reproduction of STC 1718. [BR96.B42 1979] 19 79-84087 ISBN 90-221-0907-0 : 9.00
1. Theology—Miscellanea. I. [Demaundes of Holy Scripture] II. Title. III. Series: English experience, its record in early printed books published in facsimile ; no. 907.

CLEVELAND, Edward Earl. 201'.1
Ask the prophets [by] E. E. Cleveland. [Takoma Park, Washington D.C., Review and Herald Pub. Association, c1970] 192 p. illus. 21 cm. [BR96.C57] 72-113039
1. Theology—Miscellanea. I. Title.

CUMMING, James T., 1938- 230
And, God, what about ...? / By James T. Cumming, Hans Moll ; art by Kathy Counts. St. Louis, Mo. : Concordia Pub. House, c1980. 128 p. : ill. ; 22 cm. Includes index. [BR96.C849] 80-10401 ISBN 0-570-03806-5 pbk. : 3.95
1. Theology—Miscellanea. I. Moll, Hans, 1938- joint author. II. Title.

CUMMING, James T., 1938- 230
Hey, God, what about ...? / James T. Cumming, Hans Moll ; art by Kathy Counts. St. Louis : Concordia Pub. House, c1977. 104 p. : ill. ; 22 cm. Includes index. [BR96.C85] 77-9932 ISBN 0-570-037581-1 pbk. : 2.95
1. Theology—Miscellanea. I. Moll, Hans, 1938- joint author. II. Title.

DAUGHTERS of St. Paul. 201'.1
Religion for people of today. [Boston] St. Paul Editions [1971] 109 p. illus. 18 cm. [BR96.D27] 78-160576 0.95
1. Theology—Miscellanea. I. Title.

DUDKO, Dmitrii. 230'.1'9
Our hope / Dmitrii Dudko ; translated by Paul D. Garrett ; foreword by John Meyendorff. Crestwood, N.Y. : St. Vladimir's Seminary Press, 1977, c1975. 292 p. ; 22 cm. Translation of O nashem upovanii. Includes bibliographical references. [BX512.D8213] 77-1051 ISBN 0-913836-35-4 pbk. : 6.95
1. Orthodox Eastern Church, Russian—Doctrinal and controversial works—Miscellanea. 2. Theology—Miscellanea. I. Title.

FORSTER, Roger T. 230
That's a good question; reasonable answers about living faith [by] Roger T. Forster and V. Paul Marston. Wheaton, Ill., Tyndale House [1974, c1971] 160 p. 18 cm. "First published in Great Britain under the title: Yes, but." Includes bibliographical references. [BR96.F8 1974] 72-96217 ISBN 0-8423-7030-7 1.95 (pbk.)
1. Theology—Miscellanea. I. Marston, V. Paul, joint author. II. Title.

HAMPE, Johann Christoph, 1913- 230
A book of Christian faith : questions and answers for the 20th century / Johann Christoph Hampe. Minneapolis : Augsburg Pub. House, c1980. 242 p. ; 22 cm. Translation of Was wir glauben. [BR96.H31413] 19 80-65549 ISBN 0-8066-1794-2 pbk. : 7.95
1. Theology—Miscellanea. I. Title.

HEYWARD, Isabel Carter. 234
The redemption of God : a theology of mutual relation / Isabel Carter Heyward. Washington, D.C. : University Press of America, c1982. xxvi, 240 p. ; 21 cm. Bibliography: p. 229-240. [BT75.2.H49 1982] 19 81-43706 ISBN 0-8191-2389-7 : 21.75 ISBN 0-8191-2390-0 (pbk.) : 11.00
1. Theology—Miscellanea. I. Title.

LIBBY, Raymond H. 230'.6'73
What! No God? And other brief Bible messages, by Raymond H. Libby. Mountain View, Calif., Pacific Press Pub. Association [1967] 76 p. front. 19 cm. [BX6154.L47] 66-29535
1. Seventh-Day Adventists—Doctrinal and controversial works. 2. Theology—Miscellanea. I. Title.

LONDON. Eclectic Society. 230'.3
The thought of the Evangelical leaders : notes of the discussions of the Eclectic Society, London during the years 1798-1814 / edited by John H. Pratt. Edinburgh ; Carlisle, Penn. : Banner of Truth Trust, 1978. xv, 535 p. ; 23 cm. "Prepared from memoranda made ... by Rev. Josiah Pratt, B.D." First published in 1856 by J. Nesbit under title: Eclectic notes. Includes index. [BR21.L6 1978] 79-308668 ISBN 0-85151-270-4 : 10.95.
1. London. Eclectic Society. 2. Theology—Miscellanea. I. Pratt, Josiah, 1768-1844. II. Pratt, John Henry, d. 1871. III. Title.

MARTI, Fritz, 1894- 200
Unpopular truths / Fritz Marti. Washington, D.C. : University Press of America, c1981. p. cm. Includes index. [BT78.M388] 19 81-40174 ISBN 0-8191-1671-8 : 17.75 ISBN 0-8191-1672-6 (pbk.) : 9.00
1. Theology—Miscellanea. 2. Truth—Miscellanea. I. Title.

†MORRIS, Henry Madison, 1918- 220.6
The Bible has the answer / Henry M. Morris and Martin E. Clark. Rev. & enl. San Diego : Creation-Life Publishers, c1976. xi, 380 p. ; 21 cm. Includes indexes. [BR96.M67 1976] 76-20206 ISBN 0-89051-018-0 pbk. : 4.95
1. Bible.—Examinations, questions, etc. 2. Theology—Miscellanea. I. Clark, Martin E., joint author. II. Title.

MORRIS, Henry Madison, 1918- 220.6'6
The Bible has the answer; practical Biblical discussions of 100 frequent questions, by Henry M. Morris. Grand Rapids, Mich., Baker Book House [1971] x, 256 p. 22 cm. [BR96.M67] 71-165506 3.25 (pbk)
1. Bible—Examinations, questions, etc. 2. Theology—Miscellanea. I. Title.

PRIME, Derek. 230'.076
Questions on the Christian faith answered from the Bible. [1st U.S.A. ed.] Grand Rapids, Eerdmans [1968, c1967] 128 p. 21 cm. [BR96.P73 1968] 68-18834
1. Theology—Miscellanea. I. Title.

REGAN, Cronan. 230'.2
Signpost. Chicago, Franciscan Herald Press [1972] xvii, 322 p. 22 cm. Essays originally appeared in the question and answer column "Signpost" in the monthly magazine The Sign. [BX1754.3.R4] 70-169056 ISBN 0-8199-0432-5 7.50
1. Catholic Church—Doctrinal and controversial works, Popular. 2. Theology—Miscellanea. I. The Sign. II. Title.

WIESE, Walter, fl.1966- 230'.076
Where is God? and other questions children ask. Translated by George Williams. Philadelphia, Fortress Press [1969] 54 p. illus. 19 cm. Translation of Wo ist Gott, Mutter? [BR96.W513] 78-76807 1.95
1. Theology—Miscellanea. 2. Children's questions and answers. I. Title.

WOODS, Guy N., 1908- 230
Questions and answers, open forum, Freed-Hardeman College lectures / by Guy N. Woods. Henderson, Tenn. : The College, c1976. 381 p. : ill. ; 24 cm. (Freed-Hardeman College lectures) Includes indexes. [BR96.W66] 76-359613
1. Theology—Miscellanea. I. Title. II. Series: Freed-Hardeman College. Lectures.

Theology—Outlines, syllabi, etc.

PENNSYLVANIA. State University. Center for Continuing Liberal Education. 230.02
Exploring religious ideas: the great Western faiths. [study-discussion course] by Luther H. Harshbarger, Benjamin M. Kahn, John A. Mourant. Edited by Ralph W. Condee. University Park [c1959] vi, 158p. 28cm. On the cover, Kahn's name appears first. Includes bibliographies. [BT77.P44] 59-63350
1. Theology—Outlines, syllabi, etc. I. Harshbarger, Luther H. II. Kahn, Benjamin M. III. Title.

Theology, Pastoral.

ABBOTT, Lyman, 1835-1922. 250
The Christian ministry, by Lyman Abbott. Boston and New York, Houghton, Mifflin and company, 1905. xix, 317, [1] p. 20 1/2 cm. Contents.The fundamental faiths of the ministry--The function of the Ministry.--The authority of the ministry.--The indiviual message of the ministry.--The social message of the ministry.--The minister as priest.--Qualifications for the ministry.--Some ministers of the olden time.--The ministry of Jesus Christ: His methods.--The ministry of Jesus Christ: the substance of His teaching. [BV4010.A25] 5-12378
1. Theology, Pastoral. I. Title.

ADAMS, Charles, 1808-1890. 250
Notes of the minister of Christ for the times, drawn from the Holy Scriptures. By Charles Adams. New York, Lane & Scott, 1850. 246 p. 18 1/2 cm. [BV4010.A3] 38-663
1. Theology, Pastoral I. Title.

ADAMS, Hampton. 253
The pastoral ministry, by Hampton Adams ... Nashville, Cokesbury press [c1932] 173 p. 19 cm. [BV4010.A35] 32-25804
1. Theology, Pastoral. I. Title.

ADAMS, Hampton. 250
You and your minister, by Hampton Adams ... St. Louis, Mo., The Bethany Press, 1940. 166 p. 19 1/2 cm. [BV4010.A37] 40-4927
1. Theology, Pastoral. I. Title.

ADAMS, John, 1704-1740. 250
Jesus Christ an example to His ministers. Newport, Rhode-Island; Printed and sold by J. Franklin; sold also by T. Fleet, at his printing house in Pudding-lane, Boston. MDCCXXVIII. 6 p. l., 71 p. 15 cm. Signatures: A6, B-K4. The half-title and last leaf are mounted on the original covers. "The Charge, given by the Reverend Mr. Joseph Baxter": p. 57-60; "The right hand of fellowship, given by the Reverend Mr. Richard Brown": p. 61-71. [BV4009.A4] 31-3997
1. Theology, Pastoral. 2. Sermons, American. I. Baxter, Joseph, 1676-1745. II. Brown, Richard, 1675-1732. III. Title. IV. Title: A sermon preach'd on the day of his ordination

AGAR, Frederick Alfred, 1872- 253
The minister and his opportunity, by Frederick A. Agar. New York [etc.] Fleming H. Revell company [c1932] 96 p. 19 1/2 cm. [BV4010.A5] 32-35177
1. Theology, Pastoral. I. Title.

[ANDLER, Ludwig] 1882- 262.14
The pastoral companion, by Fr. Honoratus Bonzelet, O.F.M. ... Chicagp, Franciscan herald press, 1940 vii p., 1 l., 222 p. 20 cm. "An adaptation of 'Comes pastoralls' by Fr. Louis Anler."--Pref. "Eighth edition--1889 (revised and enlarged) reprint--1940." [BX1912.A63] 41-3523
1. Theology, Pastoral. 2. Canon law. 3. Sacraments. I. Bonzelet, Honoratus, tr. II. Title.

ANLER, Ludwig, 1882- 262.14
The pastoral companion, by Fr. Louis Anler ... adapted from the German by Fr. Honoratus Bonzelet ... 3d ed. (rev and enl.) Chicago, Franciscan herald press [c1930] vii p., 1 l., 201 p. 19 1/2 cm. [BX1912.A63] 30-21306
1. Theology, Pastoral. 2. Canon law. 3. Sacraments. I. Bonselet, Honoratus, tr. II. Title.

BARTON, Levi Elder, 1870- 250
Take heed, by L. E. Barton ... Nashville, Tenn., Broadman press [1942] 182 p. 19 1/2 cm. [BV4012.B35] 43-630
1. Theology, Pastoral. I. Title.

BAXTER, Richard, 1615-1691. 262.
The reformed pastor, a discourse on the pastoral office. Designed principally to explain and recommend the duty of personal instruction and catechising. To which is added an appendix, containing some hints of advice to students for the ministry, and to tutors. Written by the reverend and pious Mr. Richard Baxter. Abridged and reduced to a new method by Samuel Palmer ... Cincinnati. Printed by J. W. Browne & co., At the office of Liberty hall, 1811. ix, [11]-179, [1] p. 17 1/2 cm. [BV4009.B3 1811] A 18
1. Theology, Pastoral. I. Palmer, Samuel, 1741-1813, ed. II. Title.

BAXTER, Richard, 1615-1691. 262.
The reformed pastor; shewing the nature of the pastoral work. By that eminent and faithful minister of Jesus Christ, the Rev. Richard Baxter. Abridged by Thomas Rutherford ... New York, Printed and sold by J. C. Totten, 1821. lxii, 63-443 p. 16 cm. [BV4009.B3 1821] 43-41746
1. Theology, Pastoral. I. Rutherford, Thomas, ed. II. Title.

BAYS, Bertie (Cole) Mrs. 251
Some preachers do! By Bertie Cole Bays. Kansas City, Mo., Western Baptist publishing cmopany, 1935. 122 p. illus. 20 1/2 cm. [BV4015.B3] 35-22650
1. Theology, Pastoral. I. Title.

BAYS, Bertie (Cole) 251
Some preachers do! By Bertie Cole Bays. Chicago, Philadelphia [etc.] The Judson press [1946] 8 p. l., 93 21 cm. [BV4015.B3 1946] 46-6034
1. Theology, Pastoral. I. Title.

BEEBE, James Albert, 1878- 250
The pastoral office; an introduction to the work of a pastor; by James Albert Beebe ... New York, Cincinnati, The Methodist book concern, 1923. 307 p. diagr. 21 1/2 cm. "Book recommended for further study" at end of most of the chapters. [B 010.B47] 24-4132
1. Theology, Pastoral. I. Title.

BENSON, Clarence Herbert, 1879- 260
Techniques of a working church, by Clarence H. Benson ... Chicago, Moody press [1946] xv, 266 p. illus. (map) diagr. 20 1/2 cm. Bibliography: p. 265-266. [BV4010.B474] 47-18184
1. Theology, Pastoral. 2. Church work. I. Title.

BITTING, William Coleman, 1857-1931. 258
The teaching pastor; the Samuel A. Crozer lectures in Crozer theological seminary, 1922-1923, by William C. Bitting, D.D. Philadelphia, Boston [etc.] The Judson press [c1923] 8 p. l., 150 p. 20 cm. [BV4012.B5] 23-17575
1. Theology, Pastoral. I. Title.

BLACKBURN, Margaret E. Mrs. 261.
Things a pastor's wife can do, by one of them. Philadelphia, American Baptist publication society, 1898. 80 p. 20 1/2 cm. [BV4305.B6] 98-444
1. Theology, Pastoral. I. Title.

BLACKWOOD,Andrew Watterson, 1882- 250
Pastoral leadership. New York, Abingdon-Cokesbury Press [1949] 272 p. 24 cm. Includes "Suggested readings." [BV4010.B484] 49-11498
1. Theology, Pastoral. 2. Church work. I. Title.

BLACKWOOD, Andrew Watterson, 1882- 250
Pastoral work, a source book for ministers [by] Andrew Watterson Blackwood ... Philadelphia, The Westminster press [1945] 252 p. 21 cm. (Half-title: The Westminster source books for ministers) Includes bibliographies. [BV4010.B485] 45-3596
1. Theology, Pastoral. I. Title.

BLAKE, Thaddeus C. 250
The pulpit and the pew; or, Preacher and people. By T. C. Blake ... Nashville, Tenn. [Printed for the author by the Cumberland Presbyterian publishing house] 1882. x p., 1 l., 11-280 p. 17 cm. [BV4010.B5] 37-39642
1. Theology, Pastoral. I. Title.

BOAZ, Hiram Abiff, bp., 1866- 250
The essentials of an effective ministry, by H. A. Boaz ... Nashville, Tenn., Cokesbury press [c1937] 137 p. 19 1/2 cm. [BV4010.B57] 37-15879
1. Theology, Pastoral. I. Title.

BOISEN, Anton Theophilus, 1876- 253
Problems in religion and life, a manual for pastors, with outlines for the co-operative study of personal experience in social situations [by] Anton T. Boisen. New York, Nashville, Abingdon-Cokesbury press [1946] 159 p. 19 1/2 cm. "The minister's professional library on the understanding of human nature": p. 152-159. "Readings" at end of most of the chapters. [BV4012.B57] 46-7910
1. Theology, Pastoral. 2. Psychology, Pastoral. 3. Social surveys. I. Title.

BONAR, Horatius, 1808-1889. 250
Words to the winners of souls. By Rev. Horatius Bonar ... Boston, American tract society, [186-?] 102 p. 15 cm. [BV4010.B6] 38-652
1. Theology, Pastoral. I. American tract society. II. Title.

BONNELL, John Sutherland, 1893- 258
Pastoral psychiatry, by John Sutherland Bonnell; with a foreword by Thaddeus Hoyt Ames, M.D. New York, London, Harper & brothers, 1938. xii, 287 p. 21 cm. "First edition." "Acknowledgments": p. 231. [BV4012.B58] 38-38024
1. Theology, Pastoral. 2. Psychology, Religious. 3. Psychology, Pathological. I. Title.

BOOTH, Henry Matthias, 1843-1899. 250
The man and his message; addresses by Henry M. Booth ... delivered before the students and alumni of the Theological seminary, of Auburn, in the state of New York. New York, Chicago [etc.] Fleming H. Revell company [c1899] 163 p. 19 cm. [BV4010.B65] 0-97
1. Theology, Pastoral. I. Title.

BROWN, Charles Reynolds, 1862- 250
The making of a minister, by Charles Reynolds Brown... New York and London, The Century co. [c1927] xv, 294 p. 19 1/2 cm. [BV4010.B75] 27-9587
1. Theology, Pastoral. I. Title.

BROWN, Ulysses Sherman, 1864- 250
If the minister is to succeed, by U. S. Brown, D.D. Grand Rapids, Mich., W. B. Eerdmans publishing company, 1937. 189 p. 20 cm. [BV4010.B76] 37-6825
1. Theology, Pastoral. I. Title.

BROWN, William Adams, 1865- 250
The minister his world and his work; a study of some pressing tasks and problems of present-day Protestantism, by William Adams Brown... Nashville, Tenn., Cokesbury press [c1937] 243 p. 25 1/2 cm. [BV4010.B78] 37-19298
1. Theology, Pastoral. I. Title.

BURDER, Henry Forster, 1783-1864. 250.
Mental discipline; or, Hints on the cultivation of intellectual and moral habits: addressed particularly to students in theology and young preachers. By Henry Forster Burder, M.A. Andover, Printed by Flagg and Gould, 1827. vi, [2] p., 1 l., [7]-126 p. 18 cm. [BV4016.B8] E10
1. Theology, Pastoral. 2. Theology—Study and teaching. 3. Conduct of life. I. Title.

BYINGTON, Edwin Hallock, 1861- 250
The minister's week-day challenge, by Edwin H. Byington ... New York, R. R. Smith, inc., 1931. v p, 1 l., 229 p. 20 cm. [BV4010.B8] 31-6899
1. Theology, Pastoral. 2. Clergy. I. Title.

CAMERON, William A. 250
The clinic of a cleric, by W. A. Cameron ... New York, R. Long & R. R. Smith, inc., 1931. 5 p. l., 3-249 p. 19 1/2 cm. [BV4012.C3] 31-34422
1. Theology, Pastoral. 2. Psychology, Religious. I. Title.

[CAMPBELL, N. W.] Mrs. 250
Why should I be a pastor! or, Conversations on the authority for the gospel ministry; its trials, importance, qualifications, duties and privileges. By the author of Why I am a Presbyterian... Philadelphia, W. S. Martien, 1852. 3 p. l., [iii]-xi, [13]-133 p. 16 1/2 cm. Dedication and preface signed: N. W. Campbell. [BV4010.C35] 38-657
1. Theology, Pastroial. I. Title.

CASHMAN, Robert, 1886- 250
The business administration of a church, by Robert Cashman ... Chicago, New York, Willett, Clark & company, 1937. x p., 1 l., 163 p. 21 cm. [The minister's professional library] [BV4012.C33] 37-27289
1. Theology, Pastoral. 2. Church work. I. Title.

CHAMBERS, Oswald, 1874-1917. 253
Workmen of God; the cure of souls, by Oswald Chambers ... New York, Dodd, Mead & company, 1938. vii, 117 p. 19 cm. "Books by Oswald Chambers": p. 117. [BV4010.C47] 39-19368
1. Theology, Pastoral. I. Title. II. Title: Cure of souls.

CHAPMAN, John Wilbur, 1859- 250
The minister's handicap, by J. Wilbur Chapman ... xii, 13-155p. 20cm. New York, N. Y. American tract society) [BV4010.C5] 18-18979
1. Theology, Pastoral. I. American tract society. II. Title. III. Series.

CHAPMAN, John Wilbur, 1859-1918. 250
The problem of the work, by Rev. J. Wilbur Chapman ... New York, Hodder & Stoughton, George H. Doran company [1911] xi, 255 p. 19 cm. [BV4010.C53] 11-29878
1. Theology, Pastoral. 2. Church work. 3. Evangelistic work. I. Title.

CLAUSEN, Bernard Chancellor, 1892- 250
The technique of a minister, by Bernard C. Clausen ... New York, Chicago [etc.] Fleming H. Revell company [c1925] 133 p. diagrs. 19 1/2 cm. [BV4010.C56] 25-20602
1. Theology, Pastoral. I. Title.

COGSWELL, William, 1787-1850. 250
Letters to young men preparing for the Christian ministry. By William Cogswell... Boston, Perkins & Marvin; Philadelphia, H. Perkins, 1837. xvi, [17]-236 p. 17 1/2 cm. [BV4020.C6] 39-429
1. Theology, Pastoral. 2. Clergy. I. Title.

COLTON, Clarence Eugene, 1914- 250
The minister's mission, a survey of ministerial responsibilities and relationships. Dallas, Story Book Press ['1951] 343 p. 20 cm. [BV4010.C57] 52-556
1. Theology. Pastoral. I. Title.

[COX, Samuel Hanson] 1793-1881, ed. 250.4
The ministry we need: three inaugural, discourses, delivered at Auburn, June 18, 1835 ... New-York, Taylor & Gould; Auburn, H. Ivison & co., 1835. 185. p. 15 cm. [BV4010.C65] 38-656
1. Theology, Pastoral. I. Adams, John Watson, 1796-1850. II. Phelps, Eilakim, 1790-1880. III. Title.
Content omitted

CULP, John. 250
The personal ministry of the gospel. As taught and exemplified by the Lord and His apostles. By John Culp ... [n. p.] c1894. 1 p. l., 204 p. 14 cm. [BV4010.C8] 38-655
1. Theology, Pastoral. I. Title.

CUSHMAN, Ralph Spaulding, bp., 1879- 250
Dear Bob; letters of a preacher to his son [by] Ralph S. Cushman ... New York, Cincinnati [etc.] The Abingdon press [c1934] 104 p. 18 cm. [BV4015.C8] 34-31967
1. Theology, Pastoral. I. Title.

CUYLER, Theodore Ledyard, 1822-1909. 250
How to be a pastor. By Theodore L. Cuyler ... New York, The Baker and Taylor co. [1890] 151 p. 18 cm. [BV4010.C85] 32-33631
1. Theology, Pastoral. I. Title.

DAVISON, Frank Elon, 1887- 250
I would do it again; sharing experiences in the Christian ministry. St. Louis, Bethany Press [1948] 158 p. 21 cm. [BV4010.D28] 48-8968
1. Theology, Pastoral. I. Title.

DAWSON, David Miles, 1885- 250
More power to the preacher; a pastoral theology. Grand Rapids, Zondervan Pub. House [1956] 153p. 20cm. [BV4010.D29] 56-41990
1. Theology, Pastoral. I. Title.

DAWSON, Lemuel Orah, 1865- 250
After fifty years [by] L. O. Dawson. Nashville, Tenn., Broadman press [c1935] 3 p. l., 5-230 p. 21 cm. [BV4010.D3] 36-4285
1. Theology, Pastoral. I. Title.

DE BLOIS, Austen Kennedy, 1886- 250
Some problems of the modern minister ... by Austen Kennedy De Blois ... Garden City, N. Y., Doubleday, Doran & company, inc., 1928. xiii, 329 p. 20 cm. (The Holland lectures for 1927, delivered at the Southwestern Baptist theological seminary) [BV4010.D35] 28-13008
1. Theology, Pastoral. 2. Clergy. I. Title.

DEXTER, Elisabeth Williams (Anthony) Mrs. 1887- 258
The minister and family troubles; a case study of the relation of the minister and the church to sex and family problems, by Elisabeth Anthony Dexter ... and Robert Cloutman Dexter ... New York, R. R. Smith, inc., 1931. xii p., 1 l., 97 p. 20 cm. "Selected reading": p. 93-97. [BV4320.D45] 31-12356
1. Theology, Pastoral. 2. Family. 3. Marriage. I. Dexter, Robert Cloutman, joint author. II. Title.

DICK, Willis V. 258
Clerical system; economics of library, periodicals, sermonology, correspondence, administration and business; a cabinet classification of literary wealth, homiletic material, special studies, and office work ... by Willis V. Dick ... Cincinnati, Jennings and Pye; New York, Eaton and Mains [c1904] 121 p. illus. 19 cm. [BV4012.D5] 4-13639
1. Theology, Pastoral. I. Title.

DICKS, Russell Leslie, 1906- 250
Pastoral work and personal counseling [by] Russell L. Dicks. New York, The Macmillan company, 1944. x, 230 p. 19 1/2 cm. "First printing." "Bibliography of pastoral aid books": p. 229-230. [BV4010.D5] 44-51358
1. Theology, Pastoral. 2. Psychology, Pastoral. I. Title.

DICKS, Russell Leslie, 1906- 250
Pastoral work and personal counseling, an introd. to pastoral care. Rev. ed. New York, Macmillan Co., 1949. xii, 195 p. 20 cm. "Pastoral aid books and pamphlets": p. 186-191. [BV4010.D5 1949] 49-7016
1. Theology, Pastoral. 2. Psychology, Pastoral. I. Title.

DOBBINS, Gaines Stanley, 1886- 250
Building better churches; a guide to the pastoral ministry. Nashville, Broadman Press [1947] ix, 465 p. 24 cm. "Classified bibliography": p. 451-458. [BV4010.D58] 47-7858
1. Theology, Pastoral. 2. Church. I. Title.

DODDRIDGE, Philip, 1702-1751. 250
Lectures on preaching, and the several branches of the miniserial office, including the characters of the most celebrated ministers among dissenters and in the establishment. By Philip Doddridge, D. D. Andover [Mass.] Flagg, Gould, and Newman, 1838. vi, [7]-144 p. 15 cm. [BV4010.D6] 38-651
1. Theology, Pastoral. 2. Preaching. I. Title.

DOLLOFF, Eugene Dinsmore 251
Maturing in the ministry, by Eugene Dinsmore Dolloff. New York, Round table press, inc., 1938. 4 p. l., 215 p. 26 cm. [BV4012.D6] 38-24881
1. Theology, Pastoral. I. Title.

DOLLOFF, Eugene Dinsomore. 258
The romance of doorbells; a guide to effective pastoral calling. [1st ed.] Philadelphia, Judson Press [1951] 197 p. 21 cm. Bibliography: p. 196-197. [BV4320.D6] 51-11459
1. Theology, Pastoral. I. Title.

DOUGLAS, Lloyd Cassel, 1877- 250
The minister's everyday life, by Lloyd C. Douglas. New York, C. Scribner's sons, 1924. xii p., 2 l., 220 p. 19 1/2 cm. [BV4010.D7] 24-7742
1. Theology, Pastoral. I. Title.

DUNN, Joseph Bragg, 1868- 250
In the service of the King; a parson's story, by Joseph B. Dunn. New York and London, G. P. Putnam's sons, 1915. ix, 158 p. 21 cm. [BV4015.D8] 15-5393
1. Theology, Pastoral. I. Title.
Contents omitted.

EAKIN, Mildred Olivia (Moody) 1890- 259
The pastor and the children, by Mildred Moody Eakin and Frank Eakin. New York, The Macmillan company, 1947. ix, 182 p. 19 1/2 cm. "First printing." "Reading suggestions and source references": p. 172-177. [BV4355.E2] 47-3413
1. Theology. Pastoral. 2. Church work with children. 3. Religious education. I. Eakin, Frank, 1885- joint author. II. Title.

EDDY, Robert Leigh. 253
Minister's Monday. Boston, Pilgrim Press [1948] 175 p. 20 cm. [BV4013.E3] 48-8543
1. Theology, Pastoral. I. Title.

EDWARDS, Richard Henry, 1877- 250
A person-minded ministry, by Richard Henry Edwards. Nashville, Cokesbury press [c1940] 253 p. 20 1/2 cm. [BV4010.E3] 40-11841
1. Theology, Pastoral. I. Title.

ELLIOTT, William Anderson. 250
D.d's for ministers, by William Anderson Elliott... Philadelphia, Boston [etc.] The Judson press [1930] 7 p. l., 3-147 p. 20 cm. Dos and don's for ministers. [BV4012.E6] 30-9985
1. Theology, Pastoral. I. Title.

FAGLEY, Frederick Louis, 1879- 253
Parish evangelism; an outline of a year's program, by Frederick, L.Fagley... introduction by Charles L. Goodell... New York, Chicago [etc.] Fleming H. Revell company [1926] 142 p. 19 1/2 cm. [BV3700.F28 1926] 26-19652
1. Theology, Pastoral. 2. Evangelistic work. I. Title.

FAUNCE, William Herbert Perry, 1859-1930. 250
The educational ideal in the ministry ... by William Herbert Perry Faunce ... New York, The Macmillan company, 1908. vii, 286 p. 20 cm. (The Lyman Beecher lecture at Yale university in the year 1908) [BV4010.F3] 3-32415
1. Theology, Pastoral. I. Title.

FOOTE, Henry Wilder, 1875- 230
The minister and his parish; a discussion of problems in church administration, by Henry Wilder Foote ... New York, The Macmillan company, 1923. xv p., 1 l., 179 p. 19 1/2 cm. [BV600.F6] 23-17132
1. Theology, Pastoral. I. Title.

FOX, Edgar Alonzo, 1858- 268.
The pastor's place of privilege and power in the Sunday school, by E. A. Fox ... Nashville, Tenn., Dallas, Tex., Publishing house of the M. E. church, South, Smith & Lamar, agents, 1907. 2 p. l., 7-210 p. 19 cm. Partly reprinted from the Sunday school times, the World evangel, and the Pilgrim teacher. [BV4360.F6] 7-39010
1. Theology, Pastoral. 2. Sunday-schools. I. Title.

FRITZ, John Henry Charles, 1874- 250
Pastoral theology; a handbook of scriptural principles written especially for pastors of the Lutheran church, by John H. C. Fritz ... St. Louis, Mo., Concordia publishing house, 1932. ix, 343 p. 24 cm. "I have used Walther's Pastoraltheologie as a bais."--Pref. [BX8071.F7] 33-1185
1. Theology, Pastoral. I. Walther, Carl Fredinand Wilhelm, 1811-1887. Amerikanisch-lutherische pastoral-theologie. II. Title.

FRITZ, John Henry Charles, 1874- 250
Pastoral theology, a handbook of Scriptural principles written especially for pastors of the Lutheran church, by John H. C Fritz ... 2d ed., rev. Saint Louis, Mo., Concordia publishing house, 1945. xii, 384 p. 23 1/2 cm. "First edition 1932. Second edition 1945." "I have used Walther's Pastoraltheologie as a basis."--Pref. [BV4010.F67 1945] 45-5709
1. Theology, Pastoral. I. Walther, Carl Ferdinand Wilheim, 1811-1887. Amerikanisch lutherische pastoral-theologie. II. Title.

FRY, Jacob, 1834-
The pastor's guide: or, Rules and notes in pastoral theology, by Jacob Fry ... Philadelphia, General council publication house, 1915. 3 p. l., 109 p. 20 cm. [BV4180.F7] 17-23305 0.75
1. Theology, Pastoral. I. Title.

GIFFORD, Frank Dean, 1891- 250
This ministry and service; a textbook of pastoral care and parish administration. New York, Morehouse-Gorham [1956] 192p. 21cm. [BV4010.G47] 56-86456
1. Theology, Pastoral. I. Title.

GLADDEN, Washington, 1836-1918. 250
... The Christian pastor and the working church, by Washington Gladden ... New York, C. Scribner's sons, 1898. xiv, 485 p. 21 cm. (Half-title: The international theological library, ed. by C. A. Briggs ... and S. D. F. Salmond) Series title in part also at head of t.-p. [BV4010.G55] 4-4181
1. Theology, Pastoral. I. Title.

GOODELL, Constans Liberty, 1830-1886. 250
How to build a church, By Rev. C. L. Goodell ... With an introduction by Rev. E. B. Webb ... Boston, Congregational Sunday-school and publishing society, [1883] 76 p. 18 cm. [BV4010.G6] 38-659
1. Theology, Pastoral. I. Congregational Sunday-school and publishing society. II. Title.

GORDON, Buford Franklin. 250
Pastor and people, dealing with problems of church administration, by Buford Franklin Gordon ... Akron, O., Pub. for the author by the Superior printing & litho. Co., 1930. 3 p. l., 173 p. 21 cm. [BV4010.G65] 31-1834
1. Theology, Pastoral. I. Title.

GOUWENS, Teunis Earl, 1886- 250
He opened the Book, by Teunis E. Gouwens ... New York [etc.] Fleming H. Revell company [c1940] 137 p. 20 cm. [BV4012.G6] 40-32849
1. Theology, Pastoral. 2. Preaching. 3. Bible--Usa. I. Title.

GRAEBNER, Theodore Conrad, 1876- 250
Pastor and people; letters to a young preacher, by Theodore Graebner. St. Louis, Mo., Concordia publishing house, 1932. viii, 163 p. 19 cm. Selected from the 1920-1930 files of the Homiletic magazine. cf. A. letter to the reader. [BX8071.G7] 32-19935
1. Theology, Pastoral. 2. Casuistry. I. Title.

GREEN, Peter, 1871- 250
The town parson, his life and work; being the substance of the pastoral theology lectures delivered before the University of Cambridge, and at King's college, London, in the year 1914; now written out and enlarged by the Rev. Peter Green ... With a preface by the Right Rev. Edward Stuart Talbot ... London, New York [etc.] Longmans, Green, and co., 1919. xi, 242 p. 20 cm. [BV4010.G75] 20-13994
1. Theology, Pastoral. I. Title.

GREGORY, Daniel Seely, 1832-1915. 250
Christ's trumpet-call to the ministry; or, The preacher and the preaching for the present crisis. By Daniel S. Gregory ... New York, London and Toronto, Funk & Wagnalls company, 1896. 4 p. l., 365 p. 20 cm. [BV4010.G77] 38-650
1. Theology, Pastoral. I. Title.

GRESHAM, Perry Epler. 253
Disciplines of the high calling. St. Louis, Bethany Press [1954] 176p. 21cm. [BV4010.G78] 54-31949
1. Theology, Pastoral. I. Title.

-GUFFIN, Gilbert Lee. 250
How to run a church; or, Guides in church administration. Birmingham, Ala., Howard College, [1948] xiii, 197 p. 22 cm. [BV4010.G84] 48-11159
1. Theology, Pastoral 2. Church work. I. Title.

GUFFIN, Gilbert Lee. 250
Pastor and church; a manual for pastoral leadership. Foreword by Davis C. Woolley. Nashville, Broadman Press [1955] 154p. 21cm. [BV4010.G85] 55-14075
1. Theology, Pastoral. I. Title.

HALL, Charles Cuthbert, 1852-1908. 250
Qualifications for ministerial power. The Carew lectures for 1895. Hartford theological seminary. By Charles Cuthbert Hall... Hartford, Conn., Hartford seminary press, 1895. 241 p. 20 cm. [BV4010.H26] 38-637
1. Theology, Pastoral. I. Carew lectures. II. Title.

HARKEY, Simeon Walcher, 1811-1889. 250
The character and value of an evangelical ministry, and the duty of the church in regard to it. By Rev. Simeon W. Harkey ... Baltimore, T. N. Kurt, 1853. vii, [9]-190 p. 15 cm. [BV4010.H3] 38-658
1. Theology, Pastoral. I. Title.

HARMON, Nolan Bailey, 1892- 250
Ministerial ethics and etiquette. Rev. ed. New York, Abingdon-Cokesbury Press [1950] 215 p. 21 cm. [BV4012.H3 1950] 50-8100
1. Theology, Pastoral. I. Title.

HARMON, Nolan Bailey, 1892- 258
Ministerial ethics and etiquette, by Rev. Nolan B. Harmon, jr., M. A. Nashville, Tenn., Cokesbury press, 1928. 180 p. 20 cm. [BV4012.H3] 28-5883
1. Theology, Pastoral. I. Title.

HARVEY, Hezekiah, 1821-1893. 250
The pastor: his qualifications and duties. By H. Harvey ... Philadelphia, American Baptists publication society [1879?] 180 p. 20 cm. [BV4010.H35] 38-638
1. Theology, Pastoral. I. American Baptist publication society. II. Title.

HATCHER, William Eldridge, 1834-1912. 268.
The pastor and the Sunday school; Sunday school board seminary lectures, course no. 1, delivered at Southern Baptist theological seminary, Louisville, Ky., Feb., 1902 [by] William E. Hatcher... Nashville, Tenn., Sunday school board, Southern Baptist convention [c1902] 180 p. front., plates, ports. 19 cm. [BV4360.H3] 2-14888
1. Theology, Pastoral. 2. Sunday-schools. I. Title.

HEDLEY, George Percy, 1899- 253.2
The minister behind the scenes. New York, Macmillan, 1956. xii, 147p. 21cm. (The James A. Gray lectures at Duke University, 1955) [GV4010.H413] 56-7305
1. Theology, Pastoral. I. Title. II. Series.

HENDRIX, Eugene Russell, bp., 1847-1927. 250
Skilled labor for the Master. By Eugene R. Hendrix ... Introduction by Bishop C. B. Galloway ... 2d thousand. Nashville, Tenn., Dallas, Tex., Publishing house of the M. E. church, South, 1901. xv, 326 p. 20 cm. [BV4010.H42 1901] 1-27085
1. Theology, Pastoral. I. Title.

HERBERT, George, 1593-1633. 210
The temple & A priest to the temple, by George Herbert. London & Toronto, J. M. Dent & sons, ltd. New York, E. P. Dutton & co. [1927] xvii p., 1 l., 304, [1] p. 17 1/2 cm. (Half-title: Everyman's library, ed. by Ernest Rhys. Poetry and the drama. [no. 309]) "First issue of this edition, 1908; reprinted, 1927." Introduction by Edward Thomas. [AC1.E8 no. 309] 36-37194
1. Theology, Pastoral. I. Title.

HEWITT, Arthur Wentworth, 1883- 250
Highland shepherds; a book of the rural pastorate [by] Arthur Wentworth Hewitt. Chicago, New York, Willett, Clark, & company, 1939. viii p., 1 l., 246 p. 21 cm. "Notes": p. 236-237. [BV4010.H44] 39-31304
1. Theology, Pastoral. 2. Rural churches. I. Title.

[HEWITT, Joses] 1847-1906. 250
Ecce clerus; or, The Christian minister in many lights, by a student of the times. New York, Eaton & Mains; Cincinnati, Curts & Jennings, 1899. 341 p. 21 cm. [BV4010.H45] 99-1693
1. Theology, Pastoral. I. Title.

HISCOX, Edward Thurston, 1814-1901. 250.
The star book for ministers. By Edward T. Hiscox ... 16th ed. Rev. and enl. Philadelphia, The Griffith and Rowland press [c1906] 299 p. 16 cm. [BV4016.H5 1906] 6-13350
1. Theology, Pastoral. 2. Liturgies. I. Title.

HOBART, Alvah Sabin, 1847-1930. 258
Pedagogy for ministers; an application of pedagogical principles to the preaching and other work of the pastor, by Alvah Sabin Hobart ... New York, Chicago [etc.] Fleming H. Revell company [c1917] 184 p. 18 1/2 cm. [BV4012.H6] 18-549
1. Theology, Pastoral. I. Title.

HOLMAN, Charles Thomas, 1882- 207
The cure of souls, a socio-psychological approach, by Charles T. Holman Chicago, Ill, The University of Chicago press [1932] xv, 331 p. 20 cm. (Half-title: The University of Chicago publications in religious education...Handbooks of ethics and religion) Bibliography: p. 321-324. [BV4012.H65] [[159.964282]] [1 [131.3482] 33-3730
1. Theology, Pastoral. 2. Personality. 3. Psychoanalysis. 4. Psychology, Religious. 5. Social psychology. I. Title.

HOLMAN, Charles Thomas, 1882- 253
Getting down to cases, by Charles T. Holman. New York, The Macmillan company, 1942. 6 p. l., 207 p. 19 1/2 cm. "First printing." [BV4012.H67] 42-8041
1. Theology, Pastoral. 2. Psychology, Religious. I. Title.

HOPPIN, James Mason, 1820-1906. 250
Pastoral theology, by James M. Hoppin ... New York, London, Funk & Wagnalls, 1884. xi, 584 p. 22 1/2 cm. [BV4010.H6] 38-3175
1. Theology, Pastoral. I. Title.

HUSS, John Ervin, 1910- 253
Ideas for a successful pastorate. Grand Rapids, Zondervan Pub. House [1953] 144p. 20cm. [BV4010.H87] 53-29145
1. Theology, Pastoral. I. Title.

IDE, George Barton, 1804-1872. 250
The ministry demanded by the present crisis. By George B. Ide ... Philadelphia, American Baptist publication society [1845] vi, [7]-102 p. 16 cm. [BV4010.I 4] 38-831
1. Theology, Pastoral. I. American Baptist publication society. II. Title.

IRION, Paul E 265.8
The funeral and the mourners; pastoral care of the bereaved. Nashville, Abingdon Press [1954] 186p. 23cm. [BV4330.I7] 53-11337
1. Theology, Pastoral. 2. Funeral service. I. Title.

JAMES, John Angell, 1785-1859. 250
An earnest ministry the want of the times. By John Angell James. With an introduction by Rev. J. B. Condit ... New York, M. W. Dodd, 1848. xii p., 2 l., [17]-288 p. 20 cm. First published, London, 1847. [BV4010.J3 1848] 38-833
1. Theology, Pastoral. I. Title.

JAMES, John Angell, 1785-1859. 250
An earnest ministry the want of the times. By John Angell James. With an introduction by Rev. Jonathan B. Condit ... Philadelphia, Presbyterian board of publication [1868] 288 p. 18 cm. First published, London, 1847. [BV4010.J3 1868] 38-834
1. Theology, Pastoral. I. Presbyterian church in the U. S. A. (Old school) Board of publication. II. Title.

JEFFERSON, Charles Edward, 1860-1937. 250
The minister as shepherd, by Charles Edward Jefferson ... New York, Thomas Y. Crowell company [1912] vii, 229 p. 18 cm. (Half-title: The George Shepard lectures on preaching, at Bengor theological seminary, 1912) "Published September, 1912." [BV4010.J4] 12-21298
1. Theology, Pastoral. I. Title.

JOHNSON, Herrick, 1832-1913. 250
The ideal ministry, by Herrick Johnson ... New York, Chicago [etc.] Fleming H. Revell company [c1908] 488 p. 22 cm. [BV4010.J65] 8-16404
1. Theology. Pastoral. 2. Preaching. I. Title.

JONES, Tiberius Gracchus. 250
Duties of a pastor to his church. By Tiberius Gracchus Jones ... Charleston, S. C., Southern Baptist publication society; Richmond, Virginia Baptist Sunday-school and publication society, 1853. 104 p. 16 cm. [BV4010.J67] 33-835
1. Theology, Pastoral. I. Southern Baptist publication society. II. Title.

JOSEPH, Oscar Loos, 1873- 250
The dynamic ministry; a study of the fourfold duty of the minister, by Oscar L. Joseph ... New York, Cincinnati, The Abingdon press [1923] 169 p. 20 cm. "Suggested reading" at end of each chapter. [BV4010.J68] 23-17443
1. Theology, Pastoral. I. Title.

JOWETT, John Henry, 1864-1923. 250
The preacher, his life and work. Yale lectures by Rev. J. H. Jowett ... New York, Hodder & Stoughton, George H. Doran company [1912] 239 p. 21 cm. The Lyman Beecher lectures on preaching, Yale university, 1911-12. [BV4010.J7] 12-25467
1. Theology, Pastoral. I. Title.

JOYNT, Robert Charles, 1856- 250
The church's real work (for clergy and laity), by R. C. Joynt ... With a foreword by the Bishop of Winchester. London, New York [etc.] Longmans, Green and co., 1934. xii, 132 p. 20 cm. [BX5175.J68] 35-3217
1. Theology, Pastoral. 2. Church work. I. Title.

JUDSON, Edward, 1844-1914. 230
The institutional church; a primer in pastoral theology, by Edward Judson, with an introductory word by Bishop Potter. New York, Lentilhon & company [c1899] 3 p. l., 5-211 p. 17 cm. (Half-title: Handbooks for practical workers in church and philanthropy, ed. by S. M. Jackson) [BV600.J8] 99-2665
1. Theology, Pastoral. 2. Church work. I. Title.

KEEDY, Edward Everett, 1869-1931. 258
Moral leadership and the ministry, by Edward E. Keedy ... Boston, Horace Worth company, 1912. vii, 200 p. 19 cm. [BV4012.K4] 12-5828

1. Theology, Pastoral. I. Title.

KEMP, Charles F. 1912- 250
Physicians of the soul, a history of pastoral counseling. New York, Macmillan Co., 1947. xiv, 314 p. 21 cm. "Notes" (Bibliographical): p. 289-306. [BV4012.K45] 47-4694
1. Theology, Pastoral. 2. Psychology, Pastoral. I. Title.

KENNEDY, Gerald Hamilton, Bp., 1907- 253
With singleness of heart. [1st ed.] New York, Harper [1951] 157 p. 20 cm. (The Slover lectures, Southwestern University, 1950) [BV4010.K42] 51-10340
1. Theology, Pastoral. I. Title.

KERN, John Adam, 1846-1926. 250
The way of the preacher; an interpretation of a calling, by John A. Kern ... Nashville, Tenn., Dallas, Tex., Publishing house of the M.E. church, South, Barbee & Smith, agents, 1902. xv, 378 p. 19 cm. [BV4010.K45] 2-18013
1. Theology, Pastoral. 2. Preaching. I. Title.

KIDDER, Daniel Parish, 1815-1891. 250
The Christian pastorate; its character, responsibilities, and duties. By Daniel P. Kidder ... Cincinnati, Hitchcock and Walden. New York, Carlton and Lanahan, 1871. 569 p. 19 1/2 cm. [BV4010.K5] 38-3177
1. Theology, Pastoral. I. Title.

KNUBEL, Frederick R 253.5
Pastoral counseling. Philadelphia, Muhlenberg Press [1952] 102p. 21cm. (The Knubel-Miller Foundation lectures) [BV4012.K58] 53-8945
1. Theology, Pastoral. 2. Psychology, Pastoral. I. Title.

KOLLOCK, Shepard Kosciuszko, 1795-1865. 258
Pastoral reminiscences; by Shepard K. Kollock, with an introduction, by A. Alexander ... New-York, M. W. Dodd, 1849. xiii, [15]-236 p. 18 1/2 cm. [BV4014.K6] 43-3562
1. Theology, Pastoral. I. Title.

LEACH, William Herman, 1888- 250
The making of the minister, by William H. Leach ... Nashville, Cokesbury press [c1938] 204 p. diagr. 20 cm. [BV4010.L36] 38-30000
1. Theology, Pastoral. I. Title.

LEIFFER, Murray Howard, 1902- ed. 250
In that case; a study of ministerial leadership in problem situations, edited by Murray H. Leiffer ... Chicago, New York, Willett, Clark & company, 1938. xvi p., 1 l., 156 p. 20 1/2 cm. [BV4005.L4] 39-31043
1. Theology, Pastoral. I. Title.

LEIFFER, Murray Howard, 1902- 250
The layman looks at the minister, by Murray H. Leiffer. New York, Nashville, Abingdon-Cokesbury press [1947] 160 p. illus. 19 1/2 cm. [BV4010.L38] 47-819
1. Theology, Pastoral. I. Title.

LICHLITER, McIlyar Hamilton, 1877- 250
The healing of souls [by] McIlyar Hamilton Lichliter ... New York, Cincinnati [etc.] The Abingdon press *1931] 175 p. 20 cm. "The Matthew Simpson lectures on 'The Christian ministry' ... delivered ... [at] De Pauw university ... April 13-15, 1931."--Foreword. "A list of helpful books": p. 173-175. [BV4010.L5] 31-30539
1. Theology, Pastoral. I. De Pauw university,Greencastle, Ind. Matthew Simpson lectureship foundation. II. Title.

LINDEMANN, Paul, 1881- 250
Ambassadors of Christ, by Paul Lindemann ... St. Louis, Mo., Concordia publishing house, 1935. iv p., 1 l., 161 p. 20 cm. [BV4010.L56] 35-5924
1. Theology, Pastoral. I. Title.

LYMAN, Albert Josiah, 1845-1915. 250
The Christian pastor in the new age, comrade--sponsor--social mediator; lectures for 1909 on the George Shepard foundation, Bangor theological seminary, by Albert Josiah Lyman ... New York, T. Y. Crowell & co. [1909] xi p., 2 l., [3]-174 p. 20 cm. "Published, November, 1909." [BV4010.L75] 9-31979
1. Theology, Pastoral. 2. Clergy. I. Title.

LYNCH, Frederick Henry, 1867-1934. 250
The new opportunities of the ministry, by Frederick Lynch ... with introduction by Professor Hugh Black ... New York, Chicago [etc.] Fleming H. Revell company [c1912] 128 p. 19 1/2 cm. [BV4010.L8] 13-799
1. Theology, Pastoral. I. Title.

MCAFEE, Cleland Boyd, 1866- 250
Ministerial practices, some fraternal suggestions, by Cleland Boyd McAfee... New York and London, Harper & brothers, 1928. vi p., 1 l., 220 p., 1 l. 19 1/2 cm. [BV4010.M215] 28-13329
1. Theology, Pastoral. I. Title.

MCCABE, Joseph E 1912- 253
The power of God in a parish program. Philadelphia, Westminster Press [1959] 164p. 21cm. [BV4015.M27] 59-6481
1. Theology, Pastoral. I. Title.

MCCLURE, James Gore King, 1848- 250
The growing pastor, by James G. K. McClure ... Chicago, The Winona publishing company, 1904. 2 p. l., [7]-138 p. 17 cm. [BV4010.M25] 4-1677
1. Theology, Pastoral. I. Title.

MCDOWELL, William Fraser, bp. 1858- 250
...In the school of Christ, by William Fraser McDowell... New York, Chicago [etc.] Fleming H. Revell company [c1910] 303 p. 20 cm. (The Cole lectures for 1910 delivered before Vanderbilt university.) [BV4010.M32] 10-20510
1. Theology, Pastoral. I. Title.

MCDOWELL, William Fraser, bp. 1858-1937. 250
...Good ministers of Jesus Christ, by William Fraser McDowell... New York, Cincinnati, The Abingdon press [c1917] 2 p. l., 7-307 p. 19 1/2 cm. (Lyman Breecher lectures on preaching, Yale university, 1917) [BV4010.M3] 17-15666
1. Theology, Pastoral. I. Title.

MCGLOTHLIN, William Joseph, 1867- 250
A vital ministry: the pastor of today in the service of man, by W. J. McGlothlin ... New York, Chicago [etc.] Fleming H. Revell company [c1913] 192 p. 19 1/2 cm. [BV4010.M33] 13-22504
1. Theology, Pastoral. I. Title.

MACGREGOR, William Malcolm, 1861- 253
For Christ and the kingdom; some chapters on the Christian ministry and the call to it, by William Malcolm Macgregor ... New York, London, and Edinburg, Fleming H. Revell company [1932] 126 p. 19 cm. "Printed in Great Britain." [BV4010.M34] 33-30694
1. Theology, Pastoral. I. Title. II. Title: The Christian ministry and the call to it.

MCKENZIE, John Grant, 1882- 258
Souls in the making; an introduction to pastoral psychology, by John G. Mackenzie... New York, The Macmillan company, 1929. 259 p. 20 1/2 cm. [BV4012.M3 1929] 29-7308
1. Theology, Pastoral. 2. Psychology, Religious. I. Title. II. Title: Pastoral psychology.

MCKINNEY, Alexander Harris, 1858- 268.
The pastor and teacher training; the Sunday school board seminary lectures course no. 4, delivered at the Southern Baptist theological seminary, Louisville, Ky., December 5-9, 1904 [by] Rev. A. H. McKinney... Nashville, Tenn., Sunday school board, Southern Baptist convention [1905] 191 p. front. (port.) 19 cm. [BV4360.M3] 5-9048
1. Theology, Pastoral. 2. Sunday-schools. I. Title.

MCNAUGHER, John, 1857- 250
Quit you like men, by John McNaugher... New York [etc.] Fleming H. Revell company [c1940] 191 p. 19 1/2 cm. [BV4010.M343] 40-10256
1. Theology, Pastoral. I. Title.

MARSHALL, Charles Clinton. 258
Church troubles; their successful management and effectual settlement. By Rev. C. C. Marshall. Warsaw, Ind., C. W. Smith publishing company, 1900. 106 p. port. 15 cm. [BV4320.M3] 0-1309
1. Theology, Pastoral. I. Title.

MARTIN, William Clyde, 1893- 250
To fulfill this ministry. New York, Abingdon-Cokesbury Press [1949] 142 p. 20 cm. [BV4010.M37] 49-7610
1. Theology, Pastoral. I. Title.

MASSILLON, Jean Baptiste, bp., 1663-1742. 253
The charges of Jean Baptiste Massillon, bishop of Clermont, addressed to his clergy. Also, two essays: the one on the art of preaching, from the French of M. Reybaz, and the other on the composition of a sermon, as adapted to the Church of England... by the Rev. Theops St. John [pseud.]... New York; Printed by D. & G. Bruce, for Brisban & Brannan, 186 Pearl-street. 1806. 1 p. l., [v]-xix p., 1 l., 23-330 p. 22 cm. [BX874.M4 1806] 34-28836
1. Theology, Pastoral. 2. Preaching. I. Reybaz, Etienne Salomon, 1737-1804. II. Clapham, Samuel, 1755-1830, tr. III. Title.

MAVES, Paul B. 259
Older people and the church [by] Paul B. Maves and J. Lennart Cedarleaf. New York, Abingdon-Cokesbury Press [1949] 272 p. 24 cm. Bibliographical references included in "Notes; (p. 257-266) [BV4012.M37] 49-8642
1. Theology, Pastoral. 2. Old age. I. Cedarleaf, J. Lennart. II. Title.

MELTON, William Walter, 1879- 250
The making of a preacher. Introd. by W. R. White. Grand Rapids, Zondervan Pub. House [1953] 150p. 21cm. [BV4010.M393] 53-36893
1. Theology, Pastoral. I. Title.

METHODIST church (United States) Commission on ministerial training. 253
The minister and human relations. William K. Anderson, editor. Nashville, Tenn., General conference Commission on courses of study, the Methodist church [1943] 160 p. 23 cm. [BV4012.M4] 43-15116
1. Theology, Pastoral. 2. Psychology, Religious. 3. Social psychology. I. Anderson, William Ketcham, 1888- ed. II. Title.

MEYER, Jack. 253
The preacher and his work; college lectures to student preachers. Athens, Ala., C. E. I. Store, c1955. 176p. 23cm. [BV4010.M46] 56-2139
1. Theology, Pastoral. I. Title.

MILLER, Rufus Wilder, 1862- 250
The minister, a man among men, with a biographical sketch of Rev. Charles F. McCauley, D.D., by Rev. Rufus W. Miller ... Philadelphia, Pa., Heidelberg press [c1917] 203 p. 2 port. (incl. front.) 20 cm. [BV4010.M5] 17-18969
1. McCauley, Charles Firey, 1816-1892. 2. Theology, Pastoral. I. Title.

THE ministry of all believers:
the pastoral role of the Christian ministry. Lexington, Ky., The College of the Bible, 1962. 56p. 23cm. (The College of the Bible spring lectures, 1961)
1. Theology, Pastoral. I. Montgomery, Riley Benjamin, 1895- II. Series.

[MONTGOMERY, Richmond Ames] 1870- 250
The triumphant ministry; letters from Timothy Kilbourn [pseud.] to Fred Gaynor ... with an introduction by Charles R. Erdman, D. D. Philadelphia, The Westminster press, 1914. x, 107 p. 18 cm. [BV4010.M55] 15-8130
1. Theology, Pastoral. I. Title.
Contents omitted.

MOORE, William Thomas, 1832-1926. 250
Preacher problems; or, The twentieth century preacher at his work, by William Thomas Moore, LL. D. New York, Chicago [etc.] Fleming H. Revell company [1907] 2 p. l., 3, [v]-vi, [2], [7]-387 p. 21 cm. [BV4010.M57] 7-13917
1. Theology, Pastoral. I. Title.

MORALS for ministers, 258
by R. E. X. New York, The Macmillan company, 1928. 151 p. 20 cm. [BV4012.M6] 28-8351
1. Theology, Pastoral. I. X., R. E. II. R. E. X.

MORGAN, George Campbell, 1863- 250
...Ministry of the Word, by G. Campbell Morgan, D.D. New York, Chicago [etc.] Fleming H. Revell company [1919] 222 p. 19 1/2 cm. (The James Sprunt lectures delivered at Union theological seminary in Virginia) [BV4010.M6] 20-2356
1. Theology, Pastoral. I. Title.

MORRISON, John Arch, 1893- 250
The preacher of today, by John A. Morrison. Anderson, Ind., The Warner press [c1937] vii, 9-136 p. 19cm. [BV4010.M64] 37-35136
1. Theology, Pastoral. I. Title.

MOTT, John Raleigh, 1865-
The pastor and modern missions; a plea for leadership in world evangelization; by John R. Mott ... New York, Student volunteer movement for foreign missions, 1904. ix p., 2 l., 249 p. 19 1/2 cm. "The general outline of the book is essentially the same as that followed in a course of lectures given in the spring of the present year at Ohio Wesleyan university (on the Merrick foundation), at Yale divinity school, and this autumn at McCormick theological seminary, and at Princeton theological seminary (on the Students' foundation)"--Pref. Appendix. The pastor's missionary library: p. [213]-226. [BV4370.M6] 4-35057
1. Theology, Pastoral. 2. Missions, Foreign. I. Title.

MUELLER, Frederick Ferdinand, 1904- 250
Ethical dilemmas of ministers, by Frederick F. Mueller ... and Hugh Hartshorne ... New York, C. Scribner's sons; London, C. Scribner's sons, ltd., 1937. xii, 250 p. 21 cm. Bibliography: p. [299]-242. [BV4012.M78] 37-21926
1. Theology, Pastoral. I. Hartshorne, Hugh, 1885- joint author. II. Title.

MURPHY, Thomas, 1823-1900. 250
Pastoral theology. The pastor in the various duties of his office. By Thomas Murphy ... Philadelphia, Presbyterian board of publication [1877] 509 p. 24 cm. [BV4010.M7] 38-817
1. Theology, Pastoral. I. Presbyterian church in the U. S. A. Board of publication. II. Title.

MURRAY, Nicholas, 1802-1861. 250
Preachers and preaching. By Rev. Nicholas Murray ... New York, Harper & brothers, 1860. xii, [3]-303 p. 20 cm. [BV4010.M75] 38-3176
1. Theology, Pastoral. I. Title.

NEILL, Stephen Charles, Bp. 250
Fulfill thy ministry. [1st ed.] New York, Harper [1952] 152 p. 20 cm. [BV4010.N4] 51-11944
1. Theology, Pastoral. I. Title.

NELSON, Peter Christopher, 1868- 253
The young minister's guide in conducting funerals, solenizing weddings, administering baptism and the Lord's supper and anointing the sick ... by P. C. Nelson ... Enid, Okla., Southwestern press [c1932] 3 p. l., 9-67 p. 20 cm. [BV4016.N4] 32-25429
1. Theology, Pastoral. I. Title.

NOEL, Samuel Lucky, 1876- 264.05
Minister's handbook; a guide for ministers in the performance of their official duties, containing helpful suggestions in ministerial decorum. By Rev. S. L. Noel ... Nashville, Tenn. [Printed by the Cumberland Presbyterian publishing house, 1932] 192 p. 18 cm. [BV4016.N6] 32-11230
1. Theology, Pastoral. I. Cumberland Presbyterian church. Liturgy and ritual. II. Title.

OATES, Wayne E 1917- 250
The Christian pastor. Philadelphia, Westminster Press [1951] 171 p. 21 cm. [BV4010.O2] 51-9873
1. Theology. Pastoral. 2. Psychology, Pastoral. I. Title.

OATES, Wayne Edward, 1917- 250
The Christian pastor. Philadelphia, Westminster Press [1951] 171p. 21cm. [BV4010.O2] 51-9873
1. Theology, Pastoral. 2. Psychology, Pastoral. I. Title.

ORTON, Job, 1717-1783. 274.
Letters to a young clergyman, from the late Reverend Mr. Job Orton ... Boston: Printed by Manning & Loring for James White, at Franklin's head, Court-street. mdccxciv. v, [7]-120 p. 20 cm. [BX5202.O6 1794] 1-10147
1. Theology, Pastoral. 2. Preaching. I. Title.

OSBORNE, Charles Edward, 1856-
The Christian priest of to-day; lectures in pastoral theology delivered in the University of Durham, 1933, by the Rev. C. E. Osborne ... with a prefatory note by the Bishop of Durham. London and Oxford, A. R. Mowbray & co. ltd.; Milwaukee, Morehouse pub. co. [1934] xi, [1], 149 p. 19 cm. A 35
1. Theology, Pastoral. I. Title.

PALMER, Albert Wentworth, 1879- 253
The minister's job, by Albert W. Palmer... Chicago, New York, Willett, Clark & company, 1937. vii p., 1 l., 102 p. 20 1/2 cm. (The minister's professional library) [BV4010.P18] 38-27059
1. Theology, Pastoral. I. Title.

PARKHURST, Charles Henry, 1842-1933. 250
The pulpit and the pew; Lyman Beecher lectures delivered 1913, before the Divinity school of Yale university, by Charles H. Parkhurst ... New Haven, Conn., Yale university press, 1913. 4 p. l., 195 p. 22 cm. [BV4010.P3] 13-18730
1. Theology, Pastoral. 2. Church work. I. Title.

PATTISON, Thomas Harwood, 1838-1904. 250
For the work of the ministry; for the classroom, the study and the street, by T. Harwood Pattison ... Elaborated by his son, Harold Pattison ... Philadelphia, American Baptist publication society, 1907. xii, 558 p. front. (port.) 20 cm. Includes bibliographies. [BV4010.P35] 7-11044
1. Theology, Pastoral. I. Pattison, Harold, 1869- II. American Baptist publication society. III. Title.

PEASE, Jay J. 253
Christian worker's manual of practical knowledge, by Rev. J. J. Pease ... Practical pointers for preachers and pastors. Grand Rapids, Mich., Zondervan publishing house [c1941] 96 p. 20 cm. [BV4012.P4] 42-6479
1. Theology, Pastoral. I. Title.

PLEUNE, Peter Henry, 1883- 250
Some to be pastors [by] Peter H. Pleune ... New York, Nashville, Abingdon-Cokesbury press [1943] 191 p. 19 1/2 cm. "War edition." [BV4010.P55] 43-16171
1. Theology, Pastoral. I. Title.

PLUMER, William Swan, 1802-1880. 250
Hints and helps in pastoral theology. By William S. Plumer ... New York, Harper & brothers, 1874. iv p., 1 l., [7]-381 p. 20 1/2cm. [BV4010.P6] 38-820
1. Theology, Pastoral. I. Title.

POND, Enoch, 1791-1882. 250
Lectures on pastoral theology. By Enoch Pond ... Andover, W. F. Draper; New York, Hurd & Houghton; [etc., etc.] 1866. 395 p. 20 cm. Published in 1844 under title: The young pastor's guide: or, Lectures on pastoral duties. [BV4010.P65 1866] 38-818
1. Theology, Pastoral. I. Title.

POND, Enoch, 1791-1882. 250
Lectures on pastoral theology. By Enoch Pond ... Boston, Draper and Halliday; Philadelphia, Smith, English, and co.; [etc., etc.] 1867. 395 p. 20 cm. Published in 1844 under title: The young pastor's guide: or, Lectures on pastoral duties. [BV4010.P65 1867] 38-35196
1. Theology, Pastoral. I. Title.

POND, Enoch, 1791-1882. 250
The young pastor's guide; or, Lectures on pastoral duties. By Enoch Pond ... Bangor, E. F. Duren; New York, E. Collier; [etc., etc.] 1844. xii, [13]-377 p. 20 cm. On cover: Pastor's guide. Published in 1866 under title: Lectures on pastoral theology. [BV4010.P65 1844] 38-819
1. Theology, Pastoral. I. Title. II. Title: Pastor's guide.

PORTER, James, 1808-1888. 250
Hints to self-educated ministers. Including local preachers, exhorters, and other Christians, whose duty it may be to speak more or less in public. By James Porter ... with an introduction, by Bishop William L. Harris ... New York, Phillips & Hunt; Cincinnati, Hitchcock & Walden [1879] 300 p. 19 cm. [BV4010.P68 1879] 38-633
1. Theology, Pastoral. 2. Preaching. I. Harris, William Logan, bp. 1817-1887. II. Title.

PORTER, James, 1808-1888. 250
Hints to self-educated ministers. Including local preachers, exhorters, and other Christians, whose duty it may be to speak more or less in public. By James Porter ... with an introduction, by Bishop William L. Harris ... 7ththousand. New York, Eaton & Mains; Cincinnati, Jennings & Graham [c1907] 299 p. 19 cm. First published in 1879. [BV4010.P68 1907] 7-25066
1. Theology, Pastoral. 2. Preaching. I. Harris, William Logan, bp., 1817-1887. II. Title.

POTEAT, Edwin McNeill, 1892- 250
Reverend John Doe, D. D., a study of the place of the minister in the modern world, by Edwin McNeill Poteat, jr. New York and London, Harper & brothers, 1935. 6 p. l., 127 p. 19 cm. "First edition." [BV4010.P7] 35-6981
1. Theology, Pastoral. I. Title.

POWELL, Sidney Waterbury, 1889- 250
Where are the people? By Sidney W. Powell. New York, Nashville, Abingdon-Cokesbury press [1942] 223 p. incl. forms. 20 1/2 cm. [BV4012.P74] 42-22922
1. Theology, Pastoral. 2. Church work. I. Title.

PYM, Thomas Wentworth, 1885- 250
A parson's dilemmas, by T. W. Pym ... Milwaukee, Wis., Morehouse publishing co. [1930] 125, [1] p. 20 cm. Printed in Great Britain. Six lectures in pastoral theology for 1929-30, delivered at the University of Cambridge. cf. Pref. [BV4010.P78] 31-33819
1. Theology, Pastoral. I. Lectures in pastoral theology, Cambridge university, 1929-30. II. Title.
Contents omitted.

RAWLINSON, Alfred Edward John, bp. of Derby, 1884- 250
The church and the challenge of to-day, a primary visitation charge to the clergy of the diocese of Derby, by A. E. J. Rawlinson ... London, New York [etc.] Longmans, Green and co., 1937. viii, 135, [1] p. 19 cm. "Some recommended books": p. 131-[136] [BX5175.R3 1937] 38-35280
1. Theology, Pastoral. 2. Church of England—Pastoral letters and charges. I. Title.

RAY, Jefferson Davis, 1860- 253
The country preacher, by Jeff D. Ray ... Nashville, Tenn., Sunday school board of the Southern Baptist convention [c1925] 132 p. 20 cm. Bibliography: p. 128-132. [BV4012.R3] 26-23224
1. Theology, Pastoral. 2. Rural churches. I. Title.

REYNOLDS, Ralph Vincent. 250
Making full proof of our ministry; a handbook of elementary pastoral studies based on the Scriptures. [Winnipeg, Columbia Press, 1953] 145p. 20cm. [BV4010.R4] 53-30886
1. Theology, Pastoral. I. Title.

RIDOUT, Daniel Lyman. 230
A young man enters the ministry, by Daniel Lyman Ridout. Boston, The Christopher publishing house [c1936] 76 p. 21 cm. [BV4010.R45] 36-16887
1. Theology, Pastoral. 2. Clergy. I. Title.

RIGGS, Ralph M 1895- 250
The spirit-filled pastor's guide. Springfield, Mo., Gospel Pub. House [1949, c1948] 287 p. 20 cm. [BV4010.R48] 49-16986
1. Theology, Pastoral. I. Title.

RILEY, William Bell, 1861- 250
Pastoral problems, by W. B. Riley ... New York [etc.] Fleming H. Revell company [c1936] 192 p. 20 cm. [BV4010.R5] 36-9447
1. Theology, Pastoral. I. Title.

ROBERTS, Benjamin Titus, 1823-1893. 250
Fishers of men; or, Practical hints to those who would win souls. By Rev. B. T. Roberts ... Rochester, N. Y., G. L. Roberts & co., 1878. 289 p. 20 cm. [BV4010.R6] 38-821
1. Theology, Pastoral. I. Title.

ROGERS, Clement Francis, 1866-
An introduction to the study of pastoral theology, by the Rev. Clement F. Rogers... Oxford, The Clarendon press, 1912. 291 p. 22 1/2 cm. A 19
I. Title.

ROGERS, Clement Francis, 1866-
Pastoral theology and the modern world, by the Rev. Clement F. Rogers... Oxford, New York, Oxford university press, Humphrey Milford; [etc., etc.] 1920. vii, 176 p. 19 cm. A 20
1. Theology, Pastoral. I. Title.

ROWE, Alexander Thomas, 1874- 250
Ideals for Christian service, by A. T. Rowe ... Anderson, Ind., The Warner press [1944] xii, 13-118 p. 19 cm. [BV4012.R67] 44-34542
1. Theology, Pastoral. 2. Church work. I. Title.

THE rural pastor:
his home and office, by C. R. McBride. Kansas City, Kan., Central Seminary press [c1956] vi, 147p. 29cm. Mimeographed.
1. Theology, Pastoral. 2. Rural churches. I. McBride, Charles R

SANGSTER, William Edwin, 1900- 250
The approach to preaching. Philadelphia, Westminster Press [1952] 112p. 20cm. [BV4010.S16] 52-7115
1. Theology, Pastoral. I. Title.

SANGSTER, William Edwin Robert, 1900- 250
The approach to preaching [by] W. E. Sangster Grand Rapids Baker Book House [1974, c1952] 112 p. 20 cm. [BV4010.S16] ISBN 0-8010-8023-1 1.95 (pbk.)
1. Theology, Pastoral. I. Title.
L.C. card no. for original edition: 52-7115.

SCARBOROUGH, Lee Rutland, 1870- 250
My conception of the gospel ministry, by Lee Rutland Scarborough ... Nashville, Tenn., The Sunday school board of the Southern Baptist convention [c1935] 101 p. 19 1/2 cm. [BV4010.S24] 36-634
1. Theology, Pastoral. I. Title.

SCHINDLER, Carl J. 258
The pastor as a personal counselor, a manual of pastoral psychology, by Carl J. Schindler... Philadelphia, Muhlenberg press [c1942] 4 p. l., 147 p. 20 cm. [BV4012.S37] 42-20406
1. Theology,Pastoral. I. Title.

SCHUETTE, Walter Erwin. 253
The minister's personal guide. [1st ed.] New York, Harper [1953] 183p. 22cm. [BV4012.S29] 53-5448
1. Theology, Pastoral. I. Title.

SHOEMAKER, Samuel Moor, 1893- 250
The church alive. [1st ed.] New York, Dutton, 1950. 160 p. 20 cm. [BV4010.S535] 50-7524
1. Theology, Pastoral. 2. Church work. I. Title.

SHOEMAKER, Samuel Moor, 1893- 250
How you can help other people, by Samuel M. Shoemaker. New York, E. P. Dutton & co., inc., 1946. 189 p. 20 cm. "First edition." Bibliographical foot-notes. [BV4012.S5] 46-319
1. Theology, Pastoral. I. Title.

SHRADER, Wesley. 250
Dear Charles; letters to a young minister. New York, Macmillan, 1954. 109p. 21cm. [BV4015.S35] 54-12798
1. Theology, Pastoral. I. Title.

SMITH, Alson Jesse. 248
Live all your life. Chicago, H. Regnery, 1955. 219 p. 22 cm. [BV4010.S545] 55-11493
1. Theology, Pastoral. 2. Psychology, Applied. I. Title.

SMITH, Henry Griggs Weston, 1890- 268.332
The pastor at work in Christian education, by Henry G. Weston Smith. Philadelphia, Boston [etc.] The Judson press [c1935] 5 p. l., 110 p. 20 cm. [BV4360.S5] 35-14702
1. Theology, Pastoral. 2. Religious education. I. Title.

SMITH, John, 1747-1807. 250
Lectures on the nature and end of the sacred office, and on the dignity, duty, qualifications and character of the sacred order. By John Smith ... Philadelphia, Sorin & Ball, 1843. xvi, [17]-284 p. 19 1/2 cm. [BV4010.S55 1843] 15-22810
1. Theology, Pastoral. 2. Clergy. I. Title.

SMITH, Karl Franklin. 250
The Scriptural view of the Christian pastorate. [Columbus? Ohio, 1951] 154 p. 19 cm. [BV4012.S56 1951] 51-39053
1. Theology, Pastoral. I. Title.

SMITH, Karl Franklin. 250
The Scriptural view of the Christian pastorate, by Karl Franklin Smith. [Columbus, O., 1944] v, 154 p. 19 cm. [BV4012.S56] 44-22356
1. Theology, Pastoral. I. Title.

SMITH, Reuben, 1789-1860. 250
The pastoral office, embracing experiences and observations from a pastorate of forty years. By the Rev. Reuben Smith. Philadelphia, Presbyterian board of publication [1859] 105 p. 15 1/2 cm. [BV4010.S6] 38-828
1. Theology, Pastoral. I. Presbyterian church in the U.S.A. (Old school) Board of publication. II. Title.

SPANN, John Richard, 1891- ed. 258
Pastoral care. New York, Abingdon-Cokesbury Press [1951] 272 p. 23 cm. [BV4010.S63] 51-13150
1. Theology, Pastoral. I. Title.

SPRING, Gardiner, 1785-1873. 250
The power of the pulpit; or, Thoughts addressed to Christian ministers and those who hear them. By Gardiner Spring ... New York, Baker and Scribner, 1848. vi, 7-459 p. front. (port.) 19 cm. [BV4010.S65] 38-830
1. Theology, Pastoral. 2. Preaching. I. Title.

STORER, James Wilson. 250
The preacher, his belief and behavior. Nashville, Broadman Press [1953] 104p. 20cm. [BV4010.S757] 53-9034
1. Theology. Pastoral. I. Title.

STOUGHTON, Clarence Charles, 1895- 250
... Set apart for the gospel, by Clarence C. Stoughton ... Philadelphia, Pa., The Board of publication of the United Lutheran church in America [1946] 3 p. l., 89 p. 21 cm. (The Knubel-Miller foundation of the United Lutheran church in America. Lectures. Second series) [BV4010.S77] 47-16593
1. Theology, Pastoral. I. Title.

SWEET, Louis Matthews, 1869- 250
The pastoral ministry in our time, by Louis Matthews Sweet and Malcolm Stuart Sweet. New York, F. H. Revell Co. [1949] 192 p. 20 cm. Bibliographical references included in "Acknowledgements" (p. 5-6) [BV4010.S83] 49-8166
1. Theology, Pastoral. I. Sweet, Malcolm Stuart, 1905- joint author. II. Title.

SWEETSER, Seth, 1807-1878. 250
The ministry we need. By S. Sweetser ... Boston, American tract society; New York,

Hurd and Houghton [1873] 123 p. 17 cm. [BV4010.S85] 38-827
1. Theology, Pastoral. I. American tract society. II. Title.

TAYLOR, William Mackergo, 1829-1895. 250
The ministry of the word. By Wm. M. Taylor ... New York, A. D. F. Randolph & company, 1876. 5 p. l., 318 p. 19 1/2 cm. "The 'Lyman Beecher lectures', for 1876."--Pref. [BV4010.T3] 38-836
1. Theology, Pastoral. I. Title.

THOMAS, William Henry Griffith, 1861-1924. 250
Ministerial life and work, by W. H. Griffith Thomas, D.D.; an abridgement of The work of the ministry, by his wife. Chicago, The Bible institute colportage ass'n. [c1927] 6 p. l., 11-236 p. 20 cm. Foreword signed: Alice Griffith Thomas. [BV4010.T4] 27-3050
1. Theology, Pastoral. I. Thomas, Mrs. Alice Griffith. II. Title.

TIDWELL, Josiah Blake, 1870- 250
Concerning preachers; what all preachers should know, by Josiah Blake Tidwell ... New York [etc.] Fleming H. Revell company [c1937] 188 p. 19 1/2 cm. [BV4010.T53] 37-14086
1. Theology, Pastoral. I. Title.

TILDEN, William Phillips, 1811-1890. 250
The work of the ministry. Lectures given to the Meadville theological school, June, 1889. By Rev. W. P. Tilden. Boston, G. H. Ellis, 1890. 138 p. 18 cm. [BV4010.T55] 38-3764
1. Theology, Pastoral. I. Title.

TOWNSEND, Luther Tracy, 1838-1922. 250
The sword and garment, by Rev. L. T. Townsend ... Boston, Lee and Shepard; New York, Lee, Shepard and Dillingham, 1871. 2 p. l., 7-238 p. 18 cm. "These pages were orginally prepared as a discourse upon ministerial education, and were delivered before the New England Methodist Episcopal conference, Boston, April, 1871."--p. 7. [BV4010.T6] 38-826
1. Theology, Pastoral. I. Title.

TREXLER, Samuel Geiss, 1877- 250
Out of thirty-five years; being leaves from the life book of a Lutheran pastor who looks out on the world and sees both good and evil. By Samuel Trexler ... New York, London, G. P. Putnam's sons, 1936. 159 p. front. (port.) 21 1/2 cm. [BV4010.T7] 36-7292
1. Theology, Pastoral. I. Title.

TUPPER, Charles B. 250
Called, in honor; ethics of the Christian ministry creatively interpreted. St. Louis, Bethany Press [1949] 158 p. facism 20 cm. "Appendix: My ministerial code of ethics," prepared by the Committee on Effective Ministry of the Home and State Missions Planning Council of Disciples of Christ: p. 155-158. [BV4012.T78] 50-1426
1. Theology, Pastoral. I. Disciples of Christ. Home and State Missions Planning Council. My ministerial code of ethics. II. Disciples of Christ. Home and State Missions Planning Council. My ministerial code of ethics. III. Disciples of Christ, Home and State Missions Planning Council. My ministerial code of ethics IV. Title.

TURNBULL, Ralph G. 253
A minister's obstacles, by Ralph G. Turnbull ... New York, London [etc.] Fleming H. Revell company [1946] 159 p. 19 1/2 cm. [BV4012.T8] 47-1163
1. Theology, Pastoral. I. Title.

TYNG, Stephen Higginson, 1800-1885. 250
The office and duty of a Christian pastor. By Stephen H. Tyng ... New York, Harper & brothers, 1874. 1 p. l., [7]-178 p. 19 1/2 cm. Lectures delivered in the School of theology, Boston university. [BV4010.T8] 38-824
1. Theology, Pastoral. I. Title.

VINET, Alexandre Rodolphe, 1797-1847. 250
Pastoral theology; or, The theory of the evangelical ministry. By A. Vinet. Translated and edited by Thomas H. Skinner ... With notes, and an additional chapter, by the translator ... New York, Harper & brothers, 1853. xix, [21]-387 p. 20 1/2 cm. "Errata" slip inserted at end. [BV4010.V5] 37-35235
1. Theology, Pastoral I. Skinner, Thomas Harvey, 1791-1871, tr. II. Title.

WALLACE, Oates Charles Symonds, 1856- 250
Pastor and people, by O. C. S. Wallace... Nashville, Tenn., Broadman press [c1936] 126 p. port. 19 1/2 cm. [BV4010.W23] 37-2514
1. Theology, Pastoral. I. Title.

WATERHOUSE, Eric Strickland, 1879- 251
Psychology and pastoral work, by Eric S. Waterhouse ... Nashville, Cokesbury press [c1940] 316 p. 22 1/2 cm. (Half-title: The London theological library, under the editorship of E. S. Waterhouse) [BV4012.W35] 40-6287
1. Theology, Pastoral. 2. Psychology, Religious. I. Title.

WAYLAND, Francis, 1796-1865. 250
The apostolic ministry: a discourse delivered in Rochester, N.Y., before the New York Baptist union for ministerial education, July 12, 1853. By Francis Wayland ... 8th thousand. Rochester, Sage & brother, 1853. 84 p. 17 cm. [BV4017.W3 1853] 33-8311
1. Theology, Pastoral. I. Title.

WAYLAND, Francis, 1796-1865. 250
Letters on the ministry of the gospel. By Francis Wayland. Boston, Gould and Lincoln; New York, Sheldon and company; [etc., etc.] 1863. xii, [13]-210 p. 18 cm. [BV4010.W35 1863] 35-23134
1. Theology, Pastoral. I. Title.

WAYLAND, Francis, 1796-1865. 250
Letters on the ministry of the gospel. By Francis Wayland. Boston, Gould and Lincoln; New York, Sheldon and company; [etc., etc.] 1864. 2 p. l., [vii]-xii, [13]-210 p. 18 cm. [BV4010.W35] 34-32832
1. Theology, Pastoral. I. Title.

WHITE, William Spottswood, 1800-1873. 250
The gospel ministry, in a series of letters from a father to his sons. By the Rev. Wm. S. White... Philadelphia, Presbyterian board of publication [1860] 204 p. 15 1/2 cm. [BV4010.W52] 38-829
1. Theology, Pastoral. I. Presbyterian church in the U.S.A. (Old School) Board of publication. II. Title.

WILLCOX, Giles Buckingham, 1826-1922. 250
The pastor amidst his flock. By Rev. G. B. Willcox... New York, American tract society [1890] 186 p. 20 1/2 cm. [BV4010.W53] 38-825
1. Theology, Pastoral. I. American tract society. II. Title.

WILLIAMS, Charles David bp 1860-1923 250
The prophetic ministry for today, by Charles D. Williams. New York, The Macmillan company, 1921. 5 p. l., 7-183 p. 19 1/2 cm. Lyman Beecher lectures on preaching. Yale university. [BV4010.W537] 21-20138
1. Theology, Pastoral. I. Title.

WILLIAMS, Ernest Swing, 1885- 250
A faithful minister; heart-to-heart talks, by Ernest S. Williams. Springifled, Mo., Gospel publishing house [c1941] 112 p. 19 cm. [BV4010.W538] 41-9813
1. Theology, Pastoral. I. Title.

WILSON, James Maurice, 1836-1931. 250
Six lectures on pastoral theology, with an appendix on the influence of scientific training on the reception of religious truth, by the Ven. James M. Wilson ... London, Macmillan and co., limited; New York, The Macmillan company, 1903. xi, 262 p. 20 cm. "Appendix I. List of books on social subjects": p. 211-213. "Appendix II. Science and theology": p. 215-262. [BV4010.W55] 3-22953
1. Theology, Pastoral. 2. Religion and science—1900- I. Title.

WOOD, Leland Foster, 1885- 258
Pastoral counseling in family relationships. New York, Commission on Marriage and the Home of the Federal Council of the Churches of Christ in America [1948] 96 p. 21 cm. "Some helps for counselors": p. 92-96. [BV4012.W62] 48-10556
1. Theology, Pastoral. 2. Counseling. 3. Family. I. Federal Council of the Churches of Christ in America. Commission on Marriage and the Home. II. Title.

WOODS, Frank Theodore, bp. of Peterborough, 1874-
Interpreters of God, by Frank Theodore Woods ... London, Society for promoting Christian knowledge; New York [etc.] Macmillan, 1922. vii, [8]-87, [1] p. 22 1/2 cm. "My first charge to the Diocese of Peterborough."--p.v. A 22
1. Theology, Pastoral. I. Title.

ZAHNISER, Charles Reed, 1873- 258
The soul doctor, by Charles Reed Zahniser. New York, Round table press, inc., 1938. viii p., 1 l., 209 p. 20 cm. [BV4010.Z3] 38-9007
1. Theology, Pastoral. 2. Psychology, Religious. I. Title.

ZIMMERMAN, Leander M., 1860- 250
The gospel minister, by L. M. Zimmerman. Baltimore, Md., Meyer & Thalheimer, 1930. 118 p. 21 cm. [BV4010.Z5] 31-1290
1. Theology, Pastoral. I. Title.

Theology, Pastoral—Addresses, Eassays, lectures.

ESSAYS on the priesthood [offered to St. Meinrad Archabbey on the occasion of its centenary (1854-1954) by members of the alumni. St. Meinrad, Ind., St. Meinrao Seminary, 1954. 100p. port. 23cm. (St. Meinrad essays, v.11, no.1) Cover title. Bibliographical footnotes. A55
1. St. Melnrao Arch. anney, Meinrao, Ind. 2. Theology, Pastoral—Addresses, Eassays, lectures. 3. [Priesthood] I. Series.
Contents omitted.

Theology, Pastoral—Anecdotes, facetiae, satire, etc.

ANDERSON, Kenneth, 1917- 250.88
It only happens to preachers. Grand Rapids, Zondervan Pub. House [1956] 185p. 20cm. [BV4015.A5] 56-41991
1. Theology. Pastoral—Anecdotes, facetiae, satire, etc. I. Title.

BRYANT, Marion S. 250.69
Parish child, by Marion S. Bryant; an informal memoir of the turn of the century. Portland, Me., Falmouth publishing house, 1940. 4 p. l., 3-74 p. 21 cm. [BV4015.B7] 41-1350
1. Theology, Pastoral—Ancedotes, facetise, satire, etc. I. Title.

HUMPHREYS, George W. 250.88
A pastor speaks out, by George W. Humphreys ... Philadelphia, The Blakiston company, distributed by Fleming H. Revell company, New York and London [c1943] 90 p. 19 cm. [BV4015.H8] 44-2043
1. Theology, Pastoral—Anecdotes, facetiae, satire, etc. I. Title.
Contents omitted.

LE MOINE, Emanuel Aaron. 250.88
A parson's crystal, by Emanuel A. LeMoine, S.T.M. [Belair, Md., The Bond street press, inc.] c1943. 3 p. l., 102 p. 18 1/2 cm [BV4015.L4] 44-26826
1. Theology, Pastoral—Anecdotes, facetiae, satire, etc. I. Title.

LORD, Daniel Aloysius, 1888- 250.883
That made me smile; a collection of incidents that have amused me "along the way," by Daniel A. Lord, S. J. St. Louis, Mo., The Queen's work [1941] 170 p., 1 l. 20 cm. [BV4015.L6] 41-25776
1. Theology, Pastoral—Anecdotes, facetise, satire, etc. I. Title.

MANN, Hames. 250
Clerical types. By The Rev. Hames Mann. New York and London, Funk & Wagnalls company, 1897. 217 p. 19 1/2 cm. [BV4010.M35] 38-832
1. Theology, Pastoral—Anecdotes, facetiae, satire, etc. I. Title.

OWENS, Loulie (Latimer) 250.88
Minnie Belle. Illustrated by Murray McKeehan. Nashville, Broadman Press [1956] 109p. illus. 22cm. [PS3529.W4419M5] 56-8671
1. Theology, Pastoral—Anecdotes, facetiae, satire, etc. I. Title.

PARTRIDGE, John A. 250.883
From a parson's diary, by John A. Partridge. Nashville, Tenn., Parthenon press [c1940] 232 p. front. (port.) illus. 20 cm. "First edition." [BV4015.P35] 41-3974
1. Theology, Pastoral—Anecdotes, facstiae, satire, etc. I. Title.

PORTER, Alyene 253.088
Papa was a preacher. Illus. by Janet Smalley. Nashville, Abingdon Pr., [1960, c.1944] 167p. (Apex Bks. E5) 1.00 pap.,
1. Theology, Pastoral—Anecdotes, facetiae, satire, etc. I. Title.

PORTER, Alyene. 253
Papa was a preacher, by Alyene Porter, illustrated by Janet Smalley. New York, Nashville, Abingdon-Cokesbury press [1944] 167 p. incl. front., illus. 20 1/2 cm. [BV4014.P6] 44-6357
1. Theology, Pastoral—Anecdotes, facetiae, satire, etc. I. Smalley, Janet, 1898- illus. II. Title.

[SMALL, James Louis] 1878- ed. 250
Within my parish; notes from the day book of a deceased parish priest, edited by James Loomis, M.D. [pseud.] Philadelphia, The Dolphin press, 1914. 4 p.l., 101 p. 17 cm. "The following sketches appeared at intervals during the year 1914 in the American ecclesiastical review."--Foreword. [BX1912.S65] 14-21767
1. Theology, Pastoral—Anecdotes, facetiae, satire, etc. I. Title.

SMITH, Daniel, 1806-1852. 248
Anecdotes and illustrations of the Christian ministry. Compiled by Rev. Daniel Smith. With an introduction by Rev. D. W. Clark, A.M. New York, Lane & Scott, 1852. 443 p. 15 1/2 cm. [BV4915.S6 1852] 7-28748
1. Theology, Pastoral—Anecdotes, facetiae, satire, etc. 2. Homiletical illustrations. I. Title.

WATSON, James V 1814-1856. 258
Tales and takings, sketches and incidents, from the intinerant and editorial budget of Rev. J. V. Watson... New York, Carlton & Porter, 1857. 1 p. l., [5]-466 p. 19 1/2 cm. [BV4014.W3] CA 12
1. Theology, Pastoral—Anecdotes, facetiae, satire, etc. I. Title.

ZIMMERMAN, Leander M., 1860- 250.883
The preacher's doorknob, by Leander M. Zimmerman. Philadelphia, Muhlenberg press [1942] 3 p. l., 58 p. 16 cm. "First printing, January 1, 1942." [BV4015.Z5] 42-9443
1. Theology, Pastoral—Anecdotes, facetiae, satire, etc. I. Title.

Theology, Pastoral—Anglican communion.

CONKLING, Wallace Edmonds, bp., 1896- 250
Priesthood in action, by Wallace Edmonds Conkling, the bishop of Chicago. New York, Morehouse-Gorham co., 1945. xv, 196 p. diagr. 21 cm. [BV4010.C58] 45-22091
1. Theology, Pastoral—Anglican communion. I. Title.

FENN, Don Frank, 1890- 250
Parish administration. 2d ed. New York, Morehouse-Gorham Co., 1951. 334 p. 23 cm. [BX5965.F4 1951] 51-8948
1. Theology, Pastoral—Anglican communion. 2. Church work. 3. Sunday-schools. I. Title.

FENN, Don Frank, 1890- 250
Parish administration by the Reverend Don Frank Fenn ... New York, Morehouse-Gorham Co., 1938. 334 p. 22 cm. [BX5965.F4] 38-15329
1. Theology, Pastoral—Anglican communion. 2. Church work. 3. Sunday-schools. I. Title.

KNOWLES, Archibald Campbell, 1865- 250
Lights and shadows of the sacred ministry. West Park, N.Y., Holy Cross Press, 1947. xii, 160 p. 20 cm. [BV4010.K6] 47-24956
1. Theology, Pastoral—Anglican communion. I. Title.

PARKER, John William, 1892- 250
The rural priesthood, by J. W. Parker ... London, The Faith press, ltd.; New York, Morehouse-Gorham co. [1939] 3 p. l., 80 p. 18 cm. "First published, September, 1939." [BV4012.P3] 42-46764
1. Theology, Pastoral—Anglican communion. 2. Rural churches—England. I. Title.

SEYZINGER, Edmund. 250
The glory of priesthood, by Edmund Seyzinger...with a foreword by the Bishop of London. London and Oxford, A. R. Mowbray & co., ltd. Milwaukee, Morehouse publishing co. [1933] xi, 167, [1] p. 19 cm. "First published in 1933." [Full name: Ernest Edmund Seyzinger] [BX5175.S4] 34-29187
1. Theology, Pastoral—Anglican communion. I. Title.

Theology, Pastoral — Catholic Church.

ANLER, Ludwig, 1882- 262.14
The pastoral companion. Formerly edited by Honoratus Bonzelet. 11th ed., rev. and amplified by Marcian J. Mathis and Clement R. Leahy. Chicago, Franciscan Herald Press [1956] 419p. 20cm. 'A translation and an adaptation of Fr. Louis Anler's German work, Comes pastoralis.' [BX1912.A63 1956] 56-14215
1. Theology. Pastoral—Catholic Church. 2. Canon law. 3. Sacraments—Catholic Church. I. Title.

[ANLER, Ludwig] 1882- 262.14
The pastoral companion, by Fr. Honoratys Bonzelet, O. F. M. 9th ed. Chicago, Franciscan herald press, 1943. vii, 228 p. 20 cm. "An adaptation of 'Comes postoralis' by Fr. Louis Anler."--Pref. [BX1912.A63 1943] 44-470
1. Theology, Pastoral—Catholic church. 2. Canon law. 3. Sacraments—Catholic church. I. Bonzelet, Honoratus, ed. and tr. II. Title.

[ANLER, Ludwig] 1882- 262.14
The pastoral companion, by Fr. Honoratus Bonzelet O. F. M. 10th ed. Chicago, Franciscan herald press, 1945. 2 p. l., iii-vii, 240 p., 1 l. 19 cm. "An adaptation of Comes pastoralis by Fr. Louis Anler."--Pref. [BX1912.A63 1945] 45-18236
1. Theology, Pastoral—Catholic church. 2. Canon law. 3. Sacraments—Catholic church. I. Bonzelet, Honoratus, ed. and tr. II. Title.

BUCHANAN, Henry Donnelly, 1887- 253
Art of persuasion in pastoral theology, based on seventy cases as concrete examples, by the Very Reverend Henry D. Buchanan. Philadelphia, Pa., The Dolphin press, 1940. 2 p. l., 96 p. 18 cm. Contents.--pt. 1. Persuasion. Motives.--pt.11. Principles of strategy. Preparation for persuasion. Errors to be avoided. Persistency. 40-34453
1. Theology, Pastoral—Catholic church. 2. Persuasion (Rhetoric) I. Title.

CARROLL, Charles Borromeo, 1872- 808.5
The priest's voice, its use and misuse [by] Rev. Charles B. Carroll ... [Baltimore, Md., Printed by Baer publicity co., inc., 1940] xiv, 177, 177a-177b, [178]-199 p. illus. (incl. music) diagrs. 23 cm. "Notes and bibliography": p. 189-192. [BX1912.C33] 40-7580
1. Theology, Pastroal—Catholic church. 2. Voice. I. Title.

FOSTER, John, 1898- 262.2
Requiem for a parish; an inquiry into customary practices and procedures in the contemporary parish. Westminster, Md., Newman, [c.]1962. 155p. 21cm. 62-16214 3.00
1. Theology, Pastoral—Catholic Church. I. Title.

GOGGINS, Ralph Damian. 271.2
Toward the clerical-religious life; a sketch of the requirements, life, and labors of the priesthood in the Dominican order, by Ralph Damian Goggins ... with a preface, by Most Reverend Martin Stanislaus Gillet ... Milwaukee, The Bruce publishing company [c1933] xii, 140 p. front., plates. 21 cm. [BX3502.G6] 34-567
1. Theology, Pastoral—Catholic church. 2. Priests. 3. Dominicans. I. Title.

GREGORIUS i, the Great Saint, Pope
King Alfred's West-Saxon version of Gregory's Pastoral care. Edited by Henry Sweet. London, New York, Published for the Early English Text Society by the Oxford University Press [1958] 2 v. facsim. 23 cm. (Early English Text Society. [Publication] Original series, no. 45, 50) Based upon manuscript Hatton 20 (formerly 88) in the Bodleian; Cotton Tiberius B. XI; Junius 53, in the Bodleian; and Cotton Otho B. II in the British Museum. 64-22702
1. Theology, Pastoral — Catholic Church. I. Alfred the Great, King of England, 849-901, tr. II. Sweet, Henry, 1845-1912, ed. III. Title.

GREGORIUS I, the Great, Saint, Pope, 540 (ca.)-604. 250
Pastoral care; translated and annotated by Henry Davis. Westminster, Md., Newman Press, 1950. 281 p. 23 cm. (Ancient Christian writers; the works of the Fathers in translation, no. 11) Bibliographical references included in "Notes" (p. [239]-270) [BR60.A35 no. 11] 50-10904
1. Theology, Pastoral—Catholic Church. I. Davis, Henry, 1866- ed. and tr. II. Title. III. Series.

HEENAN, John Carmel, 1905- 250
The people's priest. London and New York, Sheed and Ward [1951] 243 p. 21 cm. [BX1912.H36 1951] 51-8077
1. Theology, Pastoral—Catholic Church. I. Title.

HOLLAND, Cornelius Joseph, 1873- 250
His Reverence--his day's work, by Rev. Cornelius J. Holland ... with an introduction by Agnes Repplier. New York, B. Benziger & co., inc., 1921. 213 p. 19 cm. [BX1912.H6] 21-18935
1. Theology, Pastorial—Catholic church. I. Title.

HOLLAND, Cornelius Joseph, 1873- 250
The shepherd and his flock; on the duties and responsibilities of Catholic pastors. New York, D. McKay Co. [1953] 220p. 21cm. [BX1912.H63] 53-7931
1. Theology, Pastoral—Catholic Church. I. Title.

KERBY, William Joseph, 1870-1936. 250
The considerate priest, by William J. Kerby ... Philadelphia, Pa., Dolphin press, 1937. vii, 228 p. 19 1/2 cm. Reprinted from the Ecclesiastical review, 1927-1933. A companion volume to the author's Prophets of the better hope. [BX1912.K38] 37-38546
1. Theology, Pastoral—Catholic church. I. Title.

MARKOE, Ralston Joshua, 1854- 230.
Impressions of a layman, by Ralston J. Markoe. [Saint Paul, Willwerscheid & Raith, printers, c1909] 5 p. l., [9]-271 p. front. (port.) plates, plans. 20 cm. "Methods by which many different priests have been successful in their parish work ... Written from a layman's point of view."--Intord. "Some of the authorities consulted": 4th prelim. leaf. [BX1753.M3] 9-27103
1. Theology, Pastoral—Catholic church. 2. Church work. I. Title.

MICHONNEAU, G *253.5 258
The missionary spirit in parish life. Westminster, Md., Newman Press, 1952. 194 p. 22 cm. [BX2347.M48] 52-7997
1. Theology, Pastoral — Catholic Church. 2. Evangelistic work. I. Title.

MICHONNEAU, G 250
Revolution in a city parish. With a foreword by Archbishop Cushing. Westminster, Md., Newman Press, 1950. xxi, 189 p. 23 cm. [BX2347.M5] 50-9047
1. Theology, Pastoral — Catholic Church. 2. Church work. 3. Catholic Churh in France. I. Title.

MICHONNEAU, Georges, 1899- 250
Revolution in a city parish. With a foreword by Archbishop Cushing. Westminster, Md., Newman Press, 1950. xxi, 189p. 23cm. [BX2347.M5] 50-9047
1. Theology, Pastoral—Catholic Church. 2. Church work. 3. Catholic Church in France. I. Title.

THE missionary spirit in parish life. 253.5
Westminster, Md., Newman Press, 1952. 194p. 22cm. [BX2347.M48] 258 52-7997
1. Theology, Pastoral—Catholic Church. 2. Evangelistic work. I. Michonneau, Georges, 1899-

NAVAGH, James J 250
The apostolic parish. New York, P. J. Kenedy [c1950] xiii, 166 p. 20 cm. [BX1912.N3] 51-3471
1. Theology, Pastoral — Catholic Church. I. Title.

NOPPEL, Constantin, 1883- 250
Shepherd of souls; the pastoral office in the mystical body of Christ, by the Reverend Constantine Noppel, S. J., translated by the Reverend Frederic Eckhoff. St. Louis, Mo., and London. B. Herder book co., 1939. xiii, 203 p. 21 cm. Translation of Aedificatio corporis Christi, aufrisc der pastoral. [BX1912.N68] 39-31561
1. Theology, Pastorial—Catholic church. I. Eckhoff, Frederic Clement, 1899- tr. II. Title.

O'BRIEN, John Anthony, 1893- 253
The priesthood in a changing world, by Rev. John A. O'Brien...preface by Most Rev. Francis C. Kelley...introduction by Very Rev. Charles J. Callan... New York, P. J. Kenedy & sons [c1936] xx, 314 p. 21 cm. Half-title: The priesthood in a changing world; the challenge of a new day. A study in pastoral theology. [BX1912.O2] 37-2099
1. Theology, Pastoral—Catholic church. I. Title.

O'BRIEN, John Anthony, 1893- 253
The priesthood in a changing world, by Rev. John A. O'Brien ... Paterson, N.J., St. Anthony guild press, 1943. xiv p., 1 l., 326 p. 22 1/2 cm. "Second and completely revised edition."--Foreword to 2d ed. [BX1912.O2 1943] 43-15112
1. Theology, Pastoral—Catholic church. I. Title.

O'BRIEN, John Anthony, 1893- 253
The priesthood in a changing world, by Rev. John A. O'Brien ... preface by Most Rev. Francis C. Kelley ... introduction by Very Rev. Charles J. Callan ... New York, P. J. Kenedy & sons [c1936] xx, 314 p. 21 cm. Half-title: The priesthood in a changing world; the challenge of a new day. A study in pastoral theology. [BX1912.O2] 37-2099
1. Theology Pastoral—Catholic church. I. Title.

O'NEILL, Arthur Barry, 1858- 262.
Sacerdotal safeguards; casual readings for rectors and curates, by Arthur Barry O'Neill ... Notre Dame, Ind., University press [c1918] 304 p. 20 cm. [BX1912.O55] 18-23137
1. Theology, Pastoral—Catholic church. I. Title.

THE Pastoral care of souls, 250.82
by Rev. Wendelin Meyer, O.F.M., and others, translated by Rev. Andrew Green, O.S.B. St. Louis, Mo., and London, B. Herder book co., 1944. iv, 353 p. 22 cm. [BX1912.P32] 44-6336
1. Theology, Pastoral—Catholic church. I. Meyer, Wendelin, 1882- II. Green, Andrew, 1865- tr.
Contents omitted.

RULAND, Ludwig, 1873- 250.82
Ruland's Pastoral theology. St. Louis, Mo., and London, B. Herder book co., 1934-42. 3 v. 22 1/2 cm. Adapted into English form the suthor's "handbuch der praktischen seelsorge", the five volumes of which have titles: v. 1. Grenzfragen der naturwissenschaften und theologie pastoralmedizin. v.2. Die allegemeinen grundlagen des sittlichen handelns. v.3. Pslicht en gegen Gott, sich selbst; der mensch und die kreatur. v.4. Von den pslichten gegen den nachsten. v.5. Lehre vom eigentum. Contents.I. Pastoral medicine, adpated into English by T. A. Rattler, edited by Arthur Preuss.--II. Foundations of morality; God; man; lower creatures, adapted into English by T. A. Rattler, edited by Newton Thompson.--III. Morality and the social order, adapted into English by T. A. Rattler, edited by Newton Thompson. [BV4010.R8] 43-3556
1. Theology, Pastoral—Catholic church. I. Title.

RUNG, Albert. 250
Clerical courtesy [by] Rev. Albert Rung. Milwaukee, The Bruce publishing company [1931] vi p., 1 l., 86 p. illus. 18 cm. Bibliography: p. 83. [BX1912.R8] 32-1758
1. Theology, Pastoral—Catholic church. 2. Etiquette. 3. Catholic church—Clergy. I. Title.

SCHULZE, Frederick, 1855- 250
Manual of pastoral theology. A practical guide for ecclesiastical students and newly ordained priests. By Rev. Frederic Schulze ... Milwaukee, Wis., M. H. Wiltzius & co., 1899. 342 p. 21 cm. "Pastoral literature": p. 14-15. [BX1912.S48 1899] 30-34117
1. Theology, Pastoral—Catholic church. I. Title.

SLATER, Thomas, 1855-1928, tr. 250
Rules of life for the pastor of souls, from the German by Rev. T. Slater, S.J., and Rev. A. Rauch, S.J. New York, Cincinnati [etc.] Benziger brothers, 1909. viii p., 1 l., 217 p. 19 cm. [BX1912.S6] 9-10965
1. Theology, Pastoral—Catholic church. I. Rauch, A., joint tr. II. Title.

STANG, William, bp., 1854-1907. 250
Pastoral theology, by the Right Rev. Wm. Stang, D.D. Rev. according to the new Code of canon law. New York, Cincinnati [etc.] Benziger brothers [c1921] 4 p. l., 13-336 p. 20 1/2 cm. "The priest's library": p. 325-336. [BX1912.S7] 24-5959
1. Theology, Pastoral—Catholic church. I. Title.

Theology, Pastoral—Church of England.

SOUTHCOTT, Ernest William. 250
The parish comes alive. Foreword by Horace W. B. Donegan, Bishop of New York. New York, Morehouse-Gorham Co. [1957, c1956] 143 p. 21 cm. (The Annual Bishop of New York books, 1957) [BX5132.S6 1957] 57-5287
1. Theology, Pastoral — Church of England. I. Title.

Theology, Pastoral—Church of God (General assembly)

CLARK, Elijah Columbus. 253
The practical handbook of ministers, by Elijah C. Clark... Cleveland, Tenn., Church of God publishing house [c1933] 165 p. 17 cm. [BX7094.C73C5] 33-17545
1. Theology, Pastoral—Church of God (General assembly) I. Church of God (General assembly) Liturgy and ritual. II. Title.

Theology, Pastoral—Handbooks, manuals, etc.

DAVIDSON, Charles Theodore, Bp., 1905- 250.2
Minister's manual; some helps for the busy minister: funerals, dedications [and] Weddings. Cleveland, Tenn., White Wing Pub. House & Press [1952] 91p. illus. 16cm. [BV4016)06.D35] 52-64999
1. Theology Pastoral-Handbooks, manuals, etc. I. Title.

DAVIDSON, Charles Theodore, 1905- 250.2
Minister's manual; some helps for the busy minister: funerals, dedications [and] weddings. Cleveland, Tenn., White Wing Pub. House & Press [1952] 91 p. illus. 16 cm. [BV4016.D35] 52-64999
1. Theology, Pastoral—Handbooks, manuals, etc. I. Title.

EVERTS, William Wallace, 1814-1890. 250.2
Pastor's hand book. A ritual of Scriptural and poetical selections and studies for weddings, funerals, and other official duties. By W. W. Everts. Rev. ed. New York and Chicago, Sheldon and company [1883] 106 p. forms. 18 cm. [BV4016.E8 1883] 37-15932
1. Theology, Pastoral—Handbooks, manuals, etc. I. Title.

EVERTS, William Wallace, 1814-1890. 250.2
Pastor's hand book. A ritual of Scriptural and poetical selections and studies for weddings, funerals, and other official duties. By W. W. Everts. Rev. ed. New York, London, Funk & Wagnalls, 1885. 106 p. forms. 17 cm. [BV4016.E8 1885] 37-16455
1. Theology, Pastoral—Handbooks, manuals, etc. I. Title.

EVERTS, William Wallace, 1814-1890. 250.2
Pastor's hand book. A ritual of Scriptural and poetical selections and studies for weddings, funerals, and other official duties. By W. W. Everts. Rev. ed. Chicago, J. C. Buckbee & co., [1887] 115 p. forms. 17 cm. [BV4016.E8 1887] 37-15933
1. Theology, Pastoral—Handbooks, manuals, etc. I. Title.

EVERTS, William Wallace, 1814-1890. 250.2
Pastor's hand-book, comprising selections of Scripture, arranged for various occasions of official duty. Together with select formulas for marriage, etc., and rules of order for churches, ecclesiastical, and other assemblies, by W. W. Everts ... New York, Sheldon & company [c1846] 3 p. l., 72 p. forms. 18 cm. [BV4016.E8 1846] 37-18202
1. Theology, Pastoral—Handbooks, manuals, etc. I. Title.

GOULOOZE, William, 1903- 250
The Christian worker's handbook. Grand Rapids, Baker Book House, 1953. 218p. 17cm. [BV4016.G6] 53-28239
1. Theology, Pastoral—Handbooks, manuals, etc. I. Title.

HOBBS, James Randolph, 1874- 265
The pastor's manual [by] James Randolph Hobbs... [Nashville, Sunday school board. Southern Baptist convention, 1934] 2 p. l., 3-253 p. 16 1/2 cm. [BX6345.H6] 34-34411
1. Theology, Pastoral—Handbooks, manuals, etc. 2. Baptists—Government. 3. Liturgies. I. Title.

MALLORY, Orson Erskine, b. 1835. 264
Pastor's hand book with communion helps [by] O. E. Mallory ... [Worcester? Mass., 1906] 123 p. 18 cm. [BV4016.M3] 6-34258
1. Theology, Pastoral—Handbooks, manuals, etc. 2. Liturgies. 3. Sermons—Outlines. I. Title.

MURCH, James DeForest, 1892- 253
Christian minister's manual, prepared by James DeForest Murch. Cincinnati, O., The Standard publishing company [c1937] 239 p. illus., diagr. 17 cm. [BX7326.M8] 37-21629
1. Theology, Pastoral—Handbooks, manuals, etc. 2. Disciples Christ—Government. I. Disciples of Christ. Liturgy and ritual. II. Title.

OWEN, John Wilson, 1871- comp. 253
The pastor's companion; a pocket manual of forms and formulas for use in pastoral work together with selections of Scripture and helpful hymns suitable for use in visitation of the sick and on other occasions; adapted to the use of ministers of all evangelical denominations; compiled by John Wilson Owen. Dayton O., Otterbein press, c1935. 122, [6] p. 18 cm. Blank pages for "Notes" (6 at end) [BV4016.O85] 35-16617
1. Theology, Pastoral—Handbooks, manuals, etc. 2. Liturgies. I. Title.

PRIESTS' problems;
being answers to a lrage variety of questions on points of moral, canonical, liturgical and rubrical interest. Selected and edited by Rev. L. L. McReavy. New York, Benziger [1958] xix, 468p. 23cm. Responses appeared orginally in Clergy Review.
1. Theology, Pastoral—Handbooks, manual, etc. 2. Questions and answers—Pastoral theology. I. Mahoney, Edward J

Theology, Pastoral—Lutheran church.

GERBERDING, George Henry, 1847-1927. 262
The Lutheran pastor, by G. H. Gerberding ... Philadelphia. Pa., Lutheran publication society [c1902] 462 p. 23 cm. [BX8071.G43] 2-24008
1. Theology. Pastoral—Lutheran church. I. Title.

GREEVER, Walton Harlowe, 1870- 250
... The minister and the ministry, by Walton Harlowe Greever ... Philadelphia, Pa., The Board of publication of the United Lutheran church in America [1945] vii, 80 p. 20 1/2 cm. (The Knubel-Miller foundation of the United Lutheran church in America. Lectures. First series) [BV4010.G76] 46-1421
1. Theology, Pastoral—Lutheran church. I. Title.

KRETZSCHMAR, Karl,. 1877- 250
Mutual obligations of the ministry and the congregation, by Rev. Karl Kretzschmar. St. Louis, Mo., Concordia publishing house, 1934. 56 p. 23 cm. [BV4017.K7] 35-8891
1. Theology, Pastoral—Lutheran church. 2. Lutheran church—Membership. I. Title.

Theology, Pastoral—Methodist church.

BREADY, Russell H. 250
The authority of the altar, a message calling for a greater loyalty, service and organization, by Russell H. Bready ... [Greenfield, O., The Greenfield printing & publishing co., c1938] 104 p. 18 cm. [BX8345.B7] 39-2
1. Theology, Pastoral—Methodist church. I. Title.

METHODIST church (United States) Commission on ministerial training. 250
Pastor and church. Issued by the General conference commission on ministerial training by the Methodist church for undergraduate students in the first and second years. Rev. ed. William K. Anderson, editor. [Nashville] The Methodist publishing house [1947] 285 p. diagrs. 19 1/2 cm. Includes bibliographies. [BV4010.M4 1947] 47-18181
1. Theology, Pastoral—Methodist church. 2. Methodist church (United States)—Government. I. Anderson, William Ketcham, 1888-1947, ed. II. Title.

METHODIST church (United States) Commission on ministerial training. 250
Pastor and church. Issued by the General conference commission on courses of study of the Methodist church for undergraduate students in the first and second years; William K. Anderson, editor. Nashville, New York [etc.] The Methodist publishing house [1943] 320 p. diagrs. 19 1/2 cm. Includes bibliographies. [BV4010.M4] 43-5499
1. Theology, Pastoral—Methodist church. 2. Methodist church (United States)—Government. I. Anderson, William Ketcham, 1888- ed. II. Title.

METHODIST church (United States) Commission on minsterial training. 250
Pastor and church. Issued by the General conference commission on ministerial training of the Methodist church for undergraduate students in the first and second years. Rev. ed. William K. Anderson, editor. [Nashville] The Methodist publishing house [1947] 285 p. diagrs. 19 1/2 cm. Includes bibliographies. [BV4010.M4 1947] 47-18181
1. Theology, Pastoral—Methodist church. 2. Methodist church (United States)—Government. I. Anderson, William Ketcham, 1888-1947, ed. II. Title.

Theology. Pastoral — Mormon Church.

[REORGANIZED church of Jesus Christ of latter-day saints] 250
Pastoral manual. Independence, Mo., Herald publishing house [1942] 152 p. 19 1/2 cm. A companion volume to its Missionary manual. Bibliographical footnotes. [BX8671.A543] 42-152835
1. Theology, Pastoral—Mormon church. I. Title.

REORGANIZED Church of Jesus Christ of Latter Day Saints. 250
The priesthood manual; prepared under the direction of Floyd M. McDowell. Independence, Mo., Herald House, 1950 [c1949] 165 p. diagrs. 19 cm. "New edition" -- Dust jacket. [BX8671.A544 1950] 51-1175
1. Theology. Pastoral — Mormon Church. I. McDowell, Floyd Marion. II. Title.

Theology, Pastoral—Reformed church.

CANNON, James Spencer, 1776-1852. 250
Lectures on pastoral theology. By the Rev. James Spencer Cannon ... New York, C. Scribner, 1853. 3 p. l, xxxvi, 617 p. front. (port.) 23 1/2 cm. "A biographical sektch of the author. By Rev. Prof. Campbell": 2d-- 3d prelim. leaves. [BV4010. C31853] 38-66
1. Theology, Pastoral—Reformed church. I. Campbell, William Henry, 1808-1890. II. Title.

CANNON, James Spencer, 1776-1852. 250
Lectures on pastoral theology. By Rev. James Spencer Cannon ... New York, Board of publication of the Reformed Protestant, Dutch church, 1859. 3 p. l, xxxvi, 617 p. front. (port.) 24 cm. First published in 1853. "A biographical sketch of the author [by William Henry Campbell] ": 2d-3d prem. leaves. [BV4010. C3 1859] 38-665
1. Theology, Pastoral—Reformed church. I. Campbell, William Henry, 1808-1890. II. Reformed church in America. Board of publication. III. Title.

DE JONG, Peter Ymen, 1915- 253
Taking heed to the flock, a study of the principles and practice of family visitation. Grand Rapids, Baker Book House [1948] 85 p. 21 cm. [BV4012.D38] 48-6901
1. Theology, Pastoral—Reformed Church. 2. Visitations. Ecclesiastical. 3. Family—Religious life. 4. Church officers. I. Title.

DEMARST, David D. 1819-1898. 250
Pastoral theology. Outlines of lectures, printed for the use of the students of the Theological seminary of the Reformed (Dutch) church in America at New Brunswick, N. J. By David D. Demarest ... New Brunswick, N. J., Press of J. Heildingfeld, 1897. 203 p. 20 cm. [BV4010.D4] 38-660
1. Theology, Pastoral—Reformed church. I. Title.

REFORMED church in America Board of publication.
... A message to ministers, no. 2. Canons of the Synod of Dort. Christ stricken for His people. New York, Board of publication of the Reformed Protestant Dutch church [185-?] cover-title, 82, 24 p. 18 cm. Text on p. [2]-[4] of cover. "Christ stricken for His people [by James Durham] " (24 p. at end) has special t.-p. and separate paging. [BX9478.A52] 39-7840
1. Theology, Pastoral—Reformed church. 2. Presbyterian church—Sermons. I. Nationale synode te Dordrecht, 1618-1619. II. Durham, James, 1622-1658. III. Title. IV. Title: Christ stricken for His people.

Theology, Pastoral—Seventh-day Adventists.

WHITE, Ellen Gould (Harmon) Mrs., 1827-1915. 250
Gospel workers; instruction for the minister and the missionary, compiled largely from "Testimonies to the church;" together with morning talks given to the ministers of the General conference of 1883. By Mrs. E. G. White. Battle Creek, Mich.; Chicago, Ill. [etc.] Review and herald publishing co., 1892. x, 11-480 p. 19 cm. [BV4010.W5 1892] 38-634
1. Theology, Pastoral—Seventh-day Adventists. I. Title.

Theology, Pastroal.

FAGLEY, Frederick Louis, 1879- 253
Parish evangelism; an outline of a year's program, by Frederick L. Fagley ... introduction by Charles L. Goodell ... New York, Chicago [etc.] Fleming H. Revell company [1921] 121 p. 19 1/2 cm. [BV3790.F28 1921] 21-21582
1. Theology, Pastroal. 2. Evangelistic work. I. Title.

Theology, Patristic.

WRITINGS of Saint Augustine
[New York, Cima pub. co. [n. d.] v. 22cm. (The Fathers of the Church; a new translation) Half-title; each vol. has special t. p. Publisher varies. Includes bibliographies.
1. Theology, Patristic. I. Augustinus, Aurelius, Saint, Bp. of Hippo. II. Series.

Theology—Periodicals

THE Christian's magazine: 270
designed to promote the knowledge and influence of evangelical truth and order. v. 1-4; 1806-11. New York, 1806-11. 4 v. 20 1/2 - 22 1/2 cm. J. M. Mason, editor. Vols. 1-2, printed by Hopkins and Seymour; v. 3, pub. by S. Whiting & co. No more published. [BR1.C642] 2-23178
1. Theology—Period. I. Mason, John Mitchell, 1770-1829, ed.

THE Harvard theological review, v. 1- Jan. 1908- New York, The Macmillan company, 1908-09; Cambridge, Mass., Harvard university press, 1910- v. plates. plans. 25 cm. Issued quarterly by the Faculty of divinity in Harvard university. Editors: 1908-14, G. F. Moore, W. W. Fenn, J. H. Ropes.--1915- W. W. Fenn, J. H. Ropes and others. [BR1.H4] 9-3793 270
1. Theology—Period. I. Moore, George Foot, 1851-1931. II. Fenn, William Wallace, 1862-1932. III. Ropes, James Hardy, 1866-1933. IV. Harvard university. Divinity school

JOURNAL for the theology and the church. 3- Tubingen, J. C. B. Mohr; New York, Harper, 1967- v. 20cm. (Harper torchbks. TB253) Intial numbers are limited to trs. of articles from Zeitschrift fur Theologie und Kirche. [BR1.J58] 65-8933 2.95 pap., 205
1. Theology—Period. I. Zeitschrift fur Theologie und Kirche. II. as distinctive title: Distinctive Protestant and Catholic thekem reconsidered. v. 3 ed. by R. W. Funk others.

JOURNAL for theology and the church. 4- Tubingen, J. C. B. Mohr; New York, Harper 1967- v.21cm. (Harper torchbks. TB254) Initial numbers are limit ed to trs. of articles from Zeitschrift fur Theologie und Kirche. [BR1.J58] 65-8933 2.25 pap., 205
1. Theology—Period. I. Zeitschrift fur Theologie und Kirche.

THE Monthly magazine of religion and literature. Edited by W. M. Reynolds ... v. 1; Feb. 1840-jAn. 1841. Gettysburg, Printed by H. C. Neinstedt, 1840[-41] iv, 888 p. 23 cm. Caption title: Monthly magazine. No more published? [BR1.M7] 24-31550 270
1. Theology—Period. I. Reynolds, William Morton, 1812-1876, ed.

PERSPECTIVE; 205
a Princeton journal of Christian opinion. Princeton, N. J., Student Christian Association of Princeton University] v. in 26cm. 8 no. (during the school year) Began publication with Apr. 1949 issue. Cf. Union list of serials. [BR1.P38] 59-54651
1. Theology—Period. 2. Students—Period. I. Princeton University. Student Christian Association.

THEOLOGY digest. v. 1- 230.2
winter 1953- [St. Marys, Kan., St. Mary's

College] v. in 23 cm. 3 no. a year. Includes two unnumbered preliminary issues dated Dec. 1951 and May 1952. [BX801.T48] 60-17035
1. Theology — Period. 2. Catholic Church — Period. I. St. Mary's College, St. Marys, Kan. II. Title.

THE Thomist reader. 230.2
1957- [Baltimore] v. 23cm. Published by the Dominicans, Province of St. Joseph. [BX801.T52] 57-1468
1. Thomas Aquinas, Saint—Societies, periodicals, etc. 2. Theology—Period. 3. Scholasticism—Period. 4. Catholic Church— Period. I. Dominicans, Province of St. Joseph.

ZEITSCHRIFT fur Theologie and Kirche. 205
Journal for theology and the church. 1- Tubingen, J. C. B. Mohr; New York, Harper & Row, 1965- v. 20 cm. (Harper torchbooks) Initial numbers are limited to translations of articles from Zeitschrift fur Theologie and Kirche. [BR1.J58] 65-8933
1. Theology — Period. I. Title.

Theology—Periodicals—Bibliography

BRITISH Library. Lending Division. 016.2'005
Current list of serials with significant theological or religious content / compiled by G. P. Cornish. Harrogate : Theological Abstracting and Bibliographical Services, 1975. [2], 33 p. ; 26 cm. A list of serials currently received by the British Library Lending Division. [Z7753.B75 1975] [BR1.A1] 76-352357 ISBN 0-905098-01-3 : £0.75
1. Theology—Periodicals—Bibliography. 2. Religion—Periodicals—Bibliography. 3. Periodicals—Bibliography. I. Cornish, G. P. II. Title: Current list of serials ...

NEW York. Public library. 016.
List of periodicals in the New York public library, General theological seminary, and Union theological seminary, relating to religion, theology, and church history. [New York, 1905] 45 p. 26 cm. Caption title. Reprinted from N.Y.P.L. Bulletin, Jan.-Feb., 1905. "Lists of Jewish periodicals were printed in the Bulletin, vol. 6 (1902), p. 258-364, vol. 7 (1903), p. 30-31. Periodicals relating to Palestine, oriental archaeology, etc., were included in the list of periodicals relating to archaeology, vol. 1 (1897), p. 212-226. Titles of a few important religious weekly newspapers, etc., are included in this list, but both Union seminary and New York public library have incomplete files of many such papers not mentioned here."--Prefatory note. [Z7753.N63] 5-12511
1. Theology—Period.—Bibl. 2. Periodicals—Bibl.—Union lists. I. New York. General theological seminary of the Protestant Episcopal church in the U.S. Library. II. New York. Union theological seminary. Library. III. Title.

Theology—Periodicals—Bibliography—Union lists.

CHICAGO Area Theological Library Association. 016.05
Union list of serials. 1st ed. Chicago, 1974. iv, 673 p. 29 cm. [Z7753.C47 1974] 74-176319
1. Theology—Periodicals—Bibliography—Union lists. 2. Periodicals—Bibliography—Union lists. I. Title.

SOUTHEASTERN Pennsylvania Theological Library Association. 016.2
Union list of periodicals of the Southeastern Pennsylvania Theological Library Association / Donald N. Matthews, editor. 2nd key ed. Gettysburg, Pa. (66 W. Confederate Ave., Gettysburg 17235) : Copies secured through the A.R. Wentz Library, Lutheran Theological Seminary, 1981. 216 p. ; 28 cm. Title on spine: SEPTLA union list. [Z7753.S68 1981] [BR118] 19 81-132611 25.00 (pbk.)
1. Theology—Periodicals—Bibliography—Union lists. 2. Catalogs, Union—Pennsylvania. I. Matthews, Donald Nathaniel, 1930- II. Title. III. Title: SEPTLA union list.

THEOLOGICAL Education Association of Mid-America. 016.05
Team-A serials; a union list of the serials holdings of the Theological Education Association of Mid-America. Louisville, Ky., Privately published for the Team-A Libraries at Southern Baptist Theological Seminary, 1972. 4, 392 l. 28 cm. [Z7753.T375 1972] 74-151507
1. Theology—Periodicals—Bibliography—Union lists. I. Title.

Theology—Periodicals—Indexes.

CHRISTIAN periodical index. 203
1958- [Buffalo, N. Y.] Christian Librarians' Fellowship. v. 25cm. annual. A subject index to periodical literature.' [Z7753.C5] 60-36226
1. Theology—Period.—Indexes. I. Christian Librarians' Fellowship.

METZGER, Bruce Manning, ed. 016.22592
Index to periodical literature on the Apostle Paul. Grand Rapids, Mich., Eerdmans [1960] xv, 183p. 25cm. (New Testament tools and studies, v.1) 60-16310 4.00
1. Paul, Saint, apostle—Bibl. 2. Theology—Period.—Indexes. I. Title. II. Series.

REGAZZI, John J., 1948- 016.2'005
A guide to indexed periodicals in religion / by John J. Regazzi and Theodore C. Hines. Metuchen, N.J. : Scarecrow Press, 1975. xiv, 314 p. ; 22 cm. [Z7753.R34] [BR1] 75-22277 ISBN 0-8108-0868-4 : 10.00
1. Theology—Periodicals—Indexes. 2. Religion—Periodicals—Indexes. 3. Theology—Periodicals—Directories. 4. Religion—Periodicals—Directories. 5. Abstracting and indexing services. I. Hines, Theodore C., joint author. II. Title.

Theology, Practical.

BOWER, William Clayton, 1878- 260
The church at work in the modern world, written in collaboration by William Clayton Bower, editor, Edward Scribner Ames [and others] Freeport, N.Y., Books for Libraries Press [1967] xi, 304 p. maps. 22 cm. (Essay index reprint series) Reprint of the 1935 ed. Includes bibliographies. [BV3.B6 1967] 67-26717
1. Theology, Practical. 2. Church work. 3. Protestant churches—United States. I. Ames, Edward Scribner, 1870-1958. II. Title.

BOWER, William Clayton, 1878- ed. 260.82
The church at work in the modern world: written in collaboration ... William Clayton Bower, editor ... Chicago, Ill., The University of Chicago press [c1935] xi, 304 p. illus. (maps) 20 cm. (Half title: Publications of the Divinity school of the University of Chicago) A collection of studies by E. S. Ames, A. G. Baker, S. J. Case, and others. "Selected bibliography" at end of most of the chapters. [BV3.B6] 35-27395
1. Theology, Practical. 2. Church work. 3. Protestant churches—U.S. I. Ames, Edward Scribner, 1870- II. Title.

COOK, Jerry. 253
Love, acceptance & forgiveness / Jerry Cook, with Stanley C. Baldwin. Glendale, Calif. : GL Regal Books, c1979. 128 p. ; 21 cm. [BV3.C65] 79-63763 ISBN 0-8307-0654-2 : 3.50
1. Theology, Practical. 2. Christian life—1960- I. Baldwin, Stanley C., joint author. II. Title.

DEWOLF, Daniel Fowler. 220
Character, not creeds; reflections from hearth and plow beam. By Daniel Fowler Dewolf ... Cincinnati, The Robert Clarke company, 1899. xi, 258 p. 21 cm. [BR125.D59] 99-1952
1. Theology, Practical. 2. Creeds. I. Title.

DUNNING, James B. 248.4
Ministries, sharing God's gifts / by James B. Dunning. Winona, Minn. : Saint Mary's Press, c1980. 109 p. ; 23 cm. (A Pace book) Bibliography: p. 107-109. [BV3.D86] 19 80-52058 ISBN 0-88489-123-2 (pbk.) : 5.95
1. Theology, Practical. I. Title.

FEUCHT, Oscar E. 262'.15
Everyone a minister : a guide to churchmanship for laity and clergy / Oscar E. Feucht. St. Louis : Concordia Pub. House, 1974. 158 p. ; 18 cm. Includes bibliographical references. [BV3.F47] 73-90058 ISBN 0-570-03184-2 pbk. : 0.95
1. Theology, Practical. 2. Laity. 3. Christianity—20th century. I. Title.

*GERSTNER, John H. 230
Theology for everyman. Chicago. Moody [c.1965] 127p. 18cm. (Colportage lib. 512) .39 pap.,
I. Title.

HAUCK, Gary L. 253
Is my church what God meant it to be? / Gary L. Hauck. Denver : Accent Books, c1979. 160 p. ; 21 cm. [BV3.H35] 79-50811 ISBN 0-89636-029-6 : 3.95
1. Theology, Practical. 2. Church. I. Title.

HULME, William Edward, 1920- 253
Two ways of caring; a Biblical design for balanced ministry [by] William E. Hulme. Minneapolis, Augsburg Pub. House [1973] 107 p. 20 cm. [BV3.H84] 73-78270 ISBN 0-8066-1334-3 2.95 (pbk.)
1. Theology, Practical. 2. Pastoral theology. 3. Church and social problems. I. Title.

HUTTENLOCKER, Keith. 253
"Be-attitudes" for the church. Anderson, Ind., Warner Press [1971] 112 p. 19 cm. Includes bibliographical references. [BV3.H88] 70-165003 ISBN 0-87162-125-8
1. Theology, Practical. 2. Christian life—1960- I. Title.

LASHER, G[eorge] W[illiam]
Theology for plain people, by Rev. G. W. Lasher, D. D. Cincinnati, O., 1906. vi p., 1 l., 168 p. 19 cm. "The essays comprised in this volume were originally written for and published in the Journal and messenger."--Pref. 6-45728
I. Title.

MACNAIR, Donald J., 1922- 254
The birth, care, and feeding of a local church / Donald J. MacNair. Washington : Canon Press, c1973. x, 212 p. ; 24 cm. Includes index. [BV3.M3] 75-312222 ISBN 0-913686-08-5
1. Theology, Practical. I. Title.

MUELLER, Charles S. 253
What's this I hear about our church? : An action guide for congregation leaders / Charles S. Mueller. Minneapolis : Augsburg Pub. House, [1974] 104 p. : ill. ; 20 cm. (A Study of generations paperback) [BV3.M83] 74-77683 ISBN 0-8066-1434-X pbk. : 2.50 2.50
1. Theology, Practical. I. Title.

POWELL, Oliver. 248
Household of power; the task and testing of the church in our time. Boston, United Church Press [1962] 114p. 22cm. (A Pilgrim Press publication) [BV4501.2.P59] 62-18361
1. Theology, Practical. 2. Christian life. I. Title.

POWELL, Paul W. 253
How to make your church hum / Paul W. Powell. Nashville : Broadman Press, c1977. 92 p. ; 19 cm. [BV3.P68] 76-47791 pbk. : 2.50
1. Theology, Practical. 2. Pastoral theology. 3. Christian leadership. I. Title.

SCHENCK, Ferdinand Schureman, 1845-
Modern practical theology; a manual of homiletics, liturgics, poimenics, archagics, pedagogy, sociology, and the English Bible, by Ferdinand S. Schenck ... New York and London, Funk & Wagnalls company, 1903. xiv, 15-320 p. 19 1/2 cm. "Books recommended": p. xi-xiv. 3-24231
I. Title.

SCIATER, John Robert Paterson. 264
The public worship of God ... by J. R. P. Sciater ... New York, George H. Doran company [c1927] xi p., 2 l., 17-199 p. 19 cm. (The Lyman Beecher lectures on practical theology at Yale, 1927) [BV10.S4] 27-19715
1. Theology, Practical. I. Title.

SHAW, A[ngus] R[obertson] 1858-
Theology for the people. By Rev. A. R. Shaw ... Richmond, Va., Whittet & Shepperson, printers, 1902. 294 p. 21 cm. 2-19893
I. Title.

SMITH, Donald P., 1922- 253
Congregations alive / by Donald P. Smith. 1st ed. Philadelphia : Westminster Press, c1981. 198 p. ; 23 cm. Bibliography: p. 197-198. [BV3.S65] 19 81-1371 ISBN 0-664-24370-3 pbk. : 10.95
1. Theology, Practical. I. Title.

Theology, Practical—Addresses, essays, lectures.

EVANGELISM, the ministry of the Church : an introduction to the Faith to grow program / edited by Richard Hughes and Joe Serig (Program Services Division, Reorganized Church of Jesus Christ of Latter Day Saints). Independence, Mo. : Herald Pub. House, c1981. 299 p. ; 21 cm. Includes bibliographical references. [BV3.E93] 19 80-26010 ISBN 0-8309-0304-6 : 12.00 253
1. Reorganized Church of Jesus Christ of Latter-Day Saints—Doctrinal and controversial works—Addresses, essays, lectures. 2. Theology, Practical—Addresses, essays, lectures. I. Hughes, Richard, 1938- II. Serig, Joe. III. Reorganized Church of Jesus Christ of Latter-Day Saints. Division of Program Services.

PRACTICAL theology / 230
edited, with an introduction by Don S. Browning. 1st ed. San Francisco : Harper & Row, c1983. p. cm. Includes index. Contents.Contents. The foundation of practical theology / Don Browning — Theology and practice outside the clerical paradigm / Edward Farley — Schleiermacher's vision for theology / John Burkhart — The foundations of practical theology / David Tracy — Dimensions of practical theology / Thomas W. Ogletree — Practical theology and social action / Dennis McCann — Toward a theology of rhetoric/preaching / Leander E. Keck — Practical theology and the shaping of Christian lives / James Fowler — Practical theology and pastoral care / James Lapsley — Pastoral theology in a pluralistic age / Don Browning. [BV3.P69 1983] 19 82-47739 ISBN 0-06-061153-7 : 7.64
1. Theology, Practical—Addresses, essays, lectures. I. Browning, Don S.

Theology, Practical and devotional.

BELDEN, Albert David, 1883- 248
Voices of the great Creator, studies in devotion by Rev. Albert D. Belden ... Nashville, Tenn., Cokesbury press, 1929. 190 p. 19 1/2 cm. [BV4823.B43] 31-12719
1. Theology, Practical and devotional. I. Title.

GRAY, Andrew, 1633-1656. 264
The spiritual warfare; or, Some sermons concerning the nature of mortification, together with the right exercise and spiritual advantages thereof. Whereunto are added other two sermons, concerning the mystery of contentment ... Being the substance of ten sermons. By .. Mr. Andrew Gray ... Boston: in N. D. Re-rpinted by S. Kneeland, for Benj. Eliot, at his Shop in King-street, 1720. 2 p. l., 140 p. 16 cm. Preface by Thomas Manton, d. d. [BX5330.G7S6] [AC901.W3 vol. 77] 252. 6-36077
1. Theology, Practical and devotional. 2. Spiritual life. I. Title. II. Title: Mortification, of Nature of.

Theology, Practical—Anecdotes, facetiae, satire, etc.

ANDERSON, Kenneth, 1917- 202'.07
People of the steeple. Written by Ken Anderson. Drawings by Noelle. Waco, Tex., Word Books [1971] [48] p. illus. 15 cm. [BV4.A49] 72-170909
1. Theology, Practical—Anecdotes, facetiae, satire, etc. I. Title.

ANDERSON, Kenneth, 1917- 260'.2'7
Stains on glass windows, written by Ken

Anderson. Drawings by Robin Jensen. Waco, Tex., Word Books [1969] [45] p. illus. 15 cm. [BV4.A5] 74-91939 1.95
1. Theology, Practical—Anecdotes, facetiae, satire, etc. I. Title.

Theology, Practical—Bibliography

PRINCETON Theological Seminary. Library. 016.
A bibliography of practical theology. [Princeton] Theological Book Agency, 1949. 71 p. 22 cm. [Princeton Theological Seminary. Princeton pamphlets, no. 3] Cover title. [BV4070.P713 no. 3] A 51
1. Theology, Practical—Bibl. I. Title. II. Series.

Theology, Practical—Case studies.

CASEBOOK on church and society. 261.8'3 Edited by Keith R. Bridston [and others] Nashville, Abingdon Press [1974] 220 p. 22 cm. Bibliography: p. 220. [BV3.C37] 74-13419 ISBN 0-687-04709-9 5.95 (pbk.)
1. Theology, Practical—Case studies. 2. Church and social problems—Case studies. I. Bridston, Keith R., ed.

Theology, Practical—Congresses.

BERTRAM, Robert w. ed. 240
Theology in the life of the church. Philadelphia, Fortress Press [1963] v 282 p. 22 cm. Symposium planned by the Conference of Lutheran Professors of Theology. Includes bibliographical references. [BT78.B48] 63-7905
1. Theology, Practical — Congresses. I. Conferences of Lutheran Professors of Theology. II. Title.

Theology, Practical—Handbooks, manuals, etc.

BAKER'S dictionary of practical theology. 202'.02 Edited by Ralph G. Turnbull. Grand Rapids, Baker Book House [1967] xxii, 469 p. 25 cm. Includes bibliographies. [BV3.B3] 67-18199
1. Theology, Practical—Handbooks, manuals, etc. I. Turnbull, Ralph G., ed. II. Title: Dictionary of practical theology.

OTTO, Gert.
Praktisch-theologisches Handbuch / hrsg. von Gert Otto. 2., vollst. uberarb. u. erg. Aufl. Hamburg : Furche-Verlag, 1975. 657 p. ; 25 cm. Includes bibliographical references and indexes. [BV2.O88 1975] 75-511061 ISBN 3-7730-0255-6 : DM78.00
1. Theology, Practical—Handbooks, manuals, etc. I. Title.

Theology, Practical—Miscellanea.

BENSON, Dennis C. 250
Dennis C. Benson's Recycle catalogue. Nashville : Abingdon Press, [1975]. 208 p. : ill. ; 31 cm. Includes index. [BV3.B4 1975] 75-313743 ISBN 0-687-35854-X pbk. : 6.95
1. Theology, Practical—Miscellanea. I. Title. II. Title: Recycle catalogue.

BENSON, Dennis C. 250
Recycle catalogue II : fabulous flea market / Dennis C. Benson. Nashville : Abingdon, c1977. 159 p. : ill. ; 31 cm. Includes indexes. [BV3.B42] 77-23978 ISBN 0-687-35855-8 pbk. : 6.95
1. Theology, Practical—Miscellanea. I. Title.

Theology, Practical—Research.

SOUTHARD, Samuel. 230'.07'2
Religious inquiry : an introduction to the why and how / Samuel Southard. Nashville : Abingdon, c1976. 127 p. ; 19 cm. Includes index. Bibliography: p. 117-121. [BV4.S68] 76-20449 ISBN 0-687-36090-0 pbk. : 3.95
1. Theology, Practical—Research. I. Title.

Theology, Presbyterian.

THE broadening church; a study of theological issues in the Presbyterian church since 1869. Philadelphia, University of Pennsylvania Press, 1957. 195p. 22cm.
I. Loetscher, Lefferts Augustine, 1904-

GEAR, Felix B. 230'.5'1
Our Presbyterian belief / Felix B. Gear. Atlanta : John Knox Press, c1980. 90 p. ; 21 cm. Includes bibliographical references. [BX9175.2.G43] 79-23421 ISBN 0-8042-0676-7 pbk. : 4.95
1. Theology, Presbyterian. I. Title.

Theology, Protestant.

DAWE, Donald G. 230
No orthodoxy but the truth; a survey of Protestant theology, by Donald G. Dawe. Philadelphia, Westminster Press [1969] 185 p. 21 cm. Bibliographical references included in "Notes" (p. 173-180) [BX4805.2.D34] 69-10424 ISBN 0-664-20844-4 5.95
1. Theology, Protestant. 2. Theology, Doctrinal—History—Modern period, 1500- I. Title.

KING, Henry Churchill, 1858-1934. 265.
Theology and the social consciousness; a study of the relations of the the First Baptist church in Providence, by Henry Melville King, D.D. New York, The Macmillan company; London, Macmillan & co., ltd., 1902. xviii, 252 p. 20 1/2 cm. [BR115.S6K5] 2-22500
I. Title. II. Title: Social consciousness.

MCGIFFERT, Arthur Cushman, 1861-1933.
Protestant thought before Kant, by Arthur Cushman McGiffert ... New York, C. Scribner's sons, 1911. 8 p. l., 261 p. 19 cm. (On cover: Studies in theology) Bibliography: p. 255-261. A 11
I. Title.

Theology, Protestant—Collections.

SCOTT, William A., 1920- comp. 230'.08
Sources of Protestant theology. Edited by William A. Scott. New York, Bruce Pub. Co. [1971] xviii, 392 p. 23 cm. (Contemporary theology series) [BT10.S3 1971] 70-143783
1. Theology, Protestant—Collections. 2. Theology, Doctrinal—Collections. I. Title.

Theology, Protestant—Germany—History.

†RUPP, George. 230'.0943
Culture-protestantism : German liberal theology at the turn of the twentieth century / by George Rupp. Missoula, Mont. : Published by Scholars Press for the American Academy of Religion, c1977. 67 p. ; 24 cm. (AAR studies in religion ; no. 15 ISSN 0084-6287s) Includes bibliographical references. [BT30.G3R86] 77-13763 ISBN 0-89130-197-6 pbk. : 6.00
1. Theology, Protestant—Germany—History. 2. Christianity and culture—History. 3. Liberalism (Religion)—Germany—History. I. Title. II. Series: American Academy of Religion. AAR studies in religion ; no. 15.

Theology, Protestant—History.

BICKNELL, Edward John. 238.
A theological introduction to the Thirty nine articles of the Church of England, by E. J. Bicknell ... London, New York [etc.] Longmans, Green and co., 1919. xvii, [1] 560 p. 23 cm. "The book consists in the main of lectures delivered at Bishop's hostel, Lincoln, rewritten and expanded."-- Pref. [BX5137.B5] 19-14098
I. Church of England. Articles of religion. II. Title.

BICKNELL, Edward John, 1882- 238.
A theological introduction to the Thirty-nine articles of the Church of England, by E. J. Bicknell ... 2d ed. London, New York [etc.] Longmans, Green and co., 1925. xvii, [1], 565 p. 23 cm. "The book consists in the main of lectures delivered at Bishop's hostel, Lincoln, rewritten and expanded."-- Pref. Contains bibliographies. [BX5137.B5 1925] 25-25561
I. Church of England. Articles of religion. II. Title.

DORNER, Isaak August, 1809-1884. 201
History of Protestant theology; particularly in Germany, viewed according to its fundamental movement and in connection with the religious, moral, and intellectual life, by J. A. Dorner. Translated by George Robson and Sophia Taylor. With a pref. to the translation by the author. New York, AMS Press [1970] 2 v. 24 cm. Author's pref. in German and English. Reprint of the 1871 ed. Translation of Geschichte der protestantischen Theologie. Includes bibliographical references. [BX4811.D6713 1970] 72-133823 ISBN 0-404-02147-6
1. Theology, Protestant—History. 2. Germany—Church history. 3. Theology, Protestant—Germany. I. Title.

SCOTT, William A., 1920- 201
Historical Protestantism; an historical introduction to Protestant theology [by] William A. Scott. Englewood Cliffs, N.J., Prentice-Hall [1970, c1971] ix, 229 p. 23 cm. Bibliography: p. 217-224. [BT27.S35] 76-123085
1. Theology, Protestant—History. I. Title.

TILLICH, Paul, 1886-1965. 230'.4
Perspectives on 19th and 20th century Protestant theology. Edited and with an introd. by Carl E. Braaten. [1st ed. New York, Harper & Row [1967] xxiv, 252 p. 22 cm. "Lectures ... delivered at the Divinity School of the University of Chicago ... spring ... 1963." Bibliographical footnotes. [BT28.T5] 67-11507
1. Theology, Protestant—History. 2. Theology, Doctrinal—History—19th century. 3. Theology, Doctrinal—History—20th century. I. Braaten, Carl E., 1929- ed. II. Title.

Theology, Protestant—History—20th century.

CURTIS, Charles J. 200
Contemporary Protestant thought [by] C. J. Curtis. New York, Bruce Pub. Co. [1970] xiv, 225 p. 23 cm. (Contemporary theology series) Includes bibliographical references. [BT28.C87] 72-87991
1. Theology, Protestant—History—20th century. 2. Theology, Doctrinal—History—20th century. I. Title.

ZAHRNT, Heinz, 1915- 230
The question of God; Protestant theology in the twentieth century. Translated from the German by R. A. Wilson. [1st ed.] New York, Harcourt, Brace & World [1969] 398 p. 23 cm. "A Helen and Kurt Wolff book." Translation of Die Sache mit Gott. Bibliographical references included in "Notes" (p. [361]-383) [BT28.Z313 1969] 69-14847
1. Theology, Protestant—History—20th century. 2. Theology, Doctrinal—History—20th century. 3. God—History of doctrines—20th century. I. Title.

Theology, Protestant—Latin America.

WAGNER, C. Peter. 201
Latin American theology: radical or evangelical? The struggle for the faith in a young church, by C. Peter Wagner. Grand Rapids, Eerdmans [1970] 118 p. 21 cm. Bibliography: p. 110-118. [BX4811.W3] 73-88076 2.45
1. Theology, Protestant—Latin America. I. Title.

Theology, Protestant—United States

CAMPBELL, Robert, 1919- 280'.4
Spectrum of Protestant beliefs, edited by Robert Campbell. Contributors: William Hamilton [and others] Milwaukee, Bruce Pub. Co. [1968] xiv, 106 p. 22 cm. [BX4811.C3] 68-17118
1. Theology, Protestant—United States. 2. Protestantism—20th century. I. Hamilton, William, 1924- II. Title.

HOGE, Dean R., 1937- 280'.4'0973
Division in the Protestant house : the basic reasons behind intra-church conflicts / by Dean R. Hoge, with the research assistance of Everett L. Perry, Dudley E. Sarfaty, and John E. Dyble ; with the editorial assistance of Grace Ann Goodman. Philadelphia : Westminster Press, c1976. 166 p. : ill. ; 23 cm. Includes bibliographical references. [BR516.5.H64] 76-1022 ISBN 0-664-24793-8 pbk. : 3.95
1. United Presbyterian Church in the U.S.A.—Doctrinal and controversial works. 2. Theology, Protestant—United States. 3. Sociology, Christian—United States. I. Title.

SPECTRUM of Protestant beliefs, 280'.4 ed. by Robert Campbell. Contributors: William Hamilton [& others] Milwaukee, Bruce [1968] xiv, 106p. 22cm. Statements illustrating the religious, moral, and political attitudes of Amer. Protestantism, by B. Jones, Jr., representing the fundamentalist; C.F.H. Henry, the new evangelical; J. W. Montgomery, the confessional; J. A. Pike, the liberal; and W. Hamilton, the radical theologian position. [BX4811.S65] 68-17118 3.95
1. Theology, Protestant—U. S. 2. Protestantism—20th cent. I. Hamilton, William, 1924- II. Campbell, Robert, 1919- ed.

Theology, Protestant—United States—Collections.

MILLER, William Robert, comp. 280'.4'0973
Contemporary American Protestant thought, 1900-1970. Indianapolis, Bobbs-Merrill [1973] xc, 567 p. 21 cm. (The American heritage series, 84) Includes bibliographical references. [BX4811.M53] 70-151613 9.50
1. Theology, Protestant—United States—Collections. I. Title.
pap 4.75.

Theology, Protestant—United States—History—Addresses, essays, lectures—20th century.

NASH, Arnold Samuel, ed. 230
Protestant thought in the twentieth century : whence & whither? / Edited by Arnold S. Nash. Westport, Conn. : Greenwood Press, [1978] c1951. p. cm. Reprint of the ed. published by Macmillan, New York. Includes bibliographies. [BR525.N36 1978] 78-5860 ISBN 0-313-20484-5 lib.bdg. : 19.75
1. Theology, Protestant—United States—History—Addresses, essays, lectures—20th century. I. Title.
Contents omitted Contents omitted

ROBINS, Henry Burke, 1874-
... The basis of assurance in recent protestant theologies ... by Henry Burke Robins. Kansas City, Mo., C. E. Brown printing co., 1912. 92 p. 24 cm. Thesis (PH. D.)--University of Chicago, 1912. Bibliography: p. 5-10 13-2374
I. Title.

Theology, Puritan.

PETTIT, Norman. 234.1
The heart prepared; grace and conversion in Puritan spiritual life. New Haven, Yale University Press, 1966. ix, 252 p. 23 cm. (Yale publications in American studies 11) "Originally undertaken as a doctoral dissertation ... Yale University." Bibliography: p. [223]-235. [BX9322.P4 1966] 66-21530
1. Theology, Puritan. 2. Grace (Theology)—History of doctrines. 3. Conversion—Histroy of doctrines. I. Title. II. Series.

Theology, Reformed Church.

LEITH, John H. 230'.5'7
An introduction to the reformed tradition : a way of being the Christian community / John H. Leith. Atlanta : John Knox Press, c1977. 253 p., [8] leaves of plates : ill. ; 22 cm. Includes bibliographical references and indexes. [BX9422.2.L45] 76-12392 ISBN 0-8042-0471-3 : 12.95
1. Theology, Reformed Church. I. Title.

LEITH, John H. 230'.5
An introduction to the reformed tradition : a way of being the Christian community / John H. Leith. Rev. ed. Atlanta, Ga. : John Knox Press, 1981. 264 p. ; 21 cm. Includes bibliographical references and indexes. [BX9422.2.L45 1981] 19 81-5968 ISBN 0-8042-0479-9 pbk. : 8.95
1. Theology, Reformed Church. I. Title.

OSTERHAVEN, Maurice Eugene, 1915- 201'.1
The spirit of the Reformed tradition, by M. Eugene Osterhaven. Grand Rapids, Eerdmans [1970, c1971] 190 p. 22 cm. Bibliography: p. 179-187. [BX9422.2.O8] 75-127625 3.45
1. Theology, Reformed Church. I. Title.

VAN'HARN, Roger, 1932- 230'.5
Reasons IV, explaining the Reformed perspective / by Roger Van Harn. Grand Rapids, Mich. : Bible Way, c1981. p. cm. Bibliography: p. [BX9422.2.V27] 19 81-38457 ISBN 0-933140-29-0 pbk. : 3.25
1. Theology, Reformed Church. I. Title. II. Title: Explaining the Reformed perspective. Publisher's address: 2850 Kalamazoo Ave., S.E., Grand Rapids, MI 49560

Theology, Reformed Church—History.

ROGERS, Jack Bartlett. 220.6'09
The authority and interpretation of the Bible : an historical approach / by Jack B. Rogers and Donald K. McKim. 1st ed. San Francisco : Harper & Row, c1979. p. cm. Includes bibliographies and index. [BS500.R63 1979] 78-20584 ISBN 0-06-066696-X : 20.00
1. Theology, Reformed Church—History. 2. Bible—Criticism, interpretation, etc.—History. 3. Bible—Evidences, authority, etc.—History. I. McKim, Donald K., joint author. II. Title.

WOODBRIDGE, John D., 1941- 220.1'3
Biblical authority : a critique of the Rogers/McKim proposal / John D. Woodbridge. Grand Rapids, Mich. : Zondervan Pub. House, c1982. p. cm. Includes bibliographical references and index. [BS500.R633W66 1982] 19 82-8592 ISBN 0-310-44751-8 pbk. : 8.95
1. Rogers, Jack Bartlett. Authority and interpretation of the Bible. 2. Bible—Criticism, interpretation, etc.—History. 3. Bible—Evidences, authority, etc.—History. 4. Theology, Reformed Church—History. I. Title.

Theology, Reformed Church—History—19th century—Addresses, essays, lectures.

GERRISH, Brian Albert, 1931- 230
Tradition and the modern world : reformed theology in the nineteenth century / B. A. Gerrish. Chicago : University of Chicago Press, c1978. xii, 263 p. ; 24 cm. (The Andrew C. Zenos memorial lectures ; 1977) Includes index. Bibliography: p. 235-245. [BX9422.2.G47] 78-4982 ISBN 0-226-28866-8 lib. bdg. 15.00
1. Theology, Reformed Church—History—19th century—Addresses, essays, lectures. 2. Theology, Doctrinal—History—19th century—Addresses, essays, lectures. I. Title. II. Series.

Theology— Selections.

ANTHOLOGY.
Edited by Jordan Aumann, O. P. Dubuque, Priory Press, 1961. 503p. 23cm.
1. Theology— Selections. I. Jarrett, Bede, 1881-1934. II. Aumann, Jordan, 1916- ed.

NAU, Louis J. 230.
Readings on fundamental moral theology, by the Rt. Rev. Louis J. Nau ... New York, Cincinnati, Frederick Pustet company, inc., 1926. 109 p. 21 cm. [BX1758.N3] 26-21364
I. Title. II. Title: Moral theology.

Theology — Study and teaching.

ADLER, Mortimer Jerome, 1902- 230.07
Religion and theology, by Mortimer J. Adler and Seymour Cain. Prefaces by John Cogley [and others] Chicago, Encyclopaedia Britannica, 1961. 278 p. 21 cm. (The Great ideas program) Bibliography: p. 271-278. [BT77.3.A3] A 63
1. Theology—Study and teaching. 2. Religion—Study and teaching. I. Cain, Seymour, 1914- joint author. II. Title. III. Series: The Great ideas program, 4

ALLEN, Yorke. 207
A seminary survey; a listing and review of the activities of the theological schools and major seminaries located in Africa, Asia, and Latin America which are training men to serve as ordained ministers and priests in the Protestant, Roman Catholic, and Eastern churches. New York, Harper [1960] xxvi, 640 p. maps (part fold.) tables. 24 cm. Bibliography: p. 604-628. [BV4020.A6] 60-5325
1. Theology—Study and teaching. 2. Theological seminaries. I. Title.

BANGS, Nathan, 1778-1862. 250
Letters to young ministers of the gospel, on the importance and method of study. 2d ed. New-York, Published by N. Bangs and J. Emory for the Methodist Episcopal Church, 1828. 194 p. 14 cm. [BV4020.B3 1828] 50-46553
1. Theology—Study and teaching. I. Title.

BRIDSTON, Keith R. ed. 207.082
The making of ministers; essays on clergy training today. Edited by Keith R. Bridston [and] Dwight W. Culver. Minneapolis, Augsburg Pub. House [1964] xx, 275 p. 22 cm. "Written from material gathered by the Lilly Endowment study of pre-seminary education."—Dust jacket. [BV4020.B7] 64-13435
1. Theology—Study and teaching. 2. Theological seminaries. I. Culver, Dwight W., joint ed. II. Title.

COVELL, Ralph R. 207
An extension seminary primer [by] Ralph R. Covell [and] C. Peter Wagner. South Pasadena, Calif., William Carey Library [1971] xi, 140 p. illus. 23 cm. Bibliography: p. 134-138. [BV4020.C635] 72-168665 ISBN 0-87808-106-2 2.45
1. Theology—Study and teaching. I. Wagner, C. Peter. II. Title.

DORRILL, Robert L
Southern Baptist theological education study. Nashville, Tenn., Research and Statistics Department, Service Division, Baptist Sunday School Board, 1962. 1 v. 29 cm. Institutions and Sub-committee on Capitals Needs, both of the Program Committee. 64-34658
1. Theology — Study and teaching. 2. Religious education. I. Title.

DORRILL, Robert L
Southern Baptist theological education study. Nashville, Tenn., Research and Statistics Department, Service Division, Baptist Sunday School Board, 1962. 1 v. 29 cm. A report...prepared primarily for the benefit of the two Southern Baptist Convention Executive Committee sponsoring groups: Sub-committee on Institutions and Sub-committee on Capitals Needs, both of the Program Committee. 64-34658
1. Theology — Study and teaching. 2. Religious education. I. Title.

GAMBRELL, Mary Latimer. 207.74
Ministerial training in eighteenth-century New England, by Mary Latimer Gambrell ... New York, Columbia university press; London, P. S. King & son, ltd., 1937. 169 p. 23 cm. (Half-title: Studies in history, economics and public law, edited by the Faculty of political science of Columbia university, no. 428) Issued also as thesis (PH.D.) Columbia university. Bibliography: p. 148-159. [H31.C7 no. 428] [BV4033.G3 1937 a] (308.2) 38-9245
1. Theology—Study and teaching. 2. Theological seminaries—U.S. I. Title.

HAM, Wayne. 230'.9'33
More than burnt offerings : a study course on theology for adults / by Wayne Ham. Independence, Mo. : Herald Pub. House, c1978. p. cm. [BV4020.H35] 78-17646 ISBN 0-8309-0217-1 pbk. : 6.50
1. Reorganized Church of Jesus Christ of Latter-Day Saints—Doctrinal and controversial works—Study and teaching. 2. Theology—Study and teaching.

HOGAN, John Baptist.
Clerical studies, by Very Rev. J. B. Hogan... Boston, Marlier, Callahan & co., 1898. 2 p. l., iii-xiii, 499 p. 21 cm. "Re-issue, with slight alterations, of a series of articles originally printed in the American ecclesiastical review."--Pref. [BX900.H6] 98-601
1. Theology—Study and teaching. 2. Catholic church—Clergy. I. Title.

HOWE, George, 1802-1883. 207
A discourse on theological education; delivered on the bicentenary of the Westminster assembly of divines, July, 1843. To which is added, advice to a student preparing for the ministry. By George Howe ... New York, Leavitt, Trow & co.; Boston, Crocker & Brewster: [etc., etc.] 1844. 243 p. 15 1/2 cm. [BV4020.H6] 37-31983
1. Theology—Study and teaching. I. Title. II. Title: Theological education, A discourse on.

INTERNATIONAL Missionary Council. Theological Education Fund.
Issues in theological education, 1964-1965: Asia, Africa, Latin America; a report. New York, Theological Education Fund [1966?] 65 p. 67-90828
1. Theology — Study and teaching. I. Title.

JOHNSON, Elias Henry, 1841-1906.
Christian agnosticism as related to Christian knowledge, the critical principle in theology, by E. H. Johnson ... Ed., with a biographical sketch and an appreciation, by Henry C.Vadder. Philadelphia, The Griffith & Rowland press, 1907. xxxii, 302 p. front. (port.) 20 cm. 7-41093
I. Vedder, Henry Clay, 1853- II. Title.

KEMP, Charles F. 1912-
Student's guidebook; theological school study habits inventory. [Fort Worth, Texas Christian University, 1963] 1 v. (various pagings) 65-76656
1. Theology — Study and teaching. 2. Study Method of. I. Title.

MATHER, Cotton, 1663-1728. 250
Manuductio ad ministerium; directions for a candidate of the ministry, by Cotton Mather. Reproduced from the original edition, Boston, 1726, with a bibliographical note by Thomas J. Holmes and Kenneth B. Murdock. New York, Pub. for the Facsimile text society by Columbia university press, 1938. 8 p. l., xix, 151 p. 18 1/2 cm. (Half-title: Publication no. 42 of the Facsimile text society) Running title: The angels preparing to sound the trumpets. "A catalogue of books, for a young student's library": p. 150-151. [BV4009.M35 1726a] 38-8438
1. Theology—Study and teaching. 2. Theology, Pastoral. I. Holmes, Thomas James, 1874- ed. II. Murdock, Kenneth Ballard, 1895- joint ed. III. Title. IV. Title: Directions for a candidate of the ministry. V. Title: The angels preparing to sound the trumpets.

METHODIST Church (United States) Dept. of Ministerial Education.
The study of the ministry, 1960-1964. [Nashville, 1964] 128 p. (p. 121-128 blank for "Notes") 23 cm. 66-16858
1. Theology — Study and teaching. 2. Methodist Church — Education. I. Title.

NIEBUHR, Helmut Richard, 1894- 207
The purpose of the church and its ministry; reflections on the aims of theological education. In collaboration with Daniel Day Williams and James M. Gustafson. [1st ed.] New York, Harper [1956] 134p. 20cm. [BV4020.N5] 56-7026
1. Theology—Study and teaching. 2. Church. 3. Clergy. 4. Theological seminaries —U. S. I. Title.

SMITH, Gerald Birney, 1868-1929, ed. 208
A guide to the study of the Christian religion, by William Herbert Perry Faunce, Shailer Mathews ... [and others] edited by Gerald Birney Smith. Chicago, Ill., The University of Chicago press [c1916] x, 759 p. fold. diagr. 23 cm. Contains bibliographies. [BR118.S55] 16-24312
1. Theology—Study and teaching. I. Title. Contents omitted.

Theology — Study and teaching — Addresses, essays, lectures.

AMERICAN Association of Theological Schools. 230'.07
Horizons of theological education: essays in honor of Charles L. Taylor, edited by John B. Coburn, Walter D. Wagoner [and] Jesse H. Ziegler. Dayton, Ohio [1966] xvii. 133 p. 27 cm. "Published [also] in paper covers as vol. II, number 4 of Theological education." Includes bibliographical references. [BV4020.A63] 67-3969
1. Taylor, Charles Lincoln, 1901- 2. Theology — Study and teaching — Addresses, essays, lectures. I. Coburn, John B., ed. II. Wagoner, Walter D., joint ed. III. Ziegler, Jesse H., joint ed. IV. Taylor, Charles Lincoln, 1901- V. Title. Contents omitted

SOCIETY for the promotion of collegiate and theological education.
Proceedings at the quarter-century anniversary of the Society for the promotion of collegiate and theological education, at the West Marietta, Ohio, November 7-10, 1868. With an appendix. New York, The Trow & Smith book manufacturing company, 1868. vi, 182 p. 23 cm. [With its Annual report. 18th--24th, 1861-67] Includes the society's 25th annual report. [LC564.C5] [LC564.C56] 7-34502
I. Title.

SPERRY, Willard Learoyd, 1882- 261
Signs of these times; the Ayer lectures of the Colgate-Rochester divinity school for 1929, by Willard L. Sperry ... Garden City, N.Y., Doubleday, Doran & company, inc., 1929. viii p., 2 l., 3-179 p. 19 1/2 cm. [BR85.S635] 29-21277
I. Title.

Theology—Study and teaching—Africa.

INTERNATIONAL Missionary Council.
Survey of the training of the ministry in Africa; report of a survey of theological education. London, New York, 1950-54. 3 v. 23cm. Contents.pt. 1. East and West Africa, by S. Neill.--pt. 2. Angola, Belgian Congo, French West Africa, French Equatorial Africa, Liberia, Mozambique, and Ruanda-Urundi, by M. S. Bates [and others]--pt. 3. Union of South Africa, Southern and Northern Rhodesia, and Nyasaland, by N. Goodall and E. W. Nielsen. A56
1. Theology—Study and teaching—Africa. I. Neill, Stephen Charles, Bp. II. Title. III. Title: The training of the ministry in Africa.

Theology—Study and teaching—Anglican communion.

PROTESTANT Episcopal Church in the U.S.A. Special Committee on Theological Education. 207/.11/3
Ministry for tomorrow; report. Nathan M. Pusey, chairman. Charles L. Taylor, director of the study. New York. Seabury [1967] xi, 147p. 22cm. Presented to the gen. convention of the Episcopal Church in Seattle in Sept., 1967. Bibl. [BX5850.A35] 67-28443 3.95; 2.50 pap.,
1. Theology—Study and teaching—Anglican communion. 2. Theology—Study and teaching—U.S. I. Taylor Charles Lincoln, 1901- II. Protestant Episcopal Church in the U.S.A. General Convention. Seattle, 1967. III. Title.

Theology—Study and teaching—Baptists.

AMERICAN Baptist convention. Board of education. 207.73
Theological education in the Northern Baptist convention, a survey; prepared by Hugh Hartshorne and Milton C. Froyd for the Commission on a survey of theological education of the Board of education of the Northern Baptist convention. 1944-1945. [Philadelphia, The Judson press, 1954] 242p. 24cm. [BX6219.A65] 46-1218
1. Theology—Study and teaching—Baptists. 2. Theological seminaries, Baptist.

3. Baptists—Education. I. Hartshorne, Hugh, 1885- II. Froyd, Milton C. III. Title.

NORTHERN Baptist convention. Board of education. 207.73
Theological education in the Northern Baptist convention, a survey; prepared by Hugh Hartshorne and Milton C. Froyd for the Commission on a survey of theological education of the Board of education of the Northern Baptist convention. 1944-1945. [Philadelphia, The Judson press, 1945] 242 p. 24 cm. [BX6219.N6] 46-1218
1. Theology—Study and teaching—Baptists. 2. Theological seminaries, Baptist. 3. Northern Baptist convention—Education. 4. Baptists—Education. I. Hartshoren, Hugh, 1885-. II. Froyd, Milton C. III. Title.

Theology—Study and teaching—Catholic church.

CALLAHAN, Daniel J. 230
The role of theology in the university [by] Daniel Callahan, William Scott [and] F. X. Shea. Milwaukee, Bruce Pub. Co. [1967] xii, 163 p. 23 cm. (Contemporary college theology series) Bibliographical footnotes. [BT65.C3] 67-28215
1. Theology—Study and teaching—Catholic Church. 2. Theology, Doctrinal—Introductions. I. Scott, William A., 1920- II. Shea, Francis X., 1926-

COULSON, John, 1919- ed. 230.0711
Theology and the university, an ecumenical investigation [Contributors: Christopher Butler, others] Helicon [dist. New York, Taplinger, c.1964] x, 286p. 23cm. Bibl. 64-15968 4.95
1. Theology—Study and teaching—Catholic Church. 2. Religious education of adults—Catholic. 3. Catholic Church—Education. I. Title.

SMITH, John Talbot, 1855-1923.
The training of a priest; an essay on clerical education, with a reply to the critics, by Rev. John Talbot Smith ... New York, London [etc.] Longmans, Green and co., 1908. xxxix, 361 p. 19 1/2 cm. "First published under the title 'Our seminaries, etc.' in 1896; reissued, revised and enlarged, and with an article by Biship McQuald, April, 1908."--p. [ii] [BX900.S6] 8-13666
1. Theology—Study and teaching—Catholic church. I. Title.

Theology—Study and teaching—Catholic Church—Directories.

CENTER for Applied Research in the Apostolate, Washington, D.C. 207'.73
U.S. Catholic institutions for the training of candidates for the priesthood; a sourcebook for seminary reveval, 1971. Washington [1971?] xviii, 156 p. 28 cm. [BX905.C44] 72-182405
1. Theology—Study and teaching—Catholic Church—Directories. 2. Theological seminaries, Catholic—Directories. 3. Theological seminaries—United States.—Directories. I. Title.

Theology—Study and teaching—Congresses.

CONFERENCE of Baptist theological seminaries. Boston and Newton &$ Center, Mass., 1918: 268.
Conference of Baptist theological seminaries held in Boston and Newton Center, Massachusetts, March twelve and thirteen, nineteen hundred and eighteen, at the invitation of the Newton theological institution. [Chicago, University of Chicago press, 1918] [BX6219.C6] 21-2992
1. Theology—Study and teaching—Congresses. I. Newton theological institution, Newton Center, Mass. II. Title.

Theology—Study and teaching—Disciples of Christ.

DISCIPLES of Christ. Study Commission on Ministerial Education. 230'.6'6
The imperative is leadership; a report on ministerial development in the Christian Church (Disciples of Christ), by Carroll C. Cotten. With recommendations by the Study Commission on Ministerial Education, Christian Church (Disciples of Christ). St. Louis, Mo., Bethany Press [1973] 125 p. 23 cm. Includes bibliographical references. [BX7311.D57] 73-8893 ISBN 0-8272-1604-1 2.95
1. Disciples of Christ—Clergy. 2. Theology—Study and teaching—Disciples of Christ. I. Cotten, Carroll C., 1936- II. Title.

Theology-Study and teaching-Episcopal Church.

WHIPPLE, Charles Everett, 1913-
The teaching ministry of the priest in the Episcopal Church. [n.p.] 1959. ii, 159 p. Final document (Ed. D.) -- N.Y.U., School of Education, 1959. Bibliography: p. [135]-139.
1. Thelogy — Study and teaching — Episcopal Church. I. Title.

Theology—Study and teaching—Evaluation.

NELSON, Carl Ellis, 1916- 207
Using evaluation in theological education / C. Ellis Nelson. Nashville : Discipleship Resources, c1975. 121 p. ; 22 cm. Bibliography: p. [117]-121. [BV4020.N4] 75-16640
1. Theology—Study and teaching—Evaluation. I. Title.

Theology—Study and teaching—History.

GAMBRELL, Mary Latimer. 207'.74
Ministerial training in eighteenth-century New England. New York, AMS Press, 1967 [c1937] 169 p. 24 cm. (Studies in history, economics, and public law, no. 428) Originally presented as the author's thesis, Columbia University. Bibliography: p. 148-159. [BV4033.G3 1967] 71-168094
1. Theology—Study and teaching—History. 2. Theological seminaries—New England. I. Title. II. Series: Columbia studies in the social sciences, 428.

Theology-Study and teaching-Islands of the Pacific.

THEOLOGICAL Education Consultation Suva Fyi Islands 1961 207.9
Theological education in the Pacific. Report prepared and published by the Theological Education Fund Committee of the International Missionary Council. New York [1961] 82 p. 22 cm. "Sponsored by the Theological Education Fund." [BV4140.P3T5] 63-44891
1. Theology — Study and teaching — Islands of the Pacific. I. International Missionary Council. Theological Education Fund. II. Title.

THEOLOGICAL education in the Pacific; consultation (sponsored by the Theological Education Fund) at Dudley House High School. Suva, Fiji, May 7-13, 1961. Report prepared and published by the Theological Education Fund Committee ... New York, 1961. 82p. 22cm.
1. Theology-Study and teaching-Islands of the Pacific. 2. Theological seminaries-Island of the Pacific. I. International Missionary Council. Theological Education Fund.

Theology—Study and teaching—Latin America.

MULHOLLAND, Kenneth B. 207'.7283
Adventures in training the ministry : a Honduran case study in theological education by extension / by Kenneth Mulholland ; with foreword by F. Ross Kinsler. [Nutley, N.J.] : Presbyterian and Reformed Pub. Co., 1976. xvi, 219 p. : diagrs. ; 21 cm. (Studies in the world church and missions) "Grew out of an S.T.M. thesis presented to the faculty of the Lancaster Theological Seminary in 1971 ..." Bibliography: p. 209-219. [BV4140.L3M84] 76-5151 5.95
1. Seminary extension—Latin America. 2. Seminary extension—Honduras—Case studies. 3. Theology—Study and teaching—Latin America. I. Title. II. Series.

THEOLOGICAL education by extension. Edited by Ralph D. Winter. South Pasadena, Calif., William Carey Library [1969] xxvi, 589, 28 p. illus. 23 cm. Bibliography: p. 1-28 (3d group) [BV4140.L3T48] 78-96751 5.25 207'.8
1. Theology—Study and teaching—Latin America. I. Winter, Ralph D., ed.

Theology—Study and teaching—Lutheran Church.

SCHMIDT, Stephen A. 377'.8'4108 s
Powerless pedagogues; an interpretive essay on the history of the Lutheran teacher in the Missouri Synod [by] Stephen A. Schmidt. River Forest, Ill., Lutheran Education Association [1972] viii, 141 p. 21 cm. (29th LEA yearbook) Bibliography: p. 129-141. [LC573.L78 vol. 29] [LC574] 377'.8'41322 72-186108 1.95
1. Lutheran Church in Missouri—Education. 2. Lutheran Church—Missouri Synod. 3. Theology—Study and teaching—Lutheran Church. I. Title. II. Series: Lutheran Education Association. Yearbook, 29.

Theology—Study and teaching—Madagascar.

SURVEY of the training of the ministry in Madagascar; report of a survey of theological education in Madagascar undertaken in September to November, 1956, by C. W. Ranson [and others] London, New York, 1957. 51p.
1. Theology—Study and teaching—Madagascar. 2. Missions—Madagascar. I. International Missionary Council. II. Ranson, Charles Wesley.

Theology—Study and teaching—Methodist church.

HUSE, Raymond Howard, 1880- 287
Theology of a modern Methodist, by Raymond Huse. New York, Cincinnati, The Methodist book concern [c1920] 125 p. 18 cm. [BX8331.H88] 20-5057
I. Title.

SMITH, Rockwell Carter, 1908- 200
The role of rural social science in theological education; with particular application to the town and country ministry of the Methodist Church [by] Rockwell C. Smith. [Evanston, Ill., 1969] 88 p. 23 cm. Bibliography: p. 82-85. [BX8219.S6] 70-17001
1. Theology—Study and teaching—Methodist church. 2. Sociology, Rural. 3. Sociology, Christian. I. Title.

Theology—Study and teaching—Near East.

WEBSTER, Douglas, 1920- 207'.56
Survey of the training of the ministry in the Middle East; report of a survey of theological education in Iran, the Arabian-Persian Gulf, Jordan, Lebanon and Syria, and Egypt, undertaken in September to November, 1961, by Douglas Webster [and] K. L. Nasir. Geneva, New York, Commission on World Mission and Evangelism, World Council of Churches, 1962. 63 p. 22 cm. [BV4140.N4W4] 71-265080
1. Theology—Study and teaching—Near East. I. Nasir, K. L., joint author. II. World Council of Churches. Commission on World Mission and Evangelism. III. Title.

Theology — Study and teaching — Presbyterian church.

UNITED Presbyterian Church in the U.S.A. Council on Theological Education.
The United Presbyterian enterprise of theological education. [Philadelphia] 1959. viii, 83 p. 22 cm.
1. Theology — Study and teaching — Presbyterian church. I. Title.

Theology — Study and teaching — Unitarian churches

UNITARIAN Universalist Association. Committee to Study Theological Education. 207
R comprehensive plan of education for the Unitarian Universalist ministry; complete report. Boston, Unitarian Universalist Association [c1962] 137 p. 22 cm. [BX9817.U6] 63-45295
1. Theology — Study and teaching — Unitarian churches 2. Theological seminaries, Unitarian. I. Title.

Theology—Study and teaching—United States

ATLANTA theological seminary.
Catalogue. Atlanta, Ga. v. 18 cm. ca 10
I. Title.

ATLANTA theological seminary.
Catalogue. Atlanta, Ga. v. 18 cm. ca 10
I. Title.

AUBURN theological seminary. 016.
Catalogue. [Auburn,m N. Y., v. plates. 20 cm. [BV4070.A72] ca 9
I. Title.

BANGOR theological seminary, Bangor, Me.
... *Catalogue.* Bangor, 18 v. plates. 20-23 1/2 cm. CA 7
I. Title.

CUMBERLAND university, Lebanon, Tenn. Theological dept. 016.
Catalogue, Announcements, Nashville, Tenn., v. plates. 21 cm. On cover: Cumberland university bulletin ... The Lebanon theological seminary ... [BV4070.C92] ca 11
I. Title.

FUKUYAMA, Yoshio, 1921- 207'.11'5834
The ministry in transition; a case study of theological education. University Park, Pennsylvania State University Press [1972] xx, 167 p. 24 cm. Includes bibliographical references. [BX9884.A3F83] 72-1395 ISBN 0-271-01129-7 9.50
1. United Church of Christ—Clergy, Training of. 2. Theology—Study and teaching—United States. I. Title.

KENYON college, Gambier, O. Library. 016.
Catalogue of books belonging to the library of the theological seminary of the diocese of Ohio, Kenyon college and the preparatory schools. MDCCCXXXVII. Gambier, G. W. Myers, printer, 1837. 1 p. l., 76 p. 22 1/2 cm. [Z881.G182'37] 8-24401
I. Title.

LOVE, Julian Price, 1894- 207'.73
In quest of a ministry. Richmond, John Knox Press [1969] 136 p. 21 cm. [BV4030.L6] 69-12369 2.45
1. Theology—Study and teaching—U.S. 2. Seminarians. I. Title.

MASTERSON, Reginald, ed. 230.2
Theology in the Catholic college. Dubuque, Iowa, Priory Press, Asbury Rd. [c.1961] 343p. Bibl. 61-11123 3.95
1. Theology—Study and teaching—U. S. 2. Theology—Study and teaching—Catholic Church. 3. Universities and colleges—Curricula. I. Title.

MEADVILLE theological school, Meadville, Pa. Library. 016.
Catalogue of the library of the Meadville theological school. Meadville, Penn., Republican printing house, 1870. 134 p. 24 1/2 cm. [Z881.M46 1870] E 11
I. Title.

NATIONAL Council of the Churches of Christ in the United States of America. Committee on Theological Study and Teaching. 207'.73
The study of religion in college and university and its implications for church and seminary; a report on a consultation held in New York City, January 26-27, 1967. Foreword by Claude Welch. [New York?] Dept. of Higher Education, National Council of Churches [1967] xii, 100 p. 26 cm. Includes bibliographies. [BV4030.N3] 68-5492

1. Theology—Study and teaching—United States. 2. Universities and colleges—Religion. I. Title.

NIEBUHR, Helmut Richard, 1894- 207
The advancement of theological education, by H. Richard Niebuhr, Daniel Day Williams [and] James M. Gustafson. [1st ed.] New York, Harper [1957] 239p. 22cm. [BV4030.N5] 56-12071
1. Theology—Study and teaching—U. S. I. Title.

PRINCETON theological seminary. 207.
Catalogue of the officers and students of the Theological seminary of the Presbyterian church at Princeton, N. J. [Princeton, N. J., 18-19 v. pl. 24 cm. [BV4070.P72] 8-1399
I. Title.

RUDDER, William, b.1820. 016.
... Catalogue of the valuable theological, scientific and miscellaneous library of the late Rev. Dr. William Rudder, of St. Stephen's church, Philadelphia ... to be sold ... May 17th, 18th and 19th, 1880 ... M. Thomas & sons, auctioneers ... Phila[delphia] W. B. Selheimer, printer, [1880] cover-title, 82 p. 23 cm. At head of title: Private library. M. Thomas & sons, auctioneers. 1,318 entries. [Z997.R914] 13-26869
I. Title.

THEOLOGICAL education as professional education; the report of a convocation sponsored by the Episcopal Theological School during its centennial year observance. Edited by Olga Craven, Alden L. Todd [and] Jesse H. Ziegler. Dayton, Ohio, American Association of Theological Schools [1969] xi, 167 p. 26 cm. Bibliographical references included in "Footnotes" (p. 155-164) [BV4030.T48] 72-9346 207
1. Theology—Study and teaching—U.S. 2. Professional education—U.S. I. Craven, Olga, ed. II. Todd, Alden, ed. III. Ziegler, Jesse H., ed. IV. Cambridge, Mass. Episcopal Theological School.

WAGONER, Walter D 262.14
Bachelor of divinity; uncertain servants in seminary and ministry. With drawings by James Crane. New York, Association Press [1963] 150 p. illus. 21 cm. Bibliographical references included in "Notes" (p. 153-159) [BV4030.W3] 63-16044
1. Theology—Study and teaching—U.S. 2. Pastoral theology—Addresses, essays, lectures. 3. Seminarians. I. Title.

Theology, systematic — Popular works.

CHAFER, Lewis Sperry, 1871-1952.
Meigisia Meingi ma Mukanda wa Kalaga Yehowa (Major Bible Themes) Translation into Kalaga by Ernest L. Green, C. van der Ploeg and Sansago Jerome. [St. Louis] Berean Missionary Society [1962] 121 p. 64-65502
1. Theology, systematic — Popular works. I. Title.

Theology—Terminology.

ADAMS, Hampton, 1897- 230.014
Vocabulary of faith. St. Louis, Bethany Press [1956] 124p. 21cm. [BR96.5.A3] 55-12224
1. Theology— Terminology. I. Title.

BIGLER, Vernon. 230.014
Key words in Christian thinking; a guide to theological terms and ideas. New York, Association Press [1966] 125 p. 16 cm. (A Reflection book) [BR96.5.B5] 66-20477
1. Theology—Terminology. I. Title.

BURNABY, John. 204
Christian words and Christian meanings. New York, Harper [c1955] 160p. 20cm. [BR96.5.B8 1955a] 55-11477
1. Theology- Terminology. I. Title.

ELLER, Vernard. 230'.03
Cleaning up the Christian vocabulary / Vernard Eller. Elgin, Ill. : Brethren Press, c1976. 121 p. ; 18 cm. [BR96.5.E43] 76-10984 ISBN 0-87178-153-0 pbk. : 2.95
1. Theology—Terminology. I. Title.

FERGUSON, Charles Wright, 1901- 230'.01'4
A is for Advent [by] Charles W. Ferguson. [1st ed.] Boston, Little, Brown [1968] viii, 149 p. illus. 22 cm. [BR96.5.F4] 68-30879 4.95
1. Theology—Terminology. I. Title.

FURNESS, John Marshall. 220.3
Vital words of the Bible, by J. M. Furness. Grand Rapids, Eerdmans [1967, c1966] 127 p. 20 cm. [BS440.F88] 67-1707
1. Bible—Dictionaries. 2. Theology—Terminology. I. Title.

HEALEY, Frances G. 203
Fifty key words in theology, by F. G. Healey. Richmond, John Knox [1967] 84p. 20cm. (Fifty key word bks.) [BR96.5.H4] 67-16692 1.65 pap.,
1. Theology—Terminology. I. Title.

HORDERN, William. 230.014
Speaking of God; the nature and purpose of theological language. New York, Macmillan [1964] viii, 209 p. 21 cm. Includes bibliographical references. [BV4319.H6] 64-21167
1. Theology — Terminology. 2. Communication (Theology) I. Title.

RAMSEY, Ian T 230.01
Christian discourse, some ligical explorations, by Ian T. Ramsey. London, New York. Oxford University Press, 1965. 92 p. 19 cm. (Riddell memorial lectures, 35th ser.) University of Newcastle upon Tyne. Publications. Lectures delivered at the University of Newcastle upon Tyne, November 5-7, 1963. Bibliographical footnotes. [BR96.5.R29] 65-6792
1. Theology — Terminology. I. Title. II. Series.

RAMSEY, Ian T. 230.014
Religious language; an empirical placing of theological phrases. New York, Macmillan [1963] 221p. 18cm. (MP129) Bibl. 1.45 pap.,
1. Theology—Terminology. 2. Semantics (Philosophy) 3. Christianity—Philosophy. I. Title.

SARDESON, Charles Thomas. 230.014
Rediscovering the words of faith. New York, Abingdon Press [1956] 124p. 20cm. [BR96.5.S3] 56-7766
1. Theology—Terminology. I. Title.

Theophanies.

HEWLETT, Henry Charles. 231
The companion of the way. Chicago, Moody Press [1962] 159p. 22cm. [BT128.H4] 62-1315
1. Theophanies. 2. Devotional literature. I. Title.

HOUGH, Robert Ervin, 1874- 231
The ministry of the glory cloud. New York, Philosophical Library [1955] 145p. 21cm. [BT128.H6] 56-183
1. Theophanies. I. Title.

KUNTZ, John Kenneth. 231'.74
The self-revelation of God, by J. Kenneth Kuntz. Philadelphia, Westminster Press [1967] 254 p. 24 cm. Bibliography: p. [233]-243. [BT128.K8] 67-10270
1. Theophanies. 2. Revelation. I. Title.

ROSENBERG, Leon. 231.74
The various manifestations of the Deity. Los Angeles, American European Bethel Mission [c1961] 250p. 23cm. [BT128.R6] 61-18750
1. Theophanies. I. Title.

Theophanies in the Bible.

BORLAND, James A., 1944- 231'.74
Christ in the Old Testament / by James A. Borland. Chicago : Moody Press, c1978. p. cm. Includes indexes. Bibliography: p. [BS1199.T45B67] 78-10164 ISBN 0-8024-1391-9 pbk. : 4.95
1. Bible. O.T.—Criticism, interpretation, etc. 2. Theophanies in the Bible. I. Title.

Theophanies in the Bible—Prayer-books and devotions.

PATE, Don, 1951- 242
Episodes at the olive press / by Don Pate. Nashville : Southern Pub. Association, c1980. 95 p. ; 21 cm. p. cm. [BS680.T45P37] 79-24125 ISBN 0-8127-0215-8 pbk. : 4.50
1. Theophanies in the Bible—Prayer-books and devotions. I. Title.

Theophilus, William, b. 1769.

KIDDER, Daniel Parish, 1815-1891. 922.773
Recollections of William Theophilus, a pilgrim of four-score ... Edited by D. P. Kidder. New-York, Lane & Scott, for the Sunday-school union of the Methodist Episcopal church, 1852. 132 p. incl. front., plates. 15 1/2 cm. [BX8495.T.45K5] 37-7013
1. Theophilus, William, b. 1769. I. Sunday-school union of the Methodist Episcopal church. II. Title.

Theory (Philosophy)

ROTENSTREICH, Nathan, 1914- 110
Theory and practice / Nathan Rotenstreich. Atlantic Highlands, N.J. : Humanities Press, [1975] p. cm. (The Van Leer Jerusalem Foundation series) Includes index. [B842.R65] 73-85039 ISBN 0-391-00374-7 : 10.00
1. Theory (Philosophy) 2. Practice (Philosophy) 3. Idea (Philosophy) I. Title. II. Series: Van Leer Foundation for the Advancement of Human Culture. The Van Leer Jerusalem Foundation series.

Theosophical society.

AMERICAN theosophical society.
American theosophical society lodge procedure. Chicago, American theosophical society [c1925] 3 p. l., 113 p. 16 cm. "This book of procedure is compiled from the procedures, articles or suggestions of H. P. Blavatsky, Dr. Annie Besant, Rt. Rev. C. W. Leadbeater, W. J. Walters, C. F. Holland, Max Wardall, K. C. Havens,Ellen P. Talbot, Visda Stone and others."--Introd. Contains bibliographies. [BP510.A6A5 1925] 25-10606
I. Title.

FRANCIS, T. M. pseud.
Blavatsky, Besant and co. (the story of a great anti-Christian fraud) by T. M. Francis; with a preface by Herbert Thurston, S. J. ... Saint Paul, Minn., Library service guild [c1939] 5 p. l., 13-111 p. incl. front., plan. 20 cm. [BP575.F7] 10-897
1. Blavatsky, Helen Petrovna (Hahn-Hahn) 1831-1891. 2. Besant Mrs. Annie (Wood) 1847-1933. 3. Theosophical society. 4. Theosophy. I. Title.

GERARD, John, pseud. 212
Letters to friends [by] John Gerard. New York, The Quarterly book department [c1925] 4 p. l., 212 p. 19 cm. "Published under the auspices of the Theosophical society. [BP525.G4] 25-9150
I. Title.

ROBERTS, Carl Eric Bechhofer, 1894- 922.91
The mysterious madame Helena Petrouna Balavatsky: the life & work of the founder of the Theasophical society, with a note on her successor, Annie Besant, by C. E. Bechofer!-Roberts. New York, Brewer and Warren, inc., 1931. 332 p., 1 l. front. (port.) 24 cm. Bibliography: p. 323-325. [BP585.B6R6] 31-11077
1. Blavatsky, Helene Petrovna (Hahn-Hahn) 1831-1891. 2. Theosophical society. I. Title.

RYAN, Charles James. 922.91
H. P. Blavatsky and the theosophical movement, a brief historical sketch, by Charles J. Ryan. Point Loma, Calif., Theosophical university press, 1937. xxi, [1], 369, [1] p. front., illus., plates, ports., facsim. 20 1/2 cm. Facsimile accompanied by guard sheet with descriptive letterpress. "Books, magazines, etc., quoted in this volume": p. [359]-360. [BP585.B6R8] 38-6562
1. Blavatsky, Helene Petrovnn (Hahn-Hahn) 1831-1891. 2. Theosophical society. 3. Theosophy. I. Title.

SHURLOCK, Aileen Brittain. 920
Biographical sketch of Colonel Arthur Latham Conger, fifth leader of the Theosophical Society, Point Loma-Covina, philosopher. scholar, soldier, author, musician, i[Oakland? Calif, 1955] 65p. 22cm. ovina, Calif. [BP585.C6S5] 56-16956
1. Conger, Arthur Latham, 1872-1951. 2. Theosophical Society. I. Title.

THE Society for Psychical Research report on the Theosophical Society / edited, with an introd. by James Webb. New York : Arno Press, 1976. 201,-400, 60, 129-159 p., [3] fold. leaves of plates : ill. ; 23 cm. (The Occult) Reprint of Report of the committee appointed to investigate phenomena connected with the Theosophical Society, published in v. 3 of the Proceedings of the Society for Psychical Research, London, 1885; of Was she a charlatan? By W. Kingsland, published by the Blavatsky Association, London, 1927; and of The defence of the Theosophists, by R. Hodgson, published in v. 9 of the Proceedings of the Society for Psychical Research, London, 1894. Cover title: the SPR report on the Theosophical Society. [BP510.T5S6] 75-36920 ISBN 0-405-07975-3 : 20.00 147
1. Theosophical Society. 2. Theosophy. I. Society for Psychial Research, London. II. Kingsland, William, 1855-1936. Was she a charlatan? 1927. III. Series: The Occult (New York, 1976-)

SPINKS, F Pierce. *294.58 212
Theosophists: reunite! Boston, Christopher Pub. House [1958] 387 p. 21 cm. [BP510.T5S65] 58-8665
1. Theosophical Society. 2. Theosophy — Hist. I. Title.

THEOSOPHICAL society.
The Theosophical congress held by the Theosophical society at the Parliament of religions, World's fair of 1893, at Chicago, Ill., September 15, 16, 17. Report of proceedings and documents. New York, 1893. 195 p. 23 cm. 6-36971
I. Title.

THEOSOPHICAL society. American section.
... Annual convention American section T. S. ...Report of proceedings ... New York, 18 v. 23 cm. The 9th annual convention was also the 1st convention of the Theosophical society in America. [BP510.T53A3] CA 6
I. Title.

THEOSOPHICAL society in America.
... Annual convention of the Theosophical society in America ... Report of proceedings ... New York, 1895- v. 23 cm. The 1st convention was also the 9th annual convention of the American section T.S. 6-31502
I. Title.

Theosophists—Australia—Biography.

TILLETT, Gregory. 299'.934'0924 B
The elder brother : a biography of Charles Webster Leadbeater / Gregory Tillett. London ; Boston : Routledge & K. Paul, 1982. xii, 337 p., [16] p. of plates : ill. ; 24 cm. Includes index. Bibliography: p. 316-330. [BP585.L4T54 1982] 19 81-21133 ISBN 0-7100-0926-7 : 24.95
1. Leadbeater, C. W. (Charles Webster), 1847-1934. 2. Theosophists—Australia—Biography. I. Title.

Theosophists—Biography.

LEONARD, Maurice. 212'.52'0924 B
Madame Blavatsky : medium, mystic and magician / by Maurice Leonard. London ; New York : Regency Press, 1977. 115 p. ; 23 cm. [BP585.B6L43] 77-373898 £2.00
1. Blavatsky, Helene Petrovna Hahn-Hahn, 1831-1891. 2. Theosophists—Biography. I. Title.

MEADE, Marion, 1934- 299'.934'0924 B
Madame Blavatsky, the woman behind the myth / Marion Meade. New York : Putnam, c1980. 528 p., [4] leaves of plates : ill. ; 24 cm. Includes index. Bibliography: p. [499]-511. [BP585.B6M42 1980] 19 79-29648 ISBN 0-399-12376-8 : 19.95

1. Blavatsky, Helene Petrovna Hahn-Hahn, 1831-1891. 2. Theosophists—Biography. I. Title.

WACHTMEISTER, Constance. 212'.52'0924 B
Reminiscences of H. P. Blavatsky and The secret doctrine / by Countess Constance Wachtmeister et al. Wheaton, Ill. : Theosophical Pub. House, c1976. xiv, 141 p. : map ; 21 cm. (Theosophical classics series) (A Quest book) [BP585.B6W3 1976] 76-44810 ISBN 0-8356-0488-8 pbk. : 3.75
1. Blavatsky, Helene Petrovna Hahn-Hahn, 1831-1891. 2. Blavatsky, Helene Petrovna Hahn-Hahn, 1831-1891. The secret doctrine. 3. Theosophists—Biography. 4. Theosophy. I. Title.

Theosophists—Correspondence, reminiscences, etc.

JUDGE, William Quan, 1851-1896. 922.91
Practical occultism, from the private letters of William Q. Judge. Edited by Arthur L. Conger. [Pasadena, Calif.] Theosophical University Press [1951] 307 p. 22 cm. [BP585.J8A4] 52-16003
1. Theosophists—Correspondence, reminiscences, etc. I. Title.

LUTYENS, Lady Emily (Lytton) 1874- 212
Candles in the sun. Philadelphia, Lippincott [1957] 196p. plate, ports. 21cm. [BP585.L85A3 1957a] 57-12383
1. Krishnamurti, Jiddu, 1895- 2. Theosophists—Correspondence, reminiscences, etc. 3. Theosophical Society. I. Title.

Theosophy.

ALBERTSON, Edward. 147
Theosophy for the millions. Los Angeles, Sherbourne Press [1971] 165 p. 21 cm. (For the millions series, FM 43) [BP565.A38T5] 76-151861 2.50
1. Blavatsky, Helene Petrovna (Hahn-Hahn) 1831-1891. 2. Theosophy. I. Title.

ARUNDALE, George Sydney, 1878-1945. 192
You. [Slightly rev. and abridged] Wheaton, Ill., Theosophical Pub. House [1973, c1935] vi, 176 p. 18 cm. (A Quest book) [BP565.A7Y62] 73-4783 ISBN 0-8356-0434-9 1.75 (pbk.)
1. Theosophy. I. Title.

ASHISH, Madhava. 147
Man, son of man; in the stanzas of Dzyan. Wheaton, Ill., Theosophical Pub. House [1970] xiv, 352 p. illus. (part col.) 22 cm. "A companion volume to and, in fact, a continuation of Man, the measure of all things by the same author (with ... Sri Krishna Prem), which dealt with the stanzas of Dzyan relating to cosmogenesis as set forth in H. P. Blavatsky's great work, The secret doctrine."—Jacket. "The stanzas of Dzyan; excerpts from The book of Dzyan, translated by H. P. Blavatsky, in her book The secret doctrine, Book II, Part I 'Anthropogenesis.'": p. [25]-31. Bibliography: p. [xi]-xii. [BP565.A77M3 1970b] 78-98267 ISBN 0-8356-0011-4
1. Theosophy. I. Sri Krishna Prem, 1898-1965. Man, the measure of all things. II. Title.

BAILEY, Alice A. Mrs. 1881- 212
A treatise on the seven rays; the new psychology, by Alice A Bailey. New York, Lucis publishing company [1936]- v. 24 cm. "Written by Alice A. Bailey in collaboration with the Tibetan [pseud.]-- Publisher's note.. "First edition." [BP565.B3] 36-18285
1. Theosophy. I. The Tibetan. pseud. II. Title. III. Title: Seven rays. A treatise on the.

BAILEY, Alice Anne (La Trobe-Bateman), 1880- 212
A treatise on the seven rays. 2d ed. London, Lucis Press; New York, Lucis Pub. Co. [19 v. 22 cm. Contents.v. 2. Esoteric psychology. [BP565.B312] 50-2141
1. Theosophy. I. Title. II. Title: Seven rays.

BAILEY, Alice Anne (La Trobe-Bateman) 1880- 212
A treatise on the seven rays. London, Lucis Press; New York, Lucis Pub. Co. [19 v. 22 cm. Contents.v. 2. Esoteric psychology. [BP565.B312] 50-2141
1. Theosophy. I. Title. II. Title: Seven rays.

BAILEY, Alice Anne (La Trobe Bateman) 1880-1949. 212.5
A treatise on the seven rays. 4th ed. New York, Lucius Pub. Co. 1962- v. 24 cm. Contents.Contents.—v.1-2. Esoteric psychology.—v.3. Esoteric astrology.—v.4. Esoteric healing.—v.5. The rays and the initiations. [BP565.B314] 62-6365
1. Theosophy. I. Title: Seven rays.

BAILEY, Alice Anne (La Trobe-Bateman) 1880-1949. 212
A treatise on the seven rays, by Alice A. Bailey [in collaboration with the Tibetan. 1st ed.] New York, Lucis Pub. Co. [1936- v. diagrs. 24 cm. Vol. 3 lacks edition statement. Contents.[1]-2. The new psychology.--v. 3. Esoteric astrology. [BP565.B3] 36-18285
1. Theosophy. I. The Tibetan, pseud. II. Title. III. Title: Seven rays.

BAILEY, Alice Anne (LaTrobe-Bateman) 1880- 212
A treatise on the seven rays; the new psychology, by Alice A. Bailey. New York, Lucis publishing company [1936]- v. 23 1/2 cm. "Written by Alice A. Bailey in collaboration with the Tibetan."-- Publisher's note. "First edition." [BP565.B3] 36-18285
1. Theosophy. I. The Tibetan, Pseud. II. Title. III. Title: Seven rays.

BARBORKA, Geoffrey A. 212'.52
The peopling of the Earth : a commentary on archaic records in The secret doctrine / by Geoffrey Barborka. Wheaton, Ill. : Theosophical Pub. House, 1975. xiv, 233 p. : ill. ; 23 cm. (Quest books) Includes bibliographical references and index. [BP561.S43B37] 75-4243 ISBN 0-8356-0221-4 : 10.00
1. Blavatsky, Helene Petrovna Hahn-Hahn, 1831-1891. The secret doctrine. 2. Theosophy. I. Title.

BEALE, Arthur A. 212
The evolution of man-s mind, by Arthur A. Bealev... Philadelphia, The David McKay company [1939] 3 p. l., 9-96 p. 19 cm. "Printed in Great Britain." [BP565.B37] 40-900
1. Theosophy. I. Title.

BENDIT, Laurence John, 1898- 147
The mysteries today, and other essays [by] Laurence J. Bendit. London, Wheaton, Ill., Theosophical Publishing House, 1973. 154 p. 23 cm. [BP565.B417] 73-177693 ISBN 0-7229-5024-1 £1.50
1. Theosophy. I. Title.

BENDIT, Laurence John, 1898- 212'.5
Self knowledge; a yoga for the West, by Laurence J. Bendit. Wheaton, Ill., Theosophical Pub. House [1967] 100 p. 19 cm. (A Quest book) [BP565.B42] 67-7871
1. Theosophy. I. Title.

BENDIT, Laurence John, 1898- 147
The transforming mind, by Laurence J. Bendit and Phoebe D. Bendit (Phoebe Payne) Wheaton, Ill., Theosophical Pub. House [1970] iii, 161 p. 21 cm. (A Quest book original) Bibliography: p. 158-160. [BP565.B423 1970] 74-103415 1.95
1. Theosophy. I. Bendit, Phoebe Daphne (Payne) 1891- joint author. II. Title.

BESANT, Annie (Wood) Mrs. 1847-
Popular lectures on theosophy. i. What is theosophy? ii. The ladder of lives. iii. Reincarnation: its necessity. iv. Reincarnation: its answers to life's problems. v. The law of action and reaction. vi. Man's life in the three worlds. By Annie Besant ... Delivered at Adyar, India, in February and March, 1910. Chicago, The Rajput press, 1910. 1 p. l., 106 p. 20 cm. A 11
1. Theosophy. I. Title.

BESANT, Annie (Wood) Mrs. 1847- 212
Theosophy and the theosophical society, by Annie Besant. Four lectures delivered at the thirty-seventh annual convention of the Theosophical society at Adyar, on December 27th, 28th, 29th and 30th, 1912. Adyar, Madras, India, Chicago, Il., Theosophical publishing house, 1913. 2 p. l., 95 p. 19 cm. [BP563.T6] 13-12011 0.65
1. Theosophy. I. Title.

BESANT, Annie (Wood) Mrs. 1847- 212
Thought power, its control and culture, by Annie Besant. Hollywood, Los Angeles, Cal., Theosophical publishing house, Krotona, reprinted 1918. 3 p. l., 141 p. 17 cm. [BF4C1.B5 1918] 32-4061
1. Theosophy. 2. Thought and thinking. I. Title.

BESANT, Annie (Wood) 1847-1933. 212
The ancient wisdom, an outline of theosophical teachings. 2d ed. London, New York, Theosophical Pub. Society, 1899. xiv, 432, iiv p. plate. 19 cm. [BP563.A6 1899] 48-30568
1. Theosophy. I. Title.

BESANT, Annie (Wood) Mrs. 1847-1933. 212
The changing world, and lectures to theosophical students; fifteen lectures delivered in London during May, June and July 1909, by Annie Besant ... Chicago, The Theosophical book concern; London, The Theosophical publishing society. 1910. 1 p. l., vi, 333, 31 p. 19 cm. Topical index of 31 pages at end. [BP563.C5 1910] A 10
1. Theosophy. I. Title.

BESANT, Annie (Wood) Mrs. 1847-1933. 212
Esoteric Christianity; or, The lesser mysteries, by Annie Besant. New York, J. Lane, 1902. xi, 404 p. 20 cm. [BP563.E7] 1-27732
1. Theosophy. 2. Mysticism. I. Title.

BESANT, Annie (Wood) Mrs. 1847-1933. 212
... Man and his bodies, by Annie Besant. London, New York, Theosophical publishing society; [etc, etc.] 1896. 120 p. 16 x 13 cm. (Theosophical manual. no. vii) "The theosophical society": p. [115]-120. [BP563.M36] 34-13691
1. Theosophy. I. Title.

BESANT, Annie (Wood) 1847-1933.
... Man and his bodies, by Annie Besant. 3d ed. London, Theosophical publishing society; [etc., etc.,] New York, J. Lane, 1905. 114 p. 16 x 12 cm. (Theosophical manuals. No. vii) [BP563.M38] 5-37169
1. Theosophy. I. Title.

BESANT, Annie (Wood) Mrs. 1847-1933. 212
... The seven principles of man, by Annie Besant, F. T. S. 15th thousand. Rev. and cor. ed. London, New York, Theosophical publishing society; [etc., etc., 189-?] 2 p. l., 90 p. diagr. 16 x 13 cm. (Theosophical manuals. no. 1) "The theosophical society": p. 85-87. Bibliography: p. 87-89. [BP563.S4] 39-3921
1. Theosophy. I. Title.

BESANT, Annie (Wood) Mrs. 1847-1933. 212
... The seven principles of man. by Annie Besant ... 20th thousand, Rev. and cor. ed. London & Benares, Theosophical publshing soiety; New York, J. Lane; [etc., c] 1904. 2 p. l., 88 p. dags. 16 x12 cm. (Theosohical manuals. no. 1) "Theosophical socity": p. 85-87. "Books recomended for stuy": p. 87-8. [BP563.S4 1904] 5-37171
1. Theosophy. I. Title.

BESANT, Annie (Wood) Mrs. 1847-1933. 212
... The seven principles of man. By Annie Besant ... (12th thousand). London, Theosophical publishing society; New York, The Path; [etc., etc.] 1892. 88 p. diagr. 16 x 12 cm. (Theosophical manuals. no. 1) "The theosophical society": p. [83]-86. Bibliography: p. 87-88. [BP563.S39] 40-25673
1. Theosophy. I. Title.

BESANT, Annie (Wood) Mrs. 1847-1933.
Theosophy By Annie Besant... London [etc.] T. C. & E. C. Jack; New York, Dodge publishing co. [1912] 94 p. incl. front., tab. 17 cm. (Half-title: The people's books. [v. 76]) Bibliography: p. 92. 13-19
1. Theosophy. I. Title.

BESANT, Annie (Wood) Mrs. 1847-1933. 212
Thought-forms, by Annie Besant and C. W. Leadbeater. With fifty-eight illustrations. London, The Theosophical publishing society; New York, J. Lane; [etc., etc.] 1905. x, 11-84 p. col. front., illus., plates (part col.) 25 cm. "The drawing and painting of the thought-forms observed by Mr. Leadbeater or by muself, or by boh of us together, has been done by three friends--Mr. John Varley, Mr. Prince, and Miss Macfarlane."--p. [v] [BP573.T5B4] 8-29840
1. Theosophy. I. Leadbeater, Charles Webster, 1847- joint author. II. Title.

BESANT, Annie (Wood) 1847-1933.
Thought power: its control and culture, by Annie Besant. Wheaton, Ill., Theosophical Pub. House [1966] 128 p. (A Quest Book) 68-30990
1. Theosophy. 2. Thought and thinking. I. Title.

BESANT, Annie (Wood) 1847-1933. 294.58
Thought power, its control and culture. Wheaton, Ill., Theosophical Press, 1953. 128 p. 19 cm. [BF461.B5 1953] 54-965
1. Theosophy. 2. Thought and thinking. I. Title.

BESANT, Annie (Wood) 1847-1933. 212.52
Thought power, its control and culture. Wheaton, Ill., Theosophical Pub. House [1966] vi, 128 p. 18 cm. (A Quest book) [BP565] 70-1591 0.95
1. Theosophy. 2. Thought and thinking. I. Title.

BLAVATSKY, Helen Petrovna Hahn-Hahn, 1831-1891. 212'.52'0924 B
The letters of H. P. Blavatsky to A. P. Sinnett, and other miscellaneous letters. Transcribed, compiled, and with an introd. by A. T. Barker. Facsim. ed. Pasadena, Calif., Theosophical University Press [1973] xv, 404 p. facsim., port. 23 cm. [BP585.B6A47 1973] 73-84138 10.00
1. Blavatsky, Helen Petrovna Hahn-Hahn, 1831-1891. 2. Theosophy. I. Sinnett, Alfred Parcy, 1840-1921. II. Barker, Alfred Trevor, 1893-1941, ed.

BLAVATSKY, Helene Petrovna (Hahn-Hahn) 1831-1891. 212'.5
An abridgement of The secret doctrine, [by] H. P. Blavatsky. Edited by Elizabeth Preston and Christmas Humphreys. Wheaton, Ill., Theosophical Pub. House [1968, c1966] xxxii, 260 p. illus., port. 21 cm. (Theosophical classics series) (A Quest book.) Bibliography: p. [253] [BP561] 79-5835 2.25
1. Theosophy. I. Preston, Elizabeth, ed. II. Humphreys, Christmas, 1901- ed. III. Title. IV. Title: The secret doctrine.

BLAVATSKY, Helene Petrovna (Hahn-Hahn) 1831-1891. 212
An abridgment by Katharine Hillard of the Secret doctrine, a synthesis of science, religion and philosophy, by Helena Petrovna Blavatsky... New York, 1907. 2 p. l., [3]-583 p. diagrs. 21 cm. [BP561.S4 1907] 7--17357
1. Theosophy. I. Hillard, Katharine, 1839 or 40-1915. II. Title.

BLAVATSKY, Helene Petrovna Hahn-Hahn, 1831-1891. 299'.934
The esoteric writings of Helene Petrovna Slavatsky : a synthesis of science, philosophy, and religion / Helene Petrovna Blavatsky. Wheaton, Ill. : Theosophical Pub. House, c1980. p. cm. (A Quest book) Originally published in 1907 as volume 3, Occultism, of The secret doctrine. Includes indexes. Bibliography: p. [BP561.S4 1980] 79-6547 ISBN 0-8356-0535-3 pbk. : 8.75
1. Theosophy. I. Title.

BLAVATSKY, Helene Petrovna Hahn-Hahn, 1831-1891. 212'.52
Isis unveiled: a master-key to the mysteries of ancient and modern science and theology. Pasadena, Calif., Theosophical University Press [1972] 2 v. 23 cm. Reprint of the 1877 ed. Contents.Contents.—v. 1. Science.—v. 2. Theology. Includes bibliographical references. [BP561.I7 1972b] 72-186521 12.50

1. Theosophy. I. Title.

BLAVATSKY, Helene Petrovna (Hahn-Hahn) 1831-1891. 212
Isis unveiled; a master-key to the mysteries of ancient and modern science and theology. By H.P. Blavatsky... 2d Point Loma ed. Point Loma, Cal., The Theosophical publishing company 1910. 2 v. front. (port.) illus. 2 fold. diagr. 24 cm. Contents.CONTENTS--Science.--Theology. [BP561.17 1910] 15-21993
1. Theosophy. I. Title.

BLAVATSKY, Helene Petrovna (Hahn-Hahn) 1831-1891. 212
Isis unveiled; a master-key to the mysteries of ancient and modern science and theology by H.P. Blavatsky. 3d Point Loma ed.--rev. Point Loma, Calif., The Aryan theosophical press, 1919. 2 v. in 4. front, ports. 25 cm. Contents.CONTENTS--Science--Theology. [BP561.17 1919] 19-14901
1. Theosophy. I. Title.

BLAVATSKY, Helene Petrovna (Hahn-Hahn) 1831-1891. 212'.52
The key to theosophy. An abridgement, edited by Joy Mills. Wheaton, Ill., Theosophical Pub. House [1972] xv, 176 p. 21 cm. (A Quest book) (Theosophical classics series) [BP561.K4 1972] 75-181716 ISBN 0-8356-0427-6 1.95
1. Theosophy. I. Mills, Joy, ed. II. Title.

BLAVATSKY, Helene Petrovna (Hahn-Hahn) 1831-1891. 212'.52
The key to theosophy; being a clear exposition, in the form of question and answer, of the ethics, science, and philosophy for the study of which the Theosophical Society has been founded. Pasadena, Calif., Theosophical University Press [1972] xii, 373, 53 p. 20 cm. Reprint of the 1889 ed. published by Theosophical Pub. Co., London, with the addition of the glossary from the 2d ed. and a new index. [BP561.K4 1972b] 72-95701 3.50
1. Theosophy. I. Title.

BLAVATSKY, Helene Petrovna (Hahn-Hahn) 1831-1891- 212
The key to theosophy, being a clear exposition, in the form of question and answer, of the ethics, science, and philosophy for the study of which the Theosophical society has been founded. By H.P. Blavatsky. London, The Theosophical publishing company, limited. New York, W.Q. Judge, [1889] xii, 310 p. 21 x 16 1/2 cm. [BP561.K4 1889] 36-29117
1. Theosophy. I. Title.

BLAVATSKY, Helene Petrovna (Hahn-Hahn) 1831-1891. 212
The key to theosophy; being a clear exposition, in the form of question and answer, of the ethics, science, and philosophy, for the study of which the Theosophical society has been founded, with a copious glossary of general theosophical terms by H.P. Blavatsky. 2d and rev. American ed. New York, Theosophical publishing company, 1896. xiv. 344 p. 19 1/2 cm. [BP561.K4 1896] 36-29116
1. Theosophy. I. Title.

BLAVATSKY, Helene Petrovna (Hahn-Hahn) 1831-1891. 212
The key to theosophy; being a clear exposition in the form of question and answer of the ethics, science, and philosophy, for the study of which the Universal brotherhood and theosophical society has been founded, with a copious glossary of general theosophical terms, by H.P. Blavatsky. Point Loma edition, including an exhaustive index. Revised and edited by Katherine Tingley. Point Loma. Calif., The Aryan theosophical press, 1907. 3 p. l., [v]-xii, 384 p. 2 port. (incl. front.) 21 1/2 x 17 cm. [BP561.K4 1907] 36-24596
1. Theosophy. I. Tingley, Mrs. Katherine Augusta (Westcott) 1847-1929, ed. II. Title.

BLAVATSKY, Helene Petrovna (Hahn-Hahn) 1831-1891. 212
The key to theosophy; being a clear exposition in the form of question and answer of the ethics, science, and philosophy for the study of which the Universal brotherhood and theosophical society has been founded, with a copious glossary of general theosophical terms, by H.P. Blavatsky. 3d Point Loma ed. including an exhaustive index. Rev. and ed. by Katherine Tingley. Point Loma, Cal., The Aryan theosophical press, 1913. 3 p. l., [v]-xii, 384 p. 2 port. (incl. front.) 21 1/2 x 17 cm. [BP561.K4 1913] 15-
1. Theosophy. I. Tingley, Mrs. Katherine Augusta (Westcott) 1847-1929, ed. II. Title.

BLAVATSKY, Helene Petrovna (Hahn-Hahn) 1831-1891. 922.
The letters of H.P. Blavatsky to A.P. Sinnett, and other miscellaneous letters, transcribed compiled and with an introduction by A. T. Barker. New York, Frederick A. Stokes company [1924] xv, [1] 404 p. front. (port.) illus. (facsim.) 23 cm. Printed in Great Britain. The letters are intended to form a companion volume to the Mahatma letters, and should be read in conjunction with that work. Section II contains all the Miscellaneous letters of interest left by Mr. Sinnett, including some of the Mahatma letters not published in that work. [BP585.B6A25] 25-12046
1. Theosophy. I. Barker, A. Trevor, ed. II. Sinnett, Alfred Percy, 1840-1921 III. Title.

BLAVATSKY, Helene Petrovna (Hahn-Hahn) 1831-1891.
The secret doctrine, the synthesis of science, religion and philosophy. The [5th] Adyar ed. Adyar, Madras, Theosophical Pub. House; sold by Theosophical Press, Wheaton, Ill., 1962. 6 v. port. NUC65
1. Theosophy. I. Title.

BLAVATSKY, Helene Petrovna (Hahn-Hahn) 1831-1891. 212
The secret doctrine; the synthesis of science, religion and philosophy, by H.P. Blavatsky... Point Loma ed. Point Loma, Cal., The Aryan theosophical press, 1909. 2 v. diagrs. 24 1/2 cm. Contents.CONTENTS--Cosmogenesis.--Anthropogenesis. [BP561.S4 1909] 15-21992
1. Theosophy. I. Title.

BLAVATSKY, Helene Petrovna (Hahn-Hahn) 1831-1891.
The secret doctrine: the synthesis of science, religion, and philosophy. [Pasadena, Calif.] Theosophical University Press [1963] 2 v. diagrs. 24 cm. Verbatim with the original edition, 1888. Contents.Contents.-v.1. Cosmogenesis.-v.2. Anthropogenesis. Includes bibliography. 68-101966
1. Theosophy. I. Title.

BLAVATSKY, Helene Petrovna (Hahn-Hahn) 1831-1891. 212
Theosophy and the theosophical movement; some extracts from the writings of the two messengers, H.P. Blavatsky--Wm. Q. Judge... Los Angeles and San Francisco, United lodge of theosophists [n.d.] 67 p., 1 l. 18 1/2 cm. 17-14855
I. Judge, William Quan, 1851-1896. II. Los Angeles. United lodge of theosophists. III. San Francisco. United lodge of theosophists. IV. Title.

BLAVATSKY, Helene Petrovna (Hahn-Hahn) 1831-1891. 212
The voice of the silence and other chosen fragments from the Book of the golden precepts. For the daily use of lanoos (disciples). Translated and annotated by H.P.B." London, Theosophical publishing society; New York, The Path; [etc, etc.] 1892. 75 p., 1 l. 21 1/2 cm. [BP561.V7] 2-9871
1. Theosophy. I. Title.

[BLAVATSKY, Helene Petrovna (Hahn-Hahn), 1831-1891. 212
The voice of the silence and other chosen fragments from the Book of the golden precepts. For the daily use of lanoos (disciples) Translated and annotated by "H.P.B." New York, The Path; London, Theosophical publishing society, 1893. 3 p. l., iv, 107 [1] p. front. (port.) 14 cm. [BP561.V7 1893] 34-
1. Theosophy. I. Title.

BLAVATSKY, Helene Petrovna Hahn-Hahn, 1831-1891. 212'.52
The voice of the silence being chosen fragments from the "Book of the golden precepts." For the daily use of lanoos (disciples). Translated and annotated by "H.P.B." [2d. Quest book miniature ed., from original ed. of 1889] Wheaton, Ill., Theosophical Pub. House [1973] 110 p. 15 cm. (A Quest miniature.) Contents.Contents.—The voice of the silence.—The two paths.—The seven portals. [BP561.V7 1973] 73-7619 ISBN 0-8356-0380-6 1.25 (pbk.)
1. Theosophy. I. Title.

THE Brother, XII. 212
Foundation letters and teachings, by the Brother, XII. Akron, O., Sun publishing co. [c1927] xv p., 1 l., 190 p. 19 cm. [BP565.B77] 27-25793
1. Theosophy. I. Title.

BRUTEAU, Beatrice, 1930- 121
The psychic grid : how we create the world we know / by Beatrice Bruteau. Wheaton, Ill. : Theosophical Pub. House, c1979. p. cm. (A Quest book) Includes index. Bibliography: p. [BP565.B82P76] 79-64096 pbk. : 6.50
1. Theosophy. 2. Knowledge, Theory of. 3. Relativity. 4. Reality. 5. Consciousness. I. Title.

BUCK, Jirah Dewey, 1838-
Modern world movements; theosophy and the school of natural science "The venerable brotherhood of India," by Jirah Dewey Buck ... 1st ed. Chicago, Indo-American book co., 1913. 191 p. incl. facsims. front., plates, ports. 19 cm. 14-676 1.00
I. Title.

BUCK, Jirah Dewey, 1838-1916. 212
The nature and aim of theosophy. An essay. By J. D. Buck. Cincinnati, R. Clarke & co., 1889. xi, 13-55 p. front. 19 cm. Half-title: Thesophy. Psyche involved in the cycle of necessity ... [BP570.B85] 32-6518
1. Theosophy. I. Title.

*BURKS, Arthur J. 129
EN-DON: the ageless wisdom. Los Angeles, Calif., Douglas-West Publishers [1973] x, 49 p. 22 cm. ISBN 0-913264-10-5 3.25 (pbk.)
1. Theosophy. I. Title.

CLARK, James Albert.
A theosophist's point of view. [Washington] District of Columbia, Press of the Pathfinder [1901] xii, 235 p. 16 cm. 1-16417
I. Title.

[CLOUGH, Grace Evelyn] 1876- 212
"Because--" for the children who ask why. Los Angeles, Calif., The Theosophy company [1943] 4 p. l., 149 p. 19 cm. "First edition, 1916 ... Third edition, 1943." [BP565.C6 1943] 43-9594
1. Theosophy. I. Title.

CODD, Clara M. 212.'5
The ageless wisdom of life, by Clara M. Codd. [4th ed.] Wheaton, Ill., Theosophical Pub. House [1967, c1957] viii, 269 p. 18 cm. (A Quest book) [BP565.C62 1967] 67-8630
1. Theosophy. I. Title.

CODD, Clara M. 212'.52
Trust yourself to life / by Clara Codd. Wheaton, Ill. : Theosophical Pub. House, 1975, c1968. x, 116 p. ; 16 cm. (A Quest book miniature) Includes bibliographical references. [BP565.C643 1975] 75-4245 ISBN 0-8356-0464-0 pbk. : 1.75
1. Theosophy. I. Title.

COLVILLE, William Wilberforce Juvenal, 1862-1917.
A history of theosophy. By W. J. Colville. Boston, Mass., Freedom publishing company, 1896. 247 p. 19 cm. [BP530.C7] 27-21562
1. Theosophy. I. Title.

COOK, Mabel (Collins) Mrs. 1851-1927. 212
Light on the path, with notes and comments by the author. A treatise for the personal use of those who are ignorant of the eastern wisdom, and who desire to enter within its influence. Written down by M. C. Reprinted by special permission. Boston, Occult publishing company [188-] 1 p. l., 68, [3]-21 p. 18 1/2 cm. "How best to become a theosophist" ([3]-21 p.) has ms. note at head of caption title: An address delivered before the British theosophical society Jan. 6, 1880, by its president G. Wyld, M.D. [BP570.C75 1880] 21-6490
1. Theosophy. I. Wyld, George, 1821-1906 II. Title.

[COOK, Mabel (Collins)] 1851-1927. 212
Light on the path, a treatise written for the personal use of those who are ignorant of the eastern wisdom, and who desire to enter within its influence, written down by M. C., with notes by the author. Covins, Calif., Theosophical university press, 1944. 2 p. l., 96 p. 15 1/2 cm. Reprint of the 1888 edition, with Comments (p. [29]-89) taken from Luficer, vol. I, 1887-8, where they were first published. cf. Publisher's note. [BP570.C75 1944] 45-927
1. Theosophy. I. Title.

COOPER, Irving Steiger, bp., 1882-1935.
Theosophy simplified, by Irving S. Cooper ... Hollywood, Los Angeles, Cal., The Theosophical book concern, 1915. 94 p. 19 cm. "A course of reading in theosophy": p. 87-92. 15-7315
I. Title.

COOPER, Irving Steiger, Bp., 1882-1935. 212'.52
Theosophy simplified / by Irving S. Cooper. 8th ed. Wheaton, Ill. : Theosophical Pub. House, [1979] xv, 89 p. ; 21 cm. (A Quest book) Includes index. [BP565.C75T44 1979] 78-64905 ISBN 0-8356-0519-1 : 3.25
1. Theosophy. I. Title.

CROSBIE, Robert, 1849-1919. 212
The friendly philosopher, Robert Crosbie (1849-1919); letters and tanks on theosophy and the theosophical life. Los Angeles and New York city, The Theosophy company, 1934. ix, p., 2 l., 3-415 p. front. (port.) 23 cm. [BP565.C77] 35-2274
1. Theosophy. I. Title. II. Title: Letters and talks on theosophy and the theosophical life.

[CURTIS, Elizabeth Alden] 1878- 212
A handbook of theosophy, written by a pupil of a chela of the Master M. Portland, Me., Smith and Sale, 1924. 53, [1] p. 16 cm. [BP570.C78] 25-2800
1. Theosophy. I. Title.

DAS, Bhagavan, 1869- 212
The science of peace; an attempt at an exposition of the first principles of the science of the self, adhyatma-vidya, by Bhagavan Das ... (2d ed.) Madras, India; Hollywood, Cal., Theosophical publishing house; [etc., etc.] 1921. xxi p., 1 l., 432 p. 18 1/2 cm. "Index of works referred to": p. [393]-396. [BP565.D3 1921] 28-14026
1. Theosophy. I. Title.

DEWEY, John Hamlin. 133
An introduction to the theosophy of Christ; embracing the science of intuition, mental healing and spiritual supremacy. By J. H. Dewey ... [Buffalo, Carrell & Nisell, 1887] 2 p. l., [7]-88 p. 16 cm. [BF1999.D43] 20-22368
1. Theosophy. I. Title.

DEWEY, John Hamlin. 133
The open door; or, The secret of Jesus: a key to spiritual emancipation, illumination, and mastery, by John Hamlin Dewey ... New York, United States book company [1891] xxiii, 156 p. 19 cm. [BF1999.D45 1891] 18-27487
1. Jesus Christ—Spiritualistic interpretations. 2. Theosophy. I. Title.

DEWEY, John Hamlin. 232
The open door; or, The secret of Jesus: a key to spiritual emancipation, illumination and mastery, by John Hamlin Dewey ... Rev. ed. New York, J. H. Dewey publishing co., 1896. 3 p. l., [v]-xxiii, 200, [4] p. 20 cm. [Mystic science series. no. 1] [BF1999.D45 1896] 18-27488
1. Jesus Christ—Spiritualistic interpretations. 2. Theosophy. I. Title.

DEWEY, John Hamlin. 220
The way, the truth and the life; a hand book of Christian theosophy, healing, and psychic culture, a new education, based upon the ideal method of the Christ, by J. H. Dewey, M. D. Buffalo. N. Y., The

author, 1888. xiii, [1], 408 p. 20 cm. [BR125.D57] 19-20286
1. Theosophy. 2. Mental healing. I. Title.

DIXON, Herbert Allen. 261
The new theosophy, regarding man and spirit being, A book combining science and religion and saves all man-kind, by Herbert Allen Dixon. Sparks, Nev., H. A. Dixon, [c1923] 62 p. 15 cm. [BR123.D55] ca 24
I. Title.

DUTTA, Rex. 133
Reality of occult, yoga, meditation, flying saucers / Rex Dutta. London : Pelham, 1974. 199 p. : ill. ; 23 cm. Includes index. Bibliography: p. 194-195. [BP565.D87R4 1974] 75-305351 ISBN 0-7207-0789-7 : 10.00
1. Theosophy. I. Title.
Distributed by Transatlantic Arts, Levittown, N.Y.

EDGE, Henry T. 212
... The astral light, by Henry T. Edge ... Covina, Calif., Theosophical university press, 1943. 3 p. l., 67 p. 15 cm. (Theosophical manual no. X) "Second printing, 1943." [BP573.A7E3] 44-52887
1. Theosophy. I. Title.

EDGE, Henry T. 212
... Theosophy and Christianity, by H. T. Edge ... Point Loma, Calif., Theosophical university press, 1941. 3 p. l., 105 p. 15 cm. (Theosophical manual no. XII) "Second printing." [BP567.E3] 44-52888
1. Theosophy. 2. Christianity and other religions—Theosophy. I. Title.

ELEMENTARY theosophy.
Wheaton, Ill., Theosophical Press [1956] 269p. 20cm. 'Sixth edition.'
1. Theosophy. I. Rogers, Louis William, 1859-

EMMONS, Viva. 212'.5
The roots of peace; a study of human potential in relation to peace. Wheaton, Ill., Theosophical Pub. House [1969] xv, 111 p. 21 cm. (A Quest book original) Bibliography: p. 97-100. [BP573.P3E45] 73-78911 1.75
1. Theosophy. 2. Peace. I. Title.

THE Eternal verities, 212
for old souls in young bodies ... Los Angeles, Calif., The Theosophy company, 1940. vii, 296 p. 19 cm. "Revised edition." "Theosophy school songs" (with music): p. [215]-232. Teacher's manual and guide ... Los Angeles, Calif., The Theosophy company, 1941. vii, 224 p. fold. diagr. 21 x 16 cm. [BP565.E82] 41-13305
1. Theosophy.

THE Eternal verities, for the 212
teachers of children ... Los Angeles, Calif., United lodge of theosophists, 1921. 5 p. l., 237 p. 19 cm. Music: p. 153-164. [BP565.E8] 21-4095
1. Theosophy. 2. Karma.

FARNSWORTH, Edward Clarence. 212
The deeper mysteries, written down by Edward Clarence Farnsworth. Portland, Me., Smith & Sale, printers, 1921. ix, 192, [1] p. 21 cm. [BP565.F3] 21-5093
1. Theosophy. I. Title.

FARTHING, Geoffrey A. 211'.52
Exploring the great beyond : a survey of the field of the extraordinary / Geoffrey Farthing. Wheaton, Ill. : Theosophical Pub. House, c1978. xi, 214 p. ; 21 cm. (A Quest book) Bibliography: p. 203-207. [BP565.F32E94] 77-17692 ISBN 0-8356-0508-6 pbk. : 4.25
1. Theosophy. I. Title.

FARTHING, Geoffrey A. 212'.5
Theosophy: what's it all about? A brief summary of a wonderfully exciting and vitally important subject, by Geoffrey A. Farthing. London, Wheaton, Ill. [etc.] Theosophical Publishing House, 1967. x, 92 p. 18 112 cm. 10/6 Bibliography: p. 92. [BP565.F33] 67-94094
1. Theosophy. I. Title.

FARTHING, Geoffrey A. 212'.5
Theosophy: what's it all about? A brief summary of a wonderfully exciting and vitally important subject, by Geoffrey A. Farthing. London, Wheaton, Ill., Theosophical Pub House, 1967. x. 92p. 19cm. Bibl. [BP565.F33] 67-94094 1.75 pap.,
1. Theosophy. I. Title.

FIRST principles of theosophy.
10th ed. Madras, Theosophical Pub. House; [on label: Wheaton, Ill., Sold by the Theosophical Press] 1956. 473p. illus. 19cm.
1. Theosophy. I. Jinarajadasa, Curuppumullage, 1875-

GATTELL, Benoni Bernard, 212
1865-
The light of the mind, by Benoni B. Gattell and Helen Stone Gattell. Philadelphia, Dorrance and company [1938] 140 p. 20 cm. "A ... presentation in a condensed way of one of the central ideas of ... Thinking and the law of thought', by ... [H.W.] Percival."-Note. [BP565.G3] 38-5771
1. Theosophy. 2. Reincarnation. I. Gattell, Mrs. Helen (Stone) 1868- joint author. II. Percival, Harold Waldwin, 1868- III. Title.

GRANT, Terry. 212'.52
Your precious heritage; do you care? Philadelphia, Dorrance [1972] 32 p. 22 cm. [BP565.G695] 72-84849 ISBN 0-8059-1732-2 2.50
1. Theosophy. I. Title.

GRAY, Mary (Tudor) 1886- 212
The chalice of the heart; Christian teachings of the Greek adept. Boston, Christopher [1949] 110 p. 21 cm. [BP565.G698] 50-6362
1. Theosophy. I. Title.

GRAY, Mary (Tudor) Mrs. 1886- 212
... The gateway of liberation [by Mary Gray. Wheaton, Ill., The Theosophical press, 1935. 121 p. front. (port) 21 cm. [BP565.G7] 35-17070
1. Theosophy. I. Title.

HODSON, Geoffrey. 212
American lectures, by Geoffrey Hodson. Wheaton, Ill., The Theosophical press [c1929] 78 p. 18 1/2 cm. Advertisements: p. 77-78. [BP565.H55] 30-2476
1. Theosophy. I. Title.

HODSON, Geoffrey. 248'.2
The call to the heights : guidance on the pathway to self-illumination / by Geoffrey Hodson. Wheaton, Ill. : Theosophical Pub. House, 1975, c1976. 213 p. ; 21 cm. (A Quest book) Includes bibliographical references and index. [BP565.H635C3] 75-30656 ISBN 0-8356-0477-2 pbk. : 3.50
1. Theosophy. 2. Spiritual life. I. Title.

HODSON, Geoffrey. 248'.2
The call to the heights : guidance on the pathway to self-illumination / by Geoffrey Hodson. Wheaton, Ill. : Theosophical Pub. House, 1976. p. cm. (A Quest book) Includes index. [BP565.H635C3] 75-30656 ISBN 0-8356-0477-2
1. Theosophy. 2. Spiritual life. I. Title.

HODSON, Geoffrey. 212
Man, the triune God, by Geoffrey Hodson; foreword by James H. Cousins ... New York, Roerich museum press, 1932. 83 p. 19 cm. (Series: "Contemporary thought") "This book is the fourth of a series of volumes containing teachings given to the author by a member of the angelic hosts."--Author's pref. [BP573.M3H6] 32-6544
1. Theosophy. I. Title.

HODSON, Geoffrey. 212.5
Man's supersensory and spiritual powers. Madras, Theosophical Pub. House; [Label: sold by Theosophical Press, Wheaton, Ill.] 1957. 199p. 19cm. Includes bibliography. [BP573.E9H6] 59-1641
1. Theosophy. 2. Extrasensory preception. I. Title.

HODSON, Geoffrey. 212
An occult view of health & disease, by Geoffrey Hodson; preface by the Reverend Oscar Kollerstrom. Wheaton, Ill., The Theosophical press [c1930] xii, 52 p. diagrs. 18 1/2 cm. [BP573.H4H6] 30-11931
1. Theosophy. 2. Mental healing. I. Title.

HODSON, Geoffrey. 291.2'3
Reincarnation, fact or fallacy? An examination and exposition of the doctrine of rebirth. [Rev. ed.] Wheaton, Ill., Theosophical Pub. House [1967] 83 p. 18 cm. (A Quest book) [BP573.R5H6 1967] 67-4405
1. Theosophy. 2. Reincarnation. I. Title.

HOPKINS, John Goddard, 131'.3
1907-
The measure of the universe / [by] John Hopkins. Salisbury : Compton Russell, 1976. [8], 151 p. ; 19 cm. [BP565.H67M42] 76-378400 ISBN 0-900193-30-1 : £1.40
1. Theosophy. I. Title.

HUMPHREYS, Christmas, 1901- 131.3
Walk on! Wheaton, Ill., Theosophical Pub. House [1971, c1947] 101 p. 18 cm. (A Quest book) Includes bibliographical references. [BP565.H83] 74-139270 1.25
1. Theosophy. I. Title.

HYATT, Thaddeus Pomeroy, 212
1864-
A check list of some of the books and authors quoted or referred to in the two volumes of "The secret doctrine" by H. P. Blavatsky ... Compiled by Thaddeus P. Hyatt ... Stamford, Conn. 53c1940] v. 28 x 22 cm. Reproduced from type-written copy. [BP561.S4H9] 41-10618
1. Blavatsky, Helene Petrovna (Hahn-Hahn) 1831-1891. The secret doctrine. 2. Theosophy. I. Title.

JINARAJADAS, Curuppumullage, 212
1875- ed.
The early teachings of the masters, 1881-1883, edited by C. Jinarajadasa ... Chicago, The Theosophical press, 1923. 9 p. l., 245 p. front., ports., diagrs. 19 cm. [BP565.J5] 24-139
1. Theosophy. I. Title.

JINARAJADASA, Curuppumullage,
1875-
Practical theosophy, by C. Jinarajadasa, M. A (2d ed.) Adyar, Madras, India; Krotona, Los Angeles, U. S. A., Theosophical publishing house; [etc., etc.] 1919. 3 p. l., 96, [7] p. 17 cm. "The following lectures were delivered in Chicago, U. S. A., in 1910, and subsequently at the annual convention of the Burma section in 1914."--Note on verso of t.-p. [BP656.J54 1919] 25-25458
1. Theosophy. I. Title.

JINARAJADASA, 212.5
Curuppumullage, 1875-
First principles of theosophy. 10th ed. Madras, Theosophical Pub. House; [label: sold by Theosophical Press, Wheaton, Ill.] 1956. 43p. illus. 19cm. [BP565.J516 1956] 59-1558
1. Theosophy. I. Title.

JINARAJADASA, 212.5
Curuppumullage, 1875-
First principles of theosophy. 9th ed. Madras, Theosophical Pub. House; [on label: Wheaton, Ill., Sold by the Theosophical Press] 1951. 465p. illus. 19cm. [BP565.J516 1951] 54-3879
1. Theosophy. I. Title.

JINARAJADASA, Curuppumullage, 212
1875-
In his name, by C. Jinarajadasa. Chicago, The Theosophical press, 1922. 108 p. front. (port.) 16 cm. [BP565.J517 1922] 38-3068
1. Theosophy. I. Title.

JINARAJADASA, Curuppumullage, 212
1875-
Letters from the masters of the wisdom. Second series, transcribed and annotated by C. Jinarajadasa ... with a foreword by Annie Besant ... Chicago, The Theolosphical press [c1926] [BP565.J52 1926] 26-8344
1. Theosophy. I. Title.

JINARAJADASA, 212'.52
Curuppumullage, 1875-1953.
The divine vision; three lectures delivered at the Queen's Hall, London, and one lecture delivered at Palermo, Italy. Wheaton, Ill., Theosophical Pub. House [1973, c1928] 109 p. 18 cm. (A Quest book) [BP565.J54D58 1973] 72-10072 ISBN 0-8356-0433-0 1.45 (pbk.)
1. Theosophy. I. Title.

JOHNSON, Ethelbert.
The altar in the wilderness. An attempt to interpret man's seven spiritual ages. By Ethelbert Johnson. New York, Theosophical society, publishing department, 1904. 117 p. 15 cm. 9-30033
I. Title.

JUDGE, William Quan, 1851- 212
1896.
Echoes from the Orient. A broad outline of theosophical doctrines. By William Q. Judge ... 3d ed. New York, The Path; [London] Theosophical publishing society, 1893. 2 p. l., 64, [4] p. 18 cm. "Reprinted from Kate Field's Washington." [BP565.J75 1896] 40-688
1. Theosophy. I. Title.

JUDGE, William Quan, 1851- 212
1896.
The ocean of theosophy. 11th ed. Los Angeles, United Lodge of Theosophists, 1922 [c1915] xii, 153 p. port. 19 cm. [BP565.J82 1922] 49-56503
1. Theosophy I. Title.

JUDGE, William Quan, 1851- 212
1896.
The ocean of theosophy. By William Q. Judge ... New York, The Path; London, Theosophical publishing society, 1893. viii p., 1 l. 154 p. 18 cm. [BP565.J82 1893] 20-7808
1. Theosophy. I. Title.

JUDGE, William Quan, 1851- 212
1896.
The ocean of theosophy, by William Q. Judge ... 2d ed. New York, The Path; London, Theosophical publishing society, 1893. 2 p. l., [iii]-viii p., 1 l., 154, [4] p. 18 cm. "The Theosophical society: how to join it": [4] p. at end. [BP565.J82 1893a] 32-32124
1. Theosophy. I. Title.

JUDGE, William Quan, 1851- 212
1896.
The ocean of theosophy, by William Q. Judge. 10th thousand. New York, Theosophical publishing company; London, Theosophical book company, 1898. viii p., 1 l., 154 p. 18 cm. [BP565.J82 1898] 34-6356
1. Theosophy. I. Title.

JUDGE, William Quan, 1851- 212
1896.
The ocean of theosophy, by William Q. Judge. 20th thousand. Los Angeles, Calif., The United lodge of theosophists, 1915. xii, 154 p. front. (port.) 19 cm. [BP565.J82 1915] 15-19993
1. Theosophy. I. Title.

KRISHNAMURTI, Jiddu, 1895- 212
Authentic notes of discussions and talks given by Krishnamurti [at] Ojai and Sarobia, 1940. [Hollywood, Calif., The Star publishing trust, 1940. 75 p. 22 1/2 cm. [BP565.K7A78] 43-21218
1. Theosophy. I. Title.

KRISHNAMURTI, Jiddu, 1895- 212
Authentic report of eight talks, given by Krishnamurti at Ojai. [Hollywood, Calif., The Star publishing trust, c1936] 60 p. 23 cm. [BP565.K7A8] 36-14599
1. Theosophy. I. Title.

KRISHNAMURTI, Jiddu, 1895- 212
Authentic report of seventeen talks given in 1936 by Krishnamurti. [Hollywood, Calif., The Star publishing trust, c1937] 114 p. 23 cm. [BP565.K7A83] 37-16529
1. Theosophy. I. Title.

KRISHNAMURTI, Jiddu, 212'.52
1895-
The first and last freedom / by J. Krishnamurti ; with a foreword by Aldous Huxley. New York : Harper & Row, 1975, c1954. 288 p. ; 20 cm. Reprint of the ed. published by the Theosophical Pub. Co., Wheaton, Ill., in series: A Quest book. [BP565.K7F5 1975] 74-25687 ISBN 0-06-064831-7 pbk. : 2.95
1. Theosophy. I. Title.

KRISHNAMURTI, Jiddu, 1895- 147
The first and last freedom, by J. Krishnamurti. With a foreword by Aldous Huxley. Wheaton, Ill., Theosophical Pub. Co. [1968, c1954] 288 p. 21 cm. (A Quest book) [BP565] 70-1586 1.45
1. Theosophy. I. Title.

KRISHNAMURTI, Jiddu, 1895- 212
The kingdom of happiness, by Jeddu Krishnamurti. New York, Boni &

Liveright, 1927. v. p. 3 l., 13-112 p. front. (port.) 20cm. [BP565.K75] 27-7601
1. Theosophy. I. Title.

KRISHNAMURTI, Jiddu, 1895- 212
... Life in freedom. New York, H. Liveright, 1928. 96 p. 23 cm. At head of title: J. Krishnamurti. "This book has been compiled by the author from camp-fire addresses given in Benares, Ojal and Ommen during 1928." "Second printing, January, 1929." [BP565.K7L5 1929] 29-5089
1. Theosophy. I. Title.

KRISHNAMURTI, Jiddu, 1895- 212
Revised report of fourteen talks given by Kirshnamurti, Ommen comp 1937 & 1938. [Hollywood, Calif., London, etc., The Star publishing trust, c1938] 62 p. 23 cm. [BP565.K7R4] 39-4578
1. Theosophy. I. Title.

KRISHNAMURTI, Jiddu, 1895- 212
Towards discipleship (a series of informal addresses to aspirants for discipleship) by J. Krishnamurti. Chicago, The Theosophical press [c1926] 5 p. l., [9]-106 p. front. (port.) plates. 20 cm. [BP573.D5K7] 26-8749
1. Theosophy. I. Title.

KRISHNAMURTI, Jiddu, 1895- 212
Verbatim reports of talks and answers to questions by Krishnamurti ... [Los Angeles, The Star publishingtrust, c1934- v. 23 cm. [BP565.K7V4] 34-34763
1. Theosophy. 2. Religion and sociology. I. Title.

KUHN, Alvin Boyd, 1880- 212
Theosophy; a modern revival of ancient wisdom, by Alvin Boyd Kuhn. New York, H. Holt and company [1930] ix, 381 p. front. (port.) 23 cm. (Half-title: Studies in religion and culture. American religion series ii) Bibliography: p. 351-373. [BP565.K8 1930] 31-93
1. Blavatsky, Helene Petrovna (Hahn-Hahn) 1831-1891. 2. Theosophy. I. Title.

KUHN, Alvin Boyd, 1880- 212'.5
1963.
A rebirth for Christianity. Wheaton, Ill., Theosophical Pub. House [1970] xi, 218 p. 23 cm. Bibliography: p. 217-218. [BP567.K8 1970] 76-104032
1. Theosophy. 2. Christianity. I. Title.

KUNZ, Fritz. 149.3
The men beyond mankind; a study of the next step in personal and social evolution, by Fritz Kunz. Philadelphia, The David McKay company [1934] 2 p. l., 7-236 p. 20 cm. Printed in Great Britain. [BP565.K83] 35-1427
1. Theosophy. I. Title. II. Title: Evolution, Personal and social.

LAYTON, Eunice S. 212'.5
Theosophy, key to understanding, by Eunice S. Layton and Felix Layton. Wheaton, Ill., Theosophical Pub. House [1967] xi, 170 p. 18 cm. (A Quest book) [BP565.L24] 67-6516
1. Theosophy. I. Layton, Felix, joint author. II. Title.

LEADBEATER, Charles Webster, 212
1847-
The masters and the path, by the Rt. Rev. C. W. Leadbeater. Chicago, Theosophical press [c1925] 2 p. l., 354 p. 2 fold. pl. (1 col.) diagrs. 20 cm. [BP565.L525] 25-13860
1. Theosophy. I. Title.

LEADBEATER, Charles Webster, 212
1847-
The other side of death, scientifically examined and carefully described, by C. W. Leadbeater. Chicago, Theosophical book concern, 1903. 3 p. l., 9-502 p. 23 cm. Imperfect: p. 501-502 wanting. "Books quoted and mentioned": p. 499-500. [BP565.L53] 4-1628
1. Theosophy. I. Title.

LEADBEATER, Charles Webster, 212
1847-
Talks on At the feet of the Master, by the Rt. Rev. C. W. Leadbeater. Chicago, The Theosophical press [c1923] 3 p. l., [5]-522 p. 22 cm. [BP565.K7A5 1923] 23-13136
1. Krishnamurti, Jiddu, 1895- At the feet of the Master. 2. Theosophy. I. Title.

LEADBEATER, Charles Webster,
1847-
A textbook of theosophy, by C. W. Leadbeater ... [3d ed.] Krotona, Hollywood, Los Angeles, Cal., Theosophical publishing house, American branch, 1918. 4 p. l., 148, [2] p. 19 cm. A 19
1. Theosophy. I. Title.

LEADBEATER, Charles Webster, 212
1847-1934.
... The astral plane; its scenery, inhabitants and phenomena, by C. W. Leadbeater. London, New York, Theosophical publishing society; [etc., etc.] 1898. 4 p. l., 100 p. 16 cm. (Theosophical manuals. no. 5) [BP565.L3 1898] 21-1953
1. Theosophy. I. Title.

LEADBEATER, Charles Webster, 212
1847-1934.
The Christian creed, its origin and signification, by C. W. Leadbeater. 2d ed., rev. and enl. London and Benares, The Theosophical publishing society; New York, J. Lane; [etc., etc.] 1904. 3 p. l., 172 p. 4 col. pl. 22 cm. C. copy imperfect: pl. 1 wanting. [BP567.L4] 5-37782
1. Theosophy. 2. Creeds—Miscellanea. I. Title.

LEADBEATER, Charles Webster, 212
1847-1934.
... The devachanic plane, its characteristics and inhabitants, by C. W. Leadbeater. London, New York, Theosophical publishing society; [etc., etc.] 1896. 4 p. l., 88 p. 16 x 13 cm. (Theosophical manuals, no. 6) [BP565.L45 1896] 39-7024
1. Theosophy. I. Title.

LEADBEATER, Charles Webster, 128
1847-1934.
Man visible and invisible; examples of different types of men as seen by means of trained clairvoyance. Wheaton, Ill., Theosophical Pub. House, 1969. 126 p. col. plates (1 fold.) 21 cm. (Theosophical classics series) (A Quest book.) [BP565.L52 1969] 79-13922 3.25
1. Theosophy. 2. Clairvoyance. I. Title.

LEADBEATER, Charles Webster, 212
1847-1934.
The masters and the path, by the Rt. Rev. C. W. Leadbeater. 2d ed., 1925. Chicago, The Theosophical press [c1925] 3 p. l., 354 p., 1 l. fold. col. front., fold. pl., plan, diagrs. 20 cm. Folded plate accompanied by guard sheet with descriptive letterpress. [BP565.L525 1925 a] 25-27645
1. Theosophy. I. Title.

LEADBEATER, Charles Webster, 212
1847-1934.
An outline of theosophy, by C. W. Leadbeater. 2d ed. Chicago, Theosophical book concern, 1903. 2 p. l., [3]-99, [4] p. 18 cm. "Theosophical society": 4 p. at end. [BP565.L535 1903] 32-35009
1. Theosophy. I. Title.

LEADBEATER, Charles Webster, 212
1847-1934.
An outline of theosophy, by C. W. Leadbeater. 3d ed. Los Angeles, Chicago, Theosophical book concern, 1916. 2 p. l., [3]-99, [4] p. 18 cm. "Theosophical society": 4 p. at end. [BP565.L535 1916] 32-35010
1. Theosophy. I. Title.

LEADBEATER, Charles Webster, 212
1847-1934.
A textbook of theosophy, by C. W. Leadbeater ... Chicago, The Theosophical press, 1925. 3 p. l., 148 p. 20 cm. "First edition 1912." [BP565.L58] 26-5406
1. Theosophy. I. Title.

LEEUW, J. J. Van der. 212
The fire of creation, by the Rev. J. J. Van der Leeuw, L.L.D. Chicago, The Theosophical press [c1926] 220 p. front., plates. 19 1/2 cm. [BP565.L63] 26-6195
1. Theosophy. I. Title.

LEEUW, J. J. Van der. 212
Gods in exile, by J. J. Van der Leeuw ... Chicago, The Theosophical press [c1926] 5 p. l., [9]-98 p. 19 1/2 cm. [BP565.L65] 26-14522
1. Theosophy. I. Title.

LEEUW, Jacobus Johannes van 147
der, 1893-
The conquest of illusion [by] J. J. van der Leeuw. Wheaton, Ill., Theosophical Pub. House [1966] 234 p. illus. 18 cm. (A Quest book) [BP567.L418 1966] 67-2823
1. Theosophy. I. Title.

LEEUW, Jacobus Johannes 212'.52
van der, 1893-
The fire of creation / by J. J. van der Leeuw. Wheaton, Ill. : Theosophical Pub. House, 1976. xiv, 130 p. ; 21 cm. (Theosophical classics series) Reprint of the 1926 ed. published by the Theosophical Press, Chicago. "A Quest book." Includes index. [BP565.L63F57 1976] 75-26823 ISBN 0-8356-0470-5 pbk. : 2.95
1. Theosophy. I. Title.

[MCIVOR-TYNDALL, Alexander 212
J.]
Cosmic consciousness, the man-god whom we await, by Ali Nomad [pseud.] Chicago, Ill., Advanced thought publishing company; [etc., etc., c1913] vi, 310 p. 20 cm. [BP565.M14] 38-8180
1. Theosophy. I. Advanced thought publishing company. II. Title. III. Title: The man-god whom we await.

MACKENZIE, Kenneth, 1853- 239.9
Anti-Christian supernaturalism... By Rev. Kenneth Mackenzie, jr. New York, Alliance press company [190-?] 1 p. l., [v]-ix, [11]-191 p. 17 1/2 cm. [BT1240.M33] 31-11680
1. Theosophy. 2. Christian science. 3. Spiritualism. I. Title.

MACKINTOSH, Charles Henry, 212
1885-
The good way [by] Charles Henry Mackintosh. Wheaton, Ill., The Theosophical press [c1937] 63, [1] p. 16 cm. [BP565.M15] 37-14726
1. Theosophy. I. Title.

MCNEILE, E. R. 212
From theosophy to Christian faith; a comparison of theosophy with Christianity, by E. R. McNeile, with a preface by the Right Rev. Charles Gore... London, New York [etc.] Longmans, Green, and co., 1919. xi p., 1 l., 141, [1] p. 19 cm. [BP567.M2] 20-16788
I. Title.

THE Mahatma letters to A. P. 212
Sinnett from the Mahatmas M. & K. H., transcribed, compiled, and with an introduction by A. T. Barker. New York, Frederick A. Stokes company, 1924. xxxv, 492 p. facsims., diagr. 22 1/2 cm. [BP565.M3 1924] 32-4066
1. Theosophy. I. Sinnett, Alfred Percy, 1840-1921. II. Barker, A. Trevor, ed.

MASKELYNE, John Nevil, 1839-
The fraud of modern "theosophy" exposed, by J. N. Maskelyne; a brief history of the greatest imposture ever perpetrated under the cloak of religion. 2d ed. London, G. Routledge & sons, limited; New York, E. P. Dutton & co. [1913] 95, [1] p. 19 cm. A 16
1. Theosophy. I. Title.

MAVALANKAR, Damodar K. 212
... The writings of a Hindu chela, compiled by Sven Eek. Point Loma, Calif., Theosophical university press, 1940. ix, [1], 338 p. 20 cm. At head of title: Damodar. "Professor C. J. Ryan ... has contributed the valuable 'Biographical notes'."--Pref. [BP525.M3] 41-1892
1. Theosophy. I. Eek, Sven, 1900- comp. II. Ryan, Charles James. III. Title.

[MILLS, Janet Melanie Ailsa] 212
1891-
The sword and the spirit, a study of the inner meaning of the war. By H. K. Challoner [pseud.] ... including extracts from letters by P. G. Bowen ... London, New York [etc.] Rider & company [1943] 125 p. 19 cm. "Books recommended to students": p. 125. [BP567.M5] 44-51865
1. Theosophy. I. Bowen, Patrick Gillman, 1877-1940. II. Title.

MILLS, Janet Melanie 615'.852
Ailsa, 1894-
The path of healing / H. K. Challoner [i.e. J. M. A. Mills]. Wheaton, Ill. : Theosophical Pub. House, 1976, c1972. 175 p. ; 18 cm. (A Quest book) [BP573.H4M5 1976] 76-3660 ISBN 0-8356-0480-2 pbk. : 3.25
1. Theosophy. 2. Mental healing. I. Title.

MORRISH, Furze. 140.3
Outline of metaphysics [by] Furze Morrish. London, New York [etc.] Rider & co. [1945] 204 p. diagrs. 22 cm. Includes bibliographies. [BP565.M6] 45-3181
1. Theosophy. 2. Yoga. I. Title.

NEWHOUSE, Mildred (Sechler) 212
1909-
Natives of eternity; an authentic record of experiences in realms of super-physical consciousness, by Flower A. Newhouse. [4th ed.] Vista, Calif., L. G. Newhouse [1950] 96 p. illus. 25 cm. [BP573.A5N4] 50-29278
1. Theosophy. 2. Angels. I. Title.

NEWHOUSE, Mildred (Sechler) 212
1909-
Natives of eternity; an authentic record of experiences in realms of super-physical consciousness, by Flower A. Newhouse. Santa Barbara, Calif., J. F. Rowny press [c1944] xii p., 1 l., 15-96 p. front., plates. 21 cm. [BP573.A5N4 1944] 45-12610
1. Theosophy. 2. Angels. I. Title.

NEWHOUSE, Mildred (Sechler) 212
1909-
Rediscovering the angels, by Flower A. Newhouse. Illus. by Valorie Fechter and Donald Burson. [1st ed.] Vista, Calif., L. G. Newhouse [1950] 94 p. illus. 25 cm. Sequel to Natives of eternity. [BP573.A5N42] 50-13810
1. Theosophy. 2. Angels. I. Title.

OHLENDORF, William Clarence. 212
An outline of The secret doctrine; the synthesis of science, religion and philosophy by Helena P. Blavatsky ... outlined by W. C. Ohlendorf. [Chicago, Printed by Universal publisher, c1941] 75 p. diagrs. 19 cm. [BP561.S4O45] 41-15076
1. Theosophy. I. Blavatsky, Helena Petrovna (Hahn-Hahn) 1831-1891. The secret doctrine. II. Title.

OLCOTT, Henry Steel, 1832-1907.
Old diary leaves, the true story of the Theosophical society, by Henry Steel Olcott ... New York and London, G. P. Putnam's sons; [etc., etc.] 1895. xi, 491 p. front., illus., plates, ports., facsims. 20 cm. "The series of chapters which now compose this book was begun nearly three years ago in the Theosophist magazine."--Foreword. [BP540.O5] 12-37209
1. Theosophy. I. Title.

OOSTERINK, Henk, 1890- 212
Spirit in crisis [by] H. Oosterink. Covina, Calif., Theosophical university press [1946] xi, [1], 65 p. 20 cm. [BP567.O5] 47-4198
1. Theosophy. 2. Netherlands—Hist.—German occupation, 1940-1945. I. Title.

PEARSON, E. Norman 212.5
Space, time and self, by E. Norman Pearson. Wheaton. Ill, Theosophical Pub. [1967, c.1957] xi, 288p. illus. 20cm. (Quest bk.) [BP565.P33 1964] 65-7294 1.75 pap.,
1. Theosophy. I. Title.

PEARSON, E. Norman. 212*.52
Space, time, and self, by E. Norman Pearson. [Rev. ed.] Wheaton, Ill., Theosophical Pub. House [1967] xi, 288 p. illus. 21 cm. (A Quest book) [BP565] 71-1546 1.75
1. Theosophy. I. Title.

PEARSON, E Norman. 212.5
Space, time, sTheosophy. [BP565.P33] 59-1534
I. Title.

PERCIVAL, Harold Waldwin, 172'1
1868-
Democracy is self-government. [1st ed.] New York, The Word Pub. Co. [1952] 237 p. illus. 23 cm. [BP605.P365] 52-30629
1. Theosophy. 2. Occult sciences. 3. Democracy. I. Title.

PERCIVAL, Harold Waldwin, 212
1868-
Man and woman, and child. [1st ed.] New York, The Word Pub. Co. [c1951] 235 p. 21 cm. [BP605.P38] 52-6126
1. Theosophy. I. Title.

PLUMMER, L. Gordon, 1904- 110
The mathematics of the cosmic mind; a study in mathematical symbolism [by] L. Gordon Plummer. [2d ed., rev.] Wheaton, Ill., Theosophical Pub. House [1970] xv, 224 p. illus. (part col.) 28 cm. Pages 219-224, blank for "Notes and correspondences." [BP567.P56 1970] 77-114206
1. Theosophy. 2. Mathematics. 3. Symbolism. I. Title.

PLUMMER, L. Gordon, 1904- 212
... Star habits and orbits; astronomy for theosphical students. Corvina, Calif., Theosophical university press, 1944. vi p., 2 l., 162 p. diagrs. 20 cm. At head of title: L. Gordon Plummer & Charles J. Ryan. "H. P. Blavatsky's contribution to astronomy, by Charles J. Ryan" (two articles which first appeared in the Theosophical forum, September and October, 1941): p. [129]-154. Correction slip inserted. [BP573.A7P5] 44-47295
1. Theosophy. 2. Blavatsky, Helene Petrovna (Hahn-Hahn) 1831-1891. I. Ryan, Charles James. II. Title.

PURUCKER, Gottfried de. 212
Theosophy and modern science [by] G. de Purucker ... Point Loma, Calif., Theosophical university press [c1930] 2 v. 23 cm. "Lectures ... published in the Theosophical path ... during 1923-1929."--Foreword. [BP565.P8] 30-9983
1. Theosophy. I. Title.

PURUCKER, Gottfried de, 1874- 212
The esoteric tradition [by] G. de Purucker ... Point Loma, Calif., Theosophical university press, 1935. 2 v. diagrs. 25 cm. Paged continuously. "Reading reference": vol. ii, p. [61]-65 at end. [Full name: Hobart Lorenz Gottfried de Puruciker]. [BP565.P755] 35-24907
1. Theosophy. 2. Reincarnation. I. Title.

PURUCKER, Gottfried de, 1874- 212
Fundamentals of esoteric philosophy, by G. de Purucker ... edited by A. Trevor Barker. Philadelphia, David McKay company [1932] xvii p., 1 l., 555 p. diagrs. 24 cm. Printed in Great Britain. [Full name: Hobart Lorenz Gottfried de Purucker] [BP565.P76 1932 a] 32-21470
1. Theosophy. I. Barker, Alfred Trevor, 1893 ed. II. Title. III. Title: Esoteric philosophy, Fundamentals of.

PURUCKER, Gottfried de, 1874- 212
Man in evolution [by] G. de Purucker. Point Loma, Calif., Theosophical university press, 1941. x p., 1 l., 389 p. 21 cm. "This volume takes the place--at least in time--of two volumes published some years ago [1980] ... entitled Theosophy and modern science."--Pref. [Full name: Hobart Lorenz Gottfried de Purucker] Bibliography: p. [385]-389. [BP565.P78] 42-769
1. Theosophy. I. Title.

PURUCKER, Gottfried de, 1874-1942. 212
The dialogues of G. de Purucker; report of sessions, Katherine Tingley Memorial Group. Ed. by Arthur L. Conger. Covina, Calif., Theosophical Univ. Press [1948] 3 v. port. 21 cm. Full name: Hobart Lorenz Gottfried de Purucker. [BP525.P76] 48-1194
1. Theosophy. I. Title.

PURUCKER, Gottfried de, 1874-1942. 110
The esoteric tradition [by] G. de Purucker. Pasadena, Calif., Theosophical University Press [1973, c1935] 2 v. (xvi, 1109, 71 p.) 25 cm. Includes bibliographical references. [BP565.P8E8 1973] 73-81738 13.50
1. Theosophy. 2. Reincarnation. I. Title.

PURUCKER, Gottfried de, 1874-1942. 212'.52
Fountain-source of occultism : a modern presentation of the ancient universal wisdom based on The secret doctrine by H. P. Blavatsky / G. de Purucker ; edited by Grace F. Knoche. Pasadena, Calif. : Theosophical University Press, 1974. xv, 744 p. : ill. ; 24 cm. Includes bibliographical references and index. [BP565.P8F68 1974] 72-92155 ISBN 0-911500-70-7 : 12.00
1. Theosophy. I. Blavatsky, Helene Petrovna Hahn-Hahn, 1831-1891. The secret doctrine. II. Title.

PURUCKER, Gottfried de, 1874-1942. 212'.52'0924
H. P. Blavatsky : the mystery / by Gottfried de Purucker, in collaboration with Katherine Tingley. San Diego, Calif. : Point Loma Publications, [1974] xvi, 242 p. : port. ; 23 cm. Chapters of this book first appeared serially 40 years ago in The Theosophical path. [BP585.B6P87] 74-189478 pbk. : 4.95
1. Blavatsky, Helene Petrovna Hahn-Hahn, 1831-1891. 2. Theosophy. I. Tingley, Katherine Augusta Westcott, 1847-1929, joint author. II. The Theosophical path. III. Title.

PURUCKER, Gottfried de, 1874-1942. 212'.52
Man in evolution / G. de Purucker. 2d and rev. ed. / edited by Grace F. Knoche. Pasadena, Calif. : Theosophical University Press, c1977. xii, 365 p. ; 21 cm. Includes index. Bibliography: p. [277]-279. [BP565.P8M36 1977] 76-45503 ISBN 0-911500-55-3 : 5.00
1. Theosophy. I. Knoche, Grace Frances. II. Title.

PURUCKER, Gottfried de, 1874-1942. 212
The masters and the path of occultism [by] G. de Purucker. Point Loma, Calif., Theosophical university press, 1939. 4 p. l., 95, [1] p. 15 1/2 cm. Imprint on label mounted on t.-p.: Covina, Calif., Theosophical university press. "Second impression." [Full name: Hobart Lorenz Gottfried de Purucker] Bibliography: p. [96] [BP565.P785] 44-49621
1. Theosophy. I. Title.

PURUCKER, Gottfried de, 1874-1942. 212
Messages to conventions, and other writings on the policies, work and purposes of the T. S. [by] G. de Purucker. Covina, Calif., Theosophical university press, 1943. viii, 251 p., 1 l. 23 1/2 cm. [Full name: Hobart Lorenz Gottfried de Purucker] [BP525.P78] 44-35817
1. Theosophy. 2. Theosophical society in America. I. Title.

PURUCKER, Gottfried de, 1874-1942. 212
Wind of the spirit, a selection of talks on theosophy as related primarily to human life and human problems, by G. de Purucker. Covina, Calif., Theosophical university press, 1944. x p., 1 l., 254 p. 23 1/2 cm. Most of the talks and addresses were given at Point Loma, California, between the years 1930 and 1942. cf. Compiler's pref. [Full name: Hobart Lorenz Gottfried de Purucker] [BP525.P8] 44-6358
1. Theosophy. I. Title.

RANSOM, Josephine Maria (Davies) Mrs. 1879- 112
Studies in The secret doctrine, by Josephine Ransom; studies with students at Olcott sessions, summer, 1932. Wheaton, Ill., The Theosophical press, 1934. 3 p. l., 172 p. front. (port.) fold. tab., diagrs. 20 cm. [BP561.S4R3] 34-40707
1. Blavatsky, Helene Petrovna (Hahn—Hahn) 1831-1896 2. Theosophy. I. Title. II. Title: The secret doctrine.

REHAULT, Ludowic. 922.91
Krishnamurti; "Man is his own liberator", by Ludowic Rehault; translated by Ina Harper. Boston, The Christopher publishing house [c1939] 296 p. incl. front. (port.) 20 cm. [BP585.K7R383] 39-14575
1. Krishnamurti, Jiddu, 1895 2. Theosophy. I. Harper, Mrs. Ina, Tr. II. Title.

ROGERS, Louis William, 1859- 212
Elementary theosophy. 5th ed. Wheaton, Ill., Theosophical Press [1950] 269p. 20cm. [BP565.R7 1950] A51
1. Theosophy. I. Title.

ROGERS, Louis William, 1859- 212.5
Elementary theosophy, by L. W. Rogers. 6th ed. Wheaton, Ill., Theosophical Press [1956] 269 p. 20 cm. [BP565.R7] 65-8116
1. Theosophy. I. Title.

ROGERS, Louis William, 1859- 212.5
Elementary theosophy, 5th ed. Wheaton, Ill., Theosophical Press [1950] 269 p. 20 cm. [BP565.R] A51
1. Theosophy. I. Title.

ROGERS, Louis William, 1859- 212
Elementary theosophy [by] L. W. Rogers. Los Angeles, Theosophical book concern, 1917. 1 p. l., 5-214 p. 19 1/2 cm. [BP565.R7] 17-30401
1. Theosophy. I. Title.

ROGERS, Louis William, 1859- 212
Elementary theosophy. [By] L. W. Rogers. Chicago, Theo book company, 1923. 2 p. l., [7]-267 p. 19 1/2 cm. [BP565.R7 1923] 23-5378
1. Theosophy. I. Title.

ROGERS, Louis William, 1859- 212
Elementary theosophy, by L. W. Rogers. 3d ed. Chicago, Theo book company [c1929] 314 p. 19 1/2 cm. [BP565.R7 1929] 29-16390
1. Theosophy. I. Title.

ROGERS, Louis William, 1859- 212
Hints to young students of occultism, by L. W. Rogers. Albany, N.Y., The Theosophical book company, 1909. 118 p. 17 cm. [BP565.R75 1909] 9-23250
1. Theosophy. I. Title.

ROGERS, Louis William, 1859- 212
Man; an embryo god, and other lectures. [Rev. ed.] Wheaton, Ill., Theosophical Press [1950] 197 p. 19 cm. Published in 1925 under title: Gods in the making. [BP565.R74 1950] 51-334
1. Theosophy. I. Title.

RYAN, Charles James. 212'.52'0924 B
H. P. Blavatsky and the theosophical movement : a brief historical sketch / by Charles J. Ryan. [2d ed]. San Diego, Calif. : Point Loma Publications, [1975] xxii, 441 p., [5] leaves of plates ; 22 cm. Includes index. [BP585.B6R8 1975] 75-319620 ISBN pbk. : 7.00
1. Blavatsky, Helene Petrovna Hahn-Hahn, 1831-1891. 2. Theosophical Society. 3. Theosophy. I. Title.

RYAN, Charles James. 212'.52'0924 B
H. P. Blavatsky and the theosophical movement : a brief historical sketch / Charles J. Ryan. 2d and rev. ed. / edited by Grace F. Knoche. Pasadena, Calif. : Theosophical University Press, c1975. xviii, 358 p. : ill. ; 22 cm. Includes index. Bibliography: p. 325-335. [BP585.B6R8 1975b] 75-4433 ISBN 0-911500-79-0 : 8.50
1. Blavatsky, Helene Petrovna Hahn-Hahn, 1831-1891. 2. Theosophical Society. 3. Theosophy. I. Title.

RYAN, Charles James. 212'.52
What is theosophy? : A general view of occult doctrine / by Charles J. Ryan. San Diego, Calif. : Point Loma Publications, c1975. viii, 85 p. ; 18 cm. (Theosophical manual ; no. 1) [BP565.R88W46 1975] 75-321702 ISBN pbk. : 2.25
1. Theosophy. I. Title. II. Series.

RYAN, Charles James. 212
... What is theosophy? A general view for inquirers, by Charles J. Ryan. Covina, Calif., Theosophical university press, 1944. 3 p. l., [3]-131 p. 15 cm. (Theosophical manual. No. 1) "Fourth edition, third impression, 1944." [BP565.R88 1944] 45-1685
1. Theosophy. I. Title.

RYAN, Charles James. 212
What is theosophy? A general view for inquirers, by Charles J. Ryan. Point Loma, Calif., Theosophical university press, 1939. 3 p. l., [3]-131 p. 15 cm. (Theosophical manual. no. I) "Fourth edition." [BP565.R88 1939] 41-7685
1. Theosophy. I. Title.

SEILING, Max, 1852-
Theosophy and Christianity; a signpost for those who desire information concerning theosophy, by Max Seiling; with an afterword by Dr. Rudolf Steiner; translation from the German with the author's permission by "A. R." [Chicago] Rand, McNally & company, 1913. 66 p. 19 cm. $0.75 13-7806
I. Steiner, Rudolf, 1861- II. Barnett, Clara F., tr. III. Title.

SHELDON, Henry Clay, 1845-1928.
Theosophy and New thought, by Henry C. Sheldon ... New York, Cincinnati, The Abingdon press [c1916] 185 p. 17 1/2 cm. [BP575.S5] 16-16557
1. Theosophy. 2. New thought. I. Title.

SINNETT, Alfred Percy, 1840-1921. 147
Esoteric Buddhism. New ed. (revised). London, Wheaton, Ill., Theosophical Publishing House, 1972. xxiv, 181 p. 21 cm. Originally published, London, Trubner, 1883. [BP565.S4 1972] 73-159173 ISBN 0-7229-5230-9 £2.00
1. Theosophy. 2. Tantric Buddhism. I. Title.

SINNETT, Alfred Percy, 1840-1921. 212
The growth of the soul; a sequel to "Esoteric Buddhism", by A. P. Sinnett ... London, New York, The Theosophical publishing society, 1896. xv, 459 p. 20 cm. [BP565.S42] 27-21719
1. Theosophy. I. Title.

SINNETT, Alfred Percy, 1840-1921. 212
The occult world, by A. P. Sinnett. Boston, Colby & Rich, 1882. 4 p. l., 172 p. 19 1/2 cm. [BP565.S45 1882] 33-20362
1. Theosophy. I. Title.

SINNETT, Alfred Percy, 1840-1921. 212
The occult world, by A. P. Sinnett ... 2d American, from the 4th English ed., with the author's corrections and a new preface. Boston, Houghton, Mifflin and company, 1885. xvi, 228 p. 18 1/2 cm. [BP565.S45 1885] 27-21716
1. Theosophy. I. Title.

SINNETT, Alfred Percy, 1841-1921. 147
Esoteric Buddhism. 5th ed., annotated and enl. by the author. Minneapolis, Wizards Bookshelf, 1973. xxvii, 244 p. 22 cm. (Secret doctrine reference series) Reprint of the 1885 ed. Bibliography: p. 239. [BP565.S4 1973] 73-76091 ISBN 0-913510-03-3 7.00
1. Theosophy. 2. Tantric Buddhism. I. Title.

SINNETT, Patience Edensor, A. P. Sinnett," "Mrs. d.1908 212
The purpose of theosophy. By Mrs. A. P. Sinnett. Boston, Occult publishing co., 1886. 117 p. 18 1/2 cm. [BP565.S48 1886] 34-36373
1. Theosophy. I. Title.

SLOAN, Mersene Elon.
Demonosophy unmasked in modern theosophy; whence? what? whither? An exposition and a refutation with corrective Bible teaching, by Mersene Elon Sloan... 2d ed. of abridged text, rev. and enl. Saint Paul, Minn., The Way press, 1922. 1 p. l., 192 p. 18 cm. Cover-title: Modern theosophy; whence? what? whither? [BP575.S6 1922] 22-3485
1. Theosophy. I. Title. II. Title: Modern theosophy; whence? what? whither?

THE Society for Psychical Research report on the Theosophical Society / edited, with an introd. by James Webb. New York : Arno Press, 1976. 201,-400, 60, 129-159 p., [3] fold. leaves of plates : ill. ; 23 cm. (The Occult) Reprint of Report of the committee appointed to investigate phenomena connected with the Theosophical Society, published in v. 3 of the Proceedings of the Society for Psychical Research, London, 1885; of Was she a charlatan? By W. Kingsland, published by the Blavatsky Association, London, 1927; and of The defence of the Theosophists, by R. Hodgson, published in v. 9 of the Proceedings of the Society for Psychical Research, London, 1894. Cover title: the SPR report on the Theosophical Society. [BP510.T5S6] 75-36920 ISBN 0-405-07975-3 : 20.00 147
1. Theosophical Society. 2. Theosophy. I. Society for Psychial Research, London. II. Kingsland, William, 1855-1936. Was she a charlatan? 1927. III. Series: The Occult (New York, 1976-)

THE spirit of the unborn, 212
by Two workers [pseud.] Hollywood, Los Angeles, Cal., Starlight publishing co.

[c1918] 125, [2] p. 19 cm. [BP565.S5] 19-3300
1. Two workers.

SRI Ram, Nilakanta. 242
Thoughts for aspirants. Compiled from notes and writings of N. Sri Ram. Wheaton, Ill., Theosophical Pub. House [1972] vi, 145 p. 16 cm. (A Quest book) (A Quest miniature) [BP565.S515T48 1972] 73-152060 ISBN 0-8356-0431-4 1.00 (pbk.)
1. Theosophy. I. Title.

SRI RAM, Nilakanta. 147
An approach to reality, by N. Sri Ram. [Rev.] Wheaton, Ill., Theosophical Pub. House [1968] vi, 256 p. 19 cm. (A Quest book) [BP567] 74-1587 1.25
1. Theosophy. 2. Reality. I. Title.

STEINER, Rudolf, 1861-1925. 212
Initiate consciousness; truth and error in spriritual research; a cycle of lectures delivered August 11-22, 1924 at Torquay, England, by Rudolf Steiner, PH. D.: with a foreword and digest of contents by Marie Steiner; translated from the German by Olin D. Wannamaker. New York city, Anthroposophic press, 1928. 1 p. l., xxxv, 180 p. diagrs. 24 cm. [BP565.S54] 28-13007
1. Theosophy. I. Steiner, Frau Marie (von Sivers) 1867- ed. II. Wannamaker, Olin Dantzler, tr. III. Title.

STEINER, Rudolf, 1861-1925. 133.
Inititiation and its results, a sequel to "The way of Initiation", by Rudolf Steiner, PH. D.; tr. from the German by Clifford Bax. 1st American ed. New York, Macoy publishing and Masonic supply co.; [etc., etc.] 1909. 134 p. 20 cm. [BF1613.S83] 10-2135
1. Theosophy. I. Bax, Clifford, 1886- tr. II. Title.

STEINER, Rudolf, 1861-1925. 212.52
Reincarnation and karma. How karma works, Translated by Lisa D. Monges. New York, Anthroposophic Press, 1962. 57 p. 20 cm. [BP573.R5S83] 62-5124
1. Theosophy. I. Title.

STEINER, Rudolf, 1861-1925. 129
Theosophy; an introduction to the supersensible knowledge of the world and the destination of man. [Translated by Henry B. Monges and rev. for this ed. by Gilbert Church] New York, Anthroposophic Press [1971] xxiii, 195 p. 20 cm. [BP565.S72 1971] 78-135997
1. Theosophy.

STEINER, Rudolf, 1861-1925. 212
... *Theosophy,* an introduction to the supersensible knowledge of the world and the destination of man. English translation completely revised by Henry B. Monges. New York, Anthroposophic press; London,Rudolf Steiner publishing co., 1946. xxviii, 273 p. 18 cm. [BP565.S72 1946] 46-20815
1. Theosophy. I. Monges, Henry Babad, tr. II. Title.

STEINER, Rudolf, 1861-1925.
The way of initiation; or, How to attain knowledge of higher worlds, by Rudolf Steiner. [Translated from the German by Max Gysi] With a foreword by Annie Besant and some biographical notes by Edouard Schure. Mokelumne Hill, Calif., Health Research, 1960. 70 p. port. 68-12418
1. Theosophy. I. Besant, Annie (Wood) 1847-1929. II. Schure, Edouard, 1841-1929. III. Title. IV. Title: How to attain knowledge of higher worlds.

STEINER, Rudolf, 1861-1925. 212
The way of initiation; or, How to attain knowledge of the higher world, by Rudolf Steiner, PH. D. From the German by Max Gysi, with some biographical notes of the author by Edouard Schure. 1st Americanized ed. New York, Macoy publishing and masonic supply co. [c1910] 4 p. l., 7-163 p. front. (port.) 20 cm. [BP565.S6] 10-7298
1. Theosophy. I. Schure, Edouard, 1841- II. Gysi, Max, tr. III. Title.

STEINER, Rudolf, 1864-1925.
Theosophy; an introduction to the supersensible knowledge of the world and the destination of man, by Rudolf Steiner; translated, with the premission of the author, from the 3d German ed. by E. D. S. Chicago, New York, Rand, McNally & company, 1910. 2 p. l., vii-xix, 230 p. 20 cm. [DP565.S72 1910] 10-28030
1. Theosophy. I. Shields, Elizabeth Douglas, Mrs. tr. II. Title.

STOVER, Alkin J 1887- 212
Nature's magic. Covina, Calif., Theosophical Univ. Press [1948] 73 p. illus. 24 cm. [BP565.S85] 48-9732
1. Theosophy. I. Title.

TAIT, Asa Oscar.
Heralds of the morning; the meaning of the social and political problems of to-day and the significance of the great phenomena in nature ... [By] Asa Oscar Tait [New ed.] Oakland, Cal., San Francisco [etc.] Pacific press publishing company [c1899] vi, [2], 9-354 p. incl. illus., plates. front. 22 1/2 cm. 4-22272
I. Title.

TAIT, Asa Oscar.
Heralds of the morning; the meaning of the social and political problems of to-day and the significance of the great phenomena in nature. Oakland, San Francisco [etc.] Pacific press pub. co. [1899] 279 p. illus., pl. 8 cm. 99-1209
I. Title.

TAIT, Asa Oscar.
Heralds of the morning; the meaning of the social and political problems of to-day and the significance of the great phenomena in nature ... [By] Asa Oscar Tait, 160th thousand--Re-revised. Mountain View, Cal., Portland, Ore. [etc.] Pacific press publishing association [c1909] 2 p. l., vii-xi, [1], 13-419 p. incl. front., illus. 22 1/2 cm. 9-15201
I. Title.

TAIT, Asa Oscar.
Heralds of the morning; the meaning of the social and political problems of to-day and the significance of the great phenomena in nature ... by Asa Oscar Tait. Mountain View, Cal. [etc.] Pacific press publishing association, 1912. 1 p. l., vii-xi, [1], 13-419 p. illus. 22 1/2 cm. $2.00 12-18561
I. Title.

TAIT, Asa Oscar.
Heralds of the morning; the meaning of the social and political problems of to-day and the significance of the great phenomena in nature ... by Asa Oscar Tait. Mountain View, Cal., Kansas City, Mo. [etc.] Pacific press publishing association, 1915. viii, 9-398 p. incl. front., illus. 22 1/2 cm. $2.00 15-17046
I. Title.

TAYLOR, Alfred, 1896- 210
A human heritage; the wisdom in science and experience. Wheaton, Ill., Theosophical Pub. House [1975] 146 p. 22 cm. (A Quest book) [BP565.T35] 74-18360 ISBN 0-8356-0455-1 2.50 (pbk.)
1. Theosophy. I. Title.

A textbook of theosophy.
[8th ed.] Madras, India, sold by the Theosophical Press, Wheaton, Ill., 1956. 163p.
1. Theosophy. I. Leadbeater, Charles Webster, 1847-1934.

THE theosophical movement,
1875-1925; a history and survey. New York, E. P. Dutton & company [c1925] xxxii p., 1 l., 705 p. 23 cm. [BP530.T5] 25-7209
1. Theosophy. 2. Theosophical society.

THEOSOPHICAL society. American section.
... *A primer of theosophy:* a very condensed outline issued by the American section of the Theosophical society. Not copyrighted ... Second ten thousand. Chicago, The Rajput press, 1909. 126, [4] p. illus. (ports.) 17 cm. W 10
1. Theosophy. I. Title.

THEOSOPHICAL Society, 212
Blavatsky Lodge
Transactions; discussions on the stanzas of the first volume of the Secret doctrine. Covina, Calif., Theosophical University Press, 1946. 118 p. 24 cm. Transactions of the meetings of Jan. 10-Mar. 14, 1880. First ed. published in two parts, London, 1890-91. [BP561.S4T43] 52-16841
1. Blavatsky, Helene Petrovna (Hahn-Hahn) 1831-1891. The secret doctrine. 2. Theosophy. I. Title.

TINGLEY, Katherine A. 212
(Westcott) Mrs., 1852-
... *A nosegay of everlastings from Katherine Tingley's garden of helpful thoughts.* Point Loma, Calif., Pub. by the students of the Raja Yoga college, 1914. 3 p. l., 5-126 p. front., plates. 13 1/2 x 18 cm. [BP525.T5] 14-8762
1. Theosophy. I. Title.

[TINGLEY, Katherine A.
(Westcott) Mrs.] 1852-ed.
...*The pith and marrow of some sacred writings...* Point Loma, Cal., The Aryan theosophical press, c1908. 2 v. 15 cm. (New century-series) 15-28243
I. Title.

TINGLEY, Katherine A. 212
(Westcott) Mrs., 1852-
Theosophy, the path of the mystic; links for your own forging from the lectures and writings of Katherine Tingley ... comp. by Grace Knoche ... Point Loma, Calif., The Woman's international theosophical league [c1922] 6 p. l., 185 p. front. (port.) 17 1/2 cm. [BP565.T5] 22-10424
1. Theosophy. I. Knoche, Grace, comp. II. Title.

TINGLEY, Katherine A. 212
(Westcott) Mrs., 1852-
The travail of the soul, by Katherine Tingley ... Point Loma, Calif., Woman's international theosophical league [c1927] xx, 291 p. incl. front. (port.) 17 1/2 cm. [BP570.T57] 27-14549
1. Theosophy. I. Title.

TINGLEY, Katherine A. 212
(Westcott) Mrs., 1852-
The voice of the soul, by Katherine Tingley ... Point Loma, Calif., Woman's international theosophical league (c1928) xxiii, 308 p. front. 17 1/2 cm. [BP565.T52] 28-16242
1. Theosophy. I. Title.

TINGLEY, Katherine A. 212
(Westcott) Mrs., 1852-1929.
The wine of life, by Katherine Tingley; with preface by Talbot Mundy. Point Loma, Calif., Woman's international theosophical league [c1925] xxii, 332, [20] p. plates, ports. 19 1/2 cm. "A compilation from extemporaneous public addresses by Katherine Tingley...delivered in America and Europe, principally in 1923 and 1924; and from private instructions to her students." "Quotations from the author's book. 'Theosophy: the path of the mystic'": 20 p. at end. [BP565.T53] 25-8224
1. Theosophy. I. Title.

TINGLEY, Katherine Augusta 212
(Westcott) 1847-1929.
The gods await, by Katherine Tingley. Point Loma, Calif., Woman's international theosophical league [1926] x p., 2 l., 3-186 p. front., plates. 17 1/2 cm. Frontispiece and plates accompanied by leaves with descriptive letterpress. [BP565.T48] 26-8945
I. Title.
Contents omitted.

TINGLEY, Katherine Augusta 147
Westcott, 1847-1929.
Theosophy, the path of the mystic : links for your own forging / Katherine Tingley ; compiled by Grace Knoche. 3d and rev. ed. Pasadena, Calif. : Theosophical University Press, c1977. x, 159 p. ; 20 cm. [BP565.T5 1977] 77-82604 ISBN 0-911500-33-2 : 5.00 ISBN 0-911500-33-2 pbk. : 2.50
1. Theosophy. I. Knoche, Grace. II. Title.

TINGLEY, Katherine 212'.52
Augusta Westcott, 1847-1929.
The wisdom of the heart : Katherine Tingley speaks / compiled and edited by W. Emmett Small. San Diego, Calif. : Point Loma Publications, c1978. 163 p., [1] leaf of plates : port. ; 22 cm. [BP565.T5W57] 78-65338 5.75
1. Theosophy. I. Small, W. Emmett. II. Title.

TITUS, F. E. 212
The pantheism of modern science. By F. E. Titus ... A summary of recent investigations into life, force and substance, and the opinions based by scientists thereon, leading up to the conclusion that there is in nature a universal mind controlling and permeating nature's manifestations ... Chicago, Theosophical book cornern, 1900. 1 p. l., 56 p. 18 cm. [BP565.T57] 44-48439
1. Theosophy. I. Title.

VAN HOOK, Weller, 1862- 212
The cultural system [by] Weller Van Hook. Chicago The Rajput press [c1925] 3 p. l., 231 p. 20 cm. "A group of essays upon various topics of the divine wisdom" republished, with a few changes, from the Theosophist and the Messenger. cf. Foreword. [BP525.V3] 25-21886
1. Theosophy. I. Title.

VAN HOOK, Weller, 1862- 212
The future way [by] Weller Van Hook. Chicago, The Rajput press [c1928] 3 p. l., 220 p. 20 cm. [BP565.V3] 28-12839
1. Theosophy. I. Title.

VAN PELT, Gertrude Wyckoff, 212
1856-
... *Hierarchies: the ladder of life,* by Gertrude W. Van Pelt, M.D. Point Loma, Calif., Theosophical university press, 1941. 3 p. l., 95 p. 15 cm. (Theosophical manual no. IX) "Second printing." [BP573.H5V3] 45-41159
1. Theosophy. I. Title.

VAN UCHELEN, J. Croiset. 212
Healing and occult science ... Covina, Calif., Theosophical univ. press [1947] 126 p. 20 cm. [BP573.H4V3] Med
1. [Theosophy] 2. Therapeutics—Hist. 3. Occult sciences. 4. Medicine and religion. I. Title.

WACHTMEISTER, Constance. 922.91
Reminiscences of H. P. Blavatsky and "The secret doctrine" by the Countess Constance Wachtmeister ... and others, edited by a fellow of the Theosophical society. London, Theosophical publishing society: New York, The Path; [etc., etc.] 1893. 162 p. 19 1/2 cm. [BP585.B6W3] 32-6496
1. Theosophy. 2. Blavatsky, Helene Petrovna (Hahn-Hahn) 1831-1891. The secret doctrine. I. Title.

WHITTY, Michael James, 1862-
A simple study in theosophy, by Michael J. Whitty. New York, M. Kennerley, 1917. 6 p. l., 108 p. 19 cm. $1.25 "Books recommended for further study": p. 108. 17-12725
I. Title.

WILLIS, Frederick Milton, 212
1868-
... *Theosophy in outline* [by] F. Milton Willis. Girard Kan., Haldeman-Julius company [c1923] 96 p. 13cm. (Pocket series, no. 477, ed by E. Haldeman-Julius) Bibliography: p. 92-94. [BP565.W63] CA 24
1. Theosophy. I. Title.

WILSON, William Teasdale.
The eternal soul; or, The triumph of religion over science; being the last of a series of four inspired works containing the complete explanation of the plan of salvation, by William Teasdale Wilson ... London, G. Routledge & sons; New York, E. P. Dutton & co., 1920. x p., 1 l., 530 p. 22 1/2 cm. A 20
1. Theosophy. 2. Spiritualism. 3. Salvation. I. Title.

WINNER, Anna Kennedy. 147
The basic ideas of occult wisdom. Wheaton, Ill., Theosophical Pub. House [1970] 113 p. 21 cm. (A Quest book original) [BP565.W64B34] 75-116528 ISBN 0-8356-0391-1 1.95
1. Theosophy. I. Title.

WOOD, Ernest. 212
The new theosophy, by Ernest Wood ... Wheaton, Ill., The Theosophical press [c1929] 89 p. 18 1/2 cm. [BP565.W66] 30-1111
1. Theosophy. I. Title.

WOOD, Ernest. 212
The seven rays, a theosophical handbook, by Ernest Wood. Chicago, The

Theosophical press [c1925] 185 p.2 l. diagrs. 19 1/2 cm. [BP565.W67] 25-17460
1. Theosophy. I. Title.

WOOD, Ernest, 1883-1965. 212'.52
The seven rays / by Ernest Wood. Wheaton, Ill. : Theosophical Pub. House, [1976] c1925. xiv, 190 p. : ill. ; 21 cm. (A Quest book) [BP565.W67 1976] 76-4909 ISBN 0-8356-0481-0 pbk. : 2.95
1. Theosophy. I. Title.

Theosophy—Addresses, essays, lectures.

ARUNDALE, George Sydney, 1878- 212
Mount Everest, its spiritual attainment, by George S. Arundale ... Wheaton, Ill., The Theosophical press, 1933. 3 p. l., 197 p. mounted front. (port.) 19 1/2 cm. "Addresses given ... during the 1932 sessions of Wheaton institute, summer school and convention of the American theosophical society."--Foreword. [BP525.A7] 33-15277
1. Theosophy—Addresses, essays, lectures. I. Title.

BARKER, Alfred Trevor, 1893-1941. 212
The hill of discernment [by] A. Trevor Barker. Point Loma, Calif., Theosophical university press, 1941. xii p., 1 l., 388 p. front. (port.) 21 1/2 cm. Imprint on label mounted on t.p.: Covins, Calif., Theosophical university press. "Contains in large part all of the [author's] available addresses given in various parts of England."--Compilers' pref. [BP525.B3] 45-48151
1. Theosophy—Addresses, essays, lectures. I. Title.

BESANT, Annie (Wood) Mrs. 1847- 212
Some American lectures, to members of the American theosophical society during the annual convention, Chicago, 1926, by Annie Besant ... Chicago, The Theosophical press [c1927] 3 p. l., 98 p. 20 cm. [BP525.B4] 27-8213
1. Theosophy—Addresses, essays, lectures. I. Title.

[BESANT, Annie (Wood)] Mrs. 1847-1933. 212
Theosophical lectures and answers to theosophical questions; being a part of the transactions of the convention of the American section T. S., Chicago, 1907. Chicago, The Rajput press, 1907. 153 p. 20 cm. [BP563.T5] 7-37985
1. Theosophy—Addresses, essays, lectures. I. Title.

BLAVATSKY, Helene Petrovna Hahn-Hahn, 1831-1891. 299'.934
H. P. Blavatsky to the American conventions, 1888-1891 : with a historical perspective / by Kirby Van Mater. Pasadena, Calif. : Theosophical University Press, 1979. x, 74 p. ; 23 cm. Includes bibliographical references and index. [BP561.H2 1979] 19 78-74256 ISBN 0-911500-88-X pbk. : 3.75
1. Theosophy—Addresses, essays, lectures. I. Van Mater, Kirby. II. Title.

EAST meets West : 299'.934
the transpersonal approach / edited by Rosemarie Stewart. Wheaton, Ill. : Theosophical Pub. House, c1981. vii, 156 p. ; 21 cm. "A Quest book." Includes bibliographical references. [BP570.E2] 19 80-53952 ISBN 0-8356-0544-2 pbk. : 5.25 pbk. : 5.25
1. Theosophy—Addresses, essays, lectures. 2. Psychology—Addresses, essays, lectures. I. Stewart, Rosemarie, 1925-

FIVE years of theosophy 212'.52
: mystical, philosophical, theosophical, historical, and scientific essays selected from "The Theosophist" / edited by G. R. S. Mead. New York : Arno Press, 1976. p. cm. (The Occult) Reprint of the 1894 ed. published by Theosophical Publishing Society, London. [BP570.F57 1976] 75-36850 ISBN 0-405-07966-4 : 22.00
1. Theosophy—Addresses, essays, lectures. I. Mead, George Robert Stow, 1863-1933. II. The Theosophist. III. Series: The Occult (New York, 1976-)

HODSON, Geoffrey. 212.5
Theosophy answers some problems of life. [2d ed.] madras. Theosophical Pub. House; [label: sold by Theosophical Press, Wheaton, Ill.] 1955. 228p. illus. 19cm. [BP570.H6 1955] 59-1536
1. Theosophy—Addresses, essays, lectures. I. Title.

JINARAJADASA, Curuppumullage, 1875- 212
The mediator and other theosophical essays, by C. Jinarajadasa ... Chicago, The Theosophical press [c1927] 3 p. l., 79 p. front. (port.) 20 cm. [BP525.J5] 27-8214
1. Theosophy—Addresses, essays, lectures. I. Title.

JUDGE, William Quan, 1851-1896. 191 B
William Quan Judge, 1851-1896; the life of a theosophical pioneer and some of his outstanding articles. Compilers Sven Eek and Boris de Zirkoff Wheaton, Ill., Theosophical Pub. House, 1969. 96 p. facsims., ports. 24 cm. List of writings of W. Q. Judge (p. 38-40) [BP525.J8 1969] 74-263250
1. Theosophy—Addresses, essays, lectures. I. Eek, Sven, 1900- comp. II. De Zirkoff, Boris, joint comp.

KRISHNAMURTI, J. 1895- (Jiddu), 181'.4
The wholeness of life / J. Krishnamurti. 1st pbk. ed. San Francisco : Harper & Row, 1981, c1979. p. cm. [BP570.K74 1981] 19 81-2951 ISBN 0-06-064868-6 pbk. : 6.95
1. Theosophy—Addresses, essays, lectures. I. Title.

KRISHNAMURTI, Jiddu, 1895- 181'.4
The wholeness of life / J. Krishnamurti. San Francisco : Harper & Row, [1979] p. cm. [BP565.K7W48] 78-19495 ISBN 0-06-064874-0 : 7.95
1. Theosophy—Addresses, essays, lectures. I. Title.

LEADBEATER, Charles Webster, 1847-1934. 212'.52
The inner life / by Charles W. Leadbeater. [Special abridged ed.]. Wheaton, Ill. : Theosophical Pub. House, c1978. xxvii, 383 p. ; 21 cm. (A Quest book) Includes bibliographical references and index. [BP570.L38 1978] 77-17044 ISBN 0-8356-0502-7 pbk. : 4.95
1. Theosophy—Addresses, essays, lectures. I. Title.

LONG, James A 212.508
Expanding horizons [by] James A. Long. Pasadena, Calif. Theosophical University Press [1965] 246 p. 20 cm. (A Sunrise library book) [BP570.L6] 65-24093
1. Theosophy — Addresses, essays, lectures. I. Title.

MORRIS, Kenneth, 1879-1937. 909
Golden threads in the tapestry of history / by Kenneth Morris. San Diego, Calif. : Point Loma Publications, c1975. vi, 240 p., [1] leaf of plates : ill. ; 22 cm. These essays first appeared in the Theosophical path in Mar. 1915-Dec. 1916. Includes bibliographical references and index. [BP570.M65 1975] 76-369881 ISBN 0-913004-27-8 pbk. : 4.75
1. Theosophy—Addresses, essays, lectures. 2. Civilization—History—Addresses, essays, lectures. I. Title.

RUDHYAR, Dane, 1895- 218
Culture, crisis, and creativity / Dane Rudhyar. 1st Quest book ed. Wheaton, Ill. : Theosophical Pub. House, 1977. 227 p. ; 21 cm. (A Quest book) Includes bibliographical references and index. [BP570.R82] 76-43008 ISBN 0-8356-0487-X pbk. : 4.25
1. Theosophy—Addresses, essays, lectures. 2. Culture—Addresses, essays, lectures. I. Title.

TINGLEY, Katherine A. (Westcott) Mrs., 1852-
Theosophy and some of the vital problems of the day; a series of addresses delivered by Katherine Tingley ... at the Isis theater, San Diego, California ... Point Loma, Cal., Woman's international theosophical league [c1915]- v. 17 cm. 15-2903
I. Title.

Theosophy—Collected works.

BLAVATSKY, Helene Petrovna (Hahn-Hahn) 1831-1891. 212
Collected writings . [Boris De Zirkoff, compiler] 1st [American] e d. Los Angeles, Philosophical Research Society [1950- v. ports. 24 cm. Contents.[1] 1883. Bibliography: v. 1. p. 361-38 6. [BP561.A1 1950] 51-16462
1. Theosophy—Collected works. I. Title.

BLAVATSKY, Helene Petrovna (Hahn-Hahn) 1831-1891. 147
Dynamics of the psychic world; comments by H. P. Blavatsky on magic, mediumship, psychism, and the power of the spirit. Compiled with notes by Lina Psaltis. Wheaton, Ill., Theosophical Pub. House [1972] xv, 132 p. 21 cm. (A Quest book original) Bibliography: p. [122]-123. [BP561.D94] 72-78193 ISBN 0-8356-0429-2 1.95
1. Theosophy—Collected works. I. Title.

BLAVATSKY, Helene Petrovna (Hahn-Hahn) 1831-1891. 212'.52
Isis unveiled: collected writings, 1877. [New ed., rev. and corr., and with additional material] Wheaton, Ill., Theosophical Pub. House [1972] 2 v. illus. 24 cm. Contents.Contents.—v. 1. Science.—v. 2. Theology. Includes bibliographical references. [BP561.I7 1972] 78-130982 ISBN 0-8356-0193-5
1. Theosophy—Collected works. I. Title.

JINARAJADASA, Curuppumullage, 1875-1953. 212'.52
Fragments : from the world of C. Jinarajadasa / compiled by Elithe Nieswanger. Wheaton, Ill. : Theosophical Pub. House, 1980. x, 62 p. ; 15 cm. (A Quest book) [BP525.J49 1980] 79-3663 ISBN 0-8356-0533-7 : 3.50
1. Theosophy—Collected works. I. Nieswanger, Elithe. II. Title.

JUDGE, William Quan, 1851-1896. 147
Echoes of the Orient : the writings of William Quan Judge / compiled by Dara Eklund. San Diego, Calif. : Point Loma Publications, c1975- v. : ill. ; 24 cm. "The content of the first volume ... is drawn largely from the magazine the Path." Includes index. "Bibliography of W. Q. Judge's writings": v. 1, p. lvi-lviii. [BP525.J77 1975] 75-331603
1. Theosophy—Collected works. I. Title.

PURUCKER, Gottfried de, 1874-1942. 212
Studies in occult philosophy [by] G. De Purucker. Covina, Calif., Theosophical university press, 1945. xv, 744 p., 1 l. 23 1/2 cm. "Compilers' preface" signed: Helen Savage [and] W. Emmett Small. [Full name: Hobart Lorenz Gottfried de Purucker] [BP525.P79] 45-21200
1. Theosophy—Collected works. I. Savage, Helen, comp. II. Small, W. Emmett, joint comp. III. Title. IV. Title: Occult philosophy.

THEOSOPHICAL manuals ... 297
Point Loma, Calif., The Aryan theosophical press, 1907-10. 18 v. 15 cm. Copyrighted by Katherine Tingley. "These manuals are not all the product of a single pen, but are written by a number of different students at the international headquarters of the Universal brotherhood and theosophical society at Point Loma, California."--Pref. Contents.I. Elementary theosophy.--II. The seven principles of man.--III. Karma.--IV. Reincarnation.--V. Man after death.--VI. Kamaloka and Devachan.--VII. Teachers and their disciples.--VIII. The doctrine of cycles.--IX. Psychism, ghostology and the astral plane.--X. The astral light.--XI. Psychometry, clairvoyance, and thought-transference.--XII. The angel and the demon. 2 V.--XIII. The flame and the clay.--XIV. On God and prayer.--XV. Theosophy: the mother of religions.--XVI. From crypt to pronaos, an essay on the rise and fall of dogma, by Rev. S. J. Neill.--XVII. Earth: its parentage; its rounds and its races.--XVIII. Sons of the firemist, a study of man. [BP320.T5] 7-22421
I. Neill, S. J.

Theosophy—Dictionaries.

BLAVATSKY, Helene Petrovna Hahn-Hahn, 1831-1891. 212'.52'03
The theosophical glossary. London, Theosophical Pub. Society. Detroit, Gale Research Co., 1974. 389 p. 18 cm. Reprint of the 1892 ed. [BP561.T5 1974] 73-12778 15.00
1. Theosophy—Dictionaries. I. Title.

BLAVATSKY, Helene Petrovna (Hahn-Hahn) 1831-1891. 6--4152
The theosophical glossary, by H.P. Blavatsky... London, The Theosophical publishing society; New York, The Path office; [etc., etc.] 1892. 2 p. l., 389 p. 25 cm. Preface signed: G.R.S. Mead. [BP561.T5]
1. Theosophy—Dictionaries. I. Mead, George Robert Stow, 1863- II. Title.

PURUCKER, Gottfried de, 1874-1942. 212
Occult glossary; a compendium of oriental and theosophical terms. Pasadena, Calif., Theosophical University Press [1953] 193p. 22cm. [BP527.P8 1953] 53-37086
1. Theosophy—Dictionaries. I. Title.

Theosophy — History

CAMPBELL, Bruce F. 212'.52'09
Ancient wisdom revived : a history of the Theosophical movement / Bruce F. Campbell. Berkeley : University of California Press, c1980. x, 249 p., [1] leaf of plates : ill. ; 23 cm. Includes index. Bibliography: p. 227-241. [BP530.C35] 79-64664 ISBN 0-520-03968-8 : 10.95
1. Theosophy—History. I. Title.

THE Theosophical movement, 1875-1950. 212
Los Angeles, Cunningham Press [1951] xiii, 351 p. 24 cm. A continuation of The theosophical movement, 1875-1925, a history and a survey, with a "consolidation of the treatment of earlier events." Bibliography included in "notes" (p. [333]-343) [BP530.T52] 51-25094
1. Theosophy — Hist.

Theosophy. I.B., H.P.

BLAVATSKY, Helene Petrovna (Hahn-Hahn) 1831-1891.
The voice of the silence, being chosen fragments from the Book of the golden precepts. Translated and annotated by H. P. B. Pasadena, Calif., Theosophical University Press [1957] 97 p. 16 cm. "A verbatim reporduction of the original edition of 1889. At head of title: First series. NUC66
1. Theosophy. I.B., H.P. I. Title.

Theosophy—Indexes.

BENJAMIN, Elsie. 212'.52
Search and find : theosophical reference index (following the Blavatsky tradition) / compiled by Elsie Benjamin. San Diego : Point Loma Publications, c1978. 155 p. ; 23 cm. (Point Loma Publications study series ; no. 1) [Z6878.T4B46] [BP565.B427] 79-111705 pbk. : 3.95
1. Theosophy—Indexes. I. Title.

Theosophy—Miscellanea.

BESANT, Annie (Wood) Mrs. 1847-
... *Man and his bodies,* by Annie Besant. 3d ed. London, Theosophical publishing society; New York, J. Lane; [etc., etc.] 1905. 114 p. 16 x 12 cm. (Theosophical manuals. no. vii) 5-37169
I. Title.

WOOD, Ernest, 1883-1965. 212'.52
Questions on occultism / Ernest Wood. Wheaton, Ill. : Theosophical Pub. House, c1978. p. cm. (Quest books) Condensed from Ernest Wood's question and answer bulletin. [BP570.W58] 78-8791 ISBN 0-8356-0517-5 : 3.75
1. Theosophy—Miscellanea. 2. Occult sciences—Miscellanea. I. Title.

Theosophy—Periodicals

LIFE and action, the great work in America; the Indo-American magazine. v. i-The first-year's number reprinted in book form ... Chicago, The Indo-American magazine company, 1910- v. 20 cm. Vols. i-1st edition. Originally issued in parts; vol. i. no. 1, has title: The Indo-American magazine. [BF1995.L6] 11-725 212
1. Theosophy—Period.

Theotocopuli, Dominico, called El Greco, d. 1614.

BRUNO de Jesus-Marie Father, ed. 922.246
Three mystics: El Greco, St. John of the Cross, St. Teresa of Avila. New York, Sheed & Ward, 1949. 187 p. illus. 28 cm. [BV5095.A1B7] 49-6955
1. Theotocopuli, Dominico, called El Greco, d. 1614. 2. Juan de la Cruz, Saint, 1542-1591. 3. Teresa, Saint, 1515-1582. 4. Mysticism—Catholic Church. I. Title.

Therapeutae—Congresses.

CENTER for Hermeneutical Studies in Hellenistic and Modern Culture. 296.4'4
Philo's description of Jewish practices : protocol of the thirteenth colloquy, 5 June, 1977 / the Center for Hermeneutical Studies in Hellenistic and Modern Culture, the Graduate Theological Union & the University of California, Berkeley, California ; Baruch Bokser. Berkeley, CA : The Center, c1977. 41 p. ; 21 cm. (Protocol series of the colloquies of the Center ; 30 ISSN 0098-0900s) "Bibliography of Baruch M. Bokser": p. 41. [B689.Z7C4 1977b] 77-14931 ISBN 0-89242-029-4 pbk. : 4.00
1. Philo Judaeus—Congresses. 2. Jews—Rites and cermonies—Congresses. 3. Therapeutae—Congresses. 4. Qumran community—Congresses. I. Bokser, Baruch M. II. Title. III. Series: Center for Hermeneutical Studies in Hellenistic and Modern Culture. Protocol series of the colloquies ; 30.

Therapeutic cults.

KEYS to life;
a guide to the conquest of mental and physical illness, by Saint George [pseud.] New York, Exposition Press [1959] 71p.
1. Therapeutic cults. I. Katzen, Morris.

SHELTON, Herbert McGolphin, 1895-
Rubies in the sand. 1st ed. San Antonio, 1961. 330 p. port. 66-50971
1. Therapeutic cults. I. Title.

Therapeutics.

AMERICAN medical association. 615.5
The pharmacopeia and the physician; a series of articles on the use in the therapy of pharmacopeial substances which appeared in the Journal of the American medical association. Chicago, American medical association, 1939. 353 p. 19 cm. Bibliographical foot-notes. [BM122.A5] 40-9828
1. Therapeutics. 2. Pharmacology. I. Title.

Therese, Saint, 1873-1897.

AMABEL DU COEUR DE JESUS, Mother. 248
To love and to suffer; the gifts of the Holy Ghost in St. Therese of the Child Jesus. Translated by a Discalced Carmelite. Westminster, Md., Newman Press, 1953. 158p. 20cm. [BX4700.T5A74] 53-6251
1. Therese, Saint, 1873-1897. 2. Gifts, Spiritual. I. Title.

ANDERSON, Chrysostom J. 922.
An hour with the Little flower ... by Rev. Chrysostom J. Anderson ... Chicago, Ill., The Carmelite press, c1926. 3 p. l., 9-67 p. front. 14 cm. (Little flower series, no. 2) [BX4700.T5L5 no. 2] 26-12749
1. Therese, Saint, 1873-1897. I. Title.

ANTONELLIS, Costanzo J 248.0924
A saint of ardent desires; meditations on the virtues of St. Therese of Lisieux, by Costanzo J. Antonellis. [Boston] St. Paul Editions [1965] 212 p. illus. 18 cm. [BX4700.T5A78] 65-17556
1. Therese, Saint, 1873-1897. I. Title.

BEEVERS, John. 922.244
Storm of glory : Therese of Lisieux. New York, Sheed & Ward, 1950. vii, 231 p. port. 21 cm. Erratum slip inserted Bibliography: p. 229-231. [BX4700.T5B37 1950] 56-2137
1. Therese, Saint, 1873-1897. I. Title.

BEEVERS, John. 922.244
Storm of glory : St. Therese of Lisieux / byJohn Beevers. Garden City, N.Y. : Image Books, 1977c1949. 196p. ; 18 cm. (A Doubleday Image Book) Originally published by Sheed & Ward. [BX4700.T5] ISBN 0-385-12617-4 pbk. : 1.95.
1. Therese, Saint, 1973-1897. I. Title.
L.C. card no. for 1955 Image Books Ed.:55-767.

BOYLE, John, 1922- 922.244
The little one; a story of St. Therese of the Child Jesus. Illus. by Nancy Langenbahn. Notre Dame, Ind., Dujarie Press [1954] 85p. illus. 24cm. [BX4700.T5B6] 54-3702
1. Therese, Saint, 1873-1897. I. Title.

BULGER, James E 1889- 922.244
Louis Martin's daughter. Milwaukee, Bruce Pub. Co. [1952] 161p. 21cm. [BX4700.T5B8] 53-181
1. Therese, Saint, 1873-1897. 2. Martin, Louis Joseph Aloys Stanislaus, 1823-1894. 3. Martin, Zelie Marie (Guerin) 1831-1877. I. Title.

CARBONEL, J 922.244
Little Therese; the life of Soeur Therese of Lisieux for children. Translated from the French by a religious of the Society of the Holy Child Jesus. Fresno, Calif., Academy Library Guild [1955] 195p. illus. 19cm. [BX4700] 56-2435
1. Therese, Saint, 1873-1897. I. Title.

CLARKE, John Patrick, 1890- 922.
Her little way, Blessed Therese of the Child Jesus, "The Little sister of missionaries", by Rev. John P. Clarke ... New York, Cincinnati [etc.] Benziger brothers, 1924. 3 p. l, vii, 110 p. plates, 2 port. (incl. front.) 19 1/2 cm. [BX4700.T5C65] 24-8800
1. Therese, Saint, 1878-1897. I. Title.

CLARKE, John Patrick, 1890- 922.
The pilgrim's path of Saint Therese of the Child Jesus, by Reverend John P. Clarke ... Manchester, N.H. Magnificat press, 1926. xiii, 113 p. parts. 20 1/2 cm. [BX4700.T5C62] 27-6985
1. Therese, Saint, 1873-1897. I. Title.

CLARKE, John Patrick, 1890- 922.
A rose wreath for the Crowning of St. Therese of the Child Jesus, "The Little sister of missionaries", by Rev. John P. Clarke ... with a preface by Rev. Hugh F. Blunt ... New York, Cincinnati [etc.] Benziger brothers, 1925. 103 p. front. (port.) plates. 19 cm. [BX4700.T5C7] 25-10942
1. Therese, Saint, 1873-1897. I. Title.

CLARKSON, Tom. 922.244
Love is my vocation;imaginative story of St. Therese of Lisieux. New York, Farrar, Straus and Young [1953] 213p. 21cm. [BX4700.T5C715 1953] 53-9679
1. Therese, Saint, 1873-1897. I. Title.

COMBES, Andre, 1899- 922.244
The heart of Saint Therese; translated by a Carmelite nun. New York, Kenedy [1951] 196 p. 22 cm. Translation of L'amour de Jesus chex Sainte Therese de Lisieux. [BX4700.T5C723] 51-14066
1. Therese. Saint, 1873-1897. I. Title.

COMBES, Andre, 1899- 922.244
Saint Therse and her mission; the basic principles of Theresian spirituality. Translated by Alastair Guinan. New York, P. J. Kenedy [1955] 244p. 21cm. [BX4700.T5C737] 55-9611
1. Therese, Saint, 1873-1897. I. Title.

COMBES, Andre, 1899- 922.244
St. Therese and suffering; the spirituality of St. Therese in its essence. Pref. by Vernon Johnson; translated from the French ed. by Philip E. Hallett. New York, P. J. Kenedy [1952, '1951] 133 p. 22 cm. Companion volume to The spirituality of St. Therese. Translation of part of Introduction a la spiritualite de sainte Therese de l'Enfant-Jesus. [BX4700.T5C725 1952] 52-9810
1. Therese. Saint, 1873-1897. I. Title.

DALEY, Joseph John, 1875- 922.244
A saint of today: Teresian pastels, by Joseph J. Daley, s. j. New York, The Devin-Adair company [c1936] xiv p., 2 l., 285 p. 20 cm. [BX4700.T5D27] 36-7022
1. Therdee, Saint, 1873-1897. I. Title.

DAY, Michael, ed. 922.244
Christian simplicity in St. Therese; the place of St. Therese of Lisieux in Christian spirituality. With a foreword by Vernon Johnson. Westminster, Md., Newman Press, 1953. 133p. 20cm. 'First appeared as articles in Sicut parvull.' [BX4700.T5D32] 53-10272
1. Therese, Saint, 1873-1897. I. Title.

DAY, Michael, ed. 922.244
Christian simplicity in St. Therese; the place of St. Therese of Lisieux in Christian spirituality. With a foreword by Vernon Johnson. Westminster, Md., Newman Press, 1953. 133p. 20cm. 'First appeared as articles in Sicut parvull.' [BX4700.T5D32] 53-10272
1. Therese, Saint, 1873-1897. I. Title.

DE BETHUNE, Adelaide, 1914- 922.244
Saint Teresa picture book [by] A. de Bethune. New York, Sheed & Ward, 1937. [56] p. illus. 24 cm. Verse. [Full name: Marie Adelaide De Bethune] [BX4700.T5D33] 38-1806
1. Therese, Saint, 1873-1897. I. Title.

DELARUE-MARDRUS, Lucie, Mme. 1875- 922.
Sainte Therese of Lisieux; a biography, by Lucie Delarue-Mardrus; translated by Helen Younger Chase; with an introduction by Micheal Williams, LTT. D. London, New York [etc.] Longmans, Green and co., 1929. 134 p. front., plates. ports. 21 cm. Errata slip inserted before p. 5. [BX4700.T5D35] 29-10485
1. Therese, Saint, 1873-1897. I. Chase, Helen Younger, tr. II. Title.

DOLAN, Albert H. 922.
An hour with the Little flower; the Little flower, a seraph of love ... by the Rev. Albert H. Dolan ... Chicago, Ill., The Carmelite press, c1926. 3 p. l., 9-71 p. front. 14 cm. (Little flower series, no. 3) [BX4700.T5L5 no. 3] 26-12750
1. Therese, Saint, 1873-1897. I. Title.

DOLAN, Albert Harold. 922.
The living sisters of the Little flower, by the Rev. Albert H. Dolan ... edited by Robert A. Lusk ... Chicago, Ill., The Carmelite press, c1926. 4 p. l., 13-192 p. front. (port.) illus. 19 cm. [BX4700.T5D6] 27-6163
1. Therese, Saint, 1873-1897. I. Lusk, Robert A., ed. II. Title.

DOLAN, Albert Harold. 222.12
A modern messenger of purity; sermons concerning the sixth commandment, delivered at the Eastern shrine of the Little Flower, by the Reverend Albert H. Dolan ... Chicago, Ill., The Carmelite press, 1932. 3 p. l., 9-188 p. 19 cm. First printing. [BV4695.D6] 33-6352
1. Therese, Saint, 1873-1897. 2. Sexual ethics. 3. Catholic church—Discipline. 4. Catholic church—Sermons. 5. Sermons, American. I. Title. II. Title: Commandment, The sixth.

DOLAN, Albert Harold. 922.244
Roses fall where rivers meet; a description and explanation of the showers of roses of the Little Flower, by the Reverend Albert H. Dolan ... Englewood, N. J., Chicago, Ill., The Carmelite press [c1937] 4 p. l., 11-167 p. 19 cm. [BX4700.T5D62] 37-33932
1. Therese, Saint, 1873-1897. 2. Retreats. I. Title.

DOLAN, Albert Harold. 922.244
St. Therese, messenger of Mary. Chicago, Carmelite Press [1949] vii, 56 p. illus., ports. 20 cm. [BX4700.T5D625] 50-3434
1. Therese, Saint, 1873-1897. I. Title.

ERNEST, Brother, 1897- 922.244
A story of Saint Therese. Pictures by Sister M. John Vianney. Notre Dame, Ind., Dujarie Press [1957] unpaged. illus. 21cm. [BX4700.T5E7] 57-30284
1. Therese, Saint, 1873-1897. I. Title.

GARESCHE, Edward Francis, 1876- 922.
The teachings of the Little flower; St. Theresa of the Child Jesus and of the holy face, by Rev. Edward F. Garesche ... New York, Cincinnati [etc.] Benziger brothers, 1925. vi p., 1 l., 9-215 p. front. (port.) plates. 19 cm. [BX4700.T5G3] 26-274
1. Theresa, Saint, 1873-1897. I. Title.

GUITTON, Jean. 922.244
The spiritual genius of St. Therese. Translated by a religious of the Retreat of the Sacred Heart. Westminster, Md., Newman Press, 1958. 51p. 19cm. (Doctrine and life) [BX4700.T5G83] 59-2067
1. Therese, Saint, 1873-1897. I. Title.

HAUGHTON, Rosemary 271'.971'0924(B)
Therese Martin; the story of St. Therese of Lisieux. [Rev. ed.] New York, Macmillan [1967] 218p. illus., ports. 22cm. [BX4700.T5H3 1967] 67-21349 4.50
1. Therese, Saint, 1873-1897. I. Title.

HAUGHTON, Rosemary. 922.244
Therese Martin, written and illustrated by Rosemary Houghton. London, Longmans, Green Westminster, Md., Newman Press [1957] 277p. illus. 19cm. [BX4700.T5H3] 58-13638
1. Therese, Saint, 1873-1897. I. Title.

HAUGHTON, Rosemary. 271'.971'0924 B
Therese Martin; the story of St. Therese of Lisieux. [Rev. ed.] New York, Macmillan [1967] 218 p. illus., ports. 22 cm. A biography of the French woman who entered the Carmelite order at the age of fifteen, died of tuberculosis at twenty-four, and was canonized in 1925. [BX4700.T5H3 1967] 92 AC 68
1. Therese, Saint, 1873-1897. I. Title.

HUSSLEIN, Joseph Casper, 1873- 922.
The Little flower and the blessed sacrament, by Rev. Joseph Husslein, S. J. New York, Cincinnati [etc.] Benziger brothers, 1925. 2 p. l., 11-196 p. front., illus. 14 cm. [BX4700.T5H8] 26-271
1. Therese, Saint, 1873-1897. 2. Lord's supper. I. Title.

HUTTING, Albert M. 1903- 922.244
The life of the Little Flower, by Rev. Albert M. Hutting. [Royal Oak, Mich., League of the Little Flower, 1942] xi, 155 p. front., plates, ports. 21 cm. [BX4700.T5H83] 42-17406
1. Therese, Saint, 1873-1897. I. Title.

JAMART, Francois. 922.244
Complete spiritual doctrine of St. Therese of Lisieux. Translated by Walter Van de Putte. New York, St. Paul Publications [1961] 320p. 22cm. Translation of Mieux connaitre Sainte Therese de Lisieux. [BX4700.T5J313] 61-8203
1. Therese, Saint, 1873-1897. 2. Spiritual life—Catholic authors. I. Title.

JOHNSON, Vernon Cecil, 1886- 922.244
Our guiding star; a short life of St. Teresa of Lisieux, by Father Vernon Johnson, with an introduction by the Reverend Edward Towers ... [New York, Spiritual book associates, c1941] 1 p. l., v-x, 100 p. 20 cm. [With, as issued: Knox, R. A. Captive flames. New York, c1941] [BR1700.K6] 41-12706
1. Therese, Saint, 1873-1897. I. Title.

JOHNSON, Vernon Cecil, 1886- 922.244
Spiritual childhood- a study of St. Teresa's teaching. New York, Sheed and Ward, 1954. 216p. 22cm. [BX4700.T5J6] 54-8061
I. Therese, Saint, 1873-1897. II. Title.

KEYES, Frances Parkinson (Wheeler) 922.244
Therese: saint of a little way. New rev. ed. New York, Hawthorn [c.1955,1962] 186p. illus. First pub. in 1937 under title: Written in heaven. Bibl. 62-8391 3.95

1. Therese, Saint, 1873-1897. I. Title.

KEYES, Frances Parkinson (Wheeler) 1885- 922.244
Therese: saint of a little way. Garden City,N.Y., Doubleday [1966, c.1955, 1962] 193p. 19cm. (Echo bk., E27) First pub. in 1937 under title: Written in heaven. Bibl. [BX4700.T5K4] .75 pap.,
1. Therese, Saint, 1873-1897. I. Title.

KEYES, Frances Parkinson (Wheeler) 1885- 922.244
Therese: saint of a little way. New and rev. ed. New York, Hawthorn Books [1962] 186p. illus. 22cm. First published in 1937 under title: Written in heaven. Includes bibliography. [BX4700.T5K4 1962] 62-8391
1. Therese, Saint, 1873-1897. I. Title.

KEYES, Frances Parkinson (Wheeler) Mrs. 1885- 922.244
Written in heaven; the life on earth of the Little flower of Lisieux, by Frances Parkinson Keyes. [New York] J. Messner, inc., 1937. 201 p. front., plates, ports. 21 1/2 cm. Illustrated lining-papers. Bibliography: p. 199-201. [BX4700.T5K4] 37-4627
1. Therese, Saint, 1873-1897. I. Title.

KEYES, Frances Parkinson (Wheeler) Mrs. 1885- 922.244
Written in heaven; the life on earth of the Little flower of Lisieux, by Frances Parkinson Keyes. [New York] J. Messner, inc., 1937. 201 p. front., plates, ports. 21 1/2 cm. Illustrated lining-papers. Bibliography: p. 199-201. [BX4700.T5K4] 37-4627
1. Therese, Saint, 1873-1897. I. Title.

LAVEILLE, Auguste Pierre, 1856-1928. 922.244
Life of the Little Flower St. Therese of Lisieux, according to the official documents of the Carmel of Lisieux. Translated by M. Fitzsimons. New York, McMullen Books, 1952. xiv, 376p. 22cm. Bibliographical footnotes. [BX4700.T5L334] 52-14392
1. Therese, Saint, I. Title.

LEE, Michael A. 922.244
Novena to St. Therese of Lisieux, by Rev. Michael A. Lee. New York, Sheed & Ward., 1941. 3 p. l., 72 p. 16 cm. "First printing, September, 1941." [BX4700.T5L35] 41-19463
1. Therese, Saint, 1873-1897. I. Title.

MCGUINNESS, E. J. 922.
Life and devotion of Saint Therese, the Little flower of Jesus, by Rev. E. J. McGuinness, D.D. Chicago, The Extension press [c1925] 62, [2] p. illus. (incl. ports.) 16 cm. [BX4700.T5M3] 25-15859
1. Therese, Saint, 1873-1897. I. Title.

MORTEVEILLE, Blanche. 922.244
The Rose unpetaled, Saint Therese of the child Jesus; from Une parole de Dieu; sainte Therese de l'enfant-Jesus. Crowned by the French academy. [by] Blance Morteveille. Translated by Mother Paula. O.S.B. ... Milwaukee, The Bruce publishing company [1942] xii, 260 p. front., (port.) 22 1/2 cm. [BX4700.T5M63] 42-36407
1. Therese, Saint, 1873-1897. I. Paula, mother, O.S.B., tr. II. Title.

OUT of the darkness;
a story of Louis Martin. Notre Dame, Ind., Dujarie Press, [c1958] 143p. illus. 22cm.
1. Martin, Louis Joseph Aloys Stanislaus, 1823-1894. 2. Theresa of the Child Jesus, Saint, 1873-1894. I. Roberto, Brother, 1927-

PETITOT, Hyacinthe, 1870-1934.
An introduction to holiness. Translated from the French by Malanchy Gerald Carroll. Westminster, Md., Newman Press, 1950. 176 p. 19 cm. Based on the spirituality of St. Therese of Lisieux. A51
1. Therese, Saint, 1873-1897. 2. Perfection — Catholic authors. I. Title.

PHILIPON, Marie Michel, Father. 922.244
The message of Therese of Lisieux; translated by E. J. Ross. Westminster, Md., Newman Press, 1950. xv, 121 p. 18 cm. [BX4700.T5P513] 50-9053
1. Therese, Saint, 1873-1897. I. Title.

PHILIPON, Marie Michel, 1898- 922.244
The message of Therese of Lisieux; translated by E. J. Ross. Westminister, Md., Newman Press, 1950. xv, 121p. 18c4. [BX47.00.T5P513] 50-9053
1. Therese, Saint, 1873-1897. I. Title.

POWER, Albert, 1870- 230.2
The maid of Lisieux, and other papers, by the Rev. Albert Power ... New York and Cincinnati, Frederick Pustet co. (inc.) 1932. vi, p., 1 l., 142 p. 20 cm. [BX890.P6] 32-12096
1. Therese, Saint, 1873-1897. 2. Catholic church—Addresses, essays lectures. I. Title.

ROBO, Etienne. 922.244
Two-portraits of St. Teresa of Lisieux. [Rev. and enl.] Westminster, Md., Newman Press [1957] 238p. illus. 19cm. [BX4700.T5R6 1957] 57-14029
1. Therese, Saint. 1873-1897. I. Title.

ROBO, Etienne. 922.244
Two portraits of St. Therese of Lisieux. Chicago, Regnery [1955] 205p. illus. 19cm. [BX4700.T5R6] 55-13535
1. Therese, Saint, 1873-1897. I. Title.

ROHRBACH, Peter Thomas 922.244
The search for Saint Therese. [New York, Dell, 1963,c.1961] 208p. 17cm. (Chapel bk., 7690) .40 pap.,
1. Therese, Saint, 1873-1897. I. Title.

SCHMIDT-PAULI, Elisabeth von, 1882- 922.244
Little Saint Therese, by Elizabeth von Schmidt Pauli ... translated by George N. Shuster. New York, The Macmillan company, 1933. 1 p. l., 71 p. illus. 24 cm. [Full name: Elisabeth Nikoline Ida Agens Marie Von Schmidt Paul] [BX4700.T5S35] 33-7544
1. Therese, Saint, 1873-1897. I. Shuster, George Nauman, 1894- tr. II. Title. III. Title: Translation of Die geschichite der kleinen heiligen Theresia.

SHERIDAN, Doris, 1905- 922.244
The whole world will love me; the life of Saint Therese of the Child Jesus and of the Holy Face. Emeric B. Scallan, editor. New York, William-Frederick Press, 1954. 337p. illus. 23cm. [BX4700.T5S4] 53-5666
1. Therese, Saint, 1873-1897. I. Title.

TERESA, Margaret, Sister. 922.22
I choose all; a study of St. Therese of Lisieux and her spiritual doctrine. Westminster, Md., Newman Press, 1964. 252 p. 23 cm. Bibliography: p. [7]-[8] [BX4700.T4T4] 64-57885
1. Therese, Saint, I. Title.

THERESE, Saint, 1873-1897. 922.244
Autobiography; the complete and authorized text of L'histoire d'une ame. Newly translated by Ronald Knox. With a foreword by Vernon Johnson. New York, Kenedy [1958] 320 p. illus., ports. 22 cm. [BX4700.T5A5 1958] 58-7325
I. Title.

THERESE, Saint, 1873-1897. 922.244
The autobiography of St. Therese of Lisieux; the story of a soul. Newly translated, with an introd. by John Beevers. Garden City, N.Y., Image Books [1957] 159 p. 19 cm. (A Doubleday image book, D56) Translation of Histoire d'une ame. [BX4700.T5A5 1957] 57-10467
I. Title.

THERESE, Saint, 1873-1897. 922.244
Collected letters; edited by the Abbe Combes; translated by F. J. Sheed. With a foreword by Father Vernon Johnson. New York, Sheed & Ward, 1949. xvii, 398 p. 22 cm. [BX4700.T5A53] 49-11765
I. Combes, Andre, 1899- ed. II. Title.

THERESE, Saint, 1873-1897. 922.
A compendious critical life of St. Therese of Lisieux, the Little flower, by A. E. Breen ... Milwaukee, Wis., Pub. for the author by the Keystone printing service, inc., 1928. xii p., 1 l., 205, [4] p. incl. front. (port.) 23 cm. "Prayers of St. Therese": p. 180-185; "Poems of St. Therese": p. 187-203. [BX4700.T5A3] 29-15051
I. Breen, Andrew Edward, 1863- II. Title.

THERESE, Saint, 1873-1897. 922.244
"A little white flower," the story of Saint Therese of Lisieux. "The story of the springtime of a little white flower." Being the life of Saint Therese, written by herself: with notes by the editor. A revised translation of the definitive Carmelite edition of her autobiography: by the Rev. Thomas N. Taylor ... witness before the Tribunal of the beatification. 3d American Carmelite ed. Chicago, Ill., Carmelite press, Society of the Little flower [1944?] xxxii, 303, [1] p. 18 1/2 cm. The autobiography was first published under title: Soeur Therese de l'Enfant-Jesus et de la Sainte-Face. [BX4700.T5A5 1944] 44-32137
I. Taylor, Thomas Nimmo, 1873- tr. II. Title.

THERESE, Saint, 1873-1897. 922.244
Novissima verba; the last conversations and confidences of Saint Therese of the Child Jesus, May-September, 1897. With introd. by Francis Cardinal Spellman. Rev. translation by the Carmelite Nuns of New York. New York, P. J. Kenedy [1952] 152p. illus. 17cm. [BX2179.T5E5 1952] 52-14142
I. Title.

THERESE, Saint, 1873-1897. 922.244
Saint Therese of Lisieux, the Little Flower of Jesus; a revised translation of the definitive Carmelite edition of her autobiography & letters, together with the story of her canonization, and an account of several of her heavenly roses; by the Rev. Thomas N. Taylor ... New York, P. J. Kenedy & sons, 1927. viii, 456 p. front., plates, ports. 22 cm. [BX4700.T5A5] 34-23430
I. Taylor, Thomas Nimmo, 1873- tr. II. Title.

THERESE, Saint, 1873-1897. 271'.971'024 B
St. Therese of Lisieux, her last conversations / translated by John Clarke. Washington : Institute of Carmelite Studies, 1977. 332 p., [8] leaves of plates : ill. ; 22 cm. Translation of J'entre dans la vie, originally issued under title: Novissima verba. Includes bibliographical references and index. [BX2179.T5N6813 1977] 76-27207 ISBN 0-9600876-3-X pbk. : 5.95
1. Therese, Saint, 1873-1897. 2. Meditations. I. Clarke, John, 1917- II. Title.

THERESE, Saint, 1873-1897. 271'.971'024 B
Story of a soul : the autobiography of St. Therese of Lisieux / a new translation from the original manuscripts by John Clarke. 2d ed. Washington : ICS Publications, 1976. xviii, 299 p., [4] leaves of plates : ill. ; 22 cm. Translation of Histoire d'une ame. Includes bibliographical references and index. [BX4700.T5A5 1976] 76-43620 ISBN 0-9600876-4-8 pbk. : 4.95
1. Therese, Saint, 1873-1897. 2. Christian saints—France—Lisieux—Biography. 3. Lisieux, France—Biography. I. Title.

THERESE, Saint, 1873-1897. 271'.971'024 B
Story of a soul : the autobiography of St. Therese of Lisieux ; a new translation from the original manuscripts by John Clarke. Washington : ICS Publications, 1975. xviii, 288 p., [4] leaves of plates : ill. ; 22 cm. Translation of Histoire d'une ame. Includes bibliographical references. [BX4700.T5A5 1975] 74-12777 3.95
1. Therese, Saint, 1873-1897. I. Title.

THERESE Catherine Sister 271.0692
Let's talk it over: a student's text in vocational guidance. Foreword by Very Rev. Godfrey Poage. New York, Noble & Noble [c.1962] 92p. illus. (pt. col.) 22cm. 1.25 pap.,
I. Title.

ULANOV, Barry. 248.0924
The making of a modern saint; a biographical study of Therese of Lisieux. [1st ed.] Garden City, N. Y., Doubleday, 1966. ix, 372 p. port. 22 cm. [BX4700.T5U5] 65-19923
1. Therese, Saint, 1873-1897. I. Title.

VICTOR de la Vierge, Father. 922.244
Spiritual realism of Saint Therese of Lisieux; form the orginal manuscripts. Translated by teh Discalced Carmelite Nuns. Milwaukee, Bruce Pub. Co. [1961] 159 p. 23 cm. Includes bibliography. [BX4700.T5V473] 61-7492
1. Therese, Saint, 1878-1897. 2. Spiritual life — Catholic authors. I. Title.

WILLIAMS, Michael, 1878- 922.
The little flower of Carmel, by Michael Williams... New York, P. J. Kenedy & sons [c1925] 4 p. l., 108 p. front. 17 1/2 cm. [Full name: Charles Michael Williams] [BX4700.T5W5] 25-14296
1. Therese Saint 1873-1897 I. Title.

WILLIAMSON, Benedict, 1868- 922.
The sure way of St. Therese of Lisieux, by Benedict Williamson, with a foreword by the Very Rev. Patrick Murray ... London, K. Paul, French, Trubner & co. ltd.; St. Louis, B. Herder book company, 1928. xii, 264 p. 23 cm. "First edition, January 1928, second impression (with a few corrections and an epilogue), November 1928." Bibliography: p. 253-255. [BX4700.T5W5] 29-8560
1. Therese, Saint, 1873-1897. I. Title.

WINDEATT, Mary Fabyan, 1910- 922.244
Little queen; Saint Therese of the child Jesus, by Mary Fabyan Windeatt. Illustrations by Donald Walpole ... [St. Meinrad, Ind., The Grail, 1944] 4 p. l., 227, [1] p. illus. 18 cm. "First appeared in serial form in ... the Grail." [BX4700.T5W58] 45-723
1. Therese, Saint, 1873-1897. I. Title.

XAVIER, pere, 1884- 922.244
In the footsteps of Saint Teresa of the Child Jesus (Les vertus chretiennes selon sainte Therese de l'Enfant-Jesus) by the Rev. Father Xavier, O.F.M., translated from the French by Mother Mary St. Thomas. St. Louis, Mo. and London, B. Herder book co., 1932. xii, 219 p. 19 1/2 cm. [Secular name: Charles Tete] [BX4700.T5X3] 32-17779
1. Therese, Saint, 1873-1897. I. Mary St. Thomas, mother, 1867- tr. II. Title.

Therese, Saint, 1873-1897—Meditations.

NAVANTES, S. 242
The imitation of St. Therese of the Child of Jesus / by S. Navantes ; translated by Sister Mary Grace. Chicago : Franciscan Herald Press, [1979] p. cm. Translation of L'imitation de Sainte Therese de l'Enfant Jesus. [BX4700.T5N3213] 79-1132 ISBN 0-8199-0764-2 : 8.95
1. Therese, Saint, 1873-1897—Meditations. I. Title.

Therese, Saint, 1873-1897—Portraits.

THE Photo album of St. Therese of Lisieux. 922.244
Commentary by Francois de Sainte-Marie, translated by Peter Thomas Rohrbach. New York, P. J. Kenedy [1962] 224p. illus., ports. 26cm. 'This authorized edition has been made from Le visage de Therese of Lisieux.' [BX4700.T5V543] 62-10909
1. Therese, Saint, 1873-1897—Portraits. I. Francois de Sainte Marle, Father.

PHOTO album of St. Therese of Lisieux (The). 922.244
Commentary by Francois de Sainte-Marie, tr. by Peter Thomas Rohrbach. New York, Kenedy [c.1961,1962] 224p. illus. 26cm. 62-10909 12.50
1. Therese, Saint, 1873-1897—Portraits. I. Francois de Sainte Marie Father.

Theseus.

THE Quest for Theseus 398.3'52
[by] Anne G. Ward [and others] With a pref. by Reynold Higgins. New York, Praeger Publishers [1970] 281 p. illus. (part col.), maps, plans. 26 cm. Bibliography: p. 261-267. [BL820.T5Q4] 78-110285 13.50
1. Theseus. 2. Greece—Antiquities. I. Ward, Anne G., ed.

Theseus—Juvenile literature.

ESPELAND, Pamela, 1951- 398.2'2'0938
Theseus and the road to Athens / Pamela Espeland ; pictures by Reg Sandland. Minneapolis : Carolrhoda Books, c1981. [32] p. : col. ill., col. map ; 24 cm. (A Myth for modern children) When the time comes for him to join his father, King Aegeus, in Athens, Theseus decides to walk in order to test his courage. [BL820.T5E84] 19 80-27713 ISBN 0-87614-141-6 : 6.95
1. Theseus—Juvenile literature. 2. [Theseus.] 3. [Mythology, Greek.] I. Sandland, Reg. II. Title.

Thessalonica agricultural and industrial institute, Saloniki.

[HOUSE, Susan Deline (Beers) Mrs.] 1850- 922
A life for the Balkans; the story of John Henry House of the American farm school, Thessaloniki, Greece, as told by his wife to J. M. Nankivell, with an introduction by John H. Finley. New York [etc.] Fleming H. Revell company [c1939] 208 p. front., plates. ports. 21 cm. [BV3142.H6H6] 40-5686
1. House, John Henry, 1845-1936. 2. Thessalonica agricultural and industrial institute, Saloniki. I. Nankivell, Mrs. Joice M. II. Title.

Thielicke, Helmut, 1908—

DIRKS, Marvin J. 251
Laymen look at preaching; lay expectation factors in relation to the preaching of Helmut Thielicke, by Marvin J. Dirks. North Quincy, Mass., Christopher Pub. House [1972] 326 p. port. 21 cm. Bibliography: p. 317-326. [BV4211.2.D5] 79-189364 6.50
1. Thielicke, Helmut, 1908- 2. Preaching. I. Title.

Third Order Regular of St. Francis.

ESSER, Kajetan, 1913- 248.8'94
Life and rule; a commentary on the Rule of the Third Order Regular of St. Francis, by Cajetan Esser. Translated by M. Honora Hau and edited by Marion A. Habig. Chicago, Franciscan Herald Press [1967] xix, 124 p. 17 cm. "Rule of the Third Order Regular of the Seraphic Father St. Francis": p. xiii-xix. [BX3654.E813] 67-21135
1. Third Order Regular of St. Francis. I. Catholic Church. Congregatio de Religiosis. Regula Tertii Ordinis Regularis Seraphici Patris S. Franisci. English. 1967. II. Title.

Third orders.

HENNRICH, Kilian Joseph, 1880- 271
The better life; the true meaning of tertiarism, by Kilian J. Hennrich, O. F. M. Car. ... New York city, J. F. Wagner, inc.; London, B. Herder [c1942] vii p., 1 l., 326 p. 21 cm. Bibliography: p. 311. [BX2840.H4] 43-7257
1. Third orders. I. Title.

Thirlwall, Connop, bp. of St. David's, 1797-1875.

THIRLWALL, John Connop, 1904- 922.342
Connop Thirlwall, historian and theologian, by John Connop Thirlwall, jr. London, Society for promoting Christian knowledge; New York, The Macmillan company [1936] xiii, 271, [1] p. front., ports. 22 cm. Thesis (PH.D.)--Columbia university, 1936. Without thesis note. [BX5199.T45T5 1936] 37-46
1. Thirlwall, Connop, bp. of St. David's, 1797-1875. I. Society for promoting Christian knowledge, London. II. Title.

Thirlwall, Thomas, ed.

TAYLOR, Jeremy, bp. of Down and Connor, 1613-1667.
The rule and exercises of holy living, in which are described the means and instruments of obtaining every virtue, and considerations serving to the resisting all temptations. Together with prayers, containing the whole duty of a Christian, and the parts of devotion fitted for all occasions, and furnished for all necessities. 29th ed. By Jer. Taylor, D.D. ... The Rev. Thomas Thirlwall, M.A., editor. Boston, R. P. & C. Williams, 1820. xv, [17]-330 (i.e. 334) p. 18 cm. Pages 225-228 repeated. Pages 325-330, advertising matter. A 18
1. Thirlwall, Thomas, ed. I. Title.

Thoburn, James Mills, bp., 1836-

OLDHAM, William Fitzjames, bp., 1854- 922.
Thoburn--called of God, by W. F. Oldham ... New York, Cincinnati, The Methodist book concern [c1918] 188 p. incl. front. (port.) 20 cm. [BX8495.T5O5] 18-22253
1. Thoburn, James Mills, bp., 1836- I. Title.

Thomas a Becket, Saint, abp. of Canterbury, 1118?-1170.

DUGGAN, Alfred Leo, 1903- 922.242
My life for my sheep. Illus. by George Hartmann. Garden City, N. Y., Image Books [1957, c1955] 318p. illus. 18cm. (A Doubleday image book, D53) [DA209.T4D78 1957] 57-3693
1. Thomas a Becket, Saint, Abp. of Canterbury, 1118?-1170. I. Title.

DUGGAN, Alfred Leo, 1903-1964. 922.242
My life for my sheep. New York, Coward-McCann [1955] 341 p. illus. 23 cm. [DA209.T4D78] 55-10305
1. Thomas a Becket, Saint, Abp. of Canterbury, 1118?-1170. I. Title.

MASON, Arthur James, 1851-
What became of the bones of St. Thomas? A contribution to his fifteenth jubilee, by Arthur James Mason ... Cambridge [Eng.] University press, 1920. xi, [1], 196 p. front., plan. 20 cm. A 21
1. Thomas a Becket, Saint, abp. of Canterbury, 1118?-1170. 2. Canterbury cathedral. I. Title.

SPEAIGHT, Robert, 1904- 922.242
St. Thomas of Canterbury, by Robert Speaight. New York, G. P. Putnam's sons, 1938. 7 p. l., 3-244 p. 21 cm. Bibliography: p. 243-244. [DA209.T4S65 1938a] 38-13624
1. Thomas & Becket, Saint, abp. of Canterbury, 1118?-1170. I. Title.

SPEAIGHT, Robert, 1904- 922.242
Thomas Becket, by Robert Speaight ... London, New York [etc.] Longmans, Green and co. [1938] xi, 220, [2] p. incl. geneal. tab. front., pl. 22 1/2 cm. "First published, 1938." American edition published under title: St. Thomas of Canterbury. Bibliography: p. 219-220. [DA209.T4S65 1938] 39-9389
1. Thomas & Becket, Saint, abp. of Canterbury, 1118?-1170. I. Title.

Thomas a Becket, Saint, Abp. of Canterbury, 1118?-1170—Art.

BORENIUS, Tancred, 1885-1948. 704.948'6
St. Thomas Becket in art. Port Washington, N.Y., Kennikat Press [1970] xix, 122 p. illus. 24 cm. Reprint of the 1932 ed. Bibliography: p. 115-116. [N8080.B6 1970] 70-102835
1. Thomas a Becket, Saint, Abp. of Canterbury, 1118?-1170—Art. I. Title.

Thomas a Becket, Saint, Abp. of Canterbury, 1118?-1170—Juvenile literature.

CORFE, Thomas Howell. 942.03'1'0924 B
Archbishop Thomas and King Henry II / Tom Corfe Cambridge ; New York : Cambridge University Press, 1975. 48 p. : ill., facsim., geneal. tables, maps, plans, ports. ; 21 x 22 cm. (Cambridge introduction to the history of mankind : Topic book) Discusses the events surrounding the murder of Thomas a Becket, the Archbishop of Canterbury, and the living conditions in England during the reign of Henry II. [DA209.T4C63] 920 74-14442 pbk. : 2.75
1. Thomas a Becket, Saint, Abp. of Canterbury, 1118?-1170—Juvenile literature. 2. Henry II, King of England, 1133-1189—Juvenile literature. 3. [Thomas a Becket, Saint, Abp. of Canterbury, 1118?-1170.] 4. [Henry II, King of England, 1133-1189.] 5. [Great Britain—History—Henry II, 1154-1189.] I. Title.

CORFE, Thomas Howell. 942.03'1'0924
The murder of Archbishop Thomas / Tom Corfe. Minneapolis : Lerner Pub. Co., 1977, c1975. p. cm. (A Cambridge topic book) Published 1975 under title: Archbishop Thomas and King Henry II. Includes index. Discusses the events surrounding the murder of Thomas a Becket, the Archbishop of Canterbury, and the living conditions in England during the reign of Henry II. [DA209.T4C63 1977] 920 76-22419 ISBN 0-8225-1202-5 : 4.95
1. Thomas a Becket, Saint, Abp. of Canterbury, 1118?-1170—Juvenile literature. 2. Henry II, King of England, 1133-1189—Juvenile literature. 3. [Thomas a Becket, Saint, Abp. of Canterbury, 1118?-1170.] 4. [Henry II, King of England, 1133-1189.] 5. [Great Britain—History—Henry II, 1154-1189.] I. Title.

Thomas A Kempis, 1380-1471.

DE MONTMORENCY, James Edward Geoffrey, 1866-1934. 242'.1
Thomas a Kempis; his age and book. Port Washington, N.Y., Kennikat Press [1970] xxiii, 312 p. facsims. 22 cm. "First published in 1906." Contents.Contents.—Introduction.—List of manuscripts of the treatise "De imitatione Christi" in English libraries.—List of other manuscripts cited.—List of printed editions of the treatise "De imitatione Christi" cited.—The age of Thomas a Kempis.—Some fifteenth century manuscripts and editions of the Imitation.—Master Walter Hilton and the authorship of the Imitation.—The structure of the Imitation.—The content of the Imitation.—Appendix I. "De meditatione cordis," by Jean le Charlier de Gerson, chancellor of Paris.—Appendix II. Extract from the "Garden of roses," by Thomas a Kempis. [BV4829.D4 1970] 73-103183
1. Thomas a Kempis, 1380-1471. 2. Imitatio Christi. I. Gerson, Joannes, 1363-1429. De meditatione cordis.

SCULLY, Vincent Joseph, 1876- 921.
Life of the venerable Thomas Kempis, canon regular of St. Augustine, by Dom Vincent Scully, C. R. L., with introduction by Sir Francis Cruise ... London, R. & T. Washbourne; New York, Cincinnati [etc.] Benziger bros., 1901. xxi p., 1 l., 278 p. front., 2 port. 19 cm. "List of authorities": p. [xv]-xvii. [BX4705.T6S3] 3-33116
1. Thomas a Kempis, 1380-1471. I. Title.

YULE, George Udny, 1871-1951. 242'.1
The statistical study of literary vocabulary. [Hamden, Conn.] Archon Books, 1968. viii, 306 p. illus. 25 cm. Reprint of the 1944 ed. Includes bibliographies. [BV4829.Y8 1968] 68-8027 ISBN 0-208-00689-3
1. Thomas A Kempis, 1380-1471. 2. Gerson, Joannes, 1363-1429. 3. Gerson, Joannes, 1363-1429. 4. Imitatio Christi. 5. Imitatio Christi. I. Title.

YULE, Goerge Udny, 1871- 242.1
The statistical study of literary vocabulary, by G. Udny Yule ... Cambridge [Eng.] The University press, 1944. viii p., 1 l., 306 p. incl. tables, diagrs. 24 cm. A study of the vocabulary in the Imitatio Christi, the miscellaneous works of Thomas a Kempis and the works of Joannes Gerson as a basis of authorship of the Imitatio. cf. p. 3. "References" at end of each chapter. [BV4829.Y8] 44-29835
1. Thomas A. Kempis, 1380-1471. 2. Gerson, Joannes, 1363-1429. 3. Imitatio Christi. I. Title.

Thomas, Abel, d. 1816.

A brief memoir concerning 922.
Abel Thomas, a minister of the gospel of Christ in the Society of Friends, compiled from authentic documents. Philadelphia, B. & T. Kite, 1824. 51 p. 18 1/2 cm. [BX7795.T5A3] 11-5304
1. Thomas, Abel, d. 1816.

Thomas Aquinas, Saint, 1225?-1274.

THE angelic guide;
containing devotions and indulgences for those wearing the blessed cord of St. Thomas Aquinas. By a Dominican father. Boston, Marlier, Callanan & co. [c1899] 90 p. 1 l. front. 12 cm. "Hymn to St. Thomas Aquinas": 1 leaf at end. [BX2167.T6M3] 99-5682
1. Thomas Aquinas, Saint, 1225?-1274. 2. Catholic church—Prayer-books and devotions. I. [McKenna, Charles Hyacinth] 1835-1917.

BOURKE, Vernon Joseph, 1907- 922.22
Aquinas' search for wisdom. Milwaukee, Bruce [c.1965] x, 244p. 23cm. (Christian culture and phil. ser.) Bibl. [BX4700.T6B6] 65-12046 5.75
1. Thomas Aquinas, Saint, 1225?-1274. I. Title. II. Series.

BOURKE, Vernon Joseph, 1907- 922.22
Aquinas' search for wisdom [by] Vernon J. Bourke. Milwaukee, Bruce Pub. Co. [1965] x, 244 p. 23 cm. (Christian culture and philosophy series) Bibliographical footnotes. [BX4700.T6B6] 65-12046
1. Thomas Aquinas, Saint, 1225?-1274. I. Title. II. Series.

BOURKE, Vernon Joseph, 1907- 189.4
St. Thomas and the Greek moralists; under the auspices of the Aristotelian Society of Marquette Univ. Milwaukee, Marquette Univ. Press, 1947 [c1948] 63 p. 19 cm. (Aquinas lecture, 1947, Spring) Series: The Aquinas lectures, Marquette University, 1947. Spring. [B765.T54B6] 48-1776
1. Thomas Aquinas, Saint, 1225?-1274. 2. Ethics. Greek. I. Title. II. Series.

CHENU, Marie Dominique, 1895- 230.2
Toward understanding Saint Thomas. Tr. [from French] with authorized corrections, bibl. additions by A.M. Landry, D. Hughes. Chicago, Regnery [c.1964] viii, 386p. 25cm. (Lib. of living Catholic thought) Bibl. 64-14598 6.00
1. Thomas Aquinas, Saint, 1225?-1274. I. Title.

CHENU, Marie Dominique, 1895- 230.2
Toward understanding Saint Thomas [by] M.-D. Chenu. Translated with authorized corrections and bibliographical additions by A.-M. Landry and D. Hughes. Chicago, H. Regnery Co. [1964] viii, 386 p. 25 cm. (The Library of living Catholic thought) Translation of Introduction a l'etude de saint Thomas d'Aquin. Bibliographical footnotes. [[B765.T54C513]] 64-14598
1. Thomas Aquinas, Saint, 1225?-1274 I. Title.

CHESTERTON, Gilbert Keith, 1874-1936. 922.245
St. Thomas Aguinas, by G. K. Chesterton. New York, Sheed & Ward, inc., 1933. xii, 248 p. 21 cm. "First printing, November, 1933. Second printing, December, 1933." [BX4700.T6C5 1933 d] 34-5952
1. Thomas Aquinas, Saint, 1225?-1274. I. Title.

CHESTERTON, Gilbert Keith, 1874-1936. 922.245
St. Thomas Aquinas. Garden City, N. Y., Image Books [1956] 198p. 18cm. (A Doubleday image book, D66) [BX4700.T6C5 1956] 56-5405
1. Thomas Aquinas, Saint, 1225?-1274. I. Title.

COFFEY, Reginald Mary. 922.
The man from Rocca Sicca, by Reginald M. Coffey, O.P. Milwaukee, The Bruce publishing company [1944] xi, 140 p. 20 1/2 cm. [BX4700.T6C6] 44-2788

1. Thomas Aquinas, Saint, 1225?-1274. I. Title.

CONLEY, Kieran 189.4
A theology of wisdom; a study in St. Thomas. Dubuque, Iowa, Priory Pr. [c.1963] 171p. 23cm. Bibl. 63-12430 3.00
1. Thomas Aquinas, Saint, 1225?-1274. 2. Wisdom. I. Title.

CUNNINGHAM, Francis L B 231
The indwelling of the Trinity; a historico-doctrinal study of the theory of St. Thomas Aquinas. Dubuque, Priory Press, 1955. 414p. 24cm. (The Aquinas library) Includes bibliography. [BT769.C77] 55-2521
1. Thomas Aquinas, Saint, 1225?-1274. 2. Mystical union. I. Title.

DALCOURT, Gerald J 189.4
The philosophy of St. Thomas Aquinas, by Gerald J. Dalcourt. New York, Distributed by Monarch Press [1965] 126 p. 22 cm. (Monarch notes and study guides, 546-2) Bibliography: p. 125-126. 66-27749
1. Thomas Aquinas, Saint, 1225?-1274. I. Title.

D'ARCY, Martin Cyril, 922.245
1888-
St. Thomas Aquinas. Dublin, Clonmore & Reynolds; [label: Westminster, Md., Newman Press, 1953] 220p. 22cm. First ed. published in 1930 under title: Thomas Aquians. [B765.T54D3 1953] 54-1170
1. Thomas Aquinas. Saint, 1225?-1274. I. Title.

DAUGHTERS of St. Paul. 92
Pillar in the twilight; the life of St. Thomas Aquinas, written and illustrated by the Daughters of St. Paul. [Boston] St. Paul Editions [1967] 74 p. illus. 22 cm. Biography of the Christian theologian and philosopher whose beliefs and works were greatly influenced by the writings of Aristotle. [BX4700.T6D3] AC 67
1. Thomas Aquinas, Saint, 1225?-1274. I. Title.

DECOURSEY, Mary Edwin, 111.84
Sister, 1922-
The theory of evil in the metaphysics of St. Thomas and its contemporary significance, by Sister Mary Edwin DeCoursey, S. C. L. Washington, Catholic Univ. of America Press, 1948. xiii, 178 p. 23 cm. (The Catholic University of America. Philosophical studies, v. 102) Thesis--Catholic Univ. of America. Bibliography: p. 165-171. [B765.T54D37] A 49
1. Thomas Aquinas, Saint, 1225?-1274. 2. Good and evil. I. Title. II. Series.

DIGGS, Bernard James, 1916- 189.4
Love and being, an investigation into the metaphysics of St. Thomas Aquinas, by Bernard James Diggs, PH.D. New York, S. F. Vanni [1947] 4 p. l., 11-180 p. 20 1/2 cm. Bibliography: p. 173-175. [B765.T54D5] 47-2076
1. Thomas Aquinas, Saint, 1225?-1274. 2. Love. 3. Ontology. I. Title.

DUZY, Erminius Stanislaus,
brother, 1915-
... Philosophy of social change according to the principles of Saint Thomas ... by Brother E. Stanislaus Duzy ... Washington, D.C., The Catholic university of America press, 1944. x, 206 p. 23 cm. (The Catholic university of America. Philosophical studies, vol. XCI) Thesis (PH.D.)--Catholic university of America, 1944. Bibliography: p. 200-206. A 45
1. Thomas, Aquinas, Saint, 1225?-1274. 2. Civilization—Philosophy. I. Title. II. Title: Social change according to the principles of Saint Thomas.

ESSAYS in Thomism, 189.4
by Robert E. Brennan, O.P., editor, Jacques Maritain [and others] ... New York, Sheed & Ware, 1942. vii p., 1 l., 427 p. diagrs. 23 1/2 cm. [B765.T54E75] 43-4934
1. Thomas Aquinas, Saint, 1225?-1274. I. Brennan, Robert Edward, 1897- ed.

FITZPATRICK, Edmund J. 233.1
The sin of Adam in the writings of Saint Thomas Aquinas. Mundelein, Ill., Saint Mary of the Lake Seminary, 1950. 179 p. 23 cm. (Pontificia Facultas Theologica, Seminaril Sanctae Mariae ad Lacum. Dissertationes ad lauream, 20) Bibliography: p. 173-179. [BX1749.T7F5] 51-4893
1. Thomas Aquinas, Saint, 1225?-1274. 2. Fall of man—History of doctrines. I. Title. II. Series: St. Mary of the Lake Seminary, Mundelein, Ill. Dissertationes ad lauream, 20

GARRIGOU-LAGRANGE, 230.2
Reginald, Father, 1877-
Reality : Translated by Patrick Cummins. St. Louis, Herder, 1950. xiii, 419 p. 25 cm. Translation of La synthese thomiste. Bibliographical footnotes. [BX1749.T6G343] 50-14837
1. Thomas Aqulnas, Saint, 1225?-1274. I. Title.

GARRIGOU-LAGRANGE, Reginald, 231
father, 1877-
God, His existence and His nature; a thomistic solution of certain agnostic antinomies, by the Rev. R. Garrigou-Lagrange ... translated from the fifth French edition by Dom Bede Rose ... St. Louis, Mo. and London, B. Herder book co., 1934- v, 21 cm. [Secular name: Gontran Garrigou-Lagrange] [BT101.G262 1934] 35-396
1. Thomas Aquinas, Saint, 1225?-1274. I. Rose, Bede, father, 1880- tr. II. Title.

GARRIGOU-LAGRANGE, Reginald, 231
pere, 1877-
God, His existence and His nature; a Thomistic solution of certain agnostic antinomies, by the Rev. R. Garrigou-Lagrange ... translated from the fifth French edition by Dom Bede Rose ... St. Louis, Mo. and London, B. Herder book co., 1934- v. 21 cm. [BT101.G262 1934] 35-306
1. Thomas Aquinas, Saint, 1225?-1274. 2. God (Theory of knowledge) 3. Religion—Philosophy. I. Rose, Bede, father, 1880- tr. II. Title.

GERMAIN, Brother, 1912- 922.245
Knight without armor, a story of St. Thomas Aquinas. Illus. by Bernard Howard. Notre Dame, Ind., Dujarie Press [1951] 88 p. illus. 24 cm. [BX4700.T6G4] 52-15610
1. Thomas Aquinas, Saint, 1225?-1274. I. Title.

GERRITY, Benignus, Brother 189.4
1907-
Nature,knowledge and God; an introduction to Thomistic philosophy. Milwaukee, Bruce Pub. Co. [1947] xii. 662 p. 22 cm. "Readings": p. 624-642. [B765.T54G39] 48-12394
1. Thomas Aquinas, Saint, 1225?-1274. I. Title.

GILSON, Etienne Henry, 189.4
1884-
The philosophy of St. Thomas Aquinas; authorized translation from the 3d rev. and enl. ed. of Le thomisme' by Etienne Gilson ... Translated by Edward Bullough ... edited by Rev. G. A. Elrington ... St. Louis, Mo., and London, B. Herder book co., 1937. xv, 372 p. 19 cm. (The mediaeval scholastic series) "Second edition, revised 1937." [B765.T54G5 1937] 39-4162
1. Thomas Aquinas, Saint, 1225?-1274. 2. Philosophy, Medieval. I. Bullough, Edward, 1880-1934, tr. II. Elrington, G. Aldan, ed. III. Title.

GILSON, Etienne Henry, 189.4
1884-
Wisdom and love in Saint Thomas Aquinas. Under the auspices of the Aristotelian Society of Marquette University. Milwaukee, Marquette University Press, 1951. 55 p. 19 cm. (Aquinas lecture, 1951) [B765.T54G56] 51-8402
1. Thomas Aquinas, Saint, 1225?-1274. I. Title.

GRABMANN, Martin, 1875- 922.245
The interior life of St. Thomas Aquinas, presented from his works and the acts of his canonization process ; translated by Nicholas Ashenbrener. Milwaukee, Bruce [1951] 92 p. illus. 21 cm. [BX4700.T6G673] 51-7705
1. Thomas Aquinas, Saint, 1225?-1274. I. Title.

GRABMANN, Martin, 1875- 922.
Thomas Aquinas; his personality and thought, by Dr. Martin Grabmann ... Authorized translation by Virgil Micchel ... New York [etc.] Longmans. Green and co., 1928. ix p., 1 l., 191 p. 21 cm. "Literary labors of St. Thomas": p. 18-27. [BX4700.T6G7] 28-27872
1. Thomas Aquinas, Saint, 1225?-1274. I. Michel, Virgil George, father, 1890- tr. II. Title.

GRABMANN, Martin, 1875- 922.245
1949
Thomas Aquinas, his personality and thought. Authorized tr. [from German] by Virgil Michel. New York, Russel, 1963. 191p. 23cm. Bibl. 63-15160 6.00
1. Thomas Aquinas, Saint 1225? 1274. I. Michel, Virgil George, Father, 1890-1938, tr. II. Title.

HOPKIN, Charles 235'.4'0924
Edward, 1900-
The share of Thomas Aquinas in the growth of the witchcraft delusion. New York : AMS Press, [1982] p. cm. Original ed.: Philadelphia, 1940. Bibliography: p. [B765.T54H6 1982] 19 79-8103 ISBN 0-404-18415-4 : 23.50
1. Thomas Aquinas, Saint, 1225?-1274. 2. Demonology—History. I. Title.

MCINERNY, Ralph M. 230'.2'0924
St. Thomas Aquinas / by Ralph McInerny. Boston : Twayne Publishers, c1977. 197 p. : port. ; 21 cm. (Twayne's world authors series ; TWAS 408 : Italy) Includes index. Bibliography: p. 183-189. [B765.T54M244] 76-25959 ISBN 0-8057-6248-5 lib.bdg. : 8.95
1. Thomas Aquinas, Saint, 1225?-1274.

MCINERNY, Ralph M. 230'.2'0924
St. Thomas Aquinas / by Ralph McInerny. Notre Dame : University of Notre Dame Press, 1982, c1977. 197 p. ; 21 cm. Reprint ed. originally published: Boston : Twayne, c1977. Includes index. Bibliography: p. 183-189. [B765.T54M244 1982] 19 81-16293 ISBN 0-268-01707-7 pbk. : 5.95
1. Thomas, Aquinas, Saint, 1225?-1274. I. Title. II. Title: Saint Thomas Aquinas.

MARITAIN, Jacques, 1882- 922.245
The angelic doctor: the life and thought of Saint Thomas Aquinas, by Jacques Maritain ... translated by J. F. Scanlan. New York, L. MacVeagh The Dial press; Toronto, Longmans, Green & co., 1931. xviii p., 2 l., 23-300 p. 21 cm. [BX4700.T6M35] 31-9121
1. Thomas Aquinas, Saint, 1225?-1274. 2. Scholasticism. I. Scanlan, James Fr., tr. II. Title.

MARITAIN, Jacques, 1882- 922.245
St. Thomas Aquinas. [Newly translated and rev. by Joseph W. Evans and Peter O'Reilly] New York, Meridian Books [1958] 281p. 19cm. (Merdian books, M55) Includes bibliography. [BX4700.T6M345] 57-10837
1. Thomas Aquinas, Saint, 1225?-1274. 2. Scholasticism. I. Title.

MARITAIN, Raissa. Mme. 922.245
St. Thomas Aquinas, the angel of the schools, by Raissa Maritain; translated by Julie Kernan; with illustrations by Gino Severini. New York, Sheed & Ward, inc., 1935. 3 p. l., 9-127 p. illus. 22 cm. "Printed in Great Britain." [BX4700.T6M38] 35-30546
1. Thomas Aquinas, Saint, 1225?-1274. I. Kernan, Julie, 1901- tr. II. Title. III. Title: The angel of the schools.

MEYER, Charles R., 265.61
The Thomistic concept of justifying contrition. Mundelein, Ill., Apud Aedes Seminarii Sanctae Mariae ad Lacum, 1949. 236 p. 23 cm. (Pontificia Facultas Theologica, Seminarii Sanctae Mariae ad Lacum. Dissertationes ad lauream, 18) Bibliography: p. 223-236. [BX1749.T7M4] 51-28816
1. Thomas Aquinas, Saint, 1225?-1274. 2. Repentance—History of doctrines. I. Title. II. Series: St. Mary of the Lake Seminary, Mundelein, Ill. Dissertationes ad lauream, 18

MEYER, Hans, 1884- 189.4
The philosophy of St. Thomas Aquinas, by Hans Meyer; translated by Rev. Frederick Eckhoff. St. Louis, Mo., and London, B. Herder book co., 1944. viii, 581 p. 22 1/2 cm. "The writings of St. Thomas Aquinas": p. 549-554. Translation of Thomas von Aquin. [B765.T54M42] 44-6018
1. Thomas Aquinas, Saint, 1225?-1274. I. Eckhoff, Frederic Clement, 1899- II. Title.

MIRON, Cyril Harry, 189.4
father, 1906-
...The problem of altruism in the philosophy of Saint Thomas, a study in social philosophy ...by Cyril Harry Miron... Washington, D. C., The Catholic university of America press, 1939. vii p., 1 l., 130 p. 23 1/2 cm. (The Catholic university of America. Philosophical studies. Vol. XLI) Thesis (PH.D.)--Catholic university of America. Bibliography: p. 125-128. [B765.T54M5 1939] 40-1489
1. Thomas Aquinas, Saint, 1225?-1274. 2. Altruism. I. Title.

NEWLAND, Mary 271'.2'0924 B
(Reed)
St. Thomas Aquinas; a concise biography. Foreword by J. M. Donahue. New York, American R.D.M. Corp. [1967] 62 p. port. 21 cm. (A Study master publication, 961) Bibliography: p. 62. [BX4700.T6N4] 66-28705
1. Thomas Aquinas, Saint, 1225?-1274.

OLGIATI, Francesco. 189.
The key to the study St. Thomas from the Italian of Magr. Francesco Olgiati ... with a letter of approbation from His Holiness Pope Pius xi, translated by John S. Zybura. St. Louis, Mo. and London, B. Herder book co., 1925. 2 p. l., viii, 176 p. 20 cm. [B765.T54O5] 26-942
1. Thomas Aquinas, Saint, 1225?-1274. I. Zybura, John S., tr. II. Title.

O'NEIL, Charles J 189.4
Imprudence in St. Thomas Aquinas. Milwaukee, Marquette University Press, 1955. 165p. 19cm. (The Aquinas lecture. 1955) [B765.T54O53] 55-9017
1. Thomas Aquinas, Saint, 1225?-1274. I. Title.

PEGIS, Anton Charles. 189.4
... Saint Thomas and the Greeks; under the auspices of the Aristelian society of Marquette university, by Anton C. Pegis ... Milwaukee, Marquette university press, 1939. 4 p. l., 107 p. 19 cm. (The Aquinas lecture, 1939) Bibliographical references in "Notes": p. 88-107. [B765.T54P35] 39-23515
1. Thomas Aquinas, Saint, 1225?-1274. 2. Philosophy, Medieval. 3. Philosophy, Ancient. I. Title.

PEIFER, John Frederick, 189.4
1921-
The concept in Thomism. [New York] Bookman Associates [1952] 225 p. 24 cm. Bibliography: p. 216-221. [B765.T54P37] 52-12083
1. Thomas Aquinas, Saint, 1225-1274. 2. Knowledge, Theory of. I. Title.

PETITOT, Hyacinthe, 1880- 189.4 B
1934.
The life and spirit of Thomas Aquinas [by] L. H. Petitot. Translated by Cyprian Burke. Chicago, Priory Press [1966] 174 p. 21 cm. Translation of Saint Thomas d'Aquin; la vocation, l'oeuvre, la vie spirituelle. Includes bibliographical references. [BX4700.T6P42] 66-24109
1. Thomas Aquinas, Saint, 1225?-1274. I. Title.

PIEPER, Josef, 1904- 922.245
Guide to Thomas Aquinas. Tr. from German by Richard and Clara Winston [New York] w New Amer. Lib. [1964,c.1962] 160p. 18cm. (Mentor-omega MP 581) Bibl. .60 pap.,
1. Thomas Aquinas, Saint, 1225?-1274. I. Title.

PIEPER, Josef, 1904- 230'.2'0924
Guide to Thomas Aquinas / by Josef Pieper ; translated from the German by Richard and Clara Winston. New York : Octagon Books, 1982, c1962. ix, 181 p. ; 21 cm. Translation of: Hinfuhrung zu Thomas von Aquin. Reprint. Originally published: New York : Pantheon Books, 1962. Includes bibliographical references and index. [BX4700.T6P53 1982] 19 81-22501 18.00
1. Thomas, Aquinas, Saint, 1225?-1274. I.

[Hinfuhrung zu Thomas von Aquin.] English II. Title.

RAND, Edward Kennard, 1871- 1945. 189.4
Cicero in the courtroom of St. Thomas Aquinas. Milwaukee, Marquette Univ. Press, 1946. (The Aquinas lecture, Marquette University, 1945] 115 p. 19 cm. [B765.T54R25] 47-5417
1. Thomas Aquinas, Saint, 1225?-1274. 2. Cicero, Marcus Tullius. I. Title.

REGIS, Louis Marie, 1903-
St. Thomas and epistemology; under the auspices of the Aristotelian Society of Marquette Univ. Milwaukee, Marquette Univ. Press, 1946. 95 p. 19 cm. (Aquinas lecture, 1946) Bibliographical references included in "Notes" (p. 60-95) A 48
1. Thomas Aquinas, Saint, 1225?-1274. 2. Knowledge, Theory of. I. Title. II. Series: Marquette University, Milwaukee. Aquinas lecture, 1946

RICHARDSON, John T 1914- 189.4
The virtue of gratitude according to the mind of Saint Thomas. Washington, 1954. x, 78p. 23cm. 'Pars dissertationis ad lauream in Facultate S. Theologiae apud Pontificium Institutun 'Angelicum' de Urbe.' Bibliography: p. 74-76. [B765.T54R5] 55-19723
1. Thomas Aquinas, Saint, 1225?-1274. 2. Gratitude. I. Title.

ROBB, James Harry, 1918- 128
Man as infinite spirit, by James H. Robb. Milwaukee, Marquette University Publications [1974] 57 p. 19 cm. (The Aquinas lecture, 1974) Bibliography: p. 52-57. [B765.T54R57] 74-76084 ISBN 0-87462-139-9 2.50 (pbk.)
1. Thomas Aquinas, Saint, 1225?-1274. 2. Man. I. Title. II. Series.

RZADKIEWICZ, Arnold Ladislas, 1914- 123
The philosophical bases of human liberty according to St. Thomas Aquinas; a study in social philosophy. Washington, Catholic Univ. of America Press, 1949. ix (i. e. xi) 185 p. 23 cm. (Catholic University of America. Philosophical series, v. 105) Thesis--Catholic Univ. of America. Bibliography: p. 180-182. [B765.T54R9] A 49
1. Thomas Aquinas, Saint, 1225?-1274. 2. Liberty. I. Title. II. Series: Catholic University of America. Philosophical studies, v. 105

SCHARLEMANN, Robert P. 189.4
Thomas Acquinas and John Gerhard. New Haven, Conn., Yale [c.]1964. xi, 271p. 23cm. (Yale pubns. in religion, 7) Bibl. 64-12659 6.50
1. Thomas Aquinas, Saint, 1225?-1274. 2. Gerhard, Johann, 1582-1637. I. Title. II. Series.

SCHARLEMANN, Robert P 189.4
Thomas Aquinas and John Gerhard. New Haven, Yale University Press, 1964. xi, 271 p. 23 cm. (Yale publications in religion, 7) Bibliography: p. 253-258. [BX1749.T7S29] 64-12659
1. Thomas Aquinas, Saint, 1225?-1274. 2. Gerhard, Johann, 1582-1637. I. Title. II. Series.

SCHWERTNER, Thomas M.
St. Thomas Aquinas book, by Thomas M. Schwertner ... New York, N. Y., The Rosary press [c1924] 335 p. front. (port.) 13 cm. Bibliography: p. 331-335. [BX2167.T6S3] 24-7232
1. Thomas Aquinas, Saint, 1225?-1274. I. Title.

SERTILLANGES, Antonin Gilbert, 1863- 180.4
... Foundations of Thomistic philosophy, by A. D. Sertillanges, O.P.; translated by Godfrey Anstruther, O.P. London, Sands & co. St. Louis, Mo., B. Herder book co. [1931] 3 p. l., 254, [1] p. 19 cm. (Catholic library of religious knowledge. xx) [Name in religion: Dalmatius Sertillanges] [BX890.C3 vol. 20] (282.082) 35-14135
1. Thomas Aquinas, Saint, 1225?-1274. 2. Scholasticism. I. Anstruther, Godfrey, 1903- tr. II. Title.

SHERMAN, James Edward. 235
The nature of martyrdom; a dogmatic and moral analysis according to the teaching of St. Thomas Aguinas, by James Edward Sherman ... Paterson, N.J., St. Anthony guild press, 1942. xiii, 321 p. 23 cm. Bibliography: p. 239-244. [BX2325.S45] 42-24849
1. Thomas Aquinas, Saint, 1225?-1274. 2. Martyrs. I. Title.

THOMAS Aquinas Saint, 1225?- 1274. 208.1
Basic writings of Saint Thomas Aquinas ... Edited and annotated, with an introduction, by Anton C. Pegis ... New York, Random house [1945] 2 v. 23 1/2 cm. "First printing." Bibliography: v. 2, p. 1123-1129. [BX890.T62E6 1945] 45-4355
I. Theology—Collected works—Middle ages. II. Pegis, Anton Charles, 1905- ed. III. Title.
Contents omitted.

THOMAS Aquinas, Saint, 1225?- 1274.
... God and his works, being selections from Part I of the "Summa theologica" of St. Thomas Aquinas. Arranged, with an introduction, by A. G. Hebert ... London, Society for promoting Christian knowledge; New York and Toronto, The Macmillan co. [1927] xxiv, 104 p. front. (port.) 18 1/2 cm. (Texts for students no. 40) Printed in Great Britain. Text in Latin. 31-286
I. Thomas Aquinas, Saint, 1225?-1274. Summa theologica. II. Hebert, Arthur Gabriel, 1886- III. Title. IV. Title: Summa theologica.

THOMAS Aquinas Saint, 1225?- 1274. 189.4
The human wisdom of St. Thomas; a breviary of philosophy from the works of St. Thomas Aquinas, arr. by Josef Pieper, tr. by Drostan MacLaren. New York, Sheed & Ward,?1948. xii, 111 p. 21 cm. [B765.T52E5] 48-2059
I. Pieper, Josef, 1904- ed. II. MacLaren, Drostan, tr. III. Title.

THOMAS Aquinas Saint, 1225?- 1274.
On spiritual creatures (De spiritualibus creaturis) Translation from the Latin with an introd. by Mary C. Fitzpatrick in collaboration with John J. Wellmut. Milwaukee, Wis., Marquette University Press, 1949. 135 p. 22 cm. (Mediaeval philosophical texts in translation, no. 5) Cover title. Bibliography: p. 12. A 50
I. Title. II. Series.

THOMAS Aquinas Saint, 1225?- 1274. 208.1
The pocket Aquinas; selections from the writings of St. Thomas. Edited, with some passages newly translated, and a general introd., by Vernon J. Bourke. New York, Washington Square Press [1960] 372 p. 17 cm. (A Washington Square Press book, W575) [B765.T52E474] 61-923
I. Bourke, Vernon Joseph, 1907- ed. II. Title.

VANN, Gerald, 1906- 189.4
Saint Thomas Aquinas; with foreword by Charles A. Hart. New York, Benziger Bros. [1947] xxvii, 185 p. 21 cm. [B765.T54V3] 47-30708
1. Thomas Aquinas, Saint, 1225?-1274. I. Title.

VAUGHAN, Roger William Bede, abp., 1834-1883. 189.
The life and labours of Saint Thomas of Aquin. By Archbishop Vaughan ... Abridged and ed. with preface by Dom Jerome Vaughan ... 2d ed. London, Burns and Oates, Ld. New York, Catholic publication society company, 1890. 2 p. l., xi, [iii]-ix, [1], 544 p. front. (port.) 19 cm. [B765.T54V4] E 15
1. Thomas Aquinas, Saint, 1225?-1274. I. Vaughan, Jerome, ed. II. Title.

WALZ, Angelus Maria, Father, 1893- 922.245
Saint Thomas Aquinas, a biographical study. English translation by Father Sebastian Bullough. Westminister, Md., Newman Press, 1951. xi, 254 p. illus., map (on lining paper) 24 cm. Bibliography: p. 229-239. [BX4700.T6W313] 51-12488
1. Thomas Aquinas, Saint, 1225?-1274. I. Title.

WEATHERBY, Harold L., 1934- 809'.933'1
The keen delight : the Christian poet in the modern world / Harold L. Weatherby. Athens : University of Georgia Press, c1975. 167 p. ; 23 cm. Includes index. Bibliography: p. [160]-164. [PN1077.W4] 74-80043 ISBN 0-8203-0367-4 : 7.50
1. Thomas Aquinas, Saint, 1225?-1274. 2. Newman, John Henry, Cardinal, 1801-1890. 3. Religion in poetry. I. Title.

WEISHEIPL, James A. 189'.4 B
Friar Thomas D'Aquino: his life, thought, and work [by] James A. Weisheipl. [1st ed.] Garden City, N.Y., Doubleday, 1974. xii, 464 p. port. 25 cm. Bibliography: p. [355]-410. [B765.T54W35] 73-80801 ISBN 0-385-01299-3 8.95
1. Thomas Aquinas, Saint, 1225?-1274. I. Title.

WINDEATT, Mary Fabyan, 1910- 922.245
My name is Thomas, by Mary Fabyan Windeatt, illustrated by Sister Jean, O. P. ... St. Meinrad, Ind. [The Grail, 1943] 4 p. l., 86, [2] p. illus. 18 cm. [BX4700.T6W5] 43-17963
1. Thomas Aquinas, Saint, 1225?-1274. I. Title.

WULF, Maurice Marie Charles Joseph de, 1867- 189.
Mediaeval philosophy illustrated from the system of Thomas Aquinas, by Maurice de Wulf ... Cambrige, Harvard university press; [etc., etc.] 1922. 6 p. l., 3-153, [1] p. 22 cm. Bibliography: p. 153. [B734.W8] 22-19416
1. Thomas Aquinas, Saint, 1225?-1274. 2. Philosophy, Medieval. I. Title.

Thomas Aquinas, Saint, 1225?-1274—Addresses, essays, lectures.

AMERICAN Catholic Philosophical Association. 108 S
Thomas and Bonaventure : a septicentenary commemoration / edited by George F. McLean. Washington : Office of the National Secretary of the Association, Catholic University of America, c1974. iv, 344 p. ; 23 cm. (Proceedings of the American Catholic Philosophical Association ; v. 48) Includes bibliographical references. [B11.A4 vol. 48] [B765.T54] 230'.2'0922 75-319639
1. Thomas Aquinas, Saint, 1225?-1274—Addresses, essays, lectures. 2. Bonaventura, Saint, Cardinal, 1221-1274—Addresses, essays, lectures. I. McLean, George F. II. Title. III. Series: American Catholic Philosophical Association. Proceedings ; v. 48.

AQUINAS and problems of his time / edited by G. Verbeke and D. Verhelst. Louvain, Belgium : Leuven University Press, 1976. viii, 229 p. ; 25 cm. (Mediaevalia Lovaniensia ; series 1 : studia 5) English, French, or German. Includes bibliographical references and index. [B765.T54A65] 77-364753 ISBN 9-06-186050-4 230'.2'0924
1. Thomas Aquinas, Saint, 1225?-1274—Addresses, essays, lectures. I. Verbeke, Gerard. II. Verhelst, D. III. Title. IV. Series.

FAHEY, Michael Andrew, 1933- 231
Trinitarian theology East and West : St. Thomas Aquinas—St. Gregory Palamas / by Michael A. Fahey, John Meyendorff. Brookline, Mass. : Holy Cross Orthodox Press, 1977. p. cm. (Patriarch Athenagoras memorial lectures) [BT109.F34] 77-28080 ISBN 0-916586-18-9 pbk. : 2.95
1. Thomas Aquinas, Saint, 1225?-1274—Addresses, essays, lectures. 2. Palamas, Gregorius, Abp. of Thessalonica, ca. 1296-ca. 1359—Addresses, essays, lectures. 3. Trinity—History of doctrines—Addresses, essays, lectures. I. Meyendorff, Jean, 1926- joint author. II. Title. III. Series.

†GILBY, Thomas, 1902- 230'.2'08 S
Poetic experience : an introduction to Thomist aesthetic / by Thomas Gilby. Folcroft, Pa. : Folcroft Library Editions, 1977. 114 p., [1] leaf of plates : ill. ; 22 cm. Reprint of the 1934 ed. published by Sheed & Ward, London, which was issued as no. 13 of Essays in order. Includes bibliographical references. [B765.T54G45 1977] 111.8'5 77-15970 ISBN 0-8414-4438-2 lib. bdg. : 15.00
1. Thomas Aquinas, Saint, 1225?-1274—Aesthetics—Addresses, essays, lectures. 2. Experience—Addresses, essays, lectures. 3. Poetry—Addresses, essays, lectures. I. Title. II. Series: Essays in order ; no. 13.

KENNY, Anthony John Patrick, comp. 189'.4
Aquinas : a collection of critical essays / edited by Anthony Kenny. Notre Dame : University of Notre Dame Press, 1976, c1969. p. cm. Reprint of the 1st ed. published by Anchor Books, Garden City, N.Y., in series: Modern studies in philosophy. Bibliography: p. [B765.T54K43 1976] 76-22412 ISBN 0-268-00579-6 : 14.95 ISBN 0-268-00580-X pbk. :
1. Thomas Aquinas, Saint, 1225?-1274—Addresses, essays, lectures.
Contents omitted.

KENNY, Anthony John Patrick, comp. 189'.4
Aquinas; a collection of critical essays. [1st ed.] Garden City, N.Y., Anchor Books, 1969. vi, 389 p. 18 cm. (Modern studies in philosophy) Contents.—The historical context of the philosophical work of St. Thomas Aquinas, by D. Knowles.—Form and existence, by P. Geach.—Categories, by H. McCabe.—Analogy as a rule of meaning for religious language, by J. F. Ross.—Nominalism, by P. Geach.—St. Thomas' doctrine of necessary being, by P. Brown.—The proof ex motu for the existence of God; logical analysis of St. Thomas' arguments, by J. Salamucha.—Infinite causal regression, by P. Brown.—St. Thomas Aquinas and the language of total dependence, by J. N. Deck.—Divine foreknowledge and human freedom, by A. Kenny.—Intellect and imagination in Aquinas, by A. Kenny.—The immortality of the soul, by H. McCabe.—Aquinas on intentionality, by P. Sheehan.—The scholastic theory of moral law in the modern world, by A. Donagan.—The first principle of practical reason, by G. G. Grisez. Bibliography: p. [384]-389. [B765.T54K43] 79-87103 1.95
1. Thomas Aquinas, Saint, 1225?-1274—Addresses, essays, lectures. I. Title.

OWENS, Joseph. 231'.042
St. Thomas Aquinas on the existence of God : collected papers of Joseph Owens / edited by John R. Catan. Albany : State University of New York Press, c1980. p. cm. Includes index. Contents.Contents.—Aquians as Aristotelian commentator.—Aquinas on knowing existence.—Judgment and truth.—The accidental and essential character of being in the doctrine of St. Thomas Aquinas.—Diversity and community of being in the doctrine of St. Thomas Aquinas.—Aquinas and the five ways.—The conclusion of the Prima via.—The starting point of the Prima via.—Actuality in the Prima via of St. Thomas.—Immobility and existence for Aquinas.—Auqinas on infinite regress. "Selected bibliography of Joseph Owens." p. [BT100.T4O92] 79-13885 ISBN 0-87395-401-7 : 19.00
1. Thomas Aquinas, Saint, 1225?-1274—Addresses, essays, lectures. 2. God—Proof—History of doctrines—Addresses, essays, lectures. I. Catan, John R. II. Title.

PEGIS, Anton Charles, 1905- 189.4
St. Thomas and philosophy. Milwaukee, Marquette University Press, 1964. 89 p. 19 cm. (The Aquinas lecture, 1964) "Under the auspices of Wisconsin-Alpha Chapter of the Phi Sigma Tau." [BX1749.T7P4] 64-17418
1. Thomas Aquinas, Saint—Addresses, essays, lectures. I. Title. II. Series: Marquette University, Milwaukee. Aristotelian Society. The Aquinas Lecture, 1964

SAINT Thomas d'Aquin, pour le septieme centenaire de sa mort : essais d'actualisation de sa philosophie = Saint Thomas Aquinas, 700th anniversary of his death : modern interpretation of his philosophy / sous la direction de Stanislaw Kaminski, Marian Kurdzialek, Zofia J. Zdybicka. Lublin : TNKUL, 1976. 351 p. ; 25 cm. (Zrodla i monografie - Towarzystwo Naukowe Katolickiego Uniwersytetu Lubelskiego ; 100) English, French, or German. Added t.p.: W 700-lecie smierci Sw. Tomasza z Akwinu; proba uwspolczesnienia jego filozofii. Includes bibliographical references. [B765.T54S19] 77-480765 189.4
1. Thomas Aquinas, Saint, 1225?-1274—

Addresses, essays, lectures. I. Kaminski, Stanislaw. II. Kurdzialek, Marian. III. Zdybicka, Zofia Jozefa. IV. Title: Saint Thomas Aquinas, 700th anniversary of his death. V. Title: W 700 [i.e. siedemset]-lecie smierci Sw. Tomasa z Akwinu. VI. Series: Towarzystwo Naukowe Katolickiego Uniwersytetu Lubelskiego. Seria zrodel i monografij — Towarzystwo Naukowe Katolickiego Uniwersytetu Lubelskiego ; 100.

STUDIES in Maimonides and 296.61
St. Thomas Aquinas / selected with an introd. and bibliography by Jacob I. Dienstag. [New York] : Ktav Pub. House, 1975. lix, 350 p. ; 24 cm. (Bibliotheca Maimonidica ; v. 1) English, German or French. Bibliography: p. 334-345. [B765.T54S77] 75-4998 ISBN 0-87068-249-0 : 20.00
1. Thomas Aquinas, Saint, 1225?-1274—Addresses, essays, lectures. 2. Moses ben Maimon, 1135-1204—Addresses, essays, lectures. I. Dienstag, Jacob Israel. II. Series.

Thomas Aquinas, Saint. 1225?-1274 — Criticism and Interpretations.

GALLAGHER, John F
Significando causant. A study of scramental efficiency. Fribourg, University Press, 1965. xxi, 264 p. 24 cm. (Studia Friburgensia, N. F. 40) 65-108764
1. Thomas Aquinas, Saint. 1225?-1274 — Criticism and Interpretations. 2. Sacraments. I. Title.

Thomas Aquinas, Saint, 1225?-1274. De ente et essentia.

GOHEEN, John. 189.4
The problem of matter and form in the De ente et essentia of Thomas Aquinas, by John Goheon. Cambridge, Mass., Harvard university press, 1940. 5 p. l., [3]-137 p. 20 cm. [Full name: John David Maclay Goheen] Contents.--Aquinas and the problem of matter and form in the "Fons vitae."-- Augustine and the problem of matter and form--Aquinas answers Avicebron: the distinction between essence and existence.--Bibliography (p. [123]-127) [B765.T53D53] 40-6897
1. Thomas Aquinas, Saint, 1225?-1274. De ente et essentia. 2. Ibn Gabirol, Solomon ben Judah, known as Avicebron. 3. Ontology. 4. Substance (Philosophy) I. Title. II. Title: Matter and form in the De ente et essentia of Thomas Aquinas.

Thomas Aquinas, Saint, 1225?-1274— Dictionaries, indexes, etc.

DEFERRARI, Roy Joseph, 189.4
1890-
A lexicon of St. Thomas Aquinas based on the Summa theologica and selected passages of his other works, by Roy J. Deferrari and Sister M. Inviolata Barry, c. d. p. With the technical collaboration of Ignatius McGuiness, o. p. [Washington, Catholic Univ. of h America Press, 1948- v. 28 cm. [B765.T54D38] A 49
1. Thomas Aquinas, Saint, 1225?-1247—Dictionaries, indexes, etc. 2. Latin language, Medieval and modern—Dictionaries. 3. Theology—Dictionaries—Latin. 4. Philosophy—Dictionaries—Latin. I. Barry, Inviolata, Sister, joint author. II. McGuiness, Ignatius, 1914- III. Title.

STOCKHAMMER, Morris, ed. 230.203
Thomas Aquinas dictionary. With an introd. by Theodore E. James. New York, Philosophical Library [1965] xiii, 219 p. 22 cm. "Based on Aquinas' Opera omnia (1882) and on two English translations by Joseph Rickaby ... Aquinas ethicus [and] Of God and His creatures." [BX1749.T324S7] 64-21468
1. Thomas Aquinas, Saint, 1225?-1274—Dictionaries, indexes, etc. I. Title.

Thomas Aquinas, Saint, 1225?-1274— Epistemology.

RAHNER, Karl, 1904-
Spirit in the world. Trans. by William Dych. [New York] Herder and Herder [1968] 1 v., 408 p. 22 cm. Translation of Geist in Welt. 68-108831
1. Thomas Aquinas, Saint—Epistemoplogy. 2. Knowledge, Theory of. I. Title.

Thomas Aquinas, Saint, 1225?-1274— Ethics.

BRENNAN, Robert Edward, 234.1
1897-
The seven horns of the lamb; a study of the gifts based on Saint Thomas Aquinas. Milwaukee, Bruce [c.1966] ix, 169p. 22cm. Bibl. [BT767.3.B7] 66-17940 4.95
1. Thomas Aquinas, Saint, 1225?-1274—Ethics. 2. Gifts, Spiritual. I. Title.

CHERESO, Cajetan. 241.68
The virtue of honor and beaty according to St. Thomas Aquinas; an analysis of moral beauty. River Forest, Ill., 1960. xviii, 89 p. 23 cm. (The Aquinas library) Bibliography: p. 86-89. [BV4647.T4C5] 64-56370
1. Thomas Aquinas, Saint — Ethics. 2. Temperance (Virtue) I. Title.

GARRIGOU-LAGRANGE, 230.2
Reginald, 1877-
Beatitude, a commentary on St. Thomas' Theological summa, Ia IIae, qq. 1-54. Translated by Patrick Cummins. St. Louis, B. Herder Book Co. [1956] 397p. 22cm. Translation of De beatitudine, de actibus humanis et habitibus. [B765.T54G337] 56-9440
1. Thomas Aquinas, Saint, 1225?-1274—Ethics. 2. Thomas Aquinas, Saint, 1225?-1274. Summa theologics. 3. Christian ethics—Catholic authors. I. Title.

GARRIGOU-LAGRANGE, 234.1
Reginald, 1877-
The theological virtues. Translated by Thomas a Kempis Reilly. St. Louis, Herder [1965-] v. 24 cm. Contents.v. 1. On faith; a commentary on St. Thomas' Theological summa, IaIIaa qq. 62, 65, 68: IIaIIaa qq. 1-16. Bibliographical footnotes. [BV4635.G313] 64-8560
1. Thomas Aquinas, Saint, 1225?-1274 — Ethics. 2. Theological virtues. I. Title.

GERAGHTY, Richard 241'.042'0924
P.
The object of moral philosophy according to St. Thomas Aquinas / Richard P. Geraghty. Washington, D.C. : University Press of America, c1982. p. cm. Includes index. Bibliography: p. [B765.T54G368] 19 81-40713 ISBN 0-8191-2161-4 : 18.50 ISBN 0-8191-2162-2 (pbk.) : 7.75
1. Thomas, Aquinas, Saint, 1225?-1274—Ethics. 2. Christian ethics—History. I. Title.

GILSON, Etienne Henry, 171.1
1884-
Moral values and the moral life; the ethical theory of St. Thomas Aquinas. Tr. [from Latin] by Leo Richard Ward. [Hamden, Conn.] Shoe String Press, 1961[c.1931] 337p. Bibl. 61-1554 7.00
1. Thomas Aquinas, Saint—Ethics. 2. Ethics. 3. Christian ethics—Middle Ages. I. Title.

Thomas Aquinas, Saint, 1225?-1274— Exhibitions.

THE Tradition of 230'.2'0922
Aquinas and Bonaventure : text and commentary during seven centuries : [catalogue of] an exhibition of manuscripts, incunabula, and scholarly editions selected principally from the collections of the University of Chicago Library and the Newberry Library and held on the occasion of a celebration of the Medieval heritage, the University of Chicago, the Joseph Regenstein Library, November 1974 / sponsored by the University of Chicago, in cooperation with the Jesuit School of Theology in Chicago and the Catholic Theological Union. [Chicago : s.n.], c1974. [23] p. : ill. ; 28 cm. Bibliography: p. [23] [BX4700.T6T7] 75-308795
1. Thomas Aquinas, Saint, 1225?-1274—Exhibitions. 2. Bonaventura, Saint, Cardinal, 1221-1274—Exhibitions. I. Joseph Regenstein Library. II. Jesuit School of Theology in Chicago. III. Catholic Theological Union.

Thomas Aquinas, Saint, 1225?-1274— Juvenile literature.

THE ox was an angel;
a story of Saint Thomas Aquinas. Notre Dame, Ind., Dujarie Press [1961] 143p. illus. 22cm.
1. Thomas Aquinas, Saint-Juv. lit. I. Overstreet, Edward, 1938-

PITTENGER, William 271'.2'0924 B
Norman, 1905-
Saint Thomas Aquinas; the angelic doctor, by Norman Pittenger. New York, F. Watts [1969] vii, 150 p. map. 22 cm. (Immortals of philosophy and religion) Bibliography: p. 146-148. A biography of the thirteenth-century philosopher best known for his ability to reconcile the basic principles of Christian and Aristotelian thought. [BX4700.T6P565] 92 77-79849
1. Thomas Aquinas, Saint, 1225?-1274—Juvenile literature. 2. [Thomas Aquinas, Saint, 1225?-1274.] I. Title.

Thomas Aquinas, Saint, 1225-1274— Metaphysics.

BANEZ, Domingo, 1528-1604 111.1
The primacy of existence in Thomas Aquinas; a commentary in Thomistic metaphysics, by Dominic Banez. Tr., introd., notes, by Benjamin S. Llamzon. Chicago, Regnery [1966] 122p. 18cm. (Logos) Tr. of the author's commentary on Thomas Aquinas' Summa theologica, question 3, article 4, which was first pub. in 1584 in the author's Scholastica commentaria in primam partem angelici doctoris ad sexagesimam quartem questionem. [B765.T54B33] 66-26972 1.25 pap.,
1. Thomas Aquinas, Saint, 1225-1274—Ontology. 2. Thomas Aquinas, Saint, 1225-1274—Metaphysics. I. Thomas Aquinas, Saint. Summa theologica. II. Llamzon, Benjamin S., tr. III. Title.

OWENS, Joseph. 110
St. Thomas and the future of metaphysics. Milwaukee, Marquette University Press, 1957. 97p. 19cm. (The Aquinas lecture, 1957) [DD125.O87] 57-7374
1. Thomas Aquinas, Saint— Metaphysics. 2. Metaphysics. I. Title.

REITH, Herman. 189.4
The metaphysics of St. Thomas Aquinas. Milwaukee, Bruce Pub. Co. [1958] xvii, 403p. 24cm. Bibliographical footnotes. [B765.T54R44] 58-12070
1. Thomas Aquinas, Saint— Metaphysics. I. Title.

Thomas Aquinas, Saint, 1225?-1274— Moral theology.

THE obligation of almsgiving in common necessity according to St. Thomas. Lake Bluff, Ill., 1959. x, 96p. 23cm. Pars dissertationis - Pontificium Institutum 'Angelicum' de Urbe. Bibliography:p. vii-viii.
1. Thomas Aquinas, Saint-Moral theology. 2. Alms and almsgiving. I. O'Connor, Terence M

THOMAS Aquinas, Saint, 1225?- 189.
1274.
Aquinas ethicus; or, The moral teaching of St. Thomas. A translation of the principal portions of the second part of the "Summa theologica", with notes. By Joseph Rickaby ... London, Burns and Oates, limited; New York [etc.] Benziger brothers, 1896. 2 v. 19 cm. (Half-title: Quarterly series. v. 79-80) on t.-p. of v. 2: Second edition. [B765.T5R4] [BX1757.T5] E 16
I. Rickaby, Joseph John, 1845- tr. II. Title.

Thomas Aquinas, Saint, 1225?-1274— Ontology.

BANEZ, Domingo, 1528-1604 111.1
The primacy of existence in Thomas Aquinas; a commentary in Thomistic metaphysics, by Dominic Banez. Tr., introd., notes, by Benjamin S. Llamzon. Chicago, Regnery [1966] 122p. 18cm. (Logos) Tr. of the author's commentary on Thomas Aquinas' Summa theologica, question 3, article 4, which was first pub. in 1584 in the author's Scholastica commentaria in primam partem angelici doctoris ad sexagesimam quartem questionem. [B765.T54B33] 66-26972 1.25 pap.,
1. Thomas Aquinas, Saint, 1225-1274—Ontology. 2. Thomas Aquinas, Saint, 1225-1274—Metaphysics. I. Thomas Aquinas, Saint. Summa theologica. II. Llamzon, Benjamin S., tr. III. Title.

DAVIS, Gary. 081 S
What does the act of existing, esse, mean? An analysis of the act of existing as Thomas' solution to the problem of existence. Maryville, Northwest Missouri State College, 1970. 13 p. 23 cm. (The Northwest Missouri State College studies, v. 31, no. 2) (Northwest Missouri State College bulletin, v. 44, no. 11) Cover title. Includes bibliographical references. [AS36.M75 vol. 31, no. 2] [B765.T54] 111.1'092'4 72-610258 0.50
1. Thomas Aquinas, Saint, 1225?-1274—Ontology. I. Title. II. Series: Missouri. Northwest Missouri State College, Maryville. Studies, v. 31, no. 2.

KLAUDER, Francis J. 111
The wonder of the real; a sketch in basic philosophy, by Francis J. Klauder. North Quincy, Mass., Christopher Pub. House [1973] 114 p. illus. 21 cm. Includes bibliographical references. [B765.T54K553] 72-94706 4.95
1. Thomas Aquinas, Saint, 1225?-1274—Ontology. 2. Scholasticism. I. Title.

Thomas Aquinas, Saint, 1225?-1274— Philosophy.

COPLESTON, Frederick 230'.2'0924
Charles.
Aquinas / F. C. Copleston. Harmondsworth ; Baltimore : Penguin, 1975. 272 p. : 19 cm. (Pelican books ; A349) Includes index. Bibliography: p. 265-267. [B765.T54C64 1975] 75-327650 ISBN 0-14-020349-4 pbk. : 3.50
1. Thomas Aquinas, Saint, 1225?-1274—Philosophy.

COPLESTON, Frederick 189.4
Charles.
Aquinas. [Harmondsworth, Middlesex] Penguin Books [1955] 263 p. 19 cm. (Pelican books, A349) (Pelican philosophy series.) [B765.T54C64] 56-2163
1. Thomas, Aquinas, Saint, 1225?-1274—Philosophy.

GARDEIL, Henri Dominique, 189.4
1900-
Introduction to the philosophy of St. Thomas Aquinas; translated by John A. Otto. St. Louis, B. Herder Book Co. [1956- v. 21cm. [B765.T54G314] 56-9194
1. Thomas Aquinas, Saint, 1225—1274—Philosophy. I. Title.

GILSON, Etienne Henry 189.4
Elements of Christian philosophy. Garden City, N.Y., Doubleday [c.1960] 358p. Includes bibliography, p. 339-343 24cm. 60-6405 6.95
1. Thomas Aquinas, Saint—Philosophy I. Title. II. Title: Christian philosophy.

GILSON, Etienne Henry, 189.4
1884-
The Christian philosophy of St. Thomas Aquinas. With A catalog of St. Thomas's works, by I. T. Eschmann. Translated by L. K. Shook. New York, Random House [1956] x, 502 p. 24 cm. Translation of Le thomisme. Bibliographical references included in "Notes" (p. 440-493) [B765.T54G52] 56-8813
1. Thomas Aquinas, Saint, 1225?-1274—Philosophy. I. Title.

GILSON, Etienne Henry, 189'.4
1884-
The philosophy of St. Thomas Aquinas. Authorised translation from the 3d. rev. and enl. ed. of 'Le thomisme', by [Etienne Gilson. Translated by Edward Bullough. Edited by G. A. Elrington.] Freeport, N.Y., Books for Libraries Press [1971] xv, 372 p. 23 cm. Reprint of the 1937 ed. [B765.T54G5 1971] 70-157337 ISBN 0-8369-5797-0
1. Thomas Aquinas, Saint, 1225?-1274—Philosophy. 2. Philosophy, Medieval. I. Title.

GILSON, Etienne Henry, 1884- 189'.4
The philosophy of St. Thomas Aquinas / by Etienne Gilson ; authorised translation from the 3d rev. ed. of "Le thomisme." [Norwood, Pa.] : Norwood Editions, 1975. p. cm. Reprint of the 1924 ed. published by W. Heffer, Cambridge, in the Mediaeval scholastic series. Includes bibliographical references and index. [B765.T54G5 1975] 75-29121 ISBN 0-88305-236-9 lib. bdg. : 25.00
1. Thomas Aquinas, Saint, 1225?-1274—Philosophy. I. Title. II. Series: The Mediaeval scholastic series.

GILSON, Etienne Henry, 1884- 189'.4
The philosophy of St. Thomas Aquinas; authorised translation from the 3d rev. ed. of "Le thomisme", by Etienne Gilson. [Translated by Edward Bullogh. Edited by G. A. Elrington.] Folcroft, Pa.] Folcroft Library Editions, 1972. xv, 287 p. 24 cm. "Limited to 150 copies." Translation of Le thomisme. Reprint of the 1924 ed., issued in series: The Mediaeval scholastic series. Includes bibliographical references. [B765.T54G5 1972] 72-190713
1. Thomas Aquinas, Saint, 1225?-1274—Philosophy. 2. Philosophy, Medieval. I. Elrington, G. Aidan, ed. II. Title. III. Series: The Mediaeval scholastic series.

GILSON, Etienne Henry. 1884- 189.4
The spirit of Thomism. New York. Harper [1966, c.1964] 125p. 21cm. (Torchbk.; TB313F. Cathedral lib.) Bibl. [B765.T54G554] .95 pap.,
1. Thomas Aquinas, Saint—Philosophy. I. Title.

GILSON, Etienne Henry, 1884- 189.4
The spirit of Thomism, New York, Kenedy [c.1964] 127p. 22cm. (Wisdom and discovery bk.) Bibl. 64-23034 3.50
1. Thomas Aquinas, Saint—Philosophy. I. Title.

GILSON, Etienne Henry, 1884-
The spirit of Thomism, by Etienne Gibson. New York, Harper & Row [1964] 127 p. 68-97731
1. Thomas Aquinas, Saint—Philosophy. I. Title.

GILSON, Etienne Henry, 1884- 189.4
The spirit of Thomism, by Etienne Gilson, New York, P. J. Kenedy [1964] 127 p. 22 cm. (A Wisdom and discovery book) Bibliographical references included in "Notes" (p. 108-125) [B765.T54G554] 64-23034
1. Thomas Aquinas, Saint-Philosophy. I. Title.

GILSON, Etienne Henry, 1884-
The spirit of Thomism. New York, Harper & Row [1966, c1964] 125 p. 20 cm. (Harper torchbooks-the cathedral library) "First Harper torchbook editions...1966." 67-33588
1. Thomas Aquinas, Saint-Philosophy. I. Title.

GRENET, Paul Bernard. 189.4
Thomism; an introduction. Translated by James F. Ross. [1st ed.] New York, Harper & Row [1967] vii, 130 p. 22 cm. "Bibliographical note": p. 127-130. [B765.T54G783] 66-11887
1. Thomas Aquinas, Saint, 1225?-1274—Philosophy. I. Title.

KLOCKER, Harry R. 189.4
Thomism and modern thought. New York, Appleton [c.1962] 320p. 22cm. Bibl. 62-9414 4.00 bds.,
1. Thomas Aquinas, Saint—Philosophy. 2. Philosophy, Modern. I. Title.

LYNCH, Lawrence E., 1915- 201
A Christian philosophy [by] Lawrence E. Lynch. New York, Scribners [1968] xi, 277p. 23cm. Based on radio lects, given by the author in 1962 as pt. of the Canadian Broadcasting Corp. ser., Univ. of the Air, and pub. in 1963 under title: Christian philosophy. Bibl. refs. [BR100.L93 1968] 67-21341 3.95
1. Thomas Aquinas, Saint, 1225?- 1274—Philosophy. 2. Christianity—Philosophy. I. Title.

MCINERNY, Ralph M. 189.4
Thomism in the age of renewal [by] Ralph M. McInerny. [1st ed.] Garden City, N. Y., Doubledav, 1966. 206p. 22cm. Bibl. [B765.T54M245] 66-24337 4.95
1. Thomas Aquinas, Saint, 1225?-1274—Philosophy. I. Title.

MARGENAU, Henry, 1901- 189.4
Thomas and the physics of 1958: a confrontation. Milwaukee, Marquette University Press, 1958. 61p. 19cm. (The Aquinas lecture, 1958) [B765.T54M26] 58-9679
1. Thomas Aquinas, Saint—Philosophy. 2. Science—Philosophy. I. Title.

MONDIN, Battista. 189'.4
St. Thomas Aquinas' philosophy in the Commentary to the sentences / by Battista Mondin. The Hague : Martinus Nijhoff, 1975,i.e.1976 130 p. ; 24 cm. Includes bibliographical references. [B765.T54M623] 75-325051 ISBN 90-247-1733-7 pbk. 13.00
1. Thomas Aquinas, Saint, 1225?-1274—Philosophy. I. Title.
Distributed by Humanities

PHILLIPS, Richard Percival.
Modern Thomistic philosophy; an explanation for students. Westminster, Md., Newman Press, 1962-64. 2 v. Contents.v.l. The philosophy of nature.--v.2. Metaphysics. 68-21670
1. Thomas Aquinas, Saint, 1225?-1274—Philosophy. 2. Scholasticism. I. Title.

PIEPER, Josef, 1904- 189.4
The silence of St. Thomas; three essays. Translated by John Murray and Daniel O'Connor. [New York] Pantheon [1957] 122p. 22cm. 'Original German titles: Ueber Thomas von Aquin [and] Philosophia negativa.' [B765.T54P56] 57-5620
1. Thomas Aquinas, Saint—Philosophy. I. Title.

QUINN, John M 115
The doctrine of time in St. Thomas, some aspects and applications. Washington, Catholic University of America Press, 1960. xi, 54p. 23cm. (Catholic University of America. Philosophical studies, no. 198. Abstract no. 48) Abstract of thesis--Catholic University of America. Bibliography: p. 48-54. [B765.T54Q5] 61-2691
1. Thomas Aquinas, Saint—Philosophy. I. Title. II. Series.

THOMAS Aquinas Saint, 1225?-1274. 189.4
Philosophical texts, selected and translated by Thomas Gilby. New York, Oxford University Press, 1960. xxii, 405 p. 21 cm. (A Galaxy book, GB29) [B765.T52E48 1960] 60-901
1. Thomas Aquinas, Saint — Philosophy. I. Title.

WULF, Maurice Marie Charles Joseph de, 1867-1947 189.4
The system of Thomas Aquinas. Formerly titled: Mediaeval philosophy illustrated from the system of Thomas Aquinas [Gloucester, Mass., Peter Smith, 1961] 151p. (Dover bk. rebound) Bibl. 3.25
1. Thomas Aquinas, Saint—Philosophy. 2. Philosophy, Medieval. I. Title.

WULF, Maurice Marie Charles Joseph de, 1867-1947. 189.4
The system of Thomas Aquinas. Formerly titled: Mediaeval philosophy illustrated from the system of Thomas Aquinas. New York, Dover Publications [1959] 151 p. 21 cm. Includes bibliography. [B734.W8 1959] 59-65175
1. Thomas Aquinas, Saint, 1225?-1274—Philosophy. 2. Philosophy, Medieval. I. Title.

Thomas Aquinas, Saint, 1225?-1274—Philosophy—Addresses, essays, lectures.

ESSAYS in Thomism, 189'.4
by Robert E. Brennan, editor, Jacques Maritain [and others] Freeport, N.Y., Books for Libraries Press [1972] vii, 427 p. 22 cm. (Essay index reprint series) Reprint of the 1942 ed. Bibliography: p. 365-419. [B765.T54E75 1972] 72-1149 ISBN 0-8369-2834-2
1. Thomas Aquinas, Saint, 1225?-1274—Philosophy—Addresses, essays, lectures. I. Brennan, Robert Edward, 1897- ed.

Thomas Aquinas, Saint, 1225-1274—Societies, periodicals, etc.

ST. Louis university. 016.1894
St. Louis university studies in honor of St. Thomas Aquinas. v. l- 1943- [St. Louis, 1943- v. 23 cm. [B765.T54S17] 44-6116
1. Thomas Aquinas, Saint, 1225-1274—Societies, periodicals, etc. I. Title.

THE Thomist reader. 230.2
1957- [Baltimore] v. 23cm. Published by the Dominicans, Province of St. Joseph. [BX801.T52] 57-1468
1. Thomas Aquinas, Saint—Societies, periodicals, etc. 2. Theology—Period. 3. Scholasticism—Period. 4. Catholic Church— Period. I. Dominicans, Province of St. Joseph.

Thomas Aquinas, Saint, 1225?-1274—Summa contra ge ntiles.

ADLER, Mortimer Jerome, 1902- 280.2
...Saint Thomas and the gentiles, under the suspices of the Aristotelian society of Marquette university, by Mortimer J. Adler. Milwaukee, Marquette university press, 1938. 4 p. l., 111 p. front. 18 1/2 cm. (The Aquinas lecture, 1988) "Notes": p. 68-111. [BX1749.T45A3] 86-18294
1. Thomas Aquinas, Saint. Summa contra gentiles. I. Title.

RICKABY, Joseph John, 1845-1932. 230.
Studies on God and His creatures, by Joseph Rickaby... London, New York [etc.] Longmans, Green and co., 1924. vii, 205 p. 20 cm. "These studies bear on my translation of St. Thomas's Contra gentiles, published by Messrs. Burns & Oates, in the year 1905, under the title of God and His creatures...A companion volume to these studies will be found in dialogues published under the title of In an Indian abbey (Burns, Oates & Washbourne)"--Pref. [BX1749.T45R5] 24-7547
1. Thomas Aquinas, Saint. Summa contra gentiles. I. Title.

Thomas Aquinas, Saint, 1225?-1274. Summa theologica.

BRYAR, William. 231
St. Thomas and the existence of God; three interpretations. Chicago, H. Regnery Co., 1951. 252 p. 22 cm. [BX1749.T6B7] 51-14960
1. Thomas Aquinas, Saint, 1225?-1274. Summa theologica. 2. God—Proof. I. Title.

DEFERRARI, Roy Joseph, 1890- 230.2
A complete index of the Summa theologica of St. Thomas Aquinas, by Roy J. Deferrari and Sister M. Inviolata Barry. [Baltimore? 1956] ix, 386p. 28cm. [BX1749.T6D4] 56-4980
1. Thomas Aquinas, Saint, 1225?-1274. Summa theologica. 2. Thomas Aquinas, Saint, 1225?-1274 —Dictionaries, indexes, etc. I. Barry, Inviolata, joint author. II. Title.

FARRELL, Walter, 1902- 230.2
A companion to the Summa ... by Walter Farrell ... New York, Sheed & Ward, 1938-42. 4 v, 22 cm. "This whole work is not ... about the Summa, but the Summa itself reduced to popular language."--Foreword, v. 3. Contents.I. The architect of the universe (corresponding to the Summa theologica IV) 1941.--II. The pursuit of happiness (corresponding to the Summa theologica IA HAE) 1938.--III. The fullness of life (corresponding to the Summa theologica HA HAE) 1940.--IV. The way of life (corresponding to the Summa theologica IIIA and supplement) 1942. [BX1749.T6F3] 39-1667
1. Thomas Aquinas, Saint, 1225?-1274. Summa theologica. I. Title.

GARRIGOU-LAGRANGE, Reginald, Father, 1877- 232
Christ the Savior; a commentary on the third part of St. Thomas Theological summa. Translated by Dom Bede Rose. St. Louis, Herder, 1950. iv, 748 p. 25 cm. Bibliographical footnotes. [BT201.G464] 50-4482
1. Thomas Aquinas, Saint, 1225?-1274. Summa theologica. 2. Jesus Christ—Person and offices. I. Title.

GARRIGOU-LAGRANGE, Reginald, Father, 1877- 230.2
Grace; commentary on the Summa theologica of St. Thomas, Ia IIae, q. 109-14. Translated by the Dominican Nuns, Corpus Christi Monastery, Menlo Park, Calif. St. Louis, B. Herder Book Co., 1952. 535 p. 25 cm. Translation of De gratia. [BX1749T6G34] 52-13198
1. Thomas Aquinas, Saint, 1225?-1274. Summa theologica 2. Grace (Theology) I. Title.

GARRIGOU-LAGRANGE, Reginald, father, 1877- 231
The one God, a commentary on the first part of St. Thomas' Theological summa, by the Rev. Reginald Garrigou-Lagrange ... translated by Dom. Bede Rose ... St. Louis, Mo., and London, B. Herder book co., 1943. viii, 736 p. 22 1/2 cm. [Secular name: Gontran Garrigou-Lagrange] Bibliographical foot-notes. [BX1749.T6G33] 43-11888
1. Thomas Aquinas, Saint, 1225?-1274. Summa theologica. 2. God. I. Rose, Bede, father, 1880- tr. Translation of De Deo uno. II. Title. III. Title: Translation of De Deo uno.

GLENN, Paul Joseph, 1893-1957. 208.1
A tour of the Summa. St. Louis, Mo., B. Herder Book Co. [c.1960] 466p. 60-16942 5.00
1. Thomas Aquinas, Saint. Summa theologica. I. Title.

GRABMANN, Martin, 1875- 230.2
Introduction to the Theological summa of St. Thomas, by Dr. Martin Grabmann ... authorized translation from the 2d rev. and enl. ed. of the original German, by John S. Zybura ... St. Louis, Mo. and London, B. Herder book co., 1930. x, 220 p. 20 cm. [BX1749.T6G7 1930] 31-2663
1. Thomas Aquinas, Saint, 1225?-1274. Summa theologica. I. Zybura, John S., tr. II. Title.

O'CONNELL, David A 230.2
Notes from the Summa on God and His creatures. Providence, Providence College Press [1956] 187p. 28cm. [BX1749.T6O25] 56-13085
1. Thomas Aquinas, Saint, 1225?-1274. Summa theologica. 2. Thomas Aquinas, Saint, 1225?-1274—Theology. 3. God. I. Title.

PEGUES, Thomas, 1866-1936. 230.2
Catechism of the "Summa theologica" of Saint Thomas Aquinas, for the use of the faithful. Adapted from the French and done into English by Elred Whitacre. Westminster, Md., Newman Press, 1950. xvi, 314 p. 20 cm. [BX1749.T6P383 1950] 51-5980
1. Thomas Aquinas, Saint, 1225-1274. Summa theologica. 2. Catholic Church — Doctrinal and controversial works, Popular. I. Title.

SMITH, Elwood F. 230.2
A guidebook to the Summa, by Elwood F. Smith and Louis A. Ryan. New York, Benziger, 1950- v. 23 cm. Contents.v. 2. Preface to happiness. includes bibliographies. [BX1749.T6S62] 50-35716
1. Thomas Aquinas, Saint, 1225?-1274. Summa theologica. I. Ryan, Louis A., 1913- joint author. II. Title.

SYNAVE, Paul 230.2
Prophecy and inspiration; a commentary on the Summa theologica II-II, questions 171-178, by Paul Synave and Pierre Benoit. Tr. [from French] by Avery R. Dulles and Thomas L. Sheridan. New York, Desclee Co., 1961. 185p. Bibl. 60-10164 3.75
1. Thomas Aquinas, Saint, 1225?-1274. Summa theologica. 2. Bible—Inspiration. 3. Prophets. I. Benoit, Pierre, 1906- II. Title.

Thomas Aquinas, Saint, 1225?-1274—Theology.

BURRELL, David B. 231'.042
Aquinas : God and action / David B. Burrell. Notre Dame, Ind. : University of Notre Dame Press, 1978. p. cm. Includes bibliographical references. [BT100.T4B87 1978] 78-51519 ISBN 0-268-00588-5 : 11.95
1. Thomas Aquinas, Saint, 1225?-1274—Theology. 2. God—Proof—History of doctrines. I. Title.

FAIRWEATHER, Alan M. 231'.74
The word as truth : a critical examination of the Christian doctrine of revelation in the writings of Thomas Aquinas and Karl Barth / by A. M. Fairweather. Westport, Conn. : Greenwood Press, 1979. xvi, 147 p. ; 24 cm. Reprint of the 1944 ed. published by Lutterworth Press, London, which was issued as v. 18 of the Lutterworth library. Includes bibliographical references. [BT127.F3 1979] 78-26040 ISBN 0-313-20808-5 lib. bdg. : 15.00
1. Thomas Aquinas, Saint, 1225?-1274—Theology. 2. Barth, Karl, 1886-1968. 3. Revelation—History of doctrines. I. Title.

GILSON, Etienne Henry, 1884- 189'.4
Elements of Christian philosophy / Etienne Gilson. Westport, Conn. : Greenwood Press, 1978, c1960. 358 p. ; 24 cm. Reprint of the ed. published by Doubleday, Garden City, N.Y. Includes indexes. Bibliography: p. 339-343. [BX1749.G54 1978] 78-10231 ISBN 0-313-20734-8 lib.bdg. : lib. bdg. :
1. Thomas Aquinas, Saint, 1225?-1274—Theology. I. Title.

GORNALL, Thomas 211
A philosophy of God. the elements of Thomist natural theology New York, Sheed [1963, c.1962] 250p. 20cm. Bibl. 63-17140 3.95
1. Thomas Aquinas, Saint—Theology. 2. Natural theology. I. Title.

KENNY, Anthony John Patrick. 231'.0924
The five ways; St. Thomas Aquinas' proofs of God's existence. New York, Schocken Books [1969] 131 p. 23 cm. (Studies in ethics and the philosophy of religion) Bibliography: p. [123]-126. [BT98.K4 1969b] 79-77606 4.95
1. Thomas, Aquinas, Saint, 1225?-1274—Theology. 2. God—Proof. I. Title.

KENNY, Anthony John Patrick. 231'.042
The five ways : St. Thomas Aquinas' proofs of God's existence / Anthony Kenny. Notre Dame, Ind. : University of Notre Dame Press, 1980, c1969. 131 p. ; 21 cm. Reprint of the ed. published by Schocken Books, New York, in series: Studies in ethics and the philosophy of religion. Includes index. Bibliography: p. [123]-126. [BT100.T4K46 1980] 80-10416 ISBN 0-268-00952-X : 10.95
1. Thomas Aquinas, Saint, 1225?-1274—Theology. 2. God—Proof. I. Title.

MOHLER, James A. 234'.2'0924
The beginning of eternal life; the dynamic faith of Thomas Aquinas; origins and interpretation [by] James A. Mohler. New York, Philosophical Lib. [1968] 144p. 22cm. Bibl. [BT771.2.M59] 67-27267 4.95
1. Thomas Aquinas. Saint, 1225?-1274—Theology. 2. Faith—History of doctrines. I. Title.

PATTERSON, Robert Leet. 231'.042
The conception of God in the philosophy of Aquinas / by Robert Leet Patterson. Merrick, N.Y. : Richwood Pub. Co., [1976,i.e.1977] 508 p. ; 23 cm. Reprint of the 1933 ed. published by Allen & Unwin, London. Includes index. Bibliography: p. [493] [BT100.T4P3 1976] 76-49005 ISBN 0-915172-27-5 : 25.00
1. Thomas Aquinas, Saint, 1225?-1274—Theology. 2. God—History of doctrines. I. Title.

PERSSON, Per Erik, 1923- 230.20924
Sacra doctrina; reason and revelation in Aquinas. Translated by Ross Mackenzie. Philadelphia, Fortress Press [1970] xii, 317 p. 23 cm. Bibliography: p. 299-312. [BT126.5.P47 1970] 69-12992 9.75
1. Thomas Aquinas, Saint, 1225?-1274—Theology. 2. Revelation—History of doctrines. 3. Reason. I. Title.

PESCH, Otto Hermann. 231'.09
The God question in Thomas Aquinas and Martin Luther. Translated by Gottfried G. Krodel. Philadelphia, Fortress Press [1972] ix, 38 p. (p. 36-38 advertisement) 20 cm. (Facet books. Historical series (Reformation) 21) First published in Luther, Zeitschrift der Luther-Gesellschaft, v. 41 (1970) Bibliography: p. 34-35. [BT98.P48] 77-171508 ISBN 0-8006-3069-6 1.00
1. Thomas Aquinas, Saint, 1225?-1274—Theology. 2. Luther, Martin, 1483-1546—Theology. 3. God—History of doctrines. I. Title.

PRELLER, Victor. 201'.4
Divine science and the science of God; a reformulation of Thomas Aquinas. Princeton, N.J., Princeton University Press, 1967. ix, 281 p. 23 cm. "Original version ... was submitted as a doctoral dissertation to the Department of Religion at Princeton University." Bibliography: p. 273-278. [BX1749.T7P7] 66-21838
1. Thomas Aquinas, Saint, 1225?-1274—Theology. 2. Religion and language. I. Title.

PRELLER, Victor. 201'.4
Divine science and the science of God; a reformulation of Thomas Aquinas. Princeton, N.J., Princeton University Press, 1967. ix, 281 p. 23 cm. "Original version ... was submitted as a doctoral dissertation to the Department of Religion at Princeton University." Bibliography: p. 273-278. [BX1749.T7P7] 66-21838
1. Thomas Aquinas, Saint, 1225?-1274—Theology. 2. Religion and language. I. Title.

Thomas Aquinas, Saint, 1225?-1274—Theology—Congresses.

CELEBRATING the medieval heritage : a colloquy on the thought of Aquinas and Bonaventure / edited by David Tracy. Chicago : University of Chicago, 1978. ix, 239 p. ; 23 cm. "The Journal of religion, volume 58, supplement, 1978." Includes bibliographical references and index. [BX4700.T6C44] 78-113803 pbk. : 8.00 230'.2'0922
1. Thomas Aquinas, Saint, 1225?-1274—Theology—Congresses. 2. Thomas Aquinas, Saint, 1225?-1274—Philosophy—Congresses. 3. Bonaventura, Saint, Cardinal, 1221-1274—Congresses. I. Tracy, David. II. The Journal of religion.

Thomas, B. J.

THOMAS, B. J. 248'.0924
In tune : finding how good life can be / B.J. Thomas & Gloria Thomas. Old Tappan, N.J. : F.H. Revell Co., c1983. 188 p., [8] leaves of plates : ill. ; 24 cm. [BV4935.T45A34 1983] 19 82-13327 ISBN 0-8007-1325-7 : 10.95
1. Thomas, B. J. 2. Thomas, Gloria, 1949- 3. Converts—United States—Biography. 4. Singers—United States—Biography. I. Thomas, Gloria, 1949- II. Title.

Thomas, Daniel, 1778-1847. A letter written in February, 1815.

NORTON, Jacob, 1764-1858. 231
Things as they are; or, Trinitarianism developed. Second part. In reply to "A letter written in February, 1815, to the Rev. Jacob Norton, of Weymouth, and now published with an appendix, containing some notes and remarks, by Daniel Thomas, A. M., pastor of the Second church in Abington; together with a few incidental remarks on several passages of a sermon preached at the installation of the Rev. Holland Weeks, over the First church and society in Abington, the ninth of August, 1815. By Nathaniel Emmons, D. D., pastor of the church in Franklin". By Jacob Norton, A. M., pastor of the First religious society in Weymouth ... Boston: Printed for the author, by Lincoln & Edmands, no. 53, Cornhill, 1815. 112 p. 23 cm. "Serious and solemn address to Christian churches ... on the subject of the Presbyterian mode of church government and discipline": p. [101]-112. [BT111.N6] 41-33060
1. Thomas, Daniel, 1778-1847. A letter written in February, 1815. 2. Emmons, Nathanael, 1745-1840. 3. Trinity. 4. Presbyterianism. I. Title.

Thomas, David Winton, 1901- —Bibliography.

WORDS and meanings: 221.4'4
essays presented to David Winton Thomas on his retirement from the Regius Professorship of Hebrew in the University of Cambridge, 1968; edited by Peter R. Ackroyd and Barnabas Lindars. London, Cambridge U.P., 1968. xiii, 240 p. plate, port. 23 cm. "Bibliography of the writings of David Winton Thomas compiled by Anthony Phillips": p. 217-228. [BS1192.W63] 68-29649 ISBN 0-521-07270-0 45/-
1. Thomas, David Winton, 1901- —Bibliography. 2. Bible, O.T.—Criticism, interpretation, etc.—Addresses, essays, lectures. I. Thomas, David Winton, 1901- II. Ackroyd, Peter R., ed. III. Lindars, Barnabas, ed.

Thomas, Joshua, 1776-1858.

WALLACE, Adam, 1825-1903 922.773
The parson of the islands; a biography of the Rev. Joshua Thomas; embracing sketches of his contemporaries, and remarkable camp meeting scenes, revival incidents, and reminiscences of the introduction of Methodism on the islands of the Chesapeake, and the Eastern Shores of Maryland and Virginia. Introd. by James A. Massey. Cambridge, Md., Tidewater Pubs. [dist Cornell Maritime] 1961. 312p. illus. Facsimile reprint of the Philadelphia ed. of 1861. 61-17566 3.95
1. Thomas, Joshua, 1776-1853. I. Title.

WALLACE, Adam, 1825-1903. 922.773
The parson of the islands; a biography of the Rev. Joshua Thomas; embracing sketches of his contemporaries, and remarkable camp meeting scenes, revival incidents, and reminiscences of the introduction of Methodism on the islands of the Chesapeake, and the eastern shores of Maryland and Virginia. By Adam Wallace... With an introduction by the Rev. James A. Massey. Philadelphia, The author, 1861. 412 p. front. (port.) plates. 19 1/2 cm. [BX8495.T57W3] 37-7017
1. Thomas, Joshua, 1776-1858. I. Title.

Thomas, Mrs. Mary Whitall, 1836-1888.

THOUGHTS memorial of Mary 920.
Whitall Thomas, born 1836, died 1888. Arranged by E. T. G. and A. B. T. and published by direction of Woman's Christian temperance union of Maryland. Baltimore, D. W. Glass & co., 1888. 82 p. 18 1/2 cm. [HV5232.T5T5] 10-22053
1. Thomas, Mrs. Mary Whitall, 1836-1888. I. G. E. T., comp. II. T. A. B. joint comp. III. Woman's Christian temperance union. Maryland.

Thomas, Norman Mattoon, 1884-1968.

SWANBERG, W. A., 1907- 329'.81'00924 B
Norman Thomas, the last idealist / W. A. Swanberg. New York : Scribner, c1976. xii, 528 p., [17] leaves of plates : ill. ; 23 cm. Includes bibliographical references and index. [HX84.T47S9] 76-15591 ISBN 0-684-14768-8 : 15.00
1. Thomas, Norman Mattoon, 1884-1968. I. Title.

Thomas Road Baptist Church.

TOWNS, Elmer L. 286'.1755'671
Capturing a town for Christ [by] Elmer Towns. Old Tappan, N.J., Revell [1973] 191 p. illus. 21 cm. At head of title: Jerry Falwell. Includes 6 sermons by T. Falwell and a message by the author (p. 111-191) [BX6480.L94T488] 73-1869 ISBN 0-8007-0598-X 5.95
1. Thomas Road Baptist Church. 2. Evangelistic work—Lynchburg, Va. I. Falwell, Jerry. II. Title.
Pbk. 2.95

Thomas, Tay.

†THOMAS, Tay. 283'.092'4 B
My war with worry / Tay Thomas. [Lincoln, Va.] : Chosen Books ; Waco Tex. : distributed by Word Books, c1977. 154 p. : ill. ; 23 cm. [BX5995.T4A33] 77-80669 6.95
1. Thomas, Tay. 2. Episcopalians—Biography. 3. Anchorage, Alaska—Earthquake, 1964—Personal narratives. 4. Pentecostalism. I. Title.

Thomason, Thomas Truebody, 1774-1829.

SARGENT, John, 1780-1833. 922.
The life of the Rev. T. T. Thomason ... By the Rev. J. Sargent ... New-York, D. Appleton & co., 1833. xi, [13]-356 p. 19 1/2 x 11 1/2 cm. [BV3269.T55S3] 1-11047
1. Thomason, Thomas Truebody, 1774-1829. 2. Missions—India. I. Title.

Thomasville, Ga. St. Thomas Episcopal Church—History

BALFOUR, Robert C. 283'.758'98
The history of St. Thomas Episcopal Church, by R. C. Balfour, Jr. Tallahassee, Printed by Rose Print Co. [1968] 229 p. illus., ports. 24 cm. [BX5980.T4S3] 68-4292
1. Thomasville, Ga. St. Thomas Episcopal Church—Hist. I. Title.

Thompson, Anna Young, 1851-1932.

KINNEAR, Elizabeth Kelsey. 266.5'1'0924 B
She sat where they sat; a memoir of Anna Young Thompson of Egypt. Grand Rapids, Eerdmans [1971] 112 p. port. 20 cm. (Christian world mission books) [BV3572.T87K55] 76-147363 2.45
1. Thompson, Anna Young, 1851-1932. I. Title.

Thompson, Betty.

THOMPSON, Betty. 262'.7
A chance to change : women and men in the church / by Betty Thompson. 1st Fortress Press ed. Philadelphia, Pa. : Fortress Press ; Geneva, Switzerland : World Council of Churches, 1982. p. cm. Bibliography: p. [BT701.2.T484 1982] 19 82-71832 ISBN 0-8006-1645-6 pbk. : 4.95
1. Thompson, Betty. 2. Man (Theology) I. Title.

Thompson, Carroll J., 1912-

THOMPSON, Carroll J., 1912- 615.8'52
The miracle of holistic healing / by Carroll J. Thompson. Port Washington, N.Y. : Ashley Books, 1982. p. cm. [BT732.5.T48] 19 81-17589 ISBN 0-87949-203-1 : 12.95
1. Thompson, Carroll J., 1912- 2. Spiritual healing. 3. Holistic medicine. 4. Healers—Illinois—Biography. 5. Illinois—Biography. I. Title.

Thompson, Helen.

THOMPSON, Helen. 248.4'82
Journey toward wholeness : a Jungian model of adult spiritual growth / Helen Thompson. New York : Paulist Press, c1982. ix, 108 p. : ill. ; 21 cm. Bibliography: p. 107-108. [BX2350.2.T498] 19 81-83184 ISBN 0-8091-2422-X (pbk.) : 3.95
1. Thompson, Helen. 2. Spiritual life—Catholic authors. I. Title.

Thompson, Mrs. Elizabeth (Butler) 1809-1876.

[SPRING, Elizabeth (Thompson) Mrs. 922.573
Memorial of Eliza Butler Thompson. By

her daughter. New York, A. D. F. Randolph & co. [1879] 172 p. 19 1/2 cm. [BR1725.T47S6] 38-8157
1. Thompson, Mrs. Elizabeth (Butler) 1809-1876. I. Title.

Thompson, Murray Stewart, 1923-

THOMPSON, Murray Stewart, 1923- 253.5
Grace and forgiveness in ministry / Murray Stewart Thompson. Nashville : Abingdon, c1981. 174 p. ; 20 cm. Includes bibliographical references. [BV4011.T44] 19 80-23613 ISBN 0-687-15680-7 pbk. : 6.95
1. Thompson, Murray Stewart, 1923- 2. Pastoral theology. 3. Pastoral counseling. I. Title.

Thompson, Richard Wigginton, 1809-1900. The papacy and the civil power.

WENINGER, Franz Xaver, 1805-1888. 239
Reply to Hon. R. W. Thompson, secretary of the navy, addressed to the American people, by F. X. Weninger ... New York, P. O'Shea, 1877. 1 p. l., 86 p. 23 cm. [BX955.T52W4] 45-50767
1. Thompson, Richard Wigginton, 1809-1900. The papacy and the civil power. 2. Catholic church—Doctrinal and controversial works—Catholic authors. 3. Popes—Infallibility. I. Title.

Thomson, Edward, 1810-1870.

THOMSON, Edward, 1848-1870.
Life of Edward Thomson, D.D., LL.D., late a bishop of the Methodist Episcopal church. By his son, Rev. Edward Thomson, M.A. Cincinnati, Cranston & Stowe; New York, Phillips & Hunt, 1885. 336 p. front. (port.) 19 1/2 cm. 12-39517
1. Thomson, Edward, 1810-1870. I. Title.

Thornwell, James Henley, 1812-1862.

PALMER, Benjamin Morgan, 1818-1902. 285'.1'0924 B
The life and letters of James Henley Thornwell. New York, Arno Press, 1969. xi, 614 p. port. 23 cm. (Religion in America) Reprint of the 1875 ed. [BX9225.T64P3 1969] 78-83432
1. Thornwell, James Henley, 1812-1862. I. Thornwell, James Henley, 1812-1862. II. Title.

PALMER, Benjamin Morgan, 1818-1902. 922.578
The life and letters of James Henley Thornwell... ex-president of the South Carolina college, late professor of theology in the Theological seminary at Columbia, South Carolina. By B. M. Palmer... Richmond, Whittet & Shepperson, 1875. xi p., 1 l., 614 p. front. (port.) 23 cm. "Critical notice...Our danger and our duty...The state of the country" (Papers by Thornwell): p. 573-610. [LD5032.7 1852] [BX9225.T64P3] E 15
1. Thornwell, James Henley, 1812-1862. I. Title.

THORNWELL, James Henley, 1812-1862. 208.
The collected writings of James Henley Thornwell ... Ed. by John B. Adger ... Richmond, Presbyterian committee of publication; New York, Robert Cart & bros.; [etc., etc.] 1871. 2 v. front. 23 cm. Contents.--I. Theological.--II. Theological and ethical. [BX8915.T5] 22-21908
I. Adger, John Bailey, 1810-1899, ed. II. Title.

Thorp, Eli, 1816-1836.

[CHIPMAN, Richard Manning] 1806-1893. 922
Memoir of Eli Thorp. Written for the Massachusetts Sabbath school society, and revised by the Committee of publication. Boston, Massachusetts Sabbath school society, 1842. vi, [7]-162 p. 15 1/2 cm. Introduction signed: R.M.C. [i.e. Richard Manning Chipman] [BR1725.T5C5] 38-7124
1. Thorp, Eli, 1816-1836. I. Massachusetts Sabbath school society. Committee of publication. II. Title.

Thorwall, Axel Johnson, 1890-1960.

THORWALL, LaReau. 289.9'0924 B
And light new fires; the story of Axel Johnson Thorwall, an immigrant blacksmith who exchanged his forge for a frock coat, by LaReau Thorwall as told to Mel Larson. Foreword by John B. Anderson. Minneapolis, Free Church Publications [1969] 186 p. illus. 22 cm. [BX7548.Z8T48] 70-103414 4.95
1. Thorwall, Axel Johnson, 1890-1960. I. Larson, Melvin Gunnard, 1916- II. Title.

Thoth.

BOYLAN, Patrick. 299.
Thoth, the Hermes of Egypt; a study of some aspects of theological thought in ancient Egypt, by Patrick Boylan ... London, New York [etc.] H. Milford, Oxford university press, 1922. vii, [1], 215 p. 26 cm. Printed in Austria. [BL2450.T5B6] 22-17635
1. Thoth. I. Title.

Thought-transference.

EHRENWALD, Jan, 1900- 133.8'2
New dimensions of deep analysis / Jan Ehrenwald. New York : Arno Press, 1975. p. cm. (Perspectives in psychical research) Reprint of the ed. published by Grune & Stratton, New York, without date but probably published in 1955. [BF1171.E39 1975] 75-7377 ISBN 0-405-07027-6 : 18.00
1. Thought-transference. I. Title. II. Series.

FEYRER, Ernest Charles, 1877- 133
The call of the soul; a scientific explanation of telepathy and psychic phenomena, with specific instructions for developing thought-transference, psychometry, mind-reading, automatic writing, mental broadcasting and other psychic phenomena, by Dr. Ernest C. Feyrer... San Francisco, Cal., The Autoscience institute [c1926] 3 p. l., [11]-256, [1] p. illus. (ports.) 21 cm. [BF1171.F4] 26-10878
1. Thought-transference. 2. Psychical research. I. Title.

GARRETT, Eileen Jeanette (Lyttle) Mrs. 1893- 133.82
Telepathy; in search of a lost faculty [by] Eileen J. Garrett, with introduction by Eugene Rollin Corson ... New York, Creative age press, inc., 1941. xxx, 210 p. 21 cm. "A selected bibliography": p. [207]-210. [BF1171.G25] [159.96162] 41-19163
1. Thought-transference. I. Title.

HETTINGER, John, 1880- 133.82
Telepathy and spiritualism; personal experiments, experiences, and views. London, New York, Rider [1952] 150 p. illus. 22 cm. [BF1171.H4 1952] 52-3491
1. Thought-transference. 2. Spiritualism. I. Title.

WELTMER, Sidney Abram, 1858- 133
Telepathy and thought-transference. By Prof. S. A. Weltmer ... [Nevada? Mo.] 1902. [BF1171.W46] 2-19744
I. Title.

Three Oaks, Mich. Congregational church.

KUHNS, Frederick Irving, 1903- 285.8774
The Congregational church of Three Oaks, 1844-1944, by Rev. Frederick Kuhns and Frederic Chamberlain. Three Oaks, Mich., The Edward K. Warren foundation, 1944. xiii, 200 p. illus. (incl. ports.) 21 1/2 cm. Bibliographical references included in "Notes" (p. 174-195) [BX7255.T5K8] 44-9803
1. Three Oaks, Mich. Congregational church. I. Chamberlain, Frederic W., joint author. II. Edward K. Warren foundation, Three Oaks, Mich. III. Title.

Threefold refuge—Addresses, essays, lectures.

THE Threefold refuge in the Theravada Buddhist tradition / by John Ross Carter, editor ... [et al.]. Chambersburg, Pa. : Anima Publications, 1982. p. cm. Includes index. Bibliography: p. [BQ4350.T47 1982] 19 82-16467 ISBN 0-89012-030-7 : write for information. 294.3'42
1. Threefold refuge—Addresses, essays, lectures. 2. Theravada Buddhism—Addresses, essays, lectures. I. Carter, John Ross.
Contents omitted.

Throgmorton, William Pinckney, 1849-

HODGE, Clarence. 920.
W. P. Throgmorton, D.D., a biograph, by Clarence Hodge ... Marion, Ill., Egyptian press printing co., [c1917] 3 p. l., 5-244 p. front., plates, ports. 20 1/2 cm. [BX6495.T5H7] 17-20854
1. Throgmorton, William Pinckney, 1849- I. Title.

Thrower, Bob, 1927-

THROWER, Bob, 1927- 269'.2'0924 B
About face; the story of why Bob Thrower changed churches, as told to Don Christman. Washington, Review and Herald Pub. Association [1972] 128 p. illus. 21 cm. (Discovery paperbacks) [BX6189.T48A3] 72-77021
1. Thrower, Bob, 1927- I. Christman, Don R. II. Title.

The Thunder—Congresses.

CENTER for Hermeneutical Studies in Hellenistic and Modern Culture. 273'.1
The Thunder = perfect mind (Nag Hammadi Codex VI, tractate 2) : protocol of the fifth colloquy, 11 March 1973 / The Center for Hermeneutical Studies in Hellenistic and Modern Culture ; George W. MacRae. Berkeley, CA : The Center, c1975. p. cm. (Protocol series of the colloquies of the Center for Hermeneutical Studies in Hellenistic and Modern Culture ; no. 5) Includes English translation of The Thunder and bibliographical references. [BT1390.C36 1975] 75-44028 ISBN 0-89242-004-9 : 2.00
1. The Thunder—Congresses. 2. Gnosticism—Congresses. I. MacRae, George W. II. The Thunder. English. 1975. III. Title. IV. Series: Center for Hermeneutical Studies in Hellenistic and Modern Culture. Protocol series of the colloquies ; no. 5.

Thurber, Charles S., 1864-

BLAISDELL, Ethel F. 922.773
And God caught an eel. New York, Coward-McCann [1954] 242 p. illus. 21 cm. [BV2678.T5B6] 54-10140
1. Thurber, Charles S., 1864- I. Title.

Thurman, Howard, 1899-

THURMAN, Howard, 1899- 280'.4 B
With head and heart ; the autobioraphy of Howard Thurman. 1st ed. New York : Harcourt Brace Jovanovich, c1979. p. cm. Includes index. [BX6495.T53A38] 79-1848 ISBN 0-15-142164-1 : 10.00
1. Thurman, Howard, 1899- 2. Baptists—Clergy—Biography. 3. Clergy—United States—Biography. I. Title.

Thurstan, Abp. of York, 1070 (ca.)-1140.

NICHOLL, Donald, 1923- 270.4
Thurstan, Archibishop of York, 1114-1140. York, Stonegate Pr., 1964. xi, 277p. 23cm. Bibl. [BR754.T57N5] 66-6700 7.00
1. Thurstan, Abp. of York, 1070 (ca.)-1140. I. Title.
American distributor: Dufour in Chester Springs, Pa.

Thurston. Herbert, 1856-1939.

CREHAN, Joseph. 922.242
Father Thurston; a memoir, with a bibliography of his writings. London, New York, Sheed and Ward [1952] 235 p. illus. 21 cm. [BX4705.T652C7] 52-3072
1. Thurston. Herbert, 1856-1939. I. Title.

Thurston, John Lawrence, 1874-1904.

WRIGHT, Henry Burt, 1877-1923. 922.
A life with a purpose; a memorial of John Lawrence Thurston, first missionary of the Yale mission, by Henry B. Wright ... New York, Chicago [etc.] Fleming H. Revell company [c1908] 317 p. front., plates, ports. 21 cm. [BV3427.T5W8] 8-10897
1. Thurston, John Lawrence, 1874-1904. I. Title.

Thurston, Lucy Goodale, 1823-1891.

THE missionary's daughter: a memoir of Lucy Goodale Thurston, of the Sandwich islands... New York, Pub. by the American tract society [c1842] 219 p. 15 1/2 cm. (On cover: Youth's library. 29) [BV3680.H4T4 1842] [BV3680.H454 1842a] 922 7-28579 922
1. Thurston, Lucy Goodale, 1823-1891.

Thwing, Carrie Frances (Butler) 1855-1898.

CARRIE F. Butler Thwing; an appreciation by friends, together with extracts from her "Journal of a tour in Europe." Cleveland, O., The Helman-Taylor co., 1899. vii, 194 p. front. (port.) 19 1/2 cm. [BX7260.T56C3] 99-3217 920.
1. Thwing, Carrie Frances (Butler) 1855-1898.

Thwing, Mrs. Grace Welch (Barnes) 1789-1865.

THWING, Edward Payson, 1830-1893. 920.7
Memorial of Mrs. Grace W. Thwing, by her son, Rev. Edward P. Thwing. Boston, 1865. 9 (i.e. 19), [1] p. 19 1/2 cm. Page 19 incorrectly numbered 9. [BX7260.T57T5] 36-23982
1. Thwing, Mrs. Grace Welch (Barnes) 1789-1865. I. Title.

Tiara, Papal.

HALL, Kathryn Evangeline, 1924- 247.7
The papal tiara. [Palm Beach? Fla.] '1952. 74 l. 34 plates. 28 cm. Bibliography: leaves [66]-74. [CR4480.H25] 52-40960
1. Tiara, Papal. I. Title.

Tibet.

BULL, Geoffrey T., 1921- 266.65
Forbidden land; a saga of Tibet, by Geoffrey T. Bull. Chicago, Moody Press [1967, c1966] 124 p. map. 20 cm. [DS786.B8] 67-2343
1. Tibet. I. Title.

NGAWANG Lobsang Yishey Tenzing Gyatso, Dalai Lama, 1935- 951.5
My land and my people, by His Holiness, the Dalai Lama of Tibet. New York, McGraw-Hill [1962] 271 p. illus. 22 cm. [BL1489.N44A3] 62-13808
I. Title.

Tibet—History—1951-

CHOGYAM Trungpa, Trungpa Tulku, 1939- 951.5
Born in Tibet, by Chogyam Trungpa, the eleventh Trungpa Tulku, as told to Esme Cramer Roberts. With a foreword by Marco Pallis. [1st American ed.] New York, Harcourt, Brace & World [1968, c1966] 264 p. illus., maps, ports. 23 cm. "A Helen and Kurt Wolff book." [BL1490] 68-11078
1. Tibet—History—1951- 2. Surmang (Monasteries) I. Roberts, Esme Cramer. II. Title.

Tibet—Religion.

BELL, Charles Alfred, Sir 294.32
1870-
The religion of Tibet, by Sir Charles Bell ... Oxford, The Clarendon press, 1931. xv, [1] , 235, [1] p. col. front., plates, ports., 3 maps (2 fold.) 2 facsim. on 1 pl. 23 cm. "Sources": p. [193]-218. [BL1485.B4] 32-12685
1. Tibet—Religion. 2. Lamaism. 3. Tibet. I. Title.

GZI brjid. English. 299'.54
Selections.
The nine ways of bon : excerpts from gZi-brjid / edited and translated by David L. Snellgrove. Boulder, Colo. : Prajna Press, 1978, c1967. p. cm. Reprint of the ed. published by Oxford University Press, London, New York, which was issued as v. 18 of London oriental series. Includes bibliographical references. [BL1943.B6G9213 1978] 78-13010 ISBN 0-87773-739-8 pbk. : 10.00
I. Snellgrove, David L. II. Title. III. Series: London oriental series ; v. 18.

LOBSANG Rampa, pseud. 922.94
pseud.
Doctor from Lhasa. [1st U. S. ed] Clarksburg, W. Va, Saucerian Books [c1959] 239p. illus. 23cm. 'Continuation of ... [The author's] autobiography [The third eye]' [BL1490.L6A32 1959a] 60-8079
I. Title.

LOBSANG Rampa, pseud. 922.94
pseud.
The third eye; the autobiography of a Tibetan lama. Illustrated by Tessa Theobald. Garden City, N. Y., Doubleday [c1958] 256p. illus. 22cm. [BL1490.L6A3 1958] 58-11100
I. Title.

LOBSANG, Rampa T., pseud. 922.94
The third eye; the autobiography of a Tibetan lama. Illus. by Tessa Theobald. New York, Ballantine [1964 c.1956, 1958] 221p. illus. 21cm. (U5026) .60 pap.,
I. Title.

LOBSANG Rampa, Tuesday
The third eye; the autobiography of a Tibetan lama. Illustrated by Tessa Theobald. New York, Ballantine Books [1964, c1958] 221 p. illus. 18 cm. 68-259
I. Title.

LOBSANG Rampa, Tuesday FIC
The third eye; the autobiography of a Tibetan lama. Illustrated by Tessa Theobald. [1st ed.] Garden City, N.Y., Doubleday, 1957 [c1956] 256 p. illus. 22 cm. [PZ4.L797Th2] 922.94 57-6296
I. Title.

NEBESKY- 294.3'4'21109515
WOJKOWITZ, Rene de
Oracles and demons of Tibet : the cult and iconography of the Tibetan protective deities / by Rene de Nebesky-Wojkowitz. New York : Gordon Press, 1976, c1956. p. cm. English or Tibetan. Reprint of the ed. published by Mouton, 's-Gravenhage. "Tibetan sources": p. "Tibetan texts": p. [BL1945.T5N4 1976] 76-19106 ISBN 0-87968-463-1 lib.bdg. : 75.00
1. Tibet—Religion. 2. Gods, Lamaist. 3. Bon (Tibetan religion) I. Title.

SIERKSMA, Fokke, 1917- 294.3'923
Tibet's terrifying deities; sex and aggression in religious acculturation [by] F. Sierksma. [Translated from the Dutch by Mrs. G. E. van Baaren-Pape] Rutland, Vt., G. E. Tuttle Co., [1966] 283 p. illus. (part col.) 27 cm. Bibliographical references included in "Notes" (p. 237-266) [BL1945.T5S53 1966a] 67-1211
1. Tibet—Religion. 2. Demonology, Lamaist. 3. Gods, Lamaist. 4. Art, Tibetan. 5. Demonology, Tibetan. I. Title.

TUCCI, Giuseppe, 1894- 294.3'923
The religions of Tibet / Giuseppe Tucci ; translated from the German and Italian by Geoffrey Samuel. Berkeley : University of California Press, c1980. xii, 340 p., [2] leaves of plates : ill. ; 23 cm. A translation of the author's Die Religionen Tibets, published in 1970 in Tucci & Heissig's Die Religionen Tibets und der Mongolei; with additions and changes made for the 1976 Italian ed. and this ed. [BL1945.T5T815] 80-110768 ISBN 0-520-03856-8 : 19.95
1. Tibet—Religion. I. Title.

Tibet—Social life and customs

LEARNER, Frank Doggett. 275.15
Rusty hinges; a story of closed doors beginning to open in north-east Tibet, by Frank Doggett Learner ... London, Philadelphia [etc.] The China inland mission, 1933. xi, 13-157 p. front., plates, ports. 19 cm. [BV3420.T5L4] 266 35-2801
1. Tibet—Soc. life & cust. 2. Missions—Tibet. I. Title.

Tibetan literature.

**THE Tibetan Book of* 294.3809515
the Dead; the great liberation through hearing in the Bardo, by Guru Rinpoche according to Karma Lingpa; a new translation from the Tibetan with commentary by Francesca Fremantle and Chogyam Trungpa. Berkeley, London, Shambhala, 1975 xx, 119 p. 23 cm. (Clear light series) Includes index. Bibliography: p. 111-112. [BL1411.B3] 74-29615 12.50.
1. Tibetan literature. 2. Buddhist literature. Pbk. 3.95; ISBN: 0-87773-74-1 Distributed by Random House.

Ticknor, Franics Orray, 1822-1874.

MORRIS, Scott.
Confederate poets, physician and priest; Francis Orray Ticknor, Abram Joseph Ryan. Macon, Ga., Printed by Southern Press [1963] 51 p. 18 cm. "The two biographical sketches ... are parts of a larger number of sketches of Georgia writers prepared by the author in partial fulfillment of the Master of Education degree at the University of Georgia." With "selected poems" of Ticknor and Ryan. Includes bibliography. [PS3062.T8M6] 63-4516
1. Ticknor, Franics Orray, 1822-1874. 2. Ryan, Abram Joseph, 1839-1886. 3. U.S. — Hist. — Civil War — Poetry — Confederate. I. Title.

Tidwell, Josiah Blake, 1870-1946.

BAKER, Robert A. 922.673
J. B. Tidwell plus God, by Robert A. Baker ... Nashville, Tenn., Broadman press [1946] x, 111 p. 2 port. (incl. front.) 21 1/2 cm. [BX6495.T555B3] 46-2454
1. Tidwell, Josiah Blake, 1870- I. Title.

BAKER, Robert Andrew. 922.673
J. B. Tidwell plus God. Nashville, Broadman Press [1946] x. iii p. ports. 22 cm. [BX6495.T555B3] 46-2454
1. Tidwell, Josiah Blake, 1870-1946. I. Title.

Tierney, Richard Henry, 1870-1928.

TALBOT, Francis Xavier, 922.273
1889-
Richard Henry Tierney, priest of the Society of Jesus, by Francis X. Talbot ... New York, The America press, 1930. 4 p. l., 200 p. front. (port.) 19 1/2 cm. [BX4705.T655T3] 30-30118
1. Tierney, Richard Henry, 1870-1928. 2. America, a Catholic review of the week. I. Title.

Tikhon Zadonskii, Saint, Bp. of Voronezh, 1724-1783.

GORODETZKY, 281.9'092'4 B
Nadejda, 1904-
Saint Tikhon of Zadonsk, inspirer of Dostoevsky / by Nadejda Gorodetzky. Rev. ed. Crestwood, NY : St. Vladimir's Seminary Press, 1977. 318 p. ; 22 cm. Includes index. Bibliography: p. 275-295. [BX597.T53G67 1976] 76-49919 ISBN 0-913836-32-X pbk. : 6.95
1. Tikhon Zadonskii, Saint, Bp. of Voronezh, 1724-1783. 2. Christian saints—Russia—Biography. I. Title.

Tikopians.

FIRTH, Raymond William, 209'.93'5
1901-
Rank and religion in Tikopia; a study in Polynesian paganism and conversion to Christianity, by Raymond Firth. Boston, Beacon Press [1970] 424 p. illus., ports. 24 cm. Includes bibliographical references. [GN473.F47 1970b] 71-112710 10.00
1. Tikopians. 2. Rites and ceremonies—Polynesia. I. Title.

FIRTH, Raymond William, 299'.9
1901-
The work of the gods in Tikopia, by Raymond Firth. 2nd ed., with new introduction and epilogue. London, Athlone P.; New York, Humanities P., 1967. viii, 492 p. front., 8 plates, plans, diagrs. 22 1/2 cm. (Monographs on social anthropology, no 1-2) 57/6 (B67-11872) Bibliography: p. [485]-486. [GN473.F5 1967] 67-10515
1. Tikopians. 2. Rites and ceremonies — Polynesia. I. Title. II. Series.

Tilak, Narayan Vaman, 1862?-1919.

NEW lessons in love.
New York, Association press [1956?] 4v. in 1. 20cm. First published as World Christian books, nos. 9-12.
1. Tilak, Narayan Vaman, 1862?-1919. 2. Church history-Popular works. 3. Church. 4. Jesus Christ-Resurrection.

TILAK, Lakshmibai (Gokhale) 922
1873-1936.
From Brahma to Christ: the story of Narayan Waman Tilak and Lakshmibai his wife. New York, Association Press [1956] 93 p. 20 cm. (World Christian books) "The biographical material ... is drawn from [the author's] I follow after [a translation of Smrti citrem] ... The translations of poems of Narayan Waman Tilak ... are reproduced ... from a collection published under the title Bhakti Niranjana." [BV3269.T57A38 1956a] 56-6455
1. Tilak, Narayan Vaman, 1862?-1919. I. Title.

Tillett, John, 1812-1890.

PLYLER, A. W. 922.
The Iron duke of the Methodist itinerancy; an account of the life and labors of Reverend John Tillett of North Carolina. by A. W. Plyer ... Nashville, Tenn. Cokesbury press, 1925. 216 p. front. (port.) 20 cm. [BX8495.T63P6] 26-3366
1. Tillett, John, 1812-1890. I. Title.

Tillett, Wilbur Fisk, 1854-1936

COLLOMS, Lester Hubert, 922.773
1903-
Wilbur Fisk Tillett, Christian educator. Louisville, Ky., Cloister Press [1949] 234 p. port. 19 cm. A revision and rearrangement of the author's thesis, Duke University, 1942. Bibliography: p. 203-234. [BX8495.T64C6 1949] 50-362
1. Tillett, Wilbur Fisk, 1854-1936 I. Title.

Tillich, Paul, 1886-1965.

ADAMS, James Luther, 1901- 191
Paul Tillich's philosophy of culture, science, and religion. [1st ed.] New York, Harper & Row [1965] viii, 313 p. 22 cm. Revision of thesis, University of Chicago. Bibliography: p. [281]-303. [BX4827.T53A7 1965] 65-20446
1. Tillich, Paul, 1886-1965. I. Title.

ADAMS, James Luther, 1901- 200'.1
Paul Tillich's philosophy of culture, science, and religion / James Luther Adams. Washington, D.C. : University Press of America, c1982. viii, 310 p. ; 22 cm. Reprint. Originally published: New York : Harper & Row, 1965. Includes index. Bibliography: p. [280]-301. [BX4827.T53A7 1982] 19 81-43775 ISBN 0-8191-2221-1 : 21.75 ISBN 0-8191-2222-X (pbk) : 11.75
1. Tillich, Paul, 1886-1965. I. Title.

ANDERSON, James 230'.092'4 B
Francis, 1910-
Paul Tillich; basics in his thought [by] James F. Anderson. Albany, Magi Books [1972] x, 83 p. 20 cm. Includes bibliographical references. [BX4827.T53A75] 70-176127 ISBN 0-87343-040-9 4.95
1. Tillich, Paul, 1886-1965. I. Title.

ARMBRUSTER, Carl J., 230'.0924
1929-
The vision of Paul Tillich [by] Carl J. Armbruster. New York, Sheed and Ward [1967] xxii, 328 p. 22 cm. Includes bibliographical references. [BX4837.T53A8] 67-13774
1. Tillich, Paul, 1886-1965. I. Title.

BULMAN, Raymond F., 1933- 230
A blueprint for humanity : Paul Tillich's theology of culture / Raymond F. Bulman. Lewisburg : Bucknell University Press, c1981. 248 p. : port. ; 22 cm. Includes index. Bibliography: p. 225-236. [BR115.C8B84] 78-75208 ISBN 0-8387-5000-1 : 13.50
1. Tillich, Paul, 1886-1965. 2. Christianity and culture. I. Title.

CLAYTON, John Powell. 230'.044
The concept of correlation : Paul Tillich and the possibility of a mediating theology / by John Powell Clayton. Berlin ; New York : W. de Gruyter, 1980. p. cm. (Theologische Bibliothek Topelmann ; Bd. 37) Includes index. Bibliography: p. [BX4827.T53C56] 80-11208 ISBN 3-11007-914-3 : 51.25
1. Tillich, Paul, 1886-1965. 2. Theology—Methodology—History. I. Title.

FERRE, Nels Fredrick 230'.0924
Solomon, 1908-
Paul Tillich: retrospect and future. [Articles by] Nels F. S. Ferre [and others] Introd. by T. A. Kantonen. Nashville, Abingdon Press [1967, c1966] 63 p. 19 cm. "Reprinted from Religion in life, winter 1966." [BX4827.T53P3] 67-31858
1. Tillich, Paul, 1886-1965. I. Title. II. Title: Religion in life.

HAMILTON, Kenneth. 230
The system and the gospel; a critique of Paul Tillich. [1st American ed.] New York, Macmillan [1963] 247 p. 23 cm. (The Library of philosophy and theology) [BX4827.T53H3] 63-17633
1. Tillich, Paul, 1886- I. Title.

HAMILTON, Kenneth. 230'.0924
The system and the Gospel; a critique of Paul Tillich. Grand Rapids, Eerdmans [1967, c1963] 249 p. 21 cm. Bibliographical footnotes. [BX4827.T53H3 1967] 67-19318
1. Tillich, Paul, 1886-1965. I. Title.

HAMMOND, Guyton B., 1930- 230.4
The power of self-transcendence; an introduction to the philosophical theology of Paul Tillich, by Guyton B. Hammond. St. Louis, Bethany Press, 1966. 160 p. 20 cm. (The Library of contemporary theology) Bibliography: p. 148-155. [BX4827.T53H35] 66-19813
1. Tillich, Paul, 1886-1965. I. Title.

HOPPER, David. 230'.0924
Tillich; a theological portrait. [1st ed.] Philadelphia, Lippincott, 1968 [c1967] 189 p. 21 cm. [BX4827.T53H6] 68-10618
1. Tillich, Paul, 1886-1965.

THE Intellectual legacy 230'.0924
of Paul Tillich. Editor, James R. Lyons. Detroit, Wayne State University Press, 1969. 115 p. port. 22 cm. (Slaughter Foundation lectures, 1966) Contents.Contents.—Paul Johannes Tillich, biographical note, by J. R. Lyons.—The philosophical legacy of Paul Tillich, by J. H. Randall, Jr.—Paul Tillich as a contemporary theologian, by R. L. Shinn.—The psychiatric legacy of Paul Tillich, by E. A. Loomis.—Appendix, Tillich-to-Thomas Mann letter (23 May 1943) [BX4827.T53I5] 68-63714 3.95
1. Tillich, Paul, 1886-1965. I. Tillich, Paul, 1886-1965. II. Lyons, James R., ed. III. Title. IV. Series.

KEGLEY, Charles W. ed. 230.4
The theology of Paul Tillich, ed. by Charles W. Kegley, Robert W. Bretall. New York, Macmillan, 1961 [c.1952] xiv, 370p. (Library of living theology, v.1.) Bibl. 1.95 pap.,
1. Tillich, Paul, 1886- I. Bretall, Robert Walter, 1913- joint ed. II. Title.

KEGLEY, Charles W. ed. 230.4
The theology of Paul Tillich, edited by Charles W. Kegley & Robert W. Bretall.

New York, Macmillan, 1952. xvi, 370 p. port. 22 cm. (The Library of living theology, v. 1) "Bibliography of the writings of Paul Tillich to March, 1952": p. [351]-362. [BX4827.T53K4] 52-13200
1. Tillich, Paul, 1886- I. Betall, Robert Walter, 1913- joint editor.

KELSEY, David H. 230
The fabric of Paul Tillich's theology, by David H. Kelsey. New Haven, Yale University Press, 1967. x, 202 p. 21 cm. (Yale publications in religion, 13) Bibliographical footnotes. [BX4827.T53K43] 67-12994
1. Tillich, Paul, 1886-1965. I. Title. II. Series.

LEIBRECHT, Walter, ed. 230.04
Religion and culture; essays in honor of Paul Tillich. [1st ed.] New York, Harper [1959] xi, 399p. port. 25cm. Bibliographical references included in 'Notes' (p.355-363) 'A bibliography of Paul Tillich, complied by Peter H. John': p.367-396. [BR50.L38] 58-5193
1. Tillich, Paul, 1886- 2. Theology—Addresses, essays, lectures. 3. Civilization, Modern—Addresses, essays, lectures. I. Title.

LO, Samuel E. 268'.01
Tillichian theology and educational philosophy, by Samuel E. Lo. New York, Philosophical Library [1970] 126 p. 22 cm. Bibliography: p. 117-126. [BX4827.T53L6] 70-124516 6.95
1. Tillich, Paul, 1886-1965. 2. Religious education—Philosophy. I. Title.

MAHAN, Wayne W. 230'.092'4
Tillich's system / by Wayne W. Mahan. San Antonio : Trinity University Press, 1974. 148 p. ; 24 cm. Includes bibliographical references and index. [BX4827.T53M25] 73-91170 ISBN 0-911536-52-3 : 7.50
1. Tillich, Paul, 1886-1965. I. Title.

MARTIN, Bernard, 1928- 230.4
The existentialist theology of Paul Tillich. New York, Bookman [c.1963] 221p. 21cm. Bibl. 62-10275 5.00
1. Tillich, Paul, 1886- I. Title.

MARTIN, Bernard, 1928- 230.4
The existentialist theology of Paul Tillich. New Haven, Conn., Coll. & Univ.Pr. [1964, c.1963] 221p. 21cm. Bibl. 1.95 pap.,
1. Tillich, Paul, 1886- I. Title.

MAY, Rollo. 230'.092'4 B
Paulus; reminiscences of a friendship. [1st ed.] New York, Harper & Row [1973] vii, 113 p. 21 cm. Includes bibliographical references. [BX4827.T53M34] 72-78075 ISBN 0-06-065535-6 5.95
1. Tillich, Paul, 1886-1965. I. Title.

MODRAS, Ronald E. 230'.2
Paul Tillich's theology of the church : a Catholic appraisal / by Ronald E. Modras ; with a foreword by Hans Kung. Detroit : Wayne State University Press, 1976. p. cm. Includes index. Bibliography: p. [BV598.M6] 76-6082 ISBN 0-8143-1552-6 : 17.50
1. Tillich, Paul, 1886-1965. 2. Church—History of doctrines—20th century. I. Title.

O'MEARA, Thomas A. ed. 230.4
Paul Tillich in Catholic thought. Thomas A. O'Meara Celestin D. Weisser, eds. Foreword by J. Heywood Thomas, afterword by Paul Tillich. Dubuque, Iowa, Priory Pr. [c.1964] xxiii, 323p. 24cm. Bibl. 64-22796 5.95; 2.95 pap.,
1. Tillich, Paul, 1886- I. Weisser, Celestin D., joint ed. II. Title.

O'MEARA, Thomas A ed. 230.4
Paul Tillich in Catholic thought. Thomas A. O'Meara [and] Celestin D. Weisser, editors. Foreword by J. Heywood Thomas, with an afterword by Paul Tillich. Dubuque, Iowa, Priory Press [1964] xxiii, 323 p. 24 cm. Bibliographical footnotes. [BX4827.T53O45] 64-22796
1. Tillich, Paul, 1886- I. Weissner, Celestin D., joint ed. II. Title.

O'MEARA, Thomas F., 1935- 230'.4
comp.
Paul Tillich in Catholic thought. Editors: Thomas F. O'Meara [and] Donald M. Weisser. Foreword by J. Heywood Thomas; an afterword by Paul Tillich. Rev. ed. Garden City, N.Y., Image Books [1969] 395 p. 19 cm. Bibliographical footnotes. [BX4827.T53O45 1969] 78-78749 1.45
1. Tillich, Paul, 1886-1965. I. Weisser, Donald M., joint comp. II. Title.

O'MEARA, Thomas F., 211'.092'4
1935-
Paul Tillich's theology of God [by] Thomas Franklin O'Meara. [Dubuque, Iowa] Listening Press [1970] ix, 165 p. 23 cm. A revision of the author's thesis, Ludwig-Maximilian University, Munich, which had the title: Theologie und Ontologie dargestellt an der Gotteslehre von Paul Tillich. Bibliography: p. 154-162. [BT102.O46 1970] 75-304374
1. Tillich, Paul, 1886-1965. 2. God—History of doctrines—20th century. I. Title.

PAUCK, Wilhelm, 230'.092'4 B
1901-
Paul Tillich, his life & thought / Wilhelm & Marion Pauck. 1st ed. New York : Harper & Row, c1976- v. : ill. ; 22 cm. Contents.Contents.—v. 1. Life. Includes bibliographical references and index. [BX4827.T53P28 1976] 74-25709 ISBN 0-06-066474-6 (v. 1) : 15.00
1. Tillich, Paul, 1886-1965. 2. Theologians—United States—Biography. 3. Theologians—Germany—Biography. I. Pauck, Marion, joint author.

PAUL Tillich: 230'.0924
retrospect and future. [Articles by] Nels F. S. Ferre [and others] Introd. by T. A. Kantonen. Nashville, Abingdon Press [1967, c1966] 63 p. 19 cm. "Reprinted from Religion in life, winter 1966." [BX4827.T53P3 1967] 67-31858
1. Tillich, Paul, 1886-1965. I. Ferre, Nels Fredrick Solomon, 1908- II. Religion in life.

ROWE, William L. 230'.0924
Religious symbols and God; a philosophical study of Tillich's theology [by] William L. Rowe. Chicago, University of Chicago Press [1968] ix, 245 p. 22 cm. Bibliographical footnotes. [BX4827.T53R6] 68-16715
1. Tillich, Paul, 1886-1965. I. Title.

SCHARLEMANN, Robert P. 210
Reflection and doubt in the thought of Paul Tillich [by] Robert P. Scharlemann. New Haven, Yale University Press, 1969. xx, 220 p. 23 cm. Bibliography: p. [203]-209. [BX4827.T53S28] 79-81430 6.75
1. Tillich, Paul, 1886-1965. I. Title.

SCHRADER, Robert 230'.092'4
William.
The nature of theological argument : a study of Paul Tillich / by Robert William Schrader. Missoula, Mont. : Published by Scholars Press for Harvard theological review, c1975. xii, 147 p. ; 22 cm. (Harvard dissertations in religion ; no. 4) Bibliography: p. 147. [BX4827.T53S34] 75-43784 ISBN 0-89130-071-6 : 4.20
1. Tillich, Paul, 1886-1965. I. Title. II. Series.

STONE, Ronald H. 261.8'092'4
Paul Tillich's radical social thought / Ronald H. Stone. Atlanta : John Knox Press, c1980. 180 p. ; 20 cm. Includes bibliographical references and index. [BX4827.T53S76] 79-87740 ISBN 0-8042-0679-1 : 6.95
1. Tillich, Paul, 1886-1965. 2. Religion and sociology—History. I. Title.

STUMME, John R., 1942- 230'.092'4
Socialism in theological perspective : a study of Paul Tillich, 1918-1933 / by John R. Stumme. Missoula, Mont. : Scholars Press, [1978] p. cm. (AAR dissertation series ; 21 ISSN 0145-272Xs) Originally presented as the author's thesis, Union Theological Seminary. Vita. Bibliography: p. [BX4827.T53S78 1978] 78-3675 ISBN 0-89130-232-8 : 7.50
1. Tillich, Paul, 1886-1965. 2. Socialism, Christian. I. Title. II. Series: American Academy of Religion. Dissertation series — American Academy of Religion ; 21.

TAIT, Leslie Gordon, 230'.0924
1926-
The promise of Tillich, by L. Gordon Tait. [1st ed.] Philadelphia, Lippincott [1971] 127 p. 21 cm. (The Promise of theology) Bibliography: p. 123-127. [BX4827.T53T25] 79-146687 3.95
1. Tillich, Paul, 1886-1965. I. Title.

TAVARD, Georges Henri, 1922- 232
Paul Tillich and the Christian message. New York, Scribner [1962] 176 p. 22 cm. [BX4827.T53T3 1962a] 61-7227
1. Tillich, Paul, 1886-1965. 2. Catholic Church—Relations—Protestant churches. 3. Protestant churches—Relations—Catholic Church.

THATCHER, Adrian. 111'.092'4
The ontology of Paul Tillich / by Adrian Thatcher. Oxford [Eng.] ; New York : Oxford University Press, 1978. vi, 196 p. ; 23 cm. (Oxford theological monographs) Originally presented as the author's thesis, Oxford. Includes index. Bibliography: p. [178]-187. [BX4827.T53T47 1978] 77-30288 ISBN 0-19-826715-0 : 19.50
1. Tillich, Paul, 1886-1965. 2. Ontology—History. I. Title. II. Series.

THE theology of Paul Tillich; edited by Charles W. Kegley & Robert W. Bretall. New York, Macmillan, 1956. xiv, 370p. front. (port.) (The Library of living theology, v. 1)
1. Tillich, Paul, 1886- I. Kegley, Charles W ed. II. Bretall, Robert Walter, 1913- joint ed.

THOMAS, John Heywood 230.0924
Paul Tillich. [Amer. ed.] Richmond, Va., Knox [1966] 48p. 19cm. (Makers of contemp. theol.) 1st pub. in England by the Carey Kingsgate Pr., 1965. [BX4827.T53T49] 66-11072 1.00 pap.,
1. Tillich, Paul, 1886-1965. I. Title.

THOMAS, John Heywood. 230.0924
Paul Tillich, by J. Heywood Thomas. [American ed.] Richmond, John Knox Press [1966] 48 p. 19 cm. (Makers of contemporary theology) [BX4827.T53T49 1966] 66-11072
1. Tillich, Paul, 1886-1965. I. Title.

THOMAS, John Heywood. 230
Paul Tillich: an appraisal. Philadelphia, Westminster Press [1963] 216 p. 22 cm. Bibliographical references included in footnotes. [BX4827.T53T5] 63-12599
1. Tillich, Paul, 1886-1965.

TILLICH, Hannah. 910'.4
From place to place : travels with Paul Tillich, travels without Paul Tillich / Hannah Tillich. New York : Stein and Day, 1976. 223 p. : ill. ; 24 cm. [BX4827.T53T52] 75-34490 ISBN 0-8128-1902-0 : 10.00
1. Tillich, Paul, 1886-1965. 2. Tillich, Hannah. 3. Theologians—United States—Biography. 4. Wives—United States—Biography. I. Title.

TILLICH, Hannah. 230'.092'4 B
From time to time. New York, Stein and Day [1974 c1973] 252 p. 18 cm. [BX4827.T53T53] ISBN 0-8128-1742-7 1.95 (pbk.)
1. Tillich, Paul, 1886-1965. I. Title.
L.C. card no. for original edition: 73-79225

TILLICH, Hannah. 230'.092'4 B
From time to time. New York, Stein and Day [1973] 252 p. 24 cm. [BX4827.T53T53] 73-79225 ISBN 0-8128-1626-9 7.95
1. Tillich, Paul, 1886-1965. I. Title.

TILLICH, Paul, 1886-
The Church and contemporary culture: an address given before the General Board, National Council of the Churches of Christ in the U.S.A., June 8, 1955. [New York, Reproduced by and for the use fo the Department of Worship and the Art, National Council of Churches, 1956. 71. 63-79273
I. Title.

TILLICH, Paul, 1886-1965.
Dynamics of doubt; a preface to Tillich. Philadelphia, Fortress Press [1966] 128 p. 20 cm. 67-66248
I. Tillich, Paul, 1886-1965. II. Title.

TILLICH, Paul, 1886- 230.0924
1965.
The future of religions. Edited by Jerald C. Brauer. [1st ed.] New York, Harper & Row [1966] 94 p. illus., ports. 22 cm. Contents.Contents.—Tributes to Paul Tillich: Paul Tillich's impact on America, by J. C. Brauer. The sources of Paul Tillich's richness, by W. Pauck. Paul Tillich and the history of religions, by M. Eliade.—Essays by Paul Tillich: The effects of space exploration on man's condition and stature. Frontiers. The decline and the validity of the idea of progress. The significance of the history of religions for the systematic theologian. [BR123.T54] 66-15864
1. Tillich, Paul, 1886-1965. 2. Christianity—20th century—Addresses, essays, lectures. I. Brauer, Jerald C., ed. II. Title.

UNHJEM, Arne. 230.4
Dynamics of doubt; a preface to Tillich. Philadelphia, Fortress Press [1966] 128 p. 20 cm. Includes bibliographies. [BX4827.T53U5] 66-23223
1. Tillich, Paul, 1886-1965. I. Title.

WHEAT, Leonard F. 231'.0924
Paul Tillich's dialectical humanism: unmasking the God above God [by] Leonard F. Wheat. Baltimore, Johns Hopkins Press [1970] xiii, 287 p. 24 cm. Includes bibliographical references. [BX4827.T53W5 1970] 74-105365 9.00
1. Tillich, Paul, 1886-1965. I. Title.

WILLIAMSON, Rene de Visme. 261.7
Politics and Protestant theology : an interpretation of Tillich, Barth, Bonhoeffer, and Brunner / Rene de Visme Williamson. Baton Rouge : Louisiana State University Press, c1976. p. cm. Includes bibliographical references. [BR115.P7W49] 76-20817 ISBN 0-8071-0193-1 : 10.95
1. Tillich, Paul, 1886-1965. 2. Barth, Karl, 1886-1968. 3. Bonhoeffer, Dietrich, 1906-1945. 4. Brunner, Heinrich Emil, 1889-1966. 5. Christianity and politics—History. I. Title.

Tillich, Paul, 1886-1965—Addresses, essays, lectures.

THE Theology of Paul 230'.092'4
Tillich / edited by Charles W. Kegley. [2nd ed.]. New York : Pilgrim Press, c1982. xvi, 432 p. ; 21 cm. Includes indexes. Bibliography of the publications of Paul Tillich: p. 395-422. [BX4827.T53T48 1982] 19 82-301 ISBN 0-8298-0499-4 pbk. : 10.95
1. Tillich, Paul, 1886-1965—Addresses, essays, lectures. I. Kegley, Charles W.

TILLICH, Paul, 1886- 230'.092'4
1965.
The future of religions / Paul Tillich ; edited by Jerald C. Brauer. Westport, Conn. : Greenwood Press, 1976, c1966. 94 p., [8] leaves of plates : ill. ; 23 cm. Reprint of the ed. published by Harper & Row, New York. Contents.Contents.—Tributes to Paul Tillich: Brauer, J. C. Paul Tillich's impact on America. Pauck, W. The sources of Paul Tillich's richness. Eliade, M. Paul Tillich and the history of religions.—Essays by Paul Tillich: The effects of space exploration on man's condition and stature. Frontiers. The decline and the validity of the idea of progress. The significance of the history of religions for the systematic theologian. [BR123.T54 1976] 76-7566 ISBN 0-8371-8861-X lib.bdg. : 10.50
1. Tillich, Paul, 1886-1965—Addresses, essays, lectures. 2. Christianity—20th century—Addresses, essays, lectures. I. Brauer, Jerald C. II. Title.
Contents omitted.

Tillich, Paul, 1886-1965—Bibliography.

BRYAN, Lawrence D., 016.23'0092'4
1945-
The thought of Paul Tillich; a select bibliographical companion to the Systematic theology, by Lawrence D. Bryan. Evanston, Ill., Garrett Theological Seminary Library, 1973. x, 34 p. 29 cm. (Garrett bibliographical lectures, no. 9) [Z8879.75.B78] 73-168380
1. Tillich, Paul, 1886-1965—Bibliography. I. Tillich, Paul, 1886-1965. Systematic theology. II. Title. III. Series.

Tillich, Paul, 1886- Systematic theology.

MCKELWAY, Alexander J. 230
The Systematic theology of Paul Tillich, a review and analysis. Richmond, Knox [c.1964] 280p. 21cm. Bibl. 64-13969 5.50
1. Tillich, Paul, 1886- Systematic theology. 2. Theology, Doctrinal. I. Title.

Tilstra, Klaas.

TILSTRA, Albertine Klingbeil, 1905- 266'.673 B
A Dutchman bound for paradise / Albertine Klingbeil Tilstra. Washington, D.C. : Review and Herald Pub. Association, c1980. 126 p. ; 21 cm. [BV3680.N52T547] 80-18061 pbk. : 4.95
1. Tilstra, Klaas. 2. Missionaries—New Guinea—Biography. 3. Missionaries—Indonesia—Biography. 4. Missionaries—Netherlands—Biography. I. Title.

Time.

BARR, James. 220.8529
Biblical words for time. Naperville, Ill., A. R. Allenson [1962] 174p. 22cm. (Studies in Biblical theology, no. 33) [BS680.T54B3] 62-51602
1. Time. 2. Bible— Language, style. I. Title.

JORDAN, Richard Douglas. 821'.4
The temple of eternity; Thomas Traherne's philosophy of time. Port Washington, N.Y., Kennikat Press, 1972. 125 p. 24 cm. (Kennikat Press national university publications. Series on literary criticism) Bibliography: p. 119-125. [PR3736.T7J6] 70-189560 ISBN 0-8046-9019-7 8.50
1. Traherne, Thomas, d. 1674—Philosophy. 2. Time. I. Title.

Time allocation.

DAYTON, Edward R. 248'.4
Tools for time management : Christian perspectives on managing priorities / Edward R. Dayton. Grand Rapids : Zondervan Pub. House, [1974] 192 p. : ill. ; 21 cm. "Resources": p. 142-154. [BV4509.5.D35] 74-196951 4.95
1. Time allocation. 2. Christian life—1960- I. Title.

Time (Canon law)

BALZER, Ralph Francis, 1914- 271
... The computation of time in a canonical novitiate; a historical conspectus and commentary, by Ralph F. Balzer ... Washington, D.C., The Catholic university of America press, 1945. x, 227 p. 23 cm. (The Catholic university of America. Canon law studies, no. 212) Thesis (J.C.D.)--Catholic university of America, 1945. "Biographical note": p. 216. Bibliography: p. 198-203. [BX1939.T5B3] A 46
1. Time (Canon law) 2. Novitiate (Canon law) 3. Catholic church. Codex juris canonici. C. 31-35: De temporis supputatione. I. Title.

Time—Systems and standards.

DOANE, Doris Chase.
Time changes in the U.S.A. Los Angeles, Church of Light, 1966. 173 p. maps. 28 cm. 68-83434
1. Time—Systems and standards. I. Title.

Time, the weekly news-magazine.

FOX, Matthew, 1940- 200'.973
Religion USA; an inquiry into religion and culture by way of Time magazine. [Dubuque, Iowa] Listening Press, 1971. 451 p. 22 cm. Includes bibliographical references. [BR517.F64] 76-151967 3.65
1. Time, the weekly news-magazine. 2. U.S.—Religion. 3. Religion and culture. I. Title.

Time (Theology)

MOUROUX, Jean 230.01529
The mystery of time, a theological inquiry. Tr. [from French] by John Drury. New York, Desclee [1964, c.1962] 319p. 22cm. Bibl. 64-12768 5.50
1. Time (Theology) I. Title.

Time (Theology)—Biblical teaching.

BRANTLEY, Robert Augustus 1838-
Light of the world; or, A key to the Bible; especially being an explanation of the measurement of time and prophecies of the Bible, by R. A. Brantley ... [Houston, Tex., Printed by J. V. Dealy co.] 1906. 187 p. front. (port.) illus. 21 cm. 6-18572
I. Title.

DE VRIES, Simon John. 231'.7
Yesterday, today, and tomorrow : time and history in the Old Testament / Simon J. De Vries. Grand Rapids, Mich. : W. B. Eerdmans Pub. Co., [1975] 389 p. ; 24 cm. Includes bibliographical references and indexes. [BS680.T54D48] 74-31322 ISBN 0-8028-3457-4 : 10.95
1. Time (Theology)—Biblical teaching. 2. History (Theology)—Biblical teaching. I. Title.

Time (Theology)—Meditations.

ANDREASEN, Niels-Erik A. 242'.4
The Christian use of time / Niels-Erik A. Andreasen. Nashville : Abingdon, c1978. 128 p. ; 19 cm. Bibliography: p. 127-128. [BT78.A53] 78-847 ISBN 0-687-07630-7 pbk. : 3.95
1. Time (Theology)—Meditations. 2. Sabbath—Meditations. I. Title.

Times.

RAMIGE, Eldon Albert, 1894- 115
Contemporary concepts of time and the idea of God, by E. A. Ramige, PH. D. Boston, Mass., The Stratford company [c1935] 3 p. l., iv, 132 p. diagrs. 20 cm. Thesis (PH. D.) University of Iowa, 1963. Without thesis note. Thesis note on label mounted on t.-p. Bibliography: p. 129-132. [BL51.R26 1933] 35-5209
1. God. 2. Times. I. Title.

Timon, John, bp., 1797-1867.

BAYARD, Ralph Francis, 1898- 282.764
Lone-star vanguard; the Catholic re-occupation of Texas (1838-1848) with four illustrations and end-paper map, by Ralph Bayard ... Saint Louis, Mo., The Vincentian press, 1945. xiii, 453 p. 2 pl., 2 port. (incl. front.) 23 1/2 cm. Map on lining-papers. Bibliography: p. 413-432. [BX1415.T4B3] 45-10779
1. Timon, John, bp., 1797-1867. 2. Catholic church in Texas. 3. Congregation of priests of the mission in Texas. I. Title.

Timothy (Biblical character)

ALCOTT, William Andrus, 1798-1859. 225.92
The young missionary; exemplified in the life of Timothy. By Wm. A. Alcott...Written for the Massachusetts Sabbath school society, and revised by the Committee of publication. Boston, Massachusetts Sabbath school society, 1837. x, [11]-175 p. incl. front., illus. 15 1/2 cm. [BS2520.T5A6] 39-13367
1. Timothy (Bible character) I. Massachusetts Sabbath school society. Committee of publication. II. Title.

PETERSEN, William J. 227'.83'0924
The discipling of Timothy / William J. Petersen. Wheaton, Ill. : Victor Books, c1980. 186 p. ; 18 cm. [BS2520.T5P47] 19 80-50002 ISBN 0-88207-217-X (pbk.) : 2.95
1. Paul, Saint, apostle. 2. Timothy (Biblical character) I. Title.

Timothy (Biblical character)—Juvenile literature.

CALDWELL, Louise. 227'.092'4 B
Timothy, young pastor / Louise Caldwell ; illustrated by Paul Karch. Nashville, : Broadman Press, c1978. 48 p. : col. ill. ; 24 cm. (Biblearn series) Tells the story of the pastor and missionary who is thought to have been converted to Christianity by Paul. [BS2520.T5C34] 78-105195 ISBN 0-8054-4239-1 pbk. : 3.95
1. Bible. N.T.—Biography—Juvenile literature. 2. Timothy (Biblical character)—Juvenile literature. 3. [Timothy (Biblical character)] 4. [Bible stories—N.T.] I. Karch, Paul. II. Title.

LILLIE, Amy Morris 225.92
Run the good race. Illus. by Steele Savage. Nashville, Abingdon [c.1962, 1965] 72p. illus. 22cm. [BS2520T5L5] 65-14091 2.50
1. Timothy (Biblical character)—Juvenile literature. I. Title.

LILLIE, Amy Morris. 225.92
Run the good race. Illus. by Steele Savage. New York, Abingdon Press [1965] 72 p. illus. 22 cm. [BX2520.T5L5] 65-14091
1. Timothy (Biblical character) — Juvenile literature. I. Title.

Tindal, Matthew, 1657?-1733. Christianity as old as the creation.

ARSCOTT, Alexander, 1676-1737. 230
Some considerations relating to the present state of the Christian religion, wherein the nature, end and design of Christianity, as well as the principal evidence of the truth of it, are explained and recommended out of the Holy Scriptures; with a general appeal to the experience of all men for confirmation thereof. By Alexander Arscot ... London, Printed: Reprinted by B. Franklin, at the New-Printing-office, in Philadelphia, 1732. 111, [1] p. 15 1/2 cm. Part one. Differs from the edition of 1731 in imprint and advertisement only. Part II. Wherein the principal evidence of the Christian religion is explain'd and defended upon the principles of reason, as well as revelation: with observations on some passages in the book intituled, Christianity as old as the creation, so fas as concerns the doctrine herein advanced. By Alexander Arscot ... London Printed: Reprinted by B. Franklin, at the New printing office, in Philadelphia. 1732. 140, [2] p., 1 l. 15 cm. Wherein the evidence of the Christian religion is farther explain'd and defended; in answer to the objections made against it in a late vindication of the Bishop of Lichfield and Coventry; with an Appendix, containing some remarks on a passage in the second volume of Bishop Burnet's History of his own times. Part III. By Alexander Arscott ... London; Printed 1734. Philadelphia; Reprinted by Andrew Bradford at the Sign of the Bible, 1738. viii, 175 p. 16 cm. [BR120.B7 pt. III] 24-22602
1. Tindal, Matthew, 1657?-1733. Christianity as old as the creation. 2. Smalbroke, Richard, successively bp. of St. David's and of Lichfield and Coventry, 1672-1749. 3. Burnet, Gilbert, bp. of Salisbury, 1643-1715. History of my own times. 4. Franklin, Benjamin, 1706-1790—Imprints. I. Title.

Tingley, Katherine Augusta Westcott, 1847-1929.

GREENWALT, Emmett A. 212'.52 B
California utopia : Point Loma,1897-1942 / by Emmett A. Greenwalt. Rev. ed. San Diego, Calif. : Point Loma Publications, c1978. xvii, 244 p., [5] leaves of plates : ill. ; 24 cm. First ed. published in 1955 under title: The Point Loma community in California, 1897-1942. Includes index. Bibliography: p. 215-229. [BP585.T5G7 1978] 77-93816 pbk. : 5.95
1. Tingley, Katherine Augusta, 1847-1929. 2. Lomaland School, Point Loma, Calif. I. Title.

GREENWALT, Emmett A 294.58
The Point Loma community in California, 1897-1942: a theosophical experiment. Berkeley, University of California Press, 1955. 236p. illus., ports. 24cm. (University of California publications in history, v. 48) Bibliography: p. [203]-218. [E173.C15 vol. 48] 212 A55
1. Tingley, Katherine Augusta (Westcott) 1847-1926. 2. Lomaland Scholl, Point Loma, Calif. I. Title. II. Series: California. University of California publications in history, v. 48

GREENWALT, Emmett A. 212'.52
The Point Loma community in California, 1897-1942 : a theosophical experiment / by Emmett A. Greenwalt. 1st AMS ed. New York : AMS Press, 1979. 236 p., [4] leaves of plates : ill. ; 23 cm. (Communal societies in America) Rev. ed. published in 1978 under title: California utopia. Reprint of the 1955 ed. published by University of California Press, Berkeley, which was issued as v. 48 of the University of California publications in history. Includes index. Bibliography: p. 205-218. [BP585.T5G7 1979] 76-42802 ISBN 0-404-60068-9 : 26.00
1. Tingley, Katherine Augusta Westcott, 1847-1929. 2. Lomaland School, Point Loma, Calif. I. Title. II. Series: California. University. University of California publications in history ; v. 48.

Tinkling Spring Church, Augusta Co., Va.

WILSON, Howard McKnight. 285.1755
The Tinkling Spring, headwater of freedom; a study of the church and her people, 1732-1952. Fisherville, Va., Tinkling Spring and Hermitage Presbyterian Churches, 1954. xviii, 542p. illus., ports., maps (1 fold.) facsims. 24cm. Bibliography: p. [393]-409. [BX9211.T5W5] 54-11987
1. Tinkling Spring Church, Augusta Co., Va. I. Title.

Tippett, Arthur George, 1883-

[CUSDEN, Richard A J] 922
The hustling parson; or, The adventures of an unconventional evangelist. New York, Gospel car mission publishing house [c1930] 215 p. front., plates, ports. 18 cm. Frontispiece signed: Rev. Richard A. J. Cusden, author. [BV3785.T55C8] 31-994
1. Tippett, Arthur George, 1883- I. Title.

Tippit, Sammy.

TIPPIT, Sammy. 269'.2'0924 B
Sammy Tippit: God's love in action, as told to Jerry B. Jenkins. Nashville, Broadman Press [1973] 121 p. illus. 20 cm. [BR1725.T56A33] 73-78216 ISBN 0-8054-5542-6 3.95
1. Tippit, Sammy. I. Jenkins, Jerry B. II. Title. III. Title: God's love in action.

Tipple, Ezra Squier, 1861-1936.

EZRA Squier Tipple, 922.773
Christian gentleman; a record of the affection of his friends and colleagues. Madison, N. J., Drew university [c1937] 5 p. l., 3-79 p. incl. front. (port.) illus. 27 cm. [BX8495.T65E8] 37-21365
1. Tipple, Ezra Squier, 1861-1936.
Contents omitted.

TIPPLE, Ezra Squier, 1861- ed.
Drew sermons. Second series. Ed. by Ezra Squier Tipple... New York, Eaton & Mains; Cincinnati, Jennings & Graham [c1907] vii, 281 p. 21 1/2 cm. 7-14563
I. Title.
Contents omitted.

TIPPLE, Ezra Squier, 1861- ed.
Drew sermons. First series. Ed. by Ezra Squier Tipple... New York, Eaton & Mains; Cincinnati, Jennings & Graham [c1906] 5 p. l., 276 p. 21 1/2 cm. 6-16613
I. Title.
Contents omitted.

TIPPLE, Ezra Squier, 1861- ed.
Drew sermons on the golden texts for 1908, ed. by Ezra Squier Tipple... New York, Eaton & Mains; Cincinnati, Jennings & Graham [c1907] vi, 312 p. 21 1/2 cm. 7-38587
I. Title.

TIPPLE, Ezra Squier, 1861- ed.
Drew sermons on the golden texts for 1909, ed. by Ezra Squier Tipple... New York, Eaton & Mains; Cincinnati, Jennings & Graham [c1908] vii, 312 p. 21 1/2 cm. 8-29369
I. Title.

TIPPLE, Ezra Squier, 1861- ed.
Drew sermons on the golden texts for

1910, ed. by Ezra Squier Tipple... New York, Eaton & Mains; Cincinnati, Jennings & Graham [c1909] v. 311 p. 21 1/2 cm. $1.00. 9-29567
I. Title.

Tishri.

MINDEL, Nissan. 296.4
The complete story of Tishrei. Brooklyn, Merkos L'Inyonei Chinuch, 1956. viii, 231p. illus. 23cm. (His Complete festival stories) [BM693.T6M5] 57-36874
1. Tishri. I. Title.

Tithes.

CHERRY, Jeremiah Taylor, 1852-
The tithe law. Its origin: traced from paradise. Its universality; founded upon the enduring relations existing between God and man ... A lost doctrine of the church, etc. Together with five reasons why we should tithe. By Rev. J. T. Cherry ... Louisville, Ky., Pentacostal publishing company [1914] 128 p. 19 cm. 14-5177 0.25
I. Title.

CLARKE, Henry William.
A history of tithes, by the Rev. Henry William Clarke ., 2d ed. London, S. psonnenschien & co.; New York, C. Scribner's sons, 1894. xxiv, 268 p. 19 cm. [Social science series. 78]. A14
1. Tithes. I. Title.

DUNCAN, John Wesley. 254
Our Christian stewardship, by John Wesley Duncan. Cincinnati, Jennings and Graham; New York, Eaton and Maine [c1909] 4 p. l., 7-129 p. 19 cm. [BV771.D7] 11-1526
1. Tithes. 2. Stewardship, Christian. I. Title.

GASKILL, James T. 254
The home and church tithing, by Rev. Jas. T. Gaskill. Atlanta, Ga., A.B. Caldwell publishing company, 1923. 2 p. l., [9]-111 p. illus. (form) tab., diagr. 20 cm. [BV771.G3] 23-11525
I. Title.

GASKILL, James T. 254
Text book on home and church tithing, by Rev. James T. Gaskill. Boston, The Christopher publishing house [c1930] 107 p. diagr. 20 1/2 cm. Published in 1923 under title: The home and church tithing. [BV771.G32] 30-15167
1. Tithes. I. Title.

HARSHMAN, Charles William, 1858- 254
Christian giving. by the Rev. Charles William Harshman ... Cincinnati, Jennings and Graham; New York, Eaton and Mains [c1905] 118 p. 15 cm. (On cover: Little books on practice) [BV772.H3] 5-9052
1. Tithes. I. Title.

HENSEY, James Andrew, 1866- 254
Storehouse tithing; or, Stewardship up-to-date, by James A. Hensey ... New York, The Revell press [c1922] 1 p. l., 5-177 p. 19 cm. [BV771.H4] 23-6041
1. Tithes. I. Title. II. Title: Stewardship up-to-date.

HUEBSCHMANN, John Simon, 1881- 254
Three greater successes: i. You--yourself. ii. Your local church. iii. Your denomination. By J. S. Huebschmann. Cleveland, O., Central publishing house, 1922. xiii, 144 p. front., pl., ports. 20 cm. [BV771.H8] 23-5376
1. Tithes. I. Title.

JEFFREYS, Raymond John, 1896- 254
God is my landlord. Chicago, Pub. for the Dynamic Kernels Foundation by Van Kampen Press [1947] 158 p. illus., ports. 23 cm. [SB191.W5J37] [633.11] 281.2J37 Agr
1. Hayden, Perry. 2. Ford, Henry, 1863-1947. 3. Tithes. 4. Wheat. I. Dynamic Kernels Foundation. II. Title.

LANSDAIL, Henry, 1841-1919. 254
The sacred tenth; or, Studies in tithe-giving, ancient and modern, by Henry Lansdall ... containing a bibliography on tithe-giving lists of crown grantees, and modern lay-owners, of English alienated tithes, etc., etc, ... Published under the direction of the Tract committee. London, [etc.] Society for promoting Christian knowledge; New York, E. S. Gorham 1906. 2 v. 16 pl. (incl. front., ports.) 3 fold. maps, fold. tab. 22 cm. Paged continuously. "Bibliography on tithe-paying and systematic and proportionate giving": v. 1 [28] p. at end. [BV771.L3] 8-15778
1. Tithes. 2. Tithes—Gt. Brit. I. Society for promoting Christian knowledge, London. Tract committee. II. Title.

LANSDELL, Henry 254.8
The tithe in scripture. Grand Rapids, Mich., Baker Bk. [1966, c.1963] 156p. 22cm. Embodies the portions of the author's The sacred tenth which deals with the scriptural teaching on the tithe. First pub. in England in 1908. 1.50 pap.,
1. Tithes. I. Title.

LANSDELL, Henry, 1841-1919. 254.8
The sacred tenth; or, Studies in tithe-giving, ancient and modern. Grand Rapids, Baker Book House, 1955- v. 23cm. [Co-operative reprint library] [BV771.L32] 54-11072
1. Tithes. 2. Tithes—Gt. Brit. I. Title.

LANSDELL, Henry, 1841-1919 254.8
The tithe in Scripture. Grand Rapids, Mich., Baker Bk., 1963. 156p. 23cm. Embodies the portions of the author's The sacred tenth which deal with the Scriptural teaching on the tithe. 63-12030 2.95
1. Tithes. I. Title.

LOVEJOY, Luther Ellsworth, 1864-1936. 254
Speculating in futures; adventures in stewardship, by Luther E. Lovejoy ... Introduction by Bishop Edwin Holt Hughes. New York, Cincinnati, The Methodist book concern [c1927] 207 p. 18 cm. [BV772.L6] 28-4250
1. Tithes. I. Title. II. Title: Stewardship, Adventures in.

MATHER, Increase, 1639-1723. 254
A discourse concerning the maintenance due to those that preach the gospel: in which, that question whether tithes are by the divine law the ministers due, is considered, and the negative proved. By I. Mather... Boston: N.E. Printed by B. Green, 1706. 1 p. l., 60 p. 14 cm. [BV771.M38] 25-12318
1. Tithes. I. Title.

MEYER, Louis E. 254
As you tithe so you prosper, a series of four lessons in tithing, by L. E. Meyer. Kansas City, Mo., Unity school of Christianity, 1937. 59 p., 1 l. 16 1/2 cm. [BX9890.U5M4] 42-40470
I. Unity school of Christianity, Kansas City, Mo. II. Title.

ROBINSON, Arthur Thomas, 1869- 254
Tithing for juniors, by A. T. Robinson...introduction by F. A. Agar... New York, Chicago [etc.] Fleming H. Revell company [c1930] 2 p. l., 3-93 p. 19 1/2 cm. [BV772.R6] 30-9756
I. Title.

SALSTRAND, George A. E. 254.8
The tithe; the minimum standard for Christian giving. Grand Rapids, Mich., Baker Bk. [1963, c.1952] 55p. 20cm. Bibl. .85 pap.,
I. Title.

SELBORNE, Roundell Palmer, 1st earl of, 1812-1895. 254
Ancient facts and fictions concerning churches and tithes, by Roundell, earl of Selborne... London and New York, Macmillan and co., 1888. xvi, 359 p. 19 1/2 cm. [BV771.S4] 3-2193
I. Title.

SELBORNE, Roundell Palmer, 1st earl of, 1812-1895. 254
Ancient facts and fictions concerning churches and tithes, by Roundell, earl of Selborne ... 2d ed., with a supplement containing remarks on a recent history of tithes. London and New York, Macmillan and co., 1892. xvi, 413 p. 19 1/2 cm. "First edition printed 1866." [BV771.S4 1892] 44-28670
1. Clarke, Henry William. A history of tithes. 2. Tithes. I. Title.

SUTTON, Jack A. 254.8
Witness beyond barriers, by Jack A. Sutton. St. Louis, Bethany Press [1968] 158 p. 23 cm. [BV772.S87] 68-26113 4.95
1. Tithes. 2. Christian giving. I. Title.

WEATHERS, Elmer Spalding, 1880- 254
The tithing system and the change from law to grace, by E. S. Weathers. [Plainview, Tex., c1938] 2 p. l., 86 p. 19 1/2 cm. [BV771.W4] 39-2145
1. Tithes. I. Title.

Tithes—History

CONSTABLE, Giles 271.09
Monastic tithes, from their origins to the twelfth century. [New York] Cambridge. 1964. xxi, 346p. 23cm. (Cambridge studies in medieval life and thought, new ser., v.10) Bibl. 64-24317 9.50
1. Tithes—Hist. 2. Monasticism and religious orders—Finance—Hist. 3. Monasticism and religious orders—Middle Ages. I. Title. II. Series.

EASTERBY, William.
The history of the law of tithes in England. Being the Yorke prize essay of the University of Cambridge for 1887. By William Easterby ... Cambridge, University press, 1888. xiv, 110, [2] p. 22 1/2 cm. "Table of cases": p. [111] 6-29181
I. Title.
Contents omitted

RIGBY, N L.
Christ our creditor ("How much owest thou"); or, the tithe terumoth, its philosophy, history, and perptuity. 2d ed., rev. Chicago, New York [etc.] F. H. Revell co. [1899] 1 p. l., 126 p. 12 degrees. (Revell's popular religious series. no. 194) 99-1476
I. Title.

STEWART, Elmer Bryan, 1865- 254
The tithe [by] Rev. E. B. Stewart ... introduction by Layman. Chicago, Ill., Winona Lake, Ind., The Winona publishing co. [1903] xxii, 82 p. 20 cm. [BV771.S7] 3-28148
1. Tithes—Hist. I. Title.

WOOD, Samuel, 1874- 254
Tithes; a history of tithe, ancient and modern ... by Samuel Wood. [Fresno, Calif., Crown printing and engraving co., 1934. 2 p. l., [vii]-x p. 2 l., 201 p. 18 1/2 cm. Contents.pt. I. Tithes.--pt. II. Church temporalities. All things common.--Bibliography (p. 198-201) [BV771.W6] 35-3599
1. Tithes—Hist. 2. Mormons and Mormonism. I. Title.

Tithes—Ireland—Early works to 1800.

RYVES, Thomas, Sir, 1583?-1652. 262'.03'0681
The poore vicars plea : London, 1620 / Thomas Ryves. Amsterdam : Theatrum Orbis Terrarum ; Norwood, N.J. : W. J. Johnson, 1979. 152 p. ; 22 cm. (The English experience, its record in early printed books published in facsimile ; no. 953) "S.T.C. no. 21478." Photoreprint of the 1620 ed. printed by J. Bill, London. [BX5551.R9 1979] 19 79-84135 ISBN 90-221-0953-4 : 17.00
1. Church of Ireland—Clergy—Early works to 1800. 2. Tithes—Ireland—Early works to 1800. 3. Clergy—Salaries, pensions, etc.—Early works to 1800. 4. Benefices, Ecclesiastical—Early works to 1800. 5. Clergy—Ireland—Early works to 1800. I. Title. II. Series: English experience, its record in early printed books published in facsimile ; no. 953.

Tithes (Jewish law)

JAFFEE, Martin S. 296.1'23
Mishnah's theology of tithing : a study of tractate Maaserot / by Martin S. Jaffee. Chico, Calif. : Scholars Press, c1981. xxvi, 214 p. ; 23 cm. (Brown Judaic studies ; no. 19) "This study is a translation and exegesis of Mishnah's tractate Maaserot (Tithes) and its corresponding tractate of Tosefta." Includes index. Bibliography: p. xiii-xxvi. [BM506.M19J33] 19 80-29333 ISBN 0-89130-458-4 : 15.00
1. Mishnah. Ma'aserot—Commentaries. 2. Tosefta. Ma'aserot—Commentaries. 3. Tithes (Jewish law) I. Mishnah. Ma'aserot. English. 1981. II. Tosefta. Ma'aserot. English. 1981. III. Title. IV. Series.

OPPENHEIMER, Joseph, 1911- 296.7'4
Ma'aser; the precepts of tithing [by] Joseph Oppenheimer. New York, Shengold Publishers, 1971. 52 p. 22 cm. Pages 48-52 and added t.p. in Hebrew; p. 48-50: bibliographical references. Gertrude Hirschler translated the original German manuscript into English. Bibliography: p. 51-52. [BM720.T4O65] 72-24917
1. Tithes (Jewish law) I. Title.

Tithes—Mormonism.

†DOXEY, Roy Watkins, 1908- 248'.6
Tithing : the Lord's law / Roy W. Doxey. Salt Lake City : Deseret Book Co., 1976. viii, 102 p. ; 24 cm. Includes index. Bibliography: p. [96]-97. [BX8643.T5D69] 76-41587 ISBN 0-87747-615-2 : 4.95
1. Tithes—Mormonism. I. Title.

Tithes—Scotland.

CORMACK, Alexander Allan. 254
Teinds and agriculture, an historical survey, by Alexander A. Cormack ... London, Oxford university press, H. Milford, 1930. xi, 206 p., 1 l. 23 cm. Bibliography: p. [189]-193. [BR783.C6] 36-24590
1. Tithes—Scotland. 2. Agriculture—Scotland—Hist. 3. Ecclesiastical law—Scotland. I. Title.

Titicaca island—Antiquities

BANDELIER, Adolph Francis Alphonse, 1840-1914. 278.
The islands of Titicaca and Koati, illustrated by Adolph F. Bandelier. New York, The Hispanic society of America, 1910. xvi p., 2 l., 3-358 p., 1 l. front., lxxxv pl. (part col., incl. fold. maps) 24 1/2 cm. Each plate accompanied by guard-sheet with descriptive letterpress. [F3451.T6B3] 10-3392
1. Titicaca island—Antiq. 2. Koati island—Antiq. 3. Bolivia—Antiq. 4. Titcaca, Lake. I. Title.

Title.

BLACK, Hugh, 1868- 243
... "According to my Gospel", by Hugh Black ... New York, Chicago [etc.] Fleming H. Revell company [c1913] 312 p. 20 cm. At head of title: Montclair sermons. [BX9178.B62A3] 13-24880 1.25
1. Title. I. Title. II. Title: Montclair sermons.

HIFLER, Joyce 248.3
Think on these things [1st ed] Garden City, Doubleday, 1966. 116 p. 22 cm [ps3558.135t4] 66-20953 3.95
1. Title. I. Title.

HUSTON, Ruth.
Observations of God's timing in the Kentucky mountains. [Salisbury, N. C., Rowan Printing Co.] c1962. 181 p. Autobiographical. 65-55518
1. Title. I. Title.

SAUNDERS, Winnie Crandall.
The sky is God's own sonnet. Chicago, Ill., P. E. Pross, 1965. 55 p. 23 cm. Poems. 68-67504
1. Title. I. Title.

Titles of books.

PATTISON, Robert Bainbridge, 1875- comp. 011
Bible phrases used as book titles, in English novels, plays, and books of poetry, compiled by Robert B. Pattison. Ossining, N.Y., [1968?] 27 p. 29 cm. Published in 1942 under title: Book titles from the Bible. [BS432.P33 1968] 70-9332
1. Titles of books. 2. Bible in literature. I. Title.

Tittle, Ernest Fremont, 1885-1949.

MILLER, Robert 287'.1'0924 B Moats.
How shall they hear without a preacher? The life of Ernest Fremont Tittle. Chapel Hill, University of North Carolina Press [1971] xii, 524 p. illus. 24 cm. Bibliography: p. [515]-518. [BX8495.T67M5] 74-149031 ISBN 0-8078-1173-4 12.50
1. Tittle, Ernest Fremont, 1885-1949. I. Title.

TITTLE, Ernest Fremont, 252. 1885-
The foolishness of peaching, and other sermons [by] Ernest Fremont Tittle. New York, H. Holt and company [c1930] vi, 314 p. 19 1/2 cm. [BX8333.T5F6] 30-9154 *I. Title.*

Toba Indians.

METRAUX, Alfred, 1902- 980.62
Myths of the Toba and Pilaga Indians of the Gran Chaco, by Alfred Metraux. Philadelphia, American folklore society, 1946. xii, 167 p. 23 1/2 cm. (Half-title: Memoirs of the American folklore society, v. 40) Bibliography: p. 164-167. [GR1.A5 vol. 40] [F2821.3.R4M4] (398.06273) [299.8] 46-4565
1. Toba Indians. 2. Pilaga Indians. 3. Indians of South America—Religion and mythology. 4. Indians of South America—Chaco, El Gran. I. Title.

Tobin, James Edward, 1905-joint author.

DELANEY, John J. 922.2
Dictionary of Catholic biography [by] John J. Delaney, James Edward Tobin. Garden City, N. Y., Doubleday [c.1961] xi, 1245p. 27cm. [ith thumb-index, p19.95] 62-7620 18.50;
1. Tobin, James Edward, 1905-joint author. 2. Catholic Church—Biog.—Dictionaries. I. Title.

Tobin, Luke, 1908-

TOBIN, Luke, 1908- 271'.9
Hope is an open door / Mary Luke Tobin. Nashville, Tenn. : Abingdon, c1981. 143 p. ; 21 cm. (Journeys in faith) Includes bibliographical references. [BX4705.T6722A33] 19 80-21414 ISBN 0-687-17410-4 : 7.95
1. Tobin, Luke, 1908- 2. Nuns—United States—Biography. 3. Church and social problems—Catholic Church. I. Title. II. Series.

Tobit (Character in the Apocrypha)—Juvenile literature.

FADDOUL, Germain, 1912- JUV
An angel for his guide; a story of Tobit and Tobias. Illus. by Carolyn Lee Jagodits. Notre Dame, Ind., Dujarie [c.1966] 95p. illus. 24cm [PZ7.F128An] 229 66-12690 2.25
1. Tobit (Character in the Apocrypha)—Juvenile literature. 2. Tobias, son of Tobit—Juvenile literature. I. Title.

Toc H.

CLAYTON, Philip Thomas Byard, 1885- ed.
The smoking furnace and the burning lamp; a group of sermons concerning Toc H. edited by the Rev. P. B. Clayton ... With a frontispiece. London. New York [etc.] Longmans, Green and co., ltd., 1927. viii, 9-142. [1] p. front. (port.) 19 cm. [BV1280.T6C6] 27-12778 1.50
1. Toc H. I. Title.
Contents omitted.

Tocqueville, Alexis Charles Henri Maurice Clerel de, 1805-1859.

GOLDSTEIN, Doris S. 209'.44
Trial of faith : religion and politics in Tocqueville's thought / Doris S. Goldstein. New York : Elsevier, [1975] xi, 144 p. ; 24 cm. Includes index. Bibliography: p. 133-139. [BR115.P7G59] 75-4753 ISBN 0-444-99001-1 : 10.00
1. Tocqueville, Alexis Charles Henri Maurice Clerel de, 1805-1859. 2. Christianity and politics—History. 3. France—Religion. 4. France—Politics and government. 5. United States—Religion. 6. Religions. I. Title.

Todaiji, Nara, Japan.

KOBAYASHI, Takeshi, 1903- 732'.7 1969.
Nara Buddhist art, Todai-ji / by Takeshi Kobayashi ; translated and adapted by Richard L. Gage. 1st English ed. New York : Weatherhill, 1975. 157 p. : ill. (some col.) ; 24 cm. (Heibonsha survey of Japanese art ; v. 5) Translation of Todai-ji no Daibutsu. [NB1057.N36K6213] 74-22034 ISBN 0-8348-1021-2 : 12.50
1. Todaiji, Nara, Japan. 2. Sculpture, Buddhist—Nara, Japan (City) 3. Sculpture—Nara, Japan (City) I. Title. II. Series.

Todos Santos Cuchumatan, Guatemala.

OAKES, Maud van 299.7 970.62 Cortlandt, 1903-
The two crosses of Todos Santos, survivals of Mayan religious ritual. [New York] Pantheon Books [1951] xiii, 274 p. illus., ports, map. 26 cm. (Bollingen series, 27) Bibliography: p. 254-255. [F1465.2.M3O3] 51-9561
1. Todos Santos Cuchumatan, Guatemala. 2. Mam Indians. 3. Mayas—Religion and mythology. I. Title. II. Series.

Tokens.

SHIELLS, Robert, 1825-1908. 265.
The story of the token as belonging to the sacrament of the Lord's supper, by Robert Shiells ... 2d ed. ... Philadelphia, The Presbyterian board of publication and Sabbath-school work 1902. xii, 9-196 p. illus., ix pl. (incl. front.) 19 cm. Introduction to 2d edition signed: Henry C. McCook. [BV828.S5 1902] 2-16091
1. Tokens. 2. Lord's supper. I. McCook, Henry Christopher, 1837-1911. II. Title.

Tokens, Communion.

SHIELLS, Robert, 1825-1908. 265.3
The story of the token, as belonging to the sacrament of the Lord's supper. By Robert Shiells ... New York, J. Ireland [1892] vi, [2], [9]-170 p. illus. 17 1/2 cm. [BV828.S5 1892] 35-34415
1. Tokens, Communion. 2. Lord's supper—Hist. I. Title.

TENNEY, Mary (McWhorter) 265.3 Mrs., 1873-
Communion tokens, their origin, history, and use, with a treatise on the relation of the sacrament to the vitality, and revivals of the church, by Mary McWhorter Tenney ... Grand Rapids, Mich., Zondervan publishing house [c1936] 195 [9] p. front. (port.) II pl 20 cm. "The book ... gives us much interesting ... Presbyterian history."--Introd. signed: Walter L. Lingle. Full name: Mrs. Mary Francis (McWhorter) Tenney Bibliography: p. 173-195. [BV828.T45] 37-17375
1. Tokens, Communion. 2. Lord's supper—Hist. 3. Presbyterian church—Hist. I. [Full name: Mrs. Mary Frances (McWhorter) Tenney] II. Title.

Toldot Yeshu.

MEAD, George Robert Stow, 296.1'2 1863-1933.
Did Jesus live 100 B.C.? An enquiry into the Talmud Jesus stories, the Toldoth Jeschu, and some curious statements of Epiphanius, being a contribution to the study of Christian origins. New Hyde Park, N.Y., University Books [1968] xxxii, 442 p. 24 cm. Includes bibliographical references. [BM620.M4 1968] 68-18754
1. Jesus Christ—Jewish interpretations. 2. Jesus Christ—Chronology. 3. Epiphanius, Saint, Bp. of Constantia in Cyprus. 4. Toldot Yeshu. 5. Talmud—Legends. I. Title.

Toleration.

BARLOW, Richard Burgess, 274.2 1927-
Citizenship and conscience; a study in the theory and practice of religious toleration in England during the eighteenth century. Philadelphia, University of Pennsylvania Press [1963, c1962] 348 p. 22 cm. [BR1610.B35] 62-7197
1. Toleration. 2. Gt. Brit. — Church history — 18th cent. I. Title.

BELMONT, Perry, 1851- 261.
Political equality; religious toleration, from Roger Williams to Jefferson, by Perry Belmont ... New York, London, G. P. Putnam's sons, 1927. iii, 149 p. 21 cm. [BV741.B4] 27-27949
I. Title.
Content omitted.

BROOKS, Phillips bp., 1835- 261. 1893.
Tolerance, two lectures addressed to the students of several of the divinity schools of the Protestant Episcopal church by Phillips Brooks. With an introduction by Nicholas Murray Butler. [New ed.] New York, E. P. Dutton & company [1924] 4 p. l., 111 p. 18 1/2 cm. [BR1610.B6 1924] 24-15089
1. Toleration. I. Title.

CLARKE, William Francis, 261.7 1894-
The folly of bigotry: an analysis of intolerance, by William Francis Clarke ... Chicago, Non-sectarian league for Americanism [c1940] xv, 137 p. 19 cm. [BR1610.C5] 40-6508
1. Toleration. 2. Religious liberty—U.S. 3. Persecution. I. Title.

COHEN, Mortimer Joseph, 323.44 1894-
Counterattack, scapegoats or solotions, by Mortimer J. Cohen ... and Maurice B. Fagan ... Philadelphia, Pa., Philadelphia Jewish community relations council, 1945. 70 p. illus. 19 cm. [BR1610.C6] 45-56521
1. Toleration. 2. Liberty. I. Fagan, Maurice B., joint author. II. Philadelphia Jewish community relations council. III. Title.

DUSHAW, Amos Isaac, 1877- 261
No room for Him. Brooklyn, Tolerance Press [1950] 127 p. 18 cm. [BR1610.D8] 50-8526
1. Toleration. 2. Race problems. I. Title.

EISENSTEIN, Ira, 1906- 261.7
The ethics of tolerance applied to religious groups in America, by Ira Eisenstein. New York, King's crown press, 1941. viii p., 2 l., [3]-87 p. 23 cm. Issued also as thesis (PH.D) Columbia university. "Selected bibliography": p. [86]-87. [BR1610.E5 1941a] 42-3552
1. Toleration. 2. U.S.—Religion. I. Title. II. Title: Religious groups in America.

ELLIS, John Tracy, 1905- 241.4
A commitment to truth. Latrobe, Pa., Archabbey Press [c1966] vii, 93 p. 20 cm. (Wimmer lecture 19) Bibliographical references included in "Notes" (p. 79-88) [BR1610.E55] 66-18697
1. Toleration. 2. Truth. I. Title. II. Series.

HYMAN, Jacob David. 261.7
William Chillingworth and the theory of toleration, by J. D. Hyman ... Cambridge, Mass., Harvard university press, 1931. 84, [1] p. 20 cm. (Half-title: Harvard undergraduate essays, published in the year 1961 from a gift by Herbert Nathan Strans) "Honors thesis in history and literature." Bibliography: p. [81]-[85] [BR1610.H8] 31-33997
1. Chillingworth, William, 1602-1644. 2. Toleration. I. yman ... II. Title.

KAMEN, Henry Arthur 261.7'2 Francis.
The rise of toleration [by] Henry Kamen. New York, McGraw-Hill [1967] 256 p. illus. (part col.), ports. 20 cm. (World university library) Bibliography: p. 249-250. [BR1610.K3 1967b] 66-24158
1. Toleration. 2. Religious liberty—History. I. Title.

LANDIS, Benson Young, 1897- 261.7
Adventure in understanding, a handbook of discussion and source materials for Protestants, Catholics and Jews, by Benson Y. Landis; with an introduction by Henry Noble MacCracken. New York, N. Y., National conference of Christians & Jews, 1941. 63 p. 22 cm. "Selected references": p. 58-63. [BR516.L3] 41-20365
1. Toleration. 2. Catholics in the U. S. 3. Jews in the U. S. 4. Protestants in the U. S. I. National conferences of Christians & Jews. II. Title.

LECLER, Joseph 261.72
Toleration and the Reformation. 2v. Tr. [from French] by T. L. Westow. New York, Association Press [1960] 432, 544p. 25cm. Bibl. 60-12723 25.00, bxd.
1. Toleration. 2. Religious liberty—Europe. 3. Reformation. I. Title.

LOCKE, John, 1632-1704. 272
Epistola de tolerantia. A letter on toleration; Latin text edited with a preface by Raymond Klibansky; English translation with an introduction and notes by J. W. Gough. Oxford, Clarendon P., 1968. xliv, 171 p. 2 plates, 2 facsims. 23 cm. Parallel texts in English and Latin. [BR1610.L823] 70-373959 40/-
1. Toleration. I. Klibansky, Raymond, 1905- ed. II. Gough, John Weidhofft. III. Title. IV. Title: A letter on toleration.

MENSCHING, Gustav, 1901- 241'.4
Tolerance and truth in religion. Translated by H.-J. Klimkeit. Augm. in collaboration with the author. University, University of Alabama Press [1971] xii, 207 p. 22 cm. Translation of Toleranz und Wahrheit in der Religion. Bibliography: p. [196]-200. [BR1610.M413] 79-169495 ISBN 0-8173-6701-2 8.00
1. Toleration. I. Title.

MILL, James, 1773-1836. 179'.9
The principles of toleration. New York, B. Franklin [1971] iv, 44 p. 19 cm. (Burt Franklin research & source works series, 765. Philosophy monograph series, 64) Reprint of the 1837 ed., which was originally published in the Westminster review, July, 1826, under title: Essays on the formation and publication of opinions, and other subjects. Includes bibliographical references. [BR1610.M53 1971] 71-154520 ISBN 0-8337-2389-8
1. Toleration. I. Title.

MURRAY, Robert Henry, 241'.4 1874-1947.
Erasmus & Luther: their attitude to toleration, by Robert H. Murray. New York, B. Franklin [1972] xxiii, 503 p. ports. 23 cm. (Burt Franklin research and source works series. Philosophy and religious history monographs 91) Includes bibliographies. [BR350.E7M8 1972] 70-183697 ISBN 0-8337-4297-3 25.00
1. Erasmus, Desiderius, d. 1536. 2. Luther, Martin, 1483-1546. 3. Toleration. 4. Reformation. I. Title.

RUTHERFORD, Joseph F., 1869- 272
Intolerance, explained in two Bible treatises, by J. F. Rutherford... [Brooklyn, Watch tower Bible and tract society, International Bible students association, c1933] 61 p. illus. 17 1/2 cm. Contents.Intolerance; religious intolerance: why.--Value of knowledge and understanding. [BX8526.R8655] 34-2212
1. Toleration. 2. Religious liberty—New Jersey. 3. Catholic church—Doctrinal and controversial works—Protestant authors. I. Title.

SCHWAB, Paul Josiah. 922.443
... The attitude of Wolfgang Musculus toward religious tolerance, by Paul Josiah Schwab ... Scottdale, Pa., Printed by the Mennonite press, 1933. 62, [1] p. illus. (port.) 26 cm. (Yale studies in religion. no. 6) "An essay based upon a dissertation submitted to the faculty of the Graduate school of Yale university ... for the degree of doctor of philosophy [1923]" Bibliography: p. 57-[69] [BR350.M8S42 1928] 34-8173
1. Musculus, Wolfgang, 1497-1563. 2. Toleration. I. Title.

SCOTT, Nancy Elnora.
The limits of toleration within the Church of England from 1632 to 1642, by Nancy Elnora Scott ... Philadelphia [Lancaster, Pa., The New era printing company] 1912. vii, 119 p. 20 cm. Thesis (PH. D.)--University of Pennsylvania, 1909. Bibliography: p. 114-119. 12-25020

I. Title.

SEATON, Alexander Adam. 283
The theory of toleration under the later Stuarts, by A. A. Seaton ... The Prince consort prize, 1910 ... Cambridge [Eng.] University press, 1911. vii, [1], 364 p. 19 cm. (Half-title: Cambridge historical essays. no. xix) Bibliography: p. [346]-350. [BR757.S4] 11-6490
1. Toleration. 2. Gt. Brit.—Church history. 3. Religious liberty—Gt. Brit. I. Prince consort dissertation, 1910. II. Title.

TOLERANCE and the 261.7
Catholic, a symposium; translated by George Lamb. New York, Sheed and Ward, 1955. viii, 199p. 22cm. Translation of Tolerance et communaute humaine. Bibliographical footnotes. [BR1610.T615] 55-7485
1. Toleration.

VAN LOON, Hendrik Willem, 261.
1882-
Tolerance, by Hendrik Willem Van Loon ... New York, Boni & Liveright, 1925. viii p., 1 l., 11.399 p. 23 cm. [BR1610.V3] 25-22590
1. Toleration. I. Title.

VAN LOON, Hendrik Willem, 261.
1882-
Tolerance, by Hendrik Van Loon. [New York] Boni & Liveright, 1927. xi, 11-382 p. col. front., illus. 24 cm. "Ninth printing, September, 1927." [BR1610.V3 1927] 27-20682
1. Toleration. I. Title.

VAN LOON, Hendrik Willem, 261.7
1882-
Tolerance, by Hendrik Van Loon. Garden City, N.Y., Garden City publishing co., inc. [1933] xi, 11-382 p. incl. front., illus. 21 1/2 cm. [BR1610.V3 1933] 34-1028
1. Toleration. I. Title.

VAN LOON, Hendrik Willem, 261.7
1882-
Tolerance, by Hendrik Van Loon. New York, The Sun dial press, inc. [1939] xi, 11-382, p. incl. front., illus. 21 1/2 cm. [BR1610.V3 1939] 39-24334
1. Toleration. I. Title.

VAN LOON, Hendrik Willem, 261.7
1882-
Tolerance, by Hendrik Van Loon. New York, Liveright publishing corp. [1940] xi, 11-386 p. incl. col. front., illus. 22 cm. "Eleventh printing, September, 1940." [BR1610.V3 1940] 41-2054
1. Toleration. I. Title.

WHATELY, Richard, abp. of 230.3
Dublin, 1787-1863.
The use and abuse of party-feeling in matters of religion, considered in eight sermons preached before the University of Oxford, in the year MDCCCXXII, at the lecture founded by the late Rev. John Bampton... By Richard Whately... Oxford, The University press for the author, 1822. xxx, 274 p. 22 cm. (Lettered on cover: Bampton lectures. 1822) [BR45.B3 1822] (230.082) 33-21448
1. Toleration. 2. Sermons, English. I. Title. II. Title: Party feeling in matters of religion.

Toleration — Collections.

MOORE, Katharine, ed. 179.9
The spirit of tolerance. Foreword by Victor Gollancz. London, V. Gollancz [Mystic, Conn., Verry, 1966] c.1964. 256p. 21cm. [BR1610.M6] 65-85576 4.50 bds.,
1. Toleration — Collections. I. Title.

Toles, E. B.

TOLES, E. B. 286'.1'0924 B
A layman shares Jesus / E. B. Toles ; [foreword by Grady Wilson]. Nashville : Broadman Press, c1979. 158 p. : ill. ; 21 cm. [BX6495.T58A35] 78-67925 ISBN 0-8054-5506-X pbk. : 3.95
1. Toles, E. B. 2. Baptists—Biography—United States. I. Title.

Tolton, Augustine, 1854-1897.

HEMESATH, Caroline. 282'.092'4 B
From slave to priest: a biography of the Rev. Augustine Tolton (1854-1897), first Afro-American priest of the United States. Chicago, Franciscan Herald Press [1973] xiii, 174 p. illus. 21 cm. Bibliography: p. [167]-169. [BX4705.T6813H4] 73-11113 ISBN 0-8199-0468-6 5.95
1. Tolton, Augustine, 1854-1897. I. Title.

Tomas de Villanueva, Saint, 1488-1555.

DUNSTAN, Brother, 1915- 922.246
The poor rich man; a story of St. Thomas of Villanova. Illus. by Judith E. Quinn. Notre Dame, Ind., Dujarie Press [1955] 93p. illus. 24cm. [BX4700.T7D8] 55-38173
1. Tomas de Villanueva, Saint, 1488-1555. I. Title.

[MAIMBOURG, Claude] 922.
The life of St. Thomas of Villanova, archbishop of Valentia and Augustinian friar. With an introductory sketch of the men, the manners, and the morals of the sixteenth century ... 1st American ed. Philadelphia, P. F. Cunningham & son, 1874. 352 p. front. 19 cm. "Introduction and historical sketch" signed: T. C. Middleton, O.S.A. "A verbatim reprint from the London edition, translated by the Oratorian fathers, and published by Richardson and son, in 1847."--p. 74. The London edition, 1847, is accompanied by the Life of St. Francis Solano by F. Courtot; the volume was published in New York the same year (1847) by E. Dunigan. [BX4700.T7M3 1874] 30-22394
1. Tomas de Villanueva, Saint, 1488-1555. I. Middleton, Thomas Cooke, 1842-1923, ed. II. London. Oratory of St. Philip Neri. III. Title.

[MAIMBOURG, Claude] 922.
... The lives of St. Thomas of Villanova, archbishop of Valentia, and Augustinian friar; and of St. Francis Solano, apostle of Peru, of the Order of St. Francis ... New York, E. Dunigan; London [etc.] T. Richardson and son, 1847. xii, 310 p. front. (port.) 20 cm. (The saints and servants of God. [4]) Printed in Great Britain. "[The Life] of S. Thomas of Villanova is by Father Claude Maimbourg ... published at Paris in 1659; and that of S. Francis Solano by Father Francis Courtot."--Pref. Translated by the Congregation of the Oratory of St. Philip Neri, London. [BX4700.T7M3 1847] 30-22399
1. Tomas de Villanueva, Saint, 1488-1555. 2. Solano, Francisco, Saint, 1549-1610. I. Courtot, Francois, d. ca. 1705. II. Oratorians in England (London) III. Title.

Tomczak, Larry, 1949-

TOMCZAK, Larry, 1949- 248'.2 B
Clap your hands! Plainfield, N.J., Logos International [1973] 143 p. photos. 21 cm. [BX4705.T68144A33] 73-88241 ISBN 0-88270-072-3 2.50 (pbk.)
1. Tomczak, Larry, 1949- I. Title.

Tomlinson, Homer Aubrey, Bp., 1892-1968.

TOMLINSON, Homer 289'.5'0924
Aubrey, Bp., 1892-1968.
"It came to pass in those days": the shout of a king. Queens Village, N.Y., Church of God, U.S.A. Headquarters, 1968. [4], 219 p. illus. 19 cm. On spine: The shout of a king. Bibliography: 2d prelim. page. [BX7060.Z8T63] 73-172331
1. Tomlinson, Homer Aubrey, Bp., 1892-1968. 2. Church of God of Prophecy. I. Title. II. Title: The shout of a king.

Tommasini, Maria.

RICHARDSON, Mary 922.245
Kathleen, 1903-
To grow holy merrily; the life of Mother Tommasini. Fresno, Calif., Acad. Guild Pr. [1963,c.1960] 160p. 23cm. First pub. in London in 1960 under title: Tommasini. 63-12103 4.50
1. Tommasini, Maria. I. Title.

Tompkins, James J., 1870-

BOYLE, George, 1902- 922.271
Father Tompkins of Nova Scotia. New York, P. J. Kenedy [1953] 234p. illus. 21cm. [BX4705.T682B6] 53-9633
1. Tompkins, James J., 1870- I. Title.

Tong, James.

BROWNING, Mary 266.2'0924 B
Carmel.
Think big; a partial biography of Reverend James Tong, S.J. [1st ed.] Owensboro, Ky., Printed by Winkler Print. Co., 1970. 109 p. illus., ports. 28 cm. [BV3269.T67B76] 76-134943
1. Tong, James. I. Title.

Torah scrolls.

POLLAK, Michael. 222'.1'044
The discovery of a missing Chinese Torah scroll. Dallas, Bridwell Library [1973] 36 l. 28 cm. Includes bibliographical references. [BM657.T6P64] 74-177309
1. Torah scrolls. 2. Jews in Kaifeng, China. I. Bridwell Library. II. Title.

RUBENSTEIN, Shmuel. 296.7
The Sefer Torah : an illustrated analysis of the history, preparation, and use of the Sefer Torah / by Shmuel L. Rubenstein. New York : Zeirei Agudath Israel, Sefer Torah Project, [1976] 32 p. : ill. ; 23 cm. Bibliography: p. 32. [BM657.T6R82] 77-365746
1. Torah scrolls. I. Zeirei Agudath Israel of America. II. Title.

Torah (The word)

BIBLE. O.T. English. 221.5'2
Birnbaum. 1976.
The concise Jewish Bible / edited and translated by Philip Birnbaum. New York : Sanhedrin Press, c1976. 234 p. ; 24 cm. [BS895.B57] 76-49108 ISBN 0-88482-450-0 : 7.95. ISBN 0-88482-451-9 pbk. : 3.95
I. Birnbaum, Philip. II. Title.

JENSEN, Joseph, 1924- 224'.1'066
The use of tora by Isaiah; his debate with the wisdom tradition. Washington, Catholic Biblical Association of America, 1973. ix, 156 p. 26 cm. (The Catholic biblical quarterly. Monograph series, 3) Bibliography: p. 136-146. [BS1515.2.J46] 73-83134 3.00
1. Bible. O.T. Isaiah—Criticism, interpretation, etc. 2. Torah (The word) I. Title. II. Series.

MOSES, Ben Maimon 1135-1204. 296
The code of Maimonides. New Haven, Yale University Press, 1949- v. 22 cm. (Yale Judaica series, v. 2- Translation of Mishneh Torah. [BM545.M54] 49-9495
I. Title. II. Series.

Tornay, Maurice, 1910-1949.

LOUP, Robert. 922.2515
Martyr in Tibet; the heroic life and death of Father Maurice Tornay, St. Bernard missionary to Tibet. Translated from the French by Charles Davenport. New York, D. McKay Co. [1956] 238p. illus. 21cm. [BV3427.T5L62] 56-14036
1. Tornay, Maurice, 1910-1949. 2. Missions—Tibet. 3. Augustinian Canons. Congregation of the Great St. Bernard. I. Title.

Toronto. Peoples Church.

PALMER, Bernard Alvin, 289.9
1914-
Peoples : church on the go / Bernard Palmer. Wheaton, Ill. : Victor Books, c1976. 111 p. : ill. ; 21 cm. [BX9999.T666P34] 76-18626 ISBN 0-88207-656-6 pbk. : 2.50
1. Toronto. Peoples Church. I. Title.

Torquemada, Juan de, 1388-1468.

IZBICKI, Thomas M. 282'.092'4
Protector of the faith : Cardinal Johannes de Turrecremata and the defense of the institutional church / by Thomas M. Izbicki. Washington, D.C. : Catholic University of America Press, c1981. p. cm. Includes index. Bibliography: p. [BX4705.T69I93] 19 81-1400 ISBN 0-8132-0558-1 : 19.95
1. Torquemada, Juan de, 1388-1468. 2. Catholic Church—Government—History. 3. Church—History of doctrines—Middle Ages, 600-1500. I. Title.

Torquemada, Juan de, Cardinal, 1388-1468. Summa de ecclesia.

TORQUEMADA, Juan de. Cardinal
1388-1468.
John of Torquemada, O. P: The antiquity of the church; annotated text and commentary. Washington, Catholic University of America Press, 1957. 65p. 24cm. (Catholic University of America. Studies in sacred theology, 2d ser., no. 102) Includes text of chapters 22-26 of the Summa de ecclesin by John of Torquemada (p. 14-42) Bibliography: p. 62-64. Bibliographical footnotes. A60
1. Torquemada, Juan de, Cardinal, 1388-1468. Summa de ecclesia. 2. Church—Foundation. 3. umma de ecclesia. I. Title. II. Title: The autiquity of the church. III. Series: Catholic University of America. School of Sacred Theology. Studies in sacred theology, 2d ser., no. 102

Torquemada, Tomas de, 1420-1498.

LONGHURST, John Edward, 272.20946
1918-
The age of Torquemada, 2d ed. Lawrence, Kan., Bx. 32 Coronado Pr. [1964, c.1962] 146p. illus. 23cm. 3.95
1. Torquemada, Tomas de, 1420-1498. 2. Jews in Spain—Persecutions. 3. Inquisition. Spain. I. Title.

SABATINI, Rafael, 1875- 272.
Torquemada and the Spanish inquisition; a history by Rafael Sabatini ... Rev. ed. Boston and New York, Houghton Mifflin company [1924] xiv p., 2 l., [3]-466 p. front. (port.) illus. (map) plates. 19 1/2 cm. Bibliography: p. [443]-444. [BX1735.S25 1924 a] 25-362
1. Torquemada, Tomas de, 1420-1498. 2. Inquisition. Spain. I. Title.

WOOD, Clement, 1888- 272.
... Torquemada and the Spanish inquisition [by] Clement Wood. Girard, Kan., Haldeman-Julius company [c1925] 64 p. 12 1/2 cm. (Little blue book, no. 824, ed. by E. Haldeman-Julius) Advertising matter: p. 63-64. [BX1735.W6] CA 27
1. Torquemada, Tomas de, 1420-1498. 2. Inquisition. Spain. I. Title.

Torrance, David Watt, 1862-1922.

LIVINGSTONE, William 275.
Pringle.
A Galilee doctor; being a sketch of the career of Dr. D. W. Torrance of Tiberias, by W. P. Livingstone ... New York, George H. Doran company [1923] x, 283 p. front., plates, ports., map. 22 cm. Printed in Great Britain. [BV3202.T6L5] 24-5336
1. Torrance, David Watt, 1862-1922. 2. Missions—Palestine. I. Title.

Torrance, Thomas Forsyth, 1913-

CREATION, Christ, and culture 230
: studies in honour of T. F. Torrance / edited by Richard W. A. McKinney. Edinburgh : Clark, 1976. ix, 321 p., plate : port. ; 23 cm. Contents.Contents.—Clements, R. E. Covenant and Canon in the Old Testament.—Black, M. The New Creation in I Enoch.—Barbour, R. S. Creation, wisdom, and Christ.—Heron, A. Logos, image, son.—Ritschl, D. Some comments on the backbround and influence of Augustine's Lex Aeterna doctrine.—Jenson, R. W. The body of God's presence.—MacKinnon, D. M. The relation of the doctrines of the Incarnation and the Trinity.—Galloway, A. D. Creation and covenant.—Moltmann, J. Creation and redemption.—O'Donoghue, N. D. Creation and participation.—Jaki, S. L. Theological aspects of creative science.—Langford, T. A. Authority, community, and church.—Houston, J.

Precepts and counsels.—McDonagh, E. Morality and prayer.—McIntyre, J. Theology and method.—Jungel, E. The truth of life.—McKinney, R. W. A. Historical relativism, the appeal to experience and theological reconstruction.—Sykes, S. W. Life after death.—Thomas, J. H. The problem of defining a theology of culture with reference to the theology of Paul Tillich.—Newbigin, L. All in one place or all of one sort? Bibliography: p. 307-321. [BR50.C66] 76-379213 ISBN 0-567-01019-8 : £5.60
1. Torrance, Thomas Forsyth, 1913- 2. Torrance, Thomas Forsyth, 1913- — Bibliography. 3. Theology—Addresses, essays, lectures. I. Torrance, Thomas Forsyth, 1913- II. McKinney, Richard W. A.

Torres, Victor.

TORRES, Victor. 248'.2 B
Son of evil street, by Victor Torres, with Don Wilkerson. Minneapolis, Bethany Followship [1973] 160 p. 21 cm. [BV4935.T65A37] 73-10828 ISBN 0-87123-516-1 1.95
1. Torres, Victor. 2. Narcotic addicts—Personal narratives. 3. Conversion. I. Title.

TORRES, Victor. 248'.2 B
Son of evil street / Victor Torres with Don Wilkerson. 2d ed. Minneapolis : Bethany Fellowship, 1977. 166 p. ; 18 cm. (Dimension books) [BV4935.T65A37 1977] 77-150672 ISBN 0-87123-516-1 pbk. : 1.95
1. Torres, Victor. 2. Narcotic addicts—New York (State)—Brooklyn—Biography. 3. Converts—New York (State)—Brooklyn—Biography. 4. Brooklyn—Biography. I. Wilkerson, Don, joint author. II. Title.

Torrey, Charles Turner, 1813-1846.

LOVEJOY, Joseph 326'.0924 B
Cammet, 1805-1871.
Memoir of Rev. Charles T. Torrey, who died in the penitentiary of Maryland, where he was confined for showing mercy to the poor. New York, Negro Universities Press [1969] viii, 364 p. port. 23 cm. Reprint of the 1847 ed. [E449.T69 1969] 76-92749
1. Torrey, Charles Turner, 1813-1846. I. Title.

Torrey, Joseph, 1797-1867.

VERMONT. University.
Services in remembrance of Rev. Joseph Torrey, D. D., and of Geo. Wyllys Benedict, LL. D., professors in the University of Vermont. [Burlington, Free press, steam book and job office, 1874] 3 p. l., 5-66 p. 22 cm. [LD5632.2.V6] E12
1. Torrey, Joseph, 1797-1867. 2. Benedict, George Wyllys, 1796-1871. I. Title.

Torrey, Reuben Archer, 1856-1928.

DAVIS, George Thompson Brown, 922
1873-
Torrey and Alexander, the story of a world-wide revival; a record and study of the work and personality of the evangelists R. A. Torrey, D. D., and Charles M. Alexander, by George T. B. Davis ... New York, Chicago [etc.] Fleming H. Revell company [c1905] 3 p. l., [9]-257 p. front., plates, ports. 20 cm. [BV3785.T6D3] 5-39044
1. Torrey, Reuben Archer, 1856-1928. 2. Alexander, Charles McCallon, 1867-1920. I. Title.

HARKNESS, Robert. 922
Reuben Archer Torrey, the man, his message, by Robert Harkness ... Chicago, The Bible institute colportage ass'n [c1929] vii, 9-127 p. front. (port.) 20 cm. [BV3785.T6H3] 29-21154
1. Torrey, Reuben Archer, 1856-1928. I. Title.

TORREY, Reuben Archer, 1856- 220.
Is the Bible the inerrant word of God, and was the body of Jesus raised from the dead, by R. A. Torrey... New York, George H. Doran company, c1922. vii p., 2 l. 13-185 p. 19 1/2 cm. $1.50. [BS480.T65] 22-19921
I. Title.

TORREY, Reuben Archer, 1856- 243
Talks to men about the Bible and the Christ of the Bible, by R. A. Torrey... New York, Chicago [etc.] Fleming H. Revell company [c1904] 2 p. l., vii-viii p., 1 l., 138 p. 19 cm. [BV3797.T58 1904] 4-31298
I. Title.

TORREY, Reuben Archer, 1856- 243
1928.
The voice of God in the present hour, by R. A. Torrey... New York, Chicago [etc.] Fleming H. Revell company [c1917] 255 p. 19 1/2 cm. [BV3797.T6] 18-410
I. Title.

Torts (Jewish law)

MISHNAH. Baba kamma. 296
...Mishnah Baba kamma (First gate); translated and annotated by Hyman E. Goldin...with original text vocalized and annotated. New York, The Jordan publishing co., inc. 1933. 4 p. l., 193 p., 2 l., [3]-40 p. 21 cm. (Text of the Talmud) Hebrew text (2 l., [3]-40 p. at end) has special t.-p.: [BM505.A3G641] 33-38962
1. Torts (Jewish law) 2. Nuisances (Jewish law) 3. Damages (Jewish law) 4. Evidence (Jewish law) 5. Larceny (Jewish law) I. Goldin, Hyman Elias, 1881- ed. and tr. II. Title.

Toumililine. Morocco. Monastere benediction.

BEACH, Peter. 271.1096431
Benedictine and Moor; a Christian adventure in Moslem Morocco, by Peter Beach and William Dunphy. Introd. by John LaFarge. [1st ed.] New York, Holt, Rinehart and Winston [1960] 214p. illus. 22cm. [BX2740.M8B4] 60-12011
1. Toumililine. Morocco. Monastere benediction. I. Dunphy, William, joint author. II. Title.

Touraine—Description and travel

ALDRICH, Louisa M. Mrs. 726.
Six weeks in old France; or, Dr. Thom's holiday, by L. M. A. Letters from Chateau de Montagland... Albany, N.Y., American bureau of foreign travel, 1887. vi, 317 p. 12 pl., port. 17 cm. [DC28.A35] 3-29297
1. Touraine—Descr. & trav. I. A., L. M. II. Title. III. Title: Dr. Thom's holiday.

Tournier, Paul.

COLLINS, Gary R. 248'.092'4 B
The Christian psychology of Paul Tournier [by] Gary R. Collins. Grand Rapids, Mich., Baker Book House [1973] 222 p. port. 23 cm. Bibliography: p. 211-213. [BF109.T63C64] 72-93076 4.95
1. Tournier, Paul. 2. Psychology, Religious. I. Title.

PEASTON, Monroe. 248'.092'4 B
Personal living; an introduction to Paul Tournier. [1st ed.] New York, Harper & Row [1972] xvii, 107 p. 22 cm. Bibliography: p. [101]-104. [BF149.P35 1972] 70-184418 4.95
1. Tournier, Paul. 2. Psychology—Addresses, essays, lectures. I. Title.

Towers.

ALLEN, Frank James, 726.50942
1854-
The great church towers of England, chiefly of the perpendicular period; a photographic study of all the principal towers, with critical notes, records of architectural details, and exposition of the principles of tower design, by Frank J. Allen ... Cambridge [Eng.] The University press, 1932. xiii, 205 [1] p. front., illus., 52 pl. diagrs. 20 x 21 1/2 cm. "Portions of this work have been previously published in the Preceedings of the Somerset architectural and natural history society, the Cambridge antiquarian society and Harrow architectural society.". [NA5461.A55] 32-21573
1. Towers. 2. Church architecture—England. I. Title.

Towers—England.

FISHER, Ernest Arthur. 726'.597
Anglo-Saxon towers; an architectural and historical study, by E.A. Fisher. New York, A. M. Kelley [1969] 208 p. illus., plans, 5 maps. 23 cm. Bibliography: p. 193-195. [NA2930.F5] 76-77876
1. Towers—England. 2. Architecture, Anglo-Saxon. I. Title.

Towgood, Micaiah, 1700-1792.

MANNING, James. 922.342
A sketch of the life and writings of the Rev. Micaial Towgood, by James Manning ... Exeter, Printed for the author, by E. Grigg, M, DCC, XOII. 2 p. l., 191 p. 23 1/2 cm. [BX5207.T68M3] 36-32206
1. Towgood, Micaiah, 1700-1792. I. Title.

Townsend, Mass. Methodist Episcopal church.

CHARLTON, Emanuel Carlson, 287.
1849-
The Squanicook parish, by Emanuel C. Charlton. Townsend, G. A. Wilder, printer, 1917. 2 p. l., [9]-96 p. 1 illus., pl., ports. 18 cm. [BX8481.T8M4] 17-14089 0.75
1. Townsend, Mass. Methodist Episcopal church. I. Title.

Townsend. William Cameron, 1896-

HEFLEY, James C. 266'.023'0924 B
Uncle Cam : the story of William Cameron Townsend, founder of the Wycliffe Bible Translators and the Summer Institute of Linguistics / James & Marti Hefley ; photo editor, Cornell Capa. Waco, Tex. : Word Books, [1974] 272 p. : ports. ; 23 cm. [BV2372.T68H43] 73-91556 6.95
1. Townsend, William Cameron, 1896- 2. Wycliffe Bible Translators. 3. Summer Institute of Linguistics. I. Hefley, Marti, joint author. II. Title.

TOWNSEND, William 266'.023'0924 B
Cameron, 1896-
Remember all the way / by William Cameron Townsend, Richard S. Pittman. Huntington Beach, Calif. : Wycliffe Bible Translators, c1975. 144 p. ; 22 cm. Includes bibliographical references. [BV2372.T68A36] 75-329081
1. Townsend, William Cameron, 1896- I. Pittman, Richard Saunders, 1915- joint author. II. Title.

WALLIS, Ethel Emilia 266.023
Two thousand tongues to go; the story of the Wycliffe Bible Translators [by] Ethel Emily Wallis, Mary Angela Bennett. Drawings by Katherine Voigtlander. New York, Harper [c.1959, 1964] 308p. illus. 22cm. 1.95 pap.,
1. Townsend. William Cameron, 1896- 2. Wycliffe Bible Translators. 3. Missions, Foreign. I. Bennett, Mary Angela, 1906- joint author. II. Title.

WALLIS, Ethel Emilia. 266.023
Two thousand tongues to go; the story of the Wycliffe Bible Translators [by] Ethel Emily Wallis and Mary Angela Bennett. Drawings by Katherine Voiglander. [1st ed.] New York, Harper [1959] 308 p. illus. 22 cm. [BV2370.W9W3] 59-7146
1. Townsend, William Cameron, 1896- 2. Wycliffe Bible Translators. 3. Missions, Foreign. I. Bennett, Mary Angels, 1906- joint author. II. Title.

WALLIS, Ethel Emily. 266.023
Two thousand tongues to go; the story of the Wycliffe Bible Translators [by] Ethel Emily Wallis and Mary Angela Bennett. Drawings by Katherine Voigtlander. [1st ed.] New York, Harper [1959] 308 p. illus. 22 cm. [BV2370.W9W3] 59-7146
1. Townsend, William Cameron, 1896- 2. Wycliffe Bible Translators. 3. Missions, Foreign. I. Bennett, Mary Angela, 1906- joint author. II. Title.

Towson, Md. Trinity Church—Anniversaries.

A brief history of Trinity Church, Towsontown, 1860-1960. Compiled from the records of the vestry and Dr. Jackson Piper's manuscript. On the occasion of the one hundredth anniversary of the church. Towson, Md., 1960. 73p. illus., ports. 23cm.
1. Towson, Md. Trinity Church—Anniversaries. I. McIntosh, J Rieman.

Toy, Crawford, Howell, 1836-1919.

STUDIES in the history of 294.
religions, presented to Crawford Howell Toy by pupils, colleagues and friends; ed. by David Gordon Lyon [and] George Foot Moore. New York, The Masmillan company, 1912. viii p., 1 l., 373 p. 2 pl. 24 1/2 cm. [BL25.S7] 12-25968
1. Toy, Crawford, Howell, 1836-1919. 2. Religion—Addresses, essays, lectures. I. Lyon, David Gordon, 1852-1965, ed. II. Moore, George Foot, 1851-1931, joint ed.
Contents omitted.

Toys.

BOOTH, Herbert, 1862-1926. 252
Toys and things; a series of talks to parents, teachers, young people and children on the principles associated with Play-things, by Herbert Booth ... New York, Hodder & Stoughton, George H. Doran company [c1916] xviii p., 1 l., 21-235 p. 20 1/2cm. $1.00 [BV4315.B6] 16-21252
1. Toys. 2. Religious education. 3. Object-teaching. I. Title.

Tozer, Aiden Wilson, 1897-1963.

FANT, David Jones, 1897- 922.89
A. W. Tozer, a twentieth century prophet. Harrisburg, Pa., Christian Pubns., 1522 N. Third St. [1964] 180p. port. 21cm. 64-21945 price unreported
1. Tozer, Aiden Wilson, 1897-1963. I. Title.

Trabzon, Turkey (City) Ayasofya Kilisei.

RICE, David Talbot, 709'.565
1903-
The church of Haghia Sophia at Trebizond ed. by David Talbot Rice. Edinburgh, Edinburgh Univ. Pr. for the Russell Trust, 1968. xxi, 275p. 89 plates, illus. (some col. 1 fold. col. in pocket), plan. 31cm. Notes & refs. [NA5871.T7R5 1968] 68-19880 30.00
1. Trabzon, Turkey (City) Ayasofya Kilisei. I. Title.
Available from Aldine, Chicago.

Tract societies.

AMERICAN tract society.
Annual report. New York, 1826-[19 v. in. 21-23 cm. Report year ends: 1st- May 1; April 1. First issued 1826, with title: First annual report of the American tract society, instituted at New-York, 1825. With lists of ausillaries and benefactors, addresses at the anniversary &c. Title varies slightly. [BV2375.A4] 6-7873
I. Title.

AMERICAN Tract Society, Boston.
Proceedings of the first ten years. To which is added a brief view of the principal religious tract societies throughout the world. [Boston?] Printed for the American Tract Society by Flagg and Gould, 1824. 215 p. 18 cm. [BV2375.A3] 51-45983
1. Tract societies. I. Title.

MILK for babes;
or, A text and verse of a hymn for every day in the year. New York, American tract society, [18--] 128 p. 8 cm. 10-21438
I. American tract society, New York.

NEW England Tract Society. 266
Report. [Andover, Mass.] Printed by Flagg and Gould. v. 21 cm. annual. Report year ends Apr. 30. [BV2375.N44] 64-58581
I. Title.

RANNEY, David James, 1863- 922.
Dave Ranney; or, Thirty years on the Bowery; an autobiography. Introduction by Rev. A. F. Schauffler, D.D. New York, American tract society [1910] 205 p. front. (port.) plates 19 1/2 cm. [BV2657.R3A3] 10-20629

I. The American tract society. II. Title.

Tracts.

AMERICAN tract society. 240.82
The publications of the American tract society ... New York, American tract society [1826!- v. illus. 18 cm. Vol. xi includes "Alphabetical index to the ... first eleven volumes." The list of "contents" in a volume does not always correspond with the tracts. [BV4510.A1A5] 31-19013
1. Tracts. I. Title.

AMERICAN tract society, Boston. 248
The publications of the American tract society. Second series. Vol. 1. [Andover, Mass.] Printed for the society, by Ellag & Gould, 1824. 4 p. l., 5-240 p. incl. illus., plates. 14 cm. Each tract has special t.-p. No more published? [BV4510.A1A52] 39-10908
1. Tracts. I. Title.
Contents omitted.

AMERICAN Unitarian association. 288
Tracts. ser. 1, v. 1- (no. 1- Boston, 18 v. 19 cm. Issued in 10 series from 1825? to 1931? Series 11 is arbitrarily asigned in Library of Congress. Some nos. in revised editions. Ser. issued without title. [BX9813.A5] 46-28939
1. Tracts. I. Title.

CONGREGATIONAL board of publication. 248
Tracts of the Doctrinal tract and book society... Boston, Doctrinal tract and book society [185-?] 2 v. 19 1/2 cm. [BV4510.A1C65] 39-16015
1. Tracts. 2. Christianity—Addresses, essays, lectures. I. Title.

DOCTRINAL tract and book society, Boston. 248
Tracts of the Doctrinal tract and book society ... Boston, Doctrinal tract and book society [185-?] 2 v. 20 cm. [BV4510.A1D6] ISBN 39-16015
1. Tracts. 2. Christianity—Addresses, essays, lectures. I. Title.

[MARSH, Leonard] 1800-1870. 201
The apocatastasis; or, Progress backwards. A new "Tract for the times." ... By the author. Burlington [Vt.] C. Goodrich, 1854. 202 p., 1 l. 24 cm. [BL48.M3] 30-11344
I. Title.

MUDGE, James.
The life ecstatic, by the Rev. James Mudge ... New York, Boston [etc.] American tract society [c1906] 223 p. 20 cm. 6-33634
I. Title.

Tracy, Charles Chapin, 1838-1917.

WHITE, George Edward, 1861-
Charles Chapin Tracy, missionary, philanthropist, educator, first president of Anatolia collete, Marsovan, Turkey, by Rev. George E. White ... Boston, Chicago, The Pilgrim press [c1918] 2 p. l., 79, [1] p. front., plates, ports., map. 19 1/2 cm. [BV3175.M3W5] 19-2547
1. Tracy, Charles Chapin, 1838-1917. 2. Anatolia college, Marsivan, Asia Minor. 3. Marsivan, Asia Minor. I. Title.

Tracy, Leighton Stanley, 1882-1942.

TRACY, Olive Gertrude, 1908- 922.654
Tracy Sahib of India. Kansas City, Mo. Beacon Hill Press [1954] 191p. illus. 20cm. [BV3269.T7T7] 54-1974
1. Tracy, Leighton Stanley, 1882-1942. I. Title.

Trade-marks—United States

PAYNTER, Richard Henry, 1890-
A psychological study of trade-mark infringement, by Richard H. Paynter, jr. ... New York, The Science press [1920] iv, 72 p. incl. tables. 26 cm. (Archives of psychology, ed. by R. S. Woodworth. no. 42, Jan., 1920) Columbia university contributions to philosophy and psychology, vol. xxvi, no. 3-[9] Published also as thesis (PH. D.) Columbia university, 1917. [BR21.A7 no. 42] 20-11580
1. Trade-marks—U. S. 2. Psychology, Physiological. I. Title.

Tradition (Judaism)

MOSES ben Maimon, 1135-1204. 296.1'2
Maimonides' Introduction to the Talmud : a translation of the Rambam's introduction to his Commentary on the Mishna / translated and annotated by Zvi L. Lampel. New York : Judaica Press, 1975. 249, 37 p. ; 24 cm. Added t.p.: Hakdamat ha-Rambam le-ferusho la-Mishnayot. Selections from Kitab al-Siraj in English and Hebrew. Errata sheet inserted. Includes bibliographical references and indexes. [BM529.M672 1975] 74-25932 ISBN 0-910818-06-1 : 7.95
1. Mishnah—Introductions. 2. Talmud—Introductions. 3. Tradition (Judaism) I. Lampel, Zvi L. II. Title. III. Title: Introduction to the Talmud. IV. Title: Hakdamat ha-Rambam le-ferusho la-Mishnayot.

PETUCHOWSKI, Jakob Josef, 1925- 296.3
Ever since Sinai; a modern view of Torah [by] Jakob J. Petuchowski. 2d ed., rev. New York, Scribe Publications, 1968. ix, 132 p. 22 cm. Includes bibliographical references. [BM529.P36 1968] 70-5270 1.95
1. Tradition (Judaism) I. Title.

PETUCHOWSKI, Jakob Josef, 1925- 296.1
Heirs of the Pharisees [by] Jakob J. Petuchowski. New York, Basic Books, [1970] vii, 199 p. 22 cm. Includes bibliographical references. [BM529.P363 1970] 75-110776 6.95
1. Tradition (Judaism) I. Title.

SANDERS, James A., 1927- 221.1'2
Torah and canon, by James A. Sanders. Philadelphia, Fortress Press [1972] xx, 124 p. 19 cm. [BS1135.S25] 72-171504 ISBN 0-8006-0105-X 2.95
1. Bible. O.T.—Canon. 2. Tradition (Judaism) I. Title.

VERMES, Geza, 1924- 221.6'6
Scripture and tradition in Judaism. Haggadic studies. 2nd, revised ed. Leiden, Brill, 1973. x, 243 p. 25 cm. (Studia post-biblica v. 4) Includes bibliographical references. [BS1186.V47 1973] 74-157393 ISBN 9-00-403626-1
1. Abraham, the patriarch. 2. Balaam, the prophet. 3. Bible. O.T.—Criticism, interpretation, etc., Jewish. 4. Tradition (Judaism) 5. Aggada—Addresses, essays, lectures. I. Title. II. Series.
Distributed by Humanities Press; 19.25.

WEINGREEN, Jacob. 221.6'6
From Bible to Mishna : the continuity of tradition / by J. Weingreen. New York : Holmes & Meier, c1976. p. cm. Includes index. Bibliography: p. [BS1186.W44] 75-37728 ISBN 0-8419-0249-6
1. Bible. O.T.—Criticism, interpretation, etc., Jewish. 2. Mishnah—Criticism, interpretation, etc. 3. Tradition (Judaism) I. Title.

Tradition (Theology)

ALLCHIN, A. M. 230
The living presence of the past : the dynamic of Christian tradition / by A.M. Allchin. New York : Seabury Press, 1981. p. cm. [BT90.A46] 19 81-5692 ISBN 0-8164-2334-2 pbk. : 7.95
1. Tradition (Theology) 2. Church—Unity. 3. Continuity of the church. 4. Prayer. I. Title.

CHRISTIANITY in a new world. 230
Philadelphia, Boston [etc.] The Judson press [1921] 5 p. l., 3-226 p. 20 cm. Contents.Religion the basis of life, by C.W. Gitkey.--The unshaken Christ, by H.E. Fosdick.--The place of tradition in modern Christianity, by M.G. Evans.-- The liberty of the children of God, by E.D. Buxton.--The Baptist principle in a time of reconstruction, by J.R. Brown.--The modern evangel, by G. Cross.--The power of the Gospel, by G.B. Smith.--The church and social reconstruction, by W.H.P. Faunce.--Christianity and business, by G.W. Coleman.--Can a nation be moral? By S. Mathews.--Can Baptists cooperate? by R.A. Ashworth.--The ends of the earth, by J.H. Franklin. [BR479.C5] 21-4485

CLAY, Albert Tobias, 1866-1925. 222.
The origin of Biblical traditions; Hebrew legends in Babylonia and Israel; lectures on Biblical archaeology delivered at the Lutheran theological seminary, Mt. Airy, Philadelphia, by Albert T. Clay. New Haven, Yale university press; [etc., tec.] 1923. 224 p. 24 cm. (Yale oriental series. Researches. vol. xii) "Published ... on the Alexander Kohut memorial publication fund." [BS1235.C5] 23-12464
I. Yale university. Alexander Kohut memorial publication fund." II. Title.

CONGAR, Yves Marie Joseph, 1904- 230
The meaning of tradition, by Yves Congar. Translated from the French by A. N. Woodrow. [1st ed.] New York, Hawthorn Books [1964] 155 p. 22 cm. (The Twentieth century encyclopedia of Catholicism, v. 3. Section 1: Knowledge and faith) Translation of Tradition et la vie de l'eglise. [BT90.C593] 64-14159
1. Tradition (Theology) I. Title. II. Series: The Twentieth century encyclopedia of Catholicism, v. 3

CONGAR, Yves Marie Joseph, 1904- 230.09
Tradition and traditions; an historical and a theological essay, by Yves M. J. Congar. New York, Macmillan [1967, c1966] xx, 536 p. 22 cm. Bibliography: p. 521-523. [BT90.C613] 67-11630
1. Tradition (Theology) 2. Theology, Doctrinal—Hist. I. Title.

CONGAR, Yves Marie Joseph, 1904- 230.09
Tradition and traditions; an historical and a theological essay, by Yves M.-J. Congar. New York, Macmillan [1967, c1966] xx, 536 p. 22 cm. Bibliography: p. 521-523. [BT90.C613 1967] 67-11630
1. Tradition (Theology) 2. Theology, Doctrinal—History. I. Title.

GEISELMANN, Josef Rupert, 1890- 230
The meaning of tradition. [Tr. from German by W. . O'Hara. New York] Herder & Herder [c.1966] 123p. 22cm. (Quaestiones disputatae, 15) Bibl. [BT90.G413] 66-10597 2.50 pap.,
1. Tradition (Theology) I. Title.

GEISELMANN, Josef Rupert, 1890- 230
The meaning of tradition. [Translated by W. J. O'Hara. New York] Herder and Herder [1966] 123 p. 22 cm. (Quaestiones disputatae, 15) Translation of the first 3 chapters of Die Hellge Schrift und die Tradition. Bibliographical references included in "Notes" (p. 113-123) [BT90.G413 1966] 66-10597
1. Tradition (Theology) I. Title.

HINSDALE, Burke Aaron, 1837-1900. 230
Ecclesiastical tradition; its origin and early growth; its place in the churches; and its value. By B. A. Hinsdale... Cincinnati, Standard publishing co., 1879. 200 p. 19 1/2 cm. [BT90.H6] 40-22633
1. Tradition (Theology) I. Title.

JENKINS, Daniel Thomas, 1914-
Tradition, freedom, and the spirit. Philadelphia, Westminster Press [1951] 195p. 22cm. A53
1. Tradition (Theology) I. Title.

MACKEY, James Patrick 230.2
The modern theology of tradition. [New York] Herder & Herder [1963, c.1962] 219p. 23cm. Bibl. 62-19789 4.75
1. Tradition (Theology) I. Title.

MACKEY, James Patrick. 230
Tradition and change in the church [by] J. P. Mackey. Dayton, Ohio, Pflaum Press, 1968. xxiv, 192 p. 21 cm. Includes bibliographical references. [BT90.M33] 68-21238
1. Tradition (Theology) 2. Church renewal—Catholic Church. I. Title.

MEREDITH, Anthony. 262'.02
The theology of tradition. Notre Dame, Ind., Fides Publishers [1971] 95 p. 19 cm. (Theology today, no. 11) Bibliography: p. 92. [BT90.M46] 77-27746 ISBN 0-85342-257-5 0.95
1. Tradition (Theology) I. Title.

MOFFAT, James, 1870- 230
The thrill of tradition, by James Moffat ... based on the James W. Richards lectures delivered before the University of Virginia. New York, The Macmillan company, 1944. xi, 201 p. 19 1/2 cm. "First printing." Bibliographical references included in "Notes" (p. 184-193) [BT90.M6] 44-1206
1. Tradition (Theology) I. Title.

MURPHY, John L 1924- 230
The notion of tradition in John Driedo. Dissertatio ad lauream in Facultate Theologica Pontificiae Universitatis Gregorianae. Milwaukee, 1959. 321p. 23cm. At head of title: Pontificia Universitas Gregoriana. Includes bibliography. [BT90.M8] 59-9908
1. Dridoens, Jean, 1480?-1535. 2. Tradition (Theology) I. Title.

PEABODY, Francis Greenwood, 1847-1936. 230
The church of the spirit; a brief survey of the spiritual tradition in Christianity, by Francis Greenwood Peabody ... New York, The Macmillan company, 1925. 208 p. 20 cm. [BV600.P37] 25-9324
I. Title.

POWELL, Baden, 1796-1860. 230
Tradition unveiled: or, An exposition of the pretensions and tendency of authoritative teaching in the church. By the Rev. Baden Powell ... From the London edition. Philadelphia, Hooker & Agnew, 1841. 66 p. 24 cm. (On cover: Churchman's library. no. 2) [BT90.P8] 40-22634
1. Tradition (Theology) 2. Authority (Religion) I. Title.

SWIDLER, Leonard J 230
Scripture and ecumenism; Protestant, Catholic, Orthodox, and Jewish. Edited and introd. by Leonard J. Swidler. Pittsburgh, Duquesne University Press, 1965. vii, 197 p. 23 cm. (Duquesne studies. Theological series, 8) Nine papers delivered at the annual ecumenical seminar held at Duquesne University, spring, 1964. Bibliographical footnotes. [BT90.S9] 64-8867
1. Tradition (Theology) 2. Bible — Evidences, authority, etc. 3. Christian union. I. Duquesne University, Pittsburgh. II. Title. III. Series.

Tradition (Theology)—Addresses, essays, lectures.

ROMAN Catholic/Presbyterian and Reformed Conversation Group. 201
Reconsiderations; Roman Catholic/Presbyterian and Reformed theological conversations, 1966-67. Papers presented by John L. McKenzie [and others. New York, World Horizons, c1967] 157 p. 21 cm. Includes bibliographical references. [BT90.R6] 74-3313 1.25
1. Tradition (Theology)—Addresses, essays, lectures. 2. Dogma, Development of—Addresses, essays, lectures. 3. Church polity—Addresses, essays, lectures. I. McKenzie, John L. II. Title.

Tradition (Theology)—Biblical teaching—Addresses, essays, lectures.

ROWLEY, Harold Henry, 1890-
From Joseph to Joshua; Biblical traditions in the light of archaeology. London, Published for the British Academy by the Oxford University Press [1958] 200 p. 25 cm. (The Schweich lectures of the British Academy, 1948) Bibliography: p. [165]-188. 63-56646
I. Title.

TRADITION and theology in the Old Testament / edited by Douglas A. Knight ; with contributions by Walter Harrelson ... [et al.]. Philadelphia : Fortress Press, c1977. xiv, 336 p. ; 24 cm. Includes bibliographical references and indexes. 230

[BS1199.T68T73] 76-7872 ISBN 0-8006-0484-9 : 16.95
1. Bible. O.T.—Criticism, interpretation, etc.—Addresses, essays, lectures. 2. Tradition (Theology)—Biblical teaching—Addresses, essays, lectures. I. Knight, Douglas A. II. Harrelson, Walter J.

Tradition (Theology)—Early church.

HANSON, Richard Patrick Crosland 230
Tradition in the early church. Philadelphia, Westminster [1963, c.1962] 288p. 23cm. (Lib. of hist. and doctrine) Bibl. 63-7925 5.75
1. Tradition (Theology)—Early church. I. Title.

Tradition (Theology)—History of doctrines.

BIEMER, Gunter. 231'.74'0924
Newman on tradition. Translated and edited by Kevin Smyth. [New York] Herder and Herder [1967] xx, 207 p. facsim. 22 cm. Revised version of the original German edition; Uberlieferung und Offenbarung published in 1961. Bibliography: p. 193-203. [BX4705.N5B513 1967b] 66-21076
1. Newman, John Henry, Cardinal, 1801-1890. 2. Tradition (Theology)—History of doctrines. I. Smyth, Kevin, ed. and tr. II. Title.

MORRISON, Karl Frederick. 262'.8
Tradition and authority in the western church, 300-1140 [by] Karl F. Morrison. Princeton, N.J., Princeton University Press, 1969. xvii, 458 p. 25 cm. Bibliography: p. 409-443. [BT90.M67] 68-20873 ISBN 0-691-07155-1 12.50
1. Tradition (Theology)—History of doctrines. 2. Church—Authority—History of doctrines. 3. Political science—History—Europe. I. Title.

Traherne, Thomas, d. 1674.

AMES, Kenneth John. 242'.1
The religious language of Thomas Traherne's Centuries / by Kenneth John Ames. New York : Revisionist Press, 1977. p. cm. Bibliography: p. [BV4831.T73A54] 77-4000 ISBN 0-87700-260-6 lib.bdg. : 39.95
1. Traherne, Thomas, d. 1674. Centuries of meditations. 2. Devotional literature. I. Title.

Traherne, Thomas, d. 1674—Philosophy.

JORDAN, Richard Douglas. 821'.4
The temple of eternity; Thomas Traherne's philosophy of time. Port Washington, N.Y., Kennikat Press, 1972. 125 p. 24 cm. (Kennikat Press national university publications. Series on literary criticism) Bibliography: p. 119-125. [PR3736.T7J6] 70-189560 ISBN 0-8046-9019-7 8.50
1. Traherne, Thomas, d. 1674—Philosophy. 2. Time. I. Title.

Trails—United States—Indiv.—Mormon.

PETERSEN, William John, 1901-
Mormon trails in Iowa. Iowa City, 1966. 353-384 p. illus. (part col.), maps (part col.) 21 cm. (The Palimpsest. v. 57, no. 9) 68-5503
1. Trails—U.S.—Indiv.—Mormon. 2. Mormons and mormonism—Hist. 3. Mormons and mormonism—U.S.—Iowa. I. Title.

Training Union—Junior.

HARRIS, Richie.
Baptist Junior union manual II. Nashville, Convention Press [c1958] 90 p. (Teacher's edition) 68-21924
1. Training Union—Junior. I. Title.

Trance.

BOURGUIGNON, Erika, 1924- 133
Trance dance. [New York, Johnson Reprint Corp., 1973] p. Reprint of the 1968 ed., which was issued as no. 35 of Dance perspectives. Includes bibliographical references. [BF1321.B68] 73-774 ISBN 0-384-05308-4 Pap. 6.00
1. Trance. 2. Dancing (in religion, folklore, etc.) I. Title. II. Series: Dance perspectives, no. 35.

TRANCE, healing, and 291.4'2
hallucination; three field studies in religious experience [by] Felicitas D. Goodman, Jeanette H. Henney [and] Esther Pressel. New York, Wiley [1974] xxiii, 388 p. illus. 23 cm. (Contemporary religious movements) "A Wiley-Interscience publication." Each field study was originally presented as a thesis, Ohio State University. Contents.Contents.—Henney, J. H. Spirit-possession belief and trance behavior in two fundamentalist groups in St. Vincent.—Pressel, E. Umbanda trance and possession in Sao Paulo, Brazil.—Goodman, F. D. Disturbances in the Apostolic Church: a trance-based upheaval in Yucatan.—Bibliography (p. 365-380) [BV5090.T7] 74-4159 ISBN 0-471-31390-4 12.50
1. Trance. 2. Spirit possession. 3. Umbanda (Cultus) 4. Pentecostalism. I. Henney, Jeanette H. Spirit-possession belief and trance behavior in two fundamentalist groups in St. Vincent. 1974. II. Pressel, Esther. Umbanda trance and possession in Sao Paulo, Brazil. 1974. III. Goodman, Felicitas D. Disturbances in the Apostolic Church. 1974.
Contents omitted.

WAVELL, Stewart. 133.9
Trances [by] Stewart Wavell, Audrey Butt [and] Nina Epton. [1st ed.] New York, Dutton, 1967. 253 p. illus. (part col.) group ports. (part col.) 23 cm. Bibliography: p. [244]-247. [BF1321.W3 1967] 67-11941
1. Trance. I. Butt, Audrey, joint author. II. Epton, Nina Consuelo, joint author. III. Title.

WILLIAMS, Sophia. 133.83
You are psychic, by Sophia Williams. [Hollywood, Calif., Press of Murray & Gee, 1946] 96 p. port. 21 1/2 cm. [BF1321.W5] 46-4846
1. Trance. 2. Clairvoyance. I. Title.

Trance—Case studies.

TRANCE, healing, and 291.4'2
hallucination : three field studies in religious experience / Felicitas D. Goodman, Jeannette H. Henney, Esther Pressel. Huntington, N.Y. : R. E. Krieger Pub. Co., 1981, c1974. p. cm. Reprint of the ed. published by Wiley, New York, in series: Contemporary religious movements. Each field study was originally presented as a thesis, Ohio Stata University. Contents.Contents.—Henney, J. H. Spirit-possession belief and trance behavior in two fundamentalist groups in St. Vincent.—Pressel, E. Umbanda trance and possession in Sao Paulo, Brazil.—Goodman, F. D. Disturbances in the Apostolic Church. Bibliography: p. [BV5090.T7 1981] 19 80-20043 ISBN 0-89874-246-3 : 11.95
1. Trance—Case studies. 2. Spirit possession—Case studies. 3. Umbanda (Cultus) 4. Pentecostalism. I. Goodman, Felicitas D. Disturbances in the Apostolic Church. 1981. II. Henney, Jeannette H. Spirit-possession belief and trance behavior in two fundamentalist groups in St. Vincent. 1981. III. Pressel, Esther. Umbanda trance and possession in Sao Paulo, Brazil. 1981.

Trans World Radio.

FREED, Paul E. 266'.023'73
Let the Earth hear : the thrilling story of how radio goes over barriers to bring the gospel of Christ to unreached millions / Paul E. Freed. Nashville : T. Nelson, c1980. 207 p., [8] leaves of plates : ill. ; 21 cm. Includes bibliographical references. [BV2082.R3F68] 80-169 ISBN 0-8407-5199-0 : 7.95
1. Trans World Radio. 2. Freed, Paul E. 3. Radio in missionary work. I. Title.

FREED, Paul E. 253.7'8
Towers to eternity, by Paul E. Freed. Waco, Tex., Word Books [1968] 154 p. 22 cm. [BV2082.R3F7] 68-54118 3.95
1. Trans World Radio. 2. Radio in missionary work. I. Title.

Transcendence of God.

CAIRNS, David, 1904- 231
God up there? A study in divine transcendence. Philadelphia, Westminster [c.1967] 111p. 19cm. Bibl. [BT124.5.C3 1967b] 68-15906 2.95
1. Transcendence of God. I. Title.

FARLEY, Edward 231
The transcendence of God, a study in contemporary philosophical theology. Philadelphia, Westminster Press [c.1960] 255p. 21cm. Bibl.: p.223-244 60-9712 5.00
1. Transcendence of God. I. Title.

VERHALEN, Philip A. 211'.6
Faith in a secularized world : [an investigation into the survival of transcendence] / by Philip A. Verhalen. New York : Paulist Press, c1976. vii, 172 p. ; 21 cm. Bibliography: p. 166-172. [BT124.5.V47] 76-360434 ISBN 0-8091-1937-4 pbk. : 3.95
1. Transcendence of God. 2. Secularism. 3. Theology—20th century. I. Title.

Transcendence of God—Addresses, essays, lectures.

TRANSCENDENCE. 231'.4
Edited by Herbert W. Richardson and Donald R. Cutler. Boston, Beacon Press [1969] xv, 176 p. 22 cm. Based on papers presented at 2 symposiums sponsored by the Church Society for College Work, Cambridge, Mass., held Dec. 1967 at the Episcopal Theological School, and May 1968 at Endicott House. Includes bibliographical references. [BT124.5.T7] 69-14597 7.50
1. Transcendence of God—Addresses, essays, lectures. I. Richardson, Herbert Warren, ed. II. Cutler, Donald R., ed. III. Church Society for College Work.

Transcendence of God—History of doctrines.

CENTER for Hermeneutical Studies in Hellenistic and Modern Culture. 231'.7
The transcendence of God in Philo : some possible sources : protocol of the sixteenth colloquy, 20 April 1975 / the Center for Hermeneutical Studies in Hellenistic and Modern Culture, the Graduate Theological Union & the University of California, Berkeley, California ; John M. Dillon ; W. Wuellner, editor. Berkeley, CA : The Center, c1975. 44 p. ; 21 cm. (Colloquy - the Center for Hermeneutical Studies in Hellenistic and Modern Culture ; nr. 16) Includes bibliographical references. [BT100.C34 1975] 75-38047 ISBN 0-89242-015-4
1. Philo Judaeus. 2. Transcendence of God—History of doctrines. I. Dillon, John M. II. Wuellner, Wilhelm H., 1927- III. Title. IV. Series: Center for Hermeneutical Studies in Hellenistic and Modern Culture. Protocol series of the colloquies ; nr. 16.

Transcendence (Philosophy)

HAZELTON, Roger, 1909- 231'.7
Ascending flame, descending dove : an essay on creative transcendence / by Roger Hazelton. Philadelphia : Westminster Press, [1975] 128 p. ; 19 cm. Includes bibliographical references. [BD362.H38] 75-9649 ISBN 0-664-24767-9 pbk. : 3.75
1. Transcendence (Philosophy) 2. Transcendence of God. I. Title.

MORRIS, James Winston, 1949- 297'.2
The wisdom of the throne : an introduction to the philosophy of Mulla Sadra / James Winston Morris. Princeton, N.J. : Princeton University Press, c1981. p. cm. (Princeton library of Asian translations) Includes a translation of: al-Hikmah al-'arshiyah. Includes index. Bibliography: p. [B753.M83H5435] 19 81-47153 ISBN 0-691-06493-8 : 22.50
1. Sadr al-Din Shirazi, Muhammad ibn Ibrahim, d. 1641. Hikmah al-'arshiyah. 2. Transcendence (Philosophy) 3. Philosophy, Islamic—Early works to 1800. I. Sadr al-Din Shirazi, Muhammad ibn Ibrahim, d. 1641. Hikmah al-'arshiyah. English. 1981. II. Title. III. Series. IV. UNESCO collection of representative works. Arabic series

Transcendental Meditation.

*BJORNSTAD, James. 294
The transcendental mirage / by James Bjornstad. Minneapolis : Bethany Fellowship, 1976. 93p. : ill. ; 18 cm. (Dimension books) Bibliography: p. [91]-93. [BL627] 76-6614 ISBN 0-87123-556-0 pbk. : 1.50
1. Transcendental meditation. I. Title.

BLOOMFIELD, Harold H., 1944- 294
Happiness : the TM program, psychiatry, and enlightenment / Harold H. Bloomfield, Robert Kory. New York : Dawn Press : distributed by Simon and Schuster, [1976] p. cm. Includes index. [BL627.B55] 76-3754 ISBN 0-671-22269-4 : 8.95
1. Transcendental Meditation. 2. Happiness. I. Kory, Robert, joint author. II. Title.

BLOOMFIELD, Harold H., 1944- 294
Happiness : the TM program, psychiatry, and enlightenment / [by] Harold H. Bloomfield and] Robert B. Kory. New York : Pocket Books, 1977,c1976. 304p. ; 18cm. (A Kangaroo Book) Includes index. [BL627.B55] ISBN 0-671-81294-7 pbk. : 1.95
1. Transcendental Meditation. 2. Happiness. I. Kory, Robert B., joint author. II. Title.
L.C. card no. for 1976 Simon and Schuster ed.:76-3754.

BLOOMFIELD, Harold H., 1944- 294.5'43
TM discovering inner energy and overcoming stress [by] Harold H. Bloomfield, Michael Peter Cain and Dennis T. Jaffe, in collaboration with Robert Bruce Kory. Foreward by Hans Selye; introd. by R. Buckminster Fuller. [New York] Dell [1975] 317 p. illus. 18 cm. Includes index. Bibliography: p. 285-305. [BL627.B56] 1.95 (pbk.)
1. Transcendental meditation. I. Cain, Michael Peter, 1941-, joint author. II. Jaffe, Dennis T., joint author. III. Title.
L.C. no. of original edition: 74-19289

BLOOMFIELD, Harold H., 1944- 294
*TM** : discovering inner energy and overcoming stress / Harold H. Bloomfield, Michael Peter Cain, Dennis T. Jaffe, and Robert B. Kory ; foreword by Hans Selye ; introd. by R. Buckminster Fuller. Boston : G. K. Hall, 1976, c1975. p. cm. "*Transcendental meditation." "Published in large print." Includes index. Bibliography: p. [BL627.B56 1976] 76-4910 ISBN 0-8161-6366-9
1. Transcendental Meditation. 2. Sight-saving books. I. Cain, Michael Peter, 1941- joint author. II. Jaffe, Dennis T., joint author. III. Title.

BLOOMFIELD, Harold H., 1944- 294.5'43
TM: discovering inner energy and overcoming stress* [by] Harold H. Bloomfield, Michael Peter Cain [and] Dennis T. Jaffe, in collaboration with Robert Bruce Kory. Foreword by Hans Selye; introd. by R. Buckminster Fuller. New York, Delacorte Press [1975] xxvii, 290 p. illus. 22 cm. "*Transcendental meditation." Bibliography: p. [261]-280. [BL627.B56] 74-19289 ISBN 0-440-06048-6 8.95
1. Transcendental meditation. I. Cain, Michael Peter, 1941- joint author. II. Jaffe, Dennis T., joint author. III. Title.

CAMPBELL, Anthony. 158'.1
TM and the nature of enlightenment : creative intelligence and the teachings of Maharishi Mahesh Yogi / Anthony Campbell. New York : Harper & Row, 1976, c1975. 223 p. : ill. ; 18 cm. (Perennial library ; P366) First published under title: The mechanics of enlightenment. Includes index. Bibliography: p. [213]-215. [BL627.C29 1976] 76-362221 ISBN 0-06-080366-5 pbk. : 1.95

1. Mahesh Yogi, Maharishi. 2. Transcendental meditation. I. Title.

*DENNISTON, Denise. 141.3
The TM book; how to enjoy the rest of your life [by] Denise Denniston and Peter McWilliams. Illustrated by Barry Geller. [New York] Warner Books [1975] 351 p., illus. 18 cm. [BL627] 75-13848 1.95 (pbk.)
1. Transcendental meditation. I. McWilliams, Peter, joint author. II. Title.

*EBON, Martin, comp. 294
TM; how to find peace of mind through meditation, edited by Martin Ebon. [New York] New American Library [1976 c1975] 246 p. 18 cm. (A Signet Book) [BL627] 1.50 (pbk.)
1. Transcendental Meditation. I. Title.

FOREM, Jack, 1943- 141.3
Transcendental meditation; Maharishi Mahesh Yogi and the science of creative intelligence. Rev. ed. New York, Bantam Books [1976] xvii, 283 p. 18 cm. Includes bibliographical references and index. [BL627.F67] 1.95 (pbk.)
1. Transcendental meditation. I. Title.
L.C. card no. for original edition: 72-96900.

FOREM, Jack, 1943- 141'.3
Transcendental meditation; Maharishi Mahesh Yogi and the Science of creative intelligence. [1st ed.] New York, Dutton, 1973. xiii, 274 p. illus. 22 cm. Includes bibliographical references. [BL627.F67] 72-96900 ISBN 0-525-22225-1 7.95
1. Transcendental meditation.

GOLDBERG, Philip. 158'.1
The TM program : the way to fulfilment : a proven approach to developing the full human potential / Philip Goldberg. New York : Holt, Rinehart and Winston, c1976. p. cm. Includes index. Bibliography: p. [BL627.G62] 76-11747 ISBN 0-03-016631-4 : 6.95 ISBN 0-03-018231-X pbk. :
1. Transcendental Meditation. I. Title.

GOLDHABER, Nat. 294
TM : an alphabetical guide to the transcendental meditation program / by Nat Goldhaber and Denise Denniston ; with special sections by Peter McWilliams. 1st ed. New York : Ballantine Books, 1976. p. cm. [BL627.G64] 76-8830 ISBN 0-345-24096-0 : 3.95
1. Transcendental Meditation. I. Denniston, Denise, joint author. II. McWilliams, Peter. III. Title.

HEMINGWAY, Patricia Drake. 294
The transcendental meditation primer : now stop tension & start living / Patricia Drake Hemingway. New York : D. McKay Co., [1975] xviii, 264 p. ; 22 cm. Includes index. Bibliography: p. 252-254. [BL627.H43] 75-6918 ISBN 0-679-50554-7 : 8.95
1. Transcendental meditation. I. Title.

*JEFFERSON, William. 294
The story of the Maharishi. New York, Pocket Books [1976] 128 p. 18 cm. Bibliography: p. 125-128. [BL627] ISBN 0-671-80526-6 1.50 (pbk.)
1. Mahesh Yogi, Maharishi. 2. Transcendental meditation. I. Title.

JONES-RYAN, Maureen 131'.32
TM : a woman's workbook / Maureen Jones-Ryan. New York : Two Continents Pub. Group, [1976]. p. cm. Bibliography: p. [BL627.J66] 76-16206 pbk. : 4.95
1. Transcendental Meditation. I. Title.

KANELLAKOS, Demetri P. 158
The psychobiology of transcendental meditation : a literature review / by Demetri P. Kanellakos, Jerome S. Lukas. Menlo Park, Calif. : W. A. Benjamin, [1974] xiii, 158 p. : graphs ; 28 cm. Includes indexes. [BL627.K37] 74-7524 ISBN 0-8053-5205-8
1. Transcendental meditation. I. Lukas, Jerome S., 1930- joint author. II. Title.

KORY, Robert B. 294
The transcendental meditation program for business people / Robert B. Kory. New York : AMACOM, c1976. 91 p. : graphs ; 22 cm. (An AMA management briefing) Bibliography: p. 89-91. [BL627.K67] 76-3696 ISBN 0-8144-2189-X pbk. : 5.50
1. Transcendental Meditation. 2. Executive ability. I. Title. II. Series: American Management Associations. An AMA management briefing.

KROLL, Una. 294.5'43
The healing potential of transcendental meditation / Una Kroll. Atlanta : John Knox Press, 1974. 176 p. ; 21 cm. First published in 1974 under title: TM. Includes bibliographical references. [BL627.K76 1974b] 74-7615 ISBN 0-8042-0598-1
1. Transcendental meditation. I. Title.

LEWIS, Gordon Russell, 1926- 294
What everyone should know about transcendental meditation / Gordon R. Lewis. Glendale, Calif. : G/L Regal Books, [1975] 92 p. ; 18 cm. Bibliography: p. 77-79. [BL627.L49] 74-32326 ISBN 0-8307-0353-5 pbk. : 1.45
1. Transcendental meditation. I. Title.

OATES, Bob. 294 B
Celebrating the dawn : Maharishi Mahesh Yogi and the TM technique / epilogue by Maharishi Mahesh Yogi ; written by Robert Oates, Jr. New York : Putnam, c1976. 227 p. : ill. ; 24 cm. [BF637.T68017 1976] 76-14884 ISBN 0-399-11815-2 : 12.95
1. Mahesh Yogi, Maharishi. 2. Transcendental Meditation. 3. Yogis—Biography. I. Title.

ROBBINS, Jhan. 181'.45
Tranquility without pills (all about transcendental meditation); the complete how-to guide to the famous TM method of total relaxation ... [by] Jhan Robbins and David Fisher. New York, P. H. Wyden [1972] x, 142 p. 22 cm. [BL627.R6] 72-78539 4.95
1. Transcendental meditation. I. Fisher, Dave, 1946- joint author. II. Title.

*RUSSELL, Peter. 141'.3
The T M technique : an introduction to transcendal meditation and the teachings of Maharishi Mahesh Yogi / Peter Russell. London ; Boston : Routledge & Kegan Paul, 1976. xii, 13-195 p. : ill., charts, graphs ; 23 cm. Includes bibliographical references and index. [BL627] ISBN 0-7100-8345-9 : 7.50
1. Transcendental meditation. I. Title.

SHAH, Douglas. 294
The meditators / by Douglas Shah. Plainfield, N.J. : Logos International, c1975. x, 147 p. : ill. ; 21 cm. [BL627.S53 1975] 75-7478 ISBN 0-88270-125-8 : 5.95 ISBN 0-88270-126-6 pbk. : 3.50
1. Transcendental Meditation. 2. Meditation. 3. Sects. 4. Religions. I. Title.

*WHITE, John 141.3
Everything you want to know about TM - including how to do it. New York, Pocket Books [1976] 191 p. 18 cm. Bibliography: p. 189-190. [BL627.F67] 1.95
1. Transcendental meditation. I. Title.

WHITE, John Warren, 1939- 294
Everything you want to know about TM, including to do it : a look at higher consciousness and the enlightenment industry / John White. New York : Pocket Books, 1976. 191 p. ; 18 cm. Bibliography: p. 189-190. [BL627.W45] 76-351823 1.95
1. Transcendental Meditation. I. Title.

Transcendentalism.

COOK, Joseph, 1838-1901. 141
... *Transcendentalism,* with preludes on current events. By Joseph Cook ... Boston, J. R. Osgood and company, 1878. 4 p. l., 3-305 p. 19 cm. (His Boston Monday lectures) [Name originally: Flavius Josephus Cook] [B905.C7] 34-4751
1. Transcendentalism. 2. Parker, Theodore, 1810-1860. I. Title.

EMERSON, Ralph Waldo, 1803-1882.
Selected writtings of Ralph Waldo Emerson, edited and with a foreword by William H. Gilman ... New York, Toronto, New American library; London, New English library limited [1965] xxxiv, [35]-479 p. 18 cm., in case 19 cm. (A Signet classic, CQ292) On verso of t.p.: First printing, November 1965. 66-56291
I. Gilman, William Henry, 1911- ed. II. Title. III. Series.

[NORTON, Andrews] 1786-1853, ed. 141
Two articles from the Princeton review, concerning the transcendental philosophy of the Germans and of Cousin, and its influence on opinion in this country. Cambridge, J. Owen, 1840. 100 p. 23 cm. "Introductory note" signed: A. N. The second article from the January no., 1840, of the Princeton review, is a criticism of "A discourse on the latest form of infedility ..." by Andrews Norton, and of "A letter to Mr. Andrews Norton, occasioned by his discourse .." by an alumnus of the Cambridge theological school. [B823.N85] 6-44457
1. Transcendentalism. I. Alexander, James Waddel, 1804-1859. II. Dod, Albert Baldwin, 1805-1845, joint author. III. Hodge, Charles, 1797-1878. IV. Title.
Contents omitted.

Transcendentalism—Collected works.

PARKER, Theodore, 1810-1860. 288'.092'4 B
Theodore Parker: American transcendentalist; a critical essay and a collection of his writings, by Robert E. Collins. Metuchen, N.J., Scarecrow Press, 1973. v, 271 p. illus. 22 cm. Contents.Contents.—Essay: A forgotten American.—Selections from Theodore Parker: Transcendentalism. A discourse of the transient and permanent in Christianity. The position and duties of the American scholar. The political destination of America and the signs of the times. The writings of Ralph Waldo Emerson. A sermon of war.—Selected bibliography (p. 261-264) [BX9869.P3A25 1973] 73-9593 ISBN 0-8108-0641-X 7.50
1. Parker, Theodore, 1810-1860. 2. Emerson, Ralph Waldo, 1803-1882. 3. Transcendentalism—Collected works. I. Collins, Robert E., ed.

Transcendentalism (New England)

CHRISTY, Arthur, 1899- 141
The Orient in American transcendentalism; a study of Emerson, Thoreau, and Alcott, by Arthur Christy ... New York, Columbia university press, 1932. xix, 382 p., 1 l. 20 cm. (Half-title: Columbia university studies in English and comparative literature) Thesis (Ph.D.)--Columbia university, 1932. Vita. Published also without thesis note. "Books and marginalia": p. [273]-323. "Notes": p. [325]-367. [Full name: Arthur Edward Christy] [B905.C5 1932] 33-3815
1. Emerson, Ralph Waldo, 1803-1882. 2. Thoreau, Henry David, 1817-1862. 3. Alcott, Amos Bronson, 1799-1888. 4. Transcendentalism (New England) 5. Literature. Comparative—American and Oriental. 6. Literature. Comparative—Oriental and American. 7. American literature—19th cent.—Hist. & crit. I. Title. II. Title: American transcendentalism, The Orient in.

CONCORD school of philosophy. 141
Concord lectures on philosophy, comprising outlines of all the lectures at the Concord summer school of philosophy in 1882, with an historical sketch; collected and arranged by Raymond L. Bridgman, revised by the several lecturers, approved by the faculty. Cambridge, Mass., M. King [c1883] 168 p. 26 cm. [B905.B7] 11-15827
1. Emerson, Ralph Waldo, 1809-1882. 2. Transcendentalism (New England) I. Bridgman, Raymond Landon, 1848-1925, comp. II. Title.

EMERSON, Ralph Waldo, 1803-1882.
New England reformers and Divinity college address. By Ralph Waldo Emerson. New York, J. B. Alden, 1887. 3 p. l., 5-103 p. 19 cm. "The paper on Transecndentalism has been wrongly attributed to Emerson. Its author is not knows."--2d prelim. leaf. A 30
1. Transcendentalism (New England) I. Title. II. Title: Divinity college address.
Contents omitted.

FROTHINGHAM, Octavius Brooks, 1822-1895. 141
Transcendentalism in New England; a history, by Octavius Brooks Frothingham ... New York, G. P. Putnam's sons, 1876. ix, 395 p. front. (port.) 21 cm. [B905.F7] 10-28608
1. Transcendentalism (New England) I. Title.

FROTHINGHAM, Octavius Brooks, 1822-1895. 141
Transcendentalism in New England, a history by Octavius Brooks Frothingham ... New York, G. P. Putnam's sons, 1886. ix, 395 p. front. (port.) 20 cm. [B905.F7 1886] 33-6744
1. Transcendentalism (New England) I. Title.

FROTHINGHAM, Octavius Brooks, 1822-1895. 141
Transcendentalism in New England; a history, by Octavius B. Frothingham ... Boston, American Unitarian association, 1903. ix, 383 p. 21 cm. First edition, 1876. [B905.F8] 4-3985
1. Transcendentalism (New England) I. Title.

GODDARD, Harold Clarke, 1878- 141
Studies in New England transcendentalism, by Harold Clarke Goddard ... New York, The Columbia university press, 1908. x, 217 p. 24 cm. (Half-title: Columbia university studies in English. Series ii, vol. ii, no. 3) "This essay was submitted in partial fulfillment of the requirements for the degree of doctor of philosophy in Columbia university."--Pref. Bibliography: p. 207-212. [B905.G6] 8-14677
1. Transcendentalism (New England) I. Title.

HUTCHISON, William R.
The Transcendentalist ministers; church reform in the New England Renaissance. Boston, Beacon Press [1965] xiv, 240 p. ports. (Beacon paperbacks, BP 214) "This study in an earlier form was submitted in candidacy for the degree of doctor of philosophy in Yale University." Bibliography: p. 209-[223] 67-44596
1. Transcendentalism (New England) 2. Unitarians in New England. I. Title.

POCHMANN, Henry August, 1901- 141
New England transcendentalism and St. Louis Hegelianism; phases in the history of American idealism. Philadelphia, Carl Schurz Memorial Foundation [1948] 144 p. 19 cm. "Notes and references" p. 127-144. [B905.P6] 49-9251
1. Alcott, Amos Bronson, 1799-1888. 2. Brokmeyer, Henry Conrad, 1828-1906. 3. Emerson, Ralph Waldo, 1803-1882. 4. Harris, William Torrey, 1835-1909. 5. Hegel, Georg Wilhelm Friedrich, 1770-1831. 6. Transcendentalism (New England) 7. Philosophy—Hist.—Missouri—St. Louis. I. Title.

ROGERS, William Cauldwell, 1870- 141
Transcendentalism truly remarkable, by William Rogers ... Boston, The Christopher publishing house [1947] 64 p. front. (port.) 20 cm. [B905.R6] 47-21976
1. Transcendentalism (New England) I. Title.

THREE Christian transcendentalists; James Marsh, Caleb Sprague Henry, Frederic Henry Hedge [by] Ronald Vale Wells. New York, Columbia university press, 1943. x, 230 p. 23 1/2 cm. (Half-title: Columbia studies in American culture, no. 12) Bibliography: p. [217]-224. [B905.W4] 43-13153 141
1. Transcendentalism (New England) I. Marsh, James, 1794-1842. II. Henry, Caleb Sprague, 1804-1884. III. Hedge, Frederic Henry, 1805-1890. IV. Wells, Ronald Vale.

VOGEL, Stanley M 190
German literary influences on the American transcendentalists. New Haven, Yale University Press, 1955. xvii, 196p. 24cm. (Yale studies in English, v. 127) Based on thesis--Yale University. Includes bibliographies and bibliographical footnotes. [B905.V6] [B905.V6] 141 55-5520 55-5520
1. Transcendentalism (New England) 2. Literature, Comparative—American and German. 3. Literature. Comparative—German and American. 4. American literature—19th cent.—Hist. & crit. I. Title. II. Series.

Transcendentalism (New England)—Periodicals—History

GOHDES, Clarence Louis Frank, 1901- 141.05
The periodicals of American transcendentalism, by Clarence L. F. Gohdes. Durham, N. C., Duke university press, 1931. vii, 264 p. 23 cm. (Half-title: Duke university publications) Issued also as thesis (PH. D.) Columbia university. "The periodicals ... in the present study": p. 14. [B905.G65 1931a] 31-34224
1. Transcendentalism (New England)—Period.—Hist. 2. American periodicals—Hist. I. Title. II. Title: American transcendentalism, The periodicals of.

Translation of Calechisme de l'organization corporative.

ARES, Richard, 1910-
What is corporative organization? by Richard Ares...Translated and adapted by Thomas P. Fay... St. Louis, Mo., Central bureau press [1939] 95 p. 19 1/2 cm. Bibliography: p. 94-95. A40
1. Translation of Calechisme de l'organization corporative. 2. Corporate state. 3. Catholic church. Pope, 1922-2960 (Pius xi) Quadragesimo Anne (15 May, 1931) 4. Sociology, Christian—Catholic authors. I. Fay, Thomas P., 1905- tr. II. Title.

Translation of Hatha-Yoga.

SPIEGELBERG, Frederic, 1897- *181.45
Spiritual practices of India. Introd. by Alan W. Watts. [Translated from the German by Edith E. King-Fisher. San Francisco, Greenwood Press, 1951. xv, 69 p. illus. 24 cm. [B132.Y6S653] 51-13892
1. Translation of Hatha-Yoga. 2. Yoga, Ilatha. I. Title.

Translation of Lars Paul Esbjorn och Augustana-aynodens uppkomst.

RONNEGARD, Sam. 922.473
Prairie shepherd; Lars Paul Esbjorn and the beginnings of the Augustana Lutheran Church. A translation by G. Everett Arden. Rock Island, Ill., Augustana Book Concern [1952] 308 p. illus. 21 cm. [BX8080.E67R63] 52-2628
1. Esbjorn, Lars Paul 1808-1870. 2. Translation of Lars Paul Esbjorn och Augustana-aynodens uppkomst. 3. Augustana Evangelical Lutheran Church — Hist. I. Title.

Translation of Wahrhoit als begegnung.

BRUNNER, Heinrich Emil, 1889- 201
The divine-human encounter, by Emil Brunner ... translated by Amandus W. Loos. Philadelphia, The Westminster press [1943] 207 p. 21 cm. "A series of lectures, in part considerably revised, which were delivered on the Olaus Petri foundation at the University of Upsala in the fall of 1937."--Foreword. [BT78.B874] 43-16169
1. Translation of Wahrhoit als begegnung. 2. Diabetic (Theology) 3. Revelation. I. Loos, Amandus William, 1906- tr. II. Title.

Translation to heaven.

ASGILL, John, 1659-1738. 218
An argument to prove that death is not obligatory on Christians, by the celebrated John Asgill ... With introductory essay, memoir, notes, and ministerial testimony, by the Rev. Tresham D. Gregg ... New York, Ennis brothers, 1875. 135 p., 1 l. incl. front. (port.) 20 cm. On cover: The covenant of eternal life as revealed in the Scriptures. "An argument proving, that according to the covenant of eternal life revealed in the Scriptures, man may be translated from hence into that eternal life, without passing through death" (p. [57]-116) has special t.-p. (reproduction, with minor variations, of t.-p. of the 1700 edition) [BT827.A33] 36-31905
1. Translation to heaven. 2. Immortality. I. Gregg, Tresham Dames, 1799?-1881. II. Title. III. Title: The covenant of eternal life as revealed in the Scriptures.

Transmigration.

MANAS. JOHN H. 133
Metempsychosis, reincarnation; pilgrimage of the soul through matter; "solution of the riddle of life," by John H. Manas. New York city, Pythagorean-society [1941] xxii [i.e. xxiv], 23-206 [i.e. 208] p., 1 l. incl. illus., plates, ports., diagrs. 20 1/2 cm. [BF1909.M243] [159.961] 42-4580
1. Transmigration. I. Pythagorean society. II. Title.

Transmission of texts.

BEVENOT, Maurice. 230'.1'3
The tradition of manuscripts : a study in the transmission of St. Cyprian's treatises / by Maurice Bevenot. Westport, Conn. : Greenwood Press, 1979, c1961. viii, 163 p. ; 24 cm. "De ecclesiae catholicae unitate: the resultant text": p. 96-123. Reprint of the ed. published by the Clarendon Press, Oxford. Includes indexes. Bibliography: p. [151]-153. [BR65.C86B43 1979] 78-14421 ISBN 0-313-20622-8 lib. bdg. : 16.75
1. Cyprianus, Saint, Bp. of Carthage—Manuscripts. 2. Transmission of texts. I. Cyprianus, Saint, Bp. of Carthage. De ecclesiae catholicae unitate. 1978

BEVENOT, Maurice, 1897- 281.1
The tradition of manuscripts; a study in the transmission of St. Cyprian's treatises. Oxford, Clarendon Press, 1961. viii, 163 p. diagrs. 24 cm. "The treatise chosen to represent them all is the De ecclesiae catholicae unitate." "De ecclesiae catholicae unitate: the resultant text": p. 96-123. Bibliography: p. [151]-153. [BR65.C86B43] 61-19227
1. Cyprianus, Saint, Bp. of Carthage—Manuscripts. 2. Transmission of texts. I. Cyprianus, Saint, Bp. of Carthage. De ecclesiae catholi

BRACCIOLINI, Poggio, 1380-1459. 020'.75 B
Two Renaissance book hunters; the letters of Poggius Bracciolini to Nicolaus de Niccolis. Translated from the Latin and annotated by Phyllis Walter Goodhart Gordan. New York, Columbia University Press, 1974. x, 393 p. 23 cm. (Records of civilization: sources and studies, no. 91) Bibliography: p. [361]-382. [PA8477.B76Z5513] 74-1401 ISBN 0-231-03777-5
1. Bracciolini, Poggio, 1380-1459. 2. Niccoli, Niccolo, 1364 (ca.)-1437. 3. Transmission of texts. I. Niccoli, Niccolo, 1364 (ca.)-1437. II. Gordan, Phyllis Walter Goodhart, ed. III. Title. IV. Series.

Transplantation of organs, tissues, etc.—Moral and religious aspects.

MILLER, George William, 1926- 174'.25
Moral and ethical implications of human organ transplants, by George W. Miller. With a foreword by Dwight E. Harken. Springfield, Ill., Thomas [1971] xxvii, 135 p. illus. 24 cm. Originally presented as the author's thesis, Luther Rice Seminary, under the title: A critical analysis of the moral and ethical implications of human organ transplants. Bibliography: p. 121-127. [RD120.7.M55 1971] 74-149188
1. Transplantation of organs, tissues, etc.—Moral and religious aspects. 2. Medical ethics. I. Title.

Transubstantiation.

FISHER, Lizette Andrews, 1868- 809'.933'8
The mystic vision in the Grail legend and in the Divine comedy. [Folcroft, Pa.] Folcroft Library Editions, 1974. p. cm. Reprint of the 1917 ed. published by Columbia University Press, New York, in series: Columbia University studies in English and comparative literature. Originally presented as the author's thesis, Columbia University, 1916. Bibliography: p. [PN686.G7F5 1974] 74-16424 4.75
1. Dante Alighieri, 1265-1321. Divina commedia. Purgatorio. 2. Grail—Legends—History and criticism. 3. Transubstantiation. 4. Corpus Christi festival. I. Title. II. Series: Columbia University studies in English and comparative literature.

FISHER, Lizette Andrews, 1868- 809'.933'8
The mystic vision in the Grail legend and in the Divine comedy. [Folcroft, Pa.] Folcroft Library Editions, 1974 [c1917] x, 148 p. front. 26 cm. Reprint of the ed. published by Columbia University Press, New York, in series: Columbia University studies in English and comparative literature. Originally presented as the author's thesis, Columbia University, 1916. Bibliography: p. [139]-143. [PN686.G7F5 1974] 74-16424 ISBN 0-8414-4241-X (lib. bdg.)
1. Dante Alighieri, 1265-1321. Divina commedia. Purgatorio. 2. Grail—Legends—History and criticism. 3. Transubstantiation. 4. Corpus Christi festival. I. Title. II. Series: Columbia University studies in English and comparative literature.

O'NEILL, Patrick, 1795?-1879.
A sermon on the mystery of the real presence, preached in the court-house in the borough of Butler. By the Rev. P. O'Neill ... With an analysis of a sermon, said to be preached against transubstantiation, in the Associate reformed church in the borough of Butler. By the Rev. Isaiah Niblock ... Pittsburgh, Printed by Johnston and Stockton, 1831. vi, [7]-80 p. 20 1/2 cm. [BX2220.O5] 43-22042
1. Transubstantiation. I. Niblock, Isaiah. II. Title.

SCHILLEBEECKX, Edward Cornelius Florentius Alfons, 1914- 265'.3
The eucharist [by] E. Schillebeeckx. Translated by N. D. Smith. New York, Sheed and Ward [1968] 160 p. 21 cm. Translation of: Christus' tegenwoordigheid in die eucharistie. Bibliographical footnotes. [BX2220.S3513] 68-13846 3.95
1. Transubstantiation. I. Title.

Transylvania Bible School.

SHILLING, Henry, 1902- 207.748
The second seven years of faith, 1945-1952. Freeport, Pa., Fountain Press [195 --] 332 p. illus. 24 cm. [BV4070.T7S5] 58-26847
1. Transylvania Bible School. I. Title. II. Title: Seven years of faith.

Transylvania—Church history.

[CORNISH, Louis Craig] 1870- comp.
The religious minorities in Transylvania. Boston, Mass., The Beacon press, inc. [c1925] 174 p. 21 cm. On cover: Compiled by Louis C. Cornish in collaboration with the commission. "The commission was appointed by the Executive committee of the American committee on the rights of religious minorities." [BR927.T8C6] 25-6437
1. Transylvania—Church history. 2. Church and state in Transylvania. I. Anglo-American commission of 1924 to the minority churches of Transylvania. II. Title.

Trappists.

HOLMES, Frederick Lionel, 1883- 271.125
The voice of Trappist silence, by Fred L. Holmes...Harry Lorin Binsse...consulting editor. New York, Toronto, Longmans, Green and co., 1941. xi, 114 p. incl. front., illus., plates. 26 cm. "First edition." [BX4102.H6] 42-601
1. Trappist. I. Binsse, Harry Lorin,ed. II. Title.

LUDDY, Ailbe J. 922.244
The real de Rance, illustrious penitent and reformer of Notre Dame de la Trappe. By Ailbe J. Luddy ... London, New York [etc.] Longmans, Green and co., 1931. xxi, 314 p. front.)port.) 20 1/2 cm. Bibliography: p. 312-313. [BX4705.R3L8] 31-12717
1. Rance, Armand Jean le Bouthillier de, 1626?-1700. 2. Trappists. I. Title.

MERTON, Thomas, 1915- 271.125
The waters of Siloe. New York, Harcourt, Brace [1949] xxxviii, 377 p. illus. 22 cm. Bibliography: p. 353-358. [BX4102.M4 1949a] 49-6928
1. Trappists. I. Title.

MERTON, Thomas, 1915-1968. 271'.125
The waters of Siloe / Thomas Merton. New York : Harcourt Brace Jovanovich, 1979, c1949. p. cm. (A Harvest/HBJ book) Includes index. Bibliography p. [BX4102.M4 1979] 79-10372 ISBN 0-15-694954-7. : 4.95
1. Trappists. I. Title.

MERTON, Thomas [Name in religion: Father Louis] 1915- 271.125
The waters of Siloe. Garden City, N.Y., Doubleday [1962, c.1949] 399p. 18cm. (Image bk., D144) Bibl. 1.25 pap.,
1. Trappists. I. Title.

VALLEY Falls, R.I. 271.125
Monastery of Our Lady of the valley (Trappist) Valley Falls, R.I., Monastry of Our Lady of the valley [1932] 55 p. incl. illus., plates, ports. 23 cm. [BX4102.V3] 37-23395
1. Trappists. I. Title: The Cistercian monks of the strict observance (Trappists)

Trappists—Algeria—Correspondence.

FOUCAULD, Charles Eugene, vicomte de, 1858-1916. 271'.125'024
Inner search : letters (1889-1916) / Charles de Foucauld ; translated by Barbara Lucas. Maryknoll, N.Y. : Orbis Books, 1979, c1977. 151 p. : map ; 21 cm. Abridged translation of the author's Lettres a mes freres de la Trappe published in 1969. First published in English in 1977 under title: Letters from the desert. Includes index. [BX4705.F65A413 1979] 79-4353 ISBN 0-88344-281-7 : 5.95
1. Foucauld, Charles Eugene, vicomte de, 1858-1916. 2. Trappists—Algeria—Correspondence. I. Title.

Trappists—Correspondence, reminiscences, etc.

RAYMOND, Father, 1903- 208
The silent spire speaks [by] M. Raymond. Milwaukee, Bruce Pub. Co. [1966] vii, 194 p. 23 cm. [BX4705.R3744A3] 66-28857
1. Trappists—Correspondence, reminiscences, etc. I. Title.

Trappists—History

ALBERIC, father, 1881- 271.125
Compendium of the history of the Cistercian order, by a father of the Abbey of Gethsemani, Kentucky, of the Order of Cistercians of the strict observance (Trappist) [Trappist, Ky.] 1944. xv, 375 p. illus. (incl. plans) plates. 22 1/2 cm. [Secular name: Clement Ignatius Wulf] "Bibliography: Cistercian references by Cistercian authors": p. 350-351. [BX4106.A6] 45-12611
1. Trappist—Hist. I. Title.

COMPENDIUM of the history of the Cistercian order, 271.125 by a father of the Abbey of Gethsemani, Kentucky, of the Order of Cistercians of the strict observance (Trappist) [Trappsit, Ky., 1944. xv, 375 p. illus. (incl. plans) plates. 22 1/2 cm. "Bibliography: Cistercian references by Cistercian authors": p. 350-351. [BX4106.C6] 45-12611
1. Trappist—Hist. I. A father of the abbey of Gethsemani, Kentucky.

Trappists in the United States—Biography.

ADAMS, Daniel J. 271'.125'024 B
Thomas Merton's shared contemplation : a Protestant perspective / Daniel A. Adams. Kalamazoo, Mich. : Cistercian Publications, 1979. 361 p. ; 23 cm. (Cistercian studies series ; no. 62) Bibliography: p. 347-361. [BX4705.M542A64] 78-6549 ISBN 0-87907-862-6 : 17.95
1. Merton, Thomas, 1915-1968. 2.

Trappists in the United States—Biography. I. Title. II. Series.

FOREST, James H. 271'.125'024 B
Thomas Merton, a pictorial biography / by James H. Forest ; [cover photo. by Robert Lax, half title photo. by John Lyons, opposite title page photo. by John Howard Griffin]. New York : Paulist Press, c1980. 102 p., [2] leaves of plates : ill. ; 23 cm. [BX4705.M542F67] 19 80-82249 ISBN 0-8091-2284-7 (pbk.) : 5.95
1. Merton, Thomas, 1915-1968. 2. Trappists in the United States—Biography. I. Title.

FURLONG, Monica. 271'.125'024 B
Merton : a biography / Monica Furlong. 1st ed. New York : Harper & Row, c1980. p. cm. Includes index. [BX4705.M542F87] 79-3588 ISBN 0-06-063079-5 : 12.95
1. Merton, Thomas, 1915-1968. 2. Trappists in the United States—Biography. 3. Poets, American—20th century—Biography.

KELTY, Matthew. 271'.125'024 B
Flute solo : reflections of a Trappist hermit / Matthew Kelty. Kansas City, Kan. : Andrews and McMeel, c1979. 128 p. ; 23 cm. [BX4705.K375A34] 79-13335 ISBN 0-8362-3912-1 : 7.95
1. Kelty, Matthew. 2. Trappist in the United States—Biography. 3. Monastic and religious life. I. Title.

MALITS, Elena. 271'.125'024
The solitary explorer : Thomas Merton's transforming journey / Elena Malits. 1st ed. San Francisco : Harper & Row, c1980. p. cm. Includes bibliographical references and index. [BX4705.M542M34 1980] 80-7744 ISBN 0-06-065411-2 pbk. : 6.95
1. Merton, Thomas, 1915-1968. 2. Trappists in the United States—Biography. 3. Poets, American—20th century—Biography. I. Title.

MERTON, Thomas, 271'.125'024 B
1915-1968.
The seven storey mountain / Thomas Merton. New York : Harcourt-Brace Jovanovich, [1978] c1948. p. cm. (A Harvest/HBJ book) Autobiography. [BX4705.M542A3 1978] 78-7109 ISBN 0-15-680679-7 pbk. : 4.95
1. Merton, Thomas, 1915-1968. 2. Trappists in the United States—Biography. I. Title.

MERTON, Thomas, 271'.125'024
1915-1968.
The seven storey mountain / Thomas Merton. New York : Octagon Books, 1978, c1948. 429 p. ; 23 cm. Reprint of the ed. published by Harcourt, Brace, New York. Includes index. [BX4705.M542A3 1978b] 78-15504 lib.bdg. : 17.50
1. Merton, Thomas, 1915-1968. 2. Trappists in the United States—Biography. I. Title.

MERTON, Thomas, 271'.125'024
1915-1968.
The sign of Jonas / Thomas Merton. 1st Harvest/HBJ ed. New York : Harcourt Brace Jovanovich, 1979, c1953. p. cm. (A Harvest/HBJ book) [BX4705.M542A32 1979] 79-10283 ISBN 0-15-682529-5 : 4.95
1. Merton, Thomas, 1915-1968. 2. Trappists in the United States—Biography. I. Title.

RAYMOND, Father, 271'.125'024 B
1903-
Forty years behind the wall / M. Raymond. Huntington, Ind. : Our Sunday Visitor, c1979. 336 p. ; 21 cm. [BX4705.R3744A29] 79-83875 ISBN 0-87973-644-5 : 5.95
1. Raymond, Father, 1903- 2. Trappists in the United States—Biography. I. Title.

Trasher, Lillian Hunt,1887- .

SUMRALL, Lester Frank, 1913- 922
Lillian Trasher, the Nile mother. Springfield, Mo., Gospel Pub. House [1951] xiii, 177 p. illus., ports., map. 20 cm. [BV3572.T7S8] 51-5459
1. Trasher, Lillian Hunt,1887- . I. Title.

Trautmann, John, d. 1924?

TRAUTMANN, Henry. 922
Of the least of these, a character sketch by Henry Trautmann. New York, 1942. 55 p. 21 1/2 cm. An account of the lives of the author's parents, John and Maria Trautmann. [BR1725.T66T7] 43-16981
1. Trautmann, John, d. 1924? 2. Trautmann, Maria (Fohren) d. 1941. I. Title.

Travelers—Prayer-books and devotions.

CLOUD, Fred, ed. 242.8
A traveler's prayer book. Nashville, Upper Room [1965] 93p. illus. 13cm. [BV283.T7C6] 65-23851 1.00 pap.,
1. Travelers—Prayer-books and devotions. I. Title.

Travelers—Prayer-books and devotions—English.

HERNAMAN, Claudia Frances. 264.
The itinerary; a manual of devotions for travellers by land and sea. Compiled by Claudia Frances Hernaman. Published under the direction of the Tract committee. New York, E. & J.B. Young & co. [1889] 127, [1] p. 14 cm. [BV283.T7H4] 49-55500
1. Travelers—Prayer-books and devotions—English. I. Title.

Travers, Walter, 1548?-1635.

KNOX, Samuel James 285.9
Walter Travers: paragon of Elizabethan Puritanism. London, Methuen [dist. New York, Humanities, 1963, c.1962 172p. illus. 23cm. Bibl. 63-1754 6.00
1. Travers, Walter, 1548?-1635. I. Title.

Traversarius, Ambrosius, Camaldulensis, 1386-1439.

STINGER, Charles L., 282'.092'4 B
1944-
Humanism and the church fathers : Ambrogio Traversari (1386-1439) and Christian antiquity in the Italian Renaissance / Charles L. Stinger. Albany : State University of New York Press, 1977. xvii, 328 p., [4] leaves of plates : ill. ; 22 cm. Bibliography: p. 301-314. [BX4705.T737S85] 76-21699 ISBN 0-87395-304-5 : 20.00
1. Traversarius, Ambrosius, Camaldulensis, 1386-1439. 2. Fathers of the church. 3. Renaissance—Italy. I. Title.

Treacy, Gerald Carr, 1883-

CATHOLIC Church Pope (Pius 262.82
Xii), 1939-1958
Four great encyclicals of Pope Pius XII. With Christmas message of 1944: Democracy and peace; and the allocution: The world community and religious tolerance. Discussion club outlines by Rev. Gerald C. Treacy. New York, Deus Books, Paulist Press [c.1961] 224 p. Bibl. 61-8818 .95, pap.
1. Treacy, Gerald Carr, 1883- I. Title.

Treat, Richard, 1708-1778.

EVANS, David, 1688?-1751. 250
The minister of Christ, and the duties of his flock; as it was delivered in a sermon at Abington in Pensilvania, December 30, 1731. At the ordination of Mr. Richard Treat to the gospel ministry there. *With an Appendix of the questions then publickly proposed, and the charges given. Published at the request of some of the auditory. By David Evans, minister at Tredyffryn ... Philadelphia; Printed by B. Franklin, 1732. 108 p. 13 1/2 cm. Book-plate of William F. Gable [BV4009.E8] 24-6550
1. Treat, Richard, 1708-1778. I. Title.

Tree-worship.

PHILPOT, J H. Mrs.
The sacred tree; or, The tree in religion and myth, by Mrs. J. H. Philpot. London, Macmillan and co., limited; New York, The Macmillan company, 1897. xvi, 179 p. incl. front., illus. 23 cm. [BL444.P5] 291
1. Tree-worship. I. Title.

Tregian, Francis, 1548-1608.

BOYNA, Pearl Alexina. 922.242
Francis Tregian, Cornish recusant, by P. A. Boyan and G. R. Lamb. London, New York, Sheed and Ward [1955] 160p. illus. 21cm. Includes bibliography. [BX4705.T74B6] 55-4108
1. Tregian, Francis, 1548-1608. I. Lamb, George, Robert, joint author. II. Title.

Trent, Council of, 1545-1563.

BUNGENER, Laurence Louis 270.
Felix, 1814-1874.
History of the Council of Trent. From the French of L.F. Bungener ... Edited, from the 2d London ed., with a summary of the acts of the council. By John McClintock, D.D. New York, Harper & brothers, 1855. xiii, 546 p. 20 cm. Translator's preface signed: David D. Scott. [BX830.1545.B82] 41-42180
1. Trent, Council of, 1545-1563. I. McClintock, John, 1814-1870, ed. II. Scott, David Dundas, tr. III. Title.

CHEMNITZ, Martin, 1522- 262'.5'2
1586.
Examination of the Council of Trent. [St. Louis, Mo.] Concordia Pub. House [1971- v. 24 cm. Vol. 1 translated by Fred Kramer. [BX830 1545.C413] 79-143693 ISBN 0-570-03213-X
1. Trent, Council of, 1545-1563. 2. Catholic Church—Doctrinal and controversial works—Protestant authors. 3. Lutheran Church—Doctrinal and controversial works. I. Title.

[CRAMP, John Mockett] 1796- 270.6
1881.
The Council of Trent: comprising an account of the procedings of that assembly: and illustrating the spirit and tendency of popery. Philadelphia, Presbyterian board of publication, 1841. 2 p. l., 4, [9]-192 p. 16 cm. [BX830.1545.C7] 33-23852
1. Trent. Council of. 1545-1563. I. Presbyterian church in the U. S. A. (Old school) Board of publication. II. Title.

EVENNETT, Henry Outram, 270.6
1901-
The Cardinal of Lorraine and the Council of Trent; a study in the counter-reformation, by H. Outram Evennett ... Cambridge [Eng.] The University press, 1940. xvii, 536 p. 22 cm. Bibliography: p. [506]-517. [BX830.1545.E8] 31-7003
1. Lorraine, Charles, cardinal de, 1525-1574. 2. Trent, Council of, 1545-1563. 3. Counter-reformation. I. Title.

FROUDE, James Anthony, 262'.5
1818-1894.
Lectures on the Council of Trent, delivered at Oxford 1892-3. Port Washington, N.Y., Kennikat Press [1969] 339 p. 21 cm. Half title: The Council of Trent. "First published 1896; reissued." [BX830 1545.F72] 68-8244
1. Trent, Council of, 1545-1563. I. Title.

FROUDE, James Anthony, 262'.5'2
1818-1894.
Lectures on the Council of Trent, delivered at Oxford 1892-3. New York, B. Franklin [1972] p. Half title: The Council of Trent. Reprint of the 1896 ed. [BX830 1545.F73] 72-76330 ISBN 0-8337-4121-7 15.00
1. Trent, Council of, 1545-1563. I. Title.

JEDIN, Hubert, 1900- 270.6
A history of the Council of Trent. Tr. from German by Ernest Graf. St. Louis, Herder [1962, c.1957, 1961] 562p. illus. 25cm. Contents.v. 2, The first sessions at Trent, 1545-47. Bibl. A58 15.00
1. Trent, Council of, 1545-1563. I. Title.

KINSMAN, Frederick Joseph, 270.
1868-
Trent; four lectures on practical aspects of the Council of Trent, by Frederick Joseph Kinsman. New York [etc.] Longmans, Green and co., 1921. vii, 119 p. 19 cm. [BX830.1545.K5] 21-9082
1. Trent, Council of, 1545-1563 I. Title.

MCNALLY, Robert E. 262'.5
The Council of Trent, the Spiritual exercises, and the Catholic reform, by Robert E. McNally. Philadelphia, Fortress Press [1970] vii, 24 p. (p. 22-24 advertisement) 19 cm. (Facet books. Historical series, 15) "First published in Church history, 34 (1965), 36-49." Bibliography: p. 21. [BX830 1545.M3 1970] 70-96863 1.00
1. Trent, Council of, 1545-1563. 2. Loyola, Ignacio de, Saint, 1491-1556. Exercitia spiritualis. I. Title.

THEISEN, Reinold. 264.0203
Mass liturgy and the Council of Trent. Collegeville, Minn., St. John's University Press, 1965. x, 169 p. 23 cm. Includes bibliographies. [BX2230.5.T48] 66-3411
1. Trent, Council of, 1545-1563. 2. Mass — Hist. I. Title.

TRENT, Council of, 1545- 270.6
1563.
Canons and decrees of the Council of Trent; original text with English translation, by Rev. H. J. Schroeder, O.P. St. Louis, Mo., and London, B. Herder book co., 1941. xxxiii, 608 p. 23 1/2 cm. "The Latin text of the Canons and decrees given in the second part of this book [p. 279-578] and upon which the accompanying translation is based, is that of the Neapolitan edition of 1859, which was made from the Roman edition of 1834 issued by the Collegium urbanum de propaganda fide." --Translator's foreword. [BX830.1545.A3S35] 41-21651
I. Schroeder, Henry Joseph, 1875- tr. II. Title.

TRENT, Council of, 1545- 262.9
1563.
Canons and decrees of the Council of Trent / English translation by H. J. Schroeder. Rockford, Ill. : Tan Books and Publishers, 1978. xx, 293 p. ; 21 cm. Translation of Canones, et decreta. Includes bibliographical references and index. [BX830 1545.A3S35 1978] 78-66132 ISBN 0-89555-074-1 : 5.50
I. Schroeder, Henry Joseph, 1875-1942. II. Title.

TRENT, Council of, 1545- 270.6
1563.
The canons and decrees of the sacred and oecumenical Council of Trent, celebrated under the sovereign pontiffs, Paul III, Julius III and Pius IV. Translated by the Rev. J. Waterworth. Chicago, Ill., The Christian symbolic publication soc. [19--] viii, 304 p. 20 cm. [BX830.1545.A3W32] 35-31607
I. Waterworth, James, 1806-1876, tr. II. Title.

Trever, John C., 1915-

TREVER, John C., 1915- 221.4
The Dead Sea scrolls : a personal account / by John C. Trever. Rev. ed. Grand Rapids : Eerdmans, 1977. p. cm. Published in 1965 and 1966 under title: The untold story of Qumran. Includes bibliographical references and index. [BM487.T7 1977] 77-10808 ISBN 0-8028-1695-9 pbk. : 3.95
1. Trever, John C., 1915- 2. Dead Sea scrolls. 3. Qumran. I. Title.

Trexler, Samuel Geiss, 1877-1949.

DEVOL, Edmund. 922.473
Sword of the Spirit; a biography of Samuel Trexler. New York, Dodd, Mead, 1954. 298p. illus. 22cm. [BX8080.T7D4] 54-7087
1. Trexler, Samuel Geiss, 1877-1949. I. Title.

TREXLER, Samuel Geiss, 1877- 250
Out of thirty-five years; being leaves from the life book of a Lutheran pastor who looks out on the world and sees both good and evil. By Samuel Trexler ... New York, London, G. P. Putnam's sons, 1936. 159 p. front. (port.) 21 1/2 cm. [BV4010.T7] 36-7292
I. Title.

Trials (Divorce)—Great Britain.

KELLY, Henry Ansgar, 1934- 262.9'35
The matrimonial trials of Henry VIII / Henry Ansgar Kelly. Stanford, Calif. : Stanford University Press, 1976. xii, 333 p. ; 23 cm. Includes index. Bibliography: p. [299]-307. [KD378.H4K4] 75-7483 ISBN 0-8047-0895-9 : 15.00
1. Henry VIII, King of England, 1491-1547. 2. Catharine of Aragon, consort of Henry VIII, King of England, 1485-1536. 3. Anne Boleyn, consort of Henry VIII, King of England, 1507-1536. 4. Trials (Divorce)—Great Britain. 5. Marriage (Canon law) I. Title.

Trials (Heresy)—U.S.

HATCH, Carl E. 285'.1'0924 B
The Charles A. Briggs heresy trial; prologue to twentieth-century liberal protestantism [by] Carl E. Hatch. [1st ed.] New York, Exposition Press [1969] 139 p. 22 cm. (An Exposition-university book) Bibliography: p. [133]-139. [BX9193.B7H37] 70-98955 6.00
1. Briggs, Charles Augustine, 1841-1913. 2. Trials (Heresy)—U.S. I. Title.

Trials (Homicide)—California.

PARKER, Larry. 234'.2
We let our son die / by Larry Parker, as told to Don Tanner. Irvine, Calif. : Harvest House Publishers, c1980. 204 p. ; 21 cm. [KF224.P37P37] 19 80-80457 ISBN 0-89081-219-5 (pbk.) : 4.95
1. Parker, Larry. 2. Parker, Wesley, 1962-1973. 3. Trials (Homicide)—California. 4. Spiritual healing. 5. Christian life—1960- I. Tanner, Don. II. Title.

Tribes, Jewish.

SIEGEL, Jonathan Paul. 222'.1'044
The Severus scroll and 1QIs [superscript a] / by Jonathan Paul Siegel. Missoula, Mont. : Published by Scholars Press for the Society of Biblical Literature, c1975. p. cm. (Masoretic studies ; no. 2) Bibliography: p. [BS1222.5.S48S53] 75-28372 ISBN 0-89130-028-7 : 2.80
1. Bible. O.T. Pentateuch. Hebrew. Severus scroll. 2. Bible. O.T. Isaiah. Hebrew. Dead Sea scroll A. 3. Bible. O.T. Pentateuch—Criticism, Textual. 4. Sribes, Jewish. I. Title. II. Series.

Tribulation (Christian eschatology)

DUTY, Guy, 1907- 236'.3
Escape from the coming tribulation : how to be prepared for the last great crisis of history / Guy Duty. Minneapolis : Bethany Fellowship, [1975] 157 p. ; 21 cm. Bibliography: p. [154]-157. [BT888.D87] 75-17979 ISBN 0-87123-131-X : 2.45
1. Tribulation (Christian eschatology) I. Title.

MCKEEVER, James M. 236
Christians will go through the tribulation : and how to prepare for it / Jim McKeever. Medford, Or. : Alpha Omega Pub. Co., c1978. 351 p. : ill. ; 23 cm. Includes bibliographical references. [BT888.M33] 78-55091 ISBN 0-931608-01-5 : 10.95. ISBN 0-931608-02-3 pbk. : 5.95
1. Tribulation (Christian eschatology) I. Title.

WALVOORD, John F. 236'.9
The blessed hope and the tribulation : a Biblical and historical study of posttribulationism / by John F. Walvoord. Grand Rapids : Zondervan Pub. House, c1976. 167, [9] p. ; 21 cm. (Contemporary evangelical perspectives) Includes indexes. Bibliography: p. [1-5] [BT888.W34] 76-13467 pbk. : 3.95
1. Tribulation (Christian eschatology) 2. Rapture (Christian eschatology) 3. Second Advent. I. Title.

Trifa, Valerian D., 1914-

BOBANGO, Gerald J. 281.9'3 B
Religion and politics : Bishop Valerian Trifa and his times / by Gerald J. Bobango. Boulder [Colo.] : East European Monographs ; New York : Distributed by Columbia University Press, 1981. ix, 294 p. : ill. ; 23 cm. (East European monographs ; no. 92) Includes bibliographical references and index. [BX738.R69T743 1981] 19 81-65949 ISBN 0-914710-86-9 : 20.00
1. Trifa, Valerian D., 1914- 2. Orthodox Eastern Church—Bishops—Biography. 3. Bishops—United States—Biography. 4. Citizenship, Loss of—United States—Case studies. I. Title. II. Series.

Trinidad—Religion.

SIMPSON, George Eaton, 1904- 301.5'8'09729
Religious cults of the Caribbean; Trinidad, Jamaica, and Haiti. [Rev. and enl. ed.] Rio Piedras, Institute of Caribbean Studies, University of Puerto Rico, 1970. 308 p. illus. 24 cm. (Caribbean monograph series, no. 7) Bibliography: p. 289-303. [BL2530.T75S55 1970] 72-130671
1. Trinidad—Religion. 2. Jamaica—Religion. 3. Haiti—Religion. I. Title. II. Series.

Trinities.

LAWS, Samuel Spahr, 1824-1921. 232.
The at-onement by the Christian Trinity; or, The legal and spiritual salvation of man from sin makes manifest the dual philosophy of the gospel. By Samuel Spahr Laws ... [Washington, D. C.] The author, 1919. 2 p. l., 7-181 p. front. (group of ports.) 20 cm. [BT265.L35] 21-3758
I. Title.

PAINE, Levi Leonard, 1837-1902. 291.21
The ethnic trinities and thier relations to the Christian trinity; a chapter in the comparative history of religions, by Levi Leonard Paine... Boston and New York, Houghton, Mifflin and company, 1901. vii p., 2 l., [2], [3]-378 p., 1 l. 20 cm. [BL474.P3] 1-24619
1. Trinities. 2. Trinity. I. Title.

Trinity.

ARENDZEN, John Peter, 1873- 231
The holy Trinity; a theological treatise for modern laymen, by Rev. J.P. Arendzen... New York, Sheed & Ward, 1937. vii, 154 p. 20 cm. "Printed in Great Britain." [BT11.A7] 37-
1. Trinity. I. Title.

BARTLETT, Charles Norman, 1891- 231
The triune God, by C. Norman Bartlett ... New York, American tract society [c1937] 194 p. 20 cm. [BT111.B23] 37-6517
1. Trinity. I. Title.

BETTEX, Frederic. 1837-
The glory of the triune God, by F. Bettex. English translation by Andreas Bard. Burlington, Ia., The German literary board, 1914. 78p. i0cm 14-11778 0.35.
I. Bard, Andreas, 1873- tr. II. Title.

BISHOP, William Samuel, 1865- 23
The development of trinitarian doctrine in the Nicene and Athanasian creeds; a study in theological definition. by William Samuel Bishop... New York [etc.] Longmans, Green, and co., 1910. vii, 85 p. 20 cm. [BT111.B65] 10-25239
1. Trinity. I. Title.

BRUMBACK, Carl, 1917- 231
God in three Persons; a Trinitarian answer to the oneness or 'Jesus only' doctrine concerning the Godhead and water baptism. [1st ed. Cleveland, Tenn., Pathway Press, 1959] 192p. 21cm. Includes bibliography. [BT111.2.B75] 59-16846
1. Trinity. 2. Pentecostal churches—Doctrinal and controversial works. 3. Baptism. I. Title.

BURNAP, George Washington, 1802-1859. 231
Expository lectures on the principal passages of the Scriptures which relate to the doctrine of the Trinity. By George W. Burnap ... Boston, J. Munroe and company, 1845. x p., 1 l., 336 p. 19 cm. [BT111.B9] 40-22635
1. Trinity. I. Title.

BURRIS, F. Holiday. 231
The Trinity. By Rev. F. H. Burris ... with an introduction by Professor Joseph Haven ... Chicago, S. C. Griggs and company, 1874. xxvii, 216 p. 19 1/2 cm. [BT111.B95] 40-22636
1. Trinity. I. Haven, Joseph, 1816-1874. II. Title.

CANTWELL, Laurence. 231
The theology of the Trinity. Notre Dame, Ind., Fides Publishers [1969] 94 p. 18 cm. (Theology today, no. 4) Bibliography: p. 92-94. [BT111.2.C3] 78-8388 0.95
1. Trinity. I. Title.

CARROLL, Andrew, 1810- 232.8
The deity of Christ, briefly considered, by Rev. Andrew Carroll ... Cincinnati, E. Morgan and co., 1846. viii, [9]-195 p. 17 cm. [BT215.C3] 37-25862
1. Jesus Christ—Divinity. 2. Trinity. I. Title.

CLARK, Elijah Columbus. 231
Eloheim; or, The manifestation of the Godhead, by Elijah C. Clark... Cleveland, Tenn., The Church of God publishing house [c1929] 134, [2] p. 3 port. on 1 pl. 20 1/2 cm. [BT111.C6] 30-21844
1. Trinity. I. Title. II. Title: The manifestation of the Godhead. III. Title: Godhead. The manifestation of the.

COOKE, Bernard J. 231
Beyond Trinity, by Bernard J. Cooke. Milwaukee, Marquette University Press, 1969. 73 p. 19 cm. (The Aquinas lecture, 1969) "[Presented] under the auspices of the Wisconsin-Alpha Chapter of Phi Sigma Tau." Includes bibliographical references. [BT111.2.C63] 70-81373
1. Trinity. I. Title. II. Series.

CRUZ, Nicky. 231
The Magnificent Three / Nicky Cruz with Charles Paul Conn. Old Tappan, N.J. : Revell, c1976. 128 p. ; 21 cm. [BT113.C78] 76-4574 ISBN 0-8007-0788-5 : 4.95
1. Cruz, Nicky. 2. Trinity. I. Conn, Charles Paul, joint author. II. Title.

†D'ARCY, Martin C. 231
Revelation and love's architecture / Martin C. D'Arcy. Boston : Charles River Books, c1976. 48p. ; 24 cm. [BT113] 76-270990 ISBN 0-89182-010-8 : 8.00
1. Trinity. I. Title.

DAVIES, Richard N. 231
Doctrine of the Trinity; the Biblical evedence, by Richard N. Davies. Cincinnati, Cranston & Stowe; New York, Hunt & Eaton, 1891. 234 p. 20 cm. [BT111.D2] 40-22638
1. Trinity. I. Title.

DAVIS, Humphrey. 133
A treatise by way of a dialogue on cause and effect, illustrating the true science of astronomy. Also electricity, attraction, animal magnetism, repulsion and the true science of theology ... By Humphrey Davis, jr. New Bedford [Mass.] Printed for the author, 1856. 56 p. 23 cm. [X3.D28] 23-3044
I. Title.

DOW, Daniel, 1772-1849.
Familiar letters, to the Rev. John Sherman, once pastor of a church in Mansfield, in particular reference to his late anti-trinitarian treatise. By Daniel Dow ... 2d ed. Worcester: Printed by Thomas & Sturtevant, 1806. 51 p. 23 cm. (Miscellaneous pamphlets. v. 884 [no. 7]) 25-24088
1. Sherman, John, 1772-1828. One God in one person only ... 1805. 2. Trinity. I. Title.

DOW, Daniel, 1772-1849. 231
Familiar letters, to the Rev. John Sherman, once pastor of a church in Mansfield; in particular reference to his late anti-trinitarian treatise. By Daniel Dow ... Hartford: Printed by Lincoln & Gleason, 1806. 51 p. 23 cm. [BT110.D6] 25-22614
1. Sherman, John, 1772-1828. One God in one person only ... 1805. 2. Trinity. I. Title.

DOWNEY, Richard, abp., 1881- 231
The blessed Trinity, by the Most Reverend Richard Downey ... introduction by Neil McNeil ... New York, The Macmillan company, 1930. xi, 99 p. 17 1/2 cm. (Half-title: The treasury of the faith series: 4) [BT121.D75 1930a] 30-25642
1. Trinity. I. Title.

EDWARDS, Jonathan, 1703-1758. 231
An unpublished essay of Edwards on the Trinity, uith remarks on Edwards and his theology, by George P. Fisher ... New York, C. Scribner's sons, 1903. xv p., 2 l., 3-142 p. front. (port.) 21 cm. Contents.Remarks on Edwards and his theology. An unpublished essay of Edwards on the Trinity.--Appendix: Note 1. The dismissal of Edwards from the church in Northampton. Note 2. The account given by Edwards of his method of study. Note 3. Augustine on the Trinity as imaged forth in the human mind. Note 4. President T. D. Woolsey on the personal traits and the influence of Edwards. [BT110.E2F5] 3-29606
1. Trinity. 2. Edwards, Jonathan, 1703-1758. I. Fisher, George Park, 1827-1909. II. Title.

EGAR, John Hodson, 1832-1924. 231
The threefold grace of the Holy Trinity. By John H. Egar ... Philadelphia, J. B. Lippincott & co., 1870. vii, 9-304 p. 19 cm. [BT111.E3] 40-22639
1. Trinity. I. Title.

EVANS, Charles, b. 1795? 23
An exposition of the trinities of the Sacred Scriptures; or, compend of the Christian creed, as given by Christ himself as interpreted by Christ himself; His prophets, evangelists and apostles, compared and contrasted with the creeds of the different branches, respectively, of the orthodox churches in the United States of America. By Rev. Charles Evans. Montgomery, Ala., Barrett & Wimbish, printers, 1857. viii, 503, [1] p. 23 cm. [BT111.E9] 40-22640
1. Trinity. I. Title.

[FROTHINGHAM, Ephraim Langdon] 231.
A statement of the Trinitarian principle, or Law of tri-personality ... Boston, J. P. Jewett and company, 1853. 123.p. 24 cm. [BT111.F8] 40-22642
1. Trinity. 2. Personality. I. Title. II. Title: Law of tri-personality.

HAGERTY, Cornelius, 1885- 231
The Holy Trinity / by Cornelius J. Hagerty. North Quincy, Mass. : Christopher Pub. House, c1976. 359 p. : 25 cm. Includes index. Bibliography: p. 347-350. [BT111.2.H34] 73-92102 ISBN 0-8158-0316-8 : 6.95
1. Trinity. I. Title.

HALL, Francis Joseph, 1857-1932. 281
The Trinity, by the Rev. Franics J. Hall... New York, London [etc.] Longmans, Green, and co., 1910. xix, 316 p. 20 cm. (On cover: Dogmatic theology. [v. 4]) Bibliographical foot-notes. [BT75.H3 vol. 4] [(230)] 10-30166
1. Trinity. I. Title.

HARRIS, F. Donald. 231
The Trinity: is the doctrine biblical? Is it important? By F. Donald Harris and Ronald A. Harris. Neptune, N.J. Loizeaux Brothers [1971] 32 p. 17 cm. [BT113.H33] 77-123613 ISBN 0-87213-310-9 0.50
1. Trinity. I. Harris, Ronald A., joint author. II. Title.

HODGSON, Leonard, 1889- 231
The doctrine of the Trinity; Croall lectures, 1942-1943, by Leonard Hodgson ... New York, C. Scribner's sons, 1944. 237 p. 21 cm. [BT111.H6] 44-5605
1. Trinity. I. Croall lectures, 1942-1943. II. Title.

JANSSENS, Alois, 1887-1941 231
The mystery of the Trinity. Fresno, Calif., Acad. Lib. [1962, c.]1954. 168p. 23cm. (Aspect bk.) 1.95 pap.
1. Trinity. I. Title.

JEWELL, Walter Ellsworth.
Trinity science, the direct transmissional law [by] Walter Ellsworth Jewell ... Los Angeles, Cal., Trinity science church and Trinity-temple college, 1914. 453 p. illus., col. pl. 19 cm. 14-10263 3.50
I. Title.

JONES, William, 1726-1800. 231
The catholic doctrine of a Trinity, proved by above an hundred short and clear arguments, expressed in the terms of the Holy Scripture ... and digested under the four following titles: 1. The divinity of Christ. 2. The divinity of the Holy Ghost. 3. The plurality of persons. 4. The Trinity in unity. With a few reflections ... upon some of the Arian writers, praticularly Dr. S. Clarke: to which is added, A letter to the common people, in answer to some popular arguments against the Trinity. By the late William Jones ... The 1st American, from the 7th London ed. New-York: Published by Whiting and Watson, 96 Broadway. Pelsue & Gould, print. 9 Wall-street, 1813. 186 p. 18 cm. A reply to "An appeal to the common sense of all Christian people", by William Hopkins. [BT110.J7 1813] 33-16668
1. Hopkins, William, 1706-1786. An appeal to the common sense of all Christian people. 2. Clarke, Samuel, 1675-1729. The Scripture doctrine of the Trinity. 3. Trinity. I. Title.

JONES, William, 1726-1800. 231
The catholic doctrine of a Trinity, proved by above an hundred short and clear arguments, expressed in the terms of the Holy Scripture ... and digested under the four following title: 1. The divinity of Christ. 2.. The divinity of the Holy Ghost. 3. The plurality of persons. 4. The Trinity in unity. With a few reflections ... upon some of the Arian writers, particulary Dr. S. Clarke: to which is added, A letter to the common people, in answer to some popular arguments against the Trinity. By the late William Jones ... 2d American ed. New-York: Published by James Eastburn & co. at the Literary rooms, Broadway, 1818. 186 p. 18 cm. A reply to "An appeal to the common sense of all Christian people." by William Hopkins. [BT110.J7 1818] 33-17057
1. Hopkins, William, 1706-1786. An appeal to the common sense of all Christian people. 2. Clarke, Samuel, 1675-1729. The Scripture doctrine of the Trinity. 3. Trinity. I. Title.

JONES, William, 1726-1800. 231
The catholic doctrine of a Trinity, proved by above an hundred short and clear arguments, expressed in the terms of the Holy Scripture ... and digested under the four following titles: 1. The divinity of Christ. 2. The divinity of the Holy Ghost. 3. The plurality of persons. 4. The Trinity in unity. With a few reflections ... upon some of the Arian writers, particulary Dr. S. Clarke: to which is added, A letter to the common people, in answer to some popular arguments against the Trinity. By the late William Jones ... 2d American, from the 7th London ed. Philadelphia: Printed and sold by D. Dickinson, no. 100, Race street, 1818. viii, [13]-219 p. 15 cm. A reply to An appeal to the common sense of all Christian people, by William Hopkins. [BT110.J7 1818 a] 37-18486
1. Hopkins, William, 1706-1786. An appeal to the common sense of all Christian people. 2. Clarke, Samuel, 1675-1729. The Scripture doctrine of the Trinity. 3. Trinity. I. Title.

JONES, William, 1726-1880 231
The catholic doctrine of a Trinity. By the Rev. William Jones. Philadelphia, G. D. M'Cuenn, 1838. xxxvii, [39]-184 p. 17 cm. A reply to "An appeal to the common sense of all Christian people", by William Hopkins. [BT110.J7 1838] 33-16669
1. Hopkins, William, 1706-1786. An appeal to the common sense of all Christian people. 2. Clarke, Samuel, 1675-1729. The Scripture doctrine of the Trinity. 3. Trinity. I. Title.

KLEIN, Felix, 1862- 231
The doctrine of the Trinity, by Abbe Felix Klein ... translated by Daniel J. Sullivan ... New York, P. J. Kenedy & sons [c1940] ix p., 1 l., 298 p. 21 cm. Translation of Le Dieu des chretiens, notre fol en la Trinite. [Full name: Felix Phillppe Klein] [BT111.K55] 40-34099
1. Trinity. I. Sullivan, Daniel James, 1909- tr. II. Title.

LANDIS, Josiah P. 1844-
The Holy Trinity, by J. P. Landis ... Dayton, O., United brethren publishing house, 1902. 70 p. 17 cm. (Doctrinal series) 2-21591
I. Title.

LANDIS, Josiah P. 1844-
The Holy Trinity, by J. P. Landis ... Dayton, O., United brethren publishing house, 1902. 70 p. 17 cm. (Doctrinal series) 2-21591
I. Title.

LANDIS, Robert Wharton, 231
d.1883.
A plea for the catholic doctrine of the Trinity. By Robert W. Landis ... Philadelphia, 1832. ix, [1], 227 p. 21 cm. [BT111.L2] 40-22645
1. Trinity. I. Title.

THE lighted candle.
[1st ed.] New York, Vantage Press [c1959] 77p. 21cm.
1. Trinity. I. Armstrong, George T

LINFIELD, Cornelius S. 204
Science of the trinity, by Cornelius S. Linfield ... La Crosse, Wis., C. S. Linfield, 1927. 201 p. 16 cm. [BR126.L5] 27-9195
I. Title.

LOWRY, Charles Wesley. 231
The Trinity and Christian devotion. [1st ed.] New York, Harper [1946] xviii, 162 p. 20 cm. (The Presiding Bishop's book for Lent, 1946) A Lenten book selected jointly by the Presiding Bishop of the Protestant Episcopal Church and the Archibishop of Canterbury. [BT111.L6] 46-1480
1. Trinity. I. Title. II. Series.

LOWRY, Charles Wesley. 231
The Trinity and Christian devotion, by Charles W. Lowry ... New York and London, Harper & brothers [1946] xviii, 162 p. 19 1/2 cm. A Lenten book selected jointly by the Presiding bishop of the Protestant Episcopal church and the Archibishop of Canterbury. "First edition." [BT111.L6] 46-1480
1. Trinity. I. Title.

MCDONOUGH, William K. 231
The Divine Family; the Trinity and our life in God. New York, Macmillan [c.1963] 178p. 22cm. 63-9235 3.95
1. Trinity. I. Title.

MCDOWALL, Stewart Andrew, 1882-
Evolution and the doctrine of the Trinity, by Stewart A. McDowall... Cambridge, The University press, 1918. xxvii, 258 p. 19 cm. A20
1. Trinity. 2. Evolution. I. Title.

MARMION, Columba, Abbot, 231.3
1858-1923.
The Trinity in our spiritual life; an anthology of the writings of Dom Columba Marmion, compiled by Dom Raymund Thibaut. Westminster, Md., Newman Press, 1953. 284p. 23cm. Translation of Consecration a la Sainte Trinite, texte et commentaire. [BT111.M352] 53-5593
1. Trinity. I. Title.

MATTISON, Hiram, 1811-1868. 231
A Scriptural defence of the doctrine of the Trinity; or, A check to modern Arianism, as taught by Campbellities, Hicksites, New Lights, Universalists and Mormons; and especially by a sect calling themselves "Christians." By Rev. H. Mattison. New York, L. Colby & co., 1846. xii, 162 p. 16 cm. [BT111.M4] 40-37136
1. Trinity. I. Title.

MATTISON, Hiram, 1811-1868. 23
A scriptural defence of the doctrine of the Trinity; or,A check to modern Arianism, as taught by Unitarians, Hicksites, New Lights, Universalists and Mormons; and especially by a sect calling themselves "Christians." By Rev. H. Mattison. 4th ed. New York, L. Colby & co., 1850. xii, 162 p. 16 cm. [BT111.M4 1850] 20-16819
1. Trinity. I. Title.

MOHLER, John E. 1867-
The infinite in trinity and unity, by John E. Mohler ... Los Angeles, Cal., 1913. 277 p. 18 cm. $1.50 13-14294
I. Title.

MOHLER, John E. 1867-
The infinite in trinity and unity, by John E. Mohler ... Los Angeles, Cal., 1913. 277 p. 18 cm. $1.50 13-14294
I. Title.

MOLTMANN, Jurgen. 231'.044
The Trinity and the kingdom : the doctrine of God / by Jurgen Moltmann ; translated by Margaret Kohl. 1st ed. New York : Harper & Row, c1981. p. cm. Translation of Trinitat und Reich Gottes. Includes index. [BT111.2.M613 1981] 19 80-8352 ISBN 0-06-065906-8 : 14.95
1. Trinity. 2. Kingdom of God. I. [Trinitat und Reich Gottes.] English II. Title.

MOORE, Humphrey, d.1871. 231
A treatise on the divine nature, exhibiting the distinction of the Father, Son, and Holy Spirit. By Humphrey Moore ... Boston, Published by S. T. Armstrong, for the author, 1824. viii, [9]-356 p. 23 cm. [BT111.M7] 40-22646
1. Trinity. I. Title.

MYLNE, Louis George, 1843-
The holy Trinity; a study of the self-revelation of God, by Louis George Mylne ... London, New York [etc.] Longmans, Green and co., 1916. x, 286 p. 23 cm. 17-6642
I. Title.

MYLNE, Louis George, 1843-
The holy Trinity; a study of the self-revelation of God, by Louis George Mylne ... London, New York [etc.] Longmans, Green and co., 1916. x, 286 p. 23 cm. 17-6642
I. Title.

THE new discussion of the 231
Trinity; containing notices of Professor Huntington's recent defence of that doctrine, reprinted from "The Christian examiner", "The Monthly religious magazine", "The Monthly journal of the Unitarian association", and "The Christian register". Together with sermons, by Rev. Thos. Starr King, and Dr. Orville Dewey. Boston, Walker, Wise, and company, for the American Unitarian association, 1860. viii, 244 p. 19 cm. [BX9841.A1N4 1860] 252.08 33-24768
1. Trinity. 2. Unitarian church—Sermons. 3. Sermons, American. I. Huntington, Frederick Dan, bp., 1819-1904. II. King, Thomas Starr, 1824-1864. III. Dewey, Orville, 1794-1882. IV. American Unitarian association.

THE new discussion of the 231
Trinity; containing notices of Professor Huntington's recent defence of that doctrine, reprinted from "The Christian examiner", "The Monthly religious magazine", "The Monthly journal of the Unitarian association", and "The Christian register". Together with sermons, by Rev. Thos. Starr King, and Dr. Orville Dewey. Boston, American Unitarian association, 1867. viii, 244 p. 19 cm. [BX9841.A1N4 1867] 252.02 33-24769
1. Trinity. 2. Unitarian churches—Sermons. 3. Sermons, American. I. Huntington, Frederick Dan, bp., 1819-1904. II. King, Thomas Starr, 1824-1864. III. Dewey, Orville, 1794-1882. IV. American Unitarian association.

NORTON, Jacob, 1764-1858. 231
Things as they are; or, Trinitarianism developed. Second part. In reply to "A letter written in February, 1815, to the Rev. Jacob Norton, of Weymouth, and now published with an appendix, containing some notes and remarks, by Daniel Thomas, A. M., pastor of the Second church in Abington; together with a few incidental remarks on several passages of a sermon preached at the installation of the Rev. Holland Weeks, over the First church and society in Abington, the ninth of August, 1815. By Nathaniel Emmons, D. D., pastor of the church in Franklin". By Jacob Norton, A. M., pastor of the First religious society in Weymouth ... Boston: Printed for the author, by Lincoln & Edmands, no. 53, Cornhill, 1815. 112 p. 23 cm. "Serious and solemn address to Christian churches ... on the subject of the Presbyterian mode of church government and discipline": p. [101]-112. [BT111.N6] 41-33060
1. Thomas, Daniel, 1778-1847. A letter written in February, 1815. 2. Emmons, Nathanael, 1745-1840. 3. Trinity. 4. Presbyterianism. I. Title.

[ORME, William] 1787-1830. 231
Memoir of the controversy respecting the three heavenly witnesses, I John v. 7., including critical notices of the principal writers on both sides of the discussion ... By Criticus [pseud.] A new ed., with notes and an appendix, by Ezra Abbot. New York, J. Miller, 1866. xii, 213 p. 20 cm. "A series of articles which originally appeared in the Congregational magazine for 1829 ... and were published at London ... in 1880. The author [is] the Rev. William Orme."--Editorial note. [BT112.O7 1866] 41-35221
1. Trinity. 2. Bible. N. T. 1 John v, 7—Criticism, Textual. I. Abbot, Ezra, 1819-1884, ed. II. Title.

PAINE, Levi Leonard, 1837- 23
1902.
A critical history of the evolution of trinitarianism, and its outcome in the new Christology, by Levi Leonard Paine... Boston and New York, Houghton, Mifflin and company, 1900. ix p., 2 l., 387, [1] p. 20 cm. [BT111.P2] 0-2733
1. Trinity. 2. Theology, Doctrinal—Hist. 3. Athanasianism. I. Title.

PALMER, Benjamin Morgan, 1818- 23
1902.
The threefold fellowship and the threefold assurance; an essay in two parts. By B. M. Palmer... Richmond, Va., The Presbyterian committee of publication [c1902] 144 p. 20 1/2 cm. [BT111.P3] 2-9163
1. Trinity. 2. Faith. I. Title.
Contents omitted.

PANIKKAR, Raymond, 1918- 231
The Trinity and the religious experience of man; icon-person-mystery [by] Raimundo Panikkar. New York, Orbis Books [1973] xvi, 82 p. 19 cm. [BT111.2.P36] 73-77329 ISBN 0-88344-495-X 2.95 (pbk.)
1. Trinity. 2. Spirituality. I. Title.

PEASE, Aaron G. 231
Philosophy of Trinitarian doctrine: a contribution to theological progress and reform, by Rev. A. G. Pease ... New York, G. P. Putnam's sons, 1875. xii, 183 p. 19 cm. [BT111.P4] 40-22649
1. Trinity. I. Title.

PITTENGER, William Norman, 231
1905-
The divine triunity / by Norman Pittenger. Philadelphia : United Church Press, c1977. 119 p. ; 22 cm. "A Pilgrim Press book." Bibliography: p. 118-119. [BT111.2.P57] 76-55002 ISBN 0-8298-0330-0 : 5.95
1. Trinity. 2. Process theology. I. Title.

PLUMMER, Frederick. 231
A public discussion on the doctrine of the Trinity, between Elder Frederick Plummer, Christian; and the Rev. William L. M'Calla. Presbyterian. Held at Rdley, Delaware county, Pennsylvania, on the 18th, 19th, 20th, and 21st of January, 1842. Philadelphia, Kay and brother, 1842. vi, 7-288 p. 19cm. [BT111.P7] 40-22650
1. Trinity. I. M'Calla, William Latts, 1788-1859. II. Title.

POHLE, Joseph, 1852-1922. 231
The divine Trinity, a dogmatic treatise, by the Reverend Joseph Pohle ... authorized English version, with some abridgment and numerous additional references, by Arthur Preuss. St. Louis, Mo. [etc.] B. Herder, 1912. 2 p. l., iii-iv, 297 p. 21 cm. Half-title: Dogmatic theology ii. [BT111.P75] 12-1227
1. Trinity. I. Preuss, Arthur, 1871-1934 tr. II. Title.

PONTIFEX, Mark, 1896- 231.3
Belief in the Trinity. London, New York, Longmans, Green [1954] 91p. 19cm. [BT111.P78] 54-1712
1. Trinity. I. Title.

PONTIFEX, Mark, 1896- 231.3
Belief in the Trinity. New York, Harper [1954] 91p. 19cm. [BT111] 54-12211
1. Trinity. I. Title.

RAHNER, Karl, 1904- 231
The Trinity. Translated by Joseph Donceel. [New York] Herder and Herder [1970] 120 p. 21 cm. Translation of Der dreifaltige Gott als transzendenter Urgrund der Heilsgeschichte in Mysterium salutis, v. 2, chapter 5. Includes bibliographical references. [BT111.2.R3] 72-87766 4.95

1. Trinity.

RAWLINSON, Alfred Edward John, bp. of Derby, 1884- ed. 231
Essays on the Trinity and the incarnation, by members of the Anglican communion, edited by A. E. J. Rawlinson ... London, New York, [etc.] Longmans, Green and co., ltd., 1928. ix, 415 p. 23 cm. [BT111.R3] 28-13862
1. Trinity. 2. Incarnation. I. Narborough, Frederick Dudley Vaughan, 1895- II. Nock, Arthur Darby, 1902- III. Kirk, Kenneth Escott, bp. of Oxford, 1886- IV. Green, Frederick Wastle, 1884- V. Brabant, Frank Herbert, 1892- VI. Hodgson, Leonard, 1889- VII. Title.
Contents omitted.

RICHARDSON, Cyril Charles, 1909- 231
The doctrine of the Trinity. New York, Abingdon Press [1958] 159p. 20cm. Includes bibliography. [BT111.R5] 58-5393
1. Trinity. I. Title.

SERVETUS, Michael, 1509or11-1553. 231
... The two treatises of Servetus on the Trinity: On the errors of the Trinity; seven books. A.D. MDXXXI; Dialogues on the Trinity; two books; On the righteousness of Christ's kingdom; four chapters. A.D. MDXXXII. By Michael Serveto, alias Reves, a Spaniard of Aragon; now first translated into English by Earl Morse Wilbur ... Cambridge, Harvard university press. London, H. Milford, Oxford university press, 1932. xxxviii, 264 p. 23 1/2 cm. (Added t.-p.: Harvard theological studies) Series title also at head of t.-p. "Issued as an extra number of the Harvard theological review." Bibliography: p. [xxix]-xxxvi. [BT110.S55] 33-1337
1. Trinity. 2. Justification. I. Wilbur, Earl Morse, 1866- tr. II. Title.

SHINDLER, Mary Stanley Bunce (Palmer) Dana, Mrs., 1810-1883. 23
Letters addressed to relatives and friends, chiefly in reply to arguments in support of the doctrine of the Trinity. By Mary S. B. Dana ... New ed. Boston, J. Munroe and company; London, Chapman brothers, 1846. xii, 285 p. 20 cm. [BT111.S5] 27-12032
1. Trinity. I. Title.

SMITH, Ethan, 1762-1849. 232
A treatise on the character of Jesus Christ, and on the Trinity in unity of the Godhead; with quotations from the primitive fathers. By Ethan Smith ... Boston: Published by R. P. & C. Williams. Printed by N. Willis. 1814. 3 p. l., [ix]-xii, [13]-235 p. 18 cm. [BT201.S63] 37-13898
1. Jesus Christ—Person and offices. 2. Trinity. I. Title.

SMITH, William Edward. 231
Christianity and the Trinitarian doctrine, by William Edward Smith. Boston, Meador publishing company, 1936. 436 p. front. (port.) 21 cm. [BT111.S56] 37-968
1. Trinity. I. Title.

SULLIVAN, John Edward. 231
The image of God, the doctrine of St. Augustine and its influence. Dubuque, Iowa, Priory Press [1963] 356 p.. 23 cm. [BT109.S8] 63-12507
1. Trinity. 2. Augustinus, Aurelius, Saint, Bp. of Hippo. I. Title.

SUMMERBELL, Nicholas, 1816-1889. 231
Discussion on the Trinity, church constitutions and disciplines, and human depravity. Between N. Summerbell, pastor of the First Christian church, Cincinnati, Ohio, and Rev. J. M. Flood, ex-president of the Ohio conference of the M. P. church. Held in Centreville, Ohio, from August 2, to August 9, 1854. Comprising fifty-eight alternate speeches of thirty minutes each. Reported by Benn Pitman, phonographer. Examined and corrected by the parties. 3d ed. Cincinnati, Applegate & co., 1855. 432 p. 18 cm. [BT111.S9] 40-23706
1. Trinity. 2. Church polity. 3. Church discipline. 4. Sin, Original. I. Flood, J. M. II. Pitman, Benn, 1822-1910. III. Title.

VAUGHN, Ray. 231
Wallace-Vaughn debate, held at Arvada, Colorado, Septmber 5-7, 1951, between Ray Vaughn and G. K. Wallace. Wire recorded. Longview, Wash., Telegram Sermons Book Co., 1952. 194p. 22cm. [BT113.V3] 53-1093
1. Trinity. 2. Baptism. 3. United Pentecostal Church—Doctrinal and controversial works. 4. Churches of christ—Doctrinal and controversial works. I. Wallace, Gervias Knox, 1906- II. Title.

WELCH, Claude. 231.3 231
In this name; the doctrine of the Trinity in contemporary theology. New York, Scribner, 1952. 313 p. 22 cm. [BT111.W42] 52-14614
1. Trinity. I. Title.

WHITON, James Morris, 1833-1920. 231
Gloria Patri; or, Our talks about the Trinity, by James Morris Whiton... New York, T. Whittaker, 1892. 162 p. 19 cm. [BT111.W48] 40-24445
1. Trinity. I. Title. II. Title: Our talks about the Trinity.

WILSON, James, 1760-1839. 231
The doctrine of the self-existent Father, of His only begotten Son, Our Lord, and of the holy and eternal Spirit, rationally, calmly, and Scripturally considered ... By James Wilson ... Providence, Printed by Weeden and Cory, 1835. viii, [9]-68 p. 23 cm. [BT113.W5] 40-24447
1. Trinity. I. Title.

WINSLOW, Hubbard, 1799-1864. 281
Discourses on the nature, evidence, and moral value, of the doctrine of the Trinity. By Hubbard Winslow ... Boston, Perkins, Marvin & co.; Philadelphia, H. Perkins, 1834. 162 p. 16 1/2 cm. [BT111.W7] 40-24446
1. Trinity. I. Title.

WORCESTER, Noah, 1758-1837. 231
Bible news: or, Sacred truths relating to the living God His only Son and Holy Spirit; illustrated and defended in a continued series of letters and inquiries. 2d ed., cor. and enl. By Noah Worcester ... Boston, Published by Bradford & Read. Sold also by Cushing & Appleton, and T. Porter, Salem; C. Norris & co., Exeter; Lord. Hyde & co., Portland; E. Goodale. Hallowell; D. Coolidge, Concord; I. Thomas, Worcester; A. Sherman, jun, New Bedford; J. Brewer, Providence; and A. Finlay, Philadelphia 1812. xi, [13]-252 p. 17 1/2 cm. [BT115.W8 1812] 26-10893
1. Jesus Christ—Divinity. 2. Trinity. I. Title.

WORCESTER, Noah, 1758-1837. 282.
An impartial review of testimonies in favor of the divinity of the Son of God, as given by the most eminent Christian bishops and martyrs of the three first centuries, and by the Council of Nice, A.D. 325. Also, the origin of the doctrine of three persons in one God, extracted from Dr. Mosheim's "Ecclesiastical history", and confirmed by Mr. Milner's "History of the church of Christ". In letters addressed to a worthy minister of the gospel. By Noah Worcester ... [Concord, George Hough, printer] 1810. 59, [1] p. 16 1/2 cm. [BT215.W7] 25-23336
1. Jesus Christ—Dinity. 2. Mosheim, Johann Lorenz, 1694?-1755. "An ecclesiastical history, ancient and modern." 3. Milner, Joseph 1744-1797. "History of the church of Christ." 4. Trinity. I. Title.

Trinity—Addresses, essays, lectures.

ALPHA and omega : 231'.044
essays on the Trinity in honor of James A. Nichols, Jr. / edited by Caroleen Hillriegel, Lois Jones, Freeman Barton. Lenox, Mass. (200 Stockbridge Rd., Lenox, 01240) : Henceforth Publications, c1980. 140 p. ; 22 cm. Includes bibliographical references. [BT113.A46] 19 81-126219 4.50 (pbk.)
1. Nichols, James Albert—Addresses, essays, lectures. 2. Trinity—Addresses, essays, lectures. I. Nichols, James Albert. II. Hillriegel, Caroleen. III. Jones, Lois. IV. Barton, Freeman.

Trinity—Art.

MACHARG, John Brainerd, 1873-
Visual representations of the Trinity; an historical survey, by John Brainerd MacHarg ... Cooperstown, N.Y., The Arthur H. Crist publishing co., 1917. 4 p. l., 139 p. front. 23 cm. Published also as the author's thesis (PH.D.) Columbia university, 1917. Bibliography: p. 124-139. [N8040.M3] 17-29782
1. Trinity—Art. I. Title.

Trinity—Biblical teaching.

BICKERSTETH, Edward Henry bp. of Exeter, 1825-1906. 231
The rock of ages; or, Scripture testimony to the one eternal Godhead of the Father, and of the Son, and of the Holy Ghost. By Edward Henry Bickersteth ... With an introduction by the Rev. F. D. Huntington ... Boston, E. P. Dutton and company, 1860. vi, [7]-214 p. 20 cm. [BT111.B6 1860] 38-35187
1. Trinity—Biblical teaching. I. Title. II. Title: Scripture testimony to the one eternal Godhead.

BICKERSTETH, Edward Henry, bp. of Exeter, 1825-1906. 231
The rock of ages; or, Scripture testimony to the one eternal Godhead of the Father, and of the Son, and of the Holy Ghost. By Edward Henry Bickersteth ... With an introduction by the Rev. F. D. Huntington ... Boston, American tract society, 1860. v, [7]-214 p. 20 cm. [BT111.B6 1860 a] 38-37376
1. Trinity—Biblical teaching. I. American tract society, Boston. II. Title. III. Title: Scripture testimony to the one eternal Godhead.

BICKERSTETH, Edward Henry, bp. of Exeter, 1825-1906. 231
The rock of ages; or, Scripture testimony to the one eternal Godhead of the Father and of the Son and of the Holy Ghost. By the Rev. Edward Henry Bickersteth, M. A. With an introduction by the Rt. Rev. F. D. Huntington ... New York, E. P. Dutton and company, 1871. vi, [7]-214 p. 18 cm. [BT111.B6 1871] 38-35188
1. Trinity—Biblical teaching. I. Title. II. Title: Scripture testimony to the one eternal Godhead.

BICKERSTETH, Edward Henry, Bp. of Exeter, 1825-1906. 231
The Trinity; Scripture testimony to the one eternal Godhead of the Father, and of the Son, and of the Holy Spirit. Grand Rapids, Kregel Publications, 1959. 182p. 22cm. 'Companion volume to The Holy Spirit.' 'Formerly published under the title, The rock of ages.' [BT111.B6 1959] 59-13770
1. Trinity—Biblical teaching. I. Title. II. Title: Scripture testimony to the one eternal Godhead.

TRAVIS, George, 1741-1797. 907'.2'024 s
Letters to Edward Gibson, esq., 1785. New York, Garland Pub., 1974. p. cm. (The Life & times of seven major British writers. Gibboniana 13) Reprint of the 1785 ed. printed by C. F. and J. Rivington, London. [DG206.G5G52 vol. 13] [BT112] 231 74-14851 ISBN 0-8240-1349-2 22.00
1. Gibbon, Edward, 1737-1794. History of the decline and fall of the Roman empire. 2. Benson, George, 1699-1762. 3. Newton, Isaac, Sir, 1642-1727. 4. Bible. N.T. 1 John V, 7—Criticism, Textual. 5. Trinity—Biblical teaching. I. Gibbon, Edward, 1737-1794. II. Title. III. Series: Gibboniana 13.

Trinity Cathedral, Phoenix, Ariz.

LINCOLN, Joseph Colville. 748.5'9191'73
The windows of Trinity Cathedral. [1st ed. Flagstaff, Ariz.] Northland Press [1973] vii, 81 p. illus. (part col.) 26 cm. [NK5312.L56] 73-78003 ISBN 0-87358-106-7
1. Trinity Cathedral, Phoenix, Ariz. 2. Glass painting and staining—Phoenix, Ariz. I. Title.

Trinity—Congresses.

ONE God in Trinity / 231'.044
edited by Peter Toon, James D. Spiceland. Westchester, Ill. : Cornerstone Books, 1980. xiii, 177 p. : ill. ; 23 cm. Based on a conference of the historical theology group of the British Tyndale Fellowship, held at Durham, Eng., in 1978. Includes index. Bibliography: p. 173. [BT111.2.O53 1980] 19 79-57395 ISBN 0-89107-187-3 : 12.95
1. Trinity—Congresses. I. Toon, Peter, 1939- II. Spiceland, James D.

Trinity—Controversial literature.

ELLIS, George Edward, 1814-1894. 231
The Christian Trinity, the doctrine of God, the Father; Jesus Christ; and the Holy Spirit. A discourse preached in Harvard church, Charlestown, February 5, 1860. By George E. Ellis. Charlestown, Mass A. E. Cutter, 1860. 94 p. 23 1/2 cm. [BT115.E5] 40-32659
1. Trinity—Controversial literature. I. Title.

FOLSOM, Nathaniel Smith, 1806-1890. 231
The Scriptural doctrine of Our Lord Jesus Christ, and the Holy Spirit, in the relation to God the Father. By Nathaniel S. Folsom. Boston, J. Monroe and company, 1840. 2 p. l., 84 p. 19 cm. [BT115.F6] 40-22660
1. Trinity—Controversial literature. I. Title.

MILTON, John, 1608-1674. 288
... John Milton's last thoughts on the Trinity. Extracted from his posthumous work entitled "A treatise on Christian doctrine, compiled from the Holy Scriptures alone." Lately published by royal command ... Boston, W. Crosby and H. P. Nichols, 1847. 95 p. 18 cm. ([American Unitarian association. Tracts] 1st ser. no. 236) From Sumner's translation of the Latin original. cf. Pref. Also published (1908) under title, "Milton on the Son of God and the Holy Spirit." [BX9813.A5] 40-25741
1. Trinity—Controversial literature. I. Sumner, Charles Richard, bp. of Winchester, 1790-1874, tr. II. Title.

MILTON, John, 1608-1674. 231
Milton on the Son of God and the Holy Spirit : from his treatise, On Christian doctrine / with introd. by Alexander Gordon. Norwood, Pa. : Norwood Editions, 1976. xi, 136 p. ; 23 cm. Reprint of the 1908 ed. published by the British & Foreign Unitarian Association, London. Selected from the 1853 ed. of C. R. Sumner's translation of De doctrina Christiana. [BT115.M53 1976] 76-6564 ISBN 0-8482-0853-6 : 15.00
1. Trinity—Controversial literature. I. Title.

MILTON, John, 1608-1674. 231
Milton on the Son of God and the Holy Spirit, from his Treatise on Christian doctrine. With introd. by Alexander Gordon. [Folcroft, Pa.] Folcroft Library Editions, 1973. xi, 136 p. 24 cm. Reprint of the 1908 ed. published by British and Foreign Unitarian Association, London. [BT115.M53 1973] 73-4827 ISBN 0-8414-2028-9 (lib. bdg.)
1. Trinity—Controversial literature. I. Title.

[PARSONS, Benjamin] 231
The Christian layman: or, The doctrine of the Trinity fully considered, and adjudged according to the Bible. By a Christian layman ... Mobile, Doubleday and Sears; New York, C. C. Francis, and Wiley & Putnam, 1840. vii, [1], 371 p. 20 cm. [BT115.P3] 41-32804
1. Trinity—Controversial literature. I. Title.

REMARKS on the early 231
corruptions of Christianity; chiefly, so far as regards the Trinity; and on prayer. By J. W. Philadelphia, J. Campbell, 1867. v, 7-147 p. 19 cm. [BT115.R3] 40-22661
1. Trinity—Controversial literature. I. W., J. II. J. W.

SHERMAN, John, 1772-1828. 231
One God in one person only: and Jesus Christ a being distinct from God, dependent upon Him for His existence, and His various powers; maintained and defended ... By John Sherman ... Worcester [Mass.]: From the press of Isaiah Thomas, jun. September--1805. xvi, [17]-198, [2] p. 22 cm. [BT115.S5] 40-38456
1. Trinity—Controversial literature. I. Title.

SMITH, William Edward, 1881- 231.3
The faith of Jesus. Boston, Meador Pub.

Co. [1954] 697p. 22cm. [BT115.S56] 55-19726
1. Trinity—Controversial literature. 2. Holy Spirit. I. Title.

WEEKES, Robert Dodd, b.1819. 231
Jehovah-Jesus; the oneness of God: the true Trinity... By Robt. D. Weeks. New York, Dodd, Mead & company for the author, 1876. 3 p. l., [5]-140 p. 19 1/2 cm. [BT115.W3] 40-23090
1. Trinity—Controversial literature. I. Title.

WORCESTER, Noah, 1758-1837. 231
Bible news; or, Sacred truths relating to the living God, His only Son, and Holy Spirit. By Noah Worcester, A.M. 4th ed. ... New York, B. Parsons, 1851. vi, [7]-240 p. 18 1/2 cm. [BT115.W8 1851] 26-10894
1. Jesus Christ—Divinity. 2. Trinity—Controversial literature. I. Title.

Trinity—Doctrine—Sermons.

*STEWART, James Stuart, 1896- 231
The strong name, by James S. Stewart. Grand Rapids, Baker Book House [1972] viii, 260 p. 20 cm. (James S. Stewart library) First published in Edinburgh as part of the Scholar as preacher series. [BT109] ISBN 0-8010-7975-6 pap., 2.95
1. Trinity—Doctrine—Sermons. I. Title.

Trinity—Early works to 1800.

AUGUSTINUS, Aurelius, Saint, Bp. of Hippo 231
The Trinity. Tr. [from Latin] by Stephen McKenna. Washington, D.C., Catholic Univ. [c.1963] xvii, 539p. 22cm. (Fathers of the church, a new translation, v. 45) Bibl. 63-12482 7.95
1. Trinity—Early works to 1800. I. Title. II. Series.

AUGUSTINUS, Aurelius, Saint, Bp. of Hippo. 231
The Trinity. Translated by Stephen McKenna. Washington, Catholic University of America Press [1963] xvii, 539 p. 22 cm. (The Fathers of the church, a new translation, v. 45) Bibliography: p. xvii. [BT110.A813] 63-12482
1. Trinity — Early works to 1800. I. Title. II. Series.

AUGUSTINUS, Aurelius, Saint, Bp. of Hippo. 231
The Trinity [by] St. Augustine. Translated by Stephen McKenna. Edited and abridged by Charles Dollen. [Boston] St. Paul Editions [1965] 303 p. 22 cm. [BT110.A813] 64-21602
1. Trinity — Early works to 1800. I. Dollen, Charles, ed. II. Title.

AUGUSTINUS, Aurelius, Saint, Bp. of Hippo 231
The Trinity [by] St. Augustine. Tr. by Stephen McKenna. Ed., abridged by Charles Dollen [Boston] St. Paul Eds. [dist. Daughters of St. Paul, c.1965] 303p. 22cm. [BT110.A813] 64-21602 4.00
1. Trinity—Early works to 1800. I. Dollen, Charles, ed. II. Title.

EDWARDS, Jonathan, 1703-1758. 231
Observations concerning the Scripture oeconomy of the Trinity and covenant of redemption, by Jonathan Edwards. With an introduction and appendix by Egbert C. Smyth. New York, C. Scribner's sons, 1880. 3 p. l., [3]-97 p. 19 cm. [BT110.E2] 40-36584
1. Trinity—Early works to 1800. 2. Redemption. I. Smyth, Egbert Coffin, 1829-1904, ed. II. Title.

HILARIUS, Saint, Bp. of Poitiers, d.367? 231.3
The Trinity; translated by Stephen McKenna. New York, Fathers of the Church, 1954. xix, 555p. 22cm. (The Fathers of the church, a new translation, v.25) Bibliography: p. xvi-xvii. [BR60.F3H53] 54-14571
1. Trinity—Early works to 1800. 2. Arianism. I. Title. II. Series.

NOVATIANUS. 230'.1'3
The Trinity, The spectacles, Jewish foods, In praise of purity, Letters, by Novatian. Translated by Russell J. DeSimone. Washington, Catholic University of America Press [1973] p. (The Fathers of the church, a new translation, v. 67) [BR65.N62E5 1973] 73-9872 ISBN 0-8132-0066-0
1. Trinity—Early works to 1800. 2. Christian ethics—Early church. I. DeSimone, Russell J., tr. II. Title. III. Series.

SERLE, Ambrose, 1742-1812. 231
Horae solitariae: or, Essays upon some remarkable names and titles of Jesus Christ and the Holy Spirit, occurring in the Old and New Testaments, and declarative of their essential divinity and gracious offices in the redemption and salvation of men: to which is annexed, an essay, chiefly historical, upon the doctrine of the Trinity; and a brief account of the heresies relative to the doctrine of the Holy Spirit, which have been published since the Christian era. By Ambrose Serle ... New York, R. Carter, 1842. xii, 708 p. illus. 22 1/2 cm. [BT110.S4 1842] 40-37135
1. Trinity—Early works to 1800. 2. Jesus Christ—Name. 3. Holy Spirit—Name. I. Title.

Trinity Episcopal Church, Solebury, Pa.

GANTZ, Charlotte Orr. 283'.748'21
The first hundred years, Trinity Church, Solebury, Pennsylvania / by Charlotte Orr Gantz ; ill. by Barbara McArthur & Joanne McNaught. [Solebury, Pa.] : Centennial Committee of Trinity Episcopal Church, 1976, c1975. 51 p. : ill. ; 23 cm. [BX5980.S57T743] 76-352204
1. Trinity Episcopal Church, Solebury, Pa. I. Title.

Trinity Evangelical Lutheran Church, Springfield Township, Bucks Co., Pa.

BIEBER, Edmund Ellis, 1906- 284.7748
Springfield Church; a brief history of Trinity Evangelical Lutheran Church of Springfield Township, Bucks County, Pa., from 1751 to 1953. [Pleasant Valley, Pa.] Springfield Church Council [1953] 207p. illus. 22cm. [BX8076.S77B5] 53-29747
1. Trinity Evangelical Lutheran Church, Springfield Township, Bucks Co., Pa. I. Title.

Trinity—History of doctrines.

BOWIE, Walter Russell 231
Jesus and the Trinity. Nashville, Abingdon Press [c.1960] 160 p. 21 cm. (Bibl. footnotes) 60-10907 2.75
1. Trinity—History of doctrines. I. Title.

BRACKEN, Joseph A. 231
What are they saying about the Trinity? / By Joseph A. Bracken. New York : Paulist Press, c1979. v, 90 p. ; 19 cm. (A Deus book) Bibliography: p. 87-90. [BT109.B7] 78-70819 ISBN 0-8091-2179-4 pbk. : 1.95
1. Trinity—History of doctrines. I. Title.

BURTON, Edward, 1794-1836. 231
Testimonies of the ante-Nicene fathers to the doctrine of the Trinity and of the divinity of the Holy Ghost. By the Rev. Edward Burton... Oxford, The University press, 1831. xvii p., 1 l., 151 p. 23 cm. Bibliography: p. xv-xvi. [BT111.B97] 40-22637
1. Trinity—History of doctrines. 2. Holy Spirit. I. Title.

FORTMAN, Edmund J., 1901- 231
The Triune God; a historical study of the doctrine of the Trinity [by] Edmund J. Fortman. Philadelphia, Westminster [1972] xxvi, 382 p. 24 cm. (Theological resources) Bibliography: p. 347-358. [BT109.F67 1972] 73-137395 ISBN 0-664-20917-3 9.95
1. Trinity—History of doctrines. I. Title.

GRUBER, L. Franklin. 231
The theory of a finite and developing deity examined, by L. Franklin Gruber, D. D. Oberlin, O., Press of the News printing company [c1918] cover-title, p. [475]-526. 23 cm. Reprinted from Bibliotheca sacra, vol. lxxv, no. 300, October 1918. [BT101.G8] 19-5217
I. Title.

HAUGH, Richard. 231
Photius and the Carolingians : the Trinitarian controversy / Richard Haugh. Belmont, Mass. : Nordland Pub. Co., [1975] 230 p. ; 23 cm. Includes index. Bibliography: p. 207-214. [BT109.H35] 74-22859 ISBN 0-913124-05-2 : 15.00
1. Photius I, Saint, Patriarch of Constantinople, ca. 820-ca. 891. 2. Trinity—History of doctrines. I. Title.

HEDLEY, George Percy, 1899- 231
The Holy Trinity; experience and interpretation, by George Hedley. Philadelphia, Fortress [1967] xi, 147p. 18cm. [BT109.H4] 67-16468 2.00 pap.,
1. Trinity —History of doctrines. I. Title.

LONERGAN, Bernard J. F. 231
The way to Nicea : the dialectical development of trinitarian theology / Bernard Lonergan ; a translation by Conn O'Donovan of the first part of De Deo Trino. Philadelphia : Westminster Press, c1976. xxxi, 142 p. ; 23 cm. "A translation of pages 17-112, Pars dogmatica, of De Deo Trino, Rome, Gregorian University Press, 1964." Includes bibliographical references and indexes. [BT109.L6613] 76-20792 ISBN 0-664-21340-5 : 9.50
1. Trinity—History of doctrines. 2. Dogma, Development of. 3. Sects. I. Title.

MCGLOIN, Frank, 1846- 231
The mystery of the Holy Trinity in oldest Judaism, by Frank McGloin ... Philadelphia, J. J. McVey, 1916. xiii, 232 p. 20 cm. [BT111.M2] 16-9171
1. Trinity—History of doctrines. 2. Jews—Religion. I. Title.

O'CALLAGHAN, Jeremiah. 231
Atheism of Brownson's review. Unity and Trinity of God. Divinity and humanity of Christ Jesus. Banks and paper monty. By the Reverend Jeremiah O'Callahan ... Burlington, Vt., 1852. xxv, [27]-306, [2] p. 23 cm. [BT111.O2] 40-22647
1. Trinity—History of doctrines. 2. Interest and usury. 3. Brownson's quarterly review. I. Title.

PIAULT, Bernard. 231
What is the Trinity? Translated from the French by Rosemary Haughton. [1st ed.] New York, Hawthorn Books [1959] 156p. 21cm. (The Twentieth century encyclopedia of Catholicism. v. 17. Section 2: The basic truths) Translation of Le mystere du Dieu vivant, un et trine. Bibliography: p.156. [BT109.P513] 58-11595
1. Trinity—History of doctrines. 2. Creeds. I. Title. II. Series: The Twentieth century encyclopedia of Catholicism, v. 17

SLOYAN, Gerard Stephen, 1919- 231
The three Persons in One God. Englewood Cliffs, N.J., Prentice-Hall [1964] ix, 118 p. illus. 24 cm. (Foundations of Catholic theology series) Bibliography: p. 109-110. [BT109.S55] 63-22046
1. Trinity — History of doctrines. I. Title.

TAVARD, Georges Henri, 1922- 231'.044'09
The vision of the trinity / George H. Tavard. Washington, DC : University Press of America, c1981. viii, 158 p. (p. 158 blank) ; 22 cm. Includes bibliographical references and indexes. [BT109.T38] 19 80-5845 ISBN 0-8191-1412-X lib. bdg. : 17.75 ISBN 0-8191-1413-8 (pbk.) : 8.75
1. Trinity—History of doctrines. I. Title.

WARFIELD, Benjamin Breckinridge, 1851-1921. 230.1'3'0922
Studies in Tertullian and Augustine. Westport, Conn., Greenwood Press [1970] v, 412 p. 23 cm. Reprint of the 1930 ed. Includes bibliographical references. [BR1720.T3W3 1970] 73-109980
1. Tertullianus, Quintus Septimius Florens. 2. Augustinus, Aurelius, Saint, Bp. of Hippo—Addresses, essays, lectures. 3. Trinity—History of doctrines. 4. Knowledge, Theory of (Religion) 5. Pelagianism. I. Title.

Trinity—History of doctrines—Addresses, essays, lectures.

FAHEY, Michael Andrew, 1933- 231
Trinitarian theology East and West : St. Thomas Aquinas—St. Gregory Palamas / by Michael A. Fahey, John Meyendorff. Brookline, Mass. : Holy Cross Orthodox Press, 1977. p. cm. (Patriarch Athenagoras memorial lectures) [BT109.F34] 77-28080 ISBN 0-916586-18-9 pbk. : 2.95
1. Thomas Aquinas, Saint, 1225?-1274—Addresses, essays, lectures. 2. Palamas, Gregorius, Abp. of Thessalonica, ca. 1296-ca. 1359—Addresses, essays, lectures. 3. Trinity—History of doctrines—Addresses, essays, lectures. I. Meyendorff, Jean, 1926- joint author. II. Title. III. Series.

Trinity History of doctrines Early church, ca. 20-600.

THE Trinitarian 231'.044
controversy / translated and edited by William G. Rusch. Philadelphia : Fortress Press, c1980. viii, 182 p. ; 22 cm. (Sources of early Christian thought) Bibliography: p. 181-182. [BT109.T74] 79-8889 ISBN 0-8006-1410-0 : 5.95
1. Trinity—History of doctines—Early church, ca. 30-600. 2. Trinity—Early works to 1800. I. Rusch, William G. II. Title. III. Series.

Trinity Lutheran Church, Gresham, Or.

BRADFIELD, Irene. 284'.1795'49
Trinity Lutheran Church, 1899-1974 / [writer, Irene Bradfield]. Gresham, Or. : Trinity Lutheran Church, [1974] 61 p. : ill. ; 22 cm. [BX8076.G76T743] 75-308824
1. Trinity Lutheran Church, Gresham, Or. 2. Gresham, Or.—Biography. I. Trinity Lutheran Church, Gresham, Or.

Trinity Methodist Chapel, Sale, Eng.

KINDER, Arthur Gordon. 287'.1427'31
One hundred years of Trinity / [by A. Gordon Kinder]. [Sale] : [The author], [1976] 15 p. : ill. ; 22 cm. Cover title: Trinity Methodist Chapel, Sale, centenary, 1875-1975. [BX8483.S3K56] 77-353216 ISBN 0-9505228-0-5 : £0.40
1. Trinity Methodist Chapel, Sale, Eng. 2. Methodist Church in Sale, Eng. I. Title. II. Title: Trinity Methodist Chapel, Sale, centenary, 1875-1975.

Trinity—Sermons.

GAGE, William Leonard, 1832-1889. 231
Trinitarian sermons preached to a Unitarian congregation. With an introduction on the Unitarian failure, by Rev. William L. Gage. Boston, J. P. Jewett and company; Cleveland, O., H. P. B. Jewett, 1859. 5, xxi, [23]-153 p. 18 cm. [BT111.G2] 40-22643
1. Trinity—Sermons. 2. Unitarianism—Controversial literature. 3. Sermons, American. I. Title.

HALL, Arthur Crawshay Alliston, bp., 1847-1930. 231
Reasonable faith; four sermons on fundamental Christian doctrines, by Rev. A. C. A. Hall... New York, J. Pott & co., 1889. 76 p. 16 1/2 cm. [BT113.B25] 40-21816
1. Trinity—Sermons. 2. Protestant Episcoapl church in the U.S.A.—Sermons. 3. Sermons, American. I. Title.

HARROWAR, David. 231
A defence of the Trinitarian system, in twenty-four sermons; in which the leading controversial points between Trinitarians and anti-Trinitarians, are stated and discussed. By David Harrowar, A. M. Utica [N. Y.] Printed by Williams, 1822. viii, [9]-336, [6] p. 23 cm. [BT111.H3] 40-22644
1. Trinity—Sermons. 2. Sermons, American. I. Title.

O'CONNELL, Jeremiah Joseph, 1821-1894. 231
Conferences on the Blessed Trinity. By the Rev. Dr. J. J. O'Connell ... New York, The Catholic publication society co., 1882. 270 p. 19 cm. "Authors": p. [7]-8. [BT111.O25] 40-22648
1. Trinity—Sermons. 2. Catholic church—Sermons. 3. Sermons, American. I. Title.

O'CONNELL, Jeremiah Joseph, 1821-1894. 231
Conferences on the Blessed Trinity. By the Rev. Dr. J. J. O'Connell ... New York,

The Catholic publication society co., 1882. 270 p. 19 cm. "Authors": p. [7]-8 [BT111.O25] 40-22648
1. Trinity—Sermons. 2. Catholic church—Sermons. 3. Sermons, American. I. Title.

RATZINGER, Joseph. 231
The God of Jesus Christ : meditations on God in the Trinity / Joseph Cardinal Ratzinger ; translated by Robert J. Cunningham. Chicago : Franciscan Herald Press, [1978] p. cm. Translation of Le Dieu de Jesus-Christ. [BT113.R3713] 78-16275 ISBN 0-8199-0697-2 : 6.95
1. Catholic Church—Sermons. 2. Trinity—Sermons. 3. Sermons, English—Translations from French. 4. Sermons, French—Translations into English. I. Title.

REES, Paul Stromberg. 231
Stand up in praise to God. Grand Rapids, Eerdmans [1960] 117p. 20cm. (Preaching for today) [BT113.R4] 60-53088
1. Trinity—Sermons. 2. Evangelical Covenant Church of America— Sermons. 3. Sermons, American. I. Title.

Trinity United Methodist Church, Alexandria, Va.

STUKENBROEKER, Fern 287'.6755'296 C.
A watermelon for God : a history of Trinity United Methodist Church, Alexandria, Virginia, 1774-1974 / by Fern C. Stukenbroeker. Alexandria, Va. : Stukenbroeker, 1974. xiii, 268 p. : ill. ; 24 cm. Bibliography: p. 261-268. [BX8481.A53T747] 74-195119
1. Trinity United Methodist Church, Alexandria, Va. I. Title.

Trinity United Methodist Church, Richland Center, Wis.

SCOTT, Margaret 287'.6775'75 Helen.
Glory to Thy name; a story of a church. Richland Center, Wis., Richland County Publishers, 1973. 110, xiv p. illus. 26 cm. Bibliography: p. 107-110. [BX8481.R43T747] 73-76879
1. Trinity United Methodist Church, Richland Center, Wis. 2. Richland Center, Wis.—Biography. I. Title.

Tripitaka—Criticism, interpretation, etc.

NARIMAN, Gushtaspshah 294.3'82 Kaikhushro, d.1933.
Literary history of Sanskrit Buddhism (from Winternitz, Sylvain Levi, Huber) [by] J. [i.e. G.] K. Nariman. [2d ed. rep.] Delhi, Motilal Banarsidass [1972] xiv, 393 p. 23 cm. [BQ1105.N3 1972] 73-900542
1. Tripitaka—Criticism, interpretation, etc. 2. Sanskrit literature—History and criticism. I. Winternitz, Moriz, 1863-1937. II. Levi, Sylvain, 1863-1935. III. Huber, Eduard, 1879-1914. IV. Title.
Distributed by Verry, 15.00.

TRIPITAKA. English. 294.3'82 Selections
The lion's roar; an anthology of the Buddha's teachings selected from the Pali canon [by] David Maurice. [1st Amer. ed.] New York, Citadel [1967,c.1962] 255p. 21cm. "The texts herein are largely from trs. which appeared in the Light of the Dhamma. [BL1411.T82M33 1967] 67-25651 4.95
I. Maurice, David. comp. II. The Light of the Dhamma. III. Title.

TRIPITAKA. English. 294.382 Selections.
The lion's roar; an anthology of the Buddha's teachings selected from the Pali canon [by] David Maurice. New York, Citadel Press [1967, c1962] 255 p. 21 cm. "The texts herein are largely from translations which appeared...in the Light of the Dhamma." [BL1411.T82M33 1967] 67-25651
I. Maurice, David, comp. II. The Light of the Dhamma. III. Title.

TRIPITAKA. English. 294.3 Selections.
The Vedantic Buddhism of the Buddha, a collection of historical texts, tr. from the original Pali and ed. by J. G. Jennings. London, Oxford Univ. Press, 1948. cxvii, 679 p. 23 cm. [BL1411.T8E6 1948] 49-5246
I. Jennings, James George, 1866-1914, ed. and tr. II. Jatakas, Nidana-kaha. III. Title.

Tripitaka. Sutrapitaka. Lankavatarasutra—Criticism, interpretation, etc.

SUZUKI, Daisetz Teitaro, 294.3'85 1870-1966.
Studies in the Lankavatara sutra : one of the most important texts of Mahayana Buddhism, in which almost all its principal tenets are presented, including the teaching of Zen / by Daisetz Teitaro Suzuki. Boulder, Colo. : Prajna Press, 1981. xxxii, 464 p. ; 22 cm. Reprint. Originally published: London : Routledge & Kegan Paul, 1930. Includes index. [BQ1727.S87 1981] 19 81-12179 ISBN 0-87773-754-1 (pbk.) : 12.50
1. Tripitaka. Sutrapitaka. Lankavatarasutra—Criticism, interpretation, etc. I. Title.

Troeltsch, Ernst, 1865-1923.

OGLETREE, Thomas W. 230
Christian faith and history; a critical comparison of Ernst Troeltsch and Karl Barth. Nashville, Abingdon [c.1965] 236p. 23cm. Bibl. [BX4827.T703] 65-20364 4.00
1. Troeltsch, Ernst, 1865-1923. 2. Barth, Karl, 1886- 3. History—Philosophy. I. Title.

OGLETREE, Thomas W 230
Christian faith and history, a critical comparison of Ernst Troeltsch and Karl Barth [by] Thomas W. Ogletree. New York, Abingdon Press [1965] 236 p. 23 cm. Bibliographical footnotes. [BX4827.T703] 65-20364
1. Troeltsch, Ernst, 1865-1923. 2. Barth, Karl, 1886- 3. History — Philosophy. I. Title.

REIST, Benjamin A 230.0924
Toward a theology of involvement; the thought of Ernst Troeltsch, by Benjamin A. Reist. Philadelphia, Westminster Press [1966] 264 p. 21 cm. Bibliography: p. [257] -264. [BX4827.T7R4] 66-11919
1. Troeltsch, Ernst, 1865-1923. I. Title.

Troeltsch, Ernst, 1865-1923—Addresses, essays, lectures.

TROELTSCH, Ernst, 1865- 230'.08 1923.
Writings on theology and religion / Ernst Troeltsch ; translated and edited by Robert Morgan and Michael Pye. Atlanta : John Knox Press, 1977, c1976. p. cm. "The first three essays ... translated ... from Gesammelte Schriften II, Tubingen, 1913 and 1922 ... The fourth was published separately." Bibliography: p. [BR85.T7613] 77-79596 ISBN 0-8042-0554-X : 17.50
1. Troeltsch, Ernst, 1865-1923—Addresses, essays, lectures. 2. Theology—Addresses, essays, lectures. I. Title.
Contents omitted

Troeltsch, Ernst, 1865-1923—Congresses.

ERNST Troeltsch and 230'.092'4 *the future of theology* / edited by John Powell Clayton. Cambridge : Cambridge University Press, 1976. xiii, 217 p. ; 23 cm. Essays based on a colloquium sponsored by the Dept. of Religious Studies, University of Lancaster. Includes index. Bibliography: p. 196-214. [BX4827.T7E76 1976b] 76-383265 ISBN 0-521-21074-7 : 18.95
1. Troeltsch, Ernst, 1865-1923—Congresses. I. Clayton, John Powell. II. Lancaster, Eng. University. Dept. of Religious Studies.
Distributed by Cambridge University Press N.Y. N.Y.

Troll, Uschi.

HOLZER, Hans W., 133.8'092'4 B 1920-
The clairvoyant / Hans Holzer. New York : Mason/Charter, 1976. viii, 166 p. ; 24 cm. [BF1283.T76H64] 76-15165 ISBN 0-88405-370-9 : 8.95
1. Troll, Uschi. I. Title.

Tropes (Music)

CATHOLIC Church. Liturgy 783.5 and ritual.
The Winchester troper, from mss. of the Xth and XIth centuries; with other documents illustrating the history of tropes in England and France. Edited by Walter Howard Frere. London, 1894. [New York, AMS Press, 1973] xlvii, 248 p. illus. 23 cm. Reprint of the ed. printed by Harrison and Sons, which was issued as v. 8 of the Publications of the Henry Bradshaw Society. [ML3080.C32T7] 70-178507 ISBN 0-404-56530-1 18.50
1. Tropes (Music) I. Frere, Walter Howard, Bp. of Truro, 1863-1938, ed. II. [Troper (Winchester Cathedral)] III. Winchester Cathedral. IV. Title.

EVANS, Paul. 783.2'3'5
The early trope repertory of Saint Martial de Limoges. Princeton, N.J., Princeton University Press, 1970. viii, 294 p. 25 cm. (Princeton studies in music, no. 2) Transcription into modern notation of one of the 9 St. Martial tropes (now in the Bibliotheque nationale, Paris): p. 119-273. Bibliography: p. 285-290. [ML3080.E9] 66-11971 ISBN 0-691-09109-9 10.00
1. Catholic Church. Liturgy and ritual. Troper. 2. Tropes (Music) I. Paris. Bibliotheque nationale. Mss. (Lat. 1121) II. Title. III. Series.

PLANCHART, Alejandro 783.2'1 Enrique.
The repertory of tropes at Winchester / Alejandro Enrique Planchart. Princeton, N.J. : Princeton University Press, 1977. 2 v. : music ; 25 cm. A revision of the author's thesis, Harvard, 1971. Includes indexes. Bibliography: v. 2, p. [343]-360. [ML3080.P62 1977] 76-3033 ISBN 0-691-09121-8 : 22.50
1. Catholic Church. Liturgy and ritual. Troper (Winchester Cathedral) 2. Tropes (Music) I. Title.

Tropospheric radio wave propagation.

DU CASTEL, Francois. 621.38411
Tropospheric radiowave propagation beyond the horizon. Translated and edited by E. Sofaer with assistance from Dr. and Mrs. J. R. Wait. [1st English ed.] Oxford, New York, Pergamon Press [1966] [San Francisco, Sufism Reoriented, 1966] xii, 236 p. illus. (15 fold. in pocket) 24 cm. vii, 59 p. 18 cm. (International series of monographs in electromagnetic waves, v. 8) Translation of Propagation tropospherique et falsceaux hertziens transhorizon. Bibliography: p. 214-232. [TK6553.D8213] [BP570.D8] 297.4 65-16853 66-25818
1. Tropospheric radio wave propagation. 2. Theosophy — Addresses, essays, lectures. I. Duce, Ivy Oneita. II. Title. III. Title: What am I doing here? ... IV. Series. V. Series: International series of monographs on electromagnetic waves, v. 8

DUCE, Ivy Oneita. 621.38411
Tropospheric radiowave propagation beyond the horizon. Translated and edited by E. Sofaer with assistance from Dr. and Mrs. J. R. Wait. [1st English ed.] Oxford, New York, Pergamon Press [1966] xii, 236 p. illus. (15 fold. in pocket) 24 cm. (International series of monographs in electromagnetic waves, v. 8) Translation of Propagation tropospherique et falsceaux hertziens transhorizon. Bibliography: p. 214-232. [TK6553.D8213] [BP570.D8] 297.4 65-16853 66-25818
1. Tropospheric radio wave propagation. 2. Theosophy — Addresses, essays, lectures. I. Title. II. Title: What am I doing here? ... III. Series. IV. Series: International series of monographs on electromagnetic waves, v. 8

Trosse, George, 1631-1713.

TROSSE, George, 285'.092'4 B 1631-1713.
The life of the Reverend Mr. George Trosse, written by himself, and published posthumously according to his Order in 1714. Edited by A. W. Brink. Montreal, McGill-Queen's University Press, 1974. xi, 140 p. port. 23 cm. Includes bibliographical references. [BX5207.T75A33 1974] 73-79097 ISBN 0-7735-0153-3 9.75
1. Trosse, George, 1631-1713. I. Brink, A. W., ed. II. Title.
Distributed by McGill Queens University Press, New York.

Trotman, Dawson

*SKINNER, Betty Lee 248.22
Daws, the story of Dawson Trotman founder of the navigators. Grand Rapids, Zondervan [1974] 389 p. illus. 23 cm. [BP605] 73-22700 6.95
1. Trotman, Dawson I. Title.

WALLIS, Ethel Emilia. 922
Lengthened cords; how Dawson Trotman, founder of the Navigators, also helped extend the world-wide outreach of the Wycliffe Bible Translators. [Glendale, Calif., Wycliffe Bible Translators, 1958] 127 p. illus. 22 cm. [BV3785.T7W2] 58-49551
1. Trotman, Dawson. I. Title.

Trotter, Jesse M.

TROTTER, Jesse M. 248.4'83
Christian wholeness : spiritual direction for today / by Jesse M. Trotter. Wilton, Conn. : Morehouse-Barlow Co., c1982. xii, 86 p. : ill. ; 22 cm. Bibliography: p. 86. [BV4501.2.T73 1982] 19 81-84718 ISBN 0-8192-1294-6 pbk. : 4.75
1. Trotter, Jesse M. 2. Spiritual life—Anglican authors. I. Title.

Troy—Romances, legends, etc.

COLONNE, Guido delle, 879.3 13thcent.
... *Historia destructionis Troiae,* edited by Nationiel Edward Griggin. Cambridge, Mass., The Mediaeval academy of America, 1936. xvii, 293 p. 26 cm. (Half-title: The Mediaeval academy of America. Publication no. 26) At head of title: Guido de Columnia. [PA8310.C6H5 1936] 37-2294
1. Troy—Romances, legends, etc. I. Griffin, Nathaniel Edward, 1873- ed. II. Title.

SCHERER, Margaret 704.947 Roseman.
The legends of Troy in art and literature. New York, Published by the Phaidon Press for the Metropolitan Museum of Art, 1963. xviii, 304 p. illus. 26 cm. ([Phaidon art books]) Includes bibliographical references. [BL793.T7S3] 64-556
1. Troy—Romances, legends, etc. 2. Art and mythology. I. Title.

Trueblood, David Elton, 1900-

TRUEBLOOD, David 289.6'092'4 Elton, 1900-
A philosopher's way : essays and addresses of D. Elton Trueblood / edited by Elizabeth Newby. Nashville : Broadman Press, c1978. 136 p. ; 20 cm. [BX7795.T75A56] 78-57069 pbk. : 4.95
I. Newby, Elizabeth Loza. II. Title.

TRUEBLOOD, David Elton, 1900- 207
The teacher / D. Elton Trueblood. Nashville, Tenn. : Broadman Press, c1980. 131 p. ; 22 cm. [LC383.T85] 19 80-67088 ISBN 0-8054-6933-8 : 6.95
1. Trueblood, David Elton, 1900- 2. Church and college. 3. Christianity and culture. 4. Christian life—Friends authors. I. Title.

TRUEBLOOD, David 289.6'092'4 B Elton, 1900-
While it is day; an autobiography [by] Elton Trueblood. [1st ed.] New York, Harper & Row [1974] xi, 170 p. 22 cm. [BX7795.T75A37] 73-18680 ISBN 0-06-068741-X 5.95
1. Trueblood, David Elton, 1900- I. Title.

Truett, George Washington, 1867-1944.

BURTON, Joe, 1907- 922.673
Prince of the pulpit, a pen picture of George W. Truett at work, by Joe W. Burton ... Grand Rapids, Mich., Zondervan publishing house [1946] 87 p. pl., ports. 20 cm. [Full name: Joe Wright Burton] [BX6495.T7B8] 46-17816
1. Truett, George Washington, 1867-1944. I. Title.

JAMES, Powhatan Wright, 1880- 922.673
George W. Truett, a biography, by Powhatan W. James; with an introductionby Douglas Southall Freeman. New York, The Macmillan company, 19399 xv p., 1 l., 281 p. front., plates, ports. 21 cm. "First printing." [BX6495.T7J3] 39-5997
1. Truett, George Washington, 1867- I. Title.

JAMES, Powhatan Wright, 1880- 922.673
George W. Truett, a biography by Powhatan W. James. With an introduction by Douglas Southall Freeman. New and rev. ed. New York, The Macmillan company, 1945. 1 p. l., vii-xiii, 311 p. front. (port.) 20 cm. [BX6495.T7J3 1945] 45-3658
1. Truett, George Washington, 1867-1944. I. Title.

JAMES, Powhatan Wright, 1880- 922.673
George W. Truett, Biography, With an introd. by Douglas Southall Freeman. Memorial ed. Nashville, Broadman Press [1953] 311p. illus. 20cm. [BX6495.T7J3 1953] 53-7935
1. Truett, George Washington, 1867-1944. I. Title.

Trumbull, Charles Gallaudet, 1872-1941.

HOWARD, Philip Eugene, 1870- ed. 922.573
Charles Gallaudet Trumbull, apostle of the victorious life, by Philip E. Howard. Philadelphia, The Sunday school times company [1944] 4 p. l., 71 p. front. (port.) 18 cm. "Impressions of Dr. Trumbull as expressed in the words of a few friends."--Pref. [BV1518.T7H6] 44-13847
1. Trumbull, Charles Gallaudet, 1872-1941. I. Title.

Trumbull, Henry Clay, 1830-1903.

HOWARD, Philip Eugene, 1870- 922.
The life story of Henry Clay Trumbull, missionary, army chaplain, editor, and author, by Philip E. Howard; with an introduction by Charles Gallaudet Trumbull. Philadelphia, The Sunday school times co., 1905. xv, 525 p. 6 port. (incl. front.) 22 cm. "Books written by Henry Clay Trumbull": p. xi-xii. [BX7260.T7H6] 5-41785
1. Trumbull, Henry Clay, 1830-1903. I. Title.

Trungpa, Chogyam, 1939-

CLARK, Tom, 1941- 294.3'657'0924
The great Naropa poetry wars / Tom Clark ; with a copious collection of germane documents assembled by the author. 1st ed. Santa Barbara : Cadmus Editions, 1980. 87 p. ; 22 cm. [BQ990.R867C58] 79-55794 ISBN 0-932274-06-4 (pbk.) : 5.00 ISBN 0-932274-07-2 (signed) : 20.00
1. Trungpa, Chogyam, 1939- 2. Jack Kerouac School of Disembodied Poetics. 3. Lamas—United States—Biography. 4. Poets, American—20th century—Biography. 5. Poetry. I. Title.

TRUNGPA, Chogyam, 1939- 294.3'657'0924 B
Born in Tibet / by Chogyam Trungpa, the eleventh Trungpa Tulku, as told to Esme Cramer Roberts ; with a foreword by Marco Pallis. Boulder, CO : Prajna Press, 1981. p. cm. Reprint of the 3d ed. published by Shambhala, Boulder, Colo., in series: the Clear light series. Includes index. [BQ990.R867A33 1980] 19 80-20315 ISBN 0-87773-718-5 (pbk.) : 8.95
1. Trungpa, Chogyam, 1939- 2. Lamas—Tibet—Biography. I. Roberts, Esme Cramer. II. Title.
Distributed by Great Eastern Books, P. O. Box 271, Boulder, CO 80306

Truro Cathedral.

BARHAM, Fisher. 942.3'78
The creation of a cathedral : the story of St Mary's, Truro / [illustrations selected and text written] by Fisher Barham. Falmouth : Glasney Press, 1976. 88 p. : chiefly ill. (some col.), plan, ports. ; 26 cm. Plan and ill. on lining papers. [NA5471.T738B37] 76-381807 ISBN 0-9502825-2-9 : £3.95
1. Truro Cathedral. I. Title.

Truro Parish, Va.—History—Sources.

TRURO Parish, Va. Vestry. 254'.03'755291
Minutes of the Vestry, Truro Parish Virginia, 1732-1785. Lorton, Va. : Pohick Church, 1974. vi, 153 p. : ill. ; 24 cm. Includes index. [BX5980.L75T787 1974] 74-81678 12.00
1. Truro Parish, Va.—History—Sources. I. Title.

Trussville, Ala.—Biography.

HANLIN, Katherine Hale. 286'.1761'78
The steeple beckons; a narrative history of the First Baptist Church, Trussville, Alabama, 1821-1971. [Trussville, Ala., First Baptist Church, 1973] xiii, 252 p. illus. 24 cm. Bibliography: p. 207-211. [BX6480.T78F57] 72-92280
1. First Baptist Church, Trussville, Ala. 2. Trussville, Ala.—Biography. I. Title.

Trust in God.

CAMMAERTS, Emile. 248
Upon this rock [by] Emile Cammserts. New York and London, Harper & brothers [1943] ix, 118 p. 20 cm. Bibliography: p. vii. [BV4637.C3 1943] 43-2589
1. Trust in God. I. Title.

CAMMAERTS, Emile. 234.2
Upon this rock [by] Emile Cammserts. New York and London, Harper & brothers [1943] ix, 118 p. 20 cm. "Seventh edition." Bibliography: p. vii. [BV4637.C3 1943a] 45-8171
1. Trust in God. I. Title.

CAMPBELL, Dortch, 1880-1953. 248
Break those fetters of fear. New York, J. Felsberg, 1954. 166p. 23cm. [BV4637.C33] 54-34237
1. Trust in God. 2. Fear. I. Title.

CHURCH, Leslie Frederic, 1886- 248
In the storm, by Leslie F. Church. New York, Nashville, Abingdon-Cokesbury [1942] 296 p. 19 1/2 cm. [BV4637.C45] 42-14474
1. Trust in God. I. Title.

DITZEN, Lowell Russell. 248
Personal security through faith. With an introd. by Ralph W. Sockman. [1st ed.] New York, Holt [1954] 243 p. 22 cm. [BV4637.D5] 54-5446
1. Trust in God. 2. Security (Psychology) I. Title.

LEUTY, Joseph D 1909- 218
In God we trust; everyday essays on life and philosophy. [1st ed.] New York, Exposition Press [1956] 84p. 21cm. [BV4637.L46] 56-12680
1. Trust in God. I. Title.

LEUTY, Joseph D 1909- 248
In God we trust; everyday essays on life and philosophy. 1st ed. New York, Exposition Press [1956] 84p. 21cm. [BV4637.L46] 56-12680
1. Trust in God. I. Title.

LOUTTIT, Henry Irving, Bp., 1903- 248
Fear not. Foreword by Austin Pardue. Greenwich, Conn., Seabury Press, 1954. 65p. 20cm. Includes bibliography. [BV4637.L66] 54-9582
1. Trust in God. 2. Fear. I. Title.

MANN, Stella Terrill. 248
Change your life through faith and work! New York, Dodd, Mead [1953] 152p. 20cm. [BV4637.M3] 52-14113
1. Trust in God. I. Title.

MARY Bernard, Sister, 1917- 248.4'82
Who can we trust? / Sister Mary Bernard. Harrison, Ark. : New Leaf Press, c1980. 125 p. ; 18 cm. Includes bibliographical references. [BV4637.M32] 19 80-80531 ISBN 0-89221-075-3 (pbk.) : 2.50
1. Mary Bernard, Sister, 1917- 2. Trust in God. 3. Spiritual healing. I. Title.
Publisher's address: P.O. Box 1045, Harrison, Ark. 72601

TIPPETT, Harry Moyle, 1891- 248
Who waits in faith. Washington, Review and Herald Pub. Assn. [1951] 128 p. 20 cm. [BV4637.T56] 52-15009
1. Trust in God. I. Title.

Truszkowska, Maria Angela, 1825-1899.

CEGIELKA, Francis A 922.2438
The pierced heart; the life of Mother Mary Angela Truszkowska, foundress of the Congregation of the Sisters of St. Felix (Felician Sisters) Milwaukee, Bruce Press [1955] 76p. illus. 21cm. (Catholic life publications) [BX4705.T794C4] 55-3134
1. Truszkowska, Maria Angela, 1825-1899. I. Title.

Truth.

[ANLEY, Charlotte]
Miriam; or, The power of truth. A Jewish tale, by the author of "Influence." A new ed., rev. and improved, with an introduction by Rev. John Todd ... Philadelphia, Griffith & Simon, 1842. 292 p. 18 1/2 cm. [PE3.A612M] 6-2050
I. Todd, Hohn, 1800-1873. II. Title.

ASHENFELTER, Ida Goodman, 1860-
The truth; a message from the spirit, by Ida G. Ashenfelter. Covina, Cal., Ida G. Ashenfelter [c1908] 134 p. 17 1/2 cm. 8-18357
I. Title.

BAKER, Edward Mayer. 111.83
Short stories in the name of truth. [Rev. and enl. ed.] Boston, Christopher Pub. House [1958] 91p. 21cm. [BD171.B2 1958] 58-12529
1. Truth. I. Title.

FITTI, Charles J 170
A philosophy of creation. New York, Philosophical library [1963] viii, 101 p. 22 cm. [BJ1275.F5] 63-15601
1. Truth. 2. God. 3. Sacraments. I. Title.

HERSEY, Harry G. 236.
The last messenger before His face; a text book of truth ... copyright ... byHarry G. Hersey. [Guilford, Me.] 1923. 106 p. 23 cm. [BR126.H4] 23-11529
I. Title.

HERSEY, Harry G. 236.
The last messenger before his face. (2d and enl. ed.) By H. G. Hersey. Boston, The Christopher publishing house [c1925] 159 p. 21 cm. [BR126.H4 1925] 25-11446
I. Title.

JASPERS, Karl, 1883-1969. 111.83
Truth and symbol, from Von der Wahrheit. Translated with an introd. by Jean T. Wilde, William Kluback and William Kimmel. New York, Twayne Publishers [1959] 79 p. 23 cm. [BD171.J313] 59-8386
1. Truth. I. Title.

KAHLER, Erich 111.8
The true, the good, and the beautiful; a lecture delivered at Ohio State University, December 10, 1959. Columbus, Ohio State University Press [c.1960] 40p. 22cm. 60-11151 1.00 pap.,
1. Truth. 2. Good and evil. 3. Aesthetics. I. Title.

KUHNHOLD, Christa. 001.9
Der Begriff des Sprunges und der Weg des Sprachdenkens : eine Einf. in Kierkegaard / Christa Kuhnhcld Berlin ; New York : de Gruyter, 1975. xi, 183 p. : ill. ; 24 cm. Includes index. Bibliography: p. [175]-177. [B4378.T7K8] 75-514793 ISBN 3-11-004965-1 : DM68.00
1. Kierkegaard, Soren Aabye, 1813-1855. 2. Truth. I. Title.

LINES, John Davis. 111.8'3
The duality of physical truth and cause. New York, Philosophical Library [1973] 94 p. 23 cm. [BD331.L48] 72-91110 ISBN 0-8022-2105-X 6.00
1. Truth. 2. Dualism. 3. Reality. 4. Causation. I. Title.

LINK, Bessie A 248
Truth is everybody's business. Brooklyn, G. J. Rickard [1958] 100p. 22cm. [BT50.L55] 58-13152
I. Title.

MACKINNON, Edward Michael, 1928- 111.8'3
Truth and expression, by Edward M. MacKinnon. New York, Newman Press [1971] vii, 212 p. 24 cm. (The Hecker lectures, 1968) Includes bibliographical references. [BD171.M23] 70-163435 7.50
1. Truth. 2. Languages—Philosophy. 3. Analysis (Philosophy) I. Title. II. Series.

MARK, Thomas Carson, 1941- 111.8'3
Spinoza's theory of truth. New York, Columbia University Press, 1972. viii, 137 p. front. 21 cm. Bibliography: p. [129]-132. [B3999.T7M3] 72-3721 ISBN 0-231-03621-3 7.00
1. Spinoza, Benedictus de, 1632-1677. 2. Truth. I. Title.

MARSHALL, Cyril Baker. 248
Truth, by C. B. Marshall; foreword by Sir Charles Chadwick Oman ... London, New York [etc.] Skeffington & son, ltd. [1945] 82 p. 19 cm. (Half-title: New world outlook series) [BT50.M3] 45-6000
1. Truth. I. Title.

MEDICUS, Fritz Georg Adolf, 1876-1956. 111.8'3
On being human; the life of truth and its realization. Translated by Fritz Marti. New York, Ungar [1973] xii, 324 p. 22 cm. Translation of Menschlichkeit. Includes bibliographical references. [BD171.M4313 1973] 72-178170 ISBN 0-8044-5673-9 9.00
1. Truth. 2. Humanism. I. Title.

PEPPER, Stephen C. 111.83
World hypotheses; a study in evidence [Gloucester, Mass., Peter Smith] 1961[c.1942] 348p. (Univ. of Calif. Pr. paperback rebound) 4.00
1. Truth. I. Title.

PIERCE, Robert Fletcher Young, 1852-
Pictured truth; a hand-book of blackboard and object lessons. By Rev. Robert F. Y. Pierce. Introduction by Russell H. Conwell, D.D. New York, Chicago [etc.] F. H. Revell company [c1895] 208 p. illus. 20 cm. 3-22864
I. Title.

PITCHER, George, ed. 111.83082
Truth. Englewood Cliffs, N. J., Prentice Hall, [1964] viii, 118 p. 22 cm. (Contemporary perspectives in philosophy series) Bibliography: p. 113-118. [BD171.P57] 64-11556
1. Truth. I. Title.

RESCHER, Nicholas. 111.8'3
The coherence theory of truth. Oxford, Clarendon Press, 1973. xiv, 374 p. 22 cm. (Clarendon library of logic and philosophy) Bibliography: p. [366]-369. [BD171.R47] 73-173677 ISBN 0-19-824401-0 £5.50
1. Truth. I. Title.

ROBENOFF, Janeski. 248
Chimes of truth; or, Divine metaphysics ... [by] Janeski Robenoff ... Los Angeles, Calif., Society of divine metaphysics, 1937. 4 p. l., [11]-96 p. 17 cm. [BR126.R6] 38-2110
I. Society of divine metaphysics. II. Title. III. Title: Divine metaphysics.

ROBERTS, Benjamin Titus, 1823-1893.
Pungent truths; being extracts from the writings of the Rev. Benjamin Titus

Roberts ... comp. and ed. by William B. Rose. Chicago, The Free Methodist publishing house, 1912. ix, 379 p. front. (port.) 20 cm. 12-21975 1.25
I. Rose, William Brewster, 1849- ed. II. Title.

ROTHER, Aloysius Joseph, 1859- 111.
Certitude; a study in philosophy, by Rev. Aloysius Rother ... St. Louis, Mo. [etc.] B. Herder, 1911. 3 p. l., 94 p. 20 cm. [BD171.R7] 11-1664 0.50
1. Truth. 2. Evidence. I. Title.

SLEIGH, R. C., 1932- comp. 111.8'3
Necessary truth, edited by R. C. Sleigh, Jr. Englewood Cliffs, N.J., Prentice-Hall [1972] vi, 202 p. 21 cm. (Central issues in philosophy series) Contents.—pt. 1. De dicto: Necessary and contingent truths, by G. W. Leibniz. New essays concerning human understanding, by G. W. Leibniz. Introduction to the critique of pure reason, by Immanuel Kant. On the nature of mathematical truth, C. G. Hempel. Two dogmas of empiricism, by W. V. O. Quine. In defense of a dogma, by H. P. Grace and P. F. Strawson. The a priori and the analytic, by A. Quinton. The truths of reason, by R. Chisholm.—pt. 2. De re: Reference and modality, by W. V. O. Quine. De re et de dicto, by A. Plantinga. World and essence, by A. Plantinga.—Bibliography (p. 200-202) [BD171.S54] 72-172063 ISBN 0-13-610766-4 ISBN 0-13-610758-3 (pbk) 7.95
1. Truth. 2. Necessity (Philosophy) I. Title.

SMITH, Gerard. 111.83
The truth that frees. Milwaukee, Marquette University Press, 1956. 79p. 19cm. (The Aquinas lecture, 1956) [BD171.S56] 56-9140
1. Truth. 2. Liberty. I. Title.

VERSENYI, Laszlo 111
Heidegger, being and truth. New Haven, Conn., Yale 1965. xi, 201p. 22cm. [B3279.H49V4] 65-11189 5.00
1. Heidegger, Martin, 1889- 2. Truth. I. Title.

WEBBER, Walter Irving. 133
The pansophy; thirty-three formulas, embracing the eternal truths of the world's greatest faiths and philosphies, by Walter Irving Webber ... Los Angeles, Cal. [Phillips-Whittingham co.] 1919. 80 p. 20 1/2 cm. [BF1999.W4] 19-13010
I. Title.

WIDTSOE, John Andreas, 1872- 215
In search of truth; comments on the Gospel and modern thought, by Elder John A. Widtsoe ... Salt Lake City, Utah, Deseret book company [c1930] 120 p. 20 cm. [BL240.W45] 31-11188
1. Truth. 2. Religion and science—1900- 3. Mormons and Mormonism. I. Title.

Truth—Addresses, essays, lectures.

BEATTIE, James, 1735-1803.
An essay on the nature and immutability of truth, in opposition to sophistry and scepticism. By James Beattie ... 1st American from the 6th European ed. Philadelphia, S. Wicatt, 1809. iv, [5]-354 p. 18 cm. [B1403.B53E82] 11-2586
I. Title.

BURGESS, Ebenezer, 1805-1870.
What is the truth? An inquiry concerning the antiquity and unity of the human race; with an examination of recent scientific speculations on those subjects. By Rev. Ebenezer Burgess. Boston, I. P. Warren [1871] 424 p. 20 cm. Editor's notes signed: W. 5-39842
I. Title.

CROUSE, William H. 230
What is truth? Doctrine which drops as the rain and distills as the dew. Gospel truth clearly set forth in series of discourses, by William H. Crouse ... Statesboro, Ga., The Primitive herald [c1918]- v. illus., plates., 20 cm. [BR121.C7] 18-3453
I. Title.

LYNK, Frederick M., 1881- 242
Watch fires; little essays on the radiant truths of the ecclesiastical year, by Frederick M. Lynk, S.V.D. Techny, Ill., Mission press, 1931. 259 p. illus. 19 1/2 cm. [BX2182.L8] 31-3927
I. Title.

MUNSAT, Stanley, comp. 111.8'3
The analytic-synthetic distinction. Belmont, Calif., Wadsworth Pub. Co. [1971] 150 p. 22 cm. (Basic problems in philosophy series) Bibliography: p. 129-147. [BD171.M77] 76-165002 ISBN 0-534-00042-8
1. Truth—Addresses, essays, lectures. 2. Mathematics—Philosophy—Addresses, essays, lectures. 3. Empiricism—Addresses, essays, lectures. I. Title.

PARLANE, W[illiam] A[lexander] 1833-
Elements of dispensational truth, by W. A. Parlane ... 2d ed., rev. and enl. ... New York, C. C. Cook [1905] 95 p. front. (col. diagr.) 19 cm. 5-9053
I. Title.

The truth seeker.

LADD, Parish B. 211
Commentaries on Hebrew and Christian mythology, by Judge Parish B. Ladd ... New York, The Truth seeker company [c1896] x, [11]-230 p. 20 cm. --Appendix to Hebrew and Christian mythology. By Judge Parish B. Ladd ... New York, The Truth seeker company [c1898] iv, [5]-104 p. 20 cm. [BL2775.L3] 12-34972
I. Title. II. Title: Hebrew and Christian mythology.

MACDONALD, George Everett Hussey, 1857-1944. 211'.4'09
Fifty years of freethought. New York, Arno Press, 1972. 544, xviii, 657 p. illus. 21 cm. (The Atheist viewpoint) Reprint of the 1929-31 ed., which was issued in 2 v. [BL2790.M3A32] 76-161334 ISBN 0-405-03793-7
1. The truth seeker. 2. Free thought—History. 3. Rationalism—History. I. Title. II. Series.

Truth, Sojourner, d. 1883.

FAUSET, Arthur Huff, 1899- 326'.0924 B
Sojourner Truth; God's faithful pilgrim. New York, Russell & Russell [1971] viii, 187 p. port. 22 cm. Reprint of the 1938 ed. Bibliography: p. 181-182. [E185.97.T85 1971] 75-139920
1. Truth, Sojourner, d. 1883.

Truth (Theology)

ROTH, Robert P. 201'.1
Story and reality; an essay on truth, by Robert P. Roth. Grand Rapids, Eerdmans [1973] 197 p. 21 cm. [BT50.R65] 72-93621 ISBN 0-8028-1496-4 3.45
1. Truth (Theology) 2. Philosophical theology. I. Title.

SCHNACKENBURG, Rudolf, 1914- 230
The truth will make you free. [Translated by Rodelinde Albrecht. New York, Herder and Herder [1966] 126 p. 21 cm. Translation of Von der Wahrheit die Freimacht. Bibliographical footnotes. [BT50.S3913] 66-22611
1. Truth (Theology) I. Title.

Trypho, Judaeus.

JUSTINUS, Martyr, Saint. 281.3
Justin Martyr, the Dialogue with Grypho; translation, introduction, and notes, by A. Lukyn Williams ... London, Society for promoting Christian knowledge; New York and Toronto, The Macmillan co., 1930. xiii, 301 p. 19 cm. (Half-title: Translations of Christian literature Series i--Greek texts) Bibliography: p. [xii]-xiii. [BR45.T6J8] 31-8782
1. Trypho, Judaeus. I. Williams, Arthur Lykyn, 1853- ed. II. Title.

JUSTINUS, Martyr, Saint 239.2
Selections from Justin Martyr's Dialogue with Trypho, a Jew. Tr., ed. by R. P. C. Hanson. New York, Association [1964] 80p. 19cm. (World Christian bks., no. 49. 3d ser.) [BR65] 64-57268 1.25 pap.,
1. Trypho, Judaeus. I. Hanson, Richard Patrick Crosland, ed. and trans. II. Title.

Tsai, Christiana.

TSAI, Christiana. 248'.246
Christiana Tsai / by Christiana Tsai ; pictures by James N. Howard. Chicago : Moody Press, c1978. 188 p. : ill. ; 22 cm. Includes bibliographical references. [BR1725.T69A33] 77-25085 ISBN 0-8024-1422-2 pbk. : 3.50
1. Tsai, Christiana. 2. Christian biography—China. 3. Christian biography—Pennsylvania—Paradise. 4. Paradise, Pa.—Biography. 5. Malaria—Biography. I. Title.

Tsimshian Indians—Missions.

POYNTER, Margaret. 266'.023'0924 B
Miracle at Metlakatla : the inspiring story of William Duncan, a missionary / written by Margaret Poynter ; illustrated by James Padgett. St. Louis : Concordia Pub. House, c1978. 123 p. ; ill. ; 24 cm. (Greatness with faith) A biography of the Christian missionary who helped the Tsimshian Indians establish a new home in Alaska. [E99.T8D856] 92 77-29125 ISBN 0-570-07876-8 : 4.95. ISBN 0-570-07881-4 pbk. : 2.95
1. Duncan, William, 1832-1918. 2. [Duncan, William, 1832-1918.] 3. Tsimshian Indians—Missions. 4. Metlakahtla, Alaska—History. 5. Metlakatla, B.C.—History. 6. Missionaries—British Columbia—Biography. 7. Missionaries—England—Biography. 8. [Missionaries.] 9. [Tsimshian Indians.] 0. [Indians of North America.] I. Padgett, James. II. Title. III. Series.

WENTWORTH, Elaine. 266'.023'0924 B
Mission to Metlakatla. Boston, Houghton Mifflin, 1968. 194 p. illus., map. 22 cm. Records the missionary work of a nineteenth-century Englishman, who was sent to civilize the Tsimshians, a savage tribe of Alaskan Indians, and who spent a lifetime protecting and helping his adopted people in their endeavor to adjust to the modern world. [E99.T8W54] 92 AC 68
1. Duncan, William, 1832-1918. 2. Tsimshian Indians—Missions. 3. Metlakahtla, Alaska. I. Title.

Tsur, Jacob, 1906-

TSUR, Jacob, 1906- 915.694'03'40924
Sunrise in Jerusalem, by Jacob Tsur. Translated from the French by Violet M. Macdonald. [1st American ed.] South Brunswick, A. S. Barnes [1973, c1967] 286 p. 22 cm. Translation of Priere du matin; originally published in Hebrew under title: Shaharit shel etmol. [DS126.6.T75A33 1973] 72-9068 ISBN 0-498-01308-1 7.95
1. Tsur, Jacob, 1906- I. Title.

Tuamotu islands—Religion.

STIMSON, John Francis, 1883- 299.9
The cult of Kibo-tumn, by J. Frank Stimson ... Honolulu, Hawaii, The Museum, 1933. 63 p. pl. (ports.) diagrs. 25 1/2 cm. (Bernice P. Bishop museum. Bulletin 111) Tuamotuan and English in parallel columns. Supplements the author's "Tuamotuan religion" with a series of ancient chants. cf. Introd. [GN670.B4] (572.996) 34-33436
1. Tuamotu islands—Religion. 2. Io (Polynesian deity) 3. Tuamotuan language—Texts. I. Title.

STIMSON, John Francis, 1883- 299.9
Tuamotuan religion, by J. Frank Stimson ... Honolulu, Hawaii, The Museum, 1933. 1 p. l., 11, [3]-154 p. illus., 3 pl. (ports.) on 2 l. 25 1/2 cm. (Bernice P. Bishop museum. Bulletin 103) Includes Tuamotuan texts with English translations. "Literature cited": p. 153-154. [GN670.B4 no. 103] (572.996) 34-33463
1. Tuamotu islands—Religion. 2. Tuamotuan language—Texts. I. Title.

Tubingen School (Catholic theology)

FEHR, Wayne L. (Wayne Leroy) 230'.2'0924
The birth of the Catholic Tubingen School : the dogmatics of Johann Sebastian Drey / Wayne L. Fehr. Chico, CA : Scholars Press, c1981. 302 p. ; 23 cm. (American Academy of Religion academy series ; no. 37) Originally presented as the author's thesis (Ph.D.)—Yale University, 1978. Includes index. Bibliography: p. 287-295. [BX4705.D756F43 1981] 19 81-14545 14.50
1. Drey, Johann Sebastian von, 1777-1853. 2. Tubingen School (Catholic theology) I. Title. II. Series.

O'MEARA, Thomas F., 1935- 230'.2
Romantic idealism and Roman Catholicism : Schelling and the theologians / Thomas Franklin O'Meara. Notre Dame : University of Notre Dame Press, c1982. ix, 231 p. ; 24 cm. Includes index. Bibliography: p. 224-227. [BX1747.O6 1982] 19 81-40449 ISBN 0-268-01610-0 : 20.00
1. Tubingen School (Catholic theology) 2. Schelling, Friedrich Wilhelm Joseph von, 1775-1854. 3. Theology, Catholic—History—19th century. I. Title.

Tubingen School (Protestant theology)

HARRIS, Horton. 230
The Tubingen School / by Horton Harris. Oxford : Clarendon Press, 1975. viii, 288 p., [5] leaves of plates : ill. ; 22 cm. Includes index. Bibliography: p. [263]-283. [BS2350.H33] 75-328998 ISBN 0-19-826642-1 : 30.00
1. Bible. N.T.—Criticism, interpretation, etc.—History—19th century. 2. Tubingen School (Protestant theology) I. Title.
Distributed by Oxford University Press, N.Y.

HARRIS, Horton. 230
The Tubingen School / by Horton Harris. Oxford : Clarendon Press, 1975. viii, 288 p., [5] leaves of plates : ill. ; 22 cm. Includes index. Bibliography: p. [263]-283. [BS2350.H33] 75-328998 ISBN 0-19-826642-1 : £9.50
1. Bible. N.T.—Criticism, interpretation, etc.—History—19th century. 2. Tubingen School (Protestant theology) I. Title.

Tucano Indians—Religion and mythology.

REICHEL-DOLMATOFF, Gerardo. 299'.8
Beyond the Milky Way : hallucinatory imagery of the Tukano Indians / by G. Reichel-Dolmatoff. Los Angeles : UCLA Latin American Center Publications, c1978. x, 159 p. : ill. ; 29 cm. (UCLA Latin American studies ; v. 42) Includes index. Bibliography: p. 155-156. [F2520.1.T9R43] 78-620014 ISBN 0-87903-042-9 : 25.00
1. Tucano Indians—Religion and mythology. 2. Tucano Indians—Art. 3. Hallucinogenic drugs and religious experience. 4. Indians of South America—Colombia—Religion and mythology. 5. Indians of South America—Colombia—Art. I. Title. II. Series: California. University. University at Los Angeles. Latin American Center. Latin American studies ; v. 42.

Tuckahoe, N.Y. St. John's Church.

KILLEFFER, David Herbert, 1895- 283.747
The first 150 years of St. John's Church, 1798-1948. Tuckahoe, N.Y., St. John's Church [1948] 63 p. illus., plans. 24 cm. [BX5980.T8S3] 49-54
1. Tuckahoe, N.Y. St. John's Church. I. Title.

Tucker, J. W., d. 1964.

TUCKER, Angeline 266.99
He is in heaven. New York, McGraw [c.1965] 226p. illus., maps, parts. 22cm. [BV3625.C63T8] 65-25521 4.95 bds.,
1. Tucker, J. W., d. 1964. 2. Stanleyville, Congo—Massacre, 1964. 3. Missions—Congo (Leopoldville) I. Title.

Tuckerman, Joseph, 1778-1840.

CHANNING, William Ellery, 1780-1842. 922.8173
A discourse on the life and character of the Rev. Joseph Tuckerman, D. D. Delivered at the Warren street chapel, on Sunday evening, Jan. 31, 1841. By William E. Channing ... Boston, W. Crosby & co., 1841. 80 p. 17 cm. "Biographical sketch ... by Rev. E. S. Gannett ...":p. 75-80. [BX9869.T8C5] 37-8710
1. Tuckerman, Joseph, 1778-1840. 2. Unitarian churches—Sermons. I. Gannett, Ezra Stiles, 1801-1871. II. Title.

Tucuna Indians—Missions.

ROSSI, Sanna Barlow. 266'.023'0924 B
God's city in the jungle / Sanna Barlow Rossi. Wheaton, Ill. : Tyndale House Publishers, 1975. 156 p. : ill. ; 22 cm. [F2520.1.T925R67] 74-21968 ISBN 0-8423-1070-3 : 2.95
1. Anderson, Lambert. 2. Wycliffe Bible Translators. 3. Tucuna Indians—Missions. I. Title.

Tulasidasa, 1532-1623.

BAHADUR, Krishna Prakash, 1924- 294.5'922
Ramacharitmanasa : a study in perspective / K. P. Bahadur. Delhi : Ess Ess Publications, 1976. 365 p., [8] leaves of plates : ill. ; 23 cm. Includes index. [PK1947.9.T83R3318] 76-904748 Rs80.00
1. Tulasidasa, 1532-1623. Ramacaritamanasa. I. Title.

Tulpehocken Trinity United Church of Christ.

SEIBERT, Earl W. 285'.8748'19
Tulpehocken Trinity United Church of Christ, 1727-1977 / Earl W. Seibert. Richland, Pa. : Tulpehocken Trinity United Church of Christ, c1977. 100 p. : ill. ; 23 cm. On cover: Recall. Prepared under the auspices of the Tulpehocken Trinity United Church of Christ, Historical Committee. Bibliography: p. 52-53. [BX9886.Z7T847] 77-151540 4.00
1. Tulpehocken Trinity United Church of Christ. I. Tulpehocken Trinity United Church of Christ. Historical Committee.

Tulsa, Okla, First Methodist Church.

MISCH, Fannie B. 287.676686
Methodist trails to First Methodist Church, Tulsa, Oklahoma [by] Mrs. J. O. Misch. [Tulsa, Okla., 546 N. Santa Fe. Author c.1961] 141 p. illus. Bibl. 61-59842 3.00 pap.,
1. Tulsa, Okla, First Methodist Church. I. Title.

Tun-huang, Kansu.

VINCENT IRENE (VONGEH)
The sacred oasis; caves of the thousand Buddhas, Tun Huang. With a pref. by Pearl Buck. Chicago, University of Chicago Press [1953] xix, 114p. illus. (1 col.) fold. map. 25cm. Bibliography: p. 111-112. A53
1. Tun-huang, Kansu. 2. Mural painting and decoration. 3. Decoration and ornament—China—Kansu. 4. Art, Buddhist. I. Title.

Tun-huang manuscripts.

RHIE, Marylin M. 732'.4
The Fo-kuang ssu : literary evidences and Buddhist images / Marylin M. Rhie. New York : Garland Pub., 1977. xi, 274 p. : ill. ; 21 cm. (Outstanding dissertations in the fine arts) Reprint of the author's thesis, University of Chicago, 1970. "Translation of Tun-huang MS (Stein) 397": p. 47-64. Bibliography: p. 183-194. [BQ6345.W842F67 1977] 76-23690 ISBN 0-8240-2721-3 lib.bdg. : 32.50
1. Fo kuang ssu, Wu-t'ai hsien, China—History. 2. Tun-huang manuscripts. Ms. 397. 3. Sculpture, Buddhist—Wu-t'ai hsien, China. 4. Sculpture—Wu-t'ai hsien, China. I. Tun-huang manuscripts. Ms. 397. English. 1977. II. Title. III. Series.

Tune-books.

LYON, James, 1735-1794, comp. 783.9'52
Urania; a choice collection of psalm-tunes, anthems, and hymns. New pref. by Richard Crawford. New York, Da Capo Press, 1974. xxx viii, xii, 198 p. 16 x 26 cm. (Da Capo Press music reprint series) Reprint of the 1761 ed. Includes bibliographies. [M2116.L99 1974] 69-11667 ISBN 0-306-71198-2
1. Tune-books. 2. Hymns, English. 3. Anthems. I. Title.

WHITE, Benjamin Franklin, 1800-1879, comp. 783.9'52
The sacred harp, by B. F. White, E. J. King. Facsim. of the 3d ed., 1859, including as a historical introduction: The story of The sacred harp, by George Pullen Jackson. Nashville, Broadman [1968] xxxii, 432p. 16 x 24 cm. This facsimile has been made fron an orig. copy in the personal library of William J. Reynolds. Orig. t.p. reads: The sacred harp; a collection of Psalms and hymn tunes, odes and anthems, selected from the most eminent authors ... New and much improved and enl. ed. Philadelphia; Published by S. C. Collins, for the proprietors: White, Massengale, Hamilton, Ga., 1860. For 3-4 voices; shape-note notation. [M21117.W59S3 1859a] 68-18032 6.50
1. Tune-books. 2. Hymns, English. 3. Choruses, Sacred (Mixed voices), Unaccompanied. I. King, E. J. joint comp. II. Jackson, George Pullen, 1874-1953. III. Title. IV. Title: The story of The sacred harp.

Tunguses

LOPATIN, Ivan Alexis 291.23
The cult of the dead among the natives of the Amur Basin. The Hague, Mouton [dist. New York, Humanities Press, 1960] 211 p. p. [203]-206 fold. map. 24 cm. (Central Asiatic studies, 6) imprint covered by label: New york, Humanities Press. Bibl. 60-4182 pap., 9.00
1. Tunguses 2. Dead (in relig, folk-lore, etc.) 3. Indians of North America—Religion and mythology. I. Title. II. Series.

Tuno, 1930-

SHARON, Douglas. 299'.8
Wizard of the four winds : a shaman's story / Douglas Sharon. New York : Free Press, c1978. p. cm. Includes bibliographical references and index. [BL2370.S5S53 1978] 78-3204 ISBN 0-02-928580-1 : 13.95
1. Tuno, 1930- 2. Shamanism—Peru. I. Title.

Tunstall, Cuthbert, successively bp. of London and Durham, 1474-1559.

STURGE, Charles, 1867- 922.242
Cuthbert Tunstal, churchman, scholar, statesman, administrator, by Charles Sturge ... London, New York [etc.] Longmans, Green and co. [1938] xvii, 428 p. front., pl., port., facsim., fold. geneal. tab. 22 1/2 cm. "First published, 1938." Bibliography: p. [401]-413. [DA334.T8S7 1938a] 39-10962
1. Tunstall, Cuthbert, successively bp. of London and Durham, 1474-1559. I. Title.

Turin. Biblioteca nazionale. Mss. G. vii. 15

BIBLE. N. T. Gospels. Latin. 1886. Old Latin.
... Portions of the Gospels according to St. Mark and St. Matthew from the Bobbio ms. (k), now numbered G. vii. 15 in the National library at Turin; together with other fragments of the Gospels from six mss. in the libraries of St. Gall, Coire, Milan, and Berne (usually cited as n, o, p. a2, s, and t); edited with the aid of Tischendorf's transcripts and the printed texts of Ranke, Ceriani, and Hagen, with two facsimilies, by John Wordsworth ... W. Sanday ... and H. J. White ... Oxford, The Clarendon press; [etc., etc.] 1886. ccivi, 140 p. 2 facsim, (1 fold.; incl. front.) 28 x 20 cm. (Old-Latin Biblical texts: no. ii) Facsimiles: Codex bobiensis (k) fol. 41 recto. Marc. xvi, 6-0; Fragments sangallensia (n) fol. 2 verso. Matt. xvii, 25-xviii, 7. "The Oxford mss. of Cyprian": p. 123-132. For "Additions and corrections" cf. vol. iii (1888) of this series, p. [165]-166. [BS1989.A1O6 no. ii] 24-32106
1. Turin. Biblioteca nazionale. Mss. G. vii. 15 2. Bible. N. T. Gospels. Latin—Versions—Old Latin. 3. Bible. Latin—Versions—Old Latin—N. T. Gospels. I. Bible. Latin. N. T. Gospels. 1886. Old Latin. II. Bible. Manuscripts, Latin. N. T. Gospels. III. Wordsworth, John, bp. of Salisbury, 1843-1911, ed. IV. Sanday, William, 1843-1920, joint ed. V. White, Henry Julian, 1859- joint ed. VI. Title.

Turkey—Description and travel—1960- —Guide-books.

MEINARDUS, Otto Friedrich August. 915.61
St. Paul in Ephesus and the cities of Galatia and Cyprus / Otto F. A. Meinardus. New Rochelle, N.Y. : Caratzas Bros., 1979. vii, 141 p. : ill. ; 21 cm. (In the footsteps of the saints) Includes index. Bibliography: p. 139-141. [BS2506.M397 1979] 78-51246 ISBN 0-89241-071-X : 7.50 ISBN 0-89241-044-2 (pbk.) : 4.95
1. Paul, Saint, apostle—Journeys. 2. Turkey—Description and travel—1960- —Guide-books. 3. Cyprus—Description and travel—Guide-books. I. Title. II. Series.

Turkey—Foreign opinion, German.

BOHNSTEDT, John Wolfgang. 270.6
The infidel scourge of God; the Turkish menace as seen by German pamphleteers of the Reformation era [by] John W. Bohnstedt. Philadelphia, American Philosophical Society, 1968. 58 p. illus. 30 cm. (Transactions of the American Philosophical Society, new ser., v. 58, pt. 9) Bibliography: p. 52-56. [Q11.P6 ns., vol. 58, pt. 9] 68-59177 2.00
1. Turkey—Foreign opinion, German. 2. Islam—Relations—Christianity. 3. Christianity and other religions—Islam. I. Title. II. Series: American Philosophical Society, Philadelphia. Transactions, new ser., v. 58, pt. 9

Turkey—Foreign relations—Germany.

HURGRONJE, Christiaan Snouck, 1857-
The holy war "made in Germany," by Dr. C. Snouck Hurgronje ... with a word of introduction by Richard J. H. Gottheil ... New York and London, G. P. Putnam's sons, 1915. vi, 82 p. 20 cm. "Appeared originally in the Dutch periodical De Gids, 1915, no. i, under the title 'Hellige oorlog made in Germany.' It has been ... translated by Professor Joseph E. Gillet ..."--Introd., p. v. [DR588.H8] 15-7151
1. Turkey—For. rel.—Germany. 2. Germany—For. rel.—Turkey. 3. Panislamism. 4. Eastern question. I. Gillet, Joseph Eugene, 1888- tr. II. Title.

Turnbull, Bob, 1936-

STONE, Robert B. 269'.2'0924 B
Jesus has a man in Waikiki; the story of Bob Turnbull [by] Robert B. Stone. Old Tappan, N.J., F. H. Revell Co. [1973] 128 p. illus. 21 cm. [BV4447.S72] 73-3311 ISBN 0-8007-0599-8 1.95 (pbk)
1. Turnbull, Bob, 1936- 2. Church work with youth—Honolulu. I. Title.

Turner, Asa, 1799-1885.

MAGOUN, George Frederic, 1821-1896. 922.
Asa Turner; a home missionary patriarch and his times, by George F. Magoun... Introduction by A. H. Clapp, D.D. Boston and Chicago, Congregational Sunday-school and publishing society [c1889] 345 p. front., plates, ports. 20 1/2 cm. Title vignette. [BX7260.T97M3] 16-2758
1. Turner, Asa, 1799-1885. 2. Turner family. 3. Congregational churches in Iowa. I. Clapp, Alexander Huntington, 1818-1899. II. Title.

Turner, Denise.

TURNER, Denise. 253'.2
Home sweet fishbowl : confessions of a minister's wife / Denise Turner. Waco, Tex. : Word Books, c1982. 160 p. ; 23 cm. [BV4395.T85 1982] 19 81-71500 ISBN 0-8499-0301-7 : 8.95
1. Turner, Denise. 2. Clergyman's wives. I. Title.

Turner, Gladys Davis, 1914-

CARTER, Mary Ellen. 133.8'092'4 [B]
My years with Edgar Cayce; the personal story of Gladys Davis Turner. [New York] Warner Paperback Library [1974, c1972] 158 p. 18 cm. [BF1027.C3C26] 78-175159 1.25 (pbk.)
1. Turner, Gladys Davis, 1914- 2. Cayce, Edgar, 1877-1945. I. Title.

Turner, Henry McNeal, Bp., 1834-1915.

PONTON, Mungo Melanchthon, 1860- 287'.6'0924 B
Life and times of Henry M. Turner; the antecedent and preliminary history of the life and times of Bishop H. M. Turner, his boyhood, education and public career, and his relation to his associates, colleagues and contemporaries, by M. M. Ponton. New York, Negro Universities Press [1970] 173 p. port. 23 cm. "Originally published in 1917." [E185.97.T94 1970] 70-109363
1. Turner, Henry McNeal, Bp., 1834-1915.

Turner, Taos Lee, 1972-

TURNER, Dean. 242
Krinkle nose : a prayer of thanks / by Dean Turner. Old Greenwich, Conn. : Devin-Adair Co., c1979. 92 p., [2] leaves of plates : ill. ; 24 cm. [BR1725.T77T87] 77-78424 ISBN 0-8159-6002-6 : 4.95
1. Turner, Taos Lee, 1972- 2. Turner, Dean. 3. Christian biography—United States. I. Title.

Turner, Thomas Trussler, 1927-

DOWN, Goldie M. 286'.73 B
More lives than a cat / by Goldie M. Down. Nashville : Southern Pub. Association, c1979. p. cm. [BX6193.T87D68] 79-17814 ISBN 0-8127-0243-3 : 3.95
1. Turner, Thomas Trussler, 1927- 2. Seventh-Day Adventists—South Africa—Biography. 3. Clergy—South Africa—Biography. I. Title.

Turquetil, Araene Louis Eugene, bp., 1876-

MORICE, Adrian Gabriel, 1859-1938. 922.244
Thawing out the Eskimo, by Rev. Adrian G. Morice, O.M.I., translated by Mary T. Loughlin. Boston, The Society for the propagation of the faith [1943] 241 p. incl. front. (port.) 20 1/2 cm. Translation of Monseigneur Turqueill, O.M.I., apotre des Esquimaux. [E99.E7M84] 43-1878
1. Turquetil, Araene Louis Eugene, bp., 1876- 2. Eskimos—Hudson bay. 3. Eskimos—Missions. I. Loughlin, Mary T., tr. II. Society for the propagation of the faith, Boston. III. Title.

Tuskegee, Ala. First Baptist Church.

BROWN, Bessie Conner. 286'.1761'49
A history of the First Baptist Church, Tuskegee, Alabama, 1839-1971. [Tuskegee? Ala., 1972] iii l., 89 p. illus. 24 cm. [BX6480.T88F5] 73-188683
1. Tuskegee, Ala. First Baptist Church.

Tutankhamen, King of Egypt.

BUDGE, Ernest Alfred Thompson Wallis, Sir, 1857-1934. 932'.01'0924 B
Tutankhamen, Amenism, Atenism and Egyptian monotheism; with hieroglyphic

texts of hymns to Amen and Aten, translations, and illustrations. New York, B. Blom, 1971. xxii, 160 p. illus., ports. 22 cm. First published in 1923. [DT87.5.B8 1971] 79-160615
1. Tutankhamen, King of Egypt. 2. Egypt—Religion. 3. Hymns, Egyptian. 4. Egyptian language—Inscriptions. I. Title.

THE Shrines of Tut-Ankh-Amon; 299.31 texts translated with introductions by Alexandre Piankoff. Edited by N. Rambova. [New York] Pantheon Books [1955] xxi, 149p. illus., plates (part col.) 32cm. (Bollingen series, 40:2. Egyptian religious texts and representations, v. 2) Bibliographical footnotes. [PJ1551.E3 vol. 2] 55-2997
1. Tutenkhamun, King of Egypt. 2. Egyptian language—Texts. I. Plankoff, Alexandre, tr. II. Series. III. Series: Bollingen series, 40: IV. Series: Egyptian religious texts and representations, v.2)

THE Shrines of Tut-Ankh-Amon / 299.31 texts translated with introductions by Alexandre Piankoff ; edited by N. Rambova. New York : Harper & Row, 1962, c1955. xxiii, 133 p., [32] leaves of plates : ill. ; 21 cm. (The Bollingen library) (Harper torchbooks ; TB 2011) Includes bibliographical references. [BL2430.S6 1962] 75-312018
1. Tutankhamen, King of Egypt. 2. Egypt—Religion—History—Sources. 3. Egyptian language—Inscriptions. I. Piankoff, Alexandre.

THE Shrines of Tut-Ankh-Amon / 299'.3'1 texts translated with introductions by Alexandre Piankoff ; edited by N. Rambova. Princeton, N.J. : Princeton University Press, 1978, c1956. xv, 149 p., [33] leaves of plates : ill. ; 22 cm. (Princeton/Bollingen paperbacks ; 435) (Bollingen series ; 40, 2) Includes bibliographical references. [BL2430.S5 1977] 78-310474 ISBN 0-691-01818-9 : 30.00 pbk. : 5.95
1. Tutankhamen, King of Egypt. 2. Egypt—Religion—Sources. 3. Religious literature, Egyptian—Translations into English. 4. Religious literature, English—Translations from Egyptian. 5. Egyptian language—Inscriptions. I. Piankoff, Alexandre. II. Series.

SHRINES of Tut-Ankh-Amon (The) 299.31 Texts tr., with introds. by Alexandre Piankoff. Ed. by N. Rambova. NewYork, Harper [1962, c.1955] (Bollingen ser., 40: Egyptian religious texts and representations, v.2) This study is based on the work of an expedition sponsored by the Bollingen Found. . . . October, 1949, to June, 1951. 1.75 pap.,
1. Tut-Ankh-Amon, King of Egypt. 2. Egypt—Religion. 3. Egyptian literature. I. Piankoff, Alexandre, tr. II. Series: Bollingen series, 40 III. Series: Egyptian texts and representations, v.

Tutors and tutoring.

HARRISON, Grant Von. 371.39'4
Structured tutoring / Grant Von Harrison, Ronald Edward Guymon. Englewood Cliffs, N.J. : Educational Technology Publications, 1980. p. cm. (The Instructionaldesign library ; v. 34) Bibliography: p. [LC41.H3] 79-23035 ISBN 0-87778-154-0 : 13.95
1. Tutors and tutoring. I. Guymon, Ronald Edward, joint author. II. Title. III. Series: Instructional design library ; v. 34

Tuttle, James Harvey, 1824-1903.

SHUTTER, Marion Daniel, 1853- 922.
Rev. James Harvey Tuttle, D.D.; a memoir, by Marion Daniel Shutter... Boston, Universalist publishing house, 1905. ix p., 1 l., xi-xvi, 294 p. 4 pl., 2 port. (incl. front.) 20 1/2 cm. [BX9969.T855] 5-33615
1. Tuttle, James Harvey, 1824-1903. I. Title.

Tuttle, William, 1781-1847.

TUTTLE, Joseph Farrand, 1818-1901. 922.573
The life of William Tuttle, compiled from an autobiography under the name of John Homespun. Edited and continued to the close of his life by the Rev. Joseph F. Tuttle. New York, R. Carter & brothers, 1852. vi, [7]-304 p. front. (port.) 17 1/2 cm. [BR1725.T8T8 1852] 1-11949
1. Tuttle, William, 1781-1847. I. Title.

Tuxedo, N.Y.—Biography.

CROFUT, Doris. 283'.747'31
St. Mary's-in-Tuxedo, 1888-1975 / by Doris Crofut. Tuxedo Park, N.Y. : Printed by Library Research Associates for St. Mary's-in-Tuxedo, 1975. 58 p. : ill., ports. ; 23 cm. [BX5980.T89S243] 76-350022
1. St. Mary's-in-Tuxedo. 2. Tuxedo, N.Y.—Biography. I. Title.

Twana (Bantu tribe)—Church history.

PAUW, Berthold Adolf 276.87
Religion in a Tswana chiefdom. New York, Published for the International African Institute by Oxford University Press, 1960[ ] 258 p. illus., maps. tables (1 fold. col. in pocket) tables. 'A condensation of . . . [the author's] thesis accepted by the University of Cape Town for the Ph.D. degree in 1955. Bibl.: p.[249]-252. 60-3296 6.10
1. Twana (Bantu tribe)—Church history. 2. Sects—Cape of Good Hope. I. Title.

Twelve tribes of Israel.

GEUS, C. H. J., de. 309.1'33
The tribes of Israel : an investigation into some of the presuppositions of Martin Noth's amphictyony hypothesis / C. H. J. de Geus. Assen : Van Gorcum, 1977. xii, 258 p. ; 25 cm. (Studia Semitica Neerlandica ; 18) A revision of the author's thesis, Groningen. Includes indexes. Bibliography: p. 213-248. [BS1197.G47 1976] 76-359513 ISBN 9-02-321337-8 : 28.75
1. Noth, Martin, 1902-1968. 2. Bible. O.T.—Criticism, interpretation, etc. 3. Twelve tribes of Israel. I. Title. II. Series.
Distributed by Humanities Press

The Twentieth century Christ.

TWENTIETH century Christ, 230 by the Twentieth century Christ. Santa Barbara, Calif., 20th century Christ charity [c1940] 1 p. l., 3, [1], 4-67 p. front. 23 1/2 cm. [BR126.T9] 40-12756
1. The Twentieth century Christ.

Twentieth century—Forecasts.

DURKIN, Jim. 248.4
The coming world crisis : how you can prepare / Jim Durkin, Joseph Anfuso, David Sczepanski. Plainfield, N.J. : Distributed by Haven Books, c1980. 130 p. ; 21 cm. [CB161.D87] 19 80-132585 ISBN 0-88270-459-1 pbk. : 4.95
1. Twentieth century—Forecasts. 2. Christian life—1960- I. Anfuso, Joseph, joint author. II. Sczepanski, David, joint author. III. Title.
Available from Logos international, 201 Church St., Plainfield, NJ 07060

Twentieth century—Forecasts—Congresses.

FUTURISTIC Conference, Ridgecrest, N.C., 1977. 230'.6'132
Proceedings of major presentations : Futuristic Conference / sponsored by the Sunday School Board of the Southern Baptist Convention, March 21-25, 1977, Ridgecrest, North Carolina. Nashville : The Board, c1977. v, 140 leaves : ill. ; 29 cm. Includes bibliographical references. [CB161.F795 1977] 77-155217
1. Southern Baptist Convention—Congresses. 2. Twentieth century—Forecasts—Congresses. 3. Baptists—Southern States—Congresses. I. Southern Baptist Convention. Sunday School Board.

Twichell, Joseph Hopkins, 1838-1918.

STRONG, Leah A 285.87463 (B)
Joseph Hopkins Twichell, Mark Twain's friend and pastor, by Leah A. Strong. Athens, University of Georgia Press [1966] x, 182 p. port. 25 cm. Bibliography: p. 172-179. [BX7260.T99S8] 66-23072
1. Twichell, Joseph Hopkins, 1838-1918. 2. Clemens, Samuel Langhorne, 1835-1910. I. Title.

Twigg, Ena.

TWIGG, Ena. 133.9'1'0924 B
Ena Twigg, medium, by Ena Twigg with Ruth Hagy Brod; introduction by Mervyn Stockwood. London, New York, W. H. Allen, 1973. xix, 295 p. 23 cm. [BF1283.T95A3 1973] 73-158703 ISBN 0-491-00903-8 £3.00
1. Twigg, Ena. 2. Spiritualism. I. Brod, Ruth Hagy. II. Title.

TWIGG, Ena. 133.9'1'0924 B
Ena Twigg: medium, by Ena Twigg, with Ruth Hagy Brod. Introd. by Mervyn Stockwood. New York, Hawthorn Books [1972] xviii, 297 p. 22 cm. [BF1283.T95A3 1972] 72-1970 6.95
1. Twigg, Ena. 2. Spiritualism. I. Brod, Ruth Hagy. II. Title.

Twins (in religion, folk-lore, etc.)

WARD, Donald. 291'.13
The divine twins; an Indo-European myth in Germanic tradition. Berkeley, University of California Press, 1968. x, 137 p. 26 cm. (University of California publications. Folklore studies, 19) Bibliography: p. 113-127. [BL325.T8W36] 78-626557 4.50
1. Twins (in religion, folk-lore, etc.) I. Title. II. Series: California. University. University of California publications. Folklore studies, 19

Twitchell, Thomas Donn.

TWITCHELL, Thomas Donn. 285'.1'0924 B
"That they may be one" : convincing a puzzled world that God sent His Son / by Thomas Donn Twitchell. Plainfield, N.J. : Logos International, c1979. xii, 216 p. ; 21 cm. [BX9225.T84A36] 79-83792 ISBN 0-88270-360-9 pbk. : 3.95
1. Twitchell, Thomas Donn. 2. Presbyterian Church—Clergy—Biography. 3. Clergy—United States—Biography. 4. Christian union. I. Title.

Two missionaries.

THE preacher's vademecum; 248 sermon plans for Sundays, feasts of Our Lord, the Blessed Virgin and the saints, advent and lenten courses, forty hours', Sacred heart devotions, retreats, conferences, May and October devotions, special occasions, etc., by two missionaries, tr. from the French. New York, Joseph F. Wagner (inc.); [etc., etc., c1921] viii, 439 p. 21 cm. Translation of Vademecum des predicateurs. [BX1756.A1V2] 22-2497
1. Two missionaries.

Twtichell, Paul.

*STEIGER, Brad. 133.92
In my soul I am free; the incredible Paul Twitchell story. New York, Lancer [1968] 190p. 18cm. (74-952) .75 pap.,
1. Twitchell, Paul. 2. Astral projection. I. Title.

Tyndale, William. d. 1536.

CLEAVELAND, Elizabeth Whittlesey. 222'.11'052
A study of Tindale's Genesis, compared with the Genesis of Coverdale and of the Authorized version. [Hamden, Conn.] Archon Books, 1972. xliii, 258 p. 22 cm. Originally presented as the author's thesis, Yale, 1910. Reprint of the 1911 ed., which was issued as no. 43 of Yale studies in English. [PR2384.T9Z6 1972] 72-341 ISBN 0-208-01126-9
1. Tyndale, William, d. 1536. 2. Coverdale, Miles, Bp. of Exeter, 1488-1568. 3. Bible. O.T. Genesis. English—Versions. I. Title. II. Series: Yale studies in English, 43.

COOPER, William Barrett, 1857- 922.
The life and work of William Tindale, by Rev. W. B. Cooper ... Toronto, New York [etc.] Longmans, Green & company [c1924] xvii, 54 p. front., plates, ports., facsims. 17 cm. [BR350.T8C6] 25-8884
1. Tyndale, William, d. 1536. I. Title.

DE LEEUW, Cateau, 1903- 922.342
William Tyndale, martyr for the Bible. New York, Association Press [1955] 125p. illus. 20cm. (Heroes of God series) [BR350.T8D36] 55-7419
1. Tyndale, William, d.1536. I. Title.

EDWARDS, Brian H. 283'.092'4 B
God's outlaw / [by] Brian H. Edwards. Welwyn ; Grand Rapids, Mich. : Evangelical Press, 1976. 180 p. : ill., facsims., port. ; 22 cm. Includes index. Bibliography: p. 171-174. [BR350.T8E25] 77-363319 ISBN 0-85234-067-2 : £2.70. ISBN 0-85234-066-4 pbk.
1. Tyndale, William, d. 1536. 2. Christian biography—England. I. Title.

JOYE, George, 1495?-1553. 082 s
An apology made by George Joy, to satisfy, if it may be, W. Tindale. 1535. Edited by Edward Arber. Birmingham [Eng.] 1882. [New York, AMS Press, 1967] xiv, 50 p. 23 cm. (The English scholar's library of old and modern works [v. 3] no. 13) [PR1121.A72 no. 13] [BR350.T8] 283'.092'4 72-197461
1. Tyndale, William, d. 1536. 2. Bible. N.T. English—Versions. I. Title. II. Series.

JOYE, George, d.1553.
... An apology made by George Joy, to satisfy, if it may be, W. Tindale. 1535. Ed. by Edward Arber ... Birmingham [The editor] 1882. xiv, 50 p. 20 cm. (Half-title: The English scholar's library. no. 13) Series title also at head of t.-p. "This Aplogy (here first reprinted from the only copy at present known, now in Cambridge university library) ... is, for us, one of the most important contributions to the earliest bibliography of the printed English New Testament."--Introd. [PR1121.A7 no. 13] 12-17021
1. Tyndale, William. d. 1536. 2. Bible. N. T. English—Versions. 3. Bible. English—Versions—N. T. I. Title.

MOZLEY, James Frederic, 1887- 283'.0924 B
William Tyndale, by J. F. Mozley. Westport, Conn., Greenwood Press [1971] ix, 364 p. illus., ports. 23 cm. Reprint of the 1937 ed. Bibliography: p. vii. [BR350.T8M6 1971] 70-109801 ISBN 0-8371-4292-X
1. Tyndale, William, d. 1536.

MOZLEY, James Frederic, 1887- 922.342
William Tyndale, by J. F. Mozley, M. Mozley, M. A. New York, The Macmillan company [1937] ix p., 1 l., 364 p. plates, 2 port. (incl. front.) 23 cm. "First published, 1937." "Made in Great Britain." "The authorities": p. vii. "The earliest editions of the English New Testament": p. 347-352. [BR350.T8M6] 38-4874
I. Tyndale, William, d. 1536. II. Title.

Tyng, Dudley Atkins, 1825-1858.

PHILADELPHIA. Church of the Epiphany. Members. 922
A statement of the congregation of the Church of the Epiphany, Philadelphia, of facts bearing on the action of the vestry in requesting the resignation of the reactor. 2d ed., with an appendix. Published by members of the congregation. Philadelphia [Merrihew and Thompson, printers] 1856. 66 p. 23 cm. [BX5995.T87P5 1856 a] 37-18480
1. Tyng, Dudley Atkins, 1825-1858. I. Title.

Tyng, Stephen Higginson, 1800-1885.

TYNG, Charles Rockland, comp. 922.
Record of the life and work of the Rev. Stephen Higginson Tyng ... and history of St. George's church, New York, to the close of his rectorship, comp. by his son Charles Rockland Tyng. New York, E. P. Dutton & company, 1890. 682 p. front.,

plates, ports. 24 cm. [BX5995.T9T8] 22-22514
1. Tyng, Stephen Higginson, 1800-1885. I. New York. St. George's church. II. Title.

TYNG, Stephen Higginson, 1839-1898. 922.
Trial of the Rev. Stephen H. Tyng, jr., rector of the Church of the Holy Trinity, New York, in the chapel of St. Peter's church, New York, February, 1868. Reported by Warburton, Bonynge & Devine, stenographers ... New York, J. A. Gray & Green, printers, 1868. 310 p. 23 1/2 cm. [BX5960.T9A3] 1-11910
1. Protestant Episcopal church in the U.S.A. New York (Diocese) II. Title.

Typhology (Theology)

FAIRBAIRN, Patrick, 1805-1874. 220.
The typology of Scripture: viewed in connection with the entire scheme of the divine dispensations. By Patrick Fairbairn ... From the 3d Edinburgh ed. Philadelphia, W. S. & A. Martien, 1859. 2 v. 24 cm. [BS478.F3 1850] 24-10107
1. Typhology (Theology) I. Title.

Typology (Jesus Christ)

OTTS, John Martin Phillip, 1838-1901. 206
Christ and the cherubim; or, The ark of the covenant a type of Christ Our Saviour. By J. M. P. Otts ... with an introduction by Francis R. Beattie ... Richmond, Va., Presbyterian committee of publication [c1896] 63 p. 19 cm. [BT225.O8] 37-31963
1. Typology (Jesus Christ) 2. Ark of the covenant. I. Beattie, Francis Robert, 1848-1906. II. Presbyterian church in the U. S. Committee of publication. III. Title.

WARNER, Daniel Sidney, 1842-1895.
The cleansing of the sanctuary; or, The church of God in type and antitype, and in prophecy and revelation. By D. S. Warner ... and H. M. Riggle ... Moundsville, W. Va., The Gospel trumpet publishing co., 1903. 541 p. incl. front. (ports.) plans. 23 1/2 cm. 3-15426
I. Title.

Typology (Theology)

ANDERSON, Robert, Sir, 1841-1918. 227'.87'06
Types in Hebrews / by Robert Anderson. Grand Rapids, Mich. : Kregel Publications, [1978] p. cm. (Sir Robert Anderson library) (Series: Anderson, Robert, Sir, 1841-1918. Sir Robert Anderson library.) Reprint of the 2d ed. published by Pickering & Inglis, London, under title: The Hebrews Epistle in the light of the types. Includes index. [BS2775.2.A53 1978] 78-9545 ISBN 0-8254-2129-2 : pbk. : 3.50
1. Bible. N.T. Hebrews—Criticism, interpretation, etc. 2. Typology (Theology) I. Title. II. Series.

BARTLEY, David, 1827- 230.6
The Christ-man in type as prefigured by Biblical persons from Adam to David by Elder David Bartley ... [Montgomery, Ala., Press of W. E. Allred & son printing co., c1906] 181 p. 20 cm. [BT225.B3] 6-14065
1. Typology (Theology) I. Title.

BONAR, Andrew Alexander, 1810-1892. 223'.2'06
Christ and His Church in the Book of Psalms / by Andrew A. Bonar. Grand Rapids : Kregel Publications, 1978. xii, 457 p. ; 23 cm. Reprint of the 1861 ed. published by R. Carter, New York. [BT225.B6 1978] 78-5692 ISBN 0-8254-2230-2 : 12.95
1. Bible. O.T. Psalms—Criticism, interpretation, etc. 2. Typology (Theology) 3. Church—Biblical teaching. I. Bible. O. T. Psalms. English. Authorized. 1978. II. Title.

BROCK, Jefferson Columbus, 1858- 220.6
The genius of creation, by J.C. Brock. [Chicago, Rayner litho co., c1931] 76 p. 23 1/2 cm. "This treatise is an interpretation of the Scriptures which pertain to the Adam allegory."--Pref. [BS478.B7] 31-21721
1. Typology (Theology) I. Title.

BROOKS, Nathan Covington, 1809-1898. 232.1
The life and mission of Our Lord and Saviour Jesus Christ, as set forth by prophesy, history and typology. By N. C. Brooks ... Philadelphia, Geo. S. Ferguson co., 1894. 2 p. l., 3-256 p. front., illus. plates. 21 cm. Added t.-p. illustrated, has title: Christ in prophecy, history and typology. [BT225.B7 1894] 36-37998
1. Typology (Theology) 2. Messiah—Prophecies. 3. Jesus Christ—Prophecies. I. Title. II. Title: Christ in prophesy, History and typology.

BUKSBAZEN, Victor, 1903- 232.1
The Gospel in the feasts of Israel. Philadelphia, Friends of Israel Missionary and Relief Society [1954] 80p. illus. 19cm. [BT225.B8] 54-30703
1. Typology (Theology) 2. Fasts and feasts—Judaism. I. Title.

CALLAWAY, Timothy Walton, 1874- 232.1
Christ in the Old Testament. [1st ed.] New York, Loizeaux Bros. [1950] 190 p. 20 cm. [BT225.C3] 50-10256
1. Typology (Theology) 2. Messiah—Prophecies. 3. Bible. N. T.—Relation to O. T. I. Title.

CHARITY, Alan Clifford 220.64
Events and their afterlife: the dialectics of Christian typology in the Bible and Dante, by A. C. Charity. Cambridge. Cambridge Univ. Pr. 1966. xi, 288p. 23cm. Bibl. [BS478.C5] 66-18116 9.50
1. Dante Alighieri, 1265-1321—Knowledge—Bible. 2. Typology (Theology) I. Title.
Available from publisher's New York office.

DANIELOU, Jean 221.6
From shadows to reality; studies in the Biblical typology of the Fathers. [Tr. [from French] by Wulstan Hibberd] Westminster, Md., Newman Press [c.1960] 296p. Bibl. 60-14811 5.50
1. Typology (Theology) 2. Bible. O. T. Hexateuch—Hermeneutics. 3. Bible—Criticism, interpretation, etc.—Hist. I. Title.

DEHAAN, Martin Ralph, 1891- 222.11064
Portraits of Christ in Genesis, by M. R. De Haan. Grand Rapids, Mich., Zondervan [1966] 192p. 21cm. [BT225.D4] 66-21026 2.50
1. Typology (Theology) I. Title.

DE HAAN, Martin Ralph, 1891- 222.11064
Portraits of Christ in Genesis, by M. R. De Haan. Grand Rapids, Zondervan Pub. House [1966] 192 p. 21 cm. [BT225.D4] 66-21026
1. Typology (Theology) I. Title.

ESSAYS on typology 220.6
[by] G.W. H. Lampe [and] K.J.Woollcombe. Naperville, Ill., A. R. Allenson [1957] 80p. 22cm. (Studies in Biblical theology, no.22) Bibliographical footnotes. [BS478.E75] 57-3248
1. Typology (Theology) I. Lampe, Geoffrey William Hugo. II. Woollcombe, K. J. III. Series.
Contents omitted.

FORBES, Albert L. 220.6
Reading the shadows; or, Teaching from types, By Albert L. Forbes ... Stockbridge, Mich., The author, 1890. 2 p. l., [3]-110 p. 16 cm. [BS478.F6] 31-1641
1. Typology (Theology) I. Title.

FREY, Joseph Samuel Christian Frederick, 1771-1850. 220.6
Course of lectures on the Scripture types. By The Rev. Joseph Samuel C. f. Frey ... New York, D. Fanshaw [etc.] 1841. 2 v. 19 cm. Title varies; v. 2: Course of lectures on the Scripture types, with a few select sermons. [BS478.F7] 31-1648
1. Typology (Theology) I. Title.

GOD of Israel (The), the 231.4
God of Christians; the great themes of scripture [by] J. Giblet [others] Tr. [from French] by Kathryn Sullivan. Glen Rock, N.J., Paulist [1966, c.1961] vii, 261p. 18cm. (Deus bks) [BS478.G613] .95 pap.,
1. Typology (Theology) 2. Christian life—Catholic authors. I. Giblet, J.

GOD of Israel (The); the 231.4
God of Christians, the great themes of scripture [by] J. Giblet [others] Tr. by Kathryn Sullivan. New York, Desclee [c.] 1961. 261p. 61-15720 3.95
1. Typology (Theology) 2. Christian life—Catholic authors. I. Giblet, J.

GRAY, James, 1770-1824. 220.6
A dissertation, on the coincidence between the priesthoods of Jesus Christ & Melchisedec, in three parts, in which the passages of Scripture relating to that subject, in the xiv. chapter of Genesis, the cx. Psalm, the v. vi. vii. chapters of the Epistle to the Hebrews, are explained. By James Gray ... Philadelphia; Printed by Jane Aitken, no. 71, North Third street. 1810. ix, [1], 121 p. 19 cm. [BT225.G7] 37-31975
1. Jesus Christ—Priesthood. 2. Melchizedek, king of Salem. 3. Typology (Theology) I. Title.

GROOM, William Marion, 1884- 230.6
Bible men and things with their gospel meanings. By William M. Groom ... for missionary societies, Bible study classes, prayer meetings, etc. ... 2d ed. Dallas, Tex., Bible study pub. co., c1930. cover-title, 94 p. 26 cm. [BS478.G7 1930] 31-4700
1. Typology (Theology) I. Title.

HAINS, Edmont. 232.1
The Tabernacle. Introd. by Oswald J. Smith. Grard Rapids, Zondervan [1950] 120 p. 20 cm. [BT225.H3] 50-28690
1. Typology (Theology) 2. Tabernacle. I. Title.

HALL, Ona, 1894- 232.1
All the way to Calvary; the story of the Tabernacle in the wilderness and of the Savior and church which it foreshadowed. [1st ed.] New York, Greenwich Book Publishers [c1958] 74p. illus. 21cm. [BT225.H34] 58-59860
1. Typology (Theology) 2. Tabernacle. I. Title.

HARRIS, Ralph W. 232'.1
Pictures of truth : [a look at Old Testament types and their fulfillment in the New Testament] / Ralph W. Harris. Springfield, Mo. : Gospel Pub. House, c1977. 123 p. ; 18 cm. (Radiant books) [BS478.H28] 76-58081 ISBN 0-88243-905-7 pbk. : 1.50
1. Bible. N.T.—Relation to the Old Testament. 2. Typology (Theology) I. Title.

HASKELL, Stephen Nelson. 220.6
The cross and its shadow, by Stephen N. Haskell ... South Lancaster, Mass., The Bible training school, 1914. xvi p., 1 l., 19-388 p. front., illus. plates. 22 cm. [BS478.H3] 14-15442
1. Typology (Theology) I. Title.

HENDERSON, John B. 220.6
Old testament types and symbols. Notes of a series of lectures by John B. Henderson ... St. Louis, Presbyterian publishing company, 1878. viii, 9-110 p. 17 cm. [BS478.H4] 31-1646
1. Typology (Theology). I. Title.

HICKS, B R 221.93
Precious gem in the tabernacle. [Jeffersonville? Ind., 1961] 295p. illus. 23cm. [BT225.H5] 61-28193
1. Typology (Theology) 2. Tabernacle. I. Title.

HOVEN, Victor Emanuel, 1871-
Shadow and substance. St. Louis, Bethany Press [1934; Joplin, Mo., College Press, 1968] 183 p. 22 cm. (Restoration reprint library) 68-97461
1. Typology (Theology) I. Title.

HOVEN, Victor Emanuel, 1871- 220.6
Shadow and substance, by Victor E. Hoven... St. Louis, The Bethany press [c1934) xix, 183 p. front. (port.) illus. (plan) 20 cm. [BT225.H67] 35-2669
1. Typology (Theology) I. Title.

JONES, George Elliott, 1889- 232.1
The pattern, the tebernacle, the Christ. Little Rock, Ark., Baptist Publications Committee [1962] 167p. 21cm. 'Revision and enlargement of Christ revealed in the tabernacle. [BT225.J6 1962] 62-15106
1. Typology (Theology) 2. Tabernacle. I. Title.

JONES, George Elliott, 1889- 232.1
The pattern, the tabernacle, the Christ. Little Rock, Ark., 716 Main St., Baptist Pubns. Comm., c.1962. 167p. 21cm. Rev. and enlargement of Christ revealed in the tabernacle. 62-15106 1.50 pap.,
1. Typology (Theology) 2. Tabernacle. I. Title.

KETCHAM, Robert Thomas, 1889- 232.1
Old Testament pictures of New Testament truth. Des Plaines, Ill., Regular Baptist Pr., 1800 Oakton Blvd. [c.1965] 249p. illus. 20cm. [BS478.K4] 65-23587 2.95
1. Typology (Theology) I. Title.

LUCE, Alice Eveline. 220.0
Pictures of Pentecost in the Old Testament. [Springfield, Mo., Gospel Pub. House, c1950] 238 p. 20 cm. [BS478.L82] 52-20934
1. Typology (Theology) I. Title.

LUCE, Alice Eveline. 220.6
Pictures of Pentecost in the Old Testament. Second series. By Alice Eveline Luce. Springfield, Mo., Gospel publishing house [c1930] 3 p. l., 9-172 p. 19 cm. [BS478.L8] 30-34095
1. Typology (Theology) I. Title. II. Title: Pentecost, Pictures of.

MCEWEN, William, 1734-1762. 220.
Grace and truth, or, The glory and fullness of the Redeemer displayed: in an attempt to explain, illustrate, and enforce, the most remarkable types, figures, and allegories, of the Old Testament. To which is added, thoughts on various subjects. By William McEwen... Philadelphia, W. W. Woodward, 1821. xi, [13]-328 p. 15 cm. First edition. 1763. [BS478.M18 1821] 220 ISBN 31-1643
1. Typology (Theology) I. Title.

MAGNER, W. C. 220.6
Better Bible study; "Christ all and in all", by W. C. Magner... Chicago, New York [etc.] Fleming H. Revell company [1895] 191 p. 19 cm. [BT225.M2] 37-31960
1. Typology (Theology) 2. Bible—Study. I. Title.

MARIN, Louis, 1931- 232.9'6
The semiotics of the Passion narrative : topics and figures / by Louis Marin ; translated by Alfred M. Johnson, Jr. Pittsburgh, Pa. : Pickwick Press, 1980. xii, 263 p. ; 22 cm. (The Pittsburgh theological monograph series ; 25) Translation of Semiotique de la Passion. Includes indexes. Bibliography: p. 247-249. [BT414.M3513] 80-18199 ISBN 0-915138-23-9 : 12.50
1. Jesus Christ—Biography—Passion Week. 2. Typology (Theology) I. Title. II. Series: Pittsburgh theological monograph series.

MARTIN, Elmer Good. 232.96
The Lord's passover, by Elmer G. Martin ... Scottdale, Pa., Printed by the Mennonite press, 1935. 3 p. l., 9-101, [1] p. incl. pl., diagrs. 21 cm. "Regarding the day of the crucifixion of Our Lord."--p. 14. [BT430.M3] 36-4284
1. Jesus Christ—Crucifixion. 2. Jesus Christ—Chronology. 3. Typology (Theology) I. Title.

MATHER, Samuel, 1626-1671. 221'.6'4
The figures or types of the Old Testament. With a new introd. by Mason I. Lowance, Jr. New York, Johnson Reprint Corp., 1969. xxv, vii, 540 p. 23 cm. (Series in American studies) Reprint of the 2d ed., 1705. Includes bibliographical references. [BS478.M3 1969] 78-81541
1. Typology (Theology) I. Title. II. Series.

MILLER, Herbert Sumner, 1867- 282.1
The gospel in the Hebrew tabernacle, priesthood, and offerings, by Rev. H. S. Miller ... Houghton, N.Y., The Word-bearer press, 1939. vi, 234 p. incl. illus.,

plates, plan. 19 1/2 cm. [BT225.M5] 40-83413
1. Typology (Theology) I. Title.

MONSER, J. W. 220.6
Types and metaphors of the Bible. By J. W. Monser ... with an introduction by Chas. Louis Loos ... St. Louis, John Burns book co. [c1886] xiv p., 1 l., 17-320 p. 21 cm. [BS478.M6] 31-1640
1. Typology (Theology) I. Title.

NEEDHAM, George Carter, 1840- 220.6
Shadow and substance. An exposition of the tabernacle types. By Geo. C. Needham ... Philadelphia, American Baptist publication society, 1896. 199 p. incl., front. (port.) 19 cm. [BS478.N4] 30-33858
1. Typology (Theology) I. Title.

OLFORD, Stephen F. 201.1
The tabernacle: camping with God, by Stephen F. Olford. Neptune, N.J., Loizeaux Bros. [1971] 187 p. illus. 21 cm. Bibliography: p. 185-187. [BT225.O4] 78-173686 ISBN 0-87213-675-2 3.95
1. Typology (Theology) 2. Tabernacle.

PENNER, P. E. 232.1
Christ in the Scriptures, by P. E. Penner. Inman, Kan., Salem publishing house [1946] 144 p. 21 1/2 cm. "Second revised edition." [BT225.P4 1946] 46-21254
1. Typology (Theology) I. Title.

A Pseudo-Epiphanius testimony book / edited and translated by Robert V. Hotchkiss. [Missoula, Mont.] : Society of Biblical Literature, 1974. vii, 82 p. ; 24 cm. (Texts and translations - Society of Biblical Literature ; 4) (Early Christian literature series ; 1) Greek and English on opposite pages. The Greek text combines readings from the 2 available mss.: Codex Athos Iviron 28 and Codex Vaticanus Graecus 790. Includes bibliographical references. [BT200.P84] 74-15203 ISBN 0-88414-043-1 232
1. Jesus Christ—Person and offices. 2. Typology (Theology) I. Epiphanius, Saint, Bp. of Constantia in Cyprus. II. Hotchkiss, Robert V., ed. III. Title. IV. Series. V. Series: Society of Biblical Literature. Texts and translations ; 4.

ROWE, John F. 220.6
The gospel in type and antitype; also in prophecy and fulfillment. 3d. ed. by John F. Rowe ... Cincinnati, 1892. 102 p. 15 cm. "This tract formerly appeared under the title 'Analogies between the old and new institution'."--p. [3] [BS478.R6 1892] 30-33857
1. Typology (Theology) I. Title.

SABOURIN, Leopold. 220.6
The Bible and Christ : the unity of the two Testaments / by Leopold Sabourin. New York, N.Y. : Alba House, c1980. xx, 188 p. ; 21 cm. Includes index. Bibliography: p. [175]-185. [BS2387.S23] 80-14892 ISBN 0-8189-0405-4 pbk. : 6.95
1. Bible. N.T.—Relation to the Old Testament. 2. Typology (Theology) I. Title.

SHEPHERD, Coulson 296.4
Jewish holy days; their prophetic and Christian significance. New York, Loizeaux [1961] 95p. 61-16660 1.50 pap.,
1. Typology (Theology) 2. Fasts and feasts—Judaism. 3. Jews—Conversion to Christianity. I. Title.

SMITH, Austin Burns. 220.6
Gospel teacher, or, Twelve lectures on the types and shadows of the Old Testament, by Austin Burns Smith... Denison, Tex., Murray's steam printing house, 1884. 136 p. 23 cm. [BS478.S6] 30-33856
1. Typology (Theology) I. Title.

SMITH, Uriah, 1832-1903. 220.
Looking unto Jesus; or, Christ in type and antitype, by Uriah Smith ... Chicago, Ill., Battle Creek, Mich. [etc.] Review and herald publishing co. [c1898] 288 p. col. front., illus., plates. 21 cm. [BT225.S6] 38-20531
1. Typology (Theology) 2. Seventh-day Adventists—Doctrinal and controversials works I. Title.

STEVENS, Charles Hadley, 1892- 221.6'4
The wilderness journey; Christian principles illustrated by Israel's desert wanderings [by] Charles H. Stevens. Chicago, Moody Press [1971] 272 p. col. map (on lining papers) 22 cm. Bibliography: p. 271-272. [BS478.S75] 71-143474 4.95
1. Typology (Theology) I. Title.

STREET, Harold Blaine, 1899- 232.1
The believer-priest in the tabernacle furniture, by Harold B. Street ... Chicago, Ill., Moody press [1947] 160 p. illus. (plan) 20 cm. "Copyright 1946." [BS478.S8] 47-17430
1. Typology (Theology) 2. Tabernacle. I. Title.

TALBOT, Louis Thompson, 1889-1976. 296.6'5
Christ in the tabernacle / by Louis T. Talbot. Chicago : Moody Press, 1978, c1942. p. cm. [BT225.T34 1978] 78-13460 ISBN 0-8024-1393-5 : 4.95
1. Typology (Theology) 2. Tabernacle. I. Title.

TAYLOR, Thomas, 1576-1632. 232
Christ revealed / by Thomas Taylor ; a facsimile reproduction with an introd. by Raymond A. Anselment. Delmar, N.Y. : Scholars' Facsimiles & Reprints, 1979. p. cm. Reprint of the 1635 ed. printed by M. F. for R. Dawlman and L. Fawne, London. Reproduction of STC 23821. [BT225.T37 1979] 79-10885 ISBN 0-8201-1334-4 : 35.00
1. Bible. N.T.—Relation to O.T. 2. Typology (Theology) I. Title.

TRENT, Kenneth E. 232.1
Types of Christ in the Old Testament, a conservative approach to Old Testament typology. Foreword by Jacob Gartenhaus. New York, Exposition Press [c.1960] 123p. illus. 21cm. (An Exposition-Testament book) 60-50188 3.00
1. Typology (Theology) I. Title.

TRENT, Kenneth E 1927- 232.1
Types of Christ in the Old Testament, a conservative approach to Old Testament typology. Foreword by Jacob Gartenhaus. [1st ed.] New York, Exposition Press [1960] 123 p. illus. 21 cm. (An Exposition-Testament book) [BT225.T7] 60-50188
1. Typology (Theology) I. Title.

VISITS to Aunt Clement; 220.6
or, Conversations on the connection between the Old and New Testaments. New York, The General Prot. Episcopal Sunday school union, 1841. vi, [7]-172 p. 15 1/2 cm. [BS478.V5] 31-1642
1. Typology (Theology)

WIGHT, Fred Hartley, 1899- 221.6
Devotional studies of Old Testament types. Chicago, Moody Press [1956] 255p. illus. 22cm. [BT225.W53] 56-2841
1. Typology (Theology) I. Title.

ZEOLI, Anthony. 232.1
Christ the sparrow, by Anthony Zeoli ... Wyncote, Pa., A. Zeoli [c1942] 162 p., 1 l. 20 cm. [BT225.Z4] 43-4450
1. Typology (Theology) 2. Bible. O.T. Leviticus XIII-XIV—Criticism, interpretation, etc. I. Title.

Typology (Theology)—Addresses, essays, lectures.

JOHNSON, S. Lewis, 1915- 220.1'3
The Old Testament in the New : an argument for biblical inspiration / S. Lewis Johnson. Grand Rapids, MI : Zondervan Pub. House, c1980. 108 p. ; 21 cm. (Contemporary evangelical perspectives) Includes bibliographical references. [BS480.J63] 80-12194 ISBN 0-310-41851-8 pbk. : 3.95
1. Bible—Inspiration—Addresses, essays, lectures. 2. Bible. N.T.—Relation to O.T.—Addresses, essays, lectures. 3. Typology (Theology)—Addresses, essays, lectures. I. Title.

Typology (Theology)—History of doctrines.

BERCOVITCH, Sacvan, comp. 232'.1
Typology and early American literature. [Amherst] University of Massachusetts Press, 1972. 337 p. 24 cm. Includes essays which appeared in Early American literature. Contents.Contents.—Bercovitch, S. Introduction.—Davis, T. M. The traditions of Puritan typology.—Manning, S. Scriptural exegesis and the literary critic.—Rosenmeier, J. "With my owne eyes": William Bradford's Of Plymouth plantation.—Reinitz, R. The separatist background of Roger Williams' argument for religious toleration.—Lowance, M. I., Jr. Cotton Mather's Magnalia and the metaphors of Biblical history.—Reiter, Robert E. Poetry and doctrine in Edward Taylor's Preparatory meditations, series II, 1-30.—Keller, K. "The world slickt up in types": Edward Taylor as a version of Emerson.—Brumm, U. Edward Taylor and the poetic use of religious imagery.—Lowance, M. I., Jr. "Images or shadows of divine things" in the thought of Jonathan Edwards.—Bibliography (p. [245]-337) [BS478.B47] 74-181362 12.00
1. Typology (Theology)—History of doctrines. 2. American literature—Colonial period, ca. 1600-1775—History and criticism. I. Early American literature. II. Title.

BRUMM, Ursula. 230
American thought and religious typology. [Translated from the German by John Hooglund] New Brunswick, N.J., Rutgers University Press [1970]. x, 265 p. 22 cm. Translation of Die religiose Typologie im amerikanischen Denken. Bibliography: p. [253]-262. [BS478.B7713] 76-97737 9.00
1. Typology (Theology)—History of doctrines. 2. Symbolism. 3. U.S.—Intellectual life. I. Title.

FAIRBAIRN, Patrick, 1805-1874. 220.
The typology of Scripture; or, The doctrine of types investigated in its principles, and applied to the explanation of the earlier revelations of God, considered as preparatory exhibitions of the leading truths of the Gospel. By Rev. Patrick Fairbairn ... Philadelphia, Daniels & Smith, 1852. 2 v. in 1. 25 cm. Contents.--i. Patriarchal period.--ii. Mosaic period. [BS478.F3 1852] 16-12491
I. Title.

GALDON, Joseph A. 821'.009'31
Typology and seventeenth-century literature / by Joseph A. Galdon. The Hague ; Paris : Mouton, 1975. 164 p. ; 25 cm. (De proprietatibus litterarum : Series maior ; 28) Includes index. Bibliography: p. [149]-160. [BS478.G34] 76-350229 ISBN 90-279-3151-8 pbk. : 19.25
1. Typology (Theology)—History of doctrines. 2. English literature—Early modern, 1500-1700—History and criticism. I. Title. II. Series.
Distributed by Humanities Press, Atlantic Highlands, N.J.

Typology (Theology)—Meditations.

HINNEBUSCH, Paul. 232
Jesus, the new Elijah / Paul Hinnebusch. Ann Arbor, Mich. : Servant Books ; South Bend, Ind. : distributed by Servant Publications, c1978. 136 p. ; 21 cm. Includes index. [BT225.H56] 79-115638 ISBN 0-89283-062-X pbk. : 2.95
1. Elijah, the prophet—Meditations. 2. Bible, N.T. Gospels—Relation to the O.T. 1 Kings XVII—2 Kings II—Meditations. 3. Bible, N.T. Gospels—Meditations. 4. Bible, O.T. 1 Kings XVII—2 Kings II. 5. Typology (Theology)—Meditations.
Pub. Address: Servant Pubns., P. O. Box 8617, Ann Arbor MI 48107

MCNEIL, Brian. 223'.206
Christ in the Psalms / Brian McNeil. New York : Paulist Press, 1980. xiii, 90 p. ; 18 cm. [BS1430.4.M28] 19 80-82796 ISBN 0-8091-2341-X (pbk.) : 2.95
1. Bible. O.T. Psalms—Meditations. 2. Typology (Theology)—Meditations. I. Title.

Tyrrell, George, 1861-1909.

SHULTENOVER, David G., 1938- 230'.2'0924
George Tyrrell : in search of Catholicism / by David G. Schultenover. Shepherdstown [W.Va.] : Patmos Press, 1981. p. cm. Includes index. Bibliography: p. [BX4705.T9S38] 19 81-38406 ISBN 0-915762-13-7 : 32.50
1. Tyrrell, George, 1861-1909. 2. Modernism—Catholic Church—History. I. Title.
Publisher's address: P.O. Box V, Shepherdstown, WV 25443

TYRRELL, George, 1861-1909. 282'.092'2
Letters from a "modernist" : the letters of George Tyrrell to Wilfrid Ward, 1893-1908 / introduced and annotated by Mary Jo Weaver. Shepherdstown : Patmos Press ; London : Sheed and Ward, c1981. xxxiv, 192 p. ; 22 cm. Includes index. Bibliography: p. 172-185. [BX1396.T83 1981] 19 80-28372 ISBN 0-915762-12-9 : 35.00
1. Tyrrell, George, 1861-1909. 2. Ward, Wilfrid Philip, 1856-1916. 3. Newman, John Henry, Cardinal, 1801-1890. 4. Jesuits—England—Correspondence. 5. Modernism—Catholic Church—History—Sources. 6. Catholics—England—Correspondence. I. Ward, Wilfrid Philip, 1856-1916. II. Title.
Publisher's address: P.O. Box V, Shepherdstown, WV 25443

Tyson, Thornton Kelly, 1845-1912.

LOVING, Brady Antoine. 920.
Thornton Kelly Tyson, pioneer home missionary, by Bardy Antoine Loving, with a foreword by Alonzo M. Petty, D. D. Kansas City, Mo., The Western Baptist publishing company, 1915. 151 p. 2 port. (incl. front.) 20 cm. [BX6495.T85L6] 15-10845
1. Tyson, Thornton Kelly, 1845-1912. I. Title.

Tzotzil Indians—Missions.

STEVEN, Hugh. 266'.023'09727
They dared to be different / [Hugh Steven] . Irvine, Calif. : Harvest House Publishers, c1976. 160 p. ; 21 cm. [F1221.T9S74] 76-42174 ISBN 0-89081-029-X pbk. : 2.95
1. Tzotzil Indians—Missions. 2. Tzotzil Indians—Social life and customs. 3. Indians of Mexico—Missions. I. Title.

Tzotzil Indians—Religion and mythology.

HUNT, Eva, 1934- 299'.7
The transformation of the Hummingbird : cultural roots of a Zinacantecan mythical poem / Eva Hunt. Ithaca, N.Y. : Cornell University Press, 1977. 312 p. : ill. ; 22 cm. (Symbol, myth, and ritual series) Includes index. Bibliography: p. [290]-303. [F1221.T9H86] 76-12909 ISBN 0-8014-1022-3 : 18.50
1. Tzotzil Indians—Religion and mythology. 2. Symbolism. 3. Indians of Mexico—Religion and mythology. I. Title.

Tzotzil Indians—Rites and ceremonies.

VOGT, Evon Zartman, 1918- 299'.7
Tortillas for the gods : a symbolic analysis of Zinacantecan rituals / Evon Z. Vogt. Cambridge : Harvard University Press, 1976. xv, 234 p. : ill. ; 24 cm. Includes index. Bibliography: p. 221-228. [F1221.T9V59] 75-28470 ISBN 0-674-89554-1 : 16.50
1. Tzotzil Indians—Rites and ceremonies. 2. Indians of Mexico—Rites and ceremonies. 3. Tzotzil Indians—Religion and Mythology. 4. Indians of Mexico—Religion and Mythology. 5. Azinacantan, Mexico—Religion. I. Title.

Udayanacarya.

TACHIKAWA, Musashi. 110
The structure of the world in Udayana's realism : a study of the Lakasanavali and the Kiranavali / by Musashi Tachikawa. Dordrecht, Holland ; Boston : D. Reidel Pub. Co. ; Hingham, MA : Sold and distributed in the U.S.A. and Canada by Kluwer Boston, c1981. xiv, 180 p. : ill. ; 23 cm. (Studies of classical India ; v. 4) Revision of the author's thesis (Ph.D.—Harvard, 1975) Includes indexes. Bibliography: p. 163-168. [B133.U294T32 1981] 19 81-13848 ISBN 90-277-1291-3 : 39.50
1. Udayanacarya. 2. Vaisesika. 3. Nyaya. I.

Udayanacarya. Laksanavali. English & Sanskrit. 1981. II. Udayanacarya. Selections. III. Title. IV. Series.
Distributor's address: 160 Old Derby St., Hingham, MA 02043.

Uinquagesima

HERRERA Oria, Angel Bp., 1886- ed. 251.027
The preacher's encyclopedia [v.4] comp., ed. under the supervision of His Eminence Angel Cardinal Herrera, Bp. of Malaga. Eng. version tr. [from Spanish] ed. by David Greenstock. Westminster, Md., Newman [c.1955, 1965] xix, 737p. 26cm. Contents.v. 4. Advent to Quinqwagesima [BX1756.A1H43] 65-2580 15.00
1. uinquagesima p15.00 2. Church year sermons—Outlines. 3. Catholic Church—Sermons—Outlines. 4. Sermons—Outlines. I. Greenstock, David L., ed. and tr. II. Title.

Ukraine—Church history—Sources.

DRAGAN, Antin.
Our Ukrainian Cardinal. Design and layout by Bohdan Tytla. Jersey City, Ukrainian National Association and Svoboda Press [1966] ‧ [88] p. illus., ports. (part. col.) facsims. 68-27655
1. Slipyi, Osyp, Cardinal, 2. Ukraine—Church history—Sources. I. Ukrainian National Association. II. Title.

Ukrainian Orthodox Church of the United States of America.

FEDOROVICH, Nicholas. 281.9'73
My Church and my faith. [So. Bound Brook, N.J.] Ukrainian Orthodox Church of USA, 1969. 40 p. illus. map, ports. 26 cm. Enlarged and revised ed. of the author's The great Prince St. Vladimir. [BX738.U45F4 1969] 78-256441
1. Ukrainian Orthodox Church of the United States of America. 2. Vladimir, Saint, called the Great, Grand Duke of Kiev, 956 (ca.)-1015. I. Title.

Ukrainians in Canada — Education.

SKWAROK, J
The Ukrainian settlers in Canada and their schools; with reference to government, French Canadian, and Ukrainian missionary influences, 1891-1921. Edmonton, Alta., 1958. 157 p. illus. 24 cm. Includes bibliographies. [LC3734.S55] 61-40648
1. Ukrainians in Canada — Education. I. Title.

Ukrainians in the Czechoslovak Republic.

CARPATHIAN Alliance. 281.9'437
The tragedy of the Greek Catholic Church in Czechoslovakia. New York, 1971. 68 p. illus. 24 cm. Includes bibliographical references. [BX4711.77.C95C37 1971] 74-157552 2.00
1. Catholic Church. Byzantine rite (Ukrainian)—Czechoslovak Republic. 2. Ukrainians in the Czechoslovak Republic. I. Title. II. Title: The Greek Catholic Church in Czechoslovakia.

Ukrainians in the United States.

LUCIW, Theodore. 281.9'0924 B
Father Agapius Honcharenko; first Ukrainian priest in America. Introd. by Walter Dushnyck. New York, Ukrainian Congress Committee of America, 1970. xx, 223 p. illus., facsims., ports. 24 cm. Bibliography: p. 209-216. [E184.U5L77] 78-115892 7.50
1. Honcharenko, Ahapius, 1832-1916. 2. Ukrainians in the United States. I. Title.

Ulama—Addresses, essays, lectures.

SCHOLARS, saints, and 297'.0956
Sufis; Muslim religious institutions in the Middle East since 1500. Edited by Nikki R. Keddie. Berkeley, University of California Press, 1972. viii, 401 p. 25 cm. Includes bibliographical references. [BP185.S36] 77-153546 ISBN 0-520-02027-8 20.00
1. Ulama—Addresses, essays, lectures. 2. Sufism—Addresses, essays, lectures. 3. Shiites—Addresses, essays, lectures. 4. Women, Muslim—Religious life—Addresses, essays, lectures. 5. Islam—History—Addresses, essays, lectures. I. Keddie, Nikki R., ed.

Ulrich von Strassburg, d. 1277.

LESCOE, Francis J. 110
God as first principle in Ulrich of Strasburg / by Francis J. Lescoe. New York : Alba House, c1979. xvi, 276 p. : facsims. ; 23 cm. Expanded version of the author's thesis, Toronto. "The edited text Summa de bono, liber quartus, tractatus primus": p. 145-242. Includes index. Bibliography: p. 242-260. [BX1749.U383L47 1979] 79-4140 ISBN 0-8189-0385-6 : 11.95
1. Ulrich von Strassburg, d. 1277. Summa de bono. 2. Theology, Doctrinal. 3. Philosophy. I. Ulrich von Strassburg, d. 1277. Summa de bono. Book 4, tractate 1. 1979. II. Title.

Umar ibn Muhammad, al-Nasafi. al-Akaid.

MASUD IBN UMAR, Sad al-Din, al-Taftazani, 1322-1389. 297
A commentary on the creed of Islam; Sad al-Din al-Taftazani on the creed of Najm al-Din al-Nasafi. Translated with introd. and notes by Earl Edgar Elder. New York, Columbia University Press, 1950. xxxii, 187 p. 24 cm. (Records of civilization: sources and studies, no. 43) "The translation was first made as a part of the requirements for the degree of doctor of philosophy at the Kennedy School of Missions of the Hartford Seminary Foundation." Bibliography: p. [171]-175. [BP161.U55M32] 50-5160
1. Umar ibn Muhammad, al-Nasafi. al-Akaid. 2. Mohammedanism. I. Elder, Earl Edgar, 1887- ed. and tr. II. Title. III. Series.

Umbanda (Cultus)

BRAMLY, Serge, 1949- 299'.6
Macumba : the teachings of Maria-Jose, mother of the gods / by Serge Bramly ; translated by Meg Bogin. New York : St. Martin's Press, [1977] p. cm. [BL2592.U513B713] 77-76628 ISBN 0-312-50338-5 : 10.00
1. Umbanda (Cultus) I. Maria Jose, mere. II. Title.

BRAMLY, Serge, 1949- 299'.6
Macumba : the teachings of Maria-Jose, mother of the gods / by Serge Bramly ; translated by Meg Bogin. New York : Avon Books, 1979, c1977. 244p. : ill. ; 18 cm. [BL2592.U513B713] ISBN 0-380-42317-0 pbk. : 2.25
1. Maria Jose, mere. 2. Umbanda (Cultus) I. Title.
L.C. card no. for 1977 St. Martin's Press ed.:77-76628.

LANGGUTH, A. J., 1933- 299'.6
Macumba : white and black magic in Brazil / A. J. Langguth. 1st ed. New York : Harper & Row, [1975] 273 p. ; 21 cm. [BL2592.U5L34 1975] 74-1830 ISBN 0-06-012503-9 : 7.95
1. Umbanda (Cultus) 2. Magic—Brazil. I. Title.

Unas, King of Egypt.

PYRAMID texts 299'.3'1
The pyramid of Unas. Texts tr. with commentary by Alexandre Piankoff. [Princeton, N. J.] Princeton Univ. Pr. [1968] xiv, 118p. illus., fold. plans, 70 plates. 32cm. (Bollingen ser., 40:5. Egyptian religious texts & representations, v. 5) Pub. for Bollingen Found. Bibl. refs. [PJ1553.A3U5] 65-26216 10.00
1. Unas, King of Egypt. 2. Egyptian language—Inscriptions. I. Piankoff, Alexandre. ed. II. Bollingen Founadtion. III. Title. IV. Series: Bollingen series, 40:5 V. Series: Egyptian religious texts and representations, v. 5.)

Unction.

ROCCAPRIORE, Marie. 265'.7
Anointing of the sick and the elderly : a pastoral guide for home and church / by Marie Roccapriore. Canfield, Ohio : Alba Books, c1980. xvii, 142 p. : ill. ; 18 cm. Bibliography: p. 137-142. [BX2203.R6] 19 80-65722 ISBN 0-8189-1160-3 (pbk.) : 2.95
1. Unction. I. Title.

Underachievers.

CLIZBE, John A. 371.92'6
A chance for change : confronting student underachievement / John A. Clizbe, Milton Kornrich, Frances L. Reid. 1st ed. Hicksville, N.Y. : Exposition Press, c1980. x, 145 p. ; 22 cm. (Exposition-university book) Bibliography: p. 129-136. [LC4661.C564] 79-51813 ISBN 0-682-49395-3 : 8.00
1. Underachievers. 2. Motivation in education. I. Kornrich, Milton, joint author. II. Reid, Frances L., joint author. III. Title.

THE 371.9'071'273
Underachiever; a guide to tutorial, remedial, diagnostic, and academic resources in prep school programs and clinics. 1st ed. Boston, P. Sargent, 1967. 190 p. illus. 18 cm. Second ed. published in 1971 under title: The Academic underachiever. [LC3969.U58] 67-18845
1. Underachievers. 2. Education—United States—Directories. I. Sargent, Porter.

Underhill, Evelyn, 1875-1941.

ARMSTRONG, Christopher J. R., 1935- 248'.22'0924 B
Evelyn Underhill, 1875-1941 : an introduction to her life and writings / by Christopher J. R. Armstrong. Grand Rapids : Eerdmans, 1976, c1975. xxiii, 303 p. ; 22 cm. Includes index. Bibliography: p. 293-303. [BV5095.U5A75 1976] 75-33401 ISBN 0-8028-3474-4 : 7.95
1. Underhill, Evelyn, 1875-1941.

UNDERHILL, Evelyn, 1875-1941.
The miracles of our Lady Saint Mary; brought out of divers tongues and newly set forth in English, by Evelyn Underhill. New York, E. p. Dutton & co., 1906. xxviii, 308 p. front. 21 cm. Bibliography: p. xxvii-xxviii. W 6
I. Title.

UNDERHILL, Evelyn, 1875-1941.
Mysticism; a study in the nature and development of man's spiritual consciousness. Cleveland, World Publishing Co. [1963] xviii, 519 p. (Meridian books, MG-1)
I. Title.

Understanding the new religions.

NEW religious movements 200'.973
in America. [New York] : Rockefeller Foundation, 1979. viii, 146 p. ; 28 cm. (Working papers - The Rockefeller Foundation) Abridged version of discussion of conference papers which were included in rev. form in a work published 1978 under title: Understanding the new religions. [BL2530.U6N48] 79-17378 gratis
1. Understanding the new religions. 2. United States—Religion—1945- — Congresses. I. Series: Rockefeller Foundation. Working papers — The Rockefeller Foundation.

Undertakers and undertaking.

FULTON, Robert Lester.
The world stood still, by Robert L. Fulton and Howard C. Raether. 1 v. (unpaged) illus. 29 cm. 67-91447
1. Kennedy, John Fitzgerald, 1917-1964, Pres. U.S. 2. Undertakers and undertakings. 3. Funeral rites and ceremonies. I. Title.

FULTON, Robert Lester.
The world stood still, by Robert L. Fulton and Howard C. Raether. Milwaukee, Wis., National Funeral Directors Assoc. of U.S., Inc., [c1964] 1 v. (unpaged) illus. 29 cm. 67-914472
1. Kennedy, John Fitzgerald, 1917-1964, Pres. U.S. 2. Undertakers and undertakings. 3. Funeral rites and ceremonies. I. Title.

Undertakers and undertaking—Bibliography.

HARRAH, Barbara K. 016.614'6'0973
Funeral service : a bibliography of literature on its past, present, and future, the various means of disposition, and memorialization / by Barbara K. Harran and David F. Harrah. Metuchen, N.J. : Scarecrow Press, 1976. xviii, 383 p. ; 23 cm. Includes indexes. [Z5994.H3] [RA619] 76-40340 ISBN 0-8108-0946-X : 15.00
1. Undertakers and undertaking—Bibliography. 2. Undertakers and undertaking—United States—Bibliography. 3. Funeral rites and ceremonies—Bibliography. 4. Funeral rites and ceremonies—United States—Bibliography. 5. Dead—Bibliography. I. Harrah, David F., 1949- joint author. II. Title.

Undertakers and undertaking—United States—Handbooks, manuals, etc.

NATIONAL Funeral Directors Association of the United States.
NFDA U.S. reference manual. Student ed. [Milwaukee? Wis., 1966?] 1 v. (various pagings) Cover title. Includes bibliography. 68-62863
1. Undertakers and undertaking—U.S.—Handbooks, manuals, etc. 2. Funeral rites and ceremonies—U.S. 3. Military funerals—U.S. I. Title.

Underwood, Horace Grant, 1859-1916.

UNDERWOOD, Lillias (Horton) Mrs. 1851- 275.
Underwood of Korea; being an intimate record of the life and work of the Rev. H. G. Underwood, D.D., LL.D., for thirty-one years a missionary of the Presbyterian board in Korea, by his wife, Lillias H. Underwood ... New York, Chicago [etc.] Fleming H. Revell company [c1918] 350 p. front., plates, ports. 21 cm. [BV3460.U7] 18-13341
1. Underwood, Horace Grant, 1859-1916. 2. Missions—Korea. I. Title.

UNDERWOOD, Lillias (Horton) 1851-
Underwood of Korea; being an intimate record of the life and work of the Rev. H. G. Underwood, D.D., LL.D., for thirty-one years a missionary of the Presbyterian board in Korea, by His wife, Lillias H. Underwood ... New York, London [etc.] Fleming H. Revell company [1918] 350 p. front., plates, ports., facsim. 21 cm. [BV3462.U6U7] 18-13341
1. Underwood, Horace Grant, 1859-1916. 2. Missions—Korea. I. Title.

Underwood, Susan Maria, 1830-1861.

ANDERSON, Eliza H. Mrs. 922
Following after Jesus. A memorial of Susan Maria Underwood. By By Mrs. Eliza H. Anderson. Boston, American tract society [1863] 250 p. front. (port.) 17 cm. [BR1725.U6A6] 36-8155
1. Underwood, Susan Maria, 1830-1861. I. American tract society. II. Title.

Unification Church—Doctrinal and controversial works.

DURHAM, Deanna. 289.9 B
Life among the moonies : three years in the Unification Church / by Deanna Durham. Plainfield, N.J. : Logos International, c1981. x, 202 p. ; 20 cm. [BX9750.S4D87] 19 81-80395 ISBN 0-88270-496-6 pbk. : 2.95
1. Unification Church—Doctrinal and controversial works. 2. Durham, Deanna. 3. Christian biography—United States. I. Title.

KEMPERMAN, Steve, 1955- 289.9 B
Lord of the Second Advent : a rare look inside the terrifying world of the Moonies / by Steve Kemperman. Ventura, Calif. :

Regal Books, c1981. p. cm. Includes bibliographical references. [BX9750.S4K45] 19 80-54091 ISBN 0-8307-0780-8 : 8.95
1. Unification Church—Controversial literature. 2. Kemperman, Steve, 1955- 3. Christian biography—United States. I. Title.

Unification Church—Doctrinal and controversial works—Addresses, essays, lectures.

TEN theologians respond to 289.9 *the Unification Church* / edited by Herbert Richardson ; [contributors, Durwood Foster ... et al.]. 1st ed. Barrytown, N.Y. : Unification Theological Seminary ; New York, N.Y. : Distributed by Rose of Sharon Press, c1981. xv, 199 p. ; 23 cm. (Conference series / the Unification Theological Seminary ; no. 10) Includes bibliographical references. [BX9750.S4T46 1981] 19 81-70679 pbk. : 9.95
1. Unification Church—Doctrinal and controversial works—Addresses, essays, lectures. I. Richardson, Herbert Warren. II. Foster, Durwood.

Union Baptist Association (Tex.)—History.

†COMMANDER, R. G. 286'.1764
The story of Union Baptist Association, 1840-1976 / by R. G. Commander. Houston : D. Armstrong Publishers, 1977. 229 p. ; 24 cm. Includes index. Bibliography: p. 223-224. [BX6209.U63C65] 78-104909 pbk. : 4.95
1. Union Baptist Association (Tex.)—History. I. Title.
Publisher's address: 2000 B Governor's, Houston, T X 77092

Union of American Hebrew Congregations.

SPIRO, Jack D
Teacher's guide for The living Bible [by Sylvan D. Schwartzman and J. D. Spiro] New York, Union of American Hebrew Congregations [1963] 101 p. 28 cm. 66-57787
I. Schwartzman, Sylvan David. The living Bible. II. Title.

UNION of American Hebrew 296.6'7 Congregations.
Report of the president to the board of trustees. [New York?] v. 26-28 cm. annual. Title varies: 1960, Report to the UAHC board of trustees. [BM21.U43] 63-52594
I. Title.

WARSCHAUER, Heinz.
Teacher's syllabus for grade 9, according to the curriculum of the Commission of Jewish Education. Subjects included: Comparative religion; Bible: Writings. New York, Union of American Hebrew Congregations [1961] viii, 303 p. 28 cm.
1. Union of American Hebrew Congregations. I. Title.

Union Presbyterian church, Walnut township, Montgomery county, Ind.

PORTER, William 285.177248 Arthur, 1880-
A history of Union Presbyterian church, Walnut township, Montgomery county, Indiana, 1834-1934 ... Compiled by W. Arthur Porter. [Indianapolis? 1934?] 2 p. l., 47, [2] p. illus. 23 cm. "Families of Union church": p. 19-47. "Corrections and additions" slip inserted. [BX9211.U58P6] 35-12438
1. Union Presbyterian church, Walnut township, Montgomery county, Ind. 2. Montgomery co., Ind.—Geneal. I. Title.

Union United Presbyterian church, Washington township, Westmoreland co., Pa.

LUDWICK, Harry M. 285.474881
... History of Union United Presbyterian church, by Harry M. Ludwick, A. M. Scottdale, Pa., Printed by Mennonite publishing house, 1933. 2 p. l., 3-77 p. front. 20 cm. At head of title: 1858. 1963. Bibliography: p. 77. [BX9211.U6L8] 34-4740
1. Union United Presbyterian church, Washington township, Westmoreland co., Pa. I. Title.

Unison choruses, Sacred, with piano.

LESTER, William, 1889-
... Carol junior choir book with optional descants; anthems and responses, by William Lester. Chicago, New York, Clayton F. Summy co. [1938] cover-title, 14 pl. 26 cm. (The Lester junior choir series) At head of title: For unison voices. Publisher's plate no.: C. F. S. co. 3227-12. With piano accompaniment. [Full name: Thomas William Lester] [M2037.L4C3] 44-33514
1. Unison choruses, Sacred, with piano. 2. Descants. I. Title.

Unitarian.

AMERICAN Unitarian association.
Semicentennial of the American Unitarian Association with a full report of the addresses, the annual report of the executive committee, and the treasurer's statement for the year ending April 30, 1875. Boston, American Unitarian association, 1875. 101 p. 19 cm. 6-31243
I. Title.

HEYWOOD, John Healy, 1818- 230. 1880.
Unitarian views vindicated. A reply to Rev. Henry M. Denison's Review of "Unitarian views." By John H. Heywood ... Louisville, Hull & brother, printers, 1855. 156 p. 18 cm. [BX9841.H45] 24-13096
1. Denison, Henry M. Review of "Unitarian views." 2. Unitarian. I. Title.

Unitarian—Addresses, essays, lectures.

PARKER, Theodore, 1810- 230.8 1860.
Speeches, addresses, and occasional sermons, by Theodore Parker ... Boston, W. Crosby and H. P. Nichols; New York, C. S. Francis & company, 1852. 2 v. 21 cm. [BX9815.P37 1852] 33-1389
1. Unitarian—Addresses, essays, lectures. 2. Sermons, American. I. Title.

Unitarian Church of All Souls, New York.

KRING, Donald Walter. 288'.747'1
Liberals among the orthodox: Unitarian beginnings in New York City, 1819-1839. Boston, Beacon Press [1974] ix, 278 p. illus. 24 cm. Includes bibliographical references. [BX9833.6.N49K74] 73-21275 ISBN 0-8070-1662-4 12.50
1. Unitarian Church of All Souls, New York. 2. New York (City). Community Church. 3. Unitarian churches in New York (City) I. Title.

Unitarian churches.

GENERAL conference of 288.06273 Unitarian and other Christian churches.
Official report of the proceedings of the ... meeting. Boston [etc.] 18 v. 23 1/2 cm. The -23d reports. -1909, issued under the conference's earlier name: National conference of Unitarian and other Christian churches. Title varies: Report of the ... meeting. Official report of the proceedings of the ... meeting. [BX9805.A3] 44-23990
I. Title.

GENERAL conference of Unitarian and other Christian churches.
Official report of the proceedings of the ... meeting. Boston, v. 24 cm. ca 13
I. Title.

MCLACHLAN, Herbert, 1876- 287
The Methodist Unitarian movement, by H. McLachlan ... Manchester, The University press; London, New York [etc.] Longmans, Green & co., 1919. xi, 151 p. front., illus., vii pl. (incl. ports.) 19 cm. (Half-title: Publications of the University of Manchester. Historical series, no. XXXIII) On verso of t.-p.: Publications of the University of Manchester. no. CXXIII Bibliography: p. 141-144. [BX9834.M3] 20-7279
I. Title.

SERVICES of religion for 264.08 *special occasions for use in the churches of the free spirit.* Boston, The Beacon press, inc., 1938. ix, 85 p. 22 1/2 cm. Introduction signed: The Unitarian commission on hymns and services, H. W. Foote, chairman: The University commission on hymns and services, L. G. Williams, chairman. "Acknowledgments": p. vii-viii. [BX9853.S38] 38-14680
I. Unitarian churches. Liturgy and ritual. II. Universalist church. Liturgy and ritual. III. American Unitarian association. Board of directors. Commission on hymns and services. IV. Universalist general convention. Commission on hymns and services. V. Foote, Henry Wilder, 1875- VI. Williams, L. Griswold, 1893-

SERVICES of religion for 264.08 *use in the churches of the free spirit.* Boston, The Beacon press, inc., 1937. xxvi, 166 p. 22 1/2 cm. On cover: Hymns of the spirit with services. Includes music. Introduction signed: The Unitarian commission on hymns and services, H. W. Foote, chairman; The Universalist commission on hymns and services, L. G. Williams, chairman. With this is bound: Hymns of the spirit for use in the free churches of America. Boston, 1937. [BX9853.S4] [M2117.S485] 38-614
I. Unitarian churches. Liturgy and ritual. II. Universalist church. Liturgy and ritual. III. American Unitarian association. Board of directors. Commission on hymns and services. IV. Universalist general convention. Commission on hymns and services. V. Foote, Henry Wilder, 1875- VI. Williams, L. Griswold, 1898-

*UNITARIAN Church, 288.0977359 Bloomington, Illinois.
One hundred fifteen years of churchmanship (a history of Unitarianism in Bloomington-Normal) by members of the parish. Bloomington, Ill., Unitarian Church [1975] iv, 147 p. ill. 22 cm. Includes index. [BX9833.5] 6.00.
1. Unitarian churches. I. Title.
Available from publisher: 1613 E. Emerson St. 61701.

Unitarian churches—Addresses, essays, lectures.

BARTH, Joseph, 1906- 252.08
The art of staying sane. Foreword by Pierre Van Paassen. Freeport, N.Y., Books for Libraries Press [1970, c1948] viii, 192 p. 23 cm. (Essay index reprint series) Contents.Contents.—The art of staying sane.—How to lose your soul.—The God I believe in.—The fact of brotherhood.—The art of not dealing with evil.—The worst enemy of the better.—The dangers of being intelligent.—Why is mysticism?—Women in the new world to come.—Mr. Capital and Mrs. Labor.—That man, John L. Lewis.—America's most intolerant man.—Can democracy survive?—The end of the world.—The liberal looks at the cross.—When the atom bomb falls. [BX9843.B288A7 1970] 70-117757
1. Unitarian churches—Addresses, essays, lectures. I. Title.

BARTH, Joseph, 1906- 252.08
The art of staying sane; foreword by Pierre Van Paassen. Boston, Beacon Press, 1948. 192 p. 21 cm. [BX9843.B288A7] 48-1707
1. Unitarian churches—Addresses, essays, lectures. I. Title.
Contents omitted

CHRISTIANITY and modern 252. *thought.* Boston, American Unitarian associations, 1872. 5 p. l., [3]-304 p. 20 cm. "Discourses ... delivered in Boston at Hollistreet church ... during the winter of 1871-72."--Introd. Contents.Introduction.--Break between modern thought and sncient faith and worship. By H. W. Bellows.--A true theology the basis of human progress. By J.F. Clarke.--The rise and decline of the Romish church. By Athanase Coquerel, fils.--Selfhood and sacrifice. By Orville Dewey.--The relation of Jesus to the present age. By C.C. Everett.--The mythical element in the New Testament. By F.H. Hedge.--The place of mind in nature and intuition in man. By James Martineau.--The relations of ethics and theology. By A. P.]peabody-- Christianity: what it is not, and what is is. By G. V. Smith.--The aim and hope of Jesus. By Oliver Stearns. [BX9843.A1C5 1872] 16-7487
1. Unitarian church—Addresses, essays, lectures. I. American Unitarian association. II. Bellows, Henry Whitney, 1841-1882. III. Clarke, James Freeman, 1810-1888. IV. Coquerel, Athanase Josue, 1820-1875. V. Dewey, Orville, 1794-1882. VI. Everett, Charles Carroll, 1829-1900. VII. Hedge, Frederic Henry, 1805-1890. VIII. Martineau, James, 1805-1900. IX. Peabody, Andrew Preston, 1811-1893. X. Smith, George Vance, 1816?-1902.

ELIOT, Frederick May 288.081
Frederick May Eliot; an anthology; selected and edited by Alfred P. Stiernotte. With a memorial address by Wallace W. Robbins. Boston, Beacon Press [c.1959] xxxi, 300p. illus. (front.) 22cm. (bibl.: p.267-300) 59-134778 5.00
1. Unitarian churches—Addresses, essays, lectures. I. Title.

FRITCHMAN, Stephen Hole, 288 1902- ed.
Together we advance, edited by Stephen H. Fritchman. Boston, The Beacon press, 1946. ix, 209 p. plates, ports. 19 cm. Bibliographical foot-notes. Bibliography: p. 151, 207. [BX9813.F7] 47-933
1. Unitarian churches—Addresses, essays, lectures. 2. Liberalism (Religion) I. Title.
Contents omitted.

GENERAL conference of Unitarian and other Christian churches. Commission on theological education.
Report of the Commission on theological education to the General conference of Unitarian and other Christian churches, with correspondence. October, 1913. Boston, Press of G. H. Ellis co., 1913. 63 p. 24 cm. 15-600
I. Title.

HERFORD, Brooke, 1830-1903. 252.
The small end of great problems, by Brooke Herford ... New York, London [etc.] Longmans, Green, and co., 1902. 3 p. l., 306 p. front. (port.) 19 1/2 cm. [BX9843.H54S6] 2-12312
1. Unitarian churches—Addresses, essays, lectures. I. Title.

PARKER, Theodore, 1810-1860. 041
The American scholar, by Theodore Parker; ed. with notes by George Willis Cooke. Boston, American Unitarian association [c1907] vi p., 1 l., 534 p. 22 cm. [His Works. Centenary ed. v. 8] "Into this volume have been collected a number of Theodore Parker's more scholarly and critical essays."--Editor's pref. [BX9815.P3 1907 vol. 8] [AC8.P33] 204 7-39034
I. Cooke, George Willis, 1848-1923, ed. II. Title.
Contents omitted.

POWELL, Edward Payson, 230.8 1833-1915.
Liberty and life; discourses by E. P. Powell ... Chicago, C. H. Kerr & company, 1889. 208 p. 20 cm. [BX9843.P83L5] 33-17750
1. Unitarian church—Addresses, essays, lectures. I. Title.

Unitarian churches—Biography.

FRITCHMAN, Stephen 288'.0922 Hole, 1902-
Men of liberty; ten Unitarian pioneers. With illus. by Hendrik Willem Van Loon. Port Washington, N.Y., Kennikat Press [1968, c1944] xi, 180 p. illus. 21 cm. (Essay and general literature index reprint series) Contents.Contents.—Michael Servetus.—Faustus Socinus.—Francis David.—John Biddle.—Joseph Priestley.—Thomas Jefferson.—William Ellery Channing.—Ralph Waldo Emerson.—Theodore Parker.—Magnus Eiriksson. [BX9867.F7 1968] 68-15826
1. Unitarian churches—Biography. I. Title.

SCOTT, Clinton Lee 922.8173
These live tomorrow; twenty Unitarian Universalist biographies. Illus. by Robert MacLean. Boston, Beacon [1964] ix, 277p. ports. 21cm. 64-13537 price unreported
1. Unitarian Churches—Biog. 2. Universalist Church—Biog. I. Title.

WARE, William, 1797- 922.8173
1852, ed.
American Unitarian biography. Memoirs of individuals who have been distinguished by their writings, character, and efforts in the cause of liberal Christianity. Edited by William Ware ... Boston and Cambridge, J. Munroe and company; London, E. T. Whitfield, 1850-51. 2 v. front. (port.) 19 1/2 cm. [BX9867.W4] 37-9757
1. Unitarian churches—Biog. 2. Unitarian churches in the U.S.—Biog. I. Title.

Unitarian churches—Catechisms and creeds—English.

SAVAGE, Minot Judson, 1841- 238.8
1918.
Unitarian catechism, by M. J. Savage; with an introduction by E. A. Horton. Rev. ed. ... Boston, Press of G. H. Ellis, 1890. 67 p. 19 cm. "Books of reference": p. [65]-67. [BX9821.S3] 38-12924
1. Unitarian churches—Catechisms and creeds—English. I. Horton, Edward Augustus, 1843-1931, ed. II. Title.

Unitarian churches—Clergy—Biography.

FRITCHMAN, Stephen 288'.33'0924 B
Hole, 1902-
Heretic : a partisan autobiography / by Stephen H. Fritchman. [Boston] : Beacon Press, c1977. 362 p., [4] leaves of plates : ports. ; 22 cm. "A Skinner House book." Includes bibliographical references. [BX9869.F815A34] 77-70244 pbk. : 3.95
1. Fritchman, Stephen Hole, 1902- 2. Unitarian churches—Clergy—Biography. 3. Clergy—United States—Biography. I. Title.

Unitarian churches — Clergy — United States

CIRCUIT Riders.
A compilation of public records [of] 42 of the Unitarian clergymen and 450 rabbis. Cincinnati, 1961. 310 p. 22 cm. Cover title. 64-71948
1. Unitarian churches — Clergy — U.S. 2. Rabbis — U.S. 3. Clergy — U.S. I. Title.

Unitarian churches—Collected works.

CHANNING, William Ellery, 288
1780-1842.
Discourses, reviews, and miscellanies, by William Ellery Channing. Boston, Hilliard, Gray & co., 1834. ix, 603 p. 25 cm. [BX9815.C45 1834] 37-17870
1. Unitarian churches—Collected works. 2. Theology—Collected works—19th cent. I. Title.

CHANNING, William Ellery, 288
1780-1842.
Discourses, reviews, and miscellanies, by William Ellery Channing. Boston, Carter and Hendee, 1830. ix, 603 p. 26 cm. [BX9815.C45] 32-6508
1. Unitarian churches—Collected works. 2. Theology—Collected works—19th cent. I. Title.

CHANNING, William Ellery, 201'.1
1780-1842.
The works of William E. Channing. New York, B. Franklin [1970] iv, 931 p. 24 cm. (Burt Franklin research & source works series 626. American classics in history and social science 163) Reprint of the 1882 ed. [BX9815.C4 1970] 70-114815 ISBN 0-8337-0530-X
1. Unitarian churches—Collected works. 2. Theology—Collected works—19th century.

CHANNING, William Ellery, 208.
1780-1842.
The works of William E. Channing. 8th complete ed., with an introd. Boson, J. Munroe, 1848. 6 v. 20 cm. [BX9815.C4 1848] 48-40424
1. Unitarian churches—Collected works. 2. Theology—Collected works—19th cent. I. Title.

CHANNING, William Ellery, 208.1
1780-1842.
The works of William E. Channing, D. D. 1st complete American ed., with an introduction ... Boston, J. Munroe and company, 1841-43. 6 v. 21 cm. [BX9815.C4 1841] 33-1567
1. Unitarian church—Collected works. 2. Theology—Collected works—19th cent. I. Title.

CHANNING, William Ellery, 208.1
1780-1842.
The works of William E. Channing, D. D. 7th complete ed., with an introduction ... Boston, J. Munroe and company, 1847. 6 v. in 3. 21 cm. [BX9815.C4 1847] 33-1568
1. Unitarian church—Collected works. 2. Theology—Collected works—19th cent. I. Title.

CHANNING, William Ellery, 208.1
1780-1842.
The works of William E. Channing, D. D. 11th complete ed., with an introduction. Boston, G. G. Channing, 1849. 6 v. 20 cm. [BX9815.C4 1849] 33-1560
1. Unitarian churches—Collected works. 2. Theology—Collected works—19th cent. I. Title.

CHANNING, William Ellery, 208.1
1780-1842.
The works of William E. Channing, D. D. 16th complete ed. With an introduction ... Boston, Crosby, Nichols and company: New York, C. S. Francis & co., 1859. 6 v. 20 cm. [BX9815.C4 1859] 33-1570
1. Unitarian church—Collected works. 2. Theology—Collected works—19th cent. I. Title.

CHANNING, William Ellery, 208.1
1780-1842.
The works of William E. Channing, D. D. 17th complete ed. With an introduction ... Boston, American Unitarian association, 1867. 6 v. in 3. 20 cm. [BX9815.C4 1867] 33-1582
1. Unitarian churches—Collected works. 2. Theology—Collected works—19th cent. I. Title.

CHANNING, William Ellery, 208.1
1780-1842.
The works of William E. Channing, D. D., with an introduction. New and complete ed., rearranged Boston, American Unitarian association, 1875. iv, 931 p. 22 cm. [BX9815.C4 1875] 33-4127
1. Unitarian church—Collected works. 2. Theology—Collected works—16th cent. I. Title.

CHANNING, William Ellery, 208.
1780-1842.
The works of William E. Channing, D. D., with an introduction. New and complete ed. rearranged. To which is added, The perfect life. Boston, American Unitarian association, 1886. v, 1060 p. 22 cm. [BX9815.C4 1886] 6-31258
1. Unitarian church—Collected works. 2. Theology—Collected works—19th cent. I. Title.

CHANNING, William Ellery, 208.1
1780-1842.
The works of William E. Channing, D. D., with an introduction. New and complete edition, rearranged. To which is added The perfect life. Boston, American Unitarian association, 1888. v, 1060 p. 22 cm. "The perfect life, in twelve discourses ... edited ... by ... William Henry Channing":p. [925]-1020. [BX9815.C4 1888] 33-4126
1. Unitarian church—Collected works. 2. Theology—Collected works—19th cent. I. Channing, William Henry, 1810-1884, ed. II. Title. III. Title: The perfect life.

MARTINEAU, James, 1805- 208.1
1900.
Essays, reviews, and addresses. By James Martineau ... Selected and revised by the author ... London and New York, Longmans, Green and co., 1890-91. 4 v. 20 cm. Contents.I. Personal: political.--II. Ecclesiastical: historical.--III. Theological: philosophical.--IV. Academical: religious. [BX9815.M28] 35-32348
1. Unitarian church—Collected works. 2. Theology—Collected works—19th cent. I. Title.

MARTINEAU, James, 1805-1900. 204
Tides of the spirit; selections from the writings of James Martineau; edited, with an introduction, by Albert Lazenby. Boston, American Unitarian association, 1905. xxvi p., 2 l., 3-198 p. 20 cm. [BX9815.M32] 5-13046
1. Unitarian churches—Collected works. I. Lazenby, Albert, 1852- ed. II. American Unitarian association. III. Title.

PARKER, Theodore, 1810- 288.082
1860.
An anthology. Edited, with an introd. and notes, by Henry Steele Commager. Boston, Beacon Press [c.1960] viii, 391p. 22cm. 60-14677 6.00
1. Unitarian churches—Collected works. 2. Theology—Collected works—19th cent. I. Title.

WINN, Arthur Harmon, 1874- 230.8
1949.
Beyond yesterday: to the memory of Rev. Arthur Harmon Winn, A. M., his life and character, with selections from his works. Compiled and edited by Dorothy Q. Deley. [Peterborough? N. H., c1959] 251 p. illus. 23 cm. [BX9815.W52] 60-19255
1. Unitarian churches — Collected works. 2. Theology — Collected works — 20th cent. I. Daley, Dorothy Q., ed. II. Title.

Unitarian churches—Doctrinal and controversial works.

BANCROFT, Aaron, 1755-1839. 264
Sermons on those doctrines of the gospel, and on those constituent principles of the church, which Christian professors have made the subject of controversy. By Aaron Bancroft ... Worcester [Mass.] Printed by W. Manning & son, 1822. viii, [9]-10, [xi]-xvi, [17]-429, [1] p. 24 cm. [BX9841.B25] [AC901.W3 v.51, no. 1] 230. 36-33246
1. Unitarian churches—Doctrinal and controversial works. I. Title.

CARNES, Paul Nathaniel, 1921- 288
For freedom and belief; a manual for Unitarians. Boston, Beacon Press [1952] 71p. illus. 20cm. (Beacon reference series) [BX9842.C27] 53-6423
1. Unitarian churches —Doctrinal and controversial works. I. Title.

FROTHINGHAM, Octavius 230.
Brooks, 1822-1895.
The religion of humanity. By O. B. Frothingham. New York, D. G. Francis, 1873. 2 p. l., [7]-338 p. 18 cm. [BX9841.F77] 45-40609
1. Unitarian churches—Doctrinal and controversial works. I. Title.

GREELEY, Dana McLean, 288'.0924 B
1908-
25 Beacon Street, and other recollection. Boston, Beacon Press [1971] viii, 232 p. port. 21 cm. [BX9841.2.G73 1971] 78-136229 ISBN 0-8070-1666-7 10.00
1. Unitarian churches—Doctrinal and controversial works. I. Title.

MENDELSOHN, Jack, 1918- 230.8
Why I am a Unitarian. New York, Nelson [1960] 214 p. 21 cm. [BX9841.M55] 60-7294
1. Unitarian churches—Doctrinal and controversial works. I. Title.

MENDELSOHN, Jack, 1918- 288
Why I am a Unitarian Universalist. Boston, Beacon [1966, c.1964] 213p. 21cm. (BP209) First. pub. in 1960 under title: Why I am a Unitarian. 1.25 pap.,
1. Unitarian Churches—Doctrinal and controversial works. I. Title.

MENDELSOHN, Jack, 1918- 288
Why I am a Unitarian Universalist. New York, Nelson [1964] 213 p. 22 cm. First published in 1960 under title: Why I am a Unitarian. [BX9841.M55 1964] 64-25286
1. Unitarian Churches—Doctrinal and controversial works. I. Title.

PEABODY, Andrew Preston, 230.8
1811-1893.
Lectures on Christian doctrine. By Andrew P. Peabody ... 2d ed., with an introductory lecture on the Scriptures. Boston, J. Munroe and company, 1844. 2 p. l., 221 p. 20 cm. [BX9841.P4 1844 a] 38-38937
1. Unitarian churches—Doctrinal and controversial works. I. Title.

PEABODY, Andrew Preston, 230.8
1811-1893.
Lectures on Christian doctrine. By Andrew P. Peabody ... New ed., with an introductory lecture on the Scripture. Boston and Cambridge, J. Munroe and company, 1848. 227 p. 19 cm. [BX9841.P4 1848] 38-38936
1. Unitarian churches—Doctrinal and controversial works. I. Title.

PEABODY, Andrew Preston, 230.8
1811-1893.
Lectures on Christian doctrine. By Andrew P. Peabody ... New ed., with an introductory lecture on the Scriptures. Boston and Cambridge, J. Munroe and company, 1857. 263 p. 19 cm. [BX9841.P4 1857] 38-38935
1. Unitarian churches—Doctrinal and controversial works. I. Title.

SOMEN, Robert W 230.8
A Unitarian states his case. Boston, Beacon Press, 1949. vi, 149 p. 20 cm. [BX9841.S68] 50-1639
1. Unitarian churches—Doctrinal and controversial works. I. Title.

VERKUYL, Gerrit, 1872- 230.8
Reclaim those unitarian wastes, by Gerrit Verkuyl ... Grand Rapids, Mich., Zondervan publishing house, 1935. 158 p. 20 cm. [BX9847.V4] 36-13732
1. Unitarian churches—Doctrinal and controversial works. I. Title.

YATES, James, 1789-1871. 231
A vindication of Unitarianism, in reply to Mr. Wardlaw's Discourses on the Socinian controversy. By James Yates ... Boston, Wells and Lilly, 1816. iv, 294 p., 1 l., xxxv p. 23 cm. "Published ... from the Glasgow edition." [BT111.W23Y3] 44-21508
1. Wardlaw, Ralph, 1779-1853. Discourses on the principal points of the Socinian controversy. 2. Unitarian churches—Doctrinal and controversial works. I. Title.

Unitarian churches—Doctrinal and controversial works—Trinitatrian authors.

MOYSEY, Charles Abel, 1779- 230.8
1859.
The doctrines of Unitarians examined, as opposed to the Church of England. In eight sermons preached before the University of Oxford, in the year mdcccxviii, at the lecture founded by the late Rev. John Bampton ... By the Rev. C. A. Moysey ... Oxford, The University press for the author; [etc., etc.] 1818. vii, 248 p. 22 cm. Binder's title: Moysey's Bampton lectures. [1818] [BR45.B3 1818] 230.082 38-16064
1. Unitarian churches—Doctrinal and controversial works—Trinitatrian authors. I. Title.

Unitarian churches—History

WILBUR, Earl Morse, 1866- 288.09
A history of Unitarianism. Cambridge, Harvard University Press, 1945-52. 2v. 22cm. Contents.[1] Socinianism and its antecedents.--[2] In Transylvania, England, and America. Bibliographical footnotes. [BX9831.W49] A45
1. Unitarian churches—Hist. 2. Socinianism. I. Title.

WILBUR, Earl Morse, 1866- 288.09
A history of Unitarianism. Boston, Beacon Press [1965? c1945] 2 v. 22 cm. Reprint of work first published 1945-1952. Contents.Contents. -- [1] Socinianism and its antecedents. -- [2] In Transylvania, England, and America. Bibliographical footnotes. [BX9831.W492] 65-29746
1. Unitarian churches — Hist. 2. Socinianism. I. Title.

Unitarian churches—Hymns.

HYMNS of the spirit for use 783.0
in the free churches of America. Boston, The Beacon press, inc., 1937. xxi, [2], 581 p. 23 cm. [With Services of religion for use in the churches of the free spirit. Boston, 1937] With music. Preface signed: The Unitarian commission, H. W. Foote, chairman; The Universalist commission, L. G. Williams, chairman. [BX9858.S4] [M2117.S485] 38-613
1. Unitarian churches—Hymns. 2. Universalist church—Hymns. 3. Hymns, English. I. American Unitarian association. Board of directors. Commission on hymns and services. II. Universalist general

convention, Commission on hymns and services. III. Foote, Henry Wilder, 1875- IV. Williams, L. Griswold, 1893-

UNITARIAN church in Washington, D.C. 245.28
Hymns, selected from various authors, for the use of the Unitarian church in Washington ... Washington: Printed by W. Cooper. 1821. 104, [4] p. 15 cm. [With Tappan, William B. Songs of Judah, and other melodies. 1820] Without music. [PS2969.T6S6] 31-12883
1. Unitarian church—Hymns. 2. Hymns, English. I. Title.

Unitarian churches in New York (City)

KRING, Donald Walter. 288'.747'1
Liberals among the orthodox: Unitarian beginnings in New York City, 1819-1839. Boston, Beacon Press [1974] ix, 278 p. illus. 24 cm. Includes bibliographical references. [BX9833.6.N49K74] 73-21275 ISBN 0-8070-1662-4 12.50
1. Unitarian Church of All Souls, New York. 2. New York (City). Community Church. 3. Unitarian churches in New York (City) I. Title.

Unitarian churches in the United States.

[AMERICAN Unitarian association] 234.66
Services for congregational worship ... Boston, The Beacon press [c1914] 3 p. l., 81 p. 22 cm. With this in bound its New hymn and tune book (Boston [c1914]) [M2131.U5A6 1914] 81-13911
I. Title.

AMERICAN Unitarian association.
Services for congregational worship ... Boston, American Unitarian association [1914] 2 p. l., 81 p. 22 cm. 14-14931
I. Title.

LOWELL, Mass. First Unitarian society.
Semi-centennial anniversary of the South congregational society (Unitarian), in Lowell, Friday, Sept. 26, 1879. Lowell, Mass., Huse, Goodwin & co., 1880. 122 p., 1 l. 24 cm. 1-13618
I. Title.

WRIGHT, Conrad. 288'.73
The beginnings of Unitarianism in America / Conrad Wright. Hamden, Conn. : Archon Books, 1976, c1955. 305 p. : maps ; 23 cm. Reprint of the 1966 ed. published by Beacon Press, Boston. A revision of the author's thesis, Harvard University. Includes index. Bibliography: p. [292]-294. [BX9833.W7 1976] 76-20681 ISBN 0-208-01612-0 : 15.00
1. Unitarian churches in the United States. 2. Unitarianism—History. I. Title.

Unitarian churches in the United States—Addresses, essays, lectures.

A Stream of light : 288'.73
a sesquicentennial history of American Unitarianism / Conrad Wright, editor. 1st ed. Boston : Unitarian Universalist Association, 1975. xiv, 178 p. : ill. ; 23 cm. Includes bibliographical references and index. [BX9833.S74] 75-3875 6.00
1. Unitarian churches in the United States—Addresses, essays, lectures. 2. Unitarianism—History—Addresses, essays, lectures. I. Wright, Conrad.

Unitarian churches in the United States—Biography.

MCGIFFERT, Arthur Cushman, 1892- 288'.33'0924 B
Pilot of a liberal faith, Samuel Atkins Eliot, 1862-1950 / Arthur Cushman McGiffert, Jr. [Boston] : Beacon Press, 1976. 321 p. : ill. ; 23 cm. "A Skinner House book." Includes index. [BX9869.E37M28] 76-373984 12.95
1. Eliot, Samuel Atkins, 1862-1950. 2. Unitarian churches in the United States—Biography. I. Title.

Unitarian churches in the United States—Clergy.

SPRAGUE, William Buell, 1795-1876. 922.
Annals of the American Unitarian pulpit; or, Commemorative notices of distinguished clergymen of the Unitarian denomination in the United States, from its commencement to the close of the year eighteen hundred and fifty-five. With an historical introduction. By William B. Sprague, D.D. New York, R. Carter & brothers, 1865. xxv, 571, [2], 576-578 p. incl. front. (port.) 24 cm. Issued also as v. 8 of his Annals of the American pulpit. [BX9867.S6] 4-8087
1. Unitarian churches in the U.S.—Clergy. I. Title.

Unitarian churches in the United States—Hymns.

PEABODY, Andrew Preston, 1811-1893, comp.
Portsmouth Sunday school hymn book, comp. for the use of the South parish Sunday school, by their pastor, A. P. Peabody. Portsmouth [N. H.] J. W. Foster; Boston, Weeks, Jordon and company, 1840. viii, [142], [151]-165 p. 16 cm. The hymns are unpaged. "Scriptur: selections": p. [151]-165. [BV445.P4] 18-20574
1. Unitarian church in the U. S.—Hymns. 2. Hymns. I. Title.

Unitarian churches in Transylvania.

CORNISH, Louis Craig, comp.
Transylvania in 1922; report of the commission sent by the American and British Unitarian churches to Transylvania in 1922, comp. by Louis C. Cornish Boston, Mass., The Beacon press. inc., 1923. vi p., 1 l, 169 p. port. 21 cm. [BN9835.T8C6] 23-5841
1. Unitarian church in Transylvania. I. Title.

Unitarian churches—Juvenile literature.

ELGIN, Kathleen, 1923- 288
The Unitarians; the Unitarian Universalist Association. Written and illustrated by Kathleen Elgin. With a foreword by Constance H. Burgess. New York, McKay [1971] 95 p. illus. 26 cm. (The Freedom to worship series) Bibliography: p. 94. Introduces the principles of Unitarian beliefs and traces the career of Dorothea Dix, who was guided by these principles in her efforts to improve the condition of the mentally ill. [BX9841.2.E4] 75-165085 4.95
1. [Dix, Dorothea Lynde, 1802-1887.] 2. Unitarian churches—Juvenile literature. 3. [Unitarian churches.] I. Title.

Unitarian churches—Missions.

BARLETT, Laile E. 288
Bright galaxy; ten years of Unitarian fellowships. Boston, Beacon Press [1960] 255p. 21cm. [BV2595.U5B3] 60-5816
1. Unitarian churches—Missions. I. Title. II. Title: Unitarian fellowships.

BARTLETT, Laile E. 288
Bright galaxy; ten years of Unitarian fellowships. Boston, Beacon Press [c.1960] xv, 255p. 21cm. (bibl. footnotes) 60-5816 3.50
1. Unitarian churches—Missions. I. Title. II. Title: Unitarian fellowships.

Unitarian churches—Sermons.

ABBOT, John Emery, 1793-1819. 252.
Sermons, by the late Rev. John Emery Abbot, of Salem, Mass. With a memoir of his life, by Henry Ware, jr. Boston, Wait, Greene and co., 1829. xviii, [9]-329 p. 20 cm. [BX9843.A27S4] 7-39378
1. Unitarian churches—Sermons. 2. Sermons, American. I. Ware, Henry, 1794-1843. II. Title.

BRADLEE, Caleb Davis, 1831-1897.
Sermons for the church, by Caleb Davis Bradlee ... Boston, G. H. Ellis, 1893. 275 p. 21 cm. [BN9843.B7S45] 37-15962
1. Unitarian churches—Sermons. 2. Sermons, American. I. Title.

BROOKE, Stopford Augustus, 1832-1916. 252.
The gospel of joy, by Stopford A. Brooke. New York, Dodd, Mead and company, 1899. 4 p. l., 3-378 p. 19 cm. Twenty sermons, first published, 1898. [BX9843.B79G7] 4-12273
1. Unitarian churches—Sermons. 2. Sermons, English. I. Title.

BRUNDAGE, William Milton.
Some things for which the Unitarian church stands: sermons preached by Rev. William Milton Brundage ... Albany, N.Y., Gilliland bros., printers, 1895. 55 p. 23 cm. 4-32100
I. Title.

BUEHRER, Edwin T 252.08
The changing climate of religion; humanist sermon-essays, by Edwin T. Buehrer. [1st ed.] New York, Pageant Press [1965] 227 p. 21 cm. [BX9843.B98C5] 65-19370
1. Unitarian Churches — Sermons. 2. Sermons, America. I. Title.

CHANNING, William Ellery, 1780-1842. 252.
The perfect life. In twelve discourses. By William Ellery Channing, D.D. Edited from his manuscripts, by his nephew, William Henry Channing. Boston, Roberts brothers, 1873. xxi p., 1 l., 311 p. 19 cm. [BX9843.C4P4] 44-50997
1. Unitarian churches—Sermons. 2. Sermons, American. I. Channing, William Henry, 1810-1884, ed. II. Title.

CLARKE, James Freeman, 1810-1888. 252.08
Go up higher; or, Religion in common life, by James Freeman Clarke .. Boston, Lee & Shepard; New York, C. T. Dillingham, 1877. vi, 336 p. 18 cm. [BX9643.C6G6] 33-9894
1. Unitarian church—Sermons. 2. Sermons, American. I. Title.

CLARKE, James Freeman, 1810-1888. 252.08
Go up higher; or, Religion in common life, by James Freeman Clarke .. Boston, Lee & Shepard; New York, C. T. Dillingham, 1877. vi, 336 p. 18 cm. [BX9643.C6G6] 33-9894
1. Unitarian church—Sermons. 2. Sermons, American. I. Title.

CLARKE, John, 1755-1798. 252.08
Sermons, by the late Reverend John Clarke, D.D., minister of the First church in Boston, Massachusetts ... Boston: Printed by Samuel Hall, and sold at his book-store in Cornhill, July, 1799. viii, [9]-501, [3] p. front. (port.) 22 cm. "A short account of Doctor Clarke, by a late eminent, divine and author": p. [iv]-viii. [BX9643.C63S4] 36-25679
1. Unitarian churches—Sermons. 2. Sermons, American. I. Title.

DAVIES, Arthur Powell. 252.08
The faith of an unrepentant liberal, by A. Powell Davies. Boston, The Beacon press, 1946. ix, 122 p. 20 1/2 cm. [BX9843.D29F3] 46-4738
1. Unitarian churches—Sermons. 2. Sermons, America. I. Title.

DAVIES, Arthur Powell. 252.08
The temptation to be good; a book of unconventional sermons. New York, Farrar, Straus and Young [1952] 210 p. 22 cm. [BX9843.D29T4] 52-12565
1. Unitarian churches—Sermons. 2. Sermons, American. I. Title.

DIETRICH, John Hassler, 1878- 252.08
The humanist pulpit, a volume of addresses by John H. Dietrich .. Minneapolis The First Unitarian society [c1931]- v. 19 cm. Subtitle varies. "Contains series x- of the Humunist pulpit, which is a monthly publication." [BX9843D5H8 1931] [BX9843.D5H8 1931a] 32-6687
1. Unitarian church—Sermons. 2. Humaniam—20th cent. I. Title.

EMERSON, Ralph Waldo, 1803-1882. 252.08
Young Emerson speaks; unpublished discourses on many subjects. Edited by Arthur Cushman McGiffert, Jr. Port Washington, N.Y., Kennikat Press [1968, c1938] xxxix, 275 p. 23 cm. (Essay and general literature index reprint series) [BX9843.E487Y6 1968] 68-8237
1. Unitarian churches—Sermons. 2. Sermons, American. I. McGiffert, Arthur Cushman, 1892- ed. II. Title.

EMERSON, Ralph Waldo, 1803-1882. 252.08
Young Emerson speaks, unpublished discourses on many subjects, by Ralph Waldo Emerson: edited by Arthur Cushman McGiffert, jr. Boston, Houghton Mifflin company, 1938. xxxix, [1] p., 1 l., 275, [1] p. 21 cm. "Notes": p. [213]-[250]: "A list of the sermons": p. 263-[271] [BX9843.E487Y6] 38-9993
1. Unitarian churches—Sermons. 2. Sermons, American. I. McGiffert, Arthur Cushman, 1962- ed. II. Title.

FLECK, G. Peter, 1909- 252'.0833
The mask of religion / G. Peter Fleck. Buffalo, N.Y. : Prometheus Books, 1980. x, 204 p. ; 22 cm. Includes bibliographical references and index. [BX9843.F548M37] 19 79-9644 ISBN 0-87975-125-8 : 7.95
1. Unitarian churches—Sermons. 2. Sermons, American. I. Title.

GREELEY, Dana McLean, 1908- 252.08
Toward larger living, sermons on personal religion, by Dana McLean Greeley ... Boston, The Beacon press, 1944. v p., 1 l., [9]-102 p. 20 1/2 cm. [BX9843.G665TG] 44-51035
1. Unitarian churches—Sermons. 2. Sermons, American. I. Title.

HERFORD, Brooke, 1830-1903. 252.
Anchors of the soul, by Brooke Herford ... With a biographical sketch by Philip H. Wicksteed. Boston, American Unitarian association, 1905. 303 p. incl. front. (port.) 19 cm. Sermons. [BX9843.H54A5] 24-19743
1. Unitarian churches—Sermons. 2. Sermons, English. I. Wicksteed, Philip Henry, 1844-1927. II. American Unitarian association. III. Title.

JAYNES, Julian Clifford, 1854-1922. 252.
Magic wells; sermons, by Julian Clifford Jaynes. Boston, Press of Geo. H. Ellis co. (incorporated) 1922. 5 p. l., 3-303 p. front. (port.) 20 cm. [BX9843.J3M3] 22-20916
I. Title.

JONES, Jenkin Lloyd, 1843-1918. 252.
Love and loyalty [by] Jenkin Lloyd Jones ... Chicago, The University of Chicago press, 1907. xi, 454 p. 20 cm. Sermons. [BX9843.J6L6] 7-37980
1. Unitarian churches—Sermons. 2. Sermons, American. I. Title.

KING, Thomas Starr, 1824-1864. 252.
Christianity and humanity: a series of sermons, by Thomas Starr King. Edited, with a memoir, by Edwin P. Whipple. Boston, J. R. Osgood and company, 1877. lxxx, 380 p. incl. front. (port,) 18 cm. [BX9643.K4C5] 41-28176
1. Unitarian churches—Sermons. 2. Sermons, American. I. Whipple, Edwin Percy, 1819-1886, ed. II. Title.

LATHROP, John Howland, 1880- 252.08
Toward discovering a religion, by John Howland Lathrop. New York and London, Harper & brothers, 1936. 6 p. l., 3-108 p. 19 cm. "First edition." [BX9843.L365T6] 36-21048
1. Unitarian churches—Sermons. 2. Sermons, American. I. Title.

LATIMER, George Dimmick, 1856-1930.
Concerning life; sermons, by George Dimmick Latimer. Boston, American Unitarian association, 1907. 4 p. l., 190 p. 20 cm. [BX9843.L37C6] 7-15615
1. Unitarian churches—Sermons. 2. Sermons, American. I. Title.

MACKINNON, John G. 252.08'33
The MacKinnon years [by John G. MacKinnon] Indianapolis, Ind., All Souls Unitarian Church [1968] xii, 144 p. port. 24 cm. [BX9843.M23M3] 68-58353 4.95

1. Unitarian churches—Sermons. 2. Sermons, American. I. Title.

MARTINEAU, James, 1805-1900. 252.
Endeavors after the Christian life. Discourses by James Martineau ... New ed. Boston and Cambridge, J. Munroe and company, 1858. 3 p. l., [ix]-x p., 1 l., [25]-284 p.; ix p., 1 l., [285]-551 p. 19 1/2 cm. In two series, each with special half-title. [BX9843.M3E6 1853] 20-16419
1. Unitarian church—Sermons. 2. Sermons, English. I. Title.

MARTINEAU, James, 1805-1900. 252.
Endeavors after the Christian life. Discourses by James Martineau... Reprinted from the 6th English ed. Boston, American Unitarian association, 1881. xx, 449 p. 20 cm. [BX9843.M3E6 1881] 20-16417
1. Unitarian churches—Sermons. 2. Sermons, English I. Title.

MAYHEW, Jonathan, 1720- 252.08 1766.
Sermons: Seven sermons. A discourse, concerning the unlimited submission and non-resistance to the higher powers. The snare broken. New York, Arno Press, 1969. 162, 48, vii, 44 p. 23 cm. (Religion in America) Reprint of the author's works previously published separately between 1749 and 1766. [BX9843.M35S43 1969] 76-83429
1. Charles I, King of Great Britain. 2. Unitarian churches—Sermons. 3. Sermons, American. 4. Government, Resistance to. I. Mayhew, Jonathan, 1720-1766. Seven sermons. 1969. II. Mayhew, Jonathan, 1720-1766. A discourse, concerning the unlimited submission and non-resistance to the higher powers. 1969. III. Mayhew, Jonathan, 1720-1766. The snare broken. 1969. IV. Title: The snare broken.

MAYHEW, Jonathan, 1720-1766. 252.
Seven sermons upon the following subjects; viz. The difference betwixt truth and falshood, right and wrong. The natural abilities of men for discerning these differences. The right and duty of private judgment. Objections considered. The love of God. The love of our neighbour. The first and great commandment, &c. Preached at a lecture in the West meeting-house in Boston, begun the first Thursday in June, and ended the last Thursday in August, 1748. By Jonathan Mayhew... Boston, N.E., Printed and sold by Rogers and Fowle in Queen-street, MDCCXLIX. 2 p. l., 157 p. 20 cm. [BX9843.M35S5] 36-24573
1. Unitarian churches—Sermons. 2. Sermons, American. I. Title.

PALFREY, John Gorham, 1796- 252. 1881.
Sermons on duties belonging to some of the conditions and relations of private life. By John G. Palfrey... Boston, C. Bowen, 1834. 3 p. l., [v]-x, 368 p. 25 1/2 cm. [BX9843.P28S4] 42-26351
1. Unitarian—Sermons. 2. Sermons, American. I. Title.

PARK, Charles Edwards, 252.08 1873-
Creative faith. [Sermons] Foreword by Palfrey Perkins. Boston, Beacon Press [1951] 250 p. illus. 22 cm. [BX9843.P293C7] 52-6265
1. Unitarian churches — Sermons. 2. Sermons, American. I. Title.

PARKER, Theodore, 1810- 252.08 1860.
Sermons of theism, atheism, and the popular theology. By Theodore Parker ... Boston, Little, Brown and company, 1853. lxvi, 417 p. 20 cm. [BX9843.P3S5 1853] 33-409
1. Unitaran church—Sermons. 2. Sermons, American. 3. Theism. 4. Atheism. 5. Providence and government of God. I. Title.

PARKER, Theodore, 1810- 252.08 1860.
Sermons of theism, atheism, and the popular theology. By Theodore Parker ... 2d ed. Boston, Little, Brown and company, 1856. lxxv, 365 p. 21 cm. [BX9843.P3S5 1856] 33-412
1. Unitarian church—Sermons. 2. Sermons, American. 3. Theism. 4. Atheism. 5. Providence and government of God. I. Title.

PARKER, Theodore, 1810- 252.08 1860.
Sermons of theism, atheism, and the popular theology. By Theodore Parker ... 2d ed. Boston, R. Leighton, jr., 1859. lxxv, 365 p. 21 cm. [BX9843.P3S5 1859] 33-413
1. Unitarian church—Sermons. 2. Sermons, American. 3. Theism. 4. Atheism. 5. Providence and government of God. I. Title.

PARKER, Theodore, 1810- 252.08 1860.
Ten sermons of religion, by Theodore Parker ... Boston, Crosby, Nichols, and company; New York, C. S. Francis and company, 1853. vi p., 2 l., [3]-395 p. 20 cm. [BX9843.P3T5 1853] 33-15579
1. Unitarian church—Sermons. 2. Sermons, American. I. Title.

PARKER, Theodore, 1810- 252.08 1860.
Ten sermons of religion, by Theodore Parker ... 2d ed. Boston, R. Leighton, jr., 1859. vi p., 2 l., [3]-393 p. 21 cm. [BX9843.P3T5 1859] 33-414
1. Unitarian church—Sermons. 2. Sermons, American. I. Title.

PARKER, Theodore, 1810-1860. 204
The transient and permanent in Christianity, by Theodore Parker; edited with notes by George Willis Cooke. Boston, American Unitarian association [1908] 4 p. l., 482 p. 22 cm. [His Works. Centenary ed. v. 4] "A number of the earliest and latest, as well as several of the most significant, of Theodore Parker's sermons have been brought together in this volume."--Editor's pref. [BX9815.P3 1907 vol. 4] [BX9843.P3T7 1908] 252. 8-23268
1. Unitarian church—Sermons. 2. Sermons, American. I. Cooke, George Willis, 1848-1923, ed. II. Title.

PARKER, Theodore, 1810-1860. 252.
West Roxbury sermons, by Theodore Parker, 1837-1848, from unpublished manuscripts; with introduction and biographical sketch. Boston, American Unitarian association, 1902. xxiii, 235 p. 19 cm. Edited by Samuel J. Barrows. Biographical sketch by F. B. Sanborn. [BX9843.P3W5 1902] 3-32486
1. Unitarian churches—Sermons. I. Barrows, Samuel June, 1845-1909, ed. II. Sanborn, Franklin Benjamin, 1831-1917. III. Title.

PEABODY, Andrew Preston, 252. 1811-1893.
King's chapel sermons, by Andrew Preston Peabody ... Boston and New York, Houghton, Mifflin company, 1891. vi, 340 p. 20 cm. [BX9843.P5K5] 44-35816
1. Unitarian churches—Sermons. 2. Sermons, American. I. Title.

PEABODY, Andrew Preston, 252. 1811-1893.
Sermons connected with the re-opening of the church of the South parish, in Portsmouth, New Hampshire, preached Dec. 25 & 26, 1858; and Jan. 30 and Feb. 6, 1859, by Andrew P. Peabody ... Portsmouth, J. F. Shores, jun. [etc.]; Boston, Crosby, Nichols and company, 1859. 112 p. 18 cm. [BX9843.P6S57] 24-9333
1. Unitarian churches—Sermons. 2. Sermons, American. 3. Portsmouth, N. H. South church. I. Title.
Contents omitted.

PIERCE, Ulysses Grant Baker, 252. 1865-
Five sermons ... [by] Ulysses G. B. Pierce ... [Washington, D.C.] Publicity committee, All Souls church, 1924. cover-title, 67 p. 22 1/2 cm. [BX9843.P75F5] 42-2506
1. Unitarian churches—Sermons. 2. Sermons, American. I. Washington, D.C. All souls' church. Publicity committee. II. Title.
Contents omitted.

PIERCE, Ulysses Grant Baker, 252. 1865-
The religion of the Spirit; five sermons [by] Ulysses G. B. Pierce ... Washington, D.C., The Unitarian club, 1910 5 p. l., 13-96 p. 20 cm. [BX9843.P75R4] 10-8324

1. Unitarian churches—Sermons. 2. Sermons, American. I. Title.

RANKIN, David O., 1938- 252'.08
So great a cloud of witnesses / David O. Rankin. San Francisco : Strawberry Hill Press ; Harrisburg, Pa. : distributed by Stackpole Books, c1978. 192 p. : ill. ; 23 cm. Bibliography: p. 179-189. [BX9843.R26S6] 78-2584 ISBN 0-89407-014-2 pbk. : 6.95
1. Unitarian churches—Sermons. 2. Sermons, American. I. Title.

ROBBINS, Chandler, 1810- 922.8173 1882.
A discourse in commemoration of Rev. William Parsons Lunt, D. D., delivered at Quincy, Mass., on Sunday, June 7, 1857. By Chandler Robbins. Also, the last sermon preached by Mr. Lunt, December 28, 1856. With an appendix. Boston, Little, Brown and company, 1857. 71 p. 24 cm. [BX9869.L8R6] 37-10035
1. Lunt, William Parsons, 1805-1857. 2. Unitarian churches—Sermons. 3. Sermons, American. I. Title.

SAVAGE, Minot Judson, 1841- 233 1918.
Beliefs about man, by M. J. Savage ... Boston, G. H. Ellis, 1882. 5 p. l., 130 p. 19 1/2 cm. [BX9843.S3B4] 34-23401
1. Unitarian church—Sermons. 2. Sermons, American. I. Title.

SAVAGE, Minot Judson, 1841- 232.9 1918.
Jesus and modern life, by M. J. Savage. With an introduction by Professor Crawford H. Toy ... Boston, G. H. Ellis, 1893. 2 p. l., 229 p. 20 cm. A course of sermons. cf. Pref. [BS2415.S3] 38-11347
1. Jesus Christ—Teachings. 2. Unitarian churches—Sermons. 3. Sermons, American. I. Title.

SAVAGE, Minot Judson, 252.08 1841-1918.
Pillars of the temple, by Minot J. Savage ... Boston, American Unitarian association, 1908. 4 p. l., 3-226 p. 20 cm. [BX9843.S3P5 1908] 38-13597
1. Unitarian churches—Sermons. 2. Sermons, American I. Title.
Contents omitted.

SAVAGE, Minot Judson, 252.08 1841-1918.
Religion for to-day, by Minot J. Savage ... Boston, G. E. Ellis, 1900. 4 p. l., 250 p. 20 1/2 cm. First published in 1897. "Some of the sermons preached in the Church of the Messiah [New York city] during ... 1897."--Pref. [BX9843.S3R4] 4-10417
1. Unitarian churches—Sermons. I. Title.

SAVAGE, Minot Judson, 252.08 1841-1918.
The religious life, by M. J. Savage ... Boston, G. H. Ellis, 1885. 212 p. 20 1/2 cm. [BX9843.S3R42] 38-12457
1. Unitarian churches—Sermons. 2. Sermons, American I. Title.
Contents omitted.

SAVAGE, Minot Judson, 252.08 1841-1918.
... *Series on religious reconstruction* ... Boston, G. H. Ellis, 1887-88. 15 v. in 1. 19 1/2 cm. (Unity pulpit, Boston. Sermons of M. J. Savage, v. 9, no. 5-7, 10-12, 14, 17-20, 23-26) Published also under title: Religious reconstruction. [BX9841.S3 1887] 38-13606
1. Unitarian churches—Sermons. 2. Sermons, American. I. Title. II. Title: Religious reconstruction.
Contents omitted.

SEAWARD, Carl Albert. 252.08
Light on dark horizons; optimism of liberal Christianity. Boston, Beacon Press [1953] 152p. 22cm. [BX9843.S42L5] 53-7596
1. Unitarian churches—Sermons. 2. Sermons, American. 3. Liberalism (Religion) I. Title.

STEBBINS, Rufus Phineas, 922.8173 1810-1885.
Reverend Calvin Lincoln. Sermon preached in the old meeting-house, Hingham, Sunday, September 18, 1881, by Rev. Rufus P. Stebbins, D. D. Also services at the funeral, and sketch by a parishioner. Hingham [Mass.] The Parish, 1882. 66 p. front. (port.) 23 cm. [BX9869.L46S8] 37-13872
1. Lincoln, Calvin, 1799-1881. 2. Unitarian churches—Sermons. I. Title.

TUCKERMAN, Joseph, 1778- 252. 1840.
A memorial of Rev. Joseph Tuckerman. Worchester, Mass. [Private press of F. P. Rice] 1888. viii, 372 p. 19 1/2 cm. Consists of four parts, each with special t.-p. [BX9843.T8M4] 9-271
1. Unitarian churches—Sermons. 2. Sermons, American. I. Title.
Contents omitted.

UNITARIAN affirmations: 230.
seven discourses given in Washington, D.C., by Unitarian ministers. Boston, American Unitarian association, 1879. 3 p. l., 175 p. 15 1/2 cm. Contents.I. The universal and the special in Christianity. By Rev. Frederic H. Hedge, D.D.--II. The Bible. By Rev. James Freeman Clarke, D.D.--III. God. By Rev. Andrew P. Peabody, D.D.--IV. Jesus Christ. By Rev. Brooke Herford.--V. Man. By Rev. George W. Briggs, D.D.--VI. The church: the society which Jesus gathered. By Rev. Refus Ellis, D.D.--VII. The life eternal--Heaven and hell. By Rev. Samuel R. Calthrop. [BX9841.A1U5] 15-615
1. Unitarian churches—Sermons. I. Hedge, Frederic Henry, 1805-1890. II. Clarke, James Freeman, 1810-1888. III. Peabody, Andrew Preston, 1811-1893. IV. Herford, Brooke, 1830-1903. V. Briggs, George Ware, 1810-1895. VI. Ellis, Rufus, 1819-1885. VII. Calthrop, Samuel Robert, 1829-1917. VIII. American Unitarian association, pub.

WALKER, James, 1794-1874. 252.
Reason, faith, and duty. Sermons preached chiefly in the college chapel, by James Walker... Boston, Roberts brothers, 1877. xiii p., 1 l., 454 p. front. (port.) 18 1/2 cm. Introduction signed: W.O.W. [i.e. William Orne White] [BX9843.W24R4] 42-27033
1. Unitarian churches—Sermons. 2. Universities and colleges—Sermons. 3. Sermons, American. I. White, William Orne, 1821-1911, comp. II. Title.

WALKER, James, 1794-1874. 252.
Sermons preached chiefly in the college chapel. By James Walker... Two volumes in one: I. Reason, faith, and duty. (Published in 1876). II. Sermons, (Published in 1861.) Boston, American Unitarian association, 1890. 3 p. l., [v]-xiii p., 1 l., 454, v, 397 p. 19 1/2 cm. Each volume has also special t.-p. [BX9843.W24S33] 42-27033
1. Unitarian churches—Sermons. 2. Universities and colleges—Sermons. 3. Sermons, American. I. Title. II. Title: Reason, faith, and duty.

WALKER, James, 1794-1874. 252.
Sermons preached in the chapel of Harvard college. By James Walker, D.D. Boston, Ticknor and Fields, 1861. v, 397 p. 20 cm. [BX9843.W24S4] 42-27034
1. Unitarian churches—Sermons. 2. Universities and colleges—Sermons. 3. Sermons, American. I. Title.

WARE, Henry, 1794-1843. 282
Discourses on the offices and character of Jesus Christ. By Henry Ware, jr. ... Boston, Office of the Christian register, 1825. viii, [9]-217, [1] p. 20 1/2 cm. [BT250.W36] 35-31624
1. Jesus Christ—Person and offices. 2. Unitarian church—Sermons. 3. Sermons, American. I. Title.

WHITMAN, Bernard, 1796-1834. 252.
Village sermons; doctrinal and practical. By Bernard Whitman. Boston, L. C. Bowles, 1832. 202 p. 20 cm. [BX9843.W59V5] 44-50994
1. Unitarian churches—Sermons. 2. Sermons, American. I. Title.

WILSON, Lewis Gilbert, 1858- 252. 1928.
The uplifted hands and other sermons, by Lewis Gilbert Wilson ... [Hopedale, Mass.] The Women's alliance of the Hopedale memorial church [1903] 2 p. l., 136 p. front. (port.) 2 pl. 19 cm. [BX9843.W75U6] 24-13110
1. Unitarian churches—Sermons. 2. Sermons, American. I. Title.
Contents omitted.

Unitarian Sunday-school society.

HALL, Edward Henry, 1831-1912. 225.92
Lessons on the life of St. Paul, drawn from the Acts and the Epistles. By Edward H. Hall. Boston, Unitarian Sunday-School society, 1885. iv p., 1 l., [7]-114 p., 1 l., 17 1/2 cm. "References" at end of chapters. [BS2507.H3] [[922.1]] 39-11831
1. Paul, Saint, apostle—Study. 2. Unitarian Sunday-school society. I. Title.

Unitarian Universalist Association.

BARTLETT, Josiah R 288'.32
Moment of truth: our next four hundred years; an analysis of Unitarian Universalism [by] Josiah R. and Laile E. Bartlett. Berkeley, Calif. [1968] xv, 179 p. illus. 22 cm. Bibliography: p. 175-179. [BX9941.2.B3] 68-26626
1. Unitarian Universalist Association. I. Bartlett, Laile E., joint author. II. Title.

Unitarian Universalist Association—Doctrinal and controversial works—Statistics.

TAPP, Robert B. 230'.8'7
Religion among the Unitarian Universalists; converts in the stepfathers' house [by] Robert B. Tapp. New York, Seminar Press, 1973. xii, 268 p. 24 cm. (Quantitative studies in social relations) Bibliography: p. 257-259. [BX9841.2.T36 1973] 72-82127 ISBN 0-12-914650-1 10.00
1. Unitarian Universalist Association—Doctrinal and controversial works—Statistics. I. Title.

Unitarian Universalist Association—Handbooks, manuals, etc.

SCHOLEFIELD, Harry Barron, ed. 288.02
The Unitarian Universalist pocket guide. Boston Beacon [1963] 69p. 19cm. 63-18180 .50
1. Unitarian Universalist Association—Handbooks, manuals, etc. I. Title.

SCHOLEFIELD, Harry Barron, ed. 288.02
The Unitarian Universalist pocket guide. Boston, Beacon Press [1965] viii, 69 p. 19 cm. Bibliography: p. 63-68. [BX9841.2.S3 1965] 66-31585
1. Unitarian Universalist Association—Handbooks, manuals, etc. I. Title.

UNITARIAN Universalist Association. 288.73058
Directory. 1962-1963. Boston, 25 Beacon St. Author, [1963] 283p. 23cm. 62-5422 4.00; 3.00 pap., lib. ed.,
I. Title.

Unitarian Universalist Church, East Lansing, Mich.

THORNTON, Jerry. 288'.774'27
Ideas have consequences : 125 years of the liberal tradition in the Lansing area / by Jerry Thornton. [East Lansing, Mich. : Unitarian Universalist Church, 1973] 99 p. : ill. ; 28 cm. Imprint stamped on t.p. Bibliography: p. 96-97. [BX9861.E37U546] 75-303731
1. Unitarian Universalist Church, East Lansing, Mich. I. Title.

Unitarianism.

ALLEN, Joseph Henry, 1820-1898.
...An historical sketch of the Unitarian movement since the reformation. By Joseph Henry Allen ... New York, The Christian literature co., 1894. vi, 254 p. 21 cm. At head of title: American church history. Reprinted from v. 10 of American church history series. [BX9831.A4] 288 ISBN 31-25463
1. Unitarianism. I. Title. II. Title: American church history.

ALLEN, Joseph Henry, 1820-1898. 288.
Our liberal movement in theology, chiefly as shown in recollections of the history of Unitarianism in New England, being a closing course of lectures given in the Harvard divinity school by Joseph Henry Allen ... Boston, American Unitarian association [c1882] iv p., 1 l., 220 p. 19 cm. Memorial address of Rev. Frederic H. Hedge on Henry W. Bellows and Ralph Waldo Emerson: p. 208-218. [BX9833.A4 1882a] 28-20917
1. Unitarianism. I. Hedge, Frederic Henry, 1805-1899. II. Title.

AMERICAN Unitarian association. Commission of appraisal. 283
Unitarians face a new age; the report of the Commission of appraisal to the American Unitarian association. Boston, The Commission of appraisal of the American Unitarian association, 1936. x, 348 p. 24 cm. Frederick M. Eliot, chairman. H. P. Douglas, director of studies. [BX9632.A27] 36-9808
1. Unitarianism. I. Eliot, Frederick May, 1889- II. Douglas, Harian Paul, 1871- III. Title.

BARTOL, Cyrus Augustus, 1813-1900. 288
Discourses on the Christian spirit and life. New York, Arno Press, 1972 [c1850] vi, 408 p. 22 cm. (The Romantic tradition in American literature) [BX9843.B29D5 1972] 72-4951 ISBN 0-405-04622-7 20.00
1. Unitarianism. I. Title. II. Series.

BARTOL, Cyrus Augustus, 1813-1900. 252.
Discourses on the Christian spirit and life. By C. A. Bartol ... 2d ed., rev., with an introduction. Boston, W. Crosby and H. P. Nichols, 1850. vi, 408 p. 20 cm. [BX9843.B29D5 1850 a] 27-12007
1. Unitarianism. I. Title.

BURNAP, George Washington, 1802-1859. 230.
Lectures on the doctrines of Christianity, in controversy between Unitarians and other denominations of Christians. Delivered in the First independent church of Baltimore. By George W. Burnap ... Baltimore, W. R. Lucas & R. N. Wight, 1835. vii, [8]-394 p. 19 1/2 cm. [BX9841.B8] 27-12454
1. Unitarianism. I. Title.

BURNAP, George Washington, 1802-1859. 230.
Lectures on the doctrines of Christianity, in controversy between Unitarians and other denominations of Christians. Delivered in the First independent church of Baltimore. By George W. Burnap ... 2d ed. with additions. Boston and Cambridge, J. Munroe and company, 1848. viii, [13]-376 p. 20 cm. [BX9841.B8 1848] 27-12455
1. Unitarianism. I. Title.

CHADWICK, John White, 1840-1904. 288
Old and new Unitarian belief, by John White Chadwick ... Boston, G. H. Ellis, 1894. ix p., 1 l., 246 p. front. (port.) 22 cm. [BX9941.C45] 31-34946
1. Unitarianism. I. Title.

CHANNING, William Ellery, 1780-1842. 252.
Discourses, by William Ellery Channing. Boston, C. Bowen, 1832. viii, 279, [1] p. 21 cm. [BX9843.C4D5] 27-7857
1. Unitarianism. I. Title.
Contents omitted.

CHANNING, William Ellery, 1780-1842. 252.
Unitarian Christianity, a discourse on some of the distinguishing opinions of Unitarians, delivered at Baltimore, May 5, 1819 [by] William Ellery Channing. Centenary ed. Boston. Mass., American Unitarian association [1919] 1 p. l., 5-81 p. 19 cm. Introduction signed: E. M. W. [BX9843.C5S55 1919] 21-17181
1. Sparks, Jared, 1789-1866. 2. Unitarianism. I. W., E. M., ed. II. E. M. W., ed. III. Title.

CHANNING, William Ellery, 1780-1842. 288
Unitarian Christianity and other essays. Edited, with an introd. by Irving H. Bartlett. New York, Liberal Arts Press [1957] xxxii, 121 p. 21 cm. (The American heritage series, no. 21) Bibliography: p. xxxi. [BX9843.C5U5] 57-14626
1. Unitarianism. I. Title.

CLARKE, James Freeman, 1810-1888. 230.
Manual of Unitarian belief, by James Freeman Clarke. Boston, Unitarian Sunday-school society, 1884. 64 p. 18 cm. "The questions on each lessons have been prepared by Mrs. Kate Gannett Wells." cf. Pref. [BX9841.C6 1884] 24-25202
1. Unitarianism. I. Wells, Mrs. Catherine Boott (Gannett) 1813-1911. II. Title.

CLARKE, James Freeman, 1810-1888. 230.
Manual of Unitarian belief, by James Freeman Clarke ... 20th ed., rev. and published with a new list of references. Boston, The Beacon press, inc., 1924. v, 103 p. 19 cm. "References" at end of each chapter. "Questions originally prepared by Mrs. Kate Gannett Wells and now somewhat revised, are added at the close of each lesson ... The text has been ... revised by Rev. Charles T. Billings."-- Pref. [BX9841.C6 1924] 24-25201
1. Unitarianism. I. Wells, Mrs. Catherine Boott (Gannett) 1838-1911. II. Billings, Charles Towne, ed. III. Title.

CLARKE, James Freeman, 1810-1888. 230.8
Orthodoxy: its truths and errors. By James Freeman Clarke ... Boston, American Unitarian assocation; New York, J. Miller, 1866. xi, 512 p. 19 1/2 cm. "Second edition.". [BX9841.C63 1866a] 33-6285
1. Unitarianism. I. American Unitarian assocation. II. Title.

CLARKE, James Freeman, 1810-1888. 230.8
Orthodoxy: its truths and errors. By James Freeman Clarke ... 15th ed. Boston, American Unitarian association, 1884. xi, 512 p. 19 1/2 cm. [BX9641.C63] 33-32120
1. Unitarianism. I. American Unitarian association. II. Title.

CLELAND, Thomas, 1778-1858.
Unitarianism unmasked: its anti-Christian features displayed: its infidel tendency exhibited; and its foundation shewn to be untenable; in a reply to Mr. Barton W. Stone's Letters to the Rev. Dr. Blythe. By Thomas Cleland ... Lexington, Ky,. Printed by T. T. Skillman, 1825. 184 p. 17 cm. 5-41195
I. Title.

COOKE, George Willis, 1848-1923. 288'.73
Unitarianism in America. [1st AMS ed.] Boston, American Unitarian Association, 1902. [New York, AMS Press, 1971] xi, 463 p. illus., ports. 22 cm. Includes bibliographical references. [BX9833.C7 1971] 72-155153 ISBN 0-404-01699-5
1. Unitarianism. I. Title.

COOKE, George Willis, 1848-1923. 288'.73
Unitarianism in America; a history of its origin and development. Boston, American Unitarian Association, 1902. St. Clair Shores, Mich., Scholarly Press [1969?] xi, 463 p. illus., ports. 22 cm. Bibliographical footnotes. [BX9833.C7 1969] 77-8815
1. Unitarianism. I. Title.

COOKE, George Willis, 1848-1923. 288.
Unitarianism in America; a history of its origin and development, by George Willis Cooke ... Boston, American Unitarian association, 1902. xi, 463 p. front., plates. ports. 22 cm. [BX9833.C7] 3-605
1. Unitarianism. I. Title.

CROMPTON, Arnold. 288.79
Unitarianism on the Pacific coast: the first sixty years. Boston, Beacon Press [1957] 182 p. 22 cm.sUnitarian churches in the Pacific States. [BX9833.46.C7] 57-6638
I. Title.

DEWEY, Orville, 1794-1882. 230.
Discourses and discussions in explanation and defence of Unitarianism. By Orville Dewey ... Boston, J. Dowe, 1840. 1 p. l., [vii]-x p., 1 l., [13]-307 p. 20 cm. [BX9841.D4] 27-11390
1. Unitarianism. I. Title.

ELIOT, Samuel Atkins, 1862-ed. 922.
Heralds of a liberal faith; ed. with an introduction by Samuel A. Eliot. Boston, American Unitarian association, 1910. 3 v. 23 cm. Contents.i. The prophets.--ii. The pioneers.--iii. The preachers. Biographical sketches of Unitarian ministers, 1750-1900. [BX9867.E4] A 11
1. Unitarianism. I. Title.

ELIOT, Samuel Atkins, 1862-1950, ed. 288'.0922
Heralds of a liberal faith. Boston, American Unitarian Association, 1910-[52] 4 v. 23 cm. Vol. 4 has imprint: Boston, Beacon Press. Contents.1. The prophets.--2. The pioneers.--3. The preachers.--4.The pilots. [BX9867.E4] A 11
1. Unitarianism. I. Title.

ELIOT, William Greenleaf, 1811-1887. 230.
Discourses on the doctines of Christianity. By William G. Eliot... 22nd thousand. Boston, American Unitarian association, 1881. 108 p. 19 1/2 cm. [BX9841.E4 1861] 16-3280
1. Unitarianism. I. Title.

ELIOT, William Greenleaf, 1811-1887. 230.3
Discourses on the doctrines of Chrisitanity. By William G. Eliot... 13th thousand. Boston, Walker, Wise, & company, 1865. 168 p. 20 cm. [BX9841.E4 1865] 36-28616
1. Unitarianism. I. Title.

ELIOT, William Greenleaf, 1811-1887. 230.
Discourses on the doctrines of Christianity. By William G. Eliot... 13th thousand. Boston, Walker, Wise, and company, 1860. 3 p. l., [5]-168 p. 20 cm. [BX9841.E4 1860] 24-19953
1. Unitarianism. I. Title.

ELIOT, William Greenleaf, 1811-1887. 230.
Discourses on the doctrines of Christianity. By William G. Eliot... 22d thousand. Boston, American Unitarian association, 1882. 168 p. 19 1/2 cm. [BX9841.E4 1882] 16-3281
1. Unitarianism. I. Title.

ELLIS, George Edward, 1814-1894. 288
A half-century of the Unitarian controversy, with particular reference to its origin, its course, and its prominent subjects among the Congregationalists of Massachusetts. With and appendix. By George E. Ellis. Boston, Crosby, Nichols, and company, 1857. xxiv, 511 p. 22 1/2 cm. [BX9841.E5] 33-22268
1. Unitarianism. I. Title.

EMERTON, Ephraim, 1851- 230.
Unitarian thought, by Ephraim Emerton... New York, The Macmillan company, 1911. ix, 309 p. 19 1/2 cm. [BX9841.E6] 11-1127 1.50
1. Unitarianism. I. Title.

EMERTON, Ephraim, 1851- 230.8
Unitarian thought, by Ephraim Emerton... New York, The Macmillan company, 1916. ix, 309 p. 19 1/2 cm. [BX9841.E6 1916] 33-18558
1. Unitarianism. I. Title.

EMLYN, Thomas, 1663-1741. 232
An humble inquiry into the Scripture-account of Jesus Christ: or, A short argument concerning his deity and glory, according to the gospel. By the late Reverend, learned and pious Mr. Thomas Emlyn ... The 5th ed. Now re-published, with a dedication to the reverend ministers of all denominations in New-England; by a layman. Boston: Printed and sold by Edes & Gill, at their office next to the prison in Queen-street, 1756. xi, [1], 13-56 p. 21 1/2 cm. [BT200.E5 1756] 45-41152
1. Jesus Christ—Divinity—Early works to 1800. 2. Unitarianism. I. Title.

FARLEY, Frederick Augustus. 230.8
Unitarianism defined. The Scripture doctrine of the Father, Son and Holy Ghost. A course of lectures, by Frederick A. Farley. Boston, Walker, Wise & company, 1860. viii, [9]-272 p. 20 cm. [BX9841.F3 1860] 33-32108
1. Unitarianism. I. Title.

FARLEY, Frederick Augustus. 230.8
Unitarianism defined. The Scripture doctrine of the Father, Son and Holy Ghost. A course of lectures, by Frederick A. Farley ... Boston, American Unitarian

association, 1873. viii, [9]-272 p. 20 cm. [BX9841.F3 1873] 16-3273
1. Unitarianism. I. American Unitarian association. II. Title.

FRITCHMAN, Stephen Hole, 1902- 288
Unitarianism today; an eloquent protest against the forces of authority that demand blind conformity, an eloquent defense of free men who deviate from orthodoxies. Boston, American Unitarian Association, 1950. 58 p. 22 cm. "A 125th anniversary publication." "Represents, with minor editorial changes, the substance of thirteen radio talks on Unitarianism dellvered by the author over station KGFJ. Hollywood, California, from December, 1949, to February, 1950." [BX9841.F75] 50-13986
1. Unitarianism. I. Title.

GORDON, Ernest Barron, 1867- 230.
The leaven of the Sadducees; or, Old and new apostasies, by Ernest Gordon ... Chicago, The Bible institute colportage ass'sn [c1926] 268 p. 21 cm. "References" at end of each chapter. [BX9847.G6] 26-11753
1. Unitarianism. I. Title.

GRIFFIN, Richard Andrew, 1844-1909. 9228173
From traditional to rational faith; or, The way I came from Baptist to liberal Christianity. By R. Andrew Griffin. Boston, Roberts brothers, 1877. 6 p., 2 l., [9]-219 p. 18 cm. (Half-title: Town and country series) [BX9869.G83A3] 37-15491
1. Unitarianism. I. Title. II. Title: The way I came from Baptist to liberal Christianity.

HEDGE, Frederic Henry, 1805-1890. 288
Reason in religion. By Frederic Henry Hedge ... Boston, Walker, Fuller and company, 1865. iv; 458 p. 20 cm. [BX9641.H4 1865] 82-
1. Unitarianism. 2. Theism. 3. Rationalism. I. Title.
Contents omitted.

HEDGE, Frederic Henry, 1805-1890. 288
Reason in religion. By Frederic Henry Hedge ... Boston, W. V. Spencer, 1867. iv, 458 p. 19 1/2 cm. Fourth edition. [BX9841.H4 1867] 32-1020
1. Unitarianism. 2. Theism. 3. Rationalism. I. Title.
Contents omitted.

HOPKINS, Jeannette. 288
Fourteen journeys to Unitarianism; statements of religious belief prepared from personal interviews. Boston, Beacon Press [1955, c1954] 77p. 19cm. [BX9842.H78] 54-12456
1. Unitarianism. I. Title.

[HYER, G. W.] 230.
How I became a Unitarian: explained in a series of letters to a friend. By a clergyman of the Protestant Episcopal church. Boston, Crosby, Nichols, and company; New York, C. S. Francis and company 1852. 216 p. 20 cm. [BX9841.H9] 47-34164
1. Unitarianism. I. Title.

JORDAN, David Starr, 1851-
The higher sacrifice, by David Starr Jordan ... Boston, American Unitarian association, 1908. 4 p. l., [7]-54 p. 20 cm. [PS2152.J4H5] 8-23287
I. Title.

JOSLIN, James Thomas, 1834-1913.
Historical address delivered at the dedication of the remodelled church of the First Unitarian society, Hudson; Massachusetts on December nineteenth, nineteen hundred one, by James T. Joslin ... with which are included the portraits of the ministers: et cetera. Hudson, Designed and executed by E. Worcester at his print shop [1902?] 56 p. illus., plates, ports. 23 cm. "This book is n 14 of an edition limited to seventy-five copies."--On slip mounted in front. 17-8259
I. Title.

JOSLIN, James Thomas, 1834-1913.
Historical address delivered at the dedication of the remodelled church of the First Unitarian society, Hudson; Massachusetts on December nineteenth, nineteen hundred one, by James T. Joslin ... with which are included the portraits of the ministers: et cetera. Hudson, Designed and executed by E. Worcester at his print shop [1902?] 56 p. illus., plates, ports. 23 cm. "This book is n 14 of an edition limited to seventy-five copies."--On slip mounted in front. 17-8259
I. Title.

KOHLMANN, Anthony, 1771-1836.
Unitarianism philosophically and theologically examined: in a series of periodical numbers; comprising a complete refutation of the leading principles of the Unitarian system ... By the Rev. Anthony Kohlmann ... 3d ed. Washington city, H. Guegan, 1821-22. 2 v. 24 cm. Vol. 2 of 1st edition. [BX984.K7 1821 b] 25-23335
1. Jesus Christ—Divinity. 2. Unitarianism. I. Title.

MARSHALL, George N. 288'.32
Challenge of a liberal faith / George N. Marshall. Rev., updated, and enl. New Canaan, Conn. : Keats Pub., c1980. 271 p. ; 18 cm. (A Pivot paperback) Includes indexes. Bibliography: p. 242-247. [BX9841.2.M28 1980] 19 79-92445 ISBN 0-87983-214-2 (pbk.) : 1.95
1. Unitarianism. 2. Universalism. 3. Liberalism (Religion) I. Title.

MARTINEAU, James, 1805-1900.
Selections; compiled by Alfred Hall. Boston, Beacon Press, 1951. 192p. port. 19cm. 'List of references': p. xii. A53
I. Title.

MAYHEW, Jonathan, 1720-1766. 252.
Two sermons on the nature, extent and perfection of the Divine goodness. Delivered December 9, 1762., being the annual Thanksgiving of the province, &c., on Psalm 145. 9. Published with some enlargements. By Jonathan Mayhew, D. D., pastor of the West church in Boston. Boston: N.E., Printed and Sold by D. and J. Kneeland, opposite to the Probate-Office, in Queen-street, 1763. 91 p. 20 1/2 cm. [BX9843.M35T85] 6-26374
I. Title.

MONDALE, Robert Lester, 1904- 288
The Unitarian way of life, by R. Lester Mondale. Published by vote of the Trustees and of the congregation of All souls Unitarain church. Kansas City, Mo. [Westport printing co., c1943] 4 p. l., 113 p. 20 1/2 cm. [BX9841.M7] 44-10098
1. Unitarianism. I. Kansas City, Mo. All souls Unitarian church. II. Title.

NORTON, Andrews, 1786-1853. 230.
A statement for reasons for not believing the doctrines of Trinitarians, concerning the nature of God and the person of Christ. By Andrews Norton. 7th ed., with additions, and a biographical notice of the author. Boston, American Unitarian association, 1874. i, 499 p. 20 cm. "Biographical notice of Mr. Norton, by the Rev. William Newell": p. [ix]-i. [BX9841.N7 1874] 17-28559
1. Unitarianism. 2. Trinity. I. Newell, William, 1804-1881. II. Title.

NORTON, Andrews, 1786-1853. 230.
A statement of reasons for not believing the doctrines ofTrinitarians, concerning the nature of God and the person of Christ. ByAndrews Norton. 12th ed. With additions, and a biographical notice ofthe author. Boston, American Unitarian association, 1880. i, 499 p. 20 cm. Biographical notice by Rev. William Newell: p. ix-i. [BX9841.N7 1880] 26-24376
1. Unitarianism. 2. Trinity. I. Newell, William, 1804-1881. II. Title.

PARKE, David B., ed. 288
The epic of Unitarianism; original writings from the history of liberal religion. Boston, Beacon Press [1960, c.1957] xii, 164p. 21cm. (Beacon ser. in liberal religion, LR 6) (Bibl.: p.155-157) 1.45 pap.,
1. Unitarianism. I. Title.

PARKE, David B ed. 288
The epic of Unitarianism; original writings from the history of liberal religion. Boston, Starr King Press [1957] 164p. 22cm. [BX9813.P3] 57-7797
1. Unitarianism. I. Title.

PARKER, Theodore, 1810-1860. 230'.8
A discourse of matters pertaining to religion. New York, Arno Press, 1972 [c1842] vii, 504 p. 22 cm. (The Romantic tradition in American literature) [BX9841.P3 1972] 72-4968 ISBN 0-405-04639-1 24.00
1. Unitarianism. 2. Religion. 3. Christianity. I. Title. II. Series.

PARKER, Theodore, 1810-1860. 230.8
A discourse of matters pertaining to religion, By Theodore Parker ... Boston, C. C. Little and J. Brown, 1842. vii, 504 p. 24 cm. "The substances of a series of five lectures delivered in Boston during the last autumn."--Pref., dated May, 1842. [BX9841.P3 1842] 33-416
1. Unitarianism. 2. Religion. 3. Christianity. I. Title.

PARKER, Theodore, 1810-1860. 230.8
A discourse of matters pertaining to religion, by Theodore Parker ... 3d ed. Boston, C. C. Little and J. Brown, 1847. xi, [3], [3]-472 p. 20 cm. "The substance of a series of lectures delivered in Boston, during the last autumn."--Pref. to the 1st ed. dated May 1842. [BX9841.P3 1847] 33-1388
1. Unitarianism. 2. Religion. 3. Christianity. I. Title.

PARKER, Theodore, 1810-1860. 230.8
A discourse of matters pertaining to religion. By Theodore Parker ... 4th ed. Boston, Little, Brown and company, 1856. xi, 466 p. 21 cm. "The substance of a series of five lectures delivered in Boston, during the last autumn."--Pref. to 1st ed., dated May, 1842. [BX9841.P3 1856] 33-411
1. Unitarianism. 2. Religion. 3. Christianity. I. Title.

A Pocket guide to Unitarianism. Edited by Harry B. Scholefield. Boston, Beacon Press [c1954, 1956] 70p. illus. 19cm.
1. Unitarianism. I. Scholefield, Harry B., ed.

RAMANOHANA Raya raja, 1774-1833. 232.
The precepts of Jesus, the guide to peace and happiness, extracted from the books of the New Testament ascribed to the four evangelists. To which are added, the first and second appeal to the Christian public, in reply to the observations of Dr. Marshman ... By Rammohun Roy ... From the London ed. New-York, B. Bates, 1825. xix, 318 p. front. (port.) 22 cm. "The precepts of Jesus", "An appeal to the Christian public" and "Second appeal" have each special t.-p. [BT306.R63 1825] 39-3981
1. Jesus Christ—Words. 2. Unitarianism. I. Marshman, Joshua, 1768-1837. II. Title. III. Title: An appeal to the Christian public. IV. Title: Second appeal to the Christian public.

RECCORD, Augustus P. 230.
Who are the Unitarians? by Augustus P. Reccord; eight sermons delivered at the request of and published by the Board of trustees of the First Unitarian church of Detroit, Michigan. Boston, Mass., The Beacon press [c1920] 5 p. l., 134 p. 18 cm. [BX9841.R35] 20-20020
1. Unitarianism. I. Title.

RECCORD, Augustus Phineas, 1870- 230.
Who are the Unitarians! by Augustus P. Reccord; eight sermons delivered at the request of and published by the Board of trustees of the First Unitarian church of Detroit, Michigan. Boston, Mass., The Beacon press [c1920] 5 p. l., 134 p. 18 cm. [BX9841.R35] 20-20020
1. Unitarianism. I. Title.

SAVAGE, Minot Judson, 1841-1918. 230.8
My creed, by M. J. Savage. Boston, G. H. Ellis, 1887. 204 p. 20 1/2 cm. [BX9841.S24] 33-22236
1. Unitarianism. I. Title.

SECRIST, Henry T.
... Comparative studies in religion, an introduction to Unitarianism, by Henry T. Secrist. Boston, Chicago, Unitarian Sunday-school society [c1909] 3 p. l., 72 p., 1 l., 46 p. 21 cm. (The Beacon series, a graded course of study for the Sunday School) On cover: Teachers' edition with helper. 9-27110 0.65
I. Title.

SLICER, Thomas Roberts, 1847-1916. 230.
The great affirmations of religion; an introduction to real religion, not for beginners but for beginners again, by Thomas R. Slicer. Boston and New York, Houghton, Mifflin and company, 1898. ix p., 2 l., 273, [1] p. 19 1/2 cm. [BX9841.S6] 98-2307
1. Unitarianism. 2. Unitarian churches—Sermons. 3. Sermons, American. I. Title.

SLICER, Thomas Roberts, 1847-1916. 252.08
The great affirmations of religion; an introduction to real religion not for beginners but for beginners again, by Thomas R. Slicer. Boston, American Unitarian association [1911?] ix p., 1 l., 248 p. 19 1/2 cm. "Preached in the course of my work as the minister of the church of All souls, and...reported as spoken."--Pref. [BX9841.S62] 34-14476
1. Unitarianism. 2. Unitarian church—Sermons. 3. Sermons, American. I. Title.

SLICER, Thomas Roberts, 1847-1916. 230.
One world at a time; a contribution to the incentives of life, by Thomas R. Slicer... New York & London, G. P. Putnam's sons, 1902. ix, 269 p. 21 1/2 cm. [BX9841.S65] 2-8359
1. Unitarianism. I. Title.
Contents omitted.

SPRING, Samuel, 1746-1819. 232.8
Two discourses on Christ's self existence, addressed to the Second Congregational society in Newburyport, March 3, 1805. By Samuel Spring. Newburyport: Printed by Edmund M. Blunt: for sale at the bookstore of Thomas & Whipple, Market-square. 1805. 59 p. 20 cm. [BT215.S77] [AC901.W3 vol. 143, no. 9] 37-25869
1. Jesus Christ—Divinity—Sermons. 2. Unitarianism. 3. Congregational churches—Sermons. 4. Sermons, American. I. Title.

STEWART, Samuel J 230.
The gospel of law; a series of discourses upon fundamental church doctrines. Boston, G. H. Ellis, 1882. 326 p. 20 cm. [BX9841.S8] 52-48637
1. Unitarianism. I. Title.

STUART, Moses, 1780-1852. 264
Letters to the Rev. Wm. E. Channing, containing remarks on his sermon, recently preached and published at Baltimore. By Moses Stuart, associate professor of sacred literature in the Theological seminary, Andover. Andover: Published by Flagg and Gould. 1819. 167 p. 21 1/2 cm. [BX9847.S8 1819 a] [AC901.T5 vol. 61] 28-14340
1. Unitarianism. I. Channing, William Ellery, 1780-1842. A sermon at the ordination of Jared Sparks. II. Title.

STUART, Moses, 1780-1852. 264
Letters to the Rev. Wm. E. Channing, containing remarks on his sermon, recently preached and published at Baltimore. By Moses Stuart ... 2d ed. cor. and enl. Andover: Flagg and Gould, 1819. 180 p. 22 cm. [Wolcott pamphlets, v. 82] [AC901.W7 vol. 82] 28-9940
1. Channing, William Ellery, 1780-1842. A sermon at the ordination of Jared Sparks. 2. Unitarianism. I. Title.

STUART, Moses, 1780-1852. 230.
Letters to the Rev. Wm. E. Channing, containing remarks on his sermon recently preached and published at Baltimore. By Moses Stuart. 3d ed. cor. and enl. from the 2d. Andover: Published by Flagg and Gould. 1819. vi, [7]-156 p. 21 1/2 cm. [BX9847.S8 1819 b] 28-9939
1. Channing, William Ellery, 1780-1842. A sermon at the ordination of Jared Sparks. 2. Unitarianism. I. Title.

SULLIVAN, William Laurence, 1872-1935 282.0924
Under orders; the autobiography of William Laurence Sullivan. Boston, Beacon [1966, c1944] 200p. port. 21cm. Bibl. [BX9869.S8A3 1966] 66-23781 4.50 bds.,
I. Title.

SULLIVAN, William Laurence, 1872-1935. 922.8173
Under orders; the autobiography of William Laurence Sullivan ... New York, R. R. Smith, 1944. viii p., 2 l., [13]-200 p. ports. 22 1/2 cm. Bibliographical references included in "addenda" (p. 171-197) [BX9869.S8A3] 44-41899
I. Title.

TRACTS on the Unitarian controversy, published in 1815 ... Boston: Sold by Wells & Lilly, no. 97 Court street, 1816. 1 p. l., [520] p. 22 1/2 cm. Each pamphlet is paged separately. [BX9613.T8] 1-11916
1. Unitarianism. I. Belsham, Thomas, 1750-1829. II. Channing, William Ellery, 1780-1842. III. Worcester, Samuel, 1770-1821. IV. Lowell, John, 1769-1840. V. Morse, Jedediah, 1761-1826.
Contents omitted.

UNITARIAN year book. 1846- Boston, Mass., W. Crosby and H. P. Nichols [etc., 1845-53] American Unitarian association [1854-19. v. plates, maps. 19-20 1/2 cm. Publication suspended from 1859 to 1866, inclusive. Title varies: 1846-47, The Unitarian annual register. 1848-55, The Unitarian Congregational register. 1856-99, The Year-book of the Unitarian Congregational churches. 1900- Unitarian year book.--Supplement ... January 1, 1900. Boston, American Unitarian association [1900] 32 p. 19 cm. [BX9811.U5] 6-45852

WENDTE, Charles William, 1844- 922.
The wider fellowship; memories, friendships, and endeavors for religious unity, 1844-1927, [by] Charles William Wendte ... Boston, Mass., The Beacon press, inc., 1927. v. front., plates, ports. 24 1/2 cm. [BX9869.W48A3] 27-12781
1. Unitarianism. I. Title.

WENDTE, Charles William, 1844- 922.
The wider fellowship; memories, friendships, and endeavors for religious unity, 1844-1927, [by] Charles William Wendte ... Boston, Mass., The Beacon press, inc., 1927. v. front., plates, ports. 24 1/2 cm. [BX9869.W48A3] 27-12781
1. Unitarianism. I. Title.

WILBUR, Earl Morse, 1866-
Our Unitarian heritage, an introduction to the history of the Unitarian movement, by Earl Morse Wilbur ... Boston, The Beacon press, inc. [1963, c1953] xiii, 495 p. 21 cm. Maps on lining-papers. 67-26459
1. Unitarianism. I. Title.

WILBUR, Earl Morse, 1866-
Our Unitarian heritage, an introduction to the history of the Unitarian movement, by Earl Morse Wilbur ... Boston, The Beacon press, inc. c1925] xiii, 495 p. 21 cm. Maps on lining-papers. [BX9831.W5] 25-13427
1. Unitarianism. I. Title.

WILSON, John, 1802-1868. 230.8
Unitarian principles confirmed by Trinitarian testimonies; being selections from the works of eminent theologians belonging to orthodox churches. With introductory and occasional remarks. By John Wilson ... Boston, American Unitarian association, 1855. xv, 504 p. 20 cm. The introduction to the author's "The concessions of Trinitarians" forms the basis of the present volume. cf. Pref. [BX9841.W7 1855] 31-35046
1. Unitarianism. 2. Trinity. I. American Unitarian association. II. Title.

WILSON, John, 1802-1868. 230.8
Unitarian principles confirmed by Trinitarian testimonies; being selections from the works of eminent theologians belonging to orthodox churches. With introductory and occasional remarks. By John Wilson ... 5th ed. Boston, American Unitarian association, 1867. xv, 504 p. 20 cm. The introduction to the author's "The concessions of Trinitarians" forms the basis of the present volume. cf. Pref. [BX9841.W7 1867] 31-35047
1. Unitarianism. 2. Trinity. I. American Unitarian association. II. Title.

WILSON, John, 1802-1868. 230.8
Unitarian principles confirmed by Trinitarian testimonies; being selections from the works of eminent theologians belonging to orthodox churches. With introductory and occasional remarks. By John Wilson ... 10th ed. Boston, American Unitarian association, 1880. xv, 504 p. 19 1/2 cm. The introduction to the author's "The concessions of Trinitarians" forms the basis of the present volume. cf. Preface. [BX9841.W7 1880] 15-16172
1. Unitarianism. 2. Trinity. I. American Unitarian association. II. Title.

WOODS, Leonard, 1774-1854. 230.
Letters to Unitarians and Reply to Dr. Ware. 2d ed. with an Appendix. By Leonard Woods ... Andover, M. Newman, 1822. viii, 351 p. 22 1/2 cm. "Reply to Dr. Ware's letters to Trinitarians and Calvinists": p. 119-288. [BX9847.W73] 28-9941
1. Ware, Henry, 1764-1845. Letters addressed to Trinitarians and Calvinists. 2. Unitarianism. I. Title.

WOODS, Leonard, 1774-1854. 230.
Letters to Unitarians occasioned by the sermon of the Reverend William E. Channing, at the ordination of the Rev. J. Sparks. By Leonard Woods ... Andover; Published by Flagg and Gould, 1820. v. [3] -160 p. 24 cm. [BX9847.W7] 1-6707
1. Channing, William Ellery, 1780-1842. A sermon delivered at the ordination of the Rev. Jared Sparks. 2. Unitarianism. I. Title.

WORCESTER, Noah, 1758-1837. 231
An appeal to the candid, or, The Trinitarian review. To be published in several numbers ... By Noah Worcester ... Boston: Published by Cummings & Hilliard, no. 1, Cornhill. Cambridge, Hilliard & Metcalf, 1814. 3 v. 22 1/2 cm. Imperfect: v. 2 and 3 wanting. [BT115.W78] [AC901.W3 vol. 144, no. 15] [AC901.W3 vol. 144, no. 15] 40-24448
1. Unitarianism. 2. Trinity—Controversial literature. I. Title.

WORCESTER, Noah, 1758-1837.
Sacred truths relating to the Living God, His Only Son, and Holy Spirit, illustrated and defended in a continued series of letters and inquiries. The second edition, corrected and enlarged. By Noah Worcester, A.M. ... Boston, Published by Bradford & Read, 1812. 252 p. 18 cm. A 34
1. Unitarianism. I. Title.

WORCESTER, Samuel, 1770-1821. 230.8
A third letter to the Rev. William E. Channing on the subject of ultarianism. By Samuel Worcester ... Boston; Printed by Samuel T. Armstrong, no. 50, Cornhill, 1815. 80 p. 22 cm. [BX9847.W83] [BX9647.W8] [288] 32-31404
1. Channing, William Ellery, 1780-1842. Remarks on the Rev. Dr. Worcester's second letter to Mr. Channing ... 2. Unitarianism. I. Title.

Unitarianism—Addresses, essays, lectures.

CHANNING, William Ellery, 1780-1842. 230.8
A discourse, preached at the dedication of the Second Congregational Unitarian church, New York, December 7, 1826. By William Ellery Channing. New York, Second Congregational Unitarian church, 1826. 57 p., 1 l. 23 cm. [BX9643.C5D6 1826] 36-4388
1. Unitarianism—Addresses, essays, lectures. I. Title.

CHANNING, William Ellery, 1780-1842. 230.8
A discourse, preached at the dedication of the Second Congregational Unitarian church, New York. December 7, 1826. By William Ellery Channing. 2d ed. New York, Second Congregational Unitarian church, 1827. 57 p., 1 l. 23 cm. [BX9843.C5D6 1827] 36-4389
1. Unitarianism—Addresses, essays, lectures. I. Title.

CHANNING, William Ellery, 1780-1842. 208.1
A selection from the works of William E. Channing, D. D. Boston, American Unitarian association, 1855. iv p., 1 l., 480 p. 20 cm. (On cover: Theological library. A. U. A. 1.) Mainly "discourses", delivered on various occasions. [BX9615.C54] 33-32107
1. Unitarianism—Addresses, essays, lectures. I. American Unitarian association. II. Title.

CLARKE, James Freeman, 1810-1888. 252.
Essentials and non-essentials in religion. Six lectures delivered in the Music hall, Boston, by James Freeman Clarke ... Boston, American Unitarian association, 1878. 4 p. l, 148 p. 15 1/2 cm. "Delivered ... 1877 ... at the request of the American Unitarian association." Contents.Faith and belief.--Christ and Christianity.--The Bible.--The church and worship.--Christian experience.--The future life. [BX9843.C6E8] 11-13445
1. Unitarianism—Addresses, essays, lectures. I. American Unitarian association. II. Title.

CONWAY, Moncure Daniel, 1832-1907. 252.
The earthward pilgrimage, by Moncure D. Conway... New York, H. Holt and company, 1874. 2 p. l., [vii]-x, [2], [19]-406 p. 19 1/2 cm. [BX9843.C7E3 1874] 43-40956
1. Unitarianism—Addresses, essays, lectures. I. Title.

MACLEAN, Angus Hector, 1892- 288
The wind in both ears. Boston, Beacon [c.1965] viii, 144p. 22cm. [BX9841.2.M25] 65-12242 4.95
1. Unitarianism—Addresses, essays, lectures. I. Title.

PARKER, Theodore, 1810-1860. 208.1
Additional speeches, addresses and occasional sermons ... By Theodore, Parker ... Boston, Little, Brown and company, 1855. 2 v. 21 cm. [BX9815.P34] 33-415
1. Unitarianism—Addresses, essays, lectures. 2. Sermons, American. I. Title.

PARKER, Theodore, 1810-1860. 230.8
Speeches, addresses, and occasional sermons, by Theodore Parker ... Boston, R. Leighton, jr., 1860. 3 v. 21 cm. [BX9815.P37 1860] 33-1393
1. Unitarianism—Addresses, essays, lectures. 2. Sermons, American. I. Title.

SAVAGE, Minot Judson, 1841-1918. 230.8
Religious reconstruction, by M. J. Savage ... Boston, G. H. Ellis, 1888. 246 p. 20 cm. [BX9841.S3] 33-31220
1. Unitarianism—Addresses, essays, lectures. I. Title.

"SHOW us the Father" 252.
by Minot S. Savage, Samuel R. Calthrop, Henry M. Simmons [and others]... Chicago, C.H. Kerr & company, 1888. 2 p. l., 170 p. 18 1/2 cm. [BX9843.A1S6] 34-8370
1. Unitariantism—Addresses, essays, lectures. I. Savage, Minot Judson, 1841-1918.
Contents omitted.

SHUTE, John Raymond. 288
His honor the heretic; [papers] Monroe, N. C., Nocalore Press, 1950. 76p. 24cm. [BX9815.S6] 56-47838
1. Unitarianism—Addresses, essays, lectures. I. Title.

UNITARIANISM: its origin and history. A course of sixteen lectures delivered in Channing hall, Boston, 1888-89. Boston, American Unitarian association, 1890. xxviii p., 1 l., 394 p. 19 1/2 cm. [Channing hall lectures] [BX9831.U6] [BX9831.U6] A 30
1. Channing, William Ellery, 1780-1842. 2. Parker, Theodore, 1810-1860. 3. Unitarianism—Addresses, essays, lectures. 4. Transcendentalism (New England) 5. Church history. 6. Massachusetts—Church history. I. Allen, Joseph Henry, 1820-1898. II. Batchelor, George, 1836-1923. III. Beach, Seth Curtis, 1837-1932. IV. Briggs, George Ware, 1810-1895. V. De Normandie, James, 1836-1924. VI. Ellis, George Edward, 1814-1894. VII. Everett, Charles Carroll, 1829-1900. VIII. Herford, Brooke, 1830-1903. IX. Hornbrooke, Francis Bickford, 1849-1903. X. Peabody, Andrew Preston, 1811-1893.
Contents omitted.

WRIGHT, Conrad. 288'.09
The liberal Christians; essays on American Unitarian history. Boston, Beacon Press [1970] x, 147 p. 21 cm. Contents.Contents.—Rational religion in eighteenth century America.—The rediscovery of Channing.—Emerson, Barzillai Frost, and the Divinity School address.—The minister as reformer.—Henry W. Bellows and the organization of the National Conference.—From standing order to secularism. Includes bibliographical references. [BX9843.W78L5 1970] 76-84801 7.50
1. Unitarianism—Addresses, essays, lectures. I. Title.

WRIGHT, Conrad. 288.082
Three prophets of religious liberalism: Channing, Emerson, Parker. Introduced by Conrad Wright. Boston, Beacon Press [1961] 152 p. 21 cm. (Beacon paperbacks in liberal religion, LR12) Bibliographical footnotes. [BX9843.A1T5] 61-3679
1. Unitarianism—Addresses, essays, lectures. 2. Liberalism (Religion) I. Title.

Unitarianism—Controversial literature.

HENKEL, David, 1795-1831. 230.
David Henkel against the Unitarians. A treatise on the person and incarnation of Jesus Christ, in which some of the principal arguments of the Unitarians are examined ... New Market, Printed in S. Henkel's office, 1850. 119 p. 17 1/2 cm. Published by order of the Evangelical Lutherna Tennessee synod. [BX9847.H4] 44-26227
1. Jesus Christ—Person and offices. 2. Unitarianism—Controversial literature. I. Evangelical Luthern Tennessee synod. II. Title.

KOHLMANN, Anthony, 1771-1836. 230.
Unitarianism philosophically and theologically examined: in a series or periodical numbers; comprising a complete refutation of the leading principles of the Unitarian system ... By the Rev. Anthony Kohlmann ... Washington city, H. Guegan, 1821-22. 2 v. 22 cm. [BX9847.K7 1821] 25-23331
1. Jesus Christ—Divinity. 2. Unitarianism—Controversial literature. I. Title.

MILLER, Samuel, 1769-1850. 230.
Letters on Unitarianism; addressed to the members of the First Presbyterian church, in the city of Baltimore. By Samuel Miller ... Trenton, Printed by G. Sherman, 1821. vii, [9]-312 p. 23 cm. [BX9847.M55 1821] 44-13648
1. Unitarianism—Controversial literature. I. Baltimore, First Presbyterian church. II. Title.

MILLER, Samuel, 1769-1850. 230.
Letters on Unitarianism; addressed to the members of the First Presbyterian church, in the city of Baltimore. By Samuel Miller ... Lexington, Ky., T. T. Skillman, 1823. viii, [9]-312 p. 18 cm. [BX9847.M55 1823] 44-13651
1. Unitarianism—Controversial literature. I. Baltimore. First Presbyterian church. II. Title.

Unitarianism—Doctrinal and controversial works.

WARDLAW, Ralph, 1779-1853. 230.8
Unitarianism incapable of vindication; a reply to the Rev. James Yates's Vindication of Unitarianism. By Ralph Wardlaw... Andover [Mass.] Published and for sale by Mark Newman. Flagg and Gould. printers, 1817. xii, [13]-351 p. 24 1/2 x 14 1/2 cm. [BX9847.W33 1817] 35-22748
1. Yates, James, 1789-1871. Vindication of Unitarianism. 2. Unitarianism—Doctrinal and controversial works. I. Title.

Unitarianism—History

ALLEN, Joseph Henry, 1820-1898. 288'.74
Our liberal movement in theology, chiefly as shown in recollections of the history of Unitarianism in New England. New York, Arno Press, 1972 [c1882] iv, 220 p. 23 cm.

(Religion in America, series II) [BX9833.4.A43 1972] 73-38432 ISBN 0-405-04053-9
1. Unitarianism—History. I. Title.

ALLEN, Joseph Henry, 1820-1898.
Our liberal movement in theology, chiefly as shown in recollections of the history of Unitarianism in New England, being a closing course of lectures given in the Harvard divinity school by Joseph Henry Allen... Boston, Roberts brothers, 1882. iv, 1 l., 230 p. 17 cm. Memorial address of Rev. Frederic H. Hedge on Henry W. Bellows and Ralph Waldo Emerson: p. 208-218. [BX9633.A4] 26-22108
1. Unitarianism—Hist. I. Hedge, Frederic Henry, 1805-1899. II. Title.

CHEETHAM, Henry H. 288
Unitarianism and Universalism, an illustrated history. Drawings by Roger Martin. Boston, Beacon [c.1962] 124p. 21cm. 62-10818 3.95
1. Unitarianism—Hist. 2. Universalism—Hist. I. Title.

Unitarianism—History—Societies.

UNITARIAN historical society, Boston. 288.09
The proceedings. v. 1- 1925- [Boston, 1926- v. plates, ports., facsim. 22 1/2 cm. Each volume issued in 2 parts. "List of annual addresses delivered before the Unitarian historical society" since 1901, in v. 1-5, 1925-37. "The earliest New England music [by] Waldo S. Pratt" (with music): v. 1, pt. 2, 1928, p. [28]-[47] "A descriptive catalogue of American Unitarian hymn books ... by Henry Wilder Foote": v. 6, pt. 1, 1938, p. [31]-49. [BX9803.U77] 41-23750
1. Unitarianism—Hist.—Societies. I. Title.

Unitarianism in the United States

SAVAGE, Minot Judson, 1841-1918. 252.
Pillars of the temple, by Minot J. Savage ... Boston, American Unitarian association, 1904. 3 p. l., 226 p. 20 cm. [BX9843.S3P5] 4-29695
I. Title.
Contents omitted.

WRIGHT, Conrad. 288.73
The beginnings of Unitarianism in America. Boston, Starr King Press; distributed by Beacon Press [1955] 305p. maps. 22cm. 'Bibliographical appendix p.[281]-291. 'Bibliographical note': p.[292]-294. [BX9833.W7] 55-8138
1. Unitarianism in the U. S. I. Title.

Unitarianism—Periodicals

THE Monthly religious magazine and theological review. v. 1-50, v. 51, no. 1-2; Jan. 1844-Feb. 1874. Boston, L. C. Bowles, 1844-74. 51 v. in 49. 20-24 cm. Vols. 3-20 called also "2d ser., v. 1-48." Title varies: 1844-55. The Monthly religious magazine. 1856-60, The Monthly religious magazine and independent journal. 1861-69, The Monthly religious magazine. Jan.-July 1870, The Monthly review and religious magazine. Aug. 1870-1873, The Religious magazine and monthly review. Jan.-Feb. 1874, The Monthly religious magazine and theological review. Editors: 1844-58, F. D. Huntington.--1859-June 1870, E. H. Sears and R. Ellis.--July-Dec. 1870, E. H. Sears and J. W. Thompson.--1871-74, J. H. Morison. Superseded by the Unitarian review. [BX9601.M7] 2-17661
1. Unitarianism—Period. I. Huntington, Frederic Dan, bp., 1819-1904, ed. II. Sears, Edmund Hamilton, 1810-1876, ed. III. Ellis, Rufus, 1819-1885, ed. IV. Thompson, James William, 1805-1881, ed. V. Morison, John Hopkins, 1808-1896, ed.

Unitarians—Clergy—Biography.

MENDELSOHN, Jack, 1918- 288'.092'4 B
Channing, the reluctant radical : a biography / Jack Mendelsohn. Westport, Conn. : Greenwood Press, 1980, c1971. 308 p. : ports. ; 23 cm. Reprint of the ed. published by Little, Brown, Boston. Includes bibliographical references and index. [BX9869.C4M45 1980] 79-17863 ISBN 0-313-22101-4 lib. bdg. : 26.00
1. Channing, William Ellery, 1780-1842. 2. Unitarians—Clergy—Biography. 3. Clergy—United States—Biography. I. Title.

Unitarians in Boston.

HOWE, Daniel Walker. 171'.1
The Unitarian conscience: Harvard moral philosophy, 1805-1861. Cambridge, Mass., Harvard University Press, 1970. viii, 398 p. 24 cm. Originally presented as the author's thesis, University of California at Berkeley, 1966. Includes bibliographical references. [BX9833.6.B68H69 1970] 75-116737 ISBN 0-674-92121-6 15.00
1. Unitarians in Boston. I. Title.

Unitarians in India—History.

LAVAN, Spencer. 288'.54
Unitarians and India : a study in encounter and response / by Spencer Lavan. [Boston] : Beacon Press, c1977. vi, 217 p. ; 22 cm. "A Skinner House book." Includes bibliographical references and index. [BX9835.I8L38] 77-75488 3.95
1. Unitarians in India—History. I. Title.

Unitarians in Philadelphia.

GEFFEN, Elizabeth M. 288.74811
Philadelphia Unitarianism, 1796-1861. Philadelphia, Univ. of Pennsylvania Press [c.1961] 323p. illus. Bibl. 60-11411 6.00
1. Unitarians in Philadelphia. I. Title.

Unitarians in Poland.

RACOVIAN catechism.
The Racovian catechism, with notes and illustrations,translated from the Latin: to which is prefixed a sketch of the history of Unitarianism in Poland and the adjacent countries, by Thomas Rees. London, Longman, Hurst, Rees, Orme, and Brown, 1818; Lexington, Ky., American Theological Library Association, 1962.Ccviii, 404 p. 18 cm. 63-56284
1. Unitarians in Poland. I. Rees, Thomas, 1777-1864, ed. and tr. II. Title.

Unitarians—New England—Biography.

HATHAWAY, Richard D. 288'.3 B
Sylvester Judd's New England / Richard D. Hathaway. University Park [Pa.] : Pennsylvania State University Press, [1981] p. cm. Includes index. Bibliography: p. [BX9869.J8H37] 19 81-17854 ISBN 0-271-00307-3 : 16.95
1. Judd, Sylvester, 1813-1853. 2. Unitarians—New England—Biography. 3. New England—Biography. I. Title.

United brethren in Christ.

BREWBAKER, Charles W. 289.
Christian growth and conduct (a book of religious instruction for our youth) ... by Chas. W. Brewbaker ... [Dayton, O., The Otterbein press, c1922] 113 p. 17 1/2 cm. [BX9875.B7] 22-11459
1. United brethren in Christ. I. Title.

HOUGH, Samuel Strickler, 1864- ed.
tHe church in earnest; a call for the training necessary for world achievements. A word of preparation by Bishop G. M. Mathews, D.D. Ed. by S. S. Hough... Dayton, O., The Foreigh missionary society of the United Brethren in Christ [c1908] vii, 9-124 p. 18 cm. "Helpful missionary books and supplies": p. 122-124. 8-32418
I. Title.

LUTTRELL, John Lewis, 1829- 289.
History of the Auglaize annual conference of the United brethren church, from 1853 to 1891. By Rev. J. L. Luttrell... Dayton, O., United brethren publishing house, 1892. 3 p. l., iii-xv, 17-475 p. front., illus., ports., facsim. 20 cm. [BX9875.A43L8] 20-20364
1. United brethren in Christ. I. Title.

NEWCOMER, Christian, 1749-1830. 922.89
Christian Newcomer, his life, journal and achievements, edited by Samuel S. Hough, foreword by H. H. Fout ... Dayton, O., Board of administration, Church of the United Brethren in Christ [c1941] 3 p. l., 293 p. plates. 20 1/2 cm. A new edition of The life and journal of the Rev'd Christian Newcomer, published in 1834. [BX9877.N4A3 1941] 41-13127
1. United Brethren in Christ. I. Hough, Samuel Strickler, 1864- ed. II. Title.

NEWCOMER, Christian, 1749-1830. 922.
The life and journal of the Rev'd Christian Newcomer, late bishop of the church of the United brethren in Christ. Written by himself. Containing his travels and labours in the gospel from 1795 to 1830, a period of thirty-five years. Transcribed, corrected and translated by John Hildt ... Hagerstown [Md.] Printed by F. G. W. Kapp, 1834. 2 p. l., 330 p. 18 cm. [BX9877.N4A3 1834] 26-18351
1. United brethren in Christ. I. Hildt, John, tr. II. Title.

SHUEY, E[dwin] L[ongstreet] 1857-
A handbook of the United brethren in Christ. prepared by E. L. Shuey, A.M. Revised and enlarged. Dayton, O., United brethren publishing house, 1901. v. 7-80 p. 17 1/2 cm. p. 67-80, advertising matter. 6-24147
I. Title.

UNITED brethren in Christ. Board of administration. 289.
Partners in the conquering cause ... Dayton, O., Board of administration, United brethren in Christ [c1924] 114 p. incl. front., illus. 17 cm. Foreword signed: S. S. Hough, H. F. Shupe. [BX9875.A65 1924] CA 24
I. Hough, Samuel Strickler, 1864- II. Shupe, Henry Fox, 1860- III. Title.

WILMORE, Augustus Cleland, 1849- 289.
History of the White River conference of the church of the United brethren in Christ, containing an account of the antecedent annual conferences, by Rev. Augustus Cleland Wilmore ... Dayton, O., Pub. for the author by the United brethren publishing houses, 1925. ix, 504, xvi p front., plates, ports., maps. 23 1/2 cm. [BX9875.A4W5] 26-663
1. United brethren in Christ. I. Title.

United brethren in Christ—Biography

THOMPSON, Henry Adams, 1837-1920. 922.
Our bishops; a sketch of the origin and growth of the church of the United brethren in Christ as shown in the lives of its distinguished leaders, by H. A. Thompson ... With an introduction by Colonel Robert Cowden ... Chicago, Elder publishing company, 1889. 7 p. l., 7-631 p. 21 port. (incl. front.) 21 cm. [BX9877.A1T5] 24-21581
1. United brethren in Christ—Biog. I. Title.

United brethren in Christ. Conferences. Pennslyvania.

HOLDCRAFT, Paul Ellsworth. 289.9
History of the Pennsylvania conference of the Church of the United brethren in Christ, by Pual E. Holdcraft ... Susquicentennial [!] ed., 1789-1939. [Fayetteville, Pa., The Craft press, inc., 1938] xv, 17-506 p., 3 l. illus. (incl. ports., tables) 23 1/2 cm. Bibliography: p. xii. [BX9875.A4P4 1938] 39-4161
1. United brethren in Christ. Conferences. Pennslyvania. I. Title.

United brethren in Christ—Discipline.

UNITED brethren in Christ. 289.9
Disciplines of the United brethren in Christ. Part I. In English, 1814-1841. Part II. In German, 1814-1819, 1841. Translated and reprinted from the originals. Edited by Prof. A. W. Drury, D.D. Dayton, O., United brethren publishing house, 1895. x, 232, 109 p. 20 1/2 cm. Includes ten English and five German issues. Each issue after 1815 has special t.-p. English issues, with imprint dates 1816, 1817, 1819, 1822, 1826, 1829, 1833, have title: Doctrine and discipline of the United brethren in Christ: 1837 and 1841: Origin, constitution, doctrine and discipline ...: German issues, with imprint dates 1816, 1817, 1819, have title: Lehre und zucht-ordnung der Vereinigten bruder in Christo; 1841: Uraprung, lehre, constitution and sucht-ordnung ... [BX9875.A5 1895] 37-13887
1. United brethren in Christ—Discipline. I. Drury, Augustus Waldo, 1851- ed. II. Title.

UNITED brethren in Christ. 289.9
Origin, constitution, doctrine and discipline, of the United brethren in Christ. Circleville, O., Printed at the Conference office, 1837. 64 p. 12 cm. [BX9875.A5 1837] 37-15208
1. United brethren in Christ—Discipline. I. Title.

UNITED brethren in Christ. 289.9
Origin, doctrine, constitution, and discipline of the United brethren in Christ. Dayton, O., United brethren publishing house, 1889. v. 7-170 p. 14 cm. [BX9875.A5 1889] 37-15214
1. United brethren in Christ—Discipline. I. Title.

UNITED brethren in Christ. 289.9
Origin, doctrine, constitution, and discipline of the United brethren in Christ. Dayton, O., United brethren publishing house, 1893. vi, 7-224 p. 14 1/2 cm. [BX9875.A5 1893] 37-15207
1. United brethren in Christ—Discipline. I. Title.

United Brethren in Christ—History.

THE Church of the United Brethren in Christ, teachings and progress [by] Bishop W. E. Musgrave revised by Rev. R. W. Rash. Huntington, United Brethren Pub., 1956. 94p.
1. United Brethren in Christ—History. I. Musgrave, W E

DRURY, Augustus Waldo, 1851-1935. 289.9
History of the Church of the United Brethren in Christ. Rev., 1931. Dayton, Ohio, United Brethren Pub. House, 1924 [i.e. 1931] 832 p. plates, ports. 24 cm. Bibliography: p. 6-8. [BX9875.D8 1931] 50-53455
1. United Brethren in Christ—Hist. I. Title.

DRURY, Augustus Waldo, 1851-1935. 289.
History of the church of the United brethren in Christ, by A. W. Drury. Dayton, O., The Otterbein press, 1924. 821 p. front., plates, ports. 23 cm. [BX9875.D6] 24-21423
1. United brethren in Christ—Hist. I. Title.

HUBER, Samuel, 1782-1868. 922.
Autobiography of the Rev. Samuel Huber, elder in the church of the United brethren in Christ: containing sketches of his life and religious experience ... edited by John Denig Chambersburg, Pa., Printed by M. Kieffer & co., 1858. xiii [9]-256 p. 17 cm. Advertising matter: p. 255-256. [BX9877.H8A3] 5-16553
1. United brethren in Christ—Hist. I. Denig, John, ed. II. Title.

SPAYTH, Henry G. 289.
History of the church of the United brethren in Christ. By Henry G. Spayth ... 1st ed. Circleville, O., Conference office of the United brethren in & Christ, 1851. 2 v. in 1 front. (port.) 19 1/2 cm. Paged continuously. Vol. 2 has title: History of the church of the United brethren in Christ. By William Hanby. From the year 1825, to the year 1850. Vol. 2 is a continuation of Spayth's work. [BX9875.S7] 43-37705
1. United brethren in Christ—Hist. I. Hanby, William, bp. II. Title.

United brethren in Christ—Hymns.

CHURCH of the United brethren in Christ 'New constitution) 783.9

The church hymnal; the official hymnal of the Church of the United brethren in Christ, prepared by Edmund S. Lorenz, under the direction of the Board of bishops, Henry H. Fout, Arthur R. Clippinger, Arthur B. Statton [and others] ... Dayton, O., The United brethren publishing house, 1935. 496 p. 23 cm. [M2131.U6 1935] 35-13507
1. United brethren in Christ—Hymns. I. Lorenz, Edmund Simon, 1854- II. Title.

United Brethren in Christ—Missions.

MILLS, Job Smith, bp., 1848-1909.
... *Our foreign missionary enterprise,* by J. S. Mills ... W. R. Funk ... [and] S. S. Hough ... Dayton, O., United Brethren publishing house [1908] xvi, 282 p. incl. front., illus. plates, fold. map. 19 1/2 cm. (United Brethren mission study course) Bibliography: p. 263-265. [BV2590.M6] 8-33163
1. United Brethren in Christ—Missions. I. Funk, William Ross, 1861-1935, joint author. II. Hough, Samuel Strickler, 1864- joint author. III. Title.

UNITED brethren in Christ. Foreign missionary society.
The call of China and the Islands; report of the foreign deputation, 1911-1912, for every member of the United brethren church, by G. M. Mathews ... S. S. Hough ... foreword by Bishop W. M. Bell, D.D. Dayton, O., Foreign missionary society United brethren in Christ [1913?] 122 p. front., plates, ports. 19 cm. Plates printed on both sides. "Books for further investigation": p. 120-121. 14-12099
I. Mathews, George Martin, 1848- II. Hough, Samuel Strickler, 1864- III. Title.

WEEKLEY, William Marion, bp., 1851-1926. 266.
...*Our heroes;* or, United brethren home missionaries, by W. M. Weekley ...H. H. Fout... Introduction by J. P. Landis... Dayton, O., United brethren home missionary society [c1908] x, 11-340 p. front., plates, ports. 20 cm. (Denominational mission study course) [BV2766.U8W4] 8-22593
1. United brethren in Christ—Missions. 2. United Brethren in Christ—Biog. I. Fout, Henry H., 1861- joint author. II. Title. III. Title: United brethren home missionaries.

United brethren in Christ—Pennsylvania.

EBERLY, Daniel. 284.6748
Landmark history of the United brethren church... treating of the early history of the church in Cumberland, Lancaster, York and Lebanon counties, Pennsylvania, and giving the history of the denomination in the original territory, by Rev. Daniel Eberly... Rev. Isaiah H. Albright...Rev. C. I. B. Brane... [Reading, Pa., Press of Behney & Bright] 1911. viii p., 2 l., 15-292 p. front., illus. (incl. ports. facsims) 24 cm. [BX9875.E3] 33-25231
1. United brethren in Christ—Pennsylvania. I. Albright, Isaiah H. II. Brane, Commodore I. Berion. III. Title.

United brethren in Christ—Relations—Evangelical church.

JOINT commission on church federation and union of the Church of the United brethren in Christ and of the Evangelical church. 289.9
The discipline of the Evangelical united brethren church submitted by the Joint commission of church federation and union, the Church of the United brethren in Christ, the Evangelical church. [Dayton, O., The Otterbein press; Harrisburg, Pa., The Evangelical press] 1942. iv, 474 p. 17 cm. A preliminary edition, without chapter XXIX (Formulas) and index, which are "to be prepared later." [BX9875.A5 1942] 43-7073
1. United brethren in Christ—Relations—Evangelical church. 2. Evangelical church—Relations—United brethren in Christ. I. Title.

United brethren in Christ—Sermons.

DRURY, Augustus Waldo, 1851- 928.89
The life of Bishop J. J. Glossbrenner, D. D., of the United Brethren in Christ, with an appendix containing a number of his sermons and sketches, by Rev. A. W. Drury, D.D., with an introduction by Rev. James W. Hott, D.D. Dayton, O., published for J. Dodds by United brethren publishing house, 1889. xv, 17-391 p. incl. front. port. 19 cm. [BX9677.G6D7] 37-8722
1. Glossbrenner, Jacob John, bp., 1812-1887. 2. United brethren in Christ—Sermons. 3. Sermons, American. I. Title.

KEPHART, Isaiah Lafayette, 1832-1908. 922.89
Biography of Rev. Jacob Smith Kessler, of the Church of the United brethren in Christ, compiled from his autobiography, by Rev. I. L. Kephart, with a sermon by the compiler. Published by the Publishing committee of the East Pennsylvania conference, of the Church of the United brethren in Christ. Dayton, O., W. J. Shuey, publishing agent, 1867. 246 p. 19 1/2 cm. [BX9877.K45K4] 37-8723
1. Kessler, Jacob Smith, 1812-1863. 2. United brethren in Christ—Sermons. I. Title.

THE Christian as witness; conference addresses, by Rev. Wendell P. Loveless, Rev. J. A. Van Gorkom, J. A. Lyter ... [and others] Grand Rapids, Mich., Zondervan publishing house [c1936] 4 p. l., 7-91 p. 20 cm. [BX9876.C5] 36-25272 252.046
1. United Bretheren in Christ—Sermons. 2. Sermons, American. I. Loveless, Wendell Phillips, 1892.

United brethren in Christ—Virginia.

FUNKHOUSER, Abram Paul, 1853-1917. 289.9
History of the church of the United brethren in Christ, Virginia conference, by Rev. A. P. Funkhouser ... compiled by Oren F. Morton ... [Dayton, Va., Ruebush-Kieffer company, c1921] 3 p. l., 315 p. front. (port.) 23 cm. [BX9875.A4V5] 39-30720
1. United brethren in Christ—Virginia. I. Morton, Oren Frederic, 1857-1926, comp. II. Title.

United Brethren in Christ—Yearbooks.

THE Church annual; year book of the United Brethren in Christ, 1889- Dayton, Ohio. no. illus., ports. 23 cm. Title varies: 1889-1934, The Year-book of the United Brethren in Christ. [BX9875.A17] 52-33200 289.
1. United Brethren in Christ—Yearbooks. I. Church of the United Brethren in Christ (New constitution)

UNITED brethren in Christ. 289.
Year-book. Dayton, O., United brethren publishing house, v. illus., ports. 22 1/2 cm. [BX9875.A15] CA 8
I. Title.

United Christian Missionary Society.

UNITED Christian Missionary Society.
World mission of the United Christian missionary society; report of the World Mission strategy conference. [Indianapolis, Ind., U.C.M.S., 1960] 204. p.
I. Title.

WORSHIP idea book for Christian Church student groups, Disciples of Christ student fellowships, Bethany fellowships and other college age groups. Indianapolis, Student Work Office, United Christian Missionary Society [195-] 60p. 28cm.
1. United Christian Missionary Society. I. Rossman, Parker, ed.

United Church curriculum.

UNITED CHURCH BOARD FOR HOMELAND MINISTRIES. BOARD OF PUBLICATION.
Design for Christian education; an introduction to the United Church curriculum. Boston, United Church Press [1963] 80 p. illus. 26 cm. (United Church curriculum. Introduction and prospectus) Issued by United Church Board for Homeland Ministries, Division of Publication. 64-39577
1. United Church curriculum. 2. Religious education — Curricula. 3. United Church of Christ — Education. I. Title. II. Series.

United church in Japan.

IN our time, 1947-1957; ten years of experience in a cooperative program of Christian advance in Japan New York, The Interboard committee for Christian work in Japan [1957?] 80p. illus., port. 23cm.
1. United church in Japan. 2. Japan—Church history. I. Johnson, Katherine. II. Interboard Committee for Christian work in Japan.

United church of Canada.

GRANT, John Webster. 287'.92
The Canadian experience of church union. Richmond, John Knox Press [1967] 106 p. 22 cm. (Ecumenical studies in history no. 8) [BX9881.G7] 67-21481
1. United Church of Canada. 2. Christian union—Canada. I. Title. II. Series.

SILCOX, Clarice Edwin. 280
Church union in Canada; its causes and consequences, by Claris Edwin Silcox. New York, Institute of social and religious research [c1933] xvii, 493 p. diagr. 23 1/2 cm. "The Institute of social and religious research ... is responsible for this publication."--p.[11] [BX9881.S5] 33-19380
1. United church of Canada. 2. Christian union. 3. Protestant churches—Canada. 4. Canada—Church history. I. Institute of social and religious research. II. Title.

United Church of Canada—Clergy—Correspondence, reminiscences, etc.

FALLIS, George Oliver. 922
A padre's pilgrimage. Toronto, Ryerson Press [1953] 166p. illus. 22cm. Autobiographical. [BX9883.F3A3] 54-24763
1. United Church of Canada—Clergy—Correspondence, reminiscences, etc. I. Title.

United Church of Canada—Sermons.

ARCHIBALD, Frank E. 252'.07'92
An essential greatness, by Frank E. Archibald. Windsor, N.S., Lancelot Press [1968] 164 p. 21 cm. [BX9882.A8 1968] 72-180379 2.50
1. United Church of Canada—Sermons. 2. Apostles' Creed. 3. Sermons, English—Canada. I. Title.

BREWING, Willard E., 1881- 252
Faith for these times, by Willard Brewing ... Toronto, New York, Collins [1945] v, 159 p. 21 1/2 cm. "First Edition." [BX9882.B7] 45-18655
1. United church of Canada—Sermons. 2. Sermons, English—Canada. I. Title.

GRIFFITH, Arthur Leonard, 1920- 252'.07'92
Ephesians : a positive affirmation : the Ephesian letter today / Leonard Griffith. Waco, Tex. : Word Books, [1975] 173 p. ; 23 cm. Includes bibliographical references. [BS2695.4.G74] 75-3638 5.95
1. United Church of Canada—Sermons. 2. Bible. N.T. Ephesians—Sermons. 3. Sermons, English—Canada. I. Title.

LANGFORD, Norman F. 282
The two-edged sword; sermons by Norman F. Langford. Philadelphia, The Westminster press [1945] 10, 13-194 p. 21 1/2 cm. [BX9882.L3] 45-4082
1. United church of Canada—Sermons. 2. Sermons, English—Canada. I. Title.

MACLENNAN, David Alexander, 1903- 252
No coward soul. With a foreword by Lloyd C. Douglas. New York, Oxford Uiv. Press, 1949 [c1948] xi, 244 p. 22 cm. [BX9882.M33 1949] 49-9437
1. United Church of Canada—Sermons. 2. Sermons, English—Canada. I. Title.

PIDGEON, George Campbell, 1872- 252
The indwelling Christ. New York, Oxford University Press, 1949 [c1948] ix, 208 p. 22 cm. [BX9882.P494 1949] 49-9005
1. United Church of Canada—Sermons. 2. Sermons, English—Canada. I. Title.

PIDGEON, George Campbell, 1872- 252
The vicarious life, by the Very Reverend Geo. C. Pidgeon, D.D. Toronto, G. Cumberlege, Oxford university press [c1945] ix p., 1 l. 187 p. 22 cm. "Sermons from the pulpit of Bloor street United church, Toronto." [BX9882.P5] 46-16363
1. United church of Canada—Sermons. 2. Atonement—Sermons. 3. Sermons, English—Canada. I. Title.

RUSSELL, George Stanley. 252
The face of God, by G. Stanley Russell. New York and London, Harper & brothers, 1935. 3 p. l., 114 p. 19 cm. "First edition." [BX9882.R8] 35-32784
1. United church of Canada—Sermons. 2. Sermons, English—Canada. I. Title.

SHORT, John, 1896- 252
Triumphant believing. New York, Scribner, 1952. 177 p. 21 cm. [BX9882.S5] 52-8721
1. United Church of Canada—Sermons. 2. Sermons, English—Canada. I. Title.

[United Church of Christ.]

CONFIRMING our faith : 234'.162
a confirmation resource for the United Church of Christ / [editor, Larry E. Kalp ; book design and ill. by Bob and Sandy Bauer]. New York : United Church Press, c1980. p. cm. Includes bibliographical references. A confirmation course book exploring the basic ideas, concepts, and beliefs of the United Church of Christ. [BV815.C62] 19 80-22773 ISBN 0-8298-0427-7 : 4.95
1. [United Church of Christ.] 2. Confirmation—Instruction and study. 3. [Confirmation.] I. Kalp, Larry E. II. Bauer, Bob. III. Bauer, Sandy. IV. United Church of Christ.
Publishers Address: Pilgrim Press, 132 W. 31st St., NY, NY 10001

LANCASTER, Pa. Theological Seminary of the United Church of Christ. 208
Occasional papers, no. 1- Lancaster, Pa., 1962- [BR45.L25] 62-21931
I. Title.

OBENHAUS, Victor. 285'.834
And see the people; a study of the United Church of Christ [by] Victor Obenhaus with Ross Blount. [Chicago] Chicago Theological Seminary [1968] 123 p. forms. 28 cm. [BX9886.O2] 71-250
1. United Church of Christ. I. Blount, Ross, C. II. Chicago Theological Seminary. III. Title.

RONANDER, Albert C. 245
Guide to the Pilgrim hymnal [by] Albert C. Ronander [and] Ethel K. Porter. Philadelphia, United Church Press [1966] xxiv, 456 p. 22 cm. Includes music (principally unacc. melodies) Bibliography: p. 425-427. [ML3162.R65] 65-26448
1. United Church of Christ. Pilgrim hymnal. 2. United Church of Christ—Hymns—History and criticism. 3. Hymns—History and criticism. 4. Hymns—Dictionaries. I. Porter, Ethel K., joint author. II. Title. III. Title: Pilgrim hymnal.

UNITED Church of Christ. Uniting General Synod.
Minutes. Cleveland, O., The Music Hall, June 25-27, 1957. Cleveland, 1957. 192 p.
I. Title.

UNITED Church of Christ. Uniting General Synod.
The Uniting general synod of the United church of Christ. The Music Hall, Cleveland, Ohio, June 25-27, 1957. White book. St. Louis? 1957] 128 p. 23 cm. Basis of union of the Congregational Christian churches and the Evangelical and Reformed church, with interpretations:" p. 109-126.
I. Title. II. Title: White book. III. Title: Basis of union.

UNITED CHURCH OF CHRIST.
Facts concerning the work and progress of the instrumentalities toward the fulfillment of our Christian world mission. [Philadelphia? 1962] 63 p. Cover title. 68-34536
I. Title.

UNITED CHURCH OF CHRIST.
Facts concerning the work and progress of the instrumentalities toward the fulfillment of our Christian world mission. [Philadelphia? 1962] 63 p. Cover title. 68-34536
I. Title.

United Church of Christ — Addresses, essays, lectures.

HORTON, Douglas, 1891- 285.834
Reform & renewal; exploring the United Church of Christ [by] Douglas Horton [and others] Philadelphia, United Church Press [1966] 119 p. 19 cm. "Based on the Lancaster convocation lectures delivered at Lancaster Theological Seminary on April 20-21, 1965." [BX9885.A4] 66-15480
1. United Church of Christ — Addresses, essays, lectures. I. Title.

RANLETT, Louis Felix, 1896-
All Souls Congregational Church (United Church of Christ) Bangor, Maine. Bangor, 1962. 69 p. 20 cm. "Publishes ... as a part of the observance of its fiftieth anniversary March 6, 1962." 63-53136
I. Title.

REFORM & renewal; 285.834
exploring the United Church of Christ [by] Douglas Horton [others] Philadelphia, United Church Pr. [c1966] 119p. 19 cm. Based on the Lancaster convocation lects. delivered at Lancaster Theological Seminary, April 20-21, 1965. [BX9885.A4] 66-15480 1.45 pap.
1. United Church of Christ—Addresses, essays, lectures. I. Horton, Douglas, 1891-

UNITED Church Board for Homeland Ministries. Division of Publication. 285.834
The church in our world; a study of the nature and mission of the United Church of Christ. Illinois ed. New York, Produced by Division of Publication, United Church Board for Homeland Ministries [1965] 199 p. map. 29 cm. Includes bibliographies. [BX9885.A45] 66-6155
1. United Church of Christ — Addresses, essays, lectures. I. Title.

United Church of Christ—Catechisms and creeds.

CHASE, Loring D. 238
Words of faith; a resource and discussion book for youth [by] Loring D. Chase. Illustrated by Micaela Myers. Boston, United Church Press [1968] 92 p. illus. 22 cm. (Confirmation education series) "Part of the United Church curriculum, prepared and published by the Division of Christian Education and the Division of Publication of the United Church Board for Homeland Ministries." [BX9884.A3C49] 68-10038
1. United Church of Christ—Catechisms and creeds. 2. Religious education—Text-books for young people—United Church of Christ. I. United Church Board for Homeland Ministries. Division of Christian Education. II. United Church Board for Homeland Ministries. Division of Publication. III. Title.

SHINN, Roger Lincoln. 230.5834
We believe; an interpretation of the United Church Statement of faith [by] Roger Lincoln Shinn and Daniel Day Williams. Philadelphia, United Church Press [1966] 132 p. 21 cm. Statement of faith in German, Spanish, and New Testament Greek translations (p. 127-132) [BX9886.S5] 66-23992
1. United Church ,of Christ—Catechisms and creeds. I. Williams, Daniel Day, 1910- II. United Church of Christ. Statement of faith. 1966. III. Title.

United Church of Christ — Clergy.

UNITED Church of Christ. Council for Church and Ministry.
The manual on the ministry in the United Church of Christ. [1st ed.] New York [196-] 64 p. 23 cm. Cover title. "Based on the Constitution of the United Church of Christ." 65-69663
1. United Church of Christ — Clergy. I. Title.

United Church of Christ—Clergy, Training of.

FUKUYAMA, Yoshio, 1921- 207'.11'5834
The ministry in transition; a case study of theological education. University Park, Pennsylvania State University Press [1972] xx, 167 p. 24 cm. Includes bibliographical references. [BX9884.A3F83] 72-1395 ISBN 0-271-01129-7 9.50
1. United Church of Christ—Clergy, Training of. 2. Theology—Study and teaching—United States. I. Title.

United Church of Christ—Doctrinal and controversial works.

ABBOT, Carolyn T. 262'.001
One church; a grass-roots view of the Protestant ecumenical movement, by Carolyn T. Abbot. [1st ed.] New York, Exposition Press [1967] 135 p. 21 cm. Bibliography: p. [126]-135. [BX8.2.A2] 67-24257
1. United Church of Christ—Doctrinal and controversial works. 2. Christian union. I. Title.

United Church of Christ — Education.

UNITED Church of Christ. Council for Higher Education.
Colleges and academies of the Council for Higher Education. New York, Higher Education and American Missionary Association Division of the United Church Board for Homeland Ministries, 1963? 104 p. 20 cm. 65-69463
1. United Church of Christ — Education. I. Title.

United Church of Christ—History.

GUNNEMANN, Louis H. 285'.834'09
The shaping of the United Church of Christ : an essay in the history of American Christianity / Louis H. Gunnemann. New York : United Church Press, c1977. 257 p. ; 22 cm. (A Pilgrim book) Includes bibliographical references and index. [BX9884.G86] 77-4900 ISBN 0-8298-0335-1 : 8.00
1. United Church of Christ—History. I. Title. II. Series.

KOSTYU, Frank A. 285'.834'09
Adventures in faith and freedom : history of the United Church of Christ / by Frank A. Kostyu. Montclair, N.J. : Kinship Krafts Publications, 1980, c1979. 75 p. : ill. ; 22 cm. Bibliography: p. 73-75. [BX9884.K67] 79-256 ISBN 0-933274-01-7 : 3.95
1. United Church of Christ—History. I. Title.

ON the trail on the UCC : 285.8'34'09
a historical atlas of the United Church of Christ / compiled and edited by Carolyn E. Goddard ; maps on conferences drawn by John P. Wattai, Richard S. Wattai, and Joyce Petri Wattai, [UCC membership map compiled by Joseph Sellers]. New York : United Church Press, c1981. 127 p. : maps ; 28 cm. Introduces the large family of the United Church which is composed of more than 6000 churches and institutions and some dozen agencies and instrumentalities. [BX9884.O6] 19 81-290 pbk. : 8.95
1. United Church of Christ—History. 2. [United Church of Christ—History.] I. Goddard, Carolyn E., 1918-
Publishers Address: Pilgrim Press, 132 W. 31st St., NY, NY 10001

United Church of Christ in Alamance Co., N.C.

BURLINGTON-ALAMANCE County Chamber of Commerce. 285'.8756'58
Histories of United Church of Christ in Burlington and Alamance County, North Carolina. Prepared and compiled by the Burlington-Alamance County Chamber of Commerce in cooperation with the participating churches. [Burlington? N.C.] 1963. 1 v. (various pagings) 28 cm. Cover title. [BX9884.Z5N63 1963] 75-303578
1. United Church of Christ in Alamance Co., N.C. 2. United Church of Christ in Burlington, N.C. I. Title.

United Church of Christ — Missions — Yearbooks.

UNITED Church Board for World Ministeries.
Directory and calendar of prayer. 1961/62 New York [etc.] v. ports., maps. 22 cm. annual. Supersedes the Directory and calendar of prayer issued by the American Board of Commissioners for Foreign Missions. [BV2592.U5] 65-1835
1. United Church of Christ — Missions — Yearbooks. I. Title.

United Church of Christ — Prayer-books and devotions.

FROHNE, Marydel D j 242
Christians together, by Marydel D. And Victor M. Forhne. Illustrated by Eric Von Schmidt. Boston, United Church Press [1964] v. 90 p. col. illus. 23 cm. "Part of the United Church curriculum, prepared and published by the Division of Christian Education and the Division of Publication of the United Church Board for Homeland Ministries." "A hymn to read or sing, O praise ye the Lord" with keyboard acc. (p. 32) [BV85.F67] 64-19470
1. United Church of Christ — Prayer-books and devotions. 2. Lent-Prayer-books and devotions — English. 3. Children — Prayer-books and devotions — 1961- I. Frohne, Victor M. joint author. II. United Church Board for Homeland Ministries. Division of Christian Education. III. United Church Board for Homeland Ministries. Division of Publications. IV. Title.

FROHNE, Victor M., joint author. j 242
Christians togethers, by Marydel D. and Victor M. Forhne. Boston, United Church Press [1964] v. 90 p. col. illus. 23 cm. "Part of the United Church curriculum, prepared and published by the Division of Christian Education and the Division of Publication of the United Church Board for Homeland Ministries." "A hymn to read or sing, O praise ye the Lord" with keyboard acc. (p. 32) [BV85.F67] 64-19470
1. United Church of Christ — Prayer-books and devotions. 2. Lent-Prayer-books and devotions — English. 3. Children — Prayer-books and devotions — 1961- I. United Church Board for Homeland Ministries. Division of II. Title. III. Title: Christians together,

United Church of Christ—Sermons.

BRUEGGEMANN, Walter. 252'.05'834
Living toward a vision : Biblical reflections on shalom / by Walter Grueggemann. Philadelphia : United Church Press, c1976. p. cm. (A Shalom resource) Includes bibliographical references. [BX9886.Z6B78] 76-22172 ISBN 0-8298-0322-X pbk. : 4.95
1. United Church of Christ—Sermons. 2. Sermons, American. I. Title.

GLASSE, James D. 252'.0834
The art of spiritual snakehandling, and other sermons / James D. Glasse. Nashville : Abingdon, c1978. 112 p. ; 19 cm. [BX9886.Z6G562] 78-12342 ISBN 0-687-01890-0 pbk. : 3.95
1. United Church of Christ—Sermons. 2. Sermons, English. I. Title.

WAGONER, Walter D. 252'.05834
Mortgages on paradise / Walter D. Wagoner. Nashville : Abingdon, c1981. 125 p. ; 20 cm. [BX9886.Z6W335] 19 80-20138 ISBN 0-687-27220-3 pbk. : 4.95
1. United Church of Christ—Sermons. 2. Sermons, America. I. Title.

United Church of Christ — Yearbooks.

UNITED Dhurch of Christ. 285.8
Yearbook. 1962 [New York] v. 24 cm. Formed by the merger of the Year book of the Congregational Christian churches and the Year book of the Evangelical and Reformed Church. Each vol. contains statistics for the previous year. Vols. for 1962- include statistics for Congregational Christian churches which had not yet voted and for those which had voted to remain outside the United Church of Christ. [BX9884.A1U55] 65-29474
1. United Church of Christ — Yearbooks. I. Title.

United church of northern India.

PARKER, Kenneth Lawrence. 275.4
... The development of the United church of northern India, by Kenneth Lawrence Parker ... [Philadelphia, 1936] 94 p. illus. (map) diagr. 23 cm. Based on thesis (PH. D.)--University of Chicago, 1935. "Private edition, distributed by the University of Chicago libraries, Chicago, Illinois." "Reprint of Journal of the Department of history (the Presbyterian historical society) of the Presbyterian church in the U. S. A., vol. xvii, nos. 3 and 4, Sept.-Dec., 1936." [BR1155.P27 1935] 37-8990
1. United church of northern India. I. Title.

United Church Women of Minnesota.

MCKINLAY, Kathryn Thorbus.
Our story, 1936-1966, United Church Women of Minnesota; a unit within the Department of Ecumenical Relations of the Minnesota Council of Churches Minneapolis, Minnesota Council of Churches [1966] 112 p. port. 28 cm. 68-54953
1. United Church Women of Minnesota. 2. Ecumenical movement. I. Title.

United churches of Christ.

HORTON, Douglas, 1891- 285.7
The United Church of Christ: its origins, organization, and role in the world today. New York, T. Nelson [1962] 287 p. 22 cm. Includes bibliography. [BX9885.H6] 62-10371
1. United churches of Christ.

*SPEARS, Gene, Jr. 252
Seventy feet nearer the stars: sermons to help build your church. New York, Vantage [c.1964] 112p. 21cm. 2.50 bds.,
I. Title.

United evangelical church—Catechisms.

HARTZLER, Jacob.
Catechism of Christian doctrine as taught in the United evangelical church, by Rev. Jacob Hartzler ... Harrisburg, Pa., Publishing house of the United evangelical church [1901] 106 p. 15 cm. [BX9885.H3] 1-25623
1. United evangelical church—Catechisms. I. Title.

United Evangelical Lutheran Church.

JENSEN, John Martin, 1893- 284.773
The United Evangelical Lutheran Church, an interpretation, by John M. Jensen. Minneapolis, Augsburg Pub. House [1964] viii, 311 p. illus., ports. 23 cm. Bibliography: p. 296-300. [BX8058.J4] 64-21508
1. United Evangelical Lutheran Church. 2. Lutherans, Danish, in the U.S. I. Title.

United Free Church of Scotland—Clergy.

UNITED Free Church of Scotland. 285.241
Fasti, 1900-1929, edited by John Alexander Lamb. Edinburgh, Oliver and Boyd [1956] xi, 639p. 26cm. [BX9089.A53] 57-17600
1. United Free Church of Scotland—Clergy. 2. Churches—Scotland. 3. Scotland—Biog. I. Lamb, John Alexander, ed. II. Title.

United Free Church of Scotland—Sermons.

MORRISON, George Herbert 252.052
Greatest sermons. With an introd. by George M. Docherty. New York, Harper [1960, c.1959] 256p. 22cm. 60-7960 3.50 half cloth,
1. United Free Church of Scotland—Sermons. 2. Sermons, English—Scotland. I. Title.

United Lutheran Church in America.

COMPREHENSIVE index to biennial convention minutes of the United LutheranChurch in America 1918-1952. [New York?] United Luthern Publication House [1956] vi, 314p.
1. United Lutheran Church in America. I. Reinartz, Frederick Eppling, 1901- ed.

EVANGELICAL Lutheran joint synod of Ohio and other states. Northern district. 284.173
Minutes of the ... annual convention of the Northern district of the Evangelical Lutheran joint synod of Ohio and other states ... Columbus, O., Lutheran book concern, 18 -19 v. 21-22 1/2 cm. [BX8061.0315A3] 36-6861
I. Title.

EVANGELICAL Lutheran joint synod of Ohio and other states. Western district. 284.177
Minutes of the ... annual convention of the Western district of the Ev. Lutheran joint synod of Ohio and other states ... Dayton [etc.] 18 -19 v. illus. (port.) tables (part fold.) 21-22 1/2 cm. Title varies: 18 Minutes of the ... session of the Western district of the Synod and ministerium, of the Evangelical Lutheran church, in the state of Ohio. 18 Minutes of the ... annual convention of the Western district of the Evangelical Lutheran joint synod of Ohio and other states. 18 Proceedings of the ... annual convention of the Western district of the Evangelical Luth. joint synod of Ohio and other states. 1898. Minutes of the ... meeting of the Western district of the Evangelical Lutheran joint synod of Ohio and other states. 18 Minutes of the ... convention of the Western district of the Evangelical Lutheran synod of Ohio and other states. 19 Minutes of the ... regular meeting of the Western district of the Evangelical Lutheran synod of Ohio and other states. Imprint varies. [BX8061.0317A3] 36-6862
I. Title.

EVANGELICAL Lutheran Synod in the Midwest of the United Lutheran Church in America. 284.173
Synodal-Bericht. Verhandlungen. [Hastings? Neb.] v. 23 cm. Reports for issued by the synod under an earlier name: Deutsche Evangelisch-lutherische Synode von Nebraska. [BX8061.M65A3] 51-20682
I. Title.

HARKINS, George F 284.173
The church and her work. Arthur H. Getz, editor. Philadelphia, Muhlenberg Press [1960] 144p. illus. 20cm. Includes bibliography. [BX8048.H35] 60-35941
1. United Lutheran Church in America. I. Title.

ILLINOIS synod of the United Lutheran church in America. 234.1773
Minutes of the ... annual convention of the Illinois synod of the United Lutheran church in America ... Chicago, Ill., Pub. for the Synod by the United Lutheran publication society, 19 v. illus. (port.) tables. 23 cm. Includes the Minutes of the special convention of the Illinois synod ... and the Minutes of the W. H. and F. M. society of the Illinois synod; -7th incoudes the Minutes of the -fifth convention of the Synodal brotherhood ... and of the Biennial convention of the Women's missionary society of the Illinois synod; 8th- include the Minutes of the sixth-convention of the Synodal brotherhood ... [synopais only] and the directory of the Women's missionary society of the Illinois synod. [BX8061.I 32A3] ca 34
I. Title.

INDIANA Synod of the United Lutheran Church in America. 284.1772
Minutes of the annual convention. [v. p.] v. 24cm. Conventions held 19 -47 called -100th. Title varies: 19 -53, Proceedings (cover title, 1935-53, Minutes) Proceedings of the 19 convention include also the proceedings of the conventions of the Women's Missionary Society, the Lutheran Brotherhood and the Luther League. [BX806.I68A3] 56-26870
I. Title.

JOINT committee on ways and means to form the United Lutheran church in America. 284.
Minutes of Joint committee on ways and means. Feb. 6[-Nov. 14] 1918. [n. p., 1918] 64 p., 1 l., 65-107, [5] p. 23 cm. Caption title. No. 8 of a collection of pamphlets entitled: The United Lutheran church in America. First convention. The Joint committee represented the General synod of the Evangelical Lutheran church in the United States of America, the General council of the Evangelical Lutheran church in the South. [BX8048.A32 1918] 19-10971
1. United Lutheran church in America. I. Title.

KENTUCKY-TENNESSEE Synod of the United Lutheran Church in America. 284.176
Minutes of the annual convention. [Nashville?] v. illus. 23 cm. [BX8061.K4A3] 52-65851
I. Title.

KRAUSS, Paul H. 284.173
The goodly fellowship; a study of the church and its work. Philadelphia, United Lutheran Publication House [1949] 144 p. illus., port. 19 cm. "Based upon...[the author's]A lamp of burnished gold [published in 1941]" Bibliography: p. 143-144. [BX8048.K69] 50-4618
1. United Lutheran Church in America. I. Krauss, Paul H. A lamp of burnished gold. II. Title.

KRAUSS, Paul H. 284.173
... A lamp of burnished gold; a study of our church and its work [by] Paul H. Krauss. Philadelphia, Pa., The United Lutheran publication house [c1941] 144 p. fold. diagr. 20 cm. (The Lutheran leadership course) "References for additional reading" at end of each chapter. [BX8048.K7] 41-12394
1. United Lutheran church in America. I. Title.

LUFFBERRY, Henry Benner. 284.173
Thy mission high fulfilling; a study of faith and life. Arthur H. Getz, editor. Prepared and published by action of the United Lutheran Church in America in convention assembled. Philadelphia, Muhlenberg Press [1954] 129p. illus. 21cm. [BX8048.L8] 54-2977
1. United Lutheran Church in America. 2. Stewardship, Christian. I. Title.

MICHIGAN Synod of the United Lutheran Church in America. 284.1774
Minutes of the convention. [Detroit, etc.] v. 23cm. annual. Title varies: Proceedings of the convention. Vols. for include the Proceedings of the conventions of the Women's Missionary Society and the Lutheran Brotherhood. [BX8061.M6A3] 53-20706
I. Title.

MISSISSIPPI Synod of the United Lutheran Church in America. 284.1762
Proceedings of the convention. [Louisville, Miss.] v. 23cm. annual. Cover title.: Minutes of the convention. Vols. for include the Minutes of the annual convention of the Women's Missionary Society of the Mississippi Synod and also minutes of other synodical auxiillary societies. [BX8061.M68A3] 53-16394
I. Title.

PACIFIC synod of the Evangelical Lutheran church. 284.179
Minutes of the annual convention of the Pacific synod of the Evangelical Lutheran church ...) 1st- 1901- Oregon City, Or. [etc.] 1901- v. fronts., illus., plates, ports. 20 1/2-23 cm. Title varies: 1901- Minutes of the ... annual meeting. 19 Minutes of the proceedings of the ... annual convention. 19 Minutes of the ... annual convention. 1906, Record of proceedings of the ... annual meeting ... with the Minutes of the Sunday school assembly and the Record of the first meeting of the Woman's home missionary society. 1907- Minutes of the ... annual convention. Imprint varies. [BX8061.P2A2] CA 34
I. Title.

PACIFIC Synod of the United Lutheran Church in America. 284.173
The first fifty years of the Pacific Synod, 1901-1951, by Edwin Bracher, historian. Seattle, 1951. 99p. illus. 25cm. Includes bibliography. [BX8061.P2A35] 62-2436
I. Bracher, Edwin. II. Title.

PACIFIC Synod of the United Lutheran Church in America. 284.173
The first fifty years of the Pacific Synod, 1901-1951, by Edwin Bracher, historian. Seattle, 1951. 99p. illus. 25cm. Includes bibliography. [BX8061.P2A35] 62-2436
I. Bracher, Edwin. II. Title.

SYNOD of Ohio of the United Lutheran Church in America. 284.173
Minutes of the annual convention. [Columbus? Ohio] v. 24cm. [BX8061.O62A3] 54-16303
I. Title.

UNITED Lutheran Church in America. Board of Publication. 922.473
Mr. Protestant: an informal biography of Franklin Clark Fry. [Philadelphia? 1960] 76 p. ports. 21 cm. [BX8080.F74U5] 60-38562
I. Fry, Franklin Clark, 1900- II. Title.

UNITED Lutheran synod of New York. 284.174
... Minutes of the ... annual convention ... 1st- 1929- [Alabny? N.Y., etc., 1929- v. illus. (incl. ports.) tables. 23 cm. Title varies slightly. The minutes of the 1st convention include the special act of incorporation, minutes of the incorporators' meetings held January 15th and June 5th, 1929, the constitution and the certificate of merger. [BX8061.N78A3] 35-33904
I. Title.

United Lutheran Church in America. Board of Foreign Missions.

SWAVELY, C H
Mission to Church in Andhra Pradesh, India; The Andhra Evangelical Lutheran Church, 1942-1962. New York, Board of Foreign Missions of the United Lutheran Church in America, 1962. 90 p. 66-61640
1. United Lutheran Church in America. Board of Foreign Missions. I. Title.

United Lutheran church in America—Education.

COTTRELL, Donald Peery, 1902- 377'.8'41335
Instruction and instructional facilities in the colleges of the United Lutheran Church in America; a study of the organization, administration, and character of instruction and instructional facilities. New York, Bureau of Publications, Teachers College, Columbia University, 1929. [New York, AMS Press, 1972, ie. 1973] viii, 138 p. 22 cm. Reprint of the 1929 ed., issued in series: Teachers College, Columbia University. Contributions to education, no. 376. Originally presented as the author's thesis, Columbia. Published also as pt. III, chapters 1-6 of the Survey of higher education for the United Lutheran Church in America, 1929. Bibliography: p. 135-138. [LC574.C6 1972] 79-176672 ISBN 0-404-55376-1 10.00
1. United Lutheran Church in America—Education. 2. Universities and colleges—United States—Administration. 3. College teaching. I. Title. II. Series: Columbia University. Teachers College. Contributions to education, no. 376.

COTTRELL, Donald Peery, 1902- 377.
Instruction and instructional facilities in the colleges of the United Lutheran church in America; a study of the organization, administration, and character of instruction and instructional facilities, by Donald Peery Cottrell ... New York city, Teachers college, Columbia university, 1929. viii, 138 p. 24 cm. (Teachers college, Columbia university. Contributions to education, no. 376) Published also as thesis (PH. D.) Columbia university. Published also as pt. iii. chap. i-vi of the Survey of higher education for the United Lutheran church in America. Bibliography: p. 135-138. [LC574.C6 1929a] [LC5.C8 no. 376] 29-19692
1. United Lutheran church in America—Education. 2. Teaching. 3. Universities and colleges—U. S. 4. Church schools—U. S. I. Title.

KNUBEL, Frederick Hermann, 1870- ed. 284.
Our church; an official study book, the first of a series of "Key books" to the origin, principles and activities of the church, prepared under the general editorship of the Rev. F. H. Knubel ... and the Rev. M. G. G. Scherer, D. D. Philadelphia, Pa., The United Lutheran publication house [c1924] 170 p. front. (port.) plates. 19 cm. (The key books) "Intended primarily for use in the United Lutheran church in America."--Pref. [BX8048.K5] 24-28016
I. Scherer, Melanchthon Gideon Grosclose, 1861- joint ed. II. Title.

LEONARD, Robert Josselyn, 1885-1929. 377.
Survey of higher education for the United Lutheran church in America ... by R. J. Leonard ... E. S. Evenden ... and F. B. O'Rear ... with the cooperation of other members of the staff and graduate students. New York city, Teachers college, Columbia university, 1929. 3 v. illus. (incl. maps) tables, diagrs. 23 1/2 cm. Survey made at the direction of the Board of education of the United Lutheran church in America by members of Teachers college, Columbia university. cf. Introd., v. 1. [LC574.L4] 29-13611
1. United Lutheran church in America—Education. 2. Universities and colleges—U.S. 3. Church schools—U.S. I. Evenden, Edward Samuel, 1884- II. O'Rear, Floyd Barrett, 1896- III. Columbia University. Teachers college. IV. United Lutheran church in America. Board of education. V. Title.

LESOURD, Howard Marion, 1889- 377'.8
The university work of the United Lutheran Church in America; a study of the work among Lutheran students at non-Lutheran institutions. New York, Teachers College, Columbia University, 1929. [New York, AMS Press, 1973, c1972] viii, 136 p. 22 cm. Reprint of the 1929 ed., issued in series: Teachers College, Columbia University. Contributions to education, no. 377. Originally presented as the author's thesis, Columbia. Published also as pt. 7 of the Survey of higher education for the United Lutheran Church in America. [BV1610.L46 1972] 70-176990 ISBN 0-404-55377-X 10.00
1. United Lutheran Church in America—Education. 2. Church work with students. 3. Church and college. I. Title. II. Series: Columbia University. Teachers College. Contributions to education, no. 377.

LE SOURD, Howard Marion, 1889- 377.
The university work of the United Lutheran church in America; a study of the work among Lutheran students at non-Lutheran institutions, by Howard Marion Le Sourd... New York city, Teachers college, Columbia university, 1929. viii, 136 p. 23 1/2 cm. (Teachers college, Columbia university. Contributions to education, no. 377) Published also as thesis (PH.D) Columbia university. Published also as pt. vii of the "Survey of higher education for the United Lutheran church

in America.", 1929. [LC574.L45 1929a] [LB5.C8 no. 377] 371. 29-20284
1. United Lutheran church in American—Education. 2. Church and college. 3. Students—U.S. 4. Universities and colleges—U.S. I. Title.

United Lutheran church in America. Liturgy and ritual. Common service book.

HORINE, John Winebrenner, 1869- 245.2041
Sacred song; the hymns of our church, by John W. Horine ... Philadelphia, Pa., The United Lutheran publication house [c1934] 183 p. 19 cm. [BX8067.A3H6] 34-33443
1. United Lutheran church in America. Liturgy and ritual. Common service book. 2. Lutheran church—Hymns—Hist. & crit. 3. Hymns—Hist. & crit. I. Title.

UNITED Lutheran church in America. Common service book committee. 264.041
Collects and prayers for use in church; authorized by the United Lutheran church in America; prepared by the Common service book committee. Philadelphia, Pa., The Board of publication of the United Lutheran church in America [c1935] 265 p. 18 cm. L. D. Reed, chairman. "Sources and acknowledgments": p. 219-232. [BX8067.P7U6] 35-7844
I. United Lutheran church in America. Liturgy and ritual. II. Lutheran church. Liturgy and ritual. Collects. III. Reed, Luther Dotterer, 1873- IV. Title.

UNITED Lutheran church in America. Liturgy and ritual. 226
The occasional services, from the common service book of the Lutheran church. Philadelphia, The Lutheran publication society, the General council publication board; Columbia, S.C., The Lutheran board of publication, 1918. 99 p. 17 cm. "Authorized by the General synod, the General council, the United synod in the South." [BX8067.A3 1918] 18-23698
I. Title. II. Title: Common service book of the Lutheran church, The occasional services.

UNITED Lutheran church in America. Liturgy and ritual. 264.041
The occasional services, from the Common service book of the Lutheran church. Philadelphia, The Board of publication of the United Lutheran church in America [c1930] 193 p. 16 1/2 cm. "Authorized by the United Lutheran church in America." [BX8067.A3 1930] 30-12481
I. Title. II. Title: Common service book of the Lutheran church, The occasional services.

United Lutheran church in America—Missions.

DIEHL, Nona M. 266.41
Serving around the world in the United Lutheran church in America, by Nona M. Diehl ... Philadelphia, Pa., Women's missionary society, the United Lutheran church in America [c1931] 6 p. l., 156 p. incl. illus., maps. 19 cm. Bibliography at end of each chapter. [BV2540.D5] 32-14130
1. United Lutheran church in America—Missions. 2. Lutheran church—Missions. 3. Missions, Foreign. I. United Lutheran church in America, Women's missionary society. II. Title.

United Lutheran Synod of New York and New England—History

KREIDER, Harry Julius, 1896- 284.174
History of the United Lutheran Synod of New York and New England. Written at the request of the synod. Philadelphia, Muhlenberg Press, 1954- v. port., map (on lining papers) diagr. 24cm. Bibliographical footnotes. [BX8061.N78K7] 54-9180
1. United Lutheran Synod of New York and New England—Hist. I. Title.

United Methodist Church in Wayne, New Jersey.

JACKSON, Charles S. 287'.6749'23
The United Methodist Church in Wayne, New Jersey, 1853-1973, by Charles S. Jackson and F. J. Yetter. [Wayne, N.J., United Methodist Women of the United Methodist Church in Wayne, 1974] 66 p. illus. 22 cm. Cover title: Growing with a community: the story of a Christian congregation. [BX8481.W36U54] 73-93077
1. United Methodist Church in Wayne, New Jersey. I. Yetter, F. J., joint author. II. Title: Growing with a community; the story of a Christioan congregation.

United Methodist Church (United States)

COLAW, Emerson S. 230'.7'6
Beliefs of a United Methodist Christian, by Emerson Colaw. [Nashville, Tidings, 1972] 133 p. 19 cm. [BX8382.2.Z5C64] 72-95656 1.00
1. United Methodist Church (United States) I. Title.

HARMON, Nolan Bailey, 1892- 287'.6
Understanding the United Methodist Church, by Nolan B. Harmon. 2d rev. ed. Nashville, Abingdon Press [1974] 176 p. 22 cm. Published in 1955 and 1961 under title: Understanding the Methodist Church. [BX8382.2.H35 1974] 73-20001 ISBN 0-687-43005-4 2.95
1. United Methodist Church (United States) I. Title.

WALTZ, Alan K. 287'.673
Images of the future / Alan K. Waltz. Nashville : Abingdon, c1980. 80 p. ; 21 cm. (Into our third century) Includes bibliographical references. [BX8382.2.W34] 79-25028 ISBN 0-687-18689-7 pbk. : 2.95 pbk. : 2.95
1. United Methodist Church (United States) I. Title. II. Series.

WASHBURN, Paul, 1911- 287'.6
United Methodist primer. Nashville, Tidings [1969] 108 p. illus. 19 cm. Bibliographical references included in "Notes" (p. 75-77) [BX8387.W3] 68-59146
1. United Methodist Church (United States) I. Title.

United Methodist Church (United States). Baltimore Conference.

THOSE incredible Methodists; a history of the Baltimore Conference of the United Methodist Church. Edited by Gordon Pratt Baker. Baltimore, Commission on Archives and History, The Baltimore Conference, 1972. ix, 597 p. maps (on lining papers) 24 cm. Bibliography: p. 512-526. [BX8382.2.A42B357] 72-185862 287'.6'75271
1. United Methodist Church (United States). Baltimore Conference. I. Baker, Gordon Pratt, ed. II. United Methodist Church (United States). Baltimore Conference. Commission on Archives and History.

United Methodist Church (U.S.)—Clergy.

HUNT, Richard A., 1931- 262'.1476
Called to minister / Richard A. & Joan A. Hunt. Nashville : Abingdon, c1982. 124 p. : ill. ; 21 cm. (Into our third century) Includes bibliographical references. [BX8382.2.Z5H86] 19 81-22796 ISBN 0-687-04560-6 pbk. : 3.95
1. United Methodist Church (U.S.)—Clergy. I. Hunt, Joan, 1932- II. Title. III. Series.

United Methodist Church (United States)—Clergy—Statistics.

WILSON, Robert Leroy, 1925- 287'.6'0973
Trends on ministerial membership of annual conferences of the United Methodist Church, 1960-1970, by Robert L. Wilson. Dayton, Ohio, Program Council, United Methodist Church [1971] 11 p. 28 cm. (United Methodist Church. Research information bulletin, 71-3) Caption title. [BX8382.2.Z5W55] 72-184854
1. United Methodist Church (United States)—Clergy—Statistics. I. Title. II. Series: United Methodist Church (United States). Program Council. Research information bulletin 71-3

United Methodist Church (United States). Council of Bishops—History.

SHORT, Roy Hunter, Bp., 1902- 287'.673
History of the Council of Bishops of the United Methodist Church, 1939-1979 / Roy H. Short. Nashville : Abingdon, c1980. p. cm. Includes index. [BX8382.2.S46] 80-16423 ISBN 0-687-17190-3 : 10.95
1. United Methodist Church (United States). Council of Bishops—History. I. Title.

United Methodist Church (United States)—Government.

LEIFFER, Murray Howard, 1902- 262'.18
What district superintendents say—about their office and the issues confronting them; a study of professional leadership in the United Methodist Church, by Murray H. Leiffer. Evanston, Ill., Garrett Theological Seminary [1972] 123, 12 p. 23 cm. [BX8382.2.Z5L4] 72-188486 2.50
1. United Methodist Church (United States)—Government. 2. District superintendents (Methodist) I. Title.

ROGERS, Kristine M. 1946- (Kristine Malins), 287'.673
Paths to transformation : a study of the general agencies of the United Methodist Church / Kristine M. Rogers and Bruce A. Rogers. Nashville : Abingdon, c1982. 96 p. ; 20 cm. (Into our third century) Bibliography: p. 94-96. [BX8382.2.Z5R63 1982] 19 81-17565 ISBN 0-687-30094-0 pbk. : 3.50
1. United Methodist Church (U.S.)—Government. I. Rogers, Bruce A. 1941- (Bruce Alan), II. Title. III. Series.

SHERWOOD, John R., 1924- 262'.07673
Sources and shapes of power / John R. Sherwood and John C. Wagner ; Ezra Earl Jones, editor. Nashville : Abingdon, c1981. 125 p. : ill. ; 21 cm. (Into our third century) Includes bibliographical references. [BX8382.2.S53] 19 80-28125 ISBN 0-687-39142-3 pbk. : 3.95
1. United Methodist Church (United States)—Government. I. Wagner, John C., 1931- joint author. II. Jones, Ezra Earl. III. Title.

SHORT, Roy Hunter, Bp., 1902- 262'.07'6
United Methodism in theory and practice [by] Roy H. Short. Nashville, Abingdon Press [1974] 205 p. 20 cm. [BX8388.S43] 74-13016 ISBN 0-687-43009-7 5.95
1. United Methodist Church (United States)—Government. I. Title.

TUELL, Jack M., 1923- 262'.07'6
The organization of the United Methodist Church [by] Jack M. Tuell. Rev. [ed.] Nashville, Abingdon Press [1973] 175 p. 22 cm. [BX8382.2.T83 1973] 73-1056 ISBN 0-687-29442-8 3.50 (pbk)
1. United Methodist Church (United States)—Government. I. Title.

TUELL, Jack M., 1923- 262'.07'6
The organization of the United Methodist Church / Jack M. Tuell. Rev. ed. Nashville : Abingdon, 1977. 174 p. ; 22 cm. Includes index. [BX8382.2.Z5T83 1977] 76-55784 ISBN 0-687-29443-6 pbk. : 4.95
1. United Methodist Church (United States)—Government. I. Title.

TUELL, Jack M., 1923- 262'.076
The organization of the United Methodist Church / Jack M. Tuell. Rev. 1982 ed. Nashville, Tenn. : Abingdon, c1982. 173 p. ; 22 cm. Includes index. [BX8382.2.Z5T83 1982] 19 81-20633 ISBN 0-687-29444-4 pbk. : 6.95
1. United Methodist Church (U.S.)—Government. I. Title.

UNITED Methodist Church (United States) 262'.07'673
The book of discipline of the United Methodist Church, 1972. Nashville, Tenn., United Methodist Pub. House [1973] xi, 653 p. 22 cm. [BX8388.U55 1973] 73-161954 ISBN 0-687-03708-5 ISBN 0-687-03709-3 (deluxe)
1. United Methodist Church (United States)—Government. I. Title.

UNITED Methodist Church (United States) 262.9'8'76
The book of discipline of the United Methodist Church, 1976. Nashville : United Methodist Pub. House, c1976. xi, 664 p. ; 23 cm. Errata slip inserted. Includes index. [BX8388.U55 1976] 76-380158 ISBN 0-687-03707-7
1. United Methodist Church (United States)—Government. I. Title.

United Methodist Church (U.S.)—History.

PROCLAIMING grace and freedom : the story of United Methodism in America / edited by John G. McEllhenney. Nashville : Abingdon, c1982. p. cm. [BX8382.2.A4P76 1982] 19 82-8800 ISBN 0-687-34323-2 pbk. : 6.95 287'.673
1. United Methodist Church (U.S.)—History. 2. Methodist Church—United States—History. I. McEllhenney, John Galen.

United Methodist Church (U.S.)—Membership.

BUTLER, John Wesley.
Mexico coming into light, by John Wesley Butler, thirty-two years missionary in Mexico. Cincinnati, Jennings & Graham; New York, Eaton & Mains [c1907] 101 p. 16 cm. (On cover: Little books on missions) 7-14569
I. Title.

SANO, Roy I. 1931- (Roy Isao), 287'.6
From every nation without number : racial and ethnic diversity in United Methodism / Roy I. Sano. Nashville : Abingdon, c1982. 127 p. ; 21 cm. (Into our third century) Includes bibliographical references. [BX8382.2.Z5S36] 19 81-20610 ISBN 0-687-13642-3 pbk. : 3.95
1. United Methodist Church (U.S.)—Membership. 2. Church and race relations—Methodist Church. I. Title. II. Series.

United Methodist Church (United States)—Missions—Addresses, essays, lectures.

PRINCIPALITIES & powers & people : stories of oppression and hope, based on personal experiences / by eighteen mission interns ; [prepared for the Board of Global Ministries by the Education and Cultivation Division, Board of Global Ministries, the United Methodist Church]. [New York?] : The Board, c1979. 109 p. : ill. ; 22 cm. Includes bibliographical references. [BV2550.P74] 79-114054 pbk. : 2.50 261.8
1. United Methodist Church (United States)—Missions—Addresses, essays, lectures. I. United Methodist Church (United States). Board of Global Ministries. Education and Cultivation Division.
Publisher's Address : 475 Riverside Drive, New York, NY 10027

United Methodist Church (United States). South Central Jurisdiction.

AGNEW, Theodore L. 287'.676
The South Central Jurisdiction, 1939-1972; a brief history and an interpretation, by Theodore L. Agnew. Oklahoma City, Commission on Archives and History, South Central Jurisdiction, United Methodist Church [1973] 96 p. 23 cm. [BX8382.2.A42S682] 73-180924
1. United Methodist Church (United States). South Central Jurisdiction. I. Title.

VERNON, Walter N. 287'.673
One in the Lord : a history of ethnic

minorities in the South Central Jurisdiction, the United Methodist Church / authors, Walter N. Vernon, Alfredo Nanez, John H. Graham ; editor, Walter N. Vernon. Oklahoma City : Commission on Archives and History, South Central Jurisdiction, United Methodist Church, c1977. vi, 146 p. : ill. ; 23 cm. Includes bibliographical references and index. [BV4468.V47] 77-150215
1. United Methodist Church (United States). South Central Jurisdiction. 2. Church work with minorities—Methodist Church. I. Nanez, Alfredo, joint author. II. Graham, John H., joint author. III. United Methodist Church (United States). South Central Jurisdiction. Commission on Archives and History. IV. Title.

United Methodist Church. Western Pennsylvania Conference. Washington District.

BELL, Raymond Martin, 1907- 287'.6748'82
A history of United Methodism in Greene and Washington Counties, Pennsylvania (mainly the Washington District of the Western Pennsylvania Conference) / by Raymond Martin Bell. Washington, Pa. : Bell, 1977. 34 leaves ; 29 cm. [BX8382.2.A42W473] 77-378345
1. United Methodist Church. Western Pennsylvania Conference. Washington District. I. Title: A history of United Methodism in Greene and Washington Counties ...

United Methodist council on the future of faith and service, Chicago, 1938.

NALL, Torney Otto, 1900- ed. 287.666373
Vital religion; a crusading church faces its third century, edited by T. Otto Nall. New York, Cincinnati [etc.] The Methodist book concern [c1938] 150 p. 19 cm. The essence of each address delivered at the meeting of the United Methodist council in Chicago, 1938. cf. Pref. [BX8207.U6 1938] 38-14469
1. United Methodist council on the future of faith and service, Chicago, 1938. 2. Methodist Episcopal church—Congresses. I. Title.

United Missionary Church — History

STORMS, Everck Richard. 289.7
History of the United Missionary Church. Elkhart, Ind., Bethel Pub. Co. [1958] 309 p. illus. 24 cm. [BX9889.A4S8] 58-43134
1. United Missionary Church — Hist. I. Title.

United Presbyterian Church—Doctrinal and controversial works.

FRY, John R. 285'.131
The trivialization of the United Presbyterian Church / John R. Fry. 1st ed. New York : Harper & Row, [1975] x, 85 p. ; 21 cm. Includes bibliographical references. [BX8955.F79 1975] 75-9319 ISBN 0-06-063074-4 : 5.95
1. United Presbyterian Church—Doctrinal and controversial works. I. Title.

United Presbyterian Church in the U.S.A.

THE golden harvest;
the Presbyterian Town and Country Church Movement. [Boone, Iowa] United Presbyterian Church in the United States of America, Board of National Missions, Department of Town and Country Church, 1960. xv, 285p. 21cm.
I. Randolph, Henry S

HANZSCHE, William Thomson, 1891- 285.4
Know your Church; the United Presbyterian Church in the U.S.A. Rev., rewritten by Earl F. Zeigler. Philadelphia, Board of Christian Educ. of the United Presbyterian Church in the United States of America [dist. Westminister Pr., 1962, c.1961] 63p. Rev. of the author's 'Know your church! The Presbyterian Church: its history, organization, and program,' pub. in 1946, orig. pub. in 1933 under title, 'Our Presbyterian Church.' 61-14520 .85 pap.,
1. United Presbyterian Church in the U. S. A. I. Zeigler, Earl Frederick, 1889- II. Title.

HOW in the world. 285'.131
[Edited by Earl K. Larson, Jr. Philadelphia, 1966?] 283 p. illus., ports. 26 cm. "Compiled under the 177th General Assembly's call to Renewal and Extension of the Church's Ministry in the World for the study and understanding of the whole work of the United Presbyterian Church in the United States of America for 1965-1966." [BX8955.H68] 70-19337
1. United Presbyterian Church in the U.S.A. I. Larson, Earl K., ed.

MCINTIRE, Carl, 1906- 285'.131
The death of a church. Collingswood, N.J., Christian Beacon Press [1967] viii, 215 p. 18 cm. "The Confession of 1967": p. 179-195. [BX8955.M3] 78-14671
1. United Presbyterian Church in the U.S.A. Confession of 1967. 2. United Presbyterian Church in the U.S.A.—Doctrinal and controversial works. I. United Presbyterian Church in the U.S.A. Confession of 1967. 1967. II. Title.

SHANNON, Foster H., 1930- 285'.131
The growth crisis in the American church : a Presbyterian case study / Foster H. Shannon. South Pasadena, Calif. : William Carey Library, c1977. xv, 159 p. : ill. ; 22 cm. Includes index. Bibliography: p. [151]-155. [BR517.S38] 76-51359 ISBN 0-87808-152-6 pbk. : 4.95
1. United Presbyterian Church in the U.S.A. 2. Church growth—United States—Case studies. I. Title.

UNITED Presbyterian Church in the U.S.A. Board of Christian Education.
The church in Christian faith and life; a study course to prepare local churches for the use of the curriculum Christian Faith and Life, a Program for Church and Home. 3d ed. Philadelphia, 1962 63 p. 65-40417
I. Title.

United Presbyterian Church in the U.S.A. Board of Christian Education.

HUNT, George Laird.
Be what you are; a study guide on Colossians and Philemon ... [New York] United Presbyterian Women in conjunction with Division of Lay Education, Board of Christian Education, United Presbyterian Church U.S.A. [1963] 64 p. 23 cm. "Resources": p. 64. 64-73475
I. Title.

UNITED Presbyterian Church in the U. S. A. Board of Christian Education.
Handbook for Board of Christian Education and its staff. [Philadelphia, 1963] 96 p. 68-47299
1. United Presbyterian Church in the U. S. A. Board of Christian Education. I. Title.

United Presbyterian Church in the U.S.A. — Catechisms and creeds.

DOWEY, Edward A. 238'.5'131
A commentary on the Confession of 1967 and an introduction to The book of confessions, by Edward A. Dowey, Jr. Philadelphia, Westminster Press [1968] 273 p. 21 cm. "The Confession of 1967": p. 13-25. [BX8955.D68] 68-27690 2.65
1. United Presbyterian Church in the U.S.A.—Catechisms and creeds. 2. United Presbyterian Church in the U.S.A.—Doctrinal and controversial works. I. United Presbyterian Church in the U.S.A. Confession of 1967. 1968 II. Title.

MILES, O. Thomas. 238'.5'131
Crisis and creed; a contemporary statement of faith [by] O. Thomas Miles. Grand Rapids, Eerdmans [1968] 82 p. 20 cm. Bibliographical footnotes. [BX9183.M5] 68-20586
1. United Presbyterian Church in the U.S.A.—Catechisms and creeds. 2. United Presbyterian Church in the U.S.A.—Doctrinal and controversial works. I. Title.

UNITED Presbyterian Church in the U.S.A. 262'.05'131
The constitution of the United Presbyterian Church in the United States of America. Philadelphia, Office of the General Assembly of the United Presbyterian Church in the United States of America [1967] 2 v. 23 cm. Contents.Contents.—v. 1. Book of confessions.—v. 2. Book of order. [BX8955.A3 1967] 68-595
1. United Presbyterian Church in the U.S.A.—Catechisms and creeds. I. Title.

UNITED Presbyterian Church in the U.S.A. General Assembly. 238'.5'131
The proposed Book of confessions of the United Presbyterian Church in the United States of America. Philadelphia, 1966. 186 p. 23 cm. [BX8955.A27] 567
1. United Presbyterian Church in the U.S.A. — Catechisms and creeds. I. Title.

VAN TIL, Cornelius, 1895- 238'.5'132
The confession of 1967, its theological background and ecumenical significance Philadelphia, Presbyterian and Reformed Pub. Co., 1967. vi, 128 p. 23 cm. Bibliographical references included in "Publisher's note" (p. v-vi) [BX9183.V3] 66-30704
1. United Presbyterian Church in the U.S.A.—Catechisms and creeds. 2. United Presbyterian Church in the U.S.A.—Doctrinal and controversial works. I. Title.

United Presbyterian church in the U.S.A. — Church government and discipline.

UNITED Presbyterian Church in the U.S.A.
Presbyterian law for the presbytery; a manual for ministers and ruling elders [by] Eugene Carson Blake [and] Edward Burns Shaw. Rev. Philadelphia, Published for the Office of the General assembly by the General division of publication of the Board of Christian education of the Presbyterian church in the United States of America, 1960 [c1958] 156 p. diagr. 22 cm. "A treatment of Presbyterian law with special reference to the place, powers, and responsibilities of the presbytery in the United Presbyterian church in the United States of America." 63-59688
1. United Presbyterian church in the U.SA. — Church government and discipline. I. Blake, Eugene Carson, 1906- II. Shaw, Edward Burns. III. Title.

United Presbyterian Church in the U.S.A. — Doctrinal and controversial works.

HOGE, Dean R., 1937- 280'.4'0973
Division in the Protestant house : the basic reasons behind intra-church conflicts / by Dean R. Hoge, with the research assistance of Everett L. Perry, Dudley E. Sarfaty, and John E. Dyble ; with the editorial assistance of Grace Ann Goodman. Philadelphia : Westminster Press, c1976. 166 p. : ill. ; 23 cm. Includes bibliographical references. [BR516.5.H64] 76-1022 ISBN 0-664-24793-8 pbk. : 3.95
1. United Presbyterian Church in the U.S.A.—Doctrinal and controversial works. 2. Theology, Protestant—United States. 3. Sociology, Christian—United States. I. Title.

MUDGE, Lewis Seymour. 261
Why is the church in the world? [by] Lewis S. Mudge, Jr. [Philadelphia?] Board of Christian Education, United Presbyterian Church in the United States of America [1967] 95 p. 21 cm. [BR115.W6M8] 67-9285
1. United Presbyterian Church in the U.S.A.—Doctrinal and controversial works. 2. Church and the world. I. United Presbyterian Church in the U.S.A. Board of Christian Education. II. Title.

UNITED Presbyterian Church in the U.S.A.
The Constitution of the United Presbyterian Church in the United States of America. Philadelphia, Office of the General Assembly of the United Presbyterian Church in the United States of America [c1961] 351 p. 24 cm. Cover title: The Constitution of the United Presbyterian Church in the United States of America, 1961-1962.
1. United Presbyterian Church in the U.S.A. — Doctrinal and controversial works. 2. United Presbyterian Church in the U.S.A. — Discipline. 3. United Presbyterian Church in the U.S.A. — Catechisms and creeds. I. Title.

United Presbyterian Church in the U.S.A.-Education.

FRITZ, Dorothy Bertolet.
Activity programs for junior groups; a guide for adult advisers, including four expandable units of creative discovery, concerning the making and use of the Bible, worship, stewardship, and the world church. "Books and other resources": p. 197-205. A 62
1. United Presbyterian Church in the-U. S. A. — Education. 2. Activity programs in education. I. Title.

FRITZ, Dorothy Bertolet.
Activity programs for junior groups; a guide for adult advisers, including four expandable units of creative discovery, concerning the making and use of the Bible, worship, stewardship, and the world church. Philadelphia, Westminster Press [1961] 208 p. front. 23 cm. "Books and other resources": p. 197-205. A 62
1. United Presbyterian Church in the-U. S. A. — Education. 2. Activity programs in education. I. Title.

United Presbyterian Church in the U.S.A.—Government

PRESBYTERIAN Church in the U.S.A.
United Presbyterian Church in the U.S.A.: manual for ministers and ruling elders [by] Eugene Carson Blake [and] Edward Burns Shaw. Rev. 1961. Philadelphia, Published for the Office of the General Assembly by the General Division of Publication of the Board of Christian Education of the Presbyterian Church in the [united States of America [1961] 156 p. 23 cm. On cover: 1961/62. 63-36401
1. United Presbyterian Church in the U.S.A.—Govt. I. Blake, Eugene Carson, 1906- II. Shaw, Edward Burns. III. Title.

UNITED Presbyterian Church in the U.S.A. 285.173
Presbyterian law for the local church; a handbook for church officers and members, edited by Eugene Carson Blake. 6th ed., rev. [Philadelphia] Published for the Office of the General Assembly by the General Division of Publication of the Board of Christian Education of the United Presbyterian Church in the U. S. A. [dist. Westminster Press] 1960 [c.1953-1960] 144p. 20cm. 60-3669 1.50 bds.,
1. United Presbyterian Church in the U. S. A.—Government. I. Blake, Eugene Carson. II. Title.

UNITED Presbyterian Church in the U.S.A. 285.1
Presbyterian law for the local church; a handbook for church officers and members. Edited by Eugene Carson Blake. Rev. Philadelphia, 1963. 141 p. 22 cm. [BX8956.A6 1963] 262.05'132 68-2705
1. United Presbyterian Church in the U.S.A.—Government. I. Blake, Eugene Carson, 1906- ed. II. Title.

UNITED Presbyterian Church in the U.S.A.
The Presbyterian constitution and digest. Philadelphia, General Assembly of the United Presbyterian Church in the U.S.A. [c1963] 2 v. 65-25005
I. Title.

UNITED Presbyterian Church in the U.S.A. 262'.05'131
Presbyterian law for presbytery and synod : a manual for ministers and ruling elders, 1976-77 / edited by William P. Thompson. New York : Office of the General Assembly, United Presbyterian Church in the U.S.A., [1976?] 222 p. ; 23 cm. Published in 1967 under title: Presbyterian law for the presbytery. Includes index. [BX8956.U54 1976] 77-150147

1. United Presbyterian Church in the U.S.A.—Government. I. Thompson, William P., 1918- II. Title.

UNITED Presbyterian 285.173
Church in the U.S.A.
Presbyterian law for the local church; a handbook for church officers and members, edited by Eugene Carson Blake. 6th ed., rev. [Philadelphia] Published for the Office of the General Assembly by the General Divison of Publication of the Board of Christian Education of the United Presbyterian Church in the U.S.A., 1960. 144 p. 20 cm. [BX8956.A6 1960] 60-3669
1. United Presbyterian Church in the U.S.A. — Government. I. Blake, Eugene Carson, 1906- ed. II. Title.

UNITED Presbyterian Church in the U.S.A.
Presbyterian law for the local church; a handbook for church officers and members, edited by Eugene Carson Blake. Rev. 1963. Philadelphia, Office of the General Assembly, United Presbyterian Church in the U.S.A. [c1963] 141 p. 20 cm. On cover: 1963-64. 65-25777
1. United Presbyterian Church in the U.S.A. — Government. I. Blake, Eugene Carson, 1906- ed. II. Title.

UNITED Presbyterian Church in the U.S.A.
Presbyterian law for the Presbytery; a manual for ministers and ruling elders [by] Eugene Carson Blake [and] Edward Burns Shaw. Rev. 1962. Philadelphia, Published for the Office of the General Assembly by the General Division of Publication of the Board of Christian Education of the United Presbyterian Church in the United States of America [1962] 156 p. 23 cm. On cover: 1962-63. 63-59689
1. United Presbyterian Church in the U.S.A. — Govt. I. Blake, Eugene Carson, 1906- II. Shaw, Edward Burns. III. Title.

UNITED States 262'.05'131
Presbyterian Church in the U.S.A.
Presbyterian law for the local church : a handbook for church officers and members / edited by Eugene Carson Blake. 1976 revision / by William P. Thompson. New York : Office of the General Assembly, United Presbyterian Church in the U.S.A., 1976. 155 p. ; 23 cm. Includes index. [BX8956.U54 1976a] 77-150148
1. United Presbyterian Church in the U.S.A.—Government. I. Thompson, William P., 1918- II. Title.

United Presbyterian Church in the U.S.A.—History.

PARKER, Inez Moore. 377'.8'5133
The rise and decline of the program of education for Black Presbyterians of the United Presbyterian Church, U.S.A., 1865-1970 / by Inez Moore Parker. San Antonio : Trinity University Press, c1977. 319 p. ; 24 cm. (Presbyterian Historical Society publication series ; 16) Includes index. Bibliography: p. [307]-312. [LC580.P37] 76-49248 ISBN 0-911536-66-3 : 10.00
1. United Presbyterian Church in the U.S.A.—History. 2. Religious education—United States—History. 3. Presbyterians, Afro-American—United States—History. I. Title: The rise and decline of the program of education ... II. Series: Presbyterian Historical Society. Publications ; 16.

PRINCETON, Ind. United Presbyterian church.
1810-1910; centennial celebration of the United Presbyterian church Princeton, Indiana comp. by Gilbert R. Stormont... Terre Haute, Ind., The Moore-Langen printing co., 1911. xi, [13]-117 p. front., illus., ports. 23 cm. 17-8255
I. Stormont, Gilbert R., comp. II. Title.

United Presbyterian Church in the U.S.A.—Membership—Statistics.

UNITED Presbyterian 285'.131
Church in the U.S.A. General Assembly. Special Committee on Church Membership Trends.
Membership trends in the United Presbyterian Church in the U.S.A. ; research report / prepared by Special Committee of the General Assembly Mission Council to Study Church Membership Trends ; chairperson, C. Edward Brubaker .... [New York?] : The Assembly, c1976. xiv, 315 p. : ill. ; 28 cm. [BX8950.U56 1976] 76-370965 5.00
1. United Presbyterian Church in the U.S.A.—Membership—Statistics. I. Brubaker, Charles Edward, 1917- II. Title.

United Presbyterian Church in the U.S.A. — Missions.

UNITED Presbyterian Church in the U.S.A. Commission on Ecumenical Mission and Relations.
An advisory study. New York, 1961 94 p. 22 cm. "A working paper for study not to be interpreted as the policy of the Commission." Bibliography: p. 93-94. 63-59697
1. United Presbyterian Church in the U.S.A. — Missions. 2. Presbyterian Church-Missions. 3. Missions-Theory. I. Title.

United Presbyterian Church in the U.S.A. Synods. Texas—History.

PASCHAL, George H. 285'.1764
One hundred years of challenge and change; a history of the Synod of Texas of the United Presbyterian Church in the U.S.A., by George H. Paschal, Jr. and Judith A. Benner. San Antonio, Trinity University Press [1968] x, 259 p. 24 cm. Bibliography: p. [244]-249. [BX8941.P35] 68-20488 6.00
1. United Presbyterian Church in the U.S.A. Synods. Texas—History. I. Benner, Judith A., joint author. II. Title.

United Presbyterian church of North America.

MCCULLOCH, William Edward.
The United Presbyterian church and its work in America, by W. E. McCulloch ... [Pittsburgh, Pa.] Board of home missions of the United Presbyterian church of North America [c1925] 2 p. l., ix-xvi, 258 p., 1 l. front., illus., maps (1 fold.) diagr. 20 cm. [BX8982.M3] 25-11447
1. United Presbyterian church of North America. 2. United Presbyterian church of North America—Missions. 3. Missions, Home. I. Title.

UNITED Presbyterian church of North America. Foreign missionary jubilee convention, Pittsburg, 1904.
... Foreign missionary jubilee convention of the United Presbyterian church of N.A. celebrating the fiftieth anniversary of the founding of missions in Egypt and India; December 6-8, 1904, Pittsburg, Pa. Philadelphia, The Board of foreign missions of the United Presbyterian church of N.A [1905] 292, [2], 16, [42] p. illus., ports., diagrs. 23 1/2 cm. Appended: Program and music for the semi-centennial foreign missionary convention. 5-13530
I. Title.

UNITED Presbyterian 285.473
church of North America. General assembly.
The digest of the principal deliverances of the General assembly of the United Presbyterian church of North America, compiled by the Rev. O. H. Milligan ... Pittsburgh, Pa., United Presbyterian Board of publication and Bible school work, 1942. 549 p. 23 1/2 cm. [BX8986.A5 1942] 42-18145
I. Milligan, Orlando Howard, 1873- II. Title.

THE United Presbyterian directory; a half-century survey, 1903-1958, compiled for the Committee on centennial celebration ... Pittsburgh, Pa., Pickwick press [1958] 394p. 23cm. 'A supplement to the Cyclopedic manual of the United Presbyterian church of North America, by William Melancthon Glasgow ... 1903.'
I. Kelsey, Hugh Alexander, 1872- II. Glasgow, William Melancthon, 1856-1909. Cyclopedic manual. Supplement.

United Presbyterian Church of North America — Catechisms and creeds.

UNITED Presbyterian 285.173
Church of North America.
The confessional statement and The book of government and worship. [Pittsburgh, Board of Christian Education of the United Presbyterian Church of North America, 1951] 195 p. 16 cm. Cover title. In 2 pts., each with special t.p. [BX8985.A3] 51-26517
1. United Presbyterian Church of North America — Catechisms and creeds. 2. United Presbyterian Church of North America — Government. I. Title.

UNITED Presbyterian 285.173
Church of North America.
The confessional statement and The book of government and worship. [Pittsburgh, 1948] 195 p. 16 cm. Cover title. In 2 pts., each with special t-p. [BX8985.A3 1948] 48-25385
1. United Presbyterian Church of North America—Catechisms and creeds. 2. United Presbyterian Church of North America—Government. I. Title.

United Presbyterian church of North America—Education.

MCNAUGHER, John, 1857- 207.73
The history of theological education in the United Presbyterian church and its ancestries, by John McNaugher... Pittsburgh, Pa., United Presbyterian board of publication and Bible school work. 1931. 80 p. plates. 20 cm. [BX8917.M3] 32-821
1. United Presbyterian church of North America—Education. 2. Theological seminaries, Presbyterian. 3. Theological seminaries—U.S. I. Title.

United Presbyterian Church of North America—History

JAMISON, Wallace N 285.473
The United Presbyterian story; a centennial study, 1858-1958. Pittsburgh, Geneva Press [1958] 253p. illus. 21cm. Includes bibliography. [BX8982.J3] 58-1931
1. United Presbyterian Church of North America—Hist. I. Title.

United Presbyterian church of North America—Hymns.

BIBLE. O.T. Psalms. English. Paraphrases. 1872.
The Psalter. The Scottish version of the Psalms revised, and the new versions adopted by the United Presbyterian church, appropriately arranged and adapted to music by Rev. R. B. Robertson, assisted by Rev. John Gaily ... Philadelphia, Ferguson & Woodburn, 1872. 352 p. 18 cm. [M2130.B5P8 1872] 45-27791
1. United Presbyterian church of North America—Hymns. 2. Hymns, English. I. United Presbyterian church of North America. II. Robertson, R. B. III. Gaily, John. IV. Title.

BIBLE. O.T. Psalms. English. Paraphrases. 1887.
The Psalter of the United Presbyterian church of North America. With music ... Pittsburgh, United Presbyterian board of publication, 1887. iv, 508 p. 21 1/2 x 16 1/2 cm. Preface signed: Revision committee. [M2130.B5P8 1887] 45-42167
1. United Presbyterian church of North America—Hymns. 2. Hymns, English. I. United Presbyterian church of North America. Board of publication. II. Title.

UNITED Presbyterian Church 783.9
of North America. Board of Christian Education.
Sons for Christian worship; a selection of psalms and hymns for use in the church, the Bible school, the youth groups, and the home. Pittsburgh, 1950. 384 p. 22 cm. With music. Scripture readings: p. 333-374. [M2130.U5S6] 51-4162
1. United Presbyterian Church of North America — Hymns. 2. Hymns, English. I. Title.

United Presbyterian Church of North America—Missions.

FAIRMAN, Marion. 266.54
The tumbling walls, by Marion and Edwin Fairman. [Philadelphia] Board of Foreign Missions of the United Presbyterian Church of N. A. [1957] 192p. illus. 21cm. Includes bibliography. [BV2570.F2] 57-39886
1. United Presbyterian Church of North America—Missions. 2. Missions—Pakistan. 3. Missions—Africa, Northeast. I. Fairman, Edwin, joint author. II. Title.

... In the King's service. 366.
Philadelphia, Pa., The Board of foreign missions of the United Presbyterian church of N. A. [1905] 1 p. l., [5]-225, [12] p. pl., 6 port., diagrs. 19 cm. (A mission study course along biographical lines, ed. by C. R. Watson) [BV2030.I 4] 5-5919
Contents omitted.

United Reformed Church.

SLACK, Kenneth. 285'.42
The United Reformed Church / by Kenneth Slack ; foreword by Arthur L. Macarthur. Exeter [Eng.] : Religious Education Press, c1978. 52 p. : ill. ; 19 cm. (The Christian denominations series) Bibliography: p. 51. [BX9890.U254S558] 79-308672 ISBN 0-08-021414-2 pbk. : 2.25
1. United Reformed Church. I. Title. II. Series.
Distributed by British Book Center, Elmsford, NY 10523

United Society for the Propagation of the Gospel.

CALAM, John. 377'.8'373
Parsons and pedagogues: the S.P.G. adventure in American education. New York, Columbia University Press, 1971. xi, 249 p. 21 cm. Includes bibliographical references. [LC582.U53C3] 77-139603 ISBN 0-231-03371-0 10.00
1. United Society for the Propagation of the Gospel. 2. Church of England in America—Education—History. I. Title.

United Society for the Propagation of the Gospel—Archives.

MANROSS, William 016.266'3
Wilson, 1905-
S.P.G. papers in the Lambeth Palace Library; calendar and indexes. Oxford, Clarendon Press, 1974. xi, 230 p. 24 cm. [CD1069.L77M36] 74-179961 ISBN 0-19-920065-3
1. United Society for the Propagation of the Gospel—Archives. 2. Lambeth Palace. Library. I. United Society for the Propagation of the Gospel. II. Lambeth Palace. Library. III. Title.
Distributed by Oxford University Press, New York, 32.50.

United society of Christian endeavor.

CLARK, Francis Edward, 1851-
Memories of many men in many lands, an autobiography, by Francis E. Clark... Boston, Chicago, United society of Christian endeavor [1922] xxi, 704 p. incl. illus., plates, ports. front. (port.) plates. 23 1/2 cm. Appendix: List of books by Francis E. Clark, with date of issue, name of publisher,and brief comments. [BV1432.C6A5] 23-289
1. United society of Christian endeavor. I. Title.

HAGGARD, Mildreth. 287.613
The junior worker's note-book, by Mildreth Haggard... Boston, Mass., Chicago, Ill., International society of Christian endeavor [c1929] 79 p. 17 cm. "List of reference-books for junior workers": p. 44-48. [BV1429.H3] CA 30
1. United society of Christian endeavor. I. Title.

INTERNATIONAL society of 267-6131
Christian endeavor.
Official report of the ... international Christian endeavor convention ... Boston, United society of Christian endeavor [18 - 19 v. fronts., illus., plates, ports. 23-23 1/2 cm. Title varies: 10th, 1891, Narrative of

the ... annual conference of the Young people's societies of Christian endeavor ... 11th- 1892- Official report of the ... International Christian endeavor convention ... 22d, 1905, The story of the Baltimore convention; the official report of the ... international Christian endeavor convention ... 23d, 1907, The story of the Seattle convention; the official report ... 24th, 1909, The story of the St. Paul convention; the official report ... 25th, 1911, The story of the Oceanic convention; the official report ... 27th, 1915, The story of the Chicago convention; the official report of the twenty-seventh international (fifth world's) Christian endeavor convention. [BV1421.A2] 99-3867
I. Title.

SHAW, William, 1860-
The evolution of an Endeavorer; an autobiography by William Shaw ... Boston, Mass., The Christian endeavor world, 1924. 437 p. incl. plates, ports. front. 22 cm. Plates printed on both sides. [BV1423.S5A4] 24-4534
1. United society of Christian endeavor. I. Title.

WELLS, Amos Russel, 1862- 267.613
Expert endeavor; a text-book of Christian endeavor methods and principles, for the use of classes and of candidates for the title of "C.E.E."--"Christian endeavor expert", by Amos R. Wells ... Boston and Chicago, International society of Christian endeavor [c1928] 122 p., 1 l. 17 cm. On cover: Revised edition. [BV1426.W43 1928] 30-19599
1. United society of Christian endeavor. I. Title.

WELLS, Amos Russel, 1862-
The Junior text-book; a manual of questions and answers of Junior Christian endeavor work, for superintendents and members of Junior societies of Christian endeavor, by Amos R. Wells ... Boston and Chicago, United society of Christian endeavor [c1911] 100 p. 18 1/2 cm. $0.50. 12-1403
I. Title.

WELLS, Amos Russel, 1862- 240
The officers' handbook; a guide for officers in young people's societies, with chapters on parliamentary law and other useful themes, by Amos R. Wells. Boston and Chicago, United society of Christian endeavor [c1900] 143 p. 15 1/2 cm. [BV1426.W485] 0-6484
1. United society of Christian endeavor. 2. Parliamentary practice. I. Title.

WELLS, Amos Russel, 1862-
Progressive endeavor, by Amos R. Wells ... Rev. ed. Boston and Chicago, United society of Christian endeavor [c1927] 115 p. 19 1/2 cm. [BV1425.W4 1927] 28-9956
1. United society of Christian endeavor. I. Title.

WELLS, Amos Russell, 1862-
Union work; a manual for local, county, district, and state Christian endeavor unions, by Amos R. Wells ... Boston and Chicago, United society of Christian endeavor [c1916] 313 p. 19 1/2 cm. $1.00. 16-18566
I. Title.

United States.

CARR, John Foster, 1869-
Guide to the United States for the Jewish immigrant: a nearly literal translation of the 2d Yiddish ed., by John Foster Carr ... Pub. under the auspices of the Connecticut Daughters of the American revolution. New York, J. F. Carr, 1912. 63, [1] p. plates, 2 port. (incl. front.) 2 maps (1 fold.) forms. 19 cm. [JV6543.A5C3 1912] 12-29049 0.15
1. United States. I. Daughters of the American revolution. Connecticut. II. Title.

CARR, John Foster, 1869-
Guide to the United States for the Jewish immigrant; a nearly literal translation of the 2d Yiddish ed., by John Foster Carr. [3d ed.] New York, Immigrant publication society, incorporated, 1916. 64 p. plates, 2 port. (incl. front.) 2 maps (1 fold.) forms. 18 cm. [JV6545.Y5C3 1916] 16-3125 0.50
1. United States. I. Title.

HOWARD, Milford Wriarson, 1862-
If Christ came to Congress. With an introd. by Harvey Wish. New York, Living Books, 1964. xvii, 364 p. 65-69681
I. Title. II. Title: (A Clarion book)

STRONG, Josiah, 1847-1916. 277.
Our country, its possible future and its present crisis. By Rev. Josiah Strong ... with an introduction by Prof. Austin Phelps, D.D. Rev. ed. based on the census of 1890. One hundred and sixty-seventh thousand. New York, Pub. by the Baker & Taylor co. for the American home missionary society [1896?] 2 p. l., [3]-5, [vii]-x, [11]-275 p. illus. (map) 19 1/2 cm. [BV2775.S8 1896] 17-8242
1. United States. I. Title.

United States—Army—Chaplains.

PROEHL, Frederick C ed. 264.041
Service manual for Lutheran chaptams serving with the forces of the United States, prepared by Frederick C. Proehl ... Issued under auspices of the Army and navy commission of the Evangelical Lutheran synod of Missouri, Ohio, and other states. Chicago, Ill., [1942] 160 p. illus. (1 col.) 14 cm. [BV199.M5P7] 42-14677
1. U. S.—Army—Chaplains. 2. U. S.—Navy—Chaplain corps. 3. Soldiers—Prayer-books and devotions—English. I. Lutheran church. Liturgy and ritual. II. Evangelical Lutheran synod of Missouri, Ohio, and other states. Army and navy ommission. III. Title.

United States—Biography

BALDWIN, Charles Jacobs, 1841- 920
The first American and other Sunday evening studies in biography, by Charles J. Baldwin, D. D. Granville, O., First Baptist church, 1911. 3 p. l., [5]-291 p. front., ports. 20 cm. [E176.B17] 12-214 1.25
1. U. S.—Biog. 2. Biography. I. Title.
Contents omitted.

MCNAMARA, Robert Francis, 1910- 282'.092'2 B
Catholic Bicentennial profiles / by Robert F. McNamara. [Rochester, N.Y. : Christopher Press], c1975. 31 p. ; 18 cm. [BX4670.M25] 76-359391
1. Catholic Church in the United States—Biography. 2. United States—Biography. I. Title.

MALONE, Dumas, 1892- 920.073
Saints in action. Freeport, N.Y., Books for Libraries Press [1971] 178 p. 22 cm. (Essay index reprint series) Reprint of the 1939 ed. Includes bibliographical references. [E176.M26 1970] 70-142664 ISBN 0-8369-2062-7
1. U.S.—Biography. 2. Christian biography. I. Title.

MILLER, Karl Palmer, 1889- 277.3
How in the world do Americans? A biographical inquiry. [1st ed.] New York, Pageant Press [1957] 240p. 21cm. [BR569.M5] 57-8232
1. U. S.—Biog. 2. U. S.—Religion. I. Title.

United States—Biography—Study and teaching.

CLARK, Mary Ann. 282'.092'2 B
Great American Catholics / by Mary Ann Clark, Jerri Pogue, Diane Rickard ; ill. by Robert L. Mutchler. Notre Dame, Ind. : Ave Maria Press, c1976. 191 p. : ill. ; 23 cm. Includes bibliographical references. [BX4670.C48] 76-7278 ISBN 0-87793-111-9 pbk. : 3.50
1. Catholic Church in the United States—Biography—Study and teaching. 2. Catholic Church in the United States—Biography. 3. United States—Biography—Study and teaching. I. Pogue, Jerri, joint author. II. Rickard, Diane, joint author. III. Title.

United States Center for World Mission.

WINTER, Roberta H. 266'.023
Once more around Jericho : the story of the U.S. Center for World Mission / Roberta H. Winter. South Pasadena, Calif. : William Carey Library, c1978. xiv, 234 p. ; 18 cm. [BV2360.U553W56] 78-66367 ISBN 0-87808-167-4 pbk. : 2.95
1. U.S. Center for World Mission. I. Title.

United States Christian commission.

CHRIST in the army;
a selection of sketches of the work of the U.S. Christian commission, by various writers. Printed for the Ladies Christian commission. [Philadelphia, J. B. Rodgers, pr.] 1865. 144 p. l. illus. (port.) 14 1/2 cm. [E635.C54] 26-23335
1. United States Christian commission. 2. U.S.—Hist.—Civil war—Religious life, etc. I. Ladies Christian commission, Philadelphia.

CROSS, Andrew Boyd.
The war Battle of Gettysburg and the Christian commission. By Andrew B. Cross. [Baltimore] 1865. 60. 32 p. 3 fold maps. 23 cm. [E635.C95] 2-28218
1. United States Christian commission. 2. Gettysburg, Battle of 1863. I. Title.

MOSS, Lemuel, 1829-1904.
Annals of the United States Christian commission. By Rev. Lemuel Moss, home secretary to the commission. Philadelphia, J. B. Lippincott & co., 1868. 752 p. front. (port.) illus., plates. 24 cm. "Prepared in accordance with the request of the Executive committee of the ... commission, and under the superintendence of a special committee appointed for that purpose."--Pref., p. 5. "List of delegates ...": p. 602-638. [E635.M91] 2-18786
1. United States Christian commission. 2. U.S.—Hist.—Civil war—Religious life, etc. I. Title.

SMITH, Edward Parmelee, 1827-1876.
Incidents of the United States Christian commission. By Edward P. Smith ... Philadelphia, J. B. Lippincott & co., 1869. 512 p. illus., pl. 22 1/2 cm. Also published without index [Philadelphia? c1868] under title: Incidents among shot and shell. [E635.S646] 2-18787
1. United States Christian commission. 2. U.S.—Hist.—Civil war—Anecdotes. I. Title.

SMITH, Edward Parmelee, 1827-1876.
Incidents of the United States Christian commission, by Rev. Edward P. Smith ... Philadelphia, J. B. Lippincott & co., 1871. 512 p. front., illus., plates. 22 1/2 cm. First pub. in 1868, under title: Incidents among shot and shell. [E635.S647] 7-31301
1. U.S. Christian commission. 2. U.S.—Hist.—Civil war—Anecdotes. I. Title.

United States—Church history.

THE American church history series, consisting of a series of 284 denominational histories published under the auspices of the American society of church history: general editors, Rev. Philip Schaff ...Rt. Rev. H. C. Potter ... Rev. Samuel M. Jackson [and others] [New York, The Christian literature co., 1893-87] 13 v. 21 cm. Half-title. Contents.1. The religious forces of the United States, by H. K. Carroll.--v. 2. A history of the Baptist churches, by A. H. Newman.--v. 3. A history of the Congregational churches, by Williston Walker.--v. 4. A history of the Evangelical Lutheran church, by H. E. Jacobs.--v. 5. A history of Methodists, by J. M. Buckley.--v. 6. A history of the Presbyterian churches, by R. E. Thompson.--v. 7. A history of the Protestant Episcopal church, by C. C. Tiffany.--v. 8. History of the Reformed church. Dutch, by E. T. Corwin. History of the Reformed church. German, by J. H. Dubbs. A history of the United fratrum, or Moravian church, by J. T. Hamilton.--v. 9. A history of the Roman Catholic church, by Thomas O'Gorman.--v. 10. Historical sketch of the Unitarian movement since the reformation, by J. H. Allen. History of Universallsin, by Richard Eddy.--v. 11. History of the Methodist Episcopal church, South by Gross Alexander. History of the United Presbyterian church, by J. B. Scouller. A sketch of the history of the Cumberland Presbyterian church, by R. V. Foster. History of the Southern Presbyterian church, by T. C. Johnson.--v. 12. History of the Disciples of Christ, by B. B Tyler. History of the church of the United brethren in Christ, by D. Berger. History of the Evangelical association, by S. P. Spreng. A bibliography of American church history, 1820-1893. compiled by S. M. Jackson.--v.13. A history of American Christiantity, by L. W. Bacon. Contains bibliographies. [BR515.A5] 4-21612
1. U. S.—Church history. I. Schaff, Philip, 1819-1893. ed. II. Potter, Henry Codman, bp., 1834-1908. joint ed. III. Jackson, Samuel Macauley, 1851-1912, joint ed.

BACON, Leonard Woolsey, 1830-1907. 277.3
... A history of American Christianity, by Leonard Woolsey Bacon. New York, The Christian literature co., 1897. X, 420 p. 21 cm. (Half-title: The American church history series, vol. xiii) [BR515.A5 vol.13] 277.3 4-4643
1. U. S.—Church history. 2. U. S.—Religion. I. Title.

BAIRD, Robert, 1798-1863. 209'.73
Religion in America. A critical abridgement with introd. by Henry Warner Bowden. New York, Harper & Row [1970] xxxvii, 314 p. 21 cm. (Harper torchbooks, TB 1509) First published in 1844 under title: Religion in the United States of America. Bibliography: p. 304-305. [BR515.B322B3] 75-114093 2.95
1. U.S.—Church history. I. Bowden, Henry Warner, ed. II. Title.

BAIRD, Robert, 1798-1863. 277.3
Religion in America; or, An account of the origin, relation to the state, and present condition of the evangelical churches in the United States. With notices of the unevangelical demoninations. By Robert Baird. New York, Harper & brothers, 1856. xvii, [19]-696 p. 24 cm. Published in Great Britain as: Religion in the United States of America ... [BR515.B3 1856] 31-29076
1. U. S.—Church history. I. Title.

BAIRD, Robert, 1798-1863. 277.3
Religion in the United States of America. New York, Arno Press, 1969. xix, 736 p. map. 23 cm. (Religion in America) Reprint of the 1844 ed. Includes bibliographical references. [BR515.B3 1969] 70-83411
1. United States—Church history. I. Title.

BEARDSLEY, Frank Grenville, 1870- 277.3
The history of Christianity in America, by Frank Grenville Beardsley ... New York, American tract society [c1938] 244 p. 20 cm. [BR515.B47] 39-280
1. U.S.—Church history. 2. U.S.—Religion. 3. Protestant churches—U.S. I. American tract society. II. Title.

BILHEIMER, Robert S 1917- 280.1
The quest for Christian unity. New York, Association Press [1952] 181p. 20cm. (A Haddam House book) [BR516.B47] 52-14564
1. U. S.—Church history. 2. Sects—U. S. 3. Christian union—U. S. I. Title.

BODO, John R 261
The Protestant clergy and public issues, 1812-1848. Princeton, PrincetonUniversity Press, 1954. xiv, 291p. 23cm. Bibliography: p.261-284. [BR525.B63] 53-6379
1. U. S.—Church history. 2. Church and state in the U. S. I. Title.

BODO, John R. 261
The Protestant clergy and public issues, 1812-1848 / by John R. Bodo. Philadelphia : Porcupine Press, 1980, c1954. xiv, 291 p. ; 22 cm. (Perspectives in American history ; no. 45) Reprint of the ed. published by Princeton University Press, Princeton, N.J. Includes index. Bibliography: p. 261-284. [BR525.B63

1980] 79-12849 ISBN 0-87991-854-3 lib. bdg. : 19.50
1. United States—Church history. 2. Church and state in the United States—History. 3. Protestant churches—United States—Clergy. I. Title. II. Series: Perspectives in American history (Philadelphia) ; no. 45.

BROWN, William Adams, 1865- 204
The church in America; a study of the present condition and future prospects of American Protestantism, by William Adams Brown... New York, The Macmillan company, 1922. xv, 378 p. 22 1/2 cm. [BR525.B8] 22-16154
1. U.S.—Church history. 2. Protestants in the U.S. 3. Sociology, Christian. I. Title.

CAIRNS, Earle Edwin, 1910- 277.3
Christianity in the United States. Chicago, Moody [c.1964] 192p. illus. 22cm. (Christian handbks.) Bibl. 64-20990 1.75 pap.,
1. U.S.—Church history. I. Title.

CARROLL, Henry King, 1848- 284
1931.
The religious forces of the United States enumerated, classified, and described; returns for 1900 and 1910 compared with the government census of 1890: condition and characteristics of Christianity in the United States, by H. K. Carroll ... Rev. and brought down to 1910. New York, C. Scribner's sons, 1912. ixxxviii, 488 p. incl. tables, diagrs. 21 cm. [BR515.C3 1912] 12-25100
1. U. S.—Church history. 2. U. S.—Religion. 3. Sects—U. S. 4. Church statistics—U. S. I. Title.

CARROLL, Henry King, 1848- 284
1931.
... The religious forces of the United States, enumerated, classified, and described on the basis of the government census of 1890; with an introduction on the condition and character of American Christianity, by H. K. Carroll ... New York, The Christian literature co., 1893. ixii, 449 p. 21 cm. (Half-title: The American church history series, vol. i) Series title also at head of t.-p. [BR515.A5 vol. 1] 4-4646
1. U. S.—Church history. 2. U. S.—Religion. 3. Sects—U. S. 4. Church statistics—U. S. I. Title. II. Series.

CARROLL, Henry King, 1848-1931.
... The religious forces of the United States, enumerated, classified, and described on the basis of the government census of 1890; with an introduction on the condition and character of American Christianity, by H. K. Carroll ... Rev. January 1, 1896, with additional tables of statistics for the five years since the census of 1890. New York, The Christian literature co., 1893 [i. e. 1896] ixvii, 478 p. incl tables, diagrs. 21 cm. (Half-title: The American church history series ... vol. i) Series title also at head of t.-p. [BR515C3 1896] 19-12745
1. U. S.—Church history. 2. U. S.—Religion. 3. Sects—U. S. 4. Church statistics—U. S. I. Title. II. Series.

CLEBSCH, William A. 209'.73
From sacred to profane America : the role of religion in American history / by William Clebsch. [Tallahassee, Fla.] : American Academy of Religion ; Chico, CA : Distributed by Scholars Press, c1981. p. cm. (Classics and reprints series of the American Academy of Religion and Scholars Press ; no. 3) Reprint. Originally published: 1st ed. New York : Harper & Row, 1968. Includes bibliographical references and index. [BR515.C55 1981] 19 81-9142 ISBN 0-89130-519-X pbk. : 9.95
1. United States—Church history. 2. United States—Religion. I. American Academy of Religion. II. Title.

CLEVELAND, Catharine 277.
Caroline.
Great revival in the West, seventeen ninety-seven-eighteen hundred-five, by Catharine C. Cleveland. Chicago, Ill., The University of Chicago press [1916] xii, 215 p. 4 maps. 19 1/2 cm. Published also as thesis (PH.D.) University of Chicago, 1914. Bibliography: p. 206-215. [BR520.C62] 16-11053 1.00.
1. U.S.—Chruch history. 2. Revivals. I. Title.

CROWELL, Katharine Roney, 284
1854-1926.
The call of the waters; a study of the frontier, by Katharine R. Cromwell ... New York, Chicago [etc.] Fleming H. Revell company [c1908] 2 p. l., 3-157 p. front., 5 pl. 19 cm. [Home mission study course. 6] "Books of reference" at end of each chapter. [BR515.C9] 8-20327
1. U. S.—Church history. 2. U. S.—Hist. I. Title.

CURRAN, Francis X. 277.3
Major trends in American church history, by Francis X. Curran ... New York, The American press [1946] xviii p., 1 l., 198 p. 20 1/2 cm. "List of books cited": p. 182-190. [BR515.C95] 46-3025
1. U.S.—Church history. I. Title.

CURRAN, Francis Xavier, 277.3
1914-
Major trends in American church history, by Francis X. Curran ... New York, The American press [1946] xviii p., 1 l., 198 p. 21 cm. "List of books cited": p. 182-190. [BR515.C95] 46-3025
1. U. S.—Church history. I. Title.

DOMAS, Anna Wirtz. 232.91'0973
Mary-U.S.A. / Anna Wirtz Domas. Huntington, Ind. : Our Sunday Visitor, c1978. ix, 350 p. : ill. ; 29 cm. Includes index. Bibliography: p. 331-343. [BT652.U6D65] 78-69994 ISBN 0-87973-889-8 : 19.95
1. Mary, Virgin—Cultus—United States. 2. United States—Church history. 3. United States—History. I. Title.

DORCHESTER, Daniel, 1827- 284
1907.
Christianity in the United States from the first settlement down to the present time. By Daniel Dorchester, D. D. New York, Phillips & Hunt; Cincinnati, Cranston & Stowe, 1888. 795 p. incl. tables. front. (port.) 3 maps (2 double) 2 double col. charts, xi diagr. 25 cm. Contents.--i. The colonial era.--ii. The national era: Period i. From 1776 to 1800. Period ii. From 1800 to 1850. Period iii. From 1850 to 1887. [BR515.D7 1888] 17-24386
1. U. S.—Church history. I. Title.

DORCHESTER, Daniel, 1827- 284
1907.
Christianity in the United States from the first settlement down to the present time. By Daniel Dorchester, D. D. New York, Hunt & Eaton; Cincinnati, Cranston & Stowe, 1890. 799 p. incl. tables. front. (port.) 3 maps (2 double) 2 double col. charts, xi diagr. 25 cm. First edition, New York, Cincinnati, 1888. Contents.--i. The colonial era.--ii. The national era: Period i. From 1776 to 1800. Period ii. From 1800 to 1850. Period iii. From 1850 to 1887. [BR515.D7 1890] 17-24385
1. U. S.—Church history. I. Title.

DORCHESTER, Daniel, 1827- 284
1907.
Christianity in the United States from the first settlement down to the present time, by Daniel Dorchester, D. D. Rev. ed. New York, Hunt & Eaton; Cincinnati, Cranston & Curts [1895] 814 p. front. (port.) xxviii pl. (part fold., part col.; incl. maps, tables, diagrs., chart) 25 cm. Contents.--i. The colonial era.--ii. The national era: Period i. From 1776 to 1800. Period ii. From 1800 to 1850. Period iii. From 1850 to 1894. [BR515.D7 1895] 17-24384
1. U. S.—Church history. I. Title.

DRUMMOND, Andrew Landale. 284
Story of American Protestantism. Boston, Beacon Press, 1950. xii, 418 p. 23 cm. Bibliography: p. 407-413. [BR515.D8 1950] 50-12382
1. U.S.—Church history. 2. Protestant churches—U.S.

FRACCHIA, Charles A., 282'.73
1937-
Second spring : the coming of age of U.S. Catholicism / Charles Fracchia. 1st ed. San Francisco, CA : Harper & Row, c1980. p. cm. Bibliography: p. [BX1406.2.F72] 79-3599 ISBN 0-06-063012-4 : 9.95
1. Catholic Church in the United States—History. 2. United States—Church history. I. Title.

GALLOWAY, Charles Betts, 261.
bp., 1849-1909.
... Christianity and the American commonwealth; or, The influence of Christianity in making this nation. By Bishop Charles B. Galloway ... Delivered in the chapel at Emory college, Oxford, Ga., March, 1898. Nashville, Tenn., Publishing house Methodist Episcopal church, South, Barbee & Smith, agents, 1898. 213 p. 19 cm. (The Quillian lectures, 1898) [BR516.G3] C-326
1. U. S.—Church history. I. Title.

GAUSTAD, Edwin Scott 277.3
A religious history of America. New York, Harper [c.1966] xxiii, 421p. illus. (pt. col.) maps, ports. 24cm. Bibl. [BR515.G3] 66-11488 8.95
1. U. S.—Church history. I. Title.

GAUSTAD, Edwin Scott. 277.3
A religious history of America. [1st ed.] New York, Harper & Row [1966] xxiii, 421 p. illus. (part col.) maps, ports. 24 cm. Includes bibliographical references. 66-11488
1. U.S. — Church history. I. Title.

GAUSTAD, Edwin Scott. 277.3
A religious history of America. New York, Harper and Row [1974, c.1966] xxiii, 421 p. illus., maps, ports. 21 cm. Includes bibliographical references. [BR513.G3] 66-11488 ISBN 0-06-063093-0 3.95 (pbk.)
1. U.S.—Church history. I. Title.

THE great revival in the west,
1797-1805. Gloucester, Mass., Peter Smith, 1959. 215p. maps. 21cm. Originally printed in 1916 by the University of Chicago Press.
1. U. S.—Church history. 2. Revivals. I. Cleveland, Catharine Caroline.

HALL, Thomas Cuming, 1858- 277.3
The religious background of American culture, by Thomas Cuming Hall ... Boston, Little, Brown, and company, 1930. xiv, 348 p. 28 cm. "General bibliography": p. [315]-326; "Chapter bibliographies": p. [327]- 337. [BR515.H28] 30-18755
1. U.S.—Church history. 2. U.S.—Religion. 3. Dissenters—England. 4. Protestantism. I. Title.

HALL, Thomas Cuming, 1858- 277.3
1936.
The religious background of American culture. New York, Ungar [1959] 354p. 22cm. (American classics) Includes bibliography. [BR515.H28 1959] 58-59870
1. U. S.—Church history, 2. U. S.—Religion. 3. Dissenters—England. 4. Protestantism. I. Title.

HALLIDAY, Samuel Byram, 277.3
1812-1897.
The church in America and its baptisms of fire; being an account of the progress of religion in America, in the eighteenth and nineteenth centuries, as seen in the great revivals in the Christian church, and in the growth and work of various religious bodies, by Rev. S. B. Halliday ... and Rev. D. S. Gregory ... New York, London [etc.] Funk & Wagnalls company, 1896. xx, 754 p. front., ports. 24 1/2 cm. [BR515.H3] 33-38333
1. U.S.—Church history. 2. Revivals—U.S. 3. Sects—U.S. I. Gregory, Daniel Seely, 1832-1915, joint author II. Title.

HANDY, Robert T. 280'.4'0973
A Christian America; Protestant hopes and historical realities [by] Robert T. Handy. New York, Oxford University Press, 1971. x, 282 p. 22 cm. Bibliography: p. 227-236. [BR515.H354] 78-161888 ISBN 0-19-501453-7 7.95
1. U.S.—Church history. 2. Protestant churches—U.S. 3. Christianity and culture. I. Title.

HANDY, Robert T. 280'.4'0973
A christian America; protestant hopes and historical realities. New York, Oxford University Press [1974, c1971] x, 282 p., 21 cm. Bibliography: p. 227-236 [BR515.H354] ISBN 0-19-501784-6 2.95 (pbk.)
1. United States Church history. 2. Protestant churches—United States 3. Christianity and culture. I. Title.

HUMPHREY, Edward Frank, 322.10973
1878-
Nationalism and religion in America, 1774-1789. New York, Russell & Russell [1966] viii, 536p. 23cm. First pub. in 1924. Bibl. [BR520.H75] 65-17902 10.00
1. U.S.—Church history. 2. U.S.—Hist.—Revolution. 3. Church and state in the U.S. 4. Nationalism and religion—U.S. I. Title.

HUMPHREY, Edward Frank, 277.
1878-
Nationalism and religion in America, 1774-1789, by Edward Frank Humphrey ... Boston, Chipman law publishing company, 1924. 2 p. l., [vii]-viii, 536 p. 21 cm. Bibliography: p. [517]-532. [BR520.H75] 24-12770
1. U.S.—Church history. 2. U.S.—Hist.—Revolution. 3. Church and state in the U.S. I. Title.

JOYCE, Lester Douglas 277.3
Church and clergy in the American Revolution; a study in group behavior. New York, Exposition [c.1966] 224p. 22cm. Bibl. [BR520.J6] 66-3990 6.00
1. U.S.—Church history. 2. Clergy—U.S. 3. U.S.—Hist.—Revolution—Religious aspects. I. Title.

JOYCE, Lester Douglas. 277.3
Church and clergy in the American Revolution; a study in group behavior. [1st ed.] New York, Exposition Press [1966] 224 p. 22 cm. Bibliography: p. [216]-224. [BR520.J6] 66-3990
1. U.S. — Church history. 2. Clergy — U.S. U.S. — Hist. — Revolution — Religious aspects. I. Title.

KELLY, George Anthony, 282'.73
1916-
The battle for the American church / George A. Kelly. 1st ed. Garden City, N.Y. : Doubleday, 1979. xi, 513 p. ; 24 cm. Includes index. Bibliography: p. [491]-496. [BX1406.2.K43] 77-12858 ISBN 0-385-13266-2 : 14.95
1. Catholic Church in the United States—History. 2. Catholic Church in the United States—Doctrinal and controversial works—Catholic authors. 3. Vatican Council. 2d, 1962-1965. 4. United States—Church history. I. Title.

KNOX, John, 1900- ed. 261
Religion and the present crisis, edited by John Knox. Chicago, Ill., The University of Chicago press [1942] xi, 165 p. 21 cm. (Half-title: [Chicago. University] Charles R. Walgreen foundation lectures) Bibliographical references included in preface. [BR516.K63] 42-10793
1. U. S.—Church history. 2. Civilization, Christian. I. Title.
Contents omitted.

*KOLKE, Daniel. 209'.73
The church and her walls; twentieth-century parallels from the Book of Revelation. New York, Exposition Pr. [1973] 166 p. 21 cm. (Exposition-Testament Book) Bibliography: p. 163-166. [BR515] ISBN 0-682-47720-6 6.00
1. U.S.—Church history. 2. Christianity—20th century. I. Title.

LITTELL, Franklin Hamlin 209.73
From state church to pluralism: a Protestant interpretation of religion in American history. Chicago, Aldine [c.1962] 174p. 22cm. (Aldine lib. ed.) Bibl. 62-15090 5.00
1. U. S.—Church history. 2. U. S.—Religion. 3. Sects—U. S. I. Title.

LITTELL, Franklin Hamlin. 209.73
From state church to pluralism; a Protestant interpretation of religion in American history. [1st ed.] Garden City, N. Y., Anchor Books, 1962. 174 p. 18 cm. (Anchor books, A294) [BR515.L55] 61-9530
1. U.S.—Church history. 2. U.S.—Religion. 3. Sects—U.S. I. Title.

LITTELL, Franklin Hamlin. 277.3
From State church to pluralism: a Prostestant interpretation of religion in American history. New York, Macmillan [1971] xxvii, 225 p. 19 cm. Includes bibliographical references. [BR515.L55 1971] 73-127461
1. U.S.—Church history. 2. U.S.—Religion. 3. Sects—U.S. I. Title.

MEAD, Sidney Earl, 1904-. 277.3
The lively experiment : the shaping of Christianity in America. / Sidney E. Mead. New York : Harper & Row, 1976 c1963. xiii, 220 p. ; 20 cm. Includes bibliographical references and index. [BR515.M43] pbk. : 4.95
1. U.S.—Church history. I. Title.
L.C. no. for 1963 edition: 63-10750.

MEAD, Sidney Earl, 1904- 277.3
The lively experiment: the shaping of Christianity in America. [1st ed.] New York, Harper & Row [1963] 220 p. 22 cm. [BR515.M43] 63-10750
1. U.S.—Church history. I. Title.

NOBLE, William Francis Pringl, 1827-1882. 277.3
... A century of gospel-work: a history of the growth of evangelical religion in the United States; containing full descriptions of the great revivals of the century, personal sketches of eminent clergymen, narratives and incidents of Christian work, accounts of the rise of the union organizations, statistics of religious denominatons, etc. By the Rev. W. F. P. Noble ... Philadelphia, H. C. Watts & co.; San Francisco, Cal., A. L. Bancroft & co.; [etc., etc.] 1877. xxii, 25-604 p. front., plates. 23 cm. At head of title: 1776-1876. [BR515.N7] 33-38338
1. U. S.—Church history. 2. Revivals—U. S. 3. Evangelists. I. Title.

SALISBURY, William Seward. 277.3
Religion in America. New York, Oxford Book Co., 1951. iv, 60 p. illus. 19 cm. (Oxford social studies pamphlets, no. 7) Includes bibliographics. [BR515.S23] 51-4458
1. U.S. — Church history. 2. U.S. — Religion. I. Title.

SMITH, Timothy Lawrence, 1924- 269.2
Revivalism and social reform; American Protestantism on the eve of the Civil War [Gloucester, Mass., P. Smith, 1966, c.1957] 253p. 21cm. (Harper torch-bks. Acad. lib., TB1229L rebound) First pub. by Abingdon in 1957. Bibl. [BR525.S6] 4.00
1. U.S.—Church history. 2. Revivals—U.S. 3. Church and social problems—U.S. I. Title.

SMITH, Timothy Lawrence, 1924-
Revivalism and social reform; American Protestantism on the eve of the Civil War. New York, Harper [1965, c1957] 253 p. (Harper Torchbooks: The Academy Library) 68-57709
1. U.S.—Church history. 2. Revival—U.S. 3. Church and social problems—U.S. I. Title.

SMITH, Timothy Lawrence, 1924- 269.2*
Revivalism and social reform in mid-nineteenth-century America. Chapters I-XI and XIV comprise the Frank S. and Elizabeth D. Brewer prize essay for 1955, the American Society of Church History. New York, Abingdon Press [1957] 253 p. 24 cm. "Critical essay on the sources of information": p. 238-248. [BR525.S6] 57-6757
1. United States—Church history. 2. Revivals—United States. 3. Church and social problems—United States. I. Title.

SPERRY, Willard Learoyd, 1882- 277.3
Religion in America, by Willard L. Sperry. Appendices comp. by Ralph Lazzaro. Boston, Beacon [1963] 317p. 21cm. (BP162) Bibl. 2.25 pap.,
1. U. S.—Church history. 2. U. S.—Religion. I. Lazzaro, Ralph. II. Title.

SPERRY, Willard Learoyd, 1882- 277.3
Religion in America, by Willard L. Sperry ... Cambridge [Eng.] The University press, 1945. viii, [1], 317, [1] p. 21 cm. (Half-title: American life and institutions ... I) "Some of the material in the first chapters ... was used in a series of lectures delivered at King's chapel, Boston, in 1943."--Pref. "References": p. 271, 282. Bibliographical foot-notes. [BR515.S67 1945] 46-2357
1. U.S.—Church history. 2. U.S.—Religion. I. Title.

SPERRY, Willard Learoyd, 18882- 277.3
Religion in America, by Willard L. Sperry ... Appendices compiled by Ralph Lazzaro ... Cambridge [Eng.] The University press; New York, The Macmillan company, 1946. x, [1], 317, [1] p. 21 cm. (Half-title: American life and institution ... I) "Some of the material in the first chapters ... was used in a series of lectures deliverd at King's chapel, Boston, in 1943."--Pref. "References": p. 271, 282. Bibliographical foot-notes. [BR515.S67 1946] 46-7760
1. U.S.—Church history. 2. U.S.—Religion. I. Lazzaro, Ralph. II. Title.

STEPHENSON, George Malcolm, 1883- 277.3
The Puritan heritage. New York, Macmillan, 1952. 282 p. 21 cm. Bibliography: p. 271-273. [BR515.S73] 52-1108
1. U.S. — Church history. 2. U.S. — Religion. I. Title.

STEPHENSON, George Malcolm, 1883-1958. 277.3
The Puritan heritage / George M. Stephenson. Westport, Conn. : Greenwood Press, 1978, c1952. 282 p. ; 22 cm. Reprint of the ed. published by Macmillan, New York. Includes index. Bibliography: p. 271-273. [BR515.S73 1978] 78-10512 ISBN 0-313-20733-X lib.bdg. : 19.75
1. United States—Church history. 2. United States—Religion. I. Title.

SWEET, William Warren, 1881- 284
... Our American churches, by William W. Sweet ... New York, Cincinnati, The Methodist book concern [c1924] 135 p. 19 cm. (Studies in Christian faith) Bibliography: p. 129-130. [BR515.S8] 24-19997
1. U.S.—Church history. I. Title.

SWEET, William Warren, 1881- 277.3
Religion in the development of American culture, 1765-1840. Gloucester, Mass., P. Smith [1964, c.1962] xiv, 338p. 22cm. (Scribners bk. rebound) Bibl. 5.00
1. U.S.—Church history. 2. U.S.—Civilization. I. Title.

SWEET, William Warren, 1881- 277.3
Religion in the development of American culture, 1765-1840. New York, Scribner, 1952. xiv, 338 p. 22 cm. Bibliography: p. 315-332. [BR520.S882] 52-9960
1. U.S. — Church history. 2. U.S. — Civilization. I. Title.

SWEET, William Warren, 1881- 277.3
The story of religion in America, by William Warren Sweet ... New York and London, Harper & brothers [c1939] vi p., 2 l., 656 p. 22 1/2 cm. On cover: Revised edition. Published previously, 1930, under title: The story of religions in America. Bibliography: p. 599-624. [BR515.S82 1939] 39-23874
1. U.S.—Church history. 2. U.S.—Religion. I. Title.

SWEET, William Warren, 1881- 277.3
The story of religions in America, by William Warren Sweet ... New York and London, Harper & brothers, 1930. vii p., 1 l., 571, [1] p. front., plates. 22 1/2 cm. Bibliography: p. 524-542. [BR515.S82] 30-28469
1. U.S.—Church history. 2. U.S.—Religion. I. Title.

SWEET, William Warren, 1881-1959. 277.3
The story of religion in America. [2d rev. ed.] New York, Harper [1950] ix, 492 p. 22 cm. First ed. (1930) has title: The story of religions in America. Bibliography: p. 453-472. [BR515.S82 1950] 50-10239
1. United States—Church history. 2. United States—Religion.

TRACY, Joseph, 1793?-1874. 260
The great awakening. A history of the revival of religion in the time of Edwards and Whitefield. By Joseph Tracy ... Boston, Tappan and Dennet; New York, J. Adams, 1842. xviii, 433 p. front., ports. 21 1/2 cm. [BV3773.T76g] A 31
1. Whitefield, George, 1714-1770. 2. U.S.—Church history. 3. Revivals. I. Title.

WEISENBURGER, Francis Phelps, 1900- 277.3
Ordeal of faith; the crisis of church-going America, 1865-1900. New York, Philosophical Library [1959] 380 p. 22 cm. [BR525.W37] 59-16373
1. U.S. — Church history. 2. U.S. — Hist. — 1835-1898. 3. Church attendance. I. Title.

United States—Church history—19th century.

FOGDE, Myron Jean, 1934- 277.3
The church goes West / Myron Jean Fogde. Wilmington, N.C. : Consortium Books, c1977. 231 p. ; 23 cm. (Faith of our fathers ; v. 6) Bibliography: p. 226-231. [BR525.F63] 77-74856 ISBN 0-8434-0625-9 : 9.50
1. United States—Church history—19th century. I. Title. II. Series.

United States—Church history—20th century.

BAILEY, Raymond, 1938- 277.3
Destiny and disappointment / Raymond Bailey. Wilmington, N.C. : Consortium Books, [1977] p. cm. (Faith of our fathers ; v. 7) [BR525.B34] 77-9549 ISBN 0-8434-0626-7 : 9.50
1. United States—Church history—20th century. I. Title. II. Series.

HALSEY, William M., 1945- 282'.73
The survival of American innocence : Catholicism in an era of disillusionment, 1920-1940 / William M. Halsey. Notre Dame, Ind. : University of Notre Dame Press, c1979. p. cm. (Notre Dame studies in American Catholicism ; no. 2) Includes index. Bibliography: p. [BX1406.2.H25] 79-63360 ISBN 0-268-01699-2 : 16.95
1. Catholic Church in the United States—History. 2. United States—Church history—20th century. I. Title. II. Series.

KELLY, George Anthony, 1916- 282'.73
The battle for the American church / George A. Kelly. Complete and unabridged. Garden City, N.Y. : Image Books, 1981, c1979. xi, 513 p. ; 23 cm. Includes index. Bibliography: p. [491]-496. [BX1406.2.K43 1981] 19 80-22348 ISBN 0-385-17433-0 : 7.95
1. Catholic Church in the United States—History—20th century. 2. Catholic Church in the United States—Doctrinal and controversial works—Catholic authors. 3. Vatican Council. 2d, 1962-1965. 4. United States—Church history—20th century. I. Title.

QUEBEDEAUX, Richard. 262'.8
By what authority : the rise of personality cults in American Christianity / Richard Quebedeaux. 1st ed. San Francisco : Harper & Row, c1981. p. cm. Includes index. Bibliography: p. [BR526.Q4 1981] 19 81-47431 ISBN 0-06-066724-9 : 10.95
1. United States—Church history—20th century. 2. Authority (Religion) 3. Mass media in religion—United States. 4. Fame—Moral and religious aspects. 5. Christian sects—United States. I. Title.

UNDERWOOD, Kenneth Wilson. 277.8
Christianity where you live. New York, Friendship press [1945] x, 182 p. 18 cm. At head of title: Kenneth Underwood. [BR525.U5] 45-4692
1. U.S.—Church history—20th cent. 2. U.S.—Soc. condit. I. Title.

United States—Church history—Addresses, essays, lectures.

BRAUER, Jerald C. 209'.73
Reinterpretation in American church history, by R. Pierce Beaver [and others] Edited by Jerald C. Brauer. Chicago, University of Chicago Press [1968] xi, 227 p. 24 cm. (Essays in divinity, v. 5) Bibliographical footnotes. [BR515.B72] 68-20186
1. United States—Church history—Addresses, essays, lectures. I. Beaver, Robert Pierce, 1906- II. Title. III. Series.

United States—Church history—Bibliography.

BOWERMAN, George Franklin, 1868- 282.
A selected bibliography of the religious denominations of the United States, compiled by George Franklin Bowerman ... With a list of the most important Catholic works of the world as an appendix, compiled by Rev. Joseph H. McMahon. New York, Cathedral library association, 1896. v p., 1 l., 94 p. 24 1/2 cm. [Z7778.U6B7] 4-16816
1. U.S.—Church history—Bibl. 2. Catholic church—Bibl. 3. Bibliography—Best books—Catholic literature. I. McMahon, Joseph E., 1862- II. Title.

ELLIS, John Tracy, 1905- 016.282'73
A guide to American Catholic history / John Tracy Ellis and Robert Trisco. 2nd ed., rev. and enl. Santa Barbara, Calif. : ABC-Clio, c1981. p. cm. Includes index. [Z7778.U6E38 1981] [BX1406.2] 19 81-17585 ISBN 0-87436-318-7 : 27.50
1. Catholic Church—United States—History—Bibliography. 2. United States—Church history—Bibliography. I. Trisco, Robert Frederick. II. Title.

United States—Church history—Colonial period—Biography

HITT, Russell T., ed. 277.3
Heroic colonial Christians [by] Courtney Anderson [others] Ed. introd. by Russell T. Hitt. Philadelphia, Lippincott [c.1966] 255p. 22cm. Bibl. [BR569.H5] 66-19987 4.95 bds.,
1. U. S.—Church history—Colonial period—Biog. I. Anderson, Courtney. II. Title.
Contents omitted.

HITT, Russell T ed. 277.3
Heroic colonial Christians [by] Courtney Anderson [and others] Edited with an introd. by Russell T. Hitt. [1st ed.] Philadelphia, Lippincott [1966] 255 p. 22 cm. Contents.CONTENTS. -- Jonathan Edwards, by C. Anderson. -- Gilbert Tennent, by R. T. Hitt. -- David Brainerd, by C. S. Kilby. -- John Witherspoon, by H. W. Coray. Includes bibliographical references. [BR569.H5] 66-19987
1. U.S. — Church history — Colonial period — Biog. I. Anderson, Courtney. II. Title.

United States—Church history—Colonial period, ca. 1600-1775.

DE VISSER, John. 973
Pioneer churches / photos. by John de Visser ; text by Harold Kalman. New York : Norton, c1976. 192 p. : ill. (some col.) ; 32 cm. Includes index. Bibliography: p. 185-189. [BR520.D43] 76-150440 ISBN 0-393-08754-9 : 27.50
1. United States—Church history—Colonial period, ca. 1600-1775. 2. Churches—United States. I. Kalman, Harold D. II. Title.

WALLACE, Dewey D. 277.3
The Pilgrims / Dewey D. Wallace, Jr. Wilmington, N.C. : Consortium Books, c1977. iii, 240 p. ; 22 cm. (Faith of our fathers ; v. 3) [BR520.W26] 77-9507 ISBN 0-8434-0622-4 : 9.50
1. United States—Church history—Colonial period, ca. 1600-1775. I. Title. II. Series.

United States—Church history—Colonial periodicals

SHEA, Daniel B. 209'.73
Spiritual autobiography in early America, by Daniel B. Shea, Jr. Princeton, N.J., Princeton University Press, 1968. xvi, 280 p. 23 cm. Includes bibliographical references. [BR520.S5] 68-11447 7.50
1. United States—Church history—Colonial period. 2. Spiritual life—History of doctrines. 3. Autobiography. I. Title.

SWEET, William Warren, 1881- 277.3
Religion in colonial America, by William Warren Sweet. New York, Cooper Square Publishers, 1965. xiii p., 1 l., 367 p. 24

cm. "Selected bibliography": p. 341-356. [BR520.S88] 42-19309
1. U.S.—Church history—Colonial period. I. Title.

SWEET, William Warren, 1881- 277.3
Religion in colonial America, by William Warren Sweet. New York, C. Scribner's sons, 1942. xiii p., 1 l., 367 p. 24 cm. "Selected bibliography": p. 341-356. [BR520.S88] 42-193091
1. U. S.—Church history—Colonial period. I. Title.

SWEET, William Warren, 1881- 277.3
Religion in colonial America, by William Warren Sweet. New York, C. Scribner's sons, 1942. xiii p., 1 l., 367 p. 23 1/2 cm. "Selected bibliography": p. 341-356. [BR520.S88] 42-19309
1. U.S.—Church history—Colonial period. I. Title.

United States — Church history — Sources.

EARLY American Christianity 277.3 / Bill Leonard, editor. [Nashville] : Broadman Press, c1979. 415 p. ; 24 cm. (Christian classics) Includes bibliographical references. [BR514.E17] 78-59978 ISBN 0-8054-6538-3 (set) : 24.95
1. United States—Church history—Sources. I. Leonard, Bill. II. Series.

MODE, Peter George.
Source book and bibliographical guide for American church history, by Peter G. Mode ... Boston, J. S. Canner, 1964." xxiv, 735 p. 24 cm. "Reprinted from the original 1921 edition." 67-5495
1. U.S. — Church history — Sources. 2. U.S. — Church history — Bibl. I. Title. II. Title: American church history.

MODE, Peter George.
Source book and bibliographical guide for American church history, by Peter G. Mode ... Menasha, Wis., George Banta publishing company [c1921] xxiv, 735 p. 24 cm. [BR514.M6] 22-3718
1. U.S.—Church history—Sources. 2. U.S.—Church history—Bibl. I. Title. II. Title: American church history.

SMITH, Hilrie Shelton, 1893- 277.3
American Christianity; an historical interpretation with representative documents, by H. Shelton Smith, Robert T. Handy [and] Lefferts A. Loetscher. New York, Scribner [1960-63] 2 v. illus., ports. 24 cm. Includes bibliographical references. [BR514.S55] 60-8117
1. U.S.—Church history—Sources. 2. U.S.—Church history. I. Title.

United States—Church history—Sources—Bibliography

ALLISON, William Henry, 1870-1941 016.285109
Inventory of unpublished material for American religious history in Protestant church archives and other repositories. New York, Kraus Reprint, 1966. vii, 254p. 23cm. First pub. in 1910 by the Carnegie Inst. of Wash., D.C. Pubn. no.137. Papers of the Dept. of Hist. Res. 9.00 pap.,
1. U.S.—Church history—Sources—Bibl. I. Title.

ALLISON, William Henry, 1870-1941.
Inventory of unpublished material for American religious history in Protestant church archives and other repositories, by William Henry Allison ... Washington, D.C., Carnegie institution of Washington, 1910. vii, 254 p. 25 1/2 cm. (On verse of t.-p.: Carnegie institution of Washington. Publication no. 137. Papers of the Dept. of historical research) [BR514.A4] 11-10049
1. U.S.—Church history—Sources—Bibl. I. Title.

United States—Civilization.

BATES, Ernest Sutherland, 1879-1939. 277.3
American faith; its religious, political, and economic foundations [by] Ernest Sutherland Bates. New York, W. W. Norton & company, inc. [c1940] vi. [7]-479 p. 25 cm. "First edition." [E169.1.B25] 40-27258
1. U. S.—Civilization. 2. U. S.—Hist. 3. U. S.—Church history. 4. U. S.—Religion. I. Title.

COLESON, Edward P
The scriptural standard in economics and government, by Edward P. Coleson. [Spring Arbor, Mich., 1965] 183 p. 68-32294
1. U.S.—Civilization. 2. Sociology, Christian. 3. Christianity and economics. I. Title.

[INGERSOLL, Charles Jared] 1782-1862. 264
Inchiquin, the Jesuit's letters, during a late residence in the United States of America; being a fragment of a private correspondence, accidentally discovered in Europe; containing a favourable view of the manners, literature, and state of society, of the United States, and a refutation of many of the aspersions cast upon this country by former residents and tourists, By some unknown foreigner ... New-York: Printed and published by I. Riley .....1810. v, 165 p. 22 cm. [E164.I 47] [AC901.B3 vol. 57] 973. 1-16595
1. U. S.—Civilization. 2. U. S.—Soc. life & cust. 3. U. S.—Pol. & govt.—Constitutional period, 1789-1809. 4. Washington, D. C.—Descr. I. Title.

United States—Colonial question.

REUTER, Frank Theodore. 322'.1'0973
Catholic influence on American colonial policies, 1898-1904, by Frank T. Reuter. Austin, University of Texas Press [1967] xiii, 185 p. 24 cm. Bibliography: p. [169]-180. [E713.R44] 66-15701
1. Catholic Church in the United States. 2. Catholic Church—Relations (diplomatic) with the United States. 3. United States—Colonial question. I. Title.

United States Congress—Chaplains.

JOHNSON, Lorenzo Dow, 1805-1867.
Chaplains of the general government, with objections to their employment considered. Also, a list of all the chaplains to Congress, in the army and in the navy, from the formation of the government to this time. By Lorenzo D. Johnson ... New York, Sheldon, Blakeman & co., 1856. iv, [5]-82 p. 19 cm. [BV4375.J6] 19-630
1. U. S. Congress—Chaplains. 2. U. S.—Army—Chaplains. 3. U. S.—Navy—Chaplain corps. I. Title.

United States—Description and travel

WAYLEN, Edward. 922
Ecclesiastical reminiscences of the United States. By the Rev. Edward Waylen ... New-York, Wiley and Putnam, 1846. xv, 501 p. 21 1/2 cm. [E165.W35] [BX5995.W38A3] 917. 1-27886
1. U.S.—Descr. & trav. 2. U.S.—Church history. 3. Protestant Episcopal church in the U.S.A. I. Title.

U.S.—Description and travel—1848-1865.

CASWALL, Henry, 1810-1870. 283'.73
America and the American church. New York, Arno Press, 1969. xviii, 368 p. illus., map. 22 cm. (Religion in America) Reprint of the 1839 ed. [BX5880.C3 1969] 77-83413
1. Protestant Episcopal Church in the U.S.A.—History. 2. Kenyon College, Gambier, Ohio. 3. U.S.—Description and travel—1848-1865. I. Title.

United States—Economic conditions—1918—

RILEY, William Bell, 1861- 261
The philosophies of Father Coughlin, four sermons by W. B. Riley ... Grand Rapids, Mich., Zondervan publishing house [c1935] 1 p. l., 58 p. 19 cm. [BX4705.C7795R5] 36-8252
1. Coughlin, Charles Edward, 1891- 2. U. S.—Econ. condit.—1918- I. Title.

SPIVEY, Clark Dwight, 1885- 261
The coming of the peasant, by Clark Dwight Spivey. Chicago, The Christian witness, 1934. vii, 528 p. plates. 20 cm. On cover: The mystery revealed. [HN32.S7] 34-38163

1. U.S.—Econ. condit.—1918- 2. Agriculture—U.S. 3. Agriculture—Economic aspects. 4. Socialism, Christian. 5. Capitalism. 6. Antichrist. I. Title.

United States—Economic conditions—1961-

WALTON, Rus. 261.8'3
One nation under God / by Rus Walton. Washington : Third Century Publishers, [1975] 311 p. ; 21 cm. Bibliography: p. 311. [HC106.6.W24] 75-7975 3.45
1. United States—Economic conditions—1961- 2. United States—Moral conditions. 3. Church and social problems. I. Title.

United States—Emigration and immigration

LANDIS, Benson Young, 1897- 261.83
Protestant experience with United States immigration, 1910-1960, a study paper. [New York? 1961] 81p. 19cm. Includes bibliography. [BV639.I4L3] 61-11038
1. U. S.—Emig. & immig. 2. Church and social problems—U. S. I. Title.

PROTESTANT Episcopal church in the U. S. A. National council. Dept. of missions and church extension. 325.73

Neighbors: studies in immigration from the Standpoint of the Episcopal church. New York, Domestic and foreign missionary society, 1920. 3 p. l., 246 p., 1 l. plates. ports, fold. map. fold. diagrs. 19 cm. "Second edition, April, 1920." Edited by William C. Sturgis. "Reference books": p. 215-219. [BV2785.P7] 266.3 20-19514
1. U. S.—Emig. & immig. 2. Missions, Home. I. Sturgis, William Codman, 1862- ed. II. Title.
Contents omitted.

SANJEK, Louis. 922.473
In silence, by Louis Sanjek. New York, N.Y., Fortuny's [1938] 215 p. front. (port.) 21 cm. "First edition." Contents.pt. 1. Croatia, my homeland.--pt. 2. My home life and observations in Croatia.--pt. 3. United States of America, my adopted country. [BX8080.S15A3] 42-44308
I. Title.

United States engineers. 101st regt., Co. F, 1917-1919.

WEAVER, Frederic N. 213
The new creation an account of the genesis of the universe of mind and mental operations according to the Bible by F. S. Weaver ... Boston, The T. O. Metcalf company, 1924. 6 p. l., 174 p. front., illus. (incl. ports.) plates. 24 cm. [D570.31.101st.W4] 25-2790

1. U.S. engineers. 101st regt., Co. F, 1917-1919. 2. European war, 1914-1918—Regimental histories—U.S.—Engineers—101st. I. Sanborn, Philip N., joint author. II. Title.

United States. Federal Bureau of Investigation.

PRESS view the FBI raid 323.44'2'0973 : a collection of photographs and press covering the FBI raid of July 8, 1977 on the Church of Scientology. [Los Angeles : Church of Scientology of California, [1977 or 1978] 31 p. : ill. ; 28 cm. [BP605.S2P73] 78-102289 ISBN 0-915598-17-5 pbk. : 2.00
1. United States. Federal Bureau of Investigation. 2. Scientology. 3. Religious liberty—United States. 4. Church and state in the United States. I. Church of Scientology of California, Los Angeles.

United States—Foreign population.

BUHLMAIER, Marie. 277.
Along the highway of service [by] Marie Buhlmaier. Atlanta, Ga., Home mission board of the Southern Baptist convention [c1924] viii, 140 p. front. (port.) plates. 19 cm. [BV2785.B7] 25-4939
1. U. S.—Foreign population. 2. Missions, Home. 3. Baptists—Missions. I. Title.

HARKNESS, Georgia Elma. 259
The church and the immigrant, by Georgia E. Harkness ... with an introduction by G. W. Tupper ... New York, George H. Doran company [c1921] xii p., 1 l., 15-110 p. 20 cm. Bibliography: p. 103-106. [BV639.I 4H3] 21-14651
1. U. S.—Foreign population. 2. Americanization. 3. Sociology, Christian. 4. Church work. I. Title.

STOWELL, Jay Samuel, 1883- 277.
Methodism's new frontier, by Jay S. Stowell. New York, Cincinnati, The Methodist book concern, [c1924] 224 p. front., illus. (map) plates. 19 cm. [BV2766.M7S75] 24-10058
1. U.S.—Foreign population. 2. Missions, Home. 3. Methodist Episcopal church—Missions. I. Title.

United States—Foreign relations

SCHUYLEMAN, John Louis, 1875- 220.1
America, its destiny, by John L. Schuyleman ... [Portland, Or.] Priv. print. [c1935] ix p., 1 l., 127 p. 22 cm. [BS649.U6S4] 35-13658
1. U. S.—For. rel. 2. Democracy. 3. Bible—Prophecies. I. Title.

United States—Foreign relations—1797-1801.

GREEN, Ashbel, 1762-1848. 264
Obedience to the laws of God, the sure and indispensable defence of nations. A discourse, delivered in the Second Presbyterian church, in the city of philadelphia, May 9th, 1798, being the day appointed by the President of the United States, to be observed as a season for solemn humiliation, fasting and prayer. By Ashbel Green ... Philadelphia: Printed by John Ormrod, no. 41, Chestnut-street [1798] 51 p. 23 cm. [E323.G79] [AC901.H3 vol. 75] 973. 20-12765
1. U. S.—For. rel.—1797-1801. I. Title.

United States—Foreign relations—1933-1945.

FLYNN, George Q. 282'73
Roosevelt and romanism : Catholics and American diplomacy, 1937-1945 / George Q. Flynn. Westport, Conn. : Greenwood Press, 1976. xx, 268 p. ; 22 cm. (Contributions in American history ; no. 47) Includes bibliographical references and index. [E806.F55] 75-35343 ISBN 0-8371-8581-5 lib.bdg. : 13.95
1. Roosevelt, Franklin Delano, Pres. U.S., 1882-1945. 2. United States—Foreign relations—1933-1945. 3. Catholics in the United States—History. I. Title.

United States—Foreign relations—1945-

KIRKEMO, Ronald B. 261.8'7
Between the eagle & the dove : the Christian & American foreign policy / Ronald Kirkemo. Downers Grove, Ill. :

InterVarsity Press, c1976. 218 p. : ill. ; 21 cm. Includes bibliographies and index. [JX1417.K57] 76-12300 ISBN 0-87784-775-4 pbk. : 4.95
1. United States—Foreign relations—1945- 2. International relations—Moral and religious aspects. I. Title.

WHAT should be the role of 327.73
ethnic groups in U.S. foreign policy? / John Charles Daly, moderator ; Hyman Bookbinder ... [et al.] ; held on October 15, 1979, and sponsored by the American Enterprise Institute for Public Policy Research, Washington, D.C. Washington, D.C. : The Institute, c1980. 28 p. ; 23 cm. (AEI forum ; 34) [JX1417.W466] 19 80-80003 ISBN 0-8447-2171-9 pbk. : Price unreported.
1. United States—Foreign relations—1945- 2. Ethnology—United States. I. Daly, John Charles, 1914- II. Bookbinder, Hyman Harry, 1916- III. American Enterprise Institute for Public Policy Research. IV. Series: American Enterprise Institute for Public Policy Research. AEI public policy forum ; 34.

United States—Foreign relations—Catholic Church.

BABIS, Daniel George, 327.7309456
1922-
A United States ambassador to the Vatican [by] Daniel G. Babis and Anthony J. Maceli. [1st ed.] New York, Pageant Press [1952] 52p. illus. 21cm. [E183.7.B28] 53-792
1. U. S.—For. rel.—Catholic Church. 2. Catholic Church—Relations (diplomatic) with the U. S. I. Macell, Anthony J., 1923- joint author. II. Title.

FLAMINI, Roland. 327.45'634'073
Pope, Premier, President : the cold war summit that never was / Roland Flamini. New York : Macmillan, c1980. 227 p. ; 22 cm. Includes index. [BX1406.2.F52] 80-17532 ISBN 0-02-538680-8 : 10.95
1. Catholic Church—Relations (diplomatic) with the United States. 2. Catholic Church—Relations (diplomatic) with communist countries. 3. Johannes XXIII, Pope, 1881-1963. 4. Paulus VI, Pope, 1897- 5. United States—Foreign relations—Catholic Church. 6. Communist countries—Foreign relations—Catholic Church. I. Title.

United States—Foreign relations—Latin America.

MORRISON, DeLesseps 327.7308
Story, 1912-1964
Latin American mission; an adventure in hemisphere diplomacy. Ed., introd., by Gerold Frank. New York, S. & S. [c.1965] 288p. 22cm. Autobiographical [F1418.M85] 65-11977 5.95
1. U.S.—For. rel.—Latin America. 2. Latin America—Politics—1948- 3. U.S.—For. rel.—1961-1963. I. Frank, Gerold, 1907- ed. II. Title.

United States Foreign relations Near East.

GRABILL, Joseph L. 327.73'056
Protestant diplomacy and the Near East; missionary influence on American policy, 1810-1927 [by] Joseph L. Grabill. Minneapolis, University of Minnesota Press [1971] x, 395 p. illus., maps, ports. 25 cm. Bibliography: p. 351-374. [DS63.2.U5G7] 70-153504 ISBN 0-8166-0575-0 13.50
1. U.S.—Foreign relations—Near East. 2. Near East—Foreign relations—U.S. 3. Missions—Near East. 4. Missions, American. I. Title.

SHUB, Louis. 327.5'073
The United States and Israel in the Mediterranean. [Los Angeles, Center for the Study of Contemporary Jewish Life, University of Judaism, 1970] 27 p. 20 cm. (Jewish affairs, Background reports, v. 1, no. 1) [DS63.2.U5S44] 79-27993 1.00
1. U.S.—Foreign relations—Near East. 2. Near East—Foreign relations—U.S. 3. U.S.—Foreign relations—Israel. 4. Israel—Foreign relations—U.S. I. Title. II. Series.

United States—Foreign relations—Papal states.

STOCK, Leo Francis, 327.7309456
1878- ed.
Consular relations between the United States and the Papal states; instructions and despatches, edited, with introduction by Leo Francis Stock ... Washington, D.C., American Catholic historical association, 1945. xxxix, 467 p. 26 cm. (Half-title: American Catholic historical association. Documents: vol. II) "Practically all the documents here printed are copies made from the materials of the Department of state, found in that office and later in the National archives."--p. viii. Bibliographical foot-notes. [BX940.A4 vol. 2] [E183.8.P3S7] (282.082) 46-243
1. U.S.—For. rel.—Papal states. 2. Papal states—For. rel.—U.S. I. Title.

STOCK, Leo Francis, 327.7309456
1878- ed.
United States ministers to the Papal states; instructions and despatches, 1848-1868, edited with introduction by Leo Francis Stock ... Washington, D.C., Catholic university press, 1933. xxxix, 456 p. 26 1/2 cm. (Half-title: American Catholic historical association. Document vol. I) "All the documents here presented are printed from copies made at the Department of state. Futile efforts were made ... to secure for inclusion in this volume copies of such documents in the office of the papal Secretary of state as are not to be found in Washington."--Pref. [BX940.A4 vol 1] (282.082) 33-24324
1. U.S.—For. rel.—Papal states. 2. Papal states—For. rel.—U.S. I. U.S. Dept. of state. II. Title.

United States — History.

FULTON, Justin Dewey, 1828- 282
1901.
Outlook of freedom; or, The Roman Catholic element in American history. By Justin D. Fulton. Cincinnati, Printed for the author by Moore, Wilstach, Keys & Overend, 1856. viii, [9]-392 p. 19 cm. [BX1770.F8] 12-38648
1. U. S.—Hist. 2. Catholic church in the U. S. I. Title.

KLEMM, Edwin O. 231'.8
Upon request, God in action; the amazing part in the history: United States and China, by Edwin O. Klemm. [1st ed. Saginaw, Mich., 1971] xix, 406 p. illus. 24 cm. [E179.K63] 79-30883 8.80
1. U.S.—History. 2. World War, 1939-1945. 3. China—History—1900- 4. Providence and government of God. I. Title.

PETERSEN, Mark E. 973
The great prologue / Mark E. Petersen. Salt Lake City : Deseret Book Co., 1975. 136 p. ; 24 cm. Includes index. [BX8635.2.P45] 75-14997 ISBN 0-87747-557-1 : 3.95
1. Church of Jesus Christ of Latter-Day Saints—Doctrinal and controversial works. 2. United States—History. I. Title.

THOMAS, Elbert Duncan, 1881-
1953.
This nation under God, by Elbert D. Thomas. New York, Harpery & Brothers [n.d.] 1 v. (various pagings) 28 cm. Typescript (carbon copy) [incomplete] 67-6475
1. U.S. — History. 2. U.S. — Religion. 3. Presidents — U.S. I. Title.

United States—History—Civil war—Religious life, etc.

AMERICAN Unitarian association.
Tracts of the American Unitarian association. Army series. Boston, American Unitarian association, 1865. 20 no. in 1 v. 23 cm. "100 copies printed. no. 80. Charles Lowe, sec." [E635.A52] 19-1147
1. U. S.—Hist.—Civil war—Religious life, etc. 2. Conduct of life. I. Title.
Contents omitted.

BILLINGSLEY, Amos Stevens, 1818-
1897.
From the flag to the cross; or Scenes and incidents of Christianity in the war. The conversions ... sufferings and deaths of our soldiers, on the battle-field, in hospital, camp and prison; and a description of distinguished Christian men and their labors. By A. S. Billingsley ... Philadelphia, Pa., Boston, Mass. [etc.] New-world publishing company; Burlington, Ia., R. T. Root, 1872. 3 p. l., v-xvi, 15-429 p. 12 pl., 9 port. (incl. front.) 22 cm. Also published, Philadelphia, 1872, under title: Christianity in the war. [E635.B592] 19-17312
1. U. S.—Hist.—Civil war—Religious life, etc. I. Title.

GREGG, John Chandler.
Life in the army, in the departments of Virginia, and the gulf, including observations in New Orleans, with an account of the author's life experience in the ministry. By Rev. J. Chandler Gregg ... Philadelphia, Perkinpine & Higgins, 1866. 271 p. 4 pl. (incl. front.) 19 cm. The author served as chaplain of the 127th regiment, Pennsylvania volunteer infantry, 1862-1863. [E635.G8] 14-5959
1. U. S.—Hist.—Civil war—Religious life, etc. 2. U. S.—Hist.—Civil war-Religious life, etc. 3. New Orleans—Hist.—Civil war.—Regimental histories—Pa. inf.—127th. 4. Pennsylvania infantry. 127th regt. 1862-1863. 5. New Orleans—Hist.—Civil war. I. Title.

HACKETT, Horatio Balch, 1808-
1875.
Christian memorials of the war; or, Scenes and incidents illustrative of religious faith and principle, patriotism and bravery in our army. With historical notes. By Horatio B. Hackett... Boston, Gould and Lincoln; New York, Sheldon and co.; [etc., etc.] 1864. xiv, 256 p. 20 cm. [E365.H21] 2-18782
1. U.S.—Hist.—Civil war—Religious life, etc. 2. Patriotism. 3. U.S.—Hist.—Civil war—Anecdotes. I. Title.

HYMNS for the camp.
3d ed., rev. and enl. ... [Augusta, Ga., 1862] 127 p. 12 x 9 cm. On cover: Publ'd in Augusta, Ga., during the war, 1862 on war paper. Boston Athenaeum, Confederate literature ... 1917, supplies imprint: [Raleigh: 186-] [E635.H93] 21-12607
1. U. S.—Hist.—Civil war—Religious life, etc.

JONES, John William, 1836-1909.
Christ in the camp: or, Religion in Lee's army; by Rev. J. Wm. Jones ... With an introduction by Rev. J. C. Granberry ... bishop of the Methodist Episcopal church, Smith ... Richmond, Va., B. F. Johnson & co., 1887. 528 p. front. (port.) illus., plates. 22 cm. [E635.J77] 2-18784
1. U. S.—Hist.—Civil war—Religious life, etc. 2. U. S.—Hist.—Civil war—Regimental histories—Army of Northern Virginia. I. Title.

JONES, John William, 1836-1909.
Christ in the camp; or, Religion in Lee's army. Supplemented by a sketch of the work in the other Confederate armies. [By] Rev. J. Wm. Jones ... With an introduction by Rev. J. C. Granberry ... bishop of the Methodist Episcopal church, south ... Richmond, Va., B. F. Johnson & co. [1888?] 624 p. col. front., illus., col. pl. 23 cm. "Appendix no. 2. The work of grace in other armies of the confederacy": p. 535-624. [E635.J78] 2-18785
1. U. S.—Hist.—Civil war—Religious life, etc. 2. U. S.—Hist.—Civil war—Regimental histories—Army of Northern Virginia. I. Title.

JONES, John William, 1836-1909.
Christ in the camp; or, Religion in the Confederate army, by Rev. J. William Jones ... with an introduction by Rev. J. C. Granberry ... [New ed.] Atlanta, Ga., The Martin & Hoyt co. [1904] 2 p. l., 624 p. front., plates (1 col.) ports., facsims. 23 cm. Appendix: Letters from our army workers, p. 465-534. Appendix no. 2: The work of grace in other armies of the Confederacy, p. 535-624. [E635.J79] 4-25114
1. U. S.—Hist.—Civil war—Religious life, etc. 2. U. S.—Hist.—Civil war—Regimental histories—Army of Northern Virginia. I. Title.

STEWART, Bowyer.
... The work of the church in the South during the period of reconstruction, by the Rev. Bowyer Stewart ... preached at S. Chrysostom's church, Chicago, the fifteenth Sunday after Trinity, Aug. 31, 1913. Chicago, Pub. for the Western theological seminary by the Young churchman co., Milwaukee [1913?] 79 p. 23 cm. At head of title: The Hale memorial sermons, no. 8. [BX5895.S8] A 13
I. Title.

UNITED States Christian
commission.
United States Christian commission, for the army and navy. Work and incidents. First[-fourth] annual report. Philadelphia, 1863-66. 4 v. in 1. illus., pl., map, tables (part fold.) 22 1/2 cm. For the years 1862-1865; no more published, the Commission having been dissolved January 1, 1866. [E635.U55] 2-18832
1. U.S.—Hist.—Civil war—Religious life, etc. 2. U.S.—Hist.—Civil war—Hospitals, charities, etc. I. Title.

United States—History—Colonial period, ca. 1600-1775.

MARSHALL, Peter, 1940- 209'.73
The light and the glory / Peter Marshall, David Manuel. Old Tappan, N.J. : Revell, c1977. 384 p. ; 24 cm. Includes index. Bibliography: p. 371-378. [E189.M36] 77-23352 ISBN 0-8007-0886-5 : 9.95
1. United States—History—Colonial period, ca. 1600-1775. 2. United States—History—Revolution, 1775-1783. 3. United States—Church history—Colonial period, ca. 1600-1775. 4. History (Theology) 5. Providence and government of God. I. Manuel, David, joint author. II. Title.

United States—History—Colonial period, ca. 1600-1775—Outlines, syllabi, etc.

MARSHALL, Peter, 1940- 209'.73
The light and the glory study guide / [by Peter Marshall and David Manuel]. Old Tappan, N.J. : F.H. Revell Co., c1981. p. cm. [E189.M362] 19 81-15806 ISBN 0-8007-1279-X pbk. : 3.95
1. United States—History—Colonial period, ca. 1600-1775—Outlines, syllabi, etc. 2. United States—History—Revolution, 1775-1783—Outlines, syllabi, etc. 3. United States—Church history—Colonial period, ca. 1600-1775—Outlines, syllabi, etc. 4. History (Theology)—Outlines, syllabi, etc. 5. Providence and government of God—Outlines, syllabi, etc. I. Manuel, David. II. Marshall, Peter, 1940- Light and the glory. III. Title.

United States—History—Colonial period—Sources.

[PLYMOUTH, Mass, First 254
church]
Plymouth church records, 1620-1859 ... New York [New England society in the city of New York] 19 v. front., plates (part double) ports., facsim. 25 cm. [BX7255.P65F53] 44-31573
1. U.S.—Hist.—Colonial period—Sources. 2. New England—Church history. 3. Plymouth, Mass.—Hist. 4. Registers of births, etc.—Plymouth, Mass. I. New England society in the city of New York. II. Title.

United States—History, Military—Addresses, essays, lectures.

THE Wars of America 261.8'73'0973
: eight Christian views / edited by Ronald A. Wells. Grand Rapids, Mich. : Eerdmans, c1981. p. cm. Includes bibliographical references. [E181.W28] 19 81-15194 ISBN 0-8028-1899-4 : 8.95
1. United States—History, Military—Addresses, essays, lectures. 2. War and religion—Addresses, essays, lectures. I. Wells, Ronald, 1941-

United States—History—Prophecies.

CROWTHER, Duane S. 289.3'22
Prophetic warnings to modern America / Duane S. Crowther. Bountiful, Utah : Horizon Publishers & Distributors, c1977. xii, 415 p. : ill. ; 24 cm. Includes bibliographical references and index.

[BX8638.C73] 77-87431 ISBN 0-88290-016-1 : 6.95
1. Book of Mormon—Prophecies. 2. United States—History—Prophecies. I. Title.

United States—History—Revolution, 1775-1783—Addresses, essays, lectures.

THORNTON, John Wingate, 1818-1878, ed. 261.7
The pulpit of the American Revolution; or, The political sermons of the period of 1776. With a historical introd., notes, and illus. by John Wingate Thornton. New York, B. Franklin [1970] 537 p. illus., port. 23 cm. (American classics in history and social science, 109) (Research and source works series, 440.) Reprint of the 1860 ed. Contents.Contents.—Dr. Mayhew's sermon of Jan. 30, 1750.—Dr. Chauncy's thanksgiving sermon on the repeal of the Stamp act, 1766.—Mr. Cooke's election sermon, 1770.—Mr. Gordon's thanksgiving sermon, 1774.—Dr. Langdon's election sermon at Watertown, 1775.—Mr. West's election sermon, 1776.—Mr. Payson's election sermon, 1778.—Mr. Howard's election sermon, 1780.—Dr. Stiles's election sermon, 1783. [E297.T51 1970] 77-114833
1. United States—History—Revolution, 1775-1783—Addresses, essays, lectures. I. Title.

United States—History—Revolution, 1775-1783—Religious aspects.

ALBANESE, Catherine L. 209'.73
Sons of the fathers : the civil religion of the American Revolution / Catherine L. Albanese. Philadelphia : Temple University Press, 1976. xiv, 274 p. ; 23 cm. Includes bibliographical references and index. [E209.A4] 76-17712 ISBN 0-87722-073-5 : 12.50
1. United States—History—Revolution, 1775-1783—Religious aspects. I. Title.

NOLL, Mark A., 1946- 277.3
Christians in the American Revolution / Mark A. Noll. Grand Rapids : Eerdmans, [1977] p. cm. Bibliography: p. [E209.N64] 77-23354 ISBN 0-8028-1706-8 pbk. : 4.95
1. United States—History—Revolution, 1775-1783—Religious aspects. 2. United States—Church history—Colonial period, ca. 1600-1775. I. Title.

United States—History—Revolution—Addresses, sermons, etc.

SHERWOOD, Samuel, 1730-1783. 264
The church's flight into the wilderness; an address on the times. Containing some very interesting and important observations on Scripture prophecies; shewing, that sundry of them plainly relate to Great-Britain, and the American colonies; and are fulfilling in the present day. Delivered on a public occasion, January 17, 1776. By Samuel Sherwood ... New York: Printed by S. Loudon, 1776. 54 p. 22 cm. Appendix. By another hand: p. 51-54. [E297.S55] [AC901.H3 vol. 35] 973 8-11860
1. U.S.—Hist.—Revolution—Addresses, sermons, etc. I. Title.

THORNTON, John Wingate, 1818-1878, ed. 261.7
The pulpit of the American Revolution; political sermons of the period of 1776. Historical introd. and notes by John Wingate Thornton. New York, Da Capo Press, 1970. 537 p. 23 cm. (The Era of the American Revolution) Reprint of the 1860 ed. published by Gould and Lincoln, Boston. Contents.Contents.—Dr. Mayhew's sermon of Jan. 30, 1750.—Dr. Chauncy's thanksgiving sermon on the repeal of the Stamp act, 1766.—Mr. Cooke's election sermon, 1770.—Mr. Gordon's thanksgiving sermon, 1774.—Dr. Langdon's election sermon at Watertown 1775.—Mr. West's election sermon, 1776.—Mr. Payson's election sermon, 1778.—Mr. Howard's election sermon, 1780.—Dr. Stiles's election sermon, 1783. [E297.T5 1970b] 71-109611 ISBN 0-306-71907-X
1. United States—History—Revolution, 1775-1783—Addresses, sermons, etc. I. Title.

WEST, Samuel, 1731-1807. 264
A sermon preached before the Honorable Council, and the Honorable House of representatives, of the colony of the Massachusetts-Bay, in New-England. May 29th, 1776. Being the anniversary for the election of the Honorable Council for the colony. By Samuel West ... Boston, Printed by John Gill, 1776. 70 p. 22 cm. [E297.W54] [AC901.M7 Vol.102] 325 17-6710
1. U.S.—Hist.—Revolution—Addresses, sermons, etc. I. Title.

United States—History—War of 1812—Addresses, sermons, etc.

MCLEOD, Alexander, 1774-1833. 264
A scriptural view of the character, causes, and ends of the present war. By Alexander McLeod, D.D., pastor of the Reformed Presbyterian church, New York... New York: Published by Eastburn, Kirk and co.; Whiting and Watson; and Smith and Forman. Paul & Thomas, printers, 1815. viii, [9]-224 p. 21 1/2 cm. A series of sermons. [E364.5.M16] [AC901.W7 vol. 74] 811. 2-17209
1. U.S.—Hist.—War of 1812—Addresses, sermons, etc. I. Title.

United States—History—War of 1898—Personal narratives.

JONES, Harry W.
A chaplain's experience ashore and afloat; the "Texas" under fire. By Rev. Harry W. Jones ... chaplain U. S. navy. New York, A. G. Sherwood & co. [c1901] xi, 300 p. front., plates, ports. 19 cm. [E727.J77] 1-31325
1. U. S.—Hist.—War of 1898—Personal narratives. 2. Texas (Battleship) I. Title.

United States—History—War of 1898—Religious aspects.

[BACON, Thomas Scott] 1825-1904.
A new religion as revealed in three months of war ... [n.p., 1898?] 94 p. 16 cm. Preface signed: T. S. Bacon. No. [6] in a volume with binder's title: Sermons and addresses on the Spanish American war. [E735.S45 no. 6] 43-34949
1. U.S.—Hist.—War of 1898—Religious aspects. I. Title.

United States Military Academy, West Point.

PULLEY, Frank Easton, 1906- 252.5
Christ, thy Captain; sermons preached to the Class of 1952 by their chaplain. New York, Morehouse-Gorham Co., 1952. 135 p. 16 cm. [BV4316.S7P792] 52-4012
1. U.S. Military Academy, West Point. 2. Sermons, American. I. Title.

PULLEY, Frank Easton, 1906- 252.5
Help from the hills; sermons preached to the Class of 1951 by their chaplain. New York, Morehouse-Gorham Co., 1951. 127 p. 16 cm. [BV4316.S7P793] 51-4938
1. U.S. Military Academy, West Point. 2. Sermons, American. I. Title.

PULLEY, Frank Easton, 1906- 252
Soldiers of the cross; sermons preached to the Class of 1950 by their chaplain. New York, Morehouse-Gorham Co., 1950. 108 p. 16 cm. Bibliography: p. 107-108. [BV4316.S7P796] 50-8439
1. U.S. Military Academy, West Point. 2. Sermons, American. I. Title.

United States — Moral conditions.

AMERICAN Academy of Political and Social Science, Philadelphia. 170.202
Ethics in America: norms and deviations. Special editor: James C. Charlesworth. Philadelphia, 1966. ix. 227 p. 24 cm (Its Annals, v. 363) Bibliographical footnotes. [H1.A4 vol. 363] 66-15192
1. U.S. — Moral conditions. 2. Professional ethics — U.S. I. Charlesworth, James Clyde, 1900- ed. II. Title. III. Series.

BROOKS, Pat. 973
The return of the Puritans / Pat Brooks. 3rd ed. Fletcher, N.C. : New Puritan Library, 1981. 190 p. : ill. ; 21 cm. Includes bibliographical references. [HN90.M6B76 1981] 19 81-153122 ISBN 0-932050-04-2 (pbk.) : 3.50
1. United States—Moral conditions. 2. United States—Civilization—1970- 3. Puritans—United States. I. Title.

GONZALES, Carmen. 170'.973
The United States & the moral philosophy of the gutter / Carmen Gonzales. Albuquerque, N.M. : American Classical College Press, [1977] 29 leaves ; 28 cm. [HN90.M6G65] 77-7261 ISBN 0-89266-072-4
1. United States—Moral conditions. 2. Good and evil. I. Title.

GORDON, Gary.
Sins of our cities. Derby, Conn., Monarch Books [1962] 160 p. 19 cm. (Monarch human behavior series, MB525) Monarch giants. Bibliography: p. 159-160. 63-13113
1. U.S. — Moral conditions. I. Title.

HUBBARD, David Allan. 261.8'3
Right living in a world gone wrong / David Allan Hubbard. Downers Grove, Ill. : InterVarsity Press, c1981. 112 p. ; 18 cm. Includes bibliographies. [HN90.M6H8] 19 80-39671 ISBN 0-87784-470-4 pbk. 3.25
1. United States—Moral conditions. 2. Sexual ethics. 3. Christian ethics. 4. Church and social problems—United States. I. Title.

MAYO, Allen. 248'.84
Contract at Mount Horeb / Allen Mayo. [San Antonio] : Tex-Mex Books, c1977. 171 p. ; 22 cm. [HN90.M6M39] 75-13402 10.95
1. United States—Moral conditions. I. Title.

PINES, Burton Yale. 306'.0973
Back to basics : the traditionalist movement that is sweeping grass-roots America / Burton Yale Pines. 1st ed. New York : Morrow, 1982. 348 p. ; 25 cm. Includes bibliographical references and index. [HN59.2.P53 1982] 19 82-2106 ISBN 0-688-01117-9 : 13.00
1. United States—Moral conditions. 2. Conservatism—United States. I. Title.

PRICE, John Richard, 1941- 261.8'3'0973
America at the crossroads / John Price. Wheaton, Ill. : Tyndale House Publishers, c1979. 237 p. ; 18 cm. (Living books) Includes bibliographical references. [HN90.M6P74 1979] 79-65025 ISBN 0-8423-0064-3 : 2.50
1. United States—Moral conditions. I. Title.

ROBISON, James, 1943- 261.8'0973
Save America to save the world : a Christian's practical guide for stopping the tidal wave of moral, political, and economic destruction in America / James Robison, with Jim Cox. Wheaton, Ill. : Tyndale House Publishers, c1980. 112 p. ; 18 cm. [HN90.M6R6] 19 80-50189 ISBN 0-8423-5823-4 (pbk.) : 1.95
1. United States—Moral conditions. 2. Christianity—20th century. 3. Christianity and politics. I. Cox, Jimmie. II. Title.

SELLERS, James Earl. 261.8
Public ethics; American morals and manners [by] James Sellers. [1st ed.] New York, Harper & Row [1970] 349 p. 22 cm. Bibliographical references included in "Notes" (p. 313-342) [E169.12.S43 1970] 70-85049 8.95
1. U.S.—Moral conditions. 2. Church and the world. I. Title. II. Title: American morals and manners.

SELLERS, James Earl. 170'.202
Warming fires : the quest for community in America / James E. Sellers. New York : Seabury Press, [1975] xi, 207 p. ; 22 cm. "A Crossroad book." Includes bibliographical references. [HN90.M6S44] 74-28283 ISBN 0-8164-0273-6 : 7.95
1. United States—Moral conditions. 2. Social values. I. Title.

STRATON, John Roach, 1875- 261.
Fighting the devil in modern Babylon, by Dr. John Roach Straton ... Boston, The Stratford company [c1929] 1 p. l., xiii, 287 p. front. 20 cm. [BV610.S68] 29-18910
1. U.S.—Moral conditions. 2. Amusements—Moral and religious aspects. 3. Modernist-fundamentalist controversy. I. Title.
Contents omitted.

STRATON, John Roach, 1875-1929. 261.
The menace of immorality in church and state; messages of wrath and judgment, by Rev. John Roach Straton ... New York, George H. Doran company [c1920] ix p., 11-253 p. front., plates. 19 1/2 cm. [BV610.S7] 20-6996
1. U.S.—Moral conditions. I. Title.

STRONG, Josiah, 1847-1916. 277.
Our country: its possible future and its present crisis. By Rev. Josiah Strong ... With an introduction by Prof. Austin Phelps ... 65th thousand. New York, Pub. by the Baker & Taylor co., for the American home missionary society [c1885] x, 229 p. diagrs. 18 1/2 cm. This volume was prepared for the American home missionary society, for the purpose of giving facts and arguments showing the imperative need of home missionary work. cf. Prefatory note. [BV2775.S8 1885d] 18-15923
1. U.S.—Moral conditions. 2. Missions, Home. 3. U.S.—Econ. condit. I. Congregational home missionary society. II. Title.

STRONG, Josiah, 1847-1916. 309.173
Our country: its possible future and its present crisis. By Rev. Josiah Strong ... With an introduction by Prof. Austin Phelps ... 85th thousand. New York, Pub. by the Baker & Taylor co., for the American home missionary society [c1885] x, 229 p. diagrs. 18 1/2 cm. This volume was prepared for the American home missionary society, for the purpose of giving facts and arguments showing the imperative needs of home missionary work. cf. Prefatory note. [BV2775.S8 1885f] 33-39235
1. U.S.—Moral conditions. 2. Missions, Home. 3. U.S.—Econ. condit. I. Congregational home missionary society. II. Title.

SWEENEY, John F 170.973
Danger! Fraud ahead! Living and spending guideposts for the twentieth-century American. [1st ed.] New York, Exposition Press [1963] 180 p. 22 cm. (An Exposition-banner book) [HN64.S94] 62-19524
1. U.S. — Moral conditions. 2. Social ethics. 3. Conduct of life. I. Title.

VERI, Anthony. 170'.973
The new moral code of action of the large corporation's executive / Anthony Veri. [Albuquerque, N.M.] : American Classical College Press, [1977] p. cm. [HN90.M6V47] 77-7276 ISBN 0-89266-068-6 : 37.50
1. United States—Moral conditions. 2. Social ethics. 3. Executives—United States. I. Title.

YARROW, Phillip, ed. 176
Fighting the debauchery of our girls and boys. [n. p., c1923] 462p. illus. 21cm. [HQ18.U5Y3] 53-50361
1. U. S.—Moral conditions. 2. Prostitution—U. S. I. Title.

United States Moral conditions, Addresses, essays, lectures.

CAMPBELL, Robert, 1919- comp. 170'.973
New morality or no morality. New York, Bruce Pub. Co. [1969] viii, 248 p. 22 cm. [HN59.C3] 71-101719
1. U.S.—Moral conditions—Addresses, essays, lectures. I. Title.

SABINI, John, 1947- 302
Moralities of everyday life / John Sabini and Maury Silver. New York : Oxford University Press, 1982. p. cm. Includes index. Bibliography: p. [HN90.M6S2] 19 81-11004 ISBN 0-19-503016-8 : 15.95 ISBN 0-19-503017-6 (pbk.) : 6.95
1. United States—Moral conditions—Addresses, essays, lectures. 2. Social psychology—Addresses, essays, lectures. I. Silver, Maury, 1944- II. Title.

United States Naval Station, Norfolk, Va. Commodore Levy Chapel.

SOBEL, Samuel 296

I love Thy house; a keepsake of the Commodore Levy Chapel, Norfolk, 2d ed.

Norfolk, Va., 700 Spotswood Ave., Norfolk Jewish Community Council, 1963.

87p., music (31p.) illus., ports. 20cm. 62-17837 5.00: 1.50 pap.,

1. Levy Uriah Phillips, 1792-1862. 2. U.S. Naval Station, Norfolk, Va. Commodore Levy Chapel. 3. Armed Forces—Prayerbooks and devotions—English. I. Title.

SOBEL, Samuel. 296

I love Thy house; a keepsake of the Commodore Levy Chapel, Norfolk. 2d ed.

[Norfolk, Jewish Community Council] 1962. [90] p., music (31 p.) illus., ports. 20

cm. "Music of the Commodore Levy Chapel . . . [principally for the] Sabbath

eve service": 31 p. (2d group) [BM225.N7C6 1962a] 63-13730

1. U.S. Naval Station, Norfolk, Va. Commodore Levy Chapel. 2. Levy, Uriah Phillips, 1792-1862. 3. Armed Forces — Prayer-books and devotions — English. I. Title.

United States Peace Corps.

ARMSTRONG, Roger D. 266
Peace Corps and Christian mission, by Roger D. Armstrong. With a foreword by Samuel D. Proctor and a pref. by Charles W. Forman. New York, Friendship Press [1965] 126 p. 19 cm. [HC60.5.A8] 65-11435

1. U.S. Peace Corps. 2. Missions — Theory. I. Title.

United States— Religion.

ABBEY, Merrill R. 200'.973
Day dawns in fire : America's quest for meaning / Merrill R. Abbey. Philadelphia : Fortress Press, c1976. vi, 122 p. ; 20 cm. Includes bibliographical references. [BR515.A22] 75-36439 ISBN 0-8006-1218-3 pbk. : 3.25

1. United States—Religion. 2. United States—Civilization. I. Title.

ABBOTT, Ernest Hamlin, 1870- 204
1931.

Religious life in America; a record of personal observation, by Ernest Hamlin Abbott. New York, The Outlook company, 1902. xii, 370 p. 21 1/2 cm. [BR525.A5] 2-28397

1. U.S.—Religion. I. Title.

AHLSTROM, Sydney E. 200'.973
A religious history of the American people / Sydney E. Ahlstrom. Garden City, N.Y. : Image Books, 1975, c1972. 2 v. ; 18 cm. Reprint of the ed. published by Yale University Press, New Haven, with a new pref. Includes index. Bibliography: p. [621]-666. [BR515.A4 1975] 75-22362 ISBN 0-385-11164-9 (v. 1) : 3.50 ISBN 0-385-11165-7(v.2)
1. United States—Religion. I. Title.

AHLSTROM, Sydney E. 200'.973
A religious history of the American people [by] Sydney E. Ahlstrom. New Haven, Yale University Press, 1972. xvi, 1158 p. 26 cm. Bibliography: p. 1097-1128. [BR515.A4 1972] 72-151564 ISBN 0-300-01475-9 19.50
1. United States—Religion. I. Title.

AMERICAN Academy of 209.73
Political and Social Science, Philadelphia. *Religion in American society.* Special editor: Richard D. Lambert. Philadelphia, 1960. viii, 220p. illus. 24cm. (Its Annals, v. 332) Bibliographical footnotes. [H1.A4 vol. 332] 60-51981
1. U. S.—Religion. I. Lambert, Richard D., ed. II. Title. III. Series.

AMERICAN Academy of 209.73
Political and Social Science, Philadelphia. Annals.
Not many wise, a reader on religion in American society. Pilgrim Pr. [dist. Philadelphia, United Church, c.1962] 169p. 21cm. (Pilgrimbk.) Bibl. 62-13706 2.25 pap.,
1. U.S.—Religion. 2. U.S.—Church history—20th cent. I. Title.

AMERICAN Academy of 209.73
Political and Social Science, Philadelphia. Annals.
Not many wise, a reader on religion in American society. Boston, Pilgrim Press [1962] 169p. 21cm. (A Pilgrim book) 'Essays ...selected from the November 1960 issue of the Annals of the American Academy of Political and Social Science.' Includes bibliography. [BR526.A62] 62-13706
1. U. S.—Religion. 2. U. S.—Church history—20th cent. I. Title.

AMERICAN Academy of 209.73
Political and Social Science, Philadelphia. Annals, v. 332
Not many wise, a reader on religion in American society. Boston, Pilgrim Press [1962] 169 p. 21 cm. (A Pilgrim book) "Essays ... selected from the November 1960 issue of the Annals of the American Academy of Political and Social Science." Includes bibliography. [BR526.N6] 62-13706
1. U.S. — Religion. 2. U.S. Church history — 20th cent. I. Title.

ANDREEN, Paul Harold, 1891- 261
Main street today, by Paul H. Andreen ... Rock Island, Ill., Augustana book concern [1941] 211 p. 20 cm. "Suggestions for further reading": p. 199-211. [BR525.A57] 41-9817
1. U.S.—Religion. 2. U.S.—Soc. condit. I. Title.

ATKINS, Gaius Glenn, 1868- 277.3
Religion in our times, by Gaius Glenn Atkins. New York, Round table press, inc, 1932. xi, 830 p. 24 cm. [BR525.A8] 32-33927
1. U. S.—Religion. 2. U. S.—Church history. 3. Protestant churches—U. S. I. Title.

BACH, Marcus, 1906- 280
Report to Protestants; a personal investigation of the weakness, need, vision and great potential of Protestants today. [1st ed.] Indianapolis, Bobbs-Merrill Co. [1948] 277 p. 23 cm. [BR516.B265] 48-5216
1. U. S.—Religion. 2. Sects—U. S. 3. Christian union—U. S. 4. Protestantism. I. Title.

BAKER, Newton Diehl, 1871- 261
1937, ed.
The American way; a study of human relations among Protestants, Catholics, and Jews, edited by Newton Diehl Baker, Carlton J. H. Hayes [and] Roger Williams Straus. Chicago, New York, Willett, Clark & company, 1936. ix, 165 p. 20 cm. "The material is based upon the Williamstown Institute of human relations, held under the auspices of the National conference of Jews and Christians, at Williams college, August, 1935."--Introd. [BR516.B3] 36-16693
1. U. S.—Religion. 2. Sociology, Christian. 3. Protestants in the U. S. 4. Catholic in the U. S. 5. Jews in the U. S. 6. Religions—Congresses. I. Hayes, Carlton Joseph Huntley, 1882- joint ed. II. Straus, Roger Williams, 1891- joint ed. III. Institute of human relations, Williams college, 1935. IV. Title.

BEDELL, George C. 200'.973
Religion in America / George C. Bedell, Leo Sandon, Jr., Charles T. Wellborn. New York : Macmillan, [1975] xv, 538 p. ; 24 cm. Includes bibliographical references and index. [BR515.B48] 74-2867 ISBN 0-02-307920-7 : 10.95.
1. United States—Religion. I. Sandon, Leo, joint author. II. Wellborn, Charles, joint author. III. Title.

BENNE, Robert. 917.3'03'924
Defining America; a Christian critique of the American dream, by Robert Benne [and] Philip Hefner. Philadelphia, Fortress Press [1974] ix, 150 p. 22 cm. Includes bibliographical references. [BR526.B44] 73-89062 ISBN 0-8006-1075-X 3.75
1. United States—Religion. 2. United States—Civilization—1945- I. Hefner, Philip J., joint author. II. Title.

BERGER, Peter L. 209'.73
Religion in a revolutionary society; delivered at Christ Church, Alexandria, Virginia, on February 4, 1974 [by] Peter L. Berger. Washington, American Enterprise Institute for Public Policy Research [1974] 16 p. illus. 25 cm. (Distinguished lecture series on the Bicentennial) Includes bibliographical references. [BR515.B53] 74-79895 ISBN 0-8447-1306-6 1.00
1. United States—Religion. I. Title. II. Series.

BISHOP, Isabella Lucy 209'.73
(Bird) 1831-1904.
The aspects of religion in the United States of America. New York, Arno Press, 1972. 189 p. 23 cm. (Religion in America, series II) Reprint of the 1859 ed. [BR515.B57 1972] 75-38438 ISBN 0-405-04059-8
1. United States—Religion. I. Title.

BOUMAN, Walter R., 1929- 209'.73
Christianity American style, by Walter R. Bouman. Dayton, G. A. Pflaum, 1970. 128 p. illus. 18 cm. (Christian identity series) (Witness book, CI 10.) [BR515.B66] 75-114724 .95
1. U.S.—Religion. I. Title.

BRAUER, Jerald C. 209'.73
Images of religion in America, by Jerald C. Brauer. Philadelphia, Fortress Press [1967] x, 35 p. 19 cm. (Facet books. Historical series, 8) First published in Church history, v. 30, Mar. 1961, p. 3-18. Bibliographical footnotes. [BR515.B68] 67-22984
1. U.S. — Religion. I. Title.

BREWER, David Josiah, 1837- 200
1910.
The United States a Christian nation, by David J. Brewer... Philadelphia, The J. C. Winston company, 1905. 98 p. 20 cm. (Half-title: Haverford library lectures) Series title also at head of t.-p. [JK361.B8] 5-32669
1. U.S.—Religion. 2. Citizenship. I. Title. Contents omitted.

BRILL, Earl H. 209'.73
The future of the American past; a study course on American values, by Earl H. Brill. New York, Seabury Press [1974] 96 p. 21 cm. "A Crossroad book." Includes bibliographies. [BR515.B74] 73-17890 ISBN 0-8164-2086-6 2.95 (pbk.)
1. United States—Religion. 2. United States—Civilization. I. Title.

BUNDY, Edgar C. 209.73
Aposles of deceit, by Edgar C. Bundy. Wheaton, Ill., Church League of America [1966] xii, 528 p. 22 cm. [BR517.B87] 66-24178
1. U.S. — Religion. 2. Communism — U.S. I. Title.

BURLESON, Hugh Latimer, 283.
bp., 1865- ed.
How our church came to our country, a series of illustrated papers, ed. by Hugh L. Burleson ... Milwaukee, Wis., Morehouse publishing co. [c1920] 2 p. l., 280 p. illus. (incl. ports.) 24 cm. [BX5880.B8] 20-12832
I. Title.

CALIFORNIA. University. 209.73
University Extension.
Religion and the face of America; papers of the conference, presented at Asilomar, Pacific Grove, California, November 28, 29, and 3d. 1958. Edited by Jane C. Zahn. Berkeley [1959] 87p. 23cm. [BR526.C3] 59-63690
1. U. S.—Religion. I. Zahn, Jane C., ed. II. Title.

CAMPBELL, Timothy James, 209.73
1883-
Central themes of American life. Grand Rapids, Mich., Eerdmans [1959] 188p. 21cm. Includes bibliography. [BR517.C3] 59-8751
1. U. S.—Religion. I. Title.

CENTER for the Study of 208.2
Democratic Institutions.
Religion and American society, a statement of principles [by] William Clancy [and others] With an introd. by Henry P. Van Dusen. Santa Barbara, Calif. [1961] 79 p. 22 cm. (Its A contribution to the discussion of the free society) [BR517.C4] 63-91
1. U.S. — Religion. 2. Sociology, Christian. I. Clancy, William. II. Title.

CHANEY, Elmer V 277.3
The unity of science, theology, and doubt; a plea for social progress. [1st ed.] New York, Exposition Press [1957] 126p. illus. 21cm. [BR516.C45] 56-12365
1. U. S.—Religion. I. Title.

CHANEY, Elmer V 277.3
The unity of science, theology, and doubt; a plea for social progress. [1st ed.] New York, Exposition Press [1957] 126p. illus. 21cm. [BR516.C45] 56-12365
1. U. S.— Religion. I. Title.

CHAUNCY, Charles, 1705-1787. 264
A letter to a friend, containing remarks on certain passages in a sermon preached, by the Right Reverend father in God, John lord bishop of Landaff, before the incorporated Society for the propagation of the gospel in foreign parts, at their anniversary meeting in the parish church of St. Mary-le-Bow, February 20, 1767. In which the highest reproach is undeservedly cast upon the American colonies, By Charles Chauncy, D. D., pastor of the First church of Christ in Boston. Boston: Printed by Kneeland and Adams in Milk-streets, for Thomas Leverett, in Corn-hill. 1767. 56 p. 19 cm. [Hazard pamphlets, v. 14, no. 2] [AC901.H3 vol. 14] [AC901.M7 vol. 103] 264 19-10118
1. Ewer, John, bp. of Bangor, d. 1774. A sermon preached ... February 20, 1767. 2. U. S.—Religion. I. Title.

CHEEVER, George Barrell, 277.3
1807-1890.
God's hand in America. By the Rev. George B. Cheever. With an essay, by the Rev. Dr. Skinner. New-York, M. W. Dodd; London, Wiley & Putnam, 1841. xx, [21]-168 p. 19 cm. [BR515.C5] 33-388334
1. U. S.—Religion. I. Title.

CHEN, Richard M. J. 208.1
A letter to American Christians. New York, Exposition Press [c.1961] 55p. 61-3499 2.50
1. U. S.—Religion. I. Title.

CHURCH, Brooke (Peters) 280.973
1885-
A faith for you. New York, Rinehart, 1948. x, 305 p. 22 cm. Full name: Gabriella Brooke Forman (Peters) Church. Bibliography: p. 297-305. [BR516.C48] 48-8859
1. U. S.—Religion. 2. Sects—U. S. 3. Church history. I. Title.

*CLEBSCH, William A. 200.9'73
American religious thought: a history, [by] William A. Clebsch. Chicago, University of Chicago Press [1973] xxi, 212 p. 21 cm. (Chicago history of American religion.)

Bibliography: p. 197-205. [BR515] 73-82911 ISBN 0-226-10960-7 6.95
1. United States—Religion. I. Title.

CLEBSCH, William A. 209.73
From sacred to profane America; the role of religion in American history, by William A. Clebsch. New York, Harper & Row [1968] xi, 242 p. 22 cm. Bibliographical references included in "Notes" (p. 219-232) [BR515.C55] 68-11730
1. U.S.—Religion. 2. U.S.—Church history. I. Title.

COGLEY, John, ed. 261.70973
Religion in America; original essays on religion in a free society. New York, Meridian Books [1958] 288p. 18cm. (Meridian books, M60) [BR516.C68] 58-12381
1. U. S.—Religion. 2. Church and state and state in the U. S. I. Title.

COX, Claire 277.3
The new-time religion. Englewood Cliffs, N.J., Prentice-Hall [c.1961] 248p. 61-9430 3.95 bds.,
1. U.S.—Religion. I. Title.

CRAIN, Thomas Crowell Taylor, 1860- 242
A survey, by Thomas C. T. Crain. New York city, The Scribner press [c1940] 2 p. l., 67 p. front. (port.) 22 cm. [BR517.C7] 40-8175
1. U. S.—Religion. 2. Civilization. Christian. I. Title.
Contents omitted.

CROWE, Winfield Scott, 1850- 280
Phases of religion in America; a course of lectures, by W. S. Crowe ... Newark, N. J., Printed by Ward & Tichenor. 1893. 4 p. l., 144 p. 21 cm. [BR515.C85] 33-8557
1. U. S.—Religion. 2. Religion—Addresses, essays, lectures. I. Title.

CROWLEY, Dale. 200'.973
Can America survive??? : Our God-given freedoms threatened by deadly enemies within and without / by Dale Crowley. Washington : National Bible Knowledge Association, c1975. xi, 156 p. ; 22 cm. "Bicentennial special." [BR515.C93] 75-29986
1. United States—Religion. 2. United States—Moral conditions. I. Title.

DAVIES, Arthur Powell. 277.3
America's real religion. Boston, Beacon Press, 1949. 87 p. 21 cm. Based on a series of four sermons. "Sources": p. 85-87. [BR516.D27] 49-3696
1. U. S.—Religion. I. Title.

DICKS, Lee E
Religion in action; how America's faiths are meeting new challenges. Silver Spring, Md., National Observer [c1965] 211 p. illus. 28 cm. (Newsbook) 66-63589
1. U.S. — Religion. 2. Sects. — U.S. I. Title.

DIEFFENBACH, Albert Charles, 1876- 204
Religious liberty; the great American illusion, by Albert C. Dieffenbach. New York, W. Morrow & co., 1927. xiii p., 1 l., 205 p. 20 cm. [BR525.D5] 27-22169
1. U. S.—Religion. 2. Religious liberty. I. Title.

DIRKS, Lee E. 200.973
Religion in action; how America's faiths are meeting new challenges. The National observer dist. New York, Dow Jones, 1965 211p. illus., facsim., col. map, ports. 28cm. (National observer [Silver Spring, Md.] Newsbk.) [BR526.D5] 65-15132 2.00
1. U.S.—Religion. I. Title. II. Series.

EAKIN, Frank, 1885- 248
Let's think about our religion [by] Frank Eakin and Mildred Moody Eakin. New York, The Macmillan company, 1944. ix, 251 p. 19 1/2 cm. "First printing." "Source references": p. 241-243. [BR516.E3] 44-7603
1. U.S.—Religion. 2. Christianity—20th cent. I. Eakin, Mildred Olivia (Moody) 1890- joint author. II. Title.

ELSON, Edward Lee Roy, 1906- 277.3
Americas spiritual recovery Introd. by J. Edgar Hoover [Westwood, N. J.] F. H. Revell Co. [1954] 189p. 21cm. [BR516.E45] 53-10969
1. U. S.—Religion. I. Title.

FERGUSON, Charles Wright, 1901- 289
The confusion of tongues; a review of modern isms, by Charles W. Ferguson. Garden City, N.Y., Doubleday, Doran & company, inc. 1928. 7 p. l., 464 p. front., pl., ports. 23 1/2 cm. "Selected bibliography": p. 461-464. [BT1240.F4] 28-29463
1. U.S.—Religion. 2. Sects. I. Title.

FERGUSON, Charles Wright, 1901- 289
The new books of revelations; the inside story of America's astounding religious cults, by Charles W. Ferguson... Garden Ciy, N.Y., Doubleday, Doran & company, inc., 1929. 6 p. l., 464 p. 21 cm. "Plain talk edition of the Confusion of tongues. These books are printed as a special edition for Plain talk magazine. The previous edition bore the title, The confusion of tongues." "Selected bibliography": p. 461-464. [[BT1240.F]] A 39
1. U.S.—Religion. 2. Sects—U.S. I. Title.

FINKELSTEIN, Louis, 1895-. 277.3
The religions of democracy; Judaism, Catholicism, Protestantism in creed and life, by Louis Finkelstein, J. Elliot Ross [and] William Adams Brown. New York, The Devin-Adair company, 1941. 3 p. l., iii-ix, 241 p. 21cm. Contents.Preface, by R.A. Ashworth.--pt. i. The beliefs and practices of Judaism, by Louis Finkelstein.--pt. ii. The Roman Catholic religion in creed and life, by J.E. Ross.--pt. iii. Protestantism in creed and life, by W.A. Brown. Bibliography at end of each part. [BR516.F5] 41-6146
1. U.S.—Religion. 2. Jews—Religion. 3. Catholic church—Doctrinal and controversial works. 4. Protestantism. I. Ross, John Elliot, 1884-. II. Brown, William Adams, 1865-. III. Title.

FOWLER, Ira E. 261.7
Is it too late? Boston, Christopher Pub. House [c.1960] 115p. 60-15782 2.75 bds.,
1. U.S.—Religion. I. Title.

FOX, Matthew, 1940- 200'.973
Religion USA; an inquiry into religion and culture by way of Time magazine. [Dubuque, Iowa] Listening Press, 1971. 451 p. 22 cm. Includes bibliographical references. [BR517.F64] 76-151967 3.65
1. Time, the weekly news-magazine. 2. U.S.—Religion. 3. Religion and culture. I. Title.

GAER, Joseph, 1897- 917.3
The Puritan heritage; America's roots in the Bible, by Joseph Gaer and Ben Siegel. [New York,) New American Library [1964] x, 256 p. 18 cm. (A Mentor book) "MT592." Bibliography: p. 227-246. [BR517.G3] 64-25081
1. U.S. — Religion. 2. Bible — Influence. I. Siegel, Ben, 1925- joint author. II. Title.

GARRISON, Winfred Ernest, 1874- 277.3
The march of faith; the story of religion in America since 1865, by Winfred Ernest Garrison. New York and London Harper & brothers 1933. v p., 1 l., vii-viii p., 1 l., 332 p. 22 1/2 cm. "First edition." "Sources and bibliography": p. 309-316. [BR525.G3] 33-11236
1. U.S—Religion. 2. U.S.—Church history. 3. Protestant churches—U.S. I. Title.

GARRISON, Winfred Ernest, 1874-1969. 277.3
The march of faith; the story of religion in America since 1865. Westport, Conn., Greenwood Press [1971, c1933] viii, 332 p. 23 cm. Bibliography: p. 309-316. [BR525.G3 1971] 79-138112 ISBN 0-8371-5688-2
1. U.S.—Religion. 2. U.S.—Church history. 3. Protestant churches—U.S. I. Title.

GATES, John Alexander, 1898- 277.3
Christendom revisited; a Kierkegaardian view of the church today. Philadelphia, Westminster Press [1963] 176 p. 21 cm. "Selected bibliography": p. 175-176. [BX4827.K5G3] 63-10496
1. Kierkegaard, Soren Aabye, 1813-1855. 2. U.S.—Religion. I. Title.

GILMORE, Jan, comp. 280'.0973
That old-time religion; the humor, reverence, and joy of American religion in an earlier time, with just a touch of nostalgia. Edited by Jan Gilmore and Ginny Jacoby. [Kansas City, Mo.] Hallmark Editions [1972] 61 p. illus. 20 cm. [BR515.G53] 77-179715 ISBN 0-87529-259-3 2.50
1. United States—Religion. 2. Revivals—United States. I. Jacoby, Ginny, joint comp. II. Title.

GREELEY, Andrew M., 1928- 200'.973
The denominational society; a sociological approach to religion in America [by] Andrew M. Greeley. Academic advisor in sociology: Peter H. Rossi. Glenview, Ill., Scott, Foresman [1972] 266 p. 23 cm. Bibliography: p. 255-258. [BR515.G74] 70-173239
1. United States—Religion. 2. Religion and sociology. I. Title.

GREENFIELD, Robert. 200'.973
The spiritual supermarket / Robert Greenfield. 1st ed. New York : Saturday Review Press, [1975] 277 p. ; 22 cm. [BL2520.G73 1975] 74-23291 ISBN 0-8415-0367-2 : 8.95 pbk. : 3.95
1. United States—Religion. 2. East (Far East)—Religion. 3. Sects—United States. I. Title.

HARRIS, Pierce. 248
Spiritual revolution. [1st ed.] Garden City, N. Y., Doubleday, 1952. 191 p. 20 cm. [BR525.H35] 52-10400
1. U. S.—Religion. 2. Civilization, Christian. I. Title.

HEDLEY, George Percy, 1899- 277.3
The superstitions of the irreligious. New York, Macmillan, 1951. 140 p. 21 cm. [BR525.H4] 51-13953
1. U.S.—Religion. I. Title.

HEENAN, Edward F., comp. 200'.973
Mystery, magic & miracle; religion in a post-Aquarian age, edited by Edward F. Heenan. Englewood Cliffs, N.J., Prentice-Hall [1973] vii, 180 p. 21 cm. (A Spectrum book) Includes bibliographical references. [BR526.H35] 73-932 ISBN 0-13-609032-X 5.95
1. United States—Religion. I. Title.
pap 2.45

HEFLEY, James C. 209'.73
America, one nation under God / James C. Hefley. Wheaton, Ill. : Victor Books, c1975. 144 p. ; 21 cm. (An Input book) [BR515.H43] 75-12194 ISBN 0-88207-721-X pbk. : 1.95
1. United States—Religion. 2. United States—Moral conditions. I. Title.

HERTZBERG, Arthur. 277.3
The outbursts that await us, three essays on religion and culture in the United States [by] Arthur Hertzberg, Martin E. Marty [and] Joseph N. Moody. New York, Macmillan [1963] 181 p. 21 cm. [BR526.H45] 63-15684
1. U.S.—Religion. I. Title.

HIGH, Stanley, 1895- 204
... Faith for today, by Stanley High, Frank Kingdon, Gerald Groveland Walsh, S. J., Louis Finkelstein, PH. D., Swami Nikhilananda, with an introduction and postscript by George V. Denny, jr. Garden City, N.Y., Town hall press and Doubleday, Doran and company, inc., 1941. x, 266 p. 19 1/2 cm. At head of title: Five faiths look at the world. "Enlarged and amplified versions of ... [the authors'] Town hall lectures." -- Introd. "First edition." [BR516.F3] 41-18045
1. U.S. — Religion. I. Kingdon, Frank, 1894- II. Walsh, Gerald Groveland, 1892-1952. III. Finkelstein, Louis, 1895- IV. Nikhiiananda, Swami. V. Denny, George Vernon, 1899- VI. Town hall, inc., New York. VII. Title.

HOLISHER, Desider, 1901- 270
The house of God, by Desider Holisher, with 300 photographs by the author and others. New York, Crown publishers [1946] 5 p. l., 3-232 p. illus. 28 1/2 cm. Illustrations: p. 5-224. "List of picture sources": p. 231-232. [BR516.H6] 46-8359
1. U.S.—Religion. 2. Churches—U.S. 3. Synagogues—U.S. I. Title.

HOMRIGHAUSEN, Elmer George, 1900- 277.3
Christianity in America; a crisis [by] E. G. Homrighausen. New York, Cincinnati [etc.] The Abingdon press [c1936] 227 p. 20 cm. [BR525.H65] 36-18298
1. U. S.—Religion. 2. Protestant churches—U. S. 3. Christianity—20th cent. 4. Dialectical theology. I. Title.

HOWLETT, Duncan. 211'.6'0973
The fourth American faith. Boston, Beacon Press [1968] xvi, 239 p. 21 cm. (Beacon paperback no. 296) Bibliographical references included in "Notes" (p. 218-232) [BR517.H6 1968] 74-5405 1.95
1. U.S.—Religion. I. Title.

HOWLETT, Duncan. 209.73
The fourth American faith. [1st ed.] New York, Harper & Row [1964] xv, 239 p. 21 cm. Bibliographical references included in "Notes" (p. [217]-232) [BR517.H6] 64-14372
1. U.S.—Religion. I. Title.

HUDSON, Winthrop Still, 1911- 209.73
Religion in America [by] Winthrop S. Hudson. New York, Scribner [1965] xii, 447 p. 25 cm. Bibliographical footnotes. [BR515.H79] 65-28188
1. U.S.—Religion I. Title.

HUDSON, Winthrop Still, 1911- 200'.973
Religion in America; an historical account of the development of American religious life [by] Winthrop S. Hudson. 2d ed. New York, Scribner [1973] xiii, 463 p. 23 cm. (Scribners university library, SUL 1015) Bibliography: p. 442-444. [BR515.H79 1973] 72-9415 pap 5.95
1. United States—Religion. I. Title.
Hard Cover 12.50.

[INGLIS, Charles, bp. of Nova Scotia] 1734-1816. 264
A vindication of the Bishop of Landaff's sermon from the gross misrepresentations, and abusive reflections contained in Mr. William Livingston's letter to his lordship: with some additional observations on certain passages in Dr. Chauncey's Remarks, &c. By a lover of truth and decency ... New-York: Printed by J. Holt, at the Exchange, 1768. viii, 82 p. 20 cm. [Hazard pamphlets, v. 16, no. 10] [AC901.H3 vol.16] 19-10117
1. Ewer, John, bp. of Bangor, d. 1774. A sermon preached ... February 20, 1767. 2. Livingston, William, 1728 1790. A letter to ... John Lord bishop of Landaff. 3. Chauncy, Charles, 1705-1787. A letter ... containing, remarks on ... a sermon preached by ... John, lord bishop of Landaffing remarks on ... a sermon preached by ... John bishop of Landaff. 4. U. S.—Religion. I. A lover of truth and decency. II. Title.

INSTITUTE for Religious and Social Studies. Jewish Theological Seminary of America. 277.3
Patterns of faith in America today. Ed. by Ernest Johnson. New York, Collier [1962, c.1957] 192p. 18cm. (AS203) Bibl. .95 pap.,
1. U.S.—Religion. I. Johnson, Frederick Ernest, 1884- ed. II. Title.

INSTITUTE for Religious and Social Studies, Jewish Theological Seminary of America. 277.3
Patterns of faith in America today, edited by F. Ernest Johnson. New York, Institute for Religious and Social Studies; distributed by Harper [1957] 192 p. 21 cm. (Religion and civilization series) "A symposium based on lectures given at the institute ... during the winter of 1954-1955." Contents.Contents.—Classical Protestantism, by R. M. Brown.—Liberal Protestantism, by E. E. Aubrey.—Roman Catholicism, by C. Donahue.—Judaism, by S. Greenberg.—Naturalistic humanism, by J. H. Randall, Jr. Includes bibliographies. [BR515.I5 1954] 57-11160
1. U.S.—Religion. I. Johnson, Frederick Ernest, 1884- ed. II. Title. III. Series.

JENKINS, Burris Atkins, 1869- 277.3
American religion as I see it lived, by Burris Jenkins. Indianapolis, The Bobbs-Merrill company 53c19303] 281, [1] p. 21 cm. [BR525.J4] 30-25915

1. U. S—Religion. I. Title.

JOHNSON, James Wager, 1863- 261
Idolatry in America, by James W. Johnson ... New York [etc.] Fleming H. Revell company [c1937] 62 p. 19 cm. [BR525.J55] 37-10140
1. U. S.—Religion. 2. Civilization, Christian. I. Title.

JONES, Eli Stanley, 1884- 277.3
The Christ of the American road [by] E. Stanley Jones. New York, Nashville, Abingdon-Cokesbury press [1944] 255 p. 16 cm. [BR516.J74] 44-6360
1. U.S.—Religion. 2. U.S.—Church history. I. Title.

KATSH, Abraham Isaac, 1908- 973.2
The Biblical heritage of American democracy / by Abraham I. Katsh. New York : Ktav Pub. House, 1977. ix, 246 p., [1] fold. leaf of plates : ill. ; 24 cm. Includes index. Bibliography: p. 213-226. [BS538.7.K37] 76-22468 ISBN 0-87068-488-4 : 15.00
1. Bible. O.T.—Influence—United States. 2. United States—Religion. 3. United States—Politics and government—Colonial period, ca. 1600-1775. I. Title.

KENNEDY, Gerald Hamilton, 261
Bp., 1907-
The Christian and his America. [1st ed.] New York, Harper [1956] 175p. 22cm. [BR516.K4] 56-12068
1. U. S.—Religion. 2. Christianity—Addresses, essays, lectures. I. Title.

KERR, Hugh Thomson, 1871- 277.3
The Christian mission in America, by Hugh Thomson Kerr... New York, Friendship press [c1933] 5 p. l., 3-134 p. 19 1/2 cm. "Reading list": p. 173-181. [BR515.K45] 33-16861
1. U.S.—Religion. 2. Christianity. I. Title.

KOCH, Gustav Adolf, 211.50973
1900-
Republican religion; the American Revolution and the cult of reason. Gloucester, Mass., P. Smith [1965, c.1933] xvi, 334p. illus. 21cm. (Studies in religion and culture. Amer. rel. ser. vii) Bibl. [BL2760.K6] 65-2746 5.00
1. U.S.—Religion. 2. U.S.—Church history. 3. Deism—Hist. I. Title. II. Title: The American Revolution and the cult of reason. (Series) III. Series.

KOCH, Gustav Adolf, 1900- 211
Republican religion; the American revolution and the cult of reason, by G. Adolf Koch, PH. D. New York, H. Holt and company [c1933] xvi, 334 p. incl. front. 23 cm. (Half-title: Studies in religion and culture. American religion sereis. Vii) Issued also as thesis (PH. D.) Columbia university. Bibliography: p. 299-326. [BL2700.K6 1933 a] 33-21601
1. U. S.—Religion. 2. U. S.—Church history. 3. Deism. I. Title. II. Title: The American revolution and the cult of reason.

LAMPERT, Richard D ed.
Religion in American society. Philadelphia, 1960. 220 p. tables. 24 cm. Being: The Annals of the American Academy of Political and Social Science, November, 1960. Church and the Laity among Jews, by Marshall S. Sklare, p. 60-69. 68-77765
1. U.S.—Religion. I. Title.

LUCCOCK, Halford Edward, 277.3
1885-
Jesus and the American mind [by] Halford E. Luccock ... New York, Cincinnati [etc.] The Abingdon press [c1930] 224 p. 20 cm. "Approximately half of the material in this volume was delivered as the Merrick lectures of 1930 at Ohio Wesleyan university."--Foreword. "Notes": p. 221-224. [BR525.L8] 30-21081
1. U. S.—Religion. 2. National characteristics, American. I. Title.

MCDONALD, Donald John, 209.73
1920-
Religion; one of a series of interviews on the American character. Interviews by Donald McDonald with Robert E. Fitch, John J. Wright, Louis Finkelstein. [Santa Barbara, Calif.] Ctr. for the Study of Dem. Insts. [1963, c.1962] 78p. 21cm. 63-1610 gratis pap.,
1. U.S.—Religion. I. Title.

MARTY, Martin E., 1928- 270.8'2'6
The fire we can light; the role of religion in a suddenly different world [by] Martin E. Marty. [1st ed.] Garden City, N.Y., Doubleday, 1973. 240 p. 22 cm. "A Christian century projection for the 1970s." Includes bibliographical references. [BR515.M28] 73-83601 ISBN 0-385-07602-9 5.95
1. United States—Religion. I. Title.

MARTY, Martin E., 1928- 209'.73
The pro & con book of religious America : a bicentennial argument / Martin E. Marty. Waco, Tex. : Word Books, [1975] 143, 149 p. ; 23 cm. [BR515.M325] 74-27478 6.95
1. United States—Religion. I. Title.

MARTY, Martin E., 1928- 209.73
Youth considers 'do-it-yourself' religion. New York, Nelson [c.1965] 93, [2]p. 21cm. (Youth forum ser.) Bibl. [BR526.M36] 65-15404 1.50 pap.,
1. U. S.—Religion. I. Title. II. Series.

MATHENY, Ezra Stacy, 1870- 264.1
American devotion [by] E. Stacy Matheny... Columbus, O., The F. J. Heer printing co. [c1940] xi, 430 p. 21 cm. On cover: Third edition. "This edition was issued under the authority of Ohio Senate resolution no. 50, adopted May 25, 1939, at the request of the respective directors of the Department of edcuation in June 1935, March 1937, and June 1938." Previous editions have title: American patriotic devotions. Includes prayers offered in the Ohio Senate. [BR516.M3 1940] 41-524
1. U.S.—Religion. 2. U.S.—Hist.—Anecdotes. 3. Prayers. 4. Legislative bodies—Chaplains' prayers. I. Ohio. General assembly. Senate. II. Title.

MATHENY, Ezra Stacy, 1870- 277.
American devotion, [by] E. Stacy Matheny ... Columbus, O., The F. J. Heer printing co. [1943] xi, 439 p. 1 illus. 21 cm. On spine: 4th ed. Published, 1932, under title: American patriotic devotions. Includes prayers offered in the Ohio Senate. "Issued under the authority of Ohio Senate resolution no. 50, adopted May 25, 1939, at the request of the respective directors of the Department of education in June, 1935, and June 1943." [BR516.M3 1943] 43-17684
1. U.S.—Religion. 2. U.S.—Hist.—Anecdotes. 3. Prayers. 4. Legislative bodies—Chaplains' prayers. I. Ohio. General assembly. Senate. II. Title.

MATHENY, Ezra Stacy, 1870- 264.1
comp.
American patriotic devotions [compiled by] E. Stacy Matheny... New York, Association press; Col[umbu]s, O., Stoneman press, 1932. xi, 411 p. 21 cm. Includes prayers offered in the Ohio senate. [BR516.M3 1932] 32-33683
1. U. S.—Religion. 2. U.S.—Hist.—Anecdotes. 3. Prayers. 4. Legislative bodies—Chaplains' prayers. I. Ohio. General assembly. Senate. II. Title.

MATHEWS, Shailer, 1863- 922.673
New faith for old; an autobiography by Shailer Mathews. New York, The Macmillan company, 1936. vi p., 2 l., 303 p. 22 1/2 cm. [BX4827.M3A3] 36-25815
1. U.S.—Religion. 2. Protestant churches—U.S. I. Title.

MELAND, Bernard Eugene, 277.3
1899-
America's spiritual culture. [1st ed.] New York, Harper [1948] 216 p. 21 cm. [BR516.M45] 48-7613
1. U.S.—Religion. I. Title.

MISSION:
U. S. A. New York, Friendship Press [1956] x, 181p. fold. map. 20cm. Bibliography: p. 179-181.
1. U. S.—Religion. I. Hoffmann, James W

MISSION: U. S. A.
[New York, Friendship Press [1956] x, 181p. fold. map. 20cm. Bibliography: p. 179-181.
1. U. S.—Religion. I. Hoffmann, James W

MONTGOMERY, John 200'.973
Warwick.
The shaping of America : a true description of the American character, both good and bad, and the possibilities of recovering a national vision before the people perish / John Warwick Montgomery. Minneapolis : Bethany Fellowship, c1976. 255 p. : ill. ; 23 cm. Bibliography: p. [241]-255. [BR515.M57] 76-15682 ISBN 0-87123-227-8 : 5.95
1. United States—Religion. 2. United States—Moral conditions. I. Title.

MORRIS, Benjamin Franklin, 284
1810-1867.
Christian life and character of the civil institutions of the United States, developed in the official and historical annals of the republic. By B. F. Morris ... Philadelphia, G. W. Childs; Cincinnati, Rickey & Carroll, 1864. 831 p. 23 cm. "Principal authorities consulted": p. [8] [BR515.M6] 35-31537
1. U.S.—Religion. 2. U.S.—Pol. & govt. I. Title.

MOSELEY, James G. 200'.973
A cultural history of religion in America / James G. Moseley. Westport, Conn. : Greenwood Press, 1981. p. cm. Includes index. Bibliography: p. [BL2530.U6M67] 19 80-23609 ISBN 0-313-22479-X lib. bdg. : 25.00
1. United States—Religion. 2. Religion and culture. I. Title.

NICHOLS, Roy Franklin, 261.70973
1896-
Religion and American democracy. Baton Rouge, Louisiana State University Press, 1959. 108p. 21cm. (Rockwell lectures) Includes bibliography. [BR516.N5] 59-9085
1. U. S.—Religion. 2. Church and state in the U. S. I. Title.

O'KEEFE, Ruth Evans. 973
The influence of religion in American history / Ruth Evans O'Keefe. Philadelphia : Dorrance, c1975. 48 p. ; 22 cm. Bibliography: p. 45-48. [BR515.O37] 75-328527 ISBN 0-8059-2178-8 : 3.95
1. United States—Religion. I. Title.

OLMSTEAD, Clifton E. 209.73
History of religion in the United States. Englewood Cliffs, N. J., Prentice-Hall, 1960. 628 p. 24 cm. [BR515.O4] 60-10355
1. U.S.—Religion. 2. U.S.—Church history.

OLMSTEAD, Clifton E. 209.73
Religion in America, past and present. Englewood Cliffs, N. J., Prentice-Hall [1961] 172 p. 21 cm. (A Spectrum book, S-20) Includes bibliography. [BR515.O43] 61-16978
1. U.S.—Religion. 2. U.S.—Church history. I. Title.

OSBORN, Ronald E 277.3
The spirit of America Christianity. [1st ed.] New York, Harper [1958] 241p. 22cm. Includes bibliography. [BR516.O74] 57-9881
1. U. S.—Religion. 2. Religious thought—U. S. I. Title.

OTIS, George. 248'.4
The solution to crisis-America. Rev. and enl. ed. With a foreword by Pat Boone. Old Tappan, N.J., F. H. Revell Co. [1972] 120 p. illus. 18 cm. (Spire books) The original edition of The solution crisis-America published about 1970 was written by Pat Boone, George Otis, and Harald Bredesen. [BR526.O85 1972] 72-182932 ISBN 0-8007-8081-7 0.95
1. United States—Religion. 2. United States—Moral conditions. 3. United States—Civilization. I. Boone, Charles Eugene. The solution to crisis-America. II. Title.

PARRISH, Herbert. 261
A new God for America, by Herbert Parrish. New York, London, The Century co. [c1928] 2 p. l., vii-xxvii, 268 p. 20 cm. [BR525.P3] 28-5882
1. U. S.—Religion. I. Title.

PFEFFER, Leo, 1910- 291.1'77'0973
Creeds in competition : a creative force in American culture / by Leo Pfeffer. Westport, Conn. : Greenwood Press, 1978. x, 176 p. ; 23 cm. Reprint of the ed. published by Harper, New York. Includes index. [BL2530.U6P44 1978] 78-2308 ISBN 0-313-20349-0 lib.bdg. : 15.25
1. United States—Religion. 2. Religion and state—United States. I. Title.

RAAB, Earl, ed. 209.73
Religious conflict in America; studies of the problems beyond bigotry. Garden City, N.Y., Doubleday [c.]1964. viii, 231p. 18cm. (Anchor bk., A392) Bibl. 64-11733 1.25 pap.,
1. U.S.—Religion. I. Title.

RAAB, Earl, ed. 209.73
Religious conflict in America; studies of the problems beyond bigotry. [1st ed.] Garden City, N. Y., Anchor Books, 1964. viii, 231 p. 18 cm. "A392." Bibliographical footnotes. [BR516.5.R3] 64-11733
1. U. S.—Religion. I. Title.

RELIGION and American society,
a statement of principles [by] William Clancy [and others] With an introduction by Henry P. Van Dusen. Santa Barbara, Calif. [1961] 79p. 22cm. (Its A Contribution to the discussion of the free society)
1. U. S.— Religion. 2. Religion and sociology. I. Center for the Study of Democratic Institutions. II. Clancy, William.

RELIGIOUS perspectives in American culture [by Will Herberg and others] Princeton, Princeton University Press, 1961. 427p. illus. 23cm. (Religion in American life, 2) Princeton studies in American civilization, 5.
1. U. S.—Religion. 2. Church and state in U. S. I. Herberg, Will.

RICHEY, Russell E. 200'.973
American civil religion. Edited by Russell E. Richey and Donald G. Jones. [1st ed.] New York, Harper & Row [1974] viii, 278 p. 21 cm. (A Harper forum book) Bibliography: p. 273-278. [BR515.R5 1974] 73-18702 ISBN 0-06-066856-3 3.95
1. United States—Religion. I. Jones, Donald G., joint author. II. Title.

ROBERTSON, Archibald 277.3
Thomas.
That old-time religion. Boston, Houghton Mifflin, 1950. 282 p. 22 cm. [BR516.R6] 50-5680
1. U.S.—Religion. I. Title.

ROBERTSON, Archibald 277.3
Thomas.
That old-time religion / by Archie Robertson. Westport, Conn. : Greenwood Press, 1980, c1950. 282 p. ; 23 cm. Reprint of the ed. published by Houghton Mifflin, Boston. [BR515.R55 1979] 78-24159 ISBN 0-313-20823-9 lib. bdg. : 20.50
1. United States—Religion. I. Title.

ROSS, Murray G 230
Religious beliefs of youth; a study and analysis of the structure and function of the religious beliefs of young adults, based on a questionnaire sample of 1,935 youth and intensive interviews with 100 young people. Foreword by Gordon W. Allport. New York, Association Press, 1950. xviii, 251 p. 24 cm. ([Young Men's Christian Associations] National Council. Studies) Bibliography: p. 246-248. [BR516.R66] 50-7756
1. U.S. — Religion. 2. Youth — Religious life. I. Title.

ROWE, Henry Kalloch, 1869- 200
1941.
The history of religion in the United States, by Henry Kalloch Rowe ... New York, The Macmillan company, 1924. iii p., 2 l., 213 p. 20 cm. [BR515.R6] 24-23151
1. U.S.—Religion. I. Title.

ROWLAND, Stanley J 277.3
Land in search of God. New York, Random House [1958] 242p. illus. 21cm. [BR517.R6] 58-9883
1. U. S.— Religion. I. Title.

ROY, Ralph Lord. 277.3
Apostles of discord, a study of organized bigotry and disruption on the fringes of Protestantism. Boston, Beacon Press [1953] 437p. 22cm. (Beacon studies in church and state) 'Originally ... [the author's] thesis.' [BR516.R68] 53-6616
1. U. S.—Religion. 2. Protestant churches—U. S. I. Title.

ROY, Ralph Lord. 261.70973
Communism and the churches. [1st ed.]

New York, Harcourt, Brace [1960] 495p. 22cm. (Communism in American life) Includes bibliography. [BR517.R64] 60-10941
1. U. S.—Religion. 2. Communism—U. S. I. Title.

SALISBURY, William Seward. 209.73
Religion in American culture, a sociologicalinterpretation, by W. Seward Salisbury. Homewood, Ill., Dorsey Press, 1964. ix, 538 p. maps. 24 cm. (The Dorsey series in anthropology and sociology) Bibliography: p. 491-515. [BR515.S23] 64-22110
1. U.S.—Religion. I. Title.

SCHAFF, Philip, 1819-1893 277.3
America, a sketch of its political, social, and religious character. [Tr. from German] Ed. by Perry Miller. Cambridge, Belknap Press of Harvard University Press [c.]1961. 241p. (John Harvard Library) 61-8871 4.25
1. U. S.—Religion 2. U. S.—Church history. 3. U. S.—Civilization. I. Title.

SCHAFF, Philip, 1819-1893. 284
America. A sketch of the political, social, and religious character of the United States of North America, in two lectures, delivered at Berlin, with a report read before the German church diet at Frankfort-on-the- Maine, Sept., 1854. By Dr. Philip Schaff. Tr. from the German. New York, C. Scribner, 1855. xxiv, [25]-291 p. 18 1/2 cm. Contents.--pt. I. Importance, political system, national character, culture, literature, and religion of the United States.--pt. II. The churches and sects.--pt. III. Germany and America. [BR515.S3] [E166.S29] 917. 19-15051
1. U.S.—Religion. 2. U.S.—Church history. 3. U.S.—Civilization. I. Title.

SCHNEIDER, Herbert Wallace, 1892- 277.2
Religion in 20th century America. Rev. ed. New York, Atheneum, 1964 [c.1963, 1952] 285p. 19cm. (52) Bibl. 1.75 pap.,
1. U. S.—Religion. 2. U. S.—Church history—20th cent. I. Title.

SCHNEIDER, Herbert Wallace, 1892- 277.3
Religion in 20th century America. Cambridge, Harvard University Press, 1952. x, 244 p. illus. 22 cm. (The Library of Congress series in American civilization) Bibliographical references included in "Notes" (p. [200]-221) [BR525.S34] 52-8219
1. U.S. — Religion. 2. U.S. — Church history — 20th cent. I. Title. II. Series.

SCHROEDER, W. Widick 209.77
Religion in American culture; unity and diversity in a midwestern county [by] W. Widick Schroeder, Victor Obenhaus [New York] Free Pr. [c.1964] xxiii, 254p. illus. 2icm. Bibl. 64-16966 8.50
1. U.S.—Religion. 2. Religion and sociology—Case studies. 3. Middle West—Religion. I. Obenhaus, Victor, joint author. II. Title.

SCHROEDER, W Widick. 209.77
Religion in American culture; unity and diversity in a midwestern county [by] W. Widick Schroeder and Victor Obenhaus. [New York] Free Press of Glencoe [1964] xxiii, 254 p. illus. 22 cm. Bibliographical footnotes. [BR526.S3] 64-16966
1. U. S.—Religion. 2. Religion and sociology—Case studies. 3. Middle West—Religion. I. Obenhaus, Victor, joint author. II. Title.

SHEEN, Fulton John, 1895- 240
For God and country, by Rt. Rev. Fulton J. Sheen ... New York, P. J. Kenedy & sons [c1941] 5 p. l., 107 p. 16 1/2 cm. [BR525.S5] 41-9164
1. U.S.—Religion. I. Title.

SILCOX, Clarice Edwin, 1888- 277.3
Catholics, Jews and Protestants; a study of relationships in the United States and Canada, by Claris Edwin Silcox and Galen M. Fisher. New York and London, Pub. for the Institute of social and religious research by Harper and brothers [c1934] xvi, 369 p. 23 1/2 cm. "The study ... was undertaken by the Institute of social and religious research at the request of the National conference of Jews and Christians."--Pref. "First edition." [BL2520.S5] [261] 35-1151
1. U.S.—Religion. 2. Sociology, Christian. 3. Catholics in the U.S. 4. Jews in the U.S. 5. Protestants in the U.S. 6. Catholics in Canada. 7. Jews in Canada. 8. Protestants in Canada. I. Fisher, Galen Merriam, 1873- joint author. II. Institute of social and religious research. III. National conference of Jews and Christians. IV. Title.

SINGER, Charles Gregg, 1910-
A theological interpretation of American history, by C. Gregg Singer. Nutley, N.J., Craig Press, 1964. 305 p. 22 cm. Bibliographical footnotes. 65-51108
1. U.S. — Religion. 2. U.S. — Hist. — Philosophy. I. Title.

SMITH, James Ward, 1917- ed. 277.3
Religion in American life. Editors: James Ward Smith and A. Leland Jamison. Princeton, N.J., Princeton University Press, 1961- v. in illus., plans. 22 cm. (Princeton studies in American civilization, no. 5) Vol. 4 by Nelson R. Burr in collaboration with the editors. Contents.-- 1. The shaping of American religion. -- 2. Religious perspectives in American culture. -- 4. A critical bibliography of religion in America. 2 v. [BR515.S6] 61-5383
1. U.S. — Religion. 2. U.S. — Civilization. I. Jamison, Albert Leland, 1911- joint ed. II. Burr, Nelson Rollin, 1904- III. Title. IV. Series.

SMOOT, Dan. 277.3
The hope of the world. [1st ed. Dallas, Miller Pub. Co., 1958] 57 p. illus. 23 cm. [BR517.S47] 59-19517
1. U.S. — Religion. I. Title.

SNOOK, John B. 200'.973
Going further; life-and-death religion in America [by] John B. Snook. Englewood Cliffs, N.J., Prentice-Hall [1973] viii, 184 p. 21 cm. (A Spectrum book) Includes bibliographical references. [BR515.S63] 73-14532 ISBN 0-13-357814-3 6.95
1. United States—Religion. 2. Sects—United States. I. Title.
Pbk. 2.45; ISBN 0-13-357806-2.

SNYDER, Gerald S. 200'.973
The religious reawakening in America [by Gerald S. Snyder] Washington, Books by U.S. News & World Report [1972] 191 p. illus. 23 cm. [BR145.2.S66] 72-88685 2.95
1. United States—Religion. I. Title.

SOCIOLOGICAL Resources for the Social Studies (Project) 200'.973
Religion in the United States. Boston, Allyn and Bacon [1971] v, 38 p. illus. 23 cm. (Episodes in social inquiry series) Bibliography: p. 38. [BR515.S64] 77-153562 6.36
1. United States—Religion. 2. Sociology, Christian—United States. I. Title.

SONTAG, Frederick. 200'.973
God and America's future / Frederick Sontag & John K. Roth. Wilmington, N.C. : McGrath Pub. Co., c1977. xi, 224 p. ; 22 cm. "A Consortium Book". Includes bibliographical references. [BL2530.U6S66] 77-21306 ISBN 0-8434-0641-0 : 11.00. ISBN 0-8434-0642-9 pbk. : 5.95
1. United States—Religion. 2. United States—Civilization—1970- I. Roth, John K., joint author. II. Title.

SPERRY, Willard Learoyd, 1882- ed. 208.2
Religion in the post-war world, edited by Willard L. Sperry ... [Cambridge, Harvard university press, 1945] 4 v. 19 cm. Half-title. [BR525.S7] 45-6967
1. U.S.—Religion. I. Title.

STEWART, John T. 280.40973
The deacon wore spats; profiles from America's changing religious scene [by] John T. Stewart. [1st ed.] New York, Holt, Rinehart and Winston [1965] xii, 191 p. 22 cm. [BR515.S75] 65-15059
1. U.S.—Religion. 2. Clergy—Correspondence, reminiscences, etc. 3. Preaching—U.S. I. Title.

STROUT, Cushing. 200'.973
The new heavens and new earth; political religion in America. [1st ed.] New York, Harper & Row [1973, c1974] xv, 400 p. 24 cm. Includes bibliographical references. [BR515.S77 1973] 73-4128 ISBN 0-06-014171-9 12.50
1. United States—Religion. I. Title.

SWEET, William Warren, 1881- 277.3
The American Churches, an interpretation. New York, Abingdon-Cokesbury Press [1948] 153 p. 20 cm. Bibliographical footnotes. [BR515.S78 1948] 48-7227
1. U. S.—Religion. 2. U. S.—Church history. I. Title.

SWEET, William Warren, 1881- 277.3
American culture and religion; six essays. Dallas, Southern Methodist University Press, 1951. 114 p. 21 cm. (The Southwestern University lectures for 1947) Contents.Contents. -- Cultural pluralism in the American tradition. -- Protestantism and democracy. -- Natural religion and religious liberty. -- Methodist unification. -- The church, the sect, and the cult in America. -- Ecumenicity begins at home. [BR516.S95] 51-2143
1. U.S. — Religion. 2. U.S. — Civilization. I. Title. II. Series: Georgetown, Tex. Southwestern University. Southwestern University lectures. 1947

SWEET, William Warren, 1881-1959. 277.3
American culture and religion; six essays. New York, Cooper Square Publishers, 1972. 114 p. 23 cm. Reprint of the 1951 ed., which was issued as the Southwestern University lectures for 1947. Contents.Contents.—Cultural pluralism in the American tradition.—Protestantism and democracy.—Natural religion and religious liberty.—Methodist unification.—The church, the sect, and the cult in America.—Ecumenicity begins at home. Includes bibliographical references. [BR517.S95 1972] 72-78372 ISBN 0-8154-0421-2
1. United States—Religion. 2. United States—Civilization. I. Title. II. Series: Georgetown, Tex. Southwestern University. Southwestern University lectures, 1947.

THOMAS, John Lawrence. 277.3
Religion and the American people. Westminster, Md., Newman Press, 1963. 307 p. illus. 23 cm. [BR526.T5] 63-12247
1. U.S.—Religion. I. Title.

TONKS, A. Ronald. 209'.73
Faith, stars, and stripes : the impact of Christianity on the life history of America / A. Ronald Tonks and Charles W. Deweese. Nashville : Broadman Press, c1976. 124 p. ; 21 cm. Includes bibliographical references. [BR515.T66] 75-36888 ISBN 0-8054-6522-7 : 3.95
1. United States—Religion. I. Deweese, Charles W., joint author. II. Title.

VAN VLECK, Joseph, 1901- 261
Our changing churches; a study of church leadership, by Joseph Van Vleck, jr. New York, Association press, 1937. xiii, 250 p. diagrs. 22 cm. Issued also as thesis (PH.D.) Columbia university. "Acknowledgements": p. [vii] [BR525.V35 1937a] 37-28696
1. U.S.—Religion. 2. Protestant churches—U.S. 3. Clergy—U.S. I. Title.

WALDROP, W. Earl. 277.3
What makes America great? St. Louis, Bethany Press [1957] 96p. 21cm. [BR516.W3] 57-8365
1. U.S.—Religion. I. Title.

WARNER, William Lloyd, 1898- 208.1
The family of God; a symbolic study of Christian life in America. New Haven, Conn., Yale Univ. Pr. 1961 [c.1959, 1961] 451p. illus. 'Consists of sections of [the author's] The living and the dead . . . revised and supplementedr' (Yale paperbound Y-45) Bibl. 61-11400 1.75 pap.,
1. U. S.—Religion. 2. U. S.—Soc. life & cust. 3. Symbolism. I. Title.

WEAVER, Rufus Washington, 1870- 277.3
The Christian faith at the nation's capital; a series of sermons, by Rufus Washington Weaver. Philadelphia Boston [etc.] The Judson press [c1936] 6 p. l., 3-205 p. 20 cm. (Half-title: The Judson press sermons) [BR516.W4] 36-15033
1. U.S.—Religion. 2. Sociology, Christian. 3. Baptists—Sermons. 4. Sermons, American. I. Title.

WEIGLE, Luther Allan, 1880- 284
... American idealism, by Luther A. Weigle. New Haven, Yale university press; [etc., etc.] 1928. 3 p. l., 356 p. col. front., illus. (incl. ports., maps, facsim.) 26 cm. (The pageant of America. [vol. X]) "Liberty bell edition." "The Liberty bell edition of 'The pageant of America', the first to be printed, is limited to 1,500 impressions on paper expressly made for the work." Contents.Foreword: Religion in American life.--Spanish and French missionaries.--Pilgrims and Puritans.--The Church of England in the colonies.--The growth of religious freedom.--The churches and the revolution.--The development of free churches.--The maturity of the churches.--Religion on the frontier.--Elementary and secondary schools.--Colleges and universities. [E178.5.P2 vol.X] [BR515.W4] 973. 28-25825
1. U.S.—Religion. 2. U.S.—Church history. 3. Education—U.S.—Hist. 4. Universities and colleges—U.S. I. Title.

WEISENBURGER, Francis Phelps, 1900- 277.3
Triumph of faith; contributions of the church to American life, 1865-1900. [Richmond?] 1962. 221 p. 24 cm. Includes bibliography. [BR525.W38] 62-2042
1. U.S. — Religion. 2. U.S. — Civilization. I. Title.

WEISS, Benjamin. 209.73
God in American history; a documentation of America's religious heritage. Foreword by Walter H. Judd. Grand Rapids, Zondervan Pub. House [1966] 256 p. illus., ports. 23 cm. Bibliography: p. 251-253. [BR515.W42] 66-13692
1. U.S. — Religion. I. Title.

WILLIAMS, John Paul, 1900- 280
What Americans believe and how they worship. [1st ed.] New York, Harper [1952] 400 p. 22 cm. [BR516.W47] 52-5477
1. U.S.—Religion. 2. Sects.—U.S. I. Title.

WILLIAMS, John Paul, 1900- 280
What Americans believe and how they worship. Rev. ed. New York, Harper & Row [1962] 530 p. 22 cm. [BR516.5.W5 1962] 62-7308
1. U.S.—Religion. 2. Sects—U.S. I. Title.

WILLIAMS, Peter W. 200'.973
Popular religion in America : symbolic change and the modernization process in historical perspective / Peter W. Williams. Englewood Cliffs, N.J. : Prentice-Hall, c1980. xiv, 244 p. ; 23 cm. (Prentice-Hall studies in religion series) Includes bibliographical references and index. [BL2530.U6W54] 79-22986 pbk. : 7.95
1. United States—Religion. I. Title.

United States—Religion—1901-1945.

HANDY, Robert T. 209'.73
The American religious depression, 1925-1935; by Robert T. Handy. Philadelphia, Fortress Press [1968] vii, 27 p. 19 cm. (Facet books. Historical series, 9) Reprint from Church history, v. 29, 1960. Bibliography: p. 23. [BR515.H35] 68-31338 0.85
1. United States—Religion—1901-1945. 2. Protestant churches—United States. 3. Protestantism—20th century. I. Title.

KINCHELOE, Samuel Clarence, 1890- 200'.973
Research memorandum on religion in the depression, by Samuel C. Kincheloe. [New York] Arno Press [1972] ix, 158 p. illus. 23 cm. On spine: Religion in the depression. Reprint of the 1937 ed., which was issued as Bulletin 33 of the Social Science Research Council and also as no. 7 of the series: Studies in the social aspects of the depression. [BR525.K5 1972] 71-162843 ISBN 0-405-00846-5
1. United States—Religion—1901-1945. 2. United States—Economic conditions—1918-1945. I. Title. II. Title: Religion in the depression. III. Series: Social Science Research Council. Bulletin 33. IV. Series: Studies in the social aspects of the depression, no. 7.

KINCHELOE, Samuel Clarence, 1890- 200'.973
Research memorandum on religion in the depression, by Samuel C. Kincheloe. Westport, Conn., Greenwood Press [1970] ix, 158 p. illus., maps. 23 cm. Reprint of the 1937 ed. Includes bibliographical references. [BR525.K5 1970] 76-109761 ISBN 0-8371-4251-2
1. United States—Religion—1901-1945. 2. United States—Economic conditions—1918-1945. I. Title.

United States—Religion—1945-

DONICHT, Mark. 291.9
Chrysalis, "a journey into the new spiritual America" / Mark Donicht. Berkeley, Calif. : Pan Pub., [1978] p. cm. [BL2530.U6D66] 77-28335 ISBN 0-89496-011-3 pbk. : 3.95
1. Donicht, Mark. 2. United States—Religion—1945- 3. Spiritual life. 4. Religion—Biography. I. Title.

ELLWOOD, Robert S., 1933- 200'.973
Alternative altars : unconventional and Eastern spirituality in America / Robert S. Ellwood, Jr. Chicago : University of Chicago Press, 1979. xiii, 192 p. ; 21 cm. (Chicago history of American religion) Includes bibliographical references and index. [BL2530.U6E44] 78-15089 ISBN 0-226-20618-1 lib. bdg. : 12.95
1. United States—Religion—1945- 2. Cults—United States. I. Title.

HART, Roderick P. 209'.73
The political pulpit / by Roderick P. Hart. West Lafayette, Ind. : Purdue University Press, 1977. ix, 141 p. ; 23 cm. Includes index. Bibliography: p. 127-133. [BR517.H37] 76-12290 ISBN 0-911198-44-X : 8.95 ISBN 0-911198-45-8 pbk. : 3.50
1. United States—Religion—1945- 2. Church and state in the United States. I. Title.

HERBERG, Will. 277.3
Protestant, Catholic, Jew; an essay in American religious sociology. New ed., completely rev. Garden City, N.Y., Anchor Books, 1960. 309 p. 18 cm. (A Doubleday Anchor book, A195) Includes bibliography. [BR526.H4 1960] 60-5931
1. United States—Religion—1945- 2. United States—Civilization—1945- I. Title.

LINDSEY, Jonathan A., 1937- 200'.973
Change and challenge / Jonathan A. Lindsey. [Wilmington, N.C.] : Consortium Books, [1977] p. cm. (Faith of our fathers ; 8) [BL2530.U6L56] 77-9551 ISBN 0-8434-0627-5 : 9.50
1. United States—Religion—1945- I. Title. II. Series.

LITTELL, Franklin Hamlin. 277.3
The church and the body politic [by] Franklin H. Littell. New York, Seabury Press [1969] vii, 175 p. 22 cm. Bibliographical references included in "Notes" (p. 165-170) [BR526.L5] 68-29988 5.95
1. United States—Religion—1945- I. Title.

MCLOUGHLIN, William Gerald. 209.73
Religion in America, edited by William G. McLoughlin and Robert N. Bellah. Boston, Houghton Mifflin, 1968. xxiv, 433 p. illus. 24 cm. (The Daedalus library [v. 12]) Papers, by contributors chosen by the editors, based on preparatory conferences held at the American Academy of Arts and Sciences, Boston. Includes bibliographical references. [BR526.M32] 68-17174 6.50
1. United States—Religion—1945- I. Bellah, Robert Neeley, 1927- joint author. II. American Academy of Arts and Sciences, Boston. III. Title. IV. Series.

MARTY, Martin E., 1928- 200'.973
A nation of behavers / Martin E. Marty. Chicago : University of Chicago Press, c1976. xi, 239 p. ; 21 cm. Includes bibliographical references and index. [BR515.M32] 76-7997 ISBN 0-226-50891-9 : 8.95
1. United States—Religion—1945- 2. Sociology, Christian—United States. I. Title.

MARTY, Martin E., 1928- 209.73
The new shape of American religion. New York, Harper [1959] 180 p. 22 cm. Includes bibliography. [BR526.M35] 59-10336
1. United States—Religion—1945- I. Title.

MARTY, Martin E., 1928- 209'.73
What do we believe? The stance of religion in America, by Martin E. Marty, Stuart E. Rosenberg, and Andrew M. Greeley. [1st ed.] New York, Meredith Press [1968] vi, 346 p. 24 cm. Includes bibliographical references. [BR526.M355] 68-26326 6.95
1. United States—Religion—1945- 2. Public opinion—United States. I. Rosenberg, Stuart E., joint author. II. Greeley, Andrew M., 1928- joint author. III. Title.

NEUHAUS, Richard John. 200'.973
Time toward home : the American experiment as revelation / Richard John Neuhaus. New York : Seabury Press, [1975] viii, 231 p. ; 24 cm. "A Crossroad book." Includes bibliographical references and index. [BR526.N42] 75-5714 ISBN 0-8164-0272-8 : 9.50
1. United States—Religion—1945- 2. United States—Civilization—1945- I. Title.

THE Sixties: radical change in American religion. 200'.973 Special editor of this volume: James M. Gustafson. Philadelphia [American Academy of Political and Social Science] 1970. x, 250 p. 24 cm. (The Annals of the American Academy of Political and Social Science, v. 387) Includes bibliographical references. [H1.A4 vol. 387] 74-112786 3.00 (pbk.)
1. U.S.—Religion—1945- I. Gustafson, James M., ed. II. Series: American Academy of Political and Social Science, Philadelphia. Annals, v. 387

SMART, James D. 209'.73
The cultural subversion of the Biblical faith : life in the 20th century under the sign of the cross / by James D. Smart. 1st ed. Philadelphia : Westminster Press, c1977. p. cm. [BL2530.U6S63] 77-22063 ISBN 0-664-24148-4 pbk. : 4.95
1. United States—Religion—1945- 2. Christianity—United States. 3. United States—Civilization—1945- I. Title.

STARK, Rodney. 277.3
Patterns of religious commitment [by Rodney Stark and Charles Y. Glock. Berkeley, University of California Press, 1968- v. illus. 24 cm. Each vol. has also special t.p. "A publication from the Research Program in Religion and Society of the Survey Research Center, University of California, Berkeley." Contents.Contents.—v. 1. American piety: the nature of religious commitment. Bibliographical footnotes. [BR517.S73] 68-12792
1. United States—Religion—1945- I. Glock, Charles Y., joint author. II. California. University. Survey Research Center. III. Title. IV. Title: American piety: the nature of religious commitment.

STREIKER, Lowell D. 269'.2'0924 B
Religion and the new majority: Billy Graham, Middle America, and the politics of the 70s [by] Lowell D. Streiker and Gerald S. Strober. New York, Association Press [1972] 202 p. 22 cm. Includes bibliographical references. [BR515.S76] 79-189009 ISBN 0-8096-1844-3 5.95
1. Graham, William Franklin, 1918- 2. United States—Religion—1945- 3. Fundamentalism. 4. United States—Politics and government—1969-1974. I. Strober, Gerald S., joint author. II. Title.

WARNER, William Lloyd, 1898-1970. 209'.73
The family of God : a symbolic study of Christian life in America / by W. Lloyd Warner. Westport, Conn. : Greenwood Press, 1975, c1961. x, 451 p. : diagrs. ; 22 cm. Reprint of the ed. published by Yale University Press, New Haven, which was issued as A Yale paperbound, Y-45. Revised selections from the author's The living and the dead. Includes index. Bibliography: p. 431-442. [BR526.W3 1975] 75-11494 ISBN 0-8371-8206-9 lib.bdg. : 20.00
1. United States—Religion—1945- 2. United States—Social life and customs—1945- 3. Symbolism. I. Title.

WILLIAMS, John Paul, 1900- 200'.973
What Americans believe and how they worship, by J. Paul Williams. 3d ed. New York, Harper & Row [1969] x, 530 p. 22 cm. Bibliographical references included in "Notes" (p. 493-520) [BR516.5.W5 1969] 79-4791 6.00
1. U.S.—Religion—1945- 2. Sects—U.S. I. Title.

WILLIAMS, John Paul, 1900- 280
What Americans believe and how they worship. [1st ed.] New York, Harper [1952] 400 p. 22 cm. [BR516.W47] 52-5477
1. United States—Religion—1945- 2. Sects—United States. I. Title.

United States—Religion—1945-— Addresses, essays, lectures.

IN gods we trust : 301.5'8
new patterns of religious pluralism / edited by Thomas Robbins and Dick Anthony. New Brunswick, N.J. : Transaction Books, [1980] p. cm. Consists chiefly of articles from Society magazine, v. 15, May-June 1978. Includes bibliographies and index. [BL2530.U6I48] 79-66441 ISBN 0-87855-746-6 pbk. : 4.95
1. United States—Religion—1945- —Addresses, essays, lectures. 2. Cults—United States—Addresses, essays, lectures. I. Robbins, Thomas, 1943- II. Anthony, Dick, 1939- III. Society.
Contents Deleted

RELIGIONS in America / 200'.973
edited by Herbert L. Marx, Jr. New York : H. W. Wilson Co., 1977. 208 p. ; 19 cm. (The Reference shelf ; v. 49, no.6) Bibliography: p. 201-208. [BL2530.U6R43] 77-16142 ISBN 0-8242-0608-8 : 5.75
1. United States—Religion—1945-—Addresses, essays, lectures. I. Marx, Herbert L. II. Title. III. Series.

UNDERSTANDING the new religions 200'.973 / edited by Jacob Needleman and George Baker. New York : Seabury Press, 1978. p. cm. "A Crossroad book." [BL2530.U6U5] 78-14997 ISBN 0-8164-0403-8 : 14.50. ISBN 0-8164-2188-9 pbk. : 6.95
1. United States—Religion—1945- —Addresses, essays, lectures. 2. Cults—United States—Addresses, essays, lectures. I. Needleman, Jacob. II. Baker, George, 1941-

WUTHNOW, Robert. 200'.973
Experimentation in American religion : the new mysticisms and their implications for the churches / Robert Wuthnow. Berkeley : University of California Press, c1978. x, 221 p. : ill. ; 25 cm. Includes bibliographical references and index. [BL2530.U6W87] 77-71068 ISBN 0-520-03446-5 : 12.95
1. United States—Religion—1945- —Addresses, essays, lectures. 2. Cults—United States—Addresses, essays, lectures. 3. Christianity and other religions—Addresses, essays, lectures. I. Title.

United States—Religion—1945- — Case studies.

MCCREADY, William C., 1941- 200'.973
The ultimate values of the American population / William C. McCready, Andrew M. Greeley. Beverly Hills : Sage Publications, c1976. p. cm. (Sage library of social research ; v. 23) Includes bibliographical references and index. [BR526.M28] 75-40337 ISBN 0-8039-0502-5 : 12.00. ISBN 0-8039-0503-3 pbk. : 7.00
1. United States—Religion—1945- —Case studies. 2. Religion and sociology—Case studies. 3. Worth—Case studies. I. Greeley, Andrew M., 1928- joint author. II. Title.

United States—Religion—1946-

BETSWORTH, Roger G., 1933- 277.3'0826
The radical movement of the 1960's / by Roger G. Betsworth. Metuchen, N.J. : Scarecrow Press ; [Philadelphia] : American Theological Library Association, 1980. vii, 363 p. ; 23 cm. (ATLA monograph series ; no. 14) Includes index. Bibliography: p. 335-357. [BL2530.U6B46] 80-12534 ISBN 0-8108-1307-6 : 17.50
1. United States—Religion—1960- 2. Nationalism and religion—United States. I. Title. II. Series: American Theological Library Association. ATLA monograph series ; no. 14.

BROMLEY, David G. 291'.0973
Strange gods : the great American cult scare / David G. Bromley and Anson D. Shupe, Jr. Boston : Beacon Press, c1981. p. cm. Includes index. Bibliography: p. [BL2530.U6B76 1981] 19 81-65763 ISBN 0-8070-3256-5 : 12.95
1. United States—Religion—1960- 2. Christian sects—United States. 3. Cults—United States. I. Shupe, Anson D. II. Title.

CHALFANT, Paul H., 1929- 261.8'0973
Religion in contemporary society / Paul H. Chalfant, Robert E. Beckley, Eddie C. Palmer. Sherman Oaks, Calif. : Alfred Pub. Co., 1981. p. cm. Includes bibliographical references. [BL2530.U6C47] 19 80-27999 ISBN 0-88284-126-2 : 14.95
1. United States—Religion—1960- 2. Religion and sociology. I. Beckley, Robert E., joint author. II. Palmer, Eddie C., joint author. III. Title.

THE Future of the American church. 209'.73 Philip J. Hefner, editor. Contributors: Sidney E. Mead [and others] Philadelphia, Fortress Press [1968] vi, 90 p. 19 cm. The 1966 Zimmerman lectures given to commemorate the 140th anniversary of the Lutheran Theological Seminary at Gettysburg. Contents.Contents.—Preface, by P. J. Hefner.—Prospects for the church in America, by S. E. Mead.—Two requisites for the American church: moral discourse and institutional power, by J. M. Gustafson.—Freedom and the churches, by J. Haroutunian.—Schmucker and Walther: a study of Christian response to American culture, by L. D. Jordahl. Bibliographical footnotes. [BR526.F6] 68-12328
1. United States—Religion—1946- I. Hefner, Philip J., ed. II. Mead, Sidney Earl, 1904- III. Gettysburg. Theological Seminary of the United Lutheran Church in America.

GALLUP, George, 1930- 209'.73
The search for America's faith / George Gallup, Jr., David Poling. Nashville : Abingdon, c1980. 153 p. ; 22 cm. [BL2530.U6G34] 80-12619 ISBN 0-687-37090-6 : 8.95
1. United States—Religion—1960- I. Poling, David, 1928- joint author. II. Title.

HERZOG, Arthur. 277.3
The church trap. New York, Macmillan [1968] 185 p. 22 cm. [BR526.H47] 68-23064
1. United States—Religion—1946- I. Title.

United States Religion 19th century.

CARTER, Paul Allen, 1926- 209'.73
The spiritual crisis of the gilded age [by] Paul A. Carter. DeKalb, Northern Illinois University Press, 1971. xiii, 295 p. illus. 25 cm. Bibliography: p. 269-285. [BR525.C37] 72-156938 ISBN 0-87580-026-2 (hbd) ISBN 0-87580-507-8 (pbk) 8.50
1. United States—Religion—19th century. I. Title.

GRIBBIN, William, 1943- 973.5'21
THe churches militant; the War of 1812 and American religion. New Haven, Yale University Press, 1973. viii, 210 p. 23 cm. "Begun as a dissertation at the Catholic University of America." Bibliography: p. 177-197. [BR525.G7 1973] 72-91313 ISBN 0-300-01583-6 8.75
1. United States—Religion—19th century. 2. United States—History—War of 1812. I. Title.

MCLOUGHLIN, William Gerald. 200
The meaning of Henry Ward Beecher; an essay on the shifting values of mid-Victorian America, 1840-1870 [by] William G. McLoughlin. [1st ed.] New York, Knopf, 1970. xiii, 275 p. 22 cm. Includes bibliographical references. [BX7260.B3M33 1970] 77-111239 7.95
1. Beecher, Henry Ward, 1813-1887. 2.

U.S.—Religion—19th century. 3. U.S.—Civilization—19th century. I. Title.

THE Rise of Adventism; 286'.773
religion and society in mid-nineteenth-century America. Edwin S. Gaustad, editor. [1st ed.] New York, Harper & Row [1974] xx, 329 p. 24 cm. Lectures delivered during 1972-73 at the University Church, Loma Linda University, Loma Linda, Calif. Contents.Contents.—Hudson, W. S. A time of religious ferment.—Smith, T. L. Social reform.—Blake, J. B. Health reform.—Greene, J. C. Science and religion.—Hine, R. V. Communitarianism.—Moore, R. L. Spiritualism.—Sandeen, E. R. Millennialism.—McLoughlin, W. G. Revivalism.—Arthur, D. T. Millerism.—Butler, J. M. Adventism and the American experience.—Carner, V., Kubo, S., and Rice, C. Bibliographical essay (p. 207-317) [BR525.R57 1974] 74-4637 ISBN 0-06-063094-9
1. United States—Religion—19th century. 2. Adventists. I. Gaustad, Edwin Scott, ed.

United States—Religion—Addresses, essays, lectures.

THE American religious 209'.73
experiment : piety and practicality / edited by Clyde L. Manschreck and Barbara Brown Zikmund. Chicago : Exploration Press, c1976. xiii, 145 p. ; 24 cm. (Studies in ministry and parish life) Includes bibliographies. [BR515.A54] 76-7199 ISBN 0-913552-06-2 : 8.00 ISBN 0-913552-07-0 pbk. :
1. United States—Religion—Addresses, essays, lectures. I. Manschreck, Clyde Leonard, 1917- II. Zikmund, Barbara Brown. III. Series.

AMERICAN religious values 277.3
and the future of America : with contributions / by Sydney E. Ahlstrom ... [et al.] ; edited by Rodger Van Allen. Philadelphia : Fortress Press, c1978. xi, 211 p. : fold. map ; 23 cm. Map inserted. Includes bibliographical references and index. [BL2530.U6A46] 76-15894 ISBN 0-8006-0486-5 : 12.95
1. United States—Religion—Addresses, essays, lectures. I. Ahlstrom, Sydney E. II. Van Allen, Rodger.

BELLAH, Robert Neely, 1927-
Religion in America. [Articles by] Robert N. Bellah [and others Cambridge, Mass., American Academy of Arts and Sciences] 1967. 277 p. 23 cm. (Daedalus, Winter 1967) Cover title. Issued as v. 96, no. 1 of the Proceedings of the American Academy of Arts and Sciences. 68-9854
1. U. S.—Religion—Addresses, essays, lectures. I. American Academy of Arts and Sciences, Boston. II. Daedalus. III. Title.

CARROLL, Jackson W. 200'.973
Religion in America, 1950 to the present / Jackson W. Carroll, Douglas W. Johnson, Martin E. Marty ; afterword by George Gallup, Jr. 1st ed. San Francisco : Harper & Row, c1979. x, 123 p. : ill. ; 29 cm. Includes bibliographical references and index. [BL2530.U6C37 1979] 77-20451 ISBN 0-06-065433-3 : 15.00
1. United States—Religion—Addresses, essays, lectures. I. Johnson, Douglas W., 1934- joint author. II. Marty, Martin E., 1928- joint author. III. Title.

FORUM : 261.8'0973
religious faith speaks to American issues : a Bicentennial discussion stimulator / edited by William A. Norgren. New York : Friendship Press, [1975] 56 p. : ill. ; 28 cm. Bibliography: p. 55-56. [BR517.F58] 75-11874 ISBN 0-377-00044-2 pbk. : 2.95
1. United States—Religion—Addresses, essays, lectures. 2. United States—Civilization—Addresses, essays, lectures. I. Norgren, William A.
Contents omitted.

HENRY, Stuart Clark, ed. 277.3
A miscellany of American Christianity; essays in honor of H. Shelton Smith. Durham, N.C., Duke [c.]1963. viii, 390p. port. 24cm. Bibl. 63-14288 10.00
1. Smith, Hilrie Shelton, 1893- 2. U.S.—Religion—Addresses, essays, lectures. 3. Theology, Doctrinal—Hist.—U.S. I. Title.
Contents omitted.

MEAD, Sidney Earl, 1904- 200'.973
The nation with the soul of a church / Sidney E. Mead. 1st ed. New York : Harper & Row, [1975] x, 158 p. ; 21 cm. (A Harper forum book) Includes bibliographical references and indexes. [BR515.M45 1975] 75-9332 ISBN 0-06-065546-1 : 7.95 ISBN 0-06-065547-X pbk. : 3.95
1. United States—Religion—Addresses, essays, lectures. I. Title.

MICHAELSEN, Robert. 209'.73
The American search for soul / Robert S. Michaelsen. Baton Rouge : Louisiana State University Press, [1975] xii, 131 p. ; 23 cm. (Rockwell lectures) "Revised and augmented version of lectures delivered under the title The crisis in American faith and learning, at Rice University in February, 1973." Includes index. Bibliography: p. 119-128. [BR515.M5] 74-82005 ISBN 0-8071-0097-8 : 7.95
1. United States—Religion—Addresses, essays, lectures. 2. National characteristics, American—Addresses, essays, lectures. I. Title. II. Series.

MOONEY, Christopher 261.8'0973
F., 1925-
Religion and the American dream : the search for freedom under God / by Christopher F. Mooney. Philadelphia : Westminster Press, c1977. 144 p. ; 21 cm. First presented as the Bicentennial Lectures at St. Joseph's College, Philadelphia, 1975-1976. Includes bibliographical references. [BR516.M66] 76-54332 ISBN 0-664-241352 : 4.95
1. United States—Religion—Addresses, essays, lectures. 2. Church and state in the United States—Addresses, essays, lectures. 3. Justice—Addresses, essays, lectures. 4. Liberty—Addresses, essays, lectures. I. Title.

A Nation under God? / 209'.73
Edited by C. E. Gallivan. Waco, Tex. : Word Books, c1976. 136 p. ; 21 cm. (Discovery books) [BR515.N37] 75-38048 ISBN 0-87680-875-5 pbk. : 3.50
1. United States—Religion—Addresses, essays, lectures. I. Gallivan, C. E.

RELIGION in American 200'.973
history : interpretive essays / edited by John M. Mulder, John F. Wilson. Englewood Cliffs, N.J. : Prentice-Hall, [1978,i.e.1977] p. cm. Bibliography: p. [BR515.R435] 77-2883 ISBN 0-13-771998-1 : 11.95 ISBN 0-13-771980-9 pbk. : 7.95
1. United States—Religion—Addresses, essays, lectures. I. Mulder, John M., 1946- II. Wilson, John Frederick.

THE Religion of the 200'.973
Republic. Edited by Elwyn A. Smith. Philadelphia, Fortress Press [1971] viii, 296 p. 22 cm. Includes bibliographical references. [BR515.R44] 70-130326 8.95
1. U.S.—Religion—Addresses, essays, lectures. I. Smith, Elwyn Allen, 1919- ed.

SILL, Sterling W. 973
This nation under God / Sterling W. Sill. Salt Lake City : Bookcraft, c1976. viii, 248 p. : ill. ; 24 cm. Includes index. [BR515.S48] 76-8081 ISBN 0-88494-299-6 : 4.95
1. United States—Religion—Addresses, essays, lectures. 2. United States—Civilization—Addresses, essays, lectures. 3. Mormons and Mormonism—Addresses, essays, lectures. I. Title.

WHAT the religious 261.8'0973
revolutionaries are saying. Elwyn A. Smith, editor. Philadelphia, Fortress Press [1971] v, 154 p. 20 cm. Includes bibliographical references. [BR515.W48] 72-155949 ISBN 0-8006-0133-5 3.50
1. United States—Religion—Addresses, essays, lectures. I. Smith, Elwyn Allen, 1919- ed.

United States—Religion—Bibliography

BURR, Nelson Rollin, 016.2009'73
1904-
Religion in American life, compiled by Nelson R. Burr. New York, Appleton-Century-Crofts [1971] xix, 171 p. 24 cm. (Goldentree bibliographies in American history) [Z7757.U5B8] 70-136219 ISBN 0-390-15607-8(pbk.)
1. United States—Religion—Bibliography. I. Title.

A critical bibliography of religion in America, by Nelson R. Burr in collaboration with the editors: James Ward Smith and A. Leland Jamison. Princeton, Princeton University Press, 1961. 2 v. 23cm. (Religion in American life, v. 4 [pt. 1-2]) Princeton studies in American civilization, 5.
1. U. S.—Religion— Bibl. 2. U. S.—Church history—Bibl. I. Burr, Nelson Rollin, 1904-

GAUSTAD, Edwin Scott. 016.209'73
American religious history, by Edwin S. Gaustad. Washington, Service Center for Teachers of History [1967, c1966] 27 p. 23 cm. (Service Center for Teachers of History. Publication no. 65) Later ed. (c1973) published under title: Religion in America: history and historiography. Bibliography: p. 25-27. [Z7757.U5G3] 66-29229
1. United States—Religion—Bibliography. 2. United States—Religion. I. Title. II. Series.

United States—Religion—Collections.

GAUSTAD, Edwin Scott, 209'.73
comp.
Religious issues in American history. [1st ed.] New York, Harper & Row [1968] xxii, 294 p. 21 cm. (Harper forum books RD6) [BR515.G32] 68-17601 3.50
1. United States—Religion—Collections. I. Title.

MCNAMARA, Patrick H., 261'.0973
comp.
Religion American style. Edited by Patrick H. McNamara. New York, Harper & Row [1974] xiv, 408 p. 24 cm. Includes bibliographical references. [BR515.M2] 73-10686 ISBN 0-06-044377-4 4.95 (pbk.).
1. United States—Religion—Collected works. I. Title.

WRIGHT, Conrad, comp. 277.3
Religion in American life; selected readings. Boston, Houghton Mifflin [1972] x, 182 p. illus. 21 cm. (Houghton Mifflin history program) (Life in America series) Includes bibliographical references. [BR515.W75] 72-180481 ISBN 0-395-03145-1 pap. 2.60
1. United States—Religion—Collections. I. Title. II. Series.

United States—Religion—Congresses.

BICENTENNIAL Congress on 209'.73
Prophecy, Philadelphia, 1976.
America in history and Bible prophecy / edited by Thomas McCall. Chicago : Moody Press, c1976. 143 p. ; 22 cm. Includes bibliographical references. [BR515.B55 1976] 76-43049 ISBN 0-8024-0209-7 : 2.95
1. Bible—Prophecies—Congresses. 2. United States—Religion—Congresses. 3. Jews in the United States—Congresses. I. McCall, Thomas S. II. Title.

COLLEGE Theology 200'.973
Society.
America in theological perspective : proceedings of the College Theology Society / edited by Thomas M. McFadden. New York : Seabury Press, c1976. p. cm. "A Crossroad book." "All essays ... were, with two exceptions, delivered at the 1975 convention of the College Theology Society at Boston College." [BR515.C64 1976] 75-45201 ISBN 0-8164-0294-9 : 7.95
1. United States—Religion—Congresses. I. McFadden, Thomas M. II. Title.

IMMIGRANTS and religion 301.5'8
in urban America / edited by Randall M. Miller and Thomas D. Marzik. Philadelphia : Temple University Press, c1977. xxii, 170 p. ; 22 cm. Selected and rev. papers from a series of symposia sponsored by and held at Saint Joseph's College, Philadelphia, during the academic year 1975-1976. Includes bibliographical references. [BL2530.U6147] 76-62866 ISBN 0-87722-093-X : 10.00
1. United States—Religion—Congresses. 2. Cities and towns—United States—Religious life—Congresses. 3. United States—Foreign population—Congresses. 4. Minorities—United States—Congresses. I. Miller, Randall M. II. Marzik, Thomas D. III. St. Joseph's College, Philadelphia.

United States—Religion—Directories.

MELTON, J. Gordon. 200'.25'73
A directory of religious bodies in the United States / compiled from the files of the Institute for the Study of American Religion [by] J. Gordon Melton with James V. Geisendorfer. New York : Garland Pub., 1977. p. cm. (Garland reference library of the humanities ; v. 91) Bibliography: p. [BL2530.U6M44] 76-52700 lib.bdg. : 21.00
1. United States—Religion—Directories. I. Geisendorfer, James V., joint author. II. Institute for the Study of American Religion. III. Title.

United States—Religion—History—Sources.

HANDY, Robert T., comp. 200'.973
Religion in the American experience: the pluralistic style. Edited by Robert T. Handy. New York, Harper & Row [1972] xxii, 246 p. 21 cm. (Documentary history of the United States) "HR 1648." Includes bibliographical references. [BR514.H35 1972b] 70-186140 ISBN 0-06-138790-8
1. United States—Religion—History—Sources. I. Title.

HANDY, Robert T., comp. 200'.973
Religion in the American experience: the pluralistic style. Edited by Robert T. Handy. Columbia, University of South Carolina Press [1972] xxii, 246 p. 24 cm. [BR514.H35] 72-5338 ISBN 0-87249-275-3 9.95
1. United States—Religion—History—Sources. I. Title.

United States—Religion—Juvenile literature.

FLOOD, Robert. 280'.0973
America, God shed His grace on thee / Robert Flood ; illustrated by Tom Fawell. Chicago : Moody Press, c1975. 192 p. : ill. ; 29 cm. Traces the growth of christianity throughout the history of the United States. [BR515.F56] 76-356230 ISBN 0-8024-0208-9 : 9.95
1. United States—Religion—Juvenile literature. 2. Evangelicalism—United States—Juvenile literature. 3. United States—History—Juvenile literature. 4. [United States—Religion.] 5. [Evangelicalism.] 6. [United States—History.] I. Fawell, Tom. II. Title.

United States—Religion—Public opinion.

SUBURBAN 301.15'43'200973
religion : churches and synagogues in the American experience / by W. Widick Schroeder ... [et al.]. Chicago : Center for the Scientific Study of Religion, [1974] xiii, 266 p. : ill. ; 23 cm. (Studies in religion and society) Includes index. Bibliography: p. 224-230. [BL2530.U6S9] 74-82113 ISBN 0-913348-05-8 : 9.95 pbk. : 5.95
1. United States—Religion—Public opinion. 2. Suburban churches—United States—Public opinion. 3. Jews in the United States—Public opinion. 4. Public opinion—Jews. I. Schroeder, W. Widick. II. Center for the Scientific Study of Religion. III. Series: Studies in religion and society series.

United States—Religion—Statistics.

GREELEY, Andrew M., 301.5'8'0973
1928-
Ethnicity, denomination, and inequality / Andrew M. Greeley. Beverly Hills, Calif. : Sage Publications, c1976. 85 p. : ill. ; 22 cm. (Sage research papers in the social sciences ; ser. no. 90-029 : Studies in religion and ethnicity) Bibliography: p. 78-79. [BR516.5.G73] 76-2105 ISBN 0-8039-0641-2 pbk. : 3.00
1. United States—Religion—Statistics. 2. Ethnology—United States—Statistics. 3. Income distribution—United States—Statistics. I. Title. II. Series: Sage research

papers in the social sciences : Studies in religion and ethnicity.

United States—Religion—To 1800.

KOCH, Gustav Adolf, 1900- 211'.5'0973
Religion of the American enlightenment, by G. Adolf Koch. New York, Crowell [1968] xviii, 334 p. 20 cm. Originally published in 1933 under title: Republican religion. Reprint with a new foreword. Bibliography: p. 299-328. [BL2760.K6 1968] 68-29621 2.45
1. United States—Religion—To 1800. 2. United States—Church history. 3. Deism—History. I. Title.

POWELL, Milton, comp. 277.3
The voluntary church: American religious life, 1740-1865, seen through the eyes of European visitors New York, Macmillan [1967] xix, 197 p. 22 cm. Bibliography: p. 193-197. [BR515.P6] 67-19678
1. United States—Religion—To 1800. 2. United States—Religion—19th century. I. Title.

United States—Religion—To 1800—Addresses, essays, lectures.

RELIGION and the American revolution 209'.73
/ edited by Jerald C. Brauer ; with contributions by Jerald C. Brauer, Sidney E. Mead, Robert N. Bellah. Philadelphia : Fortress Press, c1976. xi, 73 p. ; 22 cm. Contents.Contents.—Brauer, J. C. Puritanism, revivalism, and the Revolution.—Mead, S. E. Christendom, enlightenment, and the Revolution.—Bellah, R. N. The Revolution and the civil religion. Includes bibliographical references. [BR520.R44] 76-9718 pbk. : 2.95
1. United States—Religion—To 1800—Addresses, essays, lectures. 2. United States—History—Revolution, 1775-1783—Addresses, essays, lectures. I. Brauer, Jerald C. II. Brauer, Jerald C. Puritanism, revivalism, and the Revolution. III. Mead, Sidney Earl, 1904- Christendom, enlightenment, and the Revolution. IV. Bellah, Robert Neely, 1927- The Revolution and the civil religion.

United States—Religious and ecclesiastical institutions—Directories.

†*DIRECTORY of religious organizations in the United States of America* 200'.25'73
/ compiled by the editorial staff of McGrath Publishing Company ; James V. Geisendorfer, editorial consultant. [Washington, N.C.] : McGrath, c1977. 553 p. ; 29 cm. "A Consortium book." Includes index. [BL2530.U6D57] 77-92346 ISBN 0-8434-0609-7 : 62.50
1. United States—Religious and ecclesiastical institutions—Directories. I. Geisendorfer, James V. II. McGrath Publishing Company.

United States—Religious life and customs.

BERGER, Peter L. 209.73
The noise of solemn assemblies; Christian commitment and the religious establishment in America. [1st ed.] Garden City, Doubleday, 1961. 189 p. 21 cm. Includes bibliography. [BR526.B45] 61-14587
1. United States—Religious life and customs. 2. United States—Church history. I. Title.

GARVIN, Philip, 1947- 209'.73
Religious America. Photos. by Philip Garvin. Text by Philip Garvin and Julia Welch. [New York] McGraw-Hill [1974] 189 p. illus. 23 x 29 cm. [BR515.G27] 74-11049 ISBN 0-07-022918-X 15.00
1. United States—Religious life and customs. I. Welch, Julia. II. Title.

PHARES, Ross. 209.73
Bible in pocket, gun in hand; the story of frontier religion. [1st ed.] Garden City, N. Y., Doubleday, 1964. 182 p. 22 cm. Bibliographical references included in "Notes" (p. [167]-182) [BR517.P5] 64-11375
1. U.S.—Religious life and customs. 2. Frontier and pioneer life—U.S. I. Title.

ZARETSKY, Irving I. 200'.973
Religious movements in contemporary America, edited by Irving I. Zaretsky and Mark P. Leone. Princeton, N.J., Princeton University Press [1974] p. cm. Bibliography: p. [BR516.5.Z37] 73-39054 ISBN 0-691-07186-1 25.00
1. United States—Religious life and customs. 2. United States—Religion—1965- I. Leone, Mark P., joint author. II. Title.

United States—Religious life and customs—Statistics.

MARANELL, Gary Michael, 1932- 200'.973
Responses to religion; studies in the social psychology of religious belief, by Gary M. Maranell. Lawrence, University Press of Kansas [1974] xvii, 313 p. illus. 25 cm. Bibliography: p. 295-304. [BR517.M37] 73-19860 ISBN 0-7006-0114-7 10.00
1. United States—Religious life and customs—Statistics. 2. Sociology, Christian—United States. 3. Christianity—Psychology. I. Title.

United States—Social conditions

ANDREWS, James F., 1936- 261.8'0973
The citizen Christian, by James F. Andrews. With an introd. by Theodore M. Hesburgh. New York, Sheed and Ward [1968] 190 p. 21 cm. Includes bibliographies. [HN58.A53] 68-26035 4.50
1. United States—Social conditions. 2. Church and social problems—United States. I. Title.

GOODWIN, R Dean, 1909- 266
There is no end. New York, Friendship Press, 1956. 126p. illus. 23cm. [BR525.G6] 275.3 56-6582
1. U. S.—Soc. condit. 2. U. S.—Religion. 3. Missions, Home. I. Title.

SCHNEPP, Gerald Joseph, brother, 1908- 282.73
...Leakage from a Catholic parish... [by] Brother Gerald J. Schnepp... Washington, D.C., The Catholic university of America press, 1942. xii, 408 p. incl. tables. diagrs. fold. form. 23 cm. Thesis (Ph.D.)--Catholic university of America, 1942. Bibliography: p. 386-391. [BX1407.S6S35] A 42
1. U.S.—Soc. condit. 2. Social surveys. 3. Catholics in the U.S. 4. Parishes—U.S. I. Title.

STRINGFELLOW, William.
Dissenter in a great society; a Christian view of America in crisis. Nashville, Abingdon Press [c1966] 164 p. 21 cm. (AB 4) 68-73800
1. U.S.—Soc. condit. 2. U.S.—Moral conditions. I. Title.

STRINGFELLOW, William. 261.83
Dissenter in a great society; a Christian view of America in crisis, [1st ed.] New York, Holt, Rinehart and Winston [1966] x, 164 p. 22 cm. [HN57.S86] 65-22472
1. U.S. — Soc. condit. 2. U.S. — Moral conditions. I. Title.

United States—Social conditions—1960- —Addresses, essays, lectures.

TASTE & see '72; 261.8'3
selections from the Liguorian (a disscussion book) Liguori, Mo., Liguori Publications [1972] 155 p. 18 cm. Contents.Contents.—Earl, R. Has the Church gone soft?—Higgins, J. J. How rich is the Catholic Church?—Weber, P. J. Is shared prayer the new devotion?—Earl, R. Why confess to a priest?—Larsen, E. Cool is dead.—Sex and the college girl.—Rick M. "Police brutality?"—Cosgrove, T. Marriage: Sacramental mystery or romantic myth?—Shanahan, L. Are marriage vows on the way out?—Hughes, J. J. Does the Church need new marriage laws?—Rue, J. J. What to look for in a marriage counselor.—Higgins, J. J. Are schools bad for kids?—Diamond, J. J. Suicide American style: the danger of birth rate decline.—Engel, R. Will your government abolish large families?—Jann, P. Questions about abortion.—Take a look at your drinking.—Miller, L. G. Busy ... but bored.—Bertha, M. K. Help is the name of the game. [HN65.T34] 72-89230 1.50
1. United States—Social conditions—1960- —Addresses, essays, lectures. 2. Church and social problems—Catholic Church—Addresses, essays, lectures. I. The Liguorian.

United States—Social conditions—Addresses, essays, lectures.

BREWSTER, John Monroe, 1904-
The cultural crisis of our time. St. Louis, Mo., Dept. of the Church in Town and Country, Division of Church Extension, United Church Board for Homeland Ministries [1963] 80 p. 20 cm. Bibliographical footnotes: p. 75-80. 68-18206
1. U.S.—Soc. condit.—Addresses, essays, lectures. 2. U.S.—Econ. condit.—1945- 3. Culture—Addresses, essays, lectures. I. United Church Board in Town and Country. Division of Church Extension. II. Title.

United States—Social policy.

THE Formation of social policy in the Catholic and Jewish traditions 261.8'3
/ Eugene J. Fisher and Daniel F. Polish, editors. Notre Dame [Ind.] : University of Notre Dame Press, c1980. xiv, 194 p. ; 21 cm. Includes bibliographical references and index. [HN65.F67] 19 80-50268 ISBN 0-268-00951-1 (pbk.) : 8.95
1. United States—Social policy. 2. Church and social problems—Catholic Church. 3. Judaism and social problems. I. Fisher, Eugene J. II. Polish, Daniel F.

United States Supreme Court. Law and religion — United States (Series)

GRISWOLD, Erwin Nathaniel, 1904-
Absolute is in the dark; a discussion of the approach of the Supreme Court to constitutional questions. [Salt Lake City, Utah Law Review Association, 1963] 1 v. (Utah. University. College of Law. William H. Leary lecture, 1963) "Reprinted from summer 1963 issue Utah law review" v. 8, no. 3. 65-3561
1. U.S. Supreme Court. Law and religion — U.S. (Series) I. Title. II. Series.

United Synagogue, London.

NEWMAN, Aubrey Norris. 296'.09421
The United Synagogue, 1870-1970 / Aubrey Newman London ; Boston : Routledge & K. Paul, 1976. xv, 239 p., [4] leaves of plates ; ill. ; 22 cm. Includes bibliographical references and index. [BM295.U5N48] 77-360194 ISBN 0-7100-8456-0 : 12.75
1. United Synagogue, London. 2. Jews in London—History. I. Title.

United Synagogue of America.

KARP, Abraham J 296.6'7
A history of the United Synagogue of America 1913-1963 [New York, United Synagogue of America, 1964] 108 p. illus., ports. 23 cm. [BM21.U665] 65-903
1. United Synagogue of America. 2. Conservative Judaism. I. Title.

United Synagogue of America. National Women's League.

UNITED Synagogue of America. National Women's League. 296'.062'1
They dared to dream; a history of National Women's League, 1918-1968. New York [1967] 107 p. illus., facsims., ports. 23 cm. [BM21.U678] 67-7880
1. United Synagogue of America. National Women's League. I. Title.

United Thank Offering—History.

YOUNG, Frances Merle, 1910- 262'.03'0681
Thankfulness unites : the history of the United Thank Offering, 1889-1979 / by Frances M. Young ; edited by Ruth G. Cheney. Cincinnati : Forward Movement Publications, c1979. 85 p. : ill. ; 22 cm. Bibliography: p. 83-84. [BX5978.Y68] 79-124170 pbk. : 1.75
1. United Thank Offering—History. I. Title.
Publisher's address :412 Sycomore st., Cincinnati, Oh 45202

Unity and plurality (in religion, folk-lore, etc.)

STEED, Ernest H. J. 291
Two be one / by Ernest H. J. Steed. Plainfield, N.J. : Logos International, c1978. ix, 160 p., [6] leaves of plates : ill. ; 21 cm. Includes bibliographical references and index. [BL270.S74] 78-50073 ISBN 0-88270-313-7 pbk. : 2.95
1. Bible—Criticism, interpretation, etc. 2. Unity and plurality (in religion, folk-lore, etc.) I. Title.

Unity church (Negro)

SMITH, B. B. 289
Unity church call. Designed for the churches of the great Christian unity, a denomination organized by the Negro race of America, November 15, 1891. First book by the evangelistic preacher, B. B. Smith & sons. Tomberlins, Lonoke co., Ark., B. B. Smith & sons, 1891. 2 p. l., [3]-64 p. 20 1/2 cm. [BX9890.U45S6] 42-42423
1. Unity church (Negro) I. Title.

Unity School of Christianity.

BACH, Marcus, 1906- 289.9
The unity way of life. [1st ed.] Englewood Cliffs, N. J., Prentice-Hall [1962] 182 p. 21 cm. [BX9890.U5B3] 62-18246
1. Unity School of Christianity. I. Title.

BUTTERWORTH, Eric. 248.4'8'99
Unity of all life. [1st ed.] New York, Harper & Row [1969] 209 p. 22 cm. Bibliographical references included in "Notes" (p. 205-209) [BX9890.U5B82] 75-85053 5.95
1. Unity School of Christianity. 2. Spiritual life. I. Title.

CADY, H Emilie, 1848- 220
Miscellaneous writings, by H. Emilie Cady ... rev. and authorized. Kansas City, Mo., Unity school of Christianity, 1917. 126, [2] p. 20 cm. [BR125.C23] 20-16807
I. Title.

CADY, H Emilie, 1848- 220
Miscellaneous writings, by H. Emilie Cady ... rev. and authorized. Kansas City, Mo., Unity school of Christianity, 1920. 128 p. 20 cm. (Lettered on cover: Unity library. vol. iii) [BR125.C23 1920] 22-6183
I. Unity school of Christianity, Kansas City, Mo. II. Title.

CADY, Harriett Emilie, 1848-1941. 131.324
How I used truth; formerly Miscellaneous writings, by H. Emilie Cady ... Revised and authorized. Kansas City, Mo., Unity school of Christianity, 1939. 132 p., 1 l. 20 cm. Essays on religious subjects. [BX9890.U5C32 1939] 159.91324 42-2839
I. Unity school of Christianity, Kansas City, Mo. II. Title.

†CLARK, Rebecca. 248'.48'89
Breakthrough / by Rebecca Clark. Unity Village, Mo. : Unity Books, c1977. xiv, 186 p. ; 20 cm. [BX9890.U5C57] 76-27494 3.95
1. Unity School of Christianity. I. Title.
Publisher's address: Unity School of Christianity, Unity Village, MO 64065

CURTIS, Donald. 230'.9'9
The Christ-based teachings / by Donald Curtis. Unity Village, Mo. : Unity Books, c1976. 156 p. ; 20 cm. [BX9890.U5C84] 75-40657 3.95
1. Unity School of Christianity. I. Title.

†CURTIS, Donald. 242
Master meditations / by Donald Curtis. Lakemont, Ga. : CSA Press, c1976 237 p. ; 21 cm. [BX9890.U5C86] 76-47422 ISBN 0-87707-185-3 pbk. : 3.25

1. Unity School of Christianity. 2. Meditations. I. Title.

CURTIS, Donald. 289.9
New age understanding. Unity Village, Mo., Unity Books [1972, c1973] 142 p. 20 cm. [BX9890.U5C87] 72-92276
1. Unity School of Christianity. I. Title.

FILLMORE, Charles, 1854- 131.324
The twelve powers of man, by Charles Fillmore. 6th ed. Kansas City, Mo., Unity school of Christianity, 1941. 188 p., 1 l., vii p., 1 l. 1 illus. 20 cm. [BX9890.U5F55 1941] [159.91324] 42-19452
I. Unity school of Christianity, Kansas City, Mo. II. Title.

FILLMORE, Lowell. 131.324
New ways to solve old problems, by Lowell Fillmore. 2d ed. Kansas City, Mo., Unity school of Christianity, 1939. 191 p. 20 cm. [BX9890.U5F58 1939] [159.91324] 42-40468
I. Unity school of Christianity, Kansas City, Mo. II. Title.

FISCHER, William L. 230'.997
Alternatives / William L. Fischer. 1st ed. Unity Village, Mo. : Unity Books, 1980. 101 p. ; 20 cm. [BX9890.U504F57] 19 79-67005 ISBN 0-87159-000-X pbk. : 3.95
1. Unity School of Christianity. I. Title.

FISCHER, William L. 248'.48'99
The master craft of living, by William L. Fischer. Unity Village, Mo., Unity Books [1974] 176 p. 20 cm. [BX9890.U5F594] 73-94281
1. Unity School of Christianity. I. Title.

FREEMAN, James Dillet. 289.9
Happiness can be a habit. Drawings by Robert Kipniss. Garden city, New York, Doubleday [1968,c.1966] 90p. 21cm. (W15) [BX9890.U5F68] 66-17396 1.95 pap.,
1. Unity School of Christianity. 2. Happiness. I. Title.

FREEMAN, James Dillet. 289.9
Happiness can be a havit. Drawings by Robert Kipniss. [1st ed.] Garden City, N.Y., Doubleday, 1966. 190 p. illus. 22 cm. [BX9890.U5F68] 66-17396
1. Unity School of Christianity. 2. Happiness. I. Title.

FREEMAN, James Dillet. 131.324
The household of faith; the story of Unity. Lee's Summit, Mo., Unity School of Christianity, 1951. 303 p. illus. 24 cm. [BX9890.U5F7] 52-20829
1. Fillmore, Charles, 1854-1948. 2. Fillmore, Myrtle (Page) d. 1961. 3. Fillmore, Myrtie (Page) d. 1961. 4. Unity School of Christianity. I. Title.

INGRAHAM, Earnest Verner, 131.324 1882-
The silence, by E. V. Ingraham. Enl. ed. Kansas City, Mo., Unity school of Christianity, 1941. 74 p., 1 l. 16 1/2 cm. [BX9890.U5I52] [159.91324] 42-19398
I. Unity school of Christianity, Kansas City, Mo. II. Title.

IUPPENLATZ, William L 1879- 289.9
Regeneration and the superman. Boston, Christopher Pub. House [1959] 118p. 21cm. [BX9890.U5 184] 59-7082
1. Unity School of Christianity. I. Title.

MCCLELLAN, Foster C. 248'.48'99
Thoughts for a friend / by Foster C. McClellan. Unity Village, Mo : Unity Books, [1975] 169 p. : ill. ; 20 cm. Includes index. [BX9890.U5M22] 75-24049 3.95
1. Unity School of Christianity. I. Title.

MCCLELLAN, Foster C. 248'.48'99
Thoughts for a friend / by Foster C. McClellan. Unity Village, Mo. : Unity Books, [1975] 169 p. : ill. ; 20 cm. Includes index. [BX9890.U5M22] 75-24049
1. Unity School of Christianity. I. Title.

MACDONALD, Elinor 289.9
Your greatest power. Lee's Summit, Mo., Unity Bks. [1966] 317p. 20cm. [BX9890.U5M24] 66-6467 2.95
1. Unity School of Christianity. I. Title.

PAULSON, J Sig
The thirteen commandments. Lee's Summit, Mo., Unity School of Christianity, 1964. 154 p. 17 cm. 65-82457
1. Unity School of Christianity. I. Title.

POUNDERS, Margaret. 230'.99
Laws of love / Margaret Pounders. 1st ed. Unity Village, Mo : Unity Books, 1979. 279 p. ; 20 cm. Includes bibliographical references. [BX9890.U504P68] 79-64898 3.95
1. Unity School of Christianity. I. Title.

ROSEMERGY, Jim. 230'.997
A recent revelation / Jim Rosemergy. 1st ed. Unity Village, Mo. : Unity Books, c1981. xi, 139 p. ; 20 cm. [BX9890.U504R65] 19 81-50146 ISBN 0-87159-002-6 pbk. : 3.95
1. Unity School of Christianity. I. Title.

ROTH, Charles, 1916- 248'.4
A new way of thinking / Charles Roth. 1st ed. Unity Village, Mo. : Unity Books, 1979. 158 p. ; 20 cm. [BX9890.U504R67] 78-64751 pbk. : 3.95
1. Unity School of Christianity. 2. Conduct of life. I. Title.
Pub. Address: Unity School of Christianity, Unity Village MO 64065

ROTH, Charles B. 230'.9'9
Mind, the master power / by Charles Roth. Unity Village, Mo. : Unity Books, [1974] 258 p. ; 20 cm. [BX9890.U5R67] 74-186980
1. Unity School of Christianity. I. Title.

ROWLAND, May. 289.9
The magic of the word. Unity Village, Mo., Unity Books [1972] 182 p. 20 cm. [BX9890.U5R68] 73-180756 ISBN 0-87159-095-6
1. Unity School of Christianity. I. Title.

SCHMELIG, Leddy. 248'.48'99
Steps in self-knowledge / Leddy and Randolph Schmelig. 1st ed. Unity Village, Mo. : Unity Books, 1979. v, 147 p. ; 20 cm. [BX9890.U504S35] 79-64038 pbk. : 3.95
1. Unity School of Christianity. I. Schmelig, Randolph, joint author. II. Title.
Pub. Address: Unity School of Christianity, Unity Village MO 64065

SCHMELIG, Randolph. 248'.48'99
Patterns for self-unfoldment / by Randolph and Leddy Schmelig. Unity Village, Mo. : Unity Books, [1975] 304 p. : ill. ; 20 cm. [BX9890.U5S34] 74-29429
1. Unity School of Christianity. I. Schmelig, Leddy, joint author. II. Title.

SIKKING, Sue. 289.9
Seed of the new age. [1st ed.] Garden City, N.Y., Doubleday, 1970. 117 p. 22 cm. [BX9890.U5S54] 79-99216 3.95
1. Unity School of Christianity. I. Title.

SMOCK, Martha. 248.4'2
Halfway up the mountain. Unity Village, Mo., Unity Books [1971] 238 p. 20 cm. [BX9890.U5S58] 70-155718 ISBN 0-87159-125-1
1. Unity School of Christianity. 2. Conduct of life. I. Title.

SMOCK, Martha. 248'.48'99
Turning points / by Martha Smock. Unity Village, Mo. : Unity Books, c1976. 206 p. ; 20 cm. [BX9890.U5S6] 75-41954
1. Unity School of Christianity. I. Title.

TAIT, Vera Dawson. 248.4'8997
Take command! / Vera Dawson Tait. 1st ed. Unity Village, Mo. : Unity Books, c1981. 174 p. ; 20 cm. [BX9890.U504T34] 19 80-53217 ISBN 0-87159-150-2 pbk. : 3.95
1. Unity School of Christianity. I. Title.

WHITNEY, Frank B. 131.324
Beginning again, a guide to taking a new hold on life, by Frank B. Whitney. Kansas City, Mo., Unity school of Christianity, 1940. 113 p., 1 l. 20 cm. [BX9890.U5W45] (159.91324) 42-40327
I. Unity school of Christianity, Kansas City, Mo. II. Title.

WORKS and wonders / 289.9
[compiled by Zelma Cook and Janna Russell ; designed by Belinda Newill ; photos. by Tony LaTona and Keith McKinney. Unity Village, Mo. : Unity Books, c1979. 62 p. : col. ill. ; 27 cm. Includes index. [BX9890.U504A45] 78-68931 3.95
1. Unity School of Christianity. I. Cook, Zelma. II. Russell, Janna. III. LaTona, Tony. IV. McKinney, Keith.

Unity School of Christianity—Addresses, essays, lectures.

BUTTERWORTH, Eric. 289.9
Unity: a quest for truth. [1st ed.] New York, R. Speller [1965] 89 p. 19 cm. [BX9890.U5B8] 65-20535
1. Unity school of Christianity—Addresses, essays, lectures. 2. Christian life. I. Title.

CADY, Harriette Emilie, 131.324 1848-1941.
Miscellaneous writings, by H. Emilie Cady ... Revised and authorized. Kansas City, Mo., Unity school of Christianity, 1917. 126, [1] p. 19 1/2 cm. Subsequently published under title: How I used truth. Essays on religious subjects. [BX9890.U5C32 1917] [159.91324] 20-16807
1. Unity school of Christianity, Kansas City, Mo. II. Title.

CADY, Harriette Emilie, 131.324 1848-1941.
Miscellaneous writings, by H. Emilie Cady ... Revised and authorized. Kansas City, Mo., Unity school of Christianity, 1920. 128 p. 20 cm. (On cover: Unity library. Vol. III) Subsequently published under title: How I used truth. Essays on religious subjects. [BX9890.U5C32 1920] [159.91324] 22-6183
I. Unity school of Christianity, Kansas City, Mo. II. Title.

CADY, Harriette Emilie, 131.324 1848-1941.
Miscellaneous writings, by H. Emilie Cady ... Revised and authorized. Kansas City, Mo., Unity school of Christianity, 1933. 128 p., 1 l. 19 1/2 cm. Subsequently published under title: How I used truth. Essays on religious subjects. [BX9890.U5C32 1933] [159.91324] 35-16971
I. Unity school of Christianity, Kansas City, Mo. II. Title.

CADY, Harriette Emilie, 131.324 1848-1941.
Miscellaneous writings, by H. Emilie Cady ... Revised and authorized. Kansas City, Mo., Unity school of Christianity, 1934. 123 p. 19 1/2 cm. Subsequently published under title: How I used truth. Essays on religious subjects. [BX9890.U5C32 1934] [159.91324] 35-3335
I. Unity school of Christianity, Kansas City, Mo. II. Title.

FREEMAN, James Dillet. 248.4'8997
Of time and eternity : a collection of the writings of James Dillet Freeman. Unity Village, Mo. : Unity Books, c1981. 187 p. ; 20 cm. [BX9890.U504F73] 19 81-51069 ISBN 0-87159-122-7
1. Unity School of Christianity—Addresses, essays, lectures. I. Title.

SIKKING, Robert P. 236
A matter of life and death / by Robert P. Sikking. Marina del Rey, Calif. : DeVorss, c1978. 112 p. ; 21 cm. [BX9890.U506S54] 77-94991 ISBN 0-87516-256-8 pbk. : 3.95
1. Unity School of Christianity—Addresses, essays, lectures. 2. Death—Addresses, essays, lectures. 3. Immortality—Addresses, essays, lectures. 4. Future life—Addresses, essays, lectures. 5. Reincarnation—Addresses, essays, lectures. I. Title.

Unity School of Christianity—Collections.

UNITY School of Christianity. 131.324
The Unity treasure chest; a selection of the best of Unity writing. [1st ed.] New York, Hawthorn Books [1956] 368p. 24cm. [BX9890.U5A626] 56-6997
1. Unity School of Christianity—Collections. I. Fillmore, Lowell, ed. II. Title.

UNITY School of Christianity. 131.324
The Unity treasury chest; a selection of the best of Unity writing. [1st ed.] New York, Hawthorne Books [1956] 363 p. 24 cm. [BX9890.U5A626] 56-6997
1. Unity School of Christianity — Collections. I. Fillmore, Lowell, ed. II. Title.

Unity School of Christianity — Dictionaries.

FILLMORE, Charles, 1854-1948.
The revealing word. Lee's Summit, Mo. Unity School of Christianity, 1959. 216 p. 17 cm. 66-23406
1. Unity School of Christianity — Dictionaries. I. Unity School of Christianity. II. Title.

Unity School of Christianity — Doctrinal and controversial works.

FILLMORE, Charles, 1854-1948.
Prosperity. Lee's Summit, Mo., Unity School of Christianity, 1960 [c1936] 204 p. 17 cm. 66-41008
1. Unity School of Christianity — Doctrinal and controversial works. I. Title.

HUNTING, Henry Gardner, 131.324 1872-
The word beyond words. New York, Dodd, Mead, 1955. 209p. 21cm. [BX9890.U5H8] 55-11794
1. Unity School of Christianity—Doctrinal and controversial works. I. Title.

KEMP, Russell A. 289.9
Live youthfully now, by Russell A. Kemp. Unity Village, Mo., Unity Books [1969] 223 p. 20 cm. [BX9890.U5K45] 79-93890
1. Unity School of Christianity—Doctrinal and controversial works. I. Title.

MACDOUGALL, Mary 131.3'2 Katherine.
Prosperity now. Lee's Summit, Mo., Unity Books [1969] 159 p. 20 cm. [BX9890.U5M25] 69-17412 2.95
1. Unity School of Christianity—Doctrinal and controversial works. 2. Success. I. Title.

SIKKING, Robert P. 289.9
Light for our age / by Robert P. Sikking. Unity Village, Mo. : Unity Books, c1976. 124 p. ; 20 cm. [BX9890.U5S53] 76-366864 3.95
1. Unity School of Christianity—Doctrinal and controversial works. I. Title.

UNITY School of 131.324 Christianity.
A more wonderful you. Lee's Summit, Mo., 1952. 185p. 17cm. [BX9890.U5A625] 55-57977
1. Unity School of Christianity—Doctrinal and controversial works. I. Title.

WHITNEY, Frank B 289.9
Be of good courage. Lee's Summit, Mo., Unity School of Christianity, 1953. 153p. illus. 17cm. Verse and prose. [BX9890.U5W44] 54-32721
1. Unity School of Christianity—Doctrinal and controversial works. I. Title.

WILSON, Ernest Charles, 1896- 248
The emerging self, by Ernest C. Wilson. Unity Village, Mo., Unity Books [1970] 191 p. 20 cm. [BX9890.U5W547] 75-120119
1. Unity School of Christianity—Doctrinal and controversial works. I. Title.

WILSON, Ernest Charles, 230'.99 1896-
Every good desire [by] Ernest C. Wilson. [1st ed.] New York, Harper & Row [1973] viii, 117 p. 21 cm. Expanded version of the 1948 ed. published by Unity Classics, Los Angeles. [BX9890.U5W553 1973] 73-6322 ISBN 0-06-069440-8 4.95
1. Unity School of Christianity—Doctrinal and controversial works. I. Title.

WILSON, Ernest Charles, 230'.9'9 1896-
Every good desire [by] Ernest C. Wilson. Boston, G. K. Hall, 1974 [c1973] 226 p. 25 cm. Large print ed. [BX9890.U5W553 1974] 74-4356 ISBN 0-8161-6217-4 7.95 (lib. bdg.)
1. Unity School of Christianity—Doctrinal and controversial works. I. Title.

WILSON, Ernest Charles, 1896- 131.324
The other half of the rainbow. Los Angeles, Unity Classics [1952] 213p. 21cm. [BX9890.U5W565] 53-15580
1. Unity School of Christianity—Doctrinal and controversial works. I. Title.

YOU can master yourself and your problems. [Atlanta, 1956] x, 131p. 20cm.
1. Unity School ofChristianity—Doctrinal and controversial works. I. Boyce, Kathryn.

Unity School of Christianity, Kansas City, Mo.

BERANGER, Clara. 131.324
You can be happy, by Clara Beranger. New York, S. Curl, inc., 1946. 162 p. 1 l. 19 cm. [Full name: Clara Kahn (Strouse) Beranger de Mille] [BX9890.U5B4] 46-20666
1. Unity school of Christianity, Kansas City, Mo. 2. New thought. I. Title.

BOATWRIGHT, Crichton Russ, 1902- 131.324
The master key to every kingdom: grace. New York, H. Paschke [1947] 111 p. 19 cm. "From talks given during the past four years, based on study of the words and life of Jesus and the writings of St. John and St. Paul." [BX9890.U5B6] 48-7007
1. Unity School of Christianity, Kansas City, Mo. 2. Grace (Theology) I. Title.

BRADEN, Charles H. 131.324
Formula divine. May man enter heaven while he lives? Los Angeles, De Vorss [1949] 139 p. 20 cm. Poems and prose. [BX9890.U5B7] 49-20894
1. Unity School of Christianity, Kansas City, Mo. I. Title.

CADY, Harriette Emilie, 1848-1941. 131.324
God a present help. 3d ed. Kansas City, Mo., Unity School of Christianity, 1942. 127 p. 20 cm. [BX9890.U5C25 1942] 49-32118
1. Unity School of Christianity, Kansas City, Mo. I. Title.

CADY, Harriette Emilie, 1848-1941. 248
God a present help, by H. Emilie Cady ... New York, Roger brothers, 1908. 117 p. 20 cm. [BX9890.U5C25 1908] 8-30153
1. Unity school of Christianity, Kansas City, Mo. I. Title.

CADY, Harriette Emilie, 1848-1941. 248
God a present help, by H. Emilie Cady ... Rev. ed. New York [The Trow press] 1912. 5 p. l., 7-117 p. 20 cm. [BX9890.U5C25 1912] 12-28372
1. Unity school of Christianity, Kansas City, Mo. I. Title.

CADY, Harriette Emilie, 1848-1941. 131.324
God a present help, by H. Emilie Cady ... 2d ed. Kansas City, Mo., Unity school of Christianity, 1941. 127 p. 19 1/2 cm. [BX9890.U5C25 1941] 159.91324 42-21920
1. Unity school of Christianity, Kansas City, Mo. I. Title.

FILLMORE, Charles, 1854- 131.324
Atom-smashing power of mind. Lee's Summit, Mo., Unity School of Christianity, 1949. 187, xvii p. 17 cm. [BX9890.U5F47] 50-28564
1. Unity School of Christianity, Kansas City, Mo. I. Title.

GATLIN, Dana. 131.324
... God is the answer. 3d ed. Kansas City, Mo., Unity school of Christianity, 1940. 154 p., 1 l. 20 cm. [BX9890.U5G3 1940] [159.91324] 42-40323
1. Unity school of Christianity, Kansas City, Mo. II. Title.

GATLIN, Dana. 289.9
Unity's fifty golden years, by Dana Gatlin. A history of the Unity movement, 1889-1939. Kansas City, Mo., Unity school of Christianity, 1939. xv p., 2 l., 135, [1] p. illus. (incl. ports.) 24 cm. [BX9890.U5G33] 42-40469
1. Unity school of Christianity, Kansas City, Mo. I. Title.

HOSCHOUER, William Isaac, 1878- 131.324
You can be prosperous; an inspiration to richer living, by W. I. Hoschouer. New York city, Landau book company [1947] 126 p. 19 1/2 cm. "Originally appeared as articles in Unity magazine." [BX9890.U5H6] 47-22188
1. Unity school of Christianity, Kansas City, Mo. I. Title.

INGRAHAM, Earnest Verner, 1882- 248
Prayer, its practice and its answer, by E. V. Ingraham ... Los Angeles, Calif., DeVorss & co. [c1935] 6 p. l., 17-173 p. 19 cm. "First edition." [BX9890.U5I5] 35-13499
1. Unity school of Christianity, Kansas City, Mo. 2. Prayer. I. Title.

LANCE, Marion T., 1892- 131.324
Spiritual equipment. Los Angeles, Willing Pub. Co. [1947] 89 p. 17 cm. [BX9890.U5L3] 47-11045
1. Unity School of Christianity, Kansas City, Mo. I. Title.

LYNCH, Richard. 131.324
Usable truth, by Richard Lynch. Kansas City, Mo., Unity school of Christianity, 1935. 154 p., 1 l. 20 cm. [BX9890.U5L9] (159.91324) 42-40324
I. Unity school of Christianity, Kansas City, Mo. II. Title.

MANN, Stella Terrill. 131.324
Change your life through love. New York, Dodd, Mead [1949] London, New York, Pub. for the British Council by Longmans, Green, 1948. vi, 186 p. 20 cm. ix, 601 p. 27 cm. Bibliography: p. vii-viii. [BX9890.U5M28] [PG9591.M32] 491.99132 49-2608 48-8848
1. Unity School of Christianity, Kansas City, Mo. 2. Love (Theology) 3. Albanian language—Dictionaries—English. I. Mann, Stuart Edward, 1905- II. Title. III. Title: An historical Albanian-English dictionary.

MANN, Stella Terrill. 264.1
Change your life through prayer, by Stella Terrill Mann. New York, Dodd, Mead & company, 1945. 148 p. 19 1/2 cm. [BX9890.U5M3] 45-7676
1. Unity school of Christianity, Kansas City, Mo. 2. New thought. 3. Prayer. I. Title.

PALMER, Clara. 131.324
You can be healed, by Clara Palmer. 3d ed. Kansas City, Mo., Unity school of Christianity, 1941. 187, [2] p. 20 cm. "Much of this book was originally published as articles in Weekly unity."--Foreword. [BX9890.U5P3 1941] [159.91324] 42-19395
1. Unity school of Christianity, Kansas City, Mo. I. Title.

POMEROY, Ella. 131.324
Powers of the soul and how to use them. New York, Island Press [1948] vii, 152 p. 23 cm. [BX9890.U5P6] 48-10654
1. Unity School of Christianity, Kansas City, Mo. I. Title.

REED, John Thomas. 131.324
Living to win, by John Thomas Reed and Della Reed. [1st ed.] Los Angeles, De Vorss [1948] 143 p. 20 cm. [BX9890.U5R4] 48-2478
1. Unity School of Christianity, Kansas City, Mo. I. Reed, Della, joint author. II. Title.

SHANKLIN, Imelda Octavia. 131.324
What are you? By Imelda Octavia Shanklin. 2d printing. Kansas City, Mo., Unity school of Christianity, 1929. 166 p. 20 cm. [BX9890.U5S47] [159.91324] 42-40326
I. Unity school of Christianity, Kansas City, Mo. II. Title.

WALTERS, Zelia Margaret. 131.324
Whatsoever ye shall ask, a book of true experiences, by Zelia M. Walters. Kansas City, Mo., Unity school of Christianity, 1941. 204 p., 1 l. 20 cm. "These stories originally appeared in Weekly unity."--Foreword. [BX9890.U5W3] (159.91324) 42-19393
I. Unity school of Christianity, Kansas City, Mo. II. Title.

WEST, Georgiana Tree. 131.324
Prosperity's ten commandments, by Georgiana Tree West. New York, T. Gaus' sons, inc. [1944] 5 p. l., 7-117 p. 19 cm. [BX9890.U5W4] 44-9871
1. Unity school of Christianity, Kansas City, Mo. 2. Commandments, Ten. I. Title.

WHITNEY, Frank B. 131.324
Mightier than circumstance, by Frank B. Whitney. 2d ed. Kansas City, Mo., Unity school of Christianity, 1939. 155 p. 1 l. front. (port.) 20 cm. [BX9890.U5W48 1939] (159.91324) 42-40628
I. Unity school of Christianity, Kansas City, Mo. II. Title.

WHITNEY, Frank B. 289.9
...Open doors, by Frank B. Whitney. Kansas City, Mo., Unity school of Christianity, 1932. 182 p., 4 l. 19 1/2 cm. [BX9890.U5W5] 35-8401
I. Unity school of Christianity, Kansas City, Mo. II. Title.

WILSON, Ernest C 131.324
Every good desire. Los Angeles, Unity Classics [c1948] 203 p. 21 cm. [BX9890.U5W553] 49-18439
1. Unity School of Christianity, Kansas City, Mo. I. Title.

WILSON, Ernest C. 131.324
The Great Physician (master class lessons) by Ernest C. Wilson. Kansas City, Mo., Unity school of Christianity, 1945. 154 p. 17 cm. "First appeared in 1935." [BX9890.U5W56 1945] 46-21086
1. Unity school of Chrisianity, Kansas City, Mo. I. Unity school of Christianity, Kansas City, Mo. II. Title.

WILSON, Ernest C. 131.324
Sons of heaven, by Ernest C. Wilson. Los Angeles, Calif., Unity classics [c1941] 5 p. l., 13-125 p., 1 l. 15 1/2 cm. [BX9890.U5W57] [159.91324] 42-7279
1. Unity school of Christianity, Kansas City, Mo. I. Title.

Universal Christian conference on life and work, Stockholm, 1925.

BRENT, Charles Henry, bp., 1862-1929. 206.
Understanding; being an interpretation of the Universal Christian conference on life and work, held in Stockholm, August 15-30, 1925 by Charles Henry Brent ... New York [etc.] Longmans, Green and co., 1925. vi, 64 p. 18 1/2 cm. [BR41.U6A5 1925 k] 25-21151
1. Universal Christian conference on life and work, Stockholm, 1925. I. Title.

SHILLITO, Edward, 1872- 206.
Life and work; the Universal Christian conference on life and work, held in Stockholm, 1925. [By] Edward Shillito ... London, New York [etc.] Longmans, Green and co. ltd., 1926. vii, 104 p. 19 cm. [BR41.U6A5 1925n] 26-11762
1. Universal Christian conference on life and work, Stockholm, 1925. I. Title.

Universal Fellowship of Metropolitan Community Churches.

ENROTH, Ronald M. 261.8'34'157
The gay church, by Ronald M. Enroth [and] Gerald E. Jamison. Grand Rapids, Eerdmans [1974] 144 p. 22 cm. Bibliography: p. 141. [BV4470.E57] 73-16483 ISBN 0-8028-1543-X 2.95
1. Universal Fellowship of Metropolitan Community Churches. 2. Church work with homosexuals. I. Jamison, Gerald E., joint author. II. Title.

Universal Life Church.

THE How-to handbook of massive tax reduction. 343.7305'23 Los Angeles, Calif. : Universal Life Church, 1982. 57, xiii, A-Z p. : ill., forms ; 28 cm. [KF6449.Z9H68 1982] 347.303523 19 81-90774 ISBN 0-960811-60-5 pbk. : 14.95
1. Universal Life Church. 2. Corporations, Religious—Taxation—United States—Popular works. 3. Taxation, Exemption from—Law and legislation—United States—Popular works. 4. Tax planning—United States—Popular works. I. Universal Life Church.

Publisher's address : 295 S. Robertson Blvd., Beverly Hills, CA 90211.

Universal Negro Improvement Association—Addresses, essays, lectures.

BURKETT, Randall K. 209'.73
Black redemption : churchmen speak for the Garvey movement / Randall K. Burkett. Philadelphia : Temple University Press, 1978. x, 197 p. : ports ; 22 cm. Includes bibliographical references. [BR563.N4B87] 77-81332 12.50
1. Universal Negro Improvement Association—Addresses, essays, lectures. 2. Garvey, Marcus, 1887-1940—Addresses, essays, lectures. 3. Afro-Americans—Religion—Addresses, essays, lectures. 4. Afro-American clergy—Biography—Addresses, essays, lectures. I. Title.

Universalism.

ADAMS, John Coleman, 1849-
Universalism and the Universalist church, by John Coleman Adams, D.D. Boston, Universalist publishing house [c1914] 115 p. 17 cm. "References" at end of each chapter. 15-16353
I. Title.

ADAMS, John Colement, 1849-
Short studies in the larger faith, by John Colman Adams, D.D. Boston, Universalist publishing house, 1907. 2 p. l., 105 p. 18 cm. A series of brief expositions of the several subjects suggested by the questions and answers of "A Universalist catechism," by Dr. G. L. Demarest. First published in "Sunday school helper." cf. Introd. 7-17911
I. Title.

ADAMS, John Greenleaf, 1810-1887. 289.
Fifty notable years. Views of the ministry of Christian Universalism during the last half-century. With biographical sketches. By John G. Adams ... Boston, Universalist publishing house, 1882. 2 p. l., viii p., 2 l., [13]-336 p. front., ports. 22 1/2 cm. [BX9933.A3] 42-51722
1. Universalism. 2. Universalist church—Biog. I. Title.

ALLEN, Timothy, 1715-1806. 230.91
Salvation for all men, put out of all dispute. By Timothy Allen, A.M. & V.D.M. Granville, Massachusetts...Hartford ct. Printed by Nathaniel Patten, a few rods north of the Court-house, [1783]. vii, [9]-56 p. 17 cm. [BX9947.A45] 34-14830
1. Universalism. I. Title.

BALFOUR, Walter, 1776-1852.
Letters to Rev. Moses Stuart ... By Walter Balfour ... Boston, B. B. Mussey, 1833. x, [11]-125 p. 16 cm. "The following letters were published in the Universalist magazine, in the years 1820 and 1821."--Introd. [BX9041.B35] 40-37664
1. Universalism. I. Stuart, Moses, 1780-1852. II. Title.

BALFOUR, Walter, 1776-1852. 288
Three inquiries. 1. Into the Scriptural doctrine concerning the devil and Satan. 2. The extent of duration expressed by the terms olim, aion, and aionios, rendered everlasting, &c. &c. in the Bible, the especially when applied to punishment. 3. The New Testament doctrine concerning the possession of devils. By Walter Balfour ... 3d ed. Providence, Z. Baker, 1842. vii, [1], [13]-420 p. 17 1/2 cm. [BX9941.B3 1842] 40-37662
1. Universalism. I. Title.

BALFOUR, Walter, 1776-1852. 288
Three inquiries on the following Scriptural subjects: I. The personality of the devil. II. The duration of the punishment expressed by the words ever, everlasting, eternal, &c. III. Demoniacal possessions. By Walter Balfour. Revised, with essays and notes, by Otis A. Skinner. Boston, A. Tompkins, 1854. vi, [7]-395, [1] p. 20 cm. [BX9941.B3 1854] 40-37663
1. Universalism I. Skinner, Otis Ainsworth, 1807-1861, ed. II. Title.

BALLOU, Hosea, 1771-1852. 252.091
Sermons on important doctrinal subjects, with critical and explanatory notes. By Rev. Hosea Ballou. Boston, J. M. Usher,

1856. viii, [9]-235 p. 19 1/2 cm. Third edition. [BX9941.B38] 33-245530
1. Universalism. 2. Sermons, American. I. Title.

BALLOU, Hosea, 1771-1852. 288
A treatise on atonement; in which, the finite nature of sin is argued, its cause and consequences as such; the necessity and nature of atonement; and its glorious consequences, in the final reconciliation of all men to holiness and happiness. By Hosea Ballou ... Randolph: (Ver.) Printed by Sereno Wright, 1805. xiii, [15]-216 p. 21 cm. [BX9941.B4 1805] 39-7004
1. Universalism. 2. Atonement. I. Title.

BALLOU, Hosea, 1771-1852. 230.91
A treatise on atonement; in which the finite nature of sin is argued, its cause and consequences as such; the necessity and nature of atonement; and its glorious consequences, in the final reconciliation of all men to holiness and happiness. By Hosea Ballou ... Bennington, Vermont, Printed for Ebenezer Walbridge, by William Haswell. 1811. xii, [13]-313 p. 16 1/2 cm. [BX9941.B4 1811] 35-28144
1. Universalism. 2. Atonement. I. Title.

BALLOU, Hosea, 1771-1852. 230.91
... A treatise on atonement: in which the finite nature of sin is argued, its cause and consequences as such; the necessity and nature of atonement; and its glorious consequences, in the final reconciliation of all men to holiness and happiness. By Hosea Ballou ... 4th ed. Boston, Marsh, Capen and Lyon, 1832. 12, [15]-228 p. 19 1/2 cm. (On cover: Universalist library, no. 3) At head of title: Stereotype edition. [BX9913.U5 no. 3] 35-82571
1. Universalism. 2. Atonement. I. Title.

BALLOU, Hosea, 1771-1852. 230.91
... A treatise on atonement: in which the finite nature of sin is argued, its cause and consequences as such; the necessity and nature of atonement, and its glorious consequences, in the final reconciliation of all men to holiness and happiness. By Hosea Ballou ... 6th ed. Boston, A. Tompkins, 1848. 9, [15]-228 p. 19 cm. At head of title: Stereotype edition. [BX9941.B4 1848] 35-23844
1. Universalism. 2. Atonement. I. Title.

BALLOU, Hosea, 1771-1852. 230.91
... A treatise on atonement; in which the finite nature of sin is argued, its cause and consequences as such; the necessity and nature of atonement, and its glorious consequences, in the final reconciliation of all men to holiness and happiness. By Hosea Ballou ... 6th ed. Boston, A. Tompkins, 1860. 9, [15]-228 p. 19 1/2 cm. At head of title: Stereotype edition. [BN9941.B4 1800] 35-32570
1. Universalism. 2. Atonement. I. Title.

BALLOU, Hosea, 1771-1852. 230.91
A treatise on atonement. By Hosea Ballou. With an introduction by A. A. Miner, 4th ed. Boston, Universalist publishing house, 1882. 286 p. 19 1/2 cm. [BX9941.B4 1882] 35-32572
1. Universalism. 2. Atonement. I. Miner, Alonzo Ames, 1814-1895, ed. II. Title.

BALLOU, Hosea, 1771-1852. 288
A treatise on atonement; in which the finite nature of sin is argued, its cause and consequences as such; the necessity and nature of atonement; and, its glorious consequences, in the final reconciliation of all men to holiness and happiness. By Hosea Ballou ... 14th ed. Boston, The Universalist publishing house, 1902. 1 p. l., xxix, 272 p. front. (port.) 20 cm. "The editions of the Treatise on atonement": p. 265-266. [BX9941.B1 1902] 2-29396
1. Universalism. 2. Atonement. I. Title.

BALLOU, Hosea, 1796-1861. 289.
The ancient history of universalism; from the time of the apostles, to its condemnation in the fifth general council, A.D. 553. With an appendix, tracing the doctrine down to the era of the reformation. By Hosea Ballou, 2d. ... Boston, Marsh and Capen, 1829. 326 p. 18 1/2 cm. [BX9931.B3 1829] 31-22707
1. Universalism. I. Title.

BALLOU, Hosea, 1796-1861. 289.1
The ancient history of universalism, from the time of the apostles to its condemnation in the fifth general council, A.D. 553. With an appendix, tracing the doctrine down to the era of the reformation. By Hosea Ballou, 2d. ... 2d ed., rev. Providence, Z. Baker, 1842. v, [2], 8-310 p., 1 l. 19 cm. [BX9931.B3 1842] 31-22709
1. Universalism. I. Title.

BALLOU, Hosea, 1796-1861. 289.
Ancient history of universalism, from the time of the apostles to the fifth general council, with an appendix, tracing the doctrine to the reformation. By Hosea Ballou, 2d., D.D. With notes, by the Rev. A. St. John Chambre, A.M., and T. J. Sawyer, D.D. Boston, Universalist publishing house, 1872. v p., 1 l., 7-313 p. 20 cm. [BX9931.B3 1872] 31-22708
1. Universalism. I. Chambre, Albert St. John. II. Sawyer, Thomas Jefferson, 1804-1899. III. Title.

BARNS, Lucy, 1780-1809.
Familiar letters and poems, principally on friendship and religion. By Lucy Barns. Also some facts concerning her father, Rev. Thomas Barns, and his descendants. Akron, O., Aunty Brown [1904] 80 p. 16 1/2 cm. [BX9915.B3] 4-36124
1. Universalism. I. Brown, Lucinda (White) b. 1822. II. Title.

BARTLETT, Samuel Colcord, 1817-1898. 230.
Lectures on modern universalism: an exposure of the system, from recent publications of its standard authors. By Samuel C. Bartlett ... Manchester, N. H., Press of Fisk & Gage, 1856. 2 p. l., iv, [5,54-229 p. 20 cm. "Errata" slip inserted at end. Bibliography included in "Introductory note". [BX9947.B35] 38-37834
1. Universalism. I. Title.

BETTS, Frederick William, 1858-
Philosophy and faith of Universalism, by Rev. Frederick W. Betts, D. D. Boston, Universalist publishing house [c1913] 62 p. 19 cm. 13-18725 0.25
I. Title.

BROWNE, Lewis Crebasa. 230.
Review of the life and writings of M. Hale Smith; with a vindication of the moral tendency of Universalism, and the moral character of Universalists. By L. C. Browne. Boston, A. Tompkins, 1847. 360 p. 19 1/2 cm. [BX9947.S7B7] 28-1485
1. Smith, Matthew Hale, 1810-1879. 2. Universalism. I. Title.

CASSARA, Ernest, 1925- 922.8173
Hosea Ballou; the challenge to orthodoxy. Boston, Universalist Historical Society [1961] 226p. 22cm. Includes bibliography. [BX9969.B3C3] 61-6545
1. Ballou, Hosea, 1771-1852. 2. Universalism. I. Title.

CASSARA, Ernest, 1925- comp. 289.1'73
Universalism in America; a documentary history. Boston, Beacon Press [1971] xi, 290 p. 21 cm. Includes bibliographical references. [BX9941.2.C38] 77-136226 ISBN 0-8070-1664-0 10.00
1. Universalism. I. Title.

CHAPIN, Edwin Hubbell, 1814-1880.
Living words, by E. H. Chapin, D. D. With an introductory letter, by Rev. T. S. King ... Boston, A. Tompkins [etc.] 1860. 360 p. front. (port.) 19 cm. [BX9915.C5 1860] 39-1482
I. Title.

CHAPIN, Edwin Hubbell, 1814-1880.
Living words, by E. H. Chapin, D. D., with an introductory letter, by Rev. T. S. King ... Boston, A. Tompkins [etc.] 1861. 360 p. front. (port.) 20 cm. [BX9915.C5] 24-11621
I. Title.

CHAUNCY, Charles, 1705-1787. 230.9'1
The mystery hid from ages and generations. New York, Arno Press, 1969. xvi, 406 p. 23 cm. (Religion in America) Reprint of the 1784 ed. The authorship of Charles Chauncy is affirmed by Richard Eddy in his Universalism in America, v. 1, 1884, p. 90-93; Dict. of Amer. biog.; Brit. Mus. Gen. cat. Erroneously attributed to Isaac Chauncy by Halkett & Laing. Includes bibliographical references. [BX9940.C5 1969] 70-83414
1. Universalism. I. Chauncy, Isaac, 1632-1712. II. Title.

COBB, Sylvanus, 1798-1866. 230.91
A compend of Christian divinity. By Sylvanus Cobb. 1st ed. Boston, The author, 1846. xii, [13]-432 p. 19 1/2 cm. [BX9941.C6] 33-39238
1. Universalism. I. Title.

DARLING, Nancy.
A brief history of the Universalist society of Hartland, Vermont, during its first century, with biographical sketches, by Nancy Darling ... [Hartland? Vt.] Northrop, printer; Castleton, publisher, 1902. 90 p. 1 l. incl. illus., port. 23 cm. 2-29381
I. Title.

DOOLITTLE, Nelson. 230.
A discussion of the subject of Universalism, held in Laport, Lorain county, Ohio; from July 29th, to August 6th, 1845; between Rev. N. Doolittle ... and Rev. John H. Power ... reported by Mr. A. A. Whetmore ... and revised by the parties. Columbus, O., Tribune office print., 1846. 300 p. 19 cm. [BX9946.D7] 38-18203
1. Universalism. I. Power, John Hamilton, 1798-1873. II. Whetmore, A. A. III. Title.

FISHER, Lewis Beals, 1859- 288
Which way? A study of Universalists and Universalism, by Lewis B. Fisher ... Boston and Chicago, Universalist publishing house [c1921] 128 p. 18 cm. Universalism. [BX9941.F5] 21-18937
I. Title.

HALL, Alexander Wilford, 1819-1902.
Universalism against itself: (revised edition) a Scriptural analysis of the doctrine, by A. Wilford Hall... New York, Hall and company, 1883. 1 p. l., [5]-336, [1] p. front. (port.) 21 cm. 15-13998
I. Title.

HANSON, John Wesley, 1823-1901. 237.
Aion-aionios; an excursus on the Greek word rendered everlasting, eternal, etc., in the Holy Bible. With appendixes. By John Wesley Hanson... Chicago, Jansen, McClurg & company, 1880. 174 p. 19 cm. [BT837.H3] 17-31603
1. Universalims. 2. Future punishment. 3. Greek language, Biblical—Semantics. 4. Greek language—Semantics. I. Title.

HANSON, John Wesley, 1823-1901. 287.
Universalism, the prevailing doctrine of the Christian church during its first five hundred years; with authorities and extracts. By J. W. Hanson... Boston and Chicago, Universalist publishing house, 1899. x, 321 p. 20 1/2 cm. [BX9941.H35] 0-494
1. Universalism. I. Title.

HUGHES, John.
Debate on Universalism and the resurrection of the dead, between Rev. John Hughes...and Eld. John R. Daily... held in the Universalist chapel at Waltonville, Illinois, Nov. 17-20, 1908...Arthur T. French, stenographer. Indianapolis, Daily & sons, 1909. 344 p. 2 port. 19 1/2 cm. 10-9950
I. Daily, John R. II. French, Arthur T. III. Title.

KNOWLTON, Isaac Case, 1819-1894. 218
Through the shadows. By Rev. I. C. Knowlton ... Boston, Universalist publishing house, 1885. 2 p. l., [iii]-v p., 1 l., [9]-210 p. 18 cm. [BX9941.K73] 41-41314
1. Universalism. 2. Future punishment—Controversial literature. I. Title.

MANNING, Stanley.
George seeks a reason, by Stanley and Ethel Manning. Boston, Mass., Universalist publishing house [c1929] 119 p. 18 1/2 cm. [BX9942.M3] 29-2387
1. Universalism. I. Manning, Ethel, joint author. II. Title.

MAYO, Amory Dwight, 1823-1907. 230.91
The balance: or, Moral arguments for Universalism. By A. D. Mayo. Boston, A. Tompkins, 1859. 155 p. 12 1/2 cm. [BX9941.M3 1859] 38-22662
1. Universalism. I. Title. II. Title: Moral arguments for Universalism.

MURRAY, John, 1741-1815.
Universalism vindicated: being the substance of some observations on the revelation of the unbounded love of God, made to the patriarch, in the field of Padanaram. Genesis, xxviii. 14. and confirmed by the joint suffrages of the prophets and apostles. Delivered some time since to the people who statedly worship the only wise God our saviour, in the meeting house in middle street, corner of Bennet street. By John Murray. Published at the request of the congregation ... Charlestown [Mass.]: Printed by J. Lamson, for the author, and sold by J. W. Folsom, in Union street, Boston, J. White, in Court street, and at various other places in town and country. [1798] xvi. 96 p. 20 cm. A 35
1. Universalism. I. Title.

MY progress in error, 922
and recovery to truth. Or, A tour through Universalism, Unitarianism, and skepticism. Boston, Gould, Kendall and Lincoln, 1842. viii, [9]-240 p. 18 cm. [BV4935.Z9M8] 36-25395
1. Universalism. 2. Unitarianism.

NORWOOD, Abraham, 1806-1880. 922.8173
The pilgrimage of a pilgrim, for forth years, as he journeyed to, and through, and from, the partialist church, into and through sixteen years' experience in the Universalist ministry--and not done yet. By Abraham Norwood ... 5th and rev. ed. Boston, Published by the pilgrim for the purchaser, 1852. viii, [9]-324 p. 15 1/2 cm. Autobiography. [BX9969.N6A3 1852] 37-30619
I. Title.

PERIN, George Landor, 1854-1921.
The heart of an optimist, from the spoken and written words of George Landor Perin, chosen and arranged by Florence Hobart Perin. New York, George H. Doran company [c1925] 396 p. 16 cm. [BX9915.P4] 25-230795
I. Perin, Florence (Hobart) Mrs. 1869-comp. II. Title.

POWER, John Hamilton, 1798-1873. 230.
An exposition of Universalism; or, An investigation of that system of doctrine which promises final holiness and happiness in heaven to all mankind, irrespective of moral character or conduct in this life. By Rev. John H. Power ... Cincinnati, Pub. by L. Swormstedt & J. H. Power, for the Methodist Episcopal church, 1850. 311 p. 19 cm. [BX9947.P8 1850] 15-24172
1. Universalism. I. Title.

ROYCE, Andrew, 1805-1854. 289.1
Universalism: a modern invention, and not according to godliness. By Andrew Royce ... 2d ed., with an examination of certain reviews. Windsor [Vt.] Printed at the Chronicle press, 1839. 207 p. 17 cm. [BX9947.R68 1839] 35-24708
1. Universalism. I. Title.

SKINNER, Dolphus. 288
A series of letters on important doctrinal and practical subjects, addressed to Rev. Samuel C. Aikin ... To which are annexed a Bible creed and six letters to Rev. D. C. Lansing ... on the subject of a course of lectures delivered by him against Universalism, in the winter of 1830. By Dolphus Skinner ... 2d ed. Utica, Office of Evangelical magazine and Gospel advocate, 1833. viii, [9]-228 p. 18 1/2 cm. "The letters to Rev. Mr. Aikin were ... published ... in the third volume (first series) of the 'Evangelical magazine' and the three first volumes (new series) of the 'Evangelical magazine and Gospel advocate'." --Pref. [BX9941.S63 1833] 39-831
1. Universalism. I. Aikin, Samuel Clark, 1790-1879. II. Lansing, Dirck Cornelius, 1785-1857. III. Title.

[SMITH, James Andrew]
The mystery solved; or, The key to the Bible: an exposition of creeds; a diagram showing why we have so many theories or denominations; and one of the factors of infidelity in this age. Nashville, Tenn., Brandon printing company, 1902. 65 p. diagrs. 19 cm. "Preface" signed: James A. Smith. [BX9942.S63] 2-13621
1. Universalism. I. Title.

SMITH, Matthew Hale, 1810-1879. 230.91
Universalism examined, renounced, exposed; in a series of lectures, embracing the experience of the author during a ministry of twelve years, and the testimony of Universalist ministers to the dreadful moral tendency of their faith. By Matthew Hale Smith. 3d ed. Boston, Tappan & Dennett; New York, Dayton & Newman; [etc., etc.] 1843. iv, 396 p. 20 cm. [BX9947.S6 1843] 35-31648
1. Universalism. I. Title.

SMITH, Matthew Hale, 1810-1879. 230.91
Universalism examined, renounced, exposed; in a series of lectures, embracing the experience of the author during a ministry of twelve years, and the testimony of Universalist ministers to the dreadful moral tendency of their faith. By Matthew Hale Smith. 12th ed. Boston, Tappan & Dennet; New York, M. H. Newman; [etc., etc.] 1844. iv, 396 p. 19 1/2 cm. [BX9947.S6 1844] 35-31647
1. Universalism. I. Title.

SMITH, Matthew Hale, 1810-1879. 230.91
Universalism not of God; an examination of the system of Universalism; its doctrine, arguments, and fruits, with the experience of the author, during a ministry of twelve years. By Matthew Hale Smith. New York, American tract society, 1847. vi, [7]-258 p. 15 1/2 cm. "'Universalism not of God' comprises the substance of the works published by the author upon Universalism, condensed, re-arranged, and in part re-written."--Advertisement. [BX9947.S65] 35-31646
1. Universalism. I. American tract society. II. Title.

STRICKLAND, William Peter, 1809-1884, ed.
Universalism against itself; or, An examination and refutation of the principal arguments claimed in support of the final holiness and happiness of all mankind. Ed. and rev. by W. P. Strickland ... Cincinnati, Applegate & company, 1855. iv, [5]-480 p. 20 cm. 7-28574
I. Title.

THAYER, Thomas Baldwin, 1812-1886. 288
Theology of Universalism: being an exposition of its doctrines and teachings, in their logical and moral relations; including a criticism of the texts cited in proof of the Trinity, vicarious atonement, natural depravity, a general judgment, and endless punishment. By Thomas Baldwin Thayer, D.D. Boston, Universalist publishing house, 1891. viii, [11]-432 p. 19 1/2 cm. [BX9941.T5] 1-24765
1. Universalism. I. Title.

[TYLER, John] 1742-1823. 252.091
The law and gospel, clearly demonstrated in six sermons ... [Norwick, Conn.] Re-printed, by Ansil Brown, for Gurdon Bill, 1815. 1 p. l., [5]-77 p. 16 1/2 cm. First published, 1796, also anonymously, under title: Universal damnation and salvation clearly proved by the Scriptures of the Old and New Testament. [BX9947.T85 1815] 37-10017
1. Universalism. 2. Law and gospel. 3. Sermons, American. I. Title.

WHITTEMORE, Thomas, 1800-1861.
The modern history of Universalism: extending from the epoch of the reformation to the present time. Consisting of accounts of individuals and sects who have believed that doctrine; sketches, biographical and literary, of authors who have written both in favor of and against it; with selections from their writings, and notes, historical, explanatory and illustrative, by Thomas Whittemore ... Vol. I. Boston, A. Tompkins, 1860. xi, [13]-408 p. 20 cm. No more published? Second edition. cf. Pref. [BX9931.W5] 43-32302
1. Universalism. 2. Universalist church—Hist. I. Title.

WHITTEMORE, Thomas, 1800-1861. 230.91
The plain guide to Universalism: designed to lead inquirers to the belief of that doctrine, and believers to the practice of it ... By Thomas Whittemore. Boston, The author, 1842. 408 p. 19 cm. [BX9941.W45] 33-37785
1. Universalism. I. Title.

WILLIAMSON, Isaac Dowd, 1807-1876. 288
An explostion and defense of Universalism, in a series of sermons delivered in the Universalist church, Baltimore, Md., by Rev. I. D. Williamson, D.D. New York, H. Lyon, 1859. vi, [7]-277 p. 15 1/2 cm. [BX9941.W5] 15-24964
1. Universalism. 2. Universalist church—Sermons. 3. Sermons, American I. Title.

WINCHESTER, Elhanan, 1751-1797. 287.7
The universal restoration. Exhibited in four dialogues between a minister and his friend ... chiefly designed fully to state, and fairly to answer the most common objections that are brought against it, from the Scriptures. By Elhanan Winchester. To this edition is prefixed, a brief account of the means and manner of the author's embracing these sentiments; intermixed with some sketches of his life during four years. Boston, B. B. Mussey, 1831. iii, [53]-301 p. front. (port.) 16 cm. [BX9941.W6 1881] 34-4746
1. Universalism. I. Title.

WINCHESTER, Elhanan, 1751-1797. 289
Universal restoration, exhibited in four dialogues between a minister and his friend; comprehending the substance of several real conversations which the author had with various persons both in America and Europe, on that interesting subject, chiefly designed fully to state, and fairly to answer the most common objections that are brought against it from the Scriptures. A new edition. By Elhanan Winchester. To this edition is prefixed, A brief account of the means and manner of the author's embracing these sentiments. Intermixed with some sketches of his life during four years. Lexington [Ky.]. Printed by J. Bradford, at the corner of Main and Cross-streets, M,DCC,XCIV. xxxi, 220 p. 22 cm. [BX9941.W] A35
1. Universalism. I. Title.

WINCHESTER, Elhanan, 1751-1797. 287.7
The universal restoration, exhibited in four dialogues between a minister and his friend; comprehending the substance of several real conversations which the author had with various persons, both in America and Europe, on that interesting subject, chiefly designed fully to state, and fairly to answer the most common objections that are brought against it, from the Scriptures. By Elhanan Winchester. To this edition is prefixed, a brief account of the means and manner of the author's embracing these sentiments; intermixed with some sketches of his life during four years. Published at Worcester, Massachusetts; by Isaiah Thomas, jun. Sold wholesale and retail by him. at his printing office in Worcester, and by Thomas & Whipple, in Newburyport. October--1803. xxxii, [33]-251 p. 17 cm. [BX9941.W6 1831] 34-4746
1. Universalism. I. Title.

Universalism—Addresses, essays, lectures.

BALLOU, Hosea, 1771-1852. 230.91
A voice to Universalists. By Hosea Ballou ... Boston, J. M. Usher; Cincinnati, J. A. Gurley, 1851. 8 p. l., [v]-viii, [13]-272 p. front. (port.) 19 1/2 cm. [BX9943.B4V6] 33-35154
1. Universalism—Addresses, essays, lectures. I. Title.

BIDDLE, Charles Wesley, 1832-1900.
Things wise and otherwise, by Charles W. Biddle, D.D. Complied by Mrs. Mary E. brown, with introduction by James M. Pullman, D.D. Boston, E. F. Endicott, 1901. xv, 287 p. front. (port.) 19 cm. "The chapters comprised in this volume are selected from articles originally published in 'The Universalist leader'."--Pref. [BX9915.B5] 1-29435
1. Universalism—Addresses, essays, lectures. I. Brown, Mary Elizabeth (Kennedy) Mrs. 1845- comp. II. Title.

MAYO, Amory Dwight, 1823-1907.
The balance; or, Moral arguments for universalism. By A. D. Mayo. Boston, B. B. Mussey and A. Tompkins, 1847. 155 p. 2 col. pl. (incl. front.) 12 cm. 15-3392
I. Title. II. Title: Moral arguments for universalism.

PARKER, Joel, 1799-1873. 289.1
Lectures on universalism. By Rev. Joel Parker ... New York, J. S. Taylor & co., 1841. xi, [13]-202 p. 19 cm. Advertising matter: p. [193]-202. [BX9941.P37] 35-25965
1. Universalism—Addresses, essays, lectures. I. Title.

Universalism—Biblical teaching.

PUNT, Neal. 234
Unconditional good news : toward an understanding of Biblical universalism / by Neal Punt. Grand Rapids : W. B. Eerdmans Pub. Co., c1980. x, 169 p. ; 21 cm. Includes bibliographical references and indexes. [BS680.U55P86] 80-10458 ISBN 0-8028-1835-8 : pbk. : 6.95
1. Universalism—Biblical teaching. 2. Universalism. I. Title.

Universalism—Controversial literature.

[HALL, Alexander Wilford] 1819-1902.
Univeralism against itself; or, An examination and refutation of the principal arguments claimed in support of the final holiness and happiness of all mankind. Edited and revised by W. P. Strickland ... Cincinnati, Applegate & company, 1855. iv, [5]-480 p. 20 cm. Edition of 1883 published under author's name. [BX9047.H3 1855] 7-28574
1. Universalism—Controversial literature. I. Strickland, William Peter, 1809-1884, ed. II. Title.

POWER, John Hamilton, 1798-1873. 230.
An exposition of Universalism: or, An investigation of that system of doctrine which promises final holiness and happiness in heaven to all mankind, irrespective of moral character or conduct in this life, By Rev. John H. Power ... Cincinnati, Pub. by L. Swormstedt & J. T. Mitchell, for the Methodist Episcopal church, 1847. 311 p. 19 cm. [BX9947.P8 1847] 40-37675
1. Universalism—Controversal literature. I. Title.

WHITMAN, Bernard, 1796-1834.
Friendly letters to a Universalist on divine rewards and punishments ... by Bernard Whitman. Cambridge [Mass.] Brown, Shattuck, and company, 1833. xi, 356 p. 18 cm. [WBX9947.W5] 44-39097
1. Universalism—Controversial literature. 2. Future life. 3. Future punishment. I. Title.

Universalism—Debates, etc.

BALLOU, Adin, 1803-1890. 230.91
Report of a public discussion, between the Revs. Adin Ballou, and Daniel D. Smith; on the question, "Do the Holy Scriptures teach the doctrine, that men will be punished and rewarded subsequently to this life, or after death, for the deeds done in this life?" Held in Boston, on Tuesday March 18, A.D. 1834, and continued through Wednesday and Thursday. Mendon [Mass.] G. W. Stacy, printer, 1834. 86 p. 24 1/2 cm. [BX9946.B8] 40-87665
1. Universalism—Debates, etc. I. Smith, Daniel D. II. Title.

BISHOP, Garry. 230.
A public controversy, upon fair investigation of doctrines; or, Universalism weighed in the balance and found wanting; being the substance of a public debate, held at the Commissioners' hall, Northern liberties, Philadelphia; between the author and the Rev. Mr. A. Kneeland ... upon the important question whether the Scriptures teach us to believe in a punishment, or condemnation after death. By G. Bishop. Philadelphia, Printed for the author, 1822. vii, [1], [5]-174 p. 18 1/2 cm. [BX9946.B5] 45-40017
1. Universalism—Debates, etc. I. Kneeland, Abner, 1774-1844. II. Title.

BRAMAN, Milton Palmer, bp., b.1799. 230.91
The Danners discussion. A report of the discussion at Danners, Mass., on November 6, 1833, between Revs. M. P. Braman, and Thomas Whittemore. Boston, B. B. Mussey, and Marsh, Capen & Lyon, 1833. 96 p. 24 cm [BX9946. B8] 40-37666
1. Universalism—Debates, etc. I. Whittemore, Thomas, 1800-1861. II. Title.

CARPENTER, George Thomas, 1834-1893. 230.91
Debate on the destiny of the wicked. Between Elder George T. Carpenter ... and Rev. John Hughes ... Reported by Rev. E. H. Waring ... Oskaloosa, Ia., Central book concern, 1875. 469 p. 20 cm. [BX9946.C3] 40-37667
1. Universalism—Debates, etc. I. Hughes, John, 1834-1916. II. Waring, E. H., reporter. III. Title.

ELY, Ezra Stiles, 1786-1861. 230.91
A discussion of the conjoint question, is the doctrine of endless punishment taught in the Bible? Or does the Bible teach the doctrine of the final holiness and happiness of all mankind? In a series of letters between Ezra Stiles Ely ... and Abel C. Thomas ... New-York, P. Price, 1835. xii, [13]-288 p. 16cm. "The letters of Dr. Ely were originally published in the Philadelphia; those of Mr. Thomas in the Messenger and Universalist, excepting the seven concluding epistles."--P. iv. [BX9946.E5] 40-37668
1. Universalism—Debates, etc. I. Thomas, Abel Charles, 1807-1880. II. Title.

FISHER, Ebenezer, 1815-1879. 230.91
The Christian doctrin of salvation. A discussion between Rev. E. Fisher, D.D., and Rev. J. H. Walden, on the proposition: "All men will be finally saved." Boston, Universalist publishing house, 1869. 70 p. 19 cm. [BX9946.F5] 40-37669
1. Universalism—Debates, etc. I. Walden, J. H. II. Title.

HOLMES, David, 1810-1873. 230.91
A debate on the doctrines of atonement, universal salvation, and endless punishment. Held in Genoa, Cayuga co., N.Y., from December 28th, 1847, to January 5th, 1848, between Rev. David Holmes...and Rev. John M. Austin...Reported by W.G. Bishop, esq. ...and revised by the parties. Auburn, N.Y., Alden & Markham, 1848. 823 p. 20 cm. "Errata": leaf inserted before t.-p. [BX9946.H7] 40-37670
1. Universalism—Debates, etc. I. Austin, John Mather, 1805-1880. II. Bishop, William, G., reporter. III. Title.

HUDSON, Charles Frederic. 230.91
Human destiny. A ciscussion. Do reason and the Scriptures teach the utter extinction of an unregenerate portion of human beings, instead of the final salvation of all! Affirmative. By Rev. C. F. Hudson. Negative. By Rev. S. Cobb. Boston, S. Cobb, 1860. xii, [xi-xiii-xvii p., 1 l., [21]-478 p. 20 cm. "Originally appeared in the Christian freeman and family visitor."--Pref. [BX9946.H8] 40-37671
1. Universalism—Debates, etc. 2. Annihilationism. I. Cobb, Sylvanus, 1796-1866. II. Title.

LOZIER, John Hogarth, 1832-1907. 230.91
Debate on universalism, between Rev. John Hogarth Lozier ... and Rev. B. F. Foster ... held at Morrison's opera hall, on July 1st, 3d, 5th, 8th, 10th, and 12th, 1867. Indianapolis, Ind., Downey & Brouse, 1867. 87 p. 20 cm. [BX9946.L8] 40-37672

1. Universalism—Debates, etc. I. Foster, Benjamin Franklin, 1820-1896. II. Title.

M'KEE, Joseph. 230.91
Theological discussion; being an examination of the doctrine of Universalism, in a series of letters between the Rev. Joseph McKee... and the Rev. Otis A. Skinner... Baltimore, 1835. xiv, 344 p. 14 1/2 cm. "A list of authors": p. [ii] [BX9946.M3] 40-37673
1. Universalism—Debates, etc. I. Skinner, Otis Ainsworth, 1807-1861. II. Title.

PETERS, Newton. 230.
Discussion between Newton Peters, predestinarian Baptist ... and M. A. Peters, Universalist ... Subjects: The death pronounced upon Adam in the garden. The resurrection of the mortal body. The eternal salvation of all mankind. Columbus, O., 1889. 1 p. l., [9]-340 p., 1 l. front. (ports.) 19 cm. [BX9946.P4] 41-83879
1. Universalism—Debates, etc. I. Peters, M. A. II. Title.

PINGREE, Enoch Merrill, 1817-1849. 230.91
A debate on Universalism: held in Warsaw, Kentucky, May, 1844, between Rev. E. M. Pingree ... and Rev. John L. Waller ... Reported by a stenographer and revised by the disputants. Cincinnati, W. L. Mendenhall, printer, 1845. iv, [5]-357 p. 18 1/2 cm. [BX9946.P5] 40-37674
1. Universalism—Debates, etc. I. Waller, John Lightfoot, 1809-1854. II. Title.

YATES, Freeman. 230.91
A discussion of the conjoint question, is the doctrine of endless punishment for any part or portion of the human family taught in the Scriptures; or, is the doctrine of the final holiness and happiness of all mankind? Between Freeman Yates ... and Eben Francis ... consisting of eight discourses, delivered in Dover, N.H., in the months of March and April, 1843. Exeter [N.H.] Printed by F. Grant, 1843. 157 p. 23 1/2 cm. [BX9946.Y3] 41-33880
1. Universalism—Debates, etc. I. Francis, Eben. II. Title.

Universalism—Doctrinal and controvesial works.

GEORGE, Nathan Dow, 1808-1896. 230.91
Universalism not of the Bible: being an examination of more then one hundred texts of Scriptures, in controversy between Evangelical Christians and Universalists, comprising a refutation of Universalist theology, and an exposure of the sophistical arguments and other means by which it is propagated; with a general and Scripture index. By Rev. N. D. George ... 2d ed. rev. New York, Nelson & Phillips; Cincinnati, Hitchcock & Walden. 1873. 458 p. 20 cm. [BX9947.G45 1873] 35-31612
1. Universalism—Doctrinal and controversial works. I. Title.

GEORGE, Nathan Dow, 1808-1896. 230.91
Universalism not of the Bible; being an examination of more than one hundred texts of Scriptures, in controversybetween Evangelical Christians and Universalists, comprising a refutation of Universalist theology, and an exposure of the sophitical arguments and other means by which it is propagated; with a general and Scripture index. By Rev. N. D. George ... 2d ed., rev. New York, Nelson and Philips; Cincinnati, Hitchcock & Walden, 1874. 458 p. 20 cm. [BX9947.G45 1874] 35-31611
1. Universalism—Doctrinal and controvesial works. I. Title.

HANSON, John Wesley, 1823-
Universalism, the prevailing doctrine of the Christian church during its first five hundred years; with authorities and extracts. Boston and Chicago. Univesalist pub. house, 1899. x, 321 p. 12 cm. Feb
I. Title.

Universalist church—Biography

HANSON, E.R. 922.6173
Our woman workers. Biographical sketches of women eminent in the Universalist church for literary, Hilanthropic and Christian work. By E.R. Hanson. Chicago, The Star and covenant office, 1889. viii, 800 p. ports. 21 1/2 x 16 1/2 cm. [BX9667.H3] 37-6733
1. Universalist church—Biog. 2. Woman—Biog. I. Title.

Universalist Church—Connecticut.

WATT, Donald. 289.1'746
From heresy toward truth; the story of Universalism in Greater Hartford and Connecticut, 1821-1971. [West Hartford] Universalist Church of West Hartford, Conn. [1971] x, 177 p. illus. 23 cm. [BX9933.5.C8W38] 76-177978 3.75
1. Universalist Church—Connecticut. I. Title.

Universalist Church—Government.

CUMMINS, Robert, 1897- 262.2
Parish practice in Universalist churches; manual of organization and administration. Boston, Murray Press [1946] 158 p. 22 cm. Bibliography: p. [151]-158. [BX9950.C8] 47-26504
1. Universalist Church—Government. I. Title.

Universalist Church—Hymns.

ADAMS, John Greenleaf, 1810-1887, comp. 245.
Hymns for Christian devotion; especially adapted to the Universalist denomination... By J. G. Adams and E. H. Chapin. 35th ed. Boston, A. Thompkins, 1856. 24, 37-642 p. 16 1/2 cm. [BV450.A6 1856] 16-1181
1. Universalist church—Hymns. 2. Hymns, English. I. Chapin, Edwin Hubbell, 1814-1880, joint comp. II. Title.

BALLOU, Hosea, 1771-1852, comp. 245.
The Universalist hymn-book; a new collection of Psalms and hymns for the use of Universalist societies. By Hosea Ballou and Edward Turner. 4th ed. Boston, Munroe and Francis, 1828. iv, [5]-396 p. 17 cm. Without music. [BV450.B3 1828] 42-43050
1. Universalist church—Hymns. 2. Hymns, English. I. Turner, Edward, joint comp. II. Title.

BALLOU, Hosea, 1796-1861, comp. 245.
A collection of Psalms and hymns for the Use of Universalist societies and families. By Hosea Ballou, 2d ... 2d ed. Boston, B. B. Mussey, 1837. xxv p., 1 l., 29-540 p. 16 cm. On spine: Universalist collection. Without music. [BV450.B33 1837] 42-43051
1. Universalist church—Hymns. 2. Hymns, English. I. Title.

BALLOU, Hosea, 1796-1861, comp. 245.
A collection of Psalms and hymns for the use of Universalist societies and families. By Hosea Ballou, 2d ... 9th ed. Boston, B. B. Mussey, 1844. 1 p. l., [5]-494 p. 12 1/2 cm. On spine: Universalist collection. Without music. [BV450.B33 1844] 42-43052
1. Universalist church—Hymns. 2. Hymns, English. I. Title.

BOSTON. First Universalist Church.
Psalms, hymns, and spiritual songs, selected and original. Designed for the use of the church universal in public and private devotion. Boston, Printed by I. Thomas and E. T. Andrews, 1792. 267p. 16cm. [BV450.B7 1792] 58-52311
1. Universalist Church—Hymns. 2. Hymns, English. I. Title.

BOSTON. First Universalist Church.
Psalms. hymns, and spiritual songs, selected and original. Designed for the use of the church universal in public and private devotion. Boston, Printed by I. Thomas and E. T. Andrews, 1792. 267p. 16cm. [BV450.B7 1792] 58-52311
1. Universalist Church—Hymns. 2. Hymns, English. I. Title.

BOSTON. First Universalist church.
Psalms, hymns, and spiritual songs; selected and designed for the use of the church universal, in public and private devotion. With an appendix, containing the original hymns omitted in the last ed. ... Boston, Munroe, Francis, & Parker, 1808. ix, [11]-388 p. 18 cm. 11-2597
I. Title.

CHURCH harmonies; 783.
a collection of hymns and tunes for the use of congregations. Prepared under the direction of the Universalist publishing house. Boston, Universalist publishing house, 1882. 318 p. 21 1/2 cm. [M2131.U7C55] 22-8753
1. Universalist church—Hymns. 2. Hymns, English.

PICKERING, David, 1789?-1859. 245.
Psalms and hymns, for social and private worship: carefully selected from the best authors. By David Pickering ... Hudson, Printed by A. Stoddard, 1822. [420] p. 14 cm. "Prayers": [9] p. at end. [BV450.P5] 19-20301
1. Universalist church—Hymns. 2. Hymns, English. I. Title.

SHOWALTER, J. Henry.
Psalms, hymns and spiritual songs. Nos. 1 and 2 combined.. By J. Henry Showalter and Geo. B. Holsinger, assisted by Sarah C. Leatherman, S. E. Duncan, W. K. Franklin, W. P. Davidson, J. C. Beahm S. J. Perry. West Milton, O., The J. H. Showalter co., c1895. 246 p. 22 1/2 cm. 3-22427
I. Title.

STREETER, Sebastian, 1783-1867, comp.
The new hymn book, designed for Universalist societies. Compiled from approved authors, with variations and additions, by Sebastian and Russell Streeter. 23d ed. Boston, T. Whittemore, 1839. 410 p. 16 cm. Without music. [BV450.S7] 64-58709
1. Universalist Church — Hymns. 2. Hymns, English. I. Streeter, Russell, joint comp. II. Title.

UNIVERSALIST general convention. 245.2091
Hymns, composed by different authors, by order of the General convention of Universalists of the New England states and others. Adapted to public and private devotion... Walpole, N.H., Printed for the committee. By George W. Nichols. 1808. 358, [2] p. 15 cm. Preface signed: Hosea Ballou, Abner Kneeland, Edward Turner, committee. Without music. [BV450.A3] [BV450.A3 1808] A 35
1. Universalist church—Hymns. 2. Hymns, English. I. Ballou, Hosea, 1771-1852. II. Kneeland, Abner, 1774-1844. III. Turner, Edward. IV. Title.

Universalist church in Ohio.

ROBINSON, Elmo Arnold, 1887- 289.1771
The Universalist church in Ohio, by Rev. Elmo Arnold Robinson. [Akron? O.] Ohio universalist convention, 1923. viii, 275 p. incl. maps. 19 1/2 cm. "Biographical notes of Ohio ministers": p. 164-224. Bibliography: p. [259]-265. [BX9933.R6] 35-28537
1. Universalist church in Ohio. I. Title.

Universalist church in the United States

FISHER, Lewis Beals, 1857- 289.
A brief history of the Universalist church for young people, by L. B. Fisher, D.D. 4th ed., rev. Prepared by the direction of the Young people's Christian union. [Boston, Universalist publishing house, 1913] 215 p. 18 cm. [BX9933.F5 1913] 26-22094
1. Universalist church in the U.S. I. Title.

UNIVERSALIST church.
The Winchester centennial, 1803-1903; historical sketch of the Universalist profession of belief adopted at Winchester, H.H., September 22, 1803, with the addresses and sermons at the commemorative services held in Winchester, Rome City, Ind., and Washington, D.C., September and October, 1903. Boston and Chicago, Universalist publishing house, 1903. xi, 218 p. front., pl., ports. 20 cm. [BX9931.W6] 4-52
I. Title.
Contents omitted.

Universalist church in the United States—Doctrinal and controversial works.

THE evangelists manual;
or, A guide to Trinitarian Universalists. Containing articles explanatory of the doctrines, tenets and faith of the associates of the primitive, apostolic church of Trinitarian Universalists, in the city of Charleston. To which is prefixed five introductory sections. And the eighteen articles of the church, concluded with thirteen propositions, and an appeal to the Christian world. With a copious index. By an associate member ... Charleston, S.C., Printed by A. F. Cunningham, 1829. vi, [7]-136 p. 19 1/2 cm. Approved and accepted by the associates, December 31, 1827. Prepared, at their request, for publication, July 23, 1829. 5-20090
I. Charleston, S.C. Association of the primitive apostolic church of Trinitarian Universalists in the city of Charleston.

ISAAC, Daniel, 1778-1834. 230.
The doctrine of universal restoration examined and refuted; and the objections to that of endless punishment considered and answered; being a reply to the most important particulars contained in the writings of Messrs. Winchester, Vidler, Wright, and Weaver. By D. Issac ... New York, Published by J. Soule and T. Mason, for the Methodist Episcopal church in the United States, 1819. xi, [13]-160 p. 18 cm. [BX9947.I7] A32
1. Universalist church in the U.S.—Doctrinal and controversial works. 2. Atonement. I. Title.

Universalist church—Massachusetts.

[LEAVITT, Percy Metcalf] 1863- 289.
Souvenir portfolio of Universalist churches in Massachusetts. Boston, Mass., The Massosoit press, 1906. 112 p. illus. 16 x 24 cm. [BX9933.5.M4L4] 6-20865
1. Universalist church—Massachusetts. 2. Churches—Massachusetts. I. Title.

ROXBURY, Mass. Universalist church.
The semi-centennial memorial of the Universalist church, Roxbury, Mass. Boston, Universalist publishing house, 1871. 108 p. 6 port. (incl. front.) 22 cm. [BX9961.R7U5] 9-12709
I. Title.

UNIVERSALIST church in the U. S. General convention, 1870.
Proceedings at the Universalist centennial held in Gloucester, Mass., September 20th, 21st, & 22nd, 1870 Boston, Universalist publishing house [c1870] 111 p. 25 1/2 cm. [BX9931.G5] 4-34304
I. Title.

UNIVERSALIST church of America.
Proceedings at the Universalist centennial held in Gloucester, Mass., September 20th, 21st, & 22nd, 1870. Boston, Universalist publishing house [c1870] 111 p. 25 1/2 cm. [BX9931.G5] 4-34304
I. Title.

Universalist Church—New York (State)

SMITH, Stephen Rensselaer, 1788-1850. 289.
Historical sketches and incidents, illustrative of the establishment and progress of Universalism in the State of New York. Buffalo, Steele's Press, 1843. 248 p. 16 cm. [BX9933.5.N4S5 1843] 48-31977
1. Universalist Church—New York (State) I. Title.

SMITH, Stephen Rensselaer, 1788-1850. 289.
Historical sketches and incidents, illustrative of the establisment and progress

of Universalism in the State of New York 2d ser. Buffalo, J. S. Leavitt, 1848. 248 p. 16 cm. [BX9933.5.N4S5 1848] 48-31980
1. Universalist Church—New York (State) I. Title.

Universalist Church of America—History

SCOTT, Clinton Lee. 289.173
The Universalist Church of America, a short history. Boston, Universalist Historical Society [c1957] 124p. 22cm. Includes bibliography. [BX9933.S3] 58-20928
1. Universalist Church of America—Hist. I. Title.

Universalist Church—Periodicals

THE Christian leader; 289.105
a journal of the Universalist fellowship. Boston [Universalist Pub. House] v. in illus., ports. 26-40 cm. Frequency varies. Began publication in 1898. Cf. Union list of serials. Vols. 3-40. no. 7 also called 82d-119th year (v. 3, no. 17-v. 40, no. 7 also called new ser.) "Continuing the Christian leader and its predecessors (1819 to 1897) the Universalist and its predecessors (1827 to 1897) the Gospelbanner (1835 to 1897)" Title varies: 189 -Dec. 26, 1925. The Universalist leader. Subtitle varies (some issues without subtitle) [BX9901.U55] 52-31755
1. Universalist Church—Period.

Universalist church—Sermons.

BALLOU, Hosea, 1771-1852. 252.
Nine sermons on important doctrinal and practical subjects, delivered in Philadelphia, November, 1834. By Hosea Ballou ... Taken in short hand. With a brief memoir of the author, and an appendix. Philadelphia, A. C. Thomas, 1835. xii, [13] -180 p. 18 1/2 cm. "The publisher ... has ... exercised the privilege of an editor."--Pref. [BX9943.B3N5] 44-36665
1. Universalist church—Sermons. 2. Sermons, American. I. Thomas, Abel Charles, 1807-1880, ed. II. Title.

BALLOU, Hosea, 1771-1852. 252.
A series of lecture sermons, delivered at the Second Universalist meeting, in Boston. By Hosea Ballou, pastor. 3d ed., stereotyped. Revised by the author. Boston, A. Tompkins, 1860. 375 p. 20 cm. Issued also semimonthly, as preached, under title: Lecture sermon. [BX9943.B3S4 1860] 45-25163
1. Universalist church—Sermons. 2. Sermons, American. I. Title.

CHAPIN, Edwin Hubbell, 1814-1880. 252.091
The church of the living God, and other sermons. By Rev. E. H. Chapin ... New York, J. Miller, 1881. 228 p. incl. front. (port.) 20 cm. [BX9943.C5C53] 33-37778
1. Universalist church—Sermons. 2. Sermons, American. I. Title.

CHAPIN, Edwin Hubbell, 1814-1880. 252.091
Discourses, on various subjects, by E. H. Chapin. 3d ed. Boston, A. Tompkins, 1858. vi, [7]-213 p. 18 cm. [BX9943.C5D5 1858] 33-37772
1. Universalist church—Sermons. 2. Sermons, American. I. Title.

CHAPIN, Edwin Hubbell, 1814-1880. 252.091
Extemporaneous discourses, delivered in the Broadway church, New York. Reported as delivered, and revised and corrected by the author. By E. H. Chapin. D. D. First series. New York, O. Hutchinson, 1860. 356 p. 19 cm. "Collected from reports in "The spiritual telegraph" and 'The banner of light.'"--Pref. [BX9943.C5E8] 32-37775
1. Universalist church—Sermons. 2. Sermons, American. I. Title.

CHAPIN, Edwin Hubbell, 1814-1880. 252.091
God's requirements, and other sermons. By Rev. E. H. Chapin ... New York, J. Miller, 1881. 4 p. l., [7]-221 p. front. (port.) 20 cm. [BX9943.C5G6] 33-37773
1. Universalist church—Sermons. 2. Sermons, American. I. Title.

CHAPIN, Edwin Hubbell, 1814-1880. 252'.09'1
Humanity in the city. New York, Arno Press, 1974 [c1854] 252 p. port. 23 cm. (Metropolitan America) Reprint of the ed. published by De Witt & Davenport, New York. [BX9943.C5H85 1974] 73-11901 ISBN 0-405-05389-4 12.00
1. Universalist Church—Sermons. 2. Sermons, American. I. Title. II. Series.

CHAPIN, Edwin Hubbell, 1814-1880. 252.091
Humanity in the city. By the Rev. E. H. Chapin. New York, De Witt & Davenport; Boston, A. Tompkins [1854] x p., 1 l., [13] -252 p. incl. front. (port.) 18 cm. [BV4501.C356] 33-37771
1. Universalist church—Sermons. 2. Sermons, American. I. Title.

CHAPIN, Edwin Hubbell, 1814-1880. 252.091
Lessons of faith and life. Discourses by E. H. Chapin. New York, J. Miller, 1877. 215 p. 19 cm. [BX9943.C5L4] 33-37776
1. Universalist church—Sermons. 2. Sermons, American. I. Title.

CHAPIN, Edwin Hubbell, 1814-1880. 252.091
Moral aspects of city life. A series of lectures by Rev. E. H. Chapin. New York, H. Lyon; Boston, A. Tompkins; [etc., etc.] 1856. 191 p. 19 cm. "Fifth thousand." [BV4501.C357] 33-37774
1. Universalist church—Sermons. 2. Sermons, American. I. Title.

CHAPIN, Edwin Hubbell, 1814-1880. 252.091
Select sermons preached in the Broadway church. By Rev. E. H. Chapin, D. D. New York, H. Lyon, 1859. v, [7]-348 p. 19 cm. [BX9943.C5S4] 33-37777
1. Universalist church—Sermons. 2. Sermons, American. I. Title.

ELLIS, Sumner, 1828-1886. 922.8173
"He being dead yet speaketh." Faith and righteousness. A memorial of Sumner Ellis, D.D., with an outline of his life and ministry by Rev. C. R. Moor. Boston, Universal publishing house, 1887. v. p. 1 l., 325 p. front. (port.) 19 cm. Preface signed: J. S. Cantwell. [BX9969.E6A3] 37-8732
1. Universalist church—Sermons. I. Cantwell, John Simon, 1837-1907, ed. II. Moor, Clark Rice, 1825-1895. III. Title.

MONTGOMERY, George Washington, 1810-1898. 230.
Sermons on doctrinal and moral subjects. By G. W. Montgomery ... Rochester [N.Y.] W. Heughes, 1850. 3 p. l., [9]-216 p. 17 cm. [BX9943.M6S4] 43-44473
1. Universalist church—Sermons. 2. Sermons, American. I. Title.

MOORE, Asher, 1810-1891. 922.8173
A memoir of the late Rev. Savillion W. Fuller, by Rev. Asher Moore. To which are added original lectures, sermons, &c., selected from the writings of Mr. Fuller. Philadelphia, J. H. Gihon & co., 1840. 214 p. front. (port.) 17 cm. [BX9969.F85M6] 37-8735
1. Fuller, Savillion Waterons, 1803-1840. 2. Universalist church—Sermons. 3. Sermons, American. I. Title.

SOULE, Caroline Augusta (White) Mrs., 1824-1903. 922.8173
Memoir of Rev. H. B. Soule. By Caroline A. Soule ... New York, H. Lyon; Auburn [N.Y.] M. W. Fish, 1852. v. p., 1 l., [9]-396 p. front. (port.) 20 cm. Selections from H. B. Soule's writings: p. 173-396. [BX9969.S7S6] 37-8739
1. Soule, Henry Birdsall, 1815-1852. 2. Universalist church—Sermons. 3. Sermons, American. I. Title.

TUTTLE, James Harvey, 1824-1903. 922.8173
The field and the fruit; a memorial of twenty-five years' ministry with the Church of the Redeemer, Minneapolis. By Rev. James H. Tuttle, D.D. Boston, Universalist publishing house, 1891. 4 p. l., [7]-362 p. front. (port.) 3 pl. 22 cm. [BX9969.T8A3] 37-8740
1. Universalist church—Sermons. 2. Sermons, American. 3. Minneapolis. Church of the Redeemer (Universalist) I. Title.

TWLEVE sermons, 252.
delivered during the session of the United States convention of Universalists, in the city of New York, September 15th and 16th, 1853. Together with a portrait of the author of each sermon. Boston, J. M. Usher, 1853. xii, [13]-285 p. ports. 20 1/2 cm. [BX9943.A1T85] 44-26456
1. Universalist, church—Sermons. 2. Sermons, American.

WILLIAMSON, Isaac Dowd, 1807-1876. 252.091
An argument for the truth of Christianity, in a series of discources. By I. D. Williamson ... New York, P. Price & co., 1836. 252 p. 15 1/2 cm. [BX9943.W45A7] 38-19326
1. Universalist church—Sermons. 2. Sermons, American. I. Title.

WILLIAMSON, Isaac Dowd, 1807-1876. 252.091
The crown of life; a series of discourses. By I. D. Williamson ... 2d ed. Boston, J. M. Usher; Cincinnati, O., J. A. Gurley; [etc., etc., 1850] x, [11]-407 p. front. (port.) 20 cm. [BX9943.W45C7] 33-37337
1. Universalist church—Sermons. 2. Sermons, American. I. Title.

Universalist church—United States

BISBEE, Frederick Adelbert, 1855-1923. 289.
1770-1920, from Good Luck to Gloucester, the book of the pilgrimage; being the record of the celebration by means of a great pageant of the one hundred and fiftieth anniversary of the landing of John Murray, his reception by Thomas Potter, and the preaching of the first Universalist sermon at Good Luck, New Jersey, and the establishing of the first Universalist Church at Gloucester, Massachusetts, by the Rev. Frederick A. Bisbee ... Boston, The Murray press, 1920. 4 p. l., 373 p. front., plates, ports. 21 1/2 cm. [BX9933.B5] 21-945
1. Murray, John, 1741-1815. 2. Universalist church—U.S. I. Title. II. Title: From Good Luck to Gloucester.

EDDY, Richard, 1828-1906. 289.
Universalism in America. A history. By Richard Eddy ... Boston, Universalist publishing house, 1884-86. 2 v. 20 cm. Contents.I. 1636-1800.--II. 1801-1886. Bibliography (p. 485-599) L. C. copy imperfect: t.-p. of v. 1. wanting. [BX9933.E3 1884] 43-32304
1. Universalist church—U.S. 2. Universalism—Bibl. I. Title.

ROBINSON, Elmo Arnold, 1887- 289.1'73
American Universalism; its origins, organization, and heritage. [1st ed.] New York, Exposition Press [1970] 266 p. 22 cm. (An Exposition-testament book) Bibliography: p. [239]-245. [BX9933.R59] 76-126375 7.50
1. Universalist Church—U.S. I. Title.

WILLIAMS, George Huntston, 1914- 289.1'73
American universalism; a bicentennial historical essay. [Boston] Universalist Historical Society [1971] v, 94 p. 23 cm. (The Journal of the Universalist Historical Society, v. 9) Includes bibliographical references. [BX9903.U524 vol. 9] [BX9933] 76-27471
1. Universalist Church—U.S. I. Title. II. Series: Universalist Historical Society. Journal, v. 9.

Universalist church—Year-books.

UNIVERSALIST church of America. 280.173
Directory, Universalist churches and ministers. Boston, Mass. v. 23 1/2 cm. [BX9911.U46] 44-31839
1. Universalist church—Year-books. I. Title.

UNIVERSALIST church of America. 289.173
Report of the Board of trustees. -1921. [Little Falls, N.Y., etc., 18 -1921] v. in plates, ports, 21-23 cm. Published under the church's earlier name: Universalist general convention. Title varies: 18 -89, Minutes. 1890-1920, Annual report of the Board of trustees (from 1891 to 19 alternate issues, Minutes) 1921, Report of the Board of trustees. Superseded by the Universalist year book. [BX9905.A3] 45-52540
I. Title.

Universalists—Washington, D.C.—Biography.

BROOKS, Seth R. 289.1'092'4 B
Recollections and reflections of Seth R. Brooks and Corinne H. Brooks / edited by William Lloyd Fox. Washington : Universalist National Memorial Church, 1977. 106 p. ; 23 cm. [BX9969.B75A35] 77-84948
1. Brooks, Seth R. 2. Brooks, Corinne H. 3. Universalists—Washington, D.C.—Biography. 4. Washington, D.C.—Biography. I. Brooks, Corinne H., joint author. II. Fox, William Lloyd.

Universals (Philosophy).

DRAVID, Raja Ram. 181'.4
The problem of universals in Indian philosophy. [1st ed.] Delhi, Motilal Banarsidass [1972 i.e. 1973] xvi, 473 p. 23 cm. Originally presented as the author's thesis, Banaras Hindu University. Bibliography: p. [465]-468. [B105.U5D7 1972] 72-906491
1. Universals (Philosophy) 2. Philosophy, Indic. I. Title.
Distributed by Verry, 14.00.

SHWAYDER, D. S. 110
Modes of referring and the problem of universal, an essay in metaphysics. Berkeley, Univ. of California Press, 1961. x, 164p. (University of California publications in philosophy, v.35) 61-63020 3.50 pap.,
1. Universals (Philosophy). I. Title. II. Series: California. University. University of California publications in philosophy, v.35

STANILAND, Hilary, 1941- 111
Universals. Garden City, N.Y., Anchor Books, 1972. x, 141 p. 18 cm. (Problems in Philosophy, PP 8) Bibliography: p. [127]-137. [B105.U5S67] 78-186055 1.45
1. Universals (Philosophy) I. Title.

Universals (Philosophy)—Addresses, essays, lectures.

AARON, Richard Ithamar, 1901- 111
Our knowledge of universals / by R. I. Aaron. New York : Haskell House Publishers, 1975. 26 p. ; 21 cm. Originally published in 1947 in the Proceedings of the British Academy, v. 31 (1945), as the 1945 Annual philosophical lecture, Henriette Hertz Trust. [B105.U5A13] 75-1309 ISBN 0-8383-0108-8 lib.bdg. 7.95
1. Universals (Philosophy)—Addresses, essays, lectures. I. Title. II. Series: British Academy, London (Founded 1901). Annual philosophical lecture, Henriette Hertz Trust ; 1945.

LOUX, Michael J., comp. 111
Universals and particulars: readings in ontology, edited by Michael J. Loux. [1st ed.] Garden City, N.Y., Anchor Books, 1970. x, 349 p. 19 cm. Contents.Contents.—The problem of universals, by M. J. Loux.—The world of universals, by B. Russell.—On what there is, by W. V. O. Quine.—Universals, by D. F. Pears.—Universals, communicable knowledge, and metaphysics, by C. A. Baylis.—Particular and general, by P. F. Strawson.—Qualities, by N. Wolterstorff.—Universals and family resemblances, by R. Bambrough.—Universals and metaphysical realism, by A. Donagan.—On the nature of universals, by N. Wolterstoff.—Particulars and their individuation, by M. J. Loux.—The identity of indiscernibles, by M. Black.—The identity of indiscernibles, by A. J. Ayer.—The identity of indiscernibles, by D. J. O'Connor.—Bare particulars, by E. B. Allaire.—Particulars re-clothed, by V. C. Chappell.—Another look at bare particulars, by E. B. Allaire.—Do relations individuate? By J. W. Meiland.—Particulars and their qualities, by D. C.

Long.—Essence and accident, by I. Copi.—Essence and accident, by H. S. Chandler.—The individuation of things and places, by D. Wiggins.—Bibliography (p. [341]-349) [B105.U5L65] 72-103791 1.95
1. Universals (Philosophy)—Addresses, essays, lectures. 2. Individuation—Addresses, essays, lectures. I. Title.

UNIVERSALS and particulars 111
: readings in ontology / edited by Michael J. Loux. Notre Dame, Ind. : University of Notre Dame Press, [1976] p. cm. [B105.U5U54 1976] 76-745 ISBN 0-268-01908-8 : 16.95 ISBN 0-268-01909-6 pbk. :
1. Universals (Philosophy)—Addresses, essays, lectures. 2. Individuation—Addresses, essays, lectures. I. Loux, Michael J.

Universals (Philosophy)—Collections.

VAN ITEN, Richard J., comp. 110
The problem of universals. Edited by Richard J. Van Iten. New York, Appleton-Century-Crofts [1970] ix, 285 p. 24 cm. "Collection of essays." Bibliography: p. 269-282. [B105.U5V34] 76-118951
1. Universals (Philosophy)—Collections. I. Title.

Universe, Creation of.

WHITNEY, Dudley J. 213
Genesis versus evolution; the problem of creation and atheistic science. New York, Exposition Press [c.1961] 61p. (Exposition-Banner bk.) 2.50
1. Universe, Creation of. 2. Atheism. I. Title.

Universe, Destruction of.

HAYNES, Carlyle Boynton, 1882- 296
On the eve of Armageddon; an account of the scriptural teaching relating to the coming war among the nations which will engulf civilization and immediately precede the universal and eternal kingdom of peace; by Carlyle B. Haynes ... Takoma Park, Washington, D.C. [etc.] Review and herald publishing association [c1924] 128 p. incl. front., illus. 19 1/2 cm. Text on p. [3] of cover. [BT875.H45] 24-7229
1. Universe, Destruction of. 2. Millennium. I. Title.

Universitah ha- 'ivrit bi-Yerushalayim—Addresses, essays, lectures.

MAGNES, Judah Leon, 1877-1948. 956.94'001
Dissenter in Zion : from the writings of Judah L. Magnes / edited by Arthur A. Goren. Cambridge, Mass. : Harvard University Press, 1982. xv, 554 [8] p. of plates : ill. ; 24 cm. Includes bibliographical references and index. [DS149.M29 1982] 19 81-7268 ISBN 0-674-21283-5 : 30.00
1. Universitah ha- 'ivrit bi-Yerushalayim—Addresses, essays, lectures. 2. Magnes, Judah Leon, 1877-1948—Addresses, essays, lectures. 3. Zionism—Addresses, essays, lectures. 4. Jewish-Arab relations—1917-1949—Addresses, essays, lectures. 5. Jews—United States—Politics and government—Addresses, essays, lectures. 6. Rabbis—United States—Biography—Addresses, essays, lectures. 7. Zionists—Palestine—Biography—Addresses, essays, lectures. I. Goren, Arthur A., 1926- II. Title.

Universities and college—Religion.

COLLEGE reading & religion; 207
a surve of college reading materials, sponsored by the Edward W. Hazen Foundation and the Committee on Religion and Education of the American Council on Education. New Haven, Yale Univ. Press, 1948. xi, 345 p. 24 cm. Includes bibliographies. [BV1610.C583] 48-6563
1. Universities and college—Religion. I. Edward W. Hasen Foundation, inc., Haddam, Conn. II. American Council on Education. Committee on Religion and Education.
Contents omitted.

Universities and colleges.

MCGRATH, Fergal, 1895-
Newman's university; idea and reality. London, New York, Longmans, Green [1951] xv. 537 p. 22 cm. "Works consulted": p. 512-522. A52
1. Newman, John Henry, Cardinal, 1801-1890. 2. Universities and colleges. 3. Education, Higher. 4. Catholic University of Ireland, Dublin. I. Title.

NEWMAN, John Henry, Cardinal, 1801-1890.
Discourses on the scope and nature of university education, addressed to the Catholics of Dublin. Dublin, J. Duffy, 1852; Dubuque, Iowa, Wm. C. Brown Reprint Library [1967] xxx, [2], 449 p. 23 cm. 68-60215
1. Universities and colleges. 2. Education, Higher. I. Title.

Universities and colleges, Catholic—Directories.

GUIA de informacion sobre las instituciones catolicas estadounidenses ... Segunda edicion, revisada ... Huntington, Indiana, Catholic Committee on Inter-American Student Problems, 1958. 128p. 23cm. illus. maps. Binder's title: Instituciones Catolicas Estadounidenses.
1. Universities and colleges, Catholic—Directories. I. Catholic Committee on Inter-American Student Problems.

Universities and colleges—Chapel exercises.

ELBIN, Paul Newell, 1905- 378
The improvement of college, worship, by Paul N. Elbin... New York city, Teachers college, Columbia university, 1932. vii, 154 p. 23 1/2 cm. (Teachers college, Columbia university, Contributions to education, no. 530) Issued also as thesis (PH.D) Columbia university. "Bibliography of materials for use in college chapels": p. 139-145; Bibliography: p. 152-154. [BV26.E5 1932a] [LB5.C3 no.580] 264 32-20609
1. Universities and colleges—Chapel exercises. 2. Liturgies. I. Title. II. Title: College worship, The improvement of.

ELBIN, Paul Nowell, 1905- 264
The improvement of college worship, by Paul N. Elbin. New York, Bureau of Publications, Teachers College, Columbia University, 1932. [New York, AMS Press, 1973, c1972] vii, 154 p. 22 cm. Reprint of the 1932 ed., issued in series: Teachers College, Columbia University. Contributions to education, no. 530. Originally presented as the author's thesis, Columbia. Bibliography: p. 152-154. [BV26.E5 1972] 72-176744 ISBN 0-404-55530-6 10.00
1. Universities and colleges—Chapel exercises. I. Title. II. Series: Columbia University. Teachers College. Contributions to education, no. 530.

Universities and colleges—China.

ASSOCIATED boards for Christian colleges in China. 377.80951
... Annual report. 19 [New York? 19 v. illus., diagr. 23 cm. Report year ends June 30. List of members in each volume. [LA1133.A87] 377
1. Universities and colleges—China. 2. Education, Higher. 3. Education, Secondary. I. Title.

[ASSOCIATED boards for Christian colleges in China] 377.80951
An impressive service: the story of the Christian colleges of China. [New York? 1940?] cover-title, 16 p. illus. (incl. map) 26 cm. Names of colleges in Chinese characters on margin. [LA1133.A9] 41-1380
1. Universities and colleges—China. 2. Church and college in China. I. Title.

UNITED Board for Christian Colleges in China. 377.80951
Annual report. [New York?] v, illus. 23 cm. Report year ends June 30. Issued by the board under its earlier name; Associated Boards for Christian Colleges in China. [LA1133.U5] 42-7936
1. Universities and colleges—China. I. Title.

Universities and colleges—China—History.

LUTZ, Jessie Gregory, 1925- 377'.8'0951
China and the Christian colleges, 1850-1950. Ithaca, Cornell University Press [1971] xiii, 575 p. maps. 24 cm. Bibliography: p. 537-556. [LC432.C5L8] 70-148022 ISBN 0-8014-0626-9 16.00
1. Universities and colleges—China—History. 2. Missions—China—Educational work. I. Title.

Universities and colleges—Curricula.

CATHOLIC University of America. Workshop on the Curriculum of the Catholic College, 1951.
The curriculum of the Catholic college, integration and concentration; the proceedings of the Workshop on the Curriculum of the Catholic College conducted at the Catholic University of America from June 12th to June 22nd, 1951. Edited by Roy J. Deferrari. Washington, Catholic University of America Press, 1952. viii, 236 p. illus. 22 cm. Includes bibliographies. A 52
1. Universities and colleges—Curricula. 2. Catholic Church—Education. I. Deferrari, Roy Joseph, 1890- ed. II. Title.

SEWANEE, Tenn. University of the South.
... The Sewanee summer school. Sewanee, Tenn., The University. v. illus. 19 1/2 cm. At head of title: Bulletin of the University of the South. [LC5752.T2S5] CA 11
I. Title.

Universities and colleges—Germany.

SCHAFF, Philip, 1819-1893. 274.
Germany; its universities, theology and religion; with sketches of Neander, Tholuck, Olshausen, Hengstenberg, Twesten, Nitzsch, Muller, Ullmann, Rothe, Dorner, Lange, Ebrard, Wichern, and other distinguished German divines of the age. By Philip Schaff ... Philadelphia, Lindsay and Blakiston; New York, Sheldon, Blakeman & co., 1857. 19 p., 1 l., [27]-418 p. front. (port.) 19 1/2 cm. [BR856.S3] 47-35445
1. Universities and colleges—Germany. 2. Germany—Church history. 3. Theologians, German. I. Title.

Universities and colleges—Iowa.

ABERNETHY, Alonzo, 1836- 377
A history of Iowa Baptist schools, by Alonzo Abernethy ... [Osage, In., Press of the Woolverton printing and publishing co.] 1907. 340 p. front., plates, ports. 20 cm. [LC562.A2] 8-8281
1. Universities and colleges—Iowa. 2. Baptists—Iowa—Education. 3. Baptists—Iowa. I. Title.

Universities and colleges—Prayers.

ADAMS, David Ernest, 1891- 264.1
A little book of college prayers, by David E. Adams. Holyoke, Mass., Unity press, inc., 1944. 70 p. 14 1/2 x 11 1/2 cm. "Three hundred copies ... No. 26." "Prepared for use in the Mount Holyoke college chapel in the years 1932-1934."--Pref. Cover-title: College prayers. [BV283.C7A3] 45-2238
1. Universities and colleges—Prayers. I. Mount Holyoke college. II. Title. III. Title: College prayers.

CUDDESDON College, Cuddesdon, Eng. 248.373
The Cuddesdon College office book. New York, Oxford [1961] xvi, 243p. 16cm. 62-151 2.40
1. Universities and colleges—Prayers. 2. Church of England—Prayer-books and devotions—English. I. Title.

FRIZZELL, John Henry, 1881- 264.1
The chapel prayer book, by John H. Frizzell ... Nashville, Cokesbury press [c 1939] 159 p. 16 cm. [BV283.C7F7] 40-1486
1. Universities and colleges—Prayers. I. Title.

GRAFTON, Thomas H. 242.8
Make meaningful these passing years; prayers, by Thomas H. Grafton on the campus of Mary Baldwin College. [1st ed.] Staunton, Va., Alumnae Association, Mary Baldwin College [1968] 80 p. 20 cm. [BV283.C7G7] 68-21671
1. Universities and colleges—Prayers. I. Mary Baldwin College, Staunton, Va. II. Title.

HARRIS, Edward George, 1917- 264.1
Prayers of a university. Philadelphia, Univ. of Pa, Pr. [1962, c.1961] 58p. 61-18520 2.75
1. Universities and colleges—Prayers. I. Title.

SEEYLE, Laurenus Clark, 1837-1924. 264.
Prayers of a college year, by L. Clark Seelye... Northampton, The Hampshire bookshop, 1925. 160 p. front. (port.) 19 1/2 cm. [BV283.C7S4] 25-11059
1. Universities and colleges—Prayers. I. Title.

VANNORSDALL, John W. 242.8'8
Campus prayers for the '70s [by] John W. Vannorsdall. Philadelphia, Fortress Press [1970] x, 118 p. 18 cm. [BV283.C7V35] 70-101425 2.50
1. Universities and colleges—Prayers. I. Title.

Universities and colleges—Religion.

AMBROSE, W. Haydn. 377
The church in the university [by] W. Haydn Ambrose. Valley Forge [Pa.] Judson Press [1968] 128 p. 20 cm. Bibliographical footnotes. [BV1610.A4] 68-13608
1. Universities and colleges—Religion. 2. Church work with students. I. Title.

BALY, Denis 248.83
Academic illusion. Foreword by Stephen F. Bayne, Jr. Greenwich, Conn., Seabury Press [c.] 1960. 179p. Bibl. footnotes. 61-5575 2.25
1. Universities and colleges—Religion. I. Title.

BALY, Denis. 248.83
Academic illusion. Foreword by Stephen F. Bayne, Jr. Greenwich, Conn., Seabury Press, 1961. 179p. 22cm. [BV1610.B25] 61-5575
1. Universities and colleges—Religion. I. Title.

BLAKEMAN, Edward William, 1880- 377.10973
The administration of religion in universities and colleges: personnel, a survey by Edward W. Blakeman ... Ann Arbor, University of Michigan press, 1942. vii, 150 p. incl. tables. 23 1/2 cm. Lithoprinted. [BV1610.B55] 42-18711
1. Universities and colleges—Religion. 2. Universities and colleges—U.S. I. Title.

BUTLER, Richard, 1918- 378
God on the secular campus. [1st ed.] Garden City, N. Y., Doubleday, 1963. 191 p. 22 cm. [BV1610.B82] 63-11217
1. Universities and colleges—Religion. I. Title.

CAMBRIDGE. University. St. John's college.
Collegium Divi Johannis Evangelistae, 1511-1911. Cambridge [Eng.] Printed at the University press, 1911. x, 126 p. illus., xxi pl. (incl. front., ports, plans, facsims.) 29 cm. "The text has been edited and seen through the press by Professor Seward. The following fellows in addition to Dr. Bonney, who wrote the account of the college buildings, have contributed notes on the illustrations: the Master (Mr. R. F. Scott), Professor Sir Joseph Larmor, Dr. J. R. Tanner, Mr. F. F. Blackman, Mr. T. R. Glover, and Mr. J. H. A. Hart."--Editorial

note. Appendix: The will of the foundress. [LF255.A4] 14-4073
I. Seward, Albert Charles, 1863- ed. II. Bonney, Thomas George, 1833-ed. III. Richmond, Margaret (Beaufort) Tudor, countess of, 1441-1509. IV. Title.

CANTELON, John E 254.2
A Protestant approach to the campus ministry. Philadelphia, Westminster Press [1964] 127 p. 19 cm. Bibliographical references included in "Notes" (p. 121-127) [BV1610.C3] 64-12142
1. Universities and colleges—Religion. I. Title.

CHAMBERLIN, John Gordon. 259
Churches and the campus. Philadelphia, Westminster Press [1963] 189 p. 21 cm. Bibliographical footnotes. [BV1610.C47] 63-9303
1. Universities and colleges—Religion. 2. Church work with students. I. Title.

COLEMAN, Albert John, 1918- 248
The task of the Christian in the university. [American ed.] Pub. for the United Student Christian Council. New York, Association Press, 1947. x, 113 p. 23 cm. (A Grey book of the World's Student Christian Federation) Includes bibliographies. [BV1610.C58 1947] 48-551
1. Universities and colleges—Religion. I. Title.

COMMUNITY on campus: 378.1'03
its formation and function. Edited by Myron B. Bloy, Jr. New York, Seabury Press [1971] 153 p. illus. 21 cm. (Church and campus books) (An Original Seabury paperback, SP 73) Evaluations and analyses from the "consultation of campus Christians" held in Nov., 1970, at the Chapel and Cultural Center, Rensselaer Polytechnic Institute, and sponsored by the Church Society for College Work and the National Center for Campus Ministry. Includes bibliographical references. [LC383.C6] 71-160585
1. Universities and colleges—Religion. 2. Christianity. I. Bloy, Myron B., ed. II. Church Society for College Work. III. National Center for Campus Ministry.

CONVOCATION on Preaching in 259
College and University Communities, 1st, Cincinnati, 1961.
On the work of the ministry in university communities [papers] Ed.: Richard N. Bender. Nashville, Div. of Higher Educ., Bd., of Educ., Methodist Church [1963] 264p. 24cm. Bibl. 63-3369 apply
1. Universities and colleges—Religion. 2. Church work with students. I. Bender, Richard N., ed. II. Methodist Church (United States) Division of Higher Education. III. Title.

CORNELL College, Mount 377
Vernon, Iowa.
Religion in higher education; report of the centennial convocation and conference on religion in higher education held at Cornell College, Mount Vernon, Iowa, November fifteenth, sixteenth, and seventeenth, nineteen hundred fifty three, as a part of the observance of the centennial year of the college. Mount Vernon, Cornell College Press, 1954. v, 104p. 23cm. Bibliographical footnotes. [BV1610.C65 1953] 54-32013
1. Universities and colleges—Religion. I. Title.

CUNINGGIM, Merrimon, 1911- 377.1
The college seeks religion. Ne Haven, Yale Univ. Pre2s, 1947. x, 319 p. 24 cm. (Yale studies in religious education, v. 20) Series: Yale studies in the history and theory of religious education, v. 20. Full name: Augustu Merrimon Cunnggim. Incldes bibliogrphical references. [BV1610.C8] 47-12248
1. Universities and colleges—Religion. I. Title. II. Series.

DONLAN, Thomas C 207
Theology and education. Dubuque, W. C. Brown Co., 1952. 134p. 24cm. (Dominican Fathers, Province of St. Albert the Great. The Aquinas library. Doctrinal studies, 2) [BV1610.D65] 53-1515
1. Universities and colleges—Religion. 2. Religious education. 3. Catholic Church—Education. 4. Theology—Study and teaching. I. Title.

THE faith, the Church and the university, A report of a conversation among university Christians. Cincinnati, Forward Movement Publications, 1959. 59p. 18cm.
1. Universities and colleges—Religion. 2. Education, Higher. I. Bayne, Stephen Fielding, Bp., 1908-

GEORGE Williams College,
Chicago:
Report of the president. [Chicago] v. illus. 23cm. annual. Report year ends June 30. [BV1130.A17] 54-28197
I. Title.

HARTT, Julian Norris. 261.5
Theology and the church in the university, by Julian N. Hartt. Philadelphia, Westminster Press [1969] 204 p. 20 cm. "Some of the material of this essay was first presented as Danforth lectures given at Brown University in the academic year 1964-1965." [BV1610.H33] 69-14198 3.25 (pbk)
1. Universities and colleges—Religion. 2. Universities and colleges—Chapel exercises. I. Title.

HINTZ, Howard William, 377.1
1903-
Religion and public higher education. [Brooklyn] Brooklyn College, 1955. 62p. 22cm. [BV1610.H5] 55-2915
1. Universities and colleges—Religion. I. Title.

INSTITUTE on Religion in 377.1
State Universities, University of Minnesota.
Institute on Religion in State Universities. [Proceedings] Minneapolis, University of Minnesota, Center for Continuation Study. v. 28 cm. [BV1610.I 5] 52-62091
1. Universities and colleges—Religion. I. Minnesota. University. Center for Continuation Study. II. Title.

JONES, George William, 1930- 377
The public university and religious practice: an inquiry into university provision for campus religious life [by] George W. Jones. Muncie, In[d.], Ball State University, 1973. v, 64 p. 25 cm. Bibliography: p. 60-62. [BV1610.J66] 73-620164
1. Universities and colleges—Religion. I. Title.

LIMBERT, Paul Moyer, 1897- 378
ed.
College teaching and Christian values. New York, Association Press, 1951. 187 p. 23 cm. [BV1610.L5] 52-1651
1. Universities and colleges—Religion. I. Title.

MAGNES, Judah Leon, 956.94'001
1877-1948.
Dissenter in Zion : from the writings of Judah L. Magnes / edited by Arthur A. Goren. Cambridge, Mass. : Harvard University Press, 1982. xv, 554 [8] p. of plates : ill. ; 24 cm. Includes bibliographical references and index. [DS149.M29 1982] 19 81-7268 ISBN 0-674-21283-5 : 30.00
1. Universitah ha- 'ivrit bi-Yerushalayim—Addresses, essays, lectures. 2. Magnes, Judah Leon, 1877-1948—Addresses, essays, lectures. 3. Zionism—Addresses, essays, lectures. 4. Jewish-Arab relations—1917-1949—Addresses, essays, lectures. 5. Jews—United States—Politics and government—Addresses, essays, lectures. 6. Rabbis—United States—Biography—Addresses, essays, lectures. 7. Zionists—Palestine—Biography—Addresses, essays, lectures. I. Goren, Arthur A., 1926- II. Title.

*MEEKS, Wayne A. 270
Go from your father's house: a college student's introduction to the Christian faith Illus by Martha F. Meeks [dist.] Richmond, Va. [Knox, c.1964] CLC Pr. 356p. 21cm. (Covenant life curriculum) 2.95 pap.,
I. Title.

MINNESOTA. University. 377.1
Institute on religion in state universities. [Proceedings] 1949- Minneapolis, University of Minnesota, Center for Continuation Study [etc.] v. 28 cm. annual. Title varies: 1949, Religion in the state university: an initial exploration. [BV1610.M55] 51-698
1. Universities and colleges—Religion. I. Minnesota. University. Center for Continuation Study. II. Title. III. Title: Religion in the state university.

MINNESOTA. University. 377.1
Institute on religion in state universities. [Proceedings] 1949- Minneapolis, University of Minnesota, Center for Continuation Study [etc.] v. 28 cm. annual. Title varies: 1949, Religion in the state university: an initial exploration. [BV1610.M55] 51-698
1. Universities and colleges—Religion. I. Minnesota. University. Center for Continuation Study. II. Title. III. Title: Religion in the state university.

NATIONAL council on 207.73
religion in higher education.
Bulletin, 1st- New York, N.Y. [etc.] 1923- v. 23 cm. Irregular. Published by the council under its earlier names as follows: 1st, Council of schools of religion: 2d-3d, National council of schools of religion. [BV1610.N32] 25-27697
1. Universities and colleges—Religion. I. Title.
Contents omitted.

NEVADA. University. 268.434
Report of statewide services. [Reno] v. illus. 29 cm. annual. [LC5301.N4A35] 64-63165
I. Title.

RELIGIOUS perspectives in 377.1
college teaching, by Hoxie N. Fairchild [and others] New York, Ronald Press Co. [1952] x, 460 pl 21 cm. "Originally ... these essays were issued ... as separate pamphlets." [BV1610.R4] 52-9464
1. Universities and colleges—Religion. I. Fairchild, Hoxie Neale, 1894-

REPORT of seminar...
June 4-23, 1956. Nashville, Tenn. [1956] 1v. illus. 28cm. Various pagings. 'Under the direction of the Department of the Christian family, The Board of Education, The Methodist Church.' Includes questionaires. Reviews of books and films: p.38-45.
I. Boston University. School of Theology. Seminar on the Church and Family Life, 1956.

ROSETTA stone 299'.31
inscription.
Report of the committee appointed by the Philonathean Society of the University of Pennsylvania to translate the inscription on the Rosetta stone. [Philadelphia, 1858] 1v. (various pagings) col. illus. 24cm. Facsimile reproduction of ms. copy. The committee consists of Chas. R. Hale. S. Huntington Jones and Henry Morton. Most of the work was done by Morton. Includes the hieroglyphic, demotic, and Greek inscriptions, with translations of each text. [PJ1531.R3 1958] 52-58748
I. Morton, Henry, 1836-1902. II. Pennsylvania. University. Philomathean Society. III. Title.

SMITH, Seymour A 377.1
Religious cooperation in State universities, an historical sketch. [Commemorating the centennial of student religious activity at the University of Michigan. Ann Arbor?, 1957. 109 p. 22 cm. [BR561.M5S6] 57-63109
1. Universities and colleges — Religion. 2. Michigan. University — Religion. I. Title.

TAYLOR, Robert N. 261.8
This damned campus; as seen by a college chaplain [by] Robert N. Taylor, Jr. Philadelphia, Pilgrim Press [1969] x, 130 p. illus. 21 cm. Bibliographical references included in "Notes" (p. 127-130) [BV639.C6T33] 77-76086 2.95
1. Universities and colleges—Religion. I. Title.

TOWNER, Milton Carsley, ed. 377.1
Religion in higher education; containing the principal papers read at the Conference of church workers, Chicago, Illinois, December 31, 1930-January 2, 1931, and other contributions to the permanent literature of higher education, edited by Milton Carsley Towner, with introductions by Shailer Mathews and Frederick J. Kelly. Chicago, Ill., The University of Chicago press [1931] xxi, 327 p. 20 cm. [BV1610.T6]
1. Universities and colleges—Religion. 2. Religious education—U.S. 3. Universities and colleges—U.S. 4. Religion—Addresses, essays, lectures. 5. Religion—Study and teaching. I. Conference of church workers in universities and colleges of the United States. Chicago, Dec. 1930-Jan. 1931. II. Title.

WALSH, Chad, 1914- 261.8
Campus gods on trial. Rev., enl. ed. New York, Macmillan, 1962 [c.1953, 1962] 154p. Bibl. 62-8559 3.00
1. Universities and colleges—Religion. 2. Apologetics—20th cent. I. Title.

WALSH, Chad, 1914- 261.8
Campus gods on trial. New York, Macmillan, 1953. 138 p. 20 cm. [BV1610.W25] 53-1048
1. Universities and colleges—Religion. 2. Apologetics—20th cent. I. Title.

WALTER, Erich Albert, ed. 377.1
Religion and the State university. Ann Arbor, University of Michigan Press [1958] vi, 321 p. 24 cm. Bibliographical references included in "Notes" (p. [311]-318) [BV1610.W28] 58-10121
1. Universities and colleges — Religion. 2. Church and state in the U.S. I. Title.

Universities and colleges—Religion—Addresses, essays, lectures.

CHRISTIAN identity on 378.1'98'1
campus. Edited by Myron B. Bloy, Jr. New York, Seabury Press [1971] 127 p. 21 cm. (Church and campus books) (An Original Seabury paperback, SP 72) "Published in collaboration with the Church Society for College Work." Includes bibliographies. [LC341.C45] 78-160584 2.95
1. Universities and colleges—Religion—Addresses, essays, lectures. I. Bloy, Myron B., ed. II. Church Society for College Work.

Universities and colleges—Religion—Societies, etc.

COLLEGE Theology Society. 230.2
The paradox of religious secularity. Katharine T. Hargrove, editor. Englewood Cliffs, N.J., Prentice-Hall [1968] x, 203 p. 22 cm. Proceedings of the 13th national convention of the College Theology Society, held in Pittsburgh, Mar. 26-28, 1967. Bibliographical footnotes. [BV1610.C584] 68-24092
1. Universities and colleges—Religion—Societies, etc. 2. Theology—Study and teaching—Societies, etc. 3. Secularism. I. Hargrove, Katharine T., ed. II. Title.

COLLEGE Theology Society. 233
To be a man; [proceedings. Edited by] George Devine. Englewood Cliffs, N.J., Prentice-Hall [1969] viii, 151 p. 22 cm. Proceedings of the national convention of the College Theology Society, held in San Francisco, 1968. Bibliographical footnotes. [BV1610.C586] 69-20489 ISBN 1-392-29639-
1. Universities and colleges—Religion—Societies, etc. 2. Theology—Study and teaching—Societies, etc. 3. Man (Theology)—Addresses, essays, lectures. I. Devine, George, 1941- ed. II. Title.

ST. Lawrence college, Mount 207.
Calvary, Wis. Alumni association.
The Laurentianum, its origin and work (1864-1924) Rev. P. Corhinian ... historian of the S. L. C. al association. [Mt. Calvary, Wis., 1924] 193 p. incl. front., illus., plates, port. 24 cm. [BX915.M66A5] 42-11952
I. Corbinian, father, 1871-1930. II. Title.

Universities and colleges—Sermons.

ALEXANDER, John Bruce. 252.6
Turning on lights, by John Bruce Alexander... Portland, Me., Falmouth publishing house, 1940. 7 p. l., 3-143 [1] p. 18 1/2 cm. [BV4310.A594] 41-1901
1. Universities and colleges—Sermons. 2. Baptists—Sermons. 3. Sermons, American. I. Title.

AMES, Edward Scribner, 1870- 252.066
The higher individualism, by Edward Scribner Ames ... Boston and New York, Houghton Mifflin company, 1915. 6 p. l., 3-161, [1] p., 1 l., 20 cm. "These sermons were delivered in Appleton chapel of Harvard university, during 1912-18 and 1913-14."--Pref. [BV4310.A65] 15-4661
1. Universities and colleges—Sermons. 2. Disciples of Christ—Sermons. 3. Sermons, American. I. Title.
Contents omitted.

BROWN, Charles Reynolds, 1862- 252.
The cap and gown, by Charles Reynolds Brown. New York, Boston [etc.] The Pilgrim press [c1910] vii, 233 p. 19 1/2 cm. [BV4310.B65] 10-22429
1. Universities and colleges—Sermons. 2. Students—Religious life. I. Title.
Contents omitted.

BROWN, Charles Reynolds, 1862- 252.
What is your name? (More "Yale talks") by Charles Reynolds Brown... New Haven, Yale university press; [etc., etc.] 1924. 6 p. l., 137 p. 19 1/2 cm. [BV4310.B7] 24-10327
1. Universities and colleges—Sermons. 2. Young men—Religious life. 3. Conduct of life. I. Title.

BROWN, Charles Reynolds, 1862- 252.
Where do you live? By Charles Reynolds Brown... New Haven, Yale university press; [etc., etc.] 1926. ix p., 1 l., 148 p. 19 1/2 cm. Addresses delivered at Yale and other colleges. cf. Pref. [BV4310.B74] 26-8342
1. Universities and colleges—Sermons. 2. Young men—Religious life. 3. Conduct of life. I. Title.

BROWN, Charles Reynolds, 1862- 252.
Yale talks, by Charles Reynolds Brown... New Haven, Yale university press; [etc., etc.] 1919. 156 p. 19 1/2 cm. [BV4310.B78] 19-25950
1. Universities and colleges—Sermons. 2. Young men—Religious life. 3. Conduct of life. I. Title.

BUTTRICK, George Arthur, 1892- 252.55
Sermons preached in a university church. New York, Abingdon Press [1959] 222p. 22cm. Includes bibliography. [BV4310.B85] 59-8194
1. Universities and colleges—Sermons. 2. Sermons, American. I. Title.

COATES, Thomas, 1910- 252.5
The chapel hour. Saint Louis, Concordia Pub. House [1955] 184p. 23cm. [BV4310.C57] 55-7714
1. Universities and colleges—Sermons. 2. Lutheran Church—Sermons. 3. Sermons, American. I. Title.

COFFIN, Henry Sloane, 1877- 252.
University sermons, by Henry Sloane Coffin ... New Haven, Yale university press: [etc., etc.] 1914. 5 p. l., 256 p. 20 cm. "First printed April, 1914. 1000 copies." [BV4310.C6] 14-7288
1. Universities and colleges—Sermons. I. Title.

DAVIES, William David, 1911- 252'.55
The new creation; university sermons [by] W. D. Davies. Philadelphia, Fortress Press [1971] iv, 107 p. 18 cm. [BV4310.D28] 78-133034 2.50
1. Universities and colleges—Sermons. 2. Sermons, American. I. Title.

DUNNING, John Wirt, 1882- 252.5
The fight for character, and other chapel talks, by John W. Dunning ... New York [etc.] Fleming H. Revell company [c1937] 186 p. 20 cm. [BV4210.D85] 37-8912
1. Universities and colleges—Sermons. 2. Presbyterian church—Sermons. 3. Sermons, American. I. Title. II. Title: Chapel talks.

DUNNINGTON, Lewis Le Roy, 1890- 252.07
Something to stand on. New York, Macmillan Co., 1949. xv, 184 p. 20 cm. [BV4310.D87] 49-4569
1. Universities and colleges—Sermons. 2. Methodist Church—Sermons. 3. Sermons, American. I. Title.

ELBIN, Paul Nowell, 1905- 252.5
The enrichment of life; ten chapel talks [by] Paul N. Elbin .. New York, N.Y., Association press [1945] v, 87 p. illus. 19 1/2 cm. "References": p. 87. [BV4310.E38] 45-8951
1. Universities and colleges—Sermons. 2. Sermons, American. I. Title.

FIFE, Robert O. 252'.55
Under the chapel spire; dynamic talks to students [by] Robert O. Fife. Grand Rapids, Mich., Baker Book House [1972] 127 p. 20 cm. [BV4310.F4] 70-188232 ISBN 0-8010-3453-1 1.95
1. Universities and colleges—Sermons. 2. Sermons, American. I. Title.

FROST, Gerhard E 252.5
Chapel time, by Gerhard E. Frost & Gerhard L. Belgum. Minneapolis, Augsburg Pub. House [1956] 149p. 21cm. [BV4310.F7] 56-9460
1. Universities and colleges—Sermons. 2. Lutheran Church—Sermons. 3. Sermons, American. I. Belgum, Gerhard L., joint author. II. Title.

HARPER, William Rainey, 1856-1906. 252.
Religion and the higher life; talks to students, by William Rainey Harper ... Chicago, The University of Chicago press, 1904. ix, 184 p. 20 cm. [BV4310.H3] 4-32682
1. Universities and colleges—Sermons. I. Title.

HASTINGS, Thomas Samuel,- 1827-1911. 252
Union seminary addresses, by Thomas S. Hastings... New York, C. Scribner's sons, 1904. vlll, 266 p. 21 1/2 cm. [BV4316.T5H3] 4-21074
1. Universities and colleges—Sermons. I. Title.

HEDLEY, George Percy, 1899- 252.5
Religion on the campus; some sermons in the chapel of Mills College. New York, Macmillan, 1955. 194p. 21cm. [BV4310.H433] 55-3565
1. Universities and colleges—Sermons. 2. Sermons, American. I. Title.

HENRY, Carl Ferdinand Howard, 1913- ed. 252.5
Not by bread alone; Wheaton chapel talks, compiled and edited by Carl F. H. Henry. Grand Rapids, Mich., Zondervan publishing house [c1940] 3 p. l., 5-153 p. 19 1/2 cm. [BV4310.H44] 40-32850
1. Universities and colleges—Sermons. I. Title.

JOHNSON, Zachary Taylor, 1897- 252.5
Sins and faults, and other addresses, by Z. T. Johnson ... Wilmore, Ky., The Asbury press [c1939] 131 p. 20 cm. [BV4310.J58] 40-4652
1. Universities and colleges—Sermons. I. Title.

JONES, Bob, 1883- 252.5
Things I have learned; chapel talks at Bob Jones College. New York, Loizeaux Bros. [1952] 224p. 20cm. [BV4310.J59] 54-40323
1. Universities and colleges—Sermons. 2. Sermons, American. I. Title.

KRUENER, Harry H 252.55
Specifically to youth; a book of sermons. [1st ed.] New York, Harper [1959] 146p. 22cm. [BV4310.K76] 59-7152
1. Universities and colleges—Sermons. 2. Sermons, American. I. Title.

MCCLELLAND, Clarence Paul, 1883- 252.5
Question marks and exclamation points, by Clarence Paul McClelland ... Chicago, Ill., and Crawfordsville, Ind., The Lakeside press, 1935. xi p. 2 l., 201 p. 19 1/2 cm. [BV4310.M125] 36-35745
1. Universities and colleges—Sermons. I. Title.

MCCONNELL, Francis John, bp., 1871- 252.
Christian focus; a series of college sermons, by Francis J. McConnell ... Cincinnati, Jennings & Graham; New York, Eaton & Mains [c1911] 229 p. 19 1/2 cm. "These sermons were delivered in Appleton chapel, Harvard university, during a two years' service as a member of the Board of preachers of the university." [BV4310.M15] 11-21879
1. Universities and colleges—Sermons. 2. Sermons, American. I. Title.

MADSEN, Thorvald Berner. 252.55
'What is your life?' and other chapel challenges. Minneapolis, Free Church Publications [1960] 88p. 18cm. [BV4310.M32] 61-21729
1. Universities and colleges—Sermons. 2. Students— Religious life. I. Title.

NEILSON, William Allan, 1869- 378.04
Intellectual honesty, and other addresses, being mainly chapel talks at Smith college, by William Allan Neilson. Litchfield, Conn., The Prospect press, 1940. xi, 134 p. 21 cm. [BV4313.N4] 41-1487
1. Universities and colleges—Sermons. I. Title.

NEILSON, William Allan, 1869-1946. 378.04
Intellectual honesty, and other addresses being mainly chapel talks at Smith College. Northampton, Mass., Hampshire Bookshop, 1956. 122p. illus. 21cm. [BV4313.N4 1956] 56-33587
1. Universities and colleges—Sermons. I. Title.

NEILSON, William Allan, 1869-1946. 378.04
Intellectual honesty, and other addresses, being mainly chapel talks at Smith College. Northampton, Mass., Hampshire Bookshop, 1956. 122p. illus. 21cm. [BV4313.N4 1956] 56-33587
1. Universities and colleges—Sermons. I. Title.

NIEBUHR, Reinhold, 1892- 352.5
Discerning the signs of the times; sermons for today and tomorrow, by Reinhold Niebuhr. New York, C. Scribner's sons, 1946. x p., 1 l., 194 p. 21 cm. [BV4310.N5] 46-39253
1. Universties and colleges—Sermons. 2. Sermons, American. I. Title.

NOONTIME messages in a college chapel; sixty-nine short addresses to young people by twenty-five well-known preachers. Boston, Chicago, The Pilgrim press [c1917] viii, 181 p. 20 cm. [BV4310.N7] 17-30764 252.
1. Universities and colleges—Sermons.

NORRIS, Louis William. 252.5
The good new days. New York, Bookman Associates [1956] 132p. 23cm. [BV4310.N74] 56-58669
1. Universities and colleges—Sermons. 2. Sermons, American. I. Title.

PARK, William Edgar, 1909- 252.5
Narrow is the way, by William E. Park ... New York, The Macmillan company, 1945. ix p., 1 l., 170 p. 19 cm. "First printing." [BV4310.P33] 45-1883
1. Universities and colleges—Sermons. 2. Sermons, American. I. Title.

PARK, William Edgar, 1909- 252.5
The quest for inner peace, by William E. Park ... New York, The Macmillan company, 1947. x p., 1 l., 207 p. 19 1/2 cm. "First printing." [BV4310.P332] 47-1971
1. Universities and colleges—Sermons. 2. Sermons, American. I. Title.

PEABODY, Francis Greenwood, 1847- 252.
Mornings in the college chapel; short addresses to young men on personal religion, by Francis Greenwood Peabody ... 2d series. Boston and New York, Houghton, Mifflin and company, 1907. xi, 233, [1] p. 18 cm. [BV4310.P47 1907] 7-37984
1. Universities and colleges—Sermons. I. Title.

PEABODY, Francis Greenwood, 1847- 252.
Sunday evenings in the college chapel; sermons to young men, by Francis Greenwood Peabody ... Boston and New York, Houghton Mifflin company, 1911. ix p., 1 l., 300 p., 1 l. 18 cm. [BV4310.P515] 11-27928
1. Universities and college—Sermons. I. Title.

PEABODY, Francis Greenwood, 1847-1936. 252.
Sundays in college chapels since the war; sermons and addresses, by Francis Greenwood Peabody ... Boston and New York, Houghton Mifflin company, 1921. ix p., 1 l., 222 p., 1 l. 18 cm. (His The college chapel series. vol. v) [BV4310.P52] 21-21622
1. Universities and colleges—Sermons. I. Title.

PRINCE, Samuel Henry. 252.5
The legacy of adoration; homiliae Columbiae. With a foreword by Grayson Kirk. [1st ed.] New York, Exposition Press [1955] 73p. 21cm. (Exposition-university book) [BV4310.P68] 54-12992
1. Universities and colleges—Sermons. I. Title.

PURDUE university, Lafayette, Ind. 252.5
Addresses and records; the convocations for worship, 1934-1940. [Lafayette, Ind.] Purdue university, 1941. 159 p. 24 cm. [BV4310.P8] 41-46204
1. Universities and colleges—Sermons. 2. Sermons, American. I. Title. II. Title: The convocations for worship, 1934-1940.

REID, Albert Clayton, 1894- 252.5
100 chapel talks. combined ed., containing the talks originally published in Invitation to Worship and Resources for Worship Nashville, Abingdon Press [c1955] 304p. 18cm. [BV4310.R43] 55-5043
1. Universities and colleges—Sermons. 2. Sermons, American. 3. Devotional literature. I. Title.

RUSSELL, Elbert, 1871- 252.5
A book of chapel talks [by] Elbert Russell ... Nashville, Cokesbury press [c1935] 222 p., 1 l. 20 cm. "Talks and addresses ... presented at Duke university."--Pref. [BV4310.R8] 35-12053
1. Universities and colleges—Sermons. I. Title. II. Title: Chapel talks.

RUSSELL, Elbert, 1871- 252.5
More chapel talks, by Elbert Russell ... Nashville, Cokesbury press [c1938] 222 p., 1 l. 20 cm. [BV4310.R83] 38-15165
1. Universities and colleges—Sermons. I. Title. II. Title: Chapel talks.

SALLMON, William Henry, 1866-1938, ed. 252.
The culture of Christian manhood; Sunday morning in Gattell chapel, Yale university, edited by William H. Salmon New York, Chicago [etc.] Fleming H. Revell company, 1897. 2 p. l., 7-309 p. 18 1/2 cm. [BV4310.S3] 44-52676
1. Universities and colleges—Sermons. 2. Sermons, American. I. Title.

SAVAGE, Thomas G. 252'.02
And now a word from our Creator [by] Thomas G. Savage. Chicago, Loyola University Press [1972] xix, 280 p. illus. 24 cm. [BX1756.Z8S28] 72-1370 ISBN 0-8294-0213-6 5.95
1. Catholic Church—Sermons. 2. Universities and colleges—Sermons. 3. Sermons, American. I. Title.

SITTLER, Joseph 252.55
The care of the earth, and other university sermons. Philadelphia, Fortress [c.1964] ix, 149p. 18cm. Bibl. 64-20114 2.45 pap.,
1. Universities and colleges—Sermons. 2. Sermons, American. I. Title.

SITTLER, Joseph. 252.55
The care of the earth, and other university sermons. Philadelphia, Fortress Press [1964] ix, 149 p. 18 cm. (The Preacher's paperback library, v. 2) Bibliographical footnotes. [BV4310.S47] 64-20114
1. Universities and colleges — Sermons. 2. Sermons, American. I. Title.

SPERRY, Willard Learoyd, 1882- 252.5
Rebuilding our world; sermons in the Harvard college chapel [by] Willard L. Sperry ... New York, London, Harper & brothers [1943] xi, 157 p. 19 1/2 cm. "First edition." [BV4310.S54] 43-16987

1. Universities and colleges—Sermons. 2. Sermons, American. I. Title.

SPERRY, Willard Learoyd, 1882- 252.5
Sermons preached at Harvard. [1st ed.] New York, Harper [1953] 188p. 22cm. [BV4310.S56] 53-8374
1. Universities and colleges—Sermons. 2. Sermons, American. I. Title.

THOBURN, Wilbur Wilson, 1859-1899. 252.
In terms of life; sermons and talks to college students, by Wilbur W. Thoburn ... Stanford University, Calif., The University, 1899. 242 p., 1 l. front. (port.) 18 1/2 cm. [BV4310.T5] 99-4024
1. Universities and colleges—Sermons. I. Title.

WARNER, Amos Griswold, 1861-1900. 252
Lay sermons. With a biographical sketch by George Elliott Howard. Baltimore, Johns Hopkins Press, 1904. [New York, Johnson Reprint Corp., 1973] p. Original ed. issued as Notes supplementary to the Johns Hopkins studies in historical and political science. Bibliography: p. [BV4310.W36 1973] 73-3355 pap. 4.00
1. Universities and colleges—Sermons. 2. Sermons, American. I. Title. II. Series: Johns Hopkins University. Studies in historical and political science. Notes supplementary.

WAYLAND, Francis, 1796-1865. 252.
Salvation by Christ. A series of discourses on some of the most important doctrines of the gospel. By Francis Wayland. Boston, Gould and Lincoln; New York, Sheldon, Blakeman & co.; [etc., etc.] 1859. viii, 386 p. 20 cm. A revised and enlarged edition of the author's "University sermons. Sermons delivered in the chapel of Brown university." published 1849. cf. Pref. [BV4310.W37 1859] 47-34687
1. Universities and colleges—Sermons. 2. Baptists—Sermons. 3. Sermons, American. I. Title.

Universities and colleges—United States

GREELEY, Andrew M., 1928- 378.73
The changing Catholic college, by Andrew M. Greeley, with the assistance of William Van Cleve [and] Grace Ann Carroll. Chicago, Aldine Pub. Co. [1967] xiii, 226 p. 23 cm. (National Opinion Research Center. Monographs in social research, 13) Bibliography: p. 221-222. [LC501.G68] 67-27393
1. Catholic Church in the United States—Education. 2. Universities and colleges—United States. I. Van Cleve, William. II. Carroll, Grace Ann. III. Title. IV. Series.

NORTH Carolina. University. University extension division. 271
... University of North Carolina extension bulletin. vol. i, no. 1- Sept. 1, 1921- Chapel Hill, N. C., The University, 1921- v. illus. 23 cm. At head of title: University extension division. "Succeeding and combining University of North Carolina extension leaflets, volumes i-iv, and the University of North Carolina record, Extension series 1-41." [LC6301.N43] [LC6301.N48 1921] 271 21-27278
I. Title.

PRESBYTERIAN Church in the U.S.A. Board of Christian Education. 377.85173
The Presbyterian college handbook, 1955-1956. Philadelphia [1955] 95 p. illus. 26 cm. [LC580.P7] 55-12680
1. Presbyterian Church in the U.S.A.—Education. 2. Universities and colleges—United States. I. Title.

WELCH, Herbert, bp., 1862- 377.
The Christian college, by Herbert Welch...Henry Churchill King...[and] Thomas Nicholson...with introduction by William H. Crawford... New York, Cincinnati The Methodist book concern [c1916] 78 p. 19 cm. [LC383.W4] 16-17378
1. Universities and colleges—U.S. I. King, Henry Churchill, 1858-1934. II. Nicholson, Thomas, 1862- III. Title.
Contents omitted.

Universities and colleges—United States—Administration.

COTTRELL, Donald Peery, 1902- 377'.8'41335
Instruction and instructional facilities in the colleges of the United Lutheran Church in America; a study of the organization, administration, and character of instruction and instructional facilities. New York, Bureau of Publications, Teachers College, Columbia University, 1929. [New York, AMS Press, 1972, ie. 1973] viii, 138 p. 22 cm. Reprint of the 1929 ed., issued in series: Teachers College, Columbia University. Contributions to education, no. 376. Originally presented as the author's thesis, Columbia. Published also as pt. III, chapters 1-6 of the Survey of higher education for the United Lutheran Church in America, 1929. Bibliography: p. 135-138. [LC574.C6 1972] 79-176672 ISBN 0-404-55376-1 10.00
1. United Lutheran Church in America—Education. 2. Universities and colleges—United States—Administration. 3. College teaching. I. Title. II. Series: Columbia University. Teachers College. Contributions to education, no. 376.

MARTIN, Theodore Krinn. 378.75
The administration of instruction in Southern Baptist colleges and universities. Nashville, Bureau of Publications, George Peabody College for Teachers, 1949. xiii, 159 p. 24 cm. (Contribution to education no. 414, George Peabody College for Teachers) Bibliography: p. 158-159. [LC562.M37] 49-49342
1. Universities and colleges—U.S.—Administration. 2. Southern Baptist convention—Education. I. Title. II. Series: George Peabody College for Teachers, Nashville. Contribution to education no. 414

Universities and colleges — United States — Directories

JESUIT Research Council Of America
Profile of Jesuit universities and colleges of America. Washington, 1964. 99 l. 30 cm. 64-52603
1. Catholic Church in the U.S. — Education — Direct. 2. Jesuits — Education — Direct. 3. Universities and colleges — U.S. — Direct. I. Title. II. Title: Jesuit universities and colleges of America.

Universities and colleges—United States—History.

GRESHAM, Perry Epler. 286'.6'0924 B
Campbell and the colleges. Nashville, Disciples of Christ Historical Society, 1973. 114 p. 22 cm. (The Forrest F. Reed lectures for 1971) Includes bibliographical references. [LB695.C352G73] 73-161134
1. Campbell, Alexander, 1788-1866. 2. Universities and colleges—United States—History. I. Title. II. Series: The Reed lectures, 1971.

Universities and colleges United States Religion.

OVERHOLT, William A. 259
Religion in American colleges and universities [by] William A. Overholt. Washington, American College Personnel Association [1970] 60 p. 28 cm. (Student personnel series, no. 14) Bibliography: p. 58-60. [BV1610.O9] 71-22569 2.50
1. Universities and colleges—U.S.—Religion. 2. College students—Religious life. I. Title. II. Series.

Universities and colleges—United States—Religion—Addresses, essays, lectures.

THE Recovery of spirit in higher education : Christian and Jewish ministries in campus life / edited by Robert Rankin, with Myron B. Bloy, Jr., David A. Hubbard, Parker J. Palmer. New York : Seabury Press, 1980. x, 340 p. ; 24 cm. "A Crossroad book." Includes bibliographical references. [LC383.R36] 19 80-20770 ISBN 0-8164-0469-0 : 14.95 378
1. Universities and colleges—United States—Religion—Addresses, essays, lectures. 2. Church and college in the United States—Addresses, essays, lectures. I. Rankin, Robert, 1915-

Universities' Mission to Central Africa.

WILSON, George Herbert, 1870- 266.3'67
The history of the Universities' Mission to Central Africa. Freeport, N.Y., Books for Libraries Press [1971] xvi, 278 p. illus. 23 cm. Reprint of the 1936 ed. [BV3520.W5 1971] 71-169781 ISBN 0-8369-6601-5
1. Universities' Mission to Central Africa. 2. Church of England—Missions. 3. Missions—Africa, Central. I. Title.

University Park, Tex. University Park Methodist church.

A history of University Park Methodist church, Dallas, Texas, 1939-1959. [Dallas, 1960] 80p. 20cm.
1. University Park, Tex. University Park Methodist church. I. Brown, Hallie Richardson.

Unmarried mothers.

TERKELSEN, Helen E. 253.5
Counseling the unwed mother [by] Helen E. Terkelsen. Philadelphia, Fortress [1967, c. 1964] 144p. 21cm. (Successful pastoral counseling ser.) [HV700.5.T4] 1.50 pap.,
1. Unmarried mothers. 2. Pastoral counseling. I. Title. II. Series.

TERKELSEN, Helen E 253.5
Counseling the unwed mother [by] Helen E. Terkelson. Englewood Cliffs, N.J., Prentice-Hall [1964] 144 p. 21 cm. (Successful pastoral counseling series) Bibliography: p. 131-135. [HV700.5.T4] 64-20746
1. Unmarried mothers. 2. Pastoral counseling. I. Title. II. Series.

Upanishads.

JOHNSTON, Charles, 1867- 294.
The song of life, by Charles Johnston. Flushing, N. Y., The author, 1901. 69 p. 17 cm. A translation of the "dialogue of Janaka and the sage," preceded by "a modern paraphrase of the Teachings". cf. Pref. Contents.--Preface.--The mystery teaching.--Drama of the mysteries (Brihadaranyaka upanishad, iv, 3-4) [BL1120.J6 1901] 1-31633
I. Upanishads. Brihadaranyaka upanished. II. Title.

MISHRA, Rammurti S., M.D. 294.54
Kena Upanisad. Ed. by Ann Adman. Orientala [dist.] N. Syracuse 12, N.Y., 102 David Dr. Yoga Soc. of Syracuse, [c.1963] 75p. 22cm. 1.75 pap.,
I. Title.

THE Upanishads. 891.21
Tr. from the Sanskrit with introductions embodying a general survey and the metaphysics and psychology of the Upanishads, and with notes and explanations based on the commentary of Sri Sankaracharya, the great ninth-century philosopher and saint of India, by Swami, Nikhilananda. [1st ed.] New York, Harper [1949- v. 22 cm. Contents.v. 1. Katha, Isa, Kena. and Mundaka. [BL1120.A3N5] 49-9558
I. Nikhilananda, Swani, ed. and tr. II. Sankaracarya. III. Upanishads. English.

UPANISHADS. 891.21
The principal Upanisads; edited with introd., text, translation, and notes by S. Radhakrishnan. New York, Harper [c1953]

958p. 22cm. [BL1120.A3R32 1953a] [BL1120.A3R32 1953a] 294.1 53-10977 53-10977
I. Upanishads. English. II. Radhakrishnan, Sarvepaill, Sir 1888- ed. and tr. III. Title.

UPANISHADS. 294.5'921
Aitareyopanisad. English & Sanskrit.
Aitareya Upanisat. Translated by Srisa Chandra Vidyarnava and Mohan Lal Sandal. Allahabad, Panini Office, 1925. [New York, AMS Press, 1974] p. Original ed. issued as v. 30, pts. 1-2 of The Sacred books of the Hindus. English and Sanskrit; commentary in English. [BL1120.A432 1974] 73-3823 ISBN 0-404-57830-6 14.50
I. Vasu, Srisa Chandra, rai bahadur, 1861-1918?, ed. II. Sandal, Mohan Lal, ed. III. Title. IV. Series: The Sacred books of the Hindus, v. 30, pts. 1-2.

THE Upanishads; breath of the eternal. Principal texts selected and translated from the original Sanskrit by Swami Prabhavananda and F. Manchester. [New York] New American Library [1957] 128p. (Menior book MD 194) A Mentor religious classics.
I. Upanishads. II. prabhavananda, Swami, 1893-

UPANISHADS. English. 294.
The great Upanishads... translated by Charles Johnston. New York, The Quarterly book department [c1927]- v. 19 1/2 cm. [BL1120.A3J6] 27-10828
I. Johnston, Charles, 1867- tr. II. Title.

UPANISHADS. English 294.5'921
The ten principal Upanishads / put into English by Shree Purohit, swami, and W. B. Yeats. New York : Macmillan, 1975, c1937. 158 p. ; 21 cm. [BL1120.A3P8 1975] 75-15999 ISBN 0-02-071550-1 pbk. : 1.95
I. Purohit, swami, 1882- II. Yeats, William Butler, 1865-1939. III. Title.

UPANISHADS. English. 891.2
The ten principal Upanishads; put into English by Shree Purohit, swami, and W. B. Yeats. New York, The Macmillan company, 1937. 2 p. l., 7-158, [1] p. 22 cm. [BL1120.A3P8 1937a] 37-20457
I. Purohit, swami, 1882- tr. II. Yeats, William Butler, 1865-1939, tr. III. Title.

UPANISHADS. English. 294.592
The Upanisads. Translated by F. Max Muller. New York, Dover Publications [1962] 2 v. 22 cm. (The Sacred books of the East, v. 1, 15) Contents.Contents.—pt. 1. Chandogya Upanisad. Talavakara (Kena) Upanisad. Aitareya Upanisad. Kausitaki Upanisad. Vajasaneyi (Isa) Upanisad.—pt. 2. Katha Upanisad. Mundaka Upanisad. Taittiriya Upanisad. Brhadaranyaka Upanisad. Svetasvatara Upanisad. Prasna Upanisad. Maitraayami Upanisad. [BL1120.A3M78 1962] 62-53180
I. Muller, Friedrich Max, 1823-1900, ed. and tr. II. Series: The Sacred books of the East (New York) v. 1, 15.

UPANISHADS. English. 294.592
The Upanishads [2 pts.] Tr. by F. Max Miiller [Gloucester, Mass., P. Smith, 1963] 2 pts. (320; 350p.) 22cm. Contents.pt. 1. Chandogya Upanisad. Talavakara (Kena) Upanisad. Aitareya Upanisad. Kausitaki Upanisad. Vajasaneyi Upanisad.--Pt. 2. Katha Upanisad. Mundaka Upanisad. Taittiriya Upanisad. Brhadaranvaka Upanisad. Svetasvatara Upanisad. Prasna Upanisad. Maitrayani Upanisad. (Sacred bks. of the East, v.1, v.15. Dover bks. rebound) 4.00 ea.,
I. Miiller. Friedrich Max, 1823-1900, ed. and tr. II. Title. III. Series: The Sacred books of the East (New York) v.1, 15

UPANISHADS English 294.5921
The Upanishads. Translations from the Sanskrit with an introd. by Juan Mascaro. Baltimore, Penguin Books [1965] 142 p. 19 cm. (The Penguin classics, L163) [BL1120.A3M32] 65-29745
I. Mascaro, Juan, ed. and tr. II. Title.

UPANISHADS. English. 294.1
The Upanishads, translated by F. Max Muller... Oxford, The Clarendon press, 1879-84. 2 v. 22 1/2 cm. (Added t.-p.: The sacred books of the East...vol. I, XV) The texts of each volume preceded by introduction. Contents.pt. I. The Khandogya-upanishad. The Talavakara-upanishad. The Altareya-aranyaka. The Kaushitaki-brahmana-upanishad and the Vagasaneyl-samhita-upanishad.--pt. II. The Katha-upanishad. The Mundaka-upanishad. The Taittiriyaka-upanishad. The Brihadaranyaka-upanishad. The Svetasvatara-upanishad. The Maitrayana-brahmana-upanishad. [BL1010.S3 vol. 1, 15] 32-5790
I. Muller, Friedrich Max, 1823-1900, tr. II. Title.

UPANISHADS. English. 891.2
The Upanishads, translated by the Rt. Hon. F. Max Muller... New York, The Christian literature company, 1897. 2 v. in 1. front. (port.) tables. 23 cm. (Half-title: The sacred books of the East...American ed., vol. I) Comprises v. 1 and 15 of the Oxford edition of the Sacred books of the East. "Transliteration of Oriental alphabets": [vol. I] p. xlviii-lv. [BL1010.S34 vol. 1] (290.8) 32-5219
I. Muller, Friedrich Max, 1823-1900, ed. and tr. II. Title.

UPANISHADS. English & 294.5'921
Sanskrit. Selections.
Isa, Kena, Katha, Prasna, Mundaka and Manduka Upanisads. Vol. 1. 2d ed. Allahabad, Panini Office, 1911. [New York, AMS Press, 1974] 320 p. 23 cm. Original ed. issued as v. 1 of The Sacred books of the Hindus. First ed., 1909-10, issued in two pts., pt. 1 with general title, The Upanisads, and pt. 2 with title, Chhandogya Upanisad. The remaining Upanishads appeared as independent vols. Includes Anandatirtha's commentary on each of the six Upanishads. Translated by Srisa Chandra Vasu. [BL1120.A3V37 1974] 73-4980 ISBN 0-404-57801-2
I. Anandatirtha, surnamed Madhvacarya, 1197-1276. II. Vasu, Srisa Chandra, rai bahadur, 1861-1918?, tr. III. Title. IV. Series: The Sacred books of the Hindus, v. 1.

UPANISHADS, English, 294.5921
Selections
The Upanishads. Tr. from Sanskrit, introd. by Juan Mascaro. Baltimore, Penguin [c.1965] 142p. 19cm. (Penguin classics, L163) [BL1120.A3M32] 65-29745 .95 pap.,
I. Mascaro, Juan, ed. and tr. II. Title.

UPANISHADS. 294.5'921
Isopanisad. English.
Sri Isopanisad / with introd., translation and authorized purports by A. C. Bhaktivedanta Swami. New York ; Bombay : The Bhaktivedanta Book Trust, 1974. xi, 139 p. : col. ill. ; 20 cm. Includes index. [BL1120.A522 1974] 75-500991 ISBN 0-912776-03-X pbk. : 1.95
I. Bhaktivedanta Swami, A. C., 1896- II. Title.

UPANISHADS. 294.5'921
Maitrayaniyopanisad. English & Sanskrit.
The Maitri Upanisat. Translated by Srisa Chandra Vidyarnava and Mohan Lal Sandal. Allahabad, Panini Office [1926. New York, AMS Press, 1974] p. cm. Original ed. issued as v. 31, pt. 2 of The Sacred books of the Hindus. [BL1120.A6252 1974] 73-3827 ISBN 0-404-57832-2 9.00
I. Vasu, Srisa Chandra, rai bahadur, 1861-1918?, ed. II. Sandal, Mohan Lal, ed. III. Title. IV. Series: The Sacred books of the Hindus, v. 31, pt. 2.

UPANISHADS. Selections. 294.1
English.
The spirit of the Upanishads; or, The aphorisms of the wise; a collection of texts, aphorisms, sayings, proverbs, etc., from "The Upanishads", or sacred writings of India, compiled and adapted from over fifty authorities, expressing the cream of the Hindu philosophical thought... Chicago, Ill., The Yogi publication society, 1907. 3 p. l., 5-85 p. 20 cm. [BL1120.A3Y6] 7-13918
I. Title.

UPANISHADS. Selections. 891.21
English.
... Three Upanishads: Aitareya upanishad, the origin of soul; Svetasvatara upanishad, sons of immortality; Prashna upanishad, the path of the self. By Swami Premananda. Washington, D.C., Self-realization fellowship [1944] 3 p. l., 13-109 p. front. (port.) 19 1/2 cm. "Translated into English from the original Sanskrit text by Swami Premananda."--3d prelim. leaf. [BL1120.A3P65] 44-26224
I. Premananda, swami, 1903- ed. and tr. II. Washington, D.C. Self-realization fellowship (Non-sectarian church) III. Upanishads. Aitareya-upanishad. IV. Upanishads. Svetasvatara-upanishad. V. Upanishads. Prasna-upanishad. VI. Title.

VASU, Srisa Chandra, 294.5'921
rai bahadur, 1861-1918?
Studies in the first six Upanisads; and the Isa and Kena Upanisads, with the commentary of Sankara. Translated by Srisa Chandra Vidyarnava. Allahabad. Panini Office, 1919. [New York, AMS Press, 1974] 152 p. 23 cm. Original ed. issued as v. 22, pt. 1 of The Sacred books of the Hindus. Includes translations in English of the Isopanisad and the Kenopanisad, with the respective commentaries of Sankaracarya, the Isopanisadbhasya and the Kenopanisadbhasya, and the commentary of Anantacarya on the Isopanisad, the Isavasyabhasya. Includes some slokas in Sanskrit. Intended to serve as an introd. to the author's translations of the Upanishads. [BL1120.V37 1974] 73-3814 ISBN 0-404-57822-5
1. Upanishads. I. Sankaracarya. Isopanisadbhasya. English. 1974. II. Sankaracarya. Kenopanisadbhasya. English. 1974. III. Anantacarya. Isavasyabhasya. English. 1974. IV. Upanishads. Isopanisad. English. 1974. V. Upanishads. Kenopanisad. English. 1974. VI. Title. VII. Series: The Sacred books of the Hindus, v. 22, pt. 1.

Upanishads—Bibliography.

UPANISHADS. English. 294.5'921
The thirteen principal Upanishads. Translated from the Sanskrit with an outline of the philosophy of the Upanishads. 2d ed., rev. London, New York, Oxford University Press [1971] xvi, 587 p. 21 cm. (A Galaxy book, GB365) Bibliography: p. 459-515. [BL1120.A3H8 1971] 71-30455 ISBN 0-19-501490-1 3.50 (U.S.)
1. Upanishads—Bibliography. 2. Philosophy, Hindu. I. Hume, Robert Ernest, 1877-1948, tr. II. Title.

Upanishads—Criticism, interpretation, etc.

DEUSSEN, Paul, 1845-1919 294.5921
The philosophy of the Upanishads. Authorized English tr. by A. S. Geden [Magnolia, Mass., P. Smith, 1967] xiv, 429p. 22cm. (Dover bk. rebound) Unabridged, unaltered repubn. of the work orig. pub. in 1906 by T. & T. Clark [BL1120.D4 1966] 4.50
1. Upanishads—Criticism, interpretation, etc. I. Title.

DEUSSEN, Paul, 1845- 294.5921
1919.
The philosophy of the Upanishads. Authorized English translation by A. S. Geden. New York, Dover Publications [1966] xiv, 429 p. 22 cm. Translation first published in 1906. "The present work forms the second part of my General history of philosophy." [BL1120.D4 1966] 66-20325
1. Upanishads—Criticism, interpretation, etc. I. Title.

PANDIT, Madhav Pundalik, 294.592
1918-
The Upanishads, gateways of Knowledge [Hollywood, Calif., Vedanta Pr., 1961, c.] 1960[ ] 174p. 25cm. 61-65699 3.00 bds.,
1. Upanishads—Criticism, interpretation, etc. I. Title.

RADHAKRISHNAN, Sarvepalli, 294.1
Sir 1888-
The philosophy of the Upanisads, by S. Radhakrishnan, with a foreword by Rabindranath Tagore and an introduction by Edmond Holmes ... London, G. Allen & Unwin ltd.; New York, The Macmillan company [1924] xv, 1431 p. 22 cm. "First published in 1924." Reprint of the section on the Upanisads from the author's Indian philosophy cf. p. [vii] [BL1120.A3R3] 25-8391
1. Upanishads—Criticism, interpretation, etc. 2. Philosophy, Hindu. I. Title.

RADHAKRISHNAN, Sarvepalli, 294.1
Sir 1888-
The philosophy of the Upanisads, by S. Radhakrishnan, with a foreword by Rabindranath Tagore and an introduction by Edmond Holmes... London, G. Allen & Unwin ltd.; New York, The Macmillan company [1935] xv, 143, [1] p. 22 cm. "Revised second edition, 1935." Reprint of the section on the Upanisads from the author's Indian philosophy. cf. p. [vii] "References": p. [9] [BL1120.A3R3 1935] 38-30039
1. Upanishads—Criticism, interpretation, etc. 2. Philosophy, Hindu. I. Title.

SANDAL, Mohan Lal. 294.5'921
Philosophical teachings in the Upanisads. [Allahabad, Panini office, 1926. New York, AMS Press, 1974] p. cm. Original ed. issued as extra v. 5 in The Sacred books of the Hindus. [BL1120.S18 1974] 73-3831 ISBN 0-404-57849-7 57.50
1. Upanishads—Criticism, interpretation, etc. I. Title. II. Series: The Sacred books of the Hindus, extra v. 5.

UPANISHADS. 294.5'921
Chandogyopanisad. English & Sanskrit.
Chhandogya Upanisad, with the commentary of Sri Madhvacharya, called also Anandatirtha. Translated by Srisa Chandra Vasu. Allahabad, Panini Office, 1910. [New York, AMS Press, 1974] p. Original ed. issued as v. 3 of The Sacred books of the Hindus. Originally published as pt. 2 of The Upanisads, issued as v. 1 of the series. English and Sanskrit; commentary in English. [BL1120.A452 1974] 73-3788 ISBN 0-404-57803-9 44.50
I. Vasu, Srisa Chandra, rai bahadur, 1861-1918?, ed. II. Anandatirtha, surnamed Madhvacarya, 1197-1276. Chandogyopanisadbhasya. English. 1974. III. Title. IV. Series: The Sacred books of the Hindus

UPANISHADS. 294.5'921
Taittiriyopanisad. English & Sanskrit.
The Tait[t]iriya Upanisat. Translated by Srisa Chandra Vidyarnava and Mohan Lal Sandal. Allahabad, Panini Press, 1925. [New York, AMS Press, 1974] p. cm. Original ed. issued as v. 30, pt. 3 of The Sacred books of the Hindus. English and Sanskrit; commentary in English. [BL1120.A732 1974] 73-3824 ISBN 0-404-57833-0 10.00
I. Vasu, Srisa Chandra, rai bahadur, 1861-1918?, ed. II. Sandal, Mohan Lal, ed. III. Title. IV. Series: The Sacred books of the Hindus, v. 30, pt. 3.

Upanishads—Criticism, interpretation, etc.—Addresses, essays, lectures.

RAMA, Swami, 1925- 128'.5
Life here and hereafter / Swami Rama. Glenview, Ill. : Himalayan International Institute of Yoga Science & Philosophy of USA, c1976. 168 p. ; 22 cm. [BD444.R25] 76-361129
1. Upanishads—Criticism, interpretation, etc.—Addresses, essays, lectures. 2. Death—Addresses, essays, lectures. 3. Atman—Addresses, essays, lectures. 4. Absolute, The—Addresses, essays, lectures. I. Title.

Upanishads. Kathaka-upanishad—Criticism, interpretation, etc.

RAJANEESH, Acharya, 294.5'9218
1931-
The supreme doctrine : discourses on the Kenopanishad / Bhagwan Shree Rajneesh ; compilation Ma Yoga Vivek ; editors, Swami Prem Chinmaya, Ma Ananda Prem. London ; Boston : Routledge & Kegan Paul, 1980. xiv, 468 p. : ports. ; 22 cm. [BL1124.7.K46R34 1980] 19 80-49960 ISBN 0-7100-0572-5 (pbk.) : 14.95
1. Upanishads. Kenopanisad—Criticism, interpretation, etc. I. Yoga Vivek, Ma. II. Yoga Cinmaya, Swami. III. Ananda Prem, Ma. IV. Title.

UPANISHADS. Kathaka- 294.1
upanishad.
... Katha unpanishad, dialogue of death and vision of immortality, by Swami Premananda. Washington, D.C., Self-realization fellowship [1943] 3 p. l., 13-75 p. 16 cm. "Translated into English from

the original Sanskrit text."--3d prelim. leaf. [BL1120.A53P7] [891.21] 43-14728
1. Premananda, swami, 1903- ed. and tr. II. Washington, D.C. Self-realization fellowship (Non-sectarian church) III. Title.

UPANISHADS. Kathaka-upanishad. 891.21
The Katha upanishad; an introductory study in the Hindu doctrine of God and of human destiny, by Joseph Nadin Rawson... London, Oxford university press, H. Milford; Calcutta, Association press, 1934. xviii, 242 p. 23 cm. Added t.-p.: ...in grateful memory of William Carey, missionary educationist, oriental scholar... The Katha upanishad: Carey centenary volume. Published by request of the senate of Scrampore college, 1934. Includes an introduction, the Sanskrit text printed in Devanagari, a transliterated text, a translation and a commentary. "Abbreviations and bibliogrpahy of works frequently cites": p. [xiii]-xviii. [PK3521.K3 1934] 35-1408
1. God (Brahmanism) 2. Carey, William, 1761-1834. 3. Upanishads. Kathaka-upanishad—Criticism, interpretation, etc. 4. Yoga. 5. Death. 6. Immortality. I. Rawson, Joseph Nadin, ed. II. Title. III. Title: Carey centenary volume.

Upanishads. Kenopanisad—Criticism, interpretation, etc.

RAJANEESH, Acharya, 1931- 294.5'9218
The supreme doctrine : discourses on the Kenopanishad / Bhagwan Shree Rajneesh ; compilation Ma Yoga Vivek ; editors, Swami Prem Chinmaya, Ma Ananda Prem. London ; Boston : Routledge & Kegan Paul, 1980. xiv, 468 p. : ports. ; 22 cm. [BL1124.7.K46R34 1980] 19 80-49960 ISBN 0-7100-0572-5 (pbk.) : 14.95
1. Upanishads. Kenopanisad—Criticism, interpretation, etc. I. Yoga Vivek, Ma. II. Yoga Cinmaya, Swami. III. Ananda Prem, Ma. IV. Title.

Upaya (Buddhism)

PYE, Michael. 294.3'92
Skilful means : a concept in Mahayana Buddhism / Michael Pye. London : Duckworth, 1979. viii, 211 p. ; 26 cm. Includes index. Bibliography: p. 198-202. [BQ4370.P93] 79-309315 ISBN 0-7156-1266-2 : 45.00
1. Upaya (Buddhism) I. Title.
Distributed by Biblio Distribution Centre, Totowa, NJ 07511

The Upper room.

SEVRE, Leif 240.5
The story of the Upper room: 30th anniversary, March--April 1935--1965 [Planned and produced by Earle H. MacLeod. Supervised by the ed.: J. Manning Potts. Nashville, Upper Room, 1965] 96p. illus. (pt. col.) col. map (on lining papers) ports. (pt. col.) 29cm. [BV4800] 65-23640 1.00 bds..
1. The Upper room. 2. Methodist Church (United States)—Period.—Hist. I. Potts, James Manning, 1895- ed. II. MacLeod, Earl Henry. III. Title.

Ur.

WOOLLEY, Charles Leonard, Sir, 1880- 221.92
Abraham; recent discoveries and Hebrew origins, by Sir Leonard Woolley, D.LITT. New York, C. Scribner's sons, 1936. 3 p. l., 5-299 p. front. (map) 20 1/2 cm. [BS580.A3W6 1936a] 36-17874
1. Abraham, the patriarch. 2. Ur. I. Title.

Urantia Foundation, Chicago.

SADLER, William Samuel, 1907-1963. 133
A study of the master universe; a development of concepts of the Urantia book. Chicago, Second Society Foundation, c1968. xvi, 150 p. illus. 24 cm. [BP605.U75S2] 68-58958
1. Urantia Foundation, Chicago. The Urantia book. I. Title.

Urban renewal.

HARVARD Colloquium, Harvard University, 1964.
Church and synagogue in Boston renewal; address delivered at a Harvard Colloquium. [Foreword by Samuel H. Miller] Cambridge, Harvard Divinity School, 1964. 90 p. 28 cm. Cover title. 66-42818
1. Urban renewal. I. Miller, Samuel Howard, 1900- II. Harvard University. Divinity School. III. Title.

SCHALLER, Lyle E
Urban renewal and the church. Cleveland, Regional Church Planning Office [1961] 72 p., plans. (Regional Church Planning Office. Report no. 5) 63-57926
I. Title.

Urban schools.

FANTINI, Mario D. 371'.009173'2
Making urban schools work; social realities and the urban school [by] Mario Fantini [and] Gerald Weinstein. New York, Holt, Rinehart and Winston [1968] x, 62 p. illus. 23 cm. Bibliographical footnotes. [LC5115.F35] 68-31654 1.50
1. Urban schools. I. Weinstein, Gerald, joint author. II. Title.

Urbana, O. St. Paul African Methodist Episcopal church.

ARNETT, Benjamin William, bp., 1838-1906. 252.6
Centennial Thanksgiving sermon, delivered by Rev. B. W. Arnett, B.D., at St. Paul A. M. E. church, Urbana, Ohio. [Urbana] 1876. 75 p. 23 cm. [BX8481.U7S3] 26-22912
1. Urbana, O. St. Paul African Methodist Episcopal church. 2. Thanksgiving day addresses. I. Title.

Urquhart, John, 1808-1827.

ORME, William, 1787-1830. 922
Memoirs, including letters, and select remains, of John Urquhart, late of the university of St. Andrew's. By William Orme ... Boston, Crocker and Brewster; New-York, J. Leavitt, 1828. 2 v. front. (port.) 17 cm. [BR1725.U7O7 1828] 38-8160
1. Urquhart, John, 1808-1827. I. Title.

[ORME, William] 1787-1830. 922
Memoirs of John Urquhart. Compiled for the American Sunday school union, and revised by the Committee of publication. Philadelphia, American Sunday school union, 1832. 174 p. 15 cm. Based on William Orme's Memoirs, including letters, and select remains, of John Urquhart. [BR1725.U7O7 1832] 38-7132
1. Urquhart, John, 1808-1827. I. American Sunday-school union. II. Title.

ORME, William, 1787-1830. 922
Memoris, including letters, and select remains, of John Urquhart, late of the university of St. Andrew's. By William Orme. With a prefatory notice and recommendation, by Alexander Duff ... Philadelphia, Presbyterian board of publication [1855] 420 p. front. (port.) 19 cm. [BR1725.U7O7 1855] 38-7133
1. Urquhart, John, 1808-1827. I. Duff, Alexander, 1806-1878. II. Presbyterian church in the U. S. A. (Old school) Board of publication. III. Title.

Ursulines.

ARON, Marguerite. 271.974
The Ursulines; tr. from the original French by Mother M. Angela Griffin. New York, D. X. McMullen Co. [1947] xiii. 208p. 20 cm. [BX4542.A7] 48-6291
1. Ursulines. I. Griffin, Angela, Mother, tr. II. Title.

BRESLIN, Mary Thomas. 922.244
Anne de Xainctonge, her life and spirituality. Kingston, NSociety of St. Ursula of the Blessed Virgin, 1957. 273p. illus. 24cm. Includes bibliography. [BX4705.X3B7] 57-9169
1. Xainctonge, Anne de, 1567-1621. 2. Ursulines. I. Title.

BRESLIN, Mary Thomas. 922.244
Anne de Xainctonge, her life and spirituality. Kingston, N. Y., Society of St. Ursula of the Blessed Virgin, 1957. 273p. illus. 24cm. Includes bibliography. [BX4705.X3B7] 57-9169
1. Xainctonge, Anne de, 1567-1621. 2. Ursulines. I. Title.

ERNEST, Brother, 1897- 922.245
To the end of time; the story of St. Angela Merici. Illus. by Rosemary Donatino. Notre Dame, Ind., Dujarie Press [1951] 103 p. illus. 24 cm. [BX4700.A45E7] 51-6622
1. Angela Merici, Saint, 1474-1540. 2. Ursulines. I. Title.

FRANCIS d'assisi mother, 1881- 922.245
Sant' Angela of the Ursulines, by Mother Francis d'Assisi, O. S. U.; the story of Angela Merici, foundress of the Ursulines, who was born in the year of Our Lord, 1474, and died in the oror of sanctity, 1540. Milwaukee, The Bruce publishing company [c1934] ix, 174 p. front., plates. 20 cm. (Secular name: Katherine Louise Myers) Bibliography: p. 174. [BX4700.A45F7] 35-399
1. Angela Merici, Saint, 1474-1540. 2. Ursulines. I. Title.

FRANCIS d'assisi mother, 1881- 922.245
Sant' Angela of the Ursulines, by Mother Francis d'Assisi, O. S. U.; the story of Angela Merici, foundress of the Ursulines, who was born in the year of Our Lord, 1474, and died in the odor of sanctity, 1540. Milwauke, The Bruce publishing company [c1934] viii p., 2 l., 3-174 p. front., plates. 20 cm. "Second printing." [Secular name: Katherine Louise Myers] Biliography: p. 174. [BX4700.A45F7 1934a] 35-13421
1. Angela Merici, Saint, 1474-1540. 2. Ursulines. I. Title.

MARY Gertrude, Sister, O. S. U., 1899- 271.974
Ursulines in training; a study based upon the counsels of Saint Angela Merici. Toledo [1956] 172p. illus. 22cm. [BX4542.M25] 57-15266
1. Ursulines. I. Angela Merici, Saint, 1474-1540. II. Title.

PARENTY, Francois Joseph, 1799-1875. 922.
Life of Saint Angela Merici. Of Brescia: foundress of the Order of Saint Ursula. By the Abbe Parenty ... With an account of the order in Ireland, Canada and the United States, by John Gilmary Shea. Published with the approbation of the Rt. Rev. Bishop of Philadelphia. Philadelphia, P. F. Cunningham [c1857] iv, [5]-251 p. 17 cm. [BX4700.A45P3 1857] 36-3414
1. Angela Merici, Saint, 1474-1540. 2. Ursulines. I. Shea, John Dawson Gilmary, 1824-1892. II. Title.

PARENTY, Francois Joseph, 1799-1875. 922.245
Life of Saint Angela Merici, of Brescia; foundress of the Order of Saint Ursula. By the Abbe Parenty ... With an account of the order in Ireland, Canada and the United States, by John Gilmary Shea. Published with the approbation of the Rt. Rev. Bishop of Philadelphia. Philadelphia, P. F. Cunningham, 1858. iv, [5]-251 p. 17 cm. [BX4700.A45P3 1858] 35-37810
1. Angela Merici, Saint, 1474-1540. 2. Ursurlines. I. Shea, John Dawson Gilmary, 1824-1892. II. Title.

Ursulines in Galveston.

JOHNSTON, Sue Mildred Lee, 1900-1970. 271'.974'0764139
Builders by the sea; history of the Ursuline community of Galveston, Texas [by] S. M. Johnston. [1st ed.] New York, Exposition Press [1971] 286 p. illus. 22 cm. (An Exposition-testament book) [BX4544.G34J64 1971] 78-164863 ISBN 0-682-47341-3 7.50
1. Ursulines in Galveston. I. Title.

Ursulines in New Orleans.

KANE, Harnett Thomas, 1910- 271.9
The Ursulines, nuns of adventure; the story of the New Orleans community. Illustrated by James J. Spanfeller. New York, Vision Books [1959] 188 p. illus. 22 cm. (Vision books, 42) [BX4544.N4K3] 59-6063
1. Ursulines in New Orleans.

Ursulines in Quebec.

REPPLIER, Agnes, 1855-1950. 922.271
Mere Marie of the Ursulines; a study in adventure. Foreword by Frances Parkinson Keyes. New York, Sheed and Ward [1957, c1931] 314p. 21cm. (A Thomas More book to live) [BX4705.M36R4 1957] 57-10178
1. Marie de l'Incarnation, Mother, 1599-1672. 2. Ursulines in Quebec. I. Title.

REPPLIER, Agnes, 1855-1950. 922.271
Mere Marie of the Ursulines, a study in adventure, by Agnes Repplier, LITT. D. Garden City, N. Y., Doubleday, Doran & company, inc., 1931. 4 p. l., 314 p. pl. 21 cm. Illustrated t.-p. "First edition." [BX4705.M36R4 1931] 31-26741
1. Marie de l'Incaration, mere, 1599-1672. 2. Ursulines in Quebec. I. Title.

REPPLIER, Agnes, 1855-1950. 922.271
Mere Marie of the Ursulines, a study in adventure, by Agnes Repplier, LITT. D. New York, The Literary guild of America, 1931. 4 p. l., 314 p. pl. 21 cm. Illustrated t.-p. "First edition." [BX4705.M36R4 1931a] 36-11316
1. Marie de l'Incarnation, mere, 1599-1672. 2. Ursulines in Quebec. I. Title.

Ursulines in the United States

[CLOTILDE Angela, sister] 1895- 271.9740979
Ursulines of the West, 1535-1935, 1880-1935, by an Ursuline of the Roman union. [Everett, Wash.] 1936. 72 p. front., plates, ports. 19 1/2 cm. [Secular name: Regina Margaret McBride] Bibliography: p. 71-72. [BX4543.U6C6] 36-19214
1. Ursulines in the U.S. I. Title.

Ursulines—Juvenile literature.

[WILLETT, Franciscus] 271.9740924
The promise to Angela; the story of St. Angela Merici [by] Pat McKern. Illus. by Suzanne Atkinson. Valatie, N. Y., Holy Cross Pr. [1966] 82p. illus. 23cm. [BX4700.A45W5] 66-8606 2.50
1. Angela Merici, Saint, 1474-1540.—Juvenile literature. 2. Ursulines—Juvenile literature. I. Title.

Usher, Mrs. Bridge (Lisle) Hoar, d. 1723.

FOXCROFT, Thomas, 1697-1769. 921
The character of Anna, the prophetess, consider'd and apply'd. In a sermon preach'd after the funeral of that honourable and devout gentlewoman, Dame Bridget Usher; who deceas'd at Boston, N. E., May 25th., 1723. Being a widow of a great age. Publis'd(with some enlargements) at the desire of the honoured executors to her will. By Thomas Foxcroft, M. A. and a pastor to the Old church in Boston. With a preface by the Rev. Mr. Wadsworth. Boston, Printed by S. Kneeland, 1723. 2 p. l., iii, 62 p. 18 cm. [CT275.U7F6] 20-7112
1. Usher, Mrs. Bridge (Lisle) Hoar, d. 1723. I. Title.

Ussher, James, Abp. of Armagh, 1581-1656.

KNOX, R. Buick. 283'.0924
James Ussher, Archbishop of Armagh, by R. Buick Knox. Cardiff, Univ. of Wales Pr., 1967. [7], 205p. plate, port. 23cm. Bibl. [BX5595.U8K5] (B) 68-75114 10.00
1. Ussher, James, Abp. of Armagh, 1581-1656. I. Title.
Distributed by Verry, Mystic, Conn.

Utah—Bibliography

EBERSTADT (Edward) and Sons, New York.
A collection of rare books, manuscripts, paintings, etc., relating to Utah and the Mormons offered for sale . . . New York [195?] 119 p. illus., port. 33 cm. Caption title. 65-32963
1. Utah—Bibl. 2. Mormons and Mormonism—Bibl. I. Title. II. Title: Rare books, manuscripts, paintings, etc., relating to Utah and the Mormons.

Utah—Description and travel

BURTON, Richard Francis, Sir 1821-1890. 922
The City of the saints, and across the Rocky mountains to California. By Richard F. Burton ... New York, Harper & brothers, 1862. 2 p. l., [ix]-xii p., 2 l., 574 p. incl. illus., plates. front., fold. map, fold. plan. 24 1/2 cm. [F826.B972] 19-5242
1. Utah—Descr. & trav. 2. Mormons and Mormonism. 3. Salt Lake City. 4. Overland journeys to the Pacific. I. Title.

CODMAN, John, 1814-1900. 922
The Mormon country. A summer with the "Latter-day saints." By John Codman. New York, United States publishing company, 1874. 2 p. l., 225 p. front. (mapy) plates. 19 cm. [F826.C67] Rc-266
1. Utah—Descr. & trav. 2. Mormons and Mormonism. I. Title.

[KANE ELIZABETH DENNISTOUN (WOOD) Mrs.] 922
Twelve Mormon homes visited in succession on a journey through Utah to Arizona. Philadelphia, 1874. 2 p. l., 159 p. 21 cm. Printed for private circulation. Published from the journal and letters of the author by her father, William Wood, with the design of commanding sympathy for the Mormons." [F826.K1] Rc-276
1. Utah—Descr. & trav. 2. Mormons and Mormonism. I. Title.

Utah-Economic conditions

ARRINGTON, Leonard J.
Great Basin Kingdom; and economic history of the Latter-Day Saints, 1830-1900. Lincoln, University of Nebraska Press [1966] xviii, 534 p. illus., ports. 21 cm. (Bison book, no. 342) Originally published, 1958, as Studies in economic history by Harvard University. Bibliography: p. [415]-515. NUC67
1. Utah-Econ. condit. 2. Mormons and Mormonism. I. Title.

Utah—History

CARLTON, Ambrose B. 922
The wonderlands of the wild West, with sketches of the Mormons. By A. B. Carlton ... [n. p.] 1891. 1 p. l., [v]-vii, [9]-346, [2] p. front., plates, ports. 23 cm. [F826.C28] Re-554
1. Utah—Hist. 2. Mormons and Mormonism. I. Title.

HICKMAN, Wiliam A 1815-1877or8. 922
Brigham's destroying angel; being the life, confession, and startling disclosures of the notorious Bill Hickman, the Danite chief of Utah. Written by Himself, with explanatory notes by J. H. Beadle ... New York, G. A. Crofutt, 1872. vii, [1], [9]-219 p. incl. front., illus. front., illus. 18 cm. [F826.H62] 17-9759
1. Utah—Hist. 2. Mormons and Moromonism. I. Beadle, John Hanson, 1840-1897, ed. II. Title.

HICKMAN, William A 1815-1877or8. 922
Brigham's destroying angel; being the life, confession, and startling disclousures of the notorious Bill Hickman, the Danite chief of Utah. Written by himself, with explanatory notes by J. H. Beadle ... Introduction by Richard B. Shepard ... Salt Lake City, Utah, Sh,pard book company, 1904. vii, [2], 10-221 p. incl. front. (port.) illus. 18 x 14 cm. [F826.H63] 4-18909
1. Utah—Hist. 2. Mormons and Mormonism I. Beadle, John Hanson, 1840-1897, ed. II. Title.

HICKMAN, William A., 1815-1877or8. 289.3'0924 B
Brigham's destroying angel: being the life, confession, and startling disclosures of the notorious Bill Hickman, the Danite chief of Utah. Written by himself, with explanatory notes by J. H. Beadle. Freeport, N.Y., Books for Libraries Press [1971] vii, 221 p. illus. 23 cm. Reprint of the 1904 ed. [F826.H63 1971] 74-165642 ISBN 0-8369-5951-5
1. Utah—History. 2. Mormons and Mormonism. I. Title.

LARSON, Gustive Olof, 1897-
Outline history of Utah and the Mormons. 3d ed. Salt Lake City, Deseret Book Co., 1965. 372 p. maps. 24 cm. Bibliography: p. [335]-357. 68-2565
1. Utah—Hist. 2. Mormons and Mormonism in Utah. I. Title.

TULLIDGE, Edward Wheelock. 922.8373
Life of Brigham Young; or, Utah and her founders. By Edward W. Tullidge. New York, 1876. 2 p. l., iv, 458, 81 p. front. (port.) 22 1/2 cm. "Biographical sketches, supplementary to "Life of Brigham Young: or, Utah and her founders"": 81 p. at end. [BX8695.Y7T8] 36-31810
1. Young, Brigham, 1801-1877. 2. Utah—Hist. 3. Utah—Biog. 4. Mormons and Mormonism. I. Title.

Utah — History — Sources.

STOUT, Hosea, 1810-1889.
Autobiography of Hosea Stout, 1810-1844. Edited by Reed A. Stout. [Salt Lake City, Utah State Historical Society] 1962. 88 p. illus., port. 24 cm. Reprinted from v. 30, 1962, Utah historical quarterly. 66-68326
1. Utah — Hist. — Sources. 2. Mormons and Mormonism — Hist. — Sources. I. Stout, Reed A., ed. II. Title.

Utah. State prison, Salt Lake City.

NICHOLSON, John, 1839-1909. 922.8373
The martyrdom of Joseph Standing; or, The murder of a "Mormon" missionary. A true story. Also an appendix, giving a succint [!] description of the Utah penitentiary and some data regarding those who had, up to date of this publication, suffered incarceration through the operations of the anti-"Mormon" crusade, begun in 1884. Written in prison, by John Nicholson ... Salt Lake City, Utah, The Deseret news co., printers, 1886. 2 p. l., [3]-160 p. 18 1/2 cm. [BX8095.S77N5] 36-31807
1. Standing, Joseph, 1855?-1879. 2. Utah. State prison, Salt Lake City. I. Title.

Utica, N. Y. Grace Church

GALPIN, William Freeman, 1890-1963. 283.74762
Grace Church; one hundred twenty-five years of downtown ministry. [Utica? N. Y., 1963] ix, 134 p. illus. (part col.) ports. 26 cm. [BX5980.U8G7] 63-19025
1. Utica, N. Y. Grace Church I. Title.

Utica, N.Y. Westminster church.

UTICA, N.Y. Westminster church. Committee of publication. 922.
Memorial addresses on the character and public services of the Rev. Samuel Ware Fisher, D.D., LL.D., delivered in the chapel of Hamilton college, on Thursday, January 29th, 1874; and in Westminster church, in Utica, on Sunday evening, February 8th, 1874, with a historical sketch of Westminster church. Utica, N.Y., Curtiss & Childs, printers, 1874. 59 p. front. (port.) 23 cm. "Historical sketch of Westminster church, Utica, N.Y., by Theodore Femeroy": p. 47-59. [LD2101.H217 1858] [BX9225.F5U7] 378. 24-23543
1. Fisher, Samuel Ware, 1814-1874. 2. Utica, N.Y. Westminster church. 3. Hamilton college, Clinton, N.Y. I. Pomeroy, Theodore. II. Title.

Utopia.

MORE, Thomas Sir Saint, 1478-1535.
Sir Thomas More's Utopia; ed., with introduction and notes, by J. Churton Collins. Oxford, Clarendon Press [1963, i.e. 1964] 283 p. 19 cm. 67-15066
1. Utopia. I. Collins, John Churton, 1848-1908, ed. II. Title.

Utopias.

NEGLEY, Glenn Robert, 1907- ed.
The quest for utopia; an anthology of imaginary societies [by) Glenn Negley [and] J. Max Patrick. Garden City, N.Y., Doubleday [1962] viii, 592 p. 18 cm. "Anchor Books edition, 1962." 65-56312
1. Utopias. I. Title.

PETERSON, Ephraim
An ideal city for an ideal people, by E. Peterson [How to build an ideal city for an ideal people, where the principles of Christianity, including economic equality, domestic virtue, and temperance in all things can become practical] [Independence, Mo., The author] 1905. 2 p. l., [3]-134 p., 1 l. port. 20 cm. 5-11075
I. Title.

PLATO.
The Republic of Plato, trans. with introduction and notes by Francis MacDonald Cornford. Oxford, Clarendon Press [1961] xxvii, 356 p. 65-93083
1. Utopias. I. Cornford, Francis MacDonald, 1874-1943. II. Title.

WILLINK, M. D. R. 220.
Utopia according to Moses; a study in the social teachings of the Old Testament, by M. D. R. Willink, s. TH. London, Society for promoting Christian knowledge; New York The Macmillan company, 1919. iv, [5]-184 p. 20 cm. [BS670.W6] 20-9927
I. Title.

WILLOUGHBY, Frank, 1866- 261
Through the needle's eye; a narrative of the restoration of the Davidic kingdom of Israel in Palestine with Jesus Christ as king. By Frank Willoughby. Based upon The bride of Christ, by Emry Davis. New York, The Palestine press, 1925. 1 p. l., 155 p. 19 1/2 cm. [HX811.1925.W5] 25-10552
1. Utopias. I. Davis, Emry. The bride of Christ. II. Title.

Utopias—Addresses, essays, lectures.

MANUEL, Frank Edward, ed.
Utopias and Utopian thought, edited by Frank E. Manuel. Boston, Beacon Press [c1966, 1967] xxiv, 321 p. 24 cm. (The Daedalus library) Includes bibliographies. 68-105425
1. Utopias—Addresses, essays, lectures. I. Title.

Utopias—Religious aspects.

HARLOW, Sarah Grace (Steves) Bear, mrs. 1854- 220
The ideal world from a Bible standpoint ... by S. Grace Harlow. Los Angeles, Calif., West Coast publishing co., 1927. 198 p. 19 cm. [BR125.H337] 27-17439
I. Title.

WEISS, Miriam Strauss. 200'.1
A lively corpse. South Brunswick [N.J.] A. S. Barnes [1969] 385 p. 25 cm. Bibliography: p. 369-374. [HX807.W4] 68-23068 10.00
1. Utopias—Religious aspects. I. Title.

Uttar Pradesh, India—Politics and government.

ROBINSON, Francis. 322'.1'09542
Separatism among Indian Muslims : the politics of the United Provinces' Muslims, 1860-1923 / Francis Robinson. London; [New York]: Cambridge University Press, 1974 [i.e. 1975] viii, 469 p., 9 p. of plates : ill., maps, ports. ; 23 cm. (Cambridge South Asian studies ; no. 16) Includes index. Bibliography: p. 440-449. [DS485.U64R54] 73-93393 ISBN 0-521-20432-1 : 27.50
1. Uttar Pradesh, India—Politics and government. 2. Muslims in India. 3. India—Politics and government—1765-1947. I. Title. II. Series.

Vacation schools.

CHAPELL, Harriet. 268.
The church vacation school; a discussion of its principles, with practical suggestion for its foundation and administration, by Harriet Chapell. New York, Chicago [etc.] Fleming H. Revell company [c1915] 160 p. illus. 20 cm. "List of works quoted or recommended": p. 157-160. [BV1585.C5] 15-23373 0.75
1. Vacation schools. I. Title.

MCDOWELL, Edith. 268.
...A first primary course for the vacation church school, by Edith McDowell New York, Cincinnati, The Abingdon press [c1924] 219 p. front. 20 cm. (The Abingdon religious education texts, David G. Downey, general editor. Daily vacation church school series, G. H. Betts, editor) Bibliography: p. 41-42. [BV1585.M3] 24-12448
1. Vacation schools. 2. Religious education. I. Title.

THE Standard vacation Bible school courses ... First year ... Cincinnati, O., The Standard publishing company [c1922] v. illus. (incl. maps, music) 31 cm. [BV1585.S7] CA 23 268.
1. Vacation schools. 2. Religious education. I. Waterman, Florence.

WEBER, William A. 268
The daily vacation Bible school, by William A. Weber ... Dayton, O., Department of Sunday school work, The Church of the United brethren in Christ [c1922] 60 p. plates. 17 1/2 cm. Bibliography: p. [58]-60. [BV1585.W4] 22-12263
I. Title.

Vacation schools, Catholic.

CONFRATERNITY of Christian doctrine. 220.
A course of study in religion for teachers of Catholic children who attend public schools. Grades I [-VIII] Developed as a manual for the use of priests, religious and lay teachers in religious vacation school classes. Prepared by a national committee under the auspices of the Confraternity of Christian doctrine: Rev. Leon A. McNeill, general chairman ... Paterson, N. J., St. Anthony guild press [1942] 3 v. 20 1/2 cm. Cover-title: Religious vacation school manual for teachers of Catholic children who attend public schools. Includes bibliographies. [BX930.C63] 43-3312
1. Vacation schools, Catholic. 2. Vacation schools, Religious—Teachers manuals. I. McNeill, Leon Aloysius, 1902- II. Title. III. Title: Religious vacation school manual.

LILLY, Edward Charles. 268.
... The Catholic religious vacation school [by] Edward C. Lilly. Washington, D. C., The Catholic education press [c1929] 51 p. 23 cm. (On cover: The Catholic university of America. Educational research bulletins ed. by the Dept. of education. vol iv, no. 3) Series title in part at head of t.-p. Bibliography: p. 47-50. [BX925.L5] 29-16873
1. Vacation schools, Catholic. 2. Vacation schools, Religious. I. Title.

Vacation schools, Christian.

ADMINISTERING a vacation Bible school. A. V. Washburn, compiler. Nashville, Convention Press [1970] viii, 136 p. illus. 20 cm. "Text for course 6305 in the subject area Bible teaching program of the New church study course." [BV1585.A44] 76-128049 268'.1
1. Vacation schools, Christian. I. Washburn, Alphonso V., ed.

FARIS, Paul Patton. 922
Modern builders of the church; twenty-five lessons for the daily vacation Bible school, prepared for use in the intermediate department, by Paul Patton Faris. Philadelphia, Board of Christian education

of the Presbyterian church in the U. S. A., 1923. 201 p. 19 cm. "Books suggested" at end of each chapter. [BR1704.F3] 23-13411
I. Title.

FLOYD, Pat, 1929- 268'.432
God made me ... to be responsible : leader's guide / by Pat Floyd ; [photos. by Barbara Withers]. Philadelphia : Published for the Cooperative Publication Association by United Church Press, [1975] 64 p. : ill. ; 28 cm. (Vacation ventures series) Bibliography: p. 56-62. [BV1585.F5] 75-14030 ISBN 0-8298-0295-9 pbk. : 1.95
1. Vacation schools, Christian. 2. Christian education—Text-books. I. Title.

THE How of vacation church school. Published for the Division of Christian Education, National Council of the Churches of Christ in the United States of America. New York, Office of Publication and Distribution [1957, c1958] 71p.

YOUR vacation church school. Anderson, Ind., Warner Press [1956] 96p.
I. Hall, Arlene Stevens.

Vacation schools, Christian—Text-books.

NICHOLSON, Dorothy. 268'.432
I can choose: leader's guide; a cooperative vacation ventures series course for use in nursery. Philadelphia, Published for the Cooperative Publication Association by United Church Press [1974] 64 p. illus. 28 cm. (Vacation ventures series) Bibliography: p. 60-61. [BV1585.N5] 74-8043 ISBN 0-8298-0280-0
1. Vacation schools, Christian—Text-books. 2. Christian education of preschool children. I. Cooperative Publication Association. II. Title.

SCHOONMAKER, Hazel K. 268'.432
Creation and me; by Hazel K. Schoonmaker. Philadelphia, Published for the Cooperative Publication Association by United Church Press [1970] iii, 92 p. illus., music. 28 cm. (The Cooperative vacation church school series) "A cooperative vacation church school course for use with kindergarten children/Teacher's course book." Bibliography: p. 90-91. [BV1585.S324] 77-132862 ISBN 0-8298-0191-X
1. Vacation schools, Christian—Text-books. 2. Christian education of pre-school children. I. Cooperative Publication Association. II. Title. III. Series.

Vacation schools, Religious.

AMERICAN Baptist publication society. Christian education dept. 268.
The church vacation school handbook; suggestions for promotion, organization, and program, compiled by Church vacation and week-day school division, Department of religious education. Philadelphia, Pa., The Judson press [1922] 4 p. l., 3-68 p. front., illus. 23 cm. Ruled pages for "Notes" (4 at end) [BV1585.A6] 22-18111
1. Vacation schools, Religious. I. Title.

ARMENTROUT, James Sylvester, 1887- 240
Administering the vacation church school; a study of the aims, organization, and administration of the vacation church school, by J. S. Armentrout ... a textbook in the Standard leadership training curriculum, outlined and approved by the International council of religious education ... Philadelphia, Printed for the Teacher training publishing association by the Westminster press, 1928. 208 p. 19 1/2 cm. (Specialization series) "Some helpful books": p. 204-205. [BV1585.A7] 28-11224
1. Vacation schools, Religious. I. Title.

BATTLE, Edith Kent. 268.
How nations share; a vacation church school unit for junior children, by Edith Kent Battle, edited by C. A. Bowen. Nashville, Dallas [etc.] Publishing house of the M. E. church, South, Lamar & Whitmore, agents [c1931] 95 p. 21 cm. Contains music. [BV1585.B36] 33-39264
1. Vacation schools. Religious. I. Bowen, Cawthon Asbury, 1885- ed. II. Title.

BLAIR, Winfrey Dyer. 268
The new vacation church school, by W. Dyer Blair ... New York and London, Harper & brothers, 1934. xiv p. 1 l., 268 p. front. 20 cm. "First edition." Includes bibliographies. [BV1585.B5] 34-12293
1. Vacation schools, Religious. I. Title.

BLAIR, Winfrey Dyer. 268
The new vacation church school, by W. Dyer Blair ... New York and London, Harper & brothers, [c1939] xiii p., 1 l., 800 p. front. 19 1/2 cm. "Fifth edition enlarged." Includes bibliographies. [BV1585.B5 1939] 39-11742
1. Vacation schools, Religious. I. Title.

BONSER, Edna Madison (MacDonald) Mrs. 268.
... Child life and religious growth, a second primary course for the vacation church school based on activities, by Edna M. Bonser, prepared in co-operation with the International association of daily vacation Bible schools. New York, Cincinnati, The Abingdon press [c1928] 380 p. front., plates. 20 cm. (The Abingdon religious education texts: D. G. Downey, general editor. Daily vacation church school series: G. H. Betts, editor) Contains bibliographies. [BV1585.B6] 28-15877
1. Vacation schools, Religious. I. International association of daily vacation Bible schools. II. Title.

BRACE, Vern Edward. 263
The what and how of daily vacation Bible school, by V. E. Brace ... Denver, Colo., W. C. Garberson, c1936. 56 p. incl. illus., form. 22 cm. "Text books": p. 37. [BV1585.B63] 36-14603
1. Vacation schools, Religions. I. Title.

BURNETT, Sibley Curtis. 268
Better vacation Bible schools. Nashville, Convention Press [1957] u50p. 20cm. [BV1585.B816] 57-13894
1. Vacation schools, Religious. I. Title.

BUTT, Elsie Miller. 268
The vacation church school in Christian education. New York, Published for the Cooperative Publication Association by Abingdon Press [1957] 192p. illus. 20cm. (The Cooperative series: leadership training texts) Includes bibliography. [BV1585.B83] 57-6754
1. Vacation schools, Religious. I. Title.

DUDLEY, Carolyn. 268.
Learning God's way; programs for the primary department, prepared for use in the daily vacation Bible school, by Carolyn Dudley, edited by John T. Faris, D. D Philadelphia, Board of Christian education of the Presbyterian church in the U. S. A., 1926. 1 p. l., 5-156 p. illus., diagrs. 24 cm. Bibliography: p. 109-110. [BV1585.D75] 26-11388
1. Vacation schools, Religious. I. Faris, John Thomson, 1871- ed. II. Title.

EDLAND, Elisabeth. 268.62
Exploring the trail with the Master Guide; a manual for use with junior groups in vacation church schools, by Elisabeth Edland and Annie Laurie Newton; John T. Faris, editor, Elizabeth S. Whitehouse, assistant editor for children's publications. Philadelphia, Board of Christian education of the Presbyterian church in the U.S.A., 1934. 267 p. illus. (incl. music) 23 1/2 cm. Includes bibliographies. "Hymns": p. 260-267. [BV1585.E3] 34-11045
1. Vacation schools, Religious. I. Newton, Annie Laurie, joint author. II. Faris, John Thomson, 1871- ed. III. Whitehouse, Elizabeth Scott, 1893- joint ed. IV. Title.

GAGE, Albert Henry, 1878- 268.
How to conduct a church vacation school, by Albert H. Gage ... Philadelphia, Boston [etc.] American Baptist publication society [c1921] 7 p. l., 167 p. front., illus., plates. 20 cm. [BV1585.G3] 21-11644
1. Vacation schools, Religious. I. Title.

GETZ, Gene A. 268
The vacation Bible school in the local church. Chicago, Moody [c.1962] 158p. illus. 62-3051 2.95
1. Vacation schools, Religious. I. Title.

GREEN, Sarah Elizabeth, 1898- 268
Planning the vacation church school for boys and girls [by] Sarah E. Green .. New York, Cincinnati [etc.] The Methodist book concern [c1937] 51 p. 20 cm. "Approved by the Committee on curriculum of the Board of education of the Methodist Episcopal church." Includes bibliographies. [BV1585.G7] 37-8518
1. Vacation schools, Religious. I. Title.

GRICE, Homer Lamar, 1883- 266
The vacation Bible school guide, by Homer L. Grice ... 1941 ed. Nashville, Tenn., Broadman press [1941] ix, 165 p. 19 cm. "fourth edition, March, 1941." [BV1585.G73 1941] 41-9445
1. Vacation schools, Religious. I. Title.

KNAPP, Ezra C.
The Community daily vacation Bible school, by E. C. Knapp ... introduction by Marion Lawrence. New York, Chicago [etc.] Fleming H. Revell company [c1922] 129 p. 20 cm. Bibliography: p. 117-120. [BV1585K6] 22-11080
1. Vacation schools, Religious. 2. Bible—Study. I. Title.

KNAPP, Ezra C. 220
Side lights on the daily vacation Bible school, by E. C. Knapp ... New York, Chicago [etc.] Fleming H. Revell company [c1923] 126 p. 20 cm. Bibliography: p. 124-128. [BS603.5.K6] 23-10935
I. Title.

KRUMBINE, Miles Henry, 1891- 268.
A summer program for the church school, by Miles H. Krumbine ... Chicago, Ill., The University of Chicago press [c1926] xi, 188 p. illus. (incl. forms) 18 cm. (Half-title: The University of Chicago publications in religious education ... Principles and methods of religious education.) Contains lists of books and stories suitable for church school use. [BV1585.K8] 26-13336
1. Vacation schools, Religious. I. Title.

NELSON, William Verner. 268
Vacation Bible school handbook; a practical guide in the conduct of daily vacation church schools, by William Verner Nelson. Cincinnati, O., The Standard publishing company [1942] 128 p. 19 1/2 cm. Bibliography: p. 123-124. [BV1585.N4] 43-16982
1. Vacation schools, Religious. I. Title.

PROTESTANT Episcopal Church in the U.S.A. National Council. Dept. of Christian Education.
Weeks of growth; a basic guide for vacation church school leaders. Illustrated by Mary Stevens. Greenwich, Conn., Seabury Press [1959] v, 106 p. illus. 27 cm. 65-66508
1. Vacation schools, Religious. I. Title.

RHODES, Bertha Marlida. 268.
A church vacation school guide for use with Religion in the kindergarten, by Marilda Rhodes. Chicago, Ill., The University of Chicago press [c1927] ix, [1], 73 p. 19 1/2 cm. (Half-title: The University of Chicago publications in religious education ... Constructive studies) [BV1585.R5] 27-16734
1. Vacation schools, Religious. I. Title.

SCHULZ, Florence 268.432
Friends and neighbors; a resource book for ministering to primary and junior boys and girls in inner-city areas Boston, 14 Beacon St. Pub. for the Cooperative Pubn. Assn. [by] Pilgrim Pr. [c.1962] 118p. 23cm. (Cooperative vacation church sch. texts) 62-21605 1.50 pap.,
1. Vacation schools, Religions. 2. Church work with children. I. Title.

SCHULZ, Florence. 248
Friends and neighbors; a resource book for ministering to primary and junior boys and girls in inner-city areas. Boston, Published for the Cooperative Publication Association [by] Pilgrim Press [1962] 118p. 23cm. (The Cooperative vacation church school texts) [BV1585.S33] 62-21605
1. Vacation schools, Religions. 2. Church work with children. I. Title.

SCHULZ, Florence. 268
Summer with nursery children. Illustrated by Lennabelle McBride Reed. Boston, Published for the Cooperative Publication Association [by] Pilgrim Press [1958] 156p. illus. 23cm. (The Cooperative series texts. Vacation church school texts) Includes bibliography. [BV1585.S35] 58-13598
1. Vacation schools, Religious. 2. Religious education of pre-school children. I. Title.

STAFFORD, Hazel (Straight) Mrs. 377.1
...Vacation religious day school, teacher's manual of principles and programs by Hazel Straight Stafford. New York, Cincinnati, The Abingdon press [c1920] 160 p. front. (port.) plates. 20 1/2 cm. [The Abdingdon religious education texts, D. G. Downey, general editor. Vacation day school series. N. E. Richardson, editor) [BV1585.S67] 20-13711
1. Vacation schools, Religious. I. Title.

STOUT, John Elbert, 1867- 268.
... The daily vacation church school, how to organize and conduct it, by John E. Stout and James V. Thompson; prepared in cooperation with the International association of daily vacation Bible schools. New York, Cincinnati, The Abingdon press, [c1923] 119 p. 20 cm. (The Abingdon religious education texts, David G. Downey, general editor. Daily vacation church school series, George Herbert Betts, editor) [BV1585.S75] 23-11054
1. Vacation schools, Religious. I. Thompson, James Voorhees, 1878-joint author II. Title.

Vacation schools, Religious—Teachers' manuals.

BAIRD, Lula Doyle, 1899- 268.61
Our daily bread; a vacation church school unit for primary children, by Lula Doyle Baird; C. A. Bowen, editor. Nashville, Cokesbury press [c1937] 76 p. 20 cm. "Songs": p. 71-76. [BV1585.B27] 37-13169
1. Vacation schools, Religious—Teachers' manuals. I. Bowen, Cawthon Asbury, 1885- ed. II. Title.

BALL, Elsie. 268.61
Friends at work [by] Elsie Ball. Prepared from a descriptive outline developed by Protestant Christian forces of the United States and Canada through the International council of religious education, and released to the constituent denominations. Leaders manual ... New York, Cincinnati [etc.] Printed for the International committee on co-operative publication of vacation church school curriculum by the Methodist book concern [c1934] 184 p. 22 cm. [The co-operative series of vacation church school texts] "Co-operative vacation church school manual for junior vacation church school groups." Includes music. Includes bibliographies. [BV1585.B35] 44-21478
1. Vacation schools, Religious—Teachers' manuals. I. International council of religious education. II. Title.

BATTLE, Edith Kent (Childs) Mrs. 1877- 268.61
What is in your Bible? A vacation church school unit for junior children, by Edith Kent Battle: C. A. Bowen, editor. Nashville, Cokesbury press [c1937] 96 p. 20 cm. "God of the earth, the sky, the sea" (words and music): p. 96. Bibliography: p. 14-15. [BV1585.B37] 37-13168
1. Vacation schools, Religious—Teachers' manuals. I. Bowen, Cawthon Asbury, 1885- ed. II. Title.

BICKEL, Lucy V. 268.432
The world about us, by Lucy V. Bickel. Vacation church school unit for beginners. Lucius H. Bugbee, C. A. Bowen, editors ... New York, Nashville, Abington-Cokesbury press, [1944] 96 p. diagrs. 23 cm. [BV1585.B48] 44-32420
1. Vacation schools. Religions—Teachers' manuals I. Bugbee, Lucius Hatfield, 1874- ed. II. Bowen, Cawthon Asbury, 1885- joint ed. III. Title.

BOWMAN, Alveretta (Warvel) Mrs. 1872- 268.61
Systematic Bible course for daily vacation Bible schools and Sunday schools, by Alveretta W. Bowman ... Grand Rapids, Mich., Wm. B. Eerdmans publishing company [c1936-37] 3 v. illus. (incl. maps) 24 cm. Contents.--i. Beginner and primary grades.--ii. Junior grades.--iii. Intermediate grades. [BV1585.B62] [220] 38-32375
1. Vacation schools,—Religious—Teachers' manuals. I. Title.

CHILDREN learn from Jesus, a co-operative vacation church school text for use with kindergarten children. Teacher's text. St. Louis, Pub. for the Co-operative Publication Assn by the Bethany Press [1957] 96p. 23cm.
1. Vacation schools, Religious—Teachers' manuals. I. Lyon, Bernice E

CLEMENS, Margaret Meyers, 1895- 268.61
God's friendly world, by Margaret M. Clemens...a vacation church school course for beginners; Miles W. Smith, editor-in-chief. Prepared in cooperation with Week-day and vacation church school division... Philadelphia, Boston [etc.] The Judson press [1938] 152 p. illus. 23 1/2 cm. Includes music. "Selected bibliography for teachers of beginners": p. 152. [BV1585.C55] 38-25902
1. Vacation schools, Religious—Teacher's manuals. I. Smith, Miles Woodward, 1889- ed. II. American Baptist publication society. Christian education dept. III. Title.

DEMAREE, Doris Clore. 268.6
Choosing God's way, a vacation church school text ... Junior department. Prepared by Doris Clore Demaree, approved by the Council on Christian education of the Northern Baptist convention for use in the unified program. Philadelphia, Chicago [etc.] The Judson press [1944] 69 p. 25 1/2 cm. (Judson keystone series) [BV1585.D38] 44-25566
1. Vacation schools, Religious—Teachers' manuals. I. Title.

DESJARDINS, Lucile. 268.433
Our living church [by] Lucile Desjaridins ... Leaders' manual Cooperative vacation church school unit for intermediates, 1936. Published for the International committee on cooperative publication of vacation church school curriculum. Philadelphia, The Westminster press, 1936. 222 p. illus., diagrs. (1 fold.) 22 cm. [The cooperative series of vacation church school texts] "Prepared from a descriptive outline developed by Protestant Christian forces of the United States and Canada through the International council of religious education, and released to the constituent denominations." "Book list": p. 210-212. [BV1585.D4] 36-22221
1. Vacation schools, Religious—Teachers' manuals. I. International council of religious ieducation. II. Title.

DUDLEY, Carolyn.
God's children living together; programs for the primary department, preapred for use in the vacation church school, by Carolyn Dudley; John T. Faris, D. D., editor. Philadelphia, Board of Christian education of the Presbyterian church in the U. S. A., 1927. 1 p. l., 5-185 p. illus. (incl. music) diagrs. 24 cm. "Helpful books": p. 178. [RV1545.D8] 27-7398
1. Vacation schools, Religious—Teachers' manuals. 2. Religious education—Text-books for children. I. Faris John Thomson, 1871- ed. II. Title.

EAKIN, Mildred Olivia (Moody) Mrs. 1890- 268.432
...Kindergarten course for the daily vacation church school, by Mildred O. Moody... New York, Cincinnati, The Abingdon press [c1925] 224 p. illus. 20 cm. (The Abingdon religious education texts, D. G. Downey, general editor. Daily vacation church school series, G. H. Betts, editor) "Prepared in cooperation with the International association of daily vacation Bible schools." Music: p. [34] [BV1540.E3] 25-4428
1. Vacation schools, Religious—Teachers manuals. 2. Kindergarten—Methods and manuals. I. International association of daily vacation Bible schools. II. Title.

EDDY, Lois B. 268.432
Friends at home and in the community, by Lois B. Eddy. A vacation church school unit for primary boys and girls. Lucius H. Bugbee, C. A. Bowen, editors ... New York, Nashville, Abingdon-Cokesbury press [1943] 89 p. 22 1/2 cm. Songs (with music) p. 88-89. "Reading books for children": p. 13-14. [BV1585.E28] 43-15829
1. Vacation schools, Religious—Teachers' manuals. I. Bugbee, Lucius Hatfield, 1875- ed. II. Bowen, Cawthon Asbury, 1885- joint ed. III. Title.

FRIEND, Edith Alice, 1903- 268.6
A ready manual for the daily vacation Bible school teacher, prepared by E. Alice Friend. Philadelphia, American Sunday-school union [c1938] 153, [6] p. illus. 18 cm. Blank pages for "Notes and clippings" ([6] at end) [BV1585.F74] 38-25909
1. Vacation schools, Religious—Teachers' manuals. I. Title.

GRICE, Homer Lamar, 1883- 268
... The first book about Jesus (Mark) by Homer Lamar Grice and Ethel Harrison Grice. A teacher's book of group-graded material for use with boys and girls, ages 13, 14, 15 and 16. To be used only in 1942, 1946, 1950. Nashville, Tenn., The Broadman press [1942] 96 p. illus. (incl. maps) diagrs. 31 x 24 cm. (Vacation Bible school textbooks, Broadman press series, intermediate-- book A) Music: p. [2] "Helps for the teachers": p. 10-11. [BV1585.G72] 42-14735
1. Vacation schools, Religious—Teachers' manuals. 2. Bible. N. T. Mark—Study—Text-books. 3. Bible—Study—Text-books—N. T. Mark. I. Grice, Ethel (Harrison) 1880- joint author. II. Title.

HAZZARD, Lowell Brestel. 268.432
Fairest Lord Jesus; a course for intermediate of junior high school groups in vacation church schools: teacher's book [by] Lowell Brestel Hazzard and Stella Tombaugh Hazzard. New York, Published for the Cooperative Publication Association by Abingdon Press [1957] 128p. illus. 20cm. (The Cooperative series: vacation church school texts) [BV1585.H39] 57-7096
1. Vacation schools, Religious— Teachers' manuals. I. Hazzard, Stella Tombaugh., joint author. II. Title.

HEFLIN, Nannie France, 1889- 268.0
Jesus and His friends, by Nan F. Hefflin, a vacation church school course for primary children; edited by Margaret M. Clemens ... Miles W. Smith, editor--in--chief. Prepared in cooperation with Week--day and vacation church school division ... Philadelphia, Boston [etc.] The Judson press [1938] 172 p. plates. 23 1/2 cm. Music: p. 168-171. "Selected biblipgraphy": p. 172. [BV1595.H4] 38-25901
1. Vacation schools, Religious—Teachers' manuals. I. Clement, Margaret Meyers, 1895- ed. II. Smith, Miles Woodward, 1889- III. American Baptist publication society. Christian education dept. IV. Title.

JENNESS, Mary. 268.61
We all need each other [by] Mary Jenness ... Leaders' manual presenting units of guided experience in Christian education for intermediate groups. New York, Cincinnati [etc.] Printed for the International committee on co-operative publication of vacation church school curriculum by the Methodist book concern [c1935] 164 p. 22 cm. [The co-operative series of vacation church school texts] "Prepared from a descriptive outline developed by Protestant Christian forces of the United States and Canada through the International council of religious education, and released to the constituent denominations." Includes bibliographies. [BV1585.J4] 35-10126
1. Vacation schools, Religious—Teachers' manuals. I. International council of religious education. II. Title.

KELSEY, Alice (Geer) 268.432
Living and working together as Christians; a vacation church school course for girls & boys of grades 4, 5 & 6. Teacher's book. Boston, Published for the Co-operative Publication Association by Pilgrim Press [1954] 172p. 20cm. (The Co-operative series: vacation church school texts) [BV1585.K38] 55-20520
1. Vacation schools, Religious—Teachers' manuals. 2. Christian life—Study and teaching. I. Title.

MARTIN, Florence, 1904- 268.61
Living in our community, by Florence Martin; units of guided experience for junior children. Leader's manual. Preguided from a descriptive outline developed by Protestant Christian forces of the United States and Canada through the International council of religious education and released to the constituent denominations. St. Louis, Mo. Pub. for the International committee on co-operative publication of vacation church school curriculum by the Bethany press. 1935 204 p. illus. 22 cm. [The co-operative series of church school texts] Includes bibliographies. [Full name: Florence Blanche Martin] [BV1585.M35] 35-13088
1. Vacation schools, Religious—Teachers' manuals. I. International council of religious education. II. Title.

MAXFIELD, Helen A. 232.3
My voyage on the blood line, lesson plans for the teacher, prepared by Helen A. Maxfield. Grand Rapids, Mich., Zondervan publishing house [c1941] 128 p. 19 1/2 cm. [BV1585.M38] 41-19794
1. Vacation schools, Religious—Teachers' manuals. 2. Atonement. I. Title.

MAXFIELD, Helen Adell, 1894- 268.6
The auction; director's manual. Grand Rapids, Zondervan Pub. House [1949] 169 p. 20 cm. A ten day program for vacation Bible schools. [BV1585.M368] 49-9377
1. Vacation schools, Religious—Teachers' manuals. I. Title.

MAXFIELD, Helen Adell, 1894- 268
The garden; director's manual, by Helen A. Maxfield ... and Alice M. Eisenhart. Grand Rapids, Mich., Zondervan publishing house [1943] 162, [4] p. 2 pl. on 1 l. 20 cm. A ten day program for vacation Bible schools. [BV1585.M37] 43-10018
1. Vacation schools, Religous—Teachers' manuals. 2. Object-teaching. I. Eisenhart, Alice M., joint author. II. Title.

MAXFIELD, Helen Adell, 1894- 232.3
My voyage on the blood line; lesson plans for the teacher, prepared by Helen A. Maxfield. Grand Rapids, Mich., Zondervan publishing house [1941] 128 p. 19 1/2 cm. [BV1585.M38] 41-19794
1. Vacation schools, Religious—Teachers' manuals. 2. Atonement. I. Title.

MAXFIELD, Helen Adell, 1894- 268.62
Temple builders; director's manual, by Helen A. Maxfield ... Grand Rapids, Mich., Zondervan publishing house [1947] 7 p. l., 13-154 p. diagrs. 20 cm. [BV1585.M39] 47-24762
1. Vacation schools, Religious—Teachers' manuals. I. Title.

MORTON, Nelle. 268.433
Making our group Christian; a text for leaders of boys and girls of junior high school age ... Teacher's book. [Rev. ed.] Richmond, Published for the Cooperative Publication Association by John Knox Press [1961] 104p. illus. 23cm. Includes bibliography. [BV1585.M58 1961] 61-6342
1. Vacation schools, Religious—Teachers' manuals. 2. Social group work (Church work) I. Title.

MOSHER, Helene K. 268.6
Understanding the Bible; a vacation church school unit for intermediate boys and girls, by Helene K. Mosier; edited by C. A. Bowen. Nashville, Cokesbury press [c1937] 1 p. l., 5-96 p. 21 1/2 cm. "Additional printed resources": p. 88-90. [BV1585.M6] 38-17811
1. Vacation schools, Religious—Teachers' manuals. 2. Bible—Study. I. Bowen, Cawthon Asbury, 1885- ed. II. Title.

ODELL, Mary (Clemens) 1904-
My family and my friends. [Teacher's book]; a cooperative vacation church school text for use with kindergarten children. [Rev. ed.] Chicago, Published for the Cooperative Publication Association by the Judson Press [1961] 112 p. 23 cm. 16 p. illus. 18 x 23 cm. Includes music. -- My family and my friends. [Pupil's book. Rev. ed.] Philadelphia, Printed for the Cooperative Publication Association by the Judson Press [1961] 65-43582
I. Title.

PROTESTANT Episcopal Church in the U.S.A. National Council. Dept. of Christian Education.
The adventure of growing. Greenwich, Conn., Seabury Press [1962] 64 p. 28 cm. The Seabury series [V-T]) (The Church's teaching) "Vacation church school primary book 2 for use with Weeks of growth." Includes bibliographies. 65-66504
1. Vacation schools, Religious—Teachers' manuals. I. Title. II. Title. III. Series.

PROTESTANT Episcopal Church in the U.S.A. National Council. Dept. of Christian Education.
Christians in action. Greenwich, Conn, Seabury Press [1961] 64 p. 28 cm. (Seabury series [V-T]) "Vacation church school older junior book 2 for use with Weeks of growth." Includes bibliographies. 65-66505
1. Vacation schools, Religious—Teachers' manuals. I. Title. II. Series. III. Series: The Church's teaching

RAUSCHENBERG, Lina (Andrews) Mrs. 1890- 268.432
To market, to market; a vacation school unit for primary children, by Lina A. Rauschenberg; C. A. Bowen, editor. Nashville, Cokesbury press [c1940] 93 p. 22 cm. Includes music. "Sources of materials": p. 11. [BV1585.R3] 40-10026
1. Vacation schools, Religious—Teachers' manuals. I. Bowen, Cawthon Asbury, 1885- ed. II. Title.

REED, Elizabeth Liggett. 268.61
Bible homes and homes today [by] Elizabeth Liggett Reed. Leader's manual presenting units of guided experience in Christian education for primary groups ... Published for the Interdenominational committee on cooperative publication of vacation church school curriculum. Boston, Chicago, The Pilgrim press [c1937] viii, 152 p. illus., 22 cm. [The cooperative series of vacation church schook texts] "Based on descriptive outlines developed by Protestant Christian forces of the United States and Canada through the International council of religious education, and released to the constituent denominations." [BV1585.R4] 37-13554
1. Vacation schools, Religious—Teachers' manuals. I. International council of religious education. II. Title.

RICE, Rebecca, 1899- 268.62
Exploring God's out-of-doors [by] Rebecca Rice. Units of guided experience for primary children ... Based on descriptive outlines developed by the Protestant Christian forces of the United States and Canada through the International council of religious education and released to the constituent denominations. Leaders' manual. Boston, Chicago, Pub. for the Interdenominational committee on cooperative publication of vacation church school curriculum, the Pilgrim press [c1935] 3 p. l., 152, [2] p. illus. 22 cm. [The co-operative series of vacation church school texts] Includes music. Bibliography: p. 151-152. [BV1585.R53] 35-14065
1. Vacation schools, Religious—Teachers' manuals. I. International council of religious education. II. Title.

ROORBACH, Harriet A. 268.432
Jesus, the Friend; a vacation church school unit for primary girls and boys. New York, Abingdon-Cokesbury [1950] 93 p. 23 cm. Hymns with music: p. [91]-93. [BV1585.R65] 50-2069
1. Vacation schools, Religious — Teachers' manuals. I. Title.

ROSENE, Myrtle Elizabeth. 268.62
What God does for me; a manual for teachers in the beginners department of the vacation Bible school, by Myrtle Elizabeth Rosene; prepared under the direction of the Commission on parish education of the American Lutheran conference. Rock Island, Ill., Augustana book concern [c1940] 120 p. illus. 24 cm. "Songs [with music]": p. 104-120. [BV1585.R7] 40-12961
1. Vacation schools, Religious—Teachers' manuals. I. American Lutheran conference. Commission on parish education. II. Title.

SHIELDS, Elizabeth McEwen, 1879- 268.482
Happy times in our church, by Elizabeth McEwen Shields. Units of guided experience for beginner children ... Leader's manual ... Richmond, Va., Published for the International committee on co-operative publication of vacation church school curriculum, by John Knox Press [c1940] 208 p. illus. 22 cm. [The co-operative series of vacation and weekday church school texts] "Prepared from descriptive outlines selected ... by the

International council of religious education, representing Protestant Christian forces of the United States and Canada, and released to the constituent denominations." Includes music. [BV1585.S5] 40-11102
1. Vacation schools, Religious—Teachers manuals. I. International council of religious education. II. Title.

SHUMATE, Aurora (Medford), Mrs., 1880- 268.61
...*The little children's world,* by Aurora Medford Shumate and Homer Lamar Grice. A teacher's book of group-graded material for use with children, ages 4 and 5... Nashville, Tenn, The Broadman press [c1938] 104 p. illus. 20 1/2 cm (Vacation Bible school textbooks, Broadman press series, beginner--book a) Music: p. 97-104. [BV1585.V25] (268.61) 38-22651
1. Vacation schools, Religious—Teachers' manuals. I. Grice, Homer Lamar, 1883- joint author. II. Title.

STEWART, Willie Jean. 268.61
... *Finding out what Jesus expects of us;* prepared by Willie Jean Stewart. A teacher's book of group-graded material for use with boys and girls, ages 9, 10, 11 and 12 ... Nashville, Tenn., The Broadman press [1941] 96 p. illus. (inc. maps) 30 1/2 x 23 1/2 cm. (Vacation Bible school textbooks. Broadman press series, junior-book D) With music. [BV1585.S72] 45-51266
1. Vacation schools, Religious—Teachers' manuals. I. Title.

STINSON, Elizabeth. 268.62
O come, let us worship, a vacation church school unit for intermediate boys and girls, by Elizabeth Stinson; C. A. Bowen, editor. Nashville, Cokesbury press [c1938] 1 p. l., 5-95 p. 21 1/2 cm. "List of books containing additional resources": p. 95. [BV1585.S73] 38-15252
1. Vacation schools, Religious—Teachers' manuals. 2. Worship (Religious education) I. Bowen, Cawthon Asbury, 1885-ed. II. Title.

TAYLOR, Florence M. 268.61
Neighbors at peace; a unit of work for grades III-IV in vacation church schools [by] Florence M. Taylor; based on experiments conducted by the Metropolitan federation of daily vacation Bible schools, 1936 and 1937. New York, Cincinnati [etc.] The Abingdon press [c1938] 134 p. 22 cm. Includes songs with music. "Books for the children's reading table": p. 131-133; "References for leaders, parents": p. 133-134. [BV1585.T27] 38-21261
1. Vacation schools, Religious—Teachers' manuals. I. Title.

TAYLOR, Florence Marian (Tompkins) 1892- 268.432
If we had lived in Bible times. For use with grades three and four in weekday church school classes. [By] Florence M. Taylor [and] Imogene M. McPherson. Teacher's book. Nashville, Abingdon-Cokesbury Press [1947- v. 19 cm. [BV1585.T266] 48-6231
1. Vacation schools, Religious—Teachers' manuals. I. McPherson, Imogene McCrary, 1892- joint author. II. Title.

WALLIS, Wilber Benson, 1912- 268
Troop school for Christian soldiers, by Lieut. and Mrs. Wilber Wallis ... Harrisburg, Pa., Christian publications, inc. [1943] 2 p. l., 67 p. incl. illus., forms, diagrs. 28 x 21 1/2 cm. [BV1585.W24] 43-18341
1. Vacation schools, Religious—Teachers' manuals. 2. Church work with children. I. Wallis, Marie (Coulombe) 1913- joint author. II. Title.

WARD, Margaret S. 268.432
Working with God in His world, by Margaret S. Ward. Philadelphia, Pa., Chicago [etc.] Pub. for the Interdenomination committee on co-operative publication of vacation church school curriculum by the Judson press [1943] 207 p. 21 1/2 cm. (Half-title: "The Co-operative series of vacation church school texts) "Prepared from a descriptive outline approved and copyrighted by the Internatioal council of religious education." "Selected books for the library": p. 205-207. [BV1585.W27] 43-13668
1. Vacation schools, Religious—Teachers' manuals. I. International council of religious education. Interdenominational committee on cooperative publication of vacation and church school curriculum. II. Title.

WARREN, Mary Sherburne. 268.432
Understanding God's world; a textbook for teachers of juniors in vacation church schools [by] Mary Sherburne Warren. Boston, Chicago, Pub. for the Interdenominational committee on cooperative publication of vacation church school curriculum by the Pilgrim press [1943] vi p., 2 l., 181 p. 22 1/2 cm. (Half-title: The Cooperative series of church school texts) "Prepared from a descriptive outline approved and copyrighted by the international council of religious education." Bibliography: p. [175]-181. [BV1585.W3] 43-12548
1. Vacation schools, Religious—Teachers' manuals. I. International council of religious education. Interdenominational committee on cooperative publication of vacation and church school curriculum. II. Title.

YOUNG, Lois Horton. 268
God and His world; a cooperative vacation school course for use with kindergarten children. Teacher's guide. Drawings by Carol Roach. Dayton, Ohio, Published for the Co-operative Publication Association by Otterbein Press [c1958] 96 p. illus. 23 cm. (The Cooperative series: vacation church school texts) Includes hymns, with music, by the author. To be used with the pupil's book, God and His world. [BV1585.Y66] 58-13374
1. Vacation schools, Religious — Teachers' manuals. I. Title.

Vacation schools, Religious—Text-books.

BARBER, Estelle Bianton. 268.61
God in our lives; a course for intermediates or junior high school groups in vacation church school. Teacher's book. New York, Published for the Cooperative Publication Associationby Abingdon-Cokesbury Press [1952] 128 p. 20 cm. (Cooperative texts for vacation church schools) [BV1585.B356] 268.432 52-2161
1. Vacation schools, Religious—Text-books. I. Title.

BIBLE outlines for vacation Bible schools, prepared for First Presbyterian church, Seattle, Washington ... 268.62
[Denver] Printed by W. C. Garberson, c1939] 2 v. illus., plates diagrs. 23 cm. Folded maps and folded diagrams in pocket at end of v. 2. Contents.--pt. 1. First and second year beginners, first, second and third year primary, by Freda Rader [and] Jane L. Rice.-pt. 2. A seven year course for advanced grades by Mary M. Fowler, Lida W. Smith N. Marie Sprinkle and others. [BV1585.B45] 39-22724
1. Vacation schools, Religious—Text-books.

BRADSHAW, Emerson Otho, 1881- 268.
... *Knights of service* (for children of 9-11 years) by Emerson O. Bradshaw ... prepared in cooperation with the International association of daily vacation Bible schools. New York, Cincinnati, The Abingdon press [c1923] 203 p. 20 cm. (The Abingdon religious eduction texts: D. G. Downet) general editor. Daily vacation church school series; G. H. Betts, editor) "This book was prepared especially to accompany Knights of service: program guide ... by Marion O. Hawtorne."--Foreword. Contents.--pt. 1. Bible stories.--pt. 2. Character stories. [BV1585.K75] 23-11103
1. Vacation schools Religious—Text-books. I. International association of daily vacation Bible schools. II. Title.

BRUMLEY, Mary Cureton. 268.432
Stories about Jesus; vacation church school unit for kindergarten children. New York, Abingdon-Cokesbury Press [1950] 96 p. illus. 23 cm. [BV1585.B73] 51-5981
1. Vacation schools, Religious—Text-books. I. Title.

DEPARTMENTALLY graded vacation Bible school textbooks ... 268.61
Springfield, Mo., Gospel publishing house [1940-42] 10 v. illus. 27 cm. Wtih music. Contents.Beginner-book I. Living in God's world, by Lorena F. Smith.--Beginner-book II. God's love and care for those in His world, by Lorena F. Smith.--Primary-book I. God's wonderful world, by Lorena F. Smith.--Primary-book II. God's wonderful gift--Jesus, by Lorena F. Smith.--Junior-books I-III, by Margaret A. Bass.--Intermediate books I-III, by Margaret A. Bass. [BV1585.D39] 45-16484
1. Vacation schools, Religious—Text-books. I. Smith, Lorena Ford. II. Bass, Margaret Ann.

DUNCAN, Charles Lee, comp. 268.6
Habit talks and missionary stories for vacation Bible schools, by Rev. Charles L. Duncan ... Published for the Department of Sunday school missions of the Board of national missions of the Presbyterian church in the U. S. A. Philadelphia, Presbyterian board of Christian education, 1933. 114 p. 19 cm. [BV1585.D83] 33-20548
1. Vacation schools, Religious—Text-books. 2. Children's stories. 3. Missionary stories. I. Presbyterian church in the U. S. A. Board of national missions. II. Title.

ECKEL, Fred L 268.432
The cathedral series; a series of Christian education courses and materials. Atlanta, c1957. 1 v. (various pagings) illus., port., plan. 29cm. Includes 'Bell ringer arrangements.' Includes bibliographical references. [BV1585.E25] 57-44560
1. Vacation schools, Religious—Text-books. I. Title.

FREIVOGEL, Esther. 266.62
Our happy world [by] Esther Freivogel; units of guided experience for kindergarten children: the child's home, the child's helpers, the child's larger world ... Leader's manual. St. Louis, Mo., Chicago, Ill., Pub. for the International committee on cooperative publication of vacation church school curriculum by Eden publishing house [c1934] 142 p. 22 cm. (Half-title: The cooperative series of vacation church school texts) "Prepared from descriptive outlines selected, approved and copyrighted in 1932 by the International council of religious education representing the Protestant Christian forces of the United States and Canada, and released to the constituent denominations, "Stories": p. 108-135; Songs, with music: p. 19-21. "The children's library": p. 19-21. [BV1585.F7] 34-10687
1. Vacation schools, Religious—Text-bok. I. International council of religious education. II. Title.

GRIFFITHS, Louise (Benckenstein) 1908-
God's world and ours; a co-operative vacation church school text for use with intermediate or junior high school groups. By Louise and Warren Griffiths. Teacher's text. Rev. Ed. St. Louis, Published for the Co-operative Publication Association by the Bethany Press [c1956] 96 p. illus. (The Co-operative series, vacation church school texts) "Suggested bibliography": p. 17-21. 64-71108
1. Vacation schools, Religious — Text-books. I. Griffiths, Carl Warren, 1907- joint author. II. Title. III. Series.

GRIFFITHS, Louise (Benckenstein) 1908- 268.433
God's world and ours; course for intermediates or junior high school groups in vacation church schools [by] Louise and Warren Griffiths. Teacher's text. St. Louis, Pub. for the Cooperative Pub. Assn. by the Bethany Press [1949] 160 p. illus. 20 cm. (The Cooperative series of vacation and weekday church school texts) [BV1585.G7] 49-18557
1. Vacation schools, Religious—Text-books. I. Griffiths, Carl Warren, 1907- joint author. II. Title. III. Series.

HAWTHORNE, Marion Olive, 1897- 268.
...*Learning to live;* a course for juniors, nine to eleven. Teacher's manual. By Marion O. Hawthorne. Prepared in cooperation with the International associaton of daily vacation Bible schools. New York, Cincinnati, The Abingdon press [c1926] 296 p. 20 cm. (The Abingdon religious education texts; D. G. Downey, general editor. Daily vacation church shool series; G. H. Betts, editor) [BV1546.H36] 27-1163
1. Vacation schools, Religious—Text-books. I. International association of daily vacation Bible schools. II. Title.

HAZELWOOD, Lola, 1897- 268.62
Discovering the lands of the Bible; a textbook for juniors in vacation church schools [by] Lola Hazelwood. New York, Cincinnati [etc.] Pub. for the International committee on cooperative publication of vacation church school curriculum by the Methodist book concern [c1939] 184 p. illus (maps) 21 1/2 cm. (Half-title: The co-operative series of vacation and weekday church school texts) Includes bibliographies. [BV1585.H38] 39-21186
1. Vacation schools, Religious—Text-books. 2. Bible—Study—Text-books. I. Title.

HUTTON, Jean Gertrude, 1871- 268.
... *Building for to-morrow;* a series of twenty-five lessons for boys and girls nine, ten, and eleven years of age, by Jean Gertrude Hutton, prepared in co-operation with the International association of daily vacation Bible schools. New York, Cincinnati, The Abingdon press [c1928] 129 p. front., plates. 20 cm. (The Abingdon religious education texts; D. G. Downey, general editor. Daily vacation church school series; G. H. Betts, editor) "Other stories to find and read" at end of each lesson. [BV1585.H8] 28-13326
1. Vacation schools, Religious—Text-books. I. International association of daily vacation Bible schools. II. Title.

JOHNSON, Olive L. 280.1
The church in today's world (a revision of One church for one world): a course for junior high school groups in vacation church schools [by] Olive L. Johnson and Frances Nall. Teacher's book. New York. Published for the Cooperative Publication Association by Abingdon Press [c.1959] 128p. illus. 23cm. (The Cooperative series: vacation church school texts) (5p. bibl.) 60-785 1.00 pap.,
1. Vacation schools. Religious—Text-books. 2. Christian union—Study and teaching. I. Nall, Frances (Mahaffie) joint author. II. Title.

JOHNSON, Olive L 280.1
The church in today's world (a revision of One church for one world); a course for junior high school groups in vacation church schools [by] Olive L. Johnson and Frances Nall. Teacher's book. New York, Published for the Cooperative Publication Assoication by Abingdon Press [c1959] 128p. illus. 23cm. (The Cooperative series: vacation church school texts. Includes bibliography. [BV1585] 60-785
1. Vacation schools, Religious—Text-books. 2. Christian union—Study and teaching. I. Nall, Frances (Mahaffle) 1902- joint author. II. Title.

JOHNSON, Olive L. 268.433
One church for one world; a course for intermediate or junior high school groups in vacation church schools. Teacher's book. [By] Olive L. Johnson and Frances M. Nall. New York, Published for the Cooperative Publication Association by Abingdon-Cokesbury Press [1951] 128 p. 20 cm. (Cooperative texts for vacation church schools) Bibliography: p. 124-127. [BV1585.J6] 51-2781
1. Vacation schools, Religious—Text-books. 2. Christian union—Study and teaching. I. Nall, Frances (Mabaffie), 1902- joint author. II. Title.

MEET your neighbors
(The Christian and others) a vacation church school course for junior boys and girls. Teacher's guide. Chicago, Published for the Cooperative Publication Association by Judson Press [c1956] 114p. illus. 23cm. 46p. illus. 26cm. (The Cooperative series vacation church school texts) Pupil's book, Illustrated by Sid Quinn. Chicago, Published for the Cooperative Publication Association by the Judson Press [c1956]
1. Vacation schools, Religious—Text-books. 2. Church and social problems-Study and teaching. I. Abernethy. Jean (Beaven) 1912- II. Series.

MERRILL, Jenny Biggs. 221.
Life stories from the Old and the New

Testament; a course of Bible lessons for daily vacation Bible schools, week day religious schools and religious training in the home, by Jenny B. Merrill ... New York, George H. Doran company [c1922] xiv p., 1 l., 17-169 p. 20 cm. [BS551.M44] 22-14835 1.00
I. Title.

NORDGREN, Julius Vincent, 1895- 268.62
Friends of Jesus; a course for juniors, ages 9-11, in vacation Bible schools and week-day schools of religion, by J. Vincent Nordgren; authorized by the Board of Christian education and literature of the Augustana synod. Rock Island, Ill., Augustana book concern [1933] 103 p. illus. (map) 18 cm. [BX8015.N57] 33-17136
1. Vacation schools, Religious—Text-books. 2. Bible stories, English—N. T. Acts. 3. Lord's prayer. 4. Lutheran church—Catechism and creeds. I. Evangelical Lutheran Augustana synod of North America. Board of Christian education and literature. II. Title.
Contents omitted.

RICE, Rebecca, 1899- 268.432
The earth is full of His riches; a vacation church school course for primary groups. Teacher's book. Boston, Published for the Co-operative Publication Association [by] Pilgrim Press [1953] 136p. 21cm. [The Co-operative series, vacation church school texts] [BV1585.R52] 53-2016
1. Vacation schools, Religious—Text-books. I. Title. II. Series.

SMITH, Ada (Wilcox) 1885- 268.432
Learning to know the Bible; junior vacation school manual. Teacher's book. New York, Published for the Cooperative Publication Association by Abingdon-Cokesbury Press [1951] 160 p. illus. 20 cm. (The Cooperative series of vacation church school texts) Full name: Ada Littleton (Wilcox) Smith. Bibliography: p. 10-11. [BV1585.S57] 51-4278
1. Vacation schools, Religious—Text-books. 2. Bible—Study. I. Title.

SQUIRES, Walter Albion, 1874- comp. 377.1
The wonderful story of Jesus the Saviour; a course of thirty lessons for vacation Bible schools, compiled by Walter Albion Squires ... in co-operation with John M. Somerndike ... Published for the Department of Sunday school missions of the Board of national missions of the Presbyterian church in the U.S.A. Philadelphia, Presbyterian board of Christian education, 1932. 256 p. 18 1/2 cm. "Hymns for use in the classes"; p. 15-40. [BV1585.S6] 33-2133
1. Vacation schools, Religious—Text-books. 2. Bible stories, English. I. Somerndike, John Mason, 1877- joint comp. II. Presbyterian church in the U.S.A. Board of national missions. III. Title.

THE Standard vacation Bible school courses. 268.
Cincinnati, Standard Pub. Co. [c1922-] v. illus., maps. 31 cm. Includes music. Contents.[1]-[2] Kindergarten, 1st-2d year, by E. B. Rowe, ed. by F. M. Waterman.--v. [3] Primary, 1st year, by F. M. Waterman.--v. [4] Primary, 2d year. Missionary stories by M. T. Applegarth, pageant by L. K. De Moss, course by F. M. Waterman.--v. [5] Intermediate, 1st year, by C. H. Benson. [BV1585.S7] 48-36730
1. Vacation schools, Religious—Text-books. I. Rowe, Edna B. II. Waterman, Florence M., ed.

SULLIVAN, Florence.
Friends everywhere. A vacation church school Text (ten sessions) . . . Philadelphia [etc.] The Judson press [1956] 128 p. illus. 26 cm. (Judson series. Primary department) Includes music.
I. Title.

TILLEY, Ethel. 268.432
Jesus is His name; a vacation school course for junior groups. Illustrated by Harold Kihl. Teacher's book. Philadelphia, Published for the Cooperative Publication Association by the Westminster Press [1957] 96 p. illus. 23 cm. (The Cooperative series: vacation church school texts) [BV1585.T5] 57-11101
1. Vacation schools, Religious—Text-books. I. Title.

VACATION church school, 268.6
manual for the teacher ... 3d series ... St. Louis, Mo., The Bethany press [c1924] 4 v. illus. 20 cm. Contains songs with music. Contents.[v. 1] Primary, group i, prepared by Jessie E. Moore, Hazel A. Lewis, editor.--[v. 2] Primary, group ii, prepared by Mrs. A. O. Kuhn, Hazel A. Lewis, editor.--[v. 3] Group iii, junior, prepared by H. Imogene McPherson, Hazel A. Lewis, editor.--[v. 4] Group iv, intermediate, prepared by W. E. Powell, H. C. Munro, editor. [BV1585.V28 3d ser.] 25-12045
1. Vacation schools, Religious—Text-books. I. Moore, Jessie Eleanor. II. Kuhn, Mrs. A. O. III. McPherson, H. Imogene. IV. Powell, Wilfred Evans. V. Lewis, Hazel Asenath, 1886- ed. VI. Munro, Harry Clyde, 1890- ed.

YOUNG, Lois Horton. j268
God's world of wonder. [Illustrated by Paul Behrens and Terry Hitt. Dayton, Ohio, Otterbein Press, c1964] Rev. Dayton, Ohio, Published for the Cooperative Publication Association by the Otterbein Press [1967] 16 p. col. illus. 18 x 23 cm. 104 p. illus., music. 23 cm. (The Cooperative series, vacation church school texts) Cover title. Includes hymns with music. "A cooperative vacation church school course for use with kindergarten children." [BV1585.Y67] 64-22741
1. Vacation schools, Religious — Text-books. 2. Religious education of pre-school children. I. Cooperative Publication Association. II. Title. III. Title: Teacher's guide.

Vacation schools, Seventh-Day Adventist.

HARRIS, William J. 268'.8'67
The challenge of vacation Bible school evangelism; the story of the beginning, growth, and effectiveness of Seventh-Day Adventist vacation Bible school evangelism, by William J. Harris. Nashville, Published for the Sabbath School Dept., General Conference of Seventh-Day Adventists, by Southern Pub. Association [1967] 214 p. illus. 22 cm. [BX6113.H3] 67-2208
1. Vacation schools, Seventh-Day Adventist. 2. Vacation schools, Religious. I. Seventh-Day Adventists. General Conference. Sabbath School Dept. II. Title.

Vacations—Moral and religious aspects.

BELGUM, Harold J. 248.42
Family vacation idea book. Illus. by Arthur Kirchhoff. St. Louis, Concordia [c.1966] 62p. illus. 28cm. [BV4599.B4] 66-21173 1.00 pap.,
1. Vacations—Moral and religious aspects. 2. Nature—Religious interpretations. I. Title.

*COOK, Roselynn 231.107
Exploring God's world. Ed.: Margaret J. Irvin. Illus.: Helen and Bill Hamilton. Designer: William 0 ol. illus. 22x28cm. (LCA vacation church sch. ser.) pap., .50; teacher's guide (to grades 3 & 4) pap., .90
I. Title.

Vacations schools, Religious—Teachers' manuals.

WHITEHOUSE, Elizabeth Scott, 1893- 268.6
Followers of Jesus, a textbook for juniors in vacation church schools [by] Elizabeth Scott Whitehouse. Philadelphia, Published for the Interdenominational committee on co-operative publication of vacation church school curriculum by the Westminster press [1942] 197 p. illus. 21 cm. (Half-title: The Co-operative series of church school texts) Includes bibliographies. [BV1585.W45] 42-12805
1. Vacations schools, Religious—Teachers' manuals. I. International council of religious education. Interdenominational committee on cooperative publication of vacation church school curriculum. II. Title.

Vaisesika.

KANADA. 181'.44
The Vaisesika sutras of Kanada, with the commentary of Sankara Misra and extracts from the gloss of Jayanarayana. Together with notes from the commentary of Chandrakanta and an introd. by the translator. Translated by Nandalal Sinha. Allahabad, Panini Office, 1911. New York, AMS Press, 1974. p. cm. Original ed. issued as v. 6, pts. 1-4, of The Sacred books of the Hindus. English and Sanskrit; introd. and explanations in English. [B132.V2K313 1974] 73-3791 ISBN 0-404-57806-3 32.50
1. Vaisesika. I. Jayanarayana Tarkapancanana. Kanadasutravivrti. English & Sanskrit. 1974. II. Candrakanta Tarkalankara. Vaisesikasutrabhasya. English & Sanskrit. 1974. III. Sinha, Nandalal, ed. IV. Sankaramisra, 15th century. Vaisesikasutropaskara. English & Sanskrit. 1974. V. Title. VI. Series: The Sacred books of the Hindus, v. 6, pts. 1-4.

TACHIKAWA, Musashi. 110
The structure of the world in Udayana's realism : a study of the Lakasanavali and the Kiranavali / by Musashi Tachikawa. Dordrecht, Holland ; Boston : D. Reidel Pub. Co. ; Hingham, MA : Sold and distributed in the U.S.A. and Canada by Kluwer Boston, c1981. xiv, 180 p. : ill. ; 23 cm. (Studies of classical India ; v. 4) Revision of the author's thesis (Ph.D.—Harvard, 1975) Includes indexes. Bibliography: p. 163-168. [B133.U294T32 1981] 19 81-13848 ISBN 90-277-1291-3 : 39.50
1. Udayanacarya. 2. Vaisesika. 3. Nyaya. I. Udayanacarya. Laksanavali. English & Sanskrit. 1981. II. Udayanacarya. Selections. 1981. III. Title. IV. Series.
Distributor's address: 160 Old Derby St., Hingham, MA 02043.

Vaishnavism.

BHANDARKAR, Ramkrishna Gopal, Sir, 1837-1925. 294.5'51
Vaisnavism, Saivism, and minor religious systems / R. G. Bhandarkar. New York : Garland Pub., 1980. 169 p. ; 23 cm. (Oriental religions) (Series: Buhler, Georg, 1837-1898, ed. Grundriss der indo-arischen Philologie und Altertumskunde ; Bd. 3, Hft. 6.) Reprint of the 1913 ed. published by K. J. Trubner, Strassburg, which was issued as Bd. 3, Hft. 6 of G. Buhler's Grundriss der indo-arischen Philologie und Altertumskunde. Includes bibliographical references and index. [BL1245.V3B4 1980] 78-74263 ISBN 0-8240-3900-9 lib. bdg. : 20.00
1. Vaishnavism. 2. Sivaism. 3. India—Religion. I. Title. II. Series.

KENNEDY, Melville T. 1882- 294.
... The Chaitanya movement; a study of the Vaishnavism of Bengal, by Melville T. Kennedy ... Calcutta, Association press (Y. M. C. A.) London, New York [etc.] H. Milford, Oxford university press, 1925. x, [2] 270 p. plates. 19 cm. (The religious life of India) [BL1245.V3K4] 25-20959
1. Vaishnavism. 2. Chaitanya, 1486-1534. I. Title.

KENNEDY, Melville T., 1882- 294.5'512
The Chaitanya movement / Melville T. Kennedy. New York : Garland Pub., 1980. p. cm. (Oriental religions) Reprint of the 1925 ed. published by Association Press (Y.M.C.A.), Calcutta, and H. Milford, Oxford University Press, London, New York, in series: The Religious life of India. Includes index. [BL1245.V3K4 1980] 78-74267 ISBN 0-8240-3904-1 lib. bdg. : 30.00
1. Chaitanya, 1486-1634. 2. Vaishnavism. I. Title. II. Series. III. Series: Religious life of India.

RAYCHAUDHURI, Hemchandra, 1892-1957. 294.5'512
Materials for the study of the early history of the Vaishnava sect / by Hemchandra Raychaudhuri. 2d ed. New Delhi : Oriental Books Reprint Corp. : distributed by Munshiram Manoharlal Publishers, 1975. viii, 146 p. ; 22 cm. "Summary of a course of lectures on the early history of the Bhagavata Vaishnava sect which ... [the author] delivered ... during the last session (1918-19)." Reprint of the 1920 ed. published by the University of Calcutta, Calcutta. Includes index. "Bibliographic index": p. [119]-124. [BL1245.V3R33 1975] 75-908076 8.50
1. Vaishnavism. I. Title.
Distributed by South Asia Books.

SCOTT, Jefferson Ellsworth, 1851- 294.55
Braj, the Vaishnava Holy Land; a jubilee volume, by Rev. J. E. Scott ... New York, Eaton & Mains; Cincinnati, Jennings & Graham [c1905] 181 p. front., 17 pl., fold. map. 19 cm. [BL1245.V3S3] 6-10935
1. Vaishnavism. 2. Missions—Muttra, India (City) 3. Muttra, India (City) I. Title.

SINHA, Jadunath, 1894- 294.5'512
The philosophy & religion of Chaitanya and his followers / by Jadunath Sinha. 1st ed. Calcutta : Sinha Pub. House, 1976. ii, ii, 151, ix p. ; 22 cm. Includes bibliographical references and index. [BL1245.V3S56] 77-901352 Rs25.00
1. Chaitanya, 1486-1534. 2. Vaishnavism. I. Title.

SREENIVASA Murthy, H. V. 294.5'512
Vaisnavism of Samkaradeva and Ramanuja; a comparative study [by] H. V. Sreenivasa Murthy. [1st ed.] Delhi, Motilal Banarsidass [1973] viii, 254 p. 23 cm. A revision of the author's thesis, Gauhati University. Bibliography: p. [236]-244. [BL1245.V3S64 1973] 73-900571
1. Sankaradeva, 1449-1569. 2. Ramanuja, founder of sect. 3. Vaishnavism. I. Title.
Distributed by Verry, 7.50

Vajiranana Varoros, Prince, Supreme Patriarch, 1859-1921.

VAJIRANANA Varoros, Prince, Supreme Patriarch, 1859-1921. 294.3'657'0924 B
Autobiography, the life of Prince-Patriarch Vajirana of Siam, 1860-1921 / Prince Vajiranana-varorasa ; translated, edited, and introduced by Craig J. Reynolds. Athens : Ohio University Press, 1979. p. cm. (Southeast Asia translation series ; 3) [BQ994.A447A3513] 79-9725 ISBN 0-8214-0376-1 : 12.00
1. Vajiranana Varoros, Prince, Supreme Patriarch, 1859-1921. 2. Priests, Buddhist—Thailand—Biography. 3. Thailand—Princes and princesses—Biography. I. Reynolds, Craig J. II. Title. III. Series.

VAJIRANANA Varoros, Prince, Supreme Patriarch, 1859-1921. 294.3'657'0924 B
Autobiography, the life of Prince-Patriarch Vajiranana of Siam, 1860-1921 / Prince Vajiranana-varorasa ; translated, edited, and introduced by Craig J. Reynolds. Athens : Ohio University Press, 1979. p. cm. (Southeast Asia translation series ; 3) [BQ994.A447A3513] 79-9725 ISBN 0-8214-0376-1 : 12.00 12.00 ISBN 0-8214-0408-3 (pbk.)
1. Vajiranana Varoros, Prince, Supreme Patriarch, 1859-1921. 2. Priests, Buddhist—Thailand—Biography. 3. Thailand—Princes and princesses—Biography. I. Reynolds, Craig J. II. Title. III. Series.

Valdes, Juan de, d. 1541.

LONGHURST, John Edward, 1918- 922.246
Erasmus and the Spanish Inquisition: the case of Juan de Valdes. Albuquerque, University of New Mexico Press, 1950. 114 p. 23 cm. (University of New Mexico publications in history. no. 1) Issued also as thesis, University of Michican, in microfilm form. Bibliography: p. 97-114. [BR350.V34L6 1950] 50-63470
1. Valdes, Juan de, d. 1541. 2. Erasmus, Desiderius, d. 1536. 3. Inquisition. Spain. I. Title. II. Series: New Mexico. University. University of New Mexico publications in history, no.1

Valdez, A. C.

VALDEZ, A. C. 269'.2'0924 B
Fire on Azusa Street / by A.C. Valdez, Sr. with James F. Scheer. Costa Mesa, Calif. :

Gift Publications, c1980, 1981. 139 p. ; 22 cm. [BX8762.Z8V348] 19 80-67301 ISBN 0-86595-003-2 pbk. : Price unreported.
1. Valdez, A. C. 2. Pentecostals—United States—Biography. 3. Pentecostalism—History. 4. Revivals—California—Los Angeles. 5. Los Angeles (Calif.)—Church history. I. Scheer, James F. II. Title. III. Title: Azusa Street.

Vale, Roy Ewing, 1885-1959.

KISSINGER, Dorothy May 285.10924 (Vale) 1916-
Say a good word; a biography of the Reverend Roy Ewing Vale, D. D., LL. D., moderator of the 156th General Assembly of the Presbyterian Church, U.S.A. [Mesa? Ariz., 1963] 243 p. port. 24 cm. [BX9225.V28K5] 63-25797
1. Vale, Roy Ewing, 1885-1959. I. Title.

Valentinians.

EVANGELIUM VERITATIS. 229.95
The Gospel of truth, a Valentinian meditation on the gospel. Translation from the Coptic and commentary by Kendrick Grobel. Nashville, Abingdon Press [c.1960] 206p. Bibliography: p.203-206 20cm. 60-5231 4.00
1. Valentinians. I. Grobel, Kendrick, ed. and tr. II. Title.

GOSPEL on truth. English 230'.99
The Gospel of truth : a Valentinian meditation on the Gospel : translation from the Coptic and commentary / by Kendrick Grobel. New York : AMS Press, [1980] i.e. 1979, c1960. p. cm. Reprint of the ed. published by Abingdon Press, New York. Bibliography: p. [BT1475.G613 1980] 78-63167 ISBN 0-404-16083-2 : 19.50
1. Valentinians. I. Grobel, Kendrick, 1908-1965.

Valle, Juan del, Bp. of Popayan, fl. 1548-1560.

FRIEDE, Juan. 922.244
Vida y luchas de don Juan del Valle, primer obispo de Popayan y protector de indios estudio documental basado en investigaciones realizadas en los archivos de Colombia, Espana y el Vaticanno. Prologo del Dr. D. Manuel Gimenez Fernandez. Popayan [Colombia, Editorial Universidad] 1961. 270 p. 25 cm. Bibliographical references included in "Notas." [BX4705.V28F72] 63-39092
1. Valle, Juan del, Bp. of Popayan, fl. 1548-1560. I. Title.

Vally, Louis, 1841-1898.

BURTON, Irwin Huntington- 922.
For the honor of the King; the life history of Louis, son of Simon and Marie Vally of Lavaudieu, in the province of Ardeche, France, by Irwin Huntington-Burton... Philadelphia, H. L. Kilner & co. [c1904] 484 p. 2 pl., 3 port. (incl. front.) 19 1/2 cm. [BX4705.V3B8] 4-35308
1. Vally, Louis, 1841-1898. I. Title.

Valmiki.

ATHAVALE, Pandurang 294.5'922 Vaijnath, 1920-
Valmiki Ramayana : a study / from the discourses of Pandurang V. Athavale. [s.l. : s.n., 1976] (Bombay : Associated Advertisers & Printers) vii, 209 p., [2] leaves of plates : ill. ; 22 cm. "Published on the occasion of the golden jubilee celebration, January 1976 of Shrimad Bhagvat Gita Pathashala." [PK3661.A8] 76-902310 Rs14.00
1. Valmiki. Ramayana. I. Title.

WURM, Alois, 1944- 294.5'922
Character-portrayals in the Ramayana of Valmiki : a systematic representation / Alois Wurm. Delhi : Ajanta Publications (India) : distributors, Ajanta Books International, 1977, c1976 xx, 570 p. ; 22 cm. A revision of a portion of the author's thesis, Karnatak University, 1972, with title: Characterization in the Ramayana of Valmiki; a textual study with a critical review of the genesis of the Ramayana. Bibliography: p. [567]-570. [PK3661.W9] 76-904969 30.00
1. Valmiki. Ramayana. I. Title.
Dist. by International Book Distributors, P.O. Box 180, Murray Hill St., New York, NY 10016

Valvin, Jean, 1509-1564—Theology.

NIESEL, Wilhelm. 230.42
The theology of Calvin. Translated by Harold Knight. Philadelphia, Westminster Press [1956] 254p. 23cm. [BX9418.N53] 56-8047
1. Valvin, Jean, 1509-1564—Theology. I. Title.

Van Cott, Mrs. Maggie (Newton) 1830-

FOSTER, John Onesimus, 922.773 1833-1920.
Life and labors of Mrs. Maggie Newton Van Cott, the first lady licensed to preach in the Methodist Episcopal church in the United States. By Rev. John O. Foster ... With an introduction by Rev. Gilbert Haven ... and Rev. David Sherman. Cincinnati, Hitchcock and Walden, for the author, 1872. xxxix, 339 p. front. (port.) pl. 18 cm. "Woman's place in the gospel. By Rev. D. Sherman": p. xxix-xxxix. [BX8495.V15F6] 37-12145
1. Van Cott, Mrs. Maggie (Newton) 1830- 2. Women as ministers. I. Sherman, David, 1822-1897. II. Title.

Van den Broek, Theodore John, 1783-1851.

[CORRY, Mary Alphonsa, 922. sister] 1842-1916.
... The story of Father Van den Broek, O. F.; a study of Holland and the story of the early settlement of Wisconsin. Chicago, Anisworth & company, 1907. 94 p. front. (port.) illus. 19 cm. (The lakeside series of English readings) Preface signed: M. A. [Secular name: Mary Ann Corry] [BV3705.V3C6] 7-15984
1. Van den Broek, Theodore John, 1783-1851. I. Title.

Van der Hurk, Pieter, 1911-

BROWNING, Norma Lee. 133.9'3'0924
Peter Hurkos : I have many lives / Norma Lee Browning. 1st ed. Garden City, N.Y. : Doubleday, 1976. 223 p. ; 22 cm. [BF1027.V3B69] 75-21213 ISBN 0-385-01508-9 : 6.95
1. Van der Hurk, Pieter, 1911- I. Title.

BROWNING, Norma Lee. 133.8'0924
The psychic world of Peter Hurkos. [1st ed.] Garden City, N.Y., Doubleday, 1970. 297 p. illus., ports. 22 cm. [BF1027.V3B7] 76-114751 6.95
1. Van der Hurk, Pieter, 1911- I. Title.

Van Dyck, Leonard B., 1802?-1877.

REMARKS on liberty of 922.573 *conscience,* human creeds, and theological schools, suggested by the facts in a recent case. By a layman of the Reformed Dutch church ... New York, Printed by J. & J. Harper, 1828. 102 p. 22 1/2 cm. [BX9543.V3R4] 36-22152
1. Van Dyck, Leonard B., 1802?-1877. 2. Reformed church in America—Doctrinal and controversial works. 3. New Brunswick, N.Y. Theological seminary of the Reformed church in America. 4. Liberty of conscience. I. A layman of the Reformed Dutch church.

Van Dyke, Henry Jackson, 1822-1891.

[VAN Dyke, Henry] 1852- 922.573 1933.
Henry Jackson Van Dyke... New York, A. D. F. Randolph & company [1892] 1 p. l., iv, 168 p. front., (port.) 19 1/2 cm. "Life and character" signed: Henry Van Dyke. Paul Van Dyke. [BX9225.V3V3] 36-22123
1. Van Dyke, Henry Jackson, 1822-1891. 2. Presbyterian church—Sermons. 3. Sermons, American. I. Van Dyke, Paul, 1859-1933, joint author. II. Title.
Contents omitted.

Van Ess, Dorothy.

VAN ESS, 266'.5'7320924 B Dorothy.
Pioneers in the Arab world, by Dorothy F. Van Ess. Grand Rapids, W. B. Eerdmans Pub. Co. [1974] 188 p. illus. 21 cm. (The Historical series of the Reformed Church in America, no. 3) Bibliography: p. 187-188. [BV2626.V36A36] 74-14964 ISBN 0-8028-1585-5
1. Van Ess, Dorothy. 2. Van Ess, John, 1879- 3. Missions to Muslims—Basra. I. Title. II. Series: Reformed Church in America. The historical series, no. 3.

Van Hornersville, N.Y. Otsquago valley larger parish.

HARRIS, Margaret J. 277.47
Life in the Larger parish, by Margaret J. Harris, director of religious education, the Otsquago valley larger parish, Van Hornersville, N.Y. 2d printing, 1944 ... New York, N.Y., Committee on town and country, Home missions council of North America and the Federal council of the churches of Christ in America [1944] 89 p. illus. 19 1/2 cm. Bibliography: p. 86-89. [BX9999.V3O8] 45-9480
1. Van Hornersville, N.Y. Otsquago valley larger parish. I. Committee on town and country. II. Title.

Van Impe, Rexella.

VAN IMPE, Rexella. 269'.2'0922 B
The tender touch : reaching out, building relationships / Rexella Van Impe. Nashville : T. Nelson, c1980. 143 p., [4] leaves of plates : ill. ; 21 cm. [BV3785.V34A36] 19 80-24593 ISBN 0-8407-5745-X pbk. : 3.95
1. Van Impe, Rexella. 2. Van Impe, Jack. 3. Evangelists—United States—Biography. I. Title.

Van Ingen, John Visger, 1806-1877.

MEMOIR of John Visger Van 922. *Ingen,* largely from his own writings ... Rochester, N. Y., For sale by Scrantom, Wetmore & co.; [etc., etc., 1878?] 2 p. l., [3]-152 p. front. (port.) 25 cm. [BX5995.V3A3] 1-2739
1. Van Ingen, John Visger, 1806-1877.

Van Name, Nettie, d. 1892.

HUGHES, George.
The sweet singer, Nettie Van Name and her seven years' work for Jesus. By Rev. George Hughes assisted by Mrs. Lidie H. Kenney. Introduction by Rev. E. I. D. Pepper. Philadelphia, National Holiness publishing house [1892?] vi, 89 p. front. (port.) 18 1/2 cm. 9-30724
1. Van Name, Nettie, d. 1892. I. Kenney, Mrs. Lidie H., joint author. II. Title.

Van Ornum, Tonl.

TONALITY Group, Salem, Or. 133.93
It's startling! Illus. by Bea Edson. New York, Comet Press Books [1955] 277p. illus. 23cm. [BF1290.T6] 55-9800
1. Van Ornum, Tonl. 2. Astrology. 3. New Thought. I. Title.

Van Orsdel, William Wesley, 1848-1919.

LIND, Robert W 287.10924
From the ground up; the story of 'Brother Van,' Montant pioneer minister, 1848-1919. [n. p., Treasure State Pub. Co., 1961] 182p. illus. 20cm. Includes bibliography. [BX8495.V2L5] 61-59891
1. Van Orsdel, William Wesley, 1848-1919. I. Title.

SMITH, Alson Jesse. 922.773
Brother Van, a biography of the Rev. William Wesley Van Orsdel. Nashville, Abingdon-Cokesbury Press [1948] 240 p. illus., ports. map (on lining-papers) 21 cm. [BX8495.V2S5] 48-6218
1. Van Orsdel, William Wesley, 1848-1919. I. Title.

Van Rensellaer, Cortlandt, 1808-1860.

MEMORIAL of Cortlandt Van 922.573 *Rensselaer.* Philadelphia, C. Sherman & son, printers, 1860. 64 p. front. (port.) 24 cm. "Funeral address. Delivered in the First Presbyterian church. Burlington, New Jersey, on the 30th of July, 1860. By the Rev. Charles Hodge, D. D.": p. 8-17. "A discourse commemorative of the life and character of the Rev. Cortlandt Van Rensselaer, D. D. Delivered ... September 30th, 1860. By Henry A. Boardman, D. D.": p. 22-39. "Part of a discourse, delivered by the Rev. W. B. Sprague, D. D.": p. 40-46. [BX9225.V35M4] 36-22143
1. Van Rensellaer, Cortlandt, 1808-1860. 2. Funeral sermons. 3. Presbyterian church—Sermons. 4. Sermons, American. I. Hodge, Charles, 1797-1878. II. Boardman, Henry Augustus, 1808-1880. III. Sprague, William Buell, 1795-1876.

Van Rensselaer, Henry, 1851-1907.

SPILLANE, Edward Peter, 922. 1859-1929.
Life and letters of Henry Van Rensselaer, priest of the Society of Jesus, by the Rev. Edward P. Spillane, S.J. New York, Fordham university press, 1908. vii p., 2 l., 293 p. 5 pl., 6 port. (incl. front.) 20 cm. [BX4705.V32S6 1908] 8-34132
1. Van Rensselaer, Henry, 1851-1907. I. Title.

SPILLANE, Edward Peter, 922. 1859-1929.
Life and letters of Henry Van Rensselaer, priest of the Society of Jesus, by the Rev. Edward P. Spillane ... 2d ed., rev. and enl. New York, The America press, 1912. xi, 331 p. 5 pl., 6 port. (incl. front.) 20 cm. [BX4705.V32S6 1912] 12-13462
1. Van Rensselaer, Henry, 1851-1907. I. Title.

Van Stone, Doris.

VAN STONE, Doris. 266'.023'0924 B
Dorie, the girl nobody loved / Doris Van Stone with Erwin Lutzer. Chicago : Moody Press, c1979. 158 p. : ill. ; 22 cm. [BV3680.N52V358] 78-17935 ISBN 0-8024-2276-4 : 5.95
1. Van Stone, Doris. 2. Missionaries—New Guinea—Biography. 3. Missionaries—United States—Biography. I. Lutzer, Irwin, joint author. II. Title.

Van Til, Cornelius, 1895-

JERUSALEM and Athens; 201'.1 critical discussions on the theology and apologetics of Cornelius Van Til. Edited by E. R. Geehan. [Nutley, N.J.] Presbyterian and Reformed Pub. Co., 1971. xv, 498 p. 23 cm. Includes bibliographical references. [BR50.J4] 78-155779 9.95
1. Van Til, Cornelius, 1895- 2. Van Til, Cornelius, 1895- —Bibliography. 3. Theology—Addresses, essays, lectures. I. Geehan, E. R., ed.

NOTARO, Thom. 239'.01
Van Til & the use of evidence / Thom Notaro. Phillipsburg, N.J. : Presbyterian and Reformed Pub. Co., 1980. 136 p. ; 18 cm. Based on the author's thesis (Th. M.—Westminster Theological Seminary) Includes bibliographical references and indexes. [BT102.N68] 19 81-112409 ISBN 0-87552-353-6 (pbk.) : 3.75
1. Van Til, Cornelius, 1895- 2. God—Proof—History of doctrines—20th century. 3. Apologetics—20th century. I. Title. II. Title: Van Til and the use of evidence.

RUSHDOONY, Rousas John. 201
By what standard? An analysis of the philosophy of Cornelius Van Til. Philadelphia, Presbyterian and Reformed Pub. Co., 1959. 209p. 22cm. Includes bibliography. [BX9225.V37R8] 58-59921
1. Van Til, Cornelius, 1895- I. Title.

RUSHDOONY, Rousas John 922.473
Van Til. Philadelphia, Presbyterian and Reformed Pub. Co., 1960. 51p. (International library of philosophy and

theology. Modern thinkers series) Bibl. 60-6805 1.25 pap.,
1. Van Til, Cornelius, 1895- I. Title.

WHITE, William, 1934- 285'.731'0924 B
Van Til, defender of the faith : an authorized biography / William White, Jr. Nashville : T. Nelson Publishers, c1979. 233 p., [4] leaves of plates : ill. ; 21 cm. Includes bibliographical references. [BX9225.V37W47] 79-9732 ISBN 0-8407-5670-4 pbk. : 4.95
1. Van Til, Cornelius, 1895- 2. Theologians—United States—Biography. I. Title.

Van, Turkey.

USSHER, Clarence Douglas, 1870-
An American physician in Turkey; a narrative of adventures in peace and in war, by Clarence D. Ussher, M.D., Grace H. Knapp, collaborating ... Boston and New York, Houghton Mifflin company, 1917. xiii, [1] p., 1 l., 338, [3] p. front., plates, ports., map, plan. 20 1/2 cm. $1.75 [BV3170.U8] 17-27881
1. Van, Turkey. 2. Missions—Van, Turkey. 3. European war, 1914-1918-Armenia. I. Knapp, Grace Higley. II. Title.

Van Wade, David.

VAN WADE, David 248'.2'0924 B
Second chance : a broken marriage restored / by David and Sarah Van Wade. Plainfield, N.J. : Logos International, c1975. 248 p. ; 21 cm. [BR1725.V27A35] 75-20899 ISBN 0-88270-137-1 : 5.95.
1. Van Wade, David. 2. Van Wade, Sarah. I. Van Wade, Sarah, joint author. II. Title.

Van Wagenen, Isabella, b. 1797?

VALE, Gilbert, 1788-1866. 922
Fanaticism; its source and influence, illustrated by the simple narrative of Isabella, in the case of Matthias, Mr. and Mrs. B. Folger, Mr. Pierson, Mr. Mills, Catherine, Isabella, &c. &c. A reply to W. L. Stone, with descriptive portraits of all the parties, while at Sing-Sing and at Third street ... By G. Vale. New York, G. Vale, 1835. 2 v. illus. (plan) 18 1/2 cm. [BR1718.M3S85] 36-31791
1. Van Wagenen, Isabella, b. 1797? 2. Matthews, Robert. 3. Stone, William Leete, 1792-1844. Matthias and his impostures. 4. Fanaticism. I. Title.

Vanamee, Parker, d. 1918.

VANAMEE, Mary Conger, Mrs. 922.
Vanamee, by Mary Conger Vanamee (Mrs. Parker Vanamee) New York, Harcourt, Brace and company [c1930] 307 p. 22 1/2 cm. [BX5199.V3V3 1930] 30-5273
1. Vanamee, Parker, d. 1918. I. Title.

Vanauken, Sheldon.

VANAUKEN, Sheldon. 248'.2'0924 B
A severe mercy / by Sheldon Vanauken. 1st U.S. ed. San Francisco : Harper & Row, c1977. p. cm. Includes index. [BX5995.V33A35 1977] 77-6161 ISBN 0-06-068821-1 : 6.95
1. Vanauken, Sheldon. 2. Lewis, Clive Staples, 1898-1963—Correspondence. 3. Anglicans—United States—Biography. 4. Anglicans—England—Biography. I. Title.

Vandeman, Herbert A.

EDWARDS, Josephine Cunnington. 286'.73 B
With an holy calling / by Josephine Cunnington Edwards. Mountain View, Calif. : Pacific Press Pub. Association, c1979. 124 p. ; 22 cm. (A Destiny book ; D-172) [BX6193.V36E38] 78-53671 ISBN 0-8163-0250-2 pbk. : 3.95
1. Vandeman, Herbert A. 2. Seventh-Day Adventists—United States—Biography. I. Title.

Vanderbilt, Mrs. Mary (Scannell) 1867-1919.

CADWALLADER, Mary E. Mrs. 133.
Mary S. Vanderbilt, a twentieth century seer, by M. E. Cadwallader ... Chicago, Ill., The Progressive thinker publishing house [c1921] vii, 126 p. front., plates. ports. 19 cm. [BF1283.N3C3] 22-8849
1. Vanderbilt, Mrs. Mary (Scannell) 1867-1919. 2. Spiritualism. I. Title.

Vann, Roger.

CHAPIAN, Marie. 280'.4 B
Escape from rage : the story of Roger Vann / by Marie Chapian ; foreword by Nicky Cruz. Plainfield, N.J. : Logos Books, c1981. x, 221 p., [14] p. of plates : ill. ; 21 cm. [BV3785.V36C48 1981] 19 81-83041 pbk. : 4.95
1. Vann, Roger. 2. Evangelists—United States—Biography. I. Title.

Vanner, Eleanor, 1828-1839.

CURWEN, John, 1816-1880. 922
The history of Eleanor Vanner, who died, April 26, 1839, aged ten years. Written for children of the same age. By John Curwen. Revised by the Committee of publication of the American Sunday-school union. Philadelphia, American Sunday-school union [1841] 68 p. 16 cm. [BR1715.V3C8] 37-19932
1. Vanner, Eleanor, 1828-1839. I. American Sunday-school union. II. Title.

Vartan, of Armenia, Saint, d. 451.

BANKER, Marie Sarrafian. 922.1
St. Vartan: hero of Armenia; the story of Armenia's early struggle for freedom to worship Christ. New York, Exposition Press [1951] 164 p. illus. 22 cm. [BX129.V3B3] 51-14405
1. Vartan, of Armenia, Saint, d. 451. I. Title.

Vass, Winifred Kellersberger.

VASS, Winifred Kellersberger. 967.5'1'03
Thirty-one banana leaves / Winifred Kellersberger Vass. Atlanta : John Knox Press, [1975] p. cm. [BV4501.2.V36] 74-7617 ISBN 0-8042-2581-8 : 3.95
1. Vass, Winifred Kellersberger. 2. Meditations. 3. Zaire—Description and travel—1951- I. Title.

Vassar, John Ellison, 1813-1878.

VASSAR, Thomas Edwin, 1834- 922.673
Uncle John Vassar; or, The fight of faith. By his nephew, Rev. T. E. Vassar. With an introduction, by Rev. A. J. Gordon ... New York, American tract society [1879] 218 p. front. (port.) 19 1/2 cm. [BV3785.V38V3] 37-36756
1. Vassar, John Ellison, 1813-1878. I. American tract society. II. Title.

VASSAR, Thomas Edwin, 1834- 922.673
Uncle John Vassar; or, The fight of faith, by Thomas E. Vassar, D.D.; revised by Rev. Howard Vassar Miller, Rev. Edwin Noah Hardy, PH.D.; introduction by Rev. Adoniram J. Gordon, D.D.; introduction to revised edition by Rev. Charles Gallaudet Trumbull, LITT.D. New York, N.Y., American tract society [c1931] 190 p. front. (port.) 19 1/2 cm. [BV2380.V3V3] 31-16573
1. Vassar, John Ellison, 1813-1878. I. Miller, Howard Vassar, 1894- II. Hardy, Edwin Noah, 1861- III. American tract society. IV. Title.

Vasubandhu.

CAUDHURI, Sukomal, 1939- 294.3'824
Analytical study of the Abhidharmakosa / by Sukomal Chaudhuri. Calcutta : Sanskrit College, 1976. xiv, 249 p., [1] leaf of plates : ill. ; 26 cm. (Calcutta Sanskrit College research series ; no. 114 : Studies ; no. 77) Title on spine: Abhidharmakosa. Originally published serially in our heritage, v. 21-23. Includes index. Bibliography: p. [233]-244. [BQ2687.C38] 76-904521 Rs35.00
1. Vasubandhu. Abhidharmakosa. 2. Abhidharma. I. Title. II. Title: Abhidharmakosa. III. Series: Calcutta. University. Sanskrit College. Dept. of Post-graduate Training and Research. Research series ; 114. IV. Series: Calcutta. University. Sanskrit College. Dept. of Post-graduate Training and Research. Research series. Studies ; 77.

Vasugupta. Sivasutra.

TAIMNI, I. K., 1898- 294.5'513
The ultimate reality and realization : Sivasutra, with text in Sanskrit, transliteration in roman, translation in English, and commentary / by I. K. Taimni. 1st ed. Madras ; Wheaton, Ill. : Theosophical Pub. House, 1976. xiv, 215 p. ; 22 cm. [BL1146.V326S527] 76-903636 Rs21.00
1. Vasugupta. Sivasutra. 2. Sivaism. I. Vasugupta. II. Title.

Vaswig, William L.

VASWIG, William L. 248'.3
I prayed, He answered / William L. Vaswig ; foreword by Agnes Sanford. Minneapolis : Augsburg Pub. House, c1977. 128 p. ; 20 cm. [BR1725.V34A34] 77-72457 ISBN 0-8066-1589-3 : 3.50
1. Vaswig, William L. 2. Vaswig, Philip. 3. Sanford, Agnes Mary White. 4. Faith-cure. 5. Prayer. I. Title.

Vatican.

HUGES De Ragnau, Edmond 1845-
The Vatican; the center of government of the Catholic world, by Rt. Rev. Edmond Canon Hugues de Ragnau. New York and London, D. Appleton and company, 1913. vii p., 1 l., 452, [1] p. front. (port.) 23 cm. $4.00 [BX1801.H8] 13-28167
I. Title.

IPSER, Karl. 709.456
Vatican art; with 160 illus. Translated from the German 'Die Kunstwerke des Vatikans' by Doireann MacDermott. New York, Philosophical Library [1953] 198p. illus. 25cm. [N2940.I413] 53-11503
1. Vatican. 2. Art—Rome. 3. Christian art and symbolism. I. Title.

LETAROUILLY, Paul Marie 1795-1885 726.640945632
The Vatican buildings [2v. in one] Pref. by A. E. Richardson. London, A. Tiranti [dist. Hollywood-by-the-Sea, Fla., Transatlantic, 1964, c.]1963. (various p.) plates, diagrs., plans. 29cm. (Precepts of art, 4) English and French. Contents.contents—1. The Pontifical Palace. 2. Belvedere. 3. Loggias. 4. Stanze. 5. Villa Pia. 6. Clementino and Chiaramonti. 7. Piazza of St. Peter. A54 19.50
1. Vatican. 2. Architecture—Rome. I. Title. II. Series.

NEVILLE, Robert 282
The world of the Vatican. New York, Harper [1962] 256p. illus. 22cm. 62-7295 4.95
1. Vatican. 2. Papacy. I. Title.

NEVILLE, Robert. 282
The world of the Vatican, [1st ed.] New York, Harper & Row [1962] 256 p. illus. 22 cm. [BX1802.N4] 62-7295
1. Vatican. 2. Papacy. I. Title.

NOGARA, Bartolomeo, 1868- 709.456
Art treasures of the Vatican. New York, Tudor Pub. Co. [1950] 308 p. illus. (part col.) 28 cm. English, Spanish, French, and Italian. [N2940.N59] 50-10579
1. Vatican. 2. Art — Rome. 3. Christian art and symbolism. I. Title.

Vatican. Archivio vaticano.

CHADWICK, Owen. 282'.09
Catholicism and history : the opening of the Vatican Archives / Owen Chadwick. Cambridge ; New York : Cambridge University Press, 1978. vi, 174 p. ; 23 cm. (The Herbert Hensley Henson lectures in the University of Oxford ; 1976) Includes index. Bibliography: p. 163-165. [CD1581.C47] 77-77740 ISBN 0-521-21708-3 : 13.95
1. Vatican. Archivio vaticano. 2. Catholic Church—Historiography. 3. Papacy—History. 4. Freedom of information in the church. 5. Church history—Historiography. I. Title. II. Series.

Vatican. Biblioteca vaticana. Mss. (Pal. Graec. 431)

WEITZMANN, Kurt, 1904- 096.1
The Joshua roll, a work of the Macedonian renaissance. Princeton, Princeton Univ. Press, 1948. vi, 119 p. 32 plates. 31 cm. (Studies in manuscript illumination, no. 3) A study of the Codex Vaticanus Palatinus Graecus 431. Bibliographical footnotes. [ND3358.J8V38] 48-8429
1. Vatican. Biblioteca vaticana. Mss. (Pal. Graec. 431) 2. Bible. O. T. Joshua—Pictorial illustrations. 3. Illumination of books and manuscripts—Specimens, reproductions, etc. I. Title. II. Series.

Vatican. Cappella sistina.

FEIN, H. Otto, 1913- illus. 726.60945632
The Sistine Chapel before Michelangelo; religious imagery and papal primacy. Photos of the frescoes by H. O. Fein. Oxford, Clarendon Pr. [New York, Oxford, c.]1965. xiii, 128p. illus. 44 plates. 29cm. (Oxford-Warburg studies) Bibl. [N2950.E8] 65-9047 12.00
1. Vatican. Cappella sistina. 2. Mural painting and decoration—Vatican City. I. Fein, H. Otto, illus. II. Title.

Vatican City. Casino di Pio IV.

SMITH, Graham, 1942- 726'.5'0945634
The Casino of Pius IV / Graham Smith. Princeton, N.J. : Princeton University Press, c1976. p. cm. Includes index. Bibliography: p. [N6920.S54] 76-3017 ISBN 0-691-03915-1 : 20.00
1. Vatican City. Casino di Pio IV. 2. Stucco—Italy—Vatican City. 3. Mural painting and decoration, Renaissance—Vatican City. 4. Mural painting and decoration—Vatican City. 5. Symbolims in art—Vatican City. I. Title.

Vatican City. Colonna di Antonino Pio.

VOGEL, Lise. 731'.76'0945634
The column of Antoninus Pius. Cambridge, Harvard University Press, 1973. xiv, 220 p. illus. 20 x 28 cm. (Loeb classical monographs) Revision of the author's thesis, Harvard, 1968. [NA9340.V3V63 1973] 74-173409 ISBN 0-674-14325-6 16.00
1. Vatican City. Colonna di Antonino Pio. I. Title. II. Series.

Vatican City—Juvenile literature.

DEEDY, John G. 282'.0904
The Vatican, by John Deedy. New York, Watts [1970] 66 p. illus., ports. 23 cm. (A First book) An introduction to the history, art, and people of the world's smallest nation, with special emphasis on the duties of the Pope. [DG800.D4] 70-102275 ISBN 5-310-06972- 3.25
1. Catholic Church—Juvenile literature. 2. [Catholic Church.] 3. Vatican City—Juvenile literature. 4. [Vatican City.] I. Title.

Vatican City. San Pietro in Vaticano (Basilica)

BERGERE, Thea. 726.50945634
The story of St. Peter's [by] Thea and Richard Bergere. Illustrated with photos., prints, and with drawings by Richard Bergere. New York, Dodd, Mead [1966] 128 p. illus., plans. 28 cm. Bibliography: p. 123. [NA5620.S9B4] 66-9799
1. Vatican City. San Pietro in Vaticano (Basilica) I. Bergere, Richard, joint author. II. Title.

GUARDUCCI, Margherita. 225.92
The tomb of St. Peter; the new discoveries

in the sacred grottoes of the Vatican. With an introd. by H. V. Morton. Translated from the Italian by Joseph McLellan. [1st ed.] New York, Hawthorn Books [1960] 198 p. illus. 24 cm. [BS2515.G813] 60-5898
1. Peter, Saint, apostle—Tomb. 2. Vatican City. San Pietro in Vaticano (Basilica) I. Title.

KIRSCHBAUM, Engelbert, 1902- 225.93
The tombs of St. Peter & St. Paul. Translated from the German by John Murray. New York, St. Martin's Press [1959] 247 p. illus. 24 cm. Translation of Die Graeber der Apostelfuersten. Includes bibliography. [BS2515.K513 1959] 59-11406
1. Peter, Saint, apostle—Tomb. 2. Paul, Saint, apostle. 3. Vatican (City) San Pietro in Vaticano (Basilica) I. Title.

LEESMILNE, James 726'.6'0945634
Saint Peter's; the story of Saint Peter's Basilica in Rome. Boston, Little, Brown [1967] 336 p. illus., col. plates 26 cm. Bibliography: p. 328. [DG816.3L4 1967b] 67-16263
1. Vatican City. San Pietro in Vaticano (Basilica) I. Title.

MATT, Leonard von 726.582
St. Peter's. Introd. by Dieter von Balthasar. New York, Universe [1962] xi p. illus. 29cm. (His Roma ser.) 62-12008 4.75
1. Vatican City. San Peitro in Vaticano (Basilica) I. Balthasar, Dieter von. II. Title.

TOYNBEE, Jocelyn M C 726.82
The shrine of St. Peter and the Vatican excavations, by Jocelyn Toynbee and John Ward Perkins. London, New York, Longmans, Green [1956] xxii, 293 p. plates, plans. 26 cm. [NA5620.S9T6] 56-1914
1. Peter, Saint, apostle — Tomb. 2. Vatican City. San Pietro in Vaticano (Basilica) I. Ward-Perkins, John Bryan, 1912- joint author. II. Title.

TOYNBEE, Jocelyn M C 726.82
The shrine of St. Peter and the Vatican excavations, by Jocelyn Toynbee and John Ward Perkins. New York, Pantheon Books [1957] xxii, 293 p. plates, plans. 26 cm. Includes bibliographical references. [NA5620.S9T6] 56-13363
1. Peter, Saint, apostle — Tomb. 2. Vatican City. San Pietro in Vaticano (Basilica) I. Ward-Perkins, John Bryan, 1912- joint author. II. Title.

Vatican council, 1869-1870.

BUTLER, Edward Cuthbert, 1858- 262.13
The Vatican council; the story told from inside in Bishop Ullathorne's letters, by Dom Cuthbert Butler ... London, New York [etc.] Longmans, Green and co., 1930. 2 v. fronts., ports. 22 1/2 cm. Bibliographical foot-notes. [BX830.1869.B8] 30-22961
1. Vatican council, 1869-1870. I. Ullathorne, William Bernard, abp., 1806-1869. II. Title.

BUTLER, Edward Cuthbert, 1858-1934. 262.5
The Vatican Council, 1869-1870, based on Bishop Ullthorne's letters. Edited by Christopher Butler. Westminster, Md., Newman Press, 1962. 510). 20cm. [BX830 1869.B822] 61-16567
1. Vatican Council, 1869-1870. I. Ullathorne, William Bernard, Abp., 1806-1889. II. Title.

BUTLER, Edward Cuthbert, 1858-1934. 262.13
The Vatican council; the story told from inside in Bishop Ullathorne's letters, by Dom Cuthbert Butler ... London, New York [etc.] Longmans, Green and co. [1936] 2 v. fronts., ports. 22 1/2 cm. [Second spring series, ii] "First published, April 1930; reissued in the "Second spring series", October, 1936." "Sources": v. 1, p. xiii-xix. [BX830.1869.B82] 38-202
1. Vatican council, 1869-1870. I. Ullathorne, William Bernard abp., 1806-1889. II. Title.

BUTLER, Edward Cuthbert, 1858-1934 262.5
The Vatican Council, 1869-1870, based on Bishop Ullathorne's letter. Ed. by Christopher Butler. Westminster, Md., Newman [c.]1962. 510p. 20cm. 61-16567 5.95; 1.95 pap.,
1. Vatican Council, 1869-1870. I. Ullathorne, William Bernard, Abp., 1806-1889. II. Title.

CHAIGNON, Pierre, 1791-1883. 723.
Das Concil und die getreuen kinder der kirche. Von Chaignon ... Einzig fur Deutschland gestattete uebers etzung aus dem franzosischen von Carl Prosp. Clasen ... Regensburg, New-York [etc.]0F. Pustet, 1870. xii, [13]-288 p. 15 cm. [BX880.1869.C56] 4132246
1. Vatican council, 1869-1870. 2. Holy year, 1869. I. Clasen, Karl Proper, 1839- tr. II. Title.

DOLLINGER, Johann Joseph Ignaz von, 1799-1890.
Letters from Rome on the Council, by Quirinus [pseud.] Reprinted from the Allgemeine zeitung. Authorized translation. London, Rivingtons, 1870. [Cleveland, Ohio, Bell & Howell, 1965?] 2 v. 19 cm. Paged continuously. A projected third volume not published? "Reproduced by duopage process ... Micro Photo Division, Bell & Howell Company." Vol. 1 of reproduction has two copies of title page; v. 2 has no title page. 67-84519
1. Vatican council, 1869-1870. 2. Popes-Infallibility. I. Title.

DOLLINGER, Johann Joseph Ignaz von, 1799-1890. 262.5'2
Letters from Rome on the Council, by Quirinus. New York, Da Capo Press, 1973. 2 v. 21 cm. (Europe, 1815-1945) Reprint of the 1870 ed. Translation of Romische Briefe vom Concil. [BX830 1869.D63] 78-127193 ISBN 0-306-70040-9 29.50 (Lib. ed.)
1. Vatican Council, 1869-1870. 2. Popes—Infallibility. I. Title. II. Series.

[DOLLINGER, Johann Joseph Ignaz von] 1799-1890. 270.
Letters from Rome on the Council, by Quirinus [pseud.] Reprinted from the Allgemeine zeitung. Authorized translation ... London [etc.] Rivingtons; New York, Pott and Amery, 1870. 2 v. 19 cm. Paged continuously. A projected third volume not published? [BX830.1869.D62] 38-31402
1. Vatican council, 1869-1870. 2. Popes—Infallibility. I. Title.

GLADSTONE, William Ewart, 1809-1898. 262.13
The Vatican decrees in their bearing on civil allegiance; a political expostulation. By the Right Hon. W. E. Gladstone, M. P. With the replies of Archbishop Manning and Lord Acton. New York, D. Appleton and company, 1874. 90 p. 23 cm. [BX830.1869.G48] 33-24557
1. Vatican council, 1869-1876. 2. Popes—Infallibility. 3. Allegiance. I. Manning, Henry Edward, Cardinal, 1806-1897. II. Acton, John Emerich Edward Daiberg Acton, 1st baron, 1854-1902. III. Title.

GLADSTONE, William Ewart, 1809-1898. 262.13
The Vatican decrees in their bearing on civil allegiance; a political expostulation. By the Right Hon. W. E. Gladstone, M. P. With the replies of Archbishop Manning and Lord Acton. New York, D. Appleton and company, 1875. 96 p. 24 cm. On cover: ... With the replies of Archbishop Manning, Lord Action, and the Right Rev. Monsignor Capel. [BX530.1869.G49] 33-6737
1. Vatican council, 1869-1870. 2. Popes—Infalibility. 3. Allegiance. I. Manning, Henry Edward, cardinal, 1806-1892. II. Acton, John Emerich Edward Dalberg Acton, 1st baron, 1834-1902. III. Capel, Thomas John, 1836-1911. IV. Title.

GLADSTONE, William Ewart, 1809-1898. 262.13
The Vatican decrees in their bearing on civil allegiance; a political expostulation. By the Right Hon. W. E. Gladstone, M. P. To which are added: A history of the Vatican council; together with the Latin and English text of the papal syllabus and the Vatican decrees. By the Rev. Philip Schaff ... New York, Harper & brothers, 1875. 3 p. l., [9]-168 p. 22 cm. "Literature": p. [53]-54. [BX830.1869.G5] 33-6733
1. Vatican council, 1869-1870. 2. Popes—Infallibility. 3. Allegiance. I. Schaff, Philip, 1819-1895. II. Catholic church, Pope, 1846-1678 (Plus ix) Syllabus errorum. III. Vatican council, 1869-1870 Acts of deerets. IV. Title.

GLADSTONE, William Ewart, 1809-1898. 265.
Vaticanism; an answer to reproofs and replies. New York, Harper, 1875. 96 p. 23 cm. [BX1767.G47 1875a] 49-56955
1. Vatican Council, 1869-1870. 2. Pope—Infallibility. I. Title.

HENNESEY, James J 262.5
The First Council of the Vatican; the American experience. [New York] Herder and Herder [1963] 341 p. 22 cm. Bibliographical footnotes. [BX8301869.H4] 63-18150
1. Vatican Council, 1869-1870. I. Title.

KENRICK, Peter Richard, Abp., 1806-1896.
An inside view of the Vatican Council, in the speech of the Most Reverend Archbishop Kenrick of St. Louis. Ed. by Leonard Woolsey Bacon, with notes and additional documents. New York, American Tract Society [1871] 250 p. 20 cm. Includes a reproduction of the original title pages of the speech. [BX8301869.K4] 49-56092
1. Vatican Council, 1869-1870. I. Bacon, Leonard Woolsey, 1830-1907, ed. II. Title.

MANNING, Henry Edward, cardinal, 1808-1892. 262.13
The Vatican council and its definitions; a pastoral letter to the clergy, by Henry Edward, archbishop of Westminster. New York, Montreal, D. & J. Sadlier, 1871. 252 p. 19 1/2 cm. [BX830.1869.M3] 33-6734
1. Vatican council, 1869-1870. 2. Popes—Infallibility. I. Title.

NEWMAN and Gladstone: 261.7
the Vatican decrees. Introd. by Alan S. Ryan. [Notre Dame, Ind.] Univ. of Notre Dame Pr. [c.]1962 xxii, 228p. (ndp 11) 62-1066 1.95 pap.,
1. Vatican Council, 1869-1870. 2. Popes—Infallibility. 3. Allegiance. I. Ryan, Alvan Sherman, 1912- II. Gladstone, William Ewart, 1809-1898. The Vatican decrees in their bearing on civil allegiance. III. Newman, John Henry, Cardinal, 1801-1890. A letter addressed to His Grace the Duke of Norfolk.

NEWMAN, John Henry, cardinal, 1801-1890. 262.13
A letter addressed to His Grace the Duke of Norfolk on occasion of Mr. Gladstone's recent expostulation. By John Henry Newman ... New York, The Catholic publication society, 1875. 171 p. 18 cm. [BX830.1869.G6N5] 33-6735
1. Gladstone, William Ewart, 1809-1898. The Vatican decrees ... 2. Vatican council, 1869-1870. 3. Popes—Infallibility. 4. Allegiance. I. Title.

WILTGEN, Ralph M., 1921- 262'.5
The Rhine flows into the Tiber; the unknown Council, by Ralph M. Wiltgen. [1st ed.] New York City, Hawthorn Books [1967] 304 p. 24 mc. [BX830 1962.W5] 67-17224
1. Vatican Council. 2d 1962-1965. I. Title.

Vatican Council, 2d.

see also Vatican Council, 2d., 1962-1965

ABBOTT, Walter M. 262.5
Twelve council fathers. New York, Macmillan [c.1963] 176p. 22cm. 63-19434 3.50 bds.,
1. Vatican Council, 2d. I. Title.

ABBOTT, Walter M 262.5
Twelve council fathers. New York, Macmillan [1963] 176 p. 22 cm. [BX830 1962.A53] 63-19434
1. Vatican Council, 2d. I. Title.

BASSET, Bernard. 262.5
Priest in the piazza; goal line tribute to a Council. With illus. by Penelope Harter. Fresno, Calif., Academy Guild Press [1963] vi, 111 p. illus. 23 cm. [BX830 1962.B3] 63-23224
1. Vatican Council, 2d. I. Title.

BERKOUWER, Gerrit Cornelis, 1903- 230.2
The Second Vatican Council and the new Catholicism, by G. C. Berkouwer. Translated by Lewis B. Smedes. Grand Rapids, Eerdmans [1965] 264 p. 23 cm. Translation of Vatikaans Concille en nieuwe theologie. Bibliographical footnotes. [BX830 1962.B453] 64-8581
1. Vatican Council, 2d. I. Title.

CAPORALE, Rock 262.5
Vatican II: last of the councils. Foreword by John J. Wright. D. D. Helicon [dist. New York, Taplinger, c.1964] 192p. 21cm. 64-23615 4.95
1. Vatican Council, 2d. I. Title.

CAPORALE, Rock. 262.5
Vatican II; last of the councils. Foreword by John J. Wright. Baltimore, Helicon [1964] 192 p. 21 cm. [BX830 1962.C3] 64-23615
1. Vatican Council, 2d. I. Title.

CATHOLIC Reporter, The 262
Kansas City, Mo. The layman and the Council; conversations between John Cogley, Daniel Callahan, Donald J. Thorman, Martin H. Work. Ed. by Michael Greene. Springfield, Ill., Templegate [1965] 128p. 19cm. Appeared serially in the Catholic reporter of the Diocese of Kansas City-St. Joseph, Mo. [BX830 1962.C35] 65-3173 3.95
1. Vatican Council, 2d. I. Cogley, John. II. Greene, Michael J., ed.

DANIEL-ROPS, Henry [Real name: Henry Jules Charles Petiot] 1901- 262.5
The Second Vatican Council; the story behind the Ecumenical Council of Pope John XXIII. Tr. [from French] by Alastair Guinan. New York, Hawthorn [c.1962] 160p. 21cm. Bibl. 62-9031 3.50
1. Vatican Council, 2d. I. Title.

FRANCK, Frederick, 1909- 262.50904
Outsider in the Vatican. New York, Macmillan [c.1965] 253p. illus., ports. 24cm. [BX830. 1962.F7] 65-22617 7.50
1. Vatican Council, 2d. I. Title.

FRANCK, Frederick, 1909-
Outsider in the Vatican. New York, Macmillan [1965] 253 p. illus., ports. 24 cm. Erratum slip inserted.
1. Vatican Council, 2d. I. Title.

FRANCK, Frederick, 1909- 262.50904
Outsider in the Vatican. New York, Macmillan [1965] 253 p. illus., ports. 24 cm. Erratum slip inserted. [BX830 1962.F6] 65-22617
1. Vatican Council, 2d. I. Title.

*FREIN, George H. 262.3
Seven lesson plans on the constitution on the Church of Vatican Council II. Glen Rock, N.J., Paulist [c.1966] 64p. illus. 21cm. .75 pap.,
I. Title.

GUITTON, Jean. 262.5
Guitton at the Council; a layman's appraisal and predictions. With pref. by Fulton J. Sheen. [Translated by Paul Joseph Oligny and Evan Roche] Chicago, Franciscan Herald Press [1964] 62 p. 21 cm. Translation of Regard sur le Concile. [BX8301962.G813] 64-24284
1. Vatican Council, 2d. I. Title.

HARING, Bernahrd, 1912- 262.5
The Johannine Council, witness to unity. Translated by Edwin G. Kaiser. [New York] Herder and Herder [1963] 155 p. 21 cm. Translation of Konzil im Zelchen der Einheit. Bibliographical footnotes. [BX830 1962.H313] 63-18151
1. Vatican Council, 2d. I. Title.

HARING, Bernhard, 1912- 262.5
The Johannine Council, witness to unity. Tr. [from German] by Edwin G. Kaiser. [New York] Herder & Herder [c.1963] 155p. 21cm. Bibl. 63-18151 3.50
1. Vatican Council, 2d. I. Title.

HORTON, Douglas, 1891- 262.5
Vatican diary; 1962, 1963 [2v.] Philadelphia, United Church Pr. [c.1964] [2v.] 206, 203p. 22cm. Contents.[1] 1962; a Protestant observes the first session of Vatican Council II.--[2] 1963; a Protestant

observes the second session of Vatican Council II. 64-23949 4.50; 3.00 ea., pap., ea.,
1. Vatican Council, 2d. I. Title.

HORTON, Douglas, 1891- 262.5
Vatican diary, 1965 Philadelphia, United Church Pr. [1966] 202p. 22cm. [BX830 1962.H6] 64-23949 4.50; 3.00, pap.
1. Vatican Council, 2d. I. Title.

JAEGER, Lorenz, Abp. 262.5
The ecumenical council, the church and Christendom. [Tr. by A. V. Littledale] New York, Kenedy [1962, c.1961] Bibl. 61-14294 3.95
1. Vatican Council, 2d. 2. Councils and synods, Ecumenical. 3. Church—History of doctrines. 4. Catholic Church—Relations. I. Title.

JAEGER, Lorenz, Cardinal, 262.5 1892-
The ecumenical council, the church and Christendom; [Translated by A. V. Littledale] New York, P. J. Kenedy [1962, c1961] 194 p. 21 cm. Includes bibliography. [BX830 1962.J313] 61-14294
1. Vatican Council, 2d. 2. Catholic Church—Relations. 3. Councils and synods, Ecumenical. 4. Church—History of doctrines—20th cent. I. Title.

KUNG, Hans, 1928- 262.5
The Council in action; theological reflections on the Second Vatican Council Translated by Cecily Hastings. New York, Sheed and Ward [1963] ix, 276 p. 22 cm. "Published in Great Britian under the title: The living church." Includes bibliographical references. [BX830 1962.K813] 63-17148
1. Vatican Council, 2d. I. Title.

KUNG, Hans, 1928- 262'.5
The living church; reflections on the Second Vatican Council Translated by Cecily Hastings and N. D. Smith. London, New York, Sheed and Ward [1963] x, 421 p. 18 cm. (Stagbooks) "Sequel to the Council and reunion." Bibliographical footnotes. [BX830 1963.K813] 63-25274
1. Vatican Council, 2d. I. Title.

LEE, Anthony D ed. 262.5
Vatican II; the theological dimension With introd. by Ferrer E. Smith. [Washington] Thomist Press, 1963. xvi, 621 p. 24 cm. "Originally published as a special issue of the Thomist, volume XXVII (complete) April, July, October, 1963." Bibliographical footnotes. [BX830 1962.L4] 63-21897
1. Vatican Council, 2d. 2. Theology — Addresses, essays, lectures. I. Title.

LINDBECK, George A., ed. 262.5
Dialogue on the way; Protestants report from Rome on the Vatican Council. Minneapolis, Augsburg [c.1965] ix, 270p. 22cm. Bibl. [BX8301962.L5] 65-12140 4.75
1. Vatican Council, 2d. I. Title.

LINDBECK, George A ed. 262.5
Dialogue on the way; Protestants report from Rome on the Vatican Council, edited by George A. Lindbeck. Minneapolis, Augsburg Pub. House [1965] ix, 270 p. 22 cm. "Bibliographical appendix": p. 269-170. [BX8301962.L5] 65-12140
1. Vatican Council, 2d. I. Title.

NATIONAL Catholic Welfare 260 Conference. Press Dept.
Council day book: Vatican II, session 3. Ed. by Floyd Anderson, director. Washington, D. C., Author, 1312 Mass. Ave. N.W., [c.1965] xv, 368p. illus., group ports. 28cm. Record of press releases at the time the Council was in session. Bibl. [BX830.1962.N3] 65-17303 5.00 pap.,
1. Vatican Council, 2d. I. Anderson, Floyd, 1906- ed. II. Title.

NATIONAL Catholic Welfare 260 Conference. Press Dept.
Council daybook: Vatican II, session 4, Sept. 14, 1965 to Dec. 8, 1965. Ed. by Floyd Anderson. Washington, D. C., Author [c.1966] xiii, 454p. illus., group ports. 28cm. A record of press releases at the time the Council was in session. Bibl. [BX830.N3] 65-17303 7.50 pap.,
1. Vatican Council, 2d. I. Anderson, Floyd, ed. II. Title.

NELSON, Claud D. 262.5
The Vatican Council and all Christians. Foreword by Roswell P. Barnes. Epilogue by Edward Duff. New York, Association [c.1962] 126p. 20cm. 62-16876 3.00 bds.,
1. Vatican Council, 2d. I. Title.

NOVAK, Michael 262.5
The open Church, Vatican II, act II. New York, Macmillan [c.1962-1964] xiii, 370p. 22cm. Bibl. 64-18270 6.50
1. Vatican Council, 2d. I. Title.

O'NEILL, Charles A ed. 280.1
Ecumenism and Vatican II. Edited by Charles O'Neill. Essays by Bernard Cooke [and others] With a foreword by Vincent T. O'Keefe. Milwaukee, Bruce Pub. Co. [1964] xii, 146 p. 22 cm. Bibliographical footnotes. [BX830 1962.O5] 64-23892
1. Vatican Council, 2d. 2. Ecumenical movement. I. Cooke, Bernard. II. Title.

PAWLEY, Bernard C. 262.5
An Anglican view of the Vatican Council. New York, Morehouse [c.1962] 116p. 20cm. 62-20222 2.90
1. Vatican Council, 2d. I. Title.

PAWLEY, Bernard C 262.5
An Anglican view of the Vation Council. [1st American ed.] New York, Morehouse-Barlow Co. [1962] 116p. 20cm. [BX830 1962.P3] 62-20222
1. Vatican Council, 2d. I. Title.

PRESBYTER Anglicanus. 264.5
The Second Vatican Council, an interim report. New York, Morehouse-Barlow [c.1963] iv, 32p. 19cm. 63-24995 .95 pap.,
1. Vatican Council, 2d. I. Title.

RYNNE, Xavier, pseud. 262.5
Letters from Vatican City; Vatican Council II, first session: background and debates. Garden City, N.Y., Doubleday [1964, c.1963] 273p. 18cm. (Image bk., D182) .95 pap.,
1. Vatican Council, 2d. I. Title.

SCHILLEBEECKE, Edward 262.15 Cornelius Florentinius Alfons, 1914-
The layman in the church, and other essays [by] E. H. Schillebeeckx. Staten Island, N. Y., Alba House [1963] 91 p. 19 cm. [BX1920.S3] 63-23157
1. Vatican Council, 2d. 2. Laity—Catholic Church. 3. Death. I. Title.

SCHILLEBEECKX, Edward 262.15 Cornelius Florentinius Alfons, 1914-
The layman in the church, and other essays. [Staten Island] N.Y. Alba House [c.1963] 91p. 19cm. 63-23157 2.95
1. Vatican Council, 2d. 2. Laity—Catholic Church. 3. Death. I. Title.

THE 2nd Vatican Council. 262.5
[New York, America Press, 1962] Essays. [BX8301962.S4] 62-4976
1. Vatican Council, 2d.

2ND Vatican Council (The) 262.5
[Essays.] New York, America, c.1962] 96p. illus. 19cm. 62-4976 .50 pap.,
1. Vatican Council, 2d.

SKYDSGAARD, Kristen E., ed. 280.1
The papal council and the gospel: Protestant theologians evaluate the coming Vatican Council Minneapolis, Augsburg [c.1961] vii, 213p. Bibl. 61-17915 3.95
1. Vatican Council, 2d, 2. Catholic Church—Relations—Lutheran Church. 3. Lutheran Church—Relations—Catholic Church. I. Title.

SPINA, Tony. 262.5
The Pope and the Council. New York, Barnes [1963] 160 p. illus. (part fold., part col.) group ports. (part col.) 31 cm. [BX830 1962.S6] 63-18254
1. Vatican Council, 2d. I. Title.

TAVARD, George Henri, 1922- 262
The church tomorrow. Garden City, N.Y., Doubleday [1966, c.1965] 152p. (Image bk., D212) p.85 pap., [BX830 1962. T3]
1. Vatican Council, 2d. 2. Theology—20th cent. I. Title.

TAVARD, Georges Henri, 1922-
The church tomorrow. Garden City, N.Y., Image Books [1966, c1965] 152 p. 18 cm. 68-17323
1. Vatican Council, 2d. 2. Theology—20th cent. I. Title.

TAVARD, Georges Henri, 1922- 262
The church tomorrow [by] George H. Tavard. [New York] Herder and Herder [1965] 190 p. 21 cm. [BX830 1962.T3] 65-13479
1. Vatican Council, 2d. 2. Theology—20th cent. I. Title.

VATICAN Council. 2d,1962- 262.5 1965.
The teachings of the Second Vatican Council; complete texts of the constitutions, decrees, and declarations. Introd. by Gregory Baum. Westminster, Md., Newman Press, 1966. xi, 676 p. 23 cm. Includes bibliographical references. [BX830 1962.A3N4] 66-19960
I. Title.

VATICAN Council II, 262.5
from John XXIII to Paul VI [Rev. ed. New York] America Pr. [c.1963] 96p. 19cm. Cover title. Essays. First pub. in 1962 under title: The 2nd Vatican Council. Bibl. 64-4928 .50 pap.,
1. Vatican Council, 2d.

VATICAN Council II, from 262.5
John XXIII to Paul VI. [Rev. ed.] New York] America Press [c1963] 96 p. 19 cm. Cover title. Essays. First published in 1962 under title: The 2d Vatican Council. Bibliography: p. 96. [BX830 1962.S42] 64-4928
1. Vatican Council, 2d.

WALL, Bernard, 1908- 262.82
Thaw at the Vatican; an account of session two of Vatican II, by Bernard & Barbara Wall. London, Gollancz [Mystic, Conn., Verry, 1965, c.] 1964. 223p. ports. 23cm. [BX830.1962.W3] 65-29695 6.00 bds.
1. Vatican Council, 2d. I. Lucas, Barbara, 1911- joint author. II. Title.

WENGER, Antoine. 262'.5
Vatican II. Translated by Robert J. Olsen. Westminster, Md., Newman Press, 1966- v. 24 cm. Contents.Contents.—v. 1. The first session. Includes bibliographical references. [BX830.1962.W413] 66-16573
1. Vatican Council, 2d. I. Title.

YZERMANS, Vincent Arthur, 262.5 1925-
A new Pentecost; Vatican Council II: session 1. Foreword by Gustave Weigel; introd. by Hans Kung. Westminster, Md., Newman Press, 1963. xx, 376 p. illus., ports. 23 cm. "A good portion of this journal ... originally appeared as weekly reports in five Catholic publications." Includes texts of many of the most important documents of the first session. [BX830 1962.Y9] 63-23099
1. Vatican Council, 2d. I. Vatican Council, 2d. II. Title.

Vatican Council, 2d, 1962-1965.

ALEXANDER, Calvert. 266'.2
The missionary dimension; Vatican II and the world apostolate. Milwaukee, Bruce Pub. Co. [1967] ix, 117 p. 22 cm. "Appendix: Decree on the missionary activity of the church": p. [69]-117. Bibliographical footnotes. [BX830.1962.A45A45] 67-18212
1. Vatican Council 2d, 1962-1965. Decretum de activitate missionali ecclesiae. 2. Catholic Church—Missions. I. Vatican Council. 2d, 1962-1965. Decree on the missionary activity of the church.

AMERICAN Jewish Committee. Institute of Human Relations.
The second Vatican Council's declaration on the Jews; a background report. New York [1965] 50 p. NUC66
I. Title.

BANKI, Judith. 261.2
Vatican Council II's statement on the Jews: five years later; a survey of progress and problems in implementing the Conciliar declaration in Europe, Israel, Latin America, the United States, and Canada. [New York, American Jewish Committee, Institute of Human Relations, 1971] 31 p. 28 cm. "[Data] compiled by the Foreign Affairs and Interreligious Affairs Departments of the American Jewish Committee." Includes bibliographical references. [BX830 1962.A45E27] 73-170483 0.25
1. Vatican Council. 2d, 1962-1965. Declaratio de Ecclesiae habitudine ad religiones non-Christianas. 2. Catholic Church—Relations—Judaism. 3. Judaism—Relations—Catholic Church. I. American Jewish Committee. Foreign Affairs Dept. II. American Jewish Committee. Interreligious Affairs Dept. III. Title.

BEA, Augustin, Cardinal, 231'.74 1881-
The word of God and mankind. Chicago, Franciscan Herald Press [1967] 318 p. 23 cm. Translation of La parola di Dio et l'umanita. Commentary on Constitution on divine revelation of Vatican Council II. Includes bibliographical references. [BX830 1962.A45C772 1967b] 68-17560
1. Vatican Council. 2d, 1962-1965. Constitutio dogmatica de divina revelatione. 2. Revelation. I. Title.

BEA, Augustin, Cardinal, 260 1881-1968.
The church and mankind. Chicago, Franciscan Herald Press [1967] vi, 282 p. 23 cm. Translation of La chiesa e l'umanita. Includes bibliographical references. [BX1746.B413] 67-8390
1. Vatican Council. 2d, 1962-1965. 2. Church. 3. Church and the world. I. Title.

BEACH, Bert Beverly. 262.5
Vatican II, bridging the abyss. Washington, Review & Herald [1968] 352p. 22cm. Bibl [BX830 1962.B424] 67-21871 6.95
1. Vatican Council. 2d, 1962-1965. 2. Catholic Church—Doctrinal and controversial works—Protestant authors. I. Title.

BLANSHARD, Paul, 1892- 282
Paul, Blanshard on Vatican Boston, Beacon [1966] 371p. 21cm. Bibl. [BX830 1962.B5] 66-23783 5.95 bds.,
1. Vatican Council. 2d, 1962-1965. I. Title. II. Title: On Vatican II.

BLANSHARD, Paul, 1892- 282
Paul Blanshard on Vatican II. Boston, Beacon [1967, c.1966] 371p. 21cm. (BP260) Bibl. [BX830.1962.B5] 66-23783 2.45 pap.,
1. Vatican Council. 2d, 1962-1965. I. Title. II. Title: On Vatican II.

BROWN, Robert McAfee, 1920- 262.5
Observer in Rome; a Protestant report on the Vatican Council. [1st ed.] Garden City, N.Y., Doubleday, 1964. xi, 271 p. 22 cm. [BX830 1962.B7] 64-184951
1. Vatican Council, 2d, 1962-1965. I. Title. II. Title: A Protestant report on the Vatican Council.

BULL, George Anthony. 262.5
Vatican politics at the Second Vatican Council, 1962-5, by George Bull. London, Issued under the auspices of the Royal Institute of International Affairs by Oxford U.P., 1966. vii, 157 p. 18 1/2 cm. (Chatham House essays, 11) 10/6 (B66-6299) [BX830 1962.B8] 66-70757
1. Vatican Counsil. 2d. 1962-1965. I. Royal Institute of International affairs. II. Title.

BULL, George Anthony 262.5
Vatican politics at the Second Vatican Council, 1962-5. London, Issued under the auspices of the Royal Inst. of Intl. Affairs [New York] Oxford [c.]1966. vii, 157p. 19cm. (Chatham House essays, 11) [BX830.1962.B8] 66-70757 1.70 pap.,
1. Vatican Council. 2d, 1962-1965. I. Royal Institute of International affairs. II. Title.

CAIRD, George Bradford. 262'.5
Our dialogue with Rome; the second Vatican Council and after [by] George B. Caird. London, New York, Oxford Univ. Pr., 1967. vii, 93p. 21cm. (Congregational lects., 1966) Oxford paperbacks, no. 124. [BX830 1962.C22] 68-89302 1.75 pap.,
1. Vatican Council. 2d. 1962-1965. 2. Christian union. I. Title. II. Series: The Congregational lectures, (London) 1966.

CAIRD, George Bradford. 262'.5
Our dialogue with Rome; the second Vatican Council and after [by] George B. Caird. [Magnolia, Mass., Peter Smith, 1968, c. 1967] vii, 93p. 21cm. (Congregational lectures, 1966) Oxford paperbacks, no. 124. rebound [BX830 1962.C22] 3.75
1. Vatican Council. 2d, 1962-1965. 2.

Christian union. I. Title. II. Series: The Congregational lectures, (London) 1966.

CARRILLO DE ALBORNOZ, Angel Francisco 1905- 262.12
Religious liberty, by A. F. Carrillo de Albornoz. Translated by John Drury. New York, Sheed and Ward [1967] xiii, 209 p. 22 cm. Translation of La libertad religiosa y el Concilio Vaticano II. Bibliography: p. 201-209. [BX830.1962.A45L523] 67-21903
1. Vatican Council. 2d, 1962-1965. Declaratio de libatate religiosa. 2. Religious liberty. I. Title.

THE Church today; 261.8'08
commentaries on the Pastoral constitution on the Church in the modern world. [Translated by John Drury, Denis Barrett, and Michael L. Mazzarese.] Edited by Group 2000. Westminster, Md., Newman Press [1967, c1968] vi, 319 p. 21 cm. Bibliographical footnotes. [BX830 1962.A45C975] 68-20847
1. Vatican Council. 2d, 1962-1965. Constitutio pastoralis de ecclesia in mundo huius temporis. 2. Church and the world. I. Group 2000.

THE Commentary on the Constitution and on the Instruction on the sacred liturgy, 270.8'2*6
by a committee of liturgical experts. Edited by A. Bugnini and C. Braga. Translated by Vincent P. Mallon. New York, Benziger Bros., 1965. xi, 441 p. 24 cm. Half title: Commentary on the sacred liturgy. On spine: The Commentary and the Instruction on the sacred liturgy. Includes the English text of the Constitution on the sacred liturgy, a commentary on each section of it, and an English translation of the Instruction for the proper implementation of the Constitution on the sacred liturgy. Bibliography: p. 439-441. [BX830 1962.A45C627] 71-2988
1. Vatican Council. 2d, 1962-1965. Constitutio de sacra liturgia. 2. Catholic Church. Congregatio Sacrorum Rituum. Instructio ad exsecutionem Constitutionis de sacra liturgia recte ordinandam (26 Sept. 1964) I. Bugnini, Annibale. II. Braga, Carlo. III. Vatican Council. 2d, 1962-1965. Constitutio de sacra liturgia. IV. Catholic Church. Congregatio Sacrorum Rituum. Instructio ad exsecutionem Constitutionis de sacra liturgia recte ordinandam (26 Sept. 1964) English. V. Title: Commentary on the sacred liturgy. VI. Title: The Commentary and the Instruction on the sacred liturgy.

COMMENTARY on the documents of Vatican II. 262'.5
[General editor: Herbert Vorgrimler New York] Herder and Herder [1967- v. 24 cm. Translation of Das zweite Vatikanische Konzil, Dokumente und Kommentare. Contents.Contents.—v. 1. Constitution on the sacred liturgy, by J. A. Jungmann.—Decree on the instruments of social communication, by K. Schmidthus.—Dogmatic constitution on the church.—Decree on Eastern Catholic churches, by J. M. Hoeck. Bibliographical footnotes. [BX830 1962.Z913] 67-22928
1. Vatican Council. 2d, 1962-1965. I. Vorgrimler, Herbert, ed.

CROSS Currents 262.5
Looking toward the council, an inquiry among Christians. Ed. by Joseph E. Cunneen. [New York] Herder & Herder [c.1962] 154p. 22cm. (Quaestiones disputatae, 5) 62-19562 3.75; 1.95 pap.,
1. Vatican Council, 2d, 1962- 2. Christian union. I. Cunneen, Joseph E., ed. II. Title.

CULLMANN, Oscar. 262'.5
Vatican Council II; the new direction. Essays selected and arr. by James D. Hester. [1st ed.] New York, Harper & Row [1968] 116 p. 22 cm. (Religious perspectives, v. 19) Translated by J. D. Hester and others. [BX830 1962.C8] 68-11981
1. Vatican Council. 2d, 1962-1965. I. Hester, James D., ed. II. Title. III. Series.

DAUGHTERS of St. Paul. 248.8'94
Religious life in the light of Vatican II. Compiled by the Daughters of St. Paul [Boston] St. Paul Editions [1967] 479 p. 21 cm. [BX2385.D3] 67-24029
1. Vatican Council. 2d, 1962-1965. 2. Monastic and religious life. I. Title.

DAVIES, Michael. 262'.5'2
Pope John's Council / by Michael Davies. New Rochelle, N.Y. : Arlington House, c1977. xvi, 336 p. ; 21 cm. (His Liturgical revolution ; pt. 2) Includes index. Bibliography: p. [325]-328. [BX830 1962.D35 1977] 77-1623 ISBN 0-87000-396-8 : 9.95
1. Vatican Council. 2d, 1962-1965. I. Title. II. Series.

DEISS, Lucien. 783'.026'2
Spirit and song of the new liturgy / by Lucien Deiss ; text for rev. ed. by Lucien Deiss. New rev. ed. Cincinnati : World Library Publications, 1976. xxi, 267 p. : music ; 22 cm. Translation of Concile et chant nouveau. Includes bibliographical references and index. [ML3082.D3213 1976] 76-9664
1. Vatican Council. 2d, 1962-1965. 2. Chants (Plain, Gregorian, etc.)—History and criticism. 3. Church music—Catholic Church—History and criticism. I. Title.

DOTY, William Lodewick, 1919- 248.4'8'2
Holiness for all; Vatican II spirituality, by William L. Doty. St. Louis, B. Herder Book Co., 1969. 142 p. 18 cm. [BX2350.2.D648 1969] 71-97236 1.45
1. Vatican Council. 2d, 1962-1965. 2. Spiritual life—Catholic authors. I. Title.

DUSHNYCK, Walter. 281.9'3
The Ukrainian-rite Catholic Church at the Ecumenical Council. 1962-1965; a collection of articles, book reviews, editorials, reports, and commentaries with special emphasis on Ukrainian-rite and other Eastern churches. New York, Shevchenko Scientific Society, 1967. 191 p. illus., ports. 26 cm. (Shevchenko Scientific Society. Ukrainian studies. English section, v. 5 (23)) Bibliography: p. [157]. [BX8301962.D78] 67-28417
1. Vatican Council. 2d, 1962-1965. 2. Catholic church. Byzantine rite (Ukrainian) I. Shevchenko Scientific Society (U. S.) II. Title.

FESQUET, Henri, 1916- 262'.5
The drama of Vatican II; the Ecumenical Council, June, 1962-December, 1965. Translated by Bernard Murchland. American introd. by Michael Novak. [1st. American ed.] New York, Random House [1967] xviii, 831 p. 25 cm. Translation of Le journal du Concile [Vatican II] [BX830.1962.F3913] 66-21475
1. Vatican Council, 2d, 1962-1965. I. Title.

FISHER, Desmond. 262'.5
The church in transition. Notre Dame, Ind., Fides Publishers [1967] 168 p. 23 cm. Bibliographical footnotes. [BX830 1962.F563] 67-24803
1. Vatican Council. 2d, 1962-1965. 2. Church renewal—Catholic Church. I. Title.

FISHER, Desmond. 262'.5
The Church in transition. Notre Dame, Ind., Fides Publishers [1967] 168 p. 23 cm. Bibliographical footnotes. [BX830.1962.F563] 67-24803
1. Vatican Council. 2d, 1962-1965. 2. Church renewal—Catholic Church. I. Title.

FULLAM, Raymond B. 262'.5
Exploring Vatican 2; Christian living today & tomorrow [by] Raymond B. Fullam. Staten Island, N.Y., Alba House [1969] xxiv, 360 p. illus. 22 cm. [BX830 1962.F8] 79-90777 5.95
1. Vatican Council, 2d, 1962-1965. 2. Christian life—Catholic authors. I. Title.

GALLI, Mario von 262.5
The Council and the future. Text by Mario von Galli, Photos. by Bernhard Moosbrugger. New York, McGraw [1966] 299p. illus., ports. 25cm. [BX830 1962.G319] 66-24564 10.95
1. Vatican Council. 2d, 1962-1965. I. Moosbrugger, Bernhard. II. Title.

GAMBARI, Elio. 248'.894
Consecration and service. Translated and abridged by Mary Magdalen Bellasis. [Boston] St. Paul Editions [1973- v. 22 cm. Translation of Manuale della vita religiosa alla luce del Vaticano II. Contents.Contents.—v. 1. The global mystery of religious life. [BX2435.G33513] 73-76311 5.00 (v. 1)
1. Vatican Council. 2d, 1962-1965. 2. Monastic and religious life. 3. Christian life—Catholic authors. I. Title. II. Title: The global mystery of religious life.

GAMBARI, Elio. 248'.894
Unfolding the mystery of religious life. Translated and abridged by Mary Magdalen Bellasis and others. [Boston] St. Paul Editions [1974] 280 p. 22 cm. (Consecration and service, v. 2) Translation of Svolgimento e pratica della vita religiosa, which was originally published as v. 2 of the author's Manuale della vita religiosa alla luce del Vaticano II. Includes bibliographical references. [BX2435.G33513 1974] 73-86210 5.00
1. Vatican Council. 2d, 1962-1965. 2. Monastic and religious life. I. Title.

GILBERT, Arthur. 282
The Vatican Council and the Jews. Cleveland, World Pub. Co. [1968] xiv, 322 p. 22 cm. Bibliographical references included in "Notes" (p. 243-261) [BX830 1962.A45G5] 68-26843 6.95
1. Vatican Council. 2d, 1962-1965. Declaratio de ecclesiae habitudine ad religiones non-christianas. 2. Catholic Church—Relations—Judaism. 3. Judaism—Relations—Catholic Church. I. Title.

HARRINGTON, Wilfrid J. 231'.74
Vatican II on revelation [by] Wilfrid Harrington and Liam Walsh. Dublin, Chicago, Scepter Books [1967] 191 p. 22 cm. "Constitutio dogmatica de divina revelatione," and its English translation: p. [156]-185. Bibliography: p. [186]-187. [BX830 1962.H36] 76-261381
1. Vatican Council. 2d, 1962-1965. Constitutio dogmatica de divina revelatione. 2. Bible—Study—Catholic Church. 3. Revelation. I. Walsh, Liam. II. Vatican Council. 2d, 1962-65. Constitutio dogmatica de divina revelatione. 1967. III. Vatican Council. 2d, 1962-65. Constitutio dogmatica de divina revelatione. English. 1967. IV. Title.

HESTON, Edward Louis, 1907- 262'.5
The press and Vatican II [by] Edward L. Heston Notre Dame, University of Notre Dame Press [1967] 134 p. illus., ports. 21 cm. [BX830.1962.H43] 66-14630
1. Vatican Council. 2d, 1962-1965. 2. Church and the press—Catholic Church. I. Title.

HOLLIS. CHRISTOPHER. 1902- 262'.5
The achievements of Vatican II. [1st ed.] New York, Hawthorn [1967] 119. [2] p. 21cm. (Twentieth cent. ency. of Catholicism; v. 1. Sect. 1: Knowledge and faith) Bibl. [BX830 1962.H58] 67-14865 3.95 bds.,
1. Vatican Council, 2d, 1962-1965. I. Title. II. Series: Twentieth century encyclopedia of Catholicism, v. 1

HORTON, Douglas, 1891- 262'.001
Toward an undivided church. With a foreword by Richard Cardinal Cushing. New York, Association Press [1967] 96 p. 20 cm. "Addresses to the Protestant and Orthodox observers and guests at Vatican II, 1962-1965, [by Pope John XXIII, Pope Paul VI, and Augustin Cardinal Bea]": (p. 63-96) Bibliographical footnotes. [BX8.2.H6] 67-10932
1. Vatican Council. 2d, 1962-1965. 2. Christian union—Catholic Church. I. Title.

HOUTEPEN, Anton W. J., 1940- 261
Theology of the Saeculum : a study of the concept of Saeculum in the documents of Vatican II and of the World Council of Churches, 1961-1972 / Anton Houtepen ; [translation, M. Goosen-Mallory]. Kampen : Kok, [1976] 170 p. ; 25 cm. Translation of Theologie van het saeculum. Includes bibliographical references and index. [BR115.W6H6713] 76-368388 ISBN 9-02-421392-4 : fl 42.00
1. Vatican Council, 2d, 1962-1965. 2. World Council of Churches. 3. Church and the world—History—Addresses, essays, lectures. 4. History (Theology)—History of doctrines—Addresses, essays, lectures. I. Title.

IMPACT of Vatican II (The) 262.5
[by] John Ford [others]. St. Louis, B. Herder. 1966. vi, 88p. 23cm. (Bellarmine Coll. studies). Lects. given before the Bellarmine Coll. Faculty Forum during 1965 and early 1966 Bibl. [BX8301962.I4] 66-19745 1.95 pap.,
1. Vatican Council. 2d. 1962-1965 I. Ford, John H. (Series: Bellarmine College, Louisville Ky. (Studies)

KAISER, Robert Blair. 262.5
Pope, Council, and world; the story of Vatican II. New York, Macmillan [1963] 266 p. 21 cm. [BX830 1962.K3] 63-161229
1. Vatican Council, 2d, 1962-1965. 2. Joannes XXIII, Pope, 1881-1963. I. Title.

KASCHMITTER, William A. 230'.2
The spirituality of Vatican II : conciliar texts concerning the spiritual life of all Christians / assembled and annotated by William A. Kaschmitter. Huntington, Ind. : Our Sunday Visitor, inc., [1975] 271 p. ; 24 cm. Includes index. [BX1747.5.K37] 74-29344 ISBN 0-87973-868-5 : 7.95
1. Vatican Council. 2d, 1962-1965. 2. Theology, Catholic—Collected works. I. Vatican Council. 2d, 1962-1965. II. Title.

KENNY, Denis. 262/.5
The Catholic Church and freedom; the Vatican Council and some modern issues. [St. Lucia, Brisbane] Univ. of Queensland Pr. [1967] 236p. 22cm. Three essays orig. delivered as lects. during Oct.-Nov. 1964 for the Univ. of New England Dept. of Univ. Extension. Bibl. [BX830 1962.K4] 67-102623 6.00 bds.,
1. Vatican Council. 2d, 1962-1965. 2. Marriage—Catholic Church. 3. 3. Religious liberty. I. Title.
American distributor: Tri-Ocean, San Francisco.

KENNY, Denis. 262'.5
The Catholic Church and freedom; the Vatican Council and some modern issues. [St. Lucia, Brisbane] University of Queensland Press [1967] 236 p. 22 cm. $4.00 Aust. (Aus 67-770) Three essays originally delivered as lectures during October-November 1964 for the University of New England Dept. of University Extension. Bibliography: p. 233-236. [BX830 1962.K4] 67-102623
1. Vatican Council. 2d, 1962-1965. 2. Marriage — Catholic Church. 3. Religious liberty. I. Title.

KLOPPENBURG, Bonaventure, 1919- 262'.02
The ecclesiology of Vatican II, by Bonaventure Kloppenburg. Translated by Matthew J. O'Connell. Chicago, Franciscan Herald Press [1974] xv, 373 p. 23 cm. Translation of A eclesiologia do Vaticano II. Includes bibliographical references. [BX830 1962.K54313 1974] 74-8035 ISBN 0-8199-0484-8
1. Vatican Council. 2d, 1962-1965. 2. Church—History of doctrines—20th century. I. Title.

KUNG, Hans, 1928- 262.5
The Council in action; theological reflections on the Second Vatican Council. Translated by Cecily Hastings. New York, Sheed and Ward [1963] ix, 276 p. 22 cm. "Published in Great Britian under the title: The living church." Includes bibliographical references. [BX8301962.K813] 63-17148
1. Vatican Council, 2d, 1962-1965. I. Title.

KUNG, Hans, 1928- 262.5
The Council, reform and reunion. Translated by Cecily Hastings. New York, Sheed and Ward [1962, c1961] 208 p. 22 cm. Translation of Konzil und Wiedervereinigung. [BX1784.K813 1962] 62-9101
1. Vatican Council. 2d, 1962-1965. 2. Catholic Church—Relations. 3. Christian union. I. Title.

LAZAR, Elmer B. 262'.5'2
The story of the century : "Jews absolved from blame of Jesus Christ's death" / by Elmer B. Lazar. New York : Philosophical Library, 1978. vii, 150 p. ; 22 cm. [BX830 1962.A45D4434] 78-50529 ISBN 0-8022-2226-9 : 7.50
1. Vatican Council. 2d, 1962-1965. Declaratio de ecclesiae habitudine ad religiones non-Christianas. 2. Catholic Church—Relations—Judaism. 3. Jesus Christ—Passion—Role of the Jeus. 4. Lazar, Elmer B. 5. Judaism—Relations—Catholic Church. 6. Christianity and antisemitism. I. Title.

LOMBARDI, Riccardo. 248.8'942
Vatican II ... and now; a retreat to the fathers of the Council, November 8-11,

1965. Washington, Movement for a Better World [1967] 144 p. 19 cm. Ten meditations translated from the Italian. [BX1912.5.L6] 73-6008
1. Vatican Council. 2d, 1962-1965. 2. Clergy—Religious life. I. Title.

MACEOIN, Gary, 1909- 262.5
What happened at Rome? The Council and its implications for the modern world. Introd. by John Cogley. Garden City, N.Y., Doubleday [1967, c.1966] 232p. 18cm. (Echo bk., E38) Bibl. [BX830. 1962. M3] .85 pap.,
1. Vatican Council, 2d, 1962-1965. I. Title.

MACEOIN, Gary, 1909- 262.5
What happened at Rome? The Council and its implications for the modern world. Introd. by John Cogley. [1st ed.] New York, Holt, Rinehart, and Winston [1966] xv, 191 p. 22 cm. Bibliographical footnotes. [BX830 1962.M3] 66-13497
1. Vatican Council. 2d, 1962-1965. I. Title.

MCMANUS, Frederick Richard, 1923- 264.02
Sacramental liturgy [by] Frederick R. McManus. [New York] Herder and Herder [1967] 256 p. 22 cm. "Text of the constitution on the sacred liturgy": p. [221] -256. [BX830.1962.A45C683] 67-18558
1. Vatican Council. 2d, 1962-1965. Constitutio de sacra liturgia. 2. Catholic Church. Liturgy and ritual. I. Vatican Council. 2d, 1962-1965. Constitutio de sacra liturgia. English. 1967. II. Title.

MCNAMARA, Kevin, 1926- 262'.5
Vatican II: the constitution on the Church; a theological and pastoral commentary, edited by Kevin McNamara. Chicago, Franciscan Herald Press [1968] 437 p. 23 cm. "Constitutio dogmatica de ecclesia": p. [365]-366. Bibliography: p. [427]-432. Bibliographical footnotes. [BX830 1962.A45C878 1968] 68-29112 7.95
1. Vatican Council. 2d, 1962-1965. Constitutio dogmatica de ecclesia. I. Vatican Council. 2d, 1962-1965. Constitutio dogmatica de ecclesia. 1968. II. Title.

MCNASPY, Clement J. 264.02
Our changing liturgy, by C. J. McNaspy. With a foreword by Godfrey Diekmann. [1st ed.] New York, Hawthorn Books [1966] 271 p. 22 cm. (Catholic perspectives) Bibliographical reference included in "Notes" (p. 237-258) [BX1970.M265] 66-10175
1. Vatican Council. 2d, 1962-1965. Constitutio de sacra liturgia. 2. Catholic Church. Liturgy and ritual. I. Title.

MANZ, James G. 262.136
Vatican II; renewal or reform? By James G. Manz. St. Louis, Concordia Pub. House [1966] 142 p. 21 cm. Bibliographical references included in "Notes" (p. [137]-142) [BX8301962.M34] 66-20499
1. Vatican Council. 2d, 1962-1965. I. Title.

MARTINDALE, Cyril Charlie, 1879- 922.
Bernard Vaughan, S.J., by C. C. Martindale ... London, New York [etc.] Longmans, Green and co., 1923. vii, [3] p., 1 l., 244 p. front., ports. 22 cm. [BX4705.V35M3] 23-14250
1. Vaughan, Bernard, 1847-1922. I. Title.

MASS means of communication. 261
[Edited by the Daughters of St. Paul. Boston] St. Paul Editions [1967] 202 p. illus., ports. 28 cm. Contents.Contents.—Foreword.—Decree on the media of social communication (p. [17]-144)—Motu proprio of Pope Paul VI, In fructibus.—Pope Pius XI on motion pictures, Vigilanti cura.—Pope Pius XII on motion pictures, radio and television, Miranda prorsus. Bibliography: p. 149. [BX830 1962.A451733] 67-25827
1. Vatican Council. 2d, 1962-1965. Decretum de instrumentis communications socialis. 2. Communication (Theology) I. Daughters of St. Paul. II. Vatican Council. 2d, 1962-1965. Decretum de instrumentis communicationis socialis. English. 1967.

MILLER, Charles Henry, 1933- 221'.6
"As it is written"; the use of Old Testament references in the documents of Vatican Council II [by] Charles H. Miller. St. Louis, Marianist Communications Center, 1973. viii, 246 p. 25 cm. Bibliography: p. [233]-246. [BX830 1962.M55] 73-161531
1. Vatican Council. 2d, 1962-1965. 2. Bible. O.T.—Criticism, interpretation, etc. I. Vatican Council. 2d, 1962-1965.

NATIONAL Council of Catholic Men. 262'.15
The spirit of renewal; [a short course in Vatican II for lay people] Washington [1967] 79 p. illus., ports. 28 cm. [BX830 1962.N33] 68-2447
1. Vatican Council. 2d, 1962-1965. 2. Laity—Catholic Church. I. Title. II. Title: A short course in Vatican II for lay people.

O'BRIEN, John Anthony, 1893- 282
Catching up with the Church: Catholic faith and practice today [by] John A. O'Brien. London, Burns & Oates; Herder & Herder, 1967 [i.e. 1968] 188p. 23cm. [BX1754.O16 1968] 68-98948 4.50
1. Vatican Council. 2d, 1962-1965. 2. Catholic Church—Doctrinal and controversial works, Popular. I. Title.

O'DEA, Thomas F. 282
The Catholic crisis [by] Thomas F. O'Dea. Boston, Beacon Press [1968] 267 p. 22 cm. Bibliographical references included in "Notes" (p. 253-261) [BX1746.O3] 68-14707
1. Vatican Council, 2d, 1962-1965. 2. Church renewal—Catholic Church. I. Title.

OUTLER, Albert Cook, 1908- 262'.5
Methodist observer atVatican II by Albert C. Outler westminster [Md.] Newman [1967] 189p. 21cm. [BX8301962.O9] 67-15717 4.50
1. Vatican Council. 2d, 1962-1965. I. Title.

PAWLEY, Bernard C. 262'.5'2
An Anglican view of the Vatican Council, by Bernard C. Pawley. Westport, Conn., Greenwood Press [1973, c1962] vi, 116 p. 20 cm. Includes bibliographical references. [BX830 1962.P32] 72-9368 ISBN 0-8371-6576-8
1. Vatican Council, 2d, 1962-1965. 2. Christian union. I. Title.

PAWLEY, Bernard C. 262'5
The Second Vatican Council: studies by eight Anglican observers; ed. by Bernard C. Pawley. [Magnolia, Mass., Peter Smith, 1968, c.1967] (Oxford Univ. Pr. bk. rebound Bibl. [BX830 1962.P38] 4.00
1. Vatican Council. 2d, 1962-1965. I. Title.

PAWLEY, Bernard C. 262/.5
The Second Vatican Council: studies by eight Anglican observers; ed. by Bernard C. Pawley. London, New York [etc.] Oxford Univ. Pr., 1967. vi, 262p. 21cm. Bibl. [BX830 1962.P38] 67-112041 3.75 pap.,
1. Vatican Council. 2d, 1962-1965. I. Title.

QUA-BECK, Warren A., ed. 262'.5
Challenge . . . and response; a Protestant perspective of the Vatican Council ed. by Warren A. Quanbeck with Friedrich Wilhelm Kantzenbach, bBibl. [BX830 1962.Q3] 66-22566 5.00
1. Vatican Council, 2d, 1962-1965. I. Title. Contents omitted.

QUANBECK, Warren A ed. 262'.5
Challenge .... and response; a Protestant perspective .of the Vatican Council, edited by Warren A. Quanbeck in consultation with Frederich Wilhelm Kantzenbach and Vilmos Vajta. Minneapolis, Augsburg Pub. House [c1966] vii, 226 p. 22 cm. Includes bibliographical references. [BX8301962.Q3] 66-22566
1. Vatican Council. 2d, 1962-1965. I. Title. - contents omitted

RATZINGER, Joseph. 262'.5
Theological highlights of Vatican 11 New York, Paulist Press [1966] vi, 185 p. 18 cm. (Deus books) [BX830.1962.R3] 66-30385
1. Vatican Council. 2d, 1962-1965. I. Title.

REGAN, Richard J. 261.7'2
Conflict and consensus; religious freedom and the second Vatican Council [by] Richard J. Regan. New York, Macmillan [1967] 212 p. 21 cm. Includes bibliographies. [BX830 1962.A45L58] 67-19679
1. Vatican Council. 2d, 1962-1965. Declaratio de libertate religiosa. I. Title.

RELIGIOUS freedom, 1965 and 1975 : 261.7'2
a symposium on a historic document / edited by Walter J. Burghardt New York : Paulist Press, 1976, c1977. v, 74 p. ; 21 cm. (Woodstock studies ; 1) Includes bibliographical references. [BX830 1962.A45L584] 76-45938 ISBN 0-8091-1993-5 pbk. : 2.45
1. Vatican Council. 2d, 1962-1965. Declaratio de libertate religiosa—Congresses. 2. Religious liberty—Congresses. I. Burghardt, Walter J. II. Title. III. Series.

RIGA, Peter J. 261
The church made relevant; a commentary on the pastoral constitution of Vatican II [by] Peter J. Riga. Notre Dame, Ind., Fides Publishers [1967] 337 p. 23 cm. [BX830.1962.A45C765] 66-30587
1. Vatican Council. 2d, 1962-1965. Constitutio pastoralis de ecclesia in mundo huius temporis. 2. Church and the world. I. Title.

RIGA, Peter J. 262'.02
The church renewed, by Peter J. Riga. New York, Sheed and Ward [1966] x, 246 p. 22 cm. Includes bibliographies. [BX1746.R52] 66-22025
1. Vatican Council. 2d, 1962-1965. Constitutio dogmatica de ecclesia. 2. Church renewal—Catholic Church. I. Title.

RYNNE, Xavier pseud pseud. 262.5
The fourth session; the debates and decrees of Vatican Council II, September 14 to December 8, 1965. New York, Farrar [c.1965, 1966] xi, 368p. 22cm. [BX830 1962.R88] 66-15322 5.50
1. Vatican Council. 2d, 1962-1965. I. Vatican Council, 2d, 1962-1965. II. Title.

RYNNE, Xavier, pseud. 262.5
The fourth session; the debates and decrees of Vatican Council II, September 14 to December 8, 1965. New York, Farrar, Straus and Giroux [1966] xi, 368 p. 22 cm. [BX830 1962.R88] 66-15322
1. Vatican Council. 2d, 1962-1965. I. Vatican Council. 2d, 1962-1965. II. Title.

RYNNE, Xavier, pseud. 262.5
Letters from Vatican City, Vatican Council II, first session: background and debates. New York, Farrar, Straus [1963] 289 p. illus. 22 cm. [BX830 1962.R9] 63-13197
1. Vatican Council, 2d, 1962-1965. I. Title.

RYNNE, Xavier, pseud. 262.5
The second session; the debates and decrees of Vatican Council II, September 29 to December 4, 1963. New York, Farrar, Straus [1964] xxiii, 390 p. facsims. 22 cm. Facsimiles in Latin. [BX830 1962.R92] 64-17815
1. Vatican Council, 2d, 1962-1965. I. Title. II. Title: The debates and decrees of Vatican Council II.

RYNNE, Xavier, pseud. 262.5
The third session; the debates and decrees of Vatican Council II, September 14 to November 21, 1964. New York, Farrar, Straus & Giroux [1965] xiii, 399 p. facsims. 22 cm. [BX830 1962.R93] 65-20915
1. Vatican Council, 2d, 1962-1965. I. Title. II. Title: The debates and decrees of Vatican Council II.

RYNNE, Xavier, pseud. 262'.5
Vatican Council II. New York, Farrar, Straus and Giroux [1968] vii, 596 p. 25 cm. A revised version of the author's earlier books covering the 4 sessions of Vatican Council II. [BX830.1962.R94] 67-21527
1. Vatican Council. 2d, 1962-1965.

SCHACHERN, Harold. 262'.5
The meaning of the Second Vatican Council; a newspaperman's report. Notre Dame, Ind., Fides Publishers [1967, c1966] 95 p. 18 cm. (A Fides dome book, D-56) [BX830 1962.S26] 67-24809
1. Vatican Council. 2d, 1962-1965. I. Title.

SCHILLEBEECKX, Edward Cornelius Florentinius Alfons, 1914- 262'.5
The real achievement of Vatican II [by] Eduard Schillebeecky. Translated by H. J. J. Vaughan [New York] Herder and Herder [1967] viii, 99 p. 21 cm. Translation of Het tweede Vaticaans Concilie. Bibliographical footnotes. [BX830 1962.S273b] 67-25884
1. Vatican Council. 2d, 1962-1965. I. Title.

SCHLINK, Edmund, 1903- 262'.5
After the Council. Translated by Herbert J. A. Bouman. Philadelphia, Fortress Press [1968] x, 261 p. 22 cm. Translation of Nach dem Konzil. Bibliographical footnotes. [BX830 1962.S2813] 68-12327
1. Vatican Council. 2d, 1962-1965.

SCHUTZ, Roger. 231'.74
Revelation, a Protestant view; the Dogmatic Constitution on divine revelation, a commentary, by Roger Schutz and Max Thurian. Pref. by Henri de Lubac. Westminster, Md., Newman Press [1968] v, 104 p. 21 cm. "The dogmatic constitution on divine revelation": p. [81]-102. Bibliography: p. 103-104. [BX830 1962.A45C774] 68-21453
1. Vatican Council, 2d. 1962-1965. Constitutio dogmatica de divina revelatione. 2. Revelation. I. Thurian, Max, joint author. II. Vatican Council, 2d, 1962-1965. Constitutio dogmatica de divina revelatione. English. 1968. III. Title.

SHERIDAN, Michael P. 377'.8'2 s
The Council on the campus, by Michael P. Sheridan. Dayton, Ohio, National Catholic Educational Association [1968] 30 p. port. 22 cm. (NCEA papers, no. 7) [LC461.N432 no. 7] 68-59293
1. Vatican Council. 2d, 1962-1965. 2. Catholic universities and colleges—U.S.—Administration. I. Title. II. Series: National Catholic Educational Association. NCEA papers, no. 7

SISTERS' Conference on Spirituality, University of Portland. 6th 1965. 248.894
Religious and the Vatican Council; lectures, edited by Joseph E. Haley. Portland, Or., University of Portland Press [1966] vi, 122 p. 22 cm. Bibliography: p. 115-116. [BX2435.S55 1965aa] 65-7107
1. Vatican Council. 2d, 1962-1965. 2. Monastic and religious life. I. Haley, Joseph Edmund ed. II. Portland, Or. University. III. Title.

STUBER, Stanley Irving, 1903- 262'.5
Implementing Vatican II in your community; dialogue and action manual based on the sixteen documents of the Second Vatican Council, by Stanley I. Stuber and Claud D Nelson Foword by Walter M. Abbot New York, Guild Press [1967] 239 p. 19 cm. (An Angelus book) Bibliography: p. [230]-232. [BX830.1962.S7] 67-10935
1. Vatican Council. 2d, 1962-1965. I. Nelson, Claud D., joint author. II. Title.

STUBER, Stanley Irving, 1903-
Implementing Vatican II in your community; dialogue and action manual based on the sixteen documents of the second Vatican Council, by Stanley I. Stuber and Claud D. Nelson ... New York, Association Press, 1967. 239 p. 19 cm. 68-88258
1. Vatican Council, 2d, 1962-1965. I. Nelson, Claud D., joint author. II. Title.

SUBILIA, Vittorio. 282
The problem of Catholicism. Translated by Reginald Kissack. Philadelphia, Westminster Press [1964] 190 p. 23 cm. (The Library of history and doctrine) Bibliographical footnotes. [BX1765.2.S853] 64-12392
1. Vatican Council, 2d, 1962-1965. 2. Catholic Church—Doctrinal and controversial works—Protestant authors. I. Title.

TAVARD, Georges Henri. 262'.5
The Pilgrim Church [by] George H. Tavard. London, Burns & Oates: [New York] Herder & Herder, 1967. 176p. 21cm. Bibl. [BX830 1962.T322] 68-96674 4.95
1. Vatican Council. 2d, 1962-1965. 2. Church. I. Title.

TRACY, Robert E. Bp. 1909- 262.5
American bishop at the Vatican Council; recollections and projections, by Robert E. Tracy. New York, McGraw [1966] viii, 242p. 22cm. [BX8301962.T7] 66-26583 6.50

1. Vatican Council. 2d, 1962-1965. I. Title.

VATICAN Council. 2d,1962- 282.08
1965.
The documents of Vatican 2; introductions and commentaries by Catholic bishops and experts, responses by Protestant and Orthodox scholars, Walter M. Abbott, general editor, Very Rev. Msgr. Joseph Gallagher, translation editor. Documents of Vatican II London, Dublin, G. Chapman, 1966. xxii, 794 p. table 18 1/2 cm. (An Angelus book) (B 66-7734) Bibliographical footnotes. [BX830 1962.A3G3] 66-74439
I. Abbott, Walter M., ed. II. Title.

VATICAN council, 2d. 262.5
Preparatory reports: Second Vatican Council. Tr. [from French] by Aram Berard. Philadelphia, Westminster [c.1965] 225p. 21cm. These reports, prepared by the preconciliar commns. and issued in l'Osservatore romano, are here tr. from the French version in la Documentation catholique. [BX8301962.A3B4] 65-19280 5.00
I. Berard, Aram, tr. II. Title.

VATICAN Council, 2d, 1962- 262/.5
1965 1962-1965
American participation in the second Vatican Council. Ed. by Vincent A. Yzermans. New York, Sheed [1967] xvi, 684p. 24cm. Contains the actual texts of the 118 addresses made by the United States' bishops in the Council. Bibl. [BX830 1962.A514] 67-13766 16.50
1. Vatican Council. 2d, 1962-1965. I. Yzermans, Vincent Arthur, 1925- ed. II. Title.

VATICAN Council. 2d, 1962- 262.9
1965.
Decree on priestly training of Vatican Council II and Decree on the ministry and life of priests of Vatican Council II. Commentary by Frank B. Norris. Glen Rock, N.J., Paulist Press, 1966. 157 p. 19 cm. (Vatican II documents) Bibliographical footnotes. [BX830 1962.A45D453] 66-29072
1. Vatican Council. 2d, 1962-1965. Decretum de institutione sacerdotali. 2. Vatican Council. 2d, 1962-1965. Decretum de presbyterorum ministerio et vita. I. Norris, Frank B. II. Vatican Council. 2d, 1962-1965. Decree on the ministry and life of priests. III. Title. IV. Title: Decree on the ministry and life of priests.

VATICAN Council. 2d, 1962- 262'.02
1965.
Vatican II on the Church. Editor: Austin Flannery. [2d ed.] Dublin, Scepter Books [1967] 363 p. 22 cm. "Constitutio dogmatica de Ecclesia" (p. [173]-335) in Latin and English on opposite pages. First ed. published in 1966 under title: Vatican II: the Church constitution. Includes bibliographical references. [BX830 1962.A45C8233 1967] 70-257873
1. Vatican Council. 2d, 1962-1965. Constitutio dogmatica de Ecclesia. I. Flannery, Austin, ed. II. Vatican Council. 2d, 1962-1965. Constitutio dogmatica de Ecclesia. English & Latin. 1967. III. Title.

VATICAN II on 262.001
ecumenism. Editor: Michael Adams. [1st ed.] Dublin, Chicago, Scepter Books [1966] 117 p. 22 cm. Contents.Contents.—The ecumenical movement, by M. Adams.—Catholic principles on ecumenism, by K. McNamara.—The practice of ecumenism, by E. McDonagh.—The separated churches and ecclesial communities, by T. F. Stransky.—Ecumenism and the missions, by B. Kelly.—Ecumenism in the light of Vatican II, by K. McNamara.—Decretum de oecumenismo—Decree on ecumenism. Includes bibliographical references. [BX830 1962.A45O462] 66-9026
1. Vatican Council. 2d, 1962-1965. Decretum de oecumenismo. 2. Christian union—Catholic Church. I. Adams, Michael, 1937- ed. II. Vatican Council. 2d, 1962-1965. Decretum de oecumenismo. English & Latin. 1966.

WALGRAVE, V. 271'.2
Dominican self-appraisal in the light of the council [by] Valentine Walgrave. Chicago, Priory Press [1968] xxxiv, 346 p. 24 cm. Translation of Essai d'autocritique d'un ordre religieux; les Dominicains en fin de concile. Bibliographical footnotes. [BX3502.2.W313] 68-29600
1. Vatican Council. 2d, 1962-1965. 2. Dominicans. 3. Church renewal. I. Title.

WILTGEN, Ralph M., 1921- 262'.5'2
The Rhine flows into the Tiber : a history of Vatican II / by Ralph M. Wiltgen. 1st British ed. Devon [Eng.] : Augustine Pub. Co., 1978. 304 p. ; 23 cm. Label mounted on t.p.: Distributed by Christian Classics, Westminster, Md. Includes index. [BX830 1962.W5 1978] 78-319985 ISBN 0-85172-721-2 : 7.95
1. Vatican Council. 2d, 1962-1965. I. Title.

WOLLEH, Lothar. 262'.5
The Council; the Second Vatican Council [by] Lothar Wolleh with the collaboration of Emil Schmitz. Introd. by Francis Cardinal Spellman. [English translation by Angus Malcolm] New York, Viking Press [1966] 120 p. col. illus., ports. (part col.) 44 cm. (A Studio book) [BX830 1962.W5913] 66-16072
1. Vatican Council. 2d, 1962-1965. I. Schmitz, Emil. II. Title.

Vatican Council. 2d, 1962-1965— Addresses, essays, lectures.

MCDONALD, William Joseph, 280'.2
ed.
The general council : special studies in doctrinal and historical background / edited and with a foreword by William J. McDonald. Westport, Conn. : Greenwood Press, 1979, c1962. viii, 182 p. ; 24 cm. Reprint of the ed. published by Catholic University Press, Washington. Includes bibliographical references. [BX825.M3 1979] 78-10099 ISBN 0-313-20753-4 lib. bdg. : lib. bdg :
1. Vatican Council. 2d, 1962-1965—Addresses, essays, lectures. 2. Councils and synods, Ecumenical—Addresses, essays, lectures. I. Title.

RAHNER, Karl, 1904- 260
The church after the council. New York, Herder and Herder [1966] 106 p. 21 cm. Translation by D. C. Herron and R. Albrecht of the author's Das Konzil: Ein neuer Beginn, Das neue Bild der Kirche, and Die Herausforderung der Theologie durch das II. Vatikanische Konzil. Contents.Contents.—The council: a new beginning.—The church: a new image.—Theology: a new challenge. [BX891.R253 1966] 66-26676
1. Vatican Council. 2d, 1962-1965—Addresses, essays, lectures. 2. Catholic Church—Addresses, essays, lectures. I. Title.

VATICAN Council. 2d, 1962- 262.5
1965.
Third session Council speeches of Vatican II. Edited by William K. Leahy and Anthony T. Massimini. Foreword by Lawrence Cardinal Shehan Glen Rock, N.J., Paulist Press [1966] xviii, 334 p. 19 cm. (Deus books) [BX830 1962.A3L4] 66-31290
I. Leahy, William K., ed. II. Massimini, Anthony T., ed. III. Title.

Vatican Council, 2d, 1962-1965—Art.

FRANCK, Frederick, 1909-
Drawings at the second Vatican Council, Edited by Columba Cary-Elwes, O.S.B. [New York, Macmillan publishing company, 1963?] vii, 52 plates, 22 cm. 68-79989
1. Vatican Council, 2d, 1962-1965—Art. I. Cary-Elwes, Columba, 1903- ed. II. Title.

Vatican Council. 2d, 1962-1965— Bibliography.

DOLLEN, Charles. 016.262'5
Vatican II: a bibliography. Metuchen, N.J., Scarecrow Press, 1969. 208 p. 23 cm. [Z7838.C7D64] 70-8394
1. Vatican Council. 2d, 1962-1965—Bibliography. I. Title.

Vatican Council. 2d, 1962-1965. Constitutio de ecclesia.

VATICAN COUNCIL. 2D, 1962- 260
1965.
Vatican II: the church constitution. Ed.: Austin Flanney. Chicago, Priory Pr. [1966] 207p. 23cm. Tr. & commentary on the constitution Constitutio de ecclesia. Appeared first in Doctrine & life. Bibl. [BX830 1962.A45 C423] 66-24108 4.95
1. Vatican Council. 2d, 1962-1965. Constitutio de ecclesia. I. Flannery, Austin, ed. II. Title.

Vatican Council, 2d, 1962-1965. Constitutio de sacra liturgia.

BOUYER, Louis, 1913- 264.02
The liturgy revived; a doctrinal commentary of the Conciliar Constitution on the liturgy. [Notre Dame, Ind.] Univ. of Notre Dame Pr. [c.]1964. 107p. 19cm. (Notre Dame pocket lib., PL-10) 64-8174 .95 pap.,
1. Vatican Council, 2d. Constituto de sacra liturgia. I. Title.

BOUYER, Louis, 1913- 264.02
The liturgy revived; a doctrinal commentary of the Conciliar Constitution on the liturgy. [Notre Dame, Ind.] University of Notre Dame Press, 1964. 107 p. 19 cm. (The Notre Dame pocket library, PL-10) [BX830.1962.A45C62] 64-8174
1. Vatican Council, 2d. Constitute de sacra liturgia. I. Title.

CHURCH and the liturgy 264.02
(The) Glen Rock, N. J., Paulist Pr. [c.1965] viii, 191p. 24cm. (Concilium theology in the age of renewal: Liturgy, v.2) Bibl. [BX830.A45C625] 65-17869 4.50
1. Vatican Council, 2d. Constitutio de sacra liturgia. 2. Catholic Church. Liturgy and ritual. I. Wagner, Johunnes, 1908- (Series: Concilium theology in the age of renewal, v.2)

CRICHTON, James D 1907- 264.02
The church's worship; considerations on the liturgical constitution of the Second Vatican Council [by] J. D. Crichton. New York, Sheed & Ward [1964] x, 246 p. 23 cm. Bibliography: p. 239-242. [BX830 1962.A45C63] 64-22998
1. Vatican Council, 2d. Constituto de sacra liturgis. I. Title.

LITURGICAL Conference, 264.02
inc.
Preaching the liturgical renewal; instructional sermons and homilies. Pref. by H. A. Reinhold. Washington [1964] 96 p. 21 cm. (Its The parish worship program) [BX830 1962.A45C65] 64-8256
1. Vatican Council, 2d. Constituto de sacra liturgia. 2. Catholic Church. Liturgy and ritual — Sermons. I. Title.

LITURGY constitution 264.02
(The); a chapter by chapter analysis of the Constitution on the sacred liturgy, with study-club questions. Glen Rock, N.J., Paulist [1965, c.1964] 191p. 18cm. (Deus bks.) Bibl. [BX830 1962.A45C68] 64-8073 .95 pap.,
1. Vatican Council. 2d. Constitutio de sacra liturgia. I. Vatican Council, 2d. Constitutio de sacra liturgia. II. Catholic Church. Pope, 1963- (Paulus VI) Motu proprio sacram liturgiam (25 Jan. 1964) English.

SLOYAN, Gerard Stephen, 1919-
Worship in a new key; what the Council teaches on the liturgy. New York, Herder and Herder, 1965. 191 p. 21 cm. (A Liturgical conference book) 67-98804
1. Vatican Council, 2d, 1962-1965. Constitutio de sacra liturgia. 2. Liturgy. I. Title.

VATICAN Council, 2d. 264.02
Constitutio de sacra liturgia.
The Liturgy constitution; a chapter by chapter analysis of the Constitution on the sacred liturgy, with study-club questions. Glen Rock, N.J., Paulist Press [1964] 191 p. 18 cm. (Deus books) "Motu proprio of Pope Paul VI": p. 179-188. Bibliography: p. 189-191. [BX830 1962.A45C68] 64-8078
1. Vatican Council, 2d. Constitutio de sacra liturgia. 2. Catholic Church. Pope, 1963-1978 (Paulus VI) Motu proprio sacram liturgiam (25 Jan. 1964) English. I. Title.

WAGNER, Johannes, 1908- 264.02
The Church and the liturgy. Glen Rock, N.J. Paulist Press [1965] viii, 191 p. 24 cm. (Concilium theology in the age of renewal: Liturgy, v. 2) Contents.Preface, by J. Wagner. -- Articles: The bishop and the liturgy, by C. Vagaggini; translated by P. Perfetti. Relation between bishop and priests according to the Liturgy Constitution, by J. Pascher; translated by T. L. Westow.The juridic power of the bishop in the Constitution on the Sacred Liturgy, by F. R. McManus. Liturgy, devotions, and the bishop, by J. A. Jungmann; translated by T. L. Westow. The role of sacred music, by J. Gelineau; translated by T. L Westow. The place of liturgical worship, by G. Diekmann. -- Bibliographical survey: Church music, by H. Hucke; translated by T. L. Westow. Concelebration, by H. Manders; translated by T. L. Westow. Communion under both kinds, by G. Danneels; translated by T. L. Westow. -- DO-C: Documentation concilium: Evolution of the concept of economic expansion, by R. Scarpati; translated by P. Perfitti and A. M. Salerno. -- Chronicle of the living Church: Introduction. International Congress on Education for the Priesthood in Western Europe; translated by T. L. Westow. Includes bibliographical references. [BX830 1962.A45C625] 65-17869
1. Vatican Council, 2d. Constitutio de sacra liturgia. 2. Catholic Church. Liturgy and ritual. I. Title. II. Series. III. Series: Concilium theology in the age of renewal, v. 2

Vatican Council, 2d, 1962-1965. De Oecumenismo.

ADAMS, Michael, ed. 262.001
Vatican II on ecumenism. [1st ed.] Dublin, Chicago, Scepter Bks. [1966] 117p. 22cm. Bibl. [BX830 1962.A45O462] 66-9026 1.50 pap.,
1. Vatican Council, 2d, 1962-1965. De Oecumenismo. I. Title.

VATICAN Council. 2d,1962- 262.5
1965.
The Vatican Council and Christian unity; a commentary on the Decree on ecumenism of the Second Vatican Council, together with a translation of the text [by] Bernard Leeming. [1st ed.] New York, Harper & Row [1966] xiv, 333 p. 22 cm. Bibliographical footnotes. [BX830 1962.A45O43] 66-15863
1. Vatican Council. 2d, 1962-1965. De Oecumenismo. I. Leeming, Bernard, ed. and tr. II. Title.

VATICAN Council, 2d, 1962- 262.5
1965
The Vatican Council and Christian unity; a commentary on the Decree on ecumenism of the Second Vatican Council, with a tr. of the text [by] Bernard Leeming. New York, Harper [c.1966] xiv, 333p. 22cm. Bibl. [BX8301962.A45043] 66-15863 7.95
1. Vatican Council, 2d, 1962-1965. De Oecumenismo. I. Leeming, Bernard, ed. and tr. II. Title.

Vatican Council. 2d, 1962-1965. Declaratio de Ecclesiae habitudine ad religiones non-Christianas.

BEA, Augustin Cardinal 261.2
1881-
The Church and the Jewish people; a commentary on the Second Vatican Councils Declaration on the relation of the Church to non-Christian religions [by] Augustin Cardinal Bea. Tr. by Philip Loretz. New York, Harper [1966] 172p. 21cm. the text of the Declaration on the relation of the Church to non-Christian religions Bibl. [BX830 1962.A45D433] 66-20790 4.50
1. Vatican Council. 2d, 1962-1965. Declaratio de Ecclesiae habitudine ad religiones non-Christianas. 2. Catholic Church—Relations—Judaism. 3. Judaism—Relations—Catholic Church. I. Title.

VATICAN COUNCIL. 2D. 1962- 261.2
1965
The Declaration on the relation of the

Church to non-Christian religions. promulgated by Pope Paul VI, October 28, 1965. Commentary by Rene Laurentin, Joseph Neuner. Study-club ed. Glen Rock. N.J., Paulist. 1966. 104p. 18cm. (Vatican II docs.) Bibl. [BX8301962.A45D353] 66-26208 .75 pap., *1. Vatican Council. 2d. 1962-1965. Declaratio de Ecclesiae habitudine ad religiones non-Christianas. 2. Catholic Church—Relations. I. Laurentin, Rene. II. Neuner, Josef. III. Title.*

Vatican Council. 2d, 1962-1965. Declaratio de liberate religiosa.

INSTITUTE on Religious 262.91 Freedom, North Aurora, Ill., 1966. *Religious liberty:* an end and a beginning; the Declaration on religious freedom.an ecumenical discussion Ed. by John Courtney Murray. New York, Macmillan 1966 192p. 21cm. Discourses given at the Inst. on Religious Freedom. organized by the Bellarmine School of Theol. of Loyola Univ. Appendix:Declaration on religious freedom': p. 162-189. Bibl. [BX830 1962.A45D423] 66-24891 4.95 *1. Vatican Council. 2d. 1962-1965. Declaratio de liberate religious. 2. Religious liberty—Addresses, essays, lectures. I. Murray, John Courtney, ed. II. Vatican Council. 2d, 1962-1965. Declaration on religious freedom. III. Loyola University, Chicago Bellarmine school of Theology, North Aurora, Ill. IV. Loyola University, Chicago. Bellarmine School of Theology, North Aurora, Ill. V. Title.*

INSTITUTE on Religious 262.91 Freedom, North Aurora, Ill., 1966. *Religious liberty:* an end and a beginning; the Declaration on religious freedom, an ecumenical discussion. Edited by John Courtney Murray. New York, Macmillan [1966] 192 p. 21 cm. Discourses given at the Institute on Religious Freedom, organized by the Bellarmine School of Theology of Loyola University. "Appendix: Declaration on religious freedom": p. 162-189. Bibliographical footnotes. [BX830 1962.A45D423] 66-24891 *1. Vatican Council. 2d, 1962-1965. Declaratio de libertate religiosa. 2. Religious liberty — Addresses, essays, lectures. I. Murray, John Courtney, ed. II. Loyola University, Chicago. Bellarmine School of Theology, North Aurora, Ill. III. Vatican Council. 2d, 1962-1965. Declaration on religious freedom. IV. Title.*

Vatican Council. 2d, 1962-1965. Decretum de presbyterorum ministerio et vita.

TARTRE, Raymond A. 253.2 *The postconciliar priest;* comments on some aspects of theDecree on the ministry and life of priests [by] Raymond A. Tartre. New York, Kenedy [1966] viii, 172p. 22cm. Includes tr. of the Decree taken from The documents of Vatican II. Bibl. [BX830 1962.A45D467] 66-25142 3.95 *1. Vatican Council. 2d, 1962-1965. Decretum de presbyterorum ministerio et vita. I. Vatican Council. 2d, 1962-1965. Decree on the ministry and life of priests. II. Title. III. Title: Decree on the ministry and life of priests.*

Vatican Council. 2d, 1962-1965. I. Title.

HARING, Bernhard, 1912- 262.5 *Road to Renewal;* perspectives of Vatican II [by] Bernhard Haring. Staten Island, N.Y., Alba House [1966] 221 p. 19 cm. "Original title: Il Concilio comincia adesso." [BX830 1962.H283] 66-27535 *1. Vatican Council. 2d, 1962-1965. I. Title. I. Title.*

Vatican Council. 2d, 1962-1965—Indexes.

DERETZ, Jacques, comp. 262'.5 *Dictionary of the Council.* Edited by J. Deretz and A. Nocent. Washington, Corpus Books [1968] 506 p. 24 cm. "Slightly abridged" translation of Synopse des textes conciliaires. [BX830 1962.A48D43] 69-14374 12.50 *1. Vatican Council. 2d, 1962-1965—Indexes. I. Nocent, Adrien, joint comp. II. Vatican Council. 2d, 1962-1965. III. Title.*

Vatican Council. 2d, 1962-65—Congresses.

INTERNATIONAL Theological 262.5 Conference, Notre Dame, Ind., 1966. *Vatican II;* an interfaith appraisal, [Participants] Barnabas Ahern [and others] Edited by John H. Miller. Notre Dame, University of Notre Dame Press [1966] xii, 656 p. 27 cm. Held at the University of Notre Dame. Half title and running title: Theological issues of Vatican II. Includes bibliographical "Notes." [BX830.1962.I5] 66-24920 *1. Vatican Council. 2d, 1962-65—Congresses. I. Miller, John H., 1925- ed. II. Notre Dame, Ind. University. III. Title. IV. Title: Theological issues of Vatican II.*

Vatican Council, 2d—Biography

NOVAK, Michael, ed. 922.2 *The men who make the Council* [vs. 7-12] Notre Dame, Ind., Univ. of Notre Dame Pr. [c.1964] 6v. (various p.) 18cm. Each v. has also special t.p. On cover: Critical portraits. [BX4664.2.N6] 64-7964 .75 pap., *1. Vatican Council, 2d—Biog. 2. Cardinals. I. Title.* Contents omitted.

Vatican Council, 2d. Constituto de sacra liturgia — Indexes.

DE MARCO, Angelus A. 264.02 *A key to the new liturgical constitution;* an alphabetical analysis. New York, Desclee [c.]1964. 132p. 19cm. 64-23899 2.95 *1. Vatican Council, 2d. Constituto de sacra liturgia—Indexes. I. Title.*

DE MARCO, Angelus A *A key to the new liturgical constitution;* an alphabetical analysis, by Angelus A. De Marco. New York, Desclee Co., 1964. 132 p. 19 cm. 264 64-23899 *1. Vatican Council, 2d. Constituto de sacra liturgia — Indexes. I. Title.*

Vatican Council, 2d. De oecumenismo.

JAEGER, Lorenz, 262.001 Cardinal, 1892- *A stand on ecumenism:* the Council's decree [by] Lorenz Cardinal Jaeger. Translated by Hilda Graef. New York, P. J. Kenedy [1965] xiii, 242 p. 22 cm. Translation of Konzilsdekret "Uber den Okumenismus." "Sources of the decree 'On ecumenism'": p. 223-236. 65-26330 *1. Vatican Council, 2d. De oecumenismo. I. Title.*

JAEGER, Lorenz, Cardinal, 262.001 1892- *A stand on ecumenism:* the Council's decree. Tr. [from German] by Hilda Graef. New York, Kenedy [c.1965] xiii, 242p. 22cm. Bibl. [BX8301962.A45D4653] 65-26330 4.95 *1. Vatican Council, 2d. De oecumenismo. I. Title.*

Vaughan, Bernard, 1847-1922.

MARTINDALE, Cyril Charlie, 922. 1879- *Bernard Vaughan, S.J.,* by C. C. Martindale ... London, New York [etc.] Longmans, Green and co., 1923. vii, [3] p., 1 l., 244 p. front., ports. 22 cm. [BX4705.V35M3] 23-14250 *1. Vaughan, Bernard, 1847-1922. I. Title.*

VAUGHAN, Bernard, 1847-1922. *What of to-day?* By Father Bernard Vaughan ... New York, McBride, Nast and company, 1915. ix p., 1 l., [xi]-xxi, 392 p. front. (port.) 21 1/2 cm. Printed in Great Britain. 15-24017 *I. Title.*

Vaughan, Curry N.

VAUGHAN, Curry N. 285'.092'4 B *Battle-ground :* a personal account of God's move upon the American military forces / by Curry N. Vaughan, Jr., with Bob Slosser. Plainfield, N.J. : Logos International, c1978. 193 p., [2] leaves of plates : ill. ; 20 cm. [BX9225.V39A33] 78-51865 ISBN 0-88270-301-3 : 2.95 *1. Vaughan, Curry N. 2. Presbyterian Church—Clergy—Biography. 3. Chaplains, Military—United States—Biography. 4. Church work with military personnel. 5. Pentecostals—United States—Biography. I. Slosser, Bob, joint author. II. Title.*

Vaughan, Henry, 1622-1695.

MARTZ, Louis Lohr. 821.409 *The paradise within;* studies in Vaughan, Traherne, and Milton, by Louis L. Martz. New Haven, Yale University Press, 1964. xix, 217 p. col. illus., facsims. 21 cm. Bibliography: p. 203-205. [PR549.R4M316] 64-20926 *1. Vaughan, Henry, 1622-1695. 2. Traherne, Thomas, d. 1674. 3. Milton, John, 1608-1674. 4. Religious poetry, English—History and criticism. I. Title.*

Vaughan, William, 1785-1877.

VAUGHAN, Henry, 1622-1695. *The sacred poems and private ejaculations of Henry Vaughan.* With a memoir by the Rev. H. F. Lyte. Boston, Little, Brown and company; New York, Evans and Dickerson; [etc., etc.] 1854. vi p., 1 l., 307 p. 17 cm. [British poets, ed. by F. J. Child] [PR3742.S4 1854] 15-10944 *I. Lyle, Henry Francis,1703-1847. II. Title. III. Title: Silex scintillaus.* Contents omitted.

VAUGHAN, Thomas M., 1825- 922.673 *Memoirs of Rev. Wm. Vaughan, D.D., by his son, Thos. M. Vaughan* ... With sketches of his character by Rev. J. M. Pendleton, D.D. and others. Also, an essay and two sermons by Dr. Vaughan. Louisville, Caperton & Cates 1878. vii, [1], [9]-336 p. 19 1/2 cm. [BX6495.V3V3] 36-21124 *1. Vaughan, William, 1785-1877. I. Pendleton, James Madison, 1811-1891. II. Title.*

Vaughn, Francis William, 1839-1913.

BLAKE, Nelson Morehouse, 268.434 comp. *The Vaughn Bible class,* Calvery Baptist church, Washington, D.C. A fifty-year history, compiled and edited by Nelson Morehouse Blake and Richard Spencer Palmer. Washington, D.C., The Franklin press [1940] 3 p. l., vi, 106 p. plates, ports. (part fold.)facsims. 23 cm. [BX6227.W3C38] 40-9535 *1. Vaughn, Francis William, 1839-1913. 2. Washington, D.C. Calvary Baptist Church. Vaughn Bible class. I. Palmer, Richard Spencer, joint comp. II. Title.*

Vaughn, Ruth.

VAUGHN, Ruth. 209'.2'4 B *My God, my God! :* answers to our anguished cries / by Ruth Vaughn. Nashville, Tenn. : Impact Books, c1982. 200 p. ; 21 cm. [BR1725.V36A35 1982] 19 81-84925 ISBN 0-86608-006-6 : 5.95 *1. Vaughn, Ruth. 2. Christian biography—United States. 3. Endocrine glands—Diseases—Patients—United States—Biography. I. Title.*

VAUGHN, Ruth. 248'.2 B *To be a graduate* / by Ruth Vaughn. Nashville : T. Nelson, c1979. 95 p. ; 21 cm. [BV4501.2.V37] 79-1404 ISBN 0-8407-4073-5 : 4.95 *1. Vaughn, Ruth. 2. Christian life—1960- I. Title.*

Vaults.

WARD, Clarence, 1884- *...Mediaeval church vaulting,* by Clarence Ward... Princeton, Princeton university press; [etc., etc.,] 1915. ix p., 1 l., 192 p. illus. 27 cm. (Princeton monographs in art and archaeology, V) Bibliography: p. 185-186. [NA5453.W3] 15-25961 *1. Vaults. 2. Chruch architecture. I. Title.*

Vaults (Architecture)

WARD, Clarence, 1884- 726'.59 *Mediaeval church vaulting.* Princeton, Princeton University Press, 1915. [New York, AMS Press, 1973] ix, 192 p. illus. 24 cm. Original ed. issued as no. 5 of Princeton monographs in art and archaeology. Bibliography: p. 185-186. [NA5453.W3 1973] 72-177847 ISBN 0-404-06836-7 10.00 *1. Vaults (Architecture) 2. Church architecture. 3. Architecture, Medieval. I. Title. II. Series: Princeton monographs in art and archaeology, 5.*

Vedanta.

ABHEDANANDA, swami. *Vendanta philosophy.* Divine heritage of man, by Swami Abhedananda. New York, The Vedanta society [1903] 215 p. front. (port.) 19 1/2 cm. 3-14879 *I. Title.*

ARYA, Usharbudh. 294.5'211 *God* / by Usharbudh Arya. Honesdale, Pa. : Himalayan International Institute of Yoga Science and Philosophy, c1979. xii, 151 p. ; 22 cm. [B132.V3A74] 79-88824 ISBN 0-89389-060-X : 4.95 *1. Vedanta. 2. Yoga. 3. God (Hinduism) I. Title.*

ASHOKANANDA, Swami. 181'.48 *My philosophy and my religion.* San Francisco, Vedanta Society of Northern California, 1970. 78 p. 24 cm. [B132.V3A76] 70-28638 *1. Vedanta. I. Title.*

BADARAYANA. 181'.48 *The Brahma Sutra* : the philosophy of spiritual life. Translated with an introd. and notes by S. Radhakrishnan New York, Greenwood Press, 1968 [c1960] 606 p. 23 cm. Text in English and Sanskrit. Bibliography: p. [565] [B132.V3B2 1968] 68-21330 *1. Vedanta. 2. Philosophy, Hindu. I. Radhakrishnan, Sarvepalli, Pres. India, 1888- ed. and tr. II. Title.*

BADARAYANA. 181.48 *The Brahma sutra,* the philosophy of spiritual life. Translated with an introd. and notes by S. Radhakrishnan. New York, Harper [1960] 606 p. 23 cm. English and Sanskrit. [B132.V3B2 1960] 60-1206 *1. Vedanta. 2. Philosophy, Hindu. I. Radhakrishnan, Sarvepalli, Sir, 1888- ed. and tr.*

BHATTACHARYYA, 181'.484 Krishnachandra, 1875-1949. *Search for the absolute in neo-Vedanta* / K. C. Bhattacharyya ; edited and with an introd. by George Bosworth Burch. Honolulu : University Press of Hawaii, [1975] p. cm. Three essays previously published in the author's Studies in philosophy. Includes index. Contents.Contents.—Place of the indefinite in logic.—The subject as freedom.—The concept of the Absolute and its alternative forms. "Bibliography of Bhattacharyya's writings": p. [B132.V3B46 1975] 75-17740 ISBN 0-8248-0296-9 : 10.00 *1. Bhattacharyya, Krishnachandra, 1875-1949—Bibliography. 2. Vedanta. 3. Absolute, The. 4. Liberty. I. Burch,George Bosworth, 1902- II. Title.*

ISHERWOOD, Christopher. 181.48 *Vedanta for Modern Man,* edited and with an introduction by Christopher Isherwood. New York, New American Library [1972] 444 p. (A Mentor Book, MW1180) Pap. 1.50 *1. Vedanta. I. Title.*

ISHERWOOD, Christopher, 181.48 1904- *An approach to Vedanta.* Hollywood, Calif., Vedanta Press [1963] 72 p. 18 cm. Full name: Christopher William Bradshaw-Isherwood. [B132.V3I75] 63-3269 *1. Vedanta. I. Title.*

ISHERWOOD, Christopher, 181.4 1904- ed. *Vedanta for the western world,* edited, and with an introduction, by Christopher Isherwood. Hollywood [Calif.] The Marcel Rodd co., 1945. viii, 452 p. 22 cm. [Full

name: Christopher William Bradshaw Isherwood] [B132.V3I8] 46-25052
1. Vedanta. I. Title.

KASHINATH. 181'.482
The scientific Vedanta. Delhi, S. Chand, 1973. xiii, 129 p. 23 cm. Bibliography: p. 124. [B132.V3K33] 73-900893
1. Vedanta. I. Title.
Available from International Publications Service, New York, for 7.50.

MAN and his becoming,
according to the Vedanta. Translated by Richard C. Nicholson. [1st Noonday paperbound ed.] New York, Noonday Press [1958] 187p. (Noonday paperbacks, N129) Bibliographical footnotes.
1. Vedanta. 2. Man. I. Guenon, Rene.

MULLER, Friedrich Max, 181.4
1823-1900.
Three lectures on the Vedanta philosophy, delivered at the Royal institutionin March, 1894, by F. Max Muller ... London and New York, Longmans, Green, and co., 1894. vii, 173 p. 23 cm. [B132.V3M7] 32-16344
1. Vedanta I. Royal institution of Great Britain, London. II. Title.

MULLER, Friedrich Max, 1823-
1900.
Three lectures on the Vedanta philosophy, delivered at the Royal institutionin March, 1894, by the Right Hon. F. Max Muller ... New impression. London, New York and Bombay, Longmans, Green, and co., 1901. vii, 173, [1] p. 20 cm. (Half-title: Collected works of the Right Hon. F. Max Muller, xvi) "First edition ... 1894. Reprinted in the collected edition ... 1901." [PJ27.M7 vol. 16] 5-19674
1. Vedanta. I. Title.
Contents omitted.

RAYAPATI, J. P. Rao. 181'.48
Early American interest in Vedanta; pre-Emersonian interest in Vedic literature and Vedantic philosophy [by] J. P. Rao Rayapati. New York, Asia Pub. House [1973] x, 133 p. 23 cm. Bibliography: p. [121]-130. [B132.V3R44 1973] 72-87302 ISBN 0-210-40508-2 5.00 (pbk.)
1. Vedanta. 2. Transcendentalism (New England) I. Title.

SANKARACARYA. supposed 181.48
author.
The Saundaryalahari; or, Flood of beauty. Edited, translated, and presented in photos. by W. Norman Brown. Cambridge, Harvard University Press, 1958. viii, 249p. plates (part col.) 27cm. (Harvard Oriental series, v. 43) Poem in English and Sanskrit. [PK2971.H3 vol.43] 57-9072
1. Vedanta. I. Title. II. Title: Flood of beauty. III. Series.

SINHA, Jadunath, 1894- 181'.482
The philosophy of Vijanaabikshu / by Jadunath Sinha. 1st ed. Calcutta : Sinha Pub. House, c1976. 73, iv, vi p. ; 23 cm. Includes bibliographical references and index. [B133.V37S56] 76-905156 Rs12.00
1. Vijnanabhiksu, fl. 1550. 2. Vedanta. 3. Sankhya. I. Title.

THORNE, Sabina. 181.48
Precepts for perfection; teachings of the disciples of Sri Ramakrishna. Hollywood, Calif., Nedanta Press [1961] 235 p. 22 cm. Includes bibliography. [B132.V3T5] 61-65951
1. Ramakrishna, 1836-1886. 2. Vedanta. I. Title.

URQUHART, William Spence, 181.
1877-
... The Vedanta and modern thought, by W. S. Urquhart ... London, New York [etc.] H. Milford, Oxford university press, 1928. xiv p., 1 l., 256 p. 23 cm. (The religious quest of India) [B132.V3U7] 29-9128
1. Vedanta. 2. Philosophy, Modern. I. Title. II. Title: Modern thought.

VEDANTA and the West. 181.4
Vedanta for modern man, ed., introd. by Christopher Isherwood. New York, Collier [1962, c.1945-1951] 446p. 18cm. Selection from material pub. between 1945 and the present day in Vedanta and the West. (BS8) 1.50 pap.,
1. Vedanta. I. Isherwood, Christopher, 1904- ed. II. Title.

VEDANTA and the West. 181.4
Vedanta for modern man, edited and with an introd. by Christopher Isherwood. [1st ed.] New York, Harper [1951] xiv, 410 p. 22 cm. "selections from...material published between 1945 and the present day" in Vedanta and the West. [B132.V3V38] 51-11293
1. Vedanta. I. Isherwood, Christopher, 1904= ed. II. Title.

VEDANTA and the West. 181.48
Vedanta for the Western World; edited, and with an introd., by Christopher Isherwood. New York, Viking [1960, c.1945] viii, 453p. 20cm. Selections from the magazine Vedanta and the West. (Compass bk. C64) 1.75 pap.,
1. Vedanta. I. Isherwood, Christopher, ed. II. Title.

VEDANTA in Southern California; anillustrated guide to the Vedanta Society. Hollywood, Calif., Vedanta Press [1956] 64p. plates, ports.
1. Vedants. I. Vedanta Society.

VEDANTA Society.
Vedanta in Southern California; an illustrated guide to the Vedanta Society. Hollywood, Calif., Vedanta Press [1956] 64 p. plates, ports.
1. Vedanta. I. Title.

VIVEKANANDA, Swami, 1863- 181.45
1902.
Jnana-yoga. [2d] rev. ed. New York, Ramkrishna-Vivekananda Center, 1955. 317p. illus. 16cm. [B132.V3V548 1955] 55-8658
1. Vedanta. 2. Yoga, Jñana. I. Title.

VIVEKANANDA, swami, 1863- 181.
1902.
Vedanta philosophy; lectures by the Swami Vivekananda on raja yoga and other subjects, also Patanjalis' yoga aphorisms, with commentaries, and glossary of Sanskrit terms. New ed., with enlarged glossary. New York, The Baker & Taylor company, 1899. xv, 381 p. incl. front. (port.) pl. 19 cm. [B132.V3V5 1899] 99-2621
1. Vedanta. 2. Yoga. I. Patañjali. II. Title.

VIVEKANANDA, swami, 1863- 181.
1902.
Vedanta philosophy; eight lectures by the Swami Vivekananda on karma yoga (the secret of work) Delivered under the auspices of the Vedanta society. 2d ed. New York, The Baker & Taylor company, 1901. 171 p. incl. front. (port.) 19 1/2 cm. [B132.V3V57 1901] 1-30853
1. Vedanta. 2. Work, Method of. I. Title. II. Title: Karma yoga.

VIVEKANANDA, swami, 1863- 181.
1902.
Vedanta philosophy; lectures by the Swami Vivekananda on jnana yoga. New York, The Vedanta society [1902] 2 p. l., 7-357 p. 19 1/2 cm. Half title-Jnana yoga. "The present volume consists chiefly of lectures which were delivered in London, England."--Pref. [B132.V3V55 1902] 2-18351
1. Vedanta. 2. Yoga. I. Title. II. Title: Jnana yoga.

VIVEKANANDA, swami, 1863- 181.
1902.
Vedanta philosophy, raja yoga, being lectures by the Swami Vivekananda; with Patanjali's aphorisms, commentaries and a glossary of terms. New ed., with enlarged glossary. New York, Brentano's, 1920. xiv, 269 p. incl. front. (port.) pl. 19 cm. [B132.V3V58 1920] 20-13335
1. Vedanta. 2. Yoga. I. Patañjali. II. Title.

VIVEKANANDA, Swami, 1863- 181.48
1902
What religion is in the words of Swami Vivekananda. Ed. by JohnYale. Biographical introd. by Christopher Isherwood. New York, Julian [c.]1962. 224p. front port. 22cm. 62-19297 5.00
1. Vedanta. 2. Yoga. I. Yale, John, ed. II. Title.

WOOD, Ernest, 1883- 181.4
The glorious presence; a study of the Vedanta philosophy and its relation to modern thought. Including a new translation of Shankara's Ode to the south-facing form. [1st ed.] New York, Dutton, 1951. 320 p. 21 cm. [B132.V3W6] 51-9111
1. Vedanta. I. Sankaracarya. Ode to the south-facing form. II. Title.

WOOD, Ernest, 1883-1965. 181'.48
The glorious presence; the Vedanta philosophy including Shankara's Ode to the south-facing form. Wheaton, Ill., Theosophical Pub. House [1974, c1951] 320 p. 21 cm. (A Quest book) Includes a translation of Shankara's Daksinamurtistotra (Ode to the south-facing form) [B132.V3W6 1974] 74-1045 ISBN 0-8356-0446-2 2.75 (pbk.)
1. Vedanta. I. Sankaracarya. Daksinamurtistotra. English. 1974. II. Title.

YALE, John, ed. 181.48
What Vedanta means to me; a symposium. With a foreword by Vincent Sheean. Garden City, N. Y., Doubleday, 1960[c.1951-1960] 215p. 60-13564 3.95
1. Vedanta. I. Title.

YALE, John 294.555
A Yankee and the swamis. Hollywood 28, 1946 Vedanta Place Calif., Vedanta Pr., [c.1961] 224p. illus., map. 61-65046 3.95
1. Vedanta. 2. Pilgrims and pilgrimages—India. I. Title.

Vedanta—Addresses, essays, lectures.

MAINKAR, Trimbak Govind. 181'.48
The making of the Vedanta / T.G. Mainkar. Delhi : Ajanta Publications : distributors, Ajanta Books International, 1980. vi, 170 p. ; 22 cm. Includes index. Bibliography: p. 165. [B132.V3M268] 19 80-903454 pbk. : 14.00
1. Vedanta—Addresses, essays, lectures. I. Title.
Distributed by South Asia Books, P.O. Box 502, Columbia, MO 65205

PRABHAVANADA, Swami, 294.5'55
1893-
Religion in practice. With an introd. by Christopher Isherwood. Hollywood, Calif., Vedanta Press [1968] 260 p. 23 cm. Bibliography: p. 252-253. [B132.V3P53] 75-4009 4.95
1. Vedanta—Addresses, essays, lectures. I. Title.

Vedanta—Collections.

DEUTSCH, Eliot. 181'.482
A source book of Advaita Vedanta [by] Eliot Deutsch [and] J. A. B. van Buitenen. Honolulu, University Press of Hawaii, 1971. ix, 335 p. 25 cm. Includes English translations of the major Sanskrit writings of the most important Vedantic philosophers. Bibliography: p. 313-318. [B132.V3D542] 75-148944 ISBN 0-87022-189-2 15.00
1. Vedanta—Collections. 2. Advaita—Collections. I. Buitenen, Johannes Adrianus Bernardus van, joint author. II. Title.

Vedanta—Comparative studies.

FAUSSET, Hugh I'Anson, 294.3'3'72
1895-
The flame and the light : meanings in Vedanta and Buddhism / Hugh I'Anson Fausset. Wheaton, Ill. : Theosophical Pub. House, 1976, c1958. 232 p. ; 21 cm. (A Quest book) Reprint of the 1969 ed. published by Greenwood Press, New York. Bibliography: p. 229-232. [B132.V3F35 1976] 76-2081 ISBN 0-8356-0478-0 pbk. : 3.75
1. Vedanta—Comparative studies. 2. Buddhism—Relations—Hinduism. 3. Hinduism—Relations—Buddhism. I. Title.

FAUSSET, Hugh I'Anson, 294.5'4
1895-
The flame and the light; meanings in Vedanta and Buddhism. New York, Greenwood Press [1969, c1958] 232 p. 23 cm. Includes bibliographical references. [B132.V3F35 1969] 69-10089
1. Vedanta—Comparative studies. 2. Buddha and Buddhism—Relations—Hinduism. 3. Hinduism—Relations—Buddhism. I. Title.

FAUSSET, Hugh I'Anson, 294.3'3'72
1895-
The flame and the light : meanings in Vedanta and Buddhism / by Hugh I'Anson Fausset. Wheaton, Ill. : Theosophical Pub. House, [1976] c1958. p. cm. (A Quest book) Reprint of the 1969 ed. published by Greenwood Press, New York. Includes bibliographical references. [B132.V3F35 1976] 76-2081 ISBN 0-8356-0478-0
1. Vedanta—Comparative studies. 2. Buddhism—Relations—Hinduism. 3. Hinduism—Relations—Buddhism. I. Title.

Vedanta—Dictionaries.

USHA, Brahmacharini 181.4803
A Ramakrishna-Vedanta wordbook. Hollywood, Calif., Vedanta Pr. [c.1962] 87p. 62-1007 1.00 pap.,
1. Vedanta—Dictionaries. I. Title.

WOOD, Ernest, 1883- 181.4803
Vedanta dictionary. New York, Philosophical [c.1964] 225p. 21cm. Bibl. 63-18059 6.00
1. Vedanta—Dictionaries. I. Title.

Vedantadesika, b. 1268. Satadusani.

SRINIVASA, Chari, S. M., 181.48
1918-
Advaita and Visistadvatta; a study based on Vedanta Desika's Satadusani. Foreword by S. Radhakrishnan. New York, Asia Pub. House [dist. Taplinger, c.1961 xvii, 204p. Bibl. 61-65906 5.00
1. Vedantadesika, b. 1268. Satadusani. 2. Advaita. I. Title.

Vedas.

BRAHMANAS. 294'.2
Aitareyabrahmana. English.
The Aitareya Brahmanam of the Rigveda, containing the earliest speculations of the Brahmans on the meaning of the sacrificial prayers, and on the origin, performance and sense of the rites of the Vedic religion. Edited, translated and explained, with pref., introductory essay, and a map of the sacrificial compound at the Soma sacrifice, by Martin Haug. Allahabad, Panini Office, 1922. [New York, AMS Press, 1974] lv, 368 p. illus. 23 cm. Original ed., a reprint of Haug's translation of 1863, minus the Sanskrit text, issued as extra v. 4 of The Sacred books of the Hindus. Includes Sayana's commentary, the Madhaviyavedarthaprakasa. [BL1119.5.A36E54 1974] 73-3830 ISBN 0-404-57848-9 27.50
I. Haug, Martin, 1827-1876, tr. II. Sayana, son of Mayana, d. 1387. Madhaviyavedarthaprakasa. English. 1974. III. Title. IV. Series: The Sacred books of the Hindus, extra

CHATTERJI, Jagadish 294.1
Chandra.
India's outlook on life; the wisdom of the Vedas, by Jagadish Chandra Chatterji ... with an introduction by John Dewey ... New York, Kailas press, 1931. 75 p. 24 cm. [BL1115.C45] 31-5133
1. Vedas. 2. Philosophy, Hindu. I. Title.

CHATTERJI, Jagadish 294'.1
Chandra.
The wisdom of the Vedas. With an introd. by John Dewey. Wheaton, Ill., Theosophical Pub. House [1973] p. (A Quest book) Published in 1931 under title: India's outlook on life. [BL1115.C45 1973b] 73-8888 ISBN 0-8356-0440-3(pbk.)
1. Vedas. 2. Philosophy, Hindu. I. Title.

CHATTERJI, Jagadish 294'.1
Chandra.
The wisdom of the Vedas / Jagadish Chandra Chatterji. Wheaton, Ill. : Theosophical Pub. House, 1980, c1973. 102 p. ; 21 cm. (Quest books) Published in 1931 under title: India's outlook on life. Includes bibliographical references. [BL1115.C45 1980] 19 80-51550 ISBN 0-8356-0538-8 pbk. : 3.95
1. Vedas. 2. Philosophy, Hindu. I. Title.

CHATTERJI, Jagadish 294'.1
Chandre.
The wisdom of the Vedas. With an introd. by John Dewey. Wheaton, Ill., Theosophical Pub. House [1973] 99 p. 23

cm. Published in 1931 under title: India's outlook on life. [BL1115.C45 1973] 73-8889 ISBN 0-8356-0214-1 3.95
1. Vedas. 2. Philosophy, Hindu.

JAGAISA-CHANDRA, Chattopadhyaya. 294.1
India's outlook on life; the wisdom of the Vedas, by Jagadish Chandra Chatterji ... with an introduction by John Dewey ... New York, Kailas press, 1931. 75 p. 24 cm. [BL1115.J3] 1-5133
1. Vedas. 2. Philosophy, Hindu. I. Title.

KEITH, Arthur Berriedale, 1879- 294.
The religion and philosophy of the Veda and Upanishads, by Arthur Berriedale Keith ... Cambridge, Mass., Harvard university press; London, H. Milford, Oxford university press, 1925. 2 v. 26 cm. (Added t.-p.: Harvard oriental series, v. 31, 32) Printed in Great Britain. 2,000 copies printed. [PK2971.H3 vol. 31, 32] 25-26743
1. Vedas. 2. Upanishads. 3. Philosophy, Hindu. 4. India—Religion. I. Title.

KEITH, Arthur Berriedale, 1879-1944. 294'.1
The religion and philosophy of the Veda and Upanishads. Westport, Conn., Greenwood Press [1971] 2 v. (xviii, 683 p.) 27 cm. Reprint of the 1925 ed. Includes bibliographical references. [BL1150.K43 1971] 71-109969 ISBN 0-8371-4475-2
1. Vedas. 2. Upanishads. 3. Philosophy, Hindu. 4. India—Religion. I. Title.

MULLER, Friedrich Max, 1823-1900. 291'.042
Physical religion / by F. Max Muller. New York : AMS Press, 1975. xii, 410 p. ; 19 cm. Reprint of the 1891 ed. published by Longmans, Green, London and New York, which was issued as Gifford lectures, 1890. Includes bibliographical references and index. [BL430.M83 1975] 73-18811 ISBN 0-404-11451-2 : 31.00
1. Vedas. 2. Religion, Primitive. 3. Natural theology. I. Title. II. Series: Gifford lectures ; 1890.

PIKE, Albert, 1809-1891. 294.1
Lectures of the Arya [by] Albert Pike, 1873. Louisville, Ky., The Standard printing co., incorporated [c1930] 3 p. l., 340 p. 26 cm. "This cloth edition ... is limited to seven hundred copies and they are numbered from 1 to 700, inclusive ... This copy is 392." "Prepared for the printer by Colonel M. W. Wood."--Foreword. "The Supreme council ordered that one edition of this manuscript be printed."--1st prelim. leaf. [BL1115.P55] 30-24323
1. Vedas. 2. Avesta. 3. Mythology, Hindu. 4. Zoroastrianism. 5. Aryans. I. Wood, Marshall William, 1846- ed. II. Freemasons. U.S. Scottish rite. Supreme council for the Southern jurisdiction. III. Title. IV. Title: Arya, Lectures of the.

Vedas—Concordances, indexes, etc.

BLOOMFIELD, Maurice, 1855-1928. 294.
A Vedic concordance, being an alphabetic index to every line of every stanza of the published Vedic literature and to the liturgical formulas thereof, that is, an index to the Vedic mantras; together with an account of their variations in the different Vedic books, by Maurice Bloomfield ... Cambridge, Mass., Harvard university, 1906. xxii p., 1 l., 1078 p. 32 cm. (Added t.p.: Harvard Oriental series ... v. 10) [PK2971.H3 vol. 10] 7-31974
1. Vedas—Concordances, indexes, etc. I. Title. II. Series.

Vedas—Criticism, interpretation, etc.

BLOOMFIELD, Maurice, 1855-1928. 294
The religion of the Veda; the ancient religion of India (from Rig-Veda to Upanishads). New York, AMS Press [1969] xv, 300 p. 23 cm. Reprint of the 1908 ed., published by J. P. Putnam's sons, London, in series: American lectures on the history of religions, 7th series, 1906-1907. Includes bibliographical references. [BL1115.B6 1969] 70-94310
1. Vedas—Criticism, interpretation, etc. 2. Brahmanism. I. Title. II. Series: American lectures on the history of religions, 7th series, 1906-1907.

PHILLIPS, Maurice, d.1910. 294.1
The teaching of the Vedas; what light does it throw on the origin and development of religion? By Maurice Phillips ... London and New York, Longmans, Green and co., 1895. viii, 240 p. 19 cm. [BL1115.P5] 1-12947
1. Vedas—Criticism, interpretation, etc. 2. Religion—Hist. I. Title.

Vedas—Criticism, interpretation, etc.—Addresses, essays, lectures.

CHATTOPADHYAYA, Kshetresh Chandra, 1896-1974. 294'.1
Studies in Vedic and Indo-Iranian religion and literature / by Kshetresh Chandra Chattopadhyaya ; edited by Vidya Niwas Misra. 1st ed. Varanasi : Bharatiya Vidya Prakasana, 1976- v. : ill. ; 22 cm. Includes bibliographical references. [BL1115.C455 1976] 76-905840 Rs45.00 (v. 1.)
1. Vedas—Criticism, interpretation, etc.—Addresses, essays, lectures. I. Misra, Vidyaniwas, 1926- II. Title.

Vedas, Rigveda—Criticism, interpretation, etc.

ARNOLD, Edward Vernon, 1857-1926. 294'.12
The Rigveda. New York, AMS Press [1972] 56 p. 19 cm. Reprint of the 1900 ed., which was issued as no. 9 of the Popular studies in mythology, romance and folklore. Bibliography: p. 39-42. [PK3017.A7 1972] 73-139172 ISBN 0-404-53509-7 5.50
1. Vedas. Rigveda—Criticism, interpretation, etc. I. Title. II. Series: Popular studies in mythology, romance and folklore, no. 9.

GRISWOLD, Hervey De Witt, 1860- 294.1
... The religion of the Rigveda, by H. D. Griswold ... London, New York [etc.] H. Milford, Oxford university press, 1923. xxiv, 392 p. 22 cm. (The religious quest of India) Bibliography: p. xxi-xxiv. [BL1115.G7] 25-1745
1. Vedas, Rigveda—Criticism, interpretation, etc. 2. Brahmanism. 3. Mythology, Hindu. I. Vedas, Rigveda. Selections, English. II. Title.

PIKE, Albert, 1809-1891. 294.1
Indo-Aryan deities and worship as contained in the Rig-Veda [by] Albert Pike, 1872. Louisville, The Standard printing co., 1930. ix, [3], 650 p. illus. (incl. chart) pl., diagrs. 26 cm. "This cloth edition ... is limited to eight hundred copies and they are numbered from 1 to 800, inclusive ... This copy is no. 392." Edited by M. W. Wood. "The Supreme council ordered that one edition of this manuscript be printed."--p. [1] [BL1115.P53] 30-243226
1. Vedas. Rigveda—Criticism, interpretation, etc. 2. Mythology, Hindu. I. Wood, Marshall William, 1846- ed. II. Freemasons. U.S. Scottish rite. Supreme council for the Southern jurisdiction. III. Title.

VEDAS, Rigveda. Selections.
Rig-veda repetitions; the repeated verses and distiches and stanzas of the Rig-veda in systematic presentation and with critical discussion, by Maurice Bloomfield ... Cambridge, Mass., Harvard university press, 1916. x v. 26 cm. (Added t.-p.: Harvard oriental series...v. 20, 24) Paged continuously. "Printed from type at the University press, Oxford, England, by Fredrick Hall, printer to the University." "First edition, 1916, one thousand copies." Contents.[v. 1] pt. 1. The repeated passages of the Rig-veda, systematically presented in the order of the Rig-veda, with critical comments and notes-- [v. 3] pt. 2. Explanatory and analytic. Comments and classifications from and lexical and grammatical and other points of view. pt. 3 Lists and indexes. 18-14390
I. Bloomfield, Maurice, 1855- ed. II. Title.

Vedas. Samaveda.

HOWARD, Wayne, 1942- 783.2'09'45
Samavedic chant / Wayne Howard. New Haven : Yale University Press, 1977. xxv, 572 p. : ill. ; 25 cm. Includes index. Bibliography: p. 559-564. [ML3197.H7] 76-49854 ISBN 0-300-01956-4 : 30.00
1. Vedas. Samaveda. 2. Chants (Hindu) 3. Music, Indic—History and criticism. I. Title.

Vedas. Yajurveda—Criticism, interpretation, etc.

DESAI, Gandabhai Girijashanker, 1896- 294'.14
Thinking with the Yajurveda [by] Gandabhai G. Desai. Bombay, New York, Asia Pub. House [1967] xxv, 184 p. 22 cm. Bibliography: p. [173]-178. [BL1115.D38] SA 68 20.00
1. Vedas. Yajurveda—Criticism, interpretation, etc. I. Title.

VEDAS, Yajurveda. Taittiriyasamhita.
The Veda of the Black Yajus schoool, entitled Taittiriya sanhita ... Tr. from the original Sanskrit prose and verse, by Arthur Berriedale Keith ... Cambridge, Mass., The Harvard university press, 1914. 2 v. 26 1/2 cm. (Added t.-p.: Harvard oriental series ... v. 18-19) Paged continuously. "Printed from type at the University press, Oxford, England, by Horace Hart, M.A., printer to the University." "First edition, 1914, one thousand copies." 17-5465
I. Keith, Arthur Berriedale, 1879- tr. II. Title.

Veddahs.

SELIGMAN, Charles Gabriel, 1873- 294
The Veddas, by C. G. Seligmann...and Brenda Z. Seligmann. With a chapter by C. S. Myers...and an appendix by A. Mendix Gunasekura... Cambridge, The University press, 1911. xix, [1], 463 p. front., illus., LXXI pl., fold. map (in pocket) 22 cm. (Half-title: Cambridge archaeological and ethnological series) "Music, by C. S. Myers": p. [341]-365. [Name originally: Charles Gabriel Seligmann] [DS489.2.S4] A 11
1. Veddahs. I. Seligman, Mrs. Brenda Z. (Salaman) joint author. II. Myers, Charles Samuel, 1873- III. Gunasekara, Abraham Mendis. IV. Title.

Vedic literature—Addresses, essays, lectures.

GOSVAMI, Satsvarupa Dasa, 1939- 294'.1
Readings in Vedic literature : the tradition speaks for itself / by Satsvarupa dasa Gosvami. New York : Bhaktivedanta Book Trust, [1977] p. cm. Includes indexes. Bibliography: p. [BL1107.G67] 76-24941 ISBN 0-912776-88-9 pbk. : 1.95
1. Vedic literature—Addresses, essays, lectures. 2. Hinduism—Addresses, essays, lectures. I. Title.

Vedic literature—History and criticism.

SANTUCCI, James A. 294'.1
An outline of Vedic literature / by James A. Santucci. Missoula, Mont. : Published by Scholars Press for the American Academy of Religion, c1976. ix, 69 p. ; 24 cm. (Aids for the study of religion series; no. 5) Bibliography: p. ix. [BL1110.S35] 76-27859 ISBN 0-89130-085-6 pbk. : 3.00
1. Vedic literature—History and criticism. 2. Vedic literature—Bibliography. I. Title. II. Series.

Vegas. Rigveda-Criticism, interpretation, etc.

AGUILAR, H. 294.5'3'4
The sacrifice in the Rgveda : doctrinal aspects / H. Aguilar ; with a pref. by R. Panikkar. Delhi : Bharatiya Vidya Prakashan, 1976. ix, 222 p. ; 23 cm. Includes bibliographical references and index. [BL1215.S2A34] 76-902122 Rs50.00
1. Vedas. Rgveda—Criticism, interpretation, etc. 2. Sacrifice (Hinduism)—History. I. Title.

DE NICOLAS, Antonio T. 181'.4
Four-dimensional man : meditations through the Rg Veda / Antonio T. de Nicolas. Stony Brook, N.Y. : N. Hays, 1977c1976 xvii, 284 p. ; 24 cm. "Selected chants from the Rg Veda": p. 193-233. Includes bibliographical references and index. [BL1115.D358] 76-39692 ISBN 0-89254-004-4 : 14.75
1. Vedas. Rgveda—Criticism, interpretation, etc. 2. Languages—Philosophy. 3. Philosophy, Comparative. I. Vedas. Rgveda. English. Selections. 1976. II. Title.

DENICOLAS, Antonio T. 181'.4
Meditations through the Rg Veda : four dimensional man / Antonio T. de Nicolas. Boulder, Colo. : Shambhala, 1978, c1976. 284p. ; 23 cm. Includes bibliographical references and index. [BL1115.D358] 77-90878 ISBN 0-87773-122-5 pbk. : 5.95
1. Vedas, Rgveda — Criticism, interpretation, etc. 2. Language — Philosophy. 3. Philosophy, Comparitive. I. Vedas. Rgveda. English. Selections. 1976. II. Title.
L.C. card no. for 1976 N. Hays ed.: 76-39692.

JOHNSON, Willard L. 294.5'9212
Poetry and speculation of the Rg Veda / Willard Johnson. Berkeley : University of California Press, c1980. p. cm. Includes index. Bibliography: p. [BL1115.A38J63] 80-14040 ISBN 0-520-02560-1 : 20.00
1. Vedas. Rgveda—Criticism, interpretation, etc. I. Title.

Vegetarian cookery.

YONEDA, Soei. 641.5'636
Good food from a Japanese temple / Soei Yoneda with Koei Hoshino, Kim Schuefftan. 1st ed. Tokyo ; New York : Kodansha International, 1982. p. cm. Includes index. [TX837.Y66 1982] 19 82-80734 ISBN 0-87011-527-8 (U.S.) : 16.95
1. Vegetarian cookery. 2. Cookery, Japanese. I. Hoshino, Koei. II. Schuefftan, Kim. III. Title.

Vegetarianism—Addresses, essays, lectures.

TREE of life : 296.7'4
an anthology of articles appearing in the Jewish vegetarian, 1966-1974 / edited by Philip L. Pick. South Brunswick, N.J. : A. S. Barnes, c1977. p. cm. Includes bibliographical references. [TX392.T73 1977] 76-18476 ISBN 0-498-01945-4 : 6.95
1. Vegetarianism—Addresses, essays, lectures. I. Pick, Philip L. II. Jewish vegetarian.

Vegetarianism—Moral and religious aspects—Judaism.

BERMAN, Louis Arthur. 296.7
Vegetarianism and the Jewish tradition / by Louis A. Berman. New York : Ktav Pub. House, 1981. p. cm. Includes index. Bibliography: p. [TX392.B44] 19 81-11729 ISBN 0-87068-756-5 : 5.95
1. Vegetarianism—Moral and religious aspects—Judaism. 2. Ethics, Jewish. I. Title.

Vegetarianism—Religious aspects—Buddhism.

KAPLEAU, Philip, 1912- 294.3'4446
To cherish all life : a Buddhist case for becoming vegetarian / Philip Kapleau. San Francisco : Harper & Row, c1982. p. cm. Bibliography: p. [BQ4570.V43K36 1982] 19 82-47746 ISBN 0-06-250440-1 pbk. : 5.72
1. Ahimsa. 2. Vegetarianism—Religious aspects—Buddhism. I. Title.

Velenus, Ulrichus.

LAMPING, A. J. 262'.13
Ulrichus Velenus (Oldrich Velensky) and his treatise against the papacy / by A. J. Lamping. Leiden : Brill, 1976. viii, 291 p. ;

24 cm. (Studies in medieval and Reformation thought : v. 19) Thesis—Leiden. "In hoc libello ... ": p. [219]-276. Includes indexes. Bibliography: p. [277]-284. [BX1805.V363L35] 76-462277 ISBN 9-00-404397-7 : fl 94.00
1. Velenus, Ulrichus. Petrum Romam non venisse. 2. Popes—Primacy—Controversial literature. I. Velenus, Ulrichus. Petrum Romam non venisse. 1976. II. Title. III. Series.

Venard, Jean Theophane, 1829-1861.

GREENE, Genard, 1921- 922.251
The hour of the dragon; a story of Blessed Theophane Venard. Illus. by Carolyn Lee Jagodits. Notre Dame, Ind., Dujarie Press [1956] 96p. illus. 24cm. [BX4705.V43G7] 56-25345
1. Venard, Jean Theophane, 1829-1861. I. Title.

VENARD, Jean Theophane, 922.
1829-1861.
A modern martyr, Theophane Venard (Blessed) revised and annotated by the Very Rev. James A. Walsh, M.A.R. [5th ed.] Maryknoll. Ossining P.O., N.Y., Catholic foreign mission society [c1913] 5 p. l., 241 p. front., plates, ports. 20 cm. [BX4705.V43A3] 14-6992
I. Walsh, James Anthony, 1867-1893, ed. II. Title.

VENARD, Jean Theophane, 1829- 922
1861.
A modern martyr. Theophane Venard (the Venerable.) Translated from the French by Lady Herbert. Revised and annotated by Rev. James Anthony Walsh ... Boston, Mass., Society for the propagation of the faith [c1905] 6 p. l. 235 p. front., plates, ports. 19 cm. [BX4705.V43A3 1905] 6-13082
I. Herbert, Mary Elizabeth (A'Court) Herbert, baroness, 1822-1911, tr. II. Walsh, James Anthony, 1867-1936, ed. III. Society for the propagation of the faith. IV. Title.

Venezuela—Church history.

WATTERS, Mary. 278.7
A history of the church in Venezuela, 1810-1930, by Mary Watters... Chapel Hill, The University of North Carolina press, 1933. ix, 260 p. 23 1/2 cm. Bibliography: p. 238-252. [BR730.W3] 34-660
1. Venezuela—Church history. 2. Catholic church in Venezuela. I. Title.

WATTERS, Mary, 1896- 282.87
A history of the church in Venezuela, 1810-1930. [1st AMS ed.] New York, AMS Press [1971] ix, 260 p. 23 cm. Reprint of the 1933 ed. Bibliography: p. 238-252. [BR730.W3 1971] 70-137303 ISBN 0-404-06877-4
1. Venezuela—Church history. 2. Catholic Church in Venezuela. I. Title.

Venezuela—Politics and government—1830-

LEVINE, Daniel H. 282'.861
Religion and politics in Latin America : the Catholic Church in Venezuela and Colombia / Daniel H. Levine. Princeton, N.J. : Princeton University Press, c1981. xii, 342 p. ; 25 cm. Includes index. Bibliography: p. 317-335. [BX1488.2.L48] 19 80-20110 ISBN 0-691-07624-3 : 22.50 ISBN 0-691-02200-3 (pbk.) : 6.95
1. Catholic Church in Venezuela. 2. Catholic Church in Colombia. 3. Venezuela—Politics and government—1830- 4. Colombia—Politics and government—1946- 5. Christianity and politics. 6. Venezuela—Church history. 7. Colombia—Church history. I. Title.

Venice. Chiesa del Redentore.

TIMOFIEWITSCH, 726'.5'094531
Wladimir.
The Chiesa del Redentore [by] Wladimir Timofiewitsch. University Park, Pennsylvania State University Press [1971] 78, [99] p. illus. (part col.), plans. 35 cm. (Corpus Palladianum, v. 3) Bibliography: p. [71]-72. [NA5621.V43T5313] 76-79838 ISBN 0-271-00090-2 17.50
1. Venice. Chiesa del Redentore. I. Title. II. Series.

Venice—Churches.

LEWIS, Douglas, 726'.5'094531
1938-
The late baroque churches of Venice / Douglas Lewis. New York : Garland Pub., 1979. p. cm. (Outstanding dissertations in the fine arts) Originally presented as the author's thesis, Yale, 1967. Bibliography: p. [NA5621.V4L48 1979] 77-94704 ISBN 0-8240-3236-5 : 42.50
1. Venice—Churches. 2. Architecture, Baroque—Italy—Venice. 3. Church architecture—Italy—Venice. I. Title. II. Series.

Venice. San marco (Basilica)

DEMUS, Otto.
The church of San Marco in Venice: history, architecture, sculpture. With a contribution by Ferdinando Forlati. Washington, Dumbarton Oaks Research Library and Collection, Trustees for Harvard University, 1960. xii, 236 p. plates. 30 cm. (Dumbarton Oaks studies, 6) Bibliography: p. 209-229. A63
1. Venice. San marco (Basilica) I. Forlati, Ferdinando. II. Title. III. Series.

TOESCA, Pietro, *738.5 729.7
1877-
Mosaics of St. Mark's. Text by Pietro Toesca and Ferdinando forlati. [Translated by Joyce Templeton and Gustina Scaglia] Greenwich, Conn., New York Graphic Society [1958] 50, [4] p. illus. (part mounted col.) 41 col. plates. 39 cm. [The Great masters of the past, 5] Bibliography: p. [51] [NA5621.V5T6] 58-5316
1. Venice. San Marco (Basilica) 2. Mosaics. I. Foriati, Ferdinando. II. Title. III. Series.

Vennard. Iva May (Durham) 1871-1945.

BOWIE, Mary Ella. 922
Alabaster and spikenard; the life of Iva Durham Vennard. Chicago, Chicago Evangelistic Institute [1947] 317 p. illus., ports. 20 cm. [BV3785.V39B6] 48-13387
1. Vennard. Iva May (Durham) 1871-1945. I. Title.

Venus (Goddess)

SUHR, Elmer George, 292'.2'11
1902-
The spinning Aphrodite; the evolution of the goddess from earliest pre-Hellenic symbolism through late classical times, by Elmer G. Suhr. [1st ed.] New York, Helios Books [1969] 218 p. illus., plates. 22 cm. Second vol. of the author's trilogy, The Column of the cosmos. Includes bibliographical references. [BL820.V5S9] 68-21940 6.95
1. Venus (Goddess) I. Title.

Verbeck, Guido Herman Fridohn, 1830-1898.

GRIFFIS, William Elliot, 922.
1843-1928.
Verbeck of Japan; a citizen of no country; a life story of foundation work inaugurated by Guido Fridolin Verbeck, by William Elliot Griffis ... New York, Chicago [etc.] Fleming H. Revell company [c1900] 376 p. front., plates, ports., facsim. 21 cm. [BV3457.V4G7] 0-6784
1. Verbeck, Guido Herman Fridohn, 1830-1898. 2. Missions—Japan. 3. Japan. I. Title.

Vereide, Abraham, 1886-

GRUBB, Norman Percy, 207'.11
1895-
Modern viking; the story of Abraham Vereide, pioneer in Christian leadership. Grand Rapids, Zondervan Pub. House [1961] 205p. illus. 23cm. [BX6.8.V4G7] 61-16751
1. Vereide, Abraham, 1886- I. Title.

Vergilius Maro, Publius. Aeneis.

BUXTON, Charles Roden, 1875-
1942.
Prophets of heaven & Hell: Virgil, Dante, Milton, Goethe; an introductory essay. New York, Haskell House, 1966. xv, 114 p. 23 cm. Completed after the author's death by Dorothy F. Buxton. 67-82509
1. 1. Vergilius Maro, Publius. Aeneis. 2. 2. Dante Alighieri. Divina commedia. 3. 3. Milton, John. Paradise lost. 4. 4. Goethe, Johann Wolfgang von. Faust. I. Buxton, Dorothy Frances (Jebb) ed. II. Title.

BUXTON, Charles Roden, 808.81
1875-1942.
Prophets of heaven & hell: Virgil, Dante, Milton, Goethe; an introductory essay, by Charles Roden Buxton. Cambridge [Eng.] The University press, 1945. xv, 115, [1] p. 19 cm. Completed after the author's death by Dorothy F. Buxton. cf. Introd. [PN1111.B8] A 45
1. Vergilius Maro, Publius. Aeneis. 2. Dante Alighieri. Divina commedia. 3. Milton, John. Paradise lost. 4. Goethe, Johann Wolfgang von. Faust. I. Buxton, Dorothy Frances (Jebb) ed. II. Title.

Vermigli, Pietro Martire, 1499-1562.

DONNELLY, John 233'.092'4
Patrick.
Calvinism and Scholasticism in Vermigli's doctrine of man and grace / John Patrick Donnelly. Leiden : Brill, 1976. x, 235 p. ; 25 cm. (Studies in medieval and Reformation thought ; v. 18) Includes indexes. "Appendix: Peter Martyr's Library": p. 211-217. [BT701.2.D64] 76-363864 fl 68.00
1. Vermigli, Pietro Martire, 1499-1562. 2. Man (Theology)—History of doctrines. I. Title. II. Series.

MCLELLAND, Joseph C 265
The visible words of God; an exposition of the sacramental theology of Peter Martyr Vermigli, A. D. 1500-1562. Grand Rapids, Eerdmans [1957] ix, 291p. 23cm. Bibliography: p. 261-266. [BX9419.V4M35] 58-9551
1. Vermigli, Pietro Martire, 1500-1562. 2. Sacraments—History of doctrines. I. Title.

MCNAIR, Philip 270.6'09224(B)
Murray Jourdan
Peter Martyr in Italy; an anatomy of apostacy, by Philip McNair. Oxford, Clarendon Pr., 1967. xxii, 325p. front. (port.) table. 23cm. Bibl. [BR350.V37M3] 67-78940 8.80
1. Vermigli, Pietro Martire, 1499-1562. I. Title.
Available from Oxford Univ. Pr. in New York.

Vermont (town, Dane County) Wis.-Vermont Lutheran Church.

VERMONT, Wis. Lutheran Church.
Vermont Lutheran Church, 1856-1956. [Kansas City, Inter-collegiate press, 1956] 1 v. (unpaged) illus., ports., map. 29 cm. Cover title.
1. Vermont (town, Dane County) Wis.-Vermont Lutheran Church. I. Title.

Veronica of the Crucifix, mother, 1820-1903.

THE hope of the 922.271
harvest; the life of Mother Veronica of the Crucifix, second superior general of the Sisters of the holy names of Jesus and Mary, 1820-1903, by a Sister of the holy names. [Portland, Or., Kilham stationery and printing company, c1944] xv, 431 p. port. 21 1/2 cm. [BX4705.V513H6] 46-14203
1. Veronica of the Crucifix, mother, 1820-1903. I. A Sister of the holy names.

Verot, Augustine, Bp., 1804-1876.

GANNON, Michael V 922.273
Rebel bishop; the life and era of Augustin Verot, by Michael V. Gannon. With a foreword by John Tracy Ellis. Milwaukee, Bruce Pub. Co. [1964] xvii, 267 p. illus., map. ports. 22 cm. Bibliographical footnotes. [BX4705.V4G3] 64-23895
1. Verot, Augustine, Bp., 1804-1876. 2. St. Augustine (Diocese) — Hist. I. Title.

Verren, Antoine.

[BARTHELEMY, Peter] 922.373
Rev. Anthony Verren, pastor of the French Episcopal church of the Saint-Esprit, at New-York, Judged by his works ... New York, Sold by the booksellers, 1840 1 p. l., 86 p. 20 cm. [BX5995.V45B3] 34-4015
1. Verren, Antoine. I. Title.

Versailles, Ky. Presbyterian Church.

SANDERS, Robert 285.1769465
Stuart.
Presbyterianism in Versailles and Woodford County, Kentucky. Louisville, Ky., Dunne Press, 1963. 220 p. illus. 24 cm. [BX9211.V4P7] 63-2045
1. Versailles, Ky. Presbyterian Church. 2. Presbyterians in Woodford Co., Ky. I. Title.

Vespers.

BACH, Marcus. 792.1
Vesper dramas, by Marcus Bach; with worship program by William H. Leach ... Chicago, New York, Willett, Clark & company, 1938. 197 p. 21 cm. [PN6120.R4B2] 39-32014
I. Leach, William Herman, 1888- II. Title.

CRANFORD, Clarence William, 248
1906-
Seekers of light; vesper messages delivered to the young people of the Pennsylvania Baptist summer assemblies by Clarence W. Cranford, and put into writing at the unanimous request of the young people of the assemblies Collegeville, Keystone, and Kiski. Philadelphia, Boston [etc.] The Judson press [c1930] 5 p. l., 3-113 p. 21 cm. [BV4310.C75] 31-2773
I. Title.

DURYEA, Joseph Tuthill, 783.
1832-1898.
Vesper services. For the use of congregations. colleges, schools, and academies, for Sunday evening worship. Edited by Rev. Joseph T. Duryea, D. D. Boston and Chicago, Congregational Sunday-school and publishing society [c1887] 2 p. l., [3]-57 p. 21 x 16 cm. [With his A morning service ... Boston and Chicago, c1888] With music. [M2123.D95] 24-27844
I. Congregational Sunday-school and publishing society. II. Title.

HAZARD, Caroline.
The college year; vesper addresses in Wellesley college chapel, by the president, Caroline Hazard. Boston and New York, Houghton Mifflin company, 1910. viii, 213, [1] p. 20 cm. 10-11930
I. Title.

STRYKER, Melancthon Woolsey,
1851-
Vesper bells, [by] Melancthon Woolsey Stryker. Rome, N.Y., Print. for the author, 1919. 4 p. l., 87, [1] p. 22 cm. "This book was printed at the Courier press, Clinton, New York ... One hundred and thirty-five copies, numbered made the edition. The paper is Fabriano handmade." This copy is no. 10. [PS2959.S63V4 1919] 19-16409
I. Title.

WEAKLAND, Rembert.
Vesper psalms according to the monastic Antiphonal. Edited by Rembert Weakland, O.S.B., [and] Alexander Deveraux, O.S.B. Latrobe, Pa., St. Vincent Archabbey, 1958. 59 p. music. 21 cm. "This booklet was edited explicitly for the Lay Brothers of the Archabbey and for the Scholastics."
1. Vespers. I. Deveraux, Alexander William, 1934- joint ed. II. Catholic Church. Liturgy and Ritual. Vesperal. III. Title.

Vester, Bertha Hedges Spafford, 1878-

†VESTER, Bertha 266'.023'095694
Hedges Spafford, 1878-
Our Jerusalem / Bertha Spafford Vester. New York : Arno Press, 1977, c1950. x,

332 p. ; 23 cm. (America and the Holy Land) Reprint of the ed. published by Doubleday, Garden City, N.J. [DS109.V3 1977] 77-70752 ISBN 0-405-10296-8 : 22.00
1. Vester, Bertha Hedges Spafford, 1878- 2. Jerusalem—Description. 3. Americans in Jerusalem—Biography. 4. Missionaries—United States—Biography. 5. Missionaries—Jerusalem—Biography. I. Title. II. Series.

Vetter, Robert J.

VETTER, Robert J. 248'.86
Beyond the exit door / Robert J. Vetter. Elgin, Ill. : D. C. Cook Pub. Co., [1974] 109 p. ; 18 cm. [BV4905.2.V47] 74-75539 ISBN 0-912692-36-7 pbk. : 1.25
1. Vetter, Robert J. 2. Consolation. I. Title.

Vianney, Jean Baptiste Marie, Saint, 1786-1859.

BETZ, Eva (Kelly) 1897- 922.244
The man who fought the Devil; the Cure of Ars. Illus. by Kathleen Voute. Paterson, N. J., St. Anthony Guild Press [1958] 144p. illus. 20cm. [BX4700.V5B4] 59-20729
1. Vianney, Jean Baptiste Marie, Saint, 1786-1859. I. Title.

CATHOLIC Church. Pope, 1958- (Joannes XXIII) Sacerdotii nostri primordia (1 Aug. 1959) English. 253.2
From the beginning of our priesthood. 'Sacerdotii nostri primordia.' As provided by N. C. W. C. [Boston] St.Paul Editions [dist. Daughters of St. Paul] [1959] 32p. 19cm. 60-197 .25 pap.,
1. Vianney, Jean Baptiste Marie, Saint, 1786-1859. 2. Clergy—Religious life. I. Title.

COYNE, Anne. 922.244
A shepherd and a king [by] Anne Coyne. Milwaukee, The Bruce publishing company [c1939] 124 p. incl. front., plates, ports. 21 cm. [BX4700.V5C6] 39-20798
1. Vianney, Jean Baptiste Marie, Saint, 1786-1859. I. Title.

GHEON, Henri, 1875- 922.244
Secrets of the saints, by Henri Gheon. New York, Sheed & Ward, 1944. 4 p. l., 406 p. 19 1/2 cm. [BX4655.G5] 44-7980
1. Vianney, Jean Baptiste Marie, Saint, 1786-1859. 2. Therese, Saint, 1873-1897. 3. Alacoque, Marguerite Marie, Saint, 1647-1690. 4. Bosco, Giovanni, Saint, 1815-1888. I. Sheed, Francis Joseph, 1897- tr. II. Attwater, Donald, 1892- tr. III. Title. IV. Title: The secret of the Cure d'Ars. V. Title: The secret of the Little Flower. VI. Title: The secret of Saint Margaret Mary. VII. Title: The secret of Saint John Bosco.
Contents omitted.

GHEON, Henri [Real name: Henri Leon Vangeon] 922.244
Secrets of the saints, by Henri Gheon. New York, Garden City, Doubleday [1963,c.1944] 395p. 18cm. 1.25 pap.,
*1. Vianney, Jean Baptiste Marie, Saint, 1786-1859. 2. Therese, Saint, 1873-1897. 3. Alacoque, Marguerite Marie, Saint, 1647-1690. 4. *Bosco, Giov)nni, Saint, 1815-1888. I. Sheed, Francis Joseph, 1897- tr. II. Attwater, Donald, 1892- tr. III. Title. IV. Title: The secret of the Cure d' Ars. V. Title: The secret of the Little Flower. VI. Title: The secret of Saint Margaret Mary. VII. Title: The secret of Saint John Bosco.*
Contents omitted.

KIRLIN, Joseph Louis J 1868-1926. 922.
Priesty virtue and zeal: a study of the life of St. John Baptist Vianney, the cure d' Ars and patron of priests, applied to the sacredotal life today, by the late Very Rev. Msgr. J. L. J. Kirlin ... with preface by Right Rev. Feancis C. Kelley ... New York, Cincinnati etc. Benziger brothers. 1928. 179 p. front. 19 cm. [BX4700.V5K5] 28-9084
1. Vianney, Jean Baptiste Marie, Saint, 1786-1859. I. Title.

LA VARENDE, Jean de, 1887- 922.244
The Cure of Ars and his cross. Translated by Jane Wynne Saul. Photos. by J. A. Fortier. Designs by R. Galoyer. New York, Desclee Co. [1959] 221p. illus. 21cm. [BX4700.V5L353] 59-12544
1. Vianney, Jean Baptiste Marie, Saint, 1786-1859. I. Title.

LOMASK, Milton. 922.244
The Cure of Ars; the priest who outtalked the devil. Illustrated by Johannes Troyer. New York, Vision Books [1958] 190p. illus. 22cm. (Vision books, 36) [BX4700.V5L6] 58-6983
1. Vianney, Jean Baptiste Marie, Saint, 1786-1859. I. Title.

O'BRIEN, Bartholomew J 922.244
Secrets of a parish priest. [Chicago, J. S. Paluch Co., c1956] 121p. 18cm. (Lumen books, 540) Includes bibliography. [BX4700.V5O2] 57-31083
1. Vianney, Jean Bartiste Marie, Saint, 1786-1859. I. Title.

OXENHAM, John, pseud. 922.244
A saint in the making; from the Valley of the singing blackbird to St. Peter's Rome (The story of the Cure d'Ars) By John Oxenham ... London, New York [etc.] Longmans, Green and co., 1931. xi, 208, [1] p. front. (port.) 19 cm. [Real name: William Arthur Dunkerley] [BX4700.V5O8] 31-31512
1. Vianney, Jean Baptiste Marie, saint, 1786-1859. I. Title.

PAULUS, Brother, 1911- 922.244
Saint of the countryside; a story of Saint John Vianney. Illus. by Bernard Howard. Notre Dame, Ind., Dujarie Press [1951] 88 p. illus. 24 cm. [BX4700.V5P3] 52-16004
1. Vianney, Jean Baptiste Marie, Saint, 1786-1859. I. Title.

PEZERIL, Daniel 922.244
Blessed and poor; the spiritual odyssey of the Cure of Ars. Tr. [from French] by Pansy Pakenham. [New York] Pantheon [1961,c.1959] 255p. Bibl. 61-7453 4.00
1. Vianney, Jean Baptiste Marie, Saint, 1786-1859. I. Title.

SAINT-PIERRE, Michel de, 1916- 922.244
The remarkable Cure of Ars: the life and achievements of St. John Mary Vianney. Tr. [from French] by A. Angeline Bouchard. Garden City, N.Y., Doubleday, 1963[c.1958,1963] 230p. 22cm. 63-8738 3.95
1. Vianney, Jean Baptiste Marie, Saint, 1786-1859. I. Title.

SAINT-PIERRE, Michel de, 1916- 922.244
The remarkable Cure of Ars: the life and achievements of St. John Mary Vianney. Translated by M. Angeline Bouchard. [1st ed.] Garden City, N. Y., Doubleday, 1963. 230 p. 22 cm. Translation of La vie prodigieuse du Cure d'Ars. [BX4700.V5S243] 63-8738
1. Vianney, Jean Baptiste Marie, Saint, 1786-1859. I. Title.

[SCHAEFER, Joseph] 1848- 922.
The life of the blessed John B. Marie Vianney, cure of Ars. With a novena and litany to this zealous worker in the vineyard of the Lord. Compiled from approved sources. New York, J. Schaefer [1911] 1 p. l., iii, [1], [5]-110 p. front. (port.) 15 cm. [BX4700.V5S3] 11-1549
1. Vianney, Jean Baptiste Marie, Saint, 1786-1859. I. Title.

TROCHU, Francis, 1877- 922.244
The cure d'Ars; a shorter biography. [Translation by Ronald Matthews] Westminster, Md., Newman Press [1955] 193p. illus. 20cm. Translation of L'admirable vie du cure d'Ars. [BX4700.V5T485] 55-8663
1. Vianney, Jean Baptiste Marie, Saint, 1786-1859. I. Title.

TROCHU, Francis, 1877- 922.244
The insight of the Cure d'Ars; selected stories. Westminster, Md., Newman Press [1957] 106p. 19cm. 'Those stories from Instutions du Cure d'Ars, series I, II et III ... were chosen and translated by V. F. Martiet.' [BX4700.V5T522] 57-14001
1. Vianney, Jean Baptiste Marie, Saint, 1786-1859. I. Title.

TROUNCER, Margaret (Lahey) 1906- 922.244
Saint Jean-Marie Vianney, cure of Ars. New York, Sheed and Ward [1959] 260 p. 22 cm. Includes bibliography. [BX4700.V5T75] 58-14452
1. Vianney, Jean Batiste Marie, Saint, 1786-1859. I. Title.

WINDEATT, Mary Fabyan, 1910- 922.244
The parish priest of Ars; the story of Saint John Marie Vianney. Illus. by Gedge Harmon. [St. Meinrad, Ind., 1947] 163 p. illus. 23 cm. "A Grall publication." --Dust jacket. [BX4700.V5W5] 47-31019
1. Vianney. Jean Baptiste Marie, Saint, 1786-1859. I. Title.

Vianney, Jean Baptiste Marie, Saint, 1786-1859—Juvenile literature.

DAUGHTERS of St. Paul. 92 (j)
The country road home; the story of St. John Vianney, the Cure of Ars, written and illustrated by the Daughters of St. Paul. [Boston] St. Paul Editions [1966] 78 p. illus. 22 cm. (Their Encounter books) [BX4700.V5D38] 66-29166
1. Vianney, Jean Baptiste Marie, Saint, 1786-1859—Juvenile literature. I. Title.

Vibhanga.

[BUDDHAGHOSA] 294.
... *Sammoha-vinodani Abhidhamma-pitake Vibhangatthakatha* edited by A. P. Buddhadatta thero ... London, New York [etc.] Pub. for the Pali text society by the Oxford university press, 1923. vii, 550, [2] p. 23 cm. (Pali text society. [Publications. 93]) Pali text translitered. "Commentary on the Vibhanga, the second book of the Abidhamma pitaka."--p. iii. [PK4541.P4 vol. 93] 27-5848
1. Vibhanga. I. Buddhadatta, A. P., 1887- ed. II. Title.

Vice.

BURKHOLDER, John David. 244
Vangel's side trip on the devil's worst roads, by Dr. John David Burkholder. Harrisonburg, Va., Pub. for Life's morning book company, by the Millersville press, Millersville, Pa. [c1931] 2 p. l., 158 p. illus. 19 cm. [BV4515.B84] 34-12557
1. Vice. I. Title.

Vicente, Gil, ca. 1470-ca. 1536. Auto de la sibila Casandra.

KING, Georgiana Goddard.
The play of the sibyl Cassandra, by Georgiana Goddard King ... Bryn Mawr, Pa., Bryn Mawr college; New York [etc.] Longmans, Green and co., 1921. 2 p. l., 55, [1] p. front. 16 1/2 cm. (Half-title: Bryn Mawr notes and monographs. II) [PQ9251.S53K5] 22-1302
1. Vicente, Gil, ca. 1470-ca. 1536. Auto de la sibila Casandra. 2. Christmas plays. I. Title. II. Title: Cassandra.

Vico, Galeazzo Caracciolo, marchese di, 1517-1586.

BALBANI, Niccolo, d.1587. 284'.2'0924 B
Newes from Italy / Niccolo Balbani. Amsterdam : Theatrum Orbis Terrarum ; Norwood, N.J. : W. J. Johnson, 1979. 82 p. ; 22 cm. (The English experience, its record in early printed books published in facsimile ; no. 905) Translation of Historia della vita di Galeazzo Caracciolo. Photoreprint of the 1608 ed. printed by H. B. for R. Moore, London. STC 1233. [BX9439.V52B3413 1979] 19 79-84085 ISBN 90-221-0905-4 : 10.00
1. Vico, Galeazzo Caracciolo, marchese di, 1517-1586. 2. Converts, Reformed Church—Biography. I. Title. II. Series: English experience, its record in early printed books published in facsimile ; no. 905.

Vico, Giovanni Battista, 1668-1743.

LION, Aline. 201
The idealistic conception of religion; Vico, Hegel, Gentile, by Aline Lion ... with a preface by Clement C. J. Webb. Oxford, The Clarendon press, 1932. xvi, 208 p. 23 cm. [BL51.L55] 32-22685
1. Vico, Giovanni Battista, 1668-1743. 2. Hegel, Georg Wilhelm Friedrich, 1770-1831. 3. Gentile, Giovanni, 1875- 4. Religion—Philosophy. I. Title.

Victoria, Australia—Church history.

HETHERINGTON, John Aikman, 1907- 279.94'5
Pillars of the faith; churchmen and their churches in early Victoria [by] John Hetherington. Melbourne, Canberra [etc.] Cheshire [1966] xii, 110 p. illus., ports. 25 cm. Bibliography: p. 107-108. [BR1483.V5H4] 66-25774
1. Victoria, Australia—Church history. I. Title.

Victoria, Australia—Religion.

KANE, Kathleen Dunlop. 271'.977'094
Adventure in faith : the Presentation sisters / [by] Kathleen Dunlop Kane. [Melbourne] : Congregation of the Presentation of the Blessed Virgin Mary, 1974. xi, 303, xxix p. : ill., diagrs., facsims., ports. ; 25 cm. Includes index. [BX4511.Z5 A84] 75-327894 ISBN 0-909246-05-X
1. Presentation Sisters in Victoria. 2. Victoria, Australia—Religion. I. Title.

Victoria, queen of Great Britain, 1819-1901—Coronation.

LEGG, John Wickham, 1843-1921. 394.
... *The coronation of the Queen,* by J. Wickham Legg ... 2d ed. Pub. under the direction of the Tract committee. London [etc.] Society for promoting Christian knowledge; New York, E. & J. B. Young & co., 1898. 54 p., 1 l. 17 cm. (The Church historical society. [Publications] xlii) [DA112.L4 1898] 20-17429
1. Victoria, queen of Great Britain, 1819-1901—Coronation. 2. Church of England. Liturgy and ritual. Coronation service. I. Title.

Vienna Presbyterian Church, Vienna, Va.

VIENNA Presbyterian Church, Vienna, Va. Centennial Committee. 285'.1755'291
Centennial 1974 / [The Centennial Committee, Vienna Presbyterian Church ; Dave LeRoy, editor ; Hal Bowman, picture editor]. Vienna, Va. : Vienna Presbyterian Church, 1974. v, 81 p. : ill. ; 23 cm. [BX9211.V5V538 1974] 75-317114
1. Vienna Presbyterian Church, Vienna, Va. I. LeRoy, Dave, 1920-

Vietnam—Prayers.

*DRAKOS, Theodore Soter. 242.4
How to pray for Vietnam. New York, 1968. 48p. 11cm. 1.00 pap.,
1. Vietnam—Prayers. I. Title.
Order from the author, 102-01 Ascan Avenue, Forest Hills New York, 11375.

Vietnam—Religion.

U.S. Bureau of Naval Personnel. 200'.9597
The religions of South Vietnam in faith and fact. [Washington] 1967. vii, 97 p. illus., maps. 26 cm. Cover title. "NAVPERS 15991." Includes bibliographies. [BL2055.U5] 67-62247
1. Vietnam—Religion. I. Title.

Vietnamese Conflict, 1961-1975—Draft resisters.

SURREY, David S. (David Sterling) 959.704'38
Choice of conscience : Vietnam era military and draft resisters in Canada / David S. Surrey. New York : Praeger, 1982. xi, 207 p. ; 24 cm. "A.J.F. Bergin Publishers book." Includes index. Bibliography: p. 189-197. [DS559.8.D7S97 1982] 19 81-18170 ISBN 0-03-059663-7 : 24.95

1. Vietnamese Conflict, 1961-1975—Draft resisters. 2. Americans—Canada. I. Title.

Vijaya-Dhama Suri, 1868-

ARDSHER Jamshedji Suravala.
...Vijaya Dharma Suri, his life and work, by A.J. Sunavala... With a prefatory note by F.W. Thomas. Cambridge, The University press, 1922. 85 p. col. front. (port.) 20 cm. At head of title: Jain literature society. [BL1335.V5A8] 22-19147
1. Vijaya-Dhama Suri, 1868- 2. Jains. I. Jain literature society. II. Title.

Vijnanabhiksu, fl. 1550.

SINHA, Jadunath, 1894- 181'.482
The philosophy of Vijanaabikshu / by Jadunath Sinha. 1st ed. Calcutta : Sinha Pub. House, c1976. 73, iv, vi p. ; 23 cm. Includes bibliographical references and index. [B133.V37S56] 76-905156 Rs12.00
1. Vijnanabhiksu, fl. 1550. 2. Vedanta. 3. Sankhya. I. Title.

Vinal, William, 1718?-1781.

FISH, Joseph, 1706-1781. 252.
Love to Christ a necessary qualification in a gospel minister. A sermon preached at the ordination of the Reverend Mr. William Vinal, to the pastoral charge of the First Congregational church of Christ in Newport on Rhode Island, October 29, 1746. With some enlargement and correction, by Joseph Fish...With the charge by the Rev. Mr. S. Checkley, and the right hand of fellowship by the Rev. Mr. J. Cotton... Newport, R. I., Printed by the Widow Franklin, at the town-school house, 1747. 55 p. 19 1/2 cm. [BX7233.F52L6] 22-2675
1. Vinal, William, 1718?-1781. 2. Ordination sermons. I. Title.

Vinayapitaka.

BUDDHAGHOSA. 294.
... *Samantapasadika.* Buddhaghosa's commentary on the Vinaya pitaka, edited by J. Takakusu ... and M. Nagai ... London, New York [etc.] Pub. for the Pali text society by the Oxford university press, 1924- v. 23 cm. (Pali text society. [Publications. v. 96]) Pali text transliterated. [PK4541.P4 vol. 96] 27-5850
1. Vinayapitaka. I. Takakusu, Junjiro, ed. II. Nagai, Makoto, joint ed. III. Title.

SUTTAPITAKA.
Some sayings of the Buddha according to the Pali canon, translated by F. L. Woodward ... London, New York [etc.] H. Milford, Oxford university press, 1925. xi. 356 p. 15 1/2 cm. A collection of passages from the Suttapitaka, with a few selections from the Vinayapitaka. [BC1410.S8] 27-18640
I. Vinayapitaka. II. Woodward, Frank Lee, tr. III. Title.

SUTTAPITAKA, Selections. 294.3
English.
Some sayings of the Buddha, according to the Pali canon; translated by F. L. Woodward, with an introduction by Sir Francis Younghusband. London, Oxford university press, H. Milford [1939] 2 p. l., vii-xxvii, 356 p. 15 1/2 cm. (Half-title: The World's classics. [483]) A collection of passages from the Suttapitaka with a few selections from the Vinayapitaka. "First published in 1925." [BL1411.S83E58 1939] 40-27469
I. Vinayapitaka. Selections. English. II. Woodward, Frank Lee, tr. III. Younghusband, Sir Francis Edward, 1863-1942. IV. Title.

VINAYAPITAKA. 294.3
Vinaya texts, translated from the Pali by T. W. Rhys Davids and Herman Oldenberg ... Oxford, The Clarendon press, 1881-85. 3 v. 23 cm. (Added t.-p.: The sacred books of the East ... Vol. XIII, XVII, XX) Contents.pt. I. The Patimokkha. The Mahavagga, I-IV.--pt. II. The Mahavagga, V-X. The Kullavagga, I-III.--pt. III. The Kullavagga, IV-XII. [BL1010.S3 vol. 13, 17, 20] (290.8) 32-34309
I. Davids, Thomas William Rhys, 1843-1922, tr. II. Oldenberg, Hermann, 1854-1920, joint tr. III. Title.

Vinayapitaka—Criticism, interpretation, etc.

MISRA, Girija Shankar 294.3'822
Prasad, 1944-
The age of vinaya, by G. S. P. Misra. With a foreword by Govinda Chandra Pande. New Delhi, Munshiram Manoharlal [1972] xvi, 298 p. 22 cm. A revision of the author's thesis, University of Rajasthan. Bibliography: p. [279]-294. [BQ1157.M57 1972] 72-906003
1. Vinayapitaka—Criticism, interpretation, etc. 2. Buddha and Buddhism—Discipline. 3. India—Social life and customs—Sources. I. Title.
Distributed by Verry; 11.50.

Vinayapitaka—Dictionaries.

UPASAK, Chandrika 294.3'822'03
Singh.
Dictionary of early Buddhist monastic terms based on Pali literature / C. S. Upasak. 1st ed. Varanasi : Bharati Prakashan, 1975. iii, 245 p. ; 26 cm. [BQ2319.U6] 75-902701 18.00
1. Vinayapitaka—Dictionaries. I. Title.
Distributed by South Asia Books.

Vincent de Paul, 1581-1660.

PURCELL, Mary 922.244
The world of Monsieur Vincent. New York, Scribners [c.1963] 243p. illus. 22cm. Bibl. 63-10449 4.50
1. Vincent de Paul, 1581-1660. I. Title.

Vincent de Paul, Saint, 1576?-1660.

ARMAUD D'AGNEL, G., 1871-
Saint Vincent de Paul, a guide for priests, translated from the French of abbe Arnaud d'Agnel, by Rev. Joseph Leonard, C.M. New York, P. J. Kenedy & sons, 1932. 2 p. l., 287 p. 19 cm. A 33
1. Vincent de Paul, Saint, 1576?-1660. 2. Catholic church—Clergy. 3. Priests. I. Leonard, Joseph, 1877- tr. II. Title.

BOUGAUD, Emile, 1824-1888 922.
History of St. Vincent de Paul, founder of the Congregation of the mission (Vincentians) and of the Sisters of charity, by Monseigneur Bougaud...translated from the 2d French ed. by Joseph Brady, C. M. With an introduction by His Eminence the cardinal archbishop of Westminster... London, New York and Bombay, Longmans, Green, and co., 1899. 2 v. fronts. (ports.) 23 cm. (Full name: Louis Victor Emile Bougaud) [BX4700.V6B6] 4-16953
1. Vincent de Paul, Saint, 1576?-1600. I. Brady, Joseph, tr. II. Title.

BOYLE, John, 1922- 922.244
Fire on the earth, a story of Saint Vincent de Paul. Illus. by Brother Bernard Howard. Notre Dame, Ind., Dujarie Press [1953] 88p. illus. 24cm. [BX4700.V6B65] 53-25515
1. Vincent de Paul, Saint, 1576?-1600. I. Title.

BROGLIE, Emmanuel, prince 922.
de, 1854-1926.
Saint Vincent de Paul, by Emmanuel de Broglie, translated by Mildred Partridge, with a preface by George Tyrrell, S.J. London, Duckworth & co.; New York, Benziger bros.; [etc., etc.] 1901. xiv, 257 p. 19cm. [The saints' series,3] Pages 251-257 wanting. [Full name: Cesar Paul Emmanuel, Prince de Broglie] [BX4700.V6B7] 4-18422
1. Vincent de Paul, Saint, 1576-1660. I. Partridge, Mildred, tr. II. Tyrrell, George, 1851-1909, ed. III. Title.

CALVET, Jean, 1874- 922.22
Saint Vincent de Paul. Translated by Lancelot C. Sheppard. New York, D. McKay [1951] 302p. 22cm. 'Bibliographical note': p. 296-298. [BX4700.V6C] A53
1. Vincent de Paul, Saint, 1576?-1660. I. Title.

CHAIGNE, Louis, 1899- 922.244
Saint Vincent de Paul. Tr. by Rosemary Sheed. New York, Macmillan, 1962 [c.1960,1962] 120p. 18cm. (Your name--your saint ser.) Bibl. 62-12422 2.50
1. Vincent de Paul, Saint, 1576?-1660. I. Title.

COSTE, Pierre. 922.244
The life & works of Saint Vincent de Paul (Monsieur Vincent: le grand saint du grand siecle) Translated from the French by Joseph Leonard. Westminster, Md., Newman Press, 1952. 3 v. illus., ports., maps. 21 cm. Bibliography: v. 3, p. 499-522. [BX4700.V6C652] 52-9978
1. Vincent de Paul, Saint, 1576?-1660. I. Title.

DANIEL-ROPS, Henry, 1901- 922.244
[RealnameHenryJulesCharlesPetiot]
Monsieur Vincent; the story of St. Vincent de Paul. Tr. from French by Julie Kernan. New York, Hawthorn Books [c.1961] 141p. illus. (part col.) 61-6711 3.95
1. Vincent de Paul, Saint, 1576?-1660. I. Title.

DELARUE, Jacques, 1914- 922.244
The holiness of Vincent de Paul. [English translation from the French by Suzanne Chapman] New York, P. J. Kenedy [c.1960] 132p. illus. 60-14108 3.50
1. Vincent de Paul, Saint, 1576?-1660. I. Title.

EMANUEL, Cyprian William, 922.
1890-
The charities of St. Vincent de Paul; an evaluation of his ideas, principles and methods, by Cyprian W. Emanuel ... Chicago, Ill., Franciscan herald press, 1923. x p., 1 l., 337 p. 23 1/2cm. Published also as thesis (ph.d.) Catholic university of America. Bibliography: p. 331-332. [BX4700.V6E6] 23-16096
1. Vincent de Paul, Saint, 1576-1660. 2. Charities—Hist. I. Title.

LAVEDAN, Henri Leon Emile, 922.
1859-1940.
The heroic life of Saint Vincent de Paul; a biography, by Henri Lavedan ... translated by Helen Younger Chase. London, New York [etc.] Longmans, Green and co., 1929. 4 p. l., 279 p. front., plates, ports. 22 cm. [BX4700.V6L33] 29-11614
1. Vincent de Paul, Saint, 1576?-1660. I. Chase, Helen Younger, tr. Translation of Monsieur Vincent, aumonier de galeres. II. Title.

MATT, Leonard von 922.244
St. Vincent de Paul [by] Leonard von Matt and Louis Cognet. Translated from the French by Emma Craufurd. Chicago, H. Regnery Co., 1960[ ] 232p. (chiefly illus.) 25cm. 60-16335 7.00 bds.,
1. Vincent de Paul, Saint, 1576?-1660. I. Cognet, Louis, joint author. II. Title.

MAYNARD, Michel Ulysse, 922.244
1814-1893.
Virtues and spiritual doctrine of Saint Vincent de Paul. Rev. by Carlton A. Prindeville. St. Louis, Vincentian Foreign Mission Press [1961] 359p. 23vm. First published in French in 1864. [BX4700.V6M36 1961] 61-3733
1. Vincent de Paul, Saint, 1576?-1660. I. Title.

MAYNARD, Theodore, 1890- 922.244
Apostle of charity; the life of St. Vincent de Paul, by Theodore Maynard. New York, The Dial press, 1939. vii, 319 p. 21 cm. [BX4700.V6M43] 39-27742
1. Vincent de Paul, Saint, 1576?-1660. 2. Daughters of charity of St. Vincent de Paul. 3. Congregation of priests of the mission. I. Title.

PURCELL, Mary 922.244
The world of Monsieur Vincent. New York, Scribners [c.1963] 243p. illus. 22cm. Bibl. 63-10449 4.50
1. Vincent de Paul, 1581-1660. I. Title.

ST. John's University, 922.244
Brooklyn
Saint Vincent de Paul, a tercentenary commemoration of his death. 1660-1960. Jamaica, N. Y., St. John's University Press [Grand Central and Utopia Parkways, c.1960] 108p. (bibl. footnotes) illus. 26cm. 'The Saint Vincent de Paul annual lectures, sponsored since 1948 by Saint John's University, Jamaica, New York.' 60-2148 3.95;1.95 pap.,
1. Vincent de Paul, Saint, 1576?-1660. I. Title.

ST. John's University, 922.244
New York.
Saint Vincent de Paul, a tercentenary commemoration of his death. 1660-1960. Jamaica, N. Y., St. John's University Press [1960] 108p. illus. 26cm. 'The Saint Vincent de Paul annual lectures, sponsored since 1948 by Saint John's University, Jamaica, New York.' Includes bibliography. [BX4700.V6S26] 60-2148
1. Vincent de Paul, Saint, 1576?-1660. I. Title.

ST. Vincent de Paul.
Jamaica, N. Y., St. John's University Press, 1961. x, 157p. 23cm. (Thought patterns, v. 9)
1. Vincent de Paul, Saint, 1576?-1660. I. Kovacs, Arpad Francis, 1898- ed.

WOODGATE, Mildred Violet, 922.244
1904-
Saint Vincent de Paul. Westminster, Md., Newman Press [1960, c1958] 136 p. 20 cm. [BX4700.V6W6] 60-3592
1. Vincent de Paul, Saint, 1576?-1660. I. Title.

Vincent de Paul, Saint, 1581-1660—Juvenile literature.

HUBBARD, Margaret Ann, 922.244
1909-
Vinent de Paul, Saint of charity. Illustrated by Harry Barton. New York, Farrar, Straus & Cudahy [1960] 190p. illus. 22cm. (Vision books, 48) Includes bibliography. [BX4700.V6H8] 60-10366
1. Vincent de Paul, Saint, 1576 -1660 — Juvenile literature. I. Title.

LOMUPO, Robert. 922.244
Fire in his name, a life of St. Vincent de Paul. Illustrated by Cajetan Holland. Valatie, N.Y., Holy Cross Press, 1964. 128 p. illus. 23 cm. (Saints who changed history series) [BX4700.V6L6] 64-2855
1. Vincent de Paul, Saint, 1581-1660 — Juvenile literature. I. Title.

LOMUPO, Robert 922.244
Fire is his name; a life of St. Vincent de Paul. Illus. by Cajetan Holland. Valatie, N. Y., Holy Cross Pr. [c.]1964. 128p. illus. 23cm. (Saints who changed hist. ser.) 64-2855 2.50
1. Vincent de Paul, Saint, 1581-1660—Juvenile literature. I. Title.

Vincent, John Heyl, bp., 1832-1920

VINCENT, Leon Henry, 1859- 922.
John Heyl Vincent; a biographical sketch, by Leon H. Vincent. New York, The Macmillan company, 1925. 5 p. l., 319 p. 3 port. (incl. front.) 23 1/2 cm. [BX8495.V5V5] 25-16278
1. Vincent, John Heyl, bp., 1832-1920 I. Title.

Vincentians in Ireland.

PURCELL, Mary, 1906- 271'.77'041
The story of the Vincentians; a record of the achievements in Ireland and Britain of the priests and lay-brothers of the Congregation of the Mission, founded by St. Vincent de Paul. Dublin, All Hallows College [1973] 214 p. 22 cm. Includes bibliographical references. [BX3770.Z5I77] 75-303854 £1.50
1. Vincentians in Ireland. 2. Vincentians in Great Britain. 3. Vincentians—Missions. I. Title.

Vincentius Ferrerius, Saint, 1350 (ca.)-1419.

ALLIES, Mary Helen 282'.0922 B
Agnes, 1852-1927.
Three Catholic reformers of the fifteenth century. Freeport, N.Y., Books for Libraries Press [1972] xii, 235 p. 23 cm. (Essay index reprint series) Reprint of the 1878 ed. Includes bibliographical references. [BX1302.A63 1972] 73-38755 ISBN 0-8369-2633-1 9.75
1. Vincentius Ferrerius, Saint, 1350 (ca.)-

1419. 2. Bernardino da Siena, Saint, 1380-1444. 3. Giovanni da Capistrano, Saint, 1385 or 6-1456. 4. Church history—15th century. I. Title.

GHEON, Henri, 1875- 922.246
St. Vincent Ferrer, by Henri Gheon; translated by F. J. Sheed. New York, Sheed & Ward, 1939. xv, 190 p. 20 cm. "Printed in Great Britain." [BX4700.V7G5] 40-3804
1. Vincentius Ferrerius, Saint, 1350 (ca.)-1419. I. Sheed, Francis Joseph, 1897- tr. II. Title.

HOGAN, Stanislaus M., 1873-
Saint Vincent Ferrer, O.P., by Fr. Stanislaus M. Hogan... New York, London [etc.] Longmans, Green and co., 1911. ix, [1] p., 1 l., 117 p. front. (port.) plates. 17 cm. (Half-title: The friar saints series) Bibliography: p. 116-117. A 12
1. Vincentius Ferrerius, Saint, 1350 (ca.)-1419. I. Title.

[MARY CATHERINE, Sister, 922.246 of the English Dominioan Congregation of Saint Catherine of Siena]
Angel of the judgement; a life of Vincent Ferrer, by S. M. C. Notre Dame, Ind., Ave Maria Press [1954] 234p. 24cm. [BX4700.V7M3] 54-5298
1. Vincentius Ferrerius, Saint, 1350 (ca.)-1419. I. Title.

ROBERTO, Brother, 1927- 922.246
The King's trumpeter; a story of Saint Vincent Ferrer. Illus. by Brother Eagan. Notre Dame, Ind., Dujarie Press [1957] 94p. illus. 24cm. [BX4700.V7R6] 58-257
1. Vincentius Ferrerius, Saint, 1850 (ca.)-1419. I. Title.

Vinet, Alexandre Rodolphe, 1797-1847.

FUHRMANN, Paul Traugott, 201 1903-
Extraordinary Christianity; the life and thought of Alexander Vinet. Pref. by John T. McNeil. Philadelphia. Westminster [c.1964] 125p. 21cm. Bibl. 64-10520 3.00
1. Vinet, Alexandre Rodolphe, 1797-1847. I. Title.

Vins, Georgii Petrovich, 1928—

VINS, Georgii Petrovich, 914.3'1 1928-
Testament from prison / Georgi Vins ; translated by Jane Ellis ; edited by Michael Bourdeaux. Elgin, Ill. : D. C. Cook Pub. Co., c1975. 283 p. ; 18 cm. [BX6495.V5A3713] 75-18986 ISBN 0-912692-84-7 : 2.50
1. Vins, Georgii Petrovich, 1928- 2. Baptists in Russia—Biography. 3. Persecution—Russia. I. Title.

Violence—Colombia—History.

OQUIST, Paul H. 303.6'09861
Violence, conflict, and politics in Columbia / Paul Oquist. New York : Academic Press, 1980. xiv, 263 p. ; 24 cm. (Studies in social discontinuity) Originally presented as the author's thesis, University of California, Berkeley, 1976. Includes index. Bibliography: p. 239-251. [HN310.V5O68 1980] 19 80-23141 ISBN 0-12-527750-4 : 25.00
1. Violence—Colombia—History. 2. Social conflict—History. 3. Colombia—Politics and government. I. Title. II. Series.

Violence in the Bible—Congresses.

VIOLENCE and 221.8'301'632
defense in the Jewish experience : papers prepared for a seminar on violence and defense in Jewish history and contemporary life, Tel Aviv University, August 18-September 4, 1974 / contributors, Yohanan Aharoni ... [et al.] ; Salo W. Baron, George S. Wise, editors, Lenn E. Goodman, associate editor. 1st ed. Philadelphia : Jewish Publication Society of America, 1977. xii, 362 p. ; 22 cm. Includes bibliographical references and index. [BS1199.V56V56] 76-52664 ISBN 0-8276-0092-5 : 12.00
1. Violence in the Bible—Congresses. 2. Violence in rabbinical literature—Congresses. 3. Antisemitism—History—Congresses. I. Aharoni, Yohanan, 1919-1976. II. Baron, Salo Wittmayer, 1895- III. Wise, George Schneiweis, 1906- IV. Goodman, Lenn Evan, 1944-

Violence—Moral and religious aspects.

BROWN, Robert McAfee, 261.8'73 1920-
Religion and violence; a primer for white Americans. Stanford, Calif., Stanford Alumni Association, 1973. xv, 112 p. illus. 23 cm. (The Portable Stanford) Bibliography: p. 104-112. [BT736.15.B76 1973b] 73-85363
1. Violence—Moral and religious aspects. I. Title.

BROWN, Robert McAfee, 261.8'73 1920-
Religion and violence; a primer for white Americans. Philadelphia, Westminster Press [1973] xv, 112 p. illus. 23 cm. Bibliography: p. 104-112. [BT736.15.B76] 73-14710 ISBN 0-664-24977-9 3.95
1. Violence—Moral and religious aspects. I. Title.

DURLAND, William R., 1931- 261.8
No king but Caesar? : A Catholic lawyer looks at Christian violence / William R. Durland ; introd. by Richard T. McSorley. Scottdale, Pa. : Herald Press, 1975. 182 p. : port. ; 23 cm. (The Christian peace shelf ; no. 7) Includes index. Bibliography: p. 175-177. [BT736.15.D87] 74-30093 ISBN 0-8361-1757-3 : 5.95
1. Violence—Moral and religious aspects. I. Title.

EDWARDS, George R. 241'.6'98
Jesus and the politics of violence [by] George R. Edwards. [1st ed.] New York, Harper & Row [1972] vi, 186 p. 22 cm. Bibliography: p. 157-169. [BT736.15.E3] 70-183635 ISBN 0-06-062124-9 5.95
1. Jesus Christ—Person and offices. 2. Violence—Moral and religious aspects. I. Title.

ELLUL, Jacques. 261.8'3
Violence; reflections from a Christian perspective. Translated by Cecelia Gaul Kings. New York, Seabury Press [1969] 179 p. 22 cm. Bibliographical footnotes. [BT736.15.E413] 69-13540 4.95
1. Violence—Moral and religious aspects. I. Title.

HENGEL, Martin. 261.8
Victory over violence, Jesus and the revolutionists. Translated by David E. Green. With an introd. by Robin Scroggs. Philadelphia, Fortress Press [1973] xxvi, 67 p. 19 cm. Translation of Gewalt und Gewaltlosigkeit. Includes bibliographical references. [BT736.15.H4513] 73-79035 ISBN 0-8006-0167-X 2.50
1. Violence—Moral and religious aspects. I. Title.

HOLLIS, Harry. 261.8'3
The shoot-'em-up society / Harry Hollis, Jr. Nashville : Broadman Press, [1974] 126 p. ; 18 cm. Includes bibliographical references. [BT736.15.H64] 74-78964 ISBN 0-8054-6113-2 pbk. : 1.50
1. Violence—Moral and religious aspects. I. Title.

JACKSON, Dave. 261.8'33
Dial 911 : peaceful Christians and urban violence / Dave Jackson. Scottdale, Pa. : Herald Press, 1981. p. cm. [BV4407.8.J3] 19 81-2541 ISBN 0-8361-1952-5 (pbk.) : 5.95 ($6.90 Can)
1. Reba Place Fellowship (Evanston, Ill.) 2. Violence—Moral and religious aspects. 3. Crime and criminals—Illinois—Evanston. I. Title. II. Title: Peaceful Christians and urban violence.

MERTON, Thomas, 1915- 261.8
Faith and violence; Christian teaching and Christian practice. [Notre Dame, Ind.] University of Notre Dame Press, 1968. x, 291 p. 21 cm. Bibliographical footnotes. [BT736.15.M4] 68-20438 1.95
1. Violence—Moral and religious aspects. I. Title.

MORRIS, Colin M. 261.8'3
Unyoung, uncolored, unpoor [by] Colin Morris. Nashville, Abingdon Press [1969] 158 p. 20 cm. Includes bibliographical references. [BT736.15.M6] 73-10321
1. Violence—Moral and religious aspects. I. Title.

SCHUTZ, Roger. 261.8'3
Violent for peace. Translated by C. J. Moore. Philadelphia, Westminster Press [1971, c1970] 144 p. 19 cm. Translation of Violence des pacifiques. Includes bibliographical references. [BT736.15.S3513 1971] 76-151348 ISBN 0-664-24922-1 2.65
1. Violence—Moral and religious aspects. I. Title.

SIDER, Ronald J. 261.8
Christ and violence / Ronald J. Sider ; introd. by John K. Stoner. Scottdale, Pa. : Herald Press, 1979. 108 p. : port. ; 20 cm. Includes bibliographical references. [BS2417.V56S55] 79-9239 ISBN 0-8361-1895-2 pbk. : 4.95
1. Jesus Christ—Teachings. 2. Violence—Moral and religious aspects. I. Title.

TOURNIER, Paul. 241
The violence within / Paul Tournier. New York : Harper & Row, [1978] p. cm. Bibliography: p. [BT736.15.T68] 78-3139 ISBN 0-06-068293-0 : 7.95
1. Violence—Moral and religious aspects. 2. Psychiatry and religion. I. Title.

Vipasyana (Buddhism)

DHIRAVAMSA. 294.3'4'43
The way of non-attachment : the practive of insight meditation / by Dhiravamsa. New York : Schocken Books, 1977, c1975. 160 p. ; 21 cm. [BQ5630.V5D48 1977] 76-48761 ISBN 0-8052-3644-9 : 6.95
1. Vipasyana (Buddhism) 2. Meditation (Buddhism) I. Title.

LEVINE, Stephen. 294.3'4'43
A gradual awakening / Stephen Levine. 1st ed. Garden City, N.Y. : Anchor Press, 1979. xv, 173 p. ; 21 cm. Includes index. Bibliography: p. [161]-163. [BQ5630.V5L48] 77-27712 ISBN 0-385-14164-5 pbk. : 3.95
1. Vipasyana (Buddhism) 2. Meditation (Buddhism) I. Title.

Virgil.

BLOCK, Elizabeth. 873'.01
The effects of divine manifestation on the reader's perspective in Vergil's Aeneid / Elizabeth Block. New York : Arno Press, 1981, c1977. 356 p. ; 23 cm. (Monographs in classical studies) Revision of thesis (Ph.D.)—University of California, 1977. Bibliography: p. 344-356. [PA6825.B55 1981] 19 80-2640 ISBN 0-405-14028-2 lib. bdg. : 39.00
1. Virgil. Aeneis. 2. Virgil—Criticism and interpretation. I. Title. II. Series.

VERGILIUS Maro, Publius.
Virgil's prophecy on the Saviour's birth, the fourth Eclogue, ed. and tr. by Paul Carus. Chicago [etc.] The Open court publishing co., 1918. 2 p. l., 97 p. 15 1/2 cm. English and Latin on opposite pages. [PA6807.B7C3] 19-13242
I. Carus, Paul, 1852-1919, ed. and tr. II. Title.

Virgil—Influence.

FICHTER, Andrew, 1945- 809.1'3
Poets historical : dynastic epic in the Renaissance / Andrew Fichter. New Haven : Yale University Press, c1982. x, 237 p. ; 22 cm. Includes bibliographical references and index. [PN1303.F5 1982] 19 81-19795 ISBN 0-300-02721-4 : 17.95
1. Virgil—Influence. 2. Epic poetry—History and criticism. 3. European poetry—Renaissance, 1450-1600—History and criticism. 4. Literature, Comparative—Classical and modern. 5. Literature, Comparative—Modern and classical. I. Title.

Virgin birth.

BIRCH, w. Grayson. 232.913
Mary and the virgin birth error, by W. Grayson Birch. Berne, Ind., Publishers Print. House [1966] 284 p. illus. 23 cm. Bibliographical footnotes. [BT317.B53] 65-28187
1. Virgin birth. I. Title.

BOSLOOPER, Thomas David, 232.921 1923-
The virgin birth. Philadelphia, Westminster Press [1962] 272 p. 24 cm. [BT317.2.B6] 62-7941
1. Virgin birth.

CONWAY, Bertrand Louis, 232. 1872-
The virgin birth, by Rev. Bertrand L. Conway, C.S.P. New York, The Paulist press [c1924] 62 p. 18 cm. Bibliography: p. 60-62. [BT317.C6] 26-1279
I. Title.

COOKE, Richard Joseph, bp., 232. 1853-1931.
Did Paul know of the virgin birth? An historical study, by the Rev. Bishop Richard J. Cooke ... New York, The Macmillan company, 1926. 152 p. 20 cm. [BT317.C65] 26-10614
1. Paul, Saint, apostle. 2. Virgin birth. I. Title.

CRAIN, Orville E. 232.
The credibility of the virgin birth, by Orville E. Crain. New York, Cincinnati, The Abingdon press [c1925] 105 p. 18 cm. Bibliography: p. 104-105. [BT317.C7] 25-18989
I. Title. II. Title: Virgin birth.

DURAND, Alfred, 1857?-1928. 232.
The childhood of Jesus Christ according to the canonical gospels, with an historical essay on the brethren of the Lord, by A. Durand, S.J.; an authorized translation from the French, edited by Rev. Joseph Bruneau ... Philadelphia, J. J. McVey, 1910. xxv, 316 p. 20 cm. [BT320.D85] 10-10343
1. Jesus Christ—Childhood. 2. Jesus Christ—Geneal. 3. Jesus Christ—Brethren. 4. Virgin birth. I. Bruneau, Joseph, 1866-1933, ed. II. Title.

GROMACKI, Robert Glenn. 232.9'21
The virgin birth: doctrine of deity. Nashville, T. Nelson [1974] 202 p. 21 cm. Bibliography: p. 199-202. [BT317.G75] 74-12250 3.50 (pbk.).
1. Virgin birth. I. Title.

GRUTZMACHER, Richard 232.921 Heinrich, 1876-
The virgin birth, by Richard H. Grutzmacher ... New York, Eaton & Mains: Cincinnati, Jennings & Graham [c1907] 80 p. 18 cm. (On cover: Foreign religious series) "The translation of the series has been made by the Rev. Bernhard Pick."--General introd. [BT317.G8] 8-264
1. Virgin birth. I. Pick, Bernhard, 1842-1917, tr. II. Title.

HALL, Arthur Crawshay Alliston, bp, 1847-1930.
The Virgin mother, retreat addresses on the life of the Blessed Virgin Mary as told in the Gospels, with an appended essay on the virgin birth of Our Lord Jesus Christ; by the Rt. Rev. A. C. A. Hall... New York and London, Longmans, Green & co., 1894. viii, 233 p. 18 cm. [BT695.H2] 15-3362
1. Mary, Virgin. 2. Virgin birth. I. Title.

HANKE, Howard A 232.921
The validity of the virgin birth. Grand Rapids, Mich., Zondervan Pub. House [1963] 121 p. 21 cm. Bibliography: p. 117-118. [BT317.H34] 63-20390
1. Virgin birth. I. Title.

KNOWLING, Richard John, 232. 1851-1919.
Our Lord's virgin birth and the criticism of to-day. By R j. Knowling .... Third issue. Published under the direction of the Tract committee. London [etc.] Society for promoting of Christian knowledge; New York, E. S. Gorham, 1907. 100 p. 19 cm. "The following papers appeared in the Churhman in the earlier part of 1903"--p. [3] [BT317.K6 1907] 39-407
1. Virgin birth. I. Society for promoting Christian knowledge, London. Tract committee. II. Title.

LAWLOR, George L. 232.9'13
Almah—virgin or young woman? By George L. Lawlor. Des Plaines, Ill.,

Regular Baptist Press [1973] 124 p. 18 cm. Bibliography: p. 119-124. [BT317.L38] 73-76072 1.50
1. Virgin birth. 2. 'Almah (The Hebrew word) I. Title.

LOBSTEIN, Paul, 1850- 1922. 232.921
The virgin birth of Christ; an historical and critical essay by Paul Lobstein ... Translated into English by Victor Leuliette ... Edited, with an introduction, by the Rev. W. D. Morrison ... London, and Oxford, Williams & Norgate; New York, G. P. Putnam's sons, 1903 138 p. 19 cm. (On cover: Crown theological library) [BT317.L7] 5-15331
1. Virgin birth. I. Leuliette, Victor, tr. II. Morrison, William Douglas, 1853- ed. III. Title.

LOBSTEIN, Paul, 1850-1922. 232.
The virgin birth of Christ, an historical and critical essay, by Paul Lobstein ... translated into English by Victor Leuliette ... Edited, with an introduction, by the Rev. W. D. Morrison ... New York, G. P. Putnam's sons; London, Williams and Norgate, 1903. 138 p. 19 cm. (On cover: Crown theological library) Bibliographical references included in "Notes" (p. 113-138) [BT317.L7 1903a] 44-14051
1. Virgin birth. I. Leuliette, Victor, tr. II. Morrison, William Douglas, 1853-1943, ed. III. Title.

MACHEN, John Gresham, 1881- 1937. 232.
The virgin birth of Christ, by J. Gresham Machen ... New York and London, Harper & brothers, 1930. vii p., 2 l., 415 p. 24 1/2 cm. "Containing in substance ... the Thomas Smyth lectures which the author had the honor of delivering at Columbia theological seminary in the spring of 1927." [BT317.M23] 30-8276
1. Virgin birth. I. Title.

MACHEN, John Gresham, D.D., 1881-1937 232.921
The virgin birth of Christ. Grand Rapids, Mich., Baker Bk., 1965[c.1930] x,415p. 22cm. [BT317] 66-839 2.95 pap.,
1. Virgin birth. I. Title.

*MIGUENS, Manuel. 232.92'1
The Virgin birth; an evaluation of scriptual evidence. Westminster, M.D., Christian Classics, 1975. iv, 169 p. 22 cm. Includes bibliographical references and scripture index. [BT317] 7.95 (pbk.)
1. Virgin Birth. 2. Mary, Virgin. 3. Immaculate Conception. I. Title.

ORR, James, 1844-1913. 232.921
The virgin birth of Christ; being lectures delivered under the auspices of the Bible teachers training school, New York, April, 1907, by James Orr ... with appendix giving opinions of living scholars ... New York, C. Scribner's sons, 1907. xiv p., 1 l., 301 p. 20 cm. [BT317.O6] 7-31231
1. Virgin birth. I. Title.

PALMER, Frederic, 1848-1932. 232.
The virgin birth, by Frederic Palmer... New York, The Macmillan company, 1924. 4 p. l., 56 p. 18 cm. [BT317.P3] 24-3291
1. Virgin birth. I. Title.

RAMSAY, Franklin Pierce, 1856- 232.
The virgin birth; a study of the argument, for and against, by F. Pierce Ramsay, PH. D. New York, Chicago [etc.] Fleming H. Revell company [c1926] 111 p. 20 cm. [BT317.R3] 26-10132
I. Title.

SCOTT, Martin Jerome, 1865- 282
The virgin birth, by Martin J. Scott, S. J. New York, P. J. Kenedy & sons, 1925. 3 p. l., 295 p. 21 cm. [BT317.S3] 25-24293
1. Virgin birth. I. Title.

STRATON, John Roach, 1875- 1929. 230
The virgin birth--fact or fiction! Third in the series of fundamentalist-modernist debates between Rev. John Roach Straton ... and Rev. Charles Francis Potter ... New York, George H. Doran company [c1924] vi p., 2 l., 11-96 p. 19 cm. [BT78.S85 3d ser.] 24-13585
1. Virgin birth. 2. Modernist-fundamentalist controversy. I. Potter, Charles Francis, joint author. II. Title. III. Title: Fundamentalist-modernist debates.

TAYLOR, Vincent. 232.
The historical evidence for the virgin birth, by Vincent Taylor ... Oxford, The Clarendon press, 1920. x p., 1 l., 136 p. 23 cm. Bibliographical foot-notes. [BT317.T3] 21-10277
I. Title.

TAYLOR, Vincent. 232.
The historical evidence for the virgin birth, by Vincent Taylor ... Oxford, The Clarendon press, 1920. x p., 1 l., 136 p. 23 cm. Bibliographical foot-notes. [BT317.T3] 21-10277
I. Title.

WORCESTER, Elwood, 1863- 232.921
Studies in the birth of the Lord, by Elwood Worcester. New York, London, C. Scribner's sons, 1932. xvi p., 1 l., 300 p. 20 1/2 cm. [BT317.W6] 32-33929
1. Virgin birth. I. Title.

Virgin birth—History of doctrines.

CAMPENHAUSEN, Hans, Freiherr von, 1903- 232.921
The virgin birth in the theology of the ancient church. [Translated by Frank Clarke] Naperville, Ill., A. R. Allenson [1964] 92 p. 22 cm. (Studies in historical theology, 2) Bibliographical footnotes. [BT317.C3] 64-55217
1. Virgin birth—History of doctrines. I. Title. II. Series.

Virgin Islands of the United States—History

LARSEN, Jens Peter Mouritz 284.172972
Virgin Islands story, by Jens Larsen. Philadelphia, Fortress [c.1950] vii, 256p. illus. 18cm. Bibl. [F2136.L3 1950b] 68-10292 2.50 pap.,
1. Virgin Islands of the United States—Hist. 2. Lutheran Church in the Virgin Islands. I. Title.

Virginia—Biography.

STEVENSON, Arthur Linwood, 1891- 287'.1'0922 B
Natives of the Northern Neck of Virginia in the Methodist ministry, by Arthur L. Stevenson. Brevard, N.C., 1973. 44 p. 22 cm. (His Native Methodist minister series, 5th) [BX8491.S72] 73-181605
1. Methodist Church—Biography. 2. Virginia—Biography. I. Title.

Virginia—Church history.

MCILWAINE, Henry Read, 1864-1934. 330.9'73 s
The struggle of Protestant dissenters for religious toleration in Virginia. Baltimore, Johns Hopkins Press, 1894. [New York, Johnson Reprint Corp., 1973] 67 p. 22 cm. Pages also numbered 175-235. Original ed. issued as no. 4 of Institutional and economic history, which forms the 12th series of Johns Hopkins University studies in historical and polictical science. Includes bibliographical references. [HC101.I54 no. 4] [BR555.V8] 277.55 72-14289 ISBN 0-384-34893-9 pap. 4.00
1. Virginia—Church history. 2. Religious tolerance. I. Title. II. Series: Johns Hopkins University. Studies in historical and political science, 12th ser., 4. III. Series: Institutional and economic history, no. 4.

MASON, George Carrington.
Colonial churches of Tidewater Virginia, by George Carrington Mason ... Richmond, Va., Whittet and Shepperson, 1945. xv, 381 p. 89 pl. (incl. maps, plans) on 46 l. 23 1/2 cm. "Based on a study ... the results of which were first published in the William and Mary quarterly historical magazine (second series), during the years 1839-1943."--Introd. Bibliographical foot-notes. A 46
1. Virginia—Church history. 2. Church architecture—Virginia. 3. Architecture, Colonial. I. Title.

MEADE, William, bp., 1789- 1862. 286.
Old churches, ministers and families of Virginia. By Bishop Meade. Philadelphia, J. B. Lippincott & co., 1857. 2 v. plates. 23 cm. An index by J. M. Toner was issued in 1898 as supplement to v. 2 of the Publications of the Southern history association. [F225.M48] [F230.M49] 923. Rc-2835
1. Virginia—Church history. 2. Virginia—Geneal. 3. Protestant Episcopal church in the U.S.—Virginia. 4. Virginia—Hist.—Colonial period. I. Title.

MEADE, William, bp., 1789- 1862. 286.
Old churches, ministers and families of Virginia. By Bishop Meade... Philadelphia, J. B. Lippincott & co., 1878. 2 v. plates, 2 ports. (incl. front.) 22 cm. Indexes to this work were published by J. M. Toner, Washington, 1898, and by J. C. Wise, Richmond, 1910. [F225.M485] 15-25677
1. Virginia—Church history. 2. Virginia—Geneal. 3. Protestant Episcopal church in the U.S.A.—Virginia. 4. Virginia—Hist.—Colonial period. I. Title.

MEADE, William, bp., 1789- 1862. 286.
Old churches, ministers and families of Virginia. By Bishop Meade ... Philadelphia, J. B. Lippincott company, 1897. 2 v. plates, 2 port. (incl. front.) 22 1/2 cm. Indexes to the work were published by J. M. Toner, Washington, 1898, and by J. C. Wise, Richmond, 1910. [F225.M49] Rc-2836
1. Virginia—Church history. 2. Virginia—Geneal. 3. Protestant Episcopal church in the U.S.A.—Virginia. 4. Virginia—Hist.—Colonial period. I. Title.

MEADE, William, bp., 1789- 1862. 286.
Old churches, minsters and families of Virginia. By Bishop Meade. Philadelphia, J. B. Lippincott & co., 1861. 2 v. plates, 2 port. (incl. front.) 24 cm. [F225.M483] 6-12268
1. Virginia—Church history. 2. Virginia—Geneal. 3. Protestant Episcopal church in the U.S.A.—Virginia. 4. Virginia—Hist.—Colonial period. I. Title.

PROTESTANT Episcopal church in the U. S. A. Virginia (Diocese) 283.755
Addresses and historical papers before the centennial council of the Protestant Episcopal church in the diocese of Virginia, at its meeting in St. Paul's and St. John's church, in Richmond, May 20-24, 1885. New York, T. Whittaker, 1885. iv p, 1 l., 195 p. 25 cm. [BX5917.V8A5 1885] 31-929
1. Virginia—Church history. I. Title.

WISE, Jennings Cropper, 1881- comp. 286.
Wise's digested index and genealogical guide to Bishop Meade's old churches, ministers and families of Virginia, embracing 6,900 proper names. Comp. by Jennings Cropper Wise ... Richmond, Va., Printed for subscribers, 1910. 114 p. 24 1/2 cm. [F225.M494] 10-10807
I. Title.

Virginia—Church history—Addresses, essays, lectures.

UP from independence : 283'.755
the Episcopal Church in Virginia : articles / by George J. Cleaveland ... [et al.]. [s.l.] : Interdiocesan Bicentennial Committee of the Virginias, 1976. iii, 125 p. : ill. ; 23 cm. Includes bibliographical references. [BX5917.V8U6] 76-380758
1. Protestant Episcopal Church in the U.S.A.—Virginia—Addresses, essays, lectures. 2. Virginia—Church history—Addresses, essays, lectures. I. Cleaveland, George Julius.

Virginia—Historic houses, etc.

LANCASTER, Robert Alexander, 1862- 277.
Historic Virginia homes and churches, by Robert A. Lancaster jr., with 316 illustrations. Philadelphia and London, J. B. Lippincott company, 1915. xviii, 527 p. incl. plates. front. 27 cm. Title vignette. "This limited edition has been printed from type and the type distributed." [F227.L24] 15-23797
1. Virginia—Historic houses, etc. 2. Churches—Virginia. 3. Virginia—Descr. & trav. 4. Virginia—Hist. I. Title.

Virginia—Religion.

RELIGIOUS life of Virginia in the seventeenth century, the faith of our fathers. Williamsburg, Virginia 350th Anniversary Celebration Corporation, 1957. 51p. illus. 21cm. (Jamestown 350th anniversary historical booklet, no. 10) 'A list of parishes in Virginia, and the clergy in them . . July 8, 1702': p. 48-51. Bibliography: p. 46.
1. Virginia—Religion. 2. Virginia—Church history. 3. Church of England in Virginia. I. Brydon, George MacLaren, 1875- II. Title: The faith of our fathers.

RELIGIOUS life of Virginia in the seventeenth century; the faith of our fathers. Williamsburg, Virginia 350th Anniversary Celebration Corporation, 1957. 51p. illus. 21cm. (Jamestown 350th anniversary historical booklet, no.10) 'A list of parishes in Virginia, and the clergy in them ... July 8, 1702': p.48-51. Bibliography: p.46.
1. Virginia—Religion. 2. Virginia—Church history. 3. Church of England in Virginia. I. Brydon, George MacLaren, 1875- II. Title: The faith of our fathers.

Virginity.

BUGGE, John M., 1941- 241'.4
Virginitas : an essay in the history of a medieval ideal / by John Bugge. The Hague : Martinus Nijhoff, 1975,i.e.1976 viii, 168 p. ; 24 cm. (Archives internationales d'histoire des idees : Series minor ; 17) Includes index. Bibliography: p. [155]-163. [BV4647.C5B84] 75-510872 ISBN 90-247-1695-0 pbk. 11.25
1. Virginity. I. Title. II. Series.
Distributed by Humanities

DUBAY, Thomas. 248'.27
A call to virginity? / Thomas Dubay. Huntington, IN : Our Sunday Visitor, inc., c1977. 63 p. ; 18 cm. [BV4647.C5D77] 76-47982 ISBN 0-87973-745-X pbk. : 1.95
1. Virginity. I. Title.

ERASMUS, Desiderius, d.1536 248.4
The comparation of vyrgin and a martyr (1523) Translated by Thomas Paynell. A facsim. reproduction of the Berthelet ed. of 1537 with an introd. by William James Hirten. Gainesville, Fla., Scholars' Facsimiles & Reprints, 1970. xlviii, 78 p. 23 cm. "Reproduced from a copy in the Lambeth Palace Library, London, England." Translation of Virginis et martyris comparatio. Includes bibliographical references. [BV4647.C5E713 1970] 70-101148 ISBN 0-8201-1072-8 6.00
1. Virginity. 2. Martyrdom (Christianity) I. Paynell, Thomas, fl. 1528-1567, tr. II. Berthelet, Thomas, d. ca. 1556. III. Hirten, William James. IV. Title.

KLIMISCH, Mary Jane, Sister 271.9069
The one bride: the church and consecrated virginity. Pref. by Ignatius Hunt. New York, Sheed [c.1965] xviii, 235p. 22cm. Bibl. [BV4647.C5K55] 65-12211 4.95
1. Virginity. I. Title.

NUGEAT, Rosamond, sister. 248
... Portrait of the consecrated woman in Greek Christian literature of the first four centuries ... by Sister M. Rosamond Nugeat ... Washington, D.C., The Catholic university of America press, 1941. xxi, 113 p. 23 cm. (The Catholic university of America. Patriotic studies and ixiv) Thesis (PH.D.)--Catholic university of America, 1941. "Select bibliography": p. xiii-xix. [BV4647.C5N8] A 42
1. Virginity. 2. Christian literature, Early—Greek authors. 3. Women in literature and art. 4. Women in Christianity. I. Title.

PERRIN, Joseph Marie, 1905- 248
Virginity. Translated by Katherine Gordon. Westminster, Md., Newman Press [1956] 161p. 19cm. [BV4647.C5P42] 56-9994
1. Virginity. I. Title.

SEGAL, Muriel. 301.41'7
Virgins reluctant, dubious, avowed / Muriel Segal. New York : Macmillan, c1977. vi, 184 p. : ill. ; 22 cm. Bibliography: p. 183-184. [BV4647.C5S43] 77-1101 ISBN 0-02-609070-8 8.95
1. Virginity. I. Title.

Virginity—Biblical teaching.

LEGRAND, Lucien, 1927- 220.8241
The Biblical doctrine of virginity. New York, Sheed & Ward [1963] 167 p. 21 cm. Includes bibliography. [BV4647.C5L4] 63-17413
1. Virginity — Biblical teaching. I. Title.

Virtue.

BALGUY, John, 1686-1748. 170
The foundation of moral goodness / John Balguy. New York : Garland Pub., 1976. 68, 102 p. ; 19 cm. (British philosophers and theologians of the 17th & 18th centuries) Reprint of the 1728-29 editions printed for J. Pemberton, London. [BJ1520.B26 1976] 75-11194 ISBN 0-8240-1750-1 lib.bdg. : 25.00
1. Virtue. 2. Ethics. I. Title. II. Series.

DE LONG, Russell Victor, 1901- 248
The game of life; specifications for character engineering, by Russell V. De Long and Mendell Taylor. [1st ed.] Grand Rapids, Eerdmans, 1954. 89p. 23cm. [BV4630.D4] 54-14528
1. Virtue. 2. Youth—Religious life. I. Taylor, Mendell, joint author. II. Title.

EDWARDS, Jonathan, 1703-1758. 170
The nature of true virtue. With a foreword by William K. Frankena. [Ann Arbor] University of Michigan Press [1960] xiii, 107 p. 21 cm. (Ann Arbor paperbacks, AA37) [BJ1520.E3] 60-1751
1. Virtue. I. Title.

GREENE, John Priest, 1849- 170
The fundamental virtues; a study of success and failure, by J. P. Greene ... Liberty, Mo., The William Jewell press, 1928. xxxi, 271, [1] p., 1 l. 19 1/2 cm. A revision of an earlier work by the author entitled "Practical morals". cf. Pref. "Supplementary readings"; 1 leaf at end. [BJ1521.G8] 29-1456
1. Virtue. 2. Ethics. 3. Conduct of life. 4. Success. I. Title.

HARNED, David Baily. 241'.4
Faith and virtue. Philadelphia, United Church Press [1973] 190 p. 22 cm. "A Pilgrim Press book." Includes bibliographical references. [BV4630.H37] 73-5686 ISBN 0-8298-0250-9 6.95
1. Virtue. 2. Virtues. 3. Christian ethics. I. Title.

HOLLINGSWORTH, Thekla. 179.9
Grains of gold. [1st ed.] New York, Vantage Press [1955] 63p. 21cm. [BJ1521.H66] 56-5530
1. Virtue. I. Title.

KANE, John A 241
The school of virtue. [1st ed.] New York, Pageant Press [1954, c1953] 168p. 21cm. [BV4630.K3] 53-11795
1. Virtue. I. Title.

KLUBERTANZ, George Peter, 1912- 170
Habits and virtues [by] George P, Klubertanz. New York, Appleton-Century-Crofts [1965] xiv, 291 p. 22 cm. Includes bibliographies. [BJ1521.K6] 65-23606
1. Virtue. 2. Habit. I. Title.

PLUS, Raoul, 1882- 248
Some rare virtues. Translated from the French by Sister Mary Edgar Meyer. Westminster, Md., Newman Press, 1950. vi, 213 p. 16 cm. [BV4630.P613] 50-8813
1. Virtue. I. Title.

RICHARDSON, Samuel, 1689-1761.
The history of Pamela; or, Virtue rewarded. A narrative, which has its foundation in truth, adapted to inculcate in the minds of both sexes, the principles of virtue and religion. By Samuel Richardson, esq. First American from the last London ed. Philadelphia, W. A. Leary & co. [185?] 1 p. l., [6]-108 p. 15 1/2 cm. A mere resume of the original story. 6-514
I. Title.

RUSSELL, William Henry, 1895- 248
Teaching the Christian virtues. Milwaukee, Bruce Pub. Co. [1952] 200p. 23cm. [BV4630.R85] 53-148
1. Virtue. 2. Christian ethics—Study and teaching. I. Title.

SHERIF, Mohamed Ahmed. 179'.9
Ghazali's theory of virtue. [1st ed.] Albany, State University of New York Press, 1975. xiii, 205 p. 24 cm. (Studies in Islamic philosophy and science) Bibliography: p. 190-199. [B753.G34S54] 71-38000 ISBN 0-87395-206-5. ISBN 0-87395-207-3 (microfiche)
1. al-Ghazzali, 1058-1111. 2. Virtue. I. Title. II. Series.

STALKER, James, 1848-1927. 170
The seven cardinal virtues, by Rev. James Stalker, D.D. New York, American tract society [1902] 1 p. l., 125 p. front. (port.) 20 cm. [BJ1521.S8] 2-26084
1. Virtue. I. Title.

THOMAS Aquinas Saint 1225?-1274. 241.4
Treatise on the virtues. Translated by John A. Oesterle. Englewood Cliffs, N.J., Prentice-Hall [1966] xvii, 171 p. 21 cm. Bibliographical footnotes. [BV4630.T473 1966] 66-18262
1. Virtue. I. Oesterle, John A., tr. II. Title.

THOMAS Aquines Saint 1225?-1274. 189.4
On the virtues, in general; translated with introd. and notes by John Patrick Reid. Providence, Providence College Press, 1951. xxix, 188 p. 21 cm. Bibliography: p. 177-181. [BV4630.T473] 51-8160
1. Virtue. I. Title.

TIEDE, David Lenz. 291.2'11
The charismatic figure as miracle worker. [Missoula? Mont.] Published by Society of Biblical Literature for the Seminar on the Gospels, 1972. vi, 324 p. 22 cm. (Society of Biblical Literature. Dissertation series, no. 1) Originally presented as the author's thesis, Harvard. Bibliography: p. 293-312. [BJ1521.T48 1972] 72-87359
1. Moses. 2. Jesus Christ—Person and offices. 3. Virtue. 4. Miracles. I. Title. II. Series.

VON HILDEBRAND, Dietrich, 1889- 179.9
Fundamental moral attitudes; translated from the German by Alice M. Jourdain. [1st ed.] New York, Longmans, Green, 1950. 72 p. 21 cm. Translation of Sittliche Grundhaltungen. [BJ1523.V613] 50-5647
1. Virtue. I. Title.

VON HILDEBRAND, Dietrich, 1889- 179'.9
Fundamental moral attitudes. Translated from the German by Alice M. Jourdain. New York, Books for Libraries Press [1969] 72 p. 23 cm. (Essay index reprint series) Reprint of the 1950 ed. Translation of Sittliche Grundhaltungen. Essays. [BJ1523.V613 1969] 77-76918
1. Virtue. I. Title.

WILLIAMS, William R., 1804-1885. 248
Religious progress; discourses on the development of the Christian character, by William R. Williams ... Boston, Gould, Kendall and Lincoln, 1850. 258 p. 19 1/2 cm. "Errata" slip inserted after last page. [BV4501.W6 1850] 38-37392
1. Virtue. 2. Baptists—Sermons. 3. Sermons, American. I. Title.

WILLIAMS, William R., 1804-1885. 248
Religious progress; discourses on the development of the Christian character, by William R. Williams ... Boston, Gould and Lincoln, 1853. 258 p. 20 cm. [BV4501.W6 1853] 38-37391
1. Virtue. 2. Baptists—Sermons. 3. Sermons, American. I. Title.

WILLIAMS, William R., 1804-1885. 248
Religious progress; discourses on the development of the Christian character, by William R. Williams ... Boston, Gould and Lincoln; New York, Sheldon, Lamport, and Blakeman, 1854. 258 p. 20 cm. [BV4501.W6 1854] 41-33858
1. Virtue. 2. Baptists—Sermons. 3. Sermons, American. I. Title.

Virtues.

[ANDERSON, Louis Francis] 1859-
Virtues; the eternal essence and form of religion ... Glen Ellyn, Ill., Society for religious education [c1923] 3 p. l., 5-297 p. 20 cm. [BV4630.A6] 23-6612
I. Title.

BOROS, Ladislaus, 1927- 241.4
Meeting God in man. Translated by William Glen-Doepel. [New York] Herder and Herder [1968] xi, 142 p. 21 cm. Translation of Im Menschen Gott begegnen. [BV4630.B613 1968b] 68-55082 4.50
1. Virtues. I. Title.

GUARDINI, Romano, 1885- 241.4
The virtues: on forms of moral life. Translated by Stella Lange. Chicago, Il. Regnery Co., [1967] vii, 163 p. 21 cm. Translation of Tugenden: Meditationen uber Gestalten sittlichen Lebens. [BV4630.G813] 67-28495
1. Virtues. I. Title.

GUARDINI, Romano, 1885-1968. 241.4
The virtues; on forms of moral life. Translated by Stella Lange. Chicago, H. Regnery Co., [1967] vii, 163 p. 21 cm. Translation of Tugenden: Meditationen uber Gestalten sittlichen Lebens. [BV4630.G813] 67-28495
1. Virtues.

LANSLOTS, Don Ildephonse, 1859- 241
The three divine virtues, by D. I. Lanslots, O. S. B. New York and Cincinnati, Frederick Pustet co. (inc.) 1925. x p., 1 l., 222 p. 20 cm. [BV4635.L3] 25-15690
I. Title.

MURPHY, John F 1922- 241
The virtues on parade. Milwaukee, Bruce Pub. Co. [1959] 144p. 23cm. [BV4630.M8] 59-7946
1. Virtues. I. Title.

PETTY, Jo, comp. 248
Wings of silver. Norwalk, Conn., C. R. Gibson Co. [1967] 89 p. illus. 21 cm. [BV4360.P47] 67-21924
1. Virtues. I. Title.

SHEEDY, Charles Edmund. 241
The Christian virtues; a book on moral theology for college students and lay readers. [2d ed.] Notre Dame, Inc., University of Notre Dame Press [1956, c1951] xi, 369 p. 24 cm. (University religion series. Texts in theology for the layman) Bibliography: p. 360-361. [BX1758] 55-8274
1. Virtues. 2. Christian ethics — Catholic authors. I. Title. II. Series: University religion series

TRAHERNE, Thomas, d.1674 241.4
Christian ethicks. General introd. commentary by Carol L. Marks. Textual introd., commentary by George Robert Guffey. Ithaca, N. Y., Cornell Univ. Pr. [1968] 1xii, 391p. 24cm. (Cornell studies in English, v. 43) The critical old-spelling text of this ed. was established after a collation of six copies of the 1675 ed. Based on doctoral dissertations written at the Universities of Wisconsin (Marks) and Illinois (Guffey) Bibl. [BV4630.T7 1968] 66-20015 10.00
1. Virtues. I. Marks, Carol L. II. Guffey, George Robert. III. Title. IV. Series: Cornell Univeristy. Cornell studies in English, v. 43)

Virtues—Addresses, essays, lectures.

GEACH, Peter Thomas. 241'.4
The virtues / Peter Geach. Cambridge : Cambridge University Press, 1977. xxxv, 173 p. ; 21 cm. (The Stanton lectures ; 1973-4) Includes index. [BV4630.G4] 76-19628 ISBN 0-521-21350-9 : 21.50
1. Virtues—Addresses, essays, lectures. I. Title. II. Series.

LESSIUS, Leonardus, 1554-1623. 242
The virtues awakened, from the Treatise on perfect happiness, by the Venerable Leonard Lessius, S.J.; translated from the original Latin by the Rev. Henry Churchill Semple, S.J. St. Louis, Mo. and London, B. Herder book co., 1924. 6 p. l., 50 p. 19 1/2 cm. [BV4830.L4] 24-21601
I. Semple, Henry Churchill, 1853- tr. II. Title.

Virtues—Juvenile literature.

CORIELL, Ron. 649'.7
A child's book of character building : growing up in God's world—at home, at school, at play / written and illustrated by Ron and Rebekah Coriell. Old Tappan, N.J. : Revell, c1981. 128 p. : ill. ; 29 cm. Presents Bible stories and situations from daily life which demonstrate the meaning of Christian values. [BV4630.C67] 19 80-148612 ISBN 0-8007-1197-1 : 7.95
1. Virtues—Juvenile literature. 2. Children—Religious life. 3. Children—Conduct of life. 4. [Conduct of life.] 5. [Christian life.] I. Coriell, Rebekah, joint author. II. Title.

VIRTUE and vice:
or, The history of Charles Careful, and Harry Heedless. Shewing the good effects of caution and prudence, and the many inconveniences that Harry Heedless experienced from his rashness and disobedience, while Master Careful became a great man, only by his merit. Boston: Printed and sold by Samuel Hall, no. 53, Cornhill. 1795. 1 p. l., [5]-61 p. front., illus. 10 1/2 cm. [PZ6.V819] 22-6760

Vishnu.

BARRACK, Howard J. 294.5'923
The thousand names of Visnu : Visnu Sahasranamam from the Mahabharata ; transliterated Sanskrit text, translation and commentary / by Howard J. Barrack ; foreword by Amritjit Singh. New York : Tara Publications, 1974. 120 p. ; 23 cm. Bibliography: p. 119-120. [BL1219.B3713] 74-194697
1. Mahabharata. Anusasanaparva. Visnusahasranama. 2. Vishnu. I. Mahabharata. Anusasanaparva. Visnusahasranama. English & Sanskrit. 1974. II. Title.

VISHNU-SMRITI. 294.2
The institutes of Vishnu, translated by Julius Jolly. Oxford, The Clarendon press, 1880. xxxvii p., 1 l., 316 p. 23 cm. (Added t.-p.: The sacred books of the East ... vol. VII) "The Vishnu-smriti ... is in the main a collection of ancient aphorisms on the sacred laws of India."--Introd. [BL1010.S3 vol. 7] 290.8 32-34304
I. Jolly, Julius, 1849-1932, ed. and tr. II. Title.

Vishnu (Hindu deity)—Poetry.

NAMMALVAR. 294.5'95
Hymns for the drowning : poems for Visnu / by Nammalvar ; translated from Tamil by A.K. Ramanujan. Princeton, N.J. : Princeton University Press, c1981. p. cm. (Princeton library of Asian translations) Translation from: Tiruvaymoli and Tiruviruttam. Includes bibliographical references and index. [PL4758.9.N3155A27] 19 81-47151 ISBN 0-691-06492-X : 15.00 ISBN 0-691-01385-3 (pbk.) : 5.95
1. Vishnu (Hindu deity)—Poetry. I. Ramanujan, A. K., 1929- II. [Tiruvaymoli.] English. Selections III. Nammalvar. English. Selections. Tiruviruttam. IV. Title. V. Series.

Visions.

BACKMAN, Milton Vaughn. 289.3'0924
Joseph Smith's first vision; the first vision in its historical context [by] Milton V. Backman, Jr. Salt Lake City, Bookcraft, 1971. xiv, 209 p. illus., maps, ports. 24 cm. Bibliography: p. [193]-204. [BX8695.S6B3] 72-149592
1. Smith, Joseph, 1805-1844. 2. Visions. 3. New York (State)—Religion. I. Title.

THE book of visions: 133
being a transcript of the record of the secret thoughts of a variety of individuals while attending church ... also, instances of the separation of the soul from the body--one individual being justified by faith, and the other condemned ... Philadelphia, J. W. Moore, 1847. 2 p. l., ix-xii, [13]-135 p. 19 1/2 cm. [BF1101.B6] 32-10529
1. Visions.

*BOUSMAN, Emma. 248.2
Christiana follows on (witness #2) [1st ed.] New York, Vantage Press [1972] 100 p. 22 cm. [BV5023] ISBN 0-533-00237-0 3.95
1. Visions. I. Title.

CHRISTIAN, William A., 1944- 248.2
Apparitions in late Medieval and Renaissance Spain / by William A. Christian, Jr. Princeton, N.J. : Princeton University Press, c1981. p. cm. Includes index. [BV5091.V6C48] 19 80-8541 ISBN 0-691-05326-X : 20.00 20.00
1. Mary, Blessed Virgin, Saint—Apparitions and miracles (Modern)—Spain. 2. Visions. 3. Apparitions. 4. Spain—Religious life and customs. I. Title.

DANIKEN, Erich von, 1935- 248.2
Miracles of the gods : a new look at the supernatural Erich von Daniken ; translated by Michael Heron. New York : Dell ,1976 c1975. xi, 291 p. : ill. ; 18 cm. Bibliography: pp. 277-291. [BF1103.D3313] pbk. : 1.95
1. Visions. 2. Miracles. 3. Bible—Miscellanea. I. Title.
L.C. card no. for 1975 Souvenir Press edition: 75-332075.

ELLSWORTH, George, 1866- 135.3
Window of God. [1st ed.] New York, Vantage Press [1955] 55p. 23cm. A record of the author's spiritual experiences. [BF1101.E4] 55-7178
1. Visions. I. Title.

GABRIELE di Santa Maria Maddelene Father. 231.73
Visions and revelations in the spiritual life. Translated by a Benedictine of Stanbrook Abbey. Westminster, Md., Newman Press, 1950. 123 p. 19 cm. [BV5091.V6G33] 51-8641
1. Visions. I. Title.

GILBERT, Levi, 1852-
Visions of the Christ, by Levi Gilbert. Cincinnati, Jennings and Pye; New York, Eaton and Mains [1903] 284 p. 18 cm. 3-61939
I. Title.

GOTTSCHALL, Amos H. comp.
Visions of heaven and hell. What men and women claim to have seen in the world beyond. Gleaned from various works by A. H. Gottschall. Harrisburg, Penn'a The Christian union, 1909. 159 p. 18 cm. 10-26371 0.75
I. Title.

HAGIN, Kenneth E., 1917- 248'.29
I believe in visions [by] Kenneth E. Hagin. Old Tappan, N.J., F. H. Revell Co. [1972] 126 p. 21 cm. [BT580.A1H3] 72-10332 ISBN 0-8007-0577-7 1.95
1. Jesus Christ—Apparitions and miracles (Modern) 2. Visions. I. Title.

HICKS, Esther L. 248.2'2
A lantern for mine anointed Jesus [by Esther L. Hicks. Roosevelt? Utah, 1971] 12 p. 23 cm. Cover title. [BV5091.V6H5] 71-26462
1. Visions. I. Title.

HUXLEY, Aldous Leonard, 1894- 135.3
The doors of perception and Heaven and hell. New York, Harper [c.1954, 1963] 185p. 21cm. (Colophon bks., CN7) 1.35 pap.,
1. Visions. I. Title.

HUXLEY, Aldous Leonard, 1894-1963. 135.3
Heaven and hell. [1st ed.] New York, Harper [1956] 103 p. 20 cm. [BF1101.H8] 55-10694
1. Visions. I. Title.

LANDRUM, L M. Mrs.
Visions of the kingdom, by Mrs. L. M. Landrum. Atlanta, Ga., Foote & Davies co., 1912. 6 p. l., [5]-310 p. 16 cm. 13-957
I. Title.

MAHURIN, S 135.3
My vision, a meditation on the spirit eternal [by] S. (Mack) Mahurin. [1st ed.] New York, Exposition Press [1955, c1954] 54p. 21cm. [BF1101.M3] 54-10340
1. Visions. I. Title.

RAHNER, Karl, 1904- 248.22
Visions and prophecies [Tr. (from German) by Charles Henkey, richard Strachan. New York] Herder & Herder [1964, c.1963] 108p. 22cm. (Quaestiones disputatae, 10) Bibl. 63-18006 2.25 pap.,
1. Visions. 2. Private revelations. I. Title.

RATHBUN, Job, b.1734.
A sign, with a looking-glass; or, A late vision opened and explained, in the light of the prophecies and revelations. In which is shown, the sudden destruction of the draggon, and beast, and false-church, and the sudden gathering in of the Jews, into their own land, and their final restoration to Christ; and the curse taken off from the earth, and the glory of the millennium.--Also, the sudden second coming of Christ ... By Job Rathbun ... Pittsfield, Printed by P. Allen, 1804. 136 p. 24 cm. 6-17548
I. Title.

SEWELL, Lisa. 248'.2
I called Jesus and He came leaping over mountains and skipping over hills. Philadelphia, Dorrance [1974] 153 p. 22 cm. [BT580.A1S48] 73-86945 ISBN 0-8059-1930-9 5.95
1. Visions. I. Title.

SEYMOUR, St. John Drelincourt. 236
Irish visions of the other-world; a contribution to the study of mediaeval visions, by St. John D. Seymour. New York, Lemma Pub. Co. [1973] p. cm. Reprint of the 1930 ed. published by Society for Promoting Christian Knowledge, London. Bibliography: p. [BT833.S4 1973] 72-87987 ISBN 0-87696-055-7 12.50
1. Visions. 2. Eschatology—History of doctrines. I. Title.

SEYMOUR, St. John Drelincourt. 237
Irish visions of the other world; a contribution to the study of medieval visions, by St. John D. Seymour... London, Society for promoting Christian knowledge. New York and Toronto, The Macmillan co. [1930] 192 p. 19 cm. "Principal authorities consulted and sources used": p. 9-12. [BT833.S4] 31-7428
1. Visions. 2. Eachatology. I. Title.

SNEAD, Martha George Tillman. 237
My soul's experience in the unseen world; or, Why I was afraid to die. Richmond, B. F. Johnson Pub. Co., 1898. 51 p. 20 cm. [BT833.S67] 48-40714
1. Visions. I. Title.

STEINER, Johannes, 1902- 248'.2 B
The visions of Therese Neumann / by Johannes Steiner. New York : Alba House, c1976. xii, 244 p. : ill. ; 22 cm. Translation of Visionen der Therese Neumann. [BX4705.N47S7513] 75-34182 ISBN 0-8189-0318-X : 5.95
1. Neumann, Therese, 1898-1962. 2. Visions. I. Title.

VISIONS of Jesus / 248'.29
[compiled by] Chet & Lucile Huyssen. Plainfield, N.J. : Logos International, c1977. xvi, 114 p. ; 18 cm. [BT580.A1V57] 77-84183 ISBN 0-88270-223-8 pbk. : 1.95
1. Jesus Christ—Apparitions and miracles (Modern) 2. Visions. I. Huyssen, Chet. II. Huyssen, Lucile.

DANIKEN, Erich von, 1935- 248'.2
Miracles of the gods : a new look at the supernatural / Erich von Daniken ; translated from the German by Michael Heron. 1st U.S. ed. New York : Delacorte Press, c1975. xiii, 291 p., [12] leaves of plates : ill. ; 22 cm. Translation of Erscheinungen. Bibliography: p. [277]-291. [BF1103.D3313 1975b] 75-29246 ISBN 0-440-05595-4 : 8.95
1. Bible—Miscellanea. 2. Visions. 3. Miracles. I. Title.

Visitations (church work)

BRYANT, Marcus David. 253
The art of Christian caring / Marcus D. Bryant. St. Louis : Bethany Press, c1979. 125 p. : ill. ; 23 cm. Includes bibliographical references. [BV4320.B79] 78-20791 ISBN 0-8272-0015-3 : 8.95
1. Visitations (Church work) I. Title.

CALLENDER, Willard D. 253
How to make a friendly call / Willard D. Callender. Valley Forge, PA : Judson Press, c1982. 111 p. ; 17 cm. [BV4320.C34] 19 81-13645 ISBN 0-8170-0947-7 pbk. : 4.95
1. Visitations (Church work) I. Title.

DICKS, Russell Leslie, 1906- 258
How to make pastoral calls, for ministers and laymen. [2d rev. ed.] St. Louis, Bethany [c.1962] 63p. 22cm. 62-17916 1.00 pap.,
1. Visitations (Church work) I. Title.

GROSS, Mynette, sister 1911- 248.89438
The contemporary sister in the apostolate of home visitation. Washington, D.C., Catholic Univ. [c.1966] vi, 121p. 22cm. Bibl. [BX4205.G7] 66-17753 2.95 pap.,
1. Visitations (church work) 2. Monasticism and religious orders for women. I. Title.

VISITATION evangelism made 269
practical; reaching your community for Christ and the church. Grand Rapids, Zondervan Pub. House [1957] 93p. illus. 20cm. [BV3793.D4] [BV3793.D4] 253 57-28032 57-28032
1. Visitations (Church work) 2. Evangelistic work. I. Dean, Horace F

WITTY, Robert Gee. 253
Church visitation: theory and practice [by] Robert G. Witty. Nashville, Broadman Press [1967] 74 p. 20 cm. [BV4320.W5] 68-12318
1. Visitations (Church work) I. Title.

Visitations (Church work)—Study and teaching.

SOUTHARD, Samuel. 259'.07
Training church members for pastoral care / Samuel Southard. Valley Forge, PA : Judson Press, 1982. 92 p. ; 22 cm. Includes bibliographical references. [BV4320.S67] 19 81-18562 ISBN 0-8170-0944-2 pbk. : 4.95
1. Visitations (Church work)—Study and teaching. 2. Lay ministry—Study and teaching. I. Title.

Visitations, Ecclesiastical.

SAVAGE, Henry Edwin. 250
Pastoral visitation, by Rev. H. E. Savage ... London, New York [etc.] Longmans, Green, and co., 1903. ix, [1], 182 p. 18 1/2 cm. (Half-title: Handbooks for the clergy, ed. by A. W. Robinson) [BV4010.S2] 3-12784
1. Visitations, Ecclesiastical. I. Title.

Visitations, Ecclesiastical—England.

CHURCH of England. 264.
... Visitation articles and injunctions of the period of the reformation ... Edited by Walter Howard Frere ... London, New York [etc.] Longmans, Green & co., 1910. 3 v. 26 1/2 cm. (Alcuin club collections, xiv, xv, xvi) Title varies slightly. Supplement by "Elizabethan episcopal administration", edited by W. P. M. Kennedy, 1924 (Alcuin club collections, xxv-xxvii) "Some principal authorities used in these volumes": v. 1, p. 205-210. [BX5141.A1A6 vol. 14-16] 11-1275
1. Visitations, Ecclesiastical—England. 2. Reformation—England. 3. Gt. Brit.—Church history—Sources. I. Frere, Walter Howard, bp. of Truro, 1863- ed. II. Kennedy, William Paul McClure, 1880- III. Title.

COURTENAY, William, Abp. of Canterbury, 1342?-1396. 282.42
The metropolitan visitations of William Courtency, Archbishop of Canterbury, 1381-1396; documents transcribed from the original manuscripts of Courteney's register, with an introd. describing the Archbishop's investigations by Joseph Henry Dahmus. Urbana, University of Illinois Press, 1950. 209 p. 27 cm. (Illinois studies in the social sciences, v. 31, no. 2) Text in Latin. [H31.I 4 vol. 31, no. 2] 50-8868
1. Visitations, Ecclesiastical—England. 2. Gt. Brit.—Church history—Sources. I. Title. II. Series: Illinois. University. Illinois studies in the social sciences, v. 31, no. 2

OXFORD (Diocese) Bishop, 1845-1869 (Samuel Wilberforce) 283.42
Bishop Wilberforce's visitation returns for the Archdeaconry of Oxford in the year 1854. Transcribed and edited by E. P. Baker. [Oxford, 1954] vi, 171p. 24cm. (Oxfordshire Record Society. [Oxfordshire record series] v.35) [DA670.O9A3 vol. 35] 57-59016
1. Visitations, Ecclesiastical—England. I. Title. II. Series.

WORCESTER, Eng. (Diocese) Bishop, 1308-1313 (Walter Reynolds) 283
The register of Walter Reynolds, bishop of Worcester, 1308-1313, edited for the Worcestershire historical society and the Dugdale society by Rowland Alwyn Wilson ... London, For the Dugdale society by H. Milford, Oxford university press, 1928. 4 p., l., xxx, 223 p. 25 cm. (Half-title: Publications of the Dugdale society ... vol. IX) Published also as a publication of the Worcestershire historical society, 1927. [DA670.W3D9 vol. IX] 29-4794
1. Visitations, Eccleslastical—England. 2. Gt. Brit.—Church history—Sources. I. Wilson, Rowland Alwyn, 1868- ed. II. Title.

Visitations, Ecclesiastical—New Mexico.

TAMARON Y ROMERAL, Pedro, Bp., 1695-1768. 271.3
Bishop Tamaron's visitation of New Mexico, 1760, Edited by Eleanor B. Adams. Albuquerque, N. M., 1954. 113p. 23cm. (New Mexico. Historical Society. Publications in history, v. 15) 'Translation ... based on Vito Alessio Robles' edition ... [of Demostracion del vastisimo obispado de la Nueva Vizcaya] published in Mexico in 1937.' Bibliographical footnotes. [F791.N45 vol.15] 57-62563
1. Visitations, Ecclesiastical—New Mexico. 2. Franciscans in New Mexico. I. Adams, Eleanor Burnham, ed. II. Title. III. Series.

Visitations, Ecclesiastical—Southwell, Eng.

SOUTHWELL CATHEDRAL 274.2
Visitations and memorials of Southwell minster. Ed. by Arthur Francis Leach. [Westminster] Printed for the Camden Soc., 1891. New York, Johnson Reprint, 1965 cxi, 234, 10p. incl. front. 22cm. (Camden Soc. Pubns. with Camden Soc. reps., list of members [DA20.C17 New Ser., No. 48] A17 13.50
1. Visitations, Ecclesiastical—Southwell, Eng. I. Leach, Arthur Francis, 1851-1915, ed. II. Title.

Visitations (Religious education)

SISEMORE, John T 268
The ministry of visitation. Nashville, Broadman Press [1954] 115p. 20cm. [BV1523.S5] 54-2969
1. Visitations (Religious education) I. Title.

Visiting teachers.

MARY Rosalita, Sister, 1874- 807
The community school visitor, by Sister Mary Salome, O.S.F. Milwaukee, Wis., New York [etc.] The Bruce publishing company [c1928] 190 p. incl. forms. 18 1/2 cm. (Half-title: The Marquette monographs on education) [Secular name: Mary Tiochemaks] Bibliography: p. 185-190. [LC485.M35] 29-1437
1. Visiting teachers. 2. Catholic church—Education. I. Title.

Visser't Hooft, Willem Adolph, 1900-

GERARD, Francois C., 1924- 262'.001
The future of the church : the theology of renewal of Willem Adolf Visser't Hooft / Francois C. Gerard. Pittsburgh : Pickwick Press, 1974. xii, 239 p. : port. ; 22 cm. (Pittsburgh theological monograph series ; 2) Bibliography: p. 232-239. [BV600.2.G42] 74-26564 ISBN 0-915138-01-8 6.95
1. Visser't Hooft, Willem Adolph, 1900- 2. Church renewal—History of doctrines. I. Title. II. Series.

MACKIE, Robert C., ed. 280.1
The sufficiency of God; essays on the ecumenical hope in honor of W. A. Visser 't Hooft. Ed. by Robert C. Mackie, Charles C. West. Philadelphia, Westminster [c.1963] 240p. group ports. 23cm. Bibl. 64-10049 5.50
1. Visser 't Hooft, Willem Adolph, 1900- 2. Ecumenical movement—Addresses, essays, lectures. 3. Christian union — Addresses, essays, lecture. I. West, Charles C., joint ed. II. Title.

Visual education.

WALDRUP, Earl. 268.635
Using visual aids in a church. Nashville, Broadman Press [c1949] xii, 178 p. illus. 20 cm. [BV1643.W3] 50-3761
1. Visual education. 2. Church work. I. Title.

Visual instruction.

FRENCH, Addie Marie. 232.9
The life of Christ; ten illustrated lessons selected from the four Gospels for use in teaching with a visual board ... Miss Addie Marie French, author, Miss Eva M. Herbert, editor, Miss Ruth I. Kiehl, illustrator, Rev. David J. Fant, publication secretary ... Harrisburg, Pa., Christian publications, inc., c1941. 2 v. illus., plates. 31 cm. Contents.--i. The earlier events of the life of Christ, from "The birth of Jesus" to "Jesus heals a sick man."--ii. The later events of the life of Christ. from "Jesus and the children" to "Jesus' assension and commission." [BT307.F7] 41-7682
1. Jesus Christ—Biog.—Study. 2. Visual instruction. I. Herbert, Eva M., ed. II. Title.

HERVEY, Walter Lowrie, 1862- 268.
Picture-work [by] Walter L. Hervey ... New York, Chicago [etc.] Fleming H. Revell company [1908] 91 p. 18 1/2 cm. "Books, pictures, and illustrative material": p. 71-81. [BV1535.H4 1908] 8-2179
1. Visual instruction. 2. Religious education—Teaching methods. I. Title.

HOCKMAN, William Smithson, 1899- 268.6352
Projected visual aids in the church. Boston, Pilgrim Press [1947] viii, 214 p. 22 cm. [BV1643.H6] 47-12092
1. Visual instruction. 2. Church work. I. Title.

INTERNATIONAL council of religious education. 268.635
... Visual method in the church curriculum ... by Protestant evangelical forces of the United States and Canada through the International council of religious education. Chicago, Ill., The International council of religious education [c1940] 59 p. illus., diagr. 23 cm. (International bulletin in religious education. Educational bulletin, no. 901) "What to read": p. 28. Available in visual education materials. [BV1535.I5] 40-10255
1. Visual instruction. 2. Moving-pictures in education. 3. Moving-pictures—Catalogs. 4. Religious education. I. Title.

JANES, Hugh Paul, 1899- 268.635
Screen and projector in Christian education; how to use motion pictures and projected still pictures in worship, study, and recreation, by H. Paul Janes. Philadelphia, The Westminster press, 1932. 160 p. illus., plates. 20 cm. [BV1643.J3] 371.335 32-23848
1. Visual instruction. 2. Moving-pictures in education. 3. Religious education. I. Title.

ROGERS, William L. 268.635
Visual aids in the church, by William L. Rogers ... [and] Paul H. Vieth ... Illustrations by Jane Martin. Philadelphia, St. Louis, The Christian education press [1946] vii, 214 p. illus., diagrs. 20 1/2 cm. "Sources of motion picture films": p. 212-214. Bibliography: p. 214. [BV1643.R6] 46-2034
1. Visual instruction. 2. Moving-pictures in education. 3. Church work. I. Vieth, Paul Herman, 1895- joint author. II. Title.

Vital force.

ATKINS, Albert James, 1868- 128
The triune principle of life and philosophy of the soul, by Albert J. Atkins, m.d. [San Francisco, The author, c1929] 3 p. l., 9-70 p. 19 cm. [BF1272.A75] ca 29
1. Vital force. 2. Soul. I. Title.

Vivekananda, Swami, 1863-1902.

MAJUMDAR, Ramesh Chandra, ed. 921.91
Swami Vivekakanda centenary memorial volume. Ed.: R. C. Majumdar. Calcutta, Swami Vivekananda Centenary [dist. Hollywood, Calif., Vendanta, 1964] xliv, 617p. illus., ports. (pt. col.) 25cm. Bibl. 64-6059 10.00
1. Vivekananda, Swami, 1863-1902. I. Vivekananda, Swami, 1863-1902. II. Title.

NIKHILANANDA, Swami. 921.9
Vivekananda, a biography. New York, Ramakrishna-Vivekananda Center, 1953. viii, 216 p. ports. 25 cm. [B133.V5N5] 53-7851
1. Vivekananda, Swami, 1863-1902.

WILLIAMS, George Mason, 1940- 294.5'6'4 B
The quest for meaning of Svami Vivekananda; a study of religious change [by] George M. Williams. [Chico, Calif.] New Horizons Press [1974] x, 148 p. 22 cm. (The Religious quest, v. 1) Bibliography: p. 141-144. [BL1270.V5W54] 74-10906 ISBN 0-914914-01-4 3.95 (pbk.).
1. Vivekananda, Swami, 1863-1902. I. Title. II. Series.

Vivekananda, Swami, 1863-1902—Addresses, essays, lectures.

SATPRAKASHANANDA, Swami. 294.5'6'4
Swami Vivekananda's contribution to the present age / by Swami Satprakashananda. St. Louis : Vedanta Society of St. Louis, c1978. 249 p., [2] leaves of plates : ill. ; 20 cm. Includes index. Bibliography: p. [241]-246. [BL1270.V5S25] 77-91628 ISBN 0-916356-58-2 : 9.50
1. Vivekananda, Swami, 1863-1902—Addresses, essays, lectures. I. Title.

Vlanney, Jean Baptise Marie, Saint, 1786-1859.

GHEON, Henri, 1875- 922.
... The secret of the cure d'Ars, with a note on the saint by G. K. Chesterton. New York-London [etc.] Longmans, Green and co., 1929. 217 p. front. (port.) 21 cm. At head of title: Translated by F. J. Sheed. "Printed in Great Britain." Bibliography: p. 217. [BX4700.V5G55] 29-16506
1. Vlanney, Jean Baptiste Marie, saint, 1786-1859. I. Sheed, Francis Joseph, 1897- tr. II. Chesterton, Gilbert Keith, 1874-1936. III. Title. IV. Title: Translation of Le saint cure d'Ars.

GHEON, Henri, 1875- 922.244
The secret of the Cure d'Ars, by Henri Gheon; translated by F. J. Sheed, with a note on the saint by G. K. Chesterton. New York, Sheed & Ward, 1938. viii, 248 p. 18 cm. (On cover: Catholic masterpieces [no. 1]) "Printed in Great Britain." Bibliography: p. 248. [BX4700.V5G55 1938] 40-4659
1. Vlanney, Jean Baptise Marie, Saint, 1786-1859. I. Sheed, Francis Joseph, 1897- tr. II. Chesterton, Gilbert Keith, 1874-1936. III. Title. IV. Title: Translation of Le saint cure d'Ars.

SHEPPARD, Lancelot Capel, 1906- 922.244
Portrait of a parish priest; St. John Vianney, the cure d'Ars. Westminster, Md., Newman Press [1958] 189 p. illus. 23 cm. [BX4700.V5S5] 58-13646
1. Vlanney, Jean Baptisic Marie, Satint, I. Title.

Vocabulary.

FULLMER, David Clarence, 1910- 201.4
... The vocabulary of religion. [By] Rev. David C. Fullmer ... Washington, D.C., The Catholic university of America. Educational research monographs. T. G. Foran, editor. Vol. XIII, May 15, 1943, no. 2) Issued also as thesis (PH.D.) Catholic university of America. Bibliography: p. 68-69. [[BX925.F]] A 45
1. Vocabulary. 2. English language—Glossaries, vocabularies, etc. I. Title.

Vocation.

BAILEY, Faith Coxe. 248
You have a talent, don't bury it! Chicago, Moody Press [1956] 128p. 19cm. [BV4740.B25] 57-2701
1. Vocation. 2. Vocational guidance. I. Title.

BARNETTE, Henlee H. 248.4
Christian calling and vocation. Grand Rapids, Mich., Baker Bk. [c.]1965. 83p. 22cm. Bibl. [BV4740.B3] 65-20754 1.50 pap.,
1. Vocation. I. Title.

BARNETTE, Henlee H 248.4
Christian calling and vocation, by Henlee H. Barnette. Grand Rapids, Baker Book House, 1965. 83 p. 22 cm. Bibliographical footnotes. Bibliography: p. 81-83. [BV4740.B3] 65-20754
1. Vocation. I. Title.

BARNETTE, Henlee H. 248
Has God called you? [By] Henlee Barnette. Nashville, Broadman Press [1969] 128 p. 21 cm. (A Broadman inner circle book) Includes bibliographies. [BV4740.B32] 69-17896
1. Vocation. I. Title.

BOGGS, Wade H 241
All ye who labor; a Christian interpretation of daily work. Richmond, John Knox Press [1961] 288p. 21cm. Includes bibliography. [BV4740.B6] 61-13480
1. Vocation. I. Title.

CALHOUN, Robert Lowry, 1896- 248
God and the day's work; Christian vocation in an unchristian world. New York, Association Press [1957] 128p. 16cm. (An Association Press reflection book) [BV4740.C3 1957] 57-11605
1. Vocation. I. Title.

CROCK, Clement Henry 248
Paths to eternal glory this is your life. [Boston] St. Paul Editions [dist. Daughters of St. Paul] [c.1960] 210p. 22cm. 60-4699 3.00; 2.00 pap.,
1. Vocation. I. Title.

DERATANY, Edward. 248'.89422
When God calls you / Edward Deratany. Nashville : T. Nelson, [1976] 206 p. ; 21 cm. Includes bibliographical references. [BV4740.D45] 76-6539 ISBN 0-8407-5601-1 pbk. : 3.95
1. Vocation. I. Title.

FERRARI, Erma Paul. 371.425
Careers for you; illustrated by Clifford Johnston. Nashville, Abingdon-Cokesbury Press [1953] 160p. illus. 20cm. [BV4740.F47] 53-10007
1. Vocation. I. Title.

FERRARI, Erma Paul. 331.702
Careers for you [by] Erma Ferrari. Rev. Nashville, Abingdon Press [1969] 160 p. 20 cm. Bibliography: p. 152-156. Discusses, from a Christian point of view, the importance of choosing and preparing for a suitable career and the proper attitude in getting and performing a job. Also includes a section on vocations in the church. [BV4740.F47 1969] 69-12770 1.75 (pbk)
1. Vocation. 2. [Vocation.] 3. [Vocational guidance.] I. Title.

FORRESTER, William Roxburgh, 1892- 250
Christian vocation; studies in faith and work, being the Cunningham lectures, 1950, in New College, Edinburgh. New York, Scribner, 1953. 223p. 21cm. [BV4740.F6 1953] 53-9436
1. Vocation. I. Title.

GRIMES, Howard 248.4
Realms of our calling. New York, Friendship [1965] 64p. 19cm. Bibl. [BV4740.G7] 65-11424 .75 pap.,
1. Vocation. I. Title.

HEIGES, Donald R. 248
The Christian's calling. Philadelphia, Muhlenberg [1962, c.1958] 114p. 18cm. Bibl. 1.00 pap.,
1. Vocation. I. Title.

HEIGES, Donald R
The Christian's calling. Philadelphia, Muhlenberg Press [c1958] 114 p. 19 cm. (Knubel-Miller lectures, 1958) "A Muhlenberg Press paperback." Includes bibliography. 67-31623
1. Vocation. I. Title.

HOHN, Hermann.
"Vocations"; conditions of admission, etc. into the convents, congregations, societies, religious institutes, etc., according to authentical information and the latest regulations. By Rev. H. Hohn ... Preface by His Eminence Cardinal Francis Bourne ... London [etc.] R. & T. Washbourne, ltd.; New York [etc.] Benziger bros., 1912. xx, 426 p., 1 l. front. (port.) 19 cm. On cover: "Vocations" (women) ... 14-8220
I. Title.

HOLLOWAY, James Y., 1927- comp. 248'.4
Callings! Edited by James Y. Holloway and Will D. Campbell. New York, Paulist Press [1974] vi, 280 p. 18 cm. (Deus books) "Most chapters in this book were originally published in the 1972 fall-winter issue of Katallagete, journal of the Committee of Southern Churchmen." [BV4740.H57] 73-90070 ISBN 0-8091-1806-8 1.95 (pbk.)
1. Vocation. I. Campbell, Will D., joint comp. II. Katallagete. III. Title.
Contents omitted.

HORTON, Dougals, 1891- 252
Christian vocation, a series of radio sermons by Douglas Horton, William Blakeman Lampe [and] Ernest Fremont Tittle; with a foreword by Lyman Bryson. Published for the Joint radio committee of the Congregational Christian, Methodist, and Presbyterian U.S.A. churches. Boston, Chicago, The Pilgrim press [1945] 72 p. 23 1/2 cm. [BV4740.H6] 45-21593
1. Vocation. 2. Sermons, American. I. Lampe, William Blakeman. 1885- II. Tittle, Ernest Fremont, 1885- III. Joint radio committee of the Congregational Christian, Methodist, and Presbyterian U.S.A. churches. IV. Title.

KLAUSLER, Alfred P 248
Christ and your job; a study in Christian vocation. Saint Louis, Mo., Concordia Pub. House [c1956] 145p. 19cm. Includes bibliography. [BV4740.K54] 56-9537
1. Vocation. I. Title.

MEEHAN, Andrew B.
A practical guide to the divine office, by Andrew B. Meehan ... [Rochester, N. Y., J. P. Smith printing co., c1912] 132 p. 17 cm. 12-18153 0.50
I. Title. II. Title: Divine office.

MILLER, Alexander, writer on Christian sociology. 248
Christian faith and my job, by Alexander Miller ... New York, Association press, 1946. xiii, 60 p. diagrs. 21 cm. "A Haddam house book." [BV4740.M5] 47-1317
1. Vocation. I. Title.

MILLER, Alexander, 1908- 248.4
Christian faith and my job. An up-to-date Reflection book ed. of the Haddam House book. New York, Association Press [1959] 128p. 16cm. (A Reflection book) Includes bibliography. [BV4740.M5 1959] 59-6838
1. Vocation. I. Title.

MILLION, Elmer G. 248.4
Your faith and your life work. New York, Friendship Press [c.1960] 80p. 19cm. Bibl.: p.78-79 illus. 60-7452 1.00 pap.,
1. Vocation. I. Title.

MINEAR, Paul Sevier, 1906- 232.9'7
To die and to live : Christ's resurrection and Christian vocation / Paul S. Minear. New York : Seabury Press, 1977. p. cm. "A Crossroad book." Includes bibliographical references and index. [BT481.M56] 77-8238 ISBN 0-8164-0340-6 : 8.95
1. Jesus Christ—Resurrection. 2. Vocation. I. Title.

NELSON, John Oliver, 1909- ed. 261.8
Work and vocation, a Christian discussion. [1st ed.] New York. Harper [1954] 224p. 22cm. Bibliography: p. 213-224. [BV4740.N4] 54-5856
1. Vocation. I. Title.

OSBORNE, William. 241.5'7
Man's responsibility; an ecumenical study. New York, Philosophical Lib. [1968] 258p. 22cm. Bibl.: p. 238-258. [BV4740.O8] 67-29201 6.00
1. Vocation. I. Title.

POAGE, Godfrey Robert, 1920- 271.0692
Parents' role in vocations, by Godfrey Poage and John P. Treacy. Milwaukee, Bruce Pub. Co. [1959] 132p. 23cm. [BX2380.P59] 59-9540
1. Vocation. 2. Vocational guidance. 3. Clergy—Appointment, call. and election. 4. Vocation (in religious orders, congregations, etc.) I. Treacy, John Patrick, joint author. II. Title.

RAND, Willard J, jr. 206.9
Call and response; an enlistment guide for church occupations. Nashville, Abingdon [c.1964] 160p. 20cm. Bibl 64-14620 1.75 pap.,
1. Vocation. 2. Church work as a profession. 3. Christian leadership. I. Title.

RAND, Willard J 206.9
Call and response; an enlistment guide for church occapations. New York, Abingdon Press [1964] 160 p. 20 cm. Bibliography: p. 154-157. [BV4740.R3] 64-14620
1. Vocation. 2. Church work as a profession. 3. Christian leadership. I. Title.

[SCHAGEMANN, John Henry] 1845-
The earthly paradise; or, The vocation to the religious state, by Rev. John Henry [pseud.] ... St. Louis, Mo. [etc.] B. Herder, 1915. 77 p. 15 cm. 15-4099
I. Title.

SCHLOSSER, Felix. 248
Forms of Christian life. Translated by R. A. Wilson. Milwaukee, Bruce Pub. Co. [1969] 96 p. 21 cm. [BV4740.S313] 69-20476
1. Vocation. I. Title.

SIGSWORTH, John Wilkins, 1915- , comp. 248
"How I found God's will for my life"; fifteen personal testimonies from choice Christian servants. Grant Rapids, Zondervan Pub. House [1960] 63 p. 20 cm. [BV4740.S55] 60-4131
1. Vocation. I. Title.

TODD, John Murray, ed. 174
Work: Christian thought and practice; a symposium. London, Darton, Longman & Todd; Baltimore, Helicon Press [1960] viii, 225 p. 23 cm. [BV4740.T6] 60-12027
1. Vocation. 2. Work. 3. Church and labor. 4. Job satisfaction. I. Title.

WENTZ, Frederick K. 248.4'2
My job and my faith; twelve Christians report on their work worlds. Frederick K. Wentz, editor. Nashville, Abingdon Press [1967] 192 p. 21 cm. [BV4740.W4] 67-22169
1. Vocation. I. Title.

ZEHRING, John William. 248'.4
Making your life count : finding fulfillment beyond your job / John William Zhering. Valley Forge, PA : Judson Press, c1980. 111 p. ; 22 cm. Includes bibliographical references. [BV4740.Z43] 79-25309 ISBN 0-8170-0869-1 pbk. :
1. Vocation. 2. Leisure. 3. Volunteer workers in social service. 4. Church work. 5. Christian life—1960- I. Title.

Vocation—Biblical teaching.

CROSBY, Michael, 1940- 234
The call and the answer. [Chicago] Franciscan Herald Press [1969] xiv, 165 p. 21 cm. Bibliographical references included in "Notes" (p. 159-165) [BX2350.2.C73] 79-94559 4.95
1. Vocation—Biblical teaching. I. Title.

Vocation, Ecclesiastical.

FISCHER, George L. 248.8'94
Generation of opportunity [by] George Fischer. [Glen Rock, N.J., Paulist Press, 1968] 96 p. illus. (part col.), ports. 29 cm. [BX2380.F53] 68-24480
1. Vocation, Ecclesiastical. I. Title.

FORD, Murray J. S. 331.702
Church vocations—a new look [by] Murray J. S. Ford. Valley Forge [Pa.] Judson Press [1971] 96 p. 21 cm. Bibliography: p. 94. [BV4740.F59] 74-160252 ISBN 0-8170-0544-7 2.50
1. Vocation, Ecclesiastical. I. Title.

HARRIS, Charles William, 1916- 253'.2
Your father's business : letters to a young man about what it means to be a priest / from Charles W. Harris. Notre Dame, Ind. : Ave Maria Press, c1978. 110 p. : ill. ; 18 cm. [BX2380.H35] 77-93018 ISBN 0-87793-146-1 : 1.75
1. Harris, Charles William, 1916- 2. Catholic Church—Clergy—Correspondence. 3. Vocation, Ecclesiastical. I. Title.

HOSTIE, Raymond, 1920- 262.14069
The discernment of vocations. Translated by Michael Barry. New York, Sheed & Ward [1963] 160 p. 22 c;. Includes bibliography. [BX2380.H613] 63-10493
1. Vocation, Ecclesiastical. I. Title.

O'DOHERTY, Eamonn Feichin. 248'.894
The psychology of vocation / E. F. O'Doherty. Dublin : Dept. of Psychology, University College, 1971. 60 p. ; 22 cm. (Thornfield series ; no. 1) [BX2380.O34] 75-309961 £0.30
1. Vocation, Ecclesiastical. I. Title.

PABLE, Martin W. 248.8'92
A call for me? : A new look at vocations / Martin W. Pable. Huntington, Ind. : Our Sunday Visitor, c1980. 110 p. ; 18 cm. Bibliography: p. 109-110. Overviews the priesthood and religious life and presents guidelines for determining if one is being called to this type of life. [BX2380.P24] 19 79-91056 ISBN 0-87973-527-9 pbk. : 2.50
1. Vocation, Ecclesiastical. 2. Vocation (in religions orders, congregations, etc.) 3. [Vocation, Ecclesiastical.] 4. [Vocational guidance.] I. Title.

SCHLECK, Charles A 271.069
The theology of vocations. Milwaukee, Bruce Pub. co. [1963] 357 p. 24 cm. [BX2380.S33] 62-20960
1. Vocation, Ecclesiastical. I. Title.

Vocation, Ecclesiastical—Addresses, essays, lectures.

EVOLVING religious careers. 253
Edited by Willis E. Bartlett. Foreword by Theodore M. Hesburgh. Washington, Center for Applied Research in the Apostolate [1970] xii, 207 p. illus. 23 cm. (CARA information service) "Based on the conference on Vocational development of religious careers, cosponsored by the Center for the Study of Man in Contemporary Society and the Department of Graduate Studies in Education, University of Notre Dame." Includes bibliographies. [BX2380.E9] 70-24375
1. Vocation, Ecclesiastical—Addresses, essays, lectures. I. Bartlett, Willis E., ed. II. Notre Dame, Ind. University. Center for the Study of Man in Contemporary Society. III. Notre Dame, Ind. University. Graduate School. Dept. of Education. IV. Center for Applied Research in the Apostolate, Washington, D.C.

Vocation, Ecclesiastical—Juvenile literature.

THATCHER, Joan. 200'.23
Church vocations / Joan Thatcher. Minneapolis : Dillon Press, c1976. 106 p. : ill. ; 24 cm. (Looking forward to a career) Includes index. Bibliography: p. [104]-106. Describes the range of careers available within church and synagogue, including those of rabbi, priest, missionary, chaplain, teacher, and others. Includes a discussion of church careers for women. [BV4740.T45] 75-33177 ISBN 0-87518-100-7 : 5.95 pbk. : 2.76
1. Vocation, Ecclesiastical—Juvenile literature. 2. [Vocation, Ecclesiastical.] 3. [Vocational guidance] I. Title.

Vocation (in religious orders, congregations, etc.)

ASSESSMENT of candidates for the religious life; 248.8'9422
basic psychological issues and procedures [by] Walter J. Coville [and others] Foreword by William C. Bier. Washington, Center for Applied Research in the Apostolate [1968] xxiii, 215 p. 22 cm. (CARA information service publication) Contains four papers originally presented at a workshop sponsored by the American Catholic Psychological Association held in New York City in 1966. Includes bibliographies. [BX2380.A75] 68-5252
1. Vocation (in religious orders, congregations, etc.) I. Coville, Walter J. II. American Catholic Psychological Association.

BIOT, Rene, 1889- 271
Medical guide to vocations, by Rene Biot and Pierre Galimard. Translated from the French and adapted into English by Robert P. Odenwald. Westminster, Md., Newman Press, 1955. 303p. 22cm. Translation of Guide medical des vocations sacerdotales et religieuses. [BX2380.B512] 54-5659
1. Vocation (in religious orders, congregations, etc.) I. Galimard. Pierre, 1912- joint author. II. Title.

BUSSARD, Paul C. 242
The living source, by Paul Bussard. New York, Sheed & Ward, inc., 1936. 3 p. l., 65, [1] p. 16 cm. "Printed in Great Britain." [BX2380.B8] 36-33423
1. Vocation (in religious orders, congregations, etc.) I. Title.

BUTLER, Richard, 1918- 271.0692
Religious vocation: an unnecessary mystery. Foreword by Edwin Vincent Byrne. [Chicago] H. Regnery Co., 1961. 167p. 21cm. [BX2380.B83] 61-7961
1. Vocation (in religious orders, congregations, etc.) I. Title.

BUTLER, Richard, 1918- 248'.89422
Religious vocation : an unnecessary mystery / by Richard Butler ; foreword by Edwin Vincent Byrne. Westport, Conn. : Greenwood Press, 1978, c1961. xiii, 167 p. ; 23 cm. Reprint of the ed. published by H. Regnery, Chicago. Includes bibliographical references. [BX2380.B83 1978] 78-14365 ISBN 0-313-21018-7 lib.bdg. : 15.00
1. Vocation (in religious orders, congregations, etc.) I. Title.

CUSHING, Richard James, Abp., 1895-- 270
That they may know Thee; selected writings on vocations. Compiled by George L. Kane. Westminster, Md., Newman Press, 1956. 217p. 22cm. [BX2380.C8] 56-8136
1. Vocation (in religious orders, congregations, etc.) 2. Catholic Church—Clergy—Appointment, call, and election. I. Title.

DAUGHTERS of St. Paul. 248.8'94
Choose your tomorrow. [Boston] St. Paul Editions [1968] 235 p. illus. 19 cm. [BX2380.D38] 68-9496 2.00
1. Vocation (in religious orders, congregations, etc.) I. Title.

FARRELL, Edward P. 271
The theology of religious vocation. St. Louis, Herder, 1951. 228 p. 22 cm. [BX2380.F3] 51-8076
1. Vocation (in religious orders, congregations, etc.) I. Title.

FICHTER, Joseph Henry, 1908- 271.0692
Religion as an occupation; a study in the sociology of professions. [Notre Dame, Ind] Univ. of Notre Dame Press [c.]1961 295p. Bibl. 61-10846 6.50
1. Vocation (in religious orders, congregations, etc.) 2. Catholic Church—Clergy—Appointment, call, and election. I. Title.

HERBST, Winfrid, father, 1891-
Girlhood's highest ideal, helpful chapters to Catholic girls at the parting of the ways, by Winfrid Herbst ... St. Nazianz, Wis., The Society of the Divine Savior, 1924. 89 p. incl. pl., port. 18 cm. [Secular name: John Anthony Herbst] [BX2380.H4] 24-15779
1. Vocation (in religious orders, congregations, etc.) 2. Monasticism and religious orders for women. 3. Girls—Religious life. I. Title.

HERR, Vincent V. 271
Screening candidates for the priesthood and religious life [by] Vincent V. Herr [and others] Chicago, Loyola University Press [1964] vii, 203 p. illus. 24 cm. Includes bibliographies. [BX2380.H44] 248'.894 68-1770
1. Vocation (in religious orders, congregations, etc.) I. Title.

INTERNATIONAL Congress on Vocations to the States of Perfection. 1st. Rome, 1961. 271.6092
Today's vocation crisis; a summary of the studies and discussions. Tr., ed. by Godfrey Poage, Germain Lievin. Westminster, Md., Newman for Pontifical Organization for Religious Vocations, Vatican City. [1963] vii, 435p. tables. 21cm. Bibl. 63-1449 5.95
1. Vocation (in religious orders, congregations, etc.) 2. Catholic Church—Clergy—Appointment, call, and election. I. Catholic. Church. Congregatio de Religiosis. II. Poage, Godfrey Robert, 1920- ed. and tr. III. Lievin, Germain, ed. and tr. IV. Title.

INTERNATIONAL Congress on Vocations to the States of Perfection. 1st, Rome, 1961. 271.0692
Today's vocation crisis; a summary of the studies and discussions. Translated and edited by Godfrey Poage and Germain Lievin. Westminister, Md., Newman Press for Pontifical Organization for Religious Vocations, Vatican City, 1962. vii, 435 p. tables. 21 cm. Sponsored by Sacra Congregazione del Religiosi. Bibliography: p. 407-435. [BX2380.I5] 63-1449
1. Vocation (in religious orders, congregations, etc.) 2. Catholic Church — Clergy — Appointment, call and election. I. Catholic Church. Congregatio de Religiosis. II. Poage, Godfrey Robert, 1920- ed. and tr. III. Lievin. IV. Title.

KANE, George Louis, 1911- ed. 271
Meeting the vocation crisis. Westminster, Md., Newman Press [1956] 204p. 21cm. [BX2380.K3] 56-7858
1. Vocation (in religious orders, congregations, etc.) I. Title.

KINNANE, John F., 1921- 248.8'9'019
Career development for priests and religious; a framework for research and demonstration [by] John F. Kinnane. Washington, Center for Applied Research in the Apostolate, 1970. vii, 134 p. illus., 5 forms. 23 cm. On cover: CARA information service. Bibliography: p. 109-112. [BX2380.K55] 78-14927
1. Vocation (in religious orders, congregations, etc.) 2. Monastic and religious life—Psychology. I. Center for Applied Research in the Apostolate, Washington, D.C. II. Title.

LECLERCQ, Jacques, 1891- 271
The religious vocation. Translated by the Earl of Wicklow. New York, Kenedy [1955] 184p. 23cm. [BX2380] 54-5656
1. Vocation (in religious orders, congregations, etc.) I. Title.

LESAGE, Germain. 248.8'942
Personalism and vocation. Staten Island, N.Y., Alba House [1966] 252 p. 22 cm. Bibliography: p. [251]-252. [BX2380.L56] 66-19718

1. Vocation (in religious orders, congregation, etc.) I. Title.

NOTRE Dame, Ind. University. 271
Vocation Institute.
Proceedings of the annual convocation. Notre Dame, University of Notre Dame Press. v. 22cm. 'Under the auspices of the Holy Cross Fathers, Notre Dame, Indiana.' [BX2380.N6] 55-2302
1. Vocation (in religious orders, congregations, etc.) I. Title.

POAGE, Godfrey Robert, 271.0692
1920-
Secrets of successful recruiting; the principles of religious vocational guidance and tested techniques of America's most successful religious recruiters. Foreword by Germain Lievin. Westminster, Md., Newman Press, 1961. 219p. 22cm. Includes bibliography. [BX2380.P63] 61-8972
1. Vocation (in religions orders, congregations, etc.) I. Title.

PRIEST and vocations 271.0692
(The). Tr. [from French] by Ronald Halstead. Westminster, Md., Newman, 1962 [c.1961] ix, 181p. 22cm. (Religious life, 11) 62-3808 4.75
1. Vocation (in religious orders, congregations, etc.)

ROSIGNOIL, Carlo Gregorio, 1631-
1707.
Choice of a state of life. By Father C. G. Rossignoli, S. T. Translated from the French ... Baltimore, J. Murphy & co., 1868. xvi, 17-252 p. 16 cm. [BX2380.R682] 38-24318
1. Vocation (in religius orders, congregations, etc.) I. Title.

SCREENING candidates for 271.0692
the priesthood and religious life [by] Magda B. Arnold [and others] Pref. by Vincent V. Herr. Chicago, Loyola University Press [1962] 203p. illus. 24cm. [BX2380.S35] 62-20462

1. Vocation (in religious orders, congregations, etc.) 2. Catholic Church—Clergy—Appointment, call, and election. 3. Mental tests. I. Arnold, Magda B.

SIKORA, Joseph John. 248.8'94
Calling; a reappraisal of religious life [by] Joseph J. Sikora. [New York] Herder and Herder [1968] 206 p. 21 cm. [BX2380.S5] 68-16995

1. Vocation (in religious orders, congregations, etc.) I. Title.

TWEEDY, Henry Hallam, 1868- 250
Christian work as a vocation, by Henry Hallam Tweedy ... Harlan P. Beach ... [and] Judson Jackson McKim ... New York, The Macmillan company, 1922. vi p., 3 l., 3-56, 50, 44 p. 19 1/2 cm. (Half-title: Christian service series, ed. by E. H. Sneath) "Available literature on the Association vocation": p. 44 (at end) [BV660.T9] 22-9651

I. Beach, Harlan Page, 1854-1933, joint author. II. McKim, Judson Jackson, joint author. III. Title.
Contents omitted.

VIGNAT, Louis. 242
'In Thy courts' (La vocation a la vie reliqieuse) translated from the French) of Louis Vignat, S. J. by Mathew L. Fortier, S. J. New York, London [etc.] Longmans, Green, and co., 1907. xiv, 61 p. 15 1/2 cm. [BX2380.V65] 7-19457
1. Vocation (in religious orders, congregations, etc.) I. Fortier, Matthew Louis, 1869- tr II. Title.

Vocation (in religious orders, congregations, etc.)—Meditations.

VOILLAUME, Rene. 248'.894
Follow me : the call to religious life today / Rene Voillaume. Huntington, Ind. : Our Sunday Visitor, c1978. 201 p. ; 21 cm. Translation of Laissez la vos filets. Includes bibliographical references. [BX2380.V713 1978] 78-60437 ISBN 0-87973-692-5 pbk. : 3.95
1. Vocation (in religious orders, congregations, etc.)—Meditations. I. Title.

Vocational guidance

BROTHERS of the Christian 242
schools.

Catechism lessons on vocation, [by] Brothers of the Christian schools; with introduction by the Most Reverend Patrick J. Hayes... New York, La Aalle bureau [c1920] 2 p., l.. 251 p. 16 1/2 cm. [BX2380.B7] 21-1168
I. Title.

WINN, Albert Curry, 1921- 206.9

You and your lifework; a Christian choice for youth, written by Albert Curry Winn in collaboration with the Dept. of the Ministry of the Commission on Higher Education, National Council of the Churches of Christ in the U.S.A. Illustrated by Nita Engle. Chicago. Science Research Associates [1963] 90 p. illus. 28 cm. [BV4740.W5] 63-11011

1. Vocational guidance. 2. Vocation. I. Title.

Vogel, Traugott, 1930-

VOGEL, Traugott, 1930- 248'.246 B
Under the SS shadow / Traugott Vogel with Shirley Stephens. Nashville : Broadman Press, 1977c1976 192 p. : ill. : 21 cm. [BX6495.V6A37] 76-27478 ISBN 0-8054-7216-9 : 6.95

1. Vogel, Traugott, 1930- 2. Baptists—Clergy—Biography. 3. Clergy—United States—Biography. 4. Converts—Germany—Biography. I. Stephens, Shirley, joint author. II. Title.

Voice of Calvary (Organization)

PERKINS, John, 261.8'3'09762
1930-

A quiet revolution : the Christian response to human need, a strategy for today / John Perkins. Waco, Tex. : Word Books, c1976. 226 p. ; 22 cm. Includes bibliographical references. [HN39.U6P47] 76-48541 ISBN 0-87680-793-7 : 4.50

1. Voice of Calvary (Organization) 2. Church and social problems—Mississippi. 3. Church and race problems—Mississippi. 4. Social action. I. Title.

Voltaire, Francois Marie Arouet de. 1694-1778.

GUENEE, Antoine] 1717-1803. 296
Letters of certain Jews to Monsieur Voltaire, Containing an apology for their own people, and for the Old Testament: with critical reflections and a short commentary extracted from a greater. In two volumes. Tr. by the Rev. Philip Lefanu, D. D. Philadelphia, Printed by William Young book-seller, no. 52, Second-street, the corner of Chestnut-street, 1795. 2 v. in 1. 22 cm. Paged continuously. Vol. 2 without t.-p. [BM648.G8 1795] 3-19042
1. Volume, Francois Marie Arouet de, 1694-1778. 2. Jews—Religion. 3. Bible. O. T.—Evidences, authority, etc. 4. Bible—Evidences, authority, etc.—O. T. I. Le Fanu, Phillip, fl. 1790, tr. II. Title.

[GUENEE, Antoine] 1717-1803. 296
Letters of certain Jews to Monsieur Voltaire, containing an apology for their own people, and for the Old Testament. With critical reflections, and a short commentary extracted from a greater; with Christian notes and additions on various parts of the work. Translated by the Rev. Phillip Lefany...2d American ed., with corrections. Paris, Ky., G. G. Moore; Covington, Ky., J. L. Newby, 1845. 2 v. in 1. 23 cm. Paged continously. Vol. 2 without t.-p. [BM648.G8 1845] 40-2726
1. Voltaire, Francois Marie Arouet de. 1694-1778. 2. Jews—Religion 3. Bible. O. T.—Evidences, authority, etc 4. Bible—Evidences, Authority, etc.—O. T. I. Le Fanu, Philip, fl. 1790, tr. II. Title.

[GUENEE, Antoine] 1717-1803. 296
Letters of certain Jews to Monsieur Voltaire, contianing and apology for their own people, and for the Old Testament. With critical reflections, and a short commentary extracted from a greater; with Christian notes and additions on various parts of the work. Translated by the Rev. Philip Lefanu ... 3d American ed., with corections. Philadelphia, H. Hooker; Cincinnati; G. G. Jones, 1848. xii, [13]-612 p. 24 cm. [BM648.G8 1848] 35-4362
1. Voluntaire, Francois Marie Arouet de, 1694-1778. 2. Jews—Religion. 3. Bible, O. T.—Evidences autority etc. 4. Bible—Evidences, authority, etc.—O. T. I. Le Fann, Phillip, fl. 1790. tr. II. Title.

VOLTAIRE, Francois Marie Arouet
de, 1694-1778.
... *Candide;* ou, L'optimisme, edited with introduction, notes, and vocabulary by Lawrence M. Levin ... New York, Prentice-Hall, inc., 1929. vii, 210 p. 19 cm. At head of title: Voltaire. Bibliography: p. 41-42. [PQ2082.C3 1929 a] 30-4022
I. Levin, Lawrence Meyer, 1898- ed. II. Title.

VOLTAIRE, Francois Marie Arouet
de, 1694-1778.
Candide; or, The optimist, by F. A. M. de Voltaire. Translated into English with an introduction by the late Henry Morley, LL.D., and nine full-page pencil-drawings, forty line-drawings, and decorative title-page by Alan Odle. London, G. Routledge and sons, ltd.; New York, E. P. Dutton and co. [1922] xvi, 223, [1] p. front., illus., plates. 26 cm. Added t.-p., illustrated; head and tail pieces. [PQ2082.C3E5 1922] 23-26062
I. Morley, Henry, 1822-1894. II. Title.

VOLTAIRE, Francois Marie Arouet
de, 1694-1778.
Candide [by] Jean Francois Marie Arouet de Voltaire, illustrated by Rockwell Kent. New York, Random house, 1928. 111, [1] p. illus. 29 cm. "Of this first book with imprint of Random house 1470 numbered copies are printed on all rag French paper and 95 coloured in the studio of the artist. Hand set in type designed by Lucian Bernhard, paragraph designs by Rockwell Kent; both cast by the Bauersche giesserei, Frankfort. The composition and press work completed by the Pynson printers in the month of April MCMXXVIII ... New York". Autographed by the artist. [PQ2082.C3E5 1928] 28-15040
I. Kent, Rockwell, 1882- illus. II. Title.

VOLTAIRE, Francois Marie Arouet
de, 1694-1778.
... *Candide,* wood engravings by Howard Simon. New York, I. Washburn, 1929. viii p., 3 l., 3-326 p., 1 l. front., plates. 24 1/2 cm. At head of title: Voltaire. "Of this edition ... one hundred sixty numbered copies ... have been printed on all rag deckle edge paper. The illustrations for these copies have been proved and signed by the artist. There have also been printed on water-marked rag paper, two thousand copies, the illustrations for which have been printed from the original wood engravings." [PQ2082.C3E5 1929] 30-1405
I. Simon, Howard, illus. II. Title.

VOLTAIRE, Francois Marie Arouet
de, 1694-1778.
Candide and other philosophical tales, by Voltaire; edited by Morris Bishop ... New York, Chicago [etc.] C. Scribner's sons [c1929] xviii, 219 p. 17 1/2 cm. (Half-title: The modern student's library. [French series]) Contents.Le monde comme il va.--Candide; ou, L'optimisme.--Histoire d'un bou bramin.--L'ingenu. [PQ2081.A23] 29-22260
I. Bishop, Morris, ed. II. Title.

Voltaire, Francois Marie Arouet de, 1694-1778—Religion and ethics.

SCHWARZBACH, Bertram 221.6
Eugene.
Voltaire's Old Testament criticism. [New York, 1968] vii, 240, 2 l. 28 cm. Thesis—Columbia University. Photocopy of typescript. Bibliography: leaves 232-240. [B2178.R4S35] 68-4929
1. Voltaire, Francois Marie Arouet de, 1694-1778—Religion and ethics. 2. Bible. O.T.—Criticism, interpretation, etc.—History—18th century. I. Title.

Voltaire, Francois Marie Arouetole, 1694-1778—Bibliography.

BARR, Mary Margaret 016.848'5'09
Harrison, 1903-
A century of Voltaire study; a bibliography of writings on Voltaire, 1825-1925, by Mary-Margaret H. Barr. New York, B. Franklin [1973 c1972] xxiii, 123 p. front. 21 cm. (Burt Franklin bibliography & reference series, 462. Philosophy & religious istory monographs, 118) Reprint of the 1929 ed., issued in series: Publications of the Institute of French Studies. [Z8945.B27 1972] 75-170189 ISBN 0-8337-3969-7 10.00 (Lib. bdg.)
1. Voltaire, Francois Marie Arouetole, 1694-1778—Bibliography. I. Title. II. Title: A bibliography of writings on Voltaire, 1825-1925. III. Series: Institut des etudes francaises. Publications.

Volunteers of America.

BOOTH, Ballington, 1859- 248
The prayer that prevails, by General Ballington Booth ... New York, The Volunteers of America [c1920] 6 p. l., [15]-94 p. 19 1/2 cm. [BV220.B55] 20-8602
I. Title.

MCMAHON, John 361.7'06'273
Francis, 1910-
The Volunteers of America [by] John F. McMahon. New York, Newcomen Society in North America, 1972 [c1971] 20 p. illus. 23 cm. ([Newcomen] address, 1971) Delivered at a national meeting of the Newcomen Society held in New York, Sept. 15, 1971. [BX9975.M3] 70-190109
1. Volunteers of America. I. Title. II. Series.

Von Nosaack, Ann, 1947-

VON NOSSACK, Ann, 1947- 286'.73 B
Diary of another Ann / Ann Von Nossack. Washington : Review and Herald Pub. Association, [1979] p. cm. [BX6193.V66A33] 79-15691 pbk. : 3.95
1. Von Nosaack, Ann, 1947- 2. Seventh-Day Adventists—United States—Biography. I. Title.

Vonier, Anscar, 1875-1938.

GRAF, Ernest, 1879- 922.242
Anscar Vonier, abbot of Buckfast, with some account of the restoration of the

Abbey and its church. Westminster. Md., Newman Press [1957] 154p. illus. 22cm. [BX4705.V75G7] 57-11814
1. Vonier, Anscar, 1875-1938. I. Title.

Vonnegut, Kurt—Religion and ethics.

SHORT, Robert L. 230'.09'04
Something to believe in : Is Kurt Vonnegut the exorcist of Jesus Christ Superstar? / Robert Short. New York : Harper & Row, [1978] p. cm. Includes bibliographical references. [BR115.C8S53] 75-36754 ISBN 0-06-067381-8 pbk. : 4.95 ISBN 0-06-067380-X : 8.95
1. Vonnegut, Kurt—Religion and ethics. 2. Blatty, William Peter. The exorcist. 3. Jesus Christ superstar [Motion picture] 4. Theology—20th century. 5. Christianity and culture. 6. United States—Popular culture. I. Title.

Voodooism.

BACH, Marcus, 1906- 133.4
Strange altars. [New York] New Amer. Lib. [1968, c.1952] 176p. 18cm. (Signet, T 3484) [BL2490.B2] .75 pap.,
1. Reser, Stanley. 2. Voodooism. 3. Folk-lore—Haiti. I. Title.

BACH, Marcus, 1906- 133.4
Strange altars. [1st ed.] Indianapolis, Bobbs-Merrill [1952] 254 p. illus. 23 cm. [BL2490.B2] 52-10690
1. Reser, Hanley. 2. Voodooism. 3. Folk-lore—Haiti. I. Title.

HASKINS, James, 1941- 299'.6
Voodoo & hoodoo : their tradition and craft as revealed by actual practitioners / Jim Haskins. New York : Stein and Day, c1978. 226 p. : ill. ; 22 cm. Includes index. Bibliography: p. 219-220. [BL2490.H37] 77-17213 ISBN 0-8128-2431-8 : 8.95
1. Voodooism. I. Title.

MARTINEZ, Raymond Joseph, 1889- 133.4
Mysterious Marie Laveau, voodoo queen, and folk tales along the Mississippi. New Orleans, Harmanson [1956] 96p. illus. 23cm. Includes bibliography. [BL2490.M32] 59-32764
1. Laveau, Marie, 1794-1881. 2. Voodooism. I. Title.

PELTON, Robert W., 1934- 133.4'4
Voodoo charms and talismans, by Robert W. Pelton. New York, Drake Publishers [1973] 220 p. illus. 24 cm. Bibliography: p. 200-209. [BL2490.P37] 73-4346 ISBN 0-87749-492-4 6.95
1. Voodooism. 2. Charms. 3. Amulets. 4. Talismans. I. Title.

PELTON, Robert W., 1934- 133.44
Voodoo charms and talismans, by Robert W. Pelton. New York, Popular Library [1973, i.e.1974] [xii] 220 p. illus. 18 cm. Bibliography: p. 201-209 [BL2490.P37] 1.25 (pbk.)
1. Voodooism. 2. Charms. 3. Amulets. 4. Talismans. I. Title.

RIGAUD, Milo, 1904- 299'.6
Ve-ve : diagrammes rituels du voudou / Milo Rigaud. Trilingual ed; French-English-Spanish. New York : French and European Publications, [1974?] 587 p. : chiefly ill. ; 27 cm. [BL2490.R54] 75-501577 ISBN 0-8288-0000-6 : 24.95
1. Voodooism. 2. Symbolism. I. Title.

TALLANT, Robert, 1909- 133.4
Voodoo in New Orleans. New York, Collier [1962, c.1946] 253p. 18cm. (AS481) Bibl. .95 pap.,
1. Voodooism. I. Title.

TALLANT, Robert, 1909- 133.4
Voodoo in New Orleans, by Robert Tallant ... New York, The Macmillan company, 1946. viii, 247, [1] p. 21 cm. Illustrated lining-papers. "First printing." Bibliography: p. [248] [BL2490.T3] 46-1837
1. Voodooism. I. Title.

Voodooism—Dictionaries.

PELTON, Robert W., 1934- 133.4'7'03
Voodoo secrets from A to Z [by] Robert W. Pelton. South Brunswick, A. S. Barnes [1973] 138 p. illus. 22 cm. Bibliography: p. [127]-138. [BL2490.P38 1973] 72-9063 ISBN 0-498-01161-5
1. Voodooism—Dictionaries. I. Title.

Voodooism—Haiti.

LAGUERRE, Michel S. 299'.67
Voodoo heritage / Michel S. Laguerre ; foreword by Vera Rubin. Beverly Hills, Calif. : Sage Publications, c1980. 231 p. : ill. ; 23 cm. (Sage library of social research ; v. 98) Includes index. Bibliography: p. 219-223. [BL2490.L27] 79-25318 ISBN 0-8039-1402-4 : 18.00 pbk. : 8.95
1. Voodooism—Haiti. I. Title.

METRAUX, Alfred, 1902-1963. 133.4'7
Voodoo in Haiti. Translated by Hugo Charteris. New introd. by Sidney W. Mintz. New York, Schocken Books [1972, c1959] 400 p. illus. 21 cm. Translation of Le vaudou haitien. Bibliography: p. 379-390. [BL2490.M453 1972] 77-185327
1. Voodooism—Haiti. 2. Folk-lore—Haiti. I. Title.

RIGAUD, Milo, 1904- 299'.6
Secrets of voodoo. Translated from the French by Robert B. Cross. Photos. by Odette Mennesson-Riguad [i.e. Rigaud] New York, Arco [1970, c1969] 219 p. illus. 24 cm. Translation of La tradition voudoo et le voudoo haitien. [BL2490.R5313 1970] 77-82128 ISBN 0-668-02008-3 7.95
1. Voodooism—Haiti. 2. Folk-lore—Haiti. I. Title.

Voodooism—Juvenile literature.

CHRISTESEN, Barbara, 1940- 299'.6
The magic and meaning of Voodoo / by Barbara Christesen. New York : Contemporary Perspectives ; Milwaukee, Wis. : Distributor, Raintree Publishers, c1977. 48 p. : some col. ill. ; 24 cm. An outline of voodoo beliefs and practices throughout the world. [BL2490.C45] 77-12781 ISBN 0-8172-1030-X lib. bdg. : 4.95
1. Voodooism—Juvenile literature. 2. [Voodooism.] I. Title.

GILFOND, Henry. 299'.6
Voodoo, its origins and practices / by Henry Gilfond. New York : Watts, 1976. viii, 114 p. : ill. ; 25 cm. Includes index. Bibliography: p. [101]-102. Discusses the history, beliefs, and rituals of voodoo, with emphasis on its practice in Haiti. [BL2490.G54] 76-16046 ISBN 0-531-00347-7 lib.bdg. : 6.88
1. Voodooism—Juvenile literature. 2. [Voodooism.] I. Title.

KRISTOS, Kyle. 299'.6
Voodoo / by Kyle Kristos. 1st ed. Philadelphia : Lippincott, c1976. 112 p. : ill. ; 21 cm. Includes index. Bibliography: p. 108. Traces the origins, cults, and practices which surround voodooism including voodoo practices in the United States and modern Haiti. [BL2490.K72] 76-18989 ISBN 0-397-31706-9 : 6.95 ISBN 0-397-31707-7 pbk. :
1. Voodooism—Juvenile literature. 2. [Voodooism.] I. Title.

Votive offerings.

ROUSE, William Henry Denham, 1863- 292
Greek votive offerings; an essay in the history of Greek religion. By William Henry Denham Rouse ... Cambridge, The University press, 1902. xv, [1], 463 p. illus., 2 pl. 23 cm. "Abbreviations": p. xiii-xv. [BL795.V6R6] 3-385
1. Votive offerings. 2. Greece—Religion. 3. Greece—Antiq. I. Title.

Votive offerings—Greece.

ROUSE, William Henry Denham, 1863-1950. 292'.3'4
Greek votive offerings / William Henry Denham Rouse. New York : Arno Press, 1975. p. cm. (Ancient religion and mythology) Reprint of the 1902 ed. published by the University Press, Cambridge, Eng. [BL795.V6R6 1975] 75-10654 ISBN 0-405-07262-7 : 27.00
1. Votive offerings—Greece. 2. Greece—Religion. 3. Greece—Antiquities. I. Title. II. Series.

Votive offerings—Pennsylvania—Philadelphia.

TESKE, Robert Thomas. 265'.9
Votive offerings among Greek-Philadelphians : a ritual perspective / Robert Thomas Teske. New York : Arno Press, 1980. xxix, 326 p., [11] leaves of plates : ill. ; 24 cm. (Folklore of the world) Originally presented as the author's thesis, University of Pennsylvania, 1974. Includes index. Bibliography: p. ix-xxvi. [BX560.T47 1980] 80-735 ISBN 0-405-13325-1 : 29.00
1. Orthodox Eastern Church—Pennsylvania—Philadelphia. 2. Votive offerings—Pennsylvania—Philadelphia. 3. Philadelphia—Religious life and customs. 4. Greek Americans—Pennsylvania—Philadelphia—Religion. I. Title. II. Series. III. Series: Folklore of the world (New York

Vows.

CARPENTIER, Rene. 248
Life in the City of God; an introduction to the religious life. Translated by John Joyce. A completely recast ed. of A catechism of the vows. New York, Benziger Bros. [1959] 192p. 22cm. Translation of Temoins de la cite de Dieu. [BX2437.C283] 59-9802
1. Vows. 2. Vows (Canon law) I. Title.

COLIN, Louis, 1884- 271
The practice of the vows. Translated by Suzanne Rickman. Chicago, H. Regnery Co., 1955. 276p. 22cm. [BX2435.C62] 55-5993
1. Vows. I. Title.

COTEL, Pierre, 1800-1884. 248
A catechism of the vows, for the use of persons consecrated to God in the religious state. By the Rev. Peter Cotel, a. j. Translated from the last French edition. Baltimore, J. B. Piet, 1893. 123 p. 14 cm. Translated by L. W. Reilly. [BX2437.C8] 33-4962
1. Vows. I. Reilly, Louis William, 1858- tr. II. Title.

COTEL, Pierre, 1800-1884. 248
Catechism of the vows for the use of religious, by Father Peter Cotel, a. j. 28th ed. carefully revised and harmonized with the Code of canon law by Father Emile Jombart, a. j., translated by Father William H. McCabe, a. j. New York, Cincinnati [etc.] Benziger brothers, 1924. 6 p. l., 15-96 p. 16 cm. [BX2437.C6 1924] 271 24-21951
1. Vows. 2. Vows (Canon law) I. Jombart, Emile, 1881- ed. II. McCabe, William Hugh, 1898- tr. III. Title.

COTEL, Pierre, 1800-1884. 248
Catechism of the vows for the use of religious, by Peter Cotel, S.J. Carefully revised and harmonized with the Code of canon law, by Emile Jombart, S.J. 2d ed. New revised translation of the thirtieth French edition (the fourth sice the Code) by William H. McCabe, S.J. New York, Boston [etc.] Benziger brothers, inc., 1945. 1 p. l., v-xv, 17-98 p. 16 cm. [BX2437.C6 1945] (271) 46-21079
1. Vows. 2. Vows (Canon law) I. Jombart, Emile, 1881- ed. II. McCabe, William Hugh, 1893- tr. III. Title.

COTEL, Pierre, 1800-1884. 248
The principles of the religious life: or, An explication of The catechism of the vows. By the Rev. Peter Cotel, S. J. Translated from the French by L. W. Reilly. Baltimore, J. B. Piet, 1894. 1 p. l., [v]-vi p., 1 l., 248 p. 20 cm. [BX2437.C64 1894] 271 33-4903
1. Vows. I. Reilly, Louis William, 1858- tr. II. Title.

COTEL, Pierre, 1800-1884. 248
Principles of the religious life; an explanation of the "Catechism of the vows", by Father Peter Cotel, S. J., carefully revised and adapted to the Code of canon law by Father Emile Jombart, S. J., translated from the 4th French ed. by Father T. Lincoln Bouscaren, S. J. New York, Cincinnati [etc.] Benziger brothers, 1926. 231 p. 19 cm. [BX2437.C64 1926] 27-269
1. Vows. 2. Vows (Canon law) I. Jombart, Emile, 1881- ed. II. Bouscaren, Timothy Lincoln, 1884- tr. III. Title.

[LOUIS, frere] 271
Instructions on vows for the use of the Brothers of the Christian schools; from the French of the first edition (Vatican press) New York, La Salle bureau of supplies, 1904. vii, 152 p. 15 cm. [BX2437.L6] 34-28831
1. Vows. I. Title.

NOTRE Dame, Ind. University. Sisters' Institute of Spirituality. 271.90698
The vows and perfection [by] Bernard I. Mullahy [others, Notre Dame] Univ. of Notre Dame Pr. [c.] 1962 vii, 232 p. (religious life in the modern world; selections from the Notre Dame Inst. of Spirituality, v. 3, NDp15) Articles...previously pub. inthe Proceedings of the Sisters' Inst. of Spirituality, 1953, 1954, and 1955 respectively. Bibl. 62-1570 pap., 1.95
1. Vows. 2. Perfection (Catholic). 3. Monastic and religious life of women. I. Mullahy, Bernard II. Title. III. Series.

THEOLOGICAL Institute for local Superiors University of Notre Dame 271.90698
The vows and perfection [by] Bernard I. Mullahy [and others. Notre Dame] University of Notre Dame Press, 1962. vii, 232 p. 21 cm. (Religious life in the modern world, v. 3) "Articles ... previously published in the Proceedings of the Sisters' Institute of Spirituality 1953, 1954, and 1955 respectively." Bibliographical footnotes. [BX2435.T45] 62-1570
1. Vows. 2. Perfection (Catholic) 3. Monastic and religious life of women. I. Mullahy, Bernard I. II. Notre Dame, Ind. University. III. Title. IV. Series.

Vows (Canon law)

FLINN, Robert J 271.069
Admission to vows; recent directives and trends [by] Robert J. Flinn. Techny, Ill., Divine Word Publications, 1965. xi, 157 p. 24 cm. "Represents somewhat more than two thirds of the author's doctoral dissertation presented to the Pontifical Gregorian University. Bibliography: p. 143-150. 65-16595
1. Vows (Canon law) I. Title.

O'NEILL, Francis Joseph, 1912- 271
... The dismissal of religious in temporary vows; an historical conspectus and commentary, by Rev. Francis Joseph O'Neill ... Washington, D.C., The Catholic university of America press, 1942. xiii, 220 p. 23 cm. (The Catholic university of America. Canon law studies, no. 166) Thesis (J.C.B.)--Catholic university of America, 1942. "Biographical note": p. [211] Bibliography: p. 191-204. [BX2427.O5] A 43
1. Vows (Canon law) 2. Monasticism and religious orders—Discipline. 3. Catholic church. Codex juris canonici. I. Title.

Voyages and travels.

THE Monks of 281'.8'0922 B
Kublai Khan, Emperor of China; or, The history of the life and travels of Rabban Sawma, envoy and plenipotentiary of the Mongol khans to the kings of Europe, and Markos who as Mar Yahbh-Allaha III became Patriarch of the Nestorian Church in Asia. Translated from the Syriac by E. A. Wallis Budge. With 16 plates and 6 illus. in the text. London, Religious Tract Society, 1928. [New York, AMS Press, 1973] xvi, 335 p. illus. 23 cm. Translation of Yish'iata demar Yahbalaha vderaban Sauma. Bibliography: p. [307]-313. [DS752.Y5513 1973] 71-38051 ISBN 0-404-56905-6 20.00
1. Sauma, Rabban, d. 1293? 2. Yabhalaha III, Patriarch of the Nestorians, 1244?-1317. 3. Voyages and travels. 4. Nestorians. I. Budge, Ernest Alfred Thompson Wallis, Sir, 1857-1934, tr.

NORTHRIP, Irene (Spencer) Mrs. 276.69
From Oklahoma City to Ogbomosho, by Irene Northrip. (Edited by Alice Routh) Oklahoma City, Okla., Baptist messenger, 1940. 64 p. incl. front. (ports.) 20 cm. [BV3625.N6N6] 266.61 40-11772
1. Voyages and travels. 2. Missions—Nigeria. I. Routh, Alice, 1909- ed. II. Title.

TYERMAN, Daniel, 1773-1828. 922.
Journal of voyages and travels by the Rev. Daniel Tyerman and Goerge Bennet, esq., deputed from the London missionary society, to visit their various stations in the South sea islands, China, India, &c. between the years 1821 and 1829. Comp. from original documents, by James Montgomery ... From the 1st London ed., rev. by an American editor. Boston, Crocker and Brewster; New York, J. Leavitt, 1832. 3 v. front. (v. 2) plates. 19 1/2 cm. (Half-title: Library of religious knowledge. I-III) Preface signed by R. A. "This first part was written in conjunction with G. Bennet, but the latter part was entirely his own. It affords a graphic picture of the state of the London society missions at the period."--Dict. nat. Biog. [BV3705.T8A3 1832] 1-24418
1. Voyages and travels. 2. Missions. I. Bennet, George, joint author. II. Montgomery, James, 1771-1854, ed. III. London missionary society. IV. Title.

Voyages around the world.

DODD, Monroe Elmon, 1878- 266.61
Girdling the globe for God; a travelogue, by M. E. Dodd ... Shreveport, La., J. S. Ramond [c1935] 184 p. front., plates. ports. 21 cm. [BV2064.D6] 35-9195
1. Voyages around the world. 2. Baptist—Missions. 3. Missions Foreign. I. Title.

Vserossilskaia evangelskaia palatochnaia missiia.

SALOF-ASTAKHOFF, Nikita Ignatievich, 1893- 274.7
Interesting facts of the Russian revolution; or, In the flame of Russia's revolution with God and the Bible, by Rev. N. I. Saloff-Astakhoff. New York, 1931. 304 p. plates, ports. 20 cm. [BV3777.R8S3] [266] 33-6051
1. Vserossilskaia evangelskaia palatochnaia missiia. 2. Dik, Iakov Iakovlevich, 1891-1919. 3. Missions—Russia. 4. Evangelistic work. 5. Russia—Religion. 6. Russia—Hist.—Revolution, 1917—Personal narratives. I. Title. II. Title: In the flame of Russia's revolution with God and the Bible.

Vsesoiuznyl sevet evangel'skikh khristian.

PROKHANOV, Ivan Stepanovich, 1869- 922.447
In the cauldron of Russia, 1869-1933; autobiography of I. S. Prokhanoff ... The life of an optimist in the land of pessimism, together with an interesting history of the Russian evangelical Christian union. New York, All-Russian evangelical Christian union, 1933. 270 p. front., plates, ports. 21 cm. [BX4849.P7] 34-29349
1. Vsesoiuznyl sevet evangel'skikh khristian. 2. Missions—Russia. 3. Evangelistic work. 4. Russia—Religion. I. Title.

Waccamaw, States C. All Saint's Church.

BULL, Henry De Saussure. 283.757
All Saint's Church, Waccamaw; the parish, the place, the people, 1739-1948. Columbia, S. C., Printed by R. L. Bryan Co., 1949. 107 p. plates. ports., fold. map 24 cm. [BX5980.W2A5] 50-12531
1. Waccamaw, S. C. All Saint's Church. I. Title.

Wach, Joachim, 1898-1955—Bibliography.

WACH, Joachim, 1898-1955. 291'.08
Understanding and believing : essays / by Joachim Wach ; edited with an introd. by Joseph M. Kitagawa. Westport, Conn. : Greenwood Press, 1975, c1968. p. cm. Reprint of the 1st ed. published by Harper & Row, New York, which was issued as no. TB1399 of the Harper torchbooks. "Bibliography of Joachim Wach (1922-55)": p. [BL27.W26 1975] 75-31987 ISBN 0-8371-8488-6 : 12.75
1. Wach, Joachim, 1898-1955—Bibliography. 2. Religion—Addresses, essays, lectures. I. Title.
Contents omitted.

WACH, Joachim, 1898-1955. 291'.08
Understanding and believing; essays. Edited with an introd. by Joseph M. Kitagawa. [1st ed.] New York, Harper & Row [1968] xviii, 204 p. 21 cm. (Harper torchbooks, TB1399) Contents.Contents.—The self-understanding of modern man.—Stefan George; poet and priest of modern paganism.—The problem of death in modern philosophy.—General revelation and the religions of the world.—The paradox of the gospel.—Redeemer of man.—Seeing and believing.—Belief and witness.—The meaning and task of the history of religions.—Religious commitment and tolerance.—The problem of truth in religion.—The Christian professor.—The crisis in the university.—Hugo of St. Victor on virtues and vices.—To a rabbi friend.—On felicity.—A prayer.—Bibliography of Joachim Wach, 1922-55 (p. 188-196) Bibliographical footnotes. [BL27.W26] 68-29897 2.95
1. Wach, Joachim, 1898-1955—Bibliography. 2. Religion—Addresses, essays, lectures. I. Title.

Waco, Tex. First Baptist church.

BURKHALTER, Frank Elisha, 1880- 286.1764
A world-visioned church; story of the First Baptist church, Waco, Texas [by] Frank E. Burkhalter ... Nashville, Tenn., Broadman press [1946] x, 301 p. plates, ports, 20 cm. Bibliographical references included in the preface. [BX6480.W25F5] 46-5091
1. Waco, Tex. First Baptist church. I. Title.

Waco, Tex. First Presbyterian church.

CALDWELL, Charles Turner, 1865- 285.1764
Historical sketch of the First Presbyterian church, Waco, Texas; written and compiled by Dr. C. T. Caldwell, pastor ... [Waco, Tex., Methodist home press, 1937] 115 p. illus. (incl. ports.) 21 cm. [BX9211.W27F5] 39-8046
1. Waco, Tex. First Presbyterian church. I. Title.

Wadhams, Edgar Prindle, bp., 1817-1891.

WALWORTH, Clarence Augustus, 1820-1900. 922.
Reminiscences of Edgar P. Wadhams, first biship of Ogdensburg. By Rev. C. A. Walworth ... With a preface by Right Rev. H. Gabriels ... New York, Cincinnati [etc.] Benziger brothers, 1893. 197 p. front., plates, ports. 19 1/2 cm. [BX4705.W25W3 1893] 36-36771
1. Wadhams, Edgar Prindle, bp., 1817-1891. 2. Converts, Catholic. I. Title.

WALWORTH, Clarence Augustus, 1820-1900. 922.
Reminiscences of Edgar P. Wadhams, first bishop of Ogdensburg. By Rev. C. A. Walworth ... With a preface by Right Rev. H. Gabriels ... 2d ed. New York, Cincinnati [etc.] Benziger brothers [c1893] 197 p. front., plates, ports. 19 1/2 cm. [BX4705.W25W3 1893a] CA 12
1. Wadhams, Edgar Prindle, bp.,1817-1891. 2. Converts, Catholic. I. Title.

Wagner inn, Poughkeepsie, N.Y.

WAGNER, Mary Swain. 247.
The inner life of an inn; being a true story of an inn near Vassar college, by Mary Swain Wagner; sketches by M.S. W. ... Poughkeepsie, N.Y., A. V. Haight co., 1919. 106 p. illus., plates. 21 1/2 cm. Illustrated lining-papers. [TX941.W3W2] 19-16642
1. Wagner inn, Poughkeepsie, N.Y. 2. Vassar college. I. Title.

Wagner, Richard, 1813-1883.

NIETZSCHE, Friedrich Wilhelm, 1844-1900.
The works of Friedrich Nietzsche ... New York, London, The Macmillan company, 18 v. 20 cm. "Vol. and x issued under the editorship of Alexander Tille; vol. xi under the supervision of the Nietzsche archiv at Naumburg." [B3312.E5T6] ca 11
1. Wagner, Richard, 1813-1883. I. Tille, Alexander, 1866-1912, ed. II. Hausemann, William A., tr. III. Gray, John, tr. IV. Common, Thomas, tr. V. Title.

Wahhabiyah—Africa, French-speaking West.

KABA, Lansine. 297'.8
The Wahhabiyya; Islamic reform and politics in French West Africa. Evanston, Ill., Northwestern University Press, 1974. xv, 285 p. map. 24 cm. (Studies in African religion) Bibliography: p. 271-285. [BP64.A4W357] 73-85874 ISBN 0-8101-0427-X 13.50
1. Wahhabiyah—Africa, French-speaking West. I. Title. II. Series.

Waikouaiti, N.Z. St. Anne's Church.

WAIKOUAITI, N.Z. St. Anne's Church. Centennial Committee. 266.2'931'57
The story of a church, its priests and its people; St. Anne's Church, Waikouaiti, 1868-1968. [Dunedin, Printed by Tablet Print, 1968] 28 p. illus. 18 x 25 cm. Cover title. [BX4644.W3S28] 78-865088
1. Waikouaiti, N.Z. St. Anne's Church. I. Title.

Wainright, Lincoln Stanhope, 1847-1929.

MENZIES, Lucy. 922.342
Father Wainright, a record. With a foreword by A. F. Winnington Ingram. London, New York, Longmans, Green [1947] xx, 124 p. ports. 19 cm. [BX5199.W2M4] 48-4709
1. Wainright, Lincoln Stanhope, 1847-1929. I. Title.

Wainwright, Jonathan Mayhew, bp., 1792-1854.

NORTON, John Nicholas, 1820-1881. 922.373
Life of Bishop Wainwright. By John N. Norton ... New York, General Protestant Episcopal Sunday school union and church book society, 1858. xii, [13]-184 p. front. (port.) pl. 15 cm. [BX5995.W3N6] 38-10405
1. Wainwright, Jonathan Mayhew, bp., 1792-1854. I. General Protestant Episcopal Sunday school union and church book society. II. Title.

Wake Baptist Association.

HISTORY of the Wake Baptist Association, its auxiliaries and churches, 1866-1966. 286'.1756'54 Raleigh, N.C. : [C. R. Trotter], c1976. [118] p. : ill. ; 29 cm. Written by C. R. Trotter and others. Includes bibliographical references. [BX6444.N8H57] 76-17376
1. Wake Baptist Association. I. Trotter, Claude Russell.

Wake, William, of Canterbury, Abp. 1657-1737.

SYKES, Norman, 1897- 922.342
William Wake, Archbishop of Canterbury, 1657-1737. Cambridge [Eng.] University Press, 1957. 2 v. port., facsims. 24 cm. Bibliography: v. 2, p. 272-278. [BX5199.W216S9] 58-1230
1. Wake, William, of Canterbury, Abp. 1657-1737. I. Title.

Wakefield Cathedral.

SPEAK, Harold. 914.28'15
For all the saints! : an outline history and guide [to] the Cathedral Church of All Saints, Wakefield / by Harold Speak and Jean Forrester. Ossett : The authors, 1976. 48 p. : ill., plans, ports. ; 21 cm. [BX5195.W27A42] 77-357778 ISBN 0-902829-05-X : £0.45
1. Wakefield Cathedral. I. Forrester, Jean F., joint author. II. Title.

Walchars, John.

WALCHARS, John. 242
Voices on fire : a book of meditations / John Walchars. New York : Crossroad, c1981. p. cm. [BX2182.2.W334] 19 81-7767 ISBN 0-8245-0094-6 pbk. : 7.95
1. Walchars, John. 2. Meditations. I. Title.

Walden, John Morgan, bp., 1831-1914.

MOORE, David Hastings, bp., 1838-
John Morgan Walden, thirty-fifth bishop of the Methodist Episcopal church, by his colleague Bishop David H. Moore, from original sources. New York, Cincinnati, The Methodist book concern [c1915] 215 p. front., plates (1 col.) ports. 20 cm. 15-18629 1.00
1. Walden, John Morgan, bp., 1831-1914. I. Title.

Waldenses.

COMBA, Emilio, 1839-1904. 284'.4
History of the Waldenses of Italy, from their origin to the Reformation / by Emilio Comba ; translated from the author's rev. ed. by Teofilo E. Comba. New York : AMS Press, 1978. viii, 357 p. ; 23 cm. Translation of Histoire des Vaudois. Reprint of the 1889 ed. published by Truslove & Shirley, London. Includes bibliographical references. [BX4881.C713 1978] 77-84713 ISBN 0-404-16119-7 : 28.50
1. Waldenses. I. Title.

MORLAND, Samuel bart., Sir 1625-1695. 284.4
The history of the Evangelical churches of the valleys of Piemont; containing a most exact geographical description of the place, and a faithfull account of the doctrine, life and persecutions of the ancient inhabitants. Together with a most naked and punctual relation of the late bloudy massacre, 1655, and a narrative of all the following transactions to the year of Our Lord, 1658. London, Printed by H. Hills for A. Byfield, 1658. [Fort Smith? Ark., 1955] [1]p., reprint: [68], 709p. illus., port., fold. map. 24cm. [BX4880.M8 1658a] 59-18661
1. Waldenses. 2. Pledmont—Hist. I. Title. II. Title: The Evangelical churches of the valleys of Plemont.

PERRIN, Jean Paul. 284.4
History of the old Waldenses, anterior to the Reformation. By Jean Paul Perrin. With illustrative notes, from modern historians and theologians. New York, Mason & co., 1843. xviii, [2], [21]-84 p. 24 cm. (On cover: History of the ancient Christians inhabiting the valleys of the Alps. pt. 1) "Catalogue of the authors cited": p. [xix-xx] [BX4881.P45] 33-37502
1. Waldenses. I. Title.

ROBINSON, Virgil E. 284'.4
Brave men to the battle; the story of the Waldenses, by Virgil E. Robinson. Cover and illus. by James Converse. Mountain View, Calif., Pacific Press Publishing Association [1967] 116 p. illus. 22 cm. (Panda book P-105) [BX4881.2.R6] 66-29350
1. Waldenses. I. Title.

SKETCHES of the Waldenses 284.4
... London, The Religious tract society; Philadelphia, American Sunday-school union [1846] vi, [7]-192 p. 15 1/2 cm. [BX4881.S6] 38-13594
1. Waldenses. I. Religious tract society, London. II. American Sunday-school union.

SMITH, Madison Monroe.
An epitome of the doctrines and practice of the old Waldenses and Albigenses. By Rev. M. M. Smith ... Nashville, Tenn., Provine & Halsell, 1866. 61 p. 22 1/2 cm. [BX1875.S55] 44-51868
1. Waldenses. 2. Albigenses. I. Title.

UTT, Walter C. 284'.4
*Home to our valleys! : True story of the incredible Glorious Return of the Waldenses to their native land / by Walter C. Utt. Mountain View, Calif. : Pacific Press Pub. Association, c1977. 160 p. : map ; 22 cm. (A Destiny book ; D-161) [BX4881.2.U87] 75-30138 pbk. : 3.50
1. Waldenses. I. Title.

WYLIE, James Aitken, 1808-1890. 284.
History of the Waldenses. By the Rev. J. A. Wylie ... 4th ed. London, New York [etc.] Cassell & company, limited [188-] xp.,119, 212 p. front. (fold. map) illus. 19cm A reprint of the 16th book of the author's "History of Protestantism". [BX4881.W9] 10-27519
1. Waldenses. I. Title.

Waldenses—History.

MONASTIER, Antoine. 284'.4
A history of the Vaudois church from its origin. New York : AMS Press, [1980] p. cm. Translation of Histoire de l'eglise vaudoise. Reprint of the 1849 ed. published by Lane & Scott, New York. Includes bibliographical references. [BX4881.M5513 1980] 19 80-24096 ISBN 0-404-16554-0 : 32.00
1. Walderness—History. 2. Persecution. I. Title. II. Title: Vaudois church.

MUSTON, Alexis. 284'.4
*The Israel of the Alps : a complete history of the Waldenses and their colonies : prepared in great part from unpublished documents / by Alexis Muston ; translated by John Montgomery, with a documentary appendix on the origin of the Waldenses, by the translator. 1st AMS ed. New York : AMS Press, 1978. 2 v. : ill. ; 23 cm. Translation of L'Israel des Alpes. Reprint of the 1875 ed. published by Blackie, London. Bibliography: v. 2, p. [397]-489. [BX4881.M8513 1978] 77-84718 ISBN 0-404-16140-5 : 75.00
1. Waldenses—History. I. Title.

Waldenses—History—Sources.

MELIA, Pius, 1800-1883. 284'.4
The origin, persecutions, and doctrines of the Waldenses / from documents, many now the first time collected and edited by Pius Melia. New York : AMS Press, 1978. xvi, 138 p. : ill. ; 24 cm. Reprint of the 1870 ed. published by J. Toovey, London. Includes index. [BX4881.M36 1978] 77-84716 ISBN 0-404-16122-7 : 19.00
1. Waldenses—History—Sources. I. Title.

Waldenses in the United States

WATTS, George Byron, 1890- 284.473
The Waldenses in the new world, [by] George B. Watts. Durham, N.C., Duke university press, 1941. xi, 309 p. plates, 2 port. (incl. front.) map. facsim. 23 1/2 cm. (Half-title: Duke university publications) Bibliography: p. [261]-278. [BX4881.5.U5W3] 42-17047
1. Waldenses in the U.S. 2. Waldenses in South America. I. Title.

WHITTIER, Isabel Mary Skolfield. 284'.4
The Waldensians. [Brunswick? Me., 1957] unpaged. illus. 23 cm. [BX4881.5.U5W5] 61-40200
1. Waldenses in the U.S. 2. Waldenses in Italy. I. Title.

Waldenses—Juvenile literature.

MANISCALCO, Joseph 284
The Waldenses. Text, illus. by Joe Maniscalco. Nashville Southern Pub. Assn. [c.1966] 1 v. (unpaged) illus. 25cm. [BX4881.2.M3] 66-4839 2.50
1. Waldenses—Juvenile literature. I. Title.

Wales—Church history.

BOWEN, Emrys George, 1900- 274.29
The settlements of the Celtic Saints in Wales. [2d ed.] Cardiff, Univ. of Wales Pr. [Mystic, Conn., Verry, 1966] xi, 175p. illus., maps. 22cm. First and 2d eds. Orig. pub. 1954 and 1956. Bibl. [BR774.B68] 3.50 bds.,
1. Wales—Church history. 2. Celtic Church. 3. Wales—Historical geography. I. Title.

A history of the Church in Wales / edited by David Walker ; foreword by the Archbishop of Wales. 274.29
Penarth : Church in Wales Publications for the Historical Society of the Church in Wales, 1976. xv, 221 p., 8 p. of plates : ill., facsim., ports. ; 23 cm. Includes index. Bibliography: p. [191]-200. [BR772.H57] 77-364750 ISBN 0-85326-010-9 : £1.75. ISBN 0-85326-011-7 pbk.
1. Wales—Church history. I. Walker, David, 1923-

WILLIAMS, Glanmor 274.29
The Welsh church from Conquest to Reformation. Cardiff, Univ. of Wales Pr. [Mystic, Conn., Verry, 1965] 602p. illus. 23cm. Bibl. [BR774.W58] 12.50
1. Wales—Church history. I. Title.

WILLIAMS, Glanmor 274.29
The Welsh church from Conquest to Reformation. Cardiff, Univ. of Wales Pr. [dist. Chester Springs, Pa., Dufour, 1963] 602p. tables (pt. fold.) 23cm. Bibl. 63-3625 12.50
1. Wales—Church history. I. Title.

WILLIAMS, Glanmor. 274.29
The Welsh church from Conquest to Reformation / by Glanmor Williams. Revised ed. Cardiff : University of Wales Press, 1976. xiv, 612 p., fold. leaf ; 23 cm. Includes index. Bibliography: p. [569]-591. [BR774.W58 1976] 77-357648 ISBN 0-7083-0084-7 : £12.00
1. Wales—Church history. I. Title.

Wales, South—Church history.

DAVIES, Ebenezer Thomas 274.29
Religion in the industrial revolution in South Wales Cardiff, Univ. of Wales Pr. [dist. Mystic, Conn., Verry, 1965] viii, 202p. 23cm. (Pantyfedwen lects., 1962) Bibl. [BR776.D3] 65-8766 4.50
1. Wales, South—Church history. I. Title. II. Series.

Walker, Charles L., 1832-1904.

WALKER, Charles L., 1832-1904. 289.3'3 B
The diary of Charles L. Walker / edited by A. Karl Larson and Katharine Miles Larson. Logan, Utah : Utah State University Press, 1980. p. cm. Includes bibliographical references and index. [BX8695.W3A32] 19 80-21200 ISBN 0-87421-106-9 (set) : 30.00
1. Walker, Charles L., 1832-1904. 2. Mormons and Mormonism in the United States—Biography. I. Larson, Andrew Karl. II. Larson, Katharine Miles. III. Title.

Walker, Charles Thomas, 1858-1921.

FLOYD, Silas Xavier, 1869- 286'.133'0924 B
Life of Charles T. Walker ... With an introd. by Robert Stuart MacArthur. New York, Negro Universities Press [1969] 193 p. illus., ports. 23 cm. Reprint of the 1902 ed. [BX6455.W3F5 1969] 70-97423
1. Walker, Charles Thomas, 1858-1921. I. Title.

FLOYD, Silas Xavier, 1869- 922.
Life of Charles T. Walker, D.D., ("The Black Spurgeon".) pastor Mt. Olivet Baptist church, New York city. By Silas Xavier Floyd, A.M. With an introduction by Robert Stuart MacArthur, D.D. Nashville, Tenn., National Baptist publishing board, 1902. 198 p. illus. (incl. ports.) 19 1/2 cm. [BX6455.W3F5] 22-6806
1. Walker, Charles Thomas, 1856- I. Title.

Walker, Dick, 1917-

WALKER, Dick, 1917- 133.9'092'4
Do not test us : one man's ventures into the psychic world / by Dick Walker. 1st ed. Portland, Or. : Binford & Mort, 1978. viii, 191 p. ; 22 cm. Bibliography: p. 189-190. [BF1031.W32] 78-57020 ISBN 0-8323-0307-0 pbk. : 4.95
1. Walker, Dick, 1917- 2. Psychical research. 3. Psychical research—Biography. I. Title.

Walker, Elkanah.

*DRURY, Clifford M. 266'.009'24
Nine years with the Spokane indians: the diary, 1838-1848, of Elkanah Walker/ by Clifford M. Drury. Glendale, Calif.: Arthur H. Clark, 1976. 547 p.: ill. (part col.), ports. (part col.); 24 cm. (Northwest historical series; XIII) Includes index. Bibliography: p. [329] [E98.M6] 75-39378 ISBN 0-87062-117-3: 26.50
1. Walker, Elkanah. 2. Indians of North America—Missions. I. Title.

Walker, George Washington, 1804-1856.

GADDIS, Maxwell Pierson, 1811-1888. 922
Brief recollections of the late Rev. George W. Walker, by Rev. Maxwell Pierson Gaddis ... With an introduction. by Rev. Charles. Elliot ... Cincinnati, Published by Swormstedt & Poe for the author, 1857. 538 p. front. (port.) 19 cm. [BX8495.W24G3] 37-7007
1. Walker, George Washington, 1804-1856. I. Title.

Walker, Guy Morrison, 1870-The things that are Caesar's.

O'CONNOR, John. 270
"Listening in" on God's radio! Being a reply to The things that are Caesar's! By J. O'Connor ... Included in this work are miscellaneous writings by the author. [Newark, N. J.] c1923. 83 p. 23 cm. [BR125.O2] ca 24
1. Walker, Guy Morrison, 1870-The things that are Caesar's. I. Title.

Walker, Jesse, 1766-1835.

PENNEWELL, Almer. 922.773
A voice in the wilderness; Jesse Walker, 'the Daniel Boone of Methodism.' Niles, Ill. [195-?] 192p. 23cm. Includes bibliography. [BX8495.W242P4] 60-45684
1. Walker, Jesse, 1766-1835. I. Title.

A voice in the wilderness.
Jesse Walker 'The Daniel Boone of Methodism. Nashville, Tenn., Parthenon Press [1958?] 192p. facsim. 23cm. Bibliography: p. 191-192.
1. Walker, Jesse, 1766-1835. 2. Methodist Episcopal Church. I. Pennewell, Almer.

Walker, John, 1674-1747.

TATHAM, Geoffrey Bulmer.
Dr. John Walker and the Sufferings of the clergy, by G. B. Tatham ... Cambridge [Eng.] University press, 1911. vii, [1], 429 p. 19 cm. (Half-title: Cambridge historical essays. No. XX) The Prince Consort prize, 1910. [BX5075.W23T3] 11-23786
1. Walker, John, 1674?-1747. An attempt towards recovering an account of the numbers and sufferings of the clergy. 2. Church of England—Hist. I. Oxford. University. Bodleian library. Mss. (Walker collection) II. Title.
Contents omitted.

Walker, Karen, 1949-1970.

WALKER, Jeanne, 1924- 133.9'013'0924 B
Always, Karen / by Jeanne Walker ; foreword by George Daisley. New York : Hawthorn Books, [1975] 137 p., [4] leaves of plates : ill. ; 22 cm. Bibliography: p. 137. [BF1301.W14 1975] 74-20288 ISBN 0-8015-2840-2 : 6.95
1. Walker, Karen, 1949-1970. 2. Spirit writings. I. Walker, Karen, 1949-1970. II. Title.

Walker, Maggie Lena.

[DABNEY, Wendell Phillips] 1865- 920.
Maggie L. Walker and the I. O. of Saint Luke; the woman and her work. Cincinnati, O., The Dabney publishing co. [1927] 137 p. front., plates, ports. 19 1/2 cm. [E185.97.W13D3] 44-50462
1. Walker, Maggie Lena. 2. Independent order of Saint Luke. I. Title.

Walker, Mary (Richardson) 1811-1897.

MCKEE, Ruth (Karr) 1874- 922.573
... Mary Richardson Walker: her book, by Ruth Karr McKee ... Caldwell, Id., The Caxton printers, ltd., 1945. 357 p. front., plates, ports., map, facsim. 23 1/2 cm. At head of title: The third white woman to cross the Rockies. [Full name: Charlotte Ruth (Karr) McKee] [F880.W25M3] 46-25010
1. Walker, Mary (Richardson) 1811-1897. 2. Missions—Oregon. I. Title.

Walker, Rollin Hough, 1865-1955.

QUIMBY, Chester Warren, 1891- 287.1'0924
Sojourner in two worlds; a memoir of Dr. Rollin Hough Walker, professor of English Bible at Ohio Wesleyan University, 1900-1936. Assembled, arranged, and edited by Chester Warren Quimby. [Long Beach? Miss.] 1967. 55 p. 28 cm. [BX8495.W2426Q5] 74-5874
1. Walker, Rollin Hough, 1865-1955. I. Title.

WALKER, Rollin Hough, 1865- 232.
Jesus and our pressing problems, by Rollin H. Walker. New York, Cincinnati [etc.] The Abingdon press [c1929] 208 p. 19 1/2 cm. [BS2415.W25] 29-28339
I. Title.

Walkertown, N.C. Love's Methodist Church.

TISE, Larry E. 287'.8756'67
A house not made with hands: Love's Methodist Church, 1791-1966, by Larry E. Tise. [Greensboro, N.C.] Piedmont Press, 1966. x, 116 p. illus., ports. 24 cm. Bibliography: p. 107-111. [BX8481.W25L68] 74-15907
1. Walkertown, N.C. Love's Methodist Church. I. Title.

Wall hangings, Hindu—Rajasthan, India.

SKELTON, Robert. 746'.3'954'4
Rajasthani temple hangings of the Krishna cult from the Collection of Karl Mann, New York. Author and guest director: Robert Skelton. An exhibition organized by the American Federation of Arts. [New York, American Federation of Arts, 1973] 112 p. illus. (part col.) 26 cm. Bibliography: p. 109-110. [NK1677.S55] 72-87726 6.00
1. Mann, Karl—Art collections. 2. Wall hangings, Hindu—Rajasthan, India. 3. Wall hangings, Hindu—New York (City) 4. Wall hangings—New York (City)—Catalogs. I. American Federation of Arts. II. Title.

Wall Street journal.

CALIAN, Carnegie Samuel. 248'.9'5
The gospel according to the Wall Street journal / Carnegie Samuel Calian. Atlanta : John Knox Press, [1975] 114 p. ; 21 cm. Includes bibliographical references. [PN4899.N42W24] 74-19971 ISBN 0-8042-0826-3 pbk : 3.95
1. Wall Street journal. 2. Christianity and economics. 3. Christian life—1960- I. Title.

Wallace, Cyrus Washington, 1805-1889.

MANCHESTER, N.H. First Congregational church. 922.573
Quarter-centennial pastorate of Rev. Cyrus W. Wallace, over the First Congregational church and society, in Manchester, N.H. [Manchester?] The Society, 1865. 56 p. 21 1/2 cm. "Discourse" by C. W. Wallace: p. [5]-26. [BX7260.W35M3] 36-21112
1. Wallace, Cyrus Washington, 1805-1889. 2. Installation (Clergy)—Anniversary sermons. I. Title.

Wallace, Robert H., 1796-

NIVEN, Archibald Campbell, 1803-1882, ed. 285.
The centennial memorial, a record of the proceedings on the occasion of the celebration of the one hundredth anniversary of the A. R. Presbyterian church, of Little Britain, N. Y. Also, of the completion of one-third of a century of the pastoral relation to this church of Rev. Robert H. Wallace ... Together with a sketch of the Clinton family, biographical notes, etc. Edited by Archibald C. Niven. New York, R. Carter & brothers, 1859. x, [xiii]-xxii, [2], 39-251 p. front. (port.) 19 cm. [BX9211.L5A8] 4-23400
1. Wallace, Robert H., 1796- 2. Clinton family. 3. Little Britain, N. Y. Associate Reformed Presbyterian church, I. Title.

Wallace, Wendell.

WALLACE, Wendell. 269'.2'0924 B
Born to burn, by Wendell Wallace with Pat King. [Special Charisma ed.] Watchung, N.J., Charisma Books [1972, c1970] 103 p. ports. 18 cm. [BR1725.W29A32 1972] 77-131116 0.95
1. Wallace, Wendell. I. King, Pat, joint author. II. Title.

Wallace, William, 1828-1915.

[WALLACE, M. S.] Mrs. 922.
Memories of William Wallace, D.D., LITT.D., Univ. Dubl., first vicar of St. Luke's, Stepney, by his wife; some problems of East London; with a preface by the Bishop of London... London, New York [etc.] Longmans, Green and co., 1919. xiv, 246 p. front., illus., plates, ports. 19 1/2 cm. [BX5199.W25W3] 19-5357
1. Wallace, William, 1828-1915. I. Title.

Wallace, William L., 1908-1951.

FLETCHER, Jesse C. 922.673
Bill Wallace of China. Nashville, Tenn., Broadman [1967, c.1963] 157p. 18cm. [BV3427.W3F5] 63-17522 1.25 pap.,
1. Wallace, William L., 1908-1951. I. Title.

Walls (in religion, folk-lore, etc.)

BACHOFEN, Johann Jakob, 1815-1887 291.35
Walls: Res sanctae, res sacrae; a passage from 'Versuch ueber die Graebersymbolik der Alten.' Tr. by B. Q. Morgan. Note on J. J. Bachofen by Lewis Mumford. Lexington, Ky., 220 Market St., Stamperia del Santuccio, 1962[c.]1961. [7]p. 29cm. (Stamperia del Santuccio. Broadside 3) 61-42168 7.00
1. Walls (in religion, folk-lore, etc.) I. Morgan, Bayard Quincy, 1883- tr. II. Title. III. Series.

Walls in the Bible.

GRAHAM, Jonathan. 220.872596
The office of a wall. Foreword by the Archbishop of Canterbury. London, Faith Press; New York, Morehouse-Barlow Co. [1966] 93 p. 19 cm. (The Archbishop of Canterbury's Lent book [1966]) [BS680.W17G7] 66-2271
1. Walls in the Bible. I. Title. II. Series.

Wallsend. St. Andrew's Presbyterian Church.

WALLSEND. St. Andrew's Presbyterian Church. 285'.294'4
St. Andrew's Presbyterian Church Wallsend centenary. [Newcastle, N.S.W., 1967] [14] p. illus. 27 cm. Cover title. [BX9215.W3S28] 75-488897
1. Wallsend. St. Andrew's Presbyterian Church.

Walmsley, John, bp. of Sierra Leone, 1867-1922.

WALMSLEY, Edgar Gwillym. 922.
John Walmsley, ninth bishop of Sierra Leone a memoir for his friends, London, Society for promoting Christian knowledge; New York and Toronto, The Macmillan co., 1923. 159 p. front. (port.) 20 1/2 cm. [BX5700.W3W3] 25-4431
1. Walmsley, John, bp. of Sierra Leone, 1867-1922. I. Title.

Walnut Hill Presbyterian Church, Fayette Co., Ky.

SANDERS, Robert Stuart. 285.1769
History of Walnut Hill Presbyterian Church, Fayette County, Kentucky. Introd. by J. Winston Coleman. Frankfort, Kentucky Historical Society, 1956. 88p. illus. 23cm. [BX9211.W28S3] 57-17932
1. Walnut Hill Presbyterian Church, Fayette Co., Ky. I. Title.

Walsh, Chad, 1914- The rough years.

DELL, Edward Thomas.
A leader's guide for use with The rough years by Chad Walsh. Prepared by Edward T. Dell, Jr. New York, Morehouse-Barlow Co. [1962, c1960] 133 p. 21 cm. "M-B." Includes bibliographies. 66-23011
1. Walsh, Chad, 1914- The rought years. 2. Religious education — Textbooks. I. Title.

Walsh, Edmund Aloyslus, 1885-1956.

GALLAGHER, Louis Joseph, 1885- 922.273
Edmund A. Walsh, S. J. a biography. New York, Benziger Bros. [1962]) 250 p. illus. 21 cm. [BX4705.W256G3] 63-2063
1. Walsh, Edmund Aloyslus, 1885-1956. I. Title.

Walsh, Gerald Groveland, 1892-1952, tr.

AUGUSTINUS, Aurelius, Saint, Bp. of Hippo. 239.3
The city of God, books VII-XVI. Translated by Gerald G. Walsh and Grace Monahan Washington, Catholic University of America Press [1963, c1952] 567 p. 22 cm. (Writings of Saint Augustine, v. 7) The Fathers of the church, a new translation, v. 14. [[BR65.A]] 83-19613
1. Walsh, Gerald Groveland, 1892-1952, tr. I. Monahan, Grace, tr. II. Title. III. Series: The Fathers of the church, a new translation, v. 14

Walsh, James Anthony, 1867-1936.

SARGENT, Daniel, 1890- 922.273
All the day long, by Daniel Sargent. James Anthony Walsh, cofounder of Maryknoll. New York, Toronto, Longmans, Green & company [c1941] x p., 2 l., 3-259 p. front., plates, ports. 23 1/2 cm. Bibliography: p. 257-259. [BX4705.W257S3] 41-26029
1. Walsh, James Anthony, 1867-1936. I. Title.

Walsh, James Edward, Bp., 1891-

KERRISON, Raymond 922.273
Bishop Walsh of Maryknoll, a biography. New York, Putnam [c.1962] 314p. 61-12733 4.95 bds.,
1. Walsh, James Edward, Bp., 1891- I. Title.

KERRISON, Raymond 922.273
Bishop Walsh of Maryknoll, a biography. New York, Lancer [1963, c.1962] 255p. 18cm. (73-413) .60 pap.,
1. Walsh, James Edward, Bp., 1891- I. Title.

WALSH, James Edward, Bp., 1891- 266'.2'0924 B
Zeal for your house / by James E. Walsh ; edited by Robert E. Sheridan. Huntington, Ind. : Our Sunday Visitor, c1976. 233 p. : ill. ; 23 cm. [BV3427.W32A35] 76-6211 ISBN 0-87973-892-8 : 7.95
1. Walsh, James Edward, Bp., 1891- 2. Missions—China. I. Title.

Walsh, John C.

WALSH, John C. 282'.092'4 B
The day after Christmas / J. C. Walsh. [s.l. : s.n., c1976] 186 leaves ; 28 cm. "Number 9 of an edition limited to twenty copies." [BX4705.W2574A33] 77-152057
1. Walsh, John C. 2. Catholic Church—Clergy—Biography. 3. Clergy—United States—Biography. I. Title.

Walsh, Mary, Mother, 1850-1922.

BOARDMAN, Anne Cawley. 922.273
Such love is seldom; a biography of Mother Mary Walsh, O. P. [1st ed.] New York, Harper [1950] xiii, 236 p. illus., ports. 22 cm. [BX4705.W2575B6] 50-10800
1. Walsh, Mary, Mother, 1850-1922. 2. Sisters of the Order of St. Dominic, New York. I. Title.

Walsh, William Francis, 1900-1930.

GLODY, Robert. 922.273
A shepherd of the far North; the story of William Francis Walsh (1900-1930) by Robert Glody ... San Francisco, Calif., Harr Wagner publishing company [c1934] xiv, 237. [1] p. front., ports. 20 cm. [BX4705.W258G5] 34-39031
1. Walsh, William Francis, 1900-1930. I. Title.

[MARY Eustolia, sister] 922.273
A shepherd of the far North; the story of William Francis Walsh (1900-1930) by Robert Glody [pseud.] ... San Francisco, Calif., Harr Wagner publishing company [c1934] xiv, 237, [1] p. front., ports. 19 1/2 cm. [Secular name: Mary Cecilia Sherry] [BX4705.W258M3] 34-39081
1. Walsh, William Francis, 1900-1930. I. Title.

Walsh, William Joseph, abp. of Dublin, 1841-1921.

WALSH, Patrick J. 922.
William J. Walsh, archbishop of Dublin, by Patrick J. Walsh, M.A. London, New York [etc.] Longmans, Green and co., 1928. xvi, 612 p. front., plates, ports. 23 cm. [BX4705.W26W3] 29-25936
1. Walsh, William Joseph, abp. of Dublin, 1841-1921. I. Title.

Walsingham. Our Lady of.

DICKINSON, John Compton. 231.73
The shrine of Our Lady of Walsingham. Cambridge [Eng.] University Press, 1956. xiii, 150p. 9 plates, plan. 21cm. 'Bibliographical note': p.143-144. [BT660.W3D5] 56-4330
1. Walsingham. Our Lady of. 2. Walsingham Priory. I. Title.

Walter Carl Ferdinand Wilhelm, 1811-1887.

POLACK, William Gustave, 1890- 922.473
The story of C. F. W. Walther, by W. G. Polack ... St. Louis, Mo., Concordia publishing house, 1935. 11, 138 p. incl. front., illus., ports., facsims. 20 cm. [BX8080.W3P6] 35-13107
1. Walther, Carl Ferdinand Wilhelm, 1811-1887. I. Title.

POLACK, William Gustave, 1890- 922.473
The story of C. F. W. Walther, by W. G. Polack. St. Louis, Concordia publishing house, 1947. vii, 167 p. incl. front., illus. (incl. ports., facsims.) 19 1/2 cm. "Revised edition." [BX8080.W3P6 1947] 47-24746
1. Walther, Carl Ferdinand Wilhelm, 1811-1887. I. Title.

SPITZ, Lewis William, 1895- 922.473
The life of Dr. C. F. W. Walther. St. Louis, Concordia [c.]1961. 117p. illus. 61-18227 2.50
1. Walther, Carl Ferdinand Wilhelm, 1811-1887. I. Title.

STEFFENS, Diedrich Henry, 1866- 922.
Doctor Carl Ferdinand Wilhelm Walther ... by the Reverend D. H. Steffens ... Philadelphia, Pa., The Lutheran publication society, 1917. 401 p. 20 cm. [BX8080.W3S8] 17-19519 1.25.
1. Walther, Carl Ferdinand Wilhelm, 1811-1887. I. Title.

WALTHER, C. F. W. 1811-1887. (Carl Ferdinand Wilhelm), 284.1'322'0924 B
Selected letters / Roy A. Suelflow, translator. St. Louis : Concordia Pub. House, c1981. 192 p. : port. ; 24 cm. (Selected writings of C.F.W. Walther) (Series: Walther, C. F. W. (Carl Ferdinand Wilhelm), 1811-1887. Selections. English. 1981.) Includes bibliographical references. [BX8080.W3A4 1981] 19 81-3228 ISBN 0-570-08279-X : 12.95
1. Walther, C. F. W. (Carl Ferdinand Wilhelm), 1811-1887. 2. Lutheran Church—Clergy—Correspondence. 3. Clergy—United States—Correspondene. I. [Correspondence.] English. Selections II. Title. III. Series.

WALTHER, Carl Ferdinand Wilhelm, 1811-1887. 284.173'0924
Letters of C. F. W. Walther; a selection. Translated, edited, and with an introd. by Carl S. Meyer. Philadelphia, Fortress Press [1969] xii, 155 p. 21 cm. (Seminar editions) Bibliographical footnotes. [BX8080.W3A413] 72-84539 2.25
I. Title.

WALTHER, Carl Ferdinand Wilhelm, 1811-1887. 230'.4'1322
Walther speaks to the church; selected letters. Edited by Carl S. Meyer. St. Louis, Concordia Pub. House [1973] 104 p. illus. 22 cm. Includes bibliographical references. [BX8080.W3A4 1973] 72-94583 ISBN 0-570-03514-7 1.95 (pbk.)
1. Walther, Carl Ferdinand Wilhelm, 1811-1887. 2. Lutheran Church—Doctrinal and controversial works. I. Title.

Walter, Florence, 1858-1944.

MURPHY, Angelina. 271'.9 B
Mother Florence : a biographical history / Angelina Murphy ; foreword by Patrick F. Flores. 1st ed. Smithtown, N.Y. : Exposition Press, c1980. xiii, 258 p., [4] leaves of plates : ill. ; 22 cm. (An Exposition-testament book) Bibliography: p. 257-258. [BX4705.W263M87] 19 80-67314 ISBN 0-682-49625-1 : 15.00
1. Walter, Florence, 1858-1944. 2. Nuns—United States—Biography. I. Title.

Walter Hoving Home.

HOBE, Laura. 248'.246 B
Try God / by Laura Hobe ; foreword by David Wilkerson. 1st ed. Garden City, N.Y. : Doubleday, 1977. 191 p. ; 22 cm. [BV4930.H6] 76-50771 ISBN 0-385-12443-0 : 6.50
1. Walter Hoving Home. 2. Converts—United States—Biography. 3. Church work with delinquent girls—New York (State)—Garrison. I. Title.

HOBE, Laura. 248'.246 [B]
Try God / by Laura Hobe ; foreword by David Wilkerson. New York : Warner Books, 1978,c1977. 207p. ; 18 cm. [BV4930.H6] ISBN 0-446-89708-6 pbk. : 1.95
1. Walter Hoving Home. 2. Converts — United States — Biography. 3. Church work with delinquent girls — New York (State) — Garrison. I. Title.
L.C. card no. for 1977 Doubleday ed.: 76-50771.

Walthari of Aquitaine.

LEARNED, Marion Dexter, 1857-1917, ed.
The saga of Walther of Aquitaine, by Marion Dexter Learned ... Baltimore, Mod. lang. association of America, 1892. vi, 208 p. 24 cm. (On cover: Publications of the Modern language association of America. vol. vii, no. i) Versions in Anglo-Saxon, Latin, Middle High German, Old Norse, and Polish. Contents.--Versions of the Saga: i. Waldere fragments. ii. Waltharius [by Ekkehardus i; (text from the ed. by Scheffel-Holder, Stuttgart, 1874)] iii. Chronicon novaliciense. iv. Walther und Hildegunde. v. Nibelungenlied. vi. Graz fragment. vii. Vienna fragment. viii. Biterolf und Dietleib. ix Alpharts tod. x. Rosengarten. xi. Dietrichs flucht. xii.

Rabenschlacht. xiii. Thidrekssaga. Old Norse version. Old Swedish version. Hlod and Angsntheow's lay. xiv. Boguphali chronicon. xv. Paprocki. xvi, Bleski. xvii. Niesleckl. xviii. Procosius. xix. Wojcicki.--Appendix (Von dem ubelen wibe. Chanson de Roland. Rolandslied)--Origin and development of the Walther Saga.--Bibliography.--Index. [PB6.M6 vol. 7 no. 1] 3-10750
1. Walthari of Aquitaine. 2. Sagas. I. Ekkehardus i, dean of St. Gall, d. 973. ii. Title. II. Title.

Waltmire, Baily, 1896-1962.

BRACE, Beverly 287'.632'0924 B Waltmire, 1924-
The Humboldt years, 1930-1939 / Beverly Waltmire Brace. Chicago : Adams Press, c1977. iv, 206 p. ; 22 cm. [BX8495.W2444B7] 77-154518 pbk. : 4.50
1. Waltmire, Baily, 1896-1962. 2. Methodist Church—Clergy—Biography. 3. Humboldt Park Community Methodist Episcopal Church, Chicago, Ill.—History. 4. Clergy—Illinois—Chicago—Biography. 5. Chicago—Biography. 6. Chicago—Church history. I. Title.

Walton, Margaret Ann, 1818-1825.

[WALTON, William Claiborne] 922 1793-1834.
Juvenile piety; illustrated in the life of Margaret Ann Walton. Daughter of the Rev. W. C. Walton, late of Hartford, Conn. With remarks on the religious education of children. Approved by the Committee of publications. Boston, Massachusetts Sabbath school society [1853] viii, [9]-126 p. incl. front. 15 1/2 cm. [BR1715.W3W3] 38-4794
1. Walton, Margaret Ann, 1818-1825. 2. Religious education. I. Massachusetts Sabbath school society. Committee of publication. II. Title.

Walton, N.Y. First Congregational church.

[MARVIN, Robert B.] 285.8747
History of the church and her organizations, commemorating the one hundred fiftieth anniversary of the organization of the First Congregational church, Walton, New York, 1793-1943. [Walton, 1943] 104 p. plates, ports. 28 cm. [BX7255.W24F5] 44-26686
1. Walton, N.Y. First Congregational church. I. Owens, Antoinette K. II. Fitch, Roderick. III. Title.
Contents omitted.

Walton, William Claiborne, 1793-1834.

DANFORTH, Joshua Noble, 922.573 1798-1861.
Memoir of William C. Walton, late pastor of the Second Presbyterian church in Alexandria, D. C., and of the Free church in Hartford, Conn. By Joshua N. Danforth ... Hartford, D. Burgess and co.; New York, J. S. Taylor, 1837. viii, [9]-319 p. front. (port.) 20 cm. [BX9225.W235D3] 36-22140
1. Walton, William Claiborne, 1793-1834. I. Title.

Walvoord, John F. Addresses, essays, lectures.

WALVOORD, a tribute / 230'.044 edited by Donald K. Campbell. Chicago : Moody Press, c1982. p. cm. Includes bibliographical references. [BR50.W33] 19 81-1688 ISBN 0-8024-9227-4 : 12.95
1. Walvoord, John F. Addresses, essays, lectures. 2. Theology—Addresses, essays, lectures. I. Walvoord, John F. II. Campbell, Donald K.

Walzer, Richard, 1900-

ISLAMIC philosophy and 181'.07 *the classical tradition;* essays presented by his friends and pupils to Richard Walzer on his seventieth birthday. Editors: S. M. Stern, Albert Hourani and Vivian Brown. Columbia, University of South Carolina Press [1972] viii, 549 p. illus. 24 cm. (Oriental studies, 5) Chiefly in English, some in French, or German. Includes bibliographical references. [B740.174 1972] 72-2497 ISBN 0-87249-271-0 25.00
1. Walzer, Richard, 1900- 2. Philosophy, Islamic—Addresses, essays, lectures. 3. Philosophy, Ancient—Addresses, essays, lectures. I. Walzer, Richard, 1900- II. Stern, Samuel Miklos, 1920-1969, ed. III. Hourani, Albert Habib, ed. IV. Brown, Vivian, ed. V. Title. VI. Series.

Wandering Jew.

[FAUST, Ambrose Jerome]
The wandering Jew: a mythical and aesthetical study ... Hartford, Church press company, 1870. vi, [7]-81 p. 18 cm. Dedicatory note signed: A. J. Faust. Reprinted, with a few changes and additions, from the Southern review, January 1870. cf. Pref. [PN687.W3F3] 3-25661
1. Wandering Jew. I. Title.

FLEG, Edmond, 1874- 232.9
... Jesus; told by the Wandering Jew, by Edmond Fleg. New York, E. P. Dutton & co., inc. [c1935] 336 p. 21 cm. At head of title: Translated by Phyllis Megros. "First edition." "Authorities, Biblical and traditional, quoted or referred to": p. [320]-336. [BT309.F62] 35-605
1. Jesus Christ—Miscellanea. 2. Wandering Jew. I. Megros, Mrs. Phyllis (Marks) tr. II. Title.

VIERECK, George Sylvester, 1884-
My first two thousand years [by] George Sylvester Viereck and Paul Eldridge. Greenwich, Conn., Fawcett [1956] 287 p. (Crest book) 67-20837
1. Wandering Jew. I. Eldridge, Paul, 1888- joint author. II. Title.

VIERECK, George Sylvester, 1884-
My first two thousand years; the autobiography of the Wandering Jew [by] George Sylvester Viereck and Paul Eldridge. New York, Sheridan House, 1963. xiii p., 1 l., [9]-501, [1] p. 21 cm. 67-81134
1. Wandering Jew. I. Eldridge, Paul, 1888- joint author. II. Title.

Wang, Mary.

WANG, Mary. 275.1
The Chinese church that will not die [by] Mary Wang, with Gwen and Edward England. Wheaton, Ill., Tyndale House Publishers [1972] 201 p. illus. 18 cm. [BR1297.W28A3 1972] 79-188533 ISBN 0-8423-0235-2 1.25
1. Wang, Mary. 2. Christianity—China. 3. Persecution—China. I. England, Gwen, joint author. II. England, Edward O., joint author. III. Title.

Wang, Ta-jun, 1917-1932.

CASTEL, Eugene, 1885- 922.251
Rose of China (Marie-Therese Wang) 1917-1932; translated from the French of Rev. E. Castel, C. M. by Rev. Basil Stegmann, O. S. B. New York, Cincinnati [etc.] Benziger brothers, 1934. x p., 1 l., 13-131 p. incl. front., illus., ports., facsim. 19 cm. [Full name: Eugene Gustave Castel] [BX4705.W28C32] 35-3448
1. Wang, Ta-jun, 1917-1932. I. Stegmann, Basil Augustine, father, 1893- tr. II. Title.

Wanless, Sir William, 1865-1933.

WANLESS, Lillian (Emery) 926.1 Havens.
Wanless of India, Lancet of the Lord [by] Lillian Emery Wanless, illustrated by Beatrice Stevens. Boston, W. A. Wilde company [1944] 366 p. front. (port.) plates, facsim. 21 cm. "Fictionized biography."--Pref. [BV3269.W25W3] 45-183
1. Wanless, Sir William, 1865-1933. I. Title.

War.

THE attitude of the 265. *Christians towards war ...* New York, N.Y., S. V. Penfold, 1915- v. 22 cm. Contents.pt. i. Lactantius. [BR115.W2A8] 17-2651
1. War. I. Lactantius, Lucius Caecilius Firmianus.

BOOTH, Herbert.
The saint and the sword; a series of addresses on the anti-christian nature of war, by Herbert Booth ... New York, George H. Doran company [c1924] 3 p. l., 344 p. 19 1/2cm. $2.00 [BR225.W2B65] 24-9481
1. War. I. Title.

CADOUX, Cecil John, 261.8'73 1883-1947.
The early Christian attitude to war : a contribution to the history of Christian ethics / by C. John Cadoux ; with a foreword by W. E. Orchard. New York : Gordon Press, 1975. xxxii, 272 p. ; 24 cm. First published in 1919. Includes bibliographical references and index. [JX1941.C3 1975] 75-3884 ISBN 0-87968-198-5 lib.bdg. : 34.95
1. War. 2. Evil, Non-resistance to. 3. Christian ethics—Early church. I. Title.

CURRIE, William, d.1803. 355
A treatise on the lawfulness of defensive war. In two parts. By William Currie. [Fifteen lines of quotation] Philadelphia: Printed and sold by B. Franklin and D. Hall, at the new printing-office, in Market-street, mdccxlviii. xviii, 102 p. 19 cm. Signatures: A-G, H. [BR115.W2C8] 30-14980
1. War. I. Title.

CURTISS, Harriette Augusta 212 (Brown) Mrs. 1856?-1932.
The philosophy of war, by Dr. and Mrs. F. Homer Curtiss ... 3d and enl. ed. Washington, D. C., The Curtiss philosophic book co., 1939. ix, 168 p. 20 cm. In first edition, 1914, the authors' names appear on t.-p as Harriette Augusta Curtiss ... and F. Homer Curtiss. [BF1999.C83 1939] 39-32501
1. War. 2. Theosophy. I. Curtiss, Frank Homer, 1875- joint author. II. Title.

DYMOND, Jonathan, 1796- 172.4 1828.
An inquiry into the accordancy of war with the principles of Christianity, and an examination of the philosophical reasoning by which it is defended. With observations on some of the causes of war and on some of its effects. By Jonathan Dymond... Philadelphia, U. Hunt and son, J. Snowdon [18--] 1 p. l., 2-6, [9]-158 p. 22 1/2 cm. [JX1949.D8 1800] 31-8577
1. War. 2. Evil, Non-resistance to. I. Title.

DYMOND, Jonathan, 1796-1828. 172.
An inquiry into the accordancy of war with the principles of Christianity; and an examination of the philosophical reasoning by which it is defended; with observations on the causes of war and some of its effects; by Jonathan Dymond. With a dedication to Sunday school teachers and scholars, and notes, by Thomas Smith Grimke...Together with an appendix... Philadelphia, Printed by I. Ashmead & co., 1834. xx, [13]-300 p. 19 cm. First published anonymously in 1823. [JX1949.D8 1834] 4-20313
1. War. 2. Evil, Non-resistance to. I. Grimke, Thomas Smith, 1786-1834, ed. II. Title.

DYMOND, Jonathan, 1796-1828. 172.
An inquiry into the accordancy of war with the principles of Christianity, and an examination of the philosophical reasoning by which it is defended. With observations on some of the causes of war and on some of it effects. By Jonathan Dymond... 4th ed. cor. and enl. Philadelphia, W. Brown, printer, 1835. 158 p. 23 1/2 cm. [JX1949.D8 1835] 4-20310
1. War. 2. Evil, Non-resistance to. I. Title.

DYMOND, Jonathan, 1796-1828. 172.
An inquiry into the accordancy of war with the principles of Christianity, and an examination of the philosophical reasoning by which it is edfended. With observations on some of the causes of war and on some of its effects. By Jonathan Dymond... 4th ed. cor. and enl. Hartford, Printed by P. Canfield, for the American peace society, 1836. 158 p. 23 cm. [JX1949.D8 1836] 4-20311
1. War. 2. Evil, Non-resistance to. I. Title.

DYMOND, Jonathan, 1796-1828. 172.
An inquiry into the accordancy of war with the principles of Christianity, and an examination of the philosophical reasoning by which it is defended. With observations on some of the causes of war and on some of its effects. By Jonathan Dymond... New York, Stereotyped for and printed by order of the trustees of the residuary estate of Lindley Murray [1847] New York, W. Wood & co. [reissued] 1872. 6, [vii]-viii, [9]-124 p. 23 cm. [JX1949.D8 1872] 35-34372
1. War. 2. Evil, Non-resistance to. I. Title.

DYMOND, Jonathan, 1796- 172.4 1828.
An inquiry into the accordancy of war with the principles of Christianity, and an examination of the philosophical reasoning by which it is defended. With observations on some of the causes of war and on some of its effects. By Jonathan Dymond... New York, Stereotyped for and printed by order of the trustees of the residuary estate of Lindley Murray [1847] New York, W. Wood & co. [reissued] 1873. 6, [vii]-viii, [9]-124. p. 23 cm. [JX1949.D8 1873] 30-34311
1. War. 2. Evil, Non-resistance to. I. Title.

DYMOND, Jonathan, 1796-1828. 172.
An inquiry into the accordancy of war with the principles of Christianity, and an examination of the philosophical reasoning by which it is defended. With observations on some of the causes of war and on some of its effects; by Jonathan Dymond... New York, Stereotyped for and printed by order of the trustees of the residuary estate of Lindley Murray [1847] [reissued] New York, W. Wood & co., 1887. 6 [vii]-viii, [9]-124 p. 23 cm. [JX1949.D8 1887] 7-2499
1. War. 2. Evil, Non-resistance to. I. Title.

ERASMUS, Desiderius, 172. d.1536.
Erasmus Against war, with an introduction, by J. W. Mackail. Boston, The Merrymount press, 1907. xxxiii, [1], 64, [2] p. 25 x 15 cm. (Half-title: The humanists' library, ed. by Lewis Einstein. II) "Of this volume, which is edited by John W. Mackall, with types & decorations by Herbert P. Horne, CCCIII copies were printed by D.B. Updie at the Merrymount press, Boston, Massachusetts, in the month of August, MCMVII." [JX1942.E86] [Z239.U6E8] 7-36263
1. War. I. Mackall, John William, 1859- ed. II. Title.

FREEMAN, Daniel Roy. 172.
God and war; an exposition of the principles underlying creative peace, by Daniel Roy Freeman. Boston, R. G. Badger; [etc., etc., c1915] 4 p. l., 11-144 p. 20 cm. (On cover: Present day problems series) [JX1953.F6] 15-13200
1. War. I. Title.

[GREEN, M. P. Miss]
The fight for dominion; a romance of our first war with Spain, by Gay Parker [psued.] With illustrations by G. B. Mitchell. New York, E. R. Herrick & co. [1899] 2 p. l., 316 p. pl. 12 degrees. May *I. Title.*

HERTZLER, Arthur Emanuel, 211 1870-
The grounds of an old surgeon's faith, a scientific inquiry into the causes of war, by Arthur E. Hertzler ... [Halstead, Kan., c1944] 2 p. l., 3-606 p. 21 cm. Bibliography: p. 571-606. [BL2790.H4A3] 44-3799
I. Title.

LEEDS, Josiah Woodward.
The primitive Christian's estimate of war and self-defense. By Josiah W. Leeds ... New Vienna, O., Peace association of Friends in America, 1876. 58, [2] p. front. 17 1/2 cm. [JX1941.L5] A 14
1. War. 2. Peace. I. Title.

MOOMAW, Daniel Crouse, 1839- 261
Christianity versus war; a presentation of Scriptural and Christian teaching upon the subject of carnal warfare and the taking of human life, together with experiences of conscientious objectors in the world war; compiled and edited by Elder D. C. Moomaw. Ashland, O., The Brethren

publishing co., 1924. v, 346 p. pl., ports., 22 cm. [BR115.W2M6] 172.4 33-8584
1. War. 2. Peace. 3. Military service, Compulsory. I. Title.

MUNNELL, Thomas. 172.
Discussion. Shall Christians go to war? by Thomas Munnell, and J. S. Sweeney ... Cincinnati, Bosworth, Chase & Hall, 1872. 247 p. 18 cm. [JX1949.M86] 10-16769
1. War. I. Sweeney, J. S., joint author. II. Title.

SHEEN, Fulton John, 1895- 261
Whence come wars, by Fulton J. Sheen ... New York, Sheed & Ward, 1940. 3 p. l., 119 p. 19 cm. [BX1753.S527] 40-11520
1. War. 2. Catholic church. I. Title.

SHULER, John Lewis, 1887- 265.
Peace or war; what the Bible says, about it, by John L. Shuler... Washington, D.C., Peekskill, N.Y. [etc.] Review and herald publishing association [c1930] 128 p. incl. front., illus. 19 cm. [BR115.W2S45] 30-6826
1. War. 2. Second advent. 3. Bible—Prophecies. I. Title.

[SMITH, John] 1722-1771. 289.
The doctrine of Christianity, as held by the people called Quakers, vindicated: in answer to Gilbert Tennent's sermon on the lawfulness of war. [Twelve lines of Biblical quotations] Philadelphia: Printed by Benjamin Franklin, and David Hall, MDCCXLVIII. iv, 56 p. 20 1/2 cm. Signatures: 2 leaves unsigned, B-H4. Preface signed: John Smith, Philadelphia, 11th Mo. 25. 1747-8. In answer to "The late association for defence, encourag'd; or, The lawfulness of a defensive war ... By Gilbert Tennent. Philadelphia [1747]" Smith's work was, in turn, answered by Tennent in "The late association for defence farther encouraged: or, Defensive war defended ... Philadelphia, 1748." [BX7748.W2S6 1748] 30-21379
1. Tennent, Gilbert, 1708-1764. The late association for defence, encourg'd; or, The lawfulness of a defensive war. 2. War. 3. Friends, Society of—Doctrinal and controversial works. I. Title.

War and religion.

ADAMS, Hampton, 1897- 261
Christian answers to war questions, by Hampton Adams. New York, London [etc.] Fleming H. Revell company [1943] 96 p. 19 1/2 cm. [BR115.W2A3] 43-5017
1. War and religion. I. Title.

ADDISON, James Thayer, 1887- 261.6
War, peace, and the Christian mind; a review of recent thought. Foreword by Henry Knox Sherrill. Greenwich, Conn., Seabury Press, 1953. 112p. 20cm. [BR115.W2A4] 53-12393
1. War and religion. I. Title.

AHO, James A. 291.1'7873
Religious mythology and the art of war : comparative religious symbolisms of military violence / James A. Aho. Westport, Conn. : Greenwood Press, c1981. p. cm. (Contributions to the study of religion ; no. 3) ISSN 0196-7053) Includes index. Bibliography: p. [BL65.W2A38] 19 80-23465 ISBN 0-313-22564-8 lib. bdg. : 27.50
1. War and religion. 2. War (in religion, folk-lore, etc.) I. Title. II. Series.

BAINTON, Roland Herbert, 1894- 261
... The churches and war; historic attitudes toward Christian participation, a survey from Biblical times to the present day, by Roland H. Bainton ... [New York, 1945] 71 p. 19 1/2 cm. At head of title: Social action. "Reprinted from January 15, 1945 Social action magazine." "Literature": p. 70-71. [BR115.W2.B316] 46-21901
1. War and religion. I. Title.

BOETTNER, Loraine. 261
The Christian attitude toward war, by Loraine Boettner ... Grand Rapids, Mich., Wm. B. Eerdmans publishing co., 1940. 119 p. 20 cm. [BR115.W2B55 1940] 44-25956
1. War and religion. 2. World war, 1939—Religious aspects. I. Title.

BOETTNER, Loraine. 261
The Christian attitude toward war, by Loraine Boettner. 2d rev. world war II ed. ... Grand Rapids, Mich., Wm. B. Eerdmans publishing co., 1942. 120 p. 20 cm. [BR115.W2B55 1942] 43-17472
1. War and religion. 2. World war, 1939—Religious aspects. I. Title.

BOORD, James A. 261
Christianity and war, can they co-exist! By J. A. Boord ... Burlington, Ia., The Lutheran literary board, 1938. 212 p. front. (port.) 22 1/2 cm. [BR115.W2B57] 38-20747
1. War and religion. I. Title.

BOOTH, Alan R. 261.8'73
Not only peace; Christian realism and the conflicts of the twentieth century [by] Alan R. Booth. New York, Seabury [1967] 141p. 23cm. Bibl. [BT736.2.B63] 67-15735 3.50 bds.,
1. War and religion. 2. Peace (Theology) I. Title.

BOWMAN, Rufus David, 1899- 261.8'73
The Church of the Brethren and war, 1708-1941, by Rufus D. Bowman. With a new introd. for the Garland ed. by Donald F. Durnbaugh. New York, Garland Pub., 1971 [i.e. 1972, c1944] 21, 348 p. illus. 23 cm. (The Garland library of war and peace) Bibliography: p. [334]-348. [BX7815.B6 1972] 75-147667 ISBN 0-8240-0425-6
1. Church of the Brethren—History. 2. War and religion. I. Title. II. Series.

BOWMAN, Rufus David, 1899- 261
Seventy times seven, by Rufus D. Bowman ... Elgin, Ill., Brethren publishing house [1945] 158 p. 20 cm. "A guided study program for young people and adults." "A brief review [of] the historical position of the church regarding war and the church's relationship to the state; the philosophical and Biblical basis for pacifism; and specific plans for a peace education program."--Introd. [BX7822.B6] 45-6376
1. War and religion. 2. Peace. 3. Church of the brethren—Doctrinal and controversial works. I. Title.

BRADEN, Charles Samuel, 1887- 291
War, communism, and world religions. [1st ed.] New York, Harper [1953] 281 p. 22 cm. [BL65.W2B7] 53-8366
1. War and religion. 2. Communism and religion. I. Title.

BUNTING, John Summerfield, 1869- 248
Christ in war time, by John S. Bunting... New York [etc.] Fleming H. Revell company [c1940] 150 p. 19 1/2 cm. [BR115.W2B85] 41-1737
1. War and religion. 2. Protestant Episcopal church in the U.S.A.—Sermons. 3. Sermons, American. I. Title.

BURKE, John James, 1857- 261.7
The Catholic at war, by Right Rev. J. J. Burke. New York, The Longfellow press [1942] 160 p. 21 cm. [BR115.W2B37] 43-4034
1. War and religion. I. Title.

CLARK, Robert Edward David. 241'.6'97
Does the Bible teach pacifism? / [by] Robert E. D. Clark ; foreword by J. Stafford Wright. [New Malden] : Fellowship of Reconciliation, 1976. [1], 70 p. ; 21 cm. Cover title. Includes index. Bibliography: p. [1] [BT736.2.C57] 76-378740 ISBN 0-900368-30-6 : £0.80
1. War and religion. 2. War—Biblical teaching. 3. Pacifism. I. Title.

COATES, John Rider, 1879-
War--what does the Bible say? By J. R. Coates. London, The Sheldon press; New York, The Macmillan company [1940] vii, 64 p. 19 cm. (Half-title: The Christian news-letter books, no. 7. General editor: Alec R. Vidler) "First published 1940." A 40
1. War and religion. 2. Bible—Criticism, interpretation, etc. I. Title.

CONFERENCE on Christian politics, economics and citizenship. Commission on Christianity and war. 261
Christianity and war; being the report presented to the conference on Christian politics, economics, and citizenship at Birmingham, April 5-12, 1924. London, New York, [etc.] Published for the conference committee by Longmans, Green and co., 1924. xi, 99, [1] p. 18 1/2 cm. (Half-title: C.O.P.E.C. commission reports. vol. VIII) "Second impression, September 1924." Alfred E. Garvie, chairman. [HN30.C6 vol. VII] 25-6842
1. War and religion. I. Title.

DODGE, David Low, 1774-1852. 261.8'73
War inconsistent with the religion of Jesus Christ. With an introd. by Edwin D. Mead. Boston, Published for the International Union [by] Ginn, 1905. [New York, J. S. Ozer, 1972] xxiv, 168 p. port. 22 cm. (The Peace movement in America) Facsim. ed. [JX1949.D7 1905a] 75-137540 9.95 (Library Ed.)
1. War and religion. 2. Peace. I. Title. II. Series.

DRESSER, Horatio Willis, 1866- 265.
The victorious faith, moral ideals in war time, by Horatio W. Dresser... New York and London, Harper & brothers [c1917] 6 p. l., 221, [1] p. 19 1/2 cm. [BR115.W2D7] 17-24116
1. War and religion. I. Title.

DRINAN, Robert F. 261.8'73
Vietnam and Armageddon; peace, war and the Christian conscience, by Robert F. Drinan. New York, Sheed and Ward [1970] vi, 210 p. 21 cm. Includes bibliographical references. [BT736.2.D7] 71-101550 ISBN 0-8362-0484-0 5.95
1. War and religion. 2. Vietnamese Conflict, 1961-1975—Moral aspects. I. Title.

DYMOND, Jonathan, 1796-1828. 261.8'73
An inquiry into the accordancy of war. With a new introd. for the Garland ed. by Naomi Churgin Miller. New York, Garland Pub., 1973. 11, 158 p. 22 cm. (The Garland library of war and peace) Reprint of the 1835 ed., which was published under title: An inquiry into the accordancy of war with the principles of Christianity. [BT736.2.D9 1973] 79-147432 ISBN 0-8240-0222-9 16.00
1. War and religion. 2. Pacifism. I. Title. II. Series.

DYMOND, Jonathan, 1796-1928. 172.
An inquiry into the accordancy of war with the principles of Christianity, and an examination of the philosophical reasoning by which it is defended. With observations on some of the causes of war and on some of its effects. by Jonathan Dymond ... [14th thousand] Philadelphia, U. Hunt and son, J. Snowdon; New York, Collins & brother [183-?] 1 p. l., 2-6, [9]-158 p. 23 cm. [JX1949.D8 1830] 10-17071
1. War and religion. 2. Evil, Nonresistance to. I. Title.

FAUNCE, William Herbert Perry, 1859-1930. 265.
... Religion and war, by William Herbert Perry Faunce ... New York, Cincinnati, The Abingdon press [c1918] 188 p. 20 cm. (The Mendenhall lectures, fourth series, delivered at DePauw university)] [BR115.W2F3] 18-16483
1. War and religion. I. Title.
Contents omitted.

FERGUSON, John, 1921- 291.1'7873
War and peace in the world's religions / by John Ferguson. New York : Oxford University Press, 1978, c1977. p. cm. Includes bibliographies and index. [BL65.W2F47 1978] 78-19191 ISBN 0-19-520073-X : 8.95. ISBN 0-19-520074-8 pbk. : 2.95 pbk.
1. War and religion. 2. Peace (Theology) I. Title.

[FISH, Samuel] 265.
An humble address to every Christian of every nation and denomination of people under Heaven; shewing an effectual means to prevent wars among all nations of the earth, and to maintain an everlasting union in families, societies, churches, towns, states, and in all the kingdoms of this lower world... Newark, New-Jersey, Printed by John Woods, MD.: cc:xciii. 68 p. 20 cm. Signed (p. 26): Samuel Fish. [(BR115.W2F)] A35
1. War and religion. I. Title.

GARDNER, Milton Bliss, 1889- 261
Christianity vs. militarism; or, The Christian's recall to foundational principles: a message for the hour, by M. B. Gardner. Philadelphia, Pa. [1942?] cover-title, 63 p. 19 cm. [BR115.W2G3] A 43
1. War and religion. 2. Christianity—20th cent. I. Title.

[GARDNER, Milton Bliss] 1889- 261
"Shall the sword devour forever?" Examination of a tract entitled "Should a Christian go to war?" Written by a well-known Bible teacher, and widely publicized by the Sunday school times. By M. B. G. [Complete ed.] Philadelphia, Pa. [1942?] cover-title, 64 p. 18 cm. [BR115.W2G33] 43-13154
1. War and religion. 2. World war, 1939—Religious aspects. I. Title.

HAUSHALTER, Walter Milton, 1889- 265.
Christ, lord of battles; by Walter M. Haushalter... Boston, R. G. Badger [c1919] 117 p. 19 1/2 cm. [BR115.W2H4] 19-15949
I. Title.

HEERING, Gerrit Jan, 1879- 261.7
The fall of Christianity; a study of Christianity, the state, and war. Translated from the Dutch by J. W. Thompson, with a foreword by E. Stanley Jones. With a new introd. for the Garland ed., by Walter F. Bense. New York, Garland Pub., 1972. 47, x, 243 p. 22 cm. (The Garland library of war and peace) Reprint of the 1930 ed. Translation of De zondeval van het Christendom. Includes bibliographical references. [BT736.2.G3613 1972] 77-147670 ISBN 0-8240-0428-0 15.00
1. War and religion. 2. Civilization, Christian. 3. State, The. 4. Church and state. I. Title. II. Series.

HERRSTROM, William Dewey, 1898- 172.4
War preparations and international suicide, by Rev. W. D. Herrstrom ... Findlay, O., Fundamental truth publishers [c1937] 71 p. 19 cm. [BR115.W2H5] 37-18018
1. War and religion. 2. Bible—Prophecies. I. Title.

HERSHBERGER, Guy Franklin, 1896- 172.4
Can Christians fight? Essays on peace and war, by Guy F. Hershberger ... Scottdale, Pa., Mennonite publishing house, 1940. 180 p. 20 cm. [Mennonite peace publications] [BX8121.H4] 40-33357
1. War and religion. 2. Peace. 3. Mennonites—Doctrinal and controversial works. 4. Evil, Non-resistance to. I. Title.

*HOLT, Glenn. 301.635
The fury of God: holy wars and sacred violence. Chatsworth, Calif. Barclay House [1974] 191 p. illus. 18 cm. Bibliography p. 189-191. [BR195.W3] ISBN 0-87682-418-1 1.95 (pbk.)
1. War and Religion. 2. War crimes. I. Title.

HORMANN, Karl. 261.873
Peace and modern war in the judgment of the church. Translated by Caroline Hemesath. Westminster, Md., Newman Press, 1966. vii, 162 p. 22 cm. Bibliographical references included in "Notes" (p. 103-158) [BT736.2H613] 66-16570
1. War and religion. 2. Peace (Theology) I. Title.

HOUSELANDER, Frances Caryll. 248
This war is the passion, by Frances Caryll Houselander, with foreword by Leonard Feeney, S.J. New York, Sheed & Ward, 1941. x, 185 p. 19 1/2 cm. [BR115.W2H75] 41-22299
1. War and religion. I. Title.

HOWARD, Harry Frank, 1872- 224.
Our next war; historic and Biblical facts, by Harry F. Howard. Rochester, N.H., Record press, 1922. 8 p. l., 404, [1] p. illus. 21 cm. Lettered on cover: Kingdom of heaven. [BS647.H67] 23-2475
I. Title.

ISBELL, Allen C 261.873
War and conscience, by Allen C. Isbell. Abilene, Tex., Biblical Research Press [1966] x, 221 p. 23 cm. Bibliography: p. 221. Bibliographical footnotes. [BT736.2.I8] 66-1666
1. War and religion. I. Title.

JONES, Rufus Matthew, 1863- 261 ed.
The church, the gospel and war. [1st ed.] New York, Harper [1948] xii, 169 p. 20 cm. Bibliographical footnotes. [BR115.W2J6] 48-2468
1. War and religion. I. Title.

KELMAN, John, 1864-1929. 265.
... Some aspects of international Christianity, by John Kelman. New York, Cincinnati, The Abingdon press [1920] 2 p. l., vii-xi, 167 p. 20 cm. (The Mendenhall lectures, 4th series, delivered at De Pauw university) [BR115.P7K4] 20-13171
1. War and religion. 2. International cooperation 3. Peace. I. Title.

KNOX, John Dunn. 261.8'73
Eternal war; the why of conscientious objection [by] John D. Knox. [Melbourne, John D. Knox, 199 Napier Street, 1967] 94 p. illus., diagrs., facsim. 19 cm. [BT736.2.K6] 70-362153 unpriced
1. War and religion. 2. Conscientious objectors. I. Title.

KREHBIEL, Henry Peter, 172.4 1862-
War, peace, amity, by H. P. Krehbiel; chapter on Women and peace by Elva Krehbiel Leisy. Newton, Kans., H. P. Krehbiel, 1937. 2 p. l., vii-xxii, 350 p. 20 cm. [BR115.W2K65] 37-16528
1. War and religion. 2. Peace. 3. Mennonites—Doctrinal and controversial works. I. Leisy, Elva (Krehbiel) Mrs. II. Title.

LEE, Umphrey, 1893- 261
The historic church and modern pacifism, by Umphrey Lee. New York, Nashville, Abingdon-Cokesbury press [1943] 249 p. 20 1/2 cm. Bibliographical references included in "Notes" (p. 225-246) [BR115.W2L4] 43-5305
1. War and religion. 2. Church and state. I. Title.

LONG, Edward Le Roy. 261.8'73
War and conscience in America. Philadelphia, Westminster Press [1968] xiv, 130 p. 19 cm. Bibliographical references included in "Notes" (p. 125-130) [BT736.2.L6] 68-22645
1. War and religion. I. Title.

LOQUE, Bertrand de. 261.8'73
Discourses of warre and single combat. Translated by John Eliot. A Renaissance library facsim. ed., with an introd. by Alice Shalvi. Jerusalem, New York, Israel Universities Press; [distributed by International Scholarly Book Services, Portland, Or., c1968] xii, 67 p. 22 cm. (Renaissance library) Original t.p. reads: Discovres of vvarre and single combat. Translated out of French by I. Eliot. London, Printed by Iohn Wolfe, and are to be solde at his shop right ouer against the great South dore of Paules, 1591. "A treatise of single combate" (p. 43-67) has special t.p. Part 1 has running title: A discourse of Christian war; pt. 2: A discourse of single combat. Translation of Deux traitez, l'un de la guerre, l'autre du duel. STC 16810. Includes bibliographical references. [BT736.2.L6413 1591a] 72-178223 ISBN 0-7065-0051-2 5.00
1. War and religion. 2. Dueling. I. Eliot, John, fl. 1593, tr. II. Title. III. Title: A treatise of single combate. IV. Title: A discourse of Christian warre. V. Title: A discourse of single combat.

MARRIN, Albert, comp. 261.8'73'08
War and the Christian conscience: from Augustine to Martin Luther King, Jr. Chicago, Regnery [1971] ix, 342 p. 21 cm. "Gateway edition." Bibliography: p. 335-342. [BT736.2.M375] 73-143855 3.95
1. War and religion. I. Title.

METHODIST Church (United 261.63 States) Commission to Study the Christian Faith and War in the Nuclear Age.
The Christian faith and war in the nuclear age. Nashville, Abingdon [c.1963] 108p. 19cm. Bibl. 63-22301 1.00 pap.,
1. War and religion. 2. Christianity and international affairs. I. Title.

METHODIST Church (United 241.6'24 States) Commission to Study the Christian Faith and War in the Nuclear Age.
The Christian faith and war in the nuclear age. New York, Abingdon Press [1963] 108 p. 19 cm. Bibliography: p. 107-108. Bibliographical footnotes. [BT736.2.M43] 261 63-22301
1. War and religion. 2. Christianity and international affairs. I. Title.

MILLER, Albert Robert Herman, 261 1893-
The church and war, by Albert R. H. Miller; introduction by Jermone Davis. St. Louis, Mo., The Bethany press [c1931] 208 p. 20 cm. "Bibliography: p. 205-206. [BR115.W2M5] 3-1
1. War and religion. I. Title.

MOELLERING, Ralph Luther. 261.6
Modern war and the American churches; a factual study of the Christian conscience on trial from 1939 to the cold war crisis of today. [1st ed.] New York, American Press [c1956] 141p. 21cm. Includes bibliography. [BR115.W2M56] 56-9006
1. War and religion. I. Title.

MOOMAW, Daniel Crouse, 1839- 261 comp.
A cloud of witnesses; an expression of the deep convictions of faithful men who are opposed to war. Compiled and edited by Eld. D. C. Moomaw. Ashland, O., The Brethren publishing co., 1925. 5 p. l., 3-180 p. port. 21 cm. [BR115.W2M62] 33-15568
1. War and religion. I. Title.

MORRISON, Charles Clayton, 261 1874-
The Christian and the war, by Charles Clayton Morrison. Chicago, New York, Willett, Clark & company, 1942. v. p., 1 l., 145 p. 19 1/2 cm. "Editorials which appeared in the Christian century in the weeks immediately following the outbreak of war between the axis powers and the United States."--Introd. [BR115.W2M65] 42-19449
1. War and religion. 2. World war, 1939—-Religious aspects. I. Title.

NEWTON, Joseph Fort, 1876- 230.
The sword of the spirit, Britain and America in the great war, by Joseph Fort Newton ... New York, George H. Doran company [c1918] 2 p. l., vii-xix p., 1 l., 23-241 p. 19 1/2 cm. $1.50 [BX9943.N4S9] 19-2199
I. Title.

NEWTON, Joseph Fort, 1876- 230.
The sword of the spirit, Britain and America in the great war, by Joseph Fort Newton ... New York, George H. Doran company [c1918] 2 p. l., vii-xix p., 1 l., 23-241 p. 19 1/2 cm. $1.50 [BX9943.N4S9] 19-2199
I. Title.

O'TOOLE, George Barry, 355.22 1886-
War and conscription at the bar of Christian morals, by Rt. Rev. Msgr. George Barry O'Toole ... New York, N.Y., The Catholic worker press [1941] 90 p. 17 1/2 cm. [BR115.W2O75] 42-25066
1. War and religion. 2. Military service, Compulsory—U.S. 3. Conscientious objectors. I. Title.

PAGE, Kirby. 265.
The sword or the cross, which should be the weapon of the church militant; By Kirby Page. Chicago, The Christian century press, 1921. 107 p., 1 l. 19 cm. [BR115.W2P25] 22-24321
1. War and religion. I. Title.

PAGE, Kirby, 1890- 265.
The sword or the cross; an examination of war in the light of Jesus' way of life, by Kirby Page ... with an introduction by Professor Harry F. Ward. [2d ed.] New York, George H. Doran company [c1923] vii p., 1 l., 11-61 p. 20 cm. (Christianity and industry, 4.) [BR115.W2P25 1923] 23-11355
1. War and religion. I. Title.

PAGE, Kirby, 1890- 171.
... The sword or the cross; an examination of war in the light of Jesus' way of life, by Kirby Page ... with an introduction by Professor Harry F. Ward. [2d ed.] New York, George H. Doran company [1922] vii p., 1 l., 11-61 p. 20 cm. (Christianity and industry, 4) [BR115.W2P25 1922] 23-11355
1. War and religion. I. Title.

PAGE, Kirby, 1890- 265.
War; its causes, consequences and cure by Kirby Page...with an introduction by Harry Emerson Fosdick. New York, George H. Dorna company [c1923] 4 ;. l., 5-80 p. 20 cm. (Christianity and world problems: no. 1) [BR115.W2P27] 23-18337
1. War and religion. 2. European war, 1914-1918—Causes. 3. European war, 1914-1918—Influence and results. I. Title.

PAGE, Kirby, 1890- 172.4
War; its causes, consequenxes and cure by Kirby Page...with an introduction by Harry Emerson Fosdick. New York, George H. Doran company [1923] xii p., 1 l., 15-215 p. 20 cm. [BR115.W2P27 1923a] 25-27778
1. War and religion. 2. European war, 1914-1918—Causes. 3. European war 1914-1918—Influence and results. I. Title.

PHELPS, William Lyon, 1865- 261
Christ or Caesar the religion of Jesus and the religion of nationalism by William Lyon Phelps ... New York, E. P. Dutton & co., inc. [c1930] "First edition." [BR115. W2P5] 30-30005
1. War and religion. 2. Peace. 3. Patriotism. I. Title.

POLING, Daniel Alfred, 1884- 261
A preacher looks at war, by Daniel A. Poling ... New York, The Macmillan company, 1943. xvi, 101 p. 19 1/2 cm. "First printing." [BR115.W2P6] 43-9215
1. War and religion. 2. World war, 1939-Religious aspects. 3. World war, 1939-$Peace. I. Title.

POTTER, Ralph B. 261.8'73
War and moral discourse [by] Ralph B. Potter. Richmond, John Knox Press [1969] 123 p. 21 cm. Includes bibliographical references. [BT736.2.P63] 69-18111 2.45 (pbk)
1. War and religion. 2. War and religion—Bibliography. I. Title.

QUIGLEY, Thomas E., 261.8'73 comp.
American Catholics and Vietnam, edited by Thomas E. Quigley. Grand Rapids, Mich., by W. B. Eerdmans [1968] 197 p. 22 cm. "Bibliographical notes": p. 9-13. [BT736.2.Q5] 68-54102 4.50
1. War and religion. 2. Vietnamese Conflict, 1961-1975—Religious aspects. 3. Catholic Church in Vietnam. I. Title.

RAMSEY, Paul. 261.63
War and the Christian conscience; how shall modern war be conducted justly? Durham, N. C., Published for the Lilly Endowment Research Program in Christianity and Politics by Duke University Press, 1961. 331 p. 22cm. [BR115.W2R25] 61-10666
1. War and religion. I. Title.

RAMSEY, Paul [Robert Paul 261.63 Ramsey]
War and the Christian conscience; how shall modern war be conducted justly? Durham, N.C., Published for the Lilly Endowment Research Program in Christianity and Politics by Duke Univ. Press [c.]1961. 331p. Bibl. 61-10666 6.00
1. War and religion. I. Title.

RAVEN, Charles Earle, 261.8'73 1885-
War and the Christian, by Charles E. Raven. With a new introd. for the Garland ed. by Franklin H. Littell. New York, Garland Pub., 1972. 9, 185 p. 22 cm. (The Garland library of war and peace) Reprint of the 1938 ed. [BT736.2.R38 1972] 75-147675 ISBN 0-8240-0432-9
1. World Conference on Church, Community and State, Oxford, 1937. 2. War and religion. I. Title. II. Series.

RAVEN, Charles Earle, 1885- 172.4
War and the Christian, by Charles E. Raven ... New York, The Macmillan company, 1938. 3 p. l., 11-185, [1] p. 20 cm. [BR115.W2R33 1938 a] 38-15159
1. War and religion. 2. World conference on church, community and state, Oxford, 1937. I. Title.

... Render unto 252.0082
Caesar, a collection of sermon classics on all phases of religion in wartime. New York, Lewis publishing company [1943] 223 p. 21 cm. At head of title: Our heritage of religious thought from the four great American wars. [BR115.W2R43] 43-16979
1. War and religion. 2. Sermons, American. 3. U.S.—Hist.—Revolution—Addresses, sermons, etc. 4. U.S.—Hist.—Civil war—Addresses, sermons, etc. 5. European war, 1914-1918—Addresses, sermons, etc. 6. World war, 1939—-Addresses, sermons, etc.

RICHARDS, Leyton Price, 265. 1879-
The Christian's alternative to war, an examination of Christian pacifism, by Leyton Richards. New York, The Macmillan company, 1929. 159 p. 19 cm. [BR115.W2R5] 29-25343
1. War and religion. 2. Peace. I. Title.

RICHARDS, Leyton Price, 172.4 1879-
Realistic pacifism; the ethics of war and the politics of peace, by Leyton Richards. Chicago, New York, Willett, Clark & company, 1935. xiv, 258 p. 19 1/2 cm. "This book combines into a single volume two separate books which were published in England, the one in 1929 and the other in 1935. They bore the titles respectively, 'The Christian alternative to war' and 'The Chrisitan's contribution to peace'."--Pref. [JX1952.R47] 36-14554
1. War and religion. 2. Peace. 3. Nationalism and nationality. I. Title.

RICHARDS, Leyton Price, 327'.172 1879-1948.
Realistic pacifism; the ethics of war and the politics of peace. With a new introd. for the Garland ed. by Charles Chatfield. New York, Garland Pub., 1972 [c1935] 12, xiv, 258 p. 22 cm. (The Garland library of war and peace) "This book combines into a single volume two separate books which were published in England, the one in 1929 and the other in 1935. They bore the titles respectively, The Christian's alternative to war and The Christian's contributions to peace." [JX1952.R47 1972] 79-147676 ISBN 0-8240-0433-7
1. War and religion. 2. Peace. 3. Nationalism. 4. Pacifism. I. Title. II. Series.

RUSSELL, J [pseud.]
The judgment of God; an historical little novel, by J. Russell ... New York, The book publishing house [1903] 3 p. l., 84 p. 14 x 12 cm. "This story deals with the taking of Jerusalem by the Christians." "The Dryden press and 'print shop' certifies that this copy is one of a limited edition of 500 copies printed on antique laid paper." 3-28134
I. Title.

RUTENBER, Culbert Gerow, 261 1909-
The dagger and the cross; an examination of Christian pacifism. [New York] Fellowship Publications [1950] 134 p. 21 cm. [BR115.W2R8] 51-7132
1. War and religion. I. Title.

SEAWARD, Carl Albert. 171.
Facing the truth, by Carl Albert Seaward ... Tufts College, Mass., The Tufts college press [c1928] 125 p. 18 cm. [BR115.W2S4] 28-6643
1. War and religion. 2. Militarism. 3. Peace. I. Title.

SHEEN, Fulton John, 1895- 248
A declaration of dependence [by] Fulton J. Sheen ... Milwaukee, The Bruce publishing company [1941] vii, 140 p. 20 cm. [BR115.W2S43] 41-21350
1. War and religion. 2. European war, 1939—-Religious aspects. 3. European war, 1939—-Catholic church. 4. Providence and government of God. I. Title.

SHEEN, Fulton John, 1895- 248
A declaration of dependence [by] Fulton J. Sheen ... Milwaukee, The Bruce publishing

company [1941] vii, 140 p. 20 cm. [BR115.W2S43] 41-21350
1. War and religion. 2. World war, 1939— Religious aspects. 3. World war, 1939— Catholic church. 4. Providence and government of God. I. Title.

SHEEN, Fulton John, 1895- 248
God and war, by Rt. Rev. Fulton J. Sheen ... New York, P. J. Kenedy & sons [1942] 5 p. l., 116 p. 16 1/2 cm. [BR115.W2S435] 42-14071
1. War and religion. I. Title.

SHEEN, Fulton John, 1895- 261
War and guilt, by Rt. Rev. Msgr. Fulton J. Sheen ... Nineteen addresses delivered in the nationwide Catholic hour (produced by the National council of Catholic men, in cooperation with the National broadcasting company), on Sundays from December 15, 1940 to April 13, 1941 ... Washington, D.C., National council of Catholic men [1941] 1 p. l., [5]-180 p., 2 l. 19 cm. [BR115.W2S44] 42-12182
1. War and religion. 2. Catholic church—Addresses, essays, lectures. I. National council of Catholic men. II. Title.

SHEERIN, John B. 261.8'73
Peace, war, and the young Catholic, by John B. Sheerin. New York, Paulist Press [1972, c1973] viii, 109 p. 18 cm. (Deus books) Bibliography: p. 108-109. [BT736.2.S46] 72-91458 ISBN 0-8091-1733-9 1.25
1. War and religion. I. Title.

SHINN, Roger Lincoln. 261
Beyond this darkness; what the events of our time have meant to Christians who face the future, by Roger L. Shinn ... New York, Association press, 1946. viii, 86 p. 21 cm. "A Haddam house book." [BR115.W2S443] 47-934
1. War and religion. 2. World war, 1939-1945—Religious aspects. I. Title.

SHRIGLEY, George Andrew Cleveland, 1902- ed. 264.1
Prayers for victory ...edited by G. A. Cleveland Shrigley. New York, T. Nelson and sons, 1942. ix, 116 p. 16 cm. [BV4897.W2S45] 42-12092
1. War and religion. 2. Prayers. 3. World war, 1839- -Religious aspects. I. Title.

SNIDER, Harold. 261
Does the Bible sanction war? (Why I am not a pacifist) By Harold Snider ... foreword by Herbert Lockyer ... Grand Rapids, Mich., Zondervan publishing house [1942] 156, [2] p. 20 cm. [BR115.W2S5] 42-16413
1. War and religion. I. Title.

SOMMER, Daniel Austen, 1878- 244
The fight of faith; an allegorical story of the struggles of an earnest Christian soldier and the company to which he belonged, by D. Austen Sommer ... Indianapolis, Ind., Apostolic review [c1918] cover-title, 1 p. l., 122 p. 23 1/2 cm. [BV4515.S6] 18-19717
I. Title.

SOMMER, Daniel Austen, 1878- 244
The fight of faith; an allegorical story of the struggles of an earnest Christian soldier and the company to which he belonged, by D. Austen Sommer ... Indianapolis, Ind., Apostolic review [c1918] cover-title, 1 p. l., 122 p. 23 1/2 cm. [BV4515.S6] 18-19717
I. Title.

SPEER, James P 211.6
For what purpose? An angry American's appeal to reason. Washington, Public Affairs Ress (1960) 86 p. 24 cm. [BT736.2.S6] 59-15845
1. War and religion. I. Title.

SPERRY, Willard Learoyd, 1882- ed.
Religion of soldier and sailor; one of a series of volumes on religion in the post-war world, edited by Dean Willard L. Sperry. By Paul D. Moody, Lucien Price, John E. Johnson [and others] ... Cambridge, Harvard university press, 1945. viii, 115 p. 19 cm. (Half-title: Religion in the post-war world, ed. by W. L. Sperry. Vol. II) A 45
1. War and religion. I. Moody, Paul Dwight, 1879- II. Title.
Contents omitted

STRATMANN, Franziskus. 265.
The church and war, a Catholic study, by Franziskus Stratmann, O.P. New York, P. J. Kennedy and sons [1928] xiii p., 1 l., 17-219 p. 19 cm. Printed in Great Britain. [BR115.W2S6] 29-14460
1. War and religion. I. Title.

STRATMANN, Franziskus Maria, 1883- 261.8'73
The church and war, a Catholic study, by Franziskus Stratmann. With a new introd. for the Garland ed. by Gerard A. Vanderhaar. New York, Garland Pub., 1971. 23, 219 p. 22 cm. (The Garland library of war and peace) Reprint of the 1928 ed. Includes bibliographical references. [BT736.2.S67 1971] 72-147677 ISBN 0-8240-0434-5
1. War and religion. I. Title. II. Series.

STRATMANN, Franziskus Maria, 1883- *261.6
War & Christianity today. Translated by John Doebele. Westminster, Md., Newman Press [1956] 134 p. illus. 22 cm. [BR115.W2S612] 57-791
1. War and religion. I. Title.

THINGS which cannot be shaken [by] Leslie D. Weatherhead, Frank H. Ballard, F. Townley Lord [and others] ... New York [etc.] Fleming H. Revell company [c1940] viii, 9-120 p. 19 1/2 cm. [BR115.W2T55] 40-5932 261
1. War and religion. 2. European war, 1939—Religious aspects. I. Weatherhead, Leslie Dixon, 1898-

TOLSTOI, Lev Nikolaevich, graf, 1828-1910. 204
...The Kingdom of God and peace essays, by Leo Tolstoy... Translated by Aylmer Maude, with an introduction by Gilbert Murray. For the Tolstoy society. London, Oxford university press, H. Milford, 1935. xxv, 591, [1] p. front. (port.) 20 cm. At head of title: "Tolstoy centenary edition." [BR125.T68] 36-9307
1. War and religion. 2. Kingdom of God. 3. Patriotism. I. Maude, Aylmer, 1858- ed. and tr. II. Murray, Gilbert, 1866- III. Title.
Contents omitted.

TOLSTOI, Lev Nikolaevich, graf, 1828-1910. 204
The kingdom of God and peace essays, by Leo Tolstoy; translated with an introduction by Aylmer Maude. London, Oxford university press, H. Milford [1936] xiii, 594, [1] p. 15 1/2 cm. (Half-title: The world's classics. CDXIV) "The kingdom of God is within you" was first published in 1898, and the essays between 1894 and 1909. In "The world's classics" they were first published in 1936." [BR125.T68] 37-27019
1. War and religion. 2. Kingdom of God. 3. Patriotism. I. Maude, Aylmer, 1858 — ed. and tr. II. Title.
Contents omitted.

VAN KIRK, Walter William, 1891- 261
Religion renounces war, by Walter W. Van Kirk ... Chicago, New York, Willett, Clark & company, 1934. vi p., 2 l., 262 p. 20 1/2 cm. "Notes" at end of each chapter. [BR115.W2V3] 35-6329
1. War and religion. 2. Protestant churches—U.s. I. Title.

VOIGT, Robert J. 191
Thomas Merton: a different drummer [by] Robert J. Voigt. Liguori, Mo., Liguori Publications [1972] 127 p. 18 cm. Bibliography: p. 125-127. [BX4705.M542V65] 72-80829 1.50
1. Merton, Thomas, 1915-1968. 2. War and religion. 3. United States—Race question. 4. Perfection. I. Title.

WEATHERHEAD, Leslie Dixon, 1893- 261
Thinking aloud in war-time [by] Leslie D. Weatherhead. New York, Cincinnati [etc.] The Abingdon press [c1940] 133 p. 19 1/2 cm. [BR115.W2W35 1940a] 40-8156
1. War and religion. I. Title.

WEBER, Theodore R. 261.8'73
Modern war and the pursuit of peace, by Theodore R. Weber. [New York] Council on Religion and International Affairs [1968] 39 p. 23 cm. (Ethics and foreign policy series) Address delivered at the World Peace Center of the Catholic Adult Education Center in 1967. Bibliographical references included in "Notes" (p. 37-39) [BT736.2.W37] 68-29422
1. War and religion. 2. Politics and war. I. Title.

WELLS, John I. 261.8'73
An essay on war. Proving that the spirit of war, existing in the rational mind, is ever inimical to the spirit of the Gospel; that the wars mentioned in the history of the Jews, were for the happiness of that people, the punishment of idolatrous nations, and the instruction of mankind generally. Also, that the spirit of war is wholly excluded from the Christian Church. Hartford, Printed by Hudson and Goodwin, 1808. [New York, J. S. Ozer, 1972] 52 p. 22 cm. (The Peace movement in America) Facsim. reprint. [BT736.2.W42 1808a] 70-137560 5.95
1. War and religion. I. Title. II. Series.

YODER, John Howard. 241
Karl Barth and the problem of war, [by] John H. Yoder. Nashville, Abingdon Press [1970] 141 p. 23 cm. (Studies in Christian ethics series) Includes bibliographical references. [BX4827.B3Y6 1970] 71-124760 ISBN 0-687-20724-X 2.95
1. Barth, Karl, 1886-1968. 2. War and religion. I. Title.

ZAHN, Gordon Charles, 1918- 261.8'73
War, conscience, and dissent [by] Gordon C. Zahn. [1st ed.] New York, Hawthorn [1967] 317p. 22cm. Bibl. [BT736.2.Z37] 67-14856 5.95 bds.,
1. War and religion. 2. War and morals. 3. Conscientious objectors. I. Title.

War and religion—Addresses, essays, lectures.

JONES, Rufus Matthew, 1863-1948, ed. 261.8'73
The church, the gospel, and war. With a new introd. for the Garland ed. by Henry Cadbury. New York, Garland Pub., 1971 [i.e. 1972, c1948] 9, xii, 169 p. 23 cm. (The Garland library of war and peace) Includes bibliographical references. [BT736.2.J65 1972] 79-147625 ISBN 0-8240-0400-0
1. War and religion—Addresses, essays, lectures. I. Title. II. Series.

MCGRATH, William R. 261.8'73
Why we are conscientious objectors to war / by William R. McGrath. Seymour, Mo. : Edgewood Press, c1980. 54 p. ; 22 cm. [BR115.W2M25] 19 80-123104 0.75 (pbk.)
1. War and religion—Addresses, essays, lectures. 2. Pacifism—Addresses, essays, lectures. I. Title.
Publisher's address :Edgewood Press 2865 East Rock Rd., Clare, MI 48617

RUTHERFORD, Joseph F., 1869- 172.4
War or peace, which? By J. F. Rutherford... Brooklyn, N.Y. [etc.] International Bible students association, Watch tower Bible & tract society, c1930. 63 p. illus. 19 cm. [BX8526.R885] 30-22066
I. Title.

WAR and Christian ethics / edited by Arthur F. Holmes. Grand Rapids : Baker Book House, c1975. 356 p. ; 22 cm. "A Canon Press book." Includes bibliographical references and index. [BT736.2.W34] 75-14602 ISBN 0-8010-4138-4 : 7.95 241'.6'24
1. War and religion—Addresses, essays, lectures. I. Holmes, Arthur Frank, 1924-

WAR or peace? : The search for new answers / edited by Thomas Shannon. Maryknoll, N.Y. : Orbis Books, [1980] p. cm. Includes bibliographical references. [BT736.2.W346] 80-15113 ISBN 088344-750-9 pbk. : 9.95 261.8'73
1. Zahn, Gordon Charles, 1918- — Addresses, essays, lectures. 2. War and religion—Addresses, essays, lectures. 3. War and morals—Addresses, essays, lectures. 4. Just war doctrine—Addresses, essays, lectures. 5. Pacifism—Addresses, essays, lectures. 6. Peace (Theology)—Addresses, essays, lectures. I. Shannon, Thomas Anthony, 1940-

WORDS of conscience : religious statements on conscientious objection / edited by Shawn Perry. 9th ed. Washington : National Interreligious Service Board for Conscientious Objectors, 1980. 133 p. : ill. ; 21 cm. Eighth ed., edited by Richard Malishchak, published in 1973. [BL65.W2W67 1980] 19 80-124020 2.00 261.8'73
1. War and religion—Addresses, essays, lectures. 2. Pacifism—Addresses, essays, lectures. I. Perry, Shawn. II. National Interreligious Service Board for Conscientious Objectors.

YODER, John Howard. 261.8'73
The original revolution; essays on Christian pacifism, by John H. Yoder. Scottdale, Pa., Herald Press [1972, c1971] 189 p. 21 cm. (Christian peace shelf series, 3) Includes bibliographical references. [BT736.2.Y6 1972] 76-181577 ISBN 0-8361-1572-4 5.95
1. War and religion—Addresses, essays, lectures. I. Title.

War and religion—Biblical teaching.

ENELOW, Hyman Gerson, 1876-1934. 296
The war and the Bible, by H. G. Enelow ... New York, The Macmillan company, 1918. 5 p. l., 115 p. 17 1/2 cm. [Full name: Hillel Hyman Gerson Enelow] [BS680.W2E6] 18-20684
1. War and religion—Biblical teaching. I. Title.

LASSERRE, Jean, of Epernay. 261.63
War and the Gospel. Translated by Oliver Coburn. Scottdale, Pa., Herald Press [1962] 243 p. 23 cm. [BT736.2.L313] 62-52667
1. War and religion—Biblical teaching. 2. Church and state. 3. Commandments, Ten—Murder. I. Title.

War and religion—Early church, ca. 30-600.

HORNUS, Jean Michel. 261.8'73
It is not lawful for me to fight : early Christian attitudes toward war, violence, and the State / Jean-Michel Hornus ; translated by Alan Kreider and Oliver Coburn. Rev. ed. Scottdale, Pa. : Herald Press, 1980. 370 p. ; 21 cm. (A Christian peace shelf selection) Original French ed. published in 1960 under title: Evangile et labarum. Bibliography: p. [343]-367. [BT736.2.H613 1980] 79-26846 ISBN 0-8361-1911-8 (pbk.) : 13.95
1. War and religion—Early church, ca. 30-600. 2. Sociology, Christian—Early church, ca. 30-600. I. Title.

War and religion—History of doctrines.

BAINTON, Roland Herbert, 1894- 261.63
Christian attitudes toward war and peace; a historical survey and critical re-evaluation. New York, Abingdon Press [1960] 299 p. illus. 24 cm. Includes bibliography. [BT736.2.B3] 60-12064
1. War and religion—History of doctrines. 2. Church history. I. Title.

JONES, Thomas Canby, 1921- 261.8'73
George Fox's attitude toward war; a documentary study, by T. Canby Jones. Annapolis, Academic Fellowship, 1972. 125, 13 p. facsim. 23 cm. Includes bibliographical references. [BT736.2.J66] 79-187544
1. Fox, George, 1624-1691. 2. War and religion—History of doctrines. I. Title.

SMITH, William Kyle. 241.6'24
Calvin's ethics of war; a documentary study. Annapolis [Published for Westminster Foundation of Annapolis by] Academic Fellowship, 1972. vii, 166 p. 23 cm. Bibliography: p. 165-166. [BT736.2.S55] 72-88871
1. Calvin, Jean, 1509-1564—Ethics. 2. War and religion—History of doctrines. I. Title.

War—Biblical teaching.

CRAIGIE, Peter C. 261.8'73
The problem of war in the Old Testament

/ by Peter C. Craigie. Grand Rapids : Eerdmans, c1978. 125 p. ; 21 cm. Includes indexes. Bibliography: p. 113-114. [BS1199.W2C72] 78-17698 ISBN 0-8028-1742-4. : 3.95
1. Bible. O.T.—Criticism, interpretation, etc. 2. War—Biblical teaching. I. Title.

ELLER, Vernard. 261.8'73
King Jesus' manual of arms for the 'armless; war and peace from Genesis to Revelation. Nashville, Abingdon Press [1973] 205 p. 23 cm. [BS680.W2E43] 72-8638 ISBN 0-687-20885-8 4.75
1. War—Biblical teaching. 2. Peace (Theology)—Biblical teaching. I. Title.

ELLER, Vernard. 261.8'73
War and peace from Genesis to Revelation : King Jesus' manual of arms for the 'armless / Vernard Eller. Scottdale, Pa. : Herald Press, 1981. 216, [4] p. ; 21 cm. Edition for 1973 published under title: King Jesus' manual of arms for the 'armless. Includes index. Bibliography: p. [219]-[220] [BS680.W2E43 1981] 19 80-26280 ISBN 0-8361-1947-9 : 8.95
1. War—Biblical teaching. 2. Peace (Theology)—Biblical teaching. I. Title.

LIND, Millard, 1918- 296.3'87873
Yahweh is a warrior : the theology of warfare in ancient Israel / Millard C. Lind ; foreword by David Noel Freedman ; introd. by John H. Yoder. Scottdale, Pa. : Herald Press, 1980. 232 p. ; 22 cm. (A Christian peace shelf selection) Includes bibliographical references and indexes. [BS1199.W2L56 1980] 80-16038 ISBN 0-8361-1233-4 (pbk.) : 9.95
1. Bible. O.T.—Criticism, interpretation, etc. 2. War—Biblical teaching. 3. God—Biblical teaching. I. Title.

MILLER, Patrick D. 296.3'87'873
The divine warrior in early Israel [by] Patrick D. Miller, Jr. Cambridge, Mass., Harvard University Press, 1973. 279 p. 22 cm. (Harvard Semitic monographs, v. 5) Includes bibliographical references. [BS1199.W2M54] 73-81264 ISBN 0-674-21296-7 5.95
1. War—Biblical teaching. I. Title. II. Series.

Warburton, William bp. of Gloucester, 1698-1779.

EVANS, Arthur William. 922.342
Warburton and the Warburtonians; a study in some eighteenth-century controversies, by A. W. Evans ... London, Oxford university press, H. Milford, 1932. viii, 315, [1] p. front. (port.) 23 1/2 cm. "Books and pamphlets connected with the Warburtonian controversies": p. [294]-306. [BX5199.W35E8] 32-22675
1. Warburton, William, bp. of Gloucester, 1698-2779. 2. Warburton, William, bp. of Gloucester, 1698-1779—Bibl. I. Title.

MILLS, William, 1793-1834. 218
The belief of the Jewish people and of the most eminent gentile philosophers, more especially of Plato and Aristotle, in a future state, briefly considered; including an examination into some of the leading principles contained in Bishop Warburton's Divine legation of Moses; in a discourse preached before the University of Oxford at St. Mary's, March 30, 1828. With notes and an appendix. By W. Mills ... Oxford, At the University press for the author, 1828. viii, 130 p. 23 cm. [BL535.M5] 31-8973
1. Warburton, William, bp. of Gloucester, 1698-1779. The divine legation of Moses. 2. Immortality. I. Title. II. Title: The belief of the Jewish people ... in a future state.

[WARBURTON, William] bp. of Gloucester, 1698-1779.
Letters from a late eminent prelate to one of his friends ... First American edition. New York, Printed for E. Sargeant, 1809. 2 p. l., 375 p. 21 1/2 cm. Letters from William Warburton to Richard Hurd, edited by the latter. "Appendix: containing letters from the Honourable Charles Yorke to Mr. Warburton": p. [364]-375. A30
I. Hurd, Richard, bp. of Worcester, 1720-1808. II. Yorke, Charles, 1722-1770. III. Title.

Ward, C. M.

WEAD, Doug. 289.9 B
The C. M. Ward story, with Doug Wead. Harrison, Ark. : New Leaf Press, c1976. 255 p. ; 23 cm. Includes index. [BX6198.A78W43] 76-22267 ISBN 0-89221-022-2 : 5.95
1. Ward, C. M. 2. Assemblies of God, General Council—Clergy—Biography. 3. Clergy—United States—Biography. I. Ward, C. M. II. Title.

Ward, John Adner.

ANDERSON, George Smith.
Adner Ward, the boy Christian; the Christ-life in childhood, by G. S. Anderson ... Little Rock, Ark. [c1910] 65, [1] p. port. 19 cm. 10-10810
1. Ward, John Adner. I. Title.

Ward, Maisie, 1889-

SHEED, Francis Joseph, 1897- 248
The instructed heart : soundings at four depths / F. J. Sheed. Huntington, Ind. : Our Sunday Visitor, inc., c1979. 128 p. ; 22 cm. [BX4705.W287S52] 79-87925 ISBN 0-87973-739-5 : 5.95 ISBN 0-87973-629-1 pbk. : 2.95
1. Ward, Maisie, 1889- 2. Mary, Virgin. 3. Heart—Biblical teaching. 4. Christian life—Catholic authors. I. Title.
Publisher's address: Noll Plaza, Huntington, Ind.

WARD, Maisie, 1889- 901.94'6 B
To and fro on the earth: the sequel to an autobiography. London, New York, Sheed and Ward, 1973, [i.e.1974] [5], 176 p. 23 cm. [BX4705.W287A29] 72-12475 ISBN 0-7220-7301-1 8.50
1. Ward, Maisie, 1889- I. Title.

Ward, Mary, 1585-1645.

MARY Oliver, Mother. 922.242
Mary Ward, 1585-1645. Introd. and epilogue by Maisie Ward. New York, Sheed and Ward [1959] 229p. 22cm. [BX4705.W29M34] 59-12092
1. Ward, Mary, 1585-1645. I. Title.

SALOME, mother. 922.242
Mary Ward; a foundress of the 17th century. By Mother M. Salome...With an introduction by the Bishop of Newport. London, Burns & Oates, limited; New York [etc.] Benziger brothers, 1901. xv, 272 p. front. (port.) 3 double pl., facsim. 19 cm. [BX4705.W29S3] 3-31114
1. Ward, Mary, 1583-1643. I. Title.

Ward, William George, 1812-1882.

WARD, Wilfrid 282'.092'4 B
Philip, 1856-1916.
William George Ward and the Catholic revival / by Wilfrid Ward. 1st AMS ed. New York : AMS Press, 1978. xlvi, 468 p. : ill. ; 23 cm. Reprint of the 1893 ed. published by Macmillan, London, New York. Includes bibliographical references and index. [BX4705.W3W3 1978] 75-29626 ISBN 0-404-14042-4 : 31.50
1. Ward, William George, 1812-1882. 2. Catholics—England—Biography. 3. Converts, Catholic. I. Title.

WARD, Wilfrid 283'.092'4 B
Philip, 1856-1916.
William George Ward and the Oxford movement / by Wilfrid Ward. New York : AMS Press, 1977. xxix, 462 p. : ill. ; 23 cm. Reprint of the 1889 ed. published by Macmillan, London, New York. [BX4705.W3W35 1977] 75-29625 ISBN 0-404-14043-2 : 31.50
1. Ward, William George, 1812-1882. 2. Catholics in England—Biography. 3. Oxford movement. I. Title.

WARD, Wilfrid Philip, 922.242
1856-1916.
William George Ward and the Oxford movement, by Wilfrid Ward. London and New York, Macmillan and co., 1889. xxix, 462 p. front. (port.) 23 cm. [BX4705.W3W35] 37-18688
1. Ward, William George, 1812-1882. 2. Oxford movement. I. Title.

WARD, Wilfrid Philip, 1856- 922.
1916.
William George Ward and the Oxford movement, by Wilfrid Ward. 2d ed. London and New York, Macmilland co., 1890. xxxi, 481 p. front. (port.) 22 1/2 cm. [BX5199.W2W2] E 10
1. Ward, William George, 1812-1882. 2. Oxford movement. I. Title.

Ward, William George, 1812-1882. Oxford movement.

WARD, Wilfrid Philip, 1856- 922.
1916.
William George Ward and the Catholic revival. London and New York, Macmilland co., 1893. xivi, 468 p. front. (port.) facsim. (4 p.) 23 cm. [BX4705.W3W3] 1-20612
1. Ward, William George, 1812-1882. Oxford movement. 2. Catholic church in England. I. Title.

Warde, Mary Francis Xavier, 1810 - 1884— Juvenile literature.

MARIE Christopher, 922.273
Sister.
Frances Warde and the first Sisters of Mercy. Illustrated by John Lawn. New York, Farrar, Straus & Cudahy [1960] 189p. illus. 22cm. (Vision books, 47) [BX4705.W35M34] 60-10365
1. Warde, Mary Francis Xavier, 1810 - 1884— Juvenile literature. 2. Sisters of Mercy—Juvenile literature. I. Title.

Warde, Mary Francis Xavier, mother, 1810?-1884.

MANCHESTER, N.H. Mount 922.273
St. Mary's convent.
Reverend Mother M. Xavier Warde, foundress of the Order of mercy in the United States; the story of her life, with brief sketches of her foundations, by the Sisters of mercy, Mount St. Mary's, Manchester, New Hampshire; preface by the Rt. Rev. Denis M. Bradley, D.D. Boston, Marlier and company, limited, 1902. xv, [1] 287 p. front., plates, ports. 19 cm. [BX4705.W32M3] 2-30097
1. Warde, Mary Francis Xavier, mother, 1810?-1884. 2. Sisters of mercy. I. Title.

Wardlaw, Ralph, 1779-1853.

YATES, James, 1789-1871. 231
A vindication of Unitarianism, in reply to Mr. Wardlaw's Discourses on the Socinian controversy. By James Yates ... Boston, Wells and Lilly, 1816. iv, 294 p., 1 l., xxxv p. 23 cm. "Published ... from the Glasgow edition." [BT111.W23Y3] 44-21508
1. Wardlaw, Ralph, 1779-1853. Discourses on the principal points of the Socinian controversy. 2. Unitarian churches—Doctrinal and controversial works. I. Title.

Ware, Harriet, 1799-1847.

[WAYLAND, Francis] 1796- 922
1865.
A memoir of Harriet Ware, first superintendent of the Children's home in the city of Providence ... Providence, G. H. Whitney, 1850. v p., 1 l., 151 p. front. (port.) 18 cm. [BR1725.W33W3 1850] 38-3186
1. Ware, Harriet, 1799-1847. I. Title.

[WAYLAND, Francis] 1796- 922
1865.
Memoir of Harriet Ware ... Philadelphia, New York [etc.] American Sunday-school union [1853] 142 p. incl. front. (port.) 15 1/2 cm. [BR1725.W33W3 1853] 38-3185
1. Ware, Harriet, 1799-1847. I. American Sunday-school union [1853] II. Title.

Ware, Henry, 1764-1845.

ROBBINS, Chandler, 1810- 922.
1882.
A discourse preached before the Second church and society in Boston, in commemoration of the life and character of their former pastor, Rev. Henry Ware, jr., D. D.; on Sunday, Oct. 1, 1843. By their minister, Chandler Robbins. With an appendix. Boston, J. Munroe and company, 1843. viii, [9]-71 p. 22 cm. Appendix: Correspondence between Mr. Ware and the parish, p. 59-62. List of the published writings of Mr. Ware: p. 66-71. [BX9869.W3R7 1843] 5-11359
1. Ware, Henry, 1794-1843. I. Title.

WARE, Henry, 1794-1843. 208.
The works of Henry Ware, jr.... Boston, J. Munroe and company; London, Chapman brothers, 1846-47. 4 v. front. (port.) 20 cm. "Advertisement" signed: Chandler Robbins. Each volume has special t.-p. Contents.v. 1-2. Miscellaneous writings.--v. 3. Sermons.--v. 4. Sermons...to which are added his work on the Formation of Christian character, and his Sequel to the same. [BX9815.W3] 27-11375
I. Robinson, Chandler, 1810-1882, ed. II. Title.

WOODS, Leonard, 1774-1854. 230.
Letters to Unitarians and Reply to Dr. Ware. 2d ed. with an Appendix. By Leonard Woods ... Andover, M. Newman, 1822. viii, 351 p. 22 1/2 cm. "Reply to Dr. Ware's letters to Trinitarians and Calvinists": p. 119-288. [BX9847.W73] 28-9941
1. Ware, Henry, 1764-1845. Letters addressed to Trinitarians and Calvinists. 2. Unitarianism. I. Title.

WOODS, Leonard, 1774-1854. 230.
A reply to Dr. Ware's Letters to Trinitarians and Calvinists, by Leonard Woods ... Andover, Flagg and Gould, 1821. iv, [5]-228 p. 23 cm. [BX9847.W72] 28-9938
1. Ware, Henry, 1764-1845. Letters addressed to Trinitarians and Calvinists. I. Title.

Ware, Mrs. Mary Lovell (Pickard) 1796-1949.

HALL, Edward Brooks, 922.6178
1800-1866.
Memoir of Mary L. Ware, wife of Henry Ware, jr. By Edward B. Hall. 12th thousand. Boston, American Unitarian association, 1880. vii, 434 p. front. (port.) 19 1/2 cm. [BX9669.W35H3 1880] 15-23666
1. Ware, Mrs. Mary Lovell (Pickard) 1798-1849. I. American Unitarian association. II. Title.

HALL, Edward Brooks, 1800- 928.
1866.
Memoir of Mary L. Ware, wife of Henry Ware, jr. By Edward B. Hall. 5th thousand. Boston, Crosby, Nichols, and company; New York, C.S. Francis and company, 1853. vii, 434 p. front. (port.) 20 cm. [BX9869.W35H3 1853] 87-9269
1. Ware, Mrs. Mary Levell (Pickard) 1796-1842. I. Title.

HALL, Edward Brooks, 1922.8178
1800-1866.
Memoir of Mary L. Wars, wife of Henry Ware, jr. By Edward B. Hall. 11th thousand. Boston, American Unitarian association, 1867. vii, 434 p. front. (port.) 19 1/2 cm. [BX9869.W35H3] 24-9831
1. Ware, Mrs. Mary Lovell (Pickard) 1796-1949. I. American Unitarian association. II. Title.

Warfield, Bernis.

JOHNSON, Lois Pheips. 922.673
I'm gonna fly; the biography of Bernis Warfield. [1st ed.] Saint Paul, Macalester Park Pub. Co. [1959] 176p. 21cm. [BX6455.W34J6] 60-19260
1. Warfield, Bernis. I. Title.

Warmer, Rose.

WARMER, Rose. 248'.246 B
The journey : the story of Rose Warmer's triumphant discovery / written by Myrna Grant. Wheaton, Ill. : Tyndale House Publishers, c1978. 207 p. ; 21 cm. [BV2623.W27A34] 78-58746 ISBN 0-8423-1970-0 pbk. : 4.95 4.95
1. Warmer, Rose. 2. Converts from Judaism—Biography. I. Grant, Myrna. II. Title.

Warner, Daniel Sidney, 1842-1895.

BROWN, Charles Ewing, 1883- 289.9
When the trumpet sounded; a history of the Church of God reformation movement. Anderson, Ind., Warner Press [1951] 402 p. ports. (on lining papers) 21 cm. [BX7094.C673B7] 51-5411
1. Warner, Daniel Sidney, 1842-1895. 2. Church of God (Anderson, Ind.)—Hist. I. Title.

BYERS, Andrew L 1869- 287.
Birth of a reformation; or, The life and labors of Daniel S. Warner, by A. L. Byers ... Anderson, Ind., Los Angeles, Cal. [etc.] Gospel trumpet company [c1921] 447 p. front., illus. (incl. music) plates, ports., facsims. 20 cm. [BX7990.H6B8] 21-9464
1. Warner, Daniel Sidney, 1842-1895. I. Title.

Warner, Rex, 1905- tr.

AUGUSTINUS, Aurelius, Saint, Bp. of Hippo. 242
Confessions. A new translation by Rex Warner. [New York] New American Library [1963] xv. 351 p. 18 cm. (A Mentor-Omega book) "MT490." Bibliography: p. 351. [BR65.A6E5] 63-11920
1. Warner, Rex, 1905- tr. I. Title.

Warner, Trevor (Hanmer) Lady, 1636-1670.

JACKSON, Frances, 1848- 922.
From hearth to cloister in the reign of Charles I I; A narrative of Sir John and Lady Warner's so-much-wondered-at resolutions to leave the Anglican church and to enter the religious life. By Frances Jackson ... From hearth to cloister in the reign of Charles the second London, Burns & Oates, limited.; New York [etc.] Benziger brothers, 1902. 3 p. l., 117 p. 20 cm. Based on "The life of Lady Warner ... By a Catholic gentleman [i. e. Edward Scarisbrick]" London, 1691. [BX4705.W35J3] 3-15777
1. Warner, Trevor (Hanmer) Lady, 1636-1670. 2. Warner, Sir John, 1640-1705. I. Scarisbrick, Edward, 1639-1709. The life of Lady Warner. II. Title. III. Title: The life of Lady Warner.

Warnke, Mike.

LEAMING, Jeremiah, 1717-1804.
A second defence of the episcopal government, of the church, containing remarks on the objections advanced by Mr. Noah Welles against the Church of England; in a piece intitled, A vindication of the validity and divine right of Presbyterian ordination. By Jeremiah Leaming... New-York, Printed by John Holt, at the Exchange, M,DCC,LXX. 1 p. l., iii, 81 (i.e. 79) p. 19 1/2 cm. [With his A defence of the episcopal government of the church. New York, 1766] "Errors" slip mounted on verso of t.-p. [BV669.L4] 43-48676
1. Welles, Noah, 1718-1776. A vindication of the validity and divine right of Presbyterian ordination. 2. Episcopacy. 3. Presbyterianism. I. Title.

WARNKE, Mike. 248'.2'0924 B
Hitchhiking on Hope Street / Mike Warnke. 1st ed. Garden City, N.Y. : Doubleday, 1979. 112 p. ; 22 cm. "A Doubleday-Galilee original." [BV4935.W34A28] 78-73197 ISBN 0-385-14540-3 : 6.95
1. Warnke, Mike. 2. Converts—United States—Biography. 3. Christian life—1960- I. Title.

Warnshuis, Abbe Livingston, 1877-1958.

GOODALL, Norman,
Christian ambassador; a life of A. Livingston Warnshuis... Manhasset, N. Y., Channel Press [c1963] xi, 174 p. 21 cm. 64-23148
1. Warnshuis, Abbe Livingston, 1877-1958. I. Title.

Warren, Ed.

BRITTLE, Gerald. 133.4'2'0922 B
The demonologist : the extraordinary careers of Ed and Lorraine Warren / Gerald Brittle. Englewood Cliffs, N.J. : Prentice-Hall, c1980. xiii, 238 p., [4] leaves of plates : ill. ; 24 cm. Includes index. Bibliography: p. 233-234. [BF1531.B75] 19 80-21065 ISBN 0-13-198333-4 : 10.95
1. Warren, Ed. 2. Warren, Lorraine. 3. Demonology—Case studies. 4. Ghosts—Case studies. I. Title.

BRITTLE, Gerald. 133.4'2'922 B
The demonologist : The extraordinary careers of Ed and Lorraine Warren / Gerald Brittle. New York : Berkley Publishing Corp., 1981, c1980. 253 p. : 18 cm. Includes index. Bibliography: p.247-248. [BF1531.B75] pbk. : 2.95
1. Warren, Ed. 2. Warren, Lorraine. 3. Demonology-Case Studies. 4. Ghosts-Case Studies. I. Title.
L.C. card no. for the 1980 Prentice Hall edition: 80-21065

Warren, Israel Perkins, 1814-1892. The parousia.

LITCH, Josiah. 232.6
Christ yet to come: a review of Dr. I. P. Warren's "Parousia of Christ." By Rev. Josiah Litch ... with an introduction by Rev. A. J. Gordon ... Boston, American millennial association, 1880. xii, [13]-192 p. 20 cm. [BT885.W32] 37-15931
1. Warren, Israel Perkins, 1814-1892. The parousia. 2. Second advent. I. American millennial association. II. Title.

Warren, Merritt.

WHEELER, Ruth Lellah (Carr) 1899- 266.6'7'0924
Light the paper lantern; the adventures of Merritt and Wilma Warren, missionaries to China, by Ruth Wheeler. Mountain View, Calif., Pacific Press Pub. Association [c1967] v, 122 p. illus. 22 cm. (A Destiny book, D-116) [BV3427.W34W5] 67-31428
1. Warren, Merritt. 2. Warren, Wilma. 3. Missions—China. I. Title.

Warren, R.I. Baptist church.

SPALDING, Amos Fletcher, 1821-1877. 267.
The centennial discourse on the one hundredth anniversary of the First Baptist church, Warren, R.I., November 15, 1864, by A. F. Spalding, A.M., pastor of the church. With an appendix containing the proceedings connected with the occasion, the addresses at the reunion, an abstract of the memorial sermon by Rev. Rufus Babcock, D.D., and historical notes. Providence, Knowles, Anthony & co., printers, 1865. 2 p. l., 76 p. 24 cm. [F89.W19S7] [BX6248.R4H5] 974. 12-11817
1. Warren, R.I. Baptist church. I. Title.

Warwick, England. Church history Sources.

WARWICK, Eng. St. Mary's Church. 283'.424'8
Ministers' accounts of the collegiate church of St. Mary, Warwick 1432-85. Transcribed and edited by Dorothy Styles, with a memoir of Philip Boughton Chatwin by Philip Styles. Oxford, Printed for the Dugdale Society at the University Press, 1969. Lv, 198 p. illus. 26 cm. (Publications of the Dugdale Society, v. 26) Includes bibliographical references. [DA670.W3D9 vol. 26] 76-531616
1. Warwick, Eng.—Church history—Sources. I. Styles, Dorothy, ed. II. Title. III. Series: Dugdale Society. Publications, v. 26

Warwick, England. St. Mary's Church. Beauchamp Chapel.

DUGDALE, William Francis Stratford, Sir bart., 1872- ed. 726.5
The restoration of the Beauchamp Chapel at St. Mary's Collegiate Church, Warwick, 1674-1742. Oxford, Printed [at University Press] for presentation to the members of the Roxburghe Club, 1956. xvi, 104 p. plates (part col.) ports. (part col.) diagr., geneal. tables. 29cm. Bibliography: p. [92] [NA5471.W33D8] 57-2733
1. Warwick, Eng. St. Mary's Church. Beauchamp Chapel. I. Title.

Washington and Jefferson college, Washington, Pa.-History

BENNETT, Daniel Miller, 1864- comp. 922.573
Life and work of Rev. John McMillan, D. D., pioneer, preacher, educator, patriot, of western Pennsylvania. Collected, compiled and published by Daniel M. Bennett. Bridgeville, Pa., 1935. xvi, 525, [3] p. incl. front., illus.. ports.. map, facsim. 24 cm. Blank pages for "Memorandum" ([3] at end) [BX9225.M28B4] [CS71.M1675 1935] 36-3981
1. McMillan, John, 1752-1833. 2. McMillan family (William McMillan, 1717-1792) 3. Washington and Jefferson college, Washington, Pa.-Hist. I. Title.

Washington, Conn. First Congregational church.

DEMING, Wilbur Stone, 1889- 285.87461
The church on the green; the first two centuries of the First Congregational church at Washington, Connecticut, 1741-1941, by Wilbur Stone Deming. Hartford, Brentano's, 1941. xvi, 235 p. front., plates, ports. 20 cm. [BX7255.W27F5] 41-20131
1. Washington, Conn. First Congregational church. I. Title.

Washington, D. C. All souls' church.

SCUDDER, Jennie W. Mrs. 288.
A century of Unitarianism in the national capital, 1821-1921, by Jennie W. Scudder, issued under the auspices of the Washington chapter, Unitarian laymen's league. Boston, Mass., The Beacon press, 1922. viii p., 2 l., 164 p. front., plates, ports., facsims. 21 cm. [BX9861.W3S4] 23-292
1. Washington, D. C. All souls' church. I. Unitarial laymen's league. Washington chapter. II. Title.

STAPLES, Laurence Carlton, 1891- 288'.753
Washington Unitarianism; a rich heritage, by Laurence C. Staples. Washington, 1970. 175 p. illus., ports. 24 cm. Bibliography: p. 174-175. [BX9861.W3S7] 74-22094
1. Washington, D.C. All Souls Church. I. Title.

WASHINGTON, D.C. All Souls' church. 289
Year book. [Washington, v. illus. 23 cm. Cover-title. [BX9861.W3A3] CA 6
I. Title.

Washington, D.C. Calvary Baptist Church. Vaughn Bible class.

BLAKE, Nelson Morehouse, comp. 268.434
The Vaughn Bible class, Calvery Baptist church, Washington, D.C. A fifty-year history, compiled and edited by Nelson Morehouse Blake and Richard Spencer Palmer. Washington, D.C., The Franklin press [1940] 3 p. l., vi, 106 p. plates, ports. (part fold.)facsims. 23 cm. [BX6227.W3C38] 40-9535
1. Vaughn, Francis William, 1839-1913. 2. Washington, D.C. Calvary Baptist Church. Vaughn Bible class. I. Palmer, Richard Spencer, joint comp. II. Title.

Washington, D.C. Cathedral of St. Peter and St. Paul.

[BRATENAHL, Florence (Brown) Mrs. 726.6
The Pilgrim steps and other cathedral landscape adventures. [Washington, D. C., All Hallows guild, c1930] cover-title, 64 p. illus. 26 cm. "By Florence Bratenahi."--p. [2] of cover. [NA5235.W3B7] 30-15547
1. Washington, D. C. Cathedral of St. Peter and St. Paul. 2. Gardens—District of Columbia. I. All Hallows guild, Washington, D. C. II. Title.

BRATENAHL, George C F ed. 726
Hand book of Washington cathedral. Published by the authority of the bishop and chapter of Washington. 5th ed., rev. and enl. Ed. by G.C.F. Bratenahl ... [Washington! D. C., c1908] v, [1], 3-85 p. front. (fold. map) illus. 24 cm. [F204.C3B8 Copyright] 8-8834
1. Washington, D. C. Cathedral of SS. Peter and Paul. I. Title.

BRATENAHL, George Carl Fitch, 1862- ed. 726.609753
Hand book of Washington cathedral. Published by the authority of the bishop and chapter of Washington. 6th ed., rev. and enl. Edited by G.C.F. Bratenahl... Handbook of washington cathedral [Washington! D. C., c1911] 3 p. l., 3-104 p. fold. front., illus. (incl. plans) port. 24 cm. [F204.C3B8 1911] 33-12870
1. Washington, D. C. Cathedral of St. Peter and St. Paul. I. Title.

FELLER, Richard T 726.609753
For Thy great glory [by] Richard T. Feller [and] Marshall W. Fishwick. [Culpepper, Va., Community Press, 1965] 111 p. 246 illus. (part col.) plans, ports. 28 cm. Bibliographical footnotes. [NA5235.W3F4] 65-16139
1. Washington, D.C. Cathedral of St. Peter and St. Paul. I. Fishwick, Marshall William, joint author. II. Title.

HARRINGTON, Ty, 1951- 726'.6'09753
The last cathedral / Ty Harrington. Englewood Cliffs, N.J. : Prentice-Hall, c1979. xiii, 156 p., [6] leaves of plates : ill. ; 29 cm. [NA5235.W3H37] 79-11976 ISBN 0-13-523878-1 : 19.95
1. Washington, D.C. Cathedral of St. Peter and St. Paul. I. Title.

MONTGOMERY, Nancy S. 746.4'4
Stitches for God : the story of Washington Cathedral needlepoint / Nancy S. Montgomery. Washington : Cathedral Church of Saint Peter and Saint Paul, [1974] 32 p. : ill. (some col.) ; 23 cm. [NK9310.M66] 74-84715
1. Washington, D.C. Cathedral of St. Peter and St. Paul. 2. Ecclesiastical embroidery—Washington, D.C. 3. Canvas embroidery. I. Title.

NATIONAL cathedral association. 726.609753
A view book of Washington cathedral, with many illustrations in full color. Washington, D. C., National cathedral association [1940] 160 p. incl. col. front., illus. (part col.) plates. plans (1 fold.) 24 cm. "First edition in color, October 1940." [NA5235.W3N27] 41-1548
1. Washington, D. C. Cathedral of St. Peter and St. Paul. I. Title.

[SATTERLEE, Henry Yates, bp.] 1843-1908, comp. 726.
The peace cross book; Cathedral of S.S. Peter and Paul, Washington. New York, R. H. Russell, 1899. 3 p. l., [11]-75 p., 1 l. plates. 21 cm. Compiled by H. Y. Satterlee. [BX5980.W3P4] 99-2154
1. Washington, D.C. Cathedral of St. Peter and St. Paul. 2. Cross and crosses—Washington, D.C. I. Title.

WASHINGTON, D.C. Cathedral of St. Peter and St. Paul. 726.
Eminent opinion regarding the cathedral at Washington: representative Americans state their views. [Washington, D.C.] Washington cathedral, Executive committee [c1929] [65] p. illus. (ports.) 23 1/2 cm. [F204.C3W24] 30-2357
I. Title.

[WASHINGTON, D.C. Cathedral of St. Peter and St. Paul] 726.
A guide book. Washington cathedral, Mount Saint Alban, Washington, D.C., A.D. 1927. (2d ed.) [Washington, D.C., National cathedral association, 1927] 81 p., 3 l. illus. (incl. plans) 23 cm. Text on p. [2]-[4] of cover. [F204.C3W25 1927] 35-30113
I. Title.

WASHINGTON, D.C. Cathedral of St. Peter and St. Paul. 726.609753
A guide book, Washington cathedral, Mount Saint Alban, Washington, D.C., A.D. 1934. (6th ed.) [Washington, D.C., National cathedral association, c1934] 140

p. illus. (incl. ports.) plans (1 fold.) 25 1/2 cm. Text on pages [2]-[4] of cover. [F204.C3W25 1934] 35-7109
I. Title.

WASHINGTON, D.C. 726.609753
Cathedral of St. Peter and St. Paul.
A guide book, Washington cathedral, Mount Saint Alban, Washington, D.C., A.D. 1937. (8th ed.) [Washington, D.C., National cathedral association, c1937] 136 p. illus. (incl. ports.) plans (1 fold.) 25 1/2 cm. Text on pages [2]-[4] of cover. [F204.C3W25] 37-15026
I. Title.

WASHINGTON, D.C. 726.609753
Cathedral of St. Peter and St. Paul.
A guide book, Washington cathedral, Mount Saint Alban, Washington, D.C. A.D. 1940. (10th ed.) Washington, D.C., The National cathedral association, 1940. 135 p. illus. (incl. ports.) plans (1 fold.) 25 1/2 cm. Text on p. [2]-[4] of cover. [F204.C3W25 1940] 40-33549
I. Title.

WASHINGTON, D.C. 726.609753
Cathedral of St. Peter and St. Paul. Executive committee.
Eminent opinion regarding the cathedral at Washington. Representative Americans state their views. [Washington, D.C.] Washington Cathedral executive committee [c1931] [68] p. illus. (ports.) 23 1/2 cm. [F204.C3W242] 34-36161
1. Washington, D.C. Cathedral of St. Peter and St. Paul. I. Title.

Washington, D.C. Chevy Chase Bpatist Church.

CLARK, Ecward Oliver, 286.1753
1893-
Faith fulfilled the story of Chevy Chase Baptist Church of Washington, D.C., 1923-1956. [Washington, 1957] 129p. illus. 22cm. [BX6480.W3C5] 58-16287
1. Washington, D.C. Chevy Chase Bpatist Church. I. Title.

Washington, D.C. Church of the Saviour.

COSBY, Gordon. 266
Handbook for mission groups / Gordon Cosby. Waco, Tex. : Word Books, c1975. 179 p. ; 23 cm. Includes bibliographical references. [BX9999.W383C67] 73-91551 ISBN 0-87680-346-X : 5.95
1. Washington, D.C. Church of the Saviour. 2. Church group work. I. Title.

O'CONNOR, Elizabeth. 289.9
Call to commitment; the story of the Church of the Saviour, Washington, D.C. New York, San Francisco, Harper and Row [1975 c1963] xiv, 205 p. 20 cm. Includes bubliographical references. [BX9999.W3C5] ISBN 0-06-066329-4 2.95 (pbk.)
1. Washington, D.C.—Church of the Saviour. I. Title.
L.C. card no. for original edition: 63-10963.

O'CONNOR, Elizabeth. 289.9
Call to commitment; the story of the Church of the Saviour, Washington, D.C. [1st ed.] New York, Harper & Row [1963] 205 p. illus. 22 cm. [BX9999.W3C5] 63-10963
1. Washington, D.C. Church of the Saviour. I. Title.

O'CONNOR, Elizabeth. 289.9
Journey inward, journey outward / Elizabeth O'Connor. New York : Harper & Row, 1975, c1968. x, 175 p., [2] leaves of plates : ill. ; 21 cm. Includes bibliographical references. [BX9999.W3C52 1975] 75-310905 ISBN 0-06-066332-4 pbk. : 3.95
1. Washington, D.C. Church of the Saviour. I. Title.

O'CONNOR, Elizabeth. 289.9
Journey inward, journey outward. [1st ed.] New York, Harper & Row [1968] x, 175 p. illus. 22 cm. [BX9999.W3C52] 68-11728
1. Washington, D.C. Church of the Saviour. I. Title.

O'CONNOR, Elizabeth. 261.8
The new community / Elizabeth O'Connor. 1st ed. New York : Harper & Row, c1976. 121 p. : ill. ; 22 cm. Includes bibliographical references. [BV4501.2.O32 1976] 76-9964 ISBN 0-06-066337-5 pbk. : 3.95
1. Washington, D.C. Church of the Saviour. 2. Christian life—1960- 3. Christian communities. 4. Church and the poor—Case studies. I. Title.

Washington, D. C.—Churches.

BROWN, Lillian Brooks. 277.53
Churches of the Presidents, a television series. Presented under the auspices of the Dept. of Radio and Television of the Washington Federation of Churches. [Washington? 1955] unpaged. illus. 22cm. [F203.2.A1B7] 55-4016
1. Washington, D. C.— Churches. 2. Presidents—U. S.—Religion. I. Churches of the Presidents (Television program) II. Title.

JONES, Olga Anna. 277.53
Churches of the Presidents in Washington; visits to sixteen national shrines. Foreword by Edward L. P. Elson. [2d enl. ed.] New York, Exposition Press [1961] 128p. illus. 21cm. [F203.2.A1J63 1961] 61-66359
1. Washington, D. C.—Churches. 2. Presidents—U. S.—Religion. I. Title.

NELMS, John Henning, ed. 277.
Where Washington worships ... editor, Rev. J. Henning Nelms ... [Washington, Acme printing co.] c1917. [5]-148 p. illus. (incl. ports., facsim.) 27 cm. Contains advertising matter. [BR560.W3N4] 17-17185
1. Washington, D. C.—Churches. I. Title.

WASHINGTON federation of 277.
churches.
Where Washington worships; a handbook of the churches of the District of Columbia, published under the auspices of the Washington federation of churches with a view to providing the community with ready information about every church and congregation ... 1st- 1923- Washington, D.C., Offices of the Federation [1923- v. illus. 27 cm. annual. [BR560.W35W3] 23-12206
1. Washington, D.C.—Churches. I. Title.

Washington, D.C.—Churches—Year-books.

WASHINGTON federation of 277.53
churches.
... Year book and church directory of the Protestant churches of the District of Columbia. 1936- Washington, The Washington Federation of churches [1936- v. illus. (incl. ports.) 23 cm. Continues Washington federation of churches. Where Washington worships. 1923, 1925 and 1926. [BR560.W35W32] 36-33581
1. Washington, D.C.—Churches—Year-books. 2. Protestant churches—Washington, D.C.—Year-books. I. Title.

Washington, D.C. Foundry Methodist Church.

CALKIN, Homer L. 287'.6753
Castings from the Foundry mold; a history of Foundry Church, Washington, D.C., 1814-1964, by Homer L. Calkin. [Nashville, Parthenon Press, 1968] 377 p. illus. 24 cm. Includes bibliographical references. [BX8481.W3F66] 68-2953
1. Washington, D.C. ?Foundry Methodist Church. I. Title.

CALKIN, Homer L 287.6753
Chronology and historical narratives of Foundry's 150 years, 1814-1964, by Homer L. Calkin. [Washington, 1965] 1 v. (unpaged) 24 cm. "Issued as supplements to the church bulletin during the twenty-two weeks of Foundry's sesquicentennial celebration [Nov. 22, 1964-Apr. 15, 1965]" [BX8481.W3F67] 66=86335
1. Washington, D.C. Foundry Methodist Church. I. Title.

Washington, D. C. Georgetown visitation convent.

LATHROP, George Parsons, 1851-
1898.
A story of courage; annals of the Georgetown convent of the Visitation of the Blessed Virgin Mary, from the manuscript records by George Parsons Lathrop and Rose Hawthorne Lathrop. Cambridge [Mass.] The Riverside press, 1895. 2 p. l., [iii]-xii p., 1 l., 380 p. front., plates, ports., double facsim. 23 cm. Edition de luxe. "Two hundred and fifty copies printed, number --.' Most of the plates accompanied by guard sheet, with descriptive letter-press. [BX4549.G4L3] 1-13625
1. Francois de Sales, Saint, bp. of Geneva, 1567-1622. 2. Washington, D. C. Georgetown visitation convent. 3. Order of the visitation. I. Lathrop, Rose (Hawthorne) Mrs. 1851-1926, joint author. II. Title.

Washington, D.C. Holy Trinity parish.

KELLY, Laurence J. 282.753
History of Holy Trinity parish, Washington, D.C., 1795-1945, by Rev. Laurence J. Kelly, S.J., on the occasion of the sesquicentennial celebration, November 4 to 11, 1945. Baltimore, Md., The John D. Lucas printing company [1945] 5 p. l., 127 p. front., illus. (incl. ports.) 24 cm. [BX4603.W32H63] 46-19818
1. Washington, D.C. Holy Trinity parish. I. Title.

Washington, D.C. Islamic Center.

ABDUL-RAUF, Muhammad, 297'.09753
1917-
History of the Islamic Center : from dream to reality / by Muhammad Abdul-Rauf. Washington : The Center, c1978. 96 p. : ill. ; 23 cm. [BP187.6.W37I742] 79-100935 pbk. : 3.00
1. Washington, D.C. Islamic Center. I. Washington, D.C. Islamic Center. II. Title.

Washington, D.C. Metropolitan Memorial United Methodist Church.

BROWN, Lillian Brooks. 287'.6753
A living centennial, commemorating the one hundredth anniversary of Metropolitan Memorial United Methodist Church. Washington [Printed by Judd & Detweiler] 1969. 88 p. illus., facsims., ports. 32 cm. [BX8481.W3M463] 78-76377
1. Washington, D.C. Metropolitan Memorial United Methodist Church. I. Title.

Washington, D. C. Mt. St. Sepulchre (Franciscan monastery)

CRANE, John de Murinelly 271.3
Cirne, 1900-
The Franciscan monastery, memorial church of the Holy Land. Washington, '1951. 1 v. (unpaged) illus., map. 26 cm. [BX2525.W3M64] 51-5369
1. Washington, D. C. Mt. St. Sepulchre (Franciscan monastery) I. Title.

[NESTERMAN, Lewis J.] ed. 271.3
The Franciscan monastery, memorial church of the Holy land. Washington [Capital souvenir company, 1946] 1 p. l., [62] p. of illus. (incl. map) 25 1/2 cm. Map continued on p. [3] of cover. "Copyrighted and edited ... by Lewis J. Nesterman." [BX2525.W3M65] 47-21742
1. Washington, D.C. Mt. St. Sepulchre (Franciscan monastery) I. Title.

Washington, D.C. National Presbyterian Church.

NANNES, Caspar Harold, 285'.1753
1903-
The National Presbyterian Church & Center, by Caspar Nannes. [Washington, Printing: Vinmar Lithographing Co., 1970] 51 p. illus. (part col.), ports. 29 cm. Bibliography: p. 51. [BX9211.W3N37] 75-17178
1. Washington, D.C. National Presbyterian Church. I. Title.

Washington, D. C. National Shrine of the Immaculate Conception.

MCKENNA, Bernard 282.753
Aloysius.
A song in stone to Mary, as told by Bernard A. McKenna to the author Victor F. O Daniel. Philadelphia [1953] ixxxvi, 509p. illus. ports. facsims. 24cm. [BX4603.W32N32] 53-20857
1. Washington, D. C. National Shrine of the Immaculate Conception. I. O'Daniel, Victor Francis, 1868- II. Title.

Washington, D.C. National Shrine of the Immaculate Conception. Slovenian Chapel.

SLOVENIAN chapel 917.53
dedication, Washington, D.C., August 15, 1971. [Editors: Cyril J. Mejac, Vladimir N. Pregelj. Washington, Slovenian Chapel Dedication Committee, c1971] 88 p. illus. 27 cm. Cover title. [BX4603.W32N34] 74-181643
1. Washington, D.C. National Shrine of the Immaculate Conception. Slovenian Chapel. I. Mejac, Cyril J., ed. II. Pregelj, Vladimir N., ed.

WASHINGTON Committee for 917.53
the Slovenian Chapel.
Slovenian Chapel in the National Shrine of the Immaculate Conception, Washington, D.C. [Washington] 1968. 16 p. illus., port. 15 x 23 cm. Cover title. [BX4603.W32N35] 70-11194
1. Washington, D.C. National Shrine of the Immaculate Conception. Slovenian Chapel. I. Title.

Washington, D. C. Saint Agnes' Episcopal Church.

BURR, Nelson Rollin, 283.753
1904-
A history of Saint Agnes' Episcopal Church Washington, D. C. [Washington? 1948] 61 p. illus. 23 cm. "Sources used in writing this history": p. [60]-61. [BX5980.W3A3] 48-11622
1. Washington, D. C. Saint Agnes' Episcopal Church. I. Title.

Washington, D.C. St. Francis Xavier Church.

THE Beacon (Washington 282.753
D.C.)
Twenty-fifth anniversary [1926-1951] St. Francis Xavier Parish, Washington, D.C. [Washington, 1951?] unpaged. illus. 28cm. 'Special silver jubilee edition.' [BX4603.W32S324] 54-34430
1. Washington, D.C. St. Francis Xavier Church. I. Title.

Washington, D.C. St. John's Church, Lafayette Square.

GREEN, Constance 283'.753
(McLaughlin) 1897-
The church on Lafayette Square; a history of St. John's Church, Washington, D.C., 1815-1970. Washington, Potomac Books [1970] ix, 116 p. illus., plans, ports. 24 cm. [BX5980.W3J62] 78-141034
1. Washington, D.C. St. John's Church, Lafayette Square. I. Title.

Washington, D. C. St. Matthew's cathedral.

PHILIBERT, Helene. 282.753
Saint Matthew's of Washington, 1840-1940, by Helene, Estelle and Imogene Philibert; foreword by the Right Reverend Edward L. Buckey. Baltimore, A. Hoen & co. [c1940] vii p., 3 l., 154 p. front., plates, ports. 26 cm. "Centennial edition (first edition, first printing)" Bibliography: p. 152-154. [BX4603.W32S33] 41-2892
1. Washington, D. C. St. Matthew's cathedral. I. Philibert, Estelle, joint author. II. Philibert, Imogene, joint author. III. Title.

Washington, D. C. St. Stephen's Church (Catholic)

GATTI, Lawrence P, 1914- 282.753
Historic St. Stephen's; an account of its eighty-five years, 1867-1952, on the occasion of the silver jubilee of the present pastor, Reverend Joseph F. Denges. Washington [1952] 144 p. illus. 23 cm. [BX4603.W32S36] 52-64453
1. Washington, D. C. St. Stephen's Church (Catholic) I. Title.

LANGLEY, Harold D. 282.753
St. Stephen Martyr Church and the community, 1867-1967 [by] Harold D. Langley. Washington [1968] vi, 131 p. illus. (part col.), facsims., ports. 29 cm. "Sponsored by the St. Stephen's Centennial Committee." Bibliography: p. 131. [BX4603.W32S4] 68-57029
1. Washington, D.C. St. Stephen's Church (Catholic) I. Washington, D.C. St. Stephen's Church (Catholic) Centennial Committee. II. Title.

Washington, D.C. St Paul's Parish.

SPAULDING, Dorothy W. 283'.753
Saint Paul's Parish, Washington, one hundred years [by] Dorothy W. Spaulding, with contributions and assistance from the rector and members of St. Paul's. Washington, 1967. vii, 101 p. illus., ports. 24 cm. Bibliography: p. 97-98. [BX5980.W3P33] 72-9547
1. Washington, D.C. St Paul's Parish. I. Title.

Washington, D. C, Way of the Cross Church of Christ.

BROOKS, Henry Chauncey, Bp., 1896- 289.9
The way of the cross leads to the crown; doctrine, life [and] sermons of Bishop Henry C. Brooks. Compiled and edited by L. Frances Hill-Watkins. [Washington? 1950] 207 p. illus., port. 20 cm. [BX9999.W3W3] 51-31771
1. Washington, D. C, Way of the Cross Church of Christ. I. Title.

Washington for Jesus rally.

GIMENEZ, John. 269'.24
Healing the fracture : America restored through the reconciliation of the church / John Gimenez ; [foreword by Pat Robertson]. Costa Mesa, CA : Gift Publications, c1981. 218 p., [9] p. of plates : ill. ; 22 cm. [BR1725.G47A33 1981] 19 81-84151 ISBN 0-86595-007-5 pbk. : Price unreported.
1. Gimenez, John. 2. Washington for Jesus rally. 3. Reconciliation—Religious aspects—Christianity. I. Title.

MANUEL, David. 269'.2'09753
The gathering / David Manuel. Orleans, Mass. : Rock Harbor Press, c1980. 230 p., [24] leaves of plates : ill. ; 21 cm. [BR526.M34] 19 80-5385 ISBN 0-932260-07-1 pbk. : 4.95
1. Washington for Jesus rally. I. Title.

Washington Street United Methodist Church, Columbia, S.C.

HEDMAN, Kathryn Pierpoint, 1916- 287'.6755'296
Washington Street United Methodist Church, Alexandria, Virginia : reflections, 1849-1974 / researcher and editor, Kathryn Pierpoint Hedman. [Alexandria? Va. : Washington Street United Methodist Church?, 1974] 348 p. : ill. ; 23 cm. [BX8481.A53W373] 75-301769
1. Washington Street United Methodist Church. 2. Alexandria, Va.—Biography.

HUFF, Archie Vernon, 1937- 287'.6757'71
Tried by fire : Washington Street United Methodist Church, Columbia, South Carolina / Archie Vernon Huff, Jr. [Greenville? S.C.] : Huff, [1975] xii, 163 p. : ill. ; 24 cm. Includes index. Bibliography: p. 133-136. [BX8481.C72W373] 75-314986
1. Washington Street United Methodist Church, Columbia, S.C. I. Title.

Wat Haripunjaya.

SWEARER, Donald K., 1934- 294.3'63
Wat Haripunjaya : a study of the Royal Temple of the Buddha's Relic, Lamphun, Thailand / by Donald K. Swearer. Missoula, Mont. : Published by Scholars Press for the American Academy of Religion, c1976. x, 94 p. : ill. ; 24 cm. (Studies in religion ; no. 10) Includes bibliographical references. [BQ6337.L352W378] 75-33802 ISBN 0-89130-052-X : 4.50
1. Wat Haripunjaya. 2. Gautama Buddha—Relics. I. Title. II. Series: American Academy of Religion. AAR studies in religion ; no. 10.

WESLEY, John, 1703-1791. 287'.092'4 B
The heart of John Wesley's Journal / with an introd. by Hugh Price Hughes, and an appreciation of the Journal by Augustine Birrell ; edited by Percy Livingstone Parker. New Canaan, Conn. : Keats Pub., 1979. xxxviii, 512 p., [12] leaves of plates : ill. ; 22 cm. (A Shepherd illustrated classic) Condensed ed. Reprint of the 1903 ed. published by Revell, New York. Includes index. [BX8495.W5A342 1979] 79-64828 ISBN 0-87983-207-X : 5.95
1. Wesley, John, 1703-1797. 2. Methodist Church—Clergy—Biography. 3. Clergy—England—Biography. I. Parker, Percy Livingstone, 1867-1925. II. Title.

Watch night.

NAGY, Paul, jr. 791.6
... In this sign conquer! A dramatic service of worship for watch night in candle light, by Paul Nagy, jr. ... Boston, Mass., Los Angeles, Cal., Baker's plays [1944] 23 p. 1 illus. 18 1/2 cm. (Baker's religious plays and pageants.) [BV50.N48N3] 44-31671
1. Watch night. I. Title.

Watch Tower Bible and Tract Society.

SCHNELL, William J., 1905- 289.9
Thirty years a Watch Tower slave; the confessions of a converted Jehovah's Witness. Grand Rapids, Baker Book House, 1956. 207 p. illus. 23 cm. [BX8526.S35] 56-13037
1. Watch Tower Bible and Tract Society. 2. Jehovah's Witnesses—Doctrinal and controversial works. I. Title.

Watch Tower Bible and Tract Society of New York.

BIBLE, N.T. German. 1963. 225.53
Neue-Welt-Ubersetzung der Christlichen Griechischen Schriften, Ubersetz nach der englischen Wiedergabe von 1961, doch unter getreuer Berucksichtigung des griechischen Urtextes [Brooklyn, N. Y., 124 Columbia Heights, Watchtower Bible & Tract Soc. of New York, c.1963] 352p. 19cm. 63-23289 .50
1. Watch Tower Bible and Tract Society of New York. I. Title.

Water.

HOUCK, Frederick Alfons, 1866- 265
Fountains of joy; or, "By water and blood," by the Rev. Frederick A. Houck... St. Louis, Mo., and London, B. Herder book co., 1931. ix, 277 p. 19 1/2 c. Contents.--pt. 1. Water.--pt. 2. Sacramental water.--pt. 3. The precious blood. [BX2203.H6] 31-10190
1. Water. 2. Holy water. 3. Lord's supper. I. Title.

Watergate Affair, 1972-

CROCKETT, H. Dale, 1933- 261.7
Focus on Watergate : an examination of the moral dilemma of Watergate in the light of civil religion / by H. Dale Crockett. Macon, Ga. : Mercer University Press, [1982], c1979. p. cm. Includes bibliographical references and index. [E860.C76 1982] 19 81-16952 ISBN 0-86554-017-9 : 14.95
1. Watergate Affair, 1972- 2. United States—Religion—1960- I. Title.

Waters, Ethel, 1900-1977.

DEKORTE, Juliann. 783.7'092'4 B
Finally home / by Juliann DeKorte. Old Tappan, N.J. : F. H. Revell Co., c1978. 128 p., [9] leaves of plates : ill ; 22 cm. At head of title: Ethel Waters. [ML420.W24D4] 78-5697 ISBN 0-8007-0934-9 : 5.95
1. Waters, Ethel, 1900-1977. 2. Singers—United States—Biography. I. Title.

WATERS, Ethel, 1900-1977. 783.7'092'4 B
His eye is on the sparrow : an autobiography / by Ethel Waters with Charles Samuels. Westport, Conn. : Greenwood Press, 1978, c1951. p. cm. Reprint of the ed. published by Doubleday, Garden City, N.Y. [ML420.W24A3 1978] 77-27496 lib.bdg. : 17.50
1. Waters, Ethel, 1900- 2. Singers—United States—Biography. I. Samuels, Charles. II. Title.

Waterston, Robert Cassie, 1812-1898.

WARE, Henry, 1794-1843. 252.
A discourse preached at the ordination of Mr. Robert C. Waterston, as minister at large, Nov. 24, 1839. By Henry Ware, jr. ... Boston, I. R. Butts, printer, 1840. 51 p. 22 cm. [BX9843.W4D5] 27-485
1. Waterston, Robert Cassie, 1812-1898. I. Title.

Watertown, Wis. St. Bernard's church.

MEAGHER, George T. 282.775
A century at St. Bernard's, by George T. Meagher, C.S.C. A history of the priests, activities, and people of St. Bernard's parish, Watertown, Wisconsin. Milwaukee, Wis., Sentinel bindery & printing company, 1946. 7 p. l., 176 p. plates, ports., facsims. 23 1/2 cm. [BX4603.W35S3] 46-18801
1. Watertown, Wis. St. Bernard's church. I. Title.

Waterville, Me. First Baptist church.

PHILBRICK, Minnie Lambert (Smith) Mrs. d.1924. 286.
... Centennial history of the First Baptist church of Waterville, Maine, by Minnie Smith Philbrick. Waterville, Me., F. B. Philbrick, 1925. 129 p. front., pl., port. 24 cm. At head of title: 1818-1918. [BX6480.W35P5] 25-23836
1. Waterville, Me. First Baptist church. I. Title.

Watson, John, 1850-1907.

EADES, Ronald W. 342.73'087
Watson v. Jones : the Walnut Street Presbyterian Church and the First Amendment / Ronald W. Eades. 1st ed. Lynnville, TN : Archer Editions Press, c1982. 144 p. ; 21 cm. Bibliography: p. 137-144. [KF228.W37E244 1982] 347.30287 19 82-1803 ISBN 0-89097-023-8 : 18.50
1. Watson, John. 2. Jones, William. 3. Walnut Street Presbyterian Church (Louisville, Ky.) 4. Church property—Kentucky. 5. Religious liberty—Kentucky. I. Title.

NICOLL, William Robertson, Sir, 1851-1923.
"Ian Maclaren"; the life of the Rev. John Watcon, D.D., by W. Robertson Nicoll. New York, Dodd, Mead and company, 1908. iv, 367 p. front. (port.) 21 cm. "List of works": p. 367. [PR5743.N5] 8-33799
1. Watson, John, 1850-1907. I. Title.

WATSON, John, 1850-1907.
Children of the resurrection, by John Watson, D.D. (Ian Maclaren) New York, Dodd, Mead and company, 1912. 190 p. front. 17 cm. $1.00 12-7797
I. Title.
Contents omitted.

[WATSON, John] 1850-1907.
The science of life: religion; by Ian Maclaren [pseud.] New York, Dodd, Mead and company, 1895. [7] p. 18 1/2 cm. CA 12
I. Title.

Watson, Richard, 1781-1833.

JACKSON, Thomas, 1783-1873. 922.
Memoirs of the life and writings of the Rev. Richard Watson, late secretary to the Wesleyan missionary society. By Thomas Jackson ... New-York, Pub. by G. Lane, for the Methodist Episcopal church, 1841. 486 p. front. (port.) 23 cm. Published also as vol. i of the Works of R. Watson, 1834-37, edited by T. Jackson. [BX8495.W323J3 1841] 15-983
1. Watson, Richard, 1781-1833. I. Title.

THE life of Rev. Richard Watson ... Compiled from authentic sources ... New-York, G. Lane & P. P. Sandford, for the Methodist Episcopal church, 1841. 312 p. 15 cm. [BX8495.W323L5] 37-9734 922.742
1. Watson, Richard, 1781-1833.

WICKENS, Stephen B. 922.742
The life of Rev. Richard Watson ... By Stephen B. Wickens ... 4th ed. New York, Carlton & Phillips, 1856. 312 p. 15 1/2 cm. [BX8495.W323W5 1856] 33-32840
1. Watson, Richard, 1781-1833. I. Title.

Watson, Richard, 1781-1833. Theological institutes.

[MCCLINTOCK, John] 1814-1870. 230
Analysis of Watson's Theological institutes. Designed for the use of students and examining committees. New York, Pub. by G. Lane & P. P. Sandford, for the Methodist Episcopal church, 1842. 228 p. 15 cm. [BR121.W4M4] 34-9075
1. Watson, Richard, 1781-1833. Theological institutes. I. Title.

Watson, Richard, bp. of Llandaff, 1737-1816.

STRICTURES on Bishop Watson's "Apology for the Bible." By a citizen of New York ... New York, Printed for J. Fellows, 1796. 1 p. l., 48 p. 18 1/2 cm. [BL2740.W4S7] 21-17183 211
1. Watson, Richard, bp. of Llandaff, 1737-1816. "Apology for the Bible." 2. Paine, Thomas, 1737-1809. Age' of reason. I. A citizen of New York.

Watters, William, 1751-1827.

WATTERS, Dennis Alonzo, 1849- 922.773
First American itinerant of Methodism, William Watters. By Rev. D. A. Watters...Introduction by Bishop Charles C. McCabe... Cincinnati, Printed for the author by Curts & Jennings, 1898. 172 p. 19 cm. [BX8495.W325W3] 37-12142
1. Watters, William, 1751-1827. I. Title.

Watts, Alan Wilson, 1915-

WATTS, Alan Wilson, 1915- 294.3'927'0924 B
In my own way; an autobiography, 1915-1965 [by] Alan Watts. [1st ed.] New York, Pantheon Books [1972] xii, 400 p. illus. 22 cm. [BL1473.W3A34] 72-3409 ISBN 0-394-46911-9 7.95
I. Title.

WATTS, Alan Wilson, 1915- 294.3'927'0924 B
In my own way; an autobiography, 1915-1965 [by] Alan Watts. New York, Vintage Books [1973, c1972] xi, 466 p. 18 cm. [BQ995.T8A33 1973] 73-5592 2.45
1. Watts, Alan Wilson, 1915- I. Title.

Watts, Isaac, 1674-1748.

[BELKNAP, Jeremy] 1744-1798. 922.
Memoirs of the lives, characters and writings of those two eminently pious and useful ministers of Jesus Christ, Dr. Issac Watts and Dr. Philip Doddridge Printed at Boston, by Peter Edes for David West, mdccxciii. 301 p. 21 cm. "An appendix is added, containing several of Dr. Watts' essays in verse and prose, which have not before been printed in America, and an authentic account of his last sentiments on the doctrine of the Trinity, by Samuel Palmer. The life of Dr. Doddridge is

written by Dr. Andrew Kippis"-Advertisement [BX5207.W3B4] 1-5167
1. Watts, Isaac, 1674-1748. 2. Doddrige, Philip, 1702-1751. I. Palmer, Samuel, 1741-1813. II. Kippis, Andrew, 1725-1795. III. Title.

BISHOP, Selma Lewis. 016.245'21
Isaac Watts's Hymns and spiritual songs, 1707 : a publishing history and a bibliography / compiled and edited by Selma L. Bishop. Ann Arbor, Mich. : Pierian Press, 1974. xxiv, 479 p., [2] leaves of plates ; 24 cm. Includes indexes. [Z7800.B57] [BS1440.W3] 73-78316 ISBN 0-87650-033-5
1. Watts, Isaac, 1674-1748. Hymns and spiritual songs—Bibliography. 2. Hymns, English—Bibliography. I. Watts, Isaac, 1647-1748. Hymns and spiritual songs. II. Title.

DAVIS, Arthur Paul. 922.342
Isaac Watts, his life and works [by] Arthur Paul Davis ... New York, The Dryden press [1943] xi, 306 p. 21 cm. "First edition." "Bibliography I. Works of Isaac Watts": p. 271-281. "Bibliography II. General": p. 282-295. [BX5207.W3D3] (928.2) 43-6707
1. Watts, Isaac, 1674-1748. I. Title.

WATTS, Isaac, 1674-1748.
The beauties of the late Rev. Dr. Isaac Watts: containing the most striking and admired passages in the works of that celebrated divine, philosopher, moralist, and poet. To which is added, the life of the author. Caldwell [N.Y.] W. Storer, jun. printer, 1821. xiv, [15]-196 p. 17 cm. [BX5200.W32 1821] 24-15958
I. Title.

WATTS, Isaac, 1674-1748.
The beauties of the late Rev. Dr. Isaac Watts; containing the most striking and admired passages in the works of that justly celebrated divine, philosopher, moralist, and poet: equally calculated for the communication of polite and useful knowledge, and the increase of wisdom and happiness. To which is added, the life of the author. Elizabeth-Town [N.J.]: Printed by Shepard Kollock, 1796. 1 p. l., xii, [13]-229, [5] p. 13 1/2 cm. [BX5200.W32 1796] 24-15959
I. Title.

WATTS, Isaac, 1674-1748.
The beauties of the late Rev. Dr. Isaac Watts: containing the most striking and admired passages in the works of that celebrated divine, philosopher, moralist, and poet. To which is added, the life of the author. Caldwell [N.Y.] W. Storer, jun. printer, 1821. xiv, [15]-196 p. 17 cm. [BX5200.W32 1821] 24-15958
I. Title.

WATTS, Isaac, 1674-1748.
The beauties of the late Reverend Dr. Isaac Watts; containing the most striking and admired passages in the works of that justly celebrated divine, philosopher, moralist, and poet: equally calculated for the communication of polite and useful knowledge, and the increase of wisdom and happiness. To which is added the life of the author. Printed at Newburyport [Mass.] By Edmund M. Blunt, for Mathew Carey, Philadelphia, 1797. viii, [9]-239 p. 18 1/2 cm. [BX5200.W32 1797] A 34
I. Title.

WATTS, Isaac, 1674-1748. 245
Childhood's songs of long ago; being some of the divine and moral songs writ by Rev. Isaac Watts, D.D. With picturings by Blanche McManus. New York, E. R. Herrick & company [1897] 87 p. incl. front., plates. 23 x 18 1/2 cm. Illustrated lining-papers. [PR3763.W2A65 1897] 14-17393
I. Mansfield, Mrs. Blanche (McManus) II. Title.

WATTS, Isaac, 1674-1748. 245
Divine songs attempted in easy language, for the use of children. By I. Watts... Newberry-Port: Printed and sold by John Mycall, 1784. vi, [7]-54 p. 12 cm. [PR3763.W2A65 1784] 22-10927
I. Title.

WATTS, Isaac, 1674-1748. 223.
Hymns and spiritual songs. In three books: I. Collected from the Scriptures. II. Composed on divine subjects. III. Prepar'd for the Lord's supper. By I. Watts, D.D. The 27th ed. ... Boston: Printed by Thomas and John Fleet, at the Heart & Crown in Cornhill, 1772. 1 p. l., viii, [12] 263 p. 16 cm. [With Bible. O.T. Psalms. English. The Psalms of David ... by I. Watts. 27th ed. Boston, 1771] [BS1440.W3 1771] 6-14392
I. Title.

WATTS, Isaac, 1674-1748. 208.1
Religuiae juveniles. Miscellaneous thoughts, in prose and verse, on natural, moral, and divine subjects; written chiefly in younger years. To which is added, Remnants of time, employed in prose and verse. By I. Watts ... 1st American ed., with large additions. Printed for William P. Blake, no. 59, Cornhill, Boston; by Charles Pierce, Portsmouth, 1796. xii, 304 p. 17 cm. Published also Elizabeth-town, N.J., 1796, under title: Miscellaneous thoughts. [BX5200.W36 1796a] 33-11050
I. Title.

WATTS, Isaac, 1674-1748. 283'.0924
Reliquiae juveniles; miscellaneous thoughts in prose and verse, 1734. A facsimile reproduction with an introd. by Samuel J. Rogal. Gainesville, Fla., Scholars' Facsimiles & Reprints, 1968. ix, xx, 350 p. 23 cm. Original t.p. has imprint: London, Printed for R. Ford and R. Hett, 1734. "Reproduced from a copy owned by Samuel J. Rogal." [BX5200.W36 1968] 68-17018
I. Title.

WATTS, Isaac, 1674-1748. 283'.092'4
The works of the reverend and learned Isaac Watts, containing, besides his sermons and essays on miscellaneous subjects, several additional pieces, selected from his manuscripts by the Rev. Dr. Jennings and the Rev. Dr. Dodridge, in 1753: to which are prefixed Memoirs of the life of the author, compiled by George Burder. London, J. Garfield, 1810-1811. [New York, AMS Press, 1971] 6 v. 28 cm. [PR3763.W2A6 1971] 70-131027 ISBN 0-404-06890-1

WILLS, Joshua Edwin, 1854- 245
Dr. Isaac Watts, "The bard of sanctuary," His birthplace and personality; his literary and philosophical contributions; his life and times; hymnology and Bible. By Rev. Joshua E. Wills ... [Philadelphia, 190-?] 66 p. incl. 2 pl., port. 20 cm. [PR3763.W2W5] 13-15393
1. Watts, Isaac, 1674-1748. I. Title.

Waverley Abbey.

WARE, Gwen. 271'.12'042219
The White Monks of Waverley / by Gwen Ware. Farnham [Eng.] : Farnham & District Museum Society, c1976. 39, [3] p. : ill., plan (on lining paper) ; 18 cm. Bibliography: p. [42] [BX2596.F37W37] 77-354226 ISBN 0-901638-06-4 : £1.10
1. Waverley Abbey. I. Title.

The Way Biblical Research Center.

WHITESIDE, Elena S. 248'.4
The Way: living in love [by] Elena S. Whiteside. [1st ed.] New Knoxville, Ohio, American Christian Press [1972] 282 p. illus. 22 cm. [BV4486.W39W44] 72-89132 ISBN 0-910068-06-2 3.95
1. The Way Biblical Research Center. I. Title.

Way, inc.

WILLIAMS, Joseph Louis, 1941- 289.9
Victor Paul Wierwille and the Way / J. L. Williams. Chicago : Moody Press, c1979. p. cm. Includes bibliographies. [BX9995.W37W54] 79-22007 ISBN 0-8024-9305-X pbk. : 1.95
1. Way, inc. 2. Wierwille, Victor Paul. I. Title.

Wayne, Pa. Central Baptist Church.

KEACH, Richard L. 261.8
The purple pulpit [by] Richard L. Keach. Valley Forge [Pa.] Judson Press [1971] 128 p. illus. 20 cm. [BX6480.W37C45] 70-147848 ISBN 0-8170-0530-7 2.95
1. Wayne, Pa. Central Baptist Church. 2. Church renewal. I. Title.

Wealth—Biblical teaching.

JOHNSON, Luke Timothy. 241'.4
Sharing possessions : mandate and symbol of faith / Luke T. Johnson. Philadelphia : Fortress Press, c1981. p. cm. (Overtures to Biblical theology ; 9) Includes index. Bibliography: p. [BS2589.J64] 19 80-2390 ISBN 0-8006-1534-4 pbk. : 8.95
1. Bible. N.T. Luke—Criticism, interpretation, etc. 2. Bible. N.T. Acts—Criticism, interpretation, etc. 3. Wealth—Biblical teaching. 4. Sharing—Biblical teaching. I. Title. II. Series.

Wealth, Ethics of.

BREIG, James. 261.8'5
Wave goodbye to the Joneses : the Christian use of wealth / James Breig. [s.l.] : Fides/Claretian, [1981] p. cm. [HB835.B73] 19 81-7828 ISBN 0-8190-0646-7 pbk. : 5.95
1. Wealth, Ethics of. 2. Church and the poor. 3. Stewardship, Christian. I. Title.
Publisher's address :333N. Lafayette. South Bend, IN 46601

BROWN, Ina Corinne, 1896- 232.
Jesus' teaching on the use of money, by Ina C. Brown ... Nashville, Tenn., Cokesbury press, 1924. 171 p. 19 1/2 cm. [BS2417.W4B7] 24-30198
1. Jesus Christ—Teachings. 2. Wealth, Ethics of. I. Title.

Wealth, Ethics of—History.

COUNTRYMAN, L. William. 261.8'5
The rich Christian in the church of the early empire : contradictions and accomodations / by L. Wm. Countryman. New York : E. Mellen Press, c1980. viii, 239 p. ; 23 cm. (Texts and studies in religion ; 7) Bibliography: p. 217-239. [HB835.C65] 19 80-81884 ISBN 0-88946-970-9 : 24.95
1. Wealth, Ethics of—History. 2. Charity—History. 3. Church history—Primitive and early church, ca. 20-600. I. Title. II. Series.

Weatherhead, Leslie Dixon, 1893-

WEATHERHEAD, Andrew Kingsley, 1923- 287'.1'0924 B
Leslie Weatherhead : a personal portrait / A. Kingsley Weatherhead. Nashville : Abingdon, [1975] 269 p. : port. ; 23 cm. [BX8495.W329W4] 75-17574 ISBN 0-687-21375-4 : 7.95
1. Weatherhead, Leslie Dixon, 1893-

Weaver, Benjamin Witwer, 1853-1928.

WENGER, Eli D. 289.7'748'15
The Weaverland Mennonites, 1766-1968, including a biography of Bishop Benjamin W. Weaver with excerpts from his diary, by Eli D. Wenger. Transcript of the Weaverland Mennonite cemeteries, by George G. Sauder. [Adamstown, Pa., Printed by Ensinger Print. Service] 1968. 363 p. illus., plan, ports. 24 cm. [BX8143.W3W35] 78-261963
1. Weaver, Benjamin Witwer, 1853-1928. 2. Mennonite Church. Lancaster County Conference. I. Sauder, George G. Transcript of the Weaverland Mennonite cemeteries. 1968. II. Title. III. Title: Transcript of the Weaverland Mennonite cemeteries.

Weaver, Jonathan, bp., 1824-1901.

THOMPSON, Henry Adams, 1837-1920. 922.
Biography of Jonathan Weaver, D.D., a bishop in the church of the United Brethren in Christ for thirty-five years, by Rev. H. A. Thompson ... with an introduction by Bishop N. Castle, D.D. Dayton, O., United Brethren publishing house, 1901. xxvii, 19-477 p. front., ports. 20 cm. [BX9877.W4T5] 2-21602
1. Weaver, Jonathan, bp., 1824-1901. I. Title.

WEAVER, Jonathan, bp., 1824-1901. 230.
The doctrine of universal restoration carefully examined. By Bishop J. Weaver ... Dayton, O., United Brethren publishing house, 1878. x, [11]-403 p. front. (port.) 19 cm. [BX9947.W4] 23-5035
I. Title.

Webb City, Mo. First Presbyterian church.

CROTTY, Henrietta M. 285.1778
The First Presbyterian church of Webb City, Missouri, commemorating sixty-five years of its history, 1877-1942 [by] Henrietta M. Crotty. Webb City, Mo [The Switzer printing company] 1942. 6 p. l., 134 p., 5 l. illus. (incl. ports.) pl. 23 1/2 cm. [BX9211.W43C7] 44-1045
1. Webb City, Mo. First Presbyterian church. I. Title.

Webb, Clement Charles Julian, 1865-

WEBB, Clement Charles Julian, 1865-
Religious experience; a public lecturedelivered in the hall of Oriel Collegeon Friday 19 May 1944. With a forwardby L. W. Grensted. Printed, togetherwith a bibliography of his published writings and presented to him by some of his friends and pupils on the occasion of his eightieth birthday, 25 June 1945. London, Oxford Univ. Press [1945] 70 p. port. 23 cm. A 48
1. Webb, Clement Charles Julian, 1865- 2. Webb, Clement Charles Julian, 1865-Bibl. 3. Religion—Philosophy. I. Title.

Webb, Robert c.

SHELDON, Henry Clay, 1845-1928. 289.
A fourfold test of Mormonism, by Henry C. Sheldon ... New York, Cincinnati, The Abingdon press [c1914] New York, Cincinnati, The Abingdon press [c1916] 151 p. 17 1/2 cm. 1 p. l., 153-192 p. 17 cm. --[Appendix] Failure of pro-Mormon apology to impair the test, by Henry C. Sheldon ... "A brief reply to the attempt of Robert C. Webb to refute my treatise in his book entitled, The case against Mormonism." [BX8645.S5] [BX8645.S5 App.] 289. 14-16787
1. Webb, Robert C. The case against Mormonism. 2. Mormons and Mormonism. I. Title.

Webber, John Boaden, 1907-1940.

EDWARDS, Henry James, 1893-
The mediumship of Jack Webber, by Harry Edwards ... New York, E. P. Dutton & co., inc., 1941. 119 p. 36 pl. (incl. ports.) on 18 l. 22 cm. Printed in Great Britain. A 42
1. Webber, John Boaden, 1907-1940. 2. Spiritualism. I. Title.

Weber, Joseph Francis, 1865-1935.

WEBER, Francis J. 189.4
Mayor of Indianapolis : Father Joseph F. Weber / [written by Francis J. Weber]. Worcester [Mass.] : Achille J. St. Onge, 1975. 26 p. ; port. ; 74 mm. 300 copies. [BX4705.W395W4] 73-90828
1. Weber, Joseph Francis, 1865-1935. 2. Indianapolis—Flood, 1913. 3. Bibliography—Microscopic and miniature editions—Specimens. I. Title.

Weber, Joseph Hulse, 1855-

KNAPP, Martin Wells, 1853-1901. 922.773
Revival tornadoes; or, Life and labors of Rev. Joseph J. Weber, evangelist, the converted Roman Catholic. By Rev. Martin Wells Knapp ... Boston, Mass., McDonald, Gill & co.; Albion, Mich., The Revivalist publishing co., 1889. 326 p. front. (port.) 20 cm. Hymns (with music): p. [8], [243] [BX8495.W33K5] 37-12171
1. Weber, Joseph Hulse, 1855- I. Title.

Weber, Max, 1864-1920.

EISENSTADT, Shmuel Noah, 1923- comp. 261.8'5
The Protestant ethic and modernization; a comparative view, edited by S. N. Eisenstadt. New York, Basic Books [1968] viii, 407 p. 25 cm. Bibliography: p. 385-400. [BR115.E3E4] 68-16156
1. Weber, Max, 1864-1920. 2. Christian ethics. 3. Social ethics. 4. Christianity and economics. I. Title.

GREEN, Robert W., ed. 261.8'5
Protestantism, capitalism, and social science; the Weber thesis controversy. Edited and with an introd. by Robert W. Green. 2d ed. Lexington, Mass., Heath [1973] xviii, 195 p. 21 cm. (Problems in European civilization) Published in 1959 under title: Protestantism and capitalism. [BR115.E3G7 1973] 72-13639 ISBN 0-669-81737-6
1. Weber, Max, 1864-1920. Die protestantische Ethik und der Geist des Kapitalismus—Addresses, essays, lectures. 2. Christianity and economics—Addresses, essays, lectures. 3. Religion and sociology—Addresses, essays, lectures. 4. Capitalism—Addresses, essays, lectures. I. Title. II. Series.
Contents omitted.

LITTLE, David. 261'.0942
Religion, order, and law; a study in pre-Revolutionary England. [1st ed.] New York, Harper & Row [1969] v, 269 p. 21 cm. (Harper torchbooks. The Library of religion and culture, TB1418.) Includes bibliographical references. [BR757.L66] 70-84041 2.95
1. Weber, Max, 1864-1920. Dieprotestantische Ethik und der Geist des Kapitalismus. 2. Church of England—Doctrinal and controversial works. 3. Sociology, Christian—Gt. Brit. 4. Religion and law. 5. Puritans. I. Title.

MARSHALL, Gordon. 261.8'5
Presbyteries and profits : Calvinism and the development of capitalism in Scotland, 1560-1707 / Gordon Marshall. Oxford : Clarendon Press ; New York : Oxford University Press, 1980. x, 406 p. ; 22 cm. Originally presented as the author's thesis, Oxford. Includes index. Bibliography: p. [373]-401. [BX9424.5.S35M37 1980] 80-40187 ISBN 0-19-827246-4 : 44.50
1. Weber, Max, 1864-1920. Die protestantische Ethik und der Geist des Kapitalismus. 2. Calvinism—Scotland—History. 3. Capitalism—History. 4. Scotland—Economic conditions. 5. Religion and sociology. 6. Christian ethics. 7. Protestantism and capitalism. I. Title.

OTSUKA, Hisao, 1907- 261.8'5
Max Weber on the spirit of capitalism / Otsuka Hisao ; translated by Kondo Masaomi. Tokyo : Institute of Developing Economies, 1976. 95 p. ; 25 cm. (I.D.E. occasional papers series ; no. 13) Includes bibliographical references. [BR115.E3W43513] 76-376652
1. Weber, Max, 1864-1920. Die protestantische Ethik und der Geist des Kapitalismus. 2. Religion and sociology—Addresses, essays, lectures. 3. Christian ethics—Addresses, essays, lectures. 4. Protestantism and capitalism—Addresses, essays, lectures. I. Title. II. Series: Ajia Keizai Kenkyujo, Tokyo. I.D.E. occasional papers series ; no. 13.

ROBERTSON, Hector Menteith. 261.8'32'5
Aspects of the rise of economic individualism; a criticism of Max Weber and his school, by H. M. Robertson. [1st ed.] Clifton [N.J.] A. M. Kelley, 1973. xvi, 223, [18] p. 22 cm. (Reprints of economic classics) "With the addition of 'European economic developments in the 16th century', reprinted from the South African journal of economics, March 1950." Based on the author's thesis, University of Cambridge, 1928-29. Reprint of the 1933 ed. published by the University Press, Cambridge, Eng. in series: Cambridge studies in economic history. Includes bibliographical references. [BR115.E3R62 1973] 73-17059 ISBN 0-678-00867-1 11.50
1. Weber, Max, 1864-1920. Die protestantische Ethik und der Geist des Kapitalismus. 2. Christianity and economics—History. 3. Religion and sociology. 4. Capitalism. I. Weber, Max, 1864-1920. Die protestantische Ethik und der Geist des Kapitalismus. II. Robertson, Hector Menteith. European economic developments in the 16th century. 1974. III. Title.

TURNER, Bryan S. 301.5'8'0917671
Weber and Islam : a critical study / [by] Bryan S. Turner. London ; Boston : Routledge & Kegan Paul, 1974. ix, 212 p. ; 23 cm. (International library of sociology) Includes bibliographical references and index. [BP173.25.W4T87] 74-77201 ISBN 0-7100-7848-X : 13.50
1. Weber, Max, 1864-1920. 2. Sociology, Islamic. I. Title.

Weber, Max, 1864-1920. Die protestantische Ethik und der geist der Kapitalismus.

ASPECTS of the rise of economic individualism; a criticism of Max Weber and his school. New York, Kelley & Millman, 1959. xvi, 223p. 22cm. 'First written in 1928-9 as a dissertation for the degree of doctor of philosophy in the University of Cambridge. 'Pref. 'First published in 1933.' Paper read to the University of Cape Town Senior Seminar, 18gh May, 1949, entitled European economic developments in the 16th century by H. M. Robertson, inserted between pages viii and [xi]
1. Weber, Max, 1864-1920. Die protestantische Ethik und der geist der Kapitalismus. 2. Religion and sociology. 3. Capitalism. I. Robertson Hector Menteith.

ROBERTSON, Hector Menteith. 261
Aspects of the rise of economic individualism; a criticism of Max Weber and his school, by H. M. Robertson ... Cambridge [Eng.] The University press, 1933. xvi, 223 p. 22 cm. (Half-title: Cambridge studies in economic history) "First written in 1928-9 as a dissertation for the degree of doctor of philosophy in the University of Cambridge ... has now been revised and rewritten."--Pref. [BR115.E3R62] 34-1239
1. Weber, Max, 1864-1920. Die protestantische ethik und der geist der kapitalismus. 2. Religion and sociology. 3. Capitalism. I. Title. II. Title: Economic individualism. Aspects of the rise of.

ROBERTSON, Hector Menteith.
Aspects of the rise of economic individualism; a criticism of Max Weber and his school. New York, Kelley & Millman, 1959. 223 p. 22 cm. "First written in 1928-9 as a dissertation for the degree of doctor of philosophy in the University of Cambridge ... has now been revised and rewritten." Bibliographical footnotes. 64-57204
1. Weber, Max, 1864-1920. Dis protestantische Ethik und der Geist des Kapitalismus. 2. Religion and sociology. 3. Capitalism. I. Title.

Webster, Samuel, 1719-1895. A winter evening's conversation upon the doctrine of original sin.

CLARK, Peter, 1694-1768. 233
The Scripture-doctrine of original sin, stated and defended. In a summer-morning's conversation, between a minister and a neighbour. Containing remarks on a late anonymous pamphlet, entitled, "A winter-evening's conversation, upon the doctrine of original sin, between a minister and three of his neighbours, accidentally met," &c. With an appendix, in reply to a supplement in the New-Haven edition of that pamphlet. By Peter Clark ... Recommended in a preface by several ministers ... Boston: Printed and sold by S. Kneeland, opposite to the Probate office in Queen-street, 1758. 2 p. l., 132, 24 p. 18 cm. [BT720.W4C6 1758] 22-12667
1. Webster, Samuel, 1719-1895. A winter evening's conversation upon the doctrine of original sin. 2. Sin, Original. I. Title.

[WEBSTER, Samuel] 1719-1796. 283.
The winter evening conversation vindicated; against the remarks of the Rev. Mr. Peter Clark of Danvers. In a piece intitled, A summer morning's conversation, &c., herein the principal arguments of said piece, from Scripture, reason and antiquity, are considered, and shown to be of no validity, by the author of The winter evening conversation ... Boston, Printed and sold by Edes and Gill, at their printing office next to the prison in Queen-street [1758?] 116 p. 20 1/2 cm. [BT720.W4C62] 23-5880
1. Webster, Samuel, 1719-1796. A winter evening's conversation. 2. Clark, Peter, 1693-1768. A summer morning's conversation. 3. Sin. I. Title.

Webster-Smith, Irene, 1888-

HITT, Russell T. 266.0924 B
Sensei; the life story of Irene Webster-Smith [by] Russell T. Hitt. [1st ed.] New York, Harper & Row [1965] 240 p. illus., ports. 22 cm. (Harper jungle missionary classics) [BV3457.W4H5] 65-20452
1. Webster-Smith, Irene, 1888- 2. Missions—Japan. I. Title.

HITT, Russell T. 266.0924
Sensie; the life story of Irene Webster-Smith. New York, Harper [c.1965] 240p. illus., ports. 22cm. (Harper jungle missionary classics) [BV3457.WH5] 65-20452 3.95 bds.,
1. Webster-Smith, Irene, 1888- 2. Missions—Japan. I. Title.

Wechsler, Hile, 1843-1894.

KIRSCH, James. 296.7'1
The reluctant prophet. Los Angeles, Sherbourne Press [1973] xii, 214 p. 24 cm. Includes bibliographical references. [BM755.W345K57] 72-96516 ISBN 0-8202-0156-1 7.50
1. Wechsler, Hile, 1843-1894. 2. Dreams—Case studies. I. Title.

Wedding etiquette.

DELL, Edward Thomas 264.035
A handbook for church weddings. New York, Morehouse-Barlow [c. 1964] 64p. 19cm. 64-16829 1.50 pap.,
1. Wedding etiquette. I. Title.

Wedding sermons.

ROGUET, A. M., 1906- 252'.1
Homilies for the celebration of marriage / by A. M. Roguet ; translated by Jerome J. DuCharme. Chicago : Franciscan Herald Press, [1977] p. cm. Translation of Homelies pour le mariage. Includes readings pertaining to marriage from the 1969 Lectionary. [BV4278.R6313] 76-53538 ISBN 0-8199-0656-5 pbk. : 3.50
1. Catholic Church—Sermons. 2. Wedding sermons. 3. Sermons, English—Translations from French. 4. Sermons, French—Translations into English. I. Catholic Church. Liturgy and ritual. Lectionary (1969, English, U.S.). Marriage. 1977. II. Title.

VINCENT, Arthur M., ed. 252.1
Join your right hands; addresses and worship aids for church weddings. St. Louis, Concordia [c.1965] 143p. 20cm. Bibl. [BV4278.V55] 65-27799 3.00
1. Wedding sermons. 2. Marriage service. I. Title.

VINCENT, Arthur M ed. 252.1
Join your right hands; addresses and worship aids for church weddings. Arthur M. Vincent, editor. St. Louis, Concordia Pub. House [1965] 143 p. 20 cm. Bibliographical reference included in "Notes" (p. 23) [BV4278.V55] 65-27799
1. Wedding sermons. 2. Marriage service. I. Title.

Wedding sermons, Jewish.

ROSENBLATT, Samuel, 1902- 296.4'44
Under the nuptial canopy : wedding sermons / by Samuel Rosenblatt. New York : P. Feldheim, 1975. x, 141 p. ; 24 cm. Includes bibliographical references. [BM744.5.R67] 74-80137 6.00
1. Wedding sermons, Jewish. 2. Sermons, Jewish—United States. 3. Sermons, American—Jewish authors. I. Title.

Weddings.

CHRISTENSEN, James L. 265.5
The minister's marriage handbook. Westwood.N.J., Revell [c.1966] 160p. 17cm. Bibl. [BV199.M3C5] 66-17045 2.95 bds.,
1. Weddings. 2. Marriage service. 3. Clergy—U.S.—Handbooks, manuals, etc. I. Title.

CHRISTENSEN, James L. 265'.5
The minister's marriage handbook / by James L. Christensen. Old Tappan, N.J. : Revell, c1974. 159 p. ; 17 cm. Bibliograph: p. 153-159. [BV199.M3C5 1974] 75-316071 4.95
1. Weddings. 2. Marriage service. 3. Clergy—United States—Handbooks, manuals, etc. I. Title.

Weed, Edward, 1807-1851.

[LILLIE, James] supposed author. 922.573
Faith and works; or, The life of Edward Weed, minister of the gospel ... New York, C. W. Benedict, 1853. xiii, 304 p., 1 l. incl. front. (port.) 18 cm. Introduction signed: J. L. [i. e. James Lillie?] [BX9225.W245L5] 36-22141
1. Weed, Edward, 1807-1851. I. Title.

Weeden, Mrs. Nettie (Hill) 1844-1889.

HILL, Francis Constantine, 1823- 922.773
Robed and crowned. A memorial of Mrs. Nettie Hill Weeden. By Rev. Francis C. Hill. With selections from her writings and sketches and papers from Rev. B. M. Adams, D.D., Rev. A. C. Bowdish, D.D. ... and others. New York, Printed by Hunt & Eaton, 1891. 272 p. front., ports., plates. 19 cm. Includes songs with music. [BV3785.W45H5] 37-36757
1. Weeden, Mrs. Nettie (Hill) 1844-1889. 2. Revivals. I. Title.

Week.

ODOM, Robert Leo. 529.2
Sunday in Roman paganism, a history of the planetary week and its "day of the sun" in the heathenism of the Roman world during the early centuries of the Christian era, by Robert Leo Odom ... Takoma Park, Washington, D.C., Review and herald publishing association [1944] 272 p. incl. front., illus., diagrs. 20 1/2 cm. (Ministerial association of Seventh-day Adventists. Ministerial reading course selection for 1944) Bibliography: p. 260-272. [CE85.O37] [292] 44-5606
1. Week. 2. Sunday. 3. Rome—Religion. I. Title.

Week-day church schools.

COPE, Henry Frederick, 1870-1923. 268.
The week-day church-school, by Henry Frederick Cope ... New York, George H. Doran company [c1921] viii p., 1 l., 11-191 p. 20 cm. "Sources of information": p. 182-1889 [BV1580.C6] 21-9802
1. Week-day church schools. I. Title.

ERB, Bessie Pehotsky. 268.432
In awe and wonder; a weekday church school course for boys and girls of grades five and six. Boston, Published for the Co-operative Publication Association by Pilgrim Press [1956] 64 p. illus. 20 cm. 140 p. illus. 20 cm. (The Co-operative series texts for weekday religious education classes and released-time religious education instruction) -- -- Teacher's book. Boston, Published for the Co-operative Publication Association [by] Pilgrim Press [BV1583.E7] 56-9757
1. Week-day church schools. 2. Religious education—Text-books for children. I. Title.

GORHAM, Donald Rex, 1903- 268
The status sof Protestant weekday church schools in the United States [by] Donald R. Gorham ... Philadelphia, Pa., The School of religious education of the Eastern Baptist theological seminary [c1934] xi, 96 p. illus. (map) diagrs. 24 cm. (Contriubtions to Christian education, no.

1) Issued also as thesis (PH. D.) University of Pennsylvania under gA study of the status of weekday church schools in the United States. Bibliography: p. 86-88. [BV1580.G55 1934a] 35-16614
1. Week-day church schools. 2. Religious education—U. S. 3. Church and education in the U. S. I. Title. II. Title: Protestant weekday church schools in the United States.

GOVE, Floyd Sherman, 1894- 268.
... *Religious education on public school time,* by Floyd S. Gove ... Cambridge, Mass., Harvard university, 1926. xvi p., 2 l., [3]-143 p. incl. tables, diagrs. 23 cm. (Harvard bulletins in education. [no. xi]) Bibliography: p. [133]-143. [BV1580.G6] 27-924
1. Week-day church schools. 2. Public schools—U. S. I. Title.

MILLER, Minor Cline, 1889- 268
Teaching the multitudes, a guidance manual in weekday religious education, by Minor C. Miller; foreword by Edward B. Paisley ... Bridgewater, Va., The Beacon publishers [1944] xviii, 230 p. 20 cm. Bibliography: p. [228]-230. [BV1580.M5] 44-39393
1. Week-day church schools. I. Title.

SHAVER, Erwin Leander, 1890- 268
The weekday church school: how to organize and conduct a program of weekday religious education on released time. Boston. Published for the Co-operative Publication Association [by] Pilgrim Press [1956] 154 p. 20 cm. [BV1580.S49] 56-8243
1. Week-day church schools. I. Title.

Week-day church schools-Teacher's manuals.

BROWN, Jeanette (Perkins) 268.
1887-
...*The knights of Anytown,* and The rest of the family, by Jeanete Eloise Perkins. Boston, Chicago, The Pilgrim press c1923] 1 p. i., 61, [3] p. illus. 21 cm. At head of title: Leader's manual. "Bird patterns and map of Anytown" in pocket. Songs with music: p. [23] and [3] p. at end. Full name: Jeanette Eloise (Perkins) Brown. [BV1580.B72] 24-11456
1. Week-day church schools—Teachrs' manuals. I. Title. II. Title: The rest of the family.

Week-day church schools—Text-books.

[BRANSTETTE, Otie G.] 260.7
The church in our community; pupil's book for work and study ... [Philadelphia, 1943] 2 pts. illus. 28 cm. Cover-title. [BV1583.B7] 44-20281
1. Week-day church schools—Text-books. I. Title.

BROWN, Jeanette (Perkins) 268.
1887-
The knights of Anytown, by Jeanette Eloise Perkins; illustrated by Florence Liley Young. Bston, Chicago, The Pilgrim press [c1923*C5 p. 1., 159 p. plates. 21 cm. 5 p. 1., 159 p. plates. 21 cm. Illustrated lining-papers. Full name: Jeanette Eloise (Perkins) Brown. [BV1580.B7] 24-3460
1. Week-day church schools—Text-books. I. Title.

BROWN, Jeanette (Perkins) 268.
1887-
The rest of the family, by Jeanette Eloise Perkins; illustrated by Florence Liley Young. Boston, Chicago, The Pilgrim press [c1923] 5 p. 1., 139 p. plates. 21 c. Full name: Jeanette Elois (Perkins) Brown. [BV1580.B76] 24-3403
1. Week-day church schools—Text-books. I. Title.

GILBERT, W Kent, ed. 268.61
The weekday church school series. Philadelphia, Muhlenberg Press [1952- v. illus. 28cm. In each vol. the main work, also published separately, is preceded by a Teacher's guide with special t. p. [BV1583.G5] 53-23897
1. Week-day church schools—Text-books. I. Title.
Contents omitted.

GRANT, Frederick Clifton, 232.9
1891-
... *The life and times of Jesus,* by Frederick C. Grant. New York, Cincinnati, The Abingdon press [1921] 222 p., 1 l. front., plates, maps., plan. 20 cm. (The Abingdon religious education texts, D. G. Downey, general editor, Week-day school series, G. H. Betts, editor) [BT307.G7] 21-4245
1. Jesus Christ—Biog—Study. 2. Week-day church schools—Text-books. I. Title.

Weeks, Philip E.

WEEKS, Philip E. 283'.092'4 B
After you receive power / Philip E. Weeks. New York : Morehouse-Barlow Co., c1974. 106 p. ; 20 cm. [BT123.W4] 74-80380 ISBN 0-8192-1185-0 pbk. : 2.95
1. Weeks, Philip E. 2. Baptism in the Holy Spirit. I. Title.

Weems, Mason Locke, 1759-1825.

KELLOCK, Harold, 283'.0924 B
1879-
Parson Weems of the cherry-tree; being a short account of the eventful life of the Reverend M. L. Weems. Ann Arbor, Mich., Gryphon Books, 1971. ix, 212 p. illus. 22 cm. "Facsimile reprint of the 1928 edition." [E302.6.W4K4 1928a] 75-107137
1. Weems, Mason Locke, 1759-1825. I. Title.

KELLOCK, Harold, 1879- 922.
Parson Weems of the cherry-tree; being a short account of the eventful life of the Reverend M. L. Weems ... first biographer of G. Washington. Faithfully set down by a latterday scrivener and writer of noteworthy lives, Harold Kellock, embellished with several superb illustrations & plates from the books & tracts of the Reverend doctor. New York & London, The Century co. [1928] ix, 212 p. plates, 2 port. (incl. front.) facsims. 21 cm. [BX5995.W43K4] 28-5887 2.00
1. Weems, Mason Locke, 1759-1825. I. Title.

Weigel, Gustave, 1906-1964.

ONE of a kind; 271'.5'0924
essays in tribute to Gustave Weigel. With an introd. by John Courtney Murray. Wilkes-Barre, Pa., Dimension Books [1967] 111 p. 21 cm. Contents.Contents.—A memorable man, by J. C. Murray.—The gringo, by J. Ochagavia.—An uncommon ecumenist, by A. C. Outler.—A living epistle of Christ, by D. Horton.—One of a kind, by J. B. Sheerin.—Unstucknes, by H. M. Jenkins.—A figure in transition, by E. Burke.—An ocumenical pioneer, by M. Brown.—Liquidator of prejudices, by R. Balkam. [BX4705.W415O5] 67-27131
1. Weigel, Gustave, 1906-1964. I. Murray, John Courtney.

Weigle, Luther Allan, 1880-

WEIGLE, Luther 285'.8'0924 B
Allan, 1880-
The glory days : from the life of Luther Allan Weigle / Luther Allan Weigle. New York : Friendship Press, [1976] p. cm. Bibliography: p. [BX7260.W444A33] 76-21779 ISBN 0-377-00058-2 pbk. : 5.95
1. Weigle, Luther Allan, 1880- 2. Weigle, Luther Allan, 1880- —Bibliography. 3. Congregational churches—Sermons. 4. Sermons, American. I. Title.

Weinstein, Jacob Joseph, 1902-

WEINSTEIN, Jacob 296.6'1'0924 B
Joseph, 1902-
Rabbi Jacob J. Weinstein, advocate of the people / edited by Janice J. Feldstein. New York : KTAV Pub. House, c1980. xii, 226 p., [8] leaves of plates : ill. ; 24 cm. Includes bibliographical references and index. [BM755.W359A37] 79-25654 ISBN 0-87068-699-2 : 15.00
1. Weinstein, Jacob Joseph, 1902- 2. Rabbis—United States—Biography. I. Feldstein, Janice J. II. Title.

Weir, Howard Robert, 1885-1937.

WEIR, Margaret (Bronson) 922.373
1886-
Howard Robert Weir, rector, by Margaret Bronson Weir. New Haven, 1947. 2 p. l. [3]-120 p. front., port. 23 cm. [BX5995.W44W4] 47-21223
1. Weir, Howard Robert, 1885-1937. I. Title.

Weiss, Paul, 1901-

LIEB, Irwin C., ed. 110.82
Experience, existence and the good; essays in honor of Paul Weiss. Carbondale, Southern Ill. Univ. Pr. [c.1961] x, 309p. 25cm. Bibl. 61-13080 10.00 bds.,
1. Weiss, Paul, 1901- 2. Metaphysics. 3. Ethics. 4. Experience. I. Title.

Welch, Thomas, 1905-

PARRICK, Jerry. 248.2
A twentieth century miracle / by Jerry Parrick. Plainfield, N.J. : Logos International, c1981. xiv, 171 p. ; 21 cm. Bibliography: p. 171. [BR1725.W36P37] 19 80-84168 ISBN 0-88270-488-5 pbk. : 4.95
1. Welch, Thomas, 1905- 2. Miracles. 3. Death, Apparent. I. Title.

Welles, Noah, 1718-1776

LEAMING, Jeremiah, 1717-1804.
A defence of the episcopal government of the church; containing remarks on two late, noted sermons on Presbyterian ordination. By Jeremiah Leaming... New-York, Printed by John Holt at the Exchange, MDCCLXVI. 73, [1] p. 19 1/2 cm. With this is bound the author's A second defence, of the episcopal government of the church. New York, 1770. A discussion of Charles Chauncy's The validity of Presbyterian ordination asserted, 1762, and Noah Welle's The divine right of Presbyterian ordination asserted, 1763. L.C. copy imperfect: t.-p. wanting; title supplied from Sabin. Bibl. Amer. [BV669.L4] 43-48677
1. Welles, Noah, 1718-1776. The divine right of Presbyterian ordination asserted. 2. Chauncy Charles, 1705-1787. The validity of Presbyterian ordination asserted. 3. Episcopacy. 4. Presbyterianism. I. Title.

Wellesley, Mass. Congregational church.

CHANDLER, Edward Herrick. 285.
The history of the Wellesley Congregational church, by Edward Herrick Chandler, pastor; with the assistance of an editorial committee. Including "The influence of the church in the making of New England"; centennial oration by William Hayes Ward ... Boston, B. H. Sanborn & co. [1898] 241 p. front., illus. (plan) plates, ports. 22 cm. [BX7255.W44C5] 98-2152
1. Wellesley, Mass. Congregational church. 2. New England—Church history. I. Ward, William Hayes, 1835-1916. II. Title.

Wellfleet, Mass. Methodist Episcopal church.

PALMER, Albert P. 287.
A brief history of the Methodist Episcopal church in Wellfleet, Massachusetts. by Rev. Albert P. Palmer. Published by the leaders and stewards. Boston, Rand, Avery & company, 1877. 84 p. 19 cm. [BX8481.W4P3] 1-5423
1. Wellfleet, Mass. Methodist Episcopal church. I. Title.

Wellons, William Brock, 1821-1877.

WELLONS, J. W. ed. 922.673
Life and labors of Rev. William Brock Wellons ... of the Christian church. Compiled and edited by his brother, Rev. J. W. Wellons, and Rev. R. H. Holland. Raleigh, N.C., Edwards, Broughton & co., printers, 1881. 448 p. front. (port.) 20 1/2 cm. [BX6793.W4W4] 36-32454
1. Wellons, William Brock, 1821-1877. I. Holland, Robert Howell, 1819-1908, joint ed. II. Title.

Wells Cathedral.

MALDEN, Richard Henry, 726.6
1879-
The story of Wells Cathedral. With a foreword by the Bishop of Bath and Wells. 3d ed. London, New York, R. Tuck, 1947. 79 p. plates. 19 cm. "Authorities": p. 77. [NA5471.W4M3 1947] 48-4781
1. Wells Cathedral. I. Title.

MALDEN, Richard 726.6094238
Henry, 1879-
The story of Wells cathedral, by Richard H. Malden ... with a foreward by the Bishop of Bath and Wells. London, New York [etc.] R. Tuck & sons, 1st [1934] viii, 9-80 p. front., plates. 19 cm. "Authorities": p. [77] [NA5471.W4M3] 34-32344
1. Wells cathedral. I. Title.

Wells (Diocese)

ROBINSON, Joseph Armitage, 1858-
1933.
... *The Saxon bishops of Wells,* a historical study in the tenth century, by J. Armitage Robinson ... London, Pub. for the British academy by H. Milford, Oxford university press [1918?] 69 p. 24 1/2 cm. (British academy. Supplemental papers. iv) [BR763.W3R6] 19-3793
1. Wells (Diocese) I. Title.

Wells, Herbert George, 1866-1946.

ARCHER, William, 1856- 231
God and Mr. Wells; a critical examination of "God the invisible king," by William Archer. New York, A.A. Knopf, 1917. vii, [1] 136 p. 19 1/2 cm. [BT101.W46.] 17-24674
1. Wells, Herbert George, 1866- God the invisible king. I. Title.

NICHOLSON, Norman, 1914- 231
H. G. Wells. Denver, A. Swallow [1950] 98 p. 19 cm. (The English novelists) [[PR5776.N]] A52
1. Wells, Herbert George, 1866-1946. I. Title. II. Series: The English novelists (Denver)

THOMAS, J. M. Lloyd. 231
The veiled being : a comment on Mr. H. G. Wells's "God, the invisible king" / by J. M. Lloyd Thomas. [Folcroft, Pa.] : Folcroft Library Editions, 1974. p. cm. Reprint of the 1917 ed. published by Cornish Bros., Birmingham. [BT101.W43T46 1974] 74-23855 ISBN 0-8414-8512-7 lib.bdg. 4.50
1. Wells, Herbert George, 1866-1946. God, the invisible king. I. Title.

WELLS, Herbert George, 1866-
The soul of a bishop, a novel (with just a little love in it) about conscience and religion and the real troubles of life, by H. G. Wells. London, New York [etc.] Cassell and company, ltd. [1917] 4 p. l., 320 p. 19 1/2 cm. "First impression September 1917." [PR5774.S6 1917] 44-10196
I. Title.

Welsh, John, 1568?-1622—Juvenile literature.

BARRETT, Ethel. 285'.23 B
John Welch, the man who couldn't be stopped / Ethel Barrett. Grand Rapids, Mich. : Zondervan Pub. House, c1980. 143 p. ; 20 cm. A biography of a dauntless Scottish preacher who in his youth belonged to a band of thieves and later married the daughter of John Knox. [BX9225.W247B37] 92 19 80-26275 ISBN 0-310-44041-6 pbk. : 2.95
1. Welsh, John, 1568?-1622—Juvenile literature. 2. Church of Scotland—Clergy—Biography—Juvenile literature. 3. [Welsh, John, 1568?-1622.] 4. Clergy—Scotland—Biography—Juvenile literature. 5. [Clergy.] I. Title.

Welz, Justinian Ernst von, Baron von Eberstein, 1621-1668.

WELZ, Justinian 266.4'1'0924 B
Ernst von, Baron von Eberstein, 1621-1668.
Justinian Welz: essays by an early prophet of mission. Translated, annotated, and with an historical introd., by James A. Scherer.

Grand Rapids, Mich., Eerdmans [1969] 111 p. 20 cm. (A Christian world mission book) Bibliography: p. 109-111. [BV2853.D9W4] 68-54103 2.45
1. Welz, Justinian Ernst von, Baron von Eberstein, 1621-1668. 2. Lutheran Church—Missions—Collected works. I. Scherer, James A., tr.

Wenceslaus, Saint, Duke of Bohemia, 907?-935?

NEWLAND, Mary Reed. 783.6'52
Good King Wenceslas / by Mary Reed Newland. New York : Seabury Press, 1980. p. cm. "A Cross road book." [BX4700.W4N4] 80-36787 ISBN 0-8164-0474-7 : 7.95
1. Wenceslaus, Saint, Duke of Bohemia, 907?-935? I. Title.

Wengatz, Mrs. Susan Moberly (Talbott) 1885-1930.

MILLER, Sadie Louise, 276.73
1870- comp.
In Jesus' name; memoirs of the victorious life and triumphant death of Susan Talbott Wengatz, compiled by Sadie Louise Miller. [Upland, Ind., Taylor university, c1932] v, 6-85 p. plates, ports. 17 cm. [BV3625.A6M5] (266.7) 32-33427
1. Wengatz, Mrs. Susan Moberly (Talbott) 1885-1930. 2. Missions—Angola. I. Title.

Wenham, Mass.—Church history—Sources.

FISKE, John, 917.44'03'208 s
1601-1677.
The notebook of the Reverend John Fiske, 1644-1675 / edited and with an introd. by Robert G. Pope. Boston : Colonial Society of Massachusetts, 1974. xlii, 256 p. ; 25 cm. (Publications of the Colonial Society of Massachusetts ; v. 47 : Collections) Incudes index. [F61.C71 vol. 47] [BX7260.F535] 285'.8'0924 B 74-81447
1. Fiske, John, 1601-1677. 2. Wenham, Mass.—Church history—Sources. 3. Chelmsford, Mass.—Church history—Sources. I. Title. II. Series: Colonial Society of Massachusetts, Boston. Publications ; v. 47.

Wenlok, Walter, de, d. 1307.

PEARCE, Ernest Harold, bp. of
Worcester, 1865-
... *Walter de Wenlok,* abbot of Westminster, by Ernest Harold Pearce ... London, Society for promoting, Christian knowledge; New York, Macmillan, 1920. vii, 236 p. front. (phot.) 22 cm. (Ecclesiastical biographies) A 21
1. Wenlok, Walter, de, d. 1307. 2. Westminster abbey. I. Title.

Werner, Eric.

WERNER, Eric. 783'.029'6
From generation to generation; studies on Jewish musical tradition. New York, American Conference of Cantors [1967?] 168 p. illus. 24 cm. "This limited edition has been published in honor of Dr. Eric Werner's forthcoming retirement from the faculty of the School of Sacred Music, Hebrew Union College-Jewish Institute of Religion." Contents.Contents.—Music in the Bible.—Musical instruments in the Bible.—The music of post-Biblical Judaism.—Role of tradition in the music of the Synagogue.—What function has Synagogue music today?—Ideas and practices of liturgical music.—Practical applications of (Jewish) musical research.—Rise and fall of American Synagogue music.—Solomon Sulzer, statesman and pioneer.—Abraham Zvi Idelsohn, in memoriam. Includes bibliographical references. [ML3195.W38] 74-182184
1. Werner, Eric. 2. Jews. Liturgy and ritual. 3. Music, Jewish—History and criticism. 4. Synagogue music—History and criticism. I. Title.

Wesberry, James Pickett.

BRYANT, James C. 286'.132'0924 B
The Morningside man : a biography of James Pickett Wesberry / by James C. Bryant. Atlanta : Morningside Baptist Church, [1975] xiv, 263 p., [4] leaves of plates : ill. ; 24 cm. [BX6495.W38B78] 75-309844 6.95
1. Wesberry, James Pickett. I. Morningside Baptist Church, Atlanta. II. Title.

Wesley, Charles, 1707-1788.

ADAMS, Charles, 1808- 922.742
1890.
The post preachers; a brief memorial of Charles Wesley, the eminent preacher and poet. By Charles Adams. Five illustrations. New York, Carlton & Porter [1859] 234 p.incl. front. (ports) plates 18 cm. [BX8495.W4A5] 37-9731
1. Wesley, Charles, 1707-1788 I. Title.

FLINT, Charles Wesley, 922.742
Bp.
Charles Wesley and his colleagues. With introductory notes by Gerald Kennedy, G. Bromley Oxnam, and Norman Vincent Peale. Washington, Public Affairs Press [1957] 221 p. 24 cm. Includes bibliography. [BX8495.W4F57] 57-9822
1. Wesley, Charles, 1707-1788.

GILL, Frederick Cyril, 922.742
1898-
Charles Wesley, the first Methodist [by] Frederick C. Gill. New York, Abingdon Press [1964] 238 p. illus., facsims., ports. 23 cm. [BX8495.W4G5] 65-3307
1. Wesley, Charles, 1707-1788.

MYERS, Elisabeth P. 287.0924
Singer of six thousand songs; a life of Charles Wesley, Drawings by Leonard Vosburgh. New York, Nelson [c.1965] 160p. illus. 21cm. Bibl. [BX8495.W4M9] 65-20772 2.95; 2.92 lib. ed.
1. Wesley, Charles, 1707-1788. I. Title.

MYERS, Elisabeth P 287.0924
Singer of six thousand songs; a life of Charles Wesley, by Elisabeth P. Myers. Drawings by Leonard Vosburgh. London, New York, T. Nelson [1965] 160 p. illus. 21 cm. Bibliography: p. 159. [BX8495.W4M9] 65-20772
1. Wesley, Charles, 1707-1788. I. Title.

WILDER, Franklin. 287'.092'4 B
The Methodist riots : the testing of Charles Wesley / Franklin Wilder. 1st ed. Great Neck, N.Y. : Todd & Honeywell, 1981. 160 p. : ill. ; 23 cm. Includes bibliographical references. [BX8495.W4W45 1981] 19 82-144959 ISBN 0-89962-237-2 : 8.95
1. Wesley, Charles, 1707-1788. 2. Methodist Church—Clergy—Biography. 3. Clergy—England—Biography. I. Title.

WISEMAN, Frederick Luke, 922.742
1858-
Charles Wesley, evangelist and poet [by] F. Luke Wiseman. New York, Cincinnati [etc.] The Abingdon press [c1932] 231 p. front. (port.) fold. map. 21 1/2 cm. [Drew lectureship in biography ... 1931] "List of books": p. 230-231. [BX8495.W4W5] 32-17067
1. Wesley, Charles, 1707-1788. I. Title.

Wesley family.

CLARKE, Adam, 1760?-1832. 922.742
Memoirs of the Wesley family; collected principally from original documents. By Adam Clarke... New York, Published by N. Bangs and T. Mason for the Methodist Episcopal church, 1824. ix, [1], [11]-432 p. front., pl., fold. facsim. 22 cm. [BX8495.W35C6 1824] 36-23404
1. Wesley family. 2. Annseley family. I. Title.

WAKELEY, Joseph Beaumont, 922.
1809-1875.
Anecdotes of the Wesleys; illustrative of their character and personal history. By Rev. J. B. Wakeley. With an introduction by Rev. J. M'Clintock ... New York, Carlton & Lanahan; Cincinnati, Hitchcock & Walden, 1869. 391 p. 3 port. (incl. front.) 18 cm. [BX8495.W33W3] 12-39764
1. Wesley family. 2. Wesley, John, 1703-1791. 3. Wesley, Charles, 1707-1788. 4. Wesley, Samuel, 1662-1735. I. Title.

Wesley Foundation, University of Illinois.

BAKER, James Chamberlain, 377.87
Bp., 1879--
The first Wesley Foundation; an adventure in Christian higher education. With a foreword by Fred P. Corson. [Nashville? Parthenon, 1960] 116p. illus. 21cm. [LD2386.5.B3] 60-28977
1. Wesley Foundation, University of Illinois. I. Title.

Wesley foundations.

METHODIST Student Workers 378.31
Association.
How to raise funds for Wesley foundations; proceedings of the fund raising conference of the Methodist Student Workers Association, October 29-30, 1951, Dallas, Texas. Nashville, Division of Educational Institutions, Board of Education, Methodist Church [1952] 110p. illus. 23cm. [LC577.M48] 53-17167
1. Wesley foundations. I. Title.

Wesley, John, 1703-1791.

AYLING, Stanley 287'.092'4 B
Edward.
John Wesley / [by] Stanley Ayling. London : Collins, 1979. 350 p., [8] p. of plates : ill., facsim., ports. ; 23 cm. Includes index. Bibliography: p. [337]-339. [BX8495.W5A94] 79-315195 ISBN 0-00-216656-9 : 12.95
1. Wesley, John, 1703-1791. 2. Methodist Church—Clergy—Biography. 3. Clergy—England—Biography.
Available from Collins Pub., 2080 W. 117th St., Cleveland, OH 44111

AYLING, Stanley 287'.092'4
Edward.
John Wesley / Stanley Ayling. Nashville, Tenn. : Abingdon, 1982, c1979. p. cm. Reprint. Originally published: Cleveland : Collins, 1979. Includes index. Bibliography: p. [BX8495.W5A94 1982] 19 82-13796 ISBN 0-687-20376-7 : 10.95
1. Wesley, John, 1703-1791. 2. Methodist Church—Clergy—Biography. 3. Clergy—England—Biography. I. Title.

BAKER, Frank, 1910- 287'.0924 B
John Wesley and the Church of England. Nashville, Abingdon Press [1970] viii, 422 p. 26 cm. Bibliography: p. 407-412. [BX8495.W5B33 1970b] 73-23809 ISBN 0-687-20445-3 14.50
1. Wesley, John, 1703-1791. 2. Church of England. I. Title.

BANFIELD, Frank. 922.742
John Wesley, by Frank Banfield. Boston, Small, Maynard & co., 1900. 4 p. l., [vii]-xvi p., 1 l., 128 p. front. (port.) 14 1/2 cm. (Added t.-p.: The Westminster biographies) Added t.-p. (Illustrated) has imprint: Boston, Small, Maynard and company; London, K. Paul, Trench, Trubner and co., limited. Bibliography: p. 126-128. [BX8405.W5B35 1900] 0-6159
1. Wesley, John, 1703-1791. I. Title.

BOND, Beverly Waugh, 922.742
1843-1920.
Life of John Wesley, By the Rev. B. W. Bond ... With an introduction by Bishop A. W. Wilson ... Nashville, Tenn., Southern Methodist publishing house, 1885. 216 p. incl. front. (port.) 16 1/2 cm. [BX8495.W5B6] 37-12141
1. Wesley, John, 1703-1791. I. Title.

BOURNE, George, 1780- 922.742
1845.
The life of the Rev. John Wesley, A. M., with memoirs of the Wesley family. To which are subjoined, Dr. Whitehead's funeral sermon: and a comprehensive history of American Methodism. By George Bourne... Baltimore: Printed by George Dobbin and Murphy, for themselves, John Hagerty and Abner Neal. 1807. viii. [9]-351, [1] p. front. (port.) 22 cm. Portrait engraved by Tiebout. Imperfect: frontispiece and t.-p. supplied (photostat negative) by Enoch Pratt Free library. [BX8495.W5b65] 37-9737
1. Wesley, John, 1703-1791. 2. Funeral sermons. 3. Methodist Episcopal church—Hist. I. Whitehead, John, 1740?-1804. II. [Bourne, George] 1780-1845. III. Title.

BREADY, John Wesley, 922.742
1887-
Faith and freedom, the roots of democracy, by J. Wesley Bready ... New York. American tract society [1946] 3 p. l., 9-149 [3] p. plates, ports. 19 1/2 cm. "Radio lectures delivered over a national hook-up for the Canadian broadcasting corporation." [BX8495.W5B695] 46-5443
1. Wesley, John, 1706-1791. I. American tract society. II. Title.

BREADY, John Wesley, 922.742
1887-
Faith and freedom, the roots of democracy, by J. Wesley Bready ... New York. American tract society [1946] 3 p. l., 9-149 [3] p. plates, ports. 19 1/2 cm. "Radio lectures delivered over a national hook-up for the Canadian broadcasting corporation." [BX8495.W5B695] 46-5443
1. Wesley, John, 1706-1791. I. American tract society. II. Title.

BREADY, John Wesley, 1887- 274.2
This freedom--whence? By J. Wesley Bready ... New York, American tract society [1942] xviii, 365 p. front., plates, ports. 20 cm. "An abridgment and a revision of my recent ... 'England: before and after Wesley'."--Pref. [BR755.B72] 42-18084
1. Wesley, John 1706-1791. 2. Gt. Brit. — Church history — modern period. 3. Gt. Brit.—Soc. condit. 4. Evangelical revival. I. American tract society. II. Title.

BREADY, John Wesley, 1887- 274.2
1953.
England: before and after Wesley; the evangelical revival and social reform. New York, Russell & Russell [1971] 463 p. illus., ports. 22 cm. Reprint of the 1938 ed. [BR755.B7 1971] 72-139906
1. Wesley, John, 1703-1791. 2. Great Britain—Church history—Modern period, 1485- 3. Great Britain—Social conditions. 4. Evangelical revival. I. Title.

CANNON, William Ragasdale, 234.7
1916-
The theology of John Wesley, with special reference to the doctrine of justification by William Ragsdale Cannon. New York, Nashville Abingdon-Cokesbury press [1946] 234 p. 21 1/2 cm. Bibliography: p. 257-273. [BX8495.W5C3] 46-5637
1. Wesley, Johh, 1708-1791. 2. Justification—History of doctrines. I. Title.

CELL, George Croft, 1875- 922.742
The rediscovery of John Wesley, by George Croft Cell ... New York, H. Holt and company [c1935] xviii, 420 p. front. (port.) 21 cm. "The data analyzed ... demonstrate ... that the Wesleyan ethic of life was ... essentially and thoroughly Calvinistic."--Pref. "Wesley's published sermons": p. 415-418. [BX8495.W5C4] 35-3965
1. Wesley, John, 1703-1791. 2. Calvinism. 3. Theology, Doctrinal—Hist.—Modern period. I. Title.

CHAPPELL, Edwin Barfield, 922.
1853-
Studies in The life of John Wesley, by E. B. Chappell ... Nashville, Tenn., Dallas, Tex., Publishing house, M. E. church, South, Smith & Lamar, agents, 1911. 239 p. front. (port.) 20 cm. (Methodist founders' series, ed. by Bishop W. A. Candler) [BX8495.W5C5] 11-32224
1. Wesley, John, 1706-1791. I. Title.

CHAPPELL, Edwin Barfield, 922.
1853-
Studies in The life of John Wesley, by E. B. Chappell ... Nashville, Tenn., Dallas, Tex., Publishing house, M. E. church, South, Smith & Lamar, agents, 1911. 239 p. front. (port.) 20 cm. (Methodist founders' series, ed. by Bishop W. A. Candler) [BX8495.W5C5] 11-32224
1. Wesley, John, 1706-1791. I. Title.

CHURCH, Leslie 287.10924
Frederic, 1886-
Knight of the burning heart; the story of John Wesley. New York, Abingdon-Cokesbury Press [1953] 185 p. 19cm. [BX8495.W5C] A53
1. Wesley, john,1703-1791. I. Title.

CLARK, Elmer Talmage, 922.742
1886-
The warm heart of Wesley, by Elmer T.

Clark. With the Aldersgate story, by John Wesley. New York, Association of Methodist Historical Societies [1950] 78 p. illus., port. 20 cm. The Aldersgate story is reprinted from Wesley's Journal. [BX8495.W5C549] 50-3500
1. Wesley, John, 1703-1791. I. Wesley, John, 1708-1791. II. Title.

CLARK, Elmer Talmage, 922.742
1886-
What happened at Aldersgate, edited by Elmer T. Clark. Addresses in commemoration of the bicentennial of the spiritual awakening of John Wesley in Aldersgate street, London, May 24, 1738. Illustrated with drawings by Ernest A. Pickup. Nashville, Tenn., Methodist publishing house [c1938] 239 p. front. (port) illus. 20 1/2 cm. "The gathering before which these addresses were delivered was the Aldersgate session of the General missionary council of the Methodist Episcopal church, South, meeting in Savannah, Ga., in the opening days of 1938." [BX8495.W5C55] 38-7037
1. Wesley, John, 1703-1791. 2. Conversion. I. Methodist Episcopal church, South. General missionary council. II. Title.

CLARK, James Osgood 922.742
Andrew, 1827-1894, ed.
The Wesley memorial volume; or, Wesley and the Methodist movement, judged by nearly one hundred and fifty writers, living or dead. Edited by Rev. J. O. A. Clark... New York, Phillips & Hunt; Cincinnati, Walden & Stowe; [etc., etc.] 1881. 743, [1] p. incl. plates, ports., facsims. front. 23 1/2 cm. "The Wesley family": p. [27]-50. Hymns, with music: p. 475-480. [BX8495.W5A15] 37-12136
1. Wesley, John. 1703-1791. 2. Wesley family. 3. Methodism. I. Title. II. Title: Wesley and the Methodist movement.

COLLIER, Frank Wilbur, 1870- 922.
Back to Wesley [by] Frank W. Collier ... New York, Cincinnati, Methodist book concern [c1924] 52 p. 19 cm. [BX8495.W5C7] 24-16334
1. Wesley, John, 1703-1791. I. Title.

COLLIER, Frank Wilbur, 1870- 922.
John Wesley among the scientists, by Frank W. Collier ... New York, Cincinnati [etc.] The Abingdon press [c1928] 351 p. front. (port.) pl. 20 cm. Bibliography: p. 323-326. [BX8495.W5C75] 28-31129
1. Wesley, John, 1703-1791. 2. Religion and science—1900- I. Title.

COOPER, Joseph, 1867- 922.742
The love stories of John Wesley, and other essays [by] Joseph Cooper. Boston, R. G. Badger [c1931] 107 p. 20 cm. [BX8495.W5C77] 31-20098
1. Wesley, John, 1703-1791. I. Title.
Contents omitted

DAVIES, Edward, 1830- 922.742
The life of Rev John Wesley, A. M. Written from a spiritual standpoint. With five illustrations. By Rev. Edward Davies ... Introduction by Dr. Charles Cullis ... Reading, Mass., Holiness book concern; New York, Willard tract repository: [etc., etc., 1887] x, [11]-261 p. front., plates, port. 18 cm. [RX8495.W5D3] 37-12143
1. Wesley, John, 1703-1791. I. Title.

DESCHNER, John 232
Wesley's Christology, an interpretation. Dallas, Southern Methodist University Press [c.] 1960. ix, 220p. 23cm. (Bibl.: p. 212-214) 60-8676 4.50
1. Wesley, John, 1703-1791. 2. Jesus Christ—History of doctrines. I. Title.

DOBREE, Bonamy, 287'.092'4 B
1891-
John Wesley. [Folcroft, Pa.] Folcroft Library Editions, 1974. p. cm. Reprint of the 1933 ed. published by Duckworth, London, which was issued as no. 4 of Great lives. Bibliography: p. [BX8495.W5D57 1974] 74-7428 10.00 (lib. bdg.).
1. Wesley, John, 1703-1791.

DOUGLASS, Paul Franklin, 922.742
1904-
Wesleys at Oxford; the religion of university men. [Bryn Mawr] Pa., Bryn Mawr Press, 1953. 107p. illus. 24cm. [BX8495.W5D6] 54-16106
1. Wesley. John, 1703-1791. 2. Wesley, Charles, 1707-1788. I. Title.

EDWARDS, Maldwyn Lloyd, 922.742
1903-
John Wesley and the eighteenth century; a study of his social and political influence [Rev. ed.] London, Epworth Pr. [dist. Mystic, Conn., Verry, 1964] 207p. 19cm. Bibl. 55-12751 3.00
1. Wesley, John, 1703-1791. I. Title.

EGERMEIER, Elsie E. 922.
John Wesley, The Christian hero, by Elsie E. Egermeier ... Anderson, Ind., Gospel trumpet company [c1923] 131 p. incl. front. (port.) illus. 19 cm. [BX8495.W5E3] 23-17579
1. Wesley, John, 1703-1791. I. Title.

ETHRIDGE, Willie 287'.0924 B
(Snow)
Strange fires; the true story of John Wesley's love affair in Georgia. New York, Vanguard Press [1971] 254 p. 24 cm. Bibliography: p. 249-254. [BX8495.W5E84 1971] 77-170902 ISBN 0-8149-0693-1 6.95
1. Wesley, John, 1703-1791. 2. Hopkey, Sophy. I. Title.

FAULKNER, John Alfred, 1857- 922.
1931.
Wesley as sociologist, theologian, churchman, by John Alfred Faulkner... New York. Cincinnati, The Methodist book concern [c1918] 173 p. 19 cm. [BX8495.W5F3] 18-19812
1. Wesley, John, 1703-1791. I. Title.

FUNSTON, John Wesley. 922.742
The Wesleys in picture and story. An illustrated history of the life and times of John and Charles Wesley. By John Wesley Funston ... [Mount Morris, Ill., Kable brothers company, printers, c1939] 5 p. l., 7-137 p. illus. (incl. ports.) 26 cm. Includes music. [BX8495.W5F8] 39-20796
1. Wesley, John 1703-1791. I. Title.

GAMBLE, Thomas, 1868- 922.
The love stories of John and Charles Wesley, by Thomas Gamble. [Savannah, Review publishing & printing co. inc., 1927] 68, [2] p. incl. illus., ports. 24 cm. [BX8495.W5G3] 27-10063
1. Wesley, John, 1703-1791. 2. Wesley, Charles, 1707-1788. I. Title.

GARBER, Paul Neff, 1899- 922.742
That fighting spirit of Methodism [by] Paul Neff Garber ... Greensboro, N.C., The Piedmont press, 1928 [i.e. 1929] viii p., 2 l., [13]-199 p. 19 1/2 cm. "First impression, October, 1928; second impression, January, 1929." "The purpose of this book is to interpret for modern Methodists the fighting spirit of John Wesley and his early followers."--Pref. [BX8495.W5G36 1929] 34-34689
1. Wesley, John, 1706-1791. 2. Methodism. I. Title.

GARBER, Paul Neff, 1899- 922.742
That fighting spirit of Methodism [by] Paul Neff Garber ... Greensboro, N.C., The Piedmont press, 1928 [i.e. 1929] viii p., 2 l., [13]-199 p. 19 1/2 cm. "First impression, October, 1928; second impression, January, 1929." "The purpose of this book is to interpret for modern Methodists the fighting spirit of John Wesley and his early followers."--Pref. [BX8495.W5G36 1929] 34-34689
1. Wesley, John, 1706-1791. 2. Methodism. I. Title.

GREEN, Richard, 1829-1907. 922.
John Wesley. By the Rev. R. Green. London, New York [etc.] Cassell, Potter, Galphin & co. [1882] viii, [9]-192 p. 16 cm. (On cover: Cassell's popular library) [BX8495.W5G69] 42-43960
1. Wesley, John, 1708-1791. I. Title.

GREEN, Vivian Hubert 922.742
Howard.
The young Mr. Wesley; a study of John Wesley and Oxford. New York, St. Martin's Press [1961] 342p. illus. 23cm. Includes bibliography. [BX8495.W5G74] 61-10197
1. Wesley, John, 1703-1791. I. Title.

HADDAL, Ingvar. 922.742
John Wesley, a biography. Translated from the original Norwegian. New York, Abingdon Press [1961] 175p. illus. 23cm. [BX8495.W5H233] 61-66826
1. Wesley, John, 1703-1791. I. Title.

HARRISON, Grace Elizabeth 922.742
(Simon) Mrs. 1886-
Son to Susanna, the private life of John Wesley, by G. Elsie Harrison. Nashville, Cokesbury press [c1938] 377 p. 23 cm. "References": p. 367-372. [BX8495.W5H33] 38-27209
1. Wesley, John, 1708-1791. I. Title.

HARRISON, Grace Elizabeth 922.742
(Simon) 1886-
Son to Susanna; the private life of John Wesley, by G. Elsie Harrison. Harmondsworth, Middlesex, Eng., New York, Penguin books [1944] vii, [1], 9-215 p., 1 l., incl. front. (port.) 1 illus. 18 cm. (On cover; Penguin books. 462) "First edition September 1937...Published in Penquin books 1944." "References": p. 207-212. [BX8495.W5H33 1944] 45-5013
1. Wesley, John, 1708-1791. I. Title.

HIGGINS, Paul Lambourne 922.742
John Wesley : spiritual witness. Minneapolis, T.S. Denison [c.1960] 134p. Bibl.: p.134. 22cm. 60-16801 3.00
1. Wesley, John, 1703-1791. I. Title.

HIGGINS, Paul Lambourne. 922.742
John Wesley: spiritual witness. Minneapolis, T. S. Denison [1960] 134p. 22cm. Includes bibliography. [BX8495.W5H48] 60-16801
1. Wesley, John. 1703-1791. I. Title.

HOLMES, David, 1810-1873 922.742
The Wesley offering; or, Wesley and his times, By Rev. D. Holmes... Auburn [N.Y.] Derby and Miller, 1852. x, [11]-308 p. front. (port.) 18 1/2 cm. [BX8495.W5H6] 37-12152
1. Wesley, John, 1708-1791. 2. Methodism. I. Title. II. Title: Wesley and his times.

[HURSTS, John Fletcher] 922.
bp., 1834-1903.
John Wesley the Methodist; a plain account of his life and work, by a Methodist preacher. With one hundred portraits, views, and facsimiles. New York, Eaton & Mains; Cincinnati, Jennings & Pye [c1903] 319 p. incl. illus., plates, ports, facisms. 23 cm. Frontispiece accompanied by guard sheet with descriptive litterpress. Extracted from Bishop Hurst's British Methodism, by Dr. Joy cf. A. Osborn, John Fletcher Hurst, New York, 1905, p. 334-335. [BX8495.W5H8] 3-9945
1. Wesley, John, 1703-1791. I. Joy, James Richard, 1863- ed. II. Title.

JEFFERY, Thomas Reed. 922.742
John Wesley's religious quest. [1st ed.] New York, Vantage Press [1960] 439p. 21cm. Includes bibliography. [BX8495.W5J4] 59-11127
1. Wesley, John, 1703-1791. I. Title.

JOY, James Richard, 1863- 922.742
John Wesley's awakening [by] James Richard Joy ... New York, Cincinnati [etc.] The Methodist book concern [c1937] 128 p. 18 cm. Bibliography: p. 125-126. [BX895.W5J6] 38-1025
1. Wesley, Johm 1703-1791. I. Title.

KERSHNER, John J. 133.
The truth about death and life hereafter, by John J. Kershner. [Chicago, Clarke-McElroy publishing co., c1924] cover-title, 2 p. l., 7-64 p. 15 cm. "The following chapters are the spirit writings of the late John Wesley." cf. Intrd. Text on p. [3] of cover. [BF1301.K4] 25-1739
1. Wesley, John, 1703-1791. I. Title.

KROLL, Harry Harrison, 922.742
1888-
The long quest; the story of John Wesley. Philadelphia, Westminster Press [1954] 192p. 22cm. [BX8495.W5K7] 53-8356
1. Wesley, John, 1703-1791. I. Title.

LARRABEE, William Clark, 922.742
1802-1859.
Wesley and his coadjutors. By Wm. C. Larrabee, A. M. Edited by Rev. B. F. Tefft ... Cincinnati, Swormstedt & Power, for the Methodist Episcopal church, 1851. 2 v. front. (port.) 17 cm. [BX8495.W5L3] 37-9732
1. Wesley, John, 1706-1791. I. Tefft, Benjamin Franklin, 1813-1885, ed. II. Title.

LARRABEE, William Clark, 922.742
1802-1859.
Wesley and his coadjutors. By Wm. C. Larrabee, A. M. Edited by Rev. B. F. Tefft ... Cincinnati, Swormstedt & Power, for the Methodist Episcopal church, 1851. 2 v. front. (port.) 17 cm. [BX8495.W5L3] 37-9732
1. Wesley, John, 1706-1791. I. Tefft, Benjamin Franklin, 1813-1885, ed. II. Title.

LAVER, James, 1899- 922.742
Wesley, by James Laver ... New York, D. Appleton and company, 1933. 3 p. l., 168, [1] p. front. (port.) 20 cm. [Appleton biographies] "Bibliographical note": p. 163-[164] [BX8495.W5L33 1933] 33-12272
1. Wesley, John, 1703-1791. I. Title.

LEE, Umphrey, 1893- 922.742
John Wesley and modern religion, by Umphrey Lee ... Nashville, Cokesbury press [c1936] xiii, 354 p. 22 1/2 cm. "Notes": p. 323-341. [BX8495.W5L34] 36-21478
1. Wesley, John, 1703-1791. 2. Methodism. I. Title.

LEE, Umphrey, 1893- 922.742
The Lord's horseman; John Wesley the man. Nashville, Abingdon Press [1954] 220 p. 22 cm. [BX8495.W5L35 1954] 54-11235
1. Wesley, John, 1703-1791. I. Title.

LEE, Umphrey, 1893- 922.
The Lord's horseman, by Umphrey Lee. New York, London, The Century co. [c1928] xi, 3-358 p. 21 cm. "An account of an amour of John Wesley": p. 267-351; "A letter to Molly": p. 352-356. [BX8495.W5L35] 28-22583
1. Wesley, John, 1706-1791. I. Title.

LEE, Umphrey, 1893- 922.
The Lord's horseman, by Umphrey Lee. New York, London, The Century co. [c1928] xi, 3-358 p. 21 cm. "An account of an amour of John Wesley": p. 267-351; "A letter to Molly": p. 352-356. [BX8495.W5L35] 28-22583
1. Wesley, John, 1706-1791. I. Title.

LEE, Umphrey, 1893-1958. 287'.142
The historical backgrounds of early Methodist enthusiasm. New York, AMS Press, 1967. 176 p. 23 cm. (Studies in history, economics and public law, no. 339) Reprint of the 1931 ed., originally presented as the author's thesis, Columbia University. Bibliography: p. 149-172. [BR112.L4 1967] 74-29899
1. Wesley, John, 1703-1791. 2. Enthusiasm. 3. Great Britain—Church history—Modern period, 1485- 4. Methodism—History. I. Title. II. Series: Columbia studies in the social sciences, no. 339.

LIPSKY, Abram, 1872- 922.
John Wesley, a portrait, by Abram Lipsky. New York, Simon & Schuster, 1928. ix p., 2 l., 305 p. 2 port. (incl. front.) 2 facsim. 21 cm. [BX8495.W5L47] 28-22586
1. Wesley, John, 1703-1791. I. Title.

LIPSKY, Abram, 1872- 287'.0924 B
1946.
John Wesley; a portrait. New York, AMS Press [1971, c1928] ix, 305 p. facsim., ports. 19 cm. Bibliography: p. 297-300. [BX8495.W5L47 1971] 76-155619 ISBN 0-404-03994-4
1. Wesley, John, 1703-1791.

LITTLE, Arthur Wilde, 1856- 922.
1910.
The times and the teaching of John Wesley, by Arthur W. Little ... 2d ed. Milwaukee, Wis., The Young churchman co., 1905. xiv, 68 p. front. (port.) 19 cm. [BX8495.W5L5 1905] 5-39042
1. Wesley, John, 1703-1791. I. Title.

LUNN, Arnold Henry Moore, 922.
1888-
John Wesley, by Arnold Lunn...with a foreword by S. Parkes Cadman, D.D. New York, L. MacVeagh, The Dial press; Toronto, Longmans, Green and co., 1929. xix, 371 p. front. (port.) 21 1/2 cm. Bibliography included in "Introduction". [BX8495.W5L8] 29-4953

1. Wesley, John, 1703-1791. I. Title.

MACARTHUR, Kathleen Walker. 922.742
The economic ethics of John Wesley [by] Kathleen Walker MacArthur. New York, Cincinnati [etc.] The Abingdon press [c1936] 166 p. 19 1/2 cm. Bibliography: p. 155-166. [BX8495.W5M23] 37-7821
1. Wesley, John, 1763-1791. 2. Sociology, Christian—Gt. Brit. 3. Sociology, Christian—Methodist authors. I. Title.

MCCONNELL, Francis John, bp. 922.742
John Wesley. Nashville, Abingdon Press [1961, c.1939] 355p. (Apex Bks. E-4) 1.75pap.,
1. Wesley, John 1703-1791. I. Title.

MCCONNELL, Francis John, bp., 1871- 922.742
John Wesley [by] Francis J. McConnell. New York, Chicago [etc.] The Abingdon press [c1939] 355 p. 24 cm. [BX8495.W5M24] 39-27458
1. Wesley, John, 1703-1791. I. Title.

MCDONALD, William, 1820-1901. 922.742
The people's Wesley, by W. McDonald. With an introduction by Bishop W. F. Mallalieu ... New York, Eaton & Mains; Cincinnati, Curts & Jennings, 1899. 1 p. l., 62 p. 18 1/2 cm. A "revised and enlarged edition" has title: The young people's Wesley. [BX8495.W5M25] 99-1319
1. Wesley, John, 1703-1791. I. Title.

MCDONALD, William, 1820-1901. 922.742
The young people's Wesley, by W. McDonald, with an introduction by Bishop W. F. Mallalieu ... New York, Eaton & Mains; Cincinnati, Jennings & Pye, 1901. 204 p. front. (port.) plates. 16 1/2 cm. "Rev. & enl. ed." of The people's Wesley.--Pref. [BX8495.W5M27] 1-22885
1. Wesley, John, 1703-1791 I. Title.

MCNEER, May Yonge, 1902- 922.742
John Wesley, by May McNeer and Lynd Ward. New York, Abingdon-Cokesbury Press [1951] 95 p. illus. (part col.) 25 cm. [BX8495.W5M28] 51-10148
1. Wesley, John, I. Ward, Lynd Kendall, 1906- illus. II. Title.

MCNEER, May Yonge, 1902- 922.742
John Wesley, by May McNeer and Lynd Ward. New York, Abingdon-Cokesbury Press [1951] 95 p. illus. (part col.) 25 cm. [BX8495.W5M28] 51-10148
1. Wesley, John, 1703-1791. I. Ward, Lynd Kendall, 1905- illus.

MARSHALL, Dorothy 922.742
John Wesley. [New York] Oxford [c.]1965. 64p. illus., ports. 21cm. (Clarendon biographies) Bibl. [BX8495.W5M29] 65-3896 1.40 bds.,
1. Wesley, John, 1703-1791. I. Title.

M'CAINE, Alexander, 1768(ca.)-1856. 262.
The history and mystery of Methodist episcopacy, or, A glance at "the institutions of the church, as we received them from our fathers." By Alexander M'Caine ... Baltimore, Printed by R. J. Matchett, 1827. v, [7]-76 p. 21 cm. [BX8345.M3] 35-23823
1. Wesley, John, 1703-1791. 2. Methodist Episcopal church—Government. 3. Episcopacy. I. Title.

MEREDITH, William Henry, 1844-1911. 922.
The real John Wesley, by William Henry Meredith ... bicentennial contribution ... Cincinnati, Jennings and Py. New York, Eaton and Mains [1903] 425 p. fold. facsim. 20 cm. [BX8495.W5M42] 3-20095
1. Wesley, John, 1706-1791. I. Title.

MEREDITH, William Henry, 1844-1911. 922.
The real John Wesley, by William Henry Meredith ... bicentennial contribution ... Cincinnati, Jennings and Py. New York, Eaton and Mains [1903] 425 p. fold. facsim. 20 cm. [BX8495.W5M42] 3-20095
1. Wesley, John, 1706-1791. I. Title.

METHODISM'S Aldersgate heritage, by four Wesleyan scholars. Nashville, [1908 Grand Ave., Methodist Evangelistic Materials c.1964] 62p. 19cm. Bibl. 64-17883 .60 pap., 287.1942
1. Wesley, John, 1703-1791. 2. Methodism—Addresses, essays, lectures.

*MILLER, Basil 287.0924(B)
John Wesley; 'I look upon the world as my parish.' Introd. by Stephen W. Paine. Minneapolis, Bethany Fellowship [1966, c.1943] 140p. 19cm. (BF150) 1.50 pap.,
1. Wesley, John, 1703-1791. I. Title.

MILLER, Basil William, 1897- 922.742
John Wesley, the world his parish, by Basil Miller; introduction by Stephen W. Paine ... Grand Rapids, Mich., Zondervan publishing house [1943] 140 p. 20 cm. [BX8495.W5M5] 43-9923
1. Wesley, John, 1703-1791. I. Title.

MITCHELL, T Crichton. 922.742
Mr. Wesley; an intimate sketch of John Wesley. Kansas City, Mo., Beacon Hill Press [1957] 96p. 19cm. Includes bibliography. [BX8495.W5M55] 57-3716
1. Wesley, John, 1703- 1791. I. Title.

MITCHELL, T Crichton. 922.742
Mr. Wesley; an intimate sketch of John Wesley. Kansas City, Mo. Beacon Hill Press [1957] 96p. 19cm. Includes bibliography. [BX8495.W5M55] 57-3716
1. Wesley, John, 1703-1791. I. Title.

MONK, Robert C. 287.0924
John Wesley; his puritan heritage; a study of the Christian life [by] Robert C. Monk. Nashville, Abingdon [1966] 286p. 24cm. Based on thesis. Priceton Univ. Bibl. [BX8495.W5M6] 66-15494 5.50
1. Wesley, John, 1703-1791. 2. Puritans. I. Title.

[MUDGE, Zachariah Atwell] 1813-1888. 922.742
Wesley and his friends: illustrating the religious spirit of their times. By the author of "Towers of Zion" ... Philadelphia [etc.] American Sunday-school union [1856] 196 p. incl. front. plates. ports. 16 cm. [BX8495.W5M8] 37-9733
1. Wesley, John, 1703-1791. I. American Sunday-school union. II. Title.

NOTT, George Frederick, 1767-1841. 287
Religious enthusiasm considered; in eight sermons, preached before the University of Oxford, in the year MDCCCII., at the lecture founded by John Bampton ... By George Frederick Nott ... Oxford, The University press, for the author; [etc., etc.] 1803. xv, 502 p. 22 cm. Binder's title: Bampton lectures. 1802. Includes "opinions ... concerning Mr. Wesley's and Mr. Whitefield's pretenstions." cf. p. [vii] Bibliography: p. viii-ix. [BR45.B3 1802] [(230.082)] 38-16048
1. Wesley, John, 1703-1791. 2. Whitefield, George, 1714-1770. 3. Enthusiasm. 4. Methodism. 5. Church of England—Sermons. 6. Sermons, English. I. Title.

OVERTON, John Henry, 1835-1903. 922.
John Wesley, by J. H. Overton, M. A. Boston and New York, Houghton, Mifflin and company, 1891. vi p., 1 l., 216 p. incl. front. (port.) 20 cm. [BX8495.W5O8] 8-23782
1. Wesley, John, 1708-1791. I. Title.

PELLOWE, William Charles Smithson. 922.712
John Wesley, master in religion; a study in methods and attitudes [by] William C. S. Pellowe ... Nashville, Methodist Episcopal church, South, for the author [1939?] 151, [1] p. 20 cm. [BX8495.W5P4] 39-22726
1. Wesley, John 1703-1791 I. Title.

PIETTE, Maximin. 922.742
John Wesley in the evolution of Protestantism, by Maximin Piette ... translated by the J. B. Howard, with forewords by Bishop F. C. Kelley [and] Dr. H. B. Workman. New York, Sheed & Ward, 1937. xlviii, 569 p. front., plates, ports., facsim. 22 cm. "Printed in Great Britain." Bibliography: p. xxxi-xlviii. [BX8495.W5P48] 38-2954
1. Wesley, John, 1703-1791. 2. Protestantism—Hist. 3. Reformation. I. Howard, Joseph Bernard, 1892- tr. II. Title.

THE Place of Wesley in the Christian tradition / edited by Kenneth E. Rowe. Metuchen, N.J. : Scarecrow Press, 1976. iii, 165 p. ; 23 cm. "Essays delivered at Drew University in celebration of the commencement of the publication of the Oxford edition of the works of John Wesley." Includes index. "A selected bibliography [by] Lawrence D. McIntosh": p. 134-159. [BX8495.W5P53] 76-27659 ISBN 0-8108-0981-8 : 6.00 287'.092'4
1. Wesley, John, 1703-1791. I. Rowe, Kenneth E.

PRINCE, John Wesley, 1892- 922.
Wesley on religious education; a study of John Wesley's theories and methods of the education of children in religion, by John W. Prince ... New York, Cincinnati, The Methodist book concern [c1926] 164 p. 24 cm. Thesis (PH. D.)--Yale university, 1924. Bibliography: p. 154-160. [BX8495.W5P7] 26-6653
1. Wesley, John, 1703-1791. 2. Religious education. I. Title.

PUDNEY, John, 1909-1977. 287'.092'4 B
John Wesley and his world / John Pudney. New York : Scribner, c1978. 128 p. : ill. ; 24 cm. Includes index. Bibliography: p. 119. [BX8495.W5P77 1978] 78-59110 ISBN 0-684-15922-8 : 10.95
1. Wesley, John, 1703-1791. 2. Methodist Church—Clergy—Biography. 3. Clergy—England—Biography. I. Title.

RATTENBURY, John Ernest, 1870- 922.
Wesley's legacy to the world; six studies in the permanent values of the evangelical revival, by J. Ernest Rattenbury ... Nashville, Tenn., Cokesbury press, 1928. 309 p. 22 cm. [The Quillian lectures, 1928] [BX8495.W5R3] 28-21917
1. Wesley, John, 1703-1791. 2. Methodism. 3. Evangelical revival. I. Title.

RIGG, James Harrison, 1821-1909. 922.742
The living Wesley, as he was in his youth and in his prime. By James H. Rigg ... With an introduction by John F. Hurst, D. D. New York, Nelson & Phillips; Cincinnati, Hitchcock & Walden, 1874. 269 p. front. (port.) 20 cm. [BX8495.W5R5 1874] 37-12170
1. Wesley, John, 1703-1791. I. Title.

SCHMIDT, Martin, 1909- 922.742
John Wesley: a theological biography; v.1. Tr. [from German] by Noran P. Goldhawk. Nashville, Abingdon [1963, c.1962] 320p. 23cm. Contents.v.1. From 17th June 1703 until 24th May 1738. Bibl. 63-3396 6.50
1. Wesley, John,1703-1791. I. Title.

SCHMIDT, Martin, 1909- 922.742
John Wesley: a theological biography. Translated by Norman P. Goldhawk. New York, Abingdon Press [1963, c1962- v. 23 cm. Contents.v. 1. From 17th June 1706 until 24th May 1738. Includes bibliography. [BX8495.W5S283] 63-3396
1. Wesley, John, 1703-1791. I. Title.

SELECMAN, Charles Claude, Bp., 1874- 287.673
The Methodist primer. Nashville, Tidings [1947] 64 p. plates, ports., map. 19 cm. Bibliography: p. 60. [BX8387.S4 1947] 48-16143
1. Wesley, John, 1703-1791. 2. Methodist Church (United States) I. Title.

SELECMAN, Charles Claude, bp.,1874- 287.673
The Methodist primer, by Bishop Charles Claude Selecman ... Nashville, Tenn., Tidings [1944] 55, [1] p. illus. (incl. ports., maps) 19 1/2 cm. [BX8387.S4] 44-12238
1. Wesley, John, 1703-1791. 2. Methodist church (United States) I. Title.

SELECTED letters;
edited by Frederick C. Gill. New York, Philosophical Library [1956] vii, 244p. 23cm.
I. Wesley, John, 1703-1791.

SHERWIN, Oscar, 1902- 922.742
John Wesley, friend of the people. New York, Twayne [c.1961] 234p. Bibl. 61-15094 5.00 bds.,
1. Wesley, John, 1703-1791. I. Title.

SHERWIN, Oscar, 1902- 922.742
John Wesley, friend of the people. New York, Twayne Publishers [1961] 284 p. 21 cm. Includes bibliography. [BX8495.W5S43] 61-15094
1. Wesley, John, 1703-1791. I. Title.

SHIELDS, James Kurtz, 1887- 922.742
Fifty years in buckles and saddle; the dramatic story of John Wesley, founder of Methodism, by James K. Shields. Newark, N.J., [c1937] 67 p. incl. pl. 19 cm. [BX8495.W5S45] 37-21913
1. Wesley, John, 1706-1791 I. Title.

SHIELDS, James Kurtz, 1887- 922.742
Fifty years in buckles and saddle; the dramatic story of John Wesley, founder of Methodism, by James K. Shields. Newark, N.J., [c1937] 67 p. incl. pl. 19 cm. [BX8495.W5S45] 37-21913
1. Wesley, John, 1706-1791 I. Title.

SHORT, Ruth Gordon. 287.10924
Affectionately yours, John Wesley. Illustrated by Jim Padgett. Nashville, Southern Pub. Association [1963] 298 p. illus. 21 cm. Bibliography: p. 297-298. [BX8495.W5S46] 63-12812
1. Wesley, John, 1703-1791. I. Title.

SIMPSON, William John Sparrow, 1859- 922.742
John Wesley and the Church of England, by W. J. Sparrow Simpson. A publication of the Literature association of the Church union. London, Society for promoting Christian knowledge; New York, The Macmillan company, 1934. xi, 100 p. 19 cm. [BX8495.W5S54] 35-4430
1. Wesley, John 1703-1791. 2. Church of England. I. The Church union. Church literature association. II. Society for promoting Christian knowledge, London. III. Title.

SLAATTE, Howard Alexander 230.7
Fire in the brand, an introduction to the creative work and theology of John Wesley. Foreword by Paul V. Galloway. New York, Exposition [c.1963] 157p. 22cm. (Exposition-univ. bk. EP41124) 63-4965 4.00
1. Wesley, John, 1703-1791. I. Title.

SLAATTE, Howard Alexander. 230.7
Fire in the brand, an introduction to the creative work and theology of John Wesley. Foreword by Paul V. Galloway. [1st ed.] New York, Exposition Press [1963] 157 p. 22 cm. (An Exposition-university book) "EP41125." [BX8495.W5S545] 63-4965
1. Wesley, John, 1703-1791. I. Title.

SNELL, Frederick John, 1862- 922.
... *Wesley and Methodism,* by F. J. Snell ... New York, C. Scribner's sons, 1900. x, 243 p. 19 cm. (The World's epoch-makers. [xxi]) [BX8495.W5S55] 2-12316
1. Wesley, John, 1708-1791. I. Title.

SNELL, Frederick John, 1863- 922.
... *Wesley and Methodism,* by F. J. Snell ... New York, C. Scribner's sons, 1900. x, 243 p. 19 cm. (The world's epoch-makers. [xxi]) [BX8495.W5S55] 2-12316
1. Wesley, John, 1703-1791. I. Title.

SNYDER, Howard A. 287'.092'4 B
The radical Wesley and patterns for church renewal / Howard A. Snyder. Downers Grove, Ill. : InterVarsity Press, c1980. p. cm. Based in part on the author's thesis, Notre Dame. Includes bibliographical references and index. [BX8495.W5S56] 80-18197 ISBN 0-87784-625-1 pbk. : 5.25
1. Wesley, John, 1703-1791. 2. Methodist Church—Clergy—Biography. 3. Clergy—England—Biography. 4. Church. 5. Church renewal. I. Title.

SOUTHEY, Robert, 1774-1843. 922.
The life of Wesley; and the rise and progress of Methodism. By Robert Southey ... New-York, Pub. by Evert Duyckinck & George Long. Clayton & Kingsland, printers, 1820. 2 v. in 1. front. (port.) 21 1/2 cm. Bibliography: p. [5]-6. [BX8495.W5S] A 33
1. Wesley, John, 1703-1791. 2. Methodism—History. I. Title.

SOUTHEY, Robert, 1774- 922.742
1843.
The life of Wesley; and rise and progress of Methodism. By Robert Southey ... With notes by the late Samuel Taylor Coleridge, esq., and remarks on the life and character of John Wesley, by the late Alexander Knox, esq. Edited by the Rev. Charles Cuthbert Southey ... 2d American ed., with notes, etc., by the Rev. Daniel Curry ... New York, Harper & brothers, 1847. 2 v. 20 cm. Bibliography: v. 1, p. [xi]-xiv. [BX8495.W5S6 1847] 37-12135
1. Wesley, John, 1708-1791. 2. Methodism—Hist. I. Southey, Charles Cuthbert, 1819-1888. II. Curry, Daniel, 1809-1887, ed. III. Knox, Alexander, 1757-1831. IV. Coleridge, Samuel Taylor, 1772-1834. V. Title.

SOUTHEY, Robert, 1774- 922.742
1843.
The life of Wesley; and rise and progress of Methodism. By Robert Southey ... With notes by the late Samuel Taylor Coleridge, esq., and remarks on the life and character of John Wesley, by the late Alexander Knox, esq. Edited by the Rev. Charles Cuthbert Southey ... 2d American ed., with notes, etc., by the Rev. Daniel Curry ... New York, Harper & brothers, 1874. 2 v. front. (port.) 20 cm. Bibliography: v. 1, p. [xi]-xiv. [BX8495.W5S6 1874] 37-12134
1. Wesley, John, 1703-1791. 2. Methodism—Hist. I. Southey, Charles Cuthbert, 1819-1888, ed. II. Curry, Daniel, 1809-1887, ed. III. Knox, Alexander, 1757-1831. IV. Coleridge, Samuel Taylor, 1772-1834. V. Title.

STARKEY, Lycurgus Monroe, 231.3
Jr.
The work of the Holy Spirit, a study in Wesleyan theology. Nashville, Abingdon [c.1962] 176p. 23cm. Bibl. 62-9996 3.00
1. Wesley, John, 1703-1791. 2. Holy Spirit—History of doctrines. I. Title.

STARKEY, Lycurgus Monroe. 231.3
The work of the Holy Spirit, a study in Wesleyan theology. New York, Abingdon Press [1962] 176 p. 23 cm. Bibliography: p. 164-169. [BT119.S75] 62-9996
1. Wesley, John, 1703-1791. 2. Holy Spirit — History of doctrines. I. Title.

STOKES, Mack B. 230'.7
The Bible in the Wesleyan heritage / Mack B. Stokes. Nashville, TN : Abingdon, 1981, c1979. 95 p. ; 20 cm. [BS500.S83 1981] 19 80-23636 ISBN 0-687-03100-1 pbk. : 3.95
1. Wesley, John, 1703-1791. 2. Bible—Criticism, interpretation, etc.—History. 3. Theology, Methodist. I. Title.

STOKES, Mack B 287.1
Our Methodist heritage. Nashville, Graded Press [1963] 128 p. 20 cm. (Basic Christian books) Bibliographical footnotes. [BX8495.W5S7] 63-5864
1. Wesley, John. 1703-1791. 2. Methodism. I. Title.

TAYLOR, Isaac, 1787-1865. 287
Wesley, and Methodism. By Isaac Taylor. New York, Harper & brothers, 1852. 1 p. l., vii-viii p., 2 l., 13-328 p. front. (port.) 20 cm. First edition, London, 1851. Frontispiece wanting. [BX8331.T3] 7-7895
1. Wesley John 1703-1791 2. Methodism. I. Title.

TELFORD, John, 1851-1936. 922.
The life of John Wesley, by John Telford ... New York, Eaton & Mains; Cincinnati, Curts & Jennings [1898?] 1 p. l., [v]-xvi, 363 p. front. (fold. facsim.) 20 1/2 cm. First published London, 1886. [BX8495.W5T4] 12-39307
1. Wesley, John, 1703-1791. I. Title.

THOMAS, George Ernest, 922.742
1907-.
Abundant life through Aldersgate. Nashville, Methodist Evangelistic Materials [c1962] 62 p. 19 cm. [BX8495.W5T45] 62-20646
1. Wesley, John, 1703-1791. I. Title.

THOMPSON, David 261.8'0924
Decamp, 1852-1908.
John Wesley as a social reformer. Freeport, N.Y., Books for Libraries Press, 1971. 111 p. port 23 cm. (The Black heritage library collection) Reprint of the 1898 ed. [BX8495.W5T5 1971] 70-164396 ISBN 0-8369-8855-8
1. Wesley, John, 1703-1791. I. Title. II. Series.

THOMPSON, David Decamp, 922.742
1852-1908.
John Wesley as a social reformer, by D. D. Thompson. New York, Eaton & Mains; Cincinnati, Curts & Jennings, 1898. 111 p. front. (port.) 19 cm. [BX8495.W5T5] 35-28997
1. Wesley, John, 1703-1791 I. Title.

TIGERT, John James, 1856- 287
1906, ed.
The doctrines of the Methodist Episcopal church in America, as contained in the disciplines of said church from 1788 to 1808, and so designated on their title-pages; compiled and edited with an historical introduction by Jno. J. Tigert ... Cincinnati, Jennings & Pye. New York, Eaton & Mains, 1902. 2 v. 15 cm. (On cover: Little books on doctrine) With reproduction of some of the original title-pages. Contents.v. 1. The Scripture doctrine of predestination, election and reprobation. Serious thoughts on the infallible, unconditional perseverance of all that have once experienced faith in Christ. Extract on the nature and subjects of Christian baptism. Against antinomianism.--v. 2. A plain account of Christian perfection, as believed and taught by the Rev. Mr. John Wesley, from the year 1725 to the year 1765. Of Christian perfection. [BX8331.T45] 2-18962
1. Wesley, John, 1703-1791. 2. Methodist Episcopal church—Doctrinal and controversial works. I. Title.

TURNER, George Allen. 287.10924
The vision which transforms; is Christian perfection scriptural? Kansas City, Mo., Beacon Hill Press [1964] 348 p. 23 cm. "A through revision under ... new title' of the author's thesis, first published in 1952 under title: The more excellent way; the MS. Thesis (Harvard University) has title: A comparative study of the Biblical and Wesleyan ideas of perfection. Bibliography: p. 329-345. [BX8495.W5T67 1964] 64-18588
1. Wesley, John, 1703-1791. 2. Perfection — History of doctrines. I. Title.

TUTTLE, Robert G., 287'.092'4 B
1941-
John Wesley : his life and theology / Robert G. Tuttle, Jr. Grand Rapids : Zondervan Pub. House, c1978. 368 p., [4] leaves of plates : ill. ; 23 cm. Includes bibliographies and index. [BX8495.W5T73] 77-27583 ISBN 0-310-36660-7 : 9.95
1. Wesley, John, 1703-1791. 2. Methodists—England—Biography. 3. Evangelists—England—Biography.

TWENTIETH century 248.487
Aldersgate, by ten Methodist bishops. Nashville, Methodist Evangelistic Materials [c1962] 64 p. 19 cm. "A collection of ... message by Methodist bishops on Wesley's Aldersgate experiences." [BX8495.W5T75] 62-20647
1. Wesley, John, 1708-1791. 2. Christian life — Methodist authors.

TYERMAN, Luke, 287'.092'4 B
1819or20-1889.
The life and times of the Rev. John Wesley, M.A., founder of the Methodists. New York, B. Franklin [1973] 3 v. ports. 23 cm. (Burt Franklin research & source works series. Philosophy & religious history monographs 132) Reprint of the 1872 ed. published by Harper & Brothers, New York. Includes bibliographical references. [BX8495.W5T8 1973] 73-14910 ISBN 0-8337-4710-X 72.50
1. Wesley, John, 1703-1791.

WADE, John Donald, 1892- 922.742
John Wesley, by John Donald Wade. New York, Coward-McCann, inc., 1930. xvii, 301 p. front., ports. 23 1/2 cm. [BX8495.W5W25] 30-28960
1. Wesley, John, 1708-1791. I. Title.

WARNER, Wellman Joel, 1897- 261.8
The Wesleyan movement in the industrial revolution, by Wellman J. Warner. New York, Russell & Russell [1967] x, 299 p. 23 cm. First published in 1930. Bibliography: p. 283-296. [HN37.M4W3 1967] 66-24768
1. Wesley, John, 1703-1791. 2. Church and social problems—Methodist Church. 3. Church and social problems—Great Britain. 4. Great Britain—Social conditions. 5. Methodism. I. Title.

WATSON, Richard, 1781- 922.742
1833.
The life of Rev. John Wesley... founder of the Methodist societies. By Richard Watson... 1st American official ed., with translation and notes, by John Emory. Cincinnati, Pub. by L. Swormstedt & A. Poe, for the Methodist Episcopal church, 1855. 384 p. front. (port.) 19 1/2 cm. [BX8495.W5W3 1855] 32-35384
1. Wesley, John, 1703-1791. I. Emory, John, bp., 1789-1835. II. Title.

WATSON, Richard, 1781-1833. 922.
The life of the Rev. John Wesley ... founder of the Methodist societies. By Richard Watson ... 1st American official ed., with translations and notes by John Emory. New-York, J. Emory and B. Waugh, for the Methodist Episcopal church, 1831. 328 p. front. (port.) 18 cm. [BX8495.W5W3 1831] 15-21481
1. Wesley, John, 1703-1791 I. Emory, John, bp., 1789-1835. II. Title.

WATSON, Richard, 1781- 922.742
1833.
The life of the Rev. John Wesley ... to which are subjoined Observations on Southey's Life of Wesley: being a defence of the character, labors, and opinions of the founder of Methodism, against the misrepresentations of that publication. By Richard Watson. A new ed., with notes, by Thomas O. Summers. Nashville, Tenn., E. Stevenson & F. A. Owen, agents, for the Methodist Episcopal church, South, 1857. x, 11-345, vi, 7-186 p. 19 cm. "Observations on Southey's Life of Wesley" (vi, 7-186 p. at end) has special t.-p. [BX8495.W5W3 1857] 34-30363
1. Wesley, John, 1703-1791. 2. Southey, Robert, 1774-1843. The life of Wesley. I. Summers, Thomas Osmond, 1812-1882, ed. II. Title.

WATSON, Richard, 1781-1833. 922.
The life of the Rev. John Wesley... founder of the Methodist societies. By Richard Watson... New York, S. Hoyt & co., 1831. viii, 328 p. front. (port.) 18 cm. [BX8495.W5W3 1831a] 15-21483
1. Wesley, John, 1703-1791. I. Title.

WATSON, Richard, 1781-1833. 922.
The life of the Rev. John Wesley... founder of the Methodist societies. By Richard Watson... 1st American official ed., with translations and notes, by John Emory. New York, G. Lane & C. B. Tippett, for the Methodist Episcopal church, 1846. 323 p. front. (port.) 18 1/2 cm. Another edition published the same year by S. Hoyt & co., New York. A "1st American official edition" also published New York, 1831. [BX8495.W5W3 1846] 15-21482
1. Wesley, John, 1703-1791. I. Emory, John, bp., 1789-1835. II. Title.

WATSON, Richard, 1781- 922.742
1833.
The life of the Rev. John Wesley... to which are subjoined Observations on Southey's Life of Wesley: being a defence of the character, labors, and opinions of the founder of Methodism, against the misrepresentations of that publication. By Richard Watson. A new ed., with notes, by Thomas O. Summers. Nashville, Tenn., E. Stevenson & F. A. Owen, agents, for the Methodist Episcopal church, South, 1857. x, 11-345, vi, 7-186 p. 19 cm. "Observations on Southey's Life of Wesley" (with special t.-p. and separate paging) is by T. O. Summers. [BX8495.W5W3 1857] 34-30363
1. Wesley, John, 1703-1791. 2. Southey, Robert, 1774-1843. The life of Wesley. I. Summers, Thomas Osmond, 1812-1882. II. Title.

WATSON, Richard, 1781- 922.742
1833.
The life of the Rev. John Wesley... to which are subjoined Observations on Southey's Life of Wesley: being a defence of the character, labors, and opinions of the founder of Methodism, against the misrepresentations of that publication. By Richard Watson. A new ed., with notes, by Thomas O. Summers. Nashville, Tenn., E. Stevenson & F. A. Owen, agents, for the Methodist Episcopal church, South, 1857. x, 11-345, vi, 7-186 p. 19 cm. "Observations on Southey's Life of Wesley" (with special t.-p. and separate paging) is by T. O. Summers. [BX8495.W5W3 1857] 34-30363
1. Wesley, John, 1703-1791. 2. Southey, Robert, 1774-1843. The life of Wesley. I. Summers, Thomas Osmond, 1812-1882. II. Title.

WESLEY, John, 1703-1791. 248
Entire Bible on holiness, John Wesley and Adam Clarke (on the New Testament) compiled and sold by John C. Capehart. Seymour, Ind., [c1923] xiv, 15-272 p. front. 19 1/2 cm. [BT767.W4] 24-9680
I. Clarke, Adam, 1760?-1832. II. Capehart, John C., comp. III. Title.

WESLEY, John, 1703-1791. 922.742
The heart of John Wesley's Journal; with an introduction by Hugh Price Hughes, M.A., and an appreciation of the Journal by Augustine Birrell, K.C., ed. by Percy Livingstone Parker. New York, Chicago [etc.] Fleming H. Revell company [1903] xxxii, 512 p. plates, ports. (incl. front.) 21 1/2 cm. Wesley bicentenary edition. "A condensation, into popular form, of John Wesley's Journal hitherto published in four volumes."--Pub. weekly. [BX8495.W5A27] 3-11328
I. Parker, Percy Livingstone, 1867-1925, ed. II. Birrell, Augustine, 1850-1933. III. Title.

WESLEY, John, 1703-1791. 922.
Interesting extracts, from the journals of the Rev. John Wesley, A. M., with a synopsis of his life and death. Boston, Printed by William S. Spear, 1918. 300 p. front. (port.) 18 1/2 cm. [BX8495.W5A4 1819] A36
I. Title.

WESLEY, John, 1703-1791. 922.
Interesting extracts, from the journals of the Rev. John Wesley, A. M., with a synopsis of his life and death. Boston, Printed by William S. Spear, 1918. 300 p. front. (port.) 18 1/2 cm. [BX8495.W5A4 1819] A36
I. Title.

WESLEY, John, 1703- 287'.092'4
1791.
John Wesley's England : a 19th-century pictorial history based on an 18th-century journal / compiled by Richard Bewes. New York : Seabury Press, 1981. ca. [110] p. : ill. ; 27 cm. [BX8495.W5A343 1981] 19 81-2008 ISBN 0-8164-2319-9 pbk. : 9.95
1. Wesley, John, 1703-1791. 2. England—Description and travel. I. Bewes, Richard. II. [Journal of the Rev. John Wesley. Selections] III. Title.

WESLEY, John, 1703-1791. 922.472
John Wesley's Journal; as abridged by Nehemiah Curnock. New York, Philosophical Library [1951] viii, 433 p. 19 cm. [[BX8495.W5A]] A51
I. Curnock, Nehemiah, 1840-1915, ed. II. Title.

WESLEY, John, 1703-1791. 922.742
Journal, as abridged by Nehemiah Curnock. With an introd. by Gerald Kennedy. New York, Capricorn Books [1963] xxii, 433 p. port. (on cover) 19 cm. (A Capricorn book, Cap89) [BX8495.W5A224] 63-4586
I. Title.

WESLEY, John, 1703-1791. 922.742
The journal of John Wesley; with an introd. by Hugh Price Hughes, appreciation of the journal by Augustine Birrell. Edited by Percy Livingstone Parker. Chicago, Moody Press, 1951. 438 p. 21 cm. (The Tyndale series of great biographies) [[BX8495.W5A]] A 52
I. Title. II. Series.

WESLEY, John, 1703-1791. 922.
The journal of John Wesley. Abridged and edited by Nora Ratcliff ... London, New York [etc.] T. Nelson & sons, ltd. [1940] v, 7-463 p. front. (port.) 19 cm. [BX8495.W] A40
I. Ratcliff, Nora, ed. II. Title.

WESLEY, John, 1703-1791. 922.
Letters of John Wesley; a selection of important and new letters with introductions and biographical notes by George Eayrs ... With a chapter on

Wesley, his times and work by the Right Honourable Augustine Birrell ... A portrait of Wesley and letters in facsimile. London, New York [etc.] Hodder and Stoughton, 1915. xxxix, 509, [1] p. front. (port.) 3 facsim. 22 cm. Of the 3 letters given in facsimile (each with a special t.-p. not included in the collation) 2 have 4 pages each and the other has 2 pages. [BX8495.W5A3] 17-6791
I. Eayrs, George, ed. II. Birrell, Augustine, 1850- III. Title.

WESLEY, John, 1703-1791, comp. 264.
Select Psalms, arranged for the use of the Methodist Episcopal church by John Wesley, with other selections and the order from the sacraments and occasional services of the church. New York, Hunt & Eaton; Cincinnati, Cranston & Stowe, 1891. iv, 284 p. 18 cm. "The shortened Psalter in Mr. Wesley's Sunday service, published in 1784."--Pref. Edited by C. S. Harrower. cf. Pref. [BX8337.W4 1891] 45-48150
I. Methodist Episcopal church. Liturgy and ritual. II. Harrower, Charles Swartz, 1842-1911, ed. III. Title.

WESLEY, John, 1703-1791, comp. 264.
Select Psalms, arranged for the use of the Methodist Episcopal church by John Wesley, with other selections. Special ed. for Syracuse university. New York, Hunt & Eaton; Cincinnati, Cranston & Curts [1894] iv, 210 p. 18 cm. "The shortened Psalter in Mr. Wesley's Sunday service, published in 1784." --Pref. Edited by C. S. Harrower. cf. Pref. With this is bound: Methodist Episcopal church. Hymnal. New York, c1878. [BX8337.W4 1894] 45-50774
I. Methodist Episcopal church. Liturgy and ritual. II. Harrower, Charles Swartz, 1842-1911, ed. III. Syracuse university. IV. Title.

WESLEY, John, 1703-1791. 922.742
Wesley his own historian. Illustrations of his character, labors, and achievements. From his own diaries. By Rev. Edwin L. Janes ... New York, Carlton & Lanshan; Cincinnati, Hitchcock & Walden; [etc., etc.] 1870. 464 p. 19 1/2 cm. [BX8495.W5A23] 37-9735
I. Janes, Edwin Lines, 1807-1875, ed. II. Title.

WESLEY, John, 1703-1791.
Wesleyana, or a complete system of Wesleyan theology; selected from the writings of the Rev. John Wesley, A.M., and so arranged as to form a miniature body of divinity. (From a London publication.) Rev., enl., and an index added. New-York, G. Lane for the Methodist Episcopal church, 1840. 326 p. front. (port.) 18 1/2 cm. Comp. by W. Carpenter. 16-23742
I. Carpenter, William, 1797-1874, comp. II. Title.

WESLEYAN university, Middletown, Conn. 922.
... *Wesley bicentennial, Wesleyan university.* Middletown, Conn., Wesleyan university, 1904. vii, 239 p. front., plates, ports. 25 cm. At head of title: 1703-1903. [BX8495.W5W55] 4-3752
1. Wesley, John, 1703-1791. 2. Methodism—Addresses, essays, lectures. I. Title.

WHITEHEAD, John, 1740?-1804. 922.
The life of the Rev. John Wesley ... Collected from his private papers and printed works; and written at the request of his executors. To which is prefixed some account of his ancestors and relations; with the life of the Rev. Charles Wesley ... Collected from his private journal, and never before published. The whole forming a history of Methodism, in which the principles and economy of the Methodists are unfolded. By John Whitehead ... With an introduction by the Rev. Thomas H. Stockton. 2d American ed. ... Philadelphia, W. S. Stockton, 1845. 2 v. in 1. fronts. (ports.) 24 cm. [BX8495.W5W6 1845] 10-7576
1. Wesley, John, 1703-1791. 2. Wesley, Charles, 1707-1788. 3. Wesley family. I. Stockton, Thomas Hewlings, 1808-1868. II. Title.

WHITEHEAD, John, 1740?-1804. 922
The life of the Rev. John Wesley ... Collected from his private papers and printed works; and written at the request of his executors. To which is prefixed some account of his ancestors and relations, with the life of the Rev. Charles Wesley, M.A. Collected from his private journal, and never before published. By John Whitehead ... Boston, Hill & Brodhead, 1846. 2 v. in 1. fronts. (ports.) 23 cm. [BX8495.W5W6 1846] 10-7575
1. Wesley, John, 1703-1791 2. Wesley, Charles, 1707-1788. 3. Wesley family. I. Title.

WILLIAMS, Colin W. 230.7
John Wesley's theology today. New York, Abingdon Press [1960] 252 p. 23 cm. Bibliography: p. 243-246. [BX8495.W5W62] 60-5238
1. Wesley, John, 1703-1791. I. Title.

WILLIAMS, Colin Wilbur, 1921- 230.7
John Wesley's theology today. New York, Abingdon Press [1960] 252 p. 23 cm. Bibliography: p. 243-246. [BX8495.W5W62] 60-5238
1. Wesley, John, 1703-1791. I. Title.

WINCHESTER, Caleb Thomas, 1847-1920. 922.
The life of John Wesley, by C. T. Winchester ... New York, The Macmillan company; London, Macmillan & co., ltd., 1906. xiii, 301 p. 3 port. (incl. front.) 22 cm. [BX8495.W5W65] 6-6747
1. Wesley, John, 1703-1791. I. Title.

WOOD, Arthur Skevington. 287'.0924
The burning heart; John Wesley, evangelist, by A. Skevington Wood. Grand Rapids, Eerdmans [c.1967] 302p. 23cm. Bibl. [BX8495.W5W7 1967b] 68-20489 4.95
1. Wesley, John, 1703-1791. I. Title.

WYNKOOP, Mildred Bangs. 230'.7'1
A theology of love; the dynamic of Wesleyanism. Kansas City, Mo., Beacon Hill Press of Kansas City [1972] 372 p. 23 cm. Bibliography: p. 369-372. [BX8495.W5W9] 72-197997
1. Wesley, John, 1703-1791. I. Title.

Wesley, John, 1703-1791—Addresses, essays, lectures.

CANDLER, Warren Akin, 1857-
Wesley and his work; or, Methodism and missions; a volume of addresses, by Warren A. Candler ... Nashville, Tenn., Dallas, Tex., Publishing house of the M.E. church, South, Smith, & Lamar, agents, 1912. 223 p. 19 1/2 cm. 12-4472 1.00.
I. Title.

OUTLER, Albert Cook, 1908- 243
Evangelism in the Wesleyan spirit [by] Albert C. Outler. Nashville, Tenn., Tidings [1971] 109 p. 19 cm. [BV3795.O94] 72-171886
1. Wesley, John, 1703-1791—Addresses, essays, lectures. 2. Evangelistic work—Addresses, essays, lectures. I. Title.

WESLEY, John, 1703-1791.
Heart religion, as described by John Wesley, selected from Wesley's works by James Mudge. Cincinnati, Jennings and Graham; New York, Eaton and Mains [c1913] 123 p. 16 cm. $0.25. (On cover: Devotional classics) $0.25. "The extracts are taken from the standard American edition of Wesley's works, published by the Methodist book concern in 1931."--Pref. 13-23244
I. Mudge, James, 1844- comp. II. Title.

Wesley, John, 1703-1791—Bibliography.

BAKER, Frank, 1910- 016.287
A union catalogue of the publications of John and Charles Wesley. Durham, N.C., Divinity School, Duke University, 1966. 230 p. 28 cm. At head of title: The Oxford edition of Wesley's works. [Z8967.B33] 70-11521
1. Wesley, John, 1703-1791—Bibliography. 2. Wesley, Charles, 1707-1788—Bibliography. I. Title.

GREEN, Richard, 1829-1907. 016.287
The works of John and Charles Wesley : a bibliography ... / by Richard Green. 2d ed., rev., and with many additional notes. New York : AMS Press, 1976. 291 p. ; 23 cm. Reprint of the 1906 (2d) ed. published by Methodist Pub. House, London. Includes indexes. [Z8967.G792 1976] [BX8495.W5] 74-26049 ISBN 0-404-12924-2 : 21.00
1. Wesley, John, 1703-1791—Bibliography. 2. Wesley, Charles, 1707-1788—Bibliography. I. Title.

STEVENSON, George John, 1818-1888. 245.
The Methodist hymn-book and its associations. By George J. Stevenson. With a chronological catalogue of the poetical works of John and Charles Wesley. [2d ed.] London, Hamilton, Adams, & co.; New York, P. Phillips, 1872. xi, 420 p. 19 cm. [BV415.S8] 17-31582
1. Wesley, John, 1703-1791—Bibl. 2. Wesley, Charles, 1707-1788—Bibl. 3. Hymns, English—Hist. & crit. 4. Methodist Episcopal church—Hymns. I. Title.

Wesley, John, 1703-1791—Congresses.

OXFORD Institute on Methodist Theological Studies, 6th, 1977. 261.8
Sanctification & liberation : liberal theologies in the light of the Wesleyan tradition / edited by Theodore Runyon ; prepared under the direction of the World Methodist Council. Nashville : Abingdon, c1981. 255 p. ; 20 cm. Papers presented at the conference held under the auspices of the World Methodist Council. Bibliography: p. 245-251. [BT765.O93 1977] 19 80-20287 ISBN 0-687-36810-3 pbk. : 6.95
1. Wesley, John, 1703-1791—Congresses. 2. Sanctification—History of doctrines—Congresses. 3. Liberation theology—Congresses. I. Runyon, Theodore. II. World Methodist Council. III. Title.

Wesley, John, 1703-1791 — Juvenile literature.

CLIFFORD, Joan. 242'.4
The young John Wesley; illustrated by Arthur Roberts. London, Parrish; New York, Roy Publishers [1966] 126 p. illus. 20 1/2 cm. 12/6 [BX8495.W5C56 1966] 67-72555
1. Wesley, John, 1703-1791 — Juvenile literature. I. Title.

Wesley, Martha, 1707-1791.

WILDER, Franklin. 287'.1'0924 B
Martha Wesley / by Franklin Wilder. 1st ed. Hicksville, N.Y. : Exposition Press, c1976. 136 p. ; 21 cm. Bibliography: p. 135-136. [BX8495.W53W54] 76-360632 ISBN 0-682-48488-1 : 6.50
1. Wesley, Martha, 1707-1791.

Wesley, Mrs. Susanna (Annesley) 1670-1742.

CLARKE, Eliza, Mrs. 922.
... *Susanna Wesley.* By Eliza Clarke. Boston, Roberts brothers, 1886. vii, [3], 12-301 p. 17 1/2 cm. (Famous women) "List of authorities": verso of leaf following p. vii. [BX8495.W55C6] 13-18874
1. Wesley, Mrs. Susanna (Annesley) 1669-1742? I. Title.

CLARKE, Eliza, Mrs. 922.
... *Susanna Wesley.* By Eliza Clarke. Boston, Roberts brothers, 1886. vii, [3], 12-301 p. 17 1/2 cm. (Famous women) "List of authorities": verso of leaf following p. vii. [BX8495.W55C6] 13-18874
1. Wesley, Mrs. Susanna (Annesley) 1669-1742? I. Title.

KIRK, John, 1813-1886. 920.7
The mother of the Wesleys, a biography. By Rev. John Kirk ... Cincinnati, Poe and Hitchcock, 1865. 398 p. front. (port.) 20 cm. [BX8495.W55K5] 30-30843
1. Wesley, Mrs. Susanna (Annesley) 1670-1742. I. Title.

STEVENS, Abel, 1815-1897. 922.7
The women of Methodism; its three foundresses, Susanna Wesley, the Countess of Huntingdon, and Barbara Heck; with sketches of their female associates and successors in the early history of the denomination. By Abel Stevens, LL. D. A centenary offering to the women of American Methodism, from the American Methodist ladies' centenary association. New York, Carlton & Porter, 1866. 304 p. 20 cm. [BX8493.S8] 36-33583
1. Wesley, Mrs. Susanna (Annesley) 1670-1742. 2. Huntingdon, Selina (Shirley) Hastings, countess, of 1707-1791. 3. Heck, Mrs. Barbara (Ruckle) 1734-1804. 4. Methodist church—Biog. 5. Woman—Biog. I. American Methodist ladies' centenary association. II. Title.

THOMAS, John Edward, 1906- 248
Susannah's sanctuary. A book for Christian mothers containing inspiration and practical suggestions for a spiritual fellowship of mother and child, by John Edward Thomas and Mazelle Wildes Thomas, with a preface by Dr. Richard C. Raines. Minneapolis, The Voyaguer press, 1939. 6 p. l., 84 p. incl. mounted front. 20 1/2 cm. Bibliography: p. 51-84. [BV1475.T5] 40-4655
1. Wesley, Mrs. Suzanna (Annesley) 1670-1742. 2. Wesley, John, 1703-1791 3. Children—Religious life. I. Thomas, Mrs. Mazelle (Wildes) 1908- joint author. II. Title.

Wesley, Samuel, 1662-1735.

WILDER, Franklin. 287'.1'0924 B
Father of the Wesleys; a biography. [1st ed.] New York, Exposition Press [1971] 220 p. port. 22 cm. Bibliography: p. 219-220. [BX5199.W396W5] 72-146917 ISBN 0-682-47238-7 6.00
1. Wesley, Samuel, 1662-1735. I. Title.

Wesleyan Church—Directories.

WESLEYAN Church. Office of the General Secretary. 287'.1'025
Church location directory for the Wesleyan Church—United States, Canada, & British Isles / prepared by the General Secretary's directory service. Marion, Ind. : Wesley Press, c1975. 95 p. : ill. ; 22 cm. Pages 88-95, blank for notes. [BX9995.W4W47 1975] 75-327421
1. Wesleyan Church—Directories. I. Title: Church location directory for the Wesleyan Church ...

Wesleyan Methodist church—Missions.

BANKER, Floyd E
From famine to fruitage; an account of fifth years of Wesleyan Methodism in Western India, by Floyd and and Hazel Banker ... Marion, Ind., Wesley Press, 1960. 188p. illus., ports., map. 21cm.
1. Wesleyan methodist Church—Missions. 2. Missions—India. I. Banker, Hazel (Rodgers) joint author. II. Title.

MARSDEN, Joshua, 1777-1837.
The narrative of a mission to Nova Scotia, New Brunswick, and the Somers islands, with a tour to lake Ontario. To which is added, The mission, an original poem, with copious notes. Also, a brief account of missionary societies, and much interesting information on missions in general. By Joshua Marsden late missionary to Nova Scotia, New Brunswick, and the Bermudas... Plymouth-Dock, Printed and sold by J. Johns, 53, St. Aubyn-street; sold also by Thomas Kaye, 42, Castle-street, Liverpool; Baynes, Paternoster-row; Williams and son, Stationer's court; Burton and Briggs, 156, Leadenhall-street; Booth, Duke-street, Manchester-square; Blanchard, City-road, London; and at all the Methodist preaching houses in town and country. 1816. [New York, Johnson Reprint Corp., 1966] xiv, 289 p. front. (port.) 2 fold. tables. 22 cm. 68-92151
1. Wesleyan Methodist church—Missions. 2. Nova Scotia—Descr. & trav. 3. New Brunswick—Descr. & trav. 4. Bermuda islands—Descr. & trav. 5. New York (State)—Descr. & trav. 6. Missions—Canada. I. Title.

Wesleyan Methodist Connection (or Church) of America.

MCLEISTER, Ira Fofd. 287.173
History of the Wesleyan Methodist Church of America. Rev. [i. e. 3d] by Roy Stephen Nicholson. Marion, Ind., Wesley Press, 1959. 558p. illus. 24cm. [BX8431.W4M3 1959] 59-2268
1. Wesleyan Methodist Connection (or Church) of America. I. Nicholson, Roy Stephen. II. Title.

MCLEISTER, Ira Ford. 287.173
History of the Wesleyan Methodist church of America, by Ira Ford McLeister ... Syracuse, N.Y., Wesleyan Methodist publishing association, 1934. xxiii, 347 p. 50 pl. (incl. front., ports.) 23 1/2 cm. Bibliography: p. xxii-xxiii. [BX8431.W4M3] 34-41994
1. Wesleyan Methodist connection (or church) of America. I. Title.

MATLACK, Lucius C. 287'.6'73
The history of American slavery and Methodism from 1780 to 1849, and History of the Wesleyan Methodist Connection of America. Freeport, N.Y., Books for Libraries Press, 1971. 2 pts. (368, 15 p.) in 1. 23 cm. (The Black heritage library collection) Reprint of the 1849 ed. [E441.M43 1971] 77-138342 ISBN 0-8369-8734-9
1. Wesleyan Methodist Connection (or Church) of America. 2. Slavery and the church—Methodist Episcopal Church. I. Title. II. Title: History of the Wesleyan Methodist Connection of America. III. Series.

WESLEYAN Methodist 287.
connection (or church) of America. Conferences. North Carolina. Minutes of the ... annual session. Syracuse, N.Y., Wesleyan Methodist publishing association v. 22 cm. [BX8431.W4A4] 44-48288

Wesleyan Methodist connection (or church) of America. Conferences. Michigan.

RENNELLS, Charles 287.1774
Stephen.
History of the Michigan conference, Wesleyan Methodist church of America, by Charles Stephen Rennels ... Centenary ed. 1840-1940 ... Introduction by Ira Ford McLeister ... Grand Rapids, Mich., Zondervan publishing house [c1940] 4 p. l., 13-169, 121 p. illus. (incl. ports.) 19 1/2 cm. "History of the Woman's home and foreign missionary society, Michigan conference, Wesleyan Methodist church of America, 1890-1940 [by] Mrs. Mabel Perrine": 121 p. at end. Bibliography: p. 168-169. [BX8431.W4R4] 41-4018
1. Wesleyan Methodist connection (or church) of America. Conferences. Michigan. 2. Wesleyan Methodist connection (or church) of America. Conferences. Michigan. Woman's home and foreign missionary society. I. Perrine, Mrs. Mabel. II. Title.

Wesleyan Methodist Connection (or Church) of America. Conferences. South Carolina.

HILSON, James Benjamin, 287.1757
1908-
History of the South Carolina Conference of the Wesleyan Methodist Church of America; fifty-five years of Wesleyan Methodism in South Carolina. Introd. by Oliver G. Wilson. [Greenville? Ill., 1950] 308 p. illus., ports. 20 cm. [BX8431.W4H5] 50-2107
1. Wesleyan Methodist Connection (or Church) of America. Conferences. South Carolina. I. Title.

Wesleyan Methodist Connection (or Church) of America—History.

MCLEISTER, Ira Ford. 287'.173
Conscience and commitment : the history of the Wesleyan Methodist Church of America / by Ira Ford McLeister, Roy Stephen Nicholson. 4th rev. ed. / edited by Lee M. Haines, Jr., Melvin E. Dieter. Marion, Ind. : Wesley Press, 1976. xviii, 693 p. : ill. ; 22 cm. (Wesleyan history series ; 1) First-3d ed. published under title: History of the Wesleyan Methodist Church of America. Includes index. Bibliography: p. 653-659. [BX8431.W4M3 1976] 76-374759
1. Wesleyan Methodist Connection (or Church) of America—History. I. Nicholson, Roy Stephen, joint author. II. Title. III. Series.

MCLEISTER, Ira Ford. 287'.173
Conscience and commitment : the history of the Wesleyan Methodist Church of America / by Ira Ford McLeister, Roy Stephen Nicholson. 4th rev. ed. / edited by Lee M. Haines, Jr., Melvin E. Dieter. Marion, Ind. : Wesley Press, 1976. xviii, 693 p. : ill. ; 22 cm. (Wesleyan history series ; 1) First-3d ed. published under title: History of the Wesleyan Methodist Church of America. Includes index. Bibliography: p. 653-659. [BX8431.W4M3 1976] 76-374759
1. Wesleyan Methodist Connection (or Church) of America—History. I. Nicholson, Roy Stephen, joint author. II. Title. III. Series.

The West.

TENNEY, Edward Payson, 1835- 377.
1916.
The new West as related to the Christian college. By E. P. Tenny 3d ed. Cambridge, Printed at the Riverside address, 1878. 106 p. incl. illus., plates, map. plan. front. 22 1/2 cm. Also published Boston, New York, 1880, under title: Colorado: and homes in the new West. [LC383.T25] [LD1133.T4 1878 b] E 9
1. The West. 2. Colorado—Description and travel. 3. Church and education (in the) U.S. 4. colorado college, Colorado Springs. I. Title.

West Chester, Pa. St. Agnes church (Catholic)

SCHUYLER, William Bishop. 282.748
The pioneer Catholic church of Chester county, Saint Agnes, West Chester, Pennsylvania, 1793-1943, by Wiliam B. Schuyler.. Philadelphia, The Peter Reilly company, 1944. xii, 283 p. front., plates, ports, maps. 23 cm. Bibliography: p. 282-283. [BX4603.W49S3] 44-24280
1. West Chester, Pa. St. Agnes church (Catholic) I. Title.

West, Daniel, 1893-1971.

YODER, Glee. 286'.5 B
Passing on the gift : the story of Dan West / by Glee Yoder. Elgin, Ill. : Brethen Press, c1978. 168 p. : ill. ; 21 cm. (Brethren biographies.) [BX7843.W46Y62] 78-6291 ISBN 0-87178-689-3 pbk. : 3.95
1. West, Daniel, 1893-1971. 2. Church of the Brethren—Biography. I. Title. II. Series.

The West—Description and travel

BROWN, James Stephens, 922.
b.1828.
Life of a pioneer; being the autobiography of James S. Brown. Salt Lake City, Utah, G.Q. Cannon & sons co,; 1900. xix, [9]-520 p. front. (port.) illus., pl. 22 cm. [BX8695.B7A3] 0-4669
1. The West—Descr. & trav. 2. Mormons and Mormonism. I. Title.

West, Edward N.

SPIRIT and light : 230
essays in historical theology / edited by Madeleine L'Engle and William B. Green. New York : Seabury Press, c1976. p. cm. "Crossroad books." [BR50.S67] 76-17834 ISBN 0-8164-0310-4 : 8.95
1. West, Edward N. 2. Theology—Addresses, essays, lectures. I. L'Engle, Madeleine. II. Green, William B., 1927-

West Hartford, Conn. First Church of Christ—History

SPINKA, Matthew, 1890- 285.87462
A history of the First Church of Christ, Congregational, West Hartford, Conn. [West Hartford, Conn., First Church of Christ, 1963?] 174 p. illus., ports. 24 cm. Includes bibliographies. [BX7255.W47F56] 68-4553
1. West Hartford, Conn. First Church of Christ—Hist. I. Title.

SPINKA, Matthew, 285'.8758'231
1890-
A history of the First Church of Christ, Congregational, West Hartford, Conn. [West Hartford, Conn., First Church of Christ, 1963?] 174 p. illus., ports. 24 cm. Includes bibliographies. [BX7255.W47F56] 68-4553
1. West Hartford, Conn. First Church of Christ—History.

West Haven, Conn. Christ Church.

KENYON, Floyd Steele, 283.746
comp.
Historical notes about Christ Church, West Haven, Connecticut, concerning its two hundred years of existance, 1723-1923. [n. p., 1945!] 156 p. illus., ports. 23 cm. Cover title: History of Christ Church, West Haven, Connecticut, 1723-1945. [BX5980.W4C45] 50-38270
1. West Haven, Conn. Christ Church. I. Title.

West Indies.

STOWELL, Jay Samuel, 1883- 277.29
Between the Americas, by Jay S. Stowell. New York, Council of women for home missions and Missionary education movement, [c1930] vi p., 1 l., 180 p. 19 1/2 cm. "Reading list: p. [177]-180. [BV2845.S75] 30-9214
1. West Indies. 2. Missions—West Indies. I. Title.

West Indies—Religion.

THE listening isles;
records of the Caribbean Consultation, May 17-24, 1957, held under the auspices of the International Missionary Council, with the cooperation of the World Council of Christian Education and Sunday School Association. [Edited by J. W. Decker] New York, International Missionary Council [1957?] 92p.
1. West Indies—Religion. 2. Caribbean area—Religion. 3. Protestant churches—West Indies. I. Caribbean Consultation, Inter-American University, San German, P. R., 1957. II. International Missionary Council.

West, Marion B.

WEST, Marion B. 248'.4
Learning to lean / Marion B. West. 1st ed. Garden City, N.Y. : Doubleday, 1980. vi, 200 p. ; 22 cm. "A Doubleday-Galilee original." [BV4501.2.W4345] 79-7514 ISBN 0-385-15088-1 : 8.95
1. West, Marion B. 2. Christian life—1960- I. Title.

†WEST, Marion B. 248'.2
No turning back / Marion B. West. Nashville : Broadman Press, c1977. 162 p. ; 18 cm. [BV4527.W44] 76-57508 ISBN 0-8054-5254-0 pbk. : 2.25
1. West, Marion B. 2. Wives—Religious life. I. Title.

West, Mary, 1816-1829.

COOLEY, Timothy Mather, 1772- 922
1859.
Memoir of Mary West, a Sabbath scholar, who died at Granville, Mass., May 19th, 1829, in the thirteenth year of her age. By Timothy M. Cooley ... Written for the Massachusetts Sabbath school society, and revised by the Committee for publication. Boston, Massachusetts Sabbath school society, 1833. 49 p. front. 15 cm. [BR1715.W4C6] 38-4785
1. West, Mary, 1816-1829. I. Massachusetts Sabbath school society. Committee of publication. II. Title.

West Point, Ga. First Baptist Church.

BARKLEY, H. E. 286'.1'758463
Links of gold; history of the First Baptist Church, West Point, Georgia, organized 1849, by H. E. Barkley. [West Point, Ga., Printed by Hester Print. Co., 1971] 190 p. illus., ports. 24 cm. Bibliography: p. 183-184. [BX6480.W42B37] 72-24925
1. West Point, Ga. First Baptist Church. I. Title.

The West—Religion.

MIYAKAWA, Tetsuo Scott. 277.8
Protestants and pioneers; individualism and conformity on the American frontier [by] T. Scott Miyakawa. Chicago, University of Chicago Press [1964] 306 p. 23 cm. Bibliography: p. 275-293. [BR545.M5] 64-22247
1. The West—Religion. 2. Protestants in The West. I. Title.

West, Samuel, 1730-1807.

EDWARDS, Jonathan, 1745- 234'.9
1801.
A dissertation concerning liberty & necessity; containing remarks on the essays of Dr. Samuel West, and on the writings of several other authors, on those subjects. New York, B. Franklin Reprints [1974] 234 p. 23 cm. (Burt Franklin research & source works series. Philosophy & religious history monographs, 140) Reprint of the 1797 ed. printed by L. Worcester at Worcester. [BJ1461.E32 1974] 73-21786 ISBN 0-8337-1003-6 15.00
1. West, Samuel, 1730-1807. Essays on liberty and necessity. 2. Free will and determinism. I. Title.

West Virginia—Religion.

PHOTIADIS, John D. 209'.754
Religion in an Appalachian state / by John Photiadis and B. B. Maurer. [Morgantown] : Division of Personal and Family Development, Appalachian Center, West Virginia University, [1974] 27 p. ; 28 cm. (Research report - Appalachian Center, West Virginia University ; 6) Caption title. Includes bibliographical references. [BR555.W4P47] 74-624112
1. West Virginia—Religion. I. Maurer, Beryl Blake, 1920- joint author. II. Title. III. Series: West Virginia. University. West Virginia Center for Appalachian Studies and Development. Research report ; 6.

West Virginia Wesleyan College, Buckhannon.

MCCUSKEY, Roy, 1883- 922.773
All things work together for good to them that love God [Buckhannon, West Va. Wesleyan Coll. Pr., 1964] 150p. illus., ports. 24cm. [LD5941.W2517] 64-7129 2.50 bds.,
1. West Virginia Wesleyan College, Buckhannon. I. Title.

Westcott, Brooks Foss, bp. of Durham, 1825-1901.

WESTCOTT, Arthur. 922.
Life and letters of Brooks Foss Westcott, D.C., D.C.L., sometime bishop of Durham; by his son, Arthur Westcott ... London, Macmillan and co., limited; New York, The Macmillan company, 1903. 2 v. fronts., (ports.) illus., 5 pl., facsim. 21 1/2 cm. Appendix III: Bibliographical, v. 2, p. 441-448. [BX5199.W4W4] 3-16354
1. Westcott, Brooks Foss, bp. of Durham, 1825-1901. I. Title.

WESTCOTT, Brooke Foss, bp. of
Durham, 1825-1901.
... The incarnation a revelation of human duties: a charge delivered to the clergy of the diocese of Durham, by Brooke Foss, lord bishop of Durham at his primary visitation, November 1892. Cambridge, Printed at the University press, 1892. 2 p. l., 66 p. 19 cm. CA 13
I. Title.

WESTCOTT, Brooke Foss, bp. 265.
of Durham, 1825-1901.
Social aspects of Christianity, by Brooke Foss Westcott ... 3d ed. London, Macmillan and co., limited; New York, The Macmillan company, 1900. xx, 202 p. 19 1/2 cm. [BR115.S6W4 1900] 3-2194

I. Title.
Contents omitted.

WESTCOTT, Brooke Foss, bp. of Durham, 1825-1901. 283.
Words of faith and hope, by the late Brooke Foss Westcott ... London, Macmillan and co., limited; New York, The Macmillan company, 1902. x, 212 p. 19 1/2 cm. Prefatory note signed: A. W. (i.e. Arthur Westcott) [BX5133.W4W6] 4-4386
1. Westcott, Arthur, ed. II. Title.

Western Reserve Historical Society, Cleveland.

WESTERN Reserve Historical Society, Cleveland. 016.2898
The Shaker collection of the Western Reserve Historical Society : a reel list of the manuscripts and a short title list of the printed materials contained in the microform collection. Glen Rock, N.J. : Microfilming Corp. of America, 1977. ix, 77 p. ; 28 cm. [Z7845.S5W47 1977] [BX9771] 77-156035 ISBN 0-667-00522-6 : 4400.00
1. Western Reserve Historical Society, Cleveland. 2. Shakers—Bibliography—Catalogs. 3. Microfilms—Catalogs. I. Title.

Western Reserve—Religion.

BADGER, Joseph, 1757-1846. 922.573
A memoir of Rev. Joseph Badger; containing an autobiography, and selections from his private journal and correspondence. Hudson, O., Sawyer, Ingersoll and company, 1851. 185 p. front. (port.) 19 cm. A record Reserve--Religion. "Rev. H. N. Day wrote the preface."--Sabin, vol. xi, p. 579. [F497.W5B24] 34-36126
1. Western Reserve—Religion. 2. Missions—Western Reserve. I. Day, Henry Noble, 1808-1890. ed. II. Title.

Western Unitarian Conference.

LYTTLE, Charles Harold, 1884- 288
Freedom moves west; a history of the Western Unitarian Conference, 1852-1952. Boston, Beacon Press [1952] xx298 p. illus. ports. 22 cm. "Bibilographical guide": p. [276]-284. [BX9807.W4L8] 52-5960
1. Western Unitarian Conference. I. Title.

Westerwoudt, Felix Johannes Maria, 1861-1898.

[RIJCKEVORSEL, E. (Westerwoudt) van] 922.2911
Felix Westerwouldt, missioner in Borneo, by E. v. R. W. (his sister) with a commendatory letter from His Eminence, Cardinal van Rossum, cardinal prefect of propaganda, translated from the Dutch by Reverend T. W. Lefeber ... edited and published by the Catholic foreign mission society of America. Maryknoll. xi, 115 p. front., plates, ports. 20 cm. Translation of Een nederlandsch missionaris Father Felix Westerwoudt. [BV3345.R5] 25-15970
1. Westerwoudt, Felix Johannes Maria, 1861-1898. 2. Catholic church—Missions. 3. Missions—Borneo. I. Lefeber, Theodore W., tr. II. Title.

Westfield Church, Westfield, Mass.

TAYLOR, Edward, 1642-1729. 285'.9'0974426
Edward Taylor's "Church records," and related sermons / edited by Thomas M. & Virginia L. Davis. Boston : Twayne Publishers, [1981] p. cm. (Twayne's American literary manuscripts series) (The Unpublished writings of Edward Taylor ; v. 1) (Series: Taylor, Edward, 1642-1729. Unpublished writings of Edward Taylor ; v. 1.) Includes bibliographical references. [BX7255.W488W477] 19 80-27925 ISBN 0-8057-9650-9 lib. bdg. : 35.00
1. Westfield Church, Westfield, Mass. 2. Taylor, Edward, 1642-1729. 3. Congregational churches—Sermons. 4. Sermons, American. I. Davis, Thomas Marion. II. Davis, Virginia L. III. Title. IV. Title: "Church records," and related sermons. V. Series.

Westfield, N.J. First Presbyterian church.

CENTENNIAL history of the First Presbyterian church and society, Westfield,N. Y.; being a compilation of historical papers, given during the centennial celebration, December, 1908. [Jamestown, N. Y., Journal press] 1910. 150 p. plates, ports. 25 cm. Some of the plates are printed on both sides. [BX9211.W52C4] 26-22910 285.
1. Westfield, N. Y. First Presbyterian church.

CENTENNIAL history of the First Presbyterian church and society, Westfield,N. Y.; being a compilation of historical papers, given during the centennial celebration, December, 1908. [Jamestown, N. Y., Journal press] 1910. 150 p. plates, ports. 25 cm. Some of the plates are printed on both sides. [BX9211.W52C4] 26-22910 285.
1. Westfield, N. Y. First Presbyterian church.

MCKINNEY, William Kerr. 285.
Commemorative history of the Presbyterian church in Westfield, New Jersey, 1728-1928, by William K. McKinney, PH.D., Chas. A. Philhoser, A.M. [and] Harry A. Kniffin. [New York, c1929] 1 p. l., 5-483 p. front., illus., plates, ports., facsims. 23 1/2 cm. [BX9211.W5F5] 29-15353
1. Westfield, N.J. First Presbyterian church. I. Philhower, Charles A. II. Kniffin, Harry A. III. Title.

TRUMP, Clara K. 285'.1747'95
First Presbyterian Church of Westfield, New York, 1808-1968; a history, by Clara K. Trump. [Westfield? N.Y., 1968] 148 p. illus., ports. 28 cm. [BX9211.W52F57] 70-1035
1. Westfield, N.Y. First Presbyterian Church.

TRUMP, Clara K. 285'.1747'95
First Presbyterian Church of Westfield, New York, 1808-1968; a history, by Clara K. Trump. [Westfield? N.Y., 1968] 148 p. illus., ports. 28 cm. [BX9211.W52F57] 70-1035
1. Westfield, N.Y. First Presbyterian Church.

WESTFIELD, N.J. Presbyterian Church. 285.174936
Commemorative history of the Presbyterian Church in Westfield, New Jersey, 1728-1962. Rev. ed. [Westfield, 1963] 253 p. illus., ports., map. 24 cm. Revised ed. of McKinney's Commemorative history of the Presbyterian Church in Westfield, New Jersey, 1728-1928, with continuations by Shelby G. Fell. [BX9211.W5W4 1963] 64-36015
1. Westfield, N.J. Presbyterian Church. I. McKinney, William Kerr. Commemorative history of the Presbyterian Church in Westfield, New Jersey, 1728-1928. II. Fell, Shelby G., ed. III. Title.

Westfield, N.J. Presbyterian Church.

WESTFIELD, N.J. Presbyterian Church. 285.174936
Commemorative history of the Presbyterian Church in Westfield, New Jersey, 1728-1962. Rev. ed. [Westfield, 1963] 253 p. illus., ports., map. 24 cm. Revised ed. of McKinney's Commemorative history of the Presbyterian Church in Westfield, New Jersey, 1728-1928, with continuations by Shelby G. Fell. [BX9211.W5W4 1963] 64-36015
1. Westfield, N.J. Presbyterian Church. I. McKinney, William Kerr. Commemorative history of the Presbyterian Church in Westfield, New Jersey, 1728-1928. II. Fell, Shelby G., ed. III. Title.

Westminister assembly of divines.

A history of the Westminster assembly of divines. 285.242
Embracing an account of its principal transactions, and biographical sketches of its most conspicuous members, compiled for the Board of publication from the best authorities. Philadelphia, Presbyterian board of publication, 1841. 1 p. l., [11]-430 p. 19 1/2 cm. [BX9053.H5] 4-20302
1. Westminster assembly of divines. I. Presbyterian church in the U.S.A. (Old school) Board of publication.

Westminister, Eng. St. Stephen's Chapel.

HASTINGS, Maurice, 1896- 726.595
St. Stephen's Chapel and its place in the development of perpendicular style in England. Cambridge [Eng.] University Press, 1955. 256p. illus. 22cm. [NA5470.S6H3] 55-14058
1. Westminister, Eng. St. Stephen's Chapel. I. Title.

Westminster abbey.

BOND, Francis, d.1918. 726.
Westminster abbey, by Francis Bond ... illustrated by 270 photographs, plans, sections, sketches and measured drawings. London, New York [etc.] H. Frowde, 1909. xvi, 332 p. incl. front., illus., ports., plans. 23 cm. Bibliography: p. [xiii]-xvi. [NA5470.W5B7] 10-35464
1. Westminster abbey. I. Title.

FARRAR, Frederic William, 1831-1903.
Westminister abbey, by the Very Rev. Dean Farrar. With a chapter on the Poets' corner, by Arthur Penrhyn Stanley ... New York, M. F. Mansfield & A. Wessels [1899] 60 p. front., plates. 20 cm. "A chronology of the poets and men of letters whose memorials have been placed in Westminster abbey": p. 55-60. A 11
1. Westminster abbey. I. Stanley, Arthur Penrhyn, 1815-1881. II. Title.

LETHABY, William Richard, 1857-1931. 726'.77'1
Westminster Abbey & the kings' craftsmen; a study of mediaeval building, by W. R. Lethaby. New York, B. Blom, 1971. xvi, 382 p. illus., plans, port. 22 cm. Reprint of the 1906 ed. [NA5470.W5L6 1971] 69-13243
1. Westminster Abbey. I. Title.

LETHABY, William Richard, 1857-1931. 726.5'09421'32
Westminster Abbey re-examined. New York, B. Blom, 1972. viii, 298 p. illus. 21 cm. Reprint of the 1925 ed. "Recent works on the Abbey": p. v-vi. [DA687.W5L4 1972] 69-13244
1. Westminster Abbey.

LOFTIE, William John, 1839-1911.
Westminster abbey, by W. J. Loftie ... With many illustrations by Herbert Railton. New ed. Philadelphia, J. B. Lippincott company., 1914. xii, 319 p. incl. illus., plates. col. front. 21 cm. A 13
1. Westminster abbey. I. Title.

PEARCE, Ernest Harold, bp. of Worcester, 1865-
... Walter de Wenlok, abbot of Westminster, by Ernest Harold Pearce ... London, Society for promoting, Christian knowledge; New York, Macmillan, 1920. vii, 236 p. front. (phot.) 22 cm. (Ecclesiastical biographies) A 21
1. Wenlok, Walter, de, d. 1307. 2. Westminster abbey. I. Title.

PERKINS, Jocelyn Henry Temple, 1870- 247.094213
... Westminster abbey, its worship and ornaments, by Jocelyn Perkins ... London, Oxford university press, H. Milford, 1938- v. front., plates, facsims. 27 cm. (Alcuin club collections, no. xxxiii) [BX5141.A1A6 no. 33] 254.03 38-10006
1. Westminster abbey. 2. Church decoration and ornament—England—London. I. Title.

ROBINSON, Joseph Armitage.
The abbot's house at Westminster, by J. Armitage Robinson ... Cambridge, University press, 1911. x, 84 p. incl. plan. pl., 2 fold. plans (col.) 27 cm. (Half-title: Notes and documents relating to Westminster abbey. no. 4) Plans in pocket at end of volume. 12-6842
1. Westminster abbey. I. Title.

TROUTBECK, G. E.
The children's story of Westminster abbey, by G. E. Troutbeck ... New York, Frederick A. Stokes company [1909] viii, v-viii, 253, [1] p. 25 pl. (incl. front.) 19 1/2 cm. A 10
1. Westminster abbey. I. Title.

Westminster Assembly of Divines.

CARRUTHERS, Samuel William, 1866- 285.242
The everyday work of the Westminster assembly, by S. W. Carruthers ... with a foreword by Thos. C. Pears, jr. ... Philadelphia, Pub. jointly by the Presbyterian historical society (of America) and the Presbyterian historical society of England, 1943. xi, 210 p. 24 cm. "A brief bibliography": p. 201-202. [BX9053.C3] 43-8095
1. Westminster assembly of divines. I. Presbyterian historical society. II. Presbyterian historical society of England. III. Title. IV. Title: Presbyterian historical society of England.

LEITH, John H. 238'.5'2
Assembly at Westminster; reformed theology in the making [by] John H. Leith. Richmond, Va., John Knox Press [1973] 127 p. facsim. 21 cm. Bibliography: p. [125]-127. [BX9183.L44] 72-11162 ISBN 0-8042-0885-9 3.95 (pbk.)
1. Westminster Assembly of Divines. 2. Westminster confession of faith. I. Title.

PRESBYTERIAN church in the United States. General assembly. 285.
Memorial volume of the Westminster assembly. 1647-1897. Containing ... addresses delivered before the General assembly of the Presbyterian church in the United States, at Charlotte, N. C., in May, 1897. In commemoration of the two hundred and fiftieth anniversary of the Westminster assembly, and of the formation of the Westminster standards. 2d ed. ... Richmond, Va., The Presbyterian committee of publication [1897] xxxviii, [2] 297 p. front.,pl., ports. 21 cm. Bibliography: p. xxxiii-xxxviii. [BX9053.A5P8] 98-180
I. Title.
Contents omitted.

ROBERTS, William Henry, 1844-1920, ed. 238.
Addresses at the celebration of the two hundred and fiftieth anniversary of the Westminster assembly, by the General assembly of the Presbyterian church in the U. S. A. Edited by the Rev. Wm. Henry Roberts ... Philadelphia, Presbyterian board of publication and Sabbath-school work, 1898. 342 p. front., pl., ports. 19 cm. [BX9053.A5R6] 98-2019
1. Westminster assembly of divines. 2. Presbyterian church in the U. S. A. General assembly, 1898. I. Title.
Contents omitted.

ROLSTON, Holmes, 1932- 230.4'2'0924
John Calvin versus the Westminster Confession. Richmond, John Knox Press [1972] 124 p. 21 cm. Includes bibliographical references. [BX9183.R63] 75-37422 ISBN 0-8042-0488-8 2.95
1. Westminster Assembly of Divines. The Confession of faith. 2. Calvin, Jean, 1509-1564—Theology. I. Title.

SHAW, Robert, of Whitburn. 238.
An exposition of the Confession of faith of the Westminster assembly of divines. By the Rev. Robert Shaw. Rev. by the Committee of publication. Philadelphia, Presbyterian board of publication [c1846] 360 p. 19 1/2 cm. [BX9183.S4] 22-21906
1. Westminster assembly of divines. I. Title.

WARFIELD, Benjamin Breckinridge, 1851-1921. 238.5
The Westminster assembly and its work, by Benjamin Breckinridge Warfield ... New York [etc.] Oxford university press, 1931. iii p., 3 l., 3-400 p. 24 cm. "Prefatory note" signed: Ethelbert D. Warfield, William Park Armstrong, Caspar Wistar Hodge, committee. "Other articles on the Westminster assembly and its work": leaf 2. [BX9053.W3] 31-18836
1. Westminster assembly of divines. I. Warfield, Ethelbert Dudley, 1861- ed. II. Title.

WILLARD, Samuel, 1640-1707. 238'.5'8
A compleat body of divinity. New York, Johnson Reprint Corp., 1969 [c1968] xii, iv, 914, [1] p. 31 cm. (Series in American studies) Reprint of the 1726 ed., with a new introd. by Edward M. Griffin. "A catalogue of the author's works": p. [915] Bibliography: p. xii. [BX9184.A5W55 1969] 68-30728
1. Westminster Assembly of Divines. Shorter catechism. 2. Congregational churches—Doctrinal and controversial works. 3. Sermons, American. I. Title. II. Series.

Westminster Assembly of Divines. shorter catechism.

[FISHER, James] 1697-1775. 238.5
The Westminster assembly's Shorter catechism explained by way of question and answer... By several ministers of the gospel ... Philadelphia, Presbyterian board of publication [185-?] 2 v. in 1. 19 cm. Preface signed: Eben. Erskine. James Fisher. Part II has half-title only. Binder's title: Fisher's catechism. [BX9184.A5F5 1850] [BX9184.A5F5 1850 a] [BX9184A5F5 18500] 33-31215
1. Westminster assemby of devines. Shorter catechism. 2. Church of Scotland—Catechisms and creeds. I. Erskine, Ebenezer, 1680-1754. II. Presbyterian church in the U.S.A. Board of publication. III. Title.

HADEN, Eric George. 238.5
The history of the use of the Shorter catechism in the Presbyterian church in the United States of America, by Eric G. Haden... [Kansas City, Kan.] Central seminary press, 1941. 101 p. 19 cm. Expanded form of thesis (PH.D.)--Yale university, 1939. Bibliographical foot-notes. [BX9184.A5H25] 41-11613
1. Westminster assembly of divines. Shorter catechism. 2. Presbyterian church in the U.S.A.—Catechisms and creeds—Hist. I. Title.

HARPER, James. 238.
An exposition in the form of question and answer of the Westminster assembly's Shorter catechism, by James Harper ... Pittsburgh, United Presbyterian board of publication, 1905. 407 p. 23 cm. [BX9184.A5H35] 5-17605
1. Westminster assembly of divines. Shorter catechism. 2. Church of Scotland—Catechisms and creeds. I. Title.

PATERSON, Alexander Smith, 1803?-1828. 238.
A concise system of theology, on the basis of the Shorter catechism. [By] Alexander Smith Paterson ... with an introductory paler, by Duncan Macfarlan ... From the 4th Edinburgh ed. New York, O. Carter & brothers, 1856. xviii, [19]-390 p. 16 cm. "1st edition, Edinburgh, 1841." [BX9184.A5P3 1856] 26-24347
1. Westminister assembly of divines. Shorter catechism. 2. Church of Scotland—Catechisms and creeds—English. I. Macfarlan, Duncan, 1771-1857. II. Title.

PATERSON, Alexander Smith, 1803!-1828. 238.
A concise system of theology, on the basis of the shorter catechism. By Alexander Smith Paterson, A. M. New York, R. Carter & brothers, 1860. xviii, [19]-390 p. 16 cm. First edition, Edinburgh, 1841. "On the history and arrangement of the shorter catechism. By the Rev. Duncan Macfarlan": p. [v]-xiii. [BX9184.A5P3 1860] 15-24161
1. Westminister assembly of divines. Shorter catechism. I. Macfarlan, Duncan, 1771-1857. II. Title.

THOMSON, John, d.1753. 238.5
An explication of the Shorter catechism, composed by the Assembly of divines, commonly called, the Westminster assembly ...By John Thomson ... Williamsburg [Va.]: Printed by William Parks, MDCCXLIX. xiv, 190, vi, 14 p. 18 cm. "An appendix, containing the Articles of the Church of England ... Williamsburg: M,DCC,XLIX", vi, 14 p. at end. [BX9184.A5T4] 5-41204
1. Westminster assembly of divines. Shorter catechism. I. Church of England. Articles of religion. II. Title.

VINCENT, Thomas, 1634-1678. 238.
An explicatory catechism: or An explanation of the Assembly's Shorter catechism ... By Thomas Vincent ... New York: Printed by Lewis Deare. 1806. 286 p. 17 cm. "A short method with the Deists. Wherein the certainty of the Christian religion is demonstrated, in a letter to a friend. By the Rev. Charles Leslie": p. [271]-286. [BX9184.A5V6 1806] 25-18754
1. Westminster assembly of divines. Shorter catechism. 2. Leslie, Charles, 1650-1722. I. Title.

VINCENT, Thomas, 1634-1678. 238.
An explicatory catechism: or, An explanation of the Assembly's Shorter catechism... By Thomas Vincent ... New Haven: Published by Walter, Austin and co. O. Steele & co. Printers. 1810. 276, 29 p. 17 1/2 cm. "Dr. Trumbull's Address on the subjects of prayer and family religion. 4th ed.": 29 p. at end. [BX9184.A5V6 1810] 25-18755
1. Westminster assembly of divines. Shorter catechism. 2. Trumbull, Benjamin, 1735-1820. 3. Prayer. I. Title.

WATSON, Thomas, d.1686. 238.
A body of practical divinity, in a series of sermons on the Shorter catechism composed by the reverend Assembly of Divines at Westminister, to which are appended, Select sermons on various subjects, including The art of divine contentment and Christ's various fulness. Philadelphia, T. Wardle, 1833 776 p. 24 cm. [BX9184.A5W3 1833] 52-53279
1. Westminster Assembly of Divines. shorter catechism. 2. Sermons, English. I. Title.

WILLARD, Samuel, 1640-1707. 238.5
A compleat body of divinity in two hundred and fifty expository lectures on the Assembly's Shorter catechism wherein the doctrines of the Christian religion are unfolded, their truth confirm'd, their excellence display'd, their usefulness improv'd; contrary errors & vices refuted & expos'd, objections answer'd, controversies, settled, cases of conscience resolv'd; and a great light thereby reflected on the present age. By the reverend & learned Samuel Willard, M.A. late pastor of the South church in Boston, and vice-president of Harvard college in Cambridge, in New England. Prefac'd by the pastors of the same church... Boston in New England: Printed by B. Green and S. Kneeland for B. Eliot and D. Henchman, and sold at their shops, MDCCXXVI. 1 p l, iv. 3, [3], 158, 177-666, 581-914 p., 1 l. 34 cm. Signatures: A3, B-V4, X2, Y1, Aa-Zz4, Aaa-Zzz4, Aaa-Ppp4, Qqq3, Aaaa-Zzzz4, Aaaa-Tttt4. Error in paging: p. 351 numbered 349. Title in red and black; initials; tail-piece. In rebinding, the t.-p. was mounted and the lower left line border restored in pencil on the paper on which the t.-p. is mounted. "The preface" signed: Joseph Sewall, Thomas Prince. "It is the first folio volume, other than Laws, and the largest work up to this time printed in the United States."--C. Evans, Amer. bibl., v. 1, p. 365, no. 2828. The protrait of Rev. Samuel Willard engraved by Van der Gucht frequently found as frontispiece is not original with the work according to a letter from Harvard college Library regarding it and other bibliographical information mounted on fly-leaf. "An exact list of the subscribers accourding to the order of the alphabet": [3] p. preceding p. 1. "A catalogue of the author's works": 1 leaf at end. Ex libris Henry B. Humphrey. [BX9184.A5W55] 32-31391
1. Westminster assembly of divines. Shorter catechism. 2. Congregational churches—Doctrinal and controversial works. 3. Sermons, American. I. Sewall, Joseph, 1688-1769, ed. II. Prince, Thomas, 1687-1758, joint ed. III. Title.

Westminster Assembly of Divines. The Confession of Faith.

CLARK, Gordon Haddon. 238.5
What do Presbyterians believe? The Westminster Confession; yesterday and today [by] Gordon H. Clark. With an introd. by John R. Richardson. Philadelphia, Presbyterian and Reformed Pub. Co., 1965. xiv, 284 p. 23 cm. First published in 1956 under title: What Presbyterians believe. Bibliographical footnotes. [BX9183.C63] 65-27481
1. Westminster Assembly of Divines. The Confession of Faith. 2. Presbyterian Church — Catechisms and creeds. I. Title. II. Title: The Westminster Confession; yesterday and today.

CLARK, Gordon Haddon. 238.5
What Presbyterians believe. With an introd. by John R. Richardson. Philadelphia, Presbyterian and Reformed Pub. Co., 1956. 130p. 23cm. [BX9183.C63] 56-8576
1. Westminster Assembly of Divines. The Confession of Faith. 2. Presbyterian Church-Catechisms and creeds. I. Title.

HENDRY, George Stuart, 1904- 238.5
The Westminster Confession for today; a contemporary interpretation. Richmond, John Knox Press [1960] 253p. 21cm. [BX9183.H4] 60-6283
1. Westminster Assembly of Divines. The Confession of Faith. I. Title.

JOPLING, Robert Ware, 1865- 238.5
Studies in the Confession of faith; or, The five points of Calvanism [!] examined, by Rev. R. W. Jopling ... [Clinton, S. C., Jacobs press, 1942] ix, 90 p. 20 1/2 cm. [BX9183.J6] 43-418
1. Westminster assembly of divines. The Confession of faith. 2. Calvanism. I. Title.

WILLIAMSON, Gerald Irvin, 1925- 238.5
The Westminster Confession of Faith, for study classes [Grand Rapids, Mich., Baker bk. 1965, c.1964] vi, 309p. 26cm. [BX9183.W5] 5.00 pap.,
1. Westminster Assembly of Divines. The Confession of Faith. I. Title.

Westminster confession of faith.

LEITH, John H. 238'.5'2
Assembly at Westminster; reformed theology in the making [by] John H. Leith. Richmond, Va., John Knox Press [1973] 127 p. facsim. 21 cm. Bibliography: p. [125]-127. [BX9183.L44] 72-11162 ISBN 0-8042-0885-9 3.95 (pbk.)
1. Westminster Assembly of Divines. 2. Westminster confession of faith. I. Title.

ROGERS, Jack Bartlett. 238'.5'131
Scripture in the Westminster Confession; a problem of historical interpretation for American Presbyterianism. Grand Rapids, W. B. Eerdmans, 1967. x, 475 p. 25 cm. Errata slip inserted. Bibliography: p. 457-475. [BX9183.R6] 67-2316
1. Westminster confession of faith. I. Title.

Westminster, England Great Martin-in-the-Fields (Parish).

NORTHCOTT, Reginald James. 922.342
Dick Sheppard and St. Martin's, by R. J. Northcott, with introduction by Pat McCormick ... London, New York [etc.] Longmans, Green and co. [1937] xvii, 109 p. front., 2 port. 19 cm. "First published, 1937; second impression, December, 1937." [BX5199.S5315N6 1937 a] 38-15980
1. Sheppard, Hugh Richard Lawrie, 1880-1987. 2. Westminster, Eng. Gt. Martin-in-the-Fields (Parish) I. McCormick, William Patrick Glyn, 1877- II. Title.

Westminster, England St. Margaret's Church.

CHURCH and parish;
studies in church problems, illustrated from the parochial history of St. Margaret's, Westminster. Greenwich, Conn., Seabury Press, 1956. xvii, 262p. front. illus. 22cm. (Paddock lectures, 1953-1954)
1. Westminster, Eng. St. Margaret's Church. 2. Church of England—Addresses, essays, lectures. I. Smyth, Charles Hugh Egerton, 1903- II. Series.

Westminster Fellowship.

PRESBYTERIAN Church in the U.S.A. Board of Christian Education. 267.625
The manual of Westminster Fellowship. [Rev. ed. Philadelphia, 1950] 106 p. illus.23 cm. [BV1430.W4P7] 50-30595
1. Westminster Fellowship. I. Title.

Westmoreland Co., Pa.—Church history.

KAUFMAN, Jean Troxell. 277.48'81
Westmoreland County's pioneer ministers, 1758-1800 / by Jean Troxell Kaufman. Greensburg, Pa. : Research Committee, Westmoreland County Historical Society, 1977. 14 leaves ; 29 cm. (Westmoreland Co. church & cemetery history ; no. 1) Bibliography: leaves 13-14. [BR555.P5W474] 77-152583
1. Westmoreland Co., Pa.—Church history. 2. Clergy—Pennsylvania—Westmoreland Co.—Biography. I. Title. II. Series.

Westover church, Harrison district, Charles City co., Va.

SAUNDERS, Caroline Kirkland (Ruffin) Mrs., 1891- 283.75544
Westover church and its environs, by Kirkland Ruffin Saunders. Richmond, Va., Printed by W. M. Brown & sons, 1937. 189 p. illus. (plan) plates. 23 1/2 cm. [BX5980.W43S3] 40-2578
1. Westover church, Harrison district, Charles City co., Va. I. Title.

Westwood, N.J. St. Andrew's Church.

REILLY, George. 282.74921
Commemorating St. Andrew's 75th anniversary and dedication of our new church. Westwood, New Jersey. History compiled and prepared by George Reilly (Westwood) c1964. 1 v. (unpaged) illus. (part col.) ports. (part col.) 28 cm. [BX4603.W54S2] 64-19837
1. Westwood, N.J. St. Andrew's Church. I. Title.

Wetumpka. Ala. Methodist Church.

PORTER, Elizabeth Gamble. 28730976152
History of the Wetumpka Methodist Church, prepared for the celebration of the centennial of the erection of the church building, 1854-1954. [By] Elizabeth Gamble Porter [and] Madora Lancaster Smith. Wetumpka, Ala., 1954. 56p. 23cm. [BX8481.W48P6] 55-18973
1. Wetumpka. Ala. Methodist Church. I. Smith, Madora Lancaster, joint author. II. Title.

Wetzell, Anne Marie.

CUNNINGHAM, Eleanor W. 248'.2 B
He touched her, by Eleanor W. Cunningham & Doris M. McDowell. Anderson, Ind., Warner Press [1973] 107 p. 19 cm. [BX8699.N38W472] 73-8854 ISBN 0-87162-159-2 2.50 (pbk.)
1. Wetzell, Anne Marie. 2. Faith-cure. I. McDowell, Doris M., joint author. II. Title.

Wharton, Charles Henry. 1748-133. A letter to the Roman Catholics of the city of Worchester.

[CARROLL, John, abp.] 1735-1815. 282
An address to the Roman Catholics of the United States of America: By a Catholic clergyman. Annapolis: Printed by Frederick Green. 1784. 116 p. 21 cm. In reply to A letter to the Roman Catholics of the city of Worcester from the late chaplain of that society [e. e. Charles H. Wharton] With this bound the author's A discourse on General Washington ... Baltimore [1800] Copy 3. [HG2611.M3T6] 36-30183
1. Wharton, Charles Henry. 1748-133. A letter to the Roman Catholics of the city of Worchester. 2. Catholic church—Doctrinal and controversial works—Catholics authors. I. Title.

CARROLL, John, abp. of Baltimore, 1735-1815.
An address to the Roman Catholics of the United States of America. Occasioned by a letter addressed to the Catholics of

Worcester, by Mr. Wharton, their late chaplain. By The Right Reverend Dr. Carroll. iPrinted at Annapolis, Maryland: and London re-printed, for P. Keating, no. 4, Air-street, Piccadilly, Printed at Annapolis, Maryland: and London reprint, for P. Keating, no. 4, Air-street, Piccadilly 1785 115, [1] p. 19 cm. A 31
1. Wharton, Charles Henry, 1748-1833. A letter to the Roman Catholics of the city of Worchester. 2. Catholic Church—Doctrinal and controversial works—Catholic authors. I. Title. II. Title: An address to the Roman Catholics of the United States of America.

CARROLL, John, abp. of Baltimore, 1735-1815.
An address to the Roman Catholics of the United States of America. Occasioned by a letter addressed to the Catholics of Worcester, by Mr. Wharton, their late chaplain. By the Right Reverend Dr Carroll. Printed at Anapolis [!] Maryland; London reprinted; and Dublin printed by Wogan (at Dr. Hay's Head) no. 23, Oldbridge, opposite Usher's-Quay, 1785. 90 p. 21 cm. Title from H. E. Hunt. A31
1. Wharton, Charles Henry, 1748-1833. A letter to the Roman Catholics of the city of Worcester. 2. Catholic church—Doctrinal and controversial works—Catholic authors. I. Title.

Whatcoat, Richard, bp., 1736-1806.

BRADLEY, Sidney Benjamin, 1901- 922.773
The life of Bishop Richard Whatcoat, by Sidney Benjamin Bradley ... 198 p. front., plates. 19 cm. [BX8495.W58B7] 36-11251
1. Whatcoat, Richard, bp., 1736-1806. II. Title.

PHOEBUS, William, 1754-1831. 922.773
Memoirs of the Rev. Richard Whatcoat, late bishop of the Methodist Episcopal church. By William Phoebus ... New York, J. Allen, 1828. 118 p. 19 cm. [BX8495.W58P5] 37-15236
1. Whatcoat, Richard, bp., 1736-1806. I. Title.

Wheat Swamp Christian Church.

HOLDER, Naomi Dail. 286'.6756'355
History of Wheat Swamp Christian Church, including the conditions in Europe and the colonies / by Naomi Dail Holder. [La Grange? N.C. : s.n.], c1977. 121 p. : ill. ; 22 cm. Includes bibliographical references. [BX7331.W47H64] 77-150024
1. Wheat Swamp Christian Church. I. Title.

Whedon, Daniel Denison, 1808-1885. Commentary on Matthew and Mark.

QUESTION-BOOK to Whedon's 226.2
Commentary on Matthew and Mark. New York, Carlton & Porter [1866] 238 p. 14 cm. [BS2556.W5] 39-25244
1. Whedon, Daniel Denison, 1808-1885. Commentary on Matthew and Mark. 2. Bible. N. T. Matthew—Examinations, questions, etc. 3. Bible. N. T. Mark—Examinations, questions, etc. 4. Bible—Examinations, questions, etc.—N. T. Matthew. 5. Bible—Examinations, questions, etc.—N. T. Mark.

Wheeler, Bonnie G.

WHEELER, Bonnie. 280'.4 B
Of braces and blessings / Bonnie Wheeler. 1st ed. Chappaqua, N.Y. : Christian Herald Books, c1980. 159 p., [2] leaves of plates : ill. ; 21 cm. [BR1725.W428A36] 19 80-65431 ISBN 0-915684-63-2 pbk. : 4.95
1. Wheeler, Bonnie G. 2. Christian biography—United States. 3. Physically handicapped children—Family relationships. 4. Children, Adopted—Family relationships. I. Title.

Wheeler, Mrs. Mercy, b. 1706.

LORD, Benjamin, 1694-1784. 922
God glorified in his works of providence and grace. A remarkable instance of it, in the various and signal deliverances, that evidently appear to be wrought for Mrs. Mercy Wheeler, of Plainfield; who was restored from extreme impotence, and long confinement ... By Benjamin Lord ... 3d ed. Boston: Printed in the year 1743. Hartford: Re-printed by Elisha Babcock, 1798. 59 p. 16 cm. "The three warnings" (verse) : p. 56-59. [BR1725.W43L6] 34-42089
1. Wheeler, Mrs. Mercy, b. 1706. I. Title.

Wheelock, Ralph, 1600-1683.

HICKS, Lewis Wilder, 1845- 922
Mr. Ralph Wheelock, Puritan; a paper read before the Connecticut historical society, November 7, 1899, by Rev. Lewis W. Hicks, M. A., a member of the society and a descendant of Mr. Wheelock; with an appendix by Thomas S. Wheelock ... [Hartford] Hartfoed press, The Case, Lockwood & Brainard company, 1899. iv, [5]-51 p. front. (coat of arms) 25 cm. [F67.W54] 21-2808
1. Wheelock, Ralph, 1600-1683. I. Wheelock, Thomas Seabury. II. Connecticut historical society. III. Title.

Wheels (in religion, folk-lore, etc.)

BLOFELD, John Eaton Calthorpe, 1913- 294.3'63 B
The wheel of life; the autobiography of a Western Buddhist [by] John Blofeld. 2d ed. Berkeley [Calif.] Shambala, 1972. 291 p. illus. 22 cm. [BQ942.L64A3 1972] 72-189854 3.95
I. Title.

SIMPSON, William, 1823-1899. 294.3'4'37
The Buddhist praying-wheel; a collection of material bearing upon the symbolism of the wheel and circular movements in custom and religious ritual. New introd. by Omar V. Garrison. New Hyde Park, N.Y., University Books [1970] ix, 303 p. illus. 24 cm. Includes bibliographical references. [BL604.W4S56 1970] 74-118597 7.95
1. Wheels (in religion, folk-lore, etc.) I. Title.

SIMPSON, William, 1823-1899. 294.32
The Buddhist praying-wheel; a collection of material bearing upon the symbolism of the wheel and circular movements in custom and religious ritual, by William Simpson ... London, Macmillan and co., ltd.; New York, The Macmillan co., 1896. viii, 303, [1] p. incl. front., illus. 23 1/2 cm. "Index to book references": p. [301]-303. [BL1475.W4S5] 32-29710
1. Wheels (in religion, folk-lore, etc.) 2. Buddha and Buddhism. 3. Symbolism. 4. Rites and ceremonies. I. Title. II. Title: Praying-wheel, The Buddhist.

Wheelwright, John, 1502?-1679.

BELL, Charles Henry, 1823-1893. 922
Memoirs of John Wheelwright. Cambridge [Mass.] Printed by J. Wilson, 1876. 148 p. facsims. 23 cm. "Fifty copies...printed." A reprint from John Wheelwright: his writings ... with a paper upon the genuineness of the Indian deed of 1629, and a memoir, by C. H. Bell, 1876. Contents.Contents.--Memoir of John Wheelwright. by C. H. Bell.--The Wheelwright deed of 1629; was it spurious? By C. H. Bell.--The Wheelwright deed. [F67.W548] 48-38523
1. Wheelwright, John, 1502?-1679. I. Title.

Whichcote, Benjamin, 1609-1683.

WESTCOTT, Brooke Foss, Bp. of Durham, 1825-1901. 209'.4
Essays in the history of religious thought in the West. Freeport, N.Y., Books for Libraries Press [1972] p. (Essay index reprint series) Reprint of the 1891 ed. [BL690.W5 1972] 72-8480 ISBN 0-8369-7338-0
1. Whichcote, Benjamin, 1609-1683. 2. Europe—Religion. 3. Philosophy and religion. I. Title.

Whipple, Henry Benjamin, Bp., 1822-1901.

OSGOOD, Phillips Endecott, 1882- 922.373
Straight tongue; a story of Henry Benjamin Whipple, first Episcopal bishop of Minnesota. Minneapolis, T. S. Denison [1958] 288p. 23cm. [BX5995.W48O8] 58-14164
1. Whipple, Henry Benjamin, Bp., 1822-1901. I. Title.

Whiston, William 1667-1753.

COLLINS, Anthony, 1676-1729. 230
A discourse of the grounds and reasons of the Christian religion / Anthony Collins. New York : Garland Pub., 1976. xlii [i.e. lxii], 284 p. ; 19 cm. (British philosophers and theologians of the 17th and 18th centuries) Reprint of the 1724 ed. Includes bibliographical references. [BL2773.C63 1976] 75-11212 ISBN 0-8240-1766-8 lib.bdg. : 25.00
1. Whiston, William, 1667-1752. An essay towards restoring the true text of the Old Testament. 2. Bible. O.T.—Quotations in the New Testament. 3. Bible. O.T.—Prophecies. 4. Christianity—Controversial literature. 5. Messiah—Prophecies. 6. Liberty. I. Title. II. Series.

FARRELL, Maureen. 509'.2'4 B
William Whiston / Maureen Farrell. New York : Arno Press, 1981. p. cm. (The Development of science) Originally presented as the author's thesis, University of Manchester, 1973, under the title: The life and work of William Whiston. Includes index. Bibliography: p. [BX5199.W52F37 1981] 19 80-2088 ISBN 0-405-13854-7 lib. bdg. : 32.00
1. Whiston, William, 1667-1752. 2. Church of England—Clergy—Biography. 3. Baptists—Clergy—Biography. 4. Clergy—England—Biography. I. Series: Development of science.

JONES, Jeremiah, 1693-1724. 225.
A new and full method of settling the canonical authority of the New Testament. To which is subjoined A vindication of the former part of St. Matthew's Gospel, from Mr. Whiston's charge of dislocations ... By the Rev. Jeremiah Jones ... Oxford, The Clarendon press, m.dcc.xcviii. 3 v. 22 cm. [BS2320.J6] 37-23398
1. Whiston, William, 1667-1752. 2. Bible. N. T.—Canon. 3. Bible—Canon—N. T. I. Title.

THIRLBY, Styan, 1686?-1753. 231.4
A defense of the Answer to Mr. Whiston's suspicions, and an answer to his charge of forgery against St. Athanasius. In a letter to Mr. Whiston. By Styan Thirlby ... Cambridge, Printed at the University-press, for C. Crownfield, 1713. 263, [5] p. 19 1/2 cm. [With Whiston, William. Athanasius convicted of forgery. London, MDCCXII] [BR1730.A7W6] 37-89
1. Whiston, William, 1667-1753. Athanasius convicted of forgery. I. Title.

WHISTON, Charles Francis, 1900-
Teach us to pray; a study of distinctively Christian praying. With an introd. by Nels F. S. Ferre. Boston, Pilgrim Press [1956, c1949] xx, 243 p. 68-26628
I. Title.

WHISTON, William, 1667-1752.
A new theory of the earth, from its original, to the consummation of all things. Wherein the creation of the world in six days, the universal Deluge, and the general conflagration, as laid down in the Holy Scriptures, are shewn to be perfectly agreeable to reason and philosophy. With a large introductory discourse concerning the genuine nature, stile, and extent of the Mosaick history of the creation. The 2d ed., with great additions, improvements and corrections. By William Whiston ... Cambridge, Printed at the University-press; [etc., etc.] 1708. 2 p. l., 453 p. front., diagrs. (1 fold.) 20 cm. 16-1200
I. Title.

Whitaker, Epher, 1820-1916.

PRESBYTERIAN church in the U. S. A. Presbytery of Long island. 285.
Epher Whitaker of Southold, published as a memorial by the Presbytery of Long island. [n. p., 1917?] 68 p. front. (port.) 19 cm. "Articles ... contributed by friends, mostly co-presbyters of Dr. Whitaker."--Foreword, signed: William Huntley Lloyd Huntley Lloyd, Charles E. Craven, committee. [BX9225.W3P7] 20-19083
1. Whitaker, Epher, 1820-1916. I. Lloyd, William Huntley. II. Craven, Charles Edmiston, 1860- III. Title.

Whitaker family.

SMELTZER, Wallace Guy, 1900- 287.674885
Homestead Methodism (1830-1933) the history of Methodism in Mifflin township, Allegheny county, Pa., being the story of the first Methodist Episcopal church in that township, variously named Whitaker church, the Franklin church, "The Neck" church, and the Anne Ashley memorial church, located at Twenty-second street, Munhall, Pa., in its background, origin, and work through the century, along with: the expansion of Methodism in the community from this original parent society; the coming of other religious communions to the vicinity; and an account of the settlement, and the industrial and social development of the Homestead district. By Wallace Guy Smeltzer...Published in connection with the centennial anniversary of the erection of the original church building, May 14th through 21st, 1933. [Pittsburg, Printed by the D. K. Murdoch company, c1933. 167 p. front., plates, ports., map. 20 cm. 32 p. incl. plan. 19 cm. Homestead Methodism supplement, being historical and informational material concerning the Anne Ashley memorial Methodist Episcopal church, Munhall, Pa., not included in the centennial volume, Homestead Methodism. Issued on May 27, 1934, on the ocassion of the 104th anniversary of the founding of the Anne Ashley memorial church [by] Wallace Guy Smeltzer...[Munhall? Pa.] The author [1943?] Autographed from typewritten copy. "A bibliography of the more important records consulted": p. 167. [BX8481.M8S5] 33-14156
1. Whitaker family. 2. Munhall, Pa. Anne Ashley memorial Methodist Episcopal church. 3. Methodist Episcopal church in Pennsylvania. I. Title.

Whitaker, Jonathan, 1771?-1835.

HOLMES, Abiel, 1763-1837.
A sermon, preached at the ordination of the Rev. Jonathan Whitaker to the pastoral care of the church and society in Sharon, Massachusetts. February 27, 1799. By Abiel Holmes. A.M., pastor of the First church in Cambridge. Dedham [Mass.]; Printed by Herman Mann. 1799. 49 p. 20 cm. Half-title: Mr. Holmes sermon. A 35
1. Whitaker, Jonathan, 1771?-1835. 2. Ordination sermons. I. Title.

Whitaker, Nathaniel, 1730-1795.

[HART, William] 1718-1784. 285.
A letter to the Reverend Nathaniel Whitaker, D.D., wherein some of his gross misrepresentations of Mr. Hart's doctrines in his dialogue, intitled, A brief examination, &c., and his false and injurious charges against him, contained in his appendix and postscript to his discourses on 2 Cor. 5. 19. lately reprinted at Salem, are detected, and justly censured. With remarks on sundry doctrines, tending to illustrate and confirm the truth, and expose the contrary errors taught by the doctor. By the author of that dialogue... New-London, Printed and sold by T. Green, 1771. 63 p. 19 cm. [BX7230.H3] 43-43185
1. Whitaker, Nathaniel, 1730-1795. 2. Congregational churches—Doctrinal and controversial works. I. Title.

Whitaker, William Force, 1853-1916.

IN loving memory of Rev. William Force Whitaker, D. D., May 6, 1853-July 9, 1916, pastor of the First Presbyterian church of Elizabeth, N. J., from May 10, 1907, to July 9, 1916. [n. p.] 1916. 61 p. 3 port. (incl. front.) 24 cm. [BX3225.W32 I 6] 28-3279

1. Whitaker, William Force, 1853-1916. 2. Elizabeth, N. J. First Presbyterian church.

White, Alma (Bridwell) 1862-1946.

PAIGE, Clara R. 1869- comp. 269
Alma White's evangelism; press reports, compiled by C. R. Paige [and] C. K. Ingler ... Zarephath, N.J., Pillar of fire, 1939-40. 2 v. fronts. (ports.) illus. 19 cm. "Drawings by Branford Clarke." Includes advertising matter. [BX8795.P5P3] 42-44306
1. White, Alma (Bridwell) 1862- 2. Pillar of fire church. I. Ingler, Clifford Knowlton, 1876- joint comp. II. Clarke, Branford, illus. III. Title.

WHITE, Alma, Mrs.
The chosen people, by Mrs. Alma White ... Bound Brook, N.J., The Pentecostal union, 1910. 313 p. front. (port.) plates. 20 cm. $1.00. 11-419
I. Title.

WHITE, Alma, Mrs., 1862- 922.
The story of my life, by Alma White. Zarephath, N.J., Pillar of fire, 1919. v. front. (port.) illus., plates. 22 cm. "Illustrated by Banford Clarke, Pillar of fire artist." [Full name: Mrs. Mollie Alma White] [BX8795.P5W6] 19-13840
I. Title.

WHITE, Alma (Bridwell) 245.2
Mrs., 1862-
Hymns and poems, by Alma White ... Zarephath, N.J., Pillar of fire, 1931. xi, 13-224 p. front., plates, ports. 19 1/2 cm. Contains music. Advertising matter: p. 220-224. [Full name: Mrs. Mollie Alma (Bridwell) White] [PS3545.H51H8 1931] [811.5] 32-555
I. Title.

WHITE, Alma (Bridwell) 922.
Mrs., 1862-
The New Testament church, by Alma White ... Rev. ed. Zarephath, N.J., Pillar of fire, 1929. 1 p. l., v-ix, 11-413 p. front. (port.) plates. 19 1/2 cm. Advertising matter: p. 407-413. [Full name: Mrs. Mollie Alma (Bridwell) White] [BX8795.P5W48 1929] 30-1110
I. Title.

WHITE, Alma (Bridwell) 922.89
Mrs., 1862-
The story of my life and the Pillar of fire, by Alma White ... Zarephath, N.J., Pillar of fire, 1935- v. front. (port.) illus., plates. 21 1/2 cm. "Drawings by Branford Clarke, Pillar of fire artist." [Full name: Mrs. Mollie Alma (Bridwell) White] [BX8795.P5W6 1935] 35-13103
I. Title.

WHITE, Alma (Bridwell) 245.2
1862-1946.
Hymns and poems, by Alma White. Zarephath, N.J., Pillar of fire, 1946. xi, 13-224 p. front. (port.) plates, 19 cm. [Full name: Mollie Alma (Bridwell) White] [PS3545.H51H8 1946] 811.5 47-18808
I. Title.

WHITE, Arthur Kent, 1889- 922.89
Some White family history. Denver, Pillar of Fire, 1948. 432 p. illus., ports. 20 cm. [BX8795.P5W66] 49-13232
1. White, Alma (Bridwell) 1862-1946. 2. White family. I. Title.

White, Andrew, 1579-1656.

... Story of Father Andrew 922.
White, S.J.; Story of St. Catherine of Alexandria; The mount and flower of the precious blood. With suggestive questions and notes. Chicago, Ainsworth & company, 1906. 2 p. l., 7-63 p. illus. 18 cm. (The lakeside series of English readings) On cover: no. 117. English readings for schools. Grammar grades. [BX4653.S8] 6-33633
1. White, Andrew, 1579-1656. 2. Catharina, Saint, of Alexandria.

White Brotherhood.

HOLY Order of MANS. 299
History of the White Brotherhood and its teachings. San Francisco : Holy Order of MANS, c1974. 182 p. ; 21 cm. [BP605.W48H64 1974] 75-315626 3.00
1. White Brotherhood. I. Title.

PROPHET, Mark. 299
The science of the spoken word : teachings of the ascended masters / given to Mark and Elizabeth Prophet. Colorado Springs : Summit Lighthouse, c1974. 82 p., [1] leaf of plates : col. ill. ; 21 cm. Includes bibliographical references. [BP605.W48P76 1974] 74-82293
1. White Brotherhood. I. Prohpet, Elizabeth, joint author. II. Title.

White, Ellen G. (Harmon) "Mrs. James White," 1827-1915.

CANRIGHT, Dudley M 1840?- 286.
Life of Mrs. E.G. White, Seventh-day adventist prophet; her false claims refuted. by D.M. Canright... Cincinnati, The Standard publishing company [c1919] 291 p. 20 cm. [BX6193. W5C3] 19-2925
1. White, Ellen G. (Harmon) "Mrs. James White," 1827-1915. I. Title.

White, Ellen Gould (Harmon) 1827-1915.

ABBOTT, George Knapp, 1880- 286.7
The witness of science to the testimonies of the spirit of prophecy; studies in the testimonies and science given at Pacific Union College. [Sanitarium, Calif.] 1947. 236 p. illus. 24 cm. Includes bibliographies. [BX6154.A56] 48-95
1. White, Ellen Gould (Harmon) 1827-1915. 2. Seventh-Day Adventists—Doctrinal and controversial works. 3. Medicine and religion. I. Title.

ABBOTT, George Knapp, 1880- 286.7
The witness of science to the testimonies of the spirit of prophecy. Rev. ed. Mountain View, Calif., Pacific Press Pub. Assn. [1948] 365 p. 23 cm. [BX6154.A56 1948] 49-2401
1. White, Ellen Gould (Harmon) 1827-1915. 2. Seventh-Day Adventists—Doctrinal and controversial works. 3. Medicine and religion. I. Title.

CANRIGHT, Dudley M 1840?- 286.
Life of Mrs. E.G. White, Seventh-day adventist prophet; her false claims refuted. by D.M. Canright... Cincinnati, The Standard publishing company [c1919] 291 p. 20 cm. [BX6193. W5C3] 19-2925
1. White, Ellen G. (Harmon) "Mrs. James White," 1827-1915. I. Title.

CHRISTIAN, Lewis Harrison. 286.7
The fruitage of spiritual gifts, the influence and guidance of Ellen G. White in the Advent movement. Washington, Review and Herald Pub. Assn. [1947] 446 p. port. 22 cm. [BX6153.C48] 48-685
1. White, Ellen Gould]Bermon:, 1827-1915. 2. Seventh-Day Adventists—Hist. I. Title.

DELAFIELD, D A 1913- 922.673
Ellen G. White and the Seventh-Day Adventist Church. Illustrated by James Converse. Mountain View, Calif., Pacific Press Pub. Association [1963] 90 p. illus. 18 cm. [BX6193.W5D4] 63-18686
1. White, Ellen Gould (Harmon) 1827-1915. I. Title.

DELAFIELD, D. A., 1913- 286'.73 B
Ellen G. White in Europe, 1885-1887 : prepared from Ellen G. White papers and European historical sources / D. A. Delafield. Washington : Review and Herald Pub. Association, [1975] 320 p. : ill. ; 22 cm. [BX6193.W5D43] 74-24318
1. White, Ellen Gould Harmon, 1827-1915. I. Title.

GILL, Mabel K., R. N. 130.1
Mind, body and religion. Nashville, Southern Pub. Assn. [c.1965] 143p. 21cm. Bibl. [BX6111.W9G5] 65-16371 3.75 bds.,
1. White, Ellen Gould (Harmon) 1827-1915. 2. Psychology, Religious. I. Title.

GRAYBILL, Ronald D. 261.8'3
E. G. White and church race relations [by] Ronald D. Graybill. Washington, Review and Herald Pub. Association [1970] 128 p. 22 cm. On spine: Church race relations. Bibliography: p. 124-128. [BX6193.W5G7] 76-122392
1. White, Ellen Gould (Harmon) 1827-1915. 2. Church and race relations—U.S. I. Title. II. Title: Church race relations.

JEMISON, T Housel. 922.673
A prophet among you. Mountain View, Calif., Pacific Press Pub. Association [1955] 505p. illus. 23cm. [BX6193.W5J4] 55-11537
1. White, Ellen Gould (Harmon) 1827-1915. I. Title.

JOHNSON, Helen M. 922.673
Stories of little Ellen and the message, by Helen M. Johnson and Evelyn Roose Dinsmore. Drawings by Peter J. Rennings. Mountain View, Calif., Pacific Press Pub. Association [1950] 95 p. illus., ports. 21 cm. [BX6193.W5J6] 50-3148
1. White, Ellen Gould (Harmon) 1827-1915. I. Dinsmore, Evelyn Roose. joint author. II. Title.

NICHOL, Francis David, 922.673
1897-
Ellen G. White and her critics; an answer to the major charges that critics have brought against Mrs. Ellen G. White. Foreword by J. L. McElhany. Takoma Park, Washington, D.C., Review and Herald Pub. Association [1951] 703 p. 23 cm. Bibliography: p. 679-703. [BX6193.W5N5] 51-2779
1. White, Ellen Gould (Harmon) 1827-1915. 2. Seventh-Day Adventists — Doctrinal and controversial works. I. Title.

NOORBERGEN, Rene 286.709
Ellen G. White, prophet of destiny. New Canaan, Conn. Keats [1974] 260 p. 18 cm. [BX6193.W5N66] 1.75 (pbk.)
1. White, Ellen Gould (Harmon) 1827-1915. I. Title.
L.C. card number for original edition: 70-190456.

NOORBERGEN, Rene. 286'.73 B
Ellen G. White, prophet of destiny. New Canaan, Conn., Keats Pub. [1972] xiv, 241 p. illus. 22 cm. Bibliography: p. 229-231. [BX6193.W5N66] 70-190456 ISBN 0-87983-014-X 6.95
1. White, Ellen Gould (Harmon) 1827-1915. I. Title.

NUMBERS, Ronald L. 286'.73 B
Prophetess of health : a study of Ellen G. White / Ronald L. Numbers. 1st ed. New York : Harper & Row, c1976. xiv, 271 p. : ill. ; 21 cm. Includes bibliographical references and index. [BX6193.W5N85 1976] 75-36752 ISBN 0-06-066325-1 : 10.00
1. White, Ellen Gould Harmon, 1827-1915. I. Title.

RICCHIUTI, Paul B. 286'.73 B
Ellen : [trial and triumph on the American frontier] / Paul B. Ricchiuti. Mountain View, Calif. : Pacific Press Pub. Association, 1976c1977 159 p. ; 22 cm. (Destiny book ; D-160) Includes bibliographical references. [BX6193.W5R5] 76-44051 pbk. : 3.50
1. White, Ellen Gould Harmon, 1827-1915. 2. Adventists—United States—Biography. I. Title.

ROBINSON, Ella May (White) 92
Stories of my grandmother; by Ella M. Robinson. Illustrated by Jim Padgett. Nashville, Southern Pub. Association [1967] 200 p. illus. 21 cm. A granddaughter's reminiscences of life with her grandmother, a Seventh Day Adventist missionary. [BX6193.W5R6] AC 67
1. White, Ellen Gould (Harmon) 1827-1915. 2. Christian life. I. Padgett, James, illus. II. Title.

SCRIPTURAL and subject 286.7
index to the writings of Ellen G. White. Mountain View, Calif., Omaha, Neb. [etc.] Pacific press publishing association [1942] 865, 104 p. 19 cm. "Supplement to the Subject index to the writings of Ellen G. White": p. [1]-94 at end. [BX6111.W9S35 1942] 42-18146
1. White, Ellen Gould (Harmon) 1827-1915. I. Pacific press publishing association.

SPALDING, Arthur 922.673
Whitefield, 1877-
Sister White, a life of Ellen G. White for primary children; illustrated by Kreigh Collins. Washington, Review and Herald Pub. Association [1950] 128 p. col. illus. 24 cm. [BX6193.W5S7] 51-792
1. White, Ellen Gould (Harmon) 1827-1915. I. Title.

SPALDING, Arthur 922.673
Whitefield, 1877--
There shines a light; the life and work of Ellen G. White. Nashville, Southern Pub. Association [1953] 96p. 19cm. [BX6193.W5S73] 53-39863
1. White, Ellen Gould (Harmon) 1827-1915. I. Title.

THE Spirit of prophecy treasure chest; an Advent source collection of materials relating to the gift of prophecy in the remenant church and the life and ministry of Ellen G. White. The textbook for Prophetic guidance in the Advent movement, a Seventh-day Adventist correspondence course. Washington, Printed by the Review and Herald Pub. Assn., for Prophetic Guidance School of the Voice of Prophecy, 1960. 192 p. illus., ports. 25 cm.
1. White, Ellen Gould (Harmon) 1827-1915. 2. Seventh-Day Adventists — Sources.

TAYLOR, Gladys (King) 922.673
Literary beauty of Ellen G. White's writings. Mountain View, Calif., Pacific Press Pub. Association [1953] 124p. 19cm. [BX6111.W9T3] 53-5688
1. White, Ellen Gould (Harmon) 1827-1915. I. Title.

WHEELER, Ruth (Carr) 922.673
Mrs. 1899-
His messenger, by Ruth Wheeler. Takoma Park, Washington, D.C., Review and herald publishing association [c1939] 192 p. incl. front., illus., ports. 21 cm. "Stories ... taken from Mrs. White's books, letters and articles ... in many cases ... the very words that Mrs. White used."--p. 7. [Full name: Mrs. Ruth Lellah (Carr) Wheeler] [BX6111.W45] 39-15992
1. White, Mrs. Ellen Gould (Harman) 1827-1915. I. Title.

WHEELER, Ruth Lellah (Carr) 92
1899-
His messenger. Washington, Review and Heald Pub. Association [1963? c1939] 188 p. col. illus. 24 cm. [BX6111] 61-13333
1. White, Ellen Gould (Harmon) 1827-1915. I. Title.

WHITE, Ellen Gould (Harmon) 922.
Mrs., 1827-1915.
Christian experience & teachings of Ellen G. White ... Volume one, with an appendix. Mountain View, Calif., Kansas City, Mo. [etc.] Pacific press publishing association, 1922. 1 p. l., 7-268 p. front., illus. (incl. ports.) 18 1/2 cm. No more published? "Sources": p. 259-260. [BX6193.W5A25] 22-16527
I. Title.

WHITE, Ellen Gould 286.70924
(Harmon) 1827-1915
I'd like to ask Sister White . . .'; the questions you might ask, answered from statements selected from the writings of Ellen G. White. Illus. by Thomas Dunbebin. Washington, D.C. Review & Herald [1965] 160p. illus. 22cm. Companion volume to His messenger. [BX6193.W5A3] 65-278601 3.95
I. Title.

WHITE, Ellen Gould (Harmon) 922.
Mrs., 1827-1915.
Life sketches of Ellen G. White, being a narrative of her experience to 1881 as written by herself; with a sketch of her subsequent labors and of her last sickness, comp. from original sources. Mountain View, Calif., Kansas City, Mo. [etc.] Pacific press publishing association, 1915. 1 p. l., 5-480 p. front. (Ort.) illus. (incl. facsims.) pl. 18 1/2 cm. [BX6193.W5A3] 15-17802
I. Title.

WHITE, Ellen Gould (Harmon) 289
Mrs., 1827-1915.
Scriptural and subject index to the writings of Mrs. Ellen G. White. Mountain View, Calif., Omaha, Neb. [etc.] Pacific press publishing association [c1926] 374 p. 18 1/2 cm. Blank pages for "Notes" (866-874) [BX6111.W9] 26-11000
I. Title.

WHITE, Ellen Gould (Harmon) 230. Mrs., 1827-1915. *Testimonies to ministers and gospel workers.* Selected from "Special testimonies to ministers and workers", numbers one to eleven; and series B, numbers one to eighteen; with numerous selections from other booklets and from periodicals. By Ellen G. White ... Mountain View, Calif., Kansas City, Mo. [etc.] Pacific press publishing association [c1923] 1 p. l., 7-544 p. 18 1/2 cm. [BX6154.W5] 23-18812
I. Title.

WILCOX, Francis McLellan. 922.673 *The testimony of Jesus;* a review of the work and teachings of Mrs. Ellen Gould White, by Francis McLellan Wilcox ... Takoma Park, Washington, D.C., Peekskill, N.Y. [etc.] Review and herald publishing association [c1934] 2 p. l., 3-127 p. incl. front. (port.) facsims. 19 1/2 cm. Bibliography: p. 96-97. [BX6193.W5W5] 34-37470
1. White, Mrs. Ellen Gould (Harmon) 1827-1915. I. Title.

WILCOX, Francis McLellan. 922.673 *The testimony of Jesus;* a review of the work and teachings of Mrs. Ellen Gould White, by Francis McLellan Wilcox ... Takoma Park, Washington, D.C., Review and herald publishing association [1944] 2 p. l., 3-160 p. incl. front. (port.) illus. (facsims) 20 cm. [BX6193.W5W5 1944] 44-44340
1. White, Ellen Gould (Harmon) 1827-1915. I. Title.

White, Ellen Gould Harmon, 1827-1915—Addresses, essays, lectures.

ROBERTSON, John J. 286.7'3 *The White truth* / John J. Robertson. Mountain View, Calif. : Pacific Press Pub. Association, c1981. 112 p. ; 18 cm. Includes bibliographical references. [BX6193.W5R58 1981] 19 82-104659 ISBN 0-8163-0466-1 pbk. : 3.95
1. White, Ellen Gould Harmon, 1827-1915—Addresses, essays, lectures. 2. Seventh-Day Adventists—Doctrinal and controversial works—Addresses, essays, lectures. I. Title.

White, Ellen Gould (Harmon) 1827-1915—Dictionaries, indexes, etc.

COMPREHENSIVE index to the writings of Ellen G. White, v.1. 286.7 Prepared under the direction of the Board of Trustees of the Ellen G. White Estate. Omaha, Nebr., Pac. Pr. Pub. [c.1962] 1064p. 22cm. Contents.v.1. Scripture index. 62-14313 12.50
1. White, Ellen Gould (Harmon) 1827-1915—Dictionaries, indexes, etc.

COMPREHENSIVE index to the writings of Ellen G. White, v.2, G-Q. 286.7 In three pts.: scripture index, topical index, quotation index. With appendix containing glossaries, tables, supplementary statements. Prepared under the direction of the Bd. of Trustees of the Ellen G. White Estate. Omaha, Neb., Pacific Pr. Pub. [c.1962] 1070-2205p. 22cm. 12.50
1. White, Ellen Gould (Harmon) 1827-1915—Dictionaries, indexes, etc.

COMPREHENSIVE index to the 286.7 writings of Ellen G. White. *Prepared under the direction of the Board of Trustees of the Ellen G. White Estate.* Omaha, Pacific Press Pub. Association [1962-63] 3 v. 22 cm. [BX6111.W9C6] 62-14313
1. White, Ellen Gould (Harmon) 1827-1915 — Dictionaries, indexes, etc. I. Title.

White, Ellen Gould Harmon, 1827-1915—Juvenile literature.

LANTRY, Eileen E. 286.7'3 B *Miss Marian's gold* / by Eileen E. Lantry. Mountain View, Calif. : Pacific Pub. Association, c1981. 80 p. : ill. ; 22 cm. (Trailblazers) Presents an account of the work of Ellen White, a prolific Seventh-Day Adventist writer, and her literary assistant, Marian Davis. [BX6193.W5L36] 920 80-15671 ISBN 0-8163-0371-1 pbk. : 5.95
1. White, Ellen Gould Harmon, 1827-1915—Juvenile literature. 2. Davis, Marian—Juvenile literature. 3. Seventh-Day Adventists—United States—Biography—Juvenile literature. 4. [White, Ellen Gould Harmon, 1827-1915.] 5. [Davis, Marian.] 6. [Seventh-Day Adventists.] 7. [Authors, American.] 8. [Christian life.] I. Title.

White Fathers.

KITTLER, Glenn D 266.2 *The White Fathers.* Introd. by Bishop Laurian Rugambwa. [1st ed.] New York, Harper [1957] 299p. illus. 22cm. [BV2300.W5K5] 276 57-6134
1. White Fathers. I. Title.

KITTLER, Glenn D 266.26 *The White Fathers.* Introd. by Laurian Cardinal Rugambwa. Garden City, N. Y., Image Books [1961, c1957] 318p. 19cm. (Image books, Diii) [BV2300] 61-66032
1. White Fathers. I. Title. II. Series.

KITTLER, Glenn D 266.2 *The White Fathers. Introd. by Bishop Laurian Rugambwa.* [1st ed.] New York, Harper [1957] 299p. illus. 22cm. [BV2300.W5K5] 276 57-6134
1. White Fathers. I. Title.

MATHESON, Elizabeth Mary 266.2676 *African apostles.* Staten Island, N.Y., Alba [c.1963] 224p. 20cm. Bibl. 63-12674 3.95
1. White Fathers. 2. Missions—Africa, East. I. Title.

White Fathers—Missions.

LINDEN, Ian. 266'.00967'571 *Church and revolution in Rwanda* / Ian Linden, with Jane Linden. Manchester : Manchester University Press ; New York : Africana Pub. Co., c1977. xvi, 304 p. : ill. ; 23 cm. Includes index. Bibliography: p. 290-296. [BR1443.R95L56 1977] 76-58329 ISBN 0-8419-0305-0 : 24.50
1. White Fathers—Missions. 2. Catholic Church in Rwanda. 3. Christianity—Rwanda. 4. Missions—Rwanda. 5. Social classes—Rwanda. 6. Rwanda—Politics and government. 7. Rwanda—Social conditions. I. Linden, Jane, joint author. II. Title.

White, Gilbert, Bp. of Willochra, 1859-1933.

WAND, John William 922.394 Charles, Bp. of London, 1885- *White of Carpentaria.* London, New York, Skeffington [1949] 112 p. illus., ports., map. 19 cm. [BX5720.W39W3] 49-51256
1. White, Gilbert, Bp. of Willochra, 1859-1933. I. Title.

White, Henry Nichols, 1847-1863—Juvenile literture.

BYERS, Carolyn. 286.7'3 B *Good night too soon* : the story of the brief life of Henry Nichols White, son of James and Ellen White / Carolyn Byers ; editor, Thomas A. Davis. Washington, D.C. : Review and Herald Pub. Association, c1980. 94 p. ; 21 cm. [BX6193.W52B93] 80-11618 4.95
1. White, Henry Nichols, 1847-1863—Juvenile literture. 2. Seventh-Day Adventists—United States—Biography—Juvenile literature. I. Davis, Thomas A. II. Title.

White, James, 1821-1881.

†ROBINSON, Virgil E. 286'.73 B *James White* / Virgil Robinson. Washington : Review and Herald Pub. Association, c1976. 316 p. : ill. ; 22 cm. Includes bibliographical references. [BX6193.W54R6] 75-16921 7.50
1. White, James, 1821-1881. 2. Seventh-Day Adventists—United States—Biography.

THIELE, Margaret 65-18670 Rossiter *By saddle and sleigh;* a story of James White's youth. Washington, D.C., Review & Hearld [1965] 128p. illus., ports. 22cm. [BX6193.W54T50286.73] price unreported
1. White, James, 1821-1881. I. Title.

White, James Edson.

GRAYBILL, Ronald D. 266.6'7762 *Mission to Black America;* the true story of Edson White and the riverboat Morning Star, by Ronald D. Graybill. Illus. [by] Dale Rusch. Mountain View, Calif., Pacific Press Pub. Association [1971] iv, 144 p. illus. 20 cm. [BX6193.W55G7] 75-154982
1. White, James Edson. 2. Morning Star (Riverboat) 3. Missions to Negroes—Mississippi. I. Title.

WHITE, James Edson. 204 *Past, present, and future...* by James Edson White. Nashville, Tenn., Ft. Worth, Tex., Southern publishing association c1909. viii p., 1 l., 11-528 p. incl. front., illus., 9 pl. 20 1/2 cm. The frontispiece and part of the illustrations and plates are colored. [BR126.W5] 9-4283
I. Title.

White, John, 1866-1933.

ANDREWS, Charles Freer, 922.76893 1871- *John White of Mashonaland,* by C. F. Andrews. New York and London, Harper & brothers, 1935. viii p., 1 l., 205 p. 19 1/2 cm. "First edition." [BV3625.M3A6 1935a] 35-19391
1. White, John, 1866-1933. I. Title.

ANDREWS, Charles 266'.7'0924 B Freer, 1871-1940. *John White of Mashonaland.* New York, Negro Universities Press [1969] 316 p. 23 cm. Reprint of the 1935 ed. [BV3625.M3A6 1969] 79-91660 ISBN 0-8371-2070-5
1. White, John, 1866 (Jan. 6)-1933.

White, Joseph, 1712 or 13-1777.

CHURCHMAN, John, 1705-1775. 922. *An account of the gospel labours,* and Christian experiences of a faithful minister of Christ, John Churchman, late of Nottingham in Pennsylvania, deceased. To which is added a short memorial of the life and death of a fellow labourer in the church, our valuable friend Joseph White, late of Bucks county ... Philadelphia. Printed by Joseph Crukshank, on the north side of Market street, between Second and Third street, mdcclxxix. vii, 256 p. 19 1/2cm. Signatures: [A]-Z', Aa-Kk'. Running title: The life and travels of John Churchman. [BX7795.C55A3 1779] 32-35152
1. White, Joseph, 1712 or 13-1777. I. Title.

White, Kent.

WHITE, Alma, Mrs., 1862- 922. *My heart and my husband* [by] Alma White. Zarephath, N.J., 1923. 94 p. front., illus., plates (music) ports. 16 cm. Partly in verse. [Full name: Mrs. Mollie Alma White] [BX8795.P5W46] 24-138
1. White, Kent. I. Title.

White, Ruthe.

WHITE, Ruthe. 242 *A spirtiual diary for saints & not-so-saintly* / Ruthe White. Irvine, Calif. : Harvest House Publishers, c1979. 142 p. : ill. ; 21 cm. [BV4832.2.W518] 78-65125 ISBN 0-89081-179-2 : 2.95
1. White, Ruthe. 2. Meditations. I. Title.

White, Tom, 1947-

WHITE, Tom, 1947- 272'.9'097291 *Missiles over Cuba* / by Tom White. Diamond Bar, Calif. : Uplift Books, c1981. p. cm. [BV2369.5.C9W54] 19 81-51935 pbk. : 2.95
1. White, Tom, 1947- 2. Christian literature—Publication and distribution—Cuba. 3. Persecution—Cuba—History—20th century. 4. Christian biography—United States. 5. Cuba—Church history. I. Title.
Publisher's address 1677 cliffbranch Dr., Diamond bar, CA 91765.

White, Wilbert Webster, 1863-1944.

EBERHARDT, Charles 922.573 Richard. *The Bible in the making of ministers;* the scriptural basis of theological education; the lifework of Wilbert Webster White. New York, Association Press, 1949. 254 p. port. 21 cm. Includes bibliographies. [BS501.W5E3] 49-5111
1. White, Wilbert Webster, 1863-1944. 2. New York. Biblical Seminary. 3. Bible—Study. I. Title.

White, William, bp., 1748-1836.

NORTON, John Nicholas, 922.373 1820-1881. *The life of the Rt. Rev. William White, D. D., bishop of Pennsilvania ...* By John N. Norton ... New York, General Protestant Episcopal S. school union, and Church book society, 1856. 103 p. front. (port.) 16 cm. [BX5995.W5N8] 32-33228
1. White, William, bp., 1748-1836. I. Title.

NORTON, John Nicholas, 922.373 1820-1881. *The life of the Rt. Rev. William White, D. D., bishop of Pennsylvania ...* By John N. Norton ... 2d ed., enl. New York. General Protestant Episcopal Sunday school union, and Church book society, 1860. 123 p. front. (port.) 17 cm. [BX5995.W5N8 1860] 32-33636
1. White, William, bp., 1748-1836. I. Title.

STOWE, Walter Herbert, 922.373 1895- *The life and letters of Bishop William White;* together with the services and addresses commemorating the one hundred fiftieth anniversary of his consecration to the episcopate. Edited by Walter Herbert Stowe ... New York and Milwaukee, Morehouse publishing co. [c1937] 3 p. l., [v]-xiii, 306 p. front. mounted illus., plates, ports, 28 1/3 cm. (Church historical society. Publication no. 9) Includes bibiolgraphies. [BX5995.W5S85] 37-23074
1. White, William, bp., 1748-1836. I. Title.

WARD, Julius Hammond, 1837- 922. 1897. *...The life and times of Bishop White,* by Julius H. Ward. New York, Dodd, Mead and company, 1892. 2 p. l., ix, [11]-199 p. front. (port.) 18 cm. ("Makers of America") [BX5995.W5W3] 9-7808
1. White, William, bp. of Pa., 1748-1836. I. Title.

WHITE, William, bp., 1748- 230.3 1836. *The common sense theology of Bishop White,* selected essays from the writings of William White, 1748-1836, first Bishop of Pennsylvania and a patriarch of the American church, with an introductory survey of his theological position, by Sydney A. Temple, jr., PH.D. New York, King's crown press, 1946. x, 169 p. front. (port.) 24 cm. Issued also as Sydney A. Temple's thesis (PH.D.) Columbia university. Bibliographical references included in "Notes" (p. [149]-159] Bibliography: p. [160]-169. [BX5845.W55 1946] A 46
1. White, William, bp., 1748-1836. 2. Protestant Episcopal church in the U.S.A.—Addresses, essays, lectures. I. Temple, Sydney Absalom, 1912- II. Title.

WILSON, Bird, 1777-1859. 922.373 *Memoir of the life of the Right Reverend William White, D.D., bishop of the Protestant Episcopal church in the state of Pennsylvania.* By Bird Wilson ... Philadelphia, J. Kay, jun & brothers; Pittsburgh, C. H. Kay & co., 1839. iv, p., 2 l., [9]-430 p. front. (port.) pl., fold. facsim. 23 cm. [BX5995.W5W5] 35-23993
1. White, William, bp., 1748-1836. I. Title.

White, William Charles, Bp., 1873-1960.

WALMSLEY, Lewis 266'.3'0924 B Calvin, 1897- *Bishop in Honan* : mission and museum in the life of William C. White / Lewis C.

Walmsley. Toronto ; Buffalo : University of Toronto Press, [1974] xi, 230 p. : ill. ; 23 cm. "Publications of the Right Reverend W. C. White": p. [217]-220. Includes index. [BV3427.W48W34] 74-82288 ISBN 0-8020-3324-5 : 10.00
1. White, William Charles, Bp., 1873-1960. I. Title.

Whitefield, George, 1714-1770.

BELCHER, Joseph, 1794-1859, comp. 285.
George Whitefield; a biography, with special reference to his labors in America. Comp. by Joseph Belcher ... New York, American tract society [pref. 1857] 514 p. front. (port.) plates. 19 1/2 cm. [BX9225.W4B4] 1-21297
1. Whitefield, George, 1714-1770. I. Title.

BELDEN, Albert David, 1883- 922.542
George Whitefield, the awakener; a modern study of the Evangelical Revival. New York, Macmillan, 1953. 302p. illus. 23cm. [BX9225.W4B45 1953a] 53-4496
1. Whitefield, George, 1714-1770. 2. Evangelical Revival. I. Title.

BILLINGSLEY, Amos Stevens, 1818-1897. 922.542
The life of the great preacher, Reverend Gerorge Whitfield, "prince of orators", with the secret of his success, and specimens of his sermons. By Rev. A. S. Billingsley ... Philadelphia, Pa., Chicago, Ill. [etc.] P. W. Ziegler & co. [c1878] vii, xx, 17-437 p. plates, 2 port. (incl. front.) 23 cm. "List of authors consulted": p. v-vii. [BX9225.W4B5] 36-31912
1. Whitefield, George, 1714-1770. 2. Presbyterian church—Sermons. 3. Sermons, English. I. Title.

BLAIR, Samuel, 1712-1751. 285.
A particular consideration of a piece, entitled, The querists: wherein sundry passages extracted from the printed sermons, letters and journals of the Rev. Mr. Whitefield are vindicated from the false glosses and erroneous senses put upon them in said Querists;... Mr. Whitefield's soundness in the true scheme of Christian doctrine maintained; and the author's disingenuous dealing with him exposed. By Samuel Blair ... Philadelphia: Printed and sold by B. Franklin, 1741. iii, 4-63 p. 16 1/2 cm. Signatures: A-D. [BX9225.W4B6] 2-11333
1. Whitefield, George, 1714-1770. 2. The querists. I. Title.

CALDWELL, Mack M. 285.
George Whitefield, preacher to millions, by Mack M. Caldwell. Anderson, Ind., The Warner press [c1929] 128 p. front., (port.) illus. 19 cm. [BX9225.W4C3] 29-23808
1. Whitefield, George, 1714-1770. I. Title.

DALLIMORE, Arnold A. 269'.2'0924 B
George Whitefield, the life and times of the great evangelist of the eighteenth-century revival / Arnold A. Dallimore. Westchester, Ill. : Cornerstone Books, 1980, c1970. 2 v. : ill. ; 23 cm. Includes index. Bibliography: p. v. 2,p. 571-579. [BX9225.W4D34 1979] 19 79-67152 ISBN 0-89107-168-7 (v. 2) : 19.95 ISBN 0-89107-167-9 (v. 1) : 19.95
1. Whitefield, George, 1714-1770. 2. Presbyterian Church—Clergy—Biography. 3. Clergy—Great Britain—Biography. I. Title.

GILLIES, John, 1712-1796. 285.
Memoirs of the life of the Reverend George Whitefield, M. A., late chaplain to the Right Honorable, the Countess of Huntingdon ... Compiled by the Rev. John Gillie ... New Haven, Printed for Andrus & Starr; Hartford, J. Barker, Printer. 1812. 316 p. front. (port.) 18 cm. [BX9225.W4G45 1812] 4-25000
1. Whitefield, George, 1714-1770. I. Title.

GLEDSTONE, James Paterson. 922.542
George Whitefield, M. A., field-preacher. By James Paterson Gledstone ... 2d ed. New York, American tract society [1901] xii, 359, [1] p. front., pl., port. 21 cm. [BX9225.W4G6 1901] 4-16960
1. Whitefield, George, 1714-1770. 2. American tract society. I. Title.

HARDY, Edwin Noah, 1861- 922.542
George Whitefield, the matchless soul winner, by Edwin Noah Hardy... New York, American tract society [c1938] 298 p. front., plates, ports. 20 cm. [BX9225.W4H23] 38-12731
1. Whitefield, George, 1714-1770. I. Title.

HARSHA, David Addison, 1827-1895. 285.
Life of the Rev. George Whitefield. Albany, J. Munsell, 1866. 65 p. port. 26 cm. [BX9225.W4H3] 48-34196
1. Whitefield, George, 1714-1770. I. Title.

HENRY, Stuart Clark. 922.542
George Whitefield: wayfaring witness. New York Abingdon Press [1957] 224p. 24cm. Includes bibliography. [BX9225.W4H4] 57-10273
1. Whitefield, George, 1714-1770. I. Title.

NEWELL, Daniel. 285.
The life of Rev. George Whitefield. By Rev. D. Newell. New York, D. Newell [c1846] 2 p. l., [iii]-viii, [7]-218 p. front., pl., ports. 18 cm. [BX9225.W4N4] 36-34771
1. Whitefield, George, 1714-1770. I. Title.

NINDE, Edward Summerfield, 1866-1935. 922.
George Whitefield, prophet-preacher, by Edward S. Ninde. New York, Cincinnati, The Abingdon press [c1924] 222 p. front., plates, ports., facsims. 21 cm. [BX9225.W4N5] 24-19434
1. Whitefield, George, 1714-1770. I. Title.

POLLOCK, John Charles. 287'.1'0924 B
George Whitefield and the Great Awakening [by] John Pollock. [1st ed.] Garden City, N.Y., Doubleday, 1972. x, 272 p. 22 cm. [BX9225.W4P65] 72-76198 ISBN 0-385-03466-0 6.95
1. Whitefield, George, 1714-1770. I. Title.

SHORT, Ruth Gordon. 269'.2'0924 B
George Whitefield, trumpet of the Lord / Ruth Gordon Short. Washington : Review and Herald Pub. Association, [1979] p. cm. [BX9225.W4S54] 79-15420 pbk. : 4.95
1. Whitefield, George, 1714-1770. 2. Evangelists—England—Biography. 3. Evangelists—United States—Biography. I. Title.

TRACY, Joseph, 1793?-1874. 260
The great awakening. A history of the revival of religion in the time of Edwards and Whitefield. By Joseph Tracy ... Boston, Tappan and Dennet; New York, J. Adams, 1842. xviii, 433 p. front., ports. 21 1/2 cm. [BV3773.T76g] A 31
1. Whitefield, George, 1714-1770. 2. U.S.—Church history. 3. Revivals. I. Title.

WAKELEY, Joseph Beaumont, 1809-1875. 285.
The prince of pulpit orators: a portraiture of Rev. George Whitefield, M.A., illustrated by anecdotes and incidents. By Rev. J. B. Wakeley ... 2d ed. New York, Carlton & Lanahan; San Francisco, E. Thomas; [etc., etc.] 1871. 400 p. front. (port.) 18 cm. [BX9225.W4W3 1871] 27-3797
1. Whitefield, George, 1714-1770. I. Title.

WAKELEY, Joseph Beaumont, 1809-1875. 285.
The prince of pulpit orators: a portraiture of Rev. George Whitefield, M.A., illustrated by anecdotes and incidents. By Rev. J. B. Wakeley ... 2d ed. New York, Eaton & Mains; Cincinnati, Curts & Jennings [1899] 400 p. front. (port.) 17 1/2 cm. Reissue of the 2d edition, 1871. [BX9225.W4W3 1899] 99-4848
1. Whitefield, George, 1714-1770. I. Title.

WHITEFIELD, George, 1714-1770.
A continuation of the Reverend Mr. Whitefield's journal during the time he was detained in England, by the embargo. v. II. Philadelphia: Printed and sold by B. Franklin, in Market-street, 1740. 2 pt. in 1 v. 13 1/2 cm. Paged continuously: [pt. 1]; iv, [5]-63 p.; [pt. 2]: 1 p. l., 67-205 (i.e. 200) p. (nos. 165-168 repeated) [Part 2] has special title: A continuation of the Reverend Mr. Whitefield's journal, from his embarking after the embargo to his arrival at Savannah in Georgia. Philadelphia: Printed and sold by B. Franklin, in Market-street, 1740. 4-19458
I. Title.

WHITEFIELD, George, 1714-1770. 285.
A continuation of the Reverend Mr. Whitefield's journal from Savannah, June 25, 1740 to his arrival at Rhode-Island, his travels in the other governments of New-England to his departure from Stanford for New-York. Boston, Printed by D. Fowle for S. Kneeland and T. Green, 1714. c96 p. 15 cm. [BX9225.W4A223] 50-50106
I. Title.

Whitehead, Alfred North, 1861-1947.

BLYTH, John W. 121
Whitehead's theory of knowledge, by John W. Blyth ... Providence, R.I., Brown university, 1941. 4 p. l., 101 p. 22 1/2 cm. (On cover: Brown university studies, vol. vii) "An analysis of the position maintained [by Whitehead] in 'Process and reality,' 'Adventures of ideas,' and 'symbolism.'"--p. 2 Lithoprinted. Bibliographical foot=notes. [B1674.W38B5] 41-15071
1. Whitehead, Alfred North, 1861- 2. Knowledge, Theory of. 3. Metaphysics. I. Title.

BLYTH, John William, 1909- 121
Whitehead's theory of knowledge, by John W. Blyth ... Providence, R.I., Brown university, 1941. 4 p. l., 101 p. 22 1/2 cm. (On cover: Brown university studies, vol. VII) "An analysis of the position maintained [by Whitehead] in 'Process and reality,' 'Adventures of ideas,' and 'Symbolism'."--p. 2. Lithoprinted. Issued also as thesis (PH.D.) Brown university. Bibliographical foot-notes. [B1674.W38B5] 41-15071
1. Whitehead, Alfred North, 1861- 2. Knowledge, Theory of. 3. Metaphysics. I. Title.

CHRISTIAN, William A., 1905- 110
An interpretation of Whitehead's metaphysics, by William A. Christian. New Haven, Yale University Press, 1959. 419 p. 24 cm. [B1674.W354C5] 59-6794
1. Whitehead, Alfred North, 1861-1947. 2. Metaphysics.

COBB, John B. 210
A Christian natural theology, based on the thought of Alfred North Whitehead, by John B. Cobb, Jr. Philadelphia, Westminster Press [1965] 288 p. 21 cm. Bibliographical footnotes. [B1674.W354C6] 65-11612
1. Whitehead, Alfred North, 1861-1947. 2. Natural theology. I. Title.

ELY, Stephen Lee. 231
The religious availability of Whitehead's God, a critical analysis by Stephen Lee Ely ... Madison, The University of Wisconsin press [1942] 2 p. l., 3-58 p. 19 cm. [B1674.W38E4] 42-37424
1. Whitehead, Alfred North, 1861- 2. God. I. Title.

HAMILTON, Peter Napier. 230'.0924
The living God and the modern world; Christian theology based on the thought of A. N. Whitehead, by Peter Hamilton. Philadelphia, United Church Pr. [1968,c.1967] 256p. 21cm. Bibl. [BT75.2.H35 1968] 67-28283 2.95 pap.,
1. Whitehead, Alfred North, 1861-1947. 2. Theology, Doctrinal. 3. Process theology. I. Title.

HARTSHORNE, Charles, 1897- 210
Whitehead's view of reality / Charles Hartshorne, Creighton Peden. New York : Pilgrim Press, c1981. 106 p. ; 23 cm. Includes bibliographical references. [B1674.W354H38] 19 80-23532 ISBN 0-8298-0381-5 pbk. : 6.95
1. Whitehead, Alfred North, 1861-1947. 2. Whitehead, Alfred North, 1861-1947—Theology. 3. Philosophical theology. 4. Methodology. I. Peden, Creighton, 1935- joint author. II. Title.

LANGO, John W. 113
Whitehead's ontology, by John W. Lango. [1st ed.] Albany, State University of New York Press, 1972. 102 p. 24 cm. Includes bibliographical references. [B1674.W353P76] 78-171184 ISBN 0-87395-093-3 6.00
1. Whitehead, Alfred North, 1861-1947. Process and reality. 2. Ontology. I. Title.

LECLERC, Ivor. 111
Whitehead's metaphysics: an introductory exposition. London, Allen and Unwin; New York, Macmillan [1958] 233p. 23cm. [B1674.W354L4] 58-4842
1. Whitehead, Alfred North, 1861-1947. 2. Metaphysics. I. Title.

LUNDEEN, Lyman T. 200'.1
Risk and rhetoric in religion; Whitehead's theory of language and the discourse of faith [by] Lyman T. Lundeen. Philadelphia, Fortress Press [1972] xii, 276 p. 23 cm. Includes bibliographical references. [BL65.L2L85] 71-171501 9.50
1. Whitehead, Alfred North, 1861-1947. 2. Religion and language. I. Title.

MELLERT, Robert B. 230
What is process theology? / By Robert B. Mellert. New York : Paulist Press, [1975] 141 p. ; 18 cm. (Deus books) Includes bibliographical references. [BT83.6.M44] 74-28933 ISBN 0-8091-1867-X pbk. : 1.95
1. Whitehead, Alfred North, 1861-1947. 2. Process theology. I. Title.

OVERMAN, Richard H. 233.11
Evolution and the Christian doctrine of creation; a Whiteheadian interpretation, by Richard H. Overman. Philadelphia, Westminster [1967] 301p. 21cm. Bibl. [BT695.O8] 67-15089 7.50 bds.,
1. Whitehead, Alfred North, 1861-1947. 2. Evolution. 3. Creation. I. Title.

PETERS, Eugene Herbert, 1929- 201
The creative advance; an introduction to process philosophy as a context for Christian faith, by Eugene H. Peters. With a comment by Charles Hartshorne. St. Louis, Bethany Press, 1966. 151 p. 20 cm. (The library of contemporary theology) Includes bibliographical references. [BR100.P386] 66-19812
1. Whitehead, Alfred North, 1861-1947. 2. Christianity—Philosophy. I. Title.

Whitehead, Alfred North, 1861-1947—Metaphysics.

ODIN, Steve, 1953- 110'.92'4
Process metaphysics and Hua-yen Buddhism : a critical study of cumulative penetration vs. interpenetration / Steve Odin. Albany : State University of New York Press, c1982. xx, 242 p. : ill. ; 24 cm. (SUNY series in systematic philosophy) Includes bibliographical references and index. [B1674.W354O34 1982] 19 81-9388 ISBN 0-87395-568-4 : 33.50 ISBN 0-87395-569-2 pbk. : 10.95
1. Whitehead, Alfred North, 1861-1947—Metaphysics. 2. Hua-yen Buddhism—Doctrines. 3. Philosophy, Comparative. 4. Process theology. 5. Metaphysics. I. Title. II. Series.

Whitfield, Joseph.

WHITFIELD, Joseph. 133.9'3
The treasure of El Dorado : featuring "the Dawn Breakers" / by Joseph Whitfield. Washington : Occidental Press, 1977. 213 p. : ill. ; 22 cm. [BF1283.W543A37] 77-89125 ISBN 0-911050-44-2 : 8.95
1. Whitfield, Joseph. 2. Spiritualists—United States—Biography. I. Title.

Whitfield, Thomas.

WHITFIELD, Thomas. 248.2'46 B
From night to sunlight / Thomas Whitfield ; foreword by Jimmy Allen. Nashville, Tenn. : Broadman Press, c1980. 189 p. : ill. ; 21 cm. [BP605.B38W48] 19 80-68874 ISBN 0-8054-5291-5 pbk. : 4.95
1. Whitfield, Thomas. 2. Whitfield, Hazel. 3. Black Hebrew Israelite Nation—Biography. 4. Converts, Baptist—Biography. I. Title.

Whitgift, John, Abp. of Canterbury, 1530?-1604.

DAWLEY, Powel Mills, 1907- 283'.092'4
John Whitgift and the English Reformation. New York, Scribner, 1954. xii, 254p. 21cm. (The Hale lectures, 1953) Bibliography: p. 231-242. [BX5199.W535D3] 54-11017
1. Whitgift, John, Abp. of Canterbury,

1530?-1604. I. Title. II. Series: Seabury-Western Theological Seminary, Evanston, Ill. The Hale lectures, 1953

WHITGIFT and the English Church... New York, The Macmillan Company [1957] 190p. 19cm. (Teach yourself history series) 'Books for further reading: p. 184.
1. Whitgift, John, Abp. of Canterbury, 1530?-1604. I. Brook, Victor John Knight, 1887-

WHITGIFT and the English Church. New York, The Macmillan Company [1957] 190p. 19cm. (Teach yourself history series) 'Books for further reading.' p. 184.
1. Whitgift, John, Aep. of Canterbury, 1530&-1604. I. Brook, Victor John Knight, 1887-

Whitham, Arthur Richard, 1863- ed.

DUCAT, William Methven Gordon, 1847-1922. 283.
Tests of vocation, and other addresses, by the late William Methven Gordon Ducat ... edited with a brief memoir by Canon A. R. Whitham ... and with a foreword by the Lord Bishop of Oxford. London, New York [etc.] Longmans, Green and co., 1924. xv, 126 p. front. (port.) 19 1/2 cm. [BX5133.D7T4] 24-23392
1. Whitham, Arthur Richard, 1863- ed. I. Title.

Whiting, Albert Bennet, 1835-1871.

WHITING, Rachel Augusta, comp. 920.
Golden memories of an earnest life. A biography of A. B. Whiting: together with selections from his poetical compositions and prose writings. Comp. by his sister, R. Augusta Whiting. Introduction by Rev. J. M. Peebles... Boston, W. White and company, 1872. 293 p. front. (port.) 18 1/2 cm. [BF1283.W55W5] 15-13518
1. Whiting, Albert Bennet, 1835-1871. 2. Spiritualism. I. Title.

Whiting, Martha, 1795-1853.

BADGER, Catharine Naomi. 923.773
The teacher's last lesson; a memoir of Martha Whiting late of the Charleston female seminary. Consisting chiefly of extracts from her journal, interspersed with reminiscences and suggestive reflections. By Catharine N. Badger ... Boston, Gould and Lincoln. New York, Sheldon, Lamport & Blakeman, 1855. xii, [13]-284 p. front. (port.) pl. 20 cm. [BR1725.W435B3] 38-7102
1. Whiting, Martha, 1795-1853. I. Title.

Whiting, Richard, Abbot of Glastonburg, d. 1539.

GASQUET, Frances Aidan, Cardinal, 1846-1929. 914.2'03
The last abbot of Glastonbury, and other essays. Freeport, N.Y., Books for Libraries Press [1970] viii, 330 p. illus., facsims. 23 cm. Reprint of the 1908 ed. Contents.Contents.—The last abbot of Glastonbury.—English Biblical criticism in the thirteenth century.—English scholarship in the thirteenth century.—Two dinners at Wells in the fifteenth century.—Some troubles of a Catholic family in penal times.—Abbot Feckenham and Bath.—Christian family life in pre-Reformation days.—Christian democracy in pre-Reformation times.—The layman in the pre-Reformation parish.—St. Gregory the Great and England. Includes bibliographical references. [BX4705.W5G32 1970] 72-137376
1. Whiting, Richard, Abbot of Glastonburg, d. 1539. 2. Catholics in England. 3. Gt. Brit.—Social life and customs. I. Title.

Whitman, Bernard, 1796-1834.

[POND, Enoch] 1791-1882. 261.
Review of Mr. Whitman's letters to Professor Stuart, on religious liberty. 2d ed. With an appendix not before published. Boston, Pierce & Parker, 1831. 84 p. 23cm. [BV741.S7W5 1831] 45-43900
1. Whitman, Bernard, 1796-1834. Two letters to the Reverend Moses Stuart. 2. Religious liberty. 3. Unitarianism—Controversial literature. I. Title.

WHITMAN, Jason, 1799-1848. 922.8173
Memoir of the Rev. Bernard Whitman. By Jason Whitman. Boston, B. H. Greene, 1837. 1 p. l., [vii]-xii p., 1 l., [13]-215 p. front. (port.) 19 cm. [BX9869.W57W5] 37-9268
1. Whitman, Bernard, 1796-1834. I. Title.

Whitman, John, 1735-1842.

WHITMAN, Jason, 1799-1843. 920.
The Christian patriarch. A memoir of Deacon John Whitman; who died at East Bridgewater, Mass., July MDCCCXLII, at the advanced age of one hundred and seven years and three months. By Rev. Jason Whitman... Boston, W. Crosby and co., 1843. 2 p. l., 101 p. front. (port.) 16 cm. [BX7260.W465W5] 1-10276
1. Whitman, John, 1735-1842. I. Title.

Whitmer, Adam Carl, 1837-1920.

WHITMER, Thomas Carl, 1873- 922.
Life of Rev. A. Carl Whitmer, a lover of man, by R. Carl Whitmer... Philadelphia, Pa., Publication and Sunday school board of the Reformed church in the United States, 1923. 4 p. l., 203 p. front. (port.) 3 facsim. 20 cm. $1.75 [BX9593.W5W5] 23-7672
1. Whitmer, Adam Carl, 1837-1920. I. Title.

Whitmore family (Thomas Whittemore, d. 1660)

WHITTEMORE, Thomas, 1800-1861. 922.
The early days of Thomas Whittemore. An autobiography: extending from A.D. 1800 to A.D. 1825. Boston, J. M. Usher, 1859. 348 p. front. (port.) 20 cm. [BX9969.W6A3] 17-14860
1. Whitmore family (Thomas Whittemore, d. 1660) I. Title.

Whitney, William Dwight, 1827-1894.

AMERICAN congress of philologists. 1st, Philadelphia, 1894. 297
The Whitney memorial meeting. A report of that session of the first American congress of philologists, which was devoted to the memory of the late Professor William Dwight Whitney. of Yale university; held at Philadelphia, Dec. 28, 1894. Ed. for the joint committees of publication, by Charles R. Lanman. Boston, Ginn and company, 1897. viii, 153 p.,1 l., front. (port.) 25 cm. (Added t.p: Journal of the American Oriental society ... v. 19. 1st half) "Chronological bibliography of the writings of William Dwight Whitney": p. 121-150. [PJ2.A6 vol.19] 5-3408
1. Whitney, William Dwight, 1827-1894. I. Lanman, Charles Rockwell, 1850- ed. II. Title.

Whittemore, Thomas, 1800-1861.

ADAMS, John Greenleaf, 1810-1887. 922.
Memoir of Thomas Whittemoore, D.D. by John G. Adams... Boston, Universalist publishing house, 1878. 2 p. l., [iii]-xii, [13]-388 p. font. (port.) 19 1/2 cm. [BX9969.W6A8] 17-17478
1. Whittemore, Thomas, 1800-1861. I. Title.

Whittingham, William Rollinson, bp, 1805-1879.

BRAND, William Francis, 1814-1907. 922.
Life of William, Rollinson Wittingham, fourth bishop of Maryland ... By William French Brand. With portrait and fac-similes ... 2d ed. with additions. New York, E. & J. B. Young & co., 1886. 2 v. front. (port.) illus., fold. facsims. 29 cm. [BX5995.W55B8 1886] 28-12140
1. Whittingham, William Rollinson, bp, 1805-1879. I. Title.

Whitwell, William, 1737-1781.

BARNARD, Thomas, 1716-1776.
A sermon preached at the ordination of the Rev. William Whitwell, to the joint pastoral care of the First church and congregation in Marblehead, with the Rev. John Barnard, August 25, 1762. By Thomas Barnard, A.M. pastor of the First church in Salem. Together with the charge given Mr. Whitwell, by the Rev. John Barnard, preceded by an introductory discourse in defence of the ecclesiastical establishment of these churches, and followed by an historical account of the First church in Marblehead. And also the Right hand of fellowship given by the Rev. Mr. Simon Bradstreet of Marblehead. Boston, New-England, Printed by J. Dpaper [1] MDCCLXII. 2 p. 1., 51 p. 22 1/2 cm. (Half-title: Mr. Barnard's sermon at the ordination of the Reverend Mt. Whitwell) A 31
1. Whitwell, William, 1737-1781. I. Barnard, John, 1681-1770. II. Bradstreet, Simon, 1709-1771. III. Title.

Wicher, Edward Arthur.

FERRIER, William Warren. 285.1794
Pioneer church beginnings and educational movements in California, comment on a California church history, by William Warren Ferrier. Berkeley, Calif., 1927. 89 p. 20 cm. Reviews The Presbyterian church in California, 1849-1927, by E. A. Wicher. New York. 1927. [BX8947.C2F4] 30-34031
1. Wicher, Edward Arthur, 1872- The Presbyterian church in California, 1849-1927. 2. California—Church history. 3. Education—California. I. Title.

Wichita, Kan. First Presbyterian church.

BRADT, Charles Edwin. 285.
A working church and its way of working. By Charles Edwin Bradt ... The story and history of the First Presbyterian church of Wichita, Kansas, after thirty three and one third years ... Wichita, Kan., Missionary messenger press, 1903. 3 p. l., [9]-181 p. illus. (incl. ports.) 16 cm. [BX9211.W55B8] 3-23387
1. Wichita, Kan. First Presbyterian church. I. Title.

Wickford, R.I. St. Paul's Church.

WHITE, Hunter C. 283.745
Old St. Paul's in Narragansett. [Wakefield? R.I., 1957. 56 p. illus. 24 cm. [BX5980.W6W5] 58-16283
1. Wickford, R.I. St. Paul's Church. I. Title.

Widows—Africa—Case studies.

KIRWEN, Michael C. 261.8'34'286
African widows : an empirical study of the problem of adapting Western Christian teachings on marriage to the leviratic custom for the care of widows in four rural African societies / Michael C. Kirwen. Maryknoll, N.Y. : Orbis Books, c1978. p. cm. Includes index. Bibliography: p. [HQ1058.5.A4K57] 78-15870 ISBN 0-88344-009-1 pbk. : 8.95
1. Widows—Africa—Case studies. 2. Levirate—Case studies. I. Title.

Widows—Prayer-books and devotions—English.

BRANDT, Catharine. 242'.4
Flowers for the living / Catharine Brandt. Minneapolis : Augsburg Pub. House, c1977. 96 p. : ill. ; 20 cm. Bibliography: p. 95-96. [BV4908.B69] 77-72449 ISBN 0-8066-1585-0 pbk. : 2.95
1. Widows—Prayer-books and devotions—English. I. Title.

Widows—Religious life.

BRITE, Mary. 248'.843
Triumph over tears / a guide for widows / Mary Brite. Nashville : T. Nelson, c1979. 143 p. ; 21 cm. Includes bibliographical references. [BV4528.B74] 78-27107 ISBN 0-8407-5680-1 pbk. : 3.95
1. Widows—Religious life. I. Title.

HSU, Dorothy. 242'.4
Mending / Dorothy Hsu. Elgin, Ill. : D.C. Cook Pub. Co., c1979. 128 p. : ill. ; 18 cm. [BV4528.H78] 78-66875 ISBN 0-89191-144-8 pbk. : 1.95
1. Hsu, Dorothy. 2. Widows—Religious life. I. Title.

Widows—Spiritual consolation.

*WEDGE, Florence 248.86
The widow. Pulaski, Wis., Franciscan Pubs. [1967] 64p. 19cm. (Help yourself ser.) .25 pap.,
1. Widows—Spiritual consolation. I. Title.

Widows—United States—Biography.

FABISCH, Judith. 248'.86 B
Not ready to walk alone / Judith Fabisch. Grand Rapids, Mich. : Zondervan Pub. House, c1978. 122 p. ; 22 cm. [BV4908.F32] 78-6724 ISBN 0-310-37070-1 : 5.95
1. Fabisch, Judith. 2. Widows—United States—Biography. 3. Christian biography—United States. 4. Consolation. I. Title.

Widtsoe, Mrs. Anna Karine (Gaarden) 1849-1919.

WIDTSOE, John Andreas, 1872- 922.8373
In the gospel net; the story of Anna K. G. Widtsoe, by John A. Widtsoe ... Independence, Mo., Press of Zion's printing and publishing co. [c1941] 118 p., 1 l. front., plates, ports, maps. 19 1/2 cm. (His Book of remembrance, no. 1) "Printed for private distribution." [BX8695.W54W5] 42-2533
1. Widtsoe, Mrs. Anna Karine (Gaarden) 1849-1919. I. Title.

WIDTSOE, John Andreas, 1872- 922.8373
In the gospel net the story of Anna Karine Gaarden Widtsoe, by John A. Widtsoe ... [Salt Lake City, The Improvement era, 1942] 140 p., 1 l. front., plates, ports., maps. 22 1/2 cm. "First edition, privately printed, December, 1941 ... Second edition, July, 1942." [BX8695.W54W5 1942] 42-209328
1. Widtsoe, Anna Karine (Gaarden) 1849-1919. I. Improvement era. II. Title.

WIDTSOE, John Andreas, 1872-1952. 289.3'0924 B
In the gospel net; the story of Anna Karine Gaarden Widtsoe, by John A. Widtsoe. [3d ed.] Salt Lake City, Bookcraft [1966] 140 p. illus., maps, ports. 24 cm. [BX8695.W54W5 1966] 67-2680
1. Widtsoe, Anna Karine (Gaarden) 1849-1919. I. Title.

Wieand, Albert Cassel, 1871-1954.

SCHWALM, Vernon Franklin, 1887- 922.673
Albert Cassel Wieand. Elgin, Ill., Brethren Press [1960] 155p. illus. 21cm. [BX7843.W55S3] 60-16194
1. Wieand, Albert Cassel, 1871-1954. I. Title.

Wiebe, Katie Funk.

WIEBE, Katie Funk. 248'.843
Alone : a widow's search for joy / Katie F. Wiebe. Wheaton, Ill. : Tyndale House Publishers, 1976. 303 p. ; 21 cm. Bibliography: p. 303. [BX8143.W43A33] 76-27572 ISBN 0-8423-0062-7 : 4.95
1. Wiebe, Katie Funk. 2. Mennonites—Kansas—Hillsboro—Biography. 3. Hillsboro, Kan.—Biography. I. Title.

Wieman, Henry Nelson, 1884-

BRETALL, Robert Walter, 1913- ed. 208.2
The empirical theology of Henry Nelson Wieman. New York, Macmillan [1963] 423 p. illus. 22 cm. (The Library of living theology, v. 4) [BX4827.W45B7] 62-21217
1. Wieman, Henry Nelson, 1884- I. Title.
Contents omitted.

EMPIRICAL theology of Henry Nelson Wieman (The) Ed. by Robert W. Bretall. New York, Macmillan [1963] 423p. illus. 22cm. (Lib. of living theology, v.4) 62-21217 8.50 208.2
1. Wieman, Henry Nelson, 1884- I. Bretall, Robert Walter, 1913- ed.
Contents omitted.

MINOR, William Sherman, 1900- 230'.092'4
Creativity in Henry Nelson Wieman / by William Sherman Minor ; with a foreword by Bernard E. Meland. Metuchen, N.J. : Scarecrow Press, 1977. xix, 231 p. ; 23 cm. (ATLA monograph series ; no. 11) Includes index. Bibliography: p. 216-224. [BX4827.W45M55 1977] 77-8087 ISBN 0-8108-1041-7 : 10.00
1. Wieman, Henry Nelson, 1884- I. Title. II. Series: American Theological Library Association. ATLA monograph series ; no. 11.

WIEMAN, Henry Nelson, 1884- 233'.7
Creative freedom, vocation of liberal religion / Henry Nelson Wieman ; Creighton Peden and Larry E. Axel, editors. New York : Pilgrim Press, c1982. p. cm. Originally published in serial form beginning 1981: American journal of theology & philosophy, ISSN 0194-3448. Includes bibliographical references. [BT810.2.W47 1982] 19 82-10182 ISBN 0-8298-0623-7 pbk. : 7.95
1. Wieman, Henry Nelson, 1884- 2. Freedom (Theology) 3. Liberalism (Religion)—History of doctrines—20th century. I. Peden, Creighton, 1935- II. Axel, Larry E., 1946- III. Title.

Wiens, Helena.

KROEKER, Nettie, 1900- 289.7'092'4 B
Far above rubies : the story of Helena Wiens / by Nettie Kroeker. Winnipeg : Christian Press, c1976. 368 p. : ill., facsims., maps, ports. ; 24 cm. Bibliography: p. 368. [BX8143.W45K76] 77-368212 10.00
1. Wiens, Helena. 2. Mennonites—Manitoba—Biography. I. Title.

Wieting, Philip, 1800-1869.

DOX, Henry L. 922473
Memoir of Rev. Philip Wieting, a pastor forty years in the same field. By Rev. H. L. Dox ... Philadelphia, Lutheran publication society, 1870. viii, [13]-316 p. front. (port.) 20 cm. The last appeal. The fortieth anniversary and valedictory sermon ... [by Rev. P. Wieting]": p. [205]-238. The funeral sermon of Rev. P. Wieting. Delivered ... by Rev. N. Van Alstine": p [276]-299. [BX8060.W5D6] 36-33026
1. Wieting, Philip, 1800-1869. 2. Installation (Clergy)—Anniversary sermons. 3. Funeral sermons. I. Van Alstine, Nicholas, 1814-1900. II. Lutheran publication society, Philadelphia. III. Title.

Wigglesworth, Michael, 1631-1705.

CROWDER, Richard 922.573
No featherbed to heaven; a biography of Michael Wigglesworth, 1631-1705. [East Lansing] Mich. State Univ. Pr. [c.1962] 299p. 22cm. Bibl. 61-16933 7.00
1. Wigglesworth, Michael, 1631-1705. I. Title.

WIGGLESWORTH, Michael, 1631-1705 248.0924
The diary of Michael Wigglesworth, 1653-1657; the consicience of a Puritan. Ed. by Edmund S. Morgan [Gloucester, Mass., P. Smith, 1966,c.1946] xv, 125p. 21cm. (Harper torchbk., Acad. lib. bk., TB1228G rebound) Orig. pub. in 1951 as pt. of Transactions, 1942-1946, v.35 of Pubns. of the Colonial Soc. of Massachusetts.bBibl. [BX7260.W48.A3] 3.25
I. Morgan, Edmund Sears, ed. II. Title.

WIGGLESWORTH, Michael, 1631-1705 248.0924
The diary of Michael Wigglesworth, 1653-1657; the conscience of a Puritan. Ed. by Edmund S. Morrgan. New York, Harper [1965, c.1946] xv, 125p. 21cm. (Harper torchbks., TB1228G. Acad. lib.) Orig. pub. in 1951 as part of Transactions, 1942-1946, v.35 of Pubns. of the Colonial Soc. of Mass. Bibl. [BX7260.W48A3] 65-25696 1.25 pap.,
I. Morgan, Edmund Sears, ed. II. Title.

WIGGLESWORTH, Michael, 1631-1705. 248'.0924
The diary of Michael Wigglesworth, 1653-1657; the conscience of a Puritan. Edited by Edmund S. Morgan. Gloucester, Mass., Peter Smith, 1970 [c1946] xv, 125 p. 21 cm. "Originally published in 1951 as part of Transactions, 1942-1946, volume XXXV of Publications of the Colonial Society of Massachusetts." Includes bibliographical references. [BX7260.W48A3 1970] 73-17093
I. Title.

Wigglesworth, Smith, 1859-1946?

FRODSHAM, Stanley Howard, 1882- 922
Smith Wigglesworth, apostle of faith. Springfield, Mo., Gospel Pub. House, 1948. 153 p. port. 21 cm. [BV3785.W42F7] 49-16052
1. Wigglesworth, Smith, 1859-1946? I. Title.

HACKING, W. (William) 269'.2'0924 B
Smith Wigglesworth remembered / by W. Hacking. Tulsa, Okla. : Harrison House, c1981. 107 p. ; 22 cm. (Harrison House classic library) Previously published as: Reminiscences of Smith Wigglesworth. [BV3785.W482H33 1981] 19 81-184385 ISBN 0-89274-203-8 (pbk.) : 3.95
1. Wigglesworth, Smith, 1859-1946? 2. Evangelists—England—Biography. 3. Pentecostal churches—Clergy—Biography. 4. Clergy—England—Biography. I. Title.

Wight, Orlando Williams, 1824-1888.

WIGHT, Jarvis Sherman, 1834-1901. 920
A memorial of O. W. Wight, A.M., M.D. Sanitarian, lawyer, and author, by J. S. Wight, M.D. Cambridge, Riverside press, 1890. 4 p. l., 266 p. 2 port. (incl. front.) 18 1/2 cm. [CT275.W558W5] 23-46
1. Wight, Orlando Williams, 1824-1888. I. Title.

Wilberforce, Robert Isaac, 1802-1857.

WILBERFORCE, Cranmer, Jewell, and the prayer book, on the incarnation. Washington, Gideon and co., printers, 1850. 56 p. 21 1/2 cm. [BT220.W7] 37-30623 232.1
1. Wilberforce, Robert Isaac, 1802-1857. The doctrine of the incarnation of Our Lord Jesus Christ. 2. Incarnation.

Wilberforce, Samuel, Bp. of Winchester, 1805-1873.

ASHWELL, Arthur Rawson, 1824-1879. 922.
Life of the Right Reverend Samuel Wilberforce, D.D., lord bishop of Oxford and afterwards of Winchester, with selections from his diaries and correspondence, by A. R. Ashwell ... and Reginald G. Wilberforce. Abridged from the English ed. ... New York, E. P. Dutton & company, 1883 xxxv, 553 p. front., plates, ports. 22 1/2 cm. [BX5199.W6A8] 12-30397
1. Wilberforce, Samuel, successively bp. of Oxford and of Winchester, 1805-1873. I. Wilberforce, Reginald Garton, 1838- joint author. II. Title.

DANIELL, George William, 1853-1931. 922.
Bishop Wilberforce, by G. W. Daniell M. A. Boston and New York, Houghton, Mifflin and company, 1891. 2 p. l., 223, [1] p. front. (port.) 20 cm. [BX5199.W6D3] 12-31847
1. Wilberforce, Samuel, Successively bp. of Oxford and of Winchester, 1805-1873. I. Title.

MARTYN, Henry, 1781-1812. 922.854
Journal and letters of the Rev. Henry Martyn ... Edited by the Rev. S. Wilberforce ... 1st American ed., abridged ... New York, M. W. Dodd, 1851. vi, [7]-466 p. 19 1/2 cm. [BV3705.M3A4 1851] 38-9768
1. Wilberforce, Samuel, successively bp. of Oxford and of Winchester, 1805-1873, ed. I. Title.

MEACHAM, Standish. 283'.0924 B
Lord Bishop; the life of Samuel Wilberforce, 1805-1873. Cambridge, Mass., Harvard University Press, 1970. x, 328 p. port. 25 cm. Bibliography: p. [ix]-x. [BX5199.W6M4] 70-102669 13.50
1. Wilberforce, Samuel, Bp. of Winchester, 1805-1873. I. Title.

Wilberforce University, Wilberforce, Ohio.

SMITH, David, 1784- 287'.83'0924 B
Biography of Rev. David Smith of the A.M.E. Church. Freeport, N.Y., Books for Libraries Press, 1971. vii, 135 p. illus. 23 cm. (The Black heritage library collection) Reprint of the 1881 ed. Includes The history of the origin and development of Wilberforce University, by Bishop D. A. Payne (p. [99]-132). [BX8449.S6A3 1971] 77-168520 ISBN 0-8369-8872-8
1. Wilberforce University, Wilberforce, Ohio. I. Payne, Daniel Alexander, Bp., 1811-1893. II. Title. III. Series.

TALBERT, Horace, 1853- 287.
The sons of Allen, by Rev. Horace Talbert, M.A. Together with a sketch of the rise and progress of Wilberforce university, Wilberforce, Ohio. Xenia, O., The Aldine press, 1906. 3 p., l., v-xiv p., 1 l., 17-286 p. front. (port.) illus. 23 cm. [BX8443.T3] 6-15719
1. Allen, Richard, bp., 1760-1831. 2. Wilberforce university, Wilberforce, O. 3. African Methodist Episcopal church—Clergy. I. Title.

Wilberforce, William, 1759-1833.

STOUGHTON, John, 1807-1897.
William Wilberforce, by John Stoughton, D.D. New York, A. C. Armstrong & son, 1880. 8 p. l., [9]-213 p. 19 cm. (Heroes of Christian history) A22
1. Wilberforce, William, 1759-1833. I. Title.

Wilbur, Isabella Sarah, 1828-1856.

SKETCHES of the life and death of Isabella Sarah Wilbur; eldest daughter of Jeremiah and Sarah R. Wilbur, and granddaughter of Thomas Masters; who died July 5th, 1856, at Blithebourne, Irvington, Westchester county, New York. New York, J. F. Trow, printer, 1858. 148 p. 17 cm. [BR1725.W45S5] 38-7111 922
1. Wilbur, Isabella Sarah, 1828-1856.

Wilcox, Brad.

WILCOX, Brad. 248'.48'933
The super baruba success book for under-achievers, over-expecters, and other ordinary people / Brad Wilcox. Salt Lake City : Bookcraft, c1979. xi, 116 p. ; 24 cm. [BX8695.W544A37] 79-53050 ISBN 0-88494-372-0 pbk. : 4.50
1. Wilcox, Brad. 2. Mormons and Mormonism—United States—Biography. I. Title.

Wilcox, William Cullen, 1850-1928.

WILCOX, Mark F. 266.5868
Proud endeavorer; the story of a Yankee New York, Graphic Pr. [1962] 144p. 23cm. 62-19484 3.00
1. Wilcox, William Cullen, 1850-1928. 2. Missions—Africa, South. I. Title.

Wilde, Oscar, 1854-1900.

SMITH, Hester Travers, Mrs. 133.
OscarWilde from purgatory, psychic messages edited by Hester Travers Smith...with a preface by Sir William F. Barrett F. R. S. New York, H. Holt and company [1926] xii, 179 p. front. (port.) illus. (facsims.) 22 cm. Printed in Great Britain. [BF1311.W5M6 1926] 27-23489
1. Wilde, Oscar, 1854-1900. 2. Spiritualism. I. Title.

Wilde, Paul.

WILDE, Carolyn. 269'.2'0922 B
We've come this far by faith / Carolyn Wilde. Plainfield, NJ : Distributed by Logos International, c1980. 163 p. ; 21 cm. [BV3780.W54] 19 80-82251 ISBN 0-88270-446-X pbk. : 4.95
1. Wilde, Paul. 2. Wilde, Carolyn. 3. Evangelists—United States—Biography. I. Title.

Wilder, Amos Niven, 1895-

CROSSAN, John Dominic. 230'.044
A fragile craft : the work of Amos Niven Wilder / John Dominic Crossan. Chico, CA : Scholars Press, c1981. 81 p. ; 23 cm. (Biblical scholarship in North America ; no. 3) Bibliography: p. [75]-81. [BS2351.W54C76] 19 80-19755 ISBN 0-89130-425-8 : 16.50
1. Wilder, Amos Niven, 1895- I. Title. II. Series.

Wilder, Robert Parmelee,

BRAISTED, Ruth Evelyn (Wilder) Mrs. 922
In this generation; the story of Robert P. Wilder, by Ruth Wilder Braisted. New York, Published for the Student volunteer movement by Friendship press [c1941] xvi, [2], 205 p. front. (port) 1 illus. 20 cm. [BV3705.W5B7] 42-3055
1. Wilder, Robert Parmelee, I. Student volunteer movement for foreign mission. II. Title.

Wilderness (Theology)

WILLIAMS, George Huntston, 1914- 248
Wilderness and paradise in Christian thought; the Biblical experience of the desert in the history of Christianity & the paradise theme in the theological idea of the university. New York, Harper & Row [c.1962] 245p. 22cm. Bibl. 62-7307 4.50 bds.,
1. Wilderness (Theology) 2. Church and college. I. Title.

WILLIAMS, George Huntston, 1914- 248
Wilderness and paradise in Christian thought the biblical experience of the desert in the history of Christianity & the paradise theme in the theological idea of the university. [1st ed.] New York, Harper [1962] 245 p. 22 cm. "The substance of this book was originally delivered at Bethel College, North Newton, Kansas, in 1958." [BV5068.W5W5] 62-7307
1. Wilderness (Theology) 2. Church and college. I. Title.

Wiley, Allen, 1789-1848.

HOLLIDAY, Fernandez C 1814-1888. 922.773
Life and times of Rev. Allen Wiley, A.M. containing sketches of early Methodist preachers in Indiana, and notices of the introduction and progress of Methodism in the state; also, including his original letters entitled, "A help to the performance of ministerial duties." By Rev. F. C. Holliday, A.M. Edited by Rev. D. W. Clark, D.D. Cincinnati, L. Swormstedt & A. Poe, for the Methodist Episcopal church, 1853. 291 p. 18 1/2 cm. [BX8495.W62H6] 37-12156
1. Wiley, Allen, 1789-1848. 2. Methodist Episcopal church in Indiana. I. Clark, Davis Wasgatt, 1812-1871, ed. II. Title.

Wiley, Isaac William, bp. 1825-1884.

RUST, Richard Sutton, 1815-1906, ed. 922.773
Isaac W. Wiley, late bishop of the M.E. church. A monograph, edited by Richard S. Rust... Cincinnati, Cranston and Stowe; New York, Phillips and Hunt, 1885. vi, 233 p. front. (port.) pl. 21 1/2 cm. [BX8495.W63R8] 37-12172
1. Wiley, Isaac William, bp. 1825-1884. I. Title.

Wilfrid, Saint, bp. of York, 634-709.

BROWNE, George Forrest, bp. of Bristol, 1833- 274.
Theodore and Wilfrith. Lectures delivered in St. Paul's in December 1896, by the Right Rev. G.F. Browne... London (etc.) Society for promoting Christian knowledge; New York, E. & J.B. Young & co., 1897. 303 p. front., illus., plates. 17 1/2 cm. [BR749.B8] 3-9238
1. Wilfrid, Saint, bp. of York, 634-709. 2. Gt. Brit.—Church history. I. Title.

EDDI, fl.669. 922.
The life of Bishop Wilfrid, by Eddius Stephanus text, translation, & notes by Bertram Colgrave. Cambridge [Eng.] The University press, 1927. xvii p., 1 l., 192 p. 22 1/2 cm. Bibliography of earlier editions of the Life: p. xvi-xvii. [BX4700.W5E4] 28-28086
1. Wilfrid, Saint, bp. of York, 634-709. 2. Gt. Brit.—Church history. I. Title.

SAINT Wilfrid at 270.2'092'4 B
Hexham / D. P. Kirby, editor. Newcastle upon Tyne [Eng.] : Oriel Press, 1974. xi, 196, 31 p. : ill. ; 24 cm. Includes bibliographical references and index. [BX4700.W5S24] 75-308585 ISBN 0-85362-155-1 : £5.50
1. Wilfred, Saint, Bp. of York, 634-709. 2. Art—Hexham, Eng. 3. Art, Anglo-Saxon—Hexham, Eng. 4. Hexham, Eng.—History. I. Kirby, D. P.

Wilhelm family.

CULAVAMSA. 294.
... *Culavamsa,* being the more recent part of the Mahavamsa, edited by Wilhelm Geiger ... London, Pub. for the Pali text society by H. Milford, Oxford university press, 1925- v. 23 cm. (Pall text society. [Publications. v. 99]) "The title Culavamsa or, in Sinhalese, Suluvamsaya is now commonly used in Ceylon to denote the young[chapters 37-100] of the Mahavamsa." The Culavamsa was written by various authors; according to Sinhalese tradition acomposed by Thera Dhammakitti of Pref. of Culavamsa, edit. by W. Geiger. [PK4541.P4 vol. 99] 27-5852
1. Dhammakitti, fl. between 1240 and 1275. II. Geiger, Wilhelm, 1856- ed. III. Title.

MEYERSDALE, Pa. St. Paul's church. Historical committee. 284.
A history of the Wilhelms and the Wilhelm charge, by the Historical committee ... Meyersdale, Pa., The Wilhelm press, 1919. 3 p. l., [9]-205 p. incl. front., plates, ports. 24 cm. [BX9569.S6M4] 20-632
1. Wilhelm family. 2. Reformed church in the United States. Classis of Somerset, Pa. I. Title.

Wilhelm, Margraf von Baden, 1593-1677.

KOHLER, Hans-Joachim. 270.6'08 s
Obrigkeitliche Konfessionsanderung in Kondominaten : eine Fallstudie uber ihre Bedingungen und Methoden am Beispiel der Baden-Badischen Religionspolitik unter der Regierung Markgraf Wilhelms (1622-1677) / von Hans-Joachim Kohler. Munster : Aschendorff, 1975. viii, 240 p. : col. maps ; 23 cm. (Reformationsgeschichtliche Studien und Texte ; Heft 110) Originally presented as the author's thesis, Tubingen, 1973. Includes index. Bibliography: p. [222]-232. [BR302.R4 Heft 110] [BR857.B3] 274.3'46 76-460411 ISBN 3-402-03717-3
1. Wilhelm, Margraf von Baden, 1593-1677. 2. Baden—Church history. 3. Baden—Politics and government. I. Title. II. Series.

Wilkerson, David R.

WILKERSON, David R. 259
Beyond the cross and the switchblade [by] David Wilkerson. Special introd. by John and Elizabeth Sherrill. Old Tappan, N.J., Chosen Books; distributed by F. H. Revell [1974] 191 p. 21 cm. [BV4470.W48] 74-12155 ISBN 0-912376-08-2
1. Wilkerson, David R. 2. Church work with narcotic addicts. I. Title.

Wilkes-Barre, Pa. St. Stephen's Church—History.

RADDIN, George Gates, 1906- 283'.748'32
The wilderness and the city; the story of a parish, 1817-1967. Wilkes-Barre, Pa., St. Stephen's Episcopal Church [1968] xviii, 777 p. illus., ports. 23 cm. [BX5980.W69S3] 68-27845
1. Wilkes-Barre, Pa. St. Stephen's Church—History. I. Title.

Wilkin, Marijohn.

HICKS, Darryl. 783.7'092'4 B
Marijohn: Lord, let me leave a song / Darryl E. Hicks. Waco, Tex. : Word Books, c1978. 159 p. : ill. ; 22 cm. [ML410.W699H5] 77-92466 ISBN 0-8499-0019-0 : 6.95
1. Wilkin, Marijohn. 2. Gospel musicians—United States—Biography. I. Title.

Wilkins, John, Bp. of Chester, 1614-1672.

SHAPIRO, Barbara J. 283'.0924 B
John Wilkins, 1614-1672; an intellectual biography [by] Barbara J. Shapiro. Berkeley, University of California Press, 1969. 333 p. port. 24 cm. Bibliographical references included in "Notes" (p. 251-320) [LF724.W5S5] 73-84042 9.50
1. Wilkins, John, Bp. of Chester, 1614-1672. 2. Religion and science—History of controversy.

Wilkinson, Asbury, 1818-1909.

CLINE, Rodney. 922.773
Asbury Wilkinson: pioneer preacher. [1st ed.] New York, Vantage Press [1956] 116p. illus. 21cm. [BX8495.W635C55] 56-9032
1. Wilkinson, Asbury, 1818-1909. I. Title.

CLINE, Rodney. 922.773
Asbury Wilkinson: pioneer preacher. [1st ed.] New York, Vantage Press [1956] 116p. illus. 21cm. [BX8495.W635C55] 56-9032
1. Wilkinson, Asbury, 1818-1909. I. Title.

Wilkinson, George Howard, 1833-1907.

MASON, Arthur James.
Memoir of George Howard Wilkinson, bishop of St. Andrews, Dunkeld and Dunblane and primus of the Scottish church, formerly bishop of Truro, by Arthur James Mason ... London, New York [etc.] Longmans, Green & co., 1909. 2 v. fronts., plates, ports. 23 cm. Title-pages in red and black. "First edition, 2 vols., 8 vo. March 1909: reprinted, June 1909." A 10
1. Wilkinson, George Howard, 1833-1907. I. Title.

Wilkinson, Jemima, 1752-1819.

HUDSON, David. 922
History of Jemima Wilkinson, a preacheress of the eighteenth century; containing an authentic narrative of her life and character, and of the rise, progress and conclusion of her ministry ... By David Hudson. Geneva, Ontario county, N.Y. Printed by S. P. Hull. 1821. x, [11]-208, xx p. 19 cm. Published later under title: Memoir of Jemima Wilkinson. [BR1719.W5H8 1821] 37-23895
1. Wilkinson, Jemima, 1752-1819. I. Title.

HUDSON, David. 289.9 B
Memoir of Jemima Wilkinson. New York, AMS Press [1972] 288 p. port. 22 cm. First published in 1821 under title: History of Jemima Wilkinson. Reprint of the 1844 ed. [BR1719.W5H8 1972] 78-134417 ISBN 0-404-08475-3 12.50
1. Wilkinson, Jemima, 1752-1819. I. Title.

[HUDSON, David] 972
Memoir of Jemima Wilkinson, a preacheress of the eighteenth century; containing an authentic narrative of her life and character, and of the rise, progress and conclusion of her ministry ... Bath, N.Y., R. L. Underhill & co., 1844. viii, [9]-288 p. front. (port.) 16 cm. Published in 1821 under title: History of Jemima Wilkenson. [BR1719.W5H8 1844] 37-24316
1. Wilkinson, Jemima, 1752-1819. I. Title.

WINSBEY, Herbert Andrew, 1919- 922.89
Pioneer prophetess: Jemima Wilkinson, the Publick Universal Friend, by Herbert A. Wisbey, Jr. Ithaca, N.Y., Cornell University Press [1964] xiv. 232 p. illus., facsim., ports. 23 cm. "Bibliographical essay": p. 217-225. [BR1719.W5W5] 64-7875
1. Wilkinson, Jemima, 1752-1819. I. Title.

WISBEY, Herbert Andrew, Jr. 1919- 922.89
Pioneer prophetess: Jemima Wilkinson, the Publick Universal Friend. Ithaca, N.Y., Cornell [c.1964] xiv, 232p. illus., facsim., ports. 23cm. Bibl. [BR1719.W5W5] 64-7875 4.95
1. Wilkinson, Jemima, 1752-1819. I. Title.

Will.

HOCHBERG, Gary M. 170
Kant, moral legislation and two senses of 'will' / Gary M. Hochberg. Washington, D.C. : University Press of America, c1982. x, 227 p. ; 23 cm. Includes bibliographical references and index. [B2799.E8H62] 19 81-40396 ISBN 0-8191-2121-5 : 20.75 ISBN 0-8191-2122-3 (pbk.) : 10.25
1. Kant, Immanuel, 1724-1804—Ethics. 2. Will. I. Title.

LUTZ, Charles P. 234'.9
You mean I have a choice? [By] Charles P. Lutz. Minneapolis, Augsburg Pub. House [1971] 127 p. 20 cm. Includes bibliographical references. [BJ1461.L84] 78-158998 ISBN 0-8066-1131-6
1. Will. I. Title.

[MARY Fortunata, sister] 1871- 377.2
Aids to will training in Christian education, by two Sisters of Notre Dame, Cleveland, Ohio. New York and Cincinnati, Frederick Pustet co. (inc.) 1943. xvi p., 1 l., 237 p. diagr. 21 cm. [Secular name: Elisabeth Aloysia Horning] Bibliography: p. 236-237. [LB1071.M3] 44-1193
1. Will. 2. Educational psychology. 3. Moral education. I. Mary Catherine, sister, 1889- joint author. II. Title.

Willard, Charlotte Richards, 1860-1930.

PYE, Ernest, ed. 923.7496
Charlotte R. Willard, of Merzifon, her life and times, edited by Ernest Pye ... New York [etc.] Fleming H. Revell company [c1933] 211 p. front., plates, ports. 20 cm. "A mosaic appreciation by those who lived and worked in her company."--Foreword. [BV3142.W5P8] 33-30545
1. Willard, Charlotte Richards, 1860-1930. 2. Missions—Turkey. I. Title.

Willard, Frances Elizabeth, 1839-1898.

CRAIG, Laura (Gerould) Mrs. 1860- comp. 220.2
Precious jewels; texts--in rosaries labeled typically as gems or topically for services--providing delightful practice in the sublime language of the Book of books while learning the supreme laws for abundant living; practical exercises for training the sadly neglected faculties--memory, meditation, application; concrete illustrations of God's word victoriously lived by Frances E. Willard. By Laura Gerould Craig ... foreword by Ida B. Wise Smith. Baffalo, N. Y. L. G. and R. Craig [c1938] x, 11-150 p., 2 l. 20 cm. "First edition." [BS432.C67] 39-23885
1. Willard, Frances Elizabeth, 1839-1898 2. Bible—Indexes, Topical. I. Title.

DILLON, Mary Earhart. 920.7
Frances Willard; from prayers to politics, by Mary Earhart. Chicago, Ill., University of Chicago press [1944] x, 417, [1] p. front., illus., pl., ports., facsim. 23 1/2 cm. Bibliography: p. 404-413. [HV5232.W6D5] A44
1. Willard, Frances Elizabeth, 1839-1898. I. Title. II. Title: From prayers to politics.

DILLON, Mary Earhart. 322.4'4'0924 B
Frances Willard, from prayers to politics / by Mary Earhart. Washington : Zenger Pub. Co., 1975, c1944. p. cm. Reprint of the ed. published by University of Chicago Press, Chicago. Includes index. Bibliography: p. [HV5232.W6D5 1975] 75-35907 ISBN 0-89201-015-0 : 13.95
1. Willard, Frances Elizabeth, 1839-1898. I. Title.

EARHART, Mary.
Frances Willard; from prayers to politics, by Mary Earhart. Chicago, Ill., University of Chicago press [1944] x, 417, [1] p. front., illus., pl., ports., facsim. 23 1/2 cm. Bibliography: p. 404-413. A 44
1. Willard, Frances Elizabeth, 1839-1898. I. Title. II. Title: From prayers to politics.

FOSTER, Judith Ellen (Horton) Mrs. 1840-1910. 178.
... *The truth in the case,* concerning partisanship and nonpartisanship in the W. C. T. U. By J. Ellen Foster ... and others ... [Clinton, Ia.] 1889. 153 p. 23 cm. [HV5227.W7F6] 39-20066
1. Willard, Frances Elizabeth, 1839-1898. 2. Woman's Christian temperance union. I. Title.

FURST, Jeffrey. 129'.4
The return of Frances Willard; her case for reincarnation. New York, Coward, McCann & Geoghegan [1971] xix, 171 p. 22 cm. [BL515.F86] 73-154778 5.95
1. Willard, Frances Elizabeth, 1839-1898. 2. Hale, Stephanie Elizabeth, 1939- 3. Reincarnation—Case studies. I. Title.

FURST, Jeffrey. 129'.4
The return of Frances Willard: her case for reincarnation. New York, Pyramid Books [1973, c.1971] 173 p. 18 cm. [BL515.F86] ISBN 0-515-03044-9 1.25 (pbk.)
1. Willard, Frances Elizabeth, 1839-1898. 2. Hale, Stephanie Elizabeth, 1939- 3. Reincarnation—Case studies. I. Title.
L.C. card no. for the hardbound edition: 73-154778.

GORDON, Anna Adams, 1853-1931. 920.
The life of Frances E. Willard, by Anna Adams Gordon; with an introduction by Lady Henry Somerset. Evanston, Ill., National woman's Christian temperance union, 1912. xiii, [1] 357 p. front., plates, ports. 21 cm. "Revised and abridged from a memorial volume issued in 1898."--Pref. [HV5232.W6G7 1912] 12-22139
1. Willard, Frances Elizabeth, 1839-1898. I. Title.

STRACHEY, Rachel (Costelloe) Mrs., 1887- 920.
Frances Willard, her life and work, by Ray Strachey. With an introduction by Lady Henry Somerset ... New York, Chicago [etc.] Fleming H. Revell company [c1912] 310 p. front., plates, ports. 21 cm. $1.50. [HV5232.W6S8 1913] 13-13982
1. Willard, Frances Elizabeth, 1839-1898. I. Title.

TROWBRIDGE, Lydia (Jones) Mrs. 920.7
Frances Willard of Evanston [by] Lydia Jones Trowbridge. Chicago, New York, Willett, Clark & company, 1938. xii p., 1 l., 209 p. front., plates., ports. 20 cm. [Full name: Mrs. Lydia Hayes (Jones) Trowbridge] Bibliography: p. 206-207. [HV5232.W6T7] 38-27677
1. Willard, Frances Elizabeth, 1839-1898. I. Title.

Willard, Samuel, 1640-1707.

LOWRIE, Ernest Benson. 230'.5'90924
The shape of the Puritan mind : the thought of Samuel Willard / Ernest Benson Lowrie. New Haven : Yale University Press, 1974. xi, 253 p. ; 21 cm. Includes index. Bibliography: p. 235-248. [BX7260.W5L68 1974] 74-76650 ISBN 0-300-01714-6
1. Willard, Samuel, 1640-1707. I. Title.

VAN DYKEN, Seymour. 285'.9'0924 B
Samuel Willard, 1640-1707; preacher of orthodoxy in an era of change Grand Rapids, Eerdmans [1972] 224 p. 23 cm. Bibliography: p. 195-211. [BX7260.W5V3] 75-168438 ISBN 0-8028-3408-6 5.95
1. Willard, Samuel, 1640-1707.

Willey, Thomas H., 1898-1968.

BALLARD, Jerry. 266'.023'0924 B
Never say can't. [1st ed.] Carol Stream, Ill., Creation House [1971] 172 p. illus. 23 cm. [BX6379.W54B34] 72-200870 4.95
1. Willey, Thomas H., 1898-1968. I. Title.

William, Catharine Downing, 1817-1860.

SEAVER, Anna Maria. 922
Gold tried in the fire; or, Some account of the life, sufferings, and death of Catharine Downing Williams. By Anna Maria Seaver ... Andover, W. F. Draper, 1861. 72 p. 18 cm. [BR1725.W457S4] 38-8159
1. William, Catharine Downing, 1817-1860. I. Title.

William, of Norwich, Saint, 1132 or 33-1144.

THOMAS of Monmouth. 922.
The life and miracles of St. William of Norwich, by Thomas of Monmouth. Now first edited from the unique manuscript, with an introduction, translation, and notes by Augustus Jessopp ... and Montague Rhodes James ... Illustrated with five plates and a map. Cambridge, University press, 1896. xv p., 1 l., 303 p. v. pl. (incl. front.) map 25 cm. Latin text with English translation at foot of page. [BX4700.W55T5] 1-25153
1. William, of Norwich, Saint, 1132 or 33-1144. I. Jessopp, Augustus, 1824-1914, ed. and tr. II. James, Montague Rhodes, 1862-joint ed. and tr. III. Title.

Williams, Charles, 1886-1945.

MOORMAN, Charles. 820.993
Arthurian triptych; mythic materials in Charles Williams, C. S. Lewis, and T. S. Eliot. Berkeley, University of California Press, 1960. ix, 163p. 23cm. (Perspectives in criticism, 5) Bibliographical references included in 'Notes'(p. 157-163) [PR6045.I5Z85] 59-14476
1. Williams, Charles, 1886-1945. 2. Lewis, Clive Staples, 1898- 3. Eliot, Thomas Stearnis, 1888- 4. Arthur, King. 5. Mythology in literature. I. Title. II. Series.

Williams, Daniel Jenkins, 1874-1952.

WILLIAMS, Daniel Jenkins, 1874-
A synopsis of the Old Testament, by Daniel Jenkins Williams... Sheboygan, Wis., The Barrett company, 1915. 56 p., 1 l. 17 cm. $0.50. 15-9683
I. Title.

WILLIAMS, Robert Hugh, 1907- 922.573
Young minister of Wisconsin, the story of Daniel Jenkins Williams and his brothers. New York, Exposition [c.1963] 75p. illus. 21cm. 63-5225 2.75
1. Williams, Daniel Jenkins, 1874-1952. I. Title.

WILLIAMS, Robert Hugh, 1907- 922.573
Young minister of Wisconsin, the story of Daniel Jenkins Williams and his brothers. [1st ed.] New York, Exposition Press [1963] 75 p. illus. 21 cm. [BX9225,W452W5] 63-5225
1. Williams, Daniel Jenkins, 1874-1952. I. Title.

Williams, Edward, 1750-1813.

OWEN, William Thomas. 922.5
Edward Williams, D.D., 1750-1813; his life, thought, and influence. Cardiff, Univ. of Wales [Mystic, Conn., Verry, 1966] xii, 171p. facsim., ports. 22cm. Bibl. [BX5207.W53O9] 66-4704 4.00
1. Williams, Edward, 1750-1813. I. Title.

Williams, Glanville Llewelyn, 1911-.

DALY, Cahal B. 241
Morals, law, and life, by Cahal B. Daly. Chicago, Scepter [1966] 228p. 19cm. Bibl. 66-21148 2.95; .95 pap.,
1. Williams, Glanville Llewelyn, 1911- The sanctity of life and the criminal law. 2. Sex and law. I. Title.

Williams, Henry, 1831-1900.

JOHNSON, William Henry, 1858- 920.
A sketch of the life of Rev. Henry Williams, D.D., late pastor of the Gilfield Baptist church, Petersburg, Virginia, with ceremonies incident to his death, and to the erection of a monument to his memory. By William H. Johnson ... Petersburg, Va., Fenn & Owen, printers, 1901. 86 p., 1 l. front., pl., 4 ports. 24 cm. [E185.97.J75] 1-20241
1. Williams, Henry, 1831-1900. I. Title.

Williams, John, 1664-1729.

WILLIAMS, Stephen West, 1790-1855. 920.
A biographical memoir of the Rev. John Williams, first minister of Deerfield, Massachusetts. With a slight sketch of ancient Deerfield, and an account of the Indian wars in that place and vicinity. With an appendix, containing the journal of the Rev. Doctor Stephen Williams, of Longmeadow, during his captivity, and other papers relating to the early Indian wars in Deerfield. By Stephen W. Williams ... Greenfield, Mass., C. J. J. Ingersoll, 1837. vi, [7]-127 p. 18 1/2 cm. Includes an abstract of Rev. John Williams' "The redeemed captive returning to Zion", first published, Boston, 1707. [E87.W7354] 7-12920
1. Williams, John, 1664-1729. 2. Deerfield, Mass.—Hist.—Colonial period. 3. Indians of North America—Captivities. I. Title.

Williams, John, 1796-1839.

MATHEWS, Basil Joseph, 1879-
John Williams, the shipbuilder, by Basil Mathews, with thirty-three illustrations, eighteen by Ernest Prater. London, New York [etc.] H. Milford, Oxford university press, 1915. viii, 298 p. col. front., illus. (incl. maps) plates (part col.) ports. 19 cm. (On verso of half-title: The pathfinder series) Illustrated lining-papers. [BV3670.M4] 17-29040
1. Williams, John, 1796-1839. 2. Missions—Polynesia. I. Title.

Williams, John Elias, 1871-1927.

WHEELER, William Reginald, 1889- 922.551
John E. Williams of Nanking, by W. Reginald Wheeler ... New York [etc.] Fleming H. Revell company [c1937] 222 p. front., plates, ports. 21 cm. [BV3427.W5W5] 37-5195
1. Williams, John Elias, 1871-1927. 2. Nanking. University. I. Title.

Williams, John Howard, 1894-1958.

BROWN, Henry Clifton, Jr., ed. 922.673
J. Howard Williams, prophet of God and friend of man. Comp., ed. by H. C. Brown, Jr., Charles P. Johnson. San Antonio, Tex., Naylor [c.1963] xv, 147p. 22cm. Bibl. 63-23376 1.95
1. Williams, John Howard, 1894-1958. I. Johnson, Charles P., joint ed. II. Title.

BROWN, Henry Clifton, ed. 922.673
J. Howard Williams, prophet of God and friend of man. Compiled and edited by H. C. Brown, Jr. and Charles P. Johnson. San Antonio, Naylor Co. [c1963] xv, 147 p. 22 cm. Bibliographical footnotes. [BX6495.W49B7] 63-23376
1. Williams, John Howard, 1894-1958. I. Johnson, Charles P., joint ed. II. Title.

Williams, Joseph, 1780-1818

HOLT, Basil Fenelon, 1902- 922
Joseph Williams and the pioneer mission to the southeastern Bantu. [Lovedale, C. P.] Lovedale Press, 1954. vii, 186p. illus., ports., facsim. 20cm. [The Lovedale Historical series, no. 1] Bibliography: p.167-172. [BV3557.W53H6] 56-22641
1. Williams, Joseph, 1780-1818 2. Missions—Africa, South. I. Title.

Williams, Lacey Kirk, 1871-1940.

HORACE, Lillian B. 286'.133 B
"Crowned with glory and honor" : the life of Rev. Lacey Kirk Williams / by Lillian B. Horace ; edited by L. Venchael Booth. 1st ed. Hicksville, N.Y. : Exposition Press, c1978. 246 p. : port. ; 22 cm. [BX6455.W54H67] 78-100358 ISBN 0-682-48939-5 : 8.00
1. Williams, Lacey Kirk, 1871-1940. 2. Baptists—Clergy—Biography. 3. Clergy—United States—Biography. I. Booth, L. Venchael. II. Title.

Williams, Mrs. Wanda (Smolinska) 1844-1931.

WILLIAMS, Thomas David, 1872- 920.7
The story of a mother, by Rev. Thomas David Williams. New York, Cincinnati [etc.] Benziger brothers, 1935. x, 374 p. pl., ports. 19 cm. [BX4705.W56W5] 35-5952
1. Williams, Mrs. Wanda (Smolinska) 1844-1931. I. Title.

Williams, Pat, 1940-

WILLIAMS, Pat, 1940- 248'.2'0924 B
The gingerbread man: Pat Williams—then and now, by Pat Williams and Jerry B. Jenkins. [1st ed.] Philadelphia, A. J. Holman Co. [1974] 119 p. illus. 21 cm. [BV4935.W54A33] 74-11309 ISBN 0-87981-038-6 5.95
1. Williams, Pat, 1940- 2. Conversion. I. Jenkins, Jerry B., joint author. II. Title.

Williams, Rebecca (Swain)

WILLIAMS, Nancy Clement. 922.8373
After 100 years. [Salt Lake City? 1951] 234 p. illus. 21 cm. [BX8695.W546W5] 51-39054
1. Williams, Rebecca (Swain) 1798-1861. 2. Williams, Frederick Granger, 1787-1842. 3. Mormons and Mormonism. I. Title.

Williams, Richard, 1815-1851.

HAMILTON, James, 1814-1867. 922.782
A memoir of Richard Williams, surgeon; catechist to the Patagonian missionary society in Terra del Fuego. By James Hamilton... New York, R. Carter & brothers, 1854. viii, 255 p. front. (port.) 17 1/2 cm. First published, London, 1854. [BV2853.P4H3 1854a] 9-22523
1. Williams, Richard, 1815-1851. 2. Missions—Patagonian. I. Title.

HAMILTON, James, 1814-1867. 922.782
A memoir of Richard Williams, surgeon; catechist to the Patagonian missionary society in Tierra del Fuego. By James Hamilton... New York, Carlton & Phillips, 1855. 270 p. 17 cm. [BV2853.P4H3 1855] 33-23868
1. Williams, Richard, 1815-1851. 2. Missions—Patagonian. I. Title.

Williams, Roger, 1604?-1683.

COTTON, John, 1584-1652. 261.7
The bloudy tenent, washed, and made white in the bloud of the Lambe / by John Cotton. New York : Arno Press, 1972. 144 p. ; 24 cm. (Research library of colonial Americana) Reprint of the 1647 ed. published by H. Allen, London. [BV741.W58C6 1972] 78-141105 ISBN 0-405-03319-2 : 20.00
1. Williams, Roger, 1604?-1683. The bloudy tenent of persecution, for cause of conscience. 2. Liberty of conscience. I. Title. II. Series.

GILPIN, W. Clark. 286'.1'0924
The millenarian piety of Roger Williams / W. Clark Gilpin. Chicago : University of Chicago Press, 1979. viii, 214 p. ; 23 cm. Includes index. Bibliography: p. 201-209. [BX6495.W55G54] 78-20786 ISBN 0-226-29397-1 lib. bdg. : 17.00
1. Williams, Roger, 1604?-1683. 2. Millennialism—History of doctrines. I. Title.

KING, Henry Melville, 1838-1919. 920.
The baptism of Roger Williams; a review of Rev. Dr. W. H. Whitsitt's inference, by Henry Melville King ... with an introduction by Rev. Jesse B. Thomas ... Providence, Preston & Rounds co., 1897. x, 145 p. 19 1/2 cm. [BX6495.W55K5] 12-34923
1. Williams, Roger, 1604?-1683. 2. Whitsitt, William Heth, 1841-1911. A question in Baptist history. I. Title.

MERRIMAN, Titus Mooney, 1822-1912. 922
The Pilgrims, Puritans, and Roger Williams, vindicated: and his sentence of banishment, ought to be revoked. By Rev. T. M. Merriman ... Boston, Bradley & Woodruff, 1892. xii, 312 p. 20 x 15 cm. [F67.M57] 1-12041
1. Williams, Roger, 1604?-1683. 2. Puritans. 3. Pilgrim fathers. 4. Massachusetts—Hist.—Colonial period. I. Title.

MERRIMAN, Titus Mooney, 1822-1912. 922
"Welcome, Englishmen"; or, Pilgrims, Puritans and Roger Williams vindicated and his sentence of banishment ought to be revoked. By Rev. T. M. Merriman ... 2d ed. Boston, Arena publishing company, 1896. xii, 320 p. 20 x 16 cm. [F67.M58] 1-12042
1. Williams, Roger, 1604?-1683. 2. Puritans. 3. Pilgrim fathers. 4. Massachusetts—Hist.—Colonial period. I. Title.

MORGAN, Edmund Sears. 322.1
Roger Williams; the church and the state[by] Edmund S. Morgan. [1st ed.] New York, Harcourt, Brace & World [1967] 170 p. 21 cm. Bibliographical references included in "Notes" (p. 145-161) [F82.W789] 67-25999
1. Williams, Roger, 1604?-1683. 2. Church and state.

POLISHOOK, Irwin H. 261.7'2'08
Roger Williams, John Cotton, and religious freedom; a controversy in new and old England [by] Irwin H. Polishook. Englewood Cliffs, N.J., Prentice-Hall [1967] vi, 122 p. 21 cm. (American historical sources series: research and interpretation) Includes bibliographical references. [F82.W792] 67-20229
1. Williams, Roger, 1604?-1683. 2. Cotton, John, 1584-1652. 3. Religious liberty. I. Title.

SEAGER, Allan, 1906- 920.02
They worked for a better world, by Allan Seager; illustrated by Theodore Haupt ... New York, The Macmillan company, 1939. 2 p. l., 123, [1] p. illus. 20 cm. (The peoples library. [4]) [Full name: John Braithwaite Allan Seager] [CT214.S4] 39-27270
1. Williams, Roger, 1604?-1683. 2. Paine, Thomas, 1737-1809. 3. Emerson, Ralph Waldo, 1803-1882. 4. Stanton, Mrs. Elizabeth (Cady) 1815-1902. 5. Bellamy, Edward, 1850-1898. I. Title.
Contents omitted.

SMYTH, Clifford, 1866- 923.273
Roger Williams and the fight for religious

freedom, by Clifford Smyth ... New York and London, Funk & Wagnalis company, 1931. 171 p. 19 cm. (His Builders of America, v. 6) [E178.S68 vol. 6] [F82.W7956] 920.073 31-35719
1. Williams, Roger, 1604!-1683 I. Title.

WHITSITT, William Heth, 1841-1911. 265'.1
A question in Baptist history / William H. Whitsitt. New York : Arno Press, 1980. 164 p. ; 21 cm. (The Baptists tradition) Reprint of the 1896 ed. published by C. T. Dearing, Louisville, Ky. [BX6231.W5 1980] 79-52611 ISBN 0-405-12476-7 : 12.00
1. Williams, Roger, 1604?-1683. 2. Baptists—History. 3. Baptists—England. I. Title. II. Series: Baptist tradition.

WILLIAMS, Roger, 1604?-1683. 277.4
Complete writings; 7v. New York, Russell [c.]1963. 7v. (various p.) facsims. 27cm. 63-11034 100.00 lim. ed., set,
I. Title.

WILLIAMS, Roger, 1604?-1683. 277.4
Complete writings. New York, Russell & Russell, 1963. 7 v. facsims. 27 cm. "The new matter ... will be found in volume seven ... in order to retain the original pagination of the first six volumes ... [of] the Narragansett edition." "Limited edition of four hundred sets." [BX6495.W55A2] 63-11034
I. Title.

Williams, Roger, 1604?-1683—Bibliography.

COYLE, Wallace. 016.9745'02'0924
Roger Williams : a reference guide / Wallace Coyle. Boston : G. K. Hall, c1977. xiii, 102 p. ; 24 cm. (Reference guides in literature) Includes indexes. [Z8976.42.C68] [F82.W] 76-44400 ISBN 0-8161-7986-7 lib.bdg. : 12.00
1. Williams, Roger, 1604?-1683—Bibliography.

Williams, Roger, Sir, 1540?-1595.

WILSON, John Dover, 1881-1969. 274.2
Martin Marprelate and Shakespeare's Fluellen; a new theory of the authorship of the Marprelate tracts. [Folcroft, Pa.] Folcroft Library Editons (sic) 1971. 74 p. 26 cm. Reprint of the 1912 ed. Includes bibliographical references. [BR757.W5 1971] 72-194068 10.00
1. Williams, Roger, Sir, 1540?-1595. 2. Shakespeare, William, 1564-1616. King Henry V. 3. Marprelate controversy. I. Title.

Williams, Samuel Wells, 1812-1884.

WILLIAMS, Frederick Wells, 1857-1928. 327.51'073
The life and letters of Samuel Wells Williams, LL.D., missionary, diplomatist, sinologue. Wilmington, Del., Scholarly Resources [1972] vi, 490 p. port. 23 cm. Reprint of the 1889 ed. published by G. P. Putnam's Sons, New York. [DS763.W5W5 1972] 72-79841 ISBN 0-8420-1355-5
1. Williams, Samuel Wells, 1812-1884. 2. Missions—China. 3. Taiping Rebellion, 1850-1864. I. Title.

Williams, Sir George, 1821-1905.

HODDER-WILLIAMS, John Ernest, Sir, 1876-1927 922
The life of Sir George Williams, founder of the Young men's Christian association, by J. E. Hodder Williams ... New York, A. C. Armstrong & son, 1906. xv, 358 p. front., plates, ports., facsim; 20 1/2 cm. [BV1085.W4H6 1906a] 6-42910
1. Williams, Sir George, 1821-1905. I. Title.

Williams, Thomas, David, 1872-ed.

MARGOT, Antoinette, 1843-1925. 922.273
The story of Antoinette Margot, a descendant of the Huguenots, by Rev. Thomas David Williams ... Baltimore, Md., John Murphy company, 1931. 216 p. front., plates, ports. 20 cm. "This story is ... told substantially in her own words."--Pre. [Full name: Henriette Antoinette Margot] [BX4705.M3252A3] 31-34503
1. Williams, Thomas, David, 1872-ed. I. Title.

Willing, William C., 1829-1894.

WILLING, Jennie (Fowler) Mrs., 1834- 922.773
A prince of the realm. Lessons from the life of Rev. W. C. Willing, D.D. By J. Fowler Willing ... Cincinnati, Cranston & Curts. New York, Hunt & Eaton, 1895. 56 p. 19 1/2 cm. [BX8495.W64W5] 37-12161
1. Willing, William C., 1829-1894. I. Title.

Willingham, Robert Josiah, 1854-1914.

WILLINGHAM, Elizabeth Walton. 922.
Life of Robert Josiah Willingham, by his daughter, Elizabeth Walton Willingham. Nashville, Tenn., Sunday school board of the Southern Baptist convention [c1917] ix, 11-282 p. front., pl., ports. 23 cm. $1.50. [BX6495.W6W6] 17-18043
1. Willingham, Robert Josiah, 1854-1914. I. Title.

Willis, Henry Milton, 1858-1885.

SIMMS, Joseph D. 922.773
Soul-saving; or, Life and labors of Henry M. Willis, evangelist and missionary, embracing an account of the revivals in which he labored in America, and of his missionary work under Bishop Taylor in Africa, together with a sketch of the life and work of Mrs. Anna Willis, his wife... By Joseph D. Simms...with an introduction by Rev. William Jones... [Philadelphia] R. E. Lynch, printer, [1887] 263 p. front. (port.) plates. map. 18 cm. [BV3785.W58S5] 37-37091
1. Willis, Henry Milton, 1858-1885. 2. Willis, Mrs. Anna (Ruddick) 1861- 3. Methodist Episcopal church—Missions. 4. Missions—Africa, Central. I. Title.

Willis, Mary Farley, 1901-

WILLIS, Mary Farley, 1901- 286.7'3 B
People of that book / Mary Farley Willis. Washington : Review and Herald Pub. Association, c1981. 127 p. ; 19 cm. [BX6193.W57A36] 19 80-25877 ISBN 0-8280-0033-6 : Price unreported
1. Willis, Mary Farley, 1901- 2. Seveth-Day Adventists—Alabama—Clanton—Biography. 3. Clanton, Ala.—Biography. I. Title.

Willis, S Miller 1839-1891

DUNLAP, W. C. 922.773
Life of S. Miller Willis, the fire baptized lay evangelist ... By Rev. W. C. Dunlap. Atlanta, Ga., Constitution publishing co., 1892. 4 p. l., [vii]-vii, [9]-299 p. front. (port.) 21 cm. [BV3785.W59D8] 37-96752
1. Willis, S Miller 1839-1891 I. Title.

Williston, Seth, 1770-1851.

BANGS, Nathan, 1778-1862. 230
The reformer reformed: or, a second part of The errors of Hopkinsianism detected and refuted: Being an examination of Mr. Seth Williston's "Vindication of some of the most essential doctrines of the reformation." By Nathan Bangs ... New-York; Printed by John C. Totten, no. 9 Bowery, 1818. viii, [9]-355 p. 17 1/2 cm. [BX7251.B3] 19-17662
1. Williston, Seth, 1770-1851. Vindication of some of the most essential doctrines of the reformation. I. Title.

BANGS, Nathan, 1778-1862.
The reformer reformed: or, A second part of the Errors of Hopkinsianism detected and refuted: being an examination of Mr. Seth Williston's "Vindication of some of the most essential doctrines of the reformation." By Nathan Bangs ... New York, Printed by John C. Totten, no. 9 Bowery. 1816. viii, [9]-353, [2] p. 18 cm. [BX7251.B3 1816] 7-39364
1. Williston, Seth, 1770-1851. Vindication of some of the most essential doctrines of the reformation. 2. New England theology. I. Title.

Willoughby, Harold Rideout, 1890-

WIKGREN, Allen Paul, 1906- ed. 208.2
Early Christian origins; studies in honor of Harold R. Willoughby. Chicago, Quadrangle Books, 1961. 160 p. illus. 22 cm. Includes bibliography. [BR129.W5] 61-7933
1. Willoughby, Harold Rideout, 1890- 2. Christianity — Origin. 3. Jesus Christ — Historicity. 4. Church history — Primitive and early church. I. Title.

Wills, Ethical—Collected works.

HEBREW ethical wills / 296.3'85
selected and edited and with an introd. by Israel Abrahams. Facsim. of original 1926 ed., two v. in one / new foreword by Judah Goldin. Philadelphia : Jewish Publication Society of America, 1976, c1954. 19, xxvi, 348, 348 p. ; 22 cm. (The JPS library of Jewish classics) English and Hebrew. 1926 ed. issued under Hebrew title: Tsava'ot ge'one Yisrael. Photoreprint ed. Opposite pages numbered in duplicate. Includes bibliographical references. [BJ1286.W59T69 1976] 76-2898 ISBN 0-8276-0081-X : 14.50 ISBN 0-8276-0082-8 pbk. : 8.50
1. Wills, Ethical—Collected works. I. Abrahams, Israel, 1858-1925. II. Series: Jewish Publication Society of America. The JPS library of Jewish classics.

Wilmer, Richard Hooker, bp., 1816-1900.

WHITAKER, Walter Claiborne, 1867- 922
Richard Hooker Wilmer, second bishop of Alabama; a biography by Walter C. Whitaker ... Philadelphia, G. W. Jacobs & co. [1907] 2 p. l., 316, [7] p. front. (port.) 20 1/2 cm. [BX5995.W63W5] 7-39218
1. Wilmer, Richard Hooker, bp., 1816-1900. I. Title.

Wilmette, Ill. Bahal Temple.

MCDANIEL, Allen Boyer, 1879- 726.2
The spell of the temple. New York, Vantage Press [1953] 96p. illus. 23cm. [NA4710.M2] 54-814
1. Wilmette, Ill. Bahal Temple. I. Title.

Wilmington, Del. Holy Trinity church.

CURTIS, Charles Minot, 1859- 284.17512
Old Swedes church, Wilmington, Delaware, 1698-1938, by Charles M. Curtis ... and Charles Lee Reese, jr. Wilmington, Del., Delaware tercentenary commission, 1938. 52 p. front. (port.) illus. (map) plates. 22 cm. "First edition." [BX8076.W5H63] 39-5108
1. Wilmington, Del. Holy Trinity church. I. Reese, Charles Lee, 1903- joint author. II. Delaware tercentenary commission. III. Title.

Wilmington, N. C.—Economic conditions

NORTH Carolina. University. 330
... Economic survey of Wilmington, North Carolina, by members of the School of commerce and the Bureau of municipal research, at the request of the city government of Wilmington. Chapel Hill, N. C., The University of North Carolina press [1927] 122 p. incl. plates. fold. front., fold. pl. 23 cm. ([North Carolina. University] University extension division. University of North Carolina extension bulletin. vol. vi, no. 14) [LC6301.N43 vol. vi, no. 14] 28-21541
1. Wilmington, N. C.—Econ. condit. I. Title.

Wilmot (N.H.)—Church history.

LANGLEY, Florence, 1902- 280'.4'09'74272
With prayer and psalm : a history of Wilmot, New Hampshire churches / Florence Langley. Canaan, N.H. : Phoenix Pub., c1981. p. cm. Includes index. Bibliography: p. [BR560.W52L36] 19 81-5116 ISBN 0-914016-77-6 : 7.95
1. Wilmot (N.H.)—Church history. I. Title.

Wilson, Alpheus Waters, bp., 1834-1916.

HARRIS, Carlton Danner, 1864-1928. 922.773
Alpheus W. Wilson, a prince in Isreal, by Carlton Danner Harris ... Louisville, Ky., Board of church extension of the Methodist Episcopal church, South [1917!] xvii, 209 p. front., plates. ports. 21 cm. [BX8495.W646H3] 34-23419
1. Wilson, Alpheus Waters, bp., 1834-1916. I. Title.

Wilson, Capt. James, 1759 or 60-1814.

GRIFFIN, John, 1769-1834.
Memoirs of Capt. James Wilson, containing an account of his enterprises and sufferings in India, his conversion to Christianity, his missionary voyage to the South Seas, and his peaceful and triumphant death. By John Griffin. 2d American ed. With an appendix, exhibiting the glorious results of the South Sea mission. Portland, J. Adams, jr., 1827. iv, [9]-220 p. 19 cm. 16-2695
1. Wilson, Capt. James, 1759 or 60-1814. I. Title.

Wilson Co., Tenn.—Biography.

PARTLOW, Thomas E. 285'.1768'54
Sugg's Creek Cumberland Presbyterian Church : an early history / by Thomas E. Partlow. Lebanon, Tenn : Partlow, 1974. 52 p. : ill. ; 27 cm. Includes index. Bibliography: p. 44-45. [BX9211.W634S936] 75-305491
1. Sugg's Creek Cumberland Presbyterian Church, Wilson Co., Tenn. 2. Wilson Co., Tenn.—Biography. I. Title.

Wilson, Daniel, bp., 1778-1858.

BATEMAN, Josiah, 1802or3-1893. 922.354
The life of Daniel Wilson, D. D.. bishop of Calcuta and metropolitan of India. By Josiah Bateman Boston, Gould and Lincoln; New York, Sheldon and company; [etc., etc. 1860. xiii. [1], 744 p. incl. illus. (incl. plans, facism.) plates. front., pl., port., fold. map. 25 cm. Page 744 numbered 744-760. [BX5680.W5B3 1860 a] 36-2438
1. Wilson, Daniel. bp., 1778-1858. 2. India—Descr. & trav. I. Title.

NORTON, John Nicholas, 1820-1881. 922.35
Life of Bishop Wilson, of Calcutta. By the Rev. John N. Norton ... New York, General Protestant Episcopal Sunday school union and Church book society, 1863. xiv, [15]-334 p. front. (port.) illus., plates. 16 cm. [BX5680.W5N6] 34-21372
1. Wilson, Daniel, bp., 1778-1858. I. General Protestant Episcopal Sunday school union and church book society. II. Title.

Wilson, David Morris, 1798-1856.

DANFORTH, Joshua Noble, 1798-1861. 922.573
The faithful elder; a memoir of David M. Wilson; for thirty years a ruling elder in the Fourth Presbyterian church, and in the Western Presbyterian church of the city of Washington. By Joshua N. Danforth ... Philadelphia, Printed for the author by C. Sherman & son, 1860. xi, [13]-179 p. 20 cm. "Funeral address. By Rev. Byron Sunderland, D. D.": p. [170]-174 [BX9225.W46D3] 36-31916
1. Wilson, David Morris, 1798-1856. 2. Funeral sermons. I. Sunderland, Byron, 1819-1901. II. Title.

HASKELL, Thomas Nelson, 1826-1906. 922.573
The life and death of a Christian are our teachers. The funeral sermon of Elder David M. Wilson, the useful layman and unassuming benefactor of Washington city; delivered in the Western Presbyterian church, March 9, 1856, by the pastor, Rev. T. N. Haskell; to which is prefixed the funeral address, by Rev. B. Sunderland, D. D., delivered on the burial day, March 1, 1856. Washington, D. C., T. McGill, printer, 1856. 52 p. 22 cm. [BX9225.W46H3] 36-31917
1. Wilson, David Morris, 1798-1856. 2. Presbyterian church—Sermons. 3. Funeral sermons. I. Sunderland, Byron, 1819-1901. II. Title.

Wilson, Edmund, 1895-1972.

WILSON, Edmund, 1895-1972. 221.4'4
Israel and The Dead Sea scrolls / Edmund Wilson. New York : Farrar, Straus, Giroux, 1978. xii, 420 p. ; 19 cm. Includes index. [BM487.W498 1978] 78-7365 ISBN 0-374-51438-0 : pbk. : 4.95
1. Wilson, Edmund, 1895-1972—Journeys—Israel. 2. Dead Sea scrolls. 3. Bible. O.T. Genesis—Criticism, interpretation, etc. 4. Israel—Description and travel. 5. Authors, American—20th century—Biography. I. Wilson, Edmund, 1895-1972. The Dead Sea scrolls, 1947-1969. 1978. II. Title: Israel. III. Title: The Dead Sea scrolls.

Wilson, Eleanor, 1891-

CORMACK, Maribelle, 1902- 922
The lady was a skipper; the story of Eleanor Wilson, missionary extraordinary to the Marshall and Caroline Islands. Foreword by Eleanor Wilson. New York, Hill and Wang, 1956. 224 p. 21 cm. [BV3678.W5C6] 56-10675
1. Wilson, Eleanor, 1891- I. Title.

Wilson, George Washington, 1853-

CALDWELL, John Walker, 1825-1890. 922.773
Evangelism and the revival work of Rev. G. W. Wilson. By Rev. J. W. Caldwell ... With an introduction by Rev. W. F. Short ... [St. Louis] Published by the author [Press of C. B. Woodward] 1884. xvi, [17]-248 p. front. (port.) plates. 20 cm. [BX8495.W65C3] 37-12162
1. Wilson, George Washington, 1853- 2. Evangelistic work. I. Title.

Wilson, Henry, 1841-1906.

WILSON, Henry, 1841-1908.
The internal Christ, by Henry Wilson ... New York city, Alliance press co. [1908] 2 p. l., [7]-92 p. 18 1/2 cm. 10-13318
I. Title.

WILSON, Madele. 922
Henry Wilson, one of God's best, by Madele Wilson and A. B. Simpson. New York, The Alliance press company [c1908] 197, [1] p. front., plates, ports. (part col.) 20 cm. Chapters V-IX inclusive, by A. B. Simpson. [BX5995.W7W6 1908a] 18-5825
1. Wilson, Henry, 1841-1906. I. Simpson, Albert B., 1844- joint author. II. Title.

Wilson, Henry Joseph, 1833-1914.

FOWLER, William Stewart. 322.4'092'4 B
A study in radicalism and dissent: the life and times of Henry Joseph Wilson, 1833-1914 [by] W. S. Fowler. Westport, Conn., Greenwood Press [1973, c1961] 192 p. port. 22 cm. Includes bibliographical references. [HN385.F6 1973] 72-11684 ISBN 0-8371-6673-X 9.50
1. Wilson, Henry Joseph, 1833-1914. I. Title.

FOWLER, William Stewart. 322.4'092'4 B
A study in radicalism and dissent: the life and times of Henry Joseph Wilson, 1833-1914 [by] W. S. Fowler. Westport, Conn., Greenwood Press [1973, c1961] 192 p. port. 22 cm. Includes bibliographical references. [HN385.F6 1973] 72-11684 ISBN 0-8371-6673-X
1. Wilson, Henry Joseph, 1833-1914. I. Title.

Wilson, Hugh, 1794-1868.

CUNNINGHAM, Thomas McHutchin, 1887. 922.573
Hugh Wilson, a pioneer saint; missionary to the Chickasaw Indians and pioneer minister in Texas; with a genealogy of the Wilson family including 422 descendents of Rev. Lewis Feuilleteau Wilson, I., by T. M. Cunningham. [Dallas, Tex., Printed by Wilkinson printing co., c1938] xi, 150 p. illus. (incl. ports.) 20 cm. Bibliography: p. 144-145. [BX9225.W463C8] 39-20800
1. Wilson, Hugh, 1794-1868. 2. Wilson family (Lewis Feuilleteau Wilson, 1753-1804) I. Title.

Wilson, James 1760-1839.

DEHUFF, Elizabeth (Willis) 1886-
Family of the Rev. James Wilson, of Barnwell County, South Carolina. [Augusta? Ga.] 1963. 55 p. facsim., maps. 23 cm. Caption title. "Records ... concerning the Wilson or Willson family in North Carolina": p. 38-40. 68-88786
1. Wilson, James, b. 1770. 2. Wilson family (James Wilson, fl. 1775) I. Title.

DEHUFF, Elizabeth (Willis) 1886-
Family of the Rev. James Wilson, of Barnwell County, South Carolina. [Augusta? Ga.] 1963. 55 p. facsim., maps. 23 cm. Caption title. "Records ... concerning the Wilson or Willson family in North Carolina": p. 38-40. 68-88786
1. Wilson, James, b. 1770. 2. Wilson family (James Wilson, fl. 1775) I. Title.

VOSE, James Gardiner, 1830-1908. 285.87452
Commemorative discourses preached in the Beneficent Congregational church, Providence, R.I., October 18, 1868, by James G. Vose, pastor. To which are appended some historical notes and reminiscences, and a list of the members of the church. Providence, Beneficent Congregational church, 1869. 135, [1] p. front., ports. 19 cm. [BX7255.P9B48] 38-14616
1. Wilson, James, 1760-1830. 2. Providence. Beneficent Congregational church. I. Title.

WILSON, Arthur Edward. 922.573
Paddy Wilson's meeting-house in Providence Plantations, 1791-1839; being an account of a genial Irish parson who shaped a community's culture and life. Boston, Pilgrim Press [1950] vii, 278 p. 22 cm. Bibliography: p.270-274. [BX7260.W55W5] 50-4825
1. Wilson, James 1760-1839. 2. Providence, Beneficent Congregational Church. I. Title.

Wilson, James Stetson, 1822-1840

HORTON, Jotham. 922.773
A tribute to James Stetson Wilson: containing an account of his life, Christian experience, happy death, miscellaneous writings and selections from H. H. White, Young, & c. also, a sermon delivered at his funeral, by Rev. Jotham Horton. Lowell, E. A. Rice and company; Boston, D. S. King, 1840. 144 p. 15 cm. [BX8495.W648H6] 32-30388
1. Wilson, James Stetson, 1822-1840 I. Wilson, James Stetson, 1822-1840. II. Title.

Wilson, Leland.

WILSON, Leland. 242'.4
Living with wonder / Leland Wilson. Waco, Tex. : Word Books, c1976. 128 p. ; 21 cm. [BV4832.2.W57] 76-19543 ISBN 0-87680-839-9 pbk. : 3.25
1. Wilson, Leland. 2. Meditations. I. Title.

WILSON, Leland. 248.4'865
Silver City / by Leland Wilson. Elgin, Ill. : Brethren Press, [1980] p. cm. [BV4501.2.W562] 80-10212 ISBN 0-87178-790-3 pbk. : 4.95
1. Wilson, Leland. 2. Christian life—Church of the Brethren authors. 3. Silver City, Calif. I. Title.

Wilson, Robert Anton, 1932-

WILSON, Robert Anton, 1932- 133
Cosmic trigger : final secret of the illuminati / by Robert Anton Wilson ; illustrated by John Thompson. Berkeley, Calif. : And/Or Press, c1977. p. cm. Includes bibliographical references and index. [BF1408.2.W54A33] 77-89429 ISBN 0-915904-29-2 pbk. : 5.95
1. Wilson, Robert Anton, 1932- 2. Occult sciences—Biography. 3. Occult sciences. I. Title.

Wilson, Samuel Thomas, 1761-1824.

O'DANIEL, Victor Francis, 1868- 922.273
A light of the church in Kentucky; or, The life, labors, and character of the Very Rev. Samuel Thomas Wilson...pioneer educator and the first provincial of a religious order in the United States, by the Very Rev. V. F. O'Daniel... Washington, D.C., The Dominicana [1932] xiv, 333 p. front., illus. (map) plates, ports. 22 1/2 cm. Bibliography: p. 322-325. [BX4705.W57O5] 34-12552
1. Wilson, Samuel Thomas, 1761-1824. 2. Catholic church in Kentucky. I. Title.

Wilson, Valere E. 1904-

WILSON, Mabel Reed, Mrs. 920.7
The ministry of Faith, by Mabel Reed Wilson ... Boston, The Christopher publishing house [c1933] 92 p. 2 port. (incl. front.) 21 cm. [CT275.W5825W5] 33-23233
1. Wilson, Valere E. 1904- I. Title. II. Title: Faith, The ministry of.

Wilton, Richard, 1827-1903.

YOUNG, Mary Blamir. 283'.0924
Richard Wilton: a forgotten Victorian. London, Allen & Unwin, 1967. 3-225p. 8 plates, illus., geneal. table, ports. 23cm. [BX5199.W69Y6] (B) 68-98929 5.25 bds.,
1. Wilton, Richard, 1827-1903. I. Title. Distributed by Fernhill House, 162 E. 23 St., New York, N.Y. 10010.

Winans, William, 1788-1857.

HOLDER, Ray. 286'.6'0924 B
William Winans : Methodist leader in antebellum Mississippi / by Ray Holder. Jackson : University Press of Mississippi, 1976. p. cm. Includes index. Bibliography: p. [BX8495.W657H64] 76-26967 ISBN 0-87805-027-2 :7.95
1. Winans, William, 1788-1857. 2. Methodist Church—Clergy—Biography. 3. Clergy—Mississippi—Biography. 4. Mississippi—Biography.

Winchelsea, Robert de, Abp. of Canterbury, d.1313-

DENTON, Jeffrey Howard. 322'.1'0924
Robert Winchelsey and the crown, 1294-1313 : a study in the defence of ecclesiastical liberty / Jeffrey H. Denton. Cambridge [Eng.] ; New York : Cambridge University Press, 1980. p. cm. (Cambridge studies in medieval life and thought : 3d series; v. 14) Includes index. Bibliography: p. [BR754.W56D46] 79-41807 ISBN 0-521-22963-4 : 32.50
1. Winchelsey, Robert, Abp. of Canterbury, d. 1313- 2. Church and state in England—History. 3. England—Church history—Medieval period, 1066-1485. I. Title. II. Series.

Winchester cathedral.

SELWYN, Edward Gordon, 1885 726.6094227
The story of Winchester cathedral, by E. G. Selwyn... London, New York [etc.] R. Tuck & sons, ltd, 1934. ix, 11-78 p., 1 l. front., plates, fold. plan. 19 cm. Bibliography: leaf at end. [NA5471.W6S4] 33-3035
1. Winchester cathedral. I. Title.

YOUNG, John, 1585-1654. 922.
The diary of John Young, S.T.P., dean of Winchester 1616 to the commonwealth; extracts transcribed and edited by Florence Remington Goodman. London, Society for promoting Christian knowledge; New York and Toronto, The Macmillan co., 1928. xi, 183 p. front. (ports.) facsims, fold. geneal. tab. 20 cm. [BX5199.Y6A3] 29-3625
1. Winchester cathedral. 2. Gt. Brit.—Chruch history—Sources. I. Goodman, Mrs. Florence Remington (Merriott) ed. II. Title.

Winchester cathedral. Chapter.

GOODMAN, Florence Remington (Merriott) Mrs. 942.27
Reverend landlords and their tenants; scenes and characters on Winchester manors after the restoration, by Florence Remington Goodman ... with a preface by A. W. Goodman ... Winchester, Warren and son, limited, 1930. 98 p. front. (phot.) 20 cm. Map on front lining-paper. [DA690.W67G6] 254 32-5892
1. Winchester cathedral. Chapter. 2. Church lands—Gt. Brit. I. Title.

Winchester, Elhanan, 1751-1797.

BENNEVILLE, George de, 1703-1793. 24-25250
Some remarkable passages in the life of Dr. George de Benneville, late of Germantown. Pennsylvania, who departed this life in March, 1793, in the ninetieth year of his age, including what he saw and heard in a trance of forty-two hours' duration. both in the regions of happiness and misery; together with a brief account of his cruel persecution in France for preaching the gospel. Translated from the French of his own manuscript. To which is prefixed a recommendatory preface by the translator, Rev. Elhann Winchester. A reprint from the American ed. of 1880. Rev. and cor. With notes and addenda not hitherto published. Germantown, Pa., C. Cleaves, 1890. 55 p. 19 cm. [BF1283.D44A5]
I. Winchester, Elhanan, 1751-1797, tr. II. Title.

REVEREND Elhanan Winchester: biography and letters. 289.1'0924 B New York, Arno Press, 1972. 252, 100 p. port. 23 cm. (Religion in America, series II) Reprint of Biography of Rev. Elhanan Winchester, by E. M. Stone, first published 1836; and of Ten letters addressed to Mr. Paine, in answer to his pamphlet, entitled The age of reason, by E. Winchester, first published 1795. [BX9969.W7R48] 72-38464 ISBN 0-405-04090-3
1. Winchester, Elhanan, 1751-1797. 2. Paine, Thomas, 1737-1809. The age of reason. I. Stone, Edwin Martin, 1805-1883. Biography of Rev. Elhanan Winchester. 1972. II. Winchester, Elhanan, 1751-1797. Ten letters addressed to Mr. Paine, in answer to his pamphlet, entitled The age of reason. 1972.

STONE, Edwin Martin, 1805-1883. 922.8173
Biography of Rev. Elhanan Winchester. By Edwin Martin Stone. Boston, H. B. Brewster, 1836. xi, [13]-252 p. 20 cm. "Mr. Winchester's publications": p. [251]-252. [BX9969.W7S8] 37-13900
1. Winchester, Elhanan, 1751-1797. I. Title.

Winchester, Eng. (Diocese)

BENHAM, William, 1831-1910.
... Winchester, By William Benham ... With map. Published under the direction of the Tract committee. London, Society for promoting Christian knowledge; New York, E. & J. B. Young & co., 1884. 2 p. l., [3]-285, [1] p. front. (fold. map) 17 cm. (Diocesan histories) [BX5107.W6B4] 4-203
1. Winchester, Eng. (Diocese) I. Title.

Winchester, Va. Grace Evangelical Lutheran Church.

EISENBERG, William Edward. 284.1755
This heritage; the story of Lutheran beginnings in the lower Shenandoah Valley, and of Grace Church, Winchester. Winchester, Va., Trustees of Grace Evangelical Lutheran Church, 1954. 395p. illus. 24cm. [BX8076.W52G7] 54-29668
1. Winchester, Va. Grace Evangelical Lutheran Church. I. Title.

Winchester, Va. Presbyterian Church.

WOODWORTH, Robert Bell, 1868- 285.1755
A history of the Presbyterian Church in Winchester, Virginia, 1780-1949, based on official documents; by Robert Bell Woodworth, with the collaboration of Clifford Duval Grim and Ronald S. Wilson. Winchester, Printed for the Church by Pifer Print. Co., 1950. 152 p. illus., ports., map. 24 cm. [BX9211.W64W6] 50-21591
1. Winchester, Va. Presbyterian Church. I. Title.

Windsor Castle. St. George's Chapel.

BLACKBURNE, Harry William, 1878- 726.6
The romance of St. George s Chapel, Windsor Castle, by Harry W. Blackburne and Maurice F. Bond. Foreword by E. K. C. Hamilton. [4th ed., rev. Windsor, Oxley, 1956] 90p. illus. 19cm. [NA5471.W73B6 1956] 57-41952
1. Windsor Castle. St. George's Chapel. I. Bond, Maurice Francis. II. Title.

BLACKBURNE, Harry William, 1878- 726.6
The romance of St. George's Chapel, Windsor Castle. New ed. rev., with additional chapters by M. F. Bond. Pref. by S. L. Ollard. London, New York, R. Tuck, 1947. 79 p. plates, plan. 19 cm. Errata slipinserted. "Books about St. George's Chapel": p. 75-76. [NA5471.W73B6 1947] 48-23803
1. Windsor Castle. St George's Chapel. I. Bond Maurice Francis, ed. II. Title.

BOND, Shelagh M ed. 726.8
The monuments of St. George's Chapel, Windsor Castle. [Windsor, Published for the Dean and canons of St. George's Chapel in Windsor Castle by Oxley, 1958] ix, 260p. 21 plates. 22cm. d(Historical monographs relating to St. George's Chapel, Windsor Castle) Bibliography: p. ivi-ix. [NA5471.W73B63] 59-41999
1. Windsor Castle. St. George's Chapel. I. Title. II. Series.

Windsor Castle. St. George's Chapel—History.

WINDSOR Castle. St. George's Chapel. 942.2'96
The Saint George's Chapel quincentenary handbook : programme of events and catalogue of the exhibition / edited by Maurice Bond [for] the Dean and Canons of Windsor. [Windsor] : Oxley and Son (Windsor) Ltd., 1975. [1], 77 p., [4] p. of plates : ill. (some col.), facsims., plan, ports. (1 col.) ; 22 cm. On cover: 500 years, Saint George's Chapel, Windsor Castle: the quincentenary handbook; programme of events and exhibition catalogue, 1975. [BX5195.W5S248 1975] 75-327374 ISBN 0-901072-23-0 : £0.50
1. Windsor Castle. St. George's Chapel—History. 2. Windsor Castle. St. George's Chapel—Exhibitions. I. Bond, Maurice Francis. II. Title.

Windsor, Conn. Congregational church.

HOLSWORTH, Dorris Campbell. 285.87462
Pathways to the light, a pageant in celectration of the tercentenary of the founding of the first church of Windsor, Connecticut, March 20, 1630; written and directed by Doris Campbell Holsworth, participated in by descendants of the founders of the church and other men, women and children of Windsor and Hartford... [Windsor, Conn.] B. S. Caster, printer, c1930. 3 p., l., [9]-52 p. plates. 23 cm. [BX7255.W6F5] 30-20994
1. Windsor, Conn. Congregational church. 2. Pageants—Windsor, Conn. I. Title.

Winebrenner, John, 1797-1860.

KERN, Richard, 1932- 289.9 B
John Winebrenner: nineteenth century reformer. Harrisburg, Pa., Central Pub. House, 1974. xi, 226 p. illus. 23 cm. Bibliography: p. 215-226. [BX7096.W5K47] 74-84501
1. Winebrenner, John, 1797-1860.

Wingren, Gustaf, 1910-

WINGREN, Gustaf, 1910- 230
Creation and Gospel : the new situation in European theology / Gustaf Wingren ; with introd. and bibliography by Henry Vander Goot. New York : E. Mellen Press, 1980, c1979. lii, 189 p. ; 21 cm. (Toronto studies in theology) "The writings of Gustaf Wingren": p. 173-189. Includes bibliographical references and index. [BT695.W54] 78-78183 ISBN 0-88946-994-6 pbk. : 19.95
1. Wingren, Gustaf, 1910- 2. Creation—History of doctrines. I. Title. II. Series.

"Wings over Jordan" (Choir)

[TOWNSEND, Leroy Clifford] 1900- 784.756
"Thunder an' lightnin' britches", the astounding truth about "Wings over Jordan" by Ommo Aummen [pseud.] St. Petersburg, Fla., Blue peninsula sanctuary [1942] [74] p. front., pl., ports. 18 1/2 cm. The story of the "Wings over Jordan" choir and its originator, Reverend Glenn T. Settle. [ML3556.T69T4] 43-2210
1. Settle, Glenn Tom. 2. "Wings over Jordan" (Choir) I. St. Petersburg, Fla. Blue peninsula sanctuary. II. Title.

Winifred, Saint.

ROBERTUS, Prior of Shrewsbury. 230'.2 s
The admirable life of Saint Wenefride / Robert, Prior of Shrewsbury. Ilkley [Eng.] : Scolar Press, 1976. 5, 5, 275 p. : ill. ; 20 cm. (English recusant literature, 1558-1640 ; v. 319) (Series: Rogers, David Morrison, comp. English recusant literature, 1558-1640 ; v. 319.) "STC 21102." Reprint of the 1635 ed. [BX1750.A1E5 vol. 319] [BX4700.W58] 270.2'092'4 B 77-351171 ISBN 0-85967-333-2
1. Winifred, Saint. 2. Christian saints—Wales—Biography. I. Title. II. Series.

Winkworth, Catherine, 1827-1878.

LEAVER, Robin A. 264'.2'0924
Catherine Winkworth : the influence of her translations on English hymnody / by Robin A. Leaver. St. Louis : Concordia Pub. House ; Ann Arbor, Mich. : distributed by University Microfilms International, c1978. xii, 198 p. ; 23 cm. (Imprint series) Includes indexes. Bibliography: p. 168-172. [BV330.W53L42] 78-11936 ISBN 0-570-03788-3 : 11.00
1. Winkworth, Catherine, 1827-1878. 2. Hymns, German—Translations into English—History and criticism. 3. Hymns, English—Translations from German—History and criticism.

Winn, Viola Schuldt.

WINN, Viola Schuldt. 940.53'161'0924 B
The escape / Viola S. Winn. Wheaton, Ill. : Tyndale House Publishers, 1975. 213 p. ; 18 cm. Autobiographical. [BV3382.W56A33] 74-19645 ISBN 0-8423-0699-4 pbk. : 1.95
1. Winn, Viola Schuldt. I. Title.

Winnebago Indians—Religion and mythology.

RADIN, Paul, 1883-
The trickster, a study in American Indian mythology, with commentaries by Karl Kerenyi and C. G. Jung. New York, Philosophical Library [1956] xi, 211p. 23cm.
1. Winnebago Indians—Religion and mythology. I. Title.

RADIN, Paul, 1883-1959. 299'.7
The trickster; a study in American Indian mythology. With commentaries by Karl Kerenyi and C. G. Jung. Introductory essay by Stanley Diamond. New York, Schocken Books [1972, c1956] xxv, 211 p. 21 cm. [E99.W7R142 1972] 73-154004 ISBN 0-8052-0351-6
1. Winnebago Indians—Religion and mythology. 2. Trickster. I. Kerenyi, Karoly, 1897- II. Jung, Carl Gustav, 1875-1961. III. Title.

RADIN, Paul, 1883-1959. 301.2'08 S
Winnebago culture as described by themselves: The or[i]gin myth of the medicine rite; three versions. The historical origins of the medicine rite. Baltimore, Waverly Press, 1950. 78 p. 26 cm. (Special publications of Bollingen Foundation, no. 2) (Indiana University publications in anthropology and linguistics. Memoir 3) "Also issued as memoir 3 of the International Journal of American Linguistics." Winnebago texts with English translations. [GN4.I5 memoir 3 1950] [E99.W7] 299'.7 74-168004
1. Winnebago Indians—Religion and mythology. 2. Winnebago Indians—Rites and ceremonies. 3. Winnebago language—Texts. I. Title. II. Series: Bollingen Foundation. Special publication, no. 2. III. Series: Indiana. University. Indiana University publications in anthropology and linguistics. Memoir 3.

THE trickster;
a study in American Indian mythology, with commentaries by Karl Kerenyi and C. G. Jung. New York, Philosophical Library [1956] xi, 211p. 23cm.
1. Winnebago Indians- -Religion and mythology. I. Radin, Paul, 1883-

Winnington-Ingram, Arthur Foley, bp. of London, 1858-

HERBERT, Charles, 1864- 922.
Twenty-five years as bishop of London, by Charles Herbert. Milwaukee, Wis., Morehouse publishing co. [1926] vii, 118 p. front. (port.) 19 1/2 cm. Printed in Great Britain. [BX5199.W7H4] 27-24572
1. Winnington-Ingram, Arthur Foley, bp. of London, 1858- I. Title.

WINNINGTON-INGRAM, Arthur Foley, bp. of London, 1858- 922.342
Fifty years' work in London (1889-1939) by Arthur Foley Winnington-Ingram ... London, New York [etc.] Longmans, Green and co. [1940] xi, 249, [1] p. front., plates, ports., facsim. 23 1/2 cm. "First published 1940." [BX5199.W7A4 1940] 41-4195
I. Title.

WINNINGTON-INGRAM, Arthur Foley, bp. of London, 1858- 922.342
Fifty years' work in London (1889-1939) by Arthur Foley Winnington-Ingram ... London, New York [etc.] Longmans, Green and co. [1940] xi, 249, [1] p. front., plates, ports., facsim. 23 1/2 cm. "First published 1940." [BX5199.W7A4 1940] 41-4195
I. Title.

WINNINGTON-INGRAM, Arthur Foley, bp. of London, 1858- 252.
Why am I a Christian? by the Right Rev. and Right Hon. Arthur F. Winnington Ingram, D.D., lord bishop of London. New York, London, G. P. Putnam's sons, 1929. xi, 193 p. 20 1/2 cm. [BX5133.W57W5] 29-22035
I. Title.

Winston-Salem, N. C. Salem congregation (Moravian)

RONDTHALER, Edward, bp., 1842-1931. 284.6756
The Memorabilia of fifty years, 1877 to 1927, by Rt. Rev. Edward Rondthaler ... pastor of Salem congregation of the Moravian church at Winston-Salem, North Carolina. Raleigh, Edwards & Broughton company, 1928. xi, 520 p. front., plates, ports. 24 cm. viii, 58 p. front. (port.) pl. 24 cm. --Appendix to the Memorabilia of fifty years; containing Memorabilia of 1928, 1929, 1930, Memoir of Bishop Edward Rondthaler, who fell asleep January 31, 1931, The distinguished community service award. Raleigh, N. C., Edwards & Broughton company, 1931. [BX8581.W7R6 App.] 29-16783
1. Winston-Salem, N. C. Salem congregation (Moravian) 2. Moravians in North Carolina. 3. Winston-Salem, N. C.—Hist. I. Title.

Winthrop, John 1588-1649.

BANKS, Charles Edward, 1854-1931.
The Winthrop fleet of 1630; an account of the vessels, the voyage, the passengers and their English homes from original authorities. Baltimore, Genealogical Pub. Co., 1961. 118p. maps. 23cm.
1. Winthorop, John, 1588-1649. 2. Puritans. 3. Arbella (Ship) I. Title.

WHEELWRIGHT, John, 1592?-1679. 285'.9'0924
John Wheelwright: his writings, including his Fast-day sermon, 1637; and his Mercurius americanus, 1645; with a paper upon the genuineness of the Indian deed of 1629, and a memoir, by Charles H. Bell. Freeport, N.Y., Books for Libraries Press [1970] viii, 251 p. facsims. 23 cm. "First published 1876." Bibliography: p. [149]-151. [F67.W547 1970] 70-128897 ISBN 0-8369-5517-X
1. Winthrop, John, 1588-1649, supposed author. A short story. 2. Massachusetts—History—Colonial period, ca. 1600-1775—Sources. 3. New Hampshire—History—Colonial period, ca. 1600-1775—Sources. 4. Antinomianism.

Wintringham, Mrs. Eliza.

PARKINSON, William, 1774-1848, defendant.
Trial of Mr. William Parkinson, pastor of the First Baptist church in the city of New-York, on an indictment for assault and battery upon Mrs. Eliza Wintringham. Taken in short hand by William Sampson ... New-York: Printed by Largin & Thompson, no. 5 Burling slip, 1811. 84 p. 22 cm. Trial in the Court of general sessions, July, 1811. 28-11939
1. Wintringham, Mrs. Eliza. I. Sampson, William, 1764-1836, reporter. II. New York (County) Court of general sessions. III. Title.

Wirt, Sherwood Eliot.

WIRT, Sherwood Eliot. 269'.2'0924 B
Afterglow : the excitement of being filled with the spirit / by Sherwood Eliot Wirt. Grand Rapids, Mich. : Zondervan Pub. House, c1975. p. cm. [BR1725.W56A32] 75-21122 4.95 pbk. : 2.95
1. Wirt, Sherwood Eliot. 2. Revivals—Canada. I. Title.

WIRT, Sherwood Eliot. 248'.4
Freshness of the spirit / Sherwood Eliot Wirt. 1st ed. San Francisco : Harper & Row, c1978. xv, 88 p. ; 21 cm. Includes bibliographical references. [BV4501.2.W57 1978] 77-20442 ISBN 0-06-069604-4 : 5.95
1. Wirt, Sherwood Eliot. 2. Christian life—1960- 3. Holy Spirit. I. Title.

Wisconsin—Church history.

PEET, Stephen, 1797-1855. 277.
History of the Presbyterian and Congregational churches and ministers in Wisconsin. Including an account of the organization of the convention, and the plan of union. By Rev. Stephen Peet. Milwaukee, S. Chapman, 1851. 208 p. 15 cm. On spine: Churches in Wisconsin. [BR555.W6P4] 44-36211
1. Wisconsin—Church history. 2. Congregational churches in Wisconsin. Conference. 3. Presbyterian church in

Wisconsin. 4. Plan of union of Presbyterian and Congregational churches. I. Title.

Wisconsin Evangelical Lutheran Synod. Minnesota District.

GOLDEN jubilee history 284'.1776
of the Minnesota District of the Wisconsin Evangelical Lutheran Synod and its member congregations, 1918-1968. [Minneapolis, Ad Art Advertising Co., c1969] 367 p. illus. 24 cm. "Authorized by the Golden Jubilee Convention of the Minnesota District at Dr. Martin Luther College, New Ulm, Minnesota, July 29-August 1, 1968." [BX8061.W6G66] 74-158379
1. Wisconsin Evangelical Lutheran Synod. Minnesota District.

Wisdom.

BIBLE. O.T. Proverbs. 223'.7'052
English. Today's English. 1974.
Ancient wisdom for modern man : Proverbs and Ecclesiastes in Today's English version. New York : Simon and Schuster, [1974] c1972. 69 p. : ill. ; 22 cm. [BS1463 1974] 75-300640 ISBN 0-671-21893-X pbk. : 3.95
I. Bible. O.T. Ecclesiastes. English. Today's English. 1974. II. Title.

*CETI, Tau 248
Wisdom. New York, Carlton [c.1964] 93p. 22cm. 3.00
I. Title.

*CETI, Tau 248
Wisdom. New York, Carlton [c.1964] 93p. 22cm. 3.00
I. Title.

CLYMER, Reuben Swinburne 133
1878-
Ancient mystic oriental masonry, its teachings, rules, laws and present usages which govern the order at the present day... By Dr. R. Swinburne Clymer... Allentown, Pa., The Philosophical publishing co. [c1907] 196 p. 18 1/2 cm. [BF1611.C56] 7-18301
I. Title.

CONLEY, Kieran 189.4
A theology of wisdom; a study in St. Thomas. Dubuque, Iowa, Priory Pr. [c.1963] 171p. 23cm. Bibl. 63-12430 3.00
1. Thomas Aquinas, Saint, 1225?-1274. 2. Wisdom. I. Title.

HAYES, Patrick Joseph, 208.1
cardinal, 1867-1938.
Cardinal Hayes; a treasury of wisdom and knowledge, by Monsignor Germano Formica ... New York, H. F. Hobson & company, inc. [c1932] xvii p., 3 l., 3-214 p. front., illus., plates, ports., facsim. 21 cm. [BX890.H3] 33-3475
I. Formica, Germano, comp. II. Title. III. Title: A treasury of wisdom and knowledge.

HOLMES, John Andrew, 1874- 220
Wisdom in small doses, by Doctor John Andrew Holmes... Lincoln, Chicago [etc.] The University publishing company, 1927. 116 p. 21 cm. [BR125.H685] 27-24909
I. Title.

HOLMES, John Andrew, 1874- 220
Wisdom in small doses, by Doctor John Andrew Holmes... Lincoln, Chicago [etc.] The University publishing company, 1927. 116 p. 21 cm. [BR125.H685] 27-24909
I. Title.

JOHNSON, Willie Harry, 1870- 248
Beginning of wisdom, by Willie H. Johnson ... Chicago, Ill., W. H. Johnson, 1928. 8 p. l., 442 p. 21 cm. [BV4501.J575] 28-29461
I. Title.

LARSEN, Ludwig B. 1864-1929. 290
Ancient prehistoric wisdom, by Ludwig B. Larsen ... Long Beach, Calif., The Virgo publishing company [c1941] ix, [11]-289 p. incl. front. (map) illus. 24 cm. [BL95.L3] 41-8949
I. Title.

MCKANE, William 221.6
Prophets and wise men. Naperville, Ill., A.R. Allenson [c.1965] 136p. 22cm. (Studies in Biblical theol., no.44) Bibl. [BS1198.M18] 65-3390 2.85 pap.,
1. Wisdom. 2. Bible. O. T.—Prophecies. I. Title. II. Series.

MAURICE, Charles, comp.
Essence of wisdom. New York, C. Maurice, 1900. 62 p. 16 cm. 0-4750
I. Title.

[MERTON, Arthur]
The book of wisdom unsealing the mental, social and physical life of man ... Chicago, R. H. Wisdom & co., 1882. 6 p. l., [3]-296 p. illus., plates (partly col.) 23 cm. [BF885.O2M54] ca 11
I. Title.

NANCE, Henry C 1887- 236.
The book of wisdom, composed by Henry C. Nance ... [Milwaukee, Krueger printing co., 1923] [52] p. illus. (port.) 20 cm. [BR126.N3] ca 23
I. Title.

RITTENHOUSE, Norman. 133
Gods in the making, by Norman Rittenhouse. [Los Angeles] Headquarters of the Father's wisdom [c1940] xi, 305 p. diagrs. 22 cm. "First edition." [BF1999.R542] [159.961] 41-26721
I. Father's wisdom, Los Angeles. II. Title.

WHEDBEE, J. William. 224'.1'06
Isaiah & wisdom [by] J. William Whedbee. Nashville, Abingdon Press [1971] 172 p. 23 cm. Bibliography: p. 155-164. [BS1515.2.W47] 75-134250 ISBN 0-687-19706-6 5.95
1. Bible O.T. Isaiah—Criticism, interpretation, etc. 2. Wisdom. I. Title.

Wisdom—Biblical teaching.

SUGGS, M. Jack. 226'.2
Wisdom, christology, and law in Matthew's Gospel [by] M. Jack Suggs. Cambridge, Harvard University Press, 1970. 132 p. 22 cm. [BS2545.W45S9] 75-95930 6.00
1. Jesus Christ—Person and offices. 2. Bible. N.T. Matthew—Criticism, interpretation, etc. 3. Wisdom—Biblical teaching. 4. Law (Theology)—Biblical teaching. I. Title.

Wisdom literature.

DE NORMANDIE, James, 1836- comp.
The beauty of wisdom; a volume of daily readings from some ancient writers for family, school, and private meditation, comp. by James De Normandie ... Boston and New York, Houghton, Mifflin and company, 1903. viii p., 1 l., 412 p., 1 l. 22 cm. 3-28854
I. Title.

HUGO, John. 208.1
The path to realization of the eternal; aphorisms and essays on the questions of life, creation and the universe. By John Hugo... Milwaukee, Wis., Students of ancient widsom, Liberty printing co. [c1933] 4 p. l., 72 p. 22 1/2 cm. [BL50.H8] 33-6345
I. Title.

MORGAN, Donn F. 221'.06
Wisdom in the Old Testament traditions / Donn F. Morgan. Atlanta, Ga. : John Knox Press, 1981. p. cm. Includes indexes. Bibliography: p. [BS1455.M67] 19 80-84653 ISBN 0-8042-0188-9 : 17.50 ISBN 0-8042-0189-7 (pbk.) : 8.95
1. Wisdom literature. I. Title.

THIND, Bhagat Singh. 211
The bible of humanity for supreme wisdom ... By Dr. Bhagat Singh Thind ... [Salt Lake City, 1928- v. ports. 19 cm. (v. 3: 21 cm.) [BL390.T45] 30-8393
I. Title. II. Title: Wisdom and the wheel.

TOLSTOI, Lev Nikolaevich, 126
graf, 1828-1910,comp.
...The pathway of life; tr. by Archibald J. Wolfe... New York, International book publishing company, 1919. 2 v. fronts. (ports.) 19 1/2 cm. (Russian author's library) At head of title: Leo Tolstoy. Cover-title: Teaching love and wisdom. "This sayings in these volumes are of varied authorship, having been gathered from Brahminical, Confucian and Buddhist sources, from the Gospels and the Epistles, and from the works of numerous thinkers both ancient and modern. Tolstoy retold [them] in his own language, arranging them under suitable captions, and interspersing them with the expressions of his own attitude to the problems of life." Author's foreword and Publisher's preface. [BD431.T65] 19-10231
I. Wolfe, Archibald John, 1878- tr. II. Title. III. Title: Teaching love and wisdom.

Wisdom literature—Criticism, Form.

MURPHY, Roland Edmund, 223'.066
1917-
The wisdom literature : Job, Proverbs, Ruth, Canticles, Ecclesiastes, and Esther / Roland E. Murphy. Grand Rapids, Mich. : W.B. Eerdmans Pub. Co., 1981. p. cm. (The Forms of the Old Testament literature ; v. 13) [BS1455.M87] 19 81-3191 ISBN 0-8028-1877-3 : 12.95
1. Bible. O.T. Job—Criticism, Form. 2. Bible. O.T. Ruth—Criticism, Form. 3. Bible. O.T. Esther—Criticism, Form. 4. Wisdom literature—Criticism, Form. I. Title. II. Series.

Wisdom literature—Criticism, interpretation, etc.

BEAUCAMP, Evode. 223
Man's destiny in the books of wisdom. [Translated by John Clarke] Staten Island, N.Y., Alba House [1970] xii, 217 p. 22 cm. Translation of La sagesse et la destin des elus, first published in 1957 as v. 2 of the author's Sous la main de Dieu. [BS1455.B3613] 73-110596 ISBN 0-8189-0159-4 4.95
1. Wisdom literature—Criticism, interpretation, etc. I. Title.

BRUEGGEMANN, Walter. 261.8
In man we trust; the neglected side of Biblical faith. Richmond, Va., John Knox Press [1973, c1972] 144 p. 21 cm. Includes bibliographical references. [BS1455.B78 1973] 72-1761 ISBN 0-8042-0199-4 4.95
1. Jews—History—To 586 B.C. 2. Wisdom literature—Criticism, interpretation, etc. 3. Theology—20th century. I. Title.

CRENSHAW, James L. 223'.06
Old Testament wisdom : an introduction / James L. Crenshaw. Atlanta : John Knox Press, c1981. 284 p. ; 21 cm. Includes indexes. Bibliography: p. [264]-272. [BS1455.C67] 19 80-82183 ISBN 0-8042-0143-9 : 16.50 (est.) ISBN 0-8042-0142-0 (pbk.) : 9.95 (est.)
1. Wisdom literature—Criticism, interpretation, etc. I. Title.

JOHNSON, L. D., 1916- 223
Israel's wisdom : learn and live / L. D. Johnson. Nashville : Broadman Press, [1975] 128 p. ; 20 cm. [BS1455.J63] 74-26312 ISBN 0-8054-8125-7 : 1.95
1. Wisdom literature—Criticism, interpretation, etc. I. Title.

*MONRO, Margaret T. 233.06
Enjoying the wisdom books. Foreword by Brendan McGrath. Chicago, Regnery [1967, c.1963] 111p. 18cm. (Lagos 61L-725) 1.45 pap.,
I. Title.

PERDUE, Leo G. 223'.06
Wisdom and cult : a critical analysis of the views of cult in the wisdom literature of Israel and the ancient Near East / by Leo G. Perdue. Missoula, Mont. : Published by Scholars Press for the Society of Biblical Literature, c1977. xiii, 390 p. ; 22 cm. (Dissertation series ; no. 30) Originally presented as the author's thesis, Vanderbilt University, 1976. Bibliography: p. 365-390. [BS1455.P4 1977] 76-47453 ISBN 0-89130-094-5 : 4.50
1. Wisdom literature—Criticism, interpretation, etc. 2. Cultus, Jewish. 3. Egyptian literature—Relation to the Old Testament. 4. Assyro-Babylonian literature—Relation to the Old Testament. I. Title. II. Series: Society of Biblical Literature. Dissertation series ; no. 30.

RAD, Gerhard von, 222'.1'066
1901-1971.
Wisdom in Israel. Nashville, Abingdon Press [1972] x, 330 p. 23 cm. Translation of Weisheit in Israel. Includes bibliographical references. [BS1455.R2313 1972b] 73-152746 ISBN 0-687-45756-4 12.95
1. Wisdom literature—Criticism, interpretation, etc. I. Title.

SCOTT, Robert Balgarnie 221.6
Young, 1899-
The way of wisdom in the Old Testament [by] R. B. Y. Scott. New York, Macmillan [1971] xv, 238 p. 22 cm. Includes bibliographical references. [BS1455.S37] 71-150075 7.95
1. Wisdom literature—Criticism, interpretation, etc. I. Title.

SHEPPARD, Gerald T., 221'.08 s
1946-
Wisdom as a hermeneutical construct : a study in the sapientializing of the Old Testament / Gerald T. Sheppard. Berlin ; New York : W. de Gruyter, 1979. p. cm. (Beiheft zur Zeitschrift fur die alttestamentliche Wissenschaft ; 151) Bibliography: p. [BS410.Z5 vol. 151] [BS1455] 229'.4'06 79-13156 ISBN 3-11-007504-0 : 42.50
1. Bible. O.T. Apocrypha. Ecclesiasticus—Criticism, interpretation, etc. 2. Bible. O.T. Apocrypha. Baruch—Criticism, interpretation, etc. 3. Bible. O.T.—Criticism, interpretation, etc. 4. Wisdom literature—Criticism, interpretation, etc. I. Title. II. Series: Zeitschrift fur die alttestamentliche Wissenschaft : Beihefte ; 151.

SKEHAN, Patrick William. 223'.06
Studies in Israelite poetry and wisdom, by Patrick W. Skehan. Washington, Catholic Biblical Association of America, 1971. xii, 265 p. 26 cm. (The Catholic Biblical quarterly. Monograph series, 1) Includes bibliographical references. [BS1455.S63] 77-153511
1. Bible. O.T. Psalms—Criticism, interpretation, etc. 2. Bible. O.T. Job—Criticism, interpretation, etc. 3. Wisdom literature—Criticism, interpretation, etc. I. Title. II. Series.

Wisdom literature—Criticism, interpretation, etc.—Addresses, essays, lectures.

ASPECTS of wisdom in Judaism 223
and early Christianity / Robert L. Wilken, editor. Notre Dame, Ind. : University of Notre Dame Press, [1975] xxii, 218 p. ; 21 cm. ([Studies in Judaism and Christianity in antiquity] ; no. 1) Papers presented at a seminar sponsored by the Dept. of theology, University of Notre Dame in 1973. Includes indexes. Bibliography: p. 201-210. [BS1455.A8] 74-27888 ISBN 0-268-00577-X : 13.95
1. Philo Judaeus. 2. Bible. N.T.—Relation to Old Testament—Addresses, essays, lectures. 3. Midrash—History and criticism. 4. Wisdom literature—Criticism, interpretation, etc.—Addresses, essays, lectures. 5. Christianity—Early church, ca. 30-600—Addresses, essays, lectures. I. Wilken, Robert Louis, 1936- II. Notre Dame, Ind. University. Dept. of Theology. III. Title. IV. Series.

ISRAELITE wisdom : 223
theological and literary essays in honor of Samuel Terrien / edited by John G. Gammie ... [et al.]. Missoula, MT : Scholars Press for Union Theological Seminary, c1977. p. cm. Includes index. Bibliography: p. [BS1455.I84] 77-17862 ISBN 0-89130-208-5 ISBN pbk. : 15.00
1. Terrien, Samuel L., 1911- —Addresses, essays, lectures. 2. Bible. O.T. Prophets—Criticism, interpretation, etc.—Addresses, essays, lectures. 3. Wisdom literature—Criticism, interpretation, etc.—Addresses, essays, lectures. I. Terrien, Samuel L., 1911- II. Gammie, John G.

STUDIES in ancient 223'.06'6
Israelite wisdom / selected with a prolegomenon by James L. Crenshaw. New York : Ktav Pub. House, 1976. xviii, 494 p. ; 24 cm. (The Library of Biblical studies) Bibliography: p. 46-60. [BS1455.S83] 75-31986 ISBN 0-87068-255-5 : 29.50
1. Wisdom literature—Criticism, interpretation, etc.—Addresses, essays, lectures. 2. Wisdom—Biblical teaching—Addresses, essays, lectures. I. Crenshaw, James L. II. Series.

Wisdom literature—Criticism, Textual.

WHYBRAY, R. N. 221'.08 s
The intellectual tradition in the Old Testament / R. N. Whybray. Berlin ; New York : De Gruyter, 1974. xii, 158 p. ; 24 cm. (Beiheft zur Zeitschrift fur die alttestamentliche Wissenschaft ; 135) Includes bibliographical references and index. [BS410.Z5 vol. 135] [BS1455] 223 73-78236 ISBN 3-11-004424-2 : 30.20
1. Wisdom literature—Criticism, Textual. 2. Wisdom—Biblical teaching. I. Title. II. Series: Zeitschrift fur die alttestamentliche Wissenschaft. Beihefte ; 135.

Wisdom literature—Relation to Egyptian literature.

BRYCE, Glendon E. 223'.7'06
A legacy of wisdom : the Egyptian contribution to the wisdom of Israel / Glendon E. Bryce. Lewisburg [Pa.] : Bucknell University Press, c1977. p. cm. Includes index. Bibliography: p. [BS1455.B79] 74-4984 ISBN 0-8387-1576-1 : 16.50
1. Bible. O.T. Proverbs—Criticism, interpretation, etc. 2. Wisdom literature—Relation to Egyptian literature. I. Title.

Wise, Isaac Mayer, 1819-1900.

HELLER, James Gutheim, 1892- 922.96
Isaac M. Wise: his life, work, and thought, by James G. Heller. [New York] Union of American Hebrew Congregations [1965] xxi, 819 p. 21 cm. Bibliography, including works of and about Rabbi Wise: p. 677-692. [BM755.W5H4] 64-24340
1. Wise, Isaac Mayer, 1819-1900. I. Title.

KNOX, Israel, 1904- 922.96
Rabbi in America: the story of Isaac M. Wise. [1st ed.] Boston, Little, Brown [1957] x. 173p. 22cm. (The Library of American biography) 'A notes on the sources':p. [165]-168. [BM755.W5K6] 57-11995
1. Wise, Isaac Mayer, 1819-1900. I. Title. II. Series.

KNOX, Israel, 1904- 922.96
Rabbi in America: the story of Issac M. Wise. [1st ed.] Boston, Little, Brown [1957] x, 173 p. 22 cm. (The Library of American biography) "A note on the sources": p. [165]-168. [BM755.W5K6] 57-11995
1. Wise, Isaac Mayer, 1819-1900. I. Title. II. Series.

LEWI, Isidor, 1850- 922.9673
Isaac Mayer Wise and Emanu-El [by] Isidor Lewi. [New York, Bloch publishing co., 1930] v, 108 numb. l. port., plates, facsims. 24 cm. Part of the plates are included in numbering. [BM755.W5L4] 30-29055
1. Wise, Isaac Mayer, 1819-1900. I. Title.

MAY, Max Benjamin, 1866-
Isaac Mayer Wise, the founder of American Judaism; a biography, by Max B. May ... New York and London, G. P. Putnam's sons, 1916. xi, 415 p. front., ports. 21 1/2 cm. "A list of the writings of Isaac Mayer Wise, prepared by Adolph S. Oke": p. 399-400. 17-6906
1. Wise, Isaac Mayer, 1819-1900. 2. Jews in the U.S. I. Title.

WILANSKY, Dena. 922.96
Sinai to Cincinnati; lay views on the writings of Isaac M. Wise, founder of reform Judaism in America, by Dena Wilansky. New York, Renaissance book company, 1937. 351 p. 22 1/2 cm. Bibliography: p. 351. [BM755.W5W5] 38-31984
1. Wise, Isaac Mayer, 1819-1900. 2. Jews—Religion. I. Title.

WISE, Isaac Mayer, 1819-1900. 301.45'19'24073 B
Reminiscences. [Translated from the German and] edited by David Philipson. New York, Arno Press, 1973 [c1901] 367 p. illus. 21 cm. (The Jewish people: history, religion, literature) Translated from the German. Reprint of the ed. published by L. Wise, Cincinnati. [BM755.W5A33 1973] 73-2233 ISBN 0-405-05294-4 20.00
1. Wise, Isaac Mayer, 1819-1900. 2. Jews in the United States. 3. Reform Judaism—United States. I. Philipson, David, 1862-1949, ed. II. Title. III. Series.

WISE, Isaac Mayer, 1819-1900. 296'.08
Selected writings of Isaac Mayer Wise. [Edited by] David Philipson and Louis Grossman[n] New York, Arno Press [1969] vi, 419 p. illus., ports. 23 cm. (Religion in America) Reprint of the 1900 ed. [BM45.W5 1969] 71-83433
1. Wise, Isaac Mayer, 1819-1900. 2. Judaism—Works to 1900.

Wise, Isaac Mayer, 1819-1900—Juvenile literature.

GUMBINER, Joseph Henry, 1906- 922.96
Isacc Mayer Wise, pioneer of American Judaism. New York, Union of American Hebrew Congregations [1959] 187p. illus. 21cm. [BM755.W5G8] 59-9711
1. Wise, Isaac Mayer, 1819-1900—Juvenile literature. I. Title.

Wise, John, 1652-1725.

COOK, George Allan. 922.573
John Wise, early American democrat. New York, King's Crown Press, 1952. 246p. 21cm. [BX7260.W565C6] 52-14615
1. Wise, John, 1652-1725. I. Title.

COOK, George Allan 285'.80924(B)
John Wise, early American democrat. New York, Octagon, 1966. ix, 246p. 21cm. Bibl. [BX7260.W565C6 1966] 66-28373 7.50
1. Wise, John, 1652-1725. I. Title.

WHITAKER, Nathaniel, 1730-1795.
A confutation of two tracts, entitled, A vindication of the New-England churches; and The churches quarrel espoused: written by the Reverend John Wise ... By Nathaniel Whitaker ... Boston: Printed by Isaiah Thomas, near the Mill-bridge. 1774. iv, 5-96 p. 20 cm. [BX7136.W62W4] 24-19711
1. Wise, John, 1652-1725. A vindication of the government of New England churches. 2. Wise, John, 1652-1725. The churches' quarrel espoused. I. Title.

Wise, Jonah Bondi, 1881-1959.

CAUMAN, Samuel. 296'.0924
Jonah Bondi Wise; a biography, by Sam Cauman. New York, Crown Publishers [1966?] ix, 214 p. illus., ports. 23 cm. [BM755.W52C3] 66-29745
1. Wise, Jonah Bondi, 1881-1959.

Wise, Karen.

WISE, Karen. 248.4
Confessions of a totaled woman / Karen Wise. Nashville, TN : T. Nelson, c1980. 128 p. : ill. ; 21 cm. [BV4501.2.W574] 80-10980 ISBN 0-8407-5725-5 pbk. : 6.95
1. Wise, Karen. 2. Christian life—1960- I. Title.

Wise, Stephen Samuel, 1874-1949.

UROFSKY, Melvin I. 296.8'346'0924 B
A voice that spoke for justice : the life and times of Stephen S. Wise / Melvin I. Urofsky. Albany : State University of New York Press, 1981. p. cm. (SUNY series in modern Jewish history) Includes index. Bibliography: p. [BM755.W53U76] 19 81-5676 ISBN 0-87395-538-2 : 49.00 ISBN 0-87395-539-0 pbk. : 16.95
1. Wise, Stephen Samuel, 1874-1949. 2. Rabbis—United States—Biography. 3. Zionists—United States—Biography. I. Title. II. Series.

VOSS, Carl Hermann. 922
Rabbi and minister; the friendship of Stephen S. Wise and John Haynes Holmes. New York Association Pr. [1968,C1964] 383p. ports., facsim. 22cm. Bibl. [BM755.W43V6] 2.75 pap.,
1. Wise, Stephen Samuel, 1874-1949. 2. Holmes, John Haynes, 1879- I. Title.

VOSS, Carl Hermann. 922
Rabbi and minister; the friendship of Stephen S. Wise and John Haynes Holmes. [1st ed.] Cleveland, World Pub. Co. [1964] 383 p. ports., facsim. 22 cm. Includes bibliographies. [BM755.W53V6] 64-12059
1. Wise, Stephen Samuel, 1874-1949. 2. Holmes, John Haynes, 1879-1964. I. Title.

VOSS, Carl Hermann. 288'.33'0924 B
Rabbi and minister : the friendship of Stephen S. Wise and John Haynes Holmes / Carl Hermann Voss. 2d ed. Buffalo, N.Y. : Prometheus Books, c1980. 383 p. ; 22 cm. (Library of liberal religion) Bibliography: p. 377-379. [BM755.W53V6 1980] 80-7453 ISBN 0-87975-130-4 pbk. : 6.95
1. Wise, Stephen Samuel, 1874-1949. 2. Holmes, John Haynes, 1879-1964. 3. Rabbis—United States—Biography. 4. Unitarian churches—Clergy—Biography. 5. Clergy—United States—Biography. I. Title. II. Series.

Wiseman, Nicholas Patrick Stephen, cardinal, 1802-1865.

FOTHERGILL, Brian. 922.242
Nicholas Wiseman, [1st ed. in the U.S.A.] Garden City, N.Y., Doubleday, 1963. 303 p. 22 cm. [BX4705.W6F6] 63-17155
1. Wiseman, Nicholas Patrick Stephen, Cardinal, 1802-1865. I. Title.

GWYNN, Dennis Rolleston, 1893- 922.242
Cardinal Wiseman. Dublin, Browne & Nolan [dist. Mystic, Conn., Lawrence Verry, River Rd., 1964] x,197p. illus., ports. 23cm. 51-5142 3.25 bds.,
1. Wiseman, Nicholas Patrick Stephen, Cardinal, 1802-1865. I. Title.

JACKMAN, Sydney Wayne, 1925- 282'.092'4 B
Nicholas Cardinal Wiseman : a Victorian prelate and his writings / [by] S. W. Jackman. [Dublin] : Five Lamps Press ; Charlottesville, Va. : [Distributed by] University of Virginia, c1977. 143 p. : port. ; 23 cm. Includes index. [BX4705.W6J33] 77-380003 ISBN 0-901072-70-2 : 7.95
1. Wiseman, Nicholas Patrick Stephen, Cardinal, 1802-1865. 2. Cardinals—England—Biography.

WARD, Wilfrid Philip, 1856-1916. 922.2
The life and times of Cardinal Wiseman, by Wilfrid Ward... 3d ed. London, New York and Bombay, Longmans, Green, and co., 1898. 2 v. 3 port. (incl. fronts.) 20 cm. [BX4705.W6W3 1898] 37-18671
1. Wiseman, Nicholas Patrick Stephen, cardinal, 1802-1865. 2. Oxford movement. I. Title.

WARD, Wilfrid Philip, 1856-1916. 922.2
The life and times of Cardinal Wiseman, by Wilfrid Ward...New impression. London, New York [etc.] Longmans, Green and co., 1900. 2 v. 3 port. (incl. fronts.) 19 cm. [BX4705.W6W3] 4-16975
1. Wiseman, Nicholas Patrick Stephen, cardinal, 1802-1865. 2. Oxford movement. I. Title.

WARD, Wilfrid Philip, 1856-1916.
The life and times of Cardinal Wiseman, by Wilfrid Ward... London, New York, Longmans, Green, and co., 1897. 2 v. fronts. (ports.) 19 cm. Vol. II, 2d edition. 16-7348
1. Wiseman, Nicholas Patrick Stephen, cardinal, 1802-1865. I. Title.

Wishard, Luther Deloraine, 1854-

OBER, Charles Kellogg, 1856- 922
Luther D. Wishard, projector of world movements, by C. K. Ober. New York, Association press, 1927. 4 p. l., 199 p. plates, ports. 22 1/2 cm. [BV1085.W5O3] 27-13397
1. Wishard, Luther Deloraine, 1854- 2. Young men's Christian associations. I. Title.

Wishes.

BARRETT, Ethel. 222'.09'505
If I had a wish ... / by Ethel Barrett. Glendale, Calif. : G/L Regal Books, c1974. 140 p. : ill. ; 20 cm. (A Regal venture book) Includes bibliographical references. [BJ1500.W55B37] 74-83139 ISBN 0-8307-0314-4 pbk. : 1.25
1. Bible. O.T.—Biography. 2. Wishes. I. Title.

Wit and humor—History and criticism

FLYNN, Leslie B. 208.8
Serve Him with mirth: the place of humor in the Christian life. Grand Rapids, Mich., Zondervan Pub. House [c.1960] 191p. 60-51823 2.95
1. Wit and humor—Hist. & crit. 2. Christian life. I. Title.

Wit and humor, Jewish.

OXENHANDLER, Bernard.
A song is borne; the story of Yankeleh, the American boy cantor. New York, Carlton press [c1963] 98 p. illus., music. 21 cm. (Geneva book) 65-75857
1. Wit and humor, Jewish. 2. Wit and humor. I. Title.

Wit and humor—Moral and religious aspects.

HYERS, M. Conrad, comp. 202'.07
Holy laughter; essays on religion in the comic perspective, edited by M. Conrad Hyers. New York, Seabury Press [1969] vi, 264 p. 22 cm. Contents.Contents.—The comic profanation of the sacred, by M. C. Hyers.—The humanity of comedy, by W. F. Lynch.—The bias of comedy and the narrow escape into faith, by N. A. Scott, Jr.—The clown as the lord of disorder, by W. M. Zucker.—The clown in contemporary art, by S. H. Miller.—The rhetoric of Christian comedy, by B. Ulanov.—Christian faith and the social comedy, by P. L. Berger.—Humour and faith, by R. Niebuhr.—The traditional roots of Jewish humour, by I. Knox.—The humour of Christ, by E. Trueblood.—Eutrapelia: A forgotten virtue, by H. Rahner.—Zen humour, by R. H. Blyth.—The dialectic of the sacred and the comic, by M. C. Hyers.—On being with it: An afterword, by C. Walsh.—Appendix: Christian sobriety, by R. Barclay. Includes bibliographical references. [PN6149.M6H9] 70-84978 6.95
1. Wit and humor—Moral and religious aspects. I. Title.

Witchcraft.

BELL, William M. 133.4
Which witch, by William M. Bell, III. [Riverside, Calif., Jurupa Mountains Cultural Center, 1971?] 17 l. 20 cm. Cover title: Witchcraft. [BF1566.B45] 73-150031
1. Witchcraft. I. Title.

[BIDDLE, Moncure] 1882- 133.4
A Christmas letter. Witches and warlocks. Philedelphia, M. Biddle & co., 1943. 61 p. front. illus., facsims. 21 cm. "Dedication" signed: Moncure Biddle. [BF1566.B5] 44-19078
1. Witchcraft. 2. Demonology. I. Title.

BLANKENSHIP, Roberta. 133.4'092'4 B
Escape from witchcraft. Grand Rapids, Zondervan Pub. House [1972] 114 p. port. 18 cm. (Zondervan books) [BF1566.B54] 72-85565 pap 0.95
1. Blankenship, Roberta. 2. Witchcraft. 3. Conversion. I. Title.

BOVET, Richard, ca. 1641- 133.4
Pandaemonium, 1684, with introd., notes by Montague Summers. Aldington, Kent, Hand & Flower Pr. [Chester Springs, Pa., Dufour, 1966] xxvii, 191p. illus. 23cm. Facsimile repro. of t.p. of orig. ed., London, 1684. Includes the author's A poem humbly presented to His Most Excellent Majesty King William the Third, and A congratulatory poem to the Honourable Admiral Russell. A53-5618 7.50 lim. ed.,
1. Witchcraft. 2. Witchcraft — England. I. Summers, Montague, 1880-1948, ed. II. Title.

BROWN, Raymond Lamont. 133.4
A book of witchcraft. With line whimsies

by Ernest Petts. New York, Taplinger [1971] 116 p. illus. 21 cm. [GR530.B7 1971] 71-143222 ISBN 0-8008-0940-8 4.50
1. Witchcraft. I. Title.

BUCKLAND, Raymond. 133.4
Witchcraft from the inside. St. Paul, Llewellyn, 1971. xiii, 141 p. illus. 21 cm. (A Llewellyn occult manual) Bibliography: p. 137-141. [BF1566.B77] 70-24986 ISBN 0-87542-049-4 2.00
1. Witchcraft. I. Title.

CARO BAROJA, Julio. 133.4
The world of the witches. Translated by O. N. V. Glendinning. [Chicago] University of Chicago Press [1964] xiv, 313 p. illus. 22 cm. (The Nature of human society series) Translation of Las brujas y su mundo. Bibliographical references included in "Notes" (p. 259-306) [BF1566.C313] 64-15829
1. Witchcraft. 2. Magic. I. Title.

COHEN, Daniel. 133.4
Voodoo, devils, and the new invisible world. New York, Dodd, Mead [1972] xii, 204 p. illus. 22 cm. Bibliography: p. 193-197. [BF1566.C57] 72-2346 ISBN 0-396-06638-0 5.95
1. Witchcraft. 2. Demonology. 3. Voodooism. 4. Prophecies (Occult sciences) I. Title.

CROWTHER, Arnold. 133.4
The secrets of ancient witchcraft with the witches Tarot / by Arnold and Patricia Crowther ; with introd. and notes by Leo Louis Martello. Secaucus, N.J. : University Books, [1974] 218 p. ; 24 cm. Bibliography: p. 216-218. [BF1566.C7] 74-80253 ISBN 0-8216-0221-7 : 7.95
1. Witchcraft. I. Crowther, Patricia, joint author. II. Title.

CROWTHER, Patricia. 133.4
The witches speak / by Patricia and Arnold Crowther ; special chapter by J. Insall-Mason ; introd. by Leo Louis Martello ; with six original ill. by Alden Cole. 1st American ed. New York : S. Weiser, 1976. ix, 145 p. : ill. ; 21 cm. [BF1566.C73 1976] 76-151279 ISBN 0-87728-285-4 : 3.50
1. Witchcraft. I. Crowther, Arnold, joint author. II. Title.

DARAUL, Arkon 133.4
Witches and sorcerers [1st Amer. ed.] New York, Citadel [1966,c.1962] 270p. illus. 22cm. [BF1566.D3] 66-16490 5.95 bds.,
1. Witchcraft. I. Title.

**EVERYTHING you always wanted to know about sorcery.* 133.4 [New York] Manor Books [1973] 190 p. 18 cm. Bibliography: p. 187-190. [BF1566] 0.95 (pbk)
1. Witchcraft. 2. Magic.

EWEN, Cecil Henry L'Estrange, 1877- 133.4
Witchcraft and demonianism [by C. L'Estrange Ewen] A facsim. reprint. New York, Barnes & Noble [1970] 495 p. illus. 23 cm. First published in 1933. Includes bibliographical references. [BF1581.E83 1970] 77-12071 11.50
1. Witchcraft. 2. Demonology. I. Title.

FAIRFAX, Edward, d.1635. 133.4'0942
Daemonologia; a discourse on witchcraft. New York, Barnes & Noble [1971] 189 p. geneal. table (on lining paper) 23 cm. "Facsimile reprint." Original t.p. reads: Daemonologia: a discourse on witchcraft as it was acted in the family of Mr. Edward Fairfax ... in the year 1621; along with the only two ecloques of the same author known to be in existence, with a biographical introduction, and notes topographical & illustrative, by William Grainge. Harrogate, R. Ackrill, Printer and publisher, Herald Office, 1882. [BF1531.F3 1882a] 70-27712 ISBN 0-389-04141-6
1. Witchcraft. I. Title.

FARRAR, Stewart. 133.4
What witches do; the modern coven revealed. With photos. by the author. [1st American ed.] New York, Coward, McCann & Geoghegan [1971] 211 p. illus. 22 cm. Bibliography: p. 197-199. [BF1571.F35 1971b] 75-154781 5.95
1. Witchcraft. I. Title.

FRANKLYN, Julian. 133.4
Death by enchantment; an examination of ancient and modern witchcraft. [1st American ed.] New York, Putnam [1971] x, 244 p. illus. 22 cm. Includes bibliographical references. [BF1566.F7 1971] 78-152769 6.95
1. Witchcraft. I. Title.

*FRITSCHER, John 133.4
Popular witchcraft. Secaucus, N.J., Citadel Press [1973] 192 p. 22 cm. Includes bibliographical references. [BF1566] 73-84152 ISBN 0-8065-0380-7 6.95
1. Witchcraft. I. Title.

FRITSCHER, John. 133.4'0973
Popular witchcraft, straight from the witch's mouth. Bowling Green, Ohio, Bowling Green University Popular Press [1972] xiii, 123 p. illus. 24 cm. Includes bibliographical references. [BF1566.F75] 71-186632 ISBN 0-87972-026-3 ISBN 0-87972-027-1 (pbk.)
1. Witchcraft. I. Title.

FROST, Gavin. 133.4'3
The magic power of witchcraft / Gavin Frost and Yvonne Frost. West Nyack, N.Y. : Parker Pub. Co., c1976. 203 p. : ill. ; 24 cm. [BF1566.F79] 75-37784 ISBN 0-13-545376-3 : 8.95
1. Witchcraft. 2. Success. I. Gavin, Yvonne, joint author. II. Title.

FROST, Gavin. 133.4
The witch's bible, by Gavin and Yvonne Frost. Los Angeles, Nash Pub. [1972] 310 p. illus. 23 cm. [BF1566.F8] 72-86673 ISBN 0-8402-1304-2 7.95
1. Witchcraft. I. Frost, Yvonne, joint author. II. Title.

*GARDNER, Helena. 133.4
Witchcraft; the path to power for those who dare to use it. Chatsworth, Calif. Brandon Books [1974] 192 p. 18 cm. Bibliography: p. 190-192. [BF1565] ISBN 0-87056-407-2 1.95 (pbk.)
1. Witchcraft. 2. Demonology. I. Title.

GIBSON, Walter Brown, 1897- 133.4
Witchcraft, by Walter B. Gibson. New York, Grosset & Dunlap [1973] 149 p. 22 cm. [BF1566.G5] 72-156327 ISBN 0-448-02182-X 4.95
1. Witchcraft.

GIFFORD, George, d.1620. 133.4
... A dialogue concerning witches and witchcrafts, 1893, by George Gifford; with an introduction by Beatrice White. [London] Pub. for the Shakespeare association by H. Milford, Oxford university press, 1931. x p., facsim. ([96] p.), 1 l. 23 cm. (Shakespeare association. Facsimiles. no. 1) "From the copy of the first edition in the British museum (c. 57 e. 43)." With facsimile of original t.-p. Bibliography: p. x. [BF1565.G5 1593 a] 32-23213
1. Witchcraft. I. White, Beatrice, 1902- ed. II. Title.

GLANVILL, Joseph, 1636-1680. 133.4
Saducismus triumphatus; or, Full and plain evidence concerning witches and appar[i] tions (1689). A facsim. reproduction, with an introd. by Coleman O. Parsons. Gainesville, Fla., Scholars' Facsimilies & Reprints, 1966. xxiv, 597 p. illus. 23 cm. "Editions of the witch book": p. xix-xxiii; "Some twentieth-century studies of Glanvill": p. xxiv. [BF1565.G58 1966] 66-60009
1. Witchcraft. 2. Apparitions. I. Title.

GREGOR, Arthur S. 133.4
Witchcraft & magic; the supernatural world of primitive man [by] Arthur S. Gregor. Drawings by Laszlo Kubinyi. New York, Scribner [1972] 148 p. 22 cm. Bibliography: p.141-144. [BF1566.G73] 72-1166 ISBN 0-684-12990-6 4.95
1. Witchcraft. 2. Magic. I. Title.

GREGOR, Arthur S. 133.4
Witchcraft and magic : the supernatural world of primitive man / Arthur S. Gregor ; drawings by Laszlo Kubinyi. New York : Charles Scribner's Sons [1976c1972] xi, 148p. : ill. ; 21 cm. Includes index. Bibliography: p. 141-144. [BF1566.G73] ISBN 0-684-14537-5 pbk. : 2.45
1. Witchcraft. 2. Magic. I. Title.
L. C. card no. for original edition: 72-1166.

GUMMERE, Amelia (Mott) Mrs. 1859- 133.
Witchcraft and Quakerism; a study in social history, by Amelia Mott Gummere ... Philadelphia, The Biddle press; [etc., etc., c1908] 4 p. l., 5-69 p. front., illus., ports. facsims. 20 cm. [BF1571.G9] 8-37756
1. Witchcraft. 2. Friends, Society of. I. Title.

GUPTA, Marie. 133
A treasury of witchcraft and devilry; a primer of the occult by Marie Gupta and Frances Brandon. Middle Village, N.Y., Jonathan David Publishers [1975] 180 p. 22 cm. [BF1566.G86] 74-6571
1. Witchcraft. 2. Demonology. 3. Ghosts. 4. Occult sciences. I. Brandon, Frances Sweeney, joint author. II. Title.

HAINING, Peter. 133.4'0904
The anatomy of witchcraft. New York, Taplinger Pub. Co. [1972] 212 p. illus. 22 cm. (The Frontiers of the unknown series) Includes bibliographical references. [BF1566.H33 1972] 72-2177 ISBN 0-8008-0201-2 6.95
1. Witchcraft. 2. Magic. I. Title.

*HAINING, Peter. 133.4
Witchcraft and black magic. Illus. by Jan Parker. Toronto, New York, Bantam Books [1973, c.1972] 159 p. col. illus. 19 cm. (Bantam knowledge through color series, no. 36) Bibliography: p. 156. [BF1566] 1.45 (pbk)
1. Witchcraft. 2. Magic. I. Title.

HANSEN, Harold A., 1924- 133.4'3
The witch's garden / Harold A. Hansen ; translated from Danish by Muriel Crofts. Santa Cruz : Unity Press, c1978. 128 p. : ill. ; 22 cm. Translation of Heksens urtegard. Includes index. Bibliography: p. 110-116. [BF1572.P43H3613] 78-5469 ISBN 0-913300-47-0 pbk. : 4.95
1. Witchcraft. 2. Plant lore. I. Title.

HART, Roger. 133.4
Witchcraft. [1st American ed.] New York, Putnam [1972, c1971] 128 p. illus. 24 cm. (Putnam documentary history series) Bibliography: p. 123. A history of the witch hunts and an examination of the folklore, superstition, and legislation pertaining to witchcraft from the fifteenth to seventeenth centuries. [BF1566.H37 1972] 71-171587 4.95
1. Witchcraft. 2. [Witchcraft.] I. Title.

HASKINS, James, 1941- 133.4'0917'496
Witchcraft, mysticism, and magic in the Black world. [1st ed.] Garden City, N.Y., Doubleday [1974] 156 p. map. 22 cm. Bibliography: p. [147]-149. [BF1566.H375] 73-11708 ISBN 0-385-02878-4 4.50
1. Witchcraft. 2. Magic. 3. Negroes—Religion.

HEATHER: 133.4'092'4 B
confessions of a witch as told to Hans Holzer. New York, Pocket Books [1975] 253 p. 18 cm. [BF1408.2H4A33] 74-19447 ISBN 0-671-802054 1.75 (pbk.)
1. Heather. 2. Witchcraft. I. Holzer, Hans W., 1920- II. Title: Confessions of a witch.

HEATHER. 133.4'092'4 B
Heather : confessions of a witch / as told to Hans Holzer. New York : Mason & Lipscomb, [1975] xii, 226 p. ; 22 cm. [BF1408.2.H4A33] 74-19447 ISBN 0-88405-096-3 : 8.95
1. Heather. 2. Witchcraft. I. Holzer, Hans W., 1920- II. Title. III. Title: Confessions of a witch.

*HILKEN, Glen A. 133.4
The best of Sybil Leek, edited by Glen A. Hilken. New York, Popular Library, [1974] 253 p. 18 cm. Bibliography: p. 252-253. [BF1566] 1.50 (pbk.)
1. Witchcraft. I. Title.

HOLZER, Hans W., 1920- 133.4
The truth about witchcraft, by Hans Holzer. [1st ed. in the U.S.A.] Garden City, N.Y., Doubleday, 1969. viii, 254 p. 21 cm. [BF1566.H65 1969] 73-78745 5.95
1. Witchcraft. I. Title.

HOYT, Charles Alva. 133.4'3
Witchcraft / by Charles Alva Hoyt ; [edited by Beatrice R. Moore]. Carbondale : Southern Illinois University Press, c1981. x, 166 p. ; 24 cm. Includes bibliographical references and index. [BF1566.H67] 19 80-24731 ISBN 0-8093-0964-5 : 19.95 ISBN 0-8093-1015-5 pbk. : 10.95
1. Witchcraft. I. Moore, Beatrice R. II. Title.

HOYT, Olga. 133.4
Witches. London, New York [etc.] Abelard-Schuman [1969] 158 p. illus. 21 cm. Bibliography: p. 151-152. Discusses the habits and practices of witches and their persecution through the ages. Includes stories of history's more infamous witches. [BF1566.H68] 68-13233 ISBN 0-200-71593-3 4.50
1. Witchcraft. 2. [Witchcraft.] I. Title.

HUEBNER, Louise. 133.4'42
Love spells from A to Z; witchy things for brewing up romance. Illustrated by William Peterson. [Kansas City, Mo.] Springbok Editions [1972] [28] p. illus. 15 cm. [BF1572.L6H8] 70-181500 ISBN 0-87529-248-8
1. Witchcraft. 2. Love. I. Title.

HUEBNER, Louise. 133.4'3
Magical candles, enchanted plants, and powerful gems; their meanings and uses in the wild world of witchcraft. Illustrated by John Overmyer. [Kansas City, Mo.] Springbok Editions [1972] [28] p. illus. 15 cm. (Her Enchantment library) [BF1566.H77] 77-179285 ISBN 0-87529-252-6
1. Witchcraft. I. Overmyer, John, illus. II. Title.

HUEBNER, Louise. 133.4
Power through witchcraft. Los Angeles, Nash Pub. Corp., 1969. 159 p. 22 cm. [BF1566.H78] 73-95367 5.95
1. Witchcraft. 2. Success. I. Title.

HUEFFER, Oliver Madox, 1877-1931. 133.4
The book of witches. Totowa, N.J., Rowman and Littlefield [1973] xi, 335 p. front. 23 cm. Bibliography: p. 334-[336] [BF1566.H48 1973] 73-2857 ISBN 0-87471-171-1 11.50
1. Witchcraft. I. Title.

HUGHES, Pennethorne. 133.4
Witchcraft. Baltimore, Penguin Books [1965] 236 p. illus. 18 cm. (Pelican books, A745) Bibliography: p. 219-222. [BF1566.H8 1965] 65-9090
1. Witchcraft. I. Title.

HUSON, Paul, comp. 133.4
The coffee table book of witchcraft and demonology. Edited with commentary by Paul Huson. New York, Putnam [1973] 224 p. illus. 28 cm. Bibliography: p. 215-217. [BF1566.H86] 72-87634 ISBN 0-399-11086-0 12.50
1. Witchcraft. 2. Demonology. I. Title.

HUSON, Paul. 133.4
Mastering witchcraft : a practical guide for witches warlocks covens / by Paul Huson ; with illustrations by the author. New York : Berkley Pub. Corp., 1977,c1970. 256p. ; 20 cm. (A Berkley Windhover Book) Bibliography: p. 253-256. [BF1566.H87] pbk. : 2.95
1. Witchcraft. I. Title.
L.C. card no. for c1970 Putnam ed.: 79-111530.

HUSON, Paul. 133.4
Mastering witchcraft; a practical guide for witches, warlocks and covens. With illus. by the author. New York, Putnam [1970] 256 p. illus. 22 cm. Bibliography: p. 253-256. [BF1566.H87] 79-111530 6.95
1. Witchcraft. I. Title.

INSTITORIS, Henricus, d.1508. 133.4
Malleus maleficarum. Translated, with an introd., bibliography and notes, by Montague Summers. New York, B. Blom [1970] xlv, 277 p. port. 26 cm. Written by H. Institoris and J. Sprenger. Reprint of the 1928 ed. "A note upon the bibliography of the Malleus maleficarum": p. xli-xlii. [BF1569.A2I5 1970] 68-57193
1. Witchcraft. 2. Demonology. 3. Criminal law. 4. Criminal procedure. I. Sprenger, Jakob, 1436 or 8-1495, joint author. II. Summers, Montague, 1880-1948, ed. III. Title.

INSTITORIS, Henricus, d.1508. 133.4
The Malleus maleficarum of Heinrich Kramer and James Sprenger. Translated with introductions, bibliography, and notes by Montague Summers. New York, Dover [1971] xiv, 277 p. 26 cm. Reprint of the 1928 ed. Includes the introd. to the 1948 reprint ed. "A note upon the bibliography of the Malleus maleficarum": p. [xli]-xlii. [BF1569.A2I5 1971] 70-176355 ISBN 0-486-22802-9 3.95
1. Witchcraft. 2. Demonology. 3. Criminal procedure (Canon law) I. Sprenger, Jakob, 1436 or 8-1495, joint author. II. Title.

JOHNSON, Frank Roy, 1911- 133.4
Witches and demons in history and folklore, by F. Roy Johnson. Murfreesboro, N.C., Johnson Pub. Co. [1969] 262 p. illus. 22 cm. Bibliographical references included in "Notes" (p. 237-252) [GR530.J6] 75-240086
1. Witchcraft. I. Title.

KINGSTON, Jeremy. 133.4
Witches and witchcraft / by Jeremy Kingston. Garden City, N.Y. : Doubleday, 1976. 144 p. : ill. ; 27 cm. (A New library of the supernatural) [BF1566.K48 1976] 76-27346 ISBN 0-385-11316-1 : 8.95
1. Witchcraft. I. Title. II. Series.

LADY Sheba. 133.4'3
The book of shadows. St. Paul, Llewellyn Publications, 1971. 155 p. 21 cm. [BF1566.L33] 72-200904 ISBN 0-87542-075-3 2.95
1. Witchcraft. I. Title.

LADY Sheba. 133.4'3
The grimoire of Lady Sheba. St. Paul, Llewellyn Publications, 1972. 219 p. illus. 26 cm. [BF1566.L334] 72-169523 ISBN 0-87542-076-1 10.00
1. Witchcraft. I. Title.

LADY Sheba. 133.4'3
The grimoire of Lady Sheba. 2d rev. ed. St. Paul : Llewellyn Publications, 1974. 227 p., [5] leaves of plates : ill. ; 24 cm. [BF1566.L334 1974] 75-308391 10.00
1. Witchcraft. I. Title.

LA VEY, Anton Szandor, 1930- 133.4
The compleat witch; or, what to do when virtue fails. New York, Dodd, Mead [1971] xiv, 274 p. col. illus. (on lining papers) 21 cm. Bibliography: p. [267]-274. [BF1566.L38] 73-135540 ISBN 0-396-06266-0 6.95
1. Witchcraft. I. Title.

LEA, Henry Charles, 1825-1909, comp. 133.409
Materials toward a history of witchcraft, collected by Henry Charles Lea ... arranged and edited by Arthur C. Howland ... with an introduction by George Lincoln Burr ... Philadelphia, University of Pennsylvania press, 1939. 3 v. 25 cm. Paged continuously. [BF1566.L4] 159.961409 39-5921
1. Witchcraft. I. Howland, Arthur Charles, 1869. II. Title.

LEEK, Sybil. 133.4
The complete art of witchcraft. [New York] New American Lib. [1973, c.1971] 205 p. illus. 18 cm. (Signet, Q5400) [BF1566L44] pap., 0.95
1. Witchcraft. I. Title.

LEEK, Sybil. 133.4
The complete art of witchcraft. New York, World Pub. Co. [1971] 205 p. illus. 22 cm. [BF1566.L44] 70-159974 6.95
1. Witchcraft. I. Title.

LEEK, Sybil. 133.4'0924
Diary of a witch. Englewood Cliffs, N.J., Prentice-Hall [1968] 187 p. 22 cm. [BF1571.L4] 68-18514
1. Witchcraft. I. Title.

LELAND, Charles Godfrey, 1824-1903. 133.4
Aradia; the gospel of the witches. [Introd. by Raymond Buckland] New York, Buckland Museum [1968] xv, 132 p. 18 cm. Bibliographical footnotes. [BF1584.I8L4 1968] 68-5407
1. Witchcraft. I. Title.

LETHBRIDGE, Thomas Charles. 133.4
Witches, by T. C. Lethbridge. [1st American ed.] New York, Citadel Press [1968, c1962] x, 162 p. illus., maps. 22 cm. [BF1567.L4 1968] 68-28449 5.95
1. Witchcraft. I. Title.

LETHBRIDGE, Thomas Charles 133.4
Witches: investigating an ancient religion. London, Routledge & Paul [dist. New York, Humanities, 1963, c.1962] 162 p. illus. 23 cm 63-3664 4.50
1. Witchcraft. I. Title.

MCGILL, Ormond. 133.4
The secret world of witchcraft. South Brunswick, A. S. Barnes [1973] 202 p. illus. 27 cm. [BF1566.M18 1973] 72-9836 ISBN 0-498-07607-5 8.95
1. Witchcraft. 2. Magic. 3. Psychical research. I. Title.

MAIR, Lucy Philip, 1901- 133.4
Witchcraft [by] Lucy Mair. New York, McGraw-Hill [1969] 255 p. illus. (part col.), facsims., col. map. 20 cm. (World university library) Bibliography: p. [248]-251. [BF1566.M26] 68-21850 4.95
1. Witchcraft.

MAPLE, Eric. 133.4
The dark world of witches. New York, A. S. Barnes [1964] 209 p. illus., ports., facsims. 22 cm. Bibliography: p. 201-203. [BF1566.M28 1964] 64-14732
1. Witchcraft. I. Title.

MASTERS, R. E. L. 133.4
Eros and evil; the sexual psychopathology of witchcraft. New York, Julian [c.]1962. xviii, 322p. 24cm. Bibl. 62-19302 8.50
1. Witchcraft. 2. Sexual perversion. 3. Demonology. I. Title.

MASTERS, R. E. L. 133.4'0942
Eros and evil; the sexual psychopathology of witchcraft. [by] R. E. L. Masters Baltimore Penguin Books [1974 c1962] xxviii., 254 p. 19 cm. Bibliography: p. 309-313 [BF1556.M35] 2.50 (pbk.)
1. Witchcraft. 2. Sexual Perversion. 3. Demonology. I. Title.
L.C. card no. for original: 62-19302

MICHELET, Jules, 1798-1874. 133.
Satanism and witchcraft, a study in medieval superstition. Tr. by A. R. Allinson. New York, Citadel Press [1946] xx, 332 p. 21 cm. Translation of La sorciere. "Principal authorities": p. 331-332. [[BF1569.M]] [[159.96140902]] [133.40902] A48
1. Witchcraft. 2. Demonomania. 3. Civilization, Medieval. I. Allinson, Alfred Richard, tr. II. Title.

MORRISON, Sarah Lyddon. 133.4
The modern witch's spellbook. New York, D. McKay Co. [1971] vii, 246 p. illus. 23 cm. [BF1566.M76] 71-135588 6.95
1. Witchcraft. I. Title.

MURRAY, Margaret Alice. 133.4
The god of the witches. New York, Oxford University Press, 1952. 212 p. illus. 23 cm. Bibliography: p. 198-207 [BF1566.M8 1952a] 53-253
1. Witchcraft. 2. Demonology. 3. Magic. 4. Cultus. I. Title.

MURRAY, Margaret Alice. 133.4
The gold of the witches. Garden City, N.Y., Doubleday [1950, c.1952] 222p. 19cm. (Anchor bk. A212) 1.45 pap.,
1. Witchcraft 2. Demonology 3. Magic 4. Cultus. I. Title.

*O'DAIR, Stan 133.4
Sex, witches, and warlocks. N. Hollywood, Calif., Brandon House [1966] 174p. 18cm. (1050) .95 pap.,
1. Witchraft. I. Title.

PAINE, Lauran. 133.4
Sex in witchcraft. London, Hale, 1972. 190, [8] p. illus., ports. 23 cm. Bibliography: p. 183-184. [BF1566.P237 1972] 72-193428 ISBN 0-7091-2899-1
1. Witchcraft. 2. Sex. I. Title.
Avail. from Taplinger. 6.50.

PAINE, Lauran. 133.4'3
Witchcraft and the mysteries / Lauran Paine. New York : Taplinger Pub. Co., 1975. 192 p., [4] leaves of plates : ill. ; 23 cm. Includes index. Bibliography: p. [190] [BF1566.P239 1975] 73-16636 ISBN 0-8008-8377-2 : 8.50
1. Witchcraft. 2. Mysteries, Religious. I. Title.

PAINE, Lauran. 133.4
Witches in fact and fantasy. New York, Taplinger Pub. Co. [1972, c1971] 188 p. illus. 22 cm. Bibliography: p. [185]-186. [BF1566.P24 1972] 74-185625 ISBN 0-8008-8374-8 6.50
1. Witchcraft. I. Title.

PARRINDER, Edward Geoffrey. 133.9
Witchcraft: European and African. New York, Barnes and Noble, 1963. 215 p. 23 cm. [BF1566.P3] 63-4000
1. Witchcraft. 2. Witchcraft—Africa.

PEPPER, Elizabeth. 133.4
The witches' almanac, Aries 1971-Aries 1972; for the first time combining the mysterious wiccan and arcane secrets of an old England witch with one from New England; prepared and edited by Elizabeth Pepper & John Wilcock. New York, Grosset & Dunlap [1971] 89 p. illus. 22 cm. [BF1566.P43] 73-29853 ISBN 0-448-00746-0 1.00
1. Witchcraft. I. Wilcock, John, joint author. II. Title.

*RAVENSDALE, Tom. 133.4
The psychology of witchcraft; an account of witchcraft, black magic and the occult. By Tom Ravensdale and James Morgan. With a foreword by Sir Alec Kirkbride. New York, Arco [1974] 200 p., illus. 23 cm. [BF1581] 74-77592 ISBN 0-668-03501-3 10.00
1. Witchcraft. 2. Black magic. 3. Occultism. I. Morgan, James, joint author. II. Title.

*RAVENSDALE, Tom. 133.4
The psychology of witchcraft; an account of witchcraft, black magic and the occult. By Tom Ravensdale and James Morgan. With a foreword by Sir Alec Kirkbride. New York, Arco [1974] 200 p., illus. 23 cm. [BF1581] 74-77592 ISBN 0-668-03501-3 10.00
1. Witchcraft. 2. Black magic. 3. Occultism. I. Morgan, James, joint author. II. Title.

ROSE, Elliot 133.4
A razor for a goat; a discussion of certain problems in the history of witchcraft and diabolism [Toronto] Univ. of Toronto Pr. [c.1962] 257p. front. Bibl. 62-3328 4.95
1. Witchcraft. 2. Devil. I. Title.

SCOT, Reginald, 1538?-1599 133.4
The discoverie of witchcraft. Introd. by Hugh Ross Williamson. Carbondale, Southern Ill. Univ. Pr. [1965, c.1964] 400p. illus. 26cm. (Centaur classics) [BF1565.S4] 64-18551 22.50
1. Witchcraft. 2. Magic. 3. Demonology. I. Title.

SCOT, Reginald, 1538?-1599. 133.4
The discoverie of witchcraft. With an introd. by Montague Summers. New York, Dover Publications [1972] xxxvii, 282 p. illus. 26 cm. Reprint of the 1930 ed. "A bibliographical note upon Scot's 'Discouerie'": p. xxxiii-xxxvii. [BF1565.S4 1972] 72-79958 ISBN 0-486-22880-0 3.95 (pbk.)
1. Witchcraft. 2. Magic. 3. Demonology. I. Title.

SEABROOK, William Buehler, 1887- 133.4
Witchcraft, its power in the world today, by William Seabrook. New York, Harcourt, Brace and company [c1940] ix, 387 p. illus. 22 cm. "First edition." [BF1571.S4 1940] 159.9614 40-31468
1. Witchcraft. I. Title.

SERGEANT, Philip Walsingham, 1872- 133.4
Witches and warlocks, by Philip W. Sergeant, with introd. by Arthur Machen. London, Hutchinson. Detroit, Gale Research Co., 1974. 290 p. illus. 24 cm. Reprint of the 1936 ed. [BF1566.S4 1974] 72-164055 11.00
1. Witchcraft. 2. Witchcraft—England. I. Title.

SERGEANT, Philip Walsingham, 1872- 133.4
Witches and warlocks, by Philip W. Sergeant. With introd. by Arthur Machen. New York, B. Blom, 1972. 290 p. illus. 21 cm. Reprint of the 1936 ed. Includes bibliographical references. [BF1566.S4 1972] 72-82208
1. Witchcraft. 2. Witchcraft—England. I. Title.

SETH, Ronald. 133.4
Witches and their craft. New York, Taplinger [1968, c1967] 255 p. illus. 22 cm. Bibliography: p. 250-251. [BF1566.S43 1968] 67-24036 4.50
1. Witchcraft. I. Title.

SIMONS, G. L. 133.4
The witchcraft world / G. L. Simons. New York : Barnes & Noble Books, 1974. 231 p. ; 22 cm. Bibliography: p. 229-231. [BF1566.S5 1974] 74-186958 ISBN 0-06-496265-2 : 10.75
1. Witchcraft. I. Title.

SMITH, Susy. 133.4'09'04
Today's witches. Englewood Cliffs, N.J., Prentice-Hall [1970] 180 p. 24 cm. Bibliography: p. 179-180. [BF1571.S63] 71-114687 ISBN 0-13-924555-3 5.95
1. Witchcraft. I. Title.

SMYTH, Frank. 133.4
Modern witchcraft; the fascinating story of the rebirth of paganism and magic. New York, Harper & Row [1973 c.1970] 125 p. photos. 18 cm. (Man, Myth & Magic Original) (Harrow Books) Further reading: p. 125-126. [BF1566.S55] ISBN 0-06-087038-9 1.25 (pbk.)
1. Witchcraft. I. Title.
L.C. no. for orig. ed.: 74-541631

STARHAWK. 299
The spiral dance : a rebirth of the ancient religion of the great goddess / Starhawk. 1st ed. San Francisco : Harper & Row, c1979. p. cm. Bibliography: p. [BF1566.S77 1979] 79-1775 ISBN 0-06-067535-7 pbk. : 6.95
1. Witchcraft. I. Title.

SUMMERS, Montague, 1880-1948. 133.4
The geography of witchcraft. Evanston, Ill. University Books [1958] 623 p. 22 cm. [BF1566.S82 1958] 58-8303
1. Witchcraft. 2. Demonology. I. Title.

SUMMERS, Montague, 1880-1948. 133.4'094
The geography of witchcraft / by Montague Summers. London ; Boston : Routledge & Kegan Paul, 1978. xi, 623 p., [4] leaves of plates : ill. ; 24 cm. Reprint of the 1927 ed. published by Kegan Paul & Co., London. Includes bibliographical references and index. [BF1566.S82 1978] 78-40094 ISBN 0-7100-7617-7 : 32.50
1. Witchcraft. 2. Demonology. I. Title.

SUMMERS, Montague, 1880-1948. 133.409
The history of witchcraft and demonology. [2d ed.] New York, University Books [1956] 353p. 22cm. [BF1566.S8 1956] 56-7838
1. Witchcraft. 2. Demonology. I. Title.

SUMMERS, Montague, 1880-1948. 133.4'09
A popular history of witchcraft. London, K. Paul, Trench, Trubner, 1937. Detroit, Gale Research Co., 1973. p. [BF1566.S84 1973] 78-110810
1. Witchcraft. I. Title.

SUMMERS, Montague, 1880-1948. 133.4
Witchcraft and black magic. London, New York, Rider. Detroit, Grand River Books, 1971. 228 p. illus. 22 cm. Reprint of the 1946 ed. [BF1566.S86 1971] 70-174114
1. Witchcraft. 2. Magic. I. Title.

SUMMERS, Montague [Alphonsus Joseph Marie Augustus Montague Summers] 1880- 133.4
Witchcraft and black magic. [dist. New York, Sterling Pub. Co., 1961‡] illus 4.95
1. Witchcraft. 2. Magic. I. Title.

TINDALL, Gillian. 133.4
A handbook on witches. [1st American ed.] New York, Atheneum, 1966. 155 p. illus., facsims. 22 cm. Bibliography: p. 151-152. [BF1566.T5 1966] 66-12995
1. Witchcraft. I. Title.

VALIENTE, Doreen. 133.4'03
An ABC of witchcraft past & present. New

York, St. Martin's Press [1973] xvii, 377 p. illus. 23 cm. Includes bibliographical references. [BF1566.V33] 78-173895 10.00
1. Witchcraft. 2. Occult sciences. I. Title.

VALIENTE, Doreen. 133.4
Witchcraft for tomorrow / Doreen Valiente. London : R. Hale ; New York : St. Martin's Press, 1978. 205 p., [4] leaves of plates : ill. ; 23 cm. Includes index. Bibliography: p. [195]-200. [BF1566.V334 1978] 77-10305 ISBN 0-312-88452-4 : 8.95
1. Witchcraft. I. Title.

WICKWAR, John Williams, 1874- 133.4
Witchcraft and the black art; a book dealing with the psychology and folklore of the witches, by J. W. Wickwar. Ann Arbor, Mich., Gryphon Books, 1971. 320 p. 22 cm. "Facsimile reprint of the 1925 edition." [BF1566.W6 1926a] 71-151817
1. Witchcraft. I. Title.

WICKWAR, John Williams, 1874- 133.4
Witchcraft and the black art; a book dealing with the psychology and folklore of the witches, by J. W. Wickwar. London, H. Jenkins Ltd. Detroit, Gale Research Co., 1973. 320 p. 18 cm. Reprint of the 1925 ed. [BF1566.W6 1973] 73-5622
1. Witchcraft. I. Title.

WILLIAMS, Charles, 1886-1945. 133.409
Witchcraft. New York, Meridian Books [1959] 316 p. 18 cm. (Meridian books, M62) [BF1566.W65 1959] 59-7178
1. Witchcraft.

WITCHES and witch-hunters. 133.4'0942
A reprint of A treatise of witchcraft, by Alexander Roberts (1616); The discovery of witches, by Mathew Hopkins (1647); [and] Scottish witchcraft trials, by J. W. Brodie (1891). With a foreword by A. E. Green. Norwood, Pa., Norwood Editions, 1973. p. Reprint of 3 works, the 1st originally printed by N. O. for S. Man, London; the 2d originally printed for R. Royston, London; and the 3d originally imprinted at the Chiswick Press, London. [BF1565.W58 1973] 73-14633 ISBN 0-88305-000-5 9.00
1. Witchcraft. 2. Trials (Witchcraft)—Scotland. I. Roberts, Alexander. A treatise of witchcraft. 1973. II. Hopkins, Matthew, d. 1647. The discovery of witches. 1973. III. Brodie-Innes, John William, 1848-1923. Scottish witchcraft trials. 1973.

WITCHES and witch-hunters. 133.4'0942
A reprint of A treatise of witchcraft, by Alexander Roberts (1616); The discovery of witches, by Mathew Hopkins (1647); [and] Scottish witchcraft trials, by J. W. Brodie (1891). With a foreword by A. E. Green. Wakefield, S.R. Publishers, 1971. [186] p. illus. 21 cm. [BF1565.W58] 72-305220 ISBN 0-85409-696-5 £0.75
1. Witchcraft. 2. Trials (Witchcraft)—Scotland. I. Roberts, Alexander. A treatise of witchcraft. 1971. II. Hopkins, Matthew, d. 1647. The discovery of witches. 1971. III. Brodie-Innes, John William, 1848-1923. Scottish witchcraft trials. 1971.

WRIGHT, Harry B 133.4
Witness to witchcraft. New York, Funk & Wagnalls [1957] 246 p. illus. 22 cm. [GN475.W7] 57-6693
1. Witchcraft. I. Title.

ZILBOORG, Gregory, 1890- 133.40902
...The medical man and the witch during the renaissance, by Gregory Zilboorg... Baltimore, The Johns Hopkins press, 1935. x, 215 p. front. (port.) illus., plates. 20 1/2 cm. (Publications of the Institute of the history of medicine, the Johns Hopkins university. 3d rev., vol. II) "The Hideyo Noguchi lectures." Contents.The physiological and psychological aspects of the Malleus malelicarum (The witch's hammer)--Medicine and the witch in the sixteenth century.--Johann Weyer, the founder of modern psychiatry. [BF1569.Z5] 159.96140902 35-12064
1. Witchcraft. 2. Psychology, Pathological. 3. Institoris, Hendricus, d. ca. 1560. Malleus maleficarum. 4. Spranger, Jokob, fl. 1404, joint author. Malleus maleficarum. 5. Wier, Johann, 1515-1568. 6. Renaissance. I. Title.

Witchcraft—Addresses essays, lectures.

THE Damned art : 133.4
essays in the literature of witchcraft / edited by Sydney Anglo. London ; Boston : Routledge & K. Paul, 1977. viii, 258. p. ; 22 cm. Includes bibliographical references and index. [BF1566.D27] 77-370448 ISBN 0-7100-8589-3 : 16.50
1. Witchcraft—Addresses essays, lectures. I. Anglo, Sydney.

Witchcraft—Africa.

SCOBIE, Alastair, 1918- 133.4
Murder for magic; witchcraft in Africa. London, Cassell [1965] x, 181 p. 21 cm. [BF1584.A53S3] 66-53647
1. Witchcraft—Africa. 2. Blood accusation. I. Title.

Witchcraft—Africa, East.

MIDDLETON, John Francis Marchment 1921- ed. 291.33
Witchcraft and sorcery in East Africa [by] John Beattie [others] Ed. by John Middleton, E. H. Winter. Foreword by E. E. Evans-Pritchard. New York, Praeger [c.1963] viii, 302p. diagrs. 23cm. Bibl. 63-18833 7.50
1. Witchcraft—Africa, East. I. Winter, Edward Henry, joint ed. II. Title.

Witchcraft and sex.

PAINE, Lauran. 133.4
Sex in witchcraft. New York, Taplinger Pub. Co. [1972] 186 p. illus. 22 cm. Bibliography: p. [182]-183. [BF1572.S4P3 1972] 72-76258 ISBN 0-8008-7151-0 6.50
1. Witchcraft and sex. I. Title.

Witchcraft—Anecdotes, facetiae, satire, etc.

PEPPER, Elizabeth. 133.4
Witches all : a treasury from past editions of the Witches' almanac / prepared and edited by Elizabeth Pepper and John Wilcock. [New York] : Grosset & Dunlap, 1977. 127 p. : ill. ; 28 cm. Bibliography: p. 89-90. [BF1566.P46] 77-73925 ISBN 0-448-12856-X pbk. : 4.95
1. Witchcraft—Anecdotes, facetiae, satire, etc. I. Wilcock, John, joint author. II. The Witches' almanac. III. Title.

Witchcraft—Basque Provinces.

HENNINGSEN, Gustav. 272'.2'09466
The witches' advocate : Basque witchcraft and the Spanish Inquisition, 1609-1614 / by Gustav Henningsen. Reno : University of Nevada Press, 1980. p. cm. (Basque series) Includes index. Bibliography: p. [BX1735.H44] 79-20340 ISBN 0-87417-056-7 : 24.00
1. Inquisition. Basque Provinces. 2. Witchcraft—Basque Provinces. I. Title.

Witchcraft—Bibliography

NEW York. Public library. 016.
... List of works relating to witchcraft in Europe. New York, 1911. 31 p. 26 1/2 cm. "Reprinted at the New York public library from the Bulletin, December, 1911." Comp. by George F. Black. [Z6878.W8N5] CA 12
1. Witchcraft—Bibl. I. Black, George Fraser, 1866- II. Title.

Witchcraft—Bibliography—Catalogs.

CORNELL University. Libraries. 016.1334
Witchcraft : Catalogue of the Witchcraft Collection in the Cornell University Library / introd. by Rossell Hope Robbins ; introd. by Russell Hope Robbons ; edited by Martha J. Crowe ; index by Jane Marsh Dieckmann. Millwood, N.Y. : KTO Press, 1977. xxcviii, 644 p. ; 31 cm. Includes index. [Z6878.W8C67 1977] [BF1566] 76-41552 ISBN 0-527-19705-X lib.bdg. : 95.00
1. Cornell University. Libraries. 2. Witchcraft—Bibliography—Catalogs. I. Title.

Witchcraft—Collected works.

WITCH, spirit, devil / 133.4'09
[compiled by] A. F. Scott. London ; New York : White Lion Publishers, 1974. 189 p., leaf of plate, [32] p. of plates : ill., facsims., port. ; 23 cm. Includes index. Bibliography: p. 183. [BF1563.W53] 75-321310 ISBN 0-7274-0050-9 : £3.75
1. Witchcraft—Collected works. I. Scott, Arthur Finley.

WOODS, William Howard, 1916- comp. 133.4'08
A casebook of witchcraft : reports, depositions, confessions, trials, and executions for witchcraft during a period of three hundred years / selected and annotated by William Woods. New York : Putnam, [1974] 216 p. ; 22 cm. [BF1563.W66] 74-79672 ISBN 0-399-11403-3 : 6.95
1. Witchcraft—Collected works. I. Title.

Witchcraft—Collections.

HAINING, Peter, comp. 133.4'08
The necromancers; the best of black magic and witchcraft. Introd. by Robert Bloch. New York, Morrow, 1972 [c1971] 255 p. illus. 22 cm. [BF1563.H34 1972] 74-166351 5.95
1. Witchcraft—Collections. 2. Magic—Collections. I. Title.

MARWICK, Max, comp. 133.4'08
Witchcraft and sorcery; selected readings, edited by Max Marwick. [Harmondsworth, Eng., Baltimore, Md.] Penguin Books [1970] 416 p. 18 cm. (Penguin modern sociology readings) Includes bibliographies. [BF1563.M3 1970] 70-18967 1.95 (U.S.)
1. Witchcraft—Collections. I. Title.

Witchcraft—Congresses.

WITCHCRAFT confessions & accusations; 133.4
edited by Mary Douglas. London, New York, Tavistock Publications [1970] xxxviii, 387 p. 23 cm. (A.S.A. monographs, 9) "Distributed in the U.S.A. by Barnes & Noble." Papers presented at the annual conference on the Association of Social Anthropologists of the Commonwealth, King's College, Cambridge, 3-6 April, 1968, which was held in honor of E. E. Evans-Pritchard. Includes bibliographies. [BF1563.W56] 133.3 78-140585 63/-
1. Witchcraft—Congresses. I. Douglas, Mary (Tew), ed. II. Evans-Pritchard, Edward Evan, 1902- III. Association of Social Anthropologists of the Commonwealth. IV. Title. V. Series.

Witchcraft—Connecticut.

TAYLOR, John Metcalf, 1845-1918. 133.4'09746
The witchcraft delusion in colonial Connecticut, 1647-1697. New York, B. Franklin [1971] xv, 172 p. facsim. 19 cm. (Burt Franklin research and source works series, 412. American classics in history and social science, 196) Reprint of the 1908 ed. Bibliography: p. [165]-166. [BF1576.T25 1971] 73-165414
1. Witchcraft—Connecticut. I. Title.

Witchcraft—Dictionaries.

NEWALL, Venetia. 133.4'03
The encyclopedia of witchcraft & magic / Venetia Newall ; introduction by Richard M. Dorson. London ; New York : Hamlyn, 1974. 192 p. : ill. (some col.), facsims., ports. ; 31 cm. Includes index. Bibliography: p. 182-185. [BF1588.N48] 74-195214 ISBN 0-600-33077-X : £3.25
1. Witchcraft—Dictionaries. 2. Magic—Dictionaries. I. Title.

NEWALL, Venetia. 133.4'03
The encyclopedia of witchcraft & magic / Venetia Newall ; introd. by Richard M. Dorson. [New York] : A & W Visual Library, c1974. 192 p. : ill. ; 29 cm. Includes index. Bibliography: p. 182-185. [BF1588.N48 1974b] 75-37317 ISBN 0-89104-031-5 : 7.95 ($8.95 Can)
1. Witchcraft—Dictionaries. 2. Magic—Dictionaries. I. Title.

Witchcraft—Dictionaries—English.

ROBBINS, Rossell Hope, 1912- 133.403
The encyclopedia of witchcraft and demonology. New York, Crown Publishers [1959] 571 p. illus. 26 cm. Includes bibliography. [BF1503.R6] 59-9155
1. Witchcraft—Dictionaries—English. 2. Demonology—Dictionaries—English. I. Title.

Witchcraft—England.

BUCKLAND, Raymond. 133.4'0942
The tree : the complete book of Saxon witchcraft / by Raymond Buckland. The Seax-Wica "Book of shadows", with annotations and additional material / by Raymond Buckland. 1st ed. New York : S. Weiser, 1974. 158 p. : ill. ; 21 cm. Bibliography: p. 156-158. [BF1581.B8] 74-79397 ISBN 0-87728-258-7 pbk. : 2.95
1. Witchcraft—England. 2. Occult sciences—England. I. Title.

DAVIES, Reginald Trevor. 133.4'0942
Four centuries of witch-beliefs, with special reference to the Great Rebellion, by R. Trevor Davies. New York, B. Blom, 1972. xii, 222 p. 24 cm. Reprint of the 1947 ed. Bibliography: p. 204-212. [BF1581.D3 1972] 74-180026 12.50
1. Witchcraft—England. I. Title.

HOLE, Christina. 133.4'0942
Witchcraft in England : some episodes in the history of English witchcraft / by Christina Hole. Totowa, N.J. : Rowman and Littlefield, 1977. p. cm. Includes index. Bibliography: p. [BF1581.H6 1977] 76-58885 ISBN 0-87471-958-5 : 8.00
1. Witchcraft—England. I. Title.

HOLE, Christina. 133.40942
Witchcraft in England, by Christina Hole, illustrated by Mervyn Peake. New York, C. Scribner's sons, 1947. 167, [1] p. front., illus., plates, ports. 24 cm. Bibliography: p. 161-163. [BF1581.H6 1947] 47-3917
1. Witchcraft—England. I. Title.

KITTREDGE, George Lyman, 1860-1941. 133.40942
Witchcraft in Old and New England New York, Russell & Russell [c1956] 641p. 22cm. Includes bibliography. [BF1581.K58 1956] 58-12929
1. Witchcraft—England. 2. Witchcraft—New England. I. Title.

KITTREDGE, George Lyman, 1860-1941. 133.4'0942
Witchcraft in Old and New England / by George Lyman Kittredge. College ed. New York : Atheneum, 1972, c1957. 641 p. ; 21 cm. (Atheneum ; 186) Includes bibliographical references and index. [BF1581.K58 1972] 76-353632
1. Witchcraft—England. 2. Witchcraft—New England. I. Title.

NOTESTEIN, Wallace, 1878- 133.4
A history of witchcraft in England from 1558 to 1718 New York, Russell & Russell, 1965 [c1911] xiv, 442 p. 23 cm. (Prize essays of the American Historical Association, 1909) Includes bibliographical references. [BF1581.N6 1965] 65-18824
1. Witchcraft—England. I. Title. II. Title: Witchcraft in England from 1558 to 1718. III. Series: American Historical Association Prize essays, 1909

NOTESTEIN, Wallace, 1878-1969. 133.4'0942
A history of witchcraft in England from 1558 to 1718 / Wallace Notestein New York : Gordon Press, 1976. p. cm. Reprint of the 1968 ed. published by Crowell, New York, which was issued as no. A-182 of Apollo editions. Includes bibliographical references and index. [BF1581.N6 1976] 76-1008 ISBN 0-87968-448-8 lib.bdg. : 44.95
1. Witchcraft—England. I. Title.

NOTESTEIN, Wallace, 1878-1969. 133.4
A history of witchcraft in England from 1558 to 1718 New York, T. Y. Crowell Co. [1968] xiv, 442 p. 20 cm. (Apollo editions, A-182) Includes bibliographical references. [BF1581.N6 1968] 68-17074
1. Witchcraft—England. I. Title. II. Title: Witchcraft in England from 1558 to 1718.

ROSEN, Barbara, comp. 133.4'0942
Witchcraft. New York, Taplinger [1972, c1969] xii, 407 p. illus. 23 cm. (The Stratford-upon-Avon library 6) Bibliography: p. [385]-391. [BF1581.R6 1972] 74-179662 ISBN 0-8008-8372-1 9.95
1. Witchcraft—England. I. Title. II. Series.

SETH, Ronald. 133.4'0942
Children against witches. New York, Taplinger Pub. Co. [1969] 190 p. illus. 23 cm. [BF1581.S35 1969] 71-83224 4.95
1. Witchcraft—England. I. Title.

Witchcraft—Europe.

MONTER, E. William, comp. 133.4
European witchcraft [by] E. William Monter. New York, Wiley [1969] xiv, 177 p. 21 cm. (Major issues in history) Contents.Contents.—Zauberwahn, Inquisition und Hexenprozess im Mittelalter, by J. Hansen.—Malleus Maleficarum, by J. Sprenger and H. Kramer.—Religion, the Reformation, and social change, by H. Trevor-Roper.—De praestigiis Daemonum, by J. Weyer.—Refutation des opinions de Jean Wier, by J. Bodin.—Law, medicine, and the acceptance of witchcraft, 1560-1580, by E. W. Monter.—Judgement on the witch Walpurga Hausmannin.—The witch-persecution at Bamberg.—Witchcraft trials in Lorraine: psychology of the judges, by E. Delcambre.—The psychology of Lorraine witchcraft suspects, by E. Delcambre.—A letter against witches, by C. de Bergerac.—Recherche de la verite, by Malebranche.—Magistrates and witches in seventeenth-century France, by R. Mandrou.—The world of the witches, by J. Caro Baroja.—I benandanti, by C. Ginzburg.—Les paysans de Languedoc, by E. Le Roy Ladurie. Bibliographical references included in "Guide to further reading" (p. 173-177) [BF1566.M66] 76-89682 ISBN 0-471-61402-5
1. Witchcraft—Europe. I. Title.

Witchcraft—Europe—History—Sources.

KORS, Alan C., comp. 133.4'094
Witchcraft in Europe, 1100-1700; a documentary history. Edited with an introd. by Alan C. Kors and Edward Petars Philadelphia, University of Pennsylvania Press [1972] viii, 382 p. illus. 26 cm. Includes bibliographical references. [BF1566.K67] 71-170267 ISBN 0-8122-7645-0 17.50
1. Witchcraft—Europe—History—Sources. I. Peters, Edward M., joint comp. II. Title.

Witchcraft—France.

BOGUET, Henri, d.1619. 133.4'0944'47
An examen of witches (Discours des sorciers) [by Henry Boguet] New York, Barnes & Noble [1971] liii, 328 p. 20 cm. A facsimile of the 1929 ed. [BF1582.A2B63 1929a] 71-27506 ISBN 0-389-04142-4
1. Witchcraft—France. 2. Demonology, French. 3. Criminal law—France. 4. Criminal procedure—France. I. Title.

Witchcraft—Germany, West—Franconia.

SEBALD, Hans. 200'943'3
Witchcraft : the heritage of a heresy / Hans Sebald. New York : Elsevier, c1978. x, 262 p. : ill. ; 23 cm. Includes index. Bibliography: p. [245]-249. [BF1583.S42] 78-10441 ISBN 0-444-99058-5 : 18.75 ISBN 0-444-99059-3 pbk. : 7.95
1. Witchcraft—Germany, West—Franconia. 2. Franconia—Religious life and customs. I. Title.

Witchcraft—Great Britain.

ASHTON, John, b.1834. 133.4'2'0941
The Devil in Britain and America / by John Ashton. New York : Gordon Press, 1976. p. cm. Reprint of the 1972 ed., published by Newcastle Pub. Co., Hollywood, Calif., of a work first published in 1896 by Ward and Downey, London. Bibliography: p. [BF1581.A8 1976] 76-1023 ISBN 0-87968-450-X lib.bdg. : 44.95
1. Witchcraft—Great Britain. 2. Witchcraft—United States. 3. Devil. I. Title.

ASHTON, John, b.1834. 133.4'0941
The devil in Britain and America / by John Ashton. San Bernardino, Calif. : Borgo Press, 1980. p. cm. Reprint of the 1972 ed. published by Newcastle Pub. Co., Hollywood, Calif., of a work first published in 1896 by Ward and Downey, London. Bibliography: p. [BF1581.A8 1980] 19 80-19692 10.95
1. Witchcraft—Great Britain. 2. Witchcraft—United States. 3. Devil. I. Title.

BRIGGS, Katharine Mary. 133.40942
Pale Hecate's team; an examination of the beliefs on witchcraft and magic among Shakespeare's contemporaries and his immediate successors. New York, Humanities Press [1962] 291 p. illus. 23 cm. [BF1581.B7] 62-6110
1. Witchcraft—Gt. Brit. 2. Magic. 3. Folklore—Gt. Brit. I. Title.

LINTON, Elizabeth (Lynn) 1822-1898, comp. 133.4'0942
Witch stories. New York, Barnes & Noble Books [1972, i.e. 1973] iv, 428 p. 23 cm. Reprint of the 1861 ed. published by Champman and Hall, London. [BF1581.L4 1973] 73-155608 ISBN 0-06-494296-1 12.50
1. Witchcraft—Great Britain. I. Title.

LINTON, Elizabeth (Lynn) 1822-1898, comp. 133.4'0942
Witch stories. London, Chapman and Hall, 1861. Detroit, Grand River Books, 1971. iv, 428 p. front. 22 cm. Contents.Contents.—The witches of Scotland.—The witches of England. [BF1581.L4 1971] 79-178642
1. Witchcraft—Gt. Brit. I. Title.

MURRAY, Margaret Alice 133.40942
The witch-cult in Western Europe [Gloucester, Mass., P. Smith, 1964] 303p. 20cm. (Oxford paperbacks, no. 53 rebound) Bibl. 3.50
1. Witchcraft—Gt. Brit. I. Title.

MURRAY, Margaret Alice 291.33
The witch-cult in western Europe. Oxford, Clarendon Pr., [dist. New York, Oxford, 1963] 303, [1] p. 20cm. Bibl. 1.50 pap.,
1. Witchcraft—Gt. Brit. 2. Ethnology. I. Title.

MURRAY, Margaret Alice. 133.40942
The witch-cult in Western Europe. Oxford, Clarendon Press [1962] 303 p. 20 cm. (Oxford paperbacks, no. 53) [BF1581.M8 1962] 63-2965
1. Witchcraft—Gt. Brit. I. Title.

Witchcraft—Handbooks, manuals, etc.

FROST, Gavin. 133.4'3
A witch's grimoire of ancient omens, portents, talismans, amulets, and charms / Gavin Frost and Yvonne Frost. West Nyack, N.Y. : Parker Pub. Co., c1979. 225 p. : ill. ; 24 cm. [BF1566.F83] 79-11745 ISBN 0-13-961557-1 : 9.95
1. Witchcraft—Handbooks, manuals, etc. 2. Magic—Handbooks, manuals, etc. I. Frost, Yvonne, joint author. II. Title.

Witchcraft—History

BURR, George Lincoln, 1857-1938. 133.4'09
New England's place in the history of witchcraft. Freeport, N.Y., Books for Libraries Press [1971] 35 p. 23 cm. Reprint of the 1911 edition. Includes bibliographical references. [BF1566.B8 1971] 71-164592 ISBN 0-8369-5876-4
1. Witchcraft—History. 2. Witchcraft—New England. I. Title.

DONOVAN, Frank Robert, 1906- 133.4'09
Never on a broomstick [by] Frank Donovan. [Harrisburg, Pa.] Stackpole Books [1971] 256 p. 23 cm. [BF1566.D65] 75-140745 ISBN 0-8117-1119-6 7.95
1. Witchcraft—History. 2. Magic—History. I. Title.

LEA, Henry Charles, 1825-1909, comp. 133.409
Materials toward a history of witchcraft; arr. and edited by Arthur C. Howland. With an introd. by George Lincoln Burr. New York, T. Yoseloff [1957, c1939] 3v. (xliv, 1548p.) 22cm. [BF1566.L4 1957] 57-59569
1. Witchcraft—Hist. I. Title.

O'CONNELL, Margaret F., 1935- 133.4'09
The magic cauldron : witchcraft for good and evil / Margaret F. O'Connell. New York : S. G. Phillips, c1975. p. cm. Bibliography: p. [BF1566.O25] 75-26757 ISBN 0-87599-187-4 : 8.95
1. Witchcraft—History. I. Title.

RUSSELL, Jeffrey Burton. 133.4'3'09
A history of witchcraft, sorcerers, heretics, and pagans / Jeffrey B. Russell. London : Thames and Hudson, 1980. 192 p. : ill. ; 25 cm. Includes index. Bibliography: p. 180-183. [BF1566.R87] 19 81-452874 ISBN 0-500-01225-3 : 15.95
1. Witchcraft—History. I. Title.
Distributed by W. W. Norton Inc., 500 Fifth Ave., New York, NY 10036

Witchcraft—History—Juvenile literature.

GARDEN, Nancy. 133.4'09
Witches / Nancy Garden. 1st ed. Philadelphia : Lippincott, [1975] 160 p. : ill. ; 21 cm. (The Weird and horrible library) Includes index. Bibliography: p. [157] Traces the history of witchcraft throughout the world from ancient times to the present. [BF1566.G28] 75-12621 ISBN 0-397-31564-3 : 5.95 ISBN 0-397-31611-9 pbk. : 2.25
1. Witchcraft—History—Juvenile literature. 2. [Witchcraft.] I. Title.

†REVESZ, Therese Ruth, 1946- 133.4'09
Witches / by Therese Ruth Revesz. New York : Contemporary Perspectives ; Milwaukee, Wis. : distributor, Raintree Publishers, c1977. 48 p. : ill. (some col.) ; 24 cm. Briefly highlights the history of witchcraft from the story of Circe and Medea, early Greek "witches," to Sybil Leek, a modern day witch. [BF1566.R44] 77-10626 ISBN 0-8172-1034-2 lib. bdg. : 4.95
1. Witchcraft—History—Juvenile literature. 2. [Witchcraft—History.] I. Title.

Witchcraft—Ireland.

SEYMOUR, St. John Drelincourt. 133.4'09415
Irish witchcraft and demonology, by St. John D. Seymour. Detroit, Singing Tree Press, 1970. vii, 255 p. 22 cm. Reprint of the 1913 ed. Includes bibliographical references. [BF1581.S4 1970] 76-99774
1. Witchcraft—Ireland. 2. Demonology. I. Title.

Witchcraft—Jamaica.

WILLIAMS, Joseph John, 1875- 133.097292
Psychic phenomena of Jamaica, by Joseph J. Williams... New York, The Dial press, 1934. 2 p. l., 309 p. 21 cm. Bibliography: p. 286-299. [BF1434.J3W5] 159.961097292 35-490
1. Witchcraft—Jamaica. 2. Magic—Jamaica. 3. Negroes in Jamaica. 4. Jamaica—Soc. life & cust. 5. Superstition. 6. Ashantis. I. Title.

Witchcraft—Jura Mountain region.

MONTER, E. William. 272'.8'09445
Witchcraft in France and Switzerland : the borderlands during the Reformation / E. William Monter. Ithaca, N.Y. : Cornell University Press, 1976. 232 p. : ill. ; 23 cm. Includes index. Bibliography: p. 201-206. [BF1582.M6] 75-31449 ISBN 0-8014-0963-2 : 15.00
1. Witchcraft—Jura Mountain region. I. Title.

Witchcraft—Juvenile literature.

ALDERMAN, Clifford Lindsey. 133.4
A cauldron of witches; the story of witchcraft. New York, Pocket Bks. [1973, c.1971] 182 p. 18 cm. Bibl. Summary: Describes the beliefs & ceremonies of witchcraft & the treatment of witches from ancient times to the present day. [BF1566.A54] ISBN 0-671-29558-6 pap., .75
1. Witchcraft—Juvenile literature. 2. [Witchcraft] I. Title.

ALDERMAN, Clifford Lindsey. 133.4
A cauldron of witches; the story of witchcraft. New York, J. Messner [1971] 190 p. 22 cm. Bibliography: p. 181-185. Describes the beliefs and ceremonies of witchcraft and the treatment of witches from ancient times to the present day. [BF1566.A54] 70-160311 ISBN 0-671-32449-7 4.50
1. Witchcraft—Juvenile literature. 2. [Witchcraft.] I. Title.

AYLESWORTH, Thomas G. 133.4
Servants of the devil [by] Thomas G. Aylesworth. [Reading, Mass.] Addison-Wesley [1970] 126 p. illus. 20 cm. "An Addisonian Press book." Traces the history of witchcraft from ancient to present times concentrating on various rituals, practices, and the trials of accused witches. [BF1566.A9] 73-118996 4.50
1. Witchcraft—Juvenile literature. 2. [Witchcraft.] I. Title.

AYLESWORTH, Thomas G. 133.4
The story of witches / by Thomas G. Aylesworth. New York : McGraw-Hill, [1979] p. cm. Includes index. Bibliography: p. Discusses how to become a witch, tests used to discover witches, tools of the trade, famous trials, and people who wanted to be witches. [BF1566.A92] 79-12321 ISBN 0-07-002649-1 : 6.95
1. Witchcraft—Juvenile literature. 2. [Witchcraft.] I. Title.

BLUE, Rose. 299
We've got the power : witches among us / by Lady Foxglove. New York : J. Messner, c1981. p. cm. "A Jem book." A brief introduction to witchcraft past and present, with biographical information on some famous modern witches. [BF1566.B56] 19 81-11098 ISBN 0-671-43604-X : 8.29
1. Witchcraft—Juvenile literature. 2. [Witchcraft.] I. Title.

BLUMBERG, Rhoda. 133.4
Witches / by Rhoda Blumberg. New York : F. Watts, 1979. 62 p. : ill. ; 22 cm. (A First book) Includes index. Bibliography: p. 57-59. Describes witches and witchcraft in history and in fiction from ancient times up to the modern resurgence of the "witch business." [BF1566.B57] 79-1427 ISBN 0-531-02948-4 : 5.90
1. Witchcraft—Juvenile literature. 2. [Witchcraft.] I. Title.

EPSTEIN, Perle S. 133.4'09
The way of witches [by] Perle Epstein. [1st ed.] Garden City, N.Y., Doubleday [1972] 175 p. illus. 25 cm. Bibliography: p. 171-172. [BF1566.E68] 72-184744 ISBN 0-385-00748-5 4.95
1. Witchcraft—Juvenile literature. 2. [Witchcraft.] I. Title.

HUNT, Bernice Kohn. 133.4
Out of the cauldron; a short history of witchcraft. [1st ed.] New York, Holt, Rinehart and Winston [1972] 119 p. illus. 22 cm. Published under the author's earlier name: Bernice Kohn. Bibliography: p. 113-114. Briefly examines the history and practices of witchcraft. [BF1566.H844] 74-150030 ISBN 0-03-080229-6 ISBN 0-03-080231-8 (lib. bdg.) 4.95
1. Witchcraft—Juvenile literature. 2. [Witchcraft.] I. Title.

STALLMAN, Birdie, 1911- 133.4'3
Learning about witches / by Birdie Stallman ; [prepared for Childrens Press by the Child's World] ; illustrated by Lydia

Halverson. Chicago, Ill. : Childrens Press, c1981. p. cm. (The Learning about series) Includes index. Briefly discusses the use of witchcraft and its practitioners. [BF1566.S76] 19 81-10011 ISBN 0-516-06536-X lib. bdg. : 9.25
1. Witchcraft—Juvenile literature. 2. [Witchcraft.] I. Halverson, Lydia, illus. II. Child's World (Firm) III. Title. IV. Series.

WILLIAMS, Selma R. 133.4
Riding the night mare : women & witchcraft / Selma Williams and Pamela J. Williams. New York : Atheneum, 1978. ix, 228 p. : ill. ; 24 cm. Includes index. Bibliography: p. 209-223. Discusses attitudes throughout history that have traditionally linked women to the practice of witchcraft. [BF1566.W73 1978] 78-6023 ISBN 0-689-30633-4 : 7.95
1. Witchcraft—Juvenile literature. 2. [Witchcraft.] I. William, Pamela J., joint author. II. Title.

Witchcraft—Lancashire, England.

CATLOW, Richard. 133.4'09427'645
The Pendle witches / [by] Richard Catlow ; [photographs by Stuart Mason]. Nelson : Hendon Publishing Co., 1976. 44 p. : ill., facsim., geneal. table, map, port. ; 21 x 29 cm. [BF1581.C38] 76-374991 ISBN 0-902907-82-4 : £1.30
1. Witchcraft—Lancashire, Eng. I. Title.

POTTS, Thomas 133.4'09427'2
fl.1612-1618.
The trial of the Lancaster witches, A.D. MDCXII; [recorded by Thomas Potts]. [1st ed. reprinted]; edited with an introduction by G. B. Harrison. London, Muller, 1971. xlvii, 188 p.; 1 illus. 23 cm. Facsimile of ed. published London, P. Davies, 1929. Originally published as The wonderfull discoverie of witches in the Countie of Lancaster, London, Barnes, 1613. Includes The arraignement and trial of Iennet Preston, of Gisborne in Craven, in the Countie of Yorke. [BF1581.P65 1971] 72-193427 ISBN 0-584-10921-0
1. Preston, Jennet, d. 1612. 2. Witchcraft—Lancashire, England. I. Harrison, George Bagshawe, 1894- ed. II. Title.
Available from Barnes and Noble, 6.50.

POTTS, Thomas, 133.4'09427'2
fl.1612-1618.
The trial of the Lancaster witches, 1612. [Edited with an introd. by G.B. Harrison New York, Barnes & Noble [1971] xlvi, 188 p. 23 cm. Facsim. reprint of the 1929 ed. Includes original t.p. which reads: The wonderfvll discoverie of witches in the covntie of Lancaster ... Together with the Arraignement and triall of Iennet Preston ... by Thomas Potts, Esquier. London, Printed by W. Stansby for Iohn Barnes, dwelling neare Holborne Conduit, 1613. The Arraignement and triall of Iennet Preston has special t.p. with imprint: London, 1612. [BF1581.P65 1929a] 75-27610 ISBN 0-389-04140-8 6.50
1. Preston, Jennet, d. 1612. 2. Witchcraft—Lancashire, Eng. I. Harrison, George Bagshawe, 1894- ed. II. Title.

Witchcraft—Maryland.

PARKE, Francis Neal. 133.409752
Witchcraft in Maryland, by Francis Neal Parke. [Baltimore?] 1937. cover-title, 50 p. 25 cm. "A paper read in part before the Round table and the Maryland historical society, and published in part in the Maryland historical magazine of December, 1936." [BF1577.M3P3] [159.961409752] 37-39102
1. Witchcraft—Maryland. I. Title.

Witchcraft—Massachusetts.

ALDERMAN, Clifford Lindsey. 133.4
The devil's shadow; the story of witchcraft in Massachusetts. New York, J. Messner [1967] 190 p. illus., map. 22 cm. Bibliography: p. 183-184. An account of the Salem witch trials and an examination of the conditions surrounding the prosecution of scores of citizens unjustly accused of witchcraft. [BF576.A4] AC 67
1. Witchcraft—Massachusetts. I. Title.

Witchcraft—Massachusetts—Juvenile literature.

DICKINSON, Alice. 272'.8
The Salem witchcraft delusion 1692. New York, Watts, 1974. 64 p. illus. 22 cm. (A Focus book) Bibliography: p. 63. Discusses the social and religious climate that led to the Salem witch hunts and describes the trials and their aftermath. [BF1576.D5] 73-12085 ISBN 0-531-01049-X 3.95 (lib. bdg.)
1. Witchcraft—Massachusetts—Juvenile literature. 2. [Witchcraft—Massachusetts.] I. Title.

Witchcraft—New England.

DANFORTH, Florence 133.4
Garrison.
New England witchcraft. New York, Pageant Press [1965] 54 p. 22 cm. Bibliography: p. 54. [BF1576.D3] 65-17620
1. Witchcraft — New England. I. Title.

DRAKE, Samuel Gardner, 133.4
1798-1875.
Annals of witchcraft in New England, and elsewhere in the United States; from their first settlement, drawn up from unpublished and other well authenticated records of the alleged operations of witches and their instigator, the devil. New York, B. Blom [1967] liii, 306 p. port. 20 cm. (Woodward's historical series, no. 8) Reprint of the 1869 ed. Includes bibliographical references. [BF1575.D7 1967] 67-13327
1. Witchcraft—New England. I. Title.

HALE, John, 1636-1700. 133.4
A modest enquiry into the nature of witchcraft / by John Hale. Facsim. reproduction with an introd. by Richard Trask. Bainbridge, N.Y. : York Mail-Print, 1973. xv, 176 p. ; 19 cm. Photoreprint of the 1702 ed. published by B. Eliot, Boston. Includes bibliographical references. [BF1575.H2 1973] 75-323418 ISBN 0-913126-05-5
1. Witchcraft—New England. I. Title.

MATHER, Cotton, 1663-1728. 133.4
On witchcraft, being The wonders of the invisible world, first published at Boston in Octr. 1692 and now reprinted with additional matter and old wood-cuts for the Library of the Fantastic & Curious. Mount Vernon, N. Y., Peter Pauper Press [1950?] 172 p. illus. 26 cm. [BF1575.M54 1950] 50-9778
1. Witchcraft—New England. I. Title. II. Title: The wonders of the invisible world.

[MATHER, Cotton] 1663-1728. 133
The vial poured out upon the sea. A remarkable relation of certian pirates brought unto a tragical and untimely end. Some conferences with them, after their condemnation. Their behaviour at their execution. And a sermon preached on that occasion. Boston: Printed by T. Fleet, for N. Belknap, and solgPaging irregular. The last leaf sign. [R] contains advertisement of "books lately printed for John Dunton". Typography and style of head-lines vary. Recto of first prelim. leaf half-title: The tryals of several vvitches, lately executed in New England published by the special command of the Governour. On verso: Imprimatur. Decem. 23 1692. Edmund Bohun. The author's defence, p. (1-2) [Letter from William Stoughton. p. [3]; prefatory note by Mather, p.[4] Enchantments encounter'd, p. 5-[17] A discourse on the wonders of the invisible world; uttered (in part) on August 4, 1692: p. 2-16, 33-80, 41-56, 89-98. First London edition. A 2d edition, greatly abridged, was published. London, J. Dunton. 1693, 62 p., and a 3d edition, London, J. Dunton, 1639, 64 p. [F2161.M42] 18-10990
1. Witchcraft—New England. I. Title.

PENNICK, Rupert. 133.4'09744
Witchcraft in New England : an investigation / by Rupert Pennick. Cambridge : Fenris-Wolf, 1976. [1], 11 p. ; 30 cm. (Megalithic visions antiquarian papers ; no. 12) Bibliography: p. 11. [BF1576.P46] 77-369745 ISBN 0-9505403-9-0 : £0.30
1. Witchcraft—New England. I. Title. II. Series.

PUTNAM, Allen, 1802-1887. 272.
Witchcraft of New England explained by modern spiritualism. By Allen Putnam ... Boston, Colby and Rich, 1880. 1 p. l., 5-482 p. 19 cm. "References": p. 20. cm. [BF1576.P88] 11-15858
1. Witchcraft—New England. I. Title.

PUTNAM, Allen, 1802- 133.40974
1887.
Witchcraft of New England explained by modern spiritualism. By Allen Putnam ... Boston, Colby and Rich, 1888. 482 p. 20 cm. "References": p. 20. [BF1576.P88 1888] 159.96140974 33-20349
1. Witchcraft—New England. I. Title.

Witchcraft—Pennsylvania.

LEWIS, Arthur H., 1906- 133.4
Hex, by Arthur H. Lewis. New York, Trident Press [1969] 255 p. 22 cm. [BF1577.P4L4] 69-14545 4.95
1. Rehmeyer, Nelson D., 1868-1928. 2. Blymyer, John H. 3. Curry, John, 1915-1962. 4. Hess, Wilbert G. 5. Witchcraft—Pennsylvania. I. Title.

Witchcraft—Rhodesia.

CRAWFORD, J. R. 133.4'09689'1
Witchcraft and sorcery in Rhodesia, by J. R. Crawford. London, pub. for the Intl. African Inst. by Oxford Univ. Pr., 1967. xi, 312p. front., 3 plates, 4. tables. 23cm. Bibl. [GN475.8.C75] 68-31932 9.50
1. Witchcraft—Rhodesia. I. International African Institute. II. Title.
Available from Oxford Univ. Pr., New York.

Witchcraft—Rhodesia, Northern.

REYNOLDS, Barrie. 291.33096894
Magic, divination, and witchcraft among the Barotse of Northern Rhodesia. Berkeley, University of California Press, 1963. xix, 181 p. illus., maps, tables. 25 cm. (Robins series, no. 3) Bibliography: p. 170-173. [BF1584.R5R4] 63-5737
1. Witchcraft—Rhodesia, Northern. 2. Lozi (African tribe) I. Title. II. Series.

Witchcraft—Salem, Mass.

HANSEN, Chadwick, 1926- 133.4
Witchcraft at Salem. New York, G. Braziller [1969] xvii, 252 p. 22 cm. Includes bibliographical references. [BF1576.H26] 69-15825 6.95
1. Witchcraft—Salem, Mass. I. Title.

JACKSON, Shirley, 133.409744
1919-1965.
The witchcraft of Salem Village. Illustrated by Lili Rethi. New York, Random House [1956] 176 p. illus. 22 cm. (Landmark books [69]) [BF1576.J3] 56-5454
1. Witchcraft—Salem, Mass. I. Title.

JACKSON, Shirley, 133.409744
1920-
The witchcraft of Salem Village. Illustrated by Lili Rethi. New York, Random House [1956] 176p. illus. 22cm. (Landmark books [69]) [BF1576.J3] 56-5454
1. Witchcraft—Salem, Mass. I. Title.

JACKSON, Shirley, 133.409744
1920-
The witchcraft of Salem Village. New York : Popular Library, 1976 c1956. 125 p. ; 17 cm. Includes index. [BF1576.J3] ISBN 0-445-03162-X pbk. : 1.50
1. Witchcraft—Salem, Mass. I. Title.
L.C. card no. for 1956 Random House edition: 56-5454.

LEVIN, David, 1924- 133.409744
ed.
What happened in Salem? Documents pertaining to the 17th-century witchcraft trials. Pref. by Thedoore Morrison. [New York] Twayne Publishers, 1952. 198p. 20cm. 'Reprinted from Handbook for English A, sixth edition, 1950.' Includes bibliography. [BF1575.L4] 52-13179
1. Witchcraft—Salem, Mass. 2. Trials (Witchcraft)—Salem, Mass. I. Title.

LEVIN, David, 1924- ed. 133.4
What happened in Salem? Documents pertaining to the seventeenth-century witchcraft trials. Young Goodman Brown [by] Nathaniel Hawthorne [and] A mirror for witches [by] Esther Forbes. 2d ed. New York, Harcourt, Brace [1960] 238 p. 24 cm. (Harbrace sourcebooks) "The introduction and parts I and II ... were first published at Harvard in the sixth edition, 1950, of the Handbook for English A." Includes bibliography. [BF1575.L4 1960] 60-8494
1. Witchcraft—Salem, Mass. 2. Trials (Witchcraft)—Salem, Mass. I. Title.

NEVINS, Winfield S. 133.4'09744'5
Witchcraft in Salem village in 1692; together with a review of the opinions of modern writers and psychologists in regard to outbreak of the evil in America. New York, B. Franklin [1971] 273 p. illus. 18 cm. (Burt Franklin research & source works series, 886. American classics in history and social science, 222) "Originally published 1916." Includes bibliographical references. [BF1576.N5 1971] 79-161383 ISBN 0-8337-4300-7
1. Witchcraft—Salem, Mass. I. Title.

NEVINS, Winfield S. 272.
Witchcraft in Salem village in 1692, together with some account of other witchcraft prosecutions in New England and elsewhere; by Winfield S. Nevins ... Salem, Mass., North shore publishing company; Boston, Lee and Shepard, 1892. 272 p. front., illus. (incl. facsim.) plates. 19 cm. [BF1576.N5] 11-8999
1. Witchcraft—Salem, Mass. 2. Witchcraft—New England. I. Title.

NEVINS, Winfield S. 272.
Witchcraft in Salem village in 1692; together with a review of the opinions of modern writers and psychologists in regard to outbreak of the civil in America. By Winfield S. Nevins. 5th ed., with new preface striking interest. Salem, Mass., The Salem press company, 1916. 2 p. l., lix, [2], 7-273 p. front., illus. (incl. facsim.) plates, ports. 18 cm. [BF1576] 17-18161
1. Witchcraft—Salem, Mass. 2. Witchcraft—New England. I. Title.

STARKEY, Marion Lena 133.409744
The Devil in Massachusetts, a modern inquiry into the Salem witch trials [Gloucester, Mass., Peter Smith, 1962, c.1940] 310p. (Dolphin bk. rebound) Bibl. 3.50
1. Witchcraft—Salem, Mass. I. Title.

STARKEY, Marion Lena 133.409744
The Devil in Massachusetts, a modern inquiry into the Salem witch trials. Garden City, N.Y., Doubleday [1961, c.1949] 310 p (Dolphin bk. C308) Bibl. 1.45 pap.,
1. Witchcraft—Salem, Mass. I. Title.

STARKEY, Marion Lena. 133.409744
The Devil in Massachusetts, a modern inquiry into the Salem witch trials. [1st ed.] New York, A. A. Knopf, 1949. xviii, 310, vii p. 22 cm. "Selected bibliography": p. 301-310. [BF1576.S8 1949] 49-10395
1. Witchcraft—Salem, Mass. I. Title.

STARKEY, Marion Lena 133.409744
The visionary girls witchcraft in salem village [by] Marion Starkey [New York-Dell 1975 c1973] 156 p. 18 cm. (Laurel Leaf Edition) [BF1576S83] 0.95 (pbk.)
1. Witchcraft—Salem, Mass. I. Title.
L.C. card no. for original edition: 72-13940.

STARKEY, Marion 133.4'09744'5
Lena.
The visionary girls: witchcraft in Salem Village, [by] Marion Starkey. [1st ed.] Boston, Little, Brown [1973] ix, 176 p. 21 cm. [BF1576.S83 1973] 72-13940 5.50
1. Witchcraft—Salem, Mass. I. Title.

TAPLEY, Charles Sutherland, 272.8
1899-
Rebecca Nurse, saint but witch victim, by Charles Sutherland Tapley. Boston, Mass., Marshall Jones company [c1930] xiii, 105 p. front. (port.) plates. 20 cm. [BF1576.T23] 30-33553
1. Nurse, Mrs. Rebecca (Towne) 1621-1692. 2. Witchcraft—Salem, Mass. I. Title.

UPHAM, Caroline E. Mrs. 272.
Salem witchcraft in outline. By Caroline E. Upham... 2d ed. Salem, Mass., The Salem press publishing & printing co., 1891. xiii,

161 p. front., 2 pl., 2 facsim. 18 cm. [BF1576.U5 1891] 17-2297
1. Witchcraft—Salem, Mass. I. Title.

UPHAM, Caroline E. Mrs. 272.
Salem witchcraft in outline. The story without the tedious detail. By Caroline E. Upham... Salem, Mass., E. Putnam, 1895. vi, ix-xiii, 161 p. front., plates, facsims. 17 1/2 cm. Nos. VII-VIII omitted in paging? [BF1576.U5 1895] 11-15968
1. Witchcraft—Salem, Mass. I. Title.

UPHAM, Charles Wentworth, 1802-1875. 272.
Lectures on witchcraft, comprising a history of the delusion in Salem, in 1692. By Charles W. Upham... Boston, Carter, Hendee and Babcock, 1831. vii, 280 p. 17 1/2 cm. [BF1576.U65] 11-14508
1. Witchcraft—Salem, Mass. I. Title.

UPHAM, Charles Wentworth, 1802-1875. 272.
Lectures on witchcraft, comprising a history of the delusion in Salem, in 1692. By Charles W. Upham... 2d ed. Boston, Carter and Hendee, 1832. v, [1], 300 p. 15 1/2 cm. [BF1576.U66] 11-14509
1. Witchcraft—Salem, Mass. I. Title.

UPHAM, Charles Wentworth, 1802-1875. 272.
Salem witchcraft; with an account of Salem village, and a history of opinions on witchcraft and kindred subjects. By Charles W. Upham... Boston, Wiggin and Lunt, 1867. 2 v. fronts., pl., fold. map, facsims. 20 1/2 cm. [BF1576.U56] 13-10002
1. Witchcraft—Salem, Mass. 2. Salem, Mass.—Hist. I. Title.

Witchcraft—Salem, Mass.—History—Sources.

RECORDS of Salem 133.4'09744'5
witchcraft, copied from the original documents. New York, B. Franklin [1972] 2 v. in 1. 22 cm. (Burt Franklin research & source works series. American classics in history and social science 236) Compiled by W. E. Woodward. Reprint of the 1864 ed., which was issued as no. 1 and 2 of Woodward's historical series. [BF1575.R3 1972] 76-178940 ISBN 0-8337-2916-0 26.50
1. Witchcraft—Salem, Mass.—History—Sources. I. Woodward, William Elliot, d. 1892, comp.

RECORDS of Salem 133.4
witchcraft, copied from the original documents. [Compiled by W. Elliot Woodward] New York, Da Capo Press, 1969. 2 v. in 1. 24 cm. (A Da Capo Press reprint edition) "Unabridged republication ... of the first edition ... published ... in 1864 and 1865." [BF1575.R3 1969] 78-75274
1. Witchcraft—Salem, Mass.—History—Sources. I. Woodward, William Elliot, d. 1892, comp.

Witchcraft—Salem, Mass.—Juvenile literature.

STARKEY, Marion Lena. 133.4'09744'5
The tall man from Boston / Marion L. Starkey ; illustrated by Charles Mikolaycak. 1st ed. New York : Crown Publishers, [1975] 46 p. : ill. ; 24 cm. An account of the Salem witch trials emphasizing the role of John Alden, one of the unjustly accused "witches." [BF1576.S82 1975] 75-9970 ISBN 0-517-52187-3 : 5.95
1. Witchcraft—Salem, Mass.—Juvenile literature. 2. [Witchcraft—Salem, Mass.] I. Mikolaycak, Charles. II. Title.

Witchcraft—Scotland.

BLACK, George Fraser, 1866- ed. 133.40941
Some unpublished Scottish witchcraft trials; transcribed and annotated by Dr. George F. Black. New York, The New York public library, 1941. 50 p. 25 cm. "The following Scottish witchcraft trials were copies in 1894-1895 from a manuscript abridgment of the Books of adjournal in the library of the Society of antiquaries of Scotland. This abridgment ... contains records ... of the Court of justiciary from 5th February, 1584, to 8th July, 1723."--p. 3. "Reprinted from the Bulletin of the New York public library of April-May-August-September 1941." [BF1581.B55] A 42
1. Witchcraft—Scotland. 2. Trials (Witchcraft) I. New York. Public library. II. Scotland. High court of justiciary. III. Title. IV. Title: Scottish witchcraft trials.

SETH, Ronald. 133.4'09415
In the name of the devil. New York, Walker [1970, c1969] 175 p. 22 cm. Bibliography: p. [171] [BF1581.S37 1970] 70-103004 4.95
1. Witchcraft—Scotland. I. Title.

SHARPE, Charles Kirkpatrick, 1781?-1851. 133.4'0941
A historical account of the belief in witchcraft in Scotland. [1st ed. reprinted]. Wakefield, S.R. Publishers, 1972. x, 266 p. 20 cm. Reprint of 1st ed., London, Hamilton, Adams, 1884. Bibliography: p. 255-262. [BF1581.S5 1972] 72-191880 ISBN 0-85409-747-3 £3.15
1. Witchcraft—Scotland. I. Title.

SHARPE, Charles Kirkpatrick, 1781?-1851. 133.4'0941
A historical account of the belief in witchcraft in Scotland. London, Hamilton, Adams, 1884. Detroit, Gale Research Co., 1974. 268 p. 22 cm. Originally published in 1819 as an introd. to Memorialls, by R. Law. Includes bibliographical references. [BF1581.S5 1974] 74-8196 ISBN 0-8103-3590-5
1. Witchcraft—Scotland. I. Law, Robert, d. 1690? Memorialls. II. Title.

Witchcraft—Scotland—Paisley.

ADAM, Isabel. 133.4'0941441
Witch hunt : a true story / Isabel Adam. New York : St. Martin's Press, c1978. 256 p. ; 22 cm. Includes index. Bibliography: p. 241-251. [BF1581.A37 1978b] 78-19427 ISBN 0-312-88429-X : 10.95
1. Paisley Abbey. 2. Witchcraft—Scotland—Paisley. I. Title.

Witchcraft—Southwest, New.

SIMMONS, Marc. 133.4'09789
Witchcraft in the Southwest; Spanish and Indian supernaturalism on the Rio Grande. [1st ed.] Flagstaff [Ariz.] Northland Press [1974] xiii, 184 p. illus. 24 cm. Bibliography: p. 181-184. [BF1577.S68S56] 74-76085 ISBN 0-87358-125-3 8.50
1. Witchcraft—Southwest, New. 2. Indians of North America—Southwest, New—Magic. I. Title.

SIMMONS, Marc. 133.4'09789
Witchraft in the Southwest : Spanish and Indian supernaturalism on the Rio Grande / by Marc Simmons. Lincoln : University of Nebraska Press, 1980, c1974. xiii, 184 p. : ill. ; 21 cm. Reprint of the ed. published by Northland Press, Flagstaff. Bibliography: p. 181-184. [BF1577.S68S56 1980] 79-18928 ISBN 0-8032-9116-7 : 4.75
1. Witchcraft—Southwest, New. 2. Indians of North America—Southwest, New—Magic. I. Title.

Witchcraft—United States.

ADLER, Margot. 133.4'.0973
Drawing down the Moon : witches, Druids, goddess-worshippers, and other pagans in America today / Margot Adler. New York : Viking Press, [1979] p. cm. [BF1573.A34] 79-12023 ISBN 0-670-28342-8 : 14.95
1. Witchcraft—United States. I. Title.

ADLER, Margot. 299
Drawing down the Moon : witches, Druids, goddess-worshippers, and other pagans in America today / Margot Adler. Boston : Beacon Press, 1981, c1979. xi, 455 p., [4] leaves of plates : ill. ; 21 cm. Originally published by Viking Press, New York. Includes bibliographical references and index. [BF1573.A34 1981] 19 80-68170 ISBN 0-8070-3237-9 (pbk.) : 8.95
1. Witchcraft—United States. 2. Cults—United States. 3. Women and religion. I. Title.

BOOTH, Sally Smith. 133.4'0973
The witches of early America / by Sally Smith Booth. New York : Hastings House, [1975] 238 p. ; 22 cm. Includes index. Bibliography: p. 231-233. [BF1573.B66] 75-2068 ISBN 0-8038-8072-3 : 9.95
1. Witchcraft—United States. I. Title.

ROBERTS, Susan. 133.4
Witches U.S.A. [Rev. ed] Hollywood, Calif., Phoenix House, 1974] 318 p. 22 cm. [BF1573.R62 1974] 74-75805 3.95 (pbk.)
1. Witchcraft—United States. I. Title.

Witchcraft—United States—Bibliography

NEW York. Public library. 016.
List of works in the New York public library relating to witchcraft in the United States. Comp. by George F. Black, of the Lenox staff. [New York, 1908] 18 p. 26 cm. Caption title. "Reprinted from the Bulletin, November, 1908." At end: 40 titles of works not in the library. [Z6878.W8N6] CA 9
1. Witchcraft—U.S.—Bibl. I. Black, George Fraser, 1866- II. Title.

Witchcraft—United States—Juvenile literature.

ALDERMAN, Clifford Lindsey. 133.4'0973
Witchcraft in America. New York, J. Messner [1974] 190 p. 21 cm. Bibliography: p. 180-185. Traces the history of witchcraft in the United States from its practice in the colonies to the present, including information on voodoo and Indian witchcraft. [BF1573.A42] 74-7586 ISBN 0-671-32685-6 5.95
1. Witchcraft—United States—Juvenile literature. 2. [Witchcraft.] I. Title.
Library binding; 5.29, ISBN 0-671-32686-4.

Witchcraft—West Indies.

BELL, Henry Hesketh Joudou, Sir, 1864-1952. 133.4
Obeah; witchcraft in the West Indies. Westport, Conn., Negro Universities Press [1970] viii, 200 p. 23 cm. Reprint of the 1889 ed. [BF1584.W5B4 1970] 78-106879
1. Witchcraft—West Indies. 2. Negroes in the West Indies. 3. West Indies—Description and travel. I. Title.

WILLIAMS, Joseph John, 1875- 133.409729
Voodoos and obeahs; phases of West India witchcraft, by Joseph J. Williams... New York, L. MacVeagh, Dial press inc., 1932. xix p., 1 l., 257 p. 23 1/2 cm. Bibliography: p. 237-248. [BF1584.W5W5] [159.961409729] 33-2130
1. Witchcraft—West Indies. 2. Voodooism. 3. Negroes in the West Indies. I. Title. II. Title: Obeahs.

WILLIAMS, Joseph John, 1875-1940. 133.4'09729
Voodoos and obeahs; phases of West India witchcraft. New York, AMS Press [1970] xix, 257 p. 24 cm. Reprint of the 1932 ed. Bibliography: p. 237-248. [BF1584.W5W5 1970] 74-111770 ISBN 0-404-06986-X
1. Witchcraft—West Indies. 2. Voodooism—West Indies. 3. Negroes in the West Indies. I. Title.

Withington, Hiram, 1818-1845.

ALLEN, Joseph Henry, 1820-1898. 922.8173
Memoir of Hiram Withington, with selections from his sermons and correspondence. Boston, W. Crosby and H. P. Nichols, 1849. 3 p. l., [3]-190 p. 18 1/2 cm. Preface signed: J. H. A. [i.e. Joseph Henry Allen] [BX9869.W6A8] 37-9267
1. Withington, Hiram, 1818-1845. 2. Unitarian churches—Sermons. 3. Sermons, American. I. Title.

Witness bearing (Christianity)

†ADAMS, James Edward, 1913- 248'.5
Three to win / James E. Adams. Springfield, Mo. : Gospel Pub. House, 1977. 125 p. ; 18 cm. (Radiant books) Adapted from Soul winning, by R. L. Brandt. [BV4520.A3] 77-72255 ISBN 0-88243-906-5 : pbk. : 1.50
1. Witness bearing (Christianity) I. Brandt, Robert L. Soul winning. II. Title.

ANDERSON, Kenneth, 1917- 248'.5
A coward's guide to witnessing [by] Ken Anderson. [1st ed.] Carol Stream, Ill., Creation House [1972] 157 p. illus. 22 cm. [BV4520.A54] 75-189627 3.95
1. Witness-bearing (Christianity) I. Title.

AUGSBURGER, David W. 248.5
Witness is withness. Chicago, Moody Press [1971] 127 p. 17 cm. [BV4520.A9] 72-143469
1. Witness bearing (Christianity) I. Title.

BARNARD, Floy Merwyn. 248
Christian witnessing. Nashville, Convention Press [1959] 111p. 19cm. [BV4520.B35] 59-9683
1. Witness bearing (Christianity) I. Title.

BARRINGTON, Porter. 248'.5
Witnessing with power and joy. [Nashville, Tenn.] T. Nelson [1972] 118 p. 21 cm. Includes bibliographical references. [BV4520.B355] 79-39590 ISBN 0-8407-5040-4
1. Witness bearing (Christianity) I. Title.

BELLET, Maurice 248.5
Facing the unbeliever. Tr. by Eva Fleischner. [New York] Herder & Herder [1967] 223p. 21cm. Tr. of Ceux qui perdent la foi. [BV4520.B3613] 67-27540 3.95
1. Witness bearing (Christianity) I. Title.

BENDER, Urie A. 248.5
The witness: message, method, motivation. Scottdale, Pa., Herald Pr. [c.1965] 159p. 21cm. [BV4520.B38] 65-18233 3.00
1. Witness bearing (Christianity) I. Title.

BENDER, Urie A 248.5
The witness: message, method, motivation, by Urie A. Bender. Scottsdale, Pa., Herald Press [1965] 159 p. 21 cm. [BV4520.B38] 65-18233
1. Witness bearing (Christianity) I. Title.

BLESSITT, Arthur. 248'.5
Tell the world; a Jesus people manual. Old Tappan, N.J., Revell [1972] 64 p. 18 cm. [BV4520.B52] 78-177397 ISBN 0-8007-0487-8 0.95
1. Witness bearing (Christianity) I. Title.

BOLIN, Gene. 248.5
Christian witness on campus. Introd. by Kenneth Chafin. Nashville, Broadman Press [1968] 95 p. 20 cm. Includes bibliographies. [BV639.C6B6] 68-20666
1. Witness bearing (Christianity) 2. Church work with students. 3. Evangelistic work. 4. College students—Religious life. I. Title.

BOND, Kingsley G. 248.5
A call to witness, by Kingsley G. Bond. Nashville, Methodist Evangelistic Materials [1965] 64 p. 19 cm. [BV4520.B57] 65-22516
1. Witness bearing (Christianity) I. Title.

BROCKWAY, Esther. 248'.5
Toward better witnessing / by Esther Brockway. Independence, Mo. : Herald Pub. House, c1976. 210 p. ; 21 cm. [BX8674.4.B76] 74-82511 ISBN 0-8309-0123-X
1. Reorganized Church of Jesus Christ of Latter Day Saints—Doctrinal and controversial works. 2. Witness bearing (Christianity) I. Title.

BRYANT, Anita. 248'.5
Fishers of men [by] Anita Bryant and Bob Green. Boston, G. K. Hall [1974, c1973] p. cm. Large print ed. [BV4520.B696 1974] 74-16001 ISBN 0-8161-6237-9 8.95 (lib. bdg.)
1. Witness bearing (Christianity) 2. Sight-saving books. I. Green, Bob, joint author. II. Title.

BRYANT, Anita. 248'.5
Fishers of men [by] Anita Bryant and Bob Green. Old Tappan, N.J., F. H. Revell Co. [1973] 156 p. illus. 21 cm. [BV4520.B696] 73-16091 ISBN 0-8007-0612-9 4.95
1. Witness bearing (Christianity) I. Green, Bob, joint author. II. Title.

CARRUTHERS, Donald Wallace, 1892- 241
How to share your spiritual discoveries; a laboratory approach to method in Christian witness, technique in Christian witness, five additional suggestions, by Donald W. Carruthers ... [State College, Pa., D. W. Carruthers, c1937] 64 p. 19 cm. [BV4520.C3] 37-14730
1. Witness bearing (Christianity) I. Title.

CHAFIN, Kenneth. 248'.5
The reluctant witness / Kenneth L. Chafin. Nashville : Broadman Press, [1975] c1974. 143 p. ; 21 cm. [BV4520.C5 1975] 74-84548 ISBN 0-8054-5550-7 : 4.50
1. Witness bearing (Christianity) I. Title.

CROSBY, John F. 240
Witness for Christ. Philadelphia, Westminster [c.1965] 96p. 19cm. Bibl. [BV4520.C7] 65-12520 1.45 pap.,
1. Witness bearing (Christianity) I. Title.

CROSBY, John F 240
Witness for Christ, by John F. Crosby. Philadelphia, Westminster Press [1965] 96 p. 19 cm. Bibliography: p. [95]-96. [BV4520.C7] 65-12520
1. Witness bearing (Christianity) I. Title.

DEVILLE, Jard. 248'.5
The psychology of witnessing / Jard DeVille. Waco, Tex. : Word Books, c1980. 126 p. ; 21 cm. [BV4520.D47] 19 80-51447 ISBN 0-8499-2922-9 (pbk.) : 4.95
1. Witness bearing (Christianity) I. Title.

DEWIRE, Harry A. 253.7
The Christian as communicator. Philadelphia, Westminster Press [c.1961] 198p. 21cm. (Westminster studies in Christian communication) Bibl.: p.191-194. 60-14681 4.50
1. Witness bearing (Christianity) I. Title.

DOBBINS, Gaines Stanley, 1886- 253
A winning witness [by] Gaines S. Dobbins ... Nashville, Tenn., The Sunday school board of the Southern Baptist convention [c1938] 4 p. l., 11-148 p. 20 cm. [BV3793.D6] 39-2584
1. Witness bearing (Christianity) 2. Evangelistic work. I. Baptist adult union. II. Title.

EIMS, Leroy. 248'.5
Winning ways; the adventure of sharing Christ. Wheaton, Ill., Victor Books [1974] 160 p. 18 cm. (An Input book) [BV4520.E35] 74-77319 ISBN 0-88207-707-4 1.75 (pbk.)
1. Witness bearing (Christianity) I. Title.

ELLIOTT, Douglas A. 248'.5
Any Christian can : a personal guide to individual ministry / Douglas A. Elliott. Waco, Tex. : Word Books, c1980. 100 p. ; 18 cm. (A Key word book) [BV4520.E44] 79-66522 ISBN 0-8499-4125-3 (pbk.) : 2.95
1. Witness bearing (Christianity) 2. Christian life—1960- 3. Sympathy. I. Title.

FEATHER, R. Othal. 248'.5
Outreach evangelism through the Sunday School [by] R. Othal Feather. Nashville, Convention Press [1972] xi, 145 p. illus. 20 cm. Bibliography: p. 141. [BV4520.F4] 70-186822
1. Witness bearing (Christianity) 2. Evangelistic work. 3. Visitations in Christian education. I. Title.

FLYNN, Leslie B. 248.5
Your influence is showing! [By] Leslie B. Flynn. Nashville, Broadman Press [1967] 127 p. 21 cm. Includes bibliographies. [BV4520.F55] 67-22027
1. Witness bearing (Christianity) 2. Christian life—Baptist authors. I. Title.

FRAZIER, Claude Albee, 1920- 248'.5
Notable personalities and their faith. Compiled by Claude A. Frazier. [Independence, Mo.] Independence Press [1972] 136 p. ports. 21 cm. [BV4520.F7] 72-89607 ISBN 0-8309-0083-7 3.50
1. Witness bearing (Christianity) I. Title.

GODFREY, George. 269'.2
How to win souls and influence people for heaven. Grand Rapids, Baker Book House [1973] 160 p. port. 22 cm. Bibliography: p. 157-158. [BV4520.G6] 72-85673 ISBN 0-8010-3666-6 2.95
1. Witness bearing (Christianity) 2. Evangelistic work. I. Title.

HITT, Russell T., comp. 248'.5
Share your faith; perspectives on witnessing. Edited by Russell T. Hitt, with William J. Petersen. Grand Rapids, Zondervan Pub. House [1973, c1970] 62 p. 18 cm. Contents.Contents.—Keiper, R. L. The secret of effective witnessing.—White, J. Witnessing is not brainwashing.—Kooiman, H. They come for coffee.—Eims, L. How to be a neighborhood witness.—Baldwin, S. C. Bashful Betty, Tacky Tom, and mistaken motives.—Barnhouse, D. G. Winning your relatives to Christ. [BV4520.H57 1973] 73-160645 0.95 (pbk)
1. Witness bearing (Christianity) I. Petersen, William J., joint comp. II. Title.

HOGUE, Richard. 248'.5
The Jesus touch. Nashville, Broadman Press [1972] 108 p. illus. 19 cm. [BV4520.H63] 72-79168 ISBN 0-8054-5524-8 1.75
1. Witness bearing (Christianity) I. Title.

HOUSTON, Jack, 1937- 267'.23
Wandering Wheels. Grand Rapids, Baker Book House [1970] 173 p. illus. 21 cm. [BV4520.H67] 75-19330 ISBN 0-8010-4009-4 3.95
1. Witness bearing (Christianity) 2. Cycling—U.S. I. Title.

ISHEE, John A. 248.5
Is Christ for John Smith? Edited by John A. Ishee. Nashville, Broadman Press [1968] 127 p. 20 cm. [BV4520.I8] 68-20677
1. Witness bearing (Christianity) I. Title.

KROMMINGA, John H 1918- 248
You shall be my witnesses; a challenge to bashful Christians. Grand Rapids, Eerdmans, 1954. 84p. 23cm. [BV4520.K7] 54-4136
1. Witness bearing (Christianity) I. Title.

KRUSE, Robert J., 1932- 248.5
To the ends of the earth; Christ here and now, by Robert J. Kruse. New York, Sheed and Ward [1969] xiv, 174 p. 21 cm. Includes bibliographical references. [BV4520.K76] 73-82596 4.50
1. Witness bearing (Christianity) I. Title.

LEAVELL, Frank Hartwell, 1884- 253
Christian witnessing [by] Frank H. Leavell... Nashville, Tenn., Broadman press [1942] 87 p. 19 1/2 cm. (My covenant series. Book 8) "My covenant" (form) on lining-paper. [BV4520.L35] 42-19312
1. Witness bearing (Christianity) I. Title.

THE Life work of George Irving; experiences in witnessing for Christ, edited by David R. Porter. New York, N.Y., Association press [1945] viii, 146 p. front. (port.) 21 cm. "Copyright ... by the International committee of Young men's Christian associations." [BV1085.I7L5] 46-763 922
1. Irving, George, 1877-1943. 2. Witness bearing (Christianity) I. Porter, David Richard, 1882- ed. II. Young men's Christian associations. International committee.

LINSLEY, Kenneth W. 248'.5'0924 B
Advocate for God : a lawyer's experience in personal evangelism / Kenneth Williams Linsley. Valley Forge, Pa. : Judson Press, c1977. 80 p. ; 22 cm. Includes bibliographical references. [BV4520.L47] 76-48749 ISBN 0-8170-0723-7 pbk. : 2.50
1. Linsley, Kenneth Williams. 2. Witness bearing (Christianity) 3. Baptists—United States—Biography. I. Title.

LITTLE, Paul E 248.5
Hou to give away your faith, by Paul E. Little. [Chicago] Inter-Varsity Press [1966] 131 p. illus. 22 cm. Bibliographical footnotes. [BV4520.L5] 66-20710
1. Witness bearing (Christianity) 2. Christian life. I. Title.

LITTLE, Paul E. 248.5
How to give away your faith, by Paul E. Little. [Chicago] Inter-Varsity [1966] 131p. illus. 22cm. Bibl. [BV4520.L5] 66-20710 3.50
1. Witness bearing (Christianity) 2. Christian life. I. Title.

METZGER, Will, 1940- 248'.5
Tell the truth : the whole gospel to the whole person by whole people : a training manual on the message and methods of God-centered witnessing / Will Metzger. Downers Grove, Ill. : InterVarsity Press, c1981. 187 p. ; 21 cm. Includes bibliographical references. [BV4520.M47] 19 80-24205 ISBN 0-87784-747-9 pbk. : 5.95
1. Witness bearing (Christianity) 2. Evangelistic work. I. Title.

MONSMA, John Clover, ed. 248
This I believe about Jesus Christ; the personal testimonies of leading Americans. [Westwood, N. J.] F. H. Revell Co. [c1955] 189p. 21cm. [BV4520.M58] 55-5389
1. Witness bearing (Christianity) I. Title.

MOREY, Robert A., 1946- 289.9'2
How to answer a Jehovah's Witness / Robert A. Morey. Minneapolis : Bethany Fellowship, c1980. p. cm. Bibliography: p. [BX8526.M66] 79-25502 ISBN 0-87123-206-5 pbk. : 2.95
1. Jehovah's Witnesses—Doctrinal and controversial works. 2. Witness bearing (Christianity) I. Title.

MORRISS, L. L. 248'.5
The sound of boldness / L. L. Morriss. Nashville : Broadman Press, c1977. 117 p. ; 20 cm. [BV4520.M63] 77-75559 ISBN 0-8054-6215-5 : 5.95
1. Witness bearing (Christianity) 2. Evangelistic work. I. Title.

NEVILLE, Joyce. 248'.5
How to share your faith without being offensive / Joyce Neville. New York : Seabury Press, 1979. vi, 152 p. ; 21 cm. "A Crossroad book." Includes bibliographical references. [BV4520.N39] 78-25885 ISBN 0-8164-2228-1 pbk. : 4.95
1. Witness bearing (Christianity) I. Title.

NILES, Daniel Thambyrajah 248.5
This Jesus . . . Whereof we are witnesses. Philadelphia, Westminister [1966, c.1965] 78p. 19cm. First pub. in Great Britain under title: Whereof we are witnesses. [BV4520.N5] 66-10503 1.25 [corrected entry] pap.,
1. Witness bearing (Christianity) I. Title. II. Title: Whereof we are witnesses.

NILES, Daniel Thambyrajah 248.5
Youth asks, what's life for; that they may see, by D. T. Niles. London, Camden, N.J. [etc.] Nelson [1968] 94 p. 20 1/2 cm. (Youth forum series) [BV4520.N52] 68-22130
1. Witness bearing (Christianity) I. Title. II. Series.

NOFFSINGER, Jack Ricks. 248.5
Heralds of Christ. Nashville, Convention Press [1966] viii, 119 p. 20 cm. "Church study course of the Sunday School Board of the Southern Baptist Convention] This book is number 0772 in category 7, section for young people." Includes bibliographies. [BV4520.N6] 66-10254
1. Witness bearing (Christianity) 2. Religious education — Textbooks for young people — Baptist. I. Southern Baptist Convention. Sunday School Board. II. Title.

PARSONS, E. Spencer 248.486
The Christian yes or no. Valley Forge [Pa.] Judson [1964, c.1963] 96p. 20cm. 64-10851 1.50 pap.,
1. Witness bearing (Christianity) 2. Christian life—Baptist authors. I. Title.

PEACE, Richard. 248'.5
Witness; a manual for use by small groups of Christians who are serious in their desire to learn how to share their faith. Foreword by Bruce Larson. Grand Rapids, Zondervan Pub. House [1971] 249 p. 21 cm. (A Zondervan horizon book) Includes bibliographical references. [BV4520.P4] 71-156253
1. Witness bearing (Christianity) I. Title.

PLEKKER, Robert J. 248'.5
Redeemed? Say so! / Robert J. Plekker. 1st ed. New York : Harper & Row, c1976. p. cm. [BV4520.P52] 76-10004 ISBN 0-06-066652-8 pbk. : 3.95
1. Witness bearing (Christianity) I. Title.

PONDER, James A. comp. 248.5
Evangelism men; motivating laymen to witness, compiled by James A. Ponder. Nashville, Broadman Press, [1975 c1974] 109 p. ports. 19 cm. [BV4520.P55] 74-20110 ISBN 0-8054-2224-2 1.95 (pbk.)
1. Witness bearing (Christianity) I. Title.

POTTHOFF, Harvey H 248.4
A theology for Christian witnessing [by] Harvey H. Potthoff. Nashville, Tidings [1964] 63 p. 19 cm. [BV4520.P6] 64-25872
1. Witness bearing (Christianity) I. Title.

PRICHARD, Ernie. 248'.5
Salesmanship for Christ [by] Ernie "Tex" Prichard. Nashville, Broadman Press [1972] 155 p. 21 cm. [BV4520.P74] 71-178064 ISBN 0-8054-5515-9 4.50
1. Witness-bearing (Christianity) I. Title.

RIDENOUR, Fritz. 248.5
Tell it like it is. Illustrated by Joyce Thimsen. Research: Georgiana Walker. Glendale, Calif., G/L Regal Books [1968] 232 p. illus. 18 cm. "The gospel of John in Living New Testament paraphrase combined with personal views and experiences of present day people." Bibliographical footnotes. [BV4520.R52] 68-29315
1. Witness bearing (Christianity) I. Title.

RINKER, Rosalind. 248'.5
Sharing God's love / by Rosalind Rinker and Harry C. Griffith. Grand Rapids : Zondervan Pub. House, c1976. p. cm. [BV4520.R53] 75-37757
1. Witness bearing (Christianity) I. Griffith, Harry C., joint author. II. Title.

RINKER, Rosalind. 253.7
You can witness with confidence. Grand Rapids, Zondervan Pub. House [1962] 105 p. 21 cm. [BV4520.R54] 63-1197
1. Witness bearing (Christianity) I. Title.

*SAMUEL, Leith. 248.5
Witnessing for Christ. Grand Rapids, Zondervan Pub. House [1974, c1962] 93 p. 18 cm. Originally published under the title Personal witness. [BV4520] 74-4955 1.25 (pbk.)
1. Witness bearing (Christianity.). I. Title.

SHELDON, Jean, 1956- 248'.5
Sharing Jesus : what witnessing is really all about / by Jean Sheldon. Mountain View, Calif. : Pacific Press Pub. Association, c1981. 144 p. ; 18 cm. Includes bibliographical references. [BV4520.S45] 79-27841 ISBN 0-8163-0350-9 pbk. : 4.95
1. Seventh-Day Adventists—Doctrinal and controversial works. 2. Witness bearing (Christianity) I. Title.
Distributed by the Greater New York Bookstore, 12 W. 40th St., New York, NY

STRACHAN, Robert Kenneth, 1910-1965. 248.5
The inescapable calling; the missionary task of the church of Christ in the light of contemporary challenge and opportunity. Grand Rapids, Mich., Eerdmans [1968] 127 p. 20 cm. (A Christian world mission book) Bibliography: p. 121-122. [BV4520.S684] 68-18841
1. Witness bearing (Christianity) I. Title.

SWEETING, George, 1924- 248'.5
How to witness successfully : a guide for Christians to share the Good News / George Sweeting. Chicago : Moody Press, c1978. 127 p. : ill. ; 22 cm. Includes bibliographical references. [BV4520.S93] 78-1959 ISBN 0-8024-3797-4 pbk. : 2.95
1. Witness bearing (Christianity) I. Title.

TERRY, Mary. 253
Winsome witnessing; how to tell your neighbors about Christ. With an introd. by M. E. Dodd. Chicago, Moody Press [1951?] 127 p. 18 cm. (Colportage library, 210) [BV4520.T4] 52-20937
1. Witness bearing (Christianity) I. Title.

TESTIMONY / 248'.5
compiled by H. Stephen Stoker & Joseph C. Muren. Salt Lake City, Utah : Bookcraft, 1980. xi, 180 p. ; 23 cm. Includes index. [BX8643.T45T46] 19 79-56174 ISBN 0-88494-391-7 : 5.95
1. Witness bearing (Christianity) 2. Mormons and Mormonism—Doctrinal and

controversial works. I. Stoker, Howard Stephen. II. Muren, Joseph C.

THOMPSON, W. Oscar, d.1980. 248'.5
Concentric circles of concern / W. Oscar Thompson, Jr. Nashville, Tenn. : Broadman Press, c1981. 168 p. : ill. ; 21 cm. [BV4520.T57 1981] 19 81-67488 ISBN 0-8054-6233-3 : 5.95
1. Witness bearing (Christianity) 2. Evangelistic work. I. Title.

ULBRICH, Armand Henry, 1915- 248'.5
Presenting the Gospel : how to do so with confidence and joy / by Armand Ulbrich. [St. Louis : Board for Evangelism, Lutheran Church-Missouri Synod, 1977] iii, 192 p. : ill. ; 23 cm. Cover title. [BV4520.U38] 77-150370
1. Witness bearing (Christianity) 2. Evangelistic work. I. Title.

WENGER, A. Grace 253.7
God builds the church through congregational witness; a resource book for the study of Christian Witnessing. Scottdale, Pa., Herald [1963, c.1962] 128p. 20cm. 62-17325 1.00 pap.,
1. Witness bearing (Christianity) I. Title.

WILLIAMS, Ethel (Hudson) Mrs. 248
Witnessing for Christ [by] Ethel Hudson Williams. Nashville, Tenn., The Sunday school board of the Southern Baptist convention [c1936] 108 p. 19 cm. [Full name: Mrs. Ethel Mae (Hudson) Williams] [BF4520.W5] 36-33926
1. Witness bearing (Christianity) 2. Youth—Religions life. I. Title.

WITMORE, Nyla. 248'.5
How to reach the ones you love : help for the family / by Nyla Witmore. San Bernardino, Calif. : Here's Life Publishers, c1981. 169 p. : ill. ; 21 cm. Bibliography: p. 168-169. [BV4520.W54] 19 81-81849 ISBN 0-89840-016-3 (pbk.) : 4.95
1. Witness bearing (Christianity) 2. Evangelistic work. 3. Family—Religious life. I. Title.

WYRTZEN, Jack, 1913- 248
Leaping flame; youth witnessing for Christ. Introd. by Charles J. Woodbridge. [Westwood, N. J.54 Revell [1954] 56p. 21cm. [BV4520.W9] 54-3174
1. Witness bearing (Christianty) I. Title.

YORK, William E. 248'.5
One to one; 15-minute Bible studies to share with a friend [by] William E. York, Jr. Downers Grove, Ill., Inter-Varsity Press [1972] 64 p. 18 cm. [BV4520.Y67] 72-78406 ISBN 0-87784-438-0 0.95
1. Witness bearing (Christianity) I. Title.

Witness bearing (Christianity)—Addresses, essays, lectures.

HITT, Russell T., comp. 248.5
Share your faith; perspectives on witnessing. Edited by Russell T. Hitt, with William J. Petersen. Grand Rapids, Zondervan Pub. House [1970] 62 p. 21 cm. (A Zondervan paperback) Contents.Contents.—The secret of effective witnessing, by R. L. Keiper.—Witnessing is not brainwashing, by J. White.—They come for coffee, by H. Kooiman.—How to be a neighborhood witness, by L. Eims.—Bashful Betty, Tacky Tom, and mistaken motives, by S. C. Baldwin.—Winning your relatives to Christ, by D. G. Barnhouse. [BV4520.H57] 76-106447 0.95
1. Witness bearing (Christianity)—Addresses, essays, lectures. I. Title.

RINKER, Rosalind 248.42
You can witness with confidence. Grand Rapids, Mich., Zondervan [c.1962] 105p. 21cm. 1.95 bds.,
I. Title.

Witness bearing (Christianity)—Biblical teaching.

BOICE, James Montgomery, 1928- 226'.5'066
Witness and revelation in the Gospel of John. Grand Rapids, Zondervan Pub. House [1970] 192 p. 21 cm. (Contemporary evangelical perspectives) Includes bibliographical references. [BS2615.2.B57] 78-106426
1. Bible. N.T. John—Criticism, interpretation, etc. 2. Witness bearing (Christianity)—Biblical teaching. 3. Revelation—Biblical teaching. I. Title.

TRITES, Allison A., 1936- 248'.5
The New Testament concept of witness / Allison A. Trites. Cambridge [Eng.] ; New York : Cambridge University Press, 1977. x, 294 p. ; 22 cm. (Monograph series - Society for New Testament studies ; 31) Includes indexes. Bibliography: p. 240-254. [BS2545.W54T74] 76-11067 ISBN 0-521-21015-1 : 23.00
1. Witness bearing (Christianity)—Biblical teaching. 2. Witnesses—Biblical teaching. I. Title. II. Series: Studiorum Novi Testamenti Societas. Monograph series ; 31.

Witness bearing (Christianity)—Case studies.

FROST, Marie. 248'.5'0924
Things happen when women care / by Marie Frost. Cincinnati : Standard Pub. Co., c1979. 143 p. ; 18 cm. [BV4520.F76] 79-63323 ISBN 0-87239-346-1 pbk. : 2.50
1. Frost, Marie. 2. Witness bearing (Christianity)—Case studies. I. Title.

Witness bearing (Christianity)—Juvenile literature.

WORRELL, George E. 248'.5
How to take the worry out of witnessing / George E. Worrell. Nashville : Broadman Press, c1976. 92 p. : ill. ; 20 cm. Includes bibliographical references. Discusses ways in which young Christians can spiritually prepare themselves for sharing their faith daily. [BV4520.W65] 76-381685 ISBN 0-8054-5568-X pbk. : 1.75
1. Witness bearing (Christianity)—Juvenile literature. 2. Youth—Religious life—Juvenile literature. 3. [Christian life.] I. Title.

Witness bearing (Christianity)—Study and teaching.

GRAYUM, H. Frank, comp. 248.5
Witnessing in today's world. H. Frank Grayum, editor. Nashville, Convention Press [1970] 57 p. 21 cm. "Text for course number 3101 of subject area Christian growth and service in the New church study course." [BV4520.G7] 75-121569
1. Witness bearing (Christianity)—Study and teaching. I. Title.

MOTT, John Raleigh, 1865- 267.
Confronting young men with the living Christ, by John R. Mott. New York, Association press, 1923. 203 p. 19 1/2 cm. [BV1090.M6] 23-9864
I. Title.

Witnesses (Canon law)

MCNICHOLAS, Timothy Joseph, 1917-
The septimae manus witness; a historical synopsis and a commentary. Washington, Catholic University of America Press, 1949. xii, 133 p. 23 cm. (The Catholic University of America. Canon law studies, no. 255) Thesis--Catholic University of America. Vita. Bibliography: p. 110-115. A 50
1. Witnesses (Canon law) 2. Marriage—Annulment (Canon law) I. Title. II. Series.

Witte, Kaaren.

WITTE, Kaaren. 248'.2
Angels in faded jeans / Kaaren Witte ; photography by Vicki Hesterman. Minneapolis : Bethany Fellowship, c1979. 158 p. : ill. ; 21 cm. [BV4531.2.W57] 79-84795 ISBN 0-87123-014-3 pbk. : 2.95
1. Witte, Kaaren. 2. Youth—Religious life. 3. Youth—Conduct of life. I. Title.

Wittenberg University, Springfield, Ohio. School of Music.

HAMMA School of Theology. 016.7839'52
Hymnbooks at Wittenberg : a classified catalog of the collections of Hamma School of Theology, Wittenberg School of Music, Thomas Library / by Louis Voigt with the collaboration of Darlene Kalke ... [et al.]. Springfield, Ohio : Chantry Music Press, 1975. [96] p. : facsims. ; 23 cm. Includes index. [Z7800.H35 1975] [BV349] 75-319617
1. Wittenberg University, Springfield, Ohio. School of Music. 2. Wittenberg University, Springfield, Ohio. Thomas Library. 3. Hymns—Bibliography—Catalogs. I. Voigt, Louis. II. Wittenberg University, Springfield, Ohio. School of Music. III. Wittenberg University, Springfield, Ohio. Thomas Library. IV. Title.

Wittgenstein, Ludwig, 1889-1951.

HALLETT, Garth. 230'.2
Darkness and light : the analysis of doctrinal statements / by Garth L. Hallett. New York : Paulist Press, c1975. vi, 174 p. ; 23 cm. Includes bibliographical references. [BX1753.H23] 75-21734 ISBN 0-8091-1897-1 pbk. : 6.95
1. Wittgenstein, Ludwig, 1889-1951. 2. Religion and language. 3. Theology, Catholic. I. Title.

HIGH, Dallas M. 149'.94
Language, persons, and belief; studies in Wittgenstein's philosophical investigations and religious uses of language [by] Dallas M. High. New York, Oxford University Press, 1967. viii, 216 p. 21 cm. Revision of the author's thesis, Duke University. Bibliographical footnotes. [B3376.W564H5 1967] 67-28127
1. Wittgenstein, Ludwig, 1889-1951. 2. Languages—Philosophy. 3. Semantics (Philosophy) I. Title.

KEIGHTLEY, Alan, 1944- 200'.1
Wittgenstein, grammar and God / [by] Alan Keightley. London : Epworth Press, 1976. 176 p. ; 22 cm. Includes index. Bibliography: p. 163-172. [B3376.W564K38] 76-374827 ISBN 0-7162-0264-6 : £1.75
1. Wittgenstein, Ludwig, 1889-1951. 2. Faith. 3. Grammar, Comparative and general. I. Title.

LOCKE, Don. 111
Myself and others: a study in our knowledge of minds. Oxford, Clarendon P., 1968. [7] 162 p. 20 cm. Bibliographical footnotes. [BD331.L77] 68-79660 27/6
1. Wittgenstein, Ludwig, 1889-1951. 2. Mind and body. 3. Cognition. 4. Personality. 5. Languages—Philosophy. I. Title.

PETERSON, Thomas D. 251'.00141
Wittgenstein for preaching : a model for communication / Thomas D. Peterson. Lanham, Md. : University Press of America, c1980. xiv, 180 p. : ill. ; 22 cm. Bibliography: p. 179-180. [B3376.W564P39] 19 80-5802 ISBN 0-8191-1342-5 : 17.00 ISBN 0-8191-1343-3 (pbk.) : 8.75
1. Wittgenstein, Ludwig, 1889-1951. 2. Semantics (Philosophy) 3. Communication (Theology) 4. Communication—Methodology. I. Title.

SHERRY, Patrick. 200'.1
Religion, truth, and language-games / Patrick Sherry. New York : Barnes & Noble Books, 1977. p. cm. (Library of philosophy and religion) Includes index. Bibliography: p. [BL51.S5226 1977] 75-41579 ISBN 0-06-496236-9 : 18.50
1. Wittgenstein, Ludwig, 1889-1951. 2. Religion—Philosophy. 3. Religion and language. I. Title.

Wittmann, George Michael, bp. of Ratisbon, 1760-1833.

MITTERMULLER, Rupert. 922.
Life and work of the Right Reverend George Michael Wittmann, bishop of Ratisbon, by Rev. R. Mittermueller, O.S.B.; translated from the German by a school sister of Notre Dame. Milwaukee, Wis., The Bruce publishing company, 1928. 202 p. front., plates, ports. 20 1/2 cm. [BX4705.W65M54] 28-15194
1. Wittmann, George Michael, bp. of Ratisbon, 1760-1833. I. A school sister of Notre Dame, tr. II. Title.

Witzlhofer, Josepha, 1817-1864.

THERESE Catherine, Sister, O.P. 271'.972'0924 B
An emerging woman [by] S. Therese Catherine. Staten Island, N.Y., Alba House [1970] xiv, 97 p., illus., coat of arms, geneal. table. 20 cm. Includes bibliographical references. [BX4705.W66T5] 71-129172 2.95
1. Witzlhofer, Josepha, 1817-1864. I. Title.

Wives.

HENDRICKS, Jeanne W. 220.9'2 B
A woman for all seasons / by Jeanne W. Hendricks. Nashville : T. Nelson, [1977] c1971. p. cm. [HQ759.H5 1977] 77-23045 ISBN 0-8407-5630-5 pbk. : 2.95
1. Wives. 2. Wives—Conduct of life. 3. Women in the Bible. I. Title.

Wives—Conduct of life.

PEALE, Ruth Stafford, 1906- 170.202'44
The adventure of being a wife : especially condensed for this gift edition by Mrs. Norman Vincent Peale. Norwalk, Conn. : C.R. Gibson Co., c1976. 120 p. ; 21 cm. [BJ1610.P292 1976] 75-16044 ISBN 0-8378-1771-4 : 4.50
1. Wives—Conduct of life. I. Title.

PEALE, Ruth (Stafford) 1906- 170.202'44
The adventure of being a wife, by Mrs. Norman Vincent Peale. Englewood Cliffs, N.J., Prentice-Hall [1971] 266 p. 22 cm. [BJ1610.P29 1971] 73-148492 ISBN 0-13-013946-7 5.95
1. Wives—Conduct of life. I. Title.

WE became wives of happy husbands : true stories of personal transformation / compiled by Darien B. Cooper, with her own comments and questions for contemplation, in collaboration with Anne Kristin Carroll. Wheaton, Ill. : Victor Books, c1976. 165 p. ; 21 cm. Bibliography: p. 165. [BJ1610.W5] 76-4314 ISBN 0-88207-731-7 pbk. : 2.50 248'.843'0922 B
1. Wives—Conduct of life. 2. Women—United States—Biography. I. Cooper, Darien B. II. Carroll, Anne Kristin.

Wives—Prayer-books and devotions.

GESCH, Roy G. 242.8'43
A wife prays, by Roy G. Gesch. St. Louis, Concordia Pub. House [1968] 104 p. 19 cm. [BV283.W6G4] 68-22575
1. Wives—Prayer-books and devotions. I. Title.

Wives—Prayer-books and devotions—English.

GRAFF, Mab. 242'.6'43
God loves my kitchen best / Mab Graff. Grand Rapids : Zondervan Pub. House, c1977. 206 p. ; 18 cm. [BV4844.G7] 77-5618 ISBN 0-310-35612-1 pbk. : 1.95
1. Wives—Prayer-books and devotions—English. I. Title.

Wives—Religious life.

BAKER, Elizabeth, 1944- 248'.843
The happy housewife / Elizabeth Baker. Wheaton, Ill. : Victor Books, [1975] 144 p. ; 18 cm. [BV4527.B3] 74-16978 ISBN 0-88207-720-1 : 1.75
1. Wives—Religious life. I. Title.

BERRY, Jo. 248.8'435
Beloved unbeliever : loving your husband into the faith / Jo Berry. Grand Rapids, Mich. : Zondervan Pub. House, c1981. 169 p. ; 21 cm. [BV4527.B46] 19 81-4518 ISBN 0-310-42621-9 pbk. : 4.95
1. Wives—Religious life. 2. Witness bearing (Christianity) I. Title.

CRANOR, Phoebe. 248'.843
How am I supposed to love myself? / Phoebe Cranor. Minneapolis : Bethany Fellowship, c1979. 144 p. ; 21 cm. Includes index. [BV4527.C72] 79-14229 ISBN 0-87123-236-7 pbk. : 2.95
1. Wives—Religious life. 2. Christian life—1960- 3. Self-love (Theology) I. Title.

DILLOW, Linda. 248'.843
Creative counterpart / Linda Dillow. Nashville : T. Nelson, c1977. 170 p. ; 21 cm. Includes bibliographical references. [BV4527.D54] 76-30387 ISBN 0-8407-5617-8 pbk. 2.95
1. Wives—Religious life. 2. Wives—Conduct of life. I. Title.

DILLOW, Linda. 248'.843
Creative counterpart : Bible study and project guide / Linda Dillow. Nashville : T. Nelson, c1978. 55 p. ; 20 cm. "Planned daily Bible reading, by Prof. J. Elwood Evans": p. 50-55. Includes index. [BV4527.D54 Suppl.] 78-675 pbk. : 1.50
1. Wives—Religious life. 2. Wives—Conduct of life. 3. Woman (Christian theology)—Biblical teaching. I. Title.

NELSON, Martha. 253'.2'0922
On being a deacon's wife. Nashville, Broadman Press [1973] 96 p. 21 cm. Includes bibliographical references. [BV4527.N382] 72-96150 ISBN 0-8054-3505-0 2.95
1. Wives—Religious life. 2. Deacons. I. Title.

NELSON, Rosanne E. 248'.842
Memo from Gabriel / Rosanne E. Nelson. 1st ed. Garden City, N.Y. : Doubleday, 1976. xii, 108 p. ; 22 cm. Includes bibliographical references. [BV4527.N387] 75-44524 ISBN 0-385-11494-X : 5.95
1. Wives—Religious life. I. Title.

†SIT, Amy Wang. 248'.843
The rib / by Amy Sit. Harrison, Ark. : New Leaf Press, 1976,c1977 140 p. ; 21 cm. Bibliography: p. 139-140. [BV4527.S47] 76-22278 ISBN 0-89221-026-5 pbk. : 2.95
1. Wives—Religious life. 2. Woman (Theology)—Biblical teaching. I. Title.

†WEST, Marion B. 248'.2
No turning back / Marion B. West. Nashville : Broadman Press, c1977. 162 p. ; 18 cm. [BV4527.W44] 76-57508 ISBN 0-8054-5254-0 pbk. : 2.25
1. West, Marion B. 2. Wives—Religious life. I. Title.

Wogen, Norris L.

WOGEN, Norris L. 284'.1'0924 B
The shadow of His hand : the dramatic account of one man's quest for fulness of life in the Spirit / Norris L. Wogen. Minneapolis : Bethany Fellowship, [1974] 127 p. ; 21 cm. [BX8080.W65A37] 74-21059 ISBN 0-87123-533-1 pbk. : 2.25
1. Wogen, Norris L. 2. Pentecostalism. I. Title.

Wold, Erling.

WOLD, Erling. 248'.86 B
Thanks for the mountain / Erling and Marge Wold. Minneapolis : Augsburg Pub. House, [1975] 111 p. ; 20 cm. [BR1725.W59A35] 74-14178 ISBN 0-8066-1461-7 pbk. 2.95
1. Wold, Erling. 2. Wold, Marge. I. Wold, Marge, joint author. II. Title.

WOLD, Erling. 248
What do I have to do - break my neck? [By] Erling and Marge Wold. Minneapolis, Minn., Augsburg Pub. House [1973, c1974] 112 p. 20 cm. [BR1725.W59A37] 73-88604 ISBN 0-8066-1407-2 2.95
1. Wold, Erling. 2. Wold, Marge. I. Wold, Marge, joint author. II. Title.

Wolf ritual.

ERNST, Alice (Henson). 970.1
The wolf ritual of the Northwest coast. Eugene, University of Oregon, 1952. ix, 107 p. illus., map. 26 cm. Bibliographical footnotes. [E98.R3E7] [299.7] 970.62 52-62258
1. Wolf ritual. 2. Makah Indians. 3. Quileute Indians. 4. Nootka Indians. I. Title.

Wolfe, Leslie E.,

ALLISON, Edith Wolfe, 1904-
Prisoner of Christ; the life story of Leslie and Carrie Wolfe. Joplin, Mo., College Press [c1960] vii, 104 p.illus., ports. 68-23226
1. Wolfe, Leslie E., 2. Wolfe, Carrie Austin, I. Title.

Wolff, Joseph, 1795-1862.

ROBINSON, Virgil E. 266.0230924
The restless missionary [by] Virgil E. Robinson. Pencil drawings by Fred Collins. Washington, Review and Herald Pub. Association [c1963] 93 p. illus., port. 22 cm. [BV3150.W7R6] 66-19419
1. Wolff, Joseph, 1795-1862. I. Title.

Wolffsohn, David, 1856-1914.

COHN, Emil, 1881- 922.96
David Wolffsohn, Herzl's successor, by Emil Bernhard Cohn. [Washington] The Zionist organization of America, 1944. xii p., 1 l., 281 p. front. (port.) 22 1/2 cm. [DS151.W7C6] 44-47715
1. Wolffsohn, David, 1856-1914. I. Zionist organization of America. II. Title.

Wolsey. Thomas, Cardinal, 1475?-1530.

CAVENDISH, George, 1500-1561? 923.242
The life of Cardinal Wolsey, by George Cavendish, his gentleman-usher; to which is added Thomas Churchyard's Tragedy of Wolsey ... With an introduction by Henry Morley ... London, G. Routledge and sons, limd. New York, E. P. Dutton and co. [1885] 284 p. 19 cm. (Half-title: Morley's universal library) [DA334.W8C35 1885] 922.242 4-17334
1. Wolsey, Thomas, cardinal, 1475?-1530. I. Churchyard, Thomas, 1520?-1604. II. Title.

FERGUSON, Charles Wright, 1901- 923.242
Naked to mine enemies; the life of Cardinal Wolsey. [1st ed.] Boston, Little, Brown [1958] 543 p. illus. 22 cm. [DA334.W8F38] 922.242 57-9320
1. Wolsey, Thomas, Cardinal, 1475?-1530. 2. Great Britain—Politics and government—1509-1547. I. Title.

POLLARD, Albert Frederick, 1869- 922.242
Wolsey. [Illustrated ed., with additional notes and corrections] London, New York, Longmans, Green [1953] xvi, 393p. ports. 22cm. Bibliographical footnotes. [DA334.W8P6 1953] [DA334.W8P6 1953] 923.242 53-10735 53-10735
1. Wolsey. Thomas, Cardinal, 1475?-1530. I. Title.

RIDLEY, Jasper Godwin. 942.05'2'0922 B
Statesman and saint / Jasper Ridley. New York : Viking Press, 1983. p. cm. Includes index. Bibliography: p. [DA334.A1R52 1983] 19 82-70122 ISBN 0-670-48905-0 : 20.75
1. Wolsey, Thomas, 1475?-1530. 2. More, Thomas, Sir, Saint, 1478-1835. 3. Great Britain—History—Henry VIII, 1509-1547. 4. Great Britain—Church history—16th century. 5. Statesmen—Great Britain—Biography. 6. Cardinals—England—Biography. 7. Christian saints—England—Biography. I. Title.

WOLSEY, 923.242
by Hilarie Belloc; with 12 illustrations and a map. Philadelphia & London, J. B. Lippincott company, 1930. viii p., 3 l., 3-336 p. front., plates, ports, map. 25 cm. [Full name: Joseph Hilaire Pierre Belloc] [DA334.W8B4] 922.242 30-31156
1. Wolsey, Thomas, cardinal, 1475-1530.

Womach, Merrill.

WOMACH, Merrill. 248'.2'0924 B
Tested by fire / Merrill and Virginia Womach, with Mel and Lyla White. Old Tappan, N.J. : Revell, c1976. 128 p. : ill. ; 21 cm. [BR1725.W595W65] 75-42789 ISBN 0-8007-0782-6 : 4.95
1. Womach, Merrill. 2. Womach, Virginia. I. Womach, Virginia, joint author. II. White, Mel, joint author. III. White, Lyla, joint author. IV. Title.

Woman.

ARMSTRONG, Frieda. 248'.843
To be free. Illustrated by Sandy Bauer. Philadelphia, Fortress Press [1974] viii, 88 p. illus. 21 cm. (Open book 9) Includes bibliographical references. [BJ1610.A75] 73-88340 ISBN 0-8006-0126-2 2.95
1. Woman. I. Title.

DEVAUX, Andre A. 201
Teilhard and womanhood, by Andre A. Devaux. Translated by Paul Joseph Oligny and Michael D. Meilach. New York, Paulist Press [1968] vii, 83 p. 19 cm. (Deus books) Translation of Teilhard et la vocation de la femme. [B2430.T374D483] 68-31259 0.95
1. Teilhard de Chardin, Pierre. 2. Woman. I. Title.

HEALY, Emma Therese, 1892- 189.4
Woman according to Saint Bonaventure. [New York?] 1956. x, 275p. 24cm. Bibliography: p. 271. [B765.B74H4] 56-1292
1. Bonaventura, Saint, Cardinal, 1221-1274. 2. Woman. I. Title.

LEWIS, Clifford, 1909- 173
God's ideal woman, by Clifford Lewis...Foreword by Mrs. William A. (Billy) Sunday. Grand Rapids, Mich, Zondervan publishing house [c1941] 86 p. incl. front. (2 port.) 19 1/2 cm. On cover: Recipes of happiness for women and girls. [Full name: John Clifford Lewis] [HQ1221.L65] 41-7998
1. Woman. I. Title.

Woman—Biography.

BACON, David Francis, 1813-1866. 920.7
Memoirs of eminently pious women of Britain and America Collected and edited by David Francis Bacon ... New Haven, D. McLeod. 1833. 2 p. l., [iii]-vii, [9]-008 p. ports. 23 cm. Added t.-p., engraved. [BR1713.B3] 37-24341
1. Woman—Biog. 2. Christian biography. I. Title.

BLUNT, Hugh Francis, 1877- 282'.0922
The great Magdalens. Freeport, N.Y., Books for Libraries Press [1969] ix, 335 p. 23 cm. (Essay index reprint series) Reprint of the 1928 ed. Contents.Contents.—Penitents of the stage.—Voices from the desert.—Magdalens of the ages of penance.—The woman Augustine loved.—Rosamond Clifford.—Saint Margaret of Cortona.—Blessed Angela of Foligno.—Blessed Clare of Rimini.—Saint Hyacintha of Mariscotti.—Cataline de Cardona, "the sinner."—Beatrice Cenci.—The Princess Palatine.—Madame de Longueville.—Louise de la Valliere.—Madame de Montespan.—Madame de la Sabliere.—Madame Pompadour.—Madame Tiquet. [BX4667.B5 1969] 71-86731
1. Catholic Church—Biography. 2. Woman—Biography. I. Title.

DEEN, Edith 922
Great women of the Christian faith Edith Deen. New York : Harper & Row, 1976 c1959. xix, 410 ; 21 cm. Includes index. Bibliography: pp. 393-397. [BR1713.D4] ISBN 0-06-061849-3 pbk. : 4.95
1. Woman—Biography. 2. Christian Biography. I. Title.
L.C. card no. for 1959 ed.: 59-12821.

FOSTER, Warren Dunham, 1886- ed. 209'.22 B
Heroines of modern religion. Freeport, N.Y., Books for Libraries Press [1970]. iv, 275 p. ports. 23 cm. (Essay index reprint series) Reprint of the 1913 ed. Contents.Contents.—Anne Hutchinson, by A. E. Jenkins.—Susannah Wesley, by W. H. Foster.—Elizabeth Ann Seton, by R. V. Trevel.—Lucretia Mott, by A. E. Jenkins.—Fanny Crosby, by W. Bradbury—Sister Dora, by G. L. Mumford.—Hannah Whitall Smith, by W. H. Foster.—Frances Ridley Havergal, by W. Bradbury.—Ramabai Dongre Medhavi, by J. C. Minot.—Maud Ballington Booth, by R. V. Trevel. Bibliography: p. 258-261. [CT3203.F75 1970] 77-107700
1. Woman—Biography. I. Title.

HARTSHORN, Leon R., comp. 289.3'092'2 B
Remarkable stories from the lives of Latter-Day Saint women. Compiled by Leon R. Hartshorn. Salt Lake City, Utah, Deseret Book Co., 1973. xi, 274 p. illus. 24 cm. Includes bibliographical references. [BX8693.H33] 73-87239 ISBN 0-87747-504-0 4.95
1. Church of Jesus Christ of Latter-Day Saints—Biography. 2. Woman—Biography. I. Title.

KER, Cecil. 266
Women who have made good, by Cecil Ker. New York, The Platt & Peck co. [c1916] vi p., 2 l., 11-91, [1] p. 16 cm. (Lettered on cover: The inspiration books) $0.35 [CT3234.K4] 16-15127
1. Woman—Biog. I. Title.
Contents omitted.

KOOIMAN, Helen W. 209'.22
Cameos, women fashioned by God [by] Helen W. Kooiman. Wheaton, Ill., Tyndale House [1969, c1968] 163 p. ports. 22 cm. [BR1713.K66] 68-56393 3.50
1. Woman—Biography. 2. Christian biography. I. Title.

MATHEWS, Winifred. 922
Dauntless women; stories of pioneer wives. Decorations by Ursula H. Bostick. New York, Friendship Press [1947] [6], 170 p. illus. 20 cm. Bibliography: 4th prelim. page. [BV3703.M3] 48-1449
1. Woman—Biog. 2. Missionaries. I. Title.
Contents omitted.

MATHEWS, Winifred, 1894- 266'.023'0922 B
Dauntless women; stories of pioneer wives. Illus. by Rafael Palacios. Freeport, N.Y., Books for Libraries Press [1970, c1947] 164 p. illus. 23 cm. (Biography index reprint series) Contents.Contents.—Ann Judson, comrade of an ambassador in chains.—Mary Moffat, mother of the tribe.—Mary Livingstone, "the main spoke in my wheel."—Christina Coillard, home-maker in the wagon.—Mary Williams, friend of the island women.—Agnes Watt, no ordinary woman.—Lillias Underwood, she followed "a red-maned star." [BV3703.M3 1970] 70-126325
1. Woman—Biography. 2. Missionaries. I. Title.

SHARP, T. 920.
The heavenly sisters; or, Biographical sketches of the lives of thirty eminently pious females, partly extracted from the works of Gibbons, Jerment, and others, and partly original: designed for use of females in general, and particularly recommended for the use of ladies' schools. By the Rev. T. Sharp ... To which is added, A sketch of the active life of Mrs. Sarah Hoffman, in her labours for the widow and the orphan, by John Stanford, A.M. New-York, H. Durell & co., 1822. vi, [7]-158 p. 15 cm. [CT3230.S5] 27-787
1. Hoffman, Mrs. Sarah (Ogden) 1742-1821. 2. Woman—Biog. I. Stanford, John, 1754- II. Title.

WILSON, William, (M.A.) 922
Heroines of the household. By the Rev. William Wilson ... With twenty-three illustrations. London, Virtue & co.; New York, Virtue and Yorston, 1869. 299, [1] p. front., illus., plates. 18 cm. [BR1713.W5] 37-25853
1. Woman—Biog. 2. Christian biography. I. Title.

Woman (Christian theology)

CARMODY, Denise Lardner, 1935- 261.8'344
Feminism & Christianity : a two-way reflection / Denise Lardner Carmody. Nashville : Abingdon, c1982 188 p. ; 22 cm. Includes bibliographical references and index. [BT704.C37 1982] 19 82-1709 ISBN 0-687-12914-1 pbk. : 8.95
1. Woman (Christian theology) 2.

Feminism—Religious aspects—Christianity. I. Title. II. Title: Feminism and Christianity.

DRAKEFORD, Robina. 261.8'357
In praise of women : a Christian approach to love, marriage, and equality / Robina and John W. Drakeford. 1st ed. San Francisco : Harper & Row, c1980. 180 p. ; 22 cm. Includes bibliographical references. [BT704.D68] 79-3000 ISBN 0-06-062063-3 : 8.95
1. Bible. O.T. Proverbs XXXI, 10-31—Criticism, interpretation, etc. 2. Woman (Christian theology) 3. Marriage. I. Drakeford, John W., joint author. II. Title.

KATOPPO, Marianne, 1943- 261.8'344
Compassionate and free : an Asian woman's theology / Marianne Katoppo. U.S. ed. Maryknoll, N.Y. : Orbis Books, 1980, c1979. vi, 90 p. : ill. ; 21 cm. Includes bibliographical references. [BT704.K37 1980] 19 80-16368 ISBN 0-88344-085-7 pbk. : 4.95
1. Katoppo, Marianne, 1943- 2. Woman (Christian theology) 3. Theology, Doctrinal—Asia—History. I. Title.

Woman (Christian theology)—Biblical teaching.

KUHNS, Dennis R. 261.8'34'12
Women in the church / Dennis R. Kuhns ; introd. by Beulah Kauffman. Scottdale, Pa. : Herald Press, 1978. 80 p. ; 20 cm. (Focal pamphlet ; 28) Bibliography: p. 75-78. [BS680.W7K83] 78-53968 ISBN 0-8361-1852-9 pbk. : 2.50
1. Woman (Christian theology)—Biblical teaching. I. Title.

SIDDONS, Philip. 261.8'344
Speaking out for women, a Biblical view / Philip Siddons. Valley Forge, PA : Judson Press, 1980. p. cm. Bibliography: p. [BS680.W7S56] 19 80-24007 ISBN 0-8170-0885-3 pbk. : 4.50
1. Woman (Christian theology)—Biblical teaching. I. Title.

Woman (Christian theology)—History of doctrines.

PHIPPS, William E., 1930- 261.8'34'12
Influential theologians on woman / William E. Phipps. Washington : University Press of America, c1980. 135 p. ; 21 cm. Includes bibliographical references and index. [BT704.P45] 79-5431 ISBN 0-8191-0880-4 pbk. : 7.25
1. Woman (Christian theology)—History of doctrines. I. Title.

Woman—Employment.

CAVAN, Ruth Shonle. 268.
Business girls: a study of their interests and problems. by Ruth Shonle Cavan ... [Chicago, Ill,[The Religious Ducation association, 1929. v. 97 p. incl. tables. diagrs. 25 cm. ([Religious education association] Religious education monograph, no. 3) Bibliography: p. 87-90. [BV1460.R53 no. 3] [BV1460.B53 no. 3] 268. E 31
1. Woman—Employment. 2. Girls. I. Title.

NELSON, Martha. 301.412
The Christian woman in the working world. New York, Pillar Books [1975 c1970] 138 p., 18 cm. Includes bibliographical references [BV4527] ISBN 0-89129-030-3 1.50 (pbk.)
1. Woman—Employment. 2. Woman—Religious life. I. Title.
L.C. card no. for original edition: 76-127198.

NELSON, Martha. 301.412'2
The Christian woman in the working world. Nashville, Broadman Press [1970] 141 p. 21 cm. Includes bibliographical references. [BV4527.N38] 76-127198 3.50
1. Woman—Employment. 2. Woman—Religious life. I. Title.

Woman—History and condition of women.

RADICALISM in religion, 081
philosophy, and social life; four papers from the Boston courier for 1858. Freeport, N.Y., Books for Libraries Press, 1972 [c1858] 79 p. 22 cm. (The Black heritage library collection) Contents.Contents.—Revival sermons.—Mr. Ralph Waldo Emerson as a lecturer.—Fair play to women.—The philosophy of abolition. [BX9869.B3R3 1972] 72-1804 ISBN 0-8369-9052-8
1. Parker, Theodore, 1810-1860. 2. Emerson, Ralph Waldo, 1803-1882. 3. Woman—History and condition of women. 4. Slavery in the United States. I. Boston daily courier. II. Title. III. Series.

Woman in church work.

WILLIAMSON, Mary (Heald) Mrs., 1901- 259
The countrywoman and her church [by] Mary Heald Willamson. New York, Nashville, Abingdon-Cokesbury press [c1940] 80 p. 19 1/2 cm. 80 p. 20 cm. 80 p. 20 cm. "Suggestions and sources for study": p. 75-80. [Full name: Mrs. Mary Louise (Heald) Williams] [BV4415.W5] 40-31670
1. Woman in church work. 2. Rural churches—U.S. I. Title.

Woman in Kongo, Belgian.

CAMPBELL, Henry D. 922.
A Congo chattel; the story of an African slave girl, by Rev. Henry D. Campbell... New York, N.Y., Christian alliance publishing company [c1917] 213 p. front (2 port.) plates 20 cm. [BV3625.K6C3] 17-11108 1.25
1. Woman in Kongo, Belgian. 2. Missions—Kongo, Belgian. I. Title.

Woman (Mormonism)

AUSTIN, Mildred Chandler, 1926- 261.8'34'12
Woman's divine destiny / Mildred Chandler Austin. Salt Lake City : Deseret Book Co., 1979. ix, 77 p. ; 24 cm. Includes bibliographies references and index. [BX8641.A9] 78-21274 ISBN 0-87747-733-7 pbk. : 3.95
1. Woman (Mormonism) I. Title.

Woman—Psychology.

HUNT, Gladys M. 261.8'34'12
Ms. means myself, by Gladys Hunt. Grand Rapids, Mich., Zondervan Pub. House [1972] 145 p. 22 cm. [HQ1206.H85] 72-85566 3.95
1. Woman—Psychology. 2. Conduct of life. I. Title.

HUNT, Gladys M. 261.8'34'12
Ms. means myself, by Gladys Hunt. New York, Bantam Books [1974, c1973] 146 p. 18 cm. [HQ1206.H85] 1.50 (pbk.)
1. Woman—Psychology. 2. Conduct of life. I. Title.
L.C. card number for original ed.: 72-85566.

Woman—Rights of women.

HAYDEN, M. P. 259
The Bible and woman; a critical and comprehensive examination of the teaching of the Scriptures concerning the position and sphere of woman. By M. P. Hayden, A.M. With an introduction by Prof. Chas. Louis Loos. Cincinnati, O., The Standard publishing company, 1902. x, 74 p. 20 cm. [HQ1395.H4] 3-15
1. Woman—Rights of women. 2. Women in the Bible. I. Title.

LAMB, Alexander. 259
Daughters who prophesy ... By Alexander Lamb. Introduction by Jennie Fowler Willing. [Philadelphia, The J. B. Rodgers printing company, c1888] 64 p. 17 cm. [HQ1395.L3] 9-5634
1. Woman—Rights of women. 2. Women in the Bible. I. Title.

TAYLOR, Isaac N. 259
The woman question? According to Moses and Paul, by Isaac N. Taylor. Boston, Arena publishing [!] co., 1894. 3 p. l., [5]-72 p. 17 x 9 cm. (On cover: Side pocket series) [HQ1395.T3] 9-5635
1. Woman—Rights of women. 2. Women in the Bible. I. Title.

Woman—Social and moral questions.

PORTER, John William, 1863- 301
Feminism, by J. W. Porter; Woman and her work, by John A. Broadus, J. B. Hawthorne, T. T. Eaton [and others] ... [Louisville, Ky., Baptist book concern, c1923] 165 p. 23 cm. [BV639.W7P6] 23-14696
1. Woman—Social and moral questions. I. Broadus, John Albert, 1827-1895. II. Title. III. Title: Woman and her work.

Woman (Theology)

MOLL, Willi 233
The Christian image of woman. Tr. by Elisabeth Reinecke, Paul C. Bailey. Notre Dame, Ind., Fides [1967] 168p. 20cm. Tr. of Die dreifache Antwort der Liebe. Bibl. [BT704.M613] 66-30592 2.95 pap.,
1. Woman (Theology) I. Title.

MOLL, Willi. 233
The Christian image of woman. Translated by Elisabeth Reinecke and Paul C. Bailey. Notre Dame, Ind., Fides Publishers [1967] 168 p. 20 cm. Translation of Die drelfache Antwort der Liebe. Bibliography: p. 165. [BT704.M613] 66-30592
1. Woman (Theology) I. Title.

MOLLENKOTT, Virginia R. 261.8'34'12
Women, men, and the Bible / Virginia R. Mollenkott. Nashville : Abingdon Press, [1977] p. cm. Includes bibliographical references. [BT704.M64] 76-40446 ISBN 0-687-45970-2 pbk. : 3.95
1. Woman (Theology) 2. Woman (Theology)—Biblical teaching. I. Title.

RABUZZI, Kathryn Allen. 248.8'43'5
The sacred and the feminine : toward a theology of housework / Kathryn Allen Rabuzzi. New York : Seabury Press, 1982. 215 p. ; 24 cm. Includes bibliographical references and index. [BL458.R26 1982] 19 81-18292 ISBN 0-8164-0509-3 : 15.95
1. Woman (Theology) I. Title. II. Title: Housework.

Woman (Theology)—Addresses, essays, lectures.

CLARK, Elizabeth, 1938- 261.8'34'12
Women and religion : a feminist sourcebook of Christian thought / Elizabeth Clark and Herbert Richardson. 1st ed. New York : Harper & Row, c1977. viii, 296 p. ; 21 cm. (Harper forum books ; RD 178) Includes bibliographical references. [BT704.C53 1977] 76-9975 ISBN 0-06-061398-X : 4.95
1. Woman (Theology)—Addresses, essays, lectures. 2. Women and religion—Addresses, essays, lectures. I. Richardson, Herbert Warren, joint author. II. Title.

Woman (Theology)—Biblical teaching.

BOLDREY, Richard. 261.8'34'12
Chauvinist or feminist? : Paul's view of women / Richard and Joyce Boldrey ; foreword by David M. Scholer. Grand Rapids : Baker Book House, c1976. 89 p. ; 22 cm. "A Canon Press book." Includes indexes. Bibliography: p. 73-82. [BS2655.W5B64] 75-38236 ISBN 0-8010-0657-0 : 2.95
1. Bible. N.T. Epistles of Paul—Theology. 2. Woman (Theology)—Biblical teaching. I. Boldrey, Joyce, joint author. II. Title.

FISCHER, James A. 261.8'34'12
God said, Let there be woman : a study of Biblical women / James A. Fischer. New York : Alba House, c1979. xiii, 115 p. ; 21 cm. Includes bibliographies. [BS680.W7F57] 78-21117 ISBN 0-8189-0378-3 pbk. : 4.95
1. Woman (Theology)—Biblical teaching. I. Title.

GUNDRY, Patricia. 262.8'34'12
Woman, be free! / Patricia Gundry. Grand Rapids : Zondervan Pub. Co., c1977. 112 p. ; 21 cm. Includes bibliographical references. [BS680.W7G86] 76-30494 4.95
1. Woman (Theology)—Biblical teaching. 2. Women in church work. I. Title.

HAGIN, Kenneth E., 1917- 233
The woman question / Kenneth E. Hagin. Greensburg, Pa. : Manna Christian Outreach, c1975. 93 p. ; 18 cm. [BS680.W7H33] 75-10513 ISBN 0-8007-8214-3 pbk. : 1.50
1. Woman (Theology)—Biblical teaching. I. Title.

HOPPIN, Ruth. 227'.87'014
Priscilla, author of the Epistle to the Hebrews, and other essays. [1st ed.] New York, Exposition Press [1969] 158 p. 21 cm. Contents.Contents.—Priscilla, author of the Epistle to the Hebrews.—The sovereignty of God and the spiritual status of women.—Four devotions.—More than a day's journey. Includes bibliographies. [BS2775.2.H6] 72-8428 6.00
1. Priscilla, Saint, wife of Saint Aquila. 2. Bible. N.T. Hebrews—Criticism, interpretation, etc. 3. Woman (Theology)—Biblical teaching. 4. Devotional exercises. I. Title.

MAERTENS, Thierry, 1921- 220.8'30141'2
The advancing dignity of woman in the Bible. [Edited by Lisa McGaw] Translated by Sandra Dibbs. De Pere, Wisc., St. Norbert Abbey Press, 1969. 241 p. 19 cm. Translation of La promotion de la femme dans la Bible. Includes bibliographies. [BT704.M313] 70-87815 4.95
1. Woman (Theology)—Biblical teaching. 2. Ordination of women. I. McGaw, Lisa, ed. II. Title.

OTWELL, John H. 296.3'87'83412
And Sarah laughed : the status of woman in the Old Testament / John H. Otwell. Philadelphia : Westminster Press, c1977. p. cm. Includes index. Bibliography: p. [BS1199.W7O88] 76-54671 ISBN 0-664-24126-3 pbk. : 7.95
1. Bible. O.T.—Criticism, interpretation, etc. 2. Woman (Theology)—Biblical teaching. I. Title.

PAPE, Dorothy. 261.8'34'12
In search of God's ideal woman : a personal examination of the New Testament / Dorothy R. Pape. Downers Grove, Ill. : Inter-Varsity Press, c1976. 370 p. ; 21 cm. Bibliography: p. 363-365. [BS2545.W65P36] 75-21453 ISBN 0-87784-854-8 : 4.95
1. Jesus Christ—Attitude towards women. 2. Woman (Theology)—Biblical teaching. 3. Women in Christianity. I. Title.

PENN-LEWIS, Jessie, 1861-1927. 248'.843
The magna charta of woman / by Jessie Penn-Lewis. Minneapolis : Bethany Fellowship, c1975. 103 p. ; 18 cm. (Dimension books) Originally published in 1919 under title: The magna charta of woman according to the scriptures. [BS680.W7P46 1975] 75-28655 ISBN 0-87123-377-0 : 1.50
1. Woman (Theology)—Biblical teaching. 2. Women—Religious life. I. Title.

SCANZONI, Letha. 261.8'34'12
All we're meant to be : a Biblical approach to women's liberation / Letha Scanzoni, Nancy Hardesty. Waco, Tex. : Word Books, [1974] 233 p. ; 23 cm. Includes bibliographical references and index. [BS680.W7S28] 74-78041 6.95
1. Woman (Theology)—Biblical teaching. 2. Women—Social conditions. I. Hardesty, Nancy, joint author. II. Title.

STAGG, Evelyn, 1914- 261.8'34'12
Woman in the world of Jesus / Evelyn and Frank Stagg. 1st ed. Philadelphia : Westminster Press, c1978. 292 p. ; 21 cm. Includes indexes. Bibliography: p. [271]-277. [BS2545.W65S72] 77-28974 ISBN 0-664-24195-6 pbk. : 5.95
1. Jesus Christ—Attitude toward women. 2. Woman (Theology)—Biblical teaching. I. Stagg, Frank, 1911- joint author. II. Title.

Woman (Theology)—History of doctrines.

KRESS, Robert. 261.8'34'12
Whither womankind? : The humanity of women / by Robert Kress. St. Meinrad, Ind. : Abbey Press, 1975. 336 p. ; 21 cm. (A Priority edition) Includes index. Bibliography: p. [321]-327. [BT704.K73] 75-207 ISBN 0-87029-045-2 pbk. : 4.75
1. Woman (Theology)—History of doctrines. 2. Feminism. I. Title.

Woman (Theology)—Sermons.

TALMAGE, Thomas DeWitt, 1832-1902. 301.41'2
Woman, her power and privileges : a series of sermons on the duties of the maiden, wife and mother, and of their influence in the home and society / by T. DeWitt Talmage. Washington : Zenger Pub. Co., 1975, c1888. p. cm. Reprint of the ed. published by J. S. Ogilvie, Chicago. [BT704.T34 1975] 75-41390 ISBN 0-89201-027-4
1. Presbyterian Church—Sermons. 2. Woman (Theology)—Sermons. 3. Sermons, American. I. Title.

Woman's American Baptist home mission society. Department of Christian friendliness.

KINNEY, Mary (Martin) Mrs. 1895- 266.61
The world at my door ... by Mary Martin Kinney. Philadelphia, Boston [etc.] The Judson press [c1938] 9 p. l., 5-185 p. front., plates, diagr. 20 cm. Illustrated lining-papers. "Published May, 1938." [Full name: Mrs. Mary Hitt (Martin) Kinney "Books that will help toward a better understanding": p. 182; "Other literature available": p. 183. [BV2766.B489K5] 38-23350
1. Woman's American Baptist home mission society. Dept. of Christian friendliness. 2. Missions, Home. 3. Baptists—Missions. I. Title.

Woman's branch of the New York city mission society.

BAINBRIDGE, Lucy (Seaman) Mrs. 1842-1928. 277.
Helping the helpless in lower New York, by Lucy Seaman Bainbridge, hon. supt. Woman's branch, New York city mission society ... Introduction by Rev. A. F. Schauffler, D. D. New York, Chicago [etc.] Fleming H. Revell company [c1917] 3 p. l., 5-172 p. front., plates. 20 cm. [BV2805.N5B3] 18-2050
1. Woman's branch of the New York city mission society. I. Title.

WHITE, Edith Hamilton, 1871- 277.471
Some life stories, by Edith Hamilton White ... New York, Chicago [etc.] Fleming H. Revell company [c1931] 83 p. 19 1/2 cm. [BV2805.N5W5] [266] 31-34723
1. Woman's branch of the New York city mission society. I. Title.

Woman's Christian temperance union.

EAST Manchester, N.H. Woman's Christian temperance union mercy home for girls.
Annual report. Bristol, N.H., v. 22 1/2 cm. Report year ends in September. 1902/03 report has title: Annual report of the W.C.T.U mercy home for girls. East Manchester, N.H. Established January 1, 1890, by the New Hampshire Woman's Christian temperance union. October, 1908. [HV1437.M2W8] CA 6
I. Title.

FOSTER, Judith Ellen (Horton) Mrs. 1840-1910. 178.
... The truth in the case, concerning partisanship and nonpartisanship in the W. C. T. U. By J. Ellen Foster ... and others ... [Clinton, Ia.] 1889. 153 p. 23 cm. [HV5227.W7F6] 39-20066
1. Willard, Frances Elizabeth, 1839-1898. 2. Woman's Christian temperance union. I. Title.

GORDON, Elizabeth Putnam, 1851-1933. 178.
Women torch-bearers; the story of the Woman's Christian temperance union [by] Elizabeth Putnam Gordon. Evanston, Ill., National woman's Christian temperance union publishing house [c1924] 5 p. l., 268 p. plates, ports., map. 21 cm. [HV5227.W6G6] 24-31815
1. Woman's Christian temperance union. I. Title.

GORDON, Elizabeth Putnam, 1851-1933. 178.062
Women torch-bearers; the first story of the Woman'sd Christian temperance union [by] Elizabeth Putnam Gordon ... 2d ed. Evanston, Ill., National woman's Christian temperance union publishing house [c1924] 5 p. l., 320 p. front., plates, ports., map, facsim. 22 cm. [HV5227.W6G6 1924 a] 33-24010
1. Woman's Christian temperance union. I. Title.

GREENE, E. G., Mrs. 178.
... Pathfinder for the organization and work of the Woman's Christian temperance union. By Mrs. E. G. Greene ... New York, The National temperance society and publication house, 1884. 183 p. 19 cm. At head of title: "For God and home and native land." [HV5227.G72] 10-35
1. Woman's Christian temperance union. I. Title.

RIVERA, Edith Mary Irvine, 1880- 178.1'062 B
Adventures for a better world. Philadelphia, Dorrance [1968] 122 p. 21 cm. [HV5232.R57A3] 68-31510 3.00
1. Woman's Christian Temperance Union. I. Title.

RIVERS, Edith M. Irvine, 1880- 178.0621
The dry blockade. Philadelphia, Dorrance [1951] 92 p. 20 cm. [HV5227.W7R5] 51-14651
1. Woman's Christian Temperance Union. 2. Liquor problem — U.S. I. Title.

WILLARD, Frances Elizabeth, 1839-1898. 178.
Woman and temperance; or, The work and workers of the Woman's Christian temperance union. By Frances E. Willard... Hartford, Conn., Park publishing co.; Chicago, J. S. Goodman & co.; [etc., etc., c1883] 648 p. incl. pl., ports. front., ports. 20 1/2 cm. "Frances E. Willard...By Mary A. Lathbury...": p. 19-38. [HV5227.W6] 9-18212
1. Woman's Christian temperance union. 2. Temperance. I. Lathbury, Mary Artemisia, 1841-1913. II. Title.

WOMAN'S Christian temperance union, New York. 178.
... W. C. T. U. handbook. Comp. by order of the executive committee of New York state Women's Christian temperance union, Lockport, N.Y., September 27th, 1888. Rev. and enl. by order of executive committee ... Chicago, Woman's temperance publishing association, 1890. 84 p. 17 cm. Committee: Mrs. Ella A. Boole, Mrs. Helen L. Bullock, Mrs. E. H. Griffith. 2d edtion. [HV5227.W8] 10-2
1. Woman's Christian temperance union. I. Title.

Woman's Christian Temperance Union. Colorado—Archives.

COLORADO. University. Libraries. Western Historical Collections. 016.178'1'062788
Guide to the Colorado Woman's Christian Temperance Union papers, 1878-1975 / compiled by Doris Mitterling ; edited by John A. Brennan. Boulder : Western Historical Collections, University of Colorado Libraries, 1976. v, 32 p. ; 28 cm. [Z6611.T24C64 1976] [HV5235.C6] 77-362161
1. Woman's Christian Temperance Union. Colorado—Archives. 2. Colorado. University. Libraries. Western Historical Collections. I. Mitterling, Doris. II. Title.

Woman's Christian temperance union—Georgia.

ANSLEY, Lula (Barnes) "Mrs. J. J. Ansley," 1861- 178.
History of the Georgia Woman's Christian temperance union from its organization, 1883 to 1907; By Mrs. J. J. Ansley, with an introduction by Miss M. Theresa Griffin ... containing the names of members of the Senate and House of representatives who voted for the prohibitory law and of the governor who signed the bill; also illustrated with a number of portraits of noted temperance men and women. [Columbus, Ga., Gilbert printing co., 1914] x. [2]. 13-262 p. front., pl., ports., map, facsim. 21 1/2 cm. [HV5235.G3A5] 14-20868
1. Woman's Christian temperance union—Georgia. I. Title.

Woman's Christian Temperance Union—History.

HAYS, Agnes Dubbs. 178'.1'06273
Heritage of dedication; one hundred years of the National Woman's Christian Temperance Union, 1874-1974. Evanston, Ill., Signal Press, 1973. 183 p. illus. 24 cm. Includes bibliographical references. [HV5227.W6H38] 73-83084
1. Woman's Christian Temperance Union—History. I. Title.

Woman's Christian Temperance Union, Indiana—History.

HENDRICKSON, Frances. 178'.1'062772
Hoosier heritage, 1874-1974: Woman's Christian Temperance Union. [Indianapolis? 1974] 206 p. illus. 23 cm. Cover title. [HV5297.I6H45] 74-171917
1. Woman's Christian Temperance Union, Indiana—History. I. Title.

Woman's Christian Temperance Union. Kansas.

HAYS, Agnes Dubbs. 178'.062'781
The white ribbon in the Sunflower State; a biography of courageous conviction, 1878-1953 [by] Agnes D. Hays (Mrs. Glenn G.) [Topeka, Woman's Christian Temperance Union of Kansas, 1953] 124 p. illus., ports. 22 cm. Includes bibliographical references. [HV5297.K2H385] 70-224571
1. Woman's Christian Temperance Union. Kansas. I. Title.

Woman's Christian temperance union. Minnesota.

SCOVELL, Bessie Lathe, Mrs. comp. 178.06273
A brief history of the Minnesota Woman's Christian temperance union from its organization, September 6, 1877 to 1939. compiled by Bessie Lathe Scovell. [St. Paul, Minneapolis, Bruce publishing company, c1939 4 p. l., 7-264 p. ports. 24 cm. Cover-title: Yesteryears. [HV5235.M6S3] 39-31308
1. Woman's Christian temperance union. Minnesota. I. Title. II. Title: Yesteryears.

Woman's Christian temperance union. New York.

GRAHAM, Frances W. 178.
Sixty years of action, 1874-1934. A history of sixty years' work of the Woman's Christian temperance union of the state of New York, by Francis W. Graham ... [n. p., 1934?] 4 p. l., [11]-150 p., 1 l. ports. 23 1/2 cm. [HV5235.N7G93] A 42
1. Woman's Christian temperance union. New York. I. Title.

GRAHAM, Frances W. Mrs. 178.
... Two decades: a history of the first twenty years' work of the Woman's Christian temperance union of the state of New York. By Frances W. Graham ... Georgeanna M. Gardiner ... Preface by Mary Towne Burt. [Oswego, N. Y., Press of R. J. Oliphant, [c1894] 83, [5] p. front., ports. 20 x 16 cm. At head of title: 1874-1894. "Written by request of the twentieth annual convention of the state Woman's Christian temperance union, held at Syracuses in October, 1893." [HV5235.N7G8] 10-4894
1. Woman's Christian temperance union. New York. I. Gardenier, Georgeanna M. (Remington) Mrs. joint author. II. Title.

Woman's Christian temperance union. Oklahoma.

HILLERMAN, Abbie B., Mrs., comp. 178.
1888-1925. History of the Woman's Christian temperance union of Indian Territory, Oklahoma Territory, state of Oklahoma, compiled by Abbie B. Hillerman... Sapulpa, Olk., Jennings printing & stationery co. [1925?] 4 p. l., [11]-111 p. incl. pl., ports. 23 1/2 cm. Running title: Oklahoma W. C. T. U. [HV5235.O5H5] 27-2526
1. Woman's Christian temperance union. Oklahoma. I. Title. II. Title: Oklahoma W. C. T. U.

Woman's Christian temperance union. Oregon.

ADDITON, Lucia H. Faxon. 178.062
Twenty eventful years of the Oregon Woman's Christian temperance union, 1880-1900. Statistical, historical and biographical. Portraits of prominent pioneer workers. [By] Lucia H. Faxon Additon... Portland, Or. Gotshall printing company, 1904. xv, 112 p. pl., ports. "Biographical": p. 87-96. [HV5235.O7A3] 33-6090
1. Woman's Christian temperance union. Oregon. 2. Oregon—Biog. I. Title.

Woman's Christian Temperance Union. Queensland.

LATHER, A. E. 178'.1
A glorious heritage, 1885-1965; history of the Woman's Christian Temperance Union of Queensland, prepared by A E. Lather [Brisbane, Woman's Christian Temperance Union of Queensland, 1968?] 62 p. ports. 22 cm. [HV5247.A82Q85] 70-423719 unpriced
1. Woman's Christian Temperance Union. Queensland. I. Title.

Woman's Christian temperance union—Salem, N.J.

VAN METER, Harriet F. 178.
... First quarter century of the Woman's Christian temperance union, Salem, New Jersey; comp. and ed. by Harriet F. Van Meter ... [Salem? N.J., c1909] 4 p. l., [7]-129 p. 22 1/2 cm. [HV5298.S32V3] 10-830
1. Woman's Christian temperance union—Salem, N.J. I. Title.

Woman's Christian Temperance Union. Tennessee.

BEARD, Mattie Carson (Duncan) 1888- 178.1062768
The W. C. T. U. in the Volunteer State, by Mattie Duncan Beard (Mrs. Samuel Clemens Beard) Kingsport, Tenn., Printed by Kingsport Press [1962] 150 p. illus. 23 cm. [HV5235.T2B4] 62-53291
1. Woman's Christian Temperance Union. Tennessee. I. Title.

Women and religion.

BRUNS, J. Edgar, 1923- 291.2'11
God as woman, woman as God [by] J. Edgar Bruns. New York, Paulist Press [1973] v, 89 p. 18 cm. (Paulist Press/Deus books) Includes bibliographies. [BL458.B78] 73-75247 ISBN 0-8091-1771-1 1.25 (pbk.)
1. Women and religion. I. Title.

CARMODY, Denise Lardner, 1935- 291.1'7834'12
Women & world religions / Denise Lardner Carmody. Nashville : Abingdon, c1979. 172 p. ; 22 cm. Includes bibliographies and index. [BL458.C37] 79-102 ISBN 0-687-45954-0 pbk. : 5.95
1. Women and religion. I. Title.

CHRIST, Carol P. 291.4
Diving deep and surfacing : women writers on spiritual quest / Carol P. Christ. Boston : Beacon Press, c1980. xvi, 159 p. ; 21 cm. Includes bibliographical references and index. [BL458.C47 1980] 79-51153 ISBN 0-8070-6362-2 : 9.95
1. Women and religion. 2. Spiritual life. I. Title.

THE Feminist mystic, and 305.4
other essays on women and spirituality / edited by Mary E. Giles. New York : Crossroad, 1982. vii, 159 p. ; 21 cm. Contents.Contents. The feminist mystic / Mary E. Giles — "Take back the night / Mary E. Giles — Immanent Mother / Meinrad Craighead — The courage to be alone—in and out of marriage / Margaret R. Miles — The feminine dimension of contemplation / Wendy M. Wright — The sexual mystic : embodied spirituality / Dorothy H. Donnelly — Armed with a burning patience : reflections on Simone Weil / Kathryn Hohlwein. Includes bibliographical references. [HQ1393.F44 1982] 19 81-22130 ISBN 0-8245-0432-1 pbk. : 8.95
1. Women and religion. I. Giles, Mary E.

GOLDENBERG, Naomi 291.1'7834'12
R.
Changing of the gods : feminism and the end of traditional religions / Naomi R. Goldenberg. Boston : Beacon Press, c1979. viii, 152 p. ; 21 cm. Includes bibliographical references and index. [BL458.G64 1979] 78-19602 ISBN 0-8070-1110-X : 9.95
1. Women and religion. 2. Religions (Proposed, universal, etc.) 3. Psychology, Religious. 4. Christianity—Controversial literature. 5. Judaism—Controversial literature. 6. Feminism—Moral and religious aspects. I. Title.

LANTERO, Erminie 291.2'11
Huntress.
Feminine aspects of divinity. [Wallingford, Pa.] Pendle Hill [1973] 32 p. 20 cm. (Pendle Hill pamphlet 191) Bibliography: p. 32. [BL458.L3] 73-84214 ISBN 0-87574-191-6 0.70 (pbk.)
1. Women and religion. 2. Sex (Theology) I. Title.

LUDER, Hope 261.8'34'12
Elizabeth.
Women and Quakerism / Hope Elizabeth Luder. Wallingford, Pa. : [Pendle Hill], 1974. 36 p. ; 19 cm. (Pendle Hill pamphlet ; 196) Bibliography: p. 35-36. [HQ1394.L84] 74-82914 ISBN 0-87574-196-7 : 0.70
1. Friends, Society of—History. 2. Women and religion. I. Title.

*MCGRATH, Sister 261.'8'34'12
Albertus Magnus.
Women and the Church. / by Sister Albertus Magnus McGrath, O. P. Garden City, N.Y. : Doubleday, 1976 c1972. 158 p. ; 18 cm. (Doubleday Image Books). Original title : What a modern Catholic believes about women Includes bibliographical references. [BL458] pbk. : 1.95
1. Women and religion. 2. Church work with women. I. Title.

MURRAY, Margaret Alice 291.213
The genesis of religion. London, Routledge & Paul [dist. New York, Philosophical, c.1963] v, 88p. 23cm. Bibl. 63-5949 3.75
1. Women and religion. I. Title.

NOBLE, Vicki. 291.2'11
Motherpeace : a way to the goddess through myth, art, and tarot / Vicki Noble. 1st ed. San Francisco : Harper & Row, c1982. p. cm. Includes index. Bibliography: p. [BL458.N63 1982] 19 82-47752 ISBN 0-06-066300-6 : 9.95
1. Women and religion. 2. Spiritual life. 3. Tarot. 4. Tarot in art. 5. Goddesses. I. Title.

OCHSHORN, Judith, 291.1'78344
1928-
The female experience and the nature of the divine / Judith Ochshorn. Bloomington : Indiana University Press, c1981. p. cm. Includes index. [BL458.O26] 19 81-47012 ISBN 0-253-31898-X : 17.50
1. Women and religion. 2. Sex and religion. 3. Sex in the Bible. 4. Polytheism. I. Title.

THE place of women in the church. By H. L. Goudge, Darwell, Stone, W. J. Sparrow Simpson, Lady Henry Somerset, Geraldine E. Hodgson, Mary Scharlieb, Mrs. Romanes, Miss E. K. Saunders. London, R. Scott; Milwaukee, Wis., Young churchman co., 1917. 204 p. 18 1/2 cm. (Half-title: Handbooks of Catholic fatiah and practice, ed. by W. J. Sparrow Simpson, D.D.) A 17
I. Goudge, Harry Leighton, 1866- II. Stone, Darwell, 1859- III. Simpson, William John Sparrow. IV. Somerset, Lady Isabella Caroline (Somers-Cocks) 1851-1921. V. Hodgson, Geraldine Emma, 1865- VI. Scharlieb, Mrs. Mary Ann Dacomb (Bird) 1845- VII. Romanes, Mrs. Ethel (Duncan) VIII. Sanders, Ella King.

SEXIST religion and 291.1'7834'12
women in the church; no more silence! Edited by Alice L. Hageman, in collaboration with the Women's Caucus of Harvard Divinity School. New York, Association Press [1974] 221 p. 22 cm. Chiefly lectures delivered at Harvard Divinity School, 1972-73. Includes bibliographical references. [BL458.S49] 73-21672 ISBN 0-8096-1840-0 6.25
1. Women and religion. I. Hageman, Alice L., ed. II. Harvard University. Divinity School. Women's Caucus.
Pbk. 3.95 Contents omitted.

SHAFFER, Wilma L. 267.4
Church women at work; a manual for church women. Cincinnati, Ohio, Standard Pub. Co. [c.1961] 106p. illus. Bibl. 1.50, pap., plastic binding
I. Title.

STONE, Merlin. 291.2'11
When God was a woman / Merlin Stone. New York : Harcourt Brace Jovanovich, 1978. p. cm. (A Harvest/HBJ book) Includes index. Bibliography: p. [BL458.S76 1978] 77-16262 ISBN 0-15-696158-X pbk. : 3.95
1. Women and religion. I. Title.

Women and religion—Addresses, essays, lectures.

BEYOND 291.1'7834'12
androcentrism : new essays on women and religion / edited by Rita M. Gross. Missoula, Mont. : Scholars Press for the American Academy of Religion, c1977. vi, 347 p. ; 24 cm. (Aids for the study of religion ; no. 6) Includes bibliographical references. [BL458.B49] 77-13312 ISBN 0-89130-196-8 pbk. : 6.00
1. Women and religion—Addresses, essays, lectures. I. Gross, Rita M. II. Title. III. Series.

WOMEN in ritual and 301.41'2
symbolic roles / edited by Judith Hoch-Smith and Anita Spring. New York : Plenum Press, c1978. xv, 289 p. : ill. ; 24 cm. Includes bibliographies and index. [BL458.W65] 77-17448 ISBN 0-306-31067-8 : 24.50
1. Women and religion—Addresses, essays, lectures. 2. Women (in religion, folk-lore, etc.)—Addresses, essays, lectures. 3. Sex role—Addresses, essays, lectures. I. Hoch-Smith, Judith. II. Spring, Anita.

Women and religion—Bibliography.

FISCHER, Clare 016.2911'78344
Benedicks.
Breaking through : a bibliography of women and religion / Clare B. Fischer ; sponsored by the Center of Women and Religion and the Graduate Theological Union Library. Berkeley, Calif. : Graduate Theological Union Library, 1981. x, 65 p. ; 24 cm. Erratum slip inserted. [Z7963.R45F57] [BL458] 80-18286 Price unreported.
1. Women and religion—Bibliography. 2. Women—Bibliography. I. Graduate Theological Union. Center of Women and Religion. II. Graduate Theological Union. Library. III. Title.

Women and religion—Congresses.

PLASKOW, Judith, 291.1'7834'12
comp.
Women and religion; papers of the Working Group on Women and Religion, 1972-73. Edited by Judith Plaskow [and] Joan Arnold Romero. Rev. ed. [Chambersburg, Pa.] American Academy of Religion; [distributed by Scholar's Press, Missoula, Mont., 1974] v, 210 p. 23 cm. Selected papers from two conferences, held in 1972 and 1973. Includes bibliographical references. [BL458.P55 1974] 74-83126 ISBN 0-88420-117-1 1.50 (pbk.)
1. Women and religion—Congresses. I. Romero, Joan Arnold, joint comp. II. Working Group on Women and Religion. III. Title.

Women—Arab countries—Bibliography.

MEGHDESSIAN, 016.3054'2'091749027
Samira Rafidi.
The status of the Arab woman : a select bibliography / compiled by Samira Rafidi Meghdessian under the auspices of the Arab Institute for Women's Studies in the Arab World, Beirut University College, Lebanon. Westport, Conn. : Greenwood Press, 1980. 176 p. ; 23 cm. Includes indexes. [Z7964.A7M43 1980] [HQ1784] 80-1028 ISBN 0-313-22548-6 lib. bdg. : 32.50
1. Women—Arab countries—Bibliography. 2. Women, Muslim—Bibliography. I. Title.

Women as ministers.

FOSTER, John Onesimus, 922.773
1833-1920.
Life and labors of Mrs. Maggie Newton Van Cott, the first lady licensed to preach in the Methodist Episcopal church in the United States. By Rev. John O. Foster ... With an introduction by Rev. Gilbert Haven ... and Rev. David Sherman. Cincinnati, Hitchcock and Walden, for the author, 1872. xxxix, 339 p. front. (port.) pl. 18 cm. "Woman's place in the gospel. By Rev. D. Sherman": p. xxix-xxxix. [BX8495.V15F6] 37-12145
1. Van Cott, Mrs. Maggie (Newton) 1830- 2. Women as ministers. I. Sherman, David, 1822-1897. II. Title.

HUNTER, Fannie McDowell, Mrs. 922
Women preachers. [By] Mrs. Fannie McDowell Hunter... Introduced by Dr. A. M. Hills... Dallas, Tex., Berachah printing co., 1905. 100 p. front. (port.) illus., pl. 23 cm. [BR1713.H8] 5-23045
1. Women as ministers. I. Title.

MEER, Haye van der. 253'.2
Women priests in the Catholic Church? A theological-historical investigation. Translated and with a foreword and afterword by Arlene and Leonard Swidler. Foreword by Cynthia C. Wedel. Philadelphia, Temple University Press [1973] xxix, 199 p. 23 cm. Translation of Priestertum der Frau? Originally presented as the author's thesis, Innsbruck, 1962. Bibliography: p. 169-191. [BV676.M4413] 73-79480 ISBN 0-87722-059-X 10.00
1. Women as ministers. I. Title.

THE office of woman in the 396.52
church; a study in practical theology. Translated with permission of Evangelischer Preszverband in Osterreich, Wien, by Albert G. Merkens. St. Louis, Concordia Pub. House [1955] 128p. 21cm. Includes bibliography. [BV676.Z45] 262.14 55-7445
1. Women as ministers. I. Zerbst, Fritz.

RAVEN, Charles Earle, 1885-
Women and the ministry, by Charles E. Raven ... with an American introduction by Elizabeth Wilson. Garden City, N. Y., Doubleday, Doran & company, inc., 1929. 3 p. l., 3-139 p. 20 cm. [BV676.R3 1929] 29-7092
1. Women as ministers. 2. Woman—Social and moral questions. I. Wilson, Elizabeth. II. Title.

Women as missionaries.

MONTGOMERY, Helen (Barrett) 266.
Mrs. 1861-1934.
Western women in eastern lands; an outline study of fifty years of woman's work in foreign missions, by Helen Barrett Montgomery ... New York, The Macmillan company, 1910. xiv, 286 p. incl. front. plates, ports., fold. tab. 19 cm. "References books" at end of most of the chapters. [BV2610.M6] 10-10345
1. Women as missionaries. 2. Women in missionary work. 3. Missions, Foreign. I. Title.

Women, Baptist—United States.

MCBETH, Leon. 261.8'34'12
Women in Baptist life / Leon McBeth. Nashville : Broadman Press, c1979. 190 p. ; 20 cm. Bibliography: p. 188-190. [BX6207.S68M32] 78-54245 ISBN 0-8054-6925-7 : 5.95
1. Southern Baptist Convention—History. 2. Women, Baptist—United States. I. Title.

Women—Biblical teaching.

STATON, Julia. 261.8'344
What the Bible says about women / by Julia Staton. Joplin, Mo. : College Press, c1980. x, 412 p. ; 23 cm. (What the Bible says series) Cover title: Women. Includes indexes. Bibliography: p. 373-374. [BS680.W7S73] 19 80-66128 ISBN 0-89900-079-7 : 13.50
1. Women—Biblical teaching. 2. Women in the Bible. I. Title. II. Title: Women. III. Series.
Publisher's address: Box 1132, 205 N. Main, Joplin, MO 64801

Women—Biography

BURDER, Samuel, 1773-1837.
Memoirs of eminently pious women. A new ed., rev. and enl. By the Rev. Samuel Burder... From a late London edition, in three volumes; now complete in one volume. Philadelphia, J.J. Woodward, 1834. 3 p. l., 730 p. front., ports. 23 1/2 cm. Complete with some omissions and additions, the work in 2 vols. by Thomas Gibbons, 1777; an additional volume added in 1804 by George Jerment, and the third volume added to a new and corrected edition by Samuel Burder in 1815. [BR768.B8 1834] 28-9917
1. Women—Biog. I. Gibbons, Thomas, 1729-1785. II. Jerment, George. III. Title.

BURDER, Samuel, 1773-1837.
Memoirs of eminently pious women. A new ed., rev. and enl. ... From a late London ed. ... Philadelphia, J.J. Woodward [1836] 2 p. l., 730 p. 2 port. (incl. front.) 23 1/2 cm. Comprises with some omissions and additions, the 2 volume work by Thomas Gibbons, 1777; an additional volume by George Jerment, 1804, and the third volume added by Samuel Burder to his edition of 1815. [BR768.B8 1836] 1-101418
1. Women—Biog. I. Gibbons, Thomas, 1720-1785. II. Jerment, George. III. Title.

DEEN, Edith. 922
Great women of the Christian faith. [1st ed.] New York, Harper [1959] 428 p. 25 cm. [BR1713.D4] 59-12821
1. Women—Biography. 2. Christian biography. I. Title.

HARDESTY, Nancy. 280'.088042
Great women of faith : the strength and influence of Christian women / Nancy A. Hardesty. Grand Rapids, Mich. : Baker Book House, c1980. 140 p. ; 23 cm. Bibliography: p. 135-140. [BR1713.H34] 19 80-65440 ISBN 0-8010-4223-2 : 9.95
1. Women—Biography. 2. Christian biography. I. Title.

Women (Christian theology)

LAHAYE, Beverly. 261.8'344
I am a woman by God's design / Beverly LaHaye. Old Tappan, N.J. : Revell, c1980. p. cm. Includes bibliographical references. [BT704.L34] 19 80-24461 ISBN 0-8007-1131-9 : 7.95
1. Women (Christian theology) I. Title.

Women (Christian theology)—History of doctrines.

BoRRESEN, Kari 261.8'344
Elisabeth, 1932-
Subordination and equivalence : the nature and role of women in Augustine and Thomas Aquinas / Kari Elisabeth Borresen

; text and citations translated from the revised French original by Charles H. Talbot. Washington, D.C. : University Press of America, 1981. p. cm. Translation of: Subordination et equivalence. Includes index. Bibliography: p. [BT704.B613 1981] 19 80-67199 ISBN 0-8191-1681-5 : 21.75 ISBN 0-8191-1682-3 (pbk.) : 12.75
1. Augustine, Saint, Bishop of Hippo. 2. Thomas Aquinas, Saint, 1225?-1274. 3. Women (Christian theology)—History of doctrines. I. [Subordination et equivalence.] English II. Title.

PLASKOW, Judith. 231
Sex, sin, and grace : women's experience and the theologies of Reinhold Niebuhr and Paul Tillich / by Judith Plaskow. Washington : University Press of America, [1980] p. cm. Based on the author's thesis, Yale, 1975. Includes index. Bibliography: p. [BT704.P56] 79-5434 ISBN 0-8191-0882-0 pbk. : 9.25
1. Niebuhr, Reinhold, 1892-1971. 2. Tillich, Paul, 1886-1965. 3. Women (Christian theology)—History of doctrines. 4. Sin—History of doctrines. 5. Grace (Theology)—History of doctrines. I. Title.

Women clergy.

BAILEY, Emma E 1844-1921. 922.
Happy day, or The confessions of a woman minister, by Reverend Emma E. Bailey. New York, European publishing company, 1901. xiv, 480 p. front., plates. ports. 21 cm. [BX9969.B26A3] 1-23281
I. Title.

BEARD, Helen. 262'.14
Women in ministry today / by Helen Beard. Plainfield, N.J. : Distributed by Logos International, c1980. xi, 248 p. ; 21 cm. Bibliography: p. 243-248. [BV676.B34] 19 80-82388 ISBN 0-88270-447-8 pbk. : 4.95
1. Women clergy. I. Title.

ELDRED, O. John. 262'.14
Women pastors : if God calls why not the church / O. John Eldred. Valley Forge, PA : Judson Press, 1981. 128 p. : ill. ; 22 cm. Includes bibliographical references. [BV676.E4] 19 80-28752 ISBN 0-8170-0901-9 : 4.95
1. Women clergy. 2. Ordination of women. I. Title.

GIBSON, Elsie. 262'.14
When the minister is a woman. [1st ed.] New York, Holt, Rinehart and Winston [1970] xviii, 174 p. 22 cm. Includes bibliographical references. [BV676.G5] 75-80361 ISBN 0-03-081846-X 4.95
1. Women clergy. I. Title.

HOWE, E. Margaret. 262'.14
Women & church leadership / E. Margaret Howe. Grand Rapids, Mich. : Zondervan Pub. House, c1982. 256 p. ; 20 cm. (Contemporary evangelical perspectives. Contemporary issues) Includes bibliographical references and indexes. [BV676.H68 1982] 19 81-16339 ISBN 0-310-44571-X pbk. : 6.95
1. Women clergy. 2. Women in Christianity. 3. Church officers. I. Title. II. Title: Women and church leadership. III. Series.

LEACH, Robert J. 262'.14
Women ministers : a Quaker contribution / Robert J. Leach ; edited by Ruth Blattenberger. Wallingford, Pa. : Pendle Hill, 1979. 29 p. ; 19 cm. (Pendle Hill pamphlet ; 227 ISSN 0031-4250s) [BX7746.L4] 79-84922 ISBN 0-87574-227-0 pbk. : 1.25
1. Friends, Society of—Clergy. 2. Women clergy. I. Blattenberger, Ruth. II. Title.
Publisher's address: 338 Plush Mill Rd., Wallingford, PA 19086.

PROCTOR, Priscilla, 1945- 253'.2
Women in the pulpit : is God an equal opportunity employer? / Priscilla and William Proctor. 1st ed. Garden City, N.Y. : Doubleday, 1976. 176 p. ; 22 cm. [BV676.P77] 75-14838 ISBN 0-385-00916-X : 6.95
1. Women clergy. I. Proctor, William, joint author. II. Title.

WILLARD, Frances Elizabeth, 1839-1898. 253'.2
Woman in the pulpit / by Frances E. Willard. Washington : Zenger Pub. Co., 1975, c1889. p. cm. Reprint of the ed. published by the Woman's Temperance Publication Association, Chicago. [BV676.W5 1975] 75-34240 ISBN 0-89201-014-2 : 11.95
1. Women clergy. I. Title.

Women clergy—Addresses, essays, lectures.

WOMEN ministers / 253'.2
edited by Judith L. Weidman. 1st ed. San Francisco : Harper & Row, c1981. p. cm. [BV676.W55 1981] 19 80-8345 ISBN 0-06-069291-X : 5.95
1. Women clergy—Addresses, essays, lectures. I. Weidman, Judith L.

Women clergy—Biblical teaching.

TETLOW, Elizabeth M. 262'.14
Women and ministry in the New Testament / Elizabeth M. Tetlow. New York : Paulist Press, c1980. 164 p. ; 21 cm. Includes indexes. Bibliography: p. 149-153. [BS2545.P45T47] 79-57398 ISBN 0-8091-2249-9 pbk. : 8.95
1. Bible. N.T.—Criticism, interpretation, etc. 2. Women clergy—Biblical teaching. 3. Pastoral theology—Biblical teaching. I. Title.

Women clergy—United States.

CARROLL, Jackson W. 262'.14
Women of the cloth : a new opportunity for the churches / Jackson W. Carroll, Barbara Hargrove, Adair T. Lummis. 1st ed. San Francisco : Harper & Row, c1982. p. cm. [BV676.C38 1982] 19 82-47740 ISBN 0-06-061321-1 : 12.45
1. Women clergy—United States. 2. United States—Church history—20th century. I. Hargrove, Barbara. II. Lummis, Adair T. III. Title.

WOMEN as pastors / 253'.2
edited by Lyle E. Schaller. Nashville : Abingdon, c1982. 127 p. ; 21 cm. (Creative leadership series) [BV676.W547] 19 81-20667 ISBN 0-687-45957-5 pbk. : 4.95
1. Women clergy—United States. I. Schaller, Lyle E. II. Series.

Women clergy—United States—Biography.

SMITH, Betsy Covington. 291.6'1'0924 B
Women in religion / by Betsy Covington Smith. New York : Walker, 1978. xix, 139 p. : ill. ; 24 cm. (Breakthrough) Describes the efforts of five women to break through the traditional male dominance of the clergy in churches and synagogues. [BV676.S64] 920 78-3016 ISBN 0-8027-6286-7 : 8.95
1. Women clergy—United States—Biography. 2. [Women clergy.] 3. [Clergy.] I. Title. II. Series: Breakthrough (New York)

Women—Conduct of life.

BLITCHINGTON, W. Peter. 248.8'43
The Christian woman's search for self-esteem / by W. Peter Blitchington. Nashville : T. Nelson, c1982. 166 p. ; 21 cm. Includes bibliographical references. [BJ1610.B55] 19 81-18963 ISBN 0-8407-5251-2 : 9.95
1. Women—Conduct of life. 2. Self-respect. I. Title.

HAWLEY, Gloria Hope. 248.3'43
Frankly feminine : God's idea of womanhood / by Gloria Hope Hawley. Cincinnati, Ohio : Standard Pub., 1981. p. cm. [BJ1610.H38] 19 81-8980 ISBN 0-87239-455-7 : 3.50
1. Women—Conduct of life. I. Title.

HEPBURN, Daisy. 248.8'43
Lead, follow or get out of the way / by Daisy Hepburn. Ventura, Calif. : Regal Books, c1982. p. cm. Includes bibliographical references. [BJ1610.H46] 19 82-295 ISBN 0-8307-0822-7 pbk. : 4.95
1. Women—Conduct of life. 2. Women—Religious life. I. Title.

LAHAYE, Beverly. 248'.843
The Spirit-controlled woman / Beverly LaHaye. Irvine, Calif. : Harvest House, c1976. 174 p. ; 21 cm. [BJ1610.L2] 76-5562 ISBN 0-89081-020-6 pbk. : 2.95
1. Women—Conduct of life. 2. Women—Religious life. I. Title.

LANDORF, Joyce. 248.8'43
Change points, when we need Him most / Joyce Landorf. Old Tappan, N.J. : Revell, c1981. 190 p. ; 22 cm. Includes bibliographical references. [BJ1610.L27] 19 81-11900 ISBN 0-8007-1257-9 : 8.95
1. Landorf, Joyce. 2. Women—Conduct of life. 3. Women—Religious life. I. Title.

ORTLUND, Anne. 248'.843
Disciplines of the beautiful woman / Anne Ortlund. Waco, Tex. : Word Books, c1977. 132 p. ; 23 cm. Includes bibliographical references. [BJ1610.O77] 77-76347 ISBN 0-8499-0000-X : 4.95
1. Women—Conduct of life. I. Title.

WILLIAMSON, Norma. 242'.6'33
Please get off the seesaw slowly / Norma Williamson. Old Tappan, N.J. : F. H. Revell Co., [1975] 127 p. ; 21 cm. [BJ1610.W54] 75-4999 ISBN 0-8007-0738-9: 4.95
1. Women—Conduct of life. 2. Women—Religious life. I. Title.

Women—Conduct of life—Addresses, essays, lectures.

WOMEN on pilgrimage / 248.8'43
edited by Shurden ... [et al.]. Nashville, Tenn. : Broadman Press, c1982. 129 p. ; 21 cm. [BJ1610.W65 1982] 19 81-70975 ISBN 0-8054-5428-4 : 4.95
1. Women—Conduct of life—Addresses, essays, lectures. I. Shurden, Kay Wilson.

Women—Employment—United States.

GILBERT, Lela. 248'.843
Just five days till Friday / Lela Gilbert. Denver : Accent Books, c1979. 127 p. ; 21 cm. [HD6053.G53] 78-74204 ISBN 0-89636-022-9 pbk. : 2.95
1. Women—Employment—United States. 2. Women—Conduct of life. I. Title.

WARD, Patricia A., 1940- 331.4'0973
Christian women at work / Patricia A. Ward and Martha G. Stout. Grand Rapids, Mich. : Zondervan, c1981. 242 p. ; 23 cm. Includes bibliographical references. [HD6095.W197] 19 81-13021 ISBN 0-310-43700-8 : 8.95
1. Women—Employment—United States. 2. Women—Control of life. 3. Women—Religious life. 4. Women in church work—United States. I. Stout, Martha G. II. Title.

Women, Friend—United States—History.

BACON, Margaret Hope. 289.6'092'2 B
As the way opens : the story of Quaker women in America / by Margaret H. Bacon. Richmond, Ind. : Friends United Press, c1980. xiv, 132 p. ; 22 cm. Bibliography: p. 129-132. [BX7635.B28] 19 80-67786 ISBN 0-913408-58-1 : 8.95
1. Women, Friend—United States—History. 2. Women, Friend—United States—Biography. 3. Social reformers—United States—Biography. I. Title.
Publisher's address: 101 Quaker Hill Dr., Richmond, IN 47374

Women hymn writers—Great Britain.

ROGAL, Samuel J. 245'.21'0922
Sisters of sacred song : a selected listing of women hymnodists in Great Britain and America / Samuel J. Rogal. New York : Garland Pub., 1980. p. cm. (Garland reference library of the humanities ; v. 223) Bibliography: p. [BV325.R63] 19 80-8482 ISBN 0-8240-9482-4 : 22.00
1. Women hymn writers—Great Britain. 2. Women hymn writers—United States. I. Title.

Women in Assam.

VICKLAND, Ellen Elizabeth. 275.
Women of Assam, by E. Elizabeth Vickland ... edited by the Department of missionary education of the Board of education of the Northern Baptist convention ... Philadelphia, Boston [etc.] The Judson press [c1928] 8 p. l., 179 p. front., plates, ports. 20 cm. Bibliography: p. 177-179. [BV3280.A8V58] 28-13229
1. Women in Assam. 2. Assam—Soc. condit. 3. Missions—Assam. I. Northern Baptist convention. Board of education. II. Title.

Women in campus ministry—Congresses.

KELLEY, Ann Elizabeth. 253
Women in campus ministry; a report from consultations with Catholic women campus ministers. [Cambridge, Mass.] National Center for Campus Ministry, 1973. xiii, 37 p. 22 cm. (National Center for Campus Ministry. Research paper no. 1) A report of the meetings held in Boston, Sept. 8-9; San Francisco, Sept. 15-16; New Orleans, Sept. 29-30; and Chicago, Oct. 6-7, 1972. [BV4376.K44] 73-158792
1. Women in campus ministry—Congresses. I. Title. II. Title: Catholic women campus ministers. III. Series.

Women in charitable work—Addresses, essays, lectures.

JAMESON, Anna Brownell Murphy, 1794-1860. 271'.9'1
Sisters of charity, Catholic and Protestant and The communion of labor / by Mrs. Jameson. Westport, Conn. : Hyperion Press, 1976. p. cm. (Pioneers of the woman's movement ; 8) Reprint of the 1857 ed. published by Ticknor and Fields, Boston. [BX4237.J35 1976] 75-15087 ISBN 0-88355-268-X : 19.75
1. Sisters of Charity—Addresses, essays, lectures. 2. Women in charitable work—Addresses, essays, lectures. 3. Nursing—Moral and religious aspects—Addresses, essays, lectures. I. Jameson, Anna Brownell Murphy, 1794-1860. The communion of labor. 1976. II. Title.

Women in Christianity.

ACHTEMEIER, Elizabeth Rice, 1926- 248.843
The feminine crises in Christian faith [by] Elizabeth Achtemeier. New York, Abingdon Press [1965] 100 p. 21 cm. "Suggested helps for Bible study": p. 153-154. [BV639.W7A3] 65-20366
1. Women in Christianity. 2. Woman — Religious life. I. Title.

ACHTEMEIER, Elizabeth Rice, 1926- 248.843
The feminine crisis in Christian faith. Nashville, Abingdon Press [c.1965] 160p. 21cm. Bibl. [BV639.W7A3] 65-20366 2.75 bds.,
1. Women in Christianity. 2. Woman—Religious life. I. Title.

COLLINS, Sheila D. 261.8'34'12
A different heaven and earth [by] Sheila D. Collins. Valley Forge [Pa.] Judson Press [1974] 253 p. 23 cm. Includes bibliographical references. [BV639.W7C57] 74-2890 ISBN 0-8170-0620-6
1. Women in Christianity. I. Title.

CROOK, Margaret Brackenbury 209
Women and religion. Boston, Beacon [1965, c.1964] x, 272p. 24cm. Bibl. [BV639.W7C7] 64-20496 5.95
1. Women in Christianity. I. Title.

CUNNEEN, Sally. 260
Sex: female; religion: Catholic. [1st ed.] New York, Holt, Rinehart and Winston [1968] xv, 171 p. 22 cm. Includes bibliographical references. [BX2347.8.W6C8] 68-10075
1. Women in Christianity. I. Title.

DALY, Mary. 261.8'34'12
The Church and the second sex / Mary Daly ; with a new feminist postchristian introd. by the author. New York : Harper & Row, 1975. 229 p. ; 21 cm. (Harper colophon books) Includes bibliographical

references and index. [BV639.W7D28 1975] 75-301799 pbk. : 3.45
1. Women in Christianity. I. Title.

DALY, Mary. 261
The church and the second sex. [1st ed.] New York, Harper & Row [1968] 187 p. 22 cm. Bibliographical footnotes. [BV639.W7D28] 68-11737
1. Women in Christianity. I. Title.

DANNIEL, Francoise 301.412
Woman is the glory of man, by E [i. e. F.] Danniel, B.Oliver. Tr. [From French] by M. Angeline Bouchard. Westminster. Md., Newman 1966 [c.1964, 1966] xiv, 137p. 22cm. Bibl. [BV639.W7D313] 66-16575 4.25
1. Women in Christianity. I. Oliver, Brigitte, joint author. II. Title.

DEMAREST, Victoria Booth-Clibborn. 262'.14
God, woman & ministry / by Victoria Booth Demarest ; photos. by Sacred Arts International, inc. Rev. ed. St. Petersburg, Fla. : Sacred Arts International, c1978. 182 p. : ports. ; 23 cm. First ed. published in 1977 under title: Sex & spirit. Bibliography: p. 180-182. [BV639.W7D45 1978] 78-103638 ISBN 0-912760-61-3: 6.95
1. Demarest, Victoria Booth-Clibborn. 2. United Church of Christ—Clergy—Biography. 3. Women in Christianity. 4. Women clergy. 5. Clergy—United States—Biography. I. Title.

DEMAREST, Victoria Booth-Clibborn. 262'.14
Sex & spirit : God, woman, & ministry / by Victoria Booth Demarest. 1st ed. [St. Petersburg, Fla. : Published by Sacred Arts International, in cooperation with Valkyrie Press, c1977] 182 p. : ill., ports. ; 22 cm. Bibliography: p. 181-182. [BV639.W7D4] 76-42915 ISBN 0-912760-29-X pbk. : 4.95 ISBN 0-912760-38-9 : 6.95
1. Demarest, Victoria Booth-Clibborn. 2. United Church of Christ—Clergy—Biography. 3. Women in Christianity. 4. Women as ministers. 5. Clergy—United States—Biography. I. Title.

ECKENSTEIN, Lina, d.1931. 270.1
The women of early Christianity, by Lina Eckenstein...Revised by Celia Roscoe. London, The Faith press, ltd.; Milwaukee, The Morehouse publishing co. [1935] xvi, 159 p. front., 1 illus., plates, facsims. 22 cm. "First published, February, 1935." "Bibliography : p. ix-xi. [BR163.E35] 922.1 35-34898
1. Women in Christianity 2. Christian biography. I. Roscoe, Celia, ed. II. Title.

ERMARTH, Margaret Sittler. 262
Adam's fractured rib; observations on women in the church. Philadelphia, Fortress Press [1970] xvi, 159 p. 20 cm. Based upon the findings of the Subcommittee on the Role of Women in the Life of the Church of the Lutheran Church in America's Commission on the Comprehensive Study of the Doctrine of the Ministry. Bibliography: p. 157-159. [BV639.W7E7] 78-117976 3.25
1. Women in Christianity. 2. Ordination of women. I. Title.

FAHERTY, William Barbey, 1914- 259
The destiny of modern woman in the light of papal teaching. Westminster, Md., Newman Press, 1950. xvii, 206 p. 21 cm. Bibliography: p. 195-199. [BV639.W7F3] 50-10660
1. Women in Christianity. 2. Church and social problems—Catholic Church. I. Title.

FITZWATER, Perry Braxton, 1871- 259
Woman, her mission, position, and ministry. Grand Rapids, W. B. Eerdmans Pub. Co., 1949. 86 p. 21 cm. [BV639.W7F5] 49-50075
1. Women in Christianity. I. Title.

HARKNESS, Georgia Elma, 1891- 261.8'34'12
Women in church and society; a historical and theological inquiry [by] Georgia Harkness. Nashville, Abingdon Press [1971, c1972] 240 p. 20 cm. Includes bibliographical references. [BV639.W7H28 1972] 76-172809 ISBN 0-687-45965-6 4.75
1. Women in Christianity. 2. Woman—History and condition of women. 3. Ordination of women. I. Title.

JOHANSEN, Ruthann Knechel, 1942- 261.8'34'1
Coming together : male and female in a renamed garden / Ruthann Knechel Johansen. Elgin, Ill. : Brethren Press, c1977. 151 p. ; 21 cm. Bibliography: p. [147]-151. [BV639.W7J64] 77-6301 ISBN 0-87178-156-5 pbk. : 3.95
1. Women in Christianity. 2. Sex role. 3. Sex discrimination against women. 4. Sex (Theology) I. Title.

MORRIS, Joan. 271'.9'009
The lady was a bishop; the hidden history of women with clerical ordination and the jurisdiction of bishops. New York, Macmillan [1973] xii, 192 p. 22 cm. [BV639.W7M63] 72-89049 6.95
1. Women in Christianity. 2. Monasticism and religious orders for women. I. Title.

PROHL, Russell C 259
Woman in the church; a restudy of woman's place in building the kingdom. Grand Rapids, Eerdmans [c1957] 86p. 23cm. Includes bibliography. [BV639.W7P7] 58-76
1. Women in Christianity. I. Title.

RICE, John R., 1895. 259
Bobbed hair, bossy wives and women preachers; significant questions for honest Christian women settled by the word of God, by John R. Rice ... Wheaton, Ill., Sword of the Lord publishers [1941] 91 p. illus. (ports.) 20 cm. "First printing, November, 1941." [HQ1395.R5] 42-7054
1. Women in Christianity. 2. Woman—Social and moral questions. 3. Women as ministers. I. Title.

RUETHER, Rosemary Radford. 261.8'34'12
Religion and sexism; images of woman in the Jewish and Christian traditions. Edited by Rosemary Radford Ruether. New York, Simon and Schuster [1974] 356 p. 22 cm. Bibliography: p. [345] [BV639.W7R8] 74-2791 ISBN 0-671-21692-9 9.95
1. Women in Christianity. 2. Women in the Bible. 3. Women in the Talmud. I. Title.
Pbk. 3.95, ISBN 0-671-21693-7.

RYRIE, Charles Caldwell, 1925- 259
The place of women in the church. Chicago, Moody [1968, c.1958] 155p. 22cm. [BR195.W6R9] 2.95
1. Women in Christianity. 2. Woman—History and condition of women. I. Title.

RYRIE, Charles Caldwell, 1925- 259
The place of women in the church. New York, Macmillan, 1958. 155p. 22cm. [BR163.R9] 58-8329
1. Women in Christianity. 2. Woman—History and condition of women. I. Title.

SWIDLER, Arlene. 261.8'34'12
Woman in a man's church; from role to person. New York, Paulist Press [1972] 111 p. 19 cm. (Deus books) Bibliography: p. 107-111. [BV639.W7S94] 72-86596 ISBN 0-8091-1740-1 1.25
1. Women in Christianity. 2. Women in church work—Catholic Church. I. Title.

TAVARD, George Henri, 1922- 261.8'34'12
Woman in Christian tradition [by] George H. Tavard. Notre Dame [Ind.] University of Notre Dame Press [1973] xi, 257 p. 24 cm. Includes bibliographical references. [BV639.W7T38] 72-12637 ISBN 0-268-00490-0 9.95
1. Women in Christianity. I. Title.

VAN SCOYOC, Nancy J., 1933- 261.8'344
Women, change, and the church / Nancy J. Van Scoyoc. Nashville, Tenn. : Abingdon, c1980. p. cm. (Into our third century) [BV639.W7V36] 80-15739 ISBN 0-687-45958-3 pbk. : 3.95
1. Women in Christianity. 2. Women—United States. I. Title. II. Series.

Women in Christianity—Addresses, essays, lectures.

CHRISTIAN freedom for 261.8'34'12
women and other human beings / Harry N. Hollis, Jr. ... [et al.]. Nashville : Broadman Press, [1975] 192 p. ; 21 cm. [BV639.W7C45] 74-21566 ISBN 0-8054-5552-3 : 4.95
1. Women in Christianity—Addresses, essays, lectures. 2. Women—Addresses, essays, lectures. I. Hollis, Harry.

SEXISM and church law 261.8'34'12
: equal rights and affirmative action / edited by James A. Coriden. New York : Paulist Press, c1977. ix, 192 p. ; 21 cm. (An Exploration book) Includes bibliographical references and index. [BV639.W7S49] 77-70638 ISBN 0-8091-2010-0 pbk. : 7.95
1. Women in Christianity—Addresses, essays, lectures. 2. Women in church work—Catholic Church—Addresses, essays, lectures. 3. Women—Legal status, laws, etc. (Canon law)—Addresses, essays, lectures. I. Coriden, James A.

WOMEN in a strange 261.8'34'12
land : search for a new image / edited by Clare Benedicks Fischer, Betsy Brenneman, and Anne McGrew Bennett. Philadelphia : Fortress Press, [1975] x, 133 p. ; 22 cm. Bibliography: p. 131-133. [HQ1394.W64] 74-26326 ISBN 0-8006-1204-3 pbk. : 3.50
1. Women in Christianity—Addresses, essays, lectures. 2. Feminism—United States—Addresses, essays, lectures. I. Fischer, Clare Benedicks. II. Brennemans, Betsy. III. Bennett, Anne McGrew.
Contents omitted.

WOMEN of spirit : 261.8'34'12
female leadership in the Jewish and Christian traditions / edited by Rosemary Ruether and Eleanor McLaughlin. New York : Simon and Schuster, c1979. 400 p. ; 22 cm. Includes bibliographical references and index. [BV639.W7W62] 78-11995 ISBN 0-671-22843-9 : 9.95
1. Women in Christianity—Addresses, essays, lectures. 2. Women in Judaism—Addresses, essays, lectures. 3. Woman (Theology)—Addresses, essays, lectures. I. Ruether, Rosemary Radford. II. McLaughlin, Eleanor.

WOMEN'S liberation 261.8'34'12
and the church: the new demand for freedom in the life of the Christian Church. Edited, with introduction by Sarah Bentley Doely. Published in co-operation with IDOC-North America. New York, Association Press [1970] 158 p. 23 cm. Bibliography: p. [149]-154. [BV639.W7W64] 70-129441 ISBN 0-8096-1814-1 5.95
1. Women in christianity—Addresses, essays, lectures. I. Doely, Sarah Bentley, ed.

Women in Christianity—Early church, ca. 30-600.

BRITTAIN, Alfred. 261.8'34'12
Women of early Christianity / by Alfred Brittain and Mitchell Carroll ; with an introd. by J. Cullen Ayre, Jr. New York : Gordon Press, 1976. p. cm. (Woman in all ages and in all countries) Reprint of v. 3 of the 1907 ed. of Woman in all ages and in all countries, published by Rittenhouse Press, Philadelphia. [BR195.W6B74 1976] [BR195.W6] 76-5490 ISBN 0-87968-268-X
1. Women in Christianity—Early church, ca. 30-600. 2. Women—Biography. 3. Christian biography. I. Carroll, Mitchell, 1870-1925, joint author. II. Title. III. Series.

LAPORTE, Jean, 1924- 270.1'088042
The role of women in early Christianity / by Jean Laporte. New York : E. Mellen Press, c1982. p. cm. (Studies in women and religion ; v. 7) Includes bibliographical references and indexes. [BR195.W6L25 1982] 19 82-8281 ISBN 0-88946-545-2 : 29.95
1. Women in Christianity—Early church, ca. 30-600. I. Title. II. Series.

MCKENNA, Mary Lawrence. 271'.9
Women of the church; role and renewal. Foreword by Jean Danielon. New York, P.J. Kenedy [1967] xvi, 192 p. 22 cm. Includes bibliographical references. [BR195.W6M3] 67-26804
1. Women in Christianity—Early church. 2. Widows. 3. Deaconesses. 4. Virginity. I. Title.

Women in Christianity—Papal documents.

CATHOLIC Church. Pope. 261
The woman in the modern world. Selected and arr. by the monks of Solesmes. [Boston] St. Paul Editions [1959] 1v. 20cm. (Papal teachings) Translation of Le probleme feminin. [BV639.W7C33] 59-16227
1. Women in Christianity—Papal documents. I. Solesmes, France. Saint-Pierre (Benedictine abbey) II. Title.

Women in Christianity—Sermons.

SPINNING a sacred 252'.0088042
yarn : women speak from the pulpit. New York : Pilgrim Press, c1982. ix, 230 p. ; 21 cm. [BV639.W7S64 1982] 19 82-569 ISBN 0-8298-0604-0 (pbk.) : 8.95
1. Women in Christianity—Sermons. 2. Sermons, American.

Women in Christianity—United States—Addresses, essays, lectures.

WOMEN in American 261.8'344
religion / Paul Boyer ... [et al.] ; edited by Janet Wilson James. Philadelphia : University of Pennsylvania Press, 1980, c1978. p. cm. [BR515.W65 1980] 79-5261 ISBN 0-8122-7780-5 : 21.95 pbk. : 9.95
1. Women in Christianity—United States—Addresses, essays, lectures. 2. Women in church work—United States—Addresses, essays, lectures. 3. Women in Judaism—United States—Addresses, essays, lectures. 4. United States—Religion—Addresses, essays, lectures. 5. Women—United States—Addresses, essays, lectures. I. Boyer, Paul. II. James, Janet Wilson, 1918-

Women in Christianity—United States—History—19th century—Addresses, essays, lectures.

WOMEN and religion in 280'.088042
America / [edited by] Rosemary Radford Ruether, Rosemary Skinner Keller. 1st ed. San Francisco : Harper & Row, c1981- v. <1 > : ill., ports. ; 24 cm. Includes bibliographical references and index. [BR515.W648 1981] 19 80-8346 ISBN 0-06-066829-6 : 15.00
1. Women in Christianity—United States—History—19th century—Addresses, essays, lectures. 2. Women in Judaism—United States—History—19th century—Addresses, essays, lectures. 3. United States—Religion—Addresses, essays, lectures. I. Ruether, Rosemary Radford. II. Keller, Rosemary Skinner.

Women in church work.

AGAR, Frederick Alfred, 1872- 259
Church women at work, by Frederick A. Agar. Philadelphia, Boston [etc.] The Judson press [1937] 5 p. l., 59 p. 20 cm. [BV4420.A28] 38-3039
1. Women in church work. I. Title.

AGAR, Frederick Alfred, 1872- 259
"Help those women"; a manual for women church workers, by Frederick A. Agar. New York, Chicago [etc.] Fleming H. Revell company [c1917] 83 p. 19 1/2 cm. [BV4420.A3] 17-26012
I. Title.

BLACKWOOD, Carolyn Philips. 259
How to be an effective church woman. With an introd. by Andrew W. Blackwood. Philadelphia, Westminster Press [1955] 189 p. 21 cm. [BV4415.B55] 55-7088
1. Women in church work. I. Title.

CAVERT, Inez M 259
Women in American church life; a study prepared under the guidance of a counseling committee of women representing national interdenominational agencies. New York, Pub. for the federal

Council of the Churches of Christ in America by Friendship Press [1949] 93 p. 23 cm. [BV4415.C3] 49-9080
1. Women in church work. I. Title.

CHURCH of England. Archbishop of Canterbury's committee on the ministry of women. 262
The ministry of women; a report by a committee appointed by His Grace the Lord Archbishop of Canterbury, with appendices and fifteen collotype illustrations. London, Society for promoting Christian knowledge: New York, The Macmillan company, 1919. xvi, 326 p. front. plates. ports. 22 cm. "Report on the sanctions and restrictions which govern the ministrations of women in the life of the church, and the status and work of deaconesses" p. 1. [BV4415.C5] 20-4477
1. Women in church work. 2. Deaconesses. I. Title.

DURKIN, Mary G., 1934- 250
The suburban woman : her changing role in the Church / Mary G. Durkin. New York : Seabury Press, c1975. p. cm. "A Crossroad book." Bibliography: p. [BV4415.D83] 75-29147 ISBN 0-8164-1200-6 : 6.95
1. Women in church work. 2. Women. 3. Suburban life. I. Title.

FEUCHT, Oscar E. 259
Guidelines for women's groups in the congregation / by Oscar E. Feucht. St. Louis, Mo. : Concordia Pub. House, c1981. 79 p. ; 23 cm. [BV4415.F4] 19 80-25111 ISBN 0-570-03828-6 pbk. : 3.95
1. Women in church work. 2. Church group work. I. Title.

KIRK, Jane. 259
Group activities for church women. [1st ed.] New York, Harper [1954] 245 p. illus. 22 cm. [BV4415.K5] 54-8961
1. Women in church work. I. Title.

MORRISON, Christine Marie (Auchinvole) "Mrs. George H. Morrison." 259
Addresses for women workers; a volume of suggested discourses for women who speak in public, by Mrs. George H. Morrison ... New York, George H. Doran company [c1926] x p., 1 l., 13-212 p. 19 1/2 cm. Includes articles signed by other authors. [BV639.W7M7] 26-5582
1. Women in church work. I. Title.

NICHOLAS, David R. 262'.15
What's a woman to do ... in the church? / by David R. Nicholas. Scottsdale, Ariz. : Good Life Productions, c1979. xiii, 150 p. ; 23 cm. Bibliography: p. 143-150. [BV4415.N53] 79-51545 7.95
1. Women in church work. 2. Woman (Christian theology)—Biblical teaching. I. Title.

NOVOTNY, Louise (Miller) Mrs., 1889- 259
Women and the church; a manual and textbook for women's organizations, by Louise Miller Novotny. Cincinnati, O., The Standard publishing company [c1940] 160 p. 19 cm. [Full name: Mrs. Louise Virgie (Miller) Novotny] [BV4415.N6] 40-9273
1. Women in church work. 2. Women in the Bible. I. Title.

[PALMER, Phoebe (Worrell) Mrs.] 1807-1874. 262
Promise of the Father; or, A neglected specialty of the last days. Addressed to the clergy and laity of all Christian communities. By the author of "The way of holiness"... Boston, H. V. Degen, 1859. xvi, 421 p. front. 19 1/2 cm. [BV639.W7P3] [396.52] 38-18180
1. Women in church work. I. Title.

POTTER, Henry Codman, bp., 1834-1908. 372.
Addresses to women engaged in church work. By the Right Reverend the Bishop of New York. New York, Published for the Church work association by E. P. Dutton & co., 1887. 106 p. 15 cm. Introductory note signed: Henry C. Potter. [BV4415.P6 1887] 38-29421
1. Women in church work. I. Title.

POTTER, Henry Codman, bp., 1834-1908. 262
Addresses to women engaged in church work, by the Right Reverend the Bishop of New York. New York, E. P. Dutton & company, 1898. vi, 149 p. 18 cm. Introductory note signed: Henry C. Potter. [BV4415.P6 1893] 396.52 39-8945
1. Women in church work. I. Title.

PROTESTANT Episcopal church in the U. S. A. National council. Woman's auxiliary. 266.3
... The Woman's auxiliary in the life of the church ... New York, The Woman's auxiliary to the National council, Church missions house, 1934. 63, [1] p. 18 cm. At head of title: W. A. 49. [BX5975.P7] 35-10682
1. Women in church work. I. Title.

SHAFFER, Wilma L
Church women at work; a manual for church women. Cincinnati, Ohio, Standard Pub. Co. [1961] 106 p. illus. 21 cm. Bibliography. 63-54321
1. Women in church work. I. Title.

WEIDENBACH, Nell L. 254'.6
Just a touch of drama : programs for women / Nell L. Weidenbach. Chicago : Moody Press, [1975] 64 p. ; 22 cm. Includes bibliographies. [BV4415.W38] 74-15346 ISBN 0-8024-4496-2 pbk. : 1.25
1. Women in church work. 2. Women—Prayer-books and devotions—English. I. Title.

WYKER, Mossie Allman. 259
Church women in the scheme of things. St. Louis, Bethany Press [1953] 117p. 20cm. [BV4415.W9] 53-3867
1. Women in church work. I. Title.

Women in church work—Addresses, essays, lectures.

WOMEN in a men's church 262'.1
/ edited by Virgil Elizondo and Norbert Greinacher ; English langauge editor, Marcus Lefebure. Edinburgh : T. & T. Clark ; New York : Seabury Press, 1980. viii, 135 p. ; 22 cm. (Concilium : religion in the eighties ; 134) Includes bibliographical references. [BV4415.W63] 19 80-50478 ISBN 0-8164-2276-1 (Seabury : pbk.) : 5.95
1. Women in church work—Addresses, essays, lectures. 2. Woman (Christian theology)—Addresses, essays, lectures. I. Elizondo, Virgilio P. II. Greinacher, Norbert, 1931- III. Lefebure, Marcus. IV. Series: Concilium (New York) ; 134.

Women in church work—Catholic Church.

TRAXLER, Mary Peter. 261.8'3
New works of new nuns, edited by Sister M. Peter Traxler. St. Louis, B. Herder Book Co. [1968] xi, 179 p. 21 cm. [BX4205.T7] 68-55600 5.95
1. Women in church work—Catholic Church. 2. Church and social problems—Catholic Church. 3. Monastic and religious life of women. I. Title.

Women in church work—Disciples of Christ.

BROWN, Phyllis G. 266'.6'6755
A century with Christian women in Virginia / by Phillis G. Brown. Richmond, Va. : Christian Women's Fellowship, Christian Church (Disciples of Christ) in Virginia, 1975. 48 p. ; 22 cm. Bibliography: p. 47-48. [BV4415.B76] 75-329725
1. Women in church work—Christian Church (Disciples of Christ) 2. Women in church work—Virginia. 3. Virginia—Biography. I. Title.

LOLLIS, Lorraine. 262
The shape of Adam's rib: a lively history of women's work in the Christian Church. Illus. by Thelma Pyatt. St. Louis, Mo., Bethany Press [1970] 219 p. illus. 23 cm. Bibliography: p. 215-219. [BV4415.L6 1970] 70-117336 3.95
1. Women in church work—Disciples of Christ. 2. Women in missionary work. I. Title.

Women in church work—General Conference Mennonite Church.

GOERING, Gladys V. 266'.97
Women in search of mission : a history of the General Conference Mennonite women's organization / Gladys V. Goering. Newton, Kan. : Faith and Life Press, c1980. vii, 128 p. : ill. ; 21 cm. Includes bibliographical references. [BX8129.G4G63] 19 80-66787 ISBN 0-8386-062-1 pbk. : 3.95
1. General Conference Mennonite Church. Women in Mission 2. Women in church work—General Conference Mennonite Church. I. Title.

Women in church work—Methodist Church—Congresses.

WOMEN in new worlds 287'.088042
: historical perspectives on the Wesleyan tradition / editors, Hilah F. Thomas, Rosemary Skinner Keller. Nashville : Abingdon, c1981. 445 p. ; 21 cm. "Women's History Project, General Commission on Archives and History, United Methodist Church"—Verso t.p. Selected papers presented at the Women in New Worlds Conference, held in Cincinnati, Ohio, Feb. 1-3, 1980. Includes bibliographical references. [BX8207.W48] 19 81-7984 ISBN 0-687-45968-0 pbk. : 12.95
1. Women in church work—Methodist Church—Congresses. 2. Methodists—United States—Congresses. I. Thomas, Hilah F. 1941- (Hilah Frances), II. Keller, Rosemary Skinner. III. Women in New Worlds Conference Cincinnati, Ohio) (1980 : IV. United Methodist Church (U.S.). Women's History Project.

Women in church work—Presbyterian Church.

VERDESI, Elizabeth Howell, 1922- 253'.2
In but still out : women in the church / Elizabeth Howell Verdesi. Philadelphia : Westminster Press, c1976. 218 p. : ill. ; 19 cm. Based on the author's thesis, Columbia University and Union Theological Seminary, New York, 1975. Bibliography: p. [209]-218. [BV4415.V45 1976] 75-34365 ISBN 0-664-24788-1 pbk. : 3.95
1. Women in church work—Presbyterian Church. I. Title.

Women in church work—Seventh-Day Adventists.

BEACH, John G. 286'.73' B
Notable women of spirit : the historical role of women in the Seventh-day Adventist Church / by John G. Beach. Nashville, Tenn. : Southern Pub. Association, c1976. 125 p. ; 21 cm. Bibliography: p. 123-125. [BV4415.B42] 76-6620 ISBN 0-8127-0115-1
1. Women in church work—Seventh-Day Adventists. I. Title.

Women in church work—United Presbyterian Church in the U.S.A.

HUMMEL, Margaret Gibson. 262
The amazing heritage. References and resources assembled by Mildred Roe. Philadelphia, Geneva Press [1970] 144 p. illus., ports. 21 cm. Bibliography: p. [142]-144. [BV4415.H77] 75-111040 2.00
1. Women in church work—United Presbyterian Church in the U.S.A. I. Title.

Women in church work—United States

CALKINS, Gladys Gilkey. 259
Follow those women ; church women in the ecumenical movement, a history of the development of united work among women of the Protestant churches in the United States. [New York, Published for United Church Women, National Council of the Churches of Christ in U.S.A. by the Office of Publication and Distribution, c1961] 108 p. 21 cm. "Presented by the officers and staff of United Church Women as the report of the triennium, 1958-1961." [BV4415.C25] 61-17252
1. Women in church work—U.S. 2. National Council of the Churches of Christ in the United States of America. Dept. of United Church Women. I. National Council of the Churches of Christ in the United States of America. Dept. of United Church Women. II. Title.

SHANNON, Margaret. 267'.43'0973
Just because : the story of the national movement of Church Women United in the U.S.A., 1941 through 1975 / by Margaret Shannon. Corte Madera, Calif. : Omega Books, c1977. 464 p. : ill. ; 21 cm. [BV4420.C483S52] 77-374035 ISBN 0-89353-027-1 pbk. : 4.50
1. Church Women United. 2. Women in church work—United States. I. Title.

Women in church work—United States—Addresses essays, lectures.

HEPBURN, Daisy. 261
Why doesn't somebody do something? / Daisy Hepburn. Wheaton, Ill. : Victor Books, c1980. 204 p. ; 21 cm. Bibliography: p. 203-204. [BV4415.H46] 19 80-51158 ISBN 0-88207-606-X (pbk.) : 3.95
1. Women in church work—United States—Addresses essays, lectures. I. Title.

Women in Hinduism.

PINKHAM, Mildreth (Worth)
Woman in the sacred scriptures of Hinduism. New York, AMS, 1967. xii, 239 p. 24 cm. Reprint of 1941 edition. Bibliography: p. [205]-220. 68-61762
1. Women in Hinduism. 2. Hinduism—Sacred books (Selections: Extracts, etc.) I. Title.

PINKHAM, Mildreth (Worth) Mrs. 204
Woman in the sacred scriptures of Hinduism [by] Mildreth Worth Pinkham, PH.D. New York, Columbia university press, 1941. xii p., 2 l., 239 p. 23 1/2 cm. Bibliography: p. [205]-220. [BL2015.W6P5] 41-7015
1. Women in Hinduism. 2. Hinduism—Sacred books (Selections: Extracts, etc.) I. Title.

Women in Judaism.

APPLEMAN, Solomon. 296.3'87'83412
The Jewish woman in Judaism : the significance of woman's status in religious culture / Solomon Appleman. 1st ed. Hicksville, N.Y. : Exposition Press, c1979. x, 141 p. ; 21 cm. [BM729.W6A66] 79-7628 ISBN 0-682-49431-3 : 7.50
1. Women in Judaism. I. Title.

LACKS, Roslyn. 296.3'87'83412
Women and Judaism : myth, history, and struggle / Roslyn Lacks. 1st ed. Garden City, N.Y. : Doubleday, 1980, c1979. xxii, 218 p. ; 22 cm. Includes index. Bibliography: p. [204]-207. [BM729.W6L32 1980] 74-25113 ISBN 0-385-02313-8 : 9.95
1. Women in Judaism. 2. Women and religion. I. Title.

MANN, Denese Berg. 296.3'87'83412
The woman in Judaism / Denese Berg Mann. Hartford, Conn. : Jonathan Publications, c1979. iii, 76 p. ; 22 cm. Bibliography: p. 74-76. [BM729.W6M36] 79-117285 pbk. : 4.50
1. Women in Judaism. 2. Sex and Judaism. I. Title.

PRIESAND, Sally. 296.3'87'83412
Judaism and the new woman / by Sally Priesand ; introd. by Bess Myerson. New York : Behrman House, c1975. xvi, 144 p. ; 19 cm. (The Jewish concepts and issues series) Bibliography: p. 135-139. [BM729.W6P74] 75-21951 ISBN 0-87441-230-7 pbk. : 2.45
1. Women in Judaism. 2. Women, Jewish. I. Title.

SWIDLER, Leonard J. 296
Women in Judaism : the status of women in formative judaism / by Leonard Swidler. Metuchen, N.J. : Scarecrow Press, 1976. vi, 242 p. ; 22 cm. Includes bibliographical references and index. [BM729.W6S9] 75-46561 9.50

1. Women in Judaism. I. Title.

Women in Judaism—Addresses, essays, lectures.

GREENBERG, Blu, 1936- 296.3'878344
On women & Judaism : a view from tradition / Blu Greenberg. 1st ed. Philadelphia : Jewish Publication Society of America, 1981. xi, 178 p. ; 24 cm. Includes bibliographical references. [BM729.W6G73] 19 81-11779 ISBN 0-8276-0195-6 : 11.95
1. Women in Judaism—Addresses, essays, lectures. I. Title.

JUNG, Leo, 1892- 301.42
Love and life / by Leo Jung. New York : Philosophical Library, c1979. 84 p. ; 22 cm. Includes bibliographical references. [BM729.W6J86] 79-87873 ISBN 0-8022-2355-9 : 7.50
1. Women in Judaism—Addresses, essays, lectures. 2. Love (Judaism)—Addresses, essays, lectures. I. Title.

THE Modern Jewish woman 296.3'878344
: a unique perspective. Brooklyn, N.Y. : Lubavitch Educational Foundation for Jewish Marriage Enrichment, c1981. xi, 179 p. : ill. ; 24 cm. (A Lubavitch women's publication) Bibliography: p. 168-169. [BM729.W6M63] 19 80-67108 ISBN 0-8266-0497-8 : 10.95
1. Women in Judaism—Addresses, essays, lectures. 2. Women, Jewish—Religious life—Addresses, essays, lectures. 3. Habad—Addresses, essays, lectures. I. Lubavitch Educational Foundation for Jewish Marriage Enrichment. II. Title. III. Series.

Women in Kongo.

KELLERSBERGER, Julia Lake (Skinner) Mrs. 1897- 276.75
Congo crosses; a study of Congo womanhood, by Julia Lake Kellersberger. Boston, Mass., The Central committee on the United study of foreign missions, 1936. 222 p. incl. illus., plates. front., plates, maps (1 fold.) facsim. 19 cm. Bibliography: p. 213-214. [BV3625.K6K4] 266 36-22376
1. Women in Kongo. 2. Missions—Kongo. 3. Kongo—Soc. life. & cust. I. Title.

Women in Kongo, Belgian.

CAMPBELL, Henry D. 922.
A Congo chattel; the story of an African slave girl, by Rev. Henry D. Campbell... New York, N.Y., Christian alliance publishing company [c1926] 213 p. plates. 20 cm. [BV3625.K6C3 1926] 26-21737
1. Women in Kongo, Belgian. 2. Missions—Kongo, Belgian. I. Title.

Women in missionary work.

BEAVER, Robert Pierce, 1906- 266
All loves excelling; American Protestant women in world mission, by R. Pierce Beaver. Grand Rapids, Mich., Eerdmans [1968] 227 p. 20 cm. Includes bibliographical references. [BV2610.B4] 68-18839
1. Women in missionary work. 2. Women as missionaries. 3. Missions, American. 4. Protestant churches—Missions. I. Title.

BEAVER, Robert Pierce, 1906- 266'.023'73
American Protestant women in world mission : a history of the first feminist movement in North America / by R. Pierce Beaver. Rev. ed. Grand Rapids, Mich. : W. B. Eerdmans Pub. Co., c1980. 237 p. ; 20 cm. First ed. (1968) published under title: All loves excelling. Includes indexes. Bibliography: p. 219-223. [BV2610.B4 1980] 80-14366 ISBN 0-8028-1846-3 pbk. : 7.95
1. Women in missionary work. 2. Women missionaries. 3. Missions, American. 4. Protestant churches—Missions. I. Title.

CROUCH, Kate C. Maddry. 266'.6'1756
The magnificent nobility : a history of Woman's Missionary Union of North Carolina, 1952-1972 / by Kate C. Maddry Crouch. Raleigh : The Union, c1977. 125 p. : ill. ; 23 cm. Includes index. Bibliography: p. 119. [BV2766.B464C76] 77-153974
1. Baptists. North Carolina. State Convention. Woman's Missionary Union. 2. Women in missionary work. 3. Baptists—Missions. I. Title.

HAYES, Florence (Sooy), 1895- 266.5
Daughters of Dorcas; the story of the work of women for home missions since 1802. New York, Board of National Missions, Presbyterian Church in the U. S. A. [1952] 158 p. 23 cm. [BV2570.H34] 52-11025
1. Women in missionary work. 2. Presbyterian Church—Missions. I. Title.

SOUTHERN Baptist Convention. Woman's Missionary Union. 266.61
Manual of Woman's Missionary Union. Auxiliary to the Southern Baptist Convennntion. Rev. by Mary Christian from the original by Kathleen Mallory. Nashville, Broadman Press [1949] 260 p.illus. 20 cm. Original ed. pub. under titletitle: Manual of W. M. U. methods. [BV25020.A8S68 1949] 49-2007
1. Women in missionary work. 2. Southern Baptist Concention—Missions. I. Mallory, Kathleen Moore, 1879- II. Title.

VANDER KAAY, Dorothy 254'.6
Women's world handbook of ideas and procedures for ladies groups. Des Plaines, Ill., Regular Baptist Press [1974] 133 p. 19 cm. [BV2610.V36] 74-79541 1.50 (pbk.).
1. Women in missionary work. I. Title.

Women in Mormonism.

MCCONKIE, Oscar Walter. 261.8'344
She shall be called woman / Oscar W. McConkie. Salt Lake City, Utah : Bookcraft, c1979. viii, 142 p. ; 24 cm. Includes index. [BX8641.M25] 79-53830 ISBN 0-88494-380-1 : 5.50
1. Women in Mormonism. 2. Woman (Theology) I. Title.

TURNER, Rodney. 230'.93'3
Woman and the priesthood. Salt Lake City, Deseret Book Co., 1972. 333 p. 24 cm. Includes bibliographical references. [BX8641.T87] 72-90345 ISBN 0-87747-487-7 4.95
1. Women in Mormonism.

WARENSKI, Marilyn. 261.8'34'12
Patriarchs and politics : the plight of the Mormon woman / Marilyn Warenski. New York : McGraw-Hill, c1978. xvi, 304 p., [8] leaves of plates : ill. ; 24 cm. Includes index. Bibliography: p. 288-289. [BX8641.W373] 78-17837 ISBN 0-07-068270-4 : 10.95
1. Women in Mormonism. 2. Feminism. I. Title.

Women in Mormonism—Congresses.

BLUEPRINTS for living 261.8'344
: perspectives for Latter-day Saint women / edited by Maren M. Mouritsen. Provo, Utah : Brigham Young University, c1980- v. ; 22 cm. Contains selected messages from the Fifth Annual Women's Conference held at Brigham Young University in early 1980, called "Blueprints for Living." Includes bibliographical references. [BX8641.B64] 19 80-138354 ISBN 0-8425-1814-2 pbk. : 5.95.
1. Women in Mormonism—Congresses. I. Mouritsen, Maren M.

Women in religion.

ARGUELLES, Miriam, 1943- 262'.14
The feminine : spacious as the sky / Miriam & Jose Arguelles. Boulder, Colo. : Shambhala ; [New York] : Distributed in the United States by Random House, 1977. 152 p. : ill. ; 26 cm. Bibliography: p. 142-149. [BL458.A73] 77-6012 ISBN 0-87773-113-6 pbk. : 6.95
1. Women in religion. I. Arguelles, Jose, 1939- joint author. II. Title.

ASHE, Geoffrey. 232.91
The virgin / Geoffrey Ashe. London : Routledge & Paul, 1976. vi, 261 p. ; 23 cm. Includes index. Bibliography: p. 251-254. [BT645.A85] 76-364472 ISBN 0-7100-8342-4 : 11.25
1. Mary, Virgin—Cultus. 2. Women in religion. I. Title.
Distributed by Routledge & Kegan Paul, Boston

HUDSON, Marshall Alonze, 1850-
The Philathea Bible class, the story of a movement for women; what it means, how it works, and secret service, the constitution, the teacher, by Marshall A. Hudson ... also a chapter on The adult Bible class teacher, by Henrietta Heron ... Philadelphia, Pa., The Sunday school times company [c1914] 3 p. l., 9-169 p. illus., pl. 18 1/2 cm. $0.50. 15-718
I. Heron, Henrietta. II. Title.

LUMMIS, Eliza O'Brien, d.1915. 267.
Daughters of the faith; serious thoughts for Catholic women (Manual) By Eliza O'B. Lummis. New York, The Knickerbocker press, 1905. xxxiii, 159 p. front. (port.) 2 p. 18 1/2 cm. [BX809.DL8] 5-23659
I. Title.

STONE, Merlin. 291.2'11
The Paradise papers : the suppression of women's rites / [by] Merlin Stone. London : Virago : Quartet Books, 1976. [15], 275, [9] p., 16 p. of plates : ill., maps ; 23 cm. American ed. published under title: When god was a woman. Includes index. Bibliography: p. 261-275. [BL458.S76 1976b] 76-374034 ISBN 0-7043-2805-4 : £4.95
1. Women in religion. I. Title.

STONE, Merlin. 291.1'7834'12
When god was a woman / by Merlin Stone. New York : Dial Press, 1976. p. cm. Includes index. Bibliography: p. [BL458.S76] 76-22544 ISBN 0-8037-6813-3 : 7.95
1. Women in religion. I. Title.

Women (in religion, folklore, etc.)

PARSONS, Elsie Worthington Clews, 1875-1941. 291.1'7834'12
Religious chastity : an ethnological study / by John Main [i.e. E. W. C. Parsons]. New York : AMS Press, [1975] xii, 365 p. ; 23 cm. Reprint of the 1913 ed. published by Macaulay Co., New York. Includes index. Bibliography: p. 325-354. [BL458.P37 1975] 72-9672 ISBN 0-404-57489-0 : 22.50
1. Women (in religion, folklore, etc.) 2. Sex and religion. 3. Chastity. I. Title.

Women in the Bible.

ADAMS, Charles, 1808-1890 230.92
Women of the Bible, By Charles Adams. Edited by Daniel P. Kidder. New York Pub. by Lane & Scott, for the Sunday-school union of the Methodist Episcopal church, 1851 225 p. 19 cm. [BB575.A15] 32-18161
1. Kidder, Daniel Parish. 1815-1891 ed. 2. Women in the Bible. 3. Bible—Biog. I. Kidder, Daniel Parish, 1815-1891 ed. II. Sunday-school union of the Methodist Episcopal church. III. Title.

ADAMS, Charlotte Hannah, 1873- 221.92
Women of ancient Israel, (by) Charlotte H. Adams... New York, National board of the Young womens Christian association of the United States of America [c1912] 104 p. 1 l. 18 1/2 cm. Bibliography: 1 leaf at end. [BS575.A2] 12-5563
1. Women in the Bible. 2. Bible. O.T.—Biog. 3. Bible—Biog—O.T. I. Title.

ADAMS, Queenie Muriel. 220.8'30141'2
Neither male nor female; a study of the Scriptures, [by] Q. M. Adams. Ilfracombe, Stockwell, 1973. 255 p. 22 cm. Includes index. Bibliography: p. [237]-[239] [BS575.A24 1973] 74-158259 ISBN 0-7223-0394-7
1. Women in the Bible. I. Title.
Distributed by Verry, 7.50.

AGUILAR, Grace, 1816-1847. 220.
The woman of Israel. By Grace Aguilar ... New York, D. Appleton and company, 1888. 2 v. in 1. fronts. 19 cm. Added t.-p., illustrated. [BS575.A3 1888] 45-53769
1. Women in the Bible. 2. Bible. O.T.—Biog. 3. Women, Jewish. I. Title.

AGUILAR, Grace, 1816-1847. 221.9'22 B
The women of Israel; or, Characters and sketches from the Holy Scriptures and Jewish history illustrative of the past history, present duties, and future destiny of the Hebrew females, as based on the Word of God. Plainview, N.Y., Books for Libraries Press [1974] p. cm. (Essay index reprint series) Reprint of the 1879 ed. published by G. Routledge, London, and E. P. Dutton, New York. [BS575.A3 1974] 74-4358 ISBN 0-518-10174-6
1. Bible. O.T.—Biography. 2. Women in the Bible. 3. Women, Jewish. I. Title. II. Title: Characters and sketches from the Holy Scriptures and Jewish history.

AGUILAR, Grace, 1816-1847. 221.92
The women of Israel. By Grace Aquilar. New York, D. Appleton & company. Philadelphia, G. S. Appleton, 1851. 2 v. 19 1/2 cm. [B8575.A3] 18-27481
1. Women in the Bible. 2. Bible. O. T.—Biog. 3. Bible—Biog.—O. T. 4. Women, Jewish. I. Title.

AGUILAR, Grace, 1816-1847. 221.93
The women of Israel. By Grace Aguilar. New York. D. Appleton & company, 1870. 2 v. fronts. 19 cm. Added t.-p., illustrated. [BS575.A3 1870] 32-32100
1. Women in the Bible. 2. Bible. O. T.—Biog. 3. Bible—Biog.—O. T. 4. Women, Jewish. I. Title.

ASHTON, Sophia (Goodrich), Mrs., 1819- 220.92
The mothers of the Bible. By Mrs. S. G. Ashton. With an introductory essay, by Rev. A. L. Stone... Boston, J. E. Tilton and company, 1859. x, [5]-335 p. 18 1/2 cm. [BS575.A8 1859] 31-21949
1. Women in the Bible. 2. Bible—Biog. I. Title.

BALDWIN, George Colfax, 1817-1899. 220.92
Representative women: from Eve, the wife of the first, to Mary, the mother of the second Adam, by Geo. C. Baldwin ... New-York, Sheldon & company; Boston, Gould & Lincoln; [etc., etc., c1855] xvi, [17]-333 p. 19 cm. [BS575.B3 1855] 31-20511
1. Women in the Bible. 2. Bible—Biblw—Biog. I. Title.

BALDWIN, George Colfax, 1817-1899. 220.92
Representative women: from Eve, the wife of the first, to Mary, the mother of the second Adam, by Geo. C. Baldwin ... New-York, Sheldon, Blakeman & co., 1857. xvi, [17]-333 p. front. 20 cm. [BS575.B3 1857] 31-20510
1. Women in the Bible. 2. Bible—Biog. I. Title.

BARKER, William Pierson. 220.9'2 B
Women and the Liberator [by] William P. Barker. Old Tappan, N.J., F. H. Revell Co. [1972] 128 p. 22 cm. [BS2445.B37] 73-186532 ISBN 0-8007-0518-1 ISBN 0-8007-0530-0 (pbk) 3.95
1. Jesus Christ—Attitude towards women. 2. Women in the Bible. I. Title.

BARNARD, David. 221.03
Biblical women. Giving a correct biographical description of every female mentioned in Scripture, with explanatory remarks, by David Barnard ... Cincinnati, O., Hart & col, 1863. 140, [3] p. 21 cm. [B3576.B35] 31-21906
1. Women in the Bible. 2. Bible. O.T.—Biog. 3. Bible—Biog. I. Title.

BATTEN, J. Rowena 248.4
Women alive; twenty-five talks on women of the Bible. Grand Rapids, Mich., Zondervan [1965, c.1964] 184p. 23cm. [BS575.B38] 65-3172 3.95 bds.,
1. Women in the Bible. I. Title.

BJERREGAARD, Carl Henrik Andreas, 1845-
The great mother, a gospel of the eternally-feminine; occult and scientific studies and experiences in the sacred and secret life, by C. H. A. Bjerregaard ... With chapters by Eugenie R. Eliscu, M.D., William F. Fraetas, Grace Gallatin Seton ... New York, N.Y., The Innerlife publishing co. [c1913] 4 p. l., 330 p. 24 1/2 cm. 13-26120

I. Eliscu, Eugenie R. II. Fraetas, William F. III. Seton, Grace (Gallatin) "Mrs. Ernest Thompson Seton," 1872- IV. Title.

BRISCOE, Jill. 220.8'30141'2
Prime Rib and Apple / by Jill Briscoe. Grand Rapids : Zondervan Pub. House, c1976. p. cm. [BS575.B67] 76-25054 5.95
1. Women in the Bible. I. Title.

BUCHANAN, Isabelia (Reid) Mrs. 1857- 220.92
Women of the Bible, by Isabella Reid Buchanan ... Minneapolis, Minn., The Colwell press, incorporated, c1924. 112, [3] p. 20 cm. [BS575.B8] 24-21697
1. Women in the Bible. 2. Bible—Biog. I. Title.

BURCHARD, Samuel Dickinson, 1812-1891. 220.92
The daughters of Zion. By Rev. S.D. Burchard, D.D., illustrated with numerous steel engravings. New York, J.S. Taylor, 1853. 4 p. l., [vii]-xii, [13]-355 p. front., plates. 19 cm. Added t.-p., illustrated. [BS575.B85] 31-20508
1. Women in the Bible. 2. Bible—Biog. I. Title.

*BURGESS, E. T. 221.92
Other women of the Bible. Little Rock, Ark., Baptist Pubns., 1964. 64p. 23cm. (Topical Bible studies, no. 31) .50 pap.,
I. Title.

BURTON, Juliette T. 220.92
The five jewels of the orient. By Juliette T. Burton. New York, Masonic publishing company, 1872. 244 p. incl. front., 1 illus., 5 pl. plates. 19 1/2 cm. [BS575.B87] 31-20507
1. Women in the Bible. I. Title.

CARMICHAEL, Calum M. 222'.1506
Women, law, and the Genesis traditions / Calum M. Carmichael. Edinburgh : Edinburgh University Press, c1979. 110 p. ; 21 cm. Includes bibliographical references and indexes. [BS575.C28] 80-467268 ISBN 0-85224-364-2 : 12.50
1. Women in the Bible. 2. Jewish law. I. Title.
Distributed by Columbia University Press, New York, NY

CHAPPELL, Clovis Gillham, 1882- 220.92
Feminine faces. Nashville, Abingdon [1966, c.1942] 219p. 20cm. (Apex bks., X3-125) [BS575.C53] 42-5030 1.25 pap.,
1. Women in the Bible. 2. Bible — Biog. I. Title.

CHAPPELL, Clovis Gillham, 1882- 220.92
Feminine faces [by] Clovis G. Chappell. New York, Nashville, Abingdon-Cokesbury press [1942] 219 p. 20 cm. [BS575.C53] 42-5030
1. Women in the Bible. 2. Bible—Biog. I. Title.

[CHARLES, Elizabeth (Rundle) "Mrs. Andrew Charles"] 1828-1896. 920.
Sketches of the women of Christendom. By the author of "Chronicles of the Schonberg-Cotta family." New York, Dodd, Mead & company [1880] vi, 334 p. 20 cm. [CT3203.C35] 6-22745
1. Women in the Bible. 2. Woman—Biog. I. Title.

CLAPP, Marie Wolcott (Welles) Mrs. 1879- 221.8396
The Old Testament as it concerns women, from Nehushta. queen-mother of the exile, to Mary, the mother of Jesus [by] Marie Welles Clapp; approved by the committee on curriculum of the Board of education of the Methodist Episcopal church. New York, Cincinnati [etc.] The Methodist book concern [c1934] 128 p. 17 1/2 cm. [DS1199.W7C6] 34-38176
1. Women in the Bible. I. Methodist Episcopal church. Board of education. II. Title.

COX, Francis Augustus, 1783-1853. 220.92
Female Scripture biography: including an Essay on what Christianity has done for women. By Francis Augustus Cox ... New-York: Published by James Eastburn & co. at the literary rooms, Broadway, corner of Pine-street. Abraham Paul, printer ... 1817. v. 19 cm. [BS575.C6 1817] ca 31

1. Women in the Bible. 2. Bible—Biog. I. Title.

DANKER, Albert. 220.92
Heroines of olden time. By the Rev. Dr. Albert Danker ... New York [Chapple & Tozer, printers] 1875. 101 p. 23 cm. [BS575.D25] 31-20506
1. Women in the Bible. 2. Bible—Biog. I. Title.
Contents omitted.

DAUGHTERS of St. Paul. 220.9'2 B
Women of the Gospel / written by the Daughters of St. Paul ; ill. by Gregori. Boston : St. Paul Editions, 1975. 134 p. : ill. ; 25 cm. [BS2445.D38] 74-32122
1. Bible. N.T.—Biography. 2. Women in the Bible. I. Title.

DEEN, Edith. 220.92
All of the women of the Bible. [1st ed.] New York, Harper [1955] xxii, 410p. 25cm. Bibliography: p.381-385. [BS575.D4] 55-8521
1. Women in the Bible. 2. Bible—Biog. I. Title.

DEEN, Edith. 220.8'30141'2
The Bible's legacy for womanhood. [1st ed.] Garden City, N.Y., Doubleday, 1969 [i.e. 1970] xviii, 340 p. 22 cm. Bibliography: p. [321]-326. [BS575.D42] 75-93203 5.95
1. Women in the Bible. 2. Woman—Religious life. I. Title.

DEEN, Edith. 248'.843
Wisdom from women in the Bible / Edith Deen. 1st ed. San Francisco : Harper & Row, c1978. p. cm. [BS575.D43 1978] 77-20460 6.95
1. Women in the Bible. I. Title.

DONE, Willard.
Women of the Bible. A series of story and character of sketches of great women who have aided in making Bible history. Salt Lake City, Utah, 1900. 224 p. front. 12 degrees. Jan
I. Title.

DRIMMER, Frederick. 220.8'30141'2
Daughters of Eve : women in the Bible / by Frederick Drimmer ; ill. by Hal Frenck. Norwalk, Conn. : C. R. Gibson Co., [1975] 88 p. : ill. ; 21 cm. [BS575.D7] 74-83776 ISBN 0-8378-1765-X
1. Women in the Bible. I. Frenck, Hal. II. Title.

EMSWILER, Sharon Neufer. 261.8'34'12
The ongoing journey : women and the Bible / by Sharon Neufer Emswiler. [New York] : Women's Division, Board of Global Ministries, United Methodist Church, c1977. 144 p. ; 19 cm. Bibliography: p. 139-142. [BS575.E55] 77-151179 1.50
1. Women in the Bible. 2. Woman (Theology)—Biblical teaching. I. Title.

FAULKNER, James, 1876- 220.92
Romances and intrigues of the women of the Bible. [1st ed.] New York, Vantage Press [1957] 162p. 21cm. [BS575.F33] 56-12197
1. Women in the Bible. I. Title.

FAXON, Alicia Craig. 225.8'30141'2
Women and Jesus. Philadelphia, United Church Press [1973] 126 p. 22 cm. "A Pilgrim Press book." Bibliography: p. 119-126. [BT590.W6F38] 72-11868 ISBN 0-8298-0244-4 4.95
1. Jesus Christ—Attitude towards women. 2. Women in the Bible. I. Title.

FRAINE, Jean de. 221.92'2
Women of the Old Testament, by J. de Fraine. Translated by Forrest L. Ingram. De Pere, Wis., St. Norbert Abbey Press, 1968. 92 p. 20 cm. Translation of Bijbelse Vrouwengestalten. [BS575.F713] 68-58524 ISBN 0-8316-1029-8
1. Bible. O.T.—Biography. 2. Women in the Bible. I. Title.

GARRISON, Webb B. 220.8396
Women in the life of Jesus. Indianapolis, Bobbs [c.1962] 192p. 22cm. 62-20683 3.95
1. Women in the Bible. I. Title.

GILLILAND, Dolores Scott. 220.9'505
Selected women of the Scriptures of stamina and courage / by Dolores Scott Gilliland ; illustrated by Gael Scott. Spearfish, SD : Honor Books, c1978. 101 p. : ill. ; 22 cm. [BS575.G47] 78-50069 ISBN 0-931446-02-3 pbk. : 3.95
1. Bible—Biography. 2. Women in the Bible. I. Title.

HALLET, Mary (Thomas) Mrs. 1892- 221.92
Their names remain, seventeen women of Old Testament days [by] Mary Hallet. New York, Cincinnati [etc.] The Abingdom press [c1938] 132 p. 17 1/2 cm. (Full name: Mrs. Mary Keller (Thomas) Hallet) [BS575.H27] 38-21542
1. Women in the Bible. 2. Bible. O. T.—Biog. 3. Bible—Biog.—O. T. I. Title.

HARRISON, Eveleen. 220.92
Little-known women of the Bible, by Eveleen Harrison. New York, Round table press, inc., 1936. 135 p. 20 cm. Contents.--Old Testament: Leah. Miriam. Deborah. Michal. The great woman of Shunem.--New Testament: Elizabeth. Anna the prophetess. The Syrophenicianwoman. Claudia Procula. Lydia of Thyatira. [BS575.H33] 36-27397
1. Women in the Bible. 2. Bible—Biog. I. Title.

HARTSOE, Colleen Ivey. 220.9'2
Dear daughter, letters from Eve and other women of the Bible / by Colleen Ivey Hartsoe. Wilton, Conn. : Morehouse-Barlow Co., c1981. 77 p. ; 19 cm. Bibliography: p. 77. [BS575.H35] 19 81-80627 ISBN 0-8192-1288-1 pbk. : 4.25
1. Women in the Bible. I. Title.

HEADLEY, Phineas Camp, 1819-1903 220.92
Historical and descriptive sketches of the women of the Bible, from Eve of the Old to the Marys of the New Testament, by P. C. Headley. Auburn, Derby, Miller & co., 1850. xii, [18]-284 p. illus. 19cm. Added t.-p., engraved. [BS575.H4] 31-20501
1. Women in the Bible. 2. Bible—Biog. I. Title.

HEAPS, Isabel (Warrington) 225.92
Five Marys [by] Isabel Warrington Heaps. New York, Nashville, Abingdon-Cokesbury press [1942] 101 p. front., plates. 25 1/2 cm. [BS2445.H4] 42-20129
1. Women in the Bible. 2. Bible. N.T.—Biog. 3. Bible—Biog.—N.T. I. Title.

HONEYWELL, Betty 248.84
Living portraits. Programs based on character studies of Bible women. Chicago, Moody [c.1965] 127p. 22cm. 1.95 pap., spiral bdg.,
I. Title.

HURLEY, James B. 261.8'344
Man and woman in Biblical perspective / James B. Hurley. 1st. ed. Grand Rapids, MI : Zondervan Pub. House, 1981. 288 p. ; 21 cm. Reprint. Originally published: Leicester : Inter-Varsity Press, 1981. Includes indexes. Bibliography: p. 272-280. [BS680.W7H87 1981] 19 81-2975 ISBN 0-310-43730-X pbk. : 6.95
1. Women in the Bible. 2. Women in Christianity. 3. Men (Christian theology)—Biblical teaching. 4. Sex role—Biblical teaching. I. Title.

JAY, William, 1769-1853. 221.
Lectures on female Scripture characters. By William Jay ... New York, R. Carter & brothers, 1854. xviii, 351 p. 21 cm. [BS575.J3] 40-23166
1. Women in the Bible. 2. Bible—Biog. I. Title.

KULOW, Nelle Wahler. 220.92
Even as you and I; sketches of human women from the Divine Book. Columbus, Ohio, Wartburg Press [1955] 72p. 20cm. [BS575.K76] 55-4428
1. Women in the Bible. 2. Bible—Biog. I. Title.

KUYPER, Abraham, 1837-1920. 225.92
Women of the New Testament; thirty meditations, by Abraham Kuyper ... translated from the Dutch by Prof. Henry Zylstra. The Scripture selection and questions for discussion have been added by "The preacher". Grand Rapids, Mich., Zondervan publishing house [c1933] 3 p. l., [5]-71 [3] p. 20 cm. Translation of the second part of author's "Vrouwen mit de Hellige Schrift". [BS575.K82] 34-6257
1. Women in the Bible. 2. Bible. N. T.—Biog. 3. Bible—Biog.—N. T. I. Zylstra, Henry, 1909- tr. II. Title.

KUYPER, Abraham, 1837-1920. 221.92
Women of the Old Testament; fifty meditations, by Abraham Kuyper ... translated from the Dutch by Prof. Henry Zylstra. The Scripture selection and questions for discussion have been added by "The preacher". Grand Rapids, Mich., Zondervan publishing house [c1933] 3 p. l., 5-120 p. 21 cm. Translation of the first part of author's "Vrouwen uit de Hellige Schrift". [BS575.K8] 34-6256
1. Women in the Bible. 2. Bible. O. T.—Biog. 3. Bible—Biog.—O. T. I. Zylstra, Henry, 1909- tr. II. Title.

LEWIS, Ethel (Clark) 220.92
Portraits of Bible women. [1st ed.] New York, Vantage Press [1956] 252p. 21cm. [BS575.L43] 55-11659
1. Women in the Bible. I. Title.

LOCKYER, Herbert. 220.92
The women of the Bible. [1st ed.] Grand Rapids, Zondervan Pub. House [1967] 321 p. 24 cm. Bibliography: p. 307-308. [BS575.L56] 67-22687
1. Women in the Bible. I. Title.

LOFTS, Norah (Robinson) 1904- 221.92
Women in the Old Testament; twenty psychological portraits. New York, Macmillan, 1949. xi, 178 p. 21 cm. [BS575.L58] 49-11604
1. Women in the Bible. I. Title.

LUNDHOLM, Algot Theodore. 220.92
Women of the Bible, by Rev. Algot Theodore Lundholm... Rock Island, Ill., Augustana book concern [c1923-26] 2 v. 20 cm. Contents.v. 1. Old Testament.--v. 2. New Testament. [BS575.L8] 23-10891
1. Women in the Bible. 2. Bible—Biog. I. Title.

LUNDHOLM, Algot Theodore, 1875- 220.92
Women of the Bible. Rock Island, Ill., Augustana Book Concern [1948] 270 p. 20 cm. [BS575.L82] 49-4068
1. Women in the Bible. 2. Bible—Biog. I. Title.

MCALLISTER, Grace Edna. 221.92
God portrays more women. Chicago, Moody Press [1956] 188p. 22cm. [BS575.M24] 56-1610
1. Women in the Bible. 2. Bible. O.T.—Biog. I. Title.

MCALLISTER, Grace Edna. 221.8396
God portrays women. Chicago, Moody Press [1954] 190p. 22cm. [BS575.M25] 54-3703
1. Women in the Bible. 2. Bible. O.T.—Biog. I. Title.

MACARTNEY, Clarence Edward Noble, 1879- 220.92
Ancient wives and modern husbands [by] Clarence E. Macartney. Nashville, Tenn., Cokesbury press [c1934] 176 p. 19 1/2 cm. [BS575.M28] 34-12014
1. Women in the Bible. 2. Presbyterian church—Sermons. 3. Sermons, American. I. Title.
Contents omitted.

MACARTNEY, Clarence Edward Noble, 1879- 220.92
Great women of the Bible, by Clarence Edward Macartney ... New York, Nashville, Abingdon-Cokesbury press [1942] 207 p. 19 1/2 cm. [BS575.M29] 42-20130
1. Women in the Bible. 2. Presbyterian church—Sermons. 3. Sermons, American. I. Title.

MCCOOK, Henry Christopher, 1837-1911. 225.92
The women friends of Jesus; a course of popular lectures based upon the lives and characters of the holy women of gospel history, by Henry C. McCook, D.D. New York, Fords, Howard & Hubert, 1886. vii, 406 p. 20 1/2 cm. [BX2445.M3] 39-10470

1. Women in the Bible. 2. Bible. N.T.—Biog. 3. Bible—Biog.—N.T. I. Title.

MARBLE, Annie (Russell) 220.92
Mrs. 1864-1936.
Women of the Bible, their services in home and state, by Annie Russell Marble. New York & London, The Century co. [c1923] viii p., 3 l., 3-315 p. front., plates. 20 cm. Bibliography: p. 298-301 [BS575.M33] 23-18289
1. Women in the Bible. 2. Bible—Biog. I. Title.

MARSHALL, Zona Bays. 220.92
Certain women; a study of Biblical women. With a foreword by James Gordon Lott, and an introd. by Robert G. Lee. [1st ed.] New York, Exposition Press [1960] 141p. 21cm. (An Exposition-Testament Book) [BS575.M337] 60-2131
1. Women in the Bible. I. Title.

[MARTYN, Sarah Towne 220.92
(Smith)] Mrs., 1805-1879.
Women of the Bible. New York, American tract society [c1868] 352 p. illus. 20 1/2 cm. Title vignette. Half-title: Women of the Bible, by Mrs. S. T. Martyn. Error in binding: pages [351]-352 bound between pages 6 and [7] [BS575.M34] 31-20499
1. Women in the Bible. 2. Bible—Biog. I. Title.

MASON, Maggie. 220.9'22
Women like us : learn more about yourself through studies of Bible women / Maggie Mason. Waco, Tex. : Word Books, c1978. 136 p. ; 21 cm. [BS575.M345] 78-57550 ISBN 0-8499-2835-4 pbk. : 3.95
1. Women in the Bible. I. Title.

MATHESON, George, 1842- 220.92
1906.
The representative women of the Bible, by George Matheson... New York, A. C. Armstrong and son; London, Hodder and stoughton, 1907. xiv, 269 p. 19 1/2 cm. [BS575.M35 1907] 7-33919
1. Women in the Bible. 2. Bible—Biog. I. Title.
Contents omitted.

MORTON, Henry Canova 220.92
Vollam, 1892-
Women of the Bible. Illustrated with a full-color front. and 18 ports. by famous old masters. [Illustrated ed.] New York, Dodd, Mead, 1956 [c1941] 204p. illus. 21cm. [BS575] 57-817
1. Women in the Bible. 2. Bible—Biog. I. Title.

MORTON, Henry Canova 220.92
Vollam, 1892-
Women of the Bible, by H. V. Morton. New York, Dodd, Mead & company, 1941. vi p., 1 l., 204 p. 21 cm. [BS575.M6 1941] 41-5256
1. Women in the Bible. 2. Bible—Biog. I. Title.

MULLIKEN, Frances 220.9'2 B
Hartman, 1924-
Women of destiny in the Bible / by Frances Hartman Mulliken and Margaret Salts. Independence, Mo. : Herald Pub. House, c1978. 187 p. ; 18 cm. Bibliography: p. 186-187. Introduces seventeen women who play a significant role in the Bible including Sarah, Esther, Mary Magdalene, and Lydia. [BS575.M83] 78-5132 ISBN 0-8309-0211-2 pbk. : 4.00
1. Bible—Biography. 2. Women in the Bible. 3. [Women in the Bible.] 4. [Bible stories.] I. Salts, Margaret, 1918- joint author. II. Title.
Publisher's address : Drawer HH, Independence, MO 64055

NEAL, Hazel G 220.92
Bible women of faith. Anderson, Ind., Warner Press [1955] 158p. 20cm. [BS575.N4] 55-3206
1. Women in the Bible. 2. Bible—Biog. I. Title.

NICHOL, Charles Ready, 220.8396
1876-
God's woman, by C. R. Nichol; the place of women in the social and religious life as revealed in the Bible. With an introduction by M. O. Daley. Clifton, Tex. Mrs. C. R. Nichol, 1938. 183 p. 20 cm. [BS680.W7N5] 38-16151
1. Women in the Bible. 2. Women—Social and moral questions. I. Title.

NOTABLE women of olden 221.92
time. Written for the American Sunday-school union. Philadelphia, New York [etc.] American Sunday-school union [c1852] 301 p. incl. front., illus. plates. 15 1/2 cm. [BS575.N6] 31-20498
1. Women in the Bible. 2. Bible. O.T.—Biog. 3. Bible—Biog.—O.T. I. American Sunday-school union.

NOTABLE women of olden 221.92
time. Written for the American Sunday-school union. Philadelphia, New York [etc.] American Sunday-school union [c1852] 301 p. incl. front., illus. plates. 16 cm. [BS575.N6] 31-20498
1. Women in the Bible. 2. Bible. O. T.—Biog. 3. Bible—Biog.—O. T. I. American Sunday-school union.

NUNNALLY-COX, Janice. 220.9'2
Foremothers : women of the Bible / Janice Nunnally-Cox. New York : Seabury Press, 1981. p. cm. [BS575.N86] 19 81-5675 ISBN 0-8164-2329-6 pbk. : 6.95
1. Women in the Bible. I. Title.

OCKENGA, Harold John, 220.92
1905-
Have you met these women? By Harold John Ockenga ... Grand Rapids, Mich., Zondervan publishing house [c1940] 146 p. 20 cm. [BS575.O25] 40-32420
1. Women in the Bible. 2. Congregational churches—Sermons. 3. Sermons, American. I. Title.

OCKENGA, Harold John, 220.92
1905-
Women who made Bible history; messages and character sketches dealing with familiar Bible women. Grand Rapids, Zondervan Pub. House [1962] 239 p. illus. 23 cm. [BS575.O27] 62-7373
1. Women in the Bible. 2. Congregational churches—Sermons. 3. Sermons, American. I. Title.

O'REILLY, Bernard, 1823- 220.92
1907.
Heroic women of the Bible and the church; narrative biographies of grand female characters of the Old and New Testaments, and of saintly women and the Christian church, both in earlier and later ages. By the Rev. Bernard O'Reilly. Illustrated with twenty-five plates in oil colors, after paintings by Raphael, Domenichino, Allori ... and others, executed by the best German and French art-printers. New York, J. B. Ford and company [c1878] 3 p. l., v-viii, 394 p. col. plates. 21 cm. Each of the four sections preceded by two unnumbered pages not included in the pagination. Plates accompanied by guard sheets with descriptive letterpress. Published in 1880 under title: Illustrious women of Bible and Catholic church history. [BS575.O7 1877] 922 31-20503
1. Women in the Bible. 2. Bible—Biog. 3. Women in literature and art. 4. Catholic church—Biog. I. Title.

O'REILLY, Bernard, 1823- 220.92
1907.
Illustrious women of Bible and Catholic church history: narrative biographies of grand female characters of the Old and New Testaments, and of saintly women of the holy Catholic church, both in earlier and later ages. By Mgr. Bernard O'Reilly ... Illustrated with twenty-five photogravures's after printings by Raphael, Domenichino, Allori ... and others. New York, J. Dewing publishing co. [c1889] 3 p. l., v-viii, 394 p. front., plates. 29 cm. Each of the four sections preceded by two unnumbered pages not included in the pagination. Published in 1877 under title: Heroic women of the Bible and the church. [BS575.O7 1889] 922 31-20505
1. Women in the Bible. 2. Bible—Biog. 3. Women in Literature and art. 4. Catholic church—Biog. I. Title.

OUTLAW, Nell (Warren) 225.92
"And certain women," by Nell Warren Outlaw. Nashville, Tenn., Broadman press [1947] 7 p. l., 3-128 p. illus. 20 1/2 cm. [BS2445.O9] 47-4383
1. Women in the Bible. 2. Bible. N.T.—Biog. I. Title.

PEABODY, Emily Clough. Mrs. 920.
Lives worth living; studies of women, Biblical and modern, especially adapted for groups of young women in churches and clubs, by Emily Clough Peabody. Chicago, Ill., The University of Chicago press [1915] xiii, 187 p. illus. (incl. ports.) 20 cm. (Half-title: The University of Chicago publications in religious education ... Constructive studies) "Reference books" at end of each lesson. [CT3203.P4] 15-16630
1. Women in the Bible. 2. Woman—Social and moral questions. I. Title.

PEABODY, Emily Clough. Mrs. 920.
Lives worth living; studies of women, Biblical and modern, especially adapted for groups of young women in churches and clubs, by Emily Clough Peabody. Chicago, Ill., The University of Chicago press [c1923] xiii, 194 p. illus. (incl. ports.) 20 cm. (Half-title: The University of Chicago publications in religious education ... Constructive studies) "Reference books" at end of each lesson. [CT3203.P4 1923] 23-12155
1. Women in the Bible. 2. Woman—Social and moral questions. I. Title.

PEASE, Alice Campbell. 220.92
Mrs.
Significant women of the Bible, by Alice Campbell Pease; introduction by Helen Barrett Montgomery. Grand Rapids, Mich., Zondervan publishing house [c1941] 135 p. 20 cm. [BS575.P4] 41-19353
1. Women in the Bible. 2. Bible—Biog. I. Title.

PRICE, Eugenia. 220.8'30141'2
The unique world of women ... in Bible times and now. Boston, G. K. Hall, 1974 [c1969] 287 p. 25 cm. Large print ed. Bibliography: p. 287. [BS575.P7 1974] 74-5126 ISBN 0-8161-6218-2 9.95 (lib. bdg.)
1. Women in the Bible. 2. Sight-saving books. I. Title.

PRICE, Eugenia. 220.8'30141'2
The unique world of women, in Bible times and now. Grand Rapids, Zondervan Pub. House [1969] 245 p. 25 cm. Bibliography: p. 245. [BS575.P7] 79-91644 3.95
1. Women in the Bible. I. Title.

PRICE, Eugenia. 220.8'30141'2
The unique world of women . . . in Bible times and now. Grand Rapids, Mich., Zondervan Pub. Co. [1973, c.1969] 175 p. 18 cm. Bibliography: p. 175. [BS575.P7] 79-91644 1.25 (pbk.)
1. Women in the Bible. I. Title.

RICHARDS, Alberta Rae 220.92
(Sune)
Women of the Bible ... [Gastonia, N. C., Geographical Pub. Co., 1962] unpaged. illus. 26cm. [BS575.R48] 62-3988
1. Women in the Bible. 2. Bible—Biog. I. Title.

RILEY, William Bell, 1861- 220.92
Wives of the Bible, a cross-section of femininity, by W. B. Riley ... Grand Rapids, Mich., Zondervan publishing house [c1938] ix p., 1 l., 13-119 p. 20 cm. [BS575.R5] 38-30642
1. Women in the Bible. 2. Bible—Biog. 3. Baptists—Sermons. 4. Sermons, American. I. Title.

ROBERTSON, Ella (Broadus) 221.
Mrs. 1872-
The ministry of women, by Ella B. Robertson. Oklahoma City, Okla., Messenger book house [c1922] 2 p. l., [7]-109 p. 19 cm. "Daily Bible readings" at end of each chapter. [BS575.R6] 22-3490 0.50
1. Women in the Bible. I. Title.

RODDY, Lee, 1921- 220.9'2 B
Women in the Bible / by Lee Roddy. 1st ed. Chappaqua, N.Y. : Christian Herald Books, c1980. p. cm. Bibliography: p. [BS575.R63] 19 80-65432 ISBN 0-915684-64-0 : 8.95
1. Bible—Biography. 2. Women in the Bible. I. Title.

RUSCHE, Helga 220.92
They lived by faith: women in the Bible. Tr. by Elizabeth Williams. Helicon[dist. New York, Taplinger, c.1963] vi, 124p. 22cm. 63-19402 2.95
1. Women in the Bible. I. Title.

RUSCHE, Helga. 220.92
They lived by faith; women in the Bible. Translated by Elizabeth Williams. Baltimore, Helicon [1963] vi, 124 p. 22 cm. [BS575.R813] 63-19402
1. Women in the Bible. I. Title.

SANGSTER, Margaret 220.92
Elizabeth (Munson) Mrs., 1838-1912.
The women of the Bible; a portrait gallery, by Margaret E. Sangster. New York, The Christian herald [c1911] 363 p.16 col. pl. (incl. front.) 21 cm. [BS575.S3] 11-27788
1. Women in the Bible. 2. Bible—Biog. I. Title.

SCHELKLE, Karl 261.8'34'12
Hermann.
The spirit and the bride : woman in the Bible / Karl Hermann Schelkle ; translated by Matthew J. O'Connell. Collegeville, Minn. : Liturgical Press, c1979. p. cm. Translation of Der Geist und die Braut. Includes bibliographical references. [BS575.S3413] 79-16976 ISBN 0-8146-1008-0 pbk. : 4.95
1. Women in the Bible. 2. Women (Theology)—Biblical teaching. 3. Marriage—Biblical teaching. I. Title.

SELL, Henry Thorne, 1854- 220.
1928.
Studies of famous Bible women, by Henry T. Sell... New York, Chicago [etc.] Fleming H. Revell company [c1925] 160 p. 19 cm. (Lettered on cover: Sell's Bible study text books) [BS575.S4] 25-9224
1. Women in the Bible. 2. Bible—Biog. I. Title.

SMITH, Judith Florence, 220.92
1882-
In Our Lady's library, character studies of the women of the Old Testament, by Judith F. Smith, with a foreword by Dom Savinien Louismet, O.S.B. London, New York [etc.] Longmans, Green and co., 1923. xii, 152 p. front. 19 cm. [BS575.S5] 23-5933
1. Women in the Bible. 2. Bible. O.T.—Biog. 3. Bible—Biog.—O.T. I. Title.

SPRAGUE, William Buell, 220.92
1795-1876,ed.
Women of the Old and New Testament; a series of portraits. With characteristic descriptions, by several American clergymen. Edited by William B. Sprague, D.D. Eighteen original designs engraved expressly for this work. 2d ed. New York, D. Appleton & company; Philadelphia, G. S. Appleton, 1851. 2 p. l., [7]-229 p. col. front., col. plates. 28 1/2 cm. [BS575.S55 1851] 31-4022
1. Women in the Bible. 2. Bible—Biog. I. Title.
Contents omitted.

SPURGEON, Charles Haddon, 221.92
1834-1892.
Sermons on women of the Old Testament; sel. and ed. by Chas. T. Cook. Grand Rapids, Zondervan Pub. House [c.1960] 256p. (Library of Spurgeon's sermons, v. 11) 61-706 2.95
1. Women in the Bible. 2. Bible. O. T.—Biog. I. Title.

STANTON, Elizabeth 220.8'30141'2
Cady, 1815-1902.
The original feminist attack on the Bible (The woman's Bible). Introd. by Barbara Welter. New York, Arno Press, 1974 [c1895-98] xlii, 217 p. 22 cm. Reprint of the ed. published by the European Pub. Co., New York. Contents.Contents.—pt. 1. Comments on Genesis, Exodus, Leviticus, Numbers, and Deuteronomy.—pt. 2. Comments on the Old and New Testaments from Joshua to Revelation. [HQ1395.S72 1974] 74-9343 ISBN 0-405-05997-3 6.95 (lib. bdg.)
1. Bible—Commentaries. 2. Women in the Bible. I. Title. II. Title: The woman's Bible.

STANTON, Elizabeth 220.8'30141'2
(Cady) 1815-1902.
The woman's Bible. New York, Arno Press, 1972 [c1895-98] 2 v. in 1. 24 cm. (American women: images and realities) Contents.Contents.—pt. 1. Comments on Genesis, Exodus, Leviticus, Numbers, and Deuteronomy.—pt. 2. Comments on the Old and New Testaments from Joshua to Revelation. [HQ1395.S72] 72-2626 ISBN 0-405-04481-X 16.00
1. Bible—Commentaries. 2. Women in the Bible. I. Bible. English. Selections. 1972. II. Title. III. Series.

STANTON, Elizabeth Cady, 1815-1902. 220.8'30141'2
The woman's Bible [by] Elizabeth Cady Stanton and the Revising Committee. Seattle, Coalition Task Force on Women and Religion [1974, c1895-98] xvii, 152, 217 p. 21 cm. Reprint of the ed. published by European Pub. Co., New York. Contents.Contents.—Comments on Genesis, Exodus, Leviticus, Numbers, and Deuteronomy.—Comments on the Old and New Testaments from Joshua to Revelation. [HQ1395.S72 1974b] 74-182269
1. Bible—Commentaries. 2. Women in the Bible. I. Bible. English. Selections. 1974. II. Title.

STARR, Lee Anna. 220.
The Bible status of woman, by Lee Anna Starr ... foreword by Lyman E. Davis ... New York, Chicago [etc.] Fleming H. Revell company [c1926] 416 p. front. (port.) 23 cm. "Probability about the address and author of the Epistle to the Hebrews, by Von A. Harnack": p. [392]-415. [BS575.S65] 26-10209
1. Women in the Bible. 2. Bible. N.T. Hebrews. I. Harnack, Adolf von, 1851- II. Title.

STEELE, Eliza R. Mrs. 221.92
Heroines of sacred history. By Mrs. Steele ... New York, J. S. Taylor and M. W. Dodd, 1841. vi, [7]-238 p. 20 cm. [BS575.S73] 31-20489
1. Women in the Bible. 2. Bible. O. T.—Biog. 3. Bible—Biog.—O. T. I. Title.
Contents omitted.

STEELE, Eliza R. Mrs. 221.92
Heroines of sacred history. By Mrs. Steele ... 2d ed. New York, J. S. Taylor, & co., 1842. vi, [7]-238 p. 16 cm. [BS575.S73 1842] 33-20575
1. Women in the Bible. 2. Bible. O. T.—Biog. 3. Bible—Biog.—O. T. I. Title.
Contents omitted.

STEPHENS, Shirley. 261.8'344
A New Testament view of women / Shirley Stephens. Nashville, Tenn. : Broadman Press, c1980. 182 p. ; 19 cm. Includes indexes. Bibliography: p. 174-177. [BS2545.W65S74] 19 80-65538 ISBN 0-8054-1524-6 pbk. : 4.95
1. Bible. N.T.—Criticism, interpretation, etc. 2. Women in the Bible. I. Title.

STOWE, Harriet Elizabeth (Beecher) Mrs., 1811-1896. 220.92
Bible heroines, being narrative biographies of prominent Hebrew women in the patriarchal, national, and Christian eras, giving views of woman in sacred history, as revealed in the light of the present day. By Harriet Beecher Stowe. Illustrations in oil colors. New York, Fords, Howard & Hulbert [c1878] [185] p. col. front., col. plates (part mounted) 26 1/2 cm. Published in 1874 under title: Woman in sacred history. [BS575.S75] 31-20487
1. Women in the Bible. 2. Bible—Biog. 3. Women in literature and art. I. Title.

STOWE, Harriet Elizabeth (Beecher) Mrs., 1811-1896. 220.92
Woman in sacred history: a series of sketches drawn from scriptural, historical, and legendary sources. By Harriet Beecher Stowe. Illustrated with sixteen chromo-lithographs, after paintings by Raphael, Batoni. Horace Vernet [etc.] ... New York, J. B. Ford and company, 1874. [189] p. col. front., col. plates 16 1/2 cm. Published in 1878 under title: Bible heroines. [BS575.S78] 31-20486
1. Women in the Bible. 2. Bible—Biog. 3. Women in literature and art. I. Title.

SUDLOW, Elizabeth (Williams) 1878- 220.92
Career women of the Bible. [1st ed] New York, Pageant Press [1951] 79 p. 21 cm. [BS575.S8] 51-14985
1. Women in the Bible. 2. Bible — Biog. I. Title.

THOMAS, Metta Newman. 220.92
Women of the Bible; a study in their life and character. Nashville, 20th Century Christian, 1956. 131p. 21cm. [BS575.T48] 57-20949
1. Women in the Bible. 2. Bible—Biog. I. Title.

THOMAS, Metta Newman. 220.92
Women of the Bible; a study in their life and character. Nashville, 20th Century Christian, 1956. 131 p. 21 cm. [BS575.T48] 57-20949
1. Women in the Bible. 2. Bible — Giog. I. Title.

THOMSON, Lucy Gertsch. 220.92
Women of the Bible: a book telling the life stories of twenty prominent women of the Old and New Testament. Salt Lake City, Deseret Book Co. [1957] 96 p. 16 cm. [BS575.T53] 57-59113
1. Women in the Bible. 2. Women in the Bible. I. Title.

TINNEY, Ethel. 220.92
Women of the Bible, in verse. [1st ed.] New York, Pageant Press [1953] 50p. 24cm. [BS575.T55] 53-12703
1. Women in the Bible. I. Title.

†TISCHLER, Nancy Marie Patterson. 220.8'301'412
Legacy of Eve : women of the Bible / Nancy M. Tischler. Atlanta : John Knox Press, c1977. 127, [1] p. ; 21 cm. Bibliography: p. [128] [BS575.T57] 76-44971 ISBN 0-8042-0074-2 pbk. : 3.95
1. Women in the Bible. I. Title.

VANDER VELDE, Frances. 220.92
She shall be called woman; a gallery of character sketches. With illus. by Dick Gringhuis. Grand Rapids, Grand Rapids International Publications; distributed by Kregel's [1957] 258 p. illus. 23 cm. (Women of the Bible) Includes bibliography. [BS575.V3] 57-13178
1. Women in the Bible. 2. Bible — Biog. I. Title.

WELD, Horatio Hastings, 1811-1888, ed. 220.92
The women of the Scriptures. Edited by Rev. H. Hastings Weld... Philadelphia, Lindsay and Blakiston [c1848] 2 p. l., [3]-240 p. front., plates. 22 1/2 cm. Added t.-p., engraved. [BS575.W4] 31-20485
1. Women in the Bible. 2. Bible—Biog. I. Title.

WHARTON, Morton Bryan. 221.92
Famous women of the Old Testament. A series of popular lectures delivered in the First Baptist church, Montgomery, Ala., by Morton Bryan Wharton ... New York, E. B. Treat, 1889. 318 p. incl. front. (port.) plates. 20 cm. [BS555.W45] 31-20484
1. Women in the Bible. 2. Bible. O.T.—Biog. 3. Bible—Biog.—O.T. I. Title.

WHITESELL, Faris Daniel, 1895- 252.027
Sermon outlines on women of the Bible. [Westwood, N.J.] Revell [c.1962] 64p. 21cm (Revell's sermon outline ser.) 62-10739 1.00 pap.,
1. Women in the Bible. 2. Sermons—Outlines. I. Title.

WILSON, Elizabeth. 259
A scriptural view of woman's rights and duties, in all the important relations of life; by Elizabeth Wilson ... Philadelphia, W. S. Young, printer, 1849. xi, [13]-376 p. 20 cm. [HQ1395.W7] 9-5636
1. Women in the Bible. 2. Woman—Rights of women. I. Title.

WOMEN of the Bible, 220.
by eminent divines ... New York & London, Harper & brothers, 1900. 6 p. l., 188 p. front., plates 23 cm. Initials on t.-p. in gold and colors. [BS575.W6] 0-6859
1. Women in the Bible. 2. Bible—Biog.

Women in the Bible—Biography.

FIELD, Faye. 225.9'22 B
Women who encountered Jesus / Faye Field. Nashville, Tenn. : Broadman Press, c1982. 128 p. ; 20 cm. [BS2445.F53 1982] 19 81-65798 ISBN 0-8054-5182-X : 3.25
1. Jesus Christ—Friends and associates—Biography. 2. Women in the Bible—Biography. I. Title.

MUSGROVE, Peggy. 220.9'2 B
Who's who among Bible women / Peggy Musgrove. Springfield, Mo. : Gospel Pub. House, c1981. 128 p. ; 18 cm. (Radiant books) [BS575.M86] 19 81-81126 ISBN 0-88243-883-2 (pbk.) : 2.50
1. Bible—Biography. 2. Women in the Bible—Biography. I. Title.

THOMPSON, Henry Adams, 1837-
Women of the Bible, consisting of biographical and descriptive sketches of the representative and more important women of Old Testament and New Testament times, as viewed in the light of our present day civilization, by H. A. Thompson ... with an introduction by Rev. Henrietta G. Moore. Illustrated with original engravings ... Dayton, O., Press of U. B. publishing house [c1914] xii, 548 p. plates. 21 1/2 cm. $3.00 14-12623
I. Title.

Women in the Bible—Biography—Juvenile literature.

STROM, Kay Marshall, 1943- 220.9'2
Special women in the Bible / written by Kay Marshall Strom ; illustrated by Ned Ostendorf. St. Louis, Mo., : Concordia Pub. House, c1980. 32 p. : ill. ; 27 cm. Presents stories about Jochebed, Rahab, Deborah, Ruth, Abigail, Queen Esther, Elizabeth and Mary, Mary and Martha, Mary Magdalene, and Dorcas. [BS575.S79] 79-27865 pbk. : 2.95
1. Women in the Bible—Biography—Juvenile literature. 2. Women—Palestine—Biography—Juvenile literature. 3. [Women in the Bible.] 4. [Bible stories.] I. Ostendorf, Ned. II. Title.

Women in the Bible—Drama.

HARE, Walter Ben, 1880- 791.6
The women of the Bible, a dramatic entertainment in three parts. by Walter Ben Hare ... Boston, Walter H. Baker company, 1922. 25 p. 19 cm. (On cover: Baker's novelty plays) [PN6120.R4H34] 37-30168
1. Women in the Bible—Drama. I. Title.

Women in the Bible—Juvenile literature.

COAKLEY, Mary Lewis, 1907- 225.92
Famous women of the New Testament. Sponsored by the Benedicitine monks of Belmont Abbey. Garden City, N. Y. [N. Doubleday, 1960] 64p. illus. 21cm. (The Catholic know-Your-Bible program) [BS2445.C6] 60-3653
1. Women in the Bible—Juvenile literature. 2. Bible. N. T.—Biog.—Juvenile literature. I. Title.

DAUGHTERS of St. Paul. 221.92'2
Women of the Bible; the Old Testament. Illus. by Gregori. [Boston] St. Paul Editions [1970] 123 p. col. illus., col. maps. 25 cm. Biblical quotations and brief narration recount the deeds of women of the Old Testament. [BS575.D34] 71-145574 5.00
1. Bible. O.T.—Biography—Juvenile literature. 2. [Bible. O.T.—Biography.] 3. Women in the Bible—Juvenile literature. 4. [Women in the Bible.] I. Gregori, illus. II. Title.

LATHAM, Judy. 220.9'2 B
Women in the Bible : helpful friends / Judy Latham ; illustrated by Paul Karch. Nashville : Broadman Press, c1979. 48 p. : col. ill. ; 24 cm. (Biblearn series) Focuses on the lives of six important women in the Old and New Testaments. Included are Deborah, Esther, Mary and Martha, Dorcas, and Lydia. [BS575.L37] 920 79-111971 ISBN 0-8054-4248-0 : 85.00 part of a set not sold separately
1. Women in the Bible—Juvenile literature. 2. [Women in the Bible.] 3. [Bible stories—O.T.] 4. [Bible stories—N.T.] I. Karch, Paul. II. Title.

MOSLEY, Jean (Bell) 1913- 225.92
Famous women of the New Testament. Garden City, N. Y. [N. Doubleday, 1960] 64p. illus. 21cm. (Know your Bible program) [BS2445.M6] 60-3654
1. Women in the Bible—Juvenile literature. 2. Bible. N. T.—Biog.—Juvenile literature. I. Title.

Women in the Bible—Study and teaching.

HERR, Ethel L. 248'.843
Chosen women of the Bible / Ethel L. Herr. Chicago : Moody Press, c1976. 96 p. ; 22 cm. Includes bibliographies. [BS575.H47] 75-36503 ISBN 0-8024-1297-1 pbk. : 1.50
1. Women in the Bible—Study and teaching. I. Title.

SMITH, Joyce Marie. 220.9'2 B
A woman's priorities / Joyce Marie Smith. Wheaton, Ill. : Tyndale House Publishers, 1976. 63 p. ; 19 cm. (New life Bible studies) Bibliography: p. 63. [BS575.S49 1976] 76-9372 ISBN 0-8423-8380-8 pbk. : 1.25
1. Bible—Biography—Study and teaching. 2. Women in the Bible—Study and teaching. I. Title. II. Series.

Women in the Catholic Church.

OHANNESON, Joan. 261.8'344
Woman : survivor in the Church / by Joan Ohanneson. Minneapolis, Minn. : Winston Press, c1980. 204 p. ; 22 cm. Includes bibliographical references. [BX2347.8.W6O38] 19 79-56865 ISBN 0-03-056671-1 pbk. : 4.95
1. Women in the Catholic Church. I. Title.

Women in the East.

YOUNG women's Christian associations. U.S. National speakers bureau. 267.
Speakers hand book; world program... New York city, National speakers bureau of the Young womens Christian associations, 1919. cover-title, 1 p. l., 93 p. diagrs. 21 cm. Contains bibliographies. [BV1375.A5 1919 a] 20-13269
1. Women in the East. 2. Women in South America. I. Title.

ZWEMER, Samuel Marinus, 1867-
Moslem women, by Dr. and Mrs. Samuel M. Zwemer. West Medford, Mass., The Central committee on the united study of foreign missions [c1926] 272 p. front., plates. 18 1/2 cm. "Reading list": p. 264. [HQ1170.Z9] 27-14201
1. Women in the East. 2. Missions—Mohammedans. I. Zwemer, Mrs. Amy E. (Wilkes) joint author. II. Title.

Women in the United States—Addresses, essays, lectures.

PETERSEN, Evelyn R., comp. 261.8'34'12
For women only; the fine art of being a woman. Edited by Evelyn R. Petersen and J. Allan Petersen. Wheaton, Ill., Tyndale [1974] 296 p. 22 cm. [HQ1420.P48] 73-93968 ISBN 0-8423-0896-2 ISBN 0-8423-0895-4 ISBN 0-8423-0896-2 (pbk.) 3.95 (pbk.).
1. Women in the United States—Addresses, essays, lectures. 2. Conduct of life—Addresses, essays, lectures. 3. Family—United States—Addresses, essays, lectures. I. Petersen, J. Allan, joint comp. II. Title.

Women—India.

HORNER, Isaline Blew, 1896- 294.3'657
Women under primitive Buddhism : laywomen and almswomen / by I. B. Horner. Delhi : Motilal Banarsidass, 1975. xxiv 391 p., 6 leaves of plates : ill. ; 22 cm. Reprint of the 1930 ed. published by G. Routledge, London. Includes bibliographical references and index. [HQ1742.H6 1975] 76-911012 ISBN 0-8426-0955-5 : 13.50
1. Women—India. 2. Women in Buddhism. I. Title.
Distributed by Verry.

Women, Jewish.

KOBLER, Franz, 1882- ed. 296
Her children call her blessed; a portrait of the Jewish mother. New York, Stephen Daye Press [1955] 392p. illus. 24cm. [BM729.W5K6] 55-6191

1. Women, Jewish. 2. Mothers in literature. I. Title.

LAZARUS, Nahida Ruth, Frau, 1849- 296
Nahida Remy's The Jewish woman. Authorized translation by Louise Mannheimer. With a preface by Prof. Dr. Lazarus. Cincinnati, Press of C. J. Krehbiel & company, 1895. 1 p. l., 7-264 p. front. (port.) 21 cm. "Works of reference": p. 264. [HQ1172.L2] 14-13641
1. Women, Jewish. I. Mannheimer, Louise Herschmann, Mrs. 1844-1920, tr. II. Title.

LEBESON, Anita (Libman) 1896- 920.073
Recall to life—the Jewish woman in America. South Brunswick, T. Yoseloff [1970] 351 p. 22 cm. Includes bibliographical references. [DS115.2.L36 1970] 77-88278 7.50
1. Women, Jewish. 2. Jews in the United States. I. Title.

LEVI, Shonie B
Guide for the Jewish homemaker [by] Shoni B. Levi [and] Sylvia R. Kaplan. Illustrated by J. B. Robinson. New York, Schocken Books [c1964] 256 p. illus. 20 cm. (Schocken paperbacks, SB87) Earlier ed. has title Across the threshold: A guide for the Jewish homemaker. 65-63486
1. Women, Jewish. 2. Jews-Social life and customs. I. Title.

LEVINGER, Elma (Ehrlich) Mrs., 1887- 922.96
Great Jewish women, by Elma Ehrlich Levinger; illustrated by Marcile Weist Stalter. New York, Behrman's Jewish book house, 1940. 7 p. l., 3-159 p. illus. 20 1/2 cm. [DS115.2.L4] 40-10875
1. Women, Jewish. I. Title.

ROSMARIN, Trude (Weiss) Mrs. 1908- 296
Jewish women through the ages, by Trude Weiss Rosmarin. New York, N. Y., The Jewish book club [c1940] 95, [1] p. 18 cm. "Selected bibliography": p. 96. [HQ1172.R6] 40-13517
1. Women, Jewish. I. Title.

WAXMAN, Meyer, 1884- 296
Blessed is the daughter [by] Meyer Waxman, Sulamith Ish-Kishor [and] Jacob Sloan. New York, Shengold Publishers [c1959] 157 p. illus. 29 cm. [BM729.W6W3] 59-11057
1. Women, Jewish. 2. Fasts anf feasts — Judaism. 3. Art, Jewish. I. Title.

Women, Jewish—Bibliography.

CANTOR, Aviva. 016.30141'2
A bibliography on the Jewish woman : a comprehensive and annotated listing of works published, 1900-1978 / compiled by Aviva Cantor. Fresh Meadows, N.Y. : Biblio Press, [c1979] 53 p. ; 28 cm. [Z7964.J4C36] [HQ1172] 78-73260 ISBN 0-9602036-0-5 pbk. : 3.00
1. Women, Jewish—Bibliography. I. Title.

CANTOR, Aviva. 016.3054'089'924
The Jewish woman, 1900-1980 : bibliography / compiled and annotated by Aviva Cantor ; editorial assistants, Susan Winter Young and Alissa Rothschild. Rev. ed. Fresh Meadows, NY : Biblio Press, c1981. 88 p. ; 28 cm. Rev. ed. of: A bibliography on the Jewish Woman. [c1979] [Z7963.J4C36 1981] [HQ1172] 19 81-67447 ISBN 0-9602036-3-X pbk. : 5.25
1. Women, Jewish—Bibliography. I. Title.
Publisher's address : P. O. Box 22, Fresh Meadows, NY 11365.

HAMELSDORF, Ora. 016.3054'089924
Jewish women and Jewish law bibliography / compiled by Ora Hamelsdorf and Sandra Adelsberg. Fresh Meadows, NY : Biblio Press, 1981, c1980. iii, 57 p. ; 28 cm. [Z7963.J4H35] [HQ1172] 19 80-69592 ISBN 0-9602036-2-1 pbk. : 3.50
1. Women, Jewish—Bibliography. 2. Women—Legal status, laws, etc. (Jewish law)—Bibliography. I. Adelsberg, Sandra. II. Title.
Publisher's address: P. O. Box 22, Fresh Meadows, NY 11365

Women, Jewish—Biography.

HENRY, Sondra. 920'.0092'924
Written out of history : a hidden legacy of Jewish women revealed through their writings and letters / by Sondra Henry and Emily Taitz. New York : Bloch Pub. Co., c1978. xi, 293 p. : ill. ; 22 cm. Includes index. Bibliography: p. 284-289. [DS115.2.H46] 77-99195 ISBN 0-8197-0454-7 : 12.50
1. Women, Jewish—Biography. I. Taitz, Emily, joint author. II. Title.

Women, Jewish—Morocco.

A study of culture stability and change: the Moroccan Jewess. Washington, Catholic University of America Press, 1956. vi, 75p. 23cm. Abstract of thesis: Catholic University of America. Bibliography: p. 70-75.
1. Women, Jewish—Morocco. 2. Jews in Morocco. 3. Acculturation. I. Jacobs, Milton, II. Title: Culture stability and change. III. Title: Moroccan Jewess.

Women. Jewish-Religious life.

LEVI, Shonie B. 296.4
Across the threshold; a guide for the Jewish homemaker, by Shonie B. Levi & Sylvia R. Kaplan. New York, Farrar, Straus & Cudahy [1959] 258 p. illus. 22 cm. Includes bibliography. [BM726.L42] 59-12039
1. Women, Jewish—Religious life. 2. Jews—Social life and customs. 3. Jews—Rites and ceremonies. I. Kaplan, Sylvia R., joint author. II. Title.

*LEVI, Shonie B. 296.4
Guide for the Jewish homemaker [by] Shonie B. Levi, Sylvia R. Kaplan [2d rev. ed.] New York, Schocken [c.1959, 1964] 256p. illus. 21cm. First pub. in 1959 by Farrar under title: Across the threshold; a guide for the Jewish homemaker. (SB87) Bibl. 1.95 pap.,
1. Women, Jewish—Religious life. 2. Jews—Soc. life & cust. 3. Jews—Rites and ceremonies. I. Kaplan, Sylvia R., joint author. II. Title.

LEVI, Shonie B.
A guide for the Jewish homemaker [by] Shonie B. Levi [and] Sylvia R. Kaplan. New York National Women's League of the United Synagogue of America [1964, c1959] xvi, 256 p. illus. 21 cm. Earlier ed. has title: Across the threshold; a guide for the Jewish homemaker. Includes bibliography. 67-76110
1. Women. Jewish-Religious life. 2. Jews-Soc. life & cust. 3. Jews-Rites and ceremonies. I. Kaplan, Slyvia R., joint author. II. Title.

Women, Jewish—United States—Biography.

SOCHEN, June, 1937- 920'.0092924073 B
Consecrate every day : the public lives of Jewish American women, 1880-1980 / by June Sochen. Albany, N.Y. : State University of New York Press, [1981] p. cm. Includes index. Bibliography: p. [DS115.2.S6] 19 80-29169 ISBN 0-87395-526-9 : 29.50 ISBN 0-87395-527-7 pbk. : 9.95
1. Women, Jewish—United States—Biography. 2. Jews in the United States—Biography. I. Title.

Women, Jewish—United States—History—Sources.

THE American Jewish woman 205.4'8
: a documentary history / by Jacob R. Marcus. New York : Ktav Pub. House ; Cincinnati : American Jewish Archives, 1981. p. cm. "Intended as a supplement to Jacob R. Marcus, The American Jewish woman, 1654-1980."—Pref. Includes index. Bibliography: p. [HQ1172.M37 Suppl] 19 81-1966 ISBN 0-87068-752-2 : 35.00
1. Women, Jewish—United States—History—Sources. 2. Jews—United States—History—Sources. 3. Women—United States—History—Sources. 4. United States—Ethnic relations—Sources. I. Marcus, Jacob Rader, 1896-

Women—Legal status, laws, etc. (Canon law)

GAGE, Matilda Joslyn, mrs. 1826-1898.
Woman, church and state: a historical account of the status of woman through the Christian ages: with reminiscences of the matriarchate: by Matilda Joslyn Gage. 2d ed. New York, The Truth seeker company [1900] 1 p. l., 554 p. 21 cm. 2-8779
I. Title.
Contents omitted.

RAMING, Ida. 262'.14
The exclusion of women from the priesthood : divine law or sex discrimination? : An historical investigation of the juridical and doctrinal foundations of the code of canon law, canon 968, 1 / by Ida Raming ; translated by Norman R. Adams ; with a pref. by Arlene & Leonard Swidler. Metuchen, N.J. : Scarecrow Press, 1976. xvii, 263 p. ; 23 cm. Translation of Der Ausschluss der Frau vom priesterlichen Amt. Includes index. Bibliography: p. [255]-257. [LAW] 76-23322 ISBN 0-8108-0957-5 : 11.00
1. Women—Legal status, laws, etc. (Canon law) 2. Clergy (Canon law) I. Title.

Women—Legal status, laws, etc. (Islamic law)

ESPOSITO, John L. 346.5601'34
Women in Muslim family law / John L. Esposito. 1st ed. Syracuse, N.Y. : Syracuse University Press, 1982. xii, 155 p. ; 22 cm. (Contemporary issues in the Middle East) Includes index. Bibliography: p. 145-148. [LAW] 345.606134 19 81-18273 ISBN 0-8156-2256-2 : 18.95
1. Women—Legal status, laws, etc. (Islamic law) I. Title. II. Series.

Women—Legal status, laws, etc. (Jewish law)

MEISELMAN, Moshe. 296.1'8
Jewish woman in Jewish law / by Moshe Meiselman. New York : Ktav Pub. House, 1978. xvi, 218 p. ; 23 cm. (The Library of Jewish law and ethics ; v. 6) Includes index. Bibliography: p. 201-209. [LAW] 77-5100 ISBN 0-87068-329-2 : 12.50
1. Women—Legal status, laws, etc. (Jewish law) 2. Women, Jewish—Religious life. I. Title.

Women ministers.

JENNINGS, Ray. 253'.2
Rev. Ms. Evelyn Morgan Jones, I love you : letters to a woman in ministry, addressed to a representative of the emerging breed of women in ministry by a middle-aged male minister / Ray Jennings. Valley Forge, Pa. : Judson Press, [1975] 64 p. ; 22 cm. Includes bibliographical references. [BV676.J46] 75-9959 ISBN 0-8170-0672-9 pbk. : 2.95
1. Women ministers. I. Title.

Women, Muslim—Near East—Biography.

MASUD-UL-HASAN. 920.72
Daughters of Islam : being short biographical sketches of 82 famous Muslim women / Masud-ul-Hasan. Lahore : Hazrat Data Ganj Baksh Academy, [1976] ii, iii, 171 p. ; 19 cm. [CT3700.M37] 77-930045 Rs15.00
1. Women, Muslim—Near East—Biography. 2. Near East—Biography. I. Title.

Women—Prayer-books and devotions.

ANDERSON, Evelyn McCullough. 242'.6'43
Devotionals for today's women. Grand Rapids, Mich., Baker Book House [1969] 79 p. 21 cm. [BV4844.A49] 75-101614
1. Women—Prayer-books and devotions. I. Title.

CARR, Jo 242.643
Too busy not to pray; a homemaker talks with God [by] Jo Carr, Imogene Sorley. Nashville, Abingdon [c.1966] 112p. 21cm. [BV4844.C35] 66-10853 2.50
1. Women—Prayer-books and devotions. I. Sorley, Imogene, joint author. II. Title.

CROWLEY, Mary C. 242'.2
A pocketful of hope : daily devotions for women / Mary C. Crowley. Old Tappan, N.J. : F.H. Revell Co., c1981. 346 p. ; 20 cm. [BV4844.C75] 19 81-11955 ISBN 0-8007-1272-2 : 9.50
1. Women—Prayer-books and devotions. 2. Devotional calendars. I. Title.

GESCH, Dorothy K. 242.8'43
Make me aware, Lord [by] Dorothy K. Gesch. Minneapolis, Augsburg Pub. House [1971] 91 p. illus. 21 cm. Free verse prayers for today's woman. [BV4844.G44] 75-135215 ISBN 0-8066-1102-2 3.50
1. Women—Prayer-books and devotions. I. Title.

GYLDENVAND, Lily M., 1917- 248.8'33
Call her blessed ... every woman who discovers the gifts of God, by Lily M. Gyldenvand. Minneapolis, Augsburg Pub. House [1967] vi, 168 p. 17 cm. [BV4844.G9] 67-11720
1. Women—Prayer-books and devotions. I. Title.

HASKIN, Dorothy (Clarks) 1905- 242'.6'
Devotions from around the world for women, by Dorothy C. Haskin. Grand Rapids, Zondervan [1967] 92p. illus., ports. 21cm. [BV4844.H3] 67-17227 price unreported. pap.,
1. Women—Prayer-books and devotions. I. Title.

HOLMES, Marjorie, 1910- 242'.6'43
I've got to talk to somebody, God; a woman's conversations with God. [1st ed.] Garden City, N.Y., Doubleday, 1969. xviii, 121 p. illus. 22 cm. [BV4844.H63] 69-10938 3.95
1. Women—Prayer-books and devotions. I. Title.

HOLMES, Marjorie, 1910- 242.8'43
Who am I, God? Illustrated by Betty Fraser. [1st ed.] Garden City, N.Y., Doubleday, 1971. x, 176 p. illus. 22 cm. [BV4844.H64] 77-139035 3.95
1. Women—Prayer-books and devotions. I. Title.

LARSON, Muriel. 242'.6'43
Devotions for women's groups. Grand Rapids, Baker Book House [1967] 105 p. 21 cm. [BV4527.L35] 67-2217
1. Women—Prayer-books and devotions. I. Title.

PELGER, Lucy J. 242'.6'33
Living for a living Lord; devotions for women's groups [by] Lucy J. Pelger. St. Louis. Concordia [1967] 97p. 22cm. [BV4844.P4] 67-14080 2.95
1. Women—Prayer-books and devotions. I. Title.

PELGER, Lucy J 242'.6'33
Living for a living Lord; devotions for women's groups [by] Lucy J. Pelger. St. Souis, Concordia Pub. House [1967] 97 p. 22 cm. [BV4844.P4] 67-14080
1. Women—Prayer books and devotions. I. Title.

SCHOENFELD, Elizabeth. 248.8'33
Thoughts for an LDS mother; to help me become a better wife, to help me become a better mother, to help me become a better person. Salt Lake City, Bookcraft [1967] 91 p. 21 cm. [BV4844.S35] 67-30256
1. Women—Prayer-books and devotions. 2. Quotations, English. I. Title.

WHALEY, Catrina Parrott 242.643
Share my devotions; living devotions for women for personal and group use. Grand Rapids, Mich., Baker Bk. [c.]1965. 120p. 20cm. [BV4844.W5] 65-27516 1.95
1. Women—Prayer-books and devotions. I. Title.

Women—Prayer-books and devotions—English.

ABERNETHY, Jean (Beaven) 1912- ed. 242.64
Meditations for women, by Edith Lovejoy

Pierce, [others] Introd. by Dorothy Canfield Fisher. Nashville, Abingdon Press [1961, c.1947] 378p. 16cm. (Apex bk. F I) .69 pap.,
1. Women—Prayer-books and devotions—English. I. Pierce, Edith Lovejoy, 1904- II. Title.

ABERNETHY, Jean (Beaven) 242
1912- ed.
Meditations for women, by Edith Love joy pierce and other, with an intro. by Dorothy Confield Fisher Nashville, Abingdon-Cokebury Press [1947] 378 p. 16 cm. [BV4844.A2] 48-286
1. Women-Prayer-books and devotions—English. I. Pierce, Edith Lovejoy, 1904- II. Title.

ANDERSON, Evelyn 242'.6'43
McCullough.
Good morning, Lord; devotions for women [by] Evelyn Anderson. Grand Rapids, Mich., Baker Book House [1971] 60 p. 19 cm. [BV4844.A493] 74-164373 ISBN 0-8010-0023-8
1. Women—Prayer-books and devotions—English. I. Title.

ANDERSON, Evelyn 242'.6'43
McCullough.
Only a woman. Grand Rapids, Baker Book House [1969] 79 p. illus. 20 cm. [BV4844.A5] 69-15663
1. Women—Prayer-books and devotions—English. I. Title.

THE Apron-pocket book of 242
meditation and prayer. Greenwich, Conn., Seabury Press, 1958. 89p. 17cm. [BV4844.A6] 58-9229
1. Women—Prayer-books and devotions—English.

BARKMAN, Alma. 242'.6'33
Sunny-side up / by Alma Barkman. Chicago : Moody Press, c1977. p. cm. [BV4844.B34] 77-7048 ISBN 0-8024-8431-X pbk. : 1.50
1. Women—Prayer-books and devotions—English. I. Title.

BENSON, Margaret H., ed. 248.374
The second Apron-pocket book of meditation and prayer, comp., written by Margaret H. Benson, Helen G. Smith. Greenwich, Conn., Seabury [c.]1963. 93p. 17cm. 63-11057 1.50, pap., plastic bdg.
1. Women—Prayer-books and devotions—English. I. Smith, Helen (Glass) 1906- joint ed. II. Title. III. Title: Apron-pocket book of meditation and prayer.

BRANSON, Mary Kinney. 242'.6'43
A woman's place / Mary Kinney Branson. Denver : Accent Books, c1975. 160 p. : ill. ; 18 cm. [BV4844.B7] 75-40909 ISBN 0-916406-14-8 pbk. : 1.95
1. Women—Prayer-books and devotions—English. I. Title.

CROWELL, Grace (Noll), 1877- 242
Meditations; devotions for women. Nashville, Abingdon-Cokesbury Press [1951] 128 p. 18 cm. [BV4844.C7] 51-10747
1. Women—Prayer-books and devotions—English. I. Title.

CROWELL, Grace (Noll) 242.64
1877-
Riches of the kigdom. Nashville, Abingdon Press [1961, c.1954] 126p. (Apex bk., F4) .69 pap.,
1. Women—Prayer-books and devotions—English I. Title.

CROWELL, Grace (Noll) 1877- 242
Riches of the kingdom. Nashville, Abingdon Press [1954] 126p. 18cm. Prose and poems. [BV4844.C72] 54-7028
1. Women—Prayer-books and devotions—English. I. Title.

DAVIDSON, Clarissa 242'.6'43
Start.
Look here, Lord; meditations for today's woman, by Clarissa Start. Illustrated by Audrey F. Teeple. Minneapolis, Augsburg Pub. House [1972] 128 p. illus. 21 cm. [BV4844.D38] 72-78550 ISBN 0-8066-1218-5 3.50
1. Women—Prayer-books and devotions—English. I. Title.

THE Days and the nights 242'.8'43
: prayers for women / collected by Candida Lund. Chicago : T. More Press, c1978. 130 p. ; 20 cm. [BX2170.W7D39] 78-104870 ISBN 0-88347-089-6 : 5.95
1. Catholic Church—Prayer-books and devotions—English. 2. Women—Prayer-books and devotions—English. I. Lund, Candida.

GIBSON, Ruth. 242'.83'3
Chipped dishes, zippers & prayer : meditations for women / Ruth Gibson. Waco, Tex. : Word Books, c1977. 94 p. : ill. ; 21 cm. [BV4844.G52] 77-76350 ISBN 0-8499-2808-7 pbk. : 3.25
1. Women—Prayer-books and devotions—English. I. Title.

GOODRICH, Donna Clark. 242'.6'43
Brighten the corner, and 45 other women's devotions. Cincinnati, Standard Pub. [1972] 96 p. illus. 18 cm. (Fountain books) [BV4844.G66] 72-82086
1. Women—Prayer-books and devotions—English. I. Title.

GRAVER, Jane, 1931- 242'.6'43
Please, Lord, don't put me on hold : meditations for women who work / Jane Graver. St. Louis : Concordia Pub. House, c1979. 64 p. ; 17 cm. [BV4844.G74] 79-4601 ISBN 0-570-03790-5 pbk. : 1.95
1. Women—Prayer-books and devotions—English. I. Title.

HOGAN, Bernice 242.64
Grains of sand. Nashville, Abingdon [c.1961] 128p. 16cm. 61-13195 2.00 bds.,
1. Women—Prayer-books and devotions—English. I. Title.

HOLMES, Marjorie, 1910- 242'.6'43
Hold me up a little longer, Lord / Marjorie Holmes ; illustrated by Patricia Mighell. 1st ed. Garden City, N.Y. : Doubleday, 1977. 120 p. : ill. ; 22 cm. [BV4844.H628] 76-42338 ISBN 0-385-12403-1 : 5.95
1. Women—Prayer-books and devotions—English. I. Title.

HOLMES, Marjorie, 1910- 242'.6'43
Hold me up a little longer, Lord / Marjorie Holmes ; illustrated by Patricia Mighell. Boston : G. K. Hall, 1977. 181 p. : ill. ; 24 cm. Large print ed. [BV4844.H628 1977b] 77-12905 ISBN 0-8161-6530-0 lib.bdg. : 8.95
1. Women—Prayer-books and devotions—English. 2. Large type books. I. Title.

HOOVER, Mab Graff. 242'.643
God still loves my kitchen / Mab Graff Hoover. Grand Rapids, MI : Zondervan Pub. House, c1981. 196 p. ; 18 cm. [BV4844.H66] 19 81-16488 ISBN 0-310-35622-9 pbk. : 3.50
1. Women—Prayer-books and devotions—English. I. Title.

IKERMAN, Ruth C. 242.643
Women's programs for special occasions [by] Ruth C. Ikerman. Nashville, Abingdon Press [1966] 159 p. 16 cm. [BV4844.I 4] 66-15003
1. Women — Prayer-books and devotions — English. I. Title.

KELLY, William L. 248.374
Women before God; prayers and thoughts. Westminster, Md., Newman [1962] 351p. illus. 'Adapted . . . from the German version 'Frauen vor Gott,' by Eleonore Beck and Gabriele Miller,' 62-7482 2.95
1. Women—Prayer-books and devotions—English. 2. Catholic Church—Prayer-books and devotions—English. I. Title.

KIELY, Martha Meister 248.37
Devotions for women at home. New York, Abingdon Press [c.1959] 127p. 18 cm. 59-5122 1.75 bds.,
1. Women—Prayer-books and devotions—English. I. Title.

LOCKERBIE, Jeanette W. 242'.643
More salt in my kitchen / Jeanette Lockerbie. Chicago : Moody Press, c1980. p. cm. [BV4844.L62] 80-12357 ISBN 0-8024-5668-5 pbk. : 1.95
1. Women—Prayer-books and devotions—English. I. Title.

MICHAEL, Phyllis C. 242'.6'43
Is my head on straight? : Meditations for women / Phyllis C. Michael. Waco, Tex. : Word Books, c1976. 120 p. : ill. ; 21 cm. [BV4844.M45] 75-19912 pbk. : 3.50
1. Women—Prayer-books and devotions—English. I. Title.

MOORE, Grace. 242'.33
The Advent of women / by Grace Moore. Valley Forge, Pa. : Judson Press, [1975] p. cm. [BV4844.M6] 75-12189 ISBN 0-8170-0691-5 pbk. : 1.00
1. Women—Prayer-books and devotions—English. 2. Advent—Prayer-books and devotions—English. I. Title.

NELSON, Ruth Youngdahl. 242.2
God's song in my heart; daily devotions for women. Rock Island, Ill., Augustana Press [1957] 418p. 22cm. Includes hymns with music. [BV4832.N345] 56-11912
1. Women—Prayer-books and devotions—English. 2. Lutheran Church— Prayer-books and devotions—English. I. Title.

NORRIS, Judy. 242'.6'43
Flowers of inspiration in God's garden. Cincinnati, Standard Pub. [1972] 95 p. illus. 18 cm. (Fountain books, 2271) [BV4844.N67] 73-190359
1. Women—Prayer-books and devotions—English. I. Title.

PATTERSON, Virginia, 1931- 242
A touch of God / Virginia Patterson. Nashville : Abingdon, c1979. 112 p. ; 21 cm. [BV4844.P34] 79-12283 ISBN 0-687-42399-6 : 6.95
1. Patterson, Virginia, 1931- 2. Women—Prayer-books and devotions—English. I. Title.

ROBERTSON, Josephine. 264.1
New prayers for a woman's day. New York, Abingdon Press [1958] 80p. 12cm.

[BV283.W6R58] 58-10461
1. Women —Prayer-books and devotions—English. I. Title. II. Title: Prayers for a woman's day.

ROBERTSON, Josephine. 264.1
Prayers for a woman's day. New York, Abingdon Press [1957] 79p. 12cm. [BV283.W6R6] 57-8355
1. Women—Prayer-books and devotions—English. I. Title.

RUSSELL, Grace. 242.8'43
Rings and things; thoughts of a man's wife. Illustrated by Gordon Haug. [Nashville] Upper Room [1970] 88 p. illus. 20 cm. [BV4844.R88] 77-115830
1. Women—Prayer-books and devotions—English. I. Title.

SHAFFER, Wilma L. 242'.6'33
Proverbs and programs for women, "a proverb for every problem," by Wilma L. Shaffer. Cincinnati, Standard Pub. [1972] 112 p. 22 cm. [BV4844.S5] 72-75097
1. Bible. O.T. Proverbs—Devotional literature. 2. Women—Prayer-books and devotions—English. I. Title.

SHAW, Jean. 242'.643
Second cup of coffee : proverbs for today's woman / Jean Shaw. Grand Rapids, MI : Zondervan Pub. House, c1981. 189 p. ; 18 cm. Includes bibliographical references. [BV4844.S53] 19 80-39577 ISBN 0-310-43542-0 pbk. : 2.95
1. Bible. O.T. Proverbs—Meditations. 2. Women—Prayer-books and devotions—English. I. Title.

WALLACE, Helen Kingsbury. 264.13
Prayers for women's meetings. Westwood, N.J., Revell [1964] 128 p. 21 cm. [BV283.W6W3] 64-20190
1. Women — Prayer-books and devotions — English. I. Title.

WILSON, Hazel Thorne, comp. 248
Women at prayer; private and universal prayers for the women of America. Boston, Pilgrim Press [1948] 96 p. 19 cm. [BV283.W6W5] 48-4036
1. Women—Prayer-books and devotions—English. I. Title.

Women-Religious life.

ALBERIONE, Giacomo Giuseppe, 1884- 248.874
Woman, her influence and zeal as an aid to the priesthood, by James Alberione. Tr. by the Daughters of St. Paul [Boston] St. Paul Eds. [dist. Daughters of St. Paul, 1964] 316p. 22cm. [BX2353.A553] 64-24361 3.50; 2.50 pap.,
1. Woman—Religious life. I. Title.

ANDERSON, Evelyn McCullough. 248.8'43
New windows for women. Grand Rapids : Baker Book House, 1976c1970. 188p. ; 20 cm. Formerly published under the title, "it's a woman's privilege." [BV4527.A5] ISBN 0-8010-0101-3 pbk. : 2.95.
1. Women-Religious life. I. Title.
L. C. card no. for original ed.71-115641.

BENNETT, Rita. 248'.833
I'm glad you asked that; timely questions women ask about the Christian life. Illustrated by Jean Beers. Edmonds, Wash., Aglow/Logos Publications [1974] xiv, 207 p. illus. 21 cm. Includes bibliographical references. [BV4527.B43] 74-81754 ISBN 0-88270-090-1 5.95
1. Woman—Religious life. I. Title.
Pbk. 2.95, ISBN 0-88270-084-7.

BENTON, Josephine Moffett. 248.84
The pace of a hen. Philadelphia, Christian Education Press [1961] 100 p. 21 cm. [BV4527.B45] 61-11487
1. Women—Religious life. 2. Family—Religious life. I. Title.

BERRY, Jo. 248'.843
Growing, sharing, serving / Jo Berry ; [edited by Sharrel Keyes]. Elgin, Ill. : D.C. Cook Pub. Co., c1979. 160 p. ; 21 cm. [BV4527.B47] 78-73461 ISBN 0-89191-073-5 pbk. : 3.95
1. Women—Religious life. I. Keyes, Sharrel. II. Title.

BIRKEY, Verna. 248'.843
You are very special / Verna Birkey. Old Tappan, N.J. : F. H. Revell Co., c1977. p. cm. [BV4527.B57] 77-23805 ISBN 0-8007-0875-X : 5.95
1. Bible—Meditations. 2. Women—Religious life. 3. Self-respect. I. Title.

BREMYER, Jayne Dickey. 248'.843
Dear God : am I important? / Jayne Bremyer. Rev. ed. Waco, Tex. : Word Books, c1976. 165 p. ; 22 cm. [BX2353.B73 1976] 76-374890 ISBN 0-87680-856-9 : 3.95
1. Women—Religious life. I. Title.

BRIGGS, Argye M 248.8
Christ and the modern woman. Grand Rapids, Eerdmans [1958] 153p. 22cm. [BV4527.B7] 58-59783
1. Woman—Religious life. I. Title.

BRIGHT, Vonette Z. 248'.843
For such a time as this / Vonette Z. Bright. Old Tappan, N.J. : F.H. Revell, c1976. p. cm. [BV4527.B72] 76-25176 ISBN 0-8007-0831-8 : 4.95
1. Bright, Vonette Z. 2. Women—Religious life. 3. Christian life—1960- I. Title.

BROOKS, Pat. 248'.843
Daughters of the King / by Pat Brooks. Carol Stream, Ill. : Creation House, c1975. 144 p. ; 22 cm. Bibliography: p. 143-144. [BV4527.B75 1975] 75-22573 ISBN 0-88419-114-1 : 2.95
1. Women—Religious life. 2. Women. I. Title.

BROOME, Connie. 248'.843
Vessels unto honor / by Connie Broome. Cleveland, Tenn. : Pathway Press, 1977,c1976 128 p. ; 21 cm. [BV4527.B76] 76-22242 ISBN 0-87148-879-5 : write for information
1. Women—Religious life. 2. Women—Conduct of life. I. Title.

*CHAPPELL, Clovis G. 248.843
Feminine faces. Grand Rapids, Baker Book House [1974, c1970] 219 p. 20 cm. (Clovis G. Chappell library) [BV4527] ISBN 0-8010-2355-6. 2.95 (pbk.)
1. Woman—Religious life. I. Title.

CLARK, Vynomma. 248.8'43
So you're a woman. Abilene, Tex., Biblical Research Press [1971] vi, 51 p. 23 cm. [BV4527.C56] 70-180790 2.95
1. Woman—Religious life. I. Title.

COOPER, Mildred. 248'.843
What every woman still knows : a celebration of the Christian liberated woman / Mildred Cooper, Martha Fanning. New York : M. Evans, c1978. x, 171 p. ; 22 cm. [BV4527.C66] 78-17182 ISBN 0-87131-271-9 : 7.95
1. Women—Religious life. 2. Women—Conduct of life. I. Fanning, Martha, joint author. II. Title.

D'ANGELO, Louise 248'.843
Too busy for God? : Think again! : A spiritual guide for working women and housewives / Louise D'Angelo. Huntington, Ind. : Our Sunday Visitor, inc., c1975. 119 p. ; 18 cm. [BX2353.D3] 75-329620 ISBN 0-87973-784-0 pbk. : 1.75
1. Women—Religious life. I. Title.

DANTUMA, Angelyn Grace 248.84

The Christian woman. Grand Rapids, Mich., Eerdmans [1962, c.1961] 144p. 61-17395 3.50 bds.,
1. Woman—Religious life. I. Title.

*DEVOS, Karen Helder. 248.8'43
A woman's worth & work : a Christian perspective. Grand Rapids : Baker Book House, 1976. 101p. ; 21 cm. [BV 4527] ISBN 0-8010-2853-1 pbk. : 2.95.
1. Women-Religious life. I. Title.

FANCHER, Wilda. 248'.833
The Christian woman in the Christian home. Nashville, Broadman Press [1972] 128 p. 21 cm. (A Broadman inner circle book) [BV4527.F36] 72-178059 ISBN 0-8054-8310-1
1. Woman—Religious life. I. Title.

FENELON, Francois de Salignac de La Mothe-, 1651-1715. 248.4'82043
Spiritual letters to women / Francois de Salignac de la Moth Fenelon ; translated by the author of Spiritual letters of S. Francis de Sales ; introduction by Elisabeth Elliot ; illustrations by Ron McCarty. Shepherd illustrated classic ed. New Canaan, Conn. : Keats Pub., 1980. 294 p., [5] leaves of plates : ill. ; 21 cm. (A Shepherd illustrated classic) Translation of: Lettres spirituelles. [BX2353.F4613 1980] 19 80-82324 ISBN 0-87983-233-9 (pbk.) : 5.95
1. Catholic Church—Prayer-books and devotions—English. 2. Women—Religious life. I. [Lettres spirituelles.] English II. Title. III. Series.

FREMANTLE, Anne Jackson, 1909- 248'.843
Woman's way to God / Anne Fremantle. New York : St. Martin's Press, c1977. xvi, 255 p. ; 22 cm. [BL624.F74] 76-10553 ISBN 0-312-88690-X : 8.95
1. Women—Religious life. 2. Religions—Biography. 3. Women—Biography. I. Title.

FROMER, Margaret. 227'.606
A woman's workshop on Philippians / Margaret and Paul Fromer. Grand Rapids, Mich. : Zondervan Pub. House, c1982. 106 p. ; 21 cm. [BS2705.5.F76 1982] 19 82-2662 ISBN 0-310-44771-2 pbk. : 2.95
1. Bible. N.T. Philippians—Study. 2. Women—Religious life. I. Fromer, Paul II. Title.

GAGE, Joy P. 248'.843
But you don't know Harry [by] Joy P. Gage. Wheaton, Ill., Tyndale House Publishers [1972] 64 p. illus. 14 cm. (A Tyndale treasure) [BV4527.G34] 72-84418 ISBN 0-8423-0195-X .50
1. Woman—Religious life. I. Title.

GRAMS, Betty Jane. 248'.843
Women of grace / Betty Jane Grams. Springfield, Mo. : Gospel Pub. House, c1978. 127 p. ; 18 cm. (Radiant books) (New studies for women on living in the Spirit) Bibliography: p. 127. [BV4527.G72] 77-93409 ISBN 0-88243-751-8 : pbk. : 1.50
1. Women—Religious life. 2. Women in the Bible. I. Title. II. Series.

GREELEY, Andrew M., 1928- 248.83
Letters to Nancy, from Andrew M. Greeley. New York, Sheed [c.1964] x, 182p. 22cm. Bibl. 64-19901 3.95
1. Woman—Religious life. I. Title.

GREELEY, Andrew M., 1928- 248.83
Letters to Nancy, from Andrew M. Greeley. Garden City, N.Y., Doubleday [1967, c.1964] x, 182p. 18cm. (Image bk., D226) Bibl. [BX2365.G7] .85 pap.,
1. Woman—Religious life. I. Title.

GREELEY, Andrew M., 1928- 248.8'3

Letters to Nancy, from Andrew M. Greeley. [New and rev.] Garden City, N.Y., Image Books [1967] 160 p. 19 cm. (Image D226) [BX2365.G7 1967] 67-8684
1. Woman—Religious life. I. Title.

GUDER, Eileen L. 248'.833
God wants you to smile [by] Eileen Guder. [1st ed.] New York, Doubleday, 1974. xi, 151 p. 22 cm. [BV4527.G79] 73-11706 ISBN 0-385-03521-7 4.95
1. Woman—Religious life. 2. Depression, Mental. I. Title.

GUDER, Eileen L. 248.833
We're never alone, Introd. by Raymond I. Lindquist. Grand Rapids, Mich., Zondervan [1966, c.1965] 148p. 21cm. (No. 29) [BV4527.G8] 65-19506 .89 pap.,
1. Woman—Religious life. I. Title.

GUNDRY, Patricia. 248.8'43
The complete woman / by Patricia Gundry. 1st ed. Garden City, N.Y. : Doubleday, 1981. 237 p. ; 22 cm. "A Doubleday-Galilee original." Bibliography: p. [235]-237. [BV4527.G86] 19 79-8928 ISBN 0-385-15521-2 : 9.95
1. Bible. O.T. Proverbs xxxi, 10-31—Criticism, interpretation, etc. 2. Women—Religious life. I. Title.

HANCOCK, Maxine. 248'.4
Love, honor, and be free / by Maxine Hancock. Chicago : Moody Press, [1975] 191 p. ; 22 cm. [BV4527.H36] 75-316072 ISBN 0-8024-5021-0 : 5.95
1. Women—Religious life. 2. Woman—Biblical teaching. 3. Women. I. Title.

HARRINGTON, Paul V. 261.83
Woman's sublime call [Boston] St. Paul Eds. [dist. Daughters of St. Paul, c.1964] 90p. 22cm. [BX2353.H3] 64-66106 1.50; 1.00 pap.,
1. Woman—Religious life. I. Title.

HAUGHTON, Rosemary. 248'.843
Feminine spirituality : reflections on the mysteries of the rosary / by Rosemary Haughton. New York : Paulist Press, c1976. ix, 93 p. ; 18 cm. [BX2353.H34] 76-24438 ISBN 0-8091-1982-X pbk. : 1.95
1. Women—Religious life. 2. Mysteries of the Rosary—Meditations. I. Title.

HENDRICKS, Jeanne W. 248'.843
Afternoon / Jeanne Hendricks. Nashvile : T. Nelson, c1979. p. cm. Includes bibliographical references. [BV4527.H46] 79-21339 ISBN 0-8407-4077-8 : 6.95
1. Women—Religious life. 2. Middle age—Religious life. 3. Hendricks, Jeanne W. I. Title.

HERTZ, Solange Strong, 1920- 248.84
Feast for a week; a retreat for housewives. Westminster, Md., Newman [c.]1964. xi, 119p. 22cm. [BX2376.W6H4] 64-66281 3.75
1. Women—Religious life. 2. Retreats. 3. Mary, Virgin—Words. I. Title.

HERTZ, Solange Strong, 1920- 248.84
Searcher of majesty. Westminister, Md., Newman [c.]1963. 283p. 23cm. 63-12245 4.75
1. Woman—Religious life. 2. Spiritual life—Catholic authors. I. Title.

HUESMAN, Rose M. 248.84
Saints in aprons. Milwaukee, Bruce [c.1962] 186p. 22cm. 62-10343 3.50
1. Woman—Religious life. I. Title.

JENNINGS, Vivien, 1934- 248'.833

The valiant woman; at the heart of reconciliation. Photography by Joseph De Caro. Photo. editor: Julie Marie. New York, Alba House [1974] xi, 112 p. illus. 22 cm. [BX2353.J46] 74-6037 ISBN 0-8189-0291-4
1. Woman—Religious life. 2. Reconciliation. I. Title.

KERIGAN, Florence. 248
Inspirational talks for women's groups. Cincinnati, Standard Pub. Co. ['1951] 124 p. 19 cm. [BV4309.K4] 52-8283
1. Woman—Religious life. I. Title.

LACY, Mary Lou. 248
A woman wants God. Richmond, John Knox Press [1959] 80p. 22cm. [BV4527.L25] 59-5120
1. Woman Religious life. I. Title.

*LANDORF, Joyce. 248'843
Every woman can be more beautiful. New York, Pillar Books [1975] 143 p. 18 cm. Original title: The Fragrance of Beauty. [BV4527.L33] 73-76813 ISBN 0-89129-029-X 1.25 (pbk.)
1. Woman—Religious life. 2. Beauty, Personal. I. Title.

LANDORF, Joyce. 248'.843
The fragrance of beauty. Wheaton, Ill., Victor Books [1973] 143 p. 18 cm. [BV4527.L33] 73-76813 0.95 (pbk.)
1. Woman—Religious life. 2. Beauty, Personal. I. Title.

MACINTOSH, Mike, 1944- 248'.843
Attributes of the Christian woman / Mike MacIntosh. Costa Mesa, Calif. : Maranatha Evangelical Association, c1977. p. cm. [BV4527.M2] 77-10431 ISBN 0-89337-003-7 pbk. : 1.50
1. Women—Religious life. I. Title.

MATHER, Cotton, 1663-1728. 248'.843
Ornaments for the daughters of Zion : a facsimile reproduction / Cotton Mather ; with an introd. by Pattie Cowell. Delmar, N.Y. : Scholars' Facsimiles & Reprints, 1978. p. cm. Reprint of the 3d ed., 1741, published by S. Kneeland and T. Green, Boston. [BV4527.M27 1978] 78-8588 ISBN 0-8201-1311-5 : 20.00
1. Women—Religious life. 2. Women—Conduct of life. 3. Women—New England. I. Title.

*MILLER, Ella May 248.833
I am a woman. Chicago, Moody [1967] 123p. 17cm. (Colportage lib., 527) .39 pap.,
1. Woman—Religious life. I. Title.

MONTGOMERY, Saphronia Geodwin. 248
The Christian woman, a religious miscellany. [1st ed.] New York, Exposition Press [c1954] 58p. 21cm. [BV4527.M6] 54-12284
1. Woman Religious life. 2. Church work—Addresses, essays, lectures. I. Title.

NELSON, Martha. 248'.833
A woman's search for serenity. Nashville, Broadman Press [1972] 140 p. 21 cm. [BV4527.N383] 78-178063 ISBN 0-8054-5214-1 3.95
1. Woman—Religious life. I. Title.

NELSON, Ruth Youngdahl. 264
The Christian woman; ten programs for women's organizations. Rock Island, Ill., Augustana Book Concern [1951] 96p. 20cm. [BV4527.N4] 51-12981
1. Woman—Religious life. I. Title.

NICHOLS, Jeannette, 1911- 248.8'43
Her works praise her; a study course for women. [Independence, Mo., Herald Pub. House, 1967] 133 p. 18 cm. Bibliography: p. 131-133. [BV4527.N5] 67-29797
1. Woman—Religious life. I. Title.

NORDLAND, Frances. 248'.833
Dear Frances ... I have a problem. Can you help me? Chicago, Moody Press [1974] 142 p. 22 cm. Includes bibliographical references. [BV4527.N67] 74-2926 ISBN 0-8024-1765-5 2.25 (pbk.).
1. Woman—Religious life. I. Title.

NYBERG, Kathleen Neill. 248.8'43
The new Eve. Nashville, Abingdon Press [1967] 476 p. 21 cm. Bibliographical references included in "Notes" (p. 173-176) [BV4527.N8] 67-22762
1. Woman — Religious life. I. Title.

POLSTON, Ruth Ann. 248'.843
You deserve to be happy : you owe it to yourself / Ruth Ann Polston. Irvine, Calif. : Harvest House Publishers, c1978. 143 p. : ill. ; 21 cm. [BV4527.P64] 77-94045 ISBN 0-89081-126-1 : 2.95
1. Women—Religious life. I. Title.

PORTER, Jean Kelleher. 242.3
Halo for a housewife; a retreat at home. Milwaukee, Bruce Pub. Co. [1962] 136p. 22cm. [BX2353.P6] 62-12430
1. Woman—Religious life. I. Title.

PRICE, Eugenia. 242.64
God speaks to women today. Grand Rapids, Zondervan Pub. House, 1964. 256 p. 24 cm. Bibliography: p. 256. [BV4527.P7] 63-9315
1. Woman—Religious life. I. Title.

PRICE, Eugenia. 248.8
Woman to woman. Grand Rapids, Zondervan Pub. House [1959] 241 p. 21 cm. [BV4527.P73] 59-4290
1. Women—Religious life. I. Title.

PRICE, Eugenia 248.374
A woman's choice; living through your problems, from confusion to peace. Grand Rapids, Mich., Zondervan [c.1962] 182p. 21cm. Bibl. 62-14439 1.50 pap.,
1. Woman—Religious life. I. Title.

ROGERS, Dale Evans. 248.833
Time out, ladies! Westwood, N. J., Revell [1966] 118 p. 21 cm. [BV4527.R6] 66-17044
1. Woman—Religious life. I. Title.

ROGERS, Dale Evans. 248.8'43
Woman / Dale Evans Rogers, with Carole C. Carlson. Old Tappan, N.J. : F. H. Revell Co., c1980. 127 p. ; 22 cm. [BV4527.R63] 79-27090 ISBN 0-8007-1115-7 : 7.95
1. Rogers, Dale Evans. 2. Women—Religious life. 3. Women—Conduct of life. I. Carlson, Carole C., joint author. II. Title.

ROGERS, Joyce. 248.8'43
The wise woman ... how to be one in a thousand / Joyce Rogers. Nashville, Tenn. : Broadman Press, 1981, c1980. 174 p. ; 22 cm. Bibliography: p. 173. [BV4527.R64] 19 80-68538 ISBN 0-8054-5289-3 : 6.95
1. Women—Religious life. I. Title.

*ROPER, Gayle G. 249
Wife, mate, mother, me! [By] Gayle G. Roper. Grand Rapids, Baker Book House [1975] 98p. 23 cm. [BV4526.2] ISBN 0-8010-7633-1 4.95.
1. Woman-Religious life 2. Conduct of life. I. Title.

SIMMONS, Patricia A. 242'.643
Everyday beginnings / Patricia A. Simmons. Nashville, Tenn. : Broadman Press, c1980. 95 p. ; 20 cm. [BV4527.S45] 19 80-65387 ISBN 0-8054-5177-3 : 5.95
1. Women—Religious life. I. Title.

SKOGLUND, Elizabeth. 248'.843
Woman beyond roleplay / Elizabeth Skoglund. Elgin, Ill. : D. C. Cook Pub. Co., c1975. 112 p. ; 18 cm. [BV4527.S55] 75-893 ISBN 0-912692-62-6 pbk. : 1.25
1. Women—Religious life. I. Title.

SPAFFORD, Belle S. 248'.843
A woman's reach [by] Belle S. Spafford. Salt Lake City, Deseret Book Co., 1974. 165 p. port. 24 cm. [BV4527.S65] 74-75032 ISBN 0-87747-518-0 4.95
1. Woman—Religious life. 2. Women in church work. I. Title.

SPAFFORD, Belle S. 301.41'2
Women in todays world [by] Belle S. Spafford. Salt Lake City, Deseret Book Co., 1971. xviii, 483 p. port. 24 cm. [BX8643.W4S67] 73-177866 ISBN 0-87747-452-4 5.25
1. Church of Jesus Christ of Latter-Day Saints. Relief Society. 2. Woman—Religious life. I. Title.

STRUCHEN, Jeanette. 248.8'43
What do I do now, Lord? Old Tappan, N.J., Revell [1971] 120 p. 21 cm. [BV4527.S75] 76-149368 ISBN 0-8007-0445-2 3.50
1. Woman—Religious life. 2. Wives—Conduct of life. I. Title.

TAYLOR, Julia Marie. 248'.843
Last, least, lowest : God's challenge for women / by Julia Marie Taylor. 1st ed. Harrison Ark. : New Leaf Press, c1979. 143 p. : ill. ; Cover title: Last, least & lowest. [BV4527.T38] 78-70663 ISBN 0-89221-058-3 pbk. : 2.95
1. Women—Religious life. I. Title. II. Title: Last, least & lowest.

TOMPKINS, Iverna. 248'.843
The worth of a woman / Iverna Tompkins. Plainfield, N.J. : Logos International, c1978. ix, 153 p. ; 21 cm. [BV4527.T65] 78-70534 ISBN 0-88270-256-4 pbk. : 2.95
1. Women—Religious life. I. Title.

WHITE, Ruthe. 248'.843
Be the woman you want to be / Ruthe White. Irvine, Calif. : Harvest House Publishers, [c1978] 175 p. : ill. ; 21 cm. [BV4527.W48] 77-88190 ISBN 0-89081-114-8 : pbk. : 2.95
1. Women—Religious life. I. Title.

WOLD, Margaret. 248'.833
The shalom woman / Margaret Wold. Minneapolis : Augsburg Pub. House, [1975] 128 p. ; 20 cm. Study guide inserted. Bibliography: p. 125-127. [BV4527.W58] 75-2828 ISBN 0-8066-1475-7 : 2.95
1. Women—Religious life. 2. Women. I. Title.

WOLD, Marge. 248'.843
The critical moment : how personal crisis can enrich a woman's life / Margaret Wold. Minneapolis : Augsburg Pub. House, c1978. 126 p. ; 20 cm. [BV4527.W57] 77-84090 ISBN 0-8066-1615-6 pbk. : 3.50
1. Women—Religious life. 2. Suffering. I. Title.

WOMEN'S correspondence Bible class, Oakland, Cal.
God's word to women. Forty-eight Bible lessons of the Women'scorrespondence Bible class. Oakland, Cal., The Women's correspondence Bible class [c1916- v. fold. pl. 21 cm. Each lesson signed: Katharine Bushnell 17-2360
I. Bushnell, Katharine. II. Title.

*WRIGLEY, Louise Scott. 248'.833
Radiance. Independence, Mo., Herald Pub. House [1973] 63 p. 18 cm. Comprises volumes previously published under titles: Your right to radiance, and Look up, heart. [BV4527]
1. Woman—Religious life. I. Title.
Available in two paperback editions, each 0.95 (pbk.) One from Independence Pr., a divn. of Herald Pr., and the other from Family Library, an imprint of Pyramid Publications, New York. L.C. card no. for the hardbound volumes: 61-12487 & 62-21992.

WRIGLEY, Louise Scott 248.843
A woman searches [Independence, Mo., Herald [c.1966] 120p. col. illus. 16cm. [BV4527.W69] 66-15424 1.95 bds.,
1. Woman—Religious life. I. Title.

WRIGLEY, Louise Scott. 248.843
A woman searches. New York, Family Library [1973, c.1966] 94 p. illus. 18 cm. [BV4527.W69] ISBN 0-515-03037-6 pap., 0.95
1. Woman—Religious life. I. Title.

WRIGLEY, Louise Scott.
Your right to radiance. Independence, Mo., Herald House [1961] 76 p. illus. 16 cm.
1. Woman — Religious life. I. Title.

ZASTROW, Nancy B. 248.843
The radiant life; reflections on a woman's life in Christ [by] Nancy B. Zastrow. St. Louis, Concordia Pub. House [1966] viii, 126 p. 19 cm. Bibliography: p. 124-126. [BV4527.Z3] 66-27385
1. Women—Religious life. I. Title.

Women—Religious life—Addresses, essays, lectures.

MATTOX, Beverly, 1929- 248'.843
Help! I'm a woman! / Beverly Mattox. Schaumburg, Ill. : Regular Baptist Press, c1977. 80 p. ; 21 cm. [BV4527.M28] 77-21631 ISBN 0-87227-053-X pbk. : 1.95
1. Women—Religious life—Addresses, essays, lectures. I. Title.

ROADS to reality : 248'.843
deeper life experiences from famous Christian women / edited and compiled by Joyce Blackburn. Old Tappan, N.J. : Revell, c1978. 159 p. ; 24 cm. [BV4527.R58] 77-16032 ISBN 0-8007-0899-7 : 6.95
1. Women—Religious life—Addresses, essays, lectures. I. Blackburn, Joyce.

UNSPOKEN worlds : 291.1'7834'12
women's religious lives in non-western cultures / [edited by] Nancy Auer Falk, Rita M. Gross. 1st ed. San Francisco : Harper & Row, c1980. xviii, 292 p. ; 21 cm. Includes bibliographical references. [BL458.U57 1980] 79-2989 ISBN 0-06-063492-8 : 5.95
1. Women—Religious life—Addresses essays, lectures. I. Falk, Nancy Auer. II. Gross, Rita M.

WOMAN / 261.8'34'12
Spencer W. Kimball ... [et al.]. Salt Lake City : Deseret Book Co., 1979. vii, 154 p. ; 24 cm. Includes index. [BX8641.W65] 79-64908 ISBN 0-87747-758-2 : 6.95
1. Women—Religious life—Addresses, essays, lectures. 2. Mormons and Mormonism—Doctrinal and controversial works—Mormon authors—Addresses, essays, lectures. I. Kimball, Spencer W., 1895-

Women—Religious life—Anecdotes, facetiae, satire, etc.

SCHWARTZ, Toby Devens. 242
Mercy, Lord! My husband's in the kitchen : and other equal opportunity conversations with god / Toby Devens Schwartz. 1st ed. Garden City, N.Y. : Doubleday, 1981. 79 p. ; 15 x 22 cm. [BV4527.S28] 19 80-715 ISBN 0-385-17058-0 : 6.95

1. Women—Religious life—Anecdotes, facetiae, satire, etc. I. Title.

Women—Social and moral questions.

GILMAN, Charlotte Perkins Stetson, 1860-1935. 261.8'341'2
His religion and hers : a study of the faith of our fathers and the work of our mothers / by Charlotte Perkins Gilman. Westport, Conn. : Hyperion Press, 1976, c1923. xi, 300 p. ; 23 cm. (Pioneers of the woman's movement) Reprint of the ed. published by Century Co., New York. [HQ1221.G53 1976] 75-29509 ISBN 0-88355-377-5 : 21.50
1. Women—Social and moral questions. 2. Religion. I. Title.

Women (Theology)

STEDMAN, Elaine. 248'.833
A woman's worth / Elaine Stedman. Waco, Tex. : Word Books, [1975] 168 p. ; 23 cm. [BT704.S73] 74-27477 4.95
1. Women (Theology) I. Title.

Women (Theology)—Addresses, essays, lectures.

WOMANSPIRIT rising 261.8'34'12
: a feminist reader in religion / edited by Carol P. Christ and Judith Plaskow. 1st ed. San Francisco : Harper & Row, c1979. xi, 287 p. ; 21 cm. (Harper forum books) Includes bibliographical references. [BL458.W657 1979] 78-3363 ISBN 0-06-061385-8 : 5.95
1. Women (Theology)—Addresses, essays, lectures. I. Christ, Carol P. II. Plaskow, Judith.

Women (Theology)—Biblical teaching.

SWIDLER, Leonard J. 261.8'34'12
Biblical affirmations of woman / Leonard Swidler. 1st ed. Philadelphia : Westminster Press, c1979. p. cm. Includes index. [BS680.W7S97] 79-18886 ISBN 0-664-21377-4 : 17.95 ISBN 0-664-24285-5 pbk. : 9.95
1. Women (Theology)—Biblical teaching. 2. Women in the Bible. 3. Women (Theology)—History of doctrines. I. Title.

Women—United States—Biography.

HOSIER, Helen Kooiman. 280'.092'2 B
Cameos, women fashioned by God / Helen Kooiman Hosier. Irvine, Calif. : Harvest House Publishers, c1979. 173 p. : ports. ; 18 cm. [BR1713.H63] 79-128734 0890810954 : 2.25
1. Women—United States—Biography. 2. Christian biography—United States. I. Title.

Wong, Sai Hee, 1857-1927.

LAI, Bessie C. 299'.514'0924 B
Ah Ya, I still remember / by Bessie C. Lai. Taipei : Meadea Enterprise Co., c1976. 173 p. ; 20 cm. Added title in Chinese romanized: Chi nien fu ch'in Huang Shih-hsi. [BL1940.W66L34] 77-358819
1. Wong, Sai Hee, 1857-1927. 2. Taoists—Hawaii—Biography. I. Title.

Wood, Allen Tate.

WOOD, Allen Tate. 289.9 B
Moonstruck : memoirs of my life in a cult / by Allen Tate Wood with Jack Vitek. 1st ed. New York : Morrow, 1979. 189 p. ; 22 cm. [BX9750.S4W668] 79-13035 ISBN 0-688-03512-4 : 9.95
1. Wood, Allen Tate. 2. Segye Kidokkyo T'ongil Sillyong Hyophoe—Biography. 3. Segye Kidokkyo T'ongil Sillyong Hyophoe—Controversial literature. 4. Moon, Sun Myung. I. Vitek, Jack, joint author. II. Title.

Wood-carving, English.

SMITH, John Colin Dinsdale. 726'.593
A guide to church woodcarvings; misericords and bench-ends [by] J. C. D. Smith. Newton Abbot [Eng.] North Pomfret, Vt., David & Charles [1974] 112 p. illus. 25 cm. Bibliography: p. 107-108. [NK9743.S62] 74-185701 ISBN 0-7153-6562-2 11.50
1. Wood-carving, English. 2. Wood-carving, Medieval—England. 3. Choir-stalls—England. I. Title.

Wood-carving, Romanesque—Auvergne.

CAHN, Walter. 726'.591
The Romanesque wooden doors of Auvergne / Walter Cahn. New York : Published by New York University Press for the College Art Association of America, 1974. xv, 168 p., [17] leaves of plates : ill. ; 29 cm. (Monographs on archaeology and fine arts ; 30) Includes bibliographical references and index. [NK9749.A3A953] 74-15291 ISBN 0-8147-1357-2
1. Wood-carving, Romanesque—Auvergne. 2. Wood-carving—Auvergne. 3. Church doors—Auvergne. I. Title. II. Series.

Wood, Christine.

WOOD, Christine. 283'.092'4 B
Exclusive by-path : the autobiography of a pilgrim / by Christine Wood. Evesham : James, 1976. 141 p. ; 19 cm. [BX5179.W74A33] 76-373348 ISBN 0-85305-183-6 : £2.80
1. Wood, Christine. 2. Church of England—Biography. 3. Plymouth Brethren—Biography. I. Title.

Wood, Harold L., 1800-1944.

OWENS, Fern Royer. 922.673
Sky pilot of Alaska. Mountain View, Calif., Pacific Press Pub. Association [1949] 176 p. illus., map. 21 cm. [BX6193.W6O8] 50-572
1. Wood, Harold L., 1800-1944. 2. Missions—Alaska. I. Title.

Wood, John 1775-1822.

[CHEETHAM, James] 1772-1810. 264
A narrative of the suppression by Col. Burr, of the History of the administration of John Adams, late president of the United States, written by John Wood ... To which is added a biography of Thomas Jefferson, president of the United States; and of General Hamilton: with structures on the conduct of John Adams, and on the character of General C. C. Pinckney. Extracted verbatim from the suppressed history. By a citizen of New-York. New-York: Printed by Denniston and Cheetham, no. 142, Pearl street, 1802. 72 p. 22 cm. [Miscellaneous pamphlets, v. 246, no. 4] [AC901.M5 vol. 246] [AC901.D8 vol.13] 264 4-1367
1. Wood, John, 1775-1822. History of the administration of John Adams. 2. Adams, John pres. U. S., 1735-1826. 3. Jefferson, Thomas, pres, U. S., 1743-1836. 4. Hamiltion, Alexander, 1757-1904. 5. Burr, Aaron, 1756-1836. I. A citizen of New York. II. Title.

Wood, Miriam.

WOOD, Miriam. 286'.73 B
Reluctant saint, reluctant sinner / Miriam Wood. Washington : Review and Herald Pub. Association, c1975. 127 p. ; 21 cm. [BX6193.W64A29] 74-25818 2.95
1. Wood, Miriam. I. Title.

Wood Samuel, 1874

SMITH, Willard J., 1858- 231
What the restoration movement teaches concerning God, by Willard J. Smith ... Port Huron, Mich. [c1935] iv, [5]-111 p. front. (port.) 19 cm. "My ... endeavor to answer the follies and foibles as set forth in Brother Wood's booklet ... "The infinite God'."--Foreword. [BT101.S627] 35-15605
1. Wood, Samuel, 1874- The infinite God. 2. Mormons and Mormonism—Doctrinal and controversial works. I. Title.

Wood, Wilford C.—Archives.

BERRETT, LaMar C. 016.2893'092'4 S
An annotated catalog of documentary-type materials in the Wilford C. Wood Collection, by LaMar C. Berrett. [1st ed. Bountiful, Utah] Wilford C. Wood Foundation, 1972. ix, 236 p. port. 29 cm. (His The Wilford C. Wood Collection, v. 1) [Z6616.W58B4 vol. 1] 016.2893'092'4 73-160582
1. Wood, Wilford C.—Archives. 2. Smith, Joseph, 1805-1844—Archives. 3. Mormons and Mormonism—History—Sources—Bibliography. I. Title. II. Series.

BERRETT, LaMar C. 016.2893'092'4
The Wilford C. Wood Collection, by LaMar C. Berrett. [1st ed. Bountiful, Utah] Wilford C. Wood Foundation, 1972- v. port. 29 cm. Catalog of the collection. [Z6616.W58B4] 73-160583
1. Wood, Wilford C.—Archives. 2. Smith, Joseph, 1805-1844—Archives. 3. Mormons and Mormonism—History—Sources—Bibliography. I. Wilford C. Wood Foundation. II. Title.

Woodbridge, John, 1784-1869.

CLARK, Sereno Dickenson. 922.
The New England ministry sixty years ago. The memoir of John Woodbridge, D.D. His method of work; his great success in powerful revivals, in high moral and educational influences; his theological views, and the theological controversies of his time, beginning with the "New departure" of Stoddard. By Rev. Sereno D. Clark... Boston, Lee and Shepard. New York, C. T. Dillingham, 1877. xxi, 473 p. 21 cm. [BX7260.W6C5] 20-17721
1. Woodbridge, John, 1784-1869. I. Title.

Woodbridge, N.J. Trinity church.

WELLES, Edward Randolph, 1907- 283.74941
A history of Trinity church, Woodbridge, New Jersey, from 1698 to 1935, by the Reverend Edward Randolph Welles ... Southborough, The Pine tree press, 1935. 96 p. front., plates. 23 1/2 cm. "One hundred copies of this book have been printed of which this is number 34." [BX5980.W8T7] 35-7225
1. Woodbridge, N.J. Trinity church. I. Title.

Woodford Methodist Church.

FULCHER, Ernest A. 287'.1421'73
The Methodist Chapel, Derby Road, Woodford, 1876-1976 / by Ernest A. Fulcher. London : Woodford Methodist Church, 1976. [4], 55 p., [4] p. of plates : ill., 2 facsims., port. ; 23 cm. [BX8483.W65F84] 77-371975 ISBN 0-9504893-0-1 : £1.00
1. Woodford Methodist Church. I. Title.

Woodforde, James, 1740-1803.

WOODFORDE, James, 1740-1803. 942.07'3'0924 B
The diary of a country parson / James Woodforde ; edited by John Beresford. Oxford : Clarendon Press ; New York : Oxford University Press, 1981. p. cm. Contents.Contents.—v. 1. 1758-1781. Includes bibliographical references. [BX5199.W755A33 1981] 19 80-49700 ISBN 0-19-811485-0 (v. 1) : 165.00 (set)
1. Woodforde, James, 1740-1803. 2. Church of England—Clergy—Biography. 3. Clergy—England—Biography. I. Beresford, John, 1888-1940. II. Title.

WOODFORDE, James, 1740-1803. 942.07'3'0924 B
The diary of a country parson, 1758-1802 / by James Woodforde ; passages selected and edited by John Beresford. Oxford [Eng.] ; New York : Oxford University Press, 1978. xviii, 622 p. ; 20 cm. (Oxford paperbacks) The present selection was published in 1935 under title: Woodforde; passages from the five volumes of The diary of a country parson, 1758-1802. Includes bibliographical references. [BX5199.W755A332 1978] 77-30569 ISBN 0-19-281241-6 pbk. : 7.50
1. Woodforde, James, 1740-1803. 2. Church of England—Clergy—Biography. 3. Clergy—England—Biography. I. Beresford, John, 1888-1940. II. Title.

Woodhouse chapel. Leicestershire.

NICHOLS, John Gough, 1806-1873.
The armorial windows erected, in the reign of Henry VI. By John, viscount Beaumont, and Katharine, duchess of Norfolk, in Woodhouse chapel, by the park of Beaumont, in Charnwood forest, Leicestershire, including an investigation of the differences of the coat of Neville. By John Gough Nichols, F. S. A. [Westminster, J. B. Nichols and sons] 1860. 2 p. l., 50 p., 1 l. illus. (incl. coats of arms) 2 geneal. tab. (incl. front.) 25 cm. "Read at the Annual meeting of the Leicestershire architectural and archaeological society of Loughborough, July 27th, 1859." Printed at the expense of William Perry Herrick. [CR1627.L4N5] 21-3222
1. Neville family. 2. Beaumont family. 3. Heraldry—England—Leicestershire. 4. Woodhouse chapel. Leicestershire. I. Herrick, William Perry, 1794-1876. II. Title.

Woodland Indians—Religion and mythology.

NATIVE North American 299'.794
spirituality of the eastern woodlands : sacred myths, dreams, visions, speeches, healing formulas, rituals, and ceremonials / edited by Elisabeth Tooker ; pref. by William C. Sturtevant. New York : Paulist Press, c1979. xvii, 302 p. : map ; 24 cm. (The Classics of Western spirituality) Includes bibliographical references and indexes. [E78.E2N37] 79-66573 ISBN 0-8091-0304-4 : 11.95 ISBN 0-8091-2256-1 pbk. : 7.95
1. Woodland Indians—Religion and mythology. 2. Indians of North America—Religion and mythology. I. Tooker, Elizabeth. II. Title. III. Series.

Woodruff, Lucile (Kates) 1895-

WOODRUFF, Leola. 922.673
Valley of decision. Illus. by Harold Munson. Mountain View, Calif., Pacific Press Pub. Association [1959] 140 p. illus. 19 cm. [BX6189.W6W6] 59-9709
1. Woodruff, Lucile (Kates) 1895- 2. Converts, Seventh-Day Adventist. I. Title.

Woodruff, Wilford, 1807-1898.

COWLEY, Matthias Foss, 1858- ed. 922.
William Woodruff, fourth president of the Church of the church of Jesus Christ of latter-day saints. history of his life and labors, as recorded in his daily journals ... prepared for publication, by Matthias F. Cowley. Salt Lake City, Utah, The Desert News; 1909. xviii, 702 p. front. (port.) 5 pl. 24 cm. [BX8695.W55C6] 9-27936
1. Woodruff, Wilford, 1807-1898. I. Title.

Woods, Leonard, 1807-1878.

PARK, Edwards Amasa, 1808-1900. 920.
The life and character of Leonard Woods ... By Edwards A. Park. Andover, W. F. Draper, 1880. 52 p. 24 cm. [BX7260.W63P3] 26-21520
1. Woods, Leonard, 1807-1878. I. Title.

Woods, Wayne.

JOHNSON, Margaret 248'.86 B Woods.
We lived with dying / Margaret Woods Johnson. Waco, Tex. : Word Books, [1975] 128 p. ; 21 cm. [RC263.J63] 74-82656 4.95
1. Woods, Wayne. 2. Cancer—Personal narratives. I. Title.

Woodson, Peggie.

WOODSON, Meg. 248'.86'0924 B
If I die at thirty / Meg Woodson. Grand Rapids, Mich. : Zondervan Pub. House, c1975. 166 p. ; 22 cm. [RJ456.C9W66] 75-6182 4.95
1. Woodson, Peggie. 2. Cystic fibrosis—Personal narratives. 3. Children—Religious life—Personal narratives. 4. Children—Death and future state. I. Title.

Woodstock College of Baltimore County, Md.

LEO X I I I. Pope, 110-1903. 871
The Latin poemsof Leo xii, done into English verse by the Jesuits of Woodstock College. With a life of the pontiff by Charles Piccirille. Baltimore, Hill & Harvey, 1887. 159 p. port. 24 cm. Latin and English on opposite pages. [PA8540.L8 1887] 49-31462
1. Woodstock College of Baltimore County, Md. I. Piccirillo, Charles. II. Title.

WOODSTOCK College of Baltimore County, Md.
Focus; Catholic background reading for the orientation of college and univerbici1cbudu4tb.)i(gppdbbobk !mkqm$nm)bp1p. lk1bn)g
I. Title.

Woodward, Augustus Brevoort, d. 1827.

BISHOP, William Warner, 1871- 112
Judge Woodward and the Catholepistemaid, by William W. Bishop ... [n.p., 1945] cover-title, [323]-336 p. illus. (facsim.) 25 1/2 cm. "Reprinted from Michigan alumnus quarterly review, July 28, 1945, vol. LI, no. 24." [BD240.W62B5] 47-26093
1. Woodward, Augustus Brevoort, d. 1827. I. Michigan. University. II. Title.

Woodward, Ellen May, 1836-1850.

MILES, George D. d.1874. 922
Memoir of Ellen May Woodward. By the Rev. Geo. D. Miles ... Philadelphia, Lindsay and Blakiston, 1850. 2 p. l., [ix]-x p., 1 l., [13]-174 p., 1 l. front. (port.) 15 1/2 cm. [BR1715.W6M5 1850] 37-19949
1. Woodward, Ellen May, 1836-1850. I. Title.

MILES, George D., d.1874. 922
Memoir of Ellen May Woodward. By the Rev. Geo. D. Miles ... 2d ed. With a preface, by the Rt. Rev. Alonzo Potter ... Philadelphia, Lindsay & Blakiston, 1852. xi, 13-161 p. front. (port.) 15 1/2 cm. [BR1715.W6M5 1852] 37-19950
1. Woodward, Ellen May, 1836-1850. I. Title.

Woodward, Walter Carleton,

EMERSON, Elizabeth (Holaday). 922.8673
Walter C. Woodward; Friend on the frontier, a biography. With a pref. by Errol T. Elliott. [Richmond? Ind., 1952] 316 p. illus. 20 cm. [BX7795.W67E5] 52-29135
1. Woodward, Walter Carleton, I. Title.

Woodworth, Ruth A.

WOODWORTH, Ruth A. 266'.6'10924 B
No greater joy / by Ruth A. Woodworth. Des Plaines, Ill. : Regular Baptist Press, [1975] 70 p. : ill. ; 19 cm. [BV3382.W66A36] 74-28952 pbk. : 1.25
1. Woodworth, Ruth A. I. Title.

Woollam, Josephine, 1944 or 5-

CHESHIRE, Geoffrey Leonard, 1917- 232.966
Pilgrimage to the Shroud. With a foreword by His Grace the Archbishop of Birmingham. New York, McGraw-Hill [c1956] 74p. illus. 20cm. [BT587.S4C45 1956a] 57-7227
1. Woollam, Josephine, 1944 or 5- 2. Holy Shroud. I. Title.

Woollcombe, Harry St. John Stirling, bp., 1869-1941.

HARRY Woollcombe, bishop; 922.342 a memoir by his friends with an introduction by Archbishop Lord Lang of Lambeth, edited by Bishop Bernard Heywood. London and Oxford, A. R. Mowbray & co. limited; New York, Morehouse-Gorham co. [1943] 133 p. front., pl., ports. 19 cm. "First published in 1943." [BX5190.W8H3] 44-26377
1. Woollcombe, Harry St. John Stirling, bp., 1869-1941. I. Heywood, Bernard Oliver Francis, bp., 1871- ed.

Woolley, Edwin Dilworth, 1897-1881.

ARRINGTON, Leonard J. 288.3'3 B
From Quaker to Latter-Day Saint : Bishop Edwin D. Woolley / Leonard J. Arrington. Salt Lake City : Deseret Book Co., 1976. xiii, 592 p. ; 24 cm. Includes index. Bibliography: p. 497-500. [BX8695.W57A77] 76-43171 ISBN 0-87747-591-1 : 6.95
1. Woolley, Edwin Dilworth, 1897-1881. 2. Mormons and Mormonism—Biography. I. Title.

WOOLMAN, John, 1720-1772. 922.
A journal of the life, gospel labours, and Christian experiences, of that faithful minister of Jesus Christ, John Woolman ... Philadelphia, T. E. Chapman, 1837. 396 p. 19 1/2 cm. [BX7795.W7A3 1837] 47-33043
I. Title.

WOOLMAN, John, 1720-1772. 922.
A journal of the life of gospel labors, and Christian experiences of that faithful minister of Jesus Christ, John Wollman: to which are added his last epistle and other writings ... New York, The Macmillan company; London, Macmillan & co., ltd., 1903. xxv, 181 p. 15 cm. [Macmillan's pocket American and English classics] [BX7795.W7A3 1903] 3-2701
I. Title.

Woolman, John, 1720-1772.

BENTON, Josephine Moffett. 289.6'0924
John woolman, most modern of ancient Friends. Philadelphia, Friends Central Bureau [195-?] 62p. 21cm. 'Publication of Religious Education Committee of Friends GeneralConference.' [BX7795.W7B4] 62-1975
1. Woolman, John, 1720-1772. I. Title.

CADY, Edwin Harrison. 922.8673
John Woolman. Author of this volume: Edwin H. Cady. New York, Washington Square Press [1965] ix, 182 p. 18 cm. (The Great American thinkers series) "W-882." Bibliography: p. 173-178. [BX7795.W7C3] 65-1754
1. Woolman, John, 1720-1772.

MOULTON, Phillips P., 1909- 289.6'092'4 B
The living witness of John Woolman [by] Phillips P. Moulton. [Wallingford, Pa., Pendle Hill Publications, 1973] 32 p. 19 cm. (Pendle Hill pamphlet 187) "Pendle Hill clusters": p. 29-32. [BX7795.W7M68] 72-94969 ISBN 0-87574-187-8 0.70
1. Woolman, John, 1720-1772. I. Title.

PEARE, Catherine Owens. 922.8673
John Woolman: child of light; the story of John Woolman and the Friends. New York, Vanguard Press [1954] 254p. illus. 22cm. [BX7795.W7P4] 54-6990
1. Woolman. John, 1720-1772. I. Title.

REYNOLDS, Reginald, 1905- 230'.96
The wisdom of Joan Woolman : with a selection from his writings as a guide to the seekers of today / Reginald Reynolds ; with a preface by Stephen Hobhouse. Westport, Conn. : Greenwood Press, 1981. p. cm. Reprint of the 1948 ed. published by G. Allen & Unwin, London. Includes index. [BX7795.W7R4 1981] 19 79-8724 ISBN 0-313-22190-1 : 22.50
1. Woolman, John, 1720-1772. 2. Friends, Society of—Doctrinal and controversial works. I. Woolman, John, 1720-1772. Selections. II. Title.

ROSENBLATT, Paul. 289.6'0924
John Woolman. New York, Twayne Publishers [1969] 163 p. 22 cm. (Twayne's United States authors series, TUSAS 147) Bibliography: p. 153-158. [PS892.R6] 68-24307
1. Woolman, John, 1720-1772. I. Title.

SISTER Ruth's stories for the young; 922. or, Evenings with John Woolman. By R. P. A. Philadelphia, T. E. Chapman, 1865. 121 p. illus. 16 cm. [BX7795.W7S5 1865] 49-38053
1. Woolman, John, 1720-1772. I. A., R. P. II. R. P. A.

SISTER Ruth's stories for the young; 922. or, Evenngs with John Woolman. By R. P. A. Philadelphia, J. B. Lippincott, 1865. 121 p. illus. 16 cm. [BX7795.W7S5 1865a] 49-38052
1. Woolman, John, 1720-1772. I. A., R. P. II. R. P. A.

WHITNEY, Janet. Mrs. 922.8673
John Woolman, American Quaker, by Janet Whitney, with illustrations by George Gillett Whitney... Boston, Little, Brown and company, 1942. x p., 2 l., [3]-490 p. illus., plates, facsims. 22 1/2 cm. Map on lining-papers. "An Atlantic monthly press book." "First edition." Bibliography: p. [435]-440. [BX7795.W7W5] 42-13313
1. Woolman, John, 1720-1772. I. Title.

WHITNEY, Janet (Payne) 1894- 922.8673
John Woolman, American Quaker, by Janet Whitney, with illustrations by George Gillett Whitney ... Boston, Little, Brown and company, 1942. x p., 2 l., [3]-400 p. illus., plates, facsims. 22 1/2 cm. Map on lining-papers. "An Atlantic monthly press book." "First edition." Bibliography: p. [435]-440. [BX7795.W7W5] 42-13313
1. Woolman, John, 1720-1772. I. Title.

WOOLMAN, John, 1720-1772. 922.8673
Journal; edited and with an introd. by Thomas S. Kepler. Cleveland, World Pub. Co. [1954] xx, 235p. 17cm. (World devotional classics) [BX7795.W7A3 1954] 54-5339
I. Title.

WOOLMAN, John, 1720-1772. 922.8673
Journal; edited by Janet Whitney. Chicago, H. Regnery Co., 1950. xv, 233 p. 22 cm. [BX7795.W7A3 1950] 50-10962

WOOLMAN, John, 1720-1772. 922.8673
The journal of John Woolman, and A plea for the poor. The John Greenleaf Whittier ed. text. Introd. by Frederick B. Tolles. New York, Corinth Books [1961] xii, 249 p. facsim. 19 cm. (The American experience series, AE2) "For further reading": p. xii. [BX7795.W7A3 1961] 61-8147
I. Woolman, John, 1720-1772. II. Title. III. Title: A plea for the poor.

WOOLMAN, John, 1720-1772. 289.6'0924 B
The journal of John Woolman, and A plea for the poor. The John Greenleaf Whittier ed. text. Introd. by Frederick B. Tolles. Gloucester, Mass., P. Smith, 1971 [c1961] xii, 249 p. 21 cm. Reprint of two works published in 1774 and 1793 respectively; the first work originally had title: A journal of the life, gospel labours, and Christian experiences of that faithful minister of Jesus Christ, John Woolman. Includes bibliographical references. [BX7795.W7A3 1971] 72-27383
I. Woolman, John, 1720-1772. A plea for the poor. 1971.

YOUNG, Mildred (Binns) 289.6'0924
Woolman and Blake: prophets for today. [Wallingford, Pa., Pendle Hill Publications, 1971] 32 p. 19 cm. (Pendle Hill pamphlet 177) "First presented as the annual John Woolman Memorial Lecture in September, 1963, at Mount Holly, New Jersey." [BX7795.W7Y65 1971] 72-170018 0.70
1. Woolman, John, 1720-1772. 2. Blake, William, 1757-1827. I. Title.

Woonsocket, R.I. Church of The Precious Blood.

KENNEDY, Ambrose, 1875- 922.273
Quebec to New England, the life of Monsignor Charles Daurey. Boston, B. Humphries [1948] 242 p. illus., ports. 22 cm. [BX4705.D278K4] 48-9338
1. Dauray, Charles, 1838-1931. 2. Woonsocket, R.I. Church of The Precious Blood. 3. Providence (Diocese) I. Title.

Worcester association (1820-Unitarian)

ALLEN, Joseph, 1790-1873. 288.
The Worcester association and its antecedents; a history of four ministerial associations: the Marlborough, the Worcester (old), the Lancaster, and the Worcester (New) associations. With biographical notices of the members, accompanied by portraits. By Joseph Allen ... Boston, Nichols and Noyes, 1868. xi, 426 p. front., ports. 19 1/2 cm. [BX9803.W8A8] 8-34560
1. Worcester association (1820- Unitarian) 2. Marlborough association. 3. Worcester association (1762-1791: Congregational) 4. Lancaster association. 5. Unitarian church—Biog. I. Title.

Worcester cathedral.

ROBINSON, Joseph Armitage, 1858- 262
... St. Oswald and the church of Worcester, by J. Armitage Robinson ... London, Pub. for the British academy by H. Milford, Oxford university press [1919] 51 p. 25 cm. (The British academy. Supplemental papers. v) Bibliographical foot-notes. [DA154.9.O7R5] 20-22067
1. Oswald, Saint, abp. of York, d. 992. 2. Worcester cathedral. I. Title.

Worcester, Eng. (Diocese)

SMITH, Isaac Gregory, 1826-1920.
...Worcester. By the Rev. I. Gregory Smith...and the Rev. Phipps Onslow...Published under the direction of the Tract committee. London, Society for promoting Christian knowledge; New York; E. & J. B. Young & co., 1883. ix p., 1 l., 367 p. front. (fold. map) 17 cm. (Diocean histories) [BX5107.W9S6] 4-205
1. Worcester, Eng. (Diocese) 2. Gt. Brit.—Church history. I. Society for promoting Christian knowledge. Tract committee. II. Onslow, Phipps, joint author. III. Title.

Worcester, Mass. Central church.

CUTLER, Uriel Waldo, 1854- 285.
The first hundred years of the Central church in Worcester, 1820-1920, by U. Waldo Cutler. Worcester, Mass., The Church, 1920. 70 p. 23 cm. "References": p. 70. [BX7255.W9C4] 21-243
1. Worcester, Mass. Central church. I. Title.

Worcester, Mass. First church. Origin and progress of difficulties, 1820.

REMARKS on the late publications of the First church in Worcester, 285. relative to the "Origin and progress of difficulties" in that church ... Worcester: Printed by Manning and Trumbull, Jan. 1821. 103 p. 22 cm. Relates to the dissension in the church regarding the pastorate of Mr. Goodrich. [BX7255.W9F5] 27-12438
1. Goodrich, Charles Augustus, 1790-1862. 2. Worcester, Mass. First church. Origin and progress of difficulties, 1820.

Worcester, Mass. First church—Poetry.

KNOWLTON, Annie I.
Good-bye, Old South, good-bye! By Annie I. Knowlton. Illustrated by Charles W. Hall. [Worcester, Mass., Bullard art publishing company, 1887] 6 l. incl. col. illus., facsim. 26 cm. Illustrated by hand in water-colors; illustrated cover. In verse. [PS2197.K34] 28-6621
1. Worcester, Mass. First church—Poetry. I. Hall, Charles W., illus. II. Title.

Worcester, Mass. Wesley Methodist Church. Social surveys.

CHURCH surveys.
A study of The Wesley Methodist Church, Worcester, Massachusetts, May, 1957. Project director, Maurice E. Culver. Boston, 1957. viii, 90 p. maps, profiles, tables, 28 cm. 64-65939
1. Worcester, Mass. Wesley Methodist Church. Social surveys. I. Culver, Maurice E. II. Title.

Worcester, Mass. Wesley Methodist Episcopal church.

MITCHELL, William Samuel, 1877- 287.
A seven-day church at work; the story of the development and program of Wesley church, Worcester, Massachusetts, by William S. Mitchell ... New York and London, Funk and Wagnalls company, 1929. xiv, 255 p. front., illus. (plans) plates. 19 1/2 cm. [BX8481.W6M5] 29-20811
1. Worcester, Mass. Wesley Methodist Episcopal church. I. Title.

Worcester, Noah, 1758-1837.

WARE, Henry, 1794-1843. 288'.092'4 B
Memoirs of the Rev. Noah Worcester, D.D., by Henry Ware, Jr. With a pref., notes, and a concluding chapter, by Samuel Worcester. Boston, J. Munroe, 1844. [New York, J. S. Ozer, 1972] xii, 155 p. front. 22 cm. (The Peace movement in America) A facsim. reprint. [BX9869.W8W3 1844a] 78-137557 8.95
1. Worcester, Noah, 1758-1837. I. Worcester, Samuel, 1793-1844, ed. II. Title. III. Series.

WARE, Henry, 1794-1843. 922.8173
Memoirs of the Rev. Noah Worcester, D.D. By the Rev. Henry Ware, jr., D.D. With a preface, notes, and a concluding chapter, by Samuel Worcester. Boston, J. Munroe and company, 1844. xii, 185 p. 20 1/2 cm. [BX9869.W3W3] 37-9273
1. Worcester, Noah, 1758-1837. I. Worcester, Samuel, 1798-1844, ed. II. Title.

Worcester, Samuel, 1770-1821.

CORNELIUS, Elias, 1791-1832. 252.
God's ways, not as our ways. A sermon, occasioned by the death of the Rev. Samuel Worcester, D.D., senior pastor of the Tabernacle church, in Salem, Mass. By Elias Cornelius... Salem, H. Whipple. 1821. 56 p. 21 1/2 cm. No. 11 in a volume lettered: Sermons. [BX9843.A1S4 no. 11] 45-52234
1. Worcester, Samuel, 1770-1821. I. Title.

WORCESTER, Samuel Melanchthon, 1801-1866. 922.573
The life and labors of Rev. Samuel Worcester, D. D., former pastor of the Tabernacle church, Salem, Mass. By his son Samuel M. Worcester ... Boston, Crocker and Brewster, 1852. 2 v. front. (port.) 21 cm. [BX7260.W64W6] 36-17207
1. Worcester, Samuel, 1770-1821. I. Title.

Worcester, Samuel Austin. 1798-1859.

BASS, Altha Leah (Bierbower) Mrs. 1892- 922.573
Cherokee messenger [by] Althea Bass. Norman, Okla., University of Oklahoma press, 1936. 348 p., 1 l. pl., 2 port. (incl. front.) map, facsims. 24 cm. [The civilization of the American Indian] [E99.C5B3] 36-7949
1. Worcester, Samuel Austin. 1798-1859. 2. Cherokee Indians—Missions. 3. Brainerd mission, Tenn. I. Title.

Word of God (Theology)

BIBLE. English. Selections. 1933. 220.52
... God's word to man ... Lock Haven, Pa., Century of progress publishing company [c1933]- v. 16 cm. Includes blank pages for "Notes". [BS195.C4] 33-34796
I. Title.

BIBLE. English. Selections. 1933. 220.52
... God's word to man ... Lock Haven, Pa., Century of progress publishing company [c1933]- v. 16 cm. Includes blank pages for "Notes". [BS195.C4] 33-34796
I. Title.

BOUYER, Louis, 1913- 232
The eternal son : a theology of the word of God and Christology / Louis Bouyer ; translated from the French by Simone Inkel and John F. Laughlin. Huntington, Ind. : Our Sunday Visitor, c1978. 431 p. ; 24 cm. Translation of Le fils eternel. Includes bibliographical references and indexes. [BT202.B673413] 77-92090 ISBN 0-87973-881-2 : 19.95
1. Jesus Christ—Person and offices. 2. Jesus Christ—History of doctrines. 3. Word of God (Theology). I. Title.

BUSHNELL, Katharine C. 296
God's word to women; one hundred Bible studies on woman's place in the divine economy, by Katharine C. Bushnell ... [2d ed.] Oakland, Calif., The author, c1923. [398] p. illus. (port.) fold. pl. 21 cm. First issued as Bible lessons of the Women's correspondence Bible class. [BS680.W7B8 1923] 24-1187
I. Title.

BUSHNELL, Katharine C. 296
God's word to women; one hundred Bible studies on woman's place in the divine economy, by Katharine C. Bushnell ... [2d ed.] Oakland, Calif., The author, c1923. [398] p. illus. (port.) fold. pl. 21 cm. First issued as Bible lessons of the Women's correspondence Bible class. [BS680.W7B8 1923] 24-1187
I. Title.

CROWE, Frederick E. 230
Theology of the Christian word : a study in history / Frederick E. Crowe. New York : Paulist Press, c1978. v, 174 p. 23 cm. Includes bibliographical references. [BT180.W67C76] 78-51595 ISBN 0-8091-2106-9 pbk. : 6.95
1. Word of God (Theology) I. Title.

*GALUSHA, Walter T. 222.1106
Fossils and the word of God. New York, Exposition [c.1964] 115p. 21cm. 3.00
I. Title.

GODS woord in mensenhandon.
Haarlem, Bohn, 1956. 1v.
I. Leendertz, Willem, 1883-

GODS woord in mensenhandon.
Haarlem, Bohn, 1956. 1v.
I. Leendertz, Willem, 1883-

GOOD, Nelson Manoah, 1856- 220
The true word of God as applied to religious principles, times, places and men, by Nelson M. Good ... [Grant Valley? Col., 1907] 196 p. 19 1/2 cm. [BR125.G6] 7-19770
I. Title.

GOOD, Nelson Manoah, 1856-
The true word of God as applied to religious principles, times, places and men, by Nelson M. Good ... [Grand Valley? Col., c1907] 196 p. 20 cm. 7-19770
I. Title.

GUILLET, Jacques. 231
A God who speaks / Jacques Guillet ; translated by Edmond Bonin. New York : Paulist Press, c1979. vi, 101 p. ; 21 cm. Translation of Un Dieu qui parle. Bibliography: p. 95-96. [BT127.2.G8413] 78-65898 ISBN 0-8091-2195-6 : 4.50
1. Word of God (Theology) I. Title.

JARRELL, Charles C.
Witnesses to the Word, by the Rev. Charles C. Jarrell ... with an introduction by Horace M. Du Bose ... Nashville, Tenn., Dallas, Tex. [etc.] Publishing house of the M. E. church, South, Smith & Lamar, agents, 1916. iii, 191 p. 20 cm. 16-14821 1.00
I. Title.

MARROW, Stanley B. 226'.06
The words of Jesus in our Gospels : a Catholic response to fundamentalism / Stanley B. Marrow. New York : Paulist Press, c1979. 152 p. ; 21 cm. (An Exploration book) Bibliography: p. 148-149. [BS2555.2.M34] 79-52105 ISBN 0-8091-2215-4 pbk. : 4.95
1. Catholic Church—Doctrinal and controversial works—Catholic authors. 2. Bible. N.T. Gospels—Criticism, interpretation, etc. 3. Word of God (Theology) 4. Fundamentalism—Controversial literature. I. Title.

*OLFORD, Stephen F. 232.2
The living word. Chicago, Moody [c.1963] 58p. 20cm. 1.75 bds.,
I. Title.

Word of God (Theology)—Addresses, essays, lectures.

ANDERSON, Bernhard W. 220.1
The living word of the Bible / Bernhard W. Anderson. 1st ed. Philadelphia : Westminster Press, c1979. 117 p. ; 21 cm. A series of lectures originally presented at theological seminaries in the U.S. and Canada. Bibliography: p. [111]-117. [BS480.A64] 78-27108 ISBN 0-664-24247-2 pbk. : 4.95
1. Bible—Evidences, authority, etc—Addresses, essays, lectures. 2. Bible—Inspiration—Addresess, essays, lectures. 3. Word of God (Theology)—Addresses, essays, lectures. I. Title.

Word of life hour (Radio program)

FORBES, Forrest Dale, 1907- 922
God hath chosen, the story of Jack Wyrtzen and the Word of life hour. Grand Rapids, Zondervan Pub. House [1948] 137 p. illus. 20 cm. [BV3785.W9F6] 48-8074
1. Wyrtzen, Jack, 1913- 2. Word of life hour (Radio program) I. Title.

SWEETING, George, 1924- 922
The Jack Wyrtzen story; the personal story of the man, his message and his ministry. Grand Rapids, Zondervan Pub. House [1960] 151 p. illus. 21 cm. [BV3785.W9S8] 60-4404
1. Wyrtzen, Jack, 1913- 2. Word of life hour (Radio program) I. Title.

Word of wisdom.

DOXEY, Roy Watkins, 1908- 230'.93
The Word of Wisdom today / Roy W. Doxey. Salt Lake City : Deseret Book Co., c1975. x,142 p. ; 24 cm. Includes index. Bibliography: p. 136-138. [BX8629.W6D68] 75-26334 ISBN 0-87747-571-7 : 4.95
1. Word of wisdom. I. Title.

OAKS, Lewis Weston, 1892- 289.
Medical aspects of the Latter-day saint Word of wisdom, by L. Weston Oaks, M. D. Provo, Utah, Brigham Young university [c1929] 4 p.l., [7]-126 p. 20 1/2 cm. Bibliography at end of each chapter except the last. [BX8629.W6O2] 29-22242
1. Word of wisdon. 2. Mormons, and Mormonism. 3. Hygiene. 4. Alcohol—Physiological effect. 5. Tobacco—Physiological effect. 6. Tea—Physiological effect. 7. Coffee. I. Title.

OAKS, Lewis Weston, 1892- 289
Medical aspects of the Latter-day saint Word of wisdom, by L. Weston Oaks, M. D. Provo, Utah, Brigham Young university, [c1929] 4 p. l., [7]-126 p. 21 cm. Bibliography at end of each chapter except the last. [BX8629.W6O2] 29-22242
1. Word of wisdom. 2. Mormons and Mormonism. 3. Hygiene. 4. Alchol—Physiological effect. 5. Tobacco—Physiological effect. 6. Tea—Physiological effect. 7. Coffee. I. Title.

OAKS, Lewis Weston 1892- 289.3
The Word of wisdom and you. Salt Lake City, Bookcraft [1958] 273p. 24cm. [BX8629.W6O23] 58-10838
1. Word of wisdom. I. Title.

WIDTSOE, John Andreas, 1872- 613.2
The Word of wisdom; a modern interpretation, by John A. Widtsoe and Leah D. Widtsoe. [Salt Lake City] Deseret book company, 1937. 263 p. front., illus., diagrs. 20 cm. "References and further reading" at end of each chapter except the last. [BX8629.W6W5] 38-7996
1. Word of wisdom. 2. Diet. 3. Nutrition. 4. Hygiene. I. Widtsoe, Mrs. Leah Eudora (Dunford) 1874- joint author. II. Title.

Wordsworth, Charles, Bp. of St. Andrews, Dunkeld, and Dunblane, 1806-1892.

WORDSWORTH, John, bp. of Salisbury, 1843-
The episcopate of Charles Wordsworth, bishop of St. Andrews, Dunkeld, and Dunblane 1853-1892; a memoir, together with some materials for forming a judgment on the great questions in the discussion of which he was concerned ... London, New York [etc.] Longmans, Green & co., 1899. xxv, [1], 402 p. front., port. 8 ° 1-6146
I. Title.

WORDSWORTH, John, Bp. of Salisbury, 1843-1911. 922.
The episcopate of Charles Wordsworth, Bishop of St. Andrews, Dunkeld, and Dunblade 1853-1892; a memoir, together with some materials for forming a judgment on the great questions in the discussion of which he was concerned. London, New York, Longmans, Green, 1899. xxv, 402 p. ports. 23 cm. "List of the principal printed writings of Charles Wordsworth in chronological order": p. 366-385. [BX5199.W85W9] 1-6146
1. Wordsworth, Charles, Bp. of St. Andrews, Dunkeld, and Dunblane, 1806-1892. I. Title.

Work.

CABOT, Richard Clarke, 1868-1939. 170
What men live by; work, play, love, worship, by Richard C. Cabot ... Boston and New York, Houghton Mifflin company, 1914. 3 p. l., [ix]-xxi, 341, [1] p. 21 cm. "Parts of several chapters have already been printed in the Atlantic monthly."--Pref. [BJ1581.C15] 14-3268
1. Work. 2. Pleasure. 3. Love. 4. Worship. I. Title.

CABOT, Richard Clarke, 1868-1939. 170
What men live by; work, play, love, worship, by Richard C. Cabot ... Boston and New York, Houghton Mifflin company [1929] 3 p. l., [lx]-xxl, 341 p. 21 cm. "Published January, 1914. Thirty-sixth impression, January, 1929." [BJ1581.C15 1929] 31-910
1. Work. 2. Pleasure. 3. Love. 4. Worship. I. Title.

CUNNINGHAM, William, 1849-1919. 240
The gospel of work; four lectures on Christian ethics, by W. Cunningham ... Cambridge, University press, 1902. xiv, 144 p. 18 cm. "Lectures ... given to Extension students in the Divinity school during the Cambridge summer meeting of 1902."--Prefatory notes. [BJ1498.C8] 3-6980
1. Work. I. Title.
Contents omitted.

HELLDORFER, Martin C. 248.4
The work trap : solving the riddle of work and leisure / Martin C. Helldorfer. Winona, Minn. : Saint Mary's Press, c1981. 96 p. ; 23 cm. Bibliography: p. 85-96. [BJ1498.H4] 19 81-113580 ISBN 0-88489-127-5 (pbk.) : 5.95
1. Work. 2. Leisure. I. Title.

LARSON, Christian Daa, 1874- 200
The new science of work, by Christian D. Larson ... New York, Thomas Y. Crowell company [c1924] 91 p. 16 cm. [BJ1498.L3] 24-4533
1. Work. 2. New thought. I. Title.

LAYMEN'S Movement for a Christian World.
Living my religion on my job; a do-it-yourself study course for the men of the church, designed by fellow laymen. Rye, N.Y., Laymen's Movement [1962] xii, 165 p. 23 cm. Includes bibliographies. 65-12957
1. Work. 2. Christian ethics — Study and teaching. I. Title.

LAYMEN'S Movement for a Christian World.
Living my religion on my job; a do-it-yourself study course for the men of the church, designed by fellow laymen. Rye, N.Y., Laymen's Movement [1962] xii, 165 p. 23 cm. Includes bibliographies. 65-12957
1. Work. 2. Christian ethics — Study and teaching. I. Title.

WALLIS, Severn Teackle, 1816-1894. 200
Leisure; its moral and political economy. A lecture, by S. Teackle Wallis...delivered before the Mercantile library association of Baltimore, 8th March, 1859. Baltimore, Printed by J.B. Rose & co., 1859. 53 p. 23 1/2 cm. [BJ1498.W2 1859] 15-10769
1. Work. I. Title.

Work, Method of.

ABHEDANANDA, swami. 2-11633
Vedanta philosophy; three lectures, by Swami Abhedananda on philosophy of work. Delivered under the auspices of the Vedanta society, in Carnegie lyceum, New York. New York, The Vedanta society, [1902] 93 p. 18 1/2 cm. Contents.Philosophy of work.--Secret of work.--Duty or motive in work.
1. Work, Method of. I. Title.

WELLS, Amos R[ussel] 1862-
How to work. Boston & Chicago, United society of Christian endeavor [1900] 152 p. 12°. (The "how" series) 6-6338
I. Title.

Work (Theology)

ILLANES, Jose Luis, 1933- 260
On the theology of work; translated [from the Spanish] by Michael Adams. 2nd ed. Dublin, Chicago, Scepter Books, 1968. 3-72 p. 22 cm. Translation of La santificacion del trabajo: tema de nuestro tiempo. Bibliographical references included in "Notes" (p. 64-72) [BT738.5.I413 1968] 74-362339 8/6
1. Work (Theology) I. Title.

KAISER, Edwin G. 1893- 261.85
Theology of work, by Edwin G. Kaiser. Westminster. Md., Newman 1966 [i.e.,1967] xxi, 521p. 24cm. Bibl. [BT738.5.K3] 66-16568 10.50
1. Work (Theology) I. Title.

SAVARY, Louis M. 261
Man, his world, and his work [by] Louis M. Savary. New York, Paulist [1967] vii, 232p. 21cm. (Exploration bks.) Bibl. [BT738.5.S3] 67-15719 4.95; 2.95 pap.,
1. Work (Theology) I. Title.

WHITE, Jerry E., 1937- 248'.88
Your job—survival or satisfaction? / By Jerry E. White and Mary A. White ; foreword by Lorne Sanny. Grand Rapids : Zondervan Pub. House, c1977. p. cm. [BT738.5.W5] 76-45191 4.95
1. Work (Theology) 2. Job satisfaction. 3. Vocation. I. White, Mary Ann, 1935- joint author. II. Title.

ZEHRING, John William. 248.8'3
Preparing for work : get ready now for life after school / John William Zehring. Wheaton, Ill. : Victor Books, c1981. 159 p. : ill. ; 18 cm. (SonPower youth publication) [BT738.5.Z4] 19 79-92001 ISBN 0-88207-582-9 (pbk.) : 2.95
1. Work (Theology) 2. Vocational guidance. I. Title. II. Series.

Work (Theology)—Addresses, essays, lectures.

WORK as praise /
editors, George W. Forell, William H. Lazareth. Philadelphia : Fortress Books, c1979. 64 p. ; 22 cm. (Justice books) Includes bibliographical references. [BT738.5.W67] 78-54549 ISBN 0-8006-1555-7 : 2.25
1. Work (Theology)—Addresses, essays, lectures. 2. Vocation—Biblical teaching—Addresses, essays, lectures. 3. Manpower policy—United States—Moral and religious aspects—Addresses, essays, lectures. 4. Unemployed—United States—Moral and religious aspects—Addresses, essays, lectures. 5. Right to labor—Moral and religious aspects—Addresses, essays, lectures. I. Forell, George Wolfgang. II. Lazareth, William Henry, 1928- III. Title. IV. Series.

Workman, George Coulson, 1848

DEWART, Edward Hartley, 1828-1903. 232.12
Jesus the Messiah in prophecy and fulfillment. A review and refutation of the negative theory of Messianic prophecy By Edward Hartley Dewart ... American ed. Cranston & Stowe: Cranston & Stowe: New York, Hunt & Eaton, 1891. xvi, [17]-256 p. 19 cm. [BT235.W63D5] 37-38009
1. Workman, George Coulson, 1848- Messianic prophecy vindicated. 2. Messiah—Prophecies. 3. Bible. O. T.—Prophecies. 4. Jesus Christ—Messiahship. 5. Bible—Prophecies—O. T. I. Title.

World Alliance of Reformed Churches (Presbyterian and Congregational)

PRADERVAND, Marcel. 262'.05
A century of service : a history of the World Alliance of Reformed Churches, 1875-1975 / Marcel Pradervand. Grand Rapids : Eerdmans, c1975. xv, 309 p. ; 23 cm. Includes bibliographical references and index. [BX8905.W63P7 1975] 75-32554 ISBN 0-8028-3466-3 : 8.95
1. World Alliance of Reformed Churches (Presbyterian and Congregational) I. Title.

World Conference of Ashkenazi and Sephardi Synagogues, 1st, Jerusalem, 1968.

KARASICK, Joseph. 296.6'5
Report to UOJCA congregations on the First World Conference of Ashkenazi and Sephardi Synagogues held in Jerusalem on 7-12 Teveth, 5728 (January 8-13, 1968). [New York] Union of Orthodox Jewish Congregations of America [1968?] 39 p. illus. 23 cm. Cover title. "Addresses of Joseph Karasick at the First World Conference of Ashkenazi and Sephardi Synagogues" (6 p.) inserted. [BM30.W57K37 1968] 74-157575
1. World Conference of Ashkenazi and Sephardi Synagogues, 1st, Jerusalem, 1968. 2. Judaism—Congresses. I. Union of Orthodox Jewish Congregations of America. II. Title.

World Conference on Church and Society, Geneva, 1966.

RAMSEY, Paul. 261
Who speaks for the church? Nashville, Abingdon Press [1967] 189 p. 22 cm. "A critique of the 1966 Geneva Conference on Church and Society." Bibliographical references included in "Notes" (p. 169-189) [BT38.W58] 67-24331
1. World Conference on Church and Society, Geneva, 1966. I. Title.

World Conference on Church, Community and State, Oxford, 1937.

LEIPER, Henry Smith, 1891- 280.631
World chaos or world Christianity, a popular interpretation of Oxford and Edinburgh, 1937, by Henry Smith Leiper. Chicago, New York, Willett, Clark & company, 1937. viii p., 1 l., 181 p. 10 1/2 cm. [BV630.L43] 38-27133
1. World conference on church, community and state, Oxford, 1937. 2. World conference on faith and order. 2d, Edinburgh, 1937. Commission on the church's unity in life and worship. 3. Christian union—Congresses. 4. Church and state. I. Title.

RAVEN, Charles Earle, 1885- 261.8'73
War and the Christian, by Charles E. Raven. With a new introd. for the Garland ed. by Franklin H. Littell. New York, Garland Pub., 1972. 9, 185 p. 22 cm. (The Garland library of war and peace) Reprint of the 1938 ed. [BT736.2.R38 1972] 75-147675 ISBN 0-8240-0432-9
1. World Conference on Church, Community and State, Oxford, 1937. 2. War and religion. I. Title. II. Series.

World conference on faith and order, Lausanne, 1927.

SOPER, Edmund Davison, 1876- 280
Lausanne: the will to understand; an American interpretation, by Edmund Davison Soper ... Garden City, N.Y., Doubleday, Doran & company, inc., 1928. xiv, 156 p. front., plates, ports. 19 1/2 cm. An interpretation of the World conference on faith and order held at Lausanne in 1927. [BX6.W75 1927 d] 28-16542
1. World conference on faith and order, Lausanne, 1927. 2. Christian union—Congresses. I. Title.

WORLD Conference on Faith and Order. Continuation Committee. 264
Intercommunion: the report of the theological commission appointed by the Continuation Committee of the World Conference on Faith and Order, together with a selection from the material presented to the commission. Edited by Donald Baillie [and] John Marsh. New York, Harper [c1952] 406p. 23cm. Bibliographical footnotes.SIntercommunion. [BX9.5.I5W6 1952a] 52-8459
I. Ballie, Donald Macpherson, 1887- ed. II. Title.

World Conference on Mission and Evangelism (1980 : Melbourne, Vic.)—Addresses, essays, lectures.

SKOGLUND, John E. 280.1
Fifty years of Faith and Order; an interpretation of the Faith and Order movement [by] John E. Skoglund, J. Robert Nelson. St. Louis, Pub. for Abbott Bks. by Bethany [1964, c.1963] 159p. 20cm. Bibl. [BX6.W7S5] 65-274 1.75 pap.,
1. World Conference on Faith and Order. I. Nelson, John Robert, 1920- II. Title.

SKOGLUND, John E 280.1
Fifty years of Faith and Order; an interpretation of the Faith and Order movement, by John E. Skoglund and J. Robert Nelson. [New York, Committee for the Inter-seminary Movement of the National Student Christian Federation, 1963] v. 113 p. 19 cm. Bibliography: p. 111-113. [BX6.W7S5] 64-28489
1. World Conference on Faith and Order. I. Nelson, John Robert. 1920- II. Title.

WITNESSING to the kingdom : 266
Melbourne and beyond / edited by Gerald H. Anderson. Maryknoll, N.Y. : Orbis Books, 1982. p. cm. Bibliography: p. [BV2070.W57] 19 82-3530 ISBN 0-88344-708-8 pbk. : 7.95
1. World Conference on Mission and Evangelism (1980 : Melbourne, Vic.)—Addresses, essays, lectures. 2. Missions—Addresses, essays, lectures. 3. Kingdom of God—Addresses, essays, lectures. I. Anderson, Gerald H.

World conferences on church, community and state, Oxford, 1937

KELLER, Adolf, 1872- 280.631
Five minutes to twelve a spiritual interpretation of the Oxford and Edinburgh conference by Adolf Keller Nashville Cokebury press 1938 127 p. 21 cm. Bibliography: p. 123-127. [BR479.K25] 38-10436
1. World conferences on church, community and stats, Oxford, 1937. 2. World conference on faith and order. 2d, Edinburgh, 1937. 3. Christianity—20th cent. 4. Church. I. Title.

World Congress of Faiths—History.

BRAYBROOKE, Marcus. 200'.6'21
Faiths in fellowship : a short history of the World Congress of Faiths and its work / [by] Marcus Braybrooke ; with a foreword by George Appleton. London : World Congress of Faiths, [1976] [8], 39 p., [4] p. of plates : ports. ; 21 cm. Includes bibliographical references. [BL21.W55B92] 77-351239 ISBN 0-905468-00-7 : £0.50
1. World Congress of Faiths—History. I. Title.

World congress of faiths, London, 1936.

YOUNGHUSBAND, Francis Edward, Sir, 1863- 290.631
...A venture of faith, being a description of the World congress of faiths held in London, 1936. New York, E. P. Dutton & company [1937] 237 p. front., ports. 22 cm. At head of title: Sir Francis Younghusband. "First published in 1937." "Manufactured in Great Britain." [BL21.W55 1936 e] 37-27377
1. World congress of faiths, London, 1936. 2. Religions. I. Title.

World Congress on Evangelism, Berlin, 1966.

HENRY, Carl Ferdinand Howard, 1913- 269
Evangelicals at the brink of crisis; significance of the World Congress on Evangelism, by Carl F. H. Henry. Waco, Tex., Word Books [1967] 120 p. 19 cm. [BR1640.H4] 67-21104
1. World Congress on Evangelism, Berlin, 1966. 2. Evangelicalism. I. Title.

World Council of Churches.

BELL, George Kennedy Allen, Bp. of Chichester, 1883- 280.1
The kingship of Christ the story of the World Council of Churches. [Harmondsworth, Middlesex, Baltimore] Penguin Books [1954] 181p. illus. 18cm. (A Penguin special, S161) [BX6.W78B4] 55-849
1. World Council of Churches. 2. Ecumenical movement—Hist. I. Title.

BELL, George Kennedy Allen, Bp. of Chichester, 1883-1958. 262'.001
The kingship of Christ : the story of the World Council of Churches / by G. K. A. Bell. Westport, Conn. : Greenwood Press, 1979. 181 p. : graphs ; 23 cm. Reprint of the 1954 ed. published by Penguin Books, Harmondsworth, Eng. Includes bibliographical references. [BX6.W78B4 1979] 78-10482 ISBN 0-313-21121-3 lib.bdg. : 15.00
1. World Council of Churches. 2. Ecumenical movement—History. I. Title.

BOCK, Paul, 1922- 261.8
In search of a responsible world society; the social teachings of the World Council of Churches. Philadelphia, Westminster Press [1974] 251 p. 21 cm. Bibliography: p. [243]-244. [HN31.B68] 74-9986 ISBN 0-664-20708-1 10.00
1. World Council of Churches. 2. Church and social problems. I. Title.

DIRKS, Lee E. 262'.001
The ecumenical movement, by Lee E. Dirks. [1st ed. New York, Public Affairs Committee, 1969] 28 p. group ports. 19 cm. (Public affairs pamphlet no. 431) [BX8.2.D5] 79-3743 0.25
1. World Council of Churches. 2. Christian union—History. I. Title.

DUFF, Edward. 280.1
The social thought of the World Council of Churches. New York, Association Press [1956] xii, 339p. diagr. 23cm. Bibliography: p. 321-331. [BX6.W78D8] 56-10665
1. World Council of Churches. 2. Church and social problems. I. Title.

GAINES, David P. 262.001
The World Council of Churches, a study of its background and history, by David P. Gaines. [1st ed.] Peterborough, N.H., R. R. Smith [1966] xviii, 1302 p. 25 cm. Bibliography: p. 1265-1281. [BX6.W78G3] 63-17177

1. World Council of Churches.

HERKLOTS, Hugh Gerard Gibson, 1903- 280
Pilgrimage to Amsterdam [by] H.G.G. Herklots and Henry Smith Leiper. New York, Morehouse-Gorham Co., 1947. 90 p. 20 cm. A revision and enlargement of the English ed. by H.G.G. Herklots, 1947. [BX6.W78H4 1947] 48-5023
1. World Council of Churches. I. Leiper, Henry Smith, 1891 joint author. II. Title.

HOEKSTRA, Harvey Thomas, 1920- 262'.001
The World Council of Churches and the demise of evangelism / Harvey T. Hoekstra. Wheaton, Ill. : Tyndale House Publishers, c1979. 300 p. : forms ; 21 cm. Bibliography: p. 289-298. [BX6.W78H7] 78-73217 ISBN 0-8423-8525-8 pbk. : 5.95
1. World Council of Churches. 2. Missions—Theory. I. Title.

KROMMINGA, John H., 1918- 260
All one body we; the doctrine of the church in ecumenical perspective, by John H. Kromminga. Grand Rapids, Eerdmans [1970] 227 p. 22 cm. Bibliography: p. 215-222. [BV598.K77] 76-120844 3.95
1. World Council of Churches. 2. Church—History of doctrines—20th century. I. Title.

LEFEVER, Ernest W. 261.8
Amsterdam to Nairobi : the World Council of Churches and the Third World / Ernest W. Lefever ; foreword by George F. Will. Washington : Ethics and Public Policy Center, of Georgetown University. c1979. xii, 114 p. ; 23 cm. Includes bibliographical references and index. [BX6.W78L43] 79-2607 ISBN 0-89633-024-9 : 5.00
1. World Council of Churches. 2. Church and underdeveloped areas. I. Georgetown Univrsity, Washington, D.C. Ethics and Public Policy Center. II. Title.

TECHNOLOGY and social justice; an international symposium on the social and economic teaching of the World Council of Churches from Geneva 1966 to Uppsala 1968. Edited by Ronald H. Preston. [1st American ed.] Valley Forge, Judson Press [1971] xx, 472 p. 24 cm. "Sponsored by the International Humanum Foundation." Includes bibliographical references. [HN31.T4 1971] 78-152584 ISBN 0-8170-0536-6 10.95 261.8
1. World Council of Churches. 2. Church and social problems—Addresses, essays, lectures. I. Preston, Ronald H., 1913- ed. II. International Foundation Humanum.

TULGA, Chester Earl, 1896- 280
The case against the World Council of Churches. Chicago, Conservative Baptist Fellowship [1949] 61 p. 18 cm. (His Little books on big subjects) [BX6.W78T8] 50-3605
1. World Council of Churches. I. Title.

*WARNER, Hugh C., comp. 242.2
Daily readings from William Temple. Ed., abridged by William Wand. Nashville, Abingdon [1965] 189p. 18cm. (Apex Bks., V-4) 1.45 pap.,
I. Title.

World Council of Churches. 1st. Assembly, Amsterdam, 1948.

AN every place a voice.
[Cincinnati, O., Woman's Division of Christian Service, Board of Missions, The Methodist Church, 1957] iv, 121p. 19cm. 'An interpretation and a commentary on a portion of 'Message' of the Amsterdam Assembly of the World Council of Churches.' -p. iii. Includes bibliographies.
I. Muelder, Walter George, 1907-

AN every place a voice.
[Cincinnati, O., Woman's Division of Christian Service, Board of Missions, The Methodist Church, 1957] iv, 121p. 19cm. 'An interpretation and a commentary on a portion of 'Message' of the Amsterdam Assembly of the World Council of Churches.' -p. iii. Includes bibliographies.
I. Muelder, Walter George, 1907-

NORTHCOTT, William Cecil, 1902- 280
Answer from Amsterdam; Congregationalism and the world church. London, Independent Press; Boston, Pilgrim Press [1948] 63 p. 19 cm. [BX6.W78N6] 49-18559
1. World Council of Churches. 1st. Assembly, Amsterdam, 1948. 2. Congregational churches—Relations. I. Title.

WORLD Council of Chuches. 1st Assembly, Amsterdam, 1948. 280
Man's disorder and God's design. New York, Harper [1949] 5 v. in 2. 22 cm. (The Amsterdam Assembly series) Vol. 5 has special t.-p. only: The First Assembly of the World Council of Churches ... edited by W. A. Visser't Hooft. Vols. 1-4, "Written in preparation for the First Assembly of the World Council of Churches in Amsterdam, Holland, August 22nd-September 4th, 1948." Each vol. also published separately. Contents.--v. 1. The universal church in God's design.--v. 2. The church's witness to God's design.--v. 3. The church and the disorder of society.--v. 4. The Church and the international disorder. First Assembly of the World Churches message.--v. 5. The First Assembly of the World Council of Churches. The offical report. [BX6.W77 1948d] 49-7873
I. Title.

World Council of Churches. 2d Assembly, Evanston, Ill.

BOSLEY, Harold Augustus, 1907- 280.1
What did the World Council say to you? New York, Abingdon Press [1955] 127p. 20cm. [BX6.W78B6] 55-5737
1. World Council of Churches. 2d Assembly, Evanston, Ill. I. Title.

NICHOLS, James Hastings, 1915- 280.1
Evanston, an interpretation. [1st ed.] New York, Harper [1954] 155p. 20cm. [BX6.W77 1954j] 54-12332
1. World Council of Churches. 2d Assembly, Evanston, Ill. I. Title.

WORLD Council of Churches. 280.1
Six ecumenical surveys: preparatory material for the Second Assembly of the World Council of Churches, North western University, Evanston, Illinois, U. S. A., 1954. New York, Harper [1954] 1v. 21cm. [BX6.W77 1954i] 54-2808
1. World Council of Churches. 2d Assembly. Evanston, Ill., 1954 (Proposed) 2. Christianity—20th cent. I. Title. II. Title: Ecumenical surveys.

WORLD Council of Churches. 2d Assembly, Evanston, Ill., 1954. 280.1
The Evanston report, the Second Assembly of the World Council of Churches, 1954. [W. A. Visser't Hooft, editor] London, SCM Press [1955] viii, 360p. 23cm. [BX6.W77 1954] 55-3616
I. Title.

WORLD Council of Churches. 2d Assembly, Evanston, Ill., 1954. 280.1
The Evanston report, the Second Assembly of the World Council of Churches, 1954. [W. A. Visser't Hooft, editor] London, SCM Press [1955] viii, 360p. 23cm. [BX6.W77 1954] 55-3616
I. Title.

WORLD Council of Churcles. Advisory Commission on the Main Theme of the Second Assembly. 280.1
Report: Christ-- the hope of the world. New York, Harper [1954] 51p. 21cm. [BX6.W77 1954h] 54-2807
1. World Council of Churches. 2d Assembly, Evanston, Ill., 1954 (Proposed) 2. Hope. I. Title. II. Title: Christ—the hope of the world.

WORLD Council of Churcles. Advisory Commission on the Main Theme of the Second Assembly. 280.1
Report: Christ-- the hope of the world. New York, Harper [1954] 51p. 21cm. [BX6.W77 1954h] 54-2807
1. World Council of Churches. 2d Assembly, Evanston, Ill., 1954 (Proposed) 2. Hope. I. Title. II. Title: Christ—the hope of the world.

World Council of Churches. 3d Assembly, Delhi, 1961.

FLETCHER, Grace (Nies) 280.1
The whole world's in His hand. New York, Dutton [c.]1962. 219p. illus. 21cm. 62-18690 4.50
1. World Council of Churches. 3d Assembly, Delhi, 1961. 2. Christianity—20th cent. I. Title.

KENNEDY, James William, 1905- 280.1
No darkness at all; a report and study guide on the Third Assembly of the World Council of Churches. New Delhi, India, November 19-December 5, 1961. Introd. by Roswell P. Barnes. St. Louis, Bethany [c.1962] 128p. 22cm.illus. Bibl. 62-12917 1.50 pap.,
1. World Council of Churches. 3d Assembly, Delhi, 1961. I. Title.

WORLD Council of Churches. 3rd Assembly,Dehli, 1961. 280.1
The New Delhi report. New York, Association [1962] viii, 448p. 23cm. 62-51170 6.50
I. Title.

World Council of Churches, 4th Assembly, Uppsala, 1968.

GOLLWITZER, Helmut. 261.8
The rich Christians and poor Lazarus. Translated by David Cairns. [New York] Macmillan [1970] xi, 108 p. 21 cm. Translation of Die reichen Christen und der arme Lazarus. Includes bibliographical references. [BR115.P7G65513] 78-107048 1.45
1. World Council of Churches, 4th Assembly, Uppsala, 1968. 2. Christianity and politics. 3. Church and social problems. I. Title.

World Council of Churches. 5th Assembly, Nairobi, 1975.

JACKSON, Joseph Harrison, 1900- 262'.001
Nairobi—a joke, a junket, or a journey? : Reflections upon the fifth Assembly of the World Council of Churches, November 27-December 8, 1975 / by J. H. Jackson. Nashville : Townsend Press, 1976. xix, 130 p. : ill. ; 23 cm. Includes index. Bibliography: p. 125-126. [BX6.W77 1975.J3] 76-27046 5.50
1. World Council of Churches. 5th Assembly, Nairobi, 1975. I. Title.

SLACK, Kenneth. 262'.001
Nairobi narrative : the story of the Fifth Assembly of the World Council of Churches, 23 November-10 December, 1975 / [by] Kenneth Slack. London : S.C.M. Press, 1976. vi, 90 p. ; 20 cm. Includes index. Bibliography: p. 88. [BX6.W77 1975.S5] 76-370414 ISBN 0-334-01096-9 : £0.90
1. World Council of Churches. Assembly, 5th, Nairobi, 1975. I. World Council of Churches. II. Title.

World Council of Churches—Addresses, essays, lectures.

POTTER, Philip. 248.4
Life in all its fullness / Philip Potter. American ed. Grand Rapids, Mich. : W.B. Eerdmans Pub. Co., 1982, c1981. p. cm. [BV4501.2.P557 1982] 19 82-5079 5.95
1. World Council of Churches—Addresses, essays, lectures. 2. Christian life—1960- —Addresses, essays, lectures. 3. Ecumenical movement—Addresses, essays, lectures. I. Title.

RELIGIOUS liberty in the Soviet Union : WCC and USSR ; a post-Nairobi documentation / edited by Michael Bourdeaux, Hans Hebly and Eugen Voss. [Keston] : Keston College, Centre for the Study of Religion and Communism, 1976. [7], 96 p. : ill., ports. ; 30 cm. (Keston book ; no. 7) Errata slip inserted. [BR936.R46] 77-354247 £1.50 ($3.50 U.S.) 322'.1'0947
1. World Council of Churches—Addresses, essays, lectures. 2. Religious liberty—Russia—Addresses, essays, lectures. I. Bourdeaux, Michael. II. Hebly, Hans. III. Voss, Eugen.

World Council of Churches. Commission on Faith and Order.

LANGE, Ernst. 270.8'2
And yet it moves : dream and reality in the ecumenical movement / by Ernst Lange. Grand Rapids : W. B. Eerdmans Pub. Co., c1979. p. cm. Translation of Die okumenische Utopie. Contains some of the papers delivered at a conference of the Commission on Faith and Order, World Council of Churches, Louvain, 1971. [BX8.2.L28513] 78-31803 ISBN 0-8028-1790-4 pbk. : 5.95
1. World Council of Churches. Commission on Faith and Order. 2. Ecumenical movement. I. World Council of Churches. Commission on Faith and Order. II. Title.

OLD and the new in the church (The) [by] World Council of Churches Commission on Faith and Order, two interim reports. Preface by Paul S. Minear. Minneapolis, Augsburg [1962, c.1961] 91p. (Faith and order studies) 1.25 pap., 261

World Council of Churches—Controversial literature.

CHURCH League of America. Research Dept. 270.8'2
Wages of sin : the World Council of Churches unmasked : a documented report from the research staff of the Church League of America. Wheaton, Ill. : The League, c1979. 176 p. (p. 176 blank) : ill. ; 28 cm. Includes bibliographical references. [BX6.W78C45 1979] 79-55335 ISBN 0-89601-025-2 : 6.00
1. World Council of Churches—Controversial literature. I. Title.
Publisher's address: 422 N. Prospect St., Wheaton, IL 60187.

SMITH, Bernard, 1925- 262'.001
The fraudulent gospel : politics and the World Council of Churches / by Bernard Smith. Wheaton, Ill. : Church League of America, 1977. 96 p. ; 21 cm. Includes bibliographical references. [BX6.W78S64] 77-84958 ISBN 0-89601-007-4 pbk. : 2.00
1. World Council of Churches—Controversial literature. I. Title.

World Council of Churches—History—20th century—Sources.

WORLD Council of Churches. 261.8'348
World Council of Churches' statements and actions on racism, 1948-1979 / edited by Ans J. van der Bent. Geneva : Programme to Combat Racism, World Council of Churches, c1980. ix, 69 p. ; 21 cm. "A special issue of PCR information." Bibliography: p. 63-69. [BT734.2.W6 1980] 19 80-154743 ISBN 2-8254-0624-4 pbk. : 2.75
1. World Council of Churches—History—20th century—Sources. 2. Church and race relations—History—20th century—Sources. I. Van der Bent, A. J. (Ans Joachim) II. World Council of Churches. Programme to Combat Racism. III. PCR information. IV. Title.
Distributed by Friendly Press, 2744 Friendly St., Eugene, OR 97405

World history—Early works to 1800.

OROSIUS, Paulus. 937
The seven books of history against the pagans. Translated by Roy J. Deferrari. Washington, Catholic University of America Press [1964] xxi, 422 p. 22 cm. (The Fathers of the church, a new translation, v. 50) Bibliography: p. xxi. [BR60.F3O7] 64-18670
1. World history—Early works to 1800. 2. History, Ancient. I. Deferrari, Roy Joseph, 1890- tr. II. Title. III. Series.

World in the Bible—Addresses, essays, lectures.

ZIMMERLI, Walther, 1907- 221.6'6
The Old Testament and the world / Walther Zimmerli ; translated by John J. Scullion. Atlanta : John Knox Press, 1976. 172 p. ; 23 cm. Translation of Die

Weltlichkeit des alten Testaments. Includes bibliographical references and indexes. [BS1199.W74Z5513 1976] 75-32946 ISBN 0-8042-0139-0 : 8.50
1. Bible. O.T.—Theology—Addresses, essays, lectures. 2. World in the Bible—Addresses, essays, lectures. I. Title.

ZIMMERLI, Walther, 1907- 221.6
The Old Testament and the world / Walther Zimmerli ; translated [from the German] by John J. Scullion. London : S.P.C.K., 1976. vii, 172 p. ; 23 cm. Translation of Die Weltlichkeit des Alten Testaments. Includes bibliographical references and indexes. [BS1199.W74Z5513 1976b] 77-350969 ISBN 0-281-02890-7 : £4.95
1. Bible. O.T.—Theology—Addresses, essays, lectures. 2. World in the Bible—Addresses, essays, lectures. I. Title.

World Jewish Congress.

SCHWARZBART, Isaac I 296
25 years in the service of the Jewish people; a chronicle of activities of the World Jewish Congress. August 1932--February 1957. New York, World Jewish Congress, Organization Dept. [1957] 56p. 23cm. [DS101.W64S4] 57-2755
1. World Jewish Congress. I. Title.

WORLD Jewish Congress. 296
Unity in dispersion; a history of the World Jewish Congress. New York, 1948. 381 p. 24 cm. [DS101.W64A5] 48-8201
1. World Jewish Congress. I. Title.

WORLD Jewish Congress. 296
Unity in dispersion; a history of the World Jewish Congress. With a foreword by A. Leon Kubowitzki. 2nd rev. ed. New York, Institute of Jewish Affairs of the World Jewish Congress, 1948. 391 p. 24 cm. [DS101.W64A5 1948a] 49-20186
1. World Jewish Congress. I. Title.

World Methodist Council.

HOLT, Ivan Lee, Bp., 1886- 287
The World Methodist movement, by Ivan Lee Holt and Elmer T. Clark. [Nashville, The Upper Room, 1956] 148p. illus. 19cm. [BX2807.W6H6] 56-58198
1. World Methodist Council. 2. Ecumenical movement. 3. Methodist Church—Stat. I. Clark, Elmer Talmage, 1886- II. Title.

World Missionary Conference, 8th, Bangkok, Thailand, 1972-1973.

BEYERHAUS, Peter. 266'.023
Bangkok '73 : the beginning or end of world mission? / Peter Beyerhaus Grand Rapids : Zondervan Pub. House, [1974] 192 p. : ill. ; 21 cm. (Contemporary evangelical perspectives) Translation of Bangkok '73. Includes selections of the 8th World Missionary Conference, held in Bangkok under the auspices of the World Council of Churches, Dec. 29, 1972-Jan. 8, 1973. Includes bibliographical references. [BV2020.W6513 1973z] 74-4949 pbk. : 3.95
1. World Missionary Conference, 8th, Bangkok, Thailand, 1972-1973. I. World Missionary Conference, 8th, Bangkok, Thailand, 1972-1973. II. Title.

World missionary conference, Edinburgh, 1910.

GAIRDNER, William Henry 266.0631
Temple, 1873-1928.
Echoes from Edinburgh, 1910; an account and interpretation of the World missionary conference, by W. H. T. Gairdner ... With an introduction by John R. Mott, L.L. D. New York, Chicago [etc.] Fleming H. Revell company [1910] 7 p. l., 3-281 p. front., plates. 20 cm. "Author's edition." [BV2391.E3 1910 h] A 10
1. World missionary conference, Edinburgh, 1910. I. Mott, John Raleigh, 1865. II. Title.

World politics—1965—

KRAMER, Leonard J ed. 261
Man amid change in world affairs. Edited with an introd. by Leonard J. Kramer. New York, Friendship Press, 1964. 175 p. 19 cm. Bibliography: p. [171]-175. [D844.K7314] 64-22938
1. World politics — 1965- 2. Christianity and international affairs. I. Title.

KRAMER, Leonard J., ed. 261
Man amid changes in world affairs. New York, Friendship [c.]1964. 175p. 19cm. Bibl. 64-22938 1.95 pap.,
1. World politics—1965- 2. Christianity and international affairs. I. Title.

World politics—1975-1985.

KENT, Maxwell. 327'.11
The United States, world Jewry, Catholic action & power politics / Maxwell Kent. [Albuquerque, N.M.] : American Classical College Press, [1976] p. cm. Cover title. [D849.5.K46] 76-40454 ISBN 0-89266-017-1 : 35.00
1. World politics—1975-1985. 2. Religion and politics. I. Title.

World Vision, Inc.

GEHMAN, Richard 275
Let my heart be broken with the things that break the heart of God. Photos. by Richard Reinhold. Grand Rapids, Mich., Zondervan [1966, c.1960] 245p. illus. 21cm. [BV2360.W88G4] .98 pap.,
1. Pierce, Robert Willard, 1914- 2. World Vision, Inc. 3. Missions—Asia. I. Title.

GEHMAN, Richard. 275
Let my heart be broken with the things that break the heart of God. Photos. by Richard Reinhold. New York, McGraw-Hill [1960] 245 p. illus. 22 cm. [BV2360.W88G4] 60-15687
1. World Vision, inc. 2. Pierce, Robert Willard, 1914- 3. Missions—Asia. I. Title.

World war, 1939-1945—Addresses, sermons, etc.

MUCKLE, Coy, 1895- 252.6
Sermons of a transport chaplain, by Coy Muckle. Bristol, Tenn., The King printing company [1946] ix, 176 p. 19 cm. [D743.9.M72] 47-15207
1. World war, 1939-1945—Addresses, sermons, etc. 2. Sermons, American. I. Title.

World War, 1939-1945—Aerial operations.

BRADDON, Russell. 922.242
New wings for a warrior; the story of Group-Captain Leonard Cheshire, v. c., D. S. O., D. F. C. New York, Rinehart [1955, c1954] 240p. illus. 22cm. First published in London in 1954 under title: Cheshire, v. c.; a story of war and peace. [BX4705.C4636B7 1955] 55-7553
1. Cheshire, Leonard. 2. World War, 1939-1945—Aerial operations. 3. Institutional missions—Gt. Brit. I. Title.

World War, 1939-1945—Civilian relief.

TO serve the present age 266'.65
: the Brethren Service story / by M. R. Zigler and other former participants ; Donald F. Durnbaugh, editor. Elgin, Ill. : Brethren Press, [1975] 224 p. : ill. ; 22 cm. Includes index. Bibliography: p. 215-218. [BX7827.3.T6] 75-6633 ISBN 0-87178-848-9 pbk. : 4.95
1. Church of the Brethren. Brethren Service Commission. 2. Church of the Brethren—Charities. 3. World War, 1939-1945—Civilian relief. I. Zigler, M. R. II. Durnbaugh, Donald F.

World War, 1939-1945—Conscientious objectors—Great Britain.

BARKER, Rachel, 355.2'24'0941
1951-
Conscience, government, and war : conscientious objection in Great Britain, 1939-45 / Rachel Barker. London ; Boston : Routledge & Kegan Paul, 1982. p. cm. Includes index. Bibliography: p. [UB342.G7B34] 19 82-3762 ISBN 0-7100-9000-5 : 14.95
1. World War, 1939-1945—Conscientious objectors—Great Britain. 2. Military service, Compulsory—Great Britain—History—20th century. I. Title.

World War, 1939-1945—Evangelical and Reformed Church.

HAFER, Harold Franklin. 284.173
1907-
The Evangelical and Reformed Churches and World War II. [Boyertown, Pa.] Boyertown Times Pub. Co., 1947. vii, 137 p. maps, 24 cm. Added t.p. (with imprint: Philadelphia, 1947) has thesis statement of Univ. of Pennsylvania. Bibliography: p. 134-137. [D810.E9H3] 48-13662
1. World War, 1939-1945—Evangelical and Reformed Church. 2. Evangelical and Reformed Church—Hist. I. Title.

World War, 1939-1945—Jews.

LESTSCHINSKY, Jacob, 1876- 296
Balance sheet of extermination. [New York, Office of Jewish Information, 1946] 2 v. illus. 19 cm. (Jewish affairs, v. 1, no. 1, Feb. 1. 1946; v. 1. no. 12, Nov. 15, 1946) Series: Jewish affairs. New York, Office of Jewish Information. v. 1, no. 1, Feb. 1, 1946; v. 1, no. 12, Nov. 15, 1946. Cover title. "Statistics in the pamphlet are based on the research of the Institute of Jewish Affairs." [D810.J4L43] 47-15553
1. World War, 1939-1945—Jews. 2. Jews—Political and social conditions. 3. Jews in Europe. I. Institute of Jewish Affairs. II. Title. III. Series.

World War, 1939-1945 — Jews — Bibliography

BRAHAM, 016.301451'924'073
Randolph L.
The Hungarian Jewish catastrophe; a selected and annotated bibliography, by Randolph L. Braham. New York, [Yivo Institute for Jewish Research] 1962. xxv, 86 p. 28 cm. (Yad Washem Martyrs' and Heroes' Memorial Authority, Yivo Institute for Jewish Research. Joint Documentary Projects. Bibliographical series, no. 4) "A multilingual bibliography." [Z6373.H8B7] 67-4478
1. World War, 1939-1945 — Jews — Bibl. 2. Jews in Hungary — Bibl. I. Title. II. Series: Jerusalem. Yad va-shem. Mirallim meshutafim sidrah bibliyografit, 4

ROBINSON, Jacob, 016.940535693
1889-
Guide to Jewish history under Nazi impact, by Jacob Robinson and Philip Friedman with forewords by Benzion Dinur and Salo W. Baron. New York [Yivo Institute for Jewish Research] 1960. xxxi, 425p. 28cm. (Yad Washem Martyrs' and Heroes' Memorial Autbority, Jerusalem. Yivo Institute for Jewish Research, New York. Joint documentary projects. Bibliographical series, no. 1) Errata leaf laid in. [Z6207.W8R56] 61-65976
1. World War, 1939-1945—Jews—Bibl. 2. Jews in Germany—Hist.—1933- —Bibl. I. Friedman, Philip, 1901-1960, joint author. II. Title. III. Series: Jerusalem. Yad va-shem. Mif'alim Meshutaflim, sidrah bibliyografit, no. 1
Contents omitted.

ROBINSON, Jacob, 016.9143'06'924
1889-
Guide to Jewish history under Nazi impact, by Jacob Robinson and Philip Friedman. With forewords by Benzion Dinur and Salo W. Baron. [New York] Ktav Pub. House, 1973 [i.e. 1974] xxxi, 425 p. 27 cm. Reprint of the 1960 ed. published by Yivo Institute for Jewish Research, New York, which was issued as no. 1 of the Sidrah bibliyografit, mif'alim meshutafim, Yad va-shem. [Z6207.W8R56 1974] 73-16300 ISBN 0-87068-231-8 35.00
1. World War, 1939-1945—Jews—Bibliography. 2. Jews in Germany—History—1933-1945—Bibliography. I. Friedman, Philip, 1901-1960, joint author. II. Title. III. Series: Jerusalem. Yad va-shem. Mif'alim meshutafim, sidrah bibliyografit, no. 1.

World War, 1939-1945-Personal Narratives, American

MAAHS, Arnold M [266.41] 279.5
Our eyes were opened. Columbus, Ohio, Warthburg Press, 1946. 110 p. plates, maps (on lining-papers) 20 cm. [D811.M17] 48-3468
1. World War, 1939-1945 — Personal narratives, American. 2. Missions — New Guines. 3. American Lutheran Church (1930-1960) — Missions. I. Title.

MASHA, Arnold M. 279.5
Our eyes were opened. Columbus, Ohio, Wartburg Press, 1946. 110 p. plates, maps (on lining-papers) 20 cm. [D811.M17] [266.41] 48-3468
1. World War, 1918-1945—Personal narratives, American. 2. Missions—New Guinea. 3. American Lutheran Church—Missions. I. Title.

World War, 1939-1945— Personal narratives, Dutch.

VAN WOERDAN, Peter. 248
In the secret place, a story of the Dutch underground. Wheaton, Ill., Van Kampen Press [1954] 64p. 20cm. [BR1725.V3A3] 54-1749
1. World War, 1939-1945— Personal narratives, Dutch. I. Title.

World War, 1939-1945—Personal narratives, German.

GOLDMANN, Gereon Karl. 940.548243
The Shadow of his wings. Translated by Benedict Leutenegger. Chicago, Franciscan Herald Press [1964] 285 p. illus., ports. 21 cm. Autobiographical. [BX4705.G5597A3] 64-14256
1. World War, 1939-1945 — Personal narratives, German. I. Title.

HARING, 940.54'75'0924 B
Bernhard, 1912-
Embattled witness : memories of a time of war / Bernard Haring. New York : Seabury Press, c1976. p. cm. "A Crossroad book." [BX4705.H14A33] 76-13556 ISBN 0-8164-0312-0 : 6.95
1. Haring, Bernhard, 1912- 2. World War, 1939-1945—Personal narratives, German. I. Title.

World War, 1939-1945—Personal narratives, Jewish.

SCHLAMM, Vera, 248'.246'0924 B
1923-
Pursued, by Vera Schlamm as told to Bob Friedman. Glendale, Calif., G/L Regal Books [1972] 212 p. 18 cm. [D810.J4S317] 72-77800 ISBN 0-8307-0153-2 1.25
1. Schlamm, Vera, 1923- 2. World War, 1939-1945—Personal narratives, Jewish. 3. Converts from Judaism. I. Friedman, Bob. II. Title.

World War, 1939-1945—Prisoners and prisons, Russian.

CISZEK, Walter J., 271'.5'3024B
1904-
He leadeth me [by] Walter J. Ciszek, with Daniel L. Flaherty. Garden City, N.Y., Image Books 1975 [c1973] 232 p., 18 cm. [BX4705.C546A34] ISBN 0-385-02805-9 1.75 (pbk.)
1. Ciszek, Walter J., 1904- 2. World War, 1939-1945—Prisoners and prisons, Russian. 3. World War, 1939-1945—Personal narratives, American. I. Flaherty, Daniel L., joint author. II. Title.
L.C. card no. for original ed.: 73-79654.

HUNT, Ruth. 940.54'72'430924 B
East wind : the story of Maria Zeitner Linke / as written by Ruth Hunt. Grand Rapids, Mich. : Zondervan Pub. House, c1976. 240 p. : ill. ; 23 cm. [BR1725.L447H86] 76-21288 6.95
1. Linke, Maria Zeitner. 2. World War, 1939-1945—Prisoners and prisons, Russian. 3. Prisoners of war—Russia—Biography. 4. Christian biography—Germany, West. I. Title.

World War, 1939-1945—Prophecies.

LUDY, Claude Edward, 1910- 224'.5'07
The vile and the holy : a commentary on the Book of Daniel / by Claude Edward Ludy. Midland, Mich. : McKay Press ; Saginaw : distributed by Ed's Starlite Books, 1978. xiv, 100 p. : ports ; 21 cm. Includes index. Bibliography: p. 98. [BS1556.L77] 77-94874 5.00
1. Bible. O.T. Daniel—Prophecies. 2. World War, 1939-1945—Prophecies. I. Bible. O.T. Daniel. English. Revised Standard. 1978. II. Title.

World war, 1939- Catholic church.

CIANFARRA, Camille Maximilian, 1907- 940.531522
The Vatican and the war, by Camile M. Cianfarra. New York, Literary classics, inc. distributed by E. P. Dutton & company, inc., 1944. 344 p. 21 cm. "First edition." [BX1378.C5] 44-860
1. Pius xii, pope, 1876- 2. World war, 1939- Catholic church. I. Title.

World war, 1939—Jews.

AMERICAN Jewish committee. Research institute on peace and post-war problems. 296
... Governments-in-exile on Jewish rights ... New York, N.Y., The American Jewish committee, 1942. 64 p. 23 cm. (Its Pahphlet series: Jews and the post-war world, ed. by A. G. Duker. No. 8) At head of title: Research institute on peace and post-war problems. [D810.J4A53] 42-25460
1. World war, 1939—Jews. 2. World war, 1939—Governments in exile. 3. Jews in Europe. I. Title.

World war, 1939—Religious aspects.

ANDERSON, Edwin Raymond. 248
A spiritual defense program, by Edwin Raymond Anderson. Grand Rapids, Mich., Zondervan publishing house [1942] 3 p. l., 9-30 p. 20 cm. [D744.4.A5] 42-18920
1. World war, 1939—Religious aspects. I. Title.

LEBER,Charles Tudor, 1898- 261
The church must win! The place, power and promise of the Christian church in the conflict of our time, by Charles Tudor Leber. New York, London [etc.] Fleming H. Revell company [1944] 185 p. 19 cm. "References suggesting a bibliography": p. 182-185. [D744.4.L4] 44-6262
1. World war, 1939—Religious aspects. 2. Reconstruction (1939-) I. Title.

WINROD, Gerald Burton. 264.1
A prayer to almighty God in time of war, by Rev. Gerald B. Winrod, D. D. Wichita, Kans., Defender publishers [c1941] 1 p. l., [5]-65, [1] p. illus. (port.) 20 cm. "First edition." [D744.4.W5] 42-19292
1. World war, 1939—Religious aspects. 2. Prayer. 3. U. S.—Religion. 4. Bible—Prophecies. I. Title.
Contents omitted.

World wide revival prayer movement.

[WOODS, Grace Winona (Kemp)] 1871- 269
Lest we forget. Atlantic City, N.J., The World wide revival prayer movement [c1942] 64 p. 18 1/2 cm. [BV3770.W57] 43-47166
1. World wide revival prayer movement. I. Title.

WOODS, Grace Winona (Kemp) "Henry M. Woods," Mrs., 1871- 269
Revival in romance and realism, by Mrs. Henry M. Woods, founder of the World-wide revival prayer movement. New York [etc.] Fleming H. Revell company [c1936] 1 p. l., 7-228 p. front., plates, ports. 19 1/2 cm. [BV3770.W58] 37-614
1. World wide revival prayer movement. I. Title.

[WOODS, Henry McKee] 1857- comp. 269
By way of remembrance. Atlantic City, N.J., The World wide revival prayer movement; London [etc.] Marshall, Morgan & Scott, ltd. [1933] 4 p. l., 11-110 p. 18 1/2 cm. Signed: H. M. and G. W. Woods. "Printed in Great Britain." A collection of letters written to encourage the World wide revival prayer movement, previously published semi-annually. cf. 3d prelim. leaf. [BV3770.W585] 38-18170
1. World wide revival prayer movement. I. Woods, Grace Winona (Kemp) "Mrs. Henry M. Woods," 1871- joint comp. II. Title.

World's Columbian Catholic Congress, Chicago, 1893.

WORLD'S Columbian Catholic Congress, Chicago, 1893. 261.8'3
The world's Columbian Catholic congresses. New York : Arno Press, 1978 [c1893] 107 42 p. : ill. ; 24 cm. (The American Catholic tradition) Reprint of v. 1 and 3 of the ed. published by J. S. Hyland, Chicago [HN37.C3W57 1893] 77-11323 ISBN 0-405-10871-0 : 10.00
1. World's Columbian Catholic Congress, Chicago, 1893. 2. Church and social problems—Catholic Church. I. Title. II. Series.

World's parliament of religions, Chicago, 1896.

BARROWS, John Henry, 1847-1902, ed. 206.
The World's parliament of religions; an illustrated and popular story of the World's first parliament of religions, held in Chicago in connection with the Columbian exposition of 1893. Ed. by the Rev. John Henry Barrows ... Chicago, The Parliament publishing company, 1893. 2 v. fronts., illus. (incl. ports.) 23 cm. Paged continuously. [BL21.W8B3] 3-31806
1. World's parliament of religions, Chicago, 1896. 2. Religions—Addresses, essays, lectures. I. Title.

World's student Christian federation.

MOTT, John Raleigh, 1865-
Strategic points in the world's conquest; the universities and colleges as related to the progress of Christianity, by John R. Mott. With map of his journey. New York, Chicago [etc.] Fleming H. Revell company [1897] 218 p. fold. map. 19 cm. [LC351.W88M8] [BV976.W8M6] E 10
1. World's student Christian federation. 2. Universities and colleges—Religion. 3. Missions, Foreign. I. Title.

World's Young Women's Christian Association.

RICE, Anna Virena, 1880- 267.59
A history of the World's Young Women's Christian Association. New York, Woman's Press [1948, c1947] 299 p. ports. 24 cm. Includes "References." [BV1340.W6R5] 48-1143
1. World's Young Women's Christian Association. I. Title.

WOODSMALL, Ruth Frances. 267.598
The Y.W.C.A. in Latin America, by Ruth F. Woodsmall ... Geneva, Switzerland, Washington, D.C., World's Young women's Christian association [1943?] 52 p. 20 1/2 cm. [BV1360.L3W6] 43-15044
1. World's Young women's Christian association. I. Title.

Worldwide Church of God.

HOPKINS, Joseph Martin, 1919- 289.9
The Armstrong empire; a look at the Worldwide Church of God. [Grand Rapids] Eerdmans [1974] 304 p. map. 21 cm. Bibliography: p. 286-291. [BR1725.A77H66] 74-8255 3.95
1. Worldwide Church of God. 2. Armstrong, Herbert W. 3. Armstrong, Garner Ted. I. Title.

Worldwide Evangelisation Crusade.

GRUBB, Norman Percy, 1895- 922
After C. T. Studd. [North American ed.] Grand Rapids, Zondervan Pub. House [1946] 185 p. illus., ports., maps. 20 cm. [BV3705.S78G68 1946] 47-4693
1. Studd, Charles Thomas, 1860-1931. 2. Worldwide Evangelization Crusade. I. Title.

Worms, Diet of, 1521.

ATKINSON, James, 1914- 270.6'0924
The trial of Luther. New York, Stein and Day [1971] 212 p. illus., facsims., ports. 23 cm. (Historic trials series) Bibliography: p. [203] [BR326.5.A8] 72-104626 ISBN 0-8128-1361-8 7.95
1. Luther, Martin, 1483-1546. 2. Worms, Diet of, 1521. I. Title.

WENTZ, Abdel Ross, 1883-
When two worlds met; "the Diet at Worms, 1521", by Abdel Ross Wentz... Philadelphia, The United Lutheran publication house [c1921] 73 p. front. 19 cm. [BR353.W4] 21-8185
1. Worms, Diet of, 1521. I. Title.

Worrall, Olga Nathalie Ripich, 1906-

CERUTTI, Edwina. 133.9'092'4 B
Olga Worrall : mystic with the healing hands / Edwina Cerutti. 1st ed. New York : Harper & Row, [1975] 169 p. ; 21 cm. [BF1027.W65C47 1975] 75-9317 ISBN 0-06-061358-0 : 7.95
1. Worrall, Olga Nathalie Ripich, 1906-

Worship.

ALLEN, J. P., 1912- 264
Reality in worship [by] J. P. Allen. Nashville, Convention Press [1955] xii, 115 p. 20 cm. [BV10.2.A35] 65-10323
1. Worship. I. Title.

ALLISON, Christopher Fitz Simmons, 1927- 241
Fear, love, and worship New York, Seabury, [1965,c1962] 144p. 21 cm. (SP17) [BV10.2.A4] 62-7473 1.45pap.,
1. Worship. 2. Fear. I. Title.

ALLISON, Christopher FitzSimons, 1927- 241
Fear, love, and worship. Greenwich, Conn., Seabury Press [1962] 143p. 20cm. [BV10.2.A4] 62-7473
1. Worship. 2. Fear. I. Title.

ALLMEN, Jean Jacques von 264
Worship, its theology and practice. New York, Oxford [c.]1965. 317p. 23cm. Bibl. [BV10.2.A44] 65-23571 6.50
1. Worship. I. Title.

ALLMEN, Jean Jacques von. 264
Worship, its theology and practice, by J. J. von Allmen. New York. Oxford University Press, 1965. 317 p. 23 cm. Bibliography: p. 315-317. [BV10.2.A44] 65-23571
1. Worship. I. Title.

ARMES, Woodson, 1912- 264
What is worship? [By] Woodson and Sybil Armes. Nashville, Convention Press [c1965] x, 68 p. 19 cm. [BV10.2.A7] 65-10322
1. Worship. I. Armes, Sybil (Leonard) joint author. II. Title.

BAYNE, Stephen Fielding, Bp., 1908- 264
Enter with joy. Greenwich, Conn., Seabury Press, 1961. 139p. 22cm. [BV10.2.B35] 61-14368
1. Worship. 2. Preaching. I. Title.

A book of common worship; prepared under direction of the New York State conference of religion, by a committee on the possibilities of common worship. New York and London, G. P. Putnam's sons, 1900. xiv, 418 p. 16°. 1-29646

BOWMAN, Clarice Marguerette, 1910- 242
Resources for worship. New York, Association Press [1961] 383p. 20cm. Includes bibliography. [BV10.2.B65] 61-8181
1. Worship. 2. Prayers. I. Title.

BOWMAN, Clarice Margurette, 1910- 264
The living art of worship. New York, Association Press [c.1964] 126p. 15cm. (Reflection bk.) An adaptation of [the author's] Resources for worship, containing part one of that book and special new material. 64-11421 .50 pap.,
1. Worship. I. Title.

BOWMAN, Clarice Margurette, 1910- 264
Restoring worship. New York, Abingdon-Cokesbury Press [1951] 223 p. 21 cm. [BV10.B6] 51-1341
1. Worship. I. Title.

BOWMAN, Clarice Margurette, 1910-
When I worship, by Clarice M. Bowman. Ray L. Henthorne, George S. Caroland, youth editors. Teacher's ed. St. Louis, Christian Board of Publication [c1957] 128 p. (Bethany graded youth books, v. 9, pt. 2; teacher's ed.) 68-77336
1. Worship. 2. Religious education—Textbooks for young people. I. Henthorne, Raymond Leasington, 1913- II. Caroland, George S. III. Title. IV. Series.

BRADLEY, Dwight. 264
Creative worship, by Dwight Bradley ... New York, N. Y., The Commission on evangelism and devotional life of the National council of the Congregational churches [c1931] 3 p. l., 74 p. 19 cm. [BV10.B7] 32-1471
1. Worship. I. Congregational churches in the U. S. National council. Commission on evangelism and devotional life. II. Title.

BRAND, Eugene, 1931- 264
The rite thing. Minneapolis, Augsburg Pub. House [1970] 119 p. 20 cm. (A Tower book) Bibliography: p. 119. [BV10.2.B67] 74-101106
1. Worship. I. Title.

BREWSTER, Edward T.
Scripture responses for worship; arranged from the authorized version... With an introduction by...J. Pearson... Dayton, Ohio, Union pub. co. (1898) 158 pp. 12 cm. cop. c-305
I. Title.

BRUNNER, Peter, 1900- 264
Worship in the name of Jesus; English edition of a definitive work on Christian worship in the congregation. Translated by M. H. Bertram. St. Louis, Concordia Pub. House [1968] 375 p. 24 cm. Translation of Zur Lehre vom Gottesdienst der im Namen Jesu versammelten Gemeinde, first published in 1954 in v. 1 of Leiturgia, edited by K. F. Muller. Bibliographical references included in "Notes" (p. 313-357) [BV10.2.B753] 68-30965 9.75
1. Worship. I. Title.

BYINGTON, Edwin Hallock, 1861- 264
The quest for experience in worship, by Edwin H. Byington ... Garden City, N. Y., Doubleday, Doran & company, inc., 1929. xii, 211 p. 20 cm. [BV10.B95] 29-11900
1. Worship. I. Title.

CAMPBELL, Edward Fay, 1894- 264
To glorify God; worship at the heart of the world community, by E. Fay Campbell, James H. Nichols, and James P. Alter, edited by Mabel H. Erdman. New York, Association press, Fleming H. Revell company, 1943. iv p., 1 l., 63 p. 19 1/2 cm. (On cover: The Pioneering church series) [BV10.C33] 44-221
1. Worship. 2. Prayer. I. Nichols, James Hastings, 1915- joint author. II. Alter, James Payne, joint author. III. Erdman, Mabel H., ed. IV. Title.

CHAMPLIN, Joseph M. 264.02
Christ present and yet to come; the priest and God's people at prayer [by] Joseph M. Champlin. Maryknoll, N.Y., Orbis Books [1971] xiii, 242 p. 21 cm. Includes bibliographical references. [BX1969.C52] 70-151180 2.50
1. Catholic Church—Ceremonies and practices. 2. Worship. I. Title.

CHICAGO. Third Unitarian church.
Church worship: in readings, songs and prayers. Chicago, Ill., Third church publishing committee, 1892. 96 p. 24 1/2 cm. Includes music. [BX9853.C5] 44-24099
I. Unitarian churches. Liturgy and ritual. II. Title.

CHRISTENSEN, James L. 264
Don't waste your time in worship / James L. Christensen. Old Tappan, N.J. : F. H. Revell Co., c1978. 127 p. ; 22 cm. [BV10.2.C44] 78-533 ISBN 0-8007-0921-7 : 5.95
1. Worship. I. Title.

CHRISTIAN worship by families; a booklet for the family. St. Louis, The Bethany Press [1957] 56p. 22cm.
I. Lentz, Richard E

CHRISTIAN worship; 264
ten lectures delivered in the Union theological seminary, New York, in the autumn of 1896, by Charles Cuthbert Hall, D.D.; Alexander V.G. Allen, D.D.; Egbert S. Smyth, D.D.; Charles C. Tiffany, D.D.; Henry Eyster Jacobs ... William Rupp, D.D.; William R. Huntington, D.D.; Allan Pollok, D.D.; George Dana Boardman ... Thomas S. Hastings ... New York, C. Scribner's sons, 1897. Chicago, Ill., The Joint committee on united youth program [1936] viii, 333 p. 18 1/2 cm. 63 p. 19 1/2 cm. [BV10.C5] 4-4639
1. Worship. 2. Liturgies. 3. Youth—Religious life. I. New York. Union theological seminary. II. Hall, Charles Cuthbert, 1852-1908. III. Christian youth conference of North America, Lakeside O., 1936. IV. Title: Report of the Christian youth conference of North America,

CHURCH of South India. 264.032
Liturgy and ritual. Book of common worship.
The book of common worship, as authorised by the synod, 1962. New York, Oxford [1964, c.]1963. xxvi, 213p. 18cm. At head of title: The Church of South India. 64-3981 1.55
I. Title.

CHURCH of South India. 264.032
Liturgy and ritual. Book of common worship.
The book of common worship, as authorised by the synod, 1962. London, New York, Oxford University Press, 1963 [i. e. 1964] Supplement, as authorised by the synod. [Madras] Published for the Church of South India by the Indian Branch, Oxford University Press, 1964- [BX5671.I55A38] 64-3981
I. Title.

CHURCH of South India. 264.032
Liturgy and ritual. Book of common worship.
The book of common worship, as authorized by the synod, 1962. London, New York, Oxford University Press, 1963 [i.e. 1964] xxvi, 213 p. 18 cm. At head of title: The Church of South India. [BX5671.I55A38] 64-3981
I. Title.

CLAPP, Mary Constance. 264
The golden quest of worship. [1st ed.] New York, Vantage Press [1957] 106p. 21cm. [BV15.C55] 57-8550
1. Worship. I. Title.

CULLEY, Iris V 264
Christian worship and church education, by Iris V. Cully. Philadelphia, Westminister Press [1967] 187 p. 21 cm. Bibliography: p. [177]-184. [BV10.2.C8] 67-20614
1. Worship. 2. Worship (Religious education) I. Title.

DAVIES, Horton. 264
Christian worship, its history and meaning. New York, Abingdon Press [1957] 128p. 21cm. Includes bibliography. [BV10.D37] 57-9784
1. Worship. I. Title.

DAVIES, Horton.
Christian worship, its making and meaning; [revised edition] Wallingford, Surrey, The Religious Education Press, Ltd. [1957] 122p. 19cm. (The Pathfinder Series)
I. Title.

DAVIS, Henry Grady 248.3
Why we worship. Philadelphia, Muhlenberg Press [c.1961] 54p. (Fortress bk.) 61-13582 1.00 bds.,
1. Worship. I. Title.

DE BARY, Richard.
The mystical personality of the church. A study in the original realism of Christ's religion, by Richard De Bary ... London, New York [etc.] Longmans, Green, and co., 1913. xxiii, 88 p. 19 cm. A 14
1. Jesus Christ—Person and offices. 2. Worship. I. Title.

DEVAN, Samuel Arthur, 1887- 264
Ascent to Zion, by S. Arthur Devan; illustrations by George F. Ketcham, jr. ... New York, The Macmillan company, 1942. xiv, 251 p. illus. 21 cm. "First printing." "Useful modern books on worship": p. 243-247. [BV10.D43] 42-22603
1. Worship. 2. Public worship. 3. Art and religion. 4. Church music—Hist. & crit. 5. Worship (Religious education) I. Title.

DUFFY, Regis A. 234'.16
Real presence : worship, sacraments, and commitment / Regis A. Duffy. 1st ed. San Francisco : Harper & Row, c1982. xiv, 206 p. ; 21 cm. Includes bibliographical references and index. [BX1969.D77 1982] 19 81-47877 ISBN 0-06-062105-2 : 8.61
1. Worship. 2. Sacraments—Catholic Church. 3. Christian life—Catholic authors. I. Title.

DUN, Angus, Bp., 1892- 264
Not by bread alone. [1st ed.] New York, Harper [1942] vii, 148 p. 20 cm. (The Presiding Bishop's book for Lent, 1942) [BV10.D8] 42-3776
1. Worship. I. Title. II. Series.

DUN, Angus, 1892- 264
Not by bread alone; the Presiding bishop's book for Lent, 1942 [by] Angus Dun. New York and London, Harper & brothers [c1942] vii p., 2 l., 148 p. 20 cm. "First edition." [BV10.D8] 42-3776
1. Worship. I. Title. II. Title: The Presiding bishop's book for Lent.

EAST Boston. Maverick
Congregational church.
Condensed history and manual of Maverick Congregational church, East Boston, Mass., from its organization, May 31st, 1836 to June 30th, 1894. [Boston] Maverick Congregational church, 1894. 8 p. l., 227 p. incl. front., ports. 20 1/2 cm. 16-7465
I. Title.

ELFORD, Homer J. R. 264
A layman's guide to Protestant worship. Nashville, Abingdon [c.1963] 64p. 17cm. .75 pap.,
I. Title.

EVANS, George, 1866- 264
The true spirit of worship, by George Evans ... Chicago, The Bible institute colportage association [c1941] 160 p. 19 1/2 cm. [BV10.E9] 41-21848
1. Worship. I. Bible institute colportage association, Chicago. II. Title.

FITCH, Florence Mary, 1875- 264
One God; the ways we worship Him, by Florence Mary Fitch; photographs chosen by Beatrice Creighton. New York, N.Y., Lothrop, Lee, & Shepard co. [1944] xi, [1], 13-144 p. illus. 25 cm. [BL550.F5] 44-47761
1. Worship. I. Title.

GALUSHA, Elinor G. 268'.61
Lift up your hearts; a resource and discussion book for youth. Elinor G. Galusha, editor. Boston, United Church Press [1968] 76 p. illus. 22 cm. (Confirmation education series) "Part of the United Church curriculum, prepared and published by the Division of Christian Education and the Division of Publication of the United Church Board for Homeland Ministries." Includes unacc. melodies with words. [BX9884.A3G3] 68-10313
1. Worship. 2. Religious education—Text-books for young people—United Church of Christ. I. United Church Board for Homeland Ministries. Division of Christian Education. II. United Church Board for Homeland Ministries. Division of Publication. III. Title.

GALUSHA, Elinor G. 268'.61
Lift up your hearts; a resource and discussion book for youth. Elinor G. Galusha, editor. [Rev. ed. New York] Herder and Herder [1968] 73 p. illus. 22 cm. (Christian commitment series) [BV10.2.G33 1968b] 68-29891 1.20
1. Worship. 2. Religious education—Text-books for young people. I. Title.

GOLD, William Jason, 1845- 264
1903.
Sacrificial worship: i. in Genesis and Exodus; ii. in the Temple; iii. in the New Testament and the Christian church, By Wm. J. Gold, S. T. D. New York, London and Bombay, Longmans, Green, and co., 1903. xiv, 112 p. front. (port.) 20 cm. [BV10.G6] 3-5153
1. Worship. 2. Sacrifice. 3. Monument. I. Title.

GUNNEMANN, Louis H. 264
The life of worship; an adult resource book [by] Louis H. Gunnemann. Boston. United Church Pr. [1966] 76p. illus. 21cm. Bibl. [BV10.2.G78] 66-12054 price unreported pap.,
1. Worship. 2. Religious education—Text-books for adults—United Church of Christ. I. Title.

HAHN, Wilhelm Traugott 264
Worship and congregation. Tr. [from German] by Geoffrey Buswell. Richmond, Va., Knox [1963] 75p. 22cm. (Ecumenical studies in worship, no. 12) Bibl. 63-8699 1.75 pap.,
1. Worship. I. Title. II. Series.

HARDMAN, Oscar, 1880- 264.009
A history of Christian worship, by Oscar Hardman... Nashville, Tenn., Cokesbury press [c1937] 263 p. 20 1/2 cm. (Half-title: The London theological library, under the editorship of Professor Eric S. Waterhouse) "A suggested library of twenty books for further study": p. 255. [BV5.H3] 37-15182
1. Worship. 2. Liturgies. 3. Lord's supper (Liturgy) I. Title.

HARTSHORNE, Hugh, 1885- 268
Worship in the Sunday school; a study in the theory and practice of worship, by Hugh Hartshorne ... New York city, Teachers college, Columbia university, 1913. vii p., 1 l., 210 p. 20 cm. Published also as thesis (PH. D.) Columbia university, 1913. Bibliography: p. 204-210. [BV1520.H36] 13-19012 1.50
1. Worship. 2. Sunday-schools. I. Title.

HATCH, Verena 264.093'3
Ursenbach.
Worship in the Church of Jesus Christ of Latter-Day Saints. [Provo, Utah, M. E. Hatch, 1968] xiv, 119 p. 26 cm. Includes bibliographical references. [BX8651.H38] 68-56831
1. Church of Jesus Christ of Latter-Day Saints. 2. Worship I. Title.

HAYMAN, Eric. 264
Worship & the common life, by Eric Hayman ... Cambridge [eng.] The University press, 1944. viii, 155, [1] p. 19 1/2 cm. Bibliographical foot-notes. [BV10.H35] 44-6019
1. Worship. I. Title.

HEDLEY, George Percy, 1899- 264
Christina worship, some meanings and means. New York, Macmillan, 1953. 306p. illus. 22cm. [BV10.H37] 53.13152
1. Worship. I. Title.

HERBERT, A S 296.4
Worship in ancient Israel. Richmond, John Knox Press [1959] 51p. 22cm. (Ecumenical studies in worship, no. 5) [BM658.H4] 59-8911
1. Worship. 2. Cultus, Jewish. I. Title.

HORTON, Douglas, 1891- 264
The meaning of worship. New York, Harper [1959] 152p. 20cm. (The Lyman Beecher lectures for 1958) [BV10.2.H6] 59-7151
1. Worship. I. Title.

HOW to plan informal worship. 264
New York, Association Press [1955] 64p. 20cm. (Leadership library) [BV259] 55-7407
1. Worship. 2. Worship programs. I. Wygal, Winnifred, 1884-

HULL, Eleanor (Means)
Let us worship God, by Eleanor Hull, Elinor G. Galusha and Sarah D. Schear. Illustrations by Shirley Hirsch. Boston, United Church Press [1964] 76 p. illus. 22 cm. 65-106502
1. Worship. I. Title.

JONES, Charlotte Chambers. 268.7
Junior worship guide, of special value to schools using the Church school closely graded courses; a bird's-eye view of the three junior courses, their objectives, activities, memory work and related worship materials as suggested in the pupil's and teacher's textbooks; with sample worship services indicating how these materials may be used in departmental worship programs ... prepared by Charlotte Chambers Jones. Boston, Chicago, The Pilgrim press [c1930] xvi, 280 p. 21 cm. [BV1522.J6] 30-10515
1. Worship. 2. Sunday-schools. I. Title.

JOYCE, J. Daniel. 265
The place of the sacraments in worship [by] J. Daniel Joyce. St. Louis, Bethany Press [1967] 159 p. 23 cm. Bibliography: p. 157-159. [BV10.2.J65] 67-27122
1. Worship. 2. Sacraments. I. Title.

KAY, J Alan. 264
The nature of Christian worship. New York, Philosophical Library [1954] 115p. 20cm. [BV10.K3] 54-2129
1. Worship. I. Title.

KEISER, Armilda Brome. 264
Come everyone and worship, by Armilda Brome Keiser. New York, Friendship press [c1941] 95, [1] p. incl. front., illus. 21 x 16 cm. [BV10.K4] 41-19443
1. Worship. I. Title.

KELLOGG, Caroline. 268.432
Forty-eight primary worship services; programs with songs, scriptures, stories and things to do, by Caroline Kellogg ... Cincinnati, O., The Standard publishing company [c1932] 208 p. illus. 22 cm. Music: p. 202-208. [BV1541.K35] 32-4874
1. Worship. 2. Sunday-schools. I. Title. II. Title: Primary worship services.

LOCKHART, William S. 264
The ministry of worship; a study of the need, psychology and technique of worship, by W. S. Lockhart ... St. Louis, Mo., Christian board of publication, 1927. 212 p. 1 illus. 20 cm. Bibliography: p. 209-212. [BV10.L6] 27-18906
1. Worship. 2. Disciples of Christ. I. Title.

MACARTHUR, Robert Stuart 1841-
The people's worship, and psalter. A complete order of service for the morning and evening worship of Christian congregations. Prepared by the Rev. Robert S. MacArthur and the Rev. Francis Bellamy ... Boston, Silver, Burdett & company, 1891. 127 p. 20 1/2 cm. 3-22866
I. Title.

MAGSAM, Charles M 264.02
The inner life of worship. St. Meinrad, Ind., Grail Publications [1958] 323p. 22cm. [BV10.M29] 58-4739
1. Worship. I. Title.

MATTOON, Laura I., ed.
Services for the open, arranged by Laura I. Mattoon and Helen D. Bragdon. New York, London, D. Appleton-Century company, incorporated, 1938. 2 p. l., vii-xxi, [3], 3-212 p. illus. 21 cm. "Hymns and songs" (with music): p. 135-212. A 41
1. Worship. 2. Public worship. I. Bragdon, Helen Dalton, 1895- joint ed. II. Title.

MAXWELL, William Delbert.
Concerning worship. London, Oxford University Press [1949] ix, 153 p. 19 cm. Bibliographical footnotes. A 52
1. Worship. I. Title.

MELAND, Bernard Eugene, 1899- 264
Modern man's worship; a search for reality in religion, by Bernard Eugene Meland ... New York and London, Harper & brothers, 1934. xix p., 2 l., 3-317 p. front., illus., plates, port., diagrs. 22 cm. "First edition." [BV10.M3] 34-37259
1. Worship. 2. Psychology, Religious. 3. Public worship. I. Title.

MICKS, Marianne H. 264
The future present; the phenomenon of Christian worship. New York, Seabury Press [1974, c1970] xiv, 204 p. 21 cm. (A Crossroad book) Includes bibliographical references. [BV10.2.M5] 75-103844 ISBN 0-8164-2109-9. 3.95 (pbk.)
1. Worship. I. Title.

MUDGE, Lewis W[ard] comp.
Carmina for social worship. New York, A.

S. Barnes & co., 1898. [240], viii, iii p. obl. 16 degree. Issued also under title "Carmina for the Sunday school." Dec
I. Turner, Herbert Barclay, 1852, joint comp. II. Title.

MUDGE, Lewis Ward, comp.
Carmina for the Sunday school. New ed. New York, A. S. Barnes & co., 1898. [240], viii, iii p. obl. 16 degree. Issued also under the title "Carmina for social worship." Dec
I. Turner, Herbert Barclay, 1852- joint comp. II. Title.

NICHOLLS, William. 264
Jacob's ladder: the meaning of worship. Richmond, John Knox Press [1958] 72p. 22cm. (Ecumenical studies in worship, no.4) [BV10.2.N5] 58-12804
1. Worship. I. Title.

PANIKKAR, Raymond, 1918- 217
Worship and secular man; an essay on the liturgical nature of man, considering secularization as a major phenomenon of our time and worship as an apparent fact of all times. A study towards an integral anthropology, by Raimundo Pannikkar. Maryknoll, N.Y., Orbis Books [1973] 109 p. 20 cm. Bibliography: p. 94-109. [BL550.P27] 72-93339 3.95
1. Worship. 2. Secularism. I. Title.

PAQUIER, Richard. 264
Dynamics of worship; foundations and uses of liturgy. Translated by Donald Macleod. Philadelphia, Fortress Press [1967] xix, 224 p. 23 cm. Translation of Traite de liturgique. Bibliographical footnotes. [BV10.2.P313] 67-19040
1. Worship. I. Title.

PARKER, Fitzgerald Sale, 1863- 264
The practice and experience of Christian worship; a study of Biblical and ecclesiastical worship practice with especial reference to the origin and development of the worship service of Episcopal Methodism, by Fitzgerald Sale Parker ... Nashville, Tenn., Cokesbury press, 1929. 272 p. 20 cm. (The Quillian lectures for 1929) [BV10.P25] 29-12223
1. Worship. I. Title.

PEARCE, J. Winston 264
Come, let us worship. Nashville, Broadman [c.1965] 127p. 20cm. Bibl. [BV10.2.P4] 65-11765 1.50 bds.,
1. Worship. I. Title.

PHIFER, Kenneth G. 264
A Protestant case for liturgical renewal. Philadelphia. Westminster [1965] 175p. 21cm. Bibl. [BV10.2.P5] 65-13493 3.95
1. Worship. 2. Liturgical movement—Protestant churches. I. Title.

PRESBYTERIAN church in the U. S. A. General assembly. 264.05
The book of common worship, prepared by the committee of the General assembly of the Presbyterian church in the United States of America. For voluntary use. Philadelphia, The Presbyterian board of publication and Sabbath-school work, 1906. x, 263, [1] p. 15 cm. Henry Van Dyke, chairman of the assembly's committee. cf. Pref., p. vi. [BX9185.A4 1906 a] 6-23081
I. Presbyterian church in the U. S. A. Liturgy and ritual. II. Van Dyke, Henry, 1852- III. Title.

PRESBYTERIAN church in the U. S. A. General assembly. 264.05
The book of common worship (revised) Approved by the General assembly of the Presbyterian church in the United States of America; for voluntary use. Philadelphia, Presbyterian board of Christian education, 1932. x, 353 p. 18 cm. Henry Van Dyke, chairman of the assembly committee. cf. Pref., p. vi-v. "A list of sources of prayers": p. [339]-353. [BX9185.A4 1932] 32-12000
I. Presbyterian church in the U. S. A. Liturgy and ritual. II. Van Dyke, Henry, 1852- III. Title.

PRESBYTERIAN church in the U.S.A. Liturgy and ritual. 264.05
The book of common worship, approved by the General assembly of the Presbyterian church in the United States of America. Philadelphia, Pub. for the office of the General assembly by the Publication division of the Board of Christian education of the Presbyterian church in the United States of America [1946] 1 p. l., v-xv, 388 p. 17 cm. Text on p. [2] and [3] of cover. "The General assembly of 1941 designated The book of common worship as an official publication ... and lodged its supervision in the office of the General assembly ... It authorized the appointment of a committee to act in collaboration with the stated clerk."--Pref. [BX9185.A4 1946] 46-16610
I. Presbyterian church in the U.S.A. General assembly. Special committee on The book of common worship. II. Title.

REAGIN, Ewell Kerr, 1900- 264
Principles of personal worship, by Ewell K. Reagin ... Nashville, Tenn., Cumberland Presbyterian publishing house, 1938. 187, [1] p. 18 cm. "List of quotations and references": p. 173-175; "Helpful books for general study": p. 175-177; "Helpful books on worship": p. 177-178. [BV10.R4] 39-31933
1. Worship. I. Title.

REX, Ruth Irwin, Mrs. 268.7
We worship; services of worship for the small church school, by Ruth Irwin Rex. New York, London, The Century co. [c1930] viii p., 2 l., 3-335 p. 19 1/2 cm. Music: p. 295-315. [BV1522.R4] 30-14584
1. Worship. 2. Sunday-schools. I. Title.

RICHTER, Dolle. 268.432
Primaries at worship, by Dolle Richter and Barbara Wade. Cincinnati, Standard Pub. Foundation, c1956. 128p. illus. 20cm. (Religious education) [BV1522.R52] 56-41916
1. Worship. I. Wade, Barbara, joint author. II. Title.

ROSS, George Alexander Johnston, 1865- 264
... Christian worship and its future; five lectures delivered at Ohio Wesleyan university, by G. A. Johnston Ross. New York, Cincinnati, The Abingdon press [c1927] 110 p. 20 cm. (The Merrick lectures for 1926) [BV10.R6] 27-18918
1. Worship. I. Title.

SCHALM, Bernard 264
The church at worship. Grand Rapids, Mich., Baker Bk. [c.]1962. 108p. 20cm. [Minister's handbk. ser.] 62-12671 1.95 bds.,
1. Worship. I. Title.

SCHROEDER, Frederick W. 264
Worship in the reformed tradition. Philadelphia, United Church Pr. [c.1966] 157p. 21cm Bibl. [BV10.2.S37] 66-16194 3.50
1. Worship. I. Title.

SEGLER, Franklin M. 264
Christian worship, its theology and practice [by] Franklin M. Segler. Nashville, Broadman Press [1967] viii, 245 p. 22 cm. Bibliography: p. 221-237. [BV10.2.S4] 67-22034
1. Worship. 2. Public worship. I. Title.

SELWYN, Edward Gordon, 1885- 264
Thoughts on worship & prayer, by Edward Gordon Selwyn... London, Society for promoting Christian knowledge; New York, The Macmillan company [1936] viii, 113, [1] p. 10 cm. "The greater part of this book consists of four lectures delivered by those attending the vacation term for Biblical study in August 1939 under the title 'Communion with God in the worship of the community and of the individual'."--Pref. "First published, 1936." [BV10.S43] 36-37280
1. Worship. 2. Prayer. I. Society for promoting Christian knowledge, London. II. Title.

SHAFER, Floyd Doud. 264.05131
Liturgy; worship and work. Philadelphia, Board of Christian Education, United Presbyterian Church U.S.A. [1966] xii, [1], 109 p. 19 cm. Bibliography: p. [xiii] [BV10.2.S48] 66-31857
1. Presbyterian Church. Liturgy and ritual. 2. Worship. I. Title.

SKOGLUND, John E 264
Worship in the free churches [by] John E. Skoglund. Valley Forge [Pa.] Judson Press [1965] 151 p. illus. 21 cm. [BV176.S56] 65-21999
1. Worship. 2. Liturgical movement—Protestant churches. I. Title. II. Title: Free churches.

SKOGLUND, John R. 264
Worship in the free churches. Valley Forge [Pa.] Judson [c.1965] 151p. illus. 21cm. [BV176.S56] 65-21999 3.95
1. Worship. 2. Liturgical movement—Protestant churches. I. Title. II. Title: Free churches.

STANFIELD, Vernon L 264
The Christian worshiping [by] V. L. Stanfield. Nashville, Convention Press [1965] ix, 110 p. 19 cm. Bibliography: p. 99-101. [BV10.2.S7] 65-10324
1. Worship. I. Title.

SWANK, Calvin P. 264
A catechism in Christian worship, by Calvin P. Swank ... Philadelphia, Pa., The United Lutheran publication house [c1927] 80 p. 19 1/2 cm. [BV10.S85] 28-4796
1. Worship. 2. United Lutheran church in America. I. Title. II. Title: Christian worship.

UNDERHILL, Evelyn, 1875-- 264
Worship, by Evelyn Underhill ... [New York and London] Harper & brothers, 1937. xxi 350 p. 22 1/2 cm. (Half-title: The library of conservative theology editors: W. R. Matthews, H. W. W. Robinson) "First edition." [BV10.U5 1937] 37-27129
1. Worship I. Title.

UNDERHILL, Evelyn, 1875-1941. 264
Worship. [1st Harper torchbook ed.] New York, Harper [1957, c1936] 350p. 21cm. (Harper torchbooks, TB 10) [BV10.U5 1957] 57-3832
1. Worship. I. Title.

UNDERHILL, Evelyn, 1875-1941. 264
Worship / by Evelyn Underhill. Westport, Conn. : Hyperion Press, 1979. p. cm. Reprint of the 1937 ed. published by Harper, New York, in series: The library of constructive theology. [BV10.U5 1979] 78-20499 ISBN 0-88355-874-2 : 25.00
1. Worship. I. Title. II. Series: The Library of constructive theology.

UNDERHILL, Evelyn, 1875-1941. 248.3
Worship / Evelyn Underhill. New York : Crossroad, 1982, c1936. xxi, 350 p. ; 23 cm. Reprint. Originally published: London : Nisbet, 1936. (The Library of constructive theology) Includes bibliographical references and indexes. [BV10.U5 1982] 19 81-70888 ISBN 0-8245-0466-6 (pbk.) : 12.95
1. Worship. 2. Public worship. 3. Liturgics. I. Title.

UNDERHILL, Francis Lees, bp. of Bath and Wells, 1878- 264
The revival of worship; a primary visitation charge to the clergy and church wardens of the diocese of Bath and Wells, by the Right Rev. Francis Underhill, D.D., bishop of Bath and Wells. London and Oxford, A. R. Mowbray & co., ltd.; New York and Milwaukee, Morehouse-Gorham co. [1938] 56 p. 1 l. 21 1/2 cm. "First published in 1938." [BV15.U5] 42-45525
1. Worship. 2. Church of England—Pastoral letters and charges. I. Title.

UNITED Presbyterian Church in the U.S.A. General Assembly.
The book of common worship: provisional services and lectionary for the christian year. Philadelphia, Westminster, 1966. 157 p. 22 cm. 68-108023
I. Title.

VERKUYL, Gerrit, 1872- 264
Adolescent worship, with emphasis on senior age, by Gerrit Verkuyl ... New York, Chicago [etc.] Fleming H. Revell company [c1929] 203 p. 19 1/2 cm. "References" at end of each chapter. [BV10.V35] 29-18754
1. Worship. 2. Adolescence. I. Title.

VERKUYL, Gerrit, 1872- 264
Devotional leadership; private preparation for public worship, by Gerrit Verkuyl ... New York, Chicago [etc.] Fleming H. Revell company [c1925] 160 p. 19 1/2 cm. "[Suggestions] for reading" at end of each chapter. [BV10.V4] 25-9318
1. Worship. I. Title.

VOGT, Von Ogden, 1879- 264
Modern worship, by Von Ogden Vogt. New Haven, Yale university press; London, H. Milford, Oxford university press, 1927. 7 p. l., [3]-153 p. 21 cm. "Four of the chapters ... are the Lowell institute lectures for 1927." [BV10.V6] 27-22858
1. Worship. I. Lowell institute lectures, 1927. II. Title.

VOGT, Von Ogden, 1879- 264
The primacy of worship. Boston, Starr King Press [1958] 175 p. 21 cm. [BV20.V6] 58-6337
1. Worship. 2. Creeds — Subscription. I. Title.

WHEATLEY, Melvin E. 248.4
The power of worship, by Melvin E. Wheatley, Jr. New York, World Pub. Co. [1970] 61 p. 22 cm. (World inspirational books) [BV10.2.W447] 75-131563 2.95
1. Worship. I. Title.

WHITE, James F. 264
The worldliness of worship [by] James F. White. New York, Oxford Univ. Pr., 1967. vii, 181p. 21cm. Bibl. [BV10.2.W45] 67-15136 5.00
1. Worship. I. Title.

WINWARD, Stephen F. 264
The reformation of our worship. Richmond, Va., John Knox [1965] ix, 126p. 22cm. Bibl. [BV10.2.W5] 65-12647 1.75 pap.,
1. Worship. I. Title.

WORLD Council of Churches. Commission on Faith and Order. Commission on Ways of Worship. 264
Ways of worship; the report of a theological commission of faith and order. Edited by Pehr Edwall, Eric Hayman [and] William D. Maxwell. New York, Harper [1951] 362 p. 23 cm. [BV10.W583 1951a] 52-8671
1. Worship. 2. Sacraments. 3. Devotion. I. Edwall, Pehr, ed. II. Title.

ZIEGLER, Edward Krusen, 1903- 264
Rural people at worship, by Edward Krusen Ziegler. New York, N.Y., Agricultural missions, inc., 1943. xvii, 118 p. 19 1/2 cm. Includes music. "Worship materials and programs collected from the rural areas of the world."--Pref. "Companion volume to his ... A book of worship ... 1939 and ... Country altars ... 1942."--Publisher's note. [BV25.Z52] 44-4540
1. Worship. 2. Liturgies. 3. Rural churches. I. Agricultural missions, inc., New York. II. Title.

ZIEGLER, Edward Krusen, 1908- 264
A book of worship for village churches, by Edward K. Ziegler...with a foreword by Bishop J. Waskom Pickett... New York, N.Y., Agricultural missions foundation, inc., 1939. 1 p. l., 130 p. 19 1/2 cm. Bibliography: p. 129-130. [RV25.Z5] 40-5745
1. Worship. 2. Liturgies. 3. Rural churches—India. 4. Missions—India. I. Title. II. Title: Village churches. A book of worship for.

Worship—Addresses, essays, lectures.

BLOY, Myron B. 264
Multi-media worship; a model and nine viewpoints. Edited by Myron B. Bloy, Jr. New York, Seabury Press [1969] 144 p. illus. 21 cm. (An Original Seabury paperback SP61) [BV10.2.B57] 78-92204 2.95
1. Worship—Addresses, essays, lectures. 2. Lord's Supper (Liturgy) 3. Youth—Religious life. I. Title.

BROWN, Leslie Abp 1912- 264.0081
Relevant liturgy. New York, Oxford [c.] 1965. vi, 86p. 19cm. (Zabriskie lects., 1964) Bibl. [BV10.2.B7] 65-17432 1.50 pap.,
1. Worship—Addresses, essays, lectures. 2. Liturgical movement—Anglican Communion. I. Title. II. Series.

BROWN, Leslie Wilfrid, Abp. 1912- 264.0081
Relevant liturgy [by] L. W. Brown, Archbishop of Uganda and Rwanda-Urundi. New York, Oxford University Press, 1965. vi, 86 p. 19 cm. (Zabriskie

lectures, 1964) Bibliographical footnotes. [BV10.2.B7] 65-17432
1. Worship — Addresses, essays, lectures. 2. Liturgical movement — Anglican Communion. I. Title. II. Series.

CHRISTIANS worship, 217
edited by Oscar E. Feucht. Saint Louis, Concordia Pub. House [1971] 146 p. illus. 21 cm. (The Discipleship series) Includes bibliographies. [BV10.2.C45] 76-161192 ISBN 0-570-06308-6
1. Worship—Addresses, essays, lectures. I. Feucht, Oscar E., ed.

HERRLIN, Olle. 264
Divine service; liturgy in perspective, by Olof Herrlin. Translated by Gene J. Lund. Philadelphia, Fortress Press [1966] 162 p. 21 cm. Translation of Liturgiska perspektiv. Bibliographical references included in "Notes" (p. [155] -- 162) [BV10.2.H4713] 66-10936
1. Worship — Addresses, essays, lectures. I. Title.

JOINT Liturgical Group 264
The renewal of worship: essays by members of the Joint Liturgical Group. Ed. by Ronald C. D. Jasper. New York. Oxford [c.] 1965. viii, 102p. 19cm. Bibl. [BV10.2.J6] 66-575 1.55 pap.,
1. Worship—Addresses, essays, lectures. I. Jasper, Ronald Claud Dudley, ed. II. Title.

JOINT Liturgical Group. 264
The renewal of worship; essays by members of the Joint Liturgical Group. Edited by Ronald C. D. Jasper. London, New York, Oxford University Press, 1965. viii, 102 p. 19 cm. Contents.The renewal of worship: introduction, by R. C. D. Jasper.--The church at worship, by R. D. Whitehorn.--Liturgy and unity, by J. A. Lamb.--Embodied worship, by S. F. Winward.--Prayer: fixed, free, and extemporary, by J. Huxtable.--Private devotion, by R. E. Davies.--Liturgy and the mission of the church, by R. A. Davies. Bibliographical footnotes. [BV10.2.J6] 66-575
1. Worship—Addresses, essays, lectures. I. Jasper, Ronald Claud Dudley, ed. II. Title.

TAYLOR, Michael J., comp. 264
Liturgical renewal in the Christian churches, ed. by Michael J. Taylor. Baltimore, Helicon [1967] 223p. 21cm. Bibl. [BV10.2T35] 67-13794 5.95 bds.,
1. Worship—Addresses, essays, lectures. 2. Liturgical movement—Addresses, essays, lectures. I. Title.
Contents omitted. Distributed by Taplinger, New York.

Worship and History

WORLD Council of Churches. 264.1
Commission on Faith and Order. Theological Commission on Worship. North American Section.
Worship in Scripture and tradition; essays by members of the Theological Commission on Worship (North American Section) of the Commission on Faith and Order of the World Council of Churches. Ed. by Massey H. Shepherd, Jr. New York, Oxford [c.] 1963 x, 178p. 21cm. Bibl. 63-19947 4.50 bds.,
1. Worship & Hist. I. Shepherd, Massey Hamilton, 1913- ed. II. Title.

Worship—Biblical teaching.

LIND, Millard, 1918- 264
Biblical foundations for Christian worship, by Millard C. Lind. Scottdale, Pa., Herald Press, 1973. 61 p. 18 cm. Based on a paper presented at the 1969 Mennonite General Conference. Includes bibliographical references. [BS680.W78L55] 72-7620 ISBN 0-8361-1701-8 0.95 (pbk.)
1. Worship—Biblical teaching. I. Title.

Worship—Comparative studies.

HILLIARD, Frederick 291.3
Hadaway.
How men worship, by F. H. Hilliard. New York, Roy Publishers [1965] ix, 184 p. illus., map. 20 cm. [BL550.H5] 66-10772
1. Worship—Comparative studies. I. Title.

MARSHALL, Romey P. 264
Liturgy and Christian unity [by] Romey P. Marshall, Michael J. Taylor. Englewood Cliffs, N.J., Prentice [c.1965] vi, 186p. 21cm. Bibl. [BV10.2.M3] 65-17534 4.95 bds.,
1. Worship—Comparative studies. 2. Catholic Church—Relations—Protestant churches. 3. Protestant churches—Relations—Catholic Church. 4. Christian union. 5. Liturgical movement. I. Taylor, Michael J. II. Title.

Worship—Dictionaries.

DAVIES, John Gordon, 264.003
1919-
A select liturgical lexicon. Richmond, Va., Knox [1966, c.1965] (Ecumenical studies in worship, no. 14) 146p. 22cm. [BV173.D3] 66-10406 2.45
1. Worship—Dictionaries. 2. Liturgies—Dictionaries. I. Title.

PODHRADSKY, Gerhard. 264'.003
New dictionary of the liturgy. Pref. by Joseph Jungmann. Foreword by Clifford Howell. English ed. edited by Lancelot Sheppard. [Original text translated by Ronald Walls and Michael Barry] Staten Island, N.Y., Alba House [1967, c1966] 208 p. illus. 24 cm. Enlarged translation of Lexikon der Liturgie. Bibliography: p. 205-208. [BV173.P613 1967] 67-5547
1. Catholic Church. Liturgy and ritual—Dictionaries. 2. Worship—Dictionaries. I. Title.

Worship—Early church.

CULLMANN, Oscar.
Early Christian worship. Translated by A. Stewart Todd and James B. Torrance. Chicago, Regnery, 1953. 124p. 21cm. (Studies in Biblical theology, no. 10) 'A translation of the second edition of Urchristeutum und Gottesdienst ... and contains also an extra chapter on 'Jesus and the day of rest' from the French translation of part 2. which appeared under the title Les sacrements dans Pevangile Johannique' Bibliographical footnotes. A55
1. Sabbath. 2. Worship—Early church. 3. Bible. N. T. John—Commentaries. I. Title. II. Series.

DELLING, Gerhard 264.009
Worship in the New Testament. Tr. by Percy Scott. Philadelphia, Westminster [c.1962] 191p. Bibl. 62-7733 4.75
1. Worship—Early church. 2. Bible. N.T.—Theology. I. Title.

HAHN, Ferdinand, 1926- 264'.01'1
The worship of the early church. Translated by David E. Green. Edited, with an introd., by John Reumann. Philadelphia, Fortress Press [1973] xxvi, 118 p. 18 cm. Translation of Der urchristliche Gottesdienst. Includes bibliographical references. [BV6.H2713] 72-87063 ISBN 0-8006-0127-0 3.25
1. Worship—Early church. I. Title.

MOULE, Charles Francis 264.01
Digby
Worship in the New Testament. [church] Richmond, Va., JohnKnox [1962] 87p. (Ecumenical studies in worship, no. 9) Bibl. 62-7174 1.75 pap.,
1. Worship—Early church. I. Title.

NIELEN, Josef Maria. 264.01
The earliest Christian liturgy, by Rev. Josef Maria Nielen;translated by Rev. Patrick Cummins ... St. Louis, Mo. and London, B. Herder book co., 1941. x, 416 p. fold. tab. 21 cm. Translation of Gebet und Gottesdienst im Neuen Testament. Bibliographical foot-notes. [BV6.N52] 41-3972
1. Worship—Early church. 2. Liturgies, Early Christian. 3. Prayer—Hist. 4. Bible. N. T.—Rites and ceremonies. 5. Bible—Rites and ceremonies—N. T. I. Cummins, Patrick, 1880- tr. II. Title.

Worship—History

BAILEY, Charles James Nice. 217
Two contemporary theologies of worship: Masure and Barth; a study in comparative dogmatics. Nashville, 1963. vii, 136 l. 28 cm. Bibliography: leaves 131-136. [BV8.B3] 63-25852
1. Worship—Hist. I. Masure, Eugene, 1882- II. Barth, Karl, 1886- III. Title.

BAILEY, Charles James Nice. 217
Two contemporary theologies of worship: Masure and Barth; an ecumenical study in comparative dogmatics [by Charles-James N. Bailey] Rev. ed. Ann Arbor, Mich., University Microfilms, 1965. xi, 165 p. (on double leaves) 22 cm. Bibliography: p. [155]-165. [BV8.B3] 65-2237
1. Worship—Hist. I. Masure, Eugene, 1882- II. Barth, Karl, 1886- III. Title.

COKE, Paul T., 1933- 264'.009'01
Mountain and wilderness : prayer and worship is the Biblical world and early church / Paul T. Coke. New York : Seabury Press, 1978. vii, 146 p. ; 21 cm. "A Crossroad book." Includes bibliographical references. [BL550.C64] 77-16154 ISBN 0-8164-2177-3 pbk. : 3.95
1. Worship—History. 2. Prayer—History. I. Title.

GWYNNE, Walker, 1845-1931. 264.
Primitive worship & the prayer book, rationale, history and doctrine of the English, Irish, Scottish and American books, by The Rev. Walker Gwynne... New York [etc.] Longmans, Green and co., 1917. xxvi, 424 p. front. (plan) 21 cm. [BX5145.G9] 17-151575
I. Title.

KALB, Friedrich. 264.041
Theology of worship in 17th-century Lutheranism. Translated by Henry P. A. Hamann. Saint Louis, Concordia Pub. House [1965] xiii, 192 p. 24 cm. Bibliography: p. 189-192. [BX8067.A1K33] 65-15934
1. Worship — Hist. 2. Lutheran Church. Liturgy and ritual — Hist. I. Title.

MITCHELL, Leonel Lake, 264'.009
1930-
The meaning of ritual / by Leonel L. Mitchell. New York : Paulist Press, c1977. xvi, 139 p. ; 19 cm. (A Deus book) Includes bibliographical references. [BV5.M57] 77-78215 ISBN 0-8091-2035-6 pbk. : 2.45
1. Worship—History. 2. Ritual—History. I. Title.

NICHOLS, James Hastings, 264.04'2
1915-
Corporate worship in the reformed tradition. Philadelphia, Westminster Press [1968] 190 p. 21 cm. Bibliographical references included in "Notes" (p. 177-182) [BX9427.N5] 68-13957
1. Reformed Church. Liturgy and ritual—History. 2. Worship—History. I. Title.

SPIELMANN, Richard M. 264.009
History of Christian worship [by] Richard M. Spielmann. New York, Seabury [1966] ix, 182p. 22cm. Bibl [BV5.S6] 66-22994 4.95
1. Worship—Hist. I. Title.

Worship—History—Early church, ca. 30-600.

CULLMANN, Oscar. 264'.009
Early Christian worship / Oscar Cullmann ; [translation by A. Stewart Todd and James B. Torrance.] Philadelphia : Westminster Press, [1978] c1953. 126 p. ; 22 cm. "A translation of the second edition of Urchristentum und Gottesdienst ... and contains also an extra chapter on 'Jesus and the day of rest' from the French translation of Part 2, which appeared under the title Les Sacrements dans l'evangile Johannique." Includes bibliographical references and index. [BV6.C8413 1978] 78-6636 ISBN 0-664-24220-0 pbk. : 4.45
1. Bible. N.T. John—Criticism, interpretation, etc. 2. Worship—History—Early church, ca. 30-600. 3. Sabbath. 4. Sacraments—Biblical teaching. I. Cullmann, Oscar. Les sacrements dans l'Evangile johannique. English. 1978. II. Title.

MARTIN, Ralph P. 264'.01'1
Worship in the early church / by Ralph P. Martin. [Rev. ed.] Grand Rapids : Eerdmans, 1974, 1975 printing, c1964. 144 p. ; 22 cm. Includes bibliographical references and index. [BV6.M37 1975] 75-14079 ISBN 0-8028-1613-4 pbk. : 3.45
1. Worship—History—Early church, ca. 30-600. I. Title.

Worship in the Bible.

HARAN, Menahem. 296.6'7
Temples and temple-service in ancient Israel : an inquiry into the character of cult phenomena and the historical setting of the priestly school / by Menahem Haran. Oxford [Eng.] : Clarendon Press, 1977. xviii, 394 p. ; 23 cm. Includes bibliographical references and indexes. [BM656.H28] 77-30069 ISBN 0-19-826318-X : 42.50
1. Jerusalem. Temple. 2. Worship in the Bible. 3. Priests, Jewish. 4. Levites. 5. P document (Biblical criticism) 6. Temples—Palestine. I. Title.

SEISS, Joseph 222'.13064
Augustus, 1823-1904.
Gospel in Leviticus / by Joseph A. Seiss. Grand Rapids, Mich. : Kregel Publications, [1981] p. cm. Reprint. Originally published: Philadelphia : Lindsay & Blakiston, 1860. [BS1255.S4 1981] 19 80-8078 ISBN 0-8254-3743-1 : 10.95
1. Bible. O.T. Leviticus—Criticism, interpretation, etc. 2. Bible. N.T.—Relation to the Old Testament. 3. Worship in the Bible. 4. Typology (Theology) I. Title.

Worship (Islam)

GHAZZALI, 1058-1111. 297'.43
Worship in Islam : being a translation with commentary and introduction of al-Ghazzal's Book of the ihya' on the worship / by Edwin Elliot Calverley. Westport, CT : Hyperion Press, 1980. p. cm. Translation of Kitab asrar al-salah wa-muhimmatiha which forms the 4th book of the 1st "quarter" of the author's Ihya' 'ulum al-din. Reprint of the 1925 ed. published by Christian Literature Society for India, Madras. Originally presented as the editor's thesis, Hartford Seminary Foundation. Includes index. Bibliography: p. [BP184.3.G513 1981] 19 79-2860 ISBN 0-8305-0032-4 : 21.50
1. Worship (Islam) I. Calverley, Edwin Elliot, 1882- II. Title.

Worship (Judaism)

HARRELSON, Walter J. 296.4
From fertility cult to worship [by] Walter Harrelson. [1st ed.] Garden City, N.Y., Doubleday, 1969. xv, 171 p. 22 cm. Six of the eight chapters included were presented as the Haskell lectures at the Graduate School of Theology, Oberlin College, in 1965. Bibliography: p. [157]-163. [BM656.H3] 66-14929 4.95
1. Worship (Judaism) I. Title.

KADUSHIN, Max, 1895- 296.4
Worship and ethics, a study in rabbinic Judaism. [Evanston, Ill.] Northwestern University Press, 1964 [c1963] x, 329 p. 23 cm. Bibliographical references included in "Notes" (p. 239-305) [BM656.K3] 63-10586
1. Worship (Judaism) 2. Jewish way of life. I. Title.

KADUSHIN, Max, 1895- 296.4
Worship and ethics : a study in rabbinic Judaism / Max Kadushin. Westport, Conn. : Greenwood Press, 1978, c1963. x, 329 p. ; 22 cm. Reprint of the ed. pubished by Northwestern University Press, Evanston, Ill. Includes bibliographical references and index. [BM656.K3 1978] 77-18849 ISBN 0-313-20217-6 lib.bdg. : 19.75
1. Worship (Judaism) 2. Jewish way of life. 3. Rabbinical literature—History and criticism. I. Title.

KRAUS, Hans Joachim 296.4
Worship in Israel: a cultic history of the Old Testament Tr. [from German]4 by Geoffrey Buswell. Richmond. Va., Knox [c.1966] xi, 246p. 23cm. Bibl. [BM656.K713] 65-16432 6.00
1. Worship (Judaism) I. Title.

KRAUS, Hans Joachim. 296.4
Worship in Israel: a cultic history of the Old Testament: translated [from the revised German ed.] by Geoffrey Buswell.

Oxford, Blackwell, 1966. xi, 246 p. 23 cm. (B66-9307) Originally published as Gottesdienst in Israel. Munich, Kaiser Verlag, 1962. [BM656.K713] 66-72621
1. Worship (Judaism) I. Title.

KRAUS, Hans Joachim. 296.4
Worship in Israel; a cultic history of the Old Testament. Translated by Geoffrey Buswell. Richmond, John Knox Press [1966] xi, 246 p. 23 cm. Bibliographical footnotes. [BM656.K713] 65-16432
1. Worship (Judaism) I. Title.

ROWLEY, Harold Henry, 1890- 296.4
Worship in ancient Israel: its forms and meaning, by H. H. Rowley: Edward Cadbury Lectures delivered in the University of Birmingham. London, S. P. C. K., 1967. xv, 307 p. tables, 22 1/2 cm. (Edward Cadbury lectures, 1966) 42/- Bibliogrpahical footnotes. [BM656.R6] 67-93885
1. Worship (Judaism) 2. Cultus, Jewish — Hist. I. Title.

ROWLEY, Harold Henry, 1890- 296.4
Worship in ancient Israel; its forms and meaning, by H. H. Rowley. [American ed.] Philadelphia, Fortress Press [1967] xv, 307 p. 23 cm. (Edward Cadbury lectures 1965) Bibliographical footnotes. [BM656.R6 1967] 67-13036
1. Worship (Judaism) 2. Cultus, Jewish—History. I. Title. II. Series.

Worship—Lutheran church.

*WEAVER, J. Bruce 284.1
Belonging to the people of God; a handbook for church members. Frank W. Klos, ed. Philadelphia, Lutheran Church Pr. [1966] 191p. illus. (pt. col.) (LCA Sch. of religion ser.) price unreported pap.,
1. Worship—Lutheran church. I. Title.

Worship programs.

"ABOUT to come forth" 264'.093'3 : sesquicentennial program for women, 1830-1980. Independence, Mo. : Herald Pub. House, c1979. 103 p. : ill. ; 28 cm. [BX8675.A23] 79-20484 ISBN 0-8309-0263-5 pbk. : 3.00
1. Worship programs. 2. Mormons and Mormonism—History—Miscellanea.

ALEXANDER, Mary Anna. 264
Begin with these; programs for worship and work [by] Mary Anna Alexander and Beverly Norman. Nashville, Broadman Press [1958] 135p. illus. 21cm. [BV198.A4] [BV198.A4] 268.7 58-8921 58-8921
1. Worship programs. I. Norman, Beverly, joint author. II. Title.

AMMERMAN, Leila Tremaine. 268.434
Inspiring develotional programs for women's groups. Natick, Mass., W. A. Wilde Co. [1960] 62p. 20cm. [BV199.W6A6] 60-15264
1. Worship programs. 2. Woman—Religious life. I. Title.

AMMERMAN, Leila Tremaine 268.434
Inspiring devotional programs for women's groups. Natick, Mass., W. A. Wilde Co. [c.1960] 62p. 20cm. 60-15264 1.95 bds.,
1. Worship programs. 2. Woman—Religious life. I. Title.

APPLEGARTH, Margaret Tyson, 268.7 1886-
Right here, right now ! [1st ed.] New York, Harper [1950] vii, 269 p. 22 cm. [BV198.A63] 50-9843
1. Worship programs. I. Title.

BAILEY, James Martin, 1929- 264.1
Worship with youth [by] J. Martin & Betty Jane Bailey. Philadelphia. Christian Education [dist. United Church, c.1962] 247p. 21cm. Bibl. 62-12679 3.95
1. Worship programs. 2. Public worship. 3. Young people's meetings (Church work) I. Bailey, Betty Jane, joint author. II. Title.

BARCLAY, William 242.63
Epilogues and prayers [Nashville] Abingdon [1964, c.1963] 227p. 23cm. 64-10678 3.25
1. Worship programs. I. Title.

BARCLAY, William lecturer 242.63 in the University of Glasgow
Epilogues and prayers. New York, Abingdon Press [1964, c1963] 227 p. 23 cm. [BV29.B33] 64-10678
1. Worship programs. I. Title.

BAYS, Alice (Anderson) 268.7 1892-
Worship programs for juniors [by] Alice Anderson Bays and Elizabeth Jones Oakberg. New York, Abingdon Press [1960] 206p. 21cm. Includes bibliography. [BV1522.B29] 60-12065
1. Worship programs. 2. Worship (Religious education) I. Oakberg, Elizabeth Jones, joint author. II. Title.

BAYS, Alice (Anderson) 268.7 1892-
Worship services for life planning. Nashville, Abingdon-Cokesbury Press [c1958] 256p. 21cm. [BV29.B355] 52-11311
1. Worship programs. 2. Young people's meetings (Church work) I. Title.

BAYS, Alice (Anderson) 268.7 1892-
Worship services for purposeful living. New York, Abingdon-Cokesbury Press [1949] 256 p. 21 cm. "Selcted bibliography": p. 251-254. [BV198.B3] 49-48227
1. Worship programs. I. Title.

BELL, Arthur Donald. 264
Worship programs [by] A. Donald Bell. Grand Rapids, Mich., Zondervan Pub. House [1971] 63 p. 21 cm. [BV198.B43] 78-146562
1. Worship programs.

BERG, Mary Kirkpatrick. 268.
More primary worship programs, by Mary Kirkpatrick Berg ... Garden City, N. Y., Doubleday, Doran company, inc., 1928. xxi p., 1 l., 182 p. front., plates. 20 cm. [BV1545.B46] 28-23818
I. Title.

BONTRAGER, John Kenneth 242
Sea rations. Nashville, Upper Room [c.1964] 88p. illus. 19cm. 64-14855 .50 pap.,
1. Worship programs. I. Title.

BREAD for the journey : 264 resources for worhsip / edited by Ruth C. Duck. New York : Pilgrim Press, c1981. 96 p. ; 23 cm. Includes bibliographical references. [BV198.B68] 19 81-5046 ISBN 0-8298-0423-4 (pbk.) : 3.95
1. Worship programs. I. Duck, Ruth C., 1947-

BRILLHART, Florence C 264
Together we praise Him group worship for women. [Westwood, N. J.] Revell [c1956] 144p. 21cm. [BV199.W6B7] 56-5238
1. Worship programs. I. Title.

BRILLHART, Florence C 268.76
Worshiping with women of the Bible a book of devotions. [Westwood, N. J.] Revell [1958] 150p. 21cm. [BV199.W6B72] 58-5341
1. Worship programs. 2. Women in the Bible. I. Title.

BROWN, John, 1934- 264'.7
New ways in worship for youth. Valley Forge [Pa.] Judson Press [1969] 224 p. illus. 27 cm. [BV29.B73] 68-20435 3.75
1. Worship programs. 2. Young people's meetings (Church work) I. Title.

BROWN, John, 1934- 264
Worship celebrations for youth / John Brown. Valley Forge, PA : Judson Press, c1980. 224 p. ; 28 cm. Includes bibliographical references. [BV29.B74] 79-20738 ISBN 0-8170-0866-7 : 7.95
1. Worship programs. I. Title.

BRYANT, Al, 1926- ed. 264
Encyclopedia of devotional programs for women's groups. Grand Rapids, Zondervan Pub. House [1956] 224p. 23cm: [BV199.W6B73] 268.7 56-25037
1. Worship programs. 2. Woman — Religious life. I. Title.

BRYANT, Al [Thomas Alton 268.7 Bryant] 1926- ed.
Encyclopedia of devotional programs for women's groups, no. 2. Grand Rapids, Mich., Zondervan [c.1961] 224p. 1.95 pap.,
1. Worship programs. 2. Woman—Religious life I. Title.

CHAPMAN, June R. 268.432
Primary worship programs. Grand Rapids, Mich., Zondervan [c.1962] 64p. 21cm. 1.00 pap.,
I. Title.

CHRISTENSEN, James L. 264
Contemporary worship services; a sourcebook [by] James L. Christensen. Old Tappan, N.J., Revell [1971] 256 p. 21 cm. Bibliography: p. 239-241. [BV198.C53] 75-137445 ISBN 0-8007-0432-0 5.95
1. Worship programs. I. Title.

CHRISTENSEN, James L. 264
Creative ways to worship [by] James L. Christensen. Old Tappan, N.J., F. H. Revell Co. [1974] 256 p. 21 cm. Includes bibliographical references. [BV198.C534] 74-3210 ISBN 0-8007-0651-X 5.95
1. Worship programs. I. Title.

CHRISTENSEN, James L. 264
The minister's church, home, and community services handbook / James L. Christensen. Old Tappan, N.J. : Revell, c1980. 192 p. ; 17 cm. Includes bibliographical references and index. [BV198.C538] 80-16857 ISBN 0-8007-1128-9 : 7.95
1. Worship programs. 2. Occasional services. I. Title.

CHRISTENSEN, James L. 264
New ways to worship; more contemporary worship services. Old Tappan, N.J., Revell [1973] 224 p. 21 cm. Bibliography: p. 217-219. [BV198.C54] 73-933 ISBN 0-8007-0583-1 5.95
1. Worship programs. I. Title.

COME, let us adore Him; 264 a book of worship services. [Westwood, N. J.] Revell [c1956] 159 p. 21 cm. [BV198.E53] [BV198.E53] 268.7 56-5239 56-5239
1. Worship programs. I. Ely, Virginia, 1899-

COOK, Virginia D. 264
Guideposts for worship. St. Louis, Bethany [c.1964] 136p. illus. 23cm. 64-12011 3.00
1. WWorship programs. I. Title.

COON, Zula Evelyn. 268.73
O worship the King; services in song. Nashville, Broadman Press [1951] 237 p. 23 cm. [BV198.C83] 51-6898
1. Worship programs. I. Title.

COUCH, Helen F., ed. 264
Worship sourcebook for youth [by] Helen F. Couch, Sam S. Barefield. Nashville, Abingdon [c.1962] 304p. Bibl. 62-8104 4.50
1. Worship programs. I. Barefield, Sam S., joint ed. II. Title.

DEVAN, S Arthur. 264
A church service book, prepared for use in public worship by S. Arthur Devan ... New York, The Macmillan company, 1924. xiii, 181 p. 18 cm. [BV198.D4] 24-7541
I. Title.

ENGSTROM, Theodore Wilhelm 268.7
Fifty-two workable junior high programs, by Ted W. Engstrom and Warren W. Wiersbe, Grand Rapids, Mich., Zondervan Pub. House. [c.1960] 116p. 20cm. 2.00 bds.,
1. Worship programs. 2. Young people's meetings (Church work) I. Title.

ENGSTROM, Theodore Wilhelm, 268.7 1916-
52 workable young people's programs. Grand Rapids, Zondervan [1950] 177 p. 20 cm. [BV29.E5] 51-16
1. Worship programs. 2. Young people's meetings (church work) I. Title.

[FLAGG, Samuel Benjamin] 1828-1900, comp.
Church service: an order for morning and evening worship. Boston, Wright & Potter, printers, 1866. 108 p. 18 1/2 cm. Compiled for the use of the First parish (Unitarian) Waltham, Mass., by its pastor Rev. S. B. Flagg. 4-13368
I. Waltham, Mass. First parish. II. Title.

[FLAGG, Samuel Benjamin] 1828-1900, comp.
Church service; an order for morning and evening worship. Boston, Wright & Potter, printers, 1866. 168 p. 18 1/2 cm. Compiled for the use of the First parish (Unitarian) Waltham, Mass., by its pastor, Rev. S. B. Flagg. [BX9853.F6] 4-13368
1. Unitarian churches. Liturgy and ritual. II. Waltham, Mass. First parish (Unitarian) III. Title.

FULTON, Mary Beth. 264
Moments of worship; resources for personal and group worship. Philadelphia, Judson Press [1953] 130p. illus. 21cm. [BV198.F8] [BV198.F8] 268.7 53-7614 53-7614
1. Worship programs. I. Title.

GUDNASON, Kay. 264
Complete worship services for the college age; in which David speaks to youth from the Psalms. Introd. by Eugenia Price. Grand Rapids, Zondervan Pub. House [1956] 153p. 21cm. [BV29.G8] 268.7 56-42839
1. Worship programs. 2. Young people's meetings (Church work) I. Title.

HALL, Donald E 1923- 268.7
Tested youth programs; 52 different young people's programs. Grand Rapids, Zondervan Pub. House [c1958] 121p. illus. 20cm. [BV29.H32] 59-29219
1. Worship programs. 2. Young peoples' meetings (Church work) I. Title.

HERSEY, Norman L. 264
Worship services for special occasions. Compiled and edited by Norman L. Hersey. New York, World Pub. Co. [1971, c1970] 214 p. 21 cm. [BV199.O3H4 1971] 70-100002 6.95
1. Worship programs. I. Title.

*HERZEL, Catherine 264.041
Christians at worship: helps for using the service book and hymnal in Sunday worship and at home. Ed.: Gustav K. Wiencke. Illus. by Bernhard and Johanna Sperl. Philadelphia, Lutheran Church [c.1964] 128p. illus. (LCA Sunday church sch. ser.) 1.25 bds.,
I. Title.

HIMMELHEBER, Diana (Martin) 264
On paths unknown; a young group's adventure in worship. St. Louis, Bethany [c.1964] 176p. illus. 21cm. Bibl. 64-23621 2.75
1. Worship programs. 2. Youth—Religious life. I. Title.

HOPPER, Myron Taggart, 1903- 264
The candle of the Lord. [Rev. ed.] St. Louis, Bethany Press [1957] 240p. 21cm. [BV29.H58 1957] 57-9776
1. Worship programs. 2. Young people's meetings (Church work) I. Title.

HOPPER, Myron Taggart, 1903- 264
The candle of the Lord. St. Louis, Bethany Press [1948] 256 p. 20 cm. [BV29.H58] 48-22755
1. Worship programs. 2. Young people's meetings (Church work) I. Title.

HOWSE, William Lewis, 1905- 264
In spirit and in truth, a book of worship programs. Rev. and enl. ed. [Westwood, N. J.] F. H. Revell Co. [1955] 96p. 20cm. [BV1522.H67 1955] 268.7 55-5392
1. Worship programs. I. Title.

HOYT, Margaret, ed. 264.0082
My heart an altar; resources for worship, edited by Margaret Hoyt and Eleanor Hoyt Dabney. Richmond, John Knox Press [1959] 189 p. 21 cm. [BV198.H67] 59-13461
1. Worship programs. I. Dabney, Eleanor Hoyt, joint ed. II. Title.

IKERMAN, Ruth C. 242
Devotional programs about people and places. Nashville, Abingdon Press [c.1947-1960] 158p. 16cm. 60-5473 2.00 bds.,
1. Worship programs. 2. Woman—Religious life. I. Title.

IRKEPMAN, Ruth C 242
Devotional programs for the changing seasons. New York, Abingdon Press [1958] 158p. 16cm. [BV199.W614] 58-10459
1. Worship programs. 2. Women—Religious life. I. Title.

MALL, E. Jane, 1920- 254'.6
Beyond the rummage sale / E. Jane Mall. Nashville : Abingdon, c1979. 64 p. : ill. ; 28 cm. Includes indexes. [BV199.W6M3] 78-26526 ISBN 0-687-03086-2 pbk. : 2.95
1. Worship programs. 2. Women—Religious life. I. Title.

MARTIN, David E. 264
Worship services for special days; forty-four complete services of worship for eighteen great days of the church. Anderson, Ind., Warner [c.1963] 96p. 22cm. 63-10213 1.25 pap.,
1. Worship programs. I. Title.

MAYNARD, Lee Carter. 264
52 worship services (with sermon outlines) / by Lee Carter Maynard. Cincinnati, Ohio : Standard Pub., c1976. 160 p. ; 22 cm. [BV198.M42] 75-27714 pbk. : 3.95
1. Worship programs. I. Title.

MURRELL, Gladys Clarke (Callahan) 1894- 264
Channels of devotion; twenty-four story worship services. New York, Abingdon-Cokesbury Press [1948] 106 p. 18 cm. [BV198.M8] 48-3682
1. Worship programs. I. Title.

MURRELL, Gladys Clarke (Callahan) 1894- 264
Patterns for devotion; twenty-seven story worship services. Nashville, Abingdon [1967,c.1950] 108p. 17cm. (Apex bks., AA6-95) Bibl. [BV198.M83] 50-8419 .95 pap.,
1. Worship programs. I. Title.

MURRELL, Gladys Clarke (Callahan) 1894- 264
Patterns for devotion; twenty-seven story worship services. New York, Abingdon-Cokesbury [1950] 108 p. 18 cm. Bibliography: p. 107-108. [BV198.M83] 50-8419
1. Worship programs. I. Title.

NELSON, Ruth Youngdahl. 248
The woman beautiful; ten programs for women's organizations. Rock Island, Ill., Augustana Book Concern [1954] 96p. 20cm. [BV199.W6N4] 56-2291
1. Worship programs. 2. Woman—Religious life. I. Title.

NORDTVEDT, Matilda. 265'.9
Women's programs for every season / by Matilda Nordtvedt and Pearl Steinkuehler. Chicago : Moody Press, c1982. 96 p. : ill. ; 22 cm. Includes bibliographical references. [BV199.W6N65 1982] 19 82-6391 ISBN 0-8024-6903-5 pbk. : 2.95
1. Worship programs. 2. Women—Religious life. I. Steinkuehler, Pearl. II. Title.

NOVOTNY, Louise (Miller) 1889- 268.7
52 practical programs for young people Grand Rapids, Zondervan Pub. House [1957] 147p. 20cm. [BV29.N6] 57-2400
1. Worship programs. 2. Young people's meetings (Church work) I. Title.

NOVOTNY, Louise [Virgie] (Miller) 246
Worship in art and music; complete programs based on great paintings and favorite hymns. Grand Rapids, Zondervan Pub. House [c.1959] 89p. illus. 20cm. 60-225 2.00 bds.,
1. Worship programs. I. Title.

ORTMAYER, Roger. 242'.8
Sing and pray and shout hurray! New York, Friendship Press [1974] 64 p. illus. 21 cm. Bibliography: p. 64. [BV198.O77] 74-3074 ISBN 0-377-00004-3 2.75 (pbk.).
1. Worship programs. 2. Prayers. I. Title.

PARROTT, Lora Lee (Montgomery) 1923- 264
Devotional programs for women's groups. Grand Rapids, Zondervan Pub. House [1952-53] 2v. 20cm. [BV198.P36] [BV198.P36] 268.7 52-7999 52-7999
1. Worship programs. I. Title.

PATTON, Kenneth Leo, 1911- 264.08'32
Services and songs for the celebration of life, by Kenneth L. Patton. Boston, Beacon Press [1967] xii, 209 p. 24 cm. [BV198.P38] 67-24897
1. Worship programs. I. Title.

PORTER, David Richard, 1882- ed. 264
Worship resources for youth. New York, Association Press, 1948. 102 p. 21 cm. "For further reading": p. 179-180. [HV29.P6] 49-7014
1. Worship programs. 2. Young people's meetings (Church work) I. Title.

REAM, Guin. 264
Come worship; forty-six short services for young people. St. Louis, Bethany Press [1957] 128p. 21cm. [BV29.R4] [BV29.R4] 268.7 57-7266 57-7266
1. Worship programs. 2. Young people's meeting (Church work) I. Title.

REST, Friedrich, 1913- ed. 264
Worship aids for 52 services. Philadelphia, Westminster Press [1951] 247 p. 21 cm. [BV198.R4] 51-12852
1. Worship programs. I. Title.

REST, Friedrich, 1913- 264
Worship services for church groups. Philadelphia, Christian Education Press [1962] 158p. 23cm. Includes bibliography. [BV198.R42] 62-9088
1. Worship programs. I. Title.

SCHROEDER, Ruth Jones. 264
Youth programs for Christian growth. New York, Abingdon Press [1957] 256p. 21cm. [BV29.S347] [BV29.S347] 268.7 57-11016 57-11016
1. Worship programs. 2. Young people's meetings (Church work) I. Title.

SCHROEDER, Ruth Jones. 264
Youth programs for special occasions. New York, Abingdon-Cokesbury Press [1950] 256 p. 21 cm. [BV29.S35] 50-7771
1. Worship programs. 2. Young people's meetings (Church work) I. Title.

SCHROEDER, Ruth Jones. 264
Youth programs on nature themes. New York, Abingdon Press [1959] 192p. 21cm. [BV29.S37] 59-8200
1. Worship programs. 2. Young people's meetings (Church work) I. Title.

SEBOLDT, Roland H A ed. 254
God and our parish; worship resources for the parish. Saint Louis, Concordia Pub. House [1963] 295 p. 21 cm. [BV198.S35] 63-14986
1. Worship programs. I. Title.

SEBOLDT, Ronald H. A., ed. 254
God and our parish; worship resources for the parish. St. Louis, Concordia [c.1963] 295p. 21cm. 63-14986 5.00
1. Worship programs. I. Title.

SHAFFER, Wilma L
Devotions and dialogs for women: "Serenity of the soul," by Wilma L. Shaffer. Cincinnati, Standard Pub. Co. [c1961] 125 p. 67-17938
1. Worship programs. I. Title. II. Title: Serenity of the soul.

SHAFFER, Wilma L
Psalms and programs for women, by Wilma L. Shaffer. Cincinnati, Standard Pub. [c1964] 128 p. 67-17149
1. Worship programs. 2. Bible. O. T. Psalms. I. Title.

SHARP, Margaret, comp. 267.626
Come into His presence; training union assembly programs for intermediates. Nashville, Tenn., Convention Press [1957] 128p. 20cm. [BV29.S4] 57-6333
1. Worship programs. 2. Young people's meetings (Church work) 3. Baptist Training Union. I. Title.

SHARP, Margaret, comp. 267.626
Come into His presence; training union assembly programs for intermediates. Nashville, Tenn., Convention Press [1957] 128 p. 20 cm. [BV29.S4] 57-6333
1. Worship programs. 2. Young people's meetings (Church work) 3. Baptist Training Union. I. Title.

SMITH, Lyndsay L., comp. 264
Creative living; fifty worship programmes for use in boys' clubs, girls' clubs, C.E. societies, Sunday Schools, Youth fellowships, compiled and edited by L. L. Smith. [Melbourne, Explorer Boys' Club Auxiliary of the Dept. of Christian Education, Churches of Christ in Victoria and Tasmania, 1968] 112 p. illus., port. 22 cm. [BV25.S6] 74-480171 unpriced
1. Worship programs. I. Churches of Christ in Victoria and Tasmania. Explorer Boys' Club Auxiliary. II. Title.

VONK, Idalee Iolf, 1913- 268.432
Growing in stature; 52 junior worship programs with object lessons, stories, playlets, and poems. Cincinnati, Standard Pub. Co. [1951] 255 p. 22 cm. [BV1546.V6] 51-25527
1. Worship programs. 2. Worship (Religious education) I. Title.

VONK, Idalee Wolf, 1913- 264 268.7
Fifty-two worship programs on Christian living. Cincinnati, Standard Pub. Co. [1952] 198 p. 21 cm. [BV198.V6] 52-28104
1. Worship programs. I. Title.

VONK, Idalee Wolf, 1913- 264
52 primary workshop programs Cincinnati, Standard Pub. Co. [1953] 285p. 21cm. [BV1545.V65] [BV1545.V65] 268.7 53-38202 53-38202
1. Worship programs. I. Title.

WALTER, Dorothy Blake 248.82
Worship time; a book of stories, finger plays, and poems for children. [Mountain View, Calif., Pacific Pr. Pub. Assn. 1962, c.1961] 165p. illus. 61-10875 3.50
1. Worship programs. 2. Children—Religious life. I. Title.

WAYLAND, John T. 264
Planning congregational worship services [by] John T. Wayland. Nashville, Tenn., Broadman Press [1972, c1971] 104 p. 21 cm. [BV198.W35] 72-178067 ISBN 0-8054-2308-7
1. Worship programs. I. Title.

WEEMS, Ann, 1934- 264'.051
Reaching for rainbows : resources for creative worship / by Ann Weems. 1st ed. Philadelphia : Westminster Press, c1980. 156 p. ; 20 cm. Bibliography: p. 156. [BV198.W38] 19 80-19330 ISBN 0-664-24355-X pbk. : 8.95
1. Worship programs. I. Title.

WHITWELL, Nevada (Miller) 1904- 266.73
At home and abroad; youth worship programs. Cincinnati, Standard Pub. Co. [1952] 216 p. illus. 22 cm. [BV29.W5] 52-27704
1. Worship programs. 2. Young people's meetings (Church work) I. Title.

WINTER, Miriam Therese. 264'.02
God with us : resources for prayer and praise Miriam Therese Winter. Nashville : Abingdon, c1979. 112 p. : music ; 28 cm. [BV198.W56] 78-13616 ISBN 0-687-15300-X pbk. : 5.95
1. Worship programs. I. Title.

WOOD, Letitia W 268.7
Dynamic worship programs for young people. Boston, Wilde [1950] 198 p. 20 cm. [BV29.W6] 51-747
1. Worship programs. 2. Young people's meetings (Church work) I. Title.

WORSHIP for the young in spirit. 264
St. Louis, Bethany Press [1957] 144p. 23cm. [BV198.E52] [BV198.E52] 268.7 57-12727 57-12727
1. Worship programs. I. Elbin, Paul Nowell, 1905-

WORSHIP services for junior highs. 264
New York, Abingdon Press [1958] 239p. 21cm. [BV29.B353] [BV29.B353] 268.7 58-10454 58-10454
1. Worship programs. I. Bays, Alice (Anderson) 1892-

YOUTH at worship. 264
Nashville, Broadman Press [1953] 167p. 21cm. [BV1522.B9] 268.7 53-11310
1. Worship programs. I. Byrd, Annie Ward.

ZION'S League annual. 267.6293
no. 1- Independence, Mo., Herald Pub. House [1947-] v. illus. 28 cm. Each vol. has also a distinctive title. "Prepared under the direction of the General Council of Zion's Leagues." [BX8671.A1Z5] 49-14554
1. Worship programs. I. Reorganized Church of Jesus Christ of Latter-day Saints. Zion's League.

Worship Religious education.

ATHEARN, Laura (Armstrong) Mrs. 264
Christian worship for America youth, by Laura Armstrong Athearn . New York, London, The Century co. [c1931] xiii, 361 p. front., illus., plates. 21 cm. "Principles, methods, and materials." "Direct correlation has been made with "The new hymnal for American youth', edited by Professor H. Augustine Smith."--Foreword. Includes music. [BV10.A7] 31-18416
1. Worship (Religious education) 2. Public worship. 3. Liturgies. I. Title.

BAKER, Edna Dean, 1883-
The worship of the little child, by Edna Dean Baker...a textbook in the standard training course outlined and approved by the International council of religious education... Nashville, Tenn., Published for the Teacher-training publishing association by Cokesbury press, 1927. 133 p. 19 cm. (Specilization series) "For further reading" at end of each chapter. [BV1525.B25] 27-15069
I. International council of religious education. II. Title.

BAN, Arline J. 264'.0088054
Children's time in worship / Arline J. Ban. Valley Forge, PA : Judson Press, c1981. 128 p. : ill. ; 22 cm. Includes indexes. [BV1522.B266] 19 81-11805 ISBN 0-8170-0902-7 pbk. : 5.95
1. Worship (Religious education) I. Title.

BARBER, Estelle Blanton. 268.73
Guiding intermediates in worship, by Estelle Blanton Barber. New York, Nashville, Abingdon-Cokesbury press [1946] 176 p. 20 1/2 cm. "References": p. 167-171. [BV1548.B34] 46-21191
1. Worship—Religious education. I. Title.

BAXTER, Edna M. 1895- 264
Learning to worship. Valley Forge, Pa. Judson [c.1965] 255p. 21cm. Bibl. [BV1522.B28] 64-20502 3.95
1. Worship (Religious education) I. Title.

BAYS, Alice (Anderson) Mrs. 1892- 268.7
Worship programs and stories for young people, by Alice Anderson Bays. Nashville, Cokesbury press [c1938] 258 p., 1 1. 20 1/2 cm. Bibliography: p. 241-244; "References and notes": p. 245-251. [BV1522.B3] 38-18514
1. Worship (Religious education) I. Title.

BAYS, Alice (Anderson) 1892- 268.73
Worship programs for intermediates, by Alice Anderson Bays. New York, Nashville, Abingdon-Cokesbury press [1942] 224 p. 20 1/2 cm. Bibliographical references included in "Notes" (p. 213-219) "Sources for hymns": p. 221-224. [BV1548.B35] 42-18087
1. Worship (Religious education) I. Title.

BAYS, Alice (Anderson, Mrs., 1892- 268.7
Worship programs in the fine arts for young people, by Alice Anderson Bays. Nashville, Cokesbury press [c1940] 256 p. 20 1/2 cm. Bibliographical references in "Notes": p. 241-249. "Sources for hymns": p. 252-256. [BV29.B35] 40-30131
1. Worship (Religious education) 2. Art and religion. 3. Hymns, English—Hist. & crit. I. Title.

BLASHFIELD, Clara (Beers) Mrs. 1889- 268.
Worship training for primary children, by Clara Beers Blashfield; a textbook in the Standard course in leadership training, outlined and approved by the International council of religious education ... [Dobbs Ferry, N.Y, Printed for the Leadership training publishing association by the Methodist book concern [c1929] 210 p. 1 illus. 19 1/2 cm. (Specialization series) Contains music. [Full name: Mrs. Clara Ora (Beers) Blashfield] Contains bibliographies. [BV1475.B5] 29-18430
1. Worship (Religious education). 2. Religious education. 3. Sunday-schools. I. International council of religious education. II. Title.

BRECK, Flora Elizabeth, 1886- 268.7
Worship services and programs for

beginners. Boston, W. A. Wilde Co. [1947] 226 p. 20 cm. [BV1522.B7] 48-15935
1. Worship (Religious education) I. Title.

BROWN, Jeanette (Perkins) 1887- 268.432
As childred worship; the leader's preparation and the child's experience .. by Jeanette E. Perkins; assisted in the music by Alton O'Steen. Boston, Chicago, The Pilgrim press [1936- v. 20 cm. *ull name: Jeanette Eloise (Perkins) Brown] [BV1522.B74] 36-16884
1. Worship (Religious education) 2. Sunday-schools. I. O'Steen, Alton, 1905- II. Title.

BROWN, Jeanette (Perkins) 1887- 268.432
As children worship; the leader's preparation and the child's experience ... by Jeanette E. Perkins; assisted in the music by Alton O'Steen. Boston, Chicago, The Pilgrim press [1936- v. 20 cm. [Full name: Jeanette Eloise (Perkins) Brown] [BV1522.B74] 36-16884
1. Worship (Religious education) 2. Sunday-schools. I. O'Steen, Alton, 1905- II. Title.

BROWN, Jeanette (Perkins) 1887- 268.7
Children's worship in the church school, by Jeanette E. Perkins ... New York and London, Harper & brothers, 1939. xix p., 1 l., 233 p. 22 cm. "First edition." Music: p. [173]-217. [Full name: Jeanette Eloise (Perkins) Brown] [BV1522.B75] 39-2574
1. Worship (Religious education) 2. Sunday-schools. I. Title.

BURGESS, Nellie V. Mrs. 264
Junior worship materials in program form, by Nellie V. Burgess, for use in junior church congregations, junior departments, vacation church schools, week-day classes and other junior groups, and for occasional use in the small or one room church school. Nashville, Tenn., Cokesbury press, 1930. 197 p. 20 cm. Music: p. 190-197. [BV199.C4B8] 30-33150
1. Worship (Religious education) I. Title.

CARR, Jo. 248'.82
Touch the wind ; creative worship with children / Jo Carr ; [ill. by Charla Honea]. Nashville : The Upper Room, [1975] x, 70 p. : ill. ; 20 cm. Bibliography: p. 69-70. [BV4571.2.C37] 74-33831 1.50
1. Worship (Religious education) 2. Children—Religious life. I. Title.

CLARKE, Maurice. 268.62
Worship and worshipers in the church; a program in Christian education for boys and girls near the age of confirmation (sixth grade) by Maurice Clarke, D.D. Pupil's workbook. Louisville, Ky., The Cloister press [1940]. iv p., 1 l, 3-114 p. incl. illus., forms. 27 1/2 cm. (The Cloister series of church school courses, Rev. Maurice Clarke ... editor). [BV1522.C54] 40-12958
1. Worship (Religion education) 2. Religious education—Text-books for children. I. Title.

CLARKE, Maurice, 1882- 238.1
We believe and worship; worship services for older members of the church school, built upon the sentences of the Apostle's creed. By the Reverend Maurice Clarke, D.D. Michigan City, Ind., Cloister press, [1938]. 6 p. l, 82 p. 1 l, 19 1/2 cm. [BX5873.C63] 38-7997
1. Worship Religious education). 2. Sunday schools—Exercises, recitations, etc. 3. Apostle's creed. I. Title.

CRANDALL, Edna M. 244
A curriculum of worship, for the junior church school... by Edna M. Crandall; with an introduction by Luther A. Weigle. New York, London, The Century co. [1925-27] 3 v. 19 1/2 cm. Includes hymns and responses with music. [BV1546.C7] 25-15860
1. Worship (Religious education) 2. Sunday-schools. I. Title.

DOAN, Eleanor Lloyd, 1914- 268.432
How to plan and conduct a primary church, with a special section for kindergarten church leaders, by Eleanor L. Doan, Frances Blankenbaker. Grand Rapids, Mich., Zondervan [c.1961] 112p. illus. 26cm. Bibl. 61-66783 1.95 pap.,
1. Worship (Religious education) 2. Church work with children. I. Blankenbaker, Frances, joint author. II. Title. III. Title: Primary church.

DOAN, Eleanor Lloyd, 1914- 268.432
How to plan and conduct a primary church, with a special section for kindergarten church leaders, by Eleanor L. Doan and Frances Blankenbaker. Grand Rapids, Zondervan Pub. House [1961] 112 p. illus. 26 cm. [BV199.C4D6] 61-66783
1. Worship (Reglious education) 2. Church work with children. I. Blankenbaker, Frances, joint author. II. Title. III. Title: Primary church.

EASTWOOD, Edna. comp. 264
Let's explore worship; an activity program created by the pupils for church school worship. New York, Morehouse-Gorham Co., 1952. 116 p. 20 cm. [BV1522.E15] 268.7 52-13439
1. Worship (Religious education) I. Title.

EIDE, Margaret (Wall) Mrs. 267.6241
...How to plan, prepare and present devotional programs and promote the crusade of prayer; a manual to gudie Luther leagues and other organizations in developing "Crusades with Christ", through prayer and worship programs, by Margaret Wall. Minneapolis, Minn., Augsburg publishing house, 1938. 72 p. illus. 23 cm. (Crusade with Christ series, manual ii) Includes bibliographies. [BX8003.Y73 Manual 2] [[267.6241]] 38-12099
1. Worship (Religious education) 2. Young people's meetings (Church work) 3. Young people's Luther league. I. Title. II. Title: Devotional programs.

FAHS, Sophia Blanche (Lyon) 1876- 268.432
Worshipping together with questioning minds. Boston, Beacon [c.1965] x, 240p. 21cm. Bibl. [BV1522.F3] 65-12241 4.95
1. Worship (Religious education) 2. Universalism—Education. I. Title.

FAHS, Sophia Blanche (Lyon) 1876- 268.432
Worshipping together with questioning minds, by Sophia Lyon Fahs. Boston, Beacon Press [1965] cx. 240 p. 21 cm. Bibliographical references included in "Notes" (p. 239-240) [BV1522.F3] 65-12241
1. Worship (Religious education) 2. Universalism — Education. I. Title.

FREESE, Doris A., 1929- 264
Children's church : a comprehensive how-to / Doris A. Freese. Chicago : Moody Press, c1982. p. cm. Bibliography: p. [BV1522.F73] 19 81-22426 ISBN 0-8024-1250-5 : 5.95
1. Worship (Religious education) I. Title.

GRICE, Ethel (Harrison) Mrs. 1880- 268.7
Junior assembly programs, by Ethel Harrison Grice. Nashville, Tenn., Broadman press [c1937] 169 p. illus. (incl. map) diagr. 23 cm. [BV1546.G68] 38-17071
1. Worship (Religious education) 2. Sunday-schools—Exercises, recitations, etc. I. Title.

GRIFFIS, Sue Randolph, Mrs. 288.7
Lamps for worship; a year of worship programs for young people, by Sue Randoloph Griffis. Cincinnati, O., The Standard publishing company [c1937] 200 p. 21 cm. [BV1522.G7] 37-6717
1. Worship (Religious education) I. Title.

GRIFFIS. SUE (RANDOLPH) Mrs. 1893- 264
Tapestry; a book of worship for youth and adults, by Sue Randolph Griffis. Cincinnati, O., The Standard publishing company [c1940] 176 p. 22 cm. [BV1522.G72] 40-7446
1. Worship (Religious education) 2. Liturgies. I. Title.

HAAS, James E. 268'.6
Make a joyful noise! By James E. and Lynne M. Haas. New York, Morehouse-Barlow Co. [1973] 40 p. illus., music. 29 cm. Includes bibliographical references. [BV1522.H24] 73-84089 ISBN 0-8192-1146-X 1.95 (pbk.)
1. Worship (Religious education) I. Haas, Lynne M., joint author. II. Title.

HAAS, James E. 268'.433
Praise the Lord! / By James E. Haas. New York : Morehouse-Barlow Co., [1974] 32 p. ; 28 cm. [BV1522.H25] 74-80388 ISBN 0-8192-1176-1 pbk. : 2.25
1. Worship (Religious education) 2. Youth—Religious life. I. Title.

HARTSHORNE, Hugh, 1885- 242
A second manual for training in worship; stories for worship and how to follow them up, by Hugh Hartshorne ... New York, C. Scribner's sons, 1921. viii, 127 p. 22 cm. [BV199.C4H3] 21-9462
1. Worship (Religious education) I. Title.

HARTSHORNE, Hugh, 1885- 268
Worship in the Sunday school; a study in the theory and practice of worship, by Hugh Hartshorne ... New York city, Teachers college, Columbia university, 1913. vii p., 1 l., 210 p., 1 l. 19 cm. Thesis (PH. D.)--Columbia university, 1913. Vita. Issued also without thesis note. Bibliography: p. 204-210. [BV1520.H35] 14-2096
1. Worship (Religious education) 2. Sunday-schools. I. Title.

HOYER, George W. 268'.432
Child of God, the Lord be with you / by George W. Hoyer. St. Louis : Clayton Pub. House, c1977. 294 p. ; 23 cm. On spine: The Lord be with you. [BV1522.H677] 77-85172 ISBN 0-915644-11-8 : 8.50
1. Worship (Religious education) I. Title. II. Title: The Lord be with you.

HOYT, Margaret. 264
Youth looking to Jesus; worship services, by Margaret Hoyt and Eleanor Hoyt Dabney. Illus. by Virginia Templin Gailey. Richmond, John Knox Press [1954] 191p. illus. 25cm. [BV1522.H68] 268.7 53-11765
1. Worship (Religious education) I. Dabney, Eleanor Hoyt, joint author. II. Title.

KOHL, Percy. 264
The Christian youth fellowship worship manual, prepared by Percy Kohl in accordance with the description and outline drafted by the Young people's section of the Curriculum committee of the United Christian missionary society, a board of missions and education. St. Louis, Mo., Christian board of publication [c1940] 64 p. illus. 19 cm. Text on p. [2] and [3] of cover. "Produced by the Division of Christian education, the United Christian missionary society, a board of missions and education." Includes bibliographies. [BV29.K6] 40-31666
1. Worship (Religious education) 2. Youth—Religious life. I. United Christian missionary society, Dept of religious education Curriculum committee. II. Title.

LAROSE, Paul F. 264'.02
Working with children and the liturgy / by Paul F. Larose. New York, N.Y. : Alba House, c1981. 93 p. ; 21 cm. [BV1522.L37] 19 81-14984 ISBN 0-8189-0428-3 pbk. : 2.95
1. Worship (Religious education) 2. Children—Religious life. I. Title.

*LAUBACH, Eugene E. 268.433
World without end: a worship anthology; for use by junior high youth in vacation church schools, youth week programs and other settings. Illus. by Linda Richmond. Nashville, Pub. for the Coop. Pubn. Assn. by Abingdon [1965, c.1964] 48p. col. illus., music 25cm. pap., .30; teacher's bk., pap., 1.75
I. Title.

LE BAR, Mary Evelyn, 1910 268'.432
Children can worship meaningfully at church and home / Mary E. LeBar. Wheaton, Ill. : Victor Books, c1976. 119 p. : ill. ; 21 cm. [BV1522.L4] 75-32884 ISBN 0-88207-173-4 pbk. : 1.95
1. Worship (Religious education) I. Title.

MCGAVRAN, Grace Winifred 268.7
Learning how children worship. Illus. by James A. Scott. St. Louis. Pub. for the Cooperative Pubn. Assn. by Bethany [c.1964] 192p. illus. 20cm. (Cooperative ser.) Bibl. 64-21304 2.95 bds.,
1. Worship (Religious education) I. Title.

MACINNES, Gordon A. 264.1
A guide to worship in camp and conference. Philadelphia, Westminster [1963, c.1962] 96p. 21cm. Bibl. 62-17570 1.50 pap.,
1. Worship (Religious education-) I. Title. II. Title: Worship in camp and conference.

MORE children's worship in the church school. [1st ed.] New York, Harper [1953] 250p. 22cm. [BV1522.B76] 268.7 53-5435 264
1. Worship (Religious education) I. Brown, Jeanette (Perkins) 1887-

MORGAN, Annie (Sewell) Mrs. 268.7
Teaching through worship; a book of junior worship programs, by Ann Morgan. Cincinnati, O., The Standard publishing company [c1940] 154 p. illus. 21 1/2 cm. [BV1522.M6] 40-30832
1. Worship (Religious education) 2. Sunday-school—Exercises, recitations, etc. 3. Religious education—Text-books for children. I. [Full name: Mrs. Annie Etta (Sewell) Morgan] II. Title.

NG, David. 264
Children in the worshipping community / David Ng and Virginia Thomas. Atlanta, Ga. : J. Knox, [1981] p. cm. Bibliography: p. [BV1522.N45] 19 80-84655 ISBN 0-8042-1688-6 pbk. : 6.50
1. Worship (Religious education) I. Thomas, Virginia, 1926- II. Title.

PARRIS, Percy Elizabeth. 268.432
Children at worship; 52 primary worship programs, by Percy Elizabeth Parris. Cincinnati, O., The Standard publishing company [1943] 121 p. 22 cm. "Worship and conduct songs" (with music): p. 95-118. [BV1545.P33] 43-3144
1. Worship (Religious education) 2. Sunday-schools—Exercises, recitations, etc. 3. Sunday-schools—Hymn-books. I. Title.

PAST, Mary Elizabeth, ed. 268.73
Intermediates' worship programs, compiled and edited by Mary Elizabeth Past. New York, London and Edinburgh, Fleming H. Revell company [1942] 205 p. 1 illus. 21 cm. Includes music ("Unafraid": p. 41) [BV1548.P3] 42-20404
1. Worship (Religious education) 2. Sunday-schools—Exercises, recitations, etc. I. Title.

PAULSEN, Irwin Guy, 1892- 268.73
The church school and worship by[Irwin G. Paulson New York The Macmillan company 1940 5 p. l., 199 p. 21 cm. "First printing." "A classified bibliography": p. 185-190 [BV1522.P3] 40-7448
1. Worship (Religious education) 2. Sunday-schools. I. Title.

PERKINS, Jeanette Eloise, 1887- 268.7
Children's workship in the church school, by Jeanette E. Perkins ... New York and London, Harper & brothers, 1939. xix p., 1 l., 233 p. 22 cm. "First edition." Music: p. [178]-217. "Acknowledgments": p. xv-xix. [BV1522.P43] 39-2574
1. Worship (Religious education) 2. Sunday-schools. I. Title.

POWELL, Marie (Cole) 1882- 268.73
Boys and girls at worship, by Marie Cole Powell. New York and London, Harper & brothers [1943] xxv, 198 p. 19 1/2 cm. "First edition." [Full name: Marie Eldredge (Cole) Powell] Bibliographical foot-notes. [BV1522.P67] 43-17293
1. Worship (Religious education) I. Title.

POWELL, Marie (Cole) Mrs. 1882- 264
Guiding the experience of worship [by] Marie Cole Powell. New York, Cincinnati [etc.] Printed for the Leadership training publishing association by the Methodist book concern [c1935] 263 p. pl., diagr. 18 cm. "Editor's introduction" signed: Erwin L. Shaver, chairman, Editorial and educational committee. "Additional reading sources" at end of most of the chapters. [Full name: Mrs. Marie Eldredge (Cole) Powell] [BV10.P6] 35-7501
1. Worship (Religious education) I. Shaver, Erwin Leander, 1899- ed. II. Title.

RABALAIS, Maria. 268'.7
Children, celebrate! Resources for youth liturgy, by Maria Rabalais [and] Howard Hall. New York, Paulist Press [1974] 137 p. 25 cm. Bibliography: p. 131-137. [BV1522.R25] 73-94212 ISBN 0-8091-1820-3 3.95 (pbk.).
1. Worship (Religious education) I. Hall, Howard, 1936- joint author. II. Title.

REX, Ruth (Irwin) Mrs., 1901- 268.7
In his holy temple; service of worship for the church school, by Ruth Irwin Rex. New York, Milwaukee, Morehouse publishing co., 1937. 128 p. front. 19 cm. Includes bibliographies. [Full name: Mrs. Ruth Elizabeth (Irwin) Rex] [BV1522.R35] 37-20554
1. Worship (Religious education) 2. Sunday-schools—Exercises, recitations, etc. I. Title.

RICHARDSON, Norman Egbert, 1878- 264
...The worship committee in action, by Norman E. Richardson...and Kenneth S. McLennan... Boston, Mass., International society of Christian endeavor [c1935] 121 p. diagr. 20 1/2 cm. (Christian youth in action) "Seventh edition." "The kingdom crusader's hymn" (words and music): p. 101. "Includes bibliographies. [BV10.R5 1935] 36-227
1. Worship (Religious education) 2. Youth—Religious life. I. McLennan, Kenneth Stewart, joint author. II. Title.

RICHARDSON, Norman Egbert, 1878- 264
The worship committee in action, by Norman E. Richardson...and Kenneth S. McLennan... Chicago, Ill., Young people's Christian union, United Presbyterian board of education [c1939] 140 p. plates, diagrs. 20 cm. "Revised edition." Includes bibliographies. [BV10.R5 1939] 39-11036
1. Worship (Religious education) 2. Youth—Religious life. I. McLennan, Kenneth Stewart, joint author. II. Title.

SHAVER, Erwin Leander, 1890- 264
Training young people in worship [by] Erwin L. Shaver and Harry T. Stock; a textbook in the Standard leadership training curriculum, outlined and approved by the International council of religious education ... Boston, Chicago, Printed for the Leadership training publishing association by the Pilgrim press [c1929] 240 p. 19 cm. (Specilization series) Contains bibliographies. [BV10.S47] 29-16087
1. Worship (religious education) I. Stock, Harry Thomas, joint author. II. International council of religious education. III. Title.

SMITH, Robert Seneca, 1880- 264
The art of group worship [by] Robert Seneca Smith... New York, Cincinnati [etc.] The Abingdon press [c1938] 105 p. 17 1/2 cm. "Editor's introduction" signed: Paul H. Vieth, editor. Bibliography: p. 87-98. [BV1522.S63] 38-32168
1. Worship [Religious education) I. Vieth, Paul Herman, 1895- ed. II. Title.

STACY, Gussie Brown, Mrs. 268.7
Worship for youth; a year of worship programs for young people, by Gussie Brown Stacy. Cincinnati, O., Powell & White [c1928- v. illus. 21 1/2 cm. "Music section": at end of each volume. Bibliography: v. 1, p. 240-241; v. 2, p. 238. [BV1570.S63] 28-19271
1. Worship (Religious education) 2. Sunday-schools. I. Title.

SULLIVAN, Jessie P. 268.077
Exciting object lessons and ideas for children's sermons [by] Jessie Sullivan Grand Rapids, Baker Book House [1975 c1970] 124 p. 19 cm. [BV1475.2.S9] ISBN 0-8010-7909-8 1.95 (pbk.
1. Worship (religious education) I. Title.
L.C. card no. for original edition: 70-129816.

SULLIVAN, Jessie P. 264
This is God speaking : 26 programs for children's church / by Jessie Sullivan ; illustrations by Lorraine Arthur. Cincinnati, Ohio : Standard Pub., c1982. 112 p. : ill., music ; 28 cm. Includes index. [BV1522.S94] 19 81-18476 ISBN 0-87239-496-4 pbk. : 6.95
1. Worship (Religious education) I. Title.

TOWNER, Vesta. 268.73
Guiding children in worship [by] Vesta Towner, C. A. Bowen, general editor. New York, Nashville, Abingdon-Cokesbury press [1946] 159 p. 19 cm. "Junior motto song" (words and music): p. [3] of cover. Bibliography: p. 154-157. "Source materials for use in worship": p. 158-159. [BV1522.T66] 46-17614
1. Worship (Religious education) I. Bowen, Cawthon Asbury, 1885- ed. II. Title.

VERKUYL, Gerrit, 1872- 268.73
Teen-age worship; with a chapter on teaching the elements of worship, by Harold E. Garner. Chicago, Moody Press, 1950. 192 p. illus. 20cm. Includes bibliographies. [BV1522.V4] 50-10998
1. Worship (Religious education) 2. Adolescence. I. Garner, Harold Eugene, 1907- II. Title.

VIETH, Paul Herman, 1895- 268.7
Worship in Christian education [by] Paul H. Vieth. Philadelphia, United Church Press [1965] 174 p. 21 cm. Bibliographical footnotes. [BV1522.V5] 65-18875
1. Worship (Religious education) I. Title.

WALLACE, John Sherman, 1877-1934. 268.
Worship in the church school, by J. Sherman Wallace. Philadelphia, Boston [etc.] The Judson press [1930] 4 p. l., 168 p. plates. 19 cm. "Reference books for teachers and pupils": verso of 4th prelim. leaf. [BV1522.W3] 30-7500
1. Worship (Religious education) 2. Sunday-schools. I. Title.

WHITWELL, Nevada Miller. 268.7
Intermediate worship services; a year of worship for intermediates in Bible schools or Christian endeavor societies, by Nevada Miller Whitwell. Cincinnati, O., The Standard publishing company [c1937] 180 p. illus. 21 1/2 cm. Includes music. [BV1522.W5] 37-6718
1. Worship (Religious education) I. Title.

WILKERSON, Barbara. 264
All about children's church / by Barbara Wilkerson. Harrisburg, Pa. : Christian Publications c1981. 175 p. : ill. ; 19 cm. (Christian life & ministry series) Bibliography: p. 168-174. [BV1522.W53] 19 80-70732 ISBN 0-87509-295-0 pbk. : 4.95
1. Worship (Religious education) I. Title. II. Series.
Publisher's address: 25 S. Tenth st., Harrisburg, PA 17101

WOODS, Sheila D. 268.433
Youth ventures toward a vital church. Nashville, Abingdon [c.1965] 238p. 23cm. Bibl. [BV1522.W58] 65-21978 3.95
1. Worship (Religious education) I. Title.

WOODS, Sheila D 268.433
Youth ventures toward a vital church [by] Sheila D. Woods. New York, Abingdon Press [1965] 238 p. 23 cm. Bibliography: p. 231-234. Bibliographical references included in "Notes" (p. 223-229) [BV1522.W58] 65-21978
1. Worship (Religious education) I. Title.

WORSHIP in my church: 268.432
junior leader's manual. Minneapolis, Minn. Augsburg [c.1963] 64p. 21cm. 1.00 pap.,

Worship services.

BUBBA Free John. 299'.93
Bodily worship of the Living God : the esoteric practice of prayer taught by Da Free John : the devotional way of life practiced by members of the Free Communion Church and students of the Laughing Man Institute / compiled and edited from the written teaching of Da Free John by the staff of the Laughing Man Institute. 2d ed. Middletown, Calif. : Dawn Horse Press, 1980. 182 p., [1] leaf of plates : ill. ; 23 cm. Includes index. First ed. published in 1978 under title: The God of the whole body. [BP610.B8115 1980] 19 80-52893 ISBN 0-913922-52-8 (pbk.) : 9.95
1. Bubba Free John. 2. Free Communion Church. 3. Worship services. I. Free Communion Church. II. Laughing Man Institute for Traditional and Esoteric Studies. III. Title.

CLARKE, Maurice. 264.
Worship services for kindergarten and primary children, by the Rev. Maurice Clarke ... with forward by the Rev. John W. Suter, jr. ... Milwaukee, Wis., Morehouse publishing co. [1929]. 6 p. l, 55, [1] p. front., pl. 23 1/2 cm. Contains music. "Books and materials recommended": verso of 1st prelim. leaf. [BX5873.C65] 29-15451
I. Title.

HICKS, William Watkin, 1837-
The sanctuary [by] William W. Hicks. [v.] 1- Boston, Publisher for The sanctuary, 1910- v. 19 cm. 10-11383
I. Title.

LITURGICAL Conference, inc.
The Book of Catholic worship. Washington, Liturgical Conference [c1966] xxii, 807 p. music. 22 cm. Liturgy and hymns in English intended for congregational use.
I. Title.

STEWART, George, 1892- 264
The sanctuary, services of prayer and praise, by George Stewart, with an introduction by the Very Reverend Howard Chandler Robbins ... New York, Association press, 1928. 118 p. 22 cm. [BV198.S67] 28-4252
I. Title. II. Title: Services of prayer and praise.

WHITING, Isabel (Kimball) Mrs., 1880- 792.1
Dramatic preludes and services of worship, by Isabel Kimball Whiting. Boston, Walter H. Baker company [c1940] 152 p. 23 1/2 cm. [PN6120.R4W52] 41-1167
I. Title.

Worship—Study and teaching.

BALDWIN, Josephine L. 264
Worship training for juniors, by Josephine L. Baldwin; a textbook in the standard course in teacher training, outlined and approved by the International council of religious education ... [New York] Printed for the Teacher training publishing association by the Methodist book concern [c1927] 219 p. 20 cm. (Specialization series) "Suggestions for additional reading" at the end of each chapter. [BV10.B3] 27-14019
I. Title.

BUTLER, Alford Augustus, 1845- 264
How shall we worship God? A non-technical introduction to the study of Christian worship. By Alford A. Butler ... New York, T. Whittaker, 1904. 161 p. incl. front. 19 1/2 cm. Bibliography: p. 159-161. [BV10.B9] 4-3926
I. Title. II. Title: Christian worship.

CLARK, Lucius Charles, 1869-
The worshiping congregation, by the Rev. Lucius C. Clark, D.D. Cincinnati, Jennings and Graham. New York, Eaton and Mains [c1912] 201 p. front. 19 1/2 cm. 12-20651 1.00
I. Title.

GUNNEMANN, Louis H. 264
Worship; a course book for adults [by] Louis H. Gunnemann. Boston, United Church Pr. [1966] 60p. 21cm. Bibl. [BV10.2.G8] 66-12053 price unreported. pap.,
1. Worship—Study and teaching. I. Title.

Worsley, Eng.—Church history.

MILLIKEN, Harold Turner. 942.7'32
Changing scene : two hundred years of church and parish life in Worsley / by H. T. Milliken ; [photography Peter Tillotson]. [Worsley] : [Worsley Parochial Church Council], 1976. 48 p. : ill., plan, port. ; 23 cm. [BX5195.W86S245] 76-379254 ISBN 0-9505113-0-7 : £0.75
1. St. Mark's Chuch, Worsley, Eng. 2. Worsley, Eng.—Church history. I. Title.

Worth.

BENETT, W. 123
Religion and free will, a contribution to the philosophy of values, by W. Benett ... Oxford, The Clarendon press, 1913. 3 p. l., 345, [1] p. 23 cm. [BF778.B46 Printed by L. C.] A 14
1. Worth. 2. Ethics. 3. Liberty of the will. 4. Philosophy and religion. I. Title.

BLECHMAN, Nathan. 121
The philosophic function of value; a study of experience showing the ultimate meaning of evolution to be the attainment of personality through culture and religion by Nathan Blechman, PH.D. Boston, R.G. Badger [c1918] 3 p. l., v-xv p., 1 l., 15-148 p. 19 1/2 cm. (Lettered on cover: Studies in philosophy) Thesis (PH.D)--New York university. Thesis note on verso of t.-p. Bibliography: p. 141-142. [BD232.B5] 18-9758 1.25
1. Worth. I. Title.

KANE, Robert Joseph, 1848- 170
Worth; lectures, by Rev. Robert Kane, S. J. London, New York [etc.] Longmans, Green and co., 1920. xii, 226 p., 1 l. 20 cm. [BJ1249.K3] 21-5842
1. Worth. 2. Ethics. I. Title.

Worth, Patience.

LITVAG, Irving. 133.9'3'0924 [B]
Singer in the shadows; the strange story of Patience Worth. New York, Popular Lib. [1973, c.1972] 319 p. 18 cm. Includes bibliographical references. [BF1301.W865L58] 0.95 (pbk.)
1. Worth, Patience. 2. Spirit writing. I. Title.
L.C. card no. for the hardbound edition: 70-165570.

LITVAG, Irving. 133.9'3'0924 B
Singer in the shadows; the strange story of Patience Worth. New York, Macmillan [1972] xiii, 293 p. 21 cm. Includes bibliographical references. [BF1301.W865L58] 70-165570 7.95
1. Worth, Patience. 2. Spirit writings. I. Title.

PRINCE, Walter Franklin, 1863- 133.
The case of Patience Worth; a critical study of certain unusual phenomena, by Walter Franklin Prince ... Boston, Boston society for psychic research, 1927. 509 p. front. (port.) 23 cm. "Books containing Patience Worth literature": p. 10. [BF1301.W865P7] 27-7975
1. Worth, Patience. 2. Psychical research. I. Worth, Patience, imputed author. II. Curran, Pearl Lenore (Pollard) Mrs. 1883- III. Title.

YOST, Casper Salathiel, 1864- 133.
Patience Worth: a psychic mystery, by Casper S. Yost. New York, H. Holt and company, 1916. iv p., 1 l., 290 p. 19 1/2 cm. [BF1301.W865Y6] 16-5963
1. Worth, Patience. 2. Spiritualism. I. Curran, Mrs. Pearl Lenore (Pullard) 1883- II. Title.

Worthington, O. Pontifical college Josephnium.

MILLER, Leo Francis, 1885- 922.273
Monsignor Joseph Jessing (1836-1899) founder of the Pontifical college Josephinum, by Leo F. Miller, D. D. Joseph C. Plumpe, PH.D.,Maurice A. Hofer, S.S.L. and George J. Undreiner, PH. D. Columbus, O., Carroll press, inc., 1936. xi, 413 p. front., plates, ports., facsims. 21 1/2 cm. Maps on lining-papers. Bibliography: p. 388-390. [BX4705.J46M5] 37-1133
1. Jessing, Joseph, 1836-1899. 2. Worthington, O. Pontifical college Josephinum. I. Plumpe, Joseph Conrad, 1901- joint author. II. Hefer, Maurice Aloysius, 1904- joint author. III. Undreiner, George Joseph, 1900- joint author. IV. Title.

Wovoka, 1856 (ca.)-1932.

BAILEY, Paul Dayton, 1906- 299'.7 B
Ghost dance Messiah [by] Paul Bailey. Los Angeles, Westernlore Press, 1970. 206 p. 22 cm. [E99.P2W58 1970] 75-135152 6.95
1. Wovoka, 1856 (ca.)-1932. 2. Indians of North America—Religion and mythology. I. Title.

Wrangham, Francis, 1769-1842—Bibliography

SADLEIR, Michael, 1888- 928.2
Archdeacon Francis Wrangham, 1769-1842, by Michael Sadleir. [Oxford] Printed at the Oxford university press for the Bibliographical society, 1937. xi, 103, [1] p. front. (port.) illus., plates, facsims. 22 x 18 cm. (Half-title: Supplement to the Bibliographical society's transactions. no. 12) [Name originally: Michael Thomas Harvey Sadler] Bibliography: p. 59-99. [Z989.W92S2] [922.342] 37-38802
1. Wrangham, Francis, 1769-1842—Bibl. 2. Wrangham, Francis, 1769-1842. I. Title.

Wren, Christopher, Sir 1632-1723.

LANG, Jane. 726.6
Rebuilding St. Paul's after the great fire of London. London, New York, Oxford University Press, 1956. xi, 269p. illus., ports. 26cm. Bibliography: p. [257]- 261. [NA5470.S5L3] 56-14474
1. Wren, Christopher, Sir 1632-1723. 2. London. St. Paul's Cathedral. I. Title.

WREN society, London. 726.6094212
... Drawings and models of the construction of St. Paul's cathedral; measured drawings of the old choir by F. C. Penrose. Thomas Malton's drawings, 1797-1800. Part I. The contract book. Part II. The minute book. Part III. The 'frauds and abuses' controversy, and Part IV. Building accounts, 1668-1675 ... Oxford, Printed for the Wren society at the University press, 1939. 3 p. l., [v]-xii, 216 p. fold. front., illus., XXII pl. (incl. plans; 1 double) 32 x 25 cm. (The Wren society. [Publications] vol. XVI) "Issued only to subscribers." Edited by A. T. Bolton and H. D. Hendry. The Malton views are reproduced from his Picturesque tour through the cities of London and Westminster. [NA997.W8A2 vol. 16] (720.62421) 39-20394
1. Wren, Sir Christopher, 1632-1723. 2. London. St. Paul's cathedral. I. Penrose, Francis Cranmer, 1817-1903. II. Malton, Thomas, 1726-1801. A picturesque tour through the cities of London and Westminster. III. Bolton, Arthur Thomas, 1864- ed. IV. Hendry, Harry Duncan, 1890- joint ed. V. Title.

Wright, Frank Lloyd, 1867-1959.

WRIGHT, Frank Lloyd, 1867-1959. 726'.3'0924
Pfeiffer Chapel, Florida Southern College, Lakeland, Florida, 1938 : Beth Sholom Synagogue, Elkins Park, Pennsylvania, 1954 / Frank Lloyd Wright ; edited and photographed by Yukio Futagawa ; text by Bruce Brooks Pfeiffer. Tokyo : A.D.A. Edita, [1976] 39 p. : chiefly ill. ; 37 cm. (Global architecture ; 40) Text in English and Japanese. [NA737.W7F8735] 77-354934
1. Wright, Frank Lloyd, 1867-1959. 2. Ann Pfeiffer Chapel, Lakeland, Fla. 3. Beth Sholom Synagogue, Elkins Park, Pa. I. Futagawa, Yukio, 1932- II. Pfeiffer, Bruce Brooks. III. Title.

Wright, George Ernest, 1909-1974.

ESSAYS in honor of George Ernest Wright / edited by Edward F. Campbell and Robert G. Boling. Missoula, MT : Scholars Press, [1976] p. cm. Essays from the Bulletin of the American Schools of Oriental Research, no. 220-221, Dec. 1975, Feb., 1976. [BS1192.E78] 76-10747 ISBN 0-89130-106-2 221.6
1. Wright, George Ernest, 1909-1974. 2. Bible. O.T.—Criticism, interpretation, etc.—Addresses, essays, lectures. 3. Bible—Antiquities—Addresses, essays, lectures. I. Wright, George Ernest, 1909-1974. II. Campbell, Edward Fay. III. Boling, Robert G. IV. American Schools of Oriental Research. Bulletin.

MAGNALIA Dei, the mighty acts of God : essays on the Bible and archaeology in memory of G. Ernest Wright / edited by Frank Moore Cross, Werner E. Lemke, and Patrick D. Miller, Jr. 1st ed. Garden City, N.Y. : Doubleday, c1976. p. cm. Includes indexes. "The bibliography of G. Ernest Wright": p. [BS1192.M34] 75-35617 ISBN 0-385-05257-X : 24.95 221.9'3
1. Wright, George Ernest, 1909- 2. Wright, George Ernest, 1909- —Bibliography. 3. Bible. O.T.—Addresses, essays, lectures. 4. Bible. O.T.—Antiquities—Addresses, essays, lectures. I. Wright, George Ernest, 1909- II. Cross, Frank Moore. III. Lemke, Werner E. IV. Miller, Patrick D.

Wright, Henry Burt, 1877-1923.

STEWART, George, 1892- 922
Life of Henry B. Wright, by George Stewart, jr., foreword by John R. Mott. New York, Association press, 1925. ix p., 3 l., 250 p. front. (port.) illus. (facsims.) 24 cm. [BV1085.W7S8] 25-20425
1. Wright, Henry Burt, 1877-1923. I. Title.

Wrottenberg, Jonas.

BACHRACH, Jeanette (Wrottenberg) Mrs. 922.96
Above rubies by Jeanette Wrottenberg Bachrach. [Los Angeles, Globe printing company, c1938] 51 p. ports., facims. 20 cm. Part 1, My mother's story retold from memories of her tales to me at bed-time and during household tasks: pt. 2, My father's story as retold by his former rabbi-instructor at one Passover feast in our home to the assembles guests, children and grand-children. [BM755.W7B3] [Wrottenberg, Mrs. Bessie (Feldman).] 34-41258
1. Wrottenberg, Jonas. I. Title.

Wurmbrand, Richard.

MOISE, Anutza. 230'.4'10924 B
A ransom for Wurmbrand. Edited by Myrtle Powley. Grand Rapids, Mich., Zondervan Pub. House [1972] 126 p. 18 cm. (Zondervan books) [BR1725.W88M6] 72-83869 0.95
1. Wurmbrand, Richard. 2. Wurmbrand, Sabina. I. Title.

Wyatt, William Edward, 1789-1864.

[WELLER, George] 1790-1841. 283.
A reply to the Review of Dr. Wyatt's sermon and Mr. Sparks' letters on the Protestant Episcopal church, which originally appeared in the Christian disciple at Boston, and subsequently, in a separate form at Baltimore in which it is attempted to vindicate the church from the charges of that review. By a Protestant Episcopalian... Boston, R. P. & C. Williams, 1821. 168 p. 1 l., 23 cm. Attributed to Rev. George Weller, presumably to John Pintard (1759-1844) in a manuscript note on the t.-p. of his copy, now in the Library of the General theological seminary, New York city. [BX5930.W4] 25-24155
1. Wyatt, William Edward, 1789-1864. 2. Sparks, Jared, 1789-1866. I. Title.

Wycliffe Associates.

KEFLEY, James C. 266'.023'06273
God's free-lancers / James C. Hefley. Wheaton, Ill. : Tyndale House Publishers, c1978. 175 p., [4] leaves of plates : ill. ; 21 cm. [BV2370.W883H43] 78-58745 ISBN 0-8423-1075-4 pbk. : 3.95
1. Wycliffe Associates. I. Title.

Wycliffe Bible Translators.

HEFLEY, James C. 266'.023'0985
Dawn over Amazonia; the story of Wycliffe Bible Translators in Peru [by] James and Marti Hefley. Waco, Tex., Word Books [1972] 193 p. illus. 23 cm. Bibliography: p. 193. [F3429.3.M6H38] 71-170914 4.95
1. Wycliffe Bible Translators. 2. Indians of South America—Peru—Missions. 3. Shapra Indians—Missions. I. Hefley, Marti, joint author. II. Title.

HEFLEY, James C. 266'.023
Miracles in Mexico, by James C. Hefley and Hugh Steven. Chicago, Moody Press [1972] 126 p. illus. 19 cm. [F1219.3.M59H4] 76-181585 ISBN 0-8024-5410-0
1. Wycliffe Bible Translators. 2. Indians of Mexico—Missions. I. Steven, Hugh, joint author. II. Title.

STEVEN, Hugh. 266'.00981
To the ends of the earth / Hugh Steven. 1st ed. Chappaqua, N.Y. : Christian Herald Books, c1978. 142 p. : ill. ; 21 cm. [F2519.3.M5S74] 77-90116 ISBN 0-915684-36-5 pbk. : 2.95
1. Wycliffe Bible Translators. 2. Indians of South America—Brazil—Missions. I. Title.

WALLIS, Ethel Emilia 266.023
Two thousand tongues to go; the story of the Wycliffe Bible Translators [by] Ethel Emily Wallis, Mary Angela Bennett. Drawings by Katherine Voigtlander. New York, Harper [c.1959, 1964] 308p. illus. 22cm. 1.95 pap.,
1. Townsend. William Cameron, 1896- 2. Wycliffe Bible Translators. 3. Missions, Foreign. I. Bennett, Mary Angela, 1906- joint author. II. Title.

WALLIS, Ethel Emilia. 266.023
Two thousand tongues to go; the story of the Wycliffe Bible Translators [by] Ethel Emily Wallis and Mary Angela Bennett. Drawings by Katherine Voiglander. [1st ed.] New York, Harper [1959] 308 p. illus. 22 cm. [BV2370.W9W3] 59-7146
1. Townsend, William Cameron, 1896- 2. Wycliffe Bible Translators. 3. Missions, Foreign. I. Bennett, Mary Angels, 1906- joint author. II. Title.

WALLIS, Ethel Emily. 266.023
Two thousand tongues to go; the story of the Wycliffe Bible Translators [by] Ethel Emily Wallis and Mary Angela Bennett. Drawings by Katherine Voigtlander. [1st ed.] New York, Harper [1959] 308 p. illus. 22 cm. [BV2370.W9W3] 59-7146
1. Townsend, William Cameron, 1896- 2. Wycliffe Bible Translators. 3. Missions, Foreign. I. Bennett, Mary Angela, 1906- joint author. II. Title.

Wycliffe College—History.

THE Enduring word : a centennial history of Wycliffe College / edited by Arnold Edinborough. Toronto ; Buffalo : Published for Wycliffe College by University of Toronto Press, 1978. ix, 129 p., [8] leaves of plates : ill. ; 24 cm. [BV4160.W92E52] 79-307142 ISBN 0-8020-3356-3 : 10.00 207'.713'541
1. Wycliffe College—History. I. Edinborough, Arnold.

Wycliffe, John, d. 1384.

BLOCK, Edward A. 270.5
John Wyclif, radical dissenter. [San Diego] San Diego State College Press, 1962. 58 p. 23 cm. (Humanities monograph series, v. 1, no. 1) Bibliographical footnotes. [BX4905.B58] 63-3841
1. Wycliffe, John, d. 1384. I. Title. II. Series.

CADMAN, Samuel Parkes, 1864-1936.
The three religious leaders of Oxford and their movements, John Wycliffe, John Wesley, John Henry Newman, by S. Parkes Cadman. New York, The Macmillan company, 1916. xvii, 596 p. 23 cm. Bibliographies: p. 171-172, 384, 588-589. [BR767.C3] 16-6226
1. Wycliffe, John, 2. Wesley, John, 3. Newman, John Henry, cardinal, I. Title.

CURRY, Daniel, 1809-1887, comp. 922.342
The life of John Wiclif, D. D., compiled from authentic sources. By Daniel Curry. George Peck, editor. New-York, Published by Lane & Tippett, for the Methodist Episcopal church, 1846. 326 p. 16 cm. A compilation from "The life and opinions of John de Wycliffe, by Robert Vaughan", and other sources, several chapters being little more than abridgements of corresponding portions of Vaughan's work. cf. Pref. [BX4905.C8] 35-35203
1. Wycliffe, John, d. 1384. I. Peck, George, ed. II. Vaughan, Robert, 1795-1868. Life and opnions of John de Wycliffe. III. Title.

DAHMUS, Joseph Henry, 1909-- 922.342
The prosecution of John Wyclyf New Haven, Yale University Press, 1952. xi, 167p. 25cm. Bibliography:p. 158-161. [BX4905.D2] 52-9262
1. Wycliffe, John, d. 1384. I. Title.

DAHMUS, Joseph Henry, 1909- 270.5'0924
The prosecution of John Wyclyf, by Joseph H. Dahmus. [Hamden, Conn.] Archon Books, 1970 [c1952] xi, 167 p. 23 cm. Bibliography: p. 158-161. [BX4905.D2 1970] 76-120371
1. Wycliffe, John, d. 1384. I. Title.

GWYNN, Aubrey Osborn. 271.40942
The English Austin friars in the time of Wyclif, by Aubrey Gwynn... London, Oxford university press, H. Milford, 1940. x, 295, [1] p. 23 cm. "Manuscripts consulted for this work": p. [288]-290. [BX2916.G92] 41-10326
1. Wycliffe, John, d. 1384. 2. Augustinians in England. I. Title.

INNIS, George Swan, 1850- 922.
... Wycliffe: the morning star, by George S. Innis ... Cincinnati, Jennings and Graham; New York, Eaton and Mains [1907] 245 p. 20 cm. (Men of the kingdom) [BX4905.I 55] 7-18306
1. Wycliffe, John d. 1884. I. Title.

KNAPP, Peggy Ann. 252'.02
The style of John Wyclif's English sermons / by Peggy Ann Knapp. The Hague : Mouton, 1977. 116 p. : diagrs. ; 24 cm. (De proprietatibus litterarum : Series practica ; 16) Bibliography: p. [111]-116. [BX4905.K62] 77-369497 ISBN 9-02-793156-9 : 19.00
1. Wycliffe, John, d. 1384. 2. Preaching—England—History. I. Title. II. Series.
Available from Mouton, 3 Westchester Plaza, Elmsford, NY 10523

LEWIS, John, 1675-1747. 270.5'092'4 B
The history of the life and sufferings of the Reverend and learned John Wiclif, D.D. ... Together with a collection of papers and records relating to the said history. A new ed., corr. and enl. by the author. Oxford, Clarendon Press, 1820. [New York, AMS Press, 1973] xxxii, 389 p. port. 23 cm. [BX4905.L45 1973] 74-178543 ISBN 0-404-56625-1 21.00
1. Wycliffe, John, d. 1384. I. Title.

LIFE and times of John de Wycliffe ... Philadelphia, American Sunday-school union; London, Religious tract society [1851?] viii, 9-192 p. 15 cm. [BX4905.L5] 32-30337 922.342
1. Wycliffe, John, d. 1384. I. American Sunday-school union.

LIFE and times of John de Wycliffe, revised by Thos. O. Summers, D. D. Nashville, Tenn., Southern., Methodist publishing house, 1885. viii, [9]-178 p. 16 cm. [BX4905.L5 1885] 41-26892 922.
1. Wycliffe, John, d. 1384. I. Summers, Thomas Osmond, 1812-1882.

MCFARLANE, Kenneth Bruce. 270.5'0924
John Wycliffe and the beginnings of English noncomformity [by] K. B. McFarlane [London] English Universities Pr. [1972, c.1952] xiii, 188 p. maps. 23 cm. ([Men & their times]) Bibliography: p. [174]-175 [BX4905.M3] A53 ISBN 0-340-16648-7
1. Wycliffe, John, d. 1384. 2. Reformation—Early movements. 3. Reformation—England. I. Title. II. Title: English nonconformity. III. Series.
Available from Verry, Mystic, Conn., for 5.00.

MCFARLANE, Kenneth Bruce. 922.342
John Wycliffe and the beginnings of English nonconformity. New York, Macmillan, 1953. 197 p. illus. 19 cm. (Teach yourself history library) [BX4905.M2] 53-4122

1. Wycliffe, John, d. 1384.

MCFARLANE, Kenneth 270.5'092'4 Bruce.
Wycliffe and English nonconformity [by] K. B. McFarlane. Harmondsworth, Penguin, 1972. xvii, 188 p. maps. 19 cm. (A Pelican book) (Teach yourself history) Originally published in 1952 under title: John Wycliffe and the beginnings of English nonconformity. Bibliography: p. [174]-175. [BX4905.M2 1972] 73-164247 ISBN 0-14-021377-5 £0.35
1. Wycliffe, John, d. 1384. I. Title.

MUDROCH, Vaclav. 270.5'092'4
The Wyclyf tradition / by Vaclav Mudroch ; edited by Albert Compton Reeves. Athens : Ohio University Press, c1979 xvii, 91 p. : port. ; 24 cm. Includes index. Bibliography: p. 81-88. [BX4905.M82] 77-92253 ISBN 0-8214-0403-2 : 8.00
1. Wycliffe, John, d. 1384. I. Reeves, Albert Compton. II. Title.

POOLE, Reginald Lane, 1857- 270.5
Wycliffe and movements for reform, by Reginald Lane Poole ... New York, A. D. F. Randolph & company [1889] 1 p. l., [v]-xi, 204 p. 19 cm. (On cover: Epochs of church history) [BR295.P8 1889] 33-6270
1. Wycliffe, John, d. 1884. 2. Papacy—Hist. 3. Reformation—Early movements. I. Title.

POOLE, Reginald Lane, 1857- 270.
Wycliffe and movements for reform, by Reginald Lane Poole ... New ed. London, New York [etc.] Longmans, Green, and co., 1896. xi, 204 p. 18 cm. (Half-title: Epochs of church history ...) [BR295.P8 1896] 3-826
1. Wycliffe, John, d. 1884. 2. Papacy—Hist. 3. Reformation—Early movements. I. Title.

POOLE, Reginald 270'.5'0924 B Lane, 1857-1939.
Wycliffe and movements for reform / by Reginald Lane Poole. New York : AMS Press, 1978. xi, 204 p. ; 19 cm. Reprint of the 1889 ed. published by A. D. F. Randolph, New York, in series: Epochs of church history. Includes bibliographical references and index. [BR295.P8 1978] 77-84729 ISBN 0-404-16129-4 : 19.00
1. Wycliffe, John, d. 1384. 2. Papacy—History. 3. Reformation—Early movements. I. Title. II. Series: Epochs of church history.

SERGEANT, Lewis, d.1902. 922.342
John Wyclif, last of the schoolmen and first of the English reformers, by Lewis Sergeant... New York, London, G. P. Putnam's sons, 1893. 2 p. l., [iii]-ix, 377 p. front., plates, ports., facsim. 20 cm. [Half-title: Heroes of the nations, ed. E. Abbott) [BX4905.S4] 4--16970
1. Wycliffe, John, d. 1384. I. Title.

SERGEANT, Lewis, 270.5'092'4 B d.1902.
John Wyclif, last of the schoolmen and first of the English reformers. Freeport, N.Y., Books for Libraries Press [1973] p. (Essay index reprint series) Reprint of the 1893 ed., issued in series: Heroes of the nations. [BX4905.S4 1973] 72-14162 ISBN 0-518-10022-7
1. Wycliffe, John, d. 1384. I. Series: Heroes of the nations.

SERGEANT, Lewis, 270.5'092'4 B d.1902.
John Wyclif, last of the schoolmen and first of the English reformers / by Lewis Sergeant. 1st AMS ed. New York : AMS Press, 1979. ix, 377 p., [31] leaves of plates : ill. ; 19 cm. Reprint of the 1893 ed. published by Putnam New York, in series: Heroes of the nations. [BX4905.S4 1978] 73-14468 ISBN 0-404-58286-9 : 30.00
1. Wycliffe, John, d. 1384. I. Title. II. Series: Heroes of the nations.

STACEY, John. 270.5
John Wyclif and reform. Philadelphia, Westminster Press [1964] 169 p. 22 cm. Includes bibliographies. [BX4905.S68] 64-19147
1. Wycliffe, John, d. 1384. I. Title.

STACEY, John, 270.5'092'4 B fl.1964-
John Wyclif and reform / by John Stacey. New York : AMS Press, 1979, c1964 p. cm. Reprint of the ed. published by Westminister Press, Philadelphia. Includes bibliographies and index. [BX4905.S68 1980] 78-63199 ISBN 0-404-16239-8 : 18.00
1. Wycliffe, John, d. 1384. I. Title.

STORRS, Richard Salter, 922. 1821-1900.
John Wycliffe and the first English Bible; an oration by Richard S. Storrs ... New York, A. D. F. Randolph & company, 1880. 85 p. 24 1/2 cm. Address given in the Academy of music, New York. December 2d, 1880. cf. p. [5] [BX4905.S7] 16-4825
1. Wycliffe, John, d. 1384. I. Title.

TYPICAL English churchmen.
Series II. From Wyclif to Gardiner. Published under the direction of the Tract committee. London, Society for promoting Christian knowledge; New York, E. S. Gorham, 1909. 190, [2] p. 22 cm. (The Church historical society ... [Publications] LXXVIII) A 10
1. Wycliffe, John, d. 1384. 2. William of Wykeham, bp. of Winchester, 1824-1404. 3. Courtenay, William, abp. of Canterbury, 1342?-1396. 4. Beaufort, Henry, cardinal, 1377-1447. 5. Gardiner, Stephen, bp. of Winchester, 1483?-1555. 6. Church of England—Biography. 7. Gt. Brit.—Church history. 8. Tunstall, Cuthbert, bp. of London and Durham, 1474-1559. I. Figgis, John Neville, 1866-1919. II. Spooner, William Archibald, 1844-1930. III. Holmes, Thomas Scott, 1852-1918. IV. Radford, Lewis Bostock, 1869- V. Ross-Lewis, George Harrison, 1846-1913. VI. Gairdner, James, 1828-1912.

VAUGHAN, Robert, 270.5'092'4 B 1795-1868.
The life and opinions of John de Wycliffe, D. D. Illustrated principally from his unpublished manuscripts; with a preliminary view of the papal system, and of the state of the Protestant doctrine in Europe, to the commencement of the fourteenth century. 2d ed. much improved. London, Holdsworth and Ball, 1831. [New York, AMS Press, 1973] 2 v. port. 23 cm. Includes bibliographical references. [BX4905.V36 1973] 71-178561 ISBN 0-404-56678-2
1. Wycliffe, John, d. 1384. I. Title.

WILD, Laura Hulda, 1870- 220.
The romance of the English Bible; a history of the translation of the Bible into English from Wyclif to the present day, by Laura H. Wild ... Garden City, N.Y., Doubleday, Doran & company, inc., 1929. xviii p., 1 l., 295 p. front., illus., plates, ports., facsim. 20 cm. "Classified bibliography": p. 276-281. [BS455.W55] 29-7094
1. Wycliffe, John, d. 1384. 2. Tyndale, William, d. 1536. 3. Bible. English—Hist. 4. Bible. English—Versions. I. Title.

WILSON, John Laird, 1832- 922. 1896.
John Wycliffe, patriot and reformer, "The morning star of the reformation"; a biography by John Laird Wilson ... New York [etc.] Funk & Wagnalls, 1884. 2 p. l., [iii]-iv, [5]-247 p. 19 cm. (On cover: Standard library. no. 126) [BX4905.W47] 12-40333
1. Wycliffe, John, d. 1384. I. Title.

WOKRMAN, Herbert Brook, 270.5 (B) 1862-
John Wyclif; a study of the English medieval church, by Herbert B. Workman. Hamden, Conn., Archon Books, 1966. 2 v. in 1. illus., facsims., ports. 23 cm. "Originally published . . . 1926." "Abbreviations and editions": v. 1, p. [xxvii]-[xxxv] [BX4905.W6 1966] 66-14608
1. Wycliffe, John, d. 1384. I. Title.

WORKMAN, Herbert Brook, 922. 1862-
John Wyclif, a study of the English medieval church, by Herbert B. Workman ... Oxford, The Clarendon press, 1926. 2 v. fronts. (ports.) plates, facsims. 23 cm. "Editions of Wyclif's works": vol. I, p. [xxxv] Bibliography: vol. I, p. [xxvii]-xxxiv. [BX4905.W6] 27-4083
1. Wycliffe, John, d. 1834. I. Title.

WYCLIFFE, John, d.1384.
John Wiclif's Polemical works in Latin, for the first time edited from the manuscripts, with critical and historical notes by Rudolph Buddensieg. English edition... London, Pub. for the Wyclif society by Trubner & co., 1883. New York, Johnson Reprint Corp. [1966] 2 v. front (facsim.) 23 cm. (On cover: Wycliff's Latin works [v. 1]) Paged continuosly. "The Wiclif--catalogues of the Vienna mss.": p. lix-lxxxiv. 68-69927
I. Buddensieg, Rudolph, 1844-1908, ed. II. Wyclif society, London. III. Title.

WYCLIFFE, John, d.1384. 208
Select English works of John Wyclif; edited from original mss. by Thomas Arnold ... Oxford, Clarendon press, 1869-71. 3 v. 23 cm. "Wyclif literatur": v. 3, p. xv-xvi. "List of English works ascribed to Wyclif":v.3,xvii-xx. Contents.I. Sermons on the Gospels for Sundays and festivals.--II. Sermons on the ferial Gospels and Sunday epistles. Treatises.--III. Miscellaneous works. [BR75.W83] 12-40256
I. Arnold, Thomas, 1823-1900, ed. II. Title.

WYCLIFFE, John, d.1384. 208
Wyclif, select English writings, edited by Herbert E. Winn, M.A., with a preface by H. B. Workman ... London, Oxford university press, H. Milford, 1929. xxxix, [1], 179, [1] p. front. (port.) 19 cm. "Manuscripts": p. [xl] [BR75.W84] 30-19601
I. Winn, Herbert Ewart, ed. II. Title.

Wyker, Bertha Park, 1893-

WYKER, Bertha 266'.66'0924 B Park, 1893-
Spanning the decades : a spiritual pilgrimage / Bertha Park Wyker. 1st ed. Smithtown, N.Y. : Exposition Press, c1981. x, 205 p., [8] p. of plates : ports. ; 21 cm. [BV3427.W93A37] 19 81-66179 ISBN 0-682-49746-0 : 8.50
1. Wyker, Bertha Park, 1893- 2. Missionaries—United States—Biography. 3. Missionaries—China—Biography. I. Title.

Wyneken, Friedrich Konrad Dietrich, 1810-1876—Juvenile literature.

WEISHEIT, Eldon. 284'.1'0924 B
The preacher's yellow pants. Art by Michael Norman. St. Louis, Concordia Pub. House [1973] [48] p. col. illus. 27 cm. Aggravated by the preacher's yellow pants, the parishoners endeavor to get him dressed in black. [BX8080.W95W44] 74-159833 ISBN 0-570-03420-5 3.25
1. Wyneken, Friedrich Konrad Dietrich, 1810-1876—Juvenile literature. 2. [Wyneken, Friedrich Konrad Dietrich, 1810-1876.] 3. [Clergy.] I. Norman, Michael, illus. II. Title.

Wynne, John Joseph, 1859-

XAVIER alumni sodality. 922
Fifty years in conflict and triumph, pub. by the Xavier alumni sodality in the city of New York. [New York, Press of Loughlin bros., c1927] 6 p. l., 3-141 p. front. (port.) 24 1/2 cm. "The third annual academy of the Xavier alumni sodality of the Blessed Virgin Mary on the occasion of the golden jubilee of Rev. John J. Wynne as member of the Society of Jesus ... Hotel Biltmore, New York, December thirteenth, nineteen hundred and twenty-six." [BX4705.W8X3] 27-11605
1. Wynne, John Joseph, 1859- I. Title.

Wyrtzen, Jack.

FORBES, Forrest Dale, 1907- 922
God hath chosen, the story of Jack Wyrtzen and the Word of life hour. Grand Rapids, Zondervan Pub. House [1948] 137 p. illus. 20 cm. [BV3785.W9F6] 48-8074
1. Wyrtzen, Jack, 1913- 2. Word of life hour (Radio program) I. Title.

*HUNTER, Jack D. 269'.2'0924 B
Word of life by Jack D. Hunter. New York, Pocket Books [1976] 192 p. 18 cm. [BV3785] ISBN 0-671-80169-4 1.95 (pbk.)
1. Wyrtzen, Jack. I. Title.

SWEETING, George, 1924- 922
The Jack Wyrtzen story; the personal story of the man, his message and his ministry. Grand Rapids, Zondervan Pub. House [1960] 151 p. illus. 21 cm. [BV3785.W9S8] 60-4404
1. Wyrtzen, Jack, 1913- 2. Word of life hour (Radio program) I. Title.

Wysox, Pa. Presbyterian church.

DETTY, Victor Charles. 285.174857
History of the Presbyterian church of Wysox, Pennsylvania, 1791-1938, by Victor Charles Detty ... Wysox, Pa., Pub. by the author, 1939. 5 p. l., [15]-244 p. front., plates. ports., maps. 21 cm. Descriptive letterpress on verso of part of the plates. [BX9211.W83W3] 30-20797
1. Wysox, Pa. Presbyterian church. 2. Presbyterians in Pennsylvania. 3. Wysox, Pa.—Geneal. 4. Registers of births, etc.—Wysox, Pa. I. Title.

Xainctonge, Anne de, 1567-1621.

BRESLIN, Mary Thomas. 922.244
Anne de Xainctonge, her life and spirituality. Kingston, NSociety of St. Ursula of the Blessed Virgin, 1957. 273p. illus. 24cm. Includes bibliography. [BX4705.X3B7] 57-9169
1. Xainctonge, Anne de, 1567-1621. 2. Ursulines. I. Title.

BRESLIN, Mary Thomas. 922.244
Anne de Xainctonge, her life and spirituality. Kingston, N. Y., Society of St. Ursula of the Blessed Virgin, 1957. 273p. illus. 24cm. Includes bibliography. [BX4705.X3B7] 57-9169
1. Xainctonge, Anne de, 1567-1621. 2. Ursulines. I. Title.

Xaverian brothers.

JULIAN, Brother. 271.79
Men and deeds; the Xaverian brothers in America, by Brother Julian, C. F. x.; with an introduction by His Grace, Michael J. Cureley, archibishop of Baltimore. New York, The Macmillan company, 1930. xx p., 1 l., 539 p. front., plates, ports. 23 cm. [BX4190.X3J8] 30-17008
1. Xaverian brothers. 2. Catholic church—Biog. I. Title.

Ya' Ityopya 'ortodoks tawahedo beta kerestiyan.

ISAAC, Ephraim. 281'.7
The Ethiopian Church. Boston, H. N. Sawyer Co., 1967. 60 p. illus., col. plates. 24 x 27 cm. [BX146.2.I8] 68-2579
1. Ya' Ityopya 'ortodoks tawahedo beta kerestiyan. I. Title.

MOLNAR, Enrico S., 281.9'63 1913-
The Ethiopian Orthodox Church; a contribution to the ecumenical study of less known Eastern Churches, by Enrico S. Molnar. Pasadena [Calif.] Bloy House Theological School, 1969. 25 p. illus., map. 24 cm. Cover title. Bibliography: p. 24-25. [BX143.2.M6] 70-7764
1. Ya' Ityopya 'ortodoks tawahedo beta kerestiyan. I. Title.

Yadin, Yigael, 1917- ed.

WAR of the Sons of Light 296 against the Sons of Darkness.
The scroll of the war of the Sons of Light against the Sons of Darkness. Ed., commentary, introd. by Yigael Yadin. Tr. from Hebrew by Batya and Chaim Rabin. New York, Oxford, [c]1962[ ] xix 387p. illus. Text of scroll in Hebrew and English. 62-3327 10.10
1. Yadin, Yigael, 1917- ed. I. Title.

WAR of the Sons of Light 296 against the Sons of Darkness.
The scroll of the War of the Sons of Light against the Sons of Darkness. Edited with commentary and introd. by Yigael Yadin. Translated from the Hebrew by Batya and Chaim Rabin. [London] Oxford University Press, 1962. xix, 387 p. illus., diagrs., facsims. 24 cm. Text of scroll in Hebrew and English. [BM488.W3A233] 62-3327
I. Yadin, Yigael, 1917- ed. II. Title.

Yakima Indians—Missions.

GARRAND, Victor. 266'.2'797
Augustine Laure, S. J., missionary to the Yakimas / by Victor Garrand ; Edward J. Kowrach, editor. Fairfield, Wash. : Galleon Press, 1977. 35 p. : ill. ; 29 cm. Translation of Le pere Augustin Laure, de la Compagnie de Jesus, missionaire aux montagnes Rocheuses. [E99.Y2G3513] 77-8126 ISBN 0-87770-176-8 : 6.95 pbk. : 3.95
1. Laure, Augustin, 1857-1892. 2. Yakima Indians—Missions. 3. Missionaries—Washington (State)—Biography. 4. Missionaries—France—Biography. 5. Indians of North America—Washington (State)—Missions. I. Title.
Publisher's address : P.O. Box 400, Fairfield, WN 99012

Yakusu, Belgian Congo.

DUNCAN, Sylvia. 266.6
Bonganga; experiences of a missionary doctor [by] Sylvia and Peter Duncan. New York, Morrow, 1960. 240 p. illus. 21 cm. [BV3625.C63B7] 59-11700
1. Browne, Stanley George. 2. Yakusu, Belgian Congo. 3. Missions, Medical—Congo, Belgian. I. Duncan, Peter, 1915- joint author.

Yale, Elisha, 1780-1853.

WOOD, Jeremiah, 1801-1876. 922.573
The model pastor. The life and character of the Rev. Elisha Yale, D.D., late of Kingsboro, drawn mostly from his own diary and correspondence. Together with the discourse preached at his funeral. January 13, 1853. By Jeremiah Wood ... Albany, J. Munsell, 1854. viii, 384 p. front., (port.) 18 cm. [BX9225.Y3W6] 36-22146
1. Yale, Elisha, 1780-1853. 2. Funeral sermons. I. Title.

Yale foreign missionary society.

TWICHELL, Joseph Hopkins, 1838-1918.
A modern knight, by Rev. Joseph Hopkins Twichell ... New Haven, Yale foreign missionary society, 1906. 1 p. l., 5-37 p. 2 port. (1 mounted) 15 1/2 x 13 1/2 cm. [BV3676.P3T9] 6-38353
1. Patterson, John Coleridge, bp., 1827-1871. 2. Yale foreign missionary society. I. Title.

Yale judaica series.

YALE university. 892.4
Judaica research at Yale university; translations and publications of Jewish classics. Report on the ... work. 1st-1944/45- New Haven [1945- v. 23 cm. annual. [PJ3001.Y3] 47-24418
1. Yale judaica series. I. Title.

Yale University. Divinity School.

BAINTON, Roland Herbert, 1894- 207.746
Yale and the ministry; a history of education for the Christian ministry at Yale from the founding in 1701. Line drawings by the author. [1st ed.] New York, Harper [1957] xiii, 297p. illus., ports. 22cm. Bibliographical references included in 'Notes' (p. 269-290) [BV4070.Y36B3] 57-7344
1. Yale University. Divinity School. I. Title.

LATOURETTE, Kenneth Scott, 1884- 286/.0924
Beyond the ranges; an autobiography. Grand Rapids, Eerdmans [1967] 161p. 23 cm. [BR139.L3A3] (B) 67-13980 3.95
1. Yale University. Divinity School. I. Title.

LATOURETTE, Kenneth Scott, 1884- 286'.0924 (B)
Beyond the ranges; an autobiography. Grand Rapids, Eerdmans [1967] 161 p. 23 cm. [BR139.L3A3] 67-13980
1. Yale University. Divinity School. I. Title.

Yale university—History

STILES, Ezra, 1727-1795. 922.
The literary diary of Ezra Stiles ... ed. under the authority of the corporation of Yale university by Franklin Bowditch Dexter ... New York, C. Scribner's sons, 1901. 3 v. front., illus., port. 24 1/2 cm. [BX7260.S8A3] 1-25841
1. Yale university—Hist. I. Dexter, Franklin Bowditch, 1842-1920. II. Title.

Yale University—History—Sources.

NISSENBAUM, Stephen, comp. 277.46'8
The great awakening at Yale College. Stephen Nissenbaum, editor. Belmont, Calif., Wadsworth Pub. Co. [1972] xii, 263 p. 23 cm. (The American history research series) Bibliography: p. 261-263. [BR520.N73] 74-167899 ISBN 0-534-00101-7
1. Yale University—History—Sources. 2. Great Awakening—History—Sources. I. Title.

Yale university. James Wesley Cooper memorial publication fund.

GLOVER, Terrot Reaveley, 1869- 294.
The influence of Christ in the ancient world, by T. R. Glover ... New Haven, Yale university press, 1929. 4 p. l., 121, [1] p., 1 19 cm. "Lectures originally delivered on the Huskell foundation at Oberlin college ... Students of Yale Divinity school heard the lectures in the session of 1928-29." "Published on the foundation established in memory of James Wesley Cooper of the class of 1865, Yale college." [BR128.A2G6] 30-7646
1. Yale university. James Wesley Cooper memorial publication fund. I. Title. II. Title: Christ in the ancient world.

Yale university—Religious history.

REYNOLDS, James Bronson, 1861-1924.
Two centuries of Christian activity at Yale; edited by James B. Reynolds, Samuel H. Fisher, Henry B. Wright, committee of publication. New York and London, G. P. Putnam's sons, 1901. xv, 367 p. fold. tables. 21 1/2 cm. Bibliography: p. 353-355. [BR561.Y3R4] 1-25471
1. Yale university—Religious history. I. Fisher, Samuel Herbert, 1867- joint ed. II. Wright, Henry Burt, 1877-1923, joint ed. III. Title.

Yamamoto, Tsunetomo, 1659-1719.

MISHIMA, Yukio, pseud. 170'.952
The way of the samurai : Yukio Mishima on Hagakure in modern life / [by Yukio Mishima] ; translated by Kathryn N. Sparling. New York : Basic Books, c1977. x, 166 p. ; 22 cm. Translation of Hagakure nyumon. [BJ971.B8Y333313] 75-36381 ISBN 0-465-09387-6 : 10.00
1. Yamamoto, Tsunetomo, 1659-1719. Hagakure. 2. Bushido. I. Yamamoto, Tsunetomo, 1659-1719. Hagakure. II. Title.

Yankton, S.D. Sacred Heart Church.

KAROLEVITZ, Robert F. 282.783'394
Pioneer church in a pioneer city; the story of Sacred Heart Parish, Yankton, South Dakota, 1871-1971, by Robert F. Karolevitz. [1st ed. Aberdeen, S.D., North Plains Press, 1971] 96 p. illus., facsims., map, ports. 31 cm. Bibliography: p. 93. [BX4603.Y3K3] 74-164645
1. Yankton, S.D. Sacred Heart Church. I. Title.

Yanoama Indians—Missions.

JANK, Margaret, 1939- 266'.023'0987
Culture shock / by Margaret Jank. Chicago : Moody Press, c1977. p. cm. [F2520.1.Y3J36] 77-22658 ISBN 0-8024-1679-9 pbk. : 3.50
1. New Tribes Mission, Chicago. 2. Yanoama Indians—Missions. 3. Indians of South America—Venezuela—Missions. I. Title.

Yantras.

KHANNA, Madhu. 294.5'3'7
Yantra, the Tantric symbol of cosmic unity / Madhu Khanna. London : Thames and Hudson, c1979. 176 p. : ill. (some col.) ; 26 cm. Includes index. Bibliography: p. 172-173. [BL1215.Y36K45] 79-318582 ISBN 0-500-01207-5 : 27.50
1. Yantras. I. Title.
Distributed by W. W. Norton, NYC

Yaqui Indians.

MCMAHON, Martin. 299'.7
Castaneda's The teachings of Don Juan, A separate reality & Journey to Ixtlan : notes, including life and background, introduction, analyses of The teachings of Don Juan, A separate reality, and Journey to Ixtlan, review questions / by Martin McMahon III ; consulting editor, James L. Roberts. Lincoln, Neb. : Cliffs Notes, c1974. 60 p. ; 21 cm. Cover title: Cliffs Notes on Castaneda's The teachings of Don Juan & other works. [E99.Y3M3] 76-353154 ISBN 0-8220-0306-6 : 1.25
1. Castaneda, Carlos. The teachings of Don Juan. 2. Castaneda, Carlos. A separate reality. 3. Castaneda, Carlos. Journey to Ixtlan. 4. Yaqui Indians. 5. Hallucinogenic drugs and religious experience. I. Title: Castaneda's The teachings of Don Juan, A separate reality ... II. Title: Cliffs Notes on Castaneda's The teachings of Don Juan & other works.

Yaqui Indians—Addresses, essays, lectures.

SEEING Castaneda : 299'.7
reactions to the "Don Juan" writings of Carlos Castaneda / edited, selected, and with introductions by Daniel C. Noel. New York : Putnam, [1975] p. cm. Bibliography: p. [E99.Y3C337 1975] 75-23146 ISBN 0-399-11603-6 : 7.95
1. Castaneda, Carlos. 2. Juan, Don, 1891- 3. Yaqui Indians—Addresses, essays, lectures. 4. Hallucinogenic drugs and religious experience—Addresses, essays, lectures. I. Noel, Daniel C.

Yaqui Indians—Art.

STAN-PADILLA, Viento, 1945- 299'.7
Dream feather / Viento Stan-Padilla ; illustated by the author. San Rafael, Calif. : Dawne-Leigh Publications, 1980. p. cm. [E99.Y3S79] 79-26213 ISBN 0-89742-035-7 : 10.95 ISBN 0-89742-034-9 (pbk.) : 7.95
1. Stan-Padilla, Viento, 1945- 2. Yaqui Indians—Art. 3. Yagui Indians—Religion and mythology. 4. Indians of North America—Religion and mythology. 5. Spiritual life. I. Title.

Yaqui Indians—Religion and mythology.

CASTANEDA, Carlos. 299'.7
The second ring of power / by Carlos Castaneda. New York : Simon and Schuster, c1977. 316 p. ; 22 cm. [E99.Y3C288] 77-22107 ISBN 0-671-22942-7 : 8.95
1. Castaneda, Carlos. 2. Yaqui Indians—Religion and mythology. 3. Hallucinogenic drugs and religious experience. 4. Indians of Mexico—Religion and mythology. 5. Anthropologists—Mexico—Biography. I. Title.

CASTANEDA, Carlos. 299'.7
The second ring of power / by Carlos Castaneda. 1st Touchstone ed. New York : Simon and Schuster, 1979, c1977. 316 p. ; 21 cm. (A Touchstone book) [E99.Y3C288 1979] 78-26557 ISBN 0-671-24851-0 pbk. : 3.95
1. Castaneda, Carlos. 2. Yaqui Indians—Religion and mythology. 3. Hallucinogenic drugs and religious experience. 4. Indians of Mexico—Religion and mythology. 5. Anthropologists—Mexico—Biography. I. Title.

CASTANEDA, Carlos. 299'.7
A separate reality; further conversations with Don Juan. New York, Simon and Schuster [1971] 317 p. 22 cm. [E99.Y3C29] 79-139617 ISBN 0-671-20897-7 6.95
1. Juan, Don, 1891- 2. Yaqui Indians—Religion and mythology. 3. Hallucinogenic drugs and religious experience. I. Title.

CASTANEDA, Carlos. 299'.7
Tales of power. New York, Simon and Schuster [1974] 287 p. 22 cm. [E99.Y3C295] 74-10601 ISBN 0-671-21858-1 7.95
1. Juan, Don, 1891- 2. Yaqui Indians—Religion and mythology. 3. Hallucinogenic drugs and religious experience. I. Title.

CASTANEDA, Carlos. 299'.7
The teachings of Don Juan; a Yaqui way of knowledge. [New York] Simon and Schuster, 1973 [c1968] 288 p. 22 cm. [E99.Y3C3 1973] 73-166188 ISBN 0-671-21555-8 7.95
1. Juan, Don, 1891- 2. Yaqui Indians—Religion and mythology. 3. Hallucinogenic drugs and religious experience. I. Title.

CASTANEDA, Carlos. 299.7
The teachings of Don Juan; a Yaqui way of knowledge. New York, Pocket Books [1974, c1968] 256 p. 18 cm. [E99.Y3C3 1974] ISBN 0-671-78748-9. 1.50 (pbk.)
1. Juan, Don, 1891- 2. Yaqui Indians—Religion & mythology. 3. Hallucinogenic drugs and religious experience. I. Title.
L.C. card number for original ed.: 68-17303.

CASTANEDA, Carlos. 299'.7
The teachings of Don Juan; a Yaqui way of knowledge. Berkeley, University of California Press, 1968. viii, 196 p. 24 cm. [E99.Y3C3 1968] 68-17303
1. Juan, Don, 1891- 2. Yaqui Indians—Religion and mythology. 3. Hallucinogenic drugs and religious experience. I. Title.

CASTENEDA, Carlos. 299.7
The second ring of power / by Carlos Castaneda. New York : Pocket Books, 1980, c1977. 328 p. ; 18 cm. [E99.Y3C288] ISBN 0-671-81650 pbk. : 2.95
1. Castaneda, Carlos. 2. Yaqui Indians — Religion and mythology. 3. Hallucinogenic drugs and religious experience. 4. Indians of Mexico — Religion and mythology. 5. Anthropologists — Mexico — Biography. I. Title.
L.C. card no. for 1977 Simon and Schuster ed.: 77-22107

CASTENEDA, Carlos. 299.7
Tales of power / Carlos Castaneda. New ork : Pocket Books, 1976c1974. 295p. ; 18 cm. [E99.Y3C295] ISBN 0-671-80676-9 pbk. : 1.95
1. Juan, Don,1891- 2. Yaqui Indians-Religion and mythology. 3. Hallucienogenic drugs and religious experience. I. Title.
L.C. card no. for 1974 Simon and Schuster edition: 74-10601

Yaqui Indians—Rites and ceremonies.

PAINTER, Muriel Thayer. 809.2'51
A Yaqui Easter. Tucson, University of Arizona Press [1971] 40 p. illus. 22 cm. Second ed. published in 1960 under title: Easter at Pascua Village. [E99.Y3P3] 74-153706 ISBN 0-8165-0168-8
1. Pascua passion-play. 2. Yaqui Indians—Rites and ceremonies. I. Title.

Yard, Edmund Jones, 1792-1876.

JAMES, Mary Dagworthy (Yard) Mrs. 1810-1883. 922.773
The soul-winner; a sketch of facts and incidents in the life and labors of Edmund J. Yard ... By his sister, Mrs. Mary D. James ... With an introduction by D. P. Kidder, D. D. New York, Phillips & Hunt; Cincinnati, Walden & Stowe, 1883. 231 p. 18 cm. [BX8495.Y3J3] 37-12160
1. Yard, Edmund Jones, 1792-1876. I. Title.

Yates, James, 1789-1871. Vindication of Unitarianism.

WARDLAW, Ralph, 1779-1853. 230.8
Unitarianism incapable of vindication; a reply to the Rev. James Yates's Vindication of Unitarianism. By Ralph Wardlaw... Andover [Mass.] Published and for sale by Mark Newman. Flagg and Gould. printers, 1817. xii, [13]-351 p. 24 1/2 x 14 1/2 cm. [BX9847.W33 1817] 35-22748
1. Yates, James, 1789-1871. Vindication of Unitarianism. 2. Unitarianism—Doctrinal and controversial works. I. Title.

Yates, Matthew Tyson, 1819-1888.

BRYAN, Ferrebee Catharine, 1886- 922.651
At the gates; the gates; life story of Matthew Tyson and Eliza Moring Yates of China. Nashville, Broadman Press [c1949] xxii. 374 p. illus., ports., facisms. 24 cm. [BV3427.Y3B7] 50-5965
1. Yates, Matthew Tyson, 1819-1888. 2. Yates, Eliza Emmeline (Moring) 1821-1894. I. Title.

TAYLOR, Charles Elisha, 1842-1916. 922.
The story of Yates the missionary, as told in his letters and reminiscences. Prepared by Charles E. Taylor ... Nashville, Tenn., Sunday school board, Southern Baptist convention, 1898. 204 p. front., plates, port., maps. 19 1/2 cm. "Dr. Yates ... in 1880-81 ... published in the Biblical recorder (Raleigh, N.C.) a series of letters entitled, 'Reminiscences of a long missionary life'. These, as well as extracts from his personal and official correspondence, constitute the main body of this volume."--Pref. [BV3427.Y3T3] 12-39305
1. Yates, Matthew Tyson, 1819-1888. 2. Baptists—Missions. 3. Missions—China. I. Title.

Ye-Su Chia-Ting.

THE 'Jesus family' in Communist China. Chicago, Moody press [1956] 126p. 19cm.
1. Ye-Su Chia-Ting. 2. Communism and religion. 3. Communism—China. I. Rees, D Vaughan.

Yeaman, William Pope, 1832-1904.

MAPLE, Joseph Cowgill, 1833-1917. 920.
Life and writings of Rev. William Pope Yeaman, S. T. D., by J. C. Maple ... Columbia, Mo., Printed for the author by the press of E. W. Stephens publishing company, 1906. 3 p. l., v-xi, 388 p. front. (port.) 21 cm. [BX6495.Y4M3] 6-6758
1. Yeaman, William Pope, 1832-1904. I. Title.

Yeats, William Butler, 1865-1939—Criticism and interpretation.

SEIDEN, Morton Irving, 1921- 821'.8
William Butler Yeats: the poet as a mythmaker, 1865-1939. New York, Cooper Square Publishers, 1975 [c1962] xiv, 397 p. front. 24 cm. Reprint of the ed. published by Michigan State University Press, East Lansing. Bibliography: p. 339-354. [PR5908.M8S4 1975] 74-79395 ISBN 0-8154-0491-3 12.50
1. Yeats, William Butler, 1865-1939—Criticism and interpretation. 2. Myth in literature.

Yeats, William Butler, 1865-1939—Religion and ethics.

MOORE, Virginia, 1903- 821'.8
The unicorn: William Butler Yeats' search for reality. New York, Octagon Books, 1973 [c1954] xix, 519 p. port. 23 cm. Reprint of the ed. published by Macmillan, New York. Bibliography: p. 476-488. [PR5908.R4M6 1973] 73-7774 ISBN 0-374-95856-4 17.50 (lib. bdg.)
1. Yeats, William Butler, 1865-1939—Religion and ethics. I. Title.

Yeats, William Butler, 1865-1939—Supernatural element.

RAINE, Kathleen Jessie, 1908- 821'.8
Yeats, the tarot, and the Golden Dawn, by Kathleen Raine. [Dublin] Dolmen Press [1972] 60, [31] p. illus. 25 cm. (New Yeats papers, 2) Imprint covered by label: Distributed in the U.S.A. by Humanities Press, New York. Includes bibliographical references. [PR5908.O25R3] 73-166426 ISBN 0-85105-195-2 £2
1. Yeats, William Butler, 1865-1939—Supernatural element. 2. Hermetic Order of the Golden Dawn. 3. Tarot. I. Title. II. Series.

Yecuana Indians—Religion and mythology.

CIVRIEUX, Marc de. 299'.8
Watunna, an Orinoco creation cycle / Marc de Civrieux ; edited and translated by David M. Guss. San Francisco : North Point Press, 1980. viii, 195 p., [10] p. of plates : ill., maps ; 23 cm. Translation from Spanish. [F2319.2.Y4C5813] 19 80-82440 ISBN 0-86547-003-0 (pbk.) : 8.50 ISBN 0-86547-002-2 : 17.50
1. Yecuana Indians—Religion and mythology. 2. Indians of South America—Venezuela—Religion and mythology. I. Guss, David M. II. [Watunna.] English III. Title.
Publisher's Address: 850 Talbot Ave. Berkeley, CA 94706.

Yezidis.

AHMED, Sami Said. 299'.1'59
The Yazidis, their life and beliefs / by Sami Said Ahmed ; edited by Henry Field. Coconut Grove, Miami : Field Research Projects, 1975. x, 485 p. : ill. ; 28 cm. Translation of al-Yazidiyah, ahwaluhum wa-mu'-taqadatuhum. Includes bibliographical references. [BL1595.A3613] 75-330953
1. Yezidis. I. Title.

Yiddish language—Composition and exercises.

GOLDIN, Hyman Elias, 1881-
The Yiddish teacher. A method for the study of Yiddish by H. E. Goldin. New York, S. Druckman [c1924] 76, [4] p. 20 cm. [PJ5115.G6] 25-4416
1. Yiddish language—Composition and exercises. I. Title.

Yiddish language—Grammar.

GOLDIN, Hyman Elias, 1881-
The Yiddish teacher; a method for the study of Yiddish, with English-Yiddish and Yiddish-English vocabularies, by H. E. Goldin. New York, Hebrew publishing company, 1928. 76, 16, [4] p. 20 cm. 28-25580
1. Yiddish language—Grammar. I. Title. II. Title: (Transliterated): Der Yiddish lehrer.

Yiddish language—Texts.

SCHWARTZ, Jacob, 1875-
Letters of a suppressed writer, by J. Schwartz. [Brooklyn, N. Y.] J. Schwartz [1913] 256 p. 18 cm. [PJ5165.S5] 14-1668
1. Yiddish language—Texts. I. Title.

Yiddish literature (Collections)

HARKAVY, Alexander, 1863-1939, ed.
The twentieth century. Literary review and almanac for the year 1900 New York, A. Harkavy, 1900. 70, 30 p. 20 cm. Thiry pages at end, advertising matter. Title transliterated: Der swanzigster yahrhundert. [PJ5125.H3] 46-43090
1. Yiddish literature (Collections) I. Title.

Yiddish literature—History and criticism

GOLDBERG, Isaac, 1887-
... The spirit of Yiddish literature [by] Isaac Goldberg. Girard, Kan., Haldeman-Julius company [c1925] 64 p. 13 cm. (Little blue book, no. 732, ed. by E. Haldeman-Julius) Advertising matter: p. 58-64. [PJ5113.G6] ca 25
1. Yiddish literature—Hist. & crit. I. Title.

Yiddish poetry.

IMBER, Samuel Jacob, 1889-1939, ed.
Modern Yiddish poetry, an anthology, edited by Samuel J. Imber. New York, The East and West publishing co., 1927. xxxi, 351, [1] p. 23 1/2 cm. Yiddish (transliterated) and English on opposite pages. "Mr. M. Licht, Miss Evelyn Markus and the editor [and others] are responsible for the English reedition of the poems."--p. ix. The translations are in press. [PJ5126.I4] 28-28178
1. Yiddish poetry. I. Title.

YMCA of Los Angeles.

WAGNER, Harold A. 267'.39794'93
As I lived it : an autobiographical history of the YMCA of Los Angeles, 1925-1966 / by Harold A. Wagner. Glendale, Calif. : A. H. Clark Co., 1979. 332 p. : ill. ; 25 cm. Includes index. [BV1050.L67W33] 79-50564 ISBN 0-87062-129-7 : 10.00
1. YMCA of Los Angeles. 2. Wagner, Harold A. 3. Young Men's Christian Associations—Biography. I. Title.

Yoder, Mrs. Rosanna (McGonegal)

YODER, Joseph Warren, 1872- 289.7748
Rosanna of the Amish, by Joseph W. Yoder ... illustrated by George Daubenspeck. Huntingdon, Pa. The Yoder publishing company, 1940. ix p., 1 l., 319 p. incl. front., illus. 20 cm. Illustrated lining-papers. Includes two Amish hymns with music (unaccompanied melodies) "All the episodes ... are based on fact. Every name ... in the real name of the person mentioned"--Pref. [BX8143.Y6Y6] 41-1744
1. Yoder, Mrs. Rosanna (McGonegal) 2. Mennonites in Pennsylvania. I. Title.

Yoga.

ACKERMAN, Dorothy. 181'.45
A Quaker looks at yoga / Dorothy Ackerman. Wallingford, Pa. : Pendle Hill Publications, 1976. 32 p. ; 20 cm. (Pendle Hill pamphlet ; 207) Bibliography: p. 30-32. [B132.Y6A33] 76-23909 ISBN 0-87574-207-6 : 0.95
1. Yoga. I. Title.

ALBERTSON, Edward. 181'.45
Spiritual yoga. Los Angeles, Sherbourne Press [1969] 154 p. 21 cm. (For the millions series, FM 22) [B132.Y6A475] 69-11837 2.50
1. Yoga. I. Title.

ALEXANDER, Mithrapuram K. 294
The Yoga system, by Mithrapuram K. Alexander. [Rev. ed.] North Quincy, Mass., Christopher Pub. House [1971, c1968] 87 p. illus. 21 cm. [B132.Y6A48 1971] 77-140373 ISBN 0-8158-0257-9 3.95
1. Yoga. I. Title.

ARCHARYA, Pundit. 181.4
Breath is life [by] Pundit Acharya. New York, Prana Press [c1930] 7 p. l., 7-66 p. 13 1/2 x 10 1/2 cm. (Yoga research institute series) "First edition." [B132.Y6A4] 40-34178
1. Yoga. 2. Respiration. I. Title.

[ATKINSON, William Walker, 1862- 181
Fourteen lessons in Yogi philosophy and Oriental occultism, by Yogi Ramacharaka [pseud.] ... 53Chicago, Ill.] The Yogi publication society [c1904] 3 p. l., 286 p. 20 cm. (On cover: Yogi philosophy. vol. i) [BF1999.A735] 24-11346
1. Yoga. I. Title.

[ATKINSON, William Walker] 1862- 181.4
Fourteen lessons in yogi philosophy and Oriental occultism, by Yogi Ramacharaka [pseud.] ... 53Chicago54 The Yogi publicationb society [c1931] 3 p. l., 288 p. 19 cm. (On cover: Yogi philosophy. vol. i) Sequel: Advanced course in yogi philosophy and Oriental occultism. [BF1999.A735 1931] 37-6440
1. Yoga. I. Title.

[ATKINSON,William Walker] 1862-
Fourteen lessons in yogi philosophy and oriental occultism, by Yogi Ramacharaka [pseud.54 ... Oak Park, Ill., The Yogi publication society, 1904. 5 p. l., 277 p. 20 cm. [NF1099] 4-84924
1. Yoga. I. Title.

[ATKINSON,William Walker] 1862-
Fourteen lessons in yogi philosophy and oriental occultism, by Yogi Ramacharaka [pseud.54 ... Oak Park, Ill., The Yogi publication society, 1904. 5 p. l., 277 p. 20 cm. [NF1999] 4-84924
1. Yoga. I. Title.

[ATKINSON, William Walker] 1862- 133
The Hindu-Yogi science of breath; a complete manual of the oriental breathing philosophy of physical, mental, psychic and spiritual development, by Yogi Ramacharaka [pseud.] Chicago, Ill., Yogi publication society, 1909. 73 p. 20 cm. [BF1909.A75 1909] 10-645
1. Yoga. 2. Respiration. I. Title.

[ATKINSON, William Walker] 1862- 181.4
The Hindu-yogi science of breath; a complete manual of the oriental breathing philosophy of physical, mental, psychic and spiritual development, by Yogi Ramacharaka [pseud.] [Chicago, Ill.] Yogi publication society; [etc., etc., 1931] 72 p., 1 l. 20 cm. [BF1999.A75 1931] 613 36-8096
1. Yoga. 2. Respiration. I. Title.

[ATKINSON, William Walker] 1862-
Mystic Christianity; or, The inner teachings of the Master, by Yogi Ramacharaka [pseud.] ... Chicago, Ill., Yogi publication society; [etc., etc., c1908] 2 p. l., 269 p. 20 cm. These lessons originally appeared in monthly form, from October, 1907, to the 12th of September, 1908. cf. Publisher's note. [BF1989.A78] 8-27508
1. Yoga. 2. Mysticism. I. Title.

[ATKINSON, William Walker] 1862-
Mystic Christianity; or, The inner teachings of the Master, by Yogi Ramacharaka [pseud.] ... Chicago, Ill., Yogi publication society; [etc., etc., c1908] 2 p. l., 269 p. 20 cm. These lessons originally appeared in monthly form, from October, 1907, to the 12th of September, 1908. cf. Publisher's note. [BF1989.A78] 8-27508
1. Yoga. 2. Mysticism. I. Title.

[ATKINSON, William Walker] 1862- 181
A series of lessons in Gnani yoga (the yoga of wisdom.) By Yogi Ramacharaka [pseud.] ... Chicago, Ill., The Yogi publication society, 1907. iv, 302 p. 20 cm. (On cover: Yogi philosophy ... vol. iv) "The lessons which compose this volume, orginally appeared in the shape of monthly lessons. the first of which was issued in October, 1906, and the twelfth in September, 1907."--Publisher's notice. [BF1999.A785 1907] 7-31387
1. Yoga. I. Title.

[ATKINSON, William Walker] 1862- 181
A series of lessons in Raja yoga, by Yogi Ramacharaka [pseud.] ... Chicago, Ill., The Yogi publication society, 1906. vi, 200 p. 20 cm. (Lettered on cover: Yogi philosophy, vol. iii) "The lessons which compose this volume, orginally appeared in the shape of monthly lessons, the first of which was issued in October, 1906, and the twelfth in September, 1906."--Publishers' notice. [BF1999.A8] 6-35999
1. Yoga. I. Title.

[ATKINSON, William Walker] 1869- 181.4
A series of lessons in Raja yoga, by Yogi Ramacharaka [pseud.] ... Chicago, Ill., The Yogi publication society [c1981] vi, 296 p., 1 l., 20 cm. (On cover: Yogi philosophy. vol. iii) "The lessons which compose this volume originally appeared in the shape of monthly lessons, the first of which was issued in October, 1906, and the twelfth in September, 1906."--Publishers' notice. [BF1999.A8 193] 37-11149

1. Yoga. I. Title.

BECK, Lily (Moresby) Adams 181
Mrs. d.1931.
A beginner's book of yoga, from the writings of L. Adams Beck; edited and with a foreword by David Merrill Bramble. New York, Farrar & Rinehart, incorporated [c1937] x, 229 p. 21 1/2 cm. [B132.Y6B33] 37-3612
1. Yoga. I. Bramble, David Merrill, ed. II. Title.

BEHANAN, Kovoor Thomas. 181.4
Yoga; a scientific evaluation, by Kovoor T. Behanan ... New York, The Macmillan company, 1937. xviii p., 2 l., 270 p. plates. 20 1/2 cm. "First printing." "Studies carried on ... at Yale (part of which is reported in the concluding chapter of this book) served to complete the dissertation for the degree of doctor of philosophy awarded in 1934."--Foreword. [B132.Y6B4] 37-27293
1. Yoga. I. Title.

BERNARD, Theos. 181.4
Heaven lies within us, by Theos Bernard ... New York, C. Scribner's sons, ltd., 1939. xiv p., 1 l., 326 p. incl. front., illus. 22 cm. "The way of life taught by yoga."--Foreword. [B132.Y6B43] 39-31183
1. Yoga. I. Title.

BESANT, Annie (Wood) Mrs. 181.4
1847-1933.
An introductin to yoga; four lectures delivered at the 32nd anniversary of the Theosophical society, Held at Benares, on Dec. 27th, 28th, 29th, 30th, 1907, by Annie Besant. (2d ed.) Adyar, Madras, India, Chicago [etc.] Theosophial publishing house, 113. vi p., 1 l., 165 p. 19 cm. [B132.Y6B435] 41-23463
1. Yoga. I. Title.

BETWEEN pleasure and pain 181'.45
: the way of conscious living. Sumas, Wa. : Dharma Sara Publications, c1976. 159 p. : ill. ; 23 cm. (Dharma sara ; 2) [B132.Y6B443] 76-11110 ISBN 0-88765-000-7
1. Yoga. I. Title. II. Series.

BHAKTIVEDANTA, A. C. 294.5'43
Swami 1896-
Krsna consciousness; the topmost yoga system [by] A. C. Bhaktivedanta Swami Prabhupada. New York, Macmillan [1972] 110 p. 18 cm. [B132.Y6B5314 1972] 72-80069 1.25 (pbk)
1. Yoga. I. Title.

BHAKTIVEDANTA, A.C., 294.5'43
Swami 1896-
Krsna consciousness: the topmost yoga system, by A. C. Bhaktivedanta Swami. Boston, Mass., Iskcon Press [1970] 57 p. 20 cm. [B132.Y6B5314] 77-127182 0.50
1. Yoga. I. Title.

BHAKTIVEDANTA, A. c Swami 181'.45
1896-
The perfection of Yoga / A. C. Bhaktivedanta Swami Prabhupada. New York : Bhaktivedanta Book Trust, 1973. 128 p. ; 18 cm. "Combines The Perfection of Yoga and Beyond birth and death." Includes index. [B132.Y6B53152] 73-6488 ISBN 0-912776-17-X
1. Yoga. I. Title.

BHAKTIVEDANTA, A.C., 181'.45
Swami 1896-
The perfection of Yoga [by] A. C. Bhaktivedanta Swami Prakhupada. New York, Iskcon Press [1972] 61 p. 18 cm. [B132.Y6B5315] 72-76302 ISBN 0-912776-36-6
1. Yoga. I. Title.

BHAKTIVEDNTA, A.C., 294.5'43
Swami 1896-
Krsna consciousness, the matchless gift / by A. C. Bhaktivedanta Swami Prabhupada. New York : Bhaktivedanta Book Trust, 1974. 118 p. ; 18 cm. At head of title: All glory to Sri Guru and Gauranga. Includes index. [B132.Y6B53136] 73-76634 ISBN 0-912776-61-7
1. Yoga. I. Title. II. Title: The matchless gift.

BHIKSHU, pseud. 181.
A series of eleven lessons in karma yoga (the yogi philosophy of thought-use) and the yogin doctrine of work, by Bhikshu ... Chicago, Yogi publication society; Tinnevelly, (S. India) The Latent light culture, 1928. 138 p. 20 cm. [B132.Y6B55] 28-30624
1. Yoga. 2. Karma. I. Title. II. Title: Karma yoga.

BRUNTON, Paul. 248
Discover yourself, by Paul Brunton, PH. D. New York, E. P. Dutton & co., inc., 1939. 315 p. 22 cm. "Published in England under the title, The inner reality." "First edition." [B132.Y6B724 1939] 39-6497
1. Yoga. I. Title.

BRUNTON, Paul. 248
The quest of the overself, by Paul Brunton. New York, E. P. Dutton & co., inc. [c1938] 304 p. 22 cm. "First edition." [B132.Y6B727] 38-8306
1. Yoga. I. Title.

BRUNTON, Paul. 181.4
A search in secret India, by Paul Brunton ... New York, E. P. Dutton & co., inc. [1935] 2 p. l., 7-312 p. front., 1 illus., plates, ports. 23 cm. "The truth behind those legends which come ever and anon to our ears, concerning a mysterious class of men called yogis by some and faqueers by others."--p. 13. [B132.Y6B73 1965] 36-950
1. Yoga. 2. Hindus. 3. India—Descr. & trav. 4. India—Religion. 5. Magic, Hindu. I. Title.

BRUNTON, Paul, 1898- 181.4
A search in secret India. London, New York, Rider [1951] 224 p. illus. 22 cm. [B132.Y6B73 1951] 51-8804
1. Yoga. 2. Hindus. 3. India—Descr. & trav. 4. India—Religion. 5. Magic, Hindu. I. Title.

BRUNTON, Paul, 1898- 181.45
The spiritual crisis of man. [1st ed.] New York, Dutton, 1953. 318 p. 21 cm. [B132.Y6B74] 52-12961
1. Yoga. I. Title.

CARRINGTON, Hereward, 1880- 181.
Higher psychical development (Yoga philosophy) an outline of the secret Hindu teachings, by Hereward Carrington ... New York, Dodd, Mead and company, 1920. 2 p. l., vii-x p., 3 l., 296 p. illus., plates. 21 cm. [B132.Y6C4] 20-17105
1. Yoga. I. Title.

CARRINGTON, Hereward, 1880- 181.
... Yoga philosophy: an outline of the secret Hinda teachings by Hereward Carrington ... Girard, Kan., Haldeman-Julius company [c1923]] 127 p. diagr. 12 cm. (Pocket series, no. 421, ed. by E. Haldeman-Julius) Advertising matter: p. 120-127. [B132.Y6C5] Ca24
1. Yoga. I. Title. II. Series.

CHAMAN Lal, 1903- 181'.45
Yoga of meditation. [Fort Lauderdale, Fla., 1971] 253 p. illus. 23 cm. [B132.Y6C545 1971] 72-179424 7.50
1. Yoga. I. Title.

CHAUDHURI, Haridas 181.45
Integral yoga; the concept of harmonious and creative living. Foreword by Pitirim A. Sorokin. London, Allen & Unwin [New York, Hillary House, 1966, c.1965] 160p. 22cm. Bibl. [B132.Y6C58] 65-6163 5.00 bds.,
1. Yoga. I. Title.

CHAUDHURI, Haridas. 181'.45
Integral yoga; the concept of harmonious and creative living. With a foreword by Pitirim A. Sorokin. [1st U.S.A. ed.] Wheaton, Ill., Theosophical Pub. House [1974, c1965] 160 p. 21 cm. (A Quest book) Includes bibliographical references. [B132.Y6C58 1974] 73-17170 ISBN 0-8356-0444-6 2.25 (pbk.)
1. Yoga. I. Title.

CHINMOY. 181'.45
Yoga and the spiritual life; the journey of India's soul [by] Sri Chinmoy. [Jamaica, N.Y., Agni Press, 1974] 210 p. 18 cm. [B132.Y6C5835] 74-81309 ISBN 0-88497-040-X 2.50 (pbk.)
1. Yoga. 2. Spiritual life (Hinduism) 3. Hinduism. I. Title.

COLLIER, Robert Gordon, *181.45
1915-
The amazing secrets of the masters of the Far East. Tarrytown, N.Y., R. Collier Publications [1956- v. 29 cm. [B132.Y6C63] 58-27510
1. Yoga I. Title.

COSGROVE, Eugene Milne, 1886- 133
The high walk of discipleship, by Eugene Milne Cosgrove. Chicago, The Ashram press, 1945. x p., 1 l., 412 p. pl. 23 1/2 cm. Bibliography: p. 411-412. [BF1999.C6965] 45-628
I. Title.

DAS, Bhagavan, 1869- 294.5'43
1958.
Mystic experiences : tales of Yoga and Vedanta from the Yoga Vasistha / [translated by] Bhagavan Das ; with notes by Annie Besant. [El Reno, OK] : Santarasa Publications, 1980. p. cm. Reprint of the 1944 ed. published by Indian Bookshop, Banaras. [BL1146.Y6213 1980] 79-28475 ISBN 0-935548-01-7 pbk. : 3.95
1. Yoga. 2. Vedanta. 3. Self-realization. 4. Mysticism—Hinduism. I. Besant, Annie (Wood) 1847-1933. II. Yogavasistharamayana. English. Selections III. Title.
Publishers Address: Mason Hall Apartments, 1420 W. Abingdon Dr., Apt. 237, Alexandria, VA 22314

DASGUPTA, Surendra Nath, 181'.452
1885-1952.
Yoga as philosophy and religion. Port Washington, N.Y., Kennikat Press [1970] x, 200 p. 21 cm. A brief exposition of the doctrines taught by Patanjali and elaborated by his commentators. [B132.Y6D27 1970] 75-102567
1. Patanjali. 2. Yoga. 3. Philosophy, Hindu. I. Title.

DASGUPTA, Surendra Nath, 181.
1887-
Yoga as philosophy and religion, by Surendranath Dasgupta ... London, K. Paul, Trench, Trubner & co., ltd; New York, E. P. Dutton & co., 1924. x p., 1 l., 200 p. 21 cm. (On cover: Trubner's oriental series) A brief exposition of the doctrines taught by Patafjalt and elaborated by his commentators. [B132.Y6D27] 25-9595
1. Yoga. 2. Philosophy, Hindu. 3. Patafjall. I. Title.

DAVIS, Roy Eugene. 181'.45
Yoga Darsana : the philosophy and light of yoga / Roy Eugene Davis. Lakemont, Ga. : CSA Press, c1976. 205 p. : ill. ; 23 cm. [B132.Y6D315] 76-44603 ISBN 0-87707-176-4 : 7.50
1. Yoga. I. Title.

DAY, Harvey. 181.45
About yoga; the complete philosophy. New York, British Book Centre [1954] 160p. 19cm. [B132.Y6D317 1954] 53-12002
1. Yoga. I. Title.

DHIRENDRA Brahmachari. 181'.45
Yogasana vijnana. The science of yoga. Bombay. New York, Asia Pub. House [1970] xvii, 313 p. (chiefly illus.) 25 cm. Bibliography: p. 305. [B132.Y6D48] 181.482 76-910816 90.00
1. Yoga. I. Title. II. Title: The science of yoga.

DONNELLY, Morwenna. 181.45
Founding the life divine; an introduction to the integral yoga of Sri Aurobindo. [1st American ed.] New York, Hawthorn Books [1956] 246p. 22cm. [B133.G5D6 1956] 56-10838
1. Ghose, Aurobindo, 1872-1950. 2. Yoga. I. Title.

ELIADE, Mircea, 1907- 181'.452
Patanjali and yoga / Mircea Eliade ; translated by Charles Lam Markmann. New York : Schocken Books, 1975, c1969. viii, 216 p. : ill. ; 21 cm. Translation of Patanjali et le Yoga. Reprint of the ed. published by Funk & Wagnalls, New York. Includes index. Bibliography: p. [205]-209. [B132.Y6E493 1975] 75-10785 ISBN 0-8052-0491-1 pbk. : 2.95
1. Patanjali. 2. Yoga. I. Title.

ELIADE, Mircea, 1907- 181.45
Patanjali and Yoga. Translated by Charles Lam Markmann. New York, Funk & Wagnalls [1969] viii, 216 p. illus. 21 cm. Bibliography: p. [205]-209. [B132.Y6E493] 69-18686 5.95
1. Patanjali. 2. Yoga.

ELIADE, Mircea, 1907- 181.45
Yoga; immortality and freedom. Translated from the French by Willard R. Trask. [New York] Pantheon Books [1958] xxii, 529 p. 25 cm. (Bollingen series, 56) Bibliography: p. 437-480. [B132.Y6E523] 58-8986
1. Yoga. I. Title. II. Series.

ELIADE, Mircea, 1907- 294.5'4
Yoga: immortality and freedom. Translated from the French by Willard R. Trask. [2d ed. with corrections and additional bibliographical notes. Princeton, N.J., Published by] Princeton University Press [for Bollingen Foundation, New York, 1969] xxii, 536 p. 25 cm. (Bollingen series, 56) Translation of Le yoga: immortalite et liberte. Bibliography: p. [433]-480. [B132.Y6E523 1969] 74-168024 7.50
1. Yoga. I. Title. II. Series.

FEUERSTEIN, Georg. 181.45
The essence of yoga : a contribution to the psychohistory of Indian civilisation / G. A. Feuerstein. 1st Evergreen ed. New York : Grove Press : distributed by Random House, 1976, c1974. 224 p. : ill. ; 21 cm. (An Evergreen book) Includes index. Bibliography: p. [215]-219. [B 132.Y6F47 1976] 75-42897 ISBN 0-8021-4004-1 pbk. : 3.95
1. Yoga. I. Title.

FEUERSTEIN, Georg. 181'.45'08
Yoga and beyond; essays in Indian philosophy [by] Georg Feuerstein & Jeanine Miller. New York, Schocken Books [1972, c1971] xiii, 176 p. 22 cm. Originally published in London in 1971 under title: A reappraisal of Yoga. Includes bibliographical references. [B132.Y6F48 1972] 73-179075 5.95
1. Yoga. I. Title.

GERVIS, Pearce. 181.45
Naked they pray. [1st American ed.] New York, Duell, Sloan and Pearce [1957, c1956] 217p. illus. 21cm. [B132.Y6G4 1957] 57-7571
1. Yoga. I. Title.

GHERWAL, Rishi Singh, 1889- 181.4
Kundalini, the mother of the universe, the mystery of piercing the six chakras, by Rishi Singh Gherwal ... Santa Barbara. Calif., Author: San Antonio, Tex., La Epoca, the Spanish printers, 1930. viii, 9-165 p. 1 illus. 19 cm. [B132.Y6G48] 212 30-15282
1. Yoga. 2. Chakras (Theosophy) I. Title.

GHERWAL, Rishi Singh, 1889- 181.4
Philosophy of peace, power and plenty; this accompanies my text of super advanced course; copyright ... by Rishi Singh Gherwal. Santa Barbara, Calif., c1932. 3 p. l., 74 p. 20 cm. "First published in 1925."-2d prelim. leaf. [B132.Y6G52 1932] 32-16305
1. Yoga. 2. Occult sciences. I. Title.

GHOSE, Aurobindo 181.45
On Yoga, [2 tomes. Westport, Conn., Associated Booksellers, 1960, i.e. 1959] 843p. 871p. 19cm. (Sri Aurobindo international university, centre collection, v.6 and 7) 60-764 6.00 ea.,
1. Yoga. I. Title. II. Series.

GHOSE, Aurobindo 181.45
A practical guide to integral Yoga; extracts compiled from the writings of Sri Aurobindo and the Mother. [2d ed.] [dist. Westport, Conn., Associated Bksellers] [1959] iv, 428p. illus. 19cm. 60-409 2.50 pap.,
1. Yoga. I. La Mere. II. Title.

GHOSE, Aurobindo, 1872- 181.45
1950.
The synthesis of yoga. New York, E. P. Dutton [1953, c1950]- v. 20cm. (The Sri Aurobindo library) Vol. 1 appeared originally in k1. The yoga of divine works. [B132.Y6] 53-11524
1. Yoga. I. Title.

GHOSE, Aurobindo, 1872- 181.45
1950.
The synthesis of yoga. New York, Sri

Aurobindo Library [c1953- v. 20cm. Copyright date in v. 1 in ms. Vol. 1 appeared originally in Arya, Jan.-Nov. 1915. [B132.Y6G569] 53-86887
1. Yoga. I. Title.

GOPI, Krishma, 1903- 181'.45
The secret of yoga. [1st ed.] New York, Harper & Row [1972] xv, 207 p. 22 cm. (Religious perspectives, v. 23) [B132.Y6G584] 77-184409 ISBN 0-06-064787-6 6.95
1. Yoga. I. Title. II. Series.

GREWAL, Singh, rishi,1889- 181.4
Philosophy of peace, power and plenty; this accompanies my text of super advanced course. Santa Barbara, Calif., c1932. 74 p. 20 cm. Name originally: Ram Rakha Singh Gherwal. [B132.Y6G67 1932] 32-16305
1. Yoga. I. Title.

GYANEE, Bhagwan Singh, 1883- 181.4
The art of living, by Bhagwan S. Gyanee. [Miami Beach, Fla., Printed by Atlantic printers, inc., c1933] 173 p. col. plates, port. 23 cm. [B132.Y6G8] 33-20549
1. Yoga. 2. Glands. 3. Mind and body. I. Occult sciences. II. Title.

HAICH, Elisabeth 181.45
Yoga and destiny [by] Elisabeth Haich, Selvaraian Yesudian. London, Allen & Unwin, 1966. 3-80p. 20cm. [B132.Y6H25] 66-74942 2.50 bds.,
1. Yoga. I. Yesudian, Selva Raja, joint author. II. Title.
Available from Hillary House in New York.

HAICH, Elisabeth. 181'.45
Yoga and destiny / Elisabeth Haich and Selvarajan Yesudian. 1st American ed. New York : ASI Publishers, 1974, c1966. 80 p. ; 19 cm. [B132.Y6H25 1974] 74-83157 ISBN 0-88231-008-9 : 4.50
1. Yoga. I. Yesudian, Selva Raja, joint author. II. Title.

HASTINGS, Stella Flowers, Mrs. 181.4
The kingdom within, by Stella Flowers Hastings.. Los Angeles, Calif.. DeVorss & co. [c1937] 3 p. l., 9-149 p. 19 1/2 cm. [B132.Y6H33] 37-8520
1. Yoga. I. Title.

JANAKANANDA Saraswati, Swami, 1939- 181'.45
Yoga, tantra, and meditation in your daily life / by Swami Janakananda Saraswati (the source of bliss) ; translated by Sheila La Farge. New York : Ballantine Books, 1976. p. cm. Translation of Yoga, tantra, och meditation i min vardag. Includes index. [B132.Y6J3513] 76-13536 ISBN 0-345-25446-5
1. Yoga. I. Title.

JOTIN, Brahmachari, 1903- 181.4
... The law of self-manifestation (karma yoga) by Bramachari Jotin. Washington, D. C., Self-realization fellowship [c1940] 5 p. l., 13-134 p. 18 cm. At head of title: Salvation is the birthright of every man. [B132.Y6J655] 40-14410
1. Yoga. I. Title.

JOTIN, Brahmachari, 1903- 181.4
... The magnetic power of love (Bhakti yoga) by Brahmachari Jotin. Washington, D. C., Self-realization fellowship [c1940] 6 p. l., 15-84 p. 18 cm. [B132.Y6J657] 41-15570
1. Yoga. 2. Love. I. Title.

JOTIN, Brahmachari, 1903- 181.4
... The path of pure consciousness (jana yoge) by Brahmachari, Jotin. Washington, D. C., Self-realization fellowship [c1939] 5 p. l., 13-124 p. 18 cm. [B132.Y6J66] 39-23770
1. Yoga. I. Title.

KIRPAL, Singh, 1894-1974. 181'.45
Surat shabd yoga : the yoga of the celestial pound : an introduction for Western readers / Kirpal Singh. Berkeley, Calif. : Images Press, 1976, c1975 71 p. ; 22 cm. (The Unity of man series) [B132.Y6K497 1975] 75-42816 ISBN 0-9600374-4-6 pbk. : 2.50
1. Yoga. I. Title.

KRISHNANANDA, Rishi, 1886- 181.4
"Let there be light!" by Rishi Krishnananda ... [New York, N. Y.] The Para-vidya center [c1940] 166 p. 20 cm. Copyright date on verse of t.-p. corrected in manuscript from 1969 to 1940. [B132.Y6K7] 40-32359
1. Yoga. 2. Reincarnation. I. Title.

KRISHNANANDA, Rishi, 1886- 181.4
The mystery of breath, by Rishi Krishnananda ... New York, N. Y., The Para-vida center [c1940] 96 p. 20 cm. Includes advertising matter. [B132.Y6K72] 40-35909
1. Yoga. 2. Respiration. I. Title.

KRISHNANANDA, Rishi, 1886- 181.4
The mystery of breath, by Rishi Krishnananda ... 2d ed. New York, N. Y., The Para-vida [i. e. Para-vidya] center [c1941] 96 p. 20 cm. Includes advertising matter. [B132.Y6K72 1941] 41-17435
1. Yoga. 2. Respiration. I. Title.

LIGHT on kriya yoga: 891.21
Kaushitaki Upanishad, The mystic way; Mundaka Upanishad, The mystic ritual; Taittiriya Upanishad, The mystic revelation. [Translated into English from the original Sanskrit text] by Swami Premananda. Washington, Self-Realization Church [1955] 109p. illus. 21cm. [BL1120.A3P64] [BL1120.A3P64] 294.1 56-15030 56-15030
1. Yoga. I. Upanishads. English. Selections. II. Premananda, Swami, 1906- ed. and tr.

MACHOVEC, Frank J. 181'.45
Yoga; an introduction to inner tranquility, by Frank J. MacHovec. Illus. by Marian Morton. Mount Vernon, N.Y., Peter Pauper Press [1972] 62 p. illus. 20 cm. [B132.Y6M246] 73-161267 1.50
1. Yoga. I. Title.

MCLAURIN, Hamish. 181.4
Eastern philosophy for western minds; an approach to the principles and modern practice of yoga, by Hamish McLaurin ... Boston, Mass., The Stratford company [c1933] 3 p. l., xii, 282 p. 21 cm. Bibliography: p. 261-279. [B132.Y6M25] 33-18494
1. Yoga. 2. Vedas. 3. Philosophy, Hindu. I. Title.
Contents omitted.

MAJITHIA, Surendra Singh, Sir. 181'.45
The great yogic sermon [by] Sir Surendra Singh Majithia [and] Y. G. Krishnamurti. Bombay, New York, Allied Publishers [1969] 212 p. illus. (part col.), facsim. 28 cm. English and Sanskrit. "Yoganusasanam" (romanized form): p. [169]-212. [B132.Y6M275] 77-911012 108.00
1. Yoga. I. Krishnamurti, Y. G., joint author. II. Yoganusasanam. 1969. III. Title.

MISHRA, Rammurti S 181.45
Fundamentals of yoga; a handbook of theory, practice, and application. Drawings by Oscar Weinland. New York, Julian Press, 1959. 255p. illus. 22cm. [B132.Y6M5] 59-10065
1. Yoga. I. Title.

MISHRA, Rammurti S. 181.45
Fundamentals of yoga; a handbook of theory, practice and application. Garden City, N.Y., Anchor Books [1974, c1959] 210 p. 18 cm. [B132.Y6M5] ISBN 0-385-00952-6. 2.50 (pbk.)
1. Yoga. I. Title.
L.C. card no. for hardbound ed.: 59-10065.

MISHRA, Rammurti S 181.452
The textbook of Yoga psychology, a new translation and interpretation of Patanjali's Yoga sutras for meaningful application in all modern psychologic disciplines. Edited by Ann Adman. New York, Julian Press [1963] xiv, 401 p. diagr. 25 cm. Includes transliterated Sanskrit text of the aphorisms. [B132.Y6M52] 63-12485
1. Yoga. I. Patanjali. Yogasutra. II. Title.

MISHRA, Rammurti S. 181'.452
Yoga sutras: the textbook of Yoga psychology [by] Rammurti S. Mishra. Garden City, N.Y., Anchor Press, 1973 [c1963] xvi, 538 p. 18 cm. First published under title: The textbook of Yoga psychology. Includes transliterated Sanskrit text of the aphorisms. [B132.Y6M52 1973] 73-161294 ISBN 0-385-08358-0 2.95 (pbk.)
1. Yoga. I. Patanjali. Yogasutra. II. Title.

MOZUMDAR, A. K.
The life and the way; the Christian yoga metaphysics, by A. K. Mozumdar ... 1st ed. New York [Printed by Modra press, c1911] 3 p. l., [9]-150 p. 21 cm. 12-927 3.00
I. Title.

MUKERJI, A P swami. 181.
Yoga lessons for developing spiritual consciousness, by Swamie A. P. Mukerji ... Chicago, Ill., Yogi publication society; [etc., etc. c1911] 191 p. 20 cm. [B132.Y6M8] 11-15605
1. Yoga. I. Title.

NARAYANANANDA, Swami. 181'.45
The primal power in man ; or, The kundalini shakti / Swami Narayanananda. 5th rev. ed. Gylling, Denmark : Narayanananda Universal Yoga Trust & Ashrama, 1976. 233 p., [3] leaves of plates : ports. ; 22 cm. [B132.Y6N36 1976] 77-150977 ISBN 8-7875-7101-3 : kr45.00 ($7.30 U.S.)
1. Yoga. I. Title.

PANDITA, Indiradevi. 181'.45
A bo[u]quet of love : yoga and meditation for everyone / by Yoga Pandita Indiradevi and R. L. Landers. [Fort Lauderdale, Fl.] : Pandita, c1975. xl, 248 p. : ill. ; 18 cm. [B132.Y6P24] 75-37396 5.00
1. Yoga. 2. Meditation. I. Landers, R. L., 1922- joint author. II. Title.

PARANJALI. 181.4
Patanjali's raja yoga; a revelation of the science of yoga, with commentary byRishi Singh Gherwal ... [Santa Barbara, Calif., R. S. Gherwal, 1935] 3 p. l., 196 p. 20 cm. [B132.Y6P26] 35-9866
1. Yoga. I. Gherwal, Rishi Singh, 1889- II. Title. III. Title: Raja yoga.

PATANJALI 181.45
How to know God: the Yoga aphorisms of Patanjali, translated with a new commentary by Swami Prabhavananda and Christopher Isherwood. [1st ed.] New York, Harper [1953] 224p. 15cm. [B132.Y6P267 1953] 52-12775
1. Yoga. I. Prabhavananda, Swami. 1896- ed. and tr. II. Isherwood, Christopher, 1904- ed. and tr. III. Title.

PATANJALI. 181.
The light of the soul, its science and effect; a paraphrases of the Yoga sutras of Pantanjali with commentary by Alice A. Bailey ... 1st ed. New York, Lucis publishing company, 1927. xvii, 426 p. 20 cm. Bibliography: p. xvil. [B132.Y6P28 1927] 27-23703
1. Yoga. I. Bailey, Allen A. Mrs. II. Title. III. Title: The Yoga sutras.

PATANJALI. 181.
The light of the soul, its science and effect; a paraphrase of the Yoga sutras of Patanjali with commentary by Alice A. Bailey ... 1st ed. New York, Lucis publishing company, 1927. xvii, 428 p. 19 1/2 cm. Bibliography: p. xvii. [B132.Y6P28 1927] 27-23703
1. Yoga. I. Bailey, Alice Anne (LaTrobe-Bateman) 1880- II. Title. III. Title: The Yoga sutras.

PATANJALI. 181'.452
Patanjali's Yoga sutras, with the commentary of Vyasa and the gloss of Vachaspati Misra. Translated by Rama Prasada, with an introd. by Srisa Chandra Vasu. Allahabad, Panini Office, 1912. [New York, AMS Press, 1974] p. cm. Cover title: Aphorisms of yoga. Original ed. issued as v. 4 of The Sacred books of the Hindus. English and Sanskrit. [B132.Y6P26413 1974] 73-3789 ISBN 0-404-57804-7 22.50
1. Yoga. I. Rama Prasada, ed. II. Vyasa. Yogabhasya. English & Sanskrit. 1974. III. Vacaspatimisra, disciple of Martandatilakasvamin. Yogatattvavaisaradi. English & Sanskrit. 1974. IV. Title: Aphorisms of yoga. V. Series: The Sacred books of

PATANJALI 181.4
Practical yoga, ancient and modern, by Ernest E. Wood; being a new, independent translation of Patanjali's Yoga aphorisms, interpreted in the light of ancient and modern psychological knowledge and practical experience. With an introd. by Paul Brunton. 1966 ed. Hollywood, Calif., Wilshire [1966, c.1948] 245p. 21cm. [B132.Y6P267] 2.00 pap.,
1. Yoga. I. Wood, Ernest, 1883- II. Title.

PATANJALI. 181.
The Yoga aphorisms of Patanjali; an interpretation by William Q. Judge, assisted by James Henderson Connelly. New York, The Theosophical publishing company of New York, 1912. xx p., 1 l., 74 p. 15 cm. Preface to 1st edition dated 1889. [B132.Y6P3] 12-8885
1. Yoga. I. Judge, William Quan, 1851-1896, ed. II. Connelly, James Henderson, 1840-1903. joint ed. III. Title.

PATANJALI 181.452
Yoga-sutra of Patanjali; [translated] by J. R. Ballantyne and Govind Sastri Deva. Calcutta, Susil Gupta (India) Private [dist. S. Pasadena, Calif., Hutchins Oriental Bks.] 114, 8p. (Bibl. notes: p.113-114) 22cm. Includes a translation of the commentary by Bhojaraja, entitled Rajamatanda. 'Sanskrit text of Yogasutram of Patanjali': 8p. at end. 60-50677 4.00 lea. cloth,
1. Yoga. I. Ballantyne, James Robert, 1813-1864, tr. II. Sastri Deva, Govind, tr. III. Bhoja-raja, King of Dhara. Rajamartanda. IV. Title.

PATANJALI 294.
The Yoga-system of Patanjali: or, The ancient Hindu doctrine of concentration of mind, embracing the mnemonic rules, called Yoga-sutras, of Patanjali, and the comment, called Yoga-bhashya, attributed to Veda-Vyasa, and the explanation, called Tattva-vaicaradi, of Vachaspati-Micra; tr. from the original Sanskrit by James Haughton Woods ... Cambridge, Mass., The Harvard university press, 1914. xii, 384 p. 26 cm. (Added t.-p.: Harvard oriental seires ... v. 17) "Printed from type at the University press, Oxford, England, by Horace Hart, M. A., printer to the University." "First edition, 750 copies, October, 1914." "Bibliography of works referred to in this volume": p. [354]-358. [PK2971.H3 vol. 17] 17-5466
1. Yoga. I. Vyasa. II. Vachaspati Misra. III. Woods, James Haughton, 1864-1935, tr. IV. Title. V. Title: Tattva-valcaradi.

PREMANANDA, swami, 1903- 181.4
... God, the universal reality, by Brahmachari Jotin. Washington, D.C. Self-realization fellowship [c1936] 5 p. l., 13-90 p. 18 cm. [Name originally: Brahmachari Jotin] [B132.Y6P68] 37-3809
1. Yoga. I. Washington, D.C. Self-realization, fellowship (Non-sectarian church) II. Title.

PREMANANDA, swami, 1903- 181.4
... The law of self-manifestation (karma yoga) by Brahmachari Jotin. Washington, D.C., Self-realization fellowship [1940] 5 p. l., 13-134 p. 18 cm. [Name originally: Brahmachart Jotin] [B132.Y6P7] 40-14410
1. Yoga. I. Washington, D.C. Self-realization fellowship (Non-sectarian church) II. Title.

PREMANANDA, swami, 1903- 181.4
... The magnetic power of love (bhakti yoga) by Brahmachari Jotin. Washington, D.C., Self-realization fellowship [c1940] 6 p. l., 15-84 p. 18 cm. [Name originally: Brahmachari Jotin] [B132.Y6P72] 41-15570
1. Yoga. 2. Love. I. Washington, D.C., Self-realization fellowship (Non-sectarian church) II. Title.

PREMANANDA, swami, 1903- 181.4
... The path of pure consciousness (jnana yoga) by Brahmachari Jotin. Washington, D.C., Self-realization fellowship [c1939] 5 p. l., 13-124 p. 18 cm. [Name originally: Brahmachari Jotin] [B132.Y6P74] 39-23770
1. Yoga. I. Washington, D.C. Self-realization fellowship (Non-sectarian church) II. Title.

PREMANANDA, swami, 1903- 181.4
... Prayers of self-realization, by Swami Premananda. Washington, D.C., Self-realization fellowship [1943] 6 p. l., 19-135 p. front (port.) 21 1/2 cm. [Name

originally: Brahmachari Jotin] [B132.Y6P76 1943] 43-14425
1. Yoga. I. Washington, D.C. Self-realization fellowship (Nonsectarian church) II. Title.

PREMANANDA, swami, 1903- 181.4
... *Realization of the self,* by Brahmachari Jotin. Washington, D.C., Self-realization fellowship [c1936] 3 p. l., [9]-37 p. 15 1/2 cm. [Name originally: Brachmachari Jotin] [B132.Y6P78] 36-8802
1. Yoga. I. Washington, D.C. Self-realization fellowship (Non-sectarian church) II. Title.

*RAWLS, Eugene S. 181.4'5
Joy of life through yoga, by Eugene S. Rawls and Eve, Diskin. [New York] Warner Paperback Library [1975] 144 p. 18 cm. [B132] 1.25 (pbk.)
1. Yoga. I. Diskin, Eve, joint author. II. Title.

RICHMOND, Sonya. 294.5'4
Common sense about yoga. New York, St. Martin's Press [1972, c1971] 171 p. 23 cm. [B132.Y6R457 1972] 70-184556 ISBN 0-261-63235-3 4.95
1. Yoga. I. Title.

RISHABHCHAND 181.45
In the mother's light. Madras, Society for the Spiritual and Cultural Renaissance of Bharat [dist. Westport, Conn., Associated Booksellers, 1960] 2v. 184p; 217p. (Bibl. footnotes) 19cm. Vol. 2 has imprint: Pondicherry, Sri Aurobindo Ashram. 60-408 1.25; 1.75 v.1., v.2,
1. Ghose, Aurobindo, 1872-1950. 2. Yoga. I. Title.

RYAN, Charles James. 181.4
... *Yoga and yoga discipline,* a theosophical interpretation, by Charles J. Ryan. Point Loma, Calif., Theosophical university press, 1940. 3 p. l., 73, [2] p. 15 cm. [Theosophical manual no. XV) [B132.Y6R9] 44-44410
1. Yoga. 2. Theosophy. I. Title.

[SABHA-PATI Svami] 1840- 181.
Esoteric cosmic yogi science; or, Works of the world teacher ... copyright ... by Prof. Wm. Estep ... Excelsior Springs, Mo., The Super mind science publications [c1929] 2 v. fronts. (ports.) illus., plates. 19 1/2 cm. "This book consists of teachings written down by disciples of the great master, Guru Yogi, Sabbapathi Swami, gnyana yogi of India ... These manuscripts were published in India in part ... in the year of 1888 ... the author-publisher now offers them to the English speaking western world students of Yoga."--Foreword. [B132.Y6S3] 29-4339
1. Yoga. I. Estep, William. II. Title.

SADHU, Mouni 181.482
Concentration. a guide to mental mastery. Hollywood, Calif., Wilshire, 1967[c.1959] 219p. 21cm. Bibl. [B132.Y6S32-181.45] 2.00 pap.,
1. Yoga. I. Title.

SADHU, Mouni. 181.45
Concentration, a guide to mental mastery. [1st ed.] New York, Harper [1959] 222 p. 22 cm. Includes bibliography. [B132.Y6S32] 59-6327
1. Yoga. I. Title.

SATYANANDA Saraswati, Swami, 1923- 181'.452
Four chapters on freedom : commentary on Yoga sutras of Patanjali / lectures delivered by Satyananda Paramahamsa ; editor, Swami Haripremananda Saraswati. Monghyr : Bihar School of Yoga, c1976. xxii, 288 p., [1] leaf of plates : ill. ; 22 cm. English and Sanskrit. Includes index. [B132.Y6S393] 76-904616 Rs35.00
1. Patanjali. Yogasutra. 2. Yoga. I. Title.

SRI Krishna Prem, 1898-1965. 181'.45
Initiation into yoga : an introduction to the spiritual life / by Sri Krishna Prem ; with a foreword by Madhava Ashish. London : Rider, 1976. 128 p. ; 20 cm. Contents.Contents.—Initiation into yoga.—Symbolism and knowledge.—The sacred marriage.—The forgotten land.—Doubts and their removal.—Past, present and future.—Superstition.—The violence of war.—Religion and philosophy. [B132.Y6S7 1976b] 76-372928 ISBN 0-09-125631-3 : £1.95
1. Yoga. I. Title.

STEARN, Jess. 181.45
Yoga, youth, and reincarnation. Photos. of Marcia Moore by Frank Stork. Drawings by Goldie Lipson. [1st ed.] Garden City, N.Y., Doubleday, 1965. 392 p. illus. 22 cm. [B132.Y6S76] 65-13265
1. Yoga. I. Title.

SUKUL, Deva Ram. 181.4
Yoga and self-culture; higher laws of spiritual dynamics including outline of philosophy of the Vedas, Upanishads, Bhagavad Gita, and the six systems of Hindu philosophy. New York, Yoga Institute of America [1948, c1947] 206 p. illus. (part col.) port. 22 cm. [B132.Y6S8 1948] 48-21663
1. Yoga. I. Title.

SUKUL, Deva Ram. 181.4
Yoga and self-culture; higher laws of spiritual dynamics, including outline of philosophy of the Vedas, Upanishads, Bhagavad Gita, and the six systems of Hindu philosophy, by Sri Deva Ram Sukul ... New York, N.Y., Yoga institute of America [1943] 3 p. l., iii-x, [11]-188 pl. incl. illus. (part col.) tables. front. (port.) pl. 21 cm. [B132.Y6S8] 43-11019
1. Yoga. I. Yoga institute of America. II. Title.

TAIMNI, I. K., 1898- 181'.45
The science of yoga; a commentary on the Yoga-sutras of Patanjali in the light of modern thought, by I. K. Taimni. Wheaton, Ill., Theosophical Pub. House [1967, c1961] xiii, 448 p. illus. 21 cm. (A Quest book) [B132.Y6T3] 67-4112
1. Yoga. I. Patanjali. Yogasutra. II. Title.

VARENNE, Jean. 181'.45
Yoga and the Hindu tradition / Jean Varenne ; translated from the French by Derek Coltman. Chicago : University of Chicago Press, 1976. x, 253 p. ; 23 cm. Translation of Le yoga et la tradition hindoue. "Yoga Darshana Upanishad": p. 200-222. Includes index. Bibliography: p. 237-240. [B132.Y6V2913] 75-19506 ISBN 0-226-85114-1 : 12.50
1. Yoga. I. Upanishads. Darsanopanisad. English. Selections. II. Title.

VASU, Srisa Chandra, rai bahadur, 1861-1918? 181'.45
An introduction to the Yoga philosophy / by Srisa Chandra Vasu. New York : AMS Press, [1974] vi, iv, 70 p. ; 23 cm. Reprint of the 1915 ed. published by the Panini Office, Allahabad, which was issued as v. 15, pt. 4 of The Sacred books of the Hindus, under the general title: Yoga sastra. [B132.Y6V36 1974] 73-3806 ISBN 0-404-57838-1 : 14.50
1. Yoga. I. Title. II. Title: Yoga sastra. III. Series: The Sacred books of the Hindus ; v. 15, pt. 4.

VISHNUDEVANANDA Swami. 181.45
The complete illustrated book of yoga. Introd. by Marcus Bach. New York, Julian Press, 1960. 359 p. illus. 26 cm. Includes bibliography. [B132.Y6V47] 59-15568
1. Yoga.

VIVEKANANDA, swami, 1863-1902. 181.
... *Eight lectures,* by the Swami Vivekananda, on Karma Yoga, (the secret of work,) delivered in New York, winter 1895-6 ... New York, Brentano's [1896] 54 p. 22 1/2 cm. Published under the auspices of the Vedanta society. [B132.V3V57 1896] 18-27498
1. Yoga. I. Vedanta society. II. Title.

VIVEKANANDA, swami, 1863-1902. 181.
Yoga philosophy; lectures delivered in New York, winter of 1895-6, by the Swami Vivekananda on raja yoga or conquering the internal nature; also Patanjali's yoga aphorisms, with commentaries. New ed. London, New York [etc.] Longmans, Green, and co., 1897. x p., 1 l., 234 p., 1 l. incl. front. (port.) 19 1/2 cm. [B132.V3 V58 1897] 40-20998
1. Yoga. I. Patañjali. II. Title.

WENTZ, Walter Yeeling Evans. 181'.45
Tibetan yoga and secret doctrines; or, Seven books of wisdom of the great path, according to the late Lama Kazi Dawa-Samdup's English rendering. Arranged and edited with introductions and annotations to serve as a commentary by W. Y. Evans-Wentz. With foreword by R. R. Marett and Yogic commentary by Chen-chi Chang, 2nd ed. [reprinted]. London, New York [etc.],Oxford U. P., 1967 [i.e. 1968]. xiiv, 389 p. 9 plates, illus., facsims., ports. 21 cm. (A Galaxy book 212) 19/p Bibliographical footnotes. [B132.Y6W4] 68-92112
1. Yoga. I. Zia-ba-Basam-grub, Kazi, 1868-1922, tr. II. Title. III. Title: Seven books of wisdom of the great path.
Contents omitted

WENTZ, Walter Yeeling Evans, ed. 181.45
Tibetan yoga and secret doctrines; or, Seven books of wisdom of the great path, according to the late Lama Kazi Dawa Samdup's English rendering. Arranged and edited with introductions and annotations to serve as a commentary by W. Y. Evans-Wentz. With foreword by R. R. Marett and Yogic commentary by Chen-chi Chang. 2d ed. London, New York, Oxford University Press, 1958. xill, 389 p. plates (part col.) ports., facsims. 23 cm. Contents.Contents.—General introduction.—The supreme path of discipleship: the precepts of the gurus.—The nirvanic path: the yoga of the great symbol.—The path of knowledge: the yoga of the six doctrines.—The path of transference: the yoga of consciousness-transference.—The path of the mystic sacrifice: the yoga of subduing the lower self.—The path of the five wisdoms: the yoga of the long hum.—The path of the transcendental wisdom: the yoga of the voidness. Bibliographical footnotes. [B132.Y6W4 1958] 58-2456
1. Yoga. I. Zla-ba-Basam-'grub, Kazi, 1868-1922, tr. II. Title. III. Title: Seven books of wisdom of the great path.

WENTZ, Walter Yeeling Evans, ed. 181.4
Tibetan yoga and secret doctrines; or, Seven books of wisdom of the great path, according to the late Lima Kazi Dawa-Samdup's English rendering; arranged and edited with introductions and annotations to serve as a commentary by W. Y. Evans-Wentz...with a foreword by Dr. R. R. Marett. London, Oxford university press H. Milford, 1935. xxiv, 389, [1] p. front., plates (1 col.) facsims. 22 1/2 cm. [B132.Y6W4] 35-23617
1. Yoga. I. Zin-ba Bsam grub, Kazi, 1868-1922, tr. II. Title. III. Title: Seven books of wisdom of the great path.

WOOD, Ernest, 1883- 181.
Raja yoga; the occult training of the Hindus, by Ernest Wood ... Sydney, Chicago [etc.] Theosophical publishing house [1927?] 68, [2] p. 18 1/2 cm. [Full name: Ernest Egerton Wood] [B132.Y6W59] 43-34509
1. Yoga. I. Title.

WOOD, Ernest, 1883-1965. 181'.45
Seven schools of yoga, an introduction. [1st U.S. ed.] Wheaton, Ill., Theosophical Pub. House [1973] 113 p. 19 cm. (A Quest book) First published in 1931 under title: The occult training of the Hindus. [B132.Y6W588 1973] 72-13120 ISBN 0-8356-0435-7 1.75
1. Yoga. I. Title.

*WOODROFFE, Sir John George, 1865-1936. 294.5'5'14
The serpent power: being the Sat-cakra-nirupana and Paduka-pancaka, two works on Laya-Yoga, translated from the Sanskrit, with introduction and commentary by Sir John Woodroffe. [8th ed.] Madras, Ganesh & Co. [1972] xii, 569 p. 9 col. plates, front port. 23 cm.
1. Yoga. 2. Shaktism. I. Avalon, Arthur, 1865-1936. II. Title.
Distributed by Vedanta Pr., Hollywood, Calif., for 12.00. ISBN 0-87481-303-4.

YESUDIAN, Selva Raja. 181.45
Yoga uniting East and West [by] Selvarajan Yesudian and Elisabeth Haich. Foreword by T. Huzella. Translated by John P. Robertson. [New York] 160p. illus. 22cm. [B132.Y4912 1956a] 55-11281
1. Yoga. I. Halch, Elisabeth, joint author. II. arper III. Title.

YESUDIAN, Selva Raja. *181.45
Yoga uniting East and West [by] Selvarajan Yesudian and Elisabeth Haich. Foreword by T. Huzella. Translated by John P. Robertson. [New York] Harper [1956] 160 p. illus. 22 cm. [B132.Y6Y4912 1956a] 55-11281
1. Yoga. I. Haich, Elisabeth, joint author. II. Title.

YOGA-VASISHTHA-RAMAYANA. 181.4
Selections. English.
Yoga Vashisht; or, Heaven found, by Rishi Singh Gherwal ... Santa Barbara, Calif., Author, 1930. 189 p. 20 1/2 cm. "We have two Yoga Vashishts, one going under the name great, the other small. This is the small book."--Introd. [B132.Y6Y6] 43-44633
1. Yoga. 2. Vedanta. 3. Buddha and Buddhism. I. Gherwal, Rishi Singh, 1889- tr. II. Title.

YOGANANDA, paramhansa. 181.4
Metaphysical meditations, by Swami Yogananda. [Los Angeles, Calif., Self-realization fellowship, c1932] 94 p. 14 cm. "Third edition." [B132.Y6Y617 1932] 40-16548
1. Yoga. I. Self-realization fellowship. II. Title.

YOGANANDA, paramhansa. 181.4
Whispers from eternity; universal scientific prayers and poems, by S. Yogananda. Los Angeles, Calif., Self-realization fellowship (Yogoda sat-sanga) 1935. 2 p. l., [9]-329 p. front. (port.) 18 1/2 cm. "Third enlarged edition." [B132.Y6Y62 1935] 35-14983
1. Yoga. I. Self-realization fellowship. II. Title.

YOGANANDA, Paramhansa, 1893-1952. 181.45
The Master said; sayings and counsel to disciples by Paramhansa Yogananda,[2d ed.] Los Angeles, Self-Realization Fellowship, 1957. 116 p. illus. 20 cm. [B133.Y6M3 1957] 59-590
1. Yoga. I. Title.

YOGANANDA, Paramhansa, 1893-1952. *181.45
Whispers from eternity. Foreword by Amelita Galli-Curci. [7th ed.] Los Angeles, Self-Realization Fellowship, 1958. 266 p. illus. 20 cm. [B132.Y6Y62 1958] 58-59965
1. Yoga. I. Title.

YOGANANDA, Paramahansa, 1893-1952. 181.45
Whispers from eternity. Foreword by Amelita Galli-Curci. [8th ed.] Los Angeles, Self-Realization Fellowship, 1959. 274 p. illus. 20 cm. [B132.Y6Y62 1959] 59-44917
1. Yoga. I. Title.

YOGANANDA, Paramhansa, 1893-1952 181'.45
Sayings of Yogananda; inspiring counsel to disciples. [3d ed.] Los Angeles, Self-Realization Fellowship, 1968. vii, 126p. illus., ports. 20cm. First-2d ed. pub. under title: The master said. [BP605.S4Y6 1968] 67-31344 2.50
1. Yoga. I. Title.
Publisher's address: 3880 San Rafael Ave., Los Angeles, Calif. 90065.

Yoga—Addresses, essays, lectures.

BHAKTIVEDANTA Swami, A. C., 1896-1977. 294.5'43
The path of perfection : yoga for the modern age / A. C. Bhaktivedanta Swami Prabhupada. Los Angeles : Bhaktivedanta Book Trust, c1979. p. cm. Includes index. Bibliography: p. [B132.Y6B53147 1979] 79-9626 ISBN 0-89213-103-9 : 9.95
1. Yoga—Addresses, essays, lectures. I. Title.

CHAMPAKLAL'S treasures / editor, M. P. Pandit. Pondicherry : Sri Aurobindo Ashram, Publication Dept., 1976. 234 p., [4] leaves of plates : ports. ; 23 cm. [B132.Y6C546] 77-900789 Rs18.00 181'.45
1. Yoga—Addresses, essays, lectures. 2. Philosophy, Indic—Addresses, essays, lectures. I. Pandit, Madhav Pundalik, 1918-

RAJANEESH, Archarya, 1931- 181'.452
Yoga, the alpha and the omega : discourses on the yoga sutras of Patanjali / Rajneesh ; compilation, Swami Amrit Pathik ; editing, Ma Ananda Prem. 1st ed. Poona : Rajneesh Foundation, 1976- v. : ill. ; 23 cm. [B132.Y6R322] 76-902396 Rs65.00 (v. 1)
1. Patanjali. Yogasutra—Addresses, essays, lectures. 2. Yoga—Addresses, essays, lectures. I. Title.

TATTWA katha : 181'.45
a tale of truth / from the teachings of Guru Purnananda Paramahansa, Guru Bhumananda Paramahansa, Guru Janardan Paramahansa, handed down from guru to disciple ; translated under the guidance of Guru Janardan Paramahansa by his disciples. New York : Ajapa Yoga Foundation, 1976- v. : ports. ; 22 cm. [B132.Y6T33313] 77-150042
1. Yoga—Addresses, essays, lectures. I. Purnananda Paramahansa. II. Bhumananda Parmamahansa. III. Janardan Paramahansa.

Yoga, Bhakti.

BHAKTIVEDANTA, A. C. Swami 1896- 294.5'43
Easy journey to other planets, by practice of supreme yoga [by] A. C. Bhaktivedanta Swami Prabhupada. Rev. ed. New York, Macmillan [1972] 96 p. 18 cm. [B132.Y6B5313 1972] 72-80068 1.25 (pbk.)
1. Yoga, Bhakti. 2. God (Hinduism) 3. Matter. I. Title.

BHAKTIVEDANTA A.C Swami 1896- 294.5'43
Easy journey to other planets (by practice of supreme yoga), by A. C. Bhaktivedanta Swami. 2d ed. Boston, Iskon Press [1970] 49 p. 19 cm. [B132.Y6B5313 1970] 70-118080 0.50
1. Yoga, Bhakti. 2. God (Hinduism) 3. Matter. I. Title.

Yoga—Congresses.

PERSPECTIVES in yoga : 181'.45
[papers] / edited by A. K. Sinha. 1st ed. Varanasi : Bharata Manisha, 1976. vi, 132 p., [8] leaves of plates : ill. ; 23 cm. (Bharata Manisha research series ; 6) Organized under the auspices of the Department of Philosophy & Psychology in Kurukshetra University, Kurukshetra in 1973." Includes bibliographical references. [B132.Y6P43] 76-901247 ISBN 0-88386-815-6 : 8.00 Rs25.00
1. Yoga—Congresses. I. Sinha, A. K. II. Series.
Distributed by South Asia Books.

Yoga—Dictionaries.

*SIVANANDA, Sri Swami 181.45
Yoga vedanta dictionary [by] Sri Swami Sivananda Jawaharnagar, Dehli Motilal Banarsidass 1973 190 p. 19 cm. [B132.Y6] ISBN 0-8426-0540-1
1. Yoga—Dictionaries. I. Title.
Distributed by Verry, Mystic, Conn. for 3.50

WOOD, Ernest, 1883-1965. 181'.45'03
Yoga wisdom. New York, Philosophical Library; [distributed by Book Sales, c1970] 101 p. 21 cm. (Castle books) [B132.Y6W595] 70-115402 ISBN 0-8022-2025-8 2.75
1. Yoga—Dictionaries. I. Title.

Yoga—Early works to 1800.

PATANJALI. 181'.452
The Yoga-system of Patanjali; or, The ancient Hindu doctrine of concentration of mind, embracing the mnemonic rules, called Yoga-sutras of Patanjali and the comment, called Yoga-bhashya, attributed to Veda-Vyasa and the explanation, called Tattva-vaicaradi, of Vachaspati-Micra. Translated from the original Sanskrit by James Haughton Woods. New York, Gordon Press, 1973. xli, 381 p. 24 cm. Reprint of the 1914 ed. published by Harvard University Press, Cambridge, which was issued as v. 17 of Harvard oriental series. Bibliography: p. [351]-358. [B132.Y6P267 1973] 73-8278 ISBN 0-87968-083-0
1. Yoga—Early works to 1800. I. Woods, James Haughton, 1864-1935, tr. II. Vyasa. Yogabhaaya. 1973. III. Vacaspatimisra, disciple of Martandatilakasvamin. Yogatattvavaisaradi. 1973. IV. Title. V. Series: Harvard oriental seri

Yoga, Hatha.

BERNARD, Theos, 1908- 181.4
Hatha yoga; the report of a personal experience, by Theos Bernard ... New York, Columbia university press, 1944. ix. [2]. 68 p. front., xxxvi pl. on 18 l. 26 cm. Issued also as thesis (PH. D.) Columbia university. "Recommended reading": p. [63]-64. [B132.Y6B425 1944 a] A 44
1. Yoga, Hatha. I. Title.

GHERANDASAMHITA. English and Sanskrit. 294.5'9
The Gheranda samhita / translated by Srisa Chandra Vasu. New York : AMS Press, [1974] ii, 59 p. ; 23 cm. Reprint of the 1914 ed. published by the Panini Office, Allahabad, which was issued as v. 15, pt. 2 of The Sacred books of the Hindus, under the general title: Yoga sastra. [B132.Y6G52413] 73-3804 ISBN 0-404-57836-5 : 14.50
1. Yoga, Hatha. I. Vasu, Srisa Chandra, rai bahadur, 1861-1918? ed. II. Title. III. Title: Yoga sastra. IV. Series: The Sacred books of the Hindus ; v. 15, pt. 2.

IYENGAR. B. K. S. 1918- 181.45
Light on yoga; yoga dipika. Foreword by Yehudi Menuhin. New York, Schocken [1966, c.1965] 342p. illus., port. 25cm. [B132.Y6195 1966] 66-11371 14.95
1. Yoga, Hatha. I. Title.

SIVASAMHITA. English and Sanskrit. 294.5'9
The Siva samhita / translated by Srisa Chandra Vasu. New York : AMS Press, [1974] 87 p. ; 23 cm. Reprint of the 1914 ed. published by the Panini Office, Allahabad, which was issued as v. 15, pt. 1 of The Sacred books of the Hindus, under the general title: Yoga sastra. [B132.Y6S56613 1974] 73-3803 ISBN 0-404-57815-2
1. Yoga, Hatha. 2. Shaktism. I. Vasu, Srisa Chandra, rai bahadur, 1861-1918? ed. II. Title. III. Title: Yoga sastra. IV. Series: The Sacred books of the Hindus ; v. 15, pt. 1.

SPIEGELBERG, Frederic, 1897- 181.45
Spiritual practices of India. Introd. by Alan W. Watts. [New York] Citadel Press, 1962 [e1951] 68 p. illus. 20 cm. Translation of Hatha-Yoga. [B132.Y6S653] 62-17829
1. Yoga, Hatha. I. Title.

SVATMARAMA, Swami. 181'.45
The Hatha yoga pradipika. Translated into English by Pancham Singh. Allahabad, Panini Office, 1915. [New York, AMS Press, 1974] v, 63 p. 23 cm. Issued separately as extra v. 2 of the Sacred books of the Hindus. Original ed. issued as v. 15, pt. 3 of the series, under the general title: Yoga sastra. English and Sanskrit; introd. in English. [B132.Y6S853 1974] 73-3805 ISBN 0-404-57837-3
1. Yoga, Hatha. I. Sing, Pancham, ed. II. Title. III. Title: Yoga sastra. IV. Series: The Sacred books of the Hindus, extra v. 2.

Yoga, Jnana.

PREMANANDA, Swami, 1903- 181.4
The path of pure consciousness (Jnana yoga) [Rev. and enl. ed.) Washington, Self-realization Fellowship [1944) 148 p. port. 20 cm. Name originally: Brahmachari Jetia. [B132.Y6P74 1944] 49-36033
1. Yoga, Jnana. I. Title.

SIVANANDA, Swami. 181'.45
Gyana yoga. [1st ed.] Delhi, Motilal Banarsidass [1973, i.e. 1974] ii, 267 p. (p. 241-267 advertisements) 19 cm. Reprint of the 1944 ed. published by the Sivananda Publication League, Rishikesh. [B132.Y6S52195 1973] 73-905191 ISBN 0-8426-0539-8.
1. Yoga, Jnana. 2. Knowledge, Theory of (Hinduism) I. Title.
Distributed by Verry, 3.75

Yoga, Karma.

VIVEKANANDA, Swami, 1863-1902. 181.45
Karma-yoga and Bhakti-yoga. Rev. ed. New York, Ramakrishna-Vivekananda Center, 1955. viii, 316p. ports. 16cm. Pref. signed: Nikhilanada. [B132.Y6V53 1955] 55-8657
1. Yoga, Karma. 2. Yoga, Bhakti. I. Nlkhllananda, Swami, ed. II. Title.

Yoga, Laya.

WOODROFFE, John George, Sir, 1865-1936, ed. and tr. 181'.45
The serpent power; being the Sat-cakra-nirupana and Paduka-pancaka: two works on Laya-yoga, translated from the Sanskrit, with introd. and commentary, by Arthur Avalon (Sir John Woodroffe). New York, Dover Publications [1974] xiv, 529 p. illus. 22 cm. Reprint of the 7th ed. published in 1964 by Ganesh, Madras; with the Sanskrit text (v, 184 p. at end) omitted. English and Sanskrit. Includes the commentary of Kalicarana on each of the texts. [B132.Y6W6 1974] 74-75259 ISBN 0-486-23058-9 5.00 (pbk.)
1. Yoga, Laya. 2. Shaktism. I. Kalicarana. II. Purnananda, fl. 1526-1577. Satcakranirupanam. English & Sanskrit. 1964. III. Padukapancakam. English & Sanskrit. 1964. IV. Title. V. Title: Sat-cakra-nirupana.

Yoga—Quotations, maxims, etc.

THE Day with yoga : 181'.45
a spiritual yoga path for thinking people / compiled and edited by Elisabeth Haich ; translated by D. Q. Stephenson ; drawings by Selvarajan Yesudian. 1st ed. New York : ASI Publishers, c1977. vii, 85 p. : ill. ; 18 cm. Translation of Der Tag mit Yoga. [B132.Y6T2813 1976] 76-42208 ISBN 0-88231-026-7 pbk. : 2.50
1. Yoga—Quotations, maxims, etc. I. Haich, Elisabeth.

PASTANJALI.
The Yoga sutras of Pantanjali, "The book of the spiritual man"; an interpretation by Charles Johnston. New York, C. Johnston, 1912. 2 p. l., [3]-118, [1] p. 22 cm. 13-5082 1.25
I. Johnston, Charles, 1867- II. Title.

Yoga, Raja.

PATANJALI 181.45
Yoga: union with the ultimate. A new version of the ancient Yoga sutras of Patanjali, by Archie J. Bahm. New York, Ungar [c.1961] 162p. bBibl. 60-53365 8.50 bds.,
1. Yoga, Raja. I. Bahm, Archie J. II. Title.

PATANJALI. 181.45
Yoga: union with the ultimate. A new version of the ancient Yoga sutras of Patanjali, by Archie J. Bahm. New York, Ungar [1961] 162p. 19cm. Bibliography: p. 159-162. [B132.Y6P267 1961] 60-53365
1. Yoga, Raja. I. Bahm, Archie J. II. Title.

VIVEKANANDA, Swami, 1863-1902. 181.45
Raja-yoga. Rev. [i.e. 2d] ed. New York, Ramakrishna-Vivekananda Center, 1955. 297 p. illus. 16 cm. [B132.V3V58 1955] 55-12231
1. Yoga, Raja.

Yogacara (Buddhism)

ASANGA. 294.3'4'2
On knowing reality : the Tattvartha chapter of Asanga's Bodhisattvabhumi / translated with introd., commentary, and notes by Janice Dean Willis. New York : Columbia University Press, [1979] p. cm. Translation of Tattvarthapatala, the 4th chapter of pt. 1 of Bodhisattvabhumi, the 15th section of Yogacarabhumi. A revision of the author's thesis, Columbia University. Bibliography: p. [BQ3062.E54W54 1979] 79-16047 ISBN 0-231-04604-9 : 20.00
1. Yogacara (Buddhism) I. Willis, Janice Dean. II. Title.

MAITREYANATHA. 294.3'4'2
Madhyanta-vibhanga; discourse on discrimination between middle and extremes, ascribed to Bodhisattva Maitreya. Commented by Vasubandhu and Sthiramati. Translated from the Sanskrit by Th. Stcherbatsky. Reprint. [Calcutta, Indian Studies: Past & Present, 1971] 223 p. 23 cm. (Soviet indology series, no. 5) (Bibliotheca Buddhica. Reprint, 30) Imprint covered by label: Sole distributors: Firma K. L. Mukhopadhyay, Calcutta. Label mounted on t.p.: Distributed by Lawrence Verry, Mystic, Conn. Includes bibliographical references. [BQ2962.E5S53 1971] 78-920098 14.00
1. Yogacara (Buddhism) I. Vasubandhu. Madhyantavibhagasutrabhasya. II. Sthiramati. Madhyantavibhagasutrabhasyatika. III. Shcherbatskoi, Fedor Ippolitovich, 1866-1942, tr. IV. Title. V. Series: Bibliotheca Buddhica, 30.

Yogi.

ABHEDANANDA, swami.
Vedanta philosophy; how to be a Yogi, by Swami Abhedananda. New York, The Vedanta society [1902] 188 p. 19 1/2 cm. 2-20063
I. Title.

[ATKINSON, William Walker] 1862-
The life beyond death, by Yogi Ramacharaka [pseud.] ... Chicago, Ill., Yogi publication society, 1912. 2 p. l., 7-192 p. 20 cm. 13-2020 1.00
I. Title.

GUPTA, Yogi. 181.45
Yoga and yogic powers. New York, Yogi Gupta New York Center [c1961] 240 p. illus. 25 cm. [B132.Y6G713] 63-14948
1. Yogi. I. Title.

Yom Kippur.

GOODMAN, Philip, 1911- comp. 296.4'32'08
The Yom Kippur anthology. [1st ed.] Philadelphia, Jewish Publication Society of America, 1971. xxix, 399 p. illus., facsims., music. 22 cm. Companion volume to the compiler's The Rosh Hashanah anthology. Bibliography: p. 387-399. [BM695.A8G66] 72-151312 7.50
1. Yom Kippur. I. Title.

Yom Kippur—Juvenile literature.

SIMON, Norma. 296.432
Yom Kippur. Illus. by Ayala Gordon. [New York 27] 3080 Bway. United Synagogue Commission on Jewish Education, c.1959. unpaged. illus. (col.) 25 x 15cm. 59-12529 .95 bds.,
1. Yom Kippur—Juvenile literature. I. Title.

Yonkers, N. Y.—Churches.

KIRKWOOD, Aghes E. 277.
Church and Sunday-school work in Yonkers: its origin and progress. By Agnes E. Kirkwood ... New York, G. L. Shearer [1891] 523 p. incl. front., illus. 24 cm. [BR560.Y7K5] 42-2195
1. Yonkers, N. Y.—Churches. I. Title.

Yonkers, N. Y. First Westminster Presbyterian Church.

SMITH, Catherine Ruth, 1906- 285.1747277
These years of grace; the history of Westminster Presbyterian Church, Yonkers, New York, 1858-1964. Yonkers, N.Y., First Westminster Presbyterian Church, 1965. xix, 582 p. illus., ports. 24 cm. Bibliography: p. 557-560. [BX9211.Y6F55] 65-26440
1. Yonkders, N.Y. First Westminster Presbyterian Church. 2. Yonkers, N.Y. Westminster Presbyterian Church. 3. Yonkers, N.Y. First Presbyterian Church. I. Title.

Yonkers, N.Y. Saint John's Evangelical Lutheran Church.

YONKERS, N.Y. 284'.1'09747277
Saint John's Evangelical Lutheran Church.
Built on the rock, 1869-1969; a history of Saint John's Evangelical Lutheran Church, Yonkers, New York. [Yonkers, 1970] 90 p. illus., facsims., ports. 29 cm. 500 copies printed. No. 486. Bibliography: p. 50. [BX8076.Y6S25] 72-119757
1. Yonkers, N.Y. Saint John's Evangelical Lutheran Church. I. Title.

Yoram.

†SACUTUS, Victor. 299
The Messiah in Sovietland : the historical openness of the revolting Yoramians / by Victor Sacutus. 1st ed. New York : Vantage Press, c1976. 316 p. ; 21 cm. [BP610.Y672S2] 77-362606 ISBN 0-533-01793-9 : 6.95
1. Yoram. 2. Georgia (Transcaucasia)—Religion. 3. Georgia (Transcaucasia)—History—1917- I. Title.

Yorgason, James, 1847-1917.

YORGASON, Blaine M., 1942- 289.3'3 B
Tall timber : the struggles of James Yorgason, a Mormon polygamist / by Blaine M. Yorgason. [Rexburg, Idaho] : Ricks College Press, 1976. xx, 315 p. : ill. ; 29 cm. Includes index. Bibliography: p. 224-228. [BX8695.Y67Y67] 76-28588 25.00
1. Yorgason, James, 1847-1917. 2. Mormons and Mormonism—Biography. I. Title.

York, Eng. (Diocese)

ORNSBY, George, 1809-1886.
... *York.* By George Ornsby ... Pub. under the direction of the Tract committee. London, Society for promoting Christian knowledge; New York, E. & J. B. Young & co. [1882] 2 p. l., 440 p. front. (fold. map) 17 cm. (Diocesan histories) [BX5107.Y6O7] 4-207
1. York, Eng. (Diocese) I. Title.

York, Eng. (Diocese)—History—Sources.

YORK, Eng. (Diocese) Archbishop, 1480-1500 (Thomas Rotherham) 282'.428'43
The register of Thomas Rotherham, Archbishop of York, 1480-1500 / edited by Eric E. Barker. [York, Eng.] : Canterbury and York Society, 1976- v. ; 25 cm. ([Canterbury and York series] ; v. 69) Cover title: Diocesis Eboracensis, registrum Thome Rotherham. [BX1495.Y67Y67 1976] 77-353537
1. York, Eng. (Diocese)—History—Sources. I. Barker, Eric Ernest. II. Title. III. Series: Canterbury and York Society. Canterbury and York series ; v. 69.

York minister.

THOMPSON, Alexander Hamilton, 1873- ed. 283.
York minister historical tracts, 627-1927, edited by A. Hamilton Thompson ... London, Society for promoting Christian knowledge; New York and Toronto, The Macmillan co., 1927. [436] p. 1 illus. 22 1/2 cm. [BX5195.Y6T5] 28-8774
1. York minister. 2. Gt. Brit.—Church history. I. Title.

York, Ray Earl, 1882-

BROWN, Bertha B. Mrs. 922
The life and sermons of Ray York, known as the boy evangelist; being a sketch of his early life, an account of his conversion, his call to the ministry, his first sermon, and his subsequent ministerial life, with a few sermons and sermon outlines. Compiled by Mrs. Bertha B. Brown, 1st ed. Kansas City, Mo., Chas. E. Brown printing co., 1898. 229 p. front., ports. 20 cm. [BV3785.Y6B7] 37-37090
1. York, Ray Earl, 1882- 2. Sermons, English. I. Title.

York, Thomas Lee.

YORK, Thomas Lee. 248'.2'0924 B
And sleep in the woods : the story of one man's spiritual quest / Thomas York. 1st ed. Toronto : Doubleday Canada Ltd. ; Garden City, N.Y. : Doubleday, 1978. x, 221 p. ; 22 cm. [BV4935.Y67A32] 77-82775 ISBN 0-385-13236-0 : 7.95
1. York, Thomas Lee. 2. Converts—Canada—Biography. 3. Vietnamese Conflict, 1961-1975—Draft resisters—Arkansas. I. Title.

Yorkshire, Eng.—Church history.

RAISTRICK, Arthur. 333.3'22'0942841
Monks & shepherds in the Yorkshire Dales / [by] Arthur Raistrick. [Leyburn] : Yorkshire Dales National Park Committee, 1976. [3], 22, [1] p. : ill., map ; 21 cm. [BX2596.F7R34] 77-363287 ISBN 0-905455-04-5 : £0.45
1. Fountains Abbey. 2. Bolton Abbey. 3. Yorkshire, Eng.—Church history. 4. Wool trade and industry—England—Yorkshire. I. Title.

Yorkshire, Eng. North Riding—Church history.

AVELING, Hugh 282.4274
Northern Catholics: the Catholic recusants of the North Riding of Yorkshire. 1558-1790. London, Dublin [etc] G. Chapman, 1966. 477p. 4 plates (incl. facsim.) 23cm. (Studies in theol. & church hist. ser.) Maps on end-papers. Bibl. [BX1494.Y6A9] 66-68727 12.50
1. Yorkshire, Eng. North Riding—Church history. 2. Catholics in Yorkshire, Eng. I. Title.
American distributor: Hillary House, New York.

Yorkshire, Eng.—Religious life and customs—Addresses, essays, lectures.

VALE, Malcolm Graham Allan. 942.8'008 s
Piety, charity, and literacy among the Yorkshire gentry, 1370-1480 / by M. G. A. Vale. [York] : [St Anthony's Press], 1976. [5], 32 p. 1 ill ; 21 cm. (Borthwick papers ; no. 50 ISSN 0524-0913s) Includes bibliographical references. [DA670.Y59B6 no. 50] [BR763.Y6] 301.5'8 77-367708 ISBN 0-900701-43-9 : £0.60
1. Yorkshire, Eng.—Religious life and customs—Addresses, essays, lectures. 2. Charities—England—Yorkshire—Addresses, essays, lectures. 3. Illiteracy—England—Yorkshire—Addresses, essays, lectures. I. Title. II. Series: Borthwick papers ; no. 50.

Yorktown, N.Y.—Biography.

LEE, Arthur C. 285'.1747'277
History of the First Presbyterian Church of Yorktown from 1906 to 1975 / by Arthur C. Lee. [s.l. : s.n.], c1976 ([Yorktown Heights, N.Y. : Mohansic Press]) 75 p. : ill. ; 22 cm. [BX9211.Y66F574] 76-368308
1. First Presbyterian Church of Yorktown. 2. Yorktown, N.Y.—Biography.

Yorktown, Va. Grace Church.

HATCH, Charles E. 283.755'42
Grace Church; general study, by Charles E. Hatch, Jr. Washington, Office of History and Historic Architecture, Eastern Service Center, 1970. v, 92 p. 23 plates. 26 cm. At head of title: Colonial National Historical Park, Yorktown, Virginia. Includes bibliographical references. [BX5980.Y6G7] 78-612222
1. Yorktown, Va. Grace Church. I. Title. II. Title: Colonial National Historical Park, Yorktown, Virginia.

Yorubas.

FARROW, Stephen Septimus. 299'.6'096692
Faith, fancies, and fetich; or, Yoruba paganism; being some account of the religious beliefs of the West African Negroes, particularly of the Yoruba tribes of Southern Nigeria, by Stephen S. Farrow. With a foreword by R. R. Marett. New York, Negro Universities Press [1969] xi, 180 p. illus. 23 cm. "Yoruba Christian lyrics" (with melodies): p. 170-173. Reprint of the 1926 ed. Bibliography: p. 9-11. [BL2480.Y6F3 1969] 76-98718
1. Yorubas. 2. Folk-lore—Nigeria—Yoruba. 3. Fetishism. I. Title.

FARROW, Stephen Septimus. 299.
Faith, fancies and fetich, or Yoruba paginism; being some account of the religious beliefs of the West African negroes, particularly of the Yoruba trives of Southern Nigeria, by Stephen S. Farrow ... With a foreword by Dr. R. R. Marett ... London, Society for promoting Christian knowledge; New York and Toronto, The Macmillan co. [1926] xi, 180 p. front., illus. (incl. music) plates. 29 cm. "A thesis approved for the degree of doctor of philosophy in the University of Edinburgh, 1924." Bibliography: p. 9-11. [BL2480.Y6F3] 27-12718
1. Yoruba. 2. Folk-lore—Nigeria—Yoruba. 3. Fetishism. I. Title.

Yorubas—Religion.

AWOLALU, J. .Omosade. 299'.683
Yoruba beliefs and sacrificial rites / J. Omosade Awolalu. London : Longman, 1979. xvi, 203 p., [4] leaves of plates : ill. ; 22 cm. Includes bibliographical references and index. [BL2480.Y6A96] 79-670588 ISBN 0-582-64203-5 : 25.00 £4.50
1. Yorubas—Religion. 2. Sacrifice. 3. Rites and ceremonies—Nigeria. I. Title.
Available from Longman, NY, NY

BASCOM, William Russell, 1912- 299'.6
Sixteen cowries : Yoruba divination from Africa to the New World / William Bascom. Bloomington : Indiana University Press, c1978. p. cm. Includes bibliographical references. [BL2480.Y6B37] 78-3239 ISBN 0-253-35280-0 : 22.50
1. Yorubas—Religion. 2. Divination—Nigeria. 3. Blacks—Latin America—Religion. 4. Cowries.

IDOWU, E. Bolaji. 299.64
Olodumare; God in Yoruba belief. New York, Praeger [1963] 222 p. illus. 23 cm. (Books that matter) [BL2480.Y6 I 3 1963] 63-12823
1. Yorubas — Religion. I. Title. II. Title: God in Yoruba belief.

Young adults—Religious life.

JONES, Rufus, 1915- 248'.83
If I were in my thirties / by Rufus Jones. Nashville : T. Nelson, c1978. 130 p. ; 21 cm. Bibliography: p. 118-130. [BV4529.2.J66] 77-27398 ISBN 0-8407-5626-7 pbk. : 2.95
1. Jones, Rufus, 1915- 2. Young adults—Religious life. 3. Christianity—20th century. I. Title.

KLINSING, P. David. 248.8'3
Is there life after high school? / Compiled by P. David Klinsing. Harrisburg, PA : Christian Publications, c1979. 116 p. ; 19 cm. [BV4529.2.K55] 19 79-53677 ISBN 0-87509-264-0 pbk. : 2.50
1. Young adults—Religious life. I. Title.

METTS, Wally. 248'.83
The life you'd love to live / Wally Metts. Denver : Accent Books, c1978. 128 p. ; 18 cm. [BV4529.2.M47] 77-87953 ISBN 0-916406-83-0 pbk. : 1.75
1. Young adults—Religious life. 2. Young adults—Conduct of life. I. Title.

†PITMAN, Thomas B. 248'.83
Reaching for the sky : a challenge to young adulthood / Thomas B. Pitman III. Cleveland, Tenn. : Pathway Press, c1976. 144 p. ; 18 cm. Bibliography: p. 143-144. [BV4529.2.P57] 75-37358 ISBN 0-87148-731-4 pbk. : 2.50
1. Young adults—Religious life. I. Title.

RUSBULDT, Richard E. 248'.83
Planning your life : understanding yourself and the person you want to become / Richard E. Rusbuldt. Valley Forge, PA : Judson Press, c1978. 88 p. : ill. ; 22 cm. Presents a program of 12 sessions for the study and planning of life goals. Includes Biblical references and suggestions for use of the material in a group setting. [BV4529.2.R87] 78-8767 ISBN 0-8170-0817-9 : pbk. : 2.50
1. Young adults—Religious life. 2. Young adults—Conduct of life. 3. Youth—Religious life. 4. Youth—Conduct of life. 5. [Christian life.] 6. [Conduct of life.] I. Title.

Young adults—United States.

DRANE, James F. 261.8'34'315
A new American reformation; a study of youth culture and religion, by James Drane. New York, Philosophical Library [1973] 166 p. 23 cm. Includes bibliographical references. [HQ799.7.D7] 73-82161 ISBN 0-8022-2123-8 7.50
1. Young adults—United States. 2. Youth—Religious life. 3. Jesus People. I. Title.

Young adults—United States—Religion life.

HARGROVE, Barbara W. 291'.0973
Religion for a dislocated generation : where will those who grew up in the sixties find faith? / Barbara Hargrove. Valley Forge, PA : Judson Press, c1980. 141 p. ; 23 cm. Includes bibliographical references. [BL2530.U6H37] 19 80-25400 ISBN 0-8170-0891-8 : 9.95
1. Young adults—United States—Religion life. 2. United States—Religion—1960- 3. United States—Civilization—1945- I. Title.

Young, Ann Eliza (Webb) b.1844.

WALLACE, Irving 922.8373
The twenty-seventh wife. New York, New Amer. Lib. [1962, c.1961] 400p. 18cm. (Signet Bk. T2133) Bibl. .75 pap.,
1. Young, Ann Eliza (Webb) b.1844. 2. Mormons and Mormonism. 3. Polygamy. I. Title.

WALLACE, Irving, 1916- 992.8373
The twenty-seventh wife. New York, Simon and Schuster, 1961. 443 p. illus. 24 cm. Includes bibliography. [BX8641.Y7W3] 61-9599
1. Young, Ann Eliza (Webb) b. 1844. 2. Mormons and Mormonism. 3. Polygamy. I. Title.

YOUNG, Anna Eliza (Webb) Mrs., 1844-
Life in Mormon bondage; a complete expose of its false prophets, murderous Danites, despotic rulers and hypnotized deluded subjects, by Ann Eliza Young, 19th wife of Brigham Young. Limited ed. Philadelphia, Boston [etc.] Aldine press, inc. [c1908] 1 p. l., 512 p. front., illus., plates, ports. 23 1/2 cm. "Edition de luxe. Copy No. A1." 8-20999
I. Title.

Young, Brigham, 1801-1877.

BURT, Olive (Wooliey) 1894- 922.8373
Brigham Young. New York, J. Messner [1956] 192p. 22cm. [BX8695.Y7B8] 56-10445
1. Young, Brigham, 1801-1877. I. Title.

BURT, Olive (Woolley) 1894- 289.3'0924 B
Brigham Young [by] Olive Burt. New York, J. Messner [1956] 192 p. 22 cm. Bibliography p. 188. A biography of the Mormon convert who later became the President of his church and led his people to the Great Salt Lake Valley to establish a large Mormon colony. [BX8695.Y7B8] 92 AC 68
1. Young, Brigham, 1801-1877. I. Title.

CANNON, Frank Jenne, 1859- 922
Brigham Young and his Mormon empire, by Frank J. Cannon and George L. Knapp ... New York, Chicago [etc.] Fleming H. Revell company [1913]. 398 p. front.,

plates, ports. 21 cm. [F826.Y7] 13-24816 1.50.
1. Young, Brigham, 1801-1877. 2. Mormons and Mormonism. 3. Utah==Hist. I. Knapp, George Leonard, 1872- joint author. II. Title.

GATES, Susa (Young) 1856-1933. 289.3'0924 B
The life story of Brigham Young: Mormon leader, founder of Salt Lake City, and builder of an empire in the uncharted wastes of Western America, by Susa Young Gates, in collaboration with Leah D. Widtsoe. Freeport, N.Y., Books for Libraries Press [1971] 287 p. illus., map, ports. 24 cm. Reprint of the 1930 ed. [BX8695.Y7G3 1971] 74-164602 ISBN 0-8369-5886-1
1. Young, Brigham, 1801-1877. 2. Mormons and Mormonism. I. Widtsoe, Leah Eudora (Dunford) 1874- joint author. II. Title.

GATES, Susa (Young) Mrs., 1856-1933. 922.83
The life story of Brigham Young, by Susa Young Gates (one of his daughters) in collaboration with Leah D. Widtsoe, with a foreword by Reed Smoot. New York, The Macmillan company, 1930. xviii p., 1 l., 388 p. front., plates. ports. 24 1/2 cm. [BX8695.Y7G3] 30-25731
1. Young, Brigham, 1801-1877. 2. Mormons and Mormonism. I. Widtsoe, Mrs. Leah Eudora (Dunford) 1871- joint author. II. Title.

GIBBONS, Francis M., 1921- 289.3'3 B
Brigham Young, modern Moses, prophet of God / Francis M. Gibbons. Salt Lake City, Utah : Deseret Book Co., 1981. 286 p. ; 24 cm. Includes index. Bibliography: p. 277-278. [BX8695.Y7G53] 19 81-7766 ISBN 0-87747-858-9 : 8.95
1. Young, Brigham, 1801-1877. 2. Mormons—United States—Biography. I. Title.

HIRSHSON, Stanley P., 1928- 289.3'0924 B
The lion of the Lord; a biography of Brigham Young [by] Stanley P. Hirshson. [1st ed.] New York, Knopf, 1969. xx, 391, xxvi p. illus. 25 cm. Bibliography: p. 377-391. [BX8695.Y7H55] 70-79334 8.95
1. Young, Brigham, 1801-1877. I. Title.

HUNTER, Milton Reed. 289.373
Brigham Young, the colonizer, by Milton R. Hunter, PH.D. Salt Lake City, Utah, The Deseret news press, 1940. xvi p., 1 l., 383 p. front., illus. (maps) plates, ports. 22 1/2 cm. Bibliography: p. [368]-378. [BX8695.Y7H8] 41-4197
1. Young, Brigham, 1801-1877. 2. Mormons and Mormonism. I. Title.

HUNTER, Milton Reed, 1902- 289.3'092'4 B
Brigham Young the colonizer, by Milton R. Hunter. [4th ed., rev.] Santa Barbara, Calif., Peregrine Smith, 1973. xviii, 399 p. illus. 23 cm. A revision of the author's thesis, University of California, Berkeley, 1935. Bibliography: p. [384]-389. [BX8695.Y7H8 1973] 73-85421 ISBN 0-87905-017-9 8.95
1. Young, Brigham, 1801-1877. 2. Mormons and Mormonism. I. Title.

NIBLEY, Preston. 922.8373
Brigham Young, the man and his work, by Preston Nebley... Salt Lake City, Utah, Deseret news press, 1936. 2 p. l., 551 p. front., ports. 23 1/2 cm. "This book is the out-growth of a series of articles which appeared in the church section of the Desert news during the years 1934 and 1935." [BX3695.Y7N5] 37-789
1. Young, Brigham, 1801-1877. 2. Mormons and Mormonism. I. Title.

SPENCER, Clarissa (Young) 1860- 922.8373
Brigham Young at home, by Clarissa Young Spencer with Mabel Harmer. Salt Lake City, Deseret Book Co., 1961 [e1940] 301 p. illus. 24 cm. [BX8695.Y7S58 1961] 61-3053
1. Young, Brigham, 1801-1877. 2. Mormons and Mormonism. I. Title.

SPENCER, Clarissa (Young) Mrs., 1860- 922.
One who was valiant, by Clarissa Young Spencer, with Mabel Harmer; illustrated with photographs. Caldwell, Id., The Caxton printers, ltd., 1940. 279 p., 1 l. front., plates, ports. 23 1/2 cm. [BX8695.Y7S6] 922 ISBN 40-3943
1. Young, Brigham, 1801-1877. 2. Mormons and Mormonism. I. Harmer, Mabel, 1894- II. Title.

TULLIDGE, Edward Wheelock. 922.8373
Life of Brigham Young; or, Utah and her founders. By Edward W. Tullidge. New York, 1876. 2 p. l., iv, 458, 81 p. front. (port.) 22 1/2 cm. "Biographical sketches, supplementary to "Life of Brigham Young: or, Utah and her founders"": 81 p. at end. [BX8695.Y7T8] 36-31810
1. Young, Brigham, 1801-1877. 2. Utah—Hist. 3. Utah—Biog. 4. Mormons and Mormonism. I. Title.

WAITE, Catharine (Van Valkenburg) Mrs. 1829-1913. 922.8373
The Mormon prophet and his harem; or, An authentic history of Brigham Young, his numerous wives and children. By Mrs. C. V. Waite ... Cambridge [Mass.] Printed at the Riverside press, and for sale by Hurd & Houghton, New York; [etc., etc.] 1866. x, 280 p. front., plates, ports., plan. 19 cm. [BX8695.Y7W3] 36-31808
1. Young, Brigham, 1801-1877. 2. Mormons and Mormonism. I. Title.

WAITE, Catharine (Van Valkenburg) Mrs., 1829-1913. 922.83
The Mormon prophet and his harem; or, An authentic history of Brigham Young, his numerous wives and children. By Mrs. C. V. Waite ... 3d ed. Cambridge [Mass.] Printed at the Riverside press, and for sale by Hurd & Houghton, New York; [etc., etc.] 1867. x, 280 p. pl., 4 port. (incl. front.) 19 1/2 cm. [F826.Y73] 19-19021
1. Young, Brigham, 1801-1877. 2. Mormons and Mormonism. I. Title.

WERNER, Morris Robert, 1897- 289.3'092'4 B
Brigham Young / by M. R. Werner. Westport, Conn. : Hyperion Press, 1975, c1925. p. cm. Reprint of the ed. published by Harcourt, Brace, New York. Includes index. Bibliography: p. [BX8695.Y7W4 1975] 75-351 ISBN 0-88355-254-X : 26.50
1. Young, Brigham, 1801-1877. 2. Mormons and Mormonism.

WERNER, Morris Robert, 1897- 922.
Brigham Young, by M. R. Werner... New York, Harcourt, Brace and company [1925] xvi, 478 p. front., illus., plates, ports. 22 1/2 cm. "First edition." Bibliography: p. 463-469. [BX8695.Y7W4] 25-11448
1. Young, Brigham, 1801-1877. 2. Mormons and Mormonism. I. Title.

WEST, Ray Benedict, 1908- 289.309
Kingdom of the saints; the story of Brigham Young and the Mormons. New York, Viking Press, 1957. 389 p. illus. 22 cm. [BX8611.W4] 57-6437
1. Young, Brigham, 1801-1877. 2. Mormons and Mormonism—History. I. Title.

YOUNG, Brigham, 1801-1877. 289.3'092'4 B
Letters of Brigham Young to his sons / edited and introduced by Dean C. Jessee ; with a foreword by J. H. Adamson. Salt Lake City : Deseret Book Co., 1974. xliv, 375 p. : ports. ; 25 cm. (The Mormon heritage series ; v. 1) Includes bibliographical references and index. [BX8695.Y7A4 1974] 74-80041 ISBN 0-87747-522-9 : 9.95
1. Young, Brigham, 1801-1877. 2. Mormons and Mormonism—Biography. I. Jessee, Dean C., ed. II. Title.

YOUNG, Brigham, 1801-1877. 289.3'0924
Manuscript history of Brigham Young, 1801-1844. Elden Jay Watson. [Salt Lake City, Smith Secretarial Service, c1968] xxxv, 274 p. illus., facsims., port. 26 cm. "From volumes 25 and 26 of Millennial Star." [BX8695.Y7A3] 75-15709
I. Watson, Elden Jay. II. Title.

YOUNG, Brigham, 1801-1877. 289.3'0924
Manuscript history of Brigham Young, 1846-1847. [Edited by] Elden J. Watson. [Salt Lake City, Utah, J. Watson, 1971] 672 p. illus. 23 cm. [BX8695.Y7A3 1971] 77-27431
I. Watson, Elden Jay. II. Title.

YOUNG, Seymour Dilworth, 1897- 922.8373
Here is Brigham; Brigham Young, the years to 1844, by S. Dilworth Young. Salt Lake City, Bookcraft [c1964] 370 p. illus., facsims., maps, ports. 24 cm. Bibliography: p. [6] [BX8695.Y7Y7] 65-1650
1. Young, Brigham, 1801-1877. I. Title.

Young, Brigham, 1801-1877—Juvenile literature.

NEELEY, Deta Petersen. 922.8373
A child's story of the prophet Brigham Young, by Deta Petersen Nelley and Nathan Glen Neeley. Salt Lake City, Deseret News Press, 1959. 171p. illus. 20cm. [BX8695.Y7N4] 60-457
1. Young, Brigham, 1801-1877—Juvenile literature. I. Neeley, Nathan Glen, joint author. II. Title.

Young Christian Students.

ANDERSON, James.
This is the Y C S; an introduction to the Young Christian Student movement for high school Y.C.S. Chicago, Ill. [1956?] 102 p. illus. 18 x 24 cm. NUC63
1. Young Christian Students. I. Title.

Young Christian workers.

DE LA BEDOYERE, Michael Anthony Maurice, 1900- 922.173
The Cardijn story; a study of the life of Mgr. Joseph Cardijn and the Young Christian Workers' movement which he founded. London, Longmans, Green [Mystic, Conn., Verry, 1965, c.1958] xi, 196p. illus., ports. 21cm. Bibl. A62 3.50 bds.,
1. Cardyn, Leon Joseph Marie, 1882- 2. Young Christian Workers. I. Title.

STEWART, Mary.
A king among men; Christ's summons to the spirit of youth to found His kingdom, by Mary Stewart ... New York, Chicago [etc.] Fleming H. Revell company [c1915] 128 p. 18 1/2 cm. $0.50. 15-21649
I. Title.

THE YCW chaplain.
Chicago, Young Christian Workers [1960] 54p. 21cm.
1. Young Christian workers. I. Hill, John J

Young Christian Workers — Handbooks, manuals, etc.

YOUNG Christian Workers.
Man in work and leisure; 1959-1960 YCW inquiry program. Chicago, Young Christian Workers [1959] 173 p. illus., forms. 22 cm. 67-20913
1. Young Christian Workers — Handbooks, manuals, etc. I. Title.

Young John Freeman, bp., 1820-1885.

PENNINGTON, Edgar Legare, 1891- 922.373
... *John Freeman Young,* second bishop of Florida, by Edgar Legare Pennington ... Hartford, Conn., Church missions publishing company, 1939. 2 pt. in 1 v. 23 cm. (Soldier and servant ... Publication no. 195-196) Paged continuously. [BX5995.Y55P4] 42-18315
1. Young John Freeman, bp., 1820-1885. I. Title.

Young Life Campaign.

CAILLIET, Emile, 1894- 267.61
Young life. New York, Harper [1964, c.1963] viii, 120p. 22cm. 64-10614 2.95
1. Rayburn, James C. 2. Young Life Campaign. I. Title.

MEREDITH, Char. 267'.13
It's a sin to bore a kid : the story of young life / Char Meredith. Waco, Tex. : Word Books, 1977, c1978. 144 p. : ill. ; 22 cm. [BV4487.Y6M47] 77-83312 ISBN 0-8499-0043-3 : 5.95
1. Young Life Campaign. I. Title.

MILLIKEN, Bill. 267'.61'0924
Tough love [by] Bill Milliken, with Char Meredith. Old Tappan, N.J., F. H. Revell Co. [1968] 160 p. 21 cm. [BV4447.M5] 68-17092 3.95
1. Young Life Campaign. 2. Church work with youth. I. Meredith, Char, joint author. II. Title.

Young men.

AINSLIE, Peter, 1867- 170
Plain talks to young men on vital issues, by Peter Ainslie ... [St. Louis] Christian publishing company, 1897. 106 p. 16 cm. [BJ1671.A2] 19-12641
1. Young men. 2. Conduct of life. I. Title.

BANKS, Louis Albert, 1855- 170
My young man, by Rev. Louis Albert Banks ... A series of addresses to young men delivered in the Young men's Christian association hall, Cleveland, Ohio. New York and London, Funk & Wagnalls company, 1899. v, [7]-123 p. 19 1/2 cm. [BJ1671.B13] 99-2493
1. Young men. I. Title.

BEECHER, Henry Ward, 1813-1887. 170
Lectures to young men, on various important subjects, by Henry Ward Beecher ... 13th thousand. Boston, J.P. Jewett & co.; New York, Saxton & Miles, 1846. 251 p. 19 cm. [BJ1671.B4 1846] 9-29948
1. Young men. I. Title.

BEECHER, Henry Ward, 1813-1887. 170
Lectures to young men, on various important subjects, by Henry Lard Beecher ... 19th thousand. Boston, J. P. Jewett; New York, M. H. Newman & co. [etc., etc.], 1851. 251 p. 19 cm. [BJ1671.B4 1851] 9-29949
1. Young men. I. Title.

BEECHER, Henry Ward, 1813-1887. 170
Lectures to young men, on various important subjects. By Henry Ward Beecher. New ed., with additional lectures. New York, J.B. Ford and company, 1873. 2 p. 1., [xv]-xvii, [1] p., 2 1., 280 p. 19 1/2 c,. [BJ1671.B4 1873] 13-11925
1. Young men. I. Title.

BEECHER, Henry Ward, 1813-1887. 170
Seven lectures to young men, on various important subjects; delivered before the young men of Indianapolis, Indiana, during the winter of 1843-4. By Henry Ward Beecher. Indianapolis, T. B. Cutler; Cincinnati, W. H. Moore & co., 1844. 4 p., 2 1., 195 p. 21 cm. [BJ1671.B4 1844] 6-44439
1. Young men. 2. Conduct of life. I. Title.

CRESSEY, Frank Graves. 259
The church & young men; a study of the spiritual condition and nature of young men, and modern agencies for their improvement, by Frank Graves Cressey, PH. D., with an introduction by Charles Richmond Henderson ... Chicago, New York [etc.] Fleming H. Revell company [c1903] xv, 233 p., 1 l. 20 cm. Bibliography: p. 228-233. [BV639.Y7C7] 4-2596
1. Young men. I. Title.

ELIOT, William Greenleaf, 1811-1887. 170
Lectures to young men, delivered in the Church of the Messiah, by William G. Eliot, jr. St. Louis, Printed at Republican office, 1852. 130 p. 15 cm. [LC261.E5] 7-37857
1. Young men. I. Title.

MAGIE, David, 1795-1865. 170
The spring-time of life; or, Advice to youth. By Rev. David Magie... New York, R. Carter & brothers, 1853. iv p., 1l., [7]-328 p. front. (port.) 17 1/2 cm. [BJ1671.M2] 10-11734
1. Young men. I. Title.

MAGIE, David, 1795-1865. 170
The spring-time of life; or, Advice to

youth. By Rev. David Magie... New York, American tract society [1855] iv p., 1 l., [7]-348 p. front. (port.) 15 1/2 cm. [BJ1671.M22] 10-11735
1. Young men. I. Title.

PORRITT, Arthur. 170
The strategy of life; a book for boys and young men, by Arthur Porritt; with a foreword by Dr. J. H. Jowett ... New York, Chicago [etc.] Fleming H. Revell company [c1920] 156 p. 20 cm. [BJ1671.P6] 20-17750
1. Young men. 2. Boys. 3. Conduct of life. I. Title.

TABOR, Edward A., 1857- 170
Danger signals for new century manhood, by Edward A. Tabor... New York, The Abbey press [c1899] 3 p. l., iii-xii, 13-318 p. front. (port.) 20 1/2 cm. [BV4541.T3] 36-32751
1. Young men. 2. Conduct of life. I. Title.

Young men—Conduct of life.

BOSWORTH, Edward Increase, 1861-
The Master's way; studies for men in the navy, by Edward Increase Bosworth...and John Leslie Lobingier... New York, National war work council of Young men's Christian associations, by Association press, 1918. vi, 168 p. 11 cm. "Certain portions of the material of this booklet were previously used in Dean Bosworth's Thirty studies about Jesus." [BV4590.B6] 21-22084
I. Lobinger, John Leslie, joint author. II. Title.

CHESTERFIELD, Philip 170'.202'232
Dormer Stanhope, 4th Earl of, 1694-1773.
Some unpublished letters of Lord Chesterfield / with an introd. by Sidney L. Gulick, Jr. Folcroft, Pa. : Folcroft Library Editions, 1977, c1937. p. cm. Reprint of the ed. published by University of California Press, Berkeley. Includes bibliographical references and index. [BJ1671.C53 1977] 77-4287 ISBN 0-8414-4590-7 lib. bdg. : 15.00
1. Chesterfield, Philip Dormer Stanhope, 4th Earl of, 1694-1773. 2. Young men—Conduct of life. I. Gulick, Sidney Lewid, 1902- II. Title.

DOLLEN, Charles. 248.8'32
Ready or not! A book for young men. [Boston] St. Paul Editions [1969] 241 p. illus. 22 cm. [BJ1671.D57] 67-29164 3.00
1. Young men—Conduct of life. I. Title.

HASSELL, Richard Burton. 246
The chums and their powwows; for young men who follow the gleam, by Richard Burton Hassell, M.A. Boston, Mass., The Stratford company, 1928. x, 118 p. pl. 2 port. (incl. front.) 19 1/2 cm. [BV4541.H3] 28-3818
I. Title.

HILDEBIDLE, Ralph G., 170.202'232
1919-
Requisites for a man, by Ralph G. Hildebidle. Philadelphia, Dorrance [1967] ix, 55p. 20cm. [BJ1671.H65] 67-16894 2.50
1. Young men—Conduct of life. I. Title.

KING, Elisha Alonzo 1870-
Helps to health and purity; a book for young men, by E. A. King ... [Rev. and enl. ed.] Des Moines, Ia., Personal help publishing co., 1903. 127 p. front. (port.) pl. 15 1/2 cm. 3-9107
I. Title.

KLEINHANS, Theodore 170.202'232
J.
Letters to John; to a young man about life, love. war, and other things [by] Theodore J. Kleinhans. St. Louis. Concordia [1967, c.1966] vii, 55p. 19cm. [BJ1671.K55] 67-13426 1.50 pap.,
1. Young men—Conduct of life. I. Title.

SEAGREN, Daniel. 248.8'32
Letters to Chip from an older brother. Introd. by Paul S. Rees. Grand Rapids, Zondervan Pub. House [1969] 87 p. 22 cm. [BJ1671.S4] 69-11655 3.50
1. Young men—Conduct of life. I. Title.

Young men—Religious life.

BROOKS, Thomas. 248
The young man's guide to duty and excellence. by Thomas Brooks. New York, W. Kerr & co., 1841. 1 p. l., 221 p. 13 1/2 cm. [BV4541.B65] 45-25149
1. Young men—Religious life. I. Title.

CONROY, Joseph P.
Out to win, by Rev. Joseph P. Conroy ... New York, Cincinnati [etc.] Benziger brothers, 1919. 181 p. 19 cm. [BX2860.C6] 19-16099
1. Young men—Religious life. I. Title.

ELMORE, Carl Hopkins, 1878- 248
Quit you like men, by Carl Hopkins Elmore ... New York, C. Scribner's sons, 1944. x p., 1 l., 180 p. 19 cm. [BV4541.E63] 44-9652
1. Young men—Religious life. 2. Conduct of life. I. Title.

ESHLEMAN, Merle W 1908- 248
Christian manhood for adolescents and young men, by Merle W. Eshleman and Noah K. Mack. Scottdale, Pa., Herald Press, 1948 [i. e. 1949] xvi, 110 p. illus. 20 cm. [BV4541.E8] 49-6398
1. Young men—Religious life. 2. Sexual ethics. I. -Mack, Noah K., 1911-joint author. II. Title.

GRAHAM, William. 248
Duty; twelve conferences to young men, by Rev. William Graham. New York, J. F. Wagner [1910] 2 p. l., 120 p. 21 cm. [BX2360.G8] 10-24730
1. Young men—Religious life. 2. Christian life—Catholic authors. I. Title.

LASANCE, Francis Xavier, 248
1860-
The young man's guide; counsels, reflections, and prayers for Catholic young men, by Rev. F. X. Lasance. New York, Boston [etc.] Benziger brothers, inc. [1944] xviii, 782 p. front., pl. 13 1/2 cm. [BX2360.L3] 44-9649
1. Young men—Religious life. 2. Christian life—Catholic authors. 3. Catholic church—Prayer-books and devotions—English. I. Title.

LASANCE, Francis Xavier, 248
1860-
The young man's guide; counsels, reflections, and prayers for Catholic young men, by Rev. F. X. Lasance. New York, Boston [etc.] Benziger brothers, inc., 1946. xviii, 782 p. front., illus., pl. 13 1/2 cm. [BX2360.L3 1946] 46-2615
1. Young men—Religious life. 2. Christian life—Catholic authors. 3. Catholic church—Prayer-books and devotions—English. I. Title.

Young Men's Christian Association—Programs.

FATHER and son Y-Indian 267.31
guides of the Young Men's Christian Association. New York, Association [c.1946-1962] 135p. illus.23cm. 1.50 pap.,
1. Young Men's Chrisian Association—Programs.

Young Men's Christian Association. International Association of Y's Men's Clubs.

DURAN, Clement A., 1902- 267.3
The Y's men's manual. New York, Association Press, 1947. 80 p. 23 cm. [BV1230.D8] 47-29988
1. Young Men's Christian Association. International Association of Y's Men's Clubs. I. Title.

Young men's Christian Association. Kansas City, Mo.

[BISHOP, Carl 267.39778411
Sidney] 1865-
More than a building; a story of the Kansas City, Missouri Young men's Christian association; published on the occasion of the diamond jubilee, 1800-1935. Kansas City, Mo., Western Baptist publishing company, 1934. 116 p. incl. front. (port.) 1 illus. 20 cm. "The author assumed entire responsibility for what he wrote, and the circulation."--Foreword, signed: C.S. Bishop. [BV1050.K35B5] 35-3560
1. Young men's Christiation. Kansas City, Mo. I. Title.

Young Men's Christian Association San Francisco.

SORENSON, Roy, 1900- 267.39794
Designing education in values; a case study in institutional change, by Roy Sorenson and Hedley S.Dimock. New York, Association Press [1955] 365p. illus. 24cm. [BV1050.S4S6] 55-7418
1. Young Men's Christian Association San Francisco. I. Dimock, Hedley Seldon, 1891- joint author. II. Title.

Young men's Christian association. Worcester, Mass.

ROE, Alfred Seelye, 1844- 267.
1917.
The Worcester Young men's Christian association. An account of its founding, development, progress, departments, objects and aims. By Alfred S. Roe. Worcester, Mass., The author, 1901. 176 p. incl. front., illus., ports., facsims. 23 1/2 cm. [BV1050.W9R7] 2-242
1. Young men's Christian association. Worcester, Mass. I. Title.

Young Men's Christian Associations.

AMES, John Quincy. 267.
Lay leadership in the Young men's Christian association, by J. Qunicy Ames ... Chicago, Ill., Young men's Christian association college [c1928] cover-title, 56 p. 23 cm. (Monograph no. vii of "The changing Young men's Christian association" series) [BV1100.A755] 26-16241
1. Young men's Christian associations. I. Title.

AMES, John Quincy. 267.
The professionalization of the secretaryship of the Young men's Christian associations of North America, by J. Quincy Ames ... Chicago, Ill., Young men's Christian association college [c1926] 83 p. 23 cm. (Monograph no. iii of "The changing Young men's Christian association" series) [BV1100.A77] 27-16736
1. Young men's Christian associations. I. Title.

ATWOOD, Jesse Howell. 267.365
The racial factor in Y.M.C.A.'s, a report on Negro-white relationships in twenty-four cities, prepared from 249 original interviews conducted and reported by Dr. J. Howell Atwood ... as summarized by Arthur W. Hardy and Owen E. Pence ... foreword by Shelby M. Harrison. Published under the auspices of the Bureau of records, studies and trends, National board of Y.M.C.A.'s, New York, N.Y. New York, Association press, 1946. xii, 194 p. 20 1/2 cm. [BV1190.A8] 47-1846
1. Young men's Christian associations. 2. U.S.—Race question. I. Hardy, Arthur W. II. Pence, Owen Earl, 1887- III. Title.

BARTLETT, Lester William, 267.
1883-
The Y.M.C.A. executive secretary; an analysis of the activities of the secretary who is responsible for the administration of the local Y.M.C.A. [by] Lester W. Bartlett ... Ralph M. Morgan ...Alden W. Boyd ... Chicago, Ill., The University of Chicago press [c1929] xiv, 104 p. 24 cm. (Half-title: Studies of the Young men's Christian association college. Chicago) [BV1100.B2] 29-24650
1. Young men's Christian associations. I. Hogan, Ralph Montague, joint author. II. Boyd, Alden W., joint author. III. Title.

BARTLETT, Lester William, 1883-
The Y.M.C.A. physical director; an analysis of the activities of the secretary who is responsible for physical education in a local Y.M.c.A. [by] Lester W. Bartlett ... [and] Alden W. Boyd ... Chicago, Ill., The University of Chicago press [c1929] xi, 104 p. 24 cm. (Half-title: Studies of the Young men's Christian association college, Chicago) [BV1145.B3] 29-28073
1. Young men's Christian associations. 2. Physical education and training. I. Boyd, Alden W., joint author. II. Title.

BOSWORTH, Edward Increase, 267.
1861-1927.
Working together. The association and the church. By Edward I. Bosworth and Reno Hutchinson. Introduction by Fred. B. Smith. [New York] New York Young men's Christian association press, 1908. 61 p. 18 1/2 cm. [BV1115.B6] 8-20163
1. Young men's Christian associations. I. Hutchinson, Reno, 1876-1906, joint author. II. Smith, Fred Burton, 1865- III. Title.

CALIFORNIA. State normal school,
San Jose.
Students' hand book. Presented by the Young women's Christian association of San Jose state normal school, San Jose, California. 1917-1918. [San Jose, Cal., Press of Wright-Eley co., inc., 1917] 68 p. illus. 14 cm. [LB1837.S22S] E 17
I. Title.

CHESLEY, Albert Meader, 1875-
Social activities for men and boys by Albert M. Chesley New York, Young men's Christian association press, 1910- xii, [4], 304 p. incl. front., illus. 20 cm. "This book is prepared as a thesis in connection with special graduate work of the Young men's Christian association training school, Springfield, Mass."--Pref. "Acknowledgement and bibliography": p. [xiv] [GV4201.C5] 11-893
1. Young men's Christian associations. 2. Amusements. I. Title.

DOGGETT, Laurence Locke, 922
1864-
Life of Robert R. McBurney, by L. L. Doggett ... Cleveland, O., F. M. Barton [1902] 12, 280 p. front., plates., map, plan. 22 cm. [BV1085.M3D7 1902] 2-19279
1. McBurney, Robert Ross, 1837-1898. 2. Young men's Christian associations. I. Title.

DOGGETT, Laurence Locke, 922
1864-
Life of Robert R. McBurney, by L. L. Doggett ... New York, London, Association press, 1912. 12, 280 p. 2 pl., 6 port. (incl. front.) 22 cm. [BV1085.M3D7 1912] 12-16649
1. McBurney, Robert Ross, 1837-1898. 2. Young men's Christian associations. I. Title.

EDDY, George Sherwood, 267.39
1871-
A century with youth, a history of the Y.M.C.A. from 1844 to 1944, by Sherwood Eddy. New York, N.Y., Association press, 1944. ix, 153 p. 19 1/2 cm. Bibliographical foot-notes. [BV1030.E3] 44-40110
1. Young men's Christian associations. I. Title.

EDUCATIONAL activities for boys
... New York, Young men's Christian association press, 1907. 52 p. illus. 18 cm. "Reprinted from Association boys." [LC589.E4] 7-22414
1. Young men's Christian associations. 2. Boys. I. Association boys.
Contents omitted

ELLENWOOD, James Lee. 267.3
... *Look at the "Y"!* ... New York, Association press [1941] 155 p. 21 cm. "First printing, December, 1940; second printing, January, 1941." [BV1090.E5 1941] 41-2745
1. Young men's Christian associations. I. Title.

FISHER, Galen Merriam, 267.3
1872-
Public affairs and the Y. M. C. A., 1844-944 with special reference to the United State. New York, Association Press, 1948. 199 p. 24 cm. "References cited": p. 187-188. [BV1090.F57] 48-8990
1. Young Men's Christian Association. I. Title.

GREGG, Abel Jones, 1890- 267.357
From building to neighborhood; a manual on the decentralization of group work, by Abel J. Gregg and Charlotte Himber. New York, Association press, 1938. 60 p. incl. form. 22 cm. Bibliography: p. 59-60. [BV1160.G7] 39-29598
1. Young men's Christian associations. I.

Himber, Charlotte, Mrs. joint author. II. Title.

HALL, Lawrence Kingsley, 1886- 267.341
Work begun; the experiences of college graduates entering the secretaryship of the Young man's Christian assocation by Lawrence Kingsley Hall... New York, Association press, 1940. xi, 222 p. diagrs., forms. 20 1/2 cm. Thesis (PH.D.)--Columbia university, 1940. Vita. Published also (160 p.) without thesis note and with only one appendix. "Appendixes": p. [157]-221. [BV1100.H27 1940] 40-30133
1. Young men's Christian associations. I. Title.

HALL, Lawrence Kingsley, 1886- 267.341
Work begun; the experiences of college graduates entering the secretaryship of the Young men's Christian association, by Lawrence Kingsley Hall... New York, Assocation press, 1940. xi, 160 p. diagrs. 21 cm. Issued also, with additional appendixes, as thesis (PH.D.) Columbia university. Bibliography: p. 155-156. [BV1100.H27 1940 a] 40-13558
1. Young men's Christian associations. I. Title.

HALL, Mary (Ross) 1890- 267
Women in the Y.M.C.A. record, by Mary Ross Hall and Helen Firman Sweet. New York, Association Press, 1947. x, 149 p. illus., ports. 21 cm. (Young Men's Christian Associations. National Council. Studies) Full name: Mary Howell (Ross) Hall. Bibliographical footnotes. [BV1090.H3] 47-11010
1. Young Men's Christian Associations. 2. Young Women's Christian Associations. I. Sweet, Helen (Firman) joint author. II. Title.

HALL, Robert King, 1912-
Report of a study of YMCA world service policies and practices, as submitted to the International Committee on YMCAs of the United States and Canada. New York, 1962. 260 p.
1. Young Men's Christian Associations. I. Young Men's Christian Associations. International Committee. II. Title.

HAMLIN, Richard Eugene. 267.35
A new look at YMCA physical education; the report of a national study. New York, Association Press [1959] 220p. illus. 24cm. [GV367.Y7H3] 59-16254
1. Young Men's Christian Associations. 2. Physical education and training—U. S. I. Title.

HARDY, James M 267'.36
Focus on the family; a national study of work with families in the YMCA [by] James M. Hardy. New York, Association Press [c1966] xii, 146 p. illus., forms. 23 cm. Bibliography: p. 144-146. [BV1172.H37] 66-25378
1. Young Men's Christian Associations. 2. Family. I. Title.

HOPKINS, Charles Howard, 1905- 267.3973
History of the Y. M. C. A. in North America. New York, Association Press, 1951. 818 p. illus. 25 cm. [BV1030.H6] 51-11674
1. Young Men's Christian Associations. I. Title.

ISRAEL, Henry, 1877 ed. 267.
Unifying rural community interests, edited by Henry Israel ... New York [etc.] Association press, 1914. 125 p. 20 cm. [BV1210.A4 1913] 14-13160
1. Young men's Christian associations. 2. Sociology, Rural I. Title. II. Title: Rural community interests.

KNEBEL, Aaron G. 1874- 922
Four decades with men and boys, by A. G. Knebel; with a foreword by C. V. Thomas. New York, Association press, 1936. vi p., 2 l., 244 p. front. (port.) 21 cm. [BV1085.K5A3] 37-21815
1. Young men's Christian association. I. Title.

LATOURETTE, Kenneth Scott, 1884- 267.3
World service; a history of the foreign work and world service of the Young Men's Christian Associations of the United States and Canada. New York, Association Press [c1957] 489p. illus. 24cm. Includes Bibliography. [BV1125.L3] 57-13143
1. Young Men's Christian Associations I. Title.

LEIBERT, Edwin Reisinger, 1903- ed. 267.3
Y.M.C.A. public relations; addresses and discussions from a short course conducted at Silver Bay, New York, July, 1941, edited by E. R. Leibert ... New York, Association press [c1941] 61 p. diagr. 27 1/2 x 21 1/2 cm. Bibliography: p. 59-60. [BV1100.L4] 42-13948
1. Young men's Christian associations. I. Title.

LIMBERT, Paul Moyer, 1897- 267.31
Christian emphasis in Y.M.C.A. program; a guide to policy and practice for Young men's Christian associations, by Paul M. Limbert. A publication of the Committee on Christian emphasis and method of the Young men's Christian associations. New York, Association press, 1944. vii p., 1 l., 147 p. plates. 21 1/2 cm. [BV1115.L5] 45-1270
1. Young men's Christian associations. I. Young men's Christian associations. Committee on Christian emphasis and method. II. Title.

LIMBERT, Paul Moyer, 1897- 267.3
New perspectives for the YMCA [by] Paul M. Limbert. New York, Association Press [1964] 255 p. 23 cm. Bibliography: p. 224-231. [BV1090.L5] 64-16124
1. Young Men's Christian Associations. I. Title.

LIMBERT, Paul Moyer, 1897- 267.3
NewPerspectives for the YMCA [by] Paul M. Limbert. New York, Association [c. 1964] 255p. 23cm. Bibl. 64-16124 3.50 pap.,
1. Young Men's Christian Associations. I. Title.

MCCANDLESS, James W. 267.
Association administration; a study of the professional task of operating a Young men's Christian association [by] James W. McCandless ... New York, Association press, 1923. v, [1], 106 p. illus., diagrs. 28 cm. "Some suggested readings": p. 106. [BV1100.M3] 24-992
1. Young men's Christian associations. I. Title.

MCCANDLESS, James W. 267.
Association administration; a study of the professional task of operating a Young men's Christian association [by] James W. McCandless ... New York, Association press, 1925. vii, 261 p. illus., diagrs. 19 1/2 cm. "Some suggested readings": p. 258-261. [BV1100.M3 1925] 25-12976
1. Young men's Christian associations. I. Title.

MCCANDLESS, James Wilbur. 267.3
Prediction, planning and control; an engineering approach to Y.M.C.A. management [by] James W. McCandless ... New York, Association press, 1933. 107 p. illus. (map) diagrs. 23 cm. (On cover: [Young men's Christian association] Occasional study, no. 15) Photolithographed. "Administrative tools and resources": p. 105. [BV1100.M35] 33-22790
1. Young men's Christian associations. I. Title. II. Title: Y.M.C.A. management.

MCCANDLESS, James Wilbur, 1884- 267.3
Developing Christian personality and building a Christian society; a study of religious effectiveness of Y.M.C.A.'s. New York, Association Press, 1949. 62 p. diagrs. 23 cm. [BV1115.M3] 50-577
1. Young Men's Christian Associations. 2. Christian life. I. Title.

MCCLOW, Loyd Levi, 1896- 267.34097731
Lay leadership; the South Chicago department, Y.M.C.A. of Chicago plan of conducting an activities program through the use of laymen, by L. L. McClow. Chicago, Ill., c1933. 59 (i.e. 63) numb. 1., 3 l. incl. forms. 28 1/2 cm. Extra numbered pages inserted. Mimeographed. Bibliography: 3 leaves at end. [BV1100.M33] CA 34
1. Young men's Christian associations. 2. Young men's Christian associations. Chicago. South Chicago dept. 3. Leadership. I. Title.

MCKIM, Judson Jackson. 267.
The operation and management of the local Young men's Christian association, by Judson J. McKim... foreword by Frederic B. Shipp... New York, Association press, 1927. xiii, 114 p. front. (2 port.) diagrs. 19 1/2 cm. Bibliography: p. 97-99. [BV1100.M35] 27-24626
1. Young men's Christian associations. I. Title.

THE ... Massasoit ... 267.
Published ... by the junior class of Springfield college. Springfield, Mass. [19 v. illus. (incl. ports.) 27 1/2 cm. annual [BV1130.A45M3] 48-36732
I. Springfield, Mass. Internation Young men's Christian association college.

THE Massasoit...
published by the junior class of Springfield college. Springfield, Mass., 19 v. illus. (incl. ports.) 27 1/2 cm. [BV1133.S82S6] CA27
I. Young men's Christian associations. Association colleges. Springfield, Mass.

MEREDITH, Frederic Charles. 267.
The Young men's Christian association and the Russian orthodox church [by] Frederic Charles Meredith. [New York, International committee of Young men's Christian associations, c1921] cover-title, 60 p. 22 cm. Report of the author's experiences in Siberia with the Young men's Christian association, submitted to the senior national secretary of the Young men's Christian association for Russia. [BV1060.S6M4] 21-6971
1. Young men's Christian association. 2. Greek church. 3. Russia—Church history. 4. Siberia—Church history. I. Title.

MEYER, William F 267.369
Organization and program of a young men's industrial club, a manual for YMCA young adult leaders. New York, Association Press [1957] 59p. 22cm. [BV1185.M4] 57-1542
1. Young Men's Christian Associations. 2. Labor and laboring classes—U. S.—1914- I. Title.

MOORE, John Ferguson, 1867- 811.5
The "Y" in rhyme, by John Ferguson Moore; foreword by John R. Mott. New York, Association press, 1940. 148 p. 21 cm. Tributes to some of the men who built the American Y. M. C. A. Errata slip mounted on lining-paper. [BV1095.M6] 267.3088 40-10024
1. Young men's Christian association. I. Title.

MORSE, Richard Cary, 1841- 922
My life with young men, fifty years in the Young men's Christian association [by] Richard C. Morse, consulting general secretary of the International committee of Young men's Christian associations. New York, Association press, 1918. xiv, 547 p. front., plates, ports. 23cm. [BV1085.M7A3] 18-6435
1. Young men's Christian associations. I. Title.

MORSE, Richard Cary, 1841-1926. 267.
Fifty years of federation of the Young men's Christian associations of North America [by] Richard C. Morse ... New York, The International committee of Young men's Christian associations, 1905. 111, [1], xxx p. 19cm. Supplement: Extracts from the early story of the confederation of the North American Young men's Christian associations, by Rev. William Chauncy Langdon, D.D., p. i-xxiii. [BV1030.M8] 5-6902
1. Young men's Christian associations. I. Langdon, William Chauncy, 1871- II. Title.

MORSE, Richard Cary, 1841-1926. 267.
History of the North American Young men's Christian associations, by Richard C. Morse ... New York [etc.] Association press, 1913. xiv p., 1 l., 290 p. incl. front. illus. (incl. ports.) 20cm. [BV1030.M83 1913] 13-15630
1. Young men's Christian associations. I. Title.

MURRAY, William D 1858- 922
As he journeyed: the autobiography of William D. Murray; foreword by Fletcher S. Brockman. New York, Association press, 1929. 2 p. l., iii-ix, 412 p. front., pl. 22 cm. [BV1085.M8A3] 29-27644
1. Young men's Christian associations. I. Title.

MURRAY, William D 1858-
Principles and organization of the Young men's Christian association [by] William D. Murray ... New York, Young men's Christian association press, 1910. 127 p. illus. 20 cm. "Bibliography for course on Association principles": p. 109-110. 10-16679
I. Title.

OATES, James Franklin, 1870- 811.
The religious condition of young men; a study by James F. Oates...with a preface by George A. Coe... Chicago, Central department, Young men's Christian association, 1901. 4 p. l., [7]-79, [1] p. diagrs. (part col.) 24 1/2 cm. [BV1095.O2] 1-15280
1. Young men's Christian associations. 2. Young men. I. Title.

OATES, James Franklin, 1870- 248.
The religious condition of young men; a study by James F. Oates ... with a preface by George A. Coe ... Chicago, Central department, Young men's Christian association, 1901. 4 p. l., [7]-79, [1] p. diagrs. (part col.) 25 cm. [BV1095.O2] 1-15230
1. Young men's Christian associations. 2. Young men. I. Title.

OBER, Charles Kellogg, 1856- 267.
The association secretaryship, by C. K. Ober. New York, Association press, 1918. 3 p. l., 98 p. 20 cm. [BV1100.O3] 18-6043
1. Young men's Christian associations. I. Title.

OBER, Charles Kellogg, 1856- 922
Luther D. Wishard, projector of world movements, by C. K. Ober. New York, Association press, 1927. 4 p. l., 199 p. plates, ports. 22 1/2 cm. [BV1085.W503] 27-13397
1. Wishard, Luther Deloraine, 1854- 2. Young men's Christian associations. I. Title.

OBER, Frank W., ed.
James Stokes, pioneer of Young men's Christian associations, by his associates in more than half a century of world service to young men. Frank W. Ober, editor... New York, Association press, 1921. x p., 1 l., 235 p. front., plates, ports. 21 1/2 cm. [BV1265.S603] 21-5547
1. Stokes, James, 1841-1918. 2. Young men's Christian associations. I. Title.

OBER, Frank W. ed.
James Stokes, pioneer of Young men's Christian association, by his associates in more than half a century of world service to young men. Frank W. Ober, editor... New York, Association press, 1921. x p., 1 l., 235 p. front., plates, ports. 22 cm. [BV1265.S6O3] 21-5547
1. Stokes, James, 1841-1918. 2. Young men's Christian associations. I. Title.

PENCE, Owen Earle, 1887- 267.31
Present-day Y.M.C.A. church relations in the United States, a diagnostic report, prepared by Owen E. Pence in consultation with the Committee of the Bureau of Records, Studies and Trends of the National Board, Y.M.C.A., as a summary and critique of studies of Y.M.C.A.-church relations conducted under the Bureau's auspices between 1940 and 1948. New York, Association Press, 1948. ix, 196 p. 23 cm. [BV1090.P4] 49-225
1. Young Men's Christian Associations. I. Young Men's Christian Associations. National Board. Bureau of Records, Studies and Trends. II. Title.

PENCE, Owen Earle, 1887- 267.34
Salary and wage policy during depression and recovery, by Owen E. Pence, prepared under the direction of the Personnel services committee and staff of the National council of the Y. M. C. As. New York, Association press, 1933. vii, 78 p. 23 cm. (On cover: [Young men's Christian associations] Occasional study, no. 14)

Photolithographed. Bibliography: p. 75-76. [BV1100.P4] 33-32397
1. Young men's Christian associations. 2. Wages—U. S. I. Young men's Christian associations. National council. II. Title.

PENCE, Owen Earle, 1887- 267.3973
The Y. M. C. A. and social need; a study of institutional adaptation, by Owen E. Pence ... foreword by William E. Speers ... New York, Association press, 1939. xiv, 360 p. diagrs. 24 cm. "Selected reference list": p. 339-345. [BV1030.P4] 39-27501
1. Young men's Christian associations. I. Title.

PHYSICAL EDUCATION SOCIETY OF THE YOUNG MEN'S CHRISTIAN ASSOCIATIONS OF NORTH AMERICA. LEADERSHIP TRAINING COMMITTEE. 267.343
Training Y.M.C.A. leaders for physical education service. New York, Association Press, 1951. 75 p. illus. 29 cm. [BV1145.A4] 52-3593
1. Young Men's Christian Associations. 2. Physical education and training. I. Title.

PIERREL, Gren O ed. 267.341
The executive role in Y.M.C.A. administration; an analysis and discussion of the administrative process in the North American Y.M.C.A.'s. Financed and supervised by the General Secretaries' Section of the Association of Secretaries. New York, Association Press, 1951. xviii, 540 p. illus. 24 cm. Bibliography; p. [503]-509. [BV1100.P5] 52-1587
1. Young Men's Christian Associations. I. Young Men's Christian Associations. Association of Secretaries. II. Title.

PIERREL, Gren O 267.34
The new executive in the smaller YMCA; developed for the General Secretaries Section of the Association of Secretaries of North America. New York, Association Press [1959] 205p. illus. 24cm. Includes bibliography. [BV1100.P55] 59-65067
1. Young Men's Christian Associations. I. Title.

PORTER, David Richard, 1882- ed. 267.
The church in the universities, edited by David R. Porter ... New York, Association press, 1925. 68 p. 20 cm. [BV1170.P6] 26-168
1. Young men's Christian association. 2. Church and college. I. Title.

RITCHIE, Frank H T comp.
Community work of the Young men's Christian association, comp. by Frank H. T. Ritchie ... New York [etc.] Association press, 1915. vii, 96 p. incl. front. (map) illus. 18 cm. "Much of the material in the following pages has appeared in various Association magazines and conference reports."--Introd. Bibliography: p. 89-96. 15-18415 0.35
I. Title.

RITCHIE, Frank Herbert Thomas, 1878-
The community and the Y. M. C. A. (revision of "Community work") [by] Frank Ritchie ... with an introduction by Ernest R. Groves ... New York, Association press, 1919. viii, 103 p. illus., plates, maps. 17 cm. "Suggestions for a community association library": p. 84-93. [BV1120.R5 1919] 19-12154
1. Young men's Christian associations. 2. Community centers. I. Title.

RITCHIE, Frank Herbert Thomas, 1878-
Community work of the Young men's Christian association, [By] Frank H. T. Ritchie ... with an introduction by Ernest R. Groves (Rev. ed.) ... New York, Association press, 1917. viii, 102 p. illus. (incl. maps) plates, diagrs. 17 cm. Bibliography: p. 83-92. [BV1120.R5 1917] 17-21970
1. Young men's Christian associations. 2. Community life. I. Title.

RITCHIE, Frank Herbert Thomas, 1878- comp. 267.
How to study your association and the community; an outline dealing with the methods and technique for making a survey, compiled by Frank Ritchie ... New York, Association press, 1926. 62 p. diagr., fold. form. 28 cm. Bibliography: p. 62. [BV1100.R45] 27-57
1. Young men's Christian associations. 2. Social surveys. I. Title.

ROBINSON, Clarence Cromwell, 1878- 267
The wage-earning boy [by] Clarence C. Robinson... New York [etc.] Association press, 1912. 108 p. 17 1/2 cm. Bibliography: p. [106]-108. [BV1160.R7] 12-6530
1. Young men's Christian associations. 2. Children—Employment. I. Title.

SAYFORD, Samuel M., d.1921.
Personal work, by S. M. Sayford ... New York, The international committee of Young men's Christian associations [1899] 134 p. 19 1/2 cm. "The worker's library": p. [131]-134. [BV1115S3] 99-3206
I. Title.

SEAMANS, Herbert Lee, 1892- ed. 267.
The work of the student Young men's Christian association; a manual of principles and methods especially for associations in colleges without employed without employed student Y M C A secretaries, edited by H. L. Seamans ... with the cooperation of C. P. Chedd. W. W. Mendenhall ... and others. [New York, c1927] 54 p. 28 cm. Bibliography: p. 51-54. [BV1170.S4] 27-25132
1. Young men's Christian associations. I. Title. II. Title: The student Young men's Christian association.

SESSIONS, John A., ed. 267
A program handbook of young men's activities, edited by John A. Sessions ... New York, Association press, 1941. 108 p. incl. tables. 23 cm. Includes bibliographies. [BV1100.S4] 41-17060
I. Young men's Christian associations. II. Title.

SMALL city secretaries' conference, Blue Ridge, N.C., 1924. 267.
Small city secretaries' conference report. Blue Ridge, N.C., May 31 to June 2, 1924. New York, Association press, 1924. 72 p. diagrs. 28 cm. "Conference...called to concentrate the constructive thought of the Young men's Christian association on the problem peculiar to the cities from 5,000 to 25,000 population." "Suggested reading, following the lines of issues raised": p. 70. [BV1010.S5 1924] 24-21486
I. Young men's Christian associations. II. Title.

SONQUIST, David Emmanuel. 267.3
The interests of young men; the discovery and meaning of interests in program building, by David E. Sonquist, PH.D. New York, Association press, 1931. x p., 1 l., 177 p. incl. diagrs., forms. III maps on 2 l. 23 1/2 cm. Largely a description and analysis of an experiment conducted in a local Young men's Christian association to determine the most adequate methods of discovering interests, with chapters on religious education and counseling written primarily for Young men's Christian associations. Bibliography: p. 167-169. [LB1065.S6] 31-19963
1. Young men's Christian associations. 2. Interviewing. 3. Personnel service in education. I. Title.

SONQUIST, David Emmanuel. 267.3
... Techniques for discovering the interests of Young men's Christian association applicants; the discovery and meaning of interests in program building ... by David Emmanuel Sonquist. New York, Association press, 1931. x p., 1 l., 177 p. incl. diagrs., forms. III maps on 2 l. 23 cm. Part of thesis (PH.D.)--University of Chicago, 1931. Published also without thesis note, under title: The interests of young men; the discovery and meaning of interests in program building. Bibliography: p. 167-169. [BV1130.S6 1931 a] 32-2859
1. Young men's Christian associations. 2. Interviewing. 3. Personnel service in education. I. Title. II. Title: The interests of Young men's Christian association applicants.

SPIRITUAL emphasis conference, New York (City) 1934. 267.306373
A Christian crusade; report of the Spiritual emphasis conference held in William Sloan house, New York city, April 14-15, 1934, under the auspices of the Commission on message and purpose of the National council of the Young men's Christian associations of the U.S.A. New York, Association press [c1934] 72 p. 23 cm. [Message and purpose paper, no. 11] "The [conference] ... here reported included in its membership representatives from all the eastern states except Maine."--Introd., signed: George Irving. [BV1010.S62 1934] 34-40129
1. Young men's Christian associations. 2. Spiritual life. I. Irving, George. II. Young men's Christian associations. Commission on message and purpose. III. Title.

SPROUL, J. Edward, ed. 267.31
The young men's Christian associations and the changing world, prepared and edited under the direction of the Executive committee, Association of employed officers, Young men's Christian association of North America, by J. Edward Sproul ... New York, Association press, 1930. xii p., 1 l., 95 p. 19 1/2 cm. "Suggestions for further study" at end of each chapter. [BV1090.S73] 30-17003
1. Young men's Christian associations. 2. Social problems. I. Young men's Christian associations. Associations of employed officers. II. Title.

STONE, Harry William, 1868- 267.
Association advertising, by H. W. Stone. Portland, Or. [Presss of Wells & company c1912] 153, [1] p. front., illus. 17 1/2 cm. "Second limited edition of 'Association advertising' of which this is no. 491." "This little book ... is a talk by a Young men's Christian association secretary to his fellows."--Pref. [BV1100.S7] 13-9184
1. Young men's Christian associations. I. Title.

SUPER, Paul. 267.
Formative ideas in the Y.M.C.A., by Paul Super ... New York, Association press, 1929. ix, 217 p. 22 cm. [BV1090.S77] 29-25157
1. Young men's Christian associations. I. Title.

SUPER, Paul. 267.
Training a staff; a manual for Young men's Christian association executives [by] Paul Super ... New York, Association press, 1920. xx, 300 p. diagr. 22 cm. "References" at end of some of the chapters. [BV1100.S93] 21-111
1. Young men's Christian associations. I. Title.

SUPER, Paul. 267.
What is the Y M C A? A study in the essential nature of the Young men's Christian association, by Paul Super ... New York, Association press, 1922. xii, 126 p. 19 1/2 cm. [BV1090.S8] 22-23799
1. Young men's Christian associations. I. Title.

TINKER, Wellington Hutchinson, ed. 267.
Life work; a statement of principles, methods, and programs that may be helpful to student Young men's Christian associations, in the conduct of their life work guidance and recruiting service, assembled and ed. by W. H. Tinker. New York, Pub. for the student department of the International committee of Y.M.C.A.'s by Association press, 1922. 51 p. 16 1/2 cm. Bibliography: p. 27-31. [BV1170.T5] 23-293
1. Young men's Christian association. I. Title.

URICE, Jay A. 267.
The theory of the Young men's Christian association; outlines for discussion studies in principles and policies [by] Jay A. Urice ... New York, Association press, 1921. 5 p. l., 60 p. 23 cm. [BV1090.U7] 21-21400
1. Young men's Christian associations. I. Title.

WILDER, Robert Parmelee, 1863- ed. 267.
The Red triangle in the changing nations, by G. Sidney Phelps, J. M. Groves, W. W. Peter [and others] ed., with an introduction, by Robert P. Wilder. New York, Association press, 1918. iv p., 1 l., 125 p. 19 1/2 cm. Describes the work of the Young men's Christian associations in other lands. cf. Introd. "References" at end of most of the chapters. [BV1125.W5] 18-17194
1. Young men's Christian associations. I. Phelps, G. Sidney. II. Title.
Contents omitted.

WILLIAMS, Paul Edgar. 267.353
The Y.M.C.A. college, by Paul Edgar Williams, PH.D. Saint Louis, Mo., Educational council of the Young men's Christian association, 1938. x, 218 (i.e. 219) numb. l. incl. map, tables, diagrs. 28 cm. Extra numbered leaf 124a inserted. Mimeographed. Bibliography: leaves 202-204. [BV1130.W5] 39-31826
1. Young men's Christian associations. 2. Universities and colleges—U.S. I. Title.

WINSOR, Wiley, ed. 267.
The leaders' handbook for the Young men's Christian associations of North America, ed. by Wiley Winsor ... New York, Association press, 1922. vi, 116 p. plates. 19 1/2 cm. Plates printed on both sides. "Books a leader should read": p. 116. [BV1100.W5] 22-8846
1. Young men's Christian associations. I. Title.

WORLD Federation of YMHA's and Jewish Community Centers. Council. 296.6'7
Report. New York. v. 28 cm. [BM21.W6] 56-46847
I. Title.

WORMAN, Eugene Clark, 1878- 367.369
Partners in victory. Y.M.C.A. policies and progress in war-industry communities, By E. C. Worman, in collaboration with Louis W. Bruemmer, Earl M. Dinger [and others] ... New York, Association press, 1943. vi, 135 p. illus., diagr. 21 1/2 cm. Bibliography:p. 133-135. [BV1185.W57] 43-16563
1. Young men's Christian associations. 2. Labor and laboring classes—U.S.—1914— I. Bruemmer, Louis W., joint author. II. Dinger, Earl Monroe, joint author. III. Title.

WORMAN, Eugene Clark, 1878- 267-3973
Soldiers in overalls; the problems and needs of young men in war-industry communities, by E. C. Worman, in collaboration with Louis W. Bruemmer, Earl M. Dinger and Herbert B. Rogers ... New York, Association press, 1942. vi, 94 p. incl. forms. 20 1/2 cm. Bibliography: p. 93-94. [BV1185.W6] 42-18296
1. Young men's Christian associations. 2. Labor and laboring classes—U.S.—1914- I. Bruemmer, Louis W., joint author. II. Dinger, Earl Monroe, joint author. III. Rogers, Herbert B., joint author. IV. Title.

WORMAN, Eugene Clark, 1878- 267.31
Working with organized labor; a study of Y.M.C.A. practice and policy, edited by E. C. Worman ... New York, Association press, 1944. 98 p. diagr. 22 cm. Bibliography:p. 98. [BV1185.W62] 45-1269
1. Young men's Christian associations. 2. Labor and laboring classes—U.S.—1914- I. Title.

YOUNG men's Christian associations.
Conference on the world-wide expansion of the Young men's Christian association held at the White House. Proceedings Ocotber 20, 1910. [n.p., 1910] 1 p. l., 63 p. fold. map. 23 1/2 cm. 11-10050
I. Title.

YOUNG men's Christian associations. 267.
The jubilee of work for young men in North America; a report of the jubilee convention of North American Young men's Christian associations; reports of the commemorative services of the Montreal and Boston associations; a world survey by countries of the association movement. New York, The International committee of Young men's Christian associations, 1901. xvi, 500 p. front., plates, ports. 25 cm. [BV1030.A5 1901] 2-11640
I. Title.

YOUNG men's Christian associations.
Year book and official roster of the Young men's Christian associations of Canada and

the United States of America ... published by the National council of Young men's Christian associations of the United States of America. New York, International committee of Young men's Christian associations [etc.] 18 -1906: Association press, 1907- v. fronts., illus., plates, ports., diagrs. 23 cm. Title varies: 18 -1891. Year book of the Young men's Christian associations of the United States and British provinces (1880/81-1891 "of the Untied States, and Dominion of Canada") 1892-1921/22, Year book of the Young men's Christian associations of North America (1901 "Jubilee year book") 1922/23- Year book and official roster of the Young men's Christian association of North America (1924/25- "of Canada and the United States of America") 1935- Year book and official rosters of the National council of the Young men's Christian associations of Canada and of the National council of the Young men's Christian associations of the United States of America. "Supplement to the official roster" [4] p. and "Toward better records": 2 l. laid in 1938 ed. [BV1005.A3] 29-15142
I. Title.

YOUNG men's Christian 267.
associations.
The Young men's Christian association in town and country; the gist of a national conference, in which various types and interests of the association and other allied agencies cooperated, held at the Edgewater Beach hotel, Chicago, Ill., October 18, 19 and 20, 1928. Edited by Henry Israel... New York, Associated press, 1929. ix, 116 p. illus. (maps) diagrs. 23 cm. [BV1210.A45 1929] 29-14365
I. Israel, Henry, 1877- ed. II. Title.

YOUNG men's Christian
associations. Association of secretaries.
Men working; the Y.M.C.A. program and the present needs of youth; being an account of the work of the Young men's Christian association as portrayed in the proceedings of the forty-sixth conference of the Association of secretaries at Silver bay on lake George. New York, June 8-13, 1936... New York, Association press [c1936] 173 p. 23 1/2 mc. Edited by L. K. Hall. "A selected bibliography": p. 171-173. A 37
1. Young men's Christian associations. 2. Youth. I. Hall, Lawrence Kingsley, 1886- ed. II. Title.

[YOUNG men's Christian 267.3
associations. Association of secretaries]
Professional competence in the Young men's Christian association. Paul M. Limbert, editor. New York, N.Y., Association press [1946] vii, 195 p. 23 1/2 cm. "Report of the 1945 triennial conference of the Association of secretaries of the United States and Canada ... Includes reports of six work groups ... The report of a seventh work group is printed separately as a supplement, entitled Personnel concerns of the Y.M.C.A. movement (New York, Association press, 1945)"--Editor's foreword. [BV1100.A44] 46-8165
1. Young men's Christian associations. I. Limbert, Paul Moyer, 1897- ed. II. Title.

YOUNG men's Christian 267.341
associations. Association of secretaries.
The traveling secretary; papers on the work of general agency secretaries of the Young men's Christian association. Committee: Guy V. Aldrich, chairman [and others] ... [New York] General agencies section of the Association of secretaries of the Young men's Christian associations of North America [1945] 58 p. 22 1/2 cm. [BV1100.A445] 47-16912
1. Young men's Christian associations. I. Aldrich, Guy V. II. Title.

YOUNG men's Christian 267.306373
associations. Association of secretaries. 47th conference, Toronto, 1939.
Toward Christian democracy; a profession takes its bearings. Summary proceedings of the forty-seventh conference of the Association of secretaries of the Young men's Christian associations of North America, May 29 to June 3, 1939, Toronto, Ontario, Canada. Edited by S. M. Keeny. New York, Association press, 1939. xiv, 212 p. 23 1/2 cm. [BV1010.A8 1939] 40-12956
1. Young men's Christian associations. 2. Youth. 3. Democracy. I. Kenny, Spurgeon Milton, 1893- ed. II. Title.

YOUNG men's Christian 267.3
associations. Association of secretaries. 48th conference, Cleveland, 1942.
In wartime and after; summary of proceedings of the forty-eighth conference of the Association of secretaries of the Young men's Christian associations of North America, May 18 to 22, 1942; Cleveland, Ohio. Edited by Paul M. Limbert. New York, Association press, 1942. 199 p. 23 1/2 cm. Bibliography included in "Editor's foreword." [BV1100.A45] 43-7829
1. Young men's Christian associations. I. Limbert, Paul Moyer, 1897- ed. II. Title.

YOUNG Men's Christian 267.30637
Associations. Association of Secretaries. 50th Conference, Grand Rapids, 1948.
Toward professional maturity; report of the 1948 Conference of the Association of Secretaries of Y. M. C. A.'s of the United States and Canada. Murray G. Ross, editor. New York, Association Press, 1948. 165 p. 24 cm. [BV1100.A44 1948] 49-4272
1. Young Men's Christian Associations. I. Ross, Murray G., ed. II. Title.

YOUNG Men's Christian 267.3063771
Associations. Association of Secretaries. 51st conference, Cleveland, 1951.
Professional perspective; the report of the 1951 triennial conference. Clement A. Duran, editor. New York, Association Press, 1951. xi, 209p. 24cm. [BV1100.A44 1951c] 53-1881
1. Young Men's Christian Associations. I. Duran, Clement A., 1902- ed. II. Title.

YOUNG Men's Christian 267.341082
Associations. Association of Secretaries. 53d conference, Kansas City, Mo., 1956.
A new look at executive responsibilities; report of the 1956 General Secretaries triennial conference of the Association of Secretaries of YMCA's in the United States and Canada, held at Kansas City, Missouri, February 29-March 4, 1956. Ernest M. Ford, editor. New York, Association Press [1956] 71 p. 23 cm. [BV1100.A44 1956c] 57-343
1. Young Men's Christian Associations. I. Ford, Ernest M., ed. II. Title.

YOUNG men's Christian 267.3
associations. Business secretaries' association.
Handbook of association business administration, compiled under the direction of the Handbook committee of the Business secretaries' association of the Young men's Christian associations of North America; G. S. Bilheimer [and] James W. McCandless--Editors. New York, Association press, 1934. vii, 486 p. incl. diagr., forms. 23 1/2 cm. Includes bibliographies. [BV1100.A5 1934] 34-5199
1. Young men's Christian associations. I. Bilheimer, Gus Stephen, 1877- ed. II. McCandless, James Wilbur, 1884- joint ed. III. Title. IV. Title: Association business administration.

YOUNG men's Christian 267.
associations. Commission on advertising and promotion.
Manual on promotion of Association educational work, prepared by the Commission on advertising and promotion... New York, Association pres, 1921. 5 p. l., 101 p. tables (1 fold.) diagrs. 28 cm. Seal of United Y.M.C.A. schools on t.-p. [BV1130.A5] 21-16061
1. Young men's Christian associations. I. Young men's Christian associations. United Y.M.C.A. schools. II. Title.

YOUNG men's Christian
associations. Drew theological seminary, Madison, N.J.
Students' hand book no. for v. 14 cm. CA 6
I. Title.

YOUNG Men's Christian
Associations. Drew Theological Seminary, Madison, N.J.
The student's handbook. [Madison] v. 14 cm. annual. [BV1051.D6A4] 58-53555
I. Title. II. Title: Title varies: — 1905/06, Drew student's handbook.

YOUNG men's Christian 267.352
associations. International committee.
Prospectus 1902-3, religious work of the city and railroad Young men's Christian associations of North America courses of Bible study topics for meetings, Biblical and missionary book, etc. New York, The International committee of Young men's Christian associations, 1902. 114 p. illus. 19 1/2 cm. Contains bibliographies. [BV1115.A3 1902] 32-30708
I. Title.

YOUNG men's Christian 267.352
associations. International committee.
Prospectus of the religious work of the Young men's Christian evangelistic, devotional and missionary meetings...etc. New York, The International committee of Young men's Christian associations [c1900] 157, viii p., illus., 19 1/2 cm. Contains bibliographies. [BV1115.A3 1900] 0-5627
I. Title. II. Title: Religious work.

YOUNG men's Christian 267.
associations. International committee. County work dept.
The Young men's Christian association in town and country; a handbook of the principles and methods of county work, prepared under the direction of the County work department of the international committee of Young men's Christian associations... New York, Association press, 1920. 94 p. 28 1/2 cm. [BV1210.A5 1920] 20-11235
I. Title.

YOUNG men's Christian
associations. International committee. Educational dept.
...Educational work for men, its field, organization, and supervision in the Young men's Christian associations. A handbook produced from the experiences of associations for the past ten years, and covering the various educational features utilized. Geo. B. Hodge, secretary. New York, The International committee of Young men's Christian associations, 1902. 1 p. l., 76 p. 20 cm. At head of title: Educational department. [LC589.Y6] 4-19173
I. Title.

YOUNG men's Christian
associations. International committee. Educational dept.
...Outlines of courses of study. (Revised prospectus) George B. Hodge, educational secretary. [6th ed.] New York, Young men's Christian association press [c1908] iv, [2], 142 p. 20 1/2 cm. [LC589.Y5] 8-11819
I. Title.

YOUNG men's Christian 267.
associations. International committee. Industrial dept.
Among industrial workers. Rev. ed. A handbook for Young men's Christian associations in industrial fields. New York city, Industrial department International committee Young men's Christian associations [c1919] 154, [10] p. illus. 23 1/2 cm. Blank pages "for memoranda" (9 at end) Bibliography: p. 150-152. [BV1185.A5 1919] 19-14088
I. Title.

YOUNG men's Christian
associations. International committee. Industrial dept.
Among industrial workers (ways and means) a hand book for Associations in industrial fields. New York city, Industrial department, International committee Young men's Christian associations [c1916] 118 p. illus., diagrs. 23 cm. $0.50. 16-22692
I. Title.

YOUNG men's Christian
associations. International committee. Railroad department.
The railroad Young men's Christian association handbook, prepared under the direction of the Railroad department of the International committee. New York, Young men's Christian association press, 1911. v. p. 1 l., 9-137 p. 20 cm. $1.00. Bibliography: p. 135-137. 11-1072
I. Title.

YOUNG men's Christian 267.
associations. International committee. Student department.
The college situation and student responsiblity; a series of discussions concerning the advance program of the Student Young men's Christian association. New York, N.Y., Student department, International committee, Young men's Christian association [c1924] 89 p. diagr. 19 1/2 cm. [BV1170.A4 1924] 24-7605
1. Young men's Christian associations. I. Title.

YOUNG men's Christian
associations. Michigan university.
The students hand book of the University of Michigan... [Ann Arbor? Mich. v. 13 1/2 x 6 cm. [LD3281.2] CA 6
I. Title.

YOUNG Men's Christian 267.3
Associations. National Board.
Association records; the official guide to YMCA program recording and reporting. New York, Association Press [1954] 88p. illus. 23cm. 'Replaces Association records and accounting, published in 1950.' [BV1100.A712] 54-10165
1. Young Men's Christian Associations. I. Title.

YOUNG men's Christian
associations. National board. Bureau of records, studies and trends.
Negro youth in city YMCAs; a study of YMCA services among Negro youth in the urban communities. New York, Bureau of records, studies and trends, National council of Young men's Christian associations [c1944] 80 p. tables. 23 cm. A45
1. Young men's Christian associations. 2. Negroes—Moral and social conditions. I. Title.

YOUNG Men's Christian 267.33
Associations. National Board. Bureau of Records, Studies and Trends.
Women and girls in the Young Men's Christian Association, a study of current practices. New York [1946] iii, 89 p. 23 cm. [BV1090.A65] 47-27994
1. Young Men's Christian Associations. I. Title.

YOUNG men's Christian
associations. National council. Bureau of records, studies and trends.
Negro youth in city YMCAs; a study of YMCA services among Negro youth in urban communities. New York, Bureau of records, studies and trends, National council of Young men's Christian associations [c1944] 80 p. tables. 23 cm. A 45
1. Young men's Christian associations. 2. Negroes—Moral and social conditions. I. Title.

YOUNG men's Christian 267.33
Associations. National Council. Bureau of Records, Studies and Trends.
Women and girls in the Young Men's Christian Association, a study of current practices. New York [1946] iii, 89 p. 23 cm. [BV1090.A65] 47-27994
1. Young Men's Christian Associations. I. Title.

YOUNG men's Christian 267.3
associations. New Jersey.
The group leaders' guide; a manual of principle and practice developed by the Young men's Christian associations of New Jersey. 9th ed., 1940. Newark, N.J., New Jersey state committee [1940] 60 p. 1 l., 20 1/2 cm. Blank leaf for "Notes" at end. [BV1100.A72 1940] 41-10405
1. Young men's Christian associations. 2. Leadership. I. Title.

YOUNG Women's Christian
Associations. U.S. National Board.
The role of the YWCA in a changing era; the YWCA study of YMCA-YWCA cooperative experiences. Dan W. Dodson, director. New York, 1960. p. 73-109. A reprint from the Work book of the 22d National Convention of the YWCA of the USA.
1. Young Men's Christian Associations. I. Dodson, Dan Willaim, 1907- II. Title.

Young men's Christian associations. Association colleges. Chicago.

THE Crucible ... the annual student publication of the Young men's Christian association college ... Chicago, Lake Geneva [c19 v. illus. (incl. ports.) 28 cm. [BV1133.C4A14] ca 30
1. Young men's Christian associations. Association colleges. Chicago.

YOUNG Men's Christian Associations. Auburn University.
Student's hand-book. [Auburn] Hand-Book Committee. v. illus. 14 x 6 cm. Vols. for 1899/1900 issued by the association under the name: Young Men's Christian Association of the Alabama Polytechnic Institute. [BV1170.A28] 62-55625
I. Title.

YOUNG men's Christian associations. Colgate university, Hamilton, N.Y.
Students' hand-book. Hamilton, N.Y., 18 v. illus., fold. plans, 13-14 cm. annual. [LD1084.2] CA 7
I. Title.

YOUNG men's Christian associations. Virginia. University.
Student's hand book. [Charlottesville, 18 v. illus., plans (fold.) 12-14 1/2 cm. [LD5679.2.Y6] CA 7
I. Title.

Young men's Christian associations. Association colleges. Springfield, Mass.

DOGGETT, Laurence Locke, 1864- 267.346
Man and a school; pioneering in higher education at Springfield college, by Laurence Locke Doggett ... New York, Association press, 1943. 4 p. l., vii-viii, 309 p. front., ports. 23 1/2 cm. Illustrated lining-papers. [BV1130.A42D6] 43-15462
1. Young men's Christian associations. Association colleges. Springfield, Mass. I. Title.

Young Men's Christian Associations—Biography.

HOPKINS, Charles Howard, 1905- 267'.392'4 B
John R. Mott, 1865-1955 : a biography / by C. Howard Hopkins. Grand Rapids : Eerdmans, c1979. xvii, 816 p., [12] leaves of plates : ill. ; 23 cm. Includes index. Bibliography: p. 779-780. [BV1085.M75H66] 19 79-15069 ISBN 0-8028-3525-2 : 19.95
1. Mott, John Raleigh, 1865-1955. 2. Young Men's Christian Associations—Biography.

Young Men's Christian Associations. Boston.

WHITESIDE, William B 267.3974461
The Boston Y.M.C.A. and community need; a century's evolution, 1851-1951. New York, Association Press, 1951. 239 p. illus. 24 cm. [BV1050.B7W5] 51-14727
1. Young Men's Christian Associations. Boston. I. Title.

Young Men's Christian Associations. Brooklyn and Queens.

WORMAN, Eugene Clark, 1878- 267.39747
History of the Brooklyn and Queens Young Men's Christian Association, 1853-1949. New York, Association Press, 1952. 256 p. illus. 24 cm. [BV1050.B8W6] 52-11534
1. Young Men's Christian Associations. Brooklyn and Queens. I. Title.

Young men's Christian associations. Buffalo.

SICKELS, Frank E. 267-3974797
Fifty years of the Young men's Christian association of Buffalo. A history by Frank E. Sickels. Buffalo, N.Y., The Association, 1902. 120 p., 1 l., front., illus. (incl. ports.) 23 cm. [BV1050.B9S5] 41-39782
1. Young men's Christian associations. Buffalo. I. Title.

YOUNG men's Christian association. Buffalo. Library.
Finding list of the Y.M.C.A. library, Buffalo, N.Y. ... Issued April 1, 1899. Buffalo, N.Y., A. T. Brown printing house, 1899. viii, 71 p. 24 1/2 cm. 4-4935
I. Title.

Young men's Christian associations—Buildings.

YOUNG men's era publishing company.
Book of Young men's Christian association buildings, containing views of all the important buildings owned and occupied by Young men's Christian associations throughout the world... Chicago, Ill., The Young men's era, 1895. 4 p. 5-108 numb. 1., 109-122 p. illus. (incl. plans) 26 x 35 1/2 cm. Pages 109-122 include advertising matter. "A brief history of the building movement in America, by I. E. Brown...[reprinted from...the Young men's era]": 5th numb. 1. [NA4900.Y7] 12-3327
1. Young men's Christian associations—Buildings. I. Title.

Young Men's Christian Associations. Chicago.

DEDMON, Emmett. 267.39773
Great enterprises; 100 years of the YMCA of Metropolitan Chicago. New York, Rand McNally [1957] 383p. illus. 22cm. [BV1050.C4D4] 57-11669
1. Young Men's Christian Associations. Chicago. I. Title.

GOODSPEED, Charles Ten Broeke, 1869- 922
Loring Wilbur Messer, metropolitan general secretary; biographical sketch by Charles Ten Broeke Goodspeed, with supplementary articles by other associates. Chicago, The Young men's Christian association, 1934. viii, 183, [1] p. front. (port.) 22 cm. [BV1085.M4G6] 35-2286
1. Messer, Loring Wilbur, 1856-1928. 2. Young men's Christian associations. Chicago. I. Title.

Young Men's Christian Associations. China.

GARRETT, Shirley S. 267'.39'51
Social reformers in urban China; the Chinese Y.M.C.A., 1895-1926 [by] Shirley S. Garrett. Cambridge, Mass., Harvard University Press, 1970. 221 p. 22 cm. (Harvard East Asian series, 56) Bibliography: p. [187]-192. [BV1060.C6G37 1970] 74-133218 ISBN 0-674-81220-4 7.50
1. Young Men's Christian Associations. China. I. Title. II. Series.

Young men's Christian associations (Colored)

ARTHUR, George Robert, 1879- 267.3650973
Life on the Negro frontier; a study of the objectives and the success of the activities promoted in the Young men's Christian associations operating in "Rosenwald" buildings [by] George R. Arthur. New York, Association press, 1934. viii, 259 p. plates, maps. 19 1/2 cm. [BV1190.A7] 35-27187
1. Young men's Christian associations (Colored) 2. Rosenwald, Julius, 1862-1932. 3. Julius Rosenwald fund. 4. Negroes—Moral and social conditions. I. Title.

Young Men's Christian Associations—Finance.

YOUNG Men's Christian Associations. National Board. 267.3
Association accounting; a guide to financial recording and reporting in the YMCA. Leslie J. Tompkins, editor. New York, Association Press [1954] 80p. illus. 23cm. [BV1100.A7117] 56-147
1. Young Men's Christian Associations—Finance. I. Tompkins, Leslie James, 1892- ed. II. Title.

Young Men's Christian Associations. Greater New York.

HALL, Robert King, 1912- 267.397471
A strategy for the inner city; a report of the program and priority study of the Young Men's Christian Association of Greater New York. [New York] Young Men's Christian Association of Greater New York, 1963. vi, 438 p. diagrs., tables. 25 cm. Bibliography: p. 192-198. [BV1050.N53H3] 64-246
1. Young Men's Christian Associations. Greater New York. I. Title.

Young Men's Christian Associations. Harrisburg. Pa.

EICHER, HuBert Clark. 267.39748
A century of service, 1854-1954: the Harrisburg Young Men's Christian Association. Harrisburg, Pa., Printed by the Evangelical Press, c1955. 312 p. illus. 21 cm. [BV1050.H2E5] 55-33685
1. Young Men's Christian Associations. Harrisburg. Pa. I. Title.

Young Men's Christian Associations. Hawaii.

ALLEN, Gwenfread Elaine, 1904- 267'.39'969
The Y.M.C.A. in Hawaii, 1869-1969, by Gwenfread E. Allen Honolulu, Young Men's Christian Association, 1969. x, 253 p. illus., ports. 24 cm. [BV1045.H3A65] 72-12603
1. Young Men's Christian Associations. Hawaii. I. Young Men's Christian Associations. Honolulu. II. Title.

Young Men's Christian Associations. Hi-Y Clubs.

HAMLIN, Richard E 267.357
Hi-Y today; a report of the national study of the Hi-Y and Tri-Hi-Y movement. New York, Association Press [1955] 150p. illus. 26cm. [BV1160.H3] 55-9119
1. Young Men's Christian Associations. Hi-Y Clubs. 2. Young Men's Christian Associations. Tri-Hi-Y Clubs sBoys—Societies and clubs. I. Title.

HAMLIN, Richard Eugene. 267.357
Hi-Y today; a report of the national study of the Hi-Y and Tri-Hi-Y movement. New York, Association Press [1955] 150p. illus. 26cm. [BV1160.H3] 55-9119
1. Young Men's Christian Associations. Hi-Y Clubs. 2. Young Men's Christian Associations. Tri-Hi-Y Clubs. 3. Boys—Societies and clubs. I. Title.

[YOUNG men's Christian associations. International committee] 267.357
The new Hi-Y tool chest, a manual for leaders and officers of Hi-Y clubs. New York, Association press, 1942. 96 p. 21 cm. "Copyright...by the International committee of Young men's Christian associations." [BV1160.A615] 42-18320
1. Young men's Christian associations, Hi-Y clubs. I. Title.

Young men's Christian associations—History.

DOGGETT, Laurence Locke, 1864- 267.39
History of the Young men's Christian association ... By L. L. Doggett ... New York, The International committee of Young men's Christian association, 1896-19 v. front., ports., facsim. 25 cm. (v. 2: 23 cm.) Vol. 1 is author's inaugural dissertation, Leipzig. Thesis note on label mounted on cover of v. 1. Vol. 2 has imprint: New York, Association press. "General and Association literature": v. 1, p. [186]-191; Bibliography: 1 leaf at end of v. 2. Contents.--i. The founding of the Association, 1844-1855.--ii. The confederation period, 1855-1861. [BV1030.D75 1896] 33-18569
1. Young men's Christian associations—Hist. I. Title.

DOGGETT, Laurence Locke, 1864- 267.
History of the Young men's Christian association ... by Laurence L. Doggett ... New York, Association press, 1922- v. front., ports., facsim. 23 cm. Bibliography at end. [BV1030.D75 1922] 22-19243
1. Young men's Christian associations—Hist. I. Title.

DOGGETT, Lawrence Locke, 1864- 267.
History of the Young men's Christian association. Vol. u. The founding of the Association, 1844-1855. By L. L. Doggett ... New York, The International committee of Young men's Christian associations, 1916. 191 p. 24 cm. "General and association literature": p. [186]-191. "I hope at some future day, if this volume meets with a kindly reception, to add others on the second and third periods of the association's history."--Pref. [BV1030.D7] A 20
1. Young men's Christian associations—History. I. Title.

HISTORY of Perth Amoby, Jersey, Young Men's Christian Association, 1912-1957. [Perth Amboy, New N. J., 1957] 164p. ports. 23cm.
I. McGinnis, William Carroll, 1884-

WILEY, Samuel Wirt, 1878- 267.31
History of Y.M.C.A.-church relations in the United States, by S. Wirt Wiley. New York, Association press, 1944. xii, 327 p. 21 cm. Bibliography: p. 211-215. [BV1040.W5] 45-981
1. Young men's Christian associations—Hist. I. Title.

ZALD, Mayer N. 338.7'61'2673
Organizational change; the political economy of the YMCA [by] Mayer N. Zald. Chicago, University of Chicago Press [1970] xvii, 260 p. illus. 24 cm. (Studies of urban society) Includes bibliographical references. [BV1040.Z3 1970] 77-101494
1. Young Men's Christian Associations—History. 2. Young Men's Christian Associations. Chicago. I. Title.

Young men's Christian associations. India.

MCCONAUGHY, David, 1860- 267.3954
Pioneering with Christ, among the young men of India and the churches of America; leaves from the life-history of David McConaughy, telling of his role in the introduction of the Young men's Christian association to India. By David McConaughy New York, Association press, 1941 2 p. l., 3-101 p. plates. ports. 21 cm. [BV1060.15M3] 42-1020
1. Young men's Christian associations. India. 2. Missions—India. I. Title.

Young Men's Christian Associations. International Association of Y's Men's Clubs.

KEITEL, George W. 267'.39
A topical history of Y'sdom: the story of the International Association of Y's Men's Clubs—The service club of the YMCA. Compiled and written by George W. Keitel. Oak Brook, Ill., International Association of Y's Men's Clubs, 1972. xi, 616 p. illus. 23 cm. Title on cover: History of Y'sdom. "Golden anniversary ed." [BV1160.K4 1972] 73-171331
1. Young Men's Christian Associations. International Association of Y's Men's Clubs. I. Title. II. Title: History of Y'sdom.

KEITEL, George W 267.3
A topical history of Y'sdom, 1920-1953; the story of the International Association Y's Men's Clubs--the service club of the YMCA. Lawrence, Mass., International Association of Y's Men's Clubs [195-] 354p. illus. 23cm. [BV1160.K4] 58-31868
1. Young Men's Christian Associations. International Association of Y's Men's Clubs. I. Title.

YOUNG men's Christian associations. International committee.
Annual survey, religious work, Young men's Christian associations [students associations excepted] year ending April 30, 1910. New York, Young men's Christian association press, 1910. 82 p. incl. tables. front., port. groups. 20 cm. $0.25. 11-762
I. Title.

Young men's Christian associations. International committee.

THE Foreign mail annual. 267. New York,, Foreign department of the International committee of Young men's Christian associations v. illus., pl., ports. 21 1/2 cm. [BV1125.F7] CA 9
1. Young men's Christian associations. International committee. Foreign dept.

HUME, Theodore Carswell, 1904-1943. 923.573
Flight to destiny! An interpretation for youth of the life of Theodore Carswell Hume. With worship material from his writings. Edited by Ruth Isabel Seabury. New York, N.Y., Association press [1945] 124 p. front. (port.) 19 1/2 cm. "Copyright ... by the International committee of the Young men's Christian associations." "Uncharted voyage, by Ruth Seabury" (also published separately): p. 5-24. [BX7260.H825A3] 45-6478
I. Young men's Christian associations. International committee. II. Seabury, Ruth Isabel, ed. III. Title.

HUME, Theodore Carswell, 1904-1943. 923.573
Flight to destiny! An interpretation for youth of the life of Theodore Carswell Hume. With worship material from his writings. Edited by Ruth Isabel Seabury. New York, N.Y., Association press [1945] 124 p. front. (port.) 19 1/2 cm. "Copyright ... by the International committee of the Young men's Christian associations." "Uncharted voyage, by Ruth Seabury" (also published separately): p. 5-24. [BX7260.H825A3] 45-6478
I. Young men's Christian associations. International committee. II. Seabury, Ruth Isabel, ed. III. Title.

NATIONAL conference of theological students, Indianapolis, 1923.
Students and the church universal; addresses delivered at the National conference of theological students, which met at Indianapolis on December 27, 1923. [New York] Theological sub-committee of Young men's Christian associations [c1924] 52 p., 1 l., 20 cm. 24-7544
I. Young men's Christian associations. International committee. Student dept. II. Title.

[PFATTEICHER, Helen Emma] 211
Come and see, by Helen Allen, pseud; New York, Association press, Fleming H. Revell company, 1943. 4 p. l., 85 p. 17 cm. "Copyright ... by the International committee of Young Men's Christian associations." [BV4515.P43] 43-17686
1. Young men's Christian associations. International committee. I. Title.

YOUNG men's Christian association. International committee.
The religious work of the Young men's Christian association; principles and methods, revised. New York, The International committee of Young men's Christian associations, 1903. 88, [2] p. 20 cm. "Bibliography of suggested books and pamphlets": 1 p. at end. 3-15184
I. Title.

YOUNG men's Christian associations. 267.3
The "Y" secretary and social issues; case studies in social leadership; editorial committee; Earl W. Brandenburg, Paul M. Limbert, Spurgeon M. Keeny, James W. McCandless [and] John R. McCurdy. Published under the auspices of the Annual conference on the association profession and the Committee on public affairs of the National board of Y.M.C.A.'s. New York, Association press, 1943. v. 65 p. 21 cm. "Copyright ... by the International committee of Young men's Christian associations." "For further study and experiment": p. 63-65. [BV1100.A43] 44-25641
I. Brandenburg, Earl W. II. Young men's Christian associations. International committee. III. Title.

[YOUNG men's Christian associations. International committee] 267
...For the millions of men now under arms. [New York, Printed by the Methodist book concern, v. plates. 21 1/2 cm. At head of title: Strictly private--not to be printed. [D627.A2Y6] 21-7205
I. Title.

[YOUNG men's Christian associations. International committee]
Principles and methods of religious work for men and boys. Atlantic City ed. New York, [etc.] Association press, 1912. 171 p. front. (port. group) 21 cm. $0.75. 12-21794
I. Title.

[YOUNG men's Christian associations. International committee]
Religious work for men; principles and methods. Bronxville ed. New York, Young men's Christian association press, 1907. 127 p. 20 cm. Bibliography: p. [109]-127. 7-21318
I. Title.

YOUNG men's Christian associations. International committee. 267.
The religious work of the Young men's Christian associations; principles and methods. New York, The International committee of Young men's Christian associations, [c1900] 79, [1] p. 19 1/2 cm. [BV1115.A5 1900] 0-5628
I. Title.

YOUNG men's Christian associations. International committee. Educational dept.
...Information, statistics and suggestions; annual report. New York, International committee [etc.] 18 v. front., illus., plates. 19 1/2 cm. Title varies: 18 ...Prospectus... ...Prospectus...and the report... ...Information, statistics and suggestions; annual report... [LC588.Y7] 8-32090
I. Title.

YOUNG men's Christian associations. International committee. Educational dept.
...Information, statistics and suggestions; annual report. New York, International committee [etc.] 18 v. front., illus., plates. 19 1/2 cm. Title varies: 18 ...Prospectus... ...Prospectus...and the report... ...Information, statistics and suggestions; annual report... [LC588.Y7] 8-32090
I. Title.

YOUNG men's Christian associations. International committee. Secretarial bureau.
The secretaryship of the Young men's Christian association, a significant life calling, prepared by the Secretarial bureau of the International committee of Young men's Christian associations. New York, Association press, 1917. vi, 70 p. 18 1/2 cm. 17-14116
I. Title.

YOUNG men's Christian associations. International committee. Student department. 267.
Student association leadership; being the Report of the Lake Forest Summer school, 1910- pub. at the direction of the student secretaries of the North American Young men's Christian associations. New York city, Student department of the International committee of the Young men's Christian associations [c1910]- v. 23 cm. [BV1170.A3] 10-27654
I. Lake Forest university. Lake Forest college. II. Title.

YOUNG men's Christian associations. Mexico (City) Railroad branch. Library.
Catalogue of books, library Railroad Young men's Christian association, Mexico city, Mexico. New York, The International committee of Young men's Christian associations, 1903. 89 p. 22 x 10 cm. [Z885.M615] 12-29667
1. Young men's Christian associations. International committee. I. Title.

Young men's Christian associations. International committee. Boys' work department

CHELEY, Frank Hobart, 1889- 267
Stories for talks to boys [by] F. H. Cheley, Boys' work department, International committee of Young men's Christian associations ... New York, Association press, 1920. x, 347 p. 18 cm. [BV1160.C4] 20-4120
I. Young men's Christian associations. International committee Boys work dept. II. Title.

PENCE, Owen Earle, 1887- 267.357
The professional boys' worker in the Young men's Christian association; an occupational study, by Owen E. Pence. New York, Association press, 1932. x p., 2 l., 108 p. diagr. 24 cm. "Reference index": p. 108. [BV1160.P4] 32-14132
1. Young men's Christian associations. International committee. Boys' work dept. 2. Boys—Societies and clubs. I. Title. II. Title: Boys' worker in the Young men's Christian association.

Young men's Christian associations. International committee. Railroad department

MOORE, John Ferguson, 1867- 267.3621
The story of the railroad "Y". by John F. Moore ... with an introduction by Fred W. Ramsey ... New York, Association press, 1930. x, 309 p. front., illus., plates (1 fold.) ports. 24 cm. [BV1200.M6] 30-31236
1. Young men's Christian associations. International committee. Railroad dept. I. Title. II. Title: The railroad "Y".

Young Men's Christian Associations—Management.

TOMPKINS, Leslie James, 1892- 267.3
Operating ratios in the YMCA. New York, Association Press [1954] 54p. illus. 22cm. [BV1100.T57] 55-12907
1. Young Men's Christian Associations—Management. I. Title.

Young men's Christian associations. Minneapolis.

WILEY, Samuel Wirt, 1878- 267.39776
Builders of men; a history of the Minneapolis Young men's Christian association: 1866-1936, by S. Wirt Wiley ... and Florence Lehmann ... Minneapolis, Minn., 1938. vii, 339 p. 23 cm. [BV1050.M6W5] 40-7847
1. Young men's Christian associations. Minneapolis. I. Lehmann, Florence. II. Title.

YOUNG men's Christian associations. Minneapolis. 267
Annual announcement. [Minneapolis? v. illus., 17 1/2 cm. On cover: The building on the corner. [BV1050.M6A4] CA 6
I. Title.

Young men's Christian associations, National council.

AMES, John Quincy. 267.
The National council of the Young men's Christian associations of the United States of America; a study in organization and admínintration, by J. Quincy Ames ... Chicago, Ill., Young men's Christian association college [c1926] cover-title. [3]-94 p. 23 cm. (Monograph iv of "The changing Young men's Christian association" series) [BV1100.A76] 27-18309
1. Young men's Christian associations, National council. I. Title.

Young men's Christian associations. New York.

BURGER, William Harold, 1883- 922
A million miles in New York state, by Billy Burger. New York, N.Y., Association press, 1946. 87 p. 2 port. (incl. front.) pl. 19 1/2 cm. Autobiographical. [BV1085.B8A3] 46-5772
1. Young men's Christian associations. New York. I. Title.

Young men's Christian associations. Phalanx fellowship. Young men's Christian associations. National council.

[YOUNG men's Christian associations. International committee) 267
Phalanx, a "Y" club for young men; a manual for club practice prepared for the National young men's council of the Y.M.C.A.'s of the Unites States ... New York, Association press [c1941] 54 p. incl. forms. 23 cm. "Copyright ... by the International committee of Young men's Christian associations." "Ray Johns, editor."--p. 7. "Program resources": p. 28-30. [BV1230.A5 1941] 44-14514
1. Young men's Christian associations. Phalanx fellowship. Young men's Christian associations. National council. I. Johns, Ray ed. II. Title.

Young men's Christian associations. Philadelphia. Pennsylvania railroad department

WILSON, William Bender, 1839-1919. 267.
History of the Pennsylvania railroad department of the Young men's Christian association of Philadelphia, by William Bender Wilson ... Philadelphia, Stephen Greene company, printers, 1911. 296 p. front., plates, ports. 25 cm. [BV1200.W5] 11-4143
1. Young men's Christian associations. Philadelphia. Pennsylvania railroad dept. I. Title.

Young men's Christian associations. Russia.

COLTON, Ethan Theodore, 1872- 267.8947
Forty years with Russian, by Ethan T. Colton, foreword by John R. Mott. New York, Association press, 1940. 192 p. 21 cm. [BV1060.R8C6] 41-6828
1. Young men's Christian associations. Russia. I. Title.

Young Men's Christian Associations. St. Paul.

ONE hundred years of fellowship and service, 1856-1956; the story of the Saint Paul Young Men's Christian Association. [St. Paul, St. Paul young men's Christian association, 1956] 60p. 22cm.
1. Young Men's Christian Associations. St. Paul. I. Bill, Alfred Hoyt, 1879-

Young Men's Christian Associations. San Francisco.

DRURY, Clifford Merrill, 1897- 267.3979461
San Francisco YMCA; 100 years by the Golden Gate, 1853-1953. Glendale, Calif., A. H. Clark [c.]1963. 256p. illus. 23cm. Bibl. 63-9295 8.00
1. Young Men's Christian Associations. San Francisco. I. Title.

Young Men's Christian Associations. Springfield, Ohio.

MCMILLEN, Theodore Clark, 1905- 267.39771
The Springfiled, Ohio, YMCA, 1854-1954. [Springfield] Ohio, 1954] 172p. illus. 24cm. [BV1050.S83M3] 54-40822
1. Young Men's Christian Associations. Springfield, Ohio. I. Title.

Young men's Christian associations. Student division.

MORGAN, William Henry, 1886- 267.3611
Student religion during firty years; programs and policies of the Intercollegiate Y.M.C.A., by William H. Morgan; with a foreword by Harrison Sackett Elliott ... New York, Association press, 1935. xiv p., 1 l., 233 p. diagrs. 21 cm. Thesis (PH. D.)--Columbia university, 1935. Issued also with vita. Bibliography: p. 228-229. [BV1170.M68 1935 a] 35-14705
1. Young men's Christian associations. Student division. 2. Students—Religious life. I. Title. II. Title: Programs and policies of the Intercollegiate Y.M.C.A.

Young men's Christian Associations. Try-Hi-Y Clubs.

YOUNG men's Christian associations. National Committee on Work with High-School Youth. 267.357
The official Tri-Hi-Y manual; a manual for leaders and officers of Tri-Hi-Y, [prepared by a commission authorized by the National Committee on Work with High-School Youth] New York, Assoc. Press, 1946 [i.e. 1947] 68 p. illus. 21 cm. [BV1170.A53] 47-7211
1. Young men's Christian Associations. Try-Hi-Y Clubs. I. Title.

Young Men's Christian Associations—Yearbooks.

YMCA year book and official rosters. 1967. New York, Association [1967] v. illus. 26cm. Pub. annually since 1875. Title varies: 18- - 1942, Year book and official rosters (varies slightly) Vols. for 1881/82, 1883/84, 1885 and 1887 were issued as an appendix to the Report of the international Y.M.C.A. convention. 1881-87. Sub. title: 1967. National Council of the Young Men's Christian Association of Canada and the United States of America. [BV1005.A3] 29-15142 15.00 bds., 369.4205
1. Young Men's Christian Associations—Yearbooks. I. Young Men's Christian Associations.

Young Men's Hebrew Associations.

RABINOWITZ, Benjamin, 1895-1948. 296
The Young Men's Hebrew Associations, 1854-1913. New York, National Jewish Welfare Board, 1948. vii, 115 p. 24 cm. "Reprinted from Publications of the American Jewish Historical Society, number 37, 1947." "Bibliography and references": p. 96-105. [BM21.A1Y8] 48-4860
1. Young Men's Hebrew Associations. I. Title.

YOUNG men's Hebrew association, New York.
Annual report. New York, Press of P. Coven. v. pl. 23 cm. Report year ends May. 26th annual report has title 1874-1900. Twenty sixth annual report of the Young men's Hebrew association of New York with membership roll. CA 6
I. Title.

Young people and the church.

THE young adolescent in the church; a guide for workers with junior highs. Philadelphia, Geneva press, [1962] 96 p. illus. 23 cm.
1. Young people and the church. 2. Adolescence.

Young people's Christian union.

MILLER, Robert Johnson, 1853- 267.
Harnessed for service; a history of the Young people's Christian union of the United Presbyterian church, 1889-1924 ... compiled by R. J. Miller ... Pittsburgh, Pa., United Presbyterian board of publication and Bible school work [c1925] viii, 245, [1] p., 1 l. illus. (incl. ports.) 20 cm. [BX8905.Y6M5] 25-17112
1. Young people's Christian union. I. Title.

SHAW, Moses M. 267
Y.P.C.U. handbook, by Moses M. Shaw ... suggestions and helps for United Presbyterian young people's societies, constitution, program and plans ... Chicago, Ill., Young people's Christian union [c1928] 64 p. 19 1/2 cm. "Books and booklets": p. 59-64. [BV1426.S45] 28-14541
1. Young people's Christian union. I. Title.

Young people's Luther league.

EIDE, Margaret (Wall) Mrs. 267.6241
...Youth points the way in membership building; a manual to assist Luther leagues and other organizations to raise the standards of membership and to overcome their fundamental problems. by Margaret Wall Eide. Minneapolis, Minn., Augusburg publishing house, 1938. 84 p. illus. 23 cm. ("Crusade with Christ" pamphlet-manual series, manual iv) "Luther league rally humn": p. 72. [BX8003.Y73 Manual 4] [[267.6341]] 38-35274
1. Young people's Luther league. I. Title. II. Title: Membership building.

EIDE, Margaret (Wall) Mrs. 267.6241
...Youth points the way to greater spiritual enlightenment; a manual to assist the educational committee in Luther leagues and other organizations to develop Christian character and an informed and intelligent church membership, by Margaret Wall Eide. Minneapolis, Minn., Augsburg publishing house, 1938. 75 p. incl. illus., forms. 23 cm. (The "crusade with Christ" pamphlet-manual series... manual v) Includes music. [BX8003.Y73 manual 5] [[267.6241]] 39-22840
1. Young people's Luther league. I. Title.

Young people's meetings.

BAPTIST young people's union of America. 267.6
... The young people's meeting, prepared by the Baptist young people's union of America ... Rev. ed. Philadelphia, Boston [etc.] The American Baptist publication society [1935] 108 p. 20 1/2 cm. (Life enrichment series) Bibliography: p. 107-108. [BV29.B3 1935] 36-10228
1. Young people's meetings. 2. Worship (Religious education) I. Title.

Young people's meetings (Church meetings work)

SUCCESSFUL youth meetings. Grand Rapids, Michigan, Baker Book House, 1960. 76p. 22cm.
1. Young people's meetings (Church meetings work) I. Phillips, Grenville W II. Title: Youth.

Young people's meetings (Church work)

BAYS, Alice (Anderson) 1892- 264
Worship services for youth, by Alice Anderson Bays. New York, Nashville, Abingdon-Cokesbury press [1946] 272 p. 20 1/2 cm. Bibliographical references included in "Notes" (p. 257-263) "Selected bibliography": p. 264-265. "Sources for hymns": p. 267-272. [BV29.B36] 46-2855
1. Young people's meetings (Church work) I. Title.

BRECK, Flora Elizabeth, 1886- 264
'Makings' of meetings; giving suggestions for meeting-planners Boston, W. A. Wilde Co. [1956] 80p. 20cm. [BV29.B67] [BV29.B67] 268.7 56-11570 56-11570
1. Young people's meetings (Church work) 2. Worhip programs. I. Title.

BURTON, Janet. 268
52 planned programs for youth and adults. Grand Rapids, Zondervan [1968] 108 p. illus. 21 cm. [BV29.B8] 68-27456
1. Young people's meetings (Church work) 2. Worship programs. I. Title.

CARLSON, Morry. 267.6
Ideas for young people's programs. by Morry Carlson and Ken Anderson. Grand Rapids, Zondervan Pub. House [1948] 84 p. 14 cm. [BV29.C3] 49-7211
1. Young people's meetings (Church work) I. Anderson, Kenneth, 1917- joint author. II. Title.

CHRISTIAN Workers' Service Bureau Inc.
Jet Cadets; a Christ-centered, challenging Program for Junior boys and girls. Calif., Christian Workers' Service Bureau Inc., c1957. 72 p. 64-12483
1. Young people's meetings (Church work) I. Title.

CUMMINGS, Oliver DeWolf, 1900-- 259
The youth fellowship, a vital church program for youth. Philadelphia, Published for the Cooperative Publication Association by the Judson Press [1956] 192p. 20cm. (The Cooperative series leadership training texts) [BV29.C8] 56-9297
1. Young people's meetings (Church work) I. Title.

FERRARI, Erma Paul. 264
Life and worship; worship services for young people, by Erma Paul Ferrari ... Cincinnati, O., The Standard publishing company [1943] 96 p. 21 1/2 cm. [BV29.F4] 43-9210
1. Young people's meetings (Church work) 2. Liturgies. I. Title.

GETTY, Frank Dales, 1890- 267.6
Building a young people's society program [by] Frank D. Getty ... Philadelphia, Chicago [etc.] The Westminster press [1936] 81 p. 19 cm. "Helpful references" at end of each chapter. "General references": p. 80-81. [BV29.G4] 43-49233
1. Young people's meetings (Church work) I. Title.

GETTY, Frank Dales, 1890- 267.6
Planning a church program for seniors and young people [by] Frank D. Getty ... Philadelphia, Chicago [etc.] The Westminster press [1939] 83, [1] p. 18 1/2 cm. "Some helpful materials" at end of each chapter except one. "General references": p. 82. [BV29.G42] 43-49234
1. Young people's meetings (Church work) I. Title.

HOGLUND, Gunnar. 259
Youth groups. Chicago, Harvest Publications [c1967] 148 p. 19 cm. (A Harvest learning-for-serving book) On cover: Success handbook for youth groups. [BV29.H54] 67-27425
1. Young people's meetings (Church work) I. Title. II. Title: Success handbook for youth groups.

HOLLAND, Richard. 267.6
The young people's meeting, by Richard Hoiland. Rev. ed. Philadelphia, Chicago [etc.] The Judson press [1943] 93 p. 19 1/2 cm. "Published August, 1935. Second revised edition ... published April 1943." Bibliography: p. 91-93. [BV29.H56 1943] 44-14248
1. Young people's meetings (Church work) I. Title.

HOWARD, John Gordon, 1899- 268.73
When youth worship [by] J. Gordon Howard ... St. Louis, The Bethany press [c1940] 254 p. 20 1/2 cm. "For the church school library": p. 26. [BV29.H6] 40-88056
1. Young people's meetings (Church work). 2. Worship (Religious education) I. Title.

HUMMEL, Margaret Gibson, ed. 267.6
The society kit; discussion topics and program suggestions for young people ... edited by Margaret Gibson Hummel. Philadelphia, The Westminster press [1943- v. illus. 20 x 27 1/2 cm. Text runs parallel with back of cover. [BV29.H8] 43-17192
1. Young people's meetings (Church work) I. Title.

JUNIOR-HI; 259
a program guide for junior high fellowships and clubs plus material for the adviser. Philadelphia, Westminster Press [19 no. illus. 28cm. annual. Editor: N. F. Langford. [BV29.J83] 54-28460
1. Young People's meetings (Church work) 2. Worship programs. I. Langford, Norman F., 1914- ed.

KLAUSLER, Alfred P 267.6241
Growth in worship; a manual for youth couselors. Saint Louis. Concordia Pub. House [1956] 108p. illus. 19cm. Includes bibliography. [BV29.K55] 55-124793
1. Young people's meetings (Church work) 2. Worship programs. 3. Worship (Religious education) I. Title.

LOTZ, Philip Henry, 1889- 264
Worship services for the church year; fifty-three worship services for the use of youth in the church school, societies for young people, summer conferences, or wherever youth gathers for Christian worship. Worship services prepared by P. Henry Lotz ... Interpretative meditations by Grace Chapin Auten ... St. Louis, The Bethany press [1944] 256 p. 20 cm. [BV29.L6] 44-34674
1. Young people's meetings (Church work) I. Auten, Grace Maude (Chapin) 1877- II. Title.

METHODIST Church (United States) Board of Education. Editorial division. 268.433
Program quarterly; for youth meetings in small churches. [Nashville, Methodist Pub. House] v. in 23 cm. Prepared by the General Board of Education of the Methodist Church through the Editorial Division. [BV29.P7] 52-19204
1. Young People's meetings (Church work) 2. Worship programs. I. Title.

MIDDLETON, Robert Lee, 1894- 248
Youth's talents for Christ; messages and program material to be used by leaders and workers with intermediates and young people, by R. L. Middleton ... Nashville, Tenn., Broadman press [c1940] 192 p. illus. 19 1/2 cm. [BV29.M5] 40-33483
1. Young people's meetings (Church work) 2. Youth—Religious life. I. Title.

PATTERSON, Ward.
A year of youth programs and activities. No. 2. Cincinnati, Ohio, Standard [c1963] 174 p. 64-51286
1. Young people's meetings (Church work) I. Title.

PICKETT, Warren Wheeler, 1895-, comp. 264
Worship services for young people, compiled by Warren Wheeler Pickett. Boston, Chicago, The Pilgrim press [c1931] x, 58 p. 20 cm. [BV29.P5] 36-10849
1. Young people's meetings (Church work) I. Title.

SANTA, George Frederick, 1914- 267.6
52 complete young people's programs, by George F. Santa and others. Grand Rapids, Zondervan Pub. House [1955] 226p. illus. 20cm. [BV29.S27] 56-17894
1. Young people's meetings (Church work) 2. Worship programs. I. Title.

SANTA, George Frederick, 1914- 267.6
Youth aid idea handbook, packed with practical tested ideas for youth workers. Grand Rapids, Zondervan Pub. House [1952] 76p. illus. 23cm. [BV29.S3] 52-14267
1. Young people's meetings (Church work) I. Title.

SHAVER, Erwin Leander, 1890- 268.
Young people and the church; a suggested plan for a project for young people's groups, by Erwin L. Shaver. Chicago, Ill., The University of Chicago press [c1925] ix, 57 p. 19 1/2 cm. (Half-title: The University of Chicago publications in religious education ... Constructive studies) Blank pages for "Notes" inserted. Contains bibliographies. [BV1475.S5Y6] 25-23421
1. Young people's meetings (Church work) I. Title.

SMITH, Esther (Mallory) Mrs., 1903- 267.61
The Moorestown plan [by] Esther M. Smith. [Moorestown, N.J., c1937] 54 p. incl. forms. 20 cm. [Full name: Mrs. Esther May (Mallory) Smith] [BV29.S5] 38-3605
1. Young people's meetings (Church work) I. Title.

VONK, Idalee Wolf, 1913- 264
Transformed; worship and expressional programs for young people and adults, by Idalee Wolf Vonk. Cincinnati, O., The Standard publishing company [1946] viii, 204 p. 20 cm. [BV29.V6] 47-30597
1. Young people's meetings (Church work) 2. Worship programs. I. Title.

WALLACE, Ray W. 267.6266
Christian youth fellowship; CYF handbook, prepared by Ray W. Wallace, produced by the Division of Christian education, the United Christian missionary society, a board of missions and education. St. Louis, Mo., Christian board of publication [1945] 64 p. illus., diagrs. 19 cm. Cover-title: CYF handbook. [BV29.W3] 45-2246
1. Young people's meetings (Church work) I. United Christian missionary society. Dept. of religious education. II. Christian board of publication, St. Louis. III. Title. IV. Title: CYF handbook.

YOUTH fellowship kit; 259
discussion topics and year-round program suggestions for young people's fellowships,societies, and clubs, v.19. Eds.: Norman F. Langford, Donald L. Leonard, J. Wilbur Patterson. Philadelphia, Westminster Press [c.1961] 232p. illus. (part col.) 28cm. Bibl. 54-2806 3.50 pap.,
1. Young people's meetings (Church work) 2. Worship programs. I. Langford, Norman F., ed.

YOUTH fellowship kit; 259
discussion topics and year-round program suggestions for young people's fellowships, societies, and clubs. Philadelphia, Westminster Press [19 v. illus. 28cm. annual. Editor: N. F. Langford. [BV29.Y6] 54-2806
1. Young people's meetings (Church work) 2. Worship programs. I. Langford, Norman F., 1914-

Young people's missionary movement of the United States and Canada.

VICKREY, Charles Vernon, 1876- 266
The young people's missionary movement, [by] Charles V. Vickrey. New York, The Young prople's missionary movement [c1906] 71, [1] p. col. pl. 19 1/2 cm. [BV2360.Y7V6] 7-25241
1. Young people's missionary movement of the United States and Canada. I. Title.

Young people's societies (Church work)

BAPTIST young people's union of America. 267.
... The commission plan for realizing the ideals of the Christian life program through the young people's society, prepared by Baptist young people's union of America. Philadelphia, Boston [etc.] The American Baptist publication society [c1928- v. diagrs. 19 1/2 cm. (Life enrichment series) [BX6205.B3A5 1928] 28-20250
I. Title.

CASE, Carl D.
The efficient young people's society; sacred literature course, by Carl D. Case, and others. [Philadelphia] American Baptist publication society and Northern Baptist convention through its Commission on young people's work [c1915] 4 p. l., 155 p. 19 cm. 15-15284 0.50
I. Title.

SHAVER, Erwin Leander, 1890- 268.
Christian world-builders; a suggested plan for a project for young people's groups, by Erwin L. Shaver. Chicago, Ill., The University of Chicago press [c1925] ix, 58 p. 19 1/2 cm. (Half-title: The University of Chicago publications in religious education ... Constructive studies) Blank pages for "Notes" inserted. Contains bibliogrpahies. [BV1475.S5C5] 25-23311
1. Young people's societies (Church work) I. Title.

Young, Virginia Custis, 1866-1933.

WATHEN, Edith. 922.373
A gallant life; memories of Virginia Custis Young, a gallant soul whose heart was pure, with courage steadfast and purpose unshaken to the end, who lived and loved and laughed that others might know life. By Edith Wathen. New York, E. S. Gorham, inc. [c1934] 4 p. l., 162 p. front. (port.) 20 cm. [BV4425.Y6W3] 34-14902
1. Young, Virginia Custis, 1866-1933. I. Title.

Young women.

MILLER, Madeleine Sweeny, Mrs. 244
... New Testament women and problems of to-day, by Madeleine Sweeny Miller]Mrs. j. Lane Miller: foreword by S. Parkes Cadman...A group of discussion studies for young women of to-day...Approved by the Committee on curriculum of the Board of education of the Methodist Episcopal church. New York, The Methodist book concern [c1926] 173 p. front. 19 cm. (Studies in Christian living) "Suggestions for bookshelf": p. 171-172. [BV4551.M5] 27-669
1. Young women. 2. Christian life. 3. Women in the Bible. I. Title.

NORRIS, Marion Lela, 1886- 244
The business girl chooses [by] Marion Lela Norris; approvedby the Committee on curriculum by the Board of education of the MethodistEpiscopal church. New York, Cincinnati [etc.] The Methodist book concern [c1930] 191 p. front. 20 cm. Song with music: p. 175. Contains bibliographies. [BV4551.N6] 30-30120
1. Young women. 2. Christian life. I. Methodist Episcopal church. Board of education. II. Title.

ROCHE, Aloysius, 1886- 248
Talks for young women, being a selection made from retreats and conferences, by Aloysius Roche. London and Glasgow, Sands & co., ltd.; St. Louis, Mo., B. Herder book co. [1938] 3 p. l., 9-153 p. 19 cm. [BX2365.R6] 40-8926
1. Young women. 2. Christian ethics—Catholic authors. I. Title.

WEST, Lillian (Clarkson) Mrs., 1869-
Aunt Hope's kitchen stove and the girls around it, by Lillian Clarkson West, cover design by Dixie Selden. Cincinnati, Stewart & Kidd company, 1911. 324 p. 1 illus. 20 1/2 cm. [BV4455.W5] 11-28828
1. Young women. I. Title.

Young women—Conduct of life.

BROWN, Patricia O'Regan. 170.202'233
Love and the teen-age girl. Englewood Cliffs, N.J., Prentice-Hall [1967] xiv, 145, 60 p. illus. 24 cm. [BJ1681.B75] 67-28308
1. Young women—Conduct of life. I. Title.

DOBBERT, John. 248.8'33
Dear Dawn, Dear Dad / John and Dawn Dobbert. Old Tappan, N.J. : Revell, c1980. 156 p. ; 22 cm. [BJ1681.D59] 80-39 ISBN 0-8007-1108-4 : 7.95
1. Young women—Conduct of life. I. Dobbert, Dawn, joint author. II. Title.

GOLD, Don. 170'.202'233
Letters to Tracy from Don Gold. New York, D. McKay Co., 1972. xv, 142 p. 21 cm. [BJ1681.G63] 72-86961 5.95
1. Young women—Conduct of life. 2. Parent and child. I. Gold, Tracy. II. Title.

GRIFFITH, Jeannette, pseud. 170
Dearest Kate; a Catholic girl meets the problems of manners and morals. [1st ed.] Philadelphia, Lippincott [1961] 172p. 21cm. [BJ1681.G7] 61-8666
1. Young women—Conduct of life. 2. Christian life—Catholic authors. I. Title.

GRIFFITH, Jeannette, pseud. 170
Dearest Kate; a Catholic girl meets the problems of manners and morals [by Jeannette Eyerly and Valeria Winkler Griffith] Philadelphia, Lippincott [c.1961] 172p. 61-8666 3.00
1. Young women—Conduct of life. 2. Christian life—Catholic authors. I. Title.

KAY, Hether, comp. 177
A new look at ourselves and others. Illus. by Kathleen Peyton. [Dist. New Rochelle, N.Y., SportShelf, c. 1961] 64p. illus. (New look ser.) 61-66333 1.50 pap.,
1. Young women—Conduct of life. I. Title.

RENICH, Jill 170.202233
So you're a teenage girl. Grand Rapids, Zondervan House [1966] 126p. 21cm. [BJ1681.R4] 66-13690 1.00 pap.,
1. Young women — Conduct of life. I. Title.

STEVEN, Norma. 248'.833
Please, can I come home? No, you can't come home! Old Tappan, N.J., F. H. Revell Co. [1973] 126 p. illus. 19 cm. Exchange of letters between the author and her daughter Wendy. [BJ1681.S73] 73-6794 ISBN 0-8007-0619-6 1.95 (pbk.)
1. Steven, Norma. 2. Steven, Wendy. 3. Young women—Conduct of life. I. Steven, Wendy. II. Title.

WHITCOMB, Helen. 170.202233
Charm; a portfolio of activities [by] Whitcomb and Lang. [New York, Gregg Division, McGraw-Hill Book Co., 1964. 287 p. illus. 20 x 24 cm. Cover title. [BJ1681.W59] 64-25156
1. Young women — Conduct of life. 2. Success. I. Lang, Rosalind, joint author. II. Title. III. Title: A portfolio of activities.

Young women — Religious life.

CALDWELL, Marge. 248.8'33
The radiant you. Nashville, Broadman Press [1968] 64 p. 20 cm. [BV4551.2.C3] 68-23559
1. Young women—Religious life. I. Title.

DESHON, George, 1823-1903. 248'.833
Guide for Catholic young women / George Deshon. New York : Arno Press, 1978 [c1892] 308 p. ; 21 cm. (The American Catholic tradition) Reprint of the 31st ed., rev. published in 1897 by the Catholic Book Exchange, New York. [BX2365.D4 1978] 77-11279 ISBN 0-405-10816-8 : 18.00
1. Young women—Religious life. 2. Young women—Conduct of life. I. Title. II. Series.

KAY, Hether, comp. 248.83
A new look at faith and loyalties. [dist. New Rochelle, N. Y., SportShelf, 1961] 48p. (New look series) Bibl. 61-1634 1.50 pap.,
1. Young women—Religious life. I. Title.

[LAY, Matthias] 1846-
The Christian maiden. Tr. from the German of Rev. Matthias von Bremscheid, O. M. CAP. [pseud.] by members of the Young ladies' sodality, Holy Trinity church, Boston. With additional prayers; preface by the Right Rev. Wm. Stang ... Boston, Angel guardian press, 1905. 3 p. l., 118 p. front. 13 cm. 5-20432
I. Boston. Holy Trinity church. Young ladies' sodality, tr. II. Title.

REDDIN OPAL. 248.8'33
Have it His way / Opal Reddin ; illustrated by Michael D. Reddin. Springfield, Mo. : Gospel Pub. House, c1980. 126 p. : ill. ; 18 cm. (Radiant books) [BV4551.2.R42] 78-73143 ISBN 0-88243-717-8 : 1.95
1. Young women—Religious life. I. Title.

RUSS, Marie. 248
... The religion of a growing person, as discussed by business girls. New York, The Womans press [c1939] 53 p. 22 cm. [Full name: Marie Elizabeth Russ] [BV4551.R8] 40-2575
1. Young women—Religious life. I. Title.

STEWART, Ora (Pate) 1910- 218
A letter to my daughter. Salt Lake City, Bookcraft [c1956] 160 p. 17 cm. [BV4451.S8] 57-31081
1. Young women — Religious life. I. Title.

ZAMBONI, Camillo 248.4
Jesus speaks to you. [Boston] St. Paul Eds. [dist. Daughters of St. Paul, c.1961] 166p. 61-14570 1.75; 1.00 pap.,
1. Young women—Religious life. 2. Christian life—Catholic authors. I. Title.

Young Women's Christian Associations.

ABEL, Barbara. 267.5
Follow the leadership and other skits, by Barbara Abel. New York, The Womans press [c1938] 1 p. l., v-xi p., 1 l., 132 p. Illus. (music) 19 1/2 cm. [BV1385.A83] 33-12983
1. Young women's Christian association. I. Title.

ABEL, Barbara. 267.5973
... Lights up [by] Barbara Abel; a playlet that gives glimpses of the war service program of the Y.W.C.A. New York, N.Y., The Womans press [1942] 23 p. 21 1/2 cm. (Program papers for today and tomorrow, XI) "Copyright ... by the National board of the Young womens Christian associations of the United States of America." [BV1385.A85] 43-10139
1. Young women's Christian associations. 2. World War, 1939—War work—Y.W.C.A. I. Young women's Christian associations. U.S. National board. II. Title.

AMES, John Quincy, comp. 267.
Co-operation between the Young women's and the Young men's Christian associations, by J. Quincy Ames ... Chicago. Ill., The Young men's Christian association college [c1929] cover-title, 2 p. l., 3-84 p. 2o cm. (Monograph no. viii of "The changing Young men's Christian association" series) Mainly a collection of source material. [BV1040.A7] 29-28335
1. Young women's Christian associations. 2. Young men's Christian associations. I. Title.

BROWN, Jean (Collier) Mrs. 267.560
Concerns of household workers; program with household workers in the Y.W.C.A [by] Jean Collier Brown. New York, N.Y., The Womans press [c1941] 167 p. 21 1/2 cm. "Annotated bibliography": p. 161-167. [BV1393.S4B7] 41-21437
1. Young women's Christian associations. 2. Servants. I. Title.

BURTON, Margaret Ernestine, 1885- 922
Mabel Cratty, leader in the art of leadership, by Margaret E. Burton. New York, The Womans press, 1929. viii p., 1 l., 3-248 p., 1 l. front., ports. 20 cm. "Miss Burton has gathered from her notebook, from the memories of friends, from letters, and from the columns of the Womans press and from Miss Cratty's own papers, the material for this book."--Foreword. [BV1370.C7B8] 29-15937
1. Cratty, Mabel, 1868-1928. 2. Young women's Christian associations. I. Title.

CAPEN, Julia Frances, 1880- 267.5
The how of volunteer training in the Y.W.C.A. [by] Julia F. Capen. New York, N.Y., The Womans press [c1941] 60 p. incl. illus., diagr., forms. 21 1/2 cm. [BV1380.C2] 41-6829
1. Young women's Christian association. I. Title.

CLARK, Margaret Logan, 1894- 267.541
The executive director on the job in a membership organization, the YWCA [by] Margaret Logan Clark and Briseis Teall. New York, Woman's Press [1947] 128 p. 20 cm. Bibliography: p. 126-128. [BV1377.C55] 47-6080
1. Young Women's Christian Associations. I. Teall, Briseis, 1900- joint author. II. Title.

ESGAR, Mildred H. 267.5
Program planning studies; a handbook on the philosophy and methods of program planning studies prepared for the use of the Y.W.C.A. by Mildred H. Esgar. New York, N.Y., The Womans press [c1940] 134 p. fold. map. 21 1/2 cm. Bibliography: p. 131-134. [BV1377.E8] 41-4190
1. Young women's Christian associations. I. Title.

GATES, Edith Mildred. 267.555
A community health program for the Y.W.C.A., by Edith M. Gates... New York, N.Y., The Womans press, [1940] 120 p. 21 1/2 cm. Includes bibliographies. [BV1390.G3] 40-33861
1. Young women's Christian associations. 2. Hygiene, Public. I. Title.

GATES, Edith Mildred. 613.7
Health through leisure-time recreation; the health education program of the Y.W.C.A. [by] Edith M. Gates... New York, The Womans press, 1931. 1 p. l., 216 p. plates, diagr. 21 cm. Appendix: Supplementary bibliography-Lists of organizations, etc.: p. [202]-216; Bibliography at end of most of the chapters. [BV1392.H4G3] [[267.555]] 31-83600
1. Young women's Christian associations. 2. Woman-Health and hygiene. 3. Physical education and training. 4. Amusements. I. Title.

GATES, Edith Mildred. 613.7
Health through leisure-time recreation; the health education program of the Y.W.C.A. [by] Edith M. Gates ... New York, The Womans press, 1931. 1 p. l., 216 p. plates, diagr. 21 cm. Appendix: Supplementary bibliography--Lists of organizations, etc.: p. [202]-216. Bibliography at end of most of the chapters. [BV1392.H4G3] [267.555] 31-33600
1. Young women's Christian associations.

2. Woman—Health and hygiene. 3. Physical education and training. 4. Recreation. I. Title.

HALLER, Frederick John, 1892- 267.551
Suggestions for an accounting plan for a non-profit organization-- the Y.W.C.A.-- [by] Frederick J. Haller ... New York, The Womans press, 1936. 5 p. l. 3-109, [6] p. incl. forms. 22 1/2 cm. [BV1377.H3] 36-11943
1. Young women's Christian associations. 2. Societies—Accounting. I. Title.

HENDEE, Elizabeth Russell. 267.591
The growth and development of the Young women's Christian association; an interpretation, by Elizabeth Russell Hendee. New York, The Womans press, 1930. ix, 83 p. fold. diagr. 20 cm. [BV1340.H4] 30-12616
1. Young women's Christian associations. I. Title.

HILLER, Margaret, 1891- 267.5
Leadership in the making; a handbook for businsess and industrial girls, by Margaret Hiller... New York, N.Y., The Womans press., 1936. 4 p. l., 142 p. 1 illus. 21 cm. "Some reference material": p. 138-142. [BV1390.H5] 36-9444
1. Young women's Christian associations. 2. Leadership. 3. Working-women's clubs. I. Title.

HILLER, Margaret, 1891- 267.5
See what you've got into! Introducing the Y. W. C. A. to new members, by Margaret Hiller; illustrations by Martha R. Colley. New York, N.Y., The Womans press [c1937] 2 p. l., 96 p. illus. (incl. map) diagr. 21 1/2 cm. "For further information": p. 96. [BV1375.H5] 37-21253
1. Young women's Christian associations. I. Title.

INTERNATIONAL survey committee. 267.391
International survey of the Young men's and Young women's Christian associations; an independent study of the foreign work of the Christian associations of the United States and Canada. New York, The International survey committee [c1932] vi, 425 p. diagrs. 23 1/2 cm. Each part preceded by leaf with half-title not included in the pagination (2 leaves) D. J. Fleming, chairman. Bibliography: p. 419-421. [BV1125.I6] 32-3575
1. Young women's Christian associations. I. Young men's Christian associations. II. Fleming, Daniel Johnson, 1877- III. Title.

LAWSON, Elizabeth (Y.W.C.A. worker) 267.5545
Music in the Young women's Christian asssociation; a guide to program planning [by] Elizabeth Lawson... New York, N.Y., The Womans press, 1934. 8 p. l., 104 p. diagrs. 21 1/2 cm. Includes bibliographies. [MT87.L38] 35-850
1. Young women's Christian associations. 2. Woman—Societies and clubs—Programs. 3. Concerts—Programs. 4. Community music. I. Title.

LIPPITT, Lucile. 267.5
The guide book for volunteers; to help leaders in the Y. W. C. A. understand the association and its methods of administration [by] Lucile Lippitt. New York, The Woman's press, 1932. 2 p. l., 59 p. illus., diagrs. 23 cm. "This guide book is the response to many requests received by the Volunteer leadership committee."--Introd. Includes bibliographies. [BV1375.L5] 33-9790
1. Young women's Christian associations. 2. Leadership. I. Young women's Christian associations. U. S. National board. Committee on volunteer leadership. II. Title.

MAINS, Frances Helen. 267'.5
From deep roots : the story of the YWCA's religious dimensions / by Frances Helen Mains and Grace Loucks Elliott. [New York : Communications, National Board. YWCA, 1974] 71 p. ; 23 cm. Bibliography: p. 70. [BV1375.M34] 75-301782 pbk. : 2.00
1. Young Women's Christian Associations. I. Elliott, Grace Loucks, 1891- joint author. II. Title.

PERKINS, Ruth. 267.553
Program making and record keeping; collected illustrations of applied educational principles and suggested tools, by Ruth Perkins ... New York, The Womans press, 1931. xi, 201 p. incl. diagrs., forms. 21 cm. "An attempt to show the present stage of program making in Young women's Christian associations."--p. v. [Full name: Ruth Shattuck Perkins] Bibliograpy: p. 200-201. [BV1377.P4] 31-24865
1. Young women's Christian associations. 2. Girls—Societies and clubs. 3. Woman—Societies and clubs—Programs. 4. Education of adults. I. Title.

PROVIDENCE evangelical young women's Christian association.
Annual report. Providence, -1901. v. 18-19 cm. Full title of report: Annual report of the Providence evangelical young women's Christian association. In 1902 united with Young women's Christian association of Providence. The 13th annual report is included in the 35th Annual report of the Young women's Christian association, 1901/02. ca 11
I. Title.

ROBINSON, Marion O. 267'.5
YWCA world mutual service; a common quest, by Marion O. Robinson. Pref. by Mary French Rockefeller. New York, National Board of the Young Women's Christian Association of the U.S.A., 1973. 48 p. illus. 22 cm. [BV1340.R6] 73-78017
1. Young Women's Christian Associations. 2. World Young Women's Christian Association. I. Young Women's Christian Associations. United States. National Board. II. Title.

SIMS, Mary Sophia Stevens, 1886- 267.59
The natural history of a social institution-- the Young women's Christian association [by] Mary S. Sims. New York, The Woman's press, 1936. x p., 1 l., 251 p. 21 cm. Bibliography at end of each chapter. [BV1340.S5] 36-4052
1. Young women's Christian associations. I. Title.

STEWART, Annabel (Murray) Mrs. 1885- 267.56
The industrial work of the Y. W. C. A. Report of a study made for the Laboratory division of the National board of the Young women's Christian association, by Annabel M. Stewart; Dorothea S. Paul, chairman of the committee for the study. New York, N. Y., The Womans press, 1937. 4 p. l., 258 p. 22 cm. [BV1392.I 6S8] 39-24404
1. Young women's Christian associations. I. Young women's Christian associations. U. S. National board. Laboratory division. II. Paul, Dorothea S. III. Title.

WASHINGTON, D.C. Young woman's Christian home.
Annual report. [Washington, D.C., v. 19 cm. [HV1437.W4Y4] CA 22
I. Title.

WILLIAMSON, Margaret, 1889- 267.5
Supervision of group leaders; outlines for study and practice, compiled by Margaret Williamson, with foreword by Bertha C. Reynolds. New York, N.Y. The Womans press [1942] 60 p. 21 1/2 cm. "Reading materials for study and reference" at end of each chapter. [BV1377.W5] 42-24846
1. Young women's Christian association. I. Title.

WYGAL, Winnifred. 267.5
Principles of religious practice in the community association program [by] Winnifred Wygal. New York, N.Y., The Womans press [c1938] 4 p. l., 72 p. 21 1/2 cm. Includes bibliographies. [BV1390.W9] 33-12733
1. Young women's Christian associations. 2. Young women—Religious life. I. Title.

WYGAL, Winnifred, 1884- 267.552
We plan our own worship services; business girls to practice the act and the art of group worship [by] Winnifred Wygal. New York, N.Y., The Womans press [c1940] 121 p. 21 1/2 cm. [Full name: Winnifred Crane Wygal] [BV1390.W93] 40-34294
1. Young women's Christian associations. 2. Young women—Religious life. 3. Worship. I. Title.
Conents omitted.

YOUNG Women's Christian Assocations. U.S. National Board. 267.5
Public affairs in the YWCA. New York, Publications Services, National Board, YWCA [1957] 52 p. 23 cm. [BV1392.P8A5] 58-27492
1. Young Women's Christian Associations. I. Title.

YOUNG women's Christian association. Binghamton, N.Y.
Annual report. Binghamton, N.Y. v. illus. 15-17 1/2 cm. Report year ends Apr. 15. Report for 1900/01 has title: Ninth annual report of the Young women's Christian association of Binghamton, N.Y. May 1900-May 1901. [BV1355.B6A3] CA 6
I. Title.

YOUNG women's Christian association, Chicago.
Annual report. Chicago, 18 v. 22 cm. Report year ends Oct. 31. Report for 1889/90 issued under title: "Fourteenth annual report of the Young women's Christian association, of Chicago, Illinois, for the year ending November 1, 1890." 6-7870
I. Title.

YOUNG women's Christian association, New York City.
Annual Report. New York. v. plates. 24 cm. 6-7869
I. Title.

YOUNG women's Christian association, Washington, D.C.
Annual reports. 1st- Feb. 1905- [Washington, D.C., 1907]- v. 18 1/2 cm. Full title: Annual reports of the Young women's Christian association of the District of Columbia. 1st and 2d reports issued combined, covering the period from Feb. 1905 to April 1, 1907. 8-2541
I. Title.

YOUNG women's Christian associations. Brooklyn, N.Y.
Report, 1st- 1888- [Brooklyn, 1889- v. 19 cm. Report for 1888 has title: First report of the Young women's Christian association of Brooklyn...presented January 26, 1889. Cover title of 1888: Young women's Christian association of Brooklyn. Year book, 1888. 10-26194
I. Title.

YOUNG women's Christian associations. New York.
Annual report of the Young women's Christian association of the city of New York ... New York, 187 -19 v. in fronts., plates. 22 1/2 cm. Report year ends Dec. 31. 187 -74 have title: Annual report of the Young ladies' Christian association. [BV1355.N5A3] 6-7869
I. Title.

YOUNG women's Christian associations. U.S. National board. 267.5973
Annual report. New York, National board, Y.W.C.A. [19 v. illus. 23-26 cm. Cover-title. 1937 has also distinctive title: The work of the National board, Y.W.C.A.; 1940: Y.W.C.A. guide posts, 1940-43, religion, democracy, world community. [BV1350.A27] 42-48693
I. Title.

YOUNG Women's Christian Associations. U.S. National Board.
Fresh perspectives on program planning. Guide for studying the role of a YWCA in its local community. Prepared by Gladys Ryland. New York, 1963. 67 p. illus. Includes bibliography. 65-50773
1. Young Women's Christian Associations. I. Ryland, Gladys. II. Title.

YOUNG women's Christian associations. U.S. National board. 267.
Light on finance, for the use of finance committees and finance workers in city, town and rural community Young women's Christian associations. New York, N.Y. The Womans press [c1925] 107 p. 23 cm. "Publications of the Womans press that help in money raising": p. 106-107. [BV1377.A5 1925] 25-11212
1. Young women's Christian associations. I. Title.

YOUNG Women's Christian Associations. U.S. National Board.
The past is prelude; fifty years of social action in the YWCA; [New York, c1963] 81 p. 23 cm. Cover title. Bibliography: p. 81. 66-8288
I. Title.

YOUNG women's Christian associations. Washington, D.C. (Colored)
...Report. Washington, D.C. v. 20 1/2 cm. Report year ends in May. Full title of 3d and 4th years' report: The Colored young women's Christian association...Report. CA 10
I. Title.

Young Women's Christian Associations—Biography

ROBINSON, Marion O. 267.50922
Eight women of the YWCA, by Marion O. Robinson. Pref. by Mary French Rockefeller. New York, National Board of the Young Women's Christian Association of the U.S.A., 1966. 118 p. ports. 25 cm. Contents.'Should women learn the alphabet?' -- Grace H. Dodge. -- Mabel Cratty.-Emma Ralley Speer.-Mary Billings French.---Vera Scott Cushman.--Martha Boyden Finley.--Florence Simms.--Theresa Wilbur Paist. Bibliography: p. [116]-118. [BV1365.R6] 66-27675
1. Young Women's Christian Associations—Biog. I. Title.

Young Women's Christian Associations. Boston.

MOORE, Sidney. 267.5974461
The heart of woman. Published in commemoration of the one hundredth anniversary of the Boston Young Women's Christian Association, March 3, 1966. [Boston? 1966] 62 p. illus. 29 cm. [BV1355.B7M6] 66-6802
1. Young Women's Christian Associations. Boston. I. Title.

Young Women's Christian Associations — History

HARPER, Elsie Dorothy, 1891- 267'.5
The past is prelude; fifty years of social action in the YWCA. [New York, Bureau of Communications, National Board, YWCA, 1963] 81 p. 23 cm. Cover title. Bibliography: p. 81. [BV1340.H3] 64-829
1. Young Women's Christian Associations — Hist. I. Title.

MORSE, Rebecca F[inley].
Chicago, The American committee of Young women's Christian associations [1901] 92 p. front., illus. 12°. 1-17689
I. Title: Young women;

SIMS, Mary Sophia Stephens, 1886- 267'.5'9
The purpose widens, 1947-1967, by Mary S. Sims. [New York, Bureau of Communications, National Board, YWCA, 1969] iv, 100 p. 21 cm. [BV1340.S515] 77-12631 2.50
1. Young Women's Christian Associations—History. I. Young Women's Christian Association. U.S. National Board. II. Title.

SIMS, Mary Sophia Stephens, 1886- 267.5973
The YWCA, an unfolding purpose. New York, Woman's Press [1950] xv, 157 p. 21 cm. Bibliography: p. 153. [BV1340.S52] 50-6074
1. Young Women's Christian Associations—Hist. I. Title.

Young women's Christian associations—Music.

LAWSON, Elizabeth. 267.5545
Music in the Young women's Christian association; a guide to program planning [by] Elizabeth Lawson ... New York, N. Y., The Womans press, 1934. 3 p. l., 104 p. diagrs. 22 cm. Includes bibliographies. [MT87.L43M8] 35-850
1. Young women's Christian associations—Music. 2. Woman—Societies and clubs—Programs. 3. Concerts—Programs. I. Title.

Young Women's Christian Associations. United States.

WILSON, Elizabeth, 1867- 267'.5'973
Fifty years of association work among young women, 1866-1916 / by Elizabeth Wilson ; with an introd. by Sheila M. Rothman. Farmingdale, N.Y. : Dabor Social Science Publications, 1978. p. cm. Reprint of the 1917 ed. published by National Board of the Young Women's Christian Associations of the United States. Bibliography: p. [BV1350.W54 1978] 78-21085 ISBN 0-89561-085-X : 15.00
1. Young Women's Christian Associations. United States. I. Title.

WILSON, Grace Hannah, 1888- 267'.5'973
The religious and educational philosophy of the Young Women's Christian Association; a historical study of the changing religious and social emphases of the association as they relate to changes in its educational philosophy and to observable trends in current religious thought, educational philosophy, and social situations, by Grace H. Wilson. New York, Bureau of Publications, Teachers College, Columbia University, 1933. [New York, AMS Press, 1972, ie 1973] 156 p. 22 cm. Reprint of the 1933 ed., issued in series: Teachers College, Columbia University. Contributions to education, no. 554. Originally presented as the author's thesis, Columbia. Bibliography: p. 149-156. [BV1350.W73 1972] 70-177632 ISBN 0-404-55554-3 10.00
1. Young Women's Christian Associations. United States. 2. Sociology, Christian. 3. United States—Social conditions. I. Title. II. Series: Columbia University. Teachers College. Contributions to education, no. 554.

WILSON, Grace Hannah, 1888- 267.5973
The religious and educational philosophy of the Young women's Christian association; a historical study of the changing religious and social emphases of the association as they relate to changes in its educational philosophy and to observable trends in current religious thought, educational philosophy, and social situations, by Grace H. Wilson ... Professor F. Ernest Johnson, sponsor. New York city, Teachers college, Columbia university, 1933. 4 p. l., 156 p. 23 1/2 cm. (Teachers college, Columbia university. Contributions to education, no. 554) Issued also as a thesis (PH.D.) Columbia university. Bibliography: p. 149-156. [BV1350.W73 1933a] [LB5.C8 no. 554] 33-14286
1. Young women's Christian associations. U.S. 2. Sociology, Christian. 3. U.S.—Soc. condit. I. Title.

YOUNG women's Christian associations. U.S. National board. 267.
The handbook of the Young women's Christian association movement. Rev. 5th ed. New York city, The Womans press, 1919. xi, 163 p. 18 1/2 cm. [BV1375.A5 1919] 19-16086
I. Title.

YOUNG women's Christian associations. U.S. National board.
The handbook of the Young womens Christian association movement; prepared under the auspices of the Department of method of the National board. New York, National board, Young womens Christian associations of the United States of America, 1914. xi, 161 p. fold. pl. map. 19 1/2 cm. $0.40. "Some of the publications of the National board": p. [159]-161. 14-5135
I. Title.

YOUNG women's Christian associations. U.S. National board.
Handbook of the Young womens Christian associations of the United States of America. New York, National board of the Young womens Christian associations of the United States of America [1910] 105 p. incl. tables, front., plates. 23 1/2 cm. 10-26259
I. Title.

YOUNG women's Christian associations. U.S. National board. 267.5
Division of community Y.W.C.A.'s.
Administration in the Y.W.C.A. ... Prepared by the administrative affairs staff, Division of community Y.W.C.A.'s, National board, Y.W.C.A. ... New York, N.Y., The Womans press [19 v. diagrs. 21 1/2 cm. Contents.[v. 2] The electorate, by Marie Russ.--[v. 3] Planning, by Belle Ingels.--[v. 4] Staff supervision, by Prisels Teall. Including bibliographies. [BV1377.A52] 44-49931
I. Title.

Young women's Christian associations. United States National board.

MACARTHUR, Kathleen Walker, 1891- 267.533
Faith for the job, by Kathleen W. MacArthur. New York, N.Y., The Woman's press [1946] 63 p. 21 1/2 cm. "Reference list" p. 62. [BV1390.M3] 46-21257
1. Young women's Christian associations. U.S. National board. I. Title.

NOURSE, Edward Everett, 1863-
The epistles of Paul; brief introductions, outlines and commentary, prepared for use in the Bible study classes of the Young women's Christian associations, by Edward Everett Nourse ... New York, National board of the Young women's Christian associations of the United States of America [1911] 190 p. 18 1/2 cm. $0.60. p. 189-190 blank. "Literature": p. 188. 11-21602
1. Young women's Christian associations. U.S. National board. I. Title.

NOURSE, Edward Everett, 1863-
The epistles of Paul; brief introductions, outlines and commentary, prepared for use in the Bible study classes of the Young women's Christian associations, by Edward Everett Nourse ... New York, National board of the Young women's Christian associations of the United States of America [1911] 190 p. 19 cm. p. 189-190 blank. "Literature": p. 188. 11-21602 0.60
1. Young women's Christian associations. U. S. National board. I. Title.

YOUNG women's Christian associations. U.S. National board.
Year book containing directory and statistical report of the Young women's Christian associations of the United States of America... New York, v. tables. 23 1/2 cm. CA 12
I. Title.

Youth.

BREWBAKER, Charles Warren, 1869- 170
Adventurous youth, by Charles Warren Brewbaker ... New York, Chicago [etc.] Fleming H. Revell company [c1930] 126 p. 19 1/2 cm. [B V 4531. B74] 30-32170
1. Youth. 2. Christian life. I. Title.

BURKHART, Roy A., ed. 242
Seeking the living way; a guide for young people in their personal worship, edited by Roy A. Burkhart ... New York, Cincinnati [etc.] The Abingdon press [c1933] 157 p. 17 1/2 cm. "For special reading": p. 155-157. [BV4850.B84] 33-33274
1. Youth. I. Title.

BURKHART, Roy A., 1895- 248
The future belongs to you; a personal message to young people who commence with seriousness the life that shall be their way of living [by] Roy A. Burkhart. New York, Cincinnati [etc.] The Abingdon press [c1937] 77 p. 19 1/2 cm. [BV4531.B85] 37-21918
1. Youth. I. Title.

CRAPULLO, George Anthony, 1890- 248
Talks to young people; thoughts on conduct and character, by George A. Crapullo ... New York [etc.] Fleming H. Revell company [c1934] 117 p. 20 cm. [BV4310.C78] 34-13526
1. Youth. 2. Christian life. I. Title.

FOOTE, Gaston, 1902- 252.07
Keys to conquest; inspirational addresses to young people, by Gaston Foote ... with an introduction by Prof. Halford E. Luccock ... New York [etc.] Fleming H. Revell company [c1933] 95 p. 19 1/2 cm. [BV4310.F6] 33-37667
1. Youth. 2. Methodism—Sermons. 3. Sermons, American. I. Title.

GILBERT, Dan. 248
Youth faces today's crisis, by Dan Gilbert, LL. D. Grand Rapids, Mich., Zondervan publishing house [1942] 112 p., 1 l. 20 cm. [Full name: Dan Wesley Gilbert] [BV4531.G53] 42-16634
1. Youth. 2. Christian life. I. Title.

GLENDINING, Marion, 1918- 170
Teen talk; illustrated by Roy Doty. [1st ed.] New York, Knopf, 1951. 146 p. illus. 22 cm. [BJ1661.G53] 51-11069
1. Youth. 2. Conduct of life. I. Title.

HOWE, Laurence Henry, 1898- 248
Finding the goal posts, addresses to youth and the leaders of youth, by Laurence H. Howe ... Nashville, Tenn., Cokesbury press [c1938] 140 p. 19 1/2 cm. [BV4310.H6] 38-5772
1. Youth. I. Title.

IRVING, Roy G. 268'.433
Youth and the church; a survey of the church's ministry to youth, ed. by Roy G. Irving, Roy B. Zuck. Chicago, Moody [1968] 422p. illus. 24cm. Bibl. [BV1475.9.17] 67-14388 5.95
I. Title.

MAUS, Cynthia Pearl, 1880- 137
Youth and creative living; a practical guide book for youth and leaders of youth in the field of character growth. By Cynthia Pearl Maus ... New York, R. Long & R. R. Smith, inc., 1932. ix p., 2 l., 3-167 p. illus. 19 1/2 cm. "Book comrades youth ought to know" at end of each chapter. [BV4531.M3] 32-13900
1. Youth. 2. Personality. 3. Character. 4. Christian life. I. Title.

NORDGREN, Julius Vincent, 1895- 248
Problems that confront young people; a series of discussions for Bible classes and young people's societies, by J. V. Nordgren ... Rock Island, Ill., Augustana book concern [1928] 120, [8] p. 19 cm. Blank pages for "Notes" *538] at end) [BV4531.N6] 28-15804
1. Youth. 2. Christian life. I. Title.

PALMER, Leon Carlos, 1883- 377.1
Youth and the church; a manual for leaders of young people in the home, the church, and the community, by Leon C. Palmer... Milwaukee, Wis., Morehouse publishing co., 1933. 3 p. l., 217, [1] p. 19 cm. Bibliography at end of most of the chapters. [BV639.Y7P3] 33-18646
1. Youth. 2. Adolescence. 3. Religious education. I. Title.

PHELPS, Edwin Philbrook, 1884- 259
The pathfinder in church work with young people, by Edwin Phelps ... with an introduction by W. Edward Raffety ... Philadelphia, Boston [etc.] The Judson press [c1928] 11 p. l., 3-220 p. incl. 1 illus., diagrs., forms. 19 cm. [BV4447.P5] 28-15197
1. Youth. 2. Church work. I. Title.

THE seven teen years. 179
Illustrated by Bill Jackson. Saint Louis, Bethany Press, 1954. 95p. illus. 21cm. [BJ1661.B75] 170 54-2559
1. Youth. 2. Conduct of life. I. Brown, Alberta Z

SPICER, William Ambrose, 1866- 922
Youthful witnesses, by W. A. Spicer ... Washington, D.C., South Bend, Ind. [etc.] Review and herald publishing association [c1921] 1 p. l., [7]-255 p. front., illus. 20 1/2 cm. [BR1704.S6] 21-6623
I. Title.

WEIL, Hans. 170
Pioneers of tomorrow, a call to American youth by Hans Weil ... New York, N.Y., Association press [1945] 2 p. l. 83 p. 19 1/2 cm. "Copyright ... by the International committee of the Young men's Christian associations." [BJ1661.W4] 45-6433
1. Youth. 2. Conduct of life. I. Young men's Christian associations. International committee. II. Title.

*WESTERVELT, Virginia 248.42
Youth's real-life problems. Illus. by Peter Petraglia. Philadelphia, Lutheran Church Pr. [c.1966] 64p. illus. (pt. col.) 23cm. .50 pap.,
I. Title.

YAXLEY, Grace 267.6
Let's be different youth meetings. Chicago, Moody [c.1963] 64p. illus. 28cm. 1.25 pap.,
I. Title.

Youth, Bahai—Conduct of life.

BAHA'I youth; 297'.894'4
a compilation. Prepared by: National Spiritual Assembly of the Baha'is of the United States. Wilmette, Ill., Baha'i Pub. Trust [1973] vii, 33 p. 22 cm. Includes bibliographical references. [BP377.B33] 73-176465
1. Youth, Bahai—Conduct of life. I. National Spiritual Assembly of the Baha'is of the United States.

Youth—Conduct of life.

ALEXANDER, Lynn. 170
Dear Lynn, I have a problem Pulaski, Wis., Franciscan Publishers, 1958. 319p. 22cm. [BJ1661.A38] 57-12622
1. Youth—Conduct of life. I. Title.

ALLEN, Charles Livingstone, 1913- 248'.83
When you graduate [by] Charles L. Allen [and] Mouzon Biggs. Old Tappan, N.J., F. H. Revell Co. [1972] 63 p. 19 cm. Advice to young people on the application of Christian principles in daily living. [BJ1661.A39] 75-189284 ISBN 0-8007-0527-0
1. Youth—Conduct of life. 2. [Youth—Conduct of life.] 3. [Christian life.] I. Biggs, Mouzon, joint author. II. Title.

*AULTMAN, Donald S. 259
Guiding youth. Cleveland, Tenn., Pathway [c.]1965. 109p. 20cm. 1.50; 1.00 pap.,
I. Title.

BOTTEL, Helen. 170.202'23
To teens with love. Illustrated by Robert Psotto. [1st ed.] Garden City, N. Y., Doubleday, 1968. xii, 276 p. illus. 22 cm. $4.95 [BJ166.B58] 68-10543
1. Youth—Conduct of life. I. Title.

BOTTEL, Helen. 170.202'23
To teens with love. Illustrated by Robert Psotto. [1st ed.] Garden City, N.Y., Doubleday, 1968. xii, 276 p. illus. 22 cm. Advice for teens in such areas as sibling rivalry, drugs, dating, popularity, etiquette, parents, jobs, and personality development. [BJ1661.B58] 68-10543
1. Youth—Conduct of life. 2. [Conduct of life.] I. Psotto, Robert, illus. II. Title.

BOZKA, Honora. 291.4
Tell me, talented teen, who are you? [1st ed.] New York, Vantage Press [1963] 87 p. 21 cm. [BJ1661] 64-57322
1. Youth — Conduct of life. I. Title.

BRAVERMAN, Katherine. 170'.202'23
Dropping in; putting it all back together. Los Angeles, Nash Pub. [1972, c1973] viii, 193 p. 23 cm. [BJ1661.B72] 72-81846 ISBN 0-8402-1294-1 6.95
1. Youth—Conduct of life. I. Title.

BRISTER, C. W. 248.4'8613203
Becoming you / C. W. Brister. Nashville, Tenn. : Broadman Press, c1980. 122 p. ; 20 cm. Includes bibliographical references. Addresses many of the personal problems facing today's teenage Christians. [BJ1661.B73] 19 79-57361 ISBN 0-8054-5332-6 pbk. : 3.50
1. Youth—Conduct of life. 2. [Conduct of life.] 3. [Christian life.] I. Title.

BRISTER, C. W. 248.8'3
It's tough growing up [by] C. W. Brister. Nashville, Broadman Press [1971] 128 p. 20 cm. Includes bibliographical references. [BJ1661.B74] 79-136134 ISBN 0-8054-5311-3 2.95
1. Youth—Conduct of life. I. Title.

CAREY, Floyd D 248.83
Teen-agers' trail guide. Cleveland, Tenn., Pathway Press [1960] 76p. 21cm. [BJ1661.C2] 60-51492
1. Youth—Conduct of life. 2. Youth—Religious life. I. Title.

CRAIG, Hazel Thompson, 1904- 170.202
Thresholds to adult living. 2d ed. Peoria, Ill., C. A. Bennett Co. [1969] 416 p. illus. (part col.) 24 cm. Bibliography: p. 411. [BJ1661.C68 1969] 70-1654
1. Youth—Conduct of life. 2. Etiquette. I. Title.

CROUNSE, Helen Louise, 1915- 170.202'23
Joyce Jackson's so happy "if" book; collection of self-help articles and stories for mid-teens and up, including parents. New Haven, College & University Press [1968] 174 p. 21 cm. Bibliographical footnotes. [BJ1661.C73] 68-22382 4.50
1. Youth—Conduct of life. I. Title: So happy "if" book.

CRUZ, Nicky. 248.8'3
The lonely now, by Nicky Cruz, as told to Jamie Buckingham. Illus. by Jim Howard. Photos. by Keith Wegeman and Stitt-Coombs-Evans Inc. Plainfield, N.J., Logos International [1971] viii, 143 p. illus. 22 cm. [BV4921.2.C78] 72-95766 ISBN 0-912106-15-8 3.95
1. Youth—Conduct of life. 2. Conversion. I. Buckingham, Jamie. II. Title.

DALY, Sheila John. 170
Questions teen-agers ask. Illustrated by Bob Kelly New York, Dodd, Mead [1963] 237 p. illus. 21 cm. [BJ1661.D32] 62-17929
1. Youth—Conduct of life. I. Title.

DETWEILER, Herbert J. 170.20223
How to stand up for what you believe: a teen-ager's action guide [by] Herbert J. Detweiler. New York, Association Press [1966] 126 p. illus. 20 cm. [BJ1661.D48] 66-20471
1. Youth—Conduct of life. I. Title.

EAKIN, Bill. 248.8'3
You know I can't hear you when you act that way [by] Bill Eakin and Jack Hamilton. Elgin, Ill., D. C. Cook Pub. Co. [1969] 95 p. 18 cm. [BJ1661.E24] 74-87319 0.95
1. Youth—Conduct of life. I. Hamilton, Jack. II. Title.

EDMUND, Ed, 1925- 170.202'23
Sex, love and life [by] E. Edmund Grand Rapids, Mich., Zondervan Pub. Co. [1973, c.1968] First published as: Teenagers; the facts of sex, love and life. [BJ1661.E3] 68-9445 0.95 (pbk.)
1. Youth—Conduct of life. I. Title.

EDMUND, Ed, 1925- 170.202'23
Teenagers; the facts of sex, love, and life. [by] E. Edmund. Grand Rapids, Zondervan [1968] 139p. 21cm. [BJ1661.E3] 68-9445 1.50 pap.,
1. Youth—Conduct of life. I. Title.

FACIUS, Johannes. 248'.83
The little white book [by] Johannes Facius, Johny Noer [and] Ove Stage. [1st American ed.] Wheaton, Ill., H. Shaw [1972, c1971] 79 p. illus. 14 cm. Translation of Den lille hvide. [BJ1668.D3F313] 72-94101 ISBN 0-87788-509-5 0.75
1. Youth—Conduct of life. I. Noer, Johny, joint author. II. Stage, Ove, joint author. III. Title.

FRANCIS, Connie 170
For every young heart. Derby, Conn., Monarch [1964, c.1962] 155p. ports. 18cm. (435) .50 pap.,
1. Youth—Conduct of life. 2. Etiquette. I. Title.

FRANCIS, Connie [Constance Franconero] 1938- 170
For every young heart. Englewood Cliffs N.J., Prentice [c.1962] 191p. illus. 21cm. 62-20919 2.95 bds.,
1. Youth—Conduct of life. 2. Etiquette. I. Title.

GARABEDIAN, John H. 290'.973
Eastern religions in the electric age [by] John H. Garabedian and Orde Coombs. New York, Grosset & Dunlap [1969] 160 p. 22 cm. [BJ1661.G28] 68-31347 4.50
1. Youth—Conduct of life. 2. Youth—Religious life. 3. Religions. I. Coombs, Orde, joint author. II. Title.

GEANEY, Dennis J. 248.482
The search for dialogue; parents, teachers and teenagers [by] Dennis J. Geaney. Notre Dame, Ind., Fides Publishers [1966] 157 p. 18 cm. (A Fides dome book, D-48) [BJ1661.G35] 66-20180
1. Youth—Conduct of life. 2. Christian ethics—Catholic authors. I. Title.

GOLLER, Edward D. 241
Trail markers by An old guide, by Edward D. Goller; cartoons by Dr. E. J. Pace. Philadelphia, The Union press [c1930] 115 p. incl. plates. 17 cm. "The messages of this book are letters ... written to individual boys and girls."--Introd. [BV4531.G6] 30-9757
I. Title.

HAGGAI, Tom. 248'.4
"Chrissie, I never had it so bad ... " Nashville, T. Nelson [1973] 160 p. 22 cm. [BJ1661.H117 1973] 72-13901 ISBN 0-8407-5044-7 4.95
1. Youth—Conduct of life. I. Title.

HEFLEY, James C. 170
Get the facts. Nashville, Broadman [c.1963] 52p. 22cm. 63-7336 .50 pap.,
1. Youth—Conduct of life. I. Title.

HEISER, Roy F. 248.8'3
Teens alive! Getting the best out of the teen years, by Roy F. Heiser and William J. Krutza. Grand Rapids, Baker Book House [1969] 114 p. 18 cm. [BJ1661.H45] 70-97510 1.50
1. Youth—Conduct of life. I. Krutza, William J., joint author. II. Title.

HUFF, Russell J., 1936- 248.8'3
The virtues; a discussion course for young people. Photo essays by Russell J. Huff. Parables [and] inquiries by Thomas F. McNally. [Edited by Russell J. Huff] Notre Dame, Ind., Fides Publishers [1968] 94 p. illus. (part col.) 27 cm. "First appeared as a series in Catholic boy and Catholic miss, 1966-67." [BX2355.H8] 68-15361 1.25
1. Youth—Conduct of life. 2. Virtues. I. McNally, Thomas Francis, 1887- II. Title.

JOINER, Verna Jones 170
What teens say; a report to parents and church youth workers on what young people are saying and a guide to dealing with questions these young people are raising. Anderson, Ind., Warner [c.1962] 95p. 21cm. 62-20181 1.25 pap.,
1. Youth—Conduct of life. I. Title.

KAYKAVUS ibn Iskandar ibn Qabus,' Unsur al-Ma'all. 1021or2-1098or9. 170.02232
A mirror for princes, the Qabus nama, by Kai Kaus ibn Iskandar, Prince of Gurgan. Translated from the Ersian by Reuben Levy. New York, E. P. Dutton [1951] xxi, [1], 265 p. 23 cm. Bibliography: p. xxi-[xxii] [BJ1678.P3K33] 51-11112
1. Youth — Conduct of life. 2. Education of princes. 3. Isiamic ethics. I. Levy, Reuben. tr. II. Title. III. Title: Qabus nama.

KINNAMON, Les. 170'.202'23
Today for youth / by Les Kinnamon. Minneapolis : T. S. Denison, c1976. 186 p. : ill. ; 23 cm. A daily program for developing character and personality. [BJ1661.K53] 76-29242 7.95
1. Youth—Conduct of life. 2. [Conduct of life.] 3. [Christian life.] I. Title.

KOLENDA, Konstantin. 170'.202'23
Ethics for the young. Houston, Tex., Tourmaline Press, 1972. vii, 111 p. 24 cm. [BJ1661.K65] 72-77241
1. Youth—Conduct of life. I. Title.

LANDIS, Paul Henry, 1901- 330.9'73 S
Coming of age: problems of teen-agers, by Paul H. Landis. [New York, AMS Press, 1973, c1956] p. (Public affairs pamphlet no. 234) Reprint of the ed. published by Public Affairs Committee, New York. Bibliography: p. [HC101.P78 no. 234] 73-11457
1. Youth—Conduct of life. 2. Dating (Social customs) I. Title. II. Series: Public affairs pamphlets (New York), no. 234.

LINK, Mark J. 248.8'3
Life in the modern world: home, parish, neighborhood, school [by] Mark J. Link. Chicago, Loyola University Press [1970] xi, 276 p. illus. 23 cm. [BJ1661.L5] 78-108376
1. Youth—Conduct of life. I. Title.

LUCEY, Dan, comp. 248'.83
The living loving generation / Dan and Rose Lucey. Huntington, Ind. : Our Sunday Visitor, [1975] 94 p. : ill. ; 21 cm. [BJ1661.L8 1975] 75-313209 ISBN 0-87973-783-2 pbk. : 1.50
1. Youth—Conduct of life. I. Lucey, Rose, joint comp. II. Title.

LUCEY, Dan, comp. 248.8'3
The living-loving generation. Edited by Dan and Rose Lucey. Milwaukee, Bruce Pub. Co. [1969] ix, 72 p. 21 cm. Contents.Contents.—Being is becoming, by A. L. Brassier.—Fish or cut bait, by T. Cole.—Sorry about your God, by J. L. Anderson.—Sex is for real! by J. and L. Bird.—Marriage—love-in for real, by G. and G. Raffo.—Talk to me, dad, by P. and P. Crowley.—Reach out my people, by W. and G. McNelly. [BJ1661.L8] 69-17322
1. Youth—Conduct of life. I. Lucey, Rose, joint comp. II. Title.

MCLEAN, Gordon R. 248.8'3
How to raise your parents [by] Gordon R. McLean. Wheaton, Ill., Tyndale House Publishers [1970] xvii, 104 p. illus. 22 cm. A youth director counsels on the traditional areas of parent-teen conflict—dating, cars, grades—as well as on the more current issues—protests, civil disobedience, and the new morality. [BJ1661.M32 1970] 73-123288 2.95
1. Youth—Conduct of life. 2. [Youth—Conduct of life.] 3. [Christian life.] I. Title.

MASON, William V. 241
Corrupt the young; a Communist plan [by] William V. Mason. [Springfield, Mo., Fellowship Publications, 1969] 48 p. illus. 19 cm. "Footnotes": p. 45-48. [BJ1661.M37] 77-12150
1. Youth—Conduct of life. I. Title.

MENNINGER, William Claire, 1899-1966. 170
Blueprint for teen-age living, by William C. Menninger and others. New York, Sterling Pub. Co. [1958] 221 p. illus. 21 cm. [BJ1661.M4] 58-12538
1. Youth—Conduct of life. 2. Etiquette for children and youth. I. Title.

MILD, Warren 248.4
Fractured questions. Valley Forge, Pa., Judson [c.1966] 125p. 22cm. [BJ1661.M54] 66-12539 1.95 pap.,
1. Youth—Conduct of life. I. Title.

MORRIS, Paul Judson. 259
Winning youth for Christ, by Paul Judson Morris. Philadelphia, Boston [etc.] The Judson press [c1930] 4 p. l., 123 p. 1 illus. 19 cm. Bibliography: 4th prelim. leaf. [BV4447.M6] 30-21311
I. Title.

NARRAMORE, Clyde Maurice, 1916- 179
Young only once; secrets of fun and success. Co-author: Ruth E. Narramore. Art illus. by Sam Pollach. Grand Rapids, Zondervan Pub. House [1957] 185p. illus. 21cm. [BJ1661.N28] 170 58-182
1. Youth—Conduct of life. I. Narramore, Ruth E., joint author. II. Title.

NATIONAL Forum Foundation. 170
Discovering myself. Prepared by the guidance staff of National Forum Foundation: Bernice L. Neugarten [and others. 3d ed.] Chicago [1961] 288 p. illus. 24 cm. (National Forum guidance series) [BJ1661,N3 1961] 63-121
1. Youth — Conduct of life. I. Neugarten, Bernice Levin, 1916- II. Title.

NESMITH, William, 1948- 170'.202'23
Congratulations, graduate! / William Nesmith. Nashville : T. Nelson, [1975] 63 p. ; 19 cm. Fourteen essays with advice to the graduate, using material drawn from the American scene. [BJ1661.N38] 75-2346 ISBN 0-8407-4044-1 : 2.95

1. Youth—Conduct of life. 2. [Conduct of life.] I. Title.

NOFFSINGER, Jack Ricks 248.83
It's your turn now! Nashville, Broadman [1964] 64p. 16cm. 65-7005 1.25
1. Youth—Conduct of life. I. Title.

PARADIS, Grace D. 170.202'23
Your life, make it count; a guide for young Americans, by Grace D. and Adrian A. Paradis. New York, Funk & Wagnalls [1968] 222 p. facsims. 22 cm. Includes bibliographies. [BJ1661.P26] 68-22149 4.95
1. Youth—Conduct of life. I. Paradis, Adrian A., joint author. II. Title.

PARR, Adolph Henry, 1900- 170
The open door to peace and happiness. New York, Fell [1964, c.1963] 80p. 21cm. 63-21660 2.00
1. Youth—Conduct of life. 2. Success. I. Title.

PENNOCK, Michael. 241'.04'2
Moral problems : what does a Christian do? / Michael Pennock. Notre Dame, Ind. : Ave Maria Press, c1979. 239 p. : ill. ; 23 cm. Includes bibliographies. Presents a systematic method, based in Catholic morality, for resolving problems concerning such issues as drugs, alcohol, premarital sex, abortion, euthanasia, poverty, prejudice, and the arms race. [BJ1661.P4] 79-51015 ISBN 0-87793-177-1 pbk. : 3.95
1. [Catholic Church.] 2. Youth—Conduct of life. 3. Christian ethics—Catholic authors. 4. [Ethics.] 5. [Conduct of life.] I. Title.

PETERS, Donald L. 170.20223
For thinking teens [by] Donald L. Peters. [1st ed.] New York, R. Rosen Press [1967] 187 p. 23 cm. [BJ1661.P4] 67-10083
1. Youth—Conduct of life. I. Title.

PETERSEN, Mark E. 248.4'8'93
Live it up! [By] Mark E. Petersen. Salt Lake City, Deseret Book Co., 1971. 115 p. 24 cm. [BJ1661.P44] 70-175717 ISBN 0-87747-450-8 3.50
1. Youth—Conduct of life. I. Title.

PRICE, Eugenia 170
Find out for yourself; young people can discover their own answers. Grand Rapids, Mich., Zondervan [c.1963] 190p. 21cm. 63-14944 2.95
1. Youth—Conduct of life. I. Title.

RAAB, Robert. 170.202'23
The teenager and the new morality. [1st ed.] New York, R. Rosen Press [1970] 172 p. 22 cm. Bibliography: p. 171-172. [BJ1661.R27] 74-116620 4.00
1. Youth—Conduct of life. I. Title.

REMENSNYDER, Junius Benjamin, 1843-
Heavenward, a guide for youth. By Rev. Junius B. Remensnyder ... A new and rev. ed. Philadelphia, Pa., Lutheran publication society [c1908] vi, 7-135 p. 19cm. 8-12178
I. Title.

RICE, F. Philip. 241
Morality and youth : a guide for Christian parents / by F. Philip Rice. 1st ed. Philadelphia : Westminster Press, c1980. 252 p. : ill. ; 21 cm. Bibliography: p. 245-252. [BJ1661.R5] 80-11433 ISBN 0-664-24315-0 : 9.95
1. Youth—Conduct of life. 2. Moral education. 3. Christian ethics—United Church of Christ authors. I. Title.

ROGNESS, Alvin N., 1906- 248'.83
Today and tomorrow / Alvin N. Rogness. Minneapolis : Augsburg Pub. House, c1978. 95 p. : ill. ; 21 cm. Discusses problems facing teenage Christians as they leave home, begin working, and fall in love. [BJ1661.R6] 77-84095 ISBN 0-8066-1621-0 pbk. : 3.95
1. Youth—Conduct of life. 2. Youth—Religious life. 3. [Conduct of life.] 4. [Christian life.] I. Title.

RYAN, Patrick James, 1902- 170
A soldier priest talks to youth. New York, Random House [1963] 205 p. 21 cm. [BJ1661.R9] 63-9352
1. Youth—Conduct of life. I. Title.

RYAN, Patrick James, 1902- 170
A solidier priest talks to youth. New York,

Random [c.1963] 205p. 21cm. 63-9352 3.95
1. Youth—Conduct of life. I. Title.

SCANZONI, Letha 248.42
Why am I here? Where am I going? Youth looks at life. Westwood, N.J., F. H. Revell Co. [1966] 127p. 21cm. [BJ1661.S3] 66-17051 2.95 bds.,
1. Youth—Conduct of life. I. Title.

SCOTT, Judith Unger. 170.202'23
The art of teenage living. Illustrated by Susan Gash. Philadelphia, MacRae Smith [1969] 189 p. illus. 22 cm. Advice to teenagers on getting the most out of clothes, money, home life, and social life, and utilizing self-potential to their best advantage. [BJ1661.S36] 69-18631 4.50
1. Youth—Conduct of life. 2. [Youth—Conduct of life.] I. Gash, Susan, illus. II. Title.

SIMON, Sidney B. 170'.202'23
Values clarification; a handbook of practical strategies for teachers and students [by] Sidney B. Simon, Leland W. Howe [and] Howard Kirschenbaum. New York, Hart Pub. Co. [1972] 397 p. 21 cm. [BJ1661.S55] 70-187023 ISBN 0-8055-1038-9 7.50
1. Youth—Conduct of life. 2. Worth. I. Howe, Leland W., joint author. II. Kirschenbaum, Howard, joint author. III. Title.

SKOGLUND, Elizabeth. 170'.202'23
Where do I go to buy happiness? Insights of a Christian counselor. Downers Grove, Ill., InterVarsity Press [1972] 157 p. 22 cm. Bibliography: p. 155-157. [BJ1661.S58] 72-84264 ISBN 0-87784-897-1 3.95
1. Youth—Conduct of life. 2. Counseling. I. Title.

SNYDER, Ross. 170.202'23
Young people and their culture. Nashville, Abingdon Press [1968, c1969] 221 p. 24 cm. [BJ1661.S63] 69-12014 4.50
1. Youth—Conduct of life. I. Title.

STILLMOCK, Martin. 248.4'8'2
Teens talk of many things [by] Martin A. Stillmock. Staten Island, N.Y., Alba House [1972] x, 177 p. port. 19 cm. A Catholic priest answers letters from teen-agers about dating, sex, interracial marriage, confession, and other topics. [BJ1661.S85] 79-39708 ISBN 0-8189-0247-7 1.65
1. Youth—Conduct of life. 2. Youth—Religious life. 3. [Youth—Religious life.] 4. [Christian life.] I. Title.

STOCK, Harry Thomas.
How to improve a young people's program [by] Harry Thomas Stock ... Boston, Chicago, The Pilgrim press [1929] 4 p. l., 7-43 p. 19 12 cm. Contains bibliographies. [BV4427.S75] 29-10487
I. Title.

STOCK, Harry Thomas.
Problems of Christian youth [by] Harry Thomas Stock ... Boston, Chicago, The Pilgrim press [c1927] 62 p. 19 cm. (Christian life series. no. II) [BV4427.S8] 28-4371
I. Title.

SUGARMAN, Daniel A. 248'.83
The Seventeen guide to you and other people [by] Daniel H. Sugarman New York, Pocket Books [1974, c1972] 159 p. 18 cm. (A Washington Square book) [BJ1661.S94] ISBN 0-671-48147-9. 1.25 (pbk.)
1. Youth—Conduct of life. I. Hochstein, Rolaine A., joint author. II. Seventeen. III. Title.
L.C. card number for original ed.: 77-187076.

SUGARMAN, Daniel A. 248'.83
The Seventeen guide to you and other people [by] Daniel A. Sugarman and Rolaine Hochstein. New York, Macmillan [1972] 196 p. 22 cm. [BJ1661.S94] 77-187076 5.95
1. Youth—Conduct of life. I. Hochstein, Rolaine A., joint author. II. Seventeen. III. Title.

20TH-CENTURY teenagers 248.83
by "A friend of youth". Foreword by John P. Carroll. [Boston] St. Paul Eds. [dist. Daughters of St. Paul, c.1961] 155 p. illus., 61-14935 2.00, 1.00, pap.
1. Youth—Conduct of life. 2. Christian ethics—Catholic authors. I. "A friend of youth"

20TH-CENTURY teenagers by 248.83
"A friend of youth." Foreword by John P. Carroll. [Boston] St. Paul Editions [1961] 155 p. illus. 21 cm. [BJ1661.T9] 61-14935
1. Youth — Conduct of life. 2. Christian ethics — Catholic authors. I. "A friend of youth."

UBALDI, Pietro. 170'.202'23
How to orient one's own life / by Pietro Ubaldi ; translated by Vasco de Castro Ferraz. 1st ed. New York : Vantage Press, c1973. 105 p. ; 21 cm. [BJ1664.U213] 74-194664 ISBN 0-533-00812-3 : 4.50
1. Youth—Conduct of life. 2. Life. I. Title.

VAN DYKE, Vonda Kay. 170.202'23
Dear Vonda Kay; questions teen-agers ask answered by a Miss America. Westwood, N.J., Revell [1968, c1967] 125 p. 21 cm. [BJ1661.V3] 68-11369
1. Youth—Conduct of life. I. Title.

VERSTEEG, John M. 171.
Christ and the problems of youth, by John M. Versteeg. New York, Cincinnati, The Abingdon press [c1924] 133 p. 17 1/2 cm. [BV4531.V4] 24-4531
I. Title.

WARNKE, David. 248.8'3
Making it big with God. North Easton, Mass., Holy Cross Press [1969] 120 p. illus. 22 cm. [BJ1661.W33] 78-89846 3.50
1. Youth—Conduct of life. I. Title.

WHEELER, Richard S. 170'.202'23
The children of darkness, by Richard S. Wheeler. New Rochelle, N.Y., Arlington House [1973] 189 p. 24 cm. [BJ1661.W44] 73-8800 ISBN 0-87000-208-2 7.95
1. Youth—Conduct of life. 2. Youth—United States. 3. United States—Religion. 4. Secularism—United States. I. Title.

WILDER, John Bunyan, 1914- 248.83
Stories to live by; true tales for young adults. Grand Rapids, Mich., Zondervan [c.1964] 87p. illus. 22cm. [BJ1661.W48] 64-15555 2.50 bds.,
1. Youth—Conduct of life. I. Title.

WILDER, John Bunyan, 1914- 248.83
Stories to live by; true tales for young adults. Grant Rapids, Zondervan Pub. House [1964] 87 p. illus. 22 cm. [BJ661.W48] 64-15555
1. Youth — Conduct of life. I. Title.

WILKERSON, David R. 248'.83
Get your hands off my throat, by David Wilkerson. Grand Rapids, Zondervan Pub. House [1971] 124 p. 22 cm. [BJ1661.W49] 76-156257 3.95
1. Youth—Conduct of life. I. Title.

WOOD, Miriam. 170
The art of living . . . when you're young. Illustrated by Ken Gunall. Washington, Review and Herald Pub. Association [1964] 160 p. illus. 22 cm. [BJ1661.W6] 64-17659
1. Youth — Conduct of life. I. Title.

Youth—Conduct of life—Case studies.

STROMMEN, Merton P. 170'.202'23
Five cries of youth [by] Merton P. Strommen. [1st ed.] New York, Harper & Row [1974] xvii, 155 p. 21 cm. Bibliography: p. 151-155. [BJ1661.S9] 73-18690 ISBN 0-06-067720-1 6.95
1. Youth—Conduct of life—Case studies. 2. Youth—Religious life—Case studies. I. Title.

Youth—Congresses.

BAPTIST Youth World 267.626
Conference, 5th, Toronto, 1958.
Christ for the world--now Official report. Edited by Cyril E. Bryant. Washington, Baptist World Alliance, Youth Dept. [1958] 211p. illus., ports. 24cm. [BX6207.A18 1958] 59-37511
1. Youth—Congresses. 2. Baptists—Congresses. I. Bryant, Cyril E., ed. II. Title.

REORGANIZED church of 268.433
Jesus Christ of latter-day saints. Youth conference. Lamoni, Ia., 1941.
The branch of today and tomorrow; official report, Youth conference, 1941, Lamoni, Iowa, June 5-16. Report prepared by Roy A. Cheville and assistants ... Independence, Mo., Published by the Youth conference committee, Herald publishing house [c1941] 160 p. 20 cm. [BX9671.A1R4 1941] 42-7053
1. Youth—Congresses. I. Cheville, Roy Arthur, 1897- II. Title.

YOUNG people's Luther 267.6241
league. 3d convention, Minneapolis, 1925.
"Forward with Christ"; sermons, addresses, reports and minutes of the third triennial convention of the Young people's Luther league at Minneapolis, Minnesota, June 6-10, 1925. Minneapolis, Minn., Augsbury publishing house, 1925. 175 p. 22 cm. [BX8003.Y75 1925] 40-20223
1. Youth—Congresses. 2. Youth—Religious life. I. Title.

YOUNG people's Luther 267.6241
league. 4th convention, Seattle, 1927.
Christ first; sermons, addresses, reports and minutes of the fourth international convention of the Young people's Luther league at Seattle, Washington, June 25-30, 1927. Minneapolis, Minn., Augsburg publishing house, 1927. 296 p. illus. 22 1/2 cm. On cover: The Y.P.L.L. year book. [BX8003.Y75 1927] 40-20224
1. Youth—Congresses. 2. Youth—Religious life. I. Title.

YOUNG people's Luther 267.6241
league. 5th convention, Duluth, 1929.
The Changeless Christ; sermons---addresses--Reports and minutes of the fifth international convention of the Young people's Luther league at Duluth, Minnesota, June 1-5, 1929. Comp. and ed. by N. M. Ylvisaker. Minneapolis, Augsburg publishing house, 1929. 7 p. l., 17-243 p. illus. 22 1/2 cm. On cover:...The Y.P.L.L. year book. [BX8003.X75 1929] 40-20225
1. Youth—Congresses. 2. Youth—Religious life. I. Ylvisaker, Nils Martin, 1882- ed. II. Title.

YOUNG people's Luther 267.6241
league. 8th convention, Sioux Falls, S.D., 1935.
Facing the world with Christ; convention addresses and panel discussion excerpts of the eighth biennial Y.P.L.L. convention. Minneapolis, Augsburg publishing house [c1935] v p. 1 l., 133 p. 19 1/2 cm. Introduction signed: N. M. Ylvisaker, executive secretary. [BX8003.Y75 1935] 38-3310
1. Youth—Congresses. 2. Youth—Religious life. I. Ylvisaker, Nils Martin, 1882- ed. II. Title.

Youth—Drug use—Religious aspects—Christianity.

REHRER, Ronald 362.2'93'088055
L., 1947-
Now what do I do? : a guide on alcohol and drugs for youth / Ronald L. Rehrer. St. Louis, Mo. : Concordia Pub. House, c1982. 79 p. : ill. ; 22 cm. [HV5824.Y68R43 1982] 19 81-22151 ISBN 0-570-03854-5 pbk. : 4.95
1. Youth—Drug use—Religious aspects—Christianity. 2. Youth—Alcohol use—Religious aspects—Christianity. I. Title.

Youth for Christ.

LARSON, Melvin Gunnard, 1916- 269
Youth for Christ, twentieth century wonder; introd. by Percy Crawford. Grand Rapids, Zondervan Pub. House [1947] 135 p. plates, ports. 20 cm. [BV3770.L35] 47-26708
1. Youth for Christ. I. Title.

Youth for Christ. Chicago.

JOHNSON, Torrey Maynard, 269
1909-
Reaching Youth for Christ, by Torrey Johnson and Robert Cook. Chicago, Ill., Moody press [1944] 95, [1] p. plates, ports., facsims. 20 cm. [BV3775.C5J6] 44-47810
1. Youth for Christ. Chicago. 2. Evangelistic work. 3. Revivals—Chicago. I. Cook, Robert, joint author. II. Title.

LARSON, Melvin Gunnard, 922.673
1916-
Young man on fire, the story of Torrey Johnson and Youth for Christ by Mel Larson. Chicago, Youth publications [1945] ix p., 1 l., 114 p. front., plates, ports. 20 cm. [BV3785.J57L3] 46-282
1. Johnson, Torrey Maynard, 1909- 2. Youth for Christ. Chicago. I. Title.

Youth for Christ International.

HEFLEY, James C. 267'.61
God goes to high school [by] James Hefley. Waco, Tex., Word Books [1970] 188 p. illus., map, ports. 23 cm. [BV1430.Y6H4] 75-85830 4.95
1. Youth for Christ International. I. Title.

Youth in church work—United Church of Christ.

ELICKER, Charles W., 1951- 248'.83
Journeys without maps ... : stories of how youth are finding their ways in the church / by Chas. W. Elicker, with Sara Ashby Sawtell, Robert W. Carlson ; foreword by Robert L. Burt. Philadelphia : Published for Joint Educational Development by United Church Press, c1976. 156 p. ; 22 cm. (A Shalom resource) [BV4427.E44] 76-7545 ISBN 0-8298-0312-2 pbk. : 4.50
1. Youth in church work—United Church of Christ. 2. Youth—Religious life. 3. Church management. I. Sawtell, Sara Ashby, 1951- joint author. II. Carlson, Robert W., 1952- joint author. III. Joint Educational Development. IV. Title.

Youth, Jewish.

AMERICAN Jewish Committee. Wilkes-Barre Chapter.
The Jewish teenagers of Wilkes-Barre; a survey of attitudes and values conducted under the sponsorship of the Wilkes-Barre chapter of the American Jewish Committee and the Jewish Community Center of Wilkes-Barre. Research consultant: Irving Jacks. [Wilkes-Barre] 1965. 25 p. 26 cm. Bibliographical footnotes. 68-41071
1. Youth, Jewish. 2. Jews in Wilkes-Barre, Pa. I. Jacks, Irving, 1925- II. Jewish Community Center, Wilkes-Barre, Pa. III. Title.

Youth, Jewish—Conduct of life.

DRESNER, Samuel H. 296.7'4
Between the generations: a Jewish dialogue, by Samuel H. Dresner. [Bridgeport, Conn.] Hartmore House [1971] 80 p. 21 cm. Includes bibliographical references. [BM727.D73] 79-172413 1.75
1. Youth, Jewish—Conduct of life. 2. Conflict of generations. I. Title.

Youth, Jewish—Religious life.

CRONBACH, Abraham, 1882- 296.42
Stories made of Bible stories. New York, Bkman. Assocs. [c.1961] 312p. 61-15675 4.50
1. Youth, Jewish—Religious life. 2. Sermons, American—Jewish authors. 3. Sermons, Jewish—U.S. I. Title.

FRANZBLAU, Abraham Norman, 1901- 296.7'4
Religious belief and character among Jewish adolescents, by Abraham N. Franzblau. New York, Bureau of Publications, Teachers College, Columbia University, 1934. [New York, AMS Press, 1973, c1972] viii, 80 p. 22 cm. Reprint of the 1934 ed., issued in series: Teachers College, Columbia University. Contributions to education, no. 634. Originally presented as the author's thesis, Columbia. Bibliography: p. 79-80. [BM727.F67 1972] 78-176783 ISBN 0-404-55634-5 10.00
1. Youth, Jewish—Religious life. 2. Faith (Judaism) I. Title. II. Series: Columbia University. Teachers College. Contributions to education, no. 634.

ROSEN, Bernard Carl 301.446
Adolescence and religion; the Jewish teenager in American society. Cambridge, Mass., Schenkman [1966, c.1965] xviii, 218p. tables. 21cm. Bibl. [BM540.Y6R6] 65-27391 4.95
1. Youth, Jewish—Religious life. I. Title.

Youth movement—Germany—History.

WALKER, Lawrence D., 1931- 322
Hitler youth and Catholic youth, 1933-1936; a study in totalitarian conquest, by Lawrence D. Walker. Washington, Catholic University of America Press [1971, c1970] x, 203 p. 24 cm. Includes bibliographical references. [HN19.W28] 75-114984 ISBN 0-8132-0499-2 10.50
1. Catholic Church in Germany—History—1933-1945. 2. Youth movement—Germany—History. 3. Church and state in Germany—1933-1945. I. Title.

Youth—Prayer books and devotions.

AHRENS, Herman C., comp. 242'.6'3
Tune in, edited by Herman C. Ahrens, Jr. Philadelphia, Pilgrim Press [1968] 93 p. illus. 21 cm. A collection of prayers from Youth magazine. [BV283.Y6A4] 68-54031 2.95
1. Youth—Prayer-books and devotions. I. Youth (Philadelphia) II. Title.

BARCLAY, William, lecturer in the University of Glasgow. 242.83
Prayers for young people. [1st ed.] New York, Harper & Row [1967, c1963] 128 p. 18 cm. Pages 122-128, blank for "Your favorite prayers." [BV4850.B3 1967] 67-10711
1. Youth—Prayer-books and devotions. I. Title.

BURKE, Carl F. 242.8'3
Treat me cool, Lord; prayers, devotions, litanies, as prepared by some of God's bad-tempered angels with busted halos, with the help of Carl F. Burke. New York, Association Press [1968] 128 p. 18 cm. [BV283.Y6B8] 68-11493
1. Youth—Prayer-books and devotions. 2. Youth—Religious life. I. Title.

COOK, Walter L. 242'.6'3
Christian friendship; youth devotions that lead to action [by] Walter L. Cook. Nashville, Abingdon Press [1967] 108 p. 16 cm. [BV4850.C57] 67-22171
1. Youth—Prayer-books and devotions. I. Title.

COOK, Walter L. 242.63
365 meditations for teen-agers, based on the sayings of Jesus. New York, Abingdon Press [1964] 222 p. 16 cm. [BV4850.C63] 64-10104
1. Youth—Prayer-books and devotions. 2. Devotional calendars. I. Title.

COOK, Walter L. 242
Youth meditations [by] Walter L. Cook. Nashville, Abingdon Press [1970] 96 p. 16 cm. [BV4531.2.C58] 72-98898 2.50
1. Youth—Prayer-books and devotions. I. Title.

COUCH, Helen F. 242.63
Devotions for young teens [by] Helen F. Couch and Sam S. Barefield. New York, Abingdon Press [1965] 111 p. 18 cm. Bibliography: p. 111. [BV4850.C66] 65-11076
1. Youth—Prayer-books and devotions. I. Barefield, Sam S., joint author. II. Title.

*MARTIN, Paul. 248.8'3
Good morning, Lord; more devotions for teens [by] Paul Martin. Grand Rapids, Mich., Baker Book House [1973] 64 p. 19 cm. (Good morning, Lord series) "The devotions in this book are selections from Get up and go, published in 1965 by Beacon Pr." [BV4850] ISBN 0-8010-5915-1 1.95
1. Youth—Prayer-books and devotions. 2. Youth—Religious life. I. Title.

*MARTIN, Paul 242
Good morning, lord devotions for young people Grand Rapids, Baker Book House [1974 c1971] 64 p. 19 cm. [BV4832] ISBN 0-8010-5958-5 1.95 (pbk.)
1. Youth—Prayer books and devotions. I. Title.

ROBINSON, Virgil E. 242.2
Reach out; a daily devotional and inspirational guide for early-teens and near-teens, by Virgil E. Robinson. Washington, Review and Herald Pub. Association [1970] 367 p. 21 cm. [BV4850.R63] 70-121416
1. Youth—Prayer-books and devotions. 2. Devotional calendars—Seventh-Day Adventists. I. Title.

SANDLIN, John Lewis. 242.83
A book of prayers for youth. Westwood, N. J., F. H. Revell Co. [1966] 120 p. 17 cm. [BV4850.S3] 66-17049
1. Youth—Prayer-books and devotions. I. Title.

SCRAGG, Walter. 242
Run this race; a daily devotional and inspirational guide for early-teens and near-teens. Washington, Review and Herald Pub. Association [1969] 367 p. 21 cm. (A Junior devotional) A scripture and devotional commentary for each day of the year. [BV4850.S35] 73-81304
1. Youth—Prayer-books and devotions. 2. Devotional calendars—Seventh-Day Adventists. 3. [Prayer books and devotions.] 4. [Devotional calendars—Seventh-Day Adventists.] I. Title.

Youth—Prayer—books and devotions—English

ALL our days; 248.373
a book of daily devotions for youth. Philadelphia. Christian Education Press [1962] 383p. illus. 17cm. [BV4850.A4] 62-12680
1. Youth—Prayer-books and devotions—English.

ANDERSON, Margaret J 249
Happy moments with God; devotions especially written for families with young children. Grand Rapids, Zondervan Pub. House [1962] 186p. illus. 21cm. [BV255.A56] 62-4925
1. Youth— Prayer-books and devotions—English. I. Title.

BARCLAY, William, lecturer in the University of Glasgow. 242'.2
Marching on : daily readings for younger people / William Barclay ; edited by Denis Duncan. Philadelphia : Westminster Press, [1975] c1974. 223 p. ; 20 cm. Companion volume to the author's Marching orders. Daily readings for six months, with suggested additional Bible readings, present the philosophies of Christian writer William Barclay. [BV4850.B28 1975] 74-30053 ISBN 0-664-24827-6 pbk. : 3.95
1. Youth—Prayer-books and devotions—English. 2. [Prayer books and devotions.] I. Duncan, Denis, ed. II. Title.

BARCLAY, William, lecturer in the University of Glasgow. 242'.2
Marching orders : daily readings for younger people / William Barclay ; edited by Denis Duncan. Philadelphia : Westminster Press, [1975] c1973. 192 p. ; 20 cm. Daily readings for six months, with suggested additional Bible readings, present the philosophies of Christian writer William Barclay. [BV4850.B29 1975] 74-26601 ISBN 0-664-24826-8
1. Youth—Prayer-books and devotions—English. 2. [Prayer books and devotions.] I. Duncan, Denis, ed. II. Title.

BEIMFOHR, Herman N 248.373
Prayers for young people, for personal or group worship. [Westwood, N. J.] Revell [1960] 128p. 27cm. [BV283.Y6B4] 60-8454
1. Youth—Prayer-books and devotions—English. I. Title.

BENNETT, Marian. 248'83
Help me, Jesus, compiled by Marian Bennett. Cincinnati, Ohio, Standard Pub. [1972] 96 p. illus. 18 cm. (Fountain books) Forty-six two page devotions concerned with teen problems such as drugs, parental pressure, and being happy. [BV4850.B45] 72-82084 Pap. 0.98
1. Youth—Prayer-books and devotions—English. 2. [Prayer books and devotions.] I. Title.

BENNETT, Marian, comp. 242'.6'3
What do I do now, Lord? Cincinnati, Ohio, Standard Pub. [1973] 96 p. illus. 18 cm. [BV4850.B46] 73-79468
1. Youth—Prayer-books and devotions—English. I. Title.

BLY, Stephen A., 1944- 242'.63
Devotions with a difference / by Stephen and Janet Bly. Chicago : Moody Press, c1982. p. cm. Presents devotions and related Bible verses on sixty-two alphabetically arranged topics from Anger to Zeal. [BV4850.B55 1982] 19 82-8304 ISBN 0-8024-1789-2 pbk. : 5.95
1. Youth—Prayer-books and devotions—English. 2. [Prayer books and devotions.] 3. [Alphabet.] I. Bly, Janet. II. Title.

BROOKE, Avery. 248.37
Youth talks with God; a book of everyday prayers. New York, Scribner [1959] 55p. 18cm. [BV283.Y6B7] 59-11606
1. Youth—Prayer-books and devotions—English. I. Title.

BRYANT, Al, 1926- 242'.2
Keep in touch : 366 day starters for young adults / Al Bryant. Waco, Tex. : Word Books, c1981. 227 p. ; 23 cm. Includes excerpts from the works of other writers as well as articles by the author. [BV4531.2.B79] 19 80-53257 ISBN 0-8499-0277-0 : 8.95
1. Youth—Prayer-books and devotions—English. 2. Devotional calendars. I. Title.

BURKHART, Roy Abram, 1895- ed. 242
Seeking the living way; a guide for young people in their personal worship, edited by Roy A. Burkhart ... New York, Cincinnati [etc.] The Abingdon press [1933] 157 p. 17 1/2 cm. "For special reading": p. 155-157. [BV4850.B84] 33-33274
1. Youth—Prayer-books and devotions—English. I. Title.

CAVERT, Walter Dudley, 1891- 248.8'3
In the days of thy youth; devotional readings for young people. Nashville, Abingdon Press [1971] 128 p. 16 cm. [BV4850.C38] 74-158674 ISBN 0-687-19355-9 2.95
1. Youth—Prayer-books and devotions—English. I. Title.

CAVERT, Walter Dudley, 1891- 248.373
Prayers for youth. New York, Abingdon Press [1962] 72p. 12cm. [BV283.Y6C3] 62-11519
1. Youth—Prayer-books and devotions—English. I. Title.

CHICAGO Christian youth council. 242
Christian youth in action; central truths of the Christian youth movement; a guide for private study and devotions. [Chicago] The Devotional committee of the Chicago Christian youth council [c1936] 56 p. 21 1/2 cm. C. K. Fewkes, chairman. cf. p. 3. [BV4850.C5] 36-7572
1. Youth—Prayer-books and devotions—English. I. Fewkes, Charles Keith, 1905- II. Title. III. Title: Central truths of the Christian youth movement.

CHURCH, Virginia Woodson Frame, 1880- 242
To meet the day [by] Virginia Church and Francis C. Ellis. Nashville, Abingdon-Cokesbury Press [1953] 128 p. 20 cm. [BV4850.C55] 53-5393
1. Youth—Prayer-books and devotions—English. I. Ellis, Francis C., joint author. II. Title.

COLEMAN, William L. 248.8'3
The great date wait, and other hazards / William L. Coleman. Minneapolis, Minn. : Bethany House Publishers, c1982. 138 p. : ill. ; 22 cm. [BV4850.C565 1982] 19 82-1233 ISBN 0-87123-348-7 (pbk.) : 4.95
1. Youth—Prayer-books and devotions—English. 2. Family—Prayer-books and devotions—English. I. Title.

COOK, Walter L. 242.63
Daily life devotions for youth. New York, Association [c.1965] 128p. 15cm. [BV4850.C58] 65-11081 1.95 bds.,
1. Youth—Prayer-books and devotions—English I. Title.

COOK, Walter L. 248.373
Daily life prayers for youth. New York, Association [c.1963] 95p. 15cm. 63-10379 1.95 bds.,
1. Youth—Prayer-books and devotions—English. I. Title.

COOK, Walter L. 242'.6'3
Devotional thoughts for youth [by] Walter L. Cook. Nashville, Abingdon Press [1975] 92 p. 16 cm. Quotations from the Bible are followed by explanations of their application in everyday life. [BV4850.C585] 74-14607 ISBN 0-687-10600-1 4.50
1. Youth—Prayer-books and devotions—English. 2. [Prayer books and devotions.] I. Title.

COOK, Walter L. 248.373
Everyday devotions for youth. Nashville, Abingdon [c.1961] 110p. 16cm. 61-11783 1.75 bds.,
1. Youth—Prayer-books and devotions—English. I. Title.

COOK, Walter L. 242.63
Meeting the test; a book of devotions for

young people. Nashville, Abingdon Press [c.1960] 112p. 16cm. 60-69291 1.75 bds.,
1. Youth—Prayer-books and devotions—English. I. Title.

COOK, Walter L. 232
Youth devotions on the Jesus who was different [by] Walter L. Cook. Nashville, Abingdon Press [1973] 96 p. 16 cm. [BT306.5.C66] 72-6643 ISBN 0-687-47144-3 3.00
1. Jesus Christ—Biography—Devotional literature. 2. Youth—Prayer-books and devotions—English. I. Title.

DOWARD, Jan S. 242'.6'3
Catch the bright dawn : the redemption story Genesis to Revelation / Jan Doward ; [editor, Bobbie Jane Van Dolson]. Washington : Review and Herald Pub. Association, c1978. 378 p. ; 21 cm. "This book is published in collaboration with the Youth Department as an enrichment of the Morning watch devotional plan." Offers devotional passages to be read day by day. [BV4850.D68] 78-5081 pbk. : 4.50
1. Seventh-Day Adventists.. 2. Youth—Prayer-books and devotions—English. 3. Devotional calendars—Seventh-Day Adventists—Juvenile literature. 4. [Prayer books and devotions.] I. Van Dolson, Bobbie Jane. II. Title.

DRESCHER, Sandra. 242'.6'3
Just between God & me / Sandra Drescher. Grand Rapids : Zondervan Pub. House, c1977. a. 250 p. ; 18 cm. Includes a meditation, Scripture verse, and short prayer for every day of the year. [BV4850.D73] 76-51295 ISBN 0-310-23940-0 : 5.95 ISBN 0-310-23941-9 pbk. : 2.95
1. Youth—Prayer-books and devotions—English. 2. [Prayer books and devotions.] I. Title.

EMSWILER, Thomas Neufer. 242'.6'3
Love is a magic penny : meditations for junior highs / Tom Neufer Emswiler. Nashville : Abingdon, c1977. 111 p. : ill. ; 19 cm. A collection of meditations for daily life, special occasions, and holidays. [BV4850.E48] 76-44384 ISBN 0-687-22815-8 pbk. :
1. Youth—Prayer-books and devotions—English. 2. [Prayer books and devotions.] I. Title.

ESTEB, Adlai Albert. 242'.2
Straight ahead; a book to help young people along the way [by] Adlai A. Esteb. Washington, Review and Herald Pub. Association [1974] 378 p. 21 cm. [BV4850.E87] 73-89469 3.95
1. Youth—Prayer-books and devotions—English. 2. Devotional calendars—Seventh-Day Adventists. I. Title.

EWING, Harold, comp. 264.1
Youth at prayer; a book of prayers for youth, compiled by Harold and Dorothy Ewing. Nashville, Upper Room [1957] 128p. 13cm. [BV245.E94] 57-13008
1. Youth— Prayer-books and devotions—English. I. Ewing, Dorothy, joint comp. II. Title.

GESCH, Roy G. 248.3
Lord of the young crowd [by] Roy G. Gesch. St. Louis, Concordia Pub. House [1971] 95 p. 18 cm. [BV4850.G43] 72-162531 ISBN 0-570-03126-5
1. Youth—Prayer-books and devotions—English. I. Title.

GILBERT, Clark R. 264
Devotions for youth, by Clark R. Gilbert. New York, Association press; New York, Fleming H. Revell company [c1943] 144 p. 20 1/2 cm. [BV4850.G5] 44-3803
1. Youth—Prayer-books and devotions—English. I. Title.

HABEL, Norman C. 242.8'3
Interrobang; a bunch of unanswered prayers and unlimited shouts, by Norman C. Habel. Illus. by Patrick Mason. Philadelphia, Fortress Press [1969] 96 p. illus. (part col.) 22 cm. (Open 2) [BV283.Y6H27] 72-84555 1.95
1. Youth—Prayer-books and devotions—English. I. Title.

HADLEY, Hazel (Mason) 242.2
Behold God's love; devotional readings for a year for junior high young people. Richmond, Published for the Cooperative Publication Association by John Knox Press [1957] 239p. 21cm. [BV4850.H25] 57-11748
1. Youth—Prayer- books and devotions—English. 2. Devotional calendars. I. Title.

HAYWARD, Percy Roy, 1884- 249
Young people's prayers; religion at work in life, by Percy R. Hayward, illustrated by Chester Bratten. New York, N.Y., Association press, Fleming H. Revell company, 1945. xi, 82 p. illus. 23 1/2 cm. "Copyright ... by the International committee of Young men's Christian associations." [BV283.Y6H3] 46-760
1. Youth—Prayer-books and devotions—English. I. Young men's Christian associations. International committee. II. Title.

HURON, Rod. 242'.6'3
Do you know who you are? : Youth devotions for the computer age / Rod Huron ; [computer symbology in collaboration with Joe Shelley]. Cincinnati : Standard Pub., c1976. 96 p. : ill. ; 18 cm. (Fountain books) Contains forty-six devotions focusing on building a personal relationship with God and dealing with problems of everyday life. [BV4850.H87] 75-38226 ISBN 0-87239-089-6
1. Youth—Prayer-books and devotions—English. 2. [Prayer books and devotions.] I. Title.

IN touch; selections from Living light. 242'.2
Wheaton, Ill., Tyndale House [1973] 1 v. (unpaged) illus. 18 cm. [BV4850.I5] 73-80923 ISBN 0-8423-1710-4 1.95
1. Youth—Prayer-books and devotions—English. 2. Devotional calendars. I. The Living light.

JOHNSON, Abigail (Acker) 264.1
Prayers for young people, with readings from the Scriptures. Philadelphia, Westminster Press [1947] 130 p. 18 cm. [BV283.Y6J6] 47-5983
1. Youth—Prayer-books and devotions—English. I. Title.

KEEP in touch : 242'.6'3
prayers, poems, images, and celebrations by and for the young / edited by Herman C. Ahrens, Jr. Philadelphia : Pilgrim Press, c1978. 93 p. : ill. ; 21 cm. Selections from Youth magazine. A collection of prayers and meditations which have appeared in "Youth" magazine. [BV283.Y6K43] 78-14912 ISBN 0-8298-0351-3 pbk. : 3.95
1. Youth—Prayer-books and devotions—English. 2. Prayers. 3. [Prayer books and devotions.] I. Ahrens, Herman C. II. Youth (Philadelphia)

KELLY, William L 248.373
Youth before God; prayers and thoughts. Westminster, Md., Newman Press [1958] 416p. illus. 15cm. 'Adapted ... from the German version 'Jugend vor Gott,' by Alfonso Pereira, S. J. and from the French version 'Rabboni,' by Fernand Leiotte, S. J.' [BX2150.K4] 58-11943
1. Youth—Prayer-books and devotions—English. 2. Catholic Church—Prayer-books and devotions—English. I. Title.

KLAUSLER, Alfred P 242.6
90 meditations for youth St. Louis, Concordia Pub. House [1959] 90p. 19cm. [BV4850.K55] 59-11121
1. Youth—Prayer-books and devotions—English. 2. Lutheran Church—Prayer-books and devotions—English. I. Title.

LARSON, Doris Linell. 248
Dear Lord; prayers for young people. Rock Island, Ill., Augustana Book Concern [1950] x, 102 p. illus. 19 cm. [BV283.Y6L3] 50-58275
1. Youth—Prayer-books and devotions—English. I. Title.

LARSON, Jeanne R. 242'.2
Climbing Jacob's ladder / Jeanne Larson and Ruth McLin. Washington : Review and Herald Pub. Association, c1979. 379 p. ; 21 cm. "Published in collaboration with the Youth Department as an enrichment of the Morning watch devotional plan." Includes index. Contains Bible verses and devotional readings for each day of the year. [BV4850.L37] 79-11820 4.95
1. Youth—Prayer-books and devotions—English. 2. Devotional calendars—Seventh-Day Adventists. 3. [Prayer books and devotions.] 4. [Devotional calendars.] I. McLin, Ruth A., joint author. II. Title.

LEBLANC, Etienne. 264'.02'00240544
How green is green? 38 eucharistic celebrations for today's youth [by] Etienne LeBlanc and Mary Rose Talbot. Notre Dame, Ind., Ave Maria Press [1973?] 180 p. 26 cm. [BV4850.L4] 73-83350 ISBN 0-87793-061-9 2.95
1. Youth—Prayer-books and devotions—English. 2. Liturgies. I. Talbot, Mary Rose, joint author. II. Title.

LOHMANN, Hartwig. 242'.8'3
I can tell you anything, God / Hartwig Lohmann ; tranlated by Ingalill H. Hjelm. Philadelphia : Fortress Press, c1978. 63 p. ; 19 cm. Translation of Dir kann ich alles sagen. [BV4850.L6313] 77-15237 ISBN 0-8006-1324-4 : pbk. : 1.95
1. Youth—Prayer-books and devotions—English. I. Title.

MCCREARY, William Burgess 248.373
When youth prays; one hundred daily devotionals for young people in the areas of faith, witness, citizenship, outreach, and fellowship. Anderson, Ind., Warner Press [dist. Gospel Trumpet Press] [1960] 112p. 19cm. 60-7925 1.25 pap.,
1. Youth—Prayer-books and devotions—English. I. Title.

MARTIN, Paul.
Get up and go; devotions for teens. Kansas City, Mo., Beacon Hill Press [1966] 96 p. 68-104805
1. Youth—Prayer—books and devotions—English I. Title.

MEYER, R Z 238.41
This faith is mine; meditations for youth on Luther's Catechism. Saint Louis, Concordia Pub. House [1960] 135p. 20cm. [BX8070.L8M4] 60-1822
1. Luther, Martin. Catechismus, Kleiner—Meditations. 2. Youth—Prayer-books and devotions—English. I. Title.

NEUFER Emswiler, Tom, 1941- 242'.63
The click in the clock : meditations for junior highs / by Tom Neufer Emswiler. New York : Pilgrim Press, c1981. p. cm. Meditations to be used alone or with a group as part of a worship time. [BV4531.2.N47] 19 81-11875 ISBN 0-8298-0470-6 pbk. : 5.95
1. Youth—Prayer-books and devotions—English. 2. [Prayer books and devotions.] I. Title.

PETERSON, Lorraine. 248.8'3
Falling off cloud nine and other high places / Lorraine Peterson ; [illustrations by LeRoy Dugan, adapted from the sketches by Neil Ahlquist]. Minneapolis, Minn. : Bethany House, c1981. p. cm. (Devotionals for teens ; 2) Addresses teen-age concerns and presents spiritual truths in a way which intends to be relevant to conduct of life. [BV4850.P45] 19 81-38465 ISBN 0-87123-167-0 (pbk.) : 3.95
1. Youth—Prayer-books and devotions—English. 2. [Prayer books and devotions.] 3. [Conduct of life.] I. Dugan, LeRoy, ill. II. Ahlquist, Neil, ill. III. Title. IV. Series.

PETERSON, Lorraine. 242'.63
If God loves me, why can't I get my locker open? / Lorraine Peterson. Minneapolis, Minn. : Bethany Fellowship, c1980. 141 p. : ill. ; 22 cm. Brief essays, Bible references, and discussion questions aid teenagers in applying Bible teachings to daily life. [BV4850.P46] 19 80-27014 ISBN 0-87123-251-0 pbk. : 3.50
1. Youth—Prayer-books and devotions—English. 2. [Prayer books and devotions.] I. Title.

PETERSON, Lorraine. 230
Why isn't God giving cash prizes? / Lorraine Peterson. Minneapolis, MN : Bethany House, 1982. p. cm. (Devotionals for teens ; #3) A thirteen-week program of devotional study exploring the existence and nature of God and other theological questions. [BV4850.P465 1982] 19 82-17866 ISBN 0-87123-626-5 (pbk.) : 3.95
1. Youth—Prayer books and devotions—English. 2. [Prayer books and devotions.] 3. [Theology.] I. Title. II. Series.

PETTY, Jo. 242'.6'3
Gifts for the graduate / Jo Petty. Old Tappan, N.J. : F. H. Revell Co., c1978. 64 p. ; 20 cm. [BV4850.P47] 77-18710 ISBN 0-8007-0929-2 : 3.95
1. Youth—Prayer-books and devotions—English. I. Title.

PIERSON, Robert H. 242'.2
In step with Jesus / Robert H. Pierson. Washington : Review and Herald Pub. Association, 1978. 375 p. ; 21 cm. "Published in collaboration with the Youth Department." Includes index. [BV4850.P53] 76-53225 pbk. : 4.50
1. Youth—Prayer-books and devotions—English. 2. Devotional calendars—Seventh-Day Adventists. I. Title.

REDDER, Ronald M. 242'.6'3
Perforated mood-swing book [by] Ronald M. Redder. St. Louis, Concordia Pub. House [1972] 79 p. illus. 23 cm. In verse. [BV4850.R4] 76-186644 ISBN 0-570-03134-6
1. Youth—Prayer-books and devotions—English. I. Title.

ROWLAND, Wilmina, comp. 264.1
When we pray. New York, Friendship Press [1955] 63p. illus. 21cm. [BV4850.R69] 55-5766
1. Youth—Prayer-books and devotions—English. I. Title.

SEWELL, Elizabeth Missing, 1815-1906, comp. 264.
Private devotions for young persons, compiled by Elizabeth M. Sewell... New York, E. P. Dutton & company, 1881. viii, 158 p. 15 cm. [BV283.Y6S4] 39-25248
1. Youth—Prayer-books and devotions—English. I. Title.

TEEN-AGERS pray. 264.1
Saint Louis, Concordia Pub. House [1956, c1955] 82p. 18cm. [BV283.Y6T4] 55-12193
1. Youth—Prayer-books and devotions—English.

TUCKER, James A. 242'.2
Windows on God's world : glimpses of the Creator through His handiwork / James A. Tucker. Washington : Review and Herald Pub. Association, c1975. 372 p. ; 21 cm. "Published by the Youth Department of Missionary Volunteers and an enrichment of the Morning watch devotional plan." [BV4850.T8] 74-29820
1. Youth—Prayer-books and devotions—English. 2. Devotional calendars—Seventh-Day Adventists. 3. [Prayer books and devotions.] 4. [Devotional calendars—Seventh-Day Adventists] I. Title.

WITT, Elmer N. 242'.8'3
Help it all make sense, Lord! By Elmer N. Witt; drawings by Jim Cummins. St. Louis, Concordia Pub. House [1972] 117 p. illus. 20 cm. [BV283.Y6W49] 72-85147
1. Youth—Prayer-books and devotions—English. 2. Prayers. I. Title.

WITT, Elmer N. 248.373
Time to pray; daily prayers for youth. Drawings by Jim Cummins. Saint Louis, Concordia Pub. House [c.1960] 116p. illus. 20cm. 60-3998 1.00 pap.,
1. Youth—Prayer-books and devotions—English. I. Title.

Youth—Religious life.

ABBOTT, Jacob, 1803-1879. 171.
The young Christian; or, A familiar illustration of the principles of Christian duty. By Jacob Abbott ... Boston, Peirce and Parker, 1832. xi, [13]-323 p. 18 1/2 cm. [BV4531.A34 1882a] 39-3957
1. Youth—Religious life. I. Title.

ABBOTT, Jacob, 1803-1879. 171.
The young Christian; or A familiar illustration of the principles of Christian duty. By Jacob Abbott. Rev. ed. New York, American tract society [c1832] 2 p. l., [3]-395 p. front. 18 1/2 cm. (On cover: Christian library [v.] 32) Added t.-p., engraved, with vignetic. [BV4531.A34 1832] 24-16574
1. Youth—Religious life. I. Title. II. Title: Principles of Christian duty.

ADAIR, James R 1923- ed. 248.83
Teen with a future, by James R. Adair.

Grand Rapids, Baker Book House, 1965. 83 p. illus., ports. 21 cm. (The Valor series, no. 12) [BV4531.2.A3] 65-25476
1. Youth — Religious life. I. Title.

ADAMS, Michael, 1937- 248'.48'2
The hard life : values for young adults / Michael Adams. Huntington, Ind. : Our Sunday Visitor, 1977. 95 p. ; 18 cm. Includes bibliographical references. [BX2355.A3 1977b] 78-60438 ISBN 0-87973-707-7 : 1.95
1. Youth—Religious life. 2. Spiritual life—Catholic authors. I. Title.

AINGER, Geoffrey. 248.8'3
Time to act. Melbourne, Methodist Federal Board of Education and Presbyterian Board of Christian Education, 1968. 36 p. 22 cm. A resource book written for the National Christian Youth Convention, Sydney, January 1969. [BV4531.2.A36] 73-411900 0.40
1. Youth—Religious life. I. Methodist Federal Board of Education. II. Presbyterian Board of Christian Education. III. National Christian Youth Convention, Sydney, 1969.

ANDERSON, Margaret J 248.83
It's your business, teen-ager! A challenge to the teenagers. Chicago, Moody Press [1960] 96p. 20cm. [BV4531.2.A5] 60-50744
1. Youth—Religious life. I. Title.

AYRES, Rollin H. 171.
The measure of a youth, by Rollin H. Ayres; introduction by Charles L. Mead ... New York, Cincinnati, The Abingdon press [c1926] 155 p. 18 cm. [BV4531.A85] 26-6677
1. Youth—Religious life. I. Title.

BADEN, Robert, 1936- 248.8'3
Teen talks with God / Robert Baden. St. Louis : Concordia Pub. House, c1980. 79 p. : ill. ; 22 cm. [BV4531.2.B23] 80-323 ISBN 0-570-03812-X pbk. : 2.50
1. Youth—Religious life. I. Title.

BALM, Catherine Atkinson (Miller), Mrs., 1896- 268.6
Leading youth to abundant life; a study of adolescent materials and methods, by Catherine Atkinson Miller. Philadelphia, Printed for the Leadership training publishing association by the Heidelberg press, 1934. vii, 235 p. 19 1/2 cm. "Editor's introduction" signed: Erwin L. Shaver, chairman, Editorial and educational committee. Includes bibliographies. [BV1533.B28] 86-1055
1. Youth—Religious life. 2. Religious education. I. Shaver, Erwin Leander, 1890- ed. II. Title.

BANKS, Louis Albert, 1855-
The problems of youth; a series of discourses for young people on themes from the book of Proverbs, by Rev. Louis Albert Banks. New York and London, Funk & Wagnalls company, 1909. iv, 393 p. 20 cm. [1909; A 251022] 9-28189 1.30
I. Title.

BARNETT, Minyard Merrell. 248
Building a life, by Minyard Merrell Barnett. Kansas City, Kan., Central seminary press, 1946. 131 p. front. (port.) 22 cm. [BV4531.B32] 46-19770
1. Youth—Religious life. I. Title.

BECK, Hubert F. 248'.83
Why can't the church be like this? [By] Hubert Beck. St. Louis, Concordia Pub. House [1973] 104 p. illus. 20 cm. "A Perspective II book." [BV4531.2.B4] 73-9111 ISBN 0-570-03171-0 1.95 (pbk.)
1. International Student Congress on Evangelism. 2. Youth—Religious life. 3. Christianity—20th century. 4. Jesus people. I. Title.

BENSON, Dennis C. 261.8'3
The now generation [by] Dennis C. Benson. Richmond, John Knox Press [1969] 143 p. 21 cm. Bibliographical references included in "Notes" (p. [137]-143) [BV639.Y7B4] 68-25012 ISBN 0-8042-1979-6 2.45
1. Youth—Religious life. 2. Youth—United States. 3. Church work with youth. I. Title.

BIETZ, Arthur Leo. 248
In quest of life. Mountain View, Calif., Pacific Press Pub. Assn. [1947] 155 p. 21 cm. Bibilography: p. 153-155. [BV4531.B5] 48-1619
1. Youth—Religious life. I. Title.

BOND, Charles Lester, 1888- 248
Adventures in Christian living, by C. Lester Bond ... Takoma Park, Washington, D.C., South Bend, Ind. [etc.] Review and herald publishing assn. [c1934] 4 p. l., 7-192 p. incl. front. (port.) 20 cm. [BV4531.B56] 34-15438
1. Youth—Religious life. I. Title.

BOON, May Ellen (Watson) Mrs. 1880- 221.
Gospel messages for boys and girls, with eight full page illustrations, by Mrs. J. Henry Boon. New York, N.Y., Christian alliance publishing co. [c1926] 115 p. front., plates. 19 cm. [BV4571.B57] 27-1372
I. Title.

BRUECKNER, Herman H.
The ideals of a young Lutheran, by Rev. Herman Brueckner ... Chicago, Ill., Wartburg publishing house, 1925. 64 p. form. 19 cm. [BX8665.B9] 25-8229
I. Title.

BUCK, Charles, 1771-1815. 240
The young Christian's guide. By Charles Buck. With an introductory essay. By T. T. Waterman ... Providence, Weeden and Cory, 1834. xxvi, [27]-180 p. 16 cm. [BV4531.B78 1834] 39-11825
1. Youth—Religious life. I. Waterman, Thomas Tileston, 1800-1873. II. Title.

BURKHART, Roy A., 1895- 248
Youth and the way of Jesus; building a philosophy of life, by Roy A. Burkhart. New York, Round table press, inc., 1939. x, 212 p. diagr. 20 cm. [BV4531.B87] 39-24332
1. Youth—Religious life. 2. Christianity—Essense, genius, nature. I. Title.

BURKHART, Roy Abram, 1895- 248
Understanding youth, his search for a way of life [by] Roy A. Burkhart. New York, Cincinnati [etc.] The Abingdon press [c1938] 176 p. diagr. 20 cm. [BV4447.B8] 38-31236
1. Youth—Religious life. 2. Adolescence. 3. Church work with youth. I. Title.

*CAREY, Floyd D.
Christian entiquette for teenagers: a handbook on Christian etiquette. Illus. by Mrs. Robert Kinsev Grand Rapids. Mich., Baker Bk. [1967, c.1963] 100p. illus. 20cm. [248.8'3] 1.50 pap.,
1. Youth—Religious life. I. Title.

CARGAS, Harry J. 248.8'3
Keeping a spiritual journal / Harry J. Cargas, Roger J. Radley. Garden City, N.Y. : Doubleday, 1981. p. cm. [BX2355.C36] 19 80-2072 ISBN 0-385-17439-X pbk. : 2.45
1. Youth—Religious life. 2. Spiritual life—Catholic authors—Juvenile literature. 3. Diaries—Juvenile literature. I. Radley, Roger J., joint author. II. Title.

CARROLL, Benajah Harvey, 1843-1914. 52.061
Ambitious dreams of youth; a compilation of discussions of life and its obligations, including the author's marvelous sermon on "Paul, the greatest man in history", by B. H. Carroll ... compiled by J. W. Crowder ... edited by J. B. Cranfill ... Dallas, Tex., Helms printing company [c1939] 205 p. incl. front. (port.) 20 cm. [BV4310.C37] 40-4926
1. Youth—Religious life. 2. Baptists—Sermons. 3. Sermons, American. I. Crowder, Joseph Wade, 1873- comp. II. Cranfill, James Britton, 1858- ed. III. Title.

CASSELS, Louis. 248'.83
Forbid them not. Illustrated by Garry R. Hood. [Independence, Mo.] Independence Press [1973] 94 p. illus. 20 cm. [BV4531.2.C34] 73-75885 ISBN 0-8309-0097-7 2.95
1. Youth—Religious life. I. Title.

CECILIA, Madame, 1852- 242
More short spiritual readings for Mary's children, by Madame Cecilia ... New York, Cincinnati [etc.] Benziger brothers, 1910. 213 p. 20 cm. [BX2198.C4] 10-25124
1. Youth—Religious life. I. Title.

CHEVILLE, Roy Arthur, 1879- 268.433
Growing up in religion; a text for explorers who are in the quest for spiritual development. Independence, Mo., Herald Pub. House [1951] 176 p. 21 cm. [BV4531.C45] 51-7974
1. Youth—Religious life. 2. Mormons and Mormonism. I. Title.

CHRISTIAN youth conference of North America, Lakeside, O., 1936. 267.61
Report of the Christian youth conference of North America, Lakeside, Ohio, June 23-28, 1936. Chicago, Ill., The Joint committee on united youth program [c1936] 63 p. 19 1/2 cm. [BV940.C55 1936] 38-7722
1. Youth—Religious life. I. Title.

CLEMENS, Bryan T. 371.4'6
The counselor and religious questioning and conflicts [by] Bryan T. Clemens [and] Darrell Smith. Boston, Houghton Mifflin Co. [1973] ix, 80 p. 23 cm. (Guidance monograph series. Series 7: Special topics in counseling) Bibliography: p. 71-77. [BV4531.2.C52] 72-1844 1.80 (pbk.)
1. Youth—Religious life. 2. Counseling. 3. Psychology, Religious. I. Smith, Darrell, joint author. II. Title.

CLEMENT, Lora Effle. 248
Let's talk it over, by Lora E. Clement... Takoma Park, Washington, D.C., Review and herald publishing assn. [c1940] 128 p. 19 cm. Head and tail pieces. [BV4531.C55] 40-8923
1. Youth—Religious life. I. Title.

COLEMAN, William L. Coleman. 248.8'3
Letters from Dad / William L. Coleman. Nashville, Tenn. : Broadman Press, c1979. 118 p. ; 20 cm. [BV4531.2.C57] 79-53430 ISBN 0-8054-5330-X pbk. : 3.50
1. Youth—Religious life. I. Title.

CONFREY, Burton, 1898- 248
Stenciled of God [by] Burton Confrey ... Manchester, N. H., Magnificat press [c1939] 212. [2] p. 23 cm. "Some ... papers are a continuation of these in "Faith and youth'," -- Foreword. [Full naem: Joseph Burton Confrey] Includes bibliographies. [B X903. C582] 39-14022
1. Youth—Religious life. 2. Christian life-Catholic authors. I. Title.

COOPER, John Charles. 248.8'3
The new mentality. Philadelphia, Westminster Press [1969] 159 p. 21 cm. Bibliographical references included in "Notes" (p. [149]-159) [BV4531.2.C6] 69-16304 2.65
1. Youth—Religious life. 2. Symbolism. 3. U.S.—Social conditions—1960- I. Title.

COTHERN, Fayly H. 177
So you want to be popular. Grand Rapids, Mich., Zondervan Pub. House [c.1960] 118p. illus. 60-51857 1.95 bds.,
1. Youth—Religious life. 2. Youth—Conduct of life. I. Title.

COX, Norman Wade, 1888- 248
Youth's return to faith, by Norman Wade Cox. Philadelphia, Boston [etc.] The Judson press [c1938] 6 p. l., 194 p. 20 cm. [BV4531.C6] 38-7721
1. Youth—Religious life. I. Title.

CRANFORD, Clarence William. 248
The devotional life of young people, by Clarence William Cranford. Philadelphia, Chicago [etc.] The Judson press [c1940] 125 p. 19 cm. "Suggested reading" at end of most of the chapters. [BV4531.C63] 40-7445
1. Youth—Religious life. 2. Devotion. I. Title.

CRANOR, Phoebe. 248'.83
Why doesn't God do something? / By Phoebe Cranor. Minneapolis : Bethany Fellowship, c1978. 143 p. ; 18 cm. (Dimension books) Includes index. Presents simple, Biblical answers to 15 questions such as "Why doesn't God heal everybody who asks?", "What will happen if I get mad at God?", and "Can I commit an unpardonable sin?" [BV4531.2.C7] 78-319166 ISBN 0-87123-605-2 : 1.95
1. Youth—Religious life. 2. [Christian life.] I. Title.

CRAPULLO, George Anthony, 1890- 248
Messages to modern youth, by George A. Crapullo ... New York [etc.] Fleming H. Revell company [c1936] 84 p. 20 cm. [BV4531.C65] 36-22368
1. Youth—Religious life. I. Title.

CUYLER, Theodore Ledyard, 1822-1909. 248
Well-built; plain talks to young people, by Theodore L. Cuyler. Boston and Chicago, United Society of Christian endeavor [1898] 53 p. front. (port.) 18 1/2 cm. (The Deeper life series) [BV4531.C8 1898] 45-50102
1. Youth—Religious life. I. International society of Christian endeavor. II. Title.

DALRYMPLE, Gwynne. 248
You and your problems, by Gwynne Dalrymple. Takoma Park, Washington, D. C., South Bend, Ind. [etc.] Review and herald publishing assn. [c1937] 107 p. 21 cm. [BV4531.D26] 37-22660
1. Youth—Religious life. I. Title.

DARE to live: 248'.83
Taize 1974; preparing for the world-wide Council of Youth. Foreword by Samuel Wylie. New York, Seabury Press [1974] vi, 161, [2] p. 21 cm. "A Crossroad book." Translation of Audacieuse aventure. Bibliography: p. [163] [BV4532.A913] 73-17912 2.95 (pbk.)
1. Communaute de Taize. 2. Youth—Religious life. I. Communaute de Taize.

DAUGHTERS of St. Paul. 248.8'3
Your right to be informed. [Boston] St. Paul Editions [1969] 430 p. illus. 24 cm. [BX2355.D38] 68-59042
1. Youth—Religious life. 2. Christian life—Catholic authors. I. Title.

DAVIES, Thomas Frederick, bp., 1872- 248
After confirmation what? By Thomas Frederick Davies ... New York, Milwaukee, Morehouse publishing co., 1936. xii, 123, [1] p. incl. front. (port.) 15 cm. Blank pages for "Notes" at end of each chapter. [BV4531.D3] 36-3124
1. Youth—Religious life. I. Title.

DEWEY, Robert D. 248'.83
Commitment; a parent-teacher manual [by] Robert D. Dewey [and] Charles Murphy. [Rev. ed. New York] Herder and Herder [1968] 76 p. illus. 22 cm. (Christian commitment series) Bibliography: p. 72-76. [BV4531.2.D48 1968] 68-29893 1.75
1. Youth—Religious life. 2. Religious education—Text-books—United Church of Christ. I. Murphy, Charles, joint author. II. Title.

DIGIACOMO, James. 232.9'01 B
Meet the Lord : encounters with Jesus / James J. DiGiacomo, John Walsh. [Minneapolis] : Winston Press, c1977. 97 p. : ill. ; 22 cm. (The Encounter series) Discusses some aspects of Jesus' life and how they relate to today's problems. [BT306.5.D48] 77-72548 ISBN 0-03-021281-2 pbk. : 2.95
1. Jesus Christ—Biography—Devotional literature. 2. [Jesus Christ—Biography.] 3. Youth—Religious life. 4. Christian life—Catholic authors. 5. [Christian life.] I. Walsh, John, joint author. II. Title.

DIGIACOMO, James. 248.4'8204
When your teenager stops going to church / James DiGiacomo. St. Meinrad, Ind. : Abbey Press, c1980. 96 p. : ill. ; 18 cm. (A When book) [BX2355.D5] 19 80-65401 ISBN 0-87029-165-3 pbk. : 1.95
1. Youth—Religious life. I. Title.

DIMMICK, Luther Fraseur, 1790-1860. 248
The claims of religion upon the young ... By L. F. Dimmick ... Newburyport [Mass.] C. Whipple, 1836. vi, [7]-72 p. 16 cm. [BV4531] 44-25655
1. Youth—Religious life. I. Title.

DODDRIDGE, Philip, 1702-1751. 252.
Sermons to young persons, on the following subjects, vix. I. The importance of the rising generation. II. Christ formed in the soul the foundation of hope. III. A dissuasive from keeping bad company. IV. The young Christian invited to an early attendance on the Lord's table. V. The

orphan's hope. VI. The reflections of a pious parent on the death of a wicked child. VII. Youth reminded of approaching judgment. By P. Doddridge, D.D. The 6th ed. Philadelphia: Printed by William Young, no. 52, Second-street the corner of Chesnut-street. M,DCC,XCIII. viii, [13]-196 p. 15 1/2 cm. [BV4310.D63 1793] 44-34545
1. Youth—Religious life. 2. Sermons, English. I. Title.

DODDS, Lois. 248.8'3
How do I look from up there? : you, from God's point of view / Lois Dodds. Wheaton, Ill. : Victor Books, c1981. 143 p. : ill. ; 18 cm. (SonPower youth publication) [BV4531.2.D62] 19 80-51160 ISBN 0-88207-584-5 (pbk.) : 2.50
1. Youth—Religious life. 2. Self-love (Theology) 3. Self-acceptance. I. Title. II. Series.

DONLE, Charles B.
How to interest the young in Bible truths [by] Charles B. Donle ... New York city, The Book stall [c1919] 113 p. incl. illus., port. 20 cm. [BS610.D6] 19-12687
I. Title.

DRESCHER, Sandra. 248'.8
Dear Jesus, love Sandy / ;by Sandra Drescher. Grand Rapids, Mich. : Zondervan Pub. House, c1982. p. cm. [BV4531.2.D73] 19 81-23997 ISBN 0-310-44841-7 pbk. : 3.95
1. Youth—Religious life. I. Title.

DUDLEY, Roger L. 248'.83
Why teenagers reject religion and what to do about it / Roger L. Dudley. Washington : Review and Herald Pub. Association, c1978. 160 p. ; 21 cm. Includes bibliographical references. [BV4531.2.D82] 78-1446 pbk. : 4.50
1. Youth—Religious life. 2. Church work with youth—Seventh-Day Adventists. I. Title.

DUNHAM, Truman Richard, 1899- 248
"In green pastures"; ten messages to young people, compiled and editedd by T. Richard Dunham ... contributors, Walter L. Wilson, Wendell P. Loveless, Rev. Percy Crawford [and others] ... Findlay, O., Fundamental truth publishers [c1937] 160 p. diagrs. 19 cm. [BV4310.D83] 39-10233
1. Youth—Religious life. I. Wilson, Walter Lewis, 1881- II. Title.

DUNN, Paul H. 248'.83
I challenge you ... by Paul H. Dunn in collaboration with Richard M. Eyre. Salt Lake City, Bookcraft [1972] 92 p. 24 cm. "I promise you ... by Paul H. Dunn in collaboration with Richard M. Eyre": p. 92-5 (text reversed and inverted with main text) [BV4531.2.D86] 72-90323
1. Youth—Religious life. I. Dunn, Paul H. I promise you. 1972. II. Title. III. Title: I promise you.

EDDY, Ansel Doane, 1798-1875. 171.
Addresses on the duties, dangers, and securities of youth: with an introductory essay by the Honourable Theodore Frelinghuysen, esq. By A. D. Eddy ... New York, Leavitt, Lord & co.; Boston, Crocker & Brewster, 1836. xxiv, [25]-266 p., 1 l. 19 1/2 cm. [BV4531.E3] 44-35428
1. Youth—Religious life. I. Title.

ELDER, Carl A. 248'.83
Youth and values : getting self together / Carl A. Elder. Nashville : Broadman Press, c1978. 168 p. ; 22 cm. [BV4531.2.E42] 78-106348 5.95
1. Youth—Religious life. 2. Youth—Conduct of life. I. Title.

ELLIS, Charles Calvert. 171.
...The Christian way of life for young people, by Charles Calvert Ellis...with an introduction by J. H. Moore. Elgin, Ill., The Elgin press [c1924] 109 p. 17 cm. (The Elgin press religious educational texts) [BV4531.E54] 24-11891
I. Title.

*EVANS, B. Hoyt 220.92
Youth programs about Bible people. Grand Rapids, Mich., Baker Bk. [c.]1964. 107p. 20cm. 1.50 pap.,
I. Title.

*EVANS, B. Hoyt 220.07
Youth programs from the Bible. Grand Rapids, Mich., Baker Bk. [1966] 119p. 20cm. (Paperback program ser.) Cover title: 37 youth programs from the Bible. 1.50 pap.,
I. Title.

EVANS, Louis Hadley, 1897- 252.051
Youth seeks a master. Westwood, N.J., Revell [c.1964] 126p. 20cm. 64-16868 2.75 bds.,
1. Youth—Religious life. 2. Presbyterian Church—Sermons. 3. Sermons, American. I. Title.

EVANS, Louis Hadley, 1897- 252.051
Youth seeks a master. Westwood, N.J., F. H. Revell Co. [c1964] 126 p. 20 cm. [BV4310.E75 1964] 64-16868
1. Youth — Religious life. 2. Presbyterian Church — Sermons. 3. Sermons, American. I. Title.

EVANS, Louis Hadley, 1897- 252.051
Youth seeks a master, by Louis H. Evans ... New York [etc.] Fleming H. Revell company [c1941] 3 p. l., 5-126 p. 19 1/2 cm. [BV4310.E75] 41-23377
1. Youth—Religious life. 2. Presbyterian church—Sermons. 3. Sermons, American. I. Title.

FAGERBURG, Frank Benjamin, 1898- 252.06
This questioning age, sermons preached to young people, by Frank B. Fagerburg. Philadelphia, Boston [etc.] The Judson press [c1936] 8 p. l., 3-178 p. 20 cm. (Half-title: The Judson press sermons) [BV4310.F25] 36-15868
1. Youth—Religion life. 2. Baptists—Sermons. 3. Sermons, American. I. Title.

FAITH in action. 248'.83
Cleveland, Tenn. : Pathway Press, c1975. 144 p. : ill. ; 18 cm. (Making life count new life series) Bibliography: p. 143-144. [BV4531.2.F28] 75-3504 ISBN 0-87148-331-9
1. Youth—Religious life. I. Pathway Press.

FEATHERSTONE, Vaughn J. 248'.83
Do-it-yourself destiny / Vaughn J. Featherstone. Salt Lake City : Bookcraft, 1977. 180 p. ; 24 cm. Includes index. The author advises young Latter-day Saints about daily living and shaping their futures. [BV4531.2.F35] 77-14716 ISBN 0-88494-329-1 : 4.95
1. [Church of Jesus Christ of Latter-day Saints.] 2. Youth—Religious life. 3. Christian life—Mormon authors—Juvenile literature. 4. [Christian life.] I. Title.

FERGUSON, Rowena. 248.83
My life; what will I make of it? Chicago, Rand McNally [1966] 159 p. 21 cm. [BV4531.2.F4] 66-18098
1. Youth—Religious life. I. Title.

FERGUSON, Rowena. 248
Youth and the Christian community. Nashville, Abingdon Press [1954] 140p. 19cm. [BV4531.F4] 54-11091
1. Youth—Religious life. 2. Church work with youth. I. Title.

FINEGAN, Jack, 1908- 248
A highway shall be there, by Jack Finegan ... St. Louis, Mo., The Bethany press [1946] 159 p. 19 1/2 cm. "Sermons ... delivered to young people in churches, colleges, and other assemblages." [BV4310.F43] 46-5057
1. Youth—Religious life. 2. Sermons, American. I. Title.

FIRNHABER, R. Paul, comp. 248.8'3
I'll let you taste my wine if I can taste yours. St. Louis, Concordia Pub. House [1969] 88 p. illus. 21 cm. (The Perspective series, 7) [BV4447.F57] 77-77627 1.25
1. Youth—Religious life. 2. Church and the world. I. Title.

FIRNHABER, R. Paul. 248.8'3
Say yes! By R. Paul Firnhaber. St. Louis, Concordia Pub. House [1968] 1 v. (unpaged) illus. (part col.) 21 cm. (The Perspective series, 6) [BV4531.2.F48] 68-25511
1. Youth—Religious life. I. Title.

FISHER, Lee. 248'.83
A time to seek. Nashville, Abingdon Press [1972] 127 p. 19 cm. [BV4531.2.F49] 75-185549 ISBN 0-687-42135-7 1.95
1. Youth—Religious life. I. Title.

FITZGERALD, Lawrence P. 248.8
One hundred talks to teen-agers. Grand Rapids, Mich., Baker Bk. House, 1961. 106p. 61-17545 1.95
1. Youth—Religious life. I. Title.

FITZPATRICK, Daniel J. 377'.8'2
Confusion, call, commitment : the spiritual exercises and religious education / Daniel J. Fitzpatrick. New York : Alba House, c1976. xx, 178 p. ; 21 cm. Bibliography: p. [169]-178. [BX2179.L8F5 1976] 76-3801 ISBN 0-8189-0327-9 : 4.95
1. Loyola, Ignacio de, Saint, 1491-1556. Exercitia spiritualia. 2. Youth—Religious life. 3. Christian education of young people. 4. Spiritual exercises. I. Title.

FOOTE, Evelyn Carter. 242'.6'3
Time with God : devotional readings for youth / Evelyn Carter Foote. Nashville : Broadman Press, c1978. 60 p. ; 19 cm. [BV4531.2.F64] 78-19970 ISBN 0-8054-5164-1 pbk. : 1.95
1. Youth—Religious life. I. Title.

FRIEND, Nellie E. Mrs. 171.
God and you; friendly talks with young people, by Nellie E. Friend ... New York, Chicago [etc.] Fleming H. Revell company [c1929] 151 p. 20 cm. [BV4531.F78] 29-8812
I. Title.

FRIEND of Youth. 248.4'8203
Teenagers today / by "A friend of youth". 2nd ed. [Boston] : St. Paul Editions, 1980. 168 p., [1] leaf of plates : ill. ; 19 cm. Edition for 1961 published under title: 20th-century teenagers. [BX2347.8.Y7F74 1980] 19 72-80448 ISBN 0-8198-7303-9 : 4.00 ISBN 0-8198-7304-7 (pbk.) : 3.00
1. Catholic Church—Doctrinal and controversial works—Catholic authors. 2. Youth—Religious life. 3. Youth—Conduct of life. I. Title.
Publisher's address 50 St. Paul's Ave., Boston, MA 02130.

GAGLIOSTRO, Vincenza. 248.4'8203
Am I ok—if I feel the way I do? / Vincenza Gagliostro. 1st ed. Garden City, N.Y. : Doubleday, 1981. 127 p. ; 18 cm. "Nazareth books." A guide to squaring one's emotions and behavior with the roots of the Christian faith. [BX2355.G26] 19 80-2077 ISBN 0-385-17437-3 pbk. : 2.75
1. Catholic Church. 2. Youth—Religious life. 3. Youth—Conduct of life. 4. Emotions—Juvenile literature. 5. [Christian life.] I. Title.

GARA, Matthew 248.42
On the road to happiness; 94 pointers along the way for teens. Illus. by Edward McDonnell. Valatie, N. Y., Holy Cross Pr. [c.]1965. 119p. illus. 23cm. [BX2355.G3] 65-21806 3.00
1. Youth—Religious life. 2. Meditations. I. Title.

GEER, Owen Meredith, 1898- 248
Christ's pathway to power: a book of personal devotion and evangelism. For individual orgru use. Especially for the use of young people in the movement, "Christin youth building a new world" [by] Owen M. Geer ... Chicago, Ill., Epworth league and young people's work [c1936] 95 p. 20 cm. Bibliography: p. 94-65. [BV4531.G4] 36-9460
1. Youth—Religious life. 2. Evangelistic work. I. Title.

GILBERT, Dan. 248
A manifesto of Christian youth, by Dan Gilbert. San Diego, Calif., The Danielle publishers [c1939] 138 p., 1 l. front. (port.) 20 cm. [Full name: Dan Wesley Gilbert] [BV4531.G5] 39-24411
1. Youth—Religious life. 2. Sociology, Christian. I. Title.

GORDON, Samuel Dickey, 1859- 248
Quiet talks with eager youth, by S. D. Gordon ... New York [etc.] Fleming H. Revell company [c1935] 160 p. 19 cm. [BV4531.G63] 35-7219
1. Youth—Religious life. I. Title.

GRAHAM, William Franklin, 1918- 248'.83
The Jesus generation, by Billy Graham. True spirituality, by Francis A. Schaeffer. Brethren, hang loose, by Robert C. Girard. A christianity today trilogy. New York, Produced for Christianity today [by] Iverson-Norman Associates, 1972. iii, 188, 180, 220 p. 22 cm. (Books for believers, v. 1) Includes bibliographical references. [BV4531.2.G74] 72-89780
1. Youth—Religious life. 2. Jesus People—United States. 3. Apologetics—20th century. 4. Church renewal. I. Schaeffer, Francis August. True spirituality. 1972. II. Girard, Robert C. Brethren, hang loose. 1972 III. Christianity today. IV. Title. V. Title: True spirituality. VI. Title: Brethren, hang loose. VII. Series.

GRANT, Dave. 248'.83
Heavy questions. Glendale, Calif., Regal Books [1972] 167 p. 18 cm. [BV4531.2.G76] 78-185800 ISBN 0-8307-0112-5 1.25
1. Youth—Religious life. 2. Christian life—Miscellanea. I. Title.

GREENWAY, Leonard, 1907- 248
Talks to teeners; chapel talks delivered during morning devotions at the Christian High School, Grand Rapids, Michigan. Grand Rapids, Zondervan Pub. House [1952] 58p. 21cm. [BV4531.G68] 53-16583
1. Youth—Religious life. I. Title.

HALLIDAY, James F. 220
Robbing youth of its religion. New York, H. Holt and company, 1929. xiv, 253 p. 21 cm. [BR125.H323] 29-23911
I. Title.

HANKS, Marion D. 284'.48'933
Now and forever [by] Marion D. Hanks. Illus. by Bill Kuhre. Salt Lake City, Bookcraft [1974] 166 p. col. illus. 24 cm. A collection of essays offering spiritual guidance to Mormon youth concerning everyday situations. [BV4531.2.H32] 74-75165 ISBN 0-88494-212-0 2.95 (pbk.)
1. Youth—Religious life. 2. [Christian life.] I. Kuhre, William, illus. II. Title.

HANSON, Cscar Conrad, 1908- 248
Live to win. Minneapolis, Augsburg Pub. House [1949] 145p. 21cm. [BV4531.H22] 49-7758
1. Youth —Religious life. I. Title.

HARE, Eric B. 252.067
Fullness of joy. Washington, Review and Herold Pub. Association [1952] 254 p. 21 cm. [BV4310.H28] 52-64332
1. Youth—Religious life. 2. Seventh-day Adventists—Sermons. 3. Sermons, American. I. Title.

HARKER, Ahimaaz.
A companion for the young people of North-America. Particularly recommended to those within the three provinces of New-York, New-Jersey, and Pennsylvania. Divided into chapters, adapted to every intelligent capacity, and calculated for the promotion and furtherance of Christian decorum among families; principally designed to excite a laudable and Christianemulation among young people, to pursue the paths which lead to real religion: by attempting to discover the beauties of a virtuous life, and to remove all objections young persons can have to being early religions. By Ahimaaz Harker ... New-York: Printed by J. Holt, at the Exchange, 1767. 3 p. l., iv. 284, [5] p. 17 cm. [BV4530.H3] 38-34611
1. Youth—Religious life. 2. Conduct of life. I. Title.

HARLOW, Samuel Ralph, 1885- 248
Honest answers to honest questions [by] S. Ralph Harlow. New York, Nashville, Abingdon-Cokesbury press [c1940] 105 p. 20 cm. [BV4531.H25] 40-34451
1. Youth—Religious life. I. Title.

HARMAN, Carl H. 248
Vital facts of life; a Christian view of sex and life, by Carl H. Harman and E. W. Marquardt. Saint Louis, Concordia Pub. House, 1949. xiii, 126 p. 23 cm. [BV4531.H26] 49-6333
1. Youth—Religious life. 2. Sexual ethics. I. Marquardt, Edward William, 1876- joint author. II. Title.

HARPER, William Allen, 1880- 171.
... *Youth and truth,* by W. A. Harper ... New York, London, The Century co. [c1927] xv, 225 p. 19 cm. (The practical Christianity series) [BV4531.H3] 27-9586 1.50
I. Title.

HARRIS, Hugh Henry.
... *Leaders of youth;* the intermediate-senior worker and work. by Hugh Henry Harris ... New York, Cincinnati, The Methodist book concern [c1922] 240 p. diagrs. 17 cm. (The worker and work series, H. H. Meyer, editor) Bibliography: p. 240. [BV1547.H3] 22-5474
I. Title.

HARTLEY, Fred. 248.8'3
Growing pains : first aid for teenagers / Fred Hartley ; illustrations by Gene Haulenbeek. Old Tappan, N.J. : Revell, c1981. p. cm. [BV4531.2.H35] 19 81-11952 ISBN 0-8007-5067-5 pbk. : 4.95
1. Youth—Religious life. 2. Youth—Conduct of life. I. Haulenbeek, Gene. II. Title.

HERRING, Clyde Lee. 248'.83
If God talked out loud ... / Clyde Lee Herring. Nashville : Broadman Press, c1977. 138 p. : ill. ; 20 cm. A youth's conversations with God help to illuminate various aspects of Christian belief. [BV4531.2.H46] 76-27479 ISBN 0-8054-5325-3 pbk. : 2.25
1. Youth—Religious life. 2. Prayer—Juvenile literature. 3. [Prayer.] 4. [Christian life.] I. Title.

HERRIOTT, Frank Wilbur, 1893- 248
Christian youth in action, by Frank W. Herriott. New York, Friendship press, 1935. 7 p. l., 169 p. 20 cm. "References" at end of some of the chapters. [BV4531.H45] 35-11735
1. Youth—Religious life. 2. Church work with youth. I. Title.

HEYER, Robert, comp. 248.8
Discovery in song. Edited by Robert Heyer. Designed by Emil Antonucci. Photographed by Ken Wittenberg. Coordinated by Richard Payne. Written by Thomas O'Brien [and others] New Glen Rock, N.J., Paulist Press [1968] 138 p. illus. 23 cm. The themes and words of some popular songs in the folk idiom are examined for their relevance to the contemporary social and individual problems of alienation, lack of communication, and the callousness of modern life. [BV4531.2.H48] AC 68
1. Youth—Religious life. I. O'Brien, Thomas E. II. Title.

HEYER, Robert. comp 248.8'3
Discovery in word; readings, ed. by Robert Heyer. Viewpoints, questions written by J. Brown. Design by Emil Antonucci. Coordinated by Richard J. Payne. New York, Paulist [c.1968] 155p. illus. 23cm. (Discovery ser.) [BV4531.2.H49] 68-31256 1.95 pap.,
1. Youth—Religious life. I. Brown, James, 1949- II. Title. III. Series: The Discovery series (New York).

HILL, John Leonard, 1878- 248
Purely personal [by] John L. Hill. [Nashville, Tenn.] The Broadman press [c1937] 230 p. 19 cm. Reprinted from the Baptist training union magazine. [BV4531.H47] 37-21920
1. Youth—Religious life. I. Title.

*HILLIS, Don W. 248.42
Get with it, man; for teens with get-up-and-go. Chicago, Moody [1967] 64p. 18cm. (Teen bk.: Compact bks., no. 58) .29 pap.,
I. Title.

HINCKLEY, Gordon Bitner, 248'.83
1910-
From my generation to yours...with love! [By] Gordon B. Hinckley. Salt Lake City, Deseret Book Co., 1973. 85 p. port. 24 cm. [BV4531.2.H54] 73-88637 ISBN 0-87747-512-1 2.95
1. Youth—Religious life. I. Title.

HODGSON, Natalie.
The church and youth; prepared by the joint youth staff. Cartoons by Walt Schoonmaker. [St. Louis, Mo., Christian Board, 1966] 160 p. 67-93443
I. Title.

HOLCOMB, Luther J. 253
Victory through youth, by Luther J. Holcomb. Nashville, Broadman press [c1938] 83 p. 18 1/2 cm. [BV3793.H6] 38-20147
1. Youth—Religious life. 2. Revivals. I. Title.

HORSTMANN, Julius Hermann 248
Edward, 1869-
Faithful unto death; a word of admonition to the confirmed youth of the Evangelical and Reformed church, by Rev. J. H. Horstmann. St. Louis, Mo., Eden publishing house [c1937] 5 p. l., 114 p. front. 15 1/2 cm. [BV4531.H6 1937] 37-22929
1. Youth—Religious life. I. Title.

HOSTY, Thomas J. 248
Straight from the shoulder [by] Rev. Thomas J. Hosty ... Preface by the Right Rev. Daniel F. Cunningham ... Milwaukee, The Bruce publishing company [1946] xiii, 114 p. 20 cm. [BX2355.H6] 46-5370
1. Youth—Religious life. 2. Christian life—Catholic authors. I. Title.

HOWE, Reuel L. 1905- 248.82
Youth considers personal moods, by Reuel L. Howe. Camden, N.J., Nelson [1966] 95p. 21cm. (Youth forum ser.) [BV4531.2.H6] 66-22000 1.50 pap.,
1. Youth—Religious life. I. Title. II. Series.

HUFFMAN, Jasper Abraham, 248
1880-
Youth and the Christ way, by Prof. J. A. Huffman ... Cincinnati, O., God's Bible school and missionary training home [c1934] 5 p. l., 13-156 p. 19 1/2 cm. Imprint covered by label: The Standard press, Marion, Indiana. [BV4531.H7] 34-12997
1. Youth—Religious life. I. Title.

HULME, William Edward, 248.8'3
1920-
When I don't like myself. New York, Popular Library [1976 c1971] 126 p. 18 cm. [BV4531.2.H83] 1.25 (pbk.)
1. Youth—Religious life. I. Title.
L.C. card no. for original edition: 79-169034.

HULME, William Edward, 248.8'3
1920-
When I don't like myself. By William E. Hulme. New York, T. Nelson [1971] v, 83 p. 21 cm. (Youth forum series YF18) Includes bibliographical references. [BV4531.2.H83] 79-169034 ISBN 0-8407-5318-7 1.95
1. Youth—Religious life. I. Title. II. Series.

HUTCHINGS, Eric 248.83
Training for triumph in victorious living. Foreword by Tom Allan. Grand Rapids, Zondervan Pub. House [1961, c.1959] 127p. 61-1588 1.95 bds.,
1. Youth—Religious life. I. Title.

I serve through Christian discipleship... Nashville, Board of Education of the Methodist Church, Youth Department [1957] 136p. 17cm. 'References': p. 134--136.
1. Youth—Religious life. I. Bennett, Thomas Russell, 1925-

I serve through Christian discipleship... Nashville, Board of Education of the Methodist Church, Youth Department [1957] 136p. 17cm. 'References': p.134-136.
1. Youth—Religious life. I. Bennett, Thomas Russell, 1925-

ICE, Orva Lee. 248
Tomorrow is yours. Nashville, Abingdon-Cokesbury Press [1953] 153p. 20cm. [BV4310.I25] 52-11317
1. Youth— Religious life. 2. Baptists—Sermons. 3. Sermons, American. I. Title.

INTERDENOMINATIONAL student 280
conference, Evanston, Ill., Dec.29,1925--Jan.1,1926.
Youth looks at the church; addresses, questions, discussions and findings, National interdenominational student conference, Evanston, Illinois, December 29, 1925--January 1, 1926, introduction by Stanley High. New York, Cincinnati, The Abingdon press [c1926] 220 p. 18 cm. [BX6.I 55A5] 26-6929
I. Title.

IVERSEN, John O. 248.83
Teen talks. Washington, D.C., 6856 Eastern Ave., N.W. Review and Herald Pub. Assn., [1962] 92p. 20cm. 61-11980 2.00
1. Youth—Religious life. I. Title.

IVERSEN, John Orville. 248.8'3
More teen talks, by J. O. Iversen. Guest writers: A teen talks back [by] Bonnie Iversen; Knocking out the "T" [by] Jerre Kent Iversen. Washington, Review and Herald Pub. Association [1968] 96 p. 20 cm. [BV4531.2.I93] 68-18743
1. Youth—Religious life. I. Title.

IVERSEN, John Orville. 248.8
More teen talks, by J. O. Iversen. Guest writers: A teen talks back [by] Bonnie Iversen; Knocking out the "T" [by] Jerre Kent Iversen. Washington, Review and Herald Pub. Association [1968] 96 p. 20 cm. A series of talks for teenagers relates Christianity to everyday life. [BV4531.2.I93] AC 68
1. Youth—Religious life. I. Title.

*JACOB, Micheal. 248.8'3
Pop goes Jesus; an investigation of pop religion in Britain and America [1st Amer. ed.] New York, Morehouse-Barlow [1973, c.1972] 92 p. 19 cm. [BV4531.2] ISBN 0-8192-1140-0 1.95 (pbk.)
1. Youth—Religious life. 2. Jesus people—United States. 3. Jesus people—Gt. Brit. I. Title.

JACOBS, James Vernon, 248.83
1898-
Starlight talks to youth. Grand Rapids, Mich., Baker Bk. House, 1961. 168p. 61-17548 2.50
1. Youth—Religious life. 2. Astronomy. I. Title.

JEFFERSON, Charles Edward, 260
1860.
Talks on high themes for young Christians, by Charles E. Jefferson ... Boston, New York [etc.] The Pilgrim press [c1909] ix, 162 p. 20 cm. [BV4531.J4] 9-26993
1. Youth—Religious life. I. Title.

JEFFERSON, Charles Edward, 252.
1860-
Under twenty; messages to big boys and girls, by Charles E. Jefferson ... New York, Chicago [etc.] Fleming H. Revell company [c1922] 192 p. 20 cm. [BV4310.J4] 23-1450
I. Title.

JEMISON, T Housel. 268.433
Facing life; guidance for Christian youth. [Mountain View, Calif.] Printed for the Dept. of Education, General Conference of Seventh-Day Adventists [by] Pacific Press Pub. Association [1958] 645p. illus. 24cm. 'A survey of the instruction contained in the writings of Ellen G. White.' [BV4531.J42] 58-10585
1. Youth— Religious life. 2. Religious education—Text-books for young people—Seventh-Day Adventists. I. White, Ellen Gould (Harmon) 1827-1915. II. Seventh-Day Adventists. General Conference. Dept. of Education. III. Title.

JENKINS, Lucy Howe, 1874- 248
Letters to my godchild, by Lucy Howe Jenkins. Boston, Mass., The Old corner book store [c1940] 81 p. 21 cm. "Edited by Caroline Schuyler Hamien."--An appreciation. "Acknowlegments": p. 80-81. [BV4531.J43] 40-33094
1. Youth—Religious life. 2. Sponsors. I. Hamlen, Caroline Schulyer (Jenkins) Mrs. 1902- ed. II. Title. III. Title: Godchild, Letters to my.

JEWETT, Dick. 248.8'3
In case you get homesick / Dick Jewett. Mountain View, Calif. : Pacific Press Pub. Association, c1980. 32 p. ; 18 cm. Presents advice for overcoming homesickness by relying on God. [BV4531.2.J48] 80-12497 ISBN 0-8163-0347-9 pbk. : 0.95
1. Youth—Religious life. 2. Homesickness. 3. [Homesickness.] 4. [Christian life.] I. Title.

JOHNSON, Mel. 248
Tips for teens. Grand Rapids, Zondervan Pub. House [c1956] 62p. illus. 20cm. [BV4531.J59] 57-2403
1. Youth—Religious life. I. Title.

JOHNSON, Paul Emanuel, 1898- 248
Who are you? [By] Paul E. Johnson. New York, Cincinnati [etc.] The Abingdon press [1937] 3 p. l., 3-204 p. 20 cm. (Half-title: The Abingdon religious education texts, J. W. Langdale, general editor; Guides to Christian leadership, P. H. Vieth, editor) "For further reading" at end of each chapter. [BV4531.J6] 37-24786
1. Youth—Religious life. 2. Personality. 3. Character. I. Title.

JOHNSTONE, Ronald L. 377.841
The effectiveness of Lutheran elementary and secondary schools as agencies of Christian education; an empirical evaluation study of the impact of Lutheran parochial schools on the beliefs, attitudes. and behavior of Lutheran youth [by] Ronald L. Johnstone. St. Louis. School for Grad. Studies. Concordia Seminary [1966] 188p. 22cm. (Concordia [Theological] Seminary, St. Louis, School for Grad. Studies. Grad. study no. 8) [BV639.Y7J57] 66-7849 3.75 pap.,
1. Youth—Religious life. 2. Lutheran Church—Missouri Synod—Education. I. Title. II. Series.

JOINER, Verna Jones 248.83
When love grows up [by] Verna J. Joiner. Anderson, Ind., Warner [1966] v, 96p. 21cm. [BV4531.2.J6] 66-23605 1.50 pap.,
1. Youth—Religious life. I. Title.

JONES, Stephen D. 268'.433
Faith shaping / Stephen D. Jones. Valley Forge, PA : Judson Press, 1980. p. cm. Includes bibliographical references. [BV4531.2.J64] 19 80-19733 ISBN 0-8170-0915-9 : 5.95
1. Youth—Religious life. 2. Church work with youth. I. Title.

KAVANAUGH, James J. 248.83
There's two of you; tempest in a teen-pot. Westminster, Md., Newman [c.]1964. xiv, 164p. 23cm. [BX2355.K3] 64-66035 3.75
1. Youth—Religious life. 2. Youth—Conduct of life. 3. Adolesence. I. Title.

KAVANAUGH, James J
There's two of you; tempest in a teen-pot, by James J. Kavanaugh. Westminster, Md., Newman Press. 1964. xiv. 164 p. 23 cm.
1. Youth — Religious life. 2. Youth — Conduct of life. 3. Adolescence. I. Title.

KELLY, George Anthony, 248.83
1916-
The Catholic youth's guide to life and love. New York, Random House [1960] 209 p. 21 cm. Includes bibliography. [BX2355.K4] 60-7680
1. Youth—Religious life. 2. Christian life—Catholic authors. I. Title.

KESLER, Jay. 248'.83
Growing places / Jay Kesler. Old Tappan, N.J. : F. H. Revell, c1978. 128 p. : ill. ; 21 cm. Bibliography: p. 128. [BV4531.2.K46] 77-26804 ISBN 0-8007-0904-7 : 5.95
1. Youth—Religious life. I. Title.

KESLER, Jay. 248'.83
I never promised you a Disneyland / by Jay Kesler, with Tim Stafford. Waco, Tex. : Word Books, c1975. 120 p., [5] leaves of plates : ill. ; 23 cm. [BV4531.2.K47] 75-10094 4.95
1. Youth—Religious life. I. Stafford, Tim. II. Title.

KESLER, Jay. 248'.4
Outside Disneyland : practical Christianity for real-life hassles / by Jay Kesler & Tim Stafford. Waco, Tex. : Word Books, c1977. 171 p. : ill. ; 23 cm. [BV4531.2.K48] 77-75465 ISBN 0-8499-0011-5 : 5.95
1. Youth—Religious life. I. Stafford, Tim, joint author. II. Title.

KLYKKEN, O.
Youth and Christianity, lectures by O. Klykken, tr. from the Norwegian by Lauritz Larsen. Decorah, Ia., Luteran publishing house, 1916. 138 p. 20 cm. 16-16153 0.50
I. Larsen, Lauritz, 1882- tr. II. Title.

KRETZMANN, Otto Paul, 248.4841
1901-
The road back to God [Rev. ed.] Saint

Louis, Concordia [1965, c.1935] xvi, 125p. 20cm. [BV4310.K7] 65-9030 2.50
1. Youth—Religious life. 2. Sermons, American. 3. Lutheran Church—Sermons. I. Title.

KRETZMANN, Otto Paul, 1901- 248.4841
The road back to God [by] O. P. Kretzmann. [Rev. ed.] Saint Louis, Concordia Pub. House [1965, c1935] xvi, 125 p. 20 cm. [BV4310.K7] 65-9030
1. Youth — Religious life. 2. Sermons, American. 3. Lutheran Church — Sermons. I. Title.

KRETZMANN, Otto Paul, 1901- 248
The road back to God; a series of self-searching devotional talks, by O. P. Kretzmann. Chicago, The Walther league] 1935. 3 p. l., ix-xvii, 120 p. 20 cm. [BV4310.K7] 36-5973
1. Youth—Religious life. 2. Devotional literature. I. Title.

KRUTZA, William J. 248'.83
Graduate's guide to success / William J. Krutza. Grand Rapids : Baker Book House, c1976. 93 p. : ill. ; 20 cm. [BV4531.2.K78] 76-375893 ISBN 0-8010-5374-9 pbk. : 2.95
1. Youth—Religious life. I. Title.

LARSEN, Earnest. 248.8'3
Don't just stand there. [Liguori, Mo., Liguorian Books] 1969. 1 v. (unpaged) illus. 18 cm. [BV4531.2.L35] 74-84648 1.75
1. Youth—Religious life. I. Title.

LARSEN, Earnest. 811'.5'4
Good old plastic Jesus. Liguori, Mo., Liguorian Books [1968?] 156 p. illus. 18 cm. [BV4531.2.L37] 68-8819 1.50
1. Youth—Religious life. I. Title.

LARSON, Bob. 248.8'3
Rock, practical help for those who listen to the words and don't like what they hear / [Bob Larson]. Wheaton, Ill. : Tyndale House Publishers, c1980. 140 p. ; 21 cm. [BV4531.2.L38] 19 79-55755 ISBN 0-8423-5685-1 (pbk.) : 3.95
1. Youth—Religious life. 2. Rock music—Moral and religious aspects.

LEDERACH, Paul M. 259
Mennonite youth; report of Mennonite youth research, by Paul M. Lederach. Scottdale, Pa., Herald Press [1971] 109 p. 22 cm. [BV639.Y7L4] 70-155174 ISBN 0-8361-1636-4
1. Youth—Religious life. 2. Church work with youth—Mennonites. I. Title.

LEE, Harold B., 1899- 248'.83
Decisions for successful living, by Harold B. Lee. Salt Lake City, Deseret Book Co., 1973. x, 265 p. port. 24 cm. Editions of 1945 and 1970 published under title: Youth and the church. [BX8643.Y6L4 1973] 73-168234 ISBN 0-87747-348-X 4.95
1. Youth—Religious life. 2. Mormons and Mormonism. I. Title.

LEE, Harold B., 1899- 248.8'3
Youth & the church, by Harold B. Lee. [Salt Lake City] Deseret Book Co., 1970. x, 261 p. col. port. 24 cm. Edition of 1973 published under title: Decisions for successful living. [BX8643.Y6L4 1970] 79-130323 ISBN 0-87747-348-X
1. Youth—Religious life. 2. Mormons and Mormonism. I. Title.

LEE, Harold B., 1899- 248
Youth and the church, by Harold B. Lee. Salt Lake City, Utah, The Deseret new press [1945] xii, 236 p. 22 cm. "Based upon a series of radio talks delivered over radio station K. S. L. at Salt Lake City...from January 1st to June 24th, 1945."--Pref. [BX8643.Y6L4] 46-13041
1. Youth—Religious life. 2. Mormons and Mormonism. I. Title.

LEIPHART, Elmer Elwood, 1895- 248
Essentials of successful living, messages to the rising generation, by Rev. Elmer E. Leiphant... Daleville, Va., Southeastern press [c1937] 182 p. 19 cm. [BV4310.L43] 38-39294
1. Youth—Religious life. 2. Evangelical and Reformed church—Sermons. 3. Sermons, American. I. Title.

LEWIS, Charles Clarke, 1857-1924. 252.
Addresses for young people; by Charles C. Lewis... College View, Neb., Union college press, 1905. 3 p. l., [17]-273 p. port. 20 cm. [BV4310.L45] 5-41617
1. Youth—Religious life. I. Title.

LLOYD, Marjorie Lewis. 248
Flickering desire. Washington, Review and Herald [1953] 95p. 21cm. [BV4531.L47] 54-1210
1. Youth—religious life. I. Title.

LONG, Jacob Avery, 1896- 261
Young people and the church: a study of the attitudes of 726 Pittsburgh Presbyterian young people toward the church and its program, by Jacob Avery Long, PH. D. Philadelphia, Pa., J. A. Long [c1940] xi, 150 p. diagrs. 21 cm. Issued also as thesis (PH. D.) Columbia university. Bibliography: p. 149-150. [BV639.Y7L65 1940 a] 40-33090
1. Youth—Religious life. 2. Church work with youth. 3. Presbyterian church in the U. S. A. I. Title.

LONG, Nat G 248
Goal posts; talks to young people on building a sound, successful life in today's troubled world. Atlanta, Tupper & Love [1953] 162p. 22cm. [BV4531.L555] 53-1532
1. Youth—Religious life. I. Title.

LORD, Daniel Aloysius, 1888- 248
Some notes on the guidance of youth, by Daniel A. Lord, S. J. St. Louis, Mo., The Queen's work [c1938] 4 p. l., [11]-174 p. 22 cm. [BX2352.L6] 38-36244
1. Youth—Religious life. I. Title. II. Title: The guidance of youth.

LORIMIER, Jacques de. 248'.83
Identity and faith in young adults, by Jacques de Lorimier, Roger Graveline, and Aubert April. Translated by Matthew J. O'Connell. New York, Paulist Press [1973] viii, 275 p. 23 cm. Translation of Identite et foi. Bibliography: p. 271-275. [BV4531.2.L5813] 73-80533 ISBN 0-8091-1766-5 4.95
1. Youth—Religious life. 2. Christian education of young people. I. Graveline, Roger, joint author. II. April, Aubert, joint author. III. Title.

LOTZ, Philip Henry, 1889- ed. 240
The quest for God through understanding, a companion volume to "The quest for God through worship." A book of fifty-two discussions especially for young people in churches, church schools, young people's meetings, summer camps, Y. M. and Y. W. C. A., colleges and universities, and leaders and counselors of youth. Edited by Philip Henry Lotz, PH. D. St. Louis, The Bethany press [c1937] x, 322 p. 21 cm. "The kingdom crusader's hymn": p. 147. Bibliography at end of most of the chapters. [BV4531.L58] 38-1804
1. Youth—Religious life. I. Title.

LUND, Gerald N. 248'.83
This is your world; four stories for modern youth, by Gerald N. Lund. Illus. by Grant L. Lund. Salt Lake City, Bookcraft [1973] viii, 91 p. illus. 24 cm. Contents.Contents.—Even as your father.—A prayer of faith.—If you love Jesus.—Foolish traditions. [BV4531.2.L84] 73-77237
1. Youth—Religious life. I. Title.

LUTHERAN youth conference. 1st, Minneapolis, 1937. 267.6241
The Lutheran youth conference and ninth international Y.P.L.L. convention Minneapolis, Minnesota, June 23-27, 1937 (main addresses and young people's panel discussion excerpts) Minneapolis, Augsburg publishing house [c1937] v, 121 p. 19 1/2 cm. Introduction signed: N. M. Yivisaker, vice-president, Youth commission, American Lutheran conference. [BX8003.L93 1937] 38-3307
1. Youth—Religious life. I. American Lutheran conference. Youth commission. II. Young people's Luther league. International convention. 9th, Minneapolis, 1937. III. Yivisaker, Nils Martin, 1882- IV. Title.

LYNN. 248'.83
Youth ask Lynn / by Lynn. Nashville, Tenn. : Broadman Press, c1978. ix, 119 p. ; 20 cm. Letters reprinted from the columns first in Upward and then in Event published by the Sunday School Board of the Southern Baptist Convention. Answers questions frequently asked by teenage Christians about dating, marriage, friendship, emotions, parents, and Christian life. [BV4531.2.L93] 77-91075 ISBN 0-8054-5328-8 pbk. : 2.75
1. Youth—Religious life. 2. Youth—Conduct of life. 3. [Conduct of life.] 4. [Christian life.] I. Southern Baptist Convention. Sunday School Board. II. Title.

MCALLISTER, Frederick Borman. 170
Frank answers to youth questions, by F. B. McAllister. New York [etc.] Fleming H. Revell company [c1935] 128 p. 19 1/2 cm. [BV4531.M25] 36-222
1. Youth—Religious life. I. Title.

MCCLUSKY, Evelyn (McFarlane) Mrs., 1890- 248
Torch and sword; a handbook for leaders of young people, by E. M. McClusky ... Oakland, Calif., The Miracle book club, 1937. 6 p. l., 143 p. 1 illus. (music) 2 pl. (incl. music) on 1 l. 19 cm. "First edition." [BV4531.M27] 37-20874
1. Youth—Religious life. I. Title.

MCGLOIN, Joseph T. 248.482
Learn a little! or, What's life all about? Illus. by Don Baumgart. Milwaukee, Bruce [c.1961] 97p. (His Love--and live, bk. 1) 61-17980 1.25 pap.,
1. Youth—Religious life. 2. Christian life—Catholic authors. I. Title.

MCGLOIN, Joseph T 248.482
Learn a little! or, What's life all about? Illustrated by Don Baumgart. Milwaukee, Bruce Pub. Co. [1961] 97p. illus. 21cm. (His Love--and live, book 1) [BX2355.M2] 61-17980
1. Youth—Religious life. 2. Christian life—Catholic authors. I. Title.

MCKAY, David Oman, 1873-1970. 248'.83
"My young friends ..." President McKay speaks to youth. Compiled by Llewelyn R. McKay. Salt Lake City, Utah, Bookcraft [1973] 84 p. port. 24 cm. [BV4531.2.M26 1973] 73-88616
1. Youth—Religious life. I. Title.

MCKEE, Bill. 248.8'3
Happy hang up! Wheaton, Ill., Tyndale House Publishers [1969]·62 p. illus. 21 cm. [BV4531.2.M27] 79-79469
1. Youth—Religious life. I. Title.

MCLEAN, Gordon R. 248'.83
Where the love is [by] Gordon R. McLean. Waco, Tex., Word Books [1973] 123 p. 23 cm. [BV4531.2.M33] 72-96352 3.95
1. Youth—Religious life. 2. Christian life—1960- I. Title.

MCPHEE, Norma. 248'.83
Discussion programs for junior highs / Norma McPhee. Grand Rapids : Zondervan Pub. House, [1974] 128 p. ; 21 cm. [BV4531.2.M34] 73-13072 1.95
1. Youth—Religious life. 2. Youth—Conduct of life. 3. Worship programs. I. Title.

MARIE Angela, Sister 248.830922
Teens triumphant [Boston] St. Paul Eds. [dist. Daughters of St. Paul, 1966, c.1965] 338p. illus. 21cm. Bibl. [BX2355.M28] 65-27249 3.50; 2.50 pap.,
1. Youth—Religious life. I. Title.

*MASHECK, Charles L. 248.4
Design for personal living. Ed. by Wilbur G. Volker. Illus. by William C. Kautz. Philadelphia, Lutheran Church Pr. [1967] 128p. illus. (pt. col.) 21cm (LCA Sunday church sch. ser.) .90 pap.,
1. Youth-Religious life. 2. Religious education—Young adults. I. Volker, Wilbur G., ed. II. Title.

MASTON, Thomas Bufford, 1897- 248
Right or wrong? Nashville, Broadman Press [1955] 146p. 21cm. [BV4531.M29] 55-14633
1. Youth—Religious life. 2. Christian ethics. I. Title.

MASTON, Thomas Bufford, 1897- 248'.83
Right or wrong? A guide for teeners and their leaders for living by Christian standards [by] T. B. Maston [and] William M. Pinson, Jr. Rev. ed. Nashville, Broadman Press [1971] 128 p. 21 cm. A guide for making decisions about such issues as drugs, dishonesty, sex, and parents. [BV4531.2.M37 1971] 75-143282 ISBN 0-8054-6101-9 3.50
1. Youth—Religious life. 2. Christian ethics. 3. [Christian life.] 4. [Conduct of life.] I. Pinson, William M., joint author. II. Title.

MAUS, Cynthia Pearl. 268
Youth and the church; a manual for teachers and leaders of intermediates, seniors and young people, by Cynthia Pearl Maus ... Cincinnati, The Standard publishing company [c1919] 186 p. illus., plates, plans, form. 19 1/2 cm. "A classified list of books for teachers of intermediate, senior and young people's classes": p. 185-186. [BV1520.M35] 19-5684
I. Title.

MAUS, Cynthia Pearl. 268
Youth and the church; a manual for teachers and leaders of intermediates, seniors and young people, by Cynthia Pearl Maus ... 5th ed., enl., and rev., with teaching outlines, discussional and examination questions for use in community training schools, leadership training schools, young people's conferences, and teacher training classes. Cincinnati, O., The Standard publishing company [c1923] 263 p. illus. (incl. plans) plates. 20 cm. "A classified list of books for teachers and leaders of intermediates, seniors and young people": p. 261-263. [BV1520.M35 1923] 23-11360
I. Title.

MAXWELL, Lawrence. 248'.83
The happy path / Lawrence Maxwell. Washington : Published for the Youth Dept. of the General Conference of Seventh-day Adventists [by] Review and Herald Pub. Association, c1975. 128 p. : ill. ; 19 cm. Sixteen anecdotes illustrating practical applications of scripture. [BV4531.2.M38] 74-27636
1. Youth—Religious life. 2. [Christian life.] I. Title.

MAXWELL, Mervyn. 248'.83
Look at it this way. Questions and answers selected from Mervyn Maxwell's column in Signs of the times magazine. Mountain View, Calif., Pacific Press Pub. Association [1972] 64 p. 19 cm. [BV4531.2.M39] 77-187400
1. Youth—Religious life. 2. Youth—Conduct of life. I. Signs of the times. II. Title.

MERIKAY. 248'.83
Huck Finn goes to church; profiles of life for young adults. Mountain View, Calif., Pacific Press Pub. Association [1972] 63 p. 19 cm. Includes brief anecdotes and articles discussing the role of religion in the lives of young people. [BV4531.2.M47] 72-83473
1. Youth—Religious life. 2. [Christian life.] I. Title.

METHODIST young people's conference, Memphis, 1935. 287.063768
Facing life with Jesus Christ; record of the proceedings of the Methodist young people's conference held in the municipal auditorium, Memphis, Tennessee, December 27-31, 1935. [Nashville, Tenn.] General board of Christian education, Methodist Episcopal church, South [c1936] 1 p. l., 5-240 p. 23 cm. "Walter Towner ... chairman ... of the Directing committee."--Historical statement. [BX8207.M4 1935] 37-2516
1. Youth—Religious life. I. Towner, Walter. II. Title.

MIDDLETON, Robert Lee, 1894- 248
The accents of life, inspirational messages for young people and illustrative material for pastors and leaders of intermediates and young people. Nashville, Broadman Press [1948] xii, 155 p. 21 cm. [BV4531.M46] 48-8417
1. Youth—Religious life. I. Title.

MIDDLETON, Robert Lee, 1894- 248
Don't disappoint God! Challenging you to live more abundantly. Nashville, Broadman

Press [1951] 174 p. 21 cm. [BV4531.M463] 51-13803
1. Youth — Religious life. I. Title.

MIDDLETON, Robert Lee, 1894- 248
Our youth for Christ: messages and program material to be used by leaders and workers with intermediates and young people, by R. L. Middleton ... Nashville, Tenn., Broadman press [c1939] 164 p. illus. 19 1/2 cm. [BV4531.M47] 39-34136
1. Youth—Religious life. 2. Religious education of adolescents. I. Title.

MIDDLETON, Robert Lee, 1894- 248
Youth conquering for Christ; inspirational messages for young people and program material for workers with intermediates and young people, by R. L. Middleton ... Nashville, Tenn., Broadman press [1944] 201 p. 19 1/2 cm. [BV4531.M474] 44-47052
1. Youth—Religious life. I. Title.

MINICH, Roy Linden, 1889- 248
Adventuring with amateur adults, by Roy Linden Minich. New York [etc.] Fleming H. Revell company [c1938] 108 p. 19 1/2 cm. [BV4531.M53] 38-34584
1. Youth—Religious life. I. Title.

MITCHELL, Joan, 1940- 248'.83
Faith : a persistent hunger / Joan Mitchell. Minneapolis : Winston Press, c1977. 96 p. : ill. ; 22 cm. The author describes searching for and living with faith in today's world. [BV4531.2.M55] 77-72201 ISBN 0-03-021261-8 pbk. : 2.50
1. Youth—Religious life. 2. Faith. 3. [Christian life.] I. Title.

MOORE, Ralph. 248.8'3
Breakout. Illustrated by John Gretzer. New York, Friendship Press [1968] 159 p. illus. 18 cm. Includes bibliographies. [BV4531.2.M6] 68-14058
1. Youth—Religious life. I. Title.

MUELLER, John Theodore, 1885- 252
Problem sermons for young people, by Rev. J. Theodore Mueller ... Grand Rapids, Mich., Zondervan publsihing house [c1939] 2 p. l., [vii]-viii p., 1 l., 13-124 p. 20 cm. [BV4310.M75] 39-10750
1. Youth—Religious life. 2. Lutheran church—Sermons. 3. Sermons. American. I. Title.

MYRA, Harold Lawrence, 1939- 248'.83
The new you; questions about this fresh newborn way of life now that you believe [by] Harold Myra. Grand Rapids, Zondervan Pub. House [1973, c1972] 115 p. illus. 18 cm. [BV4531.2.M97] 72-95527 0.95 (pbk.)
1. Youth—Religious life. 2. Questions and answers—Christian life. I. Title.

NALL, Torney Otto, 1900- 248
Young Christians at work, by T. Otto Nall and Bert H. Davis. New York, Association Press, 1949. 116 p. 21 cm. [BV4531.N3] 49-5125
1. Youth—Religious life. I. Davis, Bert Henry, 1896- joint author. II. Title.

NELSON, John Oliver, 1909- 259
Young laymen--young church; a summons to young laymen in the mid-twentieth century. New York, Association Press, 1948. 160 p. 20 cm. (A Haddam House book) "Further reading": p. 160. [BV639.Y7N4] 48-9555
1. Youth—Religious life. 2. Church work with youth. I. Title. II. Series.

OCHS, Daniel A., 1890- 248
Climbing upward, by D. A. Ochs. Washington, D.C., Review and herald publishing association [c1941] 128 p. 20 cm. [BV4531.O35] 41-19010
1. Youth—Religious life. 2. Seventh-day Adventists—Doctrinal and controversial works. I. Title.

OCHS, Daniel A 1890- 248
Climbing upward, by D. A. Ochs. Washington, D. C., Review and herald publishing association [c1941] 128 p. 20 cm. [BV4531.O35] 41-19010
1. Youth—Religious life. 2. Seventh-day Adventists—Doctrinal and controversial works. I. Title.

OLSON, David F., 1938- 248'.83
The inner revolution; a theology for people who don't understand theology [by] David F. Olson. Valley Forge [Pa.] Judson Press [1973] 120 p. illus. 21 cm. [BV4539.S9O413] 73-3088 ISBN 0-8170-0604-4 2.50 (pbk.)
1. Youth—Religious life. I. Title.

OLSON, John Helmer, 1897- 248
As children of light, by John Helmer Oslon. A letter from your pastoron your confirmation day. Rock Island, Ill., Augustana book concern [c1938] 56 p. incl. front., double form. 18 cm. [BX8074.C7O55] 38-7895
1. Youth—Religious life. 2. Confirmation. I. Title.

O'MALLEY, William J. 248'.83
Meeting the living God [by] William J. O'Malley. New York, Paulist Press [1973] ix, 197 p. illus. 28 cm. [BV4531.2.O45] 73-85135 ISBN 0-8091-9525-9 2.95
1. Youth—Religious life. 2. Religious education—Text-books for young people—Catholic. I. Title.

ORR, Dick. 248.8'3
Bible journeys, experiences for Christian growth : a youth resource / Dick Orr and David L. Bartlett ; design and ill., Baxendell Design Associates. Valley Forge, PA : Judson Press, c1980. 77 p. : ill. ; 28 cm. Includes index. A guidebook to developing Christian faith in which several Biblical characters relate their own experiences with God. Each selection is followed by thought-guiding exercises, Bible references, and suggestions for applying Christian principles in everyday life. [BS539.O77] 80-14915 ISBN 0-8170-0898-5 : 4.95
1. Bible—Juvenile literature. 2. [Bible.] 3. Youth—Religious life. 4. [Christian life.] I. Bartlett, David Lyon, 1941- joint author. II. Baxendell Design Associates. III. Title.

OSBORNE, Arthur, 1882- 248
One way streets; talks to the teen age--and other ages, by Arthur Osborne. Philadelphia, Boston [etc.] The Judson press [1935] 5 p. l., 213 p. 20 cm. [BV4531.O8] 36-4051
1. Youth—Religious life. I. Title.

PATTERSON, LeRoy, 1918- 248'.83
After you've said, "I believe" / LeRoy "Pat" Patterson. Wheaton, Ill. : Tyndale House Publishers, c1979. 118 p. : ill. ; 18 cm. [BV4531.2.P35] 78-57965 ISBN 0-8423-0056-2 pbk. : 1.95
1. Youth—Religious life. I. Title.

PEARSON, James, 1873- 244
Onward and upward. Copyright [by] James Pearson ... Shenandoah, Ia., World printing company, c1936. 158 p., 1 l. illus. (incl. ports.) 23 cm. On cover: Plain gospel in drama and illustration. Page [2] and 1 leaf at end are blank for "Greetings" and "Notes". [PN6120.R4P36] 36-25529
1. Youth—Religious life. 2. Homiletical illustrations. I. Title.

PENNOCK, Dee. 248'.83
Who is God? Who am I? Who are you? Illus. by Sally Pierone. South Canaan, Pa., Early Church Publications [1973] 160 p. illus. 21 cm. [BV4531.2.P46] 73-86196 2.50
1. Youth—Religious life. I. Title.

PETERSEN, Mark E. 248'.83
Virtue makes sense! [By] Mark E. Petersen and Emma Marr Petersen. Salt Lake City, Utah, Deseret Book Co., 1973. 105 p. 24 cm. [BV4531.2.P48] 73-81621 ISBN 0-87747-500-8 2.95
1. Youth—Religious life. I. Petersen, Emma Marr, joint author. II. Title.

PETERSON, Eugene H., 1932- 248'.83
Growing up in Christ : a guide for families with adolescents / by Eugene H. Peterson. Atlanta : John Knox Press, c1976. 93 p. ; 21 cm. Includes bibliographical references. [BV4531.2.P485] 76-12396 ISBN 0-8042-2026-3 pbk. : 3.95
1. Youth—Religious life. 2. Parent and child. I. Title.

PICKERILL, Grace Gilbert. 248
Youth adventures with God, by Grace Gilbert Pickerill. Indianapolis, Ind., United Christian missionary society [c1929] xvi, 188 p. front. 19 cm. Bibliography: p. 186-188; "Interesting books for further adventure" at end of part of the chapters. [BV4531.P45] 29-17875
I. Title.

PIKE, John Gregory, 1784-1854. 248
A guide for young disciples of the Holy Saviour, in their way to immortality; forming a sequel to Persuasives to early piety. By J. G. Pike. 1st American from the 3d London ed. ... New-York, J. Leavitt; Boston, Crocker & Brewster, 1832. viii, [9]-383 p. 20 1/2 cm. [Full name: John Deodatus Gregory Pike] [BV4531.P5 1832] 35-22120
1. Youth—Religious life. I. Title.

POLING, Daniel Alfred, 1884- 248
Youth marches! By Daniel A. Poling. Philadelphia, Boston [etc.] The Judson press [c1937] 8 p. l., 3-196 p. 20 cm. Composed chiefly of addresses delivered in the National youth radio conference. cf. Introductory note. [BV4531.P65] 37-21817
1. Youth—Religious life. 2. War and religion. I. Title.

PRATNEY, Winkie, 1944- 248'.83
A handbook for followers of Jesus / by Winkie Pratney. Minneapolis : Bethany Fellowship, c1976. p. cm. Includes indexes. Bibliography: p. [BV4531.2.P7] 76-44385 ISBN 0-87123-378-9 pbk. : 3.50
1. Youth—Religious life. I. Title.

PRIEBE, Kenneth, comp. 248
The call to youth, by Lutheran youth leaders. Minneapolis, Augsburg Pub. House [1952] 131 p. 21 cm. [BV4531.P683] 52-9408
1. Youth-Religious life. I. Title.

RANKIN, Jeremiah Eames, 1828-1904. 252.
The law of elective affinity, and other sermons, for young men and young women. By President Jeremiah Eames Rankin ... Washington, D. C., Printed at the Industrial department of Howard university, 1899. 2 p. l., 171 p. port. 20 cm. [BX7233.R3L3] 19-9831
I. Title.

THE Religious life of the adolescent / edited by Robert Heyer. New York : Paulist Press, c1974 [i.e.1975] v, 73 p. : ill. ; 19 cm. "A New Catholic world book." A collection of articles originally published in the Sept./Oct. 1974 issue of the New Catholic world. [BV4531.2.R38] 75-10113 ISBN 0-8091-1878-5 pbk. : 1.45 248'.83
1. Youth—Religious life. I. Heyer, Robert J. II. New Catholic world.

REUTER, Frederick Albert. 170
Our boys; talks to boys and young men on Catholic ethics, by Rev. Frederick A. Reuter ... New York and Cincinnati, F. Pustet co. (inc.) 1935. xii, 284 p. 22 1/2 cm. Bibliography: p. ix. [BJ1641.R4] 35-14988
1. Youth—Religious life. I. Title.

RICHARDS, Larry. 248.8'3
Are you for real? Chicago, Moody Press [1968] 160 p. illus. 19 cm. Bibliographical references included in "Footnotes" (p. 160) [BV4531.2.R45] 68-18886
1. Youth—Religious life. I. Title.

RICHARDS, Larry. 248.8'3
How do I fit in? Chicago, Moody Press [1970] 155 p. illus. 20 cm. Cover title: Youth asks: How do I fit in? Includes bibliographical references. Explores the methods one can use to establish more meaningful relationships with people and God. [BV4531.2.R452] 79-123162 1.95
1. Youth—Religious life. 2. [Christian life.] I. Title. II. Title: Youth asks: How do I fit in?

RICHARDS, Larry. 248.8'3
What's in it for me? Chicago, Moody Press [1970] 143 p. illus. 19 cm. Cover title: Youth asks: What's in it for me? Includes bibliographical references. [BV4531.2.R454] 70-104829 1.95
1. Youth—Religious life. I. Title. II. Title: Youth asks: What's in it for me?

RICHARDS, Lawrence O. 248'.83
How I can be real / Larry Richards ; ill. by Charles Shaw. Rev. ed. Grand Rapids : Zondervan Pub. House, 1979. 125 p. : ill. ; 21 cm. (Answers for youth series) Edition of 1968 published under title: Are you for real? Includes bibliographical references. A guide to finding and being oneself based on Christian values. [BV4531.2.R45 1979] 79-20735 ISBN 0-310-38971-2 pbk. : 2.95
1. Youth—Religious life. 2. [Identity.] 3. [Christian life.] I. Shaw, Charles, 1941- II. Title.

RICHARDS, Lawrence O. 248'.83
How I can fit in / Larry Richards ; ill. by Charles Shaw. Rev. ed. Grand Rapids : Zondervan Pub. House, 1979. 138 p. : ill. ; 21 cm. (Answers for youth series) Published in 1970 under title: How do I fit in? Includes bibliographical references. [BV4531.2.R452 1979] 79-18390 ISBN 0-310-38961-5 pbk. : 2.95
1. Youth—Religious life. 2. Interpersonal relations—Juvenile literature. I. Title.

RICHARDS, Lawrence O. 248'.83
How I can make decisions / Larry Richards ; ill. by Charles Shaw. New rev. ed. Grand Rapids : Zondervan Pub. House, 1979. 128 p. : ill. ; 21 cm. (Answers for youth series) First ed. published in 1970 under title: What's in it for me? Includes bibliographical references. [BV4531.2.R454 1979] 79-16212 ISBN 0-310-38981-X pbk. : 2.95
1. Youth—Religious life. I. Title.

RIDENOUR, Fritz. 248.8'3
I'm a good man, but ... Edited by Fritz Ridenour. Featuring Peanuts cartoons by Charles Schulz. Glendale, Calif., G/L Regal Books [1969] 165 p. illus. 18 cm. [BV4531.2.R46 1969] 75-96702
1. Youth—Religious life. 2. Christian ethics. I. Schulz, Charles M. II. Title.

RIEKE, Marcus. 248
Sincerely, in Him. Columbus, Ohio, Wartburg Press [1949] 140 p. 20 cm. [BV4531.R5] 49-6338
1. Youth—Religious life. I. Title.

RIESS, Walter. 248.8'3
Before they start to leave; for parents of teen-agers: some quiet directions. St. Louis, Concordia Pub. House [1967] 95 p. 19 cm. [BV639.Y7R5] 67-22998
1. Youth—Religious life. I. Title.

RIESS, Walter. 248
Teen-ager, Christ is for you. Saint Louis, Mo., Concordia Pub. House [1958, c1957] 83p. illus. 19cm. [BV4531.R53] 57-59570
1. Youth—Religious life. I. Title.

RIESS, Walter. 248.83
Teen-ager, your church is for you. St. Louis, Concordia Pub. House [1961] 100p. illus. 19cm. [BV4531.2.R48] 60-53153
1. Youth—Religious life. I. Title.

RIESS, Walter. 248.83
Teen-ager, Christ's love will make you live. St. Louis, Concordia Pub. House [1962] 102p. illus. 19cm. [BV4531.2.R47] 62-19958
1. Youth—Religious life. I. Title.

RILEY, William Bell, 1861- 252.061
Problems of youth, by W. B. Riley ... Grand Rapids, Mich., Zondervan publishing house [c1941] 5 p. l., 9-123 p. 20 cm. [BV4310.R54] 41-10322
1. Youth—Religious life. 2. Baptists—Sermons. 3. Sermons, American. I. Title.

RILEY, William Bell, 1861- 252.061
Youth's victory lies this way, by W. B. Riley ... Grand Rapids, Mich., Zondervan publishing house [c1936] 138 p. 20 cm. [BV4310.R55] 36-9301
1. Youth—Religious life. 2. Baptists—Sermons. 3. Sermons, American. I. Title.

RINKER, Rosalind. 248
The years that count; a book that lets young people think for themselves. Grand Rapids, Zondervan Pub. House [1958] 118p. 20cm. [BV4531.2.R5] 58-4706
1. Youth—Religious life. I. Title.

ROBERTS, Kenneth J., 1930- 248'.83
You better believe it : a playboy-turned-priest talks to teens / Kenneth J. Roberts. Huntington, Ind. : Our Sunday Visitor, c1977. 191 p. : ill. ; 21 cm. A priest talks with teenagers about daily living and the Catholic Church. [BX2355.R55] 77-84944 ISBN 0-87973-750-6 pbk. : 3.95

1. [Catholic Church.] 2. Youth—Religious life. 3. [Christian life.] I. Title.

ROBINSON, Ruth (Grace) 248.8'3
Seventeen come Sunday; a birthday letter, by Ruth Robinson. Philadelphia, Westminster Press, [c1966] 78 p. illus. 20 cm. [BV4531.2.R57] 67-12089
1. Youth—Religious life. I. Title.

ROGERS, Dale Evans. 248'.83
Cool it or lose it! Dale Evans Rogers raps with youth. Old Tappan, N.J., F. H. Revell Co. [1972] 96 p. 20 cm. Discusses the importance of religion in daily life and how it can help young people deal with problems. [BV4531.2.R585] 72-5348 ISBN 0-8007-0551-3 2.95
1. Youth—Religious life. 2. [Christian life.] I. Title.

ROGNESS, Alvin N 1906- 248.83
Youth asks, why bother about God? By Alvin N. Rogness. New York, T. Nelson [1965] 95. [1] p. 22 cm. (Youth forum series) Bibliography: p. [96] [BV4531.2.R6] 65-15405
1. Youth—Religious life. I. Title. II. Title: Why bother about God?

ROGNESS, Alvin N., 1906- 248.83
Youth asks, why bother about God? New York, Nelson [c.1965] 95, [1]p. 22cm. (Youth forum ser.) Bibl. [BV4531.2.R6] 65-15405 1.50 pap.,
1. Youth—Religious life. I. Title. II. Title: Why bother about God?

ROSELL, Mervin E. 243
Challenging youth for Christ, by Mervin E. Rosell ... Grand Rapids, Mich., Zondervan publishing house [1945] 4 p. l., [5]-88 p. 20 cm. [BV4531.R63] 45-19105
1. Youth—Religious life. I. Title.

RUPERT, Hoover, ed. 248
Your life counts; messages for youth. New York, Abingdon-Cokesbury Press [1950] 157 p. 20 cm. [BV4310.R78] 50-7460
1. Youth—Religious life. I. Title.

RYDGREN, John, 1932- 248.8'3
Tomorrow is a handful of together yesterdays. Minneapolis, Augsburg Pub. House [1971] 96 p. illus., ports. 17 cm. [BV4531.2.R93] 75-159004 ISBN 0-8066-9442-4 1.95
1. Youth—Religious life. I. Title.

SAYERS, Stanley E., 261.8'34'31
1933-
Bridging the generation gap and bringing it back to God / by Stanley E. Sayers. Nashville, Tenn. : Gospel Advocate Co., 1975. ix, 169 p. ; 23 cm. Bibliography: p. 166-169. [BV4531.2.S29] 75-34639 ISBN 0-89225-201-4
1. Youth—Religious life. 2. Conflict of generations. I. Title.

SEARCH for the sacred: 248'.83
the new spiritual quest. Edited by Myron B. Bloy, Jr. New York, Seabury Press [1972] viii, 180 p. illus. 21 cm. (Church and campus books) (An Original Seabury paperback, SP 75) Papers delivered at a consultation sponsored by the Church Society for College Work. Includes bibliographical references. [BV4531.2.S4] 72-76554 ISBN 0-8164-2074-2 3.75
1. Youth—Religious life. I. Bloy, Myron B., ed. II. Church Society for College Work.

SECULOFF, James F. 248'.48'2
God and the teenager / James F. Seculoff. Huntington, Ind. : Our Sunday Visitor, c1978. viii, 112 p. : ill. ; 21 cm. A Catholic priest answers 35 questions involving such topics as proper dress, drinking, drugs, finding oneself, and the Catholic Church. [BX2355.S42] 78-69732 ISBN 0-87973-651-8 pbk. : 2.95
1. [Catholic Church.] 2. Youth—Religious life. 3. Youth—Conduct of life. 4. [Christian life.] 5. [Questions and answers.] I. Title.

[SEVENTH-DAY Adventists. 248
General conference. Dept. of Education] *Youth problems,* studies in guidance, for introductory use. Washington, D.C., Review and herald, 1945. 379 p. 23 1/2 cm. Prepared by the Department of education of the General conference of Seventh-day Adventists: general editor, W. Homer Teesdale, cf. Pref. Includes bibliographies. [BV4531.S38] 45-2906
1. Youth—Religious life. 2. Seventh-day Adventists—Doctrinal and controversial works. I. Teesdale, Willaim Homer, ed. II. Title.

SIEKMANN, Theodore C. 248.83
Boys. New York, [55 Park P1., J. F. Wagner c.1961] 190p. 61-3106 3.95
1. YOuth—Religious life. I. Title.

SIEKMANN, Thodore C 248.83
Boys. New York, J. F. Wagner [1961] 190 p. 21 cm. [BX2360.S52] 61-3106
1. Youth — Religious life. I. Title.

SMITH, Frank Wade. 259
Leaders of young people, by Frank Wade Smith. New York, Cincinnati, The Methodist book concern [c1922] 224 p. 17 cm. (The worker and work series, H. H. Meyer, editor) [BV4447.S6] 22-9956
I. Title.

SMITH, Tom A. 248.8
Be! A guide for personal growth, by Tom. A. Smith, Don Knipschield. Anderson, Ind., Warner [dist. Gospel Trumpet, c.1962] 64p. 62-11102 1.00 pap.,
1. Youth—Religious life. I. Knipschield, Don, joint author. II. Title.

SMITH, Tom A 220.9'2
Be! A guide for personal growth, by Tom A. Smith and Don Knipschield. Anderson, Ind., Warner Press [1962] 64 p. 19 cm. [BV4531.2.S6] 62-11102
1. Youth — Religious life. I. Knipschield, Don, joint author. II. Title.

SPICER, William Ambrose, 922
1866-
Youthful witnesses, by W. A. Spicer ... Washington, D.C., South Bend, Ind. [etc.] Review and herald publishing association [c1921] 1 p. l., [7]-255 p. front., illus. 20 1/2 cm. [BR1704.S6] 21-6623
I. Title.

STACKEL, Robert W 248
The awakened heart; ways of cultivating the devotional life of young people, a study book, Edited by Gustav K. Wiencke. Philadelphia, Muhlenberg Press [1951] 96 p. 19 cm. [BV4531.S73] 51-13001
1. Youth — Religious life. I. Title.

STAFFORD, Tim. 248.8'3
Do you sometimes feel like a nobody / Tim Stafford. Grand Rapids, MI : Zondervan Pub. House, c1980. 139 p. ; ill. ; 21 cm. "Campus life books." Uses examples and anecdotes to help us accept ourselves. Deals with love, forgiveness, and the meaning of life. [BV4531.2.S68] 79-25556 ISBN 0-310-32951-5 pbk. : 3.95
1. Youth—Religious life. 2. Self-acceptance. 3. [Self-acceptance.] 4. [Christian life.] I. Title.

STEINKE, Peter L. 248'.83
Whose who: explorations in Christian identity [by] Peter L. Steinke. St. Louis, Concordia Pub. House [1972] 96 p. illus. 21 cm. (Perspective, 11) [BV4531.2.S78] 72-84206 ISBN 0-570-06471-6
1. Youth—Religious life. I. Title.

STEWART, Charles William. 248.8'3
Adolescent religion; a developmental study of the religion of youth. Nashville, Abingdon Press [1967] 318 p. 24 cm. Bibliography: p. 305-309. [BV4531.2.S8] 67-11712
1. Youth—Religious life. 2. Adolescence. I. Title.

THE Street people; 248.8'3
selections from "Right on," Berkeley's Christian underground student newspaper. Valley Forge [Pa.] Judson Press [1971] 62 p. illus. 28 cm. [BV4531.2.S84] 71-147962 ISBN 0-8170-0512-9 1.50
1. Youth—Religious life. I. Right on.

STREIBERT, Muriel Anne. 220
Youth and the Bible, By Muriel Anne Streibert ... New York, The Macmillan company, 1924. xv p., 1 l., 251 p. 19 1/2 cm. "Books that help":p235-246. "Books that help":p235-246. [BS600.575] 24-27610
I. Title.

STROMMEN, Merton P. 259
Profiles of church youth; report on a four-year study of 3,000 Lutheran high-school youth. Saint Louis, Concordia [c.1963] xxiv, 356p. illus., tables. 24cm. Bibl. 63-20178 5.95
1. Youth—Religious life. 2. Church work with youth—Lutheran Church. I. Lutheran Youth Research. II. Title.

SWANSON, Steve. 248'.83
What does God want me to do with my life? / Steve Swanson. Minneapolis : Augsburg Pub. House, c1979. 103 p. : ill. ; 18 cm. Discusses making decisions regarding school, friendships, sex, marriage, jobs, and other concerns in accordance with God's plan for one's life. [BV4531.2.S87] 79-50086 ISBN 0-8066-1722-5 : 2.25
1. Youth—Religious life. 2. [Christian life.] 3. [Conduct of life.] I. Title.

SWEARINGEN, Tilford Tippett. 248
Must a man live? By T. T. Swearingen. St. Louis, Mo., The Bethany press, 1941. 136 p. 20 cm. "References": p. 136. [BV4531.T8] 41-18791
1. Youth—Religious life. 2. Apologetics—20th cent. I. Title.

SWOR, Chester E. 248.8'3
Youth at bat [by] Chester E. Swor and Jerry Merriman. Westwood, N.J., F. H. Revell Co. [1968] 127 p. 21 cm. Bibliography: p. 125-127. [BV4531.2.S9] 68-17095
1. Youth—Religious life. I. Merriman, Jerry, joint author. II. Title.

TOWNSEND, Anne B 238.2
Chapel talks for school and camp. Greenwich, Conn., Seabury Press, 1961. 128 p. 22 cm. [BV4310.T6] 61-11315
1. Youth — Religious life. 2. Sermons, American. I. Title.

TYLER, Joseph Zachary, 1818- 252.
1926.
Talks to young people given before the Bethany park summer assembly, by J. Z. Tyler ... with an introduction by Francis E. Clark ... Cincinnati, O., The Standard publishing co. [1896] vi, 148 p. 20 cm. [BV4310.T78] 45-44445
1. Youth—Religious life. I. Title.

VAN DUSEN, Henry Pitney, 248
1897-
Life's meaning: the why and how of Christian living. New York, Association Press, 1951. 244 p. 21 cm. "A Haddam House book." [BV4531.V3] 51-13621
1. Youth — Religious life. I. Title.

VERSTEEG, John Marinus, 1888- 248
Christ and the problems of youth, by John M. Versteeg. New York, Cincinnati, The Abingdon press [1924] 133 p. 17 1/2 cm. [BV4531.V4] 24-4531
1. Youth—Religious life. I. Title.

WALKER, Elmer Jerry, 1918- 248.83
Seeking a faith of your own. Nashville, Abingdon Press [c.1961] 109p. 61-5560 2.00 bds.,
1. Youth—Religious life. I. Title.

WALKER, Elmer Jerry, 1918- 248.83
Seeking a faith of your own. New York, Abingdon Press [1961] 109 p. 20 cm. [BV4310.W27] 61-5560
1. Youth — Religious life. I. Title.

WARD, Hiley H. 248'.83
The far-out saints of the Jesus communes; a firsthand report and interpretation of the Jesus people movement, by Hiley H. Ward. New York, Association Press [1972] 192 p. 21 cm. Bibliography: p. [187]-190. [BV4531.2.W35] 73-189010 ISBN 0-8096-1842-7 5.95
1. Youth—Religious life. I. Title.

WARD, Ted Warren, 1930- 248'.83
Memo for the underground, by Ted Ward. [1st ed.] Carol Stream, Ill., Creation House [1971] 128 p. 23 cm. [BV4531.2.W37] 72-182853 3.95
1. Youth—Religious life. I. Title.

WEBBER, Ralph Ernest. 248
The job of living; an answer to the problems of youth, by Ralph Ernest Webber. Dayton, O., United brethren publishing house, 1934. 3 p. l., v-viii, 9-173 p. 1 illus., diagrs. 19 1/2 cm. "Other books of interest" at end of most of the chapters. [BV4531.W43] 34-18310
1. Youth—Religious life. I. Title.

WESTERHOFF, John H. 248'.83
Learning to be free, by John H. Westerhoff, III and Joseph C. Williamson. Philadelphia, United Church Press [1972] 72 p. illus. 26 cm. Includes bibliographical references. Suggests ways in which young people can work together in groups to increase, preserve, and exercise their individual and social freedoms. [BV4531.2.W45] 72-6156
1. Youth—Religious life. 2. Freedom (Theology)—Juvenile literature. 3. [Liberty.] 4. [Christian life.] I. Williamson, Joseph C., 1932- joint author. II. Title.

WESTON, Sidney Adams, 248.83
1877-
Jesus' teachings for young people [by] Sidney A. Weston [rev. ed.] Boston, Whittemore [c.1962] 93p. 19cm. .75 pap.,
1. Youth—Religious life. I. Title.

WESTON, Sidney Adams, 1877-
Jesus' teachings for young people. [Revised ed.] Boston, Whitemore Associates [1962] 93 p. 67-22356
1. Yough — Religious life. I. Title.

WESTON, Sidney Adams, 1877- 248
Jesus' teachings for young people [by] Sidney A. Weston ... Boston, Chicago, The Pilgrim press [c1927] 2 p. l., 127 p. 16 1/2 cm. [BV4531.W445 1927] 27-9253
1. Youth—Religious life. I. Title.

WESTON, Sidney Adams, 1877- 248
Jesus' teachings for young people [by] Sidney A. Weston ... Boston, Chicago, The Pilgrim press [1934] 2 p. l., 112 p. 19 1/2 cm. "Like its companion volume, Jesus and the problems of life, this is a discussion course of study."--Verso of 2d prelim. leaf. "Revised November, 1934." [BV4531.W445 1934] 35-607
1. Youth—Religious life. I. Title.

WESTON, Sidney Adams, 1877-
Life problems in a changing world. Boston, Mass., Whittemore Associates [1964] 96 p. illus. 19 cm. "Revised editions." 67-24154
1. Youth — Religious life. I. Title.

WESTON, Sidney Adams, 1877- 248
Social and religious problems of young people; a handbook for group and individual use [by] Sidney A. Weston [and] S. Ralph Harlow. New York, Cincinnati [etc.] The Abingdon press [c1934] 288 p. 20 cm. Bibliography at the end of some of the chapters. [BV4531.W45] 35-241
1. Youth—Religious life. 2. Social problems. 3. Christian life. I. Harlow, Samuel Ralph, 1885- II. Title.

WESTON, Sidney Adams, 1877- 248
Social and religious problems of young people; a handbook for group and individual use [by] Sidney A. Weston [and] S. Ralph Harlow. New York, Cincinnati [etc.] The Abingdon press [c1935] 304 p. fold. tab. 20 cm. "First edition printed December, 1934. Second printing, May, 1935." Bibliography at end of some of the chapters. [BV4531.W45 1935] 35-8534
1. Youth—Religious life. 2. Social problems. 3. Christian life. I. Harlow, Samuel Ralph, 1885- II. Title.

WIERSBE, Warren W. 248.83
Be a real teenager! Westwood, N.J., Revell [c.1965] 127p. 18cm. [BV4531.2.W5] 65-14796 .89 pap.,
1. Youth—Religious life. 2. Youth—Conduct of life. I. Title.

WIERSBE, Warren W 248.83
Be a real teenager! [By] Warren W. Wiersbe. Westwood, N.J., F.H. Revell Co. [1965] 127 p. 18 cm. [BV4531.2.W5] 65-14796
1. Youth — Religious life. 2. Youth — Conduct of life. I. Title.

WIERWILLE, Victor Paul. 248
Victory through Christ, by Victor Paul Wierwille ... Van Wert, O., The Wilkinson press, c1945. 6 p. l., 15-171 p. 16 cm. [BV4531.W483] 45-3853
1. Youth—Religious life. I. Title.

WILES, Charles Peter, 1870- 248
Upon this rock; talks with young Christians, by Charles P. Wiles, D.D. Philadelphia, Pa., The United Lutheran publication house [1939] 51 p. front. (form) 18 1/2 cm. "Revised edition." [BV4531.W5 1939] 39-19580

1. Youth—Religious life. I. Title.

WILLIAMS, Alfred E. 268'.61
Dilemmas and decisions; a resource and discussion book for youth [by] Alfred E. Williams, Jr. [Rev. ed. New York] Herder and Herder [1968] 76 p. illus. 22 cm. (Christian commitment series) Bibliography: p. 73-74. [BV4531.2.W54 1968b] 68-29892 1.20
1. Youth—Religious life. 2. Religious education—Text-books for young people—United Church of Christ. I. Title.

WILLIAMS, Alfred E. 268'.61
Dilemmas and decisions; a resource and discussion book for youth [by] Alfred E. Williams, Jr. Boston, United Church Press [1968] 76 p. illus. 22 cm. (Confirmation education series) "Part of the United Church curriculum, prepared and published by the Division of Christian Education and the Division of Christian Education and the Division of Publication of the United Church Board for Homeland Ministries." Bibliographical references included in "Notes and acknowledgements" (p. 74-76) [BV4531.2.W54] 68-10314
1. Youth—Religious life. 2. Religious education—Text-books for young people—United Church of Christ. I. United Church Board for Homeland Ministries. Division of Christian Education. II. United Church Board for Homeland Ministries. Division of Publication. III. Title.

WILLIAMSON, Audrey J 248
Your teen ager and you, guidance for the Christian home when young people are twelve to eighteen. Kansas City, Mo., Beacon Hill Press [1952] 96p. illus. 19cm. (Christian home series) [BV4531.W514] 52-11196
1. Youth— Religions life. I. Title.

WISE, Daniel, 1813-1898. 248
The path of life: or, Sketches of the way to glory and immortality. A help for young Christians. By Rev. Daniel Wise ... Boston, C. H. Peirce, 1848. 3 p. l., [v]-xii, [9]-246 p. front. 17 cm. Added t.-p., engraved. [BV4531.W53 1848] 36-3171
1. Youth—Religious life. I. Title.

WISE, Daniel, 1813-1898. 248
The path of life: or, Sketches of the way to glory and immortality, a help for young Christians. By Rev. Daniel Wise ... 29th thousand. New York, Carlton & Porter [186-?] xii, [9]-246 p. 17 1/2 cm. [BV4531.W53] 36-3175
1. Youth—Religious life. I. Title.

WITTE, Kaaren. 248'.2
Angels in faded jeans / Kaaren Witte ; photography by Vicki Hesterman. Minneapolis : Bethany Fellowship, c1979. 158 p. : ill. ; 21 cm. [BV4531.2.W57] 79-84795 ISBN 0-87123-014-3 pbk. : 2.95
1. Witte, Kaaren. 2. Youth—Religious life. 3. Youth—Conduct of life. I. Title.

WOOD, Thomas. (Wesleyan minister) 171.
Germs of thought; or, Rudiments of knowledge; intended to promote the mental and religious improvement of youth, by Thomas Wood ... First American from the first London edition. New York, Published and sold by N. Bangs & T. Mason, for the Methodist Episcopal church. William A. Mercein, printer, 1821. vii, [1] 204 p. 18 cm. "List of books ... for the use of the Methodist Episcopal church": p. [203]-204. [BV4531.W6] A 35
1. Youth Religious life. I. Title. II. Title: Rudiments of knowledge.

WRIGHT, Louis Clinton, 1879- 248
Trails for climbing youth [by] Louis C. Wright. New York, Cincinnati [etc.] The Abingdon press [c1939] 123 p. 19 1/2 cm. [BV4531.W7] 39-20408
1. Youth—Religious life. I. Title.

WYCOFF, Mary Elizabeth. 248.83
Encounter with early teens. Illustrated by John Mecray. Philadelphia, Westminster Press [1965] 92 p. illus. 23 cm. [BV639.Y7W9] 65-11611
1. Youth—Religious life. I. Title.

YEAR of youth programs and 267.6
activities, number 2. Illus. by Bill Granstaff. Cincinnati, Ohio, Standard Pub. [c.1963] 174p. illus. 28cm. 2.95 pap.,

YLVISAKER, Nils Martin, 1882- 248
Faces toward God, by N. M. Ylvisaker. Minneapolis, Augsburg publishing house, 1936. xi, 240 p. 20 1/2 cm. "The problems and difficulties of our youth."--Foreword. "First edition." [BV4531.Y6] 36-16370
1. Youth—Religious life. 2. Christian life. I. Title.

YOUNG, Howard Palmer. 248
The youth of to-day in the life of to-morrow by Howard Palmer Young... New York, Chicago [etc.] Fleming H. Revell company [c1923] 224 p. 19 1/2 cm. [BV639.Y7Y8] 23-18244
I. Title.

YOUNG people's Luther 267.6241
league. 11th convention, Billings, Mont., 1941.
Conquering with Christ; main addresses and summaries of discussions. Eleventh international convention of the Young people's Luther league at Billings, Montana, June 25-29, 1941... Minneapolis, Augsburg publishing house [c1941] 80 p. 20 cm. [BX8003.X75 1941] 41-13652
1. Youth—Religious life. I. Title.

**YOUTH kit,* 268.43
23 (formerly Youth fellowship kit) varied resources for study, discussion, action by church groups. Ed.: John C. Purdy. Ed.-in-chief: Norman F. Langford. Exec. ed.: Donald L. Leonard. Philadelphia, Geneva Pr. [dist. Westminister, c.1965] 232p. illus. 28cm. 3.50

**YOUTH kit,* 268.433
24: study, discussion, action resources. Philadelphia, Geneva Pr. [dist. Westminster. c.1946-1966] 16pts. (various p.) illus. 21cm. 5.00 pap.,

**YOUTH kit,* 268.433
22(formerly youth fellowship kit) varied resources for study, discussion, action by church groups. Ed.[of this v.] John C. Purdy. Ed.-in-chief: Norman F. Langford. Exec. ed.: Donald L. Leonard. Philadelphia, Geneva Pr. [dist. Westminster, c.1964] 232p. illus. 28cm. 3.50 pap.,

**YOUTH ministry* 268.05
notebook. 1967-1968. New York, Seabury [1967] v. illus. 28cm. Bibl. 3.00 pap.,

ZINK, Jorg. 248.8'3
Tomorrow is today: a book for young people. [Tr. by L. A. Kenworthy-Brown.] Oxford, Religious Educ. Pr., 1967. 117p. illus., ports. 29cm. Tr. of Diene zeit und alle zeit. [BV4533.Z513] 67-28788 6.00
1. Youth—Religious life. I. Title.
Order from Pergamon, New York

Youth—Religious life—Addresses, essays, lectures.

ANSWERS for young Latter- 248'.83
day Saints / [compiled from the New era] . Salt Lake City : Deseret Book Co., 1977. 113 p. ; 24 cm. Includes index. A collection of answers to doctrinal and social questions raised by young adult members of the Church of Jesus Christ of Latter-day Saints. [BX8643.Y6A57] 77-3284 ISBN 0-87747-645-4 : 4.95
1. Church of Jesus Christ of Latter-day Saints—Doctrinal and controversial works—Juvenile literature—Addresses, essays, lectures. 2. [Church of Jesus Christ of Latter-day Saints—Doctrinal and controversial works.] 3. Youth—Religious life—Addresses, essays, lectures. 4. [Conduct of life.] I. Church of Jesus Christ of Latter-day Saints. II. New era (Salt Lake City)

JOHN Paul II, Pope, 248.4'8203
1920-
You are my favorites / Pope John Paul II ; [edited by the Daughters of St. Paul] Boston, MA : Daughters of St. Paul, c1980. 187 p. : col. ill. ; 25 cm. Includes index. Talks given to youth by Pope John Paul II on a variety of topics including faith, Jesus, the Mass, Christmas, friendship, violence, sports, the sacraments, holy days, and much more. [BX2355.J56] 80-15225 ISBN 0-8198-8701-3 : 8.95
1. Youth—Religious life—Addresses, essays, lectures. 2. [Christian life—Addresses, essays, lectures.] I. Daughters of St. Paul. II. Title.

JOHN Paul II, Pope, 1920- 248'.83
"You are the future, you are my hope" to the young people of the world / Pope John Paul II compiled by the Daughters of St. Paul. Boston : St. Paul Editions, c1979. 324 p., [8] leaves of plates : ill. ; 19 cm. Includes index. [BX2355.J57] 79-24935 ISBN 0-8198-0632-3 : 4.95 ISBN 0-8198-0633-1 pbk. : 3.95
1. Youth—Religious life—Addresses, essays, lectures. I. Daughters of St. Paul. II. Title.

KNOWING and helping 268'.433
youth / G. Temp Sparkman, editor ; contributors, Dan Boling ... [et al.]. Nashville : Broadman Press, 1978,c1977. 152 p. ; 20 cm. Includes bibliographies. [BV4531.2.K6] 77-75621 ISBN 0-8054-3219-1 : 4.95
1. Youth—Religious life—Addresses, essays, lectures. 2. Church work with youth—Addresses, essays, lectures. I. Sparkman, Temp. II. Boling, Dan.

Youth—Religious life—Juvenile literature.

THE Eagle story. 248.8'3
Oak Brook, Ill. : Institute in Basic Youth Conflicts, c1982. 63 p. : ill. (some col.) ; 29 cm. [BV4531.2.E23 1982] 19 81-85536 ISBN 0-916888-07-X : 10.00
1. Youth—Religious life—Juvenile literature. 2. Nature—Religious aspects—Christianty—Juvenile literature. 3. Birds—Religious aspects—Christianity—Juvenile literature. I. Institute in Basic Youth Conflicts.

Youth—Religious life—Statistics.

ZUCK, Roy B. 248.8'3'0212
Christian youth, an in-depth study; profiles of 3,000 teenagers and their morals, values, doubts, religious practices, social characteristics, evaluations of themselves, their families, their churches, by Roy B. Zuck and Gene A. Getz. Chicago, Moody Press [1968] 192 p. illus. 26 cm. Bibliography: p. 188-189. [BV4531.2.Z8] 68-29503 5.95
1. Youth—Religious life—Statistics. 2. Youth—Conduct of life—Statistics. I. Getz, Gene A., joint author. II. Title.

Youth - Russia - Religious life.

BOURDEAUX, Michael. 248'.83'0947
Young Christian in Russia / [by] Michael Boudeaux and Katherine Murray. Minneapolis, MN : Bethany Fellowship, 1977. 156p. ; 18 cm. [BV4531.2.B68] ISBN 0-87123-663-X pbk. : 1.95
1. Youth — Russia — Religious life. I. Murray, Katherine, joint author. II. Title.
L.C. card no. for Lakeland (London) ed.: 77-359486.

Youth — Societies.

BARNES, A.M., Miss, comp.
Helps and entertainments for juvenile and young people's miissionary socities. Comp. and arranged by Miss A.M. Barnes. Nashville, Tenn., Dallas, Tex., Barbee & Smith, 1901. 206 pp. incl. front. 18 1/2 cm. Subject entries: Readers and speakers. 2-8566
I. Title.

NATIONAL Jewish Youth 296
Conference.
Proceedings. New York. v. illus. 28 cm. annual. [E184.J5N5965] 52-27198
1. Youth — Societies. 2. Jews in the U.S. I. Title.

*YAXLEY, Grace 259
Here's how youth meetings. Chicago, Moody [c.1964] 64p. illus. 28cm. 1.25 pap.,
I. Title.

Youth—United States—Religious life.

KRUMP, John. 261.8'34'3150973
Hope for the future? : Youth and the Church / by John Krump. Chicago : Thomas More Press, c1979. 110 p. ; 21 cm. Includes bibliographical references. [BX2355.K78] 79-105714 ISBN 0-88347-092-6 pbk. : 3.95

1. Youth—United States—Religious life. I. Title.

POTVIN, Raymond H. 301.15'43'2
Religion and American youth, with emphasis on Catholic adolescents and young adults / by Raymond H. Potvin, Dean R. Hoge, Hart M. Nelsen ; commissioned by Office of Research, Policy and Program Development, Department of Education, United States Catholic Conference. Washington : Publications Office, The Conference, 1976. 62 p. ; 22 cm. Bibliography: p. 55-61. [BV4531.2.P67] 77-353037

1. Youth—United States—Religious life. 2. Young adults—United States—Religious life. I. Hoge, Dean R., 1937- joint author. II. Nelsen, Hart M., joint author. III. United States Catholic Conference. Office of Research, Policy and Program Development. IV. Title.

Youth with a Mission, inc.

WILSON, R. Marshall. 248.8'3
God's guerrillas; the true story of Youth With a Mission, by R. Marshall Wilson. Illus. by Jim Howard. Plainfield, N.J., Logos International [1971] 166 p. illus. 22 cm. [BV1430.Y64W54] 71-123999 ISBN 0-912106-10-7 2.50

1. Youth with a Mission, inc. 2. Evangelistic work. 3. Youth—Religious life. I. Title.

Youville, Marie Marguerite (Dufrost de La Jemmerais) d', 1701-1771.

FITTS, Mary Pauline, 922.271
Sister.
Hands to the needy; Mother d'Youville, apostle to the poor. [1st ed.] Garden City, N. Y., Doubleday, 1950. xiii, 336 p. port., map (on lining papers) 22 cm. Bibliography: p. 327-330. [BX4705.Y6F5] 50-8150

1. Youville, Marie Marguerite (Dufrost de La Jemmerais) d', 1701-1771. I. Title.

FITTS, Mary Pauline. 271'.979 B
Hands to the needy; Blessed Marguerite d'Youville, apostle to the poor. Garden City, N.Y., Doubleday, 1971. xiii, 332 p. 21 cm. Bibliography: p. 323-326. [BX4705.Y6F5 1971] 79-182572

1. Youville, Marie Marguerite (Dufrost de La Jemmerais) d', 1701-1771. 2. Grey nuns. I. Title.

Yu, Mrs.

WHITE, Mary Culler, 1875- 922
Meet Mrs. Yu. [The true story of an outstanding Chinese Christian] New York, Abingdon-Cokesbury Press. [1948] 212 p. 19 cm. Group port on cover. [BV3427.Y8W5] 48-3631

1. Yu, Mrs. I. Title.

Yugoslavia—Economic policy—1945- — Addresses, essays, lectures. I. Stojanovic, Radmila.

Yugoslavia—Religion.

FRENCH, Reginald Michael, 1884-
Serbian church life, by R. M. French. London, Society for promoting Christian knowledge; New York, The Macmillan company [1942] vii, 64 p. front., illus. (plan) plates. 18 1/2 cm. "First published in 1942." A 43
1. Yugoslavia—Religion. 2. Orthodox Eastern church, Serbian. 3. Rites and ceremonies—Yugoslavia. 4. Yugoslavia—Soc. life & cust. I. Title.

Zacchaeus (Biblical character) — Juvenile literature.

ELLINGBOE, Betty. 225.924
The little man from Jericho. Written and illustrated by Betty Ellingboe. Minneapolis, Augsburg Pub. House [1963] unpaged. illus. 22 x 28 cm. [BS2520.Z3E4] 63-16596
1. Zacchaeus (Biblical character) — Juvenile literature. I. Title.

WARREN, Mary. 226
The great surprise Luke 19: 2-10 for children Illustrated by Betty Wind. St. Louis, Concordia Pub. House, 1964. [32] p. col. illus. 21 cm. (Arch books) Quality religious books for children. [BS2520.Z3W3] 63-23147
1. Zacchaeus (Biblical character) — Juvenile literature. I. Title.

Zachariah, Father, 1850-1936.

AN Early Soviet 281.9'092'4 B
saint : the life of Father Zachariah / translated [from the Russian MS.] by Jane Ellis ; and with an introduction by Sir John Lawrence. London : Mowbrays, 1976. xiv, 111 p. ; 23 cm. (Modern Russian spirituality series) (Keston books ; no. 6) [BX597.Z3E17] 77-361317 ISBN 0-264-66334-9 : £4.25
1. Zachariah, Father, 1850-1936. 2. Orthodox (Orthodox Eastern Church)—Biography. I. Ellis, Jane, 1951- II. Series: Modern Russian spirituality series.

Zadokite documents.

GINZBERG, Louis, 1873- 296.8'1
1953.
An unknown Jewish sect / by Louis Ginzberg. New York : Jewish Theological Seminary of America, 1976, c1970. p. cm. (Moreshet series ; v. 1) Revised and updated translation of the author's Eine unbekannte judische Sekte, 1922 ed. Includes bibliographical references and indexes. [BM175.Z3G5613 1976] 76-127636 25.00
1. Zadokite documents. I. Title. II. Series: Moreshet (New York) ; v. 1.

ZADOKITE documents. 296
The Zadokite documents; I. The admonition. II. The laws. Edited with a translation and notes by Chaim Rabin, 2d rev. ed. Oxford, Clarendon Press, 1958. xvi, 103 p. 23 cm. Hebrew and English. Includes bibliographical references. [BM175.Z3R3 1958] 58-2491
I. Rabin, Chaim, ed. and tr. II. Title.

Zaehner, R. C. (Robert Charles), 1913-1974.

NEWELL, William Lloyd. 291.4'2
Struggle and submission : R.C. Zaehner on mysticisms / by William Lloyd Newell ; foreword by Gregory Baum. Washington, D.C. : University Press of America, c1981. xvii, 383 p. ; 22 cm. Includes index. Bibliography: p. 321-343. [BL625.N4] 19 80-6295 ISBN 0-8191-1696-3 : 21.75 ISBN 0-8191-1697-1 (pbk.) : 12.75
1. Zaehner, R. C. (Robert Charles), 1913-1974. 2. Mysticism—History—20th century. I. Title.

Zaehner, Robert Charles.

MAHABHARATA 294.5'924
Bhagavadgita
The Bhagavad-Gita, with a commentary based on the original sources by R. C. Zaehner. London, Oxford, Oxford Univ. Pr. [1973, c.1969] ix, 480 p. 21 cm. (Galaxy bk., GB389) Includes transliteration of original Sanskrit. Bibl footnotes. [PK3633.B5Z3] 73-381283 ISBN 0-19-501666-1 Pap., 3.95
1. Zaehner, Robert Charles. I. Title.

Zagorsk, Russia. Gosudarstvennyi istoriko-khudozhestvennyi muzei.

ZAGORSK, Russia. 755'.2'09496
Gosudarstvennyi istoriko-khudozhestvennyi muzei.
Zagorsk : ancient Russian painting in the collection of the Zagorsk Historical and Art Museum / [compiled by Tatiana Nikolajevna Manushina]. Moscow : Pub. House "Soviet Russia", 1976. 64 p. : col. ill. ; 20 cm. [N8189.R92Z349 1976] 77-474499 0.93rub
1. Zagorsk, Russia. Gosudarstvennyi istoriko-khudozhestvennyi muzei. 2. Icons, Russian—Catalogs. 3. Icons—Russian Republic—Zagorsk—Catalogs. I. Manushina, Tat'iana Nikolaevna. II. Title.

Zahm, John Augustine, 1851-1921.

WEBER, Ralph Edward 922.273
Notre Dame's John Zahm; American Catholic apologist and educator. [Notre Dame, Ind.] Univ. of Notre Dame Press [c.] 1961. 214p. Front port. Bibl. 61-10175 5.00
1. Zahm, John Augustine, 1851-1921. I. Title.

Zahn, Gordon Charles, 1918- — Addresses, essays, lectures.

WAR or peace? : 261.8'73
The search for new answers / edited by Thomas Shannon. Maryknoll, N.Y. : Orbis Books, [1980] p. cm. Includes bibliographical references. [BT736.2.W346] 80-15113 ISBN 088344-750-9 pbk. : 9.95
1. Zahn, Gordon Charles, 1918- — Addresses, essays, lectures. 2. War and religion—Addresses, essays, lectures. 3. War and morals—Addresses, essays, lectures. 4. Just war doctrine—Addresses, essays, lectures. 5. Pacifism—Addresses, essays, lectures. 6. Peace (Theology)—Addresses, essays, lectures. I. Shannon, Thomas Anthony, 1940-

Zakarpatskaia oblast'—History.

WARZESKI, Walter C., 281.9'3
1929-
Byzantine rite Rusins in Carpatho-Ruthenia and America, by Walter C. Warzeski. [Pittsburgh, Byzantine Seminary Press, 1971] x, 332 p. illus. 23 cm. Bibliography: p. 285-315. [DB355.W37] 70-30058
1. Catholic Church. Byzantine rite (Ruthenian) 2. Zakarpatskaia oblast'—History. 3. Ruthenians in the United States. I. Title.

Zakich, Rhea.

ZAKICH, Rhea. 287'.6'0924 B
Everybody wins : the story behind the Ungame / Rhea Zakich. Wheaton, Ill. : Tyndale House Publishers, 1979. 149 p. ; 22 cm. [BX8495.Z32A33] 79-65028 ISBN 0-8423-0788-5 : 6.95
1. Zakich, Rhea. 2. Christian life—Methodist authors. 3. Ungame (Game) 4. Methodists—California—Biography. 5. California—Biography. I. Title.

Zambia—Church history.

JOHNSON, Walton R. 283'.97
Worship and freedom : a Black American church in Zambia / by Walton R. Johnson. New York : Africana Pub. Co., 1977. p. cm. Includes index. Bibliography: p. [BX8446.Z33J63 1977] 77-22388 ISBN 0-8419-0315-8 : 20.00
1. African Methodist Episcopal Church—Zambia. 2. Zambia—Church history. I. Title.

Zamucoan Indians—Missions.

WAGNER, C. Peter. 266'.023'0924 B
Defeat of the bird god / C. Peter Wagner. South Pasadena, Calif. : William Carey Library, c1975. 256 p. : ill. ; 22 cm. [F3320.2.Z3W3 1975] 75-331578 ISBN 0-87808-721-4 pbk. : 4.95
1. Pencille, Bill. 2. Zamucoan Indians—Missions. 3. Indians of South America—Bolivia—Missions. I. Title.

WAGNER, C. Peter. 266'.023'0924
Defeat of the bird god; the story of missionary Bill Pencille, who risked his life to reach the Ayores of Bolivia [by] C. Peter Wagner. Foreword by Paul S. Rees. Grand Rapids, Zondervan Pub. House [1967] 256 p. illus., map (on lining papers), ports. 23 cm. [F3320.2.Z3W3] 67-11615
1. Pencille, Bill. 2. Zamucoan Indians—Missions. 3. Santa Cruz, Bolivia (Dept.)—Description and travel. I. Title.

Zanta, Leontine.

TEILHARD de Chardin, 271'.5'0924
Pierre.
Letters to Leontine Zanta. Introd. by Robert Garric and Henri de Lubac. Translated by Bernard Wall. [1st U.S. ed.] New York, Harper & Row [1969] 127 p. 21 cm. Bibliographical footnotes. [B2430.T374A493 1969b] 69-17020 4.00
1. Zanta, Leontine. I. Title.

Zanzibar—Religious life and customs.

DALE, Godfrey. 200'.9678'1
The peoples of Zanzibar: their customs and religious beliefs. New York, Negro Universities Press [1969] 124 p. 23 cm. Reprint of the 1920 ed. [BL2470.Z35D3 1969] 78-90112
1. Zanzibar—Religious life and customs. I. Title.

Zapotec language—Texts.

BIBLE. N. T. John. Zapotec. 226.5
1912.
Spida Jesu-Cristo casi nah San Juan. New York, American Bible society, 1912. 69 p. 18 cm. Added t.-p.: El Evangelio segun San Juan. Version moderna. Zapotec and Spanish in parallel columns. Translated by Arcadio G. Molina. [BS345.Z37 John 1912] CA 17
1. Zapotec language—Texts. I. Bible. Zapotec. N. T. John. 1912. II. Bible. Spanish. N. T. John. 1912. III. Molina, Arcadio g., tr. IV. Bible. N. T. John. Spanish. 1912 V. Title.

Zealots (Jewish party)

BRANDON, Samuel George 296.8'1
Frederick.
Jesus and the Zealots; a study of the political factor in primitive Christianity, by S. G. F. Brandon. [New York] Scribner, 1967. xvi, 412 p. illus. 23 cm. Bibliography: p. 369-384. [BM175.Z4B7 1967] 68-57073 7.95
1. Zealots (Jewish party) 2. Christianity and other religions—Judaism. 3. Judaism—Relations—Christianity. I. Title.

Zebris, Joseph, 1860-1915.

WOLKOVICH- 282'.092'4 B
VALKAVICIUS, William Lawrence, 1929-
Lithuanian pioneer priest of New England : the life, struggles, and tragic death of Reverend Joseph Zebris, 1860-1915 / by William Lawrence Wolkovich-Valkavicius. Brooklyn, N.Y. (341 Highland Blvd., Brooklyn 11207) : Franciscan Press, 1980. 214 p. : ill. ; 23 cm. Includes index. Bibliography: p. 199-202. [BX4705.Z343W64] 19 80-51268 pbk. : 6.00
1. Zebris, Joseph, 1860-1915. 2. Catholic Church—Clergy—Biography. 3. Clergy—New England—Biography. 4. Lithuanian Americans—New England—Biography. 5. New England—Biography. I. Title.

Zeisberger, David, 1721-1808.

DE SCHWEINITZ, 266'.46'0924 B
Edmund Alexander, 1825-1887.
The life and times of David Zeisberger. [New York] Arno Press [1971] 747 p. 23 cm. (The First America frontier) Reprint of the 1870 ed. "Published works of David Zeisberger": p. 687-692. [E99.M9Z44 1971] 70-146391 ISBN 0-405-02844-X
1. Zeisberger, David, 1721-1808. I. Title. II. Series.

DE SCHWEINITZ, 266'.46'0924 B
Edmund Alexander, 1825-1887.
The life and times of David Zeisberger, the Western pioneer and apostle of the Indians. Philadelphia, Lippincott, 1871. New York, Johnson Reprint Corp., 1971. xii, 747 p. 23 cm. (Series in American studies) Includes bibliographical references. [E98.M6Z4 1971] 71-155745
1. Zeisberger, David, 1721-1808. I. Title.

Zen.

*WATTS, Alan W. 294.329
The way of Zen (Reissue. New York] New Amer. Lib. [1964, c.1957] 224p. illus. 18cm. (Mentor bk., MP476) Bibl. .60 pap.,
I. Title.

Zen Buddhism.

BANCROFT, Anne, 1923- 294.3'927
Zen : direct pointing to reality / [by] Anne Bancroft. London ; [New York] : Thames and Hudson, 1979. 96 p. : ill. (some col.), ports. ; 28 cm. (Art and imagination) Text on back cover. Bibliography: p. 96. [BQ9265.6.B36] 19 78-63043 ISBN 0-500-81018-4 pbk. : 7.95
1. Zen Buddhism. I. Title.
Distributed by W. W. Norton, NYC

BLYTH, Reginald Horace. 294.3'927
Games Zen masters play : writings of R. H. Blyth / selected, edited, and with an introd. by Robert Sohl and Audrey Carr. New York : New American Library, 1976. 169 p. ; 18 cm. (A Mentor book) "Classic Zen texts with ... commentaries." [BQ9265.4.B55] 75-24786 pbk. : 1.50
1. Zen Buddhism. I. Title.

CHANG, Ch'eng-chi. 294.3'927
The practice of Zen / Chang Chen-chi. Westport, Conn. : Greenwood Press, 1978, c1959. xi, 199 p. ; 23 cm. Reprint of the ed. published by Harper, New York. Includes index. Bibliography: p. 178. [BQ9265.4.C44 1978] 78-618 ISBN 0-313-20264-8 lib.bdg. : 16.00
1. Zen Buddhism. I. Title.

CHANG, Ch'eng-chi. 294.329
The practice of Zen [by] Chang Chen-chi. [1st ed.] New York, Harper [1959] 199 p. 22 cm. In English. Includes bibliography. [BL1432.Z4C5] 59-10330
1. Zen Buddhism. I. Title.

[GRAY, Terence James 294.3
Stannus]
Open secret [by] Wei Wu Wei [pseud.] [Hong Kong] Hong Kong Univ. Pr. [New York, Oxford, c.1965] xi, 194p. 24cm. [BL1493.G7] 65-8876 3.00 pap.,
1. Zen Buddhism. I. Title.

HERRIGEL, Eugen, 1884- 294.32
Zen in the art of archery. With an introd. by D. T. Suzuki. Translated by R. F. C. Hull. [New York] Pantheon Books [1953] 109 p. 21 cm. [BL1442.Z4H43] 53-9945
1. Zen Buddhism. 2. Archery. I. Title.

HERRIGEL, Eugen, 1884- 294.329
1955.
The method of Zen. Edited by Hermann Tausend. Translated by R. F. C. Hull. [New York] Pantheon Books [1960] 124 p. 21 cm. Translation of Der Zen-Weg. [BL1442.Z4H443] 59-11957
1. Zen Buddhism.

HERRIGEL, Eugen, 1884- 294.329
1955
Zen. Tr. [from German] by R. F. C. Hull. Including Zen in the art of archery, introd. by D. T. Suzuki; The method of Zen, ed. by Hermann Tausend. New York, McGraw [1964, c.1953, 1960] 109, 124p. 21cm. 64-56163 1.95 pap.,
1. Zen Buddhism. 2. Archery. I. Herrigel,

Eugen, 1884-1955. The method of Zen. II. Title.

HUANG-PO, fl.842-850. 294.329
The Zen teaching of Huang Po on the transmission of mind; being the teaching of the Zen Master Huang Po as recorded by the scholar P'ei Hsiu of the T'ang dynasty. Rendered into English by John Blofeld (Chu Ch'an) New York, Grove Press [1959, c1958] 135 p. 22 cm. "A complete translation of the Huang Po chu'an [i.e. Ch'uan] hsiu [i.e. hsin] fa yao, including the previously unpublished Wan Ling record containing dialogues, sermons and anecdotes." [BL1432.Z4H723 1959] 59-12215
1. Zen Buddhism. I. P'ei, Hsiu, fl. 842-859. II. Title.

IINO, Norimoto, 1908- 294.3'927
Zeal for Zen. New York, Philosophical Library [1967] 94 p. 22 cm. [BL1493.I4] 66-26968
1. Zen Buddhism. I. Title.

KAPLEAU, Philip, 1912- ed. 294.3'927
The three pillars of Zen : teaching, practice, and enlightenment / complied & edited, with translations, introductions & notes, by Philip Kapleau ; foreword by Huston Smith. Rev. and expanded ed. Garden City, N.Y. : Anchor Press, 1980. xxii, 400 p. : ill. ; 21 cm. Includes bibliographical references and index. [BQ9265.4.K36 1980] 78-22794 ISBN 0-385-14786-4 pbk. : 5.95
1. Zen Buddhism. I. Title.

LASSALLE, Hugo, 1898- 294.3'927
Zen—way to enlightenment, by H. M. Enomiya-Lassalle. New York, Taplinger Pub. Co. [1968, c1966] 126 p. 21 cm. Bibliographical footnotes. [BL1493.L2813 1968] 68-17642
1. Zen Buddhism. I. Title.

LU, K'uan Yu, 1898- comp. 294.3'927
Ch'an and Zen teaching. Edited, translated, and explained by Lu K'uan Yu (Charles Luk). [1st American ed.] Berkeley [Calif.] Shambala Publications, 1970- [c1960] v. 22 cm. (The Clear light series) Contents.Contents.—ser. 1. Master Hsu Yun's discourses and Dharma words. Stories of six Ch'an masters. The diamond cutter of doubts. A straight talk on the heart Sutra. [BL1493.L813] 74-146510 ISBN 0-87773-009-1 2.75
1. Zen Buddhism. I. Title.

*LU, K'uan Y, 1898- 294.3'927
Ch'an and Zen teaching, edited, translated and explained by Lu K'uan Yu (Charles Luk) [1st Amer. ed.] Berkeley [Calif.] Shambala Pubns., 1973. v. illus. 22 cm. Contents.Contents.—series 3. The Altar Sutra of the Sixth Patriarch. Yung Chia's Song of Enlightenment. The Sutra of Complete Enlightenment. [BL1493.L813] ISBN 0-87773-044-X (v. 3) 3.95 (pbk.)
1. Zen Buddhism. I. Title.
Publisher's address: 1409 Fifth St., Berkeley, CA 94710.

OGATA, Sohaku, 1901- 294.3'927
Zen for the West. For the Buddhist Society of London. Westport, Conn., Greenwood Press [1973, c1959] 182 p. illus. 22 cm. Appendices (p. [79]-[176]): 1. A new translation of the Mu mon kwan.—2. A Zen interpretation of the Tao te ching.—3. List of Chinese characters with Japanese and Chinese transliterations and dates of people, places, and technical terms in Zen for the West and in the Mu mon kwan. Includes bibliographical references. [BQ9265.4.O36 1973] 72-9543 ISBN 0-8371-6583-0 9.50
1. Zen Buddhism. I. Buddhist Society, London. II. Hui-k'ai, Shih, 1183-1260. Wu-men kuan. English. 1959. III. Lao-tzu. Tao te ching. English. 1959. IV. Title.

THE platform sutra of the sixth patriarch. 294.3'927
The text of the Tun-huang manuscript with tr. introd., notes, by Philip B. Yampolsky. New York, Columbia 1967. xii, 216, [30] p. 24cm. (Records of civilization: sources and studies. no. 76) Tr. of (romanized); Liu-tsu ta shih fa pao t'an ching) Includes ed. Chinese text based on the MS. in the Stein Collection of Chinese MSS. in the British Mus. (S5475) Prepd. for the Columbia College Program of trs. from the oriental classics. Wm. Theodore de Bary, ed. Bibliography: p. [191]-204. [BL1432.Z4H8428] 67-11847 8.50
1. Zen Buddhism. 2. 4H8428 294.3'927 I. Hui-Neng, 638-713 II. Yampolsky, Philip B. ed. III. Series.

POWELL, Robert. 294.3'927
Zen and reality : an approach to sanity and happiness on a non-sectarian basis / Robert Powell. New York : Penguin Books, [1977, c1961] p. cm. Originally published by Allen and Unwin, London. Bibliography: p. [BQ9265.6.P68 1977] 77-4379 ISBN 0-14-004532-5 pbk. : 2.95
1. Zen Buddhism. I. Title.

POWELL, Robert. 294.3'927
Zen and reality; an approach to sanity and happiness on a non-sectarian basis. New York, Viking [1975, c1961] 140, [2] p. 20 cm. Reprint of the ed. published by Allen and Unwin, London. Bibliography: p. [141]-[142] [BQ9265.6.P68 1975] 74-5808 ISBN 0-670-00588-6
1. Zen Buddhism. I. Title.

POWELL, Robert. 294.3'927
Zen and reality : an approach to sanity and happiness on a non-sectarian basis / Robert Powell. Harmondsworth, Eng. ; New York [etc.] : Penguin Books, 1977. 142 p. ; 19 cm. Bibliography: p. [141]-142. [BQ9265.4.P68 1977] 77-573996 ISBN 0-14-004532-5 pbk. : 2.50
1. Zen Buddhism. I. Title.

REPS, Paul, 1895- comp. 294.32
Zen flesh, Zen bones; a collection of Zen & pre-Zen writings. Tokyo, Rutland, Vt., C. E. Tuttle Co. [1957] 211 p. illus. 20 cm. [BL1432.Z4R4] 57-10199
1. Zen Buddhism. I. Title.

ROSS, Nancy Wilson, 1905- ed. 294.329
The world of Zen; an East-West anthology. New York, Random House [1960] 362 p. illus. 24 cm. Includes bibliography. [BL1442.Z4R6] 60-12155
1. Zen Buddhism. I. Title.

SMITH, Rosemary Dubpernell, 1929- 294.3'927
The Zen connection / by Rosemary Dubpernell Smith. Escondido, CA : Omni Publishers, c1977. 88 p. : ill. ; 28 cm. [BQ9265.4.S55] 77-19095 ISBN 0-89127-001-9 pbk. : 7.95
1. Zen Buddhism. I. Title.

SOHL, Robert, comp. 294.3'927'08
The gospel according to Zen; beyond the death of God. Robert Sohl [and] Audrey Carr, editors. New York, New American Library [1970] 133 p. illus. 18 cm. (A Mentor book) [BL1493.S64 1970] 72-20165 0.95
1. Zen Buddhism. I. Carr, Audrey, joint comp. II. Title.

*STONE, Justin F. 294.3927
The joys of meditation; a do-it-yourself book of instruction in varied meditation techniques, by Justin F. Stone. Albuquerque, New Mexico, Far West Publishing Co [1973] 94 p. illus., 23 cm. (Sun books) [BL1493] 2.95 (pbk.)
1. Zen Buddhism. I. Title.

STRYK, Lucien, ed. and tr. 294.392708
Zen: poems, prayers, sermons, anecdotes, interviews, selected and translated by Lucien Stryk and Takashi Ikemoto. [1st ed.] Garden City, N.Y., Anchor Books, 1965. xxxvii, 160 p. illus. 19 cm. "A485." [BL1493.S8] 65-20059
1. Zen Buddhism. I. Ikemoto, Takashi, 1906- joint ed. and tr. II. Title.

STRYK, Lucien, ed. and tr. 294.392708
Zen: poems, prayers, sermons, anecdotes, interviews, selected and translated by Lucien Stryk and Takashi Ikemoto. [1st ed.] Garden City, N. Y., Anchor Books, 1965. xxxvii, 160 p. illus. 19 cm. "A485." [BL1493.S8] 65-20059
1. Zen Buddhism. I. Ikemoto, Takashi, 1906- joint ed. and tr. II. Title.

SUZUKI, D. T. 294.329
Zen Buddhism & psychoanalysis. [By] D. T. Suzuki, Erich Fromm, Richard De Martino. New York, Grove [1963, c.1960] 180p. 21cm. (Evergreen E-360) Bibl. 1.95 pap.,
I. Title.

SUZUKI, Daisetz Teitaro, 1870-1966. 294.3'927
The essentials of Zen Buddhism; Selected from the writings of Daisetz T. Suzuki Edited, and with an introd., by Bernard Phillips. Westport, Conn., Greenwood Press [1973, c1962] xl, 544 p. 22 cm. Includes bibliographies. [BQ9265.4.S94 1973] 72-11306 ISBN 0-8371-6649-7 20.00
1. Zen Buddhism. I. Title.

SUZUKI, Daisetz Teitaro, 1870-1966. 294.329
The essentials of Zen Buddhism, selected from the writings of Daisetz T. Suzuki. Edited, and with an introd., by Bernard Phillips. [1st ed.] New York, Dutton, 1962. 544 p. 22 cm. Includes bibliography. [BL1442.Z4S76] 61-5041
1. Zen Buddhism.

SUZUKI, Daisetz Teitaro, 1870-1966. 294.3'927
Introduction to Zen Buddhism, including "A manual of Zen Buddhism / Daisetz Teitaro Suzuki ; foreword by C. G. Jung ; introd. to the Causeway ed. by Charles San. New York : Causeway Books, [1974] 136, 192, [7] leaves of plates : ill. ; 24 cm. Second work has separate t.p. Includes bibliographical references and indexes. [BQ9265.2.S89] 73-85123 ISBN 0-88356-022-4 : 10.00
1. Zen Buddhism. I. Suzuki, Daisetz Teitaro, 1870-1966. A manual of Zen Buddhism. 1974. II. Title.

SUZUKI, Daisetz Teitaro, 1870-1966. 294.32
Zen and Japanese Buddhism. [1st ed.] Tokyo, Japan Travel Bureau; C. E. Tuttle Co., distributors, Tokyo & Rutland, Vt. [1958] 150 p. illus. 19 cm. [BL1440.S85] 58-10641
1. Zen Buddhism. 2. Buddhism—Japan. I. Title.

SWANN, Jeffrey. 294.329
Toehold on Zen. Illustrated by Ekon. [1st ed.] Cleveland, World Pub. Co. [1963, c1962] 122 p. illus. 21 cm. [BL1442.Z4S9] 63-14784
1. Zen Buddhism. I. Title.

TSUNG-KAO, 1089-1163. 294.3'927
Swampland flowers : letters and lectures of Zen Master Ta Hui [i.e. Tsung-kao] ; translated by Christopher Cleary. 1st Evergreen ed. New York : Grove Press, 1977. xxvii, 144 p. ; 21 cm. (An Evergreen book ; E-696) Translation of chuan 31 and 32 of Chi yueh lu. [BQ9265.T77 1977] 77-77853 ISBN 0-394-17011-3 pbk. : 3.95 ISBN 0-394-42195-7 : 7.95
1. Zen Buddhism. 2. Priests, Zen—Correspondence. I. Title.

WATTS, Alan Wilson, 1915- 294.32
The way of Zen. [New York] Pantheon [1957] 236 p. illus. 22 cm. [BL1432.Z4W33] 57-7318
1. Zen Buddhism. I. Title.

WATTS, Alan Wilson, 1915-1973. 200'.8
Three / by Alan Watts. New York : Pantheon Books, [1977] p. cm. Includes bibliographies. [BQ9265.4.W37 1977] 77-76500 ISBN 0-394-41904-9 : 15.00
1. Zen Buddhism. 2. Religion—Philosophy. 3. Sex and religion. 4. Psychotherapy. 5. East and West. I. Title.
Contents omitted

WOODWORTH, Hugh M. 294.3'927
Zen; the turn towards life, by Hugh Woodworth. Boston, Branden Press [1969] 31 p. 22 cm. [BL1493.W6] 68-28824 1.00
1. Zen Buddhism. I. Title.

ZEN and the Ways / 294.3'927
[translated and edited by] Trevor Leggett. London ; Boston : Routledge and K. Paul, 1977 xiii, 258 p. : ill. ; 24 cm. Translations from the Japanese. [BQ9265.4.Z46] 77-30481 ISBN 0-7100-8598-2. 8.75 ISBN 0-7100-8599-0 pbk. : 4.50
1. Zen Buddhism. 2. Koan. I. Leggett, Trevor.

Zen Buddhism—Addresses, essays, lectures.

BLYTH, Reginald Horace. 294.3'927
Zen and Zen classics : selections from R. H. Blyth / compiled and with drawings by Frederick Franck. 1st ed. New York : Vintage Books, c1978. xviii, 289 p. : ill. ; 21 cm. [BQ9266.B55 1978] 77-92641 ISBN 0-394-72489-5 pbk. : 4.95
1. Zen Buddhism—Addresses, essays, lectures. I. Franck, Frederick, 1909- II. Title.

HERRIGEL, Eugen, 1884-1955. 294.3'4
The method of Zen [by] Eugen Herrigel. Ed. by Hermann Toausend. Tr. by R. F. C. Hull. New York, Vintage Books [1974] 124 p. 18 cm. Translation of Der Zen-Weg. Reprint of the ed. published by Pantheon Books, New York. [[BQ9266.H4713 1974]] 74-5120 ISBN 0-394-71244-7 1.95 (pbk.)
1. Zen Buddhism—Addresses, essays, lectures. I. Title.

MERTON, Thomas, 1915-1968. 294.3'927
Zen and the birds of appetite. [New York, New Directions, 1968] ix, 141 p. 21 cm. (A New Directions book) Bibliographical footnotes. [BL1442.Z4M4] 68-25546 5.25
1. Zen Buddhism—Addresses, essays, lectures. I. Title.

SEUNG Sahn. 294.3'927'08
Dropping ashes on the Buddha : the teaching of Zen master Seung Sahn / compiled and edited by Stephen Mitchell. 1st Evergreen ed. New York : Grove Press : distributed by Random House, 1976. xii, 232 p. ; 21 cm. (An Evergreen book) [BQ9266.S48] 75-37236 ISBN 0-8021-4015-7 : 4.95
1. Seung Sahn. 2. Zen Buddhism—Addresses, essays, lectures. I. Title.

SHIBAYAMA, Zenkei, 1894- 294.3'927
A flower does not talk; Zen essays. Translated by Sumiko Kudo. [1st ed.] Rutland, Vt., C. E. Tuttle Co. [1970] 264 p. illus. 19 cm. [BL1493.S48 1970] 79-109404 ISBN 0-8048-0884-8 2.75
1. Zen Buddhism—Addresses, essays, lectures. I. Title.

SUZUKI, Daisetz Teitaro, 1870-1966. 294.3'927
The awakening of Zen / Daisetz Teitaro Suzuki ; edited by Christmas Humphreys. Boulder, Colo. : Prajna Press, 1980. xv, 119 p. : ill. ; 22 cm. [BQ9266.S94 1980] 79-17444 ISBN 0-87773-715-0 pbk. : 4.95
1. Zen Buddhism—Addresses, essays, lectures. I. Humphreys, Christmas, 1901- II. Title.

SUZUKI, Daisetz Teitaro, 1870-1966. 294.329
Essays in Zen Buddhism, first series. New York, Grove Press [1961] 387 p. 21 cm. (Evergreen original,E-309) [BL1432.Z4S8 1961] 61-11477
1. Zen Buddhism—Addresses, essays, lectures.

SUZUKI, Daisetz Teitaro, 1870-1966. 294.3'927'08
The field of Zen; contributions to the Middle way, the journal of the Buddhist Society. Edited, with foreword, by Christmas Humphreys. [1st Perennial library ed.] New York, Harper & Row [1970] xvii, 105 p. ports. 18 cm. (Perennial Library, P 193) [BL1493.S88 1970] 76-17773 0.95
1. Zen Buddhism—Addresses, essays, lectures. I. The Middle way. II. Title.

†SUZUKI, Shosan, 1579-1655. 294.3'927
Selected writings of Suzuki Shosan / translated by Royall Tyler. Ithaca, N.Y. : China-Japan Program, Cornell University, c1977. 280 p. ; 28 cm. (Cornell University East Asia papers ; no. 13) Contents.Contents.—Tyler, R. Introduction.—Suzuki, S. Ninin bikuni (Two nuns).—Suzuki, S. Moanjo (A safe staff for the blind).—Suzuki, S. Bammin tokuyo (Right action for all).—Suzuki, S. Selections from Roankyo (Sayings), recorded by Echu.—Echu. Kaijo monogatari (On the sea). Includes

bibliographical references. [BQ9266.S98] 78-102006 pbk. : 6.00
1. Zen Buddhism—Addresses, essays, lectures. I. Tyler, Royall. II. Series: Cornell University. Cornell University East Asia papers ; no. 13.

Zen Buddhism and humor.

HYERS, M. Conrad. 294.3'927
Zen and the comic spirit [by] Conrad Hyers. Philadelphia, Westminster Press [1974, c1973] 192 p. illus. 21 cm. Includes bibliographical references. [BQ4570.H85H9 1974] 74-628 ISBN 0-664-20705-7 6.95
1. Zen Buddhism and humor. I. Title.
Pbk. 3.95, ISBN 0-664-24989-2.

Zen Buddhism—China.

WATTS, Alan Wilson, 1915- 294.329
The spirit of Zen; a way of life, work, and art in the Far East. New York, Grove Press [1960, c1958] 128 p. illus. 21 cm. (The Wisdom of the East) (An Evergreen book, E-219.) Includes bibliography. [BL1432.Z4W28 1960] 60-7347
1. Zen Buddhism—China. 2. Zen Buddhism—Japan. I. Title.

Zen Buddhism—Controversial literature.

CHANG, Lit-sen, 1904- 294.3'927
Zen-existentialism: the spiritual decline of the West; a positive answer to the hippies. [Nutley, N.J., Presbyterian and Rejormed Pub. Co., 1969] xi, 254 p. 24 cm. Bibliography: p. [241]-254. [BQ9269.C47] 73-156862 5.95
1. Zen Buddhism—Controversial literature. I. Title.

Zen Buddhism—Doctrines.

KASULIS, T. P., 1948- 294.3'4
Zen action/zen person / by T. P. Kasulis. Honolulu : University Press of Hawaii, c1981. xiv, 177 p. ; 22 cm. Includes index. Bibliography: p. [163]-168. [BQ9268.6.K37] 19 80-27858 ISBN 0-8248-0702-2 : 12.75
1. Zen Buddhism—Doctrines. 2. Philosophy, Buddhist. I. Title.

Zen Buddhism—Early works to 1800.

CHAO-CHOU, Shih, 778-897. 294.3'4
Radical Zen : the sayings of Joshu / translated with a commentary by Yoel Hoffmann ; pref. by Hirano Sojo ; [cover ill. and design by Karen Becker]. Brookline, Mass. : Autumn Press ; [New York] : distributed by Random House, c1978. 160 p. ; 23 cm. Includes bibliographical references. [BQ9365.C4513] 77-93523 ISBN 0-394-73512-9 : 5.95
1. Zen Buddhism—Early works to 1800. I. Hoffmann, Yoel. II. Title. III. Title: The sayings of Joshu.

EKAKU, 1686-1769. 294.3'4
The Zen Master Hakuin: selected writings. Translated by Philip B. Yampolsky. New York, Columbia University Press, 1971. xii, 253 p. 24 cm. (Records of civilization: sources and studies, no. 86) Translation of Orategama, Yabukoji, and Hebilichigo (romanized form) Bibliography: p. [235]-238. [BL1442.Z4E3613] 75-145390 ISBN 0-231-03463-6 10.00
1. Zen Buddhism—Early works to 1800. I. Title. II. Series.

HUI-NENG, 638-713. 294.3'82
The Sixth Patriarch's Dharma jewel platform sutra, with the commentary of Tripitaka Master Hua [translated from the Chinese by the Buddhist Text Translation Society]. 2d ed. San Francisco : Sino-American Buddhist Association, 1977. xxviii, 344 p., [1] leaf of plates : ill. ; 22 cm. Translation of Liu tsu ta shih fa pao t'an ching. [BQ9299.H854L613 1977] 78-100307 ISBN 0-917512-19-7 pbk. : 12.50
1. Zen Buddhism—Early works to 1800. I. Hsuan-hua, 1908- II. Title.
Available from: Buddhist Text Translation Society,Gold Mountain Monastery 1731 15th St.,San Francisco,CA 94103.

HUI-NENG, 638-713. 294.3'82
The sutra of Wei Lang (or Hui Neng). Translated from the Chinese by Wong Mou-lam. New ed. by Christmas Humphreys. Westport, Conn., Hyperion Press [1973] 128 p. 22 cm. Reprint of the 1944 ed. published for the Buddhist Society by Luzac & Co., London. [BQ9299.H854L613 1973] 73-879 ISBN 0-88355-073-3 8.50
1. Zen Buddhism—Early works to 1800. I. Wong, Mou-lam, tr. II. Humphreys, Christmas, 638-713. ed. III. Buddhist Society of Great Britain and Ireland. IV. Title.

ISHUAN, Shih, d.867. 294.3'927
The Zen teaching of Rinzai : the record of Rinzai / translated from the Chinese Lin-chi lu by Irmgard Schloegl. Berkeley, Calif. : Shambhala, 1976, c1975. 96 p. ; 23 cm. (The Clear light series) Bibliography: p. 96. [BQ9399.I554L5513 1976] 75-40262 ISBN 0-87773-087-3 pbk. : 3.50
1. Zen Buddhism—Early works to 1800. I. Title.

P'ANG, Yun, ca.740- 294.3'927
808.
The recorded sayings of Layman P'ang; a ninth-century Zen classic [compiled by Yu Ti] Translated from the Chinese by Ruth Fuller Sasaki, Yoshitaka Iriya [and] Dana R. Fraser. [1st ed.] New York, Weatherhill [1971] 109 p. illus. (part col.) 22 cm. Translation of P'ang chu shih yu lu. Bibliography: p. 99-103. [BL1432.Z3P313 1971] 77-157273 ISBN 0-8348-0057-8 5.00
1. Zen Buddhism—Early works to 1800. I. Yu, Ti, d. 818, comp. II. Title.

Zen Buddhism—Essence, genius, nature.

HUMPHREYS, 294.3'927'0942
Christmas, 1901-
A Western approach to Zen; an enquiry. [1st U.S.A. ed.] Wheaton, Ill., Theosophical Pub. House [1972, c1971] 212 p. 23 cm. Bibliography: p. 197. [BL1493.H8 1972] 72-76428 ISBN 0-8356-0211-7 5.95
1. Zen Buddhism—Essence, genius, nature. I. Title.

NHAT Hanh, Thich. 294.3'4'2
Zen keys. Translated from the French by Albert and Jean Low, with an introd. by Philip Kapleau. [1st ed.] Garden City, N.Y., Anchor Press [1974] p. cm. Translation of Clefs pour le Zen. [BQ9265.9.N4513] 74-3556 ISBN 0-385-08066-2 1.95 (pbk.)
1. Zen Buddhism—Essence, genius, nature. I. Title.

SUZUKI, Daisetz 294.3'927
Teitaro, 1870-1966.
What is Zen? Two unpublished essays and a reprint of the 1st ed. of The essence of Buddhism. New York, Harper & Row [1972] xii, 116 p. 18 cm. (Perennial Library) Contents.—Foreword by L. P. Yandell to the unpublished mss.—What is Zen?—Self and the unattainable.—The essence of Buddhism, 1st ed., 1946. [BQ9265.9.S96 1972] 72-169304 ISBN 0-06-080263-4 1.25 (pbk.)
1. Zen Buddhism—Essence, genius, nature. 2. Mahayana Buddhism—Essence, genius, nature. I. Suzuki, Daisetz Teitaro, 1870-1966. The essence of Buddhism. 1st ed. 1972. II. Title.

WIENPAHL, Paul. 294.3'927
Zen diary. New York, Harper & Row [1970] xi, 244 p. 22 cm. [BL1493.W5] 70-109059 6.95
1. Zen Buddhism—Essence, genius, nature. I. Title.

Zen Buddhism—Great Britain—Addresses, essays, lectures.

HUMPHREYS, Christmas, 294.3'4'4
1901-
Zen comes West : the present and future of Zen Buddhism in Western society / Christmas Humphreys. 2nd ed. London : Curzon Press ; Totowa, N.J. : Rowman and Littlefield, 1977. 218 p. : ill. ; 22 cm. Includes index. Bibliography: p. 211-213. [BQ9262.9.G7H85 1977] 77-380185 ISBN 0-87471-951-8 (Rowman) : 8.50
1. Zen Buddhism—Great Britain—Addresses, essays, lectures. I. Title.

Zen Buddhism—History.

DUMOULIN, Heinrich 294.3927
A history of Zen Buddhism. Tr. from German by Paul Peachey. New York, McGraw [1965, c.1963] viii, 335p. illus. 22cm. (McGraw paperbacks in religion and philosophy Bibl. [BL1493.D813] 65-8129 2.95 pap.,
1. Zen Buddhism—Hist. I. Title.

DUMOULIN, Heinrich. 294.329
A history of Zen Buddhism. Translated from the German by Paul Peachey. New York, Pantheon Books [1963] 335 p. illus. 21 cm. Translation of Zen. [BL1442.Z4D83] 62-17386
1. Zen Buddhism—History.

HOOVER, Thomas, 294.3'927'09
1941-
The Zen experience / by Thomas Hoover. New York : New American Library, c1980. 286 p. : ill. ; 21 cm. (A Plume book) Includes index. Bibliography: p. [271]-277. [BQ9262.3.H66] 79-24119 ISBN 0-452-25228-8 pbk. : 4.95
1. Zen Buddhism—History. 2. Priests, Zen—Biography. I. Title.

Zen Buddhism—Japan.

STRYK, Lucien. 294.3'927
Encounter with Zen : writings on poetry and Zen / Lucien Stryk. Chicago : Swallow Press ; Athens, Ohio : Ohio University Press, c1981. p. cm. [BQ9262.9.J3S84] 19 81-9611 21.95 ISBN 0-8040-0406-4 pbk. : 10.95
1. Zen Buddhism—Japan. 2. Priests, Zen—Japan. 3. Zen Buddhists—Japan. 4. Zen poetry—History and criticism. I. Title.

SUZUKI, Daisetz 294.3'927
Teitaro, 1870-1966.
Zen and Japanese culture / Daisetz T. Suzuki. Princeton, N.J. : Princeton University Press, 1970, c1959. xxiii, 478 p., [37] leaves of plates (3 fold.) : ill. ; 23 cm. (Princeton/Bollingen paperbacks ; 221) (Bollingen series ; 64) First ed. published in 1938 under title: Zen Buddhism and its influence on Japanese culture. Includes index. Bibliography: p. [443]-447. [BQ9262.9.J3S9 1970] 75-323168 ISBN 0-691-09849-2. ISBN 0-691-01770-0 pbk.
1. Zen Buddhism—Japan. 2. Japan—Civilization—Zen influences. I. Title. II. Series.

SUZUKI, Daisetz Teitaro, 294.329
1870-1966.
Zen and Japanese culture. [Rev. and enl. 2d ed. New York] Pantheon Books [1959] xxiii, 478 p. 68 plates (incl. ports.) 24 cm. (Bollingen series, 64) First ed. published in 1938 under title: Zen Buddhism and its influence on Japanese culture. Bibliography: p. [443]-447. [BL1442.Z4S8 1959] 58-12174
1. Zen Buddhism—Japan. 2. Japan—Civilization—Zen influences. 3. Philosophy, Japanese. I. Title. II. Series.

Zen Buddhism—Philosophy—Addresses, essays, lectures.

IZUTSU, Toshihiko, 1914- 294.3'4
Toward a philosophy of Zen Buddhism / Toshihiko Izutsu. Boulder, Colo. : Prajna Press, 1982, c1977. xii, 259 p. ; 22 cm. Reprint. Originally published: Tehran : Imperial Iranian Academy of Philosophy, 1977. (Publication / Imperial Iranian Academy of Philosophy ; no. 26) Includes bibliographical references and index. [BQ9268.6.I97 1982] 19 81-84344 ISBN 0-87773-757-6 (pbk.) : 10.00
1. Zen Buddhism—Philosophy—Addresses, essays, lectures. I. Title.

Zen Buddhism—Poetry.

SEUNG Sahn. 821
The bone of space : Zen poems / by Seung Sahn ; compiled by Stanley Lombardo. San Francisco : Four Seasons Foundation ; Eugene, Or. : Distributed by the Subterranean Co., 1982. p. cm. (Wheel series ; 2) [PR9520.9.S4B6 1982] 19 82-2476 ISBN 0-87704-053-2 (pbk.) : 4.95
1. Zen Buddhism—Poetry. I. Lombardo, Stanley. II. Title. III. Series.

Zen Buddhism—Quotations, maxims, etc.

KU tsun su yu lu. 294.3'82
English.
The transmission of the mind outside the teaching / [translated and edited by] Upasaka Lu K'uan Yu (Charles Luk). New York : Grove Press : distributed by Random House, 1975- v. ; 21 cm. (An Evergreen book) "A translation of the Chinese collection of Ch'an texts called Ku tsun su yu lu." Includes bibliographical references. [BQ9267.K8713 1975] 75-15055 ISBN 0-8021-0104-6 pbk. : 2.95 (v. 1)
1. Zen Buddhism—Quotations, maxims, etc. I. Lu, K'uan Yu, 1898- II. Title.

THE Wisdom of the Zen masters 294.3'927 / translated by Irmgard Schloegl. New York : New Directions Pub. Corp., 1976. p. cm. (A New Directions book ; 415) Companion volume to Thomas Merton's The wisdom of the desert and Geoffrey Parriner's The wisdom of the forest. [BQ9267.W57] 75-42115 ISBN 0-8112-0609-2. ISBN 0-8112-0610-6 pbk.
1. Zen Buddhism—Quotations, Maxims, etc. 2. Zen Buddhism—Japan. I. Schloegl, Irmgard.

A Zen forest, sayings 294.3'927 *of the masters* / compiled and translated, with an introd. by Soiku Shigematsu. 1st ed. New York : Weatherhill, 1981. p. cm. Translation of over 1,200 Zen phrases and koans. [BQ9267.Z46] 19 81-31 ISBN 0-8348-0159-0 : 19.95
1. Zen Buddhism—Quotations, maxims, etc. 2. Koan. 3. Zen poetry. I. Shigematsu, Soiku, 1943-

Zen Buddhism—Relations—Christianity.

CALLAWAY, Tucker N. 261.2
Zen way, Jesus way / Tucker N. Callaway. Rutland, Vermont : C. E. Tuttle, 1976. 263 p. ; 20 cm. Includes index. [BQ9269.4.C5C34] 76-6032 8.50
1. Callaway, Tucker N. 2. Zen Buddhism—Relations—Christianity. 3. Christianity and other religions—Zen Buddhism. I. Title.

EUSDEN, John Dykstra. 294.3'927
Zen and Christian, the journey between / John Dykstra Eusden. New York : Crossroad, 1981. p. cm. Includes index. [BQ9269.4.C5E97] 19 81-7837 ISBN 0-8245-0099-7 : 10.95
1. Zen Buddhism—Relations—Christianity. 2. Christianity and other religions—Zen Buddhism. I. Title.

KADOWAKI, Kakichi, 294.3'927
1926-
Zen and the Bible : a priest's experience / J. K. Kadowaki ; translated from the Japanese by Joan Rieck. London ; Boston : Routledge & Kegan Paul, 1979. xii, 180 p. ; 21 cm. Translation of Koan to Seisho no shindoku. [BQ9269.4.C5K313] 19 79-40874 ISBN 0-7100-0402-8 pbk. : 7.95
1. Bible—Criticism, interpretation, etc. 2. Zen Buddhism—Relations—Christianity. 3. Christianity and other religions—Zen Buddhism. 4. Koan. I. Title.

Zen Buddhism—Vietnam—History.

THIEN An, Thich, 294.3'09597
1926-
Buddhism and Zen in Vietnam in relation to the development of Buddhism in Asia / by Thich Thien-An ; edited, annotated, and developed by Carol Smith. Los Angeles : College of Oriental Studies, Graduate School, 1975. 301 p. : ill. ; 19 cm. Includes index. Bibliography: p. 281-289. [BQ9262.9.V5T45] 74-83391 ISBN 0-8048-1144-X : 12.50
1. Zen Buddhism—Vietnam—History. 2. Buddhism—Vietnam—History. I. Title: Buddhism and Zen in Vietnam ...

Zen Buddhists—United States—Biography.

OWENS, Claire Myers. 294.3'927'0924 B
Zen and the lady : memoirs—personal and transpersonal in a world in transition / by Claire Myers Owens. New York : Baraka Books, c1979. v, 306 p. ; 23 cm. Includes index. Bibliography: p. 299-302. [BQ976.W457A35] 79-50288 ISBN 0-88238-996-3 : 5.95
1. Owens, Claire Myers. 2. Zen Buddhists—United States—Biography. 3. Spiritual life (Zen Buddhism) I. Title.

Zen literature.

KAPLEAU, Philip, 1912- ed. 294.3927
The three pillars of Zen; teaching, practice, and enlightenment.Comp., ed., with trs., introds., notes by Philip Kapleau. Boston, Beacon [1967, c.1965] xix, 362p. 21cm. (BP 242) [BL1493.K3] 2.45 pap.,
1. Zen literature. I. Title.

KAPLEAU, Philip 1912-
The three pillars of Zen: teaching, practice, and enlightenment. Compiled and edited, with translations, introductions and notes, by Philip Kapleau. Foreword by Huston Smith. Boston, Beacon Press [1967] [xx] 363 p. illus. 24 cm. (A Beacon paperback) "First published as a Beacon paperback in 1967 from the second printing, with revisions, 1967." 68-96735
1. Zen literature. I. Title.

RYOKAN, 1758-1831. 895.6'13
The Zen poems of Ryokan / selected and translated with an introduction, biographical sketch, and notesby Nobuyuki Yuasa. Princeton, N.J. : Princeton University Press, c1981. p. cm. Bibliography: p. [PL797.6.A294 1981] 19 80-8585 ISBN 0-691-06466-0 : 20.00
I. Yuasa, Nobuyuki, 1932- II. [Poems.] English. Selections III. Title.

Zen literature—Japan.

LEGGETT, Trevor. 294.3'927
The tiger's cave : translations of Japanese Zen texts / Trevor Leggett. London : Routledge & K. Paul, 1977. 192 p., [2] leaves of plates : ill. ; 22 cm. [BQ9264.4.J3L43 1977] 78-312218 ISBN 0-7100-8636-9 pbk. : 5.50
1. Zen literature—Japan. I. Title.
Distributed by Routledge & Kegan Paul, Boston

LEGGETT, Trevor. 294.3'927
Zen and the ways / Trevor Leggett. Boulder, Colo. : Shambhala ; [New York] : distributed in the U.S. by Random House, 1978. xiii, 258 p. : ill. ; 23 cm. Includes index. [BQ9264.4.J3L44] 77-6015 ISBN 0-87773-107-1 pbk. : 5.95
1. Zen literature—Japan. I. Title.

Zen meditations.

ENCOUNTERS in yoga and Zen : meetings of cloth and stone / [compiled by] Trevor Leggett. London ; Boston : Routledge & K. Paul, 1982. p. cm. [BQ9289.5.E53 1982] 19 82-15131 ISBN 0-7100-9241-5 : 9.00 294.3'443
1. Zen meditations. 2. Meditations. I. Leggett, Trevor.

THE Grace of Zen : 294.3'4'43
Zen texts for meditation / by Ito Tenzaa Chuya ... [et al.] ; introduced by Karlfried Durckheim ; with a pref. by Dom Aelred Graham ; [translation by John Maxwell]. New York : Seabury Press, 1977,c1976. 107 p. : ill. ; 21 cm. "A Crossroad book." [BQ9289.5.G7] 76-52584 ISBN 0-8164-2151-X pbk. : 3.95
1. Zen meditations. I. Ito, Chuya.

REPS, Paul, 1895- 294.3'4'43
Juicing : Words and brushwork / by Paul Reps. Garden City, N.Y. : Anchor Books, 1978. 111 p. : ill. ; 21 cm. [BQ9289.5.R46] 77-82770 ISBN 0-385-13250-6 : 3.50
1. Zen meditations. I. Title.

Zen (Sect)

AITKEN, Robert 294.329
Zen training, a personal account. Honolulu 16, Hawaii, P. O. Box 7025 Old Island Books, [c.1960] 26p. 23cm. 60-4133 1.00 pap.,
1. Zen. (Sect) I. Title.

AMES, Van Meter, 1898- 294.329
Zen and American thought. Honolulu, Univ. of Hawaii Pr. [c.]1962. 293p. 24cm. Bibl. 62-12672 4.50
1. Zen (Sect) 2. Philosophy, American. I. Title.

BECKER, Ernest. 294.329
Zen: a rational critique. [1st ed.] New York, Norton [1961] 192p. 22cm. Includes bibliography. [BL1442.Z4B4] 61-7474
1. Zen (Sect) I. Title.

BECKER, Ernest 294.329
Zen: a rational critique. New York, Norton [c.1961] 192p. Bibl. 61-7474 4.00
1. Zen (Sect) I. Title.

BENOIT, Hubert. 294.32
The supreme doctrine; psychological studies in Zen thought. Foreword by Aldous Huxley. New York, Pantheon Books [1955] 248p. illus. 22cm. [BL1432.Z4B42] 55-10286
1. Zen (Sect) I. Title.

BLYTH, Reginald Horace 294.329
Zen and Zen classics. [Dist. New York, Perkins, 1962, c.1960] 225p. illus. 19cm. Contents.v. 7. Zen essays, Christianity, Sex, Society, etc. Bibl. 62-51117 2.75
1. Zen (Sect) I. Title.

BRIGGS, William A. 1873- ed 294.329
Anthology of Zen. Foreword by William Barrett. New York, Grove [c.1961] 301p. (Evergreen original, E-289) 61-6714 2.95 pap.,
1. Zen (Sect) I. Title.

FROMM, Erich, ed. 294.329
Zen Buddhism & psychoanalysis [by] D. T. Suzuki, Erich Fromm, and Richard De Martino. New York, Harper [c.1960] viii, 180p. 22cm. (bibl. footnotes) 60-5293 4.00 bds.,
1. Zen (Sect). 2. Psychoanalysis. I. Suzuki, Daisetz Teitaro, 1870— II. Title.

FROMM, Erich 1900-
Zen Buddism & psychoanalysis [by] D. T. Suzuki, Erich Fromm, and Richard Martino. New York, Grove Press [1963] 180 p. (Evergreen books) 64-70668
1. Zen (Sect) 2. Psychoanalysis. I. Title.

FROMM, Erich 1900-
Zen Buddism & psychoanalysis [by] D. T. Suzuki, Erich Fromm, and Richard Martino. New York, Grove Press [1963] 180 p. (Evergreen books) 64-70668
1. Zen (Sect) 2. Psychoanalysis. I. Title.

GRAHAM, Aelred, 1907- 294.329
Zen Catholicism; a suggestion. New York, Harcourt [c.1963] 228p. 21cm. Bibl. 63-10596 4.95
1. Zen (Sect) 2. Catholic Church—Relations—Buddhism. I. Title.

GRAHAM, Aelred, 1907- 294.329
Zen Catholicism: a suggestion. New York, Harcourt [1967, c.1963] xxv, 228p. 21cm. (Harvest bk., HB118) Bibl. 1.95 pap.,
1. Zen (Sect) 2. Catholic Church—Relations—Buddhism. I. Title.

HAYAKAWA, Sessue Kintaro 294.329
Zen showed me the way . . . to peace, happiness, and tranquility [tr. from te Japanese] Edited by Croswell Bowen. Indianapolis, Bobbs-Merill [c.1960] 256p. illus. 22cm. 60-13600 3.95 bds.,
1. Zen (Sect) I. Title.

HAYAKAWA, Sessue Kintaro, 1889- 294.329
Zen showed me the way ... to peace, happiness, and tranquility. Edited by Croswell Bowen. [1st ed.] Indianapolis, Bobbs-Merrill [1960] 256p. illus. 22cm. [BL1442Z4H3] 60-13600
1. Zen (Sect) I. Title.

HUI-NENG, 638-713. 294.3282
The sutra of the sixth patriarch on the pristine orthodox dharma. Translated from the Chinese by Paul F. Fung [and] George D. Fung. San Francisco, Buddha's Universal Church [1964] 187 p. 23 cm. [BL1432.Z4H843] 65-1175
1. Zen (Sect) I. Fung, Paul F., tr. II. Fung, George D., tr. III. Title.

HUMPHREYS, Christmas, 1901-
Zen Buddhism. New York, Macmillan [1962] 175 p. Includes bibliographies. 64-19896
1. Zen (Sect) I. Title.

HUMPHREYS, Christmas, [Travers Christmas Humphreys] 294.329
Zen comes West; the present and future of Zen Buddhism in Britain. New York, Macmillan, 1960[ ] 207p. illus. 23cm. 60-3885 4.75
1. Zen (Sect) I. Title.

HUMPHREYS, Christmas [Travers Christmas Humphreys 1910- 294.32
Zen Buddhism. New York, Macmillan [1962] 175p. Bibl. 1.25 pap.,
1. Zen (Sect.) I. Title.

LEGGETT, Trevor, ed. and tr. 294.329
A first Zen reader. Rutland, Vt., C. E. Tuttle Co. [1960] 236p. illus. (part col.) 60-12739 3.75 bds.,
1. Zen (Sect) I. Title.

LINSSEN, Robert 294.329
Living Zen. Pref. by Christmas Humphreys. Foreword by R. Godel. Tr. [from French] by Diana Abrahams-Curiel. London, Allen & Unwin [dist. Mystic, Conn., Verry, 1964, c.1958] 348p. illus. 23cm. Bibl. A59 6.00
1. Zen (Sect) 2. Buddha and Buddhism. I. Title.

LINSSEN, Robert 294.329
Living Zen. Pref. by Christmas Humphreys. Foreword by R. Godel. Translated [from the French] by Diana Abrahams-Curiel. New York, Grove Press [1960, c.1958] 348p. illus. 21cm. (An Evergreen book, E-203) (Includes bibliography.) 60-198 2.25 pap.,
1. Zen (Sect) 2. Buddha and Buddhism. I. Title.

LIVING Zen.
Preface by Christmas Humphreys. Foreword by Dr. R. Godel. Translated by Diana Abrahams-Curiel. New York, Macmillan [c1958] 348p.
1. Zen (Sect) 2. Buddha and Buddhism. I. Linssen, Robert.

MANUAL of Zen Buddhism.
London, New York, Published for the Buddhist Society, by Rider [1956] 192p. illus. 19cm. (His Complete works) 'First published 1950.'
1. Zen (Sect) 2. Buddha and Buddhism—China. 3. Buddha and Buddhism— Sacred books (Selections: Extracts, etc.) I. Suzuki, Daisetz Teitaro, 1870- II. Title: Zen Buddhism.

OGATA, Sohaku, 1901- 294.329
Zen for the West [Pub.] for the Buddhist Soc. of London. New York [Apollo Eds., 1962, c.1959] 182p. 20cm. (A60) 1.65 pap.,
1. Lau-tzu. Tao te ching. 2. Zen (Sect) I. Hui-Kiai, fl. 13th cent. II. Buddhist Society, London. III. Title.

OGATA, Sohaku, 1901- 294.329
Zen for the West. For the Buddhist Society of London. New York, Dial Press, 1959. 182p. illus., port. 22cm. Appendices (p. [79]- [176]): 1. A new translation of the Mu mon kwan.--2. A Zen interpretation of the Tao te ching.--3. List of Chinese characters with Japanese and Chinese transliterations and dates of people, places, and technical terms in Zen for the West and in the Mu mon kwan. [BL1442.Z4O37] 59-13401
1. Lao-tzu. Tao te ching. 2. Zen (Sect) I. Hui-k'ai. fl. 13th cent. my mon kwan II. Buddhist Society, London. III. Title.

ORYU, 1720-1813 294.329
The iron flute; 100 Zen koan. With commentary by Genro Fugai, and Nyogen. Tr. and ed. by Nyogen Senzaki, Ruth Strout McCandless. Illus. by Toriichi Murashima. Rutland, Vt., Charles E. Tuttle Co. [1961] 175p. illus. Bibl. 60-11512 3.95
1. Zen (Sect.) I. Senzaki, Nyogen, ed. and tr. II. Title.

PETER Pauper Press, Mount Vernon, N. Y. 294.329
Zen Buddhism; an introduction to Zen, with stories, parables and koan riddles of the Zen masters. Decorated with figures from old Chinese ink- paintings. Mount Vernon, N. Y. [1959] 61p. col. illus. 19cm. [BL1432.Z4P4] 59-33730
1. Zen (Sect) I. Title.

POWELL, Robert 294.329
Zen and reality; an approach to sanity and happiness on a non-sectarian basis. [Dist. New York, Taplinger, 1962, c.1961] 140p. 23cm. Bibl. 61-65668 3.95 bds.,
1. Krishnamurti, Jiddu, 1895- 2. Zen (Sect) I. Title.

REPS, Paul, 1895- comp. 294.32
Zen flesh, Zen bones: a collection of Zen & pre-Zen writings. Garden City, N.Y., Doubleday [1961] 174p. illus. (Anchor bk., A233) .95 pap.,
1. Zen (Sect) I. Title.

ROSS, Nancy Wilson, 1905- ed. 294.329
The world of Zen; an East-West anthology. New York, Random [1965, c.1960] 362p. illus. 21cm. Bibl. [BL1442.Z4R6] 3.95 pap.,
1. Zen (Sect) I. Title.

SENZAKI, Nyogen, ed. and tr. 294.32
Buddhism and Zen, compiled, edited, and translated by Nyogen Senzaki and Ruth Strout McCandless. New York, Philosophical Library [1953] 91p. 22cm. 'Sho-do-ka, by Yoka-daishi': p. 31-72. Bibliography: p. 88. [BL1442.Z4S4] 53-7898
1. Zen (Sect) I. Hauan-chileh, d, 713 Sho-do-ka. II. McCandless, Ruth Strout, joint ed. and tr. III. Title.

SENZAKI, Nyogen, comp. 294.32
101 Zen stories, transcribed by Nyogen Senzaki and Paul Reps. Philadelphia, David McKay company [1940] 126 p. 19 cm. [BL1455.S4] 40-14174
1. Zen (Sect) I. Reps, Saladin Paul, 1895- joint comp. II. Title.

THE supreme doctrine;
psychological studies in Zen thought. Foreword by Aldous Huxley. New York, Viking Press [1959, c1955] xv, 248p. 20cm. (Compass Books C43)
1. Zen (Sect) I. Benoit, Hubert.

SUZUKI, Daisetz Teitaro, 1870- 294.329
Essays in Zen Buddhism, first series. New York, Grove Press [1961] 387p. (Evergreen original, E-309) 61-11477 2.95 pap.,
1. Zen (Sect) 2. Buddha and Buddhism—China. I. Title.

SUZUKI, Daisetz Teitaro, 1870- 294.3
Essays in Zen Buddhism (second series) With 25 collotype reproductions of old masters. [Edited by Christmas Humphreys] Boston, Beacon Press, 1952. 348p. plates. 19cm. (His Complete works) Bibliographical footnotes. [BL1430.S] A54
1. Zen (Sect) 2. Buddha and Buddhism—China. I. Title.

SUZUKI, Daisetz Teitaro, 1870- 294.32
Essays in Zen Buddhism (third series) London, New York, Published for the Buddhist Society by Rider [1953] 367p. illus. 19cm. (His Complete works) [BL1430.S8 3d series 1953] 54-2080
1. Zen (Sect) 2. Buddha and Buddhism—China. I. Title.

SUZUKI, Daisetz Teitaro, 1870- 294.32
Essays in Zen Buddhism, first serins. London, New York, Published for the Buddhist Society by Rider [1949] 383 p. illus. 19 cm. (His Complete works) [BL1430.S8 1st ser. 1949] 51-17279
1. Zen (Sect) 2. Buddha and Buddhism—China. I. Title. II. Title: Zen Buddhism, Essays in.

SUZUKI, Daisetz Teitaro, 1870- 294.329
The essentials of Zen Buddhism, selected

from the writings of daisetz T. New York, Dutton, 1962. 544 p. 22 cm. Includes bibliography. [BL1442.Z4S76] 61-5041
1. Zen (Sect) I. Title. II. Title: Suzuki.

SUZUKI, Daisetz Teitaro, 1870- 294.32
An introduction to Zen Buddhism. With a foreword by C. G. Jung. London, New York, Published for the Buddhist Society by Rider [1949] 136 p. 19 cm. (His Complete works) [BL1430.S83 1949a] 51-18122
1. Zen (Sect) 2. Buddha and Buddhism—China. 3. Monasticism and religious orders, Buddhist. I. Title.

SUZUKI, Daisetz Teitaro, 1870- 294.32
An introduction to Zen Buddhism. With a foreword by C. G. Jung. New York, Philosophical Library [1949] 136 p. 19 cm. (His Complete works) [BL1430.S78 1949] 49-9310
1. Zen (Sect) 2. Buddha and Buddhism—China. 3. Monasticism and religious orders, Buddhist. I. Title.

SUZUKI, Daisetz Teitaro, 1870- 294.3
Living by Zen. London, New York, Rider [1950] 187 p. 19 cm. (His Complete works) [BL1430.S785] A51
1. Zen (Sect) 2. Buddha and Buddhism — China. I. Title.

SUZUKI, Daisetz Teitaro, 1870- 294.32
Manual of Zen Buddhism. London, New York, Published for the Buddhist Society, by Rider [1950] 192p. illus. 19cm (His Complete works) [BL1430.S84 1950] 54-25783
1. Zen (Sect) 2. Buddha and Buddhism—China. 3. Buddha and Buddhism— Sacred books (Selections: Extracts, etc.) 4. Buddha and Buddhism. 5. Monasticism and religious orders, Buddhist. I. Title. II. Title: Zen Buddhism.

SUZUKI, Daisetz Teitaro, 1870- 294.32
Manual of Zen Buddhism. London, New York, Published for the Buddhist Society, by Rider [1950] 192 p. illus. 19 cm. (His Complete works) [BL1430.S84 1950] 54-25783
1. Zen (Sect) 2. Buddha and Buddhism—China. 3. Buddha and Buddhism—Sacred books (Selection: Extractions, etc.) 4. Buddha and Buddhism. 5. Monasticism and religious orders, Buddhist. I. Title. II. Title: Zen Buddhism.

SUZUKI, Daisetz Teitaro, 1870- 294.329
Manual of Zen Buddhism. New York, Grove Press [1960] 192 p. illus. 21 cm. (Evergreen original, E-231) [BL1432.Z4S82 1960] 60-7637
1. Zen (Sect) 2. Buddha and Buddhism—China. 3. Buddha and Buddhism—Sacred books (Selections: Extracts, etc.) 4. Buddha and Buddhism. 5. Monasticism and religious orders, Buddhist. I. Title. II. Title: Zen Buddhism.

*SUZUKI, Daisetz Teitaro, 1870- 294.32
Studies in Zen. Ed. by Christmas Humphreys [New York, Dell, 1964, c.1955] 210p. 20cm. (Delta bk. 8371) 1.85 pap.,
1. Zen (Sect) I. Title.

SUZUKI, Daisetz Teitaro, 1870- 294.32
Studies in Zen. London, New York, Published for the Buddhist Society by Rider [1955] 212p. port. 19cm. (His Complete works) [BL1442.Z4S78 1955a] 56-3476
1. Zen (Sect) I. Title.

SUZUKI, Daisetz Teitaro, 1870- 294.32
Studies in Zen. Edited by Christmas Humphreys. New York, Philosophical Library [1955] 212p. illus. 19cm. [BL1442.Z4S78] 55-14253
1. Zen (Sect) I. Title.

SUZUKI, Daisetz Teitaro, 1870- 294.32
Zen Buddhism, selected writings. Edited by William Barret. [1st ed.] Garden City, N.Y., Doubleday, 1956. 294 p. 18 cm. (Doubleday anchor books, A90) [BL1430.S848] 56-9406
1. Zen (Sect) 2. Buddha and Buddhism—China. I. Title.

SUZUKI, Daisetz Teitaro, 1870- 294.32
The Zen doctrine of no-mind; the significance of the Sutra of Hui-neng (Wei-lang) London, New York, Published for the Buddist Society, by Rider [1949] 155 p. diagrs. 19 cm. (His Complete works) [BL1430.S85] 51-18119
1. Zen (Sect) 2. Buddha and Buddhism—China. 3. Hul-neng, 638-713. Liu-tsu-ta-shih-fa-pao-t,an-ching. I. Title.

WATTS, Alan Wilson, 1915- 294.32
The way of Zen. New York, Random [1965, c.1957] xvii, 236p. illus. 21cm. (Vintage Giant, v-298) [BL1432.Z4W33] 1.95 pap.,
*1. Zen. *Sect) I. Title.*

WATTS, Alan Wilson, 1915-
The way of Zen. [New York] New American Library [1959] 224 p. illus. 18 cm. (Mentor book, MD273)
1. Zen (Sect) I. Title.

ZEN
[by] D. T. Suzuki [and others. Chicago, University of Chicago Press [1958] 110p. 23cm. Its Vol. 12, no. 2, summer 1958. Cover title.
1. Zen (Sect) I. Chicago review. II. Suzuki, Daistez Daistetz Teitaro, 1870-

ZEN flesh, Zen bones;
a collection of Zen & pre- Zen writings. Garden City, N. Y., Doubleday Anchor, 1961. xv, 174p. (Doubleday Anchor book A233)
1. Zen (Sect) I. Reps, Paul, 1895-

THE Zen teaching of Huang Po on the transmission of mind; being the teaching of the Zen master Huang Po as recorded by the scholar P'ei Hsiu of the T'ang dynasty. Rendered into English by John Blofeld (Chu Ch'an) New York, Grove Press [1959, c1958] 135p. 22cm. (Evergreen books. E-171) 'A complete translation of the Huang Po chu'an [i. e. Ch'uan] hsiu [i. e. hsin] fa yao, including the previously unpublished Wan Ling Record containing dialogues, sermons and anecdotes.'
1. Zen sect. I. Huang-po, fl. 842-850. II. P'ei, Hsiu, fl. 842-859. III. Blofeld, John Eaton Calthorpe, 1913- tr.

Zen (Sect) Catholic Church—Relations—Buddhism.

GRAHAM, Aelred, 1907- 294.329
Zen Catholicism; a suggestion. [1st ed.] New York, Harcourt, Brace & World [1963] 228 p. 21 cm. [BL1442.Z4G7] 63-10596
1. Zen (Sect) 2. Catholic Church — Relations — Buddhism. I. Title.

Zen (Sect) — Dictionaries.

WOOD, Ernest, 1883- 294.329
Zen dictionary. New York, Philosophical Library [1962] 165 p. 22 cm. Bibliography: p. 163-165. [BL1403.W6] 62-12828
1. Zen (Sect) — Dictionaries. I. Title.

WOOD, Ernest, 1883-
Zen dictionary. [1st paperbound ed.] New York, Citadel Press [1962] 165 p. 22 cm. Bibliography: p. 163-165. 67-26464
1. Zen (Sect) — Dictionaries. I. Title.

Zen (Sect)—History

DUMOULIN, Heinrich 294.329
A history of Zen Buddhism. Tr. from German by Paul Peachey. New York, Pantheon [c.1959, 1963] 325p. illus. 21cm. Bibl. 62-17386 7.50
1. Zen (Sect)—Hist. I. Title.

Zeoli, Anthony.

ZEOLI, Anthony. 269'.2'0924 B
Free forever : the autobiography of Anthony Zeoli / with Gerald S. Strober. Old Tappan, N.J. : Revell, c1980. 159 p. : ill. ; 22 cm. [BV4935.Z4A34] 80-12864 7.95
1. Zeoli, Anthony. 2. Converts—United States—Biography. 3. Evangelists—United States—Biography. I. Strober, Gerald S., joint author. II. Title.

Zervas, Annella, 1900-1926.

KRITZECK, James. 922.273
Ticket for eternity; a life of Sister Annella Zervas, O. S. B. Collegeville, Minn., St. John's Abbey Press, 1957. 107p. illus. 19cm. [BX4705.Z37K7] 57-49204
1. Zervas, Annella, 1900-1926. I. Title.

Zeus.

COOK, Arthur Bernard, 1868-1952 292.211
Zeus; a study in ancient religion [v.1; v.2,pts.1&2] New York, Biblo & Tannen, 1965. 3v. (885; 1397p.) illus. (pt. fold. in pocket) plans, col. plates. 24cm. Reprint of the work first pub. 1914-40. Contents.v.1. Zeus, god of the bright sky. -- v.2. Zeus, god of the dark sky. Bibl. [BL820.J8C62] 64-25839 v.1, 37.50; v.2, pts.1&2, set, 75.00
1. Zeus. 2. Cultus, Greek. 3. Sun-worship. 4. Classical antiquities. 5. Folk literature—Themes, moties. I. Title.

HARRIS, James Rendel, 1852-
Picus who is also Zeus, by Rendel Harris. Cambridge [Eng.] University press, 1916. x p., 1 l., 76 p. 23 cm. "The present volume is a continuation of the one which was published in 1913 under the title of Boanerges, much in the same way as Boanerges was the expansion and extension of the previous volumes dealing with the Dioscuri in Christian legend and the Cult of the Heavenly Twins."--Introd. [BL442.H3] 18-5845
I. Title.

KERENYI, Karoly, 1897-1973. 292'.2'11
Zeus and Hera : archetypal image of father, husband, and wife / C. Kerenyi ; translated from the German by Christopher Holme. Princeton, N.J. : Princeton University Press, [1975] xvii, 211 p. ; 26 cm. (Archetypal images in Greek religion ; v. 5) "Translated from the original manuscript of the author. Subsequently published in German: Zeus und Hera: Urbild des Vaters, des Gatten und der Frau." Includes index. Bibliography: p. 183-195. [BL820.J8K4713] 74-23858 ISBN 0-691-09864-6 : 13.50
1. Zeus. 2. Hera. I. Title. II. Series. III. Bollingen series ; 65

PARKE, Herbert William, 1903- 292'.2'11
The oracles of Zeus: Dodona, Olympia, Ammon, by H. W. Parke. Cambridge, Harvard University Press, 1967. x, 294 p. illus. 23 cm. Includes bibliographical references. [BL820.J8] 68-1424
1. Zeus. 2. Oracles, Greek. 3. Cultus, Greek. I. Title.

PARKE, Herbert William, 1903- 292'.2'11
The oracles of Zeus: Dodona, Olympia, Ammon, by H. W. Parke. Cambridge, Harvard University Press, 1967. x, 294 p. illus. 23 cm. Includes bibliographical references. [BL820.J8] 68-1424
1. Zeus. 2. Oracles, Greek. 3. Cultus, Greek. I. Title.

Zeus (Geeek deity) Juvenile literature.

GATES, Doris, 1901- 292'.2'11
Lord of the sky: Zeus. Illustrated by Robert Handville. [1st ed.] New York, Viking Press [1972] 126 p. illus. 25 cm. A retelling of the Greek myths centered around Zeus including the tales of Europa, King Minos, and others. [PZ8.1.G1684Lo] 72-80514 ISBN 0-670-44051-5 4.95
1. Zeus—Juvenile literature. 2. [Zeus.] 3. [Mythology, Greek.] I. Handville, Robert, illus. II. Title.

Zeus (Greek deity)—Juvenile literature.

GATES, Doris, 1901- 292'.211
Lord of the sky, Zeus / Doris Gates ; illustrated by Robert Handville. Harmondsworth, Middlesex, England ; New York, N.Y. : Penguin Books, 1982, c1972. 126 p. : ill. ; 20 cm. Originally published: New York : Viking Press, 1972. A retelling of the Greek myths centered around Zeus, including the tales of Europa, King Minos, and others. [BL820.J8G37 1982] 19 82-7713 ISBN 0-14-031532-2 pbk. : 2.95
1. Zeus (Greek deity)—Juvenile literature. 2. [Zeus (Greek deity)] 3. [Mythology, Greek.] I. Handville, Robert, ill. II. Title.

Zezuru (Bantu people)—Religion.

FRY, Peter. 279'.6
Spirits of protest : spirit-mediums and the articulation of consensus among the Zezuru of Southern Rhodesia (Zimbabwe) / Peter Fry. Cambridge, Eng. ; New York : Cambridge University Press, c1976. viii, 145 p. ; 24 cm. (Cambridge studies in social anthropology ; 14) Includes index. Bibliography: p. 133-136. [BL2480.Z4F79] 75-20832 ISBN 0-521-21052-6 : 10.95
1. Zezuru (Bantu people)—Religion. 2. Spiritualism—Zimbabwe African People's Union. I. Title.

Zhabotinskii, Vladimir Evgen'evich, 1880-1940.

SCHECHTMAN, Joseph B., 1891- 922.96
Fighter and prophet; the Vladimir Jabotinsky story. New York, T.Yoseloff [c.1961] 643p. illus. Contents.[v.2,54 The last Years. Bibl. 55-11785 7.50
1. Zhabotinskii, Vladimir Evgen'evich, 1880-1940. I. Title.

Zia-ba-Bsam-'grub, Kasi, 1868-1922, tr.

BARDOTHODOE. 294.32
The Tibetan book of the dead; or, The after-death experiences on the Bardo plane, according to Lama Kazi Dawa-Samdup's English rendering, by W. Y. Evans-Wentz. With foreword by Sir John Woodroffe. 2d ed. London, New York, Oxford Univ. Press, 1949. i., 248 p. illus., plates, port., facsim. 23 cm. [BL1411.B3E6 1949] 51-4897
1. Zia-ba-Bsam-'grub, Kasi, 1868-1922, tr. I. Wentz, Walter Yeeling Evans, ed. II. Title.

Ziegenbalg, Bartholomaeus, 1683-1719.

ZORN, H. M., 1873- 922.454
... Bartholomaeus Ziegenbalg, by H. M. Zorn. St. Louis, Mo., Concordia publishing house, 1933. 150 p. illus. (incl. 2 port., map, 2 facsim.) 19 cm. (Men and missions ...x) [BV3269.Z5Z6] 33-7487
1. Ziegenbalg, Bartholomaeus, 1683-1719. I. Title.

Ziegler, Edward Krusen, 1903-

ZIEGLER, Edward Krusen, 1903- 286'.5 B
A tapestry of grace / Edward K. Ziegler. Elgin, Ill. : Brethren Press, [1980] p. cm. Includes index. [BX7843.Z53A35] 79-25331 ISBN 0-87178-834-9 pbk. : 5.95
1. Ziegler, Edward Krusen, 1903- 2. Church of the Brethren—Clergy—Biography. 3. Clergy—United States—Biography. I. Title.

Ziglar, Zig.

ZIGLAR, Zig. 248'.48'61
Confessions of a happy Christian / by Zig Ziglar ; foreword by W. A. Criswell. Gretna, La. : Pelican Pub. Co., 1978. 198 p. ; 22 cm. [BV4501.2.Z54] 78-6729 ISBN 0-88289-196-0 : 5.95
1. Ziglar, Zig. 2. Christian life—Baptist authors. I. Title.

Zimmer, Norma.

†ZIMMER, Norma. 783.7'092'4 B
Norma / Norma Zimmer. Wheaton, Ill. : Tyndale House Publishers, 1976. xii, 368 p., [18] leaves of plates : ill. ; 22 cm. Autobiographical. [ML420.Z55A3] 76-42117 ISBN 0-8423-4716-X : 7.95
1. Zimmer, Norma. 2. Gospel musicians—United States—Biography. I. Title.

Zimmerli, Walther, 1907- —Addresses, essays, lectures.

CANON and authority : 221.1'2
essays in Old Testament religion and theology / edited by George W. Coats and Burke O. Long ; with contributions by Peter R. Ackroyd ... [et al.]. Philadelphia : Fortress Press, c1977. xvi, 190 p. ; 24 cm. Includes bibliographical references and indexes. [BS480.C34] 76-62614 ISBN 0-8006-0501-2 : 13.50
1. Zimmerli, Walther, 1907- —Addresses, essays, lectures. 2. Bible. O.T.—Evidences, authority, etc.—Addresses, essays, lectures. 3. Bible. O.T.—Canon—Addresses, essays, lectures. 4. Bible. O.T.—Hermeneutics—Addresses, essays, lectures. I. Coats, George W. II. Long, Burke O.

Zinza (African people)—Religion.

BJERKE, Svein. 299'.683
Religion and misfortune : the Bacwezi complex and the other spirit cults of the Zinza of northwestern Tanzania / Svein Bjerke. Oslo : Universitetsforlaget ; New York : Columbia University Press, [distributor], c1981. vii, 318 p. : ill. ; 22 cm. Bibliography: p. 314-318. [BL2480.Z56B55 1981] 19 81-189510 ISBN 82-00-05681-3 : 27.00
1. Zinza (African people)—Religion. 2. Spirits. I. Title.

Zinzendorf, Nicolaus Ludwig, graf von, 1700-1760.

ADDISON, William George.
The renewed church of the United brethren, 1722-1930, by William George Addison...Published for the Church historical society. London, Society for promoting Christian knowledge; New York [etc.] The Macmillan co., 1932. 228 p. 22 1/2 cm. [Church historical society. Publications. New series, 8] "Thesis approved for the degree of doctor of philosophy in the University of London." Bibliographical foot-notes. A 41
1. Zirsendorf, Nicolaus Ludwig graf von, 1700-1760. 2. Moravians in Great Britain. 3. Christian union. 4. Zinsendorf, Nieslaus Ludwign, graf von, 1700-1760. I. Title.

ADDISON, William George.
The renewed church of the United brethren, 1722-1930, by William George Addison ... Published for the Church historical society. London, Society for promoting Christian knowledge; New York and Toronto, The Macmillan co., 1932. 228 p. 22 1/2 cm. [Church historical society. Publications. New series, 9] "Thesis approved for the degree of doctor of philosophy in the University of London." Bibliographical foot-notes. [BX8569.G7A3] A 41
1. Zinzendorf, Nicolaus Ludwig, graf von, 1700-1760. 2. Moravians in Great Britain. 3. Moravian church—Relations—Church of England. 4. Church of England—Relations—Moravian church. I. Title.

LEWIS, Arthur James 922.443
Zinzendorf, the ecumenical pioneer; a study in the Moravian contribution to Christian mission and unity. Philadelphia, Westminster [c.1962] 208p. illus. 23cm. Bibl. 63-7179 3.75
1. Zinzendorf, Nicolaus, Ludwig, Graf von, 1700-1760. 2. Christian union— Hist. I. Title.

MEZEZERS, Valdis. 274.7'4
The Herrnhuterian pietism in the Baltic, and its outreach into America and elsewhere in the world / by Valdis Mezezers. North Quincy, Mass. : Christopher Pub. House, c1975. 151 p., [1] leaf of plates : ill. ; 20 cm. Bibliography: p. 147-151. [BR1652.B34M49] 74-28646 ISBN 0-8158-0322-2 : 6.95
1. Zinzendorf, Nicolaus Ludwig, Graf von, 1700-1760. 2. Pietism—Baltic States. I. Title: The Herrnhuterian pietism in the Baltic ...

RITTER, Abraham, 1792-1860. 284.674811
History of the Moravian church in Philadelphia, from its foundation in 1742 to the present time. Comprising notices, defensive of its founder and patron, Count Nicholas Ludwig von Zinzendorff. Together with an appendix. By Abraham Ritter. Philadelphia, Hayes & Zell, 1857. xx, [17]-281 p., 1 l. front., plates (1 col.) ports. (1 col.) plan. 23 cm. [BX8581.P5R5] 35-36632
1. Zinzendorf, Nicolaus Ludwig, graf von, 1700-1760. 2. Philadelphia. First Moravian church. I. Title.

WEINLICK, John Rudolf. 922.443
Count Zinzendorf. illus. drawn by Fred Bees. Nashville, Abingdon Press [1956] 240p. illus. 24cm. [BX8593.Z6W4] 56-5375
1. Zinzendorf, Nicolaus Hunwig Graf von, 1700-1760 I. Title.

WEINLICK, John Rudolf. 922.443
Count Zinzendorf. Illus. drawn by Fred Bees. Nashville, Abingdon Press [1956] 240 p. illus. 24 cm. [BX8593.Z6W4] 56-5375
1. Zinzendorf, Nicolaus Ludwig, Graf von, 1700-1760. I. Title.

Zion Church, Morris, N.Y.

HALL, Lewis R. M. 283'.747'74
Zion Church, 1818-1968; historical notes, prepared for the sesquicentennial celebration, by Lewis R. M. Hall. [Gilbertsville, N.Y., V. Buday, 1968?] [15] p. illus. 24 cm. Bibliography: p. [15] [BX5980.M63Z563] 73-171824
1. Zion Church, Morris, N.Y. I. Title.

Zion Evangelical Lutheran church, Hempfield Township, Westmoreland Co., Pa.

ZUNDEL, William Arter. 284.
History of old Zion Evangelical Lutheran church in Hempfield Township, Westmoreland County, Pennsylvania. Near Harrold's By William Arter Zundel ... Pub. by the church council ... [Waverly, Ia., Wartburg Press, c1922] x p., 1 l., 266 p. front., illus. (incl. ports., facsims.) 20 cm. [BX8076.H4Z8] 22-14601
1. Zion Evangelical Lutheran church, Hempfield Township, Westmoreland Co., Pa. I. Title.

Zionism.

AMERICAN Council for Judaism. 296
Zionism vs Judaism; a collection of editorials from the Information bulletin of the American Council for Judaism. [Philadelphia. 1944?] 57 p. 18 cm. [DS149.A6S] 49-40713
1. Zionism. I. Title.

BAR-ADON, Dorothy Ruth (Kahn) 1907- 296
Spring up, O well. With an introd. by Henry W. Nevinson. New York, H. Holt [1936] 276 p. plates. 21 cm. [DS149.B323 1936a] 36-21316
1. Zionism. 2. Jews in Palestine. 3. Palestine—Soc. life & cust. 4. Tel-Aviv, Palestine. 5. Jerusalem—Soc. life & cust. I. Barradon Dorothy Ruth Kahn II. Title.

BICK, Abraham, ed. 296
Exponents and philosophy of religious Zionism, an anthology: selections from the writings of the fathers of religious Zionism, with brief biographical sketches and characterizations. Selected and edited by Abraham Bick. Brooklyn, N.Y., Hashomer hadati of North America, Misrad chinuch (Educational dept.) [c1942] 79, [1] p. ports. 21 1/2 cm. Selected from the works of Zyi Kallacher, Samuel Mohiliver, Isaac J. Reinee, Abraham I. Cook and Samuel H. Landau. [DS149.B48] 43-9486
1. Zionism. 2. Jews—Religions. I. Hashomer hadati of North America. II. Title.

BUBER, Martin, 1878-1965. 956.94'001
On Zion; the history of an idea. With a new foreword by Nahum N. Glatzer. [Translated from the German by Stanley Godman] New York, Schocken Books [1973] xxii, 165 p. 23 cm. Translation of Ben 'am le-artso. Includes bibliographical references. [BS649.J5B7713 1973] 72-88533 6.95
1. Jews—Restoration. 2. Zionism. I. Title.

FEUER, Leon Israel, 1903- 296
Why a Jewish state, by Leon I. Feuer; introduction by Abba Hillel Silver. New York, R. R. Smith, 1942. 94 p. 21 cm. [DS140.F48] 42-51090
1. Zionism. 2. Jewish question. I. Title.

FINK, Reuben, 1889- 296
America and Palestine; the attitude of official America and of the American people toward the rebuilding of Palestine as a free and democratic Jewish commonwealth, prepared and edited by Reuben Fink ... New York, American Zionist emergency council, 1944. 522 p. illus. (map, facsims.) 24 cm. [DS149.F49] 44-9169
1. Zionism. 2. Public opinion—U.S. I. American Zionist emergency council. II. Title.

FINK, Reuben, 1889- 296
America and Palestine; the attitude of official America and of the American people toward the rebuilding of Palestine as a free and democratic Jewish commonwealth. 2d rev. ed. Prepared and edited by Reuben Fink ... New York, Herald square press, inc. [1945] 538 (i.e. 544) p. illus. (map, facsims.) 22 cm. Includes extra numbered pages 24a-24f. [DS149.F49 1945] 45-2518
1. Zionism. 2. Public opinion—U.S. I. Title.

GOLDMAN, Solomon, 1893- 296.09569
Land and destiny, by Dr. Solomon Goldman; presidential address to the 42nd annual convention of the Zionist organization of America, New York, 1939. New York, Zionist organization of America [1939] 32 p. 21 1/2 cm. Published also in the author's "Undefeated," Washington, D.C., 1940. [DS149.G5458] 42-39726
1. Zionism. I. Zionist organization of America. II. Title.

GREAT Britain Palestine and the Jews, Jewry's celebration of its national charter ... New York, George H. Doran company [c1918] vii, [2], 11-93 p. 19 cm. "The charter of Zionism, letter from the British government ... to Lord Rothschild, in which Mr. A. T. Balfour, secretary of state for foreign affairs, declared the sympathy of the British government with Zionist aspirations and its favourable attitude towards the establishment in Pale [DS149.G7] 18-20393 296

GREENBERG, Simon, 1901- 956.94
Israel and Zionism, a conservative approach. [New York] National Academy for Adult Jewish Studies [of] the United Synagogue of America [1956] 38p. 22cm. [DS149.G735] 296 56-2135
1. Zionism. I. Title.

HADASSAH, the Women's Zionist Organization of America. 296
Report. [New York] v. 28 cm. annual. [DS149.A272] 51-40452
I. Title.

HELLER, Joseph. 296
The Zionist idea. New York, Schocken Books [1949] vii, 246 p. 21 cm. "Brought up to date by the author, and edited for the American reader by Carl Alpert in cooperation with the author." Bibliography: p. 229-240. [DS149.H427 1949] 49-9141
1. Zionism. I. Title.

HERZL, Theodor, 1860-1904. 296
The Jewish state; an attempt at a modern solution of the Jewish question by Theodor Herzl; foreword by Chaim Weizmann. New York, Scopus publishing company, 1943. 111 p. 19 1/2 cm. A revised version by Israel Cohen of the translation by Sylvie D'Avigdor. cf. p. 3. [DS149.H514 1943] 43-8637
1. Zionism. 2. Jewish question. I. Avigdor, Sylvia d', tr. II. Cohen, Israel, 1879- ed. III. Title.

HERZL, Theodor, 1860-1904. 296
The Jewish state; an attempt at a modern solution of the Jewish question by Theodor Herzl. Biography, based on the work of Alex Bein. Introduction by Louis Lipsky. [New York] American Zionist emergency council [1946] 160 p. front. (port.) 19 1/2 cm. "The translation ... based on a revised translation published by the Scopus publishing company [revised version by Israel Cohen of the translation by Sylvia d'Avigdor] was further revised by Jacob M. Alkow, editor of this book."--p. 5. [Full name: Theodor Benjamin Herzl] Bibliography: p. 158. [[DS149.H514] A 46
1. Zionism. 2. Jewish question. I. Avigdor, Sylvia d', tr. II. Alkow, Jacob M., ed. III. Bein, Alex, 1908- IV. American Zionist emergency council. V. Title.

LONSCHEIN, Sam.
My 83 years; the memoirs of a veteran Zionist. [New York] Zebulun [1967] 251 p. port. 22 cm.
I. Title.

A new Zionism. 956.94
New York, Theodor Herzl Foundation, Muhlenberg Press [1956] ix, 126p. 21cm. Bibliographical [DS149.K45] 296 55-28882
I. Kaplan, Mordecai Menahem, 1881-

NORDAU, Max Simon, 1849-1923. 296
Max Nordau to his people, a summons and a challenge; introduction by B. Netanyahu. New York, Published for Nordau Zionist society by Scopus publishing company, inc. [c1941] 218 p., 1 l. 20 cm. "Addresses ... reproduced, with some alterations and abbrevations, from the London Jewish chronicle, except for the address at the eighth Zionist congress": leaf at end. [Name originally: Max Simon (Simhah Meir) Sudfeld] Bibliography: p. 213-215. [DS149.N817] 42-3479
1. Zionism. 2. Jewish question. I. Netanyahu, B. II. Nordau Zionist society. III. Title.

PARTIAL documentary of tribute to Abraham Goldberg, the Zionist, and in tribute to some of his friends and associates who helped make a dream come true: The rebirth of Israel. Presented through excerpts of evaluations and tributes, photographs and some correspondence. New York, 1958. 1 v. (unpaged) illus., ports., facsims. 29cm. Caption title: cover title: Documentary, 1907-1942. Text in English, Hebrew, or Yiddish.
I. Goldberg, Abraham, 1883-1942. II. Zionism—U. S.

PINSKER, Lev Semenovich, 1821-1891. 296
Road to freedom: writings and addresses by Leo Pinsker, with an introduction by B. Netanyahn. New York, Scopus publishing company, 1944. 142 p., 1 l. 19 cm. [DS149.P56] 44-4897
1. Zionism. 2. Jewish question. I. Netanyahu, B. II. Title.

ROSENBLATT, Samuel, 1902- 296.09569
This is the land, by Samuel Rosenblatt. New York, The Mizrachi organization of America, 1940. 166 p. 24 cm. [DS149.R62] 41-7766
1. Zionism. 2. Mizrachi. I. Title.

SANKOWSKY, Shoshanna (Harris) 1906- 296
A short history of Zionism. Pictorial statistics by Itzhak Sankowsky. New York, Bloch Pub. Co., 5707-1947. 223 p. illus., ports., maps. 22 cm. First published in 1936. Bibliography:p. 220-223. [DS149.S482 1947] 47-23335
1. Zionism. I. Title.

SAVIN, Jacob. 296
The only answer, by Jacob Savin; introducted by Rev. Donald G. Lothrop ... [Boston] 1944. 74 p. incl. illus., plates, ports., facsim. 23 cm. [DS149.S4826] 44-31738
1. Zionism. I. Title.

SCHILLER, Solomon, 1862-1925. 296
... Principles of labor Zionism. [New York] The Zionist labor party "Hitachduth" of America, 1928. 31 p. 22 cm. (The Young

Jew series. No. 1) *anslated from Hebrew by Ch. A. [i. e. Chaim Arlosoroff]" [DS149.A378 no. 1] 29-29331
1. Zionism. 2. Jews in Palestine. I. Arlosoroff, Chaim, 1890-1933,- tr. II. Title.

TENNEY, Jack Breckinridge, 1898- 956.94
Zionist network; a Tenney report. Tujunga, Calif., Standard Publications, 1953. 96p. 22cm. [DS149.T4] 296 53-34529
1. Zionism. I. Title.

TENNEY, Jack Breckinridge, 1898-
Zionist network. Introd. by F. Hichborn. Sacramento, Calif., Standard Publications [1958] 96 p. (His Report on world Zionism, 2)
1. Zionism. I. Title.

WISE, Stephen Samuel, 1874- 296
The great betrayal, by Stephen S. Wise and Jacob De Haas. New York, Brentano's, 1930. xxi, 294 p. illus. 22 cm. [DS149.W5] 31-279
1. Zionism. 2. Jews in Palestine. 3. Palestine—Pol. & govt. I. De Haas, Jacob, 1872- joint author. II. Title.

WURM, Shalom. 296.09569
The kvutza; the structure, problems, and achievements of the collective settlements in Palestine, by Shalom Wurm. New York, N.Y., Habonim, Labor Zionist youth [1942] 74 p. illus. 21 1/2 cm. [DS149.W8] 42-16033
1. Zionism. 2. Agricultural colonies—Palestine. I. Habonim, Labor Zionist youth. II. Title.

ZELIGS, Dorothy Freda. 915.69
The story of modern Palestine for young people, by Dorothy F. Zeligs. New York, Bloch publishing company, 1944. xv, 339 p. incl. front. (map) illus. (incl. ports.) 23 cm. Map on lining-papers. [DS107.3.Z4 1944] 45-3942
1. Zionism. 2. Jews in Palestine. 3. Palestine—Descr. & trav. I. Title.

ZIONIST organization in America. 296
The secretary's report on the activities and achievements of the Zionist organization of America. [Washington, 19 v. 23 cm. [DS149.A3932] 46-21523
I. Title.

ZIONIST organization of America. 296
The American war Congress and Zionism; statements by members of the American war Congress on the Jewish national movement. New York, Zionist organization of America, 1919. 228 p. 20 cm. Compiled by Reuben Fink. cf. p. [3] "In addition to the letters received by the Zionist organization from the members of the war Congress, this book contains the statements of the governments pledged to support the Jewish national aspirations."--Introd. [DS149.Z7] 19-5535
1. Zionism. I. Fink, Reuben, 1889- comp. II. Title.

ZIONIST organization of America. Dept. of youth and education. 296
Jewish youth, challenge and promise. New York, N.Y., Dept. of youth and education, Zionist organization of America [1941] cover-title, 64 p. 27 1/2 x 21 1/2 cm. Errata slip inserted. "Directory of Jewish youth organizations": p. [55]-63. "Select bibliography"; p. 64. [DS149.Z786] 44-24814
1. Zionism. 2. Jews in the U.S. 3. Youth—Jews. 4. Jews—Societies. I. Title.

Zionism—Addresses, essays, lectures.

FRISCH, Daniel, 1897-1950. 296
On the road to Zion, selected writings. [Edited by Trude Weiss-Rosmarin assisted by Carl Alpert, and others] New York, Zionist Organization of America, 1950. 240 p. port. 24 cm. [DS149.F92] 50-8880
1. Zionism—Addresses, essays, lectures. I. Title.

HECHALUTZ Organization of America. 296
Hechalutz builders and fighters. [Ed. by Shmuel Ben Zvi and Shirley Lashner] New York, 1946. [5], 1, [3] 100 p. illus. 23 cm. [DS149.H422] 47-27690
1. Zionism—Addresses, essays, lectures. I. Zvi, Shmuel Ben, ed. II. Title.

MAGNES, Judah Leon, 1877-1948. 956.94'001
Dissenter in Zion : from the writings of Judah L. Magnes / edited by Arthur A. Goren. Cambridge, Mass. : Harvard University Press, 1982. xv, 554 [8] p. of plates : ill. ; 24 cm. Includes bibliographical references and index. [DS149.M29 1982] 19 81-7268 ISBN 0-674-21283-5 : 30.00
1. Universitah ha- 'ivrit bi-Yerushalayim—Addresses, essays, lectures. 2. Magnes, Judah Leon, 1877-1948—Addresses, essays, lectures. 3. Zionism—Addresses, essays, lectures. 4. Jewish-Arab relations—1917-1949—Addresses, essays, lectures. 5. Jews—United States—Politics and government—Addresses, essays, lectures. 6. Rabbis—United States—Biography—Addresses, essays, lectures. 7. Zionists—Palestine—Biography—Addresses, essays, lectures. I. Goren, Arthur A., 1926- II. Title.

SCHWARTZ, David, 1893- 296
Bitter herbs and honey. New York, Silver Palm Press, 1947. 255 p. 20 cm. [DS149.S4953] 082 47-4162
1. Zionism—Addresses, essays, lectures. I. Title.

Zionism—Congresses.

AMERICAN Zionist Council. 956.94
Proceedings of the American Zionist assembly. 1st-Dec. 1953- New York. v. 21cm. [DS149.A256] [DS149.A256] 296 55-19253 55-19253
I. Title. II. Title: American Zionist assembly.

REPORT to the annual convention. [New York] v. illus. 23cm. [DS149.A39315] 296 56-23612 956.94
I. Zionist Organization of America.

ZIONIST Organization of America. National Education Dept. 296
Reorienting Zionist education today; proceedings of conference conducted by Education Dept., Zionist Organization of America, Feb. 22-23, 1948 [Congregation Bnai Jeshurun, New York City. New York? 1948] 72 p. 28 cm. Cover title. [DS149.A3947] 48-25654
1. Zionism—Congresses. I. Title.

Zionism—Controversial literature.

RITTENHOUSE, Stan. 956.94'001
"For fear of the Jews" / Stan Rittenhouse. Vienna, Va. (P.O. Box 492, Vienna 22180) : Exhorters, 1982. vi, 257 p. ; 24 cm. Includes bibliographical references. [DS149.R535 1982] 19 81-68608 11.00
1. Zionism—Controversial literature. 2. Antisemitism. 3. Israel—Politics and government. I. Title.

ZIONISM, enemy of peace and social progress : a miscellany of papers under the general editorship of Lionel Dadiani / [compiled by G.M. Sergeyev and L. Ya. Dadiani ; Russian text edited by N.B. Maltseva]. Moscow : Progress, c1981. 159 p. ; 20 cm. Includes bibliographical references. [DS149.Z617] 19 82-133993 pbk. : 3.50 956.94'001
1. Zionism—Controversial literature. 2. Jewish-Arab relations—Addresses, essays, lectures. 3. Antisemitism—Addresses, essays, lectures. 4. Jewish capitalists and financiers—Addresses, essays, lectures. I. Dadiani, Lionel IAkovlevich. II. Sergeyev, G. M. III. Maltseva, N. B.

Zionism — Handbooks, manuals, etc.

SUGARMAN, Morris.
A program manual for Zionism on the campus. New York, Student Zionist Organization, 1963. 138 p. illus. 23 cm. Includes bibliography. 66-61768
1. Zionism — Handbooks, manuals, etc. I. Student Zionist Organization. II. Title.

Zionism—History

GOLDBERG, Israel, 1887- 296
Fulfillment: the epic story of Zionism, by Rufus Learsi [pseud. 1st ed.] Cleveland, World Pub. Co. [1951] x, 426 p. ports., maps. 25 cm. "Bibliographical note": p. 411. [DS149.G539] 51-14316
1. Zionism—Hist. I. Title.

HERTZBERG, Arthur, ed.
The Zionist idea; a historical analysis and reader. Edited and with an introd. and biographical notes. Foreword by Emanuel Neumann. Cleveland, World Pub. Co.; Philadelphia, The Jewish Publication Society of America [1964] c1959] 638 p. 21 cm. (Meridian books, JP 17) 64-73728
I. Title.

KURLAND, Samuel. 296
Biluim, pioneers of Zionist colonization, by Samuel Kurland. New York, Pub. for Hechalutz orgaanization of America by Scopus publishing company, 1943. 78 p. 21 cm. (On cover: Hechalutz library) [DS149.K85] 43-10197
1. Zionism—Hist. I. Hechalutz organization of America. II. Title.

LEVENSOHN, Lotta. 296
Outline of Zionist history, by Lotta Levensohn. Sponsored by the Keren kayemeth leisrael (Jewish national fund) and Keren hayseod (Palestine foundation fund) [New York] Scopus publishing company, inc. [c1941] 157 p. 19 1/2 cm. [DS149.L347] 42-6906
1. Zionism—Hist. I. Jewish national fund. II. Palestine foundation fund. III. Title.

ROSENBERG, Jehiol Mitchell. 296
The story of Zionism, a bird's-eye view, by J. Mitchell Rosenberg ... Preface by Ludwig Lewisohn. New York, Bloch publishing company, 1946. xiv p., 1 l., 272 p. incl. front. (map) 22 1/2 cm. "Selected bibliography": p. 229. [DS149.R597] 46-2841
1. Zionism—Hist. I. Title.

SAMUEL, Maurice, 1895- 296
Harvest in the desert [by] Maruice Samuel. Philadelphia, The Jewish Publication society of America, 1704-1944. 3 p. l., [3]-316 p. 22 cm. [DS149.S47] 44-5171
1. Zionism—Hist. I. Jewish publication society of America. II. Title.

VITAL, David. 956.94'001
Zionism, the formative years / David Vital. Oxford : Clarendon Press ; New York : Oxford University Press, 1982. xviii, 514 p. ; 23 cm. Includes index. Bibliography: p. [495]-506. [DS149.V52 1982] 19 82-147153 ISBN 0-19-827443-2 : 29.95
1. Zionism—History. I. Title.

THE Zionist idea;
a historical analysis and reader. Edited and with an introd. and biographical notes, by A. Hertzberg. Foreword by E. Neumann. New York, Meridian Books [1960] 638p. (Jewish Publication Society series, JP17)
I. Hertzberg, Arthur, ed.

Zionism — History — Sources.

HABER, Julius.
A sheaf of Zionist history. New York, Waldon press, 1964. 1 v. (various pagings, chiefly facsims.) illus. 24 cm. Added t.p. in Yiddish, with a special section in Yiddish, and several letters in Hebrew. 64-43586
1. Zionism — Hist. — Sources. I. Title.

Zionism—Poland—History.

MENDELSOHN, Ezra. 943.8'004924
Zionism in Poland : the formative years, 1915-1926 / Ezra Mendelsohn. New Haven : Yale University Press, c1981. xi, 373 p. : map ; 24 cm. Includes index. Bibliography: p. 359-364. [DS149.M44 1981] 19 81-10301 ISBN 0-300-02448-7 : 35.00
1. Zionism—Poland—History. 2. Jews—Poland—History—20th century. 3. Poland—Ethnic relations. I. Title.

Zionism—United States.

WEINSTEIN, Jacob Joseph, 1902- 296.6'1'0924 B
Solomon Goldman: a rabbi's rabbi, by Jacob J. Weinstein. New York, Ktav Pub. House, 1973. xiii, 295 p. ports. 24 cm. Bibliography: p. 287-290. [BM755.G58W45] 72-10301 ISBN 0-87068-196-6 10.00
1. Goldman, Solomon, 1893-1953. 2. Zionism—United States. 3. Judaism—United States.

Zionism—United States—History

EARLY history of Zionism in America; papers presented at the conference on the early history of Zionism in America, convened by the American Jewish Historical Society and the Theodor Herzl Foundation, in New York City, on December twenty-sixth and twenty-seventh, nineteen hundred and fifty-five. Edited by Isidore S. Meyer. New York, 1958. viii, 340p. 23cm. [DS149.A695] [DS149.A695] 296 58-14619 58-14619 956.94
1. Zionism—U. S.—Hist. I. American Jewish Historical Society. II. Meyer, Isidore S., ed. III. Theodor Herzl Foundation. IV. Title: Conference on the early history of Zionism in America.

Zionist churches (Africa)—South Africa.

SUNDKLER, Bengt Gustaf Malcolm, 1909- 289.9
Zulu Zion and some Swazi Zionists / Bengt Sundkler. London ; New York : Oxford University Press, 1976. 337 p., [6] leaves of plates : ill. ; 22 cm. (Oxford studies in African affairs) Includes index. Bibliography: p. 329-332. [BR1450.S9] 76-378094 ISBN 0-19-822707-8 : 17.50
1. Zionist churches (Africa)—South Africa. 2. Sects—South Africa. 3. Pentecostal churches—South Africa. I. Title. II. Series.

Zion's evangelical Lutheran church, East Pikeland, Chester Co., Pa.

DAPP, Charles Frederick, 1880- 284
History of Zion's or Old organ church, with a record of baptisms and biographical sketches of former pastors, founded by Muhlenberg in 1743, by the Rev. Chas. F. Dapp ... with introduction by the Rev. T. E. Schmauk ... Spring City, Pa., The Interborough press [1919] xvi, 253 p. front. (port.) plates, facsims. 23 cm. "Baptismal record": p. 122-211. [BX8076.E3D3] 19-16088
1. Zion's evangelical Lutheran church, East Pikeland, Chester Co., Pa. I. Title.

Zita, Saint, 1218-1278.

REGGIO, Edwin, 1933- 922.245
A saint in the kitchen; a story of Saint Zita. Illus. by Mary Agnes Majewski. Notre Dame, Ind., Dukarie Press [1955] 96p. illus. 24cm. [BX4700.Z5R4] 55-33691
1. Zita, Saint, 1218-1278. I. Title.

Zodiac.

GLEADOW, Rupert. 133.5'2
The origin of the zodiac. [1st American ed.] New York, Atheneum, 1969 [c1968] 238 p. illus., fold. chart. 25 cm. "Notes and references": p. 221-230. [QB803.G55 1969] 79-81501
1. Zodiac. I. Title.

HODGSON, Joan, 1913- 133.9'013
Reincarnation through the zodiac / Joan Hodgson. 1st American ed. Vancouver, Wash. : CRCS Publications, [1979] 137 p. : ill. ; 20 cm. "Originally published in England under the title: Wisdom in the stars." [BF1726.H6 1979] 79-444 ISBN 0-916360-11-3 pbk. : 4.95
1. Zodiac. 2. Astrology. 3. Reincarnation. I. Title.

MOTT, Francis John, 1901- 133.52
The meaning of the zodiac; an ancient idea reviewed in the light of a universal pattern, by Francis J. Mott. Boston, A. A. Beauchamp, 1941. xv p., 1 l., 212 p. illus., plates (1 double) diagrs. 22 1/2 cm. [BF1701.M67] (159.96152) 41-10792
1. Zodiac. 2. Astrology. I. Title.

SAMPSON, Walter Harold. 133.5'2
The zodiac : a life epitome, being a comparison of the zodiacal elements with life-principles, cosmic, anthropologic, and

psychologic / by Walter H. Sampson. New York : ASI Publishers, c1975. xxiv, 420 p. : ill. ; 21 cm. Reprint of the 1928 ed. published by the Blackfriar Press, London. [BF1726.S25 1975] 75-25826 ISBN 0-88231-019-4 : 12.50
1. Zodiac. 2. Astrology. I. Title.

Zohar.

BENSION, Ariel, 1881-1932. 296.8'2
The Zohar in Moslem and Christian Spain / by Ariel Bension ; with an introd. by Denison Ross. New York : Hermon Press, 1974. xx, 256 p., 6 leaves of plates : ill. ; 24 cm. Reprint of the 1932 ed. published by G. Routledge, London. Bibliography: p. 249-250. [BM529.B35 1974] 74-78330 ISBN 0-87203-046-6 : 12.50
1. Zohar. 2. Jews in Spain. 3. Mysticism—Spain. I. Title.

WAITE, Arthur Edward, 1857-1942. 296.1
The secret doctrine in Israel: a study of the Zohar and its connections. New York, Occult Research Press [19--] 329p. illus. 23cm. [BM525.A59W3] 57-17485
1. Zohar. 2. Cabala. I. Title.

ZOHAR. English. Selections. 296.1
The alphabet of creation, an ancient legend from the Zohar; with drawings by Ben Shahn. New York, Printed at the Spiral Press and published by Pantheon [1954] [45] p. illus. 28 cm. "Adapted by Ben Shahn from the English translation of Maurice Samuel and other sources." [BM525.A52S5] 54-11739
I. Shahn, Ben, 1898-1969, ed. and illus. II. Title.

Zollars, Ely Vaughan, 1847-1916.

OSBORN, Ronald E 922.673
Ely Vaughn Zollars, teacher of preachers, builder of colleges; a biography. St. Louis, Christian Board of Publication [1947] 287 p. 22 cm. [BX7343.Z6O8] 47-12335
1. Zollars, Ely Vaughan, 1847-1916. I. Title.

Zoology—Miscellanea—Juvenile literature.

DEVINE, Bob. 215'.74
The feathered trip-hammer / by Bob Devine. Chicago : Moody Press, c1978. p. cm. Introduces five animals whose habits illustrate fundamentals of Christian life. [QL49.D48] 78-16612 ISBN 0-8024-2537-2 pbk. : 1.50
1. Zoology—Miscellanea—Juvenile literature. 2. [Animals.] 3. [Christian life.] I. Title.

Zoology—Palestine.

CANSDALE, George Soper. 220.8'59
All the animals of the Bible lands, by George Cansdale. Foreword by John R. W. Stott. [1st ed.] Grand Rapids, Zondervan Pub. House [1970] 272 p. illus., maps, plates (part col.) 24 cm. Bibliography: p. 255-256. [BS663.C34 1970] 76-120040 6.95
1. Bible—Natural history. 2. Zoology—Palestine. I. Title.

Zoroaster.

AVESTA. Yasna. Gathas. English. 295'.63 B
The life of Zoroaster in the words of his own hymns, the Gathas, according to both documents, the priestly, and the personal, on parallel pages, (a new discovery in higher criticism) Translated by Kenneth Sylvan Guthrie. Brooklyn, Comparative Literature Press. [New York, AMS Press, 1972] 125 p. 19 cm. [BL1515.A35 1972] 73-131036 ISBN 0-404-02964-7 9.50
1. Zoroaster. I. Guthrie, Kenneth Sylvan, 1871-1940, tr. II. Title.

BIDEZ, Joseph, 1867-1945. 295.'.1'3
Les mages hellenises, Zoroastre, Ostanes et Hystaspe d'apres la tradition grecque / Joseph Bidez and Franz Cumont. New York : Arno Press, 1975. xi, 297, 409 p. ; 23 cm. (Ancient religion and mythology) Reprint of the 1938 ed. published by Societe d'editions "Les Belles lettres," Paris. Includes bibliographical references and indexes. [BL1550.B58 1975] 75-10629 ISBN 0-405-07005-5
1. Hystaspes, King. 2. Zoroaster. 3. Osthanes. 4. Iran—Religion. 5. Greece—Civilization. I. Cumont, Franz Valery Marie, 1868-1947, joint author. II. Title. III. Series.

HERZFELD, Ernst Emil, 1879- 295
Zoroaster and his world, by Ernst Herzfeld ... Princeton, Princeton university press, 1947. 2 v. illus. 23 1/2 cm. Paged continuously. Bibliographical foot-notes. [BL1555.H4] 47-1972
1. Zoroaster. I. Title.

HERZFELD, Ernst Emil, 1879-1948. 295'.63 B
Zoroaster and his world. New York, Octagon Books, 1974 [c1947] 2 v. (xvii, 851 p.) 24 cm. Reprint of the ed. published by Princeton University Press, Princeton, N.J. Includes bibliographical references. [BL1555.H4 1974] 74-6219 ISBN 0-374-93877-6
1. Zoroaster. 2. Zoroastrianism. I. Title.

THE life of Zoroaster in the words of his own hymns, the Gathas, according to both documents, the priestly, and the personal, on parallel pages, (a new discovery in higher criticism,) tr. by Kenneth Sylvan Guthrie ... Brooklyn, N. Y., The Comparative literature press [c1914] 1 p. l., 125 p. 20 cm. 14-9292 1.10
I. Guthrie, Kenneth Sylvan, 1871- tr. II. Avesta. Gathas.

WHITNEY, Lorenenzo Harper, 1834-1912. 295
Life and teachings of Zoroaster, the great Persian, including a comparison of the Persian and Hebrew religions, showing that "The word of the Lord" came to the Hebrews by way of Persia. Part second offers proof that the Jews copied heavily from the Hindu Bible. By Loren Harper Whitney... [Chicago, M. A. Donohue & co., printers, c1905] 1 p. l., 259 p. front. (port.) 20 cm. [BL1570.W5] 5-26949
1. Zoroaster. 2. Jews—Religion—Relations—Zoroastrianism. 3. Christianity and other religions—Zoroastrianism. I. Title.

Zoroastrianism.

AVESTA. Yasna. Gathas. English & Avesta. 295'.8'2
The divine songs of Zarathushtra : a philological study of the Gathas of Zarathushtra, containing the text with literal translation into English, a free English rendering, and full critical and grammatical notes, metrical index, and glossary / Irach J. S. Taraporewala. New York : AMS Press, 1977. xlii, 1166 p. ; 23 cm. Reprint of the 1951 ed. published by D. B. Taraporevala Sons, Bombay. Includes index. Bibliography: p. 1160-1166. [BL1515.5.Y3A43 1977] 74-21251 ISBN 0-404-12802-5 : 125.00
I. Taraporewala, Irach Jehangir Sorabji, 1884-1956. II. Title.

AVESTA. Yasna. Gathas. English & Avesta. 295'.8'2
The divine songs of Zarathushtra : a philological study of the Gathas of Zarathushtra, containing the text with literal translation into English, a free English rendering, and full critical and grammatical notes, metrical index, and glossary / Irach J. S. Taraporewala. New York : AMS Press, 1977. xlii, 1166 p. ; 23 cm. Reprint of the 1951 ed. published by D. B. Taraporevala Sons, Bombay. Includes index. Bibliography: p. 1160-1166. [BL1515.5.Y3A43 1977] 74-21251 ISBN 0-404-12802-5 : 125.00
I. Taraporewala, Irach Jehangir Sorabji, 1884-1956. II. Title.

CARTER, George William, 1867-
Zoroastrianism and Judaism, by George William Carter, PH. D., with an introduction by Charles Gray Shaw, PH. D. Boston, R. G. Badger [c1918] 5 p. l., 7-116 p. 21 cm. (On verso of half-title: World worships series) Bibliography: p. 107-114. [BL1566.J8C3] 18-12233 2.00
1. Zoroastrianism. 2. Jews—Religion. I. Title.

DAWSON, Miles Menander, 1863- 295
The ethical religion of Zoroaster; an account of what Zoroaster taught; as perhaps the very oldest and surely the most accurate code of ethics for man, accompanied by the Essentials of his religion, by Miles Menander Dawson ... New York, The Macmillan company, 1931. xxviii p., 1 l., 271 p. 20 cm. Bibliography: p. xvii-xix. [BL1570.D3] 31-32813
1. Zoro astrianism I. Avesta. Selections. English. II. Title.

DAWSON, Miles Menander, 1863-1942. 295
The ethical religion of Zoroaster; an account of what Zoroaster taught, as perhaps the very oldest and surely the most accurate code of ethics for man, accompanied by the essentials of his religion. New York, AMS Press [1969] xxvii, 271 p. 23 cm. Reprint of the 1931 ed. Bibliography: p. xvii-xix. [BL1570.D3 1969] 73-90100
1. Zoroastrianism. I. Avesta. Selections. English. 1969. II. Title.

DHALLA, Maneckji Nusservanji, 1875- 295
History of Zoroastrianism, by Maneckji Nusservanji Dhalla ... New York, London [etc.] Oxford university press, 1938. xxxiv, 525 p. 23 cm. Bibliography: p. xix-xxviii. [BL1570.D5] 38-20148
1. Zoroastrianism. I. Title.

DHALLA, Maneckji Nusservanji, 1875- 295
Zoroastrian theology from the earliest times to the present day. [New York, AMS Press, 1972] xxxii, 384 p. 23 cm. Bibliography: p. xxi-xxvi. [BL1571.D45 1972] 70-131038 ISBN 0-404-02123-9 17.50
1. Zoroastrianism. I. Title.

DHALLA, Maneckji Nusservanji, 1875-1956. 295
History of Zoroastrianism / by Maneckji Nusservanji Dhalla. New York : AMS Press, [1977, c1938] p. cm. Reprint of the ed. published by Oxford University Press, New York. Includes index. Bibliography: p. [BL1570.D5 1977] 74-21256 ISBN 0-404-12806-8 : 30.00
1. Zoroastrianism. I. Title.

THE divine songs of Zarathushtra, by D. J. Irani; with an introduction by Rabindranath Tagore. London, G. Allen & Unwin ltd.; New York, The Macmillan company [1924] 79, [1] p. 20 cm. [BL1515.A35 1924] 25-8395 295
I. Dinshah Jijibbai Irani, tr. II. Ravindranatha thakura, Sir, 1861- III. Avesta. Gathas.

THE divine songs of Zarathushtra, by D. J. Irani; with an introduction by Rabindranath Tagore. London, G. Allen & Unwin ltd.; New York, The Macmillan company [1924] 79, [1] p. 20 cm. [BL1515.A35 1924] 25-8395 295
I. Dinshah Jijibbai Irani, tr. II. Ravindranatha thakura, Sir, 1861- III. Avesta. Gathas.

DUCHESNE-GUILLEMIN, Jacques. 295
Symbols and values in Zoroastrianism, their survival and renewal. [1st ed.] New York, Harper and Row [1966] xvii, 167 p. plates. 22 cm. (Religious perspectives, v. 15) [BL1571.D8] 66-10234
1. Zoroastrianism. I. Title. II. Series.

DUCHESNE-GUILLEMIN, Jacques. 295
The Western response to Zoroaster, by J. Duchesne-Guillemin. Westport, Conn., Greenwood Press [1973, c1958] 112 p. 22 cm. Original ed. issued in series: Ratanbai Katrak lectures, 1956. Bibliography: p. [105]-112. [BL1571.D83 1973] 72-9593 ISBN 0-8371-6590-3
1. Zoroastrianism. I. Title. II. Series: Oxford. University. Ratanbai Katrak lectures, 1956.

JACKSON, Abraham Valentine Williams, 1862-1937. 295
Zoroastrian studies; the Iranian religion and various monographs, by A. V. Williams Jackson ... New York, Columbia university press, 1928. xxxii, 325 p. 23 cm. (Added t.-p: Columbia university Indo-Iranian series, ed. by A. V. W. Jackson ... v. 12) Bibliography: p. xx-xxxi. [BL1570.J3] [PK1.C7 vol. 12] 28-29344
1. Zoroastrianism. 2. Persia—Religion. I. Title. II. Title: Iranian religion.

LAZARUS, M. Edgeworth. 295
The Zend-Avesta, and solar religions: an historical compilation; with notes and additions. By M. Edgeworth Lazarus, M. D. New York [etc.] Published for the author by Fowlers and Wells, 1852. 132 p. 23 cm. [BL1570.L3] 32-34330
1. Zoroastrianism. 2. Sun-worship. 3. Christianity and other religions—Zoroastrianism. I. Title.

MASANI, Rustom Pestonji, Sir 1876- 295
Zoroastrianism: the religion of the good life. Foreword by John McKenzie. New York, Collier [1962] 126p. 18cm. First pub. in 1938 under title: The religion of the good life, Zoroastrianism. (AS 477v) 63-345 .95 pap.,
1. Zorastrianism. I. Title.

MILLS, Lawrence Heyworth, 1837-1918. 295'.2'3
Avesta eschatology compared with the books of Daniel and Revelations : being supplementary to Zarathushtra, Philo, the Achaemenids, and Israel / by Lawrence H. Mills. [New York : AMS Press, 1977] c1908. vii, 85 p. : port. ; 22 cm. Reprint of the ed. published by Open Court Pub. Co., Chicago. Includes bibliographies references. [BL1515.4.M53 1977] 74-24644 ISBN 0-404-12816-5 : 9.00
1. Zoroastrianism. 2. Eschatology. 3. Judaism—Relations—Zoroastrianism. 4. Christianity and other religions—Zoroastrianism. 5. Christianity and other religions—Judaism. 6. Zoroastrianism—Relations—Christianity. I. Title.

MILLS, Lawrence Heyworth, 1837-1918. 295
Avesta eschatology compared with the books on Daniel and Revelations; being supplementary to Zarathushtra, Philo, the Achaemenids and Israel, by Dr. Lawrence H. Mills ... Chicago, The Open court publishing company; London, K. Paul, Trench, Trubner & co., ltd., 1908. vii, 85 p. front. (port.) 24 cm. [BL1515.M5] 8-5564
1. Zoroastrianism. 2. Eschatology. 3. Jews—Religion—Relations—Zoroastrianism. 4. Christianity and other religions—Zoroastrianism. I. Title.

MOULTON, James Hope, 1863-1917. 295
The treasure of the Magi; a study of Zoroastrianism. London, New York, H. Milford, 1917. [New York, AMS Press, 1972] xiii, 273 p. port. 23 cm. Original ed. issued in series: The Religious quest of India. [BL1570.M67 1972] 73-173004 ISBN 0-404-04508-1
1. Zoroastrianism. 2. Parsees. I. Title.

MOULTON, James Hope, 1863-1917. 295
... The treasure of the Magi; a study of modern Zoroastrianism, by James Hope Moulton ... London, New York [etc.] H. Milford, Oxford university press, 1917. xiii, [2], 273, [1] p. front. (port.) 22 cm. (The religious quest of India) [BL1570.M8] 19-1198
1. Zoroastrianism. 2. Parsees. I. Title.

PAVRY, Jal Dastur Cursetji, 1899-
The Zoroastrian doctrine of a future life, from death to the individual judgment, by Jal Dastur Curestji Pavry ... New York, Columbia university press, 1926. xxviii, 119 p. 23 cm. (Added t.-p.: Columbia university Indo-Iranian series, ed. by A. V. W. Jackson ... v. 11) Bibliography: p. xviii-xxviii. [BL1590.F8P3] [PK1.C7 vol.11] 26-14780
1. Zoroastrianism. 2. Future life. I. Title.

PAVRY, Jal Dastur Cursetji, 1899-
The Zoroastrian doctrine of a future life, from death to the individual judgement, by Jal Dastur Cursetji Pavry ... 2d ed. New York, Columbia university press, 1929. xxviii, 126 p. 23 cm. (Half-title: Columbia university Indo-Iranian series, ed. by A. V. W. Jackson ... v. 11) Bibliography: p. xviii-

xxviii. [BL1590.F8P3 1929] [PK1.C7 vol. 11] 29-10518
1. Zoroastrianism. 2. Future life. I. Title.

SZEKELY, Edmond Bordeaux. 295
The world picture of Zarathustra. Tecate, Calif., Essene School [1954, c1953] 6v. (in portfollo) illus. 34x36cm. Inside front cover of portfolio forms board for game of Asha. 32 markers in pocket. Contents.book 1. aAvesta. English. [BL1555.S9] 54-260925
I. Title.

WATTS, Isaac, 1674-1748. 245
Divine songs attempted in easy language, for the use of children. By I. Watts... Newberry-Port: Printed and sold by John Mycall, 1784. vi, [7]-54 p. 12 cm. [PR3763.W2A65 1784] 22-10927
I. Title.

ZAEHNER, Robert Charles. 295
The dawn and twilight of Zoroastrianism. [1st American ed.] New York, Putnam [1961] 371 p. illus. 24 cm. (The Putnam history of religion) Includes bibliography. [BL571.Z3 1961] 61-8353
1. Zoroastrianism. I. Title.

ZAEHNER, Robert Charles. 295
The teachings of the magi; a compendium of Zoroastrian beliefs. London, Allen & Unwin; New York, Macmillan [1956] 156 p. 19 cm. (Ethical and religious classics of East and West, no. 14) [BL1570.Z3] 56-3626
1. Zoroastrianism. I. Title.

ZAEHNER, Robert Charles. 295
Zurvan; a Zoroastrian dilemma, by R. C. Zaehner. With a new introd. by the author. New York, Biblo and Tannen, [1973 c.1972] xvi, 495 p. 24 cm. Reprint of the 1955 ed. Bibliography: p. [453]-458. [BL1571.Z33 1972] 72-7389 ISBN 0-8196-0280-9 17.50
1. Zoroastrianism. I. Title.

Zoroastrianism—Addresses, essays, lectures.

BOYCE, Mary. 295'.0955
A Persian stronghold of Zoroastrianism / Mary Boyce. Oxford [Eng.] : Clarendon Press, 1977. ix, 284 p., [4] leaves of plates : ill. ; 23 cm. (Ratanbai Katrak lectures ; 1975) Based on the Ratanbai Katrak lectures, 1975. Includes indexes. Bibliography: p. [271]-273. [BL1525.B69] 77-7350 ISBN 0-19-826531-X 19.95
1. Zoroastrianism—Addresses, essays, lectures. 2. Sharifabad, Iran—Religious life and customs—Addresses, essays, lectures. I. Title. II. Series: Oxford. University. Ratanbai Katrak lectures ; 1975.
Distributed by Oxford University Press, NY

MOULTON, James Hope, 1863-1917. 295
Early Zoroastrianism : lectures delivered at Oxford and in London, February to May 1912 / by James Hope Moulton. New York : AMS Press, [1980] p. cm. Reprint of the 1913 ed. published by Williams and Norgate, London, which was issued as the Hibbert lectures, 2d ed ser., 1912. Includes bibliographical references and index. [BL1575.M68 1980] 77-27157 ISBN 0-404-60414-5 : 25.00
1. Zoroastrianism—Addresses, essays, lectures. I. Title. II. Series: Hibbert lectures (London) ; 1912.

Zoroastrianism—History.

BOYCE, Mary. 295'.09
Zoroastrians, their religious beliefs and practices / Mary Boyce. London ; Boston : Routledge & Kegan Paul, 1979. xxi, 252 p. : maps ; 23 cm. (Library of religious beliefs and practices) Includes index. Bibliography: p. 229-236. [BL1525.B695] 78-41104 ISBN 0-7100-0121-5 : 21.50
1. Zoroastrianism—History. 2. Parsees—History. I. Title. II. Series: Library of beliefs and practices.

GEIGER, Wilhelm, 1856-1943. 295'.09
Zarathushtra in the Gathas, and in the Greek and Roman classics / translated from the German of Drs. Geiger and Windischmann, with notes on M. J. Darmester's theory regarding Tansar's letter to the King of Tabaristan, and the date of the Avesta, with an appendix on the alleged practice of consanguineous marriages in ancient Iran, by Darab Dastur Peshotan Sanjana. 2d ed. New York : AMS Press, 1977. 307 p. in various pagings ; 23 cm. Translation of Zarathushtra in den Gathas. Reprint of the 1899 ed. published by O. Harrassowitz, Leipzig. Includes bibliographical references. [BL1525.G4313 1977] 74-21260 ISBN 0-404-12810-6 : 24.50
1. Zoroastrianism—History. 2. Zoroaster. 3. Avesta—Criticism, interpretation, etc. I. Windischmann, Friedrich Heinrich Hugo, 1811-1861, joint author. II. Sanjana, Darab dastur Peshotan, 1857-1931. III. Title.

Zoroastrianism—Relations—Christianity—Addresses, essays, lectures.

MILLS, Lawrence Heyworth, 1837-1918. 295.8'2
Our own religion in ancient Persia : being lectures delivered in Oxford presenting the Zend Avesta as collated with the pre-Christian exilic pharisaism, advancing the Persian question to the foremost position in our Biblical research / by Lawrence Mills. New York : AMS Press, 1977. xii, 193 p. ; 23 cm. Reprint of the 1913 ed. published by F. A. Brockhaus, Leipzig. [BL1515.5.M55 1977] 74-21262 ISBN 0-404-12811-4 : 45.00
1. Avesta—Addresses, essays, lectures. 2. Zoroastrianism—Relations—Christianity—Addresses, essays, lectures. 3. Christianity and other religions—Zoroastrianism—Addresses, essays, lectures. 4. Judaism—Relations—Zoroastrianism—Addresses, essays, lectures. 5. Zoroastrianism—Relations—Judaism—Addresses, essays, lectures. I. Title.

Zoroastrianism—Relations—Judaism.

CARTER, George William, 1867-1930. 295
Zoroastrianism and Judaism. With an introd. by Charles Gray Shaw. New York, AMS Press [1970] 116 p. 23 cm. Reprint of the 1918 ed. Bibliography: p. 107-114. [BL1566.J8C3 1970] 70-112489
1. Zoroastrianism—Relations—Judaism. 2. Judaism—Relations—Zoroastrianism.

Zoroastrianism.—Sacred books.

AVESTA. Yasna. Gathas. English. 295'.8'2
The hymns of Zarathustra : being a translation of the Gathas together with introduction and commentary / by Jacques Duchesne-Guillemin ; translated from the French by Mrs. M. Henning. Westport, Conn. : Hyperion Press, 1979. p. cm. Reprint of the 1952 ed. published by J. Murray, London, in series: The Wisdom of the East series. [BL1515.5.Y3A43 1979] 78-20446 ISBN 0-88355-826-2 : 16.00
I. Duchesne-Guillemin, Jacques. II. Title. III. Series: The Wisdom of the East series.

AVESTA. Yasna. Gathas. Polyglot. 295'.8'2
A study of the five Zarathushtrian (Zoroastrian) Gathas : with texts and translations, also with the Pahlavi translation for the first time edited with collation of manuscripts, and now prepared from all the known codices, also deciphered, and for the first time translated in its entirety into a European language, with Neryosangh's Sanskrit text edited with the collation of five MSS., and with a first translation, also with the Persian text contained in Codex 12b of the Munich collection edited in transliteration, together with a commentary, being the literary apparatus and argument to the translation of the Gathas in the XXXIst volume of the Sacred books of the East / by Lawrence H. Mills. New York : AMS Press, [1977] p. cm. Reprint of the 1894 ed. published by L. Mills, Oxford, available from F. A. Brockhaus, Leipsic, which was published with the assistance of the Secretary of State for India in Council and the Trustees of the Parsi Panchayet Translation Fund of Bombay. [BL1515.2.Y3A4 1977] 74-21252 ISBN 0-404-12803-3 : 57.50
I. Mills, Lawrence Heyworth, 1837-1918. II. Title.

WEST, Edward William, 1824-1905, ed. and tr. 295
Pahlavi texts, translated by E. W. West ... Oxford, The Clarendon press, 1880-97. 5 v. 23 cm. (Added t.-p.: The sacred books of the East...vol. v, XVIII, XXIV, XXXVII, XLVII) Each volume preceded by editor's introduction. Contents.pt. I. Bundahis, or, The original creation. Appendix: Selections of Zad-Sparam. Bahman Yast, or, Zand-L Vohuman Yosno. Shayast la-Shayast, or, The proper and improper.--pt. II. Dadistan-I. Dinik, or, The religious opinions of Manuskihar. Epistles of Manuskihar--pt. III. Dina-I Mainog-L Hirad, or, Opinions of the spirit of wisdom. Sikand-gumanik Vigar, or, The doubt-dispelling explanation. Saddar, or, The hundred subjects.--pt. IV. Contents of the Nasks as stated in the eighth and ninth books of the Dinkard. Details of the Nasks from other sources.--pt. V. Marvels of Zoroastrianism: Dinkard, book VII. Dinkard, book V. Selections of Zad-Sparam. [BL1010.S3 vol. 5, 18, 24, 37, 47] (290.82) 32-34303
1. Zoroastrianism.—Sacred books. 2. Pahlavi literature—Translations into English. 3. English literature—Translations from Pahiavi. I. Manuskihar, fl. 881. II. Zad-Sparam, fl., 881. III. Title.

Zorzano, Isidoro,

SARGENT, Daniel, 1890- 922.246
God's engineer; with a pref. by William P. O'Connor. Chicago, Scepter, 1954. 191p. 21cm. [BX4705.Z64S3] 54-20983
1. Zorzano, Isidoro, I. Title.

Zuck, Barb.

†ZUCK, Roy B. 248'.86'0926
"Barb, please wake up!" : How God helped a couple through their daughter's accident and long recovery from a nearly fatal auto accident / Roy B. Zuck. Wheaton, Ill. : Victor Books, c1976. 127 p. ; 18 cm. [RD594.Z8] 77-371325 ISBN 0-88207-653-1 pbk. : 1.75
1. Zuck, Barb. 2. Brain—Wounds and injuries—Biography. 3. Crash injuries—Biography. I. Title.

Zuffi Indians—Missions.

EALY, Ruth Rea, 1877- 922.573
Water in a thirsty land. [Pittsburgh?] c1955. 243p. illus. 23cm. [BX9225.E34E3] 55-44645
1. Ealy, Taylor Filmore, 1848-1915. 2. Zuffi Indians—Missions. I. Title.

Zulus—Church history.

SUNDKLER, Bengt Gustaf Malcolm, 1909- 276.8
Bantu prophets in South Africa. 2d ed. London, New York, Published for the International African Institute by the Oxford University Press, 1961. 381 p. illus. 23 cm. Includes bibliography. [SB1367.Z8S8] 61-65161
1. Zulus—Church history. 2. Sects—Africa, South. I. Title.

Zumarraga. Juan de, Abp., 1468-1548.

GREENLEAF, Richard E 272.0972
Zumarraga and the Mexican Inquisition, 1536-1543. Washington, Academy of American Franciscan History, 1961 [c1962] viii, 155 p. illus., port., facsims. 27 cm. (Academy of American Franciscan History. Monograph series, v. 4) Bibliography: p. 133-148. [BX4705.Z8G7 1962] 63-1181
1. Zumarraga, Juan de, Abp., 1468-1548. 2. Inquisition. Mexico. I. Title. II. Series.

GREENLEAF, Richard E. 272.0972
Zumarraga and the Mexican Inquisition, 1536-1543. Washington, D.C., Acad. of Amer. Franciscan Hist., 1961[c.1962] viii, 155p. illus. 27cm. (Acad. of Amer. Franciscan Hist. Monograph ser., v. 4) Bibl. 63-1181 6.50
1. Zumarraga. Juan de, Abp., 1468-1548. 2. Inquisition. Mexico. I. Title. II. Series.

Zuni Indians—Religion and mythology.

CUSHING, Frank Hamilton, 1857-1900. 299'.7
Outlines of Zuni creation myths / by Frank Hamilton Cushing. New York : AMS Press, 1976. p. 323-462 ; 23 cm. Reprinted from the 13th annual report (1891-92) of the U.S. Bureau of American Ethnology, Washington, 1896. Includes index. [E99.Z9C893 1976] 74-7947 ISBN 0-404-11834-8 : 20.00
1. Zuni Indians—Religion and mythology. I. Title.

Zunz, Leopold, 1794-1886—Addresses, essays, lectures.

GLATZER, Nahum Norbert, 1903- 296.3
Essays in Jewish thought / Nahum N. Glatzer. University : University of Alabama Press, c1978. 295 p. ; 25 cm. (Judaic studies ; 8) Includes bibliographical references and index. [BM157.G58] 76-51044 ISBN 0-8173-6904-X : 19.50
1. Zunz, Leopold, 1794-1886—Addresses, essays, lectures. 2. Buder, Martin, 1878-1886—Addresses, essays, lectures. 3. Rosenzweig, Franz, 1886-1929—Addresses, essays, lectures. 4. Judaism—History—Addresses, essays, lectures. I. Title. II. Series.

Zwemer, Samuel Marinus, 1867-1952.

WILSON, J Christy, 1891- 922
Apostle to Islam; a biography of Samuel M. Zwemer. Grand Rapids, Baker Book House, [1952] 261p. illus. 24cm. [BV2626.Z8W5] 52-13190
1. Zwemer, Samuel Marinus, 1867-1952. I. Title.

ZWEMER, Samuel Marinus, 1867- 266
The unoccupied mission fields of Africa and Asia, by Samuel M. Zwemer ... New York, Student volunteer movement for foreign missions, 1911. xx, 260 p. front., plates, ports., maps (1 fold.) 21 cm. "Select bibliography": p. 225-244. [BV3150.Z85] 11-8425
I. Title.

Zwingli, Ulrich, 1484-1531.

COURVOISIER, Jaques 238.42
Zwingli, a Reformed theologian. Richmond, Va., Knox [c.1963] 101p. 21cm. (Annie Kinkead Warfield lects., 1961) Bibl. 63-8064 1.75 pap.,
1. Zwingli, Ulrich, 1484-1531. I. Title. II. Series.

FARNER, Oskar, 1884- 922.4494
Zwingli the reformer; his life and work. Translated by D. G. Sear. New York, Philosophical Library [1952] 135 p. illus. 19 cm. Translation of Huldrych Zwingli, der schweizerische Reformator. [BR345.F295] 52-11584
1. Zwingli, Ulrich, 1484-1531. I. Title.

FARNER, Oskar, 1884- 270.6'0924 B
Zwingli the reformer; his life and work. Translated by D. G. Sear. [Hamden, Conn.] Archon Books, 1968. 135 p. facsims., ports. 18 cm. Reprint of the 1952 ed. Translation of Huldrych Zwingli, der schweizerische Reformator. [BR345.F295 1968] 68-8017 ISBN 0-208-00694-X
1. Zwingli, Ulrich, 1484-1531. I. Title.

GARSIDE, Charles 246
Zwingli and the arts. New Haven, Conn., Yale [c.] 1966. xiv, 190p. 25cm. (Yale hist. pubns. Miscellany 83) Bibl. [BR345.G3] 66-12496 7.50
1. Zwingli, Ulrich, 1484-1531. 2. Church decoration and ornament. 3. Music in churches. 4. Worship—Hist. I. Title. II. Series.

GARSIDE, Charles. 246
Zwingli and the arts. New Haven, Yale University Press, 1966. xiv, 190 p. 25 cm. (Yale historical publications. Miscellany 83) Revision of thesis, Yale University. "Bibliographical note": p. 185-186. [BR345.G3 1966] 66-12496
1. Zwingli, Ulrich, 1484-1531. 2. Church decoration and ornament. 3. Music in churches. 4. Worship — Hist. I. Title. II. Series.

GARSIDE, Charles. 246
Zwingli and the arts / Charles Garside, Jr. New York : Da Capo Press, 1981, c1966. xiv, 190 p. ; 24 cm. (Da Capo Press music reprint series) Reprint. Originally published: New Haven : Yale University Press, 1966. (Yale historical publications. Miscellany ; 83) Includes index. Bibliography: p. 185-186. [BR345.G3 1981] 19 81-4277 ISBN 0-306-76018-5 : 19.50
1. Zwingli, Ulrich, 1484-1531. 2. Christianity and the arts—History of doctrines—16th century. I. Title.

GROB, Jean.
The life of Ulric Zwingli. Translated from the German of Jean Grob. New York, Funk & Wagnalls, 1883. vi, [7]-200 p. 19 cm. (On cover: Standard library, no. 105) Translated by I. K. Loos and G. F. Behringer and edited by G. F. Behringer. cf. p. [iii]-iv. [BR345.G73] 12-82851
1. Zwingli, Ulrich, 1484-1531. I. Loos, I. K., tr. II. Behringer, George F., ed. III. Title.

HOTTINGER, Johann Jacob, 1783-1860.
The life and times of Ulric Zwingli, tr. from the German by T.C. Porter. Harrisburg, T.F. Scheffer, 1856. iv. 421 p. 19 cm. [BR345.H6] 49-31207
1. Zwingli, Ulrich, 1484-1531. I. Porter, Thomas Conrad, 1822-1901, tr. II. Title.

JACKSON, Samuel Macauley, 1851-1912.
Huldreich Zwingli, the reformer of German Switzerland, by Samuel Macauley Jackson ... together with an historical survey of Switzerland before the reformation, by Prof. John Martin Vincent ... and a chapter on Zwingli's theology, by Prof. Frank Hgh Foster ... New York and London, G. P. Putnam's sons, 1901. 3 p. l., v-xxvi, 519 p. 27 pl. (1 double) 2 port. (incl. front.) fold. map, plan, 2 fold. facsim. 20 cm. (Half-title: Heroes of the reformation. [v. 5]) Bibliography: p. xxi-xxvi. [BR345.J3] 1-30597
1. Zwingli, Ulric, 1484-1531. 2. Reformation—Switzerland. I. Vincent, John Martin, 1857- II. Foster, Frank Hugh, 1851-1935. III. Title.

JACKSON, Samuel Macauley, 1851-1912. 270.6'0924 B
Huldreich Zwingli, 1484-1531, the reformer of German Switzerland. Together with an historical survey of Switzerland before the Reformation, by Prof. John Martin Vincent ... and a chapter on Zwingli's theology, by Prof. Frank Hugh Foster. New York, Putnam, 1901. St. Clair Shores, Mich., Scholarly Press [1969] xxvi, 519 p. illus., facsims., plan, ports. 22 cm. (Heroes of the Reformation [v. 5]) Bibliography: p. xxi-xxvi. [BR345.J3 1969] 70-8883
1. Zwingli, Ulrich, 1484-1531. 2. Reformation—Switzerland. I. Vincent, John Martin, 1857-1939. II. Foster, Frank Hugh, 1851-1935.

JACKSON, Samuel Macauley, 1851-1912. 270.6'092'4 B
Huldreich Zwingli, the reformer of German Switzerland, 1484-1531. Together with an historical survey of Switzerland before the Reformation, by John Martin Vincent; and a chapter on Zwingli's theology by Frank Hugh Foster. 2d ed. rev. New York, Putnam. [New York, AMS Press, 1972] xxvi, 519 p. illus. 19 cm. Reprint of the 1901 ed., which was issued as v. 5 of Heroes of the Reformation. Bibliography: p. xxi-xxvi. [BR345.J3 1972] 75-170836 ISBN 0-404-03543-4
1. Zwingli, Ulrich, 1484-1531. 2. Reformation—Switzerland. I. Vincent, John Martin, 1857-1939. II. Foster, Frank Hugh, 1851-1935. III. Title.

LUTHER, Martin, 1483-1546. 225.
Luther's explanatory notes on the Gospels, compiled from his works, by Rev. E. Mueller...translated by Rev. P. Anstadt... York, Pa., P. Anstadt & sons, 1899. x, [11]-424 p. front. (port.) 24 cm. [BS2555.A2L8] 99-3035
1. Bible, N.T. Gospels—Commentaries. 2. Bible—Commentaries—N.T. Gospels. I. Mueller, E., comp. II. Anstadt, Peter, 1819-1903, tr. III. Title.

POTTER, George Richard, 1900- 270.6'092'4 B
Zwingli / G. R. Potter. Cambridge ; New York : Cambridge University Press, 1976. p. cm. Includes index. [BR345.P68] 75-46136 ISBN 0-521-20939-0 ; 43.50
1. Zwingli, Ulrich, 1484-1531.

RILLIET, Jean Horace 922.4494
Zwingli, third man of the Reformation, by Jean Rilliet. Tr. [from French] by Harold Knight. Philadelphia, Westminster [c.1959, 1964] 320p. 23cm. Bibl. 64-19150 6.00
1. Zwingli, Ulrich, 1484-1531. I. Title.

RILLIET, Jean Horace. 922.4494
Zwingli, third man of the Reformation, by Jean Rilliet. Translated by Harold Knight. Philadelphia, Westminster Press [1964] 320 p. 23 cm. Bibliography: p. 313-314. [BR345.R554] 64-19150
1. Zwingli, Ulrich, 1484-1531. I. Title.

SIMPSON, Smauel, 1868-
Life of Ulrich Zwingli, the Swiss patriot and reformer, by Samuel Simpson. New York, The Baker & Taylor co. [c1902] 9 p. l., [9]-297 p. front. (port.) plates. 20 cm. Bibliography: p. 280-291. [BR345.S5] 2-24755
1. Zwingli, Ulrich, 1484-1531. I. Title.

ZWINGLI, Ulrich, 1484-1531.
The Latin works and the correspondence of Huldreich Zwingli, together with selections from his German works, edited, with introductions and notes, by Samuel Macauley Jackson; translations by Henry Preble, Walter Lichtenstein, and Lawrence A. McLouth ... New York [etc.] G. P. Putnam's sons, 1912- "Of this translation of the Works of Huldreich Zwingli, seven hundred and fifty copies have been printed from type, and the type destroyed." Vol. 3 has title: The Latin works of Huldreich Zwingli, translated for the late Samuel Macauley Jackson and published under the auspices of the American society of church history ... edited, with notes, by Clarence Nevin Heller, with introductions by George Warren Richards and a preface by William Walker Rockwell. Philadelphia, The Heidelberg press, 1929. [BR346.Z23] 12-23956
I. Jackson, Samuel Macauley, 1851-1912, ed. II. Heller, Clarence Navia, ed. III. Preble, Henry, 1853-1929, tr. IV. Lictenstein, Walter, 1880- tr. V. McLouth, Lawrence Amos, 1863- tr. VI. American society of church history. VII. Title.

Zwingli, Ulrich, 1484-1531—Bibliography.

PIPKIN, H. Wayne. 016.2706'092'4 B
A Zwingli bibliography. Compiled by H. Wayne Pipkin. Pittsburgh, Clifford E. Barbour Library, Pittsburgh Theological Seminary [1972] 157 p. illus. 17 cm. (Bibliographia tripotamopolitana, no. 7) [Z8999.P56] 73-153549
1. Zwingli, Ulrich, 1484-1531—Bibliography. I. Title. II. Series.

Zyburn, John S., tr.

ZIMMERMANN, Otto, 1873-1932. 216
The problem of evil and human destiny, from the German of the Rev. Otto Zimmermann, S.J., by The Rev. John S. Zyburs ... with an introduction by the Rt. Rev. Joseph Schrembs ... St. Louis, Mo. and London, B. Herder book co., 1924. xiv, 135 p. 19 1/2 cm. [BJ1406.Z5] 24-27813
1. Zyburn, John S., tr. I. Title.